MCI

Devonshire House Prep School

A co-educational IAPS Prep and Pre-Prep School for children from 3 to 13 with its own Oak Tree Nursery for children from 2½ to 3½

Academic / Music scholarships are available for children aged 7 or 8

For more information contact Admissions: 020 7435 1916
enquiries@devonshirehouseprepschool.co.uk
www.devonshirehouseschool.co.uk

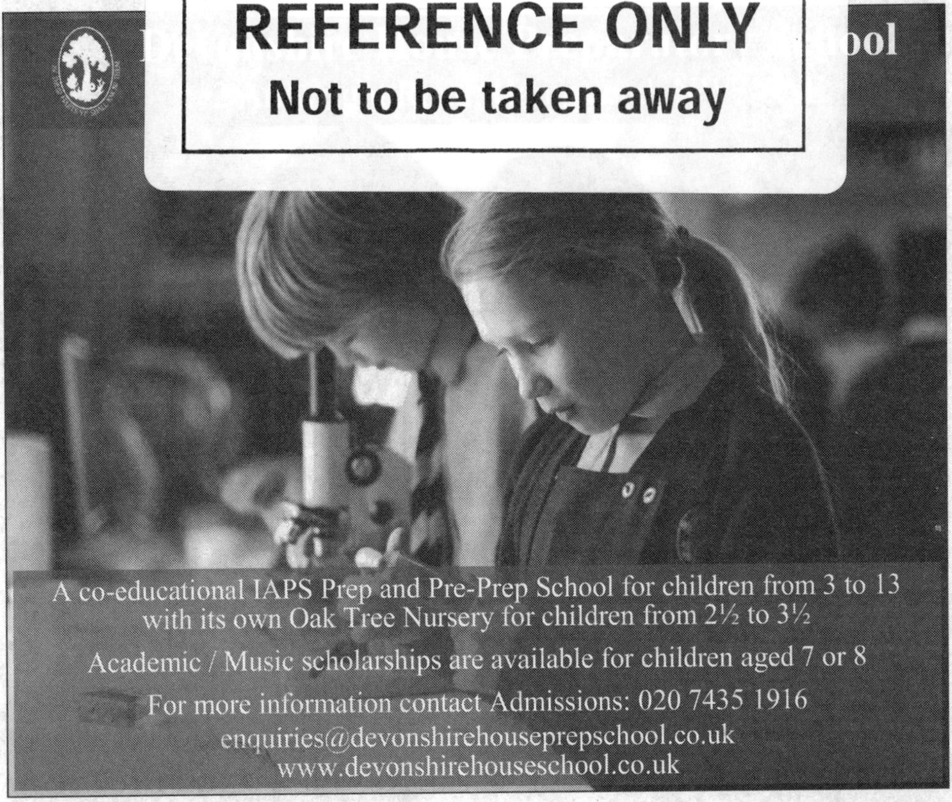

HAWKESDOWN HOUSE SCHOOL

An IAPS school for boys aged 3 to 8,
in Kensington, W8

For further details please
contact the Admissions' Secretary.

Hawkesdown House School,
27, Edge Street, Kensington,
London W8 7PN.
Telephone: 020 7727 9090.
Facsimile: 020 7727 9988.
Email: admin@hawkesdown.co.uk

A WORLD OF KNOWLEDGE
AT YOUR FINGERTIPS

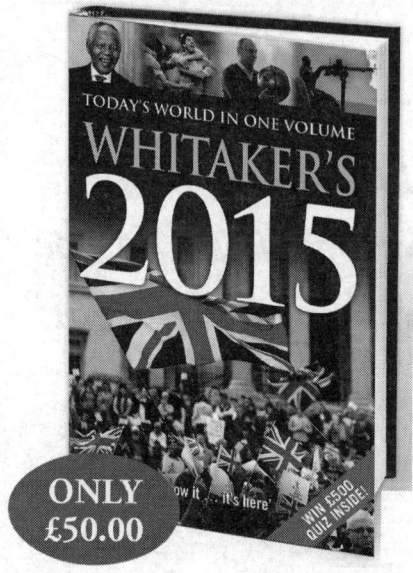

'Whitaker's remains the most comprehensive compendium of information in the English language' – JON SNOW

'A source of delight as well as a gold-mine of information'

– JONATHAN DIMBLEBY

ONLY £50.00

ALSO AVAILABLE
Whitaker's Concise 2015
All the essential UK data
in paperback
£25.00

THE ULTIMATE REFERENCE LIBRARY IN ONE VOLUME

News digests; national and local government infrastructure; guides to education, law and taxation; the royal family; overviews of the water, energy and transport industries; and reviews of the year 2013-14 covering the arts, sciences, politics and sport.

The fully updated 147th edition also includes:

- Extensive data, maps and timelines for every country of the world
- Brand new colour infographics
- Up-to-date demographics from the 2011 census

WHITAKER'S BITESIZE EBOOKS

Stay informed wherever you are with the new Whitaker's Shorts eBooks
– selected themed sections from the main print edition:

Banking & Finance

Governance

International

Law & Order

Year in Review 2013-2014

Download today from **www.bloomsbury.com**

For full details and to buy at a 10% discount, visit:
www.whitakersalmanack.com

BLOOMSBURY

INDEPENDENT SCHOOLS YEARBOOK

2014–2015

Boys Schools, Girls Schools,
Co-educational Schools and
Preparatory Schools

Details of Schools in membership of one or more
of the following Constituent Associations of the
Independent Schools Council (ISC):

Heads
Headmasters' and Headmistresses' Conference (HMC)
Girls' Schools Association (GSA)
The Society of Heads
Independent Association of Prep Schools (IAPS)
Independent Schools Association (ISA)

Overseas Schools
Council of British International Schools (COBIS)

Edited by
JUDY MOTT

Tel: 020 7631 5600; email: isyb@acblack.com
website: www.isyb.co.uk

A&C BLACK

AN IMPRINT OF BLOOMSBURY PUBLISHING PLC

LONDON • NEW YORK • NEW DELHI • SYDNEY

A&C Black
An imprint of Bloomsbury Publishing Plc

50 Bedford Square
London
WC1B 3DP
UK

1385 Broadway
New York
NY10018
USA

www.bloomsbury.com

A&C BLACK and the A&CB logo are trademarks of
Bloomsbury Publishing Plc

British Library Cataloguing-in-Publication Data
A catalogue record for this book is available from the British Library.

ISBN: PB 978-1-4729-1335-7

2 4 6 8 10 9 7 5 3 1

Typeset by A&C Black Publishers
Printed and bound in Great Britain by CPI Group (UK) Ltd,
Croydon CR0 4YY

INDEPENDENT SCHOOLS YEARBOOK 2014–2015

CONTENTS

Independent Schools Council	ix
Headmasters' and Headmistresses' Conference	x
Girls' Schools Association	xi
The Society of Heads	xii
Independent Association of Prep Schools	xiv
Independent Schools Association	xv
Council of British International Schools	xvi
Association of Governing Bodies of Independent Schools	xvii
Independent Schools' Bursars Association	xviii
Boarding Schools' Association	xviii
Independent Schools Inspectorate	xx
Methodist Independent Schools Trust	xx
Girls' Day School Trust	xxi
Independent Schools Examinations Board	xxii
Catholic Independent Schools' Conference	xxiv
Choir Schools' Association	xxv
Council for Independent Education (CIFE)	xxvi
United Learning	xxvii
ISCO	xxviii
Woodard Schools	xxix
Association for Marketing and Development in Independent Schools	xxx
Association of Representatives of Old Pupils' Societies	xxx
Montessori Schools Association	xxxi
Medical Officers of Schools Association	xxxi
English-Speaking Union	xxxii

PART I: **HEADMASTERS' AND HEADMISTRESSES' CONFERENCE**

324 schools for pupils from age 11 to 18, whose Heads are members of HMC; 63 of these are international members. They are all-boys schools (some admitting girls to the Sixth Form), co-educational schools, "Diamond" schools (girls and boys taught separately in the 11–16 age range), and some are all-girls schools. Many of the schools also have a Preparatory/Junior school or department.

Alphabetical List of Schools (UK & Ireland)	1
Geographical List of Schools (UK & Ireland)	4
Individual School Entries (UK & Ireland)	7
Entrance Scholarships	535
Bursaries	545
International Members	547
Associates	556

PART II: **GIRLS' SCHOOLS ASSOCIATION**

143 schools for pupils from age 11 to 16/18, whose Heads are members of GSA. They are all-girls schools in the 11–16 age range, some admit boys to the Sixth Form and some are "Diamond" schools (girls and boys taught separately in the 11–16 age range). Some of the schools also have a Preparatory/Junior school or department.

Alphabetical List of Schools	557
Geographical List of Schools	559
Individual School Entries	561
Entrance Scholarships	752
Bursaries	758

. . ./continued

PART III: THE SOCIETY OF HEADS

94 schools for pupils from age 11 to 18 whose Heads are members of The Society of Heads. The majority are co-educational schools, but Membership is open to boys and girls schools. Many of the schools also have a Preparatory/Junior school or department.

Alphabetical List of Schools	759
Geographical List of Schools	760
Individual School Entries	761
Entrance Scholarships	854
Bursaries	857
Additional Members	858

PART IV: INDEPENDENT ASSOCIATION OF PREP SCHOOLS

601 schools whose Heads are members of IAPS; 27 of these are overseas members. Most of the schools are co-educational; some cater for boys only or girls only. The preparatory school age range is 7 to 11/13, but many of the schools have a pre-preparatory department for children up to age 7.

Alphabetical List of Schools (UK)	859
Geographical List of Schools (UK)	864
Alphabetical List of Heads	869
Individual School Entries (UK)	872
Overseas Members	1126

PART V: INDEPENDENT SCHOOLS ASSOCIATION

253 schools in membership of ISA. Schools in this Association are not confined to one age range and can cater for any age range of pupils up to 18/19 years.

Alphabetical List of Schools	1141
Geographical List of Schools	1144
Individual School Entries	1147

PART VI: COUNCIL OF BRITISH INTERNATIONAL SCHOOLS   1225

69 British Schools abroad that are Accredited Members of COBIS and meet the UK government standards for British Schools Overseas (BSO) through a successful inspection by a government approved inspectorate. Members of this Association include primary, secondary, and all-through schools.

Index of All Schools	1233

ISC
INDEPENDENT SCHOOLS COUNCIL
www.isc.co.uk

"Working with its members to promote and preserve the quality, diversity and excellence of UK independent education both at home and abroad".

ISC is established to support the aims and objectives of its eight member associations; to protect and promote the sector with policy makers and opinion formers; to be a leading source of legal and regulatory guidance for the sector; to conduct and compile authoritative sector research and intelligence; and to provide online access to sector and school information to inform parental decisions.

The Constituent Associations of ISC are:

Association of Governing Bodies of Independent Schools (AGBIS)
Council of British International Schools (COBIS)
Girls' Schools Association (GSA)
Headmasters' and Headmistresses' Conference (HMC)
Independent Association of Prep Schools (IAPS)
Independent Schools Association (ISA)
Independent Schools' Bursars Association (ISBA)
The Society of Heads

Secretariat
Chairman
Barnaby Lenon

General Secretary
Julie Robinson

Head of Research and Deputy General Secretary
Rudolf Eliott Lockhart

Head of Press
Tracy Cook

Independent Schools Council
St Vincent House
30 Orange Street
London WC2H 7HH

Tel: 020 7766 7070 • Fax: 020 7766 7071
email: office@isc.co.uk

HMC
HEADMASTERS' AND HEADMISTRESSES' CONFERENCE
www.hmc.org.uk

The HMC dates from 1869, when the celebrated Edward Thring of Uppingham asked thirty-seven of his fellow headmasters to meet at his house to consider the formation of a 'School Society and Annual Conference'. Twelve headmasters accepted the invitation. From that date there have been annual meetings. Thring's intention was to provide an opportunity for discussion at regular intervals, both on practical issues in the life of a school and on general principles in education. He believed that his guests would discharge their practical business more effectively at a residential meeting where they could also enjoy being in the company of like-minded men. Annual Meetings of the HMC still combine formal debate on current educational questions with the second element of conversational exchanges in an agreeable environment. These gatherings, which up to 1939 were usually at individual schools, then took place at a University. Nowadays they are held in major hotels and conference centres in the Autumn term. In addition to these annual conferences attended by all members, there are local meetings each term arranged by the ten branches or Divisions into which the country is divided.

Present full membership of the HMC is a total of two hundred and sixty, which now includes headmasters and headmistresses of boys', girls' and co-educational schools. In considering applications for election to membership, the Committee has regard to the degree of independence enjoyed by the Head and his/her school. Eligibility also depends on the academic standards obtained in the school, as reflected by the proportion of pupils in the Sixth Form pursuing a course of study beyond GCSE and by the school's public examination results, including A Levels, the International Baccalaureate and the Cambridge Pre-U.

The Constitution provides that the full membership shall consist only of heads of independent schools in the UK and Ireland. At the same time, it is held to be a strength that the Conference includes heads of schools from the maintained sector as well as other influential figures from the world of education. There is provision therefore for the election of a small number of HMC Associates.

In addition the HMC has a number of International members, who are heads of high-quality schools from around the world. The International division meets on two occasions during the academic year and the Chair is a member of the HMC Committee. There is also a small number of Honorary Associates who have been elected to life membership on retirement.

The HMC is closely associated with the other independent sector associations that also belong to the Independent Schools Council (ISC), and with the Association of School and College Leaders (ASCL), which represents the Heads and senior staff of secondary schools and colleges in both the maintained and independent sectors.

The HMC Committee 2014–2015

Chairman	Richard Harman	Uppingham School
Vice-Chairman UK	Tim Hands	Magdalen College School
Chairman-Elect	Chris King	Leicester Grammar School
Treasurer	Stephen Holliday	Queen Elizabeth's Hospital
Chairman – East	Nigel Lashbrook	Oakham School
Secretary – East	Gareth Lloyd	Ratcliffe College
Chairman – Irish	Lindsay Haslett	St Columba's College, Dublin
Secretary – Irish	Moore Dickson	Belfast Royal Academy
Chairman – London	Gary Savage	Alleyn's School
Secretary – London	Michael Punt	Chigwell School
Chairman – North East	Andrew Fleck	Sedbergh School
Secretary – North East	John Hind	Dame Allan's Schools
Chairman – North West	David Cook	Merchant Taylors' School, Crosby
Secretary – North West	Andrew Chicken	Stockport Grammar School
Chairman – Scottish	Colin Mair	High School of Glasgow
Secretary – Scottish	Ken Greig	Hutchesons' Grammar School
Chairman – South Central	Julian Thould	King Edward VI School, Southampton
Secretary – South Central	Fiona Boulton	Guildford High School
Chairman – South East	Mike Buchanan	Ashford School
Secretary – South East	Shaun Fenton	Reigate Grammar School
Chairman – South West	Elizabeth Cairncross	Wells Cathedral School
Secretary – South West	Mark Moore	Clifton College
Chairman – West	Antony Clark	Malvern College
Secretary – West	Jonathan Lancashire	Dean Close School
Chairman – International	Mark Leppard	Doha College

Co-opted Members

Chairman of Academic Policy	Peter Hamilton	Haberdashers' Aske's Boys' School
Chairman of Professional Development	John Watson	Bablake School
Chairman of Universities	Chris Ramsey	King's School, Chester
Chairman of Inspection	Adam Pettitt	Highgate School
Chairman of Communications	Kevin Fear	Nottingham High School
	Tony Little	Eton College
	Mary Breen	St Mary's School Ascot

General Secretary: William Richardson, BA, DPhil (Tel: 01858 469059)
Membership Secretary: Ian Power, MA (Tel: 01858 465260)

Headmasters' and Headmistresses' Conference
12 The Point, Rockingham Road, Market Harborough, Leicestershire LE16 7QU
Tel: 01858 465260 • Fax: 01858 465759 • email: gensec@hmc.org.uk

GSA
GIRLS' SCHOOLS ASSOCIATION
www.gsa.uk.com

The Girls' Schools Association (GSA) is the professional association of the heads of independent girls' schools in the UK and overseas, and is a constituent member of the Independent Schools Council (ISC).

GSA is a member-led organisation that facilitates mutual professional support, whilst ensuring that it represents the views of practising heads of girls' schools in advising and lobbying educational policy makers. The Association is supported by a professional secretariat that directs and facilitates its work.

The aims of GSA are:
- To provide support and information to heads and their schools.
- To promote the benefits of independent schools and education in a girls-only environment.
- To influence policy and public opinion about education and independent schools for the benefit of members.

GSA schools are widely recognised for their exceptional record of examination achievements. Education, however, is not only about success in exams. Girls' schools offer wider development opportunities, and are special for a number of reasons. They provide an environment in which girls can grow in confidence and ability. In a girls' school, the needs and aspirations of girls are the main focus, and the staff are specialists in the teaching of girls. Girls hold all the senior positions in the school, and are encouraged by positive role models in the schools' teaching staff and management. Expectations are high. In GSA schools, girls do not just have equal opportunities, they have every opportunity. Members of GSA share a commitment to the values and benefits of single-sex schools for girls, and a belief that all girls, regardless of educational setting, deserve the opportunity to realise their potential, to be active and equal, confident and competent leaders, participants and contributors.

Officers 2014

President:	Alice Phillips	St Catherine's, Bramley
Vice-President:	Hilary French	Newcastle High School for Girls GDST
President Elect 2015:	Alun Jones	St Gabriel's School
Treasurer:	Christine Edmundson	Palmers Green High School

Officers 2015

President:	Alun Jones	St Gabriel's School
Vice-President:	Alice Phillips	St Catherine's, Bramley
President Elect 2016:	Caroline Jordan	Headington School
Treasurer:	Christine Edmundson	Palmers Green High School
GDST Representative:	Hilary French	Newcastle High School for Girls GDST

Committee Chairmen

Boarding:	Michael Farmer	St Teresa's Effingham
Education:	Sue Hincks	Bolton School Girls' Division
Inspections:	Claire Hewitt	Manchester High School for Girls
Membership:	Hilary Vipond	St Mary's School, Colchester
Professional Development:	Dorothy MacGinty	St Francis' College
Sports:	Jo MacKenzie	Bedford Girls' School
Universities:	Bobby Georghiou	Bury Grammar School Girls

Regional Representatives

East:	Charlotte Avery	St Mary's School, Cambridge
London:	Heather Hanbury	The Lady Eleanor Holles School
Midlands:	Gwen Byrom	Loughborough High School
North East:	Julie Lodrick	The Mount School, York
North West:	Louise Robinson	Merchant Taylors' Girls' School
Scotland:	Anne Everest	St George's School for Girls, Edinburgh
South Central:	Christina Foord	Tormead School
South East:	Paul Mitchell	Cobham Hall
South West & Wales:	Bee Hughes	The Maynard School

Secretariat

Executive Director:	Charlotte Vere
Membership Director:	Jane Carroll
PA to Executive Director:	Jeven Sharma
Membership Manager:	Kate Williams
Conference & Events Manager:	Emily Hall
Digital Manager:	Imogen Vanderpump
Communications Manager:	Rachel Kerr

Girls' Schools Association
Suite 105, 108 New Walk, Leicester, LE1 7PG
Tel: 0116 254 1619 • email: office@gsa.uk.com

THE SOCIETY OF HEADS

www.thesocietyofheads.org.uk

The Society is an Association of Heads of over 100 well-established independent schools. It was founded in 1961 at a time when the need arose from the vitality and growth of the independent sector in the 1950s and the wish of a group of Heads to share ideas and experience.

The Society continues to provide a forum for the exchange of ideas and consideration of the particular needs of the smaller independent school. These are frequently different from the issues and from the approach of the larger schools. All members value their independence, breadth in education and the pursuit of excellence, particularly in relation to academic standards.

The Society's policy is to maintain high standards in member schools, to ensure their genuine independence, to foster an association of schools which contributes to the whole independent sector by its distinctive character and flexibility, to provide an opportunity for the sharing of ideas and common concerns, to promote links with the wider sphere of higher education, to strengthen relations with the maintained sector and with local communities.

Within the membership there is a wide variety of educational experience. Some schools are young, some have evolved from older foundations, some have behind them a long tradition of pioneer and specialist education, the great majority are now co-educational but we also have all-boys and all-girls schools. A good number of the member schools have a strong boarding element and others are day schools. Some have specific religious foundations and some are non-denominational. All offer a stimulating Sixth Form experience and at the same time give a sound and balanced education to pupils of widely varying abilities and interests.

The Society is one of the constituent Associations of the Independent Schools Council. Every Full Member school has been accredited through inspection by the Independent Schools Inspectorate (or Estyn in Wales and HMIE in Scotland) and is subject to regular visits to monitor standards and ensure that good practice and sound academic results are maintained. The Society is also represented on many other educational bodies.

All members are in membership of the Association of School and College Leaders (ASCL) or other unions for school leaders and Full Member schools belong to AGBIS or an equivalent professional body supporting governance.

There are also categories of Additional, Overseas and Conference Membership to which Heads are elected whose schools do not fulfil all the criteria for Full Membership but whose personal contribution to the Society is judged to be invaluable. They are recorded separately at the end of the entries.

The Society has a one-day meeting for members in the autumn and summer terms and organises a two-day residential conference in the Easter term.

Officers 2014–2015

Chairman: Michael Windsor, Reading Blue Coat School
Vice-Chairman: Richard Palmer, St Christopher School
Chairman Designate: Dominic Findlay, Langley School
Hon Treasurer: Stephen Fairclough, Abbotsholme School

Committee 2014–2015

Kathryn Bell, Burgess Hill School for Girls
Graham Best, St John's College, Southsea
Sami Cohen, d'Overbroeck's College
Philip Cottam, Halliford School
Gregg Davies, Shiplake College
Damian Ettinger, Cokethorpe School
Gerry Holden, Dover College
Lynne Horner, Westholme School
Roland Martin, Rendcomb College
Adrian Meadows, The Peterborough School

Secretariat

General Secretary: Dr Peter Bodkin

The Society of Heads

12 The Point, Rockingham Road, Market Harborough, Leicestershire LE16 7QU
Tel: 01858 433760 • Fax: 01858 461413 • email: gensec@thesocietyofheads.org.uk

Members who are also members of the Headmasters' and Headmistresses' Conference:

Keith J Budge, Bedales Schools

David Buxton, St Columba's College

Martin G Cooke, Clayesmore School

Philip Cottam, Halliford School

Gregg Davies, Shiplake College

Damian Ettinger, Cokethorpe School

Susan Freestone, King's Ely

John Green, Seaford College

Mark Hoskins, Reed's School

Iain Kilpatrick, Sidcot School

Richard Laithwaite, Kirkham Grammar School

Patrick Lee-Browne, Rydal Penrhos School

Roderick MacKinnon, Bristol Grammar School

Anton Maree, Ackworth School

Roland Martin, Rendcomb College

Mark Mortimer, Warminster School

Joe A Peake, St George's College

Clive Rickart, Lincoln Minster School

Chris Staley, Wisbech Grammar School

Darryl Wideman, Silcoates School

Nigel Williams, Leighton Park School

Michael Windsor, Reading Blue Coat School

Members who are also members of the Girls' Schools Association:

Kathryn Bell, Burgess Hill School for Girls

Lucy Elphinstone, Francis Holland School Sloane Square

Ann Clark, King Edward VI High School for Girls

Jonathan Forster, Moreton Hall

Lynne Horner, Westholme School

Toby Nutt, Stonar School

Sarah Raffray, St Augustine's Priory School

Associate Members

S Aiano (formerly Headmaster, Bearwood College)

G Allen (formerly Headmaster, The Roman Ridge School)

J C Baggaley (formerly Headmaster, Silcoates School)

S Bailey (formerly Headmaster, The Royal Wolverhampton School)

R D Balaam (formerly Headmaster, Royal Russell School)

D J Beeby (formerly Headmaster, Clayesmore School)

N Beesley (formerly Headmaster, Beechwood Sacred Heart School)

D Boddy (formerly Headmaster, St James Senior Boys' School)

Sue Bradley (formerly Head, Stover School)

D Bryson (formerly Headmaster, St Andrew's School)

P Cantwell (formerly Headmaster, The King's School, Tynemouth)

D Chapman (formerly Headmaster, Hampshire Collegiate School)

N Chisholm, (formerly Headmaster, Yehudi Menuhin School)

R Clark (formerly Headmaster, Battle Abbey School)

A Clemit (formerly Headmaster, Longridge Towers School)

D G Crawford (formerly Headmaster, Colston's School)

N Dorey (formerly Headmaster, Bethany School)

G Doodes (formerly Headmaster, Milton Abbey School)

J Dunston (formerly Headmaster, Leighton Park School)

M Eagers (formerly Headmaster, Box Hill School)

N England (formerly Headmaster, Ryde School)

Sarah Evans (formerly Principal, King Edward VI High School for Girls)

D J Farrant (formerly Headmaster, Abbotsholme School)

R Gould (formerly Headmaster, Stanbridge Earls School)

A Graham (formerly Headmaster, Windermere St Anne's School)

C Greenfield (International College, Sherborne School)

R Hadfield (formerly Headmaster, The Read School)

T Halliwell (formerly Principal, Welbeck Defence Sixth Form College)

N Hammond (formerly Headmaster, Wisbech Grammar School)

P Harvey (formerly Headmaster, St Edward's School)

Carole Hawkins (formerly Head, Royal School, Hampstead)

R Haworth (formerly Headmaster, Hull Collegiate School)

J Hewitt (formerly Headmaster, Bredon School)

Revd P C Hunting (formerly Headmaster, St George's College)

D Jarrett (formerly Headmaster, Reed's School)

C Johnson (formerly Headmaster, The Duke of York's Royal Military School)

S Jones (formerly Headmaster, Dover College)

T Kernohan (formerly Headmaster, Fulneck School)

M A B Kirk (formerly Headmaster, Royal Hospital School)

T Kirkup (formerly Headmaster, Scarborough College)

G Link (formerly Headmaster, Stanbridge Earls School)

M Long (formerly Headmaster, Tettenhall College)

C Lumb (formerly Headmaster, St Joseph's College, Ipswich)

H MacDonald (formerly Principal, Hampshire Collegiate School)

J McArthur (formerly Headmaster, Reading Blue Coat School)

A McGrath (formerly Headmaster, Leighton Park School)

Linde Melhuish (formerly Principal, Padworth College)

E Mitchell (formerly Headmaster, Abbey Gate College)

H Moxon (formerly Headmaster, Stanbridge Earls School)

I Mullins (Licenced Victuallers' School)

T Mullins (formerly Headmaster Seaford College)

T Packer (formerly Headmaster, Teesside High School)

J Payne (formerly Headmaster, Pierrepoint School)

The Hon Martin Penney (formerly Headmaster, Bearwood College)

I Power (formerly Headmaster, Lord Wandsworth College)

M Priestley (formerly Headmaster, Warminster School)

A Reid (formerly Headmaster, Hebron School)

C Reid (formerly Headmaster, St Christopher School)

Lynne Renwick (formerly Head, Our Lady's Abingdon School)

R Repper (formerly Headmaster, Wisbech Grammar School)

D Richardson (formerly General Secretary, The Society of Heads)

D Robb (formerly Headmaster, Oswestry School)

C Robinson (formerly Headmaster, Hipperholme Grammar School)

Maureen Sheridan (formerly Headmistress, St Joseph's College Reading)

J Shinkwin (formerly Headmaster, Princethorpe College)

P Skelker (formerly Headmaster, Immanuel College)

P Spillane (formerly Headmaster, Silcoates School)

P Stockdale (formerly Headmaster, Oswestry School)

M Symonds (formerly Headmaster, Bedstone College)

Elizabeth Thomas (formerly Head, Stonar School)

N Thorne (formerly Headmaster, St John's College, Southsea)

J Tolputt (formerly Headmaster, The Purcell School)

D Vanstone (formerly Headmaster, North Cestrian Grammar School)

R Walker (formerly Headmaster, Portland Place School)

D Ward (formerly Headmaster, Saint Felix School)

N Ward (formerly Headmaster, The Royal Hospital School)

A Waters (formerly Headmaster, Kingsley School)

Ed Wesson (formerly Headmaster, The King's School, Tynemouth)

G Wigley (formerly Headmaster, Friends' School)

S Wormleighton (formerly Headmaster, Grenville College)

IAPS
INDEPENDENT ASSOCIATION OF PREP SCHOOLS
www.iaps.org.uk

Together, IAPS schools represent a multi-billion pound enterprise. Our schools educate more than 150,000 children and employ more than 15,000 members of staff.

As the voice of independent prep school education, IAPS has national influence and actively defends and promotes the interests of our members. We lobby the government on their behalf and promote prep school issues on a national and international stage. We work directly with ministers and national policy advisers to ensure the needs of the prep school sector are met.

IAPS only accredits those schools that can demonstrate they provide the highest standards of education and care. Our member schools offer an all-round, values-led, broad education, which produces confident, adaptable, motivated children with a lifelong passion for learning. In order to be elected to membership, a Head must be suitably qualified and schools must be accredited through a satisfactory inspection.

Our schools are single-sex and co-educational; boarding, day and mixed; situated in urban and rural areas. Sizes vary from more than 800 to fewer than 100 pupils per school, with the majority between 150 and 400. Most schools are charitable trusts, some are limited companies and a few are proprietary. There are also junior schools attached to senior schools, choir schools, those with a particular religious affiliation and those that offer specialist provision.

With more than 600 members, both in the UK and abroad, IAPS offers excellent opportunities for fellowship and networking. We have one of the independent sector's top training programmes, which includes a broad range of professional development courses. New members are offered an experienced Head as a mentor and members are divided into district groups by geographical location, giving them the chance to meet with fellow heads on a regular basis.

A redeveloped website with a dedicated members' log-on is packed with news, policy examples, advice and support. The site also actively promotes the prep school sector to parents and the media.

The Council and Officers for 2014–2015

President: Stuart Thackrah
Chairman: Mark Brotherton
Chairman-Elect: John Tranmer
Immediate Past Chairman: Eddy Newton
Vice-Chairman: Daphne Cawthorne

Members of Council:

Patrick Atkinson	Peter Jones
John Baugh	Huw Marshall
Heather Beeby	Andrew Potts
Justin Chippendale	Helen Skrine
Maureen Cussans	Finola Stack
Paul David	James Thompson
Andrew Donald	Tim Wheeler
Ben Freeman	Robert Williams
Mark Hartley	Ian Wright

Officers:

Chief Executive: David Hanson
Director of Education: Mark Brotherton (*from Sept 2015*)
Finance and Operations Director: Richard Flower
Courses and Conferences Manager: Larraine Curzon
Membership Officer: Jill Wharfe
Association Administrator: Christine McCrudden

Independent Association of Prep Schools
11 Waterloo Place, Leamington Spa CV32 5LA
Tel: 01926 887833 • Fax: 01926 888014 • email: iaps@iaps.org.uk

ISA
INDEPENDENT SCHOOLS ASSOCIATION
www.isaschools.org.uk

The Independent Schools Association, established in 1879, is one of the oldest of the Headteachers' Associations of independent schools that make up the Independent Schools' Council. It began life as the Association of Principals of Private Schools, which was created to encourage high standards and foster friendliness and cooperation among Heads who had previously worked in isolation. In 1895 it was incorporated as The Private Schools Association and in 1927 the word 'private' was replaced by 'independent'. The recently published History of the Association demonstrates the strong links ISA has with proprietorial schools, which is still the case today, even though the majority are now run by Boards of Governors.

Membership is open to any independent school Head or Proprietor provided they meet the necessary criteria, which includes the accreditation standards of the Independent Schools Inspectorate. ISA's Executive Council is elected by Members and supports all developments of the Association through its Committee structure and the strong regional network of Coordinators and Area Committees. Each of ISA's seven Areas in turn supports Members through regular training events and meetings.

ISA celebrates a wide ranging membership, not confined to any one type of school, but including all: nursery, pre-preparatory, junior, preparatory and senior, all-through schools, co-educational, single-sex, boarding, day, and performing arts and special schools.

Promoting best practice and fellowship remains at the core of the Association, as it did when it began 130 years ago. The 340 Members and their schools enjoy high quality national conferences and courses that foster excellence in independent education. ISA's central office also supports Members and provides advice, and represents the views of its membership at national and governmental levels. Pupils in ISA schools enjoy a wide variety of competitions, in particular the wealth of sporting, artistic and academic activities at Area and National level.

The Council and Officers for 2014–2015

President: Lord Lexden

Vice-Presidents:
Mr C J Ashby BSc PGCE
Mrs M Grant CertEd
Mr M Hewett BA CertEd
Mrs D Leek-Bailey OBE BA PGCE
Mr P Moss Cert Ed

Honorary Officers:
Mr A S Hampton BA LTCL MEd NPQH (*Chair*)
Dr S J Welch BA MA PhD (*Vice-Chair*)
Mr R M Walden MA Cert Ed MEd FCollP (*Vice-Chair*)

Elective Councillors:

Mr R H Brierly BEd
Mr A Gear BEd Cert Ed
Mr M Lloyd BA MA FCollP
Mrs J Lowe Cert Ed
Mr S Nicholson BA MA MBA PGCE
Mrs C Osborn BA MSc PGCE
Professor P Preedy PhD

Mr L Sanders BEd
Ms H Stanton-Tonner BEd
Mr J Ullmer MBE MA LRAM FRSA FCollT NPQH
Mrs S Webb BSc PGCE NPQH
Mr J T Wilding BSc
Dr P Woodroffe MMath Oxon PhD

Area Coordinators:

East Anglia: Mr K M Knight BEd Hons MA NPQH
London North: Mrs L Maggs-Wellings BEd CertEd
London South: Mrs M A Baines BA MBA FRSA
London West: Miss V S Smit BSc

Midlands: Mr M Adshead BA PGCE
North: Mr S Jandrell BA
South West: Mr P Easterbrook BEd DipEd

Officials
Chief Executive Officer: Neil Roskilly BA PGCE NPQH FRSA FRGS
Membership Officer: Carey Dickinson MA Oxon PGCE
Professional Development Officer: Alice Jeffries BA
Marketing and Communications Officer: Angie Shatford BA
Executive Assistant to the CEO: Karen Goddard BA
Accountant: Ghavini Mistry BA

Independent Schools Association
1 Boys' British School, East Street, Saffron Walden, Essex CB10 1LS
Tel: 01799 523619 • email: isa@isaschools.org.uk

COBIS
COUNCIL OF BRITISH INTERNATIONAL SCHOOLS
website: www.cobis.org.uk
twitter: @CobisDirector

COBIS is a responsive organisation, open to current and future opportunities. The association has developed markedly since its foundation, changing to meet the needs and aspirations of its growing global school membership base.

COBIS exists to serve, support and represent its member schools – their leaders, governors, staff and students by:

- Representing member schools with the British Government, educational bodies and the corporate sector
- Engaging students in challenging and rewarding inter-school competitions, events and activities
- Providing effective professional development for senior leaders, governors, teachers and support staff
- Facilitating, coordinating and supporting professional networking opportunities for British International schools
- Processing Disclosure and Barring checks to promote child protection and safer recruitment and employment practices
- Providing access to information about trends and developments in UK education
- Facilitating mentoring and support programmes for Heads and school leaders
- Promoting career opportunities within the global COBIS network
- Brokering a cost-effective consultancy service between schools and approved educational support service providers

Patron
HRH The Duke of York, KG

COBIS Executive 2014–2015
Honorary President
Sir Roger Fry CBE

Honorary Vice Presidents
The Rt Hon Lord Andrew Adonis
Sir Mervyn Brown KCMG OBE
Michael Cooper OBE
Lord Lexden OBE
The Rt Hon The Lord Macgregor OBE
Dame Judith Mayhew Jonas DBE
Sybil Melchers MBE
Jean Scott
Lord Sharman OBE

Secretariat
CEO: Colin Bell

COBIS Board
Dawn Akyurek, King's College School La Moraleja, Spain
John Bagust, Prague British School, Czech Republic
Elaine Blaus, Cambridge English Language Assessment (*co-opted*)
Jennifer Bray MBE (*Inspections and Quality Officer*)
Brian Christian, Principal, The British School in Tokyo, Japan
Anne Howells, British International School of Stavanger, Norway
Simon O'Grady, The British International School, Cairo, Egypt (*Treasurer*)
Ken Page, Headteacher, British Embassy School, Ankara, Turkey (*co-opted*)
Trevor Rowell, Governor, British School of Alicante, Spain (*Chairman*)
Peter Simpson, The British School in The Netherlands
Dr Steffen Sommer, Collège Champittet, Switzerland (*Vice Chairman*)
Teresa Woulfe, Senior Vice Principal – Head of Secondary, Doha College, Qatar (*co-opted*)

Council of British International Schools
St Mary's University, Strawberry Hill, Twickenham TW1 4SX
Tel: +44(0)20 8240 4142 · Fax: +44(0)20 8240 4255 · email: ceo@cobis.org.uk

AGBIS

ASSOCIATION OF GOVERNING BODIES OF INDEPENDENT SCHOOLS

REGISTERED CHARITY NO. 1108756

www.agbis.org.uk

The Object of the Association is to advance education in independent schools and, in furtherance of that object, but not otherwise, the Association shall have power:

(a) to discuss matters concerning the policy and administration of such schools and to encourage cooperation between their Governing Bodies;
(b) to consider the relationship of such schools to the general educational interests of the community;
(c) to consider and give guidance on matters of general or individual concern to the Governing Bodies of such schools;
(d) to promote good governance in such schools;
and
(e) to express the views of the Governing Bodies of such schools on any of the foregoing matters and to take such action as may be appropriate in their interests.

Full Membership

The Governing Body of any independent school in the United Kingdom may apply for full membership of the Association, subject to conditions determined by the Board. Admission to full membership of AGBIS will be conditional upon the educational and other standards of the school and admission of the Head to membership of the Headmasters' and Headmistresses' Conference, The Girls' Schools Association, The Society of Heads, The Independent Association of Prep Schools or The Independent Schools Association within one year. COBIS Schools and others from outside the United Kingdom should have similar characteristics to those expected of UK applicants.

Associate Membership

Any Independent School in the United Kingdom which is not a charity but whose head is a member of one of the above listed Heads' Associations or is expected to become a member within one year, may apply for Associate Membership of the Association. Such schools must show evidence of the existence of the arrangements for governance which may be in the form of an advisory board or similar.

Any independent school within the United Kingdom which meets the requirements as above, apart from membership of an ISC Heads' Association, and is in membership of either SCIS or WISC, and schools outside the United Kingdom in membership of COBIS, BISW or similar organisations and which are inspected by ISI, at the discretion of the AGBIS Board, may also apply for Associate Membership. The Membership Criteria are displayed on the AGBIS website.

Board

Chairman: Richard Green (Prior's Field School)
Deputy Chairman: Miss Margaret Rudland (St Margaret's School Bushey)
Honorary Treasurer: Michael Goolden (Benenden School)

Yvonne Burne (Berkhamsted School)
Roger Chapman (The Mill Hill School Foundation)
Lorna Cocking (Girls' Day School Trust)
Jonathan Cook (Walhampton School & Lymington Infant School)
Michael Jeans MBE (Chairman Haberdashers' Education Committee)
David Jennings (Summer Fields School)
Keith Oliver (Fettes College)
Nigel Richardson (Haileybury & Magdalen College School)
Jon Scott (Leicester Grammar School)
David Taylor (St Lawrence College, Sutton Valence School, Queen Ann's Caversham)
Paul Voller (Box Hill School)
Peter Williamson (Chairman ISI)
Ken Young (The Royal Russell School)

General Secretary: Stuart Westley
Training Secretary: Patrick Walker

Association of Governing Bodies of Independent Schools
The Grange, 3 Codicote Road, Welwyn, Hertfordshire AL6 9LY
Tel: 01438 840730 • email: gensec@agbis.org.uk

ISBA

INDEPENDENT SCHOOLS' BURSARS ASSOCIATION

www.theisba.org.uk

The Independent Schools' Bursars Association (ISBA) is the only national association to represent school bursars and business managers of independent schools, providing them with the professional support they need to manage their schools successfully and provide a world class education to their pupils.

The association can trace its history back seventy years to the founding of the Public Schools Bursars' Association which held its first general meeting on 26 April 1932 at the offices of Epsom College. Its name then changed to the Independent Schools' Bursars Association in 1983.

The ISBA now has more than 970 independent school members, covering more than 1000 schools, including some 35 overseas associate members, from smaller preparatory schools to larger and well-renowned senior schools, including both boarding and day schools. Although it is the school and not the bursar who becomes a member of the association, it is usually the bursar or equivalent who is the school's nominated representative.

The association is one of the constituent members of the Independent Schools Council (ISC) and also works closely with the other seven constituent associations of the ISC. It is represented on the ISC Governing Council and a number of ISC committees and is also often called on to represent the ISC at meetings with the Department for Education, Health & Safety Executive and Teachers' Pensions providing advice on bursarial matters.

Full membership of the ISBA is open to schools who are members of one of the constituent associations in membership of the ISC. Associate membership is open to certain other schools/organisations which are recognised as educational charities.

Day-to-day the ISBA advises many different staff within a school's senior management team including the bursar, finance director, chief operations officer, business manager, deputy or assistant with areas of responsibility encompassing accounting, financial management and reporting, risk management, regulatory compliance, facilities management, HR, technology, environmental sustainability, auxiliary services and more. As part of its range of support services the association offers schools:

- guidance and legislative briefings, and model policies to download from its online reference library;
- a comprehensive professional development programme covering finance, legal, HR, inspections and other key operational issues and tailored to suit staff at all levels;
- information, advice and networking opportunities at the ISBA Annual Conference (the 2015 conference will be held at the Celtic Manor, Newport, Wales on Wednesday 13th and Thursday 14th May 2015);
- a 'Bursar's Guide' – providing the latest information on legislation affecting schools;
- termly copies of the ISBA's magazine – The Bursar's Review – and regular e-newsletters covering the latest legal, financial and HR news and more;
- an online job vacancies page where schools can advertise any of their vacant bursary management roles for free.

The Executive Committee of the ISBA consists of the Chairman of the Association, Mark Taylor, the Bursar of The King's School, Canterbury and the bursars of eleven other leading independent schools.

The Independent Schools' Bursars Association is a Registered Charity, number 1121757,
and a Company Limited by Guarantee, registered in England and Wales, number 6410037.

General Secretary: Mr Mike Lower

Independent Schools' Bursars Association
Unit 11–12, Manor Farm, Cliddesden, Basingstoke, Hampshire RG25 2JB
Tel: 01256 330369 • email: office@theisba.org.uk

BSA

BOARDING SCHOOLS' ASSOCIATION

www.boarding.org.uk

The Boarding Schools' Association is the United Kingdom Association serving and representing member boarding schools, training boarding staff and promoting boarding education.

Full school membership of the Association is open only to schools accredited by one of the constituent associations of the Independent Schools Council or the State Boarding Schools' Association.

The Boarding Schools' Association has Associate Membership of the Independent Schools Council.

Aims

The BSA exists to:

- To help member schools provide the best quality of boarding education and meet the highest standards of welfare for boarders by providing a comprehensive programme of professional development for all staff and governors of boarding schools
- To conduct appropriate research and produce regular publications on boarding issues and good practice in boarding
- To liaise with other bodies concerned with boarding – the Independent Schools Inspectorate, the Independent Schools Council, Ofsted
- To engage in a regular dialogue with government on boarding issues
- To provide a platform informing parents and prospective boarders of the benefits of twenty-first century boarding and offer a conduit to individual member schools for further enquiry
- To forge links with associations of boarding schools worldwide
- To speak for boarding in today's world

Membership

Membership is open to all schools with boarders which are members of Associations within the Independent Schools Council (ISC), to schools in membership of the Scottish Council of Independent Schools (SCIS), and also to state-maintained boarding schools in membership of the State Boarding Schools' Association (SBSA). Membership may also be offered to boarding schools overseas at the discretion of the Executive Committee. Current membership comprises over 460 schools (fully boarding, weekly/flexi boarding, or day schools with boarding provision; co-educational or single-sex; preparatory or secondary).

Associate Membership is available to individuals, schools and other bodies at the discretion of the Executive Committee. They will be entitled to receive all Association mailings. Associate membership is open to former heads of member schools and anyone else interested in supporting the cause of boarding.

Support for Schools

The Professional Development Programme

In partnership with Roehampton University, the BSA has established a Professional Development Programme for all staff working in boarding schools. These BSA courses lead to university validated Certificates of Professional Practice in Boarding Education. There is a programme of Day Courses on a range of topics including Child Protection, Anti-Bullying strategies, the role of Gap Assistants, Boarding Legislation and Good Practice, Boarding Governance. There are also individual courses tailored to the particular needs of a school or group of schools.

BSA training is available to all staff who work in boarding schools and to the Governors of boarding schools.

BSA Training Programmes are also used by schools and boarding associations throughout the world.

Residential Conferences

Five conferences are held annually for:
Heads of Boarding Schools and representatives of their member associations
Deputy Heads & Heads of Boarding
SBSA conference
Boarding House Staff
Nurses & Matrons

Publications

These include:

- **Duty of Care**
  by Dr Tim Hawkes (amended by Tim Holgate)
- **Running a School Boarding House – A legal Guide for Housemasters and Housemistresses**
  by Robert Boyd, Revised by Veale Wasbrough Lawyers 2009
- **Parenting the Boarder**
  by Libby Purves
- **Being a Boarder**
  by Rose Heiney
- **"Boarding Now"** – an online production
- **Boarding Briefing Papers** – are published at regular intervals on matters concerning boarding legislation and good practice which includes **"A Guide for Schools on Parental Responsibility and other Family Law Issues"** by Farrer & Co 2011

National Boarding Standards

The Association meets regularly with the Department for Education to discuss issues concerned with boarding. It also liaises with Local Government, ISI (Independent Schools Inspectorate), Ofsted (Office for Standards in Education), CEAS (Children's Education Advisory Service) and all the national educational organisations.

Liaison with National Bodies

The Association meets regularly with the Department for Education to discuss issues concerned with boarding. It also liaises with Local Government, ISI (Independent Schools Inspectorate), Ofsted (Office for Standards in Education), CEAS (Children's Education Advisory Service) and all the national educational organisations.

Organisation

At the Annual General Meeting, held at the Heads' Annual Conference, Officers of the Association are elected together with the Executive Committee The Honorary Treasurer is usually a Bursar from a member school.

National Director
Robin Fletcher, email: robin@boarding.org.uk

Director of Training
Alex Thomson OBE, email: alex@boarding.org.uk

The Boarding Schools' Association
4th Floor, 134–136 Buckingham Palace Road, London SW1W 9SA
Tel: 020 7798 1580 · Fax: 020 7798 1581

THE GIRLS' DAY SCHOOL TRUST (GDST)

www.gdst.net

Vice-Presidents:	Dr Anne Hogg, MA, PhD
	Lady Warnock, DBE, MA, BPhil, Hon FBA
Chairman:	Dr Tim Miller
Deputy Chairmen:	Jane Richardson, FCA, JP
	Tom Wheare, MA, DipEd, FRSA
Chief Executive:	Helen Fraser, CBE

The GDST (Girls' Day School Trust) is the leading group of independent girls' schools in the UK, with over 3,700 staff, and nearly 20,000 students between the ages of three and 18.

One of the UK's largest educational charities, we own and run a network of 24 schools and two academies in England and Wales, reinvesting all our income into them. Founded in 1872, the GDST has a long history of pioneering innovation in the education of women, and is the largest single educator of girls in the UK.

At the GDST our aim is not just to provide an outstanding academic education, and we pride ourselves in creating a learning environment specifically designed and dedicated to the development of confident, courageous, composed and committed girls, who can meet and overcome the demands life will make of them.

While our schools and academies are all individual, the commitment to developing the whole person is part of our shared DNA. We have a strong network for sharing knowledge and for spreading best practice (whether it is excellence in sports, supporting all our medical school applicants to obtain places, or maximising our girls' potential in public exams). We can also develop and promote talented teachers through this network.

We celebrate our girls' differences, reinforce their strengths, and help them overcome their challenges. And, because we're single-sex, girls can be themselves, and grow at their own pace. They're not cloistered – far from it – but their individual characters can take shape in a way that isn't possible in a mixed environment. For example, girls at GDST schools and academies over twice as likely to study A Level physics or chemistry than girls nationally, and overall nearly half the students in GDST Sixth Forms taking at least one science A Level.

Our girls are great to talk to. In fact, they illustrate us better than anything we could write. They'll tell you how exhilarating it is. They'll tell you how much fun they have, and how much encouragement they're given. They'll almost certainly tell you how lucky they feel.

Every girl is different – good at some things, less good or less keen on others – but we make sure that, regardless, she is the best she can be, and that she tries things, reaches for things, achieves things she may have thought beyond her. And when she does this, she grows in confidence and maturity in a way that will stay with her forever.

GDST schools

Blackheath High School	Nottingham Girls' High School
Brighton & Hove High School	Oxford High School
Bromley High School	Portsmouth High School
Croydon High School	Putney High School
Howell's School, Llandaff, Cardiff	The Royal High School, Bath
Ipswich High School	Sheffield High School
Kensington Prep School	Shrewsbury High School
Newcastle High School for Girls	South Hampstead High School
Northampton High School	Streatham & Clapham High School
Northwood College for Girls	Sutton High School
Norwich High School for Girls	Sydenham High School
Notting Hill & Ealing High School	Wimbledon High School

GDST academies

The Belvedere Academy, Liverpool

Birkenhead High School Academy

Information on the schools can be found in the Yearbook or on the GDST website: www.gdst.net

The Girls' Day School Trust is a Registered Charity, number 306983.

The Girls' Day School Trust
100 Rochester Row London SW1P 1JP
Tel: 020 7393 6666 • email: info@wes.gdst.net

INDEPENDENT SCHOOLS EXAMINATIONS BOARD

www.iseb.co.uk

COMMON ENTRANCE

COMMON PRE-TESTS

COMMON ACADEMIC SCHOLARSHIP

Executive Chairman:
Mr J P Kirk, BSc Hons, FRSA

Chief Administrator:
Mrs A Entwisle, BA Hons, PGCE

COMMON ENTRANCE

The Common Entrance Examinations are used for transfer to senior schools at the ages of 11+ and 13+. The syllabuses are devised and regularly monitored by the Independent Schools Examinations Board which comprises members of the Headmasters' and Headmistresses' Conference, the Girls' Schools Association and the Independent Association of Prep Schools.

The papers are set by examiners appointed by the Board, but the answers are marked by the senior school for which a candidate is entered. A list of schools using the examination is given below. Common Entrance is not a public examination as, for example, GCSE, and candidates may normally be entered only if they have been offered a place at a senior school, subject to their passing the examination.

Candidates normally take the examination in their own junior or preparatory schools, either in the UK or overseas.

Common Entrance at 11+ consists of papers in English, Mathematics and Science. At 13+, in addition to these core subjects, a wide range of additional papers is available in modern and classical languages, and the humanities subjects. Tiered papers are available for many subjects.

Mandarin Chinese is offered as an online examination which can be taken at any age.

Dates

The 11+ examination is held in early November or mid-January.

The 13+ examination commences either on the first Monday in November, the last Monday in January or on the first Monday in June.

Entries

In cases where candidates are at schools in membership of the Independent Association of Prep Schools, it is usual for heads of these schools to make arrangements for entering candidates for the appropriate examination after consultation with parents and senior school heads. In the case of candidates at schools which do not normally enter candidates, it is the responsibility of parents to arrange for candidates to be entered for the appropriate examination in accordance with the requirements of senior schools.

Conduct of the Examination

Regulations for the conduct of the examination are laid down by the Independent Schools Examinations Board.

Past Papers and Other Resources

Copies of past Common Entrance papers can be purchased from Galore Park Publishing:

website: www.galorepark.co.uk;

email: customer.services@galorepark.co.uk;

Tel: 020 7873 6405

ISEB-endorsed Common Entrance revision guides and practice exercises are available from a number of publishers, listed on the ISEB website.

COMMON PRE-TESTS

The Common Pre-Tests are age-standardised tests used to assess pupils' attainment and potential when they are in Year 6 or Year 7, prior to entry to their senior schools. Pupils who sit the tests will normally still be required to sit the Common Entrance examinations.

ISEB commissions the tests from GL Assessment which has long been associated with providing high-quality and reliable assessments in education. The tests are taken online, usually in the child's current school, and include multiple-choice tests in Mathematics, English, verbal and non-verbal reasoning. Senior schools will inform parents if their son or daughter needs to be entered for the tests.

No special preparation is needed for the tests and no past papers are available. Examples and practice questions are provided during the testing period so that candidates understand what they have to do.

Further details are available for schools in the Schools section of the ISEB website and for parents in the Parents section of the ISEB website.

COMMON ACADEMIC SCHOLARSHIP

ISEB sets Scholarship examination papers at 13+ which a number of independent senior schools use to assess potential scholars. Papers are set in English, Mathematics, Science, History, Geography, Religious Studies, French and Latin. Questions are based on the Common Entrance syllabuses and past papers are available from Galore Park Publications.

Candidates are entered by the senior schools for which they are registered and the papers are marked by the senior schools themselves.

Fees

The Independent Schools Examinations Board decides the fees to be charged for each candidate. Schools are notified annually in the spring term of fees payable for the following three terms. Parents seeking information about current fees should look on the ISEB website or contact the ISEB office.

Correspondence

Correspondence about academic matters relating to the Common Entrance examinations and requests for further information about the administration of the examinations should be addressed (as above) to the Chief Administrator, ISEB.

Independent Schools Examinations Board

The Pump House, 16 Queen's Avenue, Christchurch, Hampshire BH23 1BZ

Tel: 01202 487538 • Fax: 01202 473728 • email: enquiries@iseb.co.uk

CATHOLIC INDEPENDENT SCHOOLS' CONFERENCE

www.cisc.uk.net

Objects

The CISC exists to:
- promote the work of Catholic independent schools throughout the UK;
- give and coordinate support and advice to member schools;
- organise activities for member schools including an annual conference, retreats and study days;
- represent the interests of CISC schools as appropriate;
- provide a help line for those seeking a Catholic Independent School for their children.

Schools

There are 140 schools currently in membership of the CISC. Schools in membership include day and boarding schools, single-sex and co-educational, senior and junior schools and special schools.

Membership

There are two categories of Members: Full Members and Associate Members.

Full Members

Full Members may be invited by the Committee to take up membership. He/She will be the Head or Principal of a school which satisfies the following seven conditions:

(a) The school shall be recognised by the local Catholic bishop as being Catholic.
(b) The school shall have been recognised as a charitable foundation by the Charity Commissioners.
(c) The school shall be independent.
(d) The school shall be in the United Kingdom.
(e) The school will have been subjected to a nationally accredited inspection and found to be in good standing.
(f) The expectation is that the head of the school will be a practising Catholic. Where governors appoint a head who is not a Catholic, CISC will expect governors to provide training and support for the head to enable the head to lead a Catholic school, and will assist them in so doing.
(g) Full members only attend the AGM.

Associate Members

Associate Members may be invited by the Chairman to take up membership, but do not attend the AGM.
The following are eligible for associate membership:

(a) Heads of proprietary-owned schools, which meet the conditions of Full Membership apart from not being recognised by the Charity Commissioners as a charitable foundation.
(b) Retired full Members.
(c) Catholics, and other Christians, who are in sympathy with the aims of CISC.
(d) Heads of Foundation or Voluntary-Aided Schools, which meet the conditions of Full Membership, apart from not being recognised by the Charity Commissioners as a charitable foundation.
(e) Heads of Catholic Independent Schools outside the United Kingdom.

Officers for 2014–2015

Chairman: Mr Chris Cleugh, MSc – St Benedict's School
Vice-Chair and Chairman Elect: Ms Antonia Beary, MPhil – St Leonards-Mayfield School
Treasurer: Mr Michael Connolly, BSc, BA, MA, MEd – Cranmore School

Committee:
Mrs Sarah Conrad, BA Hons, PGCE, NPQH – New Hall Preparatory School
Ms Sarah Gallagher, BA, MA – Marymount International School
Mr Antony Hudson, MA, PGCE, NPQH – St George's Junior School
Mr Michael Kennedy, BSc, MA, NPQH, CChem, MRSC – St Mary's College Crosby
Mr Gareth Lloyd, BA Hons, MSc, FMusTCL – Ratcliffe College
Mr Stephen Oliver, BA, MLitt – Our Lady's Abingdon

General Secretary:
Mr John Shinkwin, MA

Catholic Independent Schools' Conference
11 Osler Close, Bramley, Tadley, RG26 5QG
Tel: 01256 880209 • email: johnshinkwin@cisc.uk.net

CHOIR SCHOOLS' ASSOCIATION

www.choirschools.org.uk

Patron: The Duchess of Kent

Committee:

Chairman: Tim Cannell, Prebendal School, Chichester

Vice-Chairman: Roger Overend, King's Rochester Preparatory School

Treasurer: Robert Bacon, St Edmund's Junior School, Canterbury

Neil Blundell, Bristol Cathedral Choir School
Neil Chippington, St Paul's Cathedral School, London
Alex Donaldson, Minster School, York
Clive Rickart, Lincoln Minster School

Nick Robinson, King's College School, Cambridge
Paul Smith, Hereford Cathedral School
Stephen Yeo, Exeter Cathedral School
Richard White

CSA Full and Associate Members

Blackburn Cathedral
Bristol Cathedral Choir School
King's College School, Cambridge
St John's College School, Cambridge
St Edmund's Junior School,
 Canterbury
St John's College, Cardiff
St Cedd's School, Chelmsford
Dean Close Preparatory School,
 Cheltenham
The Prebendal School, Chichester
Croydon Minster
The Chorister School, Durham
St Mary's Music School, Edinburgh
King's Ely Junior, Ely
Exeter Cathedral School
The King's School, Gloucester
St James' School, Grimsby
Lanesborough School, Guildford
Chapel Royal, Hampton Court
Hereford Cathedral School

Leicester Cathedral
Lichfield Cathedral School
Lincoln Minster School
Runnymede St Edward's School,
 Liverpool
St Edward's College, Liverpool
The Cathedral School, Llandaff
City of London School
The London Oratory School
St Paul's Cathedral School, London
Westminster Abbey Choir School,
 London
Westminster Cathedral Choir School,
 London
Chetham's School of Music,
 Manchester
St Nicholas Cathedral, Newcastle-
 upon-Tyne
Norwich School
Christ Church Cathedral School,
 Oxford

Magdalen College School, Oxford
New College School, Oxford
The King's School, Peterborough
The Portsmouth Grammar School
Reigate St Mary's Choir School
King's Rochester Preparatory School
Salisbury Cathedral School
Sheffield Cathedral
The Minster School, Southwell
Polwhele House School, Truro
Queen Elizabeth Grammar School,
 Wakefield
Wells Cathedral School
The Pilgrims' School, Winchester
St George's School, Windsor
St Peter's Church, Wolverhampton
The King's School, Worcester
The Minster School, York
Ampleforth College, York

Overseas Members:

St Patrick's Cathedral Choir School, Dublin

The Cathedral Grammar School, Christchurch, New Zealand

National Cathedral School, Washington DC, USA

St Paul's Choir School, Cambridge, MA, USA

St Thomas Choir School, New York, USA

The 45 choir schools in the UK are all attached to cathedrals, churches or college chapels and educate over 20,000 pupils, including 1,300 choristers. Westminster Abbey Choir School is the only school to educate choristers and probationers only. The Association's associate membership includes cathedrals and churches without choir schools.

Choir schools offer a very special opportunity for children who enjoy singing. They receive a first-class academic and all-round education combined with excellent music training. The experience and self-discipline choristers acquire remain with them for life. There is a wide range of schools: some cater for children aged 7-13, others are junior schools with senior schools to 18; most are Church of England but the Roman Catholic, Scottish and Welsh churches are all represented.

Most CSA members are fee-paying schools and Deans and Chapters provide fee assistance while Government support comes in the shape of the Choir Schools' Scholarship Scheme. Under the umbrella of the Music and Dance Scheme, funds are available to help those who cannot afford even the reduced school fees. The Government funding, along with other monies in its Bursary Trust Fund, is administered by the CSA. Each application is means-tested and an award made once a child has secured a place at a choir school.

Each CSA member school has its own admissions procedure for choristers. However, every child will be assessed both musically and academically. A growing number of children are given informal voice tests which enable the organist or director of music to judge whether they have the potential to become choristers. Some are offered places immediately or will be urged to enter the more formal voice trial organised by the school. In some cases a family may be advised not to proceed. Alternatively, the child's voice may be more suitable for one of the other choir schools.

A number of special ingredients help make a good chorister: potential, a keen musical ear and an eagerness to sing. A clutch of music examination certificates is not vital – alertness and enthusiasm are! At the same time, school staff must be satisfied that a new recruit can cope with school work and the many other activities on offer as well as the demanding choir workload.

To find out more about choir schools please visit the CSA website: **www.choirschools.org.uk**

The Association publishes a newsletter – *Singing Out*

CSA members can be contacted direct or you can write, email or telephone
for further information about choir schools to:

Jane Capon, Information Officer, Village Farm, The Street, Market Weston, Diss, Norfolk IP22 2NZ
Telephone: 01359 221333; email: info@choirschools.org.uk

Mrs Susan Rees, Administrator, 39 Grange Close, Winchester, Hampshire SO23 9RS
Tel: 01962 890530; email: admin@choirschools.org.uk

COUNCIL FOR INDEPENDENT EDUCATION
(CIFE)

www.cife.org.uk

President:
Lord Lexden OBE

Vice President:
Hugh Monro, MA

Chairman:
Stuart Nicholson, MA Oxon, MBA, PGCE, NPQH
Principal, Cambridge Centre for Sixth-form Studies

Vice-Chairman:
Sally Powell, BA, PGCE, MPhil, DPhil Oxon
Principal, Collingham

Independent sixth-form colleges are extremely well placed to offer what is needed for students preparing for university and beyond. The best such colleges are members of CIFE, the Council for Independent Education, an organisation which was founded 40 years ago. There are 18 CIFE colleges, geographically spread across the country, each one offering individual features but all subject to high standards of accreditation. For example, there are some colleges that specialise in students wishing to retake in order to improve exam grades, some offering GCSE and pre-GCSE programmes as well as full A Level courses, which may be residential, homestay, day, or a mix of all three. Several colleges offer foundation programmes and are twinned with universities. In short, CIFE colleges offer a wide range of educational environments in which students can succeed.

Teaching in CIFE colleges really helps and supports students since teaching groups are small and teachers highly experienced and specialists in their subject. The 'tutorial' system derives directly from Oxbridge where it continues to be world famous. A student in a small group receives a greater degree of individual attention. Regular testing ensures that she/ he maintains good progress, and the emphasis on study skills provides essential support for the AS/A2 subjects.

It is not surprising that a student gains confidence and self-belief within such an environment. Colleges engender a strong work ethic in their student communities. Many of the minor rules and regulations essential for schools are not necessary at CIFE colleges. Good manners and an enthusiastic attitude are every bit as important, but uniform, strict times for eating or homework, assemblies or games participation are not part of the picture. It can be seen from the large numbers of students going on to higher education from CIFE colleges that universities regard our students highly.

Increasing numbers of young people are deciding to move school at the age of 16, not because they are unhappy with their school, but because they see the need for a change at this stage. It may be that they wish to study a subject which their school does not offer, such as Accounting, Law, Psychology or Photography. Perhaps they are looking for a more adult environment or one where they can focus on their academic subjects to the exclusion of other things. However, it would be misleading to suggest that CIFE colleges are lacking in extra-curricular activities of all sorts, sporting, social and creative. All colleges recognise the need for enrichment. The difference is that activities are at the choice of the student.

As with schools, choosing a college calls for careful research. CIFE colleges undergo regular inspection either by the Independent Schools Inspectorate, Ofsted and/or the British Accreditation Council, recognised bodies which regulate the provision and standards of teaching, safety and pastoral care. While each college has its own individual character, all share the desire to provide each individual student with a superb preparation for higher education.

Members of CIFE

Ashbourne Independent Sixth Form College, London
Bales College, London
Bath Academy, Bath
Bosworth Independent College, Northampton
Brooke House College, Market Harborough
Cambridge Centre for Sixth-form Studies, Cambridge
Cambridge Tutors College, London
Carfax Tutorial Establishment, Oxford
Chelsea Independent College, London
Collingham, London
DLD College, London (Belgravia Campus)
DLD College, London (Marylebone Campus)
Duff Miller Sixth Form College, London
Lansdowne College, London
Mander Portman Woodward, Birmingham
Mander Portman Woodward, London
Oxford International College, Oxford
Oxford Tutorial College, Oxford

Further information can be obtained from:

CIFE
Tel: 020 8767 8666 • email: enquiries@cife.org.uk

UNITED LEARNING

www.unitedlearning.org.uk

Our Ethos

United Learning is a group of schools committed to providing excellent education through which all pupils are able to progress, achieve and go on to succeed in life. Our approach is underpinned by a sense of moral purpose and commitment to doing what is right for children and young people, supporting colleagues to achieve excellence and acting with integrity in all our dealings within and beyond the organisation, in the interests of young people everywhere. We summarise this ethos as 'The Best in Everyone'.

This ethos underpins our core values:
- Ambition – to achieve the best for ourselves and others;
- Confidence – to have the courage of our convictions and to take risks in the right cause;
- Creativity – to imagine possibilities and make them real;
- Respect – of ourselves and others in all that we do;
- Enthusiasm – to seek opportunity, find what is good and pursue talents and interests;
- Determination – to overcome obstacles and reach success.

As a single organisation, we seek to bring together the best of independent and state sectors, respecting both traditions and learning from each. We believe that each of our schools is and should be distinctive – each is committed to developing its own strengths and identity while sharing our core values as institutions which promote service, compassion and generosity.

Academic scholarships, exhibitions and bursaries are awarded at all schools. The tuition fees vary according to age and school; for example tuition fees in the senior schools range from £9,231 to £15,600 (day), and £23,961 to £31,650 (full boarding).

United Learning comprises: UCST (Registered in England No: 2780748. Charity No. 1016538) and ULT (Registered in England No. 4439859. An Exempt Charity). Companies limited by guarantee. VAT number 834 8515 12.

Fairline House, Nene Valley Business Park, Oundle, Peterborough, PE8 4HN
Tel: 01832 864444 • Fax: 01832 864455 • email: admin@unitedlearning.org.uk

INSPIRING FUTURES

offers ISCO Membership, supporting independent and
international schools with their careers service

www.inspiringfutures.org.uk

Council of Trustees

Chairman: M E Hicks, MSc, DPhil

Hon Treasurer: R Martin

Ms E Allen	Prof D Eyre
Ms W Berliner	P Greatrix
C W Conway	K Richardson
Mrs L Croston	J Spence

Chief Executive: Mrs V Isaac

Contacts

Who to ask for information and help
Contact your Regional Director (see below) or the Information Helpline on 01276 687515

Further information on The Inspiring Futures Foundation:
Marketing Events and Impact Director: Alex de Bresser (email: a.deBresser@inspiringfutures.org.uk)

Purpose and Aims

The Inspiring Futures Foundation is a not-for-profit, careers guidance organisation. It exists to help young people make decisions and develop skills which maximize their potential, enhance their employment opportunities and allow them to make a fulfilling contribution to the world in which they live.

In order to do this, Inspiring Futures works with like-minded people and organisations to provide expert careers guidance, innovative learning resources and personal skills training to young people from all backgrounds, particularly those entering higher education.

ISCO Membership for independent and international schools provides a range of careers and higher education related services to complement and reinforce school programmes with impartial and professional expertise.

Services also include Futurewise, a personalised careers guidance programme for students aged 15 to 23. The web-based psychometric profile and one-to-one interview is followed by a wealth of resources and support for the student helping them with subject choices, routes to HE and alternative pathways to a career. The programme is flexible making it suitable for easy lesson planning. Futurewise courses and training events for students and a range of professional services to support independent schools' careers staff are also offered.

Regional Directors

Scotland & Ireland
* *Scotland & Ireland*:

Margaret Graham (Tel: 07717 530459; email: margaret.graham@inspiringfutures.org.uk)
Greta Weir (Tel: 07872 350696; email: greta.weir@inspiringfutures.org.uk)

E Scotland:
Jane Ambrose (Tel: 07887 758166; email: jane.ambrose@inspiringfutures.org.uk)

N Scotland & Central Scotland:
Greta Weir (Tel: 07872 350696; email: greta.weir@inspiringfutures.org.uk)

W Scotland:
Margaret Graham (Tel: 07717 530459; email: margaret.graham@inspiringfutures.org.uk)

England & Wales
North & Midlands
* *North & Midlands*:
Sarah Frend (Tel: 07525 805007; email: sarah.frend@inspiringfutures.org.uk)

Shropshire & Midlands:
Sally Hayward (Tel: 07887 758649; email: sally.hayward@inspiringfutures.org.uk)

North West & Yorkshire:
Rod Morley (Tel: 07702 297558; email: rod.morley@inspiringfutures.org.uk)

East:
Kate Coles (Tel: 07717 468074; email: kate.coles@inspiringfutures.org.uk)

London & South East
* *London & South East*:
Carey Irwin (Tel: 07734 569968; email: carey.irwin@inspiringfutures.org.uk)

Sussex & Kent:
Elizabeth Armstrong (Tel: 07909 972769; email: elizabeth.armstrong@inspiringfutures.org.uk)

West London:
Carol Rogers (Tel: 07702 544191; email: carol.rogers@inspiringfutures.org.uk)

South London:
Emma Fry (Tel: 07702 226271; email: emma-marie.fry@inspiringfutures.org.uk)

North London:
Helen Barham (Tel: 07917 712603; email: helen.barham@inspiringfutures.org.uk)

South West & Wales
* *South-West & Wales*:
Sarah Frend (Tel: 07525 805007; email: sarah.frend@inspiringfutures.org.uk)

Berkshire, Oxfordshire & Wiltshire:
Mark Smith (Tel: 07736 821284; email: mark.smith@inspiringfutures.org.uk)

South West:
Vicki MacDonald (Tel: 07717 496523; email: vicki.macdonald@inspiringfutures.org.uk)

International
* *International*:
John Watson (Tel: 01572 823073; email: john.watson@inspiringfutures.org.uk)

European Director:
Julia Watson (Tel: 01572 823073; email: julia.watson@inspiringfutures.org.uk)

* Area Director

High quality education in an actively Christian environment for all

Information on all of the schools can be found on the website www.woodard.co.uk

Woodard Schools form the largest group of Anglican schools in England and Wales. In addition to the above list of incorporated schools, a number of schools in the independent and maintained sectors choose to be associated or affiliated, respectively. Woodard also sponsors five academies. The schools are not exclusive and take pupils of all faiths and of none. In total some 29,000 pupils are taught in schools throughout the group. In 2011 the members of the wider Woodard family raised sufficient funds to open the Woodard Langalanga Secondary School in Gilgil, Kenya to mark the bicentenary of the birth of the Founder, Canon Nathaniel Woodard. Doors opened to the first intake of pupils in January 2012 and by February 2015 the school will be full with 480 pupils being influenced by the Woodard ethos.

This unique partnership of schools, independent and state, boarding and day, junior and senior, co-educational and single-sex, is united by a determination to provide a first-class holistic education within a distinctive Christian ethos. The schools were founded by Nathaniel Woodard in the nineteenth century and aim to prepare children from a wide variety of backgrounds for responsibility, leadership and service in today's world.

The schools seek to provide flexible, stimulating, demanding and appropriate schemes of academic study together with a rich variety of sporting, artistic and recreational opportunities. We encourage personal success, self-confidence and self-respect whilst also stressing the importance of responsible citizenship, high moral values and a commitment to use one's gifts in the service of others.

With the geographical spread and diversity of schools included in the group it is able to offer parents a wide range of educational options for their children. Woodard incorporated schools operate bursary and scholarship schemes including all classes of concession. Fees vary from school to school and are set locally.

The Woodard Corporation is a Registered Charity (No. 1096270) and Company (No. 4659710). The objects of the charity are to promote and extend education (including spiritual, moral, social, cultural and physical education) in accordance with the doctrines and principles of the Church of England/Church in Wales by directly or indirectly carrying on schools.

ASSOCIATION FOR MARKETING AND DEVELOPMENT IN INDEPENDENT SCHOOLS (AMDIS)

FOUNDED 1993

www.amdis.co.uk

Objectives:

- To promote and develop good marketing practice in admissions, marketing and development in independent education
- To help increase the effectiveness of the marketing representatives of Member Schools
- To encourage personal development within the schools' marketing profession

Achieved through:

- Seminars and workshops on a variety of marketing-led subjects held throughout the year
- Annual residential conference
- Regional networking lunches
- Training – Diploma in Schools' Marketing & Certificate in Admissions Management
- Helpline
- Website with member-only resource section
- LinkedIn Group Forum
- On-line News bulletins throughout the year
- Speakers provided for conferences, inset days and similar

Membership:

- School Membership, renewable annually by subscription
- Corporate Membership, renewable annually by subscription

The Association is directed by a Chairman, Vice Chairman and Treasurer together with a Board of Directors.

Managing Director: Tory Gillingham

AMDIS

2 St Michael's Street, Malton, North Yorkshire YO17 7LJ

Tel: 01653 699800 • email: enquiries@amdis.co.uk

ASSOCIATION OF REPRESENTATIVES OF OLD PUPILS' SOCIETIES (AROPS)

Founded in 1971

www.arops.org.uk

President: John Kidd (Old Portmuthian)

Vice-Presidents:

Guy Cliff (Old Silcoatian), Michael Freegard (Old Haileyburian),

Roger Moulton (Old Pauline)

Committee

Chairman: Bill Gillen (Old Arnoldian and Old Instonian)

Secretary: Keith Balkham (KGS Friends)

and 12 committee members

Administrator: Dina Stovell (arops@arops.org.uk)

Aim: To provide a forum for the exchange of views and experiences between representatives of old pupils' societies.

Membership: Open to representatives of any school alumni society. New members are always welcome. Details are available on the new website – www.arops.org.uk – where you can also find information on events and member societies' news, regularly updated.

Meetings:

The Conference in May is our main event and an ideal opportunity to meet up with other representatives and to share thoughts on current topics. Our very successful Conference in 2014 was held at Bristol Grammar School where sessions included 'adapting to survive', practical solutions for using free social media, an independent appraisal of alumni software, sports and music events and archiving. The Conferences always end with a lively forum and a dinner. The 2015 Conference will be held at The Leys School, Cambridge on Saturday, 9th May.

Apart from the Conference and the AGM (held in London in October), AROPS now organises a series of regional meetings around the country which allow representatives to meet neighbouring members in a less formal environment. These have proved very popular.

Subscription:

£50 per year (with discounts for smaller societies). Please email Dina Stovell, AROPS Administrator on arops@arops.org.uk or write to her at 22 Rectory Close, Guildford GU4 7AR.

MONTESSORI SCHOOLS ASSOCIATION

www.montessori.org.uk

The Montessori Schools Association (MSA) was founded to support and represent all Montessori schools across the United Kingdom. The MSA works through 10 national regions each with its own Regional Chairman, Primary Group and a Childminders' Network. The Montessori Schools Association currently has over 3,800 members and 672 Montessori schools ranging in size from 15 to 400+ pupils covering the birth to 11 age range.

It is supported and run by the Montessori St Nicholas Charity (founded in 1954). The charity today works to support Montessori across the UK in every way it can.

The mission statement of the Montessori St Nicholas Charity is to:
- facilitate the unification of the Montessori movement across the UK;
- make awards and finance initiatives that support the development of Montessori education in the fields of training grants for individuals, equipment and advice;
- fund research and development into the value and effectiveness of Montessori education.

In September 2008 the Montessori St Nicholas Charity set up the Montessori Evaluation and Accreditation Board (MEAB), a new national evaluation and accreditation scheme to raise standards within the Montessori Schools Association and put "*best practice*" at the heart of what it does. The MEAB scheme builds on Montessori's excellent track record in education. There are now 168 MEAB schools.

Chairman: Dr Martin Bradley, PhD, BEd, HMI (retired)

The Montessori Schools Association

Suites One and Two, University House 11–13 Lower Grosvenor Place London SW1W 0EX

Tel: 020 7828 7740 • Fax: 020 7793 9936 • email: head-office@montessori.org.uk

MEDICAL OFFICERS OF SCHOOLS ASSOCIATION

FOUNDED 1884

www.mosa.org.uk

Objects
It is the objective of the Association to offer guidance and support and to encourage the application of the highest of medical standards in the educational environment. MOSA offers its members mutual assistance in promoting school health and the holding of meetings for consideration of all subjects connected with the special work of medical officers of schools.

Membership
Medical officers of schools and medical and dental practitioners and nurses especially concerned with the health of the schoolchild are eligible for membership, and members of the teaching profession, and those related to independent school management, for associate membership. The membership currently stands at 400.

The work of the Association
The Council meets three times a year and is chaired by the current President, Dr Jonathan Holliday, MO to Eton College. The Hon Secretary sends out two newsletters a year and is available for advice to members and non-members. Clinical meetings are arranged each year together with an annual summer visit to a school. Research projects are carried out individually and collectively. The Association strongly recommends that all independent schools appoint medical officers to carry out preventative medicine duties which are undertaken in maintained schools by the School Health Service.

Publications
The Association publishes administrative and clinical guidelines for its Medical Officers; these are found on the Association's website and updated regularly. Members have access to a secure online discussion forum where questions and topics are discussed giving access to up-to-date resources and peer support.

For further information about the Association and other related business enquiries should in the first instance be directed to:

The Hon Secretary: Dr Rebecca Pryse, MB BS, DCH, DRCOG, DFSRH
The Swan Practice, High Street, Buckingham MK18 1NU
Tel: 01280 818600; Fax: 01280 818618
email: rebecca.pryse@nhs.net

For administrative information and background please contact:
The Executive Secretary: Mrs Louise Fortune
email: mosa.execsec@gmail.com

THE ENGLISH-SPEAKING UNION

UK REGISTERED CHARITY NO. 273136

www.esu.org/sse

Secondary School Exchange Scholarships to the USA

A gap year with a difference – since 1928 the English-Speaking Union has offered young people the opportunity to spend a life-changing year or six months at a private American high school. The ESU offers the following Secondary School Exchange Scholarships:

Three-term scholarships

- The closing date for applications is in February (in your final year of A Levels or equivalent)
- Interviews are in March
- Leave for the US in September (after completion of your A Levels or equivalent)

Two-term scholarships

- The closing date for applications is in September (after completion of your A Levels or equivalent)
- Interviews are in September/October
- Leave for the US in early January

About the Scholarship

Each scholarship covers the cost of tuition, board and lodging, worth $30,000-$50,000. Scholars are fully fledged students at their host school, with access to world class facilities and a range of extra-curricular activities. Alumni of the programme include singer KT Tunstall, Sir Ian Blair, former Metropolitan Police Commissioner, Sir Richard Dearlove KCMG OBE, former head of MI6, 'City Superwoman' Nicole Horlick, the actress and comedienne Dawn French, and former HSBC chairman, Sir John Bond.

SSE is both an academic and cultural gap year programme. Scholars study a range of subjects at their host schools including some they dropped at GCSE, subjects they will study at university, and even subjects that don't feature in UK schools. The skills that can be gained from the exchange have proven to be beneficial at University: American teaching emphasises independence of thought, and discussions play a large part in the classroom. Scholars also enjoy American rites of passage such as spring break, prom, and graduation.

Scholars are responsible for additional costs including travel, insurance, and expenses. The ESU offers means-tested assistance to help towards these additional costs to successful applicants who would otherwise be unable to take up a scholarship. It also offers one full award, designed to cover all the additional costs related to the scholarship. Grants are given in the range of £200-£2,000. Many scholars use the summer holidays or the six-month gap between finishing school and leaving the US to save money for their time abroad.

Eligibility

- You must have completed your A Levels (or equivalent) and be intending to study at a UK university on your return. Your place does not need to be confirmed or deferred, and some scholars reapply during their scholarship year.
- Applications from students intending to study at a US university at undergraduate level will not be accepted.
- You must have a minimum of 3 Grade Cs at A Level or equivalent.
- You should be under 19 years and 6 months old when you take up the scholarship.
- Scholars are expected to commit to the full term of their scholarship (two-term: 6 months; three-term: 9 months).
- You must be a British Citizen and have studied/be studying A Levels (or equivalent) at a school in the UK.

About the English-Speaking Union

Founded in 1918, the ESU is an international educational charity and membership organisation that promotes mutual understanding, and fosters friendship and exchange throughout the world.

The English-Speaking Union
37 Charles Street, London W1J 5ED
Tel: 020 7529 1550 • email: education@esu.org

Painting
a colourful
future...

www.notredame.co.uk

NOTRE
DAME
SCHOOL

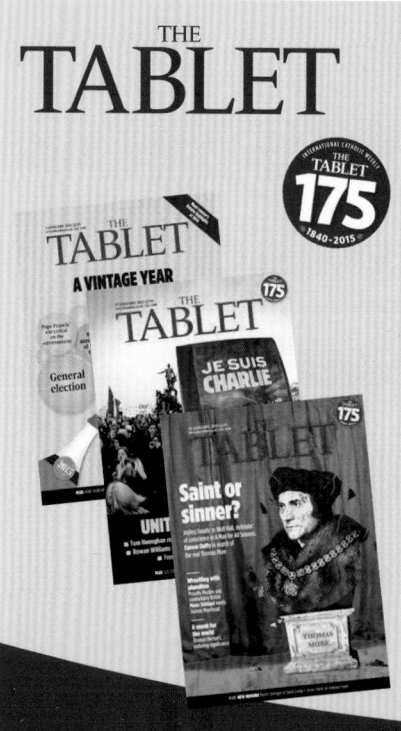

STONYHURST

![Stonyhurst building and reflection]

Developing outstanding individuals

A Co-educational Catholic Boarding and
Day School for 3–18 year olds
Tel 01254 827073   admissions@stonyhurst.ac.uk
www.stonyhurst.ac.uk

JESUIT
SCHOOLS

GapWise

Stand out from the crowd

Bringing careers into the 21st Century

GapWise is the modern, connected careers service providing interactive workshops tailored to your school:

- Understanding the modern job market
- Identifying key employability skills
- Making the most of social media

To find out more, email hello@gap-wise.co.uk
Visit gap-wise.co.uk
Or follow us on twitter @GapWise

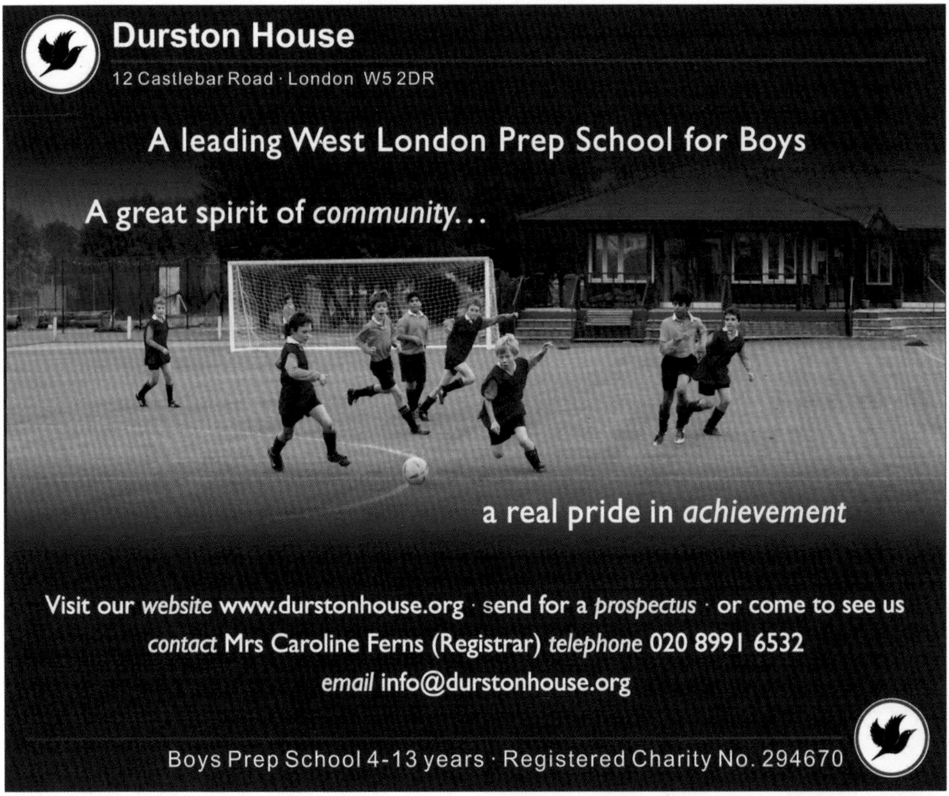

Durston House
12 Castlebar Road · London W5 2DR
A leading West London Prep School for Boys
A great spirit of community...
a real pride in achievement
Visit our website www.durstonhouse.org · send for a prospectus · or come to see us
contact Mrs Caroline Ferns (Registrar) telephone 020 8991 6532
email info@durstonhouse.org
Boys Prep School 4-13 years · Registered Charity No. 294670

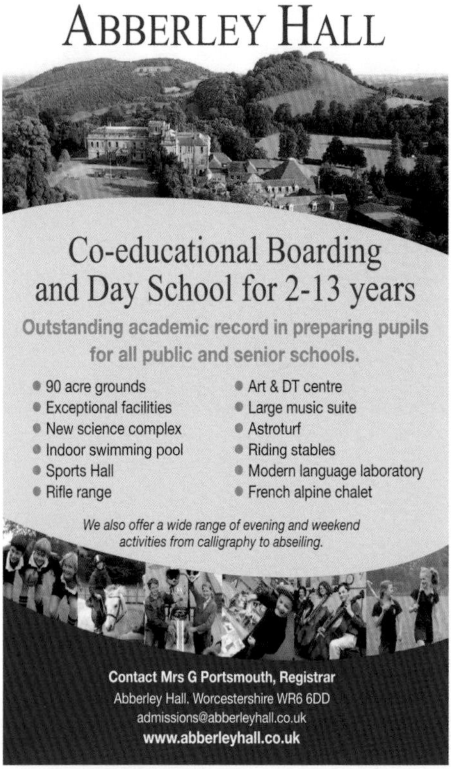

ABBERLEY HALL
Co-educational Boarding and Day School for 2-13 years
Outstanding academic record in preparing pupils for all public and senior schools.
• 90 acre grounds
• Exceptional facilities
• New science complex
• Indoor swimming pool
• Sports Hall
• Rifle range
• Art & DT centre
• Large music suite
• Astroturf
• Riding stables
• Modern language laboratory
• French alpine chalet
We also offer a wide range of evening and weekend activities from calligraphy to abseiling.
Contact Mrs G Portsmouth, Registrar
Abberley Hall, Worcestershire WR6 6DD
admissions@abberleyhall.co.uk
www.abberleyhall.co.uk

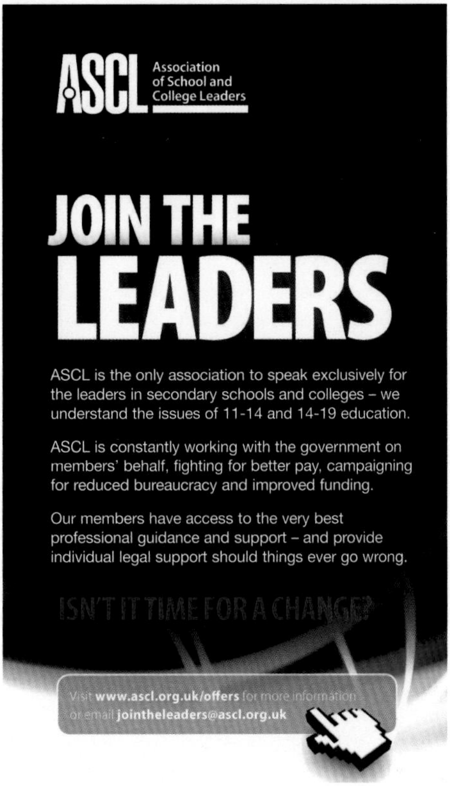

ASCL Association of School and College Leaders
JOIN THE LEADERS
ASCL is the only association to speak exclusively for the leaders in secondary schools and colleges – we understand the issues of 11-14 and 14-19 education.
ASCL is constantly working with the government on members' behalf, fighting for better pay, campaigning for reduced bureaucracy and improved funding.
Our members have access to the very best professional guidance and support – and provide individual legal support should things ever go wrong.
ISN'T IT TIME FOR A CHANGE?
Visit www.ascl.org.uk/offers for more information or email jointheleaders@ascl.org.uk

TAILORED NOT UNIFORM

When it comes to a good education, one size does not necessarily fit all.

We are one of the country's best known providers of bespoke fifth-and sixth form education, offering GCSEs and A levels in over 45 subjects.

We are distinctive in many ways, not least in our small classes of no more than eight students. We focus on exam preparation, but also offer outstanding personal support for students through our Director of Studies system. We do not patronise students by allowing low expectations of

behaviour or attainment and we help all students to raise their aspirations and give them the confidence to achieve their goals. MPW is a friendly, flexible college that offers an outstanding learning environment.

M|P|W

Mander Portman Woodward

London	Birmingham	Cambridge
020 7835 1355	0121 454 9637	01223 350158

Crowe Clark Whitehill™

A Member of Crowe Horwath International

Listening to you

Crowe Clark Whitehill is a leading national audit, tax and advisory firm with independent schools at the heart of its business. We can help you by:

▸ Giving technical expertise in a clear and pragmatic way.
▸ Focusing on your needs, investing time in understanding your school and being proactive in our approach.
▸ Always working with clear and transparent lines of communication.

To find out more about what we can offer, contact:

Tina Allison
Audit and Advisory Partner
tina.allison@crowecw.co.uk

+44 (0)20 7842 7276

Office locations and contacts

Cheltenham
Guy Biggin
guy.biggin@crowecw.co.uk

+44 (0)124 223 4421

London
Tina Allison
tina.allison@crowecw.co.uk

+44 (0)20 7842 7276

Manchester
Vicky Szulist
vicky.szulist@crowecw.co.uk

+44 (0)161 214 7500

Midlands
Helen Drew
helen.drew@crowecw.co.uk

+44 (0)121 543 1900

Thames Valley
Alastair Lyon
alastair.lyon@crowecw.co.uk

+44 (0)118 959 7222

Find out more about us at
www.croweclarkwhitehill.co.uk

Audit | Tax | Advisory

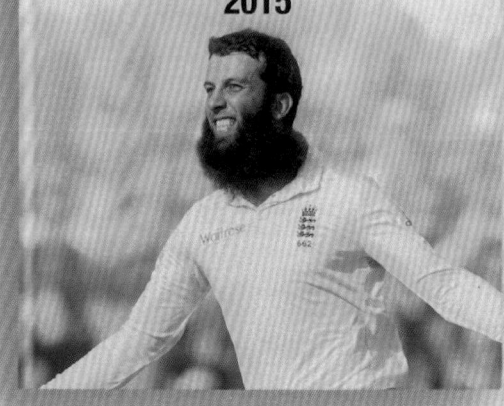

PART I
Schools whose Heads are members of the Headmasters' and Headmistresses' Conference

ALPHABETICAL LIST OF SCHOOLS
UK & Ireland

PAGE

Abingdon School, Oxon	7
Ackworth School, W Yorks	9
AKS, Lancs	10
Aldenham School, Herts	11
Alleyn's School, London	13
Ampleforth College, N Yorks	15
Ardingly College, W Sussex	17
Ashford School, Kent	18
Ashville College, N Yorks	19
Bablake School, W Midlands	21
Bancroft's School, Essex	22
Bangor Grammar School, Northern Ireland	24
Barnard Castle School, Durham	25
Bedales School, Hants	27
Bede's Senior School, E Sussex	29
Bedford Modern School, Beds	30
Bedford School, Beds	33
Belfast Royal Academy, Northern Ireland	35
Benenden School, Kent	37
Berkhamsted School, Herts	41
Birkdale School, S Yorks	44
Birkenhead School, Merseyside	46
Bishop's Stortford College, Herts	47
Bloxham School, Oxon	50
Blundell's School, Devon	52
Bolton School Boys' Division, Lancs	54
Bootham School, N Yorks	55
Bradfield College, Berks	57
Bradford Grammar School, W Yorks	59
Brentwood School, Essex	62
Brighton College, E Sussex	64
Bristol Grammar School, Bristol	66
Bromsgrove School, Worcs	68
Bryanston School, Dorset	72
Bury Grammar School Boys, Lancs	74
Campbell College, Northern Ireland	75
Canford School, Dorset	77
Caterham School, Surrey	80
Charterhouse, Surrey	83
Cheadle Hulme School, Cheshire	85
Cheltenham College, Glos	86
Chetham's School of Music, Greater Manchester	89
Chigwell School, Essex	91
Christ College, Wales	93
Christ's Hospital, W Sussex	95
Churcher's College, Hants	96
City of London Freemen's School, Surrey	98
City of London School, London	101

PAGE

City of London School for Girls, London	103
Clayesmore School, Dorset	104
Clifton College, Bristol	106
Clongowes Wood College, Ireland	108
Cokethorpe School, Oxon	109
Colfe's School, London	110
Colston's School, Bristol	112
Cranleigh, Surrey	113
Culford School, Suffolk	116
Dame Allan's Boys' School, Tyne and Wear	119
Dauntsey's School, Wilts	120
Dean Close School, Glos	121
Denstone College, Staffs	123
Dollar Academy, Scotland	125
Downe House, Berks	127
Dulwich College, London	129
The High School of Dundee, Scotland	131
Durham School, Durham	132
Eastbourne College, E Sussex	134
The Edinburgh Academy, Scotland	136
Elizabeth College, Channel Islands	138
Ellesmere College, Shropshire	139
Eltham College, London	141
Emanuel School, London	143
Epsom College, Surrey	145
Eton College, Berks	149
Exeter School, Devon	151
Felsted School, Essex	154
Fettes College, Scotland	156
Forest School, London	159
Framlingham College, Suffolk	162
Francis Holland School, London	163
Frensham Heights, Surrey	164
George Heriot's School, Scotland	167
Giggleswick School, N Yorks	169
The Glasgow Academy, Scotland	171
The High School of Glasgow, Scotland	172
Glenalmond College, Scotland	174
The Godolphin and Latymer School, London	176
The Godolphin School, Wilts	179
The Grange School, Cheshire	180
Gresham's School, Norfolk	183
Guildford High School, Surrey	186
The Haberdashers' Aske's Boys' School, Herts	188
Haileybury, Herts	191
Halliford School, Middx	194

	PAGE
Hampton School, Middx	196
Harrow School, Middx	200
Hereford Cathedral School, Herefordshire	202
Highgate School, London	203
Hurstpierpoint College, W Sussex	207
Hutchesons' Grammar School, Scotland	209
Hymers College, E Yorks	211
Immanuel College, Herts	212
Ipswich School, Suffolk	214
James Allen's Girls' School (JAGS), London	216
The John Lyon School, Middx	218
Kelvinside Academy, Scotland	219
Kent College, Kent	220
Kent College Pembury, Kent	222
Kimbolton School, Cambs	225
King Edward VI School, Hants	227
King Edward's School, Somerset	228
King Edward's School, W Midlands	231
King Edward's, Surrey	232
King Henry VIII School, W Midlands	234
King William's College, Isle of Man	235
King's College School, London	237
King's College, Somerset	241
The King's Hospital, Ireland	242
King's School, Somerset	243
The King's School, Canterbury, Kent	245
The King's School, Chester, Cheshire	248
King's Ely, Cambs	249
The King's School, Glos	252
The King's School, Macclesfield, Cheshire	255
King's Rochester, Kent	256
The King's School, Worcs	258
Kingston Grammar School, Surrey	260
Kingswood School, Somerset	262
Kirkham Grammar School, Lancs	265
Lancing College, W Sussex	266
Latymer Upper School, London	268
The Grammar School at Leeds, W Yorks	270
Leicester Grammar School, Leics	271
Leighton Park School, Berks	273
The Leys School, Cambs	275
Lincoln Minster School, Lincs	277
Lomond School, Scotland	278
Lord Wandsworth College, Hants	280
Loretto School, Scotland	281
Loughborough Grammar School, Leics	284
Magdalen College School, Oxon	287
Malvern College, Worcs	289
The Manchester Grammar School, Greater Manchester	291
Marlborough College, Wilts	293
Merchant Taylors' Boys' School, Merseyside	296
Merchant Taylors' School, Middx	297
Merchiston Castle School, Scotland	300
Mill Hill School, London	303
Millfield, Somerset	308
Monkton Combe School, Somerset	309
Monmouth School, Wales	312
Morrison's Academy, Scotland	314
Mount Kelly, Devon	316
Mount St Mary's College, Derbyshire	318
New Hall School, Essex	320
Newcastle-under-Lyme School, Staffs	322
Norwich School, Norfolk	323
Nottingham High School, Notts	326
Oakham School, Rutland	328
Oldham Hulme Grammar School, Lancs	329
The Oratory School, Oxon	331
Oundle School, Northants	333
Pangbourne College, Berks	336
The Perse Upper School, Cambs	338
Plymouth College, Devon	339
Pocklington School, E Yorks	341
The Portsmouth Grammar School, Hants	343
Princethorpe College, Warwicks	346
Prior Park College, Somerset	350
Queen Anne's School, Berks	353
Queen Elizabeth's Hospital (QEH), Bristol	354
Queen's College, Somerset	355
Radley College, Oxon	358
Ratcliffe College, Leics	360
Reading Blue Coat School, Berks	362
Reed's School, Surrey	364
Reigate Grammar School, Surrey	365
Rendcomb College, Glos	367
Repton School, Derbyshire	370
Robert Gordon's College, Scotland	372
Roedean School, E Sussex	375
Rossall School, Lancs	377
Rougemont School, Wales	379
Royal Grammar School, Surrey	380
Royal Grammar School, Tyne and Wear	382
RGS Worcester, Worcs	384
The Royal Hospital School, Suffolk	386
The Royal Masonic School for Girls, Herts	388
Royal Russell School, Surrey	389
The Royal School Dungannon, Northern Ireland	391
Rugby School, Warwicks	393
Rydal Penrhos School, Wales	396
Ryde School with Upper Chine, Isle of Wight	398
St Albans High School for Girls, Herts	400
St Albans School, Herts	402
St Aloysius' College, Scotland	404
St Bede's College, Greater Manchester	404
St Benedict's School, London	406
St Columba's College, Ireland	407
St Columba's College, Herts	408
St Columba's School, Scotland	410
St Dunstan's College, London	411
St Edmund's College, Herts	412
St Edmund's School, Kent	416

	PAGE
St Edward's, Oxford, Oxon	418
St George's College, Surrey	421
St John's School, Surrey	423
St Lawrence College, Kent	425
St Leonards School, Scotland	427
St Mary's Calne, Wilts	429
St Mary's College, Merseyside	430
St Mary's School Ascot, Berks	431
St Paul's Girls' School, London	434
St Paul's School, London	436
St Peter's School, York, N Yorks	439
Seaford College, W Sussex	440
Sevenoaks School, Kent	442
Sherborne Girls, Dorset	444
Sherborne School, Dorset	446
Shiplake College, Oxon	448
Shrewsbury School, Shropshire	450
Sidcot School, Somerset	452
Silcoates School, W Yorks	453
Solihull School, W Midlands	454
Stamford School, Lincs	457
The Stephen Perse Foundation, Cambs	458
Stewart's Melville College, Scotland	459
Stockport Grammar School, Cheshire	461
Stonyhurst College, Lancs	463
Stowe School, Bucks	465
Strathallan School, Scotland	468
Surbiton High School, Surrey	470
Sutton Valence School, Kent	474

	PAGE
Taunton School, Somerset	477
Tonbridge School, Kent	479
Trinity School, Surrey	481
Truro School, Cornwall	483
University College School, London	485
Uppingham School, Rutland	487
Victoria College, Channel Islands	491
Warminster School, Wilts	492
Warwick School, Warwicks	493
Wellingborough School, Northants	495
Wellington College, Berks	498
Wellington School, Somerset	501
Wells Cathedral School, Somerset	502
West Buckland School, Devon	504
Westminster School, London	506
Whitgift School, Surrey	508
Winchester College, Hants	511
Wisbech Grammar School, Cambs	513
Withington Girls' School, Greater Manchester	515
Wolverhampton Grammar School, W Midlands	516
Woodbridge School, Suffolk	518
Woodhouse Grove School, W Yorks	520
Worksop College, Notts	521
Worth School, W Sussex	523
Wrekin College, Shropshire	526
Wycliffe College, Glos	528
Wycombe Abbey, Bucks	531
Yarm School, Cleveland	532

GEOGRAPHICAL LIST OF HMC SCHOOLS
UK & Ireland

PAGE

ENGLAND

Bedfordshire
Bedford Modern School 30
Bedford School 33

Berkshire
Bradfield College 57
Downe House 127
Eton College 149
Leighton Park School 273
Pangbourne College 336
Queen Anne's School 353
Reading Blue Coat School 362
St Mary's School Ascot 431
Wellington College 498

Bristol
Bristol Grammar School 66
Clifton College 106
Colston's School 112
Queen Elizabeth's Hospital (QEH) 354

Buckinghamshire
Stowe School 465
Wycombe Abbey 531

Cambridgeshire
Kimbolton School 225
King's Ely 249
The Leys School 275
The Perse Upper School 338
The Stephen Perse Foundation 458
Wisbech Grammar School 513

Channel Islands
Elizabeth College 138
Victoria College 491

Cheshire
Cheadle Hulme School 85
The Grange School 180
The King's School, Chester 248
The King's School, Macclesfield 255
Stockport Grammar School 461

Cleveland
Yarm School 532

Cornwall
Truro School 483

Derbyshire
Mount St Mary's College 318
Repton School 370

Devon
Blundell's School 52
Exeter School 151
Mount Kelly 316
Plymouth College 339
West Buckland School 504

PAGE

Dorset
Bryanston School 72
Canford School 77
Clayesmore School 104
Sherborne Girls 444
Sherborne School 446

Durham
Barnard Castle School 25
Durham School 132

Essex
Bancroft's School 22
Brentwood School 62
Chigwell School 91
Felsted School 154
New Hall School 320

Gloucestershire
Cheltenham College 86
Dean Close School 121
The King's School 252
Rendcomb College 367
Wycliffe College 528

Greater Manchester
Chetham's School of Music 89
The Manchester Grammar School 291
St Bede's College 404
Withington Girls' School 515

Hampshire
Bedales School 27
Churcher's College 96
King Edward VI School 227
Lord Wandsworth College 280
The Portsmouth Grammar School 343
Winchester College 511

Herefordshire
Hereford Cathedral School 202

Hertfordshire
Aldenham School 11
Berkhamsted School 41
Bishop's Stortford College 47
The Haberdashers' Aske's Boys' School 188
Haileybury 191
Immanuel College 212
The Royal Masonic School for Girls 388
St Albans High School for Girls 400
St Albans School 402
St Columba's College 408
St Edmund's College 412

Isle of Man
King William's College 235

Isle of Wight
Ryde School with Upper Chine 398

PAGE

Kent
Ashford School 18
Benenden School 37
Kent College 220
Kent College Pembury 222
The King's School, Canterbury 245
King's Rochester 256
St Edmund's School 416
St Lawrence College 425
Sevenoaks School 442
Sutton Valence School 474
Tonbridge School 479

Lancashire
AKS 10
Bolton School Boys' Division 54
Bury Grammar School Boys 74
Kirkham Grammar School 265
Oldham Hulme Grammar School 329
Rossall School 377
Stonyhurst College 463

Leicestershire
Leicester Grammar School 271
Loughborough Grammar School 284
Ratcliffe College 360

Lincolnshire
Lincoln Minster School 277
Stamford School 457

London (see also Essex, Middlesex, Surrey)
Alleyn's School 13
City of London School 101
City of London School for Girls 103
Colfe's School 110
Dulwich College 129
Eltham College 141
Emanuel School 143
Forest School 159
Francis Holland School 163
The Godolphin and Latymer School 176
Highgate School 203
James Allen's Girls' School (JAGS) 216
King's College School 237
Latymer Upper School 268
Mill Hill School 303
St Benedict's School 406
St Dunstan's College 411
St Paul's Girls' School 434
St Paul's School 436
University College School 485
Westminster School 506

Merseyside
Birkenhead School 46
Merchant Taylors' Boys' School 296
St Mary's College 430

Middlesex
Halliford School 194
Hampton School 196
Harrow School 200
The John Lyon School 218
Merchant Taylors' School 297

PAGE

Norfolk
Gresham's School 183
Norwich School 323

Northamptonshire
Oundle School 333
Wellingborough School 495

Nottinghamshire
Nottingham High School 326
Worksop College 521

Oxfordshire
Abingdon School 7
Bloxham School 50
Cokethorpe School 109
Magdalen College School 287
The Oratory School 331
Radley College 358
St Edward's, Oxford 418
Shiplake College 448

Rutland
Oakham School 328
Uppingham School 487

Shropshire
Ellesmere College 139
Shrewsbury School 450
Wrekin College 526

Somerset
King Edward's School 228
King's College 241
King's School 243
Kingswood School 262
Millfield 308
Monkton Combe School 309
Prior Park College 350
Queen's College 355
Sidcot School 452
Taunton School 477
Wellington School 501
Wells Cathedral School 502

Staffordshire (see also West Midlands)
Denstone College 123
Newcastle-under-Lyme School 322

Suffolk
Culford School 116
Framlingham College 162
Ipswich School 214
The Royal Hospital School 386
Woodbridge School 518

Surrey
Caterham School 80
Charterhouse 83
City of London Freemen's School 98
Cranleigh 113
Epsom College 145
Frensham Heights 164
Guildford High School 186
King Edward's 232
Kingston Grammar School 260
Reed's School 364

6

	PAGE
Reigate Grammar School	365
Royal Grammar School	380
Royal Russell School	389
St George's College	421
St John's School	423
Surbiton High School	470
Trinity School	481
Whitgift School	508

Sussex (East)

Bede's Senior School	29
Brighton College	64
Eastbourne College	134
Roedean School	375

Sussex (West)

Ardingly College	17
Christ's Hospital	95
Hurstpierpoint College	207
Lancing College	266
Seaford College	440
Worth School	523

Tyne and Wear

Dame Allan's Boys' School	119
Royal Grammar School	382

Warwickshire

Princethorpe College	346
Rugby School	393
Warwick School	493

West Midlands

Bablake School	21
King Edward's School	231
King Henry VIII School	234
Solihull School	454
Wolverhampton Grammar School	516

Wiltshire

Dauntsey's School	120
The Godolphin School	179
Marlborough College	293
St Mary's Calne	429
Warminster School	492

Worcestershire

Bromsgrove School	68
The King's School	258
Malvern College	289
RGS Worcester	384

Yorkshire (East)

Hymers College	211
Pocklington School	341

	PAGE
Yorkshire (North)	
Ampleforth College	15
Ashville College	19
Bootham School	55
Giggleswick School	169
St Peter's School, York	439

Yorkshire (South)

Birkdale School	44

Yorkshire (West)

Ackworth School	9
Bradford Grammar School	59
The Grammar School at Leeds	270
Silcoates School	453
Woodhouse Grove School	520

IRELAND

Clongowes Wood College	108
The King's Hospital	242
St Columba's College	407

NORTHERN IRELAND

Bangor Grammar School	24
Belfast Royal Academy	35
Campbell College	75
The Royal School Dungannon	391

SCOTLAND

Dollar Academy	125
The High School of Dundee	131
The Edinburgh Academy	136
Fettes College	156
George Heriot's School	167
The Glasgow Academy	171
The High School of Glasgow	172
Glenalmond College	174
Hutchesons' Grammar School	209
Kelvinside Academy	219
Lomond School	278
Loretto School	281
Merchiston Castle School	300
Morrison's Academy	314
Robert Gordon's College	372
St Aloysius' College	404
St Columba's School	410
St Leonards School	427
Stewart's Melville College	459
Strathallan School	468

WALES

Christ College	93
Monmouth School	312
Rougemont School	379
Rydal Penrhos School	396

Symbols used in Staff Listings

* Head of Department	§ Part Time or Visiting
† Housemaster/Housemistress	¶ Old Pupil
‡ See below list of staff for meaning	

Individual School Entries
UK & Ireland

Abingdon School

Park Road, Abingdon, Oxfordshire OX14 1DE
Tel: 01235 521563 School
          01235 849041 Registry
          01235 849022 Bursar
Fax: 01235 849077 Head
          01235 849079 School
email: heads.pa@abingdon.org.uk
          admissions@abingdon.org.uk
          bursars.sec@abingdon.org.uk
website: www.abingdon.org.uk

The foundation of the School appears to date from the twelfth century; the first clear documentary reference occurs in 1256. After the dissolution of Abingdon Abbey, the School was re-endowed in 1563 by John Roysse, of the Mercers' Company in London. It was rebuilt in 1870 on its present site, and many further buildings have been added including extensive facilities for the arts and sport. A science centre will open in 2015. Abingdon Preparatory School is situated close by at Frilford (*see entry in IAPS section*). The total establishment numbers about 1,200 boys.

Governing Body:
Mr A Burn, FCA (*Chairman*)
Mr J R Gabitass, MA (*Vice Chairman*)
Mr A Saunders-Davies, MRICS, MBA (*Vice Chairman*)

The Mayor of Abingdon
Miss P Chapman
Miss J E Cranston
Dr O R Darbishire, MA, MSc, PhD
Lt Col A Douglas, MA
Mrs J Forrest, CertEd
Miss E J C Hohler, MA
Dr E H T Lumsden, MA, MB BS, MRCGP, DRCOG
Mr G Morris
The Hon Sir Vivian Ramsey, KT, MA, DipLaw, CEng, MICE
Mrs O Senior, MSc
Professor M C G Stevens
Mr D Tracey

Clerk to the Governors: Mr T R Ayling, MA

Head: Miss O F S Lusk, BMus

Second Master: Mr D J Dawswell, BSc
Deputy Head, Academic: Mr G May, MA
Deputy Head, Pastoral: Mr M K T Hindley, LLB, UCL, MA
Chaplain: Revd Dr S M Steer, BA, MDiv, PhD
Upper Master: Mr N J O'Doherty, BSc
Middle Master: Revd P D B Gooding, MA, DipTh, DipMin
Lower School Housemaster: Mr A J Jenkins, BA
Master of Scholars: Dr C J Burnand, MA, DPhil
Master i/c the Other Half: Mr S A Evans, BA

Housemasters:

Boarders:
School House: Mr E N F Swanwick MA
Crescent House: Mr M A Kendry
Davies's House: Mr E S Davies, BA

Dayboys:
Mr A C Christodoulou, MSc, BEng
Mr J A Cotton, MA
Mr D J T Franklin, MA

Mr H C G Morgan, MA
Mr R Southwell-Sander, BA
Mr M R Webb, BSc

Assistant Masters:

Mr D G Aitken, BA
Miss A L Atkinson, BA
Mr H Barnes, BA
Mrs D C Bennison, BSc
Mr S E Bliss, BSc
Mr E P Birkbeck, BSc
Mr D Border, BSc
Mr A Broadbent, BEd
Mr J P G Brooks, BSc
Mr A M Brown
Ms K E Byrne, BA
Mr P J E Coke, BSc
Mrs C Collins, MA
Mr J A Cotton, BA, MA
Mrs M F F Cottrell, CertEd
Mrs C Cross, CertEd
Mr M Dempsey, BSc
Mr G T Draganov, MSc
Mr M Earnshaw, BA, MA
Mr M Edgar BA
Mr A J P English, BA, MLitt
Miss M Elmore, MMath
Mr D Evans, BA
Mr N Fieldhouse, BA
Mr R M Fisher, BSc
Mr I C Fishpool, BSc, FRGS
Mrs J E Fishpool, MA
Mr C M Fletcher-Campbell, MA
Mr R Ghosh BSc
Mrs S Gibbard, BSc
Mr G M Golding, BSc
Mrs C Greenfield, BA
Mrs V Griffiths, BSc
Mr S J Grills, MSc
Mr A S Hall, BA
Mr J Hallinan, BA
Ms E Hancock, BA
Miss V E Hicks, BA
Dr R Howe, MSc, DPhil
Mr D M Hughes, BA
Mr S James, MPhys
Dr R K Jeffreys, BSc, PhD
Miss T Katic, BA
Mrs E Kaye, BSc

Miss K Lee, BSocSc
Mr M I Litchfield, BSc
Mr O T Lomax, BA
Mrs J A Mansfield, CAPES
Dr C J May, BA, PhD
Mr D R McGill, BA
Mrs S C V McRae, BSc
Mr I Middleton, MA
Mrs C Muller, BSc
Mr G R Moody, MA
Mr H C G Morgan, MMath
Mr S Newton, BSc
Mrs E O'Doherty, MA
Miss R Papadopoulos, MA
Mrs S Payne, MA
Mrs V D Penrose, BSc
Miss N Petrov, BSc
Mr B J L Phillips, BA
Mr B Ponniah, BSc, MSc
Mr M Poon, MMath
Mr M J Poynter, BA
Mrs M V Pradas Muños, BA
Mr H F C Price, BA
Mr N A F Pritchard, MA
Mr N M Revill, BA
Mr B Simmons BSc
Mrs E M-T Slatford, MA
Mr M A Stinton, MA, ARCM, LRAM
Mr E N F Swanwick, MA
Mr A P Swarbrick, BA, MPhil
Mr J H Taylor, BA
Mr R Taylor, BA
Mrs F R Tufnell, BA
Mrs A Waite, BSc
Mrs H J Wenham, MA
Mr M B Whitworth, BA
Ms A Widdern, BA
Dr J S Wiejak, MA, PhD
Mrs S Wigmore, BEd
Miss E Williamson, BA, MA
Mr J H Winters, MA
Miss R Yarrow, BA, MSc

Librarian: Mr GS Gardner, PhD

Part-time:

Mrs J Bentley, BSc
Mrs V A Clark, BSc
Mr J D E Drummond-Hay, BEd

Mrs M Pringle, MMus, FTCL, LRAM
Mrs A K Quick, BA
Miss N Spurling-Holt, BA
Mrs A M Streatfield, BEd

Director of Finance and Operations: Mr B D G Delacave, ACA
Director of Admissions and Marketing: Mrs J H Jørgensen, MA
Medical Officer: Dr M F Khan, MBChB, FRCS, DRCOG, DFFP

In the Senior School there are about 960 boys aged 11–18, of whom approximately 130 are boarders. Boarding starts from age 13.

Boarding is organised in three houses: School House (Mr E N F Swanwick), Davies' House (Mr E S Davies) and Crescent House (Mr M A Kendry). The School values its boarding element very highly and weekly boarding features strongly as part of a policy aimed at asserting a distinctive regional identity for the School.

Pastoral Care. The Lower School has a self-contained system of pastoral care, led by the Lower School Housemaster. All boys join a senior house on entering the Middle School. Within the house system there are distinct tutoring arrangements for Middle School and Upper School boys, which are coordinated by the Middle Master and Upper Master respectively. Special emphasis is placed on the value of parental involvement and also on the provision of careers guidance at appropriate points in a boy's development. Great importance is attached to pastoral care and the School's teaching philosophy is based on a tutorial approach.

Land and Buildings. The School is surrounded by 35 acres of its own grounds, yet is within a few hundred yards of the historic centre of Abingdon, which lies 6 miles down the Thames from Oxford. A further 30 acres of playing fields are located at the Preparatory School, three miles from Abingdon.

The last quarter-century has seen a considerable expansion in the School's stock of buildings. A major development in the 1990s was Mercers' Court, which celebrated the School's historical link with the Mercers' Company of London. In 2003 a £3m Arts Centre was opened providing purpose-designed facilities for music, art and drama followed in 2008 by a new Sports Centre. In 2015 the School will open a new Science Centre which will transform the science facilities and enable redevelopment of the existing science block for other subjects.

Sports facilities have been greatly enhanced by the £8m sports centre with a superb 8-lane swimming pool, fitness suites, classroom space, squash courts, climbing wall and a martial arts and fencing studio. This follows the opening in 2003 of a beautiful timber-framed boathouse situated on the River Thames a short distance from the School. In 2014 the School took over the lease for Tilsley Park Sports Centre which enhances the School's facilities still further with provision for hockey, football and athletics.

Courses of Study. The School is essentially academic in character and intention and levels of both expectation and achievement are high. Subjects taught include English, DT, History, French, German, Spanish, Mandarin Chinese, Latin, Greek, Ancient History, Economics, Business Studies, Geography, Mathematics, Physics, Chemistry, Biology, Art, Religious Studies, Psychology, Music and Theatre Studies. Over the last few years there has been increasing collaboration with the School of St Helen and St Katharine with joint tuition particularly in Theatre Studies and Government and Politics. The School is well equipped with computing facilities and audio-visual teaching aids.

All boys spend three years in the Middle School (13 to 16 year olds), in which many different subject combinations are possible, and there is no specialisation before the Sixth Form. In the Sixth Form many boys combine courses in arts and sciences; four subjects are normally taken as AS in the Lower Sixth, followed by three or four at A2 in the Upper Sixth. Classroom teaching at all levels is supplemented by a programme of specialist lectures and outside visits. In general terms, the curriculum aims to combine academic discipline and excellence with the fullest encouragement of a wide range of interests and pursuits.

Games and Activities. The School enjoys some 80 acres of playing fields and has its own sports centre, swimming pool, fitness suites, climbing wall, squash and tennis courts and a boathouse on the River Thames. The major sports are rowing, rugby, cricket, hockey, football, tennis, athletics and cross-country. Special success has been achieved recently in rowing, fencing, badminton, swimming and shooting. Other sports include sailing, golf and Real Tennis.

Importance is attached to the development of a sense of social responsibility, through voluntary membership of Community Service and the Duke of Edinburgh's Award Schemes. There is a contingent of the Combined Cadet Force based on voluntary recruitment.

There are numerous societies catering for all kinds of interests and enthusiasms. Music is particularly strong, with over half the boys taking instrumental or vocal lessons in the School. In addition to the Chapel Choir, Choral Society and three orchestras, there are excellent opportunities for ensemble playing, including jazz.

Religion. The School is Anglican by tradition, but boys of other denominations are welcome, and normally attend by year group a short non-denominational service approximately once a week.

Health. The School has its own doctor and there is a well-equipped health centre in the school grounds. In cases of emergency boys are admitted to one of the local hospitals.

Admission. The normal ages of entry to the Senior School are 11, 13 and 16; there are occasionally vacancies at other ages. About half of each year's intake enter the School at age 11 and most of the rest at age 13. Registration at age 9 or 10 is recommended. Abingdon Preparatory School has its own entrance arrangements (*see entry in IAPS section*).

Details of the entrance examination procedures for 11 and 13 year old candidates are available from the Registry. Entry to the Sixth Form, at 16, generally depends on promising GCSE grades and written tests where it is appropriate, as well as on interviews and a report from the previous school.

Term of Entry. September is the usual date of entry and is preferred by the School. Boys may be accepted in any of the three terms, if vacancies occur in their age group.

Fees per term (2014–2015). The tuition fee, for dayboys, is £5,550. This includes the cost of lunches and textbooks.

For boarders, the total fee (including tuition and all extras except for instrumental music lessons and some disbursements directly incurred by individual boys) is £9,800 (weekly) and £11,730 (full).

Scholarships and Bursaries. The School offers a number of scholarships and means-tested bursaries at ages 11, 13 and 16; Scholarships and awards categories include: Academic, All-Rounder, Music, Art and Design, Sport and Drama.

Full details are published in the spring of each year and are available, on application, from the Registry or from our website www.abingdon.org.uk/scholarships or /bursaries.

The majority of awards are made at 13+ entry and are open to external and internal candidates. Some additional awards are available on entry to Sixth Form and to the Lower School. Scholarships carry an entitlement to a nominal fee remission of £300 per year plus remission of up to 100% of the tuition fee on a means-tested bursary basis. Music Scholarships also carry an entitlement to remission on instrument tuition fees.

Honours. Numerous places are won each year at Oxford and Cambridge and on other highly selective university courses.

Old Abingdonian Club. Administrator: c/o Abingdon School.

Charitable status. Abingdon School Limited is a Registered Charity, number 1071298. It exists to provide educational opportunities which are open to talented boys without regard to their families' economic standing. Its curriculum is designed to promote intellectual rigour, personal versatility and social responsibility.

Ackworth School

Ackworth, Pontefract, West Yorkshire WF7 7LT
Tel: 01977 611401
Fax: 01977 616225
email: admissions@ackworthschool.com
website: www.ackworthschool.com
Twitter: @ackworth_school
Facebook: /AckworthSchool

This co-educational boarding and day school was founded in 1779 and occupies a large rural estate which surrounds the gracious Georgian buildings and spacious gardens and playing fields which form the School Campus. It is one of the seven Quaker Schools in England.

Governing Body:
Members appointed by The Religious Society of Friends

Clerk: Adrian Sharp

Secretary and Bursar: John Lebeter, ICSA

Full time Teaching Staff:

Head: Mr Anton Maree, BA, HED

Deputy Head (Curriculum): Jeffrey D Swales, MA, PGCE

Deputy Head (Pastoral): Guy Emmett, MA, PGCE
Director of Marketing: Marion Mitchell, BA, PGCE

Head of Sixth Form: Andrew Ward, BSc, PGCE

Heads of Subject Departments:
Art: Sarah Rose-Peirson, BA
Biology: Andrew Ward, BSc, PGCE
Business Studies: Nicola Tod, BA, PGCE
Chemistry: Nayyar Aziz, BSc, MSc, PhD
Design & Technology: Andrew Hobson, BSc, PGCE
Drama: Richard Vergette, BA, PGCE, MEd
English: Alistar Boucher, BA, MA, PGCE
French: Elizabeth Rayner, BA Hons, PGCE
Geography: Ros Noble, MPhysGeog, PGCE
German: Andrew Hilton, BA, PGCE
History: Thomas Plant, BA, PGCE
Home Economics: Brenda Hodge, BEd
Mathematics: Lucinda Hamill, MA, BEd, BA
Music: Ian Lenihan, BA, PGCE
Physical Education: Elizabeth Burrows, MSc, PGCE
Physics: Francis Hickenbottom, BSc, PGCE
Religious Studies: John Stephenson, MA, PGCE
Spanish: Gwen Casey, BA, PGCE

Heads of Boarding Houses:
Boys: Christopher Bailey, BSc
Girls: Claire Cougan, BSc, PGCE

Coram House (Junior School):
Head: Mary Wilson, BA Hons, PGCE

§*Librarian*: Erica Dean

Nursing Sister: Pamela Evans, SRN
Medical Officer: Gwenan Davenport, MBChB, MRCGP

There are 450 girls and boys aged from 4 to 18 years, 330 of whom are day pupils. Some of the pupils are from Quaker homes, but the School has long been open to boys and girls unconnected with the Society of Friends, and these pupils are now in the majority. The pattern of school life is based on the Quaker belief that religion and life are one: that spiritual conviction directly affects the way in which people behave toward each other and determines their attitude to life in general. However, while the life of the School is based on the Quakers' interpretation of Christianity, the approach is broad-based and open-minded, for the life of the community is enriched by contributions made by those of other denominations and faiths. Although all pupils attend school assemblies and Meetings for Worship, arrangements can generally be made for pupils to worship in their own churches and boys and girls can be prepared for confirmation.

Houses. Boys and girls live separately in two houses, with resident house staff and matrons responsible for their welfare.

Curriculum. Pupils follow courses leading to GCSE, IGCSE and Advanced Level examinations. A wide range of subjects can be taken. The main foreign languages taught are French, German and Spanish. There is a strong Music department and group instrumental tuition is part of the First Year (Year 7) course; Design and Technology and Art are also very well provided for, and all of these subjects are integral parts of the core curriculum. The School also has a strong sporting tradition with many successful teams, thanks to excellent coaching and first-rate facilities. The large academic Sixth Form, which offers all of the traditional subjects as well as more recent additions such as Sport and PE and Drama, prepares students extremely well for university entry and for life beyond School.

The most recent addition to our provision is our flourishing International Centre. Here, intensive English coaching is offered to students of Sixth Form age who wish to go on to follow Advanced Level courses and a one-year GCSE course.

Leisure Time. The many clubs and societies on offer cater for all ages and all tastes. The facilities for crafts, art and music are freely available outside the teaching day, and pupils participate in a huge range of team and individual sports. There is a very full programme of weekend activities and visits.

Buildings. A policy of expansion and upgrading has been maintained over the years and within the last decade wide-ranging improvements have been made to the School's facilities. Study accommodation for Sixth Formers is large and modern and the science laboratories have been re-equipped. The modern Music Centre and Fothergill Theatre provide spacious facilities for individual and ensemble music making, together with an excellent venue for concerts and School productions. The Design and Technology Centre houses a thriving department and numerous creative after-school clubs, and the spacious, well-appointed study, reference and careers library caters for all age groups. The superb, modern Sports Centre and fully resourced Information Technology Centre are in constant use. The most recent changes have been to boarding accommodation – the girls have specially designed, purpose-built furniture, while the boys' rooms have been re-designed to include en-suite facilities.

Scholarships and Bursaries. A number of awards are made each year to selected boys and girls entering the School who show high academic ability or exceptional talent in Music, Drama, Art or Sport.

Academic Scholarships are awarded annually. At ages 11+ and 13+ the awards are made on the basis of performance at the Entrance Tests and a subsequent interview. At Sixth Form level an offer of a Scholarship is made following a scholarship examination and interview in February.

Music Scholarships are usually awarded at age 11, 13 or 16+. The awards are made on the strength of a half-hour audition and recognise achievement and potential, preferably on two instruments. Free tuition on one or two instruments may be offered to promising musicians who do not gain a scholarship.

Art Scholarships are awarded at age 11 or 13. The awards are made on the strength of a 3-hour Art Scholarship examination and the submission and discussion of a portfolio of work, all of which must be supported by competent performance in the Entrance Tests.

Bursaries are available to Members or Attenders of the Society of Friends and others according to need. Travel Scholarships are available to members of the Sixth Form.

Admission. Interested parents will be sent a prospectus upon application to the Head and visits can always be promptly arranged. There are also two Open Mornings during the year, at which parents and families are welcome to tour the School and to talk to staff and pupils. Pupils for entry at age 7 and above take the School's entrance test, while entry at age 4 is based on interview. The majority of children enter the Senior School at the age of 11, but there is also a sizeable entrance at 12, 13, 14 and 16+. Entry is always possible at other ages if places are available, and there is a direct entry into the Sixth Form for pupils who are able to take the full two-year A level course.

Coram House (Junior School). Coram House caters for day boys and girls aged 4 to 11, the majority of whom move on into the Senior School. In September 2002 a nursery opened catering for pupils aged 2½ to 4 years.

Pre-prep classes are housed in new, spacious, purpose-built accommodation. From Reception onwards, emphasis is placed on a thorough understanding of the basic skills in reading, literacy, numeracy and science. In addition, a wide-ranging curriculum is provided to encourage creativity and physical ability through Art, Craft, Technology, Drama, Music and Sport.

In the Preparatory Department pupils work to a more structured timetable and are gradually introduced to special-ist subject teaching. Staffing in Coram House is generous, so a thorough grounding can be given in the core subjects of English, Mathematics and Science. A broad curriculum is provided which includes French, Art and Crafts, Technol-ogy, Drama, Music and Sport – the children thus receive a rounded education and are able to develop their individual talents.

Before-school care from 8.00 am and after-school care until 5.30 pm are both available, at no extra charge.

Fees per term (2014–2015). Coram House: £2,661–£2,738 (day); Senior School: £7,703 (boarding), £4,285 (day); International Centre: £9,312–£9,991 (boarding). The day pupil fees include lunch (and other meals if required).

The Ackworth Old Scholars' Association. This is a flourishing Association with a membership of over two thousand. Annual gatherings are held at Ackworth at Easter and there are Guild Meetings held in the regions at other times in the year.

Charitable status. Ackworth School is a Registered Charity, number 529280. It was established for the purpose of providing independent education.

AKS
United Learning

Clifton Drive South, Lytham St Annes, Lancashire FY8 1DT
Tel: 01253 784100
email: headmaster@arnoldkeqms.com
          info@arnoldkeqms.com
website: www.arnoldkeqms.com

In September 2012, Arnold (Blackpool) and KEQMS (Lytham) merged as ArnoldKEQMS (AKS), part of the United Learning group of independent schools and acade-mies. Following a year of transition in 2012–2013, where AKS operated on each respective campus, the school co-located fully from September 2013 on the refurbished and extended Lytham campus. With an outstanding reputation of academic success, our GCSE and A Level results are currently the best on the Fylde.

With over 300 years of history and tradition, the school has a reputation for high standards and excellence in achievement, both academic and non-academic, as well as encouraging participation within an inclusive and caring community environment. Hockey has triumphed at national level, while rugby and drama also hold prestigious awards, and music has an international reputation. Sports teams tour in the UK, Europe and the Southern Hemisphere, and a large number of pupils participate in the Duke of Edinburgh's Award Scheme at bronze, silver and gold level. The school also has a large CCF, with all 3 sections of RN, RAF, and army. The school has a thriving House structure, and charity features prominently in school actions, both in support of local needs as well as international needs.

Local Governing Body:
Chairman: Mr J M Wooding, OBE, BSc, CEng, FRAeS
Vice Chairman: Mrs M Towers
Mr A E P Baines, BA, BArch, RIBA
Mrs S C Carr, OBE
Mr P Cox
Mr C R Dickson
Dr J Edwards
Mrs L Hoiles
Dr I Levitt
Revd D Lyon
Mr P Maguire, ACA
Mr P M Owen, ACIB
Mr L Smith
Mr J R Taylor, LLB

Bursar and Clerk to the Governors: Commander P McCarthy, RN

Senior School Management:

Headmaster: **Mr M H P Walton**, BA, MA Ed, PGCE, NPQH

Deputy Head (*Academic*): Mr C W Jenkinson, MA Oxon
Deputy Head (*Pastoral*): Mrs J Cooper, BSc
Head of Junior School: Miss K Wright, BA
Admissions Secretary: Mrs E Wyatt
Head of Sixth Form: Mr P Hayden, BA
Head of Middle School: Mr P Rudd, BSc
Pupil Progress & Attainment, Coordinator of G&T: Mr S Collings, BA
Director of Teaching & Staff Development: Mr A McKeown, BSc
Director of E-Learning: Mr D Culpan, BSc
External Administration & Examinations Officer: Mr P Klenk, BA
Data Manager: Mrs H Salmon, BSc

Head of Art: Miss L Heap, BA
Head of Biology: Mr S Downey, BSc
Head of Business Education: Mrs S Donald, BSc
Head of Careers: Mrs M Thornton, BSc
Head of Classics: Mr I Morton, MA
Head of Computing: Mr B Smith, BSc
Head of Design & Technology: Mr P Klenk, BA
Director of Drama: Miss F Horrocks, BA
Head of English: Mr J Bridges, BA
Head of Geography & Geology: Mr N O'Loughlin, BSc
Head of History: Mr J Davey, BA
Head of Learning Support: Mrs E Luke, BEd
Head of Mathematics: Mr K Dawson, BSc
Head of MFL: Mrs F Burnett, BA
Director of Music: Mr D Chandler, BMus
Head of Physics: Mr J Riding, BEng
Head of Psychology & Sociology: Mrs D Ward
Head of PSHE: Mrs H House, BA
Head of Religious Studies: Mr M Harding, BEd
Head of Science/Head of Chemistry: Dr C Jessop, BSc, PhD
Director of Sport: Mr R Jones, BEd

Our Location. AKS dominates an impressive position in Lytham, a delightful Victorian seaside town of charming character, overlooking the sand dunes and the Fylde coast. Preston, the Ribble Valley, the Lake District and Manchester are all within easy reach by direct motorway.

Our Opportunities. Through our membership of United Learning all teaching staff benefit from a high standard of professional training. All schools within the United Learning group communicate frequently and mutual support is always available, at all levels. The Group provides tailored CPD days for schools as well as a full range of CPD courses throughout the year for individuals to attend. The school contributes in full to the Teachers' Superannuation Scheme and there is a fee remission scheme for children of staff who are educated at the school.

Our Co-curricular. Whilst the pursuit of high academic standards is undoubtedly important, all our pupils take advantage of the broad range of experience which our school offers, to nurture creativity and to encourage a spirit of voluntary contribution to the school and the wider community. In recent years pupils have raised tens of thousands of pounds to support charities both at home and abroad. Our main games are rugby, football, hockey, cricket and athletics, with strong fixture lists and several national and regional titles. This extensive programme provides competition and challenge for all pupils and touring sides have travelled as far afield as Argentina, Chile, the Caribbean, Canada, Australia and South Africa. As well as sport we also offer a Combined Cadet Force in all three sections, Duke of Edinburgh's Award at bronze to gold levels, Young Enterprise, World Challenge, debating, dance, chess and much more. Drama and music also feature prominently and inspire countless pupils each year to take part in top quality productions, concerts and recitals.

Our Facilities. The school occupies an extensive site, overlooking the coast, with superb playing fields, including an international standard artificial all-weather sports ground. Significant investment of over 9 million pounds in the last 24 months has resulted in: a brand new Junior School, a new Sports Hall, a new Library, a new drama studio, new Sixth Form facilities, new staff and administrative facilities, new ICT facilities, new D&T facilities, upgraded and new science laboratories, upgraded music facilities, improvements to internal accessibility, extended art facilities, and interactive whiteboards in each classroom.

Admission. Prospectus and Admissions forms can be obtained from the Admissions Secretary.

All entries to the Senior School are made through the Headmaster. Pupils are admitted to the Senior School on the basis of the School's own examinations in English, Mathematics and Non-Verbal Reasoning. The main intake to the Senior School is at 11, though entry at other times is possible depending on availability of places.

For entry at Sixth Form level, respectable GCSE grades in at least five subjects are normally expected in addition to a satisfactory report from the pupil's current Head.

Entry into the Junior School (2–11 years) is normally at the ages of 2, 4 and 7. Enquiries should be made to the Admissions Secretary.

Fees per term (2014–2015). Tuition (including books and stationery): Seniors £3,264; Juniors £2,331. Extras are minimal.

Entrance Scholarships. Several scholarships (including those for Music, Art and Sport) are available for entry at 11+. Music, Sport, Art and Drama scholarships are available in the Sixth Form. Bursaries and Assisted Places are also available. Further particulars from the Admissions Secretary (01253 784104).

Registration. Pupils may be registered at any time although this should be as early as possible if entry is requested at ages other than 2, 4, 7 or 11 years. Candidates will be called for examination in the year of entry, although those who live at a distance may have the papers sent to their schools.

Charitable status. AKS is part of United Learning which comprises: UCST (a Company Limited by Guarantee, Registered in England, number 2780748, and a Registered Charity, number 1016538) and ULT (a Company Limited by Guarantee, Registered in England, number 4439859, and an Exempt Charity).

Aldenham School

Elstree, Herts WD6 3AJ

Tel:	01923 858122
Fax:	01923 854410
email:	enquiries@aldenham.com
website:	www.aldenham.com

Motto: '*In God is all our Trust.*'

The School was founded in 1597 by Richard Platt, 'Cytyzen and Brewer of London.'

Governing Body:
Chairman: J S Lewis, DL, FCIS

Governor Emeritus: Field Marshal The Lord Vincent, GBE, KCB, DSO [OA]

D Bridgman	S Nokes
P Carr [OA]	Mrs C Clapper
D T Tidmarsh	I A Dewar
Col M O'Dwyer	A Hellman
Mrs D Nicholes	The Ven J Smith
Mrs V Shah	M D Thomas
A Day [OA]	B Hewetson
J T Barton [OA]	

[OA] *Old Aldenhamian*

Headmaster: **J C Fowler**, MA

Deputy Head: A M Williams, BSc
Senior Master: N D Pulman, MA
Director of Studies: D S Watts, MA, CChem, MRSC
Head of Sixth Form & Careers: R P Collins, BA, MSc

Heads of Department:
Art: Miss G Nye, BA
Biology: Mrs J Dobbin BSc
Business Studies: L M Flindall, BA
Chemistry: A Shead, BSc
Computing: M Stott, MA
Design Technology: Miss S E Nicholl, BSc
Drama: Ms J Bannister, BA
English: C R Jenkins, MA
Games and Physical Education: G Cornock, BA
Geography: Mrs J Burger, BA
History: J R Kerslake, BA
Learning Support: Mrs L V Jones, CertEd
Mathematics: D A Chorley, BSc
Languages: Srta M B Bustamante; Miss C Weber, CC
Director of Music: J R Wyatt, GRSM, LRAM, ARCO
Physics: A J R Westwood, BSc
Sciences: Dr P J Reid
Theology: Dr K Viswanathan

Head of Prep School: Mrs V Gocher, BA
Deputy Head of Prep School & Head of Foundation Stage: Mrs C J Watts, CertEd

Houses and Housemasters:

Boarding Houses:
McGill's: M I Yeabsley, BSc
Beevor's: S Pennycook, BSc
Kennedy's: C S Irish, BSc

Paull's: Miss E C Gratton, BA

Day Houses:
Paull's: Miss E C Gratton, BA
Leeman's: G L Cornock, BA
Riding's: A P Stephenson, BA
Martineau's: Mrs L Gall, BEd

Chaplain: Padre S J Chapman, BA
Librarian: A Nelson, MA, DLIS, ALA
Bursar: A W C Fraser, FCIS

Number in School. 700, of which there are 171 boarders and 529 day pupils. (There are 213 girls in the School including the Preparatory School.)

Aldenham is situated in its own beautiful grounds of more than 110 acres in the Hertfordshire green belt, with excellent access to London (First Capital Connect/Jubilee Line) and within the M25, close to the M1. Aldenham's particular reputation as a close knit, small and supportive community with a strong boarding ethos makes it the very best environment for a high-quality all-round education. The achievement of every child's academic potential remains central but the building of confidence comes too from sports, music and drama, and by living and working together within the disciplined and vigorous community that is Aldenham today.

Admission. Prospective parents are encouraged to visit the School with their sons and daughters, either individually or at one of the school's 2 open days in June and October.

At 11, entry is by tests and interview, at 13 by interview and reference, and at 16 by interview and GCSE results. Every effort is made to meet parents' wishes as regards which House is chosen for their son. All girls enter Paull's House at 13.

Registration fee £50; Deposit £1,000.

Fees per term (2014–2015). Boarders £6,431–£9,707; Day Pupils £4,669–£6,663.

Scholarships and Exhibitions. Available at each point of entry, Scholarships and Exhibitions are awarded to boys and girls who have demonstrated outstanding achievement and who have the potential to make a special contribution to the School. In addition to Academic there are also opportunities for Music, Art, Sport and Design Technology scholarships and exhibitions.

Music scholarships and exhibitions are available at 11+, 13+ and 16+ under the same terms as for academic awards. Free tuition is given to Music Scholars. Any combination of choral and instrumental ability may be offered for the audition.

Art: A small number of awards at 11+, 13+ and 16+ are available each year. These are based on the candidate's portfolio and a short exercise at the school on a mutually convenient date.

Bursaries are also available to help boys and girls who will benefit from education at Aldenham but whose parents would not otherwise be able to afford the full fees.

Curriculum. From 11 to 16 the timetable closely reflects the National Curriculum. Boys and girls are prepared for GCSEs across a range of subjects including Maths, English, French, Science and a number of other Arts and language options. Care is taken that all pupils include Art, Music, Technology and IT in their programme and there is a progressive course of Theology throughout the School with GCSE taken in Year 11. The ISCO programme of tests and interviews are used as a basis for career planning and AS/A2 Level choice in Year 11.

Those in Year 12 normally take 4 AS Levels from a range of 25 subjects, which narrows to three choices at A2 in Year 13. The majority of students go on to degree courses at universities. There are regular successes at Oxford and Cambridge. Aldenham runs a European-wide Work Experience Scheme.

Games and Other Activities. Great value is placed on the participation of every pupil in an extensive Games and Activities programme. Football, Hockey, Cricket and Athletics are the major sports for boys, whilst girls benefit from a breadth of in- and out-of-school activities including Hockey, Tennis, Badminton, Dance, Squash, Netball, Rounders, Trampolining, Aerobics and Sailing. In addition there is a full programme of House and School competitions in Squash, Eton Fives, Basketball, Tennis, Sailing, Table Tennis, Shooting, and Cross-country. Volleyball, Horse Riding, Climbing, Judo and Golf are also available. The Sports Centre provides excellent facilities for expert and novice alike and incorporates a full-size indoor hockey pitch, dance studio, martial arts room, keep-fit suite and a rifle range. Time is set apart for activities and societies; these include CCF, Adventure activities, the Duke of Edinburgh's Award scheme, Community Service, Electronics, Chess, Computing, Motor Club, Photography and Model Railway. The Debating and Philosophy societies meet regularly throughout the year

Music and Drama. Music flourishes in the School. There is a Chapel Choir, School Orchestra and wind and brass groups. A spring concert is performed annually in the School Chapel. A number of boys and girls learn to play on the fine, modern, 3-manual pipe organ in the Chapel. A music school with a recital room, practice and performance facilities and music technology classrooms was extended in September 2012.

The school theatre opened in 2007 encourages a high calibre of Drama students. In addition to an annual School Play there are Senior and Junior House Play competitions and boys and girls have the opportunity to produce and design as well as to perform in the various productions. The School's proximity to London makes possible frequent visits to theatres and concerts. Theatre Studies is offered as a full A Level subject.

Organisation. Whilst the framework of the School is contemporary, it takes as its basis the long established 'House' system. Each House creates an extended family and provides the formal and social focus of the School. There are four boarding and three day Houses together with a distinct yet fully integrated Junior House for 11–13 year olds. Each has a Housemaster or Housemistress and a team of tutors so every pupil has a personal tutor. In the Boarding Houses the Housemaster, his family, Matron and tutors live at the centre of the community ensuring the well-being of each child.

Boarding. Aldenham's unique array of day and boarding options enables it to provide the educational benefits of a boarding school to Day and Day Boarding pupils and to offer real flexibility with its arrangements for boarders, the vast majority of whom live within 20 miles of the School. Boys and girls may board from entry at 11+.

Religion. Aldenham is a Church of England foundation and seeks to maintain a strong Christian ethos to which those of other faiths are warmly welcomed.

Old Aldenhamian Society. There is a thriving Old Aldenhamian Society, details from the OA Office at the School.

Charitable status. The Aldenham Foundation is a Registered Charity, number 298140. It exists to provide high quality education and pastoral care to enable children to achieve their full potential in later life.

Alleyn's School

Townley Road, Dulwich, London SE22 8SU
Tel: 020 8557 1500
         Headmaster: 020 8557 1493
         Bursar: 020 8557 1450
Fax: 020 8557 1462
email: enquiries@alleyns.org.uk
website: www.alleyns.org.uk

Motto: '*God's Gift*'
     The School is part of the foundation known as 'Alleyn's College of God's Gift' which was founded in 1619 by Edward Alleyn, the Elizabethan actor.

The Governing Body:

Chairman: Prof the Lord Kakkar, BSc, PhD, FRCS
Mr I Barbour, BSc Econ Hons, ACIB
Dr E F Bowen, BSc, MBBS Hons, PhD, FRCP
Dr M Campbell,
Rt Revd C Chessun, Bishop of Southwark, BA
Mr T Franey, FIMI
Mr J G Lilly, BA Hons, PGCE
Mr B Martin, MA, MBA, FCMI, FRSA
Mr P Perry, BA Hons
Mr R Pinckard, BSc Econ, FCA
Mr I Pulley
Revd Dr R Waller, MA Oxford, BD London, MTh
     Nottingham, PhD London
Mr P Yetzes, BA, JP

Headmaster: Dr G J Savage, MA Cantab, PhD, FRSA

Senior Deputy Head: Mr A R Faccinello, MA (*Designated Person for Safeguarding*)

Deputy Head, Personnel & Administration: Ms S P Chandler, BSc, PGDip
Deputy Head, Academic: Mrs A McAuliffe, BA

Assistant Heads:
Mr A W A Skinnard, MA (*Head of Upper School; Religious Studies*)
Mrs M A Joel, BA (*Head of Middle School; Modern Languages*)
Mr S E Smith, BA (*Headmaster of Lower School; Classics*)
Miss N A Demain, BA (*Assistant Head Co-Curricular & Partnerships, English, Drama, PE*)

Bursar: Mr S R Born, BA

Registrar: Mrs L Aldwinckle

Teaching Staff:
* *Head of Department*
† *Head of House*
§ *Part-time*

Dr M Abdalla (*Mathematics*)
Ms A K S Ackerman, MA (**Religious Studies, Philosophy, Induction Mentor*)
Mr D S Adkins, MA, MMus (*§Music*)
Mrs D E J Aird, MA (*§Religious Studies*)
Mr R J Alldrick, BA (*†Brown's House, PE, DoE, Field Centre Coordinator*)
Mr B D Allen, BA (*Design Technology*)
Mrs G T Anderson, MA (*English*)
Mrs C M Archard, MSc (*§Chemistry*) (*maternity leave*)
Mr P Berman, BA (*§Religious Studies, History, Geography*)
Dr O J Blaiklock, BA, MA, PhD (*History*)
Miss A J Blythe, BA (*Geography 2nd in Dept*)
Miss A L Boltsa, BA (*Head of Charities, Art*)
Miss R Brett, BSc (*Biology*)

Mr A M Bruni, BSc, BEd (*Mathematics 2nd in Dept, Community Service*)
Revd A G Buckley, MA (*History, Chaplain*)
Mrs L Carey (*§Learning Support*)
Miss J R Carlsson, MA (**Geography, International Links Coordinator*)
Ms S Chaplin, BSc (*Biology*)
Mrs C A Clift, BSc (*§Girls' PE & Games*)
Mr P M Cochrane, BSc (*†Roper's House, Chemistry*)
Miss W L Collins, BSc (**Chair of Science, *Chemistry*)
Miss L F Cooper, BA, MA (*Drama, Theatre Studies*)
Miss C V Copeland, MA (**Classics, Assistant Head of Upper School*)
Mrs J C Count, MA (*§Biology*) (*maternity leave*)
Revd S C Dalwood, BA (*Examinations Officer, Mathematics*)
Mr C W E Dearmer, MA, SSt (*Director of Music*)
Dr S de Silva, PhD (*Physics*)
Mrs E C Doherty, MA (*Classics*)
Miss J E Doley, LRAM (*§Music*)
Dr S Dutta, MA, DPhil (*Classics*)
Mrs H F Eagle, BSc (*§Design & Technology*)
Mr M D Eastmond, BA, MSc (*Mathematics*)
Miss R M Edwards, BA, MA (*Art*)
Miss D N Ellis, MA (*Economics, US Enrichment*)
Mr G English, BA (*Deputy Head of Middle School, PE*)
Mr C M Fish, BA (*Music*)
Miss C E Fleming, BSc (*Biology*)
Mrs J Franco, MPhys (*Physics*)
Ms L Gardner, GRSM, LRAM, MSc (**Lower School Music*)
Mr R L Geldeard, MA (*†Spurgeon's House, Classics, *Philosophy*)
Ms J D Gibbs (*§PE*)
Miss K A Goff, BA (*Modern Languages*) (*maternity leave*)
Miss C M Goldsworthy, BA (**Art*)
Miss C S Goldthorpe, BA (*PE*)
Miss S Gore, BA (*Deputy Head of PSHE, Religious Studies*)
Mrs K M Green, BSc (*§Mathematics*)
Mr N J Green, BEd (*†Tyson's House, PE*)
Mr M F Grogan, BA, MA (**Media Studies*)
Mrs P Hall, BA (*Spanish*)
Mr R G Halladay, BA, MA (*English, Deputy Head Middle School*)
Mr D J Harley, BSc (**History, Politics, Assistant Head of Upper School*)
Mr P J Harper, BA (*Modern Languages*)
Dr D O Hawes, BA, MA, PhD (*KS3 Coordinator, History, Politics*)
Mrs M Heaton-Caffin, CertEd (*§PE*)
Miss J Hewitson, BSc (*†Tulley's House, Geography, Acting CO CCF*)
Mrs L E Higinson, MA (*Biology*)
Mr N C Hughan, BA (*History, Politics*)
Mr G L Jenkins, MA (*English*)
Miss M M Jenney, BA (*History*)
Mr D J Jewison, BA (*English*)
Mr B Jones, MSc (**Physics*)
Mr S F Keeler, BSc, MA (*Assistant of Upper School, *Psychology, Physics*)
Dr S P Kelly, BA, MA, PhD (**German, *Universities & Careers Centre, Modern Languages*)
Mrs S Kent, MA (*History, US Deputy Enrichment Coordinator*)
Ms S Kingston, MA (*Art*)
Miss S A Lane, MA, CertEd (*Deputy Head of Upper School, PE*)
Mrs S C Latham, BA (**Politics, History*)
Mrs H E Lawrence, BA (*§Deputy Head of English, Learning Support*)
Mr A J N Lea, BA (*Drama*)
Miss A M Legg, MA (**English, Media Studies*)

Miss V A Lodge, BSc (*PE*)
Mr J W Lothian, BSc (*Biology*)
Mr P M Macdonagh, BSc (**ICT*)
Mr A Macmillan, BA (**Design Technology*)
Mr E D Mann, BA (*Mathematics*)
Mrs S Mathieson, CertEd (**Food Technology*)
Miss M R McAteer, BEng (*Maths*)
Mr M McCaffrey, BA (**French*)
Mrs C A Mines, MA (§*Modern Languages*)
Mr C R Newbould BSc, PGCE (*Physics*)
Miss E M Nicoll, BA (†*Brading's House, Modern Languages*)
Mrs E O'Donnell, BA, Grad Dip LIB Science (**Librarian*)
Mr R N Ody, BEd (**Head of Games and Boys' PE*)
Dr A M O'Neill, PhD (*Chemistry*)
Miss R L Ottey, BSc (†*Cribb's House, *Physics*)
Miss K J Owens, BEd (*Deputy Head of Lower School, Design Technology, Head of PSHE*)
Mr S R Parkin, BA (*Mathematics*)
Mr R D W Payne, BSc (*Information Technology*)
Mr J S Pettigrew, BSc (*Phycology*)
Mr J S S Piper, MA (**Drama*)
Miss M M Pokorny, BSc (*CO CCF, Psychology, Biology, PSHE 2nd in Dept*)
Miss A M Poole, BSc (**Mathematics*)
Mrs K Pryse-Lloyd, MSc (*Physics*)
Miss V L Rees, BA (*Geography*)
Mr G Reid, MA (*Religious Studies*)
Miss S C Reynolds BA (*Art*)
Mr M Riedel, BSc (*Mathematics*)
Mr A W Robertson, BSc, MBA (**Economics, Deputy Head University & Careers Centre*)
Mrs H E Rowett, BA (§*Geography*)
Mr P J Ryder, BEng (*Mathematics*)
Miss A Schüller, MA (*Modern Languages*)
Mr J I Shead, BEd (*PE*)
Mr J G Shelton, BEd, RSA Dip IT (†*Dutton's House, Information Technology*)
Mrs G Silver, MA (*English*)
Mrs S C Smiddy, BSc (**Biology*)
Mr P A Smith, BMus, ARCM, LRAM (**Instrumental Studies*)
Mr K Sritharan, MSc (*Chemistry, CCF, CO RN*)
Mr V A Strain, BA (*Deputy Head of Lower School, Modern Languages*)
Mr T Strange, BA (*Classics*)
Mrs J M Tait, BA (§*Food Technology*)
Mr P Thomas, BA (§*Mathematics*)
Mr J Thompson (*Music*)
Mrs E D Thornton, BA (**Modern Foreign Languages*)
Miss S C Trotter, BA, MA (*English*)
Miss R M Twomey, BA, MA (**Spanish*)
Mrs J L van der Valk, BA (*Learning Support Coordinator*)
Miss M J Walker, BA (**Director of Sport & PE*)
Mrs A L Ward, BA, MA (§*Religious Studies*)
Mrs C L Wells, BSc (*Deputy Director of Studies, Mathematics*)
Dr S M Whitehead PhD (§*English*)
Mr M Workman, MA (*Chemistry*)

The School. Alleyn's is a co-educational day school for pupils aged 11 to 18 years, some 990 strong, of whom approximately 300 are in the Sixth Form. The Headmaster is a member of the Headmasters' and Headmistresses' Conference.

It is, with Dulwich College, the lineal descendant of "the School for twelve poor scholars" endowed by Edward Alleyn, the Elizabethan actor-manager, under a Royal Charter of 1619.

It was a Direct Grant school from 1958 until the abolition of this status in 1976. The Governors then opted for independence and at the same time opened the entry to girl pupils, making it London's first independent co-educational senior school. The School is fully co-educational.

Alleyn's Junior School, for ages 4 to 10 years, which opened in September 1992, is also on the site. (*See entry in IAPS section.*)

Entrance. A registration fee of £75* (£50 for 16+) is charged for all applications (*£200 for overseas applications).

Admission to the School is by competitive examination open to both boys and girls at age 11, the normal age for transfer from primary to secondary school. Entrance is decided on the basis of the entrance/scholarship examination held in January for entry the following September. A report is requested from the Head of the applicant's school and, if they reach a satisfactory standard in the examination, boys and girls are invited for interview. The examination consists of Reasoning papers, an English paper and a Mathematics paper. Candidates should be entered for the School before the end of November (slightly earlier for 16+), for admission the following September.

There is a smaller entry by examination open to both boys and girls at age 13. The procedure is similar to that for the 11-year-old entry, with the addition of a paper in Science.

A similar procedure operates for entry at 16+, with an examination in November including subject papers and a general paper.

Opportunities for entry at other ages occasionally occur from time to time. At age 4, 7 and 9 Junior School places are awarded on the basis of an assessment held in January for entry the following September.

Fees per term (2014–2015). £5,529 (£16,587 per annum).

Scholarships, Exhibitions and Bursaries. *Academic* Scholarships, worth up to £3,000 pa, are available at 11+, 13+ and 16+ and awarded based on the results of the entrance examination and interview.

Music Scholarships, worth up to £3,000 pa plus free tuition on principal instrument, and Music Exhibitions (free tuition on principal instrument) are available at 11+ and 13+. The Hans Keller Music Scholarship, worth up to £1,500 pa, is available at 16+.

Art Scholarships, worth up to £1,000 pa, are available at 11+.

Sports Scholarships, worth up to £3,000 pa, and Sports Exhibitions (£250 pa) are available at 11+ and 13+.

Bursaries: Academic Bursary Places (up to 100% fee remission, means-tested) are available for academically able candidates at 11+, 13+ and 16+. Means-tested bursaries (up to 100% fee remission) are also available to supplement a scholarship award.

Curriculum. All pupils follow a broad and balanced curriculum in the first three years, including English, Mathematics, Spanish, Latin and/or additional foreign languages (German or French), Biology, Chemistry, Physics, Geography, History, Religious Studies, Art, Computer Studies, Music and Design Technology. In Years 10–11, pupils take nine or ten GCSE subjects which will include English, English Literature, Mathematics, Biology, Chemistry and Physics. In addition they choose four option subjects. In Year 12, four main subjects are followed to AS Level. In Year 13, three or four A Levels are taken. In addition to those subjects listed above Classical Civilisation, Computing, Economics, Classical Greek, History of Art, Italian (ab initio), Media Studies, Philosophy, Politics, Psychology, Physical Education and Drama and Theatre Studies are also available.

Pupils go on to universities, medical and dental schools, music and art colleges. Almost all enter higher education. Selected pupils are prepared and entered for colleges at Oxford and Cambridge, where a very good record of places is maintained each year.

Organisation. The Lower School (Years 7 and Year 8) has its own separate building and its own Head. The Middle School (Years 9–11) and Upper School (Years 12–13) each has its own Head, and pupils belong to one of eight Houses. Each Head of House is responsible, not only for organised games, but also for the welfare of each of their pupils during their time in the School. This care is supplemented by a system of form tutors for supervision of academic progress and pastoral support. Parents are invited to Open Evenings during the year, at which pupils' work and progress are discussed with the teaching staff.

Games. The School stands in its own grounds of 30 acres and offers a wide variety of sports and games including Soccer, Hockey, Cricket, Swimming, Athletics, Netball, Cross-Country Running, Rugby Fives, Water Polo, Gymnastics, Badminton, Fencing, Golf, Basketball, Tennis, Rounders, Trampolining, Aerobics, Fitness and Weight Training, Table Tennis, Squash and Horse Riding.

Religious Education. The Foundation belongs to the Church of England. Religious Education of a non-denominational nature is given throughout the School, and pupils also attend regular worship in Assembly and once each term in the Foundation Chapel or in St Barnabas Church. The School Chaplain holds voluntary Holy Communion Services during term time.

Buildings. The main school building dates from 1887. The school has a fully-equipped sports hall, with cardio-vascular room, a refurbished indoor swimming pool (with a tiered viewing gallery and Olympic timing system), a technology centre, a music school, two digital language laboratories, an all-weather playing surface, a sports hall and pavilion, computer rooms, a library/resource centre and a RIBA Award-winning performing arts centre (the Edward Alleyn Building), containing a 350-seat theatre, a Sixth Form study centre, classrooms, lecture theatre, and a studio for the NYT. Some 800+ computers are networked on the school's site.

The **Fenner Library** is available to all pupils for private study. Library staff encourage reading for pleasure, with a variety of fiction and non-fiction books to borrow. Newspapers, periodicals, audio CDs and DVDs are also available.

Music, Drama and Art feature very strongly in the life of the School. There are 5 major concerts each year including an annual concert at St John's Smith Square; the School runs 3 orchestras, 3 bands, 3 choirs and has over 30 Chamber groups, chosen by ability rather than age. 5 or 6 dramatic productions are staged each year. In Art, all pupils are taught to work in different media (Painting, Drawing, Sculpture and Ceramics).

There are many clubs and societies in the school; these include, in addition to Drama groups, Debating, Dance, Photography, Chess, Politics, Science and the Christian Union.

The Combined Cadet Force has long been one of the most flourishing in the country, containing Army, Navy and RAF sections, and provides opportunities for such other activities as canoeing, rock climbing, sailing and flying. Pupils are encouraged to join at age 14 and serve for a minimum of 2 years. Pupils who do not join the CCF are expected to join either the Duke of Edinburgh's Award Scheme or the Volunteering group.

Career Guidance is given by specialised staff with the time and facilities for this important work. In Year 11 systematic aptitude testing is followed up by talks by parents themselves who give their time to talk about their own careers and who give help with offers of work experience to pupils.

An annual event, Year 12 Interview Day, is held in March. Pupils make a mock application for various and widely-ranging positions and university lecturers come in to help pupils to develop their skills.

A School Council and Learning Council, with members from each Section of the School, represents pupils' views to the Headmaster.

Relations with Parents. The Alleyn's Parents' Association is a dynamic and enthusiastic parent organisation which nurtures close links between parents and the School, and which raises considerable funds for the benefit of the School's Pupil Support Fund.

The Edward Alleyn Club. Past pupils are automatically members of the Edward Alleyn Club. This enables them to keep in touch with the school and their contemporaries, and also to take part in sporting activities if they wish. Communications should be sent to the Head of Alumni Relations, Mrs Martha Jones, c/o Alleyn's School (alumni@alleyns.org.uk).

Charitable status. Alleyn's College of God's Gift is a Registered Charity, number 1057971. Its purpose is to provide Independent Education for boys and girls from age 4 to 18.

Ampleforth College

York, North Yorkshire YO62 4ER
Tel: 01439 766000
Fax: 01439 788330
email: admin@ampleforth.org.uk
website: www.college.ampleforth.org.uk

Motto: *'Dieu le Ward'*.

Ampleforth Abbey was founded in 1607 at Dieulouard in Lorraine by English Benedictine monks who had strong links with the mediaeval Benedictines of Westminster Abbey. After the French Revolution the monastic community was resettled at Ampleforth in 1802 and the present School was started there soon after.

The Community is dedicated, first to prayer, and then to religious and charitable works. Ampleforth College and St Martin's Ampleforth are the works of St Laurence Educational Trust. The other works of the Community include parishes in Yorkshire, Lancashire and Cumbria, St Benet's Hall in Oxford and pastoral involvement both at Ampleforth and elsewhere.

Governance: The Abbot of Ampleforth is elected by the Community for eight years at a time and presides over the Community and its works.

The Abbot is Chairman of the Ampleforth Abbey Trustees, which is the legal institute that owns and governs its foundation. St Laurence Education Trust is a separate limited company formed by the Abbey Trust. This also has charitable status and is responsible for both Ampleforth College and St Martin's Ampleforth.

The governance of these works is the responsibility of the Abbot who, with structured advice, appoints the officials, monastic and lay, who are in charge of their administration.

Governing Body:
The Abbot of Ampleforth is the Chairman of Governors acting with the Council and Chapter of Ampleforth Abbey. He is assisted by a lay Advisory Body.

***Headmaster:* Mr D A Lambon**, MEng, BSc

Deputy Head: Miss D Rowe, MA
Director of Studies: Mr I F Lovat, BSc, MInstP
Director of Professional Development: Mr A S Thorpe, BSc, CChem, MRSC
Director of Admissions: Mr R F Thompson, MA
Head of Boarding: Mr A P Smerdon, BSc
Head of Sixth Form: Mr W F Lofthouse, MA
Head of Careers/Assistant Head of Sixth Form: Mrs J Campbell, BA
School Chaplain: Rev C Boulton, OSB, BA

Guestmaster: Rev H Lewis-Vivas, OSB, MA

Academic Departments:

Christian Theology:
*Mrs A M McNeill, BA
†Mr M B Fogg, BA
†Mrs G M O McGovern, MA
Mr A J J Macdonald Powney, MA
Mrs H E Pepper, BA
Mr J D Rainer, BA
Mr R M Hudson, MA

Christian Living:
†Mrs A Le Gall, MA
Mrs M B Carter, BSc
Mrs A Rogerson, BTh

Classics:
†*Mr J B Mutton, MA
Mr W F Lofthouse, MA
Mr J Layden, BA
Miss J Sutcliffe, BA

History:
*Mr P T Connor, MA
Mr H C Codrington, BEd
Mr G D Thurman, BEd
Mrs M F Rainer, BA
Miss A N Rosenberg, MA

English:
*Mr A C Carter, MA
Dr D Moses, MA, DPhil
Mr D J Davison, MA
Mrs L Roberts, MA, MPhil
Dr C G Vowles, BA, PhD
Mrs H J Burrows, BA
Dr E V Fogg, MA, PhD
    (*Head of EAL*)
Mrs A Mihkelson
    (*Learning Support*)

Modern Languages:
*Mr S R Owen, MA
Mr J P Ridge, MA
Mr M Torrens-Burton, BA
    (*EAL*)
Rev A McCabe, OSB, MA
Mrs F Garcia-Ortega, BA
Rev J Callaghan, MA
Miss A L Kimmerle, MA
Miss M V Serrano Fernandez
Mrs S M G Baseley, MA
Miss S Normand

Geography:
*Mrs C R M Dent, BSc
Mr P M Brennan, BSc, FRMetSoc
Mr A P Smerdon, BSc
Miss H K Punnett, BSc

Modern Studies:
*Mr M A Dent, BSc

PE and Games:
*Mr R J H Thorley, BA (*Director of Sport*)
Mr R W Pineo, BSc (*Assistant Director of Sport*)
Mr G D Thurman, BEd
Miss J N Horn, BA (*Head of PE*)
Mr J J Owen, BEd (*Head of Hockey*)
Mr C Booth, BSc

Miss J M C Simmonds, BSc
Mrs J Stannard, BA
Mr C S Rodda, BA

Mathematics:
*Dr H R Pomroy, BSc, PhD
Mrs P J Melling, BSc, BA
Dr R Warren, BSc, PhD
    (*Head of Middle School*)
†Mr D Willis, BEd, MEd
Mr C G O'Donovan, BSc
Dr J M Weston, BSc, DPhil
Dr J W Large, BSc, PhD
Mrs T M Jones, BSc

Physics:
*Mr J O Devitt, MPhys
Mr I F Lovat, BSc, MInstP
Dr L M Kessell, BSc, PhD
Mr B Townend, MPh
Mr J Cochrane, BSc

Chemistry:
*Mr S J Howard, BSc
Mr A S Thorpe, BSc, CChem, MRSC
Mr S J Howard, BSc
Dr M J Parker, BSc, PhD

Biology:
*Mr P W Anderson, BSc
Mr A J Hurst, BSc
Mrs J Hurst, BSc
Dr H Webster, MA
Mrs R Gibson, MSc

Music:
*Mr I D Little, MA, MusB, FRCO, ARCM, LRAM
Mr W J Dore, MA, FRCO
Mr D de Cogan, DipRCM, ARCM
Mr P J McBeth, MusB
Mr C Potts, BA

Design and Technology:
*Mr B J Anglim, BEng
†Mrs V Anglim, BEng
Miss L Follos, BA

ICT:
*Mr M A Barras, BSc

Art:
*Mr S G Bird, BA, ATC, DipAD
Mr T J W Walsh, BA
Mrs E Vowles, BA

Theatre Director:
Miss J Sutcliffe, BA

Houses and Housemasters/Housemistresses:
St Aidan's (*girls*): Mrs A Le Gall, MA
St Bede's (*girls*): Mrs V Anglim, BEng
St Margaret's (*girls*): Mrs G M O McGovern, MA
St Cuthbert's: Mr D Willis, MEd
St Dunstan's: Mr B T A Pennington, BSc
St Edward's and St Wilfrid's: Mr L W B Ramsden, BA
St Hugh's: Mr M B Fogg, BA
St John's: Dr D Moses, MA, DPhil
St Oswald's: Mr P J McBeth, MusB
St Thomas': Mr J B Mutton, MA

Counsellor: Mr J G J Allisstone, BA

Procurator: Rev W Peterburs, OSB, MA, PhD

Medical Officers:
Dr Kaye Mechie, MBChB
Dr G Black, MBChB, MRCGP, DRCOG

Headmaster's Secretary: Mrs L M Featherstone

Number in School. There are 610 students, of whom 518 are Boarders, including 190 girls, 51 are Day Boys and 41 are Day Girls.

Our aims are:

- to share with parents in the spiritual, moral and intellectual formation of their children, in a Christian community with which their families may be joined in friendship and prayer for the rest of their lives.
- to educate the young in the tradition and sacramental life of the Church and to encourage each towards a joyful, free and self-disciplined life of faith and virtue.
- to work for excellence in all our endeavours, academic, sporting and cultural. We ask students to give of their best. We ask much of the gifted and we encourage the weak. Each is taught to appreciate the value of learning and the pursuit of the truth.
- to help Ampleforth boys and girls grow up mature and honourable, inspired by high ideals and capable of leadership, so that they may serve others generously, be strong in friendship, and loving and loyal towards their families.

Organisation. St Martin's Ampleforth, an independent preparatory school at Gilling Castle, educates boys and girls from 3 to 13 years old. (*For further details, see entry in IAPS section.*)

The upper school has 7 houses for boys aged 13 to 18 and three houses for girls aged 13 to 18. Houses are kept small and are home to no more than 60 boarders and there are some day students in each.

Each house has its own separate accommodation. All students eat their lunch in separate house refectories. They eat breakfast and supper in a central cafeteria with the House staff, chaplains and tutors.

The work and games of the whole school are centrally organised. At least five tutors are allocated to each house to supervise students' work and provide the appropriate guidance at each stage in their school career. The Head of Careers provides information and assistance and can arrange expert advice for pupils, parents and tutors. Some of the non-teaching life of the school is organised around the houses. House competitions help to create a strong house loyalty. We have a central school chaplaincy that acts as a social meeting place for the middle school and a sixth form social centre, the Windmill, just off the campus.

There has been over £20m invested in the school in the last 10 years.

Curriculum. The first year (year 9) provides a broad basis from which to make informed GCSE choices. In the second and third years a core of English, Mathematics, Science and Christian Theology is studied to GCSE together with a balanced selection from a wide range of subjects. In the first year of the sixth form (year 12) up to 5 subjects may be studied to AS level. One of those subjects may be AS level Christian Theology but, if not, students follow a Christian Theology short course. Normally three subjects will be taken on to A level in the second year (year 13). A comprehensive health education programme is provided in all years.

Games and Activities. There are opportunities to play a wide variety of representative sports at all levels with excellent indoor and outdoor facilities. Many activities and games take place during the week and weekends, including drama, debating, outdoor pursuits, creative arts and a wide variety of sports. These sports range from lacrosse to rugby. The school has its own outstanding 9-hole golf course and has recently completed a new all-weather hockey surface and new tennis courts. In addition, the college has its own all-weather athletics track.

Music, which is a strong academic subject, plays a major part in the extra-curricular life of the school. The Schola Cantorum, our liturgical choir, sing for Mass in the Abbey and perform sacred music in Britain and abroad. They have been responsible for the production of several commercial CDs in recent years. The Schola Puellarum, our girls choir, sings with the Schola Cantorum on alternate Sundays and has its own repertoire. It has undertaken tours both at home and abroad and has also released its own CD.

Further enquiries may be made directly to the Director of Sport on 01439 766729 or the Director of Music on 01439 766730.

Admission. Applications may be made through the Admissions Office. Registration Fee: £75.

Fees per term (2014–2015). Boarders £10,441; Day Boys/Girls £7,047.

The fees are inclusive, the only normal extras being for individual tuition in Music: £30 per lesson, £28 for a second instrument; EAL £865 per term.

Entrance Scholarships. Academic, Music and All-Rounder scholarships are awarded at 13+ and for entry to the Sixth Form.

Scholarships are awarded annually on the results of examinations held at Ampleforth. They are honorary and carry no remission of fees. However, the award of a scholarship will support a bursary application.

Academic Scholarships at 13+: ISEB Common Academic Scholarship examinations are sat in February.

Sixth Form Entry: Academic Scholarship examinations are held in November.

Music Scholarships are available for entry to the College at ages 13 and 16. All scholarships carry free music tuition.

All-Rounder Scholarships at 13+: The Basil Hume Scholarships for candidates who have a strong commitment to extra-curricular activities.

Further details can be obtained from The Admissions Office, Tel: 01439 766863, email: admissions@ampleforth. org.uk.

Charitable status. St Laurence Educational Trust is a Registered Charity, number 1063808. Its aim is to advance Roman Catholic religion.

Ardingly College
A Woodard School

Haywards Heath, West Sussex RH17 6SQ
Tel: 01444 893000
Fax: 01444 893001
email: head@ardingly.com
website: www.ardingly.com

Motto: '*Beati Mundo Corde*'.

Ardingly is a co-educational school in the Woodard Family founded to teach the Christian Faith.

Our aim is to enable all boys and girls to develop their love of learning, academic potential and individual talents,

in a caring community which fosters sensitivity, confidence, a sense of service and enthusiasm for life.

School Council:
Mr Jim F Sloane, BSc (*Chairman, Chair of Nominations Committee*)
Mr Peter N Bryan, BA, ACA
Mrs Claire D Cater
Mr Guy Dixon, BA Hons, Dip TP, MRTPI
Mr David F Gibbs, BA (*Chair of Education Committee*)
Mrs Liz Hewer, MA, PGCE
Mr Alan A Holmes, FCA (*Governor with responsibility for Compliance*)
Mr Douglas H T Johnson-Poensgen, BEng Hons
Dr Simon Kay, PhD
The Earl of Limerick, MA
Mrs Louise E Lindsay, FCIPD, LLM, BA Hons (*Governor with responsibility for Child Protection*)
Mr Neil Mclaughlan
Mr Graham N Turner, BSc, FCIOB (*Deputy Chairman, Chair of Finance and General Purposes Committee*)
Mr Nicholas Walker, BA Comb Hons, MSc
The Right Reverend Lindsay Urwin, OGS, MA (*Provost*)

Headmaster: **Ben Figgis**, BA, MEd

Deputy Headmaster: Philip Stapleton, BSc

Chaplain: Father David Lawrence-March, BA Hons

Head of the Prep School: Chris Calvey, BEd

Director of Operations: Paddy Jackman

Medical Officer: Dr B Lambert

History and development of the College. Ardingly College, the third of Nathaniel Woodard's schools, was founded in Shoreham in 1858 and moved to its present beautiful site in Mid Sussex, about halfway between Gatwick and Brighton, in 1870. The College now consists of a Pre-Prep day School and a weekly boarding and day Prep School, for boys and girls between the ages of 2½ and 13, and a boarding and day Senior School for boys and girls aged between 13 and 18.

In the Prep School, which has been co-educational since 1986, there are 257 pupils, of whom 141 are boys and 116 are girls. There are 108 boys and girls in the Pre-Prep.

In the Senior School, which became fully co-educational in 1982, there are 557 pupils of whom 249 are in the Sixth Form. There are 334 boys and 223 girls, and 260 are boarders.

For further details about Ardingly Prep and Pre-Prep Schools, see entry in the IAPS section.

Academic. Ardingly has an extremely good academic record in both arts and science subjects achieved by boys and girls who come from a wide spectrum of ability. Both the International Baccalaureate and A Levels are offered.

In 2014 the IB students attained an average provisional point score of 37, seven points above the worldwide figure. It is the best average ever achieved in the 12 years the college has offered the IB.

In A Levels the combined results mean that nearly half of final year students achieved A*–A (47%) and three-quarters achieved A*–B.

In GCSEs the average subject grade per candidate was an A, and 25% of the 112 Fifth Form (Year 11) attained all A*s or As. 36% of grades across the cohort were A* and 65% of all grades were A*–A.

Curriculum. *First year*: A broad course in which all pupils do virtually everything: second Modern Language (German or Spanish); Expressive Arts; a trans-disciplinary 'Inquiring Curriculum' and all undertake iMind research and inquiry lessons whilst completing their own chosen personal project.

GCSE (2nd and 3rd years): All take IGCSEs in English and English Literature, Maths, Sciences, GCSEs in at least one Modern Language, and the usual wide range of options.

Sixth Form Curriculum: Standard choices in a highly flexible block system at AS/A2 or in the International Baccalaureate Diploma Programme. ICT skills are developed through AS/A2 and IB courses. All Lower Sixth students follow a development course which covers life skills, careers and HE study skills. All Sixth Form students whether following the A Level route or the IB route, complete the IB Core (Extended Essay, Theory of Knowledge, and Creativity, Action and Service) which is highly valued by universities both in the UK and around the globe.

Pastoral. There are 7 Middle School Houses, four for boys and two for girls, which contain everyone from the first year to the Lower Sixth with a separate house for the Lower Sixth girls. In the Upper Sixth all boys and girls transfer to a separate, newly built, integrated co-educational House, "Woodard" (originally opened in 1988 and the new building opened in 2013), in which they are able to concentrate more fully on their studies and can be given greater responsibility for themselves and be better prepared for life at University or in the outside world. Each House has its own Housemaster or Housemistress, Assistant and House Tutors. In addition every boy and girl will have a Tutor who has responsibility for the work, progress, choices and many other aspects of the pupil's life. Tutorials are regular, weekly group tutorials and fortnightly individual tutorials. Tutors work closely with careers staff to incorporate careers guidance into their tutorials.

In Year 9 and Year 10 pupils study and discuss personal, social and health education, careers topics in small mixed groups as part of a specially designed course called Eudaimonia meaning 'human flourishing' and through Eudaimonia days in the Fifth Form.

There is an efficient Medical Centre in the centre of the school with a residential Sister in charge. The School Doctor takes three surgeries a week in the School and is always on call.

Since September 2005 School on Saturdays has been discontinued.

Expressive Arts. *Music*: Choir, Chamber Choir, Schola Cantorum, Jazz Singers, Orchestras, Concert Band, Jazz Band, Chamber Music. Instrumental lessons taken by about half the boys and girls.

Art: Painting, drawing, printing, ceramics, sculpture, fashion & textiles, photography, etching.

Design Technology: Real design problems solved in a variety of materials and forms.

Drama: Many productions in the course of the year for all ages. Large flexible theatre and a small workshop theatre.

The expressive arts are studied throughout Year 9, are options for GCSE and A Level and offer scholarships for talented candidates, at both 13+ and for the Sixth Form.

Sport. Boys play Football, Hockey, Rugby 7s, Cricket, Tennis, Athletics; Girls play Hockey, Netball, Tennis, Rounders, Athletics. (Football and cricket are also available for girls.) The football academy caters for the elite footballers, offering an intensive training programme and competitive matches against football league academies without compromising studies.

Also (for both boys and girls) there is Cross Country, Swimming, Shooting, Golf, Volleyball, Horse Riding, Clay Pigeon Shooting, Basketball, Badminton, Karate, Croquet, Sailing, etc.

The indoor pool is open to both Prep and Senior Schools and pupils who cannot swim are taught to do so.

Activities. Combined Cadet Force (Army based), Duke of Edinburgh's Award, Beekeeping, Modern Dance, Photography, Computers, Fencing, Astronomy, Debating, Charity Focus, Amnesty International etc.

Admission to the Senior School normally takes place at 13+ or directly into the Sixth Form at 16+. Admission is also possible at 14+ but is not advisable at the beginning of the years in which GCSE or A Levels are taken unless there are very special reasons. A Pre-IB course is offered in the Sixth Form.

At 13+ entry is by written assessments in English, Mathematics and Verbal Reasoning and satisfactory results at Common Entrance. If pupils have not been prepared for Common Entrance then they will sit our own entrance papers. We also require a report and reference from the pupil's previous school. The headmaster likes to interview prospective pupils if practicable. The selection of candidates for direct entry to the Sixth Form takes place in November of the year prior to entry. All candidates are interviewed and take an English paper and a Maths paper. A report from their Head is also required. Places will then be offered subject to the candidate gaining a minimum of 6 grade Bs or above at GCSE. Modifications of these procedures and of the timing for individuals at any stage are almost always possible.

The Prep School has entry at 7+ and 11+ or at any other time between the ages of 7 and 11. Transfer into the Senior School is by entrance assessments and Common Entrance.

Scholarships. A number of Scholarships are offered for annual competition at 13+ and 16+. They include Academic, Art, Drama, Music and Sports Awards. Ashdown Awards for all-rounders are offered for those entering at 13+. The Prep School offers Academic, Art, Music and Sports Awards at 11+ with Academic Awards at 7+ and are tenable for the Prep School years only. Along with other HMC schools, the maximum value of a scholarship is 40% of the basic fees pa but all may be supplemented by a means-tested bursary if need can be shown.

A limited number of bursaries (value up to 50% of basic fees pa) are available for the children of the Clergy.

Please address all enquiries about admissions, scholarships and bursaries to the Registrar (Tel: 01444 893000; fax: 01444 893001; email: registrar@ardingly.com).

Term of Entry. Main 13+ and Sixth Form intake in September. Intake at other ages and other times on an individual basis.

Registration. The School Prospectus may be obtained from the Registrar. Registration (where a non-returnable fee of £100 is charged) can be made at any age subject to the availability of places. No separate registration is required for children transferring from the Prep to the Senior School.

Fees per term (2014–2015). Senior School: Boarding £9,570–£10,120, Day Pupils £7,115–£7,505. Casual Boarding: £40 per night. Prep School: Weekly Boarding depending on the number of days ranges from £220 per term for 1 night per week to £1,100 for 5 nights (in addition to Day Fees); Day Pupils £3,775–£4,745; Casual Boarding £30 per night. Pre-Prep: £1,975–£2,630.

Fees are inclusive. There is a surcharge of £180 per term for those entering at the Sixth Form stage.

Further Particulars. For further information, application should be made to the Registrar.

Charitable status. Ardingly College Limited is a Registered Charity, number 1076456. It exists to provide high quality education for boys and girls aged 2½ to 18.

Ashford School
United Learning

East Hill, Ashford, Kent TN24 8PB
Tel: 01233 625171
Fax: 01233 647185
email: registrar@ashfordschool.co.uk
website: www.ashfordschool.co.uk
Twitter: @AshfordSchool
Facebook: /ASA.AshfordSchoolAssociation

Chairman of School Council: Mr P Massey, MA

Vice-Chairman: Mr R I Henderson, JP, LLB

Council Members:
Mr R Coombe
Mr W Peppitt, MRICS
Mr A J Rawlins
Mr J B Rimmer, MRICS, FAAV
Mrs E Rose, MSc
Mrs L van der Bijl
Mrs J M Webb, BA
Professor P Freemont, FSB
Mr C Hendry, CBE, QSFM
Ven S Taylor, MBE

Head: **Mr Michael Buchanan**, BSc London

Head of the Prep School: Mr R Yeates, BA Exeter
Deputy Head, Director of the Senior School: Mr T Wilding, BA Exeter
School Business Manager: Mr N Cufley, MBA Cranfield

Senior School:
Deputy Head, Director of Teaching and Learning: Mrs C Allum, BA Durham, MPhil, MA Ed Warwick
Director of Upper School: Mr T Wilding, BA Exeter
Director of Sixth Form: Mr O Thomson, MA Cambridge
Director of Middle School: Mrs N Timms, BEng Loughborough

Prep School:
Deputy Head: Mrs P Willetts, BPrimEd

Ashford School was founded in 1898 as an independent, day and boarding school and provides education for boys and girls from 3 months to 18 years. There are over 450 students in the Senior School and over 350 in the Prep School (age 3–11). There are around 150 boarders in the school cared for by resident teachers and support staff in extensive accommodation that includes en-suite rooms for many. Forty nationalities are represented and specialist English tuition is provided for those who require it. There are no lessons on Saturdays.

Ashford School is a member of a group of independent schools run by United Learning which provides a first-class education for more than 25,000 pupils. United Learning aims to be at the forefront of educational development, bringing the very best resources, both human and physical, to the children in its schools.

The Senior School occupies a 25-acre site in a prominent position close to the centre of Ashford and near to the International Station. A green and secure haven in a busy and growing town, Ashford is 37 minutes from London by rail and also benefits from rapid access to Paris, Lyon, Brussels, Amsterdam, Cologne and Frankfurt on the Eurostar. With easy access to the M20 motorway and local train services, the central location and easy accessibility provides an ideally located school whether you live in the UK or anywhere across the globe.

With playing fields on site, a brand new Sports Centre, two gyms, indoor swimming pool, floodlit Astroturf, tennis and netball courts, boarding houses and dining hall, the School enjoys all the specialist teaching facilities you would expect of an independent school and has embarked on a programme to refurbish and extend the facilities. The Pre-Nursery, Bridge House, is located on the Senior School site and the Prep School is located in the nearby picturesque village of Great Chart and has recently undergone major redevelopment to double its size and further improve facilities and opportunities for pupils at the school.

Almost half of the students entering the Senior School at 11+ join direct from the Prep School and the remainder from other primary and prep schools. There are then normally three classes per year through to GCSE with additional students joining other years and the Sixth Form. All Sixth Form students go on to take degree courses at leading universities in the UK and abroad.

Over the last three years an average of two thirds of A Level students have gone to Russell Group universities and one fifth to World Top Ten such as Imperial College, LSE, Durham, Warwick, Birmingham, Bristol, UCL, Nottingham, Leeds, York and Newcastle.

An inspection by the Independent Schools Inspectorate in March 2014 found the school to be 'outstanding' or 'excellent' in every category.

The Senior School curriculum is broad and provides many opportunities in the classroom and in activities. The school has interactive whiteboards in every teaching room and modern facilities throughout. Pupils follow a broad curriculum to keep their options open and in addition to the core subjects of English, maths, the sciences and a language they may study additional languages, history, geography, religious studies, information technology, art and textiles, music, drama and physical education. Throughout the Senior School, subjects are set by ability where possible and there is a strong pastoral system based around six Houses.

External Examinations. Most pupils take 9/10 subjects at GCSE. Many A Level combinations are available to the Sixth Form, all of whom go on to Higher Education before entering a varied range of careers including music, design, advertising, banking, engineering, journalism, law, management, the media, medicine and veterinary science. There is a consistently high external examination success rate and pupils are prepared for Oxbridge in all subjects.

Entry requirements. School report, tests and interview for the Sixth Form, supporting six or more A–C grades at GCSE. Written tests at Years 7 and 9. Places are generally available throughout the year in all other year groups.

Scholarships. Academic scholarships are available at Year 5. Academic, art & design, sport and music scholarships are available in Years 7, 9 and 12 with theatre arts additionally in Year 12. Further details may be obtained from the Head.

Fees per term (2014–2015). Senior: £5,200 (day), £9,450 (weekly boarding), £10,450 (full boarding); Prep: £4,150; Pre-Prep: £2,600–£2,950; Nursery: £530 (one full day per week), £2,650 (full-time).

Charitable status. Ashford School is part of United Learning which comprises: UCST (a Company Limited by Guarantee, Registered in England, number 2780748, and a Registered Charity, number 1016538) and ULT (a Company Limited by Guarantee, Registered in England, number 4439859, and an Exempt Charity).

Ashville College

Green Lane, Harrogate, North Yorkshire HG2 9JP
Tel: 01423 566358
Fax: 01423 505142
email: ashville@ashville.co.uk
website: www.ashville.co.uk
Twitter: @AshvilleCollege
Facebook: /AshvilleCollegeHarrogate

Motto: '*Esse quam videri*'

Ashville was founded in 1877 by the United Methodist Free Church, but has been strengthened by taking under its wing at different times two older non-conformist schools: Elmfield College, founded by the Primitive Methodists in 1864, which amalgamated with Ashville in 1932; and New College, which began in 1850 with strong Baptist connections and merged with Ashville in 1930.

Ashville College offers co-educational boarding and day opportunities for girls and boys from the age of 4 years to 18 years and was voted as one of the top 100 schools in the UK in 2009.

Visitor: The President of the Methodist Conference

Governing Body:
Chairman: Mr P Whiteley, BSc, FCA
Deputy Chairman:

Headmaster: Mr D M Lauder, MA Aberdeen

Deputy Heads:
Mr G R Johnson, BSc Manchester
Mrs E Fisher, BSc Strathclyde

Assistant Head: Mr M Finch, BSc Surrey

Chaplain: Revd David Barker, BA Dunelm, BD, MPhil
  Manchester

Director of Studies: Mr P Williams, BSc Southampton

Year Heads:
Year 7: Miss J Ellis, BA Brighton
Head of Years 8 & 9: Mrs J Wilcox
Head of Years 10 & 11: Mrs L Jackson, BA Leeds
Head of Sixth Form: Mrs V Rumsey, BA East Anglia
Assistant Head of Sixth Form: Mrs K Rutter, BEd Leeds

Senior Housemaster: Mr G Coad, MA London

Heads of Departments:
Art: Mr S Brook, BA Canterbury
AVCE: Mrs C Guy, BA John Moores
Biology: Mr P D Forster, BSc Salford
Business Studies: Mrs C Guy, BA John Moores
Chemistry: Mr D J Normanshire, BSc Bangor
Classics: Mr A T Johnson, BA Dunelm
Design Technology: Mr C Pearce, BEd Leeds
Drama: Mrs J Normanshire, BA Wales
Economics: Mr D Exley
EFL: Mr P Gilmore, MA York, BSc
English: Mr G Kurczij, BA, MA Leeds
Geography: Mrs V A Simpson, BSc Salford
History: Mr A J Barker, MA St Andrews
Home Economics: Mrs L Hayes, CertEd
ICT: Mr D Taylor, BSc Sheffield, MSc Manchester
Learning Support: Mrs M G Levey, BA Leeds, BDA Di
Mathematics: Mr T Hanna & Mrs C Jennings (*Acting
  Heads*)
Modern Languages: Mr I W Kendrick, MA Leeds, BA
Director of Music: Miss A Wilby, BA Oxon, MMus RCM
PE Academic: Mr J Goldthorp, BSc Loughborough
Physics: Mr C Davies, BSc Sussex
Religious Studies: Ms C Walker
Science: Mr D J Normanshire, BSc Bangor
Director of Sport: Mr P Holmes

Junior School:
Head: Mr S Bailey, BA
Deputy Head: Mr J Thompson, BEd Dunelm
Head of Junior School Music: Miss H J Dexter, BMus
  London, LGSM

Pre-Prep:
Head: Mrs C Berrie, BEd Hull
Deputy Head: Mrs J Hopkins, BA Liverpool

Bursar: Dr Dean White

Registrar: Mrs C Butcher

Medical Officer: Ms J Tate, MS

Numbers. There are over 500 boys and girls in the Senior School, 160 in the Junior School (aged 7–11), and approximately 100 in the Pre-Prep.

Site and Buildings. The Ashville estate consists of 60 acres of land on the south side of Harrogate.

The school boasts some of the leading teaching facilities in the North of England. 2012 saw the opening of a new astroturf pitch and a £2.3 million auditorium opened in 2014. These facilities complement the specialist classrooms, sports centre, which includes the longest swimming pool in the area and extensive playing fields.

Curriculum. All pupils are prepared for the General Certificate of Secondary Education at 16, and the GCE Advanced Level examinations two years later. From the age of 11 pupils spend five years on the GCSE course, which includes the study of English Language and Literature, History, Geography, Music, Art, Religious Education, French, German, Spanish, Latin, Mathematics, Physics, Chemistry, Biology, Design Technology, Home Economics, Business Studies, and Physical Education. At A Level Economics, ICT, History of Art, English Language and Physical Education are also available. Guidance is given by the Careers Staff in the choice of Sixth Form studies and decisions are made after consultation with parents. Most pupils who complete the A Level course go on to study at university or other institution of higher education. In addition to their specialist subjects all pupils continue their general education and most offer General Studies as a subject at A Level.

Physical Education. Physical Education is a part of the curriculum for all pupils, and there are games afternoons for all during the week.

The main school games are Rugby, Hockey and Cricket for the boys, Netball, Hockey and Rounders for the girls. The school also has a very strong reputation for producing high quality swimmers and compete both regionally and nationally. There are also school fixtures in Cross-Country, Swimming, Athletics, Lacrosse, Tennis, Squash and Badminton. Many students represent the school at County level.

Careers. Careers guidance is regarded as a very important part of the service provided by the school. Ashville is in membership of the Independent Schools Careers Organisation, and parents are encouraged to share with the careers staff the responsibility for giving appropriate guidance at the Fifth and Sixth Form stage. Pupils are helped in their choice of university and degree course, and arrangements are made for them to visit universities and go on careers courses.

Religious Life. All pupils attend assembly every weekday, and there is a school service for boarders on Sunday evening. Confirmation classes are held in the Spring Term each year, and boys and girls are prepared for Joint Confirmation in the Church of England and the Methodist Church. The School Chaplain is always glad to meet parents by appointment.

Leisure Activities. There are school societies which cater for a wide range of interests, and pupils are guided in the use of their free time in the early years. The school has no cadet corps, but boys and girls are enabled to take part in the Duke of Edinburgh's Award scheme. Drama has a strong following and the school play is a highlight of the year's programme.

Music is well provided for, and pupils are encouraged to take up the study of piano, organ or an orchestral instrument. The School Choir has acquired a high reputation by its contributions at the Harrogate and Wharfedale Festivals.

Admission. The school is prepared to admit pupils at any convenient time.

Candidates for entry at the age of 11 are required to take the Ashville Entrance Examination in the January preceding the September of entry. The examination consists of papers in English, Mathematics and Reasoning. Candidates at Preparatory Schools seeking entry at the age of 13 are required to sit a similar examination.

Candidates for entry at other ages and into the Sixth Form are considered on the evidence of a headmaster's report and interview.

Registration forms and prospectus are obtainable from the Registrar. There is a registration fee of £50.

Fees per term (2014–2015). Tuition: Senior School £4,190–£4,220, Junior School £2,970–£3,590, Pre-Prep £2,475. Boarding (in addition to tuition fees): Full £2,400–£4,200, Weekly £2,200–£3,400. Lunch for Day Pupils: £250 (Junior and Senior Schools), £225 (Pre-Prep).

Scholarships and Bursaries. Discretionary Awards: Scholarships are awarded at the discretion of the Headmaster for excellence in academic performance or other disciplines, for example music. Scholarships are awarded to pupils for specific stages of their education at Ashville.

Financial Assistance: Bursaries are available at the discretion of the school and are means tested.

Forces Boarding Bursary: If a parent is serving in the armed forces and their children are boarding at Ashville, the bursary is 20% of tuition and boarding fees for junior school pupils and 10% for senior pupils.

Charitable status. Ashville College is a Registered Charity, number 529577, administered by Ashville College Trustee Ltd, company number 4552232. It aims to provide a boarding and day education for boys and girls.

Bablake School

Coundon Road, Coventry CV1 4AU
Tel: 024 7627 1200
Fax: 024 7627 1290
email: info@bablake.coventry.sch.uk
website: www.bablake.com

Bablake School was originally part of the College of the same name founded by Queen Isabella in 1344. After the dissolution of the monasteries it was refounded in 1560 by the city; it is chiefly associated with the name of Thomas Wheatley, whose indentures of 1563 put its finances on a firm foundation.

The Governing Body is Coventry School Foundation, on which are represented Sir Thomas White's Charity, the Coventry Church Charities, Coventry General Charities, Oxford and Warwick Universities and the University of Coventry. There are also several co-opted governors.

Chairman of Governors: Mr R Atkins, QC

Headmaster: Mr J W Watson, MA

Deputy Heads:
Mr C R Seeley, BA, MPhil
Mr A M Hopkins, MA (*Academic*)
Mrs G Press, BEd (*Pastoral*)

Assistant staff:
* *Head of Department*

Mrs L J Alderson, LLB (*Head of Fifth Year*)
Mrs L B Alexander, BSc
Dr P B M Archer, PhD
Mr L Atwal, BSc
Miss V Barfield, BA
Mrs K Barnacle, BSc (*Psychology*)
Mrs H M Billings, MA (*German*)
Mrs R I Bilsland, BA
Miss R M Blattner, BSc
Mrs D R Booth, BSc
Mrs A L P Bradshaw, BA
Mr M G Bull, MEng (*Director of ICT*)
Mr J M Bunce, MA
Mr R L Burdett, BSc (*Boys' PE*)
Mr J G Burns, MA (*Assistant Head*)
Mrs A S Cassell, BA
Mr A D Chowne, BSc
Mr P Cleaver, MA (*Art*)
Mr S Cooper, GLCM
Mr T Crompton, GBSM, ABSM (*Director of Music*)
Mrs C B Davey, BSc (*Food & Textiles*)
Mr J M Drury, BSc
Mr M Duerdin, BSc
Mrs K G Duke, MA (*English*)
Mr S P Enstone, BSc (*Geography*)
Ms C E Farmer, BA (*Director of Drama*)
Mrs M C Field, L-ès-L

Mrs L A French, BSc
Mr J M Grantham, BA
Mrs N D Green, BSc
Dr L S Greenway, PhD (*Learning Support*)
Mr A M Hall, BSc (*Biology*)
Mrs S V Harris, BSc (*Director of Marketing & Admissions*)
Mrs A S Heath, BEd
Mr J C Hobday, BSc (*Head of Third Year*)
Mrs E L Hollick, BSc
Miss S L Holyman, BSc
Mr T Hyde, BSc (*Physics*)
Mrs L J Jackson, CertEd (*PSHCE*)
Mrs A J Jones, BSc (*Head of Shells; First Year*)
Mr I S Kalsi, MChem
Dr P J Knight, PhD (*Chemistry*)
Miss J E Kukucska, BA
Mrs L R T Lawrence, MA
Mrs A H Learmont Henry, MA
Mrs J MacGibbon, BSc
Mrs C A Martlew, BA
Mrs J May, MA (*French*)
Mr S Memon, BSc
Mr D C Menashe, BA (*Classics*)
Mrs C Mills, CertEd
Mr C W Mohamed, BSc
Miss L J Mullan, BSc
Mr P N Neale, MA
Mr P Nicholson, BEd
Mrs M O'Neill, MA (*Spanish*)
Miss K L Ormsby, BA (*Head of Second Year*)
Mr G L Park, BA
Miss J A Payne, BSc
Mr A C Phillips, MSc
Miss R S Priest, BA
Mrs L J Reddish, BA
Mrs C A Rees, BA
Mr M Rushton, BA
Mrs H E Sawyer, BSc
Mrs C L Scott-Burt, DipTCL (*Outreach/Enrichment*)
Mr R G Sewell, BA (*Economics & Business Studies*)
Miss J L Simmons, MSc
Mrs H Skilton, MA (*History*)
Revd J S Slavic, MSE (*Chaplain*)
Mrs S M Smith, BEd (*Girls PE*)
Dr T M P Smith, PhD (*Religious Studies*)
Mrs A J Tumber, BA (*Head of Sixth Form*)
Mr K J Tyas, BEd (*Mathematics*)
Miss L C Watts, BA
Mr C R West, BEd (*Design Technology*)
Mr S E Williams, BEng
Mr B G Wilson, BEd
Mr M G A Woodward, BA (*Careers*)
Miss R F Young, BSc

Junior School

Headmaster: Mr N Price, BA

Deputy Head: Mr L Holder, BEd

Senior Master: Mr A Bogyor, Cert Ed

Assistant staff:

Mr E Benfield, BSc	Miss K Love, BSc
Mr S Cooper, GLCM	Mrs M Mason, BA, BEd
Mrs K Dawson, BA	Mr S Norman, BA
Miss G Davies, BA	Mrs K Price, BA
Mrs S Dodd, BA	Mrs M Reed, Cert Ed
Mrs K Francis, BEd	Miss H Shorter, MSc
Mrs L Knibb, MA	Mrs A Thomas, BSc
Mrs J Legate, BSc	

Headmaster's Personal Assistant: Mrs R Mohomed

Number in School. There are about 775 Day Pupils (including 350 girls) and 190 in the Junior School. There is also a Pre-Preparatory school for 100 children aged 3 to 7 on a separate site.

Buildings. In the Home Field of 11 acres stand the main buildings which have been considerably extended to include a Sports Centre, heated indoor swimming pool and a purpose-built Modern Languages block. A purpose-built English, Music and Drama block was completed in July 2000. In 1993 Bablake Junior School was opened on the Home Field site for pupils aged 7–11. The school has its own nationally recognised weather station. At Hollyfast Road there are 27 acres of playing fields, a large pavilion and two all-weather hockey pitches.

Curriculum. The Junior School is for children aged 7 to 11. There is a broad and balanced curriculum which encourages excellence and individual achievement. (*For further details, see Bablake Junior School entry in IAPS section.*)

Pupils take and must pass the Governors' Examination for entry to the Senior School. The Senior School provides courses leading to the GCSE examinations and GCE A Levels. Subjects available include: English, Mathematics, History, Geography, French, German, Spanish, Religious Studies, Latin, Classical Civilisation, Physics, Chemistry, Biology, Music, Art, Food, Design Technology, Information Technology and Textiles. Design Technology and Food and Textiles courses are followed by both boys and girls. The separate sciences or Science and Additional Science are taught up to IGCSE. Most pupils study 10 subjects at GCSE, the majority progressing into the Sixth Form where 4 subjects and sometimes 5 are taken as AS Level. At A2 Level all students take a minimum of three subjects. Most of the subjects named are available up to AS Level and A2 Level. In addition several new subjects are available, including Business Studies, Economics, Geosciences, Psychology, Sports Studies and Theatre Studies. There is a wide range of Enrichment Studies options including Art, Astronomy, Chinese, Computing, Cookery, Design, Drama, Music, Photography and many others. Some pupils take the Extended Project Qualification. All pupils follow a structured programme of PE and Games.

Games and Activities. Rugby, Hockey, Netball, Basketball, Cross-Country Running, Athletics, Rounders, Tennis, Cricket, Soccer, Squash and Swimming. The school has an extensive artificial turf games area, used mainly for hockey, but providing in the summer an additional 24 tennis courts. A wide range of extra-curricular activities is offered, and there are approximately 50 societies and clubs. Drama and Music are strong features. All pupils are involved in the charity work of the school and there is a large Community Service programme for the Senior pupils in the Fifth and Sixth Forms.

Scholarships. The Governors award annually a number (not fixed) of Entrance bursaries each year. These are dependent on academic ability and on parental means. Academic, Art and Music scholarships are also available.

Academic, Sports and Music scholarships are available in the Sixth Form.

Fees per term (2014–2015). Senior School £3,400; Junior School £2,580; Pre-Prep £2,060.

Admission. Entry is via the School's own Entrance Examination held annually in January for entrance the following September. The normal age of entry is 11 but there are smaller intakes at 12, 13 and 14. Entry to the Sixth Form is based on gaining at least 5 GCSE passes at Grade B or above and an interview with the Headmaster and Head of Sixth Form. Enquiries about admissions should be addressed to the Admissions Officer, Mrs L Baines.

Charitable status. Coventry School Foundation is a Registered Charity, number 528961. It exists to provide quality education for boys and girls.

Bancroft's School

High Road, Woodford Green, Essex IG8 0RF
Tel: 020 8505 4821
Fax: 020 8559 0032
email: head@bancrofts.org
website: www.bancrofts.org

Motto: *Unto God only be honour and glory*

By the Will of Francis Bancroft (1727) all his personal estate was bequeathed on trust to the Worshipful Company of Drapers of the City of London to build and endow almshouses for 24 old men, with a chapel and schoolroom for 100 poor boys and 2 dwelling-houses for masters. The Foundation was originally situated at Mile End, but by a scheme established by the Charity Commissioners in 1884 the almshouses were abolished and the School transferred to Woodford Green, Essex. In 1976 the School reverted to independence, and became a fully co-educational day school, with a Preparatory School being added in 1990.

The Worshipful Company of Drapers

President: The Master of the Drapers' Company

Trustees and Governors:

Appointed by the Drapers' Company:
Prof P Ogden, BA, DPhil, AcSS (*Chairman*)
J Rose
C S Tallents, BA, FCA
C Bowe, PhD

Appointed by the London Borough of Redbridge:
M J Stark

Appointed by Essex CC:
R Gooding, IEng, ACIBSE

Co-opted:
Mrs B Conroy, MA (*Old Bancroftian*)
M B Jones (*Old Bancroftian*)
Dr A V Philp, MA, MB BChir (*Deputy Chair*)
E Sautter, MA (*Od Bancroftian*)
Mrs S Siddiqui, BA, TEP
P D Southern, MA, PhD

Head: Mrs M E Ireland, BSc, DipEd, CBiol, MBS

Deputy Head: M Mikdadi, MSc

Second Deputy Head (*Academic*): M I Dixon, BSc

Assistant Heads:
Mrs E F de Renzy Channer, MA
C A F Butler, BSc

Head, Preparatory School: J P Layburn, MA, QTS

Assistant Staff:
† *Housemaster/mistress*

T R C Jones, MA	J C Pollard, BEd
C H Pearson, BA	†Miss H J Prescott-Morrin,
C J Bates, PhD	BSc
A P Macleod, BEd	S Burton, BA
L M Gibbon, MA, MPhil	Mrs J M Fryer-Green, BA
J K Lever, Essex CCC &	S A Hunn, BA, DPhil
England	N Goalby, MEng
Mrs A M Scurfield, BSc	I Moore, MA, MTh
Mrs S P Thompson, BSc	Mrs N Doctors, BA
S P Woolley, BSc	†Miss C G Edwards, BA
Mrs P R Tindall, BA	Mrs E F de Renzy Channer,
†Miss J K Robbins, BA	MA
N A Jaques, BA	†Miss A M H Wainwright,
R M Bluff, MA, FRCO	MA
†R C de Renzy Channer,	Mrs V Talbot, BA
BA	P A Caira, BSc

Mrs S Bhangal, BEd
A J Smethurst, MA
K P Gallagher, BA
Mrs A Hunter, MA
Mrs J M Hitching, BA
D J Argyle, BEd
N E Lee, BSc
M Flaherty, MA
Mrs M Baker, BA
†R M Hitching, BA
J Prole, BSc
Mrs E Tynan, MEng
†Mrs L Coyne, BA
G Ismail, BSc, PhD
Miss I Ward, BA, MA
S Oakes, PhD
M Piper, BA
Miss D Mardell, MA, MEd
Mrs K Yelverton, BA
Mrs S Jones, BA
Mrs H Chilvers, MA, BEd
Mrs M Perez, Licenciatura
  en Filología Inglesa
Miss H Gartland, MA
Mrs S O'Sullivan, BA, MA
L Brennand, BA
Miss A Moor, BA
Mrs K Dixon, Stadtexamen
R Faiers, BA
A Baum, BA
Mrs A Carter, BSc
Miss A Adams, BA
Mrs L Life, BA
Mrs E Norris, BA
Mrs C Biston, BA
Mrs S O'Sullivan, BA
A Busch, BSc, MSc
Mrs A Fryer-Green, BSc
Mrs K Dean, BA, ACA
Miss Phelps, BA
J Choy, MSc
Miss L Ellery, BSc
Mrs S Strong, BA, MA
Miss D Haynes, BA
Mrs C Foinette, BA
Miss E Middleton, BA
J Raw, MA
N Thomas, BComm

Mrs P Morton, BA
S Ahmed, MSci, PhD
A Ford, MA
Mr J Ceeraz, BSc
C Greenidge
Mrs S Cheshire
Miss D L Mugridge, BA
Mrs S Whitehead
J P Dickinson, MEng
Mrs B Rathod, BA
Miss K Stevens, BA
Miss A Grimwood, BA
Miss N Evans, BA
M Naylor, BSc
Mrs E Hewitt, BSc
C Atkinson, MA
Mrs L Whalley, BA
Mrs P Rasmussen, MA
P Edwards, BSc
A Berg, BA
A E Clay, Grad RSM
Miss J Grossman,
  Staatsexamen
Miss N Kerr-Boyle, PhD
Miss H Korcz, BSc
Miss K Lynch, BA
R Tse, MSc
Mrs N Vetta, BA
I Urreaga Gorostidi, BA
A J Mill, PhD
R M A Hay, BA
Miss H E Stewart, BA
Mrs L Dalton, BA
A M Conington, BSc
S P Taylor, BEng
Miss S Gadhvi, BA
A D Hartrup, BA
Miss L Jones, BA
P A McGuiggan, BSc
Mrs Astrid Abbott-
  Imboden, BA
Mrs Fiona M Graham, BSc
Mrs Susan C Hampson,
  BSc
Miss L R E Meaden, BSc
J D Larwood, BSc, PhD
A N Athienitis, BA

Bursar: L Green

Matron: Mrs B Sharma

Bancroft's School is a co-educational day school of about 1,100 pupils. It stands in its own grounds with about five acres of playing fields and it has a further 16 acres of playing fields near Woodford Station. Its buildings have successfully combined the spacious style of the original architecture with the constant additions demanded by developing needs. These include a swimming pool, enhanced science facilities, music resources and art rooms. In 2006 a new building, housing kitchens, additional teaching space and a new Sixth Form Centre, was opened; a new sports centre and performing arts studio were opened in 2007. A lecture theatre seating up to 120 people, digital language lab and a new ICT suite were added in 2009. 2011 saw the addition of an enhanced Sixth Form study area, new Arts and Ceramics Workshops and additional science laboratories.

Meals are taken in a well-equipped central dining room, and there is a good variety of menu with self-service on the cafeteria principle.

Pupils are grouped in four Houses – North, East, West and School. Each of the Houses has its own Housemaster or Housemistress and a tutorial system.

The School offers a wide range of subjects at GCSE and A Level and has a strong record of academic success. Virtually all Bancroftians progress to university, with about 12 each year to Oxford or Cambridge.

The major sports for girls are hockey, netball, tennis and athletics. Rugby football, hockey and cricket are the main games for boys. Swimming, soccer, badminton and basketball are also provided. The Physical Education programme includes gymnastics, trampolining, basketball and badminton.

The School has a Contingent of the CCF, a Sea Scout Unit, a branch of the Duke of Edinburgh's Award Scheme, and a Social Service Group, each of which caters both for girls and boys. The School has enjoyed considerable success in the Engineering Education Scheme. The programme of concerts and plays through the school year offers opportunities for pupils of all age groups.

Preparatory School. The School opened in September 1990 occupying purpose-built accommodation on a separate site within the school grounds. There are 12 classrooms, a hall, a library, a performing arts studio and specialist rooms for art and science. Although self-contained, the Prep School makes extensive use of the Senior School's sports, music and drama facilities.

(*For further details, see Preparatory School entry in IAPS section.*)

Admission. 65 places are available each year for boys and girls wishing to enter the Preparatory Department at 7+; entry tests take place in the January. Transfer to the Senior School is guaranteed. At 11+ there are another 60 places available for children entering Bancroft's who sit an examination in Mathematics and English in mid-January. For candidates of other ages individual arrangements are made. Applications for 7+ and 11+ entry must be made before 1 December in the year prior to entry. There is a direct entry for boys and girls into the Sixth Form dependent upon GCSE results and performance in the School's 16+ entrance examination which is sat in the November of Year 11.

Scholarships. Each year up to 15 Scholarships, worth typically one half, one third or one quarter of the full fees, are awarded to candidates at 11+ on the basis of performance in the School's own 11+ Entrance Examination. Two will generally be awarded as Music Scholarships to children of outstanding musical talent; these are worth up to 50% of fees plus extra music tuition. Five Academic Scholarships, each worth up to 50% of the full fees, are available to external candidates entering the Sixth Form. A Music Scholarship is also awarded for entrants into the Sixth Form. A further three academic awards are available to internal candidates.

Means-tested awards (including Francis Bancroft Scholarships and Foundation Scholarships) are available at age 11, which can cover the full fees. These are awarded based on disclosure of family finances and performance in the Entrance Examination. Two means-tested Francis Bancroft Scholarships are available for entrants to the Prep School at age 7; these only cover Prep School fees. Means-tested awards may also be available for entrants into the Sixth Form.

Fees per term (2014–2015). Senior School £5,016, Prep School £4,085. Fees include lunch and books.

Old Bancroftians' Association. Hon Secretary: Mr K Campbell, 46 Mayfair Gardens, Woodford Green, Essex IG8 9AB. School contact: susan.day@bancrofts.org

There is a strong Old Bancroftians' Association. The OBA also helps to organise work experience for members of the school.

Charitable status. Bancroft's School is a Registered Charity, number 1068532. It exists to provide an academic education to able children.

Bangor Grammar School

84 Gransha Road, Bangor, Co Down
BT19 7QU, Northern Ireland
Tel: 028 9147 3734
Fax: 028 9127 3245
email: info@bgs.bangor.ni.sch.uk
website: www.bangorgrammarschool.com

Motto: '*Justitiae Tenax*'
    Bangor Endowed School was founded in 1856 as a result of a bequest by the Rt Hon Robert Ward. The School is now known as Bangor Grammar School.

Governors:
The Governing Body is composed of 8 representative Governors elected by Subscribers, 6 Governors nominated by the Department of Education, 2 Parent Governors and 2 Teacher Governors.

Chairman: I G Henderson, OBE, MSc Econ

Representative Governors:
J Adrain, BSc Econ, FCA – Chartered Accountant
K Best, MSc, RIBA – Architect
P Blair, MD, FRCS – Consultant Surgeon
D W Gray, BSc Econ, LGSM, FCA – Chartered
    Accountant
JC Harper, LIB, ACIS – Senior Bank Manager
P Hatty, BSc, MSc – Insurance
I G Henderson, OBE, MSc Econ – Chief Executive
    (*Chairman*)
W McCoubrey, LLB – Solicitor

Governors nominated by the Department of Education:
A Adams – Lecturer (*Retired*)
R Bailie, BA, MSW, MBA
M Burke, MBE, MSc, BA, Vice Principal, University
    College (*Retired*)
P Kane
D G Patterson – Civil Servant (*Retired*)
A J Preston – Career Civil Servant

Parent Governors:
P Crothers – Solicitor
W Reid – Civil Servant

Teacher Governors:
G Nicholl, MA
J Todd, BSc, PGCE

Co-opted Governors:
B McKee, MA – Barrister
Geoffrey Miller, QC – County Court Judge

Bursar and Clerk to the Governors:
Mrs Fiona Woods, BSc, FCA

Principal: Mrs E P Huddleson, MSSc, BEd PQH NI

Vice-Principal: G Greer, BEd, MA, PQH NI

Assistant Principals:
S Robinson, BSc
J B Wilson, BA, PQH NI

Assistant Staff:
* *Head of Department*

Art:
*Mrs C N Steele, BA
Mrs M-C Allsopp, BA
D McShane, BSc
P Ramsey, BSc

Business Studies:
*S Sinclair, MA

Computing:
*Ms M Garland, BA, MSc

Drama:
*Mrs J K Payne, BSc, ATD
D P Cunningham, MA

English:
*H Matheson, MA (*Acting*)

W R Stevenson, BA, ATCL
Mrs M E L Cree, BA
A M Gray, BA

Geography:
*S A Beggs, BSc
M Dickson, BSc
Mrs C Greenaway, BSc,
    JEB

History:
*S Wolfenden, MA
G Bond, BA
M Robinson BA

Home Economics:
*Mrs L McDermott, BA

Languages:
*G Nicholl, MA
Mrs R Shaw, BA
Miss R Douglas, BA
Mrs C Henry, BA
Mrs K Nicholl, 1
    Staatsexamen

*Learning for Life and
    Work*:
*Mrs M Faulkner, BSc,
    PhD

Mathematics:
*Mrs K Quinn, BSc
J Todd, BSc
S Robinson, BSc
A Walker, BEng, MSc
Mrs S Forbes, BSc
Mrs C McGilton, BSc
D Hinds, MEng

Music:
*Mrs C Buchanan, BMus,
    LRSM
P O'Reilly, BMus, LRSM

Physical Education:
*D Kennedy, BSc
D Holley, BA (*also RE*)
P Cartmill, BSc

Politics:
*J B Wilson, BA

Religious Education:
*M S Nesbitt, BD
Mrs L Henry, MA, MSc
Mrs S Crawford, BTh

Science:
N A Nowotarski, BSc
    MRes (*Biology*)
Mrs M Faulkner, BSc, PhD
Mrs K Bloomfield, BSc,
    PhD
Ms C Mills, BSc, PhD
B Smith, BSc, PhD
    (*Chemistry*)
B S M Christy, BSc
Dr S Cunningham, BSc
Mrs R McKee, BSc
    (*Physics*)
F Gilmour, BSc
S Henry, BSc

Technology:
*J T Titterington, BEng
C H M Turner, BEd (*Tech
    & Design*)
M Black, BEd

Headmaster's PA: Mrs S Cordner, BA

There 880 boys in the School aged 11–18.
    School Buildings. The School moved into brand new premises in January 2013. The new school is a state-of-the-art establishment, located on the Gransha Road in Bangor.
    Admission and Curriculum. Boys are admitted to the Senior School after the age of 11 as a result of their performance in the transfer procedure using tests provided by the Association of Quality Education. All boys follow a common curriculum for the first three years. The choice of subjects for the Fourth and Fifth Forms is kept as wide as possible to enable boys to keep their future options open right up to the GCSE examinations. The School's policy is to encourage boys to undertake a wide range of studies.
    A Sixth Form of 200 plus makes possible a wide range of subjects from which boys normally take four AS Level and three or four A2 subjects.
    Activities. School games include rugby football, cricket, tennis, squash, badminton, golf, hockey, swimming, athletics, basketball and cross-country running. There are numerous societies and clubs. Both drama and music flourish. There are two major play productions in the year with further smaller-scale productions in the Summer Term. Numerous opportunities are afforded for instrumental and choral performance throughout the year, both inside and outside school. Adventure training is catered for by a flourishing contingent of the Combined Cadet Force (with Army and Naval Sections) and the Duke of Edinburgh's Award Scheme. Boys are encouraged to gain an experience of social work through the active Community Service Group. Frequent continental visits are arranged and an expedition under the auspices of World Challenge takes place every other year.
    The School has very high standards in sport. The rugby 1st XV dominated the Ulster Schools Rugby Cup in the

Eighties, with seven appearances in the final, including four victories. Other teams have been successful in the Ulster Schools Golf Championship, the major Ulster Hockey cups, the Ulster and Irish Squash and Tennis Championships and in the major Ulster Cricket cups and the Ulster Badminton Championships.

Careers. Extensive and continuous help is available to boys in connection with careers. There are five careers staff under the leadership of the Head of Careers. Careers courses, lectures, visits, interviews, work experience, work shadowing and a Challenge of Industry Conference are part of the regular careers structure for boys in Year 10 and above.

Honours. Boys from the School enter all the major universities in the British Isles. Places have been won regularly at Oxford, Cambridge and other universities.

Bangor Grammarians Association. *Hon Sec*: Norman Irwin, 10, Riverside Road, Bangor, Co Down BT20 5SA.

Barnard Castle School

Barnard Castle, County Durham DL12 8UN
Tel: 01833 690222
Fax: 01833 638985
email: secretary@barneyschool.org.uk
website: www.barnardcastleschool.org.uk

Motto: '*Parvis imbutus tentabis grandia tutus*'.

The St John's Hospital in Barnard Castle was founded in the 13th century by John Baliol, whose widow founded the Oxford College. By a Scheme of the Charity Commissioners, bequests under the will of Benjamin Flounders of Yarm were combined with the funds of the St John's Hospital and public subscriptions to build and endow the present foundation in 1883. Originally known as the North Eastern County School, the name was changed to Barnard Castle School in 1924.

The Governing Body:
Chairman: A Fielder
Vice-Chairman: P Mothersill & Mrs C J Sunley JP

M McCallum	S Crowe
D F Starr	Mrs K Pratt
C Dennis	Lt Col D Clouston
Dr N Thorpe	Dr T Winzor
M H Crosby, JP	M Airey
Mrs R Dent, JP	Dr J Elphick
D C Osborne	B Hick
P Hodges	Mrs C Newnam
Cllr G M Richardson	

Clerk to the Governors: M White

***Headmaster*: A D Stevens**, BA, MA (*History*)

Second Master: D S Gorman, BA (*History & Politics*)
Deputy Head Academic & Chaplain: Revd Dr S J Ridley, MA, EDD (*Classics & Theology*)
Head of Sixth Form: C R Butler, MSci, MA (*Physics*)
Assistant Head Pastoral: Miss A G Jackson, BA (*Geography*)

Assistant Staff:
* *Head of Department*
† *Housemaster/mistress*

†G Bishop, BA (**Economics & Business Studies*)
C P Johnson, BA (**Modern Languages*)
D C S Everall, BEd (**PE, Mathematics*)
R Child, BSc, PhD (*Biology, UCAS Adviser*)
M N R Fuller, BEd (**Biology, Careers*)
J D N Gedye, BA (**Classics*)
M H Nicholson, BSc, BA (**Mathematics*)

Miss F Cover, BEd (*PE & Geography*)
Mrs C Shovlin, BA, ALA (*Librarian*)
†Mrs A Armstrong, BEd (*PE*)
†D W Dalton, MA, BA (**Geography*)
M Donnelly, CertEd, FLCM (*Music*)
†B C Usher, BSc (*Mathematics*)
Mrs A Gorman, BA (**English*)
C H Alderson, BSc (*Geography & History*)
M P Ince, BA (**History*)
M T Pepper, BA (**Director of Sport*)
N Toyne, BSc (*Mathematics*)
A M Beaty, BSc (**Technology*)
Miss T C Broadbent, BA (*PE*)
Mrs A J Campbell, BA (*History & *Politics*)
†A J Allman, BA, MA (**Religious Studies*)
I M Butterfield, BSc, PhD (**Chemistry*)
A Jacobs, BA (*Modern Languages, *Spanish*)
Mrs K Baptist, BA (**Art*)
A M Mawhinney, MA, ARCO CHM, ARCM, LTCL (**Director of Music*)
M L West, BSc (*Chemistry*)
Mrs E E Beaty, BA (*English*)
Miss J Brown, BSc, MSc (**ICT*)
M S Atherton, MA, FTCL (*Prep School Director of Music*)
†L D Monument, BSc (*PE*)
†Mrs L Burgess, BEd (*PE*)
P C Oakley, BSc, MSc (*Technology*)
D G Goldberg, MA (*Mathematics*)
A Maude, BSc (*Mathematics*)
Mrs M Abela, BA, LLCM TD (*Music*)
N J Connor, BA (*Business Studies & ICT*)
J G Brettell, MA (*Classics & *Latin*)
Mrs C E Connor, BSc (*Biology*)
Mrs L Nicholson, Mgr, MCIL, DPSI (*ESL*)
Miss C J Snaith, LLB, LPC, MA (*Religious Studies*)
S J F Tomlinson, BA (*Modern Languages*)
Mrs S Butler, BA (*Religious Studies*)
A Dunn BSc, MSc (*Physics*)
T S Edwards, BA (*English & Theatre Studies, Director of Drama*)
H W Fairwood, BSc (*ICT, Director of ICT*)
Dr E McDermott, BSc, PhD (*Chemistry*)
Mrs M E Waddington, BEd (**Learning Support*)
Mrs E Hewlett, BA (*English*)
Miss E K McKenzie, BSc (*Sport*)
A M Wade, BA (*English & History*)
D S Walton, BSc, PhD (**Physics*)
Mrs S Rothwell, BA, MA (*Art*)
Dr S Wrathmall, PhD, MPhys, MInstP, FRAS (*Physics*)
† Miss C Burgess, MA (*Mod Languages*)
Mr A Still, BA (*Mod Languages*)
Dr K B Cosstick, JP, PhD, BSc (*Chemistry*)
Miss K Harpin, BA (*English*)
A Thompson, BA (*Sports*)
J White, BSc (*Mathematics*)

Combined Cadet Force:
Commanding Officer: Major C E Connor, BSc
SSI: WO1 M G Lewis

Preparatory School

Headmaster: C F Rycroft, BEd
Head of Pre-Prep: Mrs L E Turner, BA, MA

Deputy Head: N I Seddon, BEd
Director of Studies: Mrs R Robertson, BEd

Mrs S M Seddon, BEd	Mrs C Bale, BA
Mrs H Brown, BEd	Mrs T Michelin, BA
Mrs L Rowlandson, BA	Miss A White, BA
Mrs F M Killeen, BA	Miss E Biggart, BA
Mrs E Small, BA	Mrs J Cockerill, CertEd
Mr S T Ayres, BA	Mrs C Priestley, BEd
B Wicling, BA	

Mrs R Thompson, BEd

Dr R G Harrison PhD, BMus

Director of Operations: Mrs S Metcalf BA, FCCA

Admissions Secretary: Mrs J Simpson

Medical Officer: Dr R Carter
Medical Centre:
Mrs B Preece, RGN, BSc

Headmaster's Secretary: Mrs J A Ridley

Barnard Castle is a day and boarding school for boys and girls between the ages of 4 and 18.

Organisation and Numbers. There are 502 pupils aged 11–18 in the Senior School, of whom 153 are boarders. The Preparatory School comprises a Pre-Prep Department of 53 pupils between the ages of 4 and 7, and 155 pupils between the ages of 7 and 11, of whom 8 are boarders. (*See also Preparatory School entry in IAPS section.*) The Senior and Preparatory Schools are located on adjacent sites and operate separately on a day-to-day basis whilst enjoying the mutual benefits of being able to share a number of resources and facilities. Girls were first admitted in 1981 and the School has been fully co-educational since 1993.

Location. The School is situated in its own extensive grounds on the outskirts of an historic market town in an area of outstanding natural beauty. The area is well served by Durham Tees Valley and Newcastle airports and by Darlington railway station. The School also operates its own bus service for pupils from a wide area.

Curriculum. This is designed to provide a broad, balanced and flexible programme, avoiding undue specialisation at too early a stage. In the Prep School emphasis is given to literacy and numeracy skills, as well as Science, History, Geography, French (from age 8), Religious Education, Technology, Art, Music, Information Technology, Physical Education (including swimming) and Games. These subjects are developed further in the Senior School, with the addition of Latin or Classical Civilisation, Personal, Social and Health Education, and three separate sciences. German or Spanish is added at age 12, whilst Business Studies and Engineering increase the list of GCSE options at age 14. There are some twenty A, AS or Pre-U Level subjects which give a wide choice in the Sixth Form. Almost all Sixth Form leavers go on to University or College courses. A Learning Support Department provides specialist help for those who need it in both the Preparatory and Senior Schools, and tuition is offered in English as a Second Language.

Religious Education. The School is a Christian foundation and the Chapel stands at the heart of the School in more than just a geographical sense. The School Chaplain, who plays an important role in the pastoral structure of the School as well as being responsible for Religious Studies and Chapel worship, is an ordained member of the Church of England, but the School is a multi-denominational one which welcomes and supports pupils of all faiths and none. Pupils attend weekday morning assemblies in Chapel, and there is a Sunday service for boarders.

Boarding and Day Houses. There are eight single-sex Houses within the Senior School – three boarding and five day – each small enough for pupils to know each other well, but large enough to allow a mixture of interests, backgrounds and abilities, as well as opportunities for leadership. Housemasters and Housemistresses, each supported by a team of Tutors and Assistants, are responsible for the welfare and progress of each pupil in their charge.

Junior Boarders (boys and girls aged 7–11) and Senior Girl Boarders live in their own modern Houses in the School grounds, alongside their Houseparents, Boarding Tutors and Matrons. The two Senior Boys' Boarding Houses have recently undergone a major programme of restructuring and refurbishment, and offer comfortable accommodation within the main building of the School. The resident Housemasters are supported by resident boarding tutors and matrons, and by the School Sister in the School's Medical Centre. The School Doctor visits daily.

Cultural and other activities. The School has a flourishing music department in which the Chapel Choir, Orchestras, Wind and Jazz Bands and smaller ensembles perform regularly.

Drama is also prominent, with a regular programme of productions taking place throughout the year. There is a strong tradition of after-school activities; both day and boarding pupils take part in a wide range of clubs and societies, selecting from over 100 weekly activities.

Games. Lacrosse, Rugby, Hockey, Netball, Cricket, Athletics, Squash, Cross-Country Running, Tennis and Swimming are the main sports, and other options such as soccer, badminton, basketball and golf are available. The School has extensive playing fields, a modern Sports Hall, and Fitness Centre, squash and tennis courts, and a heated indoor swimming pool. A full-size, floodlit "astroturf-style" pitch is available for all to use. Regular inter-school matches are arranged at all levels.

Outdoor Activities. There is a strong emphasis on providing instruction, opportunity and challenge in a wide range of outdoor activities. Much of this takes place under the auspices of a flourishing Cadet Force (Army and RAF sections) or the Duke of Edinburgh's Gold and Silver Award Schemes.

Careers. There is a well-equipped Careers Room, and a team of careers staff work together with the Higher Education Coordinator to provide pupils at all stages of the School with expert advice and help in decision-making and application procedures.

Admission. Pupils are admitted at all stages either via the School's own Entrance Assessments. There is also direct entry into the Sixth Form subject to satisfactory performance at GCSE level. Details of the application procedure are obtainable from the Admissions Secretary (admissions@barneyschool.org.uk).

Scholarships and Assisted Places. Academic Scholarships and Exhibitions are awarded to entrants to the Senior School at Year 7, Year 9 and the Sixth Form, on the basis of the School's own entrance examinations held in February.

Music Scholarships and Exhibitions: There are two Music Scholarships available in Year 7, a further two in Year 9 and in the Sixth Form.

Sport Exhibitions based on potential are available at Year 7 and Scholarships are available at Year 9 and in the Sixth Form. Four Exhibitions may be awarded in Year 7, followed by up to four Scholarships in Year 9 and a further two Scholarships in the Sixth Form.

Art Scholarships and Exhibitions are available from Year 9 and in the Sixth Form.

Drama Scholarships and Exhibitions are available to candidates entering the Sixth Form.

Awards may be supplemented by means-tested Bursaries.

The School is also able to offer a small number of means-tested assisted places. Details are available from the Headmaster's Secretary.

Fees per term (2014–2015). Senior: £7,391 (Boarders), £4,117 (Day). Prep: £5,561 (Boarders), £2,875 (Day), Pre-Prep: £1,893. Fees are inclusive and subject to annual review.

Charitable status. Barnard Castle School is a Registered Charity, number 1125375, whose aim is the education of boys and girls.

Bedales School

Church Road, Steep, Petersfield, Hampshire GU32 2DG
Tel: 01730 300100
Registrar: 01730 711733
Assistant Registrar: 01730 711569
Fax: 01730 300500
email: admissions@bedales.org.uk
website: www.bedales.org.uk

Governors:
Daniel Alexander, BA, LLM, QC
Franciska Bayliss, Froebel, CertEd, FRSA
Timothy Hands, BA, AKC, DPhil
Avril Hardie, BEd, JP
Brian Johnson, FRS, FRSE, FRSC, F Accad Europa
Michele Johnson, BA
Dr Anna Keay, PhD
Rear Admiral John Lippiett, CB, MBE
Timothy Parker, MA, MSc
Mark Pyper, OBE, BA
Matthew Rice, BA (*Chair*)
Kit Thompson, BA Hons, PGCE
Nicholas Vetch, ARICS
Charles Watson, BA
Timothy Wise

Clerk to the Governors and Bursar: Richard Lushington, BA, MCIPD

Headmaster: Keith Budge, MA University College Oxford, PGCE

Managing Head of the Senior School: Louise Wilson, BA King's College London, MA Bath

Deputy Head, Pastoral and Head of Boarding: John Scullion, BA Strathclyde Polytechnic, MA London, NPQH

Deputy Head, Academic: Alistair McConville, MA Fitzwilliam College Cambridge, PGCE Gloucester

Assistant Head (Pastoral and Co-Curricular): Katie McBride, BSc Newcastle

Heads of Departments:
Art: Simon Sharp, BA
Biology: Richard Sinclair, BA St Catherine's College Oxford, PGCE London
Chemistry: Lindsey Barnes, MChem Sheffield, PGCE Manchester
Classics: Christopher Grocock, BA Royal Holloway London, PhD Bedford College London
Dance: Liz Richards, BA Chichester, MA Chichester
Design: Ben Shaw, BSc Loughborough
Drama: Phil King, BA Royal Holloway, MPhil Birmingham, PGCE Warwick
Economics: Ruth Tarrant, MA Hertford College Oxford, MA Warwick
English: David Anson, BA University College London, MA Institute of Education, PGCE Royal Academy of Dramatic Art
Geography: Kirsty Layton, BSc Plymouth, Dip HE Oceanography Southampton, PGCE Canterbury Christ Church, Kent
Global Awareness: Annabel Smith, MSc London, BA London, PGCE Lady Margaret Hall Oxford
Government and Politics: Ruth Tarrant, MA Hertford College Oxford, MA Warwick
History: Jonathan Selby, BA, PGCE Durham
Computing: Susan Robson, BSc Manchester, PGCE Portsmouth

Learning Support: Ruth Austen, BSc Swansea, PGCE Kingston, PGDip (*SEN*) Kingston, PG Dip SpLD Southampton, SpLD Assessment Practising Cert Patoss
Mathematics: Michael Truss, MPhys Balliol College Oxford, PhD Leicester, FRAS
Modern Languages: Peter Thackrey, BA Durham, PGDip City, PGCE London Institute of Education
French: Marie-Pierre Hamard, MA, PGCE Goldsmiths College London
Spanish: Ruth Carpenter-Jones, BA Queen Mary College London, PGCE Bristol
Director of Music: Nicholas Gleed, MA Cambridge, PGCE Durham
Outdoor Work: Andrew Martin, BA Manchester Metropolitan, PGCE Manchester Metropolitan
Philosophy and Religious Studies: Clare Jarmy, MA St Catharine's College Cambridge, PGCE Cambridge
Physics: Tobias Hardy, BSc York, MA Southampton, PGCE Warwick
Sport: Sonia Cartwright, BSc, PGCE Chichester Institute

Director of External Relations: Rob Reynolds, BSc, MBA, MCIM
Registrar: Janie Jarman
Secretary to the Headmaster: Pam Goff

Dunhurst (Prep School)

Head: Jane Grubb, MA Brighton, BA Newcastle, PGCE Leeds

Deputy Head, Pastoral and Head of Blocks: Nick Robinson, MSc, PGCE Portsmouth
Deputy Head, Academic: Kathy Misson, BA Liverpool, PGCE Manchester Metropolitan
Head of Boys' Boarding: Simon Kingsley-Pallant, BA Brighton
Head of Girls' Boarding: Alice Tang-Pullen, BA Newcastle, PGCE Gloucestershire
Head of Groups: Olivia Burnett-Armstrong, BA Exeter, PGCE Homerton College Cambridge

Heads of Subject Departments:
Art: Stephen York, BDes Duncan of Jordanstone College of Art & Design, Dundee
Drama: Simon Kingsley-Pallant, BA Brighton
English: Nichola Gotel, BA Winchester, PGCE Cambridge
Geography and PSHE: David Ellis, BA Portsmouth, PGCE Buckingham
History and PRE: Steve Jeggo, BA King Alfred's College, Winchester, PGCE Bath
Latin: Kathy Misson, BA Liverpool, PGCE Manchester Metropolitan
Academic Support: Sue Williams, BSc City University, PGCE, PG Cert Prof Practice
Mathematics: Darran Kettle, BEd Westminster College Oxford, Dip Educational Coaching Newcastle College
Modern Foreign Languages: Olivia Burnett-Armstrong, BA Exeter, PGCE Cambridge
Outdoor Work: Ryan Walsh, BA Northampton
Sport: Heather Lowe, BA & PGCE Manchester Metropolitan
Science: Erawin Olie, BSc Warwick, PGCE Swansea

Dunnannie (Pre-Prep School)

Head: Jo Webbern, CertEd Froebel
Senior Teacher: Julia Brown, BEd Froebel

Secretary to the Heads of Dunhurst & Dunannie: Frances Harris

Number in School. 460 in Senior School. Equal numbers of boys and girls. 70% boarders.

Bedales stands in an estate of 120 acres in the heart of the Hampshire countryside, overlooking the South Downs. Although only one hour from London by train, this is one of the most beautiful corners of rural England. Founded in 1893, Bedales is one of the oldest co-educational boarding schools. The community is a stimulating and happy one, in which tolerance and supportive relationships thrive at all levels.

The school has strong traditions in both the Humanities and the Sciences, in Art, Design, Drama and Music. The school estate supports a thriving 'Outdoor Work' programme, including the management of livestock and a variety of traditional crafts.

The school is known for its liberal values, the individualism and creativity of its students, and a sense that the students are generally at ease with who they are. The atmosphere is relaxed (first-name terms for staff and students; no uniform), but it is underpinned by a firm structure of values, rules, guidance and support.

Admission. Entry to the School is from 3+ (see Dunannie), 8+, 9+, 10+, 11+ (see Dunhurst), 13+ and 16+ (Bedales). Once in the school, pupils are assessed before proceeding to the next stage.

Entry Tests. Entry for newcomers at 10+, 11+ and 13+ takes the form of residential tests in the January preceding the September entry. Entry at 16+ is by a series of interviews spread over a single day. Write in the first instance to the Registrar.

Senior School (13 to 18). Up to 100 in each year. A new curriculum in Blocks 4 and 5 (Years 10 and 11) was introduced in September 2006. In order to promote more stimulating, varied and wide-ranging work in these years, and to reduce prescriptive external assessment, students will typically take a combination of externally moderated Bedales Assessed Courses (BACs) alongside IGCSE subjects. BACs are designed to give a strong basis for A Level study and are recognised by UCAS. A new curriculum was introduced for Block 3 (Year 9) in 2014 to prepare students better for the independent learning opportunities higher up in the school, starting with a week at an Outward Bound Centre in the Lake District.

All current IGCSE/BACs subjects (except Outdoor Work) are also offered in the Sixth Form at A Level, together with Dance, Economics, Government and Politics, Further Mathematics, Psychology and Theatre Studies. Sixth Form students can also opt for an assessed Extended Project in an area of interest. A programme of personal and social education runs in Years 9 and 10, and a general course covering a wide range of topical and personal issues is taught in the Sixth Form. Students are attached to a tutor in groups of mixed ages, and meet their tutor on a regular basis.

A series of local, national and international initiatives/ exchanges have been introduced as part of a new emphasis on Global Awareness. Geography and Biology departments run sixth form field courses, and there are special interest trips such as a History visit to Russia. IT facilities are well funded, each student having an email address and monitored access to the Internet. Students have access to desktop computers throughout the day, and those with their own laptops have wireless access to the school network across the campus. There are excellent recreational facilities including extensive playing fields, gymnasium, sports hall with multigym, indoor heated swimming pool, floodlit netball and tennis courts and a floodlit astroturf pitch. The Outdoor Work project is centred on two eighteenth-century barns reconstructed in the school grounds by students. The Bedales Gallery and Olivier Theatre run public programmes of art, drama, dance and music, and distinguished speakers visit the school to give assemblies or as part of the 'Civics' programme. Evening assemblies ('Jaw') and other talks often have a religious or moral theme, but there is no chapel; the school is non-denominational.

There are no prefects, but students take responsibility for a wide variety of aspects of school life by running activities for younger students, taking part in committees and putting forward individual initiatives. A School Council of elected representatives provides a forum for discussion including all levels of the school. Until the final year, students sleep in small mixed-age dormitories; in the final year they move to a co-educational house with exceptional facilities. This arrangement fosters very good relationships across the age range.

Bedales Prep School, Dunhurst (8 to 13). (*See entry in IAPS section*).

Bedales Pre-prep School, Dunannie (3 to 8). Entrance at 3+ is by date of registration; after this acceptances are made following informal assessments, should vacancies arise. 95 pupils. Dunannie has six classes including a nursery. Its aim is for children to develop a lifetime's love of learning in a stimulating environment.

The school has bright airy classrooms, an extensive library and an excellent ICT room. There are fabulous music rooms, hall and dining room which are shared with Dunhurst. The children at Dunannie benefit from the indoor swimming pool, tennis courts, sports hall, pitches, art gallery, farm and theatre which are all close by on the Bedales estate. The outdoor play areas include a stunning orchard with a climbing frame, Sound Garden of outdoor instruments and a hill fort.

The children have many opportunities to thrive and flourish. Dunannie offers a rich and varied curriculum that allows for rigour in basic skills, but also embraces creativity. Children are encouraged to think and be independent in their response to cross-curricular activities. First hand experiences are an integral part of learning. All children from Nursery to Year 3 go on inspiring visits that enrich the classroom experiences. There are close links between Dunannie, Dunhurst and Bedales. Children in Year 3 can automatically transfer from Dunannie to Dunhurst unless there are exceptional circumstances. There are frequent visitors to the school too. Sport is a strength with a comprehensive programme of activities including swimming, gymnastics, netball, football and orienteering. Year 3 children have sport with Dunhurst Group 1 children and have the opportunity to play inter school matches. Dunannie is a very friendly school with happy, confident children who relish being at school. Staff and parents work in partnership together and we are always pleased to welcome visitors and prospective parents to Dunannie.

Scholarships and Bursaries. Academic scholarships are available for entry to Dunhurst at 10+ and 11+. Music scholarships are awarded each year to outstanding musicians for entry to Dunhurst at 10+ and older, exceptionally at 8+. Academic and Music scholarships are available for entry to Bedales at 13+ and 16+. Art scholarships are awarded for entry at 16+.

The basic award for scholarships is £750, which can be increased through means-tested bursaries.

Means-tested bursaries are also available to those of proven need. The John Badley Foundation, launched in 2010, provides 100% bursaries for talented individuals who would not normally be able to afford a private education.

For full details of the scholarships and timing of assessment, please apply to the Registrar.

Fees per term (2014–2015). Bedales: Boarders £10,930, Day £8,590. Bedales Prep, Dunhurst: Boarders £7,510, Day £5,850–£5,915. Bedales Pre-Prep, Dunannie: £2,590–£3,200.

Charitable status. Bedales School is a Registered Charity, number 307332. Its aims and objectives are to educate children as broadly as possible in a creative and caring environment.

Bede's Senior School

Upper Dicker, East Sussex BN27 3QH
Tel: 01323 843252
Fax: 01323 442628
email: school.office@bedes.org
website: www.bedes.org

Founded in 1978 Bede's discovers the talents of each student through breadth of academic curriculum and co-curricular. It is academically ambitious for all and the pastoral care, delivered through the House and Tutor systems, is inspiring and nurturing and ensures Bede's sends its young people into the outside world self-aware, happy and confident in what they can achieve and looking forward to the challenges they will meet.

The Senior School owes its existence in part to the success and vitality of Bede's Preparatory School in East-bourne, one of the first boys' Preparatory Schools to become fully co-educational and now one of the largest co-educational Preparatory Schools in the country. The Senior School has 750 students. Of these 320 are boarders (full and weekly), 430 are day students, 340 are Sixth Formers, 60 per cent are boys and 40 per cent are girls. Bede's enjoys an enviable reputation internationally. Currently 18% of our students are from over 40 countries.

The School takes great pride in the variety of its students and the outstanding range of opportunities available to them. The breadth of choice means every student can find what they naturally excel at. Students at Bede's pick from a wide array of over 170 clubs and activities, guided by personal tutors.

Governors:
Major-General Anthony Meier, CB, OBE (*Chairman*)
Christopher Bean, LLB Hons
Andrew Corbett, MA Hons, PGCE
Jeremy Courtney, FRAgS, MBIAC
Peter Denison, OBE, CQSW
Christopher Doidge, MA Oxon
Ian Hunt, BSc
Mark MacFadden, MRICS, ACIArb
Lady Rosemary Newton, MA
Catherine Nash, BEd
Peter Pyemont (*President*)
Patrick Tobin, MA Oxon, FRSA
Xavier Van Hove, BA Hons Oxon

Senior Management:

Headmaster: **Dr R J Maloney**, MTheol Hons St Andrews, MA, PhD King's College London, PGCE

Senior Management:
Principal Deputy Headmaster: Mr J Lewis, BA Hons, MA, PGCE
Deputy Head, Academic: Mr J Tuson, MA, GTP
Deputy Head, CPD & Staff: Mr R Frame, BA Hons, HDE
Deputy Head, Co-Curricular: Ms R Woollett, BA Hons, PGCE
School Chaplain: Revd T Buckler, BA, MA Hons, PGCE
Head of Boarding: Mrs L M Belrhiti, BEd Hons, Dip TEFL
Senior Day Housemaster: Mr R Mills, BA Hons, PGCE
Principal of Summer School: Mr S Wood
Director of Curriculum Management: Mr A Hayes, BSc Hons, PGCE
Director of Marketing and Admissions: Mrs R Nairne, BA Hons

Housemasters and Housemistresses:
Bloomsbury House: Mrs M Leggett, BA Hons, MA, PGCE
Camberlot House: Mr R Jones, BA Hons
Crossways House: Mrs J Lambeth, BSc Hons, PGCE
Charleston House: Mrs S Von Riebech, BMus, PGCE

Deis House: Mr N Driver, BCom, PGCE
Dicker House: Mr T Mpandawana, BSc, DipEd, QTS
Dorms House: Mr P Juniper, BSc Hons, PGCE, CBiol, MSB
Dorter House: Mr D Leggett, BA Hons, QTS
Knights House: Mr A Waterhouse, HDE Secondary
Stud House: Mr A Walker, BA Hons, PGCE

Heads of Departments/Subjects:

Art:
Mr J Turner, BA Hons, PGCE (*Head of Faculty*)
Mr A Hammond, BA Hons, MA, GTP (*Head of Ceramics*)
Miss E Excell, BA Hons, GTP (*Head of Photography*)
Business Studies and Economics: Mr G Parfitt, MBA
Design and Technology: Mr N Potter, BSc Hons, PGCE
Drama: Mrs K Lewis, BA Hons, PGCE
EAL: Mr J Cook, RSA, TEFLA
English: Mr M Oliver, BA Hons, PGCE
Food and Nutrition: Mrs C Ballard, BEd Hons
Geography: Mrs C Buckler, BSc Hons, MA, PGCE
Higher Education and Careers: Mr P Gibbs, BA Hons, PGCE
History and Politics: Mrs K O'Hara, BA Hons, PGCE
ICT: Mr A Hayes, BSc Hons, PGCE
Learning Enhancement: Mrs S Bunyard, BSc Hons, PGCE, DMS, Adv Dip
Mathematics: Mr N Abrams, BSc Hons, PGCE
Media and Film Studies: Mr R Williams, BA Hons, GTP, Dip Media Ed
Modern Languages: Mrs J Mulligan, MA Cantab, QTS
Music: Miss L Morris, BMus Hons, PGCE
Physical Education: Mrs K Merchant, BSc, PGCE
Psychology: Mr G Rudnick, BSc, PGCE
Mr I Barr, BSc Hons, PGCE
Religious Studies and Philosophy: Mr N Stannard, BA Hons, PGCE, QTS
Science:
Mr M Costley, BSc Hons, MSc, PGCE (*Head of Faculty*)
Mrs H Tilling, BSc, PGCE (*Head of Biology*)
Dr A Cumpstey, MChem Hons, MA, PhD, PGCE (*Head of Chemistry*)
Mr C Hiscox, BSc Hons, PGCE (*Head of Physics*)
Mr S Hodges, BSc Hons, PGCE (*Head of ELBS*)
Sport: Mr Andrew Hibbert, BEd (*Director of Sport*)
Legat School of Dance:
Miss E Holland, BPhil Hons LRAD, ARAD, AISTD (*Head of Department*)
Mrs A Murphy, BA Hons, PGCE (*Head of Academic Dance*)

Year Heads:
Director of Academic Performance & Pre6th: Mr M Rimmington, BSc Hons, Dip Ind St, GTP
Head of First Year: Mr L Backler, BA Hons, PGCE
Head of Lower Fifth: Mr M Krause, BEd, QTS
Head of Upper Fifth: Ms J French, BSc, PGCE
Head of Sixth Form: Mr J Henham, BSc Hons, PGCE
Asst Head of Sixth Form: Mr B Jackson, BSc, PGCE

Aims. Bede's aims include the provision of an outstanding education, in an inclusive co-educational environment. That education is predicated on flexibility for the student; a broad and varied curriculum; personalisation of study programmes and respect for students' choices and aptitudes. Coupled with this is the provision of an extensive and exceptional variety of co-curricular activities that allows students to find, nurture and develop their interests and talents. The programme caters for everyone, from elite performers to hobbyists, and no activity is considered more important than another.

Bede's provides pastoral care that aims to support and safeguard each student, and in so doing, develops values of respect and humanity within a framework of friendly, nonconfrontational relationships between all people, adults and students alike.

Facilities. In 2007 the School opened two innovative and award-winning boarding houses and two more were opened in February 2012. The Multi-Purpose Hall, also opened in 2007, is used for School Assemblies, examinations and many sports, including basketball, badminton, cricket, football, netball and tennis. The Performing Arts Centre, in a beautiful setting next to the lake, provides studio space for both drama and dance and 2008 saw the opening of a new Music Centre. In addition, a new Multi-Purpose Games Area and water-based astro and cricket pavilion will shortly be ready for use. Bede's buildings are friendly, in enviable settings and a far cry from the overbearing, institutional character of much school architecture.

Curriculum. During the first year in the School students follow a very wide introductory course which includes the following subjects: Art and Design, Classics, Dance, Design & Technology, Drama, English, Geography, History, Home Economics, ICT, Mathematics, Modern Languages, Music, Physical Education, Science.

In the Fifth Form (Year 10) most students begin two-year courses leading to the GCSE (Key Stage 4) examinations. Students usually follow nine subjects of a possible 40 at GCSE; Mathematics, Science and English are compulsory subjects. Potential optional courses include: Art and Design, Business Studies, Dance, Design & Technology, Drama, Geography, History, Home Economics, Environmental Science, Information Technology, Latin and Greek, Media Studies, Modern Languages (French, Spanish, German), Music, Performing Arts (Dance), Physical Education, Religious Studies, Environmental and Land-Based Science, Science (Triple Award), Science (Double Award), Science (Single Award). Some IGCSEs are also offered along with some short-course GCSEs. A Pre-Sixth course is offered for those who need a year of intensive English before embarking on an A Level course.

During the first three years those with particular needs, such as those with any form of Dyslexia and those who are non-native speakers of English, can follow organised programmes within the timetable taught by suitably qualified teachers.

In the Sixth Form students can follow the traditional three or four A Level courses or a combined programme of A and AS Levels and some Pre-U courses, which can provide a broader education. Most GCSE subjects are offered at AS and A2 Level plus Accounting, Economics, Film Studies, Government & Politics, History of Art, Certificate in Professional Cookery, Performing Arts, Statistics and Theatre Studies. Bede's also offers Cambridge Pre-U in a number of subjects. Equine Studies NVQ Level 1 and 2.

Vocational provision: BTEC National Certificate in Sport, National Award in Music Performance and Music Technology, National Award in Animal Management, National Award in Business Studies.

Bede's also runs the Legat Professional Dance Course which is fully integrated with the academic programme.

Current class sizes average 16 up to GCSE level and 12 at A and AS Level.

Co-Curricular Programme including Games. The extensive programme includes the many sporting and games playing opportunities open to students, The Army Cadet Force, The Duke of Edinburgh's Award Scheme, numerous outdoor pursuits and a daily programme of activities within the fields of Art, Drama, Music, Journalism, Science, Technology, Engineering and Social Service. There are currently over 170 Club Activities running each week and an average daily choice from 40 options. Games and Sports include Aerobics, Archery, Athletics, Badminton, Basketball, Canoeing, Climbing, Cricket, Cross-Country, Fishing, Football, Golf (the School has its own practice course), Hockey, Judo, Dance, Netball, Orienteering, Photography, Riding, Rounders, Rugby, Squash, Swimming, Target Rifle Shooting, Tennis and Volleyball. Bede's has a fine sporting reputation with students past and present representing their country at cricket, football, rugby, hockey, athletics and showjumping.

Pastoral Care. There are three boys' boarding houses and two girls' houses, the numbers in each house averaging 60, with three resident staff in each. An appropriately selected tutor provides a mentor for each student during their time at the School. These tutors are responsible for ensuring that each student's academic and social well-being is carefully looked after. Tutors act in liaison with Housemasters and Housemistresses and are readily available for discussions with parents. All parents have several formal opportunities each year to meet those who teach or otherwise look after their sons or daughters.

Religion. The School maintains the Village Church for the local community. Confirmation classes are available, if requested. All students attend weekly meetings in the church which are appropriate to boys and girls of all religions and are of outstanding variety. Bede's does not impose any singular religious observance on its students but would rather either that their existing faith is further strengthened by their being full members of the congregation of local churches or that they grow to appreciate and value the importance of a strong spiritual life through the thoughtful and varied programme of 'School Meetings'. There is a choice of four types of observance on Sundays: the Multi-Religious School Meeting, Church of England, Roman Catholic and Free Church.

Admission. The normal age of entry to the School is between 12½ and 14 years. Admission is based on school reports and references and interview. Places are open each year to those wishing to join the School as Sixth Formers and at other levels in the School.

Scholarships and Bursaries. Bede's invests in excess of ten per cent of its annual income in means-tested fee remission and academic, art, dance, drama, music and sports scholarships. Prospective students who wish to join outside of the scholarship process are able to apply for means-tested fee remission.

Further details regarding scholarships and bursaries are available from the Admissions Office, email: admissions@bedes.org.

Fees per term (2014–2015). Full Boarders £10,055, Weekly Boarders £9,460, Day Pupils £6,640.

Charitable status. St Bede's School Trust Sussex is a Registered Charity, number 278950. It exists to provide quality education.

Bedford Modern School

Manton Lane, Bedford, Bedfordshire MK41 7NT
Tel: 01234 332500
Fax: 01234 332550
email: info@bedmod.co.uk
website: www.bedmod.co.uk

Bedford Modern School is one of the Harpur Trust Schools in Bedford, sharing equally in the educational endowment bequeathed for the establishment of a school in Bedford by Sir William Harpur in 1566. Bedford Modern School was a Direct Grant Grammar School which became independent in 1976. It became co-educational in September 2003.

Governors and Staff:
Chairman of the School Committee: I McEwen, BPhil, MA, DPhil

Headmaster: M Hall, BA, MA, PGCE

Senior Deputy: S E Davis, MA, PGCE
Deputy Head Academic: M R Price, MA, PGCE

Deputy Head Pastoral: I C Grainger, CertEd
Head of Junior School: J C Rex, BA, PGCE
Director of Sixth Form: J P White, Bed
Bursar: S Willis MSc BSc CDipAF
Director of External Relations: J Ridge, BA

** *Head of Faculty*
* *Head of Subject*

*Faculty of Art, Design and
  Information Technology*:
**S E Milton, BA, PGCE
Art:
S E Milton, BA, PGCE
P Edwards, BA, MA,
  PGCE
*J McGregor, BA, PG Dip,
  PGCE
Design Technology:
*P Kennington, CertEd
D Downham, HNC Eng
I C Grainger, CertEd
A Rock, BSc, PGCE
J P White, BEd
C Wiles, BA, GTP
ICT:
*J Hollingsworth, PGCE
A Leach, BA
P J Smith, BSc, CertEd

Faculty of English:
**S D Bywater, BA, MLitt,
  PGCE
Dr J P Barnes, PhD, BA
J Chumbley, BA, PGCE
J Dewar BA, PGCE
T Foster, BA, MA, PhD,
  PGCE
J Kilbey, BA, MA, PGCE
J P Sanders, BA, PGCE
E P Sheldon, BA, PGCE
Film Studies:
*J P Sanders, BA, PGCE
T Foster, BA, MA, PGCE

Faculty of Humanities:
** R Gleeson BA, PGCE
Geography:
*B W Day, BSc, PGCE
D R Mistrano, BA, PGCE
M R Price, MA, PGCE
M Ruta BSc (*Hons*)
A Vaughan MA PGCE BSc
History:
*S E Wright, MA, PGCE
S Baker, BSc, PGCE
S Boa, BA, PhD, MPhil,
  PGCE
A D Tapper, BSc, MSt
C Webb, BA, PGCE
*Religious Studies and
  Theology*:
*J Hooper, BA, PGCE
J Goodyer, MA, MPhil
J P Searle, BTh, PGCE

Faculty of Mathematics:
**N D Shackleton, BSc,
  PGCE
S A Brocklehurst, BA,
  PGCE
I R Hay, BSc, PGCE
N Hussain, BSc, PGCE
S J Jacobs, BSc, PGCE
R Kay, BSc, PGCE

D M King, BSc, PGCE
R Millar BSc and PGCE
A Slater, BEng, PGCE

*Faculty of Languages and
  Classics*:
**R Crawley, BA, PGCE,
  LGSM, MEd
Classics:
*J Newton, MA, PGCE
A D Corbett MA, PGCE
S E Davis, MA, PGCE
C W H Rees-Bidder, BA,
  MEd, PGCE
French:
*R Crawley, BA, PGCE,
  LGSM, Med (*Lings*)
German:
*R J Killen, MA, PGCE,
  TEFL, DipSp & DipFr
Spanish:
*R Reed, BA, PGCE,
  TEFL
T Le Baut Ayuso BA. MA
Languages Teachers:
G Amoros, Licence
  Civilisation Lit, PGCE
L Hendry, BA, Dip SpLD,
  PGCE
S Sobrado, Licenciatura
G Watkins BA
J Williams, BA, PGCE

Faculty of Music:
**J Mower, GRSM,
  ARCO, ARCM, Dip
  RAM
*M Perry, BMus, PGCE,
  Dip AMRSM
Music Technology:
M Gooch, BA, Dip RAM

*Faculty of Performance
  Arts*:
**H Rees-Bidder, BEd
Drama:
*L Coltman, BA, PGCE
N McLeod, BA, PGCE
Speech and Drama:
*M A Burgess, Prof Dip
S Leather, BA
Dance:
*R Bradley, AISTD, FDI

*Faculty of Politics,
  Philosophy and
  Economics (PPE)*:
**A Pollard, BA, MA,
  PGCE
Economics:
*A Pollard, BA, MA,
  PGCE
J R Ryan, BA, PGCE
M Hall, BA, MA, PGCE
Business Studies:
*R Smith, BA, PGCE
J R Ryan, BA, PGCE

Government & Politics:
*S Baker, BSc, PGCE
S Boa, BA, PhD, MPhil,
  PGCE
Philosophy:
*A Rowley, BA, MA, PhD,
  PGCE
J Morris MA
J Searle, BTh, PGCE

Faculty of Science:
**N R Else, BEd, MA
Biology:
*R J Brand, BSc, PGCE
D Donoghue BA (*Dubl.*),
  PGCE, MA
D Greenfield, BSc, PGCE
D A Jenkins, BSc, MSc,
  Dip EdTech, PGCE
H Ramji, BSc, PGCE
S Sanctuary, BSc, PGCE
S Sumal, BSc, MSc, PGCE
Chemistry:
*Dr C M Jones, BSc, PhD,
  PGCE
N K Cordell, BEd
N R Else, BEd, MA
J P Fitton, BSc, PGCE
J Sadler, BSc, PGCE
V Shehu, BSc, GTP
Physics:

Other Areas:
Careers: S Burns, DipCG
Health and Fitness Manager: L C Williams, LLB, PG Dip,
  ASCC
Librarian: M S Brown, BSc, ALA
Technical Theatre Manager: N Parker, BA

SpLD Academic Support:
**T Collins, BA, PGCE, DipSpLD
D Costello, BA, MA, Cert SpLD
L Hendry, BA, Dip SpLD, PGCE
C Setchfield, BA, Cert SpLD, PGCE
M Tew, BA, PGCE

Houses:
Senior Head of House: P Edwards, BA, MA, PGCE
Head of Bell House: A G Higgens, BSc, QTS
Head of Farrar House: J M Sadler, BSc, PGCE
Head of Mobbs House: W D Hallett, BA, MA, PGCE
Head of Oatley House: H L Gilbert, BA, MA, PGCE
Head of Rose House: A Slater, BEng, PGCE
Head of Tilden House: H Ramji, BSc, PGCE

Junior School

Head of Junior School: J C Rex, BA, PGCE

Deputy Head of Junior School: P Pacyna, BA, QTS
Head of Junior School Sports Development: T Bucktin,
  BSc, PGCE
Director of Studies, Junior School: M Capuano, BEd, QTS

*R J Turner, BSc, BA,
  PGCE
W D Hallett, BA, MA,
  PGCE
S S Harvey, BSc, CertEd
D Honnor, BA, GTP
T P Mullan, BSc, PGCE
T E Rex, BEd
Psychology:
*H J Kelly, BSc, PGCE

Faculty of Sport:
**P L Jerram, BSc
  (*Director of Sport*)
*M Bavington
*R J K Hardwick
*P J Woodroffe, BA
*P R Bignell, BEd
*D Orton, BEd, Dip ML
N J Chinneck, BEd
H L Gilbert, BA, MA,
  PGCE
A G Higgens, BSc, QTS
L Williams, LLB, PG Dip,
  ASCC
H Bodsworth BSc
H Southam BSc, PGCE,
  QTS
D Keep
C Orton B Ed
A Bygraves

H Avery, BEd
J Barlow, BEd
C Barrow, BEd
L Burton, BEd
G M Colling, CertEd
C Coyne BA
H Farrow, MA, LRAM,
  PGCE
M Fox, BA, PGCE

K Hale BA, QTS
E Hall MUSM, BA (*Hons*),
  PGCE
J Leydon, BEd
S J Nicholls, BA, CertEd
M Phillips, BEd
E Warren, BA, QTS
K Weetman, BA, PGCE

Headmaster's Assistant: J Saunders
Admissions Manager: P Heappey

Examinations Officer: M Stellman, BEd
Senior School Nurse: G Holland, RGN

Number of Pupils. There are 256 pupils in the Junior School (aged 7–11) and 945 pupils in the Senior School (aged 11–18).

(*See also Bedford Modern Junior School entry in IAPS section.*)

Facilities. The School occupies an attractive forty-acre wooded site to the north of Bedford. The main buildings date from 1974 and there have been substantial additions since that time, most notably a new assembly hall, performance arena and classrooms to the Junior School (2002); a Sixth Form Study Centre and Refectory (The Rutherford Building – 2006) and new Library Resource Centre (2007). There are extensive facilities for Science, Technology and Information Technology. There have been recent extensions to the Music School and Performing Arts Centre. Each year group has its own common room.

The playing fields are all on the School site with extensive facilities for Rugby, Football, Cricket and Athletics. There is also a large swimming pool, a fitness suite, gym and sports hall. Recent additions include two large all-weather training areas and netball courts. The School shares a large and well-stocked Boathouse with the other Harpur Trust Schools on the River Ouse.

Admissions. Pupils are admitted between the ages of 7 and 16. The School conducts its own entrance assessments which are held in January of the year prior to September entry.

Registration fee is £100.

Fees per term (2014–2015). Tuition: Junior School £2,903, Senior School £3,982.

Assistance with Fees. The School offers Modern Scholarships which are available to pupils joining the School from Year 7 (11+) upwards and have been designed to provide opportunities for children with potential academically, in sport, performance arts, music and art/design and information technology. All scholarships are means-tested and are also dependent on a pupil's academic success in the entrance assessments. Further details may be obtained from the School.

Curriculum. The Junior School (ages 7–11) curriculum covers Mathematics, English, Humanities (History, Geography and RE), Science, Information and Communication Technology (ICT), Modern Foreign Languages, PE, Art, Drama, PSHE and Games. Pupils benefit both from a purpose-built practical skills centre containing art and science rooms as well as specialist computer and technology rooms, and from the Senior School, music, PE and games facilities including the swimming pool.

In the Senior School, the curriculum includes all the core subjects, as well as Technology, IT, RE, PE, Music, Art and Drama. All pupils experience French, German, and Spanish in Year 7 and Latin in Year 8 before making choices. Pupils opt for ten GCSE subjects. For the Sixth Form, pupils select four from a wide range of 29 subjects. In addition to all the traditional options, the choice of subjects also includes Computer Science, Government and Politics, Economics, Business, Religious Studies, Philosophy, DT Systems and Control, DT Product Design, Classical Civilisation, Theatre Studies, PE, Psychology, Film Studies and Music Technology. All students will sit AS exams at the end of Year 12 in all their subjects and the majority will continue three to A Level.

ICT Facilities. The School boasts a range of ICT facilities offering both staff and pupils an individual network account and email address so that they are able to access over 400 networked PCs across the School in addition to high-speed broadband Internet access, wireless classroom laptop sets, networked printing, and an extensive subject software library including a range of training courseware material.

All standard classrooms are equipped with a computer linked to ceiling mounted data projector and speakers. There are a number of interactive whiteboards and additional presentation equipment is also available for use. The School's website can be viewed at www.bedmod.co.uk.

Religious and Moral Education. The School is multi-faith and multicultural, and religious and moral education is given throughout. Personal, social and health education is a fundamental and well-established part of the timetable.

Individual Care. Every pupil has a personal tutor, who supervises and takes an interest in his or her academic progress, co-curricular activities and sporting interests. Tutors meet with their tutees on a daily basis and there is at least one longer pastoral session each week. Each Year Group has its own common room for use at break and lunchtimes and other non-taught times with a study area and recreational facilities.

We believe that common sense and courtesy lie at the heart of pastoral care. We stress self-discipline and high standards of personal conduct. The tutorial system and the academic organisation are discrete, working in parallel to complement each other. Teaching class sizes are a maximum of twenty-four and often many fewer. We aim to provide a relaxed but purposeful environment; a culture in which all feel at ease and are ambitious to achieve their best.

Drama. There are several large-scale productions each year, a Shakespeare Festival hosted for local schools, and several smaller events. There are separate drama and dance studios and a 300-seat theatre. Speech and Drama is offered throughout the School, leading to LAMDA examinations. Ballet, tap and modern dance lessons follow the ISTD syllabus.

Music. Pupils can learn all the orchestral and band instruments as well as piano, keyboard, guitar/electric guitar and singing. The School has a large variety of choirs, orchestra, bands and ensembles. Pupils can follow courses for GCSE and A Level Music as well as A Level Music Technology. Music accommodation includes a music technology suite with ten Apple computers and state-of-the-art recording facilities.

Activities. There are many school societies and clubs catering for a variety of tastes and interests. The voluntary Combined Cadet Force is strong with Army, Navy, RAF and Marine sections. There is a structured programme of outdoor education which includes residential trips from Years 6, 7 and 8 with international expeditions available for older students. Outreach including community service and the Duke of Edinburgh's Award Scheme are very popular.

Sport. Rugby, football, cricket and rowing are major sports for boys; hockey, netball and rowing for girls. Additional activities include: table tennis, water polo, badminton, hockey (boys), equestrian, snowsports, cycling, cross-country, weights and fitness, fencing, fives, sevens, swimming, dance, athletics, rounders, tennis, climbing, shooting, and gymnastics. There is regular representation at national, divisional and regional levels.

Higher Education. The great majority of sixth form leavers go on to a degree course at their chosen university. More than 30% take courses in STEM (Science, Technology, Engineering and Mathematics) subjects.

Old Bedford Modernians' Club. Secretary: R H Wildman, c/o the School.

Charitable status. Bedford Modern School is part of the Harpur Trust which is a Registered Charity, number 1066861. It includes in its aims the provision of high quality education for boys and girls.

Bedford School

De Parys Avenue, Bedford MK40 2TU
Tel: 01234 362216
Fax: 01234 362283
email: admissions@bedfordschool.org.uk
website: www.bedfordschool.org.uk
Twitter: @bedfordschool
Facebook: /Bedford-School

Bedford School is a leading boarding and day school for boys aged 13–18. The School is situated in an extensive 50-acre estate in the heart of Bedford and is just 40 minutes from London by train.

Established in 1552, Bedford School has an established reputation for academic excellence and boys are encouraged to aspire to the highest possible standards and to exceed their expectations. The School's success is demonstrated by a long history of impressive exam results at GCSE, A Level, and in the International Baccalaureate Diploma. Bedford is also renowned for its strengths in music, the arts and sport.

From the classroom to the sports field, in laboratories and theatres, on excursions and exchanges, boys are challenged academically, socially and culturally. They learn exciting new skills and knowledge, and how to prepare themselves for a successful future as well-rounded young men with confidence, compassion and critical minds.

School Governors:
Chairman: Professor Stephen Mayson, LLB, LLM, PhD, Barrister, FRSA
Deputy Chairman: Mr David Dixon, BA Hons, MBA, FCA, AIB
Dr Anne Egan, MA, BM, BCh, MRCP, FRCR
Mr Charles Allen, BA
Mr Chris Johnson
Sir Clive Loader, KCB, OBE
Mr Ali Malek, QC, MA, BCL Oxon
Mr Hugh Maltby, BA Hons
Mr Richard Miller, MA Cantab, Dip Ed Soton, Dip HA London, RAFVR[T] (*Staff Elected Governor*)
Mrs Amanda Rea, ACMA, MBA (*Parent Elected Governor*)
Cllr David Sawyer
Mr Phil Wallace, MA, FCA, FBRP
Mr Michael Womack, MA Cantab, LLM London
Chairman of the Harpur Trust: Mr Murray Stewart
Deputy Chairman of the Harpur Trust: Mr Anthony Nutt

Head Master: J S Hodgson, BA

Vice Master: C Baker, BSc, CChem, FRSC

Deputy Head (*Academic*): A G Tighe, MA

Bursar and Clerk to the Governors: Mrs C M Godfrey, MA, FCA

Assistant Head (*External Affairs*): R J Midgley, BA Ed

Director of Admissions: Mrs V Hicks

Director of International Baccalaureate: C L Marsh, MA, MLitt

Senior Boarding Housemaster: C J Bury, BA

Undermaster: I B Armstrong, BSc, MSc

Assistant staff:
* *Head of Department*

Academic Support (*ESOL & SPLD*):
*Ms J Spir, BA, RSA Preparatory Cert TEFL
Mrs K Chevallier, MA, Cert TEFL, OCNW Level 4 Cert ESOL Subject Specialists
Mr A Fun BMus, PG Dip Ed, Cert TEFL

Mrs J Greening, BPhil, Cert TEFL
Mr B O'Connor, Cert Ed, Cert TEFL
Ms M Robinson, BA
Mrs L Patel, BA, Cert ESOL Subject Specialists
Mrs E Stillwell, BA SpLD, MEd
Miss S van Heerden, BA, Cert TEFL
Mrs D Wilkinson, BA, CELTA

Art
*Mr M Croker, BA
Mr S Chance, BA
Mrs F Whiteman, BA, MA

Biology
*Mr M Beale, BSc, MEd (*Head of Science*)
Mrs F Bell, BSc
Mr M Gunn, BSc
Mr M Mallalieu, BSc
Ms J Mainstone, BS
Mr C Palmer, BSc, MA
Ms A Swallow, BA

Chemistry
*Mr S Knight, BA
Mr C Baker, BSc, CChem, FRSC
Ms H Dimmock, BSc
Dr B Johnson, MA, MSc, PhD
Mr P Lumley-Wood, BSc, CChem, MRSC
Mr M Mitchell, MA
Dr W Suthers, BSc, MSc, PhD

Classics
*Mr A Melvill, BA
Mr N Allen, BA
Mrs F Markham, BA

Computing
*Mr P Davis, BSc

Design Technology
*Mr I Armstrong, BSc, MSc
Mr L Holt, BA
Mr M Huddlestone, BA
Mr G Waite, MEng

Economics & Business Studies
*Mr H Taylor, BSc
Mr C Bury, BA
Mr M Cassell, BSc
Mr R Heale, BSc
Mrs M Lincoln, BCom, MEd, TEFL
Mrs C Medley, BA

English
*Mr S Adams, BA
Mrs L Di Niro, BA, MPhil
Miss A Garrett, BA
Mr A Grimshaw, BA
Mrs A Smith, BA
Miss S Van Heerden, BA

Geography
*Mr W Montgomery, BSc
Mr M Gracie, BSc
Ms H Pate, BA
Mr T Rees, BSc
Ms S Spyropoulos, BA

History
*Ms E Parcell, BA
Mr N Allen, BA
Mr C Fisher, MA
Mr M Graham, BA, MA Ed
Mr M Herring, BA

Mathematics
*Mrs J C Beale, BSc, MA
Mr S Adams, MPhys
Mr B Burgess, BA Ed

Mrs R Down, BSc
Mr R Eadie, MA
Mr F Elliott, BA, MSc
Mrs T Harbinson, BSc
Mr M Hutchinson, BA
Ms E Murray, MA
Ms L Owens, BSc
Mrs N Tekell-Mellor, BSc
Mr J Watson, MA
Dr D Wild, BSc, PhD

Modern Languages
*Ms C Geneve, MA (*Head of French*)
*Mr F Graeff, BA (*Head of German*)
*Mr A Huxford, MA (*Head of Spanish*)
Mr A Braithwaite, BA
Ms E Calleja-Rubio, BA
Dr A Chen, MBA, PhD
Miss J Law, BA
Mr C Marsh, MA, MLitt
Mr J O'Neill, BA, MCIL
Miss T Trippolt, MA

Music
*Mr J Sanders, BA
Mr B Bantock, BMus, PPRNCM
Mr G Bennett, GGSM
Mr M Green, GRSM, LRAM, ARCM, Dip RAM
Mr T Rooke, BA
Mr J Rouse, MA, FRCO
Mr R Thompson, BMus, PG Dip MM
Mr A Tighe, BA
Ms E Wilson, BA

Physical Education
*Mr B Burgess, BA Ed
Mr R Midgley, BA Ed
Mr J Hinkins (*Director of Rugby*)
Mr A Meredith (*Director of Hockey*)
Mr P Mulkerrins (*Director of Rowing*)

Physics
*Mr M Crisp, MEng
Mr P Brough, BSc
Dr A Calverley, MSci, PhD, FRAS
Mr G Green, BSc
Mr L Guise, BA
Dr E Palmer, MSci, PhD
Mr S Everitt, MEng

Religious Education
*Mr A Finch, MA
Revd A Atkins, MA (*Chaplain*)
Mr M Bolton, MA
Mr W Peters, BA

Theatre Studies
*Mrs S Swidenbank, MA
Mr J Pharoah, BA
Ms J Crossley, BA (*Director of Theatre*)

Houses and Housemasters:

Boarding Housemasters:
Burnaby: R E Heale, BSc
Pemberley: Mr H Taylor, BSc
Phillpotts: A W Grimshaw, BA
Redburn: C J Bury, BA
Sanderson's: Miss J C Law, BA
Talbot's: M Gracie, BSc

Day Housemasters:
Ashburnham: S Everitt, MEng
Bromham: A J R Huxford, MA
Crescent: C Fisher, MA
Paulo Pontine: A J Braithwaite, BA
St Cuthbert's: L M Holt, BA
St Peter's: Ms E Murray, MA

Chaplain: The Revd A S Atkins, MA

Medical Officers: Dr D Fenske and Dr Murphy

Number in School. There are some 687 boys in the Upper School of whom some 232 are boarders and 455 day boys.

The Curriculum. Boys enter the Preparatory School from 7 and the Upper School at 13 years of age. The Preparatory School has its own Headmaster and specialist staff. (*See also Bedford Preparatory School entry in IAPS section.*)

A coordinated curriculum takes boys through the two Schools. The emphasis is on breadth of experience: as few doors as possible are closed at option stages. Boys are prepared for GCSE and for the new broader portfolio of AS and A Levels, and for Key Skills and General Studies. Boys also have the option to study the International Baccalaureate Diploma in the Sixth Form as an alternative to A Levels. Notably strong are Languages, Mathematics and the Sciences, and there has been heavy investment in Technology and Information Technology. Since September 2009, the School has adopted the IGCSE qualifications in the three Sciences and Design and Technology, adding English in 2010. Mandarin Chinese is also taught off timetable to those boys wishing to study the language. There is also a well-resourced Academic Support department providing valuable assistance to boys where necessary.

Boys are encouraged to make good use of non-teaching time. There are extensive departmental and central library facilities, and strong emphasis is placed upon Music, Art, Drama and IT. Clubs and Societies abound for both boarders and day boys. Concerts, plays, lectures and film performances are given in the Great Hall, the Recital Hall, the Erskine May Hall and the Theatre.

Facilities. The School's £3 million Music School is one of the largest in the country. The Recreation Centre incorporates a 250-seat theatre, state-of-the-art fitness suite, large sports hall, squash courts and a 25-metre indoor swimming pool. Other facilities include an observatory and planetarium, twin astroturf pitches and a £1.8 million library.

Classes. In the Preparatory School boys are taught in forms until age 11, and are setted for most subjects. For all post-GCSE work, a generous block system is used which enables boys to study a variety of subjects at AS and A Level, combining, if desired, Arts and Science subjects. In addition a range of subsidiary teaching is provided including Citizenship.

Information Technology. The school has a site-wide fibre optic network, including Wi-Fi access everywhere, enabling approximately 650 school computers, 350+ pupil-owned laptops, and several hundred mobile devices to use the extensive facilities provided both within and external to the site.

The school portal is used as a daily information system for staff, pupils, and parents, and provides access to our eLearning site, emails (for all staff and pupils), as well as information such as school reports. The library maintains an excellent range of online resources, including 'Clickview' that delivers teaching video clips to classroom projectors and Interactive Whiteboards.

There are 12 ICT suites with between 15 and 24 PCs each, including subject specific ones in Art, DT and Music, and three sets of classroom laptops.

Key ICT skills are taught in the first year in the Upper School, which boys use in most, if not all, of their academic subjects as they progress through GCSEs to A Levels or IB in the Sixth Form.

Careers and Higher Education. The School is a member of the Independent Schools Careers Organisation. There is a team of Careers Staff who maintain close contact with the Services and professional bodies, and commercial and industrial undertakings. There are regular contacts with local industry and Institutes of Technology and Higher Education. Annual Careers Conventions are held in Bedford.

Annually almost all of the Upper Sixth enters Higher Education, with a number of boys entering Oxford and Cambridge Universities every year.

Games. A great variety of sporting activities is offered, and senior boys in particular have a wide choice. The major sports are Cricket, Rugby, Rowing, Hockey; and there is ample opportunity also for Athletics, Swimming, Tennis, Association Football, Rugby Fives, Squash, Badminton, Fencing, Basketball, etc. In addition, there are regular PE classes. The Recreation Centre facilities include a fitness suite, large sports hall, squash courts and heated indoor swimming pool.

Services and Activities. The School offers a diverse programme of extra-curricular activities every evening between 4.15 pm and 6 pm, many of which involve girls from Harpur Trust sister school, Bedford Girls' School. Boys are expected to participate fully in this programme during their time at the School. Activities include the Combined Cadet Force (CCF), Duke of Edinburgh's Award Scheme, Community Service, fundraising groups, and more than 50 other clubs and societies from Astronomy to Young Enterprise.

Music. As well as the two Senior Symphony Orchestras, a Chamber Orchestra, a Concert Band and a large Choral Society, there is a Chapel Choir trained in the English Cathedral tradition, two Junior Orchestras, a Dance Band, Jazz Band, Rock Band, a large number of chamber music groups, and a Music Club. The Music department is situated in a £3 million, state-of-the-art, purpose-built development, which includes a fine Recital Hall.

Drama. A range of formal and informal dramatic productions are performed annually by all age groups. A new theatre is set to open in 2015 in the former St Luke's Church. The new 300-seat galleried courtyard theatre with rehearsal and teaching studios will provide a superb venue for school productions as well as visiting touring companies. House Plays are also produced on an annual basis.

Association with Bedford Girls' School. A large variety of co-educational activities are organised in association with the girls at our sister school. These include academic cooperation in minority subjects, joint seminars in major subjects, and involvement in concerts, debates, conferences and a wide range of more informal social events.

Pastoral Supervision. We have a highly developed Pastoral system. Upper School pupils are under the supervision of a Tutor within small Tutor Groups; these "family" groups are organised on a vertical structure in terms of age.

Boarders and Day Boys. In the Upper School a careful balance of Boarders and Day Boys is maintained. The organisation and tradition of the School is such as to promote mixing and to avoid any discrimination between the two groups. They are combined in work, games and all other School activities, and are equally eligible for positions of responsibility whether in House or School. There are six Senior Boarding Houses, each containing up to 51 boys; and one Junior Boarding House of up to 35. There is also a Sixth Form Boarding House.

Visits and Exchanges. Well-established language exchanges occur annually between Bedford and schools in France, Spain and Germany. There are also plentiful opportunities for educational travel including outward bound and adventure camps and expeditions, annual skiing holidays, cultural visits to a range of countries, and intercontinental sports tours.

Admission to the Upper School. Applications should be made to the Director of Admissions. The registration fee is currently £100. All applicants are expected to provide evidence of good character and suitability from their previous school. Year 9 applicants from Preparatory Schools wishing to enter the Upper School are assessed in Year 7 by an initial Pre-test and interview. Subject to performance, a computer-based test (designed to measure raw academic potential) is taken at the School during Year 8. Applicants from Maintained Schools sit tests in English and Mathematics together with the computer-based test as mentioned above.

Scholarships and Bursaries. Bedford seeks to identify boys of outstanding talent and give them access to a Bedford School education regardless of background. The school offers a range of Scholarships and Bursaries to boys who excel academically or show outstanding talent in drama, music or sport.

Awards are available for boys joining the School at our 13+ and 16+ entry points.

For more information, please visit www.bedfordschool.org.uk.

Fees per term (2014–2015). Day Boys £5,708; Full Boarders £9,654; Weekly Boarders £9,335.

Old Bedfordians Club. Tel: 01234 362262; email: obclub@bedfordschool.org.uk. For further details, see OB Club on the School's Website.

Charitable status. Bedford School is part of the Harpur Trust which is a Registered Charity, number 1066861.

Belfast Royal Academy

Belfast, Co Antrim BT14 6JL, Northern Ireland
Tel: 028 9074 0423
Fax: 028 9075 0607
email: enquiries@bfsra.belfast.ni.sch.uk
website: www.belfastroyalacademy.com

Board of Governors:
Mr S J S Warke, ACII, Dip PFS, TEP (*Warden*)
Mr D Walsh, BSc, MBA, CEng, MIME (*Senior Vice-Warden*)
Mr N W Beggs
Dr A A W Bell, BSc, BAgrSc, PhD
Dr K M Bill, MB, ChB, FCAI, FRCA, FFICM
Mrs K L Burns, BA
Ms A Chada, BA, MSc
Mrs A Clements, BA
Mr R Connolly, BSc
Ms C Dillon, BA
Mr P Dorman, BTh
Dr J A Hill, FREng, BSc, Hon DSc, CEng, FICE, FIStructE
Prof D S Jones, BSc, Hon, BA Hon, PhD, DSc, CEng, CChem, FPSNI, FIMMM, FRSS, FRSC, MIEI
Mr K A Knox, MSc (*Hon Treasurer*)
Mr J W Martin, FRICS
Mr P S McBride, BSc, MInstP
Mr B W McCormack, BSc Econ, FCA
Mrs G McGaughey, LLB, Cert Prof Legal Studies
Mr M J Neill, MSc
Mr S B Orr, LLB
Mr D E Porter, MSc, CEng, MICE, MCIHT, MCIWEM
Mr D Scoffield QC, MA, LLM
Mrs H Siberry-Hay, BA, MSc
Mr G R Simon, FRICS
Mrs J Weir, BSc, CMath, MIMA (*Hon Secretary & Junior Vice-Warden*)
Mr A J Wilkinson, FCA
Mr D Carroll, BA, MSc, MRTPI (*Co-opted Governor*)
Mr J M G Dickson, MA (*Headmaster – Non-voting member*)
Miss E Hull, BSc, Dip Acc, FCA (*Bursar – Acts as Clerk to the Board of Governors*)

Headmaster: J M G Dickson, MA

Deputy Head: Ms C N Scully, BSc, PhD, ALCM, PQH

Vice-Principals:
A R Creighton, BEd, PQH
G J N Brown, BA, PhD

Senior Mistress: Ms W E Graham, MA, PQH

Senior Masters:
M T Wilson, BSc
T M A Baldwin, BSc, MIBiol, CBiol
M C W Harte, BA

Deputy Senior Masters:
R J Jamison, BSc
M R Shields MA

Heads of School
Ms S R Ardis, BSc (*Junior School*)
T M A Baldwin, BSc, MIBiol, CBiol (*Senior School*)
T Hughes, MSc (*Middle School*)

Heads of Departments:
Mrs P Kerr, BA, ATD (*Art*)
A A W Bell, BSc, BAgrSc, PhD, AIEA (*Biology*)
Mrs G McQuiston, BEd (*Business Studies*)
Ms J R Adams, BEd (*Careers*)
B T McMurray, BSc, PhD (*Chemistry*)
J D L Reilly, MBE, BA (*Classics*)
W J W Spence, BEd, MA (*English*)
C A Stewart, BSc (*Geography*)
J Carolan, MA (*History*)
Mrs K LStuart, BSc (*ICT*)
Ms S M McIlhatton, BEng (*Mathematics*)
P C Porter, BA, BD Comm (*Modern Languages*)
Ms M McMullan, MA, MusB, LTCL, ALCM (*Music*)
W I McGonigle, BEd (*Physical Education and Boys'
   Games*)
R Budden, MSc (*Physics*)
P Dorman, BTh (*Religious Studies*)
R K Lunn, BEd (*Technology*)

Senior Subject Teachers:
Miss S Tinman, BA (*Drama and Theatre Studies*)
J M Patterson, BSc Econ, MSSc, DCG (*Economics*)
Miss R McCay, MA (*German*)
Miss K S Barnett, MA (*Government & Politics*)
Mrs R F Morrison, BA (*Home Economics*)
Mrs N S Nicholl, BA (*Physical Education*)
Mrs J Robb, BSc (*Social Science*)
Mrs S S Roberts, BA (*Spanish*)
Ms D Keenan, MSc (*Special Needs*)

Heads of Year (*Boys*):
J Buchan, BEM, MA
C R McCarey, BSc
D Morrison, MSc
M J Neill, MSc
M R Shields, MA
S C Springer, MSc PhD
P T Stretton, BEd

Heads of Year (*Girls*):
Mrs C J Adair, BA, PhD
Mrs K McIntyre, BSc
Mrs G C Morris, BEd
Mrs R F Morrison, BA
Mrs L I Nicholl, BSc
Mrs A M Reynolds, BSc
Mrs J Robb, BSc

Assistant Staff:
Mrs J C Bell, BSc
Mrs K Black, BA
Mrs N B Black, BMus
Miss K E Brady, BA
Miss B Brittain, BEd
Ms C Burns, BSc, PhD,
   MRSC
Miss V Carson, MA,
   ALCM
Mrs J M Cleland, BSc
Miss L Craig, BA
D J Creighton, BSc
Miss P R Cummings, BSc
Mrs C E Currie, BA
Miss D Currie, BSc, MSc,
   PhD
G J Forde, BMus
Mrs F A Gilmore, BSc

Mrs M L Gray, BA, MEd,
   DASE
Mrs S Graydon, BEd
Mrs N Henry, BSc
Miss J Herron, MA
Mrs C Hughes, BSc
N Irwin, BEd
C P Little, BA
P J Martin, BEd
Miss T McBeth, MA
Mrs G McCadden, Dip AD,
   ATD
Mrs S B McCoy, BA
Mrs J McGowan, MA
Miss A McMillen, BSc
Mrs H Miller, BA
O Mort, BA, PhD
Mrs D M Nicholl, BA

Mrs R O'Donnell, BA, Dip
   AD, ATD
Mrs L Patterson, BA
Miss C E Prior, BMus
Mrs J R Shaw, BA
Mrs M Sheeran, BA
Mrs J Smyth, BA
Mrs H Tate, BA
Mrs A P Terek, BSc
Miss R C Wallace, BA
Miss V S Wightman, BSc
Mrs M N Wilson, BA

Mrs G W Hanna,
Mrs C Henderson,
Mrs E Leinster, BA, PGCE
Miss P A Maxwell
Mrs B Rafferty, BA, PGCE
Mrs A Rea, BA
Mrs J Reid
Miss S Stewart
Mrs K Tepe
Mrs N Watson

Careers Advisers:
Ms J R Adams, BEd
A K Moles, BSc
S B Murphy, BEd
J M Patterson, BSc Econ,
   MSSc, DCG

Classroom Assistants:
Ms C Bernard, BA, PGCE
D R J Calvert,
Ms C Colwell, BA, PGCE

Preparatory Department:

Principal: Mrs V M McCaig, BEd, DASE
Deputy Principal: W T Wilson, BEd, LTCL

Assistant Staff:

P J Ingram, BEd, MSc
Mrs P Lennon, BEd
Mrs B Marshall, CertEd
S Patterson, BEd
Mrs S Sherrard, CertEd
Mrs E N E Wilson, BEd
Mrs R Wilson, BA, BEd,
   LTCL

Mrs E L Philpott
Mrs L Todd

Pre-Prep & Daycare Staff:
Mrs J Bradley
Miss D Davis
Mrs L Kyle
Mrs C Sempey
Mrs J Smeaton, BSc

Classroom Assistants:
Miss H E Crossan, BA

Administration:
Bursar: Miss E Hull, BSc, DipAcc, FCA
Finance Supervisor: Mrs H McClean, BA, FCA
Headmaster's Secretary: Mrs P McClintock
Headmaster's Secretary: Mrs J Sherry
General Office Manager: Ms P Ferguson
Office Administrator: Mrs L D Oliver
Receptionist/Telephonist: Mrs A Foy
Bursar's Secretary: Miss G Boyd, BA
Part-time Office Administrator: Mrs J Boyd
Part-time Finance Administrator: Mrs L Hogg, BA
Part-time Librarians: Mrs T Corcoran, BA; Miss E
   McAtamney, BA
ICT Manager: J R Cleland, BSc
Matron: Mrs N Loughran, RSCN
Alumni Officer: E G A McCamley, MA
Estates Manager: W J Thompson
Sixth Form Study Supervisor: Mrs C A Clyde
Supervisor of Grounds: M A Gaw, BTech
Swimming Pool Manager: Mrs E Alexander, BA

Belfast Royal Academy, founded in 1785, is the oldest school in the city. It moved to its present site, on the Cliftonville Road in North Belfast, in 1880, and the Gothic building erected at that time has been extensively modernised and refurbished. The fourteen Science Laboratories were opened in 1971, a 25-metre indoor heated Swimming Pool was completed in 1974, a new building for Art and Craft came into full use in 1982, and a Sports Hall was opened to mark the Bi-Centenary year. In 1989 a new Sixth Form Centre and Careers Suite were opened and a purpose-built four-room Technology Suite was completed in September 1991. An additional classroom block for English and Drama was opened in September 1994, and a new building to house the Mathematics department came into use in 1998. Since 2001 four new ICT Suites have been provided, and there is extensive provision throughout the school for teaching and learning through information technology.

The Academy is a co-educational day grammar school and there is also a preparatory and kindergarten department.

The grammar school has some 1,400 boys and girls, between the ages of 11 and 19. The kindergarten and preparatory department, known as Ben Madigan, has some 160 children, aged from 3 to 11; it is situated at 690 Antrim Road.

The curriculum has a strong academic bias and former pupils of the school are among the members of almost every university in the United Kingdom.

The work of the junior and middle Forms is directed mainly towards the GCSE examinations of the Northern Ireland Council for the Curriculum Examinations and Assessment, the Assessment and Qualifications Alliance or OCR, with a minimum of specialisation, all the usual subjects being provided and careful attention being given to the requirements of the universities and the professions. Religious studies are taught on a non-denominational basis.

There are more than 380 pupils in the Sixth Forms, where GCE Advanced Level courses are available in English, English Literature, Drama and Theatre Studies, French, German, Spanish, Latin, Mathematics (incorporating Mechanics and/or Statistics), Further Mathematics, Physics, Chemistry, Biology, Geography, History, Classical Civilisation, Economics, Politics, Art, Music, Home Economics, Business Studies, ICT, Physical Education, Religious Studies, Sociology, Technology and Moving Image Arts. Pupils are prepared for entry to Oxford or Cambridge in all the main subjects.

Much attention is given to careers guidance by the Careers Advisors, other senior members of Staff, and the Heads of Year.

The normal school day is from 8.40 am to 3.20 pm. There is no Saturday school but matches are played in the major sports on Saturdays. The school year runs from the beginning of September to the end of June, with holidays of about a fortnight at Christmas and at Easter.

There are some sixty different activities in the extra-curricular programme.

The principal games are, for boys, rugby, cricket, hockey, cross-country running, swimming and athletics; for girls, hockey, netball, tennis, swimming, cross-country running and athletics. Showjumping, water polo, golf and skiing are also available.

There is an orchestra, senior and junior choirs, a wind band, a Jazz band, several string ensembles and an Irish traditional group. Individual tuition in orchestral instruments is also provided. School organisations include Societies for Music, Drama, Chess, Bridge, Photography and Debating, an Air Training Corps, an Amateur Radio Club, Community Service and Scripture Union groups and the Duke of Edinburgh's Award Scheme.

Fees per annum (2014–2015). Parents pay a capital fee of £140 each year and a voluntary contingency charge of £27 per month.

In Ben Madigan, the annual fee is £3,438 for Years 1 to 3 and £3,642 for Years 4 to 7.

BRA Old Boys' Association. Hon Secretary: Dr L Campbell, c/o Belfast Royal Academy.

BRA Old Girls' Association. Hon Secretary: Mrs C Scoffield, 15 Glenshane Park, Newtownabbey, BT37 0QN.

Benenden School

Cranbrook, Kent TN17 4AA

Tel: 01580 240592
Fax: 01580 240280
email: registry@benenden.kent.sch.uk
schooloffice@benenden.kent.sch.uk
website: www.benenden.kent.sch.uk
Twitter: @benendenschool

Council:
Mr C A A Covell, MA (*Chairman*)
Mrs R J Johnston (*Vice Chairman*)
The Hon Mrs A Birkett, MA, MBA
Mrs W M Carey, BA Hons
Mr M C C Goolden, MA (*Chairman of the Finance Committee; AGBIS Representative*)
Mr S Green (*Chairman of the Benenden School Trust*)
Mrs S J Hayes, BA
Mr T H P Haynes, BA
Mrs S A Price, MA, PGCE
Mr H Salmon, BA (*Chairman of Health, Safety and Security Committee*)
Mr S Smart, BSc, FCA
Mr J V Strong, MRICS (*Chairman of the Building Committee*)
Mr W E H Trelawny-Vernon, BSc
Mr M K H Leung, BA, Dip Soc (*Honorary Representative for the Hong Kong Trust*)
Mr N Allen (*Secretary to the Council and School Bursar*)

Headmistress: **Mrs S A Price**, MA Edinburgh (*History of Art*)

Deputy Head: Mrs D Price, BA Open (*History*)

Assistant Head/Director of Studies: Mrs L A Tyler, MA, BD, PhD Edin, FSA Scot

Assistant Head/Director of Boarding and Pastoral Care: Miss A Steven, BA Bristol (*English*)

Housemistresses/masters:
Echyngham: Miss R Ross, BSc Exeter (*Physical Education*)
Guldeford: Miss R Johns, BSc Manchester (*Duke of Edinburgh's Award*)
Hemsted: Mrs A Roberts, BA Oxon (*English*)
Marshall: Mr C W Humphery, MA St Andrews (*English*)
Medway: Mrs E Custodio, BA Aberystwyth (*History*)
Norris: Mrs E Corry, BA Cantab (*Modern Foreign Languages*)
Founders:
Beeches: Mr A Nicol, BA Canterbury (*Religious Studies*)
Elms: Mr S Bennie, BA Surrey (*English*)
Limes: Miss K M Dobson, BA Newcastle (*Politics*)
Oaks: Mrs B Scopes, BA Kent (*History*)

School Chaplain: Revd C J Huxley, BA, QTS Canterbury

Academic Staff:
§ *Part-time/Visiting*

Assistant Director of Studies: Mr S Miller, BSc Brunel

English:
Mr A Schagen, BA York, PGCE York
Mr S Bennie, BA Surrey, PGCE London
Mrs S Carroll, BA Oxon, PGCE Canterbury
Ms J Granatt, MA UEA, BA UCL
Mr C W Humphery, MA St Andrews, PGCE Canterbury
Mr J Muir, MA, MLitt St Andrews
Mrs A Roberts, BA Oxon, GTP Canterbury
Mrs R Smith, BA, MPhil Oxon
Miss A Steven, BA Bristol
§Miss C Faram, BA Loughborough
§Miss S Watson, BA UEA

Mathematics:
Mrs G Poole, BSc Newcastle, PGCE
Mr A Fairey, BSc Hull, PGCE
Mr M Gossage, BSc, PGCE Liverpool
Mr S Miller, BSc Essex, PGCE Brunel
Ms S Roxburgh, MA Cantab, PGCE Canterbury
Mrs G Thomson, BA Open
§Mrs J Mills, BSc Reading
§Mrs J Tremble, BA Open

Science:
Ms N Marshall, MA, PGCE Oxon, MIBiol
Dr N J Dowrick, MA Oxon, DPhil Oxon, PGCE
Mr O N Hunter, BSc Durham, MA Open, PGCE
Ms S Canfield, BSc Canterbury, GTP Canterbury
Mr D Challoner, MPhys Canterbury, PGCE, MA
    Canterbury
Mr M Corry, MSc Oxon, PGCE Cantab
Mr S C Heron, BSc London, PGCE
Dr M Mahon, BSc London, PhD London
Mr N Moxham, BSc London
§Ms S Stevens, BSc Liverpool, MBA Aston, PGCE
    Liverpool
§Miss J Coombe-Jones
§Mrs W Grosvenor
§Mrs S Harris

Modern Languages:
Mrs M S Curran, BA Oxon, PGCE London
Mrs A Fuentes-Mansfield, BA, MA Caen, QTS London
Mrs M S Griffith, BA Brighton
Mrs A Jarman, MA Oxon, PGCE Reading
Mrs A Webb, BA Fuden, Shanghai, MEd
Mrs E Corry, BA, PGCE Cantab
Mr J D Crouzet, MA St Étienne
Miss V Fleitas Diaz, DTAS BA Madrid
Mrs R van der Vliet, BA UCW Aberystwyth
Ms Y Zhao, BA SOAS, PGCE London
§Mrs B Sanz, BSc Madrid
§Dr S Fra, MA Milan, PGCE Brighton
§Mrs A Hillier, BA Reading
§Miss C L Lesieur, BA, MA Amiens, PGCE Bristol)
§Mrs N Maslova-Wale, MEd Kazakhstan, TRFL Moscow
§Miss A Navarro-Silla, LLB Universidad de Valencia,
    PGCE MFL
§Mrs C G J Rennick, BA Amiens, PGCE
§Mrs D Wyles, BA Bath, PGCE Oxon, PG Cert TESOL,
    MCIL
§Miss S Cintas-Lopez, BA Jaen, Spain
§Miss A Roche

Classics:
Mr A D Matthews, BA, MLitt Newcastle
Ms P Anderson, BA Oxford
Mrs J Chapman, BA Bristol, TESOL
Mrs J Gilbert, BA Cantab
Dr B Harding, BA Kent, MA London
Ms J Howell, BA Bristol

Drama:
Ms D Caron, BA Loughborough, LGSM, AIMENTS
Mrs L Perry, BA York
Mr M S Kemp, HND Stage Mgt/Tech Theatre Bristol Old
    Vic Theatre School
Mr A D Sargeant, BEng Kent, DipStgMan UWE
§Mr G R Lee, CertEd Roehampton, Dip Design
    Bournemouth
§Ms N Thorndike, Dip LAMDA
§Mrs E Vernon, Dip Drama Studio Acting
§Miss A L Wickens, LLAM, LAMDA

Economics:
Mrs S J Northridge, BHum London, MBA Reading, PGCE
    Surrey
Miss J Eve, BA Strathclyde
§Mr C E Williams, BSc Southampton

Geography:
Mr M Dunton, BSc Bristol, PGCE Cantab, MEd Cantab
Mrs S Bosher, BHum London
Miss P A Hubbard, BSc Leicester
Miss S Jones, BSc Aberystwyth, MSc UEA

History:
Dr D Yuravlivker, BA McGill Montreal, MSc London,
    PhD Maryland, PGCE London

Mrs E C Custodio, BA Aberystwyth, CPD Surrey
Mrs A Harber, BSc Aberystwyth, MSc LSE
Mr P Hopkisson, BA Manchester, PGCE Canterbury
Mr M Loy, BA Dunelm, PGCE Dunelm
Mrs D Price, BA Open
Mrs B Scopes, BA Kent

Politics and International Relations:
Mrs A Harber, BSc Aberystwyth, MSc LSE
Miss K M Dobson, BA Newcastle

Religious Studies:
Mr A Nicol, BA Canterbury
Mr C Huxley, BA Canterbury
Mr P Sage, BA Leeds
Ms E Wheeler, BA Oxford, PGCE Chester
§Mrs K Hall, BSc Canterbury

Art & Design and History of Art:
Mrs P J Futrell, BA Middlesex Polytechnic
Mr M Gilbert, BA Glasgow, PhD Nebraska
Dr B Harding, BA Kent, MA London, PhD Essex
Miss J S Large, BA Loughborough, BTEC Diploma
Mr S H Mansfield, BA Staffs (*History of Art*)
Mrs J L Taylor, BA Nottingham Trent (*Textiles*)

Design and Technology:
Mr N Crouch, BSc Exeter, PGCE Exeter
Ms E Walsh, BA Canterbury, PGCE and QTS Greenwich
Mr C Fahy

E Technology and Computing:
Mr D Challoner, MPhys Kent, PGCE, MA Canterbury

Critical Thinking:
Mrs D Price, BA Open
Mrs H Miller, BSc Southampton, MSc Surrey, QTS
Ms S Roxburgh, MA Cantab, PGCE Canterbury
Mrs C Saint, BA Dublin
Mrs L Tyler, MA Oxon, PGCE London

Music:
Mr E Whiting, MA Oxon
Mr J Fitzgerald, BA Bristol
Mrs S Lamberton, BA Wales
Mrs V Lewis, ARCM, DipRCM (*Piano, Cello*)
§Mr S Chapman, ALCM, LLCMTO (*Guitar*)
§Mrs J M Colman, LTCL (*Piano, Double Bass*)
§Ms C Considine, MMus Perf, PGDip, MMus Hons
§Mr A Ellingworth, Military School of Music, Knellerhall
    (*Clarinet, Saxophone*)
§Mrs K Fish, LTCL, Dip TCL (*Clarinet, Saxophone*)
§Ms S Graham, GRSM, LRAM, DipRAM (*Singing*)
§Mr A W Haigh, ARCM, LRAM (*Piano*)
§Miss R J Hanson-Laurent, BMus BMus Hons
§Mr M D Hines, AGSM (*Bassoon*)
§Mr D M Manente, BMus, PGDip (*Strings*)
§Mrs H Manente, BMus, MMus RCM (*Flute*)
§Miss G A Mendes, GDipM Huddersfield, LTCL
    (*Recorder*)
§Ms S Pattinson, BMus London (*HFYO Strings Tutor*)
§Ms L Pont, LTCL (*Singing*)
§Mrs S Purton, LRAM (*Oboe, Piano*)
§Ms H Ramsay, BMus Glasgow (*Piano*)
§Mr J Raper, BMus Trinity (*Percussion*)
§Miss E J Roberts, GRNCM, PPRNCM, PDOTGSMD
    (*Horn*)
§Mrs I Sellschop, LRAM (*HFYO Strings Tutor*)
§Mrs J M Tilt, GGSM LRAM (*Singing*)
§Mrs R Waltham, PGDip RAM (*Strings*)
§Pipe Major M Wilkinson (*Bagpipes*)
§Mr M Williams, BMus Dunelm, GRSM, Hon LCM,
    FRCO (*Piano, Organ*)
§Ms A Wynne, BA Birmingham, MMus Leeds (*Harp*)

Physical Education:
Miss L K Hall, MSc Bristol

Miss V A Sawyer, MBA Keele, LLB Hons Open, BEd Hons Reading
Mr R de Wet, BSc Portsmouth REPS Level 3, NPLQ (*Lifeguard*)
Mrs J E Fahy (*Sports Centre Supervisor*)
Mrs K Jones, BA Brighton
Miss L Lynch, BSc, PGCE Loughborough (*Head Lacrosse Coach*)
Mr J B Mitchell, BA Hons Bedford
Miss R Ross, BSc Exeter
Ms J Stolworthy, BA
Mrs H Vesma (*Fitness Instructor*)
Mr D Weighton, DipPhysEd Strathclyde
§Mr N J Allen (*Rugby Coach*)
§Mr J Collins, NPLQ Level 2 (*Lifeguard*)
§Mr N Davies, USPTR, USTA (*Tennis*)
§Mrs R M Elliott, RAD, ISTD, LAMDA (*Modern & Tap Dance*)
§ADR Fricker, BSc (*Trampolining*)
§Mrs M Fricker, BSc Kent (*Trampolining*)
Mr P Hopkisson, BA Manchester (*Tennis*)
§Ms P Lane, USPTA Pro, LTA licenced, USPTR & Dip Sports Psychology (*Tennis Coach*)
§Ms C Le Gassick (*Visiting Exercise and Dance Instructor*)
§Mrs J E Marlowe-Barham, BEd Leeds
§Mrs V Mitchell, BEd Hons Bedford
§Mrs J Morris (*Lifeguard*)
§Mr M Morris (*Lifeguard*)
§Mr T Sayer (*Squash Coach*)
§Mr D Slade (*Tennis Coach*)
§Ms H Smart, BSc Portsmouth, PGCE
§Mr G Marshall England Squash Level 3 (*Squash Coach*)
§Mrs K M Steel, BEd Hons Bedford
§Mr G Turner, (*Gymnastics*)
§Miss J Wilson, ISTD, Dip LCDD (*Ballet*)

Careers & College Guidance:
Mrs C Saint, BA Dublin
§Mrs H Martin, BA Oxon

Personal, Social, Health and Economic Education:
Mrs S Bosher, BHum London

Academic Support:
Mrs A P Simpson, BSc London, Cert ADS Greenwich, ATC C&G
Mrs J Chapman, BA Bristol, DipMSE Greenwich, DipTESOL Trinity, PGCE London
Mrs D Mackinnon, LLB, Dip LA, QTS, AMBDA/ATS
Mrs H Miller, BSc Southampton, MSC Surrey
Ms S Morgan, BSc, OCR
§Mrs C M Pearson, BEd SEN CNAA
§Dr F Westcott, BSc, PhD Liverpool
§Ms C Wheat, BEd Cantab

Head of Professional Studies:
§Mrs D E Wyles, BA Bath

Librarian:
Miss A Morley, BA Brighton, MA Sussex, MCLIP, DipTEFL, DipPub

Assistant Librarians:
§Mrs A Blackmur
§Mrs M Nicol, LLB Cardiff

Administrative Staff:
Bursar: Mr N J Allen
Finance Bursar: Mr N Hollamby
Estates Bursar: Mr S Brophy
Domestic Bursar: Mrs S E Franklin, HCIMA
HR & Compliance Officer: Mrs J Card

Development Office:
Development Manager: Mrs C Saint
Deputy Development Director: Mr G E Smith
Development Executive: Mrs S Blanchard

Seniors' Officer: Mrs K H Barradell
Seniors' Officer: Mrs M Sullivan
Marketing Assistant – Events: Mrs D Bradford
Marketing Assistant – Publications: Mr S Thorneycroft
Web Assistant: Mrs S B Leathart

Registry:
Admissions Secretary: Mrs E A Ward
Admissions Assistant: Mrs S K Davies

Secretariat:
Mrs J A Sullivan (*Headmistress's Personal Assistant*)
Mrs D M Benson, LTCL, FTCL (*Music Administrator*)
Mrs D Bishop (*Head of Boarding's Secretary*)
Mrs J Crouch (*Academic Administrator*)
Mrs R Judd (*Examinations Officer*)
Mrs J McColl (*Deputy Head's Personal Assistant*)
Mrs A G Pissarro (*School Secretary – term time*)
Mrs A Molloy (*Secretary to the Housemistresses/masters*)
Mrs S Renshaw (*Bursar's Personal Assistant*)
Mrs N K Wood, BA Cornell (*Director of Studies' Secretary*)
§Mrs C Andrews (*Common Room*)
§Mrs S Cramp (*PE Administrator*)
§Mrs M E Murphy (*Careers Administrator*)

Medical:
Dr A M Wood, MBChB, MRC Psych (*Medical Officer*)
Sister J L Mallion, RGN
Mrs E O'Dell, BSc Manchester, RSCN, RGN
Mrs K Perry, RGN

Benenden School aims to give each pupil the chance to develop her potential to the full within a happy and caring environment. We want her to feel ready to take on whatever challenges lie ahead and able to make a positive difference to the world, whether that is at work or at home or both. Whilst we aim to help each girl to achieve her best possible results in public exams, we also emphasise the importance of spiritual growth and of developing as a person, most particularly in confidence, compassion and courage. We want to encourage each pupil to develop as an individual as well as a responsible and caring member of a community.
We aim to do this by providing

- a full and balanced curriculum and a very wide range of extra-curricular and co-curricular activities, designed to promote academic, cultural, creative, physical, spiritual and social development;
- well-taught lessons within facilities designed to encourage the best teaching and the best learning;
- supportive individual academic and pastoral care;
- group and individual higher education and careers guidance designed to help every student to make wise personal choices;
- a wide range of opportunities for leadership within the school;
- a culture of praise, encouragement and support within a framework designed to develop self-reliance and self-esteem;
- the experience of learning to understand other people which a full boarding school can provide;
- opportunities for a close partnership with parents so that school and home can work together to help every pupil.
In both our academic and our pastoral programme we aim to foster:
Belief in oneself: integrity, independence, courage, endeavour, reflection and self-confidence
Belief in others: trust, appreciation, consultation, understanding, generosity of spirit, respect and tolerance
Commitment to learning: an enthusiasm for and love of learning
Commitment to the community: participation, service, responsibility, leadership, initiative, compassion and commitment to equality

General Information. The School is an independent girls' boarding school standing in its own parkland of 240 acres. In the heart of the Kentish Weald, it is easily reached by road, or by rail to the neighbouring main line station at Staplehurst, and is well placed for the air terminals of Gatwick and Heathrow, the continental ferry ports of the South East coast and the Channel Tunnel (Ashford International).

Mrs Samantha Price began as Headmistress in January 2014. Previously Headmistress at Godolphin School, Mrs Price was educated at Malvern Girls' College and Edinburgh University, where she read History of Art (with modules of European History). Having graduated, she joined the Tate Britain and was responsible for marketing for Members and Patrons and became heavily involved with the Patrons of what is now the Tate Modern.

She started her teaching career in 1999 as an History of Art and History teacher at Reading Blue Coat School, where she stayed for a number of years. She then joined King's Canterbury as an Housemistress, History and History of Art teacher. Her next post was to be Deputy Head at Hereford Cathedral School and from there she became Head of Godolphin in 2010.

Samantha is married with a daughter and a son. Her husband is an Army Chaplain.

The School provides education for girls between the ages of 11 and 18 years. There are 546 students at Benenden; all are boarders and they come from a wide range of backgrounds.

Girls are taught by highly qualified full-time staff of over 100 men and women, together with some 50 part-time specialists, many of whom are leaders in their particular fields.

Each student belongs to a House in which she sleeps and spends much of her private study and leisure time: it is, in effect, her home from home. There are six Houses for 11 to 16 year olds, while Sixth Form students live in the Founders' Sixth Form Centre in one of four Sixth Form Houses.

Each House has a resident Housemistress or Housemaster, who is also a member of the teaching staff and responsible for the academic and pastoral well-being of each student in the House. Much of the day-to-day work is shared with Deputies and Day and Resident Matrons, while other non-resident members of the teaching staff are Personal Academic Tutors.

The School's facilities have been greatly improved in recent years. A new £9 million Science Centre opened in Autumn 2012. The new Science Centre represents the greatest investment in the academic life of the School since the construction of the Clarke Centre. The centre has more than doubled laboratory and teaching space an provided specialist project laboratories for A Level, as well as a 100-seat Science lecture theatre. A new eco-classroom was constructed and opened in October 2009. The classroom is completely self-sustaining, with solar power and rainwater harvesting. The School was awarded Eco-School Green Flag status in 2009. The Benenden School Theatre and Drama teaching complex was officially opened in October 2007. The Clarke Centre, a £3.5 million Study Centre, providing state-of-the-art classrooms equipped with the latest computer technology, library and IT Centre. Since 2001, a programme of extensive refurbishment has taken place in boarding houses, including a new suite of classrooms and floor of study bedrooms which opened in 2003. Extensions to the Sixth Form centre have taken place in 2006 and 2007. For physical recreation there are nine lacrosse pitches, 11 all-weather tennis courts, sports hall containing a further full-sized tennis court, an indoor heated swimming pool, a second sports hall (also used for badminton, volleyball, netball and fencing), a fitness centre and gym, two squash courts and a grass running track.

In August 2014 Benenden celebrated its best ever GCSE results. 58% of all entries were graded at A*; 88% A*–A and 99% A*–B. 44 girls achieved nothing less than an A, 25 girls at least 10 A*s and 15 girls at least 11 A*s. 12 girls took the Extended Project Qualification, a voluntary research project, and every single one gained an A*.

The School is a Christian community, based on Anglican practice, and the ethos of the School reflects Christian principles. Members of other communions and beliefs are welcomed to the School and every effort is made to help them in the practice of their own faith, in an atmosphere of respect and toleration for the views of others.

Entrance to the School is after internal assessment at Preview Weekend, but dependent upon candidates meeting the School's standard at 11+ and 13+ Common Entrance or in entrance papers. There is also a small intake at Sixth Form level, with competitive entry by the School's own examination. All of the School's students are expected to qualify for degree courses, leaving School with at least three A Levels and at least eight subjects at GCSE. A full careers programme is a key component of the Personal Development Programme, aimed to foster the widest range of skills.

The core subjects up to GCSE are English, English literature, mathematics, science and a modern language. The compulsory balanced science course ensures that all three sciences are studied (either for single sciences at GCSE or the option of Core Science plus Additional Science), and every student studies in Key Stage 3 at least two of the three modern languages offered in addition to Latin. Cross-curricular skills and the balancing of theoretical concepts with practical applications are actively encouraged. The ability to work independently is critical to enjoyment and success, and students are given every opportunity to acquire appropriate study habits. The curriculum is under constant review and development, reflecting national initiatives and the aspirations of staff and students.

Benenden believes in close cooperation between School and parents and there is regular contact with them, including a weekly email newsletter. Formal reports are sent at the end of every term. Parents are encouraged to visit the School for concerts, plays and other events, as well as to take their daughters out for meals or weekend exeats. There is a flourishing programme of social events for parents.

Curriculum. *Lower School*: English, mathematics, biology, chemistry, physics, French, German or Spanish or Classical Greek, Latin, Mandarin, geography, history, religious studies, art & design including textiles, design technology, information technology, drama, music, physical education.

GCSE Core: English, English literature, mathematics, biology, chemistry, physics, a modern foreign language.

GCSE Options: German, Spanish, Classical Greek, Latin, Mandarin, geography, history, religious studies, art, textiles, design & technology, music, drama & theatre arts.

A Level Options: English language and literature, English literature, mathematics, further mathematics, biology, chemistry, physics, French, German, Spanish, Greek, Latin, Mandarin, classical civilisation, economics, geography, history, politics, religious studies, art & design, history of art, music, theatre studies, design and technology. All Sixth Form students take Critical Thinking.

(All students' programmes also include academic extension programmes – Extend, Excel, Explore – careers education, information technology, physical education, religious education, personal, social and health education.)

Sport. Lacrosse, tennis, swimming, netball, rounders, badminton, athletics, volleyball, squash, basketball, gym, dance, fencing, trampolining, aerobics, hockey, riding.

Opportunities in Music. Tuition is available in all orchestral and keyboard instruments as well as singing. Numerous opportunities exist for instrumental and choral performance. The School is home to a full youth symphony orchestra, and in which students from other schools also play. Benenden also enjoys a strong choral tradition and hosts recitals by musicians of international calibre.

Opportunities in Speech and Drama. Students are able to pursue drama as an extra-curricular activity throughout their School career by participating in drama workshops, House and Lower and Upper School plays. Speech and drama lessons are available and students are prepared for both English Speaking Board and LAMDA examinations. There are several debating societies and students compete at the Oxford and Cambridge Union debating competitions. Sixth Formers are encouraged to run drama and debating clubs. Many pupils are involved in MUN clubs and represent the school at MUN conferences in the UK and abroad.

Optional Extras. Speech and drama, ballet, tap, modern dance, brass, guitar, percussion, piano, string, voice, woodwind, squash, tennis, fencing, judo, self-defence, yoga, riding, clay pigeon shooting, Duke of Edinburgh's Award Scheme, foreign languages.

Fees per term (2014–2015). £11,150 payable before the start of term, or by the School's Advance Payment of Fees Scheme.

Scholarships. *Academic Scholarships – Lower School Entry (11–13)*: Awards of up to 10% of fees available. The level of examination will be determined not by date of birth but by intended Form of entry (11+ for Fourth Form, 12+ for Upper Fourth, 13+ for Lower Fifth). The examinations are held in January preceding the date of entry.

Academic Scholarships – Sixth Form Entry: Examinations are held in November preceding entry in September. Candidates take three papers: a compulsory General Paper and two papers in subjects which they intend to study at A Level.

Music Scholarships – Lower School Entry (11–13): Awards of up to 10% of fees available. The examinations are held in January preceding the date of entry. Candidates should have reached the standard of Grade V (or equivalent) or show great potential. Those offering piano or singing as a principal study should be fluent in an orchestral instrument. Candidates will be required to do practical tests and will be interviewed; they are also required to show that they have reached the general academic standards of any entrant either by sitting qualifying papers, or by taking the academic scholarship examination.

Music Scholarships – Sixth Form Entry: Awards of up to 10% of fees available. Examinations are held in November preceding entry in September. The requirements for a Sixth Form Music Scholarship are very much the same as for Lower School candidates (see above entry), but candidates should have reached the standard of Grade VII (or equivalent). Candidates are also required to show that they have reached the general academic standard required of any entrant by taking two qualifying papers in subjects which they intend to study at A Level.

Art and Design: Awards of up to 10% of fees available. Examinations are held in January preceding entry in September. The examination for the Art Scholarship will consist of one hour on a set-piece drawing followed by an interview based on the candidate's portfolio on which particular emphasis will be placed for evidence of commitment and enthusiasm. Candidates are required to show that they have reached the general academic standard of any entrant by sitting two qualifying papers in subjects which they intend to study at A Level.

Design and Technology: Awards of up to 10% of fees available. Scholarships are offered to girls who show exceptional promise and commitment in this area, supported by good academic results in the normal entry papers. Applicants will be asked to produce evidence of three kinds: a record or portfolio of previous work or achievements; a response to a challenge set at Benenden; and an interview.

Candidates will be asked to identify and research the main purposes of packaging and to design and make a suitable container for a given object. They will use non-specialist materials and processes such as paper, pencils, card, scissors, glue. Research might be prepared at home or in their school, but the task of designing and making would be executed at Benenden.

Sports Scholarships: Awards of up to 10% of fees available. Scholarships are offered to girls who show exceptional promise and commitment in this area, supported by good academic results in the normal entry papers. Applicants will be asked to produce evidence of three kinds: a record or portfolio of previous work or achievements; a response to a challenge set at Benenden; and an interview. Candidates will undertake a test to measure levels of fitness, participate in a range of games to show physical ability and tactical awareness, and be given an opportunity to demonstrate their chosen specialism.

Trust Award Programme: Bursary support of up to 100% of fees (subject to means testing) to one or more local primary school pupils at 11+ or to a Sixth Form candidate at 16+.

For further information, please contact the Admissions Secretary.

Admission. Prospective parents are encouraged to visit the School, either individually or with others at a Prospective Parents' Morning. Prospectuses and full details of entry and scholarship requirements may be obtained from the Admissions Secretary.

Charitable status. Benenden School (Kent) Limited is a Registered Charity, number 307854. It is a charitable foundation for the education of girls.

Berkhamsted School

133 High Street, Berkhamsted, Hertfordshire HP4 2DJ

Tel:	01442 358000 (General enquiries)
	01442 358001 (Admissions)
Fax:	01442 358040
email:	enquiries@berkhamstedschool.org
	admissions@berkhamstedschool.org
website:	www.berkhamstedschool.org
Twitter:	@berkhamstedsch
Facebook:	/berkhamstedschool
LinkedIn:	/berkhamsted-school

In 1541 John Incent, Dean of St Paul's, was granted a Licence by Henry VIII to found a school in Berkhamsted, Incent's home town. Until the end of the nineteenth Century Berkhamsted School served as a grammar school for a small number of boys from the town but over the last century it has developed into a school of significance. In 1888 the foundation was extended by the establishment of Berkhamsted School for Girls. In 1996, these two schools and Berkhamsted Preparatory School formalised their partnership, offering the highest quality education to pupils from ages three to 19. More recently, Berkhamsted School merged with Heatherton House School to form the Berkhamsted Schools Group in 2011, and in May 2012, the Group acquired Haresfoot School, which has become the Berkhamsted Pre-Preparatory School for children aged three to seven. The existing Preparatory School focuses on the education of children aged seven to eleven. *Please refer to separate entries for Berkhamsted Preparatory, Berkhamsted Pre-Preparatory and Heatherton House.*

There are 360 pupils in the flourishing co-educational Sixth Form; between the ages of eleven and sixteen 440 boys at the Boys School (Castle) and 350 girls at the Girls School (Kings) are taught in single-sex groups.

The Principal is a member of both HMC and GSA.

Patron: Her Majesty The Queen

The Governors:
Mr G C Laws (*Chairman*)
Mrs S Turner (*Vice-Chairman*)

Mr J J Apthorp	Dr Y A Burne OBE
Mr D J Atkins	Mrs B W Canham

Ms A K Fahy
Dr M A Fenton
¶Mrs E Jeffrey
Mr A H Noel

Mr S Rolland
¶Mr M A Scicluna
Mrs S Tidey

Clerk to the Governors: Mr C Westwood
Chairman of the Berkhamsted Foundation: ¶Mrs S
   Wolstenholme OBE

¶ *Old Berkhamstedian*

Principal: Mr M S Steed, MA Cantab, MA

Vice Principal (Education): Mr M Bond, BA
Vice Principal (Business Operations): Mr P Nicholls, MA
   Cantab, FCA
Headmaster Sixth Form: Mr R Petty, BSc
Head Berkhamsted Boys (Boys 11–16): Mr R C Thompson,
   BA
Head Berkhamsted Girls (Girls 11–16): Mrs E A
   Richardson, BA
Deputy Head (Sixth Form): Mrs M C Startin, BA
Deputy Head (Sixth Form): Mr D G Richardson, BSc
Deputy Head Pastoral (Boys 11–16): Mr G Anker, BA
Deputy Head Academic (Boys 11–16): Dr N R Dennis,
   PhD, MSc, BSc
Deputy Head (Girls 11–16): Miss R L McColl, BA, MPhil
Director of Studies: Mr W R C Gunary, BSc

Chaplain: Reverend J E Markby, MA

Teaching staff:
* *Head of Department*
† *Head of House*

Art:
Mrs C M E Ferguson, MA (**Art & Design*)
Mrs K M Bly, BA (*Art*)
Miss J E Brodie, BA (*Art, Photography*)
Mr R B Garner, BA (*Art, Photography*)
Miss E L Gent, BA, MA, ATC (*Art*)
Miss A Kelway-Bamber, BA, MA (*Art, Ceramics, ICT*)

Classics:
*Mr I R Stewart, BA, MA
Miss R M Bradley, BA, MA
Mr J Cooper, BA (*also English*)
Dr A J Harker, BA, MA, PhD (*†Fry's House*)
Mrs H McCann, MA, RSA, DipTEFL, MBA (*TESL*)
Mr R K Mowbray, MA (*†Churchill House, i/c Rugby*)

Design and Technology:
*Mr S R Hargreaves, BEd
Mr M E Batchelder, CertEd, DipEd, MA (*CCF Royal Navy
   Section*)
Ms F M Garratt, BSc
Miss R Knox, BSc (*Food Technology*)
Mr A M Lansdell, BSc, DipEd
Mrs K J Pickles, BEd (*Food Technology*)
Mr D S van Noordwyk, DipEd, DipMin, MCollT (*†Bees
   House*)

Economics and Business Studies:
*Mr P C Cowie, MA
Mr D L Foster, BA (*also History, †Swift's House, Fives
   Coach*)
Mr V Fung, BSc (*Young Enterprise*)
Mr A Ottaway, BSc
Mr D R Pain, BA, BComm (*†Spencer House*)

English:
*Mr T A Grant, MA (*i/c Golf*)
Miss R Brims, BEd (*PSHE Speaker Coordinator*)
Mr J Cooper, BA (*also Classics*)
Mr A G Harrison, BA, MA, MEd
Miss A Ireland, BA
Mr T D Lines, BA, MA, MEd (*†Hawks House*)
Miss R L McColl, BA, MPhil
Mr M S Pett, BA (*†St George's House, i/c Fives*)

Mrs J F Phillips, BA, MA
Mrs L J Redman, BA (*†School House*)
Mrs E A Richardson, BA
Mrs H Rossington, BA
Mrs J Simons, BA, MA (*Senior School Careers*)
Mrs M C Startin, BA
Mrs K E Tomlin, BA, MA

Geography:
*Mr P Matthews, BSc, MA
Mr G R Burchnall, BEd (*†Reeves House*)
Mr S J Dight, BA, DipEd
Mr L Eaton, BSc
Mrs A J Murray, BSc
Mr M J Thum, MA (*CCF RAF Section*)

History and Politics:
Mr C H Savill, BA (**History*)
Mr P T Riddick, BA, MA, MSc Econ (**Politics, History, i/
   c Tennis*)
Mr G Anker, BA
Mr M Bond, BA
Mr S E Bridle, BA (*Acting †Tilman House*)
Dr N R Dennis, BSc, MSc, PhD
Mr R Falder, MA, BA
Mr D L Foster, BA (*also Economics & Business Studies,
   †Swift's, Fives Coach*)
Mr R Moseley, BA (*†Cox's House*)
Mrs N A Murphy, BA
Mr R Petty, BSc
Mr S J E Rees, BA
Miss L Spray, BA Cantab (*†Wolstenholme House*)
Miss S Afsar, BA, BSc, LLM (*also *Psychology &
   Sociology*)

Learning Support:
*Mrs A Dunmall, BSc, Dip SpLD, APC SpLD (*SENCO*)
Mrs S M Blythe, MA Cantab, OCR Dip SpLD
Mrs D Fuller, BA, MA
Mrs K Harris, BA, OCR Dip SpLD
Mrs K Warde, BSc, DipSpLD, NPQH (*†St John's
   Boarding House*)

Mathematics:
*Mr D Jeffers, BSc
Mrs W Brockie, BSc
Mrs A J Casey, BSc (*†Old Stede House*)
Mr S Fraser, BA
Mr W R C Gunary, BSc
Dr P Khare, PhD, BSc
Mr J M Mateu-Bueso, BA, MA
Mr M Middleton, BSc (*†Loxwood House*)
Mrs A K O'Clee, MA (*i/c Duke of Edinburgh's Award*)
Miss S Parsons, MA
Mr D G Richardson, BSc (**Co-curricular*)
Dr J Samuel, PhD, MMath
Mrs R H Warburton, BSc (*†Adders House*)
Mr S A Whyte, BSc, MSc

Media Studies and ICT:
Ms J D Bohitige, BA (**Media Studies, ICT*)
Mrs N A V Mateu-Bueso, BA (*Media Studies, i/c
   Community Service Pupil Development*)

Modern Languages:
*Mr N Cale, BA (*French*)
Mrs B Evans, MA Cantab (*French, German, †Russell
   House*)
Mrs L M Knight, BA (*French, Spanish, Director of
   eLearning*)
Miss A L Y Lefrançois, MFL Licence LLCE (*French,
   Spanish*)
Mrs S M Shipton, DEUG Licence (*French, Spanish, †St
   David's House*)
Mrs L C Briand, BA, DipTESOL (*German, Spanish*)
Miss J Wordie, BA (*German*)

Miss A M Ashby, BA (*Spanish*)
Mr I R Cruickshanks, BA (*Spanish*)
Mrs C A Garcia, MA (*Spanish*)
Mr T Gayton, BA (*Spanish*)
Miss E Irving, BA (*Spanish, French*)
Ms C J Moss, BA (*Spanish, French*)

Performing Arts:
*Mrs S B Gunary, BA, MA (*Director of Performing Arts*)
Mr D Curtis, BA (*Academic Drama*)
Mrs S A E Clay, Dip CSSD, CertEd, MA (*Drama*)
Mrs A Gibson, BA, MA (*Drama*)
Mr O Pengelly, BA (*Drama*)
Miss D Wylie, BA (*Drama*)
Mr A Crawford, MA, MMus (*Academic Music*)
Mr B Noithip, BA, MMus (*Director of Co-curricular Music*)
Mrs A Hatton, BA (*Music*)
Mr P J Hopkins, BA, BMus, FRCO, ARCM (*Keyboard*)

Physical Education:
Miss J Lupton, BA (*Director of Girls' Sport, *Lacrosse*)
Mr D J Gibson, BSc (*Director of Boys' Sport*)
Mrs A E Bamforth, BA (†*New Stede House*)
Miss E M Brown, BA (*i/c AS & A2 PE*)
Mr G Campbell, BA (*Football and Cricket*)
Mr F Charnock, CertEd (*CCF*)
Mrs L J Chinneck, BSc (*i/c Girls' Athletics and Cross Country*)
Mr M Coombes (*Sports Coach*)
Miss N Cresswell, BSc
Mr B P Evers, BA (†*Incents Boarding House, i/c Hockey*)
Miss D Finnigan, BSc (*i/c Netball*)
Miss E Gray (*Lacrosse Coach*)
Mr T Hockedy, BSc, MSc
Mr B R Mahoney, BEd (*Rugby, i/c Boys' Swimming*)
Miss J Osborn, BSc (*i/c Girls' Swimming and Rounders*)
Mrs D D G Pearson, BHK, BEd (*i/c Dance and Gymnastics*)
Mr R Perrie (*Sports Coach*)
Mr G Proudfoot (*Sports Coach*)
Mrs C Spooner (*Sports Coach*)
Mr A S Theodossi (*Fives Professional, Boys' Sports Administrator*)
Mr D Vila (*i/c Squash*)
Mr D Williams

Psychology and Sociology:
*Miss S Afsar, BA, BSc, LLM (*also History*)
Miss A Ali, BSc (*Psychology*)
Mrs E Taylor, BSc (*Sociology*)

Religion and Philosophy:
*Mr A Ford, BA
Mr R W D Coupe, BA, MA (*Academic Director*)
Ms H-C Burt, BTh (*Careers, *Charities*)
Miss G Ferguson, BA, MA
Mr B Hopcroft, BA
Mr A Lawrence, BA
Mr H R Maxted, BA (†*Burgh House, i/c Rowing*)
Mr M Stallard, BA

Science:
Biology:
Mr S C Robinson, BSc, FSB (*Science, *ICT*)
Mr C J Allam, BEd, BSc, MSB (*Biology*)
Mrs H A A Green, BSc
Dr P R Hatfield-Iacoponi, BA, PhD
Mr A Hopper, BSc
Dr S P S Hundal, BSc, MEd, PhD (†*Nash House*)
Ms S P Jennings, BSc (*KS3 Science Coordinator*)
Revd J E Markby, MA (*Chaplain*)
Mrs R E Miles, BSc (†*Greenes House*)
Chemistry:
Mrs M C Gould, BSc (*Chemistry*)
Mr D W Binnie, BSc

Mr P E Dobson, BSc, CChem, MRSC (*i/c Shooting*)
Mrs T A Kergon, BSc
Mr N Kirwan, BSc
Mr M Neill, BSc
Physics:
Dr S A Redman, BSc, PhD (*Physics*)
Mrs V Hyman, BSc, MSc (†*Ashby House*)
Mr D Hyman, BSc, MSc
Mr R D Matthews, BSc (†*Holme House*)
Mr P McGowan, BEng
Mr K Powell, BSc

Additional Staff:
There are 23 visiting music staff offering instrumental teaching in: acoustic guitar, bassoon, cello, clarinet, double bass, electric guitar, euphonium, flute, jazz piano, oboe, organ, percussion (including kit drumming), piano, recorder, saxophone, singing, trombone, trumpet, viola and violin. Five visiting teachers offer Speech and Drama tuition.

Director of Human Resources: Mrs T L Evans
Estates Director: Mr R Grant, MBIFM
Director of Development: Mrs S Rodwell
Director of External Relations: Mrs C Dow, BA
Admissions Manager: Mrs L T Wesley
Sports Centre Manager: Mrs V Rees
Head of Learning Resources: Mrs R Hine, BA, MA
Archivist: Mrs L Koulouris
School Counsellor: Mrs J Hennigan, MSc, BSc, MBACP Accred, MBABCP
Medical Officer: Dr V Whitbread, MB BCh, MRCGP, DCH, DRCOG
PA to Principal: Mrs N M Golder
PA to Vice Principals: Mrs N Murray
PA to Head Berkhamsted Boys: Mrs T Rawlings
PA to Head Berkhamsted Girls: Mrs S Bailey
PA to Headmaster Berkhamsted Sixth: Mrs N Seymour

Aims. At Berkhamsted we believe that excellent academic results do not have to be won at the expense of the wider attributes of a good education. All pupils are supported and encouraged to reach their full potential, with appropriate teaching environments for each age group and a structure that offers the best of both co-educational and single-sex tuition. In addition to the development of the intellect, social, sporting and cultural activities play an important part within the framework of a disciplined and creative community based on Christian values. It is important that pupils come to value both the individual and the Community through school life. The School seeks to encourage spiritual and moral values and a sense of responsibility as an essential part of the pursuit of excellence.

Location. The School stands in the heart of Berkhamsted, an historic and thriving town only thirty miles from London. It enjoys excellent communications to London, the airports, to the Midlands and the communities of Buckinghamshire, Bedfordshire and Hertfordshire.

Facilities. The original site has at its heart a magnificent Tudor Hall used as a schoolroom for over 300 years. Other buildings are from late Victorian to modern periods and of architectural interest (especially the Chapel modelled on the Church of St Maria dei Miracoli in Venice). With separate Pre-Preparatory School and Preparatory School sites, and two Senior School campuses, the School is well equipped with a range of facilities. There are new Science laboratories, Library and Learning Resources Centres, Information Technology suites, Sixth Form centres located on the two Senior School campuses, Careers libraries, Dining halls, Medical centre, House rooms, Deans' Hall (an Assembly Hall) and Centenary Theatre (a modern 500-seat theatre also used for concerts and theatre productions). Recreational and sports facilities include extensive playing fields, Fives courts, Squash courts, Tennis courts, Gymnasium, Drama studio, Music school and Art studios. A Sports Hall and 25m indoor swimming pool were opened in 2004 and a state-of-the-art Design Centre in 2008. The Nash-Harris Building at Kings was completed in 2011 comprising a new dining facility, classrooms and Chapel.

Diamond Structure. The School has a "diamond" structure that combines both single-sex and co-educational teaching. Boys and Girls are taught together until the age of 11, separately from 11 to 16, before coming back together again in a joint Sixth Form.

Curriculum. The Senior School curriculum includes: English, English Literature, Mathematics, Biology, Chemistry, Physics, History, Geography, Religious Studies, French/Spanish, Latin/Classics, Music, Art, Design and Technology. Up to eleven subjects may be taken for GCSE. In the Sixth Form, courses are offered in 27 subjects and all students benefit from an Enrichment Programme with the option to complete an Extended Project Qualification or a Business Skills course. Pupils are prepared for university entrance, including Oxbridge. All pupils are taught computer skills and have access to ICT centres. Careers guidance and personal tutoring are offered throughout.

Day and Boarding. Pupils may be full boarders, weekly/flexible boarders or day pupils. The two Boarding houses, accommodating boys and girls separately, are well equipped and within a few minutes' walk of the main campus. There are up to 60 boarding places. Day pupils come from both Berkhamsted and the surrounding area of Hertfordshire, Buckinghamshire and Bedfordshire.

Pastoral Care and Discipline. The main social and pastoral unit is the House; the Head of House and House Tutors provide continuity of support and advice and monitor each individual pupil's progress.

The aim is to encourage self-discipline so that pupils work with a sense of responsibility and trust. Pupils are expected to be considerate, courteous, honest and industrious.

There is a Medical Centre with qualified staff. The School Medical Officer has special responsibility for boarders. Qualified Counsellors are available to all pupils for confidential counselling. The School also has a full-time Chaplain.

Sport and Leisure Activities. Major sports for Girls are Lacrosse, Netball and Tennis and for Boys, Rugby, Football, Hockey and Cricket. A number of other sports are also pursued including Athletics, Badminton, Cross-Country, Equestrian, Eton Fives, Golf, Hockey, Judo, Rowing, Shooting, Squash and Swimming. Team games are encouraged and pupils selected for regional and national squads.

There is a flourishing Duke of Edinburgh's Award scheme at all levels. The CCF, community service, work experience and 'Young Enterprise' are offered. A new format to the school day allows pupils in the Senior School to choose from a wide range of clubs, societies or courses, which are attended during extended lunchtimes. Regular school theatre productions, orchestral and choral concerts achieve high standards of performance.

Careers. A team of advisors, internal and external, is directed by the Head of Careers who also arranges Careers Lunches, Business Skills training sessions and an annual Careers, Universities and GAP Year Fair. Heads of House oversee pupils' applications for higher education, together with parents and Careers advisors. The great majority of leavers proceeds to university and higher education.

Entry. Entry to the Pre-Preparatory School is from the age of three, entry to the Preparatory School from seven, and entry to the Senior School from 11. The School's Entrance Assessments and an interview are required for the Prep and Senior School. The minimum entrance requirement for the Sixth Form is 5B and 2C grades at GCSE, with A grades required to proceed to Mathematics, Science and Language A Levels, although competition amongst external candidates means that it is the norm that top grades are required.

Scholarships and Bursaries. It is the Governors' policy to award Scholarships and Exhibitions on merit to pupils whom the Governors wish to attract to Berkhamsted because of the contribution that they are able to make to School life, be that academic, musical, sporting, creative or as potential leaders.

Academic Scholarships are awarded on the basis of academic merit alone on entrance to the School.

Who can apply? Applications are welcome from pupils who qualify from their performance in the Entrance Examination and sit Scholarship Examinations in English, Mathematics and other appropriate subjects. These are usually only at 11+, 13+ and 16+.

Incent Awards are made to talented pupils from financially or socially disadvantaged backgrounds.

They are awarded to enable pupils who would not otherwise be able to attend Berkhamsted, to afford to do so.

Candidates must demonstrate academic potential or have a particular talent(s) or skill(s) so that they will make a significant contribution to some other area of School life.

The Award shall be up to 100% of the school fees, and, where appropriate, will also include financial assistance for School uniform and sports kit, travel to and from school, school trips and expeditions, extra lessons e.g. Music, Drama etc if applicable.

Whilst most applications for Incent Awards will be received from candidates who are presently in maintained sector schools, Berkhamsted does work with a number of feeder schools in the independent sector who offer awards on a similar basis and thus will entertain applications from pupils who are presently in receipt of means-tested awards of this nature.

Music, Drama, Art and Sports Scholarships are also offered.

Where there is a demonstrated need, additional means-tested funding may be available to those awarded Scholarships.

More information about Scholarships and Bursaries may be obtained from the Admissions Secretary or on the School website.

Fees per term (2014–2015). Day Pupils: £5,265–£6,180. Boarding Pupils: £9,843.33 (full), £8,271.67 (weekly 4 nights).

Further information about the School's aims, its academic curriculum, facilities, activities, admissions, scholarships and awards is published in the School's prospectus and is available on the School website. Admissions enquiries should be made in the first instance to the Admissions Secretary, who will be pleased to arrange for parents to visit the School.

Old Berkhamstedians. There is a vibrant and growing community of Old Berkhamstedians: www.theoldberkhamstedians.org. President: Mr Mike Horton.

Charitable status. Berkhamsted Schools Group is a Registered Charity, number 310630. It is a leading Charitable School in the field of Junior and Secondary Education.

Birkdale School

Oakholme Road, Sheffield S10 3DH

Tel:	0114 266 8408
	Admissions: 0114 266 8409
Fax:	0114 267 1947
email:	headmaster@birkdaleschool.org.uk
	admissions@birkdaleschool.org.uk
	enquiries@birkdaleschool.org.uk
website:	www.birkdaleschool.org.uk

Motto: '*Res non verba*'

Birkdale School is an HMC day school for 850 pupils, boys from age 4 to 18 with a co-educational Sixth Form of

200 pupils. The age 4–11 Prep School is on a separate campus nearby. (*For further details see IAPS section.*) The Governing Body is in membership of the Association of Governing Bodies of Independent Schools.

Chairman of Governors: Dr J R Goepel, MBChB, FRCPath

Bursar and Clerk to the Governors: D H Taylor, BSc

Head Master: Dr P M Owen, MA, PhD

Deputy Head: W P N Pietrek, BA

Director of Studies: P R King, BA

Heads of Departments:
Miss B Adams, MA, BSc (*Biology*)
J D Allen, BSc (*Outdoor Pursuits, Chaplain*)
Mrs S J Burt, BA (*English*)
M S Clarke, MA (*History*)
C J Cook, BSc (*Careers*)
R J Cottom, BEd (*Design & Technology*)
D Craddock, BEng (*ICT*)
Mrs M A Daly, BA (*Classics*)
R D Heaton, BEd (*Physical Education*)
Mrs K M Higham, BA, MEd (*Modern Languages*)
A M Jordan, BMus (*Music*)
Dr P C Jukes, PhD, MA (*Physics*)
Miss K J McDonnell, MA, BA (*Drama*)
Dr P D Myatt, BSc, DPhil (*Science & Chemistry*)
H Parker, BSc (*Geography*)
T J Pearson, BA (*Religious Education*)
Mrs M B Reynolds, BEd, Cert SocEd Studies, PGCert
 Dyslexia/Literacy (*Learning Support*)
M E Roach, BSc (*Mathematics*)
A Armitage, MA, Dip Ed Management (*Art*)
S B Stoddard, BA (*Economics & Business Studies*)

Prep School:
Head of Prep School: C J Burch, BA, PGCE
Deputy Head: J R Leighton, BEd
Director of Studies: A J Oakey, MScEd, BA
Senior Mistress: Mrs E J Arcari, BA/Mrs J Kitchen, MEd, BEd

Set in a pleasant residential area near the University 1.5 miles from the city centre, and 5 miles from the Peak District National Park, the school has expanded in recent years to provide for Sheffield and South Yorkshire the only independent secondary school for boys, with a co-educational Sixth Form. Birkdale Prep School for 300 boys is on a separate campus half a mile from the Senior School. School coaches bring pupils from Worksop, Chesterfield, North Derbyshire, Rotherham and Barnsley.

Birkdale is a Christian school, reflecting its foundation in the evangelical tradition. There is nothing exclusive about this: entrance is open to all, and there is no denominational emphasis. We seek to develop the full potential of each individual: body, mind and spirit. Within a framework of high academic standards, pastoral care is given a high priority, balanced by an emphasis on sport and outdoor pursuits, music and drama with a wide range of extra-curricular activities available.

At 18, over 99% of pupils go on to university, with a good proportion each year gaining places at Oxford and Cambridge.

Admission. The main ages of admission are at 4, 7, 11 and 16, although it is possible to admit pupils at other ages if a place is available. Entrance examinations for candidates at 11 are held annually towards the end of January. Entrance to the co-educational Sixth Form is subject to interview and a satisfactory performance in GCSE examinations. In the first instance, enquiries should be addressed to the Registrar.

Academic Curriculum. Over 20 subjects are offered at AS and A Level. A full range of academic subjects are offered to GCSE. All pupils study English Language and Literature, Mathematics, Double Award Science, at least one Modern Foreign Language (French, German, Spanish) and at least one of the Humanities subjects (Classical Studies, Geography, History, RE). Optional subjects include Art, DT: Electronic Products, DT: Resistant Materials, PE, Latin, Drama and Music. The wider curriculum includes ICT, Religious Education, Health Education, Careers and Economic Awareness. Latin, German and Spanish are compulsory subjects in the Lower School (11–13) in addition to the usual range of National Curriculum subjects.

Games and Outdoor Pursuits. The major games are Rugby, Soccer, Cricket and Athletics, with Cross Country, Hockey, Netball, Tennis, Squash, Basketball, Volleyball, Swimming and Golf also available. The playing fields are a short bus ride away from the school. A 10-lane cricket net facility, constructed to full English Cricket Board standards was opened in 2012. The netting system is retractable and so the area can also be fully utilised for football and hockey outside of the cricket season. All members of the school play games weekly. Additional team practices take place on Saturdays or at other times, and there is a full fixture list in the major sports. The school enjoys regular use of the university swimming pool nearby. Additionally, we use two local international venues, Ponds Forge and the English Institute of Sport for basketball, netball, dance and athletics. Birkdale's Sports Hall is at the centre of the Senior School campus.

Outdoor Pursuits play an important part in the overall leadership training programme. All members of the school participate in regular training sessions leading in each age group to a major expedition. This programme culminates in the 4th Form camp held annually in Snowdonia. Virtually all members of the Third Form undertake the Bronze Award of the Duke of Edinburgh's Award Scheme, and an increasing number progress to Silver and Gold awards.

Music and the Arts. Music, Art and Drama flourish both within and outside the formal curriculum. A full annual programme of dramatic and musical productions is arranged. Over 120 pupils receive weekly instrumental music lessons at school, and a wide range of orchestras and choirs provide opportunities for pupils to experience group musical activities at an appropriate level.

Extra-Curricular Activities. In addition to the activities above there is a broad range of clubs and societies which meet at lunchtime and outside the formal school day, providing opportunities for members of the school to explore and excel in activities such as Chess, Debating, Design and Enterprise, as well as in the usual activities such as Sport, Drama, Outdoor Pursuits, Art and Music. Awards are often won in local and national competitions.

Careers. The school is a member of the Independent Schools' Careers Organisation, and there is a well equipped Careers Centre on site. A biennial Careers Convention is held in the school and regular visits are made by services liaison officers and others to give advice and help to pupils under the guidance of the school's careers staff.

Fees per term (2014–2015). Sixth Form £3,850; Senior School: £3,800 (Years 9–11), £3,750 (Years 7 and 8); Prep School £3,150; Pre-Prep Department £2,600, including lunches, textbooks and stationery (with the exception of Sixth Form textbooks).

Scholarships and Bursaries. Academic and Music Scholarships are normally available at 11 and 16, worth up to 25% of fees. Bursaries are available to increase awards up to 100% of fees in cases of proven financial need. In addition we offer Ogden Science and Arkwright Scholarships at 16+.

Charitable status. Birkdale School is a Registered Charity, number 1018973, and a Company Limited by Guarantee, registered in England, number 2792166. It exists to develop the full potential of its members within a Christian community.

Birkenhead School

58 Beresford Road, Oxton, Birkenhead, Merseyside CH43 2JD
Tel: 0151 652 4014
Fax: 0151 651 3091
email: enquire@birkenheadschool.co.uk
website: www.birkenheadschool.co.uk
Twitter: @BirkenheadSchl
Facebook: /Birkenhead-School

Motto: *Beati mundo corde*
   Birkenhead School was opened in 1860, with the object of providing a public-school education, both Classical and Modern.

Visitor: The Rt Revd Peter Robert Forster, Bishop of Chester

President: The Rt Hon Lord Nicholls of Birkenhead, MA Cantab, LLB, Hon LLD Liverpool

Honorary Vice-Presidents:
S J Haggett
J A Gwilliam
A G Hurton
Lord Wade of Chorlton
A Whittam Smith
A L B Thomson

Emeritus Vice-Presidents:
K J Speakman-Brown
H W McCready
D A Fletcher

Governors:
Chairman: A Sutton, MA, FCA
Vice Chairman: Dr J K Moore, OBE, FRCA, MBA
I G Boumphrey
A J Cross, LLB
Mrs L Dodd, BA, FSI
G E Jones, MA
Prof Bart McGettrick
E N Rice, FRICS, MCIArb
W D C Rushworth, BA
Mrs A Walsh, BEd, Dip EFL
A F Watson, FCA

Headmaster: Dr J Grundy, MA, PhD

Deputy Headmaster: D R Edmunds, BSc
Deputy Head (Academic): Mrs K Pankhurst, BA
Assistant Head: C D McKie, MA (*Head of History*)
Bursar and Clerk to the Governors: M J Turner, BA

Assistant Teachers:
A M Aldred (*Hockey Coach*)
Mrs L D Alford-Swift, BSc
W I H Allister, MA
P G Armstrong, BSc (*Head of Biology*)
D R Bell (*Head of ICT*)
K M Britton, MA, MSc
S W Clark, PGCE
A S Davies, MA (*Network Manager*)
Miss A I Dunn, BSc
N J Frowe, BA
Miss N M Gilbride, BA
S M Gill, MA (*Head of Geography*)
Ms E A Grey, BA (*Head of Religious Education*)
S Guinness, BSc (*Head of Design and Technology*)
M J Hayward, BSc (*Head of Science*)
D A Hendry, BEd (*Head of Year 11*)
T M Higginbottom, BEng
G R Hill, BA
Ms M L Holgate, BA (*Head of Modern Languages*)

S W Hope, BSc (*Head of Mathematics*)
D K Jones, BSc
Miss F Jung, MA
Mrs H D Keenan
P Lindberg, BSc (*Head of Chemistry*)
Mrs J Lloyd-Johnson (*Head of Art*)
R E Lytollis, BSc (*Head of Physical Education and Games*)
Mrs V J Margerison, BA
Mrs A McGoldrick, BA (*Head of English*)
Miss J H Moore, BA (*Special Educational Needs Coordinator*)
G W Murdoch, MA (*Head of Year 9*)
Mrs I Nolan, BA
S J Parry, BA (*Assistant Head of Sixth Form, Assessment Manager*)
Mrs B J Parry-Jones, BSc
G Rickman (*Cricket Professional*)
C Rimmer, BA (*Head of Overdale, Assistant Head of Modern Languages*)
P F Robinson, MusB (*Director of Music*)
R A Rule, BA (*Head of Economics, Head of Year 10*)
A Rymer, BSc
Mrs S E Salter, MSc (*Assistant Head of Overdale*)
C L Smale, MA
Ms L Smeaton, BA (*Head of Sixth Form*)
Ms K P Stone, BSc
M A Turner, MA
Mrs M T Washington, BA (*Head of Classics*)
Mrs C Walker, MA
P M Webster, BEng (*Head of Physics*)
Ms E Wilday, BA

Houses and Housemasters:
Beresford House: C L Smale
Shrewsbury House: A W Rymer
Bidston House: A J Blain
Kingsmead House: Mrs S E Salter

Learning Support
Mrs B Cederholm, MA
Mrs G M Tooley, CertEd
Mrs E M Kearney, BA
Mrs P J Dale, CertEd

Headmaster's PA: Mrs D Roberts
Chaplain: Mrs Sian Howell-Jones
Librarian: Mrs E Reeve, BA
SSI: Captain J A Barnes, BSc
Nurse: Mrs J Pizer, RGN, RSCN

Prep School

Headmaster: H FitzHerbert, BA

Senior Teachers:

N J Corran, BEng	M G Stockdale, BA
Mr R A Halpin, BSc	Mrs C E Winn, BEd

Assistant Staff:

Mrs V Belchier, CertEd	Miss R J Lee, BA
Miss A C Bentley-Jones, BA	Mrs J Mayers, BEd
	Mrs S G Mills, BEd
T G Brand, BSc	Mrs G A Mudge, BSc
Mrs N A Brand, BSc	M E Pillow, BSc
Mrs B M Coyne, BA	Mrs C M Pye, BA
Miss A C Delaney, BA	Ms P Relph, BA
Mrs J E FitzHerbert, BA	Miss A E Rushton, BEd
Mrs J Goldstone, BA	Mrs H J Sewell, BA
Miss S J Harris, BA	T R Smith, BEd
Mrs A C Hendry, BSc	Mrs E Thuraisingam, BSc
Dr S M Jarvis, BSc, PhD	Mrs S L Williams, BEd
Mrs S J Keating, BA	

   Birkenhead School is Wirral's only independent day school with boys and girls aged from 3 months through to 18 years across four outstanding schools – the Nursery, the Prep, the Senior School and the Sixth Form.

Attracting students from all areas of the Wirral, Merseyside, West Cheshire and North Wales, the School enjoys a fantastic reputation for its educational successes and continues to be the best-performing school in the Wirral in terms of its public examination results.

Children thrive both academically and personally in this modern yet traditional school. Birkenhead School has a long history of providing first-class learning to its students and continues to this day to place strong emphasis on excellence in education, as well as providing a caring environment.

Our community is what binds us all; most striking is how positive and vibrant it is. Aside from our academic successes, our students succeed in the myriad opportunities available to them. Challenge and endeavour within the classroom line up alongside an exciting and varied co-curricular provision designed to enchant, excite and enable students to exceed their own potential. Everything we do is underpinned by a network of caring and supportive staff, all united in the aim of achieving the very best for our students.

School buildings are grouped around a spacious campus with a beautiful 'village green' at the centre of it. A development programme has, in recent years, extended the already extensive facilities at the School with major developments including an extension to the Prep School – the Wessex Wing – and the redevelopment of the Sixth Form Centre into a central hub for Sixth Form students to study, relax and socialise.

Unique to the School is Overdale, our entry point for Year 7 and 8 students. Students in these years enjoy a smaller community of younger students, dedicated form tutors and teachers and both separate and shared facilities to help them transition smoothly from primary to secondary years.

Curriculum. All pupils follow a common curriculum in Years 7 and 8 with a choice of two languages from French, Latin, German or Spanish in Year 8. The wide spectrum of subjects means that pupils are then ideally placed to make GCSE option choices at the end of Year 9. As well as the compulsory subjects – Mathematics, English (including for most English Literature), and three Sciences – pupils choose four more subjects from Art, French, Design and Technology, Geography, German, Greek, Spanish, Religious Studies, History, Latin, PE and Music. Almost all combinations are possible, but attention is given to ensuring at this stage that pupils opt for appropriate subjects which will not restrict their future career choices. The School has remained committed to the teaching of Biology, Chemistry and Physics as separate subjects, but also offers Dual Award Science for some pupils. A "Beyond the Curriculum" programme has been established in Years 7 and 10 and for the Sixth Form, which includes, for example, an Etiquette course, the Environment, Drama, Philosophy and Debating, and a Sports Leaders Award. A programme of Personal Social and Health Education is provided for all pupils from Year 7 to Year 11, drawing on external agencies, as well as the School's own expertise. Compulsory Games and PE lessons not only support our highly successful sports teams but are also based on a philosophy of "games for all" with students of all abilities encouraged to enjoy physical activity by specialist games teachers.

School Chapel. The School has its own Chapel and close links with St Saviour's, the local parish church. There is an outstanding Chapel Choir which sings at daily services and at the regular Sunday Evensong. Each summer the Chapel Choir performs in cathedrals and churches both in Britain and abroad.

Parents Association. There is an active Parents' Association which provides opportunities for parents to meet informally and organises social events, as well as being involved on a day-to-day basis in the life of the School and in the funding of special projects.

Extra-Curricular Activities. Involvement in extra-curricular activities is strongly encouraged and there is a wide range of clubs from which to choose, including scientific, cultural and recreational. There is a strong tradition of drama, with regular productions, and an annual House Drama and House Music competition. The School has an Orchestra, a Concert Band, Big Band and Brass Ensemble. The School has a fine reputation for choral music.

Games. Competitive sports are rugby, hockey, netball and lacrosse during the winter terms and cricket, athletics, tennis, rounders and golf during the summer. There are representative teams at all levels and the playing fields cover about 40 acres on three different sites. At McAllester Field there is a floodlit astroturf surface for hockey and tennis. A large sports complex, including a squash court, two fitness suites and a climbing wall, provides a focus for the School's comprehensive 'Sport for All' programme.

CCF and Outdoor Pursuits. The School has an active CCF contingent with Army, Navy and RAF sections. From Year 8 onwards pupils may join one of these sections. The School runs its own Duke of Edinburgh's Award Scheme. Outdoor Pursuits form part of the curriculum and from Year 6 upwards pupils spend time away from School each year on residential outdoor pursuits activities. Climbing is available as part of the PE curriculum and as a co-curricular activity.

Admission to Senior School at 11 is by progression from the Prep or by the School's own Entrance and Scholarship Examination held at the end of January. Entrance at other stages is through individual assessments and interview. Sixth Form entrants are also welcome and this selection is based on GCSE grades and interview. Prospective parents are always welcome to visit the School and the Headmaster is happy to meet parents and assist with queries over dates, methods of entry, SEN and learning support.

Fees per term (2014–2015). Senior School £3,330–£3,580; Prep £2,440–£2,714. The Birkenhead School Foundation Trust was established in 1998 to provide Bursaries and Funded Places. Scholarships are also available. Particulars may be obtained from the Headmaster's PA, Mrs Debbie Roberts.

Charitable status. Birkenhead School is a Registered Charity, number 1093419. Our charitable status means the School not only accepts fee-paying pupils but can offer places to able children from less advantaged backgrounds.

Bishop's Stortford College

Maze Green Road, Bishop's Stortford, Herts CM23 2PJ
Tel: 01279 838575
Fax: 01279 836570
email: admissions@bishopsstortfordcollege.org
website: www.bishopsstortfordcollege.org
Twitter: @BSCollege
Facebook: /bishopsstortfordcollege

Motto: '*Soli Deo Gloria*'.

Bishop's Stortford College is a friendly, co-educational, day and boarding community providing high academic standards, good discipline and an excellent all-round education. We aim to equip our pupils with the vital qualifications, skills, adaptability and, above all, confidence to thrive as adults in a rapidly changing world. A flourishing Prep School and Pre-Prep, sharing many facilities with the Senior School, give all the advantages of educational continuity whilst retaining their own distinctive characters.

When founded in 1868, it was intended that the College should provide "a liberal and religious education" acceptable to non-conformist families in the Eastern Counties. In practice, Bishop's Stortford College welcomes boys and girls of all denominations and faiths, and, while the majority of present pupils' homes are in the Home Counties and East

Anglia, a substantial number of parents work and live overseas.

Governing Council:
Dr P J Hargrave, BSc, PhD, FREng (*Chairman*)
Sir Stephen Lander, KCB, MA, PhD, LLD, DSc (*Vice Chairman*)
C Havers, MA
Mrs S Jellis, MA
L Lindop, ACMA
G E Baker, BSc, MRICS
Mrs I Pearman, MA, MRICS
Mrs L J Farrant, MSc, CPFA
G Brant, MA, BEd, CertEd
A A Trigg
G P R Bramley, LLB
Mrs M Goitiandia, BA, MBA

Headmaster: Jeremy Gladwin, BSc Dunelm

Assistant Staff:
* *Head of Department*
† *Housemaster/mistress*
# *Teacher across the College cohort*

Mrs K Adkins, CertEd (#*PE*)
N Alexander, MSc (*Mathematics*)
Dr G Allcock, BSc, PhD (*Higher Education and Careers*)
T Atkinson, BA (†*Sutton House*)
S Bacon, BSc (*Director of IT*)
Mrs H Bailey, BA (*German*)
A Baker, BSc (*Physics*)
C Bannister, MA (*Chemistry*)
S Barnard
N Barnes
P Beston, MPhil
J Birchall, MA (*Economics, Business Studies*)
Mrs J Bichara
Mrs C Bond (*English*)
B Boulden (*Chemistry, IT*)
T Borton, BA (*Sixth Form*)
G R Brooks, BA (*Deputy Head*)
Mrs R C Brown, MSc
Mrs S Brown, BA (*Religious Education*)
A M Bruce, MA (#*Director of Music*)
C de Bruyn
Ms E Chaplin, BA (†*Benson House*)
Mrs C Coates
Mrs L G Dickinson, BA (*Sixth Form*)
Mrs C Davis (*French*)
M Drury, BSc (†*Hayward House*)
P Elliston
Miss H Edwards (#*PE*)
Miss J Edworthy
Miss V Ellaway-Bell
C Fafalois
A Fulton, MA
Mrs F M Freckleton, MSc
Mrs M E P Garrett, MCLIP (*Librarian*)
Miss K Gregory
P M Griffin, BSc (†*School House*)
T A Herbert, MA (*Examinations*)
Mrs J Hewson
Mrs C Hinge, BSc
Miss R Holliday, BSc
R M Honey, MA (*Art*, †*Robert Pearce House*)
Mrs T Hood, BEd
Mrs D Huggett (#*Swimming*)
D Hughes (#*PE*)
K Irvine, BA
Mrs C Kennedy
Mrs K King, BA
J Kirton, BSc
S Lipscombe, BA
Mrs G Lynch, MA (*Latin*, †*Collett House*)

Mrs J Marshall, BSc (*Psychology*)
Dr S McPeake, PhD (*Science*)
Miss L Michell
I Morris (#*College Chaplain*)
Mrs P Mullender, MA (*Deputy, Pastoral*)
Ms C I Munck, BA
S Murtagh-Howard
R Norman, BA (*Director of Drama*)
I Nunez, BMus, PGDip, MM GSMD (#*Music*)
P W O'Connor, PhD (*Geography*)
Ms E Oakley, MSc
Mrs J Oldfield, BSc (†*Tee House*)
Mrs A Picton, BA
N J Prowse, BSc (#*PE*)
Miss C Pryce
J Reyburn, BSc (#*PE*)
Mrs S Santurri
Miss D Savva
Miss C Schalch, BA
Mrs A Self, BA (*Politics*)
Mrs H Sheehan, BA (*Senior School Music*)
Mrs L Shepherd, BEd (*Director of Sport*, #*PE*)
Mrs A N Sloman, CertEd (†*Young House*)
T Stuart, MA (*History*)
C Sutherland, BA
A Swart-Wilson
M A Tomkys, BA (*Media Studies*)
J H Trant, BA (*Design & Technology*)
Mrs J Vernon-Harcourt, BSc
Ms L Watson (#*PE*)
Mrs E A Wheeler, BSc (*Biology*)
C H Williams, BSc (*Director of Studies*)
Mrs F H M Williams, BA (*English as a Second Language, Librarian*)
Mrs J Williams, BSc
M Wilson
Mrs S J Wilson, BA (†*Alliott House*)
Mrs P Wonfor
C J Woodhouse, BSc (*Deputy Head*, *PSHE*)

Prep School

Head of Prep School: W J Toleman, BA
Mrs B Aitken (#*Music*)
Mrs H Atkinson
S Bailey, CertEd (*Geography*)
S Barnard
Miss A Beckley, BA
Mrs R Borthwick, BA
Mrs K Brooks, BA (*Head of Shell*)
Miss E Carme, MA (*French*)
R J Clough, BA
N B Courtman, BA
Mrs I Cowan (*German*)
Mrs L Davies, BA
A Donlevy, BA (*Art*)
Miss C Drury, BA
N R Eddom, BEd (*Mathematics*)
A Edwards, PhD (*Science*)
Mrs L Fraser, BA
S Gunter
A J Hathaway, BEd (†*Grimwade House*)
Mrs A Hathaway
D A Herd, BSc (*English*)
Miss E Hodgkiss
E C Jones, LLB (*PSHE*)
Mrs F Jones, BA (*Spanish*)
Mrs J Krosny-Reed
G Millard, BA (*Deputy Head*)
Mrs L Neville
Mrs J North
J Opperman
Mrs R A Pike, BA (*Librarian*)
Mrs J Prowse, BA

Mrs J Ryan, LLB
M J Self, BSocSc (*History*)
Mrs W Sharman, MSc
G Sloman, BA (*ICT*)
J Spackman, PhD
J Surrage
J Talbot Rice, BA
Miss K Taylor, BA
Mrs J Towns

Learning Support:
Mrs R J Gearing, CertEd, Dip SpLD
Mrs G Miller, CertEd, Dip SpLD

Pre-Prep

Head of Pre-Prep: Miss Belinda Callo, BEd

Miss K Boyle	Mrs C Martin, MA
Miss E Bruce, BA Hons	Miss A Strouts
Mrs A Cullum	Miss S Toward
Mrs A D Foy, RSA SpLD, CLANSA	Mrs J Windley

Bursar: M P Hemingway
Senior School Admissions Officer: Mrs M-L Gough
Prep School Admissions Officer: Mrs F Brett
Pre-Prep Admissions Officer: Mrs S McGuiness
Marketing Manager: Mrs S Gowans

There are 574 boys and girls in the Senior School (boarders and day), 451 boys and girls in the Prep School and 120 in the Pre-Prep.

Location. Bishop's Stortford is almost mid-way between London and Cambridge and is reached quickly from Liverpool Street or via the M25 and M11 motorways. Stansted Airport is just a ten minute drive. The College is situated on the edge of the town adjacent to open countryside. The gardens and grounds cover about 130 acres.

Facilities. Purpose-built Pre-Prep accommodation, Prep and Senior School libraries, extensive ICT facilities and campus-wide Wi-Fi, outstanding sports facilities, well-resourced centres for Design and Technology, the Sciences, Languages, Music and Drama and a superb Art Centre. The main school Library and state-of-the-art indoor Swimming Pool are notable features. All school Houses offer a welcoming, family-like environment.

At the centre of the campus stands the Memorial Hall, used daily for Assembly, which was erected in 1921 as a memorial to Old Boys who served and fell in the 1914–18 war.

Academic Organisation. The Curriculum is designed to give as broad a course of study as possible up to the specialisation at A and AS Level and Oxbridge entry.

In addition to the three Sciences, French, English, Maths, Geography and History, all new pupils joining the Fourth Form (Year 9) take Design and Technology, ICT, Art and Music as well as one period each of RE and PE/Swimming. Most also begin German and a significant number continue with Latin.

In the Lower and Upper Fifth Forms (Years 10 and 11), the 'core' subjects, taken by all, are English, English Literature, Maths and the three Sciences. Four other subjects, one of which must be a modern foreign language, are chosen from History, Geography, Design and Technology, Latin, French, German, Art and Design, Music, Drama and Religious Studies. Spanish will be included as a MFL for Fourth Forms (Year 9) from 2015. Pupils also have one period each of RE, PE/Swimming and ICT.

At all stages, progress is carefully monitored by Housemasters, Housemistresses and Tutors, and in Staff Meetings.

Careers. A purpose-built Higher Education and Careers Centre is open daily with three specialist staff. The College has close ties with ISCO, local commerce and industry and the Hertfordshire Careers Service. Links with local businesses are strong and there is an extensive programme of

Work Experience organised for pupils in the Upper Fifth and Lower Sixth Forms.

The Sixth Form. Pupils choose between three and five subjects at AS level in the Lower Sixth, before specialising in three or four in the Upper Sixth at A2 level. Some may take an extra AS level in the Upper Sixth. Sixth Formers select from the following subjects: Art, Biology, Business Studies, Chemistry, Classical Civilisation, Design and Technology, Drama and Theatre Studies, Economics, English Literature, French, Geography, German, History, Maths, Further Maths, Latin, Media Studies, Music, Physical Education, Physics, Politics, Psychology, Religious Studies.

An extensive PHSE programme operates throughout the school and there is a weekly Upper Sixth Form lecture.

Each Department organises visits and invites guest speakers to meetings of Societies, which are held in lunch hours or evenings. These, together with small group teaching, seminars and excellent resources, help to encourage students to develop their self-reliance, their analytical skills and their spirit of academic enquiry to equip them for Higher Education and beyond.

The progress of Sixth Formers is constantly assessed by House Masters/Mistresses and Academic Tutors, and in Staff Meetings under the overall supervision of the Head of Sixth Form. Parents are closely involved and regular Parents' Meetings are held.

Throughout the Senior School, grades for Effort and Attainment are given twice termly, and full written reports are sent home twice a year for each year group.

Worship. The Religious Instruction, Sunday Worship and occasional weekday services are interdenominational. The opportunity of exploring faith and being prepared for adult membership of particular churches (including Confirmation) is offered each year through the Chaplain.

Activities. Whether as Boarders or Day Pupils, our young people are involved in an environment of whole-hearted participation. A diverse range of extra-curricular activities alongside high academic standards provides the opportunity for every child to discover areas of interest and success that might otherwise lie untapped.

In addition to the meetings of Clubs and Societies, Wednesday and Friday sessions are set aside within the timetable for Activities, including The Duke of Edinburgh Award scheme. We thus encourage pupils to pursue their own interests and introduce them to others, so that they will wish to carry these on into their spare time and beyond the confines of the School. Projects which promote a willingness to serve others are an important aspect of the breadth of activity offered.

Music and Drama. An interest in and appreciation of all kinds of music is encouraged throughout the school. In their 1st and 2nd Forms (Years 3 & 4), all pupils in the Prep School are taught an instrument in class and those who show promise are encouraged to continue individually in the Senior School.

There are numerous ensembles including Orchestra, Wind Band, guitar and string quartets, brass group, a Choral Society, and Choirs. Pupils are also encouraged to make music in small groups from the earliest stages. There is a fully equipped Recording Studio. The Music Staff includes 27 visiting teachers of singing and all the main instruments, together with the Director of Music, 2 Assistant Directors and a Musician in Residence. The House Music Competition is a major event in the school year, involving all pupils. Pupils have regular opportunities to perform in public at Pupils' Concerts and in School Assemblies. Overseas tours also provide excellent performing experience.

Drama is an area of strength with significant developments in recent years to the theatre facilities, curriculum and performing opportunities. There are numerous opportunities for all pupils to participate. AS and A level Theatre Studies are offered, as is GCSE Drama.

Sport. The College has an excellent reputation in all areas of sporting achievement. Physical Education is taught in the Fourth and Fifth Forms and facilities include a Sports Hall, an impressive indoor swimming pool, two floodlit all-weather surface hockey pitches, hard tennis courts and 100 acres of playing fields.

Health. The Medical Centre is staffed by a resident full-time Nurse, part-time Nurse, full-time Health Care Assistant and access to a Physiotherapist. Regular Surgeries are held by the School's Medical Officer.

Varied and wholesome meals are provided in the College central Dining Hall, with plenty of choice. All day pupils take lunch at School with the cost included in the fees.

Prep School. The organisation of the Prep School (for pupils up to age 13+) is largely separate from that of the Senior School, but the curricula of the two Schools are carefully integrated. Pupils are able to share Senior School resources in Sport, Design and Technology, Music and Drama.

(*For further details see entry in IAPS section.*)

Admission. The main ages of admission are 4, 7, 11, 13 and 16, but entry at intermediate stages is possible. Entry to the Senior School at 13+ is based on school reference, interview and entry test results. Sixth Form Entry Interviews and Examinations are held in the November before year of entry.

Scholarships. The following awards are available:
Under 11 (Year 6): Academic, Music
Under 12 (Year 7): Academic, Music, Art
Under 14 (Year 9): Academic, Music, Art, Sport
Sixth Form: Academic, Music, Art, Sport

Financial Assistance. Means-tested bursaries are awarded based on individual need. Awards range from partial assistance of 5% up to (in exceptional circumstances) 100% of the full fees.

Fees per term (2014–2015). Senior School: Full Boarders £7,929–£7,967; Overseas Boarders £8,200–£8,238; Weekly Boarders £7,850–£7,888; Day £5,446–£5,484.

Prep School: Full Boarders £5,540–£6,010; Overseas Boarders £5,757–£6,227; Weekly Boarders £5,480–£5,950; Day £3,887–£4,357.

Pre-Prep £2,518–£2,561.

Fees are inclusive except for individual music tuition.

Charitable status. The Incorporated Bishop's Stortford College Association is a Registered Charity, number 311057. Its aims and objectives are to provide high quality Independent Boarding and Day education for boys and girls from age 4 to 18.

Bloxham School
A Woodard School

Bloxham, Banbury, Oxon OX15 4PE
Tel: 01295 720222
          01295 724341 Headmaster
Fax: 01295 721714 Bursar
email: registrar@bloxhamschool.com
          admissions@bloxhamschool.com
website: www.bloxhamschool.com
Twitter: @bloxhamschool
Facebook: Bloxham School

Motto: '*Justorum Semita Lux Splendens*'

Bloxham School is an independent co-educational day and boarding school for pupils aged 11–18 situated in the beautiful Oxfordshire village of Bloxham. The School was founded in 1860 by the Revd P R Egerton and it has been a member of the Woodard Corporation since 1896.

The School Council of Governors:

Provost: The Rt Revd Lindsay Urwin

Chairman: N J E Bankes, Esq

Members:

Mrs M S Brounger, LLB	C E L Mann, Esq
D R Gasson, Esq	Mrs R A H Needham
Mrs H Harper	A J P Nott, Esq
M S Hedges, Esq, MA,	M C S-R Pyper, Esq, OBE
FCA, FRSA	Ms C A Shaw
M K Higgs, Esq	J E Spratt, Esq
Mrs E L Lewis-Jones	Mrs F M Turner
R W Loades, Esq	S T Wood, Esq

Headmaster: **P W Sanderson**, BSc

Deputy Head Curriculum: M A Buckland, MEd, BSc, PGCE

Deputy Head Pastoral: M G Price, MA, MPhil

Director of Studies: D A Cooper, BSc, BEd, MSc, MCollP

Chaplain: (*to be appointed*)

Head of Exham House: T W Tuthill, BA (*Politics, History*)

Teaching Staff:
* *Head of Department*

S J Batten, MA
T M Skevington, BEd (*Design & Technology*)
G P Cruden, BA
R Hudson, BA, MA (*History*)
R D J Matthew, BA, MDes, PGCE, FRGS (*Art*)
N St J D Pigott, BA (*Geography*)
J F Berry, BSc (*Mathematics*)
D F McLellan, BA (*Modern Languages*)
Mrs J H White, BEd
M J M Moir, BSc
Mrs B M Whitehead, BA
N E C Evans, BSc (*Science*)
D R Best, BA
Mrs A L Cooper, BA, BAdmin
Miss A Hickling, BA
Dr C E Evans, PhD, MSc (*Chemistry*)
A M Goldsmith, BA
Miss G T Barbour, BA
Mrs C M McCaffrey, MA
R W F Hastings, BA (*Master i/c 6th Form*)
D K Jordan, BA (*Director of Music*)
Miss E Hicks, BA
Mrs E Moyle, MA (*English*)
Miss N C Lister, BA
D Dales, BEd (*PE*)
Dr D Herring (*Theology*)
E J Heddon, MSc, MBA, FCIPD (*ICT*)
E F Bradley, BA, PGCE
R A Devesa, BA
R J Hobley, BSc
S Thompson, BA, FRCO
Mrs F Britnell, BSc
R Dann, BA, DipM, PGCE
D Finch, BSc, PGCE (*Biology*)
Dr M J Ruck, MA, DPhil, PGCE
Miss L M Manning, BA, DMS, PG Dip
B G A Richmond, BSc
Mrs S F Westbury, BA, PGCE
L Yates, BSc
S D A Thompson, BA
S W Brassington, MA, PGCE (*Drama*)
Mrs E S Keen, BSc
Dr J H Moyle, MA, PhD, PGCE (*Head of Scholars*)
Miss R M Odlin, BSc, PGCE

There are a number of visiting Instrumental teachers.

Houses and Housemasters/mistresses:

Boys' Houses:
Crake: R A Devesa
Egerton: S D A Thompson
Seymour: D K Jordan
Wilson: T M Skevington

Girls' Houses:
Raymond: Mrs J H White
Wilberforce: Mrs C M McCaffrey

Exham House (*Lower School*):
Park Close: Mr & Mrs A N Irvine

Headmaster's PA: Mrs V Turner

Registrar: A N Irvine

Medical Officer: S A Haynes, MBBS, MRCGP, DFFP

State Registered Nurses:
Sue Edmunds, RGN
Mary Garner, RGN
Cindy Hill (*Medical Assistant*)

Bursar: N Urquhart

Organisation. There are approximately 200 boarders and 200 day pupils at Bloxham School. There are four boys' senior houses (Crake, Egerton, Seymour and Wilson) and two girls' senior houses (Wilberforce and Raymond). Day boarders are full members of their boarding houses and are allocated house rooms, studies, etc according to seniority in the same way as full boarders. They have all meals except breakfast at the School and may stay to do their homework.

Exham House (Lower School), is a mixed house which caters for all students from 11–13, be they weekly boarders or day pupils. Exham House is an integral part of the School and has its own boarding house, Park Close.

School Buildings and Grounds. The School is situated in a delightful conservation village on the edge of the Cotswolds and yet just three miles from Banbury and four miles from the M40 (J11). It is within easy reach of both Heathrow and Birmingham International airports. The attractive local Hornton stone enriches the School and the village.

The last decade has been one of major investment for the school, with facilities comparable to those offered at even the largest of schools. The Raymond Technology Centre continues to provide first-class facilities for students, with a state-of-the-art ICT suite and fully-equipped workshops for DT, Textiles and Food and Nutrition. Students are given a laptop on entering Year 10, which they may keep once they have completed their A Levels.

The boarding houses provide excellent accommodation for all, with most Sixth Form students enjoying individual studies. The junior weekly boarders from Exham House live at Park Close, which offers superb, homely facilities and lots of space for the youngest pupils to enjoy. The school has two artificial grass hockey pitches, a brand new fully-equipped sports centre (including two glass-backed squash courts, a climbing wall, gym and multi-purpose hall) and an indoor swimming pool. Equestrian sport is well catered for off campus, as is sailing and clay pigeon shooting.

Food and Nutrition is now offered as an academic subject throughout the school in a new department within the Technology Centre. Music, art and the performing arts have also benefited from recent additions to the Bloxham campus facilities.

The Sixth Form benefit from their own social centres which they manage themselves.

Admissions. We admit around 35 pupils each year at age 11+ who sit an entrance exam set by the school. These pupils can either be day pupils or weekly boarders.

Boarding and day options are available for those entering at 13+. Those joining us from prep schools are required to pass the Common Entrance Examination, while candidates from state schools are given an alternative examination specially designed to suit the National Curriculum.

Boarding and day options are available at 16+. Those who wish to start a two-year A Level course are admitted to the Sixth Form on the basis of interview, school report and GCSE results.

There is a Dyslexia Course which takes up to six pupils each year at age 13 with full scale IQs of 120+.

Applications should be made to the Headmaster.

Scholarships and Exhibitions are awarded at 11+, 13+ and at 16+ for entry into the Sixth Form. Academic awards are made on the basis of a competitive examination. Awards for Art, Design and Technology, Drama, Music (with free instrumental tuition) and Sport are also available, although we are unable to offer Sport at 11+.

Sir Lawrence Robson Scholarships and Exhibitions are awarded each year to Sixth Form entrants.

All the above awards may carry a fee remission of up to 20%, according to merit. Day boarders are eligible for all awards at equivalent value related to day-boarder fees.

Age limits for candidates on 1st September: 11+ under 12, 13+ under 14, 16+ (entry into the Sixth Form) under 17. Further details of all scholarships may be found on the school website or obtained from the Headmaster.

Bursaries. Generous support is available to children of Armed Forces parents, Clergy and teachers. Bursaries based on financial need are also considered on an individual basis.

The Roger Raymond Trust Fund sponsors the boarding education of pupils of outstanding all-round ability who would not otherwise be able to attend the school.

Fees per term (2014–2015). Boarders £10,195; Day Boarders £7,890, both inclusive and covering all meals (lunch, tea and supper) taken at School by day pupils. Lower School: Weekly Boarders £7,230, Day £5,570 (inclusive of lunch).

Information on the payment of fees by Insurance Schemes, and a School Fees Remission Scheme in case of absence, are obtainable from the Bursar.

Optional Extras. Private tuition in a particular subject may be available (POA). Instrumental Music lessons are available from £261 per term.

Curriculum. For the first three years pupils have a broad-based curriculum, which leads to nine or ten GCSEs. No choices need to be made in the Third Form and the full range of subjects is studied. In Fourth and Fifth Form, all pupils continue to study for GCSEs in English Language, English Literature, Mathematics, French, Physics, Chemistry, Biology, Religious Studies (short course). They also choose three additional options from the following, History, Geography, Spanish, German, Art, Music, Design and Technology, and Business Studies. In the Sixth Form, A Level Courses are available in Art, Biology, Business Studies, Chemistry, Design and Technology, Economics, English, French, Further Mathematics, Geography, German, History, Mathematics, Music, Physical Education, Physics, Politics, Psychology, Spanish and Theatre Studies. This broad range of options allows students to focus their studies as they choose. All pupils follow a comprehensive General Studies programme throughout the Sixth Form and the majority take General Studies A Level. Students who are interested in applying to the Oxbridge universities are given specialist advice, whilst all Sixth Form students are well supported through the UCAS application process and provided with comprehensive careers advice from the school's own Careers Department.

Tutorial System. In addition to their Housemaster or Housemistress, every pupil has a House Tutor. Each Tutor looks after about 12 pupils and is thus able to give close personal attention to the development of each, both inside and outside school. At regular intervals of three weeks the tutor reviews each pupil's Form Assessment, which gives details of standard and approach to work in all subjects as well as information on extramural activities.

Music. There is a wide range of instrumental and choral opportunities ranging from the School Orchestra and Concert Band to chamber ensembles and close harmony groups, which students are encouraged to join. These ensembles and bands often take their music outside school, with previous performances including a recital at St Paul's Cathedral, as well as frequently playing at local prep school events and performing concerts in the surrounding villages.

Games and Outdoor Activities. Boys and girls play the traditional major sports – rugby, athletics, hockey, cricket and netball – according to the season. In addition, there are good facilities for badminton, basketball, squash, fives, sailing, shooting, equestrian activities (including polo), swimming, canoeing, cross-country, fencing and tennis. Boys and girls are strongly encouraged to develop their own particular talents. In the Third Form and below, pupils are expected to participate in the major sports, with the range of choices available to students increasing as they progress up the school. All students are also given the opportunity to participate in a flourishing Community Service Organisation.

CCF. All those in the Third Form are encouraged to undertake the Duke of Edinburgh's Award Scheme training. In their second year, many students join the CCF, to which there are various challenging activities, including the annual Adventure Training Camps as well as the usual CCF Summer Camps.

Societies. There are a large number of societies offered at the school, both academic and practical. All pupils are expected to participate in some of these activities according to their interests and strengths.

Old Bloxhamist Society. *Resident Secretary*: S J Batten.

Charitable status. Bloxham School Limited is a Registered Charity, number 1076484. Its aim is to provide high quality academic education in a Christian environment.

Blundell's School

Tiverton, Devon EX16 4DN
Tel: 01884 252543
Fax: 01884 243232
email: info@blundells.org
website: www.blundells.org

The School, with its attendant connection to Balliol and Sidney Sussex Colleges, was built and endowed in 1604 at the sole charge of the estate of Mr Peter Blundell, Clothier, of Tiverton, by his executor the Lord Chief Justice, Sir John Popham. In 1882 the School was moved to its present site on the outskirts of Tiverton.

Governors:

C M Clapp, FCA (*Chairman*)
N Arnold, BA
J F Bullock, BA, MA
N P Hall, MA, FCA
B J Hurst-Bannister, MA
P M Johnson, MA, FRSA
J K Macpherson, BEd
Mrs J M A Mannix, MA
Fr R Maudsley
The Right Reverend N McKinnel BA, MA
Ms L J Smith, BA
His Honour Judge W E M Taylor
Dr M E Wood, MA
Mrs E V Heeley, BA, CertEd
Sir Christopher Ondaatje, OC, CBE (*Governor Emeritus*)

Clerk to the Governors and Bursar: D Chambers, FCA

Senior Management & Leadership Team:

Head: Mrs N Huggett, MA Oxon

Second Master: B Wielenga, BCom, BEd
Deputy Head (Academic): Mrs C V Sherwood, MA
Under Master: P F Rivett, MA
Senior Master: A J R Berrow, MA
Senior Mistress: Mrs G M L Batting, BEng
Deputy Head (Co-curricular): E K G Saunders, BA

Chaplain: The Revd T C Hunt, MTh, BD, ARICS

† *Housemaster/Housemistress*

Assistant Masters:

A J Deighton-Gibson, BSc	S J Sherwood, BA
J S Shrimpton, BA	Miss P E Turnbull, BA,
P H Gordon, BA, BEd	MSc
Mrs D Brigden, BEd	M G Lodge, BSc
M P Dyer, MSc	A J Sims, MA, MEng
Mrs N J Klinkenberg, BSc	Miss L C Elzik, BA
†P G Klinkenberg, BEd	Miss V J Gill, MEd
Dr J T Balsdon, PhD, BSc	P W Horsington, BSc
†Miss D J Hosking, BEd	Miss T E Abela, BA, MA
Miss S A Norman, BSc	Mrs G Armstrong
(Careers)	Williams, BA
Miss I G Scott, MA	Mrs L E Webster, BSc
Mrs K J Wheatley, BA	Miss R F Prescott, BA
†Mrs R J Crease, BEd	G J Baily, BSc
C L L Gabbitass, BEd	Mrs K L Corbin, BSc, MSc
R D J Matthew, BA, MDes	A J W A Fisher, BA
L Menheneott, BEd, MBA	Mrs J C Francis, BA
Miss F A Baddeley, BA	C E D Olive, BSc
†C M Hamilton, BA	Miss B E Rees, BSc
Mrs R E Milne, MA	C J Prosser, BEng
S J Dawson, BA	N M Lecharpentier
Miss C C G Rebuffet, MA	Ms J L Lee, MA
Mrs S Holman, BA	T D Pearse, BA
Mrs B A Nuttall-Owen,	J A Rochfort
BSc	Mrs E J P Moule, MA
B Wheatley, MA	P Mawson, MChem
Miss P J Black, CertEd	Mrs J K Cole, BSc
Miss H L Youngs, BTec	J D Clayton, MSc
R J Turner, BA	C F Cox, MA
Mrs T R Griffiths, BA	Miss S L Davies, BA
G A Bucknell, BSc	J P Fairclough, BSc
Mrs A T Candler, BSc	Mrs C E Francis, BA
M J Hawkins, MA	P Gordon, BA
L Wynell-Mayow, BA	Miss C R Hall, BA
Mrs L R M Stanton, BA	J M Hernandez-Garcia
†D J D Smart, BSc	Miss R S Isdell-Carpenter,
Miss K Wilson, BSc	BA
Mrs J Olive, BA	H D Jones, BSc
Mrs E V Weaver, BSc	Dr O J Leaman, BMus
H C Roffe-Silvester, MEng	Mrs R C Milne, BA
D E Morrison, MEng	Miss E P Sage, BA
A J Mead, BSc	Mlle M Schoch
Mrs T L Winsley, BA	Mrs A M Taylor-Ross, BA
T E Candler, BA	Miss C E Wilson, BA
†D P Marshman, BSc	

Director of Development: Mrs A Oliver, MInstF

Head's PA: Mrs H L Tucker

Registrars:
†P J Klinkenberg, BEd
Mrs T L Frankpitt, BEng, MBA

Medical Officer: Dr S-J Seymour, MA, MD BChir

Admission. Entry is at 11, 13 and 16 for most pupils. This is via the Blundell's Entrance Test or the Common Entrance Examination. Most join the School in September, though a January entry is welcome.

Numbers. There are 583 pupils of whom 240 are girls; 207 board or weekly board; 161 flexi board. There are three boys' Houses and two girls' Houses for Years 9–12 and a separate Upper Sixth House which was opened in 2004.

Years 7 and 8 have a separate House with separate pastoral and academic leadership. They have no lessons on Saturdays.

Fees per term (2014–2015). Full Boarding £6,950–£10,175; Weekly Boarding £6,290–£8,945; Day £4,145–£6,545. Flexi boarding is also available. A basic tuition fee is charged for those living within ten miles of Blundell's (over the age of 13).

Scholarships and Bursaries. Open Scholarships and Exhibitions: Up to half of the chosen designation fee (ie boarding, weekly, flexi, day) are offered on the basis of our own examinations held in January (13+) and November (Sixth Form). Awards for Art, Music, Drama, Sport and All-round ability are also made. At 11+ Junior Exhibitions only are awarded for academic and musical ability (January examination) and are deducted from the basic tuition fees.

Services Package available to the sons and daughters of serving members of the Armed Forces and Diplomatic Corps.

Awards may occasionally be supplemented by means-tested bursaries at the discretion of the Head.

Full details of all scholarships and bursaries are available from the Registrars.

School Work. There are four forms at age 11 and five at age 13. During the first three years most pupils will study Art, Biology, Chemistry, Design and Technology, Divinity, Drama, English, French, Geography, History, Information Technology, Mathematics, Music (Class), Personal and Social Development, Physical Education and Physics. Latin, Greek, German and Spanish are also available.

During the GCSE years the range of subjects remains broad. Extensive advice is provided by the School to assist both GCSE and A Level choices. Parents are advised to enter their children for the Independent Schools' Careers Organisation Futurewise programme and there is a comprehensive work experience scheme on offer.

Sixth Form options enable a wide combination of subjects to be taken. Four of the following are taken to AS Level and three to A Level: Art, Biology, Business Studies, Chemistry, Classical Civilisations, Design Technology, Drama, Economics, English, Film Studies, French, Geography, German, History (Modern & Early Modern options), ICT (AS only), Latin, Mathematics and Further Mathematics, Music, Photography, Physical Education, Physics, Psychology, Religious Studies (Ethics) and Spanish.

Mark Orders, Tutorial System and Reports. Good communication is a central concept. Frequent Mark Orders and Staff Meetings are held to monitor each pupil's work. All pupils have academic tutors. Parents receive termly formal written feedback in addition to receiving Mark Order summaries every few weeks. There are regular parents' meetings and information forums.

Music and Drama. Blundell's music is excellent. Based in our own music school there are several choirs, an orchestra and varying musical ensembles. These range from a jazz band through a chamber choir to brass, woodwind and string groups. The Department has a good electronic section and in addition to School concerts there are visits from professional musicians. The Choir undertakes a European tour at Christmas; recent destinations have included Prague, Paris, Oslo, and Venice.

Similarly, Drama plays a key role in the School. There are three major School Plays each year, as well as House plays. The magnificent, purpose-built Ondaatje Hall offers the combined facilities of a theatre, a concert hall and an art studio. Frequent visits are made by theatre companies and Blundell's is a cultural venue for Mid-Devon.

Games and Physical Training. Boys play rugby football in the Autumn Term whilst girls play hockey. Spring Term sports include cross-country, squash, rugby, fives, hockey, soccer, fencing, basketball, netball and rugby sevens. In the Summer Term cricket, tennis, swimming, athletics and golf take place. Clay pigeon shooting, fly fishing, canoeing and miniature range shooting are also available. The Sports Hall gives further scope to the range of sport, as does the all-weather floodlit pitch.

Computing and Technology. All Blundellians have access to the school IT network and will develop a range of skills during their time at school to support their studies.

Recent New Facilities. There have been extensive developments at Blundell's over the past two decades which include upgrading the Science Departments, provision of advanced technological and careers arrangements as part of the resources included in the redesigned Library, a new Modern Languages block, an Upper Sixth pre-university year House and an ongoing refurbishment of all boarding houses. With the relocation of St Aubyn's School (now called Blundell's Preparatory School) onto the Blundell's site, the whole campus provides education from the age of 3 to 18 years. The Blundell's Foundation has been set up to advance plans for the future and a major development plan was started to coincide with 2004, the school's quatercentenary. Two imaginative projects, a music school and an academic centre, opened in September 2007 and there are more exciting plans on the horizon.

Community Service. The School is involved in a wide variety of activities, both local and national and pupils regularly raise over £10,000 per annum for a variety of charities.

Adventure Training. Blundell's is well placed to make full use of Dartmoor and Exmoor, the coast and rivers of the area, for academic fieldwork or adventure training. For many years the School has entered teams for the Ten Tors Expedition on Dartmoor and canoes the Devizes–Westminster race.

CCF. Everyone in Year 10 serves for a year in the CCF. Thereafter it is voluntary and comprises senior pupils who provide the NCO Instructors. There are links with the 18 Cadet Training Team, Derriford, and the Rifle Volunteers.

Boarding. Blundell's is built around the ethos of boarding and all pupils (full boarding, weekly, flexi boarding and day) are accommodated in one of seven houses on the campus. A full range of weekend activities is offered including a Leadership Programme, Ten Tors, sport and a range of local trips and activities.

Religion. The School maintains a Christian tradition, while welcoming members of other faiths. All pupils are expected to attend weekday morning Chapel and boarders go to the School Service on Sundays. The Chaplain prepares boys and girls who wish to be confirmed; the Confirmation Service takes place annually in the Spring Term.

Accessibility. Blundell's is close to the M5, and is served by Tiverton Parkway Station, two hours from Paddington, London. Airports at Bristol and Exeter are close at hand.

Prospectus. Fuller details of School life are given in the prospectus, available from the Registrars. Prospective parents are invited to visit the School, when they will meet the Head and a Housemaster or Housemistress and have a full tour of the School with a current pupil. The Blundell's website (www.blundells.org) is regularly updated throughout the academic year and as well as giving details of the school and academic departments, lists the main sporting, musical and dramatic events of each term and some match results.

Preparatory School. Blundell's Preparatory School for children aged 2½ to 11 years is on its own extensive site at Blundell's. For further information apply to the Headmaster, Mr A D Southgate. (*See also entry in IAPS section*).

Charitable status. Blundell's School is a Registered Charity, number 1081249. It exists to provide education for children.

Bolton School Boys' Division

Chorley New Road, Bolton BL1 4PA
Tel: 01204 840201
Fax: 01204 849477
email: seniorboys@boltonschool.org
website: www.boltonschool.org/seniorboys
Twitter: @Philip_Britton
Facebook: /boltonschool.org
LinkedIn: /bolton-school

Motto: '*Mutare vel timere sperno'.*
Bolton School Boys' Division, founded ante 1516 as Bolton Grammar School for Boys, was rebuilt and endowed by Robert Lever in 1644. In 1913 the first Viscount Leverhulme gave a generous endowment to the Bolton Grammar School for Boys and the High School for Girls on condition that the two schools should be equal partners known as Bolton School (Boys' and Girls' Divisions).

Bolton School is a family of schools, where children can enjoy an all-through education, joining our co-educational Nursery for 3 and 4 year olds or Infant School before moving up to our single-sex Junior and Senior Schools with Sixth Forms. We are strong believers that girls and boys from 7+ perform best in a single-sex environment, but one where there are co-educational activities – the best of both worlds.

Chairman of Governors: M T Griffiths, BA, FCA

Headmaster: P J Britton, MBE, MEd

Deputy Headmaster (Pastoral): R D Wardle, BA
Assistant Head (Academic): D J Jones, BSc
Assistant Head (Activities): Dr F H Mullins, BSc, PhD

Heads of Department:
Art and Design: D McGuinness, BA
Biology: M A Tillotson, BSc
Business Studies: Mrs C M Edge, BSc
Chemistry: Dr M Yates, BSc, PhD
Classics: Dr J E Reeson, BA, MSt, PhD
Economics: D W Kettle, BA
English: M S Pollard, BA, MA
French: A C Robson, BA
Geography: P Newbold, BA
German: R A Catterall, MA
History: Miss S V Burgess, MA
ICT: P J Humphrey, BSc
Mathematics: D N Palmer, BSc
Music: J Bleasdale, BA
Physical Education:
P Fernside, BA (*Head of Games*)
M Johnson, BSc (*Head of PE*)
Physics: M R Ormerod, BSc
Religious Studies: Mrs C E Fox, BA
Russian: P G Davidson, BA
Spanish: Mrs J L Cotton, BA, MA
Technology: C J Walker, BA

Instrumental Music Staff:
Brass, Cello, Clarinet, Guitar, Oboe, Organ, Percussion, Piano, Saxophone, Singing, Viola, Violin

Junior School (Age 7–11):
Head: S Whittaker, BEd
Deputy Head: Mrs S A Faulkner, BA, MA

Headmaster's Personal Assistant: Ms M M Leather
Headmaster's Secretary & Admissions Registrar: Mrs S Yates

Situated in imposing sandstone buildings on a thirty-two acre site, Bolton School Boys' Division educates over 1,100 boys, all day pupils. Of these, 200 are members of the Junior School which is housed in an adjacent separate building close to the main site providing education for boys aged 7–11. In the Senior School of 900, 220 are in the Sixth Form.

Bolton School Boys' Division seeks to realise the potential of each pupil. We provide challenge, encourage initiative, promote teamwork and develop leadership capabilities. It is our aim that students leave the School as self-confident young people equipped with the knowledge, skills and attributes that will allow them to lead happy and fulfilled lives and to make a difference for good in the wider community.

We do this through offering a rich and stimulating educational experience which encompasses academic, extra-curricular and social activities. We provide a supportive and industrious learning environment for pupils selected on academic potential, irrespective of means and background.

Curriculum. The GCSE programme comprises a core curriculum of English Language, English Literature, Mathematics, Biology, Chemistry, Physics and Sport. In addition, pupils select a further 4 options chosen from Art, Drama, French, Geography, German, Greek, History, Latin, Music, Philosophy and Ethics, RE, Russian, Science Enrichment, Spanish and Technology. One of these choices must be a foreign language. At A Level approximately 30 different subjects are currently on offer. Boys study four subjects to AS Level, with the majority reducing to three A2 Levels in Year 13. In addition all boys have the option of taking General Studies to A2 Level. While many boys elect to take standard combinations of either Arts or Science subjects in the Sixth Form, a high degree of flexibility ensures that any desired combination of subjects can be offered. Throughout both years of the Sixth Form, there is an additional and extensive programme of academic work which supports the GCE Advanced curriculum. Some boys will take the AQA Bacc qualification and all boys do an enrichment course and take part in community service.

Facilities and Organisation. The Boys' and Girls' Divisions of Bolton School are housed in separate buildings on the same site and, though the organisation of the two Divisions provides single-sex schools, there are many opportunities for boys and girls to meet and to cooperate in the life of the school community. This is particularly so in the new Riley Sixth Form Centre, where boys and girls share a Common Room, cafe and learning areas equipped with the very latest technology. Single-sex teaching remains the norm in the Sixth Form, although in a very few subjects co-educational arrangements are in operation. The buildings of the Boys' Division include the Great Hall, two libraries, gymnasium, sports hall, swimming pool, laboratories, art rooms, sixth form common room and ICT learning centre, design technology centre, performing arts centre, MFL laboratory, classrooms and dining hall. The Junior School building has recently been extended and refurbished and contains eight form rooms and specialist rooms for ICT, art & design and science & technology together with a gymnasium, library and its own dining accommodation. Use of the sports hall, the adjacent 25-metre swimming pool and the arts centre is shared by all sections of the school.

Games and PE. The extensive playing fields which adjoin the School contain thirteen pitches. Principal games are football, rugby and cricket. Tennis, hockey, swimming, water polo, badminton, athletics, golf and orienteering are also all played at representative school level. All boys also undertake a gymnastics programme and play volleyball and basketball. The School is divided into four Houses for the purpose of internal competitions.

Art, Drama, Design, Music. In addition to timetabled sessions in each discipline there are many opportunities for extra-curricular activities in all these pursuits. Facilities in the art department include a pottery room with kiln; within the very active musical life of the School there are choral groups, orchestras and ensembles catering for all ages and abilities. In addition arrangements can be made for individual lessons on all orchestral instruments, piano, organ and in singing. Drama is an important part of the work of the English department and boys are encouraged to develop their talents in the drama studio and arts centre. The annual major school play, musical or opera is produced in cooperation with the Girls' Division. Design and technology features strongly in the curriculum in both Junior and Senior Schools with considerable success each year in the A level technology courses, many boys gaining industrial sponsorships as a result. In addition, a wide variety of extra-curricular opportunities exists in both the design technology base and the computer rooms. All boys are encouraged to take part in the extensive lunchtime programme when over 120 clubs, societies and practices are offered to different groups.

Outdoor Pursuits. All junior school pupils and all students up to and including Year 12 in the senior school undertake an annual period of outdoor education within curriculum time. In addition, camps, trips, exchanges and expeditions go to 63 destinations over two years, 17 of them abroad. The School has its own 60-bed Outdoor Pursuits Centre, Patterdale Hall in Cumbria, used by parties of boys regularly for curriculum, weekend, holiday and fieldwork expeditions. In Year 8 boys have the opportunity to undertake sail training lessons in the Irish Sea on the School's sailing ketch. There is a large and active Scout Group with its own modern headquarters on school premises.

Religion. The School is non-denominational; all boys have periods devoted to religious education. In assemblies the basic approach is Christian although a great variety of readings and methods of presentation are adopted.

Careers and Higher Education. Careers education and guidance, and life-long learning are key elements of the curriculum. In Year 8 pupils take part in a Work Sampling Day. Careers Education is part of the Year 9 curriculum including a project marked by the Headmaster. As an aid to Sixth Form choices, the Morrisby Test with follow-up interviews and extensive feedback is undertaken in Years 10 and 11. All pupils take part in Work Experience placements at the end of Year 11 and throughout the Sixth Form.

In Year 12, all pupils attend a 3 day residential business training course at Patterdale Hall and take part in an e-business competition. Mock interviews are conducted on Interview Skills Evenings. Year 13 pupils are guided through UCAS procedures and careers advice is always available from two full-time Careers Assistants in the Careers Library. The Head of Careers oversees all these events and can be consulted by all parents and pupils.

Transport. The School provides an extensive coach service which offers secure and easy access for pupils from a wide surrounding catchment area. Over twenty routes are operated by either the School's own fleet of coaches or by contract hire arrangements.

Admission. An entrance examination is held in January annually for boys over 7 and under 8 on August 31st of the year of admission and also for those over 8 and under 9 on the same date. Fifty places are available at 7+ and a few additional places thereafter. Admission to the first year of the Senior School (130 places) is by entrance examination held annually in mid-January. Boys who are over 10 and under 12 on August 31st of the year of entry are eligible. Entry to the Sixth Form is available to boys who have taken GCSE examinations elsewhere on the basis of interview and agreed levels of performance in these public examinations. Boys are also admitted at other ages when vacancies occur; in these cases admission is gained through satisfactory interview and test performances. There is a co-educational pre-preparatory section – Beech House Infants' School – which has recently moved to new purpose-built, state-of-the-art premises. Admission is from the age of 4 and enquiries should be made to infants@boltonschool.org. There is also a nursery providing facilities for children from 3 months to 4 years old.

Fees per term (2014–2015). Senior School and Sixth Form £3,632; Infant and Junior Schools £2,905. Fees include lunches.

Fee Assistance. Foundation Grants are available and one in five Senior School pupils receive assistance with fees.

Prospectus and Open Day. The School holds an annual Open Morning for the benefit of prospective candidates and their parents. This is normally in mid-October. Individual tours can be arranged on working days throughout the year. Further information concerning all aspects of the School is contained in the School Prospectus, copies of which may be obtained by writing to the Headmaster at the School, or telephoning the Headmaster's Secretary. More detail can be found on the School website. Enquiries concerning admission are welcome at any time of the School year.

Charitable status. The Bolton School is a Registered Charity, number 1110703. Under the terms of the Charity it is administered as two separate Divisions providing for boys and girls under a separate Headmaster and Headmistress.

Bootham School

York YO30 7BU

Tel: 01904 623261 (School)
              01904 623261 (Headmaster)
Fax: 01904 652106
email: office@boothamschool.com
website: www.boothamschool.com

Bootham offers Full and Weekly Boarding and Day Education to both boys and girls from 11–18, together with day education from the age of 3 at Bootham Junior School. There are now over 480 pupils in the Senior School and 150 day pupils in the Junior School (*see entry in IAPS section*).

The School was founded in 1823 by Quakers, but pupils of all denominations or none are welcomed. All pupils attend Meetings for Worship and arrangements are made for pupils to be prepared for confirmation or membership of their own churches.

Head: Jonathan Taylor, MA Oxon, MEd

Deputy Head: Suzanne Hall, BA, PhD

Academic Deputy: Ruth Crabtree, BA, MA

Head of Junior School: Helen Todd, BA Hons, MA Ed, QTS

Assistant Heads:
Andrew Bell, BA
William Lewis, MA
James Ratcliffe, BSc
Robert Tribe, BSc

Head of Boarding: Michael Shaw, BSc (†*Fox House*)

Bursar: Andy Woodland, BA, MA, MICE, MCIWEM

Assistant Staff:
* *Head of Department*
† *Housemaster/mistress*

Sarah Allen, BEd, BD (*Religious Studies*)
Rachel Antill, BA (*Art*)
Mathew D Aston, BEd (*Mathematics*)
Joan Attwell, BA (*Drama*)
Richard M Barnes, BA, MA (*Art*)
Simon Benson, BA, MA (**Drama*)
Dina Bonner (*German Language Assistant*)
Elizabeth Brown, BSc, PhD (**Geography*)
Susan Browne (*Teaching Assistant*)
Richard N Burton, BA (*Music*)
Carol L Campbell, BA (*French, Spanish, †Rowntree House*)

Angelica Coates (*Spanish Language Assistant*)
Kirsten S Cooper, MPhys (**Physics*)
Tracey Copestake, BA (**Religious Studies*)
Ben Coxon, BA (*Physical Education*)
Steve J Elsworth, BA (*Mathematics*)
Harriet Ennis, BSc (**Psychology, Biology*)
Paul Feehan, BA (**Director of Music*)
Dominic Figon, BSc (*Mathematics*)
Elizabeth Gallagher-Coates, BA (*English, Psychology*)
Robert Gardiner, BSc (**Biology*)
Emma Glover, BA (*English*)
Robert E Graham, BEd (*Physical Education, Geography*)
Sally Gray, BA (*Classics*)
Emily Harper, BA (*Art*)
Andrew Hedges, MEng, CEng (*Design & Technology*)
Elisabeth Hooley, BA (*Physical Education, Mathematics*)
Freya Horsley, BA, MA (*Art*)
Paul Irvine, BA (*Spanish, French*)
Patrick Kuntschnik, BA, MA (*Classics*)
Jack MacKenzie, BA (*Music*)
Kelly McCarthy, BA, MA (*EAL*)
Elizabeth McCulloch, MA (**History*)
Eamonn Molloy, BEd (**Design & Technology*)
Alison Moreland, BEd (**Physical Education, Geography*)
Catherine Morin (*French Language Assistant*)
Russell Newlands, MSc, BEng (*Physics*)
Sarah O'Keeffe, BSc (**Economics & Business Studies*)
Christina Oliver, BA, MA (*French, German*)
Danielle Pegg, BA (*Physical Education*)
Sue Porter, BSc (*Mathematics*)
Peter Rankin, BEng (*Information Technology, Physics*)
Melissa Raubitschek, BSc (*Science*)
Lindsey Robertson, BSc (*Chemistry*)
Mark Robinson, BA, MA (**Chemistry*)
Sarah Robinson, BA (*Classics*)
Catherine Rowell, BSc, PhD (*Biology, Chemistry, Physics*)
Catherine Rowntree, BA (*History*)
Alix Scott-Martin, BA, MA (*English & General Studies*)
Helen Sharpe, BA, MA (*English*)
Anthea Shepherdson, GMus, PGDip (*Head of Keyboard & Music Coordinator*)
Gill Simpson, BA, MA (**English*)
David Swales, BA (**Art*)
Richard Taylor, BA, MA (**Modern Foreign Languages*)
Jay Thorpe (*Outdoor Education Instructor*)
Sue Tomlinson, BSc (*Chemistry, Biology*)
Anne Whittle, BSc (*Mathematics*)
Amy Wilson, BA, MA (*Learning Support*)
Angela Woods, BEd (*Geography, Physical Education*)

Development Director: Jane Peake, BA

Registrar: Jenny Daly

Librarian: Steven Oakden, BA

Curriculum. In Years 7–9 all pupils pursue a course of study which includes English (including Drama), History, Religious Studies, Careers, Geography, Classics, Latin, French, German, Spanish, Mathematics, the three separate Sciences, Music, Art and Craft, Physical Education, Design & Technology, Computer Science, Health and the Environment and Thinking Skills.

In Years 10 and 11 pupils follow a curriculum leading to 10 subjects at GCSE.

The College Classes (Sixth Form) are preparatory to university entrance. The majority of pupils remain at school until the age of 18 and each year there is a strong Oxbridge entry. A wide choice of subjects is offered. It is usual to study 4 or 5 examination subjects and to study subjects of wider interest.

The following subjects may be taken, in many combinations, to the AS & A2 and University Entrance levels: Mathematics, Further Mathematics, Physics, Chemistry, Psychology, Biology, English, French, German, Spanish,

History, Classics, Latin, Geography, Economics, Business Studies, Music, Art, Design Technology, Religious Studies, Drama and Theatre Studies, and Sports Studies and Physical Education. To counter-balance the effects of specialisation, pupils in the College classes are required to follow courses in Religious, Physical and General Education. In General Studies pupils follow a course in a wide range of topics such as English Literature, Political History, Music Appreciation and International Affairs, given by members of the staff and, from time to time, by specialists who visit the School for this purpose. Particular emphasis is placed on the study of personal relations and the structures of communities.

Site and Buildings. The School is situated close to York Minster. From the road it appears as an impressive line of Georgian houses but behind this is the spacious main school campus. There is a steady programme of development, and the buildings now include 8 well-equipped Laboratories, an impressive Arts Centre (open 2014) with Auditorium and Darkroom (photography), 2 ICT Suites, 2 DT workshops, an Astronomical Observatory, an up-to-date Physical Education Department with Sports Hall, Indoor Swimming Pool, Fitness Suite and Squash Courts, and a modern Assembly Hall, which received a national RIBA award. There are many facilities for leisure time pursuits which are an important feature of the lives of pupils at the School. The buildings are complemented by formal gardens and a beautiful Cricket Field, overlooked by the Minster. Another large Playing Field is situated nearby, in Clifton, which also houses Bootham Junior School in a new purpose-built complex.

Pastoral Care. As a Quaker School, Bootham places great emphasis on caring relationships within a friendly community. There are three boarding houses, under the special care of House staff. Each House has its own recreational facilities. Throughout the School, both boarding and day pupils are supervised and guided by form tutors. In College, pupils have Personal Tutors who are responsible for both academic and pastoral matters, and guidance towards Higher Education.

Admission. Pupils usually enter Bootham at the age of 11. Entry is also usually possible at 12, 13 and 14. The main entrance assessment is held annually in January and this forms the basis of Scholarship and Bursary selection. Sixth form entry is welcomed and selection is on the bases of school report and GCSE performance. In special circumstances late entrants can be considered.

Leisure Time Activities. The School has long been recognised as a pioneer in the right use of leisure. The Natural History Society, founded in 1832, claims to be the oldest society of its kind with an unbroken history in this country. Other clubs and societies include Debates, Drama, Bridge, Chess, Cookery and Jazz. There are around 80 activities offered each week. Pupils follow the Duke of Edinburgh's Award scheme and are involved in Community Services.

Music. The Director of Music and his assistant are supported by 21 visiting teachers. Tuition is arranged in a wide variety of instruments and a strong tradition of music in the School is maintained. A recent leaver was named 'Young Composer of the Year' and there is a strong record of success in gaining Music College and University scholarships.

Games. Association Football, Hockey, Tennis, Fencing, Cricket, Swimming, Athletics, Netball, Basketball, Badminton, Squash, Rounders. There is no cadet force.

Fees per term (2014–2015). Boarding: £5,645–£9,495. Day: £4,995–£5,505.

Fees for instrumental music lessons are extra. Enquiries for up-to-date information are welcome.

Scholarships and Bursaries. *Academic* Scholarships (Honorary and without fee reduction) are awarded on the basis of academic performance, for entry at 11+ and 13+ (Years 7 and 9). All candidates taking the entrance assessment at the main sitting (usually held at the end of January in the year of entry) will be considered.

Sixth Form: We collaborate with the Ogden Trust to provide a means-tested Bursary to candidates who intend to study Physics at university.

Music Scholarships of up to 50% fee remission are available for candidates of good all-round musical and academic ability or potential. These are available for entry at 11+ and 13+ (Years 7 and 9) and are awarded on the basis of performance in the entrance assessment, and in tests and an audition with the Director of Music.

Means-tested Bursaries (supported by the Bootham Trust) are available:
- to assist Friend (Quaker) children, or the children of Friend (Quaker) parents, to attend the School;
- to assist children, whose families would not be able to afford an independent school education, to attend the School. Applicants will be assessed by academic performance in the entrance assessment at 11+ and 13+ and in addition, for Music Scholars, their performance at the Music Scholarship tests and audition. Applications for bursaries need to be made in the Autumn term prior to entry to the school.

Bootham Old Scholars' Association. There is an annual Reunion in York during the second weekend in May. The Bootham Old Scholars Association has branches in all parts of the country and Eire. The Secretary may be contacted through the School.

Charitable status. Bootham School is a Registered Charity, number 513645.

Bradfield College

Bradfield, Berkshire RG7 6AU
Tel: General Enquiries: 0118 964 4500
 Admissions: 0118 964 4516
 Bursar: 0118 964 4530
email: admissions@bradfieldcollege.org.uk
website: www.bradfieldcollege.org.uk
Twitter: @bradfieldcol
Facebook: /BradfieldCollege
LinkedIn: bradfield-college-enterprises-ltd

Motto: '*Benedictus es, O Domine: Doce me Statuta Tua*'. Blessed are you, our Lord; teach me your laws (from Psalm 119).

Bradfield College was founded in 1850 by Thomas Stevens, Rector and Lord of the Manor of Bradfield.

We define our ethos by the outcome of our pupils as they leave Bradfield. We actively promote personal integrity, tolerance, understanding and independence of thought. We encourage young people to work with and learn from each other, as well as to show moral courage to stand up for what they believe in. The breadth of a Bradfield education supports our pupils in challenging themselves and develops their abilities to communicate with others. The College is a co-educational boarding school dedicated to the provision of the highest possible care for all its pupils.

Visitor: The Right Revd The Lord Bishop of Oxford

Council:

M H Young (*Warden*)	G W P Barber
P G F Lowndes	Professor D Paterson
M A Jones	I M Wood-Smith
A H Scott	H P Gangsted
D Shilton	Mrs C Dibble
P B Saunders	Mrs J Scarrow
Lady Waller (*Child Protection Governor*)	I Davenport
	S Beccle
Dr S Fane	

Clerk of the Council: P C H Burrowes

Headmaster: **S C Henderson**, MA

Second Master: K J Collins, MA

Senior Deputy Head: Mrs A M C Acton, BA Hons

Deputy Heads:
N M Burch, MSci
A R MacEwen, MA

Assistant Heads:
Mrs C Kirby, BSc (*Academic*)
R J Wall, BA (*Pastoral*)

Bursar: P C H Burrowes LLB

Registrar: Mrs A H Marshall, CertEd

Director of Professional Development: Mrs C Jones, BA

Assistant Bursar: D Palmer, BSc, ACA

Director of Development: A Waddington, BA

Housemistress Representative: Miss S R Duff, MA

Housemaster Representative: C A Carlier, MA

Houses and Housemasters:
A – Loyd: J R Preston, BSc
C – Army: A S Golding, BA
D – House on the Hill: S A Long, BEd
E – Stone House: P C Armstrong, BA
F – Hillside: C A Carlier, MA
G – House on the Hill: T E Goad, BA
H – The Close: G W S Masters, BA
I – Palmer House (Girls): Mrs F D Major, BA
J – Armstrong House (Girls): Mrs S K M Ronan, CertEd
K – Stevens House (Girls): Mrs Z P Wheddon, BA
M – Stanley House (Girls): Miss S R Duff, MA
L – Faulkner's (Year 9): Mr J C Saunders and Mrs V Rae

Assistant Staff:
* *Head of Department*

Creative Arts Faculty:
*M Holmes, MA
Art:
Miss A Cowan, BA
A Fleming, BA
Miss G L Peel, BA
Mrs M R Purcell, BA
Mrs R M Swainston, MA
A Whittaker, MFA
Design & Technology:
*Miss H L Knott, BA
M K Goodwin, MA

Business Studies:
*M R Rippon, BA
S Chambers, BSc
L Webb, BSc

Careers and Higher Education:
*Mrs C J Taylor, BA

Classics:
*Mrs P M H Caffrey, MA
P C Armstrong, BA

Economics:
*T H Chaloner, MA
J C Fox, BA
R E Presley, MA

Emotional Literacy and Wellbeing:
*Mrs L K Shortland, BA
Mrs V Rae, RGN

English and Film Faculty:
*Miss A L Hatch, BA (*Head of English and Film*)
English:
D Bagnall, BA, MPhil

Miss H Brett, BA
K J Collins, MA
Mrs E V Earnshaw, BA
A S Golding, BA
J M Longmore, LLB
Miss A J Routledge, BA
J M C Saunders, BA
Ms K Terry, BA
Mrs I G Woods, BA
English Language and EAL:
*Mrs H E Bebbington, BA, MA
Mrs D Bevan, TESOL Cert
Miss S R Duff, MA
Mrs J Kingston, BA
Film Studies:
Ms J Stables, BA

Geography:
*M S Hill, BA
C B Duffell, BA
R Keeley, MA
T J Kidson, BSc
Mrs C J Kirby, BSc
R J Wall, BA

History:
*C M Best, BA
C J Booth, LLB
Mrs F D Major, BA
J P Shafe, BA
Miss M Winn, BSc
R J Veal, MA

History of Art:
*Mrs B H Bond, BA
T E Goad, BA

Mathematics and Computing Faculty:
*E J Clark, BA
Computing:
*Dr H S Shakibi, BSc, PhD
Mathematics:
Mrs N Armstrong, BA
Dr S C Beeson, BSc, PhD
D M T Brooks, BSc
C B Burgess, MA, MEng
J A Carle, BSc
Mrs J L Clubbe, BA
M J Green, BEng
A G Hill, BSc
Mrs E I Morton, BA
Mrs C Shaikh, CertEd
N J Taylor, BSc
Mrs C van der Westhuizen, MSc
S N Whalley, BSc
H Williams, MMath

Modern Languages Faculty:
*M M Etherington, BA
Mrs A M C Acton, BA
Mrs M Allusi, BA
Mrs B Benito Lozano, BA
C A Carlier, MA
Mrs I M d'Angely-Golding
Mrs B E D'Cruz, MA (*Head of German*)
J C Hanbury, BA (*Head of French*)
Mrs C Jones, BA
Mrs D J R Lyon, BA
W T Morgan, BA
Mrs K L Parker, BA (*Head of Spanish*)
Mrs J Ricci
R Somma, BA (*Head of Italian*)
Mrs F J C Wall, BA
Mrs J J Walsh, BA
Mrs Z P Wheddon, BA

Performing Arts Faculty:
Dr T Coker, PhD
Dance:
Miss M Legg
Drama:
Miss N Wilson, BA
Miss S Spencer, BA
Music:
Mrs V S Hughes, BA
J S Mountford, BA, ARCO

PE:
*R P P Sanford, BSc
D J Clark, BA
S A Long, BEd
D J Mitchell, BSc
Mrs S K M Ronan, CertEd
Mrs C Treacy, BSc

Politics:
*S H Rees, BA, PhD
A R MacEwen, MA

Religion, Philosophy and Ethics:
*Mrs M Baynton-Perret, BD Dip
J P A Ball, MA
Mrs P M Donnelly, BA
Reverend S Gray, MA (*Chaplain*)
G W S Masters, BA
S P Williams, MA, MLitt

Science Faculty:
Dr D J Brooks, BSc, PhD
Biology:
*P J J Clegg, BSc
Ms E J Appleby, BSc
F R Dethridge, BSc
Mrs C Doherty, BSc
Dr K J Ogbe, BSc, PhD
Dr L S Vat, BSc
S D Whitehead, BSc
Chemistry:
*J A F Burnside, MChem, PhD
D J Brooks, BSc
N M Burch, MSci
S Doherty BSc, PhD
A J Hardwick BSc, MA
A J Singh, BSc
Physics:
*Mrs R B Clamp, MSci, CPhys, AMInstP
P A Comerford, BSc
D Rowley, BA
Mrs N Shackell, BEng, MA

Support and Study Skills:
*Mrs F McPherson, BA, Dip SpLD
Mrs S S Bunyan, BA
Mrs K E Howells, Cert SpLD
Dr L C Hutchins, BSc, PhD
Mrs G K Mabbett, BEd, Dip SpLD
Mrs C Prior, BA, Dip SpLD
Mrs I Smith, BEd, Dip SpLD
Mrs N Bell MA, Dip.SpLD

Location. Bradfield College occupies the village of Bradfield, 8 miles west of Reading and 9 miles east of Newbury. It is 2 miles from Junction 12 of the M4 (the Theale access point). There are good road and rail communications with Reading, Oxford, London and Heathrow.

Organisation. The College is a fully co-educational boarding school with approximately 770 pupils, of whom about 100 are day pupils. At 13+ entry girls and boys spend their first year in Faulkner's, a purpose-built co-educational house with its own facilities and dining hall. Thereafter, the College is divided into 11 houses (7 for Boys and 4 for Girls). Day pupils are full members of the boarding houses.

The Housemaster/mistress is assisted by House Tutors and a Matron. Meals are served in the central Dining Hall. About sixty girls and boys join the large and vibrant Sixth Form through 16+ entry.

Admission. 13+ candidates qualify by taking either the Common Entrance Examination, the Common Academic or Bradfield College Scholarship Examination, or the Bradfield Entrance Examination (if not taking Common Entrance); candidates are interviewed by the a Housemaster/mistress and an Admissions tutor, and school reports and references are required. Admission to the Sixth Form is by Assessment; this comprises English and Maths tests and pastoral and academic interviews. In addition, school reports and references are required. Scholarships and Exhibitions are available.

A school prospectus and details of the entry procedure may be obtained from the Admissions Office or College website.

Fees per term (2014–2015). Boarders £11,100; Day pupils £8,880

A fee is payable on registration. 20 months before the date of entry a Guaranteed Place fee of £1,000, which is later credited against the final account, is payable.

Entrance Scholarships. *Academic*: At 13+ scholarships are awarded on the results of a competitive examination held at the College in the Lent Term. Candidates must be under the age of 14 on 1 September. Further Honorary scholarships conferring the status and privileges of a scholar are awarded at the end of the Year 11 (post GCSE).

At 16+ Scholarships and Exhibitions are awarded annually after competitive examinations in the Michaelmas Term.

Music Scholarships are awarded at 13+ and 16+.

Dr Gray Exhibitions are awarded at 13+ and 16+ for achievement and potential either in a specific field or in a combination of fields. Candidates may wish to offer distinction in Art, Performing Arts or Sport although other co-curricular activities will also be considered. Alternatively, they may wish to be considered for their all-round ability, which would take into account their academic achievement as well as their aptitude in any combination of other disciplines (including Music).

All awards are augmentable according to financial need. Further information and entrance forms can be obtained on application to the Admissions Office.

Academic Organisation. Pupils enter the College in September and follow a three-year course to GCSE examinations, and then a two-year course to A Level or IB.

In the first three years all the normal subjects are taught in a core curriculum, but there is also opportunity to emphasise the linguistic or the aesthetic or the practical elements through a system of options.

In the Sixth Form GCE AS and A2 Level courses are offered in all subjects studied for GCSE with the addition of Economics, Politics, History of Art, Business Studies and Computing. Sixth Formers can also choose to study the IB Diploma Programme.

A brand new state-of-the-art and environmentally-friendly Science Centre opened its doors to pupils and the local community in September 2010. It includes ten sophisticated laboratories, a living grass roof, a conservatory and a biomass boiler providing an educationally and environmentally exciting space for the teaching of science.

Academic Staff. There are 117 members of the Academic Staff who cover all the main subjects. These are almost entirely graduates recruited from British universities, although there are also native speakers of German, French and Spanish in the Modern Languages department.

Careers. The Careers Department – Bradfield Horizons – provides a wide range of careers education, information, advice and guidance to all year groups, particularly at key decision points. The College is a full member of ISCO and through them, all pupils in the Fifth Form (and new pupils in the Lower Sixth) undertake Futurewise (Morrisby) psychometric profiling, follow-up interviews and receive a detailed personal report to help them plan for the future. In the Sixth Form, pupils have opportunities to find out about various professions, industries and the Armed Services through talks, visits and courses. Specialist advice is available on University entrance in the UK and overseas, Gap Years and work-related learning.

Sports. The main Sports for girls are hockey in the Michaelmas term, netball in the Lent term and tennis and rounders in the Summer term. Girls also have the chance to play competitive lacrosse, football and cricket.

The main Sports for boys are football in the Michaelmas term, hockey in the Lent term and cricket and tennis in the Summer term.

In addition, teams represent the College at squash, fives, cross-country, fencing, athletics, golf, sailing, swimming, shooting, badminton, basketball, water polo, clay pigeon shooting, showjumping, eventing and polo. There are also opportunities to take part in dance classes, Zumba and aerobics.

There are 2 all-weather artificial grass pitches used for hockey, football and tennis, a 3-court indoor Tennis Centre, 6 other hard tennis courts, 5 netball courts, 2 fives courts, 4 squash courts and a very large and modern Sports Complex, including an indoor swimming pool. The College grounds extend to nearly 250 acres and include fine playing fields, a nine-hole golf course and fly fishing on the river Pang.

Recreation, Drama and Music. Every encouragement is given to pupils to develop their interests and talents in a wide variety of creative activities. There are modern and well-equipped studios for Art, Sculpture and Textiles, an Information Technology Centre, a purpose-built and very extensive Design and Technology Centre and a Music School with a Concert Hall and practice rooms. The Drama department stages a diverse number of productions each term and a classical Greek Play is produced every three years. In addition, there are about 30 Societies covering a wide range of other interests from Young Enterprise to Knitting.

Religion. Chapel services are those of the Church of England, and Religious Education is part of the core curriculum in Year 9. Confirmation Services are held each year for Anglicans in the College Chapel and for Catholics in the local parish.

Combined Cadet Force. The College maintains a contingent of the Combined Cadet Force which all pupils have the opportunity of joining. There is a full range of alternative activities, including Community Service and The Duke of Edinburgh's Award. All pupils take part in a programme of Adventure Training.

The Bradfield Society. The College values its links with its former pupils and parents, and a series of social and sporting occasions is held each year to enable friendships to be maintained and renewed. Address: The Bradfield Society, Bradfield College, Reading, Berkshire RG7 6AU.

Charitable status. Bradfield College is a Registered Charity, number 309089.

Bradford Grammar School

Keighley Road, Bradford, West Yorkshire BD9 4JP

Tel:	01274 542492; Headmaster: 01274 553701
Fax:	01274 548129
email:	hmsec@bradfordgrammar.com
website:	www.bradfordgrammar.com
Twitter:	@kevinjamesriley

Motto: '*Hoc Age*'

Bradford Grammar School is known to have existed in 1548 and received a title of Incorporation as 'The Free Grammar School of King Charles II at Bradford' in 1662.

Bradford Grammar School is a selective day school for boys and girls aged from 6–18 with an excellent reputation for outstanding teaching, pastoral care, sport, music and the arts.

Corporate Trustee: Bradford Grammar School Trustee Limited

Governors:
Chairman: Lady L Morrison, LLB
Vice-Chairman: Professor C Mellors, BA, MA, PhD
President: A H Jerome, MA

Ex officio:
The Very Revd Canon J Lepine, BA, Dean of Bradford

Co-optative:
W Bowser, ACIB
P Cogan, BA, FCA
A C Craig, DL, DCR
D J Davies, BEng, MA
S R Davies, BA, FRSA
C Hamilton-Stewart, MBE
His Honour Judge J A Lewis
P T Smith
C M Wontner-Smith, BA, FCA
Sir David Wootton, MA

Representative:
Professor A Francis, BSc, ACGI, FBAM, CCMI, AcSS
Professor Sir Alexander F Markham, BSc, PhD, MB, BS, DSc, FRCP, FRCPath
I McAleese, FCIPD

Governors Emeriti:
P J M Bell, JP, FCIS, CText, FTI, FRSA
R G Bowers, DL, BSc, CEng, FRSA
J D Fenton, MCSP, SRP
I Crawford, FCA
J E Barker, MA
J G Ridings, FCA

Bursar and Clerk to the Governors: I Findlay, BA, ACA

Headmaster: K J Riley, BA, MEd

Deputy Head: S Hinchliffe, BA, MEd, PhD

Pastoral Director: M J Chapman, MA
Academic Director: G P Woods, MA

Department Staff:
* *Head of Department/Subject*

Art:
*Ms J Barraclough, BA
Mrs S E Horsfield, BA
W Norman, BA
H R Thornton, BA

Biology:
*Mrs P M A Dunn, BSc
Mrs D J Chalashika, BSc
S R Hoath, BSc
Miss Z J Smeaton, BSc
K M Smith, BSc
S Thomas, BSc

Business Studies:
*D A Pullen, BSc
Ms S L Croudson, BSc

Chemistry:
*Dr D G Proctor, BSc, MSc, PhD
Mrs S J Flaherty, MA
Mrs G M Heywood, BSc
A B R Macnab, BSc

Dr D J Mouat, BSc, PhD
Mrs N S Nicholas, BSc

Classics:
*Dr K A Meakin, PhD, BA
M J A Barr, BA
T C Bateson, MA
Mrs M J Chapman, MA (*Pastoral Director*)

Design and Technology:
*S G Taylor, BSc
D Leake, BEd, MA
J I Richards, BA

Economics:
*R D Schofield, BA
M McCartney, BSc, MA

English and Drama:
*L W Hanson, BEd, MA
Miss S J Ball, BA (*Drama*)
Miss C S Bruce, MA
Miss G D'Arcy, BA, MA
Miss L A Kirk, BA
Miss A M Lancelot, BA, MA
A N Mudd, BA
S D Rees, BA
R Thompson, MA
Miss E K Trafford, BA, MA

Geography:
*A G Smith, BSc
D G Alcock, MA
Miss A C Hicks, BA (*Asst Head Years 8 & 9*)
Mrs F R Handbury, BA
Mrs H R Wong, BA

History:
*N A Hooper, MA, FRHistS
Mrs H J Baines, BA (*Joint Asst Head Sixth Form*)
Miss E A Greaves, BA
J Reed-Purvis, BA, MA (*Head of Sixth Form*)
Mrs K E Wilde, BA (*Head of Years 8 & 9*)

Computer Science:
*Mrs C M Harvey, BA, MA (*Acting *)
C R Bright, BSc
M Cottrell, BA
Ms S L Croudson, BSc

Mathematics:
*D W Fishwick, BSc, PhD
A B Baines, BSc
Mrs E C Boyes-Watson, BA
A Crabtree, BSc
Dr S Harris, MMath, PhD
P Merckx, BSc (*Head of Year 7*)
R I Page, BA, MScC Finch, BSc
V Reynolds, BSc
M A Thompson, BSc (*Head of Years 10 & 11*)
P Watson, BSc, PhD

Modern Languages:
*Mrs S L Haslam, BA (*German*)
Ms M B Cuesta-González (*Spanish*)
Mrs E J Kingsley, BA, MSc (*French*)
Miss A M Corrigan, BA
S B Davis, MA, LTCL, MCIL (*Russian*)
L C Gibbons, MA
Miss V Martí-Fernández, BA
Ms K Murach, MA
Mrs E Tomlinson, BA (*Asst Head Years 10 & 11*)
Mrs K E Whyte, BA
Mrs S Woodhead, BA
G P Woods, MA

Music:
*E M White, BA

C J Brook, BA
R McOwen, BSc
D G Roberts, LRAM, LGSM

Physics and Electronics:
*Dr P Shepherd, BEng, PhD
J D Boardman, BSc
Mrs L Leach, BA
R W Morley, BSc, MA
Miss V M Powne, BSc
O W J Theaker, MSc
I E Walker, MA (*Head of Careers*)

PE and Games:
Mrs C A Taylor, BA (*Acting Director of Sport*)
Miss D L Bloomfield, BA
Miss H E Boughton, BSc
S Darnbrough (*Rowing Coach*)
D J Dowley, BA
A J Galley, BEd
Mrs M E Harling, BSc, MA
Mrs G K Jones, BEd
S Kellett (*Cricket & Rugby Coach*)
C E Linfield, BA
J G Oakes
D R Scarbrough, BSc
B Townsend (*Swimming Coach*)
M A Wilde, BA

Politics:
*M P J Simpson, MA, DipSp
Mrs A L McOwen, BA

Psychology:
*Ms C J White, BSc

Religious Studies:
*R E Skelton, BD
M E Harling, BSc, MA
Mrs B R Reeves, BA

The Junior School:
Headmaster: N H Gabriel, BA, DipArch
Deputy Head: E M Asady, BSc

Mrs L L Alderson, BA
Mrs J S Allen, BSc
Mrs E J Green, BA
Mrs L A Hepworth-Wood, BA
Miss K L Howes, BSc, MSc
Mrs L Morris, BEd
C P Newsome, BA (*Head of Sport*)
Mrs C E Orviss, LLB
Mrs E D Rawlinson, BA
P Smales, BEd, BA
G P Smith, BEd
Miss H E Smith, BA
N J Watson, BA
Mrs A J Watts, BA
Miss D H Yates, BA

Visiting Music Teachers:
Ms A F Brown, BMus (*woodwind*)
Mrs J Bryan, GMus, CT ABRSM, LRSM (*woodwind*)
A C Cook, GLCM (*guitar*)
S Davis, MA, LTCL (*recorder*)
J P Eyre, BMus, ARCO, ATCL (*singing and organ*)
C Francis, GMus, LTCL (*upper strings*)
M Gaborak, LTCL, GDLM (*guitar*)
Ms J Harrison, GRNCM (*singing*)
Mrs E Kenwood-Herriott, GRSM, LRAM, LTCL (*double-reed instruments*)
M McGuffie, BMus (*clarinet*)
D G Roberts, LRAM, LGSM (*brass*)
A J Sherlock, BA, ALCM
B G Stevens, BA (*percussion*)

Miss A Verity, MA (*lower strings*)
A Woodrow, MA, FRCO (*singing*)

Bradford Grammar School takes pride in developing well-rounded individuals and educating pupils with the life skills that they need to achieve success in their adult lives. Its aim is to make learning a pleasure in a happy, stimulating environment and to give each student the confidence and drive to achieve their full potential.

There are currently 658 boys and 445 girls aged 6–18.

Situation and Buildings. The school stands in fine buildings and extensive grounds approximately one mile from the centre of Bradford. There are excellent transport links between the school and areas such as Wharfedale, Airedale, Leeds City Centre, Calderdale and Huddersfield.

Facilities at Bradford Grammar School include a 25m Competition Swimming Pool, a dedicated Sixth Form Centre with full Wi-Fi, a Hockney Theatre, Design Technology workshops, Computer Aided Design (CAD) Suites, Fitness Suite with rowing machines, cycling machines, treadmills and weights, a Music Auditorium, Recording Studio, Debating Chamber and dedicated Science building. The school is currently developing a state-of-the-art Library, which is due for completion in 2015. The Price Hall is the centrepiece of the main school building and provides a magnificent setting for assemblies, concerts and other major events.

Bradford Grammar Junior School occupies Clock House, a seventeenth century Manor House within the school grounds, where it enjoys its own assembly hall, Computing and Design Technology facilities and teaching accommodation. *For further details, please see separate entry in IAPS section.*

Senior School Curriculum. In Years Seven and Eight all pupils study English, Mathematics, French, German, Latin, Biology, Physics, Chemistry, Geography, History, Art, Music, Design and Technology (DT), Religious Studies (RS), Personal Development and Games.

In Year Nine pupils follow a common core of English, Mathematics, Geography, History, Physics, Chemistry, Biology, RS, Personal Development and Games, choose one core Modern Foreign Language from a choice of French, German or Spanish and choose three optional subjects from a choice of German, Russian, Latin, Greek, Art, Music, Spanish and Computer Science.

In Years Ten and Eleven pupils follow ten GCSE courses. All pupils follow a common core of English Language, English Literature, Mathematics, Biology, Chemistry, Physics, and Games, choose a core Modern Foreign Language from French, German or Spanish, and choose three optional subjects from Geography, History, German, Computer Science, Russian, Latin, Spanish, Greek, Art, Music, DT and RS.

Year 12 (Lower Sixth Form). Pupils choose four AS level subjects from Art, Biology, Business Studies, Chemistry, Classical Civilisation, DT, Economics, Electronics, English Literature, English Language, English Language and Literature, French, Further Mathematics, Geography, Geology, German, Greek, History, Computer Science, Latin, Mathematics, Music, Music Technology, Physics, Politics, Psychology, RS, Russian, Spanish and Theatre Studies. In addition, they also take two eleven-week General Studies courses from a wide range of non-examined options, or Japanese, AS Further Mathematics or the Extended Project Qualification (EPQ).

Year 13 (Upper Sixth Form). Pupils take three or four of their AS level courses through to A Level. It is possible to replace the fourth subject with another AS course. Pupils may follow a non-examinable General Studies course if they wish.

For further details please see the booklets A Guide to GCSE Courses and A Guide to Sixth Form Courses both of which can be downloaded from our website at www.bradfordgrammar.com.

Co-curricular Activities. The school strongly believes that pupils of all ages gain long term benefits from taking part in activities outside of the academic curriculum. Senior School pupils are offered an extensive range of co-curricular activities to participate in. There are many varied clubs and societies which run at lunchtimes and after school. Pupils in the Senior School currently have a choice of over 50 clubs and societies covering a wide range of sports, drama, music, academic subjects and other areas of interest. Pupils can take part in the Duke of Edinburgh's Award Scheme, the Combined Cadet Force (both RAF and Army) and World Challenge expeditions.

Pastoral Care. The Pastoral Director with her team of Year Heads and Form Teachers work closely with pupils and parents to ensure that support is available in school and at home. An extensive Peer Support scheme and a growing system of Year Group Councils are just two ways in which pupils are encouraged to take responsibility for each other and themselves in school.

Admission. Boys and girls can join the school at the ages of 6, 7, 8, 9, 10 in the Junior School or 11, 12, 13 or 16 in the Senior School. Pupils are admitted into the Sixth Form on the basis of their GCSE results, an interview and a satisfactory reference from the candidate's current school. Candidates for entry into Year 2 (6+), Year 3 (7+) and Year 4 (8+) will be invited to spend an informal day in the Junior School. Admission for all other ages is by examination in Mathematics and English in January each year.

Bursaries. Bursaries are awarded on a means-tested basis, each case being reviewed annually. The award depends on parental circumstances, the amount of capital available at the time of the examination and the academic ability of the candidate.

Fees per annum (2014–2015). Senior School £11,790; Junior School £9,225.

Old Bradfordians Association. President: Mr J R Williams, c/o Bradford Grammar School.

The Parents' Association (previously BGS Society). Chairman: Mrs L A Burke, c/o Bradford Grammar School.

Charitable status. Bradford Grammar School (The Free Grammar School of King Charles II at Bradford) is a Registered Charity, number 529113. It exists to provide education for children.

Brentwood School

Middleton Hall Lane, Brentwood, Essex CM15 8EE
Tel: 01277 243243
Fax: 01277 243299
email: headmaster@brentwood.essex.sch.uk
website: www.brentwoodschool.co.uk

Motto: '*Virtue, Learning and Manners*'.

Brentwood School was founded in 1557 and received its charter as the Grammar School of Antony Browne, Serjeant at Law, on 5th July, 1558. The Founder became Chief Justice of Common Pleas shortly before the death of Queen Mary, and was knighted a few months before his death in 1567. The Foundation Stone over the door of Old Big School was laid on 10th April, 1568, by Edmund Huddleston and his wife Dorothy, who was the step-daughter of the Founder. The Elizabethan silver seal of the School Corporation is still in the possession of the Governors. In 1622 Statutes were drawn up for the School by Sir Antony Browne, kinsman of the Founder, George Monteigne, Bishop of London, and John Donne, Dean of St Paul's.

Governors:
C J Finch, FRICS (*Chairman*)
Sir Michael Snyder, DSc, FCA, FRSA (*Vice-Chairman*)
P C Beresford, FNAEA, MARLA

Lord Black of Brentwood, MA, MCIPR, FRSA
M Bolton, MBE, BA Hons
Miss A Chapman, ACMA
Mrs S F Courage, DL
D J Elms, MA, FCA, FCSI
Professor B J W Evans, BSc Hons, PhD
Lord Flight of Worcester, MA, MBA
Mrs J M Jones, BA Hons, ARCM
M Lightowler, LLB, NP
The Venerable D Lowman, BD, AKC
Ms R Martin, MEd, NPQH
R I McLintock, MSc, DMS, DipEd
J M May, MA, LLB
Dr C Tout, MA, PhD
J Tumbridge, CC, MCIArb, LLB Hons
R J Wilson, MA, FRSA

Bursar and Clerk to the Governors: I F Bruton, BA Hons, MIOD

Headmaster: D I Davies, MA Oxon, FRSA

Second Master: D M Taylor, GRSM, LRAM, MTC, FRSA
Deputy Head: N J Carr, MA, MA EconEd, ACEM, FRSA
Deputy Head (*Pastoral*): Mrs N Jenkin, BA, MA
Deputy Head (*Academic*): J Quartermain, BA, MA MPhil

Heads of Year:
Sixth Form: Dr P Tiffen, BSc, PhD
Sixth Form Deputy Head (*Curriculum*): M McGowan, BSc
Fifth Year: Miss C Holding, BA
Fourth Year: Miss K Crane, BA
Third Year: Mrs M E Belsham, BSc
Second Year: Mr C Potter, BA
First Year: J R Brown, BA

Houses & Housemasters/mistresses:
East: J MCann, BEng
Hough: P Rees, BA & Mrs C Rees
Mill Hill: M Monro, BA & Mrs J Monro
North: S Salisbury, BA
South: C M Long, BA
Weald: S Taylor, LLB
West: Mrs L Cleaves, BA

* *Head of Department*

Art:
*Mrs M Parsons, BA
Miss N J Bixby, MA
D McAuliffe, BA, MA
Mrs S J Wells, BSc

Biology:
G Lewis, MSc
Miss J P Byrne, BSc
Mrs P Ebden, BSc, MSc
K Gray, BSc
Miss V Kerslake, BSc
M McGowan, BSc
Mrs G Robertson, BSc
Miss V Turner, BSc Hons

Business Studies:
*Miss M Sorohan, BA, MA
A Giles, BA
C A Graves, BSc
Mrs K Miller, BA
Mrs R Taker, BA

Chemistry:
*Dr A Hill, BSc, PhD
S L Gonsalves, BA
Mrs J Khush, MSc
Revd Dr A McConnaughie, BA, MA, PhD, BA
Mr R O'Rourke, BSc
A Pask, BSc

G Pye, BSc
J Seaman, BSc, CChem, MRSC

Classics:
*Mr B Clark, BA
Mrs L J Acton, BA
Miss K L Crane, BA
Miss Z Fleming, MA
Miss G Free, MA
Mrs J Gray, BA
D Hodgkinson, BA
Miss F Moore-Bridger, BA
Miss H Summerfield, BA

Computing & ICT:
*J J McCann, BEng Hons
G M Kiff, BA (*Director of Design Centre*)
Miss I Lovelock, BA
Mrs K Rajani, BSc
Miss C White, BSc Hons

Design & Technology:
*A R Eckton, BSc Hons
R T Chapman, CertEd
S Harvey, BA

Drama:
*L Jones, MA
D Brooks, BA

Mrs L Cleaves, BA

Economics:
*E Hall, BA
N J Carr, MA, MA
  EconEd, ACEM, FRSA
C A Graves, BSc
P Rees, BA
Mr S Tidball, BA

English:
*Dr S Evans, BA, PhD
Mrs H Barker, BA
Miss S Browett, BSc
Mrs M Callender, MA
Mrs S Hawkings, BA
  (*Director of Life Skills*)
Mrs S Heyn, BA
R Higgins, BA Hons
Mrs L A Hurlock, BA
R Irvine, BA
Mrs S Knowles, BEd
Miss H McMahon, BA
O Murley, BA Hons
S Salisbury, BA Hons
S Taylor, LLB

EAL:
*C Berkley, BA
Mrs E Fisher, CELTA

Food Technology:
*Mrs C Picton
Mrs B Daly, BEd
D M Taylor, GRSM,
  LRAM, MTC, FRSA

Geography:
*N S Crosby, BA
Miss G Athey, BSc
Mrs R Barford
Miss L Joseph BA Hons
C M Long, BA
J Orme, BSc

History:
*Ms B Fuller, BA
Mrs M E Belsham, BSc
C Berkley, BA
J R Brown, BA
M Clark, BA
Mrs R Coppell, MA
Mrs C Harvey, BA, PhD
Mrs J Keylock, BA
J Quartermain, BA, MA,
  MPhil
M V Willis, BA

Learning Development:
*Mrs S Heyn, BA
Mrs H Barker, BA
Mrs L Buck
Miss G Free, MA
Mrs S Knowles, BEd
Miss H McMahon, BA

Mathematics:
*Ms D Porovic, MSc
T Acton, BSc
A Barnett, BSc
T Beedell, BSc, MA
P Bolton, BSc
Mrs K Bowes, BSc
Mrs J J Coppin, BSc, MSc
A J Drake, MA
Miss J Farrow, BSc
Mrs M Hall, MSc, BA

Dr L Hubbard
J L Killilea, BEd, AIST,
  MA
B Lannigan, BSc
G J Little, MA
A Newby, BSc
J D Williams, BSc

Modern Languages:
*I Walton, MA (*German*)
Dr E Rowlands, BA, PhD
  (*French*)
Mrs C Vale, BA (*Spanish*)
Mrs J Rodgers, MSc
  (*Mandarin*)
Miss K Allen, BA
J Bowley, MA, Maîtrise,
  MIL, FCIEA, FRSA
Miss R Campbell, BA
Mrs L G M Dearmer-
  Decup, BA
Mrs F Hanley, DEUG
Mrs N Jenkin, BA, MA
Miss S Jouillerot, BA
Miss C Lacotte, DEUG
Miss A Leath, BA
Mrs I Penalver-Edwards,
  BA
R Pritchard, BA
Mrs S J Roast, BEd
Dr R M Storey, BA, PhD
Mrs M D Taylor, BA
Mrs M Watt-Jimenez, BA

Music:
Director of Music: Mrs H
  Khoo, GRSM, ARCM,
  DipRCM
F Cooper, BA
S R Rumsey, BA
W Stock, BMus

Physics:
*A Robson, MEng
Mrs N C Heelam, BSc
Dr L Hubbard BSc, MSc,
  PhD
L C Jenkins, MSc, FRAS
R O'Rourke, BSc
Dr K Stavri, BSc, PhD
J Williams, BEng

*Physical Education &
Games*:
*I Wignall, BA
W Castleman (*Rugby
  Coach*)
Miss J Bryan, BSc
Miss J Farrow, BSc
B R Hardie, NCAAC
Miss C Holding, BA
Mrs W L Juniper, BEd
M Keyte
J L Killilea, BEd, AIST,
  MA
Mrs S Knightbridge, BSc
B Lumley, BSc
C Thurston, BSc Hons

Politics:
*M V Willis, BA
J R Brown, BA
Mrs R Coppell, MA
Mrs C Harvey, BA, PhD

Psychology:
*Dr T Elder, BSc, PhD
Mrs P Ebden, BSc, MSc
M McGowan, BSc
Mrs J O'Connell, BSc

Religious Studies:
*B Clements, BA, MPhil

J Barfield, MA
Miss R Bishop, BA
Mrs S Hawkings, BA
  (*Director of Life Skills*)
R Jenkins, BA
M Monro, BA
C Potter, BA

Director of IB: J Barfield, MA
Admissions Registrar: Mrs M Henning
Headmaster's PA: Mrs S Gilder
School Medical Officer: Dr Nasif

Brentwood School is a co-educational school with a total of 1,519 pupils including 411 in the Preparatory School. The Preparatory School is fully co-educational as is the Sixth Form (of 335 pupils), but boys and girls are taught separately between the ages of 11 and 16. Boarding is available for boys and girls from 11.

Buildings and Grounds. The School occupies a 75-acre site on high ground at the northern end of the town some 20 miles north-east of London. Old Big School, the original School room, is still in regular use thus maintaining a direct link with the School's founder. Over recent years a major building programme has seen extensions to the Science and Modern Languages buildings and Dining Halls; refurbishment of the Preparatory School, Boarding Houses and Sixth Form accommodation; the building of the magnificent Brentwood School Sports Centre; a Performing Arts Centre, an all-weather pitch, an Art and Design Centre and an indoor heated swimming pool. In November 2011, HRH Prince Edward The Earl of Wessex formally opened the School's new Sixth Form Centre and Wessex Auditorium. The Sixth Form Centre, which has become the intellectual powerhouse of the School, provides an exemplary educational environment for the International Baccalaureate Diploma programme. Facilities include common rooms and private study areas, 16 additional classrooms, a dedicated computer suite and multi-purpose 400-seat auditorium.

Organisation. The School is one community within which, for good educational reasons, girls and boys are taught separately from age 11 to 16. They are encouraged to participate together in all extra-curricular activities. The Senior School is divided into Year Groups. Each Year Group has a Head of Year and Deputy who oversee it. The vast majority of pupils join the School at 11 after successfully completing our Entrance Examination. A broad curriculum is followed through the first three years and this continues through careful choice of GCSE and IGCSE subjects to the end of the Fifth Year. Entry to the Sixth Form is conditional upon success in the GCSE examinations. In the Sixth Form students take either four of the 27 AS Level subjects or follow the International Baccalaureate Diploma programme. Most go on to University. Pass rates at Advanced Level reach 100% and many pupils gain places at Oxford and Cambridge each year.

Religion. The School is an Anglican Foundation. There is a resident Chaplain and all pupils attend Chapel fortnightly. Regular Communion Services are held. Members of other faiths are welcomed and their views respected.

Boarding. There are two Boarding Houses, both of which have been thoroughly modernised. The boys reside in Hough House which can accommodate up to 42 students; the girls reside in Mill Hill House where 27 can be accommodated. The public rooms are spacious and both Houses generously staffed. Full and weekly boarding are available. A qualified Matron runs an efficient Sanatorium.

Pastoral Care. Brentwood School takes very seriously its pastoral responsibilities and provides two supportive systems. Responsibility for pastoral care is vested in the Form Tutors under the guidance of the Heads of Year and the Deputy Head, Pastoral. This system is complemented by a strong House system with Housemasters/Mistresses and

House Tutors. Partnership with parents is regarded as essential and they are encouraged to join in activities and to visit regularly.

Music, Drama and Art. Music plays an important part in the life of the School, as do Drama and Art. There are four orchestras and several ensembles and jazz groups. The Big Band is internationally acclaimed. There are at least three dramatic productions each year, together with regular Art Exhibitions.

Careers. There is an excellent University Entrance and Careers Department where students receive advice and can obtain information about courses and/or careers. Aptitude Tests; Work Experience; visits to colleges, universities and places of work; visiting speakers are all part of the provision. A careers convention is held in March each year.

CCF and CSU. All pupils either join the Combined Cadet Force or, through the Community Service Unit, engage in a wide-ranging series of activities which bring them into contact with the Community. The Duke of Edinburgh's Award Scheme runs alongside these activities.

School Societies. There are many flourishing societies covering a wide range of interests, catering for all ages. The Sir Anthony Browne Society (SABS) at Brentwood School is a society for Sixth Form pupils, which provides them with an opportunity for intellectual discussion and cultural interest.

Sports Facilities. Brentwood School was one of the official training venues for the London 2012 Games. The playing fields are part of the School complex and provide ample space for soccer, cricket, hockey, rugby and tennis. There is a world-class all-weather athletics track. The Brentwood School Sports Centre includes an indoor soccer/hockey pitch, six badminton courts, indoor cricket nets, basketball courts and a fencing salle, as well as squash courts and a fitness suite. There is a heated indoor swimming pool and an all-weather pitch. Provision is made for golf, sailing and table tennis. The two Astroturfs and netball courts are floodlit for use in winter

Preparatory School. See entry in IAPS section for details.

Entry. Entrance Examinations for both boys and girls aged 11 are held at the School in January each year. Entries are also accepted at 13 plus, following the Common Entrance Examination, vacancies permitting. Transfers at other ages are also possible. Sixth Form entry is through GCSE success, and interview.

Scholarships and Bursaries. In addition to Academic scholarships the School offers Music, Drama, Art, Sport and Choral scholarships at 11+ and for entry to the Sixth Form. These may be supplemented by means-tested Bursaries.

The School offers a considerable number of Bursaries in addition to the awards described above. Over a fifth of pupils receive such assistance.

Fees per term (2014–2015). Day £5,331; Boarding £10,463.

Old Brentwood's Society. There is a flourishing Society for pupils to stay in touch once they have left the School. The School's Alumni Relations Officer is Lucy Rome, RomeL@brentwood.essex.sch.uk

Charitable status. Brentwood School (part of Sir Antony Browne's School Trust, Brentwood) is a Registered Charity, number 310864. It is a Charitable Trust for the purpose of educating children.

Brighton College

Eastern Road, Brighton BN2 0AL

Tel:	01273 704200
	01273 704339 Head Master
	01273 704260 Bursar
	01273 704210 Prep School
	01273 704259 Pre-Prep School
Fax:	01273 704204
email:	admissions@brightoncollege.net
website:	www.brightoncollege.net

Motto: TO Δ'EY NIKATΩ (*Let the right prevail*)

The first of the Sussex public schools, Brighton College was founded in 1845 with the object of providing a 'thoroughly liberal and practical education for the sons of the local gentry in conformity with the principles of the Established Church'. With its Victorian Gothic buildings, the front quad, largely unchanged since then, has the appearance of a Cambridge court in the heart of the Kemp Town, whilst to the North of the main range many modern buildings have been added in recent years.

Over the last five years, Brighton has consistently achieved results that place the school in the top 1% of schools in England. It is for this reason that the schools has been the recipient of so many awards: The College was named 'Independent School of the Year 2011–12' by The Sunday Times, Head Master Richard Cairns was named 'Public School Headmaster of the Year 2012–13' by Tatler magazine, and Brighton was named 'United Kingdom Independent School of the Year 2013–14' at the Independent Schools Awards.

The College first admitted girls into the Sixth Form in 1973 and became fully co-educational in 1988. There are now some 875 pupils in the Upper School and 100 pupils in the Lower School, of whom a third are boarders and 40% girls. Pupils are divided into 13 houses. Pupils aged 11 were admitted to the college for the first time in August 2009.

Vice-Presidents:

The Rt Hon Sir John Chilcot	P D C Points
S J Cockburn	R J Seabrook, QC
I W Dodd	Dr A F Seldon
R F Jones	S G R Smith
Mrs J Lovegrove	C E M Snell
D A Nelson-Smith	Lady H Trafford, DSc, SRN

Chairman: Prof Lord Skidelsky, FBA

Governors:

N Abraham, CBE	The Hon Ms O Polizzi, CBE
Mrs J Aisbitt, JP	
Lady M Alexander	R Ricci
Ms J Deslandes	A J Symonds FRICS, MCI Ard
P Jackson	
Rt Hon F Maude, MP	R J S Weir, FCA, MCT
G R Miller, MBE, FCIB	P Ward
A S Pettitt	

Senior Management Team:

Head Master: R J Cairns, MA, FRSA

Director of Finance & Deputy Head (*Bursar*): P Westbrook, BA, FCA
Deputy Head: A R Bird, MSc
Deputy Head (*Common Room*): Ms A C Malloch, MSc
Deputy Head (*Pupils*): S Marshall-Taylor, BA
Deputy Headmistress (*Academic*): Mrs J A Riley, MA
Assistant Head (*Sixth Form*): D M Gabriele, MA
Assistant Head (*Middle School*): M C Sloan, BA
Assistant Head (*Lower School*): Miss L K Hamblett, MA
Assistant Head (*Co-Curriculum*): Miss N J Collins, MA
Director of Studies: J Carr-Hill, MSc (*Head of Economics*)
Director of Boarding: M I Jamieson, BA (*Housemaster, School*)
Registrar: Mrs A Withers
Director of Philanthropy: S Sheridan, BA
Director of Education, BCIS: I McIntyre

Heads of Department/Subject:
Director of Art: M J Cooper, BA
Biology: Dr B N Davies, PhD
Business Studies: Mrs S A Woodmansey, DMS, MBA
Chemistry: Dr T J Gravestock, MChem, PhD
Classics: N P Treble, MA
Director of Dance: Mrs M L Porter, BA, AISTD Dip
Design Technology: D W Currigan, MA
EAL: Ms J Dynes, BA
Economics: J Carr-Hill, MSc
English: Miss A C Smith, MA
French: Miss C Wright, BA
Geography: Miss K L Haward, BSc
German: Mrs F M Cremona, BA
Girls' Games: Ms J Langhorne, BEd
History: J A M Skeaping, BA
Director of ICT: R Ruz, MSc
Academic ICT: B L Lambe, BSc
Mandarin: T L D Godber, MA
Mathematics: G A Brocklesby, BA
Director of Music: S Chenery, MA
Academic PE: B M Frier, BSc
Physics: Dr A Baragwanath, PhD
Politics: R I Maggs, MEd
PSHE: A Wiscombe, BA
Psychology: Mrs J M Scopes, BSc
Religion & Philosophy: P Sperring, MPhil
Rugby: N Buoy, BSc
SENCO: Ms B C Walsh, BA
Spanish: R C Alvers, BA
Director of Sport: R A Nicholson, BEd
Theatre Studies: R P Messik

House Masters and Mistresses:
Abraham: P A Wilson
Aldrich: M V Lewis
Chichester: Ms E T M J Cody
Durnford: J A Cornish
Fenwick: Mrs J Hamblett-Jahn
Hampden: B M Frier
Head's: R J Grice
Leconfield: A J Merrett
New House: Mrs J M Scopes
Ryle: G J Mitchell
School: M I Jamieson
Seldon: Miss C L Davison
Williams: Ms S E Sturgeon
Lower School: Mrs K M Brown

Tutor for Admissions: C Morrissey, BA
Librarian, Head of Careers: Ms C Mayanobe, MA
Chaplain: Revd R Easton, BA, MTheol

Buildings. The College is situated in the fashionable Kemp Town district of Brighton. The original north range and Headmaster's House was designed by Gilbert Scott in 1847. The Chapel was added in 1858 and extended in 1923 as a memorial to the Old Brightonians who gave their lives in the First World War. The south and west range of boarding houses was completed to a design by Sir Thomas Jackson (an Old Brightonian) in 1886. The Great Hall (1913) and Swimming Pool are twentieth century additions. Two day boy Houses were added in September 1959. A Classroom Block was completed in 1972, and the Sports Hall in 1973. The Lester Building, for IT and Mathematics was built in 1986, and girls' day accommodation in 1990. The Hordern Room, a small theatre and concert hall was opened by Sir Michael Hordern, an Old Boy, in January 1995 as part of the College's 150th Anniversary Celebrations. A three-storey Performing Arts Centre, incorporating a Dance Studio, café and music practice rooms opened in Summer 2000.

An extensive programme of development is currently taking place which has seen many new builds win architectural awards. In 2008 the Alexander Centre for the Visual Arts and a new language laboratory opened, in 2010 the Skidelsky Building opened, home to the Lower School, a Design Technology suite and six classrooms, and the Simon Smith Building, with its new social hub and café for pupils, new medical centre and outdoor theatre space, followed in 2012, and the new sports pavilion at the college's Jubilee Ground also opened in 2012. In 2013 a new, fifth boarding house opened to meet the growing demand for boarding; 'New House' completes the east range of the quad as originally outlined in Sir Thomas Jackson's plans, and in 2015 the new Music School opens, complete with state-of-the-art recording facilities and a 150-seat Recital Hall.

The Skidelsky building, the Simon Smith building and New House all won awards from the Royal Institute of British Architects.

Admission. Pupils are admitted to the Lower Third at the age of 11 via assessments held at the College in January; to the Fourth Form between the ages of 13 and 14 via the Common Entrance examination, the Academic Scholarship examination, or by special Assessment and interview; and into the Sixth Form for a two-year A2 course, between the ages of 16 and 17, subject to a minimum of 14 points at GCSE (based on three points for an A* grade, two points for an A grade and one point for a B grade) and ideally an A grade in each subject to be studied at A Level. In all cases pupils must also produce evidence of good character and conduct from their previous school. The College Prospectus and registration form can be obtained from the Director of Admissions. A non-refundable registration fee of £120 is payable.

Entry for new Lower Third, Fourth Form and Sixth Form pupils is at the beginning of the Michaelmas Term.

Houses. Hampden, Leconfield, Aldrich, Durnford, Ryle, Chichester, Williams and Seldon are Day Houses, each with their own premises. Head's House, School House, New House, Abraham and Fenwick are Boarding Houses, which have recently had an extensive programme of refurbishment. A third of the pupils are boarders in the school. Weekly boarding is increasingly popular. Pupils may go home on Friday afternoon and return either on Sunday evening or on Monday morning.

Dyslexia Centre. The specialist Dyslexia Centre enables children who are assessed as Dyslexic, but with high intelligence, to take a suitably adjusted GCSE course within the normal College curriculum with the opportunity to proceed to A Levels in the Sixth Form.

Health. There is a Central Health Centre with a team of qualified nurses, and the Medical Officer visits regularly.

Catering. There is self-service dining room, managed by a qualified Catering Manager.

Holidays. The usual School holidays are about 3 weeks each at Christmas and Easter, and 8 weeks in the Summer. There is a half-term holiday of 1 week in all three terms.

Religion. A short morning service is held in Chapel on 2 days a week: Friday's service aims to embrace all faiths. There are services for all pupils on some Sundays to which parents and visitors are welcome. Candidates are prepared by the Chaplain for Confirmation.

Curriculum. The School is divided into 7 Forms – Lower Third, Upper Third, Fourth, Lower Fifth, Upper Fifth, Lower Sixth and Upper Sixth. In the Sixth Form some 25 subjects are available at AS or A2 level. For GCSE, pupils select their subjects – usually 10 – at the end of the Fourth Form. 98% of pupils proceed to university. Preparation for the UCAS process begins in the second term of the Lower Sixth, and pupils are guided towards appropriate choices by the Head of Sixth Form in conjunction with the individual pupil's tutor.

Sport. The College enjoys a strong record of excellence at most sports. The main playing-field (the Home Ground) is part of the College campus and the Jubilee Ground is a mile away at East Brighton Park. All pupils take part in the College's extensive games programme. The main sports for boys are rugby and cricket and for girls, netball, hockey and cricket. In addition, a host of other options are available including soccer, squash, tennis, golf, fencing, biathlon, aerobics, yoga, athletics and cross-country. There is also a flourishing Sailing Club. The College has its own indoor swimming pool.

Service. All pupils from the Lower Fifth onwards are expected to participate in a service activity on one afternoon a week. Pupils may participate in charity work or, in the Sixth Form, Community Service; alternatively they may join the Duke of Edinburgh's Award Scheme or enter one of the 3 sections of the CCF.

Music. One in three pupils learns at least one musical instrument. There is a strong musical tradition and pupils reach a very high level of performance. The Choir, Chamber Orchestra, Symphony Orchestra, Concert Band and Swing Band perform regularly both inside and outside the College. There are several Chamber groups, and the Choral Society and Orchestra usually perform major works at the annual Brighton Festival.

Drama. The College has a strong tradition of excellence in drama. There are opportunities for anyone to be involved and the College stages plays ranging from Tudor Interludes through Shakespeare, Restoration comedy and twentieth century classics. In addition to the regular calendar of a musical, Sixth Form studio production, Sixth Form play, Fourth Form play, Lower School play and House Drama festival, there are also many productions mounted entirely by pupils. There is also a junior Drama Club.

Activities. Creative activities are encouraged both in and out of school time, and the College has its own Art School and Gallery where exhibitions by leading Artists are regularly staged. Dance is an increasingly popular activity with many pupils performing in regional and national productions.

Careers. Ms Cecile Mayanobe heads a team of tutors who advise pupils on careers. The College is a member of the Independent Schools Careers Organisation.

Scholarships and Bursaries. The following awards are offered annually:

Academic Scholarships to pupils entering the College at age 11 and 13. Entries must be in by early January for 11+ and late February for 13+.

A number of scholarships and exhibitions will be offered each year to candidates showing outstanding ability in *Art, Chess, Choral, Dance, Drama, DT, Music and Sport*. Examinations and interviews will be held at the College in January (Art, Choral, Dance and Music), February (Sport), April (Chess, Drama and DT) for candidates intending to enter the College at 13+ in the following September. The value and number of the awards will depend on the calibre of the candidates.

All-Rounder Scholarships are available for entry at 11+ and 13+. Examinations and interviews will be held at the College in January (11+) and April (13+) for candidates intending to enter the College the following September. The value and number of the awards will depend on the calibre of the candidates.

Sixth Form entry Scholarships: Academic – Candidates sit a general paper, Maths and English papers, a Verbal Reasoning or EAL paper, and attend two interviews. Scholarships are also available for Sport and Expressive Arts (Art, Dance, Drama, DT and Music). All examinations take place mid-November with entries by 31st October.

The *Old Brightonian Bursary*, worth £1,000 per term, is available to a child or grandchild of an Old Brightonian who might otherwise be unable to afford independent education.

Further particulars can be obtained from the Director of Admissions.

Fees per term (2014–2015). Full Boarders £10,720–£11,320; Weekly Boarders £9,730–£10,020; Day Pupils £4,900–£7,080.

The Old Brightonians, the College's alumni network, has annual dinners and a number of flourishing sports clubs.

Preparatory School. The College has its own fully co-educational Prep School with a Pre-Preparatory department. (*For details see entry in IAPS section.*)

Charitable status. Brighton College is a Registered Charity, number 307061. It exists for the purpose of educating boys and girls.

Bristol Grammar School

University Road, Bristol BS8 1SR
Tel: 0117 973 6006
Fax: 0117 946 7485
email: headmaster@bgs.bristol.sch.uk
website: www.bristolgrammarschool.co.uk

Motto: '*Ex Spinis Uvas.*'

'The Grammar School in Bristowe' existed under a lay master in 1532 in which year, under a charter of Henry VIII, it was endowed with the estates of St Bartholomew's Hospital by the merchant and geographer Robert Thorne and others. The trust was placed in the care of the Corporation of Bristol and then the Trustees of the Bristol Municipal Charities. In September 2004 the School incorporated as a company limited by guarantee with registered charitable status and is now governed under Memorandum and Articles of Association approved by the Charity Commission in 2004.

Co-educational since 1980, today BGS provides a wide-ranging and challenging education for boys and girls aged between 11 and 18, while BGS Infants and Juniors, based on the same site, caters for those in the 4–11 age range.

Governors:
N Reeve, FCA (*Chairman*)
Mrs A J Arlidge, BA
Mr A Barr, LLB
Mrs B Bates, BA, MA, FRSA
Mrs K Case, CertEd
N Dawes, BSc Hons
N Fitzpatrick, BA, FIA, AllMR, FRSA
M Hill, BSc, FCA
Dr J D Knox, BSc, PhD
W Lee, MA, MBA, FIA
Dr J O'Gallagher, MBChB, MRCP, FRCPCH, FHEA
N Pickersgill, BSc, FCA
Prof D Stoten, BSc, PhD, DEng, CEng, FIMechE
R Vaitilingam, BA Hons Oxon, MBE
M Wilson, BSc Hons, MRICS

Senior Leadership Team:

Headmaster: R I MacKinnon, BSc

Headmaster, BGS Infants and Juniors: P R Huckle, BA, MEd
Deputy Head: P R Roberts, BSc, MSc
Deputy Head: M Bennett, BSc
Bursar: G Mitchell

Assistant Head: Miss F A Ripley, BSc
Assistant Head: P Z Jakobek, BEd
Assistant Head: Dr A J Dimberline, BSc, PhD
Assistant Head: R M Sellers, BSc
Assistant Head: D J Stone, BSc
Assistant Head: Dr M G Ransome, BA, PhD
Assistant Head: J S Harford, BSc
Assistant Head: Mrs K Jones, BSc
Assistant Head: O L Chambers, BSc

* *Head of Department*

Art:
Mrs B D Barnacle, BA
Mrs S Cooper, BA
P Z Jakobek, BEd
*J Lever, MA
Mrs J Troup, BA

Biology:
M Bennett, BSc
A Bolton, BA
Mrs R Cullen, BSc
Ms N A Diamond, BSc
  (*Head of House*)
N S Fuller, BSc, MSc,
  CBiol, MIBiol
A J Goodland, BSc
  (*Director of Studies*:
  Year 8)
J S Harford, BSc (*Director
  of Sixth Form*)
*B Schober, MA, BSc
Ms K Surry, MA

Careers:
Mrs M L Guy, CertEd
Mrs D Dutton, MA

Chemistry:
Mrs E Feasey, MSCI
Mrs A Hutchings, BSc
  (*Head of SPD*)
A Nalty, MSc
Dr H Rowlands, BSc, PhD
D J Stone, BSc
*Dr J Stone, BSc, PhD

Classics:
Miss E Cox, BA
*A J Keen, BA
G C King, MA, BA
Mrs L Ray, BA
D Watkins, BA

Dance:
*Mrs K White, BA

Design & Technology:
M Hilliard, BSc (*Head of
  House*)
Ms L-J Knights, BA
P Thomas, BA
*P M Whitehouse, BSc

Drama:
*Mrs R Johnson, BEd
L MacKenzie, BA
Mrs J Walker, BA

*Economics/Business
  Studies*:
Mrs S Biggin, BA
A J Catchpole, BSc (*Head
  of House*)
*J Williams, BSc

English:
*D L Briggs, BA
A J Jamison, BA
Mrs C V Maddock, BA,
  MEd
D S Mair, BA
Mrs C Sapsford, BA, MEd
Miss S Thomas, MA
Mrs J Whitehead, BAmS
E Yemenakis, BA
Mrs E Young, BA

EPQ:
*Mrs R Le Poer Trench,
  BSc

Food & Nutrition:
*Mrs L Bolton, Cert Ed
  Food & Nutrition

Geography:
Mrs R Atkins, BSc
Dr A J Dimberline, BSc,
  PhD
*Mrs J L Foster, BSc
L Goodman, BA (*Head of
  House*)
Mrs R Le Poer Trench, BSc
A J Short, BSc

History:
Ms S Bassett, BA
Miss E Dow, BA
O R T Edwards, BA (*Head
  of House*)
Miss L Fulton, BA
*N W Haines, BA, MA
Miss A Humphrey, BA
Mrs P Lobo, BA
Dr R A Massey, BA, PhD
  (*Director of Scholars
  and Academic
  Challenge*)

*Information Technology/
  Computing*:
G S Clark, BSc (*Head of
  Year*)
*Mrs A Finney, BA
R S Jones, BSc
I Jones, BSc

Learning Support:
Mrs J Benn
Mrs A Denny, MA
*Dr M G Ransome, BA,
  PhD

Mathematics:
C Armstrong, BSc
J Carr, BSc
O L Chambers, BSc
B Fellows, MEng
Mrs L Hancock, BSc
G R Iwi, MSc
Mrs K H Jones, BSc
Miss H Klimach, MSc
Miss A Niamir, BSc
*Miss S M Poole, BSc
P R Roberts, BSc, MSc
A Thackray, BSc
Miss J Wall, BSc

Modern Languages:
*Miss E Corrigan, BA
  (*Head of French*)
*R J Hawkins, BA (*Head
  of Russian*)
Miss C M Höelzer, MA
Mrs C Kent, BA
*Mrs A C Macro, BA
  (*Head of Spanish*)
Mrs A Pestell, BA
Dr M G Ransome, BA,
  PhD
Mrs D M G Swain, BA
Miss E J Vance, BA
*J Wall, BA (*Head of
  German*)

Miss M Whatmough, Hons
Ms L E Williamson, BA

Music:
Mrs A O Bassett, BMus
*Miss E Dobson, BA, MA
*R T Osmond, MA

PE/Games:
K R Blackburn, BSc
Mrs V L Dixon, BEd
P Z Jakobek, BEd
Mrs R E John, BA
*Mrs S A Johnson, BA
  (*Head of PE*)
L R King, BSc
Miss L Lewis, BA
Miss F A Ripley, BSc
Miss H Rhodes, BSc
Miss L Sampson, MSc,
  LABAN

PA to Headmaster: Miss C Davies

B Scott, BEd (*Head of
  House*)
*R M Sellers, BSc
  (*Director of Sport*)
Miss R Wintle, Hons

Physics:
S Carruthers, BSc
Miss L Glenn, BEng
*S Harper, BSc
R Jervis, MEng
Dr C A Rosser, BSc, PhD

Psychology:
Mrs K E Alexander, BSc,
  BA
*Mrs L Dilley, BSc

Religious Studies:
A Gunawardana, BA
Miss I M Milburn, BA
*R M Smith, BA
C P Wadey, MA

Bristol Grammar School is a day school with c 1,000 students aged between 11 and 18. Students learn in an atmosphere that motivates them to enjoy their education and as a result BGS has a deserved reputation as one of the leading academic schools in the South West. The School has a friendly and lively environment and students are encouraged to make the most of the wide-ranging opportunities available to them. Students joining at age 11 have their form rooms in the Princess Anne Building. This helps ease the transition to senior school, as well as providing an important opportunity for the year group to bond socially. This continues up the School with each year group allocated form rooms, based in separate, self-contained buildings, although teaching is spread throughout the School's specialist facilities.

Close to the city centre and adjacent to the University, Bristol Grammar School is well placed to take advantage of the city's many amenities. It is also committed to a continuing programme of investment to ensure its own facilities continue to offer the best possible opportunities to its students.

The Houses. The School is divided into six Houses, each organised by a Head of House, with the assistance of a Deputy Head of House and House Tutors. Older students become leaders within their House, whilst social, theatrical, musical, sporting and other opportunities allow those from all year-groups to work together in a friendly and cooperative atmosphere. As well as providing continuity of pastoral care and enhancing school/home links, the Houses operate as families within the school community, encouraging a real sense of belonging amongst students.

Curriculum. The school takes note of the National Curriculum but, in keeping with its academic ethos and focus on every learner being enabled to make the most of their individual ability, a far wider range of subjects and opportunities is offered. Setting is used in Maths, Science and some Modern and Classical languages to ensure optimal individual progress, but there is no streaming. In Year 7 all students follow a curriculum which includes English, Mathematics, Science, French, Spanish, History, Geography, Technology, Food & Nutrition, ICT, Latin, Religious Studies, Art, Textiles, Music, Drama, Dance and Physical Education. In Year 8 the core curriculum is continued but students are offered a further choice of languages to include German and Russian. In Year 9 students personalise their curriculum and make choices from all subjects studied thus far and other areas such as Classical Civilisation, Greek, Business Studies and Computing. From this broad base students choose their GCSE options. At the end of Year 11, most students take 10

GCSEs drawn from the core subjects of English, Mathematics, Science, a Humanities subject and a Modern Foreign Language, together with a selection of other subjects, chosen from a carefully balanced range of options.

BGS currently offers the IGCSE in Mathematics, English Language, English Literature, the Sciences, Geography, History, French, German, Spanish, Business Studies and Food & Nutrition. The Sixth Form provides a flexible range of A Level options chosen from English (Language, Literature and AS Creative Writing), Mathematics and Further Mathematics, the Sciences, Technology, French, German, Russian, Spanish, Latin, Greek, Classical Civilisation, History, Geography, Economics, Business Studies, Computing, ICT, Psychology, Religious Studies (Philosophy and Ethics), Theatre Studies, Sports Studies, Art (including Theatre Design), Music and Food & Nutrition. In addition, many students prepare for the Extended Project Qualification and Gold Duke of Edinburgh's Award; all students follow enrichment courses and attend a richly diverse programme of weekly lectures by visiting speakers; and many attend enrichment lessons to support university preparation for Russell Group and Oxbridge and including such as Medicine, Veterinary Science and Law. A highly-experienced careers and HE advisor guides students to proceed to a wide range of faculties at universities in the UK and abroad, with the majority securing places at their first-choice universities.

There are frequent opportunities for parents to consult Form Tutors, Heads of Houses and Heads of Year and regular meetings are held for parents to meet the teaching staff. The School also has three teachers to support students with SEN (including dyslexia and EAL).

Games. The games options, which vary with different age groups, include Rugby, Hockey, Football, Cross-Country, Cricket, Athletics, Swimming, Golf, Tennis, Rounders, Netball and weight training. Facilities for Orienteering, Aerobics, Climbing, Dance, Judo, Fencing, Badminton and Squash are available. There is a Pavilion and extensive playing fields at Failand, which include an all-weather netball and Tennis area and two Astroturf hockey pitches. Below the Sixth Form, all students, unless excused for medical reasons, participate in School games; the full range of sports is available to the Sixth Form on a voluntary basis. Major sports tours are run on a three year cycle: recent destinations have been New Zealand, South America and South Africa.

Activities and Societies. Students take part in a wide-ranging programme of activities (for some years this forms part of the compulsory curriculum) and there are many clubs and societies at lunchtimes and after school. There are flourishing choirs and orchestras; tuition can be arranged in a large number of instruments. Drama productions are regularly staged by different age levels of the School and by the Houses. Ski trips are offered each year. Regular excursions are made abroad, as well as cultural exchange visits, including Japan and Russia. Students may join the Duke of Edinburgh's Award Scheme in Year 10 and there is an active Community Service Unit. Overseas expeditions take place every two years and have recently visited Mongolia, Ecuador, India, Peru and Arctic Norway.

Admission. Entry to the School is normally in September at age 11+ following a satisfactory performance in the entrance examination held in the previous spring and a creditable school report or reference. In addition, all applicants are invited in to meet with a member of staff to discuss their school work, interests and hobbies. An additional 10–15 places become available each year at age 13+, with a further 20–25 places at 16+. Students may be accepted into the school during any term subject to the availability of places.

Applications should be made to the Recruitment Office at the School. Prospective entrants and their families are always welcome to visit the School. Please see the website for information about Open Days, Tours and Taster Days.

Bursaries. The School's Assisted Places Scheme is able to offer substantial financial assistance towards the fees of able students whose parents have limited means. The scheme is kept under regular review by the Governors who constantly seek to extend it. The School became a member of the Ogden Bursary Scheme in 2000.

Scholarships. Scholarships are available for entry at 11+ and 13+ and are awarded for academic ability; all applicants who sit the entrance examinations in January are automatically considered for these, there is no separate exam. Mathematics and Science Pople Scholarships are available at 14+ and 16+ and there is a separate exam for these. Scholarships are also available at 11+ and 13+ for Sports and Creative and Performing Arts.

The School runs a Scholars Programme designed to meet the educational needs of its most gifted students. This programme offers extended individual learning opportunities, group activities and mentoring in and out of School by the Director of Scholars. At 16+ students may apply to become Subject Scholars and work more closely with Heads of Subject.

Fees per term (2014–2015). Senior School £4,365. Juniors: Years 3–6 £2,960. Infants: Years 1 & 2 £2,750, Reception £2,325. Fees include the cost of most textbooks and stationery and lunch for Reception to Year 11 pupils.

BGS Infants and Juniors. The Junior School has now extended its provision to include infants, with its first Reception class in Sept 2010. The School admits children from 4–11 and is housed in its own buildings on the same site as the Senior School. (*For further details see entry in IAPS section.*)

Old Bristolians Society. Close contact is maintained with former students through the Old Bristolians Society whose honorary secretary can be contacted at the School.

Charitable status. Bristol Grammar School is a Registered Charity, number 1104425. It has existed since 1532 to provide an education for Bristol children.

Bromsgrove School

Worcester Road, Bromsgrove, Worcestershire B61 7DU
Tel: 01527 579679
Fax: 01527 576177
email: admissions@bromsgrove-school.co.uk
website: www.bromsgrove-school.co.uk
Twitter: @bromsschool
Facebook: /bromsgroveschool

Motto: '*Deo Regi Vicino.*'

The date of the School's Foundation is unknown but it was re-organised by Edward VI in 1553 and was granted a Royal Charter 6 years later. It was refounded in 1693 by Sir Thomas Cookes, Bt, at the same time as Worcester College, Oxford (formerly Gloucester Hall). The link between School and College has been maintained ever since.

Patron: A Denham-Cookes

President: V S Anthony, BSc, Hon DEd, Hon FCP, FRSA

A Vice-President: J M Baron, TD, MA
A Vice-President: Prof Sir Michael Drury, OBE, FRCP, FRCGP, FRACGP
A Vice-President: J A Hall, FCA
A Vice-President: N J Birch, MIMechE
A Vice-President: Prof K B Haley, BSc, PhD, FIMA, CMath, FIEE, CEng
A Vice-President: T M Horton, BA
A Vice-President: G R John, CBE

Governing Body:
S Towe, CBE (*Chairman*)
R D Brookes, FRICS
J Dillon
A Hodge, LLM (*Vice Chair*)

Miss F Horden
R Lane, MA
Dr C Lidbury
M Luckman
R G Noake, FCA, FCCA
Prof J G Perry, BEng, MEng, PhD, FICE, MAPM
T D Pile, BA
G Strong
Dr N Venning, BSc, PhD, MBA
D Walters, MA, FCA

Company Secretary: J Sommerville, MA

Headmaster: P Clague, BA, MBA

Bursar: Mrs L Brookes, ACMA
Deputy Headmaster: P St J Bowen, BA, PGCE
Assistant Head: Miss R M Scannell, BA, PGCE
Second Deputy (*Academic*): P S Ruben, BSc, MPhil, MBA
Second Deputy (*Co-Curricular*): P S T Mullan, BA, PGCE
Director of Staffing (*Whole School*): S Challoner, BSc, PGCE
School Medical Officer: Dr D Law MA, MBChB Oxon, MRCGP, DRCOG, DFFP
Head of Foundation: Mrs J E Rogers, BA, MSc

Staff:
* *Head of Department*
† *Houseparent*

Mrs C P M Maund, BSc, PGCE (*Assistant Pastoral Head*)
S J Kingston, BEd (*Examinations Secretary*)
Mrs C E Turner, BA, PGCE
C A Dowling MA Cantab, PGCE (*Chemistry; Academic Database Coordinator; President of the Common Room*)
Dr M R Werrett, GRSC, PhD, PGCE (*Senior Mistress*)
†M A Stone, BEng, ACGI, PGCE
†Mrs J A Holden, MA Oxon, PGCE
Mrs K Linehan, BA, MA, PGCE (*English*)
Mrs S Shinn, BSc, PGCE (*Timetabler; Head of Upper Fourth Form; Head of GCSEs*)
Dr A R Johns, BSc, PhD, PGCE (*Head of Sixth Form – Pupil Progress*)
Ms S J Cronin, BA, DMS, PGCE (*Business Studies*)
Mrs F K Bateman, BSc, PGCE (*Head of Lower Sixth Form; *Sixth Form Enrichment Curriculum*)
J W B Brogden, BA, PGCE
Mrs S E Ascough, BSc, PGCE (*i/c DofE, Head of Fifth Form*)
Miss K E Tansley, BA, MA, PGCE
†D G Wilkins, BA, SCITT (*Senior Day Houseparent*)
M A C Beet, MA Cantab, PGCE (*Modern Languages; i/c Oxbridge*)
Miss F E Diver, BA, PGCE (*Head of Lower Fourth Form, *Geography*)
†Miss Z L Leech, BA (*PSHE, *UCAS*)
N C J Riley, BSc, PGCE (*Mathematics*)
Mrs E L E Buckingham, BA (*Girls' PE & Games*)
Miss S A Franks, BSc, PGCE
Miss M M Smith, BA, PGCE (*Spanish*)
†Mrs T L Helmore, BA, PGCE
R O Knight, MA Oxon, ARCO (*Assistant Director of Music*)
A D Langlands, BSc, PGCE (*Academic PE, Master i/c Hockey*)
O A Matthews, BEng, PGCE (*Design and Technology*)
Dr M Thompson, BSc, PhD, MInstP, PGCE (*IB Coordinator*)
R Watkins, BA, PGCE (*French*)
Mrs T James, BA, PGCE (*Drama*)
Revd P Hedworth, BEd, BA (*Chaplain*)
Mrs J L Spearing, BA, PGCE (*Critical Thinking*)
Dr M K Ruben, BA, PhD, PGCE (*Gifted and Talented*)
Miss L E McCutcheon, BA
Miss S J McWilliams, BA, PGCE
Miss S Morgans, BA, PGCE, DipND (*Art*)

Mrs I Peric Crnko, BEd
Dr J May, BSc, PhD, PGCE
Ms J Comley, MSc, BA, PGCE
G N Delahunty, BA, PGCE (*Politics*)
Ms E L Densem, BA, PGCE
†H Bell, MA, PGCE
†A McClure, BA, PGCE (*Classics*)
Mrs S James, BSc, PGCE
Miss L McKee, BA, PGCE
Miss J Zafar, BA, PGCE (*History*)
S Broadbent, BA, QTS
Mrs C Wedelich-Niedzwiedz, BMus, PGCE
Ms K Garratt, MA
†G George, BSc, PGCE (*Boys' PE & Games*)
D Tamplin, BSc, PGCE
D Whiting, BSc, GTP (*Physics*)
†J D Jones, MA (*i/c Extended Project Qualification, Senior Boarding Houseparent*)
Mrs M Parkinson, BA, PGCE
†Mrs A George, BA
†Mrs T Tweddle, BSc, CertEd FE
Mrs K Hands, BA, PGCE (*Religious Studies*)
Mrs H Barton, BA, PGCE
†D Fallows (*Director of Cricket*)
Mrs J Golightly, BA
Miss R Keys, BA, PGCE (*Economics*)
S Phennah, BEd
Ms G Tyrrell, BA, PGCE
D Williams, BA, PGCE
A Carrington-Windo (*Director of Rugby*)
Miss L Davenport, BSc, PGCE
Miss F J Hardy, BA, PGCE
Mrs L I Rogers, BA, PGCE
Miss J Law, BSc, PGCE
S Noble, BSc, PGCE
N Philips, BSc, MResearch, QTS
Miss A Baker, BA, PGCE NQT
J Baldrey, BA, PGCE, NQT
M Banwell, MBE, PGCE, MEng (*i/c CCF*)
Mrs L Blain, BEng, PGCE (*i/c DofE Silver*)
Miss E Harper, BA, PGCE
A Helmore, BA, MA, PGCE
J Holdsworth, BSC, PGCE, NQT
Miss E Johnston, BSc, PGCE
Miss J Lesniak, BA, PGCE, NQT
S Matthews, BA, PGCE
Mrs D Sutherland, BA, HDipMaths, QTS
Miss J Williams, BA, PGCE
J McKelvey, BA, PGCE (*Director of Music*)
V Dal, BSc, PGCE
†Mrs K Hannah, BA, PGCE
T Clinton, BSc
Mrs J Boonnak, BA, MA, PGCE
L Mullan, BSc, PGCE
Mrs A Buckley, MA, PGCE
Miss L Hunter, BA, PGCE
M Giles, BSc, PGCE
Miss K Rankin, MA
Miss L Harrison, BA, PGCE
J Bates, BSc
Miss Brain, BSc, PGCE
Mrs G Bruce, BA, PGCE
Dr P Chatwin, BSc, PhD, PGCE
Miss C Chinn, BSc
Miss R Green, BSc, PGCE (*Science*)
Ms G Hanson, BA, PGCE
S Higgins, BEd
Miss N Langford, BA, GTTP
A Laskowski, BSc, MSc, PGCE
Miss F McCanlis, BMus, PGCE
H Pothecary, BSc, PGCE
Miss C Roye, BSc
Miss R Simmons, BA

Dr R Whitehead, MA, PhD
Mrs G Wright, BSc, PGCE (*Biology*)

Houses and Houseparents:
Boarding:
Elmshurst (*Boys*): D Fallows
Housman Hall (*Sixth Form*): J Jones
Mary Windsor (*Girls*): Mrs T Tweddle
Oakley (*Girls*): Mrs T L Helmore
Wendron-Gordon (*Boys*): H Bell

Day:
Hazeldene (*Girls*): Mrs L Rogers
Lupton (*Boys*): A L McClure
Lyttelton (*Boys*): Mr G George
School (*Boys*): Mrs J Holden
Thomas Cookes (*Girls*): Mrs K Hannah
Walters (*Boys*): D G Wilkins

Music Staff:
J McKelvey, BA, PGCE (*Director of Music*)
R O Knight, MA Oxon, ARCO (*Assistant Director of Music*)
Miss S Hyland BA, PGCE (*Music, Preparatory School*)
Miss F McCanlis, BMus, PGCE
Mrs J Russell, BA, PGCE

Visiting Music Staff:
P Badley., LLCM TD, ALCM, LLCM, FLCM, GLCM (*Voice*)
N Barry, GGSM, LTCL (*Piano*)
Miss H Bool, GBSM, ABSM, BTech Nat (*Percussion*)
M Broadhead, LTCL, DipTCL (*Cello*)
R Bull (*Guitar*)
T Bunting, BA (*Double Bass, Bass Guitar*)
Mrs S Chatt, GBSM (*Percussion*)
W Coleman, BA, LTCL (*Singing*)
J Dunlop, BA, GBSM, ABSM (*Flute*)
Mrs K Fawcett, BA, PG Dip (*Viola, Violin*)
A Gittens, BTec, HND (*Electric Guitar*)
Mrs J A Hattersley, CT ABRSM, LRSM (*Brass*)
Mrs J Hiles, GBSM, ABSM (*Flute*)
Ms A Kazimierczuk GBSM, ABSM, (*Singing*)
T Martin, BA, Dip ABRSM (*Saxophone*)
M Pearce, BMus, MA (*Clarinet*)
Mrs C Price, BA (*Violin*)
M Roberts, BA Music (*Trumpet*)
D Scally, MA, BMus, LTCL, Dip CSM (*Piano*)
Ms F Swadling, BA, ABSM, GBSM, (*Head of Strings, Viola, Violin,*)
A D C Thayer, MA, BMus, PG Dip (*Piano*)
Mrs K Thompson, PG Dip RNCM, PPRNCM (*Piano*)

Preparatory & Pre-Preparatory School

Headmistress: Mrs J Deval-Reed, BEd

Deputy Head: J Wingfield, BA, PGCE
Second Deputy: S J P Loone, MEd, BA, BTheol, PGCE, NPQH (*Religious Education*)
Director of Studies: Mrs K Ison, BEd

Mrs P Barton, CertEd
Mrs R Boardman, BA, PGCE (*Spanish*)
M Burchett, BSc, MSc, PGCE (*Resident Tutor Page House*)
Mrs G Butler, BEd (*Head of Year 3*)
Miss S Cadwallader, BA, PGCE (*Head of Year 6*)
W R Caldwell, BA, MA, MEd, PGCE (*Senior Master, *Latin*)
Miss S Cartwright, BSc, PGCE (*Science*)
G Clark, BEd (*Head of Year 7*)
Mrs C Evans, BEd
Mrs T Faulkner-Petrova, BA, BSc, MSc, PGCE
Mrs K Finnegan, BA, PCGE (*French*)
Mrs M Ford, BA, PGCE
Mrs C Goodall BA, PGCE

J P Grumball, BSc, PGCE
Miss N Harris, BSc, MSc, PGCE (*Mathematics*)
G Jones, BA, PGCE (*Boys' PE*)
Mrs S Keynes, BA, OTS
C D Kippax, BA, PGCE (*MFL*)
Mrs E Lalley, BA, PGCE
Mrs R Laurenson, BA, PGCE
Mrs C M Leather, BSc, PGCE (*Staff Appraisal and Training, joint i/c Activity Programme*)
Mrs S M Lewis, BA, PGCE
Mrs E Mullan, BEd (*Head of Year 8, *PSCHE*)
D Pover, BA, PGCE
Miss A Purver, BA, PGCE (*History*)
Miss A Read, BTec, BA, PGCE
Miss C Roskell, BEng, PGCE
Mrs J C Russell, BA, PGCE
Mrs S Stocker, BA
P Sutherland, HD Ed (*Design & Technology, Assistant Houseparent Page House*)
M J Turner, BSc, PGCE
Mrs S Webley, BSc, PGCE, MEd
Mrs J Weller, BMus, PGCE (*Girls' PE*)
†Mrs R Whiting, BA, PGCE (*Head of Year 5, *Gifted and Talented*)
R Widdop, BA, DipSpPsy (*Geography*)
Mrs N R Wingfield, BEd (*Head of Year 4*)
Miss V Ziar, MA, BA, PGCE, BIAD (*Art*)

Boarding House and Houseparents:
Page (*boys and girls*): G George & Mrs A George

Pre-Preparatory Staff:
Deputy Head (*Pastoral*), *Head of Pre-Preparatory Department*: B Etty-Leal, BSc
Deputy Head (*Academic*): Mrs K Western, BEd
Joint Head of Nursery/EYFS: Mrs S Symonds, BA

Mrs C S Abraham, BA, MA, QTS
Mrs C Cattell, BA, PGCE (*Head of Year 1*)
Mrs C Dunlop, BEd (*Head of Reception*)
Mrs L Finlay, HDip Ed (*Head of Year 2*)
Mrs R Ivison, BA, PGCE
Mrs S Kennard, BA, PGCE
Miss E Lewis, BA Ed
Mrs J Lockhart, BEd
Mrs M Martin, BA, GTP
Mrs J Townsend, BA, PGCE (*Joint Head of Nursery*)

Location. This co-educational boarding and day school is situated some 13 miles north of the Cathedral City of Worcester and an equal distance south of Birmingham. Birmingham International Airport and Station are a 20-minute drive by motorway. The M5, M6, M42 and M40 motorways provide easy access to the School.

The School stands in 100 acres of grounds on the south side and within walking distance of the market town of Bromsgrove.

Facilities. The school's £25 million building and development programme since 1994 has included a major new sports complex including an eight badminton court sized sports hall, dance studios, gym, teaching rooms and hospitality suite / sports viewing room. These new facilities enhance the existing all-weather, floodlit sports facilities. Other recently completed building projects include a state-of-the-art Library and Resources Centre, extensions to the Maths and Modern Languages facilities, an award winning Art, Design and Technology Building and a new Humanities building. Eighteen new and refurbished Science laboratories were completed in 2010. Boarding facilities have been enhanced by one completely new girls' boarding house and total refurbishment of the existing boys' and girls' houses to a very high standard. New wings have been being built at the off-campus Sixth Form boarding house, Housman Hall, and the existing building, formerly home of OB and poet A

E Housman, has been sympathetically refurbished. A new dining hall is now under construction.

Boarding. Nearly half of Bromsgrove Senior School's pupil body is made up of boarders accommodated between five houses, one of which is in the town. Loyalty to House and the traditions attendant upon it are significant factors of life at Bromsgrove. The boarding environment is happy, stable, disciplined and nurturing. House competition, day and boarding, from sport to drama, music to debating is keen.

The stability and continuity that enable boarders to thrive are provided by resident houseparents (all academic members of staff) and their families, assistant houseparents, house mothers and a team of house-based tutors. All meals are taken centrally in the School except in the case of the evening meal at Housman Hall.

Numbers. There are 950 pupils in the Senior School, of whom 545 are boys. The Preparatory, Pre-Preparatory and Nursery School has a further 700 pupils aged 3 to 13. (*See also Preparatory & Pre-Preparatory School entry in IAPS section.*)

Curriculum. In the Preparatory School and throughout the first year in the Senior School a broadly based curriculum is followed. In addition to the usual academic subjects time is given to Art, Music, ICT, Drama, Design Technology and to a full programme of Physical Education. Languages on offer include French, German, Spanish and Latin.

As pupils move up the School other options become available and some narrowing of the curriculum is inevitable. 11 subjects is the norm at GCSE, with a broad core including the three separate sciences and a further three optional subjects chosen, including if a pupil wishes the AS Level Extended Project. The minimum qualification for entry for a full programme of study in the Sixth Form is eight B grades at GCSE. Pupils may study the IB Diploma or take the A Level route and a BTEC course in Sports Performance and Excellence is also on offer. Flexibility in timetabling aims to ensure that all pupils' subject choices are catered for whatever the combination. Many subjects are available including, Art, Biology, Business, Chemistry, Classics, Design, Drama, Economics, English, French, Geography, German, Graphics, ICT, Latin, Mathematics and Further Mathematics, Music, Physical Education, Physics, Politics, Religious Studies, Spanish and Textiles. Under the IB umbrella, Italian, Environmental Systems, Mandarin and Psychology are also on offer. Over 90% stay on after Year 11 for the Sixth Form and virtually all of these pupils proceed to degree courses at university.

Music. Music flourishes as important and integral parts of the School's activities both within and outside the formal curriculum under the leadership of James McKelvey. House Music Competitions fill four afternoons, Pop & Jazz Festival two evenings and Music Scholars hold concerts twice a year. There is plenty of scope for involvement in the School Orchestra and String, Wind and Brass Ensembles, Chamber Groups, Jazz & Swing Bands, a 50-strong Chapel Choir and large Choral Society. The Music School has three floors of practice, rehearsal and concert space along with a large soundproofed recording studio for drummers and rock musicians.

The timetable is sufficiently flexible to allow special arrangements to be made for outstanding musicians. The Chapel Choir is used for broadcasts and toured major venues in New York summer 2010. Visits to St George's Chapel Windsor Castle, York Minster and St Paul's Cathedral to sing Evensong and a Senior production of Cats were recent highlights.

School musicians took part in the final gala concert of Bromsgrove Festival's 50th year at Worcester Cathedral, where they performed with the English Symphony Orchestra. The 120-strong Choral Society performed Haydn's Creation in the splendour of Birmingham Town Hall. The performing arts are well supported at Bromsgrove School and rightly thrive.

Careers. The school employs a fully qualified, full-time careers advisor and a comprehensive careers counselling programme is pursued for pupils of all ages.

Reports and Consultation. Pupils receive grades and tutor comments twice a term and there are regular reports and parents' evenings. Supervision is shared by Houseparents and House Tutors, whom parents may meet informally by appointment. There are regular parent-teacher evenings. Parents may arrange appointments to meet members of the Careers Department.

Extra-Curricular Activities. A wide range of sports and activities is offered, giving opportunities to participate at a competitive level in Rugby, Hockey, Netball, Athletics, Badminton, Basketball, Clay Pigeon shooting, Cricket, Cross-Country, Debating, Fencing, Golf, Rounders, Soccer, Squash, Swimming, Tennis and Young Enterprise.

The Saturday timetable, in conjunction with the weekday programme, allows the activities programme more flexibility to offer both recreational and academic choices. Pupils may select from a diverse range of recreational activities including Academic extension and support, Electronics AS Level, Revision for GCSE, AS and A2, Oxbridge, Biology, Chemistry and Physics Olympiad, Aerobics, Animation Creation, Art, Astronomy, Badminton, Chess, Corps of Drums, Design Technology, Drama, EPP (Economics, Politics and Philosophy) Engineering, Golf driving range, Handicrafts, Media Club, ICT, Military skills, Music, Outdoor pursuits (including climbing, high ropes, kayaking, orienteering, raft building, sailing), Mahjong, Photography, Plaster Modelling, School Magazine, Steel Pans, Table tennis, Website design and Weight training. There are opportunities to gain qualifications in Horse riding, Modern dance, Life saving, First Aid, RADA, LAMDA, Sport/Dance Leader Awards and Martial Arts. In addition to the activities programme, Year 9 pupils participate in Bromsgrove Badge, comprising a selection of activities that help to prepare them for the Bronze Duke of Edinburgh's Award and culminating in a four-day camp at the end of the year. There is a thriving Combined Cadet Force (Army and RAF), whilst approximately 100 pupils are currently involved in the Duke of Edinburgh's Award Scheme. The School's Community Action programme caters for large numbers of pupils and provides a wide range of activities; examples include working in local schools and charity shops, visiting residential homes, acting as Learning Mentors and Student Listeners, running a Fair Trade café, helping in animal sanctuaries and supporting conservation projects.

Admission. Entrance at 13 is by Bromsgrove School Entrance Examinations. Boys and Girls may be admitted to the Preparatory School at any age from 7 to 12 inclusive. 11+ Entrance Tests take place in November and in late January for entry into other years. Places are available in the Sixth Form to boys and girls who have had their GCSE education elsewhere.

Although pupils are normally accepted into the School only at the start of the Michaelmas Term of the year in which they have reached their eleventh, thirteenth or sixteenth birthdays, the Headmaster considers sympathetically applications for admission at other ages and at other times of the academic year.

Scholarships and Bursaries. Awards are made on the results of open examinations held at the school in January. A significant number of scholarships, means-tested bursaries and Foundation bursaries for pupils of academic, artistic, sporting and all-round ability are awarded at 11+, 13+ and 16+. A number of Music scholarships and exhibitions are awarded each year at ages 11, 13 and 16, offering free tuition on up to two instruments. Means-tested bursaries may be used to supplement any scholarship. Full details are available from the Admissions Department.

Fees per term (2014–2015). Senior School (age 13+): £10,395 full boarding, £6,915 weekly boarding, £4,845 day inc lunch. Preparatory School (age 7–13): £6,845–£8,440 full boarding, £4,990–£6,040 weekly boarding, £3,375–£4,385 day inc lunch. Pre-Preparatory (age 4–7): £2,200–£2,600 day. Nursery (age 3–4): £2,450 full-time.

Charitable status. Bromsgrove School is a Registered Charity, number 1098740. It exists to provide education for boys and girls.

Bryanston School

Blandford, Dorset DT11 0PX
Tel: 01258 452411
Fax: 01258 484661
email: head@bryanston.co.uk
website: www.bryanston.co.uk

Motto: '*Et nova et vetera*'.

Founded in 1928, Bryanston School aims above all to develop the all-round talents of individual pupils. A broad, flexible academic and extra-curricular programme together with an extensive network of adult support encourages pupils to maximise their particular abilities as well as to adapt positively to the demands of the society of which they are part. Creativity, individuality and opportunity are the school's key notes, but a loving community is the school's most important quality. Our aim is that Bryanstonians will leave us as well-balanced 18-year-olds, ready to go out into the wider world, to lead happy and fulfilling lives and to contribute, positively and generously. We believe a school can have no more joyful, dynamic ambition.

Governors:
Chairman: R H Cox, BA
S F Bowes
Ms S A Buxton, MA, ACA
S O Conran
M Davies, MA, BA
Mrs S Foulser, BA
J R Greenhill, MA
Mrs B Hollond, MA, FRSA
B M Irvani, MA, FCA
M A S Laurence
Mrs V M McDonaugh, MA
R A Pegna, MA
Dr H M Pharaoh, MBBS, DRCOG, MRCGP
A R Poulton, BA
Dr M L Reynolds, BA, PHD
Miss R Rogers, BMUS
D M Trick
P G E Walker, FRICS

Bursar and Clerk to the Governors: N P McRobb, OBE, MBA, BA

Head: Ms S J Thomas, BA

* *Head of Department*

Second Master: P J Hardy, JP, MA, PGCE (*Economics and Business*)
Director of Studies: P Simpson, MA (*History*)
Director of Admissions: Mrs E M Barkham, BA, MSc, PGCE (*Biology*)

Staff:
* *Head of Department*
† *Housemaster/Housemistress*

P A L Rioch, BMus, BA
D C Bourne, MA, PGCE, FRGS (*Geography; Senior Master*)
Mrs S Stacpoole, BA (*History of Art*)
G S Elliot, BA, PGCE (*Chemistry*)
M N Pyrgos, BSc, PGCE (**Economics and Business, Senior Tutor*)

Mrs F K Pyrgos, BSc, PGCE (*Careers)
J N G Fisher, BEd, PGCE (*English*)
J L Jones, MA, PGCE (*Modern Languages*)
D Fowler-Watt, MA (*Classics*)
Mrs J Ladd-Gibbon, MA (*Design*)
Mrs M F Barlow, BA (*Economics and Business*)
Mrs R A Simpson, BA (*English, Senior Tutor*)
A J Marriott, BA, PGCE (*History*)
S J Richardson, BEd, MA, FRMetS, NPQH (*Geography; Academic Registrar*)
Dr M T Kearney, MA, PhD (**Science; Physics*)
Mrs J G S Strange, BA, PGCE (*History*)
M J Owens, MA, PGCE (*Art)
S J Turrill, BSc, PGCE (*Chemistry)
N J Davies, BEd (*Design Technology*)
L C Johnson, BA, LTP (*French)
Miss J F Quan, MA (*Director of Drama*)
Mrs D M Wellesley, MA (*Modern Languages*)
C T Holland, BA (*Classics)
†Dr P S Bachra, MA (*Economics and Business*)
S H Jones, BSc, PGCE (*Biology*)
Mrs A J Gilbert, BA, PGCE (*Modern Languages*)
Mrs L C Kearney, BEd (*Geography*)
†Mrs H E Dean, BA, PGCE (*Art*)
Ms L Boothman, BA, PGCE (*English*)
†Mrs C L Miller, BEd (*Sports Studies*)
R J Collcott, MEng, MSc (*Mathematics and Physics*)
A J Barnes, BA, CertEd (*Director of Technology*)
†Dr H L Fearnley, BA, PhD (*Classics*)
D J Melbourne, BSc, PGCE (*Mathematics*)
†S M Vincent, BA, PGCE (*History*)
G M Scott, BA, ARCO, LTCL, PGCE (*Assistant Director of Music, Keyboard*)
Miss C L Bentinck, BA (*English*)
L C E Blanco Gomez, BA (*Spanish*)
N M Kelly, BA, PGCE (*English)
†J J A Beales, BA, PGCE (*Economics*)
Mrs C S Scott, BMus, PGCE, FTCL, ARCM, LTCL (*Strings)
N Welford, BSc, PGCE (*Biology)
†Mrs K J Scott, BA, PGCE (*Drama, English*)
Ms C Cava, MPhys (*Physics)
D M Emerson, BMus, PGCE (**Director of Music*)
T W Sellers, BA, PGCE, AKC (*History)
A K Tarafder, BSc (*Mathematics*)
†Mrs C L Bray, BSc, PGCE (*Sport Studies*)
N C Davies, BSc PGCE (*Chemistry*)
Mrs S L Worrall, BEd (*Mathematics*)
Mrs L M Jones, MA (*Classics*)
Mrs R Ings, BSc, PGCE (*IT, Economics*)
Revd A M J Haviland, BEd, DipCMM (*Chaplain*)
M S Deketelaere, BA, MSc, DIC (*Geography)
Miss A J Granville, BSc (*Chemistry*)
Mrs C R Chourou, BA (*Fine Art*)
C J Mills, BA, PGCE, (**Design and Technology*)
†M T Bolton, BA, GTP (*Design and Technology*)
W P Ings, MA, ARCO, PGCE (*Assistant Director of Music, Academic*)
Mrs J M I Velasco, BA, PGCE (*French)
Dr R D Heal, BSc, PhD (*Biology*)
†M S Christie, MA, PGCE (**Economics and Business*)
†J Dickson, BA, PGCE (*Art*)
A C Hartley, MMath, PGCE (*Mathematics)
R J Johnson, BSc, PGCE (*Chemistry*)
J M C Lyne, MA (*History of Art)
I W McClary, MA, PGCE (**Head of Sixth Form*)
Dr S W S Openshaw, PhD, BSc, PGCE (*Biology*)
Miss J M Pike, BA, PGCE (*Modern Languages*)
L J Pollard, MA (*Religious Studies*)
A J Sanghrajka, BA, BPP (*Classics*)
R Pinzas Balesteiro, BA, PGCE (*Spanish)
Miss C G Bloomfield, BSc (*Physics*)
Ms M T Boyd, BSc, PGCE (*Mathematics*)

Ms S D Duncker, 1/2 Staatsexamen (*German*)
P C A Dunne, BA (*History*)
R M Hallam, MPhys, PGCE (*Physics*)
Ms P L Haywood, BSc, PGCE (*Biology*)
Mrs K M Lewin, BSc, MSc, PGCE (*Mathematics*)
N M Mills, BA (*Design and Technology*)
Miss E L Pick, BSc (*Biology*)
Miss M L Sinclair-Smith, BA (*Art*)
I A McLeish, BA, MA, PGCE, MSc (*History*)
S B Green, BSc, PGCE (*Mathematics*)
T W Haysom, BSc, PGCE (*Mathematics*)
Miss F Mateo-Sanz, BA (*Spanish*)
Miss I O M White, BA, MA, PGCE (*Music*)
A Fermor-Dunman, BSc, MA (*Director of Sport*)
Miss J M Grimshaw, BSc, PGCE (*Chemistry*)
J P Heritage, BSc, PGCE (*Physics*)
Ms P Quarrell, BA, PGCE (*History*)

Admissions Registrar: Mrs S J Birkill
Head's PA: Mrs F J Howard

Situation. Occupying a magnificent Norman Shaw mansion, the School is located in beautiful Dorset countryside near the market town of Blandford. There are 400 acres of grounds, which include a stretch of river used for rowing and canoeing, playing fields, woodland and parkland.

Numbers. There are approximately 385 boys and 290 girls in the School.

Admission. Boys and girls are normally admitted between 13 and 14 years of age on the results of Common Entrance or the School's own entrance exam. Sixth Form entrants are admitted after interview, conditional upon securing at least 50 points at GCSE.

Scholarships. Academic, Art, DT, Music, Sport and Richard Hunter All-Rounder Scholarships are available annually for entry at 13+.

Academic and Music Scholarships and Udall Awards for Sport are available annually for entry to the Sixth Form.

Scholarships range in value and may be supplemented by means-tested bursaries. Music Scholarships carry free musical tuition, Alexander Technique lessons and a weekly accompaniment lesson.

Further details may be obtained from the Admissions Registrar.

Organisation. The School is organised on a House basis with 5 senior boys' houses, 5 girls' houses, and 2 junior boys' houses. All pupils have a personal tutor throughout their time in the School, with whom they meet on a one-to-one basis at least once a week. No tutor has more than 15 pupils. Feeding and medical care are organised centrally. All Sixth Form pupils in their final year have individual study-bedrooms. Lower Sixth Formers usually share study-bedrooms.

Religion. Religious instruction is widely based and is carried on throughout the School. There are two assemblies each week for the whole school. Pupils attend either assemblies or services on most Sundays during the term. Holy Communion is celebrated every Sunday and on some week days. A Chaplain is responsible for pastoral work and preparation for Confirmation.

School Work. The School aims at leading pupils, over a period of 5 years, from the comparative dependence on class teaching in which they join the school, to a state in which they are capable of working on their own, for a University degree or professional qualification, or in business. In addition to traditional class teaching, there is, therefore, increasing time given to private work as a pupil moves up the School. This is in the form of assignments to be completed within a week or a fortnight. Teachers are available to give individual help when required, and Tutors supervise pupils' work and activities in general, on a one-to-one basis.

Every pupil is encouraged to explore a range of opportunities. All pupils follow the same broad curriculum in Group D (the first year), if at all possible. This curriculum includes Latin, modern languages, three separate sciences, creative arts, technology and music. GCSE is taken after 3 years when a pupil is in Group B. There is a highly flexible choice of subjects at this level and subjects are setted independently. In the Sixth Form (Group A) pupils are expected to study up to five subjects at AS Level in the first year and to continue with three or four subjects to Advanced (A2) Level in the second year. 24 subjects are offered at AS Level and 22 at A2 Level and there are few restrictions on combinations. Alternatively, pupils may opt to study for the International Baccalaureate Diploma, which the School began teaching in September 2012. All Lower Sixth Formers follow a compulsory Personal and Social Education course and the Humanities programme provides supplementary courses to develop key skills and thinking techniques.

Music. Music plays a very important part in the life of the School. Groups and ensembles include the senior orchestra, dance band, concert band, string chamber orchestra, five choirs, choral society, brass, wind, string and vocal ensembles, informal groups, jazz and rock bands. Numerous professional and amateur concerts take place throughout the year. Tuition is available in strings, brass, wind, percussion and vocals as well as jazz piano, organ, orchestral percussion, drum kit, harp, bagpipes, classical, acoustic, electric and bass guitar, accordion and Alexander Technique. Class music is a compulsory part of the curriculum for all First Year pupils, who also receive introductory free tuition on an orchestral instrument. Over 700 one-to-one music lessons take place each week. A new music school designed by Hopkins Architects, opens in 2014.

Drama. A well-equipped, modern theatre provides the venue for the many school productions which take place during the year and for touring professional companies. In addition to acting, pupils are involved in Stage Management, Stage Lighting and Sound, and front-of-house work. There is also a large Greek Theatre in the grounds.

Sport and Leisure. A wide variety of sports is on offer at the school, including Athletics, Archery, Badminton, Canoeing, Climbing, Cricket, Cross-Country, Fencing, Fives, Hockey, Lacrosse, Netball, Riding, Rowing, Rugby, Sailing, Squash, Swimming and Tennis. Extensive playing fields between the School and the River Stour provide 46 tennis courts, 2 astroturf pitches, 9 netball courts, an athletics track and grass pitches for all major sports, an all-weather riding manège and cross-country course. A Sports Complex provides an indoor heated 25m Swimming Pool, Gymnasium, large Sports Hall, Squash courts and Fitness Centre. Sailing takes place at Poole Harbour where the School has 6 dinghies at its own base. In addition to sport, a number of clubs and societies, catering for a wide range of interests, meet in the evenings and at weekends.

Additional Activities. To encourage a sense of responsibility towards the community, a growing self-reliance and a practical training in the positive use of leisure, all pupils take part in all or some of the following:

- Community and Social Service
- Extra-curricular activities chosen from a wide range of options
- The Duke of Edinburgh's Award Scheme
- Adventure Training

Dress. There is no school uniform but there is a dress code.

Careers. There is a well-resourced Careers Room and the school maintains close links with ISCO. A full time member of staff runs a careers programme which covers the pupils' five years in the school. All pupils undertake Work Experience after their GCSEs and specific advice is given to help with A Level and University degree choices. In the Sixth Form, a mock interview course and the teaching of presentation skills ensure that pupils are well-prepared for the future.

Further Education. The vast majority of pupils in the Sixth Form gain admission to Universities or other academies of further education.

Fees per term (2014–2015). Boarders £11,162, Day Pupils £9,153.

Charitable status. Bryanston School Incorporated is a Registered Charity, number 306210. It is a charitable trust for the purpose of educating children.

Bury Grammar School Boys

Tenterden Street, Bury, Lancs BL9 0HN
Tel: 0161 797 2700
Fax: 0161 763 4655
email: info@bgsboys.co.uk
website: www.bgsboys.co.uk
Twitter: @bgsboys
Facebook: BuryGrammarSchoolBoys

Motto: *Sanctas clavis fores aperit*
   The School, formerly housed in the precincts of the Parish Church of St Mary the Virgin, was first endowed by Henry Bury in 1634, but there is evidence that it existed before that date. It was re-endowed in 1726 by the Revd Roger Kay and moved to its current site in 1966. The school is a selective grammar school which aims to provide a first-class academic and extra-curricular education; to nurture the whole person in a safe, stimulating, challenging and friendly community in which each individual is encouraged to fulfil his potential; and to prepare each boy for an adulthood of fulfilling work, creative leisure and responsible citizenship.

Governing Body:
Chair of Governors: Mrs S Henry
Vice Chair of Governors: L A Goldberg

D Baker	Mrs C A McKee
Dr G Brown	A C Murray
S N Brown	Mrs J D Pickering
M Entwistle	Dr J G S Rajasansir
The Revd Dr J C Findon	J A Rigby
Mrs D L Hampson	A H Spencer
A Marshall	Mrs S N Yule

Bursar and Clerk to the Governors: Mrs J Stevens, BFocFC, ACA

Headmaster: R N Marshall, MSc

Second Master: D P Cassidy, BSc (*Chemistry*)
Director of Studies: T J Nicholson, BA (*Head of Mathematics*)
Assistant Head – Teaching and Learning: Mrs H M Brandon, MA (*English*)
Assistant Head – Enrichment: A E Dennis, BSc (*Mathematics, Head of Outdoor Activities*)
Head of Sixth Form: N Parkinson, BA (*Economics & Business Studies*)

Assistant Staff:
M Ahmad, BSc (*Physics*)
B Alldred, MSc (*Mathematics*)
Miss E L Bailey, BSc (*Biology*)
D S Benger, MA (*Music*)
D A Bishop, BSc (*Head of Geology*)
M R Boyd, BA (*Head of French*)
Mrs R L Bradley, BA (*Classics*)
Mrs H Campion, BA (*Head of Economics & Business Studies*)
Mrs S G Cawtherley, BA (*Religious Studies*)
A P Christian, BA (*History & Politics, Learning Support Coordinator*)
M J Cooke, BEd (*CDT & Electronics, Assistant Head of Sixth Form*)
K M Cryer, BA (*French*)
P F Curry, BSc (*Head of Physics*)

Miss J H Downing, BMus (*Director of Music*)
J Eastham, BA (*History, PSHEE Coordinator*)
W Elf, BSc, MA (*Mathematics*)
G D Feely, MA (*Head of Classics*)
D A Ferguson, BA (*Computing*)
Mrs A C Gill, BSc (*Biology*)
Miss K J Gittins, BA (*Art, Head of General Studies*)
Miss K A Gore, BA (*Head of Art*)
D Hailwood, BEd (*Head of CDT & Electronics*)
G Hall, BSc (*PE & Sport*)
M J Hone, MA (*Head of History & Politics*)
Mrs S J Howard, BA (*French & German*)
D R Lee, BA (*Head of German, Head of Careers*)
P Meakin, BSc (*Head of Computing*)
D T Newbury, BSc (*Geography*)
P O'Sullivan, BA (*Head of Mathematics*)
L A Purdy, BSc (*PE & Sport*)
Mrs H C Shan, MChem (*Chemistry*)
Miss J M Solomon, BSc (*Head of Science, Head of Chemistry*)
Miss E A Stansfield, BA (*English*)
Mrs K E Stedman, BA (*Head of Religious Studies*)
Miss V Tandon, BSc (*Mathematics*)
Mrs T J Taylor, MA (*Head of Geography*)
Mrs K M Tomkinson, BA (*English*)
A D Watts, BSc (*Head of Biology*)
Miss N M Whittaker, BA (*Head of English*)
S Williams, BSc (*Director of Sport*)
B Wong, PhD (*Chemistry*)

Junior School:
R N Marshall, MSc (*Headmaster, Head of Junior School*)
Mrs C A Howard, BSc (*Assistant Head of Junior School*)
P E Burrell, BSc
Mrs F M L Hartwell, BSc
Mrs K A Marshall, BA
Miss L A Moffitt, BA
N G Robson, BA
S H Sheikh, BA
Miss C L Wheeler, BA
Mrs T H Coward (*Classroom Assistant*)

Headmaster's PA: Mrs J M McCoy

Numbers of Boys. 534, aged 7 to 18.
Admission, Scholarships and Bursaries. Admission is by examination and interview. Most boys join the school at either 7 or 11, although, subject to places being available, admission is possible at other ages. A number of means-tested bursaries, based on academic performance and financial need, are awarded each year.
Fees per term (2014–2015). Senior School £3,266; Junior School £2,427.
Facilities and Development. This ancient grammar school, proud of its historic links with the town of Bury and the surrounding area, possesses a full range of modern facilities. These facilities enable the school to offer a broad and rich academic curriculum and extra-curricular programme. Since 1993 the Junior School has occupied its own site opposite the Senior School. Junior School pupils are able to take advantage of the additional specialist facilities and resources in the Senior School. A new Learning Resource Centre, consisting of a Library, extensive ICT provision and private study facilities, was opened in 2002, and a new Art Centre in 2004. A major redevelopment of the Science facilities began in Autumn 2008.
   An Appeal was launched early in 2006 to raise funds for the new co-ed Infant School which has been built on the Girls' School site, opposite the Boys' School; for a new Sixth Form Centre, to provide study and recreational facilities for both boys and girls (due to open in October 2014); and for bursaries to extend the school's ability to welcome able boys whose parents cannot afford the fees.

Pastoral Care. Each boy has a Form Tutor who has primary responsibility for his pastoral care and for oversight of his academic progress and his extra-curricular programme. Form Tutors are led by Heads of Year who also oversee a boy's academic progress. There is also a strong House system for a wide range of sporting, musical and cultural interhouse competitions.

Curriculum. The Junior School offers a balanced and enriched curriculum in a friendly, disciplined and caring environment in which the boys' all-round development is of paramount importance.

In the Senior School, First Form boys study English, Mathematics, French, Biology, Chemistry, Physics, Geography, History, Religious Studies, Music, Computing, Art and CDT. All Second Form boys are taught German and either Latin or Classical Civilisation. At GCSE, all boys study English, Mathematics, Biology, Chemistry and Physics (all boys take separate sciences) and at least one Modern Foreign Language, and choose from a wide range of option subjects. Most boys offer ten subjects at GCSE.

In the Sixth Form, students study four subjects to AS Level and have the option of reducing to three subjects at A2 Level. A Level subjects are chosen from: Biology, Chemistry, Physics, Electronics, Mathematics, Further Maths, History, Politics, Economics, Business Studies, Geography, Geology, English Literature, English Language, French, German, Latin, Greek, Classical Civilisation, Psychology, Religious Studies, Theatre Studies, Music, PE, Art and Computing. All Lower Sixth Form students take AS General Studies, with the option of A2 General Studies in the Upper Sixth Form.

Art. The Art facility in the Senior School consists of two main studios and a separate sixth form studio. There is also a designated sculpture and pottery studio. In the first three years, all boys study Art and Pottery. Art is a popular choice at GCSE, AS and A2.

Music. Music is an important part of school life. As an academic subject it is offered at GCSE, AS and A2. At least three major musical events take place each year. Visiting peripatetic teachers teach over 170 pupils and also assist in running the wide range of extra-curricular music, including choir, orchestra, concert band, dance orchestra and several chamber groups.

Physical Education and Games. Boys participate in Games throughout the school and in Physical Education until the end of the Fourth Form. In addition, boys in the Junior School and in the First Form of the Senior School are taught swimming in the school's own pool. Indoor facilities include a sports hall, and outdoors there are extensive playing fields, a floodlit all-weather area and tennis courts. The major sports in the autumn and spring terms are Football and Rugby. In the summer term the major sport is Cricket. Other sports which are played at inter-school level are Athletics, Basketball, Cross-Country, Golf, Hockey, Swimming and Tennis.

Outdoor Education. In the Senior School, the Outdoor Activities programme includes a residential course for all First Form boys at the National Watersports Centre at Plas Menai in Wales. Boys in the Fifth, Lower Sixth and Upper Sixth Forms can choose Outdoor Activities as part of their Games programme. This includes a variety of activities and trips, including climbing, kayaking, dry-slope skiing and cycling.

CCF. Boys may join the CCF in the Third Form, and the school contingent is a strong one. The CCF helps the boys develop qualities such as self-discipline, resourcefulness and perseverance, a sense of responsibility and skills of man-management and leadership.

Careers. The Careers Department aims to provide all boys with access to the information and advice they need to make informed and sensible decisions about their futures. In addition to a very good Careers Library, guidance is provided by individual interviews. There are regular Careers Conventions. All boys are required to complete a period of work experience during the Fourth Form.

Religion. The school has a Christian foundation but is proud of its tradition of being an open and inclusive community which welcomes boys and staff from different religious faiths as well as those who belong to no faith community.

Bury Grammar School Old Boys' Association. Secretary: Martin Entwistle, 8 Greenmount Drive, Greenmount, Bury, BL8 4HA. Tel: 01204 882502.

Charitable status. Bury Grammar Schools Charity is a Registered Charity, number 526622. The aim of the charity is to promote educational opportunities for boys and girls living in or near Bury.

Campbell College

Belmont Road, Belfast, Co Antrim BT4 2ND, Northern Ireland

Tel: +44 (0)28 9076 3076
Fax: +44 (0)28 9076 1894
email: hmoffice@campbellcollege.co.uk
website: www.campbellcollege.co.uk
Facebook: /Campbell-College

Motto: '*Ne Obliviscaris*'.

Campbell College, which was opened in 1894, was founded and endowed in accordance with the will of Henry James Campbell, Esq (Linen Merchant) of Craigavad, Co Down. It has a reputation as one of the leading educational environments in the country. Our commitment is to welcome, challenge and inspire each and every pupil to be the very best they can be, to push themselves and to stand tall as contributors to a global society.

Governors:
Mr G F Hamilton, BA, FIFP (*Chairman*)
Mrs F Chamberlain, MA (*Vice-Chairman*)
Mr A J Boyd, BSc Econ, FCA
Mr G C Browne, BEng Hons, CEng, FIStructE, MICE, MaPS, MConsE
Mr M E J Graham, BSc, MSc, FCIOB
Mr A F W Devlin, LLB Barrister-at-Law
Sir Mark Horner, QC
Mr I Jordan, FCA, MA Cantab
Mr H J McKinney, BSc, CertEd (*Staff Governor*)
Mr M A D Moreland, LLB, FCA
Mr J I Taggart, ARICS
Mr W B W Turtle, LLB
Mr T R Wilcox, BSc, DipM (*Parent Governor*)
Mr J R Hassard, MA BEd DASE AdvCertEd PQH

Headmaster: Mr R M Robinson, MBE, BSc, PGCE, MEd, PQH NI

Vice-Principals:
Mr W E Keown, MA, PGCE
Mr C G Oswald, BSc, PGCE, AdvCertEd, MEd

Senior Teachers:
Mr H J McKinney, BSc, CertEd
Mr H H Robinson, BSc, PGCE

Assistant Teachers:
Mr S D Quigg, BSc
Mr D Catherwood, BMus, PGCE
Mr C G A Farr, BA, DASE, AdvCertEd, MEd, CertPD
Mr D M McKee, BA, PGCE, DipModLit
Ms B M Coughlin, BEd, PGCertComp
Mrs S Boyce, BA, PGCE
Mrs K E Sheppard, MSc, BSc, PGCE (*Learning Support*)
Mrs G E Wilson, BMus, MTD
Mr D Styles, BA, PGCE, Dip IndStudies
Mrs K P Crooks, BA, ATD

Mr B F Robinson, BA, PGCE, MSc
Mr A W Templeton, BSc, PGCE
Mrs S L Coetzee, BMus, PCGE, PGCE Careers
Mr N R Ashfield, BSc, PGCE
Mr S P Collier, BA, PGCE
Mrs R McNaught, MA, PGCE
Mr G Fry, BA, PGCE
Mr D Walker, BEd
Mrs K-A Roberts, BA, PGCE
Mr C McIvor, MA, PGCE
Mr B Meban, BSc, PGCE
Mr J McCurdy, BD, MA, PGCE
M P Cousins, BSc, PGCE
Mrs L Haughian, BA, PGCE
Miss D H Shields, MA, MSc, PGCE
Mr M G Chalkley, BA, PGCE, MEd, PQH
Mr N McGarry, BA, PGCE
Mrs M Debbadi, BA, PGCE, MSc
Dr J A Breen, BSc, PGCE, PhD
Mr R D Hall, BSc, PGCE
Mrs E McIlvenny, BA, PGCE
Mrs K Magreehan, BA, PGCE
Mrs L Brown, BA, QTS
Mrs J Bailie, BA, PGCE
Mrs C A M Irwin, BSc, PGCE
Mr P D A Campbell, BEd
Mr T R Thompson, BSc, PGCE
Mr A McCrea, BEng, PGCE
Mrs W Pearson, BEd
Mr J H Rea, BSc, PGCE
Mrs K Murphy, BSc, PGCE
Mrs V Spottiswoode, BA, PGCE
Mr F N Mukula, BSc, AssDipTh, PGCE
Miss J-A Taylor, BA, PGCE
Miss G Lamont, BEd, MSSc
Mr G P Young, BEd
Mrs C M Crozier, BSc, PGCE, MSc
Mr J P Cupitt, BSc, PGCE
Mrs W Shannon, BA, PGCE
Ms K M Marshall, MA, QTS
Mrs K McGarvey, MSci, PGCE
Mr J McNerlin, BSc, PGCE
Mr J Smyth, BSc, PGCE
Mrs E Kennedy, BA, PGDip ESL
Mrs J L Hempstead, MA, PGCE
Ms S Kirsch, BA, PGCE
Mrs R A Keown, BSc, PGCE, MSc
Dr A Dunne, MA, PhD, PGCE
Mrs E McInerney, BSC, MEd
Mr M Brown, MA, PGCE

Visiting Music Teachers:
Mrs M Fenn (*Woodwind*)
Mrs J Leslie (*Brass*)
Mrs K Lowry (*Lower Strings*)
M McGuffin (*Piano*)
Mrs H Neale (*Upper strings and Piano*)
Mr M Wilson (*Brass*)
Mr M Neale (*Percussion*)
Mr R Nellis (*Guitar*)

Bursar: J M Monteith, FCA
Headmaster's Secretary: Mrs Y J Mallon
Medical Officers:
Dr G Millar, BMSc, MBChB, MRCGP
Dr D Best, MRCGP, MRCSed, MBBch
Matron: Mrs E M Hoey, SRN

Junior School:
Head: Miss A Brown, BA, PGCE, MEd, PQH

Mrs E M Gwynne, BEd	Mrs F Mottram, BA, ATD
A P Jemphrey, BEd, DASE	Mr J S Anderson, BEd
Mrs P McGarry, BEd	Mrs H M Jennings, BEd
Mrs V A Vance, BEd	Hons, Dip PD

Mrs L M Leyland, BEd	Mrs C Glenn, MA, MEd,
Mr S Montgomery, BEd	PGCE
Miss K Courtney, MA,	Mrs S Smith, BSc, PGCE
PGCE	Miss S Busby, BSc, PGCE
Ms C Martin, BA, PGCE	Miss L Reid, LLB, PGCE
	Mr A Russell, BA, PGCE

Kindergarten:
Mrs L Wilson, BA, PGCE
Mrs H Reid

Ethos. Our commitment is to welcome, challenge and inspire each and every pupil to be the very best they can be, to push themselves and to stand tall as contributors to a global society.

Confidence, commitment and achievement are at the heart of everything we do. From the classroom to the extra-curricular activities, we are dedicated to ensuring that boys make the most of their talents within Campbell and beyond.

We nurture the individual and prepare them for the world. Academic achievements are important and we expect our pupils to strive for high grades; it is also our duty to harness the potential in every pupil whether it is academic, creative, physical or otherwise.

We want boys to leave the school with an assured set of values; we want them to believe they can truly make a difference in society. We want our boys to leave the school with things that are going to matter to them for the rest of their lives.

Pastoral Care. We believe that pupils learn best when they are happy, safe and secure and the purpose of our pastoral care is to provide such an environment. The strong, caring ethos of the College is demonstrated by its commitment to the welfare of the pupils and staff.

In Senior School all boys are allocated a Personal Tutor as the first point of contact for parents and our comprehensive Child Protection Policy is issued to all parents before their child commences school. Above and beyond this level of care we have a dedicated medical centre on campus led by the College Matron and a School Doctor who visits our boarders three times a week.

Boarding. We have a successful boarding department which brings an international dimension and unique character to the College; this will enable our pupils to thrive in the increasingly global world in which we all must live and work. We have approximately 133 boarders.

The Curriculum. This is focused upon giving our boys the maximum opportunity to produce the best possible examination results from a varied choice of subjects which meet the needs of the 21st century.

Class sizes are capped at 26 throughout Key Stage 3 to allow boys to grow in confidence and security in their learning as they make the transition from Primary School to Senior School. The teacher to pupil ratio is a generous 1:14, and the curriculum followed at Year 8 comprises English, Maths, Science, Geography, History, Religious Education, French, Art, Drama, Music, Technology, ICT, PE and Learning for Life and Work.

The Campus. Campbell College stands in a secure and impressive 100-acre wooded estate where the academic, boarding, artistic and sporting pursuits are all catered for on site. The College has its own indoor swimming pool, Astro-Turf pitches, squash courts, shooting range, running track and numerous rugby and cricket pitches. It has a variety of sports and assembly halls, drama studio, computer suites and technology areas.

Other Activities. Campbell College is able to provide boys with a host of activities which naturally complement the culture of learning promoted within the school. Whilst the College is widely acknowledged for its sporting excellence, especially in rugby, hockey and cricket, there are many other opportunities available. Alongside a diverse range of sports there are opportunities to participate in The Combined Cadet Force, Duke of Edinburgh's Award

Scheme, Drama and Music productions and the Charity Action Group.

A competitive House system allows all boys to compete, with camaraderie and collegiality, in numerous inter-House competitions so all have an opportunity to represent their House as well as their school.

Holidays. There are three annual holidays: two weeks at Christmas and Easter, and eight in the summer. In the Christmas and Easter terms there is a half-term break of one week, during which parents of boarders are required to make provision for their sons to be away from school.

Admissions. Campbell College welcomes students at a variety of entry levels. Day boys can begin in Kindergarten and stay through to Sixth Form; boarders may start at Year 8. The school structure is designed to offer our students easy transitions as they grow and mature; they begin in Junior School, then move aged 11 to Middle School, before progressing to Senior School to prepare for their public examinations (GCSE, AS and A2 Level).

There are approximately 895 students in the Senior School of whom 133 are boarders, and 300 students in the Junior School.

Fees per annum (2014–2015). Tuition (Years 8–14): £2,370 (EU citizens), £7,380 (non-EU citizens). Boarding (Years 8–14): £12,210 (EU citizens), £17,220 (non-EU citizens). Junior School: £3,680–£3,950.

As a Voluntary B Grammar School, Campbell College charges an annual fee to all pupils for development and maintenance. The Board of Governors seeks to support applications to the College by offering scholarships and bursaries, the details of which may be found in the Prospectus.

Prospectus. Further information is included in our prospectus which can be obtained from the College Office or you may download a copy from the College website.

Old Campbellian Society. There is a link from the College website.

Charitable status. Campbell College is registered with the Inland Revenue as a charity, number XN45154/1. It exists to provide education for boys.

Canford School

Wimborne, Dorset BH21 3AD
Tel: 01202 841254
Fax: 01202 881009
email: admissions@canford.com
website: www.canford.com

Motto: *Nisi Dominus Frustra*

Canford was founded in 1923. Situated among 300 acres of glorious landscaped grounds just outside Wimborne in Dorset, Canford is well served by excellent road, rail and air links, is under two hours from London and 1 hour 30 minutes' drive time from the M25/M4 junction. Examination results lead the way regionally, while the school regularly receives national recognition, most recently as a runner up as 'Public School of the Year' at the Annual Tatler School Awards 2014 and voted 'Best for Setting' by The Week magazine.

Governors:
Chairman: A J L Cottam, BSc, FCA
M Armitage, CBE, BSc, MB ChB, DM, FRCP, FRCPE
A G Boggis, MA, PGCE
A W Browning, BSc, PGCE, MA Ed, CChem, MRSC
B Coupe, BA, DipArch, RIBA
R W Daubeney, BA
Rear Admiral J M de Halpert, KCVO, CB
Rev V A Herrick, BA, MA, LTCL
M Jeffries, Dip Arch, RIBA, FICE, FRSA
M T Keats, MA

D R Levin, BEcon, MA, FRSA
J D McGibbon, FCA
R E T Nicholl, BA, PGCE
B W Richards
Miss A L R Thomas, BA
G E Vardey, MA, MSI
Mrs E T Watson, BA
M Walshe, BA

Secretary to the Governing Body: M B M Porter, MA

Headmaster: B A M Vessey, MA, MBA

Deputy Head: R J Knott, MA, ARCM
Deputy Head (Pastoral): Mrs N L Hunter, BA
Deputy Head (Co-Curricular): Dr D Neil, BSc, PhD
Director of Studies: Dr S K Wilkinson, MSc, DPhil
Head of Academic Enrichment: M H Walters, BA, MPhil
Registrar: M A Owen, BA, PGCE
Bursar: M A Clarkson, MSc, BScEng

Assistant Staff:
* *Head of Department*
† *Housemaster/mistress*

English, History, Classics, Politics, Drama, Information Technology:
*Miss C Barrett, BA, MA (*English*)
*Mrs A K R Berry, PhD, MPhil (*Classical Civilisation*)
*A C Fearnley, BA, MLitt, (*Politics*)
*J James, BA, PGCE (*Cultural Enrichment*)
*T J Marriott, BA (*History*)
*C E Thomas, BA, MA, PGCE (*Drama*)
*C A Wilson, BA, PGCE (*Classics*)
F T Ahern, MA
Miss L E E Birch, BA
Mrs M Bray, BA
Mrs S Ellis, BA, PGCE
K D R Hay, BA, Cert Ed
Mrs S J Holland, BA, PGCE
†Dr C E Ives, MA, PhD
Mrs P J Knott, MA, PGCE
Mrs K M Orpwood, BA, MA
M A Owen, BA, PGCE
L I Pearce, BSc, PCET
C M S Rathbone, MA, PGCE
†R M B Salmon, BA, PGCE
Dr F Shon, MA, DPhil
S Vandvik, MA
M H Walters, BA, MPhil
Ms K M Watts, BA, PGCE

Geography and Economics:
*Mrs K J Hoey, MA (*Geography*)
*A J Kerr, BA, PGCE (*Business Studies*)
*J Toy, MA (*Economics*)
Miss S Deblander, BSc, MA
Mrs N L Hunter, BA, PGCE
†N H Jones, BA, PGCE
Mrs C E Kilpatrick, BSc
J R Orme, MA, PGCE
R S Raumann, MA, PGCE
P D A Rossiter, MA, PGCE
Mrs J Smith, BA, PGCE

Mathematics and Science:
*R J Baldwin, BEng, MSc, PGCE (*Mathematics*)
*C L Fenwick, BSc, PGCE (*Physics*)
*E H Johnson, MSc, PGCE (*Biology*)
*G R Shaw, MChem, PGCE (*Chemistry*)
D J Allen, BSc, MSc, PGCE
†H N P Bishop, BSc, ACMA
†Mrs C D Byng, BA Ed
D H F Coles, BSc
Mrs P L Connor, MA, PGCE
†L M Corbould, BSc, PGCE
D P Culley, MA

Miss C Evans, MChem
S D Excell, BSc, PGCE
S J Gordon, BA, PGCE
R H J Hooker, BSc
Dr F G Horton, MA, DPhil
C H Jeffery, BA, MEng
Miss A Jenner, MA, PGCE
R J Knott, MA, ARCM
W J Linley-Adams, BA
Miss A L Mulley, BSc
Dr D Neill, BSc, PhD, PGCE
†O T Parkin, BSc
Miss L H Pick, BSc, PGCE
A F U Powell, MA, PGCE
S J C Rood, BSc, PGCE
Miss Z V Round, BSc, PGCE
Mrs K Salmon, BA, PGCE
T J Street, BSc, PGCE
Mrs E C Thornburrow, BSc, PGCE
A J Tyndall, MChem
Dr S K Wilkinson, MSc, DPhil

Modern Languages:
*F Compan, Licenciado en Filología Inglesa (*French and Spanish*)
*R A Wilson BA, MA, PGCE (*German and Other Languages*)
Mrs T S Ackroyd, BA, PGCE
Mrs L Harding, MA, PGCE
Mrs A S Harrison, BA, PGCE
†Mrs M Marns, Maîtrise d'Anglais, PGCE
Mrs A J Pearce, BA
Mrs E Pellejero, BA, MA
Mrs C J G Stone, Licence ès Lettres, PGCE

Music:
*C C Sparkhall, MA, ARCO, PGCE (*Director of Music*)
Miss F M McKinley, BA, LMusA (*Head of Strings*)
J Aiken, MA
Mrs L J Blake, MA, PGCE
S J Hattersley, London Academy
D A Warwick, MA, FRCO, ARCM

Art and Design:
*N Watkins, BEd (*Design Technology*)
*D H Wright, MA, PGCE (*Art*)
P A Effick, BEd, BSc
Ms R Fuller, BA
Ms J Jones, BA, PGCE
A Kirkby, BA, MA
†D F Lloyd, BA, PGCE
J V Martin, BEng, MSc, PGCE

Religious Studies:
*I Weir, BA, PGCE
The Revd P A Jack, MA
S J Millewis-Leiper, BA

Physical Education:
*M S Burley, BSocSci, MA (*Director of Sport*)
Miss H C Morrell, BSc (*Head of Girls' Games*)
†N R Baugniet, BA (*Head of Academic PE*)
T Adby (*Director of Hockey*)
D P Culley, MA (*Head of Outdoor Enterprises*)
I R Dryden (*Director of Rowing*)
M Keech (*Director of Cricket*)
P T Short, BSc (*Director of Rugby*)

Careers and Higher Education: W M Doherty, MA
Examinations Officer: Mrs V M Horwood
Archivist: F T Ahern, MA, PGCE

Houses & Housemasters/mistresses:

Boarding Houses (Boys):
Court: R M B Salmon
Franklin: H N P Bishop
Monteacute: D F Lloyd
School: L M Corbould

Boarding Houses (Girls):
Beaufort: Dr C Ives
de Lacy: Mrs M Marns
Marriotts: Mrs C D Byng

Mixed Day Houses:
Lancaster: O T Parkin
Salisbury: N H Jones
Wimborne: N R Baugniet

Medical Officers:
*Dr R Skule, MB BS, MRCP, MRCGP
P J N Dickins, MA, MB BS, DCH, DRCOG, MRCGP
B L Lear, MB BS, MRCGP

Canford is among the top co-educational, boarding and day schools in the country for pupils aged 13–18. The school has a culture which encourages participation and hard work. There is a strong sense of community, teamwork, friendliness and integrity leading to mutual trust which in turn brings achievement. Pupils are offered a wide range of opportunities inside and outside the classroom. Our aim is to provide not only an academic but also a diverse cultural, social and spiritual environment in which pupils can flourish.

Situation. Canford School stands on the edge of Wimborne, Dorset, in an enclosed park of 300 acres which includes a stretch of the River Stour used for rowing, fishing and canoeing. The main building was designed by Blore in 1825 and remodelled by Sir Charles Barry in 1846. Since the foundation of the school in 1923 there have been numerous additions on the site to provide a full range of modern facilities.

Numbers. There are currently 635 pupils of whom approximately 70% are boarders and 60% are boys.

Houses. There are 4 boarding houses for boys, 3 boarding houses for girls and 3 mixed day houses.

The Curriculum. There is considerable breadth in the lower school. In their Shell year pupils study all the subjects offered at GCSE as well as a programme developed in the school for teaching IT and Computing. There is one choice in this Shell curriculum between German and Spanish, made by pupils after a short taster course in the two languages. All pupils study for GCSEs or IGCSEs. Most take ten subjects in total of which one (Philosophy and Religion) is non-examined. Seven options, in addition to the core subjects English, Maths, Philosophy and Religion, may be chosen and must include at least two single sciences and one foreign language.

In the Lower Sixth, pupils usually choose four subjects to study at AS level. We discourage taking more than four, instead encouraging more able pupils to study in greater depth one of more of their AS subjects, perhaps extending their work with a research-based essay (EPQ). Art, French, German and Spanish are offered as Pre-U courses. Combinations of subjects are as flexible as possible. All pupils in all year groups follow a General Studies course, which includes Personal and Social Education in the first two years. Academic enrichment programmes are offered throughout the year groups, both for scholars and for all those with enquiring minds.

University Destinations. 95%+ of pupils proceed to higher education, popular destinations recently include Bath, Bristol, Cambridge, Cardiff, Durham, Edinburgh, Exeter and Oxford. On average more than a dozen places are gained at Oxford and Cambridge annually with forty-two offers in the past three years.

Tutorial System. In addition to their Housemaster/mistress and House Tutor the pupils in the Sixth Form each have an Academic Tutor who is responsible with the Housemaster/mistress for academic progress, university entry, and careers guidance. There are monthly academic assessments throughout the school which are monitored by the tutorial staff and emailed to parents.

Religion. Chapel services are held in the Norman church of Canford Magna which stands in the school grounds, and also in the Music School and the Theatre. Arrangements can be made for those of different faiths and denominations to worship independently.

Music. Music is a compulsory subject for pupils in the Shell year, and an option for GCSE and A Level. 400 individual music lessons are taken each week and more than half of pupils learn an instrument. Larger ensembles include senior orchestra, string orchestra, 2 concert bands, jazz band, Chapel Choir, Chamber Choir, Junior Choir and Choral Society while there is also a wide range of chamber ensembles. The Music School has 2 large rehearsal rooms, practice rooms and a computer suite. Regular concerts, both formal and informal, are given in the 200-seat Concert Hall as well as in prestigious outside venues.

Drama. In their first year, pupils have the opportunity to study Drama as part of the curriculum and beyond that Drama and Theatre Studies are offered at GCSE and A Level. The 300-seat Layard Theatre is home to the Drama Department and provides an exciting venue for a wide range of school productions as well as hosting work from professional companies.

Art and Design Technology. Art and Design Technology are compulsory for all pupils in their first year during which they are introduced to drawing, painting, printing, sculpture, metalwork, woodwork, plastics and CAD/CAM. They may also pursue these interests in their daily activities time and at weekends. Pupils may take GCSE and A Level.

ICT. In their Shell year all pupils follow the IAM Award which is a QCA level 2 award, equivalent to a B grade at GCSE. Thereafter the well-equipped Information Technology Centre provides cross-curricular induction courses to all, aiming to establish IT as a natural tool for learning and life, and enabling pupils to apply it to a range of academic and other work, from preps to projects, personal correspondence to school publications. Each department has a teacher assigned to the development of IT within its subject curriculum. There is open access to the centre for all pupils and staff throughout the day and in addition all houses are equipped with computers as is the library. Houses and most public areas have a wireless network for internet access.

Sport. All pupils participate in sport. The principal sports are: in the Christmas Term rugby and rowing for boys, hockey and rowing for girls; in the Easter Term hockey and rowing for boys, netball and rowing for girls; in the Summer Term cricket and rowing for boys, tennis and rowing for girls. The school also has representative teams in athletics, cross-country, sailing, swimming, golf, squash, badminton, lacrosse and royal tennis. There are other sports available. The school facilities include: a well-equipped sports centre incorporating double-sized sports hall, dance studio, physiotherapy room, two sports science classrooms and state-of-the-art fitness suite; two astroturf pitches used for hockey and tennis; three hard court areas suitable for tennis and netball; four squash courts; a royal tennis court; a nine-hole golf course, 12 grass pitches, and a new indoor 25m, 6-lane pool. There is also a climbing wall and a fully equipped boathouse on the adjacent River Stour. The school employs professional cricket, squash, royal tennis, rowing, hockey, rugby, golf and netball coaches.

Societies, Hobbies and Activities. Various societies meet on a regular basis including Debating, Literary, Science and Art. The school operates a comprehensive activity programme which is compulsory for all Shell and Fourth Form pupils. This takes place twice a week and offers a wide range of sporting, musical, drama, practical and recreational activities. There is also scope for further involvement in the senior part of the school.

Community Service. Pupils work in the local community each week, teaching in schools, volunteering at National Trust properties and other charities, helping the elderly, the disabled, and visiting patients in hospices and respite care centres. They also help to give lessons in swimming and science and look after disadvantaged children. Each year parties of Canfordians help in orphanages in Southern India, Ghana and Argentina.

Combined Cadet Force. Army, Navy and Marines sections make up a 240 strong cadet force staffed by 12 officers. About 90% of pupils join in their second year on a voluntary basis and remain in the CCF for two years. A number stay on until the end of their sixth form as NCOs. There are numerous opportunities for training exercises in the UK and abroad, including Norway and France.

Careers and Higher Education. The careers programme at Canford accelerates in the Fifth Form with testing and interviews. The whole year group has the opportunity to undergo testing for career directions and A Level choices. The Lower Sixth year starts the advice procedure for higher education applications with talks, lectures and one to one consultations. The Upper Sixth year completes these processes. A well-appointed careers room is always available and parental participation at all stages of the programme is encouraged.

Medical. The purpose-built Health Centre is staffed 24 hours a day by five fully-qualified nurses. A medical officer visits the Health Centre daily during the week and remains on call throughout and during weekends. The Health Centre also provides a physiotherapy and confidential counselling service.

Admission. It is advisable to register by the end of Year 6. £100 fee is payable. Application should be made to the Admissions Office. All registrations join the Headmaster's List and are invited to a pre-assessment during Year 7. In recent years, around 65% of those who have sat the Headmaster's List assessment have been offered conditional places. Following the offer of a conditional place, most applicants sit the Common Entrance Examination. The pass mark is currently 55%. The school uses its own entry tests for those who are not at preparatory schools. Pupils are usually admitted between their 13th and 14th birthdays or by a competitive examination at 16+.

Entrance Scholarships. *13+*: Scholarship examinations are held in January, February and March for the following awards: Academic, Music and Sport scholarships worth from 10% to 50% of the fees; Art, Drama and Design Technology scholarships worth from 10% to 20% of the fees; Armed Services scholarships, one academic and one non-academic, worth not less than 20% of the fees to the sons/daughters of serving members of UK armed services. Candidates must be in Year 8 at the time they attempt scholarships.

16+: Entrants to the school at Sixth Form level may apply for any combination of the following scholarships: Academic, Music, Assyrian (for co-curricular excellence including sport). The examinations are held in the November prior to entry. Assyrian awards are offered for a co-curricular contribution of excellent quality and are worth from 10% to 40% of the fees; Academic and Music scholarships are worth from 10% to 50% of the fees.

Financial Assistance. Means-tested bursaries worth up to 100% of the fees are available from the school where the financial need of the prospective or current parents has been established.

Further details about any awards can be obtained from the Admissions Office.

Fees per term (2014–2015). Boarders £10,374; Day £7,954.

Composition Fee. At any time in advance a composition fee at special rates may be paid to cover the cost of a pupil's education for his/her career at the school. Details may be obtained from the Admissions Office.

Insurance. There is a fees insurance scheme also covering medical and operation expenses, at the option of the parents.

The Old Canfordian Society. Enquiries to The Old Canfordian Society, Canford School.

Charitable status. Canford School Limited is a Registered Charity, number 306315. It exists to provide education for children.

Caterham School

Harestone Valley Road, Caterham, Surrey CR3 6YA
Tel: 01883 343028
Fax: 01883 347795
email: enquiries@caterhamschool.co.uk
            admissions@caterhamschool.co.uk
website: www.caterhamschool.co.uk

Motto: *Veritas Sine Timore.*

Caterham was founded in 1811 by the Revd John Townsend to provide a boarding education for the sons of Congregational ministers. Logically it was named the Congregational School. By 1884, the School had outgrown its premises, and the 114 boys with their teaching staff moved to Caterham. In 1890, the school opened its doors to the sons of laymen and to day boys. In 1995, it merged with Eothen School for Girls to create a new independent co-educational foundation. Girls had been coming to Caterham for Sixth Form education since 1981, but the merger integrated the schools and enabled co-education to be offered to pupils aged 3 years and upwards. In 1995 the School became an associate member of United Learning and benefits from the strength provided by this partnership.

Board of Trustees:
Chairman: J W Bloomer
Vice-Chairman: I R M Edwards

D P Charlesworth	Mrs S M Whittle
J Joiner	Mrs P H Wilkes
Mrs T Eldridge-Hinmers	Ms J Shadick
Revd N Furley-Smith	E Smith
G M Walter	

Bursar and Clerk to the Trustees: J C L King, MBE

The School Staff:

Headmaster: J P Thomas, BSc Hons, MBA, FRSA

Deputy Head: Mrs T B Kirnig, MA
Deputy Head (Curriculum): T J Murphy, MA Oxon
Head of Boarding: Mrs C Drummond, BA Hons
Director of Learning and Teaching: K Wells, MA Cantab
Deputy Head (External Relations and Co-curricular): M Godfrey, MA

Academic Staff:

Art and Design:
Miss A Church, MA (*Head of Textiles*)
Miss A Barnes, MA (*Head of Photography*)
Mrs C Bell, MA (*Head of Art*)
Miss C D Pateman, BA Hons (*Head of 3D Design*)
B Wilkinson, BA Hons
D Flood, BA

Biology:
*D Quinton, MA Oxon, MSB (*Head of Science*)
A P Taylor, BSc Hons (*Senior Teacher Operations & Head of Staff Development*)
S Marlow, MBiochem Oxon
Mrs A Seal, BSc Hons (*Head of First Year*)
Mrs I Whitwell, BSc (*Head of Harestone*)
J Robinson, PhD

Chemistry:
*D Keyworth, MSc
S Gilburt, MA
Miss K Handford, PhD
H Hawkridge BSc Hons
Mrs H Howgego, MChem Hons
Miss R Pilkington, BSc Hons

Classics:
*K Waite, MA Oxon
M Owen, MA Oxon
Mrs S Carpenter, BA Oxon
Mrs B Hunter, BA Oxon

Drama & Theatre Studies:
*Mrs L Fahey, BA Hons
Mrs A L T Yankova, BA Hons
Mrs J Driscoll, BA Hons

Economics and Business Studies:
*J Weiner, LLB, ACA
A Fahey, BA Hons (*Director of Sixth Form, Upper Sixth*)
C James, BSc Hons, MBA (*Director of Sixth Form, Lower Sixth*)
Mrs C Wallace, BA Hons, ACIB
A Moore, BSc (*Assistant Head of Second Year*)

English:
*Miss A O'Donnell, MA Hons
Ms A Currey, BA Hons, MTeach Distinction (*Second in Department*)
Miss A Cox, BA
Mrs C Drummond, BA Hons (*Head of Boarding*)
Mrs D Edmonds, BA Hons (*Gifted and Talented Coordinator*)
M Godfrey, MA (*Deputy Head – External Relations and Co-curriculum*)
A Van Niekerk, BA (*Head of Townsend*)
Mrs A L T Yankova, BA Hons
A Webster, BA Oxon (*Director of Digital Learning*)
Mrs H Howden, BA Hons (*Assistant Head of Fifth Year*)
Mrs L Tapley, BA Dip SpLD, AMBDA (*SENCO, Head of Lower School*)

Geography:
*S Terrell, MPhil (*Deputy Director of Sixth Form, Lower Sixth*)
A Van Niekerk, BA (*Head of Townsend*)
Mrs V Mesher, MA
R Mugridge, BA Hons

History:
*R Salem, MA Oxon (*Senior Teacher – Academic*)
T Cooper, MA, AKC
N Mills, BA Hons (*Head of Viney*)
T Murphy, MA Oxon (*Deputy Head – Curriculum*)
D Richards, BA (*Head of Rugby*)
Miss H Rogers, BA Hons
Mrs K James, BA Hons

Information Technology:
M G Bailey, BA Hons, BEd (*Head of Curricular IT*)

Mathematics:
*A Langdon, PhD
Miss N Dawrant, MA Oxon (*House Coordinator*)
Mrs P Parker, BA Hons MEd
J Ogilvie, BSc (*Examinations Officer*)
D R Todd, MA Oxon (*Head of Lewisham*)
S Lander, MA Oxon, MSc (*Second in Department, Assistant Head of Fourth Year*)
C Ware, BSc Hons (*Head of Harestone House*)
D King, BA Hons (*Senior Teacher – Pastoral*)
R Jones, BSc Hons (*Assistant Head of First Year, Assistant Head of Outdoor Learning*)
Mrs R Pearce, MA Hons

Modern Languages:
*Mrs N McVitty, DEUG, Licence d'Anglais (*Head of French, Deputy Director of Sixth Form-Lower Sixth*)
*N Parker, MSc (*Head of Spanish*)
*Mrs C M Clifton, BA Hons (*Head of German*)
Mrs J Laverick, BEd Hons Cantab
K Wells, MA Cantab (*Director of Learning & Teaching*)
C Garcia, BA Hons (*Modern Languages Coordinator*)
Mrs S Carpenter, BA Oxon
Ms A Ambles, Chartered IoLET, ASCENTIS, CELTA
Mrs Z Roberts, BA Hons
W Jones, BA Hons
Mrs C Ellis, MA

Music:
*A Assen, BMus
Mrs H Richards, BMus Hons (*Assistant Director of Music, Composer in Residence*)
R MacManus, MMus (*Head of Strings*)
T Hall, BMus
Miss J Riches, BMus (*Head of Woodwind*)
Mrs L Temple, LRAM, ACRM, Prof Cert, Dip RAM (*Head of Brass*)

Physical Education:
*R Clarke, BSc Hons (*Director of Sport, Head of Newington*)
*Miss J Leach, BSc Hons (*Head of Examination PE, Head of Netball*)
L Barnard, BSc Hons (*Assistant Head of Third Year, Head of Ridgefield*)
R Smith, CertEd (*Games Coach*)
Miss K McHugh, BA (*Head of Lacrosse, Head of Underwood*)
*Mrs N Lomas, BA Hons (*Head of Second Year*)
A Patterson, MA (*Head of Hockey, Coordinator of Clubs and Societies*)
Miss R Hart, BA Hons (*Head of Swimming, Head of Fifth Year*)
D Richards, BA (*Head of Rugby*)
A Taylor, BSc Hons (*Head of Strength and Conditioning*)

Psychology:
*D Kokott, BA (*Head of Fourth Year*)
L Barnard, BSc Hons (*Assistant Head of Third Year, Head of Ridgefield*)

Physics:
*J Mansell, BA Oxon
M Anderson, MA Cantab, MEng (*Head of Third Year*)
R Anderson, MEng
Miss C Farmer, MPhys (*Head of Aldercombe*)
A Hicks, MEng

Politics:
*T Cooper, MA, AKC (*Assistant Director of Learning and Teaching*)
D Richards, BA (*Head of Rugby*)
T J Murphy, MA Oxon (*Deputy Head – Curriculum*)
Miss H Rogers, BA Hons
Mrs K James, BA Hons

Religious Education:
*Revd Dr R Mearkle, BA, MDiv, DMin (*Chaplain*)
Mrs B Hunter, BA Oxon
Mrs T B Kirnig, MA (*Deputy Head*)
Miss H Trehane, BA Hons (*Examinations Officer*)
J Whyatt, BA, MA
Miss R Smith, BA Hons

Special Needs:
*Mrs L Tapley, BA, DipSpLD, AMBDA
Mrs C McNeice, BA Hons

EAL:
*Miss E Gibbs, MA
Mrs S Dall'Oglio, BA Ed Hons

R Stamper, BSc Hons, MA TESOL

Careers: Mrs C Brown

Registrar: Mrs A Jones

Preparatory School

Head Teacher: H W G Tuckett, MA
(*For further information see IAPS section*)

Number in School. In the Senior School there are 900 pupils, of whom 164 are boarders. In the Preparatory School there are 300 pupils.

Aims. Our aim is to provide an excellent all-round education so that every pupil can achieve his or her full potential academically and socially.

We focus on developing the whole person, aiming to ensure that each pupil leaves here ready for the challenges of life at university and beyond. We believe that truly excellent education is about more than academic achievement alone: it is also about developing a passion for learning, moral values, self-confidence without arrogance and genuine interests that extend beyond the confines of the classroom.

We are a family school with Christian values. We believe that the virtues of tolerance, understanding, respect and courtesy really matter. We strive to ensure that Caterham pupils have an understanding of their place in society – locally and globally – and seek to make a positive impact upon it.

Situation. Caterham School is in a rural location in north Surrey just 22 miles from the centre of London. The 200-acre campus is in the beautiful, wooded Harestone Valley, less than a mile from the centre of Caterham, and only five minutes drive from Junction 6 of the M25. The journey by taxi to London Gatwick airport is 20 minutes and about 50 minutes to London Heathrow.

Caterham Railway Station is a 15 minute walk. The frequent trains into London (Victoria or London Bridge) make educational and cultural visits easy to organise.

There are separate boarding houses for boys (Townsend and Viney) and girls (Beech Hanger). Common rooms, dormitories (for younger pupils) and study-bedrooms are comfortably furnished, many with en-suite facilities.

In recent years there has been a substantial building and development programme. The boarding accommodation has been extended and refurbished. The sports centre, theatre/assembly hall, language laboratory and IT facilities all benefit from extensive investment. The thirteen science labs and refectory were completed in 2007 and two additional laboratories have been built this year. The new Sixth Form Centre and Health Centre were opened in 2008.

The Preparatory School. *Please see entry in IAPS section.* Continuity of education is provided as boys and girls move from the Preparatory School to the Senior School at the age of eleven.

Admission. Intake is by selection on academic merit and on assessment of a pupil's likely positive contribution through good behaviour to the aims, ethos and co-curricular life of the School. All candidates must sit our examinations.

For day pupils the main intake ages are 11+ years, 13+ years and for the Sixth Form. All day pupil candidates are required to attend an interview and a report from the pupil's current school will be required prior to an offer of a place being made.

Places in the Sixth Form are offered subject to a minimum of six GCSE passes (or equivalent) at Grade A. Additionally, pupils will be expected to meet the specific subject entry requirements for their AS and A Level choices. This is a pass at grade A or B (or equivalent) depending on the subject.

All international applicants for boarding places must pass our examinations which are usually taken at the offices of the British Council or one of our overseas agents. For all international applicants we require a school report at registration.

For further details please contact the Registrar, Mrs A Jones, Tel: 01883 335058, email: admissions@ caterhamschool.co.uk.

Details concerning the admission of pupils to the Pre-Preparatory and Preparatory School are published separately (*see entry in IAPS section*).

Term of Entry. Pupils are normally accepted for entry in September each year, but vacancies may occur at other times.

Scholarships. Scholarships are assessed with a view to encouraging pupils. The breadth and depth of the awards can vary each year depending on the quantity and quality of applicants.

Academic Scholarships: These are awarded at 11+, 13+ and 16+ and can represent up to 50% of the fees

At 11+ and 13+: All external candidates who have registered, and those pupils progressing from Caterham Preparatory School, are automatically considered for an Academic Scholarship. The scholarships are awarded solely on the basis of our entrance examinations, interviews and Head Teacher reports.

At 16+: Candidates applying for Academic Scholarships are required to sit a general paper and two other papers in subjects of their choice that they will be studying at A Level. Examinations and interviews take place in the November preceding entry the following academic year. These scholarships are available to all external candidates, and to internal candidates not already holding an award. Candidates must still satisfy the entry requirement for Sixth Form. In addition to Academic Scholarships, awards may be made for specific subjects, eg languages.

All Rounder Scholarships: These are awarded at 11+ and 13+ and can represent up to 25% of the fees. These scholarships are awarded to candidates who are academically sound and achieve scholarship standard in two of the following subjects: Art, Drama, Music or Sport. They should be a genuine 'all-rounder' with real evidence of potential leadership.

Art & Design Scholarships: These are awarded at 11+, 13+ and 16+ and can represent up to 25% of the fees. Candidates wishing to be considered for a scholarship will initially be asked to submit a portfolio of their work for assessment by the Head of Department. The portfolio should reflect the breadth and depth of personal interest and may include paintings, prints, drawings and photographs of three-dimensional work. Portfolios will be returned. Successful candidates will be invited to attend a scholarship interview and to undertake a practical examination. Sketchbooks and a selection of the work from the portfolio should be made available at the interview. All Art & Design Scholars are expected to be fully committed to the school's Art & Design programme.

Music Scholarships & Awards: Music Scholarships are awarded at 11+, 13+ and 16+ and can represent up to 25% of the fees. In addition, up to four exhibitions may be offered, each to the value of free instrumental music tuition on one or more instruments in school. These awards are made on the basis of musical potential as well as actual achievement. As a guide we would expect students to have achieved grade 4 or above aged 11+; grade 5 or above at 13+ and grade 7/8 at 16+ on their principal instrument. Auditions take place early in the Spring Term during which candidates are required to perform one substantial piece (or two shorter pieces) on their principal instrument, and one piece on a second instrument (if studied). There are also sight-reading, aural tests and an informal viva voce with members of the Music department.

All Music award holders are expected to be ambassadors for the music department taking part in the annual music award holders concert and playing active roles in the co-curricular music programme.

Performing Arts Scholarships: These are awarded at 11+ and 13+ and can represent up to 25% of the fees. They are awarded on the basis of performance in the entrance examination and interview, together with performance in the following disciplines: dance, drama or music. Candidates will be expected to excel in two of these disciplines, with potential to develop the third.

Sports Scholarships: These are awarded at 11+, 13+ and 16+ and can represent up to 25% of the fees. Candidates are expected to show exceptional promise in at least one sport and have an established record of achievement in one of Caterham School's major sports at their current school, and at club/county level. Candidates will be required to take part in drills and game situations to show evidence of their positional and tactical awareness as well as skill, agility and fitness level. Records of achievement and school recommendations will be taken into consideration. All Sports Scholars are expected to be fully committed to the School's annual sports programme.

Boarding/International Scholarships: We are prepared to consider awarding a scholarship of up to 25% of the fees to a pupil who is judged to have the potential to make a significant contribution to the boarding community. If applicable at 16+, arrangements can be made for Academic Scholarship assessments to take place overseas. Please contact the Registrar for details.

Science Scholarships: These are awarded at 16+ and can represent up to 25% of the fees. Candidates are expected to show exceptional promise in at least two subjects (chosen from Biology, Physics, Chemistry or Maths) and have an established record of achievement in the subjects at their current school. The Head of Science will interview candidates. All Science Scholars are expected to be fully committed to the School's curricular and co-curricular science activities.

Drama Scholarships: These are awarded at 16+ and can represent up to 25% of the fees. Candidates will be required to perform and discuss two contrasting monologues, one of which must be from the classical repertoire. They will be required to attend an interview to which they should bring a portfolio of their experiences and achievements.

Bursaries. We wish to ensure that Caterham School is accessible to talented students, irrespective of parental income. Therefore, any prospective pupil from a low-income family is eligible to apply for a Caterham Bursary to obtain means-tested financial support in respect of day fees. Bursaries do not preclude pupils from holding a scholarship award.

Bursaries can be offered to new pupils and those who are already in the school and whose families have suffered sudden and unexpected financial hardship. All Bursaries are reassessed annually.

A fully-funded day place for a Sixth Form student is provided by a Wilberforce Bursary. Bursaries are also available for the sons and daughters of URC Clergy, Regular Forces and FCO personnel.

Fees per term (2014–2015). Boarding £9,488–£10,003; Day £5,122–£5,361. Lunch for Day Pupils: £210.

Curriculum. Preparatory School: A wide range of subjects is provided following National Curriculum guidelines. (*For further details see entry in IAPS section.*)

Senior School: For GCSE the core curriculum is English Language and Literature, Mathematics, Physics, Chemistry, Biology and a Modern Language as well as PE and Games and RPSE. To this core is added three further subjects from Latin, Greek, Modern Languages (French, German, Spanish, Italian), Art, 3D Design, Music, Drama, GCSE PE, Economics and Business Studies, History, Geography and Religious Studies. All of the subjects offered at GCSE are available at A Level, as well as Further Mathematics, Economics, Business Studies, Photography, Psychology, Politics and Textiles. The curriculum is supplemented by an innovative, non-examined 'Forum' programme that includes expert led lectures and seminars designed to prepare students for the opportunities and responsibilities of adult life. Sixth Form students can also participate in the Caterham Award which recognises public speaking, community service and leadership development.

Music, Drama and Creative Arts. Music is an important feature of the life of the School. Individual lessons are given on the piano, in string, brass and wind instruments, and the organ. The Choral Society performs at least one major choral work each year. Each term there are several School concerts and a programme of recitals is arranged. Drama is also well-supported and popular. Each year there are three major productions which involve a large number of pupils both on and off stage. The expertise within the Art Department is broad, including painting, printmaking, textiles, fashion, ceramics, photography, digital media and sculpture and pupils are encouraged to pursue their interests in creative work, as diverse as ceramics, textiles, digital manipulation, drypoint etching and mixed media.

Societies and Hobbies. All pupils are encouraged to pursue a hobby or constructive outside interest, and there are a large number of active School Societies, including: Art, CCF, Chess, Amnesty International, Astronomy, Dance, Debating, Duke of Edinburgh's Award, Film, Greek, ICT Club, Kit Car Club (Caterham 7), Moncrieff-Jones (Sixth Form Science), Music, Circus, Textiles, Young Enterprise. The School has an active charity committee and significant funds are raised annually to support partner schools in Tanzania and Ukraine.

Games. Most of the playing fields adjoin the School including an all-weather synthetic grass pitch for Lacrosse, Hockey and Tennis. Overall there are many sporting activities, but in each term at least one major game is played. For boys it is Rugby in the Autumn Term, Hockey in the Spring Term and Cricket in the Summer. Girls play Lacrosse, Netball, Rounders and Tennis. Pupils can also participate in Athletics, Fencing, Equestrian, Swimming, Badminton, Basketball, Cross-Country, Squash, Soccer, Taekwondo and, in the Summer Term, Sailing, Windsurfing and Canoeing.

Health. There is a well-equipped Health Centre with a SRN Sister. The School Doctor attends regularly.

Careers. The Careers staff are available to give advice. The School has membership of the Independent Schools Careers Organisation and parents are encouraged to enter their sons or daughters for the ISCO Aptitude Test in the Sixth Form year. The School arranges Careers and Higher Education Forums and the Headmaster and Careers staff are available to discuss careers with parents.

Old Caterhamians' and Parents' Associations. The School has flourishing Old Caterhamians' and Parents' Associations. Information about these may be obtained from the School.

Charitable status. Caterham School is a Registered Charity, number 1109508. Its aim is to develop the academic and personal potential of each pupil in a Christian context.

Charterhouse

Godalming, Surrey GU7 2DX

Tel:	Admissions: +44 (0)1483 291501
	Headmaster: +44 (0)1483 291601
	Bursary and Enquiries: +44 (0)1483 291500
Fax:	Admissions: +44 (0)1483 291507
	Headmaster: +44 (0)1483 291647
email:	reception@charterhouse.org.uk
	admissions@charterhouse.org.uk
website:	www.charterhouse.org.uk
Twitter:	@CharterhouseSch

Motto: '*Deo Dante Dedi*'

Charterhouse is a beautiful school and a wonderful place to live and work. It was founded in 1611 and moved to its present magnificent 250-acre site near Godalming in Surrey in 1872. Few schools can offer such a splendid backdrop for teaching and learning, and the school community is very strong, with excellent relationships between pupils and staff.

Charterhouse accepts only boys at 13+, but it has welcomed girls at 16+ for over forty years. There are currently almost 140 girls out of a total of 415 sixth formers.

The curriculum follows the normal path to (I)GCSEs in Year 11, followed by a choice of Cambridge Pre-U / A Level courses or the IB Diploma Programme thereafter. We have high expectations of both pupils and teachers and aim to stretch and challenge all our pupils, in many cases well beyond the demands of the syllabus. The university destinations of our leavers reflect both their abilities and the quality of the education we provide.

Governing Body:
Chairman: W S M Robinson, BA

The Archbishop of Canterbury
M J Collins, MA, DPhil
Lady Toulson, CBE, LlB, FRSA
Mrs C M Oulton, MA
Professor K R Willison, BSc, PhD
R A Henley, FCA
P M R Norris, MA
N J Kempner, BSc
M L Everett, MA
DF Jennings, MA, Dip Arch, RIBA
C W V Wright, MA
Cllr Mrs C Curran, BSc
J N B Bovill, BA

Clerk to the Governing Body and Bursar: D A E Williams, BA, FCA

Headmaster: **R T F Pleming**, MA

Second Master: A J Turner, BA, LLM

Deputy Headmaster (*Academic*): J H Kazi, MA

Deputy Headmaster (*Pastoral*): J S Wilson, BA

Head of Girls: Mrs M H Swift, BDS

Head of Pupil Development: S P M Allen, MA

Assistant Staff:
T J Aberneithie, BA (*Head of Design & Technology*)
Miss P Aguado, BA
A Aidonis, MA, PhD (*Head of Classics and Master of the Scholars*)
Mrs S C Allen, MA
G Balasubramanian, MSc, PhD
Miss L F Batty, BSc
P A Bagley, MA
W Baugniet, LLM
N Beasant, BA (*Director of Sport*)
M Begbie, MA (*Director of Culture*)
M P Bicknell
J A Bingham, MA
M L J Blatchly, MA, FRCO
R A Bogdan, MA
S F C Brennan, BA (*Head of Spanish*)
K D Brown, BSc
R Brown, MPhys, PhD
O W Choroba, MA, PhD, CSci, CChem, MRSC (*Head of Chemistry*)
Miss S H Clarke, BA
Miss S Clarkson, MSt
Mrs C F Clive, DipTEFL
N L Coopper, MSc
M J Crosby
P D Dixon, BBus, BSc
M K Elston, BSc (*Head of Mathematics*)

O P Elton, BA
Major R N D Follett, BA (*CO, CCF*)
Miss E J Fox, BA (*Head of French*)
J D Freeman, BA (*Director of Drama*)
J P Freeman, MA
P Funcasta, BA, MSc
H D Gammell, MA
N S Georgiakakis, MSc
G H M Gergaud, L-ès-L
M R Gillespie, BA (*Head of History*)
N Hadfield, MA
E Hadley, BA (*Head of Theology, Philosophy & Ethics*)
C R G Hall, MA
I J M Hamilton
The Revd S J Harker, MA
R W T Haynes, MA
J S Hazeldine, BA
S T Hearn, MSc, MInstP
A D Hemery, MA, PhD
Miss A L Hoek, MSci
I A Hoffmann de Visme, MSc
Mrs E H H Holloway, BSc, PhD, MinstP
Miss J J Hughes, BSc, MEd (*Head of Careers*)
A R Hunt, MA
S D James, MA
A G Johnson, MSc (*Master of Examinations*)
A Johnston, MA, PhD
M D Kinder, MChem
J J Knight, BA (*Head of Government & Politics*)
D N Lancefield, CPhys, MInstP, MIEE, MIEEE (*Head of Physics*)
P J Langman, PhD
C W D Marsh, MA
T Marlow, PhD
S P Marshall, MMath, DPhil
D P Martucci, BSc
Miss H J Maxfield, BA
D J McCombes, BA
Mrs C L McDonald, MA (*Master of the Specialists*)
Ms E McGowan
R C D Millard, MA, MPhil (*Head of Academic Music*)
P Monkman, MA (*Director of Art*)
M W Nash, BA
Mrs E P Nelson, BSc, MSc (*Head of Biology*)
S J Northwood, BA, PhD
Mrs M D B Olive, HS Dip AD, MCLIP (*Librarian*)
The Revd C J B O'Neill, MA, PhD, DCH, Dip Psych, Cert Couns ECP
Mrs M H Orson, BA
Mrs D Osborn, BA, Dip SpLD (*Head of SEN*)
J N Parsons, BA, LRAM, ARCM
N S Pelling, MA
Miss H E Pinkney, BA
A Polunin
E F Poynter, BA
P A Price, MA (*Head of Geography*)
J Price
Miss J Puri, BA (*Head of Business Management*)
P J Rand, BA, PhD
E J Reid, MMath (*Master of the Under School*)
A N Reston, BA, MSt
T E Reynolds, MA, MSc
I S Richards, MA
Miss E J Richardson, BA
J M Richardson, BA
R D Sarre, BSc, DPhil (*Director of Academic IT Strategy*)
M N Shepherd, MA, FRCO, ARCM (*Director of Music*)
J M Silvester, BSc
R W Smeeton, ARCM, LRPS, MLC
Mrs C R I Smith, BA, MArAd (*Archivist*)
I C Smith, MA, MSci, CChem, MRSC (*Head of Science*)
R H Snell, BSc, MChem, DPhil
C M Sparrow, MA (*Master of the Yearlings*)

P S Stimpson, MEng
Miss S Taylor, BA
Miss J Tod, MSc (*Master of the Specialists*)
J C Troy, BSc (*Head of Economics*)
J F Tully, BEng, FICS, FRGS
Mrs E J Turner, BSc (*Head of Higher Education*)
N P Wakeling, MA (*Head of English*)
S Wood, BA
D G Wright, LTCL
Miss R E Wright, BA
M G Yeo, MA, PhD, FRHistS
E H Zillekens, BA, DPhil (*Head of Modern Languages*)

Senior Chaplain: The Revd Clive Case, BA, MTh

Admissions Registrar: H D Gammell, MA

Estate Bursar: Mrs E Humphreys, RIBA
Accountant: Mrs V Western, BA, FCA
Medical Officer: Dr A Borthwick, MA, MB, BChir

Counsellors:
The Revd C J B O'Neill
Mrs V Gordon-Graham, MA

Cricket Professional: M Bicknell
Football Professional: D Howells
Rackets Professional: M J Crosby

Houses and Housemasters:
Saunderites: Mrs S C Allen
Verites: N Hadfield
Gownboys: A N Reston
Girdlestoneites: P J Langman
Lockites: A Johnston
Weekites: E F Poynter
Hodgsonites: D G Wright
Daviesites: J F Tully
Bodeites: J S Hazeldine
Pageites: N S Pelling
Robinites: S T Hearn
Fletcherites: I A Hoffmann de Visme

Admission. Parents wishing to enter their sons for the School should contact the Admissions Registrar at least 3 years before they are due to come to the School.

Parents wishing their sons or daughters to enter Charterhouse in the Sixth Form should contact the Registrar at the beginning of the summer term in the year before the September entry.

At least one term's notice is required before the removal of a pupil from the School.

Details of the School's admissions policies can be found on the website.

Date of admission. Boys and girls are accepted for September entry only.

Fees per term (2014–2015). Inclusive fees: £11,415 for Boarders, £9,433 for Day Boarders, £8,273 for Sixth Form day pupils (Fletcherites). The Governing Body reserves the right to alter the School fee at its discretion.

Scholarships, Exhibitions and Bursaries.
13+ entry:
Ten Foundation Scholarships and up to five Exhibitions are offered. The examination is held in May.

A Benn Scholarship is offered for proficiency in Classics.

Up to five Music Scholarships and two Exhibitions are offered. The examinations are held at the School at the end of January. Music tuition on two instruments is free for Music Scholars and on one or two instruments for Exhibitioners.

Two Art Scholarships are offered as a result of an examination held at the School at the end of January.

Five Peter Attenborough Awards are made annually to candidates who demonstrate all-round distinction.

Up to two Sports Awards are made annually to exceptional sportsmen.

Sixth Form entry:

Up to six Sir Robert Birley Academic Scholarships and seven Academic Exhibitions are offered annually on the basis of performance in the entrance examination and interview.

Five Music Scholarships are offered annually, normally awarded in December. Music tuition on two instruments is free for Music Scholars. In addition, there is the John Pilling Organ Scholarship.

Two Art Scholarships are offered; the examinations for these awards will normally be held in November.

The Fletcher Scholarship is offered to a pupil from the local area to attend Fletcherites, the sixth form House at Charterhouse.

Bursaries. All Awards (except Exhibitions) may be increased to the value of the full School fee in cases of proven financial need.

Two Entrance Bursaries are offered to boys in Year 6 after a selection day in May.

Music. A tradition of musical excellence at Charterhouse is maintained and enhanced with six full-time staff and 30 visiting staff. 400 music lessons a week are taught, and orchestral and choral standards are enviable. Music IGCSE and Cambridge Pre-U are offered.

Art. The Studio offers excellent facilities to study painting, print-making, ceramics, sculpture, photography and film-making. Art GCSE and Cambridge Pre-U are offered. Life-drawing and the study of art history and architecture complement the practical work.

Design. The John Derry Technology Centre provides facilities for the teaching of GCSE, AS and A Level Design and Technology. The Centre offers boys and girls the opportunity to work in a wide range of materials.

Drama. The School has its own modern Theatre which is used extensively by pupils in term time, as well as by the public in school holidays. AS and A Level Theatre Studies are offered.

Golf. A 9-hole golf course was given to the school in July 1988 by the Old Carthusian Golfing Society.

Sports Centre. The Queen's Sports Centre was opened by The Queen in February 1997. It includes a 25m x 6 lane Swimming Pool, a multi-purpose Sports Hall, Fitness Suite, an Activities Room and an internal Climbing Tower.

Athletics Track. An all-weather Athletics Track was opened during the autumn of 1996.

Old Carthusian Club. All enquiries should be made to Mrs M F Mardall, The Recorder, Charterhouse, Godalming, Surrey GU7 2DX.

Prospective parents and their children are warmly invited to visit Charterhouse where they normally meet the Headmaster or Registrar, other staff and members of the School.

Charitable status. Charterhouse School is a Registered Charity, number 312054. Its aims and objectives are the provision of education through the medium of a secondary boarding school for boys, and girls in the Sixth Form.

Cheadle Hulme School

Claremont Road, Cheadle Hulme, Cheadle, Cheshire SK8 6EF

Tel: 0161 488 3330
             0161 488 3345 Registrar
Fax: 0161 488 3344
email: admissions@chschool.co.uk
website: www.cheadlehulmeschool.co.uk
Twitter: @CheadleHulmeSch

Motto: '*In loco parentis*'

A challenging, dynamic and relevant education for every student lies at the heart of Cheadle Hulme School. Set in 83 acres of Cheshire countryside, near Manchester, the School offers Bursaries, Scholarships in Music and Sport and an outstanding education founded upon academic challenge, personal and social development, physical health, emotional well-being, the practice of leadership and a commitment to service. Confidence is instilled in each student, helping them to become more effective learners by challenging them to think, to experience, to act and to share. Above all else,, every student is encouraged to develop and fulfil his or her potential. The skills and personal qualities nurtured through involvement in co-curricular activities enhance the quality of life of students throughout the School, developing interests and passions and supporting classroom study to ensure that every boy and girl at CHS is capable of greatness.

Governing Body:
Mr Philip R Johnson (*Chairman*)

Mr Michael Birchall	Mr Robin Cridland
Mrs Catherine Boyd	Mr Peter Driver
Mr Hans van Mourik Broekman	Dr David Riley
	Mr Chris Roberts
Mr Barney Brown	Mr David Shipley
Dr Stella Butler	Mrs Joanne Squire

Bursar and Clerk to the Governors: Mrs Sue Kershaw (*from April 2014*)

Head: Miss Lucy C Pearson, BA Oxon

Senior Deputy Head: Mr John Winter, BA

Deputy Heads:
Mr Andy D Nolan, BSc (*Pastoral*)
Mr Lee Richardson, BA (*Co-Curricular*)

Head of Junior School: Mrs Barbara Bottoms, BSc

Head of Infants: Mrs Anneliese Pye, BSc

Heads of Departments:
Art & Design: Mr Keith Yearsley, BA
Biology: Mr Jonathan Hedwat, BSc
Careers: Mrs Alison Hoverstadt, MSc
Chemistry: Mr Ian Chippendale, BA
Classics: Mrs Ann Johnson, BA
Design Technology: Mrs Fiona Buxton, BA
Director of Sport: Mr Matthew Higgins, BSc
Economics Business Management: Mr Gareth Matthews, BSc
English: Mr Nigel Westbrook, BA
Food & Nutrition: Mrs Rachel Dalton-Woods, MSc
Geography: Mrs Corrie Shallcross, BSc
History & Politics: Mr Nick Axon, MA
ICT Curricular Development Mrs Louise Hayes
Learning Support Mrs Sue Matthews, BSc
Mathematics Mr Steven Norton, MSc
Modern Languages, French: Mrs Francoise Lucas, BA
Modern Languages, German: Mrs Nicole Meredith, BA
Modern Languages, Spanish: Mr John Wilson, MPhil
Music: Mr Philip Dewhurst, BA
Philosophy, RS: Mrs Helen Firth, BA
Physics: Dr Jade Johnstone, MPhys, PhD
Psychology: Mrs Kris Gilbertson, BSc
Sixth Form Diploma: Mrs Nicole Meredith, BA
Sports Science: Mr Andy Wrathall, BSc
Theatre Studies & Drama: Ms Clare Harms, BA

Registrar: Mrs V Gray

Number in School. 1,420 (785 boys 635 girls) of whom 309 are in the Junior School and 279 in the Sixth Form.

Location. The School which is about 10 miles south of Manchester, 3 miles from the Airport and 10 miles from the Derbyshire Hills consists of the original Victorian and many new buildings in its own 83 acres of open land.

Admission. There are four main points of entry to Cheadle Hulme School.

The Junior School takes pupils from 4 years of age into Reception and there are a few places available to join at age 7 into Year 3.

In the Senior School the largest intake is at 11+ into Year 7 and there are a limited number of places available at 13+ into Year 9. We also welcome academically-able students to join us in the Sixth Form at 16+. There may be opportunities to join CHS in other Year groups, subject to places being available.

The entrance test, which is competitive because many more children apply than places exist, is designed to determine that the child can profit from the type of education provided.

Organisation and Curriculum. For pastoral care and administrative purposes the School is divided into Sixth Form; Upper School (Years 9–11); Lower School (Years 7 and 8); Junior and Infant. The curriculum is kept as broad as possible to KS3 and students choose 9 subjects at GCSE. In the Sixth Form pupils choose their 4 AS subjects and 3/4 A2 subjects or Cambridge Pre-U exams from a wide range of subjects. Special provision is made for those who wish to enter Oxford or Cambridge. Extensions classes form part of the Year 13 curriculum in all subjects.

On leaving the majority of pupils progress to University.

Clubs and Societies. There are many co-curricular activities which students are encouraged to participate in. These include a variety of music groups such as Concert Band, Big Band, Rock School, Wind and Guitar ensembles, Sinfonia and choirs, and there are many annual dramatic and musical productions. Among the societies and clubs catering for those interested are The Ezekiel Browne Society, Multimedia ICT, Go Sushi, Geography, Language clubs including Russian, Chinese, Spanish and German, Eco Soc, DT 'Come Design with Me', Science, Chess, Go Board Game, Classics, War Gaming, Climbing, Astronomy star gazing, orienteering, a wide range of Sports clubs, Dance and Fitness Clubs, Philosophical Society, Jewish Society, Amnesty International, Model United Nations Debating, Young Enterprise, Think Tank, 'Diggers' History, Volunteer and Community Groups and many others. Large numbers of pupils undertake the Duke of Edinburgh's Award Scheme which introduces them to a variety of new skills and expeditions to develop organisational and leadership abilities. 'Student Leader schemes' in over 50 co-curricular clubs give older pupils the opportunity to gain experience and skills working with and coaching younger pupils.

Games and Physical Activities. There is a full range of the field and team games, and, additionally, in Year 11 and Sixth Form, Yoga, Badminton, Volleyball and Basketball. Swimming is for all in the School's heated indoor pool. Students are encouraged to participate in all sports and to perform to the highest standard.

Fees per term (2014–2015). Subject to termly review: Junior School £2,565–£2,756; Senior School £3,552.

New parents, who are not already in membership of the Foundation Scheme, will automatically be enrolled in it. The aim of the scheme is to assist pupils to remain in the School in the face of financial difficulty following the incapacitation or the death of a parent. Benefits cannot be guaranteed, but in recent years no deserving case has been refused.

Scholarships and Bursaries. Music Scholarships are available for entry at 11+ and Sixth Form. Sports Scholarships are available for entry at 11+.

Bursaries are offered at 11+ based on academic merit and financial eligibility. A number of other Bursaries are available for entry to the Sixth Form on the same basis.

Charitable status. Cheadle Hulme School is a Registered Charity, number 1077017.

Cheltenham College

Bath Road, Cheltenham, Gloucestershire GL53 7LD
Tel: College: 01242 265600
          Admissions: 01242 265662
          Bursar: 01242 265686
Fax: College: 01242 265630
          Headmaster: 01242 265685
          Bursar: 01242 265687
email: info@cheltenhamcollege.org
website: www.cheltenhamcollege.org

Motto: *Labor Omnia Vincit*

Situated in 72 acres of beautiful grounds in the heart of the Cotswolds, Cheltenham College is one of the country's leading co-educational independent schools for boarding and day pupils aged 13–18. Combining a strong academic record with a considerable reputation for sport, drama, music and outward-bound activities, College offers an outstanding all-round education. Founded in 1841, it was the first of the great Victorian schools.

Visitor: The Rt Revd The Lord Bishop of Gloucester

The Council:
President: The Revd J C Horan
Deputy President: Dr R Acheson

Mr P Badham	Mr E L Rowland
Reverend P Bernhard	Ms K Sayer
Mrs J Blackburn	Mr T Smith
Mr P Brettell	Mr C Smyth
Professor C Chilvers	Mr W Straker-Nesbit
Dr M Crispin	Dr P Wingfield
Mrs R Lewis	Mr M Wynne
Brigadier D J R Martin	

Headmaster: Dr A L R Peterken, BA Durham, MA London, EdD Surrey

Bursar & Secretary to Council: Mr J Champion, FCIB

Deputy Head (Pastoral): Mr C N B Dawson, BA Bristol
Deputy Head (Academic): Mr D J Byrne, BA Cambridge, MA Cambridge
Senior Chaplain: The Reverend Dr A J Dunning, BA Oxford, PhD Birmingham
Assistant Head (Co-curricular): Mr A J Gasson, MA Dundee
Director of Admissions and Marketing: Mrs C Wood, BSc Sheffield
Development Director: Mrs C Dickens, BA Nottingham
Assistant Development Director: Mr S F Bullock, BA Exeter

Special Responsibilities:
Director of Learning: Dr M P Plint, BEd Johannesburg, MEd, PhD Gloucestershire
Head of Upper College: Mr S M F McQuitty, BSc Nottingham (*Head of Higher Education and Careers*)
Deputy Head of Upper College: Mr D M A Evans, BA Manchester
Head of Lower College: Mr G J Cutts, BA Sheffield City
Head of Third Form: Mr S E Conner, BSc Durham
Tutor for International Pupils: Ms S L Proudlove, BA Durham, MA York
Scholarships Coordinator: Mrs A J Eldred, BA Durham
Head of Prep School Liaison and Parental Relations: Mr S E Conner, BSc Durham
Director of Studies: Mr S J Brian, MA Edinburgh
Director of Extra-Curricular: Mr D R Faulkner, BSc Imperial
Director of Student Welfare: Mr B J Lambert, BSc Brunel
Head of Critical Thinking: Dr S J C Morton, MSc, PhD Birmingham

Coordinator of PSHCE: Mr T P F Carpenter, BSc Bristol

Duke of Edinburgh's Award Coordinator: Mr J L Jones, BSc Swansea, MSc Surrey, CChem, MRSC

Head of Community Service & 2 i/c PSHCE: Mr J C Stubbert, BEng Cardiff

Head of Leadership and Charities: Mr M C Todd, BComm Natal London Business School, CA South Africa

Examinations Officer: Mr D Meason, BA Gloucestershire

Induction Tutor Coordinator: Mrs C E Harrison, BSc Warwick

Housemasters and Housemistresses:

Ashmead Girls: Mrs A V Cutts, BEd Middlesex (*English & Drama*)

Boyne House Boys: Mr R J Penny, BSc Swansea (*Head of Geography*)

Chandos Girls: Mrs A J Poulain, BSc Brunel (*Sports Science*)

Christowe Boys: Mr N Nelson, BA East Anglia (*History of Art*)

Hazelwell Boys: Mr A J Coull, BA Thames Valley (*Modern Languages*)

Leconfield Boys: Mr C L Reid, BA Portsmouth, MA Ed Anglia Ruskin (*History & Politics*)

Newick House Boys: Mr F Llewellyn, BA London (*English and Theatre Studies*)

Queen's Day Girls:
Mr W Bates, BA Exeter (*Geography*)
Mrs W Bates, BA, MA Nanterre, Paris (*Modern Languages*)

Southwood Day Boys: Mr M K Coley, BSc Leeds (*Sports Science*)

Westal Girls: Mrs J O'Bryan, MSc Nottingham (*Biology*)
Mrs S M Jackson, TTD Johannesburg, FDE South Africa (*Assistant Housemistress*)

Common Room:

Art:
Miss J S Wallace-Mason, BA Brighton (*Head of Art*)
Mr N Nelson, BA East Anglia (*Head of History of Art*)
Mr D M A Evans, BA Manchester
Mr P J Lelliott, BA Coventry, MA RCA
Mrs S L Enright, BA Gloucestershire

Classics:
Mr T A Lambert, BA, MPhil King's College Cambridge (*Head of Classics*)
Miss E J Rawkins, MA St Andrews
Mr D J McCombie, BA Oxford
Mrs T V Penny, BA Birmingham

Design Technology:
Mr D J M Lait, BSc Brunel (*Head of Design Technology*)
Mr G J Cutts, BA Sheffield City
Mr B J Lambert, BSc Brunel
Ms B M Kaja, BA Bretton Hall College, West Yorkshire
Mr C P M McKegney, BA Loughborough
Miss H Hubbard, BA Gloucestershire

Economics & Business Studies:
Mr J R Mace, BA Durham, MSc Leicester (*Head of Business Studies*)
Dr G Mallard, MA Cambridge (*Head of Economics*)
Mr S F Bullock, BA Exeter
Mrs Z la Valette-Cooper, BA London Guildhall
Dr S J C Morton, MSc, PhD Birmingham (*Head of Critical Thinking*)
Mr M Todd, BComm Natal London Business School, CA South Africa
Mr M J Evetts, BSc Bath
Mrs A D Cross, BA Humberside

English and Drama:
Mr T E Brewis, BA Exeter (*Head of English*)
Ms J E Brodigan, BA Reading (*Second in Department*)
Mr F J Llewellyn, BA Royal Holloway

Mr K A Cook, BA Southampton
Mrs A V Cutts, BEd Middlesex
Mrs S M McBride, BA, MA Warwick (*Director of Drama*)
Mr C Runciman, MA Warwick (*Director in Residence*)
Mr L Davidson, BA York, MA York, PhD York
Miss C J Rowland, BA Salford
Mr J C P Kelway, BA Exeter, MA King's College London

English as an Additional Language:
Ms S L Proudlove, BA Durham, MA York (*Head of Department*)
Miss H C Davies, BA Lancaster

Geography:
Mr R J Penny, BSc Swansea (*Head of Geography*)
Mr S E Conner, BSc Durham
Mr A J Gasson, MA Dundee
Mr W Bates, BA Exeter
Mr F A Dobney, MA Aberdeen
Miss E R C Hartley, MA St Andrews

History & Politics:
Miss J E Doidge-Harrison, BA, MA Cantab (*Head of History*)
Dr M D Jones, MA Cantab, PhD London
Dr R D A Woodberry, MA Oxon, MLitt, PhD Bristol, FRSA
Mrs A J Eldred, BA Durham
Mr R Moore, BA Manchester (*Head of Politics*)
Mr C L Reid, BA Portsmouth, MA Ed Anglia Ruskin
Mr D M A Evans, BA Manchester

Information Technology:
Mr A H Isaachsen, BEd Deakin, Melbourne (*Director of ICT*)

Learning Support:
Dr M P Plint, BEd Johannesburg, MEd, PhD Gloucestershire (*Director of Learning*)
Mrs J Todd, BA Durham
Miss S J Marquis, BSc Bath (*Learning Mentor*)

Library:
Mrs G Doyle, MCLIP (*Librarian*)

Mathematics:
Dr B E Enright, BSc, PhD Hull (*Head of Department*)
Mr J R Card, BSc Birmingham, MEd Birmingham (*Second in Department*)
Mr S M F McQuitty, BSc Nottingham
Mr J S Morton, BEng Imperial
Mr R Peacock, BSc Bristol
Mr J C Stubbert, BEng Cardiff
Dr G A Ward, MEng Durham
Mr O W Packer, BSc Loughborough

Modern Languages:
Mrs E Leach, BA UWE (*Head of Department*)
Mrs S L Checketts, BA Cardiff
Mr D J Byrne, MA Cambridge
Mr S J Brian, MA Edinburgh
Mrs W A Bates, BA, MA Nanterre, Paris
Mrs G I J Fryer, Baccalaureat Serie A2, Nantes (*French Assistant*)
Mrs I T M Pemberton, BA Oxford Brookes
Ms A S Lopez Reyes
Mr J Coull, BA Thames Valley
Miss C A Smith, BA Cambridge, MPhil Cambridge (*Head of French*)
Mrs H Powell, BA Durham
Mrs V A Gonzalez, BA Georgetown University USA
Dr E A A Gerry, BA Oxford
Mr J C Chaloner, BA Oxford

Music:
Mr D P J McKee BA, MA Exeter (*Director of Music*)
Mr A J McNaught, GRSM, LRAM, ARCM
Mr A M M Ffinch, MA Oxon, ARCM

Psychology:
Dr T A Norman, BSc Durham, PhD Reading (*Head of Department*)
Miss L L Beere, BSc Open University
Mrs J E McQuitty, BSc Nottingham

Theology, Philosophy & Ethics:
The Reverend Dr A J Dunning, BA Oxford, PhD Birmingham (*Head of Department*)
The Reverend Dr A Samuel, BA Essex, MA Warwick
Dr A L R Peterken, BA Durham, MA London, EdD Surrey
Mr C B Dawson, BA Bristol

Science:
Mrs I C M Mech, BSc Johannesburg, MA Johannesburg (*Head of Department and Head of Biology*)
Mr S R Cooper, BEng Nottingham (*Head of Physics*)
Mr J L Jones, BSc Wales, MSc Surrey, CChem, MRSC (*Head of Chemistry*)
Mrs C E Harrison, BSc Warwick
Mrs S Ramsay, BEd Durban
Mr T P F Carpenter, BSc Bristol
Mrs J M O'Bryan, BSc Nottingham
Mrs J L Smith, BSc Nottingham
Mr S Rice, BSc Open University
Miss L L Beere, BSc Open University
Mr D R Faulkner, BSc Imperial
Miss P J Hoskins, BSc Loughborough
Mrs A Rowan, BA Cambridge
Mrs P E Aitken, BSc Dundee
Miss C Knowles, BSC Cardiff
Miss R Kramer, BSc King's College, London
Miss A M Haddock, BEng Durham
Mr R J H jones, BEng Newcastle, MSc Newcastle

Sports Science:
Mrs R K Faulkner, BSC Exeter (*Head of Girls' Games*)
Mrs A J Poulain, BSc Brunel (*Head of Sports Performance*)
Mr M K Coley, BSc Leeds
Miss P J Hoskins, BSc Loughborough (*Head of Netball*)
Mr R Shepherd (*Squash & Tennis Professional*)
Mr M P Briers (*Cricket & Rackets Professional*)
Mr J Cload, ACHE Portsmouth (*Officer i/c Shooting*)
Mr G H Williams, BSc Cheltenham & Gloucester College of HE, MA Gloucestershire (*Head of Hockey*)
Mr R J H Jones, BEng Newcastle (*Head of Rowing*)
Mr T Mayglothling (*Rowing Professional*)
Mr T Richardson, BSc Gloucestershire (*Head of Rugby*)
Mr M A Walton (*Rugby Coach*)
Mr M J Fairburn (*Hockey Professional*)
Miss C Roberts (*Hockey Coach*)
Mrs K Hornsby, BEd Sussex (*i/c Girls' Tennis*)
Mrs S Styler (*Head of Polo*)
Mr O. Morgan (*Rugby Coach*)
Mr N. Runciman (*Rugby Coach*)
Mr T Woodman (*Rugby Professional*)

CCF:
Mr R J Penny, BSc Swansea (*Contingent Commander*)
Mr J P Gwynne, WO2, QMSI (*Schools Staff Instructor*)

Archives:
Mrs C A Leighton, BA London, DAA Aberystwyth (*Archivist*)
Mrs J Barlow, BA Cardiff, MA Illinois (*Assistant Archivist*)

Preparatory School

Headmaster: Mr J F Whybrow, BEd Exeter

Deputy Head (Academic): Mrs V M Jenkins, BA
Deputy Head (Pastoral): Mr O A Jenkins, BA
Director of Studies: Mr P J Williams, BEd, BA
Director of Learning: Mrs G Barrett, MA, Adv Dip SEN, Cert SpLD

Director of Upper School: Mrs S Reid, BA
Director of Middle School: Mrs D Bond, BEd, MA
Head of Lower School: Mrs D J Isaachsen, BEd
Head of Kingfishers: Mrs R Buttress, BSc
Boarding House Parents: Mr R M Wells, BSc and Mrs F E Wells, BSc
Director of Music and Head of Co-Curricular: Mr K W Perona-Wright, BA

Location. Stunning buildings and first-class playing fields provide a magnificent setting near the centre of Regency Cheltenham. Situated in the heart of the beautiful Cotswolds with excellent road and rail connections with London and the major airports, Cheltenham College offers all the advantages of life in a thriving town community, whilst maintaining a separate campus life.

Numbers. Boys: 330 boarders; 68 day boys. Girls: 206 boarders; 56 day girls.

Admission. Entry to College is into Third Form at 13+ or Lower Sixth at 16+. Able pupils may also be admitted into the Fourth Form at 14+. Entry at 13+ can be secured in three ways: Common Entrance, College Entrance papers or College Academic Scholarship papers. Entry at 16+ can be secured by scholarship and entry tests in November or March, good GCSE predictions and a testimonial from previous school. Full details, prospectuses and application forms can be obtained from the Admissions Department who will always be glad to welcome parents who wish to see College. There is a registration fee of £100 and a final acceptance fee of £1,000 (for pupils aged 13–16) or £1,350 (for Sixth Form entrants) which is deducted from the final term's account.

Scholarships and Bursaries. Scholarships and Exhibitions are available for entry at both 13+ and 16+ (as well as 11+ into Cheltenham Prep). They are offered in Academic, Art, Design Technology, Drama (13+ only), Music (including 16+ Organ and Choral awards) and Sport. Discounts for Services Families and bursaries are also available.

Fees per term (2014–2015). Boarders £10,938, Day pupils £8,196. Sixth Form: Boarders £11,238, Day pupils £8,496.

Chapel. There is a ten-minute service in the Chapel most weekday mornings and a main service each Sunday. There is a Confirmation service every year.

Houses. The 10 Houses, eight boarding and two day, are at the heart of College life and all located around the College campus. Girls are in four houses and boys are in six houses. Accommodation and pastoral care is outstanding for both boys and girls.

Planned Developments. In line with our development plan we've already completed significant refurbishment of the College Library, Big Classical Theatre and, most recently, the Science Building. These are all facilities that we're very proud of and that's true too of Westal, our new girls' boarding house opened in September last year. Looking forward, we'll continue the rolling programme of boarding house refurbishment whilst at the same time completing many exciting new development projects including the creation of a new rowing base, renewal of our synthetic sports pitches and a major extension of the Sports Hall.

Curriculum. On entry at 13+, pupils follow a broad course for one year, before embarking upon GCSE in the Fourth Form. The core of the curriculum comprises: IGCSE English Language and English Literature, IGCSE Mathematics, and all three Sciences (either as Dual Award or Triple Award). All then choose at least one Modern Language (French, German, Spanish); and four options from Art, Classical Civilisation, Design Technology (Resistant Materials, Textiles), Drama, Geography, Greek, History, Latin, Music, PE and Theology, Philosophy & Ethics. In the Sixth Form, twenty-five AS and full A Level subjects as well as EPQ are offered. Boys and girls and given extensive preparation for entrance to Oxford, Cambridge and other top Russell Group universities. Over 95% of leavers go on to university.

Cultural Activities. The Arts are central to the life of College, with at least six plays being staged each year in the school's various theatres. Boys and girls are encouraged to attend concerts, plays, films and lectures not only in Cheltenham but in nearby Oxford, Stratford, Bristol and London. College is also significantly involved in Cheltenham's Jazz, Science, Literature and Music Festivals. Art is housed in Thirlestaine House, a beautifully elegant early nineteenth century mansion, with a Gallery that houses an exhibition of current Art and that also serves as an excellent chamber music concert hall, housing the superb Bösendorfer Imperial Concert grand pianoforte. The beautiful Chapel houses a magnificent 3-manual Harrison & Harrison organ. Music plays a vital part in College life, with pupils able to learn just about every orchestral instrument imaginable, even bagpipes. The Chapel Choir, Chamber Choir and Barbershop groups enable singers to reach very high standards and many achieve university Choral Scholarships. The numerous instrumental groups and ensembles, from the Orchestra, Chamber Orchestra and Wind Band to the Jazz Bands and String Quartets, regularly perform in Cheltenham Town Hall, the town's Pump Rooms, as well as in the College Chapel and other venues. Both the top Jazz Band 'JIG' and the Chamber Choir have recorded CDs in the last few years.

Sports. Cheltenham College is one of the strongest schools nationally in a wide cross section of sports and benefits from top-level sports professionals and coaches. The main boys' games are rugby, hockey, tennis, cricket and rowing. The main girls' games are hockey, netball, tennis and rowing. In addition to the two astroturf pitches, the Sports Hall and swimming pool, there are excellent facilities for other sports available, which include rackets, squash, golf, basketball, dance, athletics, cross country, badminton, basketball, polo, climbing and shooting.

Activities. On entry to College, a structured programme of outdoor pursuits, team building exercises and leadership initiatives are provided for one year. Following this, CCF is compulsory for one year at age 14, optional thereafter. The Duke of Edinburgh's Award Scheme operates at Bronze and Gold level and a wide range of expeditions is available, including an annual trip to Nepal. College offers a full range of activities in the period after GCSEs. Up to 30 clubs operate weekly, including shooting, dance, pottery, film-making and drama.

Service. There is a strong Community Service scheme which serves the town, and an Industrial Link scheme enables all College Sixth-formers to experience the world of work. The College's Humanitarian Aid Project raises funds for building and refurbishment work in a number of orphanages and schools and the members of the group regularly visit Romania and Kenya to provide practical assistance. Wherever possible, all College facilities are made available to the town, especially the festivals, and other schools.

University entry and Careers. There is a full-time teacher in charge of Careers, and another responsible for University and Higher Education advice. In addition, every Sixth-former has a tutor who is charged with ensuring that he or she is fully aware of the opportunities and challenges available.

Cheltonian Association. Tel: 01242 265694.

Cheltenham College Preparatory School. *For details see entry in IAPS section.*

Charitable status. Cheltenham College is a Registered Charity, number 311720. As a charity it is established for the purpose of providing an efficient course of education for boys and girls.

Chetham's School of Music

Long Millgate, Manchester M3 1SB
Tel: 0161 834 9644
Fax: 0161 839 3609
email: chets@chethams.com
website: www.chethams.com

Chetham's is a co-educational school for boarding and day students aged eight to eighteen. The School teaches a broad curriculum set within a framework of music. At the centre of every child's course is a 'musical core' of experiences rooted in a determination to educate the whole person. Originally founded in 1653, through the Will of Humphrey Chetham, as a Bluecoat orphanage, the School was reconstituted in 1969 as a specialist music school.

Governors:
Dame A V Burslem, DBE (*Chairman*)
R Bailey
Ms A Corcoran
M Edge
The Very Revd Rogers Govender, Dean of Manchester Cathedral
Prof E Gregson, BMus, GRSM, LRAM, FRAM
Dr D Hill
Mrs J Pickering
A Simpkin
J Wainwright, BA

Staff:

Head: Mrs Claire Moreland, MA

Director of Music: S Threlfall, GRNCM Hons, FRSA
Bursar: Mrs S C Newman, BSc Hons, FCA
Deputy Head, Pastoral: Ms C Rhind, BA
Deputy Head, Curriculum: C Newman, MA, MSc

Music:

PA to the Director of Music: Mrs J Scott
Music Department Coordinator: I Mayer
Concert Administrator: Ms H Bull
Music Department Timetabler: Miss N Prestt
Auditions and Administration Secretary: Mrs A Herbert
Music Department Secretary: Mrs C Booth

Key:
Chamber Music Tutor
(Hallé) *Member of Hallé Orchestra*
(BBC) *Member of BBC Philharmonic*
* *Tutor at Royal Northern College of Music*
(O.North) *Member of Opera North Company*
(RLPO) *Member of Royal Liverpool Philharmonic Orchestra*
X *Manchester Camerata*
(CBSO) *Member of City of Birmingham Symphony Orchestra*

Brass:
Head of Department: David Chatterton
Euphonium Tutors: Bill Millar #, David Thornton #*
Horn Tutors: Elizabeth Davis #*, Julian Plummer (*Hallé*)
Percussion Tutors: Sophie Hastings (*Latin percussion and Kit*), David Hext (*Hallé*), Paul Patrick (*BBC*)#*
Trombone Tutors: Robert Burtenshaw #(*O.North*), Philip Goodwin (*BBC*)#, Les Storey #
Trumpet Staff: David Chatterton #
Tutors: John Dickinson *#, Murray Greig *#(*O.North*), Tracey Redfern #X, Gareth Small (*Hallé*)#
Tuba Tutors: Brian Kingsley *#(*O.North*)

Keyboard:
Head of Department: Dr Murray McLachlan *

Staff: Susan M Bettaney #, Simon Bottomley #, Peter Lawson *
Tutors: Ruth Aldred, Graham Caskie, Hazel Fanning, Benjamin Frith #, Duncan Glenday, John Gough, Alison Havard, Marta Karbownicka, Helen Krizos *, Jonathan Middleton, Dina Parakhina *, Marie-Louise Taylor, Masa Tayama, Kathleen Uren #, Jeremy Young #
Harpsichord Tutor: Charlotte Turner
Jazz Piano Tutor: Les Chisnall
Organ Tutors: Christopher Stokes, Joshua Hales
Chamber Tutors: Benjamin Frith, Jeremy Young

Strings:
Head of Department: Nicholas Jones
Assistant: Owen Cox
Senior Chamber Music Tutor: Graham Oppenheimer
Violin Staff: Owen Cox
Tutors: Joafeng Chen, Connie del Vecchio (*RLPO*), Kristoffer Dolatko, Mikhail Gurevitch, Ruth Hahn, Benedict Holland *, Linda Janowska, Adrian Levine #, Sebastian Mueller, Jan Repko *, Yumi Sasaki, Katie Stillman, Deirdre Ward, Qian Wu #
Viola Tutors: Adrian Levine, Graham Oppenheimer #
Cello Staff: Nicholas Jones # *, Stephen Threlfall #
Tutors: Barbara Grunthal X, Anna Menzies, David Smith #, Gillian Thoday, Elinor Gow
Double Bass Tutor: Yi Xin Salvage (*Hallé*), Steve Berry (*jazz*)
Harp Tutor: Eleanor Hudson, Marie Leenhardt (*Hallé*)
Guitar Tutors: Jim Faulkner (*jazz*), Wendy Jackson #, Rory Russell
Lute Tutor: Hugh Cherry

Woodwind:
Head of Department: Belinda Gough
Recorder/Baroque Ensembles Tutor: Chris Orton
Baroque Flute and Historical Performance: Martyn Shaw
Oboe Tutors: Rachael Clegg X, Stephane Rancourt (*Hallé*), Valerie Taylor *
Flute Tutors: Katherine Baker (*Hallé*), Rachel Forgreive *, Belinda Gough #, Laura Jellicoe #*, Linda Verrier #*
Clarinet Tutors: Rosa Campos-Fernandez (*Hallé*), Lynsey Marsh *, Jim Muirhead (*Hallé*)#, Andrew Wilson #
Saxophone Tutors: Iain Dixon (*Jazz/improvisation*), Jim Muirhead (*Hallé*), Carl Raven * (*Jazz/improvisation*), Andrew Wilson #
Bassoon Tutors: Ben Hudson (*Hallé*), Graham Salvage *
Contra-Bassoon Tutor: Steve McGee *(*Hallé*)

Vocal Department:
Tutors: Helen Francis #, Margaret McDonald, Stuart Overington, Diana Palmerston #

Staff Accompanists:
Heads of Department: Brenda Blewett, Nicholas Oliver
Staff: Elena Namilova, Martyn Parkes, Hilary Suckling

Composition:
Head of Department: Dr Jeremy Pike, MA, MPhil, PhD, LRAM, HonARAM
Staff: Dr Gavin Wayte

Music Technology:
Head of Department: Dr Jeremy Pike, MA, MPhil, PhD, LRAM, HonARAM
Staff: Adrian Horn, BMus

Practice Team Leaders:
Charlotte Turner
Lulu Yang

Big Band:
Directors: Richard Iles, Jim Muirhead (*Hallé*)

Improvisation:
Steve Berry *, Les Chisnall (*Keyboard*), Iain Dixon

Alexander Technique:
Patrick Grundy-White, Anne Whitehead

Academic Music:
S King, BA, MA, MPhil, PhD
Ms R Aldred, BMus
Miss C Campbell Smith, MA
J LeGrove, BA
D Mason, BA
Dr S Murphy, PhD, BA
Mrs S Oliver, BA

Art:
Miss A Boothroyd, BA
Mrs J Jones, BA

Compensatory Education/Special Needs:
Mrs B L Owen, BEd, RSA Dip SpLD
Miss L Fogg, MA
Miss C Lynch, BA
A Saunders, BMus (*Learning Support Assistant*)

Drama & Theatre Studies:
P Dougal, MA

English:
Mrs J Harrison, MA
P Dougal, MA
Miss L Jones, BA
J Runswick-Cole, MEd

Humanities & PSHE:
A Kyle, BA
M Clarke, BSc
Mrs S Cox, BA
C Newman, MA

Information Technology:
Mrs F Holker, BSc
Miss C Whittaker, BA

Junior Department:
D Harris, BA

Languages:
C Law, PhD, MA
P Chillingworth, BA
Ms S Grossova, BA
Mrs S Hales, BA

Mathematics:
Miss A Hayward, BSc
C Bramall, BA
Mrs F Holker, BSc

Music Technology:
Head of Department: Dr Jeremy Pike, MA, MPhil, PhD, LRAM, HonARAM
Staff: Adrian Horn, BMus

Recreation:
Ms I Staszko, BEd, MA
Miss C Whittaker, BA

Sciences:
P Przybyla, BSc
J Blundell, BSc
Mrs A Dack, BSc
Mrs L Gartside, BSc
A Henderson, BA

Librarian: Mrs G Wood, BMus

Careers:
Dr S Murphy, PhD, MMus, BA (*Music Colleges*)
C Newman, MA (*Universities*)

Houses:
Mr & Mrs J Runswick-Cole (*Boys' House*)
Mrs I Merrett (*Girls' House*)
Mr G Taylor (*Victoria House*)

School Doctor: Dr J Tankel
Nurse: Mrs K Scott, RGN
Head's PA: Mrs L Haslam

The School numbers 294 students, of whom 149 are girls. There are 215 boarders. Admission is solely by musical audition, and any orchestral instrument, plus keyboard, guitar, voice or composition, may be studied. Each student studies two instrumental studies, or voice and one instrument, as well as following academic courses which lead to GCSE and A Levels and to university entrance and music college. The School stands on the site of Manchester's original 12th century Manor House adjacent to the Cathedral, and is housed partly in the fine 15th century College Buildings, and partly in the New School (2012) which houses all the instrumental, musical and academic teaching, an Outreach Centre and two performance spaces.

Music. Instrumental tuition is guided and monitored by the advisers in each specialism, who visit regularly to survey students' work, conduct internal examinations and give masterclasses. Internationally renowned musicians hold residences at the School for string, wind, brass, percussion and keyboard players. The Director of Music has responsibility for the full-time Music Staff and also for about 100 visiting tutors. All students receive three sessions of individual instrumental tuition each week. Practice is rigorously set and supervised. Academic Music is normally studied at A Level.

Boarding. There are two boarding houses for girls and boys aged 13 to 18 and one for Juniors aged 8 to 13. Each House is run by House Parents in residence, with resident assistants. All full-time teachers act as Tutors and are involved with pastoral care. In addition, when necessary, students have open access to the School Counsellors.

Recreation. Serious attention is paid to recreation, PE and games and the students' physical well-being. On-site facilities include an indoor swimming pool, gym, multi-gym and a squash court.

Applications, Visits. Entry is by audition only. Preliminary assessment auditions are held throughout the year, with final auditions in the Christmas and Spring terms.

The Prospectus and application forms are sent on request and are available on the School's website. Parents and prospective students are welcome to visit the School by arrangement with the Head's PA.

Fees, Grants. All entrants from the United Kingdom are eligible for grants under the Department for Education's Music and Dance Scheme. Parental contributions are calculated according to means and parents on low incomes qualify automatically for full fee remission. The Bursar will be glad to advise about the scales.

Choristers. The School is a member of the Choir Schools' Association and Choristerships at Manchester Cathedral for day boys and girls are available under a separate scheme. Choristers' Fee: £9,480 pa (subject to Cathedral Bursaries).

Charitable status. Chetham's School of Music is a Registered Charity, number 526702. It exists to educate exceptionally gifted young musicians.

Chigwell School

Chigwell, Essex IG7 6QF

Tel:	020 8501 5700
Fax:	020 8500 6232
email:	hm@chigwell-school.org
website:	www.chigwell-school.org

Motto: *'Aut viam inveniam aut faciam'*, *'Find a Way or Make a Way'*.

The School was founded in 1629 by Samuel Harsnett, Archbishop of York, "to supply a liberal and practical education, and to afford instruction in the Christian religion, according to the doctrine and principles of the Church of England". William Penn, founder of Pennsylvania, is the most famous Old Chigwellian.

Today the School welcomes boys and girls from all backgrounds and is a lively, happy community in which pupils are encouraged to develop all their talents to the full.

The School became co-educational in September 1997 and currently there are over 885 pupils aged 4 to 18 pupils, including 27 international boarders.

Governing Body:
Chair: Mrs S L Aliker, BA, MBA, ACMA
Vice Chairman: D Morriss, Esq, BSc, CEng, FIET, FBCS, CITP
Mrs E Brett, ACA
J Cullis, Esq, MBE, BA, MSc
Sir Richard Dales, KCVO, CMG, MA
Dr G Dixon, MA, BMus, PhD, ARAM, FRCO, FRSA
N Garnish, Esq, BSc, MBA, MCMI
Mrs J Gwinn, BSc
A N Howat, Esq
M Higgins, Esq
R Howard, Esq, MA
The Revd M Lambert, BSc, MA, MPhil
Dr A Pruss, BSc, PhD, MBBS
The Revd G R Smith, AKC
R H Youdale, Esq, MA

Clerk to the Governors: G Norman, Esq, BSc Econ

Bursar: D N Morrison, MA, PGCE

Headmaster: M E Punt, MA, MSc, PGCE

Deputy Head: D J Gower, BSc, PGCE

Deputy Head, Staff and Systems: Mrs A Savage, FTLC, GTCl, PGCE

Head of the Junior School: S C James, BA, PGCE

Deputy Head of the Junior School: A Stubbs, BA

Head of the Pre Prep School: Mr E Gibbs, BA, PGCE, NPQH

Assistant Staff:
* *Head of Department*
† *Housemaster/mistress*

Mrs A M Aitken, MA
E Aitken, MA (*Art and Design)
Ms S Bell, BA
Mrs L E Bengtson, BSc, PDAP (†*Lambourne*)
Mrs K S Bint, BSc
Mrs J M Botham, BSc
Mrs J M Boughton, BA
The Revd M L Bradley, BA, MMus, MLitt
S M Chaudhary, MA (*Mathematics)
Mrs L Chery, MA
Miss R M Childs, MA
Dr P G Clayton, BSc, PhD
Miss E C Conway, BA
S Coppell, MA (*Modern Languages)
Ms E Creber, BSc
Miss S L Dick, BSc (†*Swallow's*)
W P Eardley, BSc (*Biology)
H J G Ebden (*Music)
K Farrant, BEd (*Boys Games)
Mrs E M P Feeney, L-ès-L
Dr E M Ferreira, PhD, MSc
P R Fletcher, MA, DipTEFL
Miss J R Foster, BA
Mrs A L Gehrke, BA
I C Goddard, BA (*History)

S J Goodfellow, MA (*Religious Studies*)
J W Harley, BA
D J L Harston, MA
D W Hartland, MA (*Geography; †Caswalls*)
G S Inch, BA (*Senior Master*)
Mrs S Inch, BEd
Mrs V C James, BEd
Mrs N A Jermyn, MEd, BA (*Design & Technology*)
Mrs N J Jones, BA
C K Lawrence, BSc (*A Level PE*)
Miss F M Leach, BMus
A Long, MSc (*Head of Sixth Form*)
R A F Lonsdale, MA
C J Lord, MA (*Classics*)
H J Lukesch, 1st & 2nd STEX (*German*)
J L Maingot, BA (*Drama*)
Dr T Martin, PhD
Mrs C E Matthews, BA
Ms J Meadows, BSc
F Meier, BA (*Boarding*)
Mrs V G Meier, BA
J P Morris, BSc (†Penns*)
D N Morrison, MA
D J Morse, BA (*Academic IT*)
J A Muse, MA
Ms C M Nairac, BA
Miss A M J Ochana MSc
Ms J Osborne, BEd (*Learning Support*)
D I Patel, BSc
The Revd S N Paul, BA (*Chaplain*)
S B Pepper, BA (*Government & Politics*)
Miss Y A Peterson, BA
Mrs P Pewsey, BSEd, TEFL
Mrs R J Philip, BEd
B W Porter, BSc
D P Rabbitte, BA, LLB
Mrs E R Rawlings, BA
Mrs E R Rea, MA (*English*)
Ms P S Rex, BA
Mrs M A Saunders, BA
N M Saunders, BSc (*Director of Studies*)
Miss M F Smith, BA
Miss H E Spark, BSc
R S Spicer, BA (*Economics*)
Mrs J Summers, BEd
Ms M C Teichman, BSc
Mrs L M Thurtle, BA
Mrs C E Tilbrook, BEd, DipSEA
W Tomset, BSc
J J Twinn, BA
Mrs T Tyson, BA
Miss A D van Bergen, BEd
Miss S E Wales, BA (* Girls' Games*)
Miss M Weeks, BSc
Mrs S E Welsford, BEd
B Wille, BSc
S C Wilson, MEd, BSc (*Science*)
Dr G Winfield, PhD

Admissions Registrar: Mrs J S Long

Medical Officer: Dr S Rebel, MBBS, DRCOG, MRCGP, DFFP, BSc

Location. Chigwell School stands in a superb green belt location in 100 acres of playing fields and woodlands, midway between Epping and Hainault Forests and enjoys excellent communications. It is easily accessible from London (by Central Line Undergound network). Both the M25 and M11 motorways are close by, while Heathrow, Gatwick, City of London, Stansted and Luton Airports are all reachable from the School within the hour.

Buildings. The original building is still in use and houses the Senior School Swallow Library. There has been a con-

siderable amount of building in the past years and all the older buildings have been modernised while retaining their character. New facilities include a Junior School classroom block, a new Junior School library, a state-of-the-art Drama Centre, new catering facilities, a Sixth Form coffee shop, upgraded boys' boarding houses and a superb floodlit all-weather pitch. The latest addition is the purpose-built Pre-Prep School which opened in September 2013.

Organisation. The School is divided into the Senior and Junior Schools but is administered as a single unit with a common teaching staff.

The Head of the Junior School is responsible for all pupils between the ages of 7 and 13, although teaching from Year 7 upwards is coordinated by the Senior School. The Junior School is on the same site as the Senior School and all facilities and grounds are used by Junior pupils. Assembly, Games and Lunch are all arranged separately from the Senior School. (For further details, see Junior School entry in IAPS section.)

The Head of Pre-Prep is responsible for children aged 4 to 7 and they are largely self-contained in the new Pre-Prep School.

In the Senior School, all the day pupils and boarders are divided into four Day Houses. Each House has a large House room and a Housemaster's or Housemistress's study.

Curriculum. Pupils follow a broad based course leading to GCSE. Maths, English, Science and one modern language form the common core of subjects. Science is taken either as three separate subjects (Physics, Biology, Chemistry) or as Coordinated Science. In addition, a wide range of options is taken at GCSE including Art and Design, Graphic Design, Design Technology, French, German, Spanish, Latin, Greek, Geography, History, Religious Studies, Drama and Music.

Sixth Form. Students take 4 AS Level subjects in the first year and 3 or 4 A2 Level subjects in the second year. Subjects taken include, Latin, Greek, Classical Civilisation, French, German, Spanish, English, Economics, History, Geography, Maths, Further Maths, Physics, Chemistry, Biology, Music, Art, Design and Technology, Psychology, Religious Studies and Theatre Studies.

Games and Activities. Cricket, Football, Netball, Hockey (Boys and Girls), Athletics, Cross-Country Running, Swimming, Squash, Tennis, Golf, Basketball and Badminton. There are numerous School Societies and an Explorer Scout Troop. Many pupils join The Duke of Edinburgh's Award scheme. There is a swimming pool, two Sports Halls and extensive playing fields on site.

Art & Design, Ceramics, and D & T. Art is taught throughout the School and there is excellent provision for Ceramics and D & T which form part of the curriculum for all pupils between the ages of 10 and 14.

Music. There are three Orchestras, two Wind Bands, one Swing Band and six Choirs. Many other ensembles flourish and perform at major concerts during the year, some of which take place in the local community. Pupils may learn any instrument (including the Organ).

Boarding. Boy Boarders are accommodated in Church House, run by Mr and Mrs Meier, and Harsnett's House, run by Mr and Mrs Saunders. Sandon Lodge, set in the middle of the beautiful School Grounds, accommodates Sixth Form Girl Boarders under the care of Dr and Mr Lord. Hainault House, under the supervision of Mr and Mrs Goddard, lies adjacent to the Junior School and offers accommodation for girls.

Fees per term (2014–2015). Full boarding £8,560; Day pupils £3,215–£5,115. Fees vary depending on age. Fees are inclusive of all tuition, meals (lunch and afternoon tea), textbooks, societies and most clubs.

Admission. Pupils usually join Chigwell School at 4+, 7+, 11+, 13+ or 16+.

Scholarships and Bursaries. Academic scholarships are awarded each year, primarily at 11+ and 16+. They are awarded in recognition of academic merit, irrespective of financial means. A competitive examination for Academic scholarships is held each year during the Lent Term for pupils aged 11+ and during the Michaelmas Term for pupils aged 16+.

Music scholarships are offered each year at 11+ and sometimes at 13+ and 16+ and these make a substantial contribution to school fees. In return, scholars are expected to play a full role in the performing life of the department. Currently, two scholars attend the Junior Guildhall School of Music on Saturdays.

Art and Drama scholarships are available at 16+.

Chigwell has always tried to ensure that children who would benefit from an education at the School are not excluded for financial reasons. A number of means-tested Bursaries are offered.

Further details can be obtained from the Admissions Registrar (email: admissions@chigwell-school.org).

The Old Chigwellians' Association. c/o Development Office, Chigwell School, Essex.

Charitable status. Chigwell School is an Incorporated Charity, registration number 1115098. It exists to provide a rounded education of the highest quality for its pupils.

Christ College
Brecon

Brecon, Powys LD3 8AF
Tel: 01874 615440 (Head)
           01874 615440 (Bursar)
Fax: 01874 615475
email: enquiries@christcollegebrecon.com
website: www.christcollegebrecon.com

Motto: '*Possunt quia posse videntur.*'
Founded by Henry VIII, 1541. Reconstituted by Act of Parliament, 1853.

Visitor: Her Majesty The Queen

Governing Body:
E P Silk (*Chairman*)
The Rt Revd The Lord Bishop of Swansea and Brecon
The Venerable The Archdeacon of Brecon
J Bartlett
W R M Chadwick, JP
D G Clarke, TD, OBE, DL
Prof R B Davies
M Gittins
Mrs S A E Gwyer Roberts, BA, MEd, NPQH, FRSA
R J Harbottle, BA
D James
Mrs J James
Mrs H Johnson
The Hon Mrs E S J Legge-Bourke, LVO, Lord Lieutenant of Powys
Mrs A Mathias
A Whittall

Head: **Mrs Emma Taylor**, MA Oxon

Deputy Head: S A Spencer, BA (*English*)

Director of Studies: J D Bush, MA (*English*)

Assistant Staff:
* *Head of Department*
† *Housemaster/mistress*

Mrs R E Allen, BA (*History)
The Revd S A Baker, BEd (*Chaplain & RS*)
†Mrs E Blatt, BSc (*Biology*)
N C Blackburn, BSc (*Mathematics*)
T Bolderstone, BA (*Modern Languages*)
†Mrs H A Caithness, BSc Hons (*Mathematics*)

†M J Caithness, BSc Hons (*Chemistry*)
P Chandler, BA (*EAL, Careers*)
J T Cooper, BA, ARCO (*Director of Choral Music*)
†A Copp, BSc (*Economics*)
M Cornish, MA (*RS)
P E Curran, BSc (**Information Technology*)
P K Edgley, ARPS (*Photography*)
R Evans, BSc (*Geography*)
Miss H Evans, BA (*Modern Languages*)
Mrs U Feldner, BA (*Art*)
†Mrs C N Forde-Halpin, BA (*Mathematics*)
†B Goodrich, MSc (*Geography)
†Mrs R Goodrich, MA (*Psychology)
D R Grant, BSc (*Chemistry*)
†G Halpin, BSc (*Business Studies*)
Miss H Evans, BA (*Modern Languages*)
Mrs D Houghton, BA (*Art)
G Hope, BEng, MSc (**Physics & Science*)
Mrs J Hope, MA (*English*)
Miss S Hunter, BA (*PE)
J S Johnson, MA (*Drama)
Miss S E Jones, BSc (*Biology)
Mrs F Kilpatrick, BA, RSA Dip SpLD, AMBDA (*Learning Support)
J Ling, BA (**Director of Music*)
Mrs L McLean, BA (*Modern Languages)
G Meredith, BSc, PhD (*Chemistry)
I J Owen, BSc (*Mathematics)
Miss L Perez Garcia, BA Hons (*Modern Languages*)
Dr D Phelps, MA, PhD (*History*)
A Reeves, BSc (*Physics*)
C Rees, BA (*Modern Languages*)
R G Rogers, BA (**Design & Technology*)
Mrs R Sandhu, BA (*History*)
†M P Sims, BSc (*Biology*)
Mrs M K E Tanner, MA (*English)
C Thomas, BSc (*Physics*)
T J Trumper, BEd (*Director of Sport*)
Mrs S E Warwick, MA (*DT, ICT, PSE*)
Mrs L Webber, Cert Ed, Dip Psych, MEd Psych (*PE*)

Junior Section
Mrs J Lewis, BA Ed (*Head of Juniors*)
G Kerr, BA Ed (*KS2*)
Miss A Hallinan, BSc (*KS2*)
H Jones (*Sports Assistant*)
Mrs J Gardner (*Classroom Assistant*)

Visiting Music Staff:
T Cronin
A S Davies, GWCMD
G Hamlin
J C Herbert
P Israel
R Johnston
Miss E Priday, LRAM, ARAM
Mrs D Taylor
Miss K Thomas
Mrs C E Walker, MA Oxon, ARCM

Bursar: M Allen
Admissions Registrar: Mrs M L Stephens
SSI: WO2 M Bevan
OBA Liaison: H L P Richards
Development Director: S Maggs, BA, GCGI, PMICS, MInstF

Christ College, Brecon lies in a setting of outstanding natural beauty at the foot of the Brecon Beacons on the edge of the small market town of Brecon, two minutes walk away on the opposite side of the river. The River Usk flows alongside the playing fields providing good canoeing and fishing while the nearby Llangorse Lake is available for sailing and windsurfing.

The school was founded by King Henry VIII in 1541 when he dissolved the Dominican Friary of St Nicholas. The 13th Century Chapel and Dining Hall are at the centre of school life and the school's mix of important, historic buildings and modern architecture represents the continuity of education at the school. In the last ten years additional boarding capacity has been added to a girls house, all of the houses have been refurbished, an Astroturf built as well as Fitness Suite, the Art School re-located and expanded while a Sixth Form Centre renovated as well as extensive landscaping of the school campus. In recent years, new additions to the built environment include a £1.5m Science Centre and a new Centre for the Creative Arts – Y Neuadd Goffa: The Memorial Hall. In September 2014, St Nicholas House, a junior day house for pupils aged 7–11 years, was opened.

Estyn, Her Majesty's Inspectorate for Education & Training in Wales, inspected the school in 2011 and rated the school's current performance as 'Excellent' with 'Excellent prospects for improvement'.

Organisation. Christ College was a boys' only school until 1987 when girls were admitted to the Sixth Form. In 1995 the school became fully co-educational. There are 380 pupils in the school of whom 219 are boys and 161 girls. Approximately 60% of pupils board and there are three senior boys' houses, School House, Orchard House and St David's House, two senior girls' houses, Donaldson's House and de Winton House, and a lower school house, Alway House, for 11–13 year old boys and girls. St Nicholas House is a junior day section for boys and girls aged 7–11 years.

Chapel. Chapel services are conducted in accordance with the liturgy of the Anglican church, but entrance to Christ College is open to boys and girls of all faiths. The ownership of Chapel by the boys and girls, demonstrated through their participation in services and their singing, is a feature of the school. Pupils are prepared for Confirmation by the School's Chaplain who lives on site.

Curriculum. Up to the Form 5 (Year M11) pupils follow a balanced curriculum leading to GCSE at which most pupils take 10 subjects. Options are chosen at the end of Form 3 (Year M9). Current subjects taught include English Language, English Literature, Mathematics, French, Spanish, Physics, Chemistry, Biology, History, Geography, Latin, Religious Studies, Art, Music, Design & Technology, Physical Education, Photography, Drama, PSE, Information Technology and Welsh. Greek is sometimes available as an extra subject outside the timetable.

In the Sixth Form a similar range of subjects is taken at AS and A2 Level plus opportunities to take Economics, Further Maths, Business Studies and Psychology. All pupils have timetabled tutorial periods and in the Sixth Form periods are set aside for Careers advice. The Extended Project Qualification (EPQ) is also available for Sixth Form pupils.

Class sizes rarely exceed 20 up to GCSE and average fewer than 10 at A Level.

Games. The main school games are Rugby Football, Cricket, Hockey, Soccer, Netball, Cross-Country and Athletics. Tennis, Badminton, Squash, Volleyball, Basketball, Golf, Fishing, Swimming, Shooting, Mountain Biking, Canoeing, Fencing, Indoor Cricket, Climbing, Triathlon and Aerobics are also available. The playing fields are extensive and lie adjacent to the school. Christ College has entered into a corporate partnership with Cradoc Golf Club, two miles outside of Brecon, to encourage pupils of all ages and experience in the fundamentals of the game of golf. The opportunity to play at Cradoc Golf Club and receive professional instruction is also extended to all parents of pupils attending Christ College. A recent initiative with The Pony Club also means that equestrians now have access to a British Eventing standard course at the nearby Glanusk Estate.

Thursday Afternoons. On Thursday afternoons the CCF Contingent meets. There is a choice between Army and Royal Air Force sections and the CCF has its own Headquarters, Armoury and covered 30m Range in the school grounds. Pupils take their proficiency certificate after two years and may then choose to continue as Instructors, undergo training for the Duke of Edinburgh's Award Scheme or leave the CCF and may become involved in community service.

Music. The Chapel Choir is large and enjoys an excellent reputation with radio and television broadcasts as well as overseas tours to its credit. As befits a school in Wales singing on all school occasions is committed, energetic and frequently with natural harmony. The school has a Jazz Band, Chamber Choir, plus multiple wind, brass and string ensembles and its pupils play a prominent role in the South Powys Youth Orchestra. There are many other opportunities to play in ensemble groups throughout the school. Individual instrumental and singing lessons are delivered by visiting musicians.

Activities. In addition to sporting pastimes a wide range of activities are available to pupils including Sixth Form Film Society, Advanced Chemistry, Art, Badminton, Basketball, Brass Group, Canoeing, Chamber Choir, Chess, Choir, Climbing, Community Service, Disability Sport, Drama, Female Choir, Fencing, Fitness, Golf, Indoor Cricket, IT Projects, Jazz Band, Male Voice Choir, Mandarin Chinese, Modern Dance/Jazz, Modern Language Film Society, Music Practice, Music Theory, Percussion Group, Project Science, Railway Modelling, Shooting, Stage Management, String Group, String Quartet, Technology, Wado Kai Karate, Wind Sinfonia, and Young Enterprise. The Duke of Edinburgh's Award Scheme has been popular for many years and the majority of pupils gain at least a Bronze award, and a significant number go on to achieve the Gold award.

Overseas Travel is frequent and extensive. In recent years tours, expeditions and exchanges have taken place to Beijing, Canada, Japan, Nepal, New York, Shanghai, Tibet and Barbados as well as a number of European destinations.

Careers. Two members of staff also serve in the Careers department which also enlists the help of the Independent Schools Careers Organisation as well as the local Careers organisations. Former pupils return annually for Careers evenings and in this the Old Breconian Association is very helpful.

Entrance. Pupils are admitted at the age of 7+, 11+, 13+ and 16+ following the school's own entrance papers in English and Mathematics plus an IQ test, school report and interview. These tests are usually held in Jan/Feb, but individual arrangements can be made. The majority of 11 year old entrants come from local State Primary Schools, those at 13 from Preparatory schools when, instead of the Common Entrance examination, pupils face the same entrance procedures as at 11. Boys and girls also enter the Sixth Form on the basis of GCSE grade estimates, an IQ test and an interview. Although these are standard entry points, pupils will be considered for entry in Year 8 and Year 10.

Term of Entry. Pupils are accepted in the Michaelmas, Lent and Summer terms.

Scholarships. Scholarships are available for entry at age 11, 13 and 16.

Academic: Up to 10 Academic scholarships and exhibitions, tenable at 11+, 13+ and 16+ and ranging in value from 10 to 50% of the fees, are offered annually.

Music: Up to 8 Music scholarships in total are available each year, for award at 11+, 13+ or 16+ ranging in value from 10 to 50% of the fees, together with free tuition on one instrument.

Art: One Art exhibition may be awarded each year at 13+, up to the value of 20% of the fees.

Science scholarships are available at 13+ and 16+, also ranging from 10 to 50% of the fees.

Sports scholarships are available annually at 11+, 13+ and 16+ to candidates showing outstanding talent ranging in value from 10% to 50% of the fees.

All-Rounder: W G Fryer All-Rounder Scholarships are available at 13+ and 16+ each year.

In addition, three scholarships are awarded each year to those entering the Sixth Form each worth £1,500 a year: a Lord Brecon, a Roydon Griffiths and a G John Herdman Scholarship.

The value of any award may be augmented in case of need.

Bursaries are available at all ages and are subject to a means test.

There is a 25% fee remission for sons and daughters of the Clergy, and 10% bursaries are available each year for the children of serving members of the Armed Forces.

Fees per term (2014–2015). Years 3–6: Day £2,665–£3,500; Years 7 and 8: Day £4,515; Boarders £6,210. Years 9–11: Day £5,140; Boarders £7,935; Years 12–13: Day £5,395; Boarders £8,335.

Charitable status. Christ College, Brecon is a Registered Charity, number 525744. Its aims and objectives are to provide a fully rounded education for boys and girls between the ages of 7 and 18.

Christ's Hospital

Horsham, West Sussex RH13 0LJ
Tel: 01403 211293
Fax: 01403 255283
email: hmsec@christs-hospital.org.uk
website: www.christs-hospital.org.uk

Christ's Hospital was founded in the City of London by King Edward VI in 1552. In 1902 the boys moved to Horsham, where they were joined by the girls from their Hertford school in 1985.

Christ's Hospital is now a fully co-educational 11–18 boarding and day school for up to 870 pupils set in over 1000 acres of magnificent Sussex countryside.

Head Master: **John Franklin**, BA, MEd

Deputy Heads:
T N M Lawson, MA (*Economics*)
Mrs J Thomson, BA (*English*)

Chaplain:
Revd S Golding, BA, MA (*Theology & Philosophy*)

Assistant Staff:
* *Head of Department*

Miss R A Ahmed (*English*)
R Allcorn, MSc (*Biology*)
P A Andersen, BA (*History*)
Miss J Azancot, BA (*Design & Technology*)
Mrs M Bloor-Black, MA (**Drama*)
Dr R Brading, BA, MA, PhD (*English*)
Mrs T Brassington (*Mandarin and Chinese*)
P W Broomfield, BSc (*Mathematics*)
Miss L Brown, MA (*French and English*)
Mrs E A Callaghan (*Theology & Philosophy*)
T J Callaghan, BMus, LRAM (*Music*)
J B Callas, BSc (**Biology*)
K Camburn, BA (*Economics & Mathematics*)
Miss E C Cattle, MA (*Classics*)
G N Chandler, BA (*German, French*)
J W Cherry, BA, MPhil (*Theology & Philosophy*)
Mrs C Cherry, MA (*English*)
A M C Cleary, BA (**Music*)
M Commander, BEng (*Physics*)
Miss J A C Copley, BA (*History*)
S A Cowley, BA (*Art*)
Mrs C C C Cowley, BA (*EFL*)
P Deller, BA (**Art*)

Mrs A K Dewhurst, BSc (*Geography*)
Mrs A Domec (*French & Spanish*)
Mrs N D Dotor Cespedes, BSc (*Biology*)
Mr J D Duffield, BSc (*Mathematics*)
P L Dutton, MA, ARCO (*Music*)
Mrs V C Dutton, BEng, MSc (*Physics*)
S T Eason, BA, MIL (*Languages*)
D J Farnfield, BA (*Geography*)
Mrs M A Fleming, BA (*Classics*)
N M Fleming, BA, DipArch, LRPS (**Archaeology*)
Mrs A K Franklin, BA, MA (*English*)
Miss S Gamba, BMus (*Music*)
A H Goddard, BA, MA, PhD (*History*)
Mrs M K Golding, BA, MA (*SEN*)
Mr J-M Gonzalez (*Spanish*)
Miss S M Gorman, BSc (*Physics*)
Mrs J I Green, BSc (*Chemistry*)
D Griffiths, BSc (*Mathematics*)
P H Hall-Palmer, BA (**Design & Technology*)
Dr K H Hannavy, BSc, DPhil (*Chemistry*)
Miss A H Hart, BA (*Art*)
E W G Hatton, BA (**Classics*)
Mr EJ Hawkins, BSc (*Mathematics*)
Mrs C M Hennock, MA (*Mathematics*)
Miss A E Henry (*Physical Education*)
A E Henocq, BSc (*Chemistry*)
H P Holdsworth, BA, CertEd (*English*)
Miss E F Holmes, BA (*Mathematics*)
I B Howard, MA (*Languages*)
M R Jennings, BA, PhD (*History*)
E Jones, MA (*Music*)
Mrs C E Kelley, BA (*Drama*)
D M L Kirby, BA (*English, Theology & Philosophy*)
Mrs J F Lawson, MA, MSc (*Biology*)
Miss F MacKenzie, MA (*Librarian*)
Mrs I M Mainwaring, BA (*Mandarin*)
R B Malpass, PhD (*English, Classics*)
E A Marquez, BSc (**Spanish*)
S Mason, BSc (**Physics*)
K McArtney, BA (**Computer Studies*)
Mrs D McCulloch, MSc (*Mathematics*)
F McKenna, BTech (*Computer Studies, Design & Technology*)
G C McPheat, BSc (*Learning Support*)
M I Medley, MSc, PhD (**Chemistry*)
D H Messenger, BA (**Director of Sport*)
Mrs I J Morgan, MA (*Classics*)
D Mulae, BSc (*Biology, General Science*)
S J O'Boyle, BSc, ARCS (*Mathematics*)
P O O'Regan, BSc (*Physics*)
M J Overend, MA (**Languages/French*)
Mrs C E P Page, BSc (**PE & Sport*)
H Parker, BSc (*Mathematics*)
A R B Phillips, BA (*Languages*)
Mrs L V Ransley, BA (**Modern Languages*)
A A Reid, BA (**History*)
Mrs E A Robinson, BA (**Food & Nutrition*)
Mrs H Rowland-Jones (*Asst Director of Sport*)
Mrs L B Russell, MA (*Biology*)
A Saha, MA, BA (*English*)
J P Salisbury, BSc (*Chemistry*)
Mr R D Sharkey, BA (**Economics*)
Mrs D J Stamp, BEd (*Mathematics*)
I N Stannard, BA (**Theology & Philosophy*)
Mr M S Stephens, BSc (*Mathematics*)
T G Stokes, BSc (**Sports Science & Physical Education*)
R W Stuart, MA, PhD (*English*)
J Tamvarkis, BEd, (*Science, Mathematics*)
F J Thomson, BEd (*Geography*)
Miss L E A Thornton, MA (*History*)
S M Titchener, BA, MMus (*Music*)
S W Walsh, MA (**English*)
Ms R L Watson, BSc (*Design & Technology*)

W P Wearden, BA (*Economics with Mathematics*)
Miss G M Webster, BA, PG Dip (*Music*)
G P Whitely, BA (*Art*)
T W Whittingham, BA, LTCL (*Music, Bandmaster*)
Mrs S H Wilson, BSc (*Biology*)
A R Wines, MA, PhD (*History*)
Mrs M E Young, BSc (**Geography*)
S C Young, MSci (*Chemistry*)

Clerk: G Andrews
Bursar: K J Willder, MBE
Admissions Registrar: Mrs J Howard
Head Master's PA: Mrs C Clark

Christ's Hospital is in many ways unique, offering an independent education of the highest calibre to children with academic potential, from all walks of life in a caring, boarding and day environment.

Pupils' fees are assessed according to family income, so that it is a child's ability and potential to benefit from a Christ's Hospital education that determines their selection. This results in a social and cultural diversity that enriches our school community and offers our pupils unique opportunities as we prepare them to take their place in the modern world.

We believe in the benefits of a rounded and balanced education for our pupils. In practice, this means that as well as a challenging academic programme, pupils are also involved in music, art, drama, public speaking, community action and sport.

The School has an impressive history of high academic achievement with an average of 10 pupils each year taking up places at Oxford or Cambridge, and 98% of leavers going on to top Universities in this country and abroad.

Facilities. The Christ's Hospital campus is nothing short of majestic. From the moment you arrive you'll see that it is a very special place. Sweeping sports fields, beautiful buildings and our spectacular Quad are immediately visible.

We also have 16 boarding houses, two Upper Sixth Form residences, our own purpose-built theatre, modern sports centre, music school and art school. The School has recently implemented a major programme of refurbishment, which has included a complete modernisation of the boarding houses.

The majority of pupils and teachers live on site, creating a community where children are happy and secure, with a wide range of activities on their doorstep. The seven-day week boarding school environment provides the time and space for pupils to develop their interests and talents, and to live and work successfully with others from a diverse range of backgrounds.

Christ's Hospital welcomes day pupils who are within a commutable distance from the School. Day pupils enjoy all the advantages of a top boarding school with access to an exceptional co-curricular programme.

Admission. Normally entry to Christ's Hospital is at Year 7, Year 9 or Sixth Form. Occasionally, we can admit children at Year 8 or 10. The Admissions Office will be able to advise you if places are available.

We encourage you to visit CH on one of our termly Open Mornings to enable you to see the school in action.

Our selection process is designed to determine whether a child will flourish in a busy boarding school environment with a strong academic ethos, enjoying the wide range of opportunities on offer, and feel at home at Christ's Hospital.

Parents are advised to start the Admissions process as early as possible and ideally at least eighteen months before their child would be due to enter the school.

Places at the school are academically selective and are offered on the basis of Christ's Hospital's own assessments.

Year 7 Entry. As a guide, children entering at age 11 into Year 7 need to show evidence of academic potential, working towards the higher end of the ability range in both the Mathematics and English National Curriculum syllabuses (ie predicted level 5 in the Key Stage 2 SATs tests).

Year 9 Entry. Entrants will be expected to be working at SATs level 6/7 across the board or to be predicted to achieve an average of 60% at Common Entrance.

Candidates for entry at age 13 into Year 9 who are coming from independent prep schools or choir schools may choose to apply to be tested at age 11 and have their places deferred. Offers will be made on the basis of Christ's Hospitals own assessments but will be subject to satisfactory completion of Common Entrance.

Alternatively candidates from independent prep schools or choir schools may choose to apply during Year 8 for a Year 9 place following the same assessment process and subject to places remaining available.

Sixth Form Entry. Offers of places at age 16 into Year 12 (Sixth Form) are conditional upon an applicant achieving 6 As or A*s in their GCSE exams.

Additional Entry Information. In all cases reports will be requested from a candidate's current school and it is recommended that parents contact their child's current school early in the admissions process to ask about their child's predicted SATs/Common Entrance/GCSE results.

Fees per term (2014–2015). Boarding £9,850; Day £5,100 (Years 7–8), £6,400 (Years 9–13).

Charitable status. Christ's Hospital School is a Registered Charity, number 1120090, supported by the Christ's Hospital Foundation, Registered Charity number 306975.

Churcher's College

Petersfield, Hampshire GU31 4AS
Tel: 01730 263033
Fax: 01730 231437
email: enquiries@churcherscollege.com
website: www.churcherscollege.com

Motto: *'Credita Cælo'* – Entrusted to Heaven

The College was founded in 1722 by a local philanthropist, Richard Churcher, who provided an endowment for boys to be taught English, Mathematics and Navigation in preparation for apprenticeships with the East India Company. The school relocated to more spacious grounds and accommodation in 1881. The College roll is 1079 pupils. The Sixth Form totals 213 and the Junior Department (ages 4 to 11 years) totals 229.

The school is fully co-educational.

Governing Body:
M J Gallagher, DipArch Hons, RIBA, MIOD, FIMgt (*Chairman*)
Mrs J Bloomer, LLB (*Vice-Chairman*)
S Barrett
S Beecham
Mrs D Cornish, BA, MLitt
P Dacam, BA
S Flint, BSc, MBA
R Hastings, LLB Hons
Mrs C Herraman-Stowers
W A Jones, MA
R May, MIOD
Mrs D Moses, FCA
C J Saunders, MA
Ms A J Spirit, BA
Mrs L Warner, FCA, CTA

***Headmaster*: S H L Williams**, BSc, MA

Deputy Heads:
Mrs S M J Dixon, BSc (*Staff and Co-curricular*)
C D P Jones, MA (*Pastoral*)
I G Knowles, BSc (*Academic*)

Head of Sixth Form: W Baker, BA, MSc

Senior Teacher (Pastoral): Mrs J E Jamouneau, BEd, MSc (*Head of Collingwood House*)

Senior Teacher (Public Relations): Mrs J B Millard, BSc, MSc, ARCS (*5th Year Pastoral Coordinator*)

Academic Registrar: I M Crossman, BA

Creative Arts Faculty:
Head of Faculty/Art: A Saralis, BA
M Grubb, BA
Mrs G Heath, BA
Miss G Hosker, BA

English Faculty:
Head of Faculty: Dr D P Cave, BA, PhD
Miss S Brunner, MA (*Assistant Head of Sixth Form*)
Mrs S Herrington, BA (*Head of Drake House*)
Mrs C Lilley, BA
S Reeves, MA
Ms C Reynolds, BEd (*Coordinator of Springboard*)
Mrs L Wade, BA
Mrs B Williams, BEd (*maternity cover*)

Humanities Faculty:
Head of Faculty/Classics: J Hegan, BA
Head of Economics & Business Studies: M Hill, BA (*Deputy Head of Sixth Form*)
Head of Geography: D J Nighy, BSc (*PSHE Coordinator*)
Head of History: Miss C Letherby, MA
Head of Religion & Philosophy: T Ostersen, BA
W Baker, BA, MSc (*Head of Sixth Form*)
Mrs S M J Dixon, BSc (*Deputy Head Staff and Co-curricular*)
J Harris, BSc
M Hoebee, MA (*Assistant Head of House*)
Miss T Houlden, BA (*Assistant Head of House*)
C D P Jones, MA (*Deputy Head Pastoral*)
Miss L Jenkinson, BA
Mrs H Jolliffe, MA
J Lofthouse, BA, MMus, PGDip
M Murray, MA
Mrs N Plewes, BSc (*Deputy Head of Sixth Form*)
Mrs D Pont, BA, DMS
B Seal, BA (*Assistant Head of House*)
P Shipley, BA (*EPQ Coordinator*)

Mathematics Faculty:
Head of Faculty: Mrs T L Greenaway, BSc
Miss L A Cox, BSc, ACA
Miss S Hunt, BSc
Dr N Jackson, DPhil, MSc
Miss A Scudder, BSc
Mrs A Ladbury-Webb, MA (*Assistant Head of Sixth Form*)
R J Lynn, BA, AMusTCL (*Deputy Head Academic*)
J Seaton, BA (*Head of Grenville House*)
Mrs L J Selby, BSc
Mrs R Tindal, BSc (*Assistant Head of House*)

Modern Languages Faculty:
Head of Faculty/French: Mrs K A Shaw, BA
Head of German: Mrs P Sykes, BSc
Head of Spanish: Mrs A-M Giffin, BA
I M Crossman, BA (*Academic Registrar*)
J Jones, LLB, CEM
Miss A Loten, BA (*Assistant Head of House*)
Mrs S Schofield, BA (*Head of PSHE*)
Mrs N Sparks, BA (*OSCA Admin*)
H Sutherland, BA

Performing Arts Faculty:
Head of Faculty: R M Hoe, BSc (*Head of Nelson House*)
Head of Drama: Ms S Stokes, BA
Director of Music: Mrs H J Purchase, BA, LTCL
Mrs L Cox, BA
P Cree, BA (*Assistant Director of Music Academic*)

M Greenwood, BA (*Assistant Director of Music Performance*)
Miss E Hughes, BA
H Newport, BMus

Science Faculty:
Head of Faculty: Mrs J B Millard, BSc, MSc, ARCS (*Senior Teacher Marketing & Public Relations; 5th Year Pastoral Coordinator*)
Head of Chemistry: D J Dunster, MA
Head of Physics: M C Kelly, BSc
Head of Biology: Ms M J Westwood, BSc
Mrs S L Cockerill, BSc (*Assistant Director of Studies*)
Dr T J K Dilks, BSc, BA Ed, DPhil, CBiol, MIBiol (*Alumni Relations Officer*)
R M Hoe, BSc (*Head of Nelson House*)
Mrs J E Jamouneau, BEd, MSc (*Head of Collingwood House; Senior Teacher Pastoral*)
I Knowles, BSc (*Deputy Head Academic*)
Dr V Raeside, BSc, PhD
Ms F J Pope, BSc
Mrs N Rivett, BSc
Mrs E Smith, BSc
Miss L Smith, BSc
Mrs M Thorpe, BSc (*sabbatical cover*)
R West, BEng
J G Yugin-Power, BSc (*Head of Rodney House*)

Sports Faculty:
Director of Sport: D R Cox, BA, MSc (*Head of Boys' PE*)
Head of Girls' PE: Mrs C Eaton, Cert Ed
Head of A Level PE: Miss L K Howe, BSc (*Acting Fifth Year Pastoral Coordinator*)
Miss E Chambers, BSc
J Daniel (*First Challenge*)
M A Eaton, BEd (*Director of Adventure*)
Miss E Hughes, BA
Mrs T Jenkins
K Magurie, BA
R Maier

Technology Faculty:
Head of Faculty: M Parrish, BSc, Dip Arch
Head of Design & Technology: Mrs C Lines, BA
Head of Computing: G Bradshaw, BSc
D Fellows, BSc
S Reid, BSc

Adventure Faculty:
Head of Faculty: M A Eaton, BEd, ML (*Director of Adventure, Hockey, Expeditions, Ten Tors, OC CCF, Photography and Press*)
M J B Adams, BEd (*i/c CCF Navy Section*)
I M Crossman, BA (*CCF RAF*)
J Daniel (*First Challenge*)
Mrs C Eaton, Cert Ed (*Netball, Rounders, 2i/c CCF, i/c Expedition Medicine and First Aid*)
Miss L K Howe, BSc, ML (*OSCA, Elite Skiing*)
Mrs C Knowles, BSc Ecn (*DofE and OSCA Admin Support*)
A Olle (*CCF School Staff Instructor*)
P Pearson, ML, SPA, DofE Manager, OSCA, Climbing Wall Manager, QM for Adventure Stores
Mrs N Sparks, BA (*OSCA*)
Mrs P Utting, BA (*DofE Administrator, Assistant Head of Sixth Form, CCF Navy*)

Curriculum Support:
Mrs L Blackman, BEd, Dip SpLD (*Head of Curriculum Support, School Counsellor*)

Junior School

Head of Junior School: I Adams, BSc, MBA

Deputy Head: Mrs P Yugin-Power, BSc, MA Ed, QTS
Head of Infant Department: Miss K M Humphreys, BEd

Senior Teacher Middle School: Mrs S J Moore, ARCM, GRSM
Senior Teacher Upper School: N Rushin, BSc, MSc
Senior Teacher Staffing: Mrs S Roberts, BEd

Miss H Parry, BA (*Class R Teacher*)
C Taylor, BSc (*Class 1 Teacher*)
Miss K M Humphreys, BEd (*Class 2 Teacher*)
Mrs S J Moore, ARCM, GRSM (*Class 3M Teacher*)
Mrs J Gillard (*Class 3G Teacher*)
M Forbes, BSc (*Class 4F Teacher*)
Ms K Pendry, BA (*Class 4P Teacher*)
Miss R Morris, BA, MSc (*Class 5M Teacher*)
Mrs K Tkaczynska, BEd (*Class 5T Teacher*)
Mrs L M Eddy, BA (*Class 6E Teacher*)
N Rushin, BSc, MSc (*Class 6R Teacher*)
Mrs S Roberts, BEd
Mrs S Bint, GMus RNCM, MA (*Head of Music*)
Mrs R Cameron, CertEd, DipSpLD (*Learning Support*)
Mrs A C Chilton, BEd (*Head of PE*)
W Pook, BSc (*ICT*)
Mrs P Clemens, BEd (*Maths, PE*)
J Daniel (*Assistant Sports Teacher*)
Mrs C Foley (*Art*) (*maternity cover*)
Mrs F Little (*French*)
H Newport, BMus (*Music*)

Librarians:
Mrs L M Robbins, BSc, MIEH (*Junior School*)
Miss P Harper, BA
Mrs V Johnson, BSc

Bursar: D T Robbins, BSc, FCCA

Admission. The normal ages of admission to the Senior School are 11+ and 16+, and 4+ and 7+ in the Junior School after Churcher's assessment in the Spring Term. However, if vacancies exist, pupils are considered for admission at other ages.

A prospectus and application form, with details of fees, are available from the Headmaster.

The Sixth Form. Students are prepared for GCE A and AS Levels.

A wide combination of choices is offered from English, History, Geography, Economics, French, German, Spanish, Latin, Art & Design, Music, Drama, Philosophy & Ethics, Business Studies, Mathematics, Further Mathematics, Physics, Chemistry, Biology, Classical Civilisation, Design & Technology, Sport and Physical Education and Computing. All students take a course to prepare them for AS Level General Studies.

There is a fully-equipped Sixth Form Centre, for both study and recreation, a floor of the Library dedicated to Sixth Form private study, an excellent Careers Library and full-time Careers Officer and specialist Sixth Form teaching rooms and ICT facilities.

Years 1–5. From the 11+ entry all pupils follow a common academic programme comprising Mathematics, English, French, Physics, Chemistry, Biology, Latin, Classical Civilisation, Geography, Religion and Philosophy, Music, Art, Design & Technology, ICT, Drama and PE. In Year 2 an additional Modern European language (German or Spanish) is added to the programme. All pupils follow a broad curriculum and are not asked to specialise until they reach GCSE. All pupils follow GCSE courses in Mathematics, English, Language and Literature, Biology, Chemistry, Physics, a Modern Language, a Humanity and at least 2 additional optional subjects.

Pupils are tested and examined regularly with formal assessment procedures each half term and each end of term.

Facilities. Churcher's academic facilities include impressive purpose-built teaching accommodation, ICT suites, drama studios, art and design studios, design technology workshops, music centre and science block. Sports facilities include a swimming pool, sports halls and on-site tennis courts, netball courts, rugby pitches, all-weather hockey pitches and cricket squares. Churcher's has the facilities and resources to support an extensive range of extra-curricular activities. The Sixth Form enjoys extensive recreational and teaching facilities. The Junior School is situated on its own spacious 10 acre site in Liphook, close to Petersfield.

Games and other Activities. The major sports played are Rugby, Hockey, Netball, Cricket and Rounders. There are also facilities for Badminton, Basketball, Volleyball, Tennis, Athletics, Aerobics and Cross-country, to name but a few. The School has a strong CCF unit with Army, Air Force and Naval Sections, and a flourishing Duke of Edinburgh's Award programme. Other activities include Mountain Biking, Canoeing, Gliding, Climbing, Adventurous Training, Young Enterprise Companies, Dance, Karate, Fencing, Football, Sailing, Horse Riding, Bridge, Chess, Debating, Drama and Photography.

Music, drama and dance are very strong in the school with School and House plays produced regularly and a wide range of out-of-school activities. The school also has a significant range of orchestras, wind bands and choirs and many more ensembles.

Careers. The College has a full-time Careers Adviser on the staff and regular visits are made by other professional Career Advisers. Talks are given to pupils in the Third Form and above, and individual interviews are arranged.

A **Parents' Association** was formed in 1967 and meetings are held each term.

Fees per term (2014–2015). Senior School £4,352; Junior School £2,769–£2,954. Fees include charges for examination fees and textbooks, but exclude lunches and individual music lessons.

Charitable status. Churcher's College, Petersfield, Hampshire is a Registered Charity, number 307320. Its aims and objectives are to provide a school for boys and girls between the ages of 4 and 18 in the Parish of Petersfield.

City of London Freemen's School

Ashtead Park, Surrey KT21 1ET
Tel: 01372 277933
Fax: 01372 276165
email: headmaster@clfs.surrey.sch.uk
website: www.clfs.surrey.sch.uk

Motto: '*Domine dirige nos*'

The City of London Freemen's School is an independent co-educational day and boarding school which provides continuity of education for children aged 7 to 18. The School was founded in Brixton in 1854 by the Corporation of the City of London to provide 'a religious and virtuous education' for the orphaned children of Freemen of the City of London; Christian principles remain at the heart of its ethos, although the School is non-denominational. It is one of 3 schools governed and maintained by the City of London Corporation.

In 1926 the School moved to Ashtead Park, its present site and now educates approximately 890 girls and boys. Most of these pupils are day pupils, but the School remains firmly committed to the provision of boarding for a number of its pupils.

Alongside excellent academic results, our innovative enrichment programme is at the heart of our commitment to developing the whole person. We have the facilities, staff and grounds to ensure our students are happy, secure and fulfilled. We place particular emphasis on the individual and their needs and in providing the opportunities to identify and develop their skills to flourish throughout their time at Freemen's, and beyond.

The School has a rich history and a bright future as we continue to shape the minds of tomorrow's leaders.

The Board of Governors:

Chairman: S J Fraser, CBE
Deputy Chairman: R A H Chadwick

Aldermen:
P Hewitt, FCSI, FRSA
Dr A C Parmley, MusM, Hon FGS
J R White

Common Councilmen:

J A Bennett	Miss J L Pleasance, MA
B N Harris	Hons
M Hudson	Ms E Rogula
Mrs V Littlechild, JP	Dr G Shilson, Deputy (*ex*
H F Morris	*officio*)
G D Packham	Sir M Snyder (*ex officio*)
	P Woodhouse

Co-opted:

F M Bramwell	D J L Mobsby, MBE
Sir Clive Martin	Councillor C Townsend
A McMillan	Ms G Yarrow

Clerk to the Governors: Gemma Stockley

Headmaster: P MacDonald, MA Oxon

Deputy Head: Mrs V E Buckman, BSc

Second Deputy Head: R J Alton, MA Cantab, MPhys

Head of Junior School: M W G Robinson, BA, MA
Head of Upper School: Mrs E E Guest, BA
Head of Sixth Form: G C Hughes, BA

Assistant Staff:
* Head of Department/Subject

Art & Design:
*Ms G Humphreys, HD Fine Arts, Dip Theatre Design
Miss J Ayre, BA, MA
Mrs R Houseman, BA

Business Studies & Economics:
*R Dolan, BA
Mrs J Marvin, BSc

Classics:
*A Chadwick, BA
M G Hearne, MA Cantab

Computing & Information Technology:
*R Flook, BSc
Miss H L Crow, BSc, MEd

Design Technology:
M J Collier, BEd (*Electronics & Technology*)
M S Hicks, BA
Mrs M A Smith, BEd (*Food Technology*)
D F Treloar, BEd

Drama:
* Miss J M Warburton, BA
Ms S M Chamberlain-Webber, BA

English:
*Mrs S E Parkin, BA, MA Ed
C E Bloomer, BA
Miss R Butterwick, BA
Ms S Chamberlain-Webber, BA
Mrs E E Guest, BA
G C Hughes, BA
Mrs A M Sloper, BA
Mrs S A Stewart, BA, MA

Geography:
*R Bustin, BSc
Miss G Hill, BSc
Mrs H Pennington, BA
Mrs P Whiteley, BSc

History & Politics:
*A J Wright, MA Oxon, MA
J A Brooke, BA
Mrs K S Edwards, BA
Mrs R E Joss, BA

Mathematics:
*E Bramhall, BSc
M J Belcher, BSc
Mrs M A Cast, BSc
R Chiba, BEng
Mrs C A Inns, BA
Mrs E C Newhouse, MA (*Sixth Form Enrichment Studies*)
A Parkin, BSc (*Assistant Head of Sixth Form*)
R G Retzlaff, BSc, BEd, MPhil
Mrs E J Rowlands, BSc

Modern Languages:
*Mrs S E Hankin, BA (*German*)
Mrs L A Headon, BA
Mrs C J Leighton, BA
Mrs J I Rosin, MagPhil
Mrs C A Salisbury, BA (*Spanish*)
Miss L R Vickers, MA
Mrs B C Wheatley, BA
Miss R E Willis, BA
Mrs M Willis-Jones, LFL

Music & Music Technology:
*P M Dodds, BA (*Director of Music*)
Mrs I Ashworth, BA
Ms N Z Eaglestone, BMus

Physical Education:
*J Shore Nye, BSc (*Director of Sport*)
A Bird, BSc
A Buhagiar, BSc
Mrs N C Clark, BSc
Miss K Crook, BA
J G Moore, BA (*A Level Sports Studies*)
Miss F L Paul, BSc (*Hockey*)
Mrs L J Shaill, BEd

Psychology:
*Miss J C Vinall, BSc, MSc

Religious Education:
*T Wright
Miss N L Bax, MA
A N Illingworth, BA

Science:
*J D Hallam, BSc (*Physics*)
Mrs V E Buckman, BSc
R T Calladine, BSc
Mrs J E Dickson, BA
Mrs R M Fox, BSc
Mrs S Fraser, BEd
J C Graham, BSc
Mrs H M Irwin, BEd
Dr J M Lister, MSc
Mrs S Meek, BSc
J E Newell, BSc (*Chemistry*)
M A Newcome, BSc, MA Ed
M Shields, BSc
P Thornton, BEng, MSc
Mrs J P Vatcher, BSc (*Biology*)

Junior School:

Mrs J E Cooper, BEd	Ms F I Moncur, BEd
S P Davies, BA	Mrs M Restall, BA
Mrs S J Gillespie, BA	Mrs A J Richardson, BEd
Mrs J Heafford, Cert Ed	Mrs R S Samson, BA
Mrs V E Ielpi, BEd	Mrs N S Sanderson, BA
Mrs L J Jowitt, MA	Mrs E C Smith, LLB
Miss R J Kempster, BA	Mrs V C Symonds, BSc
R A Metcalf, BA	M P Valkenburg, HDE

Mrs P G Whiteley, BSc   Mrs J Wilby, BA
                             Mrs C A Williams, BEd

Sixth Form Careers Advisor: A J Wright, MA Oxon, MA

Learning Support Manager: A Illingworth, BA

Visiting Instrumental Staff:
Mrs V Brockless, MMus, BA
Ms N Berg, BA, MA, ARCM
Mrs A Bishop, ARAM
Ms N Berg, BA, MA, ARCM
Miss R Chappell, AGSM
D Eaglestone, AdDip
G Gottlieb, BA, MMus
Ms J Janse, MA, BA, MA Music, Dip Ram, LRAM
Ms A Lovett, MMus, BMus Hons, LRAM
Mrs M MacDonald, BA, Dip ABRSM
J O'Carroll, BMus
Miss E Pappalardo, BMus, MMus
T Peake, GGSM
N Perona-Wright, LRAM, LTCL, LLCM TD
P Price, LRAM, LTCL, ALCM
P Smith
Mrs G Wallace, LRAM, GRSM
J Wallace
D Ward, AGSM

Music Department Administrator: Mrs S Grover

Cricket Professional: N M Stewart
Swimming Coach: D Cross

Bursar: Mrs S Williams, BA, MBA

Administrative Staff:
Assistant Bursar: Mrs A J Atkins, BCom, MCIPD
Finance Manager: Mrs G Bilsland
Registrar: Miss J R Atkins, BA
General Services Manager: G Heffer
Head of Boarding: A G Bird, BSc
Assistant Head of Boarding: Mrs L J Retzlaff
House Tutor: M C Belcher, BSc
House Tutor: C E Bloomer, BA
House Tutor: J A Brooke, BA
House Tutor: Mrs R E Joss, BA
House Tutor: Miss A Kaufmann
House Tutor: Miss R J Kempster, BA
House Tutor: Dr J M Lister, MSc
Headmaster's Secretary: Mrs K Montague
Administrative Assistant, Headmaster's Office: Mrs A
    Caprano-Wint
Deputy Head's Secretary: Miss J Ford
Second Deputy Head's Secretary: Mrs A Moss
Senior School Secretary: Mrs L Ryckaert
Senior School Receptionist: Ms C Taylor
Junior School Secretary: Mrs G Anklesaria
Junior School Administrator: Mrs A Tindall
Admissions Officer: Mrs J L Shalgosky
Reprographics Officer: N Fairhurst
Reprographics Assistant: S Butcher
Finance Officer – Fees: Mrs D Widmer
Finance Officer – Creditors: Mrs M Ilbert
Finance Administrator: Mrs J Arnett
Lettings Administrator: Mrs S Wilding
School Doctor: Dr C Avellini, MB, BCh
School Sisters: Mrs K Utchanah, RGN; Mrs A Corbett,
    RGN; Mrs B O'Connor, BA, Dip Nursing
Senior Librarian: Mrs S Dawes, BLib, MCLIP
Assistant Librarians: Mrs L J Retzlaff
HR Administrator: Miss H Lambert
Marketing & Admissions Administrator: Mrs H Sareen
Sports Administrator: Mrs R Young (*maternity leave*)
Sports Administrator: Mrs M Scott (*maternity cover*)
Examinations Administration Officer: Mrs N Williams
ICT Manager: A Cohen
Systems Engineer: A Richmond

ICT Technician: N Foot
ICT Technician: S Miller

There are 889 pupils in the School, approximately equal numbers of boys and girls, including up to 25 girl and 25 boy boarders. There are 498 pupils over the age of 13, including a Sixth Form of approximately 212.

The School stands in 57 acres of playing fields and parkland between Epsom and Leatherhead with easy access to Heathrow and Gatwick via the M25. Buildings include a central Georgian Mansion, an Assembly Hall a floodlit all-weather pitch and a Sports Hall complex completed in 1995. A multimillion pound building programme in the 1990s saw the addition of a Sixth Form Centre, an Art and Design Centre and a Science and Technology Centre. New teaching facilities for all subject Departments including Library and IT facilities were completed with the opening of the Haywood Centre in September 2000. A Studio Theatre was opened in October 2001, providing an auditorium for all productions, recitals, concerts and lecture facilities. The all-weather pitch has been replaced, bringing both up to modern national representative standards. A state-of-the-art music school, including a Steinway-D concert grand piano, and a co-educational boarding house for 60 pupils were completed and opened in 2014. This will be followed by the re-building of the swimming pool and the refurbishment of Main House.

Junior School. Since September 1988 the Junior School, ages 7–13, has been accommodated in a new complex in Ashtead Park. This provides 18 classrooms for up to 360 pupils. The Junior School is fully integrated within the framework and policies of the whole school and other facilities include specialist rooms for Art and Design, Science, Music and an integrated Technology Centre as well as an Assembly Hall and recently extended Library.

See Junior School entry in IAPS section.

Organisation and Entry. The School is divided into 2 sections but is administered as a single unit. The Junior Department has its own specially trained staff and its own self-contained building, but otherwise all staff teach throughout the School.

Junior entry is by the School's own competitive examination at 7+ or 11+ (normally in January).

Senior School entry is by passing the Common Entrance examination, normally at the age of 13+, or by the School's own 13+ examination. Screening tests for Senior School entry have been introduced for Year 6 and Year 7 pupils; these take place in January. CLFS Junior School pupils may expect to transfer satisfactorily to the Senior School at 13+ without sitting a special examination.

Sixth Form entry is by obtaining good GCSE grades with a minimum of 55 points from 10 subjects (or equivalent average for fewer subjects) with at least 8 passes at GCSE (grade C or better) including English and Mathematics. In addition, most subjects have specific entry requirements. At least four grade B passes must be obtained at GCSE in appropriate subjects if new subjects are being studied at AS Level. (A*=8, A=7, B=6, C=5)

Foundation entry is open to orphan children of Freemen at any age from 7+ to 16+, subject to satisfactory academic potential.

(Except for Foundationers, it is not necessary for applicants to be children of Freemen of the City.)

Curriculum. The first four years (7+ to 10+ in Years 3 to 6) are largely taught by class teachers up to Key Stage 2 following the broad outlines of the National Curriculum. Up to the age of about 14 all pupils have substantially the same curriculum which comprises English, French/German/Spanish, Mathematics, Physics, Chemistry, Biology, History, Geography, Religious Education, Latin, Design Technology, Information Technology, Food Technology, Art and Music. Thereafter, apart from a common core of English, French or German or Spanish, Mathematics and the 3 separate Sciences, selection is made for the course to GCSE from 15 other subjects including Spanish, German, French, Computer Studies, Drama, Electronics, Latin, Sociology and Design Technology so that the average pupil will offer 10 subjects. The principles of the National Curriculum are followed at all levels. Physical Education and Personal, Social and Health Education are included in the curriculum at all levels and all age groups have an Enrichment afternoon.

Sixth Form courses include the following main AS and A Level subjects: Mathematics, Further Mathematics, Physics, Chemistry, Biology, Electronics, History, Geography, Politics, Classical Civilisation, French, German, Spanish, Business Studies, Computing, Drama, Art, Music, Physical Education, Food Technology, Design Technology, Music Technology, Information Technology, Economics, Psychology and Philosophy and Theology. Pre-U courses are also offered in Literature in English, Biology, History and Art & Design. All pupils follow an Enrichment Curriculum which consists of Critical Thinking, an Extended Project, Physical Education, Leadership Skills and Community Service.

The School has an excellent academic record. Recent GCSE results have been excellent, with more than 80% of examinations awarded A* or A grades. A Level results have been equally impressive with over 90% of examinations awarded A or B grades, and nearly all leavers go on to degree courses at universities or other higher education institutes.

Computer Studies is well equipped and established, with specialist rooms in each of the Junior and Senior Schools, as well as substantial departmental IT resources as appropriate.

Each pupil is allocated to a House comprising a cross-section of boys and girls, both day and boarding, throughout the School. House teams compete in all forms of sport as well as music, drama and debating.

Games. *For Boys*: Principally Rugby, Cricket, Athletics, Fencing and Swimming. Badminton, Basketball, Hockey, Squash, Tennis are also available.

For Girls: Principally Hockey, Tennis, Athletics and Swimming. Badminton, Fencing, Horse Riding, Netball and Squash are also available.

There is a very wide choice of extra-curricular activities throughout the School. The Duke of Edinburgh's Award Scheme is a very popular option in the Senior School.

Fees per term (2014–2015). Senior School: £5,175 (day), £8,370 (boarding); Junior School: £3,864–£4,122 (day). Instrumental Music lessons: £205.

Scholarships and Bursaries. City of London Scholarships, open to both internal and external applicants, are awarded as follows:

At 11+ up to 3 Scholarships of not more than 50% of the tuition fee, tenable for seven years. These Scholarships are awarded on the basis of performance in the School's Entrance Examination, school reports and an interview.

At 13+ up to 5 Scholarships of not more than 50% of the tuition fee, tenable for five years. These Scholarships are awarded on the basis of performance in the 13+ Scholarship examinations, school reports and an interview.

At 16+ (Sixth Form entry) up to 10 Scholarships are awarded of not more than 50% of the tuition fee tenable for two years. These Scholarships are awarded on the basis of performance in the Sixth Form Scholarship papers, school reports and an interview.

Music Scholarships are awarded as follows:

At 11+ up to 2 awards of not more than 25% of the tuition fee. Applicants must have reached Grade 3 in one instrument and be able to offer a second study. Auditions and interviews are held with the Director of Music.

At 13+ up to 2 awards of not more than 50% of the tuition fee. Applicants must have reached Grade 5 in one instrument and be able to offer a second study. Auditions and interviews are held with the Director of Music.

At 16+ (Sixth Form) up to 2 awards of not more than 50% of the tuition fee. Applicants must have reached Grade 7 in one instrument and be able to offer a second study. Auditions and interviews are held with the Director of Music.

In all cases, music scholarships include free tuition in one instrument provided by teachers at the School.

A significant number of Bursaries from Livery Companies are also available.

City of London School

Queen Victoria Street, London EC4V 3AL
Tel: 020 7489 0291
Fax: 020 7329 6887
email: admissions@clsb.org.uk
          head@clsb.org.uk
website: www.clsb.org.uk

The City of London School occupies a unique Thameside location in the heart of the capital and has 925 day boys between the ages of 10 and 18 from all parts of the capital. It traces its origin to bequests left for the education of poor boys in 1442 by John Carpenter, Town Clerk of the City. The Corporation of London was authorised by Act of Parliament in 1834 to use this and other endowments to establish and maintain a School for boys. This opened in 1837 in Milk Street, Cheapside, and moved to the Victoria Embankment in 1883. In 1986 the School moved again, to excellent purpose-built premises provided by the Corporation on a fine riverside site in the City, to which a new Technology building was added in 1990. The School lies on the riverside next to the Millennium Bridge with St Paul's Cathedral to the north and the Globe Theatre and Tate Modern across the Thames to the south. The School's Board of Governors is a committee of the Court of Common Council, the Corporation of London's governing body and four independent co-opted members.

Chairman of Governors: Deputy Dr Giles Shilson

Head: Mrs S K Fletcher, MA

Second Master: G S Griffin, BA
Assistant Headmaster: C B Fillingham, BA, MA
Director of Studies: Miss N H Murphy, BA
Director of Admissions: D R Heminway, BD
Head of Professional Development: A J V McBroom, BA
Head of Management Information Systems: E Whitcomb, BSc
Finance Director: P J Everett, BSc, MA, FCA

Head of Sixth Form: A J V McBroom, BA
Deputy Head of Sixth Form: Miss Z L Connolly, MA
Deputy Head of Sixth Form: N P McMillan, BEd
Head of Fifth Form: S S Fernandes, BSc, MA
Deputy Head of Fifth Form: Miss E M A Earl, BA
Head of Fourth Form: B L Jones, BA
Deputy Head of Fourth Form: G W Dawson, BSc
Head of Third Form: G P L Farrelly, BA
Deputy Head of Third Form: Mr M C Chataway, BA
Head of Second Form: J Norman, MA
Deputy Head of Second Form: Miss K A Saunt, BA
Head of First Form and OG: M P Kerr, BA
Deputy Head of First Form and OG: Miss C A Hudson, BSc

* *Head of Department*

Classics:	Design & Visual Arts:
*W Ellis-Rees, MA	*R G Pomeroy, BA
B L Jones, BA	G P L Farrelly, BA
Miss C L Rose, BA	Miss A E Gill, BA
Miss Z L Connolly, MA	Miss B Easton, BA
J E Pile, BA	S R Lewington
S A Swann, BA, MPhil	

Drama:
*Miss S H Dobson, BA
Miss M L Franklin, BA

Economics:
*D P Rey, BSc, MA
N P McMillan, BEd
M Wacey, BSc

English:
*R A Riggs, BA, MA
J Norman, MA
J S Williams, BA
Miss H M Sénéchal, MA
M Hilton-Dennis, BA
J P Clayton, BA, MA
B Bellak, BA
Miss J N Rush, BA, PhD
N C Hudson, BA

Geography:
*O J Davies, BSc, MSc
P S Marshall, MA
Miss V J Robin, MA
Miss A E Low, BA

History and Politics:
*A J Bracken, BA
G S Griffin, BA
Miss N H Murphy, BA
A J V McBroom, BA
Mrs F N Carter, BA
Mrs V W Arnold, BA
Miss K A Saunt, BA
S M Jones, BSc, MPhil
S J Brown, BA, MA
M C Chataway, BA, MA
J T Crowther, MA

Information Technology:
*Mrs S L Ralph, BA
Mrs A M MacDonagh, BSc, BSc

Mathematics:
*D R Eade, BA
D J Chamberlain, BSc, MSc
Miss C A Hudson, BSc
S S Fernandes, BSc, MA
Mrs C S Musgrove, MA
Miss J C L Mesure, BA
Miss E L McCallan, MA
A D Blake, BSc
S J Dugdale, BSc, PhD
Ms N Bigden, BSc, Msc
Mr B P Broadhurst, MA

There are Visiting Music Teachers for Bassoon, Cello, Double Bass, French Horn, Flute, Guitar, Jazz, Oboe, Organ, Percussion, Piano, Saxophone, Singing, Trombone, Trumpet, Tuba, Viola, Violin.

Learning Support:
*Ms A C DiStefano Power, BAH, BEd
D W Dyke, BA
Mrs A J Fountaine, MSci, MA
Mrs J de Stacpoole, Hornsby Diploma SpLD
M C Biltcliffe, BA

Library:
*D A Rose, BA, Dip Lib, ALA
Ms J Grantham, MA
Miss R Stocks, BA

Modern Languages:
*R Edmundson, MA
A T Laidlaw, MA
    (*French*)
P A Allwright, MA
G J Dowler, JP, MA
Mrs A J Heaf, BA, MA
Miss V Vincent, MA
Mrs A L Robinson, BA
C B Fillingham, BA, MA
Mrs E Morgan, BA
P R Eteson, BA
Ms M J Ciechanowicz, MA
I Emerson, BSSc, MA

Music:
*P Harrison, GLCM, MA
Miss J E Jones, BA
J Harrison, BA

Physical Education:
*N F Cornwell, BEd
M P Kerr, BSc, MSc
B J Silcock, BPE
J P Santry, BEng
C E Apaloo, BSc

Religious Education:
*J T Silvester, BA
D R Heminway, BD
Miss K E Wratten, MA, MA
Mrs E M Bugilimfura, BA
Mrs A Giannorou, BSc, BA, MPhil

Science:
H R S Jones, BSc
    (*Physics, *Science*)
Mrs P C McCarthy, BSc
    (*Chemistry*)
A Zivanic, BA, MA
    (*Biology*)
J Easingwood, CertEd, BA
N O Mackinnon, BSc, PhD
R Mackrell, BSc
G W Dawson, BSc
E Whitcombe, BSc
K P Rogers, MChem
P J Naylor, BSc
Miss R A Norman, BSc
Miss C Weller, BSc
Mrs K L Pattison, BSc, PhD
M V Pereira, BSc, BEng
G H Browne, BA, BSc
A A Wood, MSci
M N Pennell, MChem, PhD

Admissions Secretary: Mrs J Brown
Human Resources Manager: Miss S F Denbow, BA, PG Dip

Admissions. Pupils are admitted aged 10, 11 and 13 (as on 1st September of year of entry), on the results of the School's own entrance examinations held each year in January. All candidates are examined for entry when they are in Year 6 – including boys applying for entry at age 13. Those admitted at 16 into the Sixth Form are selected by test and interview in November. Application forms for admission may be obtained from the Admissions Secretary at the School or from the website.

Fees per term (2014–2015). £4,771.

Entrance Scholarships. At least 30 Academic, Music and Sports Scholarships, with a value of up to half of the school fees, and a number of minor awards, are awarded annually. These Scholarships are available at any of the normal entry points. For ages 10+, 11+ and 13+ a Scholarship interview is awarded on the strength of a candidate's performance in the School's normal entrance examinations. At 16+ an Academic Scholarship may be awarded on the strength of a candidate's GCSE results.

Candidates for entry to the School may also apply for Choristerships at the Temple Church or the Chapel Royal, St James's (the choristers of both choirs are pupils at the School). Choristers receive Choral Bursaries whose value is two-thirds of the school fee. Potential choristers may also take auditions and academic tests at the age of 8 or 9; successful applicants will be offered an unconditional place in the School for the year after their 10th birthday.

Sponsored Awards. The School offers a number of Sponsored Awards, up to full fees, to assist those parents of academically very bright boys, who otherwise could not contemplate private education. These awards are only available at 11+ and 16+.

Curriculum. All boys follow the same broad curriculum up to and including the Third Form. The First Form curriculum includes an introduction to the use of computers, and in the Third Form boys spend some eight afternoons throughout the year on educational visits to institutions and places of interest in and around the City. Latin and French are started by all in the First Form and two choices from Greek, Classical Civilisation, Drama, German and Spanish may be added as options in the Third Form. Fourth and Fifth Form boys take a core of English, Mathematics, three Sciences (the core subjects are all IGCSEs), and at least one Modern Foreign Language (which can include Russian), and choose three other subjects from a wide range of subjects available for study to GCSE/IGCSE. In the Sixth Form boys take a combination of AS or A2 Level subjects together with the ECDL. A majority of the Senior Sixth finish with four A Levels and usually over fifty per cent get four grade As. Virtually all boys leaving the Sixth Form proceed to their first or second choice of Russell Group University or Medical School.

Games. The School's 20 acres of playing fields, at Grove Park in south-east London, offer excellent facilities for football, cricket, athletics, and tennis. Sporting facilities on the School site include a sports hall, a gymnasium with conditioning room, three squash courts, a fencing salle, and a 25-metre swimming pool. Particular success has been achieved in football, water polo, fencing, table tennis, basketball and badminton.

School Societies. There is a large number of School Societies, catering for a very wide range of interests. Every encouragement is given to benefit from the School's central position by participation in the cultural and educational life of London and of the City in particular. The School has a strong musical tradition; tuition is available in any instrument, and membership of the School choirs and orchestras is encouraged. Choristers of the Temple Church and of the Chapel Royal are educated at the School as bursaried scholars provided that they satisfy the entrance requirements. There is much interest in Drama, and the staff includes a full-time Director of Drama: the School has a fully-equipped and recently refurbished Theatre and also a Drama Studio. There is a large CCF Contingent which boys may join from the age of 13 until 18, with Army, Navy and RAF Sections. There is also a successful Community Service programme. Boys frequently take part in the Duke of Edinburgh's Award Scheme.

Alumni Association. There is a flourishing Old Boys' Society known as the John Carpenter Club, website: www.jcc.org.uk. The Alumni Relations Officer can be contacted at the School.

City of London School for Girls

St Giles' Terrace, Barbican, London EC2Y 8BB
Tel: 020 7847 5500
Fax: 020 7638 3212
email: info@clsg.org.uk
website: www.clsg.org.uk
Twitter: @CLSGgirls
Facebook: /clsggirls

Motto: *Domine Dirige Nos*

School Governors:
Chairman: Sir Michael Snyder, Deputy
Deputy Chairman: Mrs Clare James, MA, CC

Headmistress: Mrs E Harrop, BA Salamanca, MA Munich, MPhil Cantab, MA London

Deputy Head: Mr W A Douglas, BA Hons Oxon
Deputy Head Staff Development: Mrs C Tao, BSc Surrey, MSc LSE
Director of Studies: Mr N Codd, BA Hons Oxon

Head of Sixth Form: Miss R Lockyear, BA Hons Cantab
Assistant Head of Sixth Form: Mrs C Williamson, BA Cantab

Head of Senior School: Mrs S Gilham, BA Oxon
Assistant Heads of Senior School:
Miss N Ispahani, BSc York
Mr A Wright, BSc Bournemouth

Head of Lower School: Mrs K N Brice, MA Cantab
Assistant Head of Lower School:
Mrs J Norman, BEd De Montfort [Maternity Leave]
Ms E Obiri-Darko, BSc British Columbia, Canada [Maternity Cover]

Head of Preparatory School: Miss J Rogers, MPhil, BA London
Deputy Head of Preparatory Department: Mrs D Mallett, BAEd Hons Reading

Heads of Department:

Art:
Miss J Curtis, BA Hons London, St Martin's School of Art, ATC London

Classical Languages:
Mr D Themistocleous, BA Oxon

Drama:
Mr S Morley, Dip Acting CCSD

Economics:
Mr A Kanwar, BA Oxon

Politics:
Miss R Lockyear, BA Hons Cantab

English:
Mr B Ward, BA The New University of Ulster

Geography:
Miss E A Moore, BA Liverpool, FRGS

History:
Mrs K N Brice, MA Cantab

Mathematics:
Mr K Latham, BSc Liverpool

Modern Languages:
French: Mr G Tyrrell, BA Oxford Brookes, MA
German: Mrs A Marett, BA Oxon
Spanish: Miss M Leturia, BA Granada, MA London
Italian: Miss E Perkins, BA Leeds
Chinese: Ms E Garner, BA Hons York, MA SOAS, MSc Manchester

Music:
Mrs M Donnelly, BEd London

Physical Education:
Ms C Castell, BA Loughborough

Religion, Philosophy and Ethics:
Mrs K Bullard, MA Cantab

Sciences:
Biology: Miss N Brown, BSc Hons Edinburgh, MRes Edinburgh
Chemistry: Mr A Stylianou, BSc Hons London
Physics: Mr M Wilkinson, BSc Hons Nottingham

Technology:
Miss S McCarthy, BSc Brunel

ICT:
Mr D Libby, BSc West of England

Careers and PSHCEE:
Miss E Perkins, BA Leeds

Library:
Mrs R Trevor, BA Hons, MCLIP

Bursar: Colonel E L Yorke
Premises Manager: Mr J Valentine
Finance Manager: Mr R Woodvine, MA RCA
Admissions Officer: Miss R Ford, MA Dunelm
Marketing & Development Officer: Miss J Jones, BA UNSW, Australia
Bursar's Secretary & HR Assistant: Mrs V Pyke

Health & Support Network:
School Doctor: Dr D Soldi, MB, ChB, DCH
School Nurse: Miss G Walshe, BSc London
School Counsellors:
Ms D Marcus, BA Counselling Tavistock Institute, Dip Psychodynamic Counselling Westminster Pastoral Foundation
Ms C Nancarrow
Learning Support Coordinators:
Mrs C Cole, BA East Anglia, RSA Dip London
Miss E Herbert, BA London, PGCE Secondary

City of London School for Girls is an academically selective, non-denominational, independent day school for girls aged 7–18. There is an infectious vibrancy and energy at "City". Its distinctive location in the Barbican Centre provides immediate access to the wealth of London's educational and cultural opportunities, while the teaching staff and girls imbue the place with a sense of happiness, purpose, enthusiasm and fulfilment.

The School Course includes English Language and Literature, History, Geography, Religion, Philosophy and Ethics, Latin, Greek, French, German, Spanish, Mathematics, Biology, Chemistry, Physics, Economics and Politics, Art, Music, Physical Education, Classical Civilisation, Design and Technology, Theatre Studies, and Chinese.

Pupils are prepared for GCSE, AS and A2 Level Examinations offered by Edexcel, OCR and AQA. They are also prepared for entrance to Oxford, Cambridge and other Universities. The Sixth Form courses are designed to meet the needs of girls wishing to proceed to other forms of specialised training.

Facilities are provided for outdoor and indoor games and the school has its own indoor swimming pool and an all-weather sports pitch. Extra-curricular activities before school, in the lunch hour or at the end of afternoon school include Debating, Football, Drama, Science, Technology, Fencing, Netball, Gymnastics, Swimming, Tennis, Climbing and classes in Chinese, as well as many more. Guest speakers are frequently invited to the school, especially in the Sixth Form. There are also Junior and Senior Choirs, a Madrigal group, a Barbershop group, Junior and Senior Orchestras, a Wind Ensemble, a Chamber Orchestra and a Swing Band. Lunch hour music recitals, with visiting professional players, are encouraged. Many girls take the Duke of Edinburgh's Award Scheme at bronze, silver and gold level.

Admission. Main entry points to the school are at 7 and 11 and 16 years of age. For girls over 11 years old, vacancies are only occasional. The entrance examinations for age 11 admission in September will usually be held in the previous January. For age 7 the entrance exam is held in the Autumn Term. Admission to the Sixth Form is also by written examination and interview during the Autumn Term.

Applications for 11+ and 16+ should reach the Admissions Officer by the start of the previous October. Specific deadlines can be found on the website.

Scholarships and Bursaries. The School has a variety of art, music and drama scholarships and means-tested bursaries for entry at 11+ and 16+.

Further details may be obtained from the Admissions Officer.

Fees per term (2014–2015). Preparatory Department: £4,803 (including lunch); Main School: £4,803 (excluding lunch).

Senior School lunches are paid for with a cashless system based on credited payment cards. Pupils in the Preparatory Department are expected to take school lunch for which there is no extra charge. After-school supervision is also available at £169 per term.

Extra Subjects: Pianoforte, Violin, Cello, Flute, Clarinet, Organ, Guitar and a wide variety of other instruments, including Singing: £240 per term (fees are all payable in advance).

Clayesmore School

Iwerne Minster, Blandford Forum, Dorset DT11 8LL
Tel: 01747 812122
Fax: 01747 813187
email: hmsec@clayesmore.com
website: www.clayesmore.com
Twitter: @clayesmore

Developing the unique gifts of every girl and boy

Council of Governors:
Mr J Andrews, LLB (*Chairman of F&GP*)
Mr D M Green, MA, FRSA (*Vice Chairman – Education*)
Mr A Beaton (*OC*)
Mr P Dallyn, FRICS, FAAV
Mrs F Deeming, BA, PGCE
Mrs D Geary, CertEd
Mr D Haywood, MA, FRGS
Mr T Ingram, MA, MBA, FCIB
Mrs R Stiven
Major General J Stokoe, CB, CBE
Dr J Traill, BA, MMus, DPhil Oxon, FRSM
Dr R Willis, MA, BM, BCh

Governors Emeritus:
Mr R C Kingwill, BSc, MS
Mrs J H Lidsey

***Headmaster*: Mr M G Cooke**, BEd, FCollP

Deputy Head: Mr J R Carpenter, BA, FRSA

Second Deputy: Mrs E M Bailey, BA, PGCE

Director of Teaching & Learning: Mr A R West, BA, MA, PGCE

Head of Sixth Form & Senior Master: Mr R A Chew, MA

Head of Learning Support: Mrs A Cowley, BSc, PGCE, MEd SEN, Dip SpLD, AMBDA

Director of Co-curriculum: Mr J A Reach, BEng, PCGE

Bursar: Mr M J M Dyer

House Staff:
Mr C R Middle, BA
Mr M McKeown, BA, PGCE
Mrs J A Murphy
Mrs H N Christmas, BA
Mr D I Rimmer, MA

Assistant Staff:
Mr T M Andrews, BA
Ms B Barrie, BA, MA
Mr R G Berry, BSc, PGCE
Mrs I Browse, BA, MA
Miss S Buckland, BSc, PGCE
Mr C L Burton, BSc, PGCE
Miss A L Cheverton, BSc, PGCE
Mrs L Chmielewski, BA
Mrs H N Christmas, BA, PGCE
Miss T S Cook, BA
Miss E C Cummings, BA, MA, PGCE
Mr C B A Didier, MFLE, PGCE
Mrs E L Dorey, BA, PGCE
Mrs L Downton, BA
Mrs B Eckhardt-Potter, BA, MA, PGCE
Mr C B W Ellis, BA, PGCE
Mrs H B Forster, MA, PGCE
Mr M S Fraser, BA, PGCE
Mr H J Gibbons, BSc, PGCE, CPhys, CSci, MinstP
Mr W H Gibbs, BSc, PGCE
Mrs C Godfree, BA, PGCE
Mr A Hanson-Stewart, BSc, PGCE
Miss J E Hayes, BEd
Mrs C E Hayter, BA, PCGE
Mrs M Herry, BA, PGCE
Mr D A Humphreys, BSc Tech
Mr A Jancis, BSc, PGCE
Dr A P G Jancis, BSc, PhD, CBiol, MIBiol, PGCE
Mr M I Jones, BA, PGCE
Mr R Kerr, MA
Mrs K R Mareau-Jones, BA, PGCE
Mrs J M Martin, Dip SteinerEd, RSA DipSpLD
Miss S E May, MA, PGCE
Mr M McKeown, BA, PGCE
Mr C R Middle, BA
Mr R S Miller, BSc, PGCE
Mrs T J Mousalli, BSc
Mrs J A Murphy
Mr M I Newland, BSc, MA, PGCE
Mrs S J Newland, BSc, PGCE
Miss K E O' Rourke, BA, PGCE
Mrs H A Perrett, BA, PGCE
Ms A K Pilgrim, BA, PGCE
Mrs N L Potter, BSc, PGCE
Revd J C E Pottinger, MA, MTh, PGCE
Mr A K Powell-Young, BSc, PGCE, MRSC
Mr P J Randall, BA, PGCE
Miss R V Readman, BA, PGCE

Miss S-J Rhead, BSc, PGCE
Mr K A Richards, BA, PGCE
Mr D I Rimmer, MA
Mr E R Robeson, MA, PGCE
Mr K A Samoluk, BA, PGCE
Mrs M J Simpson, BCom, PGCE
Mr H C Smith, BA, PGCE
Mr S A Smith, BSc, PGCE, MinstPhys
Mr H P Stevenson, BA, PGCE
Dr F M Thomason, BSc, PhD, OCN Cert SpLD, PGCE
Ms A E Turner, MA
Mr T E Wansey, BA
Miss C L Waples, BSc, PGCE
Mrs J Willoughby, BSc, PGCE
Miss T F Woolford, BSc, PGCE

Administrative Staff:
Headmaster's Secretary & Registrar: Mrs M B McCafferty
Assistant Registrar: Mrs H de Bie
Marketing Manager: Mrs E A Cooke, BEd, AdvDipEd
Development Officer: Mrs L Smith, BA
Marketing and Development Assistant: Mrs N E Cassin, BA
School Secretary: Mrs R Rutherford
Transport Manager: Mrs H Horley
Pupil Registration/Absence: Mrs S J Lockwood
Exams Officer: Mr A Jancis, BSc
Assistant Exams Officer: Mr J Goodman, BA

House Matrons:
Mrs E Reed (*Wolverton*)
Mrs W Everest (*Gate*)
Mrs A Goates (*King's*)
Mrs J Dalton (*Manor*)
Mrs L Miskin (*Devine*)
Mrs A West (*Wolverton/The Bower*)

Medical Officers:
Dr N Berry, BM, BS, BMedSc, DRCOG, MRCGP
Dr S Nixon, BA, MB, BChir

Nurses:
Mrs D J Amphlett, RGN
Mrs J Morris, RGN, RSCN, HV
Mrs H Berry, RNLD
Mrs G Hakimzadeh, RGN
Mrs M Sandiford, RGN
Medical Centre Assistant: Mrs C McKeown

Director of Sport & Enterprise: C Humpage, BH, PGCE
Assistant Directors of Sport & Enterprise: Mr R S Miller, BSc, PGCE; Miss T S Cook
CCF School Staff Instructor: Mr C Evans
Buildings & Estates Manager: Mr J Handley
Building & Estates Secretary: Mrs V McKinley
Catering Manager: Mr A Croft
Head Groundsman: Mr R Norris, BSc, Dip EnvDev
Librarians: Mrs J A Murphy, Mrs MA McCrow

Clayesmore Prep School

Headmaster: Mr W G Dunlop, BA

Deputy Head: Mr S Reeves, BA, QTS
Director of Teaching & Learning: Miss S Weber, BA, PGCE
Head of LSU: Mrs A Cowley, BSc, PGCE, MEd SEN, PG Dip SpLD, AMBDA
Head of Pre-Prep & Nursery: Mrs J E Jackson, CertEd
Head of Boarding: Mr D J Browse, BA, QTS
Head of Nursery: Mrs E Stewart, BA, PGCE

Assistant Staff:
Miss G Ankers, BA, PGCE
Mrs H Bignold, BLib, MA, MCLIP
Dr S Bragg, BA, PhD
Mrs I J Browse, BA, MA
Mrs S Bunnell, BA, Cert Ed, RSA Dip TEFL, HND, MlfL

Mrs C Caiger, BA, PGCE, PGDip
Mrs F Carless, BA
Mrs S M Chinnock, BA, PGCE
Mrs A Coombes, BEd, PCES SpLD
Mrs J E Coplan, BMus, MA, PGCE
Mr D A Harrison, BSc, PGCE
Mrs S Hart, BA, PGCE
Mrs S L Hart, BA
Mrs M Herry, BA, PGCE
Mr T Manley, BSc
Miss S May, MA
Mrs P-A Middle, BA, PGCE
Mr R S Miller, BSc, PGCE
Mr N Moore, BEd
Mrs M M Oakley, CertEd, RSA SpLD
Mrs S Panton, BSc, MA, PGCE
Mrs E F Pogson, BEd, Cert RSA SpLD
Mrs P Price, CertEd
Mrs E L Reach, BEd
Mrs C Ritchie, BA, MA
Mrs I Rose, BA, PGCE
Miss N Rowse, BEd, RSA Cert SpLD
Mr J Smith, BMus, PGCE
Mrs D Spokes, BSc, PGCE
Mrs C Townsend, MA, PGCE
Mr G Weaver, BA, PGCE
Mr R Wilson, BA

Nursery Staff:
Miss R Howell, Diploma in Childcare
Mrs H Martin, City & Guilds NVQ3

Administrative & Pastoral:
Head's Wife: Mrs C Dunlop, BA, PGCE
School Secretary: Mrs H Young, BA
Registrar: Mrs R Johnson, BA
Office Secretary: Mrs H Garrett

Sister in charge: Mrs S Hillyard, RN
Deputy Sisters: Mrs R Flute, RGN
Matrons: Mrs H Galley

Librarian: Mrs H Bignold, BLib, MA, MCLIP

Infused with an atmosphere of warmth and friendliness, Clayesmore is a flourishing co-educational school with Senior and Preparatory sharing the same stunning 62-acre site. The Senior School was founded in 1896 and in 1975 was joined by the Prep at Iwerne Minster. Despite Clayesmore being one big happy family, the two schools each have their own Headmaster, staff and separate teaching areas.

Clayesmore has been deemed 'excellent' across the board following a recent Independent Schools Inspectorate Inspection that included pupils' achievements, quality of teaching and quality of boarding. The report strongly praised the school's remarkable achievements and its rise to becoming one of the South West's premier independent boarding and day schools.

Buildings and Grounds. The excellent facilities have been radically improved in recent years providing even greater opportunities for pupils. The attractive main building functions as the school's HQ with the upper floors used as a girls' boarding house. The ground floor features a charming library complete with computer facilities for private study and research, as well as delightful reception rooms for a variety of uses.

Recent development has included a £2.8m state-of-the-art Business School and a girls' boarding house to accommodate growing pupil numbers. The stylish Business School houses teaching facilities for Business Studies, Economics, Psychology and a brand new Careers Centre. Future development plans include the building of a new theatre, sports pavilion, English & Drama faculty and boys' boarding house.

The Sports Centre has a 25m indoor pool, squash courts, fitness suite, four badminton courts and indoor cricket nets. Outside, as well as the many pitches and netball courts, there is a floodlit, all-weather hockey pitch that provides 12 tennis courts for summer use.

There is a dedicated Music School and self-contained Art School, as well as a Chapel, built in 1956, as a memorial to the Old Clayesmorians who gave their lives in two World Wars. The parkland grounds are quite outstanding, with extensive playing fields, a lake, and wonderful views towards Hambledon Hill with its Saxon fort.

Houses and Pastoral Care. The Senior School has five houses (three for boys and two for girls) each with resident, married house staff, and resident tutor, who provide nurturing pastoral care. Boarding pupils and day pupils live and learn together – there are no day houses and all pupils have a tutor to oversee academic progress and support them through school. Clayesmore has a real family feel and its comparatively small size enables the Headmaster and the staff to really get to know the pupils.

Academic work. Year 9 serves as a useful foundation year prior to GCSE courses starting in Years 10 and 11. Sixth Form students study four AS Levels in the Lower Sixth, taking three of these on to A2 in the Upper Sixth. The school has also introduced new A Level subjects and a number of BTEC options to broaden choice. The Sixth Form really helps to prepare students for life after Clayesmore, with supportive tutors, work experience opportunities and expert careers advice.

Clayesmore pays close attention to the needs of individual pupils, both in academic as well as other spheres, and the school has earned a strong reputation for successfully helping pupils with dyslexia.

Scholarships. A wide range of bursaries and scholarships really open doors, including those for HM Forces families.

The wider life at Clayesmore. Sport is well supported at Clayesmore with rugby, hockey, cricket, athletics, netball, swimming and cross-country complemented by popular subsidiary sports such as badminton, squash, sailing and orienteering.

Year 10 and 11 pupils can experience the challenges and excitement of the Combined Cadet Force with many enthusiasts continuing as NCOs into the Sixth Form. Clayesmore also offers the chance to achieve the well-respected Duke of Edinburgh's Award, as well as a marvellous mix of other activities.

Music and drama play a vibrant role in the life of the school and provide pupils with numerous opportunities to perform. Encouragement is given to pupils of all ages to learn instruments and sing in the choirs. There are all sorts of ensembles and new ones are formed to match different pupil interests. The purpose-built theatre is a practical, intimate space, used with great imagination, not only for various termly productions, but also for GCSE and A Level Theatre Studies.

Entry arrangements. Entrance to Clayesmore Senior School is at 13 with those from preparatory schools taking the Common Entrance examination. For entrants from maintained schools, there are tests in English, Mathematics, Science and French. Girls and boys may join Clayesmore earlier if they attend Clayesmore Preparatory School and it is quite normal for new pupils to arrive at age 11 and undertake Years 7 and 8 at the Prep School. Each year, between 10 and 20 young people join as Sixth Formers, and the total number in the Sixth Form is roughly 170.

Clayesmore Preparatory School. Clayesmore is an 'all-through' school with both Prep and Senior sharing the same idyllic setting and offering a seamless transition at 13 that is perfect for parents, particularly of boarders, who are keen to keep siblings together. Entrance to the Preparatory School may take place into any year group assuming a place is available, and is dependent upon an interview with the Headmaster and a report from the pupil's present school.

Fees per term (2014–2015). Senior School: £10,639 (boarding), £7,783 (day). Preparatory School: £6,954–£7,622 (boarding), £2,317–£5,661 (day).

Charitable status. Clayesmore School Limited is a Registered Charity, number 306214.

Clifton College

College Road, Clifton, Bristol BS8 3JH

Tel: +44 (0)117 315 7000
            +44 (0)117 315 7503 (Preparatory School)
Fax: +44 (0)117 315 7101
email: admissions@cliftoncollege.com
            prepadmissions@cliftoncollege.com
website: www.cliftoncollege.com
Twitter: @Clifton_College
Facebook: /CliftonCollegeUK
LinkedIn: /clifton-college

Motto: '*Spiritus intus alit*'

Clifton College was founded in 1862 and is a Corporation by Royal Charter granted 16 March 1877.

Council:
President: Dr J Cottrell, PhD, MA, FCA
Chairman: Mr R M Morgan, MA
Vice-Chairman: Mrs A Streatfeild-James, MA
Treasurer: Mr S Smith, BSc, DPhil, FCA

Dr C K Beale, MBA, FIMechE, FRAeS
Ms T Fisk, MA, FCA
Mr L Gray, MA, PGCE, ARCO, FRSCM
Mr H Harper, MA
Mrs L Harradine, BA
Mrs C Lear, BA
Mr D Maggs, MA
Mr P McCarthy, BSc, MBA, CEng, FI ET
Brig R J Morris, BA
Mr C Pople, ACA, ATII
Sir H Sants, MA
Mr N Tolchard, BSc
Mr C Trembath, BSc

Secretary and Bursar: Mrs L K J Hanson, BSc, FCA

Head Master: Mr M J Moore, MA

Deputy Head (Pastoral): Miss A Tebay, BSc
Deputy Head (Academic): Mr T M Greene, BA, DPhil
Chaplain: Revd K Taplin, BA, MTh, FRSA
Director of Admissions: Mr J S Tait, BA, MA
Head of Sixth Form: Mr J H Greenbury, MA

Heads of Department:
Mr P Askew, BEd (*Director of Sport*)
Miss C Bloor, BA (*French*)
Mr J C Bobby, BA (*Boys' Games*)
Mrs L A Catchpole, BA (*Girls' Games*)
Miss S A Clarke, MA (*English*)
Ms E L Cordwell, BA (*Mandarin*)
Mr D Dean, MA, PhD (*Information Technology*)
Mrs J M Greenbury, BA (*Religious Studies and Philosophy*)
Ms S Griffin, BSc (*PSHE and Psychology*)
Miss N O Hall, MA (*Design & Technology*)
Miss M Harris, BA (*Spanish*)
Mr A Hasthorpe, MSc (*Physics and Science*)
Mr O G Lewis, MA (*German*)
Mr P G Lidington, BA (*Politics*)
Mr N Mills, BA, MA (*History*)
Mr J Older, BA, PhD (*Chemistry*)
Mr T Patrick, MA, DPhil (*Classics*)

Mrs K J Pickles, BA (*Director of Drama*)
Dr R Poland, MA, PhD (*Biology*)
Mr D Robson, BA (*Director of Music*)
Mr W Scott, BSc (*Economics & Business Studies*)
Mr L Siddons, MA (*Modern Languages*)
Mr G E Simmons, BSc (*Mathematics*)
Mr A Wagstaff, MA (*Physical Education*)
Mr A J Wilkie, BA (*Art*)
Mr M Williams, BA (*Geography*)

Houses and Housemasters/mistresses:

Boys Boarding:
Moberly's: Mr G J Catchpole, MEng
Watson's: Mr S Heard, BA
School House: Mr J H Hughes, MA
Wiseman's: Mr W J Huntington, MA

Girls Boarding:
Worcester: Mrs A J Ballance, BSc
Oakeley's: Mrs K A Jeffery, BSc
Hallward's: Mrs K J Pickles, BA

Boys Day:
North Town: Mr D Janke, BA
South Town: Mr J T J Hills, BA
East Town: Mr J H Thomson-Glover, BA

Girls Day:
West Town: Mrs L A Catchpole, BEd

Clifton College was founded in 1862, and incorporated by Royal Charter in 1877. It is situated in the City of Bristol, on the edge of Clifton Down and not far from open country. The School is well placed to take advantage of the many cultural and educational activities of the City, and to gain much else of value from its civic and industrial life. There are friendly links with the Universities and with other schools of various types.

Admission. Boy and girl boarders and day pupils are normally admitted in September between the ages of 13 and 14, and most are required to pass the Common Entrance examination, which can be taken at their Preparatory Schools. Credentials of good character and conduct are required. Registration Forms can be obtained from the Director of Admissions, 32 College Road, Clifton, Bristol BS8 3JH.

Houses. It is usual for a pupil to be entered for a particular House, but where parents have no preference or where no vacancy exists in the House chosen, the Head Master will make the necessary arrangements.

Day Pupils and Day-Boarders. Day boys are divided into Houses: North Town, South Town and East Town. Day girls enter West Town or Hallward's. The town Houses have the same status as Boarding Houses and day pupils are encouraged to take a full part in the various activities of the School. A small number of day-boarder places are available for boys and girls.

Catering is managed by our own experienced caterers and boarders take all meals in the School Dining Hall. Day pupils and day-boarders are required to have their midday meal at School, and arrangements are made for their tea and supper at the School when necessary.

Fees per term (2014–2015). Boarders £10,800–£11,125; Day Boarders (4 nights) £9,825–£10,110; Day Pupils £7,450–£7,575. Sixth Form Joiners (from other schools): Boarders £11,450; Day Boarders (4 nights) £10,350; Day Pupils £7,875.

Scholarships, Bursaries and Awards. All awards on merit are limited to 25% of the fees, but they may be augmented by means-tested bursaries. The following awards are offered each year:

13+ entry: Academic, Music, Art scholarships and Sport awards. Boys and girls who are already in the School may compete for all 13+ scholarships and awards.

Sixth Form entry: Up to 10 Academic scholarships per year are available for entrants from other schools to the Sixth Form. A limited number of Sport awards, Music scholarships and an Organ scholarship are also available. A further Sixth Form award is offered to sons or daughters of Old Cliftonians.

All Music awards include free tuition in two instruments (one of which may be singing).

The Birdwood Award, for sons and daughters of serving members of HM Forces, is awarded on the results of the Entrance Scholarship exam.

Bursaries: these are means-tested awards and may be awarded in addition to scholarships (or in their own right). In exceptional circumstances, bursaries may be awarded up to 100% of the fees.

Academic structure. Boys and girls enter the School in the Third Form, following a general course for their first year. Most GCSEs are taken at the end of the Fifth Form.

Thereafter boys and girls enter Block I (Sixth Form) and take an advanced course consisting of 4 subjects at AS Level, then 3 at A Level. A great many combinations of subjects are possible. Boys and girls are prepared for entrance to Oxford and Cambridge.

Service. All pupils are given a course in outdoor pursuits and other skills in the Third Form. In the Fourth Form they are given more advanced training, which may include involvement in the Duke of Edinburgh's Award Scheme, and at the end of the year they decide whether to join the Army, Navy or Air Force sections of the CCF or to take part in Community Service. There is regular use of a property owned by the school in the Brecon Beacons for all these activities.

Societies. Voluntary membership of Scientific, Historical, Literary, Dramatic, Geographical, Debating and many other Societies is encouraged.

Music and Art. The Musical activities of the School are wide and varied, and are designed for musicians of all standards. They include the Chapel Choir, Choral Society and Chamber Choir, a full orchestra, 2 string orchestras, 2 wind bands, a jazz band, as well as numerous chamber music activities. Visiting concert artists regularly run masterclasses, and there are wide opportunities for performance. Teaching is available on virtually all instruments and in all styles. Instrumental and vocal competitions are held at House level and individually annually. The well-equipped and recently refurbished Music School includes practice facilities, computers, recording studio, an extensive sheet music library and a large record/compact disc library.

Drawing, Painting, Sculpture, Pottery, Textiles and various Crafts are taught under the supervision of the Director of Art in the Art School. There is an annual House Art Competition and various exhibitions throughout the year.

Theatre. Drama and Dance play an important part in the life of the School with an increasing number of pupils achieving success in LAMDA, PCERT LAM and RAD examinations. The Redgrave Theatre is used for School plays, the House Drama Festival, and for other plays that may be put on (eg by individual houses, the staff or the Modern Language Society). Each House produces a play each year. It is also used for teaching purposes, and in addition for concerts, lectures and meetings.

Information and Communication Technology. The ICT Centre at the heart of the School houses the most advanced internet facility of any school in the South West.

Physical Education. Physical Education is part of the regular School curriculum and games are played at least twice per week by all age groups.

In the Michaelmas Term, boys play Rugby and girls play Hockey. There is a multi-sport option for seniors who are not in team squads. In the Lent Term, Hockey and Soccer are the main options for the boys whilst the girls mostly play Netball. Rowing, Running, Squash, Swimming, Shooting, Tetrathlon and Fives are among the alternative options for senior boys and girls. In the Summer Term, Cricket is the main sport for the boys and Tennis for the girls, with Tennis,

Athletics, Rowing, Swimming and Shooting as alternatives for seniors. The Clifton College playing fields in Abbots Leigh include three floodlit all-weather Hockey and Football pitches, six floodlit Tennis courts, a 3G artificial pitch for Soccer and Rugby, a water-based Hockey pitch with training D, and a Real Tennis court. An indoor facility for Tennis and Netball is one of the best in the region.

Careers. Careers advice is the shared responsibility of the Head Master, Housemasters, Housemistresses, Heads of Departments and the Head of Sixth Form. The School is a subscribing member of the Independent Schools Careers Organisation and of the Careers Research and Advisory Centre at Cambridge. The proximity of the City of Bristol enables the Careers Department and other members of the staff to keep in close touch with Universities, business firms and professional bodies about all matters affecting boys' and girls' careers.

Clifton College Preparatory School. *Headmaster*: J Milne, BA, MBA

The Preparatory School has separate buildings (including its own Science laboratories, Arts Centre, ICT Centres and Music School) and is kept distinct from the Upper School. The two Schools nevertheless work closely together and share some facilities, including the Chapel, Theatre, Sports complex, all-weather playing surfaces and swimming pool. Most boys and girls proceed from the Preparatory School to the Upper School. Pupils are also prepared for schools other than Clifton. There is a Pre-Prep School for day pupils aged between 3 and 8. Boys and girls are accepted at all ages and scholarships are available at age 11.

For further details see entries for Clifton College Preparatory School in IAPS section.

Old Cliftonian Society. *Secretary*: S J M Reece, The Garden Room, 3 Worcester Road, Clifton, Bristol BS8 3JL (Tel: 0117 3157 156).

Charitable status. Clifton College is a Registered Charity, number 311735. It is a charitable trust providing boarding and day education for boys and girls aged 3–18.

Clongowes Wood College

Clane, Co Kildare, Ireland
Tel: 00 353 45 868202
Fax: 00 353 45 861042
email: reception@clongowes.net
website: www.clongowes.net

Motto: '*Aeterna non Caduca*'

Clongowes Wood College was founded in 1814 in a rebuilt Pale castle – Castle Brown in North Kildare, about 25 miles from Dublin. A boarding school for boys from 12–18, the school has developed steadily ever since and now has 500 pupils on the rolls, all of whom are boarders.

Trustee of the School: Fr Tom Layden, SJ, Provincial of the Society of Jesus in Ireland

Chairman of the Board of Management: Mr David Dilger

Headmaster: Fr Leonard Moloney, SJ, BA, HDip, MDiv, MPhil (*Ecum*)

Assistant Headmaster: Mr Martin Wallace, BA, HTE

Deputy Assistant Headmaster: Mr Frank Kelly, BComm, HDip

The College is situated on 150 acres of land, mostly comprising sports fields and a 9-hole golf course. It is surrounded by about 300 acres of farmland. Clongowes is listed as an historic building.

Admission. Application for admission should be made to the Headmaster. There is a registration fee of €50. An assessment day is held in early October prior to the year of entry and entry is determined by a variety of factors including family association, geographical spread including Northern Ireland and abroad, date of registration, and an understanding of the values that animate the College. Normal entry is at the age of 12; entry in later years is possible in exceptional circumstances if a place becomes available.

Curriculum. A wide choice of subjects is available throughout the school and pupils are prepared for the Irish Junior Certificate and the Irish Leaving Certificate. This latter is the qualifying examination for entry to Irish Universities and other third-level institutions. It is acceptable for entry to almost all Universities in the United Kingdom, provided the requisite grades are obtained. All pupils take a Transition Year programme following the Junior Certificate. This programme is recommended by the Department of Education in Ireland. Work experience modules, social outreach programmes, exchanges with other countries and opportunities to explore different areas of study are all included in this programme.

Religious Teaching. Clongowes is a Jesuit school in the Roman Catholic tradition and there are regular formal and informal liturgies. Boys are given a good grounding in Catholic theology and are encouraged to participate in retreats, prayer groups and pilgrimages (Taize, Lourdes). Social Outreach is part of the curriculum in Transition Year and is encouraged throughout the school. A small number of boys of other faiths are pupils in the school.

Sport. All boys play rugby in their first year in school. They then have the choice to continue in that game or to play other games. Rugby pitches, a golf course, tennis courts, soccer pitches, squash courts, a cross-country track, an athletics and cricket oval, a gymnasium and a swimming pool provide plenty of opportunity for a variety of activities. Athletics, Gaelic football and cricket are popular activities in the third term. Clongowes has a strong rugby tradition and has won the Leinster Championship twice in the last decade.

Other activities. Following the Jesuit tradition, the school has a fine reputation for debating and has won competitions in three different languages (English, Irish, French) in the last decade. A large school orchestra and school choir gives a formal concert at Christmas and another before the summer holidays. Drama productions take place at every level within the school. A large-scale summer project for charity has been undertaken each year. A residential holiday project for children with disabilities takes place in the school each summer and is animated by teachers and pupils. The College has recently created link programmes with schools in Hungary and Romania.

Pastoral Care. The school is organised horizontally into Lines. Two 'prefects', or housemasters look after each year within a Line, composed of two years, with a Line Prefect in charge of the Line itself. In addition, an Academic Year Head oversees the academic work of each of the 70 pupils within each year. A Spiritual Father or Chaplain is attached to each line. There is a strong and positive relationship with parents and a good community spirit throughout the school. The school seeks to foster competence, conscience and compassionate commitment in each of the boys in its care.

Fees per annum (2014–2015). €17,800. Parents are also asked to support the continuing development of the College through various fundraising activities.

Clongowes Union. This association of past pupils of the school can be contacted through: The Secretary, The Clongowes Union, Clongowes Wood College, Clane, Co Kildare; email: development@clongowes.net.

Cokethorpe School

Witney, Oxfordshire OX29 7PU
Tel: 01993 703921
email: hmsec@cokethorpe.org
            admissions@cokethorpe.org
website: www.cokethorpe.org.uk
Twitter: @cokethorpe

Motto: *Inopiam Ingenio Pensant*

Cokethorpe School, founded in 1957, is a vibrant and dynamic day school for around 660 girls and boys aged 4 to 18. It is set in 150 acres of parkland, two miles from Witney and ten from Oxford. There are 137 children in the Junior School and 521 pupils in the Senior School (including 130 Sixth Formers).

Governing Body:
Chairman: Sir John Allison, KCB, CBE, FRAeS
Vice-Chairman: Mr S K Dexter Esq, FCA
Mr A Bark, ACIB
Mrs C Bartlett, MA
Mr M Booty
Mrs D Fairweather, BA
Mrs R Gunn, MA Cantab
Mr R F Jonckheer Esq, LLB Hons
Mr P G Riman Esq, BA, LL Dip
Mr R Walker Esq, BSc, PGCE, CChem, CSci, FRSA
Prof J Wood, CBE, FREng
Governor Emeritus: M St John Parker Esq, MA

Headmaster: D J Ettinger, BA, FRSA, MA, PGCE

Deputy Headmaster: J C Stevens, BEng
Bursar: Mrs S A Landon, BA, ACMA
Head of Junior School: Mrs C A Cook, BEd
Director of Studies: Dr A P Willis, BSc, PhD
Registrar: Mrs S M L Copeland, BA, PGCE, AdvDipPsych
Senior Administrator: E J Fenton, BD, AKC, PGCE
Head of Sixth Form: G J Sheer, BA, PGCE

Deputy Head of Sixth Form: Mrs S Howells, BA, PGCE
Deputy Head of Sixth Form: J E Bown, BSc, PGCE
Deputy Head of Sixth Form: Mrs H M Kenworthy, BSc, PGCE
Third Master: C Maskery, MSc, BA, PGCE, FBAPT
School Nurse: Mrs J E Homewood
Chaplain: Revd R Turner

Housemasters and Housemistresses:
Feilden: Miss P S M Townsend, BA, MBA, PGCE
Gascoigne: Mrs E Semenzato, DLit, PGCE
Harcourt: W G Lawson, BA, PGCE
Queen Anne: A P Gale, BSc, PGCE
Swift: Mrs M H D Cooper, BA, PGCE
Vanbrugh: T J Walwyn, BA
Lower House: Mrs J L Pratley, BA, MCertSpLD

Heads of Departments:
Miss M Bennett, BA, PGCE (*Modern Foreign Languages*)
T J Bostwick, BA, PGCE (*History*)
Mrs H V Brown, BA, PGCE (*Design Technology*)
Dr C Flaherty, PhD, MSc, PGCE, MRSC (*Science*)
J E Hughes, BA, BMus (*Music*)
Mrs C L Hooper, Dip Act, DCL (*Drama*)
R D Hughes, BA (*Business Studies and Economics*)
Miss D C H Jackson, BEd, Dip EFL, FRSA (*English*)
Mrs C M McCormick, BA, PGCE (*Learning Support*)
J A W Capel, MA, PGCE (*Geography*)
Mrs A B Hughes, BSc, PGCE, MA (*Psychology*)
Mrs C S Scaysbrook, BSc, PGCE (*Mathematics*)
Miss F S O'Hagan, BA, PGCE (*Philosophy, Religion and Ethics*)
Miss M M Taylor, BA, PGCE, NDDA, PGDC (*Art*)

Mr P A R Goulding, BA (*Classics*)
Miss A M Woodcock, BSc (*Physical Education*)

74 full-time academic teaching staff, plus 17 part-time.
13 visiting teachers for Piano, String, Wind and Brass instruments, Timpani and Singing.
20 part-time sports coaches.

Curriculum. A curriculum is offered that gives pupils the chance to pursue individual passions, with both traditional and modern subjects, those that are highly academic and others that are more practical. The National Curriculum is broadly followed up to GCSE. All pupils study core subjects of English, Maths and Science at GCSE and have a wide choice of subject options. There is also a full programme of personal, social and health education.

Sixth Formers typically choose four subjects to study at AS Level and continue with three of these subjects to A2 Level. The small size of teaching groups is particularly conducive to individual attention and encouragement. The usual courses are supplemented by Economics, Photography, Government and Politics, Philosophy and Classical Civilisation.

The Junior School offers a fully balanced curriculum with the focus on developing high standards and providing intellectual challenges. Whilst the National Curriculum is followed, the freedom to offer breadth is embraced. (*See Cokethorpe Junior School entry in IAPS section.*)

Parents are kept closely informed of their child's progress and achievement, both academically and socially.

Facilities. Teaching takes place in a range of modern buildings set around the elegant Queen Anne Mansion House. The most recent addition is the Dining Hall and dedicated Sixth Form Centre that sit alongside the contemporary glass and stone library. A 200-seat auditorium is the centre for Performing Arts and a perfect setting for visiting speakers. As well as extensive sport pitches, astroturf pitches, tennis and netball courts, a nine-hole golf course, climbing tower and clay pigeon shoot, Cokethorpe also has a full-size Sports Hall with a fitness suite. The Sports facilities are rounded off with the Boat House situated close to the School on the River Thames.

Pastoral. The House system, personal tutoring (including day-to-day care, pastoral welfare and academic progress), year-group specific social and health programmes and a joint Anglican and Roman Catholic foundation creates an excellent support structure. Small classes and dedicated teachers help pupils champion their strengths and challenge their weaknesses.

Sport. The School has a strong and successful sporting tradition. Principal sports include rugby, hockey, netball, soccer, cricket, tennis, kayaking and clay pigeon shooting. A wide variety of subsidiary sports are also available including badminton, athletics, cross-country, golf, judo, squash, swimming and sailing, designed to suit all tastes and abilities. All pupils do PE as part of the curriculum. There are regular county, national and international successes. The most talented pupils will be considered for the School Sports Academy.

Other Activities. The extra-curricular programme (known as 'AOB') plays a prominent part in a pupil's timetable and includes over 40 clubs such as Dance, Engineering, Graphic Novels, Gardening, Web Design, Chess, Debating, Climbing and Duke of Edinburgh's Award Scheme. There is a strong tradition of fundraising. Other activities include language exchanges, ski trips, sports tours abroad and cultural trips to Africa and Greece.

Music, Drama and Creative Arts. The Arts are extremely important at Cokethorpe. All pupils are encouraged to learn a musical instrument and join the choir or one of the range of orchestras and ensembles. Peripatetic teachers cover a very wide range of instruments, and there are regular concerts and recitals during the year. Drama flourishes with two to three whole-School productions and the

Inter-House competition annually, numerous GCSE and A Level performances, a programme of lunchtime recitals from all years and frequent trips to the theatre. Art, Textiles and Design Technology (Resistant Materials and Graphic Design) are all offered at GCSE and A Level, with Photography also offered at A Level. There is also a vibrant and varied range of art, design and craft activities as part of the extended curriculum.

Higher Education and Careers. The majority of Sixth Form leavers go on to Higher Education, enrolling in a wide variety of foundation courses, degrees or apprenticeships. A careers programme is followed throughout the Senior School, including work experience, careers conventions and psychometric profiling. Help and advice is given by experienced Careers teachers and the latest literature is available in the Careers Library.

Admission. Pupils usually enter the Junior School at age 4 or 7 (the latter based on an assessment day in January) and the Senior School either at age 11, 13 or 16. There are occasionally vacancies at other ages. Candidates at age 11 are required to sit assessments in Maths and English, at age 13 either assessments or Common Entrance and at age 16 GCSEs or equivalent. Places are offered on the basis of these results, plus interviews and school reports. There is a registration fee of £75. Registration forms and details of entrance examination procedures are available from the Registrar.

Scholarships. Scholarships are assessed separately and awarded annually. Academic, All Round, Art and Design, Music, Sport, Drama and Modern Languages scholarships and awards are available.

Bursaries. Financial assistance is available, through the award of means-tested bursaries, to those families entering the School from ages 11 through to 18 (and occasionally into the Junior School). The value of the bursary can be up to 100% of fees.

Fees per term (2014–2015). Junior School £3,825; Senior School £5,550. Fees include lunch. Extras are kept to a minimum.

The Cokethorpe Society. c/o Events and Alumni Administrator: Nicole Rolfe, Cokethorpe School (society@cokethorpe.org).

Charitable Status. Cokethorpe Educational Trust Limited is a Registered Charity, number 309650. It aims to provide a first-class education for each individual pupil.

Colfe's School

Horn Park Lane, London SE12 8AW
Tel: 020 8852 2283
Fax: 020 8297 1216
email: head@colfes.com
website: www.colfes.com

Colfe's is one of the oldest schools in London. The parish priest of Lewisham taught the local children from the time of Richard Walker's Charity, founded in 1494, until the dissolution of the monasteries by Henry VIII. Revd John Glyn re-established the school in 1568 and it was granted a Charter by Queen Elizabeth in 1574. Abraham Colfe, Vicar of Lewisham, became a Governor in 1613 and the School was re-founded bearing his name in 1652. Colfe declared that the aim of the School was to provide an education for "pupils of good wit and capacity and apt to learn", reflecting the School's emphasis on sound learning and academic achievement since the earliest times. Colfe's original vision was to educate the children of "the hundred of Blackheath" and although today our pupils travel to the School from all parts of London, a strong sense of local community remains, with most of the pupils coming from the four boroughs which surround the school. One of Abraham Colfe's wisest moves was to invite the Leathersellers' Company, one of the oldest of the city Livery Companies, to be the Trustee of his will. Links between the School and the company are strong.

Mottos: 'Soli Deo honor et gloria' (Leathersellers) 'Ad Astra per Aspera' (Colfe)

Visitor: HRH Prince Michael of Kent

The current Governors provide between them a broad range of relevant experience and qualifications. A majority are Members or appointees of the Leathersellers' Company to which Abraham Colfe entrusted the School in his will when he died in 1657.

The activities of the Leathersellers are many and varied but the School and its fortunes continue to feature prominently on the Company's agenda. The Master of the Company is, *ex officio*, a member of the Board of Governors.

Board of Governors:
Dr Anthony Watson, CBE (*Master of the Leathersellers' Company*)
Mr Ian A Russell, MBE (*Chairman*)
Mr Andrew B Strong, BSc
Mr Nigel R Pullman, JP
Mr Simon W Polito, MA, LLB
Mr Sean Williams, MA Oxon, MPA Harvard
Miss Serena Cheng, MA, LLB
Mr Mark Williams
Dr Angela Brueggemann, DPhil
Dr Sara Owen, DPhil
Mr John Guyatt, MA Oxon
Mr Andrew Grant, MA Cantab
Mrs Belinda Canham, BA

Headmaster: R F Russell, MA Cantab

Deputy Head – Pastoral: Mrs A Cobbin, BA Hons, Dip Ed, NPQH
Deputy Head – Administrative: J King, BSc, MA
Director of Studies: A Pearson, BSc
Director of Sixth Form: S Drury, BA, MA
Head of Preparatory School: Mrs S Marsh, BEd Hons, MA
Head of Pre-Prep & Nursery: Mrs S Redman, BEd
Bursar: Mrs J Lerbech, MA Cantab, MSci, CA

Director of Admissions: Mrs S Walker, BA Hons

Academic Staff, Senior School:
* *Head of Department*

Art:	Design & Technology:
*Ms S Beetlestone, BA Hons, MA	*Mrs C Matthews, BA Hons
Mrs J Burton, BA Hons	Miss C Quinton, BA Hons
S Zivanovic, BA Hons	S Zivanovic, BA Hons

Biology:	Drama:
*Mr C Morriss, BSc Hons	*Mis L Atkinson, BA Oxon, MA
Miss I Ackers, BSc Hons	Mrs R Medhurst, MA Cantab
Miss R Hargrave, BEd Hons	
Dr J Lea, PhD, BSc Hons	Economics & Business Studies:
Dr E Nicholls, BSc Hons, PhD	*R Otley, BA Hons
Mr M Stamp, BSc Hons	J King, BSc, MA
	Miss S Price, BA Hons, MSc
Chemistry:	
*Mr J Worley, BSc Hons, DIS	English:
Mr D Sawyer, BSc Hons	*Miss M Schramm, BA, MA
	Ms M Brack BA Hons, MA
Classics:	Mrs A Cobbin, BA Hons, Dip Ed, NPQH
*A Corstorphine, MA Cantab, MPhil	C Dunsmore, MA Oxon, G Dip Law
Mrs N Herbert, MA Cantab	
Miss C Le Hur, MA, MPhil	
R Russell, MA Cantab	

Mrs E Karavidas, BA Hons, MA
J Smith, BA Hons

General Studies:
*C Foxall, BA Hons

Geography:
*O Snell, BSc Hons, MSc
Miss J Lawton, BSc Hons
Mrs F McAuliffe, BSc Hons
A Newell, BSc Hons
Mrs A Tickner, BSc Hons, AIEAM

History:
*J Patterson, BA Hons
A Foster, MA Cantab
Miss L Lechmere, BA Hons
S Varley, BA Hons, MA

IT:
*C P Smith, BSc Hons, MInstP

Learning Support:
*Miss A Coode, BA Hons, DTLLS – Literacy

Mathematics:
*Mrs J Sansome, BSc Hons, MSc
Dr C Buescu, BSc Hons, MA, PhD
Mrs E Cordell, BSc Hons
Mrs O Hamidzadeh, BSc Hons
A Pearson, BSc Hons
Mr J Smith BA Hons
U Vijapura, PhD

Media Studies:
*C Foxall, BA Hons
Miss Li-Sue, BA Hons, Dip NFTS

Modern Foreign Languages:
*Mrs E Biggs, BSc Hons, MA
Miss E Harris, BMus with French (*French*)

M Koutsakis, MA (*German*)
A Seddon, BA Hons, MIL (*Spanish*)
Mrs A Chapman, BA Hons
Miss F Deutsch, SE
Mrs J German, BA Hons

Music:
Miss K Collinson, MA Cantab
P Gobey, GRSN, MMus Cantab, ARCO, FRSA
Mrs M Metherell, BA Hons

Outdoor Education:
*Major C Cherry, BSc Hons

Physical Education:
*Mrs N Rayes, BEd Hons, EMBA
Mr A Bateson, BA Hons
Mr F Berridge, BA Hons
Major C Cherry, BSc Hons
Mr G Clinton IB
Miss E Cordell, BSc Hons
Mr L Fielden, BA Hons
Miss S Holder
Miss S Manzi

Physics:
*Mr J Fishwick, BSc Hons
Miss M Danielewicz, BA Hons, MSci
M Hillmer, BSME, MS

Politics:
*S Drury, BA Hons, MA
A Collier, BA Hons, MA
O Snell, BSc Hons, MSc

Psychology:
*Dr J Lea, PhD, BSc Hons
Mr M Stamp, BSc Hons

Religious Studies & Philosophy:
*Miss E Henderson, BA Hons
Revd J Chuter, MA
Mrs R Conway MA

Academic Staff, Preparatory School:

Head of Preparatory School: Mrs S Marsh, BEd Hons, NA
Deputy Head: Miss D Lemprière, BA
Director of Studies: M Heil, BEd

Miss C Blair, BA
Mrs J Dunmore, BA
Mrs K Eggins, BSc
Mrs G Fisher, HND, OCR Level 5 & 7 CertSpLD
Mr J Ford, BA
Mrs E Higgs, BA
Mr C Kitchen, BA
Mrs H Lowth, BSc

Miss A Manning, BA
Mr B Medhurst, BA
Mrs J Pearson, BSc
Ms D Santos, BEd
Miss C Tullis, BA, MA
Mrs S Watts, BEd, LTCL, Dip Perf Stds Opera
Mrs V Welch, BA, DipEd

Pre-Preparatory and Nursery School:

Head of Pre-Prep and Nursery: Mrs S Redman, BEd

Miss L Evans, BA
Mrs E Frost, BEd
Mrs S Gurr, BEd
Mrs R Hall, BA

Miss C Harknett, BA Early Years Leadership with Early Years Teaching Status
Mrs D Hills, BA

Mrs L Jennings, BA
Mrs M Moody, BEd, NNEB
Mrs E Otley, TCert, DipSpLD
Mrs N Pearce, BA
Mrs C Russell, BA Hons, NNEB

Mr J Sadzik, BA
Mrs S Walsh, BA
Ms D Wheater, BEd
Miss N Williams, BA
Mrs S Williams, BSc
Mrs C Zahra

Admissions. There are 625 pupils in the Senior School, including 170 in the Sixth Form. The Preparatory School and Nursery and Pre-Preparatory School cater for a further 397 pupils. All sectors of the school are fully co-educational. The main points of entry to the Preparatory School are 3+ and 4+ (Nursery and Pre-Prep) and 7+. The majority of the Prep School pupils transfer to the Senior School at 11. Approximately 65 pupils from a range of local state primary and Prep schools enter the Senior School directly at 11 and there are a limited number of places available to pupils wishing to join in the Sixth Form at Year 12.

Buildings. All the teaching accommodation is modern and purpose built. Specialist on-site facilities include the Leisure Centre, comprising sports hall, swimming pool and fitness suite. The Leathersellers' Sports Ground, located less than a mile from the main school campus, provides extensive playing fields and related facilities. A Visual and Performing Arts centre was built in 2003 and an extensive all-weather pitch was completed in 2006. The Preparatory School and Nursery and Pre-Preparatory Schools are housed in separate modern buildings on the main school site. A large building project is on-going which provided extended provision for the Pre-Prep and Nursery from September 2014 and will provide a new Sixth Form Centre in September 2015.

Curriculum. The curriculum follows the spirit of the National Curriculum in both Preparatory and Senior Schools. Pupils are entered for the separate Sciences at GCSE and follow the IGCSE Maths course. A wide range of subjects is available at A Level, 26 in total, including Drama, Government and Politics, Media Studies, Psychology and Philosophy.

Physical Education and Games. Physical Education and Games are compulsory for all pupils up to and including Year 11. Full use is made of the wide range of facilities available on-site, including a fully-equipped Sports Centre, swimming pool and all-weather surface.

The main sports for boys are rugby, football and cricket. Girls play hockey, netball, tennis and athletics. Other sports available include badminton, basketball, cross-country running, squash and swimming. Girls' cricket introduced in 2013. Girls' teams national champions in netball and county champions in cricket (2013).

Music and Drama. Music and Drama thrive alongside each other in the purpose-built Performing Arts Centre. The music department is home to a wide range of performance groups ranging from beginners to advanced ensembles in both classical and contemporary genres. There are regular performance opportunities given throughout the year, some held in the purpose-built recital hall and others in external venues. A team of 20 visiting instrumental teachers provide further opportunities for pupils to enjoy making music. Drama is a popular subject at both GCSE and A Level, with large numbers of pupils also involved outside the classroom. We recently staged a full-scale production of *One Flew Over The Cuckoo's Nest* at the Greenwich Theatre, London.

Careers. The Careers and Higher Education Department is staffed on a full-time basis. Regular events include University Information Evenings and Careers Fairs.

Fees per term (2014–2015). Senior School £4,917 (excluding lunch); Preparatory School £3,987 (excluding lunch); Pre-Preparatory £3,768 (including lunch); Nursery £3,609 (including lunch).

Scholarships and Bursaries. Academic Scholarships are awarded mainly on the basis of outstanding performance in the Entrance Examinations. The exams are designed to identify and reward academic potential, as well as achievement.

Means-tested bursaries are also available at 11+. Bursaries may, in exceptional circumstances, cover the total cost of tuition fees. Application forms are available from the Director of Admissions.

A limited number of Music, Drama and Sports awards are also available at 11+. In the case of Music scholars, free instrumental tuition may accompany the award. Details of Music and Sports awards can be obtained from the Director of Admissions.

A number of scholarships, bursaries and other awards are also available to candidates entering the school at 16+. Details can again be obtained from the Director of Admissions.

Preparatory School. The purpose-built Preparatory School was opened by HRH Prince Michael of Kent in 1988. Specialist rooms of the Senior School are also used. While the curricular emphasis is on high standards in basic Mathematics and English, a wide range of other subjects is taught, including Science and French. There is also a range of activities similar to those enjoyed by the Senior School and all pupils are expected to participate. All pupils proceed to the Senior School if they achieve the qualifying standard. It is expected that virtually all pupils from the Prep school will proceed to the Senior school at 11.

(*For further details see entry in IAPS section.*)

Nursery and Pre-Prep. A co-educational nursery and pre-preparatory school for pupils aged 3 to 7 is housed in modern accommodation (substantially expanded in 2013) adjacent to the Prep School.

The Colfeian Society. Enquiries to the Alumni Relations Officer, Colfe's School, London SE12 8AW. Tel: 020 8463 8119.

Charitable status. Colfe's School is a Registered Charity, number 1109650. It exists to provide education for boys and girls.

Colston's School

Stapleton, Bristol BS16 1BJ
Tel: 0117 965 5207
Fax: 0117 958 5652
email: admissions@colstons.bristol.sch.uk
website: www.colstons.bristol.sch.uk

Motto: '*Go, and do thou likewise.*'

Colston's School is a thriving co-educational day school for pupils aged 3 to 18 located on a spacious 30-acre site at Stapleton village in north Bristol. Our traditional pastoral structures and house system promote a sense of community and belonging amongst pupils.

A Colston's education extends far beyond the classroom with opportunities for sport, music, service and extra-curricular activities all playing their part in creating the unique experience on offer at the school.

The Governors of the school are The Society of Merchant Venturers, Merchants' Hall, Bristol BS8 3NH.

Governors:
Mr R Bernays (*Chair*)

Mr N Baker	Mr J McGeehan
Mr N Bhadresa	Mrs P Morris
Mrs K Curling	Mr R Morris
Mr I Gunn	Mr T Pearce
Mr J Hunt	Dr A Seddon
Mr T Kenny	Mr J Webb
Mr D Mace	Mr N Wilson

¶ *Old Colstonian*

Headmaster: Mr J McCullough, MA Oxon

Deputy Headmaster: Mr P Goodyer, BSc
Deputy Headmaster (*Academic*): Dr P Hill, BSc, PhD

Miss T Anderson, BSc (*PE/Games*)
Mr C Banning, BSc Hons (*Head of Roundway House, PE*)
Mr B Berry, BA (*Head of Psychology*)
Mr M Castle, BA (*Music*)
Mrs K Connolly, BSc Hons (*Biology*)
Mrs D Currie, BA (*Senior Teacher, Head of MFL*)
Dr K Dawson, BA, PhD (*Examinations Officer, Geography*)
Miss O De Zarate, BA (*Spanish*)
Mr N Drew, BA (*Head of History*)
Mr L Evans, BSc (*PE/Games*)
Mr M Eyles, BSc (*Head of Geography*)
Miss C Flay, BA Hons (*Head of Aldington House, RS, Geography*)
Mr R Gash, BSc (*Head of Computing*)
Mrs L Goodyer, BSc (*Biology*)
Mr P Goodyer, BA (*Psychology*)
Miss R Green (*PE/Games*)
Mr J Gwilliam, BA Hons (*MFL*)
Mrs C Hambley, BA (*MFL*)
Mr J Harper, MA (*Physics*)
Mr O Harris, BSc (*Mathematics, Games*)
Mrs A Hart, BSc (*Biology*)
Mrs E Hayett (*Mathematics*)
Miss S Hill, MA (*English*)
Dr P Hill, BSc, PhD (*Chemistry*)
Mrs R Johnson, BA (*Head of Mathematics*)
Mr P Jones, BSc (*Head of Sixth Form, Mathematics*)
Mr D Kaye, BA Hons (*Head of Dolphin House, History*)
Mr J Layland BA Hons (*Head of Business Studies*)
Dr A Martin, BSc, PhD (*Acting Head of Science, Biology*)
Mr D Mason, BSc (*Senior Teacher Academic Management, Mathematics*)
Mr L Masters, BSc (*Head of King's House, RS & PSHE*)
Mr M Mullings, BSc Hons (*Chemistry*)
Mrs D Panaho, BSc (*PE/Games, Assistant Head of Roundway House*)
Mrs J Poppy, BA (*English*)
Mr S Pritchard, MA (*Head of Drama*)
Mr S Proudman, BA Hons (*Head of English*)
Mr C Pullen, BA Hons (*Drama*)
Mr T Richardson BA Hons (*Head of Music, Commander CCF*)
Mr T Rounds, BA (*Head of RS/Philosophy*)
Mrs K Snell, BA (*Head of DT*)
Mr P Temple, BSc (*Head of Chemistry*)
Mr P Thornley, BEd (*Director of Physical Education*)
Dr J A Tovey, BA, PhD (*Senior Teacher, English*)
Miss S Victor, BEd (*MFL*)
Mr N Vittle BA Hons (*History, Management of DofE*)
Mr D Wall, BEd (*Head of PE/Games*)
Mrs S Ward, BA Hons (*Head of Girls PE/Games*)
Ms L Wight, BEd (*Head of Learning Support*)
Miss A Willis, BA (*Drama*)
Ms C Wyatt, BA (*Art*)
Mr N Yaxley, BEd (*Head of Art, Community and Service Coordinator*)

Lower School

Head of Lower School: Mr S Smart, BA Hons, MSc, PGCE

Deputy Head: Mr M Weavers, BEd Hons
Head of Pre-Prep: Mrs R Wyles, CertEd
EYFS Coordinator: Mrs S Howlett, BEd Hons
Special Needs Coordinator: Mrs N Whitaker, BA Hons, MA, ATS

Junior Department:
Mrs J Barwell, BA Hons, PGCE

Mr O Barwell, BA Hons
Mrs H Fitzpatrick, BSc
Mr T George, BSc Hons, Cert TEFL
Mrs C Hambley, BA Hons, Cert TEFL
Mr O Harris, BSc Hons
Miss V Hawkings, BSc Hons
Miss K Jones, BA
Mr N Kerry, BHum Hons
Mrs S Lake, Cert Ed
Mrs M May, BEd Hons
Mr K Watts, BEd

Pre-Prep:
Mrs K Bates, BEd Hons
Miss H Dennehy, BSc Hons
Mrs H Pendrey, BEd Hons
Mrs S Lake, CertEd
Miss H Pendrey, BEd Hons
Miss L Sharp, BA Hons
Mrs S Shafi, BA Hons
Miss H Williams, BEd Hons

Assistants:
Mrs C F Bastin, NNEB
Mrs R Butler, CACHE III
Mrs N Clarke, CACHE 111
Mrs Y Lewis, CACHE 111 (*Breakfast Club and After Care*)
Mrs R Nowak, NVQIII
Mrs S Quilter, LLB Hons, CACHE II
Mrs S Roberts, BSc Hons, NCFE 111
Miss L Sears, LLB Hons
Mrs N Stuckey, NCFE III

Director of Finance: Mrs N Prosser,BSc, ACA
Marketing and Communications Manager: Mrs K Hassan, BA Hons, MSc
Headmaster's PA: Mrs D Sollis
Lower School Head's Secretary: Mrs C Pullin
School Administrator: Mrs D Thomas
Receptionist: Mrs E Hughes
Librarian: Miss J Boyce
Careers & HE Adviser: Mrs M Hall
Accounts Manager: Ms S Hemmings
Facilities Director: Mr A Meakin
Matron: Mrs D Head
Commander CCF: Dr K Dawson, BA, PhD
SSI CCF: Sgt R Cain
Catering Manager: Mr J Dier

Organisation. There are approximately 800 pupils at Colston's. The Lower School which caters for the 3–11 age range includes a nursery and is adjacent to the main site which accommodates the Upper School (11–18 years).
For details of the Lower School, see entry in IAPS section.

Admission. Pupils are admitted at 11+ and 13+ through the school's own examination or at 13+ through the Common Entrance Examination if appropriate. Scholarships are available for those excelling in areas including: academic, music, art, drama and sports. Bursaries are also available which are means tested.

Work. Colston's offers a wide ranging and engaging curriculum which avoids premature specialisation and is in line with the provisions of the National Curriculum. German, Spanish, Religious Knowledge, Drama, Art, Music, Technology, Design Technology and ICT are optional subjects. There is a wide choice of A Level subjects available in the Sixth Form.

Chapel. Colston's is a Church of England Foundation, and use is made of neighbouring Stapleton Parish Church for morning assemblies and other services. Pupils of other denominations are also warmly welcomed.

Sport and Games. Colston's has a shining sporting legacy, perhaps unsurprisingly given our impressive on site facilities that are unique in Bristol. Sport plays a huge part in the life of our pupils and while excellence is pursued for those with talent, we encourage all, regardless of ability to get involved. Opportunities to represent the school are abundant and an impressive number of teams are fielded each week. The main sports for boys are rugby, hockey and cricket and hockey, netball and rounders for girls.

Music and Drama. Our drama department is one of the most successful in the country. It is based in the Harry Crook Theatre which offers an exceptionally well-equipped 200-seat auditorium. Music is vibrant and inclusive, with one third of pupils taking individual instrumental lessons. Performances are given regularly in our dedicated concert hall.

Careers. Colston's is proud of its dedicated careers provision which is available to all pupils. We are a member of the Independent Schools Careers Organisation. Through a highly successful programme of careers guidance, we help pupils make the right decisions to ensure success. Our careers library and interactive resources help pupils think about career options and our Head of Careers and Employability meets with each pupil regularly throughout their time at Colston's.

Service and Community. Our pupils are given many opportunities to contribute to the wider community. Our Combined Cadet Force, one of the most successful in the South West, allows cadets to regularly take part in expeditions and activities. Pupils also undertake the Duke of Edinburgh's Award which seeks to develop lifelong skills. Pupils relish the opportunity to get involved in a diverse range of volunteering projects across the city.

Fees per term (from January 2015). £4,045 (Lunch £195).

Modernisation. An extensive building programme has been carried out to provide new teaching classrooms, a 210-seat concert hall and purpose-built CCF headquarters. Additionally the library, laboratories and Sixth Form facilities have been completely refurbished to create a 21st century learning environment.

Situation. Colston's is located in Stapleton village which is within the city of Bristol, and enjoys the advantage of having all its playing fields and facilities on site. Our 30-acre campus, which is unique within Bristol, provides a wonderful environment for our pupils to explore, learn and excel.

The school is large enough to sustain a wide range of activities at a high level and yet small enough for each boy or girl to contribute actively and be known as an individual. Every effort is made to provide for and develop pupils' abilities in academic, cultural and other extra-curricular activities. The school aims to encourage a strong sense of community and service, and to fully develop and extend the talents of every boy and girl.

Charitable status. Colston's School is a Registered Charity, number 1079552. Its aims and objectives are the provision of education.

Cranleigh

Horseshoe Lane, Cranleigh, Surrey GU6 8QQ
Tel: 01483 273666; 01483 276377 (Headmaster)
Fax: 01483 267398; 01483 273696 (Headmaster)
email: enquiry@cranleigh.org
website: www.cranleigh.org

Motto: *'Ex cultu robur'*
Cranleigh School was founded in 1865.

Visitor: The Rt Revd The Lord Bishop of Winchester

Governing Body:
Chairman: J A V Townsend, MA
Deputy Chairman: A J Lajtha, MA, FCIB

Dr R Chesser, MA, MB, BChir, MRCP
R A de Blaby, BSc, MRICS
Mrs M M S Fisher, MA
Mrs N A Huggett, MA
R L Johnson, BSc, MRAes
J A M Knight, BA
Mrs A J Lye, BA
M J Meyer
Mrs L A Muirhead, BA
The Revd Canon N P Nicholson, DL
R A Robinson, FCA, MBA
The Revd Dr T J Seller, BSc, PhD
Mrs E Stanton, BSc, ACA
N D L Sweet, Dip LA, MA, MLI
J C Turley
J G M Wates, BA, MBA
S J Watkinson
O A R Weiss, MA
Dr T D Wilkinson, BEng, PhD, MIET
Mrs M J Williamson

Bursar and Clerk to the Governors: P T Roberts, MBE

Headmaster: Martin Reader, MA Oxon, MPhil, MBA

Deputy Headmaster: A J Griffiths, BSc, MSc, DIC, CGeol, FGS, QTS
Director of Studies: D R Boggitt, BEng, PGCE
Assistant Deputy Headmaster: S D Bird, BA
Head of Admissions: Mr S J Batchelor
Head of School Administration: Ms A J Russell-Price

Members of Common Room:
† *Housemaster/mistress*

Mrs M C Allison, BEd
Miss M Baffou, LLCE
Mr A K B Barker, BSc, PGCE
Mr J Bartlett, BA
Mr S J Batchelor
Mrs S E Baumann, BA, PGCE
Mr S D Bird, BA
Mr C H D Boddington, BA, PGCE (†*Cubitt*)
Mr M J Brookes, BA
Mr B W Browne, BSc, PGCE
Mr E M Burnett, BSc, PGCE (†*North*)
Mrs H K E Burns, BEd
Mrs O Burt, BA, MA
Mr S T Cooke, BA
Miss E M Coule, BA, MA
Mrs E G M Dellière, BA
Mr N Drake, BA
Mrs E L Ellin, BA, PGCE
Mr T R Fearn, BSc, PGCE
Mrs H B Fearn, BA
Mr A P Forsdike, MA
Mrs R E Frett, MA, PGCE (†*South*)
Mr D J Futcher, BSc
Mr R B Gale, BSc, DPhil
Miss R S Gibson, BTh
Mr T R D Goddin, BA
Miss G L Greenwood, BSc, MSc
Miss S L Greenwood, BA Ed
Mr E J Griffiths, BSc
Dr D A W Hogg, MA, DPhil
Mr A R Houston, BSc
Miss L J Hyett, BA
Mr M R Jenkins, BA
Mr R C E K Kefford, BSc, PGCE
Dr S L Kemp, BSc, PhD, PGCE
Mr R Lailey, MA
Mr R G Lane, BEng
Mr T G Leeke, BSc
Revd T M PLewis, MA, Mth
Mr P Leggitt, MA
Mr P F Lewthwaite, BA

Mr A A G Logan, BA, PGCE (†*Loveday*)
Mr P J Longshaw, MA
Miss H Mallory, BSc
Dr J C E Mann, BSc, PhD, CBiol, MIBiol, QTS
Mrs S E McLaughlin, BEd
P A McNiven, DipAD, QTS
Miss H K Merry, BSc
Miss A W A C Mitropoulos, BA, MPhil
Mr J B Nairne, BFA, PGCE
Mrs C Neill, BA, PGCE
Mr G J N Neill, BA, PGCE
Miss C E Nicholls, MA, PGCE
Ms R P F Nicholson, BA, PGCE
Mrs N L Odhams, BA, MEng
Miss K O'Hara, BA
Mr R Organ
Miss C Osner-Clark, BSc, PGCE
Mr B E Page, BA, PGCE
Miss D E Parkes, BA
Miss S R Parry, BA, PGCE
Mr M C Pashley, BMus
Mrs J A Pimm, BEd
Ms N Plowman, BA, QTS
Mrs O D Ravilious, BA, PGCE
Mrs A E Reader, BA, PGCE
Mr D C Reed, BA, MSc
Mr A D Robinson, BS, PGCE
Mr I P Rossiter, BSc
Dr A P Saxel, BSc, PhD (†*West*)
Mr R J Saxel, BA, DipRam, LRAM
Mr P N Scriven, BA, MA, LRAM, MM (*Organist in Residence*)
Mr W Sherrington-Scales, BA, PGCE
Mrs A Simpson, BA, PGCE
Ms E Sinclair, BA, PGCE
Mr C P Stearn, BA, MPhil
Ms L E C Sturdee, MA, PGCE
Mrs N R Sutton, BA
Mrs S D Thomson, BSc
Dr B R Tyrrell, MChem, DPhil
Ms A Ventress, BA
Mr R Verdon, BA, MBA
Dr M Ward, BA, PhD, LGSM, MMus, Dip RCM
Miss H R F Warner, BA, MA
Mr K W Weaver, BA Music, PGDip
Miss S L Webb, BA
Mr S D Welch
Miss J D Wiles, BSc
Mrs R A Williams, BMus, PGDip, PGCert, PGCE
Mr R A Wilson, LTCL
Mr J M Witcombe, BSc, PGCE († *East*)
Mrs U C Yardley, BA, PGCE
Ms W Yates, Cert. Ed
S A H Young, BSc, MSc, PhD, PGCE

Medical Officer: Dr G Tyrrell, MB BS, DObstRCOG

Preparatory School
(*see entry in IAPS section*)

Headmaster: Mr M T Wilson, BSc Keele

Deputy Headmaster: Mrs S D Gravill, BA, PGCE

Members of Common Room:
Mr E T Batchelor, BSc
Mrs C A Beddison, BMus, PGCE
Miss E Blackmore, BA, MA
Mr D Britt, BA, PGCE
Mrs J Brown, HND
Miss Z Burrell, BSc
Mr R B P Carne, MA, PGCE
Mr J Dale-Adcock, BA, PGCE
Mr B M Dixon, BA, CertEd
Mrs C Elliott, BA, PGCE, OCR Dip SpLD
Mrs L Everett, BA

Mrs A Fenton, BA
Mr N French, BSc
Miss C Gibson, BSc, PGCE
Mr N Green, BA
Mr M J Halstead, BSc, PGCE
D Hitchen, GRSM, ARMCM
M S F Howard, BA, CertEd
Mrs S Johnston, BSc, PGCE
Mrs A Jolly, BSc, PGCE
Ms K Laidler, BA
Mr D S Manning, EDE
MrsJ J Marriott, BA, PGCE
Miss L R Martin, BA, PGCE
Mrs N M C McCormack, BSc
Mrs H McNiven, BA
Mrs P R Meadows, BEd
Miss J Moore, BSc
Mrs H L H Pakenham-Walsh, BA
Mr M Poeti, BSc
Mrs E Reed, BSc, PGCE
Ms V Sandford
Mrs K Schutte, BA, MA
Mrs R Sharpe
Mrs L J Smith, BA
Mr P B Storey, DipEd
Mr T M Stroud, BSc
Mrs T Thistlethwaite, BEd, CertEd
Mr H Thomas
Mr M Till, BSc
Ms L Turner
Mr P G Waller, MA, PGCE
Ms V Wild
Mrs C J Wilson, BEd, RSA Dip SpLD
Mrs J M Witcombe, BSc

Registrar: Mrs F M J Bundock
School Secretary: Mrs J M Cooke

Cranleigh School's principal aim is to provide an environment in which pupils can flourish, enabling them to capitalise on the diverse range of opportunities offered by the School and to achieve to the best of their ability within a framework of shared values and standards. The School's 240-acre site, situated eight miles from Guildford on the Surrey-West Sussex border, lies on the outskirts of Cranleigh Village and within 45 minutes of London. The School is fully co-educational, with some 200 girls and 400 boys between the ages of 13 and 18, including a Sixth Form of about 240. It is a predominantly boarding community, attracting boarders from both the local area and further afield; it also, however, welcomes day pupils, who are fully integrated into the Cranleigh community, playing their part in the activities of their respective Houses and benefiting from the advantages thereby offered.

Each House (separate for boys and girls) has a resident Housemaster or Housemistress, a resident Deputy, a Warden, two Matrons and a team of tutors for both the Lower School and Sixth Form. There is also a strong and active partnership between parents and the School.

Cranleighans are encouraged to relish challenge, to feel they are known as individuals, and to become talented and wise adults with an inherent ability to adapt to a fast-changing world. Aligned with this, the School boasts an impressive record in academic achievement. Almost all pupils achieve three A2 Levels (with a record number of A*s in 2014), plus at least one additional AS Level, and in recent years more than 99% have gone on to university, with 90% to their first-choice university – including an impressive number of Oxbridge offers being received.

Academic Patterns. Our aim is to act within the spirit of the National Curriculum, but to offer more, taking full advantage of our independence and the extra time available to a boarding school. We therefore retain a very broad curriculum in the Fourth Form, and have an options system in

the Lower and Upper Fifth Forms which enables a pupil to take between nine and eleven GCSE subjects before moving on to AS Levels in the Sixth Form. We offer the opportunity to do Double or Triple Award Science, as well as giving good linguists the chance to take two foreign languages (with Latin if they wish). In the Sixth Form pupils can select from a wide choice of around twenty AS Level subjects.

Work on languages, with an emphasis on commercial and colloquial fluency, is encouraged for non-specialist linguists, and much use is made of the Language Laboratory. Exchanges take place with pupils in schools in France, Spain and Germany. We have comprehensive facilities for Science, with an emphasis on experimental work. All members of the Lower Sixth Form study a course in Critical Thinking, or attend a series of lectures on a variety of topics, to help broaden their education.

Information Technology is incorporated into the teaching of all other subjects, with each academic department having its own IT policy, coordinated by the Director of IT. Most teaching rooms have networked PCs, and every House and academic department has PCs available for use, all linked to the School's network and the Internet.

Creative and Performing Arts. Cranleigh has maintained an enviable reputation for Music over many years, and the Merriman Music School offers pupils some of the finest facilities available. We send Choral Scholars to Oxford, Cambridge and major Music Departments and Colleges elsewhere; boys and girls of all ages successfully take part in national competitions and well over a third of the School learns a musical instrument. Keyboard players have access to a new Mander two-manual tracker organ, purposefully designed for versatility and teaching, and to two Steinway concert grand pianos. Cranleigh's exciting Cranleigh Music initiative is now well established, bringing together the Music Departments of Cranleigh School and Cranleigh Preparatory School under a single performing, management and administrative structure. Whilst facilities remain on separate sites (both sides of Horseshoe Lane), the ethos is that of a single Music Faculty encompassing the full 7–18 age range, whose cohesive structure will help to nurture and progress talent from a very young age, so ensuring that all pupils are able to perform in an environment commensurate with their individual ability.

Cranleigh also boasts a strong Drama tradition. Regular large-scale productions take place in the Devonport Hall, to which is linked a studio theatre, the Vivian Cox Theatre, while a flourishing Technical Theatre department encourages the development of 'backstage' skills. The School's proximity to London allows for regular attendance at professional theatre, music and opera productions.

Art & Design are brought together under one Faculty, housing a talented mix of practising artists, teachers and designers. The spectacular Rhodes Art & Design School is spread over several buildings, with a mix of dedicated airy studios and manufacturing and prototyping areas. A comprehensive range of disciplines across drawing, painting, sculpture, printmaking, ceramics, graphics, product and industrial design, prototyping and CAD/CAM are delivered. The studios are open every day and appropriate use is made of the Faculty library, ICT and digital video and photo facilities. External visits are encouraged (both nationally and internationally). All students exhibit throughout the year.

Sport. Cranleigh provides an extremely diverse range of sporting activities for all pupils.

The School possesses an impressive array of sports facilities, including four full-size Astroturf pitches (one of which is floodlit), a 9-hole golf course, an Equestrian Centre with floodlit sand-school, 4 squash courts, 6 fives courts, 24 tennis courts, 8 netball courts and an indoor swimming pool. The large Sports Hall complex (the Trevor Abbott Sports Centre) provides a popular venue for netball, tennis, badminton and basketball, and also includes a separate dance studio and a fully equipped fitness suite. There is also a separate Indoor Cricket Bubble for year-round development. High standards are set for the numerous competitive teams, with an extensive programme of fixtures at all levels and for all ages. 'Sport for All' is a key philosophy at the School, supported by an experienced and talented team of coaches, many of whom have competed themselves at county, national and Olympic level. The School has witnessed some outstanding team and individual successes in recent years, including recently winning the Nationals in boys' hockey; having several current pupils picked for National representation in hockey, rugby and cricket; taking National titles in horse riding (showjumping and dressage), and also seeing several recent Old Cranleighans continue to compete in the international arena – including in the Cricket World Cup – and as Olympic hopefuls.

In the Michaelmas Term the majority sports are hockey for girls and rugby for boys; in the Lent Term the majority sports are netball for girls and hockey for boys. During the winter terms, pupils can also compete in lacrosse, cross-country, golf, water polo, soccer, fives, rugby-sevens, basketball, riding and squash, plus badminton and canoeing for the Sixth Form. All pupils in the Fourth and Lower Fifth Forms take part in the majority sport, while an element of choice is gradually introduced for the older pupils. All pupils in the School take part in sport, even in the Sixth Form.

In the Summer Term, the main team sport for boys is cricket, whilst some boys compete in tennis, swimming, athletics and golf. For girls the main sport is tennis, with competitive swimming, athletics, rounders and cricket popular additional offerings.

Service Activities. There are opportunities for pupils to take part in a range of 'service' activities. Boys and girls may join the CCF or get involved with community service, ecology or first-aid training. Cranleighans help local elderly people in their homes and also have links with local schools for children with learning difficulties and with a home for adults with similar problems. Many Houses and the Fundraising Group raise money for various charities. Wider initiatives also include Amnesty and Environmental Awareness groups, and the School's 'Beyond Cranleigh' initiative – a key partnership between Cranleigh School and Beyond Ourselves, a London-based charity that works to improve the lives of disadvantaged young people in both London and in Zambia. This partnership offers pupils various opportunities beyond Cranleigh – such as trips out to the Kawama School in the Copperbelt region of Zambia, to build much-needed classrooms, assist with teaching and set up a Social Enterprise Scheme, and to help in a variety of other ways. Such initiatives are designed to focus pupils' thoughts on life beyond the School.

Outdoor Education. Cranleigh operates a large Duke of Edinburgh's Award Scheme group, with many pupils completing the Gold Award before leaving school. By way of introduction, all Year 9 pupils undergo an Outdoor Education programme in order to improve their self-awareness and confidence. There are many other opportunities for Outdoor Education through the CCF, there is a well-attended climbing club (which has its own bouldering wall), and the School enters the annual International Devizes-to-Westminster Canoe Race (with both the boys' and the girls' team taking first place among Schools in the country in 2010).

Religion. The striking, neo-Gothic Chapel was built as a central point of the School, and Cranleigh maintains its concern to present the Christian way of life.

Developments. The latest in a line of major building projects, the Emms Centre houses the Modern Languages, Science and Mathematics Departments, while the new Faculty of Art & Design offers fabulous work spaces for these disciplines (*see Creative and Performing Arts section*). A timber-pole Workshop, designed using sustainable principles, has won numerous Awards. A premier 1st XV rugby pitch and additional cricket pitches have recently been added to the School's impressive sporting facilities.

Planning for our Pupils' Future. Cranleigh takes the future of its pupils very seriously. It maintains good contacts with the professions, industry and commerce, through links developed as part of the careers advice structure. All pupils are regularly assessed during their time at the School, and this process includes a period of Work Experience at the end of the Upper Fifth year. On a personal level, the Old Cranleighan Society enables current and past boys and girls to maintain lasting links with one another.

Admission and Registration. Parents wishing to enquire about places at the School or to request a copy of the detailed Prospectus should contact the Admissions team via 01483 273666, or visit the website at www.cranleigh.org. If you wish to visit the School, the Headmaster would be delighted to welcome you: please telephone to make an appointment. Pupils between the ages of 13 and 14 are admitted in September, via the Common Entrance or the Scholarship examinations. There may be vacancies at other levels and there is a smaller intake at Sixth Form level. The entrance procedure at Sixth Form level includes a series of interviews and a written test for candidates for Academic Awards.

Awards. The Master of Scholars has a specific responsibility for all Scholars. They are members of their Houses and attend normal lessons, but also have an additional programme throughout their time at the School that covers a wide variety of academic, cultural, social and commercial areas beyond the syllabus and which encourages independent thinking and research.

At age 13, Academic, Music and Art Awards are available, along with Eric Abbott Awards for candidates of good academic ability with at least one other clearly established area of excellence and the potential to have a positive impact on life at Cranleigh. Music Awards include free musical tuition. In certain circumstances, additional consideration may be given to sons or daughters of public servants, members of the armed forces and the clergy of the Church of England.

At Sixth Form level, Academic, Music, Art and Eric Abbott Awards are offered.

Fees per term (2014–2015). Boarders £10,930, Day Pupils £8,910.

It is the policy of the School to keep extras down to an absolute minimum, and limited to such charges as individual music tuition. Textbooks are supplied until the Sixth Form, at which point pupils are encouraged to buy their own so that they may take them on to university. A scheme is available for the payment of fees in advance.

Preparatory School. The School has its own Preparatory School and boys and girls are normally admitted at seven or eight, but also at other ages. For further information, apply to the Headmaster of the Preparatory School (*see entry in IAPS section*).

Charitable status. Cranleigh School is a Registered Charity, number 1070856. It exists to provide education for children aged 13–18 and the Preparatory School for those aged 7–13.

Culford School

Bury St Edmunds, Suffolk IP28 6TX

Tel:	01284 728615
Fax:	01284 728631
email:	admissions@culford.co.uk
website:	www.culford.co.uk
Twitter:	@CulfordSchool
Facebook:	/culfordschoolocs

Motto: '*Viriliter Agite Estote Fortes*'

Culford School was founded in 1881 in Bury St Edmunds and moved to its present site in 1935. Culford School is under the overall control of the Methodist Independent Schools Trust, but is administered by a Board of Governors, to whom local control is devolved.

Visitor: The President of the Methodist Conference

Patron: The Rt Hon Viscount Chelsea

Governors:
Chairman: Air Vice Marshall S Abbott, CBE, MPhil, BA
Mrs P Abbott, BEd, ECP
Mrs J Anderton, BA
N J Bristow, FCA
Prof S Challacombe, BDE, PhD, FRC Path, FDSRC Ed, FMedSci, DSc hc, FKC
A P Crane, BSc, CEng, FIET
N Gillis, MA
J M Hammond, MA
M King
T C Matthews, BSc, FRICS
S Pott, FRICS, FRAgS, FinstCPD FRAU
The Revd J M Pursehouse
Professor R Swanston, DSc, FRICS, FCMI
Mrs C Whight, FCIPD

Headmaster: J F Johnson-Munday, MA, MBA

Deputy Heads:
Dr J Guntrip, BSc, PhD
J Williams, BA, PGCE

Assistant Head: D V Watkin, BEd

Chaplain: The Revd Simon Crompton-Battersby, BTh

Members of the Common Room:
* *Head of Department*
† *Housemaster/mistress*

Art:
*Mrs B A Hunt, BA
L Hoggar, BA
Miss K Noorlander

Business Studies and Economics:
*D Tomalin, BSc, MA, PGCE
†S Arbuthnot, MSc

Classics:
*Miss S Smith, MA

Design Technology:
*I C Devlin, BEd
Miss J Cooke, BA

EAL:
*Mrs H F Baker, BSc
Mrs A Burge, BA
Mrs C Byrne, MA
Mrs B Recknell, BA, MA

English:
*Mrs A Glassbrook, BA
Mrs C Byrne, MA
Dr J M Byrne, PhD, MA
Mrs C De Vito, BA
J D J Williams, MCGI

Drama:
*Miss M Jackson, MA

Geography:
*M H Barber, MA
†Miss H Mayhew, BSc
Mrs A Burge, BA

History:
*P M Jones, MA
G E Draper, BA
†Miss J Kaye, MSc

Information & Communication Technology:
*J W Tyler, MA, BSc

Mathematics:
*N J Tully, BSc
R J Hamilton, BPhil, BSc
†P Massey, BA, MA, MMath
†G Reynolds, BEng
J Veitch, BA, BSc

Modern Languages:
*A R Deane, BA
Ms C Alfaro, BA
Ms J Loco, BA

Music:
*P R Burge, MusB, ALCM
D Bolton, Dip Mus
Mrs H Medlock, GRSM, LRAM, Dip RAM
J D Recknell, MA, FRCO

Physical Education:
*Mrs K Kemp, BEd
Mrs C Almond, FISTC
†M Copping, BSc
Miss L Kammerijer
M Bolton, BSc
Mrs E Long, BSc
A H Marsh, Cert Ed

†Miss C Olley
Mrs C Reynolds, BEd
D Hall (*Director of Tennis*)
J D Yates

Religious Studies:
*Revd Dr A G Palmer, MTh, PhD
Revd S C Crompton-Battersby, BTh

Science:

Chemistry:
*D Rees, BSc
Mrs S L Antonietti, BSc
Mrs H F Baker, BSc

Physics:
*J Bauer, MA, MSc
J Christopher, BSc

Finance Director: Mrs E Boardley, BA, FCCA
Operations Director: C Muir, BSc, MRICS
Medical Officer: Dr N Harpur, MB BS, MRCGP, DRCOG
Headmaster's PA: Mrs K Hudson Leet
Registrar: Mrs K Tompkinson

Preparatory School
(*see entry in IAPS section*)

Headmaster: M Schofield, BEd

Deputy Head: Miss J Hatton, BEd
Deputy Head (*Academic*): Mrs C Bentley, BEd

Miss S Ahrens, MA
Mrs K Allum, BEd
*Mrs C Alston, BA
Mrs D Barker, Maître FLE
Mrs T Black
Mrs C Blake
*M Bolton, BSc
Miss P Buis, BSc
Mrs A Bunting, BA
Mrs S Burrell, BA
J Calvert, BA
Mrs S Combes
M Copping, BSc

Mrs C Currie, BSc
*Mrs C Dunnell-Paley, BA
Mrs S Guntrip, BSc
*P Harrison, BEd
Mrs E Herd, BA
†J Herd, BSc
Mrs J Nuttall
Miss S Smith, MA
Miss S Smye, BA
*Miss T Stinson, BSc
Mrs E Veitch, BEd
Mrs K Waghorn
Mrs P Weyers, BMus
*Mrs H Whiter, BA

Pre-Preparatory School:

Headmistress: Mrs S Preston, BA

Nursery Manager: Mrs E Grey, DPP

Mrs K Absolon
Mrs M Anderson
Mrs M Bainbridge
Mrs S E Combes, BA
Miss K Harrison, BEd
Mrs A McKenzie, TFL Dip French
Mrs A Morrell, BEd

Mrs D Rampling
Mrs R Ratcliffe, BEd
Miss N Rodwell, BTEC
Miss C Rossiter, BEd
Mrs J Suckling
Miss K Trow, BTEC
Miss S Widger, BSc

†J Fox, BSc

Biology:
*A P Fisk, MSc, BSc
Ms R Ainscough, BSc, MBA
Dr J Guntrip, BSc, PhD

Psychology:
*Dr A Butler, PhD, BSc

Learning Development:
*†Mrs B Murray, TTHD, Dip SpLD
Mrs J Cope, BA, Cert SpLD
Miss R Stevens, Dip SpLD

Library:
Mrs L Martin, MA, MCLIP

About Culford School. Culford is an Ofsted rated 'Outstanding' independent, co-educational boarding and day school for pupils aged between 2¾–18. Culford is divided into three schools; the Pre Prep & Nursery, Prep and Senior Schools, all of which are situated within 480 acres of beautiful parkland.

Where is Culford School? Culford is conveniently located four miles north of Bury St Edmunds, Suffolk, and is within easy reach of Cambridge and Norwich (to which the school will be running a daily shuttle service to and from, from 2015), Ipswich and Stansted Airport, and Heathrow and Gatwick airports are within two hours of Culford.

Teaching & Learning. At Culford we believe education should be challenging, enriching and fun. We're committed to helping our pupils achieve excellence in all areas of school life. Hard work in the classroom is complemented by full sporting and extra-curricular programmes, including sport, drama, music and creative and performing arts.

Culford pupils are imbued with a sense of Integrity and respect for the individual alongside a commitment towards the wider community. Our well-founded House and tutorial systems ensure that the pastoral care is personal and effective, something that is made possible by our pupil-staff ratio of 10:1. We have a deep respect for our Christian heritage and are inclusive and welcoming to pupils of all faiths and of none.

Curriculum. We aim to give a broad and balanced education that enables every pupil to fulfil their academic potential. Core subjects at GCSE are English Language and Literature, Mathematics, the three sciences and a foreign language. Pupils can choose additional subjects from a wide range of options and receive guidance from the Director of Studies, their teachers and House Tutor who, with the Housemaster or Housemistress, has responsibility for their academic and social progress. To support this Culford pupils also experience Personal, Social, Health and Citizenship Education (PSHCE) courses.

Culford Sixth Formers usually study four subjects at AS Level, followed by three at A2. Each year several Sixth Formers gain admission to Oxford and Cambridge and many others go on to prestigious Russell Group universities. Culford Sixth Formers may also study for an EPQ (Extended Project Qualification).

Facilities. Culford is centred on the magnificent Culford Hall, an 18th century mansion formerly the seat of Marquis Cornwallis and Earl Cadogan. The Hall enjoys glorious views across Culford Park and houses Culford's renowned Music School and purpose-built Studio Theatre. In September 2015 the School's facilities will be further enhanced by a brand new £2.2m landmark library which will become the academic hub of Culford.

Teaching Facilities. Culford's curriculum is extremely broad and affords pupils a range of opportunities for education and learning. Our staff are specialists in their fields and are united by a passion to help the children in their care achieve their goals, whatever they may be. Classrooms are modern and well equipped, and in the case of specialist subjects, such as languages and sciences, have the latest learning aid technologies installed. The School also has excellent Art, Design and Technology facilities in the Pringle Centre which boasts its own gallery.

Sports Facilities. Culford's fantastic £2m Sports and Tennis Centre is a short walk from the Hall and is a real favourite with day and boarding pupils alike. This state-of-the art facility comprises of four indoor tennis courts, a 25m indoor pool, gym, squash courts and a large sports hall in which badminton, netball, climbing and football are regularly played. Outside there are six further tennis courts, an Astroturf pitch and numerous rugby and hockey pitches. Our coaching facilities are just as impressive, including as they do the likes of former Davis Cup star, Andrew Richardson, and international rugby player, Mark Bolton.

Away from the Sports and Tennis Centre pupils can pursue athletics, canoeing, sailing, diving, golf or even fishing in our own lake.

Boarding. Culford accepts boarders aged 7 to 18 and for a whole host of reasons, including an 'Outstanding' ISI rating, boarding is extremely popular with over half of Senior pupils boarding. Boarders enjoy an amazing range of weekend activities and have full access to Culford's impressive Sports and Tennis Centre.

Culford's boarding houses Cadogan, Edwards, Fitzgerald and Jocelyn offer children a comfortable, secure and fun place to live during term time. Boarders in their first year share study-bedrooms and move into single rooms in the Upper Sixth. Culford offers flexible arrangements for other boarders where possible: weekly and occasional boarding is available providing space is free. We do not have an enforced exeat at the weekends; children may stay at school throughout the term, going home at the weekend or to stay with friends only when they or their parents wish them to.

All pupils have access to our fully-equipped Medical Centre, supervised by a resident nurse, and this includes provision for residential care when necessary.

Culford Pre-Prep & Nursery School. Our purpose-designed Nursery accepts children from 2¾ and work on the Early Years Foundation Stage which perfectly prepares them for School life. Culford's Nursery is located close to the heart of the School and is housed in its own purpose-built building with its own well-equipped play area and secure garden.

Culford Pre-Prep occupies its own area of the Culford Estate in Fieldgate House. A combination of new and entirely refurbished buildings, it provides teaching for 80 children from Reception through to age seven in a delightful setting within the grounds.

Both Pre Prep and Nursery schools take part in Forest School activities, a way of learning outdoors that helps children to develop personal, social and technical skills in a woodland setting.

Music & Drama. Music plays an important part in the life of the School. There are numerous choirs, orchestras and bands and regular concerts are held to give pupils the chance to perform in public. Individual music tuition is offered in voice, piano, organ and all orchestral instruments. Drama is also very popular and there are regular house plays and concerts as well as major productions: these include musicals and plays for different sections of the School.

Activities. There is a huge array of clubs and societies on offer – from academic and creative to sporting and community. Pupils are encouraged to take part in Community Service Activities, which covers a wide range of services to the School and the local community. Many participate in the Duke of Edinburgh's Award Scheme or choose to join the Combined Cadet Force (CCF).

Staff regularly take pupils out on visits and expeditions too, and every summer a group of Sixth Formers and teachers spend 3 weeks in Malawi helping with various development projects something that is universally viewed as a life-changing experience. Other recent trips have included tours to China, New York, skiing in France, scuba diving as well as sports tours worldwide.

Entry. The majority of pupils join in September at ages 2¾–7 (Pre-Prep), 7+, 8+ and 11+ (Preparatory School); and at 13+ and 16+ (Senior School). Entrance examinations are held in January and February of the year of entry or pupils may enter having passed Common Entrance in June. Entry to the Sixth Form is on the basis of GCSE performance or its equivalent for overseas candidates.

Entry to Culford Pre-Preparatory School is by informal assessment just prior to enrolment.

Applications are welcome from individuals throughout the year, subject to places being available.

Visiting Culford School. If you would like to visit Culford, the Headmaster will be delighted to welcome you. Please contact the Admissions Office to arrange an appointment and a tour on 01284 385308 or to request a copy of the School prospectus. We also hold regular Open Mornings each term, please visit www.culford.co.uk to find out more.

Scholarships and Exhibitions. Culford holds its Scholarship examinations between November (Sixth Form) and January/February for entry in the following September. Scholarships and Exhibitions are awarded according to merit in the following categories:

10+: Swimming and Tennis

11+: Academic, Music, Swimming and Tennis

12+: Swimming and Tennis

13+: Headmaster's Foundation Scholarship, Academic, Art, Design & Technology, Drama, Music, Hockey, Rugby, Swimming, Tennis and Sport

16+: Headmaster's Foundation Scholarship, Professor Watson Scholarship, Academic, Art, Drama, Music, Design & Technology, Hockey, Rugby, Swimming, Tennis and Sport

11+, 13+ and 16+: Jubilee Scholarships for all-rounders who board are worth up to 25% of boarding fees

16+: The William Miller Scholarship for a pupil studying sciences is worth up to 25% of tuition fees. The Arkwright Scholarship for a pupil studying Design & Technology allows an amount over two years to be shared between the pupil and the School.

Swimming and Tennis Scholarships and Exhibitions may be available at any age from 10+.

The Headmaster's Foundation Scholarship is worth up to 50% of tuition fees; the Professor Watson Scholarship (restricted to pupils coming from state schools) is worth 25% of day or boarding fees; all other scholarships are worth up to 25% of tuition fees, and Exhibitions are worth up to 10%.

Bursaries are available to those in genuine financial need.

A generous Forces Allowance is available to parents who are serving members of the Armed Forces and are in receipt of the MOD CEA.

For further details please apply to The Registrar, Tel: 01284 385308, Fax: 01284 385513 or email: admissions@ culford.co.uk.

Fees per term (2014–2015). Day £2,830–£5,780; Boarding £6,760–£9,330.

Charitable status. Culford School is a Registered Charity, number 310486. It exists to provide education for boys and girls.

Dame Allan's Boys' School

Fenham, Newcastle-upon-Tyne NE4 9YJ
Tel: 0191 275 1500 (School); 0191 274 5910
            (Bursar)
Fax: 0191 275 1502 (School); 0191 275 1501
            (Bursar)
email: enquiries@dameallans.co.uk
website: www.dameallans.co.uk
Twitter: @dameallans
Facebook: /Dame-Allans-Schools

The School was founded in 1705 by Dame Eleanor Allan and in 1935 was moved to Fenham on a site of 13 acres.

Governors:
Chairman: Mr E Ward
Vice-Chairman: Mr B W Adcock

Dr B Bevitt   Prof R Plummer
Mrs K Bruce   Mrs P Robinson
Prof E Cross   Mrs M E Slater
Mr M Davison   Mr A M Stanley
Mrs M Nicholson   Mr D Tait Walker

Ex officio:
The Lord Mayor of Newcastle upon Tyne
The Dean of Newcastle

Clerk to the Governors and Bursar: Mrs M Lant

Principal: **J R Hind**, MA Downing College Cambridge, MEd Newcastle, PhD Durham

Vice-Principal (Pastoral): N Shaw, BSc Liverpool
Vice-Principal (Academic): A Hopper, MA Merton College Oxford
Head of Boys (Years 7–11): P Wildsmith, BSc Birmingham, CBiol, MIBiol, MBES

Head of Sixth Form: D C Henry, BSc Heriot-Watt, FIMLS

J A Benn, BA Newcastle
H R Borland, MA Aberdeen
K Clark, BA Leicester
G Cockburn, MA Edinburgh
A Cranley, BA Belfast
J L Devine, BA Liverpool
J Downie, BA Durham
J C Downie, BSc Lancaster, MA Newcastle
M J Dutton, BA Huddersfield
J Etherington, BSc Manchester
L J Friel, BA Hull
J P Gardner, MA Girton College Cambridge
F Gold, BA Oxford
E Hopkinson, BSc Loughborough
W P Hudson, BSc Loughborough
A M Hughes, MA St Hilda's College Oxford
D N Leese, BSc Nottingham, MSc Warwick, PhD
    Newcastle
M V Lynch, BA Manchester
E Marsh, BSc Hull
E A Midcalf, BSc Brunel
D F O'Connor, BSc Durham
R Oliver BA Manchester
L Phillips, MA University College Oxford, BSc Middlesex
J P E Procter, BA York
C Pulford, BA Leeds
E Renshaw, BSc Nottingham
M J Salisbury, BA Swansea
G Sharp, BSc Durham
P Surrage, BSc Durham
C N Tuck, BSc, PhD Aston
H Walton, BA Leeds
S Watt, BA Newcastle
B J Whitehouse, BA Liverpool
K Wilkinson, MA, BA, PhD Sheffield
G J M Witney, BSc London
T J Wood, BA Newcastle
S E Wright, BA Northumbria

Junior School:
Head: A J Edge, MA St Andrews
Deputy Head: D M Farren, BA Warwick
A Bodfield, BTEC
A Brown, BSc Northumbria
K Carruthers, BSc Loughborough
J Dennis, BTEC
K Ellis, BA Liverpool
T E Fox, Cert Early Years
A L Jackson, LLB Sheffield
C Henderson, BA Manchester
J Loraine, BEd Newcastle
B Metcalf, BSc York
J Needham, BA Durham
R Johnson, BA Northumbria
C Peacock, BA York St John
P Pollock, CertEd Leeds
B Shaw, BA Newcastle
R Watson, BA Leeds
G Williams, BA Ripon & York St John

There are approximately 550 boys in the School, which has a three-form entry at 11+. With the Girls' School, which is in the same building, it shares a mixed Sixth Form and a mixed Junior School for pupils aged 3–11.

The Main School follows the normal range of subjects, leading to examination at GCSE. German is introduced in Year 8 and Spanish is offered in Year 9.

Most boys stay on into the Sixth Form and from there normally go on to Higher Education.

Buildings. In recent years, developments have included additional classrooms, a new Library, Computer Resource Centre, Technology Centre, ICT network, a new Sixth Form

Centre, and a Drama and Dance Studio. The Schools opened a new, state-of-the-art junior school in September 2012.

School Societies. The current list includes: outdoor pursuits (including Duke of Edinburgh's Award scheme and our own in-house expedition award for younger pupils), choirs, Ceilidh Band, drama, computing, art, chess, Christian Fellowship, Cookery Club, history, science, electronics, mathematics, dance, public speaking, and debating.

Pastoral. Each boy is placed in the care of a Form Teacher who oversees his progress and development. In the Sixth Form he has a Tutor who is responsible for both academic and pastoral care.

Careers. There is a structured programme, beginning in Year 9, with a contribution from Connexions.

Sixth Form. In 1989 the Sixth Form was merged with that of our sister School, giving both Schools the rare constitution of single-sex education (11–16) with a co-educational Sixth Form. The Head of Sixth Form is Mr D C Henry who will welcome enquiries concerning admission.

Games. The principal games are Rugby Football and Cricket. The School playing field adjoins the premises. Cross-Country, Swimming, Football and Athletics are also available. Hockey and Tennis are introduced as options from Year 9 and older boys may also participate in a range of other sporting activities including weight training, golf, rock climbing, squash, table tennis, volleyball, basketball and trampolining.

Admission. Governors' Entrance Scholarships are awarded on the results of the Entrance Examinations held annually in the Spring Term at all ages from 11+ to 13+. Bursaries are available to pupils aged 8 and over on entry. Assessments for entry to the junior school take place throughout the year.

Fees per term (2014–2015). Senior School £3,756; Junior School £2,309–£3,025.

Dame Allan's Allanian Society. President: Mr B Sanderson, c/o Dame Allan's Schools.

Charitable status. Dame Allan's Schools is a Registered Charity, number 1084965. It exists to provide education for children.

Dauntsey's School

West Lavington, Devizes, Wiltshire SN10 4HE
Tel:　　01380 814500
Fax:　　01380 814501
email:　　info@dauntseys.org
website:　　www.dauntseys.org

"Steadily improving results and facilities are putting Dauntsey's among the front-runners in the area. Its friendliness, breezy campus and outdoorsy image belie a focused academic purpose, which encompasses arts and sciences, though it doesn't inhibit the pupils from having a pretty good time. Dauntsey's is fab." (Good Schools Guide 2013).

Founded in 1542 by Alderman William Dauntesey of the Mercers' Company. New School buildings erected in 1895 and extended regularly from 1919 to the present.

Governors:
Mr R G Handover, CBE
Mr R M Bernard, CBE
Mr A G P Dudgeon
Mr N B Elliott, QC
Mr N J S Fisk, BA, ACA
Mrs P L P Floyer-Acland, BSc
Mrs S E S Gamble, BA
Professor L M Harwood, MA, BSc, MSc, PhD, CSci, CChem, FRSC
The Venerable A P Jeans, BTh MA
Air Chief Marshal Sir Richard Johns, GCB, KCVO

Mr M J H Liversidge, BA, FSA, FRSA
Mr P J Lough, MA
Mr C H de N Lucas, FRICS, FAAV
Mr A S Macpherson, BA, ACA
Mrs V P Nield, BSc, MBA
Dr R E L Quarrel, BA, MA, DPhil
Brigadier P P Rawlins, MBE
Mr F W Scarborough
Mr N W Smith
Mrs L F Walsh Waring, BA

Head Master: **Mark Lascelles**, BA

Deputy Head: Mrs J F E Upton, BSc

Second Master: Mr M C B McFarland, BA

Director of Studies: Mr M A C Neve, BSc

Head of Lower School: Miss E S Conidaris, BSc

Heads of Department:
Art: Mrs V A Rose, BA Bath Spa
Careers: Mr J F O'Hanlon, BSc Wales
Classics: Mrs A Webb, MA Cambridge
Design Technology: Mr A Pickford, BA Wales
Drama and Dance: Mr R M Jackson, BA Warwick
Economics and Business Studies: Mr A Poole, BA West of England
English: Mrs L Lloyd-Jukes, BA York
EFL: Mrs A Whitchurch, BA Swansea, TESOL
Geography: Mr A J Palmer, BSc London, FCIEA
History: Mr B H Sandell, BA Exeter
Information Technology: Mr G R Parry, BSc London
Language Development: Mr C W W Wilson, BA Exeter, Dip SpLD
Mathematics: Mr P A Mobbs, BSc Bath, MSc LSE
French: Ms P J Harrison, BA Birmingham
German: Mrs V A H Wilks, BA Exeter
Spanish: Mrs A L Jackson, BA Nottingham and Mrs A L Evans, BA Portsmouth
Music: Mr B D Gudgeon, BA Bristol, MA Washington State
Physical Education: Mr M D Collison, BSc Bath
PSE: Mr A J Sheffield, BSc Leeds
Religious Studies: Mrs S B M Gifford, MA Exeter, BD Wales
Science: Mr A J Crossley, BSc Newcastle
Biology: Mr V R Muir, BSc Canterbury NZ, BSc Open, MIBiol
Chemistry: Mr A J Crossley, BSc Newcastle
Physics: Dr R V Lewis, BSc, PhD Wales, FRAS
Sailing: Mr T R Marris, DTP, YME
A Level PE: Mr S J Hardman, BEd Loughborough

Houses and Housemasters/Housemistresses:

Upper School:
Evans: Mr & Mrs N Yates
Farmer: Mr W P J Whyte
Fitzmaurice: Mr J A Spencer
Hemens: Mr S J Hardman
Jeanne: Mrs A L Jackson
King-Reynolds: Mrs E Crozier
Lambert: Mrs K S Clark
Mercers: Mr & Mrs P J Thomas

Lower School:
Manor: Mr T W Butterworth
Forbes: Mrs E C Gardiner
Rendell: Mr M Olsen
Scott: Mrs G S Ward

Chaplain: Revd D R Johnson, MA, BSc
Bursar: Air Cdr S Lilley, RAF Retd
Registrar: Mrs J H Sagers, BA
Head Master's Secretary: Mrs D Caiger

Medical Officers:
Dr N Swale, MA, FRCS, DRCOG
Dr C C Cowen, MA, FRCS, DRCOG

Number. 788 Pupils aged between 11–18 years: 401 boys, 387 girls, approximately 40% boarders.

Situation. The School is set in an estate of over 100 acres in the Vale of Pewsey in Wiltshire. The Manor House, a mansion with its own woodland and playing fields, is the co-educational Junior boarding house for pupils in the First to Third Forms.

The Community. Our house system is the cornerstone of our community, giving pupils a secure source of support and guidance on every aspect of life, as well as the chance to get together and have fun. Every pupil joins either a boarding or day house, which are co-educational in the Lower School (ages 11 to 13) and single sex in the Upper School (ages 14 to 18). Each house is run by a housemaster or housemistress and a team of tutors who take a close and active interest in pupils' academic and social development, as well as encouraging them to make the most of the activities on offer. Above all, they really do make sure that the house is a home from home.

Curriculum. Throughout the School, the curriculum is broad and balanced, offering the opportunity to study an extensive range of subjects. The academic curriculum is well balanced, very wide ranging and offers a good amount of choice. The timetable offers a great deal of flexibility, with well-structured weekly lessons and extensive options that cater for the different interests and aptitudes of all our pupils. Dauntsey's especially promotes independent learning, enabling pupils to fulfil their potential and develop the key skills they will need in later life. Gifted and talented pupils have access to work and experiences at the higher cognitive levels, to stimulate interest and develop advanced thinking skills, while pupils with mild learning difficulties get expert help and support from a dedicated team of specialist teachers.

Games. The major sports are Rugby, Football, Hockey, Cricket and Netball. Other games options include Tennis, Squash, Athletics, Swimming, Soccer, Water Polo, Fencing, Badminton and Basketball. In the Sixth Form further options include Triathlon training, Canoeing, Basketball, Rifle-shooting, Yoga, Cross-Country, Ballet, Dance, Conditioning and Riding. Sixth Formers can also choose to do volunteer work within the community. Special attention is given to Physical Education.

Extra-Curricular Activities. Our adventure education and extra-curricular programmes set us apart, encouraging pupils to try new experiences. From drama, dance, music, sport and a huge range of clubs and societies, to our lecture series, adventure programmes and volunteering initiatives – there are opportunities to suit everyone. We aim to push our pupils out of their comfort zone, inside and outside the classroom, and we bring that spirit of adventure to everything we do.

Fees per term (2014–2015). Boarders £9,380; Day Pupils £5,600; International Pupils £10,850. There are no compulsory extras.

Admission. Boys and girls are admitted at 11 on the results of a competitive examination; at 13 on the results of Scholarship and Common Entrance examinations; to the Sixth Form dependent upon academic record and reports, with a minimum of six GCSE passes, three at grade A and three at grade B.

Scholarships and Bursaries. Academic Scholarships are awarded on merit following examinations held in January (First Form), February (Third Form), and November (Sixth Form) for entry the following September.

There is a wide range of Scholarships and Awards available for entry to the First, Third and Sixth Form:

First Form (Year 7): Academic, Music, All Rounder.

Third Form (Year 9): Available to all Boarding applicants: Academic, Art, Design Technology, Drama, Music, Science, Sport, Jolie Brise All-Rounder.

Sixth Form (Year 12): Academic, Sport, Performing Arts (Music, Drama, Dance), Boarding.

Bursaries: The school funds three new, 100% bursary places each year to pupils whose parents would otherwise be unable to fund any portion of the school fees. In addition, there is a fund to provide short-term bursarial support for current pupils whose parents or guardians who meet financial difficulties.

For further details please contact the Registrar.

Charitable status. Dauntsey's School is a Registered Charity, number 1115638. It is dedicated to the education of boys and girls.

Dean Close School

Shelburne Road, Cheltenham, Gloucestershire GL51 6HE
Tel: 01242 258000
Fax: 01242 258004
email: registrar@deanclose.org.uk
website: www.deanclose.org.uk
Twitter: @DeanCloseSchool
Facebook: /DeanCloseSchool

Motto: '*Verbum Dei Lucerna.*'

Sitting on a beautifully landscaped 50-acre site in the Regency town of Cheltenham, Dean Close School is an attractive mixture of old, traditional buildings and modern, hi-tech structures. The School was opened in 1886 in memory of Francis Close, Rector of Cheltenham 1826–55 and later Dean of Carlisle, and has been co-educational since 1967. Dean Close is a Christian school which believes that education is as much about building character and relationships as it is about gaining knowledge. An independent Preparatory School was established in 1949.

Visitor: The Rt Revd Michael Perham, The Lord Bishop of Gloucester

President of Council of Members: The Baroness Cox of Queensbury

Board of Trustees:
N C J Bewes, BA
Dr W E Bowring, BEd, ADB Ed, MEd
Dr T Brain, OBE, QPM, BA, PhD, FRSA
Mrs K Carden, MPhil, BA (*Chairman*)
J M Carter
M J Cartwright, BA, FCA (*Treasurer*)
The Revd R M Coombs, BSc, MA
Mrs H Daltry, BA
Mrs R Dick, BA, ACA
C S S Drew, MA
R S Harman, MA
Mrs S L Hirst, BEd
The Revd D J S Munro, MA, MBA

The Trustees are elected by the Members of Council and oversee the overall governance of the School. They carry a substantial burden of financial and legal responsibility on an entirely voluntary basis and the School is greatly indebted to them.

Headmaster: **J M Lancashire**, MA, ACA

Deputy Head: B J Salisbury, BA, PGCE
Senior Master (Communications): D R Evans, MA
Deputy Head Pastoral: Mrs J A Davis, MA, PGCE
Deputy Head Academic: M D Tottman, MA, MBA
Director of Sixth Form Studies: J E Talbot, MA, PGCE
  (**Geography*)

Director of Middle School Studies: B P Price, BSc, PGCE
Director of Fourth Form Studies: A J George, MA, PGCE
Common Room President: D J R Pellereau, MA, PGCE

Housemasters & Housemistresses:
Brook Court: J Slade (*2004*)
Dale: J P Watson (*2004*)
Fawley: Mrs J Abbott (*2011*)
Field: P S Montgomery (*2005*)
Gate: M D Tottman (*2008*)
Hatherley: Mrs K E Milne (*2011*)
Mead: Mrs P S Watson (*2001*)
Shelburne: Mrs J D Kent (*2001*)
Tower: B W Williams-Jones (*2008*)

Heads of Department:

J M Allen, MA, PGCE (*Classics*)
L S Allington, BA (*Drama*)
G N Baber-Williams, BA, PGCE (*Sport*)
S A Bell, MMUs, BMus, FRCO (*Choral Music*)
Miss R J Donaldson, BSc, PGCE (*Academic PE, Assistant
    Director of Studies*)
Mrs C J Evans, BA, PGCE (*Art & Design*)
D D Evans, BSc (*Design Technology*)
Mrs C M Feltham, MA, PGCE (*History & Politics*)
D M Fullerton, MA (*Careers & UCAS*)
P J J Garner, MA, PGCE (*Mathematics*)
P Harvey, BA, PGCE (*Physics*)
C J Hooper, BA, PGCE (*Modern Languages*)
Mrs K Ledlie, MA, PGCE (*English*)
I V McGowan, BCom, TDip (*Economics & Business
    Studies*)
A R Needs, BSc, PGCE, AMRSC (*Chemistry*)
Mrs H L Porter, BA, LRAM, PGCE (*Music*)
Miss D-M Richards, (*PSHE*)
Z Suckle (*Librarian*)
J Talbot (*Geography*)
Mrs H Tookey, BA (*Religious Studies*)
Mrs R E Tottman, MA (*Learning Support*)
Miss R J Vest (*English Language Training*)
Miss R M O Vines, BA, FVCM, LALAM, ALAM (*Speech
    & Drama*)
Mrs P S Watson (*Equestrianism*)
M M Wilkes (*Biology*)
Miss T L Williams, BSc, PGCE, GTP (*Psychology*)

Medical Officers (*both Schools*):
Dr J Wilson & Partners, MBBS, DRCOG, Dip Pall Med,
    FRCGP
Overton Park Surgery

SSI, CCF: WO2 B Lloyd

Preparatory School:
(*see entry in IAPS section*)
Headmaster: Roger Jones,
Deputy Head: A S Brown, BEd
Deputy Head Academic: Mrs V M Beevers, BEd
Senior Mistress: Mrs E Bailey, BSc, PGCE

Pre-Preparatory School:
(*see entry in IAPS section*)
Headmistress: Dr C A Shelley, PhD
Deputy Head: J E Cowling, BA, PGCE
Early Years Foundation Stage Coordinator: Mrs R
    Cowling

Bursar: A P Bowcher
Deputy Bursar (*Finance*): R G Perry, ACA
Deputy Bursar (*Estates*): P L Bray
Admissions Tutor: Mrs M-A McClaran, MA
Registrars (*Senior*): Mrs S F H Smith, BSc and Mrs B J
    Holley, BSc
Head of Marketing (*Senior*): Mrs T C Colbert-Smith, BA,
    MCIM
Admissions/Marketing (*Prep*): Mrs R Chaplin, BSc

Headmaster's PA (*Senior*): Mrs J Lynton
Headmaster's PA (*Prep*): Mrs E Materacki

Admission and Withdrawal. Admission to the Senior School at 13 is through Common Entrance or direct entrance tests in English, Maths and Verbal Reasoning. Sixth Form: examination and interview, 4 A/Bs and 2 Cs minimum at GCSE. Prospectus and application forms are available from the Registrar who is also happy to arrange a visit at a time to suit. There is a non-returnable fee of £100 and a returnable deposit of £750 payable one year before entry. One term's notice is required before a pupil is withdrawn from the School.

Fees per term (2014–2015). Boarders £10,680, Day Boarders £8,135, Day Pupils £7,360.

Term of Entry. We prefer to accept pupils in September but will make exceptions at any time of year, even in the middle of a term, if a good reason exists.

Scholarships and Bursaries. The School offers scholarships, exhibitions and bursaries at age 13 and for entry into the Sixth Form. The six areas of talent which are recognised are academic, music, sport, drama, art and design technology. An all-rounder award is also available at 13. The size of award is set according to performance. Dean Close Prep School also offers scholarships at age 7.

Academic: The 13+ ISEB Common Scholarship Examination, for which specimen papers are available from the ISEB, is held annually at the school in February. Candidates for academic scholarships from state schools should contact the Admissions Tutor. The Sixth Form Scholarship examination takes place in November.

Music (including Choral and Organ) and Drama Scholarships are based on audition, interviews and exam (Drama). Individual specialist tuition is free to all scholars and exhibitioners.

Carducci Strings Scholarship: linked to the Carducci Quartet.

Art and Design Technology Scholarships may be awarded, based on portfolio, drawing / technical test and interview.

Sports Scholarships are awarded to reflect all-round sporting ability and commitment. Assessment by conditioning tests, skills tests in two or more sports and interviews.

Colin Cocks and All-Rounder Awards: assessed by exams, activities and candidates' description of service or roles of responsibility.

Means-tested bursaries for sons and daughters of clergy and missionaries. Automatic discounts, known as Thierry Awards, are offered to parents serving in HM Armed Forces on a scale according to rank. Foundation Bursaries for families in the locality unable otherwise to benefit from a Dean Close education.

Number and Organisation. There are 484 in the Senior School (13–18). The Sixth Form comprises approximately 40% of the School. There are nine Houses: three for boarding boys, two for day boys, two for boarding girls and two for day girls. Housemasters take immediate responsibility for pupils' work, careers, applications for universities and further education. A tutorial system ensures that all pupils have a member of the teaching staff who takes a particular interest in them, both academically and pastorally. There is a Careers department. The Prep School (2½–13) has approximately 381 pupils of whom 163 are girls.

Work. In the lower part of the School pupils are set rather than streamed. Included in the Lower School timetable is a Creative Studies course introducing pupils to a wide range of artistic and creative subjects, embracing DT, Art, Drama, Music and Physical Education. The language centre, high-tech seminar room, music school, art school, sports hall, modern laboratories, computer, electronics and creative workshops combine excellent teaching and leisure facilities which are available both in timetabled and extra-curricular time. Much of the accommodation has been built in the last twenty years and is modern and purpose-built. A professional 550-seat theatre houses an ambitious programme of productions. There is also an open-air theatre. As well as several orchestras, wind band, many ensembles and the Chapel Choir, the School has a Choral Society which performs a major work at least once a year. The Strings Department is headed up by the internationally renowned Carducci Quartet. Tuition in any number of musical instruments is available as an extra. Free tuition is provided for music award holders and high-grade musicians. The theatre also affords first-class concert facilities.

Religious Education. The teaching and Chapel services are in accordance with the Church of England and the School's strong Evangelical tradition is maintained. The Chaplain prepares members of the School for confirmation each year. Most services are in the School Chapel. There is a thriving Christian Union and each House hosts voluntary weekly bible studies groups.

Games. The School has a 25m indoor swimming pool and a £3m sports hall, both used all the year round. There are two astroturf pitches and a large number of tennis courts. Hockey, rugby, cricket, basketball, netball, rounders, badminton, athletics, tennis, squash and cross-country are the main sports.

Health. The School has three qualified Sisters with Assistants and visiting Doctors. There is a surgery and a medical centre.

Outside Activities. There is a huge range of clubs, activities and societies, from climbing to creative writing, salsa dancing to Warhammer, theatre tech to horse riding. A very active Combined Cadet Force with RN, RAF and Army sections trains every Wednesday afternoon and some pursue Bronze and Gold Duke of Edinburgh's Awards. There is an active outward bound club and a large Community Action group gets involved with projects on a local, national and international level, particularly with a link school in Uganda.

Denstone College
A Woodard School

Uttoxeter, Staffs ST14 5HN
Tel: 01889 590484
Fax: 01889 591295
email: admissions@denstonecollege.org
website: www.denstonecollege.org

Motto: '*Lignum Crucis Arbor Scientiae.*'

Achievement, Confidence and Happiness are central to the College philosophy, through which girls and boys are always encouraged to aim high and so reach their full potential. Founded in 1868, the College is rich in tradition and history, but combines this with a forward thinking approach to education.

Denstone College offers a rounded education, where proper emphasis is placed on academic achievement and high standards are the top priority. A wide range of other opportunities, however, ensures that every individual finds and develops his or her own special talents. Denstonians emerge with a degree of self-esteem and confidence, possible only as a result of so much opportunity and challenge. They have the qualifications, skills and personality to make their mark in today's competitive world.

Visitor: The Bishop of Lichfield

School Council:
G Gregory, MA, BA (*Custos*)
The Revd Canon B D Clover MA, LTCL (*Senior Provost*)
A D Coley
His Honour Judge R T N Orme, LLB (*Vice Custos*)

J S F Cash, BSc, MRICS
Mrs B C Hyde, BA Hons, Dip MS, MBA
K P Threlfall
C J Lewis
Mrs Z Raybould, BA
Mrs H Mason, LLB
B W Hinton, MBA, FCIPD, MCIM
G R Bowe, BA, PGCE
D T Brown, ACA

Headmaster: **D M Derbyshire**, BA, MSc

Second Masters:
M R M Norris, BA
J Hartley, BA (*Registrar*)

Chaplain: The Revd R C M Jarvis, MA, MPhil, Cert Th

Masters and Mistresses:

Miss J R Morris, GMus	Mrs C L Burrows, BA
T P S O'Brien, DA	Mrs C G Bailey, MA
R C Menneer, BSc, CNAA	A D Pearson, BSc
(*Head of Senior School*)	Miss G K Brown, BSc
M P Raisbeck, BA, CNAA	J I Young, BA (*Selwyn*
Mrs S A Leak, BEd	*House*)
Miss J H Plewes, BA	Miss S Jones, BA
A J Wray, BA	Miss L Finat-Duclos, MSc
J M Tomlinson, BSc	N Horan, BA
(*Heywood House*)	R Lightfoot, MSc
Mrs V A Derbyshire, BA	Mrs L A Gater, BA, MA
Mrs P A Provan	R C Neal, BSc, MEd
A C Bonell, BEd (*Head of*	C M Ashurst, BA (*Head of*
Junior School)	*Middle School*)
Mrs K Hood, BSc (*Senior*	Mrs C L Ashurst, BA
Mistress)	Mrs S J Burrows, BA
M S Skipper, BMus	Mrs R E Maddocks, BA
P D Brice, BA (†*Meynell*)	J A Taylor, BA
C J Sassi, MA (†*Philips*)	T A H Williams, BSc
B J R Duerden, BSc	Mrs R C Abson, BA
Mrs K Rylance, BSc	Dr D P Baker, BA, MA,
S R Francis, BSc	MPhil, PhD
(*Shrewsbury House*)	Miss O J Barraclough, BA
T J Bell, BA (*Director of*	Mrs M J Davies, BA
Studies)	R H W Hinton, BA
Mrs M Moore, BA	Miss V Leicester, MSc,
Mrs M Silvey, BA	BSc
Mrs J A Teather (*Head of*	P Nye, BSc
Moss Moor)	Miss J R Pitt, BA, MA
Mrs C A Tuxford, BA	M E H Rankin, BA
I A K Sherwani	Mrs L E Stanley, BSc
J M Tyler, BA	Mrs J Westacott, MSc

Visiting Music Staff:
Mrs A O'Brien, DRSAMD, PGDip RSAMD, ARCM (*Piano, Singing, Recorder*)
D Gore (*Guitar*)
Mrs S Stewart, GRNCM (*Violin*)
Mrs A Hardy, GBSM, ABSM (*Flute*)
R Shaw, BA, GRSM, PGDip, ARCM, ABSM (*Saxophone, Clarinet*)
S J Ryde, ARCM, ARCO (*Piano*)
Ms C M Thomson, LRAM, GRSM, PGCE, CDRS (*Piano, Flute, Singing*)
W Raffle, BA, LVCM, AVCM (*Guitar*)
Ms L Kaniewski, BA (*Cello, Guitar*)
Mrs R Theobald, LRAM, ALCM (*Voice, Piano, Oboe*)
Mrs R Melland, GRSM, PG Dip (*Brass*)
J Broberg (*Drums, Percussion*)

Chapel Organist: G Walker, MA, ARCO, FRSA
Finance Bursar and Clerk to the School Council: D M Martin, ACIB
HR Manager: Mrs V L Astley
Headmaster's Secretary: Mrs T F Wedgwood, BA
Admissions Secretary: Mrs V J Carman

*Denstone College Preparatory School at Smallwood
  Manor*:

Headmaster: J Gear, BEd

(*For further details about the Preparatory School, see
  entry in IAPS section.*)

Location. Denstone College is situated on the Staffordshire/Derbyshire border, 6 miles north of Uttoxeter in 100 acres of grounds. The site is located in magnificent countryside, but is well served by road, rail and air.

Organisation. The College is divided into the following units: Junior School (ages 11–14, Years 7, 8 and 9), Middle School (ages 14–16, Years 10 and 11), and Senior School (ages 17–18, Sixth Form which typically numbers around 200 pupils).

All girls and boys are in one of the six houses, each numbering about 100 members, with a total roll of 615. Weekly boarding is a popular option. Just over a quarter of our pupils board, and one third are girls, who have separate boarding accommodation. The College does not believe in vertical boarding.

Denstone College Preparatory School at Smallwood Manor, also a Woodard School, is 9 miles away. Age range 3–11.

Buildings. The main building contains classrooms, day and boarding areas, studies, Dining Hall, Chapel, Theatre and resident staff accommodation. A great deal of school life is thus centred in this main block, which also includes IT facilities, library, and a language laboratory.

The Sports Hall, laboratories, other classrooms, indoor heated swimming pool, Art Centre, Design and Technology Centre, and other buildings, such as the Medical Centre and School Shop, are elsewhere in the grounds.

Recent and Future Developments. Over £7 million has been spent on improving our buildings and on building new facilities in recent years.

The most recent development is the College Library, which was refurbished and extended and opened in September 2013. A purpose-built 9-classroom block, Tookeys, which houses English and RS classrooms, was completed in June 2012. Other developments include a second Astroturf and £750,000 invested in the kitchens and dining area, and the updating of boarding facilities, including the development of a Sixth Form girls' boarding house.

A £2 million Music School and classroom block was completed in May 2010. As well as practice rooms and two music classrooms with interlinking recording studio, there are also two History classrooms, a Psychology classroom and three IT classrooms in the building.

Curriculum. In the Junior School (ages 11 to 14, Years 7, 8 and 9) all follow roughly the same spread of subjects: English, Drama, French, Spanish, Mathematics, Physics, Chemistry, Biology, History, Geography, Art, Music, DT, Religious Studies, Information Technology, and PE.

Girls and boys enter the Middle School at the beginning of Year 10. Subjects are studied in option blocks. Mathematics, English Language and Literature, a Modern Language, RS and Science are core subjects, and three others are chosen from those listed above, along with Business and Economics GCSE.

Girls and boys then specialise in AS and A2 Levels, chosen in an option system appropriate to the current discussions regarding Sixth Form Curriculum nationally. Four AS Levels will normally be taken in the Lower Sixth. Subjects offered are Mathematics, Further Maths, Physics, Chemistry, Biology, English Language, English Literature, French, Spanish, History, Geography, Economics, Psychology, Politics, Art, Theatre Studies, PE, and DT. There will also be a minority who will study, in varying numbers from year to year, Music and Religious Studies. An extremely flexible timetable is possible and we aim to offer as many combinations of subjects as possible.

The vast majority of pupils take A Levels, with the aim of going on to University. Each year, some girls and boys are prepared for Oxford or Cambridge entrance. A majority of the Upper Sixth are typically accepted into one of the Russell Group Universities and almost all to their first-choice or second-choice university.

The School is well-equipped with computer rooms, laboratories, and a 200-seat Theatre. Each department remains up-to-date with subject development and members of staff regularly attend courses and conferences.

Class sizes are relatively small. Up to Year 11, 20 is an average class size, and in the Sixth Form sets vary from 6 to 14.

In addition to having a Head of School and Head of House each pupil has a Tutor with whom he or she meets regularly to discuss work and progress, and both half termly and end of term grades and reports are issued.

Pupils in both Junior and Middle School have a number of staff supervised Homework sessions incorporated into the school day. Boarding members of Fifth Form, Lower Sixth and Upper Sixth have shared or single studies.

Out of Class Activities. The aim is to provide as wide a variety of opportunities for pupils of differing aptitudes and inclinations as possible.

Games: The College has 2 full-size all-weather hockey pitches, one of which is floodlit and provides 9 tennis courts in the Summer Term. A nine-hole handicap-standard golf course has been laid out to the west of the College. There is an indoor heated swimming pool, and the main Sports Hall accommodates indoor sports as well as a fitness room. The Drill Hall provides further games space and a CV gymnasium, with cycle machines and rowing machines.

The main sports in the Michaelmas Term are rugby for the boys and hockey for the girls, with opportunities for other games. In the Lent Term these change to hockey and football for the boys and netball for the girls, along with swimming, cross country, aerobics, and others. In the summer there is a degree of choice between cricket, athletics, swimming, golf, and tennis and rounders for girls.

In the course of the year there is opportunity for boys and girls to take part in a wide variety of sports, in which they can represent both their House and the School.

CCF and Pioneers: There is also a Combined Cadet Force with Army and Royal Air Force sections and The Duke of Edinburgh's Award Scheme.

The Arts: There are set times each week when priority is given to non-sporting clubs and activities, giving pupils opportunities in a wide range of experiences. Music plays a central role in College life. There is a School Orchestra, Swing Band, and Jazz Ensemble. There is a Girls chamber choir, and the Chapel choir sings at the main service each Friday. In addition, there are also other specialist ensembles and small instrumental groups. Music is included in the curriculum of Years 7–9 and in addition tuition in most instruments from both resident and visiting staff is available. A number of musical events takes place annually, including the Junior School Music concert, and the Summer Serenade, the showcase concert, held in May.

Traditionally there is a major play or musical at the end of the Michaelmas term. The College has a proud record of 104 Shakespearean productions. The 2014 School Play will be *Arabian Nights*. Each year there is also a Junior School Play (*Alice in Wonderland* in 2013), the Junior Drama Festival and performances from GCSE Drama and A Level Theatre Studies students.

The DT Department is fully equipped with Art and Pottery centres. These facilities are housed in the Centenary Building and allow pupils to fulfil abilities in design, woodwork, metalwork, painting, drawing, ceramics, and printing.

Entrance. Pupils wishing to join Year 7 (age 11+) or Year 9 (age 13+) sit examinations at the College in January and February. Pupils wishing to join Year 9 (age 13+) from Independent Preparatory Schools offering Common

Entrance, sit the Common Entrance examination in June. There is also entry in the Sixth Form, an increasingly popular option for girls and boys after their GCSEs.

Occasionally pupils enter at other ages and times. They need to show that they have attained the necessary academic standard either by public examination results or by sitting papers set by the College.

The Registration Fee is £50 and the deposit is £400.

Scholarships, Exhibitions and Bursaries. Scholarships and Exhibitions are available in the following categories – Academic, Art, Design and Technology, Drama, Music (instrumental and choral), Sport and All-Rounder – and are at the discretion of the Headmaster. They are awarded at the ages of 11, 13 and for Sixth Form entry. Scholarships carry a remission of up to 20% of the fees which may be supplemented by means-tested Bursaries. Recently launched awards, which are usually made annually, are the Alastair Hignell Scholarship and the Governors' Award.

In all Scholarships, in addition to academic excellence, all-round ability and out-of-school activities and interests are taken into account.

A number of bursaries may be awarded to those in genuine financial need. Special consideration is given to the children of Clergy, Old Denstonians and members of the Armed Forces.

Fees per term (2014–2015). Boarding: £5,475 (Year 7), £7,256 (Years 8 & 9), £7,954 (Years 10–13) including items of board and education other than music lessons and extra tuition.

Day: £3,780 (Years 7–9), £4,568 (Years 10–13).

The Old Denstonian Club. *Secretary*: Mr M S Smith, Denstone College, Uttoxeter, Staffs. Regional Clubs based in London, Manchester and at the College.

Charitable status. Denstone College is a Registered Charity, number 1102588. It exists to provide Christian education for children.

Dollar Academy

Dollar, Clackmannanshire FK14 7DU
Tel: 01259 742511
Fax: 01259 742867
email: rector@dollaracademy.org.uk
website: www.dollaracademy.org.uk

Motto: '*Juventutis veho fortunas*'

The Academy, founded in 1818 and the oldest co-educational boarding and day school in Britain, is situated in forty acres of its own grounds on the southern slopes of the Ochil Hills, 30 miles from Edinburgh, 38 from Glasgow, 40 from St Andrews and 10 miles east of Stirling. The Academy is renowned for its academic reputation, for its inclusive international outlook, and for its range of co-curricular activities. In recent years, all the boarding houses have been extensively refurbished, and the quality of the facilities throughout the school campus is of the highest order; a Sixth Form Centre was opened in 2010 and a new Modern Languages centre is under construction for 2015–2016. The A-listed Playfair Building of 1821 is surrounded by a number of impressive modern buildings named after distinguished Scots.

Governors:
Chairman: J B Cameron, CBE, FRAgS, AIAgE

Vice-Chairmen:
Professor J McEwen, MBChB, FRCP, FFPH, FFOM, FDSRCS, FMEdSci
Professor R E Morris, MA, DPhil

Members:
M W Balfour, BCom, CA
K M Brown, MA
Mrs D A Burt, MCSP
Cllr A D Campbell, CA
D M Clark, MA, LLB, WS
Dr G B Curry, BA Mod, PhD, DIC
W E Gibson, BA, LLB
I C Glasgow, BSc, Dip Surv, Dip IA, ASIP
R P S Harris, BCom, Dip Com, CA
Dr M A Hogg, LLB, LLM, PhD, NP, FRSA
C J Milne, BSc
M J Rice
Mrs J M Smith, BA
D C Walker, BArch, Dip Arch, ARB
A G Webb, BCom
Dr D D Weir, MBChB
E D White, BCom

Bursar and Clerk to Governors: J StJ Wilkes, MA
Assistant Bursar: Mrs J Johnson, MA, ACA
Bursar's PA: Mrs M Campbell, BA

Rector: D J Knapman, BA, BSc, MPhil

Deputy Rector: G P Daniel, MA, MA

Assistant Rectors:
Dr J T Brooks, BSc, PhD
Mrs L H Hutchison, BA
S P Johnson, MA
Mrs A M Morrison, BA (*also Head of Prep & Junior School*)

Director of Music: J McGonigle, Dip Mus RSAMD

* *Head of Department*
† *Houseparent*
‡ *Head of Year*

Prep & Junior School:
Deputy Head, Prep & Junior School: Mrs M Barbour, BEd
Assistant Head, Junior School: Miss S Horne, BEd

Mrs L Barlow, MA	Mrs N M Letford, BEd
Ms K Cleghorn, MA, MLitt	†Mrs G A McFadyean, BA
Mrs V Currie, DipCE	A Mills, BEd
T A Dann, BEd	Mrs J W Moffat, BEd
Mrs O Dunn, BA	Mrs J Montgomery, BA,
Miss R E Foster, MA	Cert FPS
Mrs M E Hamilton, BA,	Miss L S Pollock, BEd,
Dip CE	AVCM
Mrs M Harewood, MA,	Ms L E O' Sullivan, BEd
BEd	Mrs K Thomson, BEd
Mrs L Hudson, BA	Mrs L L Thomson, BEd

Mrs K Bunyan (*Prep Assistant*)
Mrs E Beveridge (*Prep Assistant*)
Mrs L Taylor (*Prep Assistant*)
Mrs E Hamilton (*Prep Assistant*)

Senior School:

Art & Design:
*A K MacLean, DA
Mrs C L Kelly, BA
Ms S C Kennedy, BA
Mrs T L Livingstone, BA
M T MacDermot, BA
Mrs C MacLean, DA
F G Muirhead, BSc, BA

Biology:
*C K Ainge, BSc
P J Arnold, MA, BSc
J B Fraser, BSc
Ms S Hussain, BSc
Mrs F McDonald, BSc
Dr L A Payne, BSc, PhD

Business Education:
*M C Moore, BSc, IDM Dip
*Ms T Spencer, BA
Mrs H M Duncan, BA
Mrs L McMartin, BA
Mrs A L Robinson, MA
J A Simpson, BA
Mrs M A Waddell, Dip Com

Chemistry:
*D J Lumsden, BSc
‡N F Blezard, BSc, MRSC
Mrs H Cook, MChem
‡Dr R Johnson, BSc, PhD

Dr S Scheuerl, BSc, PhD,
  MRSC
‡C Smith, BSc

Classics:
*Mrs H S Lumsden, MA
Dr E Macleod, MA, PhD
E M Duncan, BA
Miss M Zikou, BA, MSc

Computing:
Ms R McGuinness, MSc
Mrs J Greenlee, BSc

Drama:
P G Russell, BA

*Engineering, Design &
  Technology*:
*Dr D A Keys, BA, PhD
S W Cochrane, BEdTech
J Delaney, BEdTech
Mrs P Webster, BEdTech

English:
*Mrs C Murray, MA,
  MPhil
Ms C Abel, BA, MLitt
Ms R J Halden, BA
D A H Johnston, BA,
  MLitt, MPhil
Miss E M Langley, MA
Miss R J Meiklejohn, BA
Mrs J E M Monk, MA
Mrs H K Moore, BA, MLitt
Mrs J Nozedar, MA
Mrs E A Taylor, MA

Geography:
*A M McConnell, BSc
Miss G Dean, MA
Mrs S A Scott, BSc

History & Modern Studies:
*Miss M D Sharp, MA
R Lindsay, MA
N G McEwan, MA
‡Miss G McCord, MA
†N J McFadyean, MA,
  MPhil (*World Studies*)
†R W Welsh, MA

Home Economics:
Mrs C Maciver, Dip
  HomeEc
Mrs S Malcolm, Dip
  DomSci
Mrs N O'Donnell, BA

Mathematics:
Mrs F G Stewart, BSc
  (*Acting*)
Miss S G Cannon, BSc
Mrs C M Childs, BSc
R W Durran, BA

Pupil Counsellor: Mrs L A Jeffrey, BA
Librarian: Miss T Hepburn, MA
Rector's PA: Ms E C Gallagher
Registrar: Ms C Gair
Marketing & Liaison Manager: Mrs E Gunn, MA, Dip
  IDM
School Office Manager: Ms L Elrick
IT Manager: J L Tracey
Building & Contracts Manager: D R Yuill-Kirkwood
Music Technologist: I H Campbell, BMus
CXO (*CCF*): M Scott
Janitor: W Anderson

Miss K Ely, BSc
D H M Gibb, BSc
Mrs L A Jeffrey, BA
P McKay, MA
I Mackenzie, BSc, CEng,
  MIET
Mrs V Mason, BSc

Modern Languages:
*D Delaney, MA
Miss C Bowie, BA,
  Maîtrise FLE
Mrs S Brooks, MA
Mrs A R Bryce, BA
Dr J M Fotheringham, BA,
  PhD
C W S Prior, BA
Miss F Sieger, BA
S K Young, BA
Mrs J Young, MA

Assistants:
Madame N Marec (*French*)
Herr M Hipp (*German*)
Signor A Bacciu (*Italian*)
Señorita I Lopez (*Spanish*)
Miss L Wang (*Mandarin*)

Music:
*Mrs K Fitzpatrick, MSc,
  BMus
D M Christie, BA, LLCM,
  ALCM
Mrs M Leggatt, MusB,
  DipMTh, LGSM, LLCM
Mrs L Timney, MA

Physical Education:
*S R Newton, BSc
Ms L Allan, BEd (*Director
  of Hockey*)
D W Caskie, BEd (*Director
  of Rugby*)
Miss S E Davidson, BEd
J G A Frost, BEd, MSc
P N Gallagher, BEd
Mrs C C Galloway, BEd
M I Hose, BEd
Mrs G M Robb, BEd
Mrs V A Smith, BA

Physics:
*J T A Fulton, BSc
Dr S Fulton, BSc, PhD
‡A N Johns, BSc, CPhys,
  MInstP
Miss C Malley, BSc

Support for Learning:
*Mrs L S McDougall, MA
Mrs W J Ainge, MA
Mrs A Gibson, DipCE
Mrs J Smith, BA

Head of Grounds: R W Meldrum
Piping Instructor: C Stewart
Pool Manager / Swimming Instructor: R W Kidd, FIOS,
  MSTA, TEAQ

Houseparents:
Argyll: Mr & Mrs R W Welsh
Heyworth: Mr & Mrs E Duncan
McNabb & Tait: Mr & Mrs N J McFadyean

Organisation. The Academy is divided into the Senior
School (ages 12–18, 850 pupils); the Junior School (ages
10–12, 162 pupils) and the Prep School (ages 5–9, 204
pupils). It is fully co-educational throughout, and has been
from 1818.

Academic. Pupils follow a course of study based upon
the Scottish Curriculum for Excellence, leading to qualifications that are highly regarded and which are valid for entry
to all world universities. In the Senior School, pupils are
prepared for examinations at National 5 level (generally in 7
or 8 subjects) and Higher Grades (usually in 5 subjects); and
then afterwards for a range of Advanced Highers, further
Highers or wider interest modules. Three Modern Languages are offered from age 10, with Mandarin optional at
age 12, and co-curricular Japanese. The separate sciences
are available from 13. The timetable is created around the
needs of the pupils rather than requiring them to slot into
pre-arranged subject blocks.

Beyond Dollar. Senior staff offer advice on Careers and
Higher Education to current and former pupils. In addition,
all pupils are offered the services of a professional careers
adviser, and both Planitplus and Centigrade programmes are
used. The Academy has a flourishing Work Experience programme for seniors locally, and in France, Germany and
Spain. Volunteering, community service and charitable
activities are widely supported throughout the school.

International links. Contact with other countries has
increased notably in recent years. For example, the Art
department visits Paris, Berlin, London and Madrid; the
geographers visit USA, Iceland and the Swiss Alps; the biol-
ogists visit Costa Rica; the Modern Languages department
runs exchange programmes and trips to France, Germany,
Spain and China, while sporting links are firmly established
elsewhere in Europe, in Japan, Ireland, Australia and South
Africa. The Pipe Band has toured in Sri Lanka, the Far East
and mainland Europe. The boarding community includes
boys and girls from throughout the world.

Games and Activities. The extensive playing fields and
new all-weather playing surface are immediately adjacent to
the school, as are the Games Halls, the Sports Centre with
fully-equipped Fitness Suite, 25-metre indoor heated swimming pool and the rifle range.

Teams represent the school in rugby, hockey, cricket, tennis, athletics, swimming, skiing, shooting, curling, football,
golf, badminton, basketball and ultimate frisbee.

The Duke of Edinburgh's Award Scheme is widely supported at all three award levels. The Combined Cadet Force
has equal numbers of boys and girls in a Royal Signals
troop, an Infantry section, a REME section, an RAF section,
an RN section and two Pipe Bands.

Dollar follows the principle of allowing pupils to opt into
co-curricular activities as well as games, and an extraordi-
narily wide variety of clubs is on offer, from surfing and croquet to climbing and childcare.

The Arts. Music is taught as part of the curriculum, and
tuition is offered as an extra in most orchestral instruments,
besides bagpipes, guitar, drums and clarsach. There are six
choirs, four orchestras, two Jazz bands and one Celtic Rock
Orchestra. Junior and Senior Musical productions are performed annually. Drama productions and clubs are found
throughout the age range; a range of performance spaces is
used including the purpose-built Studio Theatre. Many Art
Clubs take place outwith the timetabled lessons and exhibitions are held throughout the year. Dance – whether it be

Scottish Country or Latin American – is taught at all levels. Debating and Public Speaking are popular and competitive activities both within Dollar and in national competitions, where success is regularly achieved.

Boarding. Boarding pupils are accepted from the age of nine. There is one Boys' and two Girls' Houses. Weekly or flexible boarding arrangements can be made to suit pupils' and parents' needs.

Fees per term (2014–2015). Tuition: £2,751 (Prep), £3,162 (Junior), £3,678 (Senior). Boarding fee: £4,830 (full), £4,368 (weekly).

Admission. This is by interview and/or test with the Head of the Prep and Junior School for ages 5–14; and by interview and current school report for ages 14–18. The biggest single intakes are at age 5, and at 10 and 11 to the Junior School; there are intakes in other years as vacancies occur.

Charitable status. The Governors of Dollar Academy Trust is a Registered Charity; it exists to provide education for boys and girls.

Downe House

Cold Ash, Thatcham, Berks RG18 9JJ
Tel: 01635 200286
Fax: 01635 202026
email: correspondence@downehouse.net
website: www.downehouse.net
Twitter: @DowneHouse1
Facebook: /downehouse

Founded 1907.

Governors:
Chairman: Mr R Parry, BA
Mr S Creedy-Smith, BA, ACA
Mrs V Exelby
Mr R C Farquhar
Mr N Gold, FCA
Mrs J M Grant Peterkin, BA
Ms F Hazlitt
Dr C Hewitt [Mrs C Cunningham], BSc, FRCP
Mr N Hornby, BSc
Mr C D Keogh
Mr M J Kirk, MA
Mr C Radford, BSc Hons, FRICS
Mr S J Robinson, BA, FRSA, PGCE
Mr J Stephen, BSc, FRICS
Mrs B N Wheeler, BSc

Headmistress: Mrs E McKendrick, BA Liverpool, PGCE, FRSA

Deputy Head: Mrs A Bizior, BSc, PGCE, BEd University of South Africa
Academic Deputy: Mr M Hill, BA Hull, MA Reading, MEd Open, PGCE
Boarding Deputy: Mrs T MacColl, MA Hons Aberdeen, PGCE
Head of Sixth Form: Ms M Stimson, MA Edinburgh, PGCE
Head of Upper School: Mrs G Ford, BA Bristol, PGCE
Head of Lower School: Mrs J Gilpin-Jones, LWCMD
Assistant Headmistress (Foundation): Mrs M Scott, BEd Brisbane
Finance Bursar: Mr C Cockburn, FCCA
Director of Information Systems: Mr S Finch
Director of HR: Mrs K Tuttle, MCIPD
Director of Estates, Property and Services: Mr A Heath

Director of Admissions: Mrs L Ogilvie-Jones, BSc, PGCE, PGDip CEG, QCG
Director of Operations: Mrs Y J Charlesworth, BSc Reading, PGCE *(also Head of Science)*

Director of Studies (Assessment and Reporting): Mrs P Toogood, BA Hons, MSt Oxon, PGCE
Director of Studies (Data Management): Mrs K Henson, BA, MA, PGCS, MEd

Heads of Department:
Art: Mrs S J Scott, BA Central England, PGCE
Biology: Miss C M Pugsley, BSc Warwick, PGCE
Careers & Guidance: Mrs M Ahktar, BA, MA, PGCE, PG Cert
Chemistry: Mr A Reynolds, BSc Loughborough, PGCE
Classics: Mrs L Dakin, MA Cantab
Co-Curricular: Mrs J Dell
Design & Technology: Miss S Singh, HDE Natal, South Africa, QTS
Drama: Miss S Hannibal, BA Hons, PGCE
English: Mr L McBratney, BA, MA, MPhil, PGCE
Geography: Mr R Barnes, BSc Bristol, PGCE
Global Perspectives & Research: Mr I Vallance, BEd, MA
History: Mr W Lane, MA, PGCE
ICT: Mrs D Evans, BSc Oxford Brookes, PGCE
Learning Skills: Mrs T Evans, BA, PG Dip SpLD, RSA TEFL, AMBDA
Library: Ms L Scott-Picton, BA, MLib, PGCE, MCLIP
Mathematics: Mr R S Barnes, BSc East Anglia, PGCE
Modern Languages: Mrs J Basnett, BA Westminster, MA, PGCE
Music: Dr C Exon, BMus, PhD Birmingham, PGCE
Physical Education: Mrs L J M Rayne, BEd Hons
Physics: Mr M Rivers, MA, PGCE
PSHE: Mrs N Riddle, B PhysEd, Dip T
Religious Studies: Mr P Evans, BD London, MA London, PGCE
Science: Mrs Y J Charlesworth, BSc Reading, PGCE
Social Science: Dr A R Mickleburgh, BA ANU, MPhil Sussex, PhD Cantab
Speech & Drama: Mrs R Watson, BA Hons, AVCM

Housemistresses/Housemaster:
Hermitage House: Mrs A Nash, BTchg, Lng Canterbury, NZ
Hill House: Mrs F V Capps, CertEd Bedford College
Darwin: Miss F Smith, BSc, PGCE
Veyrines (France): Mrs D Scotland
Aisholt: Mrs R Wilson, MA Cantab, PGCE
Ancren Gate North: Miss K Anger, BMus Hons, GSMD
Ancren Gate South: Mrs S McClymont, LLB, PG Dip LPC
Holcombe: Miss B Evans, BA, PGCE
Tedworth: Mrs S Barnard, MA
Willis House East: Mrs T Reeve, MA, PG Dip
Willis House West: Mrs V Ryan, BA Bangor, PGCE
York House North: Mrs C Walton-Walters, BSc Open, Cert Ed
York House South: Dr A Roberts, BSc, PGCE, PhD

Chaplain: Revd Andrew Taylor
Nurse Manager: Mrs G Murray, BSc RGN, BSc RM

Numbers on roll. 557 Boarding girls, 22 Day girls.
Age Range. 11–18.
Downe House is situated in 110 acres of wooded grounds, five miles from Newbury and within easy reach of Heathrow Airport. The school's proximity to London allows the girls to take part in a rich variety of cultural activities outside the school.

Buildings. There are Junior Houses for girls aged 11+ and 12+, which are currently being renewed, and five recently refurbished mixed-age Houses for those between 13 and 16. When girls enter the Sixth Form they move into one of two Sixth Form Houses, where they have twin-shared or single study-bedrooms and facilities appropriate to their needs. All the Housemistresses are members of the teaching staff and are responsible for the coordination of the academic, pastoral, social and moral development of the girls in their care.

The school buildings include up-to-date Science Laboratories, an Art School, Design and Technology suite, a Music School, an indoor Swimming Pool and Squash Courts and a Library. The games facilities are excellent; a Sports Centre and all-weather pitch. The school also has a Performing Arts Centre and a Concert Room which are used for lectures, concerts and plays, and a recording studio.

Religion. Downe House is a Church of England school with its own chapel, which girls attend for prayers and for a service of either Matins or Evensong on Sunday. Holy Communion is celebrated once a week and girls are prepared for confirmation if they wish. Other denominations are welcome. Girls can go to mass on Sundays and are prepared for Roman Catholic Confirmation.

Curriculum and Activities. The curriculum includes the study of English, History, Geography, Religious Studies, French, German, Spanish, Italian, Latin, Greek, Mathematics, Physics, Chemistry, Biology, Design and Technology, Information & Communication Technology, Music, Art, Drama and Theatre Studies, Food and Nutrition and Textiles. In addition, Classical Civilisation, Business Studies, Sports Science, Politics, Economics, Photography and History of Art are offered at A Level or Pre-U, as well as Global Perspectives and writing a 5000-word Independent Research Report. Leiths Food & Wine Certificate is also offered to girls in the Sixth Form. Girls are prepared for GCSE, IGCSE, AS, A Level and Pre-U examinations, with the vast majority of girls going on to University or some other form of Higher Education.

ICT skills are developed across the years with all girls following a general ICT course. All girls have their own Downe House email address.

All girls in the Lower Fourth, aged 12, spend a term at the School's House in France in the Dordogne, to study French and increase their awareness of themselves as global citizens.

Careers Specialists give help to the girls in selecting their careers and a Careers Resource Centre is available to all ages.

There are many extra-curricular activities, including a variety of musical instruments, Fencing, Drama, Sub Aqua, Pottery, Photography, Art, Craft, Singing, Speech & Drama Training, Cookery, Dance (Tap, Modern, Ballet, Hip Hop, Street) and Self-Defence. There is a regular programme of varied weekend activities, including the Duke of Edinburgh's Award Scheme. Expeditions abroad such as World Challenge, which develops leadership qualities, are offered alongside Young Enterprise which offers an insight into business practice in the UK.

Fees per term (2014–2015). £10,930 for boarders and £7,910 for Day Girls.

Admissions. Girls may enter the school at 11+, 12+ or 13+ after assessment, interview and Common Entrance. A few girls annually are given places in the Sixth Form after interview and entrance test.

Application for entry should be made well in advance. Prospective parents are asked to make an appointment to see the Headmistress, at which time they are offered a comprehensive tour of the school.

Scholarships. Scholarships are awarded to recognise girls with strong academic, musical, artistic, sporting or dramatic potential from a variety of backgrounds and who will benefit from the overall education offered by Downe House.

The School offers a number of Academic Scholarships at 11+, 12+, 13+ and for entry into the Sixth Form. Scholarships are also awarded in Music, Art and Sport (11+ and 13+) and Drama (13+ and 16+) and there are Headmistress's Awards for outstanding all-round performers.

All Academic, Art, Sport and Drama Scholars receive recognition in the form of £750 per annum remission in fees. Exhibitioners receive a remission of £450 per annum.

Music Scholars will receive free tuition in two instruments, which may include the voice, up to a maximum of 30 lessons per year. Exhibitioners will receive free tuition in one instrument, up to a maximum of 30 lessons per year.

Candidates who are successful in gaining an award, but require greater remission in fees in order to be able to take up their place may apply for an Academic, Art, Music, Sport or Drama means-tested Bursary, as appropriate.

Academic Awards. The Olive Willis 13+ Scholarships, 12+ and 11+ Downe House Scholarships are awarded on the results of examinations and interviews with the Headmistress, Head of Upper School and Head of Lower School, held each year in January. In addition to these major awards, Exhibitions may be awarded in each age group. Further Minor Awards for excellence in specific fields may be made if candidates of sufficient merit present themselves. Candidates sit papers in English, Mathematics, Science, French (12+ and 13+ only), a General Paper, plus Latin (optional).

Sixth Form Scholarships are year round and candidates sit papers in two subjects of their choice, together with a General Paper. Candidates will also be required to undertake an interview with the Headmistress and Head of Sixth Form.

Age of entry will normally be in line with general entry, ie 11+, 12+, 13+ and Sixth Form (16+). Candidates must be under 12, under 13 or under 14 on the 1st September following the examination. Girls sitting for entry to the Sixth Form must be in the final year of their GCSE studies or equivalent.

Music Awards will be made on the results of auditions and aural tests held at Downe House in February each year.

Art Awards will be made on the results of a girl's portfolio and a practical test held at Downe House in June each year.

Drama Awards will be made on the results of a one-hour written paper and a one-hour practical examination held at Downe House in May/June each year.

Sports Awards are made at in March each year. It is expected that potential candidates will be at the top level of their year group in a minimum of two major sports. Candidates will be invited to undertake a programme that will test general principles of fitness and skill acquisition. All candidates will also be assessed in swimming and gymnastics.

A number of *Headmistress's Awards* may be awarded, at the discretion of the Headmistress, to reward outstanding all-round performers.

For Music, Art, Sport and Drama awards junior candidates must be under 14 on the following 1st of September of the year of entry. Potential award holders are required to reach a satisfactory standard in the Common Entrance examinations for their age group before taking up their Award. Senior candidates (i.e. those entering the Sixth Form) must achieve Grade B or above in seven IGCSE subjects before taking up their Award and at least an A/A* grade in the subjects they wish to pursue in the Sixth Form.

Bursaries. The School is able to award a small number of full means-tested Bursaries for girls to join the School at 11+, 12+ or 13+. Girls should be able to meet the entry requirements and benefit from a busy boarding environment.

Alumnae Bursaries are available for the daughters of alumnae if their parents are in need of financial assistance.

Charitable status. Downe House School is a Registered Charity, number 1015059. Its aim is the provision of a sound and broadly based education for girls, which will fit them for University Entrance and subsequently for a successful career in whatever field they choose.

Dulwich College

Dulwich Common, London SE21 7LD
Tel: 020 8693 3601
Fax: 020 8693 6319
email: info@dulwich.org.uk
website: www.dulwich.org.uk
Twitter: @DulwichCollege
Facebook: /DulwichCollege

Motto: '*Detur gloria soli Deo*', ('Let Glory be given to God alone')

The Governing Body:
Chairman: Lord Turnbull, KCB, CVO
Vice Chairman: Mr V P Bazalgette, MA (*OA*)
Sir Brian Bender, KCB
Dr I Bishop, CBE, BEd, MA, LLD
Ms V Flind, BA
Mr R J Foster, BEd
Mr B Ghosh, BA, MA
Mrs J M Hill, MA
Mr P L Hogarth, CA, MSI
Dr A H Köttering, BSc, MSc, DPhil
Mr J D Lovering, BA, MBA (*OA*)
The Rt Hon P J R Riddell, CBE, MA, FRHistS
Mr P M Thompson, RD, MB BS, FRCS (*OA*)
Mr G N C Ward, CBE, MA, FCA

Honorary International Advisor to the Governors:
His Excellency Khun Anand Panyarachun, Hon KBE, MA (*OA*)

Special Advisor to the Governors: Sir John H Riblat, FRICS, Hon FRIBA (*OA*)

(*OA*) *Old Alleynian*

Clerk to the Governors: Ms K Jones, LLB

Master of the College: Dr J A F Spence, BA Hons, PhD

Deputy Masters:
Mr S R Northcote-Green, BA (*Pastoral*)
Mr A J S Kennedy, BA (*Academic*)
Mr R I Mainard, BA, MA Theol, MA Ed (*External*)

Chief Operating Officer: Mr S J Yiend, MA
Director of Finance: Mr N Prout, BA, ACA
Director of Communications: Ms J M Scott, MA, MBA
Head of Upper School: Dr C S B Pyke, MA, MMus, PhD
Head of Middle School: Dr N D Black, BA, PhD
Head of Lower School: Mr I L H Scarisbrick, BSc
Head of Junior School: Dr T G A Griffiths, PGCE, MA, MSc, DPhil
Head of DUCKS (*Kindergarten and Infants' School*): Mrs H M Friell, DipEd
Registrar: Mrs S Betts
Archivist: Mrs C M Lucy, BA, MCLIP
Head of Academic Administration: Mr N P Young, BSc
Director of Co-Curricular: Miss S G Wood, BSc
Examinations Officer: Mr M Grantham-Hill, BSc
Head of Curriculum and Learning: Mrs F M Angel, BA
Staff Tutor: Mr A J Threadgould, BSc
Head of Lower School Learning: Mr S Tanna, BA

Heads of Department:
Mr R S Baylis, MA, MA (*Modern Languages*)
Mrs J Briggs, BA (*Italian*)
Mr J G Brown, BA (*French*)
Mr M Burdekin, BA (*PE*)
Dr J Carnelley, BMus, MMus, ARCO (*Academic Music*)
Mr J D Cartwright, MA (*Computer Science*)
Dr N T Croally, MA, PhD (*Scholars and General and Liberal Studies*)
Miss S E Horsfield, BA (*EAL*)

Dr P J Cue, BSc, PhD (*Biology*)
Miss K Cutler, BA (*Spanish*)
Mr W Dugdale, BA (*German*)
Mr P J Fletcher, BA, DipLib, MCLIP (*Libraries*)
Mr D Flower, BA (*History and Politics*)
Mr J H Fox, BA (*Religion and Theology*)
Mr P C Greenaway, BSc (*Director of Sport*)
Dr J-M Hulls, MPhil, PhD (*Classics*)
Mrs K Johnstone MA, Dip SpLd (*Joint Head of Learning Support*)
Mrs A J Owen, CertEd SpLd (*Joint Head of Learning Support*)
Mr P V Jolly, BA, DipRSA (*Director of Drama*)
Dr J Kinch, BA, BPhil, DPhil (*Critical Thinking*)
Mr D King, MA (*Director of Science*)
Mr N Mair, BA (*Director of Languages*)
Mr R G Mayo, MA, MusB, FRCO (*Director of Music*)
Mrs S Mulholland, BA (*Director of Art*)
Mr M Nash, MA (*Acting Director of University Admissions*)
Mrs K Norton-Smith, BA (*Academic Drama*)
Mr C J Ottewill, BA, MPhil (*Mathematics*)
Miss L V A Rand, MChem (*Chemistry*)
Mr M Ross, BA (*Design & Technology*)
Miss A C Smith, BA (*Acting Head of Economics*)
Mrs E H Soare (*Careers*)
Mr A M Stark, BA, DMS, MA (*Chinese*)
Dr A C Storey, BA, MSc, PhD (*Director of ICT*)
Mr R F Sutton, BA (*English*)
Mr R Weaver, BA, MA, FSA Scot (*Keeper of the Fellows' Library*)
Mr S T Whittaker, BA, MSc (*Physics*)
Mr I L Williams, BSc (*Science Coordinator*)
Mr Graham Wilson, MPhys (*Lower School Science*)
Miss J K Woolley, BA (*Geography*)

DUCKS (*Dulwich College Kindergarten and Infants' School*):
Miss S Donaldson, NNEB, MA (*Head of Kindergarten*)
Mrs N Black, BA (*Deputy Head of DUCKS*)

Medical Centre Charge Nurse: Miss P Heaton, RGN, RM, RSN, BSc Hons Specialist Community Practitioner, Dip Counselling
College Counsellor: Ms J De Heger, BEd, Dip Art Therapy
Medical Officer: Dr R A Leonard, MBE, MA, MB, BChir, MRCGP, DRCOG
PA to the Master and to the Clerk: Mrs M Wood

Dulwich College was founded in 1619 by Edward Alleyn, the Elizabethan actor, and is approaching its 400th anniversary.

The College is an academically selective, independent day and boarding school for boys aged 7–18; full and weekly boarding is available for boys aged 13–18. Situated in over 70 acres of grounds and playing fields, the campus is just 10 minutes by train from London Victoria. A Dulwich education ensures each pupil fulfils their academic potential whilst taking advantage of the wide range of sporting, cultural and adventurous activities on offer.

Boys move on to universities, medical and dental schools, music and art colleges. Almost all enter higher education, but an increasing number of boys are following vocational paths. Pupils are prepared for entry to the most competitive universities such as Oxford, Cambridge and Imperial, where a very good record of places is maintained each year.

The College's principal aims for all its boys are:
- to offer an appropriate academic challenge which enables each pupil to realise his potential;
- to create an environment which promotes an independent work ethic and encourages all boys to acquire a love of learning;

- to provide a wide range of co-curricular activities through which boys can learn to take the lead and to work cooperatively;
- to nurture a supportive community which encourages social responsibility and spiritual and personal development and in which boys from a variety of cultural and social backgrounds can feel secure and equally valued.

Organisation. The College, comprising some 1,500 boys, has four specific schools: Junior School, Lower School, Middle School and Upper School. Each of these has its own Head who is responsible to the Master for that part of the College. Within each School there are Heads of Year and form tutors who have daily contact with boys in their care. These teams are responsible for overseeing the pastoral and academic welfare of the boys and they ensure that close links are fostered between parents and the College.

DUCKS. Dulwich College's Kindergarten and Infants' School is the only co-educational element of the College providing a secure foundation for future learning and development. Most children from DUCKS enter leading independent schools in south London, and many boys will pass the entrance examination for the College.

Day House system. A thriving Day House system offers boys the opportunity to take part in a wide range of competitive activities including art, chess, poetry, general knowledge, debating, drama and music. They can also compete in a number of sports throughout the academic year, including rugby, soccer, hockey, cricket and athletics.

Curriculum. All boys follow a broad and balanced curriculum in Years 7 and 8, including all standard core subjects and French or Spanish, Chinese, Latin, Well-being, Computing, Drama, DT, Art and Music for all pupils. In Year 9, boys continue with French or Spanish and choose a second language from German, Chinese, French, Spanish or Latin. All pupils continue with all humanities, creative subjects and Well-being as in Years 7 and 8. In Years 10 and 11, boys take between nine and eleven GCSE subjects which will include English, English Literature, Mathematics, Biology, Chemistry and Physics and French or Spanish. In addition they choose three option subjects and continue with a Wellbeing lesson each week. In Year 12, there is a free choice of four main subjects and every pupil opts for a Liberal Studies course with regular lectures for the whole year group. In Year 13, three or four A Levels (or Pre-U in two subjects) are continued, along with a Liberal Studies course in conjunction with James Alleyn's Girls' School. In addition to those subjects already mentioned above, Ancient History, Computing, Economics, Classical Greek, History of Art, Italian, Politics, Physical Education and Theatre Studies are also available.

Facilities. Over the years the College has developed its complex of buildings to meet the needs of boys' education in the twenty-first century, and this development continues. The latest addition, which was completed in February 2009, is the Lord George Building which houses a new Sixth Form Centre with adjoining suites for economics and careers, a café and a suite of changing rooms.

Construction of a new landmark science laboratory is underway, with completion scheduled for 2016, which will house 21 new science laboratories, IT suites and a 240 seat auditorium which will be available to the whole Dulwich community for events and exhibitions. The Laboratory has been designed by Grimshaw architects who are renowned for their work at the Eden Project and Cutty Sark in Greenwich.

Extensive IT facilities are available to all pupils. The IT network gives pupils and staff access to a wide range of centrally stored learning resources through the College's own virtual learning environment, 'MyDulwich'. Three separate libraries, all staffed by professional librarians, cater to the specific needs of different age groups. Exhibitions, drawn from the College archive, are regularly mounted in the Wodehouse Library.

The College has two separate dining areas which provide a wide choice of food, including a vegetarian option, on a cafeteria basis for both pupils and staff. The College also has its own shop, the Commissariat, where uniform, equipment and stationery can be purchased. The Richard Penny Medical Centre provides professional nursing care on a round-the-clock basis for boarders and day boys. The College Counsellor, based in the Medical Centre, provides confidential consultation for pupils and parents.

Sport is integral to life at Dulwich College both within the curriculum and as part of the wider co-curricular programme. There are over 70 acres of playing fields. The PE Centre includes a substantial sports hall and a modern indoor 25-metre swimming pool. The College owns a boathouse on the Thames, accommodating the thriving Boat Club, and an Outdoor Centre in the Brecon Beacons which is used for a variety of activities and residential courses. The sports programme provides a continuity and breadth of experience across the age range, with 24 different sports on offer, giving all boys the opportunity to reach their sporting potential.

Music and Drama. A professionally equipped, purpose-built Music School provides all pupils with the opportunity to study a musical instrument. More than 500 pupils receive individual tuition every week from 35 experienced specialist musicians, led by the Heads of Strings, Wind, Brass, Keyboard and Singing. The College Chapel Choir, an ancient foundation, leads regular services in the Foundation Chapel and also at other venues throughout the country. The Edward Alleyn Theatre is a fully rigged auditorium with a capacity of 250; over 50 events are staged annually and the facility includes rehearsal and teaching spaces, as well as dressing rooms.

Clubs and Societies. A wide variety of clubs and societies, many run by the boys themselves, take place during the lunch break and after school. These range from Lego for the younger boys to the Political Society which is responsible for inviting prominent public figures to speak. The College encourages boys to take part in expeditions as well as many community-based activities which can include membership of the Combined Cadet Force, Scouts, the Duke of Edinburgh's Award Scheme and Community Service. Academic, cultural and sporting excursions take place at various points throughout the school year.

Careers. Specialist careers staff, professional external advisors, dedicated IT facilities and an accredited library provide an up-to-date service assisting boys in planning higher education and careers. Boys and their parents attend the annual Courses and Careers Convention to consult with representatives from key employers, professional institutes and around 25 universities. Upper School boys receive guidance on how degree course choices might influence their future careers.

Boarding. There are three boarding houses in Dulwich College, all situated within or close to the campus. Each house has a Housemaster who is resident with his family. Younger boys (aged up to 16) live in The Orchard, sharing comfortable study-bedrooms. Boys in the Upper School live in Blew House and Ivyholme, where each boy has his own room with en-suite facilities. At present, there are around 130 boarders. Boarding at Dulwich is truly international with boys coming from all over the world and this adds to an atmosphere of cultural tolerance and intellectual curiosity.

ISI Inspection November 2014. ISI Inspectors awarded Dulwich College, Dulwich College Junior School and DUCKS 'Excellent' in every category, 'Exceptional' for 'the quality of pupils' achievements and learning' for the senior school – the only category for which this grading can be given – and 'Outstanding' for the EYFS (Kindergarten, Nursery and Reception).

Entry. Boys are admitted to the College as day boys, boarders or weekly boarders. Places are available at age 7, 11, 13 and 16. Casual vacancies occur from time to time at ages 8, 9, 10 and 12. At age 7 places are awarded on the basis of interview, report and practical assessment during the Lent Term. At age 11 places are awarded on the results of the Combined Entrance and Scholarship Examination held in the Lent Term. Candidates take papers in English and Mathematics and also a Verbal/Non-Verbal Reasoning test. At age 13 boys may take the College's own Entrance Examinations held in the Lent Term. Entrance is by examination and interview. At 16+ places are offered on the results from subject specific tests, interview and GCSE grades. Application should generally be in the year before desired date of entry. For further information please see the Admissions section on the College website. A non-refundable registration fee of £100 is charged for all applications and £200 for overseas applications.

Fees per term (2014–2015). Day £5,801 (includes lunch for Junior and Lower School pupils); Full Boarding £12,108; Weekly Boarding £11,353.

Scholarships and Bursaries. A significant number of academic scholarships are awarded each year up to one-third of the tuition fee. There are also scholarships for music, art and sports. Scholarships can be enhanced by Bursaries in cases of financial need. A substantial number of Bursaries are awarded annually to new boys entering Year 3, Year 7 or Year 9 where parents are unable to pay the full tuition fee. Bursaries are means-tested and reviewed annually. All applicants will be considered on the basis of their performance in the entrance examination and interview.

Old Alleynians. Founded in 1873, The Alleyn Club is a flourishing former pupils' association with over 10,000 Old Alleynian (OA) members. The club's name acknowledges the founder, Edward Alleyn, actor, theatre manager and contemporary of William Shakespeare.

Charitable status. Dulwich College is a Registered Charity, number 1150064.

The High School of Dundee

Euclid Crescent, Dundee, Tayside DD1 1HU
Tel: 01382 202921
Fax: 01382 229822
email: enquiries@highschoolofdundee.org.uk
website: www.highschoolofdundee.org.uk
Twitter: @HSofDundee
Facebook: /highschoolofdundee

Motto: '*Prestante Domino*'.

The present School traces its origins directly back to a 13th century foundation by the Abbot and Monks of Lindores. It received a Royal Charter in 1859. Various Acts of Parliament in the 19th Century were finally consolidated in an Order in Council constituting the High School of Dundee Scheme 1965, which was revised in 1987.

The Board of Directors comprises:
Chairman, 2 ex officiis Directors, viz, The Lord Dean of Guild and The Parish Minister of Dundee. The Guildry of Dundee, the Nine Trades of Dundee, the Old Boys' Club and the Old Girls' Club and the Parents' Association each elect one Director. Six Directors are elected by Friends of the High School and up to 6 co-opted by the Board.

School Staff:

Rector: Dr J D Halliday, BA Hons, PhD

Deputy Rectors:
Mrs L A M Hudson, MA
Mrs V A Vannet, MA, DipEd, FRGS, FRSGS

Assistant Rector – Junior Years and Nursery: Mrs J Rose, BEd

Bursar: C M Sharp, FCCA

Deputy Heads – Senior School:
Mr D A Brett, BSc
Mr D G Smith, BSc
Mrs S J Watson, MA

Deputy Heads – Junior Years:
Mr R Petrie, BA
Mrs C E Proudfoot, MA, DELL

Director of ICT: Mr W Wilson, BSc

Junior Years:

Mrs P L Hourd, BSc, AUPE, MEd (*Junior/ Senior Transition Coordinator*)	Mrs L Coupar, MA
	Mrs C Reid, BEd
	Mrs S Fish, BEd
	Miss K A Reith, MEd
Mrs L J Mooney, DipCE, IE	Miss L Carrie, MA, MPhil
	Mrs K Goldie, BEd
Mrs L Docherty, DipCE	Mrs M R Leburn, MA
Mrs M A Mordente, BEd	Miss J Wallace, BEd
Miss M Cardno, MA, CEEd	Mrs D Sager, MA
	Mrs J Coull, DipCE
Mrs L Smith, BEd	Mrs G Johnson, BEd
Mrs A Davie, MEd	Mrs M R Leburn, MA
Mrs P J Halliwell, BEd	Mrs C E Proudfoot, MA, DELL
Mrs C Powrie, BSc	
Mrs F S Wilson, BEd	Mr R Petrie, BA
Miss G Alexander, BEd	

Nursery:
Manager: Mrs S C Tosh, MA

Mrs L C Yule, BA	Miss C Cosgrove
Mrs D M Irving, BA	Miss N V Whyte
Miss A A Balfour	

Senior School:
* *Head of Department*

English:
*Mrs J Phillips, MA
Mrs D M MacDonald, MA
Mrs D E Keogh, MA
Mrs M Ovenstone-Jones, MA
Miss E Whatley-Marshall, MA
Mr D P Campbell, MA

Drama and Media Studies:
*Mrs L M Drummond, Dip Drama
Miss L Shand, BA

History and Modern Studies:
*Mr G Fyall, BA, DipEd
Miss K McKie, MA
Miss L Hegan, MA
Mrs L A Hudson, MA
Mr C Melia, MA

Geography:
*Miss J L Stewart, BSc
Mr C R McAdam, MA
Mrs S B Williams, MA
Mrs V A Vannet, MA, DipEd, FRGS, FRSGS
Mrs R Lloyd, MA, MSc
Mrs S J Watson, MA

Philosophy and Religion:
*Mr D J Goodey, BA, MA
A W Cummins, BD, DipMin

Business Studies:
*Mrs C A Laird-Portch, BA

*Mr N S Higgins, BSc (*acting*)
Mr J C Hendry, BA

Classics:
*Mr E Faulkes, BA
Mrs C Meeuwsen-Findlater, MA

Modern Languages:
*Mr N A MacKinnon, MA
Mrs I M McGrath, MA
Mrs F M Cram, MA, DipEd
Mrs G A Mackenzie, MA
Mrs L Smith, MA
Mrs J Brown, BA
Ms A Aguero, BA, BEd
Mr F M McAvinue, MA, MSc
Dr J D Halliday, BA, PhD
Mr J P Nolan, MA

Mathematics:
*Mr G A Mordente, BSc
Mr A G Blackburn, BSc
Mrs M A Oliver, BSc
Mr R C Middleton, BSc
Miss D MacDonald, BSc
Mrs L A Craig, BSc
Dr F Spiezia, MSc, PhD

Chemistry:
*Mrs R J Broom, BSc
Mr D A Brett, BSc

Mrs G Spinks, BSc, MRSC, CChem
Dr P Taylor, PhD, BSc, MRSC, CChem

Biology:
*Dr E Duncanson, BSc, PhD
Dr M W Fotheringham, MA, PhD
Mr G M S Rodger, BSc
Mr R H Bunting, BSc

Physics:
*Mr J Darby, BSc
Dr D G Brown, BSc, PhD
Mr T Guild, BSc
Dr G MacKay, BSc, MSc, PhD

Technology:
*Mr F Walker, BSc
Mr D F Preston, MEd, BEd

Computing:
*Mr S McBride, BSc
Mr C P Stuart, BSc
Mr D G Smith, BSc

Art and Design:
*Mr A Kerr, BA
Mrs M Angus, BA
Miss A Douglas, BDes
Miss J Campbell, MDes
Miss R J Jordan, BA

Music:
*Mr L S Steuart Fothringham, MA, FRCO
Mr D G Love, DipMusEd, DRSAMD
Mrs M Scott-Brown, LTCL
Ms G Simpson, DipMus, ALCM
Mr S Armstrong, DRSAMD
Mrs S Sneddon, LTCL, ALCM
Miss A Evans, BA, LTCL
Mr J McAuley, BA
Ms S Morgan, BMus
Mrs J Petrie, BA, CPGS

Learning Skills:
*Mrs P A Maxwell, BEd, DPSE, Cert SpLD

Mrs M A Mordente, BEd
Mrs J Downie, MA
Mrs J Chalmers, DPE SIQ
Mrs L Batchelor, BEd
Mrs L Duff

Physical Education:
*Mr A A Campbell, BEd, MSc, DipEd
Mr G W Spowart, BEd
Mrs J A Hutchison, DipPE
Mrs P M Spowart, BEd
Mr G R Merry, BSc
Miss V Bunce, BSc (*Coach*)
Mr W Nicol (*SSI/Instructor in Outdoor Activities*)
Mr E D Jack, BEd
Mrs L Christie, BA
Mrs S McKenzie, BEd
Mr G Black (*cricket/rugby coach*)
Miss J McMullen, BSc
Mr I Strachan (*hockey/sports coach*)

Home Economics:
*Mrs L J Ross, MA
Mrs O Anderson, BSc

Guidance:
Principal Teachers:
Mr C P Stuart, BSc
Mr C R McAdam, MA
Mr G W Spowart, BEd
Mrs P M Spowart, BEd

Assistant Principal Teachers:
Mrs F Cram, MA, DipEd
Mrs J Hutchison, DipPE
Mrs J Brown, BA
Mrs S B Williams, MA

Head of Careers:
Mr G M S Rodger, BSc

Outdoor Activities Coordinator:
Mr G M Ross, BA

Admission. The School comprises three sections:
The Nursery.
The Junior School – 313 pupils (Primary 1 to Primary 7).
The Senior School – 670 pupils (Form 1 to Form 6).
The normal stages of entry are Nursery, Primary 1 and Form 1. Entry to Primary 1 (age 4½ to 5½ years) is by interview held in January and to Form 1 (age 11 to 12 years) by an Entrance Examination held in January. Where vacancies exist entrance is usually available at all other stages subject to satisfactory performance in an entrance assessment.

Bursaries. A limited number of bursaries are provided to pupils in P6/7 and those entering Form 1.

Fees per term (2014–2015). Junior School: £2,600 (L1 to L3), £2,725 (L4 to L5), £3,095 (L6 to L7); Senior School £3,690. Nursery varies according to the number of sessions selected.

Buildings. The 5 main school buildings are in the centre of the city and form an architectural feature of the area. Two excellent playing fields – Dalnacraig and Mayfield – are situated some 1½ miles to the east of the school. This incorporates an international standard synthetic water-based hockey surface and a sand-dressed synthetic hockey pitch up to national standard. The school's Mayfield Sports Centre,

comprising state-of-the-art games hall, dance studio, gymnasium and fitness suite, is adjacent to the playing fields. The Nursery is also located at Mayfield.

Curriculum. The Junior School follows a wide-ranging primary curriculum. Subject specialists are employed in Physical Education, Art, Home Economics, Music, French, Information Technology.

In the Senior School, after two years of a general curriculum, some specialisation takes place with pupils currently being prepared for the Scottish Qualifications Authority Examinations at National 5, Higher and Advanced Higher which lead directly to university entrance.

Co-Curricular Activities. A wide range of activities is offered. There is a flourishing contingent of the Combined Cadet Force including a pipe band. Drama, Public Speaking and Debating, Chess and The Duke of Edinburgh's Award Scheme are examples of the wide variety of activities available.

Music plays an important part in the life of the school. Special tuition is provided in a wide variety of instruments.

Charitable status. The Corporation of the High School of Dundee is a Registered Charity, number SC011522. The school is a charity to provide quality education for boys and girls.

Durham School

Quarry Heads Lane, Durham City DH1 4SZ
Tel: 0191 386 4783
Fax: 0191 383 1025
email: enquiries@durhamschool.co.uk
website: www.durhamschool.co.uk
Twitter: @dunelmia
Facebook: /Durham School (1414-present)

Motto: *Floreat Dunelmia – Let Durham Flourish*

Durham School is one of the oldest in England. It probably has a continuous history from Saxon times and has always been closely associated with the Diocese of Durham. As the Bishop's School it was re-organised and endowed by Cardinal Langley in 1414 and was re-founded in 1541 by Henry VIII as a Lay Foundation under the control of the Dean and Chapter of Durham. In 1995 it left the Cathedral Foundation to become a separate body. The school is now fully co-educational 3–18, incorporating Bow, Durham School (3–11). 2014 marks 600 years of providing outstanding education.

Governing Body:
Mr A MacConachie, OBE, DL, FRSA (*Chairman*)
Mr F Nicholson (*Vice Chairman*)
Canon D Kennedy
Mrs M Coates
Mr S Hackett
Miss G Kerr
Mr R A Langdon
Mrs S Langridge
Mr A Martell
Mr D Welsh

Clerk to the Governors: Ms M Bagshaw

Headmaster: Mr K J McLaughlin, MA, PGCE

Deputy Head: Mr J Webb, BA, PGCE
Deputy Head (*Pastoral*): Dr J M Burns, BA, PhD
Bursar: Mrs D J Leigh, BA, FCA
Senior Master, Head of Boarding: Dr M P Alderson, BA, MA
Head of Bow, Durham School: Mr R N Baird, BA, PGCE
Director of Sixth Form Studies: Mr P C Gerrard
Director of Marketing: Mrs A N McCann, Dip CIPR, MCIPR

Admissions Officer: Mrs E Cathrae
Headmaster's PA: Mrs S Spence

Heads of Department – Senior School:
Art and DT: Mr M C T Baldwin, BA, PGCE
Biology: Mr M F Burke, BSc, PGCE
Boys' Games: Mr M Bedworth, BA
Chemistry: Mrs T Moore, BSc
Classics: Mr C Hope, BA, MA, M Phil
Co-curriculum: Mrs K L Rochester, BA
Drama: Miss A Parkin, BA
EAL, Chemistry: Miss K Lowery, BSc, PGCE
Economics and Business Studies: Mr O J Hughes, BA
English: Mrs F Swan, BA, PGCE
Geography: Mr J C Renshaw, BA, PCGE
Girls' Games: Mrs K E Dougall, BA, QTS
History: Mr D Tyreman, BA, MA, PGCE
ICT: Mr M A Gardner, BSc, MA
Learning Support: Mrs E J Ross, BA, MA Ed
Mathematics: Mr C S Fordyce, BSc
Modern Languages: Mr M P Alderson, BA, MA
Music: Mr R A Muttitt, BMus, MA, ARCO, FRSA
Physics: Mr I J Campbell, BEng, PGCE
Politics: Mr S McNair, BA, MA
Psychology: Mr B Brownlee, BA
Religious Studies, PSHE and General Studies: Mrs M F Proud, MA, PGCE
Director of Sport: Mr B M Mason, BEd

Location. The School is magnificently situated above the steep banks of the River Wear, overlooked by the west towers of Durham Cathedral on the opposite bank, and has occupied its present site since 1844. The School is physically compact – all the buildings are within 5 minutes' walk of each other; the playing fields and the river are adjacent. The School still has connections with Durham Cathedral and all pupils attend Chapel on a regular basis and the cathedral once a term.

Aims. While pursuing the highest academic standards, the School has an intellectual range which includes both prospective Oxford or Cambridge entrants and pupils who will succeed at A Level with the careful teaching and support the School provides. The School's main objective is to bring out the best in every pupil. Everyone is expected to contribute fully to the life of the School and thus to develop all their talents to the full. The School provides the care, the teaching and the facilities to do this in happy and attractive surroundings.

Size. Numbers are relatively small, around 480, with an excellent staffing ratio. The Preparatory School (age 3–11) currently caters for a further 140 day girls and boys.

The House System. The House system is one of the great strengths of the School, enabling pastoral care of the highest order. There are 5 Houses at the Senior School: three for boys (School House, Poole House and Caffinites House) and two for girls (Pimlico House and MacLeod House). Junior House staff look after the interests of Years 7 and 8 and in the boys' Houses Assistant/Deputy Housemasters are in charge of Years 9, 10 and 11. The School offers full, weekly or occasional boarding and has some 120 boarders (girls and boys). Day pupils enjoy all the benefits of a "boarding style" education during the day (including breakfast and supper, included in the fee), the same leisure facilities as the boarders and space for private study.

Admission. At the Prep School, admission is possible at any age and entry is based on an interview with the Headmaster and (if appropriate) an assessment test. Entry at age 11 is by way of the Durham School 11+ Entrance Examination. Pupils joining at age 13 sit the School's 13+ Entrance Examination. It is also possible to join in the Sixth Form. Such admission is by interview, testimonial and GCSE results. Entrance and Scholarship examinations and interviews generally take place in late January/early February, although Sixth Form scholarships take place in December

(see scholarships below). A prospectus with full details can be obtained on application to the Admissions Office.

Academic. Academic courses are followed to GCSE, AS and A2 Levels. A broad programme is pursued during the years up to GCSE and there is a wide choice and flexible programme for the Sixth Form. There is a fully developed Careers Advisory Service as well as a dedicated EPQ coordinator and Elite-Course coordinator.

Extra-Curricular Activities. A very wide and growing variety of musical, dramatic, sporting and other activities is available. Sports on offer include rugby, hockey, rowing, cricket, netball, rounders, squash, swimming, athletics, cross-country, tennis and water polo. The School has an all-weather sports pitch. Various types of Adventure Training are pursued through the Combined Cadet Force (CCF) and pupils can take part in World Challenge expeditions and the Duke of Edinburgh's Award scheme. The Durham School Boat Club is proudly the 3rd oldest Boat Club in the world and the School is also the 5th oldest Rugby Club in the world.

Scholarships and Bursaries. A range of prestigious Academic, Drama, Music, Art, Design and Technology and Sports Scholarships is available at 11+, 13+ and 16+ entry. The King's Scholarship award can be awarded to top performing candidates at 11+ and 13+ entry and the Burkitt Scholarship is awarded at 16+. Adamson Scholarships are available at Years 3 and 4 and the Peter Lee Scholarship for applicants of Chinese origin is available for academic entry to the Sixth Form.

Financial support in the form of means-tested Bursaries is available at all ages where appropriate and bursaries can be held alongside academic and non-academic awards. Langley Foundation Bursaries are available for entry at Reception, 7+, 11+, 13+ and 16+. These are means-tested awards which can be up to 100% of the school fee.

Music Scholarships are available at 11+, 13+ and 16+ entry. At least one scholarship is available at each age group in each of the following categories: strings, brass, woodwind, piano. A Sixth Form organ scholarship is available annually. All holders of Music Awards receive some free music tuition.

Drama, Sports, Art and DT Scholarships are also available at 11+, 13+ and 16+ entry.

Fee concessions are available for brothers and sisters and children of clergy and the Armed Forces (in addition to the CEA Boarding allowance).

Fees per term (2014–2015). Nursery: £2,331, Reception, Years 1 & 2: £2,640, Years 3–6: £3,195, Years 7–8: £7,025 (full boarder), £7,350 (overseas full boarder), £6,180 (weekly boarder), £4,310 (day pupil). Years 9–13: £8,215 (full boarder), £8,645 (overseas full boarder), £7,450 (weekly boarder), £5,280 (day pupil). The overseas fee includes a Saturday Language Activity Programme and EAL teaching as required. Extras are kept to a minimum.

Bow, Durham School is Durham School's Preparatory School and caters for around 140 girls and boys from age 3–11. It is situated in its own beautiful grounds half a mile away from the Senior School and makes full use of the Senior School facilities. It has been situated on its present site, half a mile from the Senior School and overlooking the cathedral, since 1888. Bow has its own extensive facilities including a fully-equipped science laboratory, IT suite, sports hall and library. Pupils also benefit from all the excellent facilities at the senior site, such as the swimming pool, all-weather sports pitch, the chapel and the theatre.

Bow has a fine record of academic achievement over the years and results in externally-marked examinations, such as the Key Stage I and 2 tests, are regularly impressive. The overwhelming majority of pupils move into the Senior School at the age of 11 at which point a range of prestigious awards are available. A high pupil-teacher ratio is maintained and small classes are considered vital as we seek to ensure that each child fulfils his or her academic potential.

Bow has an outstanding tradition in competitive sport, many former pupils having represented their country. A wide range of sports is on offer to all pupils. Music and drama form an integral part of life at Bow, with an active choir, ceilidh band and fiddle group performing regularly. There are three drama productions each year. Pupils are encouraged to take part in these productions whether it is on the stage or behind the scenes. Bow offers a wide range of extra-curricular activities which are seen as a vital ingredient in the daily diet of every Bow pupil. In addition further activities and hobbies are available as voluntary after-school clubs.

Charitable status. Durham School is a Registered Charity, number 1023407. It exists to provide a high quality education for boys and girls.

Eastbourne College

Old Wish Road, Eastbourne, East Sussex BN21 4JX
Tel: Headmaster: 01323 452320
           Bursar: 01323 452300
Fax: Headmaster: 01323 452327
           Bursar: 01323 452307
email: reception@eastbourne-college.co.uk
website: www.eastbourne-college.co.uk
Facebook: /EastbourneCollege

Founded 1867; Incorporated 1911.

Board of Governors:
President: His Grace The Duke of Devonshire, KCVO, CBE, DL

Vice-Presidents:
The Bishop of London
The Earl of Burlington

Members:
¶ *Former Pupil*

¶Mr M T Barford, MA, FCA
¶Mr P A J Broadley, MA Oxon, FCA, FRSA (*Vice-Chairman*)
¶Mr C D Cracknell
Dr C R Darley, MD, FRCP
Mr C M Davies, FRICS, ACIArb
Mrs N L Eckert, BA, PGCE
¶Mrs V J Henley, BA
Mr G Marsh, MA Oxon
¶Dr R A McNeilly, MBBS, DCH, MRCGP, DOccMed, MBA
¶General Sir Kevin O'Donoghue, KCB, CBE (*Chairman*)
¶General The Lord Richards of Herstmonceux, GCB, CBE, DSO, DL
Mrs M J Richards
Mr T S Richardson, FRICS
Mr A M Robinson, BA, ACA (*Treasurer*)
¶Mr J H Ryley, BA Dunelm, AMP
Mrs A M Saunders, CB, LLB
¶Dr D L Smith, MA Cantab, PhD, PGCE, FRHistS
Ms C Stokes, BA
¶Mr J P Watmough, LLB
¶Mr D Winn, OBE, MInstM
Mr A W L Wolstenholme, OBE, BSc, CEng, FICE

In attendance:
Mr S P Davies, MA Oxon, PGCE
Mr S Severino, MA Oxon, PGCE
Mr C W Symes, BSc, MCGI, PGCE
Mr G Ferguson, BSc, PGCE

Bursar and Clerk to the Board of Governors: Mrs C Meade, MA Cantab

Senior Management Team:

Headmaster: Mr S P Davies, MA

Deputy Head: Mr C W Symes, BSc, MCGI
Bursar to the Eastbourne College Charity: Mrs C Meade, MA
Assistant Head (*Curriculum*): Mr J M Gilbert, BSc, MRSC, CChem
Assistant Head (*Co-curricular*): Mr A T Lamb, BA
Assistant Head (*Teaching and Learning*): Mr D J Ruskin, BA
Assistant Head (*Pastoral*): Mrs G E Taylor-Hall, BA
Registrar: Mr L Chu, BA
Marketing and Communications Director to the Eastbourne College Charity: Mrs J S B Lowden, BA
Eastbournian Society Director: Mr D A Stewart

* *Head of Department*
† *Housemaster/mistress*
§ *Part-time*
¶ *Former Pupil*

Art:
*Mrs J L A Harriott, BA
Miss K M Hobden, MA
¶§Ms J Lathbury, DipFA
Mrs S A Martin, BA

Classics:
*Mr P J Canning, MA
Mr S T Baddeley BA
†Mr M J Banes, BA
§Mr S J Beal, BA
Miss V J Boorman, BA
†Mr H B Jourdain, BA
¶†Mr I P Sands, MA

Dance:
Dr J R M Gabelman, MA, PhD

Design and Technology:
*Mr M B Wilders, BSc, DipArch
Mr N J Clark, BA
Ms Z B Cosgrove, BA, MA, LTI (*Textiles)
Mr G L McDonald, BEd
Mr W L Trinder, BEd, EITB
†Mrs A Young, MA

Drama:
*Mr T W Marriott, BA
Mrs A F Marriott, BA, MA Ed

Economics / Business:
*Mr G R Bowmer, BA
¶Mr J M Bathard-Smith, MA
Mrs L A Salway, BA, MA
Mr R D Earnshaw, MA
Mr T J Holgate, BA
Mr M C Tonkin BSc

English:
*Mr C A Davies, BA
§Mrs LJ Ablewhite, BA
§¶Mrs J E Bathard-Smith, BA, MA
Mr T S Fisher, BA, MA
§Mrs L J Jourdain, BA
Mr P H Lowden, MA
†Mrs L J C Mackenzia, BA
Mr O K Marlow, MA
Miss P M H Squire, BA

English as an Additional Language:
§*Miss K Briedenhann, BSecEd Sci, CELTA
§Mrs G L Williams, BA, RSA Dip TEFL

Geography:
*Mr R K Hart, BA
§Miss J E B Henman, BA, MA
†Mr R W Hill, HND
Mr A T Lamb, BA, FRGS
Mr W M Longden, BA
§Mrs L Price, BSc
Miss E F Reed, BA
Mr C W Symes, BSc, MCGI

History:
*Mr S A Gent, MA
†Mr R H Bunce, MA
Revd C K Macdonald, BA, DipTheo
†Mr J C Miller, MA
Mr T J Spiers, BA

Information and Communication Technology:
*Mr I R Shakespeare, BSc
Mrs M A Ambler, BSc

Learning Support:
*Mr M L Saul, BEd
Mrs E B Miller, MBBS
§Mrs H J Williams, BA, CELTA

Life and Learning Skills:
*Mr E V Protin, MA

Mathematics:
*Mr J R Wooldridge, MA
¶Mr S E Beal, BA (*Deputy HoD*)
Mr O L Dennis, MA, LRAM, ARAM
Ms C E Hewson, BSc, MSc
¶§Mr L G Karunanayake, MA
Miss J K Lusty, BSc
Mrs K F MacGregor, MA, MSc, MBA
Mrs E M Sheridan, BSc

†Mrs J C Wood, MA

Modern Languages:
*Mrs G A Webb, BA
Mrs M C Tripp, BA, CMIL, DipTrans IoL (*Deputy HoD*)
†Miss V E Burford, MA
Mr L Chu, BA
Mrs M J De La Torre, BA
§Ms A G Del Angel, BA, MA
§Mrs R Entwisle, MA
Ms A-L Lafargue, M
Mr N G A Miller, BA
Mr E V Protin, MA
§Mrs H R Rünger-Field, BA
Mr D J Ruskin, BA
§Miss M G A Thaëron, BA
Mr J Thornley, BA

Music:
*Mr N J Parrans-Smith, DipTCL
Mr D R S Force, BA (*Academic Music*)
Mr T J G Gilbert, BA
Ms P E Walker, ARCM, DipRCM

Physical Education:
§*Mrs J M Simmonds, BA
Mr M T Harrison, BSc
¶§Mrs J M Kirtley, BA
Mrs G E Taylor-Hall, BA
Mr O M Torri, BAS, MBA

Visiting Music Staff:
Mrs A Boothroyd, MA, ARCM (*Piano*)
Miss S Carter, GMus (*Flute*)
Mr J R Cruttenden, BA, ABSM (*Double Bass*)
Miss M M Davis, BA, Dip RCM (*Strings*)
Miss R K Dines, ARAM, MMus, BMus, LRAM, ARCM (*Piano*)
Mr P Edwards, MMus, GRSM (*Woodwind*)
Mr M D Fields, AGSM, LRAM (*Guitar*)
Mr D Fuller, BMus, LGSMD (*Horn*)
Mrs N Fuller, BMus, LGSMD (*Piano*)
Mr K Goddard (*Guitar, Bass Guitar*)
Mrs J P Goss-Turner, PPRNCM (*Vocal Studies*)
Mr P T Greatorex (*Drums*)
Mr C D Greenwood, BA (*Jazz Piano*)
Mr S A Hollamby, ARCM, Dip RCM (*French Horn, Trumpet, Trombone*)
Mr H Jones, AGSM, PG Dip GSMD (*Bassoon, Percussion*)
Mr J L Kotz, BA (*Oboe*)
Mrs J H Lakin, GRSM, ARCM, LRAM (*Piano*)
Mr R C Lakin, GRSM, Dip RCM piano, Dip RCM violin (*Keyboard*)
Mr T J Lees (*Guitar*)
¶Mr A R Mackenzie-Wicks, BA (*Vocal Studies*)
Mrs E J Mansergh, FTCL, LTCL, ARCO (*Piano*)
Miss C S Mumford, Dip ABRSM (*Cello*)
Ms L P Wigmore, GRSM, ARCM (*Violin*)
Mr T A Williams (*Guitar*)

Mrs C Whiddett-Adams, BA

Religious Studies and Philosophy:
*Revd D J Peat, BA, MA (*Chaplain*)
Mrs C Dixon, MTheol
Dr D P Gabelman, BA, MA, PhD
Dr J R M Gabelman, MA, PhD

Biology:
*Mr D J Beer, BSc
Miss C S Arnold, BSc
Mrs R N Cooke, BSc
Mr C C Corfield, BSc
¶Mr P J Fellows, MBioMedSc

Chemistry:
*Mrs A R Bunce, BSc
Mr J M Gilbert, BSc, MRSC, CChem
¶Mr D C Miller, BSc, MRSC, CChem
Miss H L Simmons, BA
Mr A D Swift, BSc

Physics:
*Mr D J Hodkinson, BSc (*also *Science*)
Dr A Ball, BSc, PhD
Mr J M Hall, BSc, CPhys, MInstP
Mrs E J Livingstone Greer, BSc

Situation. The College is situated 400 metres from the sea in the prime residential part of the town of Eastbourne, adjacent to the national Tennis Centre at Devonshire Park, the Congress Theatre, and at the heart of the cultural quarter of the town. There is easy access to a wide range of cultural opportunities. The train to Gatwick Airport and London Victoria is under ten minutes walking distance; it is 1½ hours travel to London. The College links closely with the local community in a variety of ways including assisting people through its extensive S@S (Service at School) programme. There are a number of successful partnership schemes with local schools in the maintained sector. We also have a partnership with Glyndebourne and host rehearsals, auditions, masterclasses and performances.

Organisation and Pastoral Care. The College is a medium-sized boarding and day community where the ethos is of full boarding education. The College is co-educational with a ratio of girls to boys of 43:57. In 2014–2015 there are 636 pupils, of whom nearly a half are boarders. There are five boarding houses, three of which are for boys (Gonville, Pennell and Wargrave) and two are for girls (Nugent and School). There are six day houses, three of which are for boys (Craig, Powell and Reeves) and three are for girls (Arnold, Blackwater and Watt). Day and boarding houses have similar facilities and are run on similar lines with resident house staff and full tutorial teams. All day pupils can take supper at school and do prep in houses. School buses leave at two different times in the evening and pupils choose which time best suits their programme for the day. There is great commitment from staff and pupils in all areas and there is strong system of pastoral care.

Curriculum. Pupils study the full range of subjects in their first year which includes the opportunity to study both Latin and Classical Greek along with a second or even third modern language. For GCSE, pupils study biology, chemistry, English, a modern foreign language, mathematics and physics, as well as four other subjects from a choice of 16. At AS level, most pupils select four subjects from a choice of 24. Life and Learning skills are available in addition. Sixth Form students are encouraged to pursue individual research through extended projects, calling upon their teachers and tutors to support and encourage as needed. At A2 level most pupils study three subjects and all follow an extensive General Studies programme. ICT is central to the teaching and learning experience and the College is networked with its own Intranet.

Sport. A wide variety of sports is offered: major sports are cricket, hockey and rugby for boys; and hockey, netball and tennis for girls. Athletics, basketball, badminton, cross-country running, equestrian (show jumping), fencing, fives, football, golf, rowing, sailing, squash, swimming and tennis all have fixtures as well. All games pitches are within a short walking distance including two Astroturf hockey pitches, seven rugby pitches, four highly maintained cricket squares, four netball courts and 28 tennis courts in the summer including professional quality grass courts at Devonshire LTC. The school has its own 25-metre indoor swimming pool, a sports hall and two fitness suites. Most major sports enjoy international tours at regular intervals (for example, cricket to Sri Lanka and netball to Barbados in 2012, hockey to Holland in 2013, and rugby to South Africa in 2014). Sport is offered to all pupils; almost the whole College is involved in fixtures. There are also current and former pupils achieving county, regional and national recognition. In September 2015 the College will be a team base for South Africa during the Rugby World Cup.

Religion. The College is a Church of England registered school with an Anglican Chapel and Chaplain. All pupils experience Christian worship at least once a week. There is a long choral tradition and the Chapel Choir continues to contribute to the worshipping life of the community. Religious studies is compulsory in Year 9, with many pupils opting for the subject at GCSE and A Level.

Developments. All boarding and day houses continue to be refurbished on a rolling programme. The Birley Centre, a whole-school performing arts facility that includes a new music school, was opened in September 2011 and is much in demand from within the school and from outside groups including Ballet Rambert and Culture Shift. College pupils and those from other schools reap the benefits of collaborations with such organisations. A new day-girl house

(Arnold) opened September 2014. The College is currently working towards a game-changing development to be completed in celebration of the 150th anniversary of its founding which falls in 2017. This development will include a new dining hall, a classroom block and a new sports centre.

Activities. A wide variety of activities are undertaken as part of the junior school programme and numerous and diverse clubs and societies flourish throughout the school. All pupils are encouraged to do something well and standards in art, drama, dance and music are all high. The Birley Centre (opened in September 2011) provides state-of-the-art facilities for the performing arts. The school has three other theatres: Big School Theatre, the Le Brocq Studio and the Dell Theatre for outdoor productions. The CCF, Duke of Edinburgh's Award Scheme and S@S (Service at School) all offer opportunity for leadership, initiative testing and service to the community. There are regular College expeditions abroad while a wide range of other outdoor activities thrive on the Sussex "Sunshine Coast".

Admission. Boys and girls are generally admitted between the ages of 13 and 14 years in Year 9 or for the Sixth Form in Year 12 after GCSE examinations. A prospectus and application form may be obtained from the Admissions Officer. The website contains more information and parents and prospective pupils who wish to visit the school are welcomed. Early registration for a place is recommended, preferably a year in advance; a registration fee (£75) is charged and places are confirmed with a guaranteed place deposit (£750 for UK; a term's fees for overseas) within a year of entry. All pupils start in September, although exceptional cases are occasionally considered at other times.

Scholarships and Bursaries. At 13+, academic, art, drama, music and sports scholarships are offered. In line with most top independent schools, the great majority of awards given at the College are between 5% and 20% of the day or boarding fees but more may be offered in exceptional circumstances (up to a maximum of 50%). Applicants must be under 14 on 1 September in the year they are due to enter the College. At 16+, academic scholarships (including the Scoresby-Jackson Science Award and the Bernard Drake Award), art, drama, design and technology, music, and sports scholarships are offered to pupils who join the school in Year 12 after GCSEs. A 10% boarding discount is available to HM Forces and Diplomatic Service families.

Bursaries are awarded in appropriate circumstances. All are means tested according to the Charity Commission criteria.

Entry forms for scholarships can be obtained from The Registrar.

Fees per term (2014–2015). Boarding: £10,295 (Years 9–11), £10,410 (Sixth Form); Day £6,745 (Years 9–11), £6,860 (Sixth Form). An additional supplement for overseas pupils of £150 per term applies. Fees include meals and most extras.

Preparatory School. The charitable bodies governing Eastbourne College and the independent prep school, St Andrew's, amalgamated in February 2010 to become one charity. Collaboration between the two schools had always been extremely close but, until then, there had been no formal financial or governance links between them. This was a change of governance and not of the school. The schools continue to operate independently and St Andrew's prepares boys and girls for a variety of schools including the College.

The **Eastbournian Society** brings together all those with a College connection: parents of current and former pupils, current and former staff, Old Eastbournians, friends, neighbours and local businesses. In particular, strong links are maintained with former pupils who offer careers assistance to current pupils (there is a convention every year to support the careers and higher education programme). The Society provides a series of social events and career and business networking opportunities. It comprises also the College's fundraising activity, providing funds for bursaries and new developments.

The **Devonshire Society** (legacy club) meets annually.

Charitable status. Eastbourne College Incorporated is a Registered Charity, number 307071. It exists for the purpose of educating children.

The Edinburgh Academy

42 Henderson Row, Edinburgh EH3 5BL
Tel: 0131 556 4603
            0131 624 4987 (Admissions)
Fax: 0131 624 4990
email: enquiries@edinburghacademy.org.uk
            admissions@edinburghacademy.org.uk
website: www.edinburghacademy.org.uk

The Edinburgh Academy is a co-educational day school for pupils aged 3 to 18 with a proud history and outward vision. Founded in 1824 with the aspiration to create a school where excellence could always be achieved, leading to the School motto of 'Always Excel', it carries forward strong traditions whilst also constantly striving to innovate.

Court of Directors:

Chairman: M W Gregson, MBA, BSc (*Chair EA Foundation*)

Extraordinary Directors:
Lord Cameron of Lochbroom, PC, FRSE
Professor J P Percy, CBE, LLD, CA
J H W Fairweather, MA
S A Mackintosh, MA, LLB, WS

Elected Directors:
B E Beveridge, LLB, Dip LP, NP
A M Duncan, MA, BPhil, Dip Ed, FEA
Dr A E Gebbie, MB ChB, FRCOG, FFSRH, DCH
C S Gillies, LLB, ACA, MBA
Dr B A Hacking, MA Hons, D Clin Psychol
G T Hartop
Dr A Huntingdon, BA, PhD, FSI
M McNeill, LLB, LLM, Dip LP
P H Miller, BLE, MRICS
C C R Robertson, MA
Sheriff Principal CAL Scott, QC
J F Smith, MA Hons, BSc Hons
L M Watson, Ace, MEd
S J M Whitley, MA
V Skene, MCIPD
R Karling, MA, MBA

Co-opted Members:
The Rector
The Senior Deputy Rector
The Headteacher of Junior School

Bursar and Clerk to the Court:
G G Cartwright, MA CA

Rector: M G Longmore, MA, FRSA

Senior Deputy Rector: Mrs D K Birrell, BSc Hons
Deputy Rector (Director of Studies): Dr R Wightman, BSc, PhD
Deputy Rector (Pastoral and Personnel): M Bryce, BSc

Head of Sixth Form: Mrs F B Slavin, MA

Senior School Staff:

Heads of Departments:
Art: D L Prosser, BA
Biology: A W MacPherson, BSc, MSc, PhD
Business Studies/Economics: W J Turkington, BA

Careers: Mrs Y D Harley
Chemistry: Dr J R Coutts, BSc, DPhil
Classics: A K Tart, MA
Computing: D G Stewart, BSc
Design & Technology: Miss S M Hennessy, BA, MA
Drama: Miss G D M Henderson, BA
English: J R Meadows, BA
Geography: Dr D J Carr, BSc, PhD
History, Politics and Modern Studies: J Lisher, BA Hons
Mathematics: C A Brookman, BSc, PhD, GRSC, MInstP
Modern Languages: Mrs T J Irving, MA
Music: P N Coad, MA, PhD, FRCO (*Director*)
Physical Education: M J de G Allingham, MSc
Curriculum PE: M E Appleson, BA
Physics: N Armstrong, MA, CPhys, MInstP
Religious Education: H Jarrold, M Theol
Support for Learning: Mr C Gerrard

Librarian: Mrs S Phillips

Junior School Staff:
Headteacher: G Calder, MA
Deputy Head: Mrs L Htet-Khin, LLB Hons

Assistant Heads:
Mrs L A Paterson, DCE, INSC (*Head of Early Years*)
Mrs B Robertson, BEd, DPSE (*Head of Middle Primary*)
P Bertolotto, BEd Hons, PGCE (*Head of Upper Primary*)

Admissions Registrar: Mrs J Murray Brown

The Edinburgh Academy consists of a Senior School of 534 pupils (ages 11–18), a Junior School of 374 pupils (ages 4–11) and a Nursery Department of 98 pupils. The School's size allows us to cater for the individual needs and ambitions of each child whilst high staff ratios allow us to tailor the teaching and pastoral care to the needs of each pupil, giving them the best possible chance to develop their unique talents. Through a rounded education, Academy pupils enhance their social, emotional and spiritual capacities, equipping them for citizenship in a challenging and changing world.

Campus. The Senior School is situated in the heart of Edinburgh's New Town and is a stunning architectural blend of traditional and modern buildings. The most recent additions have been the purpose-built Science Centre and Performing Arts Centre. Significant investment will continue to ensure the best of facilities for our pupils.

The Junior School, Nursery and Playing Fields are on Arboretum Road next to the renowned Royal Botanic Gardens. The recently opened McTavish Wing at the Junior School has created a new library, learning resource centre and four additional classrooms while the purpose built Nursery provides a bright, functional and fun environment with play areas, sensory gardens, Nursery allotments and Forest School outdoor classroom.

Academic. The Academy has an ambitious programme of a mixed economy of exams, using both English and Scottish Examination Boards. The curriculum is designed to provide challenge and progression as pupils move up the school. At each successive stage we seek to build on previous foundations, developing new skills and knowledge.

As the pupils move through these stages, the number of subjects studied decreases and the course become increasingly specialised in nature. In the Sixths and Sevenths, pupils have the flexibility to choose to study for Scottish Highers, Advanced Highers or English A Levels, meaning every pupil can find the programme that best suits their needs and targets beyond school.

Class Sizes. We keep our class sizes small to allow teachers to identify and nurture each child's strengths. In the Junior School class sizes are 20 (P1–P3) and 22 (P4–P6). In the Senior School, no teaching group is larger than 24 pupils, and most are substantially smaller.

Courses of Study. A wide range of courses, following the Curriculum for Excellence, is followed with French introduced in Nursery, Mandarin in P5, and then German or Spanish in the second year of Senior School.

Eight subjects are taken for GCSE and again balance across a range of subjects is recommended. English, Maths, a foreign language and a science must be taken and we recommend that pupils complete the balance by adding either History or Geography, and one of Art, Music, Drama, PE or a technical subject.

In the final years of the Senior School the emphasis moves increasingly towards preparing young people for higher education and working life, and there is a choice between breadth (with Scottish Highers) and depth (with Advanced Highers). In the majority of subjects pupils can study for Highers in the Sixths and move on to Advanced Highers in Sevenths. The direct two-year A Level course is offered in Art and Music, where we feel the A Level course is better suited to the needs of our pupils.

Physical Education. The Academy has over 25 acres of sports pitches, squash, tennis and fives courts, a running track and two full sized all weather pitches and a sports centre. All Academy pupils are encouraged to stay active and healthy, and we provide top-class coaching and facilities to help them enjoy their chosen sports. Pupils can choose from full range of winter and summer sports and teams represent the School in rugby, hockey, football, cricket, tennis, squash, badminton, fives, athletics, skiing, shooting, golf, shooting, sailing, swimming, basketball, netball and dance.

Music, Drama, Art. The Creative Arts are an important part of Edinburgh Academy life and pupils are encouraged to take part from Junior School and beyond. Many pupils learn a musical instrument, are involved with the dramatic productions each year or are members of the various choirs, orchestras, bands and ensembles.

In Art, a large number of pupils take the A Level and the success rate for being accepted into Art College is very high. A number of students join the Academy each year with their primary objective being to study Fine Art with the teachers here and in Design and Technology there is a fully furnished Jewellery Studio. At the end of each year there is a major exhibition in these subjects where pupils work is displayed and even sold.

Extra-Curricular. The Academy also recognises that learning takes place outside the formal classroom and we believe in a balance to academic and co-curricular activities, offering a wide range of opportunities to participate and represent the Academy in sport, music and a variety of expressive and creative arts.

There is an extremely broad range of extra-curricular activities available including Debating, Photography, Computing, Model United Nations, Modern Languages, Jazz, Politics, Scripture Union, Film Club, Bridge, Chess, CCF, Eco Group and many, many more.

Combined Cadet Force and The Duke of Edinburgh's Award Scheme. All pupils over the age of 14 must participate in either the CCF (Army, RAF or Pipe Band sections) or The Duke of Edinburgh's Award Scheme for a period of three terms after which time participation is voluntary. The CCF sections offer pupils training in field craft, weapons handling, orienteering, drill and first aid and affords young people the opportunity to develop their leadership potential.

Fees per term (2014–2015). Nursery £1,603–£2,514. Junior School P1–P6 £2,472–£3,076. Senior School: £3,353 (Geits), £4,164 (2nds–7ths).

When 3 or more siblings are in attendance at the School at the same time, a reduction of one-third of the tuition fees is made for each sibling after the first two.

Scholarships and Bursaries. At key stages from 11+, means-tested Bursaries of up to 100% of fees are offered to pupils who are most able to benefit from an Edinburgh Academy education, irrespective of financial means.

A number of Scholarships are offered from age 11 to candidates of very high ability either academically or in Art, Music or Sport. Examinations and assessments are held in January.

Admissions. The majority of new pupils are admitted at the beginning of the Autumn Term in late August, although they can be accepted at any time places are available. All candidates for admission to the Edinburgh Academy must first be assessed by the School and assessment days are held in January, although The Academy is always delighted to welcome families outwith this time. Initial enquiries should be made to the Admissions Department on 0131 624 4987 or by email to admissions@edinburghacademy.org.uk.

Edinburgh Academical Club. There is a strong former pupil community and the Club work hard to remain in contact with former pupils all over the world. They host events each year, both from a social and career perspective, and have established a career mentoring and internship service to help former pupils, no matter what stage in their career they are at. Contact: Ms Eve Macdonald, Tel: 0131 624 4958, email: accies@edinburghacademy.org.uk.

Charitable Status. The Edinburgh Academy is a Registered Charity, number SC016999. It exists for the advancement of education and the contribution to the educational life of Scotland in its widest sense.

Mrs E J Chamberlain, BSc, MEd	D R L Inderwick, BA, MA
Miss K F Conroy, BA	J Krishna, BSc
G S Cousens, BA	T C Le Lacheur, MPhys
P G Davis, BSc	Miss P S Le Poidevin, BA
R M Davis, BA	S R Le Prevost, BA, ARCM
A T Debney, BSc	R G Le Sauvage, BSc
Miss A C M Demongeot, BA, MA	Mrs S Lee, Mgr
T R de Putron, BSc	D R Loweth, MA, MEd
Mrs J-A Dittmar, BSc	A B Lumley, BA
T P Edge, BA, MA	Mrs H M Mauger, BA
T P Eisenhuth, BPhysEd	R A Morris, BA
Miss J Flood, BA, MA	S G D Morris, BSc
M Garnett, BA	Mrs P J Read, MSci, MA
Mrs N M Gava, BA	Miss M Schofield, BA
A J Good, BSc	Mrs K M Shaw, BA
Mrs M E Gordon, MA	Miss H Shepherd, MChem
M N Heaume, BSc	T C Slann, Dip NEBSS
D S Herschel, BSc	M A G Stephens, BA
L Hudson, BA	S S Tansey, BA
S J Huxtable, MA	E H A Vincent, BA

Chaplain: The Revd Dr R G Harnish, BSc, MA
Director of Music: Miss E D Willcocks, BMus, MA
Games and Physical Education: D Wray, BEd

Head of the Junior School: J E Walton, BA
Prep:
Deputy Head Pastoral: Mrs E Bott, BEd
Deputy Head Academic: Miss E J Brooker, BSc

Mrs M Boyle, BSc	R Sutton, BA
Mrs S Crittell, BA	C Veron, BEd
Mrs D Dowding, BA	
Mrs M Kinder, CertEd	*Pre-Prep:*
Mrs K Le Guilcher, CertEd	*Deputy Head:* Mrs J Atkinson, BEd
Mrs O McEwan, BA	
Mrs D M McLaughlin, BSc	Mrs C Bowden, BEd
Mrs E Parkes, BEd	Mrs J Chauhan, BA
Mrs A M Pollard, BEd	Miss C Gillman, BA Ed
Mrs K Reed, BA	Mrs E Jones, BA Ed
P Sargent, BA	Miss G Smith, BA
Mrs N Stevens, BEd	Miss L Wadley, BA Ed

Bursar and Clerk to the Directors: M F Spiller, MSc, BSSc, FCILT

Elizabeth College

The Grange, St Peter Port, Guernsey, Channel Islands GY1 2PY

Tel:	01481 726544
Fax:	01481 714839
email:	office@elizabethcollege.gg
website:	www.elizabethcollege.gg
Twitter:	@Eliz_Coll

Motto: *Semper Eadem*

Elizabeth College was founded in 1563 by Queen Elizabeth I in order to provide education for boys seeking ordination in the Church of England. It is one of the original members of HMC and has Direct Grant status. It provides a broad education while maintaining the Christian aspirations of its Foundress. There are approximately 790 pupils in the College, of whom about 280 are in the Junior School. Girls are accepted into the Junior School. The Sixth Form is mixed through a partnership with nearby Ladies' College.

Visitor: The Assistant Bishop of Winchester

Directors:
R Clark (*Acting Chairman*)
A H Langlois
J D Perkins
D G Le Marquand
D E Preston
M R Buchanan
Mrs A-M Collivet
K Roberts

Principal: G J Hartley, MA Cantab, MSc

Vice-Principal (Academic): R J W James, BA
Vice-Principal (Pastoral): J M Shaw, BA, MA
Assistant Principal (Sixth Form): C R W Cottam, MA, CT ABRSM
Assistant Principal (Pupil Progress and Inspection Compliance): Mrs P E Cross, BA, ARCM

Members of Teaching Staff:

D A Akam, BSc	Mrs C S Buchanan, BA
B E H Aplin, BSc	M A M Buchanan, BA
Dr A S Bargery, MESci	Mrs M Campbell, BA, MA
A M Brown, BA, MA	A P Carey, BA, MA

Buildings and Grounds. The Upper School (for pupils over 11 years) is situated in imposing buildings dating from 1829 which stand on a hill overlooking the town and harbour of St Peter Port. The classrooms and laboratories, all of which are equipped with appropriate modern teaching aids, the Hall, Sports Hall and Swimming Pool are accommodated on this site. Improvements in recent years have included a new Refectory, Performing Arts Suite and an additional classroom at the Junior School. Six new Mathematics classrooms were opened at the start of Michaelmas Term 2014. There are two large games fields, one of which includes an artificial pitch for hockey. Elizabeth College Junior School comprises Beechwood, a prep school, and Acorn House, a pre-prep and nursery school. The Junior School has its own site some ten minutes' walk from Elizabeth College. It takes boys and girls from 7 to 11 years old. Acorn House accepts boys and girls from 4 to 7 years old and also has a pre-school facility for younger children.

Academic Curriculum. In their first three years in the Upper School boys follow a broad curriculum which is common to all – covering arts, sciences, creative and practical subjects. Information Technology is timetabled in all three years to develop the skills needed for the demands of GCSE and A Level courses. Opportunity is also afforded to boys to sample both Latin and a second Modern Foreign Language in addition to French. PSHE, RS, PE, Games and Drama are timetabled throughout. In Years 10 and 11 the aim is to produce a high level of achievement and choice at GCSE by offering flexibility wherever possible. Three separate sciences or Core and Additional Science are studied. At least one modern language should be taken, although two are available as an option. English Literature is studied within the English teaching groups, but is not compulsory for all. Other GCSE options combine the traditional with the contemporary. Art, Business Studies, Ancient History, Drama, Graphics or Resistant Materials, History, Latin, Music, and PE are currently offered. Alongside the GCSE courses PSHE and PE continue to be taught. The Sixth Form is run in partnership with The Ladies' College, with interchange of pupils between schools and shared teaching of many groups. The Sixth Form offers a very broad array of subjects across the two schools enabling a wide variety of choices, with subjects ranging from the traditional to the new and now including Computing. Tutorial periods enable vocational, careers and pastoral guidance to be available.

Music. There is a lively extra-curricular music programme which includes the College Orchestra, Wind Ensemble and Brass Jazz Band, with numerous small ensembles running alongside these larger groups. There is a variety of choral groups, with the College choir making regular visits to the French mainland to sing in Cathedrals and at concerts. Individual instruction is available in instrumental and vocal studies, catering for a wide range of interests including piano, organ and traditional orchestral studies as well as contemporary and jazz styles. The Junior School has its own choirs, orchestra, recorder group and steel pan band. Each summer holiday the College hosts a week-long orchestral course when tuition is provided by eminent professionals to over two hundred and fifty boys and girls drawn from the islands, the mainland and other parts of Europe.

Games. The sports fields cover some 20 acres. The Junior School has its own small playing field, and also has access to the facilities of the Upper School. The major College games are Association Football, Hockey and Cricket. Athletics, Badminton, Basketball, Cross-country Running, Fencing, Golf, Rugby Football, Sailing, Shooting, Squash and Swimming also flourish. Physical Education forms a regular part of the curriculum for all boys up to the end of Year 11. Some seniors specialise in Outdoor Pursuits as their "sport". This is under the guidance of a fully qualified expert. Despite the size of the Island, plentiful opposition is available. The College competes against other Island schools, has a traditional rivalry with Victoria College in Jersey, makes regular tours to the mainland and hosts return visits from UK schools.

Combined Cadet Force. This is voluntary and optional from Year 10, and is Tri-Service. Cadets travel regularly to the UK and beyond for proficiency training, camps, courses, qualifications and competitions, as well as adventurous training. Competition shooting forms a major part of the CCF and there is a long and distinguished record at Bisley. The CCF has an important role in providing Guards of Honour for Island ceremonial occasions.

Duke of Edinburgh's Award. Boys are encouraged to participate in this scheme. Both Bronze and Gold Awards are offered as extra-curricular activities. Bronze expedition work takes place locally in the Channel Islands whilst the expedition work necessary for the Gold Award takes place on the mainland during the Easter and Summer holidays.

Community Service Unit. This Unit draws boys from Year 10 and above. It serves those in need and those who are handicapped throughout the Island community.

Scouts. There is an active Scout Group, whose headquarters are situated on the College Field. At the Junior School there is a Cub Scout Group.

Clubs and Societies. The College stresses the importance of extra-curricular activity. Among currently active clubs are those which foster Art, Bell Ringing, Chess, Circus Skills, Climbing, Coding, Debating, Fencing, Life Saving, Model Railways, Sailing, Shooting and Squash.

Pastoral Care. In the Upper School each year has a Head of Year assisted by four Tutors. Acorn and Beechwood have Form Tutors. All these staff provide pastoral care and academic guidance for their own sections of the College. They are supported by a full-time Chaplain who conducts services in all three schools as well as preparing boys for Confirmation.

Parental Involvement. Parents are strongly encouraged to take an active part in their child's education. There are regular assessments and reports, parents' evenings, pastoral information evenings and parent workshops. Heads of Year keep in regular contact with parents through newsletters and email. The Heads of Year and pupils' tutors are always available to meet with parents to discuss any concerns.

Admission. The principal ages for admission into the school are 4, 7, 11, 13 and 16, but there are usually vacancies for entry at other ages. Entry is by means of tests and/or interview which are adapted to the age of the applicant. There is a £110 non-refundable registration fee. Applications for entry should be addressed to the Principal.

Scholarships to the College. The Gibson Fleming Trust provides Scholarships for current pupils. The award value depends to some extent upon the needs of the applicant's parents. The Trustees review their Scholars each year.

Choral and Instrumental Scholarships. The Gibson Fleming Trust provides Choral and Instrumental Scholarships to current pupils. Details of the scholarships may be obtained from the Principal.

Scholarships to the Universities. The College Exhibitions, Scholarships and Prizes include the Queen's Exhibition, the Lord de Sausmarez Exhibition, the Mainguy Scholarship, the Mansell Exhibition and the Mignot Fund. The Gibson Fleming Trust can also provide awards to its Scholars for their future education.

Travel. There are several flights each day from Southampton (half an hour), Gatwick (about three quarters of an hour) and Stansted (about one hour). There are also regular flights to the West Country and to Midlands and northern airports. There are frequent sailings to and from Portsmouth, Poole and Weymouth, which offer vehicle transportation.

Old Boys. The Honorary Secretary of the Old Elizabethan Association is James Ovenden who may be contacted via www.oea.org.gg.

Fees per term (2014–2015). Acorn House (Pre-Prep): £2,875; Beechwood (Prep): £3,215; Upper School (11–18): £3,205.

Ellesmere College
A Woodard School

Ellesmere, Shropshire SY12 9AB
Tel: 01691 622321
Fax: 01691 623286
email: hmsecretary@ellesmere.com
website: www.ellesmere.com
Twitter: @ellesmerecoll
Facebook: /EllesmereColl

Motto: '*Pro Patria Dimicans.*'

Ellesmere College is a fully co-educational school set in the beautiful English countryside. Founded in 1884, the school offers students between the ages of 7 to 18 the chance to achieve success in both their studies and a wide range of activities, including music, art, sport and drama, in a happy, friendly atmosphere. We prepare students for their GCSEs, A Levels and the International Baccalaureate as well as giving them the opportunity to enjoy a full and varied sports and social programme. Standing in its own stunning grounds covering more than 50 hectares, the school is conveniently located near the small, historic town of Ellesmere, and is less than 100 kilometres from both of England's second major cities, Manchester and Birmingham.

Founder: The Revd Nathaniel Woodard, DCL, then Dean of Manchester

Visitor: The Rt Revd The Lord Bishop of Lichfield

College Council:

D C Brewitt	C E Lillis
Mrs F M Christie	J A Mathias, FCA
The Reverend Canon B C Clover	A L Morris
	Mrs C S Newbold, BA
Mrs S Connor	Mrs R E Paterson
J S Hopkins	The Reverend M J Rylands
R A K Hoppins	M D T Sampson

Headmaster: B J Wignall, BA, MA, MCMI, FRSA

Deputy Head (*Pastoral*): Dr R Chatterjee, BSc, MSc, PhD, Cert SpLD
Deputy Head (*Academic*): Mrs S V Pritt-Roberts, BEd, MEd, NPQH
Head of Sixth Form: P A Wood, MA (*General Studies*)
Head of Middle School: Dr T Gareh BSc, MSc, PhD, CSci, CChem, MRSC
Head of Lower School: Mrs S Owen, BEd
Director of Activities: Mrs D Joynson-Brooke, BEd
Chaplain: The Revd David Slim, MEd
Director of Finance: N Haworth, ACMA, BA
Director of Operations: M McCarthy, BSc, DMS

Teachers:
* *Head of Department*
† *Housemaster/mistress*

Ms S M Abbots, MA
Ms C Allen, BA (*EAL*)
†J J Baggaley, BA
Mrs S J Bogue, BSc
M P Clewlow, BSc
M Coats, BSc Hons (*Information Technology*)
Dr J K Collins, BSc PhD
T Coupe (*Music*)
J H Cowley, BSc, NPQH (*Mathematics*)
D W Crawford, MA, MSc, MPhil
Miss A C Darrant, BSc (*Physics*)
Mrs H L Davenport, BSc (*Physical Education*)
T Davidson (*English*)
C R Davies, BA
Mrs J M Davies, BA
†Mrs J K Evans, BA
Mrs V Hart, MA
P J Hayes, MA
Miss G Heald, BA
Mrs J M Hibbott, BA
Mrs V M Howle, BEd, Cert SpLD, Dip RSA
Mrs M E Hutchings, MA, MA (*Media Studies*)
W J Hutchings, BEd
G Hutchinson, MA
Mrs D Joynson-Brooke, BEd
Miss E A Killen, BEd
Ms D Lensing, BA
G Macdonald, BSc
R J Macintosh, BSc
Miss J M Manion, BA, NPQH (*Support for Learning*)
†D J Morgan, BSc
Mrs S E Morgan, BEd
Miss R Morris, BSc
S B Mullock, BA (*Business Studies and Careers*)
A Murphy, BSc
Mrs J R Nicolson, MA
H B Orr, BD (*Religious Studies and Sociology*)
†G Owen, BEd
Mrs L A Paton, BA (*History & Classics*)
Mrs R Paul, BA

Mrs E Phillips, BSc
Mrs S Phillips, MA (*Art and Design Technology*)
R J Purnell, BSc
D M Roberts, BSc, MEd
†I Roberts
Ms R Schubert (*Director of Drama*)
P E Swainson, BSc (*Chemistry*)
Ms M J Tarrega, MA
Miss M Thomas, MA
Dr I G Tompkins, MA, BD, DPhil (*IB Coordinator*)
J Underhill, MA
Mrs R Waddams (*Geography*)
S Welti, LTA Club Coach
Mrs C Westwood, BA (*MFL*)
I L Williams, BEd

Registrar: Mrs D Smith

School Medical Officer: Dr E A M Greville, MBChB
Sanatorium Sisters:
Mrs J Slim, RGN
Mrs M Moore, RGN
Mrs M Haynes, SEN

The College Building. The main school building contains three boys' Boarding and Day Houses, as well as a mixed 10–12 junior Boarding and Day House, bachelor and married accommodation for Housemasters and Housemistresses and/or Assistant Housemasters and Housemistresses, the Chapel and the Dining Hall. St Luke's Boarding House completes the main quadrangle. A 13–16 girls' Boarding and Day house has its own wing in the main building and was opened in response to demand in 1996. The girls' Sixth Form Boarding and Day House which accommodates girls in a combination of shared and single study bedrooms and dayrooms was completed in 1986. A Gymnasium, Big School (Assembly Hall) which houses the Schulze Organ, and three subject Departments are also located in the main building. September 2004 saw the opening of the College's new Sports Hall, which adds to facilities that include two other gymnasia and squash courts.

Additional wings contain the Library and Sixth Form Centre. Other subjects are taught in their own Departmental blocks close to the main building, and include Science Laboratories, a Modern Languages Department with a Language Laboratory, an Art School, a Design & Technology Centre, and a Business Studies Department with its own computer suite. A purpose-built Lower School for Years 3–8 was opened in 1999.

The House System. The Lower School (ages 7–13) has a competitive system based on 3 Houses. The Senior School has a competitive system based on 4 Houses all of which are co-educational and combine boarding and day pupils. Separate from the competitive Houses is the residential House system for living arrangements. There are 2 Girls' Houses, catering for age 13–16 and Sixth Form respectively; there are 4 Boys' Houses: two for age 13–16 and two Sixth Form Houses; there is also a Mixed House catering for boarders of ages 10–12.

Curriculum. In the first year in the Senior School a full range of fourteen subjects is studied, including Art, Design and Technology, Computing and Technical Drawing. This curriculum is designed to give all pupils a comprehensive introduction before reducing to a basic eight subjects for GCSE. At GCSE all pupils take English, Mathematics, and either Dual Award Science or the three Sciences studied separately. Other subjects depend on individual aptitude and choice.

In the Sixth Form over 20 different academic subjects are available for study to A Level or IB Diploma to prepare for University Entrance or entry to the Services and the Professions.

Music. The College has a very strong musical tradition. It possesses two of the finest organs in the country, including the internationally renowned St Mary Tyne Dock Schulze Organ. The Chapel Choir has a wide repertoire of Church Music. There is a Big Band, a Choral Society, a Jazz Group and other ensembles, all of which give regular concerts. There are House Music Competitions every year.

An annual programme of Celebrity Concerts brings distinguished musicians to the College.

The Music School is part of the College Arts Centre which provides first-class facilities, including 8 Practice Rooms, a Recording Studio, Teaching Rooms and a Studio Theatre designed for small concerts and seating 220 people.

The department has 2 full-time and 16 part-time teachers.

Arts Centre. This purpose-built complex was opened in 1976 for Drama, Dance, Film, Music and Art Exhibitions. A programme is organised in which international artists in all these fields visit the Centre, which shares its facilities with the local community.

Careers. At all levels pupils are encouraged to seek advice from the College careers masters and mistresses as well as representatives from the Independent Schools Careers Organisation. The ISCO aptitude tests are available for all pupils in their GCSE level year. A Careers' Convention is held each year for pupils in Year 11.

Games and Physical Education. Ellesmere has a long tradition of sporting excellence particularly in rugby and tennis. The sporting excellence is supported by the Rugby Academy programme (3 leavers turned professional in 2008), the Tennis Academy, and the joint College and Community Ellesmere College Titans Swimming Team. The Cricket Academy was launched in 2009 and the Shooting Academy in 2010.

All members of the School are required to participate in a regular programme of games, though particular inclinations and aptitudes are taken fully into consideration. Facilities include a sports hall, a floodlit multi-sports area, a fitness centre, squash courts, a heated indoor swimming pool, indoor and outdoor shooting range, a gymnasium, 6 floodlit all-weather tennis courts, a golf course, rugby pitches, all-weather hockey pitches, cricket squares, and an athletics track. Ellesmere has a long tradition of sporting excellence, particularly in rugby and tennis.

Ellesmere is superbly placed for outdoor pursuits. Easily accessible lakes, rivers and hills provide opportunities to develop talents and interests.

Sailing takes place on Whitemere. The School owns six boats and pupils are allowed to bring their own craft. Canoeing takes place on the Ellesmere canal and on local rivers such as the Dee and the Severn.

All pupils are expected to join one of the following: Outdoor Training Unit; CCF; Social Service. These activities occur on one full afternoon a week, but, in order to extend their activities, twice a year 3 days are set aside when all members of the School participate in 48-hour expeditions. In the Lent Term a single day is devoted to expeditions.

Admission. Boys and girls are admitted at all points of entry into the school. Entrance examinations are held in February for Lower School entry. Scholarships for Prep School candidates are held in May, while others take the Common Entrance Examination in June.

Scholarships and Bursaries. A wide range of Awards recognising a range of talents is available:

Academic: Available at 8+, 9+, 11+, 13+ and 16+ entry worth up to a maximum of 50% fee remission.

All-Rounder: Available at 11+, 13+ and 16+ entry worth up to a maximum of 25% fee remission.

Art: Available at 13+ and 16+ entry worth up to a maximum of 25% fee remission.

Drama: Available at 13+ and 16+ entry worth up to a maximum of 25% fee remission.

Music: Available at 8+, 9+, 11+, 13+ and 16+ entry. Scholarships are worth up to a maximum of 50% fee reduction and free tuition in two instruments. Exhibitions are

worth up to a maximum of 25% fee reduction and free tuition in one instrument.

The *Schulze Organ Award* is reserved for Sixth Form candidates and is valued at 50% of fees.

Sports: Available at 13+ and 16+ entry and may be worth up to a maximum of 50% fee remission. (Awards below Sixth Form level are unlikely to exceed 25% fee reduction.)

In cases of need, all awards may be supplemented by means-tested bursaries.

There are reduced fees for children of the Clergy. Foundation and Regional awards are available for children of parents of limited means.

Fees per term (2014–2015). Upper School: Boarders £9,717, Weekly Boarders £7,230, Day £5,598. Lower School: Boarders £7,773, Weekly Boarders £7,032, Day £3,417–£3,927. Fees are inclusive of general School charges.

Music lessons are given at a charge of £262 for ten lessons and individual tuition for dyslexic pupils also incurs an extra cost. A scheme of insurance is in force under which the School Fees may be insured for a small termly premium for any number of years and which enables a pupil to remain at Ellesmere to complete his/her education free of all board and tuition fees, if a parent dies before the pupil's School career is ended. There is also a School Fees Remission Scheme for insurance of fees in cases of absence through illness and of surgical and medical expenses. Arrangement can be made for a single advance payment of fees.

'Old Boys and Girls'. Former pupils of the school normally become members of the Old Ellesmerian Club, which in turn enables them to take part in a number of societies and activities. For further information contact: Nick Pettingale, Director of Development, Ellesmere College, Ellesmere, Shropshire, SY12 9AB.

Charitable status. Ellesmere College is a Registered Charity, number 1103049. It exists to provide education for children.

Eltham College

Grove Park Road, London SE9 4QF

Tel:	020 8857 1455
Fax:	020 8857 1913
email:	mail@eltham-college.org.uk
website:	www.eltham-college.org.uk
Twitter:	@ElthamHead
Facebook:	/ElthamCollegeOfficial
LinkedIn:	/Ole Elthamians

Founded originally for the education of the sons of missionaries, Eltham College is an independent day school for 830 boys aged 7 to 18 with a co-educational Sixth Form. An academically selective school, its aim is to provide a balanced and stimulating education based on Christian principles and practice. An education at Eltham College stresses the Christian values upon which the school is founded to shape and build character, and individuals who can take their place in society.

Eltham College is an academically rigorous school where every pupil is known individually throughout their time here. Teachers inspire and motivate students to discover new passions and to develop their talents. It is committed to academic achievement of the highest standards, but its yardstick is always the individual's potential. Students are encouraged to perform at their highest level both academically and in the breadth of school life. In the range of activities here, from sport, through outdoor pursuits, to our justly celebrated music, art and drama, there is scope for everyone to realize that potential.

Governors:
The Governing Body comprises the Chairman and Vice Chair, ten Trust Governors and eight Nominated Governors representing the Baptist Missionary Society, the Council for World Mission, the United Reformed Church, the London Boroughs of Bexley and Bromley, the Parents (two representatives elected by the parental body) and the Staff Common Room (one representative elected by the Teaching staff).

Chairman of the Board: S Wells, RIBA

Headmaster: G R Sanderson, MA Oxon, FRSA

Deputy Head – Academic: L Watts, BSc
Deputy Head – Pupils: D J Cooper, BSc, MA
Bursar: M Darlington, BSc
Development Director: S J McGrahan, MSc

Academic Staff:
J Baldwin, BSc (*Mathematics*)
J L Batty, BSc (*Geology*)
A D Beattie, MA (*Geography*)
Mrs N Bilsby, BSc (*Head of Mathematics, Assistant Head of Sixth Form – Girls*)
Mr R D Booth, MEng (*Chemistry*)
D Boudon, L-ès-L (*French, Head of Community Service*)
D J Boydell, MSc (*Head of D & T*)
Ms E R Brass, BA, MA (*Director of Art*)
V Broncz, BSc (*Mathematics*)
J P Chesterton, BSc (*Head of Geography*)
J P Crowley, BEng (*Mathematics*)
M E R Chesterton, BA (*History*)
D K Cotterill, BSc (*Registrar, Geography*)
Mrs A C Dickinson, BA (*English*)
Ms S Dunne, BA (*Spanish, French*)
Mrs K Evans, BSc (*Economics and Business Studies*)
Mr M E Gennari, BSc (*Design and Technology*)
Miss R Gordon, BSc (*Mathematics, Head of Teaching and Learning*)
D R Grinstead, BA (*Head of History*)
M Hamblin, BA (*English*)
Ms E G Haste, BA (*Head of Religious Studies*)
Dr J N Hill, BSc (*Chemistry*)
Mrs C M Hobbs, BSc (*Head of Biology*)
T A Hotham, BA (*Head of Classics*)
P A Howls, BA (*French, German, Russian*)
Mr K A Hughes, BA (*Music*)
Mr R D Jukes, BA (*Physics*)
N A Levy, GGSM, Cert Mgmt (*Music*)
M M MacKenzie, BSc (*Head of Physics*)
P J Mander, BA (*Head of Sixth Form, Politics, History*)
Dr S M McClellan, BA, MSc (*English*)
N W Miller, BSc (*Head of PE*)
N R Miller, BA (*Musician-in-Residence*)
S G Milne, MA (*Head of Economics & Business Studies, Deputy Head of Sixth Form*)
T C Mitchell, BA (*Head of English, Drama*)
Dr F Morris, BSc (*Chemistry, Biology*)
Dr J Munn, MA, PhD (*Chief Examinations Officer, Mathematics*)
Ms F Nicolson (*Artist-in-Residence*)
Mrs L E Oldfield, BA (*Director of Music*)
P J Ormanczyk, BSc (*Biology*)
Ms J Perry, BSc (*Biology, Chemistry*)
B Pollard, MA (*Head of Modern Languages, German and French*)
J P Pringle, BSc (*Head of Computing*)
Mrs K Robinson, BA, MA (*Head of Drama*)
Mrs C M Roche, MA (*Librarian*)
Ms L U Scarantino, BA (*Head of French*)
Revd P Swaffield, BA (*Chaplain, Religious Studies*)
A Thomas, BEd (*Physical Education*)
S Thomson, BSc (*Physical Education*)
E T Thorogood, BSc (*Physical Education*)

D P Tuck, BA, MA (*Head of Politics, Head of Liberal Studies, History*)
M P Wearn, BA (*History*)
J A Willatt, BA (*Geography*)
P J Wren, TEng, BSc (*Design and Technology*)
E B Wright, MA (*Head of Data and Pupil Progress, Physics*)
P Zdarzil, LLM (*Director of IT Services*)

Part-time:
P D Agate, BA (*Sculpture and Ceramics*)
P G Cheshire, MA (*German, RS*)
Ms A M Classen (*German*)
Mrs H C Clough, BSc (*Biology*)
Ms R J Deluce, BA (*Drama*)
Mrs M Franklin, BA (*Art*)
Mrs C D Green, DipEd (*English*)
Miss M Mateos, BA (*Spanish*)
Mrs A McCullough, BA (*Mandarin*)
Mrs S Potter, BA (*Economics and Business Studies, Head of PSHE*)
Mrs A C E Richards, BA (*Art and Design*)
Miss I Sadler, BSc (*Spanish*)
Mrs A Senior, L-ès-L (*French*)
Mrs C W Shipp, BA, MA, CertSpLD, DipSpLD, AMBDA (*Learning Support*)
Miss M Su, BA (*Mandarin*)
Mrs C Taylor, BA (*Latin*)
Ms S Wood, BSc (*Mathematics*)
J Zablocki, BSc (*Chemistry*)

Junior School:

Master: E R Cavendish, MA
Deputy Master: P McIntyre, BA, MA, MSc
Director of Studies: Mrs L Evelyn-Rahr, BA Ed, MA

Mr M Alexander, BA
Mrs N Chamberlain, BA Ed
Mrs A Hallett, BA Ed
Miss M Johnson, BA
Miss L Kanellis, MA
M O'Dwyer, BEd
J Poole, BA Ed
W Schaper, BA Ed
Miss N Tutchings, BA Ed
Mrs L Wrafter, CertEd

Part-time:
D Boudon, L-ès-L
Mrs A McCullough, BA (*Mandarin*)
Mrs K Newham, Bed
Mrs J Smith, BSc
Miss M Su, BA (*Mandarin*)

Buildings and Grounds. The school sits in an oasis of almost 70 acres of playing fields, providing excellent facilities for the core sports of rugby, hockey and cricket with newly refurbished pavilions and a sport centre with swimming pool, conditioning room, dance studio and sports hall. The purpose-built Music School provides extensive teaching and practice facilities supporting the excellent music programme. The Performing Arts Centre is used for curricular drama, plays and concerts. In 2012, Gerald Moore Gallery for modern and contemporary art was opened and is used as a new centre for learning for both the school and wider community use. The students benefit from an extensive modern and bright library, providing huge amounts of resource which extends online to the virtual library and online resource links. Plans are being finalised for a new Sixth Form centre to further support the transition from school to university.

Curriculum. In the Lower and Middle School the curriculum is broad based and forms are composed of around 25 boys. There is some setting in languages and mathematics. In the Middle School boys normally take ten subjects for the

GCSE or IGCSE examinations, always including a range of both Arts and Science studies, before entering the Sixth Form in which they specialise in courses leading to the AS and A Level. Subjects available include Art, Biology, Business Studies, Chemistry, Design and Technology, Drama, Economics, English, French, Geography, Geology, German, History, Latin, Mathematics (Pure, Mechanics, Statistics and Further Mathematics), Music, Politics, Physical Education, Physics, Religious Studies and Spanish. On average, over the last four years, 80% of pupils have been successful in obtaining places at Oxford, Cambridge or other Russell Group universities.

Extra-Curricular. Great emphasis is placed on the non-examined or extra-curricular activities. **Sport** has three major games: rugby, hockey and cricket for boys, but many other sports are offered such as football, cross country, basketball, netball (for girls), swimming, tennis and athletics, as well as fencing, water polo and chess. **Music** excels in the school with over 25 different ensembles and choirs, and high-quality visiting music teachers: choral singing is a particular strength, and a music project providing free instrumental lessons to all Junior School pupils has set down excellent foundations for the future. **Drama** is part of the curriculum for all in Years 7–9, and productions at every age range (including musicals) are very popular. **Art** also runs many out-of-hours activities, including study trips abroad. There are many Clubs and Societies linked to subject disciplines, many of which are student led. The school's Travel Club oversees a large range of trips in the UK (DEAS expeditions, Geography and Geology field trips) and abroad (language exchanges, sports and music tours, adventure expeditions to Borneo, China, the Amazon and the Galapagos).

A proportion of the Sixth Form timetable is given to non-examined opportunities: Games, Community Service and Liberal Studies.

Admission. Boys are admitted by entrance examination to the Senior School at the age of 11 and a few places may be available at 13 and other ages. Sixth Form places are available by examination for both boys and girls.

Bursaries and Scholarships. As befits a school founded for the sons of missionaries and a former Direct Grant School, many pupils receive financial support to attend. Bursaries are available up to 100% of fees subject to ISBA confidential means test. Community Scholarships (for 11+ boys from the immediate neighbourhood) are assessed on financial need.

Scholarships of not more than 50% of fees are awarded on Academic performance at 11+, 13+ and 16+. Awards are also made for Music (11+, 13+ and 16+), Sport and Art (11+ and 16+), and Drama (16+ only). The Leverhulme Trust Scholarship is also available for Sixth Form entry.

Term of Entry. The School normally accepts pupils only for the beginning of the academic year in September but, if gaps in particular year groups occur, it is willing to interview and test at any point in the year with a view to immediate or subsequent entry.

Junior School. The Grange, a large house on the school estate has been converted and extended to accommodate about 200 day boys in classes of not more than 25. The form rooms are complemented with an Assembly Hall, Science Room, Music Room, and Art, Design and Technology Room. With an emphasis on English and Mathematics, the curriculum, which includes Mandarin as the main Modern Foreign Language along with French in Year 6, provides an excellent foundation. Extra-curricular activities (sport, music, drama, art, scouts and day and residential trips) ensure the boys are buzzing! The school is managed by its own Master who is responsible to the Headmaster. Admission is at the age of 7, though a small number of candidates are admitted at 8, and Junior School boys almost always qualify for admission to the Senior School at 11.

The School thus provides an opportunity for 11 years' uninterrupted education in healthy surroundings.

Junior School applications should be made to the Junior School Secretary.

Fees per term (2014–2015). Senior School £4,916; Junior School £4,340. Lunch: £245.

Charitable status. Eltham College is a Registered Charity, number 1058438. It exists to provide education for boys and girls.

Emanuel School

Battersea Rise, London SW11 1HS
Tel: 020 8870 4171
Fax: 020 8877 1424
email: enquiries@emanuel.org.uk
website: www.emanuel.org.uk

Motto: *Pour bien désirer*

The School was founded in Westminster by Lady Anne Dacre in 1594, and moved to its present site on the north side of Wandsworth Common in 1883 as one of the three schools of the United Westminster Schools Foundation.

Governing Body:

Chairman: F R Abbott, Esq, BA
Vice Chairman: C F Scott, Esq
B F W Baughan, Esq
Mrs S Chambers
Ms M A D'Mello, BSc, MSc
Dr F Lannon, MA, DPhil, LMH University of Oxford
M Jaigirder, Esq, MA
R Naylor, Esq
Mrs M M Parsons, MA
The Very Reverend V A Stock, OAM, AKC, FRSA
J G M Wates, Esq, CBE
Dr P Zutshi, MA, PhD, FSA, University of Cambridge

Clerk and Receiver: R W Blackwell, MA

Headmaster: M D Hanley-Browne, MA Oxon

Deputy Headmaster: J A Hardy, MA
Director of Studies: W M Rogers, BSc
Assistant Head, Registrar: J F W Benn, BA, MBA
Assistant Head, Co-Curricular: J P Layng, BSc, MCIEA, MSB
Assistant Head, Pastoral: Mrs S M Williams-Ryan, L-ès-L, MA
Assistant Head, Academic: Mrs J L Peters, MA Oxon
Head of the Lower School: S J Gregory, MA, ARCO
Head of Middle School: S P Andrews, BA
Head of Sixth Form: Ms K Bainbridge, MA
Senior Chaplain: Revd P M Hunt, MA, MTh

Teaching staff:
* Head of Department

R J Arnott, BA
A C Ball, BA (*DT*)
R Berlie, MA Cantab (*Humanities*)
E Braun, BEng
Mrs M E Brennand, MMath, ACA
Ms H Burnett, BA
Miss L Butler, BSc
Ms U S Casais, BA
Miss C R Cheers, BA
Miss L A Christie, BA
A E Clay, BA (*Music*)
S R L Clayton, MA Oxon (*History*)
Miss L C Cleveland, BTh Oxon, MTh
D Conington, BSc
Ms R Cottone, MA

C Csaky, BSc, MA Ed
Dr M Dancy, BSc, PhD
Mrs B M Dawson, BA (*Drama*)
J Dunley, BA
Ms C Easton, BA (*Classics*)
N Fazaluddin, BSc (*Mathematics*)
Miss L Fitzgibbon, BSc
H G Flower, BA
Miss C F Forrest, BA
Mrs V C Gill, BA
M Girvan, BSc
D Gundersen, PDip (*PE*)
T Gwynne, BSc
D C Hand, BA
Mrs G Hanlan, BSc (* *Chemistry*)
R Hardy, BA
Miss L Hayward, BA
M Healy, BSc (*Biology*)
Miss J O Henderson, BA
Miss L A Holden, BA
N D House, MA
M P Hughes, BA
Miss E Hunter, BSc
H Jackson, BA (*German*)
Miss J A Johnson, MA Oxon (*English*)
Miss A Jordon, BSc
Mrs G I Kazi-Fornari, BA
A F S Keddie, MA Oxon, ACIB
P King, BEd
Miss J O Knowles, BA Cantab
C O Labinjo, BSc
W Lai, BA, MEng
A J Leadbetter, BSc
Ms C Lepetre, Licence d'Anglais
Mrs R A Lewis, MA
Miss O Lopez, MA (*Geography*)
Miss S E MacMillan, BA (*Art*)
Miss H Malik, BSc
R R Marriott, MA
P McMahon, MA Cantab
Miss K Z Moore, BA
Mrs J Morrison-Bartlett, BSc (*Science, *Physics*)
N M Mullen, MA Cantab
N Nilsson, BA
S E O'Neill, MA Oxon (*Modern Languages, *French,
   German)
Miss S Potts, BMus
R Price, BSc
Dr B A Reynolds, BSc, PhD
Mrs N A Ridge, BA
S J Rowley, BA, MA
Mrs S Shaw, DipSpLD
R Skinner, BSc
M Swift, BA
R Tong, LLB (*Business Studies & Economics*)
D J Traynor, BSc
The Rev R F Walker, BSc, BD (*Chaplain*)
D J Walshe, BA
Miss H C Windsor, BA
Miss R Wills, BSc
Mrs G M Wright, BSc (*Psychology*)
Miss C Yeoman, BSc
Ms A Zaratiegui, MA (*Spanish*)

Visiting Music Teachers:
F Baird, Dip TCL, ARCM (*Percussion*)
Ms C Boushell, MMus, PG Dip, ArtDipOp, RCM (*Singing*)
A Brookshaw, MA Cantab, ARM, RCM (*Singing*)
Mrs Y Burova, BMus, GSMD (*Viola/Violin*)
W Cole, BMus, RAM (*Double Bass*)
F Crowther, BMus (*Jazz Piano*)
M Crowther, Dip GGSM (*Brass*)
Mrs P Crowther, Dip AGSM (*Brass*)
Ms L Easton, BA (*Singing*)

R B Harker, MA Cantab, MA RAM, LRSM (*Music
   Theory/Piano/Organ*)
Miss Harwood-White, BMus, PG Dip, DAAD Scholar,
   (*Oboe*)
Ms J Hayter, BMus RAM, LRAM, PG Dip RCM (*Bassoon,
   Flute, Clarinet*)
Ms K Lauder, BMus RNCM, PPRNCM (*French Horn/
   Piano*)
M Livingstone, BA (*Drums*)
J McCredie, MMus, BMus, CertEd (*Guitar*)
Ms A Mowat, BMus RAM, LRAM (*Cello*)
J Oldfield, MA Cantab, PG Dip RCM, ArtDipOp RCM
   (*Singing*)
G Philips, BMus GSMD (*Clarinet, Saxophone*)
Ms P Sharda (*Guitar*)
Dr F Tarli, MMus, PhD (*Piano*)
D Watts, BMus RNCM (*Flute*)

Librarian: T Jones, BA
Assistant Librarian: G J Dibden
Director of Finance and Administration: J E Sharp, MA,
   ACA
Development Officer: Miss E Symmonds, BA
Headmaster's Secretary: Mrs J Wood
Admissions Secretary: Ms D Shuttleworth

Emanuel is a fully co-educational day school. We have approximately 775 pupils, with about 180 in the Sixth Form.

Admission. Each September about 20 pupils are admitted at age ten, 90 pupils at age eleven and about 15 to 20 at age thirteen. There are also about 10 external candidates admitted into the Sixth Form each year.

Entry at age ten and eleven is by competitive examination, held at the school each year in January. Applications for 10+ and 13+ entry should be made before the middle of November of the preceding year. 11+ entry is capped at 600 registrations and this was reached by early July 2014 for 2015 entry, so early registration is a must.

Entry at age thirteen is by an Emanuel examination in January.

Entry to the Sixth Form is by interview and tests held in the November before entry. Unconditional or conditional offers may be made.

Prospective parents are warmly encouraged to visit the school and there are many opportunities to do so. Please see our website or telephone for details.

Fees per term (2014–2015). £5,468 covering tuition, some stationery, books and lunch. Extras charged are for individual instrumental tuition and some external visits and trips.

Site and Buildings. Emanuel was founded in 1594. In 1883 it moved from Westminster to the present site in Wandsworth. The original building is the core of the school, with most of its classrooms and a fine library and chapel. The first addition made was the new building of 1896, which now houses our concert hall and music rooms and the science laboratories. These have been completely refurbished in the last few years to a very high standard.

Over the last century many further additions have been made, including a large sixth form centre. The school's playing fields adjoin the school buildings together with a full-sized indoor swimming pool. Our facilities include fives courts and a sports hall. The new library and theatre are superb resources for the whole school. The school has a boathouse on the Thames by Barnes Bridge and further pitches on the A3 near Raynes Park.

Scholarships, Exhibitions and Bursaries. There are three types of scholarship at Emanuel: Foundation Scholarships (50% reduction in fees), Dacre Scholarships (25%) and Normal scholarships (10%).

All types of scholarship can be topped up using school bursaries to a maximum of 100% of the school fee, depending on financial need. It is also possible for a pupil to apply for and be awarded a scholarship in more than one category. Categories can be added together.

Academic scholarships are awarded at 10+, 11+ and 13+ on the basis of outstanding performance in the school entrance examinations held in January. At 16+ Academic scholarships are awarded to internal candidates on the basis of internal tests and to external candidates on the basis of their performance in the interviews and assessment tests.

Candidates applying for Music, Art, Drama and Sports scholarships must meet the general criteria for admission to Emanuel (eg reach the required standard in the academic entrance examinations) before a scholarship can be awarded. Thereafter each department has specific criteria for their scholarship requirements.

Exhibitions are awards of up to £500 on the basis of a pupil's high attainment in the entrance exams.

Bursaries are intended to help parents of pupils who can demonstrate financial need. Most bursaries are used to top up scholarships.

Full details of Scholarships, Exhibitions and Bursaries can be found on the School Website (www.emanuel.org.uk) or by contacting the Admissions Secretary.

Organisation. There is one form for pupils who join at age ten (Year 6). Pupils joining at age eleven (Year 7) are streamed by ability in five forms. Primary responsibility for their care rests with the form teacher and the head of year, under the overall supervision of the Head of the Lower School, who deals with Years 6, 7 and 8. As all pupils move from Year 9 into Year 10 there is a re-grouping along the lines of the subjects chosen for GCSE examinations. In the Sixth Form a tutor system operates.

Pupils are placed in houses when they join the school and they stay in these houses throughout their school career. Although originally intended as a means of fostering competition in games, these houses have developed over many years a strong community spirit.

For fuller details please ask for the school prospectus or go to the website (www.emanuel.org.uk).

Times. The normal school day runs from 8.30 am to 3.45 pm, but many activities extend into the late afternoon after school. Many school activities, especially games, also take place on Saturday mornings.

Curriculum. Pupils are prepared for the GCSE. There is a wide range of options with most pupils taking nine subjects.

Thereafter, in the Sixth Form, there is a further range of options from which pupils choose four AS Level subjects leading to examination at the end of the Lower Sixth. They can then choose to continue with all four or to take 3 through to A Level. The vast majority of Sixth Form leavers go on to university, art college or other forms of higher education.

Religious Education. There are two Chaplains who work in the school, whose general religious tenor is that of the Church of England. A daily service is held in the school chapel. Pupils in Years 6, 7, 8 and 9 receive one or two periods per week of religious education, which continues into Years 10, 11 and Sixth Forms as a GCSE or A Level option.

The Arts. Emanuel has a long-standing tradition of excellence in these areas and all pupils are encouraged to participate in one or more of these activities. The school has a chapel choir and a chamber choir, an orchestra and ensemble groups and a major musical production is presented each year.

There is a specialist suite of art rooms with facilities for all kinds of creative activity. A great deal of high quality work is displayed around the school and several pupils a year go on to foundation courses at art college.

Drama is taught throughout the school and there is a major school production every year, usually in the autumn term, with many smaller-scale events during the year. The Theatre has been rebuilt and opened in September 2013.

We have an annual arts festival in July with an art exhibition, summer serenade, performances by pupils and visitors and a series of talks by visiting speakers.

Games and Activities. At present cricket, rowing, rugby and athletics are the main school games for the boys. For the girls the main activities are netball, hockey, rowing, tennis, athletics, and swimming. Many other activities become available as a pupil moves up the school. Each pupil will have one games afternoon each week and other opportunities for physical education and swimming. The school has its own playing fields, sports hall, swimming pool, fives courts and boathouse on the Thames.

The Duke of Edinburgh's Award scheme is offered at all levels to pupils from Year 9 upwards. Community service is arranged for senior pupils and can involve hospital visiting or voluntary work in local primary schools, charity shops or our local hospice. More formal work experience is offered as part of an extensive careers and further education advice programme from Year 9 upwards. There is a very strong Young Enterprise programme in the Lower Sixth.

Careers. Careers and further education advice is readily available from an experienced team. There is an annual careers convention for the senior school when many representatives from the professions and commerce visit the school to talk about career options. All pupils become members of the Independent Schools Careers Organisation (included in the fees).

Old Emanuel Association. *Membership Secretary*: Mr R Udall, 43 Howard Road, Coulsdon, Surrey CR5 2EB.

Charitable status. Emanuel School (administered by the United Westminster Schools' Foundation) is a Registered Charity, number 309267. Its aims and objectives are for "the bringing up of children in virtue and good and laudable arts".

Epsom College

College Road, Epsom, Surrey KT17 4JQ
Tel: 01372 821004 (Headmaster)
           01372 821234 (Admissions Registrar)
           01372 821133 (Bursar)
Fax: 01372 821237
email: admissions@epsomcollege.org.uk
website: www.epsomcollege.org.uk

Motto: '*Deo non Fortuna*'.

Founded in 1855, Epsom College is situated in 84 acres of parkland estate close to Epsom Downs and 15 miles from central London. Epsom has become one of the most successful co-ed boarding and day schools for able all-round girls and boys aged 13–18. Almost all leavers go onto degree courses, especially at the research led universities, with historic strengths in Medicine, but now in all subjects. Art, music, drama and sport are very strong, with national representatives at Rugby, Netball, Hockey, Cricket, Golf and Target Rifle Shooting. Boarding is central to the College with over 380 boarders, many living within 25 miles; the House system ensures a strong sense of community and support. Academic results are high; 83% of A2 results at A* to B, with 54% at A*-A, 70% of all University places secured at Russell and 1994 Group Universities with 15% taking medicine from a stimulating Sixth Form curriculum of A Levels.

Patron: Her Most Gracious Majesty The Queen

President: Lord McColl, CBE, MS, FRCS, FACS

Visitor: The Right Reverend The Lord Bishop of Guildford

Governing Body:
Chairman: Dr A J Vallance-Owen, MBE, MBA, FRCS Edin

Vice Chairman: Dr A J Wells, MBBS, DRCOG, MRCGP
Treasurer: Ms S J Williams, MEng, FCA
Dr J Bolton, MA, MB BChir, FRCPsych
Mrs F Boulton, BSc, MA
Dr H H Bowen-Perkins, LMSSA, MRCS Eng, LRCP London, MBBS
Mr K Budge, MA Oxon
Mrs B Dolbear, LLB
Mr J A Hay
Dr S Lipscomb, MA Oxon, MSt Oxon, DPhil Oxon
Mr D Maunder, MA Oxon
Mr G B Pincus, MBE, MBA, MIPA
Mrs S Piper, BA, MA
Mr M A Ralf, MBA, CDir
Mrs K Thomas, BM Soton, FRCS Orth
Mr C Watson, ACA

Bursar and Clerk to the Governing Body: Mrs S E Teasdale, BSc London, ACA

Staff:

Headmaster: Mr J A Piggot, BA Cardiff, MA Liverpool

Deputy Head: Mr P J Williams, BSc Dunelm
Deputy Head Academic: Mr R J Alton, BSc Cantab
Assistant to Deputy Head Academic: Mrs T M Muller, MA Oxon

Director of Admissions: Mrs C Kent
Assistant Head – Senior Master: Mr A J Bustard, BA Swansea
Assistant Head – Teaching Staff: Dr M A L Tod, MA, PhD Glasgow, FSA Scot

Heads of Year:
Head of Sixth Form: Mr N Russell, MA Liverpool
Head of L6: Mr G R Watson, BA Cantab
Head of 5th Form: Mrs H E Keevil, BA Exeter
Head of U4: Mr M Zacharias, BA Dunelm
Head of Transition: Mrs F C Drinkall, BSc Loughborough

Director of Information Technology: Mr M Blahut, BSc Matej Bel, Slovakia
Head of Higher Education and Careers Guidance: Mrs R J B Harrop, BA Bristol
Personal and Social Development Coordinator: Mrs H E Keevil, BA Exeter
Activities Coordinator: Mr B G MacDowel, MTheol St Andrews

Housemasters/Housemistresses:

Carr (boys' day):
Mr L Matthews, BSc Exeter
Matron: Ruth Boyce

Crawfurd (girls' boarding):
Mrs H H Hynd, BA Nottingham, MA Dunelm, FRSA
Matron: Jill Ballinger

Fayrer (boys' boarding):
Mr S J Head, BSc West of England
Matron: Corinne Roy

Forest (boys' boarding):
Mr J F Stephens, BSc Liverpool
Matron: Yvette Tolson

Granville (boys' boarding):
Mr R C G Young, BSc Bath
Matron: Karen Clarke

Holman (boys' boarding):
Mr C I Holiday, BEd Leeds, ACP (*Senior Housemaster*)
Matron: Silvana Ispani

Propert (boys' day):
Mr A J Wilson, BSc, MSC Warwick
Matron: Lesley Angus

Raven (girls' day):
Dr R L Stone, BSc Bristol, PhD Birmingham
Matron: Gina Frost

Robinson (boys' day):
Mr M C Conway, MA Cantab
Matron: Tracey Pointing

Rosebery (girls' day):
Mrs R J B Harrop, BA Bristol
Matron: Patricia Martins

White (girls' VI form boarding & day):
Mrs C C Winmill, MA Bordeaux
Matron: Diane Liquorish

Wilson (girls' boarding):
Mrs K R Tod, BA London (*Senior Housemistress*)
Matron: Tania Moore

Chaplain: Revd Fr P Thompson, BA Oxon (*Senior Chaplain*)

* *Head of Department*

Art:
*Mrs K H P Lenham, BA Soton
Mr N Arvanitis, MA University of the Arts, London
Miss J Moore, MA Cantab

Biology:
*Mr W Keat, MA London
Mr P E D Green, BSc Manchester, MA London, CBiol, MSB
Mr M D Hobbs, BSc London, CBiol, MSB
Dr V Patel, BSc Leeds, PhD London
Dr R L Stone, BSc Bristol, PhD Birmingham
Dr R Storey, BSc Dunelm, PhD King's College London
Mrs P S Woolmer, BSc Hull

Chemistry:
*Mr J Styles, BSc University College London
Miss S Heyes, BSc Newcastle
Mr L Matthews, BSc Exeter
Mrs T M Muller, MA Oxon
Mrs M Odendaal, BSc Newcastle, MPhil Zimbabwe
Mr N S A Payne, BSc Salford
Mrs S E Williams, MA Cantab

Classics:
Mr E Cori, MA University of L'Aquila

Design Technology:
*Miss A M R Wickham, BEd Exeter, MEd Open
Mr M Day, BEd Trent Polytechnic
Mr P G Lewsey, BSc Coventry

Economics & Business Studies:
*Mr P J Gillespie, BA Exeter
Mr S J Head, BSc West of England
Mr M Hipperson, BSc Loughborough
Mrs E G Irvine, MA Aberdeen, PG Dip Tourism Surrey
Mr D N Rice, BSc Econ London, DLC Loughborough
Mr G R Watson, BA Cantab
Mr J M Whatley, BSc Cardiff
Mr R C G Young, BSc Bath

English:
*Mr W M A Burn, BA London
Mrs C E Jeens, MA Soton
Miss H P McCullough, BA Soton
Mr N Russell, MA Liverpool
Mrs S H Wilson, BA Nottingham
Mr R M Wycherley, BA Leeds
Mr M Zacharias, BA Dunelm

Geography:
*Mr S Powell, BSc Dunelm, MEd Cantab
Mr C J Baverstock, BSc Soton
Mrs A Venables, BSc Bristol

Mr R I Whiteley, MA Cantab

History, Government & Politics:
*Dr H R Meier, BA, MSc Oxon, DPhil Oxon
Mr A J Bustard, BA Swansea
Mr M C Conway, MA Cantab
Mr B S H Jerrit, BA Bristol
Mrs A O'Dwyer, BA Dublin, MSc Edinburgh
Mrs K R Tod, BA London
Dr M A L Tod, MA Glasgow, PhD Glasgow, FSA Scot

ICT and Computing:
*Miss S Biletchi, BSc Bucharest
Mr C J Davies, BSc Cardiff, CEng, CITP, MBCS, CMath, MIMA
Mr R A Johnstone, BTheol Brunel
Mr I M Winmill, BSc London

Learning Support:
*Mrs R Doyle, BEd Glasgow, BA Open, BPhil Birmingham, RSA Dip TEFL, Adv Dip Sp Ed
Mrs M-A Barnett, BA Manchester, TEFL Adv Dip (*EAL*)
Mrs A Davies, CertEd, CTEFLA Wales

Mathematics:
* Mr T A Stone, BSc Plymouth
Ms F G Buzzacott, BSc Exeter
Mr J Farrelly, BA, MSc Nottingham
Mrs K Hancock, BSc London
Miss S Hassan, BSc London, MSc Cass Business School
Mr S Hibbitt, BA York
Dr E Shanson, BSc Imperial College London, MPhil Birmingham
Mr J F Stephens, BSc Liverpool
Mr P J Williams, BSc Dunelm
Mr A J Wilson, BSc, MSc Warwick

Modern Languages:
*Mr M Fries, BA Open University
Mrs N Cholet, BA Open University (*French Assistante*)
Miss C L Creevey, BA Nottingham
Mrs C Guyon, Teacher's Cert (*French Assistante*)
Mrs C Hearne, BA Royal Holloway London
Mr M P Hynd, MA Glasgow
Mrs M Jones, Teacher's Cert (*Spanish Assistante*)
Mrs H E Keevil, BA Exeter
Mrs Z Liu, BEd Shenyang
Mr N Mayer, BA Ruhr, Bochum
Mrs D Y Shi, BA Yun Normal, China
Mrs C C Winmill, MA Bordeaux

Music:
*Mr G A Lodge, MA, BMus Cardiff, LTCL, ACIEA
Mr M Hampshire, BA Hull, FRSA
Mr C I Holiday, BEd Leeds, ACP

Visiting Instrumental Tutors:
Mr M E Allsop, BA RSAMD (*electric/acoustic guitar and music technology*)
Mr P S Beecher, BA ACM (*electric/acoustic guitar*)
Mr T Carey, MA BMus ARCM LTCL (*organ and piano*)
Mr A Dennant (*violin*)
Mrs L Egan, BMus, Cert Ed, LRAM, LTCL (*oboe, bassoon*)
Mr P G Evans (*bass guitar*)
Miss G Ford (*piano*)
Ms L Geldard DipRCM ARCM PGRM (*flute*)
Mr C Goldsack MA, PGCE (*singing*)
Miss A Goldy, PGCPerfTCL Dip-TCL, PGCE (*singing*)
Miss N Harling, BMus (*harp*)
Mr N Hassall, BMus, PGDip RCM (*saxophone and clarinet*)
Mrs K Humphries, GRSM (*piano*)
Mr P Johnson-Hyde, BMus (*piano*)
Mr M Kruk, H Dip Contemporary Music (*drum kit*)
Mr D C Marrion (*clarinet, saxophone, flute*)

Miss B Meek, DipMus, Cert Ed RSAM, DRSAM Performers, Cert Ed (*singing*)
Mr C Moore (*trumpet*)
Miss D Morley, BMus (*singing*)
Miss S D'Oliveira Teixeira, BMus MSTAT (*Alexander Technique*)
Mr J O'Carroll (*drum kit*)
Mr M W Osborn (*drum kit, percussion*)
Miss S Pedley, BSc, BA, BTEC National Diploma Music (*beatbox*)
Mr N Perona-Wright, LRAM, LTCL, LLCM TD (*flute, recorder*)
Mr G R D Rowland, ARCO, ARCM (*piano, harpsichord*)
Mr R H W Slade, MA Cantab, Cert Ed (*singing*)
Mr D Smith, AGSM (*electric and acoustic guitar*)
Mr R Smith, BMus, PGDip RCM (*violin*)
Dr J Spooner, MA Cantab, MA, PhD London, ARCM, LRAM, DipRAM (*cello*)
Mrs B Stevens, ARCM (*violin*)
Mrs C Stewart, BMus, PGCE (*piano*)
Mr G Straw, BA (*trumpet, french horn*)
Mr J S D Taylor, LRAM, Teachers Professional Cert (*classical guitar*)
Mrs H Taylor, BA, LGSM (*piano*)
Mr A Waterson, BSc, EBOR (*electric/acoustic guitar*)
Mrs J Whatley, BMus, Dip ABRSM (*clarinet and saxophone*)
Mr D Whitson, LRAM, ARCM, ARAM (*trombone*)

Physical Education:
*Mrs F C Drinkall, BSc Loughborough (*Director of Sport*)
Mrs S L Church-Jones, BA Exeter (*Head of Girls' Games*)
Mr A Wolstenholme, BEd Exeter (*Head of Rugby and Athletics*)
Mr N Taylor (*Head of Cricket*)
Mr D Charles, BSc Sheffield (*Head of Hockey*)
Mr R Ashton (*Sports Coach*)
Miss J Bennett (*Sports Coach*)

Visiting Coaching Staff:
Mr D Bangerter (*Table Tennis and Badminton*)
Mrs B Bostok (*Netball*)
Mr R Barcellona (*Strength and Conditioning*)
Mr R Chappell, MA London, MEd Kentucky, MSc Leicester (*Athletics & Basketball*)
Mr J Culver, Licensed CCA LTA (*Tennis*)
Mr R Dennis, ITF 5th Degree (*Taekwon-do*)
Mr D Donovan (*Rugby, Athletics and Strength & Conditioning*)
Mr N Frankland (*Squash*)
Mr C Hanson-Khan (*Badminton*)
M Homes (*Rugby, Football & Cricket*)
Ms E Robertson (*Netball*)
Mr J Shackell, BAF, NSAC (*Fencing*)
Mr S White (*Hockey*)

Physics:
*Mr C Telfer, BSc, MEd West of England
Mr R J Alton, BSc Cantab
Mr R D B Burgess, BSc Soton, ACMA
Mr J M Drinkall, BSc Dunelm
Mr J R L Hartley, BSc Dunelm
Mr M W D Perrins, MEng Oxon
Mr V Singh, MSc IIT Roorkee, India

Theatre Studies:
*Miss K Chandley, BA Birmingham
Mr P Henson, MA De Montfort

Theology and Philosophy:
*Mrs A Martineau, BA Bristol
Mrs H H Hynd, BA Nottingham, MA Dunelm, FRSA
Mr B G MacDowel, MTheol St Andrews
Revd Fr P Thompson, BA Oxon

Headmaster's Office:
Headmaster's PA: Mrs C Beesley
Deputy Heads' Secretary: Mrs S Lawrence
Mrs E Bauchop
Database and Exams Administrator: Mrs N Elliott

Admissions Office:
Director of Admissions: Mrs C Kent
Admissions Manager: Mr M Day, BEd Trent Polytechnic
Admissions Assistant: Mrs D Upot
Marketing & Events Assistant: Ms J Busby

Epsom College Education Trust:
Education Trust Coordinator: Miss V Ward

Old Epsomian Club:
Secretary: Mrs S Croucher

The Royal Medical Foundation:
Administrator: Mr C Titman

Other Staff:
Archivist: Mr A G Scadding, BA Newcastle
Examinations Officer: Mr A P Thompson, BSc Newcastle
Medical Officer: Dr M Sevenoaks, BSc, MBBS, MRCGP, DRCOG, DFFP
Dr K A Bryce, BSc, MBBS, MRCP, MRCGP
Music Administrator: Mrs J Bustard, BSc Swansea
Senior Sister: Mrs L Hendry, RN, DPNS
School Counsellor: Mrs E Baxter, Dip Couns
Sports Centre Manager: Mr C Field
CCF Instructor: WO1 RLS Bonner IG Combined Cadet Force

Numbers and Houses. The College has been fully co-educational from September 1996. There are 740 pupils in the School, 376 full and weekly boarders and 364 day pupils, divided among 7 boarding houses and 5 day houses. There are 337 in the Sixth Form. The College has 18% of pupils from overseas and a spread of 38 nationalities. The boy/girl ratio is 2:1 in the junior year groups and 1:1 in the Sixth Form.

There are 5 separate houses for girls: two boarding houses, Crawford and Wilson; two day houses, Raven and Rosebery; and a Sixth Form house, White, for both boarding and day girls.

The boys' boarding houses are: Fayrer, Forest, Granville and Holman. All boarding Sixth and Fifth Formers and Upper Fourth Formers have study-bedrooms in the modernised Houses. In the Michaelmas Term there are two weekend exeats roughly halfway through each half of term, in addition to a two week half-term holiday. In each of the other two terms there is one exeat in the first half followed by a one week half-term holiday. Weekly boarders can go home every weekend.

The day boy Houses are: Carr, Propert and Robinson. Day boys and girls are full members of the School community and have lunch and tea in College. All members of the School, boarders and day, eat centrally in the Dining Room which makes for efficiency and strengthens the sense of community.

Pupils who are ill are looked after in the School Medical Centre which has 8 beds with a qualified sister always on duty. One of the two (one male, one female) School Doctors visits daily except Sundays.

Academic Work. In the Middle Fourth (Year 9) pupils take English, French, Mathematics, Physics, Chemistry, Biology, Religious Studies, Drama, Geography, History, Art, Music, Information Technology and Design Technology. Latin, Spanish, German, Mandarin and English as an Alternative Language are offered as options. The normal programme is to enter the Middle Fourth at the age of thirteen and take the main block of GCSEs at the end of the Fifth Form (Year 11) but pupils take AS modules in Mathematics, Latin and Critical Thinking at the end of the Fifth Form. Almost everyone then enters the Sixth Form of approximately 330 pupils. A wide range of A Level subjects is offered. New options in Business Management, Politics and Government, Photography and Economics are introduced to complement the broad range of subjects already available at GCSE. In addition to the usual four AS subjects, Sixth Formers may opt to study AS Critical Thinking or join the Young Enterprise scheme. A large number of pupils take on independent learning through Extended Project Qualifications, with over 90 percent gaining A*-A. There are excellent facilities for work in one's own study, in the main Library or one of the specialist Departmental Libraries. The school is fully networked and has the latest Wi-Fi router system, including all Houses, and has over 600 computers alongside a further 600 BYOD, as well as digital projectors and electronic whiteboards used across the curriculum. There are five fully-equipped Information Technology rooms and Design Technology is housed in award-winning buildings, with state-of-the-art, industrial-standard CAD and CAM facilities.

Higher Education. Almost all students go on to university, with the occasional student choosing to follow another path, such as Art Foundation. In recent years, Medicine, Law, Engineering, Economics and Business degrees have proved particularly popular degree options, but Epsom students have been successful in gaining places on a broad variety of competitive courses. Approximately 70% of all pupils go to Russell Group or 1994 Group universities each year.

Careers. Careers education is offered from the first term at Epsom and is particularly well developed in the Sixth Form. Epsom has an experienced team of careers tutors with specialists in Medicine, Oxbridge Entrance, Engineering and American University Entrance. There is a well-stocked Careers Room attached to the Library, and much care is taken to assess a pupil's potential and aptitude and to provide proper guidance on careers. All pupils belong to the ISCO Scheme and all Fifth Form pupils take careers aptitude tests through Futurewise. There is a well-established work experience programme and a Careers Convention is organised each year for the Fifth Form and Lower Sixth. The College also hosts a GAP Year Fair.

The **Religious Teaching** and the Chapel Services follow the doctrines of the Church of England, but there are always pupils of other denominations and faiths. Multi-faith services take place regularly. There is a Senior Chaplain who works together with a visiting Rabbi and a Hindu priest to ensure a multi-faith approach. Muslim pupils attend prayers at the College.

Games and other Activities. Games contribute much to the general physical development of girls and boys at Epsom and the College has a strong tradition of high standards in many sports. The very large number of teams means that almost all pupils are able to represent the School each year. A wide range of sports is available: Rugby, Hockey, Netball, Cricket, Tennis, Athletics and Swimming, Squash (6 courts), Target Rifle Shooting (with an indoor range), Soccer, Cross-Country, Fencing, Golf, Badminton, Rounders, Basketball, Judo, Sailing and Lacrosse. The Indoor Sports Centre, housing two sports halls, a fencing salle and climbing wall, was opened in 1989 by the Patron of Epsom College, Her Majesty the Queen. In January 2007 a new extensive fitness suite was completed. The Target Rifle Team has been National Champions at Bisley winning the Ashburton Shield a record breaking 15 times in the years between 1990 and 2011.

The CCF has Naval, Army and RAF Sections and pupils over the age of 14 are expected to join for 2 years when much time is spent on camping and expeditions. Older boys and girls may join instead the Duke of Edinburgh's Award Scheme, while others are involved with Social Service work in Epsom.

The College ensures that all pupils take advantage of an extensive range of activities from Dance to Design Textiles.

Music, Art and Drama. There are three full-time Music teachers and a large staff of visiting music teachers. Over one-third of the pupils learn musical instruments and virtually any instrument can be taught, and many take singing lessons. There are four Choirs, a School Orchestra and seven major instrumental ensembles, including Big Band, Clarinet, Saxophone and Classical Guitar. Visits are arranged each term to concerts in London and elsewhere. The Music School has a Concert Hall and 18 practice rooms. Recent productions have included *The Coronation of Poppea, Sweeney Todd* and *Les Misérables*.

Art, which includes pottery, printing and sculpture as well as painting and drawing, is housed in a spacious building with 8 studios, a Library, an Exhibition Room and an Exhibition Hall. There are two full-time Art teachers and one part-time, and Art is studied up to GCSE and A Level.

There are several major Drama productions each year, from classical theatre to the modern musical, produced by a range of staff and pupils. These give boys and girls an opportunity to develop their talents and interests in Drama. In 2004 staff and pupils wrote their own show which was performed at the Royal Albert Hall, with over 1,000 performers, to mark the 150th Anniversary of the College.

Admission. Almost all pupils enter Epsom College in September. Most pupils come at the age of 13 after reaching a satisfactory standard in the Common Entrance or Scholarship Examination or the Epsom College January Entry Test examination set specially for those who are not prepared for Common Entrance. All boys and girls will be expected to sit a Pre-Test Examination in their Year 6 of corresponding entry at 13+. If the required standard is achieved, a pupil will be offered a place for entry at 13+, conditional upon maintaining the same standards at the present school and to a test being taken in the year of entry for setting purposes. Some enter the school later than this and there is always a direct entry into the Sixth Form, both for girls and boys.

A boy or girl may be registered at any age by sending in the registration form and fee. All enquiries should be sent to the Director of Admissions from whom a prospectus may be obtained.

Fees per term (2014–2015). Boarders £10,730; Weekly Boarders £9,795; Day Pupils £7,335.

The fees are inclusive and cover the normal cost of a pupil's education. The main extras are for examination fees, private tuition and a pupil's personal expenses. Fees for day pupils include lunch and tea.

There is a College Store for the provision of uniform, clothing and other requirements.

Entrance Scholarships. Scholarships are available at both 13+ and 16+ entry in the following areas: Academic, Art, Design/Technology, Drama/Dance, Music, Sport and the new Headmaster's Award for talented all-rounders at 13+.

Music candidates compete for all Open Scholarships. Music can be offered at a lower level as part of a candidature for an All-Rounder Award.

Drama/Dance awards are based upon a performance audition, interview and authorised record of achievement.

Art candidates compete for all Open Scholarships. They should submit a varied portfolio of about 15 pieces of work and they will then be invited to Epsom to discuss their work at interview and, at 13+, to do a timed drawing test.

Design Technology awards are based upon a portfolio presentation composing several contrasting items and, at 13+, a timed design test.

Sport awards are based upon a combination of skills' tests and authorised records of achievement.

Headmaster's Awards (All-Rounder) at 13+ require applicants to offer an academic element plus two or more elements to be selected from Art, Design Technology, Drama/Dance, Music and Sport. The latter are assessed through tests and interviews.

Scholarships and bursaries are available for children of the medical profession.

Bursaries. Over the past six years, Epsom has reduced the value of non means-tested Scholarships and Awards, which can be worth up to 10% per annum. This has enabled us to double the bursary fund which is allocated to families with demonstrable financial need. In turn this has helped us, with Educational Trust support, to 'Widen our access' to disadvantaged families which is one of the College's declared aims in line with both Government and HMC guidance. Potential scholarship applicants are encouraged to seek extra financial support, if appropriate, by way of a means-tested Bursary. Application forms are available on request from the Bursar or Admissions Registrar.

Old Epsomians. The Old Epsomian Club promotes sporting activities, social gatherings and networking events among its former pupils, with eight international chapters and an online database. On leaving the College, all pupils automatically become life-long members of the OE Club and they are invited back regularly for reunions, the OE Dinner and Founder's Day. They also receive several publications each year, including the OE magazine. Bursaries are available for the sons and daughters of OEs who wish to attend the College.

Charitable status. Epsom College is a Registered Charity, number 312046. It exists for the advancement of education.

Eton College

Windsor, Berkshire SL4 6DW

Tel:	01753 370611 (Admissions)
	01753 370800 (Head Master)
	01753 370540 (Bursar)
email:	admissions@etoncollege.org.uk
website:	www.etoncollege.com

Motto: '*Floreat Etona*'.

The King's College of our Lady of Eton beside Windsor was founded by Henry VI in 1440. The College Foundation comprises a Provost, 11 Fellows, Head Master, Lower Master, Bursar, Chaplain and 70 Scholars. There are some 1,240 Oppidans, or boys not on the Foundation.

Visitor: The Rt Revd The Lord Bishop of Lincoln

Provost and Fellows (Governing Body):
The Lord Waldegrave of North Hill, PC (*Provost*)
Dr Andrew Gailey, CVO, MA, PhD (*Vice-Provost*)
Professor Michael Proctor, SCD, FRS, FRAS, FIMA
Hamish Forsyth, MA
Professor Christopher Dobson, MA, DPhil, FRS, SCD
Sir Michael Burton, MA
The Marchioness of Douro, OBE, BA
David Reid Scott, MA
Professor Kim Nasmyth, PhD, FRS
Dr Caroline Moore, MA, PhD
Brent Hoberman, MA
John Varley, MA

Honorary Fellows:
John Butterwick, TD
Sir Simon Robertson
Sir Eric Anderson, KT, MA, MLitt, DLitt, FRSE
Lady Smith, OBE, BA

Steward of the Courts: The Rt Hon the Lord Carrington, KG, GCMG, CH, MC, PC

Conduct: The Revd Canon K H Wilkinson, MA

Precentor and Director of Music: T J Johnson, MA

Bursar: Miss J S Walker, MA, FCA

Assistant Bursars:
I C Mellor, ARICS, DipProjMan
Miss K Bradley, MA
A Harris, BSc, FRICS

Director of Development: Mrs R Henshilwood
College Librarian & Keeper of College Collections: Mrs R Bond, MA
Curator of Modern Collections: M C Meredith, MA
College Archivist: Miss E Cracknell, MARM

Head Master: A R M Little, MA

Lower Master: R M Stephenson, BSc, PhD

Director of Curriculum: G J D Evans, MA

Director of School Administration & IT: Dr P R Harrison, MA, DPhil

Senior Tutor: I Harris, MA

Tutor for Admissions: P J McKee, MA

School Office Manager: R A Hutton

School Doctor: J J C Holliday, MB BS, MRCS, LRCP, MRCGP, DCH, DRCOG, DFFP

Assistant Masters:
* *Head of Department/Subject*
† *House Master*

Art:
I Burke, MA *
A Forsyth, BA
C Gibbons, BA, MFA
E J V Parker, MA
D Reid, BA
S J Sharrard, MA

Classics:
K M Allott, MA
A J Chirnside, MA †
I Harris, MA
T E W Hawkins, MA †
M T Holdcroft, BA
J C A Jackson, MA
H G P Jones, BA
S A Lambert, BA †
J D Macartney, MA
A J Maynard, MA
R D Oliphant-Callum, MA †
J R B Scragg, BA †
R E C Shorrock, BA, MPhil, PhD
C J Smart, MA *
B E Smith, MA
P B Smith, MA, MSt †

Computing:
J W F Stanforth, MA*

Design:
S E Hearsey, BSc
H M Park, BSc
K R N Ross, BSc *

Divinity:
J D Breadon, BD, PhD
Revd R E R Demery, BTh, MA (*Chaplain*)
W I N Griffith, MA
Revd N G Heap, BA, DPhil (*Roman Catholic Chaplain*) *
Revd P A Hess, BA, MTh (*Chaplain*)

Revd C M Jones, MA (*Chaplain*)
G A J Rice, MPhil
E J N Russell, MA, PhD
R Stewart, MA †
M L Wilcockson, MA
Revd Canon K H Wilkinson, MA (*Conduct*)

Economics:
R E Bahr, BA
P R K Bird, BA
D J Fox, BA
J R Ginsberg, BA
D M Gregg, BSSc *
L J Purshouse, MA, PhD
G B Riley, MA
P S Smith, MA

English:
S-J Bentley. BA
B B Cooper, MA, MPhil, PhD *
A P Ford, BA
J E Francis, BA
A C D Graham-Campbell, MA
M A Grenier, MA, FRSA †
T J Howe, BA
D J Jackson, BA
W S Knowland, BA
M Liviero, Dott Ling, PhD †
S M McPherson, BComm, MA †
N J Mortimer, MA, DPhil
J D Newton, MA †
J M Noakes, MA
J M O'Brien, MA †
H-E Osborne, MA (*Director of Drama*)
R G Steel, BA (*Head of Theatre Studies*)
N H Zimbelius, MA

Geography:
D E Anderson, BA, DPhil *
E L Anderson, MA, MSc
T F X Eddis, BA
A B Henshilwood, MA
C M M Jenkinson, MA
A S Jennings, BA
P I Macleod, BEd, BA
M G H Mowbray, MA †

History & History of Art:
V S J Clark, BA
K C Davies, MA, MSt
S E Frew, BA
J A G Fulton, MA *
J D Harrison, MA
N A E Jeffery, BA
J P Murrin, MA
T E J Nolan, MA †
H S J Proctor, MA
J M Rainey, BA
A S Robinson, MA, MLitt †
J L Sillery, MA, DPhil †
D J Sullivan, BA
P E P Walsh, BA

Mathematics:
N Adams, BSc
D W B Anderson, BSc
J P Barker, BSc
S J Dean, MA
N J Fowkes, BSc
R J Gazet, MA *
L J Henderson, BA
B J Holdsworth, MA
P J McKee, MA
W F Moore, BSc †
J Moston, BSc, PhD
R S Oliver-Jones, MA, MMath
M J Salter, MA, MMath
C K Squires-Parkin, BA, MSc
J M Stone, MA
M Strutt, BSc
I R Swan, MEng, PhD
J E Thorne, BSc
S P Vivian, MA, MSc, CStat
A Warnes, BSc, PhD †
C M B Williams, MA, MSc
P G Williams, MA †

Modern Languages:
T E Beard, BA, PhD
M Bruna, BA
J M Burrows, BA
R A A Coward, MA
M G Doran, BA
G J D Evans, MA
R A Fletcher, BA, MPhil
J M Gibbons, BA, MPhil, DPhil †
A D Halksworth, MA, MLitt
N C Hulme, MA
T Hulks, MA
A P Iltchev, BA
M-L Lin, BA (*Chinese*)
K S K Pierce, MA (*German*)

M J Polglase, MA †
M Porcel Martin, MA
A Powles, BA (*French*)
P V Reznikov, BA (*Russian*)
N J Roberts, MA (*Italian*)
N C W Sellers, MA †(*Portuguese*)
H A Shirwani, MA (*Arabic*)
D M Stanford-Harris, MA (*Japanese*)
J W F Stanforth, MA
Y Zhao

Music:
E J Burgess, BA, PG Dip RAM
T M Foster, BMus, PG Dip RAM, LRAM
N D Goetzee, MSc, LRAM
D W Goode, BA, MPhil, FRCO
T J Johnson, MA *
M A O'Donovan, MA, MMus, ARCO
E C Yeo, BA

Physical Education:
N W Flanaghan, BSc
L S Harris, BSc
P I Macleod, BEd, BA
W E Norton, BA *
G J Pierce, BEd

Science:

Biology:
H W T Adams, BA, BSc
A Z Bridges, MA, MSc *
K Frearson, MA (*Science*)
G D Fussey, BSc
P M Gillam, MA
K L Hicks, BA
N P T Leathers, BSc
J H Owen, BSc, PhD
P S T Wright, MA

Chemistry:
D L Brewis, MChem
A K Copsey, BSc
R N Edmonds, BA, PhD
S P Hermes, MChem
N P T Leathers, BSc
A M Miles, BSc
R R Montgomerie, MA
G R Pooley, BSc, PhD †
A J Saunders, MChem, DPhil *
J A Steadman, MA, PhD

Physics:
W E S Casson, BSc
H G C Clarke, BA
J D Dangerfield, MSc *
M N Fielker, BSc
R P D Foster, MA †
I R Gray, BSc, PhD
P R Harrison, MA, DPhil
P D A Mann, MSc, PhD
S P Martin, BSc
S M Wright, BA

Jewish Tutor: J M Paull, MA, DIPM, MCIM

Muslim Tutor: Imam M Hussain, BTh

Hindu Tutor: J Lakhani, MSc

Roman Catholic Chaplain: Revd N G Heap, BA, DPhil

The King's Scholars (Collegers) normally number 70 and are boarded in College, each in his own room, under the care of the Master-in-College. About 14 Scholarships are awarded each year. Candidates need to be registered by the 1st March of the year of entry. For information apply to *The College Examination Secretary, Admissions Office, Eton College, Windsor SL4 6DB*.

The Scholarship Examination is held at Eton in May. Candidates must be aged 13 on 1st September of the year of entry. All candidates take English, Mathematics A, General I (general questions requiring thought rather than knowledge) and Science. They must also offer three or more of the following: French (written, aural and oral), Latin, Greek, Mathematics B, General II (Literature, the Arts, moral and religious issues, etc), and a paper combining History, Geography and Divinity.

Scholarships are to the value of 10% of the full fee, and all of them will be supplemented up to the value of full fees (subject to means-testing).

A Scholarship is normally tenable for five years.

Term of Entry. All boys enter in September.

Fees per term (2014–2015). £11,478. The Entrance fee is £1,900 with £1,250 being refunded when a boy leaves with all fees settled.

Oppidans. There are about 1,240 Oppidans (non-Collegers) housed in 24 Boarding Houses, each under the care of a House Master, and every boy has his own room. A boy enters the school in the September following his 13th birthday, and must pass the Common Entrance unless granted exemption on his performance in the Scholarship Examination. Details of arrangements for boys entering Eton directly from the maintained sector can be obtained from the Admissions Office.

Parents wishing to send their sons to Eton as Oppidans should apply to *The Tutor for Admissions, Eton College, Windsor SL4 6DB* for a copy of the Prospectus, which gives full details of the registration procedure. Information is also available on the website at www.etoncollege.com. Boys may be registered at any time between birth and the age of ten and a half and take a preliminary assessment at eleven.

Music Scholarships. Up to eight scholarships can be awarded annually, each to the value of 10% of the full fee, and all of them supplemented up to the value of full fees (subject to means-testing). All awards carry remission of instrumental lesson fees up to 135 minutes tuition per week. In addition there are up to six Music Exhibitions, carrying remission of instrumental lesson fees up to 135 minutes tuition per week. One also carries a place in the school, the other five being open only to boys who already have Conditional Places following the assessment at 11. Two Honorary Exhibitions may also be awarded, carrying no financial remission. Special consideration will be given to cathedral choristers who would still be able to sing treble in the College Chapel Choir. Further particulars and entry forms may be obtained from *The Tutor for Admissions, Eton College, Windsor SL4 6DB*.

Bursaries. Eton has substantial financial provision designed to widen access by enabling boys to come to the school who could not otherwise do so, and to allow boys to remain in the event of a change in family circumstances. For boys with scholarships, supplementary bursaries will be awarded up to full fees depending on need. For boys without scholarships, the normal maximum level of assistance is half the school fee, but growing funds are now enabling us to make a number of bursary awards beyond that level and indeed to subsidise the fee entirely in cases of need. No parents with a talented boy should feel that Eton is necessarily beyond their means. Further details are available on the website at www.etoncollege.com.

New Foundation Scholarships. Currently up to four scholarships by examination and interview are awarded to boys who have been educated in the UK maintained (state) sector for at least Years 6, 7 and 8 of their schooling up to age 13. It is aimed at boys who would not be able to attend Eton without very substantial financial assistance (in certain cases full remission may be given). The intellectual standard expected will be very high and comparable with the King's Scholarship, but the emphasis in the New Foundation Scholarship is on potential rather than knowledge, and all-round talents and personality will be taken into account.

The closing date for entries is in November of Year 8. Applicants will normally be in that school year. A boy who will become 14 before September 1st is too old to enter. Further information can be obtained from the Access Adviser, f.moultrie@etoncollege.org.uk.

Sixth Form Scholarships. Up to 12 Sixth Form Scholarships are offered each year to enable boys attending schools in the state sector to have two years of Sixth Form education at Eton. Each year in February, selected candidates are invited to attend interviews in those subjects which they intend to offer at A Level or Pre-U. All those attending the interviews will sit a written General Paper and verbal and non-verbal reasoning tests. Candidates must register on, or before, a date specified in mid-December. Two of the scholarships may be awarded to boys with exceptional talents in music or drama. The scholarships will cover the whole or part of the fees, and other educational expenses depending on the Scholar's financial need. An Open Afternoon is held in the Michaelmas term for anyone interested in coming to visit the school. For information apply to *The School Office Manager, Eton College, Windsor SL4 6DW*.

Charitable status. Eton College is a Registered Charity, number 1139086.

Exeter School

Victoria Park Road, Exeter, Devon EX2 4NS

Tel:	01392 273679 (Headmaster/Registrar)
	01392 258712 (Bursar/Office)
Fax:	01392 498144
email:	admissions@exeterschool.org.uk
website:	www.exeterschool.org.uk

Motto: ΧΡΥΣΟΣ ΑΡΕΤΗΣ ΟΥΚ ΑΝΤΑΞΙΟΣ

Founded in 1633, Exeter School occupies a 25-acre site, located within a mile of the city centre, having moved from its original location in the High Street in 1880. Some of its well-designed buildings date from that time but many new buildings have been added over the past twenty years and the school now enjoys first-rate facilities on a very attractive open site.

The school is fully co-educational and offers education to boys and girls from 7 to 18. It has its own Junior School of around 200 pupils, nearly all of whom transfer to the Senior School at the age of 11. The Senior School has around 720 pupils, including a Sixth Form of 220. (*For further information about Exeter Junior School, see entry in IAPS section.*)

Exeter School is a well run school with high all-round standards and very good academic results. It prides itself on strong cultural, sporting and extra curricular achievement. Its music is outstanding and there is a strong tradition of performance drawn from all age groups in the School. It offers a very wide range of sports and maintains consistently high standards especially in hockey, rugby and cricket. It is well placed for outdoor pursuits (eg Duke of Edinburgh's Award Scheme and Ten Tors on Dartmoor) and has its own very large voluntary CCF unit. The School is closely involved with the life of the City of Exeter and its university and it has a substantial commitment to support the local community.

Patrons:
The Lord Lieutenant of the County of Devon
The Right Reverend the Lord Bishop of Exeter
The Right Worshipful the Lord Mayor of Exeter

Governors:
Appointed by the Devon County Council:
Mrs R Brook

Appointed by the Exeter City Council:
G J Prowse

Appointed by the Governors of St John's Hospital:
¶A C W King (*Vice-Chairman*)
Mrs M Giles, LLB

Representatives of the Universities of Exeter and Oxford:
Exeter: Dr S C Smart, PhD
Oxford: Dr M C Grossel, MA, PhD

Co-opted Governors:
¶T E Hawkins (*Vice-Chairman*)
Mrs H Clark
J D Gaisford, BSc, ACA
Mrs B Meeke, LLB (*Chairman*)
T D Wheare, MA, FRSA
¶A P Burbanks, BA
Dr P R Scott, MA, DPhil
¶Mrs G A Hodgetts, BA, MSc
Prof A F Watkinson, MSc, FRCS

Headmaster: R Griffin, MA

Deputy Headmaster: P M Šljivić, MA
Deputy Headmaster: M J Hughes, MA
Assistant Head: Miss L J Hilton, MSc
Director of Alumni Relations: J W Davidson, MA, MSc

Assistant Staff:
* *Head of Department*
† *Housemaster/mistress*
§ *Part-time or Visiting*
¶ *Former pupil*

Art & Design:
*Mrs A J Dyer, BA
Mrs R A Smith, BA

Biology:
*Mrs J H Metcalf, MA
†P J C Boddington, BSc
B D Kirsch, BSc
M K Chitnavis, BSc, CSci, FRSC (*Universities Adviser*)
Mrs P Smith, BSc
Miss J M Booth, BSc

Chemistry:
*R F J Tear, BSc
Miss L J Hilton, MSc (*Assistant Head*)
M K Chitnavis, BSc, CSci, FRSC (*Universities Adviser*)
Dr S P Smale, BSc, PhD
Dr A M Rowland, PhD
§Mrs F J Tamblyn, BSc

Classical Subjects:
*N P L Keyes, MA
Mrs S Shrubb, MA

Computing & Information Systems:
*Mrs R Cull, BSc, MIITT, CMath, MIMA
N F Howard, BA
§D E Sims, BSc

Design Technology:
*N W Moon, BSc
I R Lowles, BA

Drama:
*J S Brough, BSc

Electronics:
*Dr A W Houghton, MA, MSc, PhD
M E Schramm, BSc

English:
*A S Dobson, MA
Mrs J H Daybell, MA
†Mrs E K J Dunlop, MA, MPhil
Mrs E A Whittall, BA, MEd
Miss K L Ridler-Murray, MA
B J J Masters, MA

Geography:
*Mrs H M Sail, BA
J W Davidson, MA, MSc (*Director of Alumni Relations*)
§Miss M J Vaggers, MA
P M Šljivić, MA (*Deputy Headmaster*)
Mrs A Roff, BSc
Miss J D Horsford, BSc

History:
*G N Trelawny, BEd, MA
Mrs A-J Culley, BA, BSc
Miss M F Dunn, BA
Ms J R Hodgetts, BA

Languages:
*M F Latimer, MSt
†M C Wilcock, BEd
Mrs A M Francis, MA
§Mrs S C Wilson, BA
R A Charters, BA
J C Hatton, BA
Mrs D D S Masters, BA

Mathematics:
*Miss E V Marshall, BSc
†G R Willson, BSc
†Dr P M Smallwood, BSc, PhD
A J Reynolds, BSc
†W J Daws, BA
M J Hughes, MA (*Deputy Head*)
Dr G J D Chapman, BSc, MSc, PhD (*CCF Contingent Commander*)
Mrs A J James, BSc
F E Malone-Lee, BA
Miss M McCluskey, MSc

Music:
*P Tamblyn, MA, MMus (*Director of Music*)
T P Brimelow, MA
Mrs R Mitchell, BA, Dip Mus, LTCL
§A Gillett, ARCM
§D Bowen, BEd
§P Painter, DipMusEd, Cert Ed
§B Moore, BA

Physical Education and Games:
*A C F Mason, BA (*Director of Sport*)
Mrs A J Marsh, BEd (*Head of Sixth Form*)
J W Fawkes, BSc
E P M Jones, BSc
Miss R A Carter, BSc
§F L Smith (*CCF SSI*)
§G Skinner, BEd

Physics:
*G S Bone, BSc, CSci (*Director of Science*)
T J Clark, BSc
Dr A W Houghton, MA, MSc, PhD
Dr J L Wilson, MPhys, DPhil
M E Schramm, BSc
M K Chitnavis, BSc, CSci, FRSC (*Universities Adviser*)

Religious Studies:
*†M H R Porter, BA
†Mrs J M K Murrin, BA
§J A Allan, BA (*Chaplain*)

Mrs A J Marsh, BEd

Social Studies:
*S K Mackintosh, BA (*Economics)
Miss M F Dunn, BA (*Politics)
†R J Baker, BA
P Bell, MA

Learning Support:
§Mrs A Southcott, BEd
§Mrs S E Oliver, BEd

Junior School

Headmistress: Mrs A J Turner, MA

Assistant Head: J S Wood, BA

Assistant Staff:
R Bland, BEd
¶G E L Ashman, BA
Mrs P A Goldsworthy, BA, LTCL
R J Pidwell, BA
§Mrs R M Parkin, CertEd
Mrs V K Randerson, CertEd
Ms J A Barnes, MSc
§Mrs C H Handley, BEd
Mrs L L Hardy, MA
Miss K J Ballard, BA
Mrs R E Pettet, BA

Bursar and Clerk to the Governors: Cdre R C Hawkins
RN, BA
Deputy Bursar and Company Secretary: Mrs G M Robins,
BA, ACCA
Registrar: Mrs W M Drake
Headmaster's PA: Mrs A C Goswell
Head of Information Systems: W R T Lines, MSc, CEng
Librarian: Mrs E G Taylor, BSc, DipLib
School Nurse: Mrs M R Sanders, RGN

Buildings, Grounds and General Facilities. The Senior
School block includes a large multi-purpose assembly hall, a
library, a private study area, dining hall and Sixth Form Centre as well as many well-appointed classrooms. A major
refurbishment of the former boarding accommodation to
include a new Library and Study Centre was completed for
September 2006. There are separate buildings on the site
housing the Chapel, the Music School, the Science Centre,
Art Studios, Drama Studio, Design and Technology Centre
and Exonian Centre. The Science Centre provides 14 laboratories and there are four fully-equipped computer rooms. All
departments have access to their own computers and the
School has a wide, controlled access to the internet. In 2005
the school opened a new dance studio and a fitness suite to
add to the existing sports facilities of a large modern well-
equipped Sports Hall with its own squash courts and access
to on-site floodlit all-weather sports arena, top-grade all-
weather tennis/netball courts and a heated swimming pool.
The playing fields, which are immediately adjacent to the
School buildings are well kept and provide, in season,
rugby, cricket, hockey, football, rounders and athletics areas.
The Junior School, which was extended in 2012 to provide
four new modern classrooms, has access to all the Senior
School facilities but is self-contained on the estate.

Admission. The majority of pupils enter the Junior
School at 7 or 8 and the Senior School at 11 or 13. Admission is also possible at other ages where space allows and a
significant number of pupils join at the age of 16 for Sixth
Form Studies.

Entrance to the Junior School is by assessment in January. This includes a report from the child's previous school,
classroom sessions in the company of other prospective
pupils, and literacy, numeracy and general intelligence
tasks.

Entrance examinations for the Senior School are held in
January.

Assessment for entry to the Sixth Form at 16 is by interview and a report from the applicant's previous school. Dedicated interview days are held monthly from December to
March each year and the entry requirement is a minimum of
3 A and 3 B grades at GCSE, including English and Mathematics, with normally an A grade in the subjects chosen for
study.

Registration Fee £100.

Fees per term (2014–2015). Junior School: £3,395
(includes lunch which is compulsory). Senior School:
£3,765.

Sibling discount of 10% for the second child and 20% for
the third or subsequent child attending concurrently.

Scholarships and Financial Awards. Academic Scholarships and Exhibitions, in the form of an individual prize,
are offered annually to pupils who excel in the school's
entrance tests at 7+, 11+ and 13+. Music Scholarships and
Exhibitions are offered at 11, 12, 13 and 16 following an
audition and interview. One Ogden Science Scholarship,
means-tested, offering up to 100% discount off tuition fees
is available for a pupil joining the Sixth Form studying
Maths and Physics.

The School annually makes available a number of means-
tested Governors' Awards. These are for external candidates
joining the School, who meet the academic entry requirements and whose parents could not afford to send them to
Exeter School without financial assistance. As a general
guide, gross parental income will need to be below £60,000
per annum to allow consideration for a Governors' award. In
addition, there are also a number of special awards made
possible by donations from local benefactors for able pupils
whose parents require financial assistance. The School is
supported by the Ogden Trust and the Rank Foundation.

Curriculum. In the first 3 years in the Senior School all
pupils take English, History, Geography, a carousel of
French, German, Spanish and Latin, Mathematics, IT, Physics, Chemistry, Biology, Art, Design Technology, Drama,
Music and Religious and Physical Education. After this
there is a wide choice of subjects at GCSE level, including
English, one compulsory Modern Foreign Language, Mathematics, dual or triple award Science, Religious Studies and
3 of the following: Latin, French, German, Spanish, Classical Civilisation, History, Geography, Music, Drama, Art,
Design and Technology, and Information Technology.

Pupils enter the Sixth Form choosing from 26 different
subjects for AS or A Level study and are prepared for university scholarships, university entrance and admission to
other forms of further education or vocational training. Over
95% go on annually to Degree Courses.

Houses. There are nine Pupil Houses. Each is under the
personal care of a Head of House and his/her deputy, with
whom parents are invited to keep in touch on any matter
affecting their child's general development and progress
throughout the school.

Religion. All pupils attend Religious Education classes,
which include Sixth Form discussion groups. Pupils may be
prepared for Confirmation.

Games. Rugby, Hockey, Cricket, Swimming, Athletics,
Dance, Cross Country, Tennis, Badminton, Squash, Shooting, Basketball, Netball, Fencing, Cycling and Golf. Further
activities are available for the Sixth Form, including Football and Multi-Gym sessions.

Community and other Service. All pupils learn to serve
the community. Many choose to take part in Social Service,
helping old people and the handicapped young. There is a
voluntary CCF Contingent with thriving RN, Army and
RAF Sections. The CCF offers a large variety of Outdoor
Activities, including Adventure Training Camps, Ten Tors
Expedition Training as well as specialist courses. Pupils are
encouraged to participate in the Duke of Edinburgh's Award
Scheme.

Music. Pupils are taught Singing and Musical appreciation and are encouraged to learn to play Musical Instruments. More than one third of all pupils have individual lessons on at least one instrument. There are 4 Orchestras, a Choral Society which annually performs a major work in Exeter Cathedral and 4 Choirs, 3 jazz bands, and numerous smaller groups from string quartets to rock bands. There are over 30 visiting instrumental teachers. Over 20 public concerts are given each year. Recent Summer Music trips have included Lake Garda and Barcelona.

Drama. Drama is developed both within and outside the curriculum. The School Hall with its large and well-equipped stage provides for the dual purpose of studio workshop and the regular production of plays, operas and musicals. The recently refurbished Drama Studio is used for smaller productions.

Art and Design. Art lessons are given to junior and senior forms. Apart from the formal disciplines of GCSE and A Level, which can be taken by those who choose, all pupils have opportunity for artistic expression in painting, print-making, photography, pottery, construction in many materials and carving wood and stone. All younger pupils learn to develop craft skills in wood, metal and plastic and to use them creatively in design work. Some then follow GCSE or A Level courses in Design and Technology. There is an annual art exhibition in July.

Expeditions. Throughout the school a large number of residential field trips and expeditions take place each year including a Third Form new pupils' Dartmoor weekend, various departmental excursions, several foreign exchanges and Duke of Edinburgh's Award expeditions. Pupils are also encouraged to compete for external expeditions and, following years of representation on its expeditions, the school has been awarded Star status by the British Exploring Society (BES). In recent summers, the school has run its own adventure trips to Chile, Namibia, Peru and the Himalayas and canoeing trips to Peru and Slovenia. There is a programme of major and minor sports tours.

Societies and Clubs. Pupils are encouraged to pursue their interests by joining one of the School Societies. Groups of enthusiasts can form new Societies or Clubs, but the following are at present available: Art, Badminton, Basketball, Canoeing, Chess, Choral Society, Christian Union, Computing, Dance, Debating, Drama, Electronics, Model Railway, Music, Politics, Sailing, Shooting and Squash.

Social. Close contact is maintained with the City and the University. Association between members of the School and the wider society outside is fostered wherever opportunity offers.

The staff believe strongly in the value of association with parents, who are invited to meetings annually throughout their sons' or daughters' time at the School. A termly lecture by a visiting speaker is provided for parents. The Exeter School Parents' Association exists to promote closer relations between the School and its parents.

Careers. Careers education begins at the age of 13 and continues on a progressive programme until students leave the school. Careers evenings are held annually when pupils and their parents have the opportunity to consult representatives of the professions, industry and commerce. A work experience programme is organised for Year 11 pupils each summer, and a scheme of mock interviews with career professionals for pupils in the Sixth Form. A major Careers Convention is held at the school each Autumn for pupils from Years 9 to 13.

Honours. Pupils regularly gain admission to Oxford and Cambridge. The School encourages application to the leading universities, including the Russell and 1994 Groups.

Leading musicians have recently gained places at the Royal College of Music and the Royal Academy of Music.

Charitable status. Exeter School is a Registered Charity, number 1093080, and a Company Limited by Guarantee, registered in England, number 04470478. Registered Office: Victoria Park Road, Exeter, Devon EX2 4NS.

Felsted School

Felsted, Essex CM6 3LL
Tel: 01371 822606 (Headmaster)
01371 822605 (Admissions Registrar)
Fax: 01371 822697 (School)
01371 822607 (Headmaster)
email: info@felsted.org
website: www.felsted.org
Twitter: @FelstedSchool
Facebook: /FelstedSchool
LinkedIn: /Felsted Network

Founded in 1564 by Lord Richard Riche, Felsted celebrated its 450th anniversary in 2014, and was honoured by a visit from Her Majesty The Queen. Educating boys and girls aged 4 to 18, Felsted is is ideally situated in a picturesque North Essex village, close to both London and Cambridge, and within easy reach of Stansted and other international airports. Felsted is a Church of England foundation but welcomes pupils from all Christian denominations and those from other religious traditions. The Senior School, for 13 to 18 year olds, has around 540 pupils; the majority are boarders and weekend arrangements are flexible. The Preparatory School boasts 480 pupils, with a buoyant boarding house, home to full, weekly and flexible boarders.

The School is a Global Member of the Round Square Organisation offering international exchanges and collaboration, and offers both A Levels and the International Baccalaureate in the Sixth Form. Felsted's prospectus can be found online at www.felsted.org along with much other information and news, details of forthcoming events and location maps. Each Boarding House has its own web page and several videos, including one called 'Boarding at Felsted', can be downloaded. Felsted had an Ofsted boarding and welfare inspection in 2011 and was rated 'outstanding' in every aspect, with no recommendations for improvement. This is a rare accolade. Felsted also received an 'excellent' in all aspects rating by the Independent Schools Inspectorate in 2013, details of which are available from their website.

Governing Body:
J H Davies (*Chairman*)

K M R Foster	O Stocken
P G Lee	J Tibbitts
P J Cooper	Mrs J Crouch
S J Ahearne	W Sunnucks
Mrs J Simpson	B Grindlay
P J Hutley	N Stuchfield
Mrs B Davy	Mrs A Carrington
Dr J Nicholson	

Bursar & Clerk to the Governors: Mrs Margaret McKenna

Headmaster: Dr Michael J Walker, MA, PhD, CertEd, FRSA

Deputy Headmaster (*Pastoral*): Mr Christopher J Townsend, MA (*Classics*)
Deputy Headmaster (*Academic*): Mr Jeremy Westlake, MA, NPQH (*Modern Languages*)
Deputy Head (*Welfare*): Mrs Karen A Megahey, BSc (*Mathematics; Designated Safeguarding Officer; *PSHE*)

Assistant Head: Mrs Sarah R Capewell, MA (*Classics*)

Staff:
* *Head of Department*
p/t *Part-time*
† *Housemaster/mistress*
AHM *Assistant Housemaster/mistress*

Mr G Charles Allen, BA, MA (*Classics*)

Mr J Andrews, MA (*Mathematics*)

Miss C Ardoino, BA, MA (*Italian and French*)

Mrs Vanessa Balch BA (*Mathematics; p/t*)

Mrs Julie Balchin, BEd (*Support for Learning; p/t*)

Mr Francis M Barrett, BBS (*Economics and Business Studies; †Windsor's*)

Mrs Lucy T Barrett, BSc (*Chemistry; p/t*)

Mrs Sarah Barrett, BSc (*PE; Director of Girls' Sport; †Garnetts*)

Mr Peter G Bennett, AGSM (*Music; *Music Technology; †Gepp's*)

Mrs Mandy J Bonnett, MSc (*Biology; AHM Manor*)

Ms Maria E Burns, BA (*English; Felsted Diploma; Round Square Coordinator*)

Mr Barny J Bury, BA Ed (*PE; *PE; AHM Windsor's*)

Mrs Melissa Cacace, BA (*Psychology i/c Community Services*)

Mr Michael J Campbell, MSci (*Mathematics; *Mathematics*)

Mr Alan G Chamberlain, MA (*Modern Foreign Languages*)

Mrs Caroline Croydon, MSc Hons (*ICT; *ICT; Timetabler*)

Ms Z Defoe, BA, HLTA (*EAL*)

Miss Constance Donaldson, BSc (*Mathematics; p/t*)

Maj William H Eke, MBE (*CCF Adjutant*)

Ms A Fazekas, MA (*German; Modern Languages*)

Mr Richard L Feldman, MSc (*Mathematics; Monitoring & Evaluation Advisor*)

Mr Edward Fenning, MA (*Mathematics; AHM Elwyn's*)

Mrs Helen A Fenning, MA (*Chemistry*)

Miss Lucy Fox, BSc (*Physics; Resident Tutor Follyfield*)

Mr Jason E R Gallian (*Geography; Director of Cricket; AHM Montgomery's*)

Mr T Galvin, BSc (*Geography*)

Ms Helen Giles, BA (*German; p/t*)

Miss Hannah Grace, MA (*Theatre Studies (Technical); Theatre Manager*)

Mrs Rebecca Grant, BA (*Modern Foreign Languages*)

Mrs Dianne K Guerrero, BA (*ESL; *ESL; International Coordinator*)

Mr Thomas J Hietzker, FSB (*Biology; *Biology; Deputy Designated Safeguarding Officer*)

Mr Jeff Hipkin, BA, QTS, MEd (*SfL; Geography*)

Miss J Hodges, BA (*Art*)

Mr A Martin Homer, MA, (*English; Drama; *Theory of Knowledge; Director IB*)

Mrs Catriona M James, BA (*English; *English; p/t*)

Ms Nicola J Johnson, CDip (*Teaching Assistant*)

Mr Charles S Knightley, BA (*PE; Director of Sport; †Deacon's*)

Mrs Rebecca J P Lagden, BA (*English; ACT & MUN*)

Mr Andrew Le Chevalier (*PE; Director of Rugby; †Montgomery's*)

Dr Charles R S Lee, BA, MA, PhD, MMC (*Drama; English; *Drama and Theatre Studies*)

Madame Beatrice J Lemoine-Chicoine, L-ès-L (*Modern Foreign Languages; †Garnetts*)

The Revd Nigel Little, BA (*Chaplain; Charities*)

Mr James D Lowry, MA, ALCM (*Music; Director of Music*)

Miss L Macey, BA (*Drama & English*)

Ms Janine K Mallett, BA (*French; *French*)

Mrs Frances Marshall, BSc (*History*)

Mrs Nichola Martin, BA, DipLib, MCLIP (*Learning Resources Manager*)

Mr J McArdle, MA (*Classics*)

Mrs Joy E McArdle, BA, MBA (*Business Studies and Economics*)

Ms Ingrid McCrudden (*French Language Assistant*)

Dr Sophie McGuire, BSc, MSc, PhD (*Chemistry & Biology; †Thorne*)

Mr Luke McIlvenna, BA (*Economics and Business Studies; *Economics and Business Studies; Acting Assistant Head*)

Miss Elizabeth M McLaren, BA (*Classics; Non-Resident Tutor*)

Mr Chris J Megahey, MA (*Mathematics*)

Dr Peter H Milner, BSc, PhD, CChem, MRSC (*Teaching Assistant*)

Mrs Katherine Moir-Smith, BA (*Geography*)

Mrs H Mollison, BSc (*Chemistry; *Science*)

Mrs Tina Oakley-Agar, BSc (*ICT*)

Ms Nicola F S O'Brien, MA (*Spanish; †Follyfield*)

Mr Clifford H Palmer, MA (*Physics; Mathematics*)

Mr Rakesh Pathak, BA (*History; *History; Senior Scholarship Coordinator*)

Mr Ben R Peart, BSc (*Biology; †Elwyn's*)

Mrs Carolyn M Phillips, MCLIP (*Learning Support; †Manor; Careers*)

Mr Nicholas J Phillips, BA (*PE; Head of Boys Hockey; Geography*)

Mr Mick A Pitts, BEng (*Design Technology; *Design Technology*)

Ms Y Quintana Naranjo (*Spanish Language Assistant*)

Mrs Beth S Roberts Jones, BSc (*RE; *RE; †Thorne*)

Ms Elizabeth K Rose, BA (*Geography; *Geography*)

Mrs Anna L Salmon, BA (*Support for Learning; *Support for Learning; †Stocks's*)

Mr Felix Sanchez del Rio, Licenciatura (*Spanish; *Modern Languages; *Spanish*)

Miss Tatjana Schror (*German Language Assistant*)

Ms Loren Sherer, BSc, MA (*PE; Biology; Head of Girls Hockey; AHM Follyfield*)

Miss Katie Shirtcliffe, BA (*Artist in Residence*)

Miss Alex L F Simpson, BSc (*Biology; Director of Work Education; Sixth Form Coordinator*)

Mr Jonny Sloman, MSc, BSc (*Graduate Assistant – Sport; Resident Tutor Gepp's & Deacon's*)

Mr David J Smith, BA (*Art; *Art*)

Mr David T Smith, BSc (*Physics; *Physics*)

Miss E Smith (*Graduate Resident Assistant – Theatre Support*)

Mrs Vicky L Smith, BSc (*Psychology; *Psychology*)

Miss Rebecca Speight, BA (*English; Lower School Academic Coordinator*)

Mr Nicholas J Spring, MA (*English; Careers & Universities; President of Common Room*)

Mrs L Stefanini, BSc, MA (*Religious Studies*)

Mrs G Stringer, BSc (*Geography*)

Mrs A Thomson, BEd (*Sports Coach*)

Mrs K Truiggs (*English*)

Sra Marta M Valls, BA (*Spanish*)

Mrs Lucy Vignoles, BA (*Design Technology; p/t*)

Miss R Ward, BA (*History*)

Miss Rebecca Warner, MSc (*Graduate Assistant – Sport*)

Mr William Warns, BA, FNCM (*Choirmaster & Organist*)

Mr Christian L Watkinson, BSc (*Chemistry; *Chemistry*)

Mr K Wells, BSc (*Geography*)

Mrs Sarah A Wells, MA (*Geography & History*)

Mrs K Westlake, BA (*History*)

Mrs Dee L Whittock (*DofE Manager; Educational Visits & CAS*)

Miss L Wigglesworth, BA (*Religious Studies*)

Ms Sonia D Wilson, BA (*Business Studies and Economics; AHM Garnetts*)

Miss M Wood, BA, MA (*History of Art*)

Houses and Housemasters/mistresses:

Boys' Houses:
Deacon's: Charlie Knightley
Elwyn's: Ben Peart
Gepp's: Peter Bennett
Montgomery's: Andrew Le Chevalier
Windsor's: Francis Barratt

Girls' Houses:
Follyfield: Nicola O'Brien
Garnetts: Sarah Barratt
Manor: Carolyn Phillips
Stocks's: Anna Salmon
Thorne: Sophie McGuire

Head of the Preparatory School: Mrs Jenny M Burrett, BA

Director of Marketing: Mrs Sophy Aitken

Admissions Registrar: Mr Ed Peters

School Chaplain: Reverend Nigel Little

Medical Officer: Mrs Alison Grayson

The Houses. There are ten Houses at Felsted, a day house for boys, a day house for girls, three boarding houses for boys, three boarding houses for girls, an Upper Sixth House for boys and an Upper Sixth House for girls. Each House is under the direction of a resident Housemaster or Housemistress.

Each Housemaster/Housemistress is supported by a pastoral team comprising a resident Assistant Housemaster/Housemistress, a matron responsible for overseeing the domestic arrangements, and several House tutors.

The Curriculum. All pupils study English Language, English Literature, Mathematics and Sciences (Science/Additional Science) to GCSE and choose a further five subjects from the following: History, Geography, Religious Studies, French, German, Spanish, Latin, Classical Civilisation, Art and Design, Music, Drama, Triple Science (instead of Science/Additional Science), Design & Technology (Resistant Materials or Graphic Products), Physical Education and Computing.

One of the options must be a Modern Foreign Language and one must be a Humanities subject.

In the Sixth Form pupils have a choice between A Levels and the International Baccalaureate.

Those studying A Levels choose four subjects to study to AS Level and then continue with either three or four subjects to A Level. The following subjects are offered: Art and Design, Business Studies, Classical Civilisation, Computing, Design Technology, Drama and Theatre Studies, Economics, English Literature, Geography, Government and Politics, History, History of Art, Latin, Mathematics, Mathematics (Further), Modern Foreign Languages (French, German, Spanish), Music, Music Technology, Physical Education, Psychology, Religious Studies, Sciences (Biology, Chemistry, Physics).

IB pupils study six subjects, one from each of the following categories: Language and Literature (English, German, Italian, Self-Study Language, Spanish and French), Language Acquisition (French, German, English, Spanish, Latin. Mandarin, Spanish and Italian 'ab initio'), Individuals and Societies (Economics, Geography, History, Philosophy, Psychology), Sciences (Biology, Chemistry, Design Technology, Physics, Sports Exercise and Health Science), Mathematics (Maths, Maths Studies), The Arts (Visual Arts, Music). They also follow a course on the Theory of Knowledge, write an extended essay and are fully involved in the Creativity, Action and Service Programme.

Scholarships and Bursaries. Academic, Music, Drama, Art, Design & Technology and Sports Scholarships are awarded annually for entry at 13+ and to the Sixth Form, up to the value of 20% of the fees.

The examinations for the 13+ Scholarships take place in February and May and for the Sixth Form Scholarships in November and February.

Mary Skill Awards, which recognise all-round ability or a specific ability in one area, are also available.

Means-tested Bursaries may be available to increase an award.

Up to two Open Bursaries (100%) each year are available to those who might otherwise not be able to consider Felsted, due to financial circumstances.

Talented students in Design are also entered at 16+ for Arkwright Foundation Scholarships.

Scholarships are also awarded at 11+ at Felsted Preparatory School and these may be carried through to the Senior School.

Fee reductions are available for children of those serving in the Armed Services.

Full details are available at www.felsted.org and from the Admissions Registrar.

Registration and entry. Boys' and girls' names can be registered at any time.

Before admission to Felsted all pupils at other preparatory schools must pass the Common Entrance or Common Academic Scholarship Examination. Entry from other schools is by Head Teacher's Report and Verbal Reasoning Test, or, for Sixth Form entry, 6 B Grades at GCSE, Head Teacher's report, Verbal Reasoning Test and interview.

Fees per term (2014–2015). Senior School: £9,990 boarders, £6,975 day pupils.

Preparatory: £3,995–£5,250; Pre-Preparatory: £2,750; Boarding £6,690–£6,895.

Registration fee £75.

Felsted Preparatory School, whose Head is in membership of IAPS (The Independent Association of Prep Schools), shares the same governing body with Felsted School. It has its own campus, with approximately 470 pupils aged 4 to 13. There is a dedicated teaching centre for 11–13 year-olds and a brand new state-of-the-art Pre-Preparatory Department, which opened in November 2011. (*For further information, see entry in IAPS section.*)

Old Felstedian Society organises both social and sporting activities. The Secretary is: P G Norton, Ultima Dimora, 172 Braunston Road, Oakham, Rutland LE15 6RU. The Old Felstedian Liaison Master, Mr N S Hinde, would be pleased to answer queries about the Alumni and further information can be found at www.archives.felsted.essex.sch.uk.

Charitable status. Felsted School is a Registered Charity, number 310870. The charity is based upon the Foundation established by Richard Lord Riche in 1564 with the objective of teaching and instructing children across a broad curriculum as ordained from time to time by its Trustees.

Fettes College

Carrington Road, Edinburgh EH4 1QX
Tel: 0131 311 6744
Fax: 0131 311 6714
email: enquiries@fettes.com
website: www.fettes.com
Twitter: /Fettes_College

Motto: '*Industria*'.

Founded in 1870 by Sir William Fettes and designed by David Bryce, Fettes College is uniquely situated in extensive grounds and woodland close to the heart of Edinburgh, and enjoys a reputation as one of the pre-eminent co-educational boarding schools in the UK. Fettes College has 755 pupils aged 7–18 (197 in the Prep School and 558 in The College), boarders and day pupils at a ratio of 80:20 in the Senior School and 30:70 in the Prep School. Fettes Students are drawn from all over the British Isles and from abroad and this diverse and healthy mix of backgrounds provides a richness that contributes to the stimulating, warm and energetic community that is Fettes College.

Governors:
[1]The Hon Lord Tyre, CBE, QC (*Chairman*)
¶A E H Salvesen, Esq, CBE (*Deputy Chairman*)

[1]B Aird, Esq
[1]Mrs D Atkins
Councillor J Balfour
[1]Professor I W Campbell, FRCP
Mrs J A Campbell
A G H Davidson, Esq, FInstD, MCMI
¶[1]B Dingwall, Esq, CBE
Reverend N N Gardner
¶[1]C Grassie, Esq
R S Keen, QC
Mrs I Keith
¶[1]J C Lang, Esq
A A McCreath, Esq, MCIPD, MIED
¶[1]C K Oliver, WS
I M Osborne, Esq
Professor K Whaler, FRSE
¶[1]E Young, Esq
¶[1]A G Fox, WS (*Clerk*)

¶ *Old Fettesian*
[1] *Parent/Former Parent*

Senior Management Team:

Headmaster: M C B Spens, MA Selwyn College Cambridge

Deputy Head: Mrs H F Harrison, MA Cambridge
Assistant Headmaster & Director of Studies: A Shackleton, MA Cambridge
Headmaster of the Preparatory School: A A Edwards, BA London
Director of Extra-Curricular Activities & Director of Sport: S M Bates, BSc London
Director of ICT & Communications: A M Hall, MA, PhD St Andrews
Director of Teaching & Learning: A J Armstrong, MA St Andrews
Bursar: P J F Worlledge, BSc Bristol
Director of Marketing and PR: Mrs G G Gray, MA Edinburgh
Foundation Director: Mrs E H M Anderson, BA Los Angeles
Assistant Director of Studies: L J Whyte, BSc PhD Norwich

Chaplain: Revd Dr A Clark, BA York, PhD St Andrews

Heads of Departments/Subjects:

Art: Miss B J Conway, BA Edinburgh College of Art
Biology: Dr S A Lewis, BSc London, PhD Glasgow (*Head of Science*)
Business Studies and Economics: P F Heuston, BSc Cape Town (*i/c Outdoor Pursuits*)
Chemistry: L J Whyte, BSc, PhD Norwich
Classics: Miss C L Nicholls, BA Oxford
Drama: E M J Boulter-Comer, BA Edinburgh
English: A J Speedy, BA Durham
Geography: Mrs R C O Nicol, BA Ripon & York St John
Government and Politics: D B McDowell, MA Oxford
History: Miss T J McDonald, BA Salford
History of Art: R E Hughes, MA Edinburgh, MPhil London
ICT: A M Hall, MA, PhD St Andrews
Mathematics: Dr N J Granger, MSc St Andrews, PhD Heriot-Watt
Modern Languages: M Delveaux, PhD, MA Exeter
Music: D A Goodenough, GGSM, FTCL, ARCO, ALCM (*Director of Music*)
Bagpipe Music: C R Drummond, BA RSAMD
Physical Education:
S M Bates, BSc London, MBA Durham (*Director of Sport*)
Miss F Ermgassen, BSc Bath (*Head of Girls' Games*)
J D Pillinger, BSc Surrey (*Head of PE*)
Physics: N C R Ward, BSc Manchester
Support For Learning: Miss P Bailey, MA Lancaster

Preparatory School:

Headmaster: A A Edwards, BA London

Deputy Headmaster: A A Rathborne, BA University of East Anglia (*Deputy CPO*)
Director of Studies: Mrs J A Hudson-Price, BA Durham (*Head of Geography*)
D Bywater, Cert Maths Cambridge (*Head of Mathematics, 1st Form Tutor*)
M Bywater, BA Stirling (*T Form Tutor*)
Revd Dr A Clark, BA York, PhD St Andrews (*School Chaplain, Head of Religious Studies*)
Miss E R Davies, BA Warwick (*Child Protection Officer, PHSE Coordinator, S Form Tutor*)
D Dawson, BSc Edinburgh (*Houseparent Iona House, 1st Form Tutor*)
Mrs C R Dawson (*Houseparent Iona House, Classroom Assistant*)
Mrs T E Deacon, BSc Southampton (*M Form Tutor*)
Mrs J Edwards, BA UEA (*Head of Modern Languages*)
Mrs J E Fletcher, BSc Chester (*Director of Sport, 2nd Form Tutor*)
D G Hall, BEd Liverpool John Moores (*Housemaster Arran House, Head of Science, 1st Form Tutor*)
Mrs R L Heuston, BA Natal (*Head of English, T Form Tutor*)
Mrs J A Hudson-Price, BA Durham (*Director of Studies, Head of Geography, 2nd Form Tutor*)
Miss E J G Kidd, BA Durham (*General Studies, M Form Tutor*)
Miss A A F Mair, MA Glasgow (*Head of History, 2nd Form Tutor*)
Mrs R Millburn, MA St Andrews (*1st Form Tutor*)
Miss K Moodie, BA Stirling (*General Studies, P Form Tutor*)
Mrs J O'Shea, BA Edinburgh (*Head of IT, General Studies, S Form Tutor*)
G Pettinger, BA RSAMD (*Director of Music, 1st Form Tutor*)
Mrs S C Quaile, MA Edinburgh (*Head of Latin, 2nd Form Tutor*)
Ms C M Tainsh, BEd Aberdeen BA Gray's (*Head of Art*)
Miss M Walker, BSc Cape Town (*Head of Support for Learning, 2nd Form Tutor*)
Miss D Whitcombe, BEd London (*Head of Drama*)
G Wood, BSc Heriot-Watt (*Head of Boys Games, P Form Tutor*)

Registrar: Mrs H F Marshall
Preparatory School Secretary: Miss M L Walls

Fettes College has over 5,000 Old Fettesians who remain in touch with us for one very compelling reason: being educated at Fettes was one of the most important and beneficial aspects of their lives.

Fettes is where their confidence was built, horizons broadened, talents nurtured and lifelong friendships made, where they achieved exam success, broke sporting records, were inspired by teachers and learnt the skills which would equip them for later life.

Fettes is where they were enthused, praised and encouraged to work hard and achieve the very best they could, while being surrounded by like-minded peers and caring staff.

To this day, a Fettes education is an incredible start to life.

Situation and Buildings. Fettes stands in 80 acres of parkland close to the centre of Edinburgh. Being just 20 minutes' walk to the city centre, means that Fettes students can take full advantage of the wealth of cultural resources on offer in Scotland's Capital city such as galleries, museums and theatres. Students also have every opportunity to enjoy the majestic Scottish outdoors with a full programme of trips and experiences from hillwalking to canoeing, camping to white water rafting. Regular national and international school trips further broaden the experience Fettes students are offered.

Transportation links by road, rail and air are excellent.

Organisation. Each member of the School is the responsibility of a Housemaster or Housemistress. In the Senior School there are four Houses for boys, four for girls, and a co-ed Upper Sixth Form house. The Upper Sixth Form boarding house provides individual and twin study-bedrooms with en-suite facilities for all boarders. There is a strong tutorial system for the encouragement and guidance of each pupil.

Aims. Our mission at Fettes is to develop broadly educated, confident and thoughtful individuals. The hopes and aspirations of each and every one of our students are of central importance to us, and the happy, purposeful environment of the College encourages the boys and girls to flourish and develop fully the skills and interests that they possess.

Curriculum. For GCSE all students take English, Mathematics, Physics, Chemistry and Biology. Students then choose four subjects from the following list: Art & Design, Classical Civilisation, Classical Greek, Drama, Economics, French, Geography, German, History, Latin, Mandarin, Music, PE and Spanish. Students must choose at least one modern foreign language.

Fettes offers a very broad range of subjects in the Sixth Form with students choosing either A Levels or International Baccalaureate, therefore allowing a choice of curriculum to best suit the needs of the individual student. Over 98% of pupils gain university entry with up to 15 students securing places at Oxford and Cambridge each year.

Careers. The School is a member of the Independent Schools Careers Organisation, and a team of Staff are responsible for providing specialist advice on careers and Higher Education and for developing links with industry and commerce. Fettes Community was launched in 2014 providing business networking links between Old Fettesians, current parents, past parents, Fettes students and recent Fettes graduates.

Chapel. The College Chapel, situated in the heart of the School, is central to life at Fettes with the daily Chapel service forming the core of the moral and spiritual guidance offered at Fettes. Fettes has a strong Christian tradition but members of other faiths and those with no faith are warmly welcomed, and this is reflected in the tolerant and questioning character of the School.

Games. All students are involved in sports at least 3 afternoons per week. All major sports are offered at Fettes in fact there are very few sports you cannot pursue. Rugby, cricket, hockey, lacrosse, netball, athletics, tennis, squash, fives, swimming, badminton, fencing, basketball, volleyball are an example of what is on offer. Fettes College is very proud of the individual and team success at school and national levels across a range of sports including rugby, fencing, sailing and cross-country. Fettes College also has excellent sporting facilities including a purpose-built sports centre, all-weather pitches, indoor swimming pool, climbing wall, courts for fives and squash, shooting range and a separate specialist gym for Sixth Form pupils.

Other activities. There are 50+ societies, clubs and extra-curricular activities, and each pupil is encouraged to develop cultural interests. On Saturday evenings, in addition to lectures, plays and concerts, there are regular dances and discos, and committees of pupils, with the assistance of members of Staff, are responsible for planning and organising social events for different age groups.

Music. The College possesses a strong musical tradition, and many pupils receive instrumental tuition. In addition to the orchestras there are ensembles, a swing band, Chapel Choir and Concert Choir. A major concert is held at the end of every term. Standards are very high and the Chapel Choir has achieved notable success, being recorded by the BBC and performing by invitation at Westminster Abbey and St Paul's Cathedral.

Drama. Drama is lively and of a high standard. Each year the School Play and House plays offer great opportunities for large numbers of boys and girls to act and to participate in Lighting and Stage Management.

Art. The Art School is flourishing, and the standards of pupil attainment are very high. Regular House art competitions and gallery display of current work occur.

Combined Cadet Force, Duke of Edinburgh's Award Scheme, Outside Service. Pupils are members of the CCF for two years and may choose to extend their service while they are in the Sixth Form. Training is offered in Shooting, Vehicle Engineering, Canoeing, Rock-Climbing, Skiing, Sub-Aqua and Sailing.

In the Sixth Form many pupils pursue the Gold Standard of the Duke of Edinburgh's Award Scheme, and some 70 members of the School join the Outside Service Unit which provides help for others in difficult circumstances and raises funds for Charities.

Outdoor Activities. The School aims to make full use of its proximity to the sea, the Dry Ski Slope, and the rivers and mountains of Scotland. Outdoor activities are encouraged for the enjoyment that they give and the valuable personal qualities which they help to develop. A number of members of Staff are experts in mountaineering, skiing and watersports, and all pupils have opportunities for receiving instruction in camping, canoeing, sailing, hillwalking and snow and rock climbing. There are regular expeditions abroad.

Preparatory School. The Preparatory School for 195 boys and girls aged 7 to 13 is situated in the School grounds. Boarders stay in the modern purpose-built Houses. Pupils in the Prep School share the facilities of the senior school and participate in the full range of activities enjoyed by the College as a whole. (*For further details see entry in IAPS section.*)

Admission. Personal interviews assess the promise of each individual and determine those who will gain most from a Fettes education. Entrance exams are also required for entry. Pupils may join the Preparatory School at any stage (7–13) with students normally joining the Senior School at 13+, 14+ and 16+. Further details are available from the Registrar.

Scholarships and Bursaries. All applicants can apply for a means-tested bursary which can cover up to 100% of the fees. There is a finite amount of funding available each year and therefore not all applicants will be successful. Bursaries are awarded independently of any Scholarship or Award. The process for applying for a bursary is completely separate to the admissions process and must be done through the Bursar's Office.

There is a wide range of Scholarships and Awards available at 13+ and/or 16+ including Academic, All-Rounder, Sport, Music, Art and Piping. There is great kudos associated with being a scholar or award holder of The College. Scholarships also attract reductions of up to 10% of the fees while Awards can also attract reductions of up to 5% of the fees unrelated to parents' financial circumstances.

Children of members of HM Forces qualify for a reduction in fees and Special Bursaries (Todd) are available for descendants of Old Fettesians.

Past papers are available and further enquiries should be made to the Registrar.

Fees per term (2014–2015). Senior School: Boarders £10,060, Day Pupils £7,730. The fees cover all extras except books and stationery, music lessons and subscriptions to voluntary clubs and activities.

Registration Fee £50.

Old Fettesian Association. *Liaison:* Mrs D A Beaumont, Old Fettesian Association Office, Fettes College (Telephone 0131 311 6741).

Charitable status. The Fettes Trust is a Registered Charity, number SC017489. Fettes aims to provide a quality education at Junior and Senior level.

Forest School

London E17 3PY
Tel: 020 8520 1744
Fax: 020 8520 3656
email: info@forest.org.uk
website: www.forest.org.uk
Twitter: @ForestSchoolE17

Motto: '*In Pectore Robur*'.
    Established in 1834, Forest School is a diamond structure school located on the edge of London's largest open space, Epping Forest.

Council:
Chairman of the Governors: J W Matthews, FCA

Members of the Council:
Prof J E Banatvala, CBE
B M de L Cazenove, TD
The Venerable Elwin Cockett, Archdeacon of West Ham
G S Green, MA
Mrs G Jenkinson, AGSM, Dip Ed
His Honour Judge W Kennedy
Mrs P Oates, BEd
Dr E M Sidwell, CBE, PhD, FRSA, FRGS
D Wilson, LLB
W Fuller

Warden: **Mrs S J Kerr-Dineen**, MA

Bursar and Clerk to the Governors:
Mrs D Coombs, BSc, MBA

Deputy Warden and Head of the Boys' School:
M Cliff Hodges, MA

Deputy Warden and Head of the Girls' School:
Mrs P A Goodman, MA

Head of Preparatory School:
A M Noakes, MA

Director of Teaching and Learning:
J W J Mitchell, MA

Director of Co-Curriculum:
J E R Sanderson, BA, BMus

Director of Sixth Form:
Mrs S M Clarke, BSc

Chaplain:
Reverend P K Trathen, MA

Assistant Staff:
[B] *Boys' School*
[G] *Girls' School*
[P] *Prep School*
HM *Housemaster or Housemistress*

B D Adams, BSc Exeter [B] (*Boys' Games, HM*)
A Amirthananthar, BSc Queen Mary & Westfield London [B] (*Chemistry*)
F J Andrews, MA Royal College of Art [B] (*Art*)
F Anwar, BA Huddersfield [G] (*Learning Support*)
R K Appleyard, BA University College London [B] (*Classics*)
M Arnold, BSc Open University [P]
T J Arnold, BSc Exeter [B] (*Boys' Games and PE, Boys' Prep School Games*)
P T S Aspery, BA Lady Margaret Hall Oxford [B] (*Head of Physics*)

L M Baber, BSc Baylor, MSc Harvard [G] (*Biology*)
L D Barker, BA Brighton [B] (*Head of Design and Technology*)
T A Barlow, MA Birmingham [B] (*English*)
G R Barton, BA University College London [G] (*Mathematics*)
A N Bergès, Lic-ès-Lettres Paris [B] (*Modern Languages*)
A J Birkhamshaw, MSc Birmingham [B] (*Geography*)
L S Bishop, BSc London [G] (*Food and Nutrition, Examinations Officer*)
C D Brant, MA Queens' College Cambridge [G] (*Head of History*)
C P A Browne, BEd Surrey, MA Institute of Education London [P] (*Deputy Head of Preparatory School*)
M D Bullock, BSc Nottingham [G] (*Mathematics, Assistant Timetabler*)
T J Burnside, MA Manchester [B] (*English*)
S L Campbell, BA Worcester [P] (*RE Subject Leader*)
J Chan, BEd Leeds, MEd Open University, AMBDA [P] (*English Subject Leader*)
K L Clark, BEd Homerton College Cambridge [P] (*Head of Prep School Girls' Pastoral Care*)
N Coghlan, BA Roehampton Institute [B] (*Head of Special Education Provision*)
H Cole, BA Wales, Lampeter [G] (*Geography*)
J Connell, BA Warwick [B] (*English*)
K L Cooper, BA Middlesex [P]
P Cordón, BA Vigo, Spain [B] (*Spanish*)
A L Cossey, MA Worcester College Oxford, MA King's College London, PG Dip Law BPP Law School [G] (*Religious Studies and Philosophy, HM*)
Joanna Cumming, BEd Northampton [P] (*Music Subject Leader*)
A R Dainton, BSc Loughborough [B] (*Director of Physical Education*)
B R d'Arcy, MA The Queen's College Oxford, Grad Dip Law BPP Leeds, BPTC [G] (*Classics*)
C A Davies, MBiochem The Queen's College Oxford, MEd Homerton College Cambridge [G] (*Biology, Head of Inclusion*)
M Dean, MA Stellenbosch, South Africa [B] (*Economics and Business Studies*)
O Dhani, BSc City University London [B] (*Mathematics*)
S Dhanjal, BSc University College London [B] (*Art and Design*)
P Drennan, Digby Stuart College, Dip DT Middlesex [B] (*Design and Technology*)
M Lee Duraku, BSc East London [B] (*Computing*)
H Edwards, MA Edinburgh [G] (*Classics*)
S Edwards, BA Birmingham [P] (*Head of Prep School Boys' Pastoral Care*)
P M Faulkner, BSc Leeds, MSc Edinburgh [P] (*Master i/c of Pre-Preparatory School*)
A L Feldman, BA Newcastle [B] (*Mathematics, Assistant Director of Sixth Form – Higher Education*)
S F Firek, BSc Leicester, PhD Portsmouth Polytechnic [B] (*Head of Biology*)
A E Foinette, MA Nottingham [B] (*Classics*)
C A Forsdyke, MA St John's College Cambridge, PG Dip Law City University, PG Dip Classical Studies King's College London [B] (*Classics, Assistant Examinations Officer*)
S J Foulds, BA Royal Holloway London [B] (*Modern Languages, HM*)
E F Golden, BA Williams College USA [G] (*History, HM*)
A G Gould, MA Balliol College Oxford [B] (*Head of Classics*)
F J Grace, BSc Sussex [G] (*Chemistry*)
D F Graham, Royal Academy of Music, GRSM, LRAM [G] (*Music, Senior Mistress, Girls' School*)
M Gray, BA Lancaster, MA Middlesex [B] (*Design and Technology, Senior Master, Boys' School*)
N V Gray, MA St John's College Cambridge [G] (*History*)

R Greasley, BEd Liverpool John Moores [B] (*Design and Technology*)

S M Harris, BA Southampton, MA East London [G] (*Modern Languages, Child Protection Officer*)

K Hawkins, BA Nottingham [B] (*RS and Philosophy*)

C A Heath, BA Queen Mary & Westfield London [G] (*Head of French, HM*)

P Henley-Smith, BSc, PhD Nottingham [B] (*Chemistry, HM*)

K Hersey, BSc Brunel [G] (*Girls' PE and Games, Educational Visits Coordinator*)

T C Hewitt, BA Cardiff College Wales [B] (*English*)

B Holmes, BA Fitzwilliam College Cambridge [B] (*Graduate Assistant Teacher Music*)

I R Honeysett, MA Selwyn College Cambridge [B] (*Head of Science*)

D Hordok, BA Liverpool [B] (*Modern Languages*)

F Hoxha, BSc Royal Veterinary College London [G] (*Biology*)

K A Hughes, MA Edinburgh [B] (*History*)

J E Hunt, BSc London Metropolitan [G] (*Food and Nutrition, HM*)

Karen Ip, BA Middlesex [P]

M S Jalowiecki, BA Queen Mary London [B] (*Computing*)

J J Kay, BA Leeds [B] (*English, HM*)

R H Kay, MA Warwick [G] (*History, HM*)

J H Kayne, BSc Nottingham Trent [B] (*Deputy Head of Boys' School*)

S C Keating, BEd Chelsea College of PE [G] (*Head of Girls' PE and Games*)

A Kelly, BSc Surrey [G] (*Physics*)

M C Kelly, MA Cork [B] (*Spanish*)

J I Kleiner, BA Middlesex [G] (*Design and Technology*)

C Leckie, BA Nottingham Trent [G] (*Graduate Teaching Assistant Sport*)

I M Leitão, MSc Glamorgan [G] (*Physics*)

O E Ling, BA Queen Mary & Westfield London [B] (*Government and Politics, HM*)

R Mackie, MA, MEd Fitzwilliam College Cambridge [G] (*RS and History*)

Anna Manlangit, BA British Columbia [P] (*Head of Pre-Preparatory School Teaching and Learning*)

L A McAllister, BA Brighton [P] (*Geography Subject Leader*)

I A McGregor, MA Fitzwilliam College Cambridge, MA Keele [B] (*Director of Music*)

J T McGurran, BA St Catherine's College Oxford [G] (*Economics and Business Studies*)

A J McIlwaine MA Sidney Sussex College Cambridge [G] (*Director of Drama*)

D Meredith [B] (*Art and Textiles*)

H P R Miller, BA University College London [B] (*Head of German*)

J Miller, BA Exeter [B] (*Modern Languages, HM*)

A H Moor [P] (*Drama*)

R Moore, BSc Stafford [G] (*Head of Computing*)

L A R Morrell, BA Brighton [G] (*Girls' PE and Games*)

E W Morris, BSc Cheltenham & Gloucester College of HE [G] (*Head of Geography*)

S P Morris, BSc York [B] (*Head of Chemistry*)

G Moss, BA Worcester [P] (*History Subject Leader*)

Z A Munir, BA Westminster [G] (*Economics and Business Studies*)

C Murphy, BA Liverpool John Moores [G] (*Head of Food and Nutrition, HM*)

L E Murray, BA Sheffield College of Art [G] (*Director of Art*)

Z H Nazir, BSc, DPhil Sussex [B] (*Mathematics*)

E Newman, MA Sheffield [B] (*History and Religious Studies*)

C M Nortier, BSc Free State, S A [B] (*Mathematics, Timetabler*)

B O'Brien-Blake, BA St Anne's College Oxford [G] (*Economics and Government & Politics*)

J F O'Riordan, BA College of Marketing and Design, Dublin [G] (*Design and Technology*)

C J A Palmer, BA University College London [G] (*Head of Modern Foreign Languages*)

L P Parnham, BA Exeter [P] (*Art Subject Leader*)

J S Pell, BA St John's College Cambridge [P] (*ICT Subject Leader*)

C R E Pepys, BA Durham [G] (*Head of Religious Studies and Philosophy*)

F M Pereira, MA Middlesex [G] (*Computing, Assistant Head of e-Learning*)

B M J Phillips, BSc Cardiff Metropolitan [B] (*Graduate Teaching Assistant – Sport*)

M M Pickwick, BSc City of London Polytechnic [P] (*SEND*)

D R Potter, BA Birmingham, PG Dip Acting Webber Douglas Academy [B] (*Drama*)

D Rathod, MSci Imperial College London [B] (*Mathematics*)

M J Raybould, MSc Imperial College London [G] (*Physics*)

S Razzaq, BSc King's College London [G] (*Biology*)

A J Redpath, BMus Royal College of Music [B] (*Assistant Director of Music*)

C Risk, BSc, BPhD Otago, Dunedin, NZ [G] (*Girls' PE and Games, Girls' Prep School Games*)

J B Scott, BA Reading [P] (*Maths Subject Leader*)

K Scott, BA Ulster [P] (*Coordinator Extra-Curricular Activities*)

T F Shah, BSc Kent [B] (*Chemistry*)

B J Shuler, BEng Durham [B] (*Physics*)

K C Skelding, BA Exeter [G] (*Head of Spanish*)

J T Sloan, BA Royal Holloway London [B] (*History, HM*)

M J Smith, BSc University College Swansea, MBA Open University, FRGS [B] (*Geography*)

K Spencer Ellis, MA Christ Church Oxford [G] (*Head of English*)

M H A Stern, PhD Kent [G] (*English*)

D J Supperstone, MA Gonville and Caius College Cambridge [G] (*Modern Languages*)

Charlotte Taylor, BA Bristol [P]

J V Taylor, CertEd I M Marsh College of PE Liverpool [G] (*Girls' PE and Games*)

M J Taylor, MA Jesus College Oxford, MSc Manchester [G] (*Head of Mathematics*)

C F Thompson, BSc Newcastle [G] (*Mathematics*)

A H Todd, BSc Royal Holloway London, PhD King's College London [G] (*Chemistry*)

D L Tubb, BEd I M Marsh College of PE Liverpool [G] (*Girls' PE and Games*)

S E Veitch, BSc Durham [B] (*Biology*)

J K Venditti, BEng University College Swansea [G] (*Deputy Head of Girls' School*)

K Vidos, BSc Nottingham [G] (*Biology*)

E P Watson, MEng York [B] (*Design and Technology, Assistant Director of Sixth Form – Careers*)

A M Weston, BA East Anglia [G] (*Mathematics*)

K White, MA Canterbury Christ Church [P] (*Preparatory School Music Coordinator*)

J A C Whitmee, BA Sheffield [B] (*Geography, HM*)

J J Whitton, BBusSci Cape Town, MA Oxford [B] (*Head of Economics and Political Science*)

S M Wiles, BA Kent, MA Open University [B] (*Music, Head of e-Learning*)

T E Wilson, MSci Imperial College London [G] (*Physics and Mathematics*)

S M Wood, BA Canterbury University, NZ [G] (*English*)

M A Wyatt, MA Cambridge [G] (*Religious Studies and Philosophy, Project Qualification Coordinator*)

L Yardley, BA Newcastle upon Tyne [G] (*Textiles*)

J Clifton (*Teacher's Assistant, Reception*)

L Crisp (*Classroom Assistant*)

B Eiras Reboiras (*Spanish Language Assistant*)
H Fellowes (*Y3 Teacher's Assistant*)
D Groves (*Teacher's Assistant, Reception*)
G Henze (*German Language Assistant*)
K Kelsey (*Y2 Teacher's Assistant*)
F Matson (*Y1 Teacher's Assistant*)
N Messalti (*French Language Assistant*)
J Randall (*Y4 Teacher's Assistant*)
S Sahins (*Y2 Teacher's Assistant*)
D Young (*Y1 Teacher's Assistant*)

There are currently about 1300 pupils in the School (515 boys in the Boys' School, 515 girls in the Girls' School, 270 boys and girls in the Pre-Preparatory and Preparatory School). All pupils share the main School campus and facilities such as Chapel, Sports Hall, Theatre and Computer Centre. The Sixth Form is co-educational with a dedicated Sixth Form Centre including collaborative IT work spaces and group study areas. The School site and playing fields cover nearly 27 acres.

Diamond Structure. Boys and girls are taught in co-educational classes when they join Forest School in the Pre-Prep, then in single-sex classes within the Prep School from Y3. At 11 pupils join the Boys' or Girls' School, separate divisions of Forest School with their own Houses and pastoral systems, which look after the boys and girls until they leave at 18. Single-sex teaching persists until the Sixth Form, where classes are once again co-educational. Co-curricular activities are largely co-educational although boys and girls follow different sports programmes. We believe this gives pupils the best of all worlds.

While the existence of the diamond structure at Forest is a result of evolution rather than initial design, the Forest School of today regards the mix of single-sex and co-educational teaching as an educational model of which to be proud, and thought and effort goes into making it a structure that we might indeed have designed from scratch.

Curriculum. The Forest curriculum parallels the National Curriculum, although the School exercises its independence to enable teachers to exploit the high academic ability of the pupils. In Y7–Y9 a range of core subjects is taught, including Modern and Classical Languages and the three Sciences. Options in Y9 include Computing, Ancient Greek and Food & Nutrition, as well as more mainstream subjects. At GCSE, all pupils follow a core curriculum of English Language & Literature, a Modern Foreign Language, Maths and Science (separate or Double Award, according to preference) as well as a choice from around 15 optional subjects. A distinctive feature of the curriculum is that all pupils also submit work for the Higher Project Qualification (HPQ) – a research-based dissertation on a subject of the pupil's own choosing, following a taught course of critical thinking and project skills, assessed at GCSE level.

In the Sixth Form, pupils can choose three A Levels from 27 different subjects, taught by subject specialists in small teaching groups of around ten to fifteen pupils and examined at the end of the two-year course. All Sixth Form pupils begin a course in Project Skills in Year 12, and most will continue to produce an EPQ project by the November of Year 13. This may take the form of a dissertation-style essay, or perhaps a 'creative artefact', like a film, composition or even a computer program.

The School places considerable emphasis on teaching the effective use of Information and Communications Technology. After Y7, the teaching of ICT skills is embedded in the work of all subjects, and pupils in the Sixth Form are encouraged to use internet-enabled devices in lessons or in collaborative working environments in the Sixth Form Centre. Computing, with an emphasis on programming, is available from Y9 as an academic subject.

The curriculum is augmented by a wide range of popular academic co-curricular activities which supplement timetabled subjects. Lessons in Brazilian Portuguese, Italian, Mandarin Chinese and Russian are offered, as well as opportunities to develop skills in Music Technology, Science and other academic disciplines.

Co-Curriculum. The School has a large Music Department with more than 50 visiting staff teaching a wide range of instruments and voice, regular concerts in school venues and outside, House Music and Classical competitions. Drama offers two major plays and House Drama Competitions as well as regular showings for curricular drama. Art presents regular exhibitions and cross-curricular projects with English and other departments. Other activities include Forest's Combined Cadet Force, which is linked to the Royal Green Jackets and the Duke of Edinburgh's Award which offers Bronze, Silver and Gold levels delivered by Forest staff. Other activities include raising money for charity, taking part in public speaking competitions, community work – such as visiting the elderly and riding for the disabled – student-led societies and publications, video techniques, theatre lighting, additional languages, musical theatre, dance, speech & drama and journalism. The Forest Portfolio monitors pupil involvement and encourages a rounded approach to co-curricular involvement.

Games. The main games are Association football, Hockey, Cricket, Netball, Athletics, Basketball and Swimming. The sporting facilities are extensive and include tennis and netball courts, indoor and outdoor cricket nets, gym, sports hall and two swimming pools.

Fees per term (2014–2015). Years 7–13 £5,238, Years 4–6: £4,109, Year 3 £3,797, Reception–Year 2 £3,543. Lunch included.

Admission. Examinations for pupils at 7+ and 11+ take place in January for entry in the following September. Places are available at 16+, 13+ and occasionally at other ages.

Careers. Almost all pupils go on to Universities to take Degree Courses, including 5–6 each year to Oxford and Cambridge. Careers advice is given to all pupils.

Scholarships and Bursaries. Scholarships and Bursaries are available by competitive process for entry at 11+, 13+ and 16+. The maximum non-means tested fee remission awarded in respect of any one pupil is 50% of full fees, whether in one area of excellence or in combination of one or more areas of excellence. Bursaries are means-tested and are awarded in addition to Scholarships, up to and including the total remission of fees.

Up to the equivalent of 12 places may be given annually to pupils at 11+, following Scholarship assessment in January of the year of entry, of which 2 are reserved for excellence in Music.

Up to the equivalent of 2 Forest Exhibitions are awarded at 11+ to those showing all-round promise but who have not been awarded an Academic Scholarship. In the case of Music, Forest Exhibitions meet the cost of lessons in one or more instrument.

Up to the equivalent of 2 places are awarded at 13+ to internal or external applicants, as Excellence Scholarships in recognition of exceptional attainment or potential in curricular or co-curricular areas.

Up to the equivalent of 6 places may be given annually to both internal and new entrants to the Sixth Form, of which up to 2 are reserved for Academic excellence and 1 in Music. Scholarships are also awarded for outstanding ability in Art, Drama and Sport.

Up to the equivalent of 2.25 places are generally available to new entrants to the Sixth Form, sponsored by the Ogden Trust, Mulalley and Co, the Old Foresters, and the 175th Anniversary appeal.

Fee reductions are available for children of the Clergy.

For full details visit www.forest.org.uk.

Old Foresters Club. *Hon Secretary*: Mrs K Hersey, c/o Forest School.

Charitable status. Forest School, Essex is a Registered Charity, number 312677. The objective of the School is Education.

Framlingham College

Framlingham, Woodbridge, Suffolk IP13 9EY

Tel: 01728 723789
Fax: 01728 724546
email: admissions@framcollege.co.uk
website: www.framcollege.co.uk
Twitter: @framcollege
Facebook: /framcollege
LinkedIn: /framlingham-college

Motto: '*Studio Sapientia Crescit.*'

Chairman of Governors: A W M Fane, MA, FCA

Headmaster: **Mr P B Taylor**, BA Hons

Senior Deputy Head: Mrs S M Wessels, MA, BSc, NDip
Deputy Head Academic: D G Ashton, BA Hons, Dip Ed
Deputy Head Co-Curricular: M D Robinson, MA, BEd Hons (*Head of History*)
Deputy Head Pastoral: C E Hobson, BA Hons, PGCE

Heads of Department:
Art: Mrs C E Mallett, BA Hons, AdvDipT
Business Studies & Economics: C Caiger, BA, MSc, PGCE
Careers: Miss C Cranmer, BA Hons, PGCE, Dip Speech & Drama
Universities: R W Skitch, BSc, ACCEG, ACIB, PGCE
Design & Technology: M B Brown, Cert Ed
Drama: Ms D Englert, BA Hons, PGCE, Dip Speech & Drama
ESL: Mrs K Cavalcanti, BEd Hons, RSA Dip EFL
English: L Goldsmith, BA Hons, MBA, PGCE
Geography: D Lyon, MSc, BA, PGCE
Languages: B Dyer, BA Hons
Learning Support: Mrs L Wrigglesworth, BA Hons
Mathematics: K R S Hoyle, BSc, PGCE
Director of Music: T Rhodes, BMus Hons
PSHE: D J Boatman, BA Hons, PGCE
Psychology: Mrs J S Hobson, BA Hons, PGCE
Religious Studies: J E Holland, BA, PGCE
Science: Dr D R Higgins, MA, PhD, PGCE
Director of Sport: S Sinclair

Finance Director: N J Chaplin, BA Hons, FCCA
Operations Director: A L Payn, Chartered FCIPD
Admissions Registrar: Miss E Rutterford, BA Hons
Headmaster's Personal Assistant: Mrs H Alcoe

Location. The school is situated close to the wonderful Suffolk Coast, in the historic market town of Framlingham, overlooking the Mere and Castle, and is served by good road and rail links to London, Cambridge, Colchester, Norwich and all the main London airports.

History. The School was founded in 1864 by public subscription as the Suffolk County Memorial to Prince Albert and was incorporated by Royal Charter.

Organisation. Mr Taylor became Headmaster in September 2009; he was formerly Lower Master (Deputy Head) at King's School in Canterbury. He now leads a school that has recently received an excellent ISI Inspection Report, which described the College as highly successful in meeting its stated aims and mission of providing a first-class, holistic education, in a safe and inspiring environment, accessible to a broad range of boys and girls. The Senior School numbers some 415 pupils of whom 236 are boarders. All students are accommodated in seven fully-integrated boarding and day houses: three for girls and four for boys.

Preparatory School. Brandeston Hall, located less than 5 miles away, is a leading preparatory school for boys and girls aged 2½–13. All students are prepared for the ISEB Common Entrance Examination. (*See entry in IAPS section.*)

Facilities. An imaginative buildings programme has produced an exciting range of facilities which include the Headmaster Porter Theatre, a state-of-the-art drama and music facility. Science, Technology and Art enjoy purpose-built accommodation, and the Leisure Centre houses an indoor swimming pool and fitness suite, thereby enhancing the superb range of sports facilities. The flourishing Sixth Form is 200 strong and students enjoy their own Centre, which overlooks an attractive central concourse used extensively for informal gatherings. There are further plans to improve the warm and friendly boarding houses.

Curriculum. The College has a fine record in stretching the most able, while the 'value added' rating for those pupils who are not automatically destined to achieve A grades at GCSE and A Level stands among the very best in the country. Department for Education figures covering recent years confirmed this when placing the College among the top 5% in the country at improving pupils' grades between GCSE and A Level, and this is reflected in the ISI Inspection report which describes much of the teaching as *outstanding*.

Extra-Curricular Activities. Our academic success rates are mirrored by outstanding sporting achievements, commitment to the popular and extremely successful Duke of Edinburgh's Award Scheme and the outward-bound work of the voluntary Combined Cadet Force. From the cut and thrust of the debating society there are visiting speakers and musical performances, charity competitions, formal house suppers and many cultural, educational and recreational visits. Whether it is cookery or the choral society, equestrianism or aero-modelling, a round of golf on campus or trekking in Nepal, there is something for everyone.

Games. Framlingham College enjoys an enviable reputation for sport and fields a large number of teams, with students benefiting from an Elite Athlete programme where one student has been selected for the 2012 Olympic K4 Kayaking Development Squad and another for the U16 Great Britain skiing team. The major games are rugby, hockey, cricket, athletics and tennis for boys, and hockey, netball, tennis and athletics for girls. There is a wide range of other sporting opportunities, including squash, football, badminton, basketball, rounders, swimming, archery, shooting, volleyball and table tennis. The immaculately tended grounds include four rugby pitches, two floodlit artificial pitches, a golf course and one of the finest cricket squares in the East of England. The facilities also include a sports hall, indoor swimming pool, fitness centre, gym, squash courts, netball courts and tennis courts.

Music and Drama. Framlingham has a very strong choral tradition, and there is a wide range of orchestras and instrumental ensembles. In the past seven years, three pupils have reached the finals of BBC Radio 2 Chorister of the Year. The College's dramatic productions enjoy a very high reputation. The main productions each year generally include one musical, a major drama and a junior play.

Religion. The College has a strong Christian foundation, but students of all backgrounds are welcomed.

Admission. Common Entrance and interview form the normal means of entry to the College at 13+, but special provision is made for students for whom this is not appropriate. Entrance at 16+ is normally on the basis of GCSE results and interview or testing, but special arrangements are made for overseas students who are not following the British Curriculum. Visits from interested parties are welcomed; please contact us to make an appointment.

Scholarships and Bursaries. A wide range of scholarships are awarded every year at the following points of entry:

11+ (Brandeston Hall): Academic, Music, and Sports.

13+: Academic, Art, Design & Technology, Drama, Music, and Albert Memorial (All-Rounder including Sport). The Porter Science Scholarship is awarded at 13+ for excellence in Science.

Sixth Form: Stapleton (Academic) Scholarships are available to students who are attaining academic excellence and have the potential to achieve at least 3 Grade As at A Level. Art, Design & Technology, Drama, Music, and Albert Memorial (All-Rounder including Sport) Scholarships are also available.

Successful candidates can be offered further assistance through bursaries in cases of proven financial need.

Special bursaries are available for the children of serving members of HM Forces.

Fees per term (2014–2015). Boarding £9,222.58, Day £5,929.91 (including lunch).

Charitable status. Albert Memorial College (Framlingham College) is a Registered Charity, number 1114383.

Francis Holland School
Regent's Park

Clarence Gate, Ivor Place, London NW1 6XR
Tel: 020 7723 0176
Fax: 020 7706 1522
email: admin@fhs-nw1.org.uk
website: www.francisholland.org.uk

Founded 1878.

Patron: The Right Revd and Right Hon The Lord Bishop of London

Council:
Chairman: Mrs M Winckler, MA
Vice Chairman: Mrs A Edelshain, BA, MBA, MCIPD
Mr P Ashton, BSc, ACA
Mr A Beevor, BA, MBE
Miss E Buchanan, CVO, LLD, ARAgS
Mr D Dowley, MA, QC
Mr J Dunston, MA, ACIL, FRSA
Mrs S Graham Campbell
Dr M Harrison, BA
Mrs S Honey, BA
Mrs C Longworth, BA
Mrs B Mathews, BA, FCA
Professor J Parry, MA, PhD
Mr S Pitchford, MA
Miss S Ross, BSc, FInstP (*Safeguarding Children – Child Protection*)
Dr H Spoudeas, MBBS, DRCOG, FRCPCH, FRCP, MD
Professor J Yeomans, MA, DPhil

Locum Bursar: Mr G Wilmot, BA, ACA
Clerk to the Governors: Mrs G Shaw, BSc

Headmistress: Mrs V M Durham, MA Oxon

Senior Deputy Head : Mrs K Whiteman, MA Oxon
Academic Deputy Head: Miss J Zugg, BSc Cape Town South Africa
Pastoral Deputy Head: Miss C Mahieu, BEd Sydney Australia
Director of Extra-Curricular Studies: Miss C MacDonnell, MA London
Head of Sixth Form: Mrs A Francisco, BA Sydney Australia
Director of Higher Education and University Applications: Ms A Slocombe, MA Cantab

Head of Year 7: Mr M Chiverton, MA Oxon
Head of Year 8: Mrs S Bexon, BA King's College London
Head of Year 9: Miss J Laytham, BEd Newcastle Australia

Head of Year 11: Miss J Tucker, BEd Queensland Australia
Head of Year 10: Miss M Gustave, BA MA Montpellier

Teaching Staff:
* *Head of Department*
Art:
*Miss J Orr, BA NkU, MA Sussex
Miss H Gardner, BA Hons Nottingham
Mrs R North, BA Byam Shaw School of Art
Miss R Thomson, MA Edinburgh

Classics:
*Mrs H Packford, BA Cantab
Mrs J Cohen, MA Oxon
Mrs A Hillier, MA Cantab
Mrs C Wood, BA Oxon

Economics:
*Miss A M Conway, MA St Andrews

English:
*Miss E Williams, BA Leeds
Mrs N Foy, MA London
Mrs K F Oakley, BA London
Dr F De Bono, PhD London
Miss A Hine, BA Goldsmiths
Mr A Smith, BA York

Geography:
*Miss S Hack, BA Portsmouth
Miss J Hallett, BA Nottingham
Mrs P Freeley, BA Durham

History and Politics:
*Mr H Clayton, BA Liverpool
Mr M Chiverton, MA Oxon
Miss F Barton, BA Cantab
Miss K Lewis, BA Cantab
Mrs K Whiteman, MA Oxon

History of Art:
*Mrs A Montgomery, BA Newcastle
Mrs A Francisco, BA Sydney Australia
Miss C MacDonnell, MA London

Information Technology:
*Miss V Rusu, BEd Alberta
Mrs M Anastasi, BSc Open University

Learning Enhancement:
*Mrs F Forde, CertEd Dartford College
Mrs J Denniston, BA Edinburgh
Mrs M Wynne, BA Dunedin New Zealand

Librarian:
Ms L Barlow, MA Loughborough

Mathematics:
*Mrs A Martin, BSc UCL
Miss N Murugan, BSc Heriot-Watt
Miss R Le Roux, BSc Nottingham Trent, MSc Essex
Miss P Shah, BA Oxon
Miss J Zugg, BSc Cape Town South Africa

Modern Languages:
*Mr N Gridelli, BA Bologna Italy
Mrs B Edwards, BA Hull
Miss A Spera, B Pisa
Herr R Diesel, Technische Universitat Berlin (*German*)
Miss M Gustave, MA Montpellier
Miss N Lamas, MA KCL
Miss J Laurent, MA Victor Segalen
Mrs R Pithouse, BA Lyon France
Ms A Slocombe, MA Cantab
Mrs F Boschi, AVCE
Ms G Tomsett-Rowe, BA Exeter

Music:
*Mr R Patterson, MA Cantab, FRCO
Mrs S Kenyon, BMus RNCM

Mr A Smith, BA York

Visiting Music Staff:
Mr K Abbs, FTCL (*Clarinet/Saxophone*)
Ms F Firth, LTCL (*Voice*)
Ms K Bennett, MMus (*Flute*)
Mr E Hackett, LRAM (*Percussion & Kit*)
Mrs C Hall, LRAM (*Voice*)
Miss C Graham, MMus (*Cello*)
Miss J Harris, BMus (*Trumpet*)
Mr O Lallemant, MA Cantab (*Organist, Accompanist and Piano*)
Ms J McLeod, ARCM (*Theory*)
Mr D Parsons, ARCM (*Guitar*)
Miss C Parker, BMus (*Violin*)
Mr S Queen, MA Cantab (*Voice*)
Mr P Robinson, MA Cantab (*Voice*)
Ms J Schloss, BMus Qld (*Piano*)
Ms A Thwaite, BMus Guildhall (*Piano*)

Also visiting teachers for:
aerobics, kick boxing, self-defence, pottery, cookery, fencing, yoga and Alexander Technique, according to demand.

Physical Education:
*Miss J Tucker, BEd Queensland Australia
Mrs S Drummond, CertEd Nevilles Cross Durham
Mrs K Lombard, BEd Canterbury New Zealand
Miss C Mahieu, BEd Sydney Australia
Miss J Laytham, BEd Newcastle Australia
Ms C Bain, BEd Queensland Australia
Mrs F Forde, CertEd Dartford College

Psychology:
*Miss A Langley, BSc UWE

Religious Education:
*Miss J Farthing, BA Bristol
Mrs S Bexon, BA King's College

Speech and Drama:
Ms K Mount, BA Rose Bruford College

Science:
*Mr D Ward, BSc Nottingham Trent, MA Open University (*Physics*)
Mr J Peters, BSc Swinburne
Miss K Hotchkiss, MChem Oxon
Mrs R Grant, BSc Sheffield (*Biology, Chemistry*)
Miss S Fernandez, BSc Nottingham
Miss M Lockwood, BA Oxon
Mrs S Drummond, CertEd Nevilles Cross Durham
Miss B Shah, MSc Queen Mary's
Miss T Ahmed, MSc Strathclyde

Non-Teaching Staff:
Admissions Registrar: Mrs S Bailey
PA to the Headmistress: Miss G Hogarth, MA King's College London
Assistant to the SLT: Ms R Smith, MSc Edinburgh
School Secretary, Admissions: Miss S Clarke
Art Technician: Miss R Oloumi, BA Edinburgh
Systems Manager: Mr T Oladuti, MBCS, BA Winchester
ICT Technician: Mr S Andrews
Database Manager: Mrs M Anastasi, BSc Open University
Examination Administration Officer: Mrs J Cohen, MA Oxon
Assistant Examination Administration: Mrs S Gurini
Science Technicians:
Mrs G Unwin, BSc Greenwich
Mrs N Kazemi, BSc North London
Mrs M Shah, BA Tribhuwan University Nepal
Caretakers:
Mr C Alarcon Mejia
Mr J Saguiguit
Mr K Bright

Catering Manager: Mr S King
School Counsellor: Mrs A Salter, MA School of Psychotherapy and Counselling

There are 465 day girls and entry by examination and interview is normally at 11+, with a number joining at 16+ for the Sixth Form. The school was founded in 1878 and is affiliated to the Church of England, but girls of all Christian denominations and other faiths are accepted.

Curriculum. Girls are prepared for GCSE, A and AS Levels, and for admission to Universities, and Colleges of Art, Education and Music. Games are played in Regent's Park and full use is made of the museums, theatres and galleries in central London. Extra lessons are available including fencing, music, pottery, Speech and Drama, Alexander Technique, kickboxing, Mandarin Chinese and cookery. For the first five years, to GCSE, girls follow a broad curriculum and normally take 10 GCSE subjects. Careers advice is given from the third year, and all pupils receive individual guidance through to the Sixth Form. In the Sixth Form a wide choice of A Level subjects is combined with a general course of study, including the opportunity to take the Extended Project. All girls are expected to stay until the end of the A Level course.

Scholarships and Bursaries. We will consider awarding a bursary to girls who demonstrate the ability to succeed at Francis Holland, but whose parents might not have sufficient financial resources.

A bursary is a means-tested award and is determined by the family's financial circumstances, taking into account income, realisable assets and other relevant circumstances. The level of assistance provided will depend on individual circumstances, which will be reviewed annually. The number of bursaries awarded each year is at the discretion of the Governors and may vary.

Remission of a third of the fees is available to places offered to daughters of the clergy.

Fees per term (2014–2015). £5,560.

Situation. The school is situated just outside Regent's Park and is three minutes from Baker Street and Marylebone stations. Victoria and Hampstead buses pass the school.

Charitable status. The Francis Holland (Church of England) Schools Trust Limited is a Registered Charity, number 312745. It exists to provide high quality education for girls.

Frensham Heights

Rowledge, Farnham, Surrey GU10 4EA
Tel: 01252 792561
Fax: 01252 794335
email: admissions@frensham-heights.org.uk
website: www.frensham.org

Patrons:
¶Professor T Sherwood, MB, MA, FRCP, FRCR (*Emeritus Professor of Radiology, Cambridge, Fellow of Girton College*)
¶Mrs J Read, BA, FCIPD (*Semi-retired HR Consultant*)
Chairman: Mr M Chadwick, ACA, ATII (*former Head of Group Taxation, Friends Provident plc*)
Vice Chairman: Mr D Haywood MA (*Retired Headmaster of City of London Freemen's School*)
Treasurer: Mr R Lowther, CIMA, MSc (*Finance Consultant*)
Company Secretary and Clerk to the Governors: Mr P Lane, MBA, BSc, FCIPD, FCMI

Governors:
Mrs M Coltman, BA LLB (*Group General Counsel and Company Secretary Prudential*)
¶Mr D Eley (*CEO of The Dan Eley Foundation*)

Mr J Hynam Cert Ed, ACP, BEd, MPhil (*Former Bursar of Winchester College*)
Mr A Lawman, AFA, FIAB, FCMA (*Finance Director*)
Mr M Lupton, MRCOG, MBBS, MA, Cert MEd, Dip MEd, MEd (*Consultant Physician*)
¶Mr W Marriott, BA (*Partner with Meadows Fraser LLP*)
Mrs S Palfreyman, SRN, SCM, MSc, CertEd (*Lecturer in health and education*)
Mrs K Poulsom (*Managing Director of an Agricultural Contracting and Plant Hire Company*)
Mrs J Sullivan (*Chartered Surveyor*)
Mr P Ward BEd (*Headmaster of Thomas's Preparatory School, Clapham*)

Head: **Andrew Fisher**, BA, MEd, FRSA

Deputy Head: Becks Scullion, BSc, PGCE
Deputy Head (*Academic*): Rachel Burnett, BA, MSc, PGCE

Heads of Schools:
Sixth Form: Peter Unitt, BSc, PGCE
Middle School: Andy Spink, BSc, QTS
Junior School: Nic Hoskins, BA, QTS

Departments:
* *Head of Department*
TiC *Teacher in Charge*

English:
*Lisa Graham, BA, PGCE
Deirdre Gannon, BA, Dip Ed
Jennifer Hodge, MA, PGCE
Hannah Manton, BSc, PGCE
Rachel Burnett, BA, MSc, PGCE
Alison Bundy, BEd

Mathematics:
*Steve Powell, BSc, PGCE
Russell Crew, BEng, PGCE
Andrew Ellison, BSc, QTS
David Stevenson, BA, PGCE
Paul Hughes, BEng, PGCE
Karen McCathie, BSc, QTS

Sciences:
*Tom Bacon, BSc, PGCE
Peter Unitt, BSc, PGCE
Nick Arnell, BSc, PGCE (*TiC Biology*)
Charlotte Douglass, BA, PGCE (*TiC Chemistry*)
Susan Millerchip, BSc, PGCE (*TiC Physics*)
Andrew Ellison, BSc, QTS
Jeff Loomis, PhD, QTS
Andrew Melbourne, BSc, PGCE
Janette Wiggs (*Senior Science Technician*)
Rene Bachmann (*Science Technician*)

Modern Foreign Languages:
*Tim Seys, BA, PGCE (*Spanish/French*)
Angela Schock-Hurst, MA (*TiC German*)
Richard Arthur, BA, PGCE
Kate Godeseth, BA, PGCE
Emma Wyld, BA, Dip TESOL TiC EAL
Valerie Taylor-Meysonnet, BA, PGCE
Nia Tkhelidze (*HMC Teacher*)

History:
*Matthew Burns, BA, PGCE
Charles Bennett, BA, PGCE
Sophia Colley, MA, PGCE
Amanda McCallum, BSc, PGCE

Geography:
*Nicola O'Donnell BA, MEd, PGCE
Karen McBride, BSc, PGCE
Will Paskell, BSc, PGCE
Amanda McCallum BSc, PGCE

Economics & Business Studies & Sociology:
*Hugh Robertson, BSc, PGCE, MBA
Barry Carr, MA, PGCE
Becks Scullion, BSc, PGCE
Hannah Manton, BSc, PGCE

Psychology:
Hannah Manton, BSc, PGCE

IT:
*Karen McCathie BSc, QTS

PE & Games:
*Jeremy Belas BSc, QTS
Andy Spink, BSc, QTS
Sian Owens, BSc, QTS
Lucy Fox, BSc, PGCE
David Lloyd Coach

Co-curricular and Outdoor Education:
Linn Kathenes

Art & Design:
*Brendan Horstead, BA, PGCE
Alexander Allan, BA, PGCE (*TiC Design Technology*)
John Atkinson, BSc, PGCE, CertTheol (*TiC Photography*)
Michele Rickett, BA, PGCE
Ashley Howard, MA
Steffi Cottle-Bailey, BA
Beatrice Espinosa (*Ceramics Technician*)
Robert Russell (*Art Technician*)
Tom Armour (*DT Technician*)

Dance:
*Robert Keane
Lynn Goodburne, BPhil, Dip LCDD, QTS

Drama:
*Amanda Liddle, BA
Clare Marsh, MA, PGCE
Sara Winthrop

Music:
*Rupert Gardner, BA, PGCE
Shelagh Harris, GGSM, ARCM, PGCE
Laura Eaton, BMus

Learning Support:
Beverley Wrigglesworth (*Senior SENCO*)
Chris Vardy, BEd (*Junior SENCO*)

PSME:
Kate Godeseth, BA, PGCE

RE:
Karen McBride, BSc, PGCE

Librarian:
Noel Rasmussen

Junior School:
Nic Hoskins, BA, QTS (*Head of Junior School*)
Nick Oram-Tooley, BA (*Class Teacher Year 6*)
Rosemary Giraudet, BEd (*Class Teacher Year 5*)
Sally Heighington, BEd (*Class Teacher Year 4*)
Rosemary McMillan, CertEd (*Class Teacher Year 3*)
Clive Esterhuysen, BA (*Class Teacher Year 2*)
Olivia Aylott, BEd (*Class Teacher Year 1*)
Esme Lee, BEd (*Class Teacher Year 1*)
Lucinda Edwards, BA, PGCE (*Class Teacher Reception*)
Cristina Pecetta (*Nursery Teacher*)
Lydia Hardcastle, LLB, PGCE (*Forest Class Teacher*)
Samantha Pole (*Teaching Assistant*)
Debbie Hunt (*Teaching Assistant*)
Penny Gibbs (*Teaching Assistant*)
Sanya Birch (*Teaching Assistant, Extended Day Supervisor*)

Boarding House Staff:

Becks Scullion (*Deputy Head, Director of Boarding*)

Hamilton House (Years 7 to 9):
Clive Esterhuysen (*Housemaster*)
Lucy Fox (*Deputy Housemistress*)
Brendan Horstead (*Visiting Tutor*)
Rupert Gardner (*Visiting Tutor*)
Debbie Hunt (*House Parent*)
Thomas Cox (*Resident Staff*)

Main House (Years 10 and 11):
Lynn Goodburne (*Senior Housemistress*)
Deirdre Gannon (*Girls' Deputy Housemistress*)
William Paskell (*Boys' Housemaster*)
David Lloyd (*Boys' Deputy Housemaster*)
Sian Owens (*Visiting Tutor*)
Sarah Dedman (*House Parent – West Wing*)
Colette Hill (*House Parent – East Wing*)

Roberts House (Sixth Form):
Steve Powell (*Housemaster*)
Cristina Pecetta (*Deputy Housemistress*)
Jenny Hodge (*Resident Tutor*)
Matthew Burns (*Assistant Housemaster*)
Peter Unitt (*Visiting Tutor*)
Amanda Liddle (*Visiting Tutor*)
Norma Scholey (*House Parent*)

Medical Centre:
Sarah Burton (*Senior School Nurse*)
Charlotte Lee (*School Nurse*)
Debbie Huddlestone (*School Nurse*)
Vanessa Edworthy (*School Counsellor*)
Dr Paul Adams (*Medical Officer*) (*visiting*)
Dr Liz Colyer (*Medical Officer*) (*visiting*)

Support Staff:
Headmaster's Office:
Lindsey Boyce (*Headmaster's PA*)
Helen Evans, BA (*School Secretary*)
Samantha Moulton (*Junior School Administrator*)
Lulu Spurling (*Receptionist*)
Vicki Maule (*Receptionist*)
Sally Vivian (*Receptionist*)
Marketing & Admissions:
Emily Wood, BA (*Director of Marketing & Admissions*)
Peter German, BA (*Marketing & Admissions Manager*)
Sarah Windsor, BA (*Admissions Registrar*)
Florence Hibbert,, BA (*Marketing & Admissions*)
Bursary:
Paul Lane MBA, BSc, FCIPD, FCMI (*Bursar & Clerk to Governors*)
Susie Birdsall, BA (*Bursar's Secretary*)
Karen Anderson, FCCA (*Finance Manager*)
Rachel Goddard, MATT (*Senior Financial Administrator*)
Julie Cox (*Accounts Assistant*)
Barbara Smale (*Accounts Assistant*)
Louise Moore BEng (*IT Manager*)
Sean Connor, BA (*Theatre Manager*)
Ruth Wilde (*Resources*)
Karen Heath (*Resources & IT Support*)
Kerry Guy (*Enterprises Manager*)
Adiyta Thapa (*Gen Manager, Catering*)
Sarah Bryant (*Asst Manager, Catering*)
Christine Barrett (*Housekeeper*)
Gordon Duncan (*Estate Bursar*)
Liz Bownass-Clark (*School Administrator/Assistant Exams*)
Michael Hoy (*Head of Maintenance*)
Kevin Barrett (*Plumber*)
Russell Finbow (*Carpenter*)
Doug Paine (*Maintenance Assistant*)
Robert McGuigan (*Maintenance Assistant*)

Founded in 1925, Frensham Heights is a highly distinctive school in a world of educational conformity. We have developed from the progressive school movement and are acknowledged as one of the most successful liberal day and boarding schools in the country. We believe every child is an individual and we will feed their imaginations, expect them to ask questions – and indeed pursue their own answers, and therefore help them grow into confident, generous and happy young adults. At the heart of this is personal development and responsibility alongside excellent academic achievements.

Pupil numbers. 500 boys and girls aged 3 to 18 years. Average class size: 18.

Entry. Children entering from Nursery to Year 6 have an assessment day. Children entering the school at the age of 11+ and 13+ sit the Frensham Heights Entrance Examination, held in January. Entrance to the Sixth Form is by examination and interview with a minimum of six GCSE passes at Grade C or above (A/B grades in A Level subjects). The school recommends that parents first visit on an Open Day, after which individual appointments tailored to their specific requirements can be made through the Admissions Registrar.

Curriculum. Most students take 9 GCSE subjects of which the compulsory elements are English Language and Literature, mathematics and triple or double award science. The top set take triple award science. Students then choose from geography, history, business studies, a second modern language, art, 3D design, dance, design technology, drama, music, music technology or PE. Photography is taught to GCSE as an extra-curricular activity and as part of the curriculum at A Level. There are 22 subjects to choose from at A Level. The AQA Extended Project Qualification is offered for suitable candidates. PSME is taught throughout the school.

Academic Results. Examination results are very good. There is a strong Sixth Form, the vast majority of whom go on to further education, including Oxford, Cambridge and Russell Group. Public examination results 2014: A Level – 12% A*, 47% A*/A, 88% A*–C grades; GCSE – 12% A*, 31% A*/A, 89% A*–C.

Sport. The school's excellent sporting facilities include an astroturf, playing fields, swimming pool, tennis courts and an indoor sports centre. Sports include basketball, football, netball, hockey, rounders and cricket. Annual ski and surfing trips take place abroad in the holidays.

Outdoor Education. Outdoor education is part of the curriculum for all pupils in Year 7 and above. Training takes place in the school's extensive adventure centre and leads to weekend and holiday expeditions in camping, climbing, caving, canoeing, scuba-diving and trekking, including World Challenge and Duke of Edinburgh's Awards.

Extra-curricular Activities. All pupils are expected to take part in extra-curricular activities. An extensive and varied selection of activities includes sports of all sorts, art, music, dance, drama, hobbies and clubs and sailing.

Facilities. 100 acres of parkland in beautiful countryside, a Performing Arts Centre (the Aldridge Theatre), drama studios, music school with recital room and recording facilities, state-of-the-art photography suite (opened Sept 2013), science laboratories, art & design centre, Mac and PC computer suites, junior and senior libraries, sixth form centre and boarding house, completely refurbished Middle School boarding houses (separate houses for younger and older students).

Music. Music is held in high esteem at the school and regarded as an essential part of a student's education. It is studied by all students until the end of Year 9. The school has an impressive record for its choral and instrumental music. There are senior and junior choirs, two orchestras and a large number of instrumental groups. Concerts are put on regularly.

Boarding. Boarders are housed in small and friendly boarding houses. Each has a resident housemaster or housemistress and house tutor. There is a varied programme of weekend activities for the boarders. Weekly boarders may leave on Friday afternoon, returning on Sunday evening or Monday morning. The School organises a coach to London at weekends.

Religion. Frensham Heights is non-denominational and there are no religious services during the school day.

Dress. There is no uniform but students follow a dress code based on respect for others.

Welfare and Discipline. The school's discipline is firmly based on good relationships between staff and students and reflects the values of the school, including respect, tolerance, self-discipline, cooperation and creativity. Every student has a personal tutor. Senior pupils act as mentors to younger members of the school. A thriving School Council, consisting of elected representatives from all age groups, meets regularly to discuss matters of mutual interest and concern. The boarding house staff are supported by a school nurse and a part-time counsellor.

Learning Difficulties. The school is sympathetic to those with dyslexia and other specific learning difficulties and offers limited support.

Overseas Students. The school admits a small number of boarders from overseas each year and provides tuition in English as a Second Language as part of their curriculum.

Frensham Heights Junior School. Nursery to Year 3 students aged 3–8 are in their own recently enlarged buildings and gardens within the main school grounds. Years 4–6 are situated in new purpose-built classrooms. The Junior School provides firm foundations in English and Mathematics, supported by a well-balanced curriculum that includes Science, French, Information Technology, Music, Drama and Dance at a level appropriate to the year group. Students have access to all the main school's facilities.

Fees per term (2014–2015). Nursery (EYFE Scheme): £17.25 (morning session, including lunch), £30.63 (afternoon session, including lunch); Reception £2,075; Years 1–2 £2,550; Year 3 £3,050; Year 4 £3,115; Years 5–6 £3,850; Years 7–8: £5,540 (day), £7,770 (boarding); Years 9–13: £5,805 (day), £8,755 (boarding); Sixth Form: £6,110 (day), £9,045 (boarding).

Scholarships and Bursaries. Scholarships will be awarded for Academic distinction or exceptional promise in Music, Art, Dance, Drama and Sport at 11+, 13+ and for Sixth Form entry. These do not have monetary value but they recognise and celebrate excellence. Bursaries are awarded on the basis of a means-tested assessment.

Charitable status. Frensham Heights Educational Trust is a Registered Charity, number 312052. It exists to provide high quality education for boys and girls.

George Heriot's School

Lauriston Place, Edinburgh EH3 9EQ
Tel: 0131 229 7263
Fax: 0131 229 6363
email: enquiries@george-heriots.com
website: www.george-heriots.com

Motto: '*I distribute chearfullie*'

Heriot's Hospital was founded in 1628 to care for the fatherless sons of Edinburgh burgesses. Today it is a fully co-educational day school, deeply rooted in the Scottish tradition.

The School is attractively situated in its own grounds close to the city centre and within easy walking distance of bus and rail terminals. A number of bus routes also service the School. Edinburgh Castle forms a magnificent backdrop, and Edinburgh's flourishing financial centre, the University of Edinburgh, the College of Art, the National Library and the Royal Scottish Museum are located close by.

The original building, described as a "bijou of Scottish Renaissance Architecture", has been carefully preserved and, as a historic monument, is open at certain times to the public during school holidays. The Chapel, Council Room and Quadrangle are particularly notable.

Over the years a succession of new buildings has provided the full complement of educational facilities. The most recent additions include the purchase of an adjoining site to extend facilities. A state-of-the-art Sports Centre was opened in 2012. Similarly, improvements and additions have been made over the years to provide excellent sports fields and facilities at Goldenacre. The School has sole use of an outdoor centre in the Scottish Highlands.

Governors of George Heriot's Trust:

Chairman: M J Gilbert, CA
Vice-Chairman: A Paton, MCIBS, FRSA
Finance Convener: J D M Hill, CA
Education Convener: Dr P Sangster, MA, PhD
Buildings Convener: Dr N M Irons, CBE, JP, DL
Miss J Armstrong
Mrs K Cherry
Ms K Fitzgerald
Revd Dr R Frazer, BD, PhD
I Herok
N Jamieson
G Robertson
N Robertson
Councillor C Rose
Prof M W J Strachan
J Thomson

Bursar: Mrs J A Alexander

Acting Principal: C D Wyllie, MA

PA to the Principal: Miss C Macleod

Head of Senior School: C D Wyllie, MA

Depute Headteachers, Senior School:
Mrs C W Binnie, BA
R C Dickson, MA
Mrs M Lannon, BA
Miss K A Macnab, MA
K J Ogilvie, MA
N J Seaton, MA

Chaplain: Mrs A G Maclean, BD, DCE

Art:
*Mrs A J E Thomson, BA
Mrs R E Billett
Mrs J R Coombs, MA
Mrs C M Fraser, BA
Ms N L Garriock, BA
Mrs S L Jamieson, BA
Mrs C J McGirr, BA

Biology:
*Miss A McKenzie, BSc
Ms D Barnaby, BSc
Miss J Burgess, PGCE
Miss J Fraser
Miss M E Gralewicz, BSc
Mrs G Lippok, DipEd
Mrs A Macleod, BSc
A A N Ramage, BSc

Business Education:
*Mrs J Arnott
Miss K C Coltart, BA
Mrs A Donaldson, BA
Mrs M Lannon, BA
Mrs G Line, BA

Miss K A Macnab
J Payne, BA

Chemistry:
*F I McGonigal, BSc
Mrs J Blaikie, HND
Mrs F Donaldson, BSc
Miss E L Maclean, BSc
J Wilson, BSc

Citizenship:
*Mrs G K Hay

Classics:
*D Carnegie
Mrs L C Williams

Computing:
*J T Scott, BSc
A Semmler, BA
Ms J McColgan, MA
Miss F Ramsey, PGDE

Drama:
*Mrs J H Arya, BA
Miss K Henderson, MA

Mrs E R Mackie, MA
Miss K H Morgan, MA

English:
*K Simpson, MA, LLB
R C Dickson, MA
N H Grant, MA
R Gray, MA, MSc
Mrs G K Hay, MA
Mrs D Keohane, MA, CIM
    Dip
P J Lowe, MA
Mrs M C Massie, BA, MA
Miss K H Morgan, MA
Dr A Neilson, MA
C D Wyllie, MA

Geography:
*Mrs A Hughes, MA
D Armstrong, BSc
Miss M E Gralewicz, BSc
Mrs S E A Harris, MA
K J Ogilvie, MA
E Watson, BSc
Miss J Woodhead, PGCE

History and Modern
Studies:
*M A McCabe, MA, MTh,
    PhD, BD
Miss M Buchanan, MA
T J Clancey, MA
Ms A Connor, MA
Miss L P Robertson, MA
N J Seaton, MA
Miss T Peters, MA

Food, Health & Consumer
Studies:
Miss L Ballentyne, PGDE

Support for Learning:
*Ms V Higson, BSc,
    DipSpLD
Ms M Churches
Mrs H R Fennell, BA
Ms S G Gallacher, MA
Mrs S C Harrod
Mrs J Jackson, MA, MSc,
    PGCE, CPsych
Mrs H A Staines, MA
D Thain, BEd

Mathematics:
*G A Dickson, BSc
*D C Porteous, BSc
Mrs J H Dickson, BSc
Mrs P E Hart, BSc
Miss K Henry, PGDE

Head of Junior School: Mrs L M Franklin, MA

Deputy Head of Junior School: Mrs K S O'Hagan, BEd

Depute Headteachers, Junior School:
C McCloghry, PGCE
Mrs L K Reid, MA
Mrs K L Stevens
Miss L Waddell, MA

Principal Teachers:
Miss S Gordon, MA
Miss E F Hay
Miss M Thomson, MA

Junior School Teachers (*including Nursery*):

Miss B Aitken, PGCE
Miss M E Beteta, BEd

Mrs K Lydon, BSc
Miss F Moir, BA
C Walker, BSc

Modern Languages:
*M G Grant, BA
Mrs C W Binnie, BA
Miss C Boscher, MA
Ms E Bottaro, MA
Ms E M Brown, MA
Mrs H Davies
Miss C Gatenby
Mr A G Hector
F Hédou, DEUG, MA
Ms E R Mackie, MA
Mrs D M Mullen, BA
Ms J Murphy

Music:
*G C W Brownlee, BA,
    LLCM, ALCM
Mrs J Buttars, BA
Mrs S C Lovell, DRSAMD
G D Maclagan, BMus
Mrs R S J Weir, BMus

PE/Games:
*M Mallinson, BEd
Miss L Brown, BEd
G Hills, BEd
Mrs N Kesterton, BEd
Mrs G Mollison, BEd
Mrs K F Rutherford, BEd
R Stevenson, BEd
K M Yuille, DipPE

Physics:
*R M Bush, BSc
Miss R D Connell, BSc
Ms W C Morgan, BSc
I Oliphant, BSc
Dr K Ward, BSc, PhD

Philosophy and Religion:
*R H Simpson, BD,
    MTheol
Mrs L Beilby, MA
Mrs A G Maclean, BD
Miss O Williams

Design & Technology:
*Mrs E L Watson-Massey,
    BSc
Mrs A Johnson, BA
I Purves, BEd
D W Urquhart, HNDEng,
    DipTechEd,
    CertEdComp

J Caton, MA
Mrs K Duncan, BSc

Mrs V E J Clark, MA
Mrs E S Clarke, DipEd,
    INSC
G Cockburn, BA
Mrs L Gilmour, BA
W Hamilton, BSc
Mrs G Happs, BEd
Miss E Hay, MA
Mrs B I S Hunt, BEd
Miss R Jackson-Hutt, MA
C Johnstone, PGDE
Ms A Josiffe, BA
Mrs R McKinnon
Mrs A Millar, MA
Miss H Oliver, MA
G Rand, MA

E P Santer
Miss K H Shannon, BEd
P Swierkot, BA
B Tyler, BSc
Miss F Walker, BEd
R J Waters, MA
I J A S Woolley, DipEd

Learning Enhancement:
Miss J Attenborough, BEd
Ms H A Bassam
Miss E J Bidwell
Ms S G Gallacher, BA
Mrs H Murphy
Mrs S Wilken, BEd

Our aim is to introduce all our pupils to the broadest possible spectrum of academic, spiritual, cultural and sporting interests and experiences, which will enable them as articulate, self-reliant adults to play a full part in an ever-changing society.

Heriot's has long enjoyed a reputation for academic excellence, and we strive to help pupils to attain the highest possible level of competence. In the same spirit, every pupil is encouraged to participate in an extensive array of extracurricular activities. We value sporting achievement, particularly in team games, and we encourage activity in art, music and design. In addition, pupils are introduced to religious, moral and philosophical concepts in the search for the answers to the more abstract questions that life poses.

The Nursery (32 children). The Nursery accommodates children in their pre-school year. It is part of the Early Years Department. Admission to the Nursery is open to all.

The Junior School (613 pupils). The Junior School curriculum enshrines the central aims of Curriculum for Excellence, with a focus on academic rigour and solid subject content, particularly with regard to literacy, numeracy and science, and great is taken over the academic progression of our Junior School pupils into the Senior School. Art, Drama, Modern Languages, Music and all areas of Physical Education are taught by specialists, and Junior School staff liaise closely with their secondary colleagues to provide curricular continuity throughout a pupil's time here.

A very active Junior School extra-curricular programme includes music, drama, adventure weeks and support for charities.

The Senior School (1036 pupils). For the first two years a system of flexible streaming provides a broad curriculum for all. An extensive choice of subjects is available from S3 to S6 in preparation for Scottish Qualifications Agency examinations at every level. Most pupils stay on for a Sixth Year and proceed to university or other forms of tertiary education.

Our vast Senior School extra-curricular programme is designed to suit all interests and abilities, and it provides recreation, enjoyment and excellence. Pupils achieve national and international recognition in their chosen activities, and many Former Pupils have pursued their interests with similar success in adult life.

Music and drama are very strong. Performances are given annually in our two halls, our Chapel, in the adjoining Greyfriars Church, in the Usher Hall and other venues.

The CCF is active and thriving, our Duke of Edinburgh's Award Scheme is one of the largest in Scotland, and an award winning Voluntary Service programme is a key feature of the Sixth Year at Heriot's. The main sports are cricket, cross-country running, hockey, rowing, rugby and tennis but most other sports are available in school or at Goldenacre.

Heriot's enjoys a reputation as a caring community. The greatest importance is given to pastoral care and a sophisticated careers advisory programme is in place. The Support for Learning Department provides invaluable help to all Junior School and Senior School pupils, be it that they have a specific learning difficulty or are outstandingly gifted.

Admission. Admission (other than for Nursery) is by assessment or examination. Application for occasional places is welcome at any time, but for the main stages should normally be submitted by the end of November.

Fees per annum (2014–2015). Junior School: £7,131 (Nursery, P1 & P2), £8,655 (P3 to P7). Senior School: £10,695.

A limited number of Bursaries is available in Senior School and there are Scholarships for entry at S1. Fatherless and motherless children may qualify for free education and other benefits through the Foundation and James Hardie Bursaries. Full information is available from the Finance and Business Office on request.

Charitable status. George Heriot's Trust is a Registered Charity, number SC011463. It exists to provide education for children.

Giggleswick School

Giggleswick, Settle, North Yorkshire BD24 0DE
Tel: 01729 893000 Headmaster's Office
01729 893012 Bursar's Office
Fax: 01729 893150
email: admissions@giggleswick.org.uk
website: www.giggleswick.org.uk

Giggleswick School, founded by 1512, was granted a charter by Edward VI on 26 May, 1553, at the instance of John Nowell, then Vicar of Giggleswick, and one of the King's Chaplains. Fully co-educational since the 1980s, continuous investment in facilities and staff has created a modern learning environment with first-class sports and creative facilities.

The Governing Body:
Chairman: Mrs H J Hancock, MA, LVO
Vice-Chairman: A R Mullins Esq, BSc, MBA, ACA

R A P Brocklehurst Esq, MA, MBA
Miss L M Campbell, OBE, BEd
Mrs S L Capstick
Dr M Dörrzapf, DPhil
¶J L Ellacott Esq, MA
¶Miss S C Fox, BMus, ARCM
¶Mrs G M Harper
The Rt Revd and The Rt Hon Lord Hope of Thornes, KCVO
Miss A L Hudson, MA, MRICS
A M Jarman Esq, MA
The Hon W J Kay-Shuttleworth, BA
D S Lowther Esq, BA
Dr P M Neumann, OBE, BA, MA, DPhil, DSc
M H O'Connell Esq, BA, FCA
¶His Honour Judge D A Stockdale Esq, QC, MA
P J S Thompson Esq, LLB, Hon D Laws, MCI Arb
¶ Dr V L Turner, MA, MB, BChir

¶ *Old Giggleswickian*

Headmaster: M M Turnbull, BA, MA

Deputy Heads:
N A Gemmell, BA West London Inst of HE
Ms S L Williamson, BA Liverpool

Director of Learnng: Miss A L Wood, MA New College Oxford

* *Head of Department/Subject*
† *Housemaster/mistress*

Art:
*C D Knight, BA Loughborough College
Miss E M Rowles, BA Canterbury Christ Church
Mrs N L McGoldrick, BA St Martin's College, Lancaster
M Wilcock, BA, UCLWN (*Artist in Residence*)

Business Studies & Economics:
*W S Robertson, BA Lancaster
P Adams, MBA London

Design:
*J Huxtable, BA Coventry
G Wigfield, College of Ripon and York St John
A J Scholey, BSc City of London Polytechnic (†*Shute*)

Drama:
*J G Warburton, Bolton Inst of HE (*Director of Drama*)
Miss B K L Stoll, BA Aberystwyth

English:
*Mrs J E Farmer, BA Leeds
N A Gemmell, BA West London Inst of HE
Sarah L Williamson, BA Liverpool
A J Pickles, BA Durham (†*Catteral*)
J M C Giles, BA Strathclyde (†*Morrison*)
Mrs K J Peacock, MA York

Geography:
*C D Richmond, BSc, MA London
J P Bellis, BA Salford

History & Politics:
*Mrs M M Davidson, BA Durham
Mrs A L Coward, MA London
S C Griffiths, MSc Edinburgh (†*Paley*)
Miss J C Landon, MA Durham

Home Economics:
*Mrs C Gemmell, BEd Manchester Polytechnic

ICT:
*Mrs S C Watts-Wood, BA Leeds
S Heap, BEd Madeley College, Staffordshire
P C R Andrew, BEng Warwick, MIEE (†*Nowell*)

Languages:
*C A Meneses, BA Antioquia, Colombia
Miss A L Wood, MA New College Oxford
Mrs E-J Wharton, BA Aberystwyth (†*Carr*)
Miss J C Landon, MA Durham
Mrs D A Taylor, BA Manchester Polytechnic
Mrs L J R Ladds, BA Aberystwyth (†*Style*)
S F Kenchington, MA St Andrews

Learning Support:
*J M Curry, BA Wadham College Oxford, AMBDA
Mrs K R Haynes, MA Lancaster
Mrs J R Maguire, BEd HLTA Bangor

Mathematics:
*J D Western, BSc Bristol
S Heap, BEd Madeley College, Staffordshire
Mrs S J Ayari, BEd De Montfort
P A Keron, BSc, MSc Nottingham
S F Rudsdale, BSc Open
J P Taylor, MEng Newcastle, MA Durham

Music:
D C Chapman, MA Keble College Oxford, LRAM
Mrs L M Stott, Royal Northern College of Music
J M Lowe, BMus, ARCO, RNCM (*Chapel Organist*)
H J Lorriman, Dip Mus, Cert Ed Huddersfield Polytechnic
N C Young, BA Birmingham Conservatoire
Miss A E Grant, BA Leeds College of Music

PE:
*Mrs M H Wright, BSc Worcester (*Head of Academic PE*)
D J Cook, BSc Hull (*Director of Sport*)
F D G Ogilvie, BEd Jordanhill College of Education, Glasgow

Mrs S J Ayari, BEd De Montfort
R Bunday, BSc UWIC
Miss E R Whyte, BSc Leeds Metropolitan

RS:
*A J Ladds, BD Aberystwyth
M D O Davies , BD Glasgow

Science:
*P K Hucknall, BSc, PhD Leeds (*Science, *Physics*)
N M Walker, BSc, PhD Hull, CBiol, MIBiol (*Biology*)
R M Taylor, BSc, PhD Manchester (*Chemistry*)
C D P Wright, BSc, MSc, PhD Hughes Hall Cambridge
J M Curry, BA Wadham College Oxford
Miss K E Arnold, BSc York
F E Davies, MA St Edmund Hall Oxford

Bursar and Clerk to the Governors: G R Bowring, MA
Director of Admissions & Marketing: Mrs S Hird
Foundation Director: A Beales. MSci, MInstF Dip
Commercial Manager: J A Wright, BA, MBA
Headmaster's PA: Mrs C A Jowett

Junior School:

Head: M S Brotherton, BEd Hons De Montfort, NPQH

Deputy Head: J R Mundell, LLB, PGCE University of
    Wales, Newport

Early Years Unit:
Mrs J A Middleton, BA QTS Lancaster
Miss E Monks (*Early Years Practitioner*)
Mrs L Shepherd, BA EYPS
Miss M Ford (*Early Years Practitioner*)
Miss D Magson (*Early Years Practitioner*)
Mrs K Hall, HLTA
Years 1 & 2: Mrs D A Horsman, BEd Hons London
Years 3 & 4: Miss G C Sismey, BA Leeds
Year 5: J R Mundell, LLB, PGCE University of Wales,
    Newport
Year 6:
F D G Ogilvie, BEd Jordanhill College of Education,
    Glasgow
Miss H S Pritchard, BSc Leeds

Specialist Subject Teachers:
Sport: F D G Ogilvie, BEd Jordanhill College of Education,
    Glasgow
Music: Miss A E Grant, BA Leeds College of Music
Art and Design: Mrs N L McGoldrick BA St Martin's
    College, Lancaster
Food Technology: Mrs C Gemmell, BEd Manchester
    Polytechnic
English and Drama: Mrs S M Butler, ALCM
Languages: Mrs H D Brotherton, BA Wolverhampton
    Polytechnic
Learning Support: Miss G C Sismey, BA Leeds
Science: Mrs H J Davies, BSc Glasgow

Registrar & Head's PA: Mrs S E Driver

Giggleswick provides boarding and day education for
about 400 boys and girls aged from 11–18. It also has its
own Junior School for children aged 3–11. The School is situated in beautiful Yorkshire Dales' scenery, close to the borders of Cumbria and Lancashire and is an hour's drive from
Leeds, Manchester and The Lakes. It can be reached from
the M6 or M1 motorways or by rail via Settle or Giggleswick stations. Overseas students fly to Leeds/Bradford or
Manchester Airports.

Senior School. For eleven year olds admission is usually
based on performance in Giggleswick's own entrance examination. At thirteen, entrance is based on performance in the
Common Entrance Examination for pupils in Preparatory
Schools. However, for pupils being educated either abroad
or in the maintained sector, other appropriate forms of
assessment are used.

Admission direct to the Sixth Form is on the basis of
reports and interviews, and is conditional upon the applicant
obtaining a minimum of five GCSE passes with Grade B
passes in subjects to be taken at AS/A Level. There are
approximately 150 pupils in the Sixth Form. Generous Academic, Music, Art, Design & Technology, Drama, Sport and
All-Rounder Scholarships are available for entry to Year 7,
Year 9 and L6.

Boarding. 60% of Senior School pupils are boarders and
the School's routine is entirely geared to boarding education. There are seven Houses, four for boys and two for girls
in Years 9–U6, with 50–60 pupils in each, and one for boys
and girls in Year 7–8. The Housemaster or Housemistress is
responsible for the well-being and progress of pupils in the
House and is assisted by House Tutors.

Most Sixth Formers have their own Study-Bedroom;
other pupils share Study-Bedrooms or small Study Dormitories.

Day Pupils. Day pupils are fully integrated with boarders; they arrive before Morning Registration, share studies
and use all School facilities. They have lunch and tea at
School and return home after prep. There are bus services
from Skipton, Grassington, Colne, Ilkley, Clitheroe, Lancaster and Levens via Kirkby Lonsdale.

Courses of Study. From Years 7–9 the curriculum comprises English, French, German, Spanish, Latin, Mathematics, Sciences, History, Geography, Arts (including Drawing
and Ceramics), Music, Drama, Technology (including
Home Economics, Graphics and Design), Religious Studies,
Physical Education and PSHE. In Years 10 and 11 a pupil
takes 9 or 10 subjects leading to the GCSE examinations.

In the Sixth Form, a pupil normally studies four subjects
leading to GCE AS Level and three to A2 Level examinations. The subjects available are Mathematics, Further
Mathematics, Physics, Chemistry, Biology, Business Studies, English, French, German, Classical Civilisation, Spanish, Latin, History, Geography, Art, Design, Music,
Economics, Theatre Studies, PE and Information Technology.

Pupils are prepared for Oxford and Cambridge University
Entrance.

Religion. The religious life of the School is supervised by
a resident Anglican Chaplain. At their own wish pupils may
be prepared for Confirmation into the Church of England.
Catholic pupils are excused certain Chapel services in order
to attend Mass. The School respects and allows for other
religious convictions.

Health. There is a surgery in the charge of a resident
SRN with a Deputy who is also an SRN. The School Doctor
visits regularly 4 or 5 days a week and is available in emergencies.

Games. In the Autumn Term the main games are rugby
for boys and hockey for girls and in the Spring Term hockey
for boys and netball for girls. In the Summer Term the main
sports are cricket for boys and tennis for girls, but athletics,
swimming, and tennis are available for boys and girls. In
addition, there are excellent facilities for soccer, squash,
fives, golf, badminton, basketball, netball, cross-country and
fell running etc. There are regular overseas tours by the
sports teams. A Quincentenary Rugby, Hockey and Music
tour to Australia took place in July 2012. A cricket tour to
India took place in April 2014.

Outdoor Education. This is an important part of the
School's extra-curricular life. All pupils have introductory
courses in map reading, orienteering and camp craft, and
train for the Giggleswick Certificate at the end of Year 9.
Many go on to the Silver Award and some each year to the
Gold. Trained and qualified members of staff lead these
activities.

Music. Tuition, given by four full-time musicians and a
number of visiting teachers, is available in all keyboard and
orchestral instruments. The Music School has excellent
recital, rehearsal, teaching and practice rooms. Concerts are

given by the School Orchestra, the Concert Band, Ensembles and the Choral Society. Concert tours have been undertaken in the USA, Holland, Prague and Italy.

Drama. There is a major production each year, as well as public performances of GCSE, AS and A Level work. Drama is a timetabled subject in Years 7- 9 and the subject is offered at GCSE and A Level. The School has an extensive theatre wardrobe of its own. Drama tours are a regular feature of school life, the most recent being a Drama and Music Tour to Italy.

Art. The Art Department is fine-art-based concentrating on drawing, painting, print-making and ceramics. It boasts excellent examination results.

CCF. All pupils follow a structured course in Year 10, divided equally into military and non-military skills. The contingent has Army, RAF and Royal Marine Sections. At the end of the year, pupils may opt to leave or remain in the CCF. Advanced training is given in a variety of skills. The contingent fields strong teams for the District competitions and sends many cadets on further training at camp and on various courses.

Societies. There is a wide variety of societies. Sixth Formers have their own Social Centre.

Recent Developments. More than £13m has been invested in facilities since 1999, including a new dining hall, a Learning and Information centre, a floodlit synthetic hockey pitch, a new Art School, completely refurbished Science laboratories and a Sports Hall. In 2010 the Richard Whiteley Theatre was opened.

Careers Advice and Staff-Parent Conferences. Two experienced Careers Advisors supplement the advice of House Staff and Heads of Academic Departments in guiding academic choices and career decisions. The School is a member of ISCO and uses the ISLO/Morrisby Scheme of Careers Education and guidance. Regular Staff-Parent conferences are held at School to enable discussion of pupils' past, present and future progress and needs. Parents are always welcome at other times, especially at Chapel, sports fixtures, concerts, plays, etc.

Junior School. Giggleswick Junior School stands in its own grounds on a site adjacent to the Senior School. It has its own staff but also has the advantage of specialist teachers and facilities of the Senior School. Recent improvements include a new Library, teaching and IT centre and a new Sports Hall. There is a Nursery for children aged 3 and above.

Admission is possible at any age between 3–11. At eleven, pupils transfer in the Autumn Term to the Senior School, enjoying continuity of environment, curriculum and friendships.

(*For further information see Giggleswick Junior School entry in IAPS section.*)

Entrance. Most pupils enter in the September term, but a few are admitted in January and April. Registration fee £150 (Senior), £50 (Junior).

Scholarships, Exhibitions and Bursaries. Generous scholarships and exhibitions are available to boys and girls entering Year 7 (11+), Year 9 (13+), and Sixth Form (16+) as boarding or day pupils. The scholarship exams/assessments are taken in the spring term preceding entry. The following categories are available: Academic, All-Rounder, Music, Sport, Art (13+ and 16+ only), Design and Drama (16+ only). A leaflet containing full details of the awards and examinations can be obtained from the Registrar.

Means-tested bursaries are available to successful candidates where the award is not sufficient to enable the child to take up the place.

Discounts are available for members of HM Forces.

Fees per term (2014–15) The fees are fully inclusive. Senior School: Boarders £7,136 (Years 7 & 8), £9,884 (Years 9–U6); Flexi Boarders £6,422 (Years 7 & 8), £7,924 (Years 9–U6); Day Pupils £5,496 (Years 7 & 8), £6,769

(Years 9–U6). Junior School: Boarders £6,205 (full), £4,787 (3-night flexi); Day Pupils £2,329–£3,726.

Further details are available in the Prospectus which may be obtained from the Headmaster, to whom applications for entry should be made.

Charitable status. Giggleswick School is a Registered Charity, number 1109826. It exists to provide education for boys and girls.

The Glasgow Academy

Colebrooke Street, Glasgow G12 8HE
Tel: 0141 334 8558
Fax: 0141 337 3473
email: enquiries@theglasgowacademy.org.uk
website: www.theglasgowacademy.org.uk

Motto: '*Serva Fidem.*'

Founded in May 1845, The Glasgow Academy is the oldest continuously independent school in the west of Scotland. It has been co-educational since 1991, when it joined forces with Westbourne School for Girls. Mergers with Atholl Preparatory School in Milngavie (1999) and Dairsie House School in Newlands (2005) have given parents a choice of three locations for their children in the Nursery to Prep 4 age group, contributing to the school's enduring success as a school covering the whole of west central Scotland. Children from TGA Milngavie and Dairsie transfer to the main Academy site at Kelvinbridge at Prep 5. The school's affairs are managed by the Glasgow Academicals' War Memorial Trust, formed to commemorate the 327 former pupils killed in the war of 1914–18.

Chairman of Governors: Graham Scott, FCIBS

Nominated and Elected Governors:
Mrs C F Abercrombie, BAcc, CA
A Barr
B G Duncan, MBA, MRICS
Jeremy Glen, LLB, Dip LP, NP
G W Henry, CA
M J Lee, MA
S J McCaffer, BCom, CA
Dr M J McDonald, MBChB, MRCP, FRCPath
R I McNaught, BAcc, CA
Mrs N Mahal, MA, DCG
G Scott, FCIBS
I G Shankland, CA, MCT
W Sinclair, MA, MFB, MIDE, MIOD, MSExpE, MICM, MAPS
G Smith, MRICS
A Waddell, MA, CA, ASIP

Secretary: T W Gemmill, LLB, NP

Rector: P J Brodie, MA Oxon, MA Management of Education, Canterbury Christ Church University College

Deputy Rector: A J Williams, BSc Dunelm

Deputy Heads:
Dr J Andrews, BSc Glasgow, PhD London
A L Evans, BSc Strathclyde
A N Macrae, BSc Strathclyde

Heads of Department:
English: Mrs A F Watters, MA St Andrews
Mathematics: Mrs L S Moon, BSc Southampton, CMath, FIMA, CertGuid
Modern Languages: Mrs E B Holland, MA Glasgow
Biology: J M Shields, BSc Glasgow
Chemistry: Dr R J Sowden, MChem St Andrews, DPhil Oxon
Physics: S M Brunton, BSc Glasgow

Art/Craft & Design: J M McNaught, BA Glasgow
Classics: S A A McKellar, MA Glasgow
Computing Science: Mrs J E McDonald, MA Glasgow
Drama: G E Waltham, MA Glasgow
Economics & Business Studies: Mrs S McKenzie, MA
   Glasgow, PGDip BusAdmin Strathclyde
Food Technology: Ms C Dolan, BSc Manchester
   Metropolitan University
Geography: Miss V Barton, MA Glasgow
History & Modern Studies: S M Wood, MA St Andrews
Music: M B Marshall, BA Southampton, ARCO, DipMus
Physical Education/Sport:
S W McAslan, BEd Jordanhill (*Head of PE*)
Miss R I Simpson, BEd Heriot-Watt (*Director of Sport*)
PSE: Mrs M T Muirhead, BA East Anglia, Dip Guid &
   Pastoral Care Glasgow
Outdoor Education: Miss R Goolden, Mountain Instructor
   Certificate, Outdoor Education Diploma & National
   Governing Awards, Newbury College
Learning Support: Mrs A A Harvie, BA Strathclyde,
   PGDip Ind Admin Glasgow Caledonian
Careers: A J McCaskey, MA Glasgow

Preparatory School:
Head: A M Brooke, BEd Southampton
Deputy Head: Mrs H A Kirkhope, BEd Strathclyde
Depute: AW Mathewson BEd Strathclyde

TGA Milngavie:
Head: Miss J McMorran, DCE, PGDip, DipTEFL

Dairsie:
Head: Miss H J Logie, BEd Oxon

After-school Care:
After-school Care Manager: Mrs C Bremridge, BA
   Childhood Practice, Glasgow
--
Chaplains:
Revd D J M Carmichael, MA, BD
Revd A Frater, BA, BD
Revd G Kirkwood, BSc, BD, PGCE
Revd S Matthews BD, MA
Revd J D Whiteford, MA, BD, Dip Soc Wk
--
Combined Cadet Force:
OC CCF: Captain A W Mathewson
SSI: WO2 C J Duff

Administration/Finance:
General Manager: Dr W R Kerr, LLB Glasgow
   Caledonian, PhD Strathclyde, MBA Glasgow, MSc
   Glasgow Caledonian, FCIS, FCIM, FHCIMA

Rector's PA: Ms E McGowan, BA Strathclyde
Administration Manager: Miss I Kovacs, BA Strathclyde
School Secretary: Mrs A M Farr
Database Coordinator/Administration Secretary: Mrs D
   Hegedus, BA Budapest, MA Pecs

Development:
Director of Admissions and External Relations: M R
   McNaught, MA Glasgow
Director of Development: M G Taylor, MA Aberdeen

Organisation. The Preparatory School contains some
662 pupils (362 boys, 300 girls) between the ages of 3 and
11 and educates pupils from the earliest stages for the work
of the Senior School. The Senior School contains 679 pupils
(356 boys, 323 girls). They are prepared for the National
Qualifications at Higher and Advanced Higher at the end of
Fifth and Sixth year. The Sixth Form provides courses in
most subjects leading to presentation at Advanced Higher.
Pupils are prepared for entrance to Oxford and Cambridge.
The Academy has a fine record at Oxford, Cambridge and
the Scottish Universities. It aims to offer a unique combination of academic, musical, dramatic, sporting, co-curricular,

social and outdoor education opportunities, backed up by
high levels of pastoral care. There are numerous opportunities for children to develop leadership skills and take on
responsibilities.

Buildings. The magnificent main building (1878) contains the Senior School library as its centrepiece and classrooms. Recent purpose-built facilities include a Music
School (1994), Art and Design School (1998), Preparatory
School (2008) and extensive sports facilities (featuring
astros, rugby pitches and a water-based hockey pitch (2013)
used for the 2014 Commonwealth Games). A new Science
and Food Technology Centre and Auditorium open in 2015.
The school's Wi-Fi network covers the entire campus and
supports pupils' own laptops, smart phones and tablets. The
Academy VLE is continually developing and is used to
engage pupils and parents in the learning experience.

Music and Drama. Music tuition is offered in a wide
range of instruments by 24 tutors. There are Senior, Junior
and Theatre Choirs, a Concert Band, Pipe Band, Brass
Group, Percussion Ensemble, Orchestra and various Prep
School groups. Concerts and large-scale drama productions
take place regularly and are supplemented by plays mounted
by smaller groups.

Societies and Activities. These range from Basketball,
Chess, Debating and Public Speaking to Engineering, Fair-
trade and Research clubs. Very large numbers of pupils
undertake each section of the Duke of Edinburgh's Award
and there is a thriving Young Enterprise group. Residential
education is an integral part of the curriculum at various
stages of both the Prep and Senior schools. These experiences augment the PSE programme by promoting team
building and personal and social development through outdoor challenges.

Games. Teams represent the school in Hockey, Rugby,
Cricket, Swimming, Golf, Tennis, Athletics, Rowing, Foot-
ball, Shooting and Squash. Options include Badminton,
Cross-Country running and Dance.

Combined Cadet Force. The Academy has a strong voluntary contingent with RN, Army, Signals and RAF Sections.

Childcare outside school hours. The Academy provides
care before and after school for its younger pupils. There is
also provision for children between the ages of 3 and 12
throughout the holidays.

Entrance. Pupils may be registered at any age. The main
entry points are (a) in the Preparatory School: age 3, 4 and
10; (b) in the Senior School: age 11 or 12 or for Sixth Form.
Bursaries are available for P7–S6.

Fees per term (2014–2015). Preparatory School: P1
£2,490/£2,710, P2 £2,565/£2,790, P3–P4 £2,835/£3,045, P5
£3,045, P6–P7 £3,630. Senior School: S1–S2 £3,405, S3–S5
£3,695, S6 £3,695 (Autumn & Spring Terms), £3,015 (Summer Term).

Charitable status. The Glasgow Academy is a Registered Charity, number SC015638. It exists to provide education for girls and boys.

The High School of Glasgow

637 Crow Road, Glasgow G13 1PL
Tel: 0141 954 9628
Fax: 0141 435 5708
email: rector@hsog.co.uk
website: www.glasgowhigh.com

Motto: '*Sursum semper*'.

The new, independent, co-educational High School of
Glasgow came into being at Anniesland in 1976 following a
merger involving the Former Pupil Club of the High School,
a maintained school previously in the State system, and
Drewsteignton School in Bearsden.

Governing Body:
Honorary President: Lord Macfarlane of Bearsden, KT
Chairman: B C Adair, TD, LLB
P M A Forgie, MCIBS
Mrs P Galloway, FCA
A Horn, MA, LLB
E W Hugh, CA
Mrs L Keith, MA, Cert Ed, ITQ
S J MacAulay
C M Mackie, BSc, FFA
D J Maclay, BSc, CA
S C Miller, LLB Hons, Dip L
Professor V A Muscatelli, MA, PhD, FRSE, FRSA
K M Revie, LLB Hons
Dr A C E Short, MBChB, FRCGP, DRCOG
Mrs M A Stewart, LLB Hons, Dip LP, DFM
R M Williamson, MA, LLB, FRSA, FRSAMD
R G Wishart, FCMA

Rector: C D R Mair, MA

Senior Deputy Rector: J O'Neill, MA

Deputy Rectors:
Mrs M E R Price, MA
K J A Robertson, BSc
I S Leighton, BSc

Staff:
* *Head of Department*

English:
*P A Toner, MA
†G Baynham, BA
Miss R A Davies, MA
†P D C Ford, MA
†T Lyons, MA
Miss S L McCaffer, MA
Mrs J Muir, MA
Mrs M E R Price, MA
Mrs M Noonan, BA
    (*Drama*)
Miss L Fenton, BA
    (*Drama*)

Mathematics:
*S Welsh, BEng
†Mrs C V M Anderson,
    BSc
T Lockyer, LLB
†J G MacCorquodale, BSc
D MacGregor, BSc
Mrs H S Mills, MEng
P Moon, BSc
Mrs N Morrison, BSc

Computer Studies:
*N R Clarke, BSc
D Muir, BSc
I R Purdie, BSc

Science:
A E Baillie, BSc (*Physics*)
N M E Dougall, MSc, BSc
    (*Biology*)
Mrs K S M O'Neil, BSc
    (*Chemistry*)
Mrs A E McNeil, BSc,
    MSc
Dr L A A Nicholl, BSc,
    PhD
Dr N J Penman, BSc, PhD
K J A Robertson, BSc
Miss M Robertson, MSc
I J Smith, BSc
Dr D R Went, MSci, PhD

Modern Languages:
*N F Campbell, MA, LLB
Miss M Cranie, BA
Mrs K Evans, MA
†Mrs J M Horne, MA
†Miss K J McAllister, BA
Mrs A M T Drapeau-
    Magee, L-ès-L, M-ès-L
Mrs V MacCorquodale,
    MA
Mrs H O'Driscoll, BA,
    MA, MPhil
Miss H Agustí Goméz, BA
Mrs A Hilt, MA

Classics:
*A H Milligan, MA
T W Ingham, MA
C McCay, LLB, MLitt

*Economics and Business
    Studies*:
*T J Jensen, MEd, BComm
Mrs E A Milne, BA,
    MCIBS

*Geography and Modern
    Studies*:
*Miss N L Cowan, MA
K F FitzGerald, BSc
I S Leighton, BSc
Miss J A McAteer, BA
Mrs L McFarlane, BSc
J O'Neill, MA

History:
*G K Sinclair, MA
R J Broadbent, BA, MEd
    (*Careers*)
Miss N Sutherland, MA
Mrs G A Lindsay, MA

Art:
*Mrs C J Bell, BA
Mrs J Waldron, BA
Ms N Henderson, BDes

Home Economics:
*Miss K Moore, BA
Mrs S MacLean, Dip HE
Mrs J Sellar, BA TQFE

Learning Support:
*Mrs R E Hamilton, BA
Mrs N Morrison, BSc

Music:
*Mrs S C Stuart, MMus
    Oxon, MSt Oxon,
    PGAdvDip RCM
L D Birch, BA, LRAM,
    DRSAMD
M Duncan, DRSAMD
Ms W MacDougall, MMus,
    BA, LLCM TD
N G McFarlane, BA
R McKeown, DRSAMD
Mrs C Mitchell, MMus,
    BMus, PGDM, PGDE
Mrs J Tierney, BMus
F Walker, BA, ARCO

Junior School Staff:
Head Teacher: Mrs K R Waugh, BA, DCE
Mrs J MacKay, BSc, SQH (*Deputy Head*)
Mrs A Kiyani, BEd, Masters in TEYL (*Deputy Head, Early
    Years*)
Mrs M Moreland, DCE, AEE (*Acting Deputy Head*)
Mrs C Brown, NNEB
Miss C E Carnall, BMus, MA
Mrs L Cowan, BEd
Mrs A M T Drapeau-Magee, L-ès-L, M-ès-L (*French*)
Mrs H M Eustace, BEd
Mrs S A Foster, MA
Mrs E Gibson, BEd
Mrs M J Gillan, DPE, Dip Sfl, ATQ
I Hallahan, BA, PG Dip (*Educational Support*)
Mrs J Jackson, DCE
Mrs L A Lambie, BEd
S Leggat, BEd (*Physical Education*)
Mrs E J McConechy, BEd (*Physical Education*)
Mrs E McCormick, DCE
Mrs S E MacDougall, DCE, ACE
Miss M MacLean, BA
Mrs F McNaught, MA
Mrs I W McNeill, DA (*Art*)
A Meikle, BA
Mrs J Moir, DCE
Mrs J O'Neill, NNEB
Mrs G Reid, MA
Mrs C Ritchie, DCE
Miss I Skinner, MSc (*Principal Teacher*)
G J Walker, BSc
Mrs M C Watt, DCE

Bursar: Mrs J M Simpson, BAcc, CA

Rector's PA: Mrs J McGlone

Religion & Philosophy:
*C F Price, MTheol
Mrs G A Lindsay, MA

Physical Education:
*D N Barrett, BEd
Mrs A Cox, BEd (*Girls'
    PE*)
Mrs H Cannon, BEd
K F FitzGerald, BSc
Mrs R Owen, BEd
Mrs S Dougan, BEd
Mrs M Gillan, DPE
S Leggat, BEd
J McConnell, UKCC Level
    2 (*Rugby*)
Mrs C MacKay, BEd
Mrs D McCluskey, BSc
Mrs S Mitchell, BEd
Mrs M Stevenson, DPE
C Muir, BEd
A Maclay, BEd

Buildings. The Senior School occupies modern purpose-built buildings at Anniesland on the western outskirts of the city immediately adjacent to twenty-three acres of playing fields. The Junior School is in the extended and modernised former Drewsteignton School buildings in Bearsden about three miles away. New facilities opened during the last few years include a purpose-built Science extension, a Junior School extension, a Drama Studio, a Refectory, a Fitness Centre, a Grandstand and an Information and Communications Technology building.

Organisation. The School is a day school with about 1,040 boys and girls. The Junior School, which includes a pre-school Kindergarten, has some 359 pupils (ages 3–10). Primary 7 pupils are included in the Senior School which has about 681 pupils (ages 11–18). A general curriculum is followed until the Third Year of the Senior School when, with the Scottish Qualifications Authority examinations in view, a measure of choice is introduced. In Fifth Year Higher examinations are taken and in Sixth Year courses for Advanced Highers are offered. Whilst the majority of pupils are aiming for the Scottish universities, places are regularly gained at Oxford, Cambridge and other English universities.

Throughout the School, time is allocated to Art, Music, Personal, Social and Health Education, Physical Education and Religion and Philosophy. All pupils will also take courses in Computing Studies, Drama and Home Economics at various stages in their school careers.

Games. The main sports are hockey, rugby, athletics, cricket, tennis and swimming. Pupils participate in a wide variety of other sports, including badminton, basketball, netball, volleyball, golf, cross-country running and skiing.

Activities. Pupils are encouraged to participate in extra-curricular activities. Clubs and societies include debating, Scripture Union groups, computer, table tennis, chess, art, bridge, chemistry, electronics, drama and film clubs. Pupils take part in the Duke of Edinburgh's Award Scheme and the Young Enterprise Scheme, and parties regularly go on tour. There are choirs, orchestras, jazz and concert bands and a pipe band and tuition in Instrumental Music is arranged as requested. Each year there are several concerts and dramatic productions. The Chamber Choir was BBC Songs of Praise Senior School Choir of the Year 2013.

Admission. Entrance tests and interviews are held in January. The principal points of entry are at Kindergarten (age 4), Junior 1 (age 5), Transitus (age 11) and First Year (age 12) but pupils are taken in at other stages as vacancies occur.

Fees per term (2014–2015). Junior School: £1,187–£3,143; Senior School: £3,184–£3,659.

Bursaries. The School operates a Bursary Fund to give assistance with fees in cases of need.

Former Pupils' Club. The Glasgow High School Club Limited is the former pupils' association of the old and new High Schools. Former pupils all over the world maintain an interest in the life and work of the School. *Secretary:* Murdoch C Beaton, LLB.

Charitable status. The High School of Glasgow Limited is a Registered Charity, number SC014768. It is a recognised educational charity.

Glenalmond College

Glenalmond, Perth PH1 3RY
Tel: 01738 842000
              Admissions Office: 01738 842144
Fax: 01738 842063
email: registrar@glenalmondcollege.co.uk
website: www.glenalmondcollege.co.uk
Twitter: @GlenalmondColl
Facebook: /Glenalmond College

Motto: '*Floreat Glenalmond*'
Glenalmond College, was founded by Mr W E Gladstone and others in 1841 and opened as a School in 1847.

Council:
*President of Council: The Primus of the Episcopal Church in Scotland, The Most Reverend David Chillingworth, Bishop of St Andrews, Dunkeld & Dunblane
*Chairman of Council: The Rt Hon Lord Menzies PC (*OG*)
*Chairman of Committee of Council: N S K Booker, BA Hons (*OG*)
The Earl of Home, CVO, CBE
*I R Wilson Esq, CBE
D J C MacRobert Esq, LLB (*OG*)

*D G Sibbald Esq, BArch Hons, RIBA, FRIAS (*OG Club Secretary*)
Mrs C S C Lorenz, AA Dipl
*J M Squire Esq, MBA, MSc
J V Light Esq, MA
*M A J Miller Esq, BSc, MRICS
*J G Thom Esq, LLB, Dip LP, NP, TEP (*OG*)
P A A Mackenzie Smith Esq, BSc (*OG Club Chairman*)
D M S Johnston Esq
Prof A McCleery, MA, PhD
J Smelt Esq, MA, FCSI
*K R Cochrane Esq, BAcc Hons, CA, DSC
T J O Carmichael Esq
Mrs L White, LLB
The Rt Revd Dr G D Duncan, Bishop of Glasgow and Galloway

* *Committee of Council*
(OG) *Old Glenalmond*

Warden: G C Woods, MA Oxon, PGCE

Sub-Warden: C G Henderson, BSc, PhD St Andrews
Deputy Head – Academic: Dr S N Kinge, BSc, PhD
Director of Boarding and Child Protection: Mrs S Sinclair, BSc Edinburgh, PGCE
Registrar: M T Jeffers, BSc, PGCE
Chaplain: The Revd G W Dove, MA, MPhil, BD
Director of Finance and Secretary to the Council: Ms L A Kennedy, BA, CA
Director of Development: Dr C Fleming, BSc, PhD
Director of Alumni Relations: Mrs M Marshall, MBA, MInstF (*Cert*)
Head of Marketing: Ms L M Nowell, BA, DipM, Dip DigM, MCIM
Bursar (Facilities and Estates): Lt Col K H Montgomery, BSc, MBA, MCMI, MInstRE, MBIFM
Head of Sixth Form and Careers: A Norton, BA, BEd
Director of Pupil Development: C D B Youlten, BA, PGCE
Matron: Mrs J Duguid, RGN

Teaching Staff:
* *Head of Department*
† *Housemaster/mistress*

English:
*M Watson, BA, MEd, PGCE
J D G Lugton, MA, PGCE
Miss V M Dryden, BA, PGDE
Mrs C M Gillespie, MA Oxon, PGCE (†*Lothian*)
Mrs W Youlten, MA, PGCE
Miss L Kirk, RSAMD Glasgow, PGCE

Mathematics:
*G G O'Neill, BSc, PGCE
M T Jeffers, BSc, PGCE
M Allnutt, BSc, CertEd (*Director of Studies*)
S P Erdal, BSc, PGCE
Mrs S Sinclair, BSc, PGCE
M A Orviss, MA Cantab, PGCE
Mrs S Smith, BSc, PGCE

Classics:
*G W J Pounder, MA Oxon, PGCE
J D Wright, MA Oxon
Miss V M Dryden, BA, PGDE

Modern Foreign Languages:
*Mrs J Davey, MA, PGCE
J A Gardner, BA, PGCE
J B M Poulter, MA Cantab, PGCE
Mrs K A Watson, BA Hons (†*Home*)
W R Davidson, MA, PGCE (†*Skrine's*)
Mrs S Baldwin, MA Cantab, PGCE
Mrs I Reynolds, MA

Geography:
*S Smith, MA, PGDE

C S Swaile, MA, PGCE
M Gibson, BSc, PhD, PGCE, FRGS (†*Reid's*)
Mrs G Armitage, BA, PGCE

History:
*R R Mundill, MA, PhD, PGCE, DipEd, FIHGS
L W R Rattray, MA, MLitt, PGDE (†*Matheson's*)
C D B Youlten, BA, PGCE
Mrs L Donaldson, BA

Biology:
*A C Hughes, BSc, PGCE
C G Henderson, BSc, PhD, PGCE
Dr S Colby, BSc, PhD, PGCE
Miss L Howden, BSc, PGCE

Chemistry:
*Dr T S Wilkinson, BSc, PhD, PGCE
Dr S N Kinge, BSc, PhD
Mrs T T Hughes, BSc, PGCE
Miss L Howden, BSc, PGCE

Physics:
*R Benson, BSc, PGCE
Dr S N Kinge, BSc, PhD
D M Smith, BSc, MEng, PGCE
W G R Bain, MA Cantab, PGCE

Economics and Business Studies:
*J C Robinson, BA, PGCE
P J Golden, BSocSc, MA, PGCE (†*Goodacre's*)

Computing:
*Mrs I Cox, BA, PgD, DipEd
W A S MacAulay, BA, PgD
G Collins HND
I Hems

Politics:
*A Norton, BA, BEd

Drama:
*C D B Youlten, BA, PGCE (*Head of Academic Theatre Studies*)
*Miss L Kirk, RSAMD, PGCE (*Head of Drama and Performance*)

Music:
*T J W Ridley, GRSM, PhD, LRAM, FRSA
B J Elrick, LLB
Ms J Neufeld, BA, BEd

Art and Design:
*B Wang, BA, MA
Mrs C V Norton, BA
Mrs N J Beaumont, BA, PGCE (†*Cairnies*)
Mrs C J R Butler, MA

History of Art:
*Mrs C J R Butler, MA

Divinity and Religious Studies:
*Revd G W Dove, MA, MPhil, BD

Library and Archives:
Mrs E Mundill, MA, DipLib, MCILIP, Cert TM, TESOL

Design Technology:
*A A Purdie, BSc, BEd
W G R Bain, MA Cantab, PGCE
Mrs N J Beaumont, BA, PGCE (†*Cairnies*)

Physical Education:
*M J Davies, BA, PGCE (*Director of Sport*)
Miss C Bircher, BEd
H G Thomas, BSc (†*Patchell's*)
Miss G Douglas, BPE

Learning Support:
*Mrs N Henderson, BSc, PGCE
Mrs E Critchley, Montessori Diploma

Miss G Douglas, BPE
Mrs W Youlten, MA, PGCE

English as an Additional Language:
J A Gardner, BA Hons, PGCE
Mrs M Gardner, BA, PGDE
Mrs E Mundill, MA, DipLib, MCILIP, Cert TM, TESOL

The College is built on the south bank of the River Almond, from the north bank of which rise the Grampian mountains. It is about 50 miles north of Edinburgh and 10 miles from both Perth and Crieff.

The College Buildings, grouped round a cloistered quadrangle, comprise the Chapel, Hall, Library, houserooms and studies, study bedrooms, classrooms and laboratories. A separate block houses additional laboratories and a Theatre. A few metres away are the Art School and the Design and Technology Centre. Next to these are the Music practice rooms and a Concert Hall.

The Sports Complex consists of squash courts, a gymnasium, an indoor sports hall and a heated indoor swimming pool and fitness suite.

The College also has a state-of-the-art Science Block and IT Resources Centre.

Houses. There are 5 houses for boys, and 3 for girls. Each house has married accommodation for resident Housemaster or Housemistress. Senior boys and girls have study-bedrooms of their own.

Religion. The College has an Episcopalian foundation and has a splendid Chapel. However pupils from a wide range of ethnic, religious and cultural backgrounds are welcomed; the needs of other religious groups and recognised faiths will be observed and supported.

Admission. In line with the College's foundation and tradition, entry to Glenalmond is academically selective. Boys and girls may be registered for admission at any time after birth and enter the College between the ages of 13 and 14 via the Common Entrance Examination or Entrance Scholarship papers. Pupils leaving Primary Schools may qualify by tests and examinations for junior entry at age 11 or 12. Girls and boys may also qualify for entry into the Lower Sixth, or at other points during their school career. Boarding and Day pupils are accepted throughout the school.

For those applying from overseas, or whose first language is not English, we expect, as a minimum, an Intermediate standard of written and spoken English (IELTS Grade 4 or equivalent).

Curriculum. In the Second and Third Form (Years 8 and 9, S1 and S2) all pupils take a wide range of subjects including English, Mathematics, History, Geography, French, Spanish or German, Latin or Ancient Civilisation, Biology, Chemistry, Physics, Technology, Music, PSHCE, Drama, Art and ICT. In the 4th and 5th Form pupils may choose three options, including Greek, along with the core subjects of Mathematics, English Language and Literature, French and the three Sciences. Each pupil is guided by an academic tutor who meets regularly with their tutor group.

The Sixth Form curriculum is designed to allow pupils as wide a choice as possible with 24 A Level subjects being offered ranging from Business Studies and Music Technology to Physics and Philosophy. There are weekly lectures from outside speakers on social, economic and cultural subjects which foster academic excellence across the age ranges. The more able pupils are encouraged to join the William Bright Society which promotes cross year group discussion on relevant academic and moral issues.

Careers. Over 98% of pupils continue to university; some go direct to professional careers, industry, the Services, etc. Great emphasis is placed on careers guidance: careers talks, visits and advice along with a well-stocked careers room assist pupils in their choice. All pupils are encouraged to take psychometric careers aptitude tests at age 16.

The computer network extends to all parts of the campus. ICT is available in libraries and all classrooms, and all pupils have access to email and the internet within their Houses.

Art, Drama and Music. Music plays a central part in the life of the school: there is an Orchestra as well as smaller String, Woodwind and Brass Groups. A large Choir and Choral Society perform at the College, in Perth and in Edinburgh. A new Harrison and Harrison pipe organ supports Glenalmond's central Chapel tradition. The Concert Society arranges recitals and concerts at the College; frequent visits are made to concerts in Perth and elsewhere. There are currently two Pipe Bands.

The Drama and Art departments flourish, in conjunction with the well-established Design and Technology Centre. Both Art and Music as well as Design/Technology form part of the normal curriculum and can be taken at GCSE and A Level.

Sport and Recreation. Rugby (boys) and Hockey (girls) are played in the Michaelmas Term and there is a wide variety of activities to choose from in the Lent Term, including Lacrosse and Netball for girls and Hockey, Football and Cross-Country for boys, with Cricket, Athletics, Shooting, Sailing, Tennis and Golf in Summer. Shooting on the Miniature Ranges takes place during the two winter terms. There is a large indoor heated Swimming Pool and pupils are trained in personal survival and Lifesaving. Instruction in Sub-aqua and Canoeing is given. There are also Squash Courts, Tennis Courts, a nine-hole (James Braid) Golf Course, and two full-size all-weather pitches for hockey, netball and tennis.

During the Summer, pupils have the opportunity to explore the hills and the neighbouring countryside. There is also a Sailing and Windsurfing Club which uses a neighbouring loch. Weekend camping expeditions are arranged to encourage self-reliance and initiative.

Glenshee is just over an hour away and there are opportunities for skiing in the Lent Term.

Combined Cadet Force. There is a contingent of the Combined Cadet Force which has strong links with the Armed Forces and the Royal Regiment of Scotland (Black Watch Battalion) in particular. The ceremonial dress, as worn by the Pipe Band for example, is the Highland dress with the Murray of Atholl tartan.

Army and Air sections, with a Pre-Service section for Junior Pupils, are organised on the basis of the Duke of Edinburgh's Award. Shooting and Adventure Training figure prominently; pupils may also be engaged on Conservation, Community Service Work or Mountain Awareness Group.

Fees per term (2014–2015). £10,100 Boarders; £6,880 Day Pupils (for whom free transport is arranged); £7,570 Junior Boarders; £5,160 Junior Day.

These fees include extras common to all pupils, such as membership of the CCF, Games, Subscriptions, journeys to matches, the use of the Golf Course, etc.

Sibling discounts are available. Children of serving members of the Armed Forces and members of the Clergy receive an automatic 10% fee discount.

Term of Entry. Entry is normally in September. Entry in January or April can be considered where special circumstances exist.

Scholarships and Bursaries. Academic Scholarships and Exhibitions are awarded. Junior Scholarship candidates must be under 14 on 1 September of the year of entry. A short statement showing the scope of the examination will be forwarded on application, and copies of last year's papers may be obtained. Scholarship candidates will be examined at Glenalmond. The Entrance Scholarships Examinations are usually held in March for younger pupils and in November for entrants to the Sixth Form.

Music Scholarships may be available to entrants at 12+, 13+ or Sixth Form. Candidates will usually offer two instruments at least to Grade V. Promising string players and singers will be considered with great interest. Award holders receive free musical tuition.

An Organ Scholarship, Piping Awards and Art & Design Scholarships are also available. There are also Outstanding Talent Awards for Sport.

All-Rounder Awards are available to 13+ entrants only; candidates must demonstrate strength in at least two of the following areas: Drama, Sport, Music, Art.

All Awards can be increased in cases of need. A number of means-tested bursaries are available each year for up to 100% of fees. Applications should reach the Director of Finance no later than 1 February in the year of entry.

The Old Glenalmond Club. *Hon Secretary*: D Sibbald, 21 Ravelston Park, Edinburgh EH4 3DX.

Charitable status. Glenalmond College is a Registered Charity, number SC006123. It exists for the all-round education of Boys and Girls in the tranquillity of a rural setting.

The Godolphin and Latymer School

Iffley Road, Hammersmith, London W6 0PG

Tel: 020 8741 1936; 020 8563 7649 (Bursar)
Fax: 020 8735 9520
email: office@godolphinandlatymer.com
website: www.godolphinandlatymer.com

Motto: *Francha Leale Toge*

Foundation: Godolphin and Latymer, originally a boys' school, became a girls' day school in 1905. It was aided by the London County Council from 1920 onwards and by the Inner London Education Authority when it received Voluntary Aided status after the 1944 Education Act. Rather than become part of a split-site Comprehensive school it reverted to Independent status in 1977.

Governors:
Chairman: Mr Clifford Hampton, BA, FCA
Ms Julia Barfield, MBE, AA, Dip RIBA
Mr Sean Carney, BEcon, LLB
Miss Julia Collins, BA, ACCA
Miss Sarah Davies, MA
Mr Simon Davies, BA Oxon
Mr Jonathan Eley, MA
Mr Jon Gabitass, MA
Mr Timothy Howe, QC
Professor Dame Julia Higgins, DBE, FRS, FREng
Dr Leonard Magrill, PhD, BSc, MCom
Mrs Alison Paines, MA, BA
Mrs Penelope Stout-Hammar, BA
Mr Matthew Streets, BA
Miss June Taylor, BSc
Mrs Elizabeth Watson, BA

Clerk to the Governors: Mrs Diana Lynch, BSc Kingston, FCCA

Staff:

Head Mistress: **Mrs Ruth Mercer**, BA London, PGCE Oxford

Deputy Head: Mrs Anna Paul, BA

Senior Teachers:
Mr John Carroll, BSc Durham
Miss Caroline Drennan, MA Oxon, MA UEA
Miss Julia Hodgkins, MA Brunel, BEd CNAA
Mrs Sue Kinross, BA Exeter
Ms Amanda Triccas, MA, BA London

Teaching Staff:
Miss Zoe Abrahams, BA Nottingham
Ms Sarah Adams, BEd Melbourne
Miss Sue Adey, BEd Brighton
Mrs Genevieve Andrade, MA UEL, BSc Imperial College
Mrs Svetlana Andreyeva, BA Leningrad
Mr Richard Arch, MA London, MSc York, BA Keele
Mrs Anna Armstrong, BA York
Mrs Sylvie Banks, L-ès-L Paris
Miss Karen Barac, BSc, BEd British Columbia
Miss Ella Barden, BSc Durham
Mr Anthony Belfrage, CertEd Leeds, Dip Computer Ed WLIHE
Mr Julian Bell, BA Cantab, MA Sussex
Dr Pamela Bickley, PhD London, BA London
Ms Diana Blease, MA Oxon, BA Open
Mrs Ebiere Bolu, BSc Loughborough
Mr Frederick Bosanquet, BA Oxon
Mrs Sancha Briffa, MA Kingston, BA Central St Martins
Dr Aimee Bunting, PhD Soton, MA Soton, BA Soton
Miss Clare Butterworth, MA London, BA Oxon
Miss Karen Casterton, BSc Keele
Mrs Emma Chorley, PhD Bristol, BA Bristol
Miss Alison Clark, BA Oxon
Mrs Matilda Cockbain, MA Oxon
Miss Lucy Cooper, MA Wimbledon School of Art, BA Staffordshire
Mrs Celine Corcoran, MA Soton
Mr Peter Cosgrove, BA Bristol College of Art & Design
Dr Morven Creagh, PhD Exeter, MA Nottingham, BA Exeter
Mrs Genevieve Cuming, MA Sorbonne
Mr Adrian Davies, BA Cardiff Institute
Mr Quintin Davies, MA Keele
Miss Tara Dean, BSc Edinburgh
Mrs Amertha Devadoss, BSc London
Mr Nikhil Dholakia, MBA, MEng London
Miss Audrey Dubois, Maîtrise FLE, LLCE Boulogne-sur-mer
Mrs Louise Duffett, MA London, BA Oxon
Miss Natalie Earl, BA Manchester
Miss Ellen Elfick, BEd Exeter
Mrs Sara Farago, BA Winchester School of Art
Mrs Ursula Fenton, Diploma PH Freiburg
Miss Elizabeth Fox, MA Oxon, MSc LSE
Miss Sarah Fryer, BA Bristol
Mrs Jennifer Garcia, BMus Surrey
Mrs Clare Gatward, BA Oxon
Mrs Penny Gilbert, BA Durham
Mr Miles Golland, BA London
Miss Ruth Gordon, BA Durham
Mrs Veronique Halls, BA Sorbonne
Miss Nicola Hanger, BA Oxon
Dr Eilis Harron-Ponsonby, PhD, BA, MSci Cantab
Ms Rachel Hart, BA Oxon
Miss Faye Hasteley, BA Falmouth
Miss Kate Healy, BA Leicester
Mrs Rachel Hollis, PhD Birmingham, BSc Portsmouth
Miss Isabell Jacobson, BA Bristol
Dr Ian Jones, PhD CNAA, MSc Cardiff, BSc Liverpool
Mr Mark Laflin, MA Oxon, ARCO, ATCL
Mrs Katherine Laurence, MA Cantab
Mrs Christine Lee, MA London, BEd Exeter
Miss Jennifer Lloyd, MChem Cardiff
Miss Emma Lorys, BA Exeter
Miss Francesca Mabley, BSc Bath
Mr David Mahoney, BSc London
Mrs Harsha Mason, MA London, BA Durham
Miss Helena Matthews, BA Cantab
Miss Nicola McDonald, BA Bristol
Mr Justin McGrath, MSc Cranfield, BSc Wales
Mrs Fiona Meyers, BA Kent
Miss Amanda Newton

Miss Sophie Nicholas, BA Loughborough
Miss Louise Ockenden, MA RCA, BA Central St Martins
Mrs Caroline Osborne, MA Sussex
Miss Luigia Padalino, BA Bologna
Mrs Christine Preston, BSc Bath
Mrs Sylvia Rendall, BA Manchester
Mr Stephen Ridgwell, BA, MPhil Swansea
Mrs Victoria Robinson, BA Durham
Miss Madeline Row, MSc Brunel, BSc Brunel
Miss Lucy Shackleton, BA Cantab
Mr Avinash Shah, MEd Sheffield, BA City
Dr Ben Snook, PhD Cantab, MPhil Cantab, BA Cantab
Dr Jenny Stevens, PhD London, MA London
Mrs Susan Sutherland, BA Aberystwyth
Miss Katherine Tallett-Williams, MA Cantab
Miss Jennifer Taylor, BA Durham
Mr Carl Thomas, LPC Westminster, LLB North London, BSc London
Miss Helen Tomlinson, BSc Durham
Mrs Thania Troya, BA Santa Cruz de Tenerife
Miss Sarah Valentine, BSc Wellington
Mr Alastair Vettese, BA Oxon
Miss Stephanie von Haniel, MA Edinburgh
Miss Lucy Wallace, BA Reading
Ms Jane Waltham, BSc Manchester
Miss Alice Weldon, BSc Durham
Dr Rik Werker, PhD Cantab, BSc Bangor
Mr Neil White, BSc London
Mrs Susan Whittaker, BA Durham
Miss Camilla Williams, BA Kent
Miss Helena Wittwer, BA Oxon
Mrs Jennifer Wright, BA Bristol, BEd Bath College
Miss Wendy Zhang, MSc Birmingham, BSc Manchester

Visiting teachers in Music and Speech Training:
Miss Rebecca Austen-Brown, BMus RAM
Mrs Christina Birchall-Sampson, BA Cantab
Ms Elizabeth Bradley, MMus London
Miss Ruth Buxton, BMus RCM, LGSM Guildhall
Miss Davina Clarke, BMus Manchester
Mrs Jane Clark-Maxwell, BMus London, LTCL
Mrs Harriet Davey, BMus Guildhall
Miss Eva Doroszkowska, BMus Manchester, RNCM
Miss Meryl Drower, ARCM
Miss Claire Egan, BMus London, PgDip Birmingham
Mrs Kasia Feltrin, MA Cracow, PGDip Guildhall
Miss Victoria Galer, BA York
Miss Rachel Latham, BMus, ARCM
Mr Martyn Lewington, Dip RCM
Miss Ching-Ching Lim, MMus RCM, LRSM, FRCL, LTCL
Miss Annie Lower, MMus, BMus, BA, Queensland
Mr Alex Mitchell, GMus RNCM, PPRNCM
Miss Catherine Morphett, BMus Sydney
Ms Vivien Munday, BMus Sydney
Mr David Neville, BA RCM
Miss Camilla Pay, BMus RAM, LRAM
Mrs Jaimi Rainsford, BSc Birmingham
Mrs Rosie Richardson, MMus Guildhall
Ms Catherine Riley MMus Auckland NZ, LRSM
Mrs Kate Ryder, MMus London, DSCM NSW Conservatorium
Miss Julia Staniforth, Virtuosité DipRAM, GRSM, DipALCM
Mr Christopher Stell, LRAM DipRam RAM
Miss Emma Tingey, LWCMD, ACC WCMD, TCM
Miss Lindsay Tricker, BEd CSSD
Mrs Penny Whinnett, GMus RNCM
Mr Ryan Williams, MMus Guildhall, BMus Exeter
Miss Emilia Zakrzewska, BMus RAM, RSAMD, DipRAM, LRAM

Bursar: Mrs Diana Lynch, BSc Kingston, FCCA
Registrar: Mrs Felicity Lundberg

Head Mistress's PA: Mrs Vivienne Cox, BA
School Doctor: Dr Louise Miller, MA Cantab, MB, BChir, MRCGP
School Nurse: Mrs Tessa Vardigans, RN, SpCPHN-SN, Mrs Victoria Dickins, RN, BSc, Dip SpLD

Godolphin and Latymer is an independent day school for 780 girls, aged 11 to 18. The school stands in a four acre site in Hammersmith, near Hammersmith Broadway and excellent public transport. The original Victorian building has been extended to include a pottery room, computer studies room, language laboratory, science and technology laboratories, art studios, a dark room and an ecology garden. The girls benefit from a recently renewed all-weather surface for hockey and tennis, as well as netball courts and a Sixth Form Centre. Since September 2006, the school has leased St John's Church and its Vicarage, both adjacent to the existing site. The Vicarage, renamed the Margaret Gray Building, provides additional classrooms. The new Rudland Music School opened in the Autumn Term 2008 and the renovated church, The Bishop Centre, for the performing arts was completed in early Spring 2009. These state-of-the-art developments provide a range of teaching and performance spaces, recording studios and a music technology suite. The Bishop Centre provides an auditorium to seat over 800.

The Godolphin and Latymer School aims to provide a stimulating, enjoyable environment and to foster intellectual curiosity and independence. We strive for a love of learning and academic excellence, emphasising the development of the individual, within a happy, supportive community.

While girls are expected to show a strong commitment to their studies they are encouraged to participate in a range of extra-curricular activities. We aim to develop the girls' self-respect and self-confidence, together with consideration and care for others so that they feel a sense of responsibility and are able to take on leadership roles within the school and the wider community.

Pastoral Care. The school has a close relationship with parents, and every member of the staff takes an interest in the girls' academic and social welfare. Each girl has a form teacher and a deputy form teacher and there is a Head of Lower School, Head of Middle School and a Head of Sixth Form, each with at least one deputy.

Curriculum. We offer a broad, balanced curriculum including appropriate education concerning personal, health, ethical and social issues. During the first three years Philosophy and Religion, English, French, Spanish or German, Mandarin, Latin, History, Geography, Mathematics, Physics, Chemistry, Biology, Food Technology, Design Technology, Art, Music, and Physical Education are studied. In Year 10 Italian, Russian, Greek, Classical Civilisation and PE and Drama become available. Girls take ten or eleven subjects to GCSE. Drama is studied in Years 7, 8, 9 and 10.

In the Sixth Form there is a choice of curriculum between the Advanced Level (AS and A2) and the International Baccalaureate Diploma. All subjects offered to GCSE can be continued into the Sixth Form with the addition of Ancient History, Drama and Theatre Studies, Economics, Government and Politics and History of Art. Sixth Formers also undertake the Extended Project Qualification (AL) or Extended Essay and Theory of Knowledge (IB) and attend lectures given by outside speakers.

The Sixth Form. The Sixth Form facilities include a Common Room, Work Room and Terrace. The 220 girls in the Sixth Form play a leading role in the school, taking responsibility for many extra-curricular activities, producing form plays and organising clubs. They undertake voluntary work and lead our Raising and Giving programme.

Higher Education and Careers Advice. A strong careers team offers advice to girls and parents. Our specialist room is well stocked with up-to-date literature and course information, and lectures and work shadowing are arranged. Almost all girls proceed to Higher Education degree courses

(including an average of 15 a year to Oxford and Cambridge).

The Creative Arts. Music and Drama flourish throughout the school. The Rudland Music School has outstanding facilities for music: 20 soundproofed rooms for individual or group work, a recording studio, ICT suite and two classrooms which open out into a very large rehearsal space for choirs and orchestras. There are four choirs, two orchestras and several small ensembles, and a joint orchestra and choral society with Latymer Upper School. Individual music lessons are offered in many different instruments. Each year there is a pantomime, Year 10 and Sixth Form plays as well as the school productions. The refurbished church, known as The Bishop Centre, offers a superb performing arts space for music, drama and dance. Venues out of school have included the Cochrane Theatre, Lyric Theatre, Riverside Studios and the Edinburgh Festival.

Physical Education is a vital part of a girl's development as an individual and as a team member. Younger girls play netball, hockey, tennis and rounders and have gymnastic and dance lessons. In the senior years there is a wider range of activities offered, including rowing and squash off site. We are currently in the process of replacing our gymnasium, with a new Sports and Fitness Centre which will greatly enhance our sports provision.

Extra-Curricular Activities. The many opportunities for extra-curricular activities include the British Association of Young Scientists, Computing, Chess, the Young Enterprise Scheme, Debating, Creative Writing, Classics Club and the Duke of Edinburgh's Award Scheme, as well as a wide range of sporting activities such as karate, fencing, rowing and canoeing.

Activities outside the School. We organise language exchanges to Germany, France and Russia, a musical exchange to Hamburg and Sixth Form work experience in Versailles and Berlin. There is also an exchange with a school in New York. Each year, Year 9 girls ski in the USA and there are study visits to Spain, Italy and France and History of Art visits to Paris, Bruges, Venice and Florence and, for the Upper Sixth, a visit to Jordan.

We take advantage of our London location by arranging visits to conferences, theatres, exhibitions and galleries. Field courses are an integral part of study in Biology and Geography.

Admission. Girls are normally admitted into Year 7 (First Year Entrance) or into our Sixth Form. Examinations for First Year entrance are held in January and for the Sixth Form in November. There are occasional vacancies in other years. Entry is on a competitive basis.

Fees per term (from January 2015). £6,060. Fees may be raised after a term's notice. Private tuition in music and speech and drama are extra. Most girls have school lunch, but it is an option from Year 8.

Scholarships. Music scholarships are available on entry to Year 7 and in the Sixth Form and include free tuition in one instrument.

An Art scholarship is available in the Sixth Form.

All scholarships are worth up to 30% of fees and may be topped up by means-tested bursaries in cases of need. For all awards, candidates must satisfy the academic requirements of the school.

Bursaries. A number of school bursaries are available annually.

Uniform. Uniform is worn by girls up to and including Year 11.

Charitable status. The Godolphin and Latymer School is a Registered Charity, number 312699. It exists to provide education to girls aged 11 to 18.

The Godolphin School

Milford Hill, Salisbury SP1 2RA
Tel: 01722 430500
             Preparatory School: 01722 430652
Fax: 01722 430501
email: admissions@godolphin.wilts.sch.uk
website: www.godolphin.org

Motto: *Franc Ha Leal Eto Ge* (Frankness and Loyalty be Yours)
    Founded by Elizabeth Godolphin in 1707; date of the will of the Foundress, 24 June 1726; a new scheme made by the Charity Commissioners and approved by HM, 1886, and re-issued by the Charity Commissioners in February 1986. The Godolphin School is an independent boarding and day school for girls aged 11–18, with its own purpose-built preparatory day school for girls from the age of 3. Of the 350 girls in the senior school, over 100 are in the Sixth Form.

Governing Body:
M J Nicholson Esq (*Chairman*)
Lady Ruth Hawley
Mrs S Herd
G W Green Esq
S Hill Esq
J S Lipa Esq, LLB, MJur, FINZ, ICFM
The Revd C Mitchell-Innes
Mrs K Browne
Mrs T Watkins, BA
Dr R Griffiths
J Kelly Esq
Mrs J Forrest
J Booker Esq
A F R Boys Esq
R Franks Esq
N Huggett Esq
Mrs C J M Jenkinson

Bursar and Clerk to the Governors: K G M Flynn Esq, BSc, FCMA

Headmistress: **Mrs Emma Hattersley**, BA Hons Dunelm

Deputy Head: R T W Dain Esq, MA Oxon
Academic Deputy: Mrs H Portas, BA Wales
Pastoral Deputy: Mrs N Green, MA Sussex
Director of Admissions and Marketing: Mrs M Rowney

Registrar: Mrs C Heritage, BA Manchester

Staff:
* *Head of Department/Subject*

Religious Studies:
*F R Spencer Esq, BA Essex, BTh Southampton
P Sharkey Esq, BA London
Mrs E Hattersley, BA Hons Dunelm, PG RAM

English:
*M Ryan-East Esq, BA Hons Plymouth
Mrs M Edouard, BA London
Mrs T Nicholls, MA Keele, BEd Cambridge
Mrs R Carville, BA Hons Birmingham
R T W Dain Esq, MA Oxon

History:
*Dr A Dougall Esq, LLB London, MA, PhD Southampton
Miss J Miller, BA Belfast, MEd Open
Mrs S Eggleton, MA Aberdeen
Mrs H Portas, BA Wales

Psychology:
Miss A Bowler, BA Manchester, BA Wimbledon
J Larcombe Esq, BSc Durham

Business Studies and Economics:
*D J Miller Esq, BA Nottingham
Mrs N Owers, BA Nottingham

Geography:
*Miss S L Collishaw, BSc Swansea
Mrs J Morris, MA Bath

Classics:
*A Mackay Esq, MA Cantab
C Gilham Esq, BA London
Mrs S Radice, BA Reading

Modern Languages:
*Mrs S Smith, MA Cantab
Mrs J Gilham, BA Cape Town
Ms M A Cibis, BA, MA Sheffield
Dr L Rojas-Hindmarsh, DPhil Leeds
Miss M Reyes Avila Cabrera, Lda Alicante
C Gilham Esq, BA London
Miss P Clement, BEd Angers
Mrs E Bally (*Assistentin*)
Sr J-M Verdu Cortes (*Assistentin*)

Mathematics:
*Mrs K Healey, BSc Bristol
*Mrs J L Robson, BSc Bristol
Mrs R C Stratton, BSc Exeter
Mrs N Owers, BA Hons Nottingham, PGCE
Mrs A Bacon, BSc Hons Southampton PGCE

Science:
*Dr C Thrower, PhD, MSc, BSc Manchester (*Chemistry*)
Dr B Medany, BSc London, PhD Nottingham (*Biology*)
C Hillman Esq, MS, PhD Southampton (*Physics*)
Mrs M Foster, BA London
P Hill Esq, BSc London
Miss A E Masson, BA Cambridge
J McNulty Esq, MSc Leicester
R Pocklington Esq, BEd Southampton

Design and Food Technology:
*M Berry Esq, BEd Leeds, MA Open
Mrs P Parry-Jones, BSc Bath College of Higher Education
Mrs C Complin, BSc Bath College of Higher Education

Information and Communication Technology:
*N Everett Esq, BSc South Bank
Mrs W Laptain, BEd Manchester

Art and Design:
*N Eggleton Esq, BA London, ATC
Mrs S Duggan, BA Winchester
Miss E Findley, BA Leeds Metropolitan
C Wright Esq, BA Napier
Mrs J Josey, C&G TCert Basingstoke

History of Art:
*Mrs S Radice, BA Reading

Music:
*R A Highcock Esq, BMus London
Mrs O Sparkhall, BA Dunelm
C Guild Esq, BMus Royal College of Music

Drama:
*D Hallen Esq, BA Hons Middlesex, PGCE
Miss N Strode, BA Cardiff
Mrs M Ferris, LGSM, LTCL (*Speech and Drama Coach*)

Instrumental Staff and Ensemble Coaches:
Miss S Cox, BA
Mrs G Cullingford
N Ellis Esq
C Hobkirk Esq, BA MusEd, ARCO
R Leighton Boyce Esq
Mrs J Littlemore, BMus, LRAM
Mrs C Long, GTCL, LTCL
Ms S McKenzie-Park

Miss S Stocks, LRAM, LGSM
M Wilkinson Esq, CertEd
C Holmes Esq, ARCM
Mrs F Brockhurst, ARCM
J Gilbert Esq
H Hetherington Esq, MA Cantab
Mrs E Huntriss, GNSM, LRAM
C Hurn Esq, LGSM, BA
Ms E Innes, GGSM, AGSM

Physical Education:
*Mrs S Pokai, BA Brighton
Mrs L Edwards, BSc Hons Loughborough
Mrs A J Venn, BA Manchester, PGSC Physical Education
Miss L Christian, BA Wagner College, New York
Mrs S C Harvey, BEd Exeter
Miss S Oor (*Lacrosse Coach*)

Chaplain: Dr S Wood, MA, DPhil Oxford
Librarian: Ms D Jones, BA Oxford
Head of Sixth Form and Higher Education Adviser: Dr A Dougall, LLB London, MA, PhD Southampton
Upper School Tutor: D Hallen Esq, BA Middlesex
Middle School Tutor: Mrs S Eggleton, MA Aberdeen
Lower School Tutor: Mrs W Laptain, BEd Manchester
Careers Adviser: Mrs B Ferguson, BA Hons Newcastle upon Tyne

Learning Support:
Mrs C Firth, BA, BSc Open, MSc, SpLD Southampton
Mrs J Dunne, BEd Oxon, CELTA
Mrs A Eccles, BA Hons Exeter
R Tarlton Esq, MA Leicester

Sixth Form Centre:
School House:
Ms S Jones, BA Wales (*Housemistress*)
D Hallen Esq, BA Middlesex (*Deputy Housemaster*)
Jerred House:
Miss E Findley, BA Leeds Metropolitan (*Housemistress*)
Mrs V Wilson (*Assistant Housemistress*)
Ms M Cibis (*Assistant Housemistress*)

Houses:
Cooper:
Mrs L Cotterell, MA Oxford (*Housemistress*)
Mrs Y Meek (*Deputy Housemistress*)
Walters:
Mrs W Laptain, BEd Manchester (*Housemistress*)
Mrs M Reyes Avila Cabrera, Lda Alicante (*Deputy Housemistress*)
Sayers:
Mrs S Ramsdale, BEd Liverpool (*Housemistress*)
Miss J Tatem, BEd Southampton (*Deputy Housemistress*)

Sanatorium:
Mrs G Davey, RGN
Mrs V Block, RGN
Mrs R Nicholls, RGN
Mrs V Coupe, RGN
Mrs J Palk

The Godolphin School stands in 16 acres of landscaped grounds on the edge of the historic cathedral city of Salisbury, overlooking open countryside.

A strong academic life combines with thriving art, drama, music and sport. A five-studio art centre provides excellent art and design facilities, while the Blackledge Theatre provides a professional environment for drama and music performance. Other notable developments include the Baxter Pool and Fitness Centre, a new boarding house and a dedicated Sixth Form Centre, the latter providing a focus for careers and higher education advice, and the Sixth Form social programme, as well as study-bedrooms, work space and recreational areas. Sciences are taught within the well-equipped laboratories and have a strong tradition of Oxbridge success. The whole site is served by a wireless network.

Religious Instruction. Godolphin has strong affiliations with the Church of England, but religious instruction covers all the major world faiths.

Curriculum. High academic standards (90% A* to C grades at A Level and 98% A* to C grades at GCSE and IGCSE in 2014) are combined with a wide range of clubs, societies and weekend activities; also an outstanding programme of trips and expeditions. Activities include: cookery, photography, Duke of Edinburgh's Award, Combined Cadet Force, community service, debating, creative writing, academic societies and wide ranging opportunities in art, drama, music and sport. 24 subjects are available at A Level, and virtually all students continue to higher education, most to universities, including Oxbridge; some to art colleges, drama schools and music conservatoires. There is considerable emphasis on Careers guidance, including an excellent work shadowing scheme.

Physical Education. Strong sporting record with pupils regularly selected for county and regional teams; also at national level. 22 sporting options include lacrosse, hockey, netball, tennis, athletics, swimming, gymnastics, dance, rounders and cross-country. Each girl is encouraged to find at least one sport she really enjoys during her time at Godolphin.

Entrance Examination. Godolphin's own assessment and interview at 11+ and Common Entrance Examination at 13+. Examination and interview at all other levels, including Sixth Form.

Scholarships and Bursaries. 11+ and 13+ Academic, Art, Music and Sports Scholarships are awarded for outstanding merit and promise. Candidates for music awards should have attained at least Grade 4 at 11+ (Grade 6 at 13+) on one instrument. They are also expected to reach an acceptable academic standard.

Sixth Form Academic, Art, Drama, Music and Sports scholarships are also available.

Six means-tested Foundation Bursaries, each worth 70% of the fees, are available from time to time to boarding candidates from single parent, divorced or separated families who have been brought up as members of the Church of England.

The Old Godolphin Bursary, a means-tested bursary worth up to 50% of the boarding fees, is awarded from time to time by the Old Godolphin Association to the daughter of an Old Godolphin.

Fees per term (2014–2015). Senior School: Full Boarding £7,972–£9,359, 5-day Boarding £7,739–£9,085, 3-day Boarding £7,460–£8,759, Day £5,558–£6,176.

Prep School: Full Boarding £7,234, 5-day Boarding £6,177, 3-day Boarding £5,367, Day £2,069–£3,997.

Fees include tuition, textbooks, stationery, sanatorium, laundry, and most weekday and weekend clubs and activities.

Extra Subjects. Individual tuition in music, speech and drama, Italian, tennis, fencing, judo, EFL and learning support.

Old Godolphin Association. *Secretary*: Miss H Duder, Keith Cottage, Cold Ash, Thatcham, Berkshire RG18 9PT, or via Development Office, Tel: 01722 430570.

Charitable status. The Godolphin School is a Registered Charity, number 309488. Its object is to provide and conduct in or near Salisbury a boarding and day school for girls.

The Grange School

Bradburns Lane, Hartford, Northwich, Cheshire CW8 1LU
Tel:　　01606 74007
Fax:　　01606 784581

email: office@grange.org.uk
website: www.grange.org.uk
Twitter: @GrangeHartford
Facebook: /tbegrangeschool

Motto: *E Glande Robur*
The Grange was founded in 1933 as a Preparatory School, the Senior School opening in 1978. The School is co-educational, with 1,177 pupils from 4–18 years, and is situated in the village of Hartford, half an hour away from Chester and Manchester and eight miles from the M6 motorway.

Governing Body:
Chairman: Mr C Stubbs, CEng, MIMechE, MBA

Mrs A Arthur	Mrs S Dawson
Mr S Batey	Mr C Oglesby
Mrs S Hudson	Mrs K Williams
Mr C P Jackson, BSc,	Mrs C Stanton
MIHT	Mr N Brougham
Mrs K Jones, BA, ACA	Mrs C Bregal
Mr N Parkinson, BSc	Mr L Fairclough
Mr J Stamer, FRCS	

Head: **Mr C P Jeffery**, BA, FRSA

Deputy Head (*Staff & Pupils*): Mr A Testard, BA
Deputy Head (*Communications & Enrichment*): Mrs P Duke, BA
Deputy Head (*Academic*): Mr A Crook, MA, MPhil
Head of Sixth Form Studies: Mr A Reeve, BA York, MCIEA
PA to the Head: Mrs J Ward, BA
Bursar: Mrs L Foxley, ACA
Estates Manager: Mr I Grant, MRICS
Employee Support and Compliance Manager: Mrs R Rigden, Chartered MCIPD

Assistant staff:
* *Head of Department*

Mr P J Ackerley, BA (*English*)
Mrs P Allison, BA (*History*)
Mrs N Beardsall, BA (*Art and Technology*)
Mrs J Bloor, BA (*Director of Performing Arts, *Speech & Drama*)
Mr A Boardman, MA (*History*)
Mrs J Breton, BEd (*Food and Nutrition*)
Mrs B A Broderick, BSc (*Chemistry, Geography, *Outdoor Pursuits*)
Miss E Brooke, BA (*Art*)
Mrs S Brunt, BA (*Economics*)
Mr P Buckley, BA (**Classics*)
Miss S Chapman, BA (*Spanish*)
Mrs G Clough, MA (*English*)
Mrs J Corrigan, BA, CertEd (*PE & Games, English*)
Mr N Cusick, BSc (*PE & Games*)
Miss A Dostalova, BSc (*Biology*)
Mrs H Eaton, MA (*Geography*)
Mrs M Ellis, BSc (*Mathematics*)
Mr T H Giles, BA (*PE & Games*)
Mr M Goff, BA (*English*)
Mr P Grattage, BSc (*Director of Sport*)
Mrs L Goldstone, BA (*French*)
Mrs H Hackett, BA, MSc (*German & French*)
Mrs J Hardy-Kinsella, BA (*Drama & English*)
Mr R A Hibbert, BA (**Modern Languages*)
Mrs C Hill, BSc (**Mathematics*)
Mrs H Horsley, BSc (*Physics*)
Mr R A Hough, BA (*Religious Studies, *Philosophy*)
Mr C Howe, BSc (**Chemistry*)
Mr S Howells, BA (**French*)
Mrs S Hoyle, BA (*Religious Studies, Philosophy*)
Miss A Jackson, BSc (*Biology*)
Ms P H Janson, MA (*Mathematics*)

Mr D W Jones, MA (*History & Politics*)
Mr G Jump (**Rowing*)
Mr M Jump (*Rowing*)
Mr H Kelly, MA (*English*)
Mr S Kenyon, BSc (*Geography*)
Mr D Kereszteny-Lewis, BA (*Director of Art & Design, *Art*)
Mrs V Kereszteny-Lewis, BA (**German*)
Mrs H Kerr, BA (*History, *Politics*)
Mr M Lambert, BSc (*Mathematics*)
Mrs M Kaipainen, MA (*English*)
Mr R Latham, BA (**Religious Studies*)
Miss H R Lawson, BA (**Girls' Games*)
Mrs G Lewis, BSc (*Mathematics*)
Mr A Lumley, BSc (*Mathematics*)
Mr B Madden, BA (*Music*)
Mr A Masters, BA (**ICT*)
Mrs J Masters, BA (*Biology and Maths*)
Mr P McAleny, BA (**Graphic Design*)
Mr A J Millinchip, MA, FRCO CHM (*Director of Music*)
Mr A Milne, BSc, MSc (**Science, *Biology*)
Mr W Morrison, BA (**Economics & Business Studies*)
Mrs J S Oakes, BSc (*Biology*)
Mrs C J Osborne, BSc (*Mathematics*)
Mrs K Osorio, BA (**Spanish*)
Mr J M Pearson, BA (**Geography*)
Mr S Petts, BA (**Physics*)
Mrs M Plant, MA (*French & German*)
Mr A Reeve, BA (*Economics*)
Mr R K Robson, BA (**History*)
Mr G Sgroi, BA (*Classics*)
Miss S Sharp, BA (*Art*)
Mr D Shaw, BSc, MSc (*Chemistry*)
Mr L Snelson, BSc (*ICT*)
Mrs A Stewart (*Food & Nutrition*)
Miss J Stockton (**English*)
Mrs L Sunners, BA (*Drama*)
Mrs J Thayer, BSc (*Mathematics*)
Mrs S Thornes, BSc (*Physics*)
Miss S Thorp, BA (*Philosophy, Graphic Design*)
Mrs K Tomlin, BA (*Drama*)
Dr S Wharton, BSc (*Chemistry*)
Mr R Williams, BSc (*Chemistry*)

Junior School

Head of Junior School: Mr G Rands, BSc
Senior Deputy Head of Junior School: Mrs K J Hill, BEd
Head of Pre-Prep: Miss A Evans, BEd
Head of Prep: Mr J Land, BEd
PA to the Headmaster/Admissions Secretary: Mrs M Shaw

Mrs A Basnett, BA	Mr D Heine, BSc
Ms K Blakeley, BA	Mrs V Houghton, MA, BEd
Mrs L Broster-Jones,	Mr D Jackson, BEng
CertEd	Mrs C Jones, BSc
Mrs D Bull, MEd	Mrs E Jones, CertEd, BEd
Mrs C Carson, CertEd	Mr H Jones, BEd
Mrs L Collier, BA	Mrs S Jones, BEd
Mrs A Connolly, BEd	Mr J P Land, BEd
Mrs A Copping, BA	Miss J Lloyd, MA
Mrs K Dakin, BA	Mrs S Lucchesi, BA
Mrs R Davies, BA	Mrs G Montague
Mrs M Dewhurst, BEd	Mrs H Oliver, BA
Miss H Elleray, BA	Mrs Z A Pidcock, BA
Mr G H Evans, BEd	Mrs J Ratcliffe, BEd
Mrs J Haynes, BEd	Mrs G L Rosa, BA
Mrs V Heath, BEd	Miss C Sales, BA

Peripatetic Staff:
Ms C Barker, BA, LGSM (*Cello*)
Mrs A Barnett, BMus, LRAM (*Clarinet, Saxophone*)
Mrs N Boardman, Dip RNCM (*Violin*)
Mrs M Bushnell-Wye, ARCM, LGSM, GRSM (*Clarinet, Saxophone*)

Mr C Gandee, ARCM, LLCM TD, SFLCM (*Brass*)

Miss L Hibberd, BMus (*Piano*)

Mrs S Hoffman, BMus (*Flute*)

Mr G Hogan, BA, LRAM, LGSM, LLCM (*Keyboard, Piano*)

Ms R Holt, GMus RNCM, PPRNCM (*Flute*)

Mrs C Hughes, GNSM, ARCM (*Piano*)

Mr M Jackson, Grad Dip Jazz & Cont Music (*Guitar*)

Mr B Madden, BA (*Cello, Piano*)

Mrs J Martin, CT ABRSM (*Violin*)

Miss P MacMillan, BMus, PG Dip RNCM, ALCM [TD] (*Percussion and Drum Kit*)

Mrs A Powell, BMus, PG Dip RNCM, PPRNCM (*Oboe*)

Mr S Watkiss, CT ABRSM (*Guitar*)

Miss S Wilkes, GMus RNCM (*Singing*)

The Kindergarten and Junior School (449 pupils). 1996 saw the opening of a brand new, purpose-built Kindergarten and Preparatory School for children aged 4–11. In 2010 an additional extension was added incorporating a sports hall, Music Department, Science, Design Technology and Art rooms. These developments have brought together all the children of this age group on to one attractively landscaped eleven acre site which is within walking distance of the Senior School. The main teaching takes place in 21 large, self-contained classrooms on two floors, with the younger children located on the ground floor separated from the older children. The school has its own extensive playing fields and generous play areas while three large halls provide facilities for dining, teaching, sports and school productions. Rooms are provided for specialist teaching in Science, Art, Design Technology and a Music Department with no fewer than 6 individual music practice rooms. As well as a broad curriculum, junior pupils study ICT and a modern language; they have regular swimming lessons and compete in sport with other schools. Close attention is given to each child's progress with two parents' evenings each year. Children learn to use computers from Kindergarten, there is a junior orchestra, and opportunities for private music and drama lessons. Extra-curricular activities are held both at lunchtimes and after school. Before and after school care is available from 7.30 am and until 5.45 pm during term time.

The Senior School (728 pupils). The pupils benefit from excellent extra-curricular and study facilities. There is an ambitious but realistic building programme which saw the opening of a state-of-the-art Science and Information Technology Centre in 2001. This superb facility complements such recent developments as a Modern Languages suite, including Language Laboratory and satellite television and new study and leisure facilities for the Sixth Form. A new teaching centre for the Mathematics Faculty was completed recently and a Library and suite of classrooms opened in May 2003. A 300-seater theatre and classroom facilities for Music and Drama were completed in August 2005.

Curriculum. Years 1, 2 and 3 follow a broad curriculum with all Third Year pupils studying two modern languages. In the Third Year pupils continue to study English, Mathematics, Biology, Chemistry, Physics, History, Geography, Classical Civilisation or Latin, Religious Studies, Information Technology, PE/Games, two Modern Languages, and select three of five practical subjects. At the end of the Third Year pupils opt for nine subjects which must include Mathematics, English, at least one science and at least one modern language. Personal and Social Education is taught in Years 1 to 5.

From the Third Year advice and assistance is available to all pupils on a wide range of career possibilities. The careers team arrange a biannual careers convention supplemented with regular visits and talks when advice is given by consultants from a variety of professions. There is a fully equipped careers room.

Pastoral Care. The School provides a disciplined, caring and secure environment in which pupils may work and play without being subjected to harm or distress, in which they may develop their personalities to the full and enjoy their time at school. The Form Teacher is the key figure in each pupil's academic and pastoral welfare and is the first point of contact with parents. The Form Teacher is supported by Heads of Year and regular meetings are held to ensure that the pastoral needs of all our pupils are met. The system is enhanced by a Peer Support scheme which allows trained senior students to listen to younger pupils' concerns.

House Activities. Each pupil is allocated to one of four Houses on entry to the school; siblings are allocated to the same House. A House Convener arranges meetings with Heads of House to discuss policy, procedure and House activities. These activities range from sporting competitions to an art and a literary competition. Each year the pupils produce their own play for the drama competition and their own repertoire for the music competition. The organisation of such activities is carried out by the pupils themselves with staff providing support and guidance. All pupils are actively encouraged to participate in the full range of activities in order to raise their self-esteem and to allow each to shine; they gain much from the experience. Junior, Intermediate and Senior House Assemblies are held on a weekly basis.

Sixth Form and Higher Education. Students take four or five subjects plus General Studies to AS Level in the Lower Sixth. They continue with three or four of those subjects plus General Studies to A2 Level in the Upper Sixth. The subjects are chosen from an extensive range with 27 presently available. All Sixth Formers participate in Games lessons, where a wide choice of activities is provided. Supplementary courses provided include Information Technology, Application of Number and Communication and ab initio language courses.

Careers guidance is given considerable emphasis in the Grange Sixth. Each student is attached to a member of the careers team and linguists are given the opportunity to undertake their work experience abroad. Almost all the students progress to higher education, with around 15% going on each year to Oxford and Cambridge.

Sixth Formers are expected to play a leading role in school life. They also participate in the extensive programme of House activities as well as in the Duke of Edinburgh's Award Scheme, outward bound courses, Young Enterprise, and the Engineering Council Award Scheme.

All students are required to participate in the execution of duties around school and there is a Sixth Form Council, run by the Head Girl and Head Boy, to coordinate the various aspects of Sixth Form life. Students have the use of their own common rooms.

Reporting to Parents. The School recognises that our pupils are best served when parents and the School work together and to this end we consider it important to report to parents fully and regularly. We encourage full discussion of the pupils' progress and well being. Each pupil receives at least two full reports per year. Each half term brings a progress report with academic grades and a profile of the pupil's extra-curricular involvement and pastoral welfare. There are two parents' evenings each year for all Junior School pupils and Years 1, 4 and Lower Sixth in the Senior School, and one for all other year groups. If parents have any concerns, they are encouraged to discuss these with the relevant staff at the earliest opportunity and the School will always contact parents and invite them to discuss issues should we feel it necessary.

Games. The School has 22 acres of sports fields across both schools, an all-weather sports area including a 60m athletics track and a low ropes course. The principal games are hockey, netball, rugby, rowing, football, cricket, cross country, athletics and tennis. There are four all-weather tennis courts as well as three badminton courts.

Art, Design, Drama, Music. In addition to timetabled lessons for these subjects there are numerous opportunities to participate in extra-curricular activities.

In the music department no less than 15 peripatetic teachers provide 420 private lessons a week. There are two orchestras, jazz, string, wind and saxophone ensembles, senior choir and choral society. Cantores Roborienses, the School's senior singing group, and the Chamber Orchestra perform at the many informal concerts held during the year and at numerous public events.

Considerable emphasis is placed on Drama in the school with two part-time and two full-time members of staff and pupils participate in a number of drama festivals with a high degree of first and second placings. Over 80 private Speech and Drama lessons take place each week, with all these pupils entering Trinity-Guildhall examinations, from Junior Preliminary to Grade 8. Regular school productions take place each year with frequent theatre trips.

Religion. The School is Christian based but pupils of all faiths and none are accepted as long as they are prepared to take a full part in the life of the School. Full School Assemblies take place twice a week.

Transport. Hartford is served by two main line stations, Manchester to Chester and Crewe to Liverpool. The majority of children travel to and from school by car or by one of the private buses which cover a 25-mile radius.

Admission. Kindergarten by informal assessment at the end of January; Senior School by entrance assessment on the first Saturday in February; Sixth Form by interview and good GCSE results.

Pupils are also admitted at other ages as vacancies occur. Admission is gained by interview and test performance. Enquiries for admission are welcome at any time of the year and a copy of the school prospectus may be obtained by contacting the Admissions Secretary.

Open Morning. The School holds two Open Mornings in the Autumn term when prospective parents and pupils are welcome to see the facilities available and to talk to the pupils and staff. Appointments to view the school can be made at other times by contacting the Admissions Secretary.

Fees per term (from January 2015). £2,570 (Kindergarten & Form 1); Junior School £2,785 (Forms 2–6); Senior School £3,435.

Scholarships. Several scholarships are offered for entry to the Senior School for exceptional academic ability and music. A number of Sixth Form Scholarships are awarded for outstanding academic potential after an examination held at the end of spring term preceding Sixth Form entry.

Bursaries worth up to full fees and assessed according to means are available to new entrants to the Senior School.

Charitable status. The Grange School is a Registered Charity, number 525918. It exists to provide high quality education for boys and girls.

Gresham's School

Cromer Road, Holt, Norfolk NR25 6EA

Tel: 01263 714500
Fax: 01263 712028
email: reception@greshams.com
website: www.greshams.com

Motto: *Al Worship Be To God Only*

The School was founded in 1555 by Sir John Gresham Kt and the endowments were placed by him under the management of the Fishmongers' Company.

Governors:
Mr James fforde (*Prime Warden of Fishmongers' Company*)
Mr A Martin Smith, BA Hons (*Chairman of Governors*)

Mr N Bankes (*Chairman of Policies & Procedures Committee*)
Mr Colin Boag, CB, CBE (*Clerk to Fishmongers' Company*)
Mr S Gorton
Mr D Jones
Mr C Spicer, MA Cantab
The Bishop of Lynn, The Rt Revd Jonathan Meyrick
Mr P Peal
Mrs S Smart, MA Oxon, PGCE
Mr K Waters, BA, FCA (*Deputy Chairman of Governors, Chairman of Property Sub and Audit, Risk and Compliance Committees*)
Mr G Able, MA Cambs, PGCE (*Chairman of the Remuneration Committee*)
Mr E Gould, MA Oxon
Mrs A MacNicol, DL
Mr P Marriage
Mr P Mitchell, MEng Cambs (*Chairman of Finance & Enterprises and Chairman of GSEL*)
Mrs R Monbiot, OBE (*Chairman of Education and Health & Safety Committees*)
Mr J Morgan, LLB (*Chairman of Property Development Committee*)
Mr S Oldfield
Mrs D Scott, BSc Hons
Dr I M Waterson, FRCP, MD

Clerk to the Fishmongers' Company: C Boag, Fishmongers' Hall, London Bridge, EC4R 9EL

***Headmaster*: D Robb**, MA, MEd

Second Master: N C Flower, BA, PGCE
Deputy Head – Teaching & Learning: S A Kinder, BA, PGCE
Chaplain: The Revd B Roberts, BD, DipTheol
Business & Finance Director: J Stronach, ACA

Assistant Staff:
* *Head of Department*
† *Housemaster/mistress*

S Adams, BEd (**Sport*)
Dr B Aldiss, BSc, PhD, QTS (*Biology*)
D Atkinson, BA, PGCE (*Geography, †Farfield*)
D Bailey, ONC/HND (*Design & Technology*)
Mrs L Barden, BA, PGCE (**MFL, French*)
A Bealey, BA, PGCE (*English*)
Mrs S Botley, BSc, PGCE (**Mathematics*)
Mr S Brown, BA, PGCE (**Geography*)
G J Burnell, BA, MEd, FRGS (**Latin*)
Mrs A Colley, BSc, CertEd (*Mathematics*)
N Colley, BEng, DipEM, PGCE (*Physics, Electronics*)
Dr A K Cormack, BA, MA, PhD, PGCE (**English*)
A Coventry, BA, PGCE (*Business Studies*)
C Cox, BA, PGCE (**History*)
S Curtis, BSc, PGCE (*Mathematics*)
P Detnon, BSc, PGCE (**Economics*)
Mrs S L Ellis-Retter, BA, PGCE (**ESL*)
Mrs V English, BEd (*Careers Coordinator, Learning Support*)
Dr E Fern, BA, MA, PhD, PGCE (*History, †Edinburgh*)
Mrs J Flower (*Games, †Britten*)
S B Gates, BA, MA, PGCE (**Religious Studies, *Philosophy*)
Miss F Gathercole, BA (*Biology, Environmental Systems and Societies*)
M Gillingwater, MSc, BSc, PGCE (*Head of Sixth Form, *Biology*)
A Gray, BA, PGCE (**Art*)
C Halsall, BA, MA, DipRSA, DipMS, PGCE (*German*)
Mrs C Halsall, BA, PGDip, RSHDipTEFL (*ESL*)
Dr C Hammond, MPhil, PhD (*French, Spanish*)
R Hensen, BCom, HDE (*Mathematics*)
N Humphrey, BA, PGCE (**Design Technology*)

Mrs C Jefford, BA (*French*)
A Jenkins, BSc, MA (**ICT, Physical Education*)
M H Jones, GRSM, FRCO, ARCM (**Music*)
T Keen, CertEd (*Learning Support*)
P R Kelsey, BEd (*Design Technology*)
M Kemp, BSc, PGCE (*Chemistry*)
Miss S King, BSc, PGCE (*Geography*)
P Laidler, BSc, PGCE (*Biology, †Tallis*)
J Lewis, BA (**Physical Education*)
S Lowe, BA, QTS (*Mathematics*)
J P B Martin, BSc (*Chemistry*)
M Matthams, BSc, MA, PGCE (**Science*)
J McCullough, BSc, MSc (*Economics*)
Mrs K Mousley, BA, PGCE (*French, Spanish, †Oakeley*)
Mrs M Myers, BEd, RSACertTEFL, CertSpLD (*Learning Support*)
C Nichols, BSc, PGCE (*Religious Studies*)
J Norris, BA, MA, MSc, PGCE (**Chemistry*)
Miss B O'Brien, BA, PGCE (**Drama*)
T O'Donnell, BS, QTS (*History*)
Mrs K Patilas, BSc, PGCE (**Psychology*)
Miss S Pink, BA, PGCE (*Art*)
Mrs S Radley, BEd (*Biology, PSHE*)
C Reed, BEng, PGCE (*Physics*)
F J V Retter, BA, PGCE (**German, †Woodlands*)
Revd B R Roberts, BD, DipTheol (*Religious Studies*)
Miss L B Roberts, BA, ARCM, AGSM, DipNCOS (*Assistant Director of Music*)
Mrs H Robinson, BA, MA (*History of Art*)
Mrs K Robinson, BA, PGCE (*English, ESL*)
Mrs L Rose, BEd, DipSpLD (**Learning Support*)
D Saker, BSc, MSc, PGCE (**Physics*)
Ms T Sampy, BA (*Art*)
S Satchwell, BA PGCE (*Art*)
M Seldon, BA, MA (*IB Diploma Coordinator, English*)
Mrs V Seldon, BA, PGCE (**Spanish*)
A Smith, BA, PGCE (**Business Studies*)
A Stromberg, BEng, MSc, AFRIN, PGCE (*Mathematics, †Howson's*)
J R P Thomson, BEng, PGCE (*Mathematics*)
L Tao, BA, PGCE (*Music, Organist*)
Miss E Thornbury, BA, PGCE (*Games*)
Miss K Truman, BA, PGCE (*CAS Coordinator, Geography*)
Dr K C Tsai, MA, PhD, DipEd (*Mandarin*)
Mrs C van Hasselt, BA, PGCE (*English*)
Mrs K Walton (*DofE Coordinator, Games*)
Dr J Ward, BA, PhD (*English*)
Mrs A Watt, BA, PGCE (*French*)
R West, MMath, PGCE (*Japanese*)
M Whitaker, BA, PGCE (*Mathematics*)
Mrs G Wiley, BA, MLitt, Cert TEFL, PGCE (*English*)
Mrs M Wilkes, BA, PGCE (*ESL*)
Miss H Wilson, BA, PGCE (*English*)
Miss M Zechiel, Staatsexamen Degree, QTS (*German*)

Prep School:
Headmaster: J H W Quick, BA Hons, PGCE
Deputy Head: R T N Brearley, CertEd (**Geography*)
Director of Studies: P A J Hawes, MEd, CertEd, FRGS, FCollT (*History, Geography*)

Assistant Staff:
Mrs J M Andrews, BA, QTS (*Learning Support*)
Mrs E Ashcroft, BA, PGCE (*Modern Languages*)
Dr L Betts, MB, BS, MS (*Science*)
Mrs J Brearley, BA, Dip ELS (*Librarian, English, Learning Support*)
N P Cornell, BSc, PGCE (*Science*)
Mrs C Cozens-Hardy MTD (*Art, Design Technology*)
Mrs E Curtis, BSc (*Sport*)
Mrs K Edwards, MA, BA (**Performing Arts*)
Mrs S Fairbain-Day, BA, PGCE (*Science, Religious Studies, PSHE Coordinator*)

Mrs J Fenn, MEd, DipHD (*English, *Learning Support*)
Mrs K Fields, BEd (*Geography, History, †Crossways*)
S Fields, BSc, QTS (**Mathematics, Religious Studies, †Crossways*)
Mrs K Gill, BA, PGCE (*Mathematics, English, Science, Hockey*)
Mrs H Hall (*Sport*)
Miss V Harvey, BA (**English, Performing Arts*)
A Horsley, BA, PGCE (*Mathematics*)
Ms J Howard, BA (*Modern Languages, Learning Support*)
Mrs G Kretchetov, MA, RSA CTEFLA (*EAL, Learning Support*)
P M Laycock, BA, BSc, PGCE (**Design Technology*)
Mrs S Li-Rocchi, MA, BA, PGCE (**Art*)
Miss J Lister (*Games*)
Mrs P Matthams, BSc (*Games*)
P Moore, BSc, PGCE, PGDAA (*Physics*)
Mrs A Nash, BA, PGCE (**Religious Studies, Modern Languages*)
Mrs S O'Leary, BA (**History, English*)
Mrs A Pitkethly, BA, PGCE, PG Dip (*Learning Support*)
Mrs K Quick, BA, PGCE (*Special Projects and Outreach Coordinator, English, History, Latin*)
Miss L B Roberts, BA, ARCM, AGSM, DipNCOS (*Assistant Director of Music*)
Mrs C Sankey, BA, PDSEN (*Learning Support*)
Mrs C Smith, BA, PGCE (*English, Mathematics*)
M Smith, BA (*Mathematics, Sport*)
N Thomas, BA, PGCE (*English, Modern Languages, †Kenwyn*)
Mrs F Thomas (*†Kenwyn*)
Mrs S Vare, BA (*Assistant Head, *Classics, PSHE, Modern Languages*)
Mrs K Walton (*Sport*)
N Waring, BMus, MMus (**Director of Music*)
Mrs D West, BA (*English, *Girls' PE*)
Mrs H E Witton, BA (**ICT, Learning Support, Sport*)
Mrs L Worrall (*Sport*)
S C Worrall, BA, PGCE (*Geography, *Boys' PE*)

Pre-Prep School:
Headmistress: Mrs J Davidson, DipEd Scot
Deputy Head: Mrs C A Burchell, BEd, MEd

Assistant Staff:
Mrs K Heal, BA, PGCE
Mrs K Kinder, BSc, PGCE
Mrs A King, CertEd
Mrs E Langton, BEd
Miss S MacDonald, BEd
Mrs E Richardson, NVQ4 (*Nursery Leader*)
Miss J Sandford, BSc, PGCE (*EYFS Coordinator*)
Miss A Scott, BEd
Mrs C Welham, MontDip

Medical Officer: Dr J Farthing
School Counsellor: Mrs R Lubbuck
SSI: C C Scoles, MBE

There are 472 pupils in the Senior School, 265 boys and 207 girls, of whom 221 are in the Sixth Form, and 289 are boarders.

The School is situated some 4 miles from the North Norfolk coast, in one of the most beautiful parts of England. The School has a spacious setting in 200 acres including 50 acres of woodland. Numbered amongst its alumni are W H Auden, Benjamin Britten, Stephen Spender, Lord Reith, Ben Nicholson and Olivia Colman on the Arts side, Christopher Cockerell, inventor of the hovercraft, Ian Proctor, yacht designer, Leslie Everett Baynes, who first patented swing-wing variable aircraft geometry, Sir Martin Wood, co-founder of Oxford Instruments, and Sir James Dyson of more recent fame on the engineering side, as well as the bio-physicist and 1963 Nobel Prize winner in Physiology or Medicine, Sir Alan Lloyd Hodgkin. It offers excellence in a wide range of fields, from which pupils gain an outstanding, balanced education.

Gresham's is a Church of England foundation but all religious denominations are welcomed. The School has its own Chaplain and a Counsellor. Both are available to advise and help pupils throughout their time at Gresham's.

In the Senior School there are four boys' boarding houses and three girls' houses. Students joining in Year 9 share a small dormitory, while older pupils share study-bedrooms, and most Sixth Formers have their own room.

Curriculum. In their first year (Year 9) all students follow a broad curriculum covering all the traditional subjects, including separate lessons in the three sciences. There is a comprehensive language tuition programme and pupils can select up to three languages from French, Spanish, German, Latin, Mandarin and Japanese. The curriculum is designed to allow students to experience the full range of subjects prior to making their choices for their two year GCSE programme. For GCSE all students follow a compulsory curriculum of English, Maths, a language and either dual award or all three sciences, together with an option system allowing for up to a further four subject choices (including further languages) to be made. The flexibility built into our option system allows for virtually all subject combinations to be accommodated.

Since September 2007, we have offered a one year Pre IB course to a small number of students each year. This course is specifically designed to integrate overseas students into life at Gresham's and most students will gain approximately 8 full GCSEs as a result. The course offers the ideal preparation for the IB Diploma and students follow an individually tailored curriculum centred on English Language, Maths, (usually) two sciences and two or three other option subjects.

Entry into the Sixth Form is dependent on students achieving a minimum of six GCSE passes at A* to B grade, to include passes in Maths and English. Students can either opt for A Levels or the IB Diploma. All students receive advice, information and guidance on academic choices and full support for university entrance.

For those students following the A Level course, four subjects are normally taken in the Lower Sixth year with three of these subjects continued to full A Level in the Upper Sixth year. Students are also taught a Theory of Knowledge (TOK) course and encouraged to complete an Extended Essay and participate in a Creativity, Action & Service programme.

For those students entering our IB Diploma, six subjects have to be taken, at least three at higher level and three at standard level. In addition, a Theory of Knowledge (TOK) course is taken, a Creativity, Action and Service (CAS) course followed and an Extended Essay (effectively a research project on a subject of the student's choosing) has to be written. This rigorous programme helps pupils become life-long and independent learners and the IB qualification is recognised by universities throughout the world.

Throughout their time with us, all pupils receive appropriate careers advice and computerised aptitude tests are taken by the majority of our Year 11 and Lower Sixth Form students. A varied programme of enrichment is offered across the school. In Year 9, students select an area of specialism – academic, drama, art, music or sport. In Year 10, all pupils experience an academic enrichment carousel, whilst there is a stimulating Friday night lecture programme for Sixth Formers. Lower Sixth pupils also experience a successful wellbeing programme. A large number of Academic and discussion groups are also available for any Sixth Form student to attend and these include The Auden Society (literature appreciation and discussion) and a large number of other societies based around languages, Economics, Science, Philosophy/Ethics and History.

Sport, Music and Drama. The School has abundant playing fields. The main sports are rugby football, hockey, cricket and athletics for boys, and hockey, netball, rounders, athletics and tennis for girls. Shooting, sailing, swimming, squash, badminton, cross-country running, athletics and golf are also very popular, and national and international success has been consistently achieved in shooting and sailing, and recently in hockey.

There is a flourishing CCF contingent and Duke of Edinburgh's Award section and approximately 25 gold awards are achieved each year. The School has a very strong choir which tours internationally and performs regularly in East Anglia. Several of its members have recently sung in the National Youth Choir. Art and drama are also exceptionally strong, and Drama and Theatre Studies are offered at GCSE and A Level.

Entrance. Those entering at Year 9 from Preparatory Schools take Entrance Examinations in January. Gresham's Prep pupils take a Year 8 exit examination. Tests in Maths, English and a General Paper are given to those entering from independent schools and from the maintained sector. Able international pupils are welcomed.

Scholarships and Bursaries. The School is extremely grateful to benefactors, in particular the Fishmongers' Company, for financing many of the awards below.

There are several Academic Scholarships available for Year 9 and Sixth Form entry, as well as scholarships for Music, Art, Drama and Sport. All-Rounder Scholarships may also be awarded for Year 9 entry.

Year 9 Scholarships: Examinations are held each year at Gresham's in February.

Scholarships represent a reduction of fees of up to 20%; in certain cases such scholarships may be increased, by way of a bursary, up to 100%.

Some awards are restricted to pupils who are from state schools or pupils resident in Africa.

Sixth Form Scholarships: Candidates are assessed in November each year for acceptance into the Sixth Form in the following September and Academic Scholarships, as well as scholarships for those who are exceptional in Music, Art, Drama or Sport may be awarded.

Year 7 Scholarships at Gresham's Prep School: Assessment takes place in the January preceding entrance to Year 7. Academic, Art, Music, Drama and Performing Arts and Sport Scholarships are available for entry into Year 7. These scholarships are available to children currently at Gresham's Prep School and to children applying from other schools.

Fees per term (2014–2015). Senior School: £10,230 (boarding), £7,620 (day). Prep School: £7,450 (boarding), £5,500 (day). Pre-Prep School: £2,900–£3,300 (day).

These are inclusive fees; no extra charge is made for laundry, games, medical attention, etc, although some areas, such as individual music tuition, English as a Second Language and learning support, attract extra charges.

Day pupils' meal charges are included in the fees. Necessary extras are very few.

Honours. In 2014 the A Level pass rate was 99% with 68.3% A*-B grades. The average score attained by our IB Diploma students was 34.2, with one score of 45 and five over 40. We consistently send 95% of our Upper Sixth leavers on to higher education, most of these going to their first-choice courses. At GCSE in 2014, we achieved 47% A* and A grades.

Gresham's Prep School is a flourishing boarding and day co-educational prep school of 210 pupils within half a mile of the Senior School. Its Headmaster is a member of IAPS. (*For further details see entry in IAPS section.*) There is also a Pre-Prep School of 104 pupils.

Scholarships are available at Year 7 and enquiries should be directed to the Headmaster at the Prep School.

The Old Greshamian Club. The Club is active on behalf of present and former members of the School and it can be contacted through its Coordinator, Mrs J Thomas-Howard, at Gresham's School.

Charitable status. Gresham's School is a Registered Charity, number 1105500. The School is a charitable trust for the purpose of educating children.

Guildford High School
United Learning

London Road, Guildford, Surrey GU1 1SJ
Tel: 01483 561440
Fax: 01483 306516
email: guildford-admissions@guildfordhigh.co.uk
website: www.guildfordhigh.surrey.sch.uk
Twitter: @GuildfordHigh

Motto: *As one that serveth*
  Established in January 1888.

Governing Body: The Council of United Learning

Patron: The Most Revd and Rt Hon Justin Welby, Archbishop of Canterbury

Local Governing Body:
Chairman: Mr Dan Perrett
Dr David Ashton
Revd Robert Cotton
Mrs Jane Hellier
Mrs Anna Lise Gordon
Prof Ortwin Hess
Miss Zip Jila
Mr John Rigg
Mr Robert Turnbull

Staff:

Headmistress: Mrs F J Boulton, BSc Hons Cardiff, MA London (*Biology*)

Deputy Heads:
Mrs V M Bingham, BA Hons Keble College Oxford (*Classics*)
Mrs K J Laurie, BA Hons Leeds (*History*)
Mr W H Saunders, BA Hons Bristol, MA St Mary's Twickenham (*History*)

Head of Junior School: Mrs S J Phillips, BA Hons Reading

* *Head of Department*

Art & Design:
Mr I A Charnock, BA Hons Bangor, MA London
*Mrs S Kew, BA Hons Kingston
Mr R C R Laughton, BA Hons Liverpool John Moores

Classics:
Mrs V Bingham, BA Hons Keble College Oxford
Mrs A George, MA St Hugh's College Oxford, PGCE Cambridge
Mr A James, MA Worcester College Oxford
*Mrs S N Merali-Smith, BA Hons, MA Manchester (*maternity leave*)
Miss C L Weightman, BA Capetown, MA Capetown
Mrs O Wulffen-Thomas, MA Merton College Oxford

Computer Science:
Mr J Gonzalez Abia, BA Hons Valladolid Spain

Critical Thinking:
Mrs S J Buxton, BA Hons Cardiff
Mr W H Hack, BA Hons, MSci Cambridge
Mrs K M C Perrin, BA Hons, MPhil Trinity Hall Cambridge
*Miss K M Sloan, BA Hons Reading

Design & Technology:
*Mrs W A Bengoechea, BEd Hons Bath (*Head of Year 7, Head of Faculty*)

Mrs L C Cartwright, BA Hons Newcastle upon Tyne
Mrs H P Gowers, BSc Surrey
Mrs J Wilkinson, BA Hons Sheffield Hallam

Economics:
*Mrs C L Jones, BA Hons Sheffield

English & Theatre Studies:
Miss J P Davis, BA Hons Homerton College Cambridge (*NQT*)
Ms A L Fenton, BA Hons Aberystwyth (*Head of Drama*)
Mrs J A Gibson, BA Hons Liverpool
Mrs S L Glyn-Davies, BA Hons East Anglia
Ms A E Gray, BA Hons Leeds
Mrs J E Holt, BA Hons York, MA London
Miss J Kettle, BA Hons Keble College Oxford
Mrs N J Lewis, BA Hons York
*Miss F H S Mackay, BA Hons Ulster
Miss H A Stephens, MA Hons St Andrews

Geography:
Mrs K N Banks, MA Oxon (*Assistant Head of Sixth Form*)
Mrs S R Howitt, BA Hons Belfast
*Mrs S P B Wilson, MA Hons St Andrews, DMS Oxford Brookes

History:
Mrs S Darbar, BA Hons Cambridge (*NQT*)
Mrs K J Laurie, BA Hons Leeds
*Mrs A Minear, BA Hons Exeter
Mrs K M C Perrin, BA Hons, MPhil Trinity Hall Cambridge
Mr W H Saunders, BA Hons Bristol, MA St Mary's Twickenham
Miss K M Sloan, BA Hons Reading

Mathematics:
Mrs C Butler-Gates, BComm, HED Bloemfontein SA
*Mrs K M Denny, BSc Hons London
Mr W G Forse, BSc Hons Southampton
Miss S E Holliday, MEng Gonville & Caius College Cambridge (*Curriculum Assistant*)
Mr M W Holtham, BA St John's College Cambridge (*Examinations Officer*)
Mrs C L Joyce, BA Hons St Hilda's College Oxford
Mrs E Mulgrew, MA Oxford
Mrs K Perryman, BSc Hons York
Mrs G T Rackham, BSc Hons Sheffield
Miss L A Rolls, BSc Surrey
Mrs A Worthington, BSc Hons London

Modern Languages:
Miss K A Buckley, BA Hons Exeter (*Head of Sixth Form*)
Mrs V A Callaghan, BA Hons Portsmouth (*Head of French*)
Miss F L Cramoisan, MA Homerton College Cambridge
Mr J Gonzalez Abia, BA Hons Valladolid Spain
Ms C Igoe, BSc Hons Georgetown Washington DC
Mr A James, BA Hons Worcester College Oxford
Mrs A J Lewis, MA Université François-Rabelais France
Mr T G M'Clelland, BA Hons King's College London
Mrs Z N Rowe, BA Hons Exeter
Mrs J F Vickerman, BA Hons Southampton (*Head of German*)
Mrs G Wang-Luis, MSc Sterling, Teaching Mandarin Chinese Taipei Language Institute
*Mrs R P Watters, BA Hons Ulster (*Head of Modern Languages*)
Mrs C H Wilkinson, MA Queens' College Cambridge (*Head of Spanish*)

Music:
Mrs E M Forrest-Biggs, MA Downing College Cambridge (*Deputy Head of Sixth Form*)
Mr A C Hadfield, BA Hons St Catharine's College Cambridge
*Mr G T Jones, BMus Hons Birmingham

Mr N A H Tudor, BA York

Physical Education:
Mrs R E Byrne, BEd Hons De Montfort (*Assistant Director of Sport*)
Miss C H Coutts-Wood, BA Durham
Miss M T Folley, BA Hons Edinburgh
Mr G S Groom, BA Hons Manchester (*Head of Outdoor Education*)
Mrs K M Harper, BSc Hons Loughborough (*Head of Year 8*)
Miss K E Hoffman, BA North Carolina
Mrs Helen Le Page, BA Hons East Anglia
Mrs T J Oxley, BSc Hons Birmingham
*Mrs L Stone, BEd Hons Bedford College (*Director of Sport*)
Mrs A J Whybro, BA Hons Chichester

Politics:
*Mr D Cleaver, MSc Econ Swansea, MA Econ Manchester

Psychology:
*Mrs C A Benson, BA Hons Manchester
Dr J E Boyd, BSc Newcastle, PhD King's College London

Religious Studies:
Mrs S J Buxton, BA Hons Cardiff
Miss R L Cocksworth, BA Hons Durham
Mrs A E Gillingham, BA Hons Westminster College, Oxford
*Mrs J A Shopland, BA Hons Lampeter

Science:
Mrs R L Batchelar, MA St Hilda's College Oxford
*Mrs J Blatchford, BSc Hons Kent, MA Kingston (*Head of Chemistry*)
Mrs F J Boulton, BSc Hons Cardiff, MA London
*Dr J E Boyd, BSc Hons Newcastle, PhD London
Miss T Cardon, BA Hons Cambridge, MA Cambridge (*Head of Biology*)
Mrs C Gilmore, BSc Hons Bath (*Head of Year 9*)
Mr W H Hack, BA Hons, MSc Cambridge
Mr T A Helliwell, BSc Hons Southampton
Miss S E Holliday, MA MEng Gonville & Caius College Cambridge
Mrs R J Ling, MChem, MSc Oxford
Dr L Lockett, BA Hons Oxford, MSc London, DPhil York
Miss S Quiney, BSc Hons Nottingham
Dr G Robb, MSc Corpus Christi College Oxford, PhD Southampton
*Mr B J Russell, BEng UCL (*Head of Science*)
Mrs G A Scott, BSc Hons Surrey
Miss K F Walrond, BSc Hons London (*Head of Physics*)

Junior School:
Mrs J A Bottomley, BA Hons Birmingham
Mrs C J Burch, BA Hons Exeter
Miss L Cartwright, BA Hons Newcastle upon Tyne
Miss H A Collins, BA Hons Southampton
Mrs M B Crowley, BSc Hons London
Miss J Drayton, BA Hons Nottingham
Miss V L Ellis, BSc Hons Cardiff
Mrs L P Fishburn, BA Hons Canterbury
Miss C Flint
Miss S H Graveston, BSc Hons Lancaster
Miss H Green, BSc Hons Exeter
Mrs D Hall, BEd Joint Hons Exeter
Miss K L Holland, BSc Hons Brunel
Mrs R F Kemp, BSc Hons Exeter
Mrs J E Kinch, BEd Birmingham
Mrs C Kirkham, BA Hons Leeds
Miss A Langfield, BA Hons Bournemouth
Miss M Mager, BA Hons St Mary's College Durham
Miss L Matthews, BA Hons Brighton
Mrs K L Nanson, BEd Bedford College
Mr T Pearne

Miss J Rowell, BA Hons Cardiff
Miss H Shaw, BA Hons Prim Ed Durham
Mrs H M Stamp, BEd Hons East Anglia
Mrs L Sunckell, BSc Hons Leeds
Mrs R J Wardell, BMus Hons London
Miss S C Wright, BA Hons UWE

Library:
Mrs Y A Skene
Mrs A Hewson, BA Hons, CILIP

Music Administrator:
Mrs D R G Baumann, MA, MusB St Catharine's College Cambridge

Visiting Staff:
Music:

Bassoon:
Miss R Cow, MMus, BMus Hons

Cello:
Mr R Bridgemont, TCL, ARCM, LTCL
Miss J Kimber, BMus

Clarinet:
Miss CHenry, ARCM, LRAM

Double Bass:
Miss N Bailey, ARCM, LRAM

Flute:
Mrs D Ball, LTCL
Miss R E Chappell, AGSM
Mrs F J Howe, ARCM

French Horn and Trumpet:
Miss F Moore-Bridger, MA Cantab, Dip RAM, LRAM

Guitar:
Mr P L Howe, ARCM

Harp and Piano:
Mrs J Carr, BMus

Oboe:
Miss J Lees

Percussion:
Mr J Morley, BA Hons

Piano:
Mrs I Bridgmont, BMus, LTCL, ARCM
Miss H Dives, LTCL
Miss G Young, LRAM, ARCM, DipMT Nordoff-Robbins, Grad Dip Mus

Saxophone:
Mr S D West, GTCL, LTCL

Singing:
Mrs S M Hellec-Butcher
Miss K Walker, BMus Hons, LRAM
Miss J Ward, AGSM

Trombone, Trumpet and Tuba:
Mr R Whitehead, BMus, MA

Violin and Viola:
Miss L Hill, LTCL, FTCL
Miss C Jackson, GGSM
Mrs C A Woehrel, Grad Lucerne (*Head of Strings*)

Director of Marketing: Mrs L E Miles, BA Hons Warwick, MA Swansea
Director of Admissions: Mrs H E Moffat, BSc Econ Cardiff
Assistant Registrar: Mrs J Bak, BA Hons Bath
Marketing and Admissions Assistant: Mrs S Saunders, BA Hons Bristol
Teaching Schools Coordinator: Miss M Bednarek
Accounts Administrator: Mrs V M Livermore
PA to the Headmistress: Mrs H J Thompson

HR Administrator: Mrs S M Mooney, BSc Hons Leicester, PG Dip Personnel Mgt Kingston
Facilities Manager: Mr I Hazell

Number of Girls. 700 Day Girls aged 11–18 years.

Guildford High School is a successful school in which high expectations are set for all pupils, with learning as its key focus. It is a community in which everyone is known, valued and feels secure. Pupils are supported and encouraged to reach their potential.

The school has outstanding pastoral care: it is key to its happy and successful environment. It has a system of Form Tutors, Heads of Year and, of course, a Deputy Head responsible for pastoral matters. When the girls arrive in Year 7, they are assigned a 'buddy' from Year 8 who will steer them through the first term and beyond.

Guildford High School has an extensive extra-curricular and curriculum-enrichment programme, encompassing sport, drama, music, debating and much more besides.

As a result, the girls achieve outstanding success at all levels from SATs to GCSE and A Level. Last year, the A Level pass rate was 100%, with 86% of girls achieving A* or A grades and 40% of all grades were A* grade. At GCSE, 96% of the results were A or A* with 74% being A*. Most importantly, the vast majority of leavers go on to their first-choice university with an average of 20% gaining offers from Oxford or Cambridge each year.

Sixth Form. There is a strong Sixth Form and most girls take four AS Level subjects from the wide range offered and continue with 3 of these subjects to A Level. They also follow a non-examined General Studies course. All girls proceed to University or to other areas of Higher Education. The Sixth Form has its own accommodation, which has been extended and refurbished as part of a major development plan.

Music. There is a lively musical tradition and girls are encouraged to play musical instruments and to join one of the orchestras, choirs, chamber groups or the wind bands.

Drama. Drama is taught as part of the curriculum. GCSE Drama is available as well as AS Theatre Studies. There are major productions every term which are actively participated in by girls of all ages taking on acting, directing, producing and backstage roles.

The Duke of Edinburgh's Award Scheme. Around 90% of girls take part in this fun and challenging scheme, which is run jointly by parents and teachers and which offers opportunities for developing character through service, skills and expeditions.

Physical Education. Lacrosse, netball, tennis, rounders, athletics, gymnastics, dance and swimming take place within games lessons. A wide range of sports including cross-country running, rowing, taekwondo, yoga, badminton, indoor climbing, football, hockey, golf, fencing and trampolining are also available as extra-curricular activities. The girls compete locally, nationally and internationally with excellent results and a 'sport for all' policy provides many opportunities to take part for fun and recreation. Sixth Formers can select from a wide choice of activities for their timetabled games lesson.

Situation and Facilities. The school is pleasantly situated near the centre of Guildford on a bus route and close to London Road Station; frequent trains to the main station provide links over a wide area. Facilities include libraries, eleven well-equipped laboratories, whiteboards in every classroom, an Information Technology Centre, a Design Technology Centre, Art and Design Studios, a Food Technology Room, Music Rooms, Music Technology Studio, a Careers Room and Dining Hall. The school also opened a £5 million Sports Hall and indoor swimming pool in October 2006.

The Junior School at Guildford High School combines a warm, caring atmosphere with a stimulating environment,

and offers careful preparation for entry to the Senior School. (*See Junior School entry in IAPS section.*)

Normal ages of entry. 11 years and Sixth Form level (the Junior School takes girls at age 4 and 7).

Admissions. The school sets its own entrance examination. Academic standards are high.

Fees per term (2014–2015). £4,988. Fees exclude lunches. Textbooks and stationery are provided.

Extra Subjects. Instruments (orchestral) £199.

Scholarships and Bursaries. Academic Scholarships are offered at 11+ and 16+. Academic Exhibitions (lesser award) are also available at 7+, 11+ and 16+. Music Scholarships are also offered at 11+ and 16+. United Learning Assisted Places are available at 11+. These places are awarded on the basis of financial need. Bursaries are available throughout the School for daughters of Clergy.

Charitable status. Guildford High School is part of United Learning which comprises: UCST (a Company Limited by Guarantee, Registered in England, number 2780748, and a Registered Charity, number 1016538) and ULT (a Company Limited by Guarantee, Registered in England, number 4439859, and an Exempt Charity).

The Haberdashers' Aske's Boys' School

Butterfly Lane, Elstree, Hertfordshire WD6 3AF
Tel: 020 8266 1700
Fax: 020 8266 1800
email: office@habsboys.org.uk
website: www.habsboys.org.uk

Motto: *Serve and Obey*.

The School was founded in 1690, endowed by an estate left in trust to the Haberdashers' Company by Robert Aske, Citizen of London and Liveryman of the Haberdashers' Company. In 1898 it was transferred from Hoxton to Hampstead and in 1961 to Aldenham Park, Elstree, Hertfordshire.

Governing Body:
The Governing Body consists of representatives of the Worshipful Company of Haberdashers, the world of education, the catchment area of the school and former pupils.

Chairman: Sir Robert Fulton, KBE
Chairman of the Boys' School Committee: D A Hochberg
Chairman of the Girls' School Committee: T Haden-Scott

R Gokhale	T Jackson-Stops
L Goldman	A Kirk
M Pereira-Mendoza	S Ajitsaria
N R Scarles	

Clerk to the Governors: C M Bremner

Headmaster: P B Hamilton, MA

Second Master: M L S Judd, BA
Deputy Head Academic: J Maguire, BSc
Deputy Head Pastoral: Mrs M J C Jones, BEd
Bursar: S B Wilson, MSc

Director of Staff Development: Mrs C B Lyons, MA
Assistant Head (Director of ICT): I R Phillips, MA
Registrar: Mrs D L Robertson, BSc
Head of the Sixth Form: Mrs K R Pollock, MA
Head of the Middle School: M Lloyd-Williams, BA
Head of the Junior School: Mrs D J Bardou, BA
Head of the Preparatory School: Miss Y M Mercer, BEd

Teaching Staff – Main School:
* *Head of Department*

Art:
*A K Keenleyside, BA
Miss L M Bird, BA
Mrs J E Gleeson, CertEd
S N Todhunter, BA

Classics:
*R C Whiteman, MA
Dr C J Joyce, PhD
Ms E M Simons, BA

Computing & ICT:
*I R Phillips, MA
Miss D F Blyth, BSc
M C Yu, BSc

Design & Technology:
*N P Holmes, BEd
P I Dathan, BEd
T B W Hardman, BEd
P I Roncarati, BA, MSc
G Cox (*Design Technician*)

Drama:
*T J P Norton, BA
Mrs D H Morris-Wolffe, BA
H Silver, BA (*Drama Technician*)

Economics:
*Dr S Koestlé-Cate PhD
P H Bartlett, MA
M Desai, BSc
G J Hall, MBA
Mrs K Shah, MPhil

English:
*I D Wheeler, BA
R Amlot, MA
C R Bass, BA
W J Brotherston, BA
T Eyre-Maunsell, MA
W D Hall, BA
Mrs C B Lyons, MA
Mrs D H Morris-Wolffe, BA
T J P Norton, BA
A E O'Sullivan, BA
S Pinkus, MA
Mrs M Platt, MA
Mrs K R Pollock, MA

Geography:
*J S Bown, BA
Mrs M A Carrick, BA

Music:
*C D Muhley, GRSM, ARCO CHM, ARCM, LRAM, FRSA
A J Simm, BA
Miss C Cousens, BA, FRCO
Miss R Gozzard, MA
Mrs E Leutfeld, MA
Miss H Watts, BA (*Music Asst*)

Instrumental Staff:
P Bainbridge, ARCM, DipRCM (*Trumpet*)
B Bantock, BMus, PPRNCM (*Cello*)
D Bentley GGSM (*French Horn*)
S J Byron, BMus (*Trombone and Tuba*)
R A Carter, FRCO CHM, FTCL, ARCM, LRAM (*Pianoforte and Organ*)
Miss S L Core, GTCL, LTCL (*Flute*)
Miss K Cox, BMus, PGDip, LRAM (*Viola*)
Miss U Galuszka, MMus (*Guitar*)
L Gee, BA, GBSM, ABSM (*Violin*)
Dr O Gledhill PhD MA ARCM (*Cello*)

Ms C Ezekiel, BSc
M L S Judd, BA
Mrs E J Lemoine, BA
J Maguire, BSc
D C Taberner, MSc

History:
*Dr A Courtney, PhD
Mrs D J Bardou, BA
S P H Clark, BA
T M Handley, MA
N P Saddington, BA
A P A Simm, BA
Dr I St John, DPhil

Mathematics:
*N P Hamshaw, MMath
J A Barnes, BSc
Mrs A C C Baron, BSc
Dr P A Barry, PhD, ARCS, DIC
Mrs J E Beeson, BSc
Ms M Brock, BSc
S D Charlwood, BSc, CMath, MIMA
V Gathani, BSc
J Hails, BSc
S Haring, BA
Dr I B Jacques, DPhil
T I Jones, BSc
N Jovanovic, BSc
G P Kissane, BSc
A Lee, BSc
R D Oldfield, BSc
Mrs D L Robertson, BSc
Mrs A Thakar, BSc
A M Ward, BSc
Mrs R M Wright, BA

Modern Languages:
*R J Thompson, BA
Mrs E Childerstone, BA
M J Donaghey, BA
Mrs E Gomez, BA
H Haldane, BA
P B Hamilton, MA
Mrs S E Hanlon, MA
Ms L Lakobachvili, MA
Miss A McKenzie, BA
Mrs J Robson, BA
Mrs J B Swallow, BA
J C Swallow, MA
Miss L von Truchsess, BA

Miss G Harvey, BMus (*Saxophone*)
Mrs R Heathcote, BMus, LGSMD (*Oboe*)
H J Legge, LRAM (*Bassoon*)
S D Lyon, GRSM, MA (*Pianoforte*)
Miss C Maguire, LRAM (*Double Bass*)
Miss I C Mair, GRSM, MMus, LRAM, ARCM (*Pianoforte*)
J E Ormston, MA, LRAM (*Percussion*)
Miss M B Parrington, ARCM (*Violin*)
M P Pritchard, DipRCM (*Clarinet*)
Miss L M Rive (*Violin*)
Miss P Worn, LRAM, ABSM, ALCM (*Viola*)

Physical Education:
*R J McIntosh, BA
Miss K Brandon, BSc
D Cooper, BA
D H Kerry, BSc
A F M Metcalfe, BSc
P D Stiff, BSc

Games:
S D Charlwood (*i/c Cricket*)
D Cooper (*i/c Hockey*)
T B W Hardman (*i/c Sailing*)
J Hails (*i/c Tennis*)
S Lowe (*i/c Athletics*)
A F M Metcalfe, BSc (*i/c Rugby*)
R D Oldfield (*i/c Orienteering*)
P D Stiff, BSc (*i/c Swimming & Water Polo*)
A M Ward (*i/c Association Football & Golf*)
C K Whalley (*i/c Badminton*)

Politics:
*S P H Clark, BA

Science:
*Dr G R Hobbs, PhD
A C Bagguley, BSc, CBiol, MIBiol
Dr G Chapman, PhD
Dr A Citron, PhD

D R Delpech, BSc, CBiol, MIBiol
Mrs L I Dixon, BSc
D S Endlar, MChem
Dr C Gannarelli, PhD
Mr H Gauntlett, BSc
C Glanville, BSc, BA (*i/c Biology*)
Dr C L Harrison, PhD
Ms G R Haskall, MSc
Mrs M J C Jones, BEd
R O Kerr, BSc (*i/c Physics*)
R J Kingdon, MSc, CPhys, MInstP
Mrs J Letts, BSc
Dr M J Lawless, PhD
E Pauletto, BSc
Dr A D S Perera, PhD
Miss A Pindoria, BSc
Dr S J Pyburn, PhD (*i/c Chemistry*)
Miss K R Sander, BSc
J Teague, MSc
J B Ward, BSc
C K Whalley, BSc

Theology and Philosophy:
*R J Cawley, MA
J Bronson, MA
R C Garvey, MA
Revd J Goodair, PhD
Dr J S Green, PhD
M Lloyd-Williams, BA

Combined Cadet Force:
WO2 J Sandercock (*School Staff Instructor*)

Teaching Staff – Preparatory School:
*M G Brown, BSc (*Deputy Head*)
Mrs S Adat, BA
Mrs K Bruce-Green, BEd
J J Evans, BA (*Senior Teacher*)
Miss R Gozzard, MA
Mrs C M Griggs, CertEd, DipS&D (*Deputy Head-Pastoral*)
Miss C A Grimes, BEd
Mrs S M E Herbert, BEd
Dr C A Lessons, PhD
S S Lipscomb, BA
S Lowe, BEd
Mrs J I Magnus, BA
Miss S E McLeigh, BA
Mrs J Valente, PGCE
G M Zucker, BA

Teaching Staff – Pre-Preparatory School:
*Mrs A Fielden, CertEd (*Senior Teacher*)
Mrs J Barber
Mrs D A McKever
Mrs N Patel, BA
Miss V G Peck, BSc

Mrs H M R Pullen, BEd

Chaplain: The Revd Dr J Goodair, BA

Library:
Mrs S Stanbury MA MCLIP
Ms C Wright BA, ACLIP
Mrs A Sellen
Mrs A Leith

Administrative Staff:
PA to Headmaster: Mrs C Russell
Development Officer: Miss Z Okpara, MSc
Admissions & Database Officer: Miss C Allison
PA to Bursar: Miss T Phipps
PA to 2nd Master: Miss J Woodham
Secretary to Deputy Head (*Pastoral*): Mrs S Muller
Secretary to Deputy Head (*Academic*): Miss K Mamaril
Preparatory School Secretary/Receptionist: Mrs D Jones
Catering Manager: E Johnson
Estates Manager: R A Hamzat
Finance Manager: P Spence
Grounds Manager: M Kemmett
HR Manager: Mrs R Titley
ICT Support Director: I R Phillips, MA
Payroll: Mrs L Meighan
School Counsellor: Ms L Nolte
School Nurses: Mrs G McGrath, RGN; Ms M McGrath, RGN
School Office Manager: Mrs S Vithlani
School Shop Manager: Miss S Lewis
Transport Manager: Ms R Caterer
Assistant Director: ICT: G Byrne

The aim of the School is the fullest possible development of the varied talents of every boy within it, and to this end a broad curriculum is provided, together with extensive facilities for the development of each boy's cultural, physical, personal and intellectual gifts. The School sets out to achieve high academic standards and sets equally high standards in cultural and other fields. In matters of behaviour a large degree of self-discipline is expected, and of mutual tolerance between members of the School community.

Organisation. The School, which is a day school, has 70 boys in the Pre-Prep (ages 5–7) and over 200 boys in the Preparatory School (ages 7–11), 300 in the Junior School (ages 11–13), 500 in the Middle School (ages 13–16) and over 300 in the Sixth Form (over 16). There are 6 Houses. The School regards pastoral care as important; all the Housemasters and Deputy Housemasters and Heads of Section have a large responsibility in this field but so also do House Tutors, the Senior Master and the Chaplain, as well as other members of the staff.

Forms. In the Pre-Prep school there are two forms in Years 1 and 2 with approximately 18 boys in each form. In the Preparatory School there are three forms in Years 3, 4, 5 and 6 each with about 18 boys. In the Main School there are 6 forms in Years 7 and 8 with approximately 25 boys in each form. There are 12 forms in Year 9 each with about 14 boys. Years 10 and 11 are divided amongst 18 forms each with 17–18 boys. The usual size of teaching groups in the Sixth Form is about 10–15.

Facilities. The School and its sister Girls' School, the Haberdashers' Aske's School for Girls, enjoy the use of a campus of over 140 acres with extensive woodlands. The playing fields surround the buildings, which in the Boys' School include the following: Assembly Hall, Dining Hall, Sixth Form Common Room, Music Auditorium, special accommodation for Classics, English (including a Drama Room), History, Geography, Mathematics, Information Technology, Modern Languages including 2 Languages Laboratories, Music School, Science and Geography Centre with 19 laboratories and 8 classrooms, a Design Centre for Art, Craft and Technology, Sports Centre, Gymnasium,

Indoor Swimming Pool, two Artificial Grass Pitches and School Shop.

The Preparatory School is situated on the same campus in a new building of its own. (*For further details, see Preparatory School entry in IAPS section.*) The Pre-Prep is situated on its own nearby campus.

The Curriculum up to the age of 13 is common for all, with no streaming or setting except in Mathematics in Year 8. From the age of 11 in addition to the usual subjects it includes three separate Sciences and two foreign languages which are taught as a carousel to ensure all boys have sampled all languages before making informed choices. From the age of 13, subjects are taught in sets of mixed abilities. GCSE courses start in Year 10, when boys take ten subjects. In the Sixth Form students study four subjects to AS in the Lower Sixth, narrowing to three A2 subjects in the Upper Sixth. The School takes seriously its commitment to Enrichment and Enhancement; this non-examined part of the curriculum occupies 10% of the week in both Upper and Lower Sixth. Boys are entered for the GCE examination at A Level at the age of 18 and are prepared for entry to degree courses at Universities. The wide scope of the School's curriculum gives ample opportunity for all its boys whether preparing for University (overwhelmingly their primary interest), for a profession, for the services, or for commerce or industry. The University Applications and Careers Departments have their own modern facilities, and careers advice is readily available to parents and to boys.

Religious Education. The School is by tradition a Church of England school, but there are no religious barriers to entry and no quotas. It is part of the ethos of the School that all its members respect the deeply-held beliefs and faith of other members. The School Chaplain is available to, and holds responsibility for, all boys in the School of whatever faith. She prepares for Confirmation those who wish it, and there are weekly celebrations of Holy Communion and an annual Carol Service in St Albans Abbey. The morning assembly and class teaching, however, are non-denominational in character. Faith assemblies are held on Thursday mornings, and comprise separate meetings for Christians, Jews, Muslims, Hindus, Jains and Sikhs.

Physical Education. A wide variety of sports is available, including Athletics, Badminton, Basketball, Cricket, Cross-country running, Fencing, Golf, Gymnastics, Hockey, Rugby Football, Sailing, Soccer, Squash, Shooting, Swimming, Tennis, Table Tennis and Water Polo. All boys are expected to take part in physical education unless exempt on medical grounds.

Out of School Activities. The extensive range includes a period of 2 hours on Friday afternoon when boys can choose one of a large variety of activities of a service nature. This includes Community Service, both on the School campus and among those who need help in the surrounding district. It also includes the Combined Cadet Force, which has Royal Navy, Army and Royal Air Force sections, and Adventure Training.

Music and Drama. Both have a prominent place in the School. The Music School has a Recital Hall and some 12 other rooms; 20 visiting instrumental teachers between them teach 500 instrumental pupils each week covering all the normal orchestral instruments together with Piano and Organ. There is a Choir of 250, and several orchestras. For Drama the facilities include a generously equipped stage and a separate Drama Room with its own lighting and stage equipment.

School Societies. School Societies and expeditionary activities in term time and holidays include Amnesty, Archery, Art, Badminton, Bridge, Canoeing, Chess, Choral, Classical, Crosstalk, Debating, Duke of Edinburgh's Award, Dramatics, English, Football, History, Jazz, Jewish Society, Life-saving, Life Drawing, Modern Languages, Mountaineering, Philosophical, Photography, Politics, Puzzles and

Games, Rifle, Sailing, Science, Squash, Stamp Club, Windsurfing.

Transport. There is a joint schools coach service providing an extensive network of routes and some 130 pick-up points, to enable boys and girls to attend the School from a wide area, and to remain for after-School activities.

Admission. Boys are admitted only at the beginning of the school year in September. They may be admitted at the age of 5 and may remain in the School until the end of the academic year in which the age of 19 is attained, subject to satisfactory progress at each stage of the course and to compliance with the School Rules currently in force. Each year approximately 36 boys are admitted at age 5, a further 18 boys at age 7, approximately 100 at age 11, approximately 25 at age 13 and a very small number at age 16. There are competitive examinations including written and oral tests of intelligence, literacy and numeracy at the ages of 7 and 11, held in January for admission in the following September. Applicants aged 13 also take examinations at the beginning of January and are interviewed later in the month for entry in September. At 16 admission is by GCSE and interview. An Open Day for prospective parents is held each year early in October. Registration Fee: £100.

Scholarships and Bursaries. A number of Academic Scholarships are awarded annually to pupils entering the Main School. A smaller number of Music Scholarships are also awarded each year to candidates showing special promise in music.

A significant number of means-tested Governors' Bursaries are awarded at age 11+, valued from a few hundred pounds to full fees (and in some cases coach fares), depending upon financial need. Open equally to boys progressing from the Prep School and to those applying from other Schools.

Full details of all these awards are included in the prospectus available from the School Registrar who is glad to answer enquiries. Alternatively you can request a prospectus via the school's website: www.habsboys.org.uk.

Fees per term (2014–2015). Main School £5,554 exc lunch; Preparatory School (Years 3–6) £5,554 exc lunch; Pre-Preparatory (Years 1 & 2) £4,187 inc lunch.

Piano, Organ and Orchestral instruments (individual tuition) £210 per instrument; Orchestral classes £138; Aural classes £67; Instrument hire £30. Speech & Drama group lessons £25.

Honours. In 2014, 37 boys secured a place at Oxford or Cambridge, 100% of the year group accepted a university place and 86% of those commencing university courses secured their first-choice offer.

Charitable status. The Haberdashers' Aske's Charity is a Registered Charity, number 313996. It exists to promote education.

Haileybury

Hertford, Hertfordshire SG13 7NU

Tel:	Reception: 01992 706200; Master: 01992 706204
	Bursar: 01992 706216; Admissions: 01992 706353
Fax:	01992 470663
email:	registrar@haileybury.com
website:	www.haileybury.com

Motto: *Fear God. Honour the King. Sursum Corda (Lift up your hearts)*

Visitor: The Most Revd and Rt Hon the Lord Archbishop of Canterbury

President of the Council: The Rt Revd The Bishop of St Albans

Council:
Mrs S Beazley, MA Oxon, PGCE (*Chair*)
Colonel C I Darnell, MDA, BA Hons MBE
M R B Gatenby, FCA
D F Gibbs, BA
Dr W S Harvey, BA, MPhil, PhD
J C Lowe, JP, MA Oxon, PGCE
D F Macleod, FCA
D S McMullen, MA, DL
The Venerable Luke Miller, Archdeacon of Hampstead
The Revd Dr Gerard G Moate, BA, PhD, FRSA
R P Munn, MA Hons
A J T Pilgrim, BSc FCA
Miss S E Pope, MA, MBA, FCIS
Mrs C M Rawlin, BSc Hons, FCA, MAE, MCIArb
Dr N P V Richardson, MA, PGCE, PhD
Mrs J G Scott, BSc, PGCE
C N C Sherwood, MA Cantab, MBA
Mrs S T Tomlinson, LLB
J C G Trower, MA
S W Urry, LLB, FCA
The Revd P R Wadsworth

Secretary and Bursar: P Watkinson, BSc, MBA

Master: J S Davies, MA

Deputy Master: Dr R M Sullivan, BSc, MSc, PhD

Deputy Head (Co-Curricular): A J H Head, BSc, MA

Deputy Head (Academic): S R Smith, BA

Head of Lower School: Dr L B Pugsley, MA, PhD
Assistant Head of Lower School: Mrs C J Gandon, BA

Marketing Director: D Cresswell, BA, DipM

Full staff list:
Daniel Addis, BA (*Classics*)
Lizzie Alexander, BA (*Head of Careers, PHSE, English*)
Julian Alliott, BSc, PGCE (*Economics*)
Alison Baker, MA, PGCE (*Religious Studies*)
Harry Baxendale, BA, PGCE (*English*)
Rachel Beggs, BA, PGCE, MEd (*Director of Drama*)
Anna Bell, BEd (*Design & Technology*)
Peter Blair, MA, PGCE (*English*)
Charlotte Blake, BA, PGCE (*Head of French, Modern Languages*)
Edward Bond, BA, MA, PGCE (*History*)
Adrian Box, MA, ATC (*Dance Coordinator, Art*)
Dr Kate Brazier, PhD, PGCE (*IB Coordinator, Chemistry*)
Revd Chris Briggs, BD, AKC, PGCE (*Chaplain, Religious Studies*)
Maggie Brooking, BEd (*PE, PHSE*)
Linzi Burstein, BA (*Head of Lacrosse*)
Dora Callington, BA, MA, PGCE(*Modern Languages*)
Mike Cawdron, BSc (*Rackets Professional, Mathematics*)
Dirkie Chamberlain, BA (*Hockey Coach*)
Clare Cohen, BSc, PGCE (*Head of PHSE Chemistry; PHSE*)
Jonathan Cohen, BSc, PGCE, MEd (*Director of Professional Development, Economics*)
Annalisa Conway, BA (*Italian Assistant, Modern Languages*)
Kate Corney, MA (*History*)
Emily Coutts, MA (*English*)
Joe Davies, MA, PGCE (*The Master, History*)
Nicholas Davies, BA, QTS GTP (*Geography*)
Nicola Dawson, BA, QTS Teach First (*Religious Studies*)
Dr Thomas Day, BA, MA, PhD (*Head of English*)
James Deveson, BMus, MMus, PGCE (*Head of Academic Music*)
Dr Lucy Dexter, MChem, PhD (*Chemistry*)
Elizabeth Dow, MA, PGCE (*Music*)
Jennifer Evans, BSc, PGCE (*Geography*)

Ruth Everness, MA, PGCE (*Director of Model United Nations, Physics*)
Christopher Filbey, BA, PGCE (*Head of Modern Languages*)
Olivia Firek, BSc, PGCE (*Biology*)
Cahan Flint Sue, BSc (*Tutor*)
Cahan Flint William, MA (*GCSE Examinations Officer, Modern Languages*)
Mark Forth, MChem, PGCE (*Head of Chemistry*)
Kathryn Galbraith, MA (*Head of History*)
Carole Gandon, BA, PGCE (*Assistant Head of Lower School, Classics*)
Stephanie Gates, BA, PGCE, OCR Dip SpLD, Cert TESOL (*Head of Learning Support*)
Ian George, Dip PE, CertEd (*Director of Sport, Geography*)
Ryan Glass, MSc, PGCE (*Mathematics*)
James Gough, BA, MA, FRCO, LRAM (*College Organist*)
Richard Greenberg, BA (*Biology*)
Grace Griffiths, BA (*Lacrosse Coach*)
Dr Duncan Harvey, GSTD London, MSc, DPhil (*A Level Examinations Officer, Mathematics*)
Elspeth Harvey, BA (*Librarian*)
Angus Head, BSc, MA (*Deputy Head Co-Curricular, Psychology*)
Ryan Hepburn, MA, ARCO, Cert GSMD [P], QTS GTP (*Director of Music*)
Michelle Hillen, BSc, PGCE (*Mathematics*)
Katie Howell, BSc (*Biology*)
Max Humberstone, BSc, QTS GTP (*Mathematics*)
Richard Hunter, BA (*Head of Classical Civilisation*)
Joe Hyam, MA (*Modern Languages*)
Carl Igolen-Robinson, BA, PGCE (*Modern Languages*)
Nicola Ilott, BA
Lee Ilott, BEd (*PE*)
William Irving, BSc, MSc, PGCE (*D of E Coordinator, Physics*)
Jocelyn Jennings, BSc, PGCE (*Head of Mathematics*)
Peter Johns, BEd (*Head of Boarding, Technology*)
Dale Johnson, MChem, DPhil, PGCE (*UCAS Adviser, Chemistry*)
Anthanasios Karapatsias, BEd, MSc (*Mathematics*)
Arthur Kattavenos, BEd, MSc (*Physics*)
Dr Cheryl Loughton, BSc, PGCE, MEd, PhD (*Biology*)
Angus MacDonald, BSc, PGCE (*Head of Psychology*)
Graeme Macpherson-Smith, Cert Ed (*Head of Design & Technology*)
Russell Matcham, BEd, PGCE (*Outreach & Partnerships, English*)
Niall McCarthy, BEng, PGCE (*Mathematics*)
Dr Katherine Mair, BA, MA, PhD (*English*)
Sarah McDonald, MA, MEd, PGCE (*Head of Religious Studies*)
Clare McTernan, BA, LLB, PGCE (*Oxbridge Coordinator, English*)
Alasdair McWhirter, BA, PGCE (*Internal Exams Coordinator, Head of Classics*)
Alison McWhirter, BA, PGCE (*Head of Academic Drama, English*)
Jonathan Medcraft, BSc, PGCE (*Head of Economics*)
William Mieville-Hawkins, BA, PGCE (*History*)
Ben Miller, BA, PGCE (*Biology*)
Emma Millo, BA, MSc (*Psychology*)
Graham Mitchell (*Technology*)
Jutta Mueller-Leighton (*German*)
Charlotte Orford, BA, PGCE (*Head of Art*)
Michael Owen, BSc, QTS GTP (*Director of Rugby*)
Maggie Pagliarulo, LAM Equity, ISTD (*LAMDA*)
Toby Parker, BA, PGCE, FSA Scot, FRAS, FLS (*IB Core Coordinator, Honorary Archivist, Art*)
Ruth Parkes, BSc, PGCE (*Mathematics*)
Helene Pavan, CertEd HE, MA (*French Assistant, Modern Languages*)
Daniel Payne-Cook, BEd, PGCE (*Head of PE*)

Nicola Payne-Cook, BSc, PGCE (*Tutor*)
Anthoula Petrovic, BSc, PGCE (*Biology*)
Jennifer Pilgrim, BSc (*Mathematics*)
Chris Pitchford, BA, PGCE (*English*)
Hester Pretorius, BSc, MEd (*Technology*)
Dr Laura Pugsley, MA, PhD (*Head of Lower School History*)
Matthew Radley, MA, PGCE, MEd (*History*)
Tim Reade, BSc, PGCE, AKC (*Head of Physics Physics*)
Ben Richards, BA, PGCE (*Drama*)
Ben Sadler, BA, PGCE (*History, Politics*)
Maria Sanchez, BA, PGCE (*Modern Languages*)
Ian Sanders, BSc, PGCE (*New Staff Mentor, Chemistry*)
Claudia Schmitz, MA, PGCE (*German*)
Andrew Searson, BA, PGCE (*Head of Academic Analysis, Assistant Director of Sport, Modern Languages*)
Dr Sian Searson, BSc, PhD, PGCE (*Biology*)
George Seccombe, BA, PGCE (*Head of Geography*)
Pippa Simou, BA, BSc, PGCE (*Religious Studies*)
Alexandra Smith, BA, PGCE, MEd (*Head of Spanish*)
Simon Smith, BA, PGCE (*Deputy Head Academic, History*)
Ann Spavin, MSc (*ICT, Geography, PE, PHSE*)
Jonathan Spavin (*Head of ICT*)
Andrew Stout (*Rackets Coach*)
Angela Suarez, BA (*Spanish Assistant, Modern Languages*)
Dr Ruth Sullivan, BSc, MSc, PhD, PGCE (*Deputy Master, Geography*)
Andrew Thomas, BSc, PGCE, OCR DipSPLD (*Learning Support*)
Miles Tomkins, MMath (*School Timetabler, Mathematics*)
Bunge van Daan, BEd (*Director of Cricket*)
Catherine Vincent, Dip ABRSM, BA, PGCE (*Classics*)
Caroline Walker, BA, PGCE (*Modern Languages*)
John Whitworth, BA, PGCE (*Economics; Politics*)
Richard Williams, BSc, PGCE (*Head of Biology*)
Roger Woodburn, BSc, PGCE (*Senior Higher Education Adviser, Biology*)
Helen Woolley, BSc, PGCE (*Biology*)

Plus 20 Visiting Music Staff

Counsellor: Lindsey Othen-Price, MSc, BA, BACP

Head of Boarding: P Johns, BEd

Houses and Housemasters/mistresses:
Albans: Mrs E Alexander, BA
Allenby: Mrs C Cohen, BSc, PGCE
Bartle Frere: E R L Bond, BA, MA, PGCE
Batten: M R J Radley, MA, PGCE, MEd
Colvin: Dr L Dexter, MChem, PhD
Edmonstone: P Blair, MA, PGCE
Hailey: Mrs A J Baker, MA, PGCE
Highfield: L Ilott, BA
Kipling: H Baxendale, BA, PGCE
Lawrence: C E Igolen-Robinson, BA, PGCE
Melvill: Mrs O Firek, BSc, PGCE
Thomason: N Davies, BA, QTS GTP
Trevelyan: W Irving, BSc, MSc, PGCE

Registrar: Mrs I Hutchinson, BA

Number in School. 774.
Location. Haileybury is situated near Hertford, approximately 20 miles north of central London and 30 miles south of Cambridge. It is easily accessible by motorway and train from London and its airports. Set in 500 acres of beautiful rural Hertfordshire, the spectacular grounds are home to outstanding facilities, excellent teaching and superb pastoral care.
History. Many of Haileybury's buildings were designed by William Wilkins in the early 1800s for the East India Company's training college. The East India College was closed in 1858 after the Mutiny and re-opened as a school in 1862. During the Second World War the Imperial Service

College at Windsor was amalgamated with Haileybury to become Haileybury and ISC, but the school is known simply as Haileybury. The Imperial Service Junior School at Windsor served as Haileybury's junior school until 1997 when it amalgamated with Lambrook School in Bracknell to form Lambrook Haileybury School. Haileybury celebrated its 150th anniversary in 2012.

Co-education. Haileybury welcomed girls into its Sixth Form in 1973 and since September 1998 has admitted girls at 11+ and 13+. The school is fully co-educational with girls currently making up 43% of the school roll.

Student Profile. There are three main points of entry: at age 11, 13 and 16. In addition to this pupils are admitted into Lower School 2 (Year 8) and Middles (Year 10) when space allows. Around two-thirds of Haileyburians are boarders.

Campus Life. Pupils joining at 11 enjoy the benefits of self-contained teaching and recreational space in Lower School together with access to all the specialist facilities of the Main School. Newly refurbished, small dormitory-style boarding accommodation exists exclusively for boys and girls in Lower School (Years 7 and 8).

Accommodation for 13 to 18 year olds is centred around the Quadrangle and Houses are either recently built, or are newly refurbished older buildings providing a high-quality living and working environment. In the Fifths (Year 11) pupils can expect to share a room, although many benefit from single accommodation, and in their final two Sixth Form years Haileyburians usually enjoy a single room.

Haileybury is a boarding school with day pupils, with a boarding to day ratio of around 2:1. In 1999 there were 372 boarders at the school, rising to 516 in 2013, an almost 40% increase. The Master, Joe Davies, attributes Haileybury's success to the fact that the school provides its boarders with a fulfilling, happy experience.

Day pupils integrate fully with boarding pupils in each House to form communities of around 55–60 in each. Day pupils in Main School are expected to remain in school until 6.30pm each school day, although they are welcome to stay longer if they choose. By arrangement with their Housemaster or Housemistress day pupils may undertake a two-week trial of boarding, allowing for an easy transition into full boarding.

Welfare. Housemasters and Housemistresses (HMs) live alongside their charges, ensuring ready, natural and easy contact for all parties. Mutually supportive relationships involving pupils, parents, tutors and the HMs are central to life at Haileybury and there is a real sense of community – over 90% of all teaching staff live on site.

Children in the Lower School are supervised and supported by their tutors, teaching staff who undertake this pastoral role. Once they join a House in Main School at 13 a pupil's Housemaster or Housemistress undertakes primary responsibility for his or her care and is regarded as the first point of contact for pupils and parents alike. Housemasters and Housemistresses are supported by house tutors.

Haileybury is one of very few independent schools in the UK with its own full-time doctor resident at school, who attends to all medical and health education matters and is based in the Health Centre. The doctor is available to listen and counsel pupils confidentially, as are both the School Counsellor and Chaplain.

Tuition and Curriculum. Pupils are taught in small class sizes: typically 15 pupils per class in Years 7 and 8 in Lower School, usually fewer than 20 from Years 9 to 11. A Level classes average 14, IB classes 12. Pupils' progress is formally monitored by regular reports and tutorials and communication between subject teachers and tutors, Housemasters and Housemistresses ensure all involved are mindful of every pupil's performance.

Academic standards are high and the principles of both challenging the most able and encouraging those in need of support apply. Pupils are setted where appropriate. Years 7 and 8 study English, Mathematics, Science, ICT, History, Geography, French, Spanish, Latin, Music, Art, Drama, Religious Studies, Design Technology, PE and PHSE (Personal, Health and Social Education). Prep is set daily and day pupils are able to complete it with supervision in Prep before going home if they choose.

Removes (Year 9) pupils study the core curriculum which includes all the subjects required at Key Stage 3 of the National Curriculum: Mathematics, English, Biology, Chemistry, Physics, History, Geography, French or Spanish, Art, Design Technology, Religious Studies, ICT, PE, Haileybury Horizons (current affairs, cultural awareness, debating, ethics, and leadership) and PHSE. In addition, pupils choose two optional subjects from Classical Civilisation, Drama, Greek (Classical), Italian, Latin, Music and Spanish (if French is chosen as the core Modern Foreign Language).

Middles (Year 10) pupils begin a two-year (I)GCSE course in a variety of subjects leading to examinations. Compulsory (I)GCSEs at Haileybury are English Language, Mathematics, a Modern Foreign Language, Religious Studies and Science (either as a dual certificate or as three separate sciences). Optional subjects are: Art, Classical Civilisation, Drama, DT Graphics, DT Systems, DT Resistant Materials, English Literature, French, Geography, Greek (Classical), History, ICT, Latin, Music, Physical Education and Triple Science (which provides space for a third science to be taught). All pupils are expected to take a minimum of ten (I)GCSEs. Entry into the Sixth Form is subject to a minimum matriculation requirement of six (I)GCSEs at grade B or above or equivalent.

Sixth Form pupils can choose to follow either the International Baccalaureate (IB) Diploma Programme or the traditional A Level course. A Level pupils study four or five A Level subjects and are required to specialise in at least three in the Upper Sixth, from a range of 23 subjects. Those who choose the IB Programme study six subjects, three at Standard Level and three at Higher Level combined with the core elements of Theory of Knowledge, Extended Essay and Creative, Action and Service (CAS). The vast majority of Haileyburians gain a place at their first choice university, including a number of Oxbridge places every year. Comprehensive university and careers advice is available and the school is a member of the Independent Schools Careers Organisation.

Co-curricular Activities. Haileybury is not a one-dimensional school and happiness and success are not just about academic achievement. By engaging with the extensive programme outside the classroom, Haileybury pupils develop key life skills and a concern for others, encouraging them to give something back to society. Community Service is incredibly important at Haileybury; all sixth form pupils are involved in service to the community.

Sport at Haileybury benefits from professional coaches and superb facilities. There are opportunities for pupils to represent the school at every level, in a wide range of sports including lacrosse, hockey, netball, rugby, football, rackets, squash, basketball, cross-country, cricket, tennis, athletics, swimming, shooting, sailing, rowing, rounders and golf.

Haileybury's Sports Complex features a swimming pool, gym and large sports hall adjacent to two floodlit all-weather surfaces for tennis and hockey. Legends Tennis Academy is located on site and provides a world-class playing surface and professional coaching in partnership with the school.

Every Haileybury pupil is involved in Wednesday afternoon Activities – a key component of the co-curricular provision – giving pupils a huge range of opportunities from swing dance to Community Service, the Duke of Edinburgh's Award Scheme to the Combined Cadet Force. The College has an indoor .22 rifle range. Co-curricular options differ from Lower School to Upper Sixth but the choice is enormous – canoeing to Chinese, dance to debating, Economics Society to multi-media – there is something for everyone. An extended 'Field Weekend' takes place each term when longer periods of time are devoted to D of E and CCF as well as educational trips within the UK and overseas.

The school offers an extensive and varied range of lectures and events featuring world-class speakers and performers, many of which are open to the wider Haileybury community. Academic societies enhance the intellectual life of the school beyond the academic syllabuses; others will build transferable skills in teamwork, leadership and social awareness. The Model United Nations programme runs for all ages throughout the school and the annual Haileybury MUN Conference is the largest in the UK, hosting hundreds of delegates from around the world.

Haileybury has a formidable reputation for music, staging over 30 concerts each year and hosting over 400 individual instrumental lessons a week. The College has won the BBC Songs of Praise School Choir of the Year Competition, reached the final of the BBC Proms composition competition and pupils regularly secure places in national youth orchestras and music scholarships to prestigious universities.

The Art School has extensive facilities for work in fine art, design and ceramics and the department stages regular exhibitions of an extremely high standard.

Drama at Haileybury has always been strong and there are three or four major productions during the year. The Ayckbourn Theatre provides fully-equipped studio facilities and tiered seating; the auditorium in Big School also has a comprehensive lighting and sound system.

Admission. Pupils join at 11 (Lower School), 13 (Removes) and 16 (Lower Sixth). Lower School candidates are asked to complete tests in English, Mathematics and Reasoning and are interviewed. A report and reference from their current school are required. Pupils joining the school at 11 are expected to graduate to the Main School automatically at age 13.

The 13+ entrance procedure usually starts when a child is in Year 5, but Haileybury welcomes later applications for as long as spaces remain available. Candidates are required to sit exams in Mathematics, English and Reasoning, have an interview and submit a satisfactory report and reference from their current school.

Sixth Form entry is by entrance exams in English, Mathematics and Reasoning along with a personal interview. The selection procedure takes place at Haileybury in November prior to the year of entry. Unconditional offers are made in December to candidates based on the November examination results, successful interview, satisfactory current school report and school reference.

Applications are registered with a non-refundable registration fee of £100. An Acceptance Deposit of £1,000 is requested upon acceptance of a place for those whose parents live in England and Wales. For all other candidates the Acceptance Deposit is equivalent to one term's fee.

All enquiries and applications for admission should be addressed to the Admissions Department who are happy to discuss any aspect of the admissions procedure, and from whom Open Morning details and individual appointments to visit are available.

Fees per term (2014–2015). Main School (13–18): £10,046 Boarders, £7,546 Day; Lower School (11–13): £6,373 Boarders, £5,014 Day. The fees are reviewed annually. There are extra charges for music lessons, private tuition and coaching and equipment for some sports, e.g. sailing.

Scholarships. Scholarships are available at 11+, 13+ and 16+ and entries are encouraged from candidates who demonstrate excellence, talent, outstanding achievement and promise. A Haileybury Scholarship carries 10% fee remission – in exceptional circumstances, Haileybury can raise this to 30% for an outstanding candidate. A Scholarship will normally be held for the duration of a pupil's

career at the College, subject to the pupil continuing to meet the standards expected of Scholars.

Academic, Music and *Sport* Scholarships are available at 11+, 13+ and 16+ entry.

Art and/or *Design Technology* Scholarships are available at 13+ and 16+ entry.

All-Rounder Scholarships are available at 11+ entry, requiring candidates to exhibit outstanding achievement in two or more areas.

The Registry team will be pleased to discuss with parents any aspects of the Scholarships procedure.

Bursaries are offered to make it possible for talented pupils of those in significant pastoral need, whose parents could not otherwise afford the fees, to benefit from an education at Haileybury. Any successful recipient must satisfy the school's entry requirements and expectations. Bursary applications must be made 18 months prior to intended entry. Application forms may be obtained from the Registry.

Please contact the Registrar for all Admissions enquiries: registrar@haileybury.com

Charitable status. Haileybury is a Registered Charity, number 310013. It exists to provide education for boys and girls.

Halliford School

Russell Road, Shepperton, Middlesex TW17 9HX

Tel:	01932 223593
Fax:	01932 229781
email:	registrar@halliford.net
website:	www.hallifordschool.co.uk

Halliford School was founded in 1921, moved to its present site in 1929 and was registered as a charity in 1966.

Brothers of existing pupils are usually accepted as long as they can benefit from a sound academic education. This policy creates a strong feeling of a family community and helps reinforce the close partnership that exists with parents.

Girls are admitted into the Sixth Form at Halliford.

The Governors are in membership of the Association of Governing Bodies of Independent Schools.

Governors:
Mr K Woodward, QPM (*Chairman*)
Mr C S Squire, FIHort (*Deputy Chairman*)
Mrs N F Cook, BA
Mr M A Crosby, BSc, DipArch RIBA
Mr R Davison, MA
Mrs K Gulliver
Mr W J Hargan, BSc
Mr B T Harris, FIPD
Mrs T Harrison, BA
Mrs P A Horner, BA, LLB
Mr A Lenoel
Mr R J Parsons
Professor J P Phillips, BA, PhD, FRHS
Mr P Roberts, BSc
Major General A P V Rogers, OBE, LLM, FRSA
Dr M Sachania, MA Cantab, MPhil, PhD, FRSA

Headmaster: Mr Simon G Wilson, BSc, LRAM

Bursar: Mr P Godfrey, MA, BSc, CEng, CPhys, MIET, MInstP
Deputy Head: Mr R C Talbot, BHum West London Institute, PGCE
Director of Teaching and Learning: Mrs T Bartholomew, BA Rhodes, GTP
Director of Studies: Mr A F Nelson, BSc Brunel, Cert Ed, CM, DMS, MBA
Senior Tutor: Mr J E Carrington, BEng Loughborough, PGCE

Head of Sixth Form: Mr S Slocock, BEd South Africa

Academic Staff:
* *Head of Department*

Art:
*Mr N Moseley, MA Brighton, PGCE
Mrs S Regan, Cert Ed Westhill

Business Studies:
*Mr S Slocock, BEd South Africa
Mrs D Duffy, BSc Glasgow, MBA London Business
 School, PGCE

Classics:
*Mrs B McCrea, MA Cantab
Mr M Shales, BA Warwick

Critical Thinking:
*Dr R Singh, LLB, PhD Warwick, PGCE

Design Technology:
*Mr J E Carrington, BEng Loughborough, PGCE
Mr H Verling

Drama:
*Miss A Stowe, BA Winchester, PGCE
Miss P Hitt

Economics:
*Mr S Slocock, BEd South Africa

English:
*Ms M Hodgson, BA Harvard, MA London, MLitt Oxon,
 MSt Oxon, PGCE
Mrs T Bartholomew, BA Rhodes, GTP
Miss A Cordingley, PGCE Oxford
Mr N De Cata, Cert Ed Madeley
Mr R C Talbot, BHum West London Institute, PGCE
Mrs M Rogers, BA Hons Surrey
Miss P Hitt

Geography:
*Mrs K Gilbert, BEd London
Mr J Willcox, BA Exeter, PGCE

Government & Politics:
*Mr C Bartlett, BA Keele, PGCE
Mr J da Costa, BA Exeter, MA

History:
*Mr C Bartlett, BA Keele, PGCE
Mr P V Cottam, MA Oxon, FRGS
Mr M Woolard, RSA Cert EFL Cambs
Mr J da Costa, BA Exeter, MA King's College London
Mr M Shales, BA Warwick

ICT:
*Mrs D Duffy, BSc Glasgow, MBA London Business
 School, PGCE
Mr A F Nelson, BSc Brunel, Cert Ed, CM, DMS, MBA

Mathematics:
*Mr P Diamond, BEng UMIST, PGCE
Mr P N Booth, BSc Exeter, MSc London, PGCE
Mr L Cupido, BEd University of the Western Cape
Mr G Benjamin, MSc Bath, PGCE
Mr B M Sunderji, BSc Newcastle, MSc W Indies, Dip Ed,
 AFIMA, CMath, MIMA
Mr P Hodgkinson, BSc St Mary's Twickenham
Mr T Ackroyd, BSc Durham, Cert Ed
Mr J E Carrington, BEng Loughborough, PGCE
Mr I Roslan, MChem Oxon, PGCE

Media Studies:
*Mr N De Cata, Cert Ed Madeley

Modern Languages:
*Mr M Gruner, BA QTS Münster
Mrs A Wain, BA Sorbonne, PGCE (*French*)
Miss T Whittall, MA Aberdeen, PGCE (*French & Spanish*)

Mr I Arriandiaga, MA Swansea, PGCE (*French & Spanish*)
Miss C E Wilcockson, BA North London University,
 PGCE (*French & German*)
Mr M Gruner, BA QTS Münster (*French & German*)
Mr P A Sweeting, BSc Salford (*French, German &
 Spanish*)
Mrs M Moon, BA Universidad del Valle (*Spanish*)

Music:
*Mrs R L Greaves, BMus Huddersfield, PGCE
Mr A Williams, MA London
Mrs H Head, MA Surrey, BMus, LTCL

PE:
*Mr I P Bardgett, BA Surrey
Mr P Hodgkinson, BSc St Mary's Twickenham
Mr J Newbery, BA Brighton
Mr R C Talbot, BHum West London Institute, PGCE

Religious Studies:
*Dr R Singh, LLB, PhD Warwick, PGCE
Mr M Woolard, RSA Cert EFL Cambs
Mr J Willcox, BA Exeter, PGCE
Mr R C Talbot, BHum West London Institute, PGCE

Science:
*Mrs D Samarasinghe, BSc Warwick, GTP

Biology:
*Mr D P Howard, BSc North East Surrey, PGCE
Miss C Wood, BSc MTeach Sydney, OTT
Mrs D Samarasinghe, BSc Warwick, GTP
Mr T Ackroyd, BSc Durham, Cert Ed

Chemistry:
*Mrs D Samarasinghe, BSc Warwick, GTP
Dr J Dunlop, BSc Brunel, PhD, PGCE, NPQH, CPhys
Mr Ishmael Roslan, MChem Oxon, PGCE
Miss C Wood, BSc, MTeach Sydney, OTT
Mr T Ackroyd, BSc Durham, Cert Ed

Physics:
*Mr V Harden-Chaters, BEng Kingston, PGCE
Miss C Wood, BSc, MTeach Sydney, OTT
Mrs D Samarasinghe, BSc Warwick
Mr T Ackroyd, BSc Durham, Cert Ed
Mr W Davies, BSc Nottingham, QTS

Visiting Staff:

Mrs S Blandford (*Trombone*)	Mr J Fryer (*Woodwind*)
	Mr P Savides (*Guitar*)
Mr I Brener (*Singing*)	Mr S Tanner (*Piano*)
Mr W Brown (*Percussion*)	

Administrative Staff:
Registrar: Mrs F Clatworthy
Headmaster's Secretary: Mrs K Davis
Bursar's Secretary: Mrs T Trevorrow, ICSA Dip
Accounts: Mrs S O'Hara
Facilities Assistant: Mrs L Gabb (*part-time*)
School Fee Clerk: Mrs J Egginton
School Administrator: Mrs M Hammond
Alumni Secretary: Mrs K Smallbone
School Receptionist (*am*): Mrs A Grainger
School Receptionist (*pm*): Mrs L Gabb
Librarian: Mrs E Wilson, BA
Marketing & Publicity: Mrs A Cottam, BA
Matron: Mrs C Brooks
Lab Technicians:
Dr V Harrison, BSc, PhD
Mrs S Luterbacker
Mrs H Spellman, BSc, PGCE
IT Technicians: Mrs S Bryant, T Hext-Stephens
DT Technician: Mr R Wiedemann
Lighting: Mr P Abbott
Teaching Assistant: Ms N Kritzinger
Caretaker: Mr R Knight

Catering Manager: Mr A Murphy

Visiting Chaplain: The Revd Christopher Swift, MA, Rector of Shepperton

Facilities. Halliford School is situated on the Halliford bend of the River Thames. The old house, a graceful eighteenth century building, which stands in six acres of grounds, is the administrative centre of the school. Some 500 yards from the school gate there are six additional acres of sports fields. Over the years there has been a steady development programme which has resulted in the addition of a state-of-the-art Sixth Form Centre, along with Music and Art studios, in September 2012.

In September 2001 the school opened an exciting new 320-seat theatre. Incorporated into this development is a kitchen, dining room and music practice facilities. In the Spring of 2003 three new classrooms and a new Science laboratory were added to the new teaching block. In September 2005 a new Sports Hall with new changing facilities, Library and additional classrooms were opened.

Admission. There are 429 pupils on roll with a four-form entry at 11+ through Halliford's own entrance examination. There is a further entry at 13+ through Common Entrance and admission is possible at other times dependent on the availability of places. Entrance is by examination and interview.

Curriculum. During Years 7, 8 and 9 all boys study a broadly based curriculum which includes Drama, Religious Studies, PE and Careers.

In Year 8 Maths and Languages are set in four groups to provide even smaller group teaching. In Year 9 all subjects are divided into four groups whether set or not. At least nine subjects are taken at GCSE with the top Maths set taking GCSE a year early and then starting on AS Maths in Year 11. The most academic also start a Critical Thinking AS course in parallel with their GCSE course.

In the Sixth Form some 25 subjects are available at A/AS Level and all teaching is co-educational.

Games. Rugby, Football, Cricket, Athletics, Rowing, Basketball, Badminton, Tennis, Volleyball, Swimming and Golf are available. There is also a Climbing Club which makes use of the climbing wall in the new Sports Hall.

Pastoral Organisation. There are four Houses and pupils are tutored in House groups. Parents receive six communications each year on their son's progress and there is a Prep Diary which parents are requested to sign each week. Tutors are always willing to see parents and the Headmaster can usually be seen at very short notice.

Out of School Activities. These include a very successful Drama Department which mounts some eight productions a year including a major whole school production at the start of the Spring Term. There are also lively Music and Art Departments.

There is a long list of clubs including Chess, Design, IT, Film, Creative Writing, Modern Languages, Science and Art. In addition there are Senior and Junior Debating and Academic Societies and Interhouse Public Speaking and Unison Singing Competitions. The Duke of Edinburgh's Award is available as an additional activity.

School Council. Each Tutor group elects a representative to the School Council (19 members). This is not a cosmetic exercise and in recent times the School Council has effected real changes. Halliford believes that pupils do have good ideas which can be utilised for the well-being of the School as a whole.

Prospective Parents. In the Summer Term each year the School holds Open Days in March and May when the School is in session. In the Autumn Term the School holds an Open Day on a Saturday morning at the beginning of October and two days in November. Prospective parents are welcome at other times by appointment.

Fees per term (2014–2015). £4,315.

Scholarships and Bursaries. The School offers up to six scholarships to the value of 10% of the annual school fees for entry at 11+. The scholarships are awarded for academic, artistic, musical and sporting excellence. All those taking the 11+ entrance examination will be considered for the academic scholarships. Means-tested Bursaries are available on application.

Sixth Form Scholarships and Bursaries: Three scholarships to the value of 10% of the annual school fees are available for external candidates showing excellence whether musical, artistic, dramatic or sporting. In addition there are means-tested Bursaries. These are available on application and are awarded either to support scholarships or to candidates with potential.

Old Hallifordians. *Chairman*: Darren Allen, 53 Fullerton Road, Byfleet, Surrey, KT14 7TA.

Charitable status. Halliford School is a Registered Charity, number 312090. It exists to provide high-quality education.

Hampton School

Hanworth Road, Hampton, Middlesex TW12 3HD
Tel: 020 8979 5526
Fax: 020 8783 4035
email: headmaster@hamptonschool.org.uk
          admissions@hamptonschool.org.uk
website: www.hamptonschool.org.uk

Motto: *Praestat opes sapientia.*

Founded in the academic year of 1556/57 by Robert Hammond, a Hampton merchant, and re-established in 1612. From 1910 the School was administered by the local authority, latterly as a voluntary aided school, but in 1975 reverted to independent status.

Governors:
Chairman: N J Spooner, BA
Vice-Chairman: J S Perry, BA
S A Bull, BSc, ACA
R C Davison, MA, LRPS
Mrs M Ellis, Cert Ed
R C Kelly
His Honour Judge S E Kramer, MA, QC
L R Llewellyn, BSc, MMus, MBA, FCMA, FRSA
J A Livingston, MA, Dipl Arch RIBA
A H Munday, LLB, QC
A J Roberts, CBE, BA, FRSA, FColl
S C Naidu
Air Vice Marshal [Retd] G Skinner, CBE, MSc, CEng, FIMecchE, FILT, FRAeS
R M Walker, MA
R J K Washington, MA Oxon, MBA
The Revd D N Winterburn, BSc, MA (*Vicar of Hampton*)

Clerk to the Governors: M A King, BSc

Senior Management Team:

Headmaster: K Knibbs, MA Oxon

Deputy Heads:
Ms P Z S Message, BSc (*Safeguarding Designated Person*)
P D Hills, MA, MPhil, PhD Cantab
J O Morris, MA Cantab

Assistant Head: Mrs E T Watson, BA
Bursar: M A King, BSc
Director of Studies: A N R McBay, BSc, MSc

Senior Tutors:
D R Clarke, BHum
S Paraskos, MA Oxon
S A Wilkinson, BA Oxon

Departmental Staff:
* *Head of Department*

Art:
*Mrs K A Williams, BA
J Baker, BA
A J Bannister, BA, MA
Mrs S J Kirby, BA

Biology:
*P H Langton, BSc, Dip EnvSci
C J Barnett, MA Oxon (*Assistant Head of Lower Sixth*)
R J Davieson, BSc (*Head of Upper Sixth*)
Miss P A Holmes, BSc (*Head of Fifth Year*)
M I Johnstone, BSc, MSc (*Deputy Head of Examinations*)
Mrs K L Martin, MA Oxon
Ms P Z S Message, BSc (*Deputy Head, Safeguarding Designated Person*)
G Ryan, BSc (*Assistant Head of Third Year*)
M J Williams, BSc (*Assistant Head of Fifth Year*)
G K Baker, MBiochem Oxon
Mrs L A Holmes, BSc

Careers and UCAS:
*P J Talbot, BA, MA (*Director of Careers and UCAS*)
R D Worrallo, MA Oxon (*Assistant Director of Careers and UCAS, Talk!*)

Chemistry:
*Ms C J Gilfillan, MSc
P A Coleman, BSc
N J Double, BSc (*Assistant Head of Fifth Year*)
Miss P A Holmes, BSc (*Head of Fourth Year*)
Mrs J F Knibbs, BSc
J Neville MChem (*Assistant Head of Fourth Year*)
W D Partridge, MChem Oxon (*Asst Head of Second Year*)
Mrs J Cooper, BSc
Dr M G Stuart, DPhil Oxon
Dr S R Langdon
Miss J C Erasmus, BSc
Mrs C Mackey, MSc

Classics:
*J W Barber, MA Oxon
Ms Helen Carmichael, BA Cantab
N A Coyle, BA Oxon
M D Haswell, BA, MA Cantab
P D Hills, MA, MPhil, PhD Cantab (*Deputy Head*)
T J Leary MLitt, PhD Oxon, PG Cert ARM, (*Keeper of the Archives*)
Miss A H Jacobs, MA Cantab

Design & Technology:
*G Nicholls, MSc
R Alvarez, BA
M Richards, BA
J O Sarpong, BSc
Ms D C Woodward, BSc

Drama:
*Miss V K Buse, BA (*Director of Performing Arts*)
M J Duda, BA
R K Kothakota, BA (*Head of Fourth Year*)

Economics:
**S Paraskos, MA Oxon (*Senior Tutor*)
Z A Higgins, BSc (*Director of Rugby*)
T F Rigby, BA
J D Slater, BA
D Walter, MSc

English:
*Miss C E Goddard, BA
Mrs C M O'Hanlon, BA, MA
S Timbs, BA (*Master i/c Sporting Conduct*)
P D Thomas, BA
M M Baker, MA
J J Brookes, BA

D C Phillips
N Collins, MA
Miss L A Teunissen, BA Oxon
Mrs H Booker, BA
Ms A C McLusky, BA
P Smith, BA, MA
M Payne, BA, MA

Geography:
*B S Bett, BA, MA
Miss L J Farrell, BA (*Assistant Head of Upper Sixth*)
J R Partridge, MA Oxon (*Head of First Year*)
P J Talbot, BA, MA (*Director of Careers and UCAS*)
D Saul, BSc
T E Hill, BA
Mrs A J Boulton, MA (*Work Experience Coordinator*)

History:
*A J Cook, MA Oxon
D R Clarke BHum (*Senior Tutor*)
A J Lawrence, MA Oxon
J O Morris, MA Cantab (*Deputy Head*)
J Parrish, BA (*Head of Lower Sixth*)
Mrs H E Partridge, BA (*Assistant Head of Fifth Year*)
Mrs J L Peattie, BA (*Assistant Head of First Year, Form Charity Coordinator*)
Miss V M Smith, BA (*Head of Tennis, Assistant Head of Upper Sixth*)
R D Worrallo, BA Oxon (*Assistant Director of Careers and UCAS, Talk!*)
M P Cross, BA
D Grossel, BA

Information Technology:
I Trevena, MCSA, MCP (*Security & IT Network Manager*)
N Hutchins (*IT Technician*)
A Cornell, MCP XP/2003 (*Assistant Network Manager*)
S W Clark (*Asst Systems Manager*)
J A Hutchins (*Apple Systems Administrator*)

Learning Support:
*Ms C Conway
Mrs S Harradine, Cert Ed BDA, Dip SpLD, PG DipEd

Library:
*K Hemsley, MA
Miss H Hansell (*Asst Librarian*)

Mathematics:
*E B S Bowles, MEng Oxon, MSc
C G Aubrey, MA Oxon (*Head of Key Stage 4 Maths*)
A Banerjee, BSc
S Boret
Mrs H Clarke, BSc (*Assistant Head of Third Year*)
Miss J R Condon, MMath Oxon
M Curtis, MSc, PhD Oxon
Miss B Flatt, BSc
D Griller, BA Cantab
A W Kershaw, BSc
Ms F D Latulipe, BSc, MA
J J Lee, MA Cantab
A N R McBay, BSc, MSc (*Director of Studies*)
B C Murphy, MEng (*Head of Junior Football*)
J P Orr, MA Oxon (*Senior Mathematician*)
T Passmore, MEng
W Quayle, BSc
Miss A Schröder, BA (*Assistant head of First Year*)
Mrs V Short, MA Cantab
R R Trivedi, MA Cantab
Miss M Watson, BSc
A L Blyth, MSc Oxon
Mrs A Burke, MA Oxon
Mrs M W Field, BSc
Mrs C H Reyner, MA, MSc Oxon

Modern Languages:
*D E Peel, BA (*Head of German*)

M J Passey, BA (*Head of Spanish*)
F C Chaveneau, BA (*Head of French*)
Miss H Zhang, BA (*Head of Mandarin*)
Mrs K N Dubova, BA (*Head of Russian*)
T R Aucutt, BA
C J Blachford, BA (*Form Charity Coordinator*)
M Boardman, BA Oxon
Ms S A Buckley, BA
Miss F Byrne, MA
Ms S Garrido-Soriano, BA
Miss H Oliphant, BA
Mrs J C Owen, BA (*Head of Second Year*)
Miss A Schröder, BA (*Assistant Head of First Year*)
P Studt, BA, MA
P G Turner, BA
Mrs J Wilberforce, BA Cantab
Mrs S C D Yoxon, MA
Mrs M A Chandler, MA
Mrs P Croucher, MA
Mrs S E May, BA
Mrs E McIntyre, MA
Mrs E T Watson, BA (*Assistant Head*)
Ms H Zhou, BA, MA
Miss J Iredale, BA, Dip IM (*Languages Resources Supervisor*)

Language Assistants:
Miss A Marchand (*French Assistant*)
Miss M Seret (*Junior French Assistant*)
C Knedeisen (*German Assistant*)
Miss L Pla-Miro (*Spanish Assistant*)
B San Sebastian (*Junior Spanish Assistant*)
Mrs Y Isaeva (*Russian Conversation*)
Mrs L Wilson (*Russian Conversation*)

Music:
*I C Donald, BA (*Director of Music*)
Ms H M Lucas, BA
D E Roland, MusB
M Ward, BA, MPhil, PhD Cantab
Ms K Ford, BA (*Performing Arts Administrator*)

Personal Health and Social Education:
*J H Talman, BA
Mrs R Nicholson, MPhys Oxon

Physical Education and Games:
*P Bolton, BSc (*Head of PE Athletics*)
D R Clarke, BHum (*Senior Tutor*)
C Greenaway (*Director of Rowing*)
C T Mills, BSc (*Head of Games, Football*)
B O Ruse, BA
M K Sims, BSc (*Sports Rehabilitation, Assistant Head of Second Year*)
S Timbs, BA (*Master i/c Sporting Conduct*)
P O Walsh, BA (*Outdoor Pursuits*)

Physics:
*M G Yates, PhD
P Armstrong, BSc
C Arnold, DPhil Oxon
G H Clark, BSc
Miss J C Erasmus, BSc
D J Fendley, BEng (*Induction Tutor*)
S Gray, BSc
Ms K E Millar BEng (*Head of Third Year*)
W Pope, BEng
L O Rouse, BSc
A R Tilling, MA
N D Woods, MA, MEng Cantab (*Head of Third Year*)
Mrs J L Boon, MA
Mrs R J Nicholson, MPhys Oxon (*Asst Head of PHSE*)

Politics:
*Miss J A Field, BA Cantab
Miss H E Partridge, BA (*Asst Head of Fourth Year*)

T F Rigby, BA
Miss V M Smith, BA (*Head of Tennis, Assistant Head of Upper Sixth*)
R D Worrallo, BA Oxon (*Assistant Director of Careers and UCAS, Talk!*)
M P Cross, BA
D Grossel, BA

Psychology:
*S J Wakefield, BSc
Miss A Goodman, BSc

Religious Studies:
*M A J Nicholson, BA (*Asst Head of Fifth Year*)
N K Carrier, BA, MPhil Oxon, PhD Cantab
Miss A R Parker, BA
P D Rowntree BEd
J H Talman, BA (*Head of PHSE*)
S A Wilkinson, BA Oxon (*Senior Tutor*)
Mrs J A Perkins, BA, MPhil, MA Oxon

Combined Cadet Force:
Captain Mike Haswell, BA, MA Cantab (*Commanding Officer CCF Contingent*)

Administrative Staff:
Examinations Officer: Mrs M Barnes
Headmaster's PA: Mrs J Simmons
Admissions Manager: Mrs D Jones, BA DipMar
Deputy Admissions Manager: Mrs C Elia
Admissions Assistant: Mrs R Binns

Hampton is a day school of around 1,250 boys aged from 11 to 18, including a Sixth Form of about 340. The School achieves all-round excellence, encouraging academic ambition, personal responsibility and independent thinking in an energetic, happy and well-disciplined community. It aims to provide a challenging and stimulating education for boys of high academic promise from the widest possible variety of social backgrounds.

The most recent ISI inspection (February 2010) found Hampton to be a school at which pupils are exceptionally well educated in accordance with the School's holistic educational aims. The School achieves excellence in its pastoral care and moral and spiritual guidance and also in the quality of the pupils' academic and other achievements. The pupils' personal development was deemed outstanding. The teaching at the School, described as dedicated, committed and often inspiring, makes an excellent contribution to pupils' educational progress. It was also noted that the curriculum is enriched by an extensive, varied range of co-curricular activities and strong links with the community. The inspection report confirmed the School's success in meeting its aim of producing mature, confident yet unpretentious young people who aim for personal success while supporting those around them.

Hampton is academically selective and virtually all boys go on to elite universities, the Russell Group and Oxbridge with increasing numbers to American Ivy League Universities. Examination results in 2014 at A Level (93.4% A*, A and B grades) and GCSE (88% A*/A grades) were extremely strong with the number of A* grades at record levels (32% at A Level, 55% at GCSE). 25 boys achieved their Oxbridge offers, another record. The Sixth Form has a strong emphasis on deep academic enquiry, breadth of study, critical thinking and independent learning.

An annual exchange programme offers boys the chance to visit Spain, Germany, France, Italy and Russia as well as Asia, Africa and the Far East. Boys visit many other countries through academic and sporting initiatives and there is an extraordinary range of trips available.

The extensive co-curricular programme forms an essential part of the balanced education which Hampton provides. Music and drama are central to the character of the School and concerts, musicals and plays involve all age groups throughout the year. Over half the boys learn musical instruments and there are frequent music and choir tours abroad. A notable number of Organ and Choral Scholarships to Oxbridge colleges have been won over recent years.

Drama is included in the curriculum, in addition to regular School and Year group productions. There are major joint musical and drama productions regularly with The Lady Eleanor Holles Girls' School. Recent highlights including *Jekyll & Hyde, Chicago, Les Misérables*, Shakespeare's *The Tempest*, Joseph Kesselring's *Arsenic and Old Lace*, Jez Butterworth's *Jerusalem* and *Oliver Twist*, a joint production with Waldegrave School for Girls.

Hampton has an outstanding reputation for sport and standards are very high indeed; many boys play at county and national level in a wide range of sports. Particular strengths are cricket, football, rowing, rugby, tennis and chess. Boys benefit from superb facilities and specialist coaching. Hampton has produced many schoolboy internationals in a wide range of sports and also Olympic rowers; the School shares a nearby boathouse on the River Thames with The Lady Eleanor Holles School.

Integrity and social conscience are encouraged implicitly through the daily interaction of boys and teachers, as well as explicitly through School assemblies, PSHE lessons, extensive Charity, Environment and Community Service programmes, and long-standing links with the Hampton Safe Haven in Malawi. The School became the first 'climate neutral' school in the country by offsetting all of its carbon emissions. The School was one of the two founding schools of the 'Mindfulness in Schools Project' promoting pupil well-being and emotional resilience.

Hampton School and The Lady Eleanor Holles School are served by 21 coach routes across south-west London, Surrey and Berkshire.

Buildings and Grounds. The School has been situated on its present site since 1939. Its premises and facilities for both academic work and co-curricular activity have been greatly improved and extended since 1975 when the School, formerly Hampton Grammar, reverted to independence.

Set within grounds of some 27 acres all facilities (with the exception of the Boat House) are on site including four rugby pitches, seven football pitches, six cricket squares and six hard tennis courts. Buildings include an Assembly Hall, Dining Hall, large multi-purpose Sports Hall, fully-equipped Library and specialist facilities for Art, Science, Technology, ICT and Languages.

The Millennium Boat House, located on the nearby River Thames and shared with The Lady Eleanor Holles School, was opened in 2000 by Sir Steve and Lady Redgrave and provides the focal point for the popular and highly successful Boat Club.

The magnificent 450 Hall was opened in September 2009 to commemorate the School's 450th anniversary and provides exceptional facilities for the performing arts, doubling as a theatre and concert hall.

A rigorous development programme ensures that all boys continue to benefit from excellent facilities. A new three-storey Atrium extension opened in September 2011, comprising 11 classrooms, a new Biology lab and a large display area. The latest addition is a state-of-the-art, all-weather 3G sports ground, opened in 2013, for football, rugby and recreational use. The 3G area is a unique facility for a school and has dual accreditation from FIFA and the Rugby Football Union.

Community. Hampton School has developed extensive partnerships both locally and internationally. The School enjoys particularly strong links with two neighbouring schools, Hampton Academy and The Lady Eleanor Holles School (LEH). These two schools participate in various activities with Hampton pupils, especially Drama and Music, Combined Cadet Force and the very popular visiting speakers '*Talk*!' programme. A 'United Nations Youth & Student Association' (UNYSA) branch involves pupils

meeting to discuss issues of national and international significance. Strong links are maintained with the numerous local state primary schools which provide around 70% of the First Year intake. Year 5 and Year 6 pupils from a number of local state primary schools attend teaching sessions in a range of subjects on Saturday mornings. The School also works in partnership with other local independent and state secondary schools offering GCSE revision courses and a range of academic and co-curricular activities.

In addition, Hampton School has a busy Community Service programme and also hosts many events for schools in Richmond Borough. All members of the Lower Sixth undertake a placement in a local primary school as part of their Curriculum Enrichment Programme, working with young children on literacy, numeracy, computing and sport. Many boys in the Fourth Year and above volunteer their assistance in primary schools, residential homes for the elderly, or the local Barnardo's project. Various joint activities are run with LEH, including an annual Christmas Party for the elderly, and a trip to the Science Museum for children with special needs. Several senior boys participate in holiday schemes for young people from more deprived parts of East London each summer.

Curriculum. Boys in the Lower School follow a wide curriculum, including Technology, Coding and Computing, Physics, Chemistry, Biology, a Modern Language (French, German or Spanish) and Latin. Mandarin has recently been added to the curriculum; Greek, Classical Civilisation and Russian are optional subjects begun in the Third Year. In the Fourth and Fifth Years all boys continue to study, in addition to PE, Games and Religious Studies, the following: English Language, English Literature, a Modern Language, Mathematics and the three sciences for either GCSE or IGCSE. They choose three subjects from the following: Art, Classical Civilisation, Drama, French, Geography, German, Greek, History, Latin, Mandarin, Music, Religious Studies, Russian, Spanish and Technology. Most of these GCSEs/IGCSEs are taken at the end of the Fifth Year. The most able mathematicians take GCSE/IGCSE at the end of the Fourth Year and then move on to AS Level study in the Fifth Year.

The Sixth Form offers a free choice of A and AS Level subjects, in addition to a wide range of courses leading to A Level General Studies, and the option to enter for Critical Thinking. The Cambridge Pre-U is offered in addition to the standard AS/A2 in Physics, Chemistry, History, German, Mandarin and Philosophy. Additional teaching and preparation is provided for boys seeking entrance to Oxford or Cambridge, to which around twenty to twenty-five boys are admitted each year. About fifty boys a year also opt for the Hampton Extended Project, a substantial piece of independent research of around 5,000 words.

Games. Sport and Physical Education are part of every boy's School week. A very large number of boys also take part in voluntary sport on Saturdays; fixtures, at a range of ability levels, are arranged for each age group. Whenever possible boys are able to choose which sport to follow, with a wider range of options available to Sixth Form boys. In winter, the major games are Rugby, Association Football and Rowing; in summer, Cricket, Athletics and Rowing. Other sports include Tennis, Real Tennis, Fencing, Squash, Skiing, Windsurfing, Sailing, Climbing, Cycling and Swimming.

Careers. Each boy receives advice from the careers staff at those points when subject choices should be made. The School is a member of ISCO, who provide Morrisby testing as part of the Fifth Year advice programme. A Careers Convention is held annually, there are advice evenings for parents on A Level choice and on university decision-making, and comprehensive work experience is arranged.

Pastoral Care. This is one of the strongest features of the School. A boy's Form Tutor is responsible in the first instance for his academic and pastoral welfare and progress. The work of Form Tutors is supported and coordinated by

Assistant Heads of Year and Heads of Year under the direction of one of the Deputy Heads. The School works in partnership with parents who are always welcome to discuss their son's work with any of these tutors; Parents' Evenings provide an opportunity to meet subject teachers. Year group Pastoral Forums provide parents with an opportunity to meet staff responsible for pupil welfare and to discuss a variety of pastoral issues. There is also an active Parents' Association.

Societies. The School's large CCF contingent, run jointly with LEH, and more recently an intake from Hampton Academy, comprises Army and RAF sections and has a programme which includes adventurous training, orienteering and gliding. The very active Adventure Society provides opportunities for kayaking, climbing, orienteering, camping and expeditions both in the UK and abroad. A very large number of boys regularly take the Duke of Edinburgh's Award Gold, Silver and Bronze awards.

The Music Department fosters solo and ensemble performance as well as composition, and offers pupils an opportunity to perform in the School's orchestras, bands and choirs including National Choir of the Year Finalists, Voices of Lions. Singing is very popular and there are eight different choral groups. The Joint Choral Society, with the neighbouring LEH, gives a performance of a major choral work annually. The number of drama productions is increasing. There is at least one dramatic production each term, and also an annual musical. In all these activities, as in the Community Service work, the School enjoys close cooperation with The Lady Eleanor Holles Girls' School. Hampton has recently become only the seventh school in the country to be *All-Steinway* in its provision of pianos.

A programme of visiting speakers, '*Talk*!', holds lunchtime and evening meetings and offers boys the opportunity to hear and question distinguished politicians, writers, academics and scientists.

There is also an extensive range of co-curricular societies, among which Chess, Debating, the Technology Club and the Creative Writing Society are particularly strong.

Admission. Boys are usually admitted to the School into the First Year (Year 7), Third Year (Year 9) and the Sixth Form. Approximately 120 boys join the First Year at 11+ each September and a further 60–70 join the Third Year at 13+. A small number join the Sixth Form each year.

Entry at 11+ is via the School's own entrance examination, which is held in the January of Year 6. Entry at 13+ is through the Common Entrance examination following a Pre-test which candidates sit in the January of Year 6. A further Pre-test is held in Year 7 for those who sat the Year 6 Pre-test without gaining an offer, as well as to those who have not sat before.

Boys may also be admitted to fill occasional vacancies at other ages at the discretion of the Headmaster. Further details may be obtained from the Admissions Manager (Tel: 020 8979 9273).

Fees per term (2014–2015). £5,585 inclusive of books and stationery.

Scholarships and Bursaries. Scholarships (remitting up to 25%) are awarded for academic, musical, artistic and all-round merit at 11+ and 13+. Choral Scholarships, awarded in conjunction with the Chapel Royal, Hampton Court Palace, are also available at 11+ entry.

The School also has a Bursary Fund from which awards are made according to parental financial circumstances. A number of free places are also awarded each year.

Further details on all Awards may be obtained from the Admissions Manager.

Old Hamptonians' Association. Leavers are entitled to life membership of this association which provides regular communication with members and has active sporting and dramatic sections. The OHA Office is located at School and can be contacted by email: oha@hamptonschool.org.uk.

Charitable status. Hampton School is a Registered Charity, number 1120005.

Harrow School

Harrow on the Hill, Middlesex HA1 3HP

Tel:	020 8872 8000 (Enquiries)
	020 8872 8003 (Head Master)
	020 8872 8007 (Admissions)
	020 8872 8320 (Bursar)
Fax:	020 8423 3112 (School)
	020 8872 8012 (Head Master)
email:	harrow@harrowschool.org.uk
website:	www.harrowschool.org.uk

Harrow School was founded in 1572 by John Lyon under a Royal Charter from Queen Elizabeth.

Mottos: *Stet Fortuna Domus; Donorum Dei Dispensatio Fidelis*

Visitors:
The Archbishop of Canterbury
The Bishop of London

Governors:
R C Compton (*Chairman*)
J F R Hayes, MA, FCA
Professor D J Womersley, PhD
S J G Doggart, MA
V L Sankey, MA
C H St J Hoare, BAK
W B Gilbert, BA, FCA
E J H Gould, MA
R C W Odey, BA
Mrs H S Crawley, BA
J P Batting, MA, FFA
Professor G Furniss, BA, PhD
M K Fosh, BA, MSI
Professor Sir David Wallace, CBE, FRS, FREng
The Hon Robert Orr-Ewing
Mrs S Whiddington, AB
Rear Admiral G M Zambellas, DSC, BSc
Professor P Binski, MA, PHD, FSA, FRSA
C Stonehill, MA
A P McClaran, BA, FCMI
Dr Isis Dove-Edwin, BSc, MD, MRCP
G W J Goodfellow, QC, MA, LLM
J M P D Stroyan, MA
Mrs M S Brounger, LLB
A Goswell, BSc Hons, MRICS

Clerk to the Governors: The Hon Andrew Millett, MA, 45 Pont Street, London SW1X 0BX

Head Master: J B Hawkins, MA

Deputy Head Master: W M A Land, MA

Senior Tutor: A R McGregor, MA

Director of Studies: J R Elzinga, BA

Senior Master and Director of Boarding: P J Bieneman, MA

Bursar: N A Shryane, MBE, BA, MPhil

Registrar: E R Sie, BSc, PhD, CChem

Surmaster: A K Metcalfe, MA, FRGS, CGeog

Academic and Universities Director: N Page, BA, MCIL

Head of Departments:
Director of Art: L W Hedges, BA, MA
Biology: N S Keylock, MSc
Chemistry: Dr A F Worrall, MA, MSc, PhD

Classics: Dr J L Roberts, BA, MA, PhD
Computing: N J Marchant, BEng
Critical Thinking: C D Barry, BSc
Design and Technology: T M Knight, BA
Drama and Theatre Studies: S L Mackrory, BA
EAL: H E Rhodes, BA
Economics and Business Studies: C T Pollitt, BA
English: Dr J K Bratten, BA, PhD
French: W Turner, BA
Geography: S M Sampson, BSc
German: O Syrus, BA
Government and Politics: Dr M E P Gray, BA, MA, PhD
History: A D Todd, BA, MPhil
History of Art: L W Hedges, BA, MA
ICT: Dr C D O'Mahony, BA, DPhil
Mathematics: I Hammond, BSc
Modern Languages: W Turner, BA
Director of Music: D N Woodcock, MA, FRCO
Oriental Languages: R M Tremlett, BA, MA
Painting: S N Page, BEd
Photography: D R J Bell, BA
Physical Education: J J Coulson, BA, MA
Physics and Astronomy: C D Barry, BSc
Religious Studies: R J Harvey, BA
Sculpture: I A Stroud, BA
Director of Sport: J J Coulson, BA

Houses & House Masters:
Bradbys: Dr D R Wendelken
Druries: Mr M J M Ridgway
Elmfield: Mr M J Tremlett
Lyon's: Mr N J Marchant
Moretons: Mr P J Evans
Newlands: Mr E W Higgins
Rendalls: Mr S N Taylor
The Grove: Mr C S Tolman
The Head Master's: Dr S A Harrison
The Knoll: Dr S J Abbott
The Park: Mr B J D Shaw
West Acre: Mr M G J Walker

The School. Harrow is a full-boarding school for boys in northwest London, founded in 1572 under a royal charter granted by Elizabeth I. Distinguished Old Harrovians include seven British prime ministers and the first prime minister of India, Pandit Nehru, as well as poets and writers as diverse as Byron, Sheridan and Richard Curtis. As stewards of many cherished traditions, boys at Harrow benefit from an education that develops their unique talents and a love of learning, alongside a keenness to contribute their strengths to the world. There are many unique Harrow traditions, not least Songs, nameboards and straw hats, and many recent innovations too. For example, we have recently installed an observatory in our Physics Schools and now offer Astronomy GCSE.

Academic. Our Masters' Room comprises an array of highly qualified academics, who are each experts in their field and who also have the ability to inspire young men. In 2014, in light of major examination reforms that saw national deflation in the A*/A and B grade brackets, the number of A* grades at Harrow continued on its upward trajectory, with a rate of nearly 26%. 56% of the examinations taken in English Literature were of A* standard, while six Modern Foreign Language subjects saw 100% attainment of A*/A grades. This includes French, which bucked the national trend of deflation year on year. At (I)GCSE, 85.2% of all examinations taken were awarded A* or A grades. The A* rate of the last two years has been recording-breaking, at 56% in 2014. 37 boys achieved 10 A* grades, joining the ranks of Honorary Academic Scholars. Two Harrovians secured 13 A* grades and one, 15. There was a strong performance in the core subjects of Mathematics (92% A*/A) and English (84% A*/A). Three Modern Foreign Language subjects saw 100% attainment of A*/A grades. Visit http://www.harrowschool.org.uk/1527/academic-life/the-curriculum/ for details of the curriculum.

The Super-Curriculum. Beyond the examination syllabus, our Super-Curriculum focuses on the aspects of scholarship that are not formally assessed: habitual reading, independent research, reflection and debate. Central to this is the electives system, in which boys select a challenging off-syllabus course that is taught in small groups. These courses promote lateral thinking, problem-solving and the articulation of profound thought, while also allowing boys to lead their own learning. This eclectic academic diet is not just for the intellectual elite. We think every Harrow boy, wherever he stands in the spectrum of ability, should find learning both enormously stimulating and great fun. On virtually every night of the week, there are seminars and society meetings to pique every interest. Thanks to the School's reputation and close proximity to London, we attract eminent speakers from all walks of life to enrich and broaden the boys' experience of academic and cultural life.

Boarding. Our leafy 260-acre estate contains 12 Boarding Houses. The buildings are quite individual with their own gardens and facilities, helping to set each house apart. The Houses inspire fierce loyalty from the boys and old boys, who take pride in their own part of Harrow. Common to every house is the highest quality of pastoral care, which is a major strength of the School. House Masters and their families live in the houses, and are assisted by an Assistant House Master, Matron, Year Group Tutors and Health Education Tutors. In addition, the chaplaincy, full-time psychologist and pastoral support committee provide further layers of nurturing and support. On average, there are about 60–70 boys in each house. There are no dormitories: a boy shares his room with a boy of the same age for the first three to six terms and thereafter has a room to himself. Every boy has a computer in his room and each house has common rooms and shared kitchens. All teachers live in the School, and this makes possible the extraordinary diversity of worthwhile activities on offer in the evenings and at weekends. Typically, for the first two weekends of a term, all pupils are in the School. If they are able to, parents come and visit. On the third weekend, all pupils go home or to friends; the weekend starts at 12 noon on Friday and ends at 9 pm on Sunday. The next two weekends are followed by a nine-day half term.

Sport. Sport enriches the life of every boy throughout his time at Harrow. With afternoon games five times a week, sporting fixtures against other schools and the chance to compete regularly in house matches, boys are kept healthy and active. Under the expert guidance of some of the country's leading coaches, boys develop their skills, character and confidence. Through games such as rugby, soccer, cricket and Harrow football, they learn how to be team players. Equal emphasis is placed on the many individual sports offered here that cultivate resilience, self-discipline and enjoyment. Surrounded by acres of sports fields, AstroTurf pitches, a golf course, swimming pool, sports centre, tennis, rackets and fives courts, Harrow has a breadth of sporting opportunities to match every interest and ability. Our elite sportsmen have an impressive record of achieving excellent standards and some go on to enjoy successful, professional sporting careers. Unique occasions like the annual cricket match versus Eton at Lord's provide memorable highlights in the School year.

The Arts. The arts are an extremely important part of Harrow's packed calendar of activities. Whether it's learning a musical instrument, playing in orchestras and ensembles, singing in choirs or in houses, performing in plays or discovering beauty in fine art, sculpture and ceramics, the opportunity for creative expression at Harrow not only sets our boys on a lifetime of personal enrichment and enjoyment, but also teaches them to be more self-disciplined, attentive and better at planning and organising their busy lives. Boys who participate in the vast spectrum of Harrow's creative and performing arts also find that this involvement has a broader, more beneficial effect on their overall academic performance. By encouraging boys to perform in the highest-quality School and house concerts, plays and competitions, we see them finding their own voice and the confidence to express their individual creativity, regardless of innate talent.

After Harrow. Virtually all of our boys take up places at selective universities. Boys who are heading towards Oxbridge, Ivy League and other competitive institutions are given specific guidance and preparation from their House Masters and our dedicated Universities Team. The Harrow Association, Harrow's Old Boys' Society, has a thriving membership of over 10,000. Director: C J A Virgin, Tel: 020 8872 8200, email: virginj@harrowschool.org.uk.

Admission. Application for admission should be made to the Registrar. Boys are admitted between the ages of 13 and 16, but most in the September before their fourteenth birthday. Most candidates take the Pre-Selection Test at Harrow at the age of 11. The Common Entrance Examination is taken at their Preparatory Schools usually in the term preceding entrance to Harrow. There are also some vacancies for Sixth Form boys. For details on admission to Harrow, visit http://www.harrowschool.org.uk/1563/admissions/.

Fees per term (2014–2015). £11,530. A small number of optional charges are not covered by the consolidated fee (for private tuition in music, for example).

Scholarships and bursaries. A large number of scholarships are awarded every year. Scholarships have a value of 5% of the fee and are held throughout a boy's time at Harrow, subject to satisfactory performance. Boys may apply for more than one of the different types of scholarship, which include Academic, Music, Art, Sport and Outstanding Talent. Scholarships can often be supplemented by a means-tested bursary of up to 100% for parents who might not otherwise be able to afford the fees.

Charitable status. The Keepers and Governors of the Free Grammar School of John Lyon is a Registered Charity, number 310033. The aims and objectives of the Charity are to provide education for the pupils at the two schools in the Foundation, Harrow School and The John Lyon School.

Hereford Cathedral School

Old Deanery, The Cathedral Close, Hereford HR1 2NG
Tel: 01432 363522
Fax: 01432 363525
email: schoolsec@herefordcs.com
website: www.herefordcs.com
Twitter: @Herefordcs1
Facebook: /HerefordCathedralSchool

Founded ante 1384. No record of the School's foundation survives, although its close association with the Cathedral is indicated by Bishop Gilbert's response to the long-standing right of the Chancellor to appoint the Headmaster in a letter of 1384, and it is probable that some educational institution was always associated with the Cathedral, which was founded in 676.

Governing Body:
President: The Very Revd M Tavinor, Dean of Hereford, MA, MMus
Chairman: R Haydn Jones, BSc, MRICS
C D Hitchiner, LLB, ACIS
Mrs D Bradshaw, MA
C R Potter, FCCA (*OH*)
Prof E Ellis, MA, PhD
Lady Mynors, BA, CertEd
Mrs V Oliver-Davies, JP
A Teale, BSc, PGCE
Ms K Skerrett, BA, Dip Law, BVC

W Hanks, BDS Lond

Clerk to the Governors: R Pizii, MA, BSc

Headmaster: P A Smith, BSc

Deputy Head: B G Blyth, BA

Deputy Head (*Academic*): J P Stanley, MA, MBA

Head of Sixth Form: J R Terry, BSc

Chaplain: Canon Revd P A Row, MA

Heads of Department:
Art: C A Wilkes, BA
Biology: Mrs E Segalini-Bower, MSc
Chemistry: Mrs A J Burdett, MSc
Classics: Miss A M Wright, MA
Drama: Ms L D A Zammit, BEd
Economics: M R Jackson, BA
English: J B Petrie, BA
Geography: Mrs R M Floyd, BSc
History: P A Wright, BA
Junior ICT: M P Jackson, BA
Learning Support: Miss L R Stevens, BA
Mathematics: M Taylor, BSc, ARCM
Modern Languages: Mrs N J Teale, BA
Music: D R Evans, MA, GBSM
PE and Games: R P Skyrme, BA
Physics: Dr S J B Rhodes, BEng, PhD
Religious Studies: Mrs A E D Locke, MA
Technology: C J Howells, BA

Careers Adviser: Mrs M McCumisky, BA
OC CCF: Gp Capt J Andrews RAFVR(*T*)
Director of Finance and Resources: R Pizii, MA, BSc
Headmaster's PA: Mrs S Gurgul
Marketing & Engagement Director: C J Townend, BA, ACIM
Development Director: Mrs C M Morgan-Jones
Admissions Officer: Mrs S D A Fortey
Tel: 01432 363506, email: admissions@herefordcs.com
Examinations Officer: Mrs C J Notley
School Office Administrator: Mrs L G Harding

The Junior School
Headmaster: C Wright, BSc, MSc, PGCE
Deputy Headmaster: J M Debenham, BEd
Head of Pre-Prep: Mrs E Lord, Bed
Head of Nursery: Mrs J Windows, BA

Heads of Department:
English: J Bond, BA
Maths: Miss N Jeynes, BEd
Science: Dr I Barber, BSc
French: Miss C Lambert, BA
Humanities: T Brown, BA
Drama: Miss A Sutton, BA
ICT: T Hutchinson, BSc, CertEd
Art: Mrs K Gummerson, BA
Music: Miss R Toolan, BMus, PG Dip Perf Hons
PSHE: Mrs S Price, LLB, PGCE
Learning Development: Mrs S Bristow, PGCE
Boys Games: S Turpin, BA
Girls Games: Miss K A Davies, BEd
Gifted & Talented: Mrs M Cadman-Davies, BA, CertEd

Secretary: Mrs S Stick
Admissions Secretary: Mrs A Phillips
Tel: 01432 363511, email: enquiry@herefordcs.com
Nurses:
Mrs S Warner, RGN
Mrs F Jennings

It is a fully co-educational 11–18 day school of 505 pupils.

Admission. Pupils are normally admitted at the ages of 11, 13 or 16. Admission at ages 11 to 14 is by sitting the

Senior School Entrance Examination at the School. Suitably qualified boys and girls may be admitted at Sixth Form level. The School operates a Deferred Entry Scheme at 11 for 13+ entries.

Facilities. The School is situated in the lee of the Cathedral. It occupies many historic buildings and some later ones, all adapted for School use, as well as purpose-built facilities. On the main campus are, in addition to some of the main departments, eight science departments, five which are new, a large music school, an Art, Design and Technology and Computer Centre (that gained Hereford's first RIBA award for architecture), the Gilbert Library and a refurbished Dining Hall. The Zimmerman Building provides 20,000 square feet of robust working space for Classics, Modern Languages, examination/functions hall, Geography and Drama departments and the Sixth Form Centre. A new on-site Sports Hall was opened in April 2009, which has first-class facilities for badminton, five-a-side football, netball, basketball and four sets of cricket nets. Rugby and outdoor cricket is held at the School's Wyeside sports ground, alongside the HCS rowing club.

Curriculum. Pupils are divided on entry at 11 into 4 forms (a maximum of 24 pupils per form) for academic and pastoral purposes. Below the Sixth Form, pupils take a broad range of subjects. Option choices are made at the end of the Third year (Year 9).

In the Sixth Form pupils are prepared for A (AS/A2) Levels, for which there is a wide choice of subjects: Latin, Greek, English Literature/Language (Combined), English Literature, French, Philosophy and Ethics, Classical Civilisation, Spanish, Economics, History, Geography, Mathematics, Further Mathematics, Biology, Physics, Chemistry, Design and Technology, Fine Art, Textiles, Business Studies, Music, Drama and Theatre Studies and Physical Education. Almost all students go on to Higher Education degree courses and the vast majority to the university course of their choice.

Religious instruction throughout is in accordance with the doctrines of the Church of England. The School is privileged to have the daily use of Hereford Cathedral for Chapel.

Sports/Activities include Rugby, Cricket, Football, Badminton, Tennis, Hockey, Netball, Athletics, and Rowing. There is a CCF Group and a wide range of societies active within the School. The School is an Operating Authority for the Duke of Edinburgh's Award Scheme. Drama flourishes, with several productions each year. The School has a national reputation in debating.

Music. The School is also particularly strong in Music: over half the pupils receive tuition in the full range of orchestral instruments, piano, organ and classical guitar. There is a Senior Symphony Orchestra, Senior Wind Quintet, Junior and Senior String Quartet, a Jazz Ensemble, Senior Chamber Choir, a Chapel Choir and a Junior Choir and many chamber music groups. There is at least one Concert each year and operas are produced from time to time. The musical tradition is strengthened by the presence of the Cathedral Choristers (and former Cathedral choristers) in the School.

Fees per term (2014–2015). £4,213.

Extras. CCF £22 per term from Year 11; DoE from £210 Bronze level; Instrumental Tuition £16.90 per lesson, plus public examination fees; PTA £20 per family annually.

Scholarships. Up to 8 Dean's Scholarships are awarded as a result of the Senior School Entrance and 11+ Scholarship Examination. Up to 3 Dean's Scholarships are also awarded at 13+. Up to 8 Dean's Scholarships are competed for entry to the Sixth Form. Art and Drama Scholarships are available at 13+ and 16+ entry. Sports and All-Rounder Scholarships are available at 11+, 13+ and 16+ entry. All Scholars are admitted to the Foundation by the Dean of Hereford each Autumn term.

Up to four Music Exhibitions are awarded each year as a result of auditions held in the first half of the Spring Term. 11+, 13+ and Sixth Form Music Scholarships are also available. Details are available from the Director of Music.

Cathedral choristers are members of the School from entry. They are accepted from the age of 8 as probationers following voice and educational tests held in May each year, and are educated initially at the Junior School. The Governors and the Chapter award choral scholarships jointly annually. Two-thirds reductions in tuition fees are available for Cathedral Choristers.

Bursaries. A number of means-tested bursaries are awarded competitively to able children from families of limited means.

Old Herefordian Club. *Alumni Coordinator*: Mrs Helen Pearson.

The Junior School. This is situated close by the main school. (*For details, please see Junior School IAPS entry*).

Charitable status. Hereford Cathedral School is a Registered Charity, number 518889. Its aims and objectives are to promote the advancement of education by acquiring, establishing, providing, conducting and carrying on residential and non-residential schools in which boys and girls of all sections of the community may receive a sound general education (including religious instruction in accordance with the doctrines of the Church of England).

Highgate School

North Road, London N6 4AY

Tel:	020 8340 1524 (Office)
	020 8347 3564 (Admissions)
Fax:	020 8340 7674
email:	office@highgateschool.org.uk
	admissions@highgateschool.org.uk
website:	www.highgateschool.org.uk

Motto: *Altiora in votis.*

Highgate School was founded in 1565 by Sir Roger Cholmeley, Knight, Chief Justice of England, and confirmed by Letters Patent of Queen Elizabeth in the same year. The School has three principal aims: to be a place for learning and scholarship; to be an exemplar for the healthy life; and to be a reflective community.

Visitor: Her Majesty The Queen

Governors:

J F Mills, CBE, MA, BLitt (*Treasurer and Chairman*)
R M Rothenberg, MBE, BA, FCA, CTA, MAE (*Deputy Chairman*)
Mrs G Aitken, BA
M Clarke, MA, FCA
J Claughton, MA
Mrs J Coleman
M Danson, MA
B Davidson, MD, FRCS
Miss R Langdale, QC, LLB, MPhil
Dr K Little, MB BS, BSc
P E Marshall, BSc, MRICS
K Panja, BA
A Patel, BA
J D Randall, BSc
P Rothwell, MArch

Bursar and Secretary to the Foundation: J C Pheasant, BSc, LLDip, Barrister

Head Master: A S Pettitt, MA

Deputy Heads:
T J Lindsay, MA (*Principal Deputy Head, Senior School*)

S M James, BA, MA (*Principal of the Junior School, Deputy Head and Director of Admissions*)
D M Fotheringham, MA (*Deputy Head, Academic*)

Assistant Heads:
P R Aston, BEd (*Assistant Head – Health & Safety; Co-Curricular*)
S N Brunskill, MA (*Head of Sixth Form*)
S Evans, BA (*Head of Lower School*)
Mrs C L Heindl, BA (*Assistant Head, Teaching and Learning*)
J R Lewis, BA, PhD, FRGS (*Community Partnerships Director*)
Miss L M Shelley, BA (*Head of Middle School*)
M J Short, MA (*Assistant Head – Staff*)
B S Weston, BSc, PhD, FSB, CBiol (*Assistant Head, Teaching and Learning*)

Teachers:
* *Head of Department*
† *Housemaster*

Art:
J L Allchin, BFA
C M Finnegan, BA
Ms J L Hendra, BA, MA
Ms S Keay, BA, MA
[Mrs T A Jay, MA]
*Mrs M J Nimmo, BA

Classics:
*G A Waller, MA
Mrs A J Brunner, BA
T L Corcoran, BA
D M Fotheringham, MA
Ms H J P Isaksen, BA
J S Morrow, BA
†H E Shepherd, MA
J J Shinkwin, MA
Miss V L Smith, BA, MA

Design Technology Engineering:
P R Aston, BEd
A B H Sursok, BA
J J Taylor, BA
*A F Thomson, BSc

Drama and Theatre Studies:
Ms J E Fehr, BA (**Theatre Studies*)
Mrs K A Hale, BA
T J A Hyam, BA

Economics:
Miss E L Cowell, BA, MPhil
*M J Feven, BSc, MA
†Miss K P Norris, BA

English:
S G Appleton, MA
G J H Catherwood, BA
Mrs C L Heindl, BA
*Mrs R J Hyam, BA
[Dr K L Kramer, BA, MA, DPhi]
†Miss J E McLoughlin, BA
A J Miles, BA
M E Morgan, MA, MSt
Miss O R Orlans, BA
A J Plaistowe, MA
R J Powell, BA
†M W M Seymour, BA
Miss L M Shelley, MA

Miss S K Wijesuriya, BA, MA

Geography:
W J C Blackshaw, BA
†D G Brandt, BA
[Mrs H J Broadbent, BA]
P J Harrison, MA
*Miss R E Joss, BA
Miss G S Y Kwong, BA, MPhil
J R Lewis, BA, PhD, FRGS

History:
Miss C A Burch, BA
B J Dabby, MA, MPhil, PhD
A T Davies, BA, MA, PhD
T J Lindsay, MA
P P McClory, BA, MA
Ms E L Milton, BA, MA
*Mr J P R Newton, BA, MSc
Miss E A Worthen, BA

History of Art:
*Ms J E W Jammers, MA, PhD
Miss S K Wijesuriya, BA, MA

Information Technology:
*M A O'Connor, BA

Learning Support:
Mrs S M Bambrough, BA
*P Johnston, BSc, PhD
Ms J Hamilton, BA

Mathematics:
T E Bateup, BSc
A D Bottomley, MMath, MRes
Miss J R Brewin, MMath
Miss P F D Brownlee, BSc, MSt
C R Cockerill, BSc
A G Dales, MA
T J Dessain, MMath, PhD
P A Davison, MMathPhil
J S Galdal-Gibbs, BA, BA
†Miss H Gardiner, BA
Miss S L Johnson, MMath
B M W Lane, BSc
Mrs N S Levin, MA, MBA

L C Mulcahy, BA
D J Noyce, MMath
S D Powell, BSc
M P Streuli, MA, MBA
*D J Vaccaro, MA
J Wright, MMath
Mrs L A Wright, MMath

Modern Languages:
Miss N Arosemena Manso, BA
[Mrs N Y Arnold, BA]
Ms M R Bolster, BA, MA
S N Brunskill, BA
J A Brydon, BA, MSt, DPhil
G D C Creagh, BA (**German*)
J H Houghton, MA (**Spanish*)
Mrs J F Morelle, BA
Mrs C B Pettitt, L-ès-L
Miss C Pottier, L-ès-L
Mrs R J Russell, MA (**Russian*)
F J Santaniello, L-ès-L
Mrs J E C Spencer, L-ès-L, MA
†Mrs C Walker, BA
Mrs Q W Wallis, BA (**Mandarin*)
Miss Y Wang, BA, MA
J J Werbicki, BA

Music:
V J Barr, LRAM
A Cannière, BM, MM
G Hanson, BMus, LRAM, FRSM
Miss C D Harrison, BA
S J King, BMus
J P Murphy, GRNCM
Miss E C Price, BMus, MA
*T Wiggall, MA

Politics:
*R R X Miller, MA
Mrs K B Shapiro, MA

Sport and Exercise:
S Evans, BA
*C L M Henderson, BEd (*Co-Director of Sport and Exercise*)
J Humphrey (*Head of Football*)
Miss K T Johnston, BSc

*Miss S Pride, BSc (*Co-Director of Sport and Exercise*)
Mrs L Sursok, BA
†A G Tapp, BEd

Religious Education and Philosophy:
C M Ajmone-Marsan, BMus, BA
S Bovey, BA
R N Davis, BA
The Revd N H Lamb, BA
*Miss E A Shipp, MA
[Mrs J T Stone, BA]
Miss P C Voute, BA, MA
Revd RSS Weir BA, Dip TH, MTh

Science:
K Agyei-Owusu, MSci, PhD
W J Atkins, BA
†R C J Atkinson, MA, MSci, PhD, DIC
K S Bains, BSc, ARCS (**Chemistry, *Science*)
†J T M Barr, MEng
Miss L I Batten, BA, MSc
A C Cheung, BA, MSci, PhD (**Physics*)
S R Crawford, BA, PhD (**Biology*)
Ms C L Cunningham, MPhys
†A R Dabrowski, MSci
P D Davey, MChem
†P Doyle, BSc
Mrs C A Gruer, BSc (*Ogden Teaching Fellow*)
Miss G V Gulliford, BA
P Johnston, BSc, PhD
P A Liebman, BA
K E Quinn, BSc, PhD (*Ogden Teaching Fellow*)
M J Short, BA
Miss C E Steers, MChem
Miss C C Stimmler, BSc, MEd
Dr V E C Stubbs, BSc, PhD
A Z Szydlo, MSc, PhD
J M Tomasi, BSc, MPhil
Mrs V Vaccaro, BA
Mrs J C Y Welch, BSc, MSc, PhD
B S Weston, BSc, PhD

Highgate Junior School
Cholmeley House, 3 Bishopwood Road, London N6 4PL
Tel: 020 8340 9193; Fax: 020 8342 8225
email: jsoffice@highgateschool.org.uk

Principal of the Junior School: S M James, BA, MA
(*For further details, see entry in IAPS section.*)

Highgate Pre-Preparatory School
7 Bishopswood Road, London N6 4PH
Tel: 020 8340 9196; Fax: 020 8340 3442
email: pre-prep@highgateschool.org.uk

Principal: Mrs D Hecht, DCE

There are 1,100 boys and girls in the Senior School. The Junior School has some 345 boys and girls, aged 7 to 11, and prepares them for entry to the Senior School. The Pre-Prepa-ratory School has 140 boys and girls aged 3 to 7. The School is fully co-educational and admits girls and boys at each entry point.

Situation and Grounds. The academic centre of the Senior School is in the heart of old Highgate, which has retained much of its village atmosphere. In addition to the Victorian buildings, such as the Chapel and Central Hall classrooms, the pupils have the benefit of modern facilities such as Dyne House, with its 200-seat auditorium and dedi-cated recital space, an Art, Design & Technology Centre opened in 2005 and the Charter Building, housing the English and Geography Departments, a science laboratory and ICT suite which opened in 2012; the Sir Martin Gilbert Library opened in Big School in 2013, and an extension to the Garner Building, providing two new science laboratories and three new modern languages classrooms, opened for use in September 2014.

Highgate underground station, on the Northern line, is a short walk away and there is also easy access to the School by bus. It is four miles to central London (City or West End).

A few hundred yards along Hampstead Lane in Bishop-swood Road lie more than twenty acres of playing-fields together with the Mallinson Sports Centre, indoor swim-ming pool and other extensive sporting facilities, the dining hall, the Junior School and the Pre-Preparatory School. Hampstead Heath and Kenwood, the largest expanse of open country in London, are adjacent.

Pastoral Care. In the Senior School, pastoral care for Years 7 and 8 is organised by form, with a Head of Year in overall charge. From Year 9, each pupil is a member of a House. There are twelve Houses based on particular areas of North London. A Housemaster, helped by five tutors, is responsible for monitoring the day-to-day progress and wel-fare of the fifty or so pupils in his or her care and for liaising with their parents.

Academic Curriculum. Pupils enter the Senior School at 11+ (Year 7); there is a further, limited, entry at 13+. There are seven or eight forms in Years 7 and 8 and the cur-riculum is broad. At present, in addition to the usual range of subjects in Years 7 to 9, Art, Music and Design Technology are taken by all; the vast majority of pupils take Latin, and two sets study both Latin and Greek in Year 9 as a single timetable option; all pupils take a second modern language option in Year 9. Mandarin has been offered at GCSE since 2011 and is offered as a Pre-U in the Sixth Form. By the time they start their GCSEs, pupils have developed an appropriate pattern of work, both in the classroom and out of school. Homework is an integral part of each pupil's pro-gramme of study.

The two-year GCSE courses begin in Year 10. The core subjects, studied by all, are: English, English Literature, Mathematics, Biology, Chemistry and Physics as single award separate sciences. A further four subjects (including a modern language) are then chosen from: Ancient History, Art, Classical Civilisation, Design Technology, Drama, Geography, French, German, Greek, History, Latin, Manda-rin, Music, Religious Studies, Spanish and Russian. In addi-tion to their GCSE subjects, all pupils take courses in Religion and Philosophy and Sport and Exercise. All GCSEs are taken at the end of Year 11. The IGCSE qualifi-cation is taken in English Language, English Literature, Sciences, History, French, German and Spanish.

The teaching staff are experienced and well-qualified subject specialists and the teacher/pupil ratio is about 1:9. Class sizes are generally in the low twenties in Years 7 to 9 and just under twenty in Years 10 and 11, although for some subjects they will be much smaller; in the Sixth Form classes of 6–14 are usual.

Educational resources include a new learning platform, HERO, which enables pupils to access learning materials and extension work and to submit assignments and receive feedback on them. This complements an extensive intranet on a large information technology network and parent and pupil portals for remote access. The use of all these is guided by trained professionals and they complement the facilities available in the academic departments, which have specialist teaching rooms, equipment and, where appropri-ate, technicians, computers and libraries. Fieldwork and vis-its to galleries, museums, exhibitions and lectures are an integral part of the academic programme.

When they enter Year 12, girls and boys choose four sub-jects from the wide range of AS and A Level courses on offer. Prospective Sixth Formers are assisted in selecting the best programme of study according to their known ability and future plans. A booklet listing the options available and containing details of the courses is published each year and given to Year 11 and their parents before those choices are made. Both new and old-style A Levels will be taught in a linear fashion from 2015 and pupils will not take any public examinations at the end of Year 12.

All Year 12 pupils follow a Critical Method programme which introduces them to the criticism and formation of log-ical argument. This is followed by a Critical Independence course for one term in Year 13, which pursues the aims of the Year 12 course at a higher level. The Extended Project has been introduced as an additional option in Year 12.

Emphasis is placed on learning to work independently and to develop more advanced study skills. At this stage a pupil will for the first time have a number of private reading periods. Two Sixth Form Common Rooms act as a social and recreational base for senior pupils.

Each Sixth Former has a tutor who, in conjunction with the Housemaster, exercises supervision over general aca-demic progress and who advises on and monitors higher education applications in conjunction with the Director of Higher Education.

Religion. Highgate has a Christian tradition but pupils from all faiths and denominations or none are welcome. Pupils attend Chapel once a week, by houses, and there are weekly voluntary celebrations of Holy Communion; Choral Evensong is sung on some Sundays, at which parents are welcome. Greek Orthodox and Roman Catholic services are also held each term and there are weekly meetings of the Jewish Circle and an assembly for those of other faiths.

Knowledge Curriculum. A structured programme of academic extension is in place in each year group. Particular themes have been identified, to which each department con-tributes. The curriculum is delivered in lesson time and through a dedicated week once a year which focuses on the relevant theme. The purpose is to expand pupils' cultural and academic knowledge and to develop their critical think-ing skills.

Music, Drama and Art. Highgate music has a long and distinguished tradition and many former pupils are now leading composers, conductors or performers. A wide range of musical activities is designed both to encourage the beginner and to stimulate and further the skills of the tal-ented musician. State-of-the-art performance spaces for orchestral and chamber music, complete with computerised recording facilities, are available in Dyne House.

There are five main instrumental ensembles: a symphony orchestra, a chamber orchestra, a symphonic wind band, and string orchestra and a concert band. Two choirs provide music for Choral Evensong on Sundays, with a further three choirs covering a wide range of sacred and secular reper-toire. There are four main concerts each year, one taking place in a major central London venue. Numerous chamber groups rehearse weekly and regular concerts are arranged, together with masterclasses, workshops and an annual house music competition.

Individual music lessons are available with specialist vis-iting teachers in all the main instruments and in singing. Certain orchestral instruments can be hired by beginners who may be offered a free term's trial of lessons.

Every encouragement is given to participate in drama, as actors, in stage management, or by assisting with sound and lighting. Major productions in recent years have included *West Side Story, Midsummer Night's Dream, Sweeney Todd, Les Misérables, Blood Wedding, The Bacchae, Medea, Bugsy Malone, Skellig, Oklahoma, Much Ado about Nothing* and *The Tempest*. Small-scale plays are staged in most terms, some by younger pupils, and there is a biennial play performed in French. A separate drama studio provides additional rehearsal and performance space. Regular visits to the professional theatre are also arranged. In 2014, Highgate held its first Festival, celebrating excellence in the performing arts and sport, which culminated in a show at Camden's Roundhouse.

The excellent Art department has facilities for painting, print-making, life drawing, sculpture, pottery, photography, and film-making. Whether taking part in formal classes or working in their free time boys and girls are encouraged to explore their own ways of expressing ideas visually. Their work is regularly exhibited, both in the department and elsewhere in the school.

Sport and Exercise. Highgate is exceptionally fortunate in its sports facilities. The extensive playing fields are complemented by the Mallinson Sports Centre and by courts for squash, tennis and Eton fives, and a new all-weather pitch which opened for use in 2009.

The Sport and Exercise (Games and PE) curriculum aims to maximise participation, promote enjoyment and ensure progression. Sport (one afternoon per week) and exercise (a double period in Years 7–10) are integrated to ensure pupils develop skills and strength relevant to the sport which, from Year 8 onwards, they choose from a wide range, including the team games of football, rugby, cricket (boys) and netball, hockey and rounders (girls), and the following options: athletics, aquatics, cross-country, climbing, fives, fencing, golf, gym and dance, kayaking, martial arts, rowing, sailing, softball, squash and tennis. Specialist sports coaches lead the teaching which is complemented by early-morning, lunch-time and after-school training. There is a High Performance Programme for outstanding sports pupils. Tours take place annually, either to short- or to long-haul destinations.

Activities. We aim to provide as many opportunities as possible in which pupils will develop qualities of self-reliance, endurance and leadership, in which they can serve the community and in which they can develop their own interests and enthusiasms. There are a large number of societies and clubs, usually meeting in the lunch-hour or after school. The School is an operating authority for the Duke of Edinburgh's Award scheme and each year many gain the bronze award and often go on to gain the silver and gold awards. There is also a Community Service scheme and an Urban Survival award scheme.

Admission. Normal entry to the Junior School is at the age of 7. All candidates take an entrance examination in January and a proportion are recalled for interview shortly thereafter, for entry the following September. Application should be made in writing to the Principal of the Junior School, 3 Bishopswood Road, London N6 4PL.

Boys who enter the Senior School at 11+ are mainly from primary schools while girls come from prep and primary schools; those who enter at 13+ are usually from preparatory schools. The remainder enter from Highgate Junior School. Places for the limited entry at 13+ will be offered on the basis of pre-tests in the September of Year 7, conditional on passing Common Entrance. 13+ pupils not in preparatory schools should contact the Admissions Office for advice. Girls and boys from other schools are also admitted to the Sixth Form at Highgate following a thinking skills test and interviews. Only occasionally are there vacancies at other levels of the School. All enquiries concerning admission to the Senior School should be addressed to the Director of Admissions, admissions@highgateschool.org.uk.

Fees per term (2014–2015). Senior School: £6,055; Junior School: £5,555; Pre-Preparatory School: £5,245 (Reception–Year 2), £2,620 (Nursery).

Fees are inclusive of lunch (exc Nursery) and the use of books.

Scholarships and Bursaries.

Bursaries: The Outreach and Access Officer (sam.keeble @highgateschool.org.uk) can provide information about the process for bursary applications and on the number of bursaries held by pupils in the school at any one time. Preference will be given to bursary candidates who currently attend state schools. There would need to be particular and unusual circumstances for us to award a bursary to a child attending an independent school.

Scholarships: Academic scholarships are honorary and do not bring with them any remission of the school fee. We do not award academic scholarships on the strength of the entrance tests alone. We believe that we gain a much more accurate picture of a child's academic ability after we have had an opportunity to see the quality of their work within the School. Therefore we award academic scholarships towards the end of Years 7, 8, 9 and 10, and then again in the Sixth Form. In Year 7, usually six of these are awarded to external 11+ entrants and six to those coming from the Junior School. Two further scholarships are awarded at the end of Years 8, 9 and 10 on the basis of examination results, the pupil's class work and homework, and teachers' assessment of the pupil's effort and performance. There are also a small number of lesser awards, Academic Exhibitions, awarded at the end of each year.

Music awards: We make music awards (scholarships and exhibitions) for pupils joining the school at 11+ and 13+, by means of audition at the point of entry. Awards are also made to pupils already in the school at these points, too, where they have met the standard for a scholarship or exhibition. Music scholarships bring up to a maximum of 10% remission of the school fee and free tuition on two instruments, provided tuition is given by instrumental teachers employed at Highgate. More detailed guidance may be obtained from the Admissions Office (admissions@ highgateschool.org.uk) or the Music Department (natasha. creed@highgateschool.org.uk).

Old Cholmeleian Society. Former pupils are known as Cholmeleians. Enquiries should be addressed to the Foundation Office at the School, oc@highgateschool.org.uk.

Charitable status. Sir Roger Cholmeley's School at Highgate is a Registered Charity, number 312765, committed to meeting its responsibilities to the society that lies beyond the school gates. The importance that Sir Roger Cholmeley's School at Highgate attaches to its social responsibilities has become more focused, but is not new; the objects stated in the charity's constitution are:

- the advancement of education by the provision of a school in or near Highgate, the provision of incidental or ancillary educational activities, and the undertaking of associated activities for the benefit of the public;
- in so far as the Governors think fit (and so long as they in their discretion consider that the first object is being properly provided for) the relief of the poor.

The principal ways in which the charity meets these objects are:

- the provision of bursaries and scholarships;
- training teachers;
- running educational summer schools;
- supporting applications to selective universities;
- partnerships with local primary and secondary schools;
- sharing our facilities with community groups;
- an extensive programme of community service;
- events in support of other charities.

More detailed information can be found on the School's website.

Hurstpierpoint College
A Woodard School

College Lane, Hurstpierpoint, West Sussex BN6 9JS
Tel: 01273 833636
Fax: 01273 835257
email: registrar@hppc.co.uk
website: www.hppc.co.uk

Motto: *Beati mundo corde*
Founded 1849 by Nathaniel Woodard, Canon of Manchester.

Visitor:
The Rt Revd The Lord Bishop of Chichester

Provost: The Rt Revd Lindsay Urwin, MA, OGS, DD Hons

School Council:
Chairman: A Jarvis, BEd, MA, FRSA

Members:
Professor J P Bacon, MA, MSc, PhD
Dr S Brydie, MBBS, MD, MRCGP
P M Dillon-Robinson, BAFCA, MBA
¶R J Ebdon, BSc, MAPM, MCIOB, FRSA
Mrs F M Hampton
M S Harrison, FCA
The Revd J B A Joyce, BA, DipEd
K S Powell FCA
¶J P Ruddlesdin, FCA
G A Rushton
¶G J Taysom, BSc, FRSA
Mrs C M A Turnbull, BA

Headmaster: T J Manly, BA, MSc

* *Head of Department*
† *Housemaster/mistress*
§ *Part-time*
¶ *Former Pupil*
\# *Head of Year*

Deputy Head (*Academic*): Mrs K J Austin, BSc, CSci, FRSC
Deputy Head (*Head of Sixth Form*): T Firth, BA
Deputy Head (*Head of Middle School*): R Taylor-West, MA, AKC
Chaplain: Revd Jeremy Sykes, MA
Bursar: S A Holliday, BSc, ACIB, MAPM

Staff:
L J Agate, BA
R J Ashley, MA (**Geography, Director of Learner Development*)
Mrs V I Bacon, BEd (*Director of Digital Strategy*)
Miss K S E Barker, MA (*Classics)
N D D Beeby, BA (**Director of Drama,* †*St John's House*)
Miss L N Blackstone, BA
Ms H K Bray, BMus
Mrs A Browne (†*St John's House*)
P A Browne, BSc
W Carroll, BSc
N P Chapman, BA
C J Chilton, MPhys
Ms A E D Chinn, BA
Miss J C Clarke, BA (*History)
M F Clay, MBA
Miss E V Coffey, BA
Ms J G Coleman, MA
Ms D B Collins, MA (*Head of Library*)
Mrs N Coxon, BSc (*Biology)
R J S Cooke, BSc (**Computing/IT Sixth Form*)
¶N Creed, BA (†*Crescent House, Assistant Director of Sport*)

Mrs S Crickmore, MA (*Chemistry)
S J Crook, BSc (**Computing/IT Middle School*)
L P Dannatt, MEng (*Director of Studies*)
T T Davies, BA
A G Daville, MA (**Science/Physics*)
Ms A De Britt, BEng
Mrs K V Doehren, BEd, RSA Dip SpLD (*Director of Learning Support*)
Miss N C Dominy, BA (**Dance, Acting*† *Shield House*)
C J Eustace, MA (†*Eagle House*)
Miss T C I Farrell, BA
Mrs J L Firth, BA
Mrs C A Forman, BSc
L A Gasper, MA
Miss J C Gillick, MA (*English)
Mrs K L B Goddard, MA (*ESL)
O J J Gospel, BEng (#*Fifth Form*)
S M Graham, BSc
Mrs H A Harper, MSc
Mrs A K Higazi, BA
S N Higazi, BSc
D M Higgins, BA (*Director of Operational Technology*)
§Mrs H E Higgins, BA (†*Phoenix House*)
A J Hopcroft, MEng (†*Red Cross House*)
§Mrs A Hurst, BA
Miss K L Husher, MA
Mrs S Hyman, BA (†*Fleur de Lys House*)
Mrs D C Jackson, BA
D Jameson, MA (*Academic Music)
Miss A N Jayne, BEng
Ms J Jedamzik, BA, MA (**Business Studies & Economics*)
R M Johnson, BSc (**Design & Technology*)
Mrs R J Jutson (*Acting Asst Director of Sport – Girls*)
R M Kift, BEd (**Director of Sport*)
Ms A C Kilpatrick (†*Pelican House*)
T Kingston, BA (*French)
M Lamb, BSc (†*Chevron House*)
Mrs K Lea, BSc (†*Martlet House*)
Mrs S A Lear, MA
Mrs J Leeper, BA (*Senior Mistress i/c Discipline/Director of Child Protection and Pastoral Welfare*)
T F Q Leeper, BSc (*Senior Master i/c Discipline/Director of Child Protection and Pastoral Welfare*)
Mrs L J Mackinder, BSc (*Mathematics)
Miss P Maple, BA (†*Pelican House*)
Miss A S Masson, BSc
N K Matthews, BA (**Director of Music*)
S J May, BSc
Miss S O K McCrohan, BSc
P J McKerchar, MA, CChem, MRSC
Miss S T Miller, BA
Miss B J Mowlam, BSc
Miss A Morgan, BA
J O'Dowd, BSc
D E Parry, MA (#*Shell*)
Ms K Pattison, BA (#*Remove*)
Ms E M Paull, BA
Mrs M Payeras-Cifre, TFL (*Spanish)
S P Poole, BEd (*Psychology)
A J Presland, BSc
A J Ritter, BEng
Miss C L Roberts, BA
J R Rowland, BA
B Schofield, BA (#*UVI*)
J Scott, BA, MBA (#*LVI*)
Mrs R J Scott, BA (*Asst Director of Sport – Girls*)
§Mrs C A Shearman, BA
R L Shearman, MSc, BA (†*Star House*)
E W R Short, BA
Mrs J C Silvey, BA
F J Simkins (*Director of Outdoor Education*)
A J Smith, BA (**Academic Drama,* †*Woodard House*)
P G Statter, BSc (**Academic Administration*)

Miss M A Tait, BSc
Miss A L Taylor, BSc
Mrs D Treyer-Evans, BA (*Senior School Registrar*)
Mrs S N M Watson-Saunders, BA
Dr S Waugh, MA, PhD
P C Wells, BA
Mrs J West, BA (**Art*)
R L White, BA (**PSHE*)
D J Wickenden, BA
Mrs F Williams, BA
J Williams, BSc (*Director of Hockey*)
A P Wood, MA, MSc (**Philosophy and Theology, Director of Academic Enrichment*)
Miss L R Woolgar, BSc
Mrs M Zeidler, MEd (*Director of Professional Development and Performance*)

O J Bell (*Sports Coach*)
S J Blount (*Outdoor Pursuits Instructor*)
M Brigden (*Fencing Coach*)
Miss S D Brown, BA (*Girls' Games Coach*)
A T Bygraves (*Gym Manager*)
§M J Carter (*Playwright in Residence*)
Ms R Caufield, BA (*Resident Coach*)
§A L Drummond (*Interpersonal & Empathy Coach*)
§Mrs T Fielden (*Careers Advisor*)
§Miss E M Franks (*Girls' Games Coach*)
Mrs K L Goldfinch (*Tennis Coach*)
T Hariki (*Tai Chi Teacher*)
P M Harrap, BA (*Art Instructor*)
S A Hartman, BA (*CCF RAF Officer*)
J R P Heath (*Cricket Coach*)
S M Heaton, BA, BSc (*Rugby Coach*)
C J Marchant (*Games Coach*)
Ms B S McMullen (*Aerobics Instructor*)
Miss N E Miller, BSc (*Resident Coach*)
Miss K Money (*Games Coach*)
§Mrs M Simkins (*Outdoor Pursuits*)
S A Simkins (*Resident Coach*)
Miss L S Skates, BSc (*Assistant Girls' Games Coach*)
Mrs C Ticktum (*Ballet Teacher*)
§Mrs T M Towler (*Girls' Cricket Coach*)
Mrs H Turier (*Goal Mapping Coach*)
D Valentine (*Sports Coach*)
E J Waagenaar (*Life Skills*)

There are 23 visiting Music Teachers.

Prep/Pre-Prep School

Head: I D Pattison, BSc
Deputy Head: N J Oakden, BA
Deputy Head (*Pastoral/Discipline*): Mrs D K Stoneley, BEd

Staff:
Mrs C Adams (**Girls' Games*)
Miss A E Albury, MA (*#3–6, *History*)
J O Baldwin, BSc (**PE*)
Mrs L M Brunjes, BA
T A Cattaneo, BEd, CertEd (**Mathematics*)
Mrs S L Deelman, BSc
Miss C Dilley BA
R J Egan, BSc, MSc(**Boys' Sport*)
Mrs A J Filkins, BA (**MFL*)
A A Gardner, BA (**Enrichment, Philosophy & Theology*)
Mrs P Gordon-Stewart, BA (**English*)
Ms A E Hawley (**Drama*)
A J Hopcroft, MEng (**KS3 Physics*)
Mrs L S Johnson, BA
Mrs H L Kitson, BSc (**KS3 Biology, KS2 Science*)
Mrs L A Lane, BA (**Art*)
Miss A L Megahey, BA
Miss G R Merridan, BA (*#7–8*)
Mrs S H Miles, BEd (**PSHCE*)
§Mrs L A Moakes, BA

§Mrs C P Owen, BEd
Mrs T-A Preen, BSc (**KS2 Mathematics*)
Mrs D A Ross, BEd (*#Reception–Year 2*)
A M J Reeder, BA
Mrs Z Taylor-West, BA
A M Travers, MA, GCLCM (**Director of Music*)
Ms E K Warbey, BSc
T B B Williams, BSc (**Geography*)
Mrs K J Woodward, BA (**Learning Support*)
Miss L R Woolgar, BSc (**KS3 Mathematics*)

Teaching Assistants:
Mrs K L Ford, NNEB
Mrs K Hayles, CACHE Level 3
Mrs L Melling, NVQ 3
Mrs D J Murray, HNC

Hurstpierpoint College is a co-educational day and boarding school for boys and girls aged between 4 and 18 years. Pre-Prep, Prep and Senior Schools are linked by common values and a common academic and administrative framework, to provide a complete education. There are currently 406 boys and 332 girls. 51% of the pupils are boarders. The Preparatory School has a further 292 boys and girls and the Pre-Prep currently has 54 pupils.

The school is truly co-educational throughout and offers boarding for boys and girls in the Senior School. Boarding is a particularly popular option at the school with many day pupils and flexi-boarders later opting to become weekly boarders. In their Upper Sixth year at Hurst, pupils join St John's House, a co-educational day and boarding house where, appropriately supervised, they enjoy greater freedom and are encouraged to further develop their independent learning skills in preparation for university.

Buildings and Facilities. At the heart of the school's large country campus lie the core school buildings and Chapel arranged around three attractive quadrangles built of traditional Sussex knapped flint. Key facilities nearby include two floodlit Astroturfs, art school, sports hall, music school, dance and drama studios, 250-seat theatre, indoor swimming pool and Medical Centre. Other facilities include a new Library and fully-equipped IT Centre. The extensive grounds are laid mainly to playing fields and include one of the largest and most attractive school cricket pitches in the country.

Chapel. As a Woodard School, Hurstpierpoint is a Christian foundation and underpinned by Christian values, although pupils of other faiths or of no faith are warmly welcomed. Pupils attend up to three assemblies during the week. The main Eucharist, which parents and friends are most welcome to attend, takes place early on Friday evenings, although there are also occasional Sunday services in addition to voluntary celebrations of the Holy Communion. Pupils who wish to do so are prepared in small classes for the annual Confirmation taken by one of the Bishops of the diocese.

Curriculum. The five-day academic week is structured to allow boys and girls to study a variety of subject options that can be adapted to suit their natural ability. The entry year (Shell) gives pupils the chance to experience most of our GCSE subjects before they choose their options. It involves the study of English, History, Geography, French, Spanish, Latin, Ancient Greek, Mathematics, Physics, Chemistry, Biology, Religious Studies, Art, Design & Technology, Music, Drama, Physical Education and IT. In the second (Remove) and in the third (Fifth) years students study between 8 and 10 GCSE subjects. In addition to the core subjects there are five option blocks offering a choice of 17 subjects, including Ancient Greek, Applied Business and Dance.

Students entering the Lower Sixth are able to choose between A Levels and the International Baccalaureate (IB) Diploma Programme.

The majority of Sixth formers who opt for A Levels study four AS Levels in the Lower Sixth. The choice is wide, with 28 AS subjects to choose from. Art & Design (Photography), Business Studies, Classical Civilisation, Computing, Dance, Economics, Further Maths, Music Technology and Psychology are introduced in addition to the GCSE options. There is also a General Studies programme. The Upper Sixth can take a varied programme with the most able studying four or five full A Levels, whilst others build a valuable qualifications portfolio by studying a varying number of AS subjects along with at least two full A Levels.

Students who opt for the IB Diploma Programme choose six subjects in total, three at Higher Level and three at Standard Level, from the following six groups: English Literature or German Language and Literature; English, French, Spanish, German, Latin; History, Geography, Economics, Psychology, Philosophy; Physics, Chemistry, Biology; Mathematics or Mathematical Studies, Music, Visual Arts and Theatre. In addition to completing three core elements as an integral part of the course: Theory of Knowledge; Creativity, Action and Service; Extended Essay.

All pupils' work is overseen by academic tutors and we take particular care to ensure that university applications are properly targeted to suit the students' aspirations and talents.

Games. The School operates a "Sport for All" policy that seeks to place pupils in games most suited to their tastes and abilities. During the first two years they are expected to take part in at least some of the major sports but thereafter a greater element of choice occurs. The major sports are Rugby, Hockey, Cricket and Athletics for boys; Hockey, Netball, Athletics and Tennis for girls. Recent tours for major sports include Rugby (Italy), Netball (Barbados), Dubai (Cricket), South Africa (Hockey). In addition there are teams in Basketball, Cross Country, Football, Golf, Polo, Rounders, Shooting, Squash, Swimming, Triathlon, boys' Tennis, girls' Cricket and girls' Rugby. The Sports Hall and indoor Swimming Pool provide opportunities for many other pursuits such as Aerobics, Badminton, Equestrian, Fencing, Gymnastics, Power Walking, Weight Training and Water Polo, while the Outdoor Pursuits enable pupils to enjoy challenges such as Rock Climbing, Mountain Biking, Sailing, Kayaking and Canoeing.

Service Afternoons. On Wednesdays all pupils other than the Shell (Year 9) are expected to take part in The Duke of Edinburgh's Award activities alongside the Combined Cadet Force (Army, RN or RAF sections), Community Service or Environmental Conservation.

Music. There has always been a strong musical tradition at Hurstpierpoint with an orchestra and other more specialised ensembles. A large proportion of the pupils, currently 160, take individual instrumental lessons and give frequent recitals. The Chapel Choir plays a major part in regular worship and there are several other choral groups.

Drama. The Shakespeare Society is the oldest such school society in the country and organises an annual production and an annual musical. Drama covers a wide range and varies from major musicals to more modest House plays and pupil-directed productions. The 250-seat Bury Theatre also gives the more technically minded ample opportunity to develop stage management, lighting and sound skills.

Other Activities. The Thursday afternoon activity programme is for Shell and Remove pupils (Years 9 & 10) and includes Art, Climbing, Dance, Self-Defence, Car Maintenance, Girls' Football, Hurst Farm, Robotics, Japanese, LAMDA, Ningitsu, Shooting, Horse Riding, Polo, Karate, Golf Range, Squash, Clay Pigeon Shooting, Dinghy Sailing and Surfing alongside a variety of music clubs and literary clubs. Other activities also take place during the school week.

Hurst Johnian Club. In addition to providing facilities and events for Old Pupils, the Club also assists with careers and supports the current pupils in various ways, eg Gap Year

travel fund and tour sponsorship contributions. Contact the Hon Secretary, c/o Hurstpierpoint College.

Fees per term (2014–2015). Senior School: Full Boarding: £10,375 (Overseas students including ESL), £9,840 (UK students); Weekly Boarding £8,795; Flexi Boarding £8,250; Day £6,975.

Scholarships and Bursaries. Awards available at 13+: Academic, 'Hurst' All-Rounder, Art, Drama, Music and 'Downs' Sports. Please note that candidates entering for awards other than Academic are not eligible to apply for All-Rounder awards. Such candidates will be considered for All-Rounder awards as part of their other applications. Awards available at 16+: Academic, Art, Drama, Music and 'Downs' Sports.

Academic Award examinations are held annually in May for 13+ candidates. Assessments for All-Rounder, Art, Drama and Sports Awards are held in February.

Music Award assessments are held in January for entrants to the Prep School the following September and in February for entrants to the Senior School the following September. Awards are offered with free musical tuition in two instruments. Informal auditions are encouraged and may be held at any time by arrangement with the Director of Music. The Awards are given subject to satisfactory Scholarship or Common Entrance results or the College's own entry tests.

Art Scholarships: A folio of work is presented and there is an objective test as well as an interview.

Assessment for Sixth Form awards takes place in November of the year preceding entry.

Means-tested bursaries may be available to supplement awards.

Admission. For 13+ entry, pupils must be registered on the School's list and pass Common Entrance or Scholarship examinations. Entry from Hurst Prep school is by the College's own examinations. Entrants from maintained schools and from overseas undergo separate tests and interviews.

Places in the Sixth Form are available to students who achieve an A/A* grade at GCSE in the subjects (or, if a new subject, then in a subject closely related to it) that they intend to study, whether they choose the A Level or the IB Diploma programmes of study. Students should also have a minimum of a C grade at GCSE in Mathematics and English.

Please contact the Senior School Admissions Officer for further information.

Preparatory School. *See entry in IAPS section.*

Charitable status. Hurstpierpoint College is a Registered Charity, number 1076498. It aims to provide a Christian education to boys and girls between the ages of four and eighteen in the three schools on the campus.

Hutchesons' Grammar School

21 Beaton Road, Glasgow G41 4NW
Tel: 0141 423 2933
Fax: 0141 424 0251
email: rector@hutchesons.org
website: www.hutchesons.org

Motto: *Veritas.*

Founded in the 17th Century and endowed by the brothers George and Thomas Hutcheson (Deed of Mortification 1641). The School is governed by Hutchesons' Educational Trust.

Governors:
Not more than 17 in number.
Representatives of the following Bodies:
Glasgow Presbytery of the Church of Scotland (2), Senatus Academicus of Glasgow University (1), Merchants' House of Glasgow (1), Trades House of Glasgow (1), Patrons of

Hutchesons' Hospital (2), Glasgow Educational Trust (1), Senate of the University of Strathclyde (1), FP Club (1), School Association (1) and not more than 9 persons co-opted by the Governors.

Chairman: Prof Brian Williams, CBE, MD, Hon DSc, FRCP, FRCS

Rector: **Dr K M Greig**, MA Oxon, PhD Edinburgh

Senior Depute Rector: Mr M Martin, BSc Hons

Bursar: Mr I T Keter, BA, CA

Depute Rectors (Secondary School):
Mr C Bagnall, MA, MA
Mr D G Campbell, MA Hons, MEd Hons, MSc
Mrs G Fergusson, MA, MEd
Mr J McDougall, MA Hons

Depute Rectors (Primary School):
Miss F Macphail, BA, MBA
Mrs C Hatfield, BEd Hons
Miss H Gibson, BEd

Heads of Departments:
Art: Mrs S Breckenridge, BA Hons
Biology: Mr A Kerr, BSc Hons
Chemistry: Mr P H B Uprichard, BSc Hons
Classics: Mrs E Carey, MA Hons, BA
Drama: Mrs V Alderson, DipSD
Economics & Business Studies: Mrs C Keddie, BA Hons
English: Mr M J Symington, MA Hons
Geography: Mr C C Clarke, BSc Hons
History: Mrs M Windows, BA Hons
ICT: Ms R Housley, BSc Hons, DipCompEd
Law: Miss R Hems, MA, MEd
Mathematics: Mrs M T Fyfe, BSc Hons
Modern Languages: Mrs E M Bertram, MA Hons
Modern Studies: Mr G F Broadhurst, BA Hons
Music – Curriculum: Mr E W M Trotter, BMus Hons
Music – Performance: Mr K D Walton, BMus Hons
Philosophy: Dr P Tonner, MA Hons, MA, PhD
Physical Education:
Director of Sport: Mr S Lang, BEd Hons
Head of Boys' PE: Mr R Dewar, BEd Hons
Head of Girls' PE: Mrs K Robertson, BSc Hons
Head of Girls' Hockey: Mrs G Green, BEd Hons
Physics: Dr S Lonie, BSc Hons, MSc, PhD
Religious Studies: Mr S J Branford, MA Hons
Technology: Mr C McCormick, BTechEd Hons

Rector's Secretary & Admissions: Mrs S Burrowes and Mrs A Burns
Development Manager: Mrs C Biggart
Communications & Marketing Manager: Mrs M Campbell

Hutchesons' Grammar School is now a dynamic place of tremendous vitality and diversity, open to intelligent children from any background.

The School is situated on two campuses a mile apart in the South side of Glasgow. Approximately 900 boys and girls from 12 to 18 years attend the Secondary School in Beaton Rd and around 450 children aged 5 to 12 attend the Primary School in Kingarth Street. There is an automatic progression from Primary to Secondary for current pupils.

The last decade has seen substantial development on both sites, including a new Infant Block, Science Wing, Sports Hall, Library, dining room and classrooms. The School acquired and converted the Fotheringay Church and extended it to form a stunning new centre for ICT and music, as well an auditorium and a multi-purpose studio/ meeting room.

2009 saw the opening of the world-class Alix Jamieson Stadium, home to a floodlit Hockey pitch and an international standard athletics track, which provides an outstanding opportunity for Primary and Secondary pupils to develop sporting excellence. The nearby Auldhouse Sports Ground has additional pitches for rugby, hockey and cricket.

The curtain went up on a state-of-the-art Drama Studio with spacious practice rooms, an adaptable theatre and a cutting-edge technical gallery for Beaton Rd in 2012. This year a new purpose-built infant playground and stunning outdoor classroom was unveiled at Kingarth St.

The School prides itself on academic excellence and a welcoming family ethos. Experienced teachers produce the highest possible standards at every age group and, year upon year, results are among the best in the country. Life experience is expanded with a wealth of co-curricular activities which encourage children to grow as individuals, developing valuable skills and friendships that can extend past the school gates into university and beyond.

Admission. Pupils are normally admitted on interview at age 4/5 and by examination at age 9/10 to the Primary School or at age 11/12 to the Secondary School, but applications for vacancies at other stages are welcomed.

New pupils normally start at the beginning of the academic year, but intermediate entries are possible from time to time where circumstances dictate.

Fees per term (2014–2015). Primary £2,798.33–£3,212.67. Secondary 1–2 £3,566.67. Secondary 3–6 £3,476.67. All fees from Primary 1 to Secondary 2 include books.

Financial Assistance. The School offers financially means-tested bursaries by competitive entry for entry to S1.

Religion. The School is non-denominational, but many pupils opt to attend regular Christian, Muslim and Jewish assemblies. The School also hosts interfaith events and Religious Studies are taught in S1 and S2.

Curriculum. We aim to provide a happy, purposeful environment for the academic, social and emotional development of all pupils at Hutchesons'.

The foundation for excellence starts at Primary 1 with a tailored and comprehensive curriculum.

In the early years, a strong emphasis on Mathematics and Language forms the foundation for confident and successful development and subjects include Social Studies, Health and Well-Being, Science, Technology and Religious and Moral Education. Pupils benefit from specialist teaching in Art, PE and Music from Primary 1. ICT specialists teach P4–P7 and a range of Modern Languages is introduced in P5–P7.

The rich mix of drama, musical productions, sport and many extra-curricular activities enriches the more formal areas of the curriculum, providing all pupils with the confidence and skills to move on to the next stage of their educational careers.

A natural passion for discovery and love of learning is carefully nurtured creating a strong platform for academic success at the Secondary school.

At the first year of Secondary pupils take Art, Biology, Chemistry, Drama, English, Geography, History, Computing, Latin, Mathematics, Modern Language, Music, Physics, Religious Education, Personal and Social Education, PE/ Games and at the beginning of S1, pupils will choose a Modern Language from French, German or Spanish on which to focus in S1 and S2. In S2 the core subjects are expanded to include Product Design and Marketing, RMPS and Technology.

Pupils then follow more specialised courses leading to presentation for SQA Highers in S5. Most pupils continue into S6, which offers a wide range of courses, including further Highers (such as Philosophy and Psychology), Advanced Highers and options at A Level.

In general, pupils are prepared for universities and higher education, including Oxbridge. They are given vocational and pastoral guidance throughout the Secondary School.

Games. Rugby, Football, Hockey, Cricket, Rowing, Netball, Tennis, Golf, Badminton and Athletics. Senior years can enjoy Aerobics/Cheerleading, Basketball, Fitness, Kick-boxing and Climbing.

There is an extensive programme of after-school sports, notably Rugby, Boys and Girls Hockey, Football, Cricket and Cross-Country Running. The PE department offers a range of lunchtime drop-in sessions at the Games Hall, to which any pupil may turn up. This includes Basketball, Net-ball, Badminton and Volleyball.

Activities, Clubs and Societies. There are many co-curricular activities available to pupils throughout their time at Hutchesons', including Art, Archaeology, Chess, Chemistry, Climbing, Creative Writing Bridge, Debating, Model United Nations, J8, Photography, Film and Scripture Union. Sports include Hockey, Rugby, Table Tennis, Volleyball, Basketball, Netball, Kickboxing and Running, while Drama and Music offer various clubs, choirs, Ceilidh Band, Orchestra, Wind Band and Guitar Ensemble. A major highlight is the end-of-session Senior Show, a joint Music and Drama production involving up to 100 pupils on stage, in the orchestra and backstage. More than 500 pupils receive specialist instrumental and vocal tuition. There is also a very strong tradition of fundraising for charity, community service, Young Enterprise and The Duke of Edinburgh's Award. School pupils publish the School magazine, "The Hutchesonian", every June.

Charitable status. Hutchesons' Educational Trust is a Registered Charity, number SC002922.

Hymers College

Hymers Avenue, Hull, East Yorkshire HU3 1LW
Tel: 01482 343555
Fax: 01482 472854
email: enquiries@hymers.org
website: www.hymerscollege.co.uk

Hymers College in Hull was opened as a school for boys in 1893, when the Reverend John Hymers, Fellow of St John's College, Cambridge, and Rector of Brandesburton, left money in his Will, for a school to be built 'for the training of intelligence in whatever social rank of life it may be found among the vast and varied population of the town and port of Hull'. Although the school has remained true to its Founder's intentions, the catchment area now stretches across East Yorkshire and North Lincolnshire and the school became fully co-educational in 1989.

Governors:
Chairman: M de-V Roberts, FCA
Vice Chairman: District Judge P J E Wildsmith, LLB
S Martin, MA, FCA
J R Wheldon, LLB, MRICS, ACI ArB
Mrs B E Elliott, MSc, BN, RGN, RSCN, RHV, NNDNCert
Mrs G Greendale
Cllr J G Robinson, BA
D J Stone, BA
S G West, BA
M C S Hall, BSc
P A B Beecroft, MA, MBA
Mrs T A Carruthers
D A Gibbons, BSc, MRICS
C M Read
J M V Redman
W H Gore
Prof P G Burgess
Dr A Pathak
Mrs J Lloyd, MSc, FCIPD
R Crampton

***Headmaster*: D C Elstone**, MA Ed Mgt

Deputy Head (*Management*): A N Holman, MA Cantab

Deputy Head (*Pastoral*): Mrs A Singleton

Head of Junior School: P C Doyle, BSc

Teachers:
* *Head of Department*

Ms D Bache, BA
Miss N Batch (**Geography*)
Dr R Bennett, BSc Hons
Mrs J M Brown, BA (**Art*)
A D Cadle, BSc
Mrs C Cook, BA
P Cook, BA (**ICT*)
Mrs C Copeland, BSc
Miss L R Crawley, BA
Dr J Denton, MA (**History & Politics*)
P C Doyle, BSc
Mrs J I Duffield, BA
Mrs R Elstone, MA (**English*)
Mrs A Exley, BA
N Exley, BA
Miss H L Ferguson, BEd
Mrs J Fillingham
S R Fincham, MSc
C J Fitzpatrick, BA Ed
Dr I Franklin, BSc, PhD
Mr N Gandy, BA Hons, PGDip (**Director of Sport*)
C Gaynor-Smith, BA (**Sixth Form, *RE*)
Mme N Gibson, DEUG Lic Lyon (**Modern Languages*)
Mrs Z L Gillett, BSc
Mrs J Godber
G R Hambleton, BA
D Harrison, MA
Mrs H L Harrison, BA
D Hickman, BSc
Mr B Hollis, BSc Hons (**Psychology*)
Mrs J Huntsman
R P Huntsman, BEd
Mr A Irving, BA
Mrs H Jackson, BSc
Dr J M Jarvis, BSc
A Z Javed, MSc
M Jones, BSc
Mrs S Lord, BA
Mr J Lucas
Mrs C McDonough-Bradley, BSc
D McPherson, BA (**Latin*)
M McTeare, BA
P Meadway, BSc
Mr D Mills, BEd (**Design Technology*)
J Mutter (**Business Studies & Economics*)
Miss C Myers, BA
I Nicholls, BA (**German*)
Mrs K R Oatridge, MChem
R O'Hara, BSc
A Penny, GRNCM, ARNCM
Dr M J Pickles, MEng, ACGI, PhD
Mrs A J Powell
G Prescott, MA (**Chemistry*)
M Pybus, BMus (**Director of Music*)
Dr R Pybus, BSc Hons, MRSC
R Quick, ALCM, ARCM
A Raspin, BSc
Mrs L Raymond
Mrs T Redhead
Mrs F Rix, BA Hons
Mrs L L Roberts, MSc
P J Roberts, MA (**Biology*)
Mrs S E Rogers, BA
C J Ryan, BA, MBA
Mr I R Sanderson, MA Cantab
Mr R Shaw
Mrs S E Sinkler, BPharm
Dr A H Smith

R J Summers, BSc
E Tame, MMath (*Mathematics*)
Mrs J Tapley, BEd
N A Taylor, BA
D Thompson, BSc
Mrs L A Walmsley, BA
S J Walmsley, BA
Mrs A Webb, BA
A Whittaker, BA
Ms J Willan, MA Hons
B J Young (*Physics*)

Number of Pupils. 972.

The Junior School has 198 pupils aged 8–11. There is a full range of academic, sporting, music and extra-curricular activities.

The Senior School has 537 pupils in Years 7–11 and the Sixth Form has 237 pupils.

Admission is by competitive examination at ages 8, 9 and 11, together with an interview with the Headteacher. Most pupils proceed at age eleven into the Senior School by an examination taken also by pupils from other schools. Almost all pupils qualify for the Sixth Form through GCSE results. Pupils from other schools are admitted to the Sixth Form on the basis of good GCSE results.

Pupils are prepared for the GCSE in a broad curriculum including music, business-related subjects, computer studies, technology and the arts.

There is a full range of courses leading to AS and Advanced Level examinations, and special preparation is given for Oxford and Cambridge entrance.

Facilities. The buildings consist of 35 classrooms, 11 specialist laboratories, a 30-booth language laboratory, extensive ICT facilities, audio-visual room, art rooms, theatre, Art/Design Technology Centre, a gymnasium and very large sports hall. A new Music Block opens in September 2014 providing a full range of music facilities including a Recital Hall, Rehearsal and Music Technology Rooms and a Recording Studio. The Junior School building contains 9 classrooms and specialist rooms for music, DT, art, ICT and science, along with a library, hall and changing rooms. The grounds, which extend for over 40 acres, include an all-weather hockey pitch, 12 tennis courts and a swimming pool/sports centre.

Extra-Curricular Activities. All pupils are strongly encouraged to participate in the very wide range of extra-curricular activities. The main school games are rugby, cricket, hockey, netball, tennis and athletics. There are also school teams in swimming and fencing. The school regularly competes at national level in these sports and provides members of county and national teams. Many pupils take part in the Duke of Edinburgh's Award Scheme and the school has an impressive track record in Young Enterprise. Other clubs include ACF, chess, debating, photography, community service and journalism. Drama is particularly strong, with several productions a year. Music is a major school activity; there are three full orchestras, a large choir, and several chamber groups in each part of the school. Individual tuition is available in most instruments.

Fees per term (2014–2015). (including textbooks) Senior School £3,333; Junior School £2,775–£2,931. Hymers Bursaries are awarded at ages 8, 9, 11 and 16.

The Old Hymerians Association, c/o Alumni Relations Manager, Hymers College, Hull HU3 1LW.

Charitable status. Hymers College is a Registered Charity, number 529820-R. Its aims and objectives are education.

Immanuel College

Elstree Road, Bushey, Hertfordshire WD23 4EB
Tel: 020 8950 0604
Fax: 020 8950 8687
email: enquiries@immanuel.herts.sch.uk
website: www.immanuelcollege.co.uk

Motto: *Torah im Derech Eretz* (Jewish learning leading to secular success)

Immanuel College is a selective, co-educational day school founded in 1990 by the late Chief Rabbi, Lord Jakobovits to fulfil his vision of an educational establishment that affirms orthodox Jewish values and practice in the context of rigorous secular studies. The College aims at giving its pupils a first-class education that encourages them to connect Jewish and secular wisdom, to think independently and to exercise responsibility. Its ethos is characterised by attentiveness to individual pupils' progress, high academic achievement and the integration of Jewish and secular learning. There are both Jewish and non-Jewish teachers at the school, the common element being enthusiasm for their work and concern for their pupils.

Board of Governors:
Mr Edward Misrahi, BA Econ Hons (*Co-Chairman*)
Professor Anthony Warrens, BM, PhD, FRCP, FRCPath, FEBS, FHEA (*Co-Chairman*)
Mr Richard Werth, BSc Hons, ACA (*ViceChairman*)
Mr Anthony Pins, FCA (*Treasurer*)
Mrs Lynda Dullop, BA Hons (*Director of Admissions, Parental Liaison / Fundraising & PR*)
Mrs Annette Koslover, LLB (*Designated Child Protection Governor*)
Mr Andrew Baker, MA
Mr Michael Dangoor, BSc Hons
Mrs Ruth Hoyland, BSc Hons
Mr Tim Isaacs, BSc Econ, ACA
Dr David Kennard, PhD, MBA, MRPharmS
Mrs Erica Marks, BA Comb Hons, MBA
Lord Jonathan Mendelsohn, BA Hons
Mrs Michelle Sint, MA
Rabbi Eliezer Zobin, MA

Bursar & Clerk to the Governors: Mr Adam Harris, BSc, FCCA

Head Master: Mr Charles Dormer, MA Cantab

Deputy Head, Pastoral Care and Pupil Progress: Mrs Beth Kerr, BSc
Deputy Head, Jewish Life & Learning: Rabbi David Riffkin, BA, MA

Assistant Masters and Mistresses:
* *Head of Department/Subject*
§ *Part-time*

§ Mrs Rosina Abrahams, BSc (*Specialist Mathematics Tutor*)
Mr Paul Abrahams, BA (*Assistant Head – Operations & Examinations, French & Spanish*)
Mrs Naomi Amdurer, BA (*English, French, Spanish, Deputy Head of Middle School*)
§Mrs Elisa Angel, BA (*English*)
§Mrs Alison Ardeman, BA (**Art & Design – Fine Art*)
Rabbi Amos Azizoff (*Jewish Studies*)
Mr Danny Baigel, BA (*Jewish Studies*)
Miss Laura Beer, BA (*Year 1 Teacher, Prep School*)
Mrs Anna Blain, MA (*Geography*)
Mrs Saadia Bokhari, BSc (*Chemistry*)
Mr Mario Brzezinski, BSc (**ICT, Senior Teacher*)
Mrs Gemma Buckland, BSc (*Prep School*)
Mrs Samantha Childs, (*Prep School*)

Mr Nicky Cleaver, MSCi (*Mathematics*)
*Mrs Lorraine Conetta, BEd (*PE*)
Mr Bradley Conway (*Jewish Studies, DoE Coordinator*)
Mr Alex Coope, MA (*Philosophy and Ethics*)
Mrs Kirsti Cullen, BSc (*STEM Coordinator*)
*Mr Steven Da Costa, BA (*Business Studies*)
§Mrs Ruth Davis, BA (*Mathematics*)
Mr Nick De Carpentier, BA (*Geography*)
Miss Talya Dullop (*Prep School*)
Mr David Dwyer, BA (*D&T, Electronics*)
§Ms Laurel Endelman, BA, MA (*PSHE, Drama &
Theatre Studies, Head of Middle School*)
*Mrs Nicola Fahidi, BA (*Modern Languages*)
Mrs Elizabeth Feigin (*Jewish Studies*)
Mr Richard Felsenstein, BA (*Assistant Head – Community
& Communication, History*)
Mrs Naama Fialkov, Montessori Certified
Mrs Nerys Fielden, BSc (*Geography*)
§Mrs Sue Fishburn, BA, RSA Dip SpLD (*Teaching &
Learning*)
Miss Katie Fisher, BSc (*Year 2 Teacher, Prep School*)
§Mrs Joanna Fleet, BA (*Drama & Theatre Studies, Head
of Upper School*)
Mrs Rochelle Freedman (*Prep School*)
Miss Jacyn Fudge, BSc (*Phase Leader for Early Years &
Key Stage 1, Prep School*)
Mrs Alexis Gaffin, BEd Cantab (*Head of Prep School*)
§Mr Nicholas Garman, BA (*Music*)
Mrs Maureen Gatsky, Sp LSA (*Teaching and Learning*)
Mr Mark Gavin, BA, MA (*Economics*)
§Mrs Alison Gellman, BEd (*Reception Teacher*)
Mr Joshua Gershuny, FdA (*Mediat Studies Teaching
Assistant*)
§Mr Michael Gillis, BSc, MA (*Biblical Hebrew*)
Mr Zach Gold (*Informal Jewish Studies*)
Mr Adam Gooch (*Teaching and Learning*)
Mrs Amanda Goodman (*Assistant Librarian*)
§Mrs Yaffit Gordon, BSc (*Mathematics*)
Mrs Dawn Goulde (*Photography*)
Mrs Judith Graham, BA (*Director of Sixth Form, History,
Government & Politics*)
§Miss Naomi Grant, BA (*English*)
Mrs Laura Hill, BA (*History, Government & Politics*)
§Mrs Bettina Jacobs, BA (*Art & Design – Fine Art*)
Mrs Susan Jager, NNEB (*Prep School*)
§Mrs Naina Kanabar, BSc (*ICT*)
Mrs Leora Kaye, BA (*Informal Jewish Studies*)
Mr Jonathan Kerridge-Phipps, MA (*English*)
Mrs Sheerelle Labi, (*Informal Jewish Studies*)
§Ms Natalie Lancer, MA (*Director of Higher Education*)
Ms Janine Lewinton, BA (*English & Learning Support*)
§Dr Eleanor Lipman, PhD, BSc (*Science*)
Mr Daniel Littlestone, MSc, (*Deputy Head of Mathematics*)
Miss Helen Lord, BSc (*Girls' Physical Education*)
Mr Eli Mamane, BSc (*Physics, Mathematics, Electronics*)
Mrs Jane Marks (*Prep School*)
Mr Samuel Millunchick (*Informal Jewish Studies*)
§Mrs Jaime Minter-Green, BSc (*Physical Education*)
Mr Phil Monaghan, BA (*PE*)
Mrs Sue Muswell, BSc, MSc, MSB (*Physics*)
§Mrs Mazal Nisner, BEd (*Modern Hebrew*)
Ms Kalpana Patel, BA, MBA (*Mathematics*)
Mrs Anne Pattinson, BA (*Deputy Head of English*)
Mrs Loukia Peara, BSc (*Science*)
Ms Sarah Perlberg, BA (*French*)
§Mrs Emma Phillips, BSc (*Sociology*)
Mr Felix Posner, BSc (*Head of Science*)
Mr Lee Raby, BA (*Physical Education*)
Mr Stephen Radford, MA (*Science*)
§Mrs Melissa Resnick, BSc (*Psychology*)
Mrs Rosalind Reindorp (*Teaching and Learning*)
Miss Susan Ribeiro, BA (*Deputy Head of Lower School
Art, Joint Head of Year 7*)

Mr Lee Rich, BA (*Assistant Head – Teaching Quality,
Pupil Tracking & Staff Development, History*)
§Mrs Sara Russell (*Prep School*)
§Mrs Michelle Sacker, BSc (*Science*)
Mrs Vardit Sadeh-Ginzburg, BA, MA (*Modern Hebrew*)
Mrs Lily Schonberg, BA, BSc Ed (*French*)
Mrs Sharron Shackell, BA (*History*)
Mr Ellis Sharpe (*Teaching and Learning*)
§Mrs Claire Shooter, BA (*Spanish*)
Mr Gordon Spitz, BA, HDipEd, MA (*English*)
§Mrs Helen Stephenson-Yankuba, BSc (*Psychology*)
Mr Jonathan Sumroy, BA (*Year 3 Teacher prep school*)
Mrs Martine Travers (*Careers*)
Mrs Dawn Trober, Sp LSA (*Teaching and Learning*)
Mrs Camilla Turze, BSc (*Biology*)
Mrs Deborah Unsdorfer, BSc (*Deputy Head of Jewish
Studies*)
Miss Neha Vadera, BA (*Art & Design – Photography*)
Mr Charles Wakely, BSc (*Assistant Head – Timetable &
Curriculum, Physics*)
§Mrs Annette Weinberg, BSc (*Mathematics*)
Mrs Sara Wolman, BSc (*Mathematics*)

Librarian: Mrs Janet Leifer, MA, MCLIP

*Director of the Beit HaMidrash and Sixth Form Jewish
Studies (Jewish Study Centre)*:
Rabbi Eliezer Zobin

Visiting Music Staff:
Mrs Samantha Cooper, BA (*Singing*)
Mr Lewis Fisher, BA Hons, ATCL (*Pianoforte*)
Mr Richard Herdman, BA (*Guitar & Guitar Ensemble,
Bass Guitar, Acoustic/Electric*)
Mrs Noam Lederman (*Percussion*)
Mrs Rebecca Randall, FTCL (*Violin, Viola and String
Quartet*)

Age Range. 4–8 and 11–18. The Preparatory School
opened in September 2011 and now includes Reception,
Year 1, Year 2 and Year 3 classes.

School Roll. There are 475 pupils on roll, of whom 210
are girls and 265 are boys. There are 105 pupils in the Sixth
Form.

Buildings and Grounds. The College is situated in a
tranquil 11-acre site dominated by Caldecote Towers, a
Grade II listed 19th-century mansion. Facilities include The
Joyce King Theatre, a suite of science laboratories, a fitness
suite, a large all-weather surface for tennis and netball,
cricket and football pitches, and grounds for field events and
athletics. Professor Lord Winston opened a new multi-functional 8-classroom building in September 2010, and a further building programme commenced in 2013 for an
enhanced Jewish Learning facility (Beit Midrash), additional classrooms and state-of-the-art laboratories.

Admission (Senior School). Most boys and girls enter in
September, though pupils are accepted in all three terms.
Admission into the Senior School is on the basis of performance in the College's entrance examination and interview.
The principal entry is at 11+, but the school considers pupils
for admission into all year groups. A number of boys and
girls join the College in the Sixth Form; offers of places are
gained by interview and are conditional upon GCSE results.

Admission (Preparatory School). Admission into
Reception and Year 1 is on the basis of informal assessment
consisting of a play session and a focus activity. For Year 2
there will be a short maths activity and a reading/writing
task. During the academic year 2014–15 the College will be
considering applications for admission into Reception, Year
1, Year 2 and Year 3 for the academic year 2015–16.

Fees per term (2014–2015). Senior School: £4,999;
Lunch £258. Preparatory School: £2,800; Lunch £162.

Scholarships and Bursaries. Immanuel Jakobovits
Scholarships are awarded up to the value of 100% of fees on
a competitive basis to ten outstanding 11+ entrants. These

awards are subject to a yearly review throughout a pupil's time at the College. Exhibitions to the value of £2,000 per annum are awarded to pupils who show exceptional promise in Art or Music. Means-tested bursaries are awarded to a number of boys and girls from less affluent families who are academically and personally suited to the education the College provides.

Curriculum. The articles of the College's faith are that Jewish and secular learning shed light on one another, that the study of each is deepened and appreciated by study of the other, and that the life of the mind and spirit should not be compartmentalised but embraced. As such, the school offers a wide range of secular subjects, including English, Mathematics and the Sciences, as well as Art and Design, Drama, Geography, Modern and Biblical Hebrew, Electronics, History, ICT, French, Spanish, Music, Personal, Social and Health Education, Photography, and Physical Education. At A Level, additional subjects include Business Studies, Computing, Economics, Further Mathematics, Government & Politics, History of Art, Media Studies, Psychology and Sociology. Throughout a pupil's time at Immanuel, Jewish Studies forms part of her or his core curriculum. Jewish philosophy, history and religion are studied principally by way of close textual learning but there are also guest speakers and seminars developing *Chochma* (wisdom) and Israel Education. All members of the College have informal and formal opportunities to deepen their understanding of Jewish faith and practice with members of the school's Jewish study centre, the Beit Midrash.

Pastoral Care. The College prides itself on its attentiveness to the needs of individual pupils. The Pastoral Team includes Form Tutors and Heads of Section, who in Years 7 to 11 work under the direction of the Deputy Head for Pastoral Education and Pupil Progress. The Director of Sixth Form is in charge of a team of Form Tutors. Parental consultation evenings take place regularly. The School Council, which meets fortnightly with the Deputy Head for Pastoral Education and Pupil Progress and the Head Master, gives pupils the opportunity to express their views and make suggestions about improving school life.

Religious Life. The College commemorates and celebrates landmarks in the Jewish and Israel calendar such as Purim, Chanukah, Succot and Yom Ha'atzmaut. Each January, on Holocaust Memorial Day, Lower Sixth Form students share the knowledge and insights that they have gained on their trip to Poland with pupils in the first five years of the Senior School. The College also commemorates Yom Hazikaron. Pupils attend morning and afternoon prayers on a daily basis.

The **Academic Support Department** offers courses that enable pupils to become independent and successful learners. In addition to the programme followed by all pupils, the department provides small group teaching to a range of pupils whose learning needs are more specific. Pupils with a variety of learning profiles are thereby helped to develop confidence and do justice to their potential.

Art, Music and Drama. The College enjoys a tradition of excellence in the visual arts (the annual Gottlieb Art Show being the highlight of the artistic year) and drama (recent school productions have included *Macbeth, An Inspector Calls, The Happiest Days of Your Life, Pygmalion, The Trojan Women* and *Twelfth Night*). There is a yearly Music Festival and the calendar includes a number of concerts and recitals involving soloists, ensembles and orchestra.

Games. The PE and Games staff involve pupils in activities that range from aerobics, golf, and trampolining to athletics, cricket, football, hockey, table tennis, netball, badminton and tennis. Over twenty sports clubs meet weekly. Physical Education may be studied for GCSE and A Level. Sports facilities include an all-weather surface and a fitness suite.

Enrichment activities. The many co-curricular activities on offer include opportunities for pupils to participate in leadership programmes, volunteering schemes, the Duke of Edinburgh's Award, public-speaking and debating competitions. There are also clubs in philosophy, chess, art, science and modern European languages.

Educational Journeys. In Year 7 pupils visit Amsterdam; in Year 8 they visit Paris; in Year 9 they spend four weeks in Israel; in Year 10 they visit Jewish families in Strasbourg and Madrid; and in the Lower Sixth they spend eight days in Poland. These experiences encourage pupils to bond with one another and help them to understand the forces that have shaped contemporary Jewry. History of Art and Photography students benefit from trips to Florence and Paris.

Careers. The careers guidance provided by the College enables pupils to research the choices open to them after completing their formal education. Year 11 pupils may undertake testing for the Morrisby Profile, which assists the decision-making process by identifying their innate abilities and strengths, whilst students in the Lower Sixth Form undertake two weeks' work experience. Year 8 pupils participate in the 'Take Your Child to Work' scheme. Language students may undertake work experience in Strasbourg and Madrid.

Charitable status. Immanuel College is a Registered Charity, number 803179. It exists to combine academic excellence and Jewish tradition in a contemporary society.

Ipswich School

Henley Road, Ipswich, Suffolk IP1 3SG
Tel: 01473 408300
Fax: 01473 400058
email: enquiries@ipswich.suffolk.sch.uk
website: www.ipswich.suffolk.sch.uk

Motto: *Semper Eadem.*

The School was founded in about 1390 by the Ipswich Merchant Guild of Corpus Christi. Its first Charter was granted by Henry VIII and this was confirmed by Queen Elizabeth I.

At Ipswich School we pride ourselves on a passion for learning, and the care and attention we give to our pupils. Through these we help our pupils to unlock their potential and develop their talents.

Visitor: Her Majesty The Queen

Governing Body:
K Daniels (*Chairman*)
N C Farthing, LLB, (*Vice Chairman*)
D E Bertram-Ralph, BSc Econ
C D Brown, MA
J A Caudle, LLB
D A Chivers, BA, DipPM
The Revd Dr G M W Cook, MSc, PhD, FIBiol, FRSC
Mrs Elizabeth Garner, MEd, BA, PGCE
Dr Orla Goble, MBBS, DRCOG, DFFP, JCPTGP
Mrs R E Gravell, MEd, BA
E B Hyams, BSc Eng, ACGI, CDIPAF, MIET
J W Poulter, MA
A C Seagers, BA
N H H Smith, MA, FCA
Dr A M Spencer, BA, MPhil, PhD
H E Staunton, BA, FCA
Rt Revd Dr D Thomson, MA, DPhil, FSA, FRSA, FRHists
   (*Acting Bishop of St Edmundsbury & Ipswich*) (*ex officio*)
Professor C M Temple, BSc, MA, DPhil, CPsychol, AsFBPS
Dr R A Watts, MA Oxon, DM Oxon, FRCP

R P E Wilson, MA, ARCM

Headmaster: N J Weaver, BA, MA

Senior Deputy Head (Pastoral): Mrs A Cura, BSc
Deputy Head (Academic): T Allen, BSc
Head of Sixth Form: L G D'Arcy, MChem
Head of Middle School: A R Bradshaw, BA
Head of Lower School: B Cliff, MA
Chaplain: The Revd A C Winter, BSc

Heads of Houses:
J W Orbell, BSc
S J Blunden, BA
D J Beasant, BA
Mrs P M Adcroft, BEng
Ms A Caston, BSc
Mrs J B Christie, BSc

Heads of Department:
Mrs Z Austin, MA (Psychology)
S J Boyle, BA (Middle School Careers)
A M Calver, BSc (Sixth Form Careers)
Ms J S Clarke, BA (English)
Miss S Holden, BA (Curriculum PE)
M J Core, BSc (Mathematics)
Miss K Hutton, BA, MEd (Classics)
Mrs M O Davis, BEd (Art and Design)
S J Duncombe, BA (Design Technology)
Mrs O Tollemache, BA (History)
A M Dejonwo, BSc (Biology)
D J P Halford-Thompson, BSc (Chemistry & Science)
D J Hacker (Director of Sport)
S W Parry, BMus (Music)
J A Thompson, MA (Modern Languages)
S A Arthur, BEng (Physics)
E Wilson, BEd (Economics & Business Studies)
Ms T Walker, BA (Religious Studies)
Mrs L Ward, BEd (Drama)
R G Welbourne, BA, FRGS (Geography)

Head of Preparatory School: Mrs A H Childs, BA QTS,
    PGC PSE, DipEd, MA

Bursar: P Wranek
Director of Admissions: Mrs Y M Morton
Headmaster's PA: Mrs R G Connor

Ipswich School occupies an attractive site adjacent to Christchurch Park. The cricket field lies within the perimeter of the school buildings and a further two sports sites, Notcutts playing fields and Ipswich School Sports Centre (Rushmere) are owned by the school locally.

There are 749 pupils in the Senior School (11–18), including 41 boarders. Of these, 226 boys and girls are in the Sixth Form. There are 283 pupils in the Preparatory School (2–11).

The Boarding House stands in its own grounds a short distance from the school. There is a choice of full, weekly and occasional boarding for pupils in the Senior School.

All academic subjects have been housed in new or refurbished rooms in the last few years and visitors comment on the quality of the buildings, which are grouped around one of the School's playing fields.

The Preparatory School is housed in purpose-built accommodation on an adjacent campus; it benefits from all the amenities of the Senior School including the Sports Hall, Swimming Pool, Performing Arts Centre and Playing Fields. (For further details, see entry in IAPS section.)

Admission. Entry to the Preparatory School after Nursery is by means of an assessment. Pupils must show language and number skill levels that are above their chronological age and acceptable behaviour. The main entry to the Senior School at 11 is by examination in English, Mathematics and a Reasoning test, taken in late January/ early February. At 13, more pupils enter the Senior School,

taking the Common Entrance Examination in June or the School's own Entrance and Scholarship Examination in March. Admission to the Sixth Form for girls and boys from other schools is by attainment of the required grades at GCSE, a report from the previous Head and an interview in November. Application forms may be obtained from the Director of Admissions. A registration fee of £50 is payable (£25 for brothers or sisters).

Religious Education. There is religious education throughout the age range and weekly chapel services for different sections of the school; pupils normally attend one Sunday service a term at which their parents are also most welcome.

Careers. Computer analyses of interests and aptitudes complement carefully planned advice about GCSE and A Level choices, higher education and professional training.

Curriculum. In the Preparatory School pupils study English, Mathematics, Languages, French, ICT, History, Geography, Philosophy, Religion & Ethics, Science, Music, PE, Art and Design Technology and PSHE.

Senior School pupils follow a common curriculum in the first two years with a choice between French and Spanish, plus Classical Civilisation in Year 7 and Latin in Year 8. German or Russian are introduced in Year 9. Mathematics and English are taken at IGCSE, one or more Modern Foreign Languages and separate Sciences are taken by all pupils to GCSE level. Apart from these compulsory subjects, pupils are examined in three other subjects chosen from French, Latin, History, Geography, German, Russian, Spanish, Drama, Design and Technology, Classical Civilisation, Art and Design, Philosophy, Religion and Ethics, and Music.

In the Sixth Form AS and A Level subjects are chosen from the following:

Mathematics, Further Mathematics, Physics, Chemistry, Biology, Latin, Classical Civilisation, Economics, Business Studies, Art, Design Technology, Music, History, Geography, English, French, German, Russian, Spanish, Psychology, PE, Philosophy, Religion and Ethics, and Theatres Studies.

In addition to their A Level studies, all Sixth Formers participate in an Enrichment Programme designed to complement and broaden the conventional curriculum. Students are also able to gain qualifications in a range of subjects such as Critical Thinking, ICT, Mandarin, Politics, Photography, Law and Spanish, and the Extended Project Qualification (EPQ).

Clubs, Trips and Activities. All are encouraged to participate in a variety of co-curricular activities which take place in lunchtimes, after school, at weekends and during the holidays. One afternoon a week is devoted to a host of community service activities, such as music and drama in the community, conservation work, CCF (Army and RAF contingents) and a variety of sports and other pursuits. Sixth Formers may participate in the School's Leadership Programme at this time.

Drama in the school is particularly strong; continuous activity in this sphere maintains a succession of productions throughout the year, in all age groups. Productions in 2013–2014 included: Medea, Beauty and the Beast, The 39 Steps and The Long Road.

Ipswich School Britten Faculty of Music has an impressive reputation as a place where musicians thrive, finding unstinting support from expert staff. There are ample opportunities for music-making, including Symphony, Intermediate and Chamber Orchestras; Chapel Choir; Schola Cantorum; Show Choir; Choral Society; Chamber Music Groups; Ensembles for Brass, Flutes, Clarinets and Saxophones; Big Band, Stage Band, Jazz and Rock Bands. Tours have taken the Chapel Choir to residencies in Durham, Salisbury, Winchester and Wells Cathedrals, and visits to Poland, Switzerland and Italy as well as singing Evensong in St Paul's Cathedral, London. In 2014 the Chapel Choir became the first visiting school choir to sing Evensong at King's College, Cambridge. Our annual concerts at Snape Maltings have featured Britten's Spring Symphony and St Nicolas, Elgar's Dream of Gerontius ("a towering achievement"), Duruflé's Requiem and Alexander L'Estrange's "Ahoy!" and "Zimbe", acclaimed by the composer himself as "superb". The Music Faculty offers an annual residential Summer Music Course, while the Preparatory School runs its own Summer Strings course. Our annual Festival of Music brings world-renowned musicians into the school environment. Highlights in 2014 include Vivaldi's The Four Seasons performed by La Serenissima, The Full English Quartet with guests Megson and a Jazz Night with Alan Barnes.

The School runs a successful Duke of Edinburgh's Award Scheme. In 2014 there were 79 pupils who entered the Bronze Award, our highest-ever number of participants from one year group. A number of pupils in 2014 completed their residential section of the Gold Award, participating in a community project in Leh, Northern India. In 2015, there will be Silver expeditions to the Wye Valley and Gold expeditions to Southern Snowdonia.

Games. The main team games for boys are rugby, hockey and cricket and for girls, hockey, netball and athletics. Alternatives for many in the Senior School include rounders, cross-country, golf, tennis, Eton fives, football, squash, polygym, sailing, badminton, swimming and windsurfing. Skiing parties travel overseas each year. The Mermagen Sports Hall provides facilities for a wide range of indoor sports and is part of a complex which includes a cricket gallery, whose indoor nets function as a centre of excellence for the county as well as the school. There is a heated indoor swimming pool, three covered Eton fives courts, two squash courts and a twenty-two station fitness suite. Within a short distance from the School are the School's other sports grounds. Notcutts has extensive pitches for rugby, football, rounders and cricket. At our Rushmere Sports Centre there are three new (Sept 2014) state-of-the-art hockey astroturf pitches, two of which are floodlit and two in the Olympic blue and pink colours, plus six netball courts (Sept 2014), four of which are floodlit, and six tennis courts (four floodlit); the Centre also has the school's second sports hall. There is a further astroturf pitch for hockey at Westwood, the school's Boarding House.

Fees per term (2014–2015). Day: Senior School £4,351; Lower School £3,969; Preparatory School: £3,448 (Years 4–6), £3,626 (Year 3 inc lunch); Pre-Preparatory School (Reception, Years 1 & 2) £3,309 (inc lunch); Nursery (inc lunch): £28.96 (am/pm session), £54.75 (whole day).

Boarding (inclusive of tuition fees): Full Boarding: £8,054 (Years 9–13); £7,024 (Years 7 and 8); Weekly Boarding: £7,296 (Years 9–13); £6,487 (Years 7 and 8).

Scholarships. These are available for external candidates at 11, 13 and 16. Academic Scholarships, known as Queen's Scholarships commemorating the Royal Charter granted to the School by Queen Elizabeth I in 1566, of up to half fees are awarded on the basis of examinations and interviews at 11 and 13. Music and Art Scholarships at 11 and 13 are awarded on the basis of excellence in these areas as demonstrated by audition or portfolio. Music auditions for promising instrumentalists entering Years 7 and 9 are held in January/February. A Sports Scholarship at 11 is awarded to a pupil who will make a significant contribution to the quality of sport at the school and an All-rounder Scholarship is available at 13.

Sixth Form Scholarships are awarded for academic excellence, for exceptional musical talent and for an all-rounder who will do well academically and contribute outstandingly in other areas of school life such as sport or drama. Academic Scholarships are awarded on the basis of school reports, predicted GCSE grades, interview and scholarship essay. Sixth Form Music Scholarship auditions are held in November. A Sports Scholarship is also available at 16. We also offer Arkwright Scholarships, which focus on Design Technology, and Ogden Trust awards, which are open to pupils from State Schools wishing to study Maths and Physics. The Ogden Trust awards are restricted to those whose parents have a relatively low income.

Awards may be supplemented by bursaries in cases of proven need.

Bursaries. These are available on a means-tested basis, up to full fee remission, for entry at 11, 13 and 16.

The Old Ipswichian Club. Annual dinners are held in London and Ipswich. There are clubs for cricket, fives and golf. Teams are fielded against the school in several sports and the Club holds many social events each year.

Charitable status. Ipswich School is a Registered Charity, number 310493. It exists for the purpose of educating children.

James Allen's Girls' School (JAGS)

East Dulwich Grove, London SE22 8TE
Tel: 020 8693 1181
Fax: 020 8693 7842
email: enquiries@jags.org.uk
website: www.jags.org.uk

Governing Body:
Sir Hugh Taylor, BA Hons, KCB (*Chair*)
Ms Simonetta Agnello Hornby, Dr Juris, Solicitor
Mr David Levin, BEcon, MA Hons, FRSA
Mr David Miller, MA Hons, FCSI
Professor John Moxham, MD, FRCP
Ms Helen Nixseaman, MA Hons, FCA
Mrs Jane Onslow, MA Hons
Mrs Frances Read, MA Hons, FCA, MSI
Ms Sarah Tunstall, BA Hons
The Hon Dr Rema Kaur Wasan, MA Hons, MBBS, MRCP, FRCR

Clerk to the Governors and Bursar: Miss Sarah Buxton, MA Hons, ACA

Headmistress: Mrs Marion Gibbs, CBE, BA Hons, MLitt, PGCE Bristol, FRSA

Deputy Head: Mrs Deborah Bicknell, BSc Hons Durham, MEd Belfast (*Biology*)

Teaching Staff:
* Head of Department

Mr Christopher Adams, BSc Hons KCL (*Physics*)
Miss Helen Adie, BA Hons London (*Drama and English*)
Mrs Luisa Alonso, BA Hons Durham (*Spanish*)
Mr Arvind Arora, Staatsexamen Germany (**German*)
Mrs Vikki Askew, MA Hons Edinburgh (*History, Head of Sixth Form*)
Miss Eleanor Baker, BA Hons Oxford (*Chemistry*)
Miss Rachel Barnes, BA Hons Belfast (*Religious Studies*)
Miss Sarah Barr, BSc Hons London (*Geography*)
Mrs Wendy Barratt, BSc Hons Kent (*Biology*)
Mrs Corrine Barton, BA Hons Sheffield
Miss Charline Besançon, Licence-Maîtrise Strasbourg
Mrs Joanna Billington, BA Hons Middlesex (**Drama*)
Mr Timothy Billington, BA Hons London (*German, Critical Thinking, ICT*)
Ms Katherine Bishop, BA Hons Cambridge (*English*)
Ms Kirsty Bradley, MChem, BSc Hons Leeds (*Chemistry*)
Mrs Monica Buckley, BA Hons Oxford (**History & Politics*)
Dr David Burns, BSc Hons London (*Economics*)
Mr Andrew Carter, BA Hons Central St Martin's (*Art*)
Mrs Fabienne Collombon-Branson, Licence-Maîtrise France (*French*)

Miss Louise Cook, BA Hons Wolverhampton
(*Technology*)
Miss Elinor Corp, BA Hons Bristol (*Music*)
Mr Paul Davies, BSc Hons Newcastle (*Physics*)
Mrs Caroline Davis, ARCM (*Music*)
Ms Kay Dickson, GRSM, Dip RCM London (*Music*)
Ms Melanie Duignan, MA Manchester (*English*)
Dr Matthew Edwards, BA Hons, PhD Bristol (*English*)
Mrs Rachel Edwards, BA Hons Cambridge (*English*)
Mrs Catherine Ferrar, MA Hons Cambridge (*English*)
Mrs Katharine Firth, BA Hons CNAA (*Art*)
Miss Rachel Furlonger, BA Hons Oxford (*Classics*)
Mrs Clare Gene, Licence LCA Paris (*French*)
Mrs Sally George, BA Hons London, MA London
(*Russian*)
Ms Karen Giles, BSc Hons York (*Biology*)
Miss Chantal Gilou, BA Hons Norwich School of Art (*Art*)
Ms Sara Glover, BSc London (*Mathematics*)
Mrs Clare Grant, BSc Hons Sussex (*Chemistry*)
Mr Michael Grant, MA Royal College of Art (*Art*)
Mr Peter Gravell, BA Hons Oxford (*Physics*)
Mr Peter Gritton, BA Hons Cambridge (*Music*)
Mr Thomas Hamilton-Jones, BA Hons Oxford
(*Economics*)
Mrs Saltanat Hanif, BA Hons Cambridge (*Classics*)
Mrs Elizabeth Head, BA Hons Brighton (*Physical
Education*)
Mr Andrew Hicklenton, BSc Hons Southampton (*Physics*)
Miss Joanna Hill, BSc Chichester (*PE*)
Ms Alison Holmes-Milner, BA Hons York (*English*)
Miss Yihuan Huang, MSci Imperial (*Chemistry*)
Mrs Nicola Hunt, BSc Hons UCL (*Biology*)
Miss Wendy Johnson, BEd Hons London (*Physical
Education*)
Mrs Anna Jones, BA Hons Nottingham (*English*)
Mrs Ruth Jones, BA Hons Durham, MA Southampton
(*Classics*)
Mr Stuart Labran, BA Hons Leeds (*Religious Studies*)
Ms Georgina Legg, BA Hons Sussex (*French*)
Mrs Deborah Lewis, BA Hons Sheffield (*Religious
Studies*)
Ms Lorna Macleod, BA Hons Bristol, MBA Warwick
(*French*)
Ms Sarah Macpherson, MA Hons Edinburgh (*History &
Politics*)
Mrs Giulia Marchini, Dottoressa Bari (*Italian*)
Mrs Ann Massey, BA Hons Oxford (*History, SENCO*)
Mrs Emma Mayo, MA Cambridge (*History, Head of Years
7–9*)
Ms Paula McCormick, BA Hons London (*Design
Technology*)
Mrs Sonia McGarr, BA Hons KCL (*Classics*)
Miss Holly McKinlay, BA Hons Bristol (*Drama*)
Mrs Lara Meeran, BEng Hons London (*Design
Technology, *Careers*)
Ms Lola Merino, BSc Hons London (*Spanish*)
Mrs Jessica Millar, BSc Hons Nottingham (*Mathematics*)
Miss Lucy Mitchell, BA Hons Oxford (*Geography*)
Mrs Alice Mollison, MA Hons Edinburgh (*Geography*)
Mr Daniel Monks, BA Hons Keele (*Music*)
Miss Fiona Murray, BEd Hons London (*Physical
Education, Assistant Head*)
Miss Catherine Newsam, BSc Hons Bristol (*Mathematics*)
Miss Angela Newton, MSc LSE (*Chemistry*)
Mr Roger Nicholls, BSc London, MSc London
(*Mathematics*)
Mr Hiroshi Okura, BA Waseda, Tokyo (*Japanese*)
Mrs Gillian Oxbrow, BSc Hons Exeter (*Mathematics*)
Miss Elizabeth Parker, BSc Hons London (*Biology*)
Mr John Pattison, BSc Hons Newcastle, MA Lancaster
(*Mathematics*)
Miss Jessica Payne, BA Hons Hull (*Drama*)

Miss Samantha Payne, BA Hons Central St Martins (*Art,
Head of Years 10 & 11*)
Dr Howard Peacock, BA Hons Oxon, MPhil London
(*Classics & Philosophy*)
Mrs Natalie Plant, BSc Hons Bristol (*Mathematics*)
Miss Jane Quarmby, BA Hons Bristol (*English*)
Mr Kenelm Richardson, MA Cambridge (*History &
Politics*)
Ms Irene Riddell, BA Hons Glasgow (*Art*)
Miss Nicola Roden, BSc Hons Bristol (*Biology*)
Mrs Sally Ann Rosier, BSc Hons Durham (*Physics*)
Ms Natalia Rukazenkova-Cleverly, MPhil Cambridge, BA
Cambridge (*Mathematics & *PSHCE*)
Miss Cristina Sanchez-Satoca, BA Hons Barcelona, MA
London (*Spanish*)
Mrs Frances Shaw, MA Oxford (*Classics & Philosophy*)
Mr Andrew Tait, MA Middlesex (*Music*)
Miss Gina Thomson, BA Hons Brighton (*Physical
Education*)
Mrs Marta Totten, BA Hons Bergamo (*Italian*)
Mrs Kate Trefusis, BA Hons Manchester (*History of Art*)
Miss Stella Turner, BSc Hons Nottingham (*Mathematics*)
Ms Anne-Marie von Lieres, BA Hons Paris (*French*)
Mr Robert Wallace, MA Birmingham, MBA Nottingham
(*Design Technology, Assistant Head*)
Mrs Tracey Walton, BSc Hons Cambridge (*Mathematics*)
Miss Heather Webb, MA Oxford (*Chemistry*)
Mrs Ksenia Wesson, BEd Hons Krasnoyarsk (*Russian*)
Mr Laurence Wesson, BSc Hons London (*Biology &
Science*)
Miss Angela White, BA Hons Brighton (*PE*)
Miss Roberta Zuric, BA Hons Greenwich (*Drama*)

Librarians:
Mrs Elen Curran, BA Hons Reading, Dip Lib, MCLIP
(*Senior Librarian*)
Mrs Susan Stacey, BA Hons Manchester (*Library
Assistant*)
Mrs Nel Yiend, BA Hons Exeter, ACLIP (*Library
Assistant*)

Head of Finance: Mr Kevin Barry, ACA
Registrar: Mrs Henrietta Kiezun, BA Hons Keele
PA to Headmistress: Ms Sarah Thomson
Communications Director: Mrs Alison Venn, BEd Hons
Cambridge
IT Operations Manager: Ms Justine Addison

School Nurses:
Mrs Karen Cattanach, RGN
Ms Jacqui Martin, RGN
Mrs Helen Mandefield-Chang, RGN

The school was founded in 1741 as part of the Foundation of Alleyn's College of God's Gift and is the oldest independent girls' school in London.
JAGS is set in 22 acres of grounds in North Dulwich,
with extensive playing fields and long-established Botany
gardens. The school buildings include a well-equipped modern library, 13 science laboratories, a purpose-built suite of
language laboratories, 6 art rooms, 4 computer rooms,
design technology workshops, new indoor swimming pool,
floodlit artificial turf pitch, dance studio, sports hall with
squash court, fitness studios and a climbing wall, a profes-
sionally-managed theatre and a music school. The Sixth
Form Centre has its own tutorial rooms, common rooms and
lecture theatre. A new two-storey dining hall and teaching
block opened in 2008.
There is a four-form entry at 11 and JAGS senior school
has about 800 pupils with 200 in the Sixth Form. About a
third of girls come up from our junior department, James
Allen's Preparatory School (qv) with about two-thirds entering from other preparatory and state primary schools.
Girls follow a broad curriculum with a wide choice of
GCSE/IGCSE options, structured to ensure a balanced pro-

gramme. Advanced Level courses are available in all the usual subjects as well as Classical Civilisation, Greek, Latin, Russian, Spanish, Italian, Japanese, Economics, Philosophy, Physical Education, Politics, Music and Theatre Studies. Art is a particular strength throughout the school. The Pre-U English course is followed.

The extra-curricular programme is a key part of the JAGS education. The excellent Prissian Theatre enables first class, full scale drama productions, while the active music department plays a central role, offering some 30 ensembles including 6 choirs, 4 orchestras, brass ensembles, wind ensembles plus jazz and big bands. A great variety of other interests is encouraged, from The Duke of Edinburgh's Award, debating, photography, and the Literary Society, to Politics and Amnesty International. Study visits to Russia, France, Germany, Italy, and Spain are regularly organised. The choirs, orchestras and sports teams also visit overseas. Community Action plays an important part in school life, and there are extensive partnership activities with other local schools and community groups.

Sports: Hockey, netball, football, aerobics, basketball, gymnastics, dance, tennis, rounders, swimming, athletics and self-defence are taught in the curriculum, with opportunities for yoga, fencing, rugby, badminton, sailing, ice skating and golf.

Individual lessons in Instrumental Music and Speech and Drama are available (fees on application).

Fees per term (2014–2015). £5,080.

Admission. Girls are mainly admitted at 11+ and also into the Sixth Form. Casual vacancies at other ages. Registration fee: £50.

Entrance Examination. Every candidate for admission will be required to pass an examination, graduated according to age. For details and method of admission, please visit www.jags.org.uk.

Scholarships and Bursaries. Up to twenty Foundation Scholarships are awarded every year to girls of 11 years of age on entry to the School. There are also Scholarships on entry into the Sixth Form. Scholarships are awarded for academic ability, but are also available for Music and Art. Music Scholarships are on the same basis as academic scholarships but also include instrument tuition. Candidates must satisfy the academic requirements of the school and pass an audition. All Scholarships are augmented by a means-tested element where there is need. Major and Minor Sports Exhibitions are also awarded at 11+ each year.

Following the demise of the Government Assisted Places Scheme, the School has introduced James Allen Bursaries to continue to enable talented girls from families of limited means to enter JAGS. Fee support up to 100% is available.

Charitable status. James Allen's Girls' School is a Registered Charity, number 1124853 and exists for the purpose of educating girls.

The John Lyon School

Middle Road, Harrow, Middlesex HA2 0HN
Tel: 020 8515 9400
Fax: 020 8515 9455
email: enquiries@johnlyon.org
website: www.johnlyon.org

Motto: *Stet Fortuna Domus.*

The John Lyon School was established as a Day School in 1876 under the Statutes made by the Governors of Harrow School, in pursuance of the Public Schools Act, 1868.

Foundation Governors: The Governors of Harrow School

Governors:
Mr J F R Hayes, MA, FCA (*Chairman*)

Mr A P McClaran, BA Hons
Prof J S Chadha, BSc, MSc
Mr J R Davies, MRICS
Mr J H Dunston, MA, ACIL, FRSA
Mr R Fox, LLB Hons
Mr A R C Fraser, MBE
Mr K W B Gilbert, BA, FCA
Mr J B Hawkins, MA (*Head Master, Harrow School*)
Dr S Jollyman, MB ChB, DCH, DRCOG, DFFP, MRCGP
Mr I Kendrick, BEd Hons
Mr G Stavrinidis, BSc, MBA, DipM
Mr J Mark Stroyan, MA, LLB
Mrs S Symonds
Mr D Tidmarsh, BSc Hons, PGCE

Clerk to the Governors: The Hon Andrew C Millett, MA, 45 Cadogan Gardens, London SW3 2AQ

Head: Miss K E Haynes, BA Hons, MEd, NPQH

Bursar: Mr M E Gibson, BA, MSc

Deputy Head: Mr S Miles, BMus, ARCO, ARCM, AMusLCM, NPQH

Assistant Staff:
Mr J E Ahsan, BA (*Classics*)
Mr S J K Andon, BA, MSc (*Mathematics*)
Mr J A Armstrong, BA, MA (*Politics*)
Mrs F Attar, BA (*Learning Support*)
Miss F J Baldwin, BA (*Religious Studies*)
Mr P D Berry, BA (*Spanish*)
Ms S C Blanchard, Bac (*Learning Support*)
Miss A R Bolland, BA Hons (*Classics*)
Mr D P Boylan, BEd (*Business Studies*)
Mr M L Broughton, BA Hons (*Physical Education*)
Mr K R Brown, BMus, ALCM, FRSA (*Music*)
Mr J D Bruce, BSc (*Geography*)
Mr L D Budd, BA, MA, Dip SpLD AMBDA (*Learning Support*)
Mr M A Bulmer, BA (*Drama*)
Ms S L Capponi (*English*)
Mr P M Clarke, BA, MSc (*Mathematics*)
Dr C J Clews, BA, MA, PhD (*History*)
Mr E R Collard-Walker (*Art*)
Mr P J Cowie, BA, MA (*Classics*)
Mr O Damree, BSc (*Chemistry*)
Mr T P Dennehy, BA (*Physics*)
Ms A Y Douglas, BA (*Spanish and French*)
Mr L E M Evans, Dip Mus (*Music*)
Mr A K Ferguson, BA (*French and Spanish*)
Mr P T Fernando, BA Hons, MLitt (*Economics*)
Mr R J Finch, BA Hons (*Economics*)
Mr C M Grey, BMus, MA, LRAM (*Music*)
Miss C Harrison, BA, MA (*English*)
Ms L Hope, Dip VA (*Art*)
Mr A Hurst, BSc (*Biology*)
Mr G R Iveson, BA, MA (*English*)
Miss A N James, BSc Hons (*Chemistry*)
Mr C D James, BSc (*Biology*)
Mr A L Jones, BSc (*Physical Education*)
Mr T J Lewis, MA (*Mathematics*)
Mr A S Ling, BSc (*Physical Education*)
Ms J C Lin, MA, BA (*Chinese*)
Miss K M Littlefield, BSc Hons (*Geography*)
Mr C K Longhurst, BA (*History*)
Mr T J Mahon, BSc, MA, BSc (*Physics*)
Mr R E Marshall, BND (*Music Technology*)
Mrs E M McMillan, BSc, MSc (*Psychology*)
Mr J M McNaughton, BSc (*Mathematics*)
Dr M A Mellor, BA, MA, PhD (*English*)
Mr J C A Moore, BA, MA (*History*)
Mr M J Noble, BA (*French and Spanish*)
Mr K G Paradise, BSc (*Physical Education*)
Mr I R Parker, BSc (*Physical Education*)
Mr J W Peel, BA (*English*)

Mr J O Pepperman, MA (*History*)
Mrs L S Plummer, BA (*Religious Studies*)
Mr S Rana, MSc (*Biology*)
Dr K S Sudhakar, BSc, PhD (*Mathematics*)
Mr F Troublé, BA, MA (*French*)
Miss A M C Twomey, BA Hons (*Drama*)
Mr L A Ulakanathan, BSc, MSc (*Biology*)
Mr M W Vickery, BEng (*Mathematics*)
Mr J F Walker, BSc, MSc (*Physics*)
Mr D F Weedon, MA (*Chemistry*)
Mr A S Westlake, BA, MA (*Religious Studies*)

Visiting Music Staff:
Mr C Avison, BMus (*trumpet*)
Mr R Boyle, AGSM (*guitar, guitar ensemble*)
Mr V E Davies, BMus (*horn, euphonium, trombone, tuba*)
Mrs S Evans (*flute*)
Mr T Godel, Dip (*bass guitar*)
Mr C M Grey, MA, BMus, LRAM (*piano, violin, Chamber
   Ensemble, String Ensembles, Grade V Theory*)
Mr T Hooper, BMus Hons Perf, LRAM (*drums &
   percussion*)
Mr P Huntington, BA (*drums & percussion*)
Mr J Kingston, BMus Hons, PGCE, DipMusCH FCSM
   (*Piano*)
Mr R E Marshall, BND (*drums & percussion, electric
   guitar*)
Mr L Rao (*electric/acoustic guitar*)
Mr H Ridgeon, BMus Hons, PG Dip LRAM (*violin, viola*)
Mrs J Warren, Dip TCL, PGTCL (*cello*)
Mr R Whitehead, MA, BMus Hons (*trombone, trumpet*)
Ms E Armour (*voice*)
Miss K Samways, BMus Hons (*saxophone, clarinet*)
Mrs V Koleva-Burova, BMus Hons, AVCE/BTEC (*piano*)

PA to the Head: Mrs J Blake

There are 580 boys in the School, all day boys.

Admission. The School is open to boys residing within reasonable travelling distance.

There are places each September for boys at 11+ for Year 7 and 13+ for Year 9. An entrance examination is set in January. There is also automatic entry into the Sixth Form for boys who have six A*–B grades at GCSE.

Registration Fee: £100.

Fees per term (2014–2015). Years 7 to 11: £5,386 (including lunch); Sixth Form: £5,188. Key textbooks are covered within these figures.

Curriculum. The School Curriculum at present includes Religious Studies, English, History, Geography, Economics, French, Spanish, Latin, Ancient Greek, Business Studies, Mathematics, Chemistry, Physics, Biology, Art and Design, Music, Drama and Theatre Studies, ICT, Government and Politics, Classical Civilisation, Psychology and PE. Religious teaching is non-denominational.

Examinations. Boys are prepared for GCSE and IGCSE. In the Sixth Form four subjects are normally chosen to be studied for AS level in the first year leading to three (or four) A2 levels in the second.

Scholarships. Scholarships normally provide for £500–£2,000 remission of tuition fees.

All boys who sit the 11+ and 13+ entrance examination in January will be considered for Academic and All-Rounder Scholarships; their performance in the examination, current school report and interview will all be taken into consideration. Additional Academic Scholarships are available to Sixth Form entrants on the basis of outstanding performance at GCSE.

Consideration is given to candidates at 11+, 13+ and 16+ of outstanding potential and ability in Art & Design, Drama, Music and Sport. Separate applications need to be made for 11+ and 13+ awards by 31st October for entry the following September and for 16+ awards by 31st January for entry the

following September. Potential candidates are called for selection interviews and tests as appropriate.

Bursaries. Bursaries up to the value of a full place are available, subject to financial assessment.

Term of Entry. Normal entry date is in the September term.

School Buildings. The School Buildings are on the West side of Harrow Hill and include the usual facilities. Regular additions have been made. In 1973 a wing was built as part of a Development Plan, allowing for the reorganisation and modernisation of existing buildings, which was completed in 1974. In 1981 Oldfield House was built to accommodate the first two years and in 1989 a new assembly hall/theatre/classroom complex called the Lyon Building came into use. A Sports Complex comprising an indoor swimming pool and sports hall was opened by HRH The Duke of Edinburgh in February 1997. Recent developments include a new catering extension in January 2012. A new Sixth Form Centre was opened in September 2012 in the restored Old Building, the original 1876 School house.

Games. The School playing fields are within 10 minutes' walk on the south side of the Hill. In addition, the School is able to use the Harrow School Athletic Track, Golf Course and Tennis Courts.

The main games are Association Football in the Winter Terms, Cricket and Athletics in the Summer Term, supported by Badminton, Tennis, Basketball, Archery, and other games. PE and Swimming are in the curriculum.

Out of School Activities. Boys are strongly encouraged to play an active part in a wide range of activities. There is a School Orchestra, a Junior Orchestra, a Wind Band, a Jazz Band, large and small choirs. Drama, as well as being taught in the curriculum, is developed through House and School Plays. There is the normal range of School Clubs and Societies.

The School takes an active part in the Duke of Edinburgh's Award Scheme and has a full-time Head of Outdoor Education. The School's CCF operates in conjunction with Harrow School.

Community Service has been developed through various projects which are undertaken in the Harrow Area. Each year the school devotes considerable time to fundraising for a Charity chosen by the boys.

Careers. Advice on Careers is given by the Head of Careers. Specialist advice concerning entrance to Higher Education is given. Morrisby testing is undertaken.

The Old Lyonian Association. The Old Lyonians' Association was founded in 1902. All boys on leaving the school from the Sixth Form become life members of the Association. The Association has its own ground and pavilion at Pinner View, Harrow.

Entries to Universities. The Upper Sixth on average consists of 70 boys who will usually apply for Degree courses at leading Universities and of these the great majority are successful.

Charitable status. The Keepers and Governors of the free Grammar School of John Lyon is a Registered Charity, number 310033. The purpose of the charity is the education of boys living within reach of Harrow between the ages of 11–18.

Kelvinside Academy

33 Kirklee Road, Glasgow G12 0SW
Tel: 0141 357 3376
Fax: 0141 357 5401
email: rector@kelvinsideacademy.org.uk
website: www.kelvinsideacademy.org.uk

Motto: ΑΙΕΝ ΑΡΙΣΤΕΥΕΙΝ

The Academy was founded in 1878. Since May 1921, it has been controlled by the Kelvinside Academy War Memorial Trust, which was formed in memory of the Academicals who gave their lives in the War of 1914–18. The affairs of the Trust are managed by a Board of Governors, mainly composed of Academicals and parents.

The Governing Body:
Chairman: Mr N Fyfe
Mr C Neill, BA (*ex officio*)
Mr K Cairnduff
Mrs E M Davis, BA Hons, PGCE
Mr C J MacKenzie, LLB, DIP LP, NP
Mr N J McNeill, CA
Mr C Rutherford, FCIBS, MBA
Mrs A McDowall, LLB Hons, Dip LP
Mrs J Rowand, FIRP
Professor W Cushley, BSc, PhD, FSB
Mr D Wilson

Secretary to the Governors: Mr D Pocock, FInstAM, MCGI

Rector: **Mr R J Karling**, MA, MBA

Deputy Rector: Mr A J Gilliland, BSc

Academic Deputy: Ms L Thrippleton,

Senior School Staff:

Mrs J Cunningham, BMus Hons	Mrs B Meikle, BA
Mr R W J Moir, BEd	Mrs J Hardy, MA
Mr A G Mulholland, BSc	Mrs N Mathews, BA
Mr D J Wilson, BEd	Mrs J Rynn, BSc Hons
Miss S Crichton, BMus	Mrs F Kennedy, BEd
Mr J Gilius, MA	Mrs L Fitzgerald, BSc
Mrs J B Shields, MA	Mr N Reid, BSc
Mr J I O Cuthbertson, BSc	Miss L Bruce, BSc
Mrs A Schneeberger, MA	Mrs J Clark, BA
Mrs H Jephson, MA	Mr G Guile, BSc Hons
Mr I Nicholson, BSc	Mr B Parham, BSc Hons
Mr S Connor, BEng	Mr B FitzGerald, MSci
Mrs J L Hannah, BA	Miss S Jeen, MA Hons
Mr S Klimowicz, MA	Mrs A Gallie, BA Hons
Mr C Lawson, BEd	Mr J Calder, MA Hons, PG Dip, PGCE
Mrs A Mullan, BA Hons	Miss R Fleming, MA Hons
Miss K Leckie, BSc Hons	Miss L Preston, BA Hons
Mrs F Caffola, BA Hons	Mr C Simpson
Mrs F Whittle, BMus	Mr D O'Neil
Mrs D Macgregor, BSc	

Head of Junior School: Mr A Dickenson, MA Hons

Junior School Staff:

Mrs M Jeffrey, DPE	Mrs E Laird-Jones, BSc
Mrs A Stevenson, BEd	Mrs L Hill, BEd
Mrs L L McColl, BEd	Mrs G Flanigan, BEd
Mrs A McAllister, BEd	Mrs S Marshall BEd
Mrs E Henderson, BEd	Ms L Jackson, BEd
Mrs S Paterson, BEd Hons	Mr C MacDonald, BEd
Mrs S Rodger, BEd Hons	Mrs N Anderson
Mr N Armet, BSc	

Nursery School Staff:
Mrs T Nugent, BEd Hons (*Nursery Leader*)

Mrs J Hartley	Mr A Docherty
Mrs P Argue	Mrs J Pettigrew
Miss M McNeil	

Bursar: Mr D Pocock, FInstAM, MCGI
Director of Admissions and Communications: Mrs K Bottomley
Development Manager: Mrs E Solman
Marketing Officer: Mrs C Howison / Mrs L Young
Head of Digital Learning: Mrs J S Maclean, BEd Hons
SSI: Sgt M McAlister

Kelvinside Academy is a co-educational day school for some 580 pupils, aged 3 to 18.

The main building is in neo-classical style and Grade A listed but has been extensively modernised within. Further buildings and extensions provide excellent facilities for all subjects and interests, and are symptomatic of the school's progressive approach. Recent additions include state-of-the-art IT and multimedia suites, custom-built nursery and new sports pavilion.

Curriculum. Junior School pupils (from J1) benefit from specialist input in Art, Music, PE and Modern Languages. The Senior Prep (P7) year is a transitional year with a core curriculum taught by the class teacher but science, languages, art, music and PE are delivered by secondary specialists. Computing is a core compulsory subject up to S4.

Senior 3 and 4 pupils follow eight National 4 or 5 courses, followed by Higher and Advanced Higher courses in Senior 5 and 6.

Combined Cadet Force. The hugely popular CCF is compulsory for one year in Senior 3. Pupils embark upon the Duke of Edinburgh's Award Scheme at this stage.

Games. Rugby and hockey are the principal team games in the winter terms with athletics, tennis and cricket in the summer. A range of additional sports and games, from football to basketball and dance, is offered.

Activities. A rich programme of extra-curricular and House activities contributes significantly to the broad educational experience enjoyed by all pupils.

The Expressive Arts. Music, drama, dance and the visual arts have a central role in both the curriculum and the co-curriculum.

Fees per term (2014–2015). Nursery £1,430–£2,670, Junior School £2,320–£3,360, Senior School £3,510–£3,720.

Admission. For Nursery and P1, children undergo an informal assessment. For P2 to Senior 3, children sit an entrance test and informal interview. For Senior 4 to Senior 6, entry is by interview, school report and exam results.

Bursaries. Financial support with fees (ranging from 10%–100%) is available to P7 and Senior School pupils.

Charitable status. The Kelvinside Academy War Memorial Trust is a Registered Charity, number SC003962. The purpose of the Trust is to run a combined primary and secondary day school in memory of those former pupils of the school who gave their lives in the war of 1914–18.

Kent College

Canterbury, Kent CT2 9DT
Tel:	01227 763231
Fax:	01227 787450
email:	admissions@kentcollege.co.uk
website:	www.kentcollege.com
Twitter:	@kentcollegehm
Facebook:	/kentcollege
LinkedIn:	/kent-college-canterbury

Motto: *Lux tua via mea*
Kent College App – free to download at the appstore.

This outstanding boarding and day school is situated on the rural edge of the beautiful City of Canterbury. Students come to the school from the age of three through to eighteen. The majority of students live within an hour of the school. However, the school also has a strong and fully integrated boarding community of children from the age of seven; these children come from all over the world and add an exciting international aspect to the school. Academic, sporting and musical achievements are nationally acclaimed. Parents choose the school for its warm, friendly and welcoming nature where their children are encouraged to achieve all that they can, in a happy and supportive environment.

Governors:
Chairman: Dudley Shipton, CertEd Oxon, Dip MathsEd, Mathematical Assoc (*OC*)
Secretary to the Governors and Bursar: Mrs A C Hencher, AInstAM

(OC) *Old Canterburian*

Head Master: Dr D J Lamper, EdD Hull, BMus, MA London, AKC

Deputy Head Master: J G Waltho, MA Oxon

Director of Studies: G Letley, BA Kent

Chaplain: Revd Dr P Glass, BA Leeds, MA Cantab, PhD Leeds

Registrar: Mrs J Simpson
Head Master's PA: Miss M Lucas

Infant and Junior School:
Head Master: A J Carter, BEd
(*See entry in IAPS section*)

Facilities. The Junior and Senior schools occupy two independent sites. All of the six boarding houses are situated on site. Both of the schools are surrounded by extensive playing fields which are used throughout the school day. Modern classrooms and provision of laptops to senior school students, distinguishes Kent College as a market leader in education. Excellent sport, music and drama facilities are augmented by the highest level of teaching and coaching. The school also runs its own farm and equine unit.

Curriculum. The curriculum is aligned to the National Curriculum but a greater range of subjects is provided. It is not the aim to specialise in any one group of subjects but to provide a balanced curriculum which will give full opportunity for students to get a good grounding of general knowledge and later to develop particular talents to a high standard. We pride ourselves on being able to provide a personalised learning experience, where we can organise the curriculum to suit the child.

The International Baccalaureate is offered alongside A Levels in the Sixth Form with outstanding results in both.

Dyslexia Unit. The Dyslexia Support Centre is a haven of help for those amongst the school intake that need extra support. Students are taught all the mechanisms that they need to access the whole curriculum. Support remains a constant throughout the child's time here.

International Study Centre. Small group lessons and specific language assistance provide a useful platform for those students who arrive without an adequate level of English. These students are then integrated into the main stream classes at a pace that suits them.

Pastoral Care. The school operates closely with each student and the student's parents to ensure that there is an open line of communication. Each student is individually supported by a strong team: house parents; year heads; tutors; teachers and peer mentors all of whom take a significant interest in looking after the needs of each individual.

Religion. As a Methodist school a strong Christian ethos purveys all that the school does. Students of all faiths and no faith are welcomed in the school.

Games and Activities. The school possesses 28 acres of playing fields and a floodlit all-weather hockey pitch. The major games for boys are Rugby, Hockey, Tennis, Cricket and Athletics and for girls Netball, Hockey, Tennis, Athletics and Rounders. Hockey is a particular strength with teams regularly attaining National championship status. Representative honours is a common occurrence in all sports. The boarding community enjoys full use of the facilities in the evening with regular activities in Basketball, Football and Fitness Training. Senior pupils take part in various forms of community service in the City and the school also has its own Duke of Edinburgh's Award group. There is a full range of optional school activities, including Art, Debating, Chess, Conservation, CDT and Photography. The School has its own farm and developing equine unit which provides countless opportunities for outdoor adventure and agricultural experiences.

Music and Drama. Music and drama play an important part in the life of the school.

There are four choirs, two orchestras, a jazz band, rock groups and a variety of other specialist ensembles and singing groups. Many concerts are given each year, including the annual Carol Service in Canterbury Cathedral. The last whole-school production was *42nd Street*, which was a great success!

Admission. The usual ages of admission to the Senior School are 11, 13 and 16. Entrance Examinations usually take place in the Spring Term for admission the following September.

Fees per term (2014–2015). Day Pupils: £5,096–£5,613; Boarders: £10,132–£10,358 (full). International Study Centre: £1,300 extra.

Entrance Scholarships. The school awards academic, music, sport, drama and art scholarships to pupils for entry into Years 7, 9 and 12. Scholarships normally carry a value equivalent to a percentage remission of the tuition fees which would not exceed a maximum of 50% and would be at the discretion of the Head Master. Full particulars may be obtained from the Registrar.

Academic scholarships for Years 7 and 9 are awarded as a result of performance in our Entrance Test, usually held in the Spring Term, for entry the following September. Sixth Form academic scholarships are awarded on the basis of existing performance, a detailed report from the Head of Year or current school, and confirmation of high levels of performance in the final GCSEs.

Music/Drama scholarships of up to half the tuition fee are offered in conjunction with the Entrance Test to candidates for entry into Years 7, 9 and 12. Free tuition on two instruments is offered to Music Scholars.

Sports scholarships of up to half the tuition fee are awarded to pupils for entry into Years 7, 9 and 12. For Years 7 and 9 these will be awarded in the Spring Term in conjunction with the Entrance Test and on the basis of assessment at Kent College. For Year 12, Sports scholarships will be based on current performance and other assessment methods during the year.

Bursaries will be awarded in accordance with, and after consideration of, the financial circumstances of parents. Parents will be invited to complete a financial assessment form and the scale of bursary awarded will be based on the information provided and the financial criteria which the school applies to all bursary awards. All bursaries are reviewed annually.

In addition, the school operates an awards system for the children of HM Forces, NATO and War Graves Commission personnel, whereby the parents pay a set figure, normally 10% of the inclusive fee, plus the amount of Boarding School Allowance which they receive. The balance is treated as a Bursary Award.

Exhibitions. Means-tested awards for academic, music, sport, drama and art achievement and potential are available to children entering Year 4.

Honours. Most school leavers go on to university and a number of pupils secure offers of places at Oxford and Cambridge colleges each year.

Charitable status. Kent College, Canterbury is a Registered Charity, number 307844. The School was founded to provide education within a supportive Christian environment and is a member of the Methodist Independent Schools Trust.

Kent College Pembury

**Old Church Road, Pembury, Tunbridge Wells, Kent
TN2 4AX**
Tel: 01892 820218
Fax: 01892 820239
email: admissions@kentcollege.kent.sch.uk
website: www.kent-college.co.uk

Kent College Pembury is a leading day and boarding school for girls aged 3 to 18. A happy thriving school with high academic standards and an ethos of providing a bespoke education and outstanding opportunities for enrichment and success. The school provides for the educational and cultural needs of day students and boarders from all over the world. Set in beautiful countryside, just 35 miles from London, students benefit from innovative teaching and excellent resources in a superbly equipped environment, within a caring Christian community. All girls participate in the imaginative and extensive programme of extra-curricular activities which include various music, drama and sports clubs and other exciting activities such as film-making, scuba-diving, canoeing and clay pigeon shooting amongst others. Performing Arts and Science are major strengths of the school and the school was delighted to open a state-of-the-art Library and Art Centre in March 2013 and a Fitness Suite in September 2013. The school is accredited by HMC, GSA and IAPS.

Board of Governors:
Chairman: Mr E Waterhouse
Vice-Chair: Mrs H Alleyne

Mr R J Bamford	Mrs G Morgan
Mr J Harrison	Mr I Pattenden
Dr A Hayward	Mr D Robins
Revd J Hellyer	Mrs J Stevens
Mr J Ingram	Mr T Sturgess
Mrs G Langstaff	Revd T Swindell
Mr I Leroni	Mrs E Thomas
Mr G MacKichan	Mrs C Veall
Revd S Mann	Dr C Williams

Headmistress: Mrs S A Huang, MA Oxon, MSc, PGCE

Bursar: Mrs A Jenkins, BA Hons Aberystwyth, ACA

Deputy Head: Mr A Kirk-Burgess, BSc Bath, PGCE Oxford

Senior School Staff:

** *Head of Subject Group*
* *Head of Department*
§ *Part-time*

Mr B Allberry, HND University College Chichester (*PE*)
§Mr N Ashton, BA Hons Worcester College, PGCE London (**Drama*)
§Mr T Bailey, BSc Hons Plymouth, MSc London, PGCE Canterbury (*Science*)
Ms E A Benfield, BA Birmingham, MA London, Dip TEFL, Dip TESOL (*EAL*)
§Mrs L Bright, BTec, Dip Design (*Art*)
§Miss H Bruce, BMus Hons Edinburgh, MMus GSM, PGCE London (*Music*)
§Mrs S Caird, BA Hons Stirling, PGCE Cambridge (*History*)
§Miss A M C Church, BA Oxford, PGCE Birmingham (**English*)
§Mrs E Cliff, MBiol Bath, PGCE Wales (*Biology, Science*)
Mrs E Coddington, BA New College Oxford, PGCE Kingston (*German, Latin, Japanese*)
Dr A Cowie, BSc Hons St Andrews, DPhil Sussex, QTS (*Science*)

§Mrs J Cox (*PE, Gym & Aerobics Coach*)
Mrs C Davidson, BA Hons QTS Kent, AEP Dib Brighton (*PSHE, Head of Pastoral & Outdoor Education, Senior School Deputy DCPO*)
§Mrs J Denman, BA Hons, PGCE Durham, PG Dip Courtauld Inst (**Director of Art, History of Art, German*)
Mrs L Denning, BA QTS Roehampton (*Art*)
§Mrs N Denton, BSc Hons Loughborough QTS (*Second In Dept PE*)
Mr A Dixon, BA Hons Kingston, PGCE Canterbury (**Art & Photography*)
§Mrs J Dooley, BA Hons Kent, MA Nottingham, PGCE Chichester (*Film Studies, English*)
§Mr K Fitzell, BEd Hons Reading (*English*)
Miss S Fuller, BA Hons London, PGCE (*Geography & Head of Danes*)
§Dr J Glasspool, BSc Hons Warwick, PhD Bristol, PGCE OU (*Physics*)
Miss J Hall, BSc Hons Hertfordshire, QTS (*GTP PE*)
Mrs L Hallam, BA Hons Southampton (*Assistant Head (Lower School), Spanish*)
§Mrs M Hambleton, BA Hons Reading, PGCE London (**Geography*)
§Mrs M Haslett, CertEd London (*Food Technology*)
Mrs R A Havard, BSc Hons Roehampton (*Dyslexia Specialist*)
Miss E Hayes, MA Manchester, BA Hons Manchester, PGCE King's College London (*Classics, Latin*)
§Mr C Hayward, PGCE Leigh City, MIBiol Bromley College (*Science*)
Mrs J Hill, BSc Hons, PGCE Hertfordshire (*Second in Dept, Mathematics*)
§Mr K Hoffmann, Dip Speech & Drama Scottish Academy of Music, PGCE Glasgow (**Film Studies, English*)
§Mrs E Hooper, MA Sheffield, BA Hons Loughborough (*Film Studies, English*)
Ms D Hopper, BSc Hons Canterbury Christ Church, QTS (***Head of Sciences,*Biology*)
§Mrs A Hutchinson, BA, MA, PGCE Oxon (**Classics, Latin, Greek*)
§Mrs L Jeal, BSc Hons Exeter, PGCE Reading (*Mathematics, *Ecology & Sustainability Issues*)
Mrs J Jenkins, BEd Hons Exeter (**Mathematics*)
Mrs T Karalius, BA Hons Aberystwyth, PGCE Canterbury Christ Church (**Economics and Business Studies*)
Mr M Kent-Davies, BMus Hons Sheffield, PGCE Manchester Polytechnic (**Director of Music, Boarders Band & Services*)
§Mrs S Kruschandl, BA Hons Lancaster, PGCE Nottingham (*English*)
Mrs R Leach, BSc Plymouth, PGCE Exeter (*Mathematics, Assistant Housemistress Hawkwell & Hargreaves*)
Mr D Lee, BSc London Guildhall, QTS (***Humanities and Social Sciences,*Psychology, Gifted and Talented coordinator*)
Mrs H Levett, BA Hons, PGCE Leeds, MA York, MEd OU (**SENCO*)
§Mrs L Lewis, BSc Hons Leeds, GDL London, PGCE Greenwich (*Science*)
Miss G Lucy, BSc Hons Southampton, PGCE (*PE*)
Ms C Lusher, BA Hons Middlesex (**Food Technology*)
Mrs D Mackenzie, BSc Hons Aberdeen/George Washington, PGCE East London (*PE*)
Mrs S Mahillon-Goddard, Licence de Langues Poitiers, PGCE Hertfordshire (*French, German*)
§Mrs P Mardon BA Hons, HED, QTS CCRS (*Geography*)
Mr J Marshall, MA, BA Oxon, PGCE (*French, *German, DofE Assistant Unit Leader, Assistant Director of Studies*)
Mr H Matthews, BSc Leeds, BA Hons Cambridge, PGCE London (*Science*)
Mrs L Maule, BSc Hons Greenwich (*ICT*)
§Mrs V McVickers (*English*)

Mrs J Medcalf, BSc Hons Staffordshire, PGCE Brighton (*Science, *Chemistry*)

Mrs B Mitchell, BA Hons Durham, MA London, PGCE London (*RS, PHSCE*)

§Mrs R Mitchell, BA Hons Keele. PGCE Manchester (*Mathematics & Science Tutor*)

§Mrs C Morrice, BSc Aberdeen, PGCE OU (*Mathematics*)

Miss C Mortlock (**ICT and Business Studies, Assistant Exams Officer*)

Mr J Mossman, BA Hons, MA, PGCE King's College London (***Linguistics, *Classics, Assistant Head Sixth Form*)

§Mrs A Nieto, BA Madrid, PGCE London (**MFL, *Spanish*)

§Miss C Noyek, BA Hons Surrey, PGCE (*Dance*)

Mrs L J Oliver-Murphy, BEd Bedford College (*Weekend Boarders' Activities Director; PE; Head of Boarding, Senior Housemistress James & Osborn*)

§Mrs S Overy, BSc Hons, PGCE Cambridge (*PE*)

Mrs K Pusey, GGSM, PGCE Middx (*Second in Dept, Head of Prep School Music*)

§Mrs A Quiqley, MA Oxon, PGCE London (**Physics*)

§Mrs C Rook, BA Hons Canterbury Christ Church (*Economics and Business Studies*)

Ms K Russell, BA Hons Guildhall, QTS (*Geography*)

§Mrs E Sharnock-Smith, BA (*Drama, Peri Speech & Drama*)

Mrs C Skinner, BA Hons Kent, PGCE Lancaster (*Second In Dept, English*)

Mrs C Smith, BA Hons Somerset, PGCE Cardiff (**Textiles*)

§Mr R Starkey, BA Hons Cambridge QTS (*Mathematics*)

§Mrs D Stein, BA Hons, PGCE (*Spanish, French*)

§ Mrs C Sutton, BA Ed Hons Exeter (*PE*)

Mrs E Thacker, BA & MA Warwick, PGCE Worcester (*History*)

§Ms S Tidey (*Trampoline Tutor*)

Miss G Thorpe, BA Hons Lancaster, QTS (***Performing and Creative Arts, Second in Dept Drama, Theatre Manager, Assistant Head of Years 7–9*)

Mrs J Tobin, BA Hons, PGCE Canterbury Christ Church (**Religious Studies, DofE Assistant Unit Leader, Assistant Head of Years 10–11*)

§Ms C Waller, Acting Dip Mountview Theatre School (*Drama*)

Mr J Watson, BSc Canterbury QTS, BA Open (*Assistant Head Middle School, Science, Psychology, Housemaster James & Osborn, DCPO*)

Mrs A Wharton, BA Hons, PGCE Leeds (**Politics & History, Assistant Head of Years 12–13*)

Mr C Whyld BSc St Martin's, PGCE St Mary's (*Drama*)

§Ms W Yang, BSc Guangxi Normal University China, MSc Reading (*Chinese Tutor*)

§Mrs W Young Min, BA Hons London, PGCE Nottingham (**MFL, *French*)

plus 12 Visiting Instrumental Staff.

Chaplain:
§Revd H Matthews, BSc Leeds, BA Hons Cambridge, PGCE London

Head of Careers:
§Mrs G E Shukla, BEd Bradford College, PGCE Reading

Library & ICT:
Mrs S Waller, BA Hons Anglia Ruskin, MCLIP (***Learning & Life Skills, Librarian*)

Mrs J Manning, BA Hons (*Report Data Manager, Library & ICT Support Assistant*)

Mrs C Songhurst (*Library and ITC Support Assistant*)

Duke of Edinburgh's Award Scheme:
Mrs Carol Davidson, BA Hons QTS Kent, AEP Dib Brighton

House Staff:
Mrs L J Oliver-Murphy, BEd Bedford College (*Head of Boarding, Senior Housemistress, James & Osborn*)

Miss G Lucy, BSc Hons Southampton, PGCE (*Senior Housemistress, Hawkwell & Hargreaves*)

Mrs R Leach (*Housemistress, Hawkwell & Hargreaves*)

Miss J Hall (*Assistant Housemistress, Hawkwell & Hargreaves*)

Mr J Watson, BSc Canterbury QTS (*Housemaster, James & Osborn*)

Miss I Stafford (*Assistant Housemistress, James & Osborn*)

§Mrs V Cowan (*Relief Housemistress*)

Medical Staff:
Medical Officer: Dr P Lautch, MB BS, MA, MRCGP
Nursing Sister: Mrs J M Devine, RGN
Medical Assistant: Mrs S Greenhalgh
School Counsellor: Mrs S Jenkins

Administrative Staff:
Head of External Relations: Miss E Donovan, ACIM, BA Hons Surrey Institute (*maternity leave*)
Acting Head of External Relations: Miss K Minihane, BSc Hons Oxford Brookes, ILM Level 2
Director of Admissions: Mrs D Sainsbury
School Secretary & Cover Assistant: Mrs A Masters
Assistant School Secretary: §Mrs M Wakeford
Admissions Officer: §Mrs N Sneddon, BEd Hons Cheltenham
Marketing & Admissions Assistant: Mr D MacDonnell, BA Hons Canterbury Christ Church
Lettings and PE Administrator: Mrs A Stone, BEd I M Marsh
Receptionist: §Mrs J Gowen-Smith
Afternoon Receptionist: §Mrs L Bone
Examinations Officer, Senior Attendance Officer & Cover Supervisor: Ms A Linford
HR Administrator & Database Manager: Miss M Gow, CIPD
Secretary to the Senior Leadership Team: Mrs L Roberts

Bursar's Office:
Bursar: Mrs A Jenkins, BA Hons Aberystwyth, ACA
Finance Manager: Mrs I Scinteie, BA Bucharest
Bursar's PA: §Mrs A West, BA Hons Central St Martins
Finance Assistant: Mrs V Carter, AAT Level 3
Purchase Ledger Clerk: §Mrs N Foster, AAT Intermediate NVQ3 (*maternity leave*)
Purchase Ledger Clerk: §Ms C Krasniqi (*maternity cover*)

Technical Support Staff:
Ms J Hinton (*Senior Laboratory Technician*)
Mr C Hayward, PGCE, MIBiol Bromley College (*Laboratory Technician*)
Mr G Hougham HND Northbrook College (*Theatre Technician*)
§Mrs P Mulhere (*Design & Technology Technician*)
§Mrs S Percival (*Design & Technology Technician*)
§Mrs L Bright, BTec, Dip Design (*Design and Technology Textiles Technician*)
Miss R Boxall (*Art & Design and Technology Textiles Technician*)

Catering Manager: Mrs S Stone

Kent College Preparatory School:

Headmistress: Mrs A Lawson, BEd Hons Exeter

Deputy Head: Mr O Snowball, BA Hons Nottingham, MA Goldsmiths, PGCE London

Miss V Armstrong, BA Hons Warwick, PGCE London (*Assistant Head KS1, Year 1, ICT Coordinator*)
§Mrs S Beazleigh, BA Hons Brighton (*PE*)
Mrs S Bishop, BA Hons, PGCE Loughborough (*Learning Support Teacher*)
§Mrs L Bon, BEd Cert Hons Brighton (*Learning Support*)

§Miss L Budden, National Diploma in Counselling, NNEB Croydon College (*Play Therapist*)

Mrs H Chapman, BEd Brighton, London College of Music (*Early Years + KS1 Music Coordinator, RE Coordinator, Year 6*)

Mrs C Corp, BEd Derbyshire (*Year 3, KS1 & Early Years History & Drama Coordinator*)

Mrs A Crotty, BEd Hons (*Year 4 Teacher*)

Mrs P Dabin, CertEd London, BSc Hons OU (*Early Years Coordinator, Reception Class*)

Miss R Dalby, BA Hons Wales, BA Hons OU, PGCE (*Year 6*)

Mrs J Dearlove, BEd Hons Montreal, CertEd Canterbury (*KS2 English Coordinator, KS2 Drama, Year 4*)

§Mrs E Graham, CACHE Level 3, BA Hons Oxford Brookes (*Nursery Practitioner*)

Mrs S Hall, BSc Hons Wales, PGCE Canterbury (*Assistant Head KS2, Year 5*)

§Ms R Hood, BSc Durham, PGCE London (*Learning Support, KS2*)

§Mrs R Hunton, BSc, PGCE Goldsmiths (*KS1 Maths Coordinator, Mathematics, Year 4*)

§Mr A Knowles, BSc, MSc (*ICT*)

§Miss P Lamb, BA Hons Staffordshire, Cert Ed Keele (*KS2 Science Coordinator, KS1 Coordinator, Year 5*)

§Miss S Lawson-Wood, BA Hons Croydon (*Drama*)

Mrs A Lees, CertEd London (*Art Coordinator, Year 1*)

Mrs H Levett, BA Hons, PGCE Leeds, MA York, MEd OU (*SENCO*)

Miss G Lucy, BSc Hons Southampton, PGCE (**Prep School PE*)

§Mrs C Marnane, BA Ed Goldsmiths (*Geography Coordinator, Year 3*)

§Mrs C Snowball, BA Hons Leeds (*Drama, Head of Prep School Peri Speech & Drama*)

Miss K Soutter, Dip Montessori (*Nursery*)

Mrs K Whittle, BA Hons London College of Fashion, PGCE Southbank (*Reception, KS1 Science Coordinator, Prep School Deputy DCPO*)

§Mrs C Williams, BEd Hons (*Year 2*)

Mrs C Wilson, BEd Hons London (*French*)

Mrs T Youdale, CertEd Brighton, BA Hons Manchester (*Assistant Head Pastoral, PSHE Coordinator, Year 5*)

§Mrs E Andrews, City & Guilds Learning Support (*Early Years & KS1 ICT Coordinator, Teaching Assistant, After School Care*)

Mrs S Beard (*Early Years Teaching Assistant*)

Mrs M Cuttill, ASA Cert (*Swimming*)

Mrs A Cyster (*School Secretary*)

§Mrs B Davison, BSc Hons Southampton (*Teaching Assistant*)

§Mrs J Rhoades, NVQ Level 3 (*Teaching Assistant*)

§Mrs C Spink (*Teaching Assistant Yr 1, After school Care*)

§Ms K Warren (*Early Years Teaching Assistant*)

§Mrs J Wolton (*After School Care, Teaching Assistant*)

Administrative Staff:
Headmistress's PA: Mrs D Shepherd
School Secretary: Mrs A Cyster
Assistant School Secretary: §Mrs A Knapp

Ethos and Aims. The Prep School (ages 3–11) and the Senior School (ages 11–18) are part of a group of Methodist Schools, which have an ethos of being caring, Christian environments, and welcoming pupils from all faiths or none. Kent College is a happy school with high academic standards and pupils achieve excellent results in public examinations. With 200 girls in the Prep School and 470 in the Senior School there is a real community feel and teaching staff know each girl as an individual. Building self-esteem is at the heart of our ethos. All girls get a chance to shine, try something different, feel good about themselves and develop new and existing talents. Exciting opportunities to develop confidence are an integral part of school life: overseas music, drama and sports tours, an Australian exchange, 80 extra-curricular activities, Kent College Gym, Theatre and Swimming Academies to name a few. Our aim is to equip students with the confidence, skills and positive attitude to succeed in their examinations, at university, in their chosen career and in life ahead.

Location and Facilities. The Prep School and the Senior School share the site which is set in 75 acres of beautiful green countryside in Pembury, three miles from Royal Tunbridge Wells. It is just forty minutes to London by train and within easy reach of Gatwick, Heathrow and Luton airports, channel ports and the Channel Tunnel. The Senior School campus comprises an elegant Victorian manor house, used for offices and boarding, and purpose-built facilities include language laboratories, a music school, Sixth Form Centre, science laboratories, dance studio and onsite outdoor adventure confidence course. The Susanna Wesley Arts and Library Centre opened in March 2013 and provides an open-plan Library space, ICT areas and a coffee shop on the ground floor with art studios and offices above. The two schools benefit from an excellent range of shared facilities including a large sports hall, state-of-the-art theatre, an indoor heated swimming pool and dining hall; excellent ICT facilities include Apple Mac suite, wireless laptops and smart boards in the majority of the teaching rooms. The boarding house Hawkwell and Hargreaves is home to all boarders in Year 9 and below while James and Osborn is home to all boarders in Year 10 and above. The Prep School is based in its own modern, purpose-built building with spacious playgrounds. The Preparatory School has its own range of after school clubs and also offers supervised prep, late after prep care facility including supper and an early morning breakfast club.

(*See also Prep School entry in IAPS section.*)

Curriculum. In the first years of the Senior School all girls follow a wide curriculum which includes academic as well as creative and practical subjects. They learn keyboard skills and develop confidence in the use of computers and technology. At GCSE level, all girls take English language, English literature, mathematics, science, and select other GCSE option subjects. At 16+, girls take the two-year Advanced Level course in four subjects and all follow a structured Curriculum Enrichment programme. In addition to A Levels, students can take the prestigious Leith School's Basic Certificate in Food and Wine. All students are given extensive careers and higher education advice and academically able students are prepared for admission to Oxford and Cambridge. The majority of students proceed directly to their first-choice universities and colleges of higher education.

Sport. Sporting activities include hockey, netball, rounders, football, basketball, athletics, cross-country, fencing, horse riding, swimming, tennis, trampolining, dance and gymnastics. The school has a reputation for achievement in inter-school matches and talented athletes can enter county and national competitions. The superb facilities include an indoor heated swimming pool, sports hall, dance studio and spacious grounds with a variety of courts and pitches. The school also runs its own Gymnastics Academy.

Extra-Curricular Activities, Music and Drama. The school prides itself on offering an extensive programme of extra-curricular activities at lunchtimes, after school and at weekends which are open to day girls and boarders. Senior School pupils are expected to take part in at least two activities from an extensive list. There are frequent visits to London theatres and overseas trips and exchange visits in the holidays. The school has a reputation for high standards in music and drama. There are opportunities for girls of all ages to take part in drama productions.

Christian Community. Kent College was founded by the Wesleyan Methodist Schools' Association in 1886. The school continues to benefit from having its own resident

Chaplain. There are Christian assemblies on certain weekdays and a school service each Sunday.

Entrance. Main intakes to the Prep School are to the Nursery (aged 3) and Reception (aged 4) classes. The school will take girls into other year groups subject to places being available. Entrance is based on a place being available; however entrance into Years 3–6 pupils is based on the school's own entrance tests.

The main entries to the Senior School are at 11+, 13+ and 16+. Entrance is by the school's own Entrance Examinations, interview and a report from the previous school. At 13+ entry we also accept the Common Entrance as a means of entry. Girls wishing to study A Levels are required to gain at least six GCSE passes at grade C or above. Boarders are welcomed from age 10.

Scholarships and Bursaries. Academic, Drama, Music and Sport Scholarships are awarded to outstanding entrants at 11+. Academic, Drama, Music, Art and Sport Scholarships are awarded to outstanding entrants at 13+ and 16+. A maximum of two practical scholarships may be applied for and these may be worth up to 10% of the tuition fees.

Bursaries: Fee assistance may be offered to those applying to the senior school. This fee assistance is for those girls who would benefit from all the school offers but whose parents cannot meet full fees. Such fee assistance is means tested on application.

Fees per term (2014–2015). Senior: Day £5,975, Boarders £9,633. Prep: Day: £2,720–£4,098, Boarders £7,408. Sixth Form Entrant: £6,515. 20% discount for Forces' personnel. Discounts for sisters.

Charitable status. Kent College Pembury is a Registered Charity, number 307920. It exists for the education of children.

Kimbolton School

Kimbolton, Huntingdon, Cambs PE28 0EA

Tel:	01480 860505
Fax:	01480 860386
email:	headmaster@kimbolton.cambs.sch.uk
website:	www.kimbolton.cambs.sch.uk
Twitter:	@KimboltonSchool
Facebook:	/KimboltonSchool

Motto: *Spes Durat Avorum.*

The School was founded in 1600 and was awarded Direct Grant status as a boys' day and boarding school in 1945. Girls were first admitted in 1976. The Preparatory School (ages 4–11) and the Senior School are fully co-educational with day boys and girls (4–18) and boarding boys and girls (11–18). As a result of the withdrawal of the Direct Grant the School assumed fully independent status in 1978. There are around 300 pupils in the Prep School and 660 pupils in the Senior School. There is almost a 50:50 ratio of girls to boys.

Governing Body:
Mr C A Paull, MPhil, FCA (*Chairman*)
Mr J W Bridge, OBE, DL (*Vice Chairman*)
Mr P F R D Aylott, MA, MNI
Mr C R Boyes
Prof F Broughton Pipkin, MA, DPhil, FRCOG
Miss E M C Coles [Colonel]
Mrs S E Duberly, DL
Mr PJ Farrar, BA Hons, MA
Cllr J A Gray
Cllr Mrs S Hawkes, BSc, DIC, MBA
Mrs D A Hellett
Dr T P Hynes, BA, MA, PhD
Mrs K E S Lancaster, MC Cantab, LPC/CPE
Mr M C Neale, LLB, PG Dip

Mr S J F Page, BA Hons, Cert Ed
Mr G K Peace

Headmaster: **Mr J Belbin**, BA, FRSA

PA to the Headmaster: Mrs J Nelson-Lucas

Senior School:

Senior Deputy Headmaster: Mr M J Eddon, BSc
Deputy Headmaster (Academic): Mr C J A Bates, BA, MA
Assistant Head (Extension & Enrichment): Mr J C Newsam, MA, MEd
Assistant Head (Pastoral): Mrs C A Stokes, BEd
Assistant Head (Staff): Mrs L A Hadden, BA
Director of Activities: Mr R E Knell, BA
Head of Sixth Form: Mr A J Bamford, MA

School Chaplain: Revd L N Bland, BEd
Head of Careers: Mrs A J Bates, BA

Heads of Departments:
Art: Mrs L D Bamford, BA, MA
Design & Technology: Mr K Spencer, BEd, MSc, MInstMI
Digital Learning: Mr M Reed, MEng
Drama: Mrs B L Copeland-Jordan, BA
Economics & Business Studies: Mr J R Saunders, BA
English: Mr S K Pollard, MA
Food & Nutrition and Textiles: Mrs C E Bennett, BSc
French: Mr R E Knell, BA
Geography: Mr S Wilson, BA
History: Mr A J Bamford, MA
Maths: Mr A S Jessup, BSc, MA
Music: Mr S C Ball, MA, PGRNCM
Physical Education: Mr M S Gilbert, BEd
Politics: Mr F W B Leadbetter, MA, BD, AKC, FRSA, FRHistS
Religious Studies: Mrs L Stone, BEd
Spanish: Mr J C Gomez, BA
Director of Science: Mr A Gray, BSc
Biology: Mr A J Treharne, MBE, BSc, PhD, CBiol, FSB, FLS, FRSA
Chemistry: Mr E C Drysdale, BSc
Physics: Mr C A M Holmes, BSc, BA
Academic Support: Ms R Stewart, BEd
Outdoor Pursuits: Mr T Webster

Preparatory School:

Headmaster of Preparatory School: Mr R J Wells, BEd, BA
Deputy Headmaster: Mr O C Stokes, BEd, MEd
Director of Studies: Mrs F Y Tavares, BA, MAEd
Lower Prep Coordinator: Mrs P M Binham, BSc

Bursar & Clerk to the Governors: Mr E F P Valletta, MBIFM
Registrar: Mrs J Simpson

Mission Statement. Kimbolton School creates a caring, challenging environment in which all pupils are encouraged to fulfil their potential and are given opportunities to flourish in a wide variety of curricular and extra-curricular interests.

It provides a close family environment where young people are educated to be tolerant, socially responsible and independent of mind, equipping them for our changing world. It is a community that challenges pupils to discover their talents, develop socially and excel.

Facilities. The Senior School facilities are situated in and around the main school building, Kimbolton Castle, once the home of Queen Katharine of Aragon and for three centuries the home of the Dukes of Manchester. Now, with its Vanbrugh front and Pellegrini murals, it is a building of considerable beauty and architectural importance. The former Staterooms are study areas for senior pupils and the Castle Chapel is used each day for prayers.

The Queen Katharine Building is a state-of-the-art teaching and learning centre, complete with a 120-seat multimedia lecture theatre and six new classrooms. The School is currently constructing a complementary new two-storey Science and Maths building, and refurbishing another teaching block – both projects will be completed by September 2015. The Lewis Hall caters for the performing arts and daily assemblies and provides modern theatre and concert facilities. The Design Technology Centre is up-to-date and well-equipped, as is the ICT Centre and the Music School.

A large sports complex, incorporating squash courts, gymnasium, sports hall, multi-gym and changing rooms stands in the Castle's parkland. Closer to the Castle itself, lie a modern Art Centre, Library and an indoor swimming pool. The School has two fine all-weather hockey pitches, one of which is floodlit.

One girls' and one boys' boarding houses stand adjacent to the grounds in the picturesque Kimbolton High Street. The boarding community is an important part of the School.

The Prep School is located on its own site. A major rebuilding programme was completed in 2007 providing new classrooms, changing rooms and a hall for music and drama. There is also a gymnasium plus specialist science and information technology rooms. The 4–7 age range is housed in the purpose-built Aragon House.

Admission and Organisation. The Prep School admits children at the age of 4 or 7 (as day pupils) who are expected to complete their education in the Senior School. Entry at other ages is sometimes possible. Tests for entry at the Prep School are held in February. Entry into the Senior School at the age of 11 is open to boarders and day pupils; the Senior School Entrance examinations are also held in February. There are significant entries at 13+ usually by the Common Entrance Examination in June. Those not preparing for Common Entrance may sit the School's own 13+ examination in February. Entry into the Sixth Form is based on interview and GCSE results.

Arrangements can be made for overseas candidates to take the Entrance Examination at their own schools.

Pupils are accepted in September at the start of the academic year, but a few places may be available for entry in other terms.

The relationship between the Prep and Senior Schools is a close one and contributes to the strong 'family' atmosphere of the whole School. In the Senior School, there are four senior houses and one junior house. It is an important element of our pastoral care that boarding pupils and day pupils are together – there are no day houses. Housemasters/ Housemistresses, assisted by Tutors, look after the general well-being and progress of their charges.

Work and Curriculum. For the first two years in the Senior School there are four parallel forms; in each of the third, fourth and fifth years there are five smaller forms with sets for some subjects. Boys and girls aged at 13 join one of the five Third Forms. An option scheme is introduced in the Fourth Form. In the Sixth Form specialisation occurs, and pupils will usually study four subjects from the following list: English Language and Literature; English Literature: History; Geography; French; Spanish; Maths; Further Maths; Physics; Chemistry; Biology; Music; Art (Fine Art); Art (Critical and Contextual); Food, Nutrition and Health; Design Technology; Drama and Theatre Studies; Physical Education; Economics; Business Studies; and Politics. All Sixth Formers follow a 'Preparation for Citizenship' series of lectures, seminars and debates and may opt to take A Level General Studies. In the Upper Sixth pupils usually continue with three subjects to A Level.

Almost all leavers go on to University or to Further Education. In 2013, almost 10% of the Upper Sixth received offers from Oxbridge.

Religious Teaching. Pupils attend Chapel once a week and have RS lessons each week in the 1st to 3rd Form. Other services are held in the School Chapel during each term for pupils and parents to attend. Sunday Services are held in the Chapel and occasionally the School worships in the Parish Church.

Sport and Activities. The School owns over 120 acres of land, more than 20 of which are laid out as playing fields. The major sports for boys are Association Football, Hockey and Cricket. For girls the main sports are Hockey, Netball and Tennis. Other sports include Athletics, Gymnastics, Dance, Climbing, Archery, Swimming, Golf, Fitness Training, Rifle Shooting, Clay Pigeon Shooting, Squash, Badminton, Rowing, Basketball and Rounders. Swimming is popular with before and after school sessions and numerous galas. Extensive use is also made by the Sailing Club of nearby Grafham Water, both for recreational sailing and inter-school matches. Canoeing is popular and each year a team competes in the highly demanding 125-mile Devizes-Westminster challenge. The Equestrian Club competes in around twenty fixtures during the course of the year. The aim is to find a sport that each pupil loves and will continue to enjoy long after leaving Kimbolton.

Music and Drama play an important part in the life of the School and almost half of the pupils take lessons in a great variety of instruments. There is a Choral Society, two orchestras, several bands and many ensemble groups. The School stages plays, musicals or concerts each term.

The School contingent of the CCF is a voluntary, keen and efficient body, divided into Navy, Army and RAF Sections with a national reputation for excellence; Community Service is an alternative. There is a successful Duke of Edinburgh's Award scheme with a growing number of participants.

There are many other activities and societies that meet on a regular basis, such as debating, public speaking, Latin, Young Enterprise, forensic science, photography, chess, robotics, bookworms, beekeeping, gardening, modelling, pottery and philosophy.

All pupils are able to participate in the large number of trips in the UK and abroad.

Careers. Advice can be sought at any time by pupils or their parents from the Careers Staff, three of whom specialise in university entrance. There is a well-stocked Careers Room, and the School is a member of the Independent Schools Careers Organisation. Fifth formers take the Morrisby careers tests administered by ISCO. An annual Careers Fair is held for fourth to sixth formers.

Dress. The School colours are purple, black and white. Boys wear blazers and grey flannels (shorts until the final year in the Prep School). The girls' uniform includes a standard skirt, blouse and blazer. Sixth Formers wear a black suit.

Scholarships and Bursaries. A number of scholarships are awarded at 11+ and 13+ to candidates who perform with distinction in the Entrance Examination or in Common Entrance.

Further Scholarships, known as William Ingram Awards, may be awarded at 13+ to external candidates with strengths in music, art, games or leadership.

Sixth Form Scholarships and Exhibitions are awarded to those who achieve outstanding results in GCSE. Two Sir Brian Corby bursaries, available for pupils entering the Sixth Form from state schools, cover up to 100% of fees and may include extras.

There is a bursary scheme for deserving candidates aged 11 or over.

Fees per term (2014–2015). £2,970 (Lower Prep), £3,770 (Upper Prep), £4,615 (Senior Day), £7,685 (Senior Full Boarding), £7,185 (Senior Weekly Boarding). A 2% discount is applied if fees paid by termly direct debit.

The fees are inclusive of lunches and there is no charge for laundry, books, stationery and examination entries.

There is a reduction of 2½% in tuition fees when siblings attend at the same time.

Music Tuition Fee: £218–£245 per term for individual lessons. (Half a term's notice must be given in writing before a pupil discontinues music lessons.)

Old Kimboltonians Association. All correspondence to: Mrs H M Hopperton, Alumni Officer, OKA, Kimbolton School, Kimbolton, Huntingdon, Cambridgeshire PE28 0EA; email: alumni@kimbolton.cambs.sch.uk.

Charitable status. Kimbolton School Foundation is a Registered Charity, number 1098586.

King Edward VI School
Southampton

Wilton Road, Southampton SO15 5UQ
Tel: 023 8070 4561
Fax: 023 8070 5937
email: registrar@kes.hants.sch.uk
website: www.kes.hants.sch.uk

King Edward VI School was founded in 1553, under Letters Patent of King Edward VI, by the will of the Revd William Capon, Master of Jesus College, Cambridge, and Rector of St Mary's, Southampton. The original Royal Charter, bearing the date 4th June 1553, is preserved in the School. The first Head Master was appointed in 1554.

Patron: The Lord Lieutenant for the County of Hampshire

Governors:
B E Gay (*Chair*)
P W Brazier, BSC, FCIOB (*Vice-Chair*)
Incumbent Team Rector City Centre Parish Southampton, Revd Dr J E Davies, MA, DPhil
Dr Y Binge, MBChB
Dr R B Buchanan, FRCP, FRCR, MBBS
Dr N J England, MA, DPhil, DL
Mrs S J Mancey
Miss J C May
M H Mayes, MSc, MA, MBA
J W J Mist, FCA
A J Morgan, MA Oxon, FCA, ATII
Councillor R Perry, BA
Mrs C Pierce, DCH, DRCOG, MRCGP
B W Richards
M J Rowles, FCA
Alderman A Samuels, BA Cantab
Mrs A Steele Arnett, CertEd, PGDip, MBA
Dr A L Thomas, MA, PhD
K St J Wiseman, MA

Bursar and Clerk to the Governors: R V Maher, BA Econ, ACA

Head: A J Thould, MA

Deputy Heads:
Mrs E J Thomas, BSc
A F Dellar, BSc

Assistant Heads:
R W Allen, BSc
Mrs P E Burrows, MSc
S G Hall, BSc
Ms H Smith, BSc
Mr B M Waymark, MA

Teaching Staff:

S T Aellen, BSc	Mrs J Barnes-Wardlow,
Ms S L Allen, MA	BSc
Miss I M Anderson, MA	Miss J M Barron, BA
S J B Ayers, BA	J M R Belassie, MA
Miss E F Ball, BA	L B Berryman, MA, MM,
S H Barker, MA	PhD

Miss H G Birks, BA
D T Blow, BSc
D Brown, BA
Mrs S Burt, BA
Miss C Campbell, BA
Mrs E J Coker, BSc
P D Collins, BSc
Miss C J Costello, BSc
K P Coundley, MA
C S Crichton, BA
R J Cross, BSc
N D Culver, MA
S Z Cutherbertson, BSc
Mrs H Dean, BSc, PhD
N J Diver, MA
Miss R L Enfield
Mrs S Evans, BA
G A Eyssens, BEd
Mrs J D M Ferrand, BA
D W Filtness, MA
K A Fitzpatrick
J M Foyle, BSc
Mrs H Freemantle, MA, LLCM, ALCM
S D Gamblin, BSc, PhD
A W Gilbert, BA
C E Giles, BA
Dr V A Green, MSc, PhD
Ms R M Greenwood, MA
Mrs J Gunton, BA
J C Halls, BA
I Hardwick, BA
Mrs J M Hardwick, BA
G P Havers, BSc
Mrs L C Henderson, BEd
L J Herklots, BSc
Miss L Hewitt, BSc
G S Hunt, BSc
Srta L Ibanez Manzano
Mrs J V Jones, BA
Miss R L Jones, BA, MA, MPhil
P G Kay-Kujawski, BA
L J Kelsey, MA
D Kent, BA
M G Kukla, MA
Miss E M Ladislao, BA
G S P Lawson, MA

E T Lewis, BA
Miss M Lindebringhs, BA
M W Long, DipAD
P A Mapstone, BSc
Mrs J M Meredith, BA
Mrs L S D Millar, BSc
M P Miller, MA, MPhil
M G Mixer, BSocSc
Mrs N A Moxon, BA
R G Patten, BA
M A Paver, BSc, PhD
Mrs A H Penfold, BA
Mrs C L Piggott, BA
G L Piggott, BA
Revd J G Poppleton, BA, DipRS
Mrs R K Potter, BA
A L Powell, BSc
C W Prowse, BSc
G T Purves, MPhys, PhD
Mrs S Quinn, BA
Mrs L J Race, BA
Miss E S Ridley, BSc
P J Robinson, BEng
Mrs S Rugge-Price, MA
A J Schofield, MA
Mrs H Searles, MA
Mrs E L Sheppard, BSc
P Sheppard, BSc
R S Simm, BSc
J H H Singleton, BSc
Mrs K S Skipwith, BSc
S J Smart, BA, MPhil
Mrs S M Smart, BA
Miss G S Stenning, BA
Miss A M L Stone, BSc
J D Tesseyman, BSc
Mrs E L Thomas, BSc, PhD
Mrs S J I Thould, BA
T H Tofts, MA, DipPhil
M A Walter, BSc, MPhil
G S Westwater, BSc
Mrs C E Wikeley, MA, PhD
Mrs C F Williams, BSc
R J L Wood, BEd
Miss K J Yerbury, BSc

There are about 970 pupils in the School, of whom over 250 are in the Sixth Form.

Admission. An entrance examination is held in January for boys and girls seeking to enter the First Form at age 11 or the Third Form at age 13 last September. Applications from able under-age candidates will also be considered. Smaller numbers of entrants are accepted into the other school years if there is space, provided the applicants are of suitable academic ability. Students may also apply to join the Sixth Form. In order to qualify for entrance to the Sixth Form a student will normally be required to have grade B or above in six subjects at GCSE, including English Language and Mathematics, and A grades in the subjects to be studied at A Level.

Registration for entry may be made at any time on a form obtainable via the school website or from the Registrar, who can supply current information about fees, bursaries and scholarships.

Class sizes average 22; the average size of Sixth Form sets is 11.

Curriculum. All pupils follow a common course in the first two years: this includes French or German or Spanish with Latin, Mathematics, Science and an Extended Studies programme. In years 3, 4 and 5 all pupils study eight 'core'

subjects to IGCSE: Biology, Chemistry, English Language, English Literature, a Modern Foreign Language, Mathematics, Religious Studies and Physics. In addition there is a range of 'option' subjects: Art, Computing, Design and Technology, Economics, Geography, German, Greek, History, Italian, Music, PE, Philosophy, Sports Science, Theatre Studies and Spanish. The syllabus leading to the IGCSE Examinations, in which most pupils take eleven subjects, is designed to avoid any premature specialisation. In the Sixth Form, students may either take 3 Advanced Level subjects along with one AS course or four full Advanced Level subjects. In addition, all have an afternoon of games in both years and follow a Foundations Studies programme in both the Lower and Upper Sixth Year.

On entering the First Year pupils join a form of about 22, with a Form Tutor responsible for their general welfare and progress. The other years are organised on a system of pastoral groups of about 16. Each group has its own Year Head. In addition there is a Head of Lower School who has general responsibility for the first three years; a Head of Upper School and a Director of the Sixth Form have similar responsibilities in their respective areas.

Our aim is to provide a congenial atmosphere and a disciplined environment in which able pupils can develop as individuals.

School Activities. 10% of a student's timetable is devoted to physical education as sport and games are regarded as forming an integral part of life at King Edward's. The major sports played in the three terms are rugby, hockey, cricket and tennis for boys; and netball, hockey, tennis and rounders for girls; other sporting activities include athletics, basketball, badminton, fencing, squash, swimming and a number of other games. The School has a large sports hall and a fully equipped fitness studio and an all-weather pitch for Hockey and similar games which provides twelve Tennis Courts in Summer. There are a further 33 acres of off-site sports fields which include a second astro pitch and floodlit netball and tennis courts.

A considerable range of clubs and societies meets during lunchtime, after school, at weekends and in school holidays, catering for pupils of all ages and many differing tastes. All are encouraged to join some of these societies, in order to gain the greatest advantage from their time at the School.

In addition to a large number of sporting teams representing the School, there are such activities as charitable and community work, dance, drama, debating, chess, Duke of Edinburgh's Award Scheme, International Expeditions, sailing, collectors' clubs and music. The School has flourishing choirs, as well as orchestras and a large number of smaller instrumental groups. Art and Design and Technology occupy up-to-date premises. The studios and workshops are usually open during lunchtimes and after school. Over the past 6 years the whole school has been expanded and refurbished with modern classrooms and specialist rooms. A new 400-seat theatre is due for completion in November 2015.

Fees per term (2014–2015). £4,605. Fees can be reduced in appropriate cases by the award of Bursaries and Scholarships. Scholarships are available on entry at age 11, 13 and 16. Further Scholarships may be awarded during a pupil's career in the School. Some Scholarships are awarded for proficiency in the Creative Arts. Foundation Bursaries are available at age 11, 13 and into the Sixth Form.

Charitable status. King Edward VI School Southampton is a Registered Charity, number 1088030. The object of the Charity is to advance education and training in or near Southampton or elsewhere, including the carrying on of school or schools or other educational establishments and ancillary or incidental educational or other associated activities for the benefit of the community.

King Edward's School
Bath

North Road, Bath BA2 6HU

Tel:	Senior School: 01225 464313
	Junior School: 01225 463218
	Pre-Prep School: 01225 421681
Fax:	Senior School: 01225 481363
	Junior School: 01225 442178
	Pre-Prep School: 01225 428006
email:	headmaster@kesbath.com
website:	www.kesbath.com

King Edward's School was founded in 1552 by King Edward VI. Originally a Grammar School, the School was fully independent until 1920, when it accepted Direct Grant status, reverting to full independence in 1976. King Edward's is fully co-educational, with girls and boys from age 3–18.

King Edward's School is a busy day school, with a proud record of sustained academic achievement (98% of its pupils regularly proceed to universities and institutions of higher education). It is also committed to providing the broadest possible range of opportunities for all its pupils and a multiplicity of extra-curricular activities, trips and expeditions are on offer. The School has a strong commitment to sport, both recreational and competitive, and the arts flourish, with the Annual Arts Festival providing a showcase for talented pupils in art, music and drama.

There are currently 744 pupils in the Senior School, 185 pupils in the Junior School, and 57 pupils in the Nursery and Pre-Prep.

For over 400 years, the School occupied various premises in the city centre, but in 1961 the Senior School moved to a fine fourteen-acre site on North Road, on the south-eastern slopes of the city. This site has been extensively developed in recent years and now boasts superb facilities. The Junior School moved into outstanding new premises here in 1990.

The Pre-Prep School is situated in an elegant Victorian house on the western side of the city.

Chairman of Governors: Mrs W Thomson, MEd, BEd Hons, LLCM TD

Headmaster: Mr M Boden, MA

Second Master: Mr M J Horrocks-Taylor, BSc, MEd
Deputy Head, Academic: Mr T D Burroughs, BA
Deputy Head, Pastoral: Ms C Losse, MA
Assistant Head: Mr D J Chapman, BA
Assistant Head: Mr A M Bougeard, BSc
Assistant Head: Mrs P Bougeard, MA
Assistant Head: Mr D Middleborough
Assistant Head: Mr P H Simonds, BSc

* *Head of Department*
§ *Part-time*

Miss F Bains, BA	*Mrs B Charlton
Mr M Barber, BA	Miss T Costanza, BSc
Mr N P C Barnes, MA	§Mrs M N Davis, MA
Mrs J Blair, BMus	*Ms R Davies, BA
Mrs H Blamire, BDes	Mrs O Doughty, BA
Mr D Bloower, BSc, MBA	Mr R J S Drury, BA
Mr M Boden, MMus	Dr A M Fewell, PhD, BSc
*Mrs E Brown, BA	Mr J Garner-Richardson,
Mr G Browning, BA, BSc	BSc
Mrs L Browning, BA	Miss S Gilbert, BA
§Mrs C Bruton, BA	Miss C Goodall, BA
Mr M Bull, MA	Mrs H Graham, MA
Mr M Buswell, ME	Mrs E Grainger, BA
Mr G Butterworth, BA	*Mrs L Gwilliam, BSc
§Mrs J Chapman, BA	Mr D Hall, BA

Mr M Harrison, BSc
Miss C Hartket, BA
*Mr M Hawker, BEd
*Mr R Haynes, MA
Dr M Heywood, BSc, PhD
Miss L Hughes
*Mr J Holdaway, BEng
Miss Z Kayacan, BA
Mr J Kean, MA
Mrs A Kean, BSc
*§Dr J Knight, BSc, PhD
*Mr T W L Laney, BSc
Mrs B Lang, BSc
Mr R Lang, BSc
Mrs J Maguire
Mr M Mairis, BA
Mr P Mason, BSc
Mr J Mawer, BSc
Miss S McCronie
*Mr T G Medhurst, BEd
Miss L Miners, MSc
§Mrs T Minty, BA
Miss A Molineaux, BSc
*Mrs A Munn, BA
Mr M Oehler, BSc
*Mr R Pagnamenta, MEng
*Mr M R Pell, BA

Mr J Pendred, BA
Miss A Perrio, BSc
Mrs A Phillips, MA
Mr N D Purcell, BA, MA
Miss A Robertson, BA, MSc
Mr M Ruxton, BSc
*Mr W R Satterthwaite, MA
*Mrs J Scott-Palmer, BSc
Mrs K Simonds, BSc
*Miss V Stevens-Craig, BA
Mrs D Tamblyn, BEd
*Mr R Thomas, BA, MA
Mr J E G Tidball, BSc
*Mr A I M Vass, MA
Mr N A Vile, BSc
Dr L Wainer, MSc, PhD
Mr T West, BA
§Mrs J Wilcox, BSc
Mrs Willoughby, MSc, MEng
§Mr D Willison, BA
§Dr M Wood, PhD
§Mr D Wright, BSc
*Miss E Young, BEd

Ms L Williams, BSc, PGCE

Pre-Prep Administrator: Mrs A Fairlie

Senior School Chaplain: Revd Caroline O'Neill
Bursar and Clerk to the Governors: Mr J Webster, BSc, ACA
Registrar: Ms A Rashid
Head's Personal Assistant: Mrs L Wolfe, BA
School Nurse: Mrs C Morris, RGN
Head of PSHE and School Librarian: Mrs L Bowman, BA, MA, MLS
Finance Manager and School Accountant: Mrs N Rowlands, AAT
HR Officer and Bursar/Second Master's PA: Mrs J Howard
Development Office: Mrs C Davies, BA
Communications Officer: Mrs K Gentle, BA
Development Director: Ms K Teague, BA, MinstF
Examinations Officer: Mrs S Moles
PE Administrator: Mrs R Worsdall, BA

Junior School:
Head of Junior School: Mr G Taylor, BA Ed, NPQH
Deputy Head: Mr M Innes, BA, PGCE
Deputy Head (Pastoral): Mrs R Hardware, BEd
Mrs R Barrett, MA
Mr S Carr, BEd
Miss L Chapman, MA
Mr J Corp, BSc
Mr E Heaney, BEd
Mr M Howarth, ECB Level 3, RFU Level 2, EHB Level 1
Mrs A Jabarin, BA, PGCE
Mrs C Lewis, CertEd
Mrs E MacFarlan, BEd
Mrs G Oliver, CertEd, ASM
Mrs E Pike, BA Hons, PGCE
Mr J Roberts-Wray, BA
Mrs A Sellick, BSc
Mrs S Taylor, FD Education Studies, UKCC Level 1 Netball and Hockey, STA Level 2 Swimming, NRATCA

Junior School Administrator: Mrs N Carr

Pre-Prep School Staff:
Head of Pre-Prep & Nursery: Mrs J Gilbert, BEd Hons, NPQH
Deputy Head: Mrs D Bright, BA Hons QTS
Mr S Boydell, BA Hons, PGCE
Mrs H Blakey, BSc
Mrs J Carter, BA Hons

Buildings. The Senior School is housed in a complex of buildings. Nethersole, dating from 1830, provides accommodation for Economics and Business Studies, History, Classics and Religious Studies. The Main Teaching building comprises a Music block, the Wroughton Theatre, Physics and Chemistry laboratories and classrooms. From September 2009 a new building was added creating suited departments for the Biology Department with 3 new biology laboratories and preparation room; the Geography Department; a new ICT laboratory; and a Modern Languages suite which includes two dedicated Modern Language Laboratories. The Holbeche House houses a Sixth Form Centre with adjoining kitchen, an extended and modernised Careers and Higher Education Centre, a new Drama Studio and Art Gallery, Library and classrooms. There is also a magnificent Sports Hall, together with an artificial playing surface for hockey and tennis. A new three-storey replacement for the Willett Hall is being developed (to be completed by Easter 2015) and will combine a state-of-the-art dining room and servery on the first floor and a multifunctional second floor venue for assemblies, presentations, concerts, dance, cookery and social gatherings. The pavilion at Bathampton, completed in 1998, is surrounded by 17 acres of playing fields with a Club House.

Admission. While half the pupils come from the City of Bath or its immediate environs, nearly half are resident in the counties of Gloucestershire, Somerset and Wiltshire – a wide catchment area made possible by excellent public transport services and coaches organised by the School.

Methods of Entry. *Nursery and Pre-Prep*: From the age of 3, according to the availability of places. There is an informal assessment for entry into Year 1 and Year 2.

Junior School: From our own Pre-Prep by internal assessment and interview.

Pupils from other Primary Schools and Preparatory Schools may be offered places by examination and interview. The main entry is in Year 3 but other vacancies may occur.

Senior School: From our own Junior School by passing the Senior School Entrance Examination for 11 year-olds.

Pupils from other Primary and Preparatory Schools may be offered places on the results of the same examination held in January of each year.

Older pupils may enter the Senior School, if and where places are available, by sitting an entrance examination appropriate to their age.

Students may also seek direct entry into the Sixth Form. Such students are expected to acquire a sound set of GCSE passes before transfer for advanced study. Applicants are interviewed and a reference is sought from their present schools.

Application forms and further information concerning entry are obtainable from the Registrar. Open Days are held in the Autumn and Spring Terms.

Fees per term (2014–2015). Senior School: £4,135–£4,200; Junior School: £3,265; Pre-Prep £2,950; Nursery £2,430.

Scholarships. Scholarships to a maximum of £500 per annum are awarded at Year 7, either for academic excellence or for an outstanding special talent in art, drama, music and sport. Students who perform outstandingly at GCSE may also receive a Scholarship award. Further details are obtainable from the Registrar.

Bursaries. Income-related entrance Bursaries may be awarded to children entering Years 7 and 12, whose parents are unable to pay the full fee. A general Bursary fund is also available to assist parents during times of unforeseen family circumstances, when they may find themselves unable to fund full school fees. Further details are obtainable from the Bursaries Administrator.

Curriculum. The School is committed to breadth in education. In Years 7 and 8 all pupils are taught nineteen subjects. An options scheme in Year 9 allows some choice to be made whilst also offering the opportunity to try new subjects. By the time choices for GCSE are made, pupils have been able to find subjects which suit their strengths and enthusiasms. At A Level, additional subjects are on offer, allowing pupils to choose from around 30 courses. The AS/A2 subjects on offer are: Art, Biology, Business Studies, Chemistry, Classical Civilisation, Classical Greek, Computing, Design & Technology, Economics, Electronics (AS Level only) English Language, English Literature, French, Further Mathematics, Geography (Human and Physical) German, History, Latin, Mathematics, Music, Philosophy, Photography, Physical Education & Sports Studies, Physics, Politics, Psychology, Religious Studies, Spanish and Theatre Studies.

Music and Drama. There is a healthy musical tradition in the School. Many instrumental and choral groups afford opportunities to explore differing musical styles. The School is a centre for the examinations of the Associated Board of the Royal Schools of Music and these are held termly.

The School has an outstanding dramatic tradition, with two or more major productions a year. The splendid Wroughton Theatre, supported by a full-time technical manager, provides an outstanding facility for productions and concerts of every kind. There is in addition a purpose-built Drama Studio.

Art and Photography. Housed in an extended and modernised custom-built suite of studios, the Art and Photography Department is a centre of excellence. Teaching covers fine art, drawing and painting, ceramics and three-dimensional work, printmaking and photography. Art History and critical studies are taught as an integral part of the course and field trips and visits to galleries along with links to practising artists, are encouraged. Sixth Form Art Tours are planned annually. Every year students are prepared for interview at Art School and related courses.

Games. The main playing fields at Bathampton, comprising 17 acres, are attractively situated at one end of the Limpley Stoke valley, about a mile from the School. An All-Weather Synthetic Pitch on the main School site has proved to be invaluable for hockey and tennis, and as an intensively used practice area for all games.

The major games are Rugby Football, Hockey, Cricket and Netball. Minor sports include Athletics, Cross-Country, Tennis, Soccer, Rounders, Badminton, Golf, Basketball, Dance, Gymnastics, Table Tennis and Trampolining. Each boy or girl has a full games session per week and has ample opportunities to represent the School or to participate in a wide range of inter-Form activities.

Activities. In Year 9, pupils may opt to join the School CCF, founded in 1896 and the oldest in the West Country. The contingent has a fine record of success in regional and national competitions. The CCF provides many opportunities for adventure training and leadership and there is an Annual Easter and Summer Camp. Students can also participate in the Duke of Edinburgh's Award Scheme.

There is also a strong tradition of mountain walking and adventure training for pupils with trips to Dartmoor and the Welsh mountains. The School enters the Ten Tors Competition each year.

School Societies and Clubs. Pupils are actively encouraged to engage in the many Societies and Clubs which cater for every interest and for every age group. Frequent opportunities for travel abroad, especially during the Easter vacation, are provided by School tours or exchanges conducted by members of Staff. All pupils in Years 7–10 are involved in a residential trip during Activities Week in the Summer Term.

Pastoral Care The Deputy Head (Pastoral) coordinates the pastoral team. Every child has a Form Teacher who is at the centre of their daily life at school. Tutors work in teams managed by Heads of Year or Senior Tutors who are in turn assisted by Heads of Sector (Lower, Middle School and Sixth Form). The pastoral staff are ably supported by a School Nurse and Counsellor. The School prides itself on its family atmosphere and the excellent relationships between pupils of all ages and staff. Advice on Careers and entry to Higher Education is readily available. Parents meet Staff at regular intervals to discuss academic progress, or at social functions. Many of the latter are organised by a very active parents' group.

Dress. Boys in the Main School wear a dark blue blazer and flannels. Younger girls wear a Lindsay tartan kilt, a white open-neck blouse and the school blazer, whilst Middle School girls wear a grey skirt or grey trousers. In the Sixth Form, boys and girls wear suits of their own choosing, appropriate for formal work. Girls may wear trouser suits.

Junior School. The Junior School is an integral part of the foundation and is governed by the same Board. It joins with the Senior School in major events, such as the Founder's Day Service in Bath Abbey, and shares various games facilities and teaching staff. The curriculum is organised in close consultation with the Senior School and the Pre-Prep to ensure that education provided is continuous and progressive from the age of 3 to 18.

Its curriculum comprises English, Mathematics, Science, DT, History, Geography, Art, Music, Religious Education, Physical Education, French, German, Spanish, Drama, ICT taught to all years and Learning Skills, including Philosophy.

All children learn the strings (violin, viola, cello, double bass) in Year 3, recorder in Year 4, whole class orchestra/band and Gamelan in Year 5 and authentic Steel Pans in Year 6. Well over half of the children learn additional instruments under the tutelage of a strong peripatetic music staff. A mixture of French, German and Spanish is taught throughout the School while purpose-built facilities in Art, Science, Technology and IT, coupled with specialist teaching, ensure high standards of achievement in those areas. The Junior School has developed a reputation in the past few years for dramatic productions of the highest quality and a drama club, which runs throughout the year, is always a popular choice. This School is a very busy one renowned for its extra-curricular activities programme. The wide variety of activities on offer include table tennis, gymnastics, fencing, judo, Lego, chess and craft club. This is not to mention the various musical and instrumental groups and the many opportunities to play rugby, football, hockey, netball, cricket, basketball, tennis, rounders, cross country and athletics. All children throughout the School also go swimming at a local pool. A large number of competitive fixtures are played against other schools in a wide variety of sports and activities and each year group has their own programme of fixtures. Frequent educational trips are arranged in and around the local area and during the summer Activities Week; residential trips for Years 3–6 include destinations such as France and Devon. Sporting tours also take place each year.

The House system plays a central role in the life of the School. All children belong to one of four Houses and take part in many events and competitions during the year.

Pre-Prep School. Children are encouraged to develop academic abilities as well as personal qualities such as enthusiasm, self-motivation, persistence, empathy with other people and social skills which are vital for success in life.

The creative curriculum is designed to develop well-motivated, independent learners who have a love of learning. High staff to pupil ratios ensure learning is personalised so children can flourish. Teaching and learning is connected through exciting projects that capture the children's imagination. The children are encouraged to ask critical and challenging questions, to share their ideas and collaborate, test options and explore. Investigations, problem solving and imaginative play form part of everyday learning. Specialist teaching is provided in French, music, physical education/dance, gymnastics, games and swimming.

A large emphasis is placed on breadth of learning and first-hand experiences. School trips and visiting experts are encouraged. The children take part in two whole-school dramatic productions each year and a number of festival events.

The Pre-Prep is a Forest School. The outdoor environment is seen as an extension of the classroom and used continually throughout the day to support teaching and learning. Every child has the opportunity to visit a local forest and participate in engaging activities in a woodland environment.

A wide variety of extra-curricular activities are offered to children in addition to the broad and balanced curriculum.

The Pre-Prep caters for children from 3 to 7. The Nursery, which takes girls and boys from 3, has its own self-contained unit and playground to cater specifically for the needs of the very young child. Structured play offers children rich opportunities for controlling and shaping what they do. Children may stay all day or attend separate morning or afternoon sessions. Children in the Nursery and Reception work towards the Early Years Foundation Stage goals and beyond.

Honours. In 2014 pupils performed exceptionally in their A Levels: 25% at A*, 60% at A* or A and 86% at A*–B. At GCSE: 51% at A*, 81% at A* or A and 95% at A*–B.

The Association of Old Edwardians of Bath. c/o The Development Office.

Charitable status. King Edward's School at Bath is a Registered Charity, number 310227. It is a charitable trust for the purpose of educating children.

King Edward's School
Birmingham

Edgbaston Park Road, Birmingham B15 2UA
Tel: 0121 472 1672
Fax: 0121 415 4327
email: admissions@kes.org.uk
website: www.kes.org.uk

Motto: '*Domine, Salvum fac Regem*'.

King Edward's School, Birmingham, was founded in 1552 and occupied a position in the centre of the city until 1936 when it moved to its present 50 acre site in Edgbaston, surrounded by a golf course, lake and nature reserve and adjacent to the University. It is an independent day school with 855 boys aged 11 to 18. Approximately 50 boys in each year receive financial assistance with fees from scholarships and the Assisted Places Scheme. The school belongs to the Foundation of the Schools of King Edward VI in Birmingham (two independent, five grammar schools and one academy), and its sister-school, King Edward VI High School for Girls, is on the same campus. Academically one of the leading schools in the country, King Edward's is also renowned for the scale of its provision and its excellence in sport, music, drama, outdoor pursuits and trips and expeditions.

Governing Body:
Mr Tim Clarke (*Chairman*)

Dr B Adab	Mr P Christopher
Mr G Andronov	Mr I Metcalfe
Mrs G Ball, OBE	Ms L Pearson
Mr J Beeston	Dr J Sherwood
Mr P Burns	Mr S M Southall
Mr S Campbell	Ms S Stobbs

Chief Master: Mr J A Claughton, MA

Deputy Head (*Administration and Pupil Discipline*): Mr K D Phillips, BA

Deputy Head (*Pupil Welfare/Health & Safety*): Mr R D Heathcote, BSc

Deputy Head (*Academic*): Mr J C Fern, MA

Assistant Teachers:

Mr S E Lampard, BSc	Mr D H Corns, MA, MPhil
Dr T F P Hosty, BA, PhD	Mr H M Coverdale, BScEcon
Mr L W Evans, BA	
Mr J P Davies, MA	Mrs E J Wareing, BA
Mr J C S Burns, MA	Dr D C Wong, BEng, PhD
Mr L M Roll, BA	Ms L C Seamark
Mr T Mason, BSc	Mr T J M Arbuthnott, BA, MPhil
Mr E J Milton, BA	
Mr B M Spencer, BA	Mr M P Barratt, BA, MA
Mrs G A Ostrowicz, BA	Ms H A Ferguson, BSc, MSc
Mr C D Boardman, BSc	
Mr S J Tinley, BSc	Mr C G Irvine, BA
Mrs C M L Duncombe, BA	Mrs G J Babb, BA, MA
Mr J Porter, BSc	Mr T J Wareing, BA
Mr T A McMullan, BSc	Dr C Arico, MSc, PhD
Dr G Galloway, PhD	Miss F C Lee, BA
The Revd D H Raynor, MA, MLitt	Dr M Romon Alonso, MSc, PhD
Mr M J Monks, GRSM, Dip RCM	Mr J Abrahams, BSc
Mr R W James, BA	Mr J J W Fair, BSc
Mr S L Stacey, MA	Dr T S Miles, MSc, PhD
Mr T F Cross, BSc	Mr P R Ollis, BSc, MA
Mr D J Ash, MA	Dr L A L Rackham, MA, MSc, PhD
Ms R Leaver, MEng	
Mr J P Smith, BA	D L N Tuohey, BSc
Mr R E Turner, BA, MPhil	Mrs K S Charlesworth-Jones, BA
Ms D E McMillan, BSc	
Mr P A Balkham, BA	Mr J M Pavey, BSc
Mr D M Witcombe, MSc	Ms D K Poole, BA
Mr I J Connor, BSc	Mr S Loughrey, BSc
Mr R D Davies, BSc	Mr T Burdett, BSc
Ms S-L Jones, BSc	Dr H M Cocksworth, MA, PhD
Dr J L Amann, BA, PhD	
Ms E K Sigston, BA	Mr A M Dutch, BMus
Mr P W L Golightly, BA	Dr J Fennell, BSc, PhD
Mrs J L Parkinson-Mills, BA, MSc	Mrs C L Gillow, BA
	Miss E J Gorle, BA
Mr M J Bartlett, BA	Dr S P Kulkarni, BSc, MPhil, PhD
Mrs P J R Esnault, MA	
Senora A Estevez, BA, MA	Dr M D Leigh, MA, PhD
Mr C A P Johnson, BA	Mr A Mason, BA
Mr M E Johnson, BSc	Mr B A Orlin, BA
Dr M R Follows, BSc, PhD	Mr N A Shepherd, BSc
Mrs F M Atay, BA	Ms E Wood, MA

Part-time Teachers:

Mr D C Dewar, BSc	Miss J Helm, BA
Dr R T Bridges, MA, PhD	Mrs K M Buxton, BSc
Mrs G Hudson, BEd	Mrs C Smith, BA, MA
Mrs C R Bubb, BA	Mr R W Symonds, BSc
Mr C W Walker, CertEd	Mr J C Howard, BEd
Mrs H J Cochrane, BA	Mr R J Deeley, MA
Mrs S Thorpe, BSc, MEd	Mr E J Aston, BSc

Librarian: Ms K A Fletcher-Burns, BA, MSc Econ

School Medical Officer: Dr M Forrest, MBChB, DRCOG, MRCGP

Admission. Most boys enter the school at 11+, although a small number join at 13+. In addition, applications at 16+ to enter the Sixth Form are encouraged. At both 11+ and 13+ candidates take papers in Mathematics, English and Verbal Reasoning at a level appropriate to the National Curriculum. A large number of pupils are also interviewed as part of the admissions process. At 16+ entry is decided by interview, report from current Headteacher and predicted GCSE grades.

The names of candidates must be registered at the School before the closing date as stated in the prospectus. Evidence of date of birth and a recent photograph must be produced when the name of a candidate is registered for the examination.

Term of Entry: Autumn term only.

Scholarships and Assisted Places. Approximately 15–20 Academic scholarships varying in value from 15% to 50% of the fees are awarded each year. Most of these scholarships are awarded at 11+, but awards are also made to outstanding candidates at 16+ and, very occasionally, at 13+. Music scholarships are also available.

Scholarships may be increased to full fees in cases of financial need.

The Assisted Places Scheme offers means-tested support to up to 35 boys a year. The scheme targets primarily 11+ entrants but 16+ entrants are also eligible to apply.

Fees per term (2014–2015). £3,860.

Academic Success. In 2014 the school's third International Baccalaureate results were outstanding with over a quarter gaining 40 points or over, the equivalent of 4 A*s at A Level. Almost all leavers go on to University, some after a gap year. 11 pupils gained places at Oxford and Cambridge. Additionally, 13 boys will study Medicine.

At GCSE the school broke all previous records with 68% of results at A* and 91% A* or A grades, the highest percentage of A*/A grades ever achieved by a boys' school in Birmingham. Furthermore 27 pupils gained 10 A* grades and a further 15 gained 9 A*s.

Curriculum. *Lower School*: The following subjects are studied by all boys to the end of the third year: English, Mathematics, French, Geography, History, Physics, Chemistry, Biology, (General Science in first year), Latin, Art, Design, Drama, Music, PE and Religious Studies. All boys study one of German, Spanish or Classical Greek in the third year and may take their choice to GCSE or IGCSE and beyond. In addition, boys are required to undertake familiarisation courses in Information Technology. In the Fourth and Fifth year all boys study Mathematics, English, English Literature, a Modern Foreign Language and either Physics, Chemistry, Biology plus three other optional subjects, or two Sciences plus four other optional subjects, which are taken to GCSE or IGCSE. At present, the school offers IGCSE in Mathematics, Biology, Chemistry, Physics, English, English Literature, History, Modern Languages and Music.

Sixth Form: Since September 2010, A Levels have been replaced entirely with the International Baccalaureate Diploma. The school believes that this diploma provides a more challenging and broad Sixth Form education with greater opportunity for independent learning and is a better preparation for university study and life thereafter.

The school's curriculum goes beyond preparation for examinations. For example, PE and games are compulsory for all and Friday afternoon is set aside for the entire school to pursue non-academic activities: Combined Cadet Force, Leadership, service in the community, outdoor pursuits, Art, Information Technology etc.

Music and Drama. The school has a very rich musical and dramatic life. Many of the musical groups and theatrical productions take place jointly with King Edward VI High School for Girls. There are ten different musical groups and choirs. The school has recently opened a Performing Arts Centre with a main hall seating up to 500 and excellent facilities for music and drama.

Games. Rugby, Cricket, Hockey, and Athletics are the major team games in the school. However, many other games prosper including archery, badminton, basketball, chess, cross-country, cycling, fencing, Fives, golf, kayaking, squash, swimming, table tennis, tennis, water polo. The School has extensive playing fields for all these activities

plus its own swimming pool, AstroTurf, all-weather athletics track, sports hall, gymnasia and squash courts.

Societies and Clubs. The school has a very wide range of clubs and societies including Christian Union, Islamic Society, Literary Society, Classical and Junior Classical Societies, Historical and Junior Historical Societies, Living History Society, Economics Society, Musical Society, Senior and Junior Dramatic Societies, Shakespeare Society, Art Society, Geographical Society, Debating and Junior Debating Societies, Scientific Society, Biological Society, Mathematical Society, Meteorological Society, Modern Language Society, Chess Club, Photographic Section, School Chronicle, Film Society, Hard Rock Society.

CCF, Outdoor Pursuits and Expeditions. The Royal Naval, RAF and Army Sections of the Combined Cadet Force are very popular amongst pupils. In addition, the KES Award and the Duke of Edinburgh's Award Scheme have grown substantially in recent years, so that the majority of pupils in the third year gain the KES Award and about 20 each year gain the Gold Duke of Edinburgh's Award. All of this forms part of a strong tradition of trips and expeditions, ranging from cycling and caving and walking and skiing trips, to language trips to Europe to major expeditions to Honduras, Venezuela, Peru, Egypt, Morocco. There have also been very successful rugby tours to Australia, South Africa and China.

Forms and Houses. In the first five years there are five forms in each year, with an average of 24 pupils. In the Sixth Form, forms are on average 12 in number, and often comprise pupils together from the Lower and Upper Sixth. There is also a house system, comprising eight houses, which continues to provide an important element of pastoral support and competition in sport, music, debating and general knowledge.

Charitable status. The Schools of King Edward VI in Birmingham is a Registered Charity, number 529051. The purpose of the Foundation is to educate children and young persons living in or around the City of Birmingham.

King Edward's
Witley

Petworth Road, Godalming, Surrey GU8 5SG

Tel: 01428 686700
Fax: 01428 682850
email: admissions@kesw.org
website: www.kesw.org
Twitter: @KESWNews

King Edward's Witley was founded in 1553 by King Edward VI as Bridewell Royal Hospital. Originally housed at the Bridewell Palace, which was given under Royal Charter to the City of London, the School moved to Witley in 1867, simultaneously changing its name; it became co-educational again in 1952. The School is an independent boarding and day school for girls and boys aged 11–18. The School has 400 pupils; approximately a third are day pupils. There are a substantial number of bursaries, currently over 100, available to help boys and girls whose home circumstances make a boarding style of education a particular need. For 2015, King Edward's Witley will also offer the new A Level course as an alternative to the IB, ensuring pupils have a choice of routes to secure a place at University.

Treasurer and Chairman of Governors: P K Estlin, BSc

Headmaster: J Attwater, MA

Senior Deputy Head: S J Pugh, MA

Academic Staff:
* *Head of Department*

† *Housemaster/mistress*

Mrs J A Abraham, BSc (*Mathematics, †Elizabeth*)
Miss S J Brown, BA (*Modern Languages*)
N J Budden, BSc, MA (**Modern Languages*)
Mrs S Butler, BA (**Learning Support*)
Miss L Carey, MA (*Philosophy, Religious Education*)
J G Culbert, BSc (**Physics*)
A Day, BSc (*ICT, †Edward*)
Miss H Duncan, BA Ed (*Science, †Queens*)
Mrs J Edney, CPE BA (**Director of Sport*)
L Edney, BMus (*Music*)
N Emsley, BSc, Dip Com, PGCE (*Science, Physics*)
Mrs E J Esdon (*Learning Support, Religious Education*)
K B Forster, BA (*Modern Languages, Careers
   Coordinator*)
Dr E K Foshaugen, BA, MPhil (**Philosophy/Critical
   Thinking*)
D G Galbraith, BSc (*Science, *Chemistry*)
Miss G Gammons, BSc (*Chemistry, †Tudor*)
Mrs K M Goundry, BA (*Food & Textiles Technology*)
Mrs C Green, BA (*Learning Support*)
J Haigh, MA (*ICT*)
Mrs H Hanley, BSc (*Geography*)
Miss E Harman, BSc (**Economics & Business Studies*)
Mrs J Harris (**Library, Extended Essay Coordinator*)
P W Head, BSc (**Mathematics*)
Mrs A E Hill, BSc (**Science, Biology*)
Mrs J A Hinton, BSc (*Mathematics*)
J Hole, BA, MA (*Deputy Head Academic*)
P Humphreys, BSc, MEd (**Geography*)
Miss I Ilic (*Teaching Assistant, Modern Languages*)
A N K Johnson, BSc, MSc (**Design & Technology, ICT*)
J C Langan, BA (**English & Drama*)
Dr A Lennard, PhD, BSc (**ICT*)
Mrs J Lyttle, BA (*English*)
S McDonald, MA (*Classics*)
Mrs C J Meharg, BA (*Director of IB, Modern Languages*)
Dr H Mir, PhD (*Mathematics*)
Mrs L Moore (*Art and Photography*)
Mrs P V Nash, BEd (*Science*)
Mrs J H Pearce, BA (**Religious Studies*)
D G K Pennell, BEd (*Physical Education, †Wakefield*)
S D Pentreath, BSc (*Head of Lower School, Chemistry,
   †QMH*)
D K Poulter, BSc, FRGS (*Deputy Head-Co-curriculum,
   Geography*)
S J Pugh, MA (*Senior Deputy Head, Classics*)
N Rendall, BA (*History, †Grafton*)
Mrs E V Rooyen, BA, BSc (*Learning Support*)
Mrs A S Saunders, BA (*Head of Sixth Form, History*)
C R Saunders, BSc (**Biology*)
Mrs C Shouksmith (**Art*)
Mrs N Skau, BAc (*Library*)
A Sibacher (*Mathematics*)
D Slater, BA (*English*)
S Sliwka, BMus, FRCO (**Director of Music*)
Mrs P Slater, BSC (*Modern Languages*)
Miss L Tattersall, BA (*English & Drama*)
Mrs A J Tinsley, CertEd (**Design & Technology*)
S L Todd, BSc (*Examinations Officer, Physical Education,
   Science*)
Mrs L M Vitagliano, MA (**History*)
Mrs B Waters, BEd (*Mathematics*)
J K Webster, BSc (*Mathematics*)
Mrs H A White, BSc (*Mathematics*)
C A Wilson, BSc (*Design & Technology, Mathematics*)
Mrs K A Wilson, DipM, ACIM (*Economics and Business
   Studies, †Copeland*)

Houses and Housemasters/Housemistresses:

Queen Mary House (*Junior Boys*): S D Pentreath
Copeland House (*Junior Girls*): Mrs K A Wilson
Senior Paired Houses:

Wakefield (*Boys*): D G K Pennell and Elizabeth (*Girls*):
   Mrs J A Abraham
Edward (*Boys*): A Day and Tudor (*Girls*): Miss G
   Gammons
Grafton (*Boys*): N Rendall and Queens (*Girls*): Miss H
   Duncan

Medical Officer: P R Wilks, MA, MB, BChir
Director of Finance and Administration: A Lewis
Director of Admissions & Communication: J Benson
Head of Marketing: Miss N Dimmock
Development Manager: Mrs E Harrison
Headmaster's Secretary: Ms C Todd

King Edward's Witley is an independent boarding and day school for girls and boys aged 11–18, sited within a 100-acre campus in an Area of Outstanding Natural Beauty in the Surrey countryside. The School is approximately ten miles south of Guildford, with Heathrow and Gatwick international airports both within a 45-minute drive.

Founded in 1553 and with established links with the City of London, King Edward's Witley is steeped in history, but combines its traditional strengths with a modern outlook. The School prides itself on its ability to provide a school community that reflects the real world, but admitting pupils from a broad range of academic, social, economic and cultural backgrounds – 65% are English native speakers and over 43 countries are represented. All children are nurtured to encourage independent thinking and a spirit of respect and understanding for others, resulting in a mature and well-rounded outlook on life and a commitment to upholding the strongest moral values.

King Edward's Witley is proud to be one of the first English boarding schools in the area to offer the IB Diploma Programme and in 2014 celebrates 10 years of the IB. In those ten years pupils have achieved close to a 100% success rate and King Edward's has evolved to become one of the top IB schools in the country, as acknowledged by an award from Best Schools UK this year.

For 2015, King Edward's will also offer the new A Level course as an alternative to the IB, ensuring pupils have a choice of routes to secure a place at university. The School also runs a one-year Pre Sixth Form course for overseas pupils, representing an opportunity to improve English language skills and trial both IB and A Level subjects on offer, allowing for more Sixth Form choices.

Renowned for its ability to nurture pupils so they excel in their academic studies, King Edward's Witley also provides a highly motivating and inspiring environment for children to equally thrive in other sporting / creative activities. The School has an excellent reputation for its welcoming community and the provision of high-quality pastoral care.

The 1st and 2nd Forms constitute the Lower School and, from September 2015, will be accommodated in Queen Mary House with shared communal facilities for boys and girls. From the 3rd Form upwards boys and girls live in seven modern, purpose-built paired houses where the accommodation and study areas are completely separate but everyone can come together in the shared communal facilities on the ground floor.

Facilities at the School are second to none and include a brand new state-of-the-art Business and Finance Centre, indoor swimming pool, all-weather hockey and tennis playing fields and a newly refurbished central dining hall, which delivers an outstanding standard of catering. The School pioneered paired boarding houses with communal areas, where everyone can come together in their spare time to enjoy games, TV, music and conversation in the common rooms, kitchen, music and television rooms. For the Sixth Form, a lively common room and new study area and careers library provide an environment for independent learning and recreation.

Admission. Children are normally admitted at 11+, 13+ and 16+ but if there is room they may be admitted at other times, and occasionally a child who should clearly be working alongside older children is admitted at 10+. Admission is by the School's own entrance examination and interview taken normally in the January prior to entry.

Fees per term (2014–2015). Boarders: Lower School £7,300, Forms 3–5 £9,150, (Pre) Sixth Form £9,500, including all boarding and tuition fees, books and games equipment, and the provision of school uniform and games clothing.

Day Pupils: Lower School £4,995, Forms 3–5 £6,245, (Pre) Sixth Form £6,650, including meals and uniform. Individual music tuition in piano, organ, singing and all orchestral instruments is available.

Bursaries. Bursaries are available for both boarding and day pupils. The School has an endowment providing support for children whose circumstances make boarding a particular need. Awards are reviewed annually with regard to parental circumstances and to school fees. They may be given in conjunction with Local Education Authority grants or help from a charitable trust. The School has a dedicated Bursaries officer who works with applicants to source the financial support needed to enable worthy candidates to join the School.

Scholarships. Academic, Art, Drama, Music Scholarships and Sports Exhibitions are offered at 11+, 13+ or 16+ for entry to the Sixth Form. These awards will be up to a maximum of 30% of full fees but may be augmented in case of financial need. A discount of 10% of full fees is available to children from service families. There is a special IB Sixth Form Day scholarship available, awarding 100% of fees.

Charitable status. King Edward's Witley is a Registered Charity, number 311997. The Foundation exists to provide boarding education for families whose circumstances make boarding a particular need, though the excellent facilities and the high standards of academic achievement and pastoral care make it attractive also to any family looking for a modern and distinctive education.

King Henry VIII School
(Part of the Coventry School Foundation)

Warwick Road, Coventry CV3 6AQ
Tel: 024 7627 1111
Fax: 024 7627 1188
email: info@khviii.net
website: www.khviii.com
Twitter: @KHVIIISchool

Founded in 1545 by John Hales, Clerk of the Hanaper to the King, under Letters Patent of King Henry VIII, King Henry VIII School has a deserved reputation as one of the finest independent, co-educational day schools in the UK.

"Success, responsibility and enjoyment – these are our prime aims", states Jason Slack, Headmaster.

The school is represented on the Headmasters' Conference and on the Association of Governing Bodies of Independent Schools. The governing body is the Coventry School Foundation, on which are represented Sir Thomas White's Charity, the Coventry Church Charities, Coventry General Charities and Birmingham, Coventry, Oxford and Warwick Universities. There are also several co-opted Governors.

There are 407 boys and 317 girls in the Senior School, and 258 boys and 230 girls in the Prep School.

Chairman of Governors: Mr Richard Atkins, QC

Senior School

Headmaster: **Mr Jason Slack**, BSc, MA Ed

Deputy Heads:
Mr Warren Honey, BSc, MEd
Mr David Morton, BA
Miss Ann Weitzel, MA, NPQH

Teaching Staff:

Mr Tom Andrews, BSc
Mr Conn Anson-O'Connell, BA
Miss Marysia Bancroft, MA
Dr Steven Barge, BA
Miss Julie Bassett, BMus
Mr Matthew Blake, MPhys
Mrs Sally Bradley, BA
Mr Ben S Bramley, BSc
Miss Hannah Bredin, BA
Miss Sally Burton, BA
Dr Helen Buttrick, MA, MSCi
Mr James Carlyle, BA
Mrs Anna Clegg, BA
Dr Michele Cuthbert, BSc, MEd, HDipEd, WITS
Mrs Clare Dempsey, BSc
Mr Niall Doherty, BA, LTCL
Mrs Carrie Dowding, BSc
Mrs Tracy Ferguson, BSc
Miss Laura Garcia, BA
Miss Angelique Giordano, BA
Mr Richard Harrington, MA
Dr Debbie Hayton, BSc
Mrs Anna Heathcote, BA
Mr John Henderson, BA
Mrs Julie Holland, BA
Dr Tim Honeywill, MMath
Mrs Linda Horton, MA
Mr Robert Howard, BA
Mrs Karen Hunt, BEd
Mrs Kathryn Hunt, BSc
Mr Peter Huxford, MA
Mrs Anna Jewell, BA
Mr Nicholas Jones, MA
Mrs Victoria Kaczur, BA
Mr Alistair Kennedy, BA, BA Mus
Mr Peter Manning, MA
Mrs Rachel Mason, BSc
Mrs Jaynita Mattu, BSc
Dr Mary McKenzie, MA
Mr Nick Meynell, BA
Mrs Pip Milton, BSc
Mr Peter Milton, BA

Miss Sarah Mould, BA
Mrs Cindy Neale, MA
Dr Donna Norman, BSc
Miss Jenny Norton, MA
Mr Francis O'Reilly, BA
Mrs Michelle Oxtoby, BSc, BSc
Mrs Kulwinder Pabla, MSc
Mrs Denise Pandya, BMus
Mr Andrew Parker, BEd
Miss Ruth Partington, BMus
Dr Noel Phillips, BSc
Mrs Dolores Pittaway, BA, PG Dip
Mrs Amanda Pontin, CertEd
Mrs Debra Quinn, BA
Dr Michael Reddish, LLM
Mr Alastair Rendle, BEng
Dr Lynn Reynolds, BSc
Ms Sally Ridley, BA, MBA
Mr Paul Robbins, MEng
Miss Tajinder Sanghera, MA
Mrs Helen Savage, BEd, CertEd, Dip TEFL
Miss Jessica Shapiro, BA
Mr Thomas Spillane, BSc
Mrs Chris Spriggs, BSc
Miss Grace Spring, BA
Dr Robert Stephen, BA, BD, MTh, FSA Scot, FRSA
Mr Dan Super, BSc
Mr Stuart Sweetman, MA
Mr Sukhbir Tandy
Mr Neil Tingle, BA
Mrs AJ Tracey, BSc
Mrs Mary Tynan, BSc
Mrs Anne Wade, BSc, MA, CBiol, ML
Mrs Kate Whitehead, BSc
Mrs Lisa Whiteman, Nat Dip Perf Arts, Higher Nat Dip Dance
Mr Chris Wilde, BA
Mr Steve Wilkes, BEd
Mr Paul Wilkins, BA

Administrative Staff:
Bursar: Mr Michael Shaw
School Administrator: Mrs Julie Goodwin, HND
Headmaster's PA/Admissions Secretary: Mrs Amanda Skinner
Examinations Officer: Mrs Belinda Leslie, MBA
Careers Advisor: Mrs Sally Pike, BA, Dip Careers Guidance
School Nurse: Mrs Wendy Bolland, RGN
School Network Manager: Mr Tim Lees
Office Manager: Mrs Jacky Matthews
Sports Centre Manager: Mr Rob Phillips, BSc
Librarian: Ms Helen Cooper, LLB, PGCE
Alumni Relations Officer: Mrs Amanda Garman, BSc

King Henry VIII Preparatory School

Headmaster: Mr Nicholas Lovell, BA

Deputy Head (Swallows): Miss Caroline Soan, GMus, PGCE
Deputy Head (Hales): Mrs Helen Higginson, BSc, MA
Director of Studies: Mr Steven Dhaliwal, BEd, MSc

Teaching Staff:

Mrs Rachel Avlonti, BEd	Mrs Lesley McKenzie, BEd
Ms Emma Barwell, BA	Mrs Helen Mellor, BEd
Miss Nicola Bawcutt, BMus, PGCE	Mrs Ruth Morris, BA
	Mr Neil Mosedale, BSc
Mr Greg Beaufoy, BSc	Mrs Elizabeth Ochieng,
Mrs Sarah Brand, BEd	BEd
Mrs Claire Brindley, BSc	Mrs Kelly Osman, BA,
Miss Lynn Brown, BSc	PGCE
Mrs Jane Coles, CertEd, BPhil, MSc	Mrs Manisha Patel, MA, PGCE
Mrs Emma Curran, BEd	Mr Ken Pearson, BEd
Mr Steve Dhaliwal, BEd, MSc	Mrs Beverley Piercy, BTEC Dip
Mrs Lucy Duckers, BA, PGCE	Mrs Amanda Pontin, CertEd
Mrs Jane Duffield, BSc, PGCE	Miss Jenna Sainsbury, BA
	Mr Phil Savage, BA
Mrs Charlotte Ferguson, BA	Miss Tamsin Slack, BSc
Mr Steve Hall, BA	Mrs Jill Sutherland, BA, QTS
Mrs Julia Halstead, BA	Mrs Sian Westmancoat, BA
Mrs Helen Harvey, BA	Ed
Mr Brian Hewetson, BA	Mrs Helen Williamson,
Mrs Catherine Jeffcoat, BA	BSc
Mr Lau Langkilde	Miss Nicola Wood, BA
Mrs Jane Lovell, BEd	Mrs Karen Wormald, BEd
Miss Emily Manship, BSc, PGCE	Miss Kate Wozencroft, HND, BEd Hons
Mr Philip McGrane, BSc	Mrs Sophia Wright, BA

Administrative Staff:
Bursar: Mr Michael Shaw
School Administrator: Mr Alan Shaw
Headmaster's PA/Admissions Secretary: Mrs Lesley Batson
School Nurse: Mrs Wendy Bolland, RGN
School Network Manager: Mr Tim Lees
Librarian: Mrs Kate Batchelor

Facilities. The school moved to its present extensive site in a pleasant part of Coventry in 1885. The Governors have continually improved, extended and restored the buildings which are well equipped to cope with the demands of an up-to-date, relevant and challenging curriculum. The school has extensive playing fields, some of which are located on the main site. Other playing fields are five minutes away by minibus.

The Governors have committed themselves to a major building programme at the school. A new Prep School, Art facility, Sixth Form Centre and Sports Hall have recently been completed. Both Senior and Prep Schools have a first-rate computer network available to all pupils. A six-lane, 25m swimming pool (and fitness suite) opened in 2009. An Archive was opened in 2014 containing a timeline from 1545 to 2014 and original Tudor artefacts.

Curriculum. The curriculum is broad and balanced, integrating National Curriculum principles and practices where appropriate. The Senior School curriculum provides courses leading to the GCSE examinations and GCE AS and A Levels. Subjects available currently are Art, Biology, Business Studies, Chemistry, Classical Civilisation, Computing, Design and Food Technology, Drama and Theatre Studies, Economics, English, French, Geography, German, Greek, History, Information and Communication Technology, Latin, Law, Mathematics, Music, Photography, Psychology, Physics, Religious Studies and Spanish. Physical Education and Sport are also considered to be a vital part of the curric-

ulum and are available as an AS and A2 Level option. All students follow a structured PSHE course.

Courses in Key Skills/Complementary Studies and Critical Thinking are offered in the Sixth Form. The Extended Project Qualification was introduced for Year 13 in 2012.

Examination results at all levels are excellent.

Games. Rugby, Hockey, Netball, Basketball, Cross-Country Running, Athletics, Rounders, Tennis, Cricket, Swimming, Golf, Orienteering and Fencing. Prep School games include Tag Rugby, Swimming, Soccer, Rounders, Athletics, Cricket and Cross-Country Running. In 1986 the largest artificial turf games area in the country was created, and refurbished in 2014, used mainly for hockey, but providing an additional 24 tennis courts in the summer. This facility is shared with Bablake School.

Extra-Curricular Activities. The School is noted for the excellence of its sport, music, drama, debating, public speaking and outdoor pursuits. All pupils are encouraged to make a contribution to the extra-curricular life of the school. The School has close connections with many universities including Oxford and Cambridge.

Admission. Admission is via the School's own Entrance Examination, held annually in January for entrance the following September. The normal age of entry is 11, but there are additional intakes at other ages and also at Sixth Form level. All enquiries about admission to the school should be addressed to the Headmaster.

Scholarships. The Governors award annually a number (not fixed) of entrance bursaries and scholarships. Full details regarding financial assistance are available from the Headmaster at the school.

Old Coventrians Association. Contact: Mrs Jay Mattu; email: webALUMNUS@khviii.com; website: www.khviii.com.

Fees per term (2014–2015). Senior School £3,400; Prep School £2,580–£2,750.

Prep School. The Prep School is based on two nearby sites and enjoys excellent facilities which include an Early Years Centre, a Library, ICT rooms with networked PCs, an Art and Design rooms, a Science room, Astroturf and Sports Hall and a Music room. Children are accepted by competitive examination from 7+ to 10+. The emphasis is on a broad education based upon the National Curriculum and children are prepared for the Entrance Examination for entry to the Senior School.

(*For further information about the Prep School, see entry in IAPS section.*)

Charitable status. Coventry School Foundation is a Registered Charity, number 528961. Its aim is to advance the education of boys and girls by the provision of a school or schools in or near the City of Coventry.

King William's College

Castletown, Isle of Man IM9 1TP

Tel:	01624 820400
Fax:	01624 820401
email:	barbara.kniveton@kwc.im
website:	www.kwc.im

Motto: '*Assiduitate, non desidia.*'

King William's College owes its foundation to Dr Isaac Barrow, Bishop of Sodor and Man from 1663 to 1671, who established an Educational Trust in 1668. The funds of the Trust were augmented by public subscription and the College was opened in 1833 and named after King William IV, 'The Sailor King'.

In 1991, the College merged with the Isle of Man's other independent school, The Buchan School, Castletown, which had been founded by Lady Laura Buchan in 1875 to provide education for young ladies. The Buchan School has been reformed as the junior section of the College for boys and girls up to age 11. (*For further details of The Buchan School, see entry in IAPS section*).

The Isle of Man, being internally self-governing, has a very favourable tax structure and the independence of College would not be affected by changes in UK legislation.

Visitor: The Most Revd and Right Hon Dr J Sentamu, Lord Archbishop of York

Trustees:
Chairman: His Excellency Mr Adam Wood, Lieutenant Governor of the Isle of Man
S G Alder, BA, FCA
The Ven Andrew Brown, MA, Archdeacon of Man
T W B Cullen, MA
Professor Ronald Barr, Chief Executive Officer, Department of Education and Children
M J Hoy, MBE, MA
The Rt Revd Robert Paterson, MA, The Lord Bishop of Sodor and Man

Secretary to the Trustees and Bursar: J V Oatts, BA, MSc, Dip Surv

Governors:
Chairman: N H Wood, ACA, TEP
Prof R J Berry, RD, MA, DPhil, MD, FRCP
Mr S Billinghurst, BA Hons, ACA
A C Collister
Miss J M Crookall, BSc, FSI
M Grace, BSc Hons, MRICS
Mrs E J Higgins, BSc, ACA
Dr L Hulme, LRCP, MRCS
Miss S J Leahy, LLB, DipLP
Mr R T F Pleming, MA
N T Westlake, LLB Hons, PGCE

Principal: M A C Humphreys, MA

Vice-Principal: J H Buchanan, BA (*IB Coordinator*)
Head of Senior School: S Miller, BA

* *Head of Department*
† *Housemaster/mistress*

J M Allegro, BA
Mrs M Bailey-Barnes, BA (*Spanish, Head of Fourth Form*)
Mrs E J Ballantyne, BSc
Mr G Blasco, BA
Mrs K E Brew, BEng
Miss C L Broadbent, BA (*PSHE*)
Miss A J Clark, BA
Mrs A Z A Clarke, MA (*English*)
S N Cope, BA (*Geography*)
M C Crabtree, BSc (*Boys PE & Games*)
Mrs D J Currie, BA (*Religious Studies, History*)
C Davidson, MA
Miss E F Drane, BA
Mrs B Dunn, BEd (*Director of Sport*)
Miss S Elliott, BA
Mrs S M Ellson, MA
Mrs R J Foxon, BSc
Miss C Ganzo Perez, BA
Miss B C Harkin, BA
Miss F Heckel, MA (*French, *Modern Languages*)
Mr N A Howell-Evans, BA (*Head of Science*)
E J Jeffers, BA (*Head of Boarding, †Colbourne House*)
Mrs S A Jeffers, BA
S P Kelly, BA (*Art*)
Miss A Kerr, MA
Mrs B Kneen, BSc (*Head of Fifth Form*)
Miss C V Ledger, BA (*Drama*)
D M C Matthews, BSc (*Mathematics*)
Mrs Z A McAndry
D McConnell, BSc

G E Moore, BMus
Mrs A L Morgans, BA Ed, BSc (*Head of Sixth Form*)
Dr P H Morgans, BSc, PhD (*Science, *Chemistry*)
Mrs J Munro, BA
Mrs G R Murphy, MCLIP (*Librarian*)
R C Parry, BSc
Mrs S Parry, BA (†*School House*)
R Riekert, BComm (*Economics*)
Mrs A M Schreiber, MA
Miss K K Teare, BSc
A D Ulyett, BSc (*Biology*)
P Verschueren, MSc
Ms M Westall, BSc
D S Winrow, MSc
Mr J J Wood, MSc
J Wright, MA, MMus (*Director of Music*)

Part-time Staff:
Miss C R Beswick, MSci
D Cowley, BSc
Miss D Espinosa
Miss R Lloyd, BMus
Miss S Havet
Miss R R Pate
Ms S Roper, BA
Mrs S A Ross, BEd
Reverend E J Scott, BA (*Chaplain*)
Mrs O Stone, BA

Principal's PA: Mrs J Bateson
Admissions Secretary: Mrs B Kniveton
School Medical Officer: Castletown Medical Centre

The College is set in superb countryside on the edge of Castletown Bay and adjacent to Ronaldsway Airport. The Isle of Man is approximately 33 miles long and 13 miles wide and is an area of diverse and beautiful scenery. The Isle of Man is an unusually safe environment with a very low crime rate.

There are approximately 400 pupils at College and a further 200 pupils at the Preparatory School. There is also a Nursery School for 2 to 4 year olds on the Buchan site. Both King William's College and The Buchan School are fully co-educational.

Entry. New pupils are accepted at any time, but most begin at the start of the September Term. Boys and girls are admitted to the Preparatory School up to the age of 11 at which point transfer to King William's College is automatic. Entry to College, including Sixth Form level, is by Head's report and, where possible, by interview.

Further details and a prospectus may be obtained from the Admissions Office to which applications for entry should be made.

Organisation. The school is divided into three sections: Fourth Form (Years 7 & 8), Fifth Form (Years 9, 10 & 11) and Sixth Form (Years 12 & 13). Each section is led by a Head of Year, assisted by a team of tutors who monitor the academic progress and deal with all day-to-day matters relating to the pupils in their charge. In addition, all pupils are placed in one of three co-educational Houses for internal competitive purposes, which provides an important element of continuity throughout a pupil's career at the School.

Boarders. There are two houses: one for boys and the other for girls. The living and sleeping accommodation is arranged principally in study-bedrooms for senior pupils with junior pupils sharing dormitories in small groups. Each House has its own Houseparent who is responsible for the pastoral welfare of the pupils. He or she is assisted by two or three tutors, of whom at least two are resident.

Chapel. The College is a Church of England foundation but pupils of all denominations attend Chapel; the spirit of the services is distinctly ecumenical.

Curriculum. Pupils at both Schools follow the National Curriculum in its essentials.

The curriculum is designed to provide a broad, balanced and challenging form of study for all pupils. At 11–13 pupils take English, Mathematics, French and Spanish or Latin, Science, History, Geography, Design Technology, ICT, Art, Music, Drama, Religious Studies, Physical Education, PSHE. Pupils then go on to study typically 9 subjects at GCSE/IGCSE level from a wide number of options.

In the Sixth Form King William's College offers the **International Baccalaureate**. Students choose 6 subjects, normally 3 at higher level and 3 at standard level, which must include their first language, a second language, a science, a social science and Mathematics. In addition, students write an extended essay (a research piece of 4,000 words), follow a course in the Theory of Knowledge (practical philosophy) and spend the equivalent of one half day a week on some form of creative aesthetic activity or active community service (e.g. Duke of Edinburgh's Award fulfils this requirement).

Music and Drama. There are excellent facilities for drama with House plays and at least one major school production each year, together with regular coaching in Speech and Drama. There are Junior and Senior Bands and Choirs, and a very flourishing Chapel Choir. The House Music competition is one of the many focal points of House activity.

Games. The College has a strong tradition and a fine reputation in the major games of rugby, hockey and cricket. There are regular fixtures with Isle of Man schools and schools in other parts of the British Isles. Netball, athletics, soccer, cross-country and swimming all flourish and there are both House and College competitions. Senior pupils may opt to play golf on the magnificent adjoining Castletown Golf Links or to sail as their major summer sport. There are approximately thirty acres of first class playing fields, an indoor heated swimming pool which is in use throughout the year, a miniature rifle range, a gymnasium for basketball and badminton with an indoor cricket net, hard and grass tennis courts, two squash courts and a sand dressed all-weather pitch.

Other Activities. There is a wide range of societies and activities to complement academic life. The Duke of Edinburgh's Award Scheme flourishes and expeditions are undertaken regularly both on the Island and further afield. There is a thriving Combined Cadet Force and Social Services group. There are strong links with the Armed Services who help regularly with Cadet training. There are regular skiing trips, choir tours and educational trips to the UK and abroad.

Travel. King William's College is easily accessible from the UK and from abroad. Some boarders come by sea from Heysham or Liverpool using the regular service to Douglas but the majority of boarding pupils and parents come by air from the British Isles and much further afield. There are direct flights to London, Belfast, Dublin, Liverpool, Manchester, Bristol and other UK cities. Boarding House staff are fully experienced in arranging international flights and younger pupils are met at the airport.

Health. The health of all pupils is in the care of the School Doctor. There is a sanatorium supervised by a qualified nursing sister and high standards of medical care are available at Noble's Hospital in Douglas.

Fees per term (2014–2015). Day: £4,763 (Years 7 & 8), £5,949 (Years 9–11), £6,773 (Years 12 & 13). Boarding Fee: £3,087 in addition to Day Fee.

A reduction of one-third of the fee for boarders and one half of the fee for day pupils is allowed to children of clergy holding a benefice or Bishop's licence and residing in the Isle of Man. There is a similar arrangement for children of Methodist Ministers.

A reduction of 15% is allowed for serving members of the Armed Forces of the Crown. Once a pupil is accepted, the reduction continues even though the parent may leave the Services.

A reduction of 10% is made for the second, third and fourth child.

Scholarships and Bursaries. Year 7 Academic Scholarships are offered up to the value of 20% of the current tuition fee and examinations take place in late January. There are papers in English and Mathematics and an interview.

Sixth Form Academic Scholarships are offered up to the value of 20% of the current tuition fee and examinations are normally held in November of the year prior to entry. There are papers in Mathematics, English, one other subject chosen by the candidate and an interview.

Music Scholarships, Drama and Sports Awards to the value of 20% of the tuition fee are available to candidates entering either the Lower Fourth or the Lower Sixth Form who demonstrate exceptional talent or potential. Examinations and auditions take place by arrangement.

There is also a Bursary fund to support students if the financial circumstances of parents make this necessary.

Further details of all scholarships may be obtained from the Admissions Office and on the website.

Charitable status. King William's College is a Manx Registered Charity, number 615 and is operated as a Company limited by guarantee.

King's College School

Wimbledon Common, London SW19 4TT
Tel: 020 8255 5300
Fax: 020 8255 5309 (Porters' Lodge)
email: admissions@kcs.org.uk
website: www.kcs.org.uk

Motto: *Sancte et Sapienter.*

King's College School was founded as the junior department of King's College in 1829. According to the resolutions adopted at the preliminary meeting of founders in 1828, "the system is to comprise religious and moral instruction, classical learning, history, modern languages, mathematics, natural philosophy, etc., and to be so conducted as to provide in the most effectual manner for the two great objects of education the communication of general knowledge, and specific preparation for particular professions"". In 1897 it was removed from the Strand to its present site on Wimbledon Common.

Governing Body:
The Archbishop of Canterbury (*Visitor*)
The Rt Revd Christopher Chessun, Bishop of Southwark
   (*Ex Officio*)
Mrs P L Hughes, CBE (*Chairman*)
Mrs F R Cahill, BA Hons
R J Cairns, MA
O L Carlstrand, BSc, CEng, MICE
A J M Chamberlain, MA, FIA
T A Clark, CBE, MA, MSc
G D Connell, MA, FCA
P G S Evitt, MA
Dr P A Fraser
G W James, MA
Sir Robert Jay, BA, QC
Professor D A Lievesley, CStat, AcSS, CBE
R S Luddington, MA, MPhil
Mrs P Reed-Boswell, CertEd
M D J Sharp, BA
D R J Silver, MA
G C Slimmon, MA, MBA
P J L Strafford, BA, MBA

Bursar & Secretary to the Governing Body: Mr D S
   Armitage, MBE, MSc

Senior School

Head Master: Mr A D Halls, MA, FRSA

Principal Deputy: Miss M Hunnaball, BSc, MA
Deputy Head (Pastoral): Mr R Milne, BA
Deputy Head (Academic): Mr W Brierly, BSc
Senior Master (Learning Resources): Mr B J Driver, MA

Assistant Heads:
Mr M D Allen, MA (*Teaching & Learning*)
Mr J A Galloway, BA (*Head of Middle School*)
Dr S A Hendry (*Head of Sixth Form*)
Mr R J Mitchell, MA (*Public Occasions*)
Mr M P Stables, MA (*Director of Studies*)

Chaplain: The Revd J W Crossley, BA, MA, PhD
Assistant Chaplain: Mr G D Kennedy, BEng

Biology:
Dr R C Clark (*Head of Science*)
Mr N E Edwards, MSc (*Head of Examinations*)
Mr J E Grabowski, BSc
Dr S A Hendry
Mr P M Lavender, BSc
Mrs A Abbott, BA
Dr A Stewart

Chemistry:
Dr A M Hayes
Dr I I F Boogaerts
Mr I M Davies, MA
Mr M Gibson, BSc
Dr P M Lloyd (*Deputy Head of IB*)
Miss H L McKissack, BSc, MA (*Senior Teacher*)
Mr R J Mitchell, MA
Dr R A L Winchester

Physics:
Mr T S Banyard, BA
Mr G E D Bennett, MA
Mr G Cawley, BSc
Miss M Hunnaball, BSc, MA
Mr R W M Hughes, MSc
Miss N J Kersley, BSc (*Assistant Head of PSHE*)
Mr D J Lavender, MA, ALCM
Mr D Miller, BSc
Ms M A G Spottiswoode, BSc

Classics:
Mr B M Baulf MA
Mr G E Bennett, BA
Mr J R Carroll, MA (*Head of Maclear House*)
Miss V R Casemore, BA
Miss J E S Lewis, BA (*maternity cover*)
Miss C L Tedd, MA (*Head of Sixth Form Girls*)
Mr S L C Young, BA

Economics & Social Sciences:
Mr A G Hepworth, BSc
Miss M V Anthony, BSc (*maternity cover*)
Mr W P Brierly, BSc
Miss A Croft, BA
Mrs S M Danaher, BBS
Mrs S Williams, BCom

English:
Dr J P D Cannon
Miss P Alisse, MSt
Mr M D Allen, MA
Mrs K L Bird, MA, MPhil
Mr B L Bransfield, MA (*Assistant Director of Partnerships*)
Miss E C Collin, BA
Miss C F Crothers, BA
Mrs L J Hobbs, MA
Mr R Milne, BA, MSc

Drama:
Mr J L B Trapmore, MA (*Head of Curriculum Drama*)
Mr A P Cross, MA (*Director of Drama*)
Mr D R Antorbus, BS (*Theatre Director in Residence*)

Geography:
Dr E Laurie (*Head of Glenesk House*)
Mr M C Christou, BA
Mr J A Galloway, BA
Miss C J Goodwin, BA
Miss J M Lawton, BSc
Mr J M Stanley, BSc (*OC CCF Army Section*)

History:
Mr A W Thomas, MA
Miss R M Davis, BA
Miss L E Kay, BA
Mr J G Lawrence, MA, MLitt (*Director of Co-Curricular Education*)
Mr J G Ryan, BA
Miss A Simonow
Mr M A Stephenson, MA
Mrs S E Wiseman, MA
Mrs J I Woodward, MA

Mathematics:
Mr S J Nye, BSc
Mr H Bond, BSc
Mr S M Borio, MPhil
Mr B J Driver, MA, ARCO
Mr A D Gradon, BSc
Mr J A Harris, MEng
Mr T P Howland, BA (*Deputy Head of Examinations*)
Mr G D Kennedy, BEng
Mrs E C Nicholl, BSc
Mrs A J Panaite, BSc (*Chaplaincy Associate*)
Mr M P Stables, MA
Dr T Squires (*Acting Head of Alverstone House*)
Ms S J Walker, BEng (*Head of IB Diploma*)
Mr I C Wilson, MA

Modern languages:
Mr S Tint, MA, FCIL
Mr B P Andrews, BA (*Deputy Head of Middle School*)
Mrs A J Ansbro, MA
Miss B P Cerda Drago, BA
Mr H Chapman, MA (*Director of Partnerships and Outreach*)
Miss A V Eilert, MA (*Coordinator of Chinese Studies*)
Mr C C D Fowler, BA (*Head of Kingsley House*)
Mr S C Kent, MA
Dr E Keys
Miss M M E Kidwell, MA (*maternity cover*)
Mrs H M Lindsey-Noble, BA
Mrs D McBride, Pol Sci Int, Florence University
Mrs H M Mulcahy, BA
Miss R C Peel, BA (*Head of Major House*)
Mrs J E Purslow, MA
Ms C O H Robinson, BA
Mr J M A Ross, BA (*Head of Layton House*)
Mr J R C Saxton, BA
Miss J Turquin, BA
Ms R Cagigas (*Spanish Assistant*)
Miss S Faou (*French Assistant*)
Mr E Gomez Sanchez (*Spanish Assistant*)
Mr W Makolle Mouelle (*French Assistant*)
Mr M Schiebel (*German Assistant*)

Psychology:
Dr G M Bamford
Mr S B Costello, BSc

Theology & Philosophy:
Mr J H Renwick, BA
Mrs R R Catterall, MA, MPhil
Rev Dr J W Crossley

Miss J J MacDonald, BSc
Mr M J Owen, BA (*Chaplaincy Associate*)

Memorial Library:
Miss H J Pugh, BA, MCLIP
Mrs H I Mavin, BSc Econ

Junior School
Tel: 020 8255 5335; Fax: 020 8255 5339;
email: jsadmissions@kcs.org.uk; HMJSsec@kcs.org.uk

Headmaster: Dr G A Silverlock, BEd Hons, MLitt, PhD

Deputy Heads:
Mrs H J Morren, MA (*Pastoral*)
Mr D Jones, BA (*Academic*)
Mr R S Brambley, BA (*Public Occasions*)

Assistant Head: Mr J E A Hipkiss, BSc Hons (*Outreach & Head of Science*)

Head of Rushmere: Mrs C Madge, BEd

Junior School Staff:
Mr R D Anderson, BComm (*Head of Windsor House*)
Miss V J Attié, BA (*Head of Tudor House*)
Mr N G Attwood, BA (*Head of English*)
Mr A Baker, BEd (*Professional Tutor*)
Miss C M Bitaud, BA (*Head of Years 7 & 8*)
Mrs J C Blight, BEd
Mr P K Brady, BA (*Head of Stuart House*)
Mr J R Chesworth, BA (*Head of Games & PSHE*)
Mr S F Connolly, BSc
Mrs S J de Montfort, MA
Mr J M Egan, BA (*Head of Maths & Academic Administrator*)
Miss E J Emmott, BA
Miss C Fillis, BEd
Miss L S Gillard, MA, ATC (*Head of Art & Design*)
Mrs O M Hamilton, MA (*Head of Religious Studies*)
Mr M J Hortin, MA (*Head of Classics*)
Mrs S V D Howes, BA (*Head of Drama*)
Mrs A Huckerby, BA
Miss F C Hutchison, BA
Mrs L A Jones, BEd (*Head of Music*)
Mr R Lang, BSc
Mrs J C Lewis, BA Ed
Mr E H Lougher, BA (*Head of Modern Languages*)
Mrs S J Martineau Walker, BA
Miss J E May, BMus
Mrs S F McKay, MA
Mr I D Morris, BA
Mr P Nash, BEd (*Head of Years 5 & 6*)
Mr M L Nixon, BMus (*Head of Keyboard*)
Mrs S K Phillips, BEd Hons
Mrs R F A Rose, BSc
Miss E Savitt, MEd
Mr M N Sayer, MA
Mrs C L Sanderson, BSc Hons (*maternity leave*)
Mr M N Sayer, MA
Mr J A Streatfeild, BA (*Head of Geography*)
Mrs A C Tingle, BA, Dip SpLD
Mr P P Thomas, MA (*Head of ICT*)
Mr E T Watkins, BA (*Head of History*)

Joint Junior and Senior Departments

Art:
Mr R A Carswell, MA
Miss E-J Emmott, BA
Miss L S Gillard, MA, ATC (*Head of Junior School Art & Design*)
Mrs S J Martineau Walker, BA
Mr N A Pollen, MA

Design Technology:
Miss D Langenberg, BA
Mr J D Broderick, BA

Miss L E L Spicer, BA

ICT & Computing:
Miss C A Ramgoolam, BEd, MA (*Senior School ICT Coordinator*)

Learning Enrichment:
Mrs E Goodchild, BSc, Dip SpLD
Mrs L Charlesworth, MA
Mrs A C Tingle, BA

Music:
Mr D G Phillips, MA, FRCO (*Director of Music*)
Mr P A Hatch, MusB (*Assistant Director of Music and Head of PSHE*)
Mr C A Jackson, MA (*Organist and Teacher of Academic Music*)
Mr M L Nixon, BMus (*Head of Keyboard*)
Mr L Silvera, BMus (*Head of Strings*)
Mrs L A Jones, BEd (*Head of Junior School Music*)
Mr J Begbie (*Gap year student*)

Physical Education:
Mr L B D Kane, BSc (*Director of Sport and Head of Football*)
Mr G P Butcher (*Sports Coach*)
Mr J R Chesworth, BA (*Head of Junior School Games & PE*)
Mr J G Clark, BSc (*Deputy Director of Sport*)
Mr M P Culverhouse, BA
Mr P Duggan (*Director of Rowing*)
Mrs N L Edwards, BA (*Head of Girls' Games*)
Mr J S Gibson, BA (*Teacher of PE & Games*)
Mr N C Roberts (*Director of Rugby*)
Mr R M Schilling (*Head of Hockey and Basketball*)
Mr A C Young (*Swimming Instructor*)
Mr J Jordan Ortiz (*Sports assistant*)
Mr J R Fearnside (*Gap year student*)
Mr D S Ruba (*Gap year student*)

Support Staff:
Bursar & Secretary to the Governors: Mr D S Armitage, MBE, MSc
PA to the Head Master: Mrs S Carrett
Admissions Registrar: Ms S J W Dowling, BA Hons
PA to Junior School Headmaster: Mrs S Richards

Organisation. King's College School is a day school. Boys only are admitted below the Sixth Form. The Sixth Form is co-educational. The School consists of a Senior School of 840 pupils aged 13 to 18 (11–18 from September 2016) and a Junior School of 460 pupils aged 7 to 13 who are prepared for entry to the Senior School. On entry to the Senior School pupils are placed in one of the six Houses. Every pupil has a Tutor who is responsible for their progress and welfare throughout their school career.

Admission. Entrance at 13+ to year 9 is via a pre-test which boys sit in year 6 followed by the CE or scholarship in year 8. From 2016 a new lower school will admit boys in year 7 after 11+ testing. Candidates from King's College Junior School sit either the Transfer Examination or the Scholarship Examination. Places for girls and boys are available each year for entry to the Sixth Form. Preliminary enquiries about entry should be made to the Admissions Registrar. A non-refundable Registration Fee of £150 is charged.

Junior School. Entrance examinations, graded according to the ages of the pupils, are held in the January of the year of entry. Enquiries should be made to the Junior School Secretary. (*For further details of the Junior School refer to entry in IAPS section.*)

Scholarships and Bursaries. A system of scholarships helps to set high academic standards and create opportunities for pupils from a variety of backgrounds to benefit from what the school offers at both 11+ and 13+.

11+ scholarships for entrance into the lower school, will be available in 2016. Further information will be available closer to the entrance exam.

13+ Academic scholarships: Up to twenty academic scholarships may be awarded. The number will vary according to the quality of the candidates. Candidates must be under 14 years of age on 1 September of the year in which they sit the examination. This is held at King's College School in early May. The maximum award for major scholarships will be £1,500. Smaller awards will be fixed sums of £1,000, or £500. If a pupil is awarded two or more scholarships, the maximum fee remission will be £2,000 pa. All additional financial benefits will be means tested, so that any award would be supplemented by fee remission of up to 100% inclusive of the scholarship.

13+ Art scholarships: One or more art scholarship and/or exhibition worth up to £1,500 of the school tuition fee per annum may be awarded annually to a boy of high artistic ability or potential. Selection will be by folio inspection and by invitation to a half-day of practical work in an informal and friendly atmosphere in the King's studios.

13+ Drama scholarships: One or more drama scholarships or exhibitions worth up to £1,500 of the school tuition fee per annum may be awarded annually. The school's intention is to offer awards to drama enthusiasts of outstanding ability and potential as performers, technicians or practitioners.

13+ Music scholarships: Three or more music scholarships or exhibitions worth up to £1,500 of the school tuition fee, in addition to free instrumental tuition on two instruments, may be awarded annually. The school's intention is to offer awards to instrumentalists of outstanding ability and potential. As a guideline, a boy of at least Grade 6 standard would be considered a promising candidate.

13+ Sports scholarships: One or more scholarships or exhibitions worth up to £1,500 of the school tuition fee per annum may be awarded annually to boys of exceptional ability or potential, determination and enthusiasm. Sports scholars should have exceptional talent in one or more sports, normally at least two. Candidates for all scholarships must be under 14 years of age on 1 September in the year of entry.

It is a condition of the award that the scholar achieves the King's pass mark in the common entrance examination, the King's scholarship examination or the transfer examination.

Sixth Form Academic scholarships: Rossetti and Fawcett scholarships which recognise academic performance in the entry examinations are available for boys and girls entering the Sixth Form.

Sixth Form Music scholarships: One or more music scholarships and exhibitions worth up to £1,500 may be awarded annually following auditions in November. The school also awards an organ scholarship. Recipients of these awards additionally receive free tuition on two instruments.

Sixth Form Drama scholarships: One or more drama scholarships or exhibitions worth up to £1,500 of the school tuition fee per annum may be awarded annually. The school's intention is to offer awards to drama enthusiasts of outstanding ability and potential as performers, technicians or practitioners. Selection takes place in the summer term of Year 11 through auditions and a workshop day.

Sixth Form Sport scholarships: We will consider awarding sports scholarships to Sixth Form entrants based on the pupil's track record and/or impact in their first term at King's.

Bursaries: The school is making increasing provision for Bursaries both from its own resources and as a result of the generosity of its many benefactors. Bursaries may be awarded at any of the points of entry to the junior and senior schools. Bursaries are means tested and may offer up to 100% fee remission, inclusive of any scholarships. Parents should make their initial application in advance of any entrance examination.

Fees per term (2014–2015). Tuition: Senior School £6,485, Junior School £5,175–£5,840.

The Curriculum – Junior School. The curriculum of the Junior School is designed to lead naturally into that of the senior school in content and style. All boys within a year group follow the same timetable.

Transition, First and Second Forms (Years 3, 4 & 5): English; Mathematics; History; Geography; Science and Technology; French (from year 5); Art; Drama; Music; Religious Studies; Writing Skills; ICT; Personal, Social & Health Education and three sessions of PE & Games.

Third and Remove Forms (Years 6, 7 & 8): English; Mathematics; French; Latin; History; Geography; Science; Art; Drama (year 6 only); Music; Design Technology; ICT; Religious Studies; Personal, Social & Health Education; PE and two afternoons of Games.

Homework in the Junior School: Homework is graduated according to age, starting with enough to form a regular discipline.

The Curriculum – Senior School. In the first three years the curriculum offers a wide range of options whilst keeping open the maximum choice of subjects in the Sixth Form. A very wide range of subjects is available at GCSE and IGCSE (International GCSE), with the majority of subjects now being taken at IGCSE. In the Sixth Form pupils choose to study either A Levels or the International Baccalaureate.

Religious Education. King's is an Anglican foundation but welcomes pupils from all churches and faiths. The practice of other faiths is encouraged. The School has a Chaplaincy through which pupils are prepared for confirmation and there is a Chapel for voluntary worship and communion.

Music. There is a purpose-built music school. Four orchestras, three choirs and two wind bands, as well as various smaller groups and jazz groups, perform a number of major choral and orchestral works each year. There are regular performances at major London venues including Westminster Abbey, Cadogan Hall, St Paul's Cathedral and St John's Smith Square. Also, the choir and orchestra undertake international tours. Some 30% of the pupils have individual music lessons at the School.

Games. After an introduction to a range of games in the fourth form, pupils have a free choice of termly sports. The major sports are rugby, hockey, soccer and cricket and the games programme also includes athletics, badminton, basketball, cross-country running, fencing, fives, hockey, karate, rowing, sailing, shooting, squash, swimming, tennis and water polo. The School has its own indoor heated swimming pool. The sports hall has a floor area providing 4 badminton courts, as well as volley and basketball, indoor tennis and cricket nets, together with a fitness training room and four squash courts. There are two all-weather surfaces for hockey and tennis at the Kingsway ground. The School's boathouse is on the Tideway at Putney Bridge.

School societies and activities. Every pupil is encouraged to take part in extra-curricular activities. Societies meet in the two extended lunch breaks and after school. Friday school finishes early to allow pupils to participate in a range of activities such as the CCF and community service. The school runs an impressive outreach programme supporting a number of neighbouring state schools. There are active drama and debating societies, together with a wide range of other societies.

Honours. Places offered at Oxford and Cambridge for 2013: 55, 2014: 54, 2015: 52.

Charitable status. King's College School is a Registered Charity, number 310024. It exists to provide education for children.

King's College
A Woodard School

South Road, Taunton, Somerset TA1 3LA
Tel: Headmaster: 01823 328210
          Reception: 01823 328200
Fax: 01823 328202
email: admissions@kings-taunton.co.uk
website: www.kings-taunton.co.uk

Motto: *Fortis et Fidelis*

A Woodard school, Canon Nathaniel Woodard renamed the school King's College in memory of King Alfred, when he bought it in 1879, but its historical links go back to the medieval grammar school which was founded by Bishop Fox of Winchester in 1522.

King's College, Taunton is an independent co-educational boarding and day school for 460 boys and girls aged 13–18 years.

Situated on the outskirts of Taunton, the county town of Somerset, on a splendid 100-acre site, King's College offers high academic standards, a friendly and caring day and boarding community, and has an enviable reputation for music, drama and sport. Kindness, consideration for others, honesty and self-discipline are the values which King's hopes will provide its pupils with the inner resources not just for school, but for life.

Senior Provost: The Revd Canon Brendan D Clover, MA, FRSA, LTCL

School Council:
R D V Knight, OBE, MA, DipEd (*Custos*)
Dr R A K Mott, BA, PhD (*Vice-Custos*)
The Revd Canon Mrs L M Barley, BA, MSc, PGCE
S J Carder, MA, MBA
Mrs C A Cavaghan-Pack, BEd, JP
C F B Clark, MA, MRICS, FAAV
T A Close, FCA
Mrs C Cooper
G P Davis, FCA
Sir Harry Farrington Bt, MRICS
C H Hirst, MA
J E R Houghton, MA
R D A Lloyd, BSc, MRICS
Mrs R Price
M F Trimble, BSc, ACA, FCSI

Headmaster: **R R Biggs**, BSc Cape Town, MA Oxon

Chaplain: The Revd M A Smith, BA, DipTh St Paul's

Deputy Head (*Academic*): J J B Lawford, BA
Deputy Head (*Pastoral*): Mrs K L McSwiggan, BA
Assistant Head (*Administration*) & *Director of Music*: C J Albery, BMus
Director of Extra-Curricular Activities: D J Cole, BSc
Director of Finance: M C MacEacharn, BSc, FCA
Director of Operations: A J Prosser, BSc
Director of Marketing: Mrs J M Hake, ACIM
Director of Development: Mrs L M Lavender, MBE
Administration Manager and Exams Officer: Ms F Buchanan, Dip RSA
Admissions Registrar: Mrs K J Rippin

Assistant Teachers:
* *Head of Department*
† *Housemaster/mistress*

Ms H Agg-Manning, BA
J Arliss, BA (*Philosophy of Religion and Ethics*)
Mrs C Bianco de Kellaway
J Bird, MA (*Geography*)
Mrs S Brownlee, MBA, BA, DipHM

Mrs A M Butler, BA (†*Taylor*)
O Butterworth, BSc
Mrs L S Cashmore, BA (*Classics, *Induction*)
Mrs L M M Cruttenden, MA (*Modern Languages*)
Mrs K E Cole, BA (*Learning Support, †Carpenter*)
Mrs P Corke, BA
Mrs J M Currie, LLB, Cert TEFL
Miss K M Davies, BA (*Careers*)
Mrs K A Dewberry, BA, MA (*Art*)
Mrs M V Duckham
Miss G Fagan, MA (†*Meynell*)
S Florey, BSc (†*King Alfred*)
Miss E Forward, BA
Ms J Geoffroy, BA
B M Greedy, MChem, DPhil (*Chemistry*)
Mrs L Gregory (*Economics and Business Studies*)
Mrs J A Gresswell, BSc (*Physics*)
N S Gresswell (*Co-Director of Sport*)
J H Griffiths, BTech (*Boarding*)
J W Grindle, BSc (*Design and Technology*)
Miss R L Grove, BSc, MPhys, AMInstP
Miss I S Hobday, BSc (*Senior Tutor*)
C K Holmes, BA
Mrs A M Kelly, BA
M M Lang, BSc, MPhil (*ICT*)
Mrs S Lawson
Mrs C H Lewis, BSc
P D Lewis, BSc (†*Tuckwell*)
Miss C S Mann, BSc
C R Mason, MMath
T McHenry, MA, BA
Miss M R Menheneott, BSc
Ms V K Morgan, BA
Mrs K M Mulligan, BA, RSA Dip
Mrs K J Paul, BA (*Assistant Director of Music*)
O Ridley, BA (*Sixth Form*)
J K Round, MA (*Mathematics*)
Miss K Rowe, BSc
P J Scanlan, MA (*History, *Teaching Strategies*)
Mrs C Schmidt, BA
J A Scott, BSc (*Biology*)
T D H Smith, MA (*English*)
Dr D J Snell, BSc, PhD (†*Woodard*)
Miss E Stevens, BA
M J Taylor, BA
Mrs N Williams
A J Wood, BA (*Drama, †Bishop Fox*)
Mrs L D Wrobel, BA
G Wrobel, BSc

CCF:
Lt Col D J Cole (*Officer Commanding*)
S Sgt R Mason (*SSI*)
Lt M A Smith, BA
Lt S J Shaw (*Army*)
Capt S King (*RM*)
Dr B M Greedy (*Chindits*)

Medical Officers:
Dr Yvonne L Duthie, MB BS, DCH, MRCGP
Dr A F C Fulford, MB ChB, DRCOG, MRCGP
Dr J Martin, MB BS, MRCPCH, DRCOG, MRCGP

ICT Manager: M M Lang, BSc

King's College, Taunton, delivers success at all ages whilst offering a friendly, happy and safe living and working environment. The school provides an extraordinary breadth of opportunities to pupils and has very high academic standards. As well as the school's academic success, pupils also enjoy the highest levels of achievement in sports, art, drama and music. The school won the 2007 BBC Songs of Praise Senior School Choir of the Year title, as well as the Rosslyn Park 7s Rugby Cup – a taste of the breadth of opportunity available to pupils.

King's College has produced a large number of Oxbridge entrants over the years and is well regarded by the top universities in the UK. Pupils can join the Third Form (Year 9) at 13, going on to take GCSE exams, or in the Sixth Form (Year 12) at 16 or 17 to study for A Levels. The school is blessed with highly-qualified and committed members of staff who see their role as ensuring the happiness and successful development of each individual member of the school community. The word community is very prominent at King's: Boarders and day pupils benefit from a strong Christian ethos: an environment where self-respect and kindness to others are highly-regarded qualities.

Admission. All entries are made through the Headmaster. Pupils normally enter at 13 years in the Michaelmas term and are admitted via Common Entrance or the Scholarship Examination.

The registration fee is £75.

Fees per term (2014–2015). Boarders £9,800 Day Pupils £6,650. The fees are inclusive of all extra charges of general application.

Scholarships. Scholarships are available to boys and girls going into the Third Form (13+) and Sixth Form. Major Academic scholarships are awarded, as well as scholarships for Music, Drama, Art, DT and Sport.

The Somerset Scholarship, for academic achievers from the state maintained sector, is for entry into the Sixth Form, and is available for competition in November.

Auditions for Music and Drama Scholarships and Awards are held in February (13+), and in November for Sixth Form.

Applicants for Art and Design & Technology Scholarships are invited to visit the school during the Lent term with a portfolio of work.

13+ Sports Scholarships are available for competition each February and Sixth Form Sports Scholarships are available in November.

Old Aluredian's Association. *Secretary*: P J Scanlan, MA, c/o King's College.

Charitable status. Woodard Schools Taunton Ltd is a Registered Charity, number 1103346. King's College exists to provide high quality education for boys and girls aged 13–18.

The King's Hospital

Palmerstown, Dublin 20, Ireland

Tel: 00 353 1 643 6500
Fax: 00 353 1 623 0349
email: admissions@kingshospital.ie
website: www.kingshospital.ie

Voluntary Church of Ireland (Anglican), co-educational, secondary school for boarders and day pupils aged 12–18 with 720 pupils, of whom 140 boys and 131 girls are boarders and 268 boys and 181 girls are day pupils.

The King's Hospital, one of the oldest boarding schools in Ireland, was founded in 1669 as The Hospital and Free School of King Charles II. In 1971 the School moved from the centre of Dublin to its present, modern setting in spacious, scenic grounds of over 100 acres on the banks of the River Liffey in Palmerstown, yet remains only 15 minutes from Dublin International Airport. The King's Hospital attracts pupils from all over Ireland as well as from overseas.

The fundamental values of a Christian conscience, a sense of duty and loyalty and a love of learning are actively promoted.

The school offers five day teaching with quality 5 and 7 day boarding options at extremely competitive rates. Our Saturday Programme of activities is designed to support the school curriculum and offer the pupil the opportunity to expand his/her knowledge base. Workshops in Art and Dance, Extra English classes, Indoor Sports, Zumba classes are a sample of the options available on Saturday mornings.

Chairman of Governors: Mr Ken Peare

Headmaster: **John Rafter**, BA MOD, BSc, HDipEd

Deputy Head: Louise Marshall, BEd

Assistant Heads:
John Huggard, BA, HDipEd (*Games & Recreations*)
Siobhán Daly, BA, HDipEd (*Academic Affairs*)
John Aiken, BA, HDipEd (*Pastoral Care*)

Chaplain: The Revd Canon Peter Campion, MPhil, MA, PGCE

Subject Coordinators:
Detta Brennan, Dip Fine Arts, Dip ADT (*Art*)
Orla Cummins, BA, HDipEd (*Mathematics*)
Dean Maguire, BComm, HDipEd (*Mathematics*)
The Revd Canon Peter Campion, MPhil, MA, PGCE (*Religious Education*)
Jean Atkinson, BBS, HDipEd (*Business*)
Annabel Browne, BA, HDipEd (*Geography and CSPE*)
Glenda Ua Bruadair, BA, PGCE (*English*)
Janet Nelson, MSc, BA, HDipEd, DSEN (*Special Education Needs*)
John Huggard, BA, HDipEd (*History*)
Emma Ryan, BSc QTS (*Physical Education*)
Caroline Brady, BEd (*Home Economics*)
Dymphna Morris, BA, DipComp (*Information Technology*)
Michelle Murray, MEd Mgt, BA Special, HDipEd (*Irish*)
Patrick O'Shea, BTechEd (*Design and Communication Graphics*)
Aileen Polke, BA, HDipEd (*Modern Languages*)
Miriam Wright, BMus, HDipEd (*Music*)
Susan Tanner, BSc, HDipEd, HDCG (*Career Guidance and SPHE*)
Ciaran Whelan, BSc, HDipEd (*Science*)
Cormac Ua Bruadair, BA, HDipEd (*Transition Year*)

Housemasters/mistresses:
Bluecoat (*Sixth Form boy boarders*):
Raymond McIlreavy, MEd, BA, HDipEd
Bluecoat (*Sixth Form girl boarders*):
Amy Fitzgerald, BA, HDipEd
Grace (*Girl boarders*):
Rachelle van Zyl, BComm, HDipEd
Mercer (*Girl boarders*):
Caroline Brady, BEd
Ormonde (*Boy boarders*):
Niall Mahon, BSc, HDipEd
Morgan (*Boy boarders*):
Cormac Ua Bruadair, BA, HDipEd
Bluecoat / Desmond (*Senior School day pupils*):
Yvonne Duggan, BSc, BComm, HDipEd
Swift (*Middle School day pupils*):
Noel Cunningham, MSc, BSc, HDEnvEng, HDipEd
Blackhall (*Middle School day pupils*):
Alison Gill, BA, PGCE
Stuart (*Middle School day pupils*):
Elizabeth Peoples, MA, BA, HDipEd
Desmond (*Middle School day pupils*):
Dean Maguire, BComm, HDipEd
Ivory (*Junior School day pupils*):
David Plummer, BSc, PGCE
Denise Farrelly, BA, HDipEd

Bursar: Ronald Wynne

Headmaster's P.A.: Lorraine Walker

The King's Hospital believes that every child should achieve his or her true potential intellectually and socially, through personal endeavour and the encouragement and support of our staff, parents and governors. Through our academic, pastoral and extra-curricular programmes, we strive to develop core values of:

- a love of learning which makes all study a discovery and a joy, and which leads to standards of academic excellence appropriate to each child's ability;
- a Christian conscience and awareness which enables our pupils to develop a personal faith in God, to lead fulfilling lives which will enrich the communities in which they live, to uphold truth and show respect for others as well as for themselves, and to accept responsibility for their own actions;
- a sense of duty and loyalty which encourages participation in, and commitment to, every aspect of school life.

Academic. The school has an excellent academic record (98% progression to Higher Education in 2014).

Most pupils pursue a 6 year course on entering the school at the age of 12. The first three years lead to the Junior Certificate Examination, followed by a Transition Year, and the final two years are devoted to the Irish Leaving Certificate Examination (equivalent to 4 A Levels) providing access to universities in the UK and throughout the World. Streaming is not a policy at The King's Hospital and the consistently high level of academic achievement is a reflection of the manner in which the School has always adapted to the ever-evolving education process and the ever-changing needs of its pupils by providing a comprehensive and progressive range of subjects, extensive specialist facilities and a highly qualified teaching staff.

The specialist facilities range from laboratories, workshops and computers to technical equipment and instruments, with Computer/PowerPoint facilities in all classrooms. A highly trained and well-equipped Special Needs department is available for both gifted children and those with learning difficulties. Media technology in the Harden Library provides access to national and international databases for project work as well as a computerised resource centre for information and guidance on careers.

Extra-Curricular. In addition to academic pursuits, The King's Hospital is renowned for its choice of recreational activities and offers a wide variety of sporting, music, drama and academic clubs and societies with unrivalled facilities. Pupils are encouraged to participate and all have the opportunity to represent the School at various levels in the activities of their choice.

An ultra-modern Sports Hall incorporating a fully-equipped fitness centre, a 25-metre indoor heated swimming pool and a floodlit astroturf pitch are among the outstanding facilities providing ample opportunity for Rugby, Hockey, Athletics, Swimming, Canoeing, Rowing, Cricket, Soccer, Basketball, Badminton and Tennis.

The promotion of cultural activities is catered for through Arts and Crafts, Choirs, Orchestras and Drama and Musical productions. A dedicated Performing Arts Centre is a recently built facility with the School's Assembly Hall/Theatre.

A diverse array of recreational activities is covered with clubs and societies, a Student Council, social work and European Studies, theatre and concert trips and trips abroad, both sporting and cultural.

Pastoral. Cooperation and mutual respect between pupils and staff, as well as a specified code of behaviour, are central to the daily life of the School. There are ten houses whose Housemaster or Housemistress has specific responsibility for the general welfare and development of pupils under his or her care. The diverse aspects of health education are included in the School's programme and 24 hour nursing care and a counsellor are available. Worship, according to the rites of the Church of Ireland and led by the resident Chaplain, is an integral part of daily life and pupils gain an understanding of and respect for all religious persuasions.

The Future. A vision for the future of the School is embodied in an ever-evolving School Plan and the Board of Governors is committed to implementing the development strategies within that plan. The School maintains its position as one of Ireland's leading educational institutions through this ambitious development programme, the most recent addition being the completion of a new Form 6 Centre, complete with ensuite accommodation for boarders. The King's Hospital is a school firmly rooted in tradition while continuing to be at the cutting edge of modern education.

Fees per annum (2014–2015). Boarders €14,774 (7-day Boarding), €13,750 (5-day Boarding); Day €6,674.

King's School
Bruton

Bruton, Somerset BA10 0ED

Tel: 01749 814200
Fax: 01749 813426
email: office@kingsbruton.com
website: www.kingsbruton.com
Twitter: @kingsbruton
Facebook: /kings.bruton

Motto: *Deo Juvante.*

The School was founded in 1519 by Richard Fitzjames, Bishop of London, John Fitzjames, his nephew, Attorney-General, afterwards Chief Justice of the King's Bench, and John Edmonds, DD, Chancellor of St Paul's. It was closed in 1538 on the suppression of the Monasteries, and re-founded by Edward VI in 1550.

An HMC, co-educational, 13 to 18 school based in the lovely town of Bruton, Somerset.

Governors:
Lt Gen [Retd] A M D Palmer (*Senior Warden*)
Mr R I Case, CBE, DL, FREng, FRAeS, MSc (*Chairman of Finance*)
Mr R F Badham-Thornhill, BA, PGCE
Mr C R S Birrell, MA, FCA, MCT
Mr R A E Davey, MA
Professor W P H Duffus, BVSc, MA, PhD, MRCVS
Mrs M A Edwards, BA, MA, PGCE, ARCM
Mr E G Hobhouse, BSc Eng, MBA
Mrs T G Jones, OBE, JP
Mr K L Lawes, CBE, FCA
Mrs A L Lee, RGN, RNT, BEd, MA
The Revd Canon B McConnell, Dip Th
Mr P J Phillips, FIPA
Ms H R Sampson, BA, MA, MBA
Ms Y Spencer, MA, LLB

Clerk to the Governors: Col S G Adlington

Headmaster: Mr I S Wilmshurst, MA Cantab

Deputy Headmaster: Mr G J Evans, BSc Econ
Second Deputy Head: Mrs A J Grant, BA
Director of Studies: Mr A Kok, BEng, CEng
Head of Teaching and Learning: Mr D J Cupit, MA

Heads of Departments/Subjects:
Mr S W Spilsbury, BEdTech (*Head of Art*)
Mr T Fletcher, BA (*Head of History*)
Revd N H Wilson-Brown, BSc (*Chaplain, Head of Religious Studies*)
Mr C A Barrow, BA (*Head of Boys' PE and Boys Games*)
Ms M H King, BA (*Head of Theatre Studies*)
Mr J B Slingo, BSc (*Head of Economics & Business Studies*)
Mrs G de Mora, BSc (*Head of Mathematics, Designated Deputy Child Protection Officer*)
Mrs R A Vigers-Belgeonne, BSc (*Head of Food Science*)

Mrs A L Ashworth, BSc (*Head of Physics*)
Mr D J Gorodi, GRSM, LRAM (*Director of Music*)
Mrs A C Sherrard, BA (*Head of Learning Support Unit*)
Mr D R Cowley, BEd (*Head of Design and Technology*)
Dr S D Osborne, BSc, MSc, PhD (*Head of Chemistry*)
Mrs P G Atkinson-Kennedy, BSc (*Director of Sport*)
Mrs S L Wilson-Brown, BEd (*Head of PHSEE*)
Mr A J Marshfield, BMus (*Director of Choral Studies*)
Mrs A Maistrello, BA (*Head of English as a Foreign Language*)
Mrs E Loveless, BA (*Head of Modern Foreign Languages*)
Mr D J Hodder, BSc (*Head of Geography*)
Mr D J Cupit, MA (*Head of Biology*)
Mr M S J Hambleton (*Head of English*)
Mrs N Archer, MSc (*Head of Psychology*)
Mrs L J Bray, BA (*Head of Spanish*)

Designated Child Protection Officer: Mr R J P Lowry, BA
Examinations Officer: Mr T R N Walker, MA

Housemasters/mistresses:
Lyon House: Mr R S Hamilton, BEd
New House: Mr W R Dawe, BA
Blackford House: Mr N P Bunday, BA, MA
Wellesley House: Mrs J L Deaney
Arion House: Mrs B Griffiths, BSc
Old House: Mr M K W Jeffrey, BSc
Priory House: Mrs E J Simper, MA

Bursar: Mrs H Feilding, MA, ACA
Finance Bursar: Mrs S L Blundy, BSc, ACCA
Registrar: Mrs C S E Oulton
Headmaster's PA: Mrs S L Carpenter
Bursar's PA: Mrs E Milln
School Administrator: Mrs J L Deaney
School Receptionist: Mrs T D Shean
Estates Manager: Mr P J Cloney, MBE

School Doctors:
Dr J Dolman, BSc, MBBCh, MRCGP
Dr U Nauman, DRCOH, MRCGP
Dr N Gompertz, BSc, MB ChB, MRCGP
Dr S Franks, ChB, MB, MRCGP
Dr C M William, MBBS, DRCOG, MRCGP

Hazlegrove (King's Bruton Preparatory School)
Sparkford, Yeovil, Somerset BA22 7JA
Telephone: 01963 440314 (*Headmaster and Secretary*)
Fax: 01963 440569
email: office@hazlegrove.co.uk
website: www.hazlegrove.co.uk

Headmaster: Mr R B Fenwick, MA

Deputy Head: Mr M Davis, BEd Hons
Director of Studies: Mr D Edwards, BA Hons, MEd
Head of Pre-Prep: Miss E Lee, BEd Hons
Assistant Head (Admin): Mr C J Smith, CertEd
Assistant Head (Pastoral): Mr D Floyd
Headmaster's Secretary: Mrs S Newton
Head of Admissions: Mrs F O'Neill

Number of Pupils. 329. Boarders: 72 girls, 156 boys. Day: 47 girls, 54 boys. Sixth Form: 129.

Pastoral Care. When pupils first arrive at King's, they are welcomed into a genuinely caring community, where individuals and individuality are valued. At the centre of this community are the boarding houses which are in the care of a Housemaster or Housemistress who has overall responsibility for each pupil and who is that pupil's first and last supporter throughout his or her time at King's. In addition, pupils have their own tutor, who will keep an eye on academic progress, ensure that any problems are resolved, and offer advice and friendship. Housemasters, Housemistresses, matrons, tutors and senior pupils all work to ensure that each new pupil settles in quickly and successfully.

From the very beginning our pupils lead busy lives, full of work, activities and friends. The size of the School is a particular strength; in a community where everyone is known, pupils cannot drift, hide or get lost.

We believe that close communication between school and parents is very important, and the Housemaster/Housemistress will be the first point of contact for parents, who are kept informed of progress through reports and more informal contacts.

Day pupils are fully integrated into the life of the boarding houses and it is often hard to dislodge them from King's. They will frequently stay late into the evenings and come into school at weekends. For them, and for our many boarders, the friendships they build at King's become of great value to them, both while they are at school and after they have moved on.

Co-education. Girls have been admitted since 1969 to Sixth Form courses subject to GCSE level success, either as boarders or day girls. Junior girls from age 13 have been welcomed since 1997 when two girls' houses were opened and a third was added in 2007. King's was full for girls for the first time in its history in 2012.

Buildings. The oldest portion of the buildings date from the early part of the 16th century. This, with numerous additions and alterations, forms Old House. New House was begun in 1872 and has been considerably extended since. Priory House was acquired in 1942. Lyon House was opened in 1954, and extended in 1976 and 1986, and Blackford House in September 1960. Wellesley was opened in 1984 and Arion in 1997. There is a Medical Centre, staffed by a senior nurse. The Memorial Hall, built by Old Brutonians after the First World War, incorporates a classroom wing, a recital and meeting room and the refurbished and extended Music School. A development programme, completed in 1979, included the extension of the Music School, a large Sports Hall with a theatre in the same building, and the self-service Dining Hall, built in 1974, which has classrooms and the Norton Library on the first floor. A classroom block, Chemistry, Maths and Modern Languages, lead to the splendid Design Centre opened in 1989 and incorporating all facilities for Design, Technology, Art and Information Technology. An extension to the Design Centre housing a Physics Department and extended ICT facilities was opened in September 1994. A new Science Centre for Biology, Chemistry and Home Economics was opened in September 1999 and a new Library/Learning Centre built in 2004. 2007 saw the completion of a Sixth Form Social Centre and a third girls' boarding house. The stunning Basil Wright Reception Centre was opened in September 2008. A new synthetic playing surface for hockey was opened in December 2010. An accelerated programme of boarding house refurbishment is under way with all houses to be completed by September 2014. The Wi-Fi system has been fully upgraded and a second hockey astroturf was opened in October 2013.

Curriculum. King's is divided into Upper and Lower Sixth, Fifth, Fourth and Third forms. The subjects taught include Art, Biology, Business Studies, Chemistry, Design & Technology, Drama & Theatre Studies, Economics, English Language, English Literature, French, Geography, German, History, Information Technology, Latin, Mathematics, Further Mathematics, Music, Music Technology, Personal, Social, Health and Economic Education, Philosophy & Ethics, Physical Education, Physics, Psychology, Religious Studies, and Spanish. National Curriculum GCSE courses are followed up to the Fifth Form, after which, in the Sixth Form, pupils are able to specialise for subjects at A Level, for entry to Universities, the Services and other Careers. BTecs in Health Hospitality and Sport are offered from September 2013. There is a Learning Support department. Gifted & Talented activities include the Extended Project Qualification. Philosophy 4 Children and the Level 1 Project Qualification have been introduced at Third form.

Games. The main school sports are Cricket, Rugby, Hockey and Netball. There is a wide variety of other sports available as options. Boys play Rugby in the Christmas Term, Hockey in the Easter Term; Cross-Country Running for both girls and boys takes place in both. Boys Cricket is played in the summer, but Athletics and Tennis are also encouraged. Girls play hockey in the Christmas term, Netball in the Easter term, and Tennis in the summer. There are 2 main playing fields, 17 Tennis Courts, 2 Squash Courts, 2 Fives Courts, and a Sports Hall. A Physical Education course is provided for all pupils. Judo, Basketball, Badminton, Fencing and Golf are also part of the School sports provision. Hockey is now sponsored and the Head of Hockey is supported by an additional hockey professional. Hockey is played on two full-size astroturf surfaces and indoor in the Sports Hall.

There is a Combined Cadet Force which all boys and girls are expected to join for a definite period, after which they can undertake other forms of Service in the community. There is a Rifle Range, and Army ranges are nearby. Pupils are also engaged in the Duke of Edinburgh's Award Scheme (with 19 pupils now undertaking cycling expeditions) and Ten Tors.

Music. Vocal and Instrumental Music has for many years been one of the strong features in education at the School, and pupils are strongly encouraged to learn and appreciate music. Frequent concerts are given by Choir, Orchestra, Dance, Jazz and Military bands. The School has Full, Chapel and Chamber Choirs as well as a Boys' Barbershop and a Girls' Close Harmony Group.

Societies and other activities. There is time every day devoted to a wide range of activities, including Acting, Archery, Art, Chess, Computer Programming, Debating, Drama, Electronics, Horse Riding, Music, Printing, and Photography. Design, Technology, Art and Computing are all provided in the Design Centre. A Community Service activity provides help in the town and the neighbourhood.

Worship. Assembly takes place in the Memorial Hall. A weekly, whole school service takes place in the large parish church of St Mary, Bruton. Pupils are prepared by the Chaplain for Confirmation in the Autumn Term. There is a flourishing Christian fellowship group and many Bible study groups. TGI Friday is a voluntary, weekly chaplaincy activity, hosted by the Chaplain. Around 50/60 attend each week. A Lenten Address team visit annually for a week.

Careers. Careers and Higher Education materials are readily available in the library and via the school intranet. Most of our pupils go on to university so the main thrust of the work of the Higher Education and Careers is aimed at university application. Lower Sixth pupils and parents are invited to a Higher Education and Careers Convention in January while sixth formers are also put in contact with Old Brutonians and parents via King's Connect – a social media forum to help with careers advice, university choice and work placement. Younger pupils are well briefed on the importance of topics such as subject choice, CV writing and work experience. Psychometric testing and consequent advice is available for fifth formers. The King's Bruton Gap Year programme is organised over two years. The first year is spent fundraising, and culminates in an expedition. When they leave school, those involved in the programme will spent time serving in an orphanage in Salam, India during their GAP year.

Admission. No child is admitted to the Senior School before age 13. Entry is via the Common Entrance or Scholarship Examinations.

Scholarships and Bursaries. Scholarships are awarded annually for competition. The number and value of awards are at the Headmaster's discretion. The maximum financial value of any non means-tested scholarship or award or combination of awards is 20% of fees. Scholarships and awards may be augmented by means-tested Bursaries.

13+ Entry: All scholarship and award candidates need the support of their current school for their application. The form must be signed by their current Head Teacher. All candidates for awards other than the Academic Scholarships should be of good Common Entrance standard. Scholarships available are Academic, All Rounder, Sport, Art and Technology and Music. Please see the school website for more details.

Sixth Form Entry: A report will be requested from the current school in support of the candidate's application. Scholarships available are Academic, Art, Sport, Drama and Music. Please see the school website for more information.

Further details of specific entry requirements can be obtained from the Registrar on 01749 814251.

Fees per term (2014–2015). Boarding £9,642, Day £6,868.

The fees are inclusive of necessary extras, eg Medical Attendance, Games.

The School offers a 20% remission of fees to all boarding students with one or both parents serving in the Armed Forces. The maximum combined value of Forces remission plus other awards is 25%. Other awards may be subsumed within the Forces remission. Forces fee remission may be augmented by means-tested bursaries.

The Preparatory School is at Hazlegrove, Sparkford, 9 miles from Bruton, and takes pupils from age 2½–13. The fullest cooperation and continuity are ensured between the Preparatory and Senior School, boys and girls passing from one to the other having obtained a pass in Common Entrance.

(For further details, see Hazlegrove's entry in IAPS section.)

Old Brutonian Association. Contact with the Old Brutonian Association can be made via the school.

Charitable status. King's School, Bruton is a Registered Charity, number 1071997. It exists to provide education for boys and girls from 13–18.

The King's School
Canterbury

Canterbury, Kent CT1 2ES
Tel: 01227 595501
            Bursar: 01227 595544
            Admissions: 01227 595579
Fax: 01227 766255
email: headmaster@kings-school.co.uk
website: www.kings-school.co.uk

Visitor: The Lord Archbishop of Canterbury

Governors:

Chairman: The Very Revd Dr R A Willis, BA, Dip Th, FRSA, Dean of Canterbury Cathedral
Vice-Chairman: N S L Lyons, MA
Dr C R Prior, DPhil, PhD
The Ven S A Watson, Archdeacon of Canterbury, MA, MPhil
A M L Stewart
Mrs E McKendrick, BA
The Revd Canon D C Edwards
Sir Roger De Haan, CBE, DL
The Revd Canon C P Irvine
J D Tennant, MRICS
R C A Bagley, LLB
Mrs C Evelegh, Dip CE, Dip SpLD
Miss F J Judd, QC
M W S Bax, FRICS
T M Steel, MA, DL
The Revd Canon N Papadopulos, MA
Dr M Sutherland, BSc, MSc, PhD

Clerk to the Governors: M R Taylor, FRSA

Governors Emeriti:
The Very Revd J A Simpson, OBE, MA, DD
The Very Revd D L Edwards, DD
The Lady Kingsdown, OBE, DCL

Headmaster: P J M Roberts, MA

Headmaster's PA: Mrs A Kelly, BA; Mrs P Picarelli
Headmaster's Office PA: Miss C J M Finch
PA/Receptionist: Miss J M Henderson, BA

Senior Deputy Head: Mrs E A Worthington, MA

Deputy Head Academic: G R Cocksworth, BA, MA
Deputy Head Pastoral: Miss T Lee, BA

PA to Senior Deputy Head/Deputy Head Pastoral: Miss F Lillie, BA
Academic Assistant: Mrs G V Hone, BSc Econ
Examinations Officer: Mrs L A Renault

Head of Sixth Form: Mrs C D Cornell, BA, MA
Head of Middle School: A S D Stennett, BSc
Head of Lower School: R P Cook, BSc, and Mrs K J Newsholme, BA
Head of Oxbridge: Mrs E J Kornicki, MA
Head of Extended Projects: Miss A K Fraser, MA, MPhil

Bursar: M R Taylor, FRSA
Estates Bursar: L Dudas, BSc, Dip Surv, Associate RICS
Deputy Finance Bursar: D Rogers, MAAT
Human Resources Manager: J Hadlow, BA, Associate CIPD

Foundation Director: P C J Sheldon, BA

Head of Strategy and Planning: I S MacEwen, MA

Registrar: G E Sinclair, AGSM, FRSA
Assistant Registrar: Mrs B Skilton

Senior Tutor: M J Miles, MA
University and Careers Adviser: Ms P D Williams, MA, DipCG

Senior Chaplain: The Revd Canon C F Arvidsson, DipTheol
Assistant Chaplain: The Revd M Robbins, BA, BTh

Librarian: Mrs S A L Gray, BSc Econ, MCLIP

Medical Officers:
Dr W Lloyd Hughes, MB BS
Dr T Crook, MB BS, MRCGP, DRCOG

* *Head of Department*
† *Housemaster/mistress*

Art:
Mrs G C Burrows, BA
*P K Cordeaux, BA
M McArdle, BA
Mrs J Taylor-Goodman, BA, MA
I S Wallace, BA
D K Willis, BA

S C Pleasants, BA
G E Sinclair, AGSM

Economics:
*S N Chester, BA
Mrs L A Horn, BSc
†R W Ninham, MA
H J Phillips, BSc

Classics:
M W Browning, BA
Mrs H Johnson, BA
Miss K M M Synge, MA
*Miss J Taylor, BA

English:
†Mrs J M Cook, BA
Mrs C D Cornell, BA, MA
*A J W Lyons, BA, MA, FRSA
Ms E V Nairne, BA
Mrs K J Newsholme, BA
Miss K E O'Connor, BA, MSt
Dr C E Pidoux, MA, PhD, ALCM
Miss L W K Pinching, BA
†Mrs C J Shearer, BA

Design:
M J Franks, BEd
*M J Rolison, BEd
G J Swindley, BSc

Drama:
*Mrs R J Beattie, BA, FRSA

†Mrs A L Young, MA

Geography:
†S E Anderson, BA
†A J Holland, BSc
†N L Phillis, MA
Mrs C F B V Roberts, BSc
*R P Sanderson, BA
M C E Turner, BSc

History:
Miss C E Anderson, BA, MA
Mrs D J Ardley, BA
J P Bass, BA
S J Graham, MA
E G Immink, BA
Miss E Park, BA
*D J C Perkins, BA, MA, DipLaw, PhD
Mrs E A Worthington, MA

History of Art:
*D J Felton, BA, MA
Miss D M Francis, BA, DipEcol, Cert Vis

ICT and Computing:
Mrs L M Cousins, BA
*†A J Holland, BSc
B D M Katz, BA, MSc
Dr S Kerridge, BA, BSc, PhD
M C E Turner, BSc

Mathematics:
M O Cox, MA, MEng, Dip ITEC
M P H Dath, L-ès-ScM, M-ès-ScM
J P E Dickson, BSc, MSc, RN
Miss E R Laughlin, MSci
†Mrs J Gorman, BSc
B D M Katz, BA, MSc
Dr S Kerridge, BA, BSc, PhD
A McFall, BSc
*S P Ocock, BA
Dr K J Palmer, BSc, PhD
R C Stuart, BSc
R N Warnick, MA

Learning Support:
Mrs D J Ardley, BA
Mrs P J Brown, BA, MA
Mme M-D Bradburn, BA
Miss C J Grannell, MA
*Ms G R Moorcroft, BEd, MA

Modern Languages:
†Mrs Z T Allen, MA
*T J Armstrong, MA, MA Ed
Miss L N Bernardo Otamendi, Lda, MPhil, MA
Mrs A Browne, LSc
Mrs M B Garcés-Ramón, Lda
Mrs N Geoffroy, L-ès-ScEd
*Mrs R E Heskins, BA
T I Jennings, BA
*Mrs L Liu, BA, MPhil
Miss J M Maréchal, BA, MSc

M J Miles, MA
C P Newbury, BA
Miss A M Pedraza Rascado, BA, MA
D P Rowlands, MA
Miss L Salter, MA Ed
Mrs L J Warnick, MA
Mrs C L Kelly, MA, BEd
Miss F Zanardi, MA

Music:
K Abbott, DipRCM
P R Barton Hodges, BMus
*W Bersey, BMus
S J R Matthews, MA
N Parvin, BMus
A Pollock, MA
N G Todd, MA

Politics:
Mrs D J Ardley, BA
I S MacEwen, MA
*O T Moelwyn-Hughes, BA, LLB, MSt

Physical Education:
Miss H Barley, BA, PGCE
T G Hill, BSpSt
*M E Lister, BSc, MSc
R A L Singfield, BEd (*Sport)

Religious Studies and Philosophy:
The Revd Canon C F Arvidsson, DipTheol
G R Cocksworth, BA, MA
*Mrs C A Cox, BA, MPhil
Miss A K Fraser, MA, MPhil
Miss T Lee, BA
†J W Outram, BA
The Revd M Robbins, BA, BTh
Miss C A Tyndall, BA

Science:

Biology:
Miss K Budden, BSc
†J M Hutchings, BA
Mrs E J F Kornicki, MA
Miss S A Rajska, BSc
M J W Smiley, MA
*M J Thornby, BSc
Mrs J A Watson, BA, MSc, MIBiol
*S J Winrow-Campbell, BSc, MIBiol, CBiol

Chemistry:
D M Arnott, BSc, PhD
R P Cook, BSc
Miss A R Donkin, MChem
F Elias Schliserman, Ldo, PhD
*S T Hayes, MSci, PhD, MRSC
L W Hynes, BSc PhD
D A Scott, BSc, MSc, MA Ed, MRSC (*Science)
A S D Stennett, BSc

Physics:
C B Burson-Thomas, MEng

*Miss L M Comber BSc
  (*Science*)
Mrs D M Pollitt, BSc
†Mrs E S Ladd, BEng
†M C Orders, BSc

D M Tanton, MA, MSc,
  DipD'I, PhD

Geology:
*M R Mawby, BSc

Houses and Housemasters/mistresses:

School House: M J Thornby
The Grange: M C Orders
Walpole: Mrs A L Young
Meister Omers: R W Ninham
Marlowe (*day*): S E Anderson
Luxmoore: Ms L Cousins
Galpin's: J M Hutchings
Linacre: J W Outram
Tradescant: N L Phillis
Broughton: Mrs C J Shearer
Mitchinson's (*day*): Mrs E S Ladd
Jervis: Mrs J Gorman
Harvey: Mrs J M Cook
Bailey (*Sixth Form*): Mrs Z T Allen
Carlyon (*day*): A J Holland

The Junior King's School
Milner Court, Sturry, Nr Canterbury, CT2 0AY.
Tel: 01227 714000

Headmaster: P M Wells, BEd

(*For further details see King's Junior School entry in IAPS section.*)

St Augustine's foundation of a monastic school in Canterbury in 597 AD marks the origin of The King's School: hence, its claim to be the oldest school in the country. It was re-founded by King Henry VIII in 1541. More recently, a Junior School has been established on the former estate of Lord Milner outside the city. The close relationship with the Cathedral Foundation has been there throughout.

King's Scholars. Many schools cherish the notion that they are the oldest school in the country, but there is little doubt that there has been a school on the present World Heritage site of King's School, Canterbury since the Augustinian mission to England in 597 AD. The name of the school and its intimate relationship with the Cathedral community of the mother church of the Anglican Communion date from the Henrician settlement, as do the King's scholars who, along with the Headmaster and the Senior Deputy Head, form part of the original Foundation of Christchurch, Canterbury. So much for the history, the King's scholars continue to occupy buildings and be taught in classrooms that predate the Reformation. Besides their function in the Cathedral, the King's scholars are at the heart of the vibrant and open-ended academic life of the school. Each year, some of the King's scholars are on full means-tested bursaries, keeping alive the original vision of the school. The modern King's scholar discovers a school which is fully coeducational, diverse in its catchment and intentions, as well as in tune with the wider life of the city of Canterbury and national/international context beyond its immediate compass.

Scholarships and Bursaries. Up to twenty King's Scholars and Exhibitioners are elected each year following competitive examinations and interviews in February. A further group of King's Scholars are added at the Sixth Form entrance stage (competitive examination and interviews in the November preceding entry). These academic awards have a meritocratic value of 10%, but the crucial thing is that they can be augmented by means-tested bursaries up to 100%. The extremely strong tradition of music at King's, both instrumental and choral, means that music scholarships (up to 12) are generously provided for. The school is particularly welcoming for those who have come on to King's from the choir schools of Cathedrals and Colleges. There are further Music Scholarships made for Sixth Form entry.

There are further Scholarships and Exhibitions at 13+ for exceptional ability in Art, Sport – the Gower Sports Scholarships named after the former England cricket captain, and the school welcomes applications from pupils with an outstanding interest for CDT.

Academic Life. The King's curriculum is distinct for its combination of striving for the very highest standards in the most appropriate Public Examinations (IGCSEs at the end of Year 10 for a few subjects, but mainly at the end of Year 11, AS Levels at the end of Year 12 and A2s at the end of Year 13) on the one hand, and the pursuit of learning and the development of the intellect for its own sake (self-standing courses, tutorials and lectures in the evenings and extended project qualifications, as well as independent research). The school puts particular emphasis on studying Mandarin, German and Russian, as well as 'new' subjects like Photography and Dance. A wide degree of choice of subject in the Sixth Form (Geology and Philosophy, for example) is often an engine for academic success.

Some 25 offers of admission to Oxford and Cambridge are received each year.

All round vision. Christopher Marlowe, William Harvey and Thomas Linacre number amongst King's pupils and the pursuit of the Renaissance ideal still resonates in the contemporary school. The strongest encouragement is given to music, drama, sport, CCF and the visual arts. This stems from belief in the value of these activities in themselves, but also since recreation and success in these fields leads to growth in self-confidence and better academic performance. Alongside these activities are opportunities to get involved in outreach programmes and pursue the Duke of Edinburgh's Award.

Numbers and Organisation. There are currently 825 pupils on the school roll, 453 boys and 368 girls, of whom 76% are boarders. There are 6 boys' boarding houses, 6 girls' boarding houses and 3 (mixed) day houses. Junior King's School, the prep school of King's, occupies a site on the River Stour, in Sturry, 3 miles from Canterbury. There are currently 384 pupils at Junior King's, 213 boys and 171 girls of whom 76 are boarders. To the east of the main school buildings in the cathedral precincts is St Augustine's, home to 5 boarding houses, the original Medieval Hall and magnificent school library. There are 2 major sites for sport, Birley's and Blore's, each with extensive sports facilities.

Admission. Application should be made to the Assistant Registrar. It is advisable to register pupils at an early age. Admission is normally through the Common Entrance Examination, the King's School entrance examination (for non-CE candidates) or, if academically able, through the School's own Scholarship Examination. The age of entry is about 13.

Fees per term (2014–2015). Senior School: £11,120 for boarders and £8,430 for day pupils. Junior School: £7,635 for boarders and £5,015–£5,580 for day pupils.

OKS (Old King's Scholars). *Secretary*: Mrs S Tingle, OKS & Foundation Office, Tel: 01227 595669; email: oks@kings-school.co.uk.

The King's Society exists for all parents, past and present. A termly programme of social and cultural events is open to all members and is published on the school website.

Charitable status. The King's School of the Cathedral Church of Canterbury is a Registered Charity, number 307942. It exists to provide education for boys and girls.

The King's School
Chester

Chester CH4 7QL
Tel: 01244 689500
Fax: 01244 689501
email: info@kingschester.co.uk
website: www.kingschester.co.uk

Motto: '*Rex Dedit, Benedicat Deus.*'
  The School was founded AD 1541 by King Henry VIII, in conjunction with the Cathedral Church of Chester. It was reorganised under the Endowed Schools Act in 1873, and by subsequent schemes of the Ministry of Education. The School is now Independent. The aim of the School is to prepare pupils for admission to Universities and the professions, and at the same time provide a liberal education.

Patron: His Grace the Duke of Westminster, KG, CB, CVO, OBE, TD, CD, DL

Governors:
Mrs E M Johnson, JP (*Chairman*)
The Rt Revd the Lord Bishop of Chester
The Very Revd the Dean of Chester
Prof J H P Bayley, MA, PhD, FRS
Prof J Billowes, MA, DPhil, FInstP
Mrs J L Clague, BA, ACA
J C Davies, MSc, CEng, FICE, MCIOB, MIWM
K Hassett, BA, MSc
Revd Canon P Howell-Jones, MA
K James, FCA
P M H Jessop, BA
Mrs K Kerr, MBA, BA
I O'Doherty, BE, MSc, MBA
Dr D Pawson, BSc, PhD
Mrs R J Phillipson, BA, FCIPD
G P Ramsbottom, BSc, MSc, MRICS
R A Storrar
W J Timpson, OBE

Clerk to the Governors: S P Cross, MSc, LLB

Headmaster: C D Ramsey, MA, late scholar of Corpus Christi, Cambridge

Deputy Head: Dr J M Byrne, BA, PhD
Deputy Head (Academic): J E Millard, BA
Deputy Head (Pastoral): M J Harle, BSc
Head of Sixth Form: J P Carter, MA
Head of Academic Administration: S Neal, BA
Head of Learning Support: Mrs S Glass, BA
Head of Co-curricular: R G Wheeler, BA

Assistant staff:
* *Head of Department*

Art and Design:
*S Downey, BA
Ms L Black, BA
Mrs A L Hollingworth, BA

Biology:
*Dr H C Faulkner, BSc, DPhil
R D J Elmore, BSc, MIBiol, CBS
Mrs P Housden, BEd
R H Jones, BSc, PhD
L A Parkes, BSc, MSc

Chemistry:
*A Cook, BSc, PhD
Dr C A Gleave, BSc, PhD
M J Harle, BSc

Mrs J E Jepson, BSc
Dr J R Macnab, BSc, PhD
Mrs K L Russon, BSc

Classics:
*P R Wilcock MA
Mrs S H Gareh, BA, MA
M J P Punnett, MA

Design Technology:
*R J Curtis, BSc
N J Dudderidge, BA, MSc
Miss E Hodgson, BA

Drama:
*Mrs C L Howdon, BA

Economics:
*S D Walton, BA, MSc

Mrs S Glass, BA
Miss E M Rowley, BSocSc
Miss E J Tappin, BA, MA, LLB

English:
*R J Aldridge, BA
Mrs H C Lydon, BA
Dr A M McMahon, MA, DPhil
Mrs A E Richards, BA
Miss A C Tedford, MA
R G Wheeler, BA

Geography:
*J H King, MA, MSc
Mrs R H Aldridge, BA
J A D Blackham, BA
J F Day, MSc

History & Politics:
*P G Neal, BA
Miss S E Butler, MA
J P Carter, MA
Mrs G K Chadwick, BA
S Neal, BA

Information Technology:
*R J Higgins, MSc
Mrs E E Simpson, BA, MBA

Mathematics:
Miss H E Bannaghan, MMath (*Acting Head of Maths*)
S D Bibby, BSc
C J Canty, BSc
Mrs S Cooper, BSc
Dr P Dello Stritto, PhD
Mrs A Ignata, BSc
Mrs C E Lanceley, BSc
Mrs C Plass, BSc
Mrs C N Ranson, BSc
Miss D Roberts, BSc

Junior School:
Head: S A Malone, BEd
Deputy Head: A Griffiths, BA
Director of Studies: T W Griffin, BA

Assistant Staff:

Miss J M Anderson, BA, CertEd
Mrs J Benson, BA
Mrs K Dickson, BA
H J Duncalf, BEd
Mrs M M Griffin, BEd, MEd
K A Hollingworth, BEd
Mrs N C M Moffatt, BA
Mrs M D O'Leary, BA

Peripatetic Staff:
W Armstrong, BA, PGRNCM (*Oboe*)
Miss C Barker, BA (*Cello*)
Mrs F Cooke, MA, LRAM (*Voice*)
S J Hall, BSc (*Bass Guitar*)
Mrs V L Ierston, LTCL (*Piano & Flute*)
Miss R Jones, GMus, RNCM, LRAM, ARCM, FLCM (*Piano*)
G Macey, ATCL (*Woodwind*)
Ms S Marrs, FTCL (*Voice*)
D Ortiz, BMus (*Head of Brass*)
A Parker, MA (*Saxophone*)

Modern Languages:
*P D Shannon, MA
Mrs C E Irvine, BA
Miss R E Lindesay, BA
Mrs K L Shapland, MA
Mrs K J Thurlow-Wood, BA
Mme F Vergnaud, MA

Music:
*T M Harvey, BA, ARCO (*Director of Music*)
Ms K Z Andrews, BMus, MA (*Head of Academic Music*)
Mrs V L S Latifa, BMus
J E Millard, BA

Personal & Social Education:
*M S Lee, MA

Physical Education:
*R Lunn, BEd (*Director of Sport*)
Mrs K Jones, BA (*Assistant Director of Sport*)
R I D Hornby, BA
B Horne, BSc (*Director of Football*)
Ms J Huck, BA
C Morris, BEd
Mrs C Sumner, BA

Physics:
*N Heritage, MSc, PhD, MInstP, CPhys
S Bosworth, MA, DPhil, FRAS
Ms H M Davies, BSc, MSc
N A Grisedale, MPhys
B Horne, BSc

Religious Studies:
*J R Rees, BA
M S Lee, MA
Ms J E Rutberg, MA

D M O'Neil, BSc
Mrs S Parker BEd
J H Pownall, BEd
Mrs D L Rudd, BA
Miss K A Savage, BA
J N Spellman, BEd
Mrs N J Stevens, BMus
Mrs N M Tomlinson, BA
Mrs S Tomlinson, BEd

M Reynolds BA (*Piano*)
Mrs J Riekert, ATCL (*Flute*)
S A Rushforth (*Head of Strings*)
Mrs S E Tyson, MA (*Woodwind, Voice*)
C J Wharton, BA (*Drums & Music Technology*)
Mrs J Williams, BA (*Bassoon*)
P J Williams, BEng (*Electric Guitar*)
T Wyss, ARCM, LRAM, LTCL (*Brass*)

Extra-Curricular Staff:
Director of Rowing: J A D Blackham, BA
Contingent Commander, CCF: Maj M S Lee, MA
Duke of Edinburgh's Award Coordinator: D A Brown
Educational Visits Coordinator: R I D Hornby, BA

Bursar: Mrs J H Beer, ACMA, CGMA, CIPS
Director of Marketing: Ms V M Titmuss, BA
Admissions Manager: Mrs E R Sears, BA
Estates Manager: P N Cotter
Head Librarian & Archivist: Mrs R Harding, MA
Examinations Officer: R D J Elmore, BSc
School Nurse: Sister S J Catherall, RGN
Care Scheme Supervisor: Mrs L Hornby

Headmaster's PA: Mrs A M E Wilson, BA

Organisation. The School, which at present numbers 987, consists of (i) a Junior School for pupils aged 7 to 11 years, which is housed in a separate building, but is run in collaboration with (ii) the Senior School.

Admission. Boys and girls are admitted to the Senior School aged between 11 and 12, and may remain till the end of the year in which they become 18. Pupils in the Junior School normally move into the Senior School at the age of 11 on the evidence of academic ability tracked during their years at the Junior School. Students are admitted to the Sixth Form on the basis of GCSE results.

The Entrance Examinations for the Junior and Senior Schools are held in the Lent Term. Applications are made on a form obtainable from the School and on the website.

Academic. The subjects offered for study in the Sixth Form are – on the Arts side: Art, Business Studies, Classical Studies, Economics, English, English Language, French, Geography, German, History, Latin, Music, Philosophy, Politics, Religious Studies, Spanish; and on the Science side: Biology, Chemistry, Computing, Further Mathematics, Mathematics, Physics, Sports Science and Technology. It is possible to take most combinations of subjects at AS and A Level. All pupils in the Sixth Form take four subjects at AS Level but may drop to three subjects at A Level if they wish.

Spiritual life. The School is part of the Cathedral Foundation and regularly holds its own services in the Cathedral. Spiritual assemblies are held regularly in school.

Music. Music is part of the general curriculum for all pupils up to the age of 14. After this music may be taken at GCSE and A Level. Private tuition in orchestral instruments, piano and organ is available. There are many musical ensembles and choral groups including the Schola Cantorum which leads the worship in Cathedral services.

Cadet Corps. There is a CCF contingent which gives pupils opportunities to develop leadership skills and to undertake adventurous training.

Outdoor Education. Opportunities are provided both within and outside the curriculum for outdoor education, and all pupils in each of the first three years of the senior school spend some days away at centres specialising in outdoor activities. In addition many pupils participate in the Duke of Edinburgh's Award Scheme at all levels.

Games. Soccer, Rugby, Hockey, Cricket, Rowing, Swimming, Badminton, Basketball, Athletics, Netball, Tennis, Squash, Golf, Rounders.

Buildings. Formerly situated adjacent to the Cathedral, the school moved into new buildings in 1960 situated in rural surroundings nearly 2 miles from the centre of Chester. Though the Junior and Senior Schools are on the same site

of 32 acres, they are housed in separate buildings each having its own playing fields. In 1960 the new school was formally declared open by Her Majesty Queen Elizabeth the Queen Mother. In 1964 a new indoor Swimming Pool and Pavilion were opened. More new buildings were added in the course of the 1980s and 1990s.

A major development plan was launched in October 2002 with the aim of providing an all-weather playing surface, improvements to the Art and Design / Technology centres and a new medical room. The new Music School was completed in 2005. An exciting new performance centre, The Vanbrugh Theatre, opened in 2011 and a newly refurbished and expanded Sixth Form Centre opened the following year. In September 2014 the Junior School was extended to provide a new Library and Learning Centre.

A purpose-built Infant School (Willow Lodge) will open on the same site in September 2015 when King's will welcome 120 pupils aged 4–7 years old.

Alumni associations. Please see the website (www.kingschester.co.uk/kings-alumni) for details of OAKS (the Organisation for the Alumni of the King's School) and CAOKS (Chester Association of Old King's Scholars).

Fees per term (2014–2015). Tuition: Senior School £3,986, Junior School £3,056. Lunches: £240.

The School offers a small number of bursaries annually.

Scholarships. Academic scholarships of up to £500 are awarded to pupils during their early years in the Senior School. Scholars carry the title 'King's Scholar' throughout their time at the school.

Tenable in the Sixth Form: A number of scholarships are awarded to students on entry to the Sixth Form and during their Sixth form years. These include: (1) Alfred McAlpine Scholarship of £1,000; (2) Keith Oates Scholarship of £1,000; (3) Investec Scholarship of £1,000; (4) King's School Parents' Association Scholarship: £500.

Tenable at Universities: (1) Old King's Scholars Exhibition: £750 over 3 years; (2) Robert Platt Exhibition: £500; (3) John Churton Exhibition: £500; (4) Haswell Exhibition: £500; (5) Finchett Maddock Exhibition: £500; (6) King's School Parents' Association: two exhibitions of £600 over 3 years.

Charitable status. The King's School, Chester is a Registered Charity, number 525934. The aim of the charity is to provide a sound education to all boys and girls who can benefit from it regardless of their economic and social background.

King's Ely

Ely, Cambridgeshire CB7 4EW
Tel: 01353 660701 (Principal's PA)
             01353 660707 (Director of Recruitment & Communications)
Fax: 01353 667485
             01353 662187 (Business Manager)
email: admissions@kingsely.org
website: www.kingsely.org

Energy, Courage, Integrity

An independent, co-educational school, with day and boarding facilities, offering a seamless education for students from 3 to 18. With over 1000 years of experience educating young people, King's Ely is a school that is innovative, challenging and inspiring. Boasting as its school chapel one of the world's finest cathedrals, with easy access to London, King's Ely offers a very special and very tranquil environment, with one of the best stretches of training river in the UK.

King's Ely is a school where education really is an adventure. Students of all ages are encouraged to take risks in their learning, pushing themselves beyond the boundaries of their expectations, discovering more about the world around them, and, in so doing, more about themselves. What makes us special is our determination to instil in the young people in our care a real enthusiasm for learning and a belief that drives us all, that all students can achieve if the teaching is approached in a way that suits the learning style of each student. This is not easy necessarily; it is challenging, often uncomfortable, but King's Ely students know that they are well supported, that their teachers believe in them, and so they are willing to step out of their 'comfort zone' and take the very risks that will bring about high-level learning.

Our long and illustrious past provides a dynamic springboard to the future; our confidence is born of tradition, our aspirations reach for the stars.

Visitor: The Rt Revd S Conway, Bishop of Ely

Governors:
Chairman: Mr J Hayes
Vice-Chairman: ¶Mr R Phillips, QC
Chairman of Executive and Finance Committee: ¶Mr A J Morbey
Chairman of Education Committee: The Revd Canon D Pritchard, BA, FRCO, LTCL
¶Air Vice-Marshal C Bairsto, CBE, CMgr, FRAeS, FCMI, RAF
The Revd Canon M Bonney, Dean of Ely
Mr D Day
Mrs A East
Mr B D Fraser, BSc, MBA
Mrs A Kenna, MEd, LRAM
Mrs F Martin-Redman
Mrs I Newport-Mangell
Rt Hon Sir J Paice, MP
Prof M Proctor, FRS
¶Dr K Skoyles, LLB, LLM, PhD
Professor A Wyllie, FRS

¶ Old Elean

Principal: Mrs S E Freestone, MEd, GRSM, LRAM, ARCM, FRSA

Head of King's Ely Senior: Mr A McGrath, MA, PGCE
Deputy Head of King's Ely Senior: Miss S E Knibb, BA, PGCE
Deputy Head (Academic): Mrs J R Thomas, MA, PGCE
Director of Recruitment and Communications: Mrs F A Blake, BA, PGCE

Head of King's Ely Junior: Mr R J Whymark, BA Ed
Deputy Head of King's Ely Junior: Mr A Marshall, BSc, PGCE
Director of Studies, King's Ely Junior: Mr J A Lowery, BA, PGCE

Head of King's Ely Acremont: Dr L Brereton, BSc, PhD, PGCE
Head of Nursery and Deputy Head of King's Ely Acremont: Mrs A G Wynn, BEd, MA

Academic Manager of King's Ely International: Mr M Norbury, BA

Chief Operating Officer: Mr M Hart
Business Manager: Mr S Drew
Medical Officer: Dr A S Douglas, BMedSci, BMBS, DRCOG, FP Cert; Dr J Kitson, MBCLB, DRCOG, DFFP, MRCGP
PA to the Principal: Mr T Kingsnorth, BA
Admissions Coordinator: Mrs D Burton

King's Ely Senior Heads of Department:
Art: Mrs A J Rhodes, BA, MA
Business Studies: Mr D Kittson, HND, CertEd, FETC, ACIS, PACA
Chemistry: Mr M Newman, BSc, PGCE

Classics: Mr J Burden, MA Oxon
Design & Technology: Mrs C Poole, BEng, MA, PGCE
Economics: Mr N Williams, MEd, BA, PGCE
English: Mr F Danes, BA, PGCE
Film & Media Studies: Mr S Merrell, BA, TCert
French: Mr A Reall, BA
Geography: Miss C Kyndt, BA, MSc, PGCE
German: Miss K Walter, BSc, MEd, PGCE
History: Mr C Currie, MA, PGDE
Government & Politics: Mr A J Thomas, BA, MEd, PGCE
ICT & Computing: Mr M G Hawes, BA, PGCE
Mathematics: Dr C P Skeels, BSc, DPhil, PGCE
MFL & Spanish: Mrs E Salgado, BA, PGCE
Music: Mr J Kingston, BMus, PGCE
Performance Studies: Miss A C Charlton, BEd
Personal Development: Mr T Humphry, BA, MA
Physical Education: Mr K R Daniel, BA, PGCE
Physics: Mr E W M Kittoe, BSc, PGCE
Psychology: Mr S Quinn, BSc, MSc
Religious Studies: Ms G Smith, MA, MTh, PGCE
Science & Biology: Mrs P Maitland, BSc, PGCE
KS3 English: Miss R Watkins, MEd, BEd
KS3 Mathematics: Ms A Bezzina, BSc, MSc
KS3 MFL: Mrs M Delaveau-Fillmore, BA, CPLP2, PGCE

King's Ely Junior Heads of Department:
English: Miss R Watkins, MEd, BEd
Geography: Miss C Kyndt, BA, MSc, PGCE
Girls' Games: Miss A E Kippax, BSc, HND, Dip SpLD
History: Mr E J Davis, BA, MA, PGCE
Information Technology: N M Ovens, BA, CertEd
Mathematics: Ms A Bezzina, BSc, MSc
MFL: Mrs M Delaveau-Fillmore, BA, CPLP2, PGCE
Music: Mr N Porter-Thaw, LTCL, Dip TCL
Physical Education: Mr D A Boothroyd, BEd
PSHE: Mrs K Prior, DipSpLD, CertEd
Religious Studies: Mrs K Pearce, BA, PGCE
Science: Mrs L H F Roberts, BSc, PGCE

King's Ely Acremont Staff:
Mrs C M Burgess, BA, PGCE
Ms J H Lyall, BA, PGCE
Miss T Miller, BSc, PGCE
Mrs H Monk, BMus, PGCE
Mrs J Thompson, BA, PGCE
Mrs A G Wynn, BEd, MA

In addition, 29 visiting music teachers and 18 external sports coaches.

Organisation. The school is fully co-educational from the ages of 2 to 18. The total roll is 981 and more than a quarter of pupils over the age of eight are boarders.

The school is divided into four parts: King's Ely Acremont, the Nursery and Pre-Prep for children from age 2 years to Year 2, standing in its own grounds at Acremont House; King's Ely Junior for Years 3–8; King's Ely Senior for Years 9–13 and King's Ely International.

Buildings. The Old Palace on Palace Green, home for centuries to the Bishops of Ely, now serves as the entrance to the school, housing the new Sixth Form Centre, the Head's Offices and Admissions as well as the new Development Office. The school still uses many of Ely's medieval monastic buildings – as boarding houses, as classrooms and as the dining hall. The 14th century Porta, the great gateway to the monastery, has been converted into a magnificent new Senior School library. Other recent buildings show the continuing and substantial investment in modern facilities: the renovated Georgian villa that now houses the Nursery and Pre-Prep section of King's Acremont; a brand new Art School and Performance Studies block, housing the new Dance Studio and 'Black Box' Drama Studio; a Technology Centre; a senior Music School and Recital Hall and a self-contained, two-storey accommodation including seven classrooms and a science laboratory for Years 7 and 8.

King's Ely Acremont. At King's Ely Acremont, children thrive in a happy, safe environment where they feel secure and valued and quickly develop a sense of belonging. Children from 2 to 7 are encouraged to question, explore and have the confidence and security to take risks in their learning. A rich, creative curriculum sets the children on the road to becoming lifelong thinkers and learners. Courage and courtesy are valued, encouraged and celebrated publicly.

Children may start in King's Ely Nursery in the term in which they turn two. The Nursery is sessional and we recommend three sessions a week from the outset. However, we strive to be flexible to suit the needs of each individual child. Please contact us to discuss suitable sessions for your child. As children progress through the Nursery, the number of sessions increase to a minimum of five sessions per week. The children are very well prepared for a smooth transition into Reception through regular visits ensuring that they are very familiar with both staff and setting in the next stage of their journey through King's Ely.

Children start Reception in the September following their fourth birthday. Reception, Year 1 and Year 2 are all taught in Acremont House. Small class sizes, with a Teacher and Teaching Assistant in each, allow children to flourish, preparing them well for the transition to King's Ely Junior.

King's Ely Acremont offers working parents the option of an 8 am Breakfast Club, After School Care until 6 pm and Holiday Club.

King's Ely Junior. In King's Ely Junior, we celebrate the many ways that our students learn and we are keen to embrace different learning styles. Students are encouraged to develop their autonomy as they mature and we expect an ever-increasing use of information literacy, technology and study skills during the students' time at King's Ely Junior. Individual responses, such as films being made for homework, or a computer generated response to a task are equally as welcome as a formal written piece of work. Our students can be characterised by their flexibility of approach and we see this as an important life skill for the next generation.

Ensuring that every student is challenged to fulfil their potential and encouraged along the way, requires that the progress of each student is measured and supported well at all times. Form Tutors shoulder this role on a day to day basis. However, each student has a Head of Year who monitors their work and considers how well they are progressing against our predictions. Weekly meetings ensure that speedy intervention is offered to support or extend students appropriately.

From Year 5 onwards, students are set for Maths and English. At this point the students are split between four sets of about 14. These groups are reviewed frequently by the subject teachers and the Head of Year and any adjustments to the sets are made by the Director of Studies, following discussion with parents. As students progress through the school more subjects are set, such as languages and Science. In Years 7 and 8 subjects are linked according to the English, Maths and Science or Language sets. Students are taught in four or five groups, depending on subject.

Every term is punctuated by a host of academic challenges that serve to inspire the pupils and encourage them to push the parameters of their learning. The overtly enriching activities this year have all been provided as additional activities beyond the timetabled lessons:

- King's Ely awarded Gold medals in the Biology Olympiad
- King's Ely Junior takes part in their first ever Big Outdoor Day
- A week of Masterchef Finals concluded in a cook-along session for Jamie Oliver's Food Revolution Day
- Visit from Rt Hon John Bercow MP – The Speaker of the House of Commons
- Breakfast Week goes International – Students take part in Shake Up Your Wake Up's Breakfast Week

- King's Ely International students visit Free the Children's We Day at Wembley as part of the We Act programme
- King's Ely Crews bring home 10 trophies from the Bedford Star Regatta
- Year 9 students win the Modern Foreign Languages round of the Real Business Challenge
- King's Ely Sixth Form launches The Big Thinking Club

Examination results are high and the school prides itself on being at the forefront of developments in the educational world.

During the school day all children are divided among four co-educational Houses for pastoral and competitive purposes; each of these houses is staffed by male and female members of the teaching staff. King's Ely Junior has one co-educational boarding house and one for the boy choristers of Ely Cathedral who are all pupils of King's Junior School. There is a wide range of extra-curricular opportunities both at lunch times and after school.

King's Ely Senior. The amount of academic choice that pupils can exercise grows as they move through the Senior School: options in the Sixth Form are very flexible, and the sets are often small. Up to GCSE (Year 11) there is a compulsory core of English, Mathematics, Religious Studies and Sciences. In addition every pupil chooses up to four option subjects from: Art, Business Studies, Classical Civilisation, Design & Technology (Resistant Material Technology, Food and Nutrition), Drama, English as a Foreign Language, French, Geography, German, History, Latin, Music, Physical Education, Spanish.

The entry qualification for the Sixth Form is not less than six C grades with B grades in subjects selected for A Level. Twenty-seven AS/A2 Level subjects are offered in Years 12 and 13.

King's Ely International. At King's Ely International, students are welcomed from all over the world to engage with the unique community that is King's Ely. The aim is to ensure a smooth and successful transition into the vibrant environment of a UK boarding school, steeped in history but offering an innovative educational experience.

King's Ely International offers effective support academically for international students between the ages of 14 and 16 who may be studying for the first time in the UK. The one-year intensive GCSE course suits students who wish to complete their GCSEs in a year. The Pre-GCSE programme is for students between the ages of 14 and 15 who need support in their English. It is also a "stand-alone" course and may be seen as a sabbatical year, especially for European students who wish to return to their home countries after a year abroad improving their English.

Extra-Curricular Activities. Music, art, drama, outdoor pursuits, sports, practical hobbies and interests – all are catered for in a large range of lunchtime and after-hours activities.

The Ely Scheme. All pupils in Year 9 are introduced to the school's distinctive outdoor pursuits programme, the Ely Scheme, which provides a training in practical and personal skills and in teamwork, initiative and leadership. For some pupils it leads on to the Duke of Edinburgh's Award Scheme or to specialised activities such as climbing.

Art, Drama and Music. Music is strong, as one would expect in a school that is so closely linked to the Cathedral. There is a full programme of performances for school and public audiences, and regular tours overseas. Nearly half of all pupils have personal tuition in a musical instrument; many learn two or even three. An outstanding new Art School, opened in March 2010, inspires fine art, sculpture, ceramics, photography and textiles. All parts of the school present plays every year in addition to productions by year or ad hoc groups.

Games. The main sports are rowing, rugby, soccer, netball, hockey and cricket. Athletics, badminton, basketball, tennis, sailing, squash, swimming, golf and horse riding are also available. All pupils are encouraged to take part in team games, and there is a full programme of fixtures against other schools.

Religious Worship. The Junior and Senior Schools worship regularly in Ely Cathedral. Other services weekly are also in accordance with the principles of the Church of England. The Bishop conducts a confirmation service for pupils in the Lent term. However, all denominations (or none) are warmly welcome.

Exeats. Boarders are granted weekend exeats on the written request of a parent or guardian. Weekly boarding is increasingly popular.

Admission. Application forms can be obtained from the Admissions Department. Admission to King's Ely Acremont is by interview; to King's Ely Junior by interview and INCAs and Lucid screening for dyslexia; and to King's Ely Senior at 13+ by the school's entrance examination. A £65 fee is payable at first registration. Pupils may enter the school at any time, depending on availability.

Scholarships and Exhibitions. Entrance Scholarships and Exhibitions up to a cumulative total of 25% (15% in King's Ely Junior) of tuition fees are awarded for achievement and potential in academic work, music, art, design technology, drama and sports.

King's Ely Junior Academic Awards are for the two final years (Years 7 and 8). A competitive examination is held in January each year and successful candidates enter Year 7 the following Michaelmas term. These Scholarships will be continued until the end of Year 11, subject to satisfactory progress, after which an application for a Sixth Form Scholarship may be made.

King's Ely Senior Academic Scholarships are for the three years from Year 9 leading to the GCSE examinations and are made on the basis of a competitive examination set by the school in February.

Sixth Form Scholarships are for the two years of the AS/A2 course and are made following an examination in November and an interview with the Head and Director of Sixth Form. Candidates should be on course for at least six A* or A passes at GCSE.

Music Scholarships are available for choral and/or instrumental excellence, including organ-playing, and may include free weekly tuition on two musical instruments. Candidates for entry into Year 7 and Year 9 are invited to the school for auditions in February and in November for entry into Year 12 the following September.

All boy Choristers of Ely Cathedral are full boarders of King's Ely Junior and receive a choristership worth 50% of fees while they remain in the choir and a bursary worth 33% of fees on transfer to King's Ely Senior. Members of the Cathedral Girls' Choir are all boarders in King's Ely Senior and receive a bursary worth 33% of boarding fees. Additional means-tested funding may be available. Chorister auditions are held in February for boys who will be aged 8 and for girls who will be 13 by the following September.

Sports Awards, for entry into Years 7, 9 and 12, are open to boys and girls with potential for major county, regional or national representation or with all-round sporting excellence. Reports will be sought from the candidates' coach(es) and practical tests, if required, will be held at the school in February.

Art and Drama Exhibitions are available for entry to Years 7 and 9 and a Design Technology Exhibition fee is available for entry to Year 9. Interviews are held in late January or early February.

Full particulars of all awards are available on the King's Ely website.

Bursaries. Awards may be supplemented by a means-tested Bursary if there is genuine financial need. Bursary support may be available to new pupils over the age of three whose parents are unable to pay the full tuition fee.

Fees per term (2014–2015). *King's Ely Acremont Nursery and Pre-Prep*: Nursery places are booked by the session (morning or afternoon) and the day of the week; full care for five days a week would be £2,695. The fee for Pre-Prep Reception to Year 2 is £2,900 (no boarding). Pre- and after-school care and holiday club are available at extra charge.

King's Ely Junior: Years 3 and 4: £4,097 (day); £6,533 (boarding); Years 5 to 8: £4,471 (day); £6,896 (boarding). There is no Saturday morning school for Years 3 and 4. There is an optional programme on Saturday mornings for pupils in Years 5 and 6. From Year 7 Saturday morning school is a compulsory part of the school week.

King's Ely Senior: Years 9 to 13: £6,177 (day); £8,942 (boarding).

Flexi boarding: It may be possible to offer overnight accommodation for day pupils on an occasional basis at a cost of £34.92 per night. The cost of extended flexi boarding will be quoted in advance upon application to the Bursar.

Concessions: A 10% discount in fees is available from age 4 for children of clergy serving the Christian faith and boarders who are children of Services personnel in receipt of CEA. Sibling discounts may be available.

Old Eleans. Former pupils receive news of the school and of their contemporaries and are invited annually to events.

Charitable status. The King's School, Ely is a Registered Charity, number 802427. Its aims and objectives are to offer excellence in education to day and boarding pupils.

The King's School
Gloucester

Gloucester GL1 2BG

Tel:	01452 337337
Fax:	01452 337314
email:	office@thekingsschool.co.uk
website:	www.thekingsschool.co.uk

Motto: *Via Crucis via Lucis.*

A hidden gem with around 520 girls and boys aged three to eighteen, King's is a successful co-educational independent day school offering academic excellence, small class sizes, outstanding pastoral care and a unique 'Keystones' programme to identify and develop individual talents.

Established by Henry VIII and set within the Cathedral grounds, the school offers an inspiring setting and provides a special sense of identity and powerful community unlike any other. While the Choristers and Choral music are intrinsic to life at King's, the school nurtures and is also extremely proud of both its acting and sporting talent. King's has a Gifted and Talented Sports programme which is designed to support and develop talented athletes, with one of English rugby's greatest players, Phil Vickery (MBE) as the programme mentor.

From Monday to Friday a varied academic and extra-curricular programme including music, art and drama is presented with a vibrant culture of endeavour and scholarship, which continues to thrive since the school was founded in 1541. King's twelve dedicated bus services enable access countywide.

Governing Body:
Chairman:
Mr C L Major, LLB Retired Solicitor and District Judge
The Dean of Gloucester: The Very Reverend Stephen Lake
The Canons Residentiary of Gloucester Cathedral:
Canon N Arthy, MA
Canon NC Heavisides, MA
Canon C Thomson, MA

Lay Governors:
Mr T F Heal, FRICS (*Chartered Surveyor, Alder King*)
Mr C Collier FCIB (*Former Manager, Lloyds Bank*)

Mr J H Holroyd, CB, CVO, MA (*Former Crown Appointments Secretary*)
Mr P Markey, BA, ACA (*Chartered Accountant*)
Mr P Lapping, BA, MA (*Former Headmaster, Sherborne School*)
Mr R Slawson, RIBA (*Former Architect*)
Mr A Brett, BSc, PSC, MInst RE (*Former Bursar, Headington School, Oxford*)
Mr P Lachecki, BSc (*Marketing Consultant, Lachecki Consulting Limited*)
Mr L Rake, BA, FLS (*Vice Principal, Hartpury College*)
Mr M Hurrell (*Managing Editor, BBC Radio Gloucestershire*)
Mr P Dancey (*Company Director, Woodward & Co Environmental Limited*)
Mrs G Brook, CBE (*Assistant Director of Nursing*)
Mrs A Gillespie, BA Hons York, PGCE CertMusEd Trinity (*Music Teacher*)

Headmaster: Mr A K J Macnaughton, MA

Senior Management (Academic):
Mr D J Evans, MA, PGCE (*Deputy Head – Academic*)
Mrs M J Phillips, BA, PGCE (*Deputy Head – Pastoral*)
Mrs A C Haas, BPrimEd (*Head of Junior School*)
Mr J S Collins, BA, PGCE (*Director of Staff Development*)

* Head of Department

English and Drama:
*Dr M C Craddock, BA, DPhil, QTS
Mr J C Hammond, MA, PGCE
Mr J D Hathaway, MA, MSc, PGCE
Mrs M Luchesa, MA, PGCE
Mrs S E Massey, BA, DipLaw, QTS
Mr A K J Macnaughton, MA (*Headmaster*)
Mrs K O'Sullivan, BA, PGCE

Religious Studies:
Mr D J Griffiths, BEd, DipRS (*Coordinator of PSHE*)
*Mr J M Webster, MA, BD, PGCE

History and Politics:
Miss E A Bartlett, MA, PGCE
*Miss H Colson, BA, PGCE
Mr D J Evans, MA, PGCE (*Deputy Head – Academic*)
Mrs T Grime, BA, PDip AARM, PGCE
Mrs S J Hobbs, MA, PGCE

Geography:
*Miss R Lewis, BSc, PGCE
Mrs L A Rowe, LLB, PGCE

Classics:
Mrs P M Fayter, BA, PGCE, Cert Sp LD
Mr T P Hinde, MA
*Mr P O'Brien, BA, PGCE

Modern Languages:
Mr P Arnison, BA, PGCE
Miss H P Cleland, MA, MSc, QTS
*Mrs S M Mitchell, MIL, PGCE
Miss A F Williams, BA, PGCE

Mathematics:
Miss L J Comens, BSc
Dr W Gibson, BEng, PhD, PGCE
*Mrs C S A Miskin, MA, PGCE
Mrs S Rodford, BEd (*Examinations Officer*)
Mr J Withers, BA, PGCE

Science:
Mr J L Auld, MPhys, MPhil, QTS
Mrs J A Burden, BSc, PGCE
Mr B T Hogg, MSc, PGCE
*Mr A G Moore, BSc, PGCE
Mrs B J Rouan-North, BSc, PGCE
Mr C D Sharp, BSc, PGCE
Miss A E Talbot, BSc, MPhil, PGDE

Art and Design Technology:
*Miss C L Billingsley, BA
Mr J S Collins, BA, PGCE (*Director of Staff Development*)
Miss K M Dale, BEd
Miss J Fowler, BA
Mr R A Gadd, BA, QTS
Mrs L A J Lewis, BDes, PGCE

Information Technology:
*Mr B R Calderwood, BEd
Mrs F C Lucas, BA, PGCE

Economics and Business:
Mr D H Butler, BA, PGCE
*Mr D A Lloyd, BSc Econ, PGCE

Music:
Mr L C Hills, LLB
*Mr J Pennington, BMus, DipRCM, ARCM, ARCO, ALCM, PGCE

Physical Education and Games:
Mr A Barr, BA
Mr A N Bressington, BSc, QTS
Mr I Davies, BSc
Mrs J D Fenn, BEd
Mrs G A Pearce, BSc, GTP
*Mr A J Phillips, BA, PGCE
Mrs M J Phillips, BA, PGCE (*Deputy Head – Pastoral*)
Miss L A Pike, BSc, PGCE
Mr L E Robson, BEd

Psychology:
Mrs L Sutton

Learning Skills:
Mrs A B Clancy, BEd, PGCSpLD

Junior School:
Mrs E A Berry, BA, PGCE
Mrs N J Coates, BEd
Mr R A Cooper, BEd
Mrs A C Haas, BPrimEd (*Head of Junior School*)
Mrs C J Hadfield, BEd
Mrs C A McKane, MEd, BA, PGCE (*Head of Wardle House*)
Mrs H M McVittie, BA Ed, QTS
Mrs E I S Tuffill, BA, QTS (*Junior School Director of Studies*)
Mr S P Williams, BSc, PGCE (*Junior School Pastoral Tutor*)
Mrs J C Johnson, BA, PGCE
Mrs C J Sawyer, BA
Mrs G S Southgate, BEd
Mrs R H Woodliffe, Dip Ed, AISTD
Mrs H J Wright, BEd
Mrs J E Wheeler, BA, PGCE
Mrs A M Wyman, BEd

Library :
Mrs E A Houghton, BA, MCLIP

Visiting Music Staff:
Mrs J M Beddoe, LTCL, ATCL (*Clarinet and Saxophone*)
Dr H Crown, MA, PhD, FTCL, LTCL, Dip ABRSM (*Flute and Piano*)
Mr S Field, BA (*Singing*)
Mr S Gerard BSc (*Percussion and Kit*)
Mrs H Green, BA, ABSM (*Violin*)
Miss S J Honeywill, CT ABRSM, Dip ABRSM (*Piano and Chorister Theory*)
Mr I Russell (*Brass*)
Miss J Tomlinson, LRAM (*Violoncello*)
Mr J M Trim, BMus (*Violin, Viola and Senior Strings*)
Mrs J Walker, BMus (*Singing*)
Mr C White, BA Mus (*Guitar*)

Welfare Centre:
Dr I Jarvis, MB, BCh
Mrs M Johnson

Administrative Staff:
Bursar: Ms J Millar, ACMA
Clerk of Works: Mr A Spencer

Development Office:
Registrar and Marketing Manager: Mrs S Bird, BA
Marketing Executive: Miss E Vandervell, BA
Foundation and Alumni Relations Coordinator: Miss A K
   Mayhew
Database and Admissions Coordinator: Mrs E Thorne, BA

Headmaster's Office:
Headmaster's Personal Assistant: Mrs A McMeeken

Receptionists:
Mrs W Courtenay
Mrs S Hall
Mrs E Newth
Mrs D Swanston
Mrs A Baldwin
Mrs S Hall

Structure of the School. The school provides a day education for boys and girls aged 3–18 years. The most common ages for entry are at 3, 7, 11, 13 and 16 years, however, children are welcomed across all year groups with provision for entrance at any point during the academic year. For administrative purposes, the school is divided into the following sections:
Junior School: aged 3–11 (incorporating the Nursery, Wardle House, ages 3–5).
Senior School: aged 11–18.

Junior School (including the Nursery). As the only Independent Junior School in Gloucester, King's provides a happy, secure and stimulating education for boys and girls aged 3–11, enhanced by the inspiring cathedral setting which develops a rich sense of community.

The unique 'Keystones' approach to learning and pastoral care fosters an inner strength and passion for discovery where children are encouraged to think creatively and explore their potential both inside and outside the classroom – skills which last a lifetime. King's Junior School shares the grounds with the Senior School and benefits from use of the Design Technology Centre, ICT Suite, brand new Sports Hall and Cookery Centre, as well as taking part in full school assemblies in the Cathedral. There is a close liaison with the specialist teachers in the Senior School to ensure continuity in teaching and the curriculum. After school care is available and Holiday Club which runs for 50 weeks of the year.

Senior School. The transition from class teaching to subject based set teaching is carried out gradually to enable the pupils to feel secure in their educational environment. Pastoral care is form-based with Tutors and Year Heads monitoring the progress of each pupil and liaising closely with parents.

While the classrooms, set within the Cathedral grounds afford a sense of history and excellent learning, the grounds also boast a wealth of modern facilities such as the laboratories, ICT and Design Technology suites and brand new Cookery centre.

The school playing fields, home to premiership cricket squares and Rugby pitches, are nearby at Archdeacon Meadow, which now boasts a 2.5 million pound Sports Hall. Here, other facilities are also available including indoor a swimming pool, gym, squash and tennis courts.

The school is proud of its tradition of personal discipline which is based on mutual respect and self esteem. The relationship between pupils and staff is at the same time friendly and well defined. A coordinator of Personal and Social Education oversees the cross curricular themes essential to the development of the whole person in this challenging world.

The Sixth Form Centre in Dulverton House provides an academic and social focus for senior students.

The Curriculum. The principal foundations on which the curriculum of The King's School rests "to stimulate all pupils to the greatest possible academic, creative and extra-curricular achievement".

Through the core curriculum in Junior School and up to the end of the Fifth Form (Y11) a clear emphasis is placed on acquiring skills in speaking and listening, literacy and numeracy. The GCSE core curriculum includes English Language and Literature, Mathematics, Religious Studies and a minimum of one Science subject, with the majority of pupils studying two or three Sciences. All pupils are encouraged to include at least one foreign language, but the key focus is on genuine choice based on personal aptitudes and interests.

Although mindful of the national requirements, we also value the freedom to develop our own curriculum in ways that suit the needs of our pupils. With our commitment to small class sizes, we are able to go well beyond the confines of the National Curriculum by offering:
- A flexible and wide choice of subject options, a timetable which is uniquely tailored to individual choices
- A strong moral and spiritual perspective fostered through Chapel, Religious Studies and PSHE
- A commitment to areas of study which are not included in National Curriculum arrangements
- An emphasis on open-ended independent learning and cross-curricular work through special project weeks
- Lessons which are engaging, providing many opportunities for oral participation and encouraging pupils to think for themselves.

Pupil progress is assessed formally through end of unit tests in Junior School and half-termly assessments in Senior School. We also hold examinations in both Junior and Senior School and operate our own internal tracking based on standardised tests. Progress is encouraged through a school ethos which is purposeful without being unduly pressurised or overly competitive.

Junior School is non-selective and caters for a wide range of abilities. Senior School has a more restricted range, since its curriculum is designed for those of high or average academic ability. Within that broad remit, we welcome all those who can access our curriculum and make the most of the opportunities on offer in the school. Treating every pupil as an individual is important to us. We have high expectations of achievement and seek to encourage intellectual curiosity and ambition in our more able pupils through the enrichment programme which operates in both Junior School and Senior School.

Games and Activities. A full range of games is available with the main games being Rugby, Hockey and Cricket for boys and Hockey, Netball, Tennis and Rounders for girls. Senior pupils are able to participate in a whole range of minor games including Squash and Badminton, and Athletics is also available. A well-equipped Gymnasium at The Riverside Sports and Leisure Club at Archdeacon Meadow, where the school's Sports Hall is situated, provides the focus for Physical Education. Dance and Drama are fully integrated in the curriculum. Swimming lessons are an important part of the curriculum throughout the school, the annual House swimming gala being a very competitive event.

The School's main playing field, Archdeacon Meadow, is an approved county cricket ground. The King's School is a Junior Academy of Gloucestershire County Cricket Club and a Partnership School with the Gloucester and England RFU Junior Academy.

Its proximity to Kingsholm and its special relationship with Gloucester Rugby Club, for example being part of the Community Connection Scheme, has enabled the school to become a centre of excellence in the sport. Overseas sports tours are held regularly for boys and girls.

A new Gifted and Talented Sports programme designed to support, develop and nurture talented pupils was launched in 2012 and the school offers the Duke of Edinburgh's Award scheme, a comprehensive outdoor pursuits programme plus a wide and varied range of extra-curricular clubs and societies are offered daily. Annual overseas expeditions go as far afield as Ecuador and Mongolia.

Music and the Performing Arts. There is a strong tradition of musical excellence as befits a Cathedral Choir School, where all pupils are encouraged to appreciate music. A good proportion of the school receives instrumental tuition and the various choirs, orchestras and ensembles play regularly in the Cathedral, and in the local area. Music Technology includes sequencing and music publishing software (Sibelius) and portable digital recording equipment. The school is a Choir School and as such provides the trebles for the Cathedral choir, and has a number of music scholarships and bursaries endowed for that purpose. As well as providing a succession of Oxbridge organ scholars, the school provides a full range of musical activities.

Religious Worship. Whilst pupils from all denominations are warmly welcomed, the religious services are in accordance with the principles of the Church of England. Most days start with an assembly, usually in the Cathedral and of a nature to suit each age group. A strong chaplaincy team, led by the School Chaplain, supports the spiritual development of pupils and staff alike.

Admission. Junior School: a Taster Day and low-key assessment of each child. Senior School: entrance tests are given for each pupil. At key entry points: 11+ or 13+ examinations, Common Entrance Examination or other tests appropriate to a child's previous education. However, applications for entrance are welcomed and accommodated throughout the Academic year.

Fees per term (2014–2015). These are staged according to age. Junior School £2,135–£4,075; Senior School £4,740–£5,575; Sixth Form £5,895.

Scholarships. Academic Scholarships may be awarded to outstanding boys and girls at age 11, 13 and 16. A number of lesser Exhibitions are also available at these ages. Scholarship examinations are held annually in November for 11+ and March for 13+ and 16+. Awards in Sport, Music, Art, and Drama are available at age 11, 13 and in the Sixth Form.

At this Cathedral School Choral Scholarships worth 75% of tuition fees for Cathedral Choristers are available for boys aged between 7 and 9 and a half.

Governors' Bursaries are also available.

Gloucester King's School Society. Email: alumni@ thekingsschool.co.uk.

Charitable status. The King's School, Gloucester is a Registered Charity, number 1080641. It exists to provide for the education of Cathedral Choristers and others, within a co-educational environment.

The King's School
Macclesfield

Cumberland Street, Macclesfield, Cheshire SK10 1DA

Tel: 01625 260000
Fax: 01625 260022
email: mail@kingsmac.co.uk
website: www.kingsmac.co.uk

Situated in rolling Cheshire countryside on the edge of the Peak District, the King's School is the top performing independent school in Cheshire East for both GCSE and A Level results and is in The Telegraph Top 150 Independent Schools for exam results in 2014.

Founded in 1502, King's offers an academic education through a unique combination of mixed and single-sex education (known as a diamond structure school). It places an emphasis on excellent teaching and academic standards combined with an extensive range of extra-curricular activities and exceptional pastoral care.

Chairman of the Governors: J Kennerley
Vice-Chair of Governors: J Sugden, MA, FIMechE, CEng

Senior Management Team:

Head of Foundation: Dr S Hyde, MA, DPhil

Deputy Headmaster (*Development*): T Seth, MA Cantab
Deputy Headmaster (*Academic*): R Griffiths, MA Cantab
Director of External Relations: Mrs C Johnson, BSc, DipM
Director of Finance: J M Spencer Pickup

Principal of Boys: I J Robertson, BSc
Principal of Girls: Mrs J Anderson, BA, MEd, PGCE
Principal of Infants & Juniors: Mrs C J Hulme-McKibbin, BEd
Principal of Sixth Form: Mrs R H Roberts, BA

Vice-Principal of Boys: P M Edgerton, MA
Vice-Principal of Girls: Mrs J Seth, BA, MA, PGCE
Vice-Principal of Juniors: Mrs A Lea, BMus
Vice-Principal of Infants: Mrs E L Warburton, BEd

Heads of Departments:
Art & Design: Mrs D Inman, BA
Biology: Miss E Hall, BSc, MSc, PGCE
Chemistry: Miss L C Watkins, BSc
Classics: M T Houghton, BA
Design & Technology: J Nichols, BEd
Drama: D A Forbes, BA
Economics & Business Studies: J S MacGregor, MA
English: Miss L C Derby, BA
Geography: A S Puddephatt, BA
Geology: Dr J A Fitzgerald, BSc, MSc, PhD
German: Mrs J Houghton, BA
History: M S Robinson, BA
Information Technology: C O'Donnell, BSc
Learning Support: Mrs N S Davis, BA, Dip Psych, PG Cert
Modern Languages: I E Dalgleish, BA
Director of Music: I Crawford, BMus
Physical Education (*Director of Sport*): C S Thompson, BA, PGCE
Physics: Dr S J Hartnett, BSc, DPhil, PGCE
Psychology: M J Brown, MSc, BSc
Religion & Philosophy: R N Jackson, BA
Science: J Street, BSc, PGCE
Spanish: Miss H L Connaughton, BA (*Acting Head*)

Number in School. Infants 3–7: 42 boys, 41 girls. Juniors 7–11: 124 boys, 84 girls. Boys (11–16) 400; Girls (11–16) 311. Sixth Form: 148 boys, 109 girls. Total: 1,259.

Organisation and Curriculum. The King's School Foundation is organised into four Divisions: on one site, an Infant & Junior Division (co-educational 3–11) and a Senior Girls' Division (11–16); on the other, a Senior Boys' Division (11–16) and a Sixth Form (co-educational 16–18). Each Division is run by a Principal, who is responsible for day-to-day organisation, and the pupils in the 11–16 divisions of the school are taught separately but undertake a number of joint extra-curricular activities (e.g. music, drama, trips abroad etc.)

The Foundation has one Board of Governors, one Head and two Deputy Heads who manage the school and plan regularly with the Division Principals to carry out the aims and objectives of the school. Girls and boys from 3–18 enjoy the same opportunities.

The curriculum is rich throughout all year groups offering pupils of all ages choice and a breadth of experience.

Pastoral care is a very high priority. The divisional structure is key to enabling each unit to be small and operate as a community.

Students are assigned to a personal tutor responsible for a group of 10 or so pupils throughout their Sixth Form course. Any justifiable combination of available A and AS Level subjects may be pursued, complemented by General Studies, EPQ and Recreational Activity. In addition to compulsory core units in General Studies, students choose from a wide range of options designed to extend their breadth of cultural interest and intellectual inquiry, whilst Recreational Activities are designed to encourage the positive use of leisure time and offers initial experience in sports and activities new to the individual. Pupils are also prepared for University Entrance Examinations where appropriate.

Arts and Craft. Well-equipped art rooms and Design & Technology (DT) workshops are also available for use by the members of the Art Club and Craft Societies outside the timetable.

Music. Over 400 pupils receive tuition in the full range of orchestral instruments, the Piano, Organ, Classical Guitar and Singing. An introductory tuition scheme enables all new entrants to assess their talent. There are three orchestras, a Concert-band, two Jazz bands, three Choirs and many ensembles, all of which provide regular performing experience. The Foundation Choir was the first BBC Songs of Praise Choir of the Year in 2003. Pupils regularly enter music profession in addition to those pursuing academic training.

Drama. Theatre Studies is an important creative option at GCSE and AS Level and covers all aspects of the theatre. Great importance is attached to the regular school plays and musicals, which involve large numbers of pupils and enjoy a distinguished reputation. Pupils regularly take examinations and study for LAMDA qualifications in performance and public speaking.

Games. All pupils take part in games and athletic activity appropriate to the season. Junior School sports include Soccer, Cricket, Netball, Hockey, Tennis, Rounders, Athletics and a wide range of individual games. In the Senior School, boys' sports include Rugby, Hockey, Cross-Country, Squash, Badminton, Cricket, Tennis, Athletics, Swimming and Basketball; the girls' sports include Hockey, Netball, Tennis, Football, Cross-Country, Volleyball, Cricket, Rugby and Athletics. In addition there is a varied programme of sports in the Sixth Form, including Rugby and such activities as Hillwalking, Caving and Rock Climbing which are actively pursued by boys and girls. The school opened new netball courts, Junior cricket wickets and an adventure playground in September 2012. In March 2014, it will open new astro pitches for hockey, as well as new tennis courts, netball courts and cricket nets.

Outdoor Pursuits. This is a thriving part of the school. There is a regular programme of activity weekends including canoeing, gorge scrambling, surfing etc. In addition, numerous expeditions are arranged in the many favourable areas near the school and also abroad. Sailing and orienteering are popular and the Duke of Edinburgh's Award scheme attracts 60 pupils each year.

Clubs and Societies. There is a wide range of other clubs catering for most interests and hobbies, ranging from Astronomy, Debating, Chess and Fencing to Sailing, Zoology Club and Taekwondo.

Fees per term (2014–2015). Senior School £3,770, Junior School £3,055, Infants Department £2,840.

Scholarships and Bursaries. Bursaries are available for entry at 11, 13 and 16. In addition seven or more Academic Scholarships are given on performance in the Entrance Examination. Senior School Music Scholarships are available for instrument or singing. Academic, Music and Organ scholarships are also available in the Sixth Form. Funds are available to assist pupils attending courses and field trips and to help in cases of urgent need.

Admissions. Admission is normally for September each year through competitive examination for boys and girls aged 7–10, and 11–14 years. Girls and boys are admitted to the Sixth Form subject to academic attainment, interview and course requirement. Admission arrangements are advertised and available on request. Immediate admission, eg for new arrivals in the area, is possible.

Former Pupils' Association. Chairman: David Barratt; email: formerpupils@kingsmac.co.uk. An annual magazine and termly newsletter are provided to former pupils.

Visit the Website. The award-winning website is found at www.kingsmac.co.uk.

Charitable status. The King's School, Macclesfield is a Registered Charity, number 1137204. It exists for the education of boys and girls between the ages of 3 and 18.

King's Rochester

Satis House, Boley Hill, Rochester, Kent ME1 1TE

Tel:	01634 888555
Fax:	01634 888505
email:	admissions@kings-rochester.co.uk
website:	www.kings-rochester.co.uk
Twitter:	@Kings_Rochester

The School traces its history to 604 AD, when St Justus, the first Bishop of Rochester, formed a school in connection with his Cathedral; it was reconstituted and endowed by Henry VIII as the King's School in 1541. The School has been fully co-educational since 1993.

Patron: The Lord Bishop of Rochester, The Rt Revd James Langstaff

Governing Body:
Chairman: The Dean of Rochester, The Very Revd Dr M H F Beach
Mr B Bell, BSc Hons, CIMDIP, FCIM
The Venerable S Burton-Jones, MA, BTh
Mr M J Chesterfield
Mr J K Daffarn, FRICS
Mr J Franklin, BA Med Admin
Mrs J Glew, BA, CIMDIP, MA
The Revd Canon Dr P Hesketh, PhD, BD, AKC
Mr R W Hoile, MS, FRCS
The Revd Canon J Kerr, MA, CertEd
Mr J W Lord, FCA, ATII
Mr B Owen, BSc, CEng, FICE, FRSA
Mr P L Rothwell, LLB Hons
Mrs R A Rouse, MSc
Mr C R Shepherd, BSc, CEng, FICE, FRSA
Miss J A Shicluna, MA Oxon
The Revd Canon N Thompson, BEd, MA
Mr P J Webb, MS, FRCS

Executive Board:

Principal: **Mr J Walker**, MA Oxon, MA London

Headmaster of the Senior School: Mr J Walker, MA Oxon, MA London
Headmaster of the Preparatory School: Mr R P Overend, BA, FTCL, ARCM, FRSA
Headmistress of the Pre-Preparatory School: Mrs S E J Skillern, MA, NPQH, BA Hons QTS
Finance Director and Clerk to the Governors: Mr G R Longton, BSc, FCMA
Director of Marketing and Communications: Mrs J E Shilling, BA Joint Hons

Senior School:

Headmaster of the Senior School: Mr J Walker, MA Oxon, MA London

Deputy Head (*Academic*): Miss N Steel, BSc
Deputy Head (*Pastoral*): Mr C H Page, BA
Deputy Head (*Operations*): Miss H L Catlett, BA
Chaplain: The Revd J A Thackray, BSc, ACIB

Heads of Department:
Art: Mr A J Robson, BA
Biology: Mr B Liddle, BSc
Chemistry: Mr N J McMillan, BSc Hons
Classics: Mr S C Janssens, MA
Design & Technology: Mr S J Johnson, BEd
English: Mr W E Smith, BA
French: Mrs A Warne, Maître
Geography: Miss L Costelloe, BA
German & Russian: Mr B W Richter, BA
History: Mr C M Hoile, BA Hons
ICT: Miss C Welch, BA
Mathematics: Mr P G Stevens, BSc
Music: Mr D B McIlwraith, BA Hons, ARCO, PGCE
Physics: Miss E L Rein, BSc
Physical Education: Mrs A J Richter, BSc
Religious Studies: Mrs L A Rogers, BA
Sport: Mr J Halls, BA

Registrar: Mrs L Davies
Marketing Officer: Mrs J Moore, BA Hons
Librarian: Mrs X Guo, MA
CCF Contingent Commander: Major S Short

Preparatory School:
Headmaster: Mr R P Overend, BA, FTCL, ARCM, FRSA
Deputy Headmaster: Mr P N Medhurst, BA, MA

Pre-Preparatory School:
Headmistress: Mrs S E J Skillern, MA, NPQH, BA Hons
QTS
Deputy Headmistress: Mrs L A MacDonald, BA, PGCE
Honorary Pre-Preparatory School Lay Chaplain: Dr S
Hesketh, MB BS, MRCGP, AKC, PRCOG, DCH,
DFSRH

Music Department:
Director of Music: Mr D B McIlwraith, BA Hons, ARCO,
PGCE
Preparatory School Director of Music & Head of Strings:
Mrs J M Hines, BA
Head of Woodwind: Mr G Vinall, BA, LRAM
Cathedral Director of Music: Mr S Farrell, BMus Hons,
ARCO, ARCM, PGCE

Medical Officer: Dr M Ojedokun, MB BS, MRCGP

The School is situated close to the Cathedral and Castle in the centre of the city and in a secluded conservation area; it enjoys the open spaces of the Precincts, the Vines and the Paddock, which is one of the School's playing fields. The other playing field, the Alps, is 10 minutes from the School. The School recently acquired a local Sports Centre which it is currently refurbishing at a cost of half a million pounds. This new facility will expand the School's current sporting facilities with 9 additional external tennis/netball courts, a large gymnasium, a fitness gym, physio suite and changing rooms in addition to the indoor swimming pool and playing fields already on the 1400 year-old school's town centre site.

The Main School dates from the mid-nineteenth century but the School also has a number of fine listed buildings from the eighteenth century, and considerable extensions of more recent date. Recent additions include a £3 million Conference Centre and dining facility, a girls' boarding house, and a Pre-Prep building with Sports Hall and a modern, self-contained nursery was added in 2010. There is an indoor swimming pool and a well-equipped language laboratory.

The School numbers about 650 pupils, including a small but significant community of 70 boarders from the local

area, London and overseas. The School is fully co-educational and divided into a Pre-Preparatory School of approximately 130 pupils (4–8 years), plus 30 in the nursery, a Preparatory School of approximately 200 pupils (8–13 years) and a Senior School of approximately 300 pupils (13–18 years); this provides 3 units of an intimate size, which are regarded as a single community working closely together. While catering for the whole of a pupil's career from 3 to 18, there is a large entry of pupils at 11, 13 and 16 who bring experience from other backgrounds, and enjoy the advantages of coming into a stable community with a strong family atmosphere.

The boarders, some of whom are weekly, play an important part in the life of the School. Although a small community, they are a large enough part of the School to make a very significant contribution of their own, and enjoy a more intimate atmosphere than is possible in a larger boarding environment.

King's is the Cathedral School. The Dean and Chapter are ex officio Governors, the Principal and King's Scholars are members of the Cathedral Foundation, and the Cathedral Choristers are members of the Preparatory School. The School uses the Cathedral for worship.

Work. In the Pre-Preparatory School, the pupils follow a four year curriculum of Maths, Science, English, Divinity, Geography, History, Information Technology, Art and Craft, Design & Technology, Music, and Physical Education. Daily spoken German lessons taught by native German teachers form part of the curriculum from the age of 4 with German fun and games sessions twice weekly in the nursery.

In the Preparatory School, the syllabus covers Art, Religious Studies, English, General Science, History, Geography, Mathematics, Information Communication Technology, Latin, French, Music, Physical Education and Design & Technology.

In the Senior School, all pupils continue with the same range for the first year. In the Fifth Forms, a core of subjects is continued and pupils add a balanced choice of options in preparation for the GCSE and IGCSE examinations at the end of the two-year course.

In the Sixth Form, a wide range of AS and A Level subjects are available. Pupils study 4, or occasionally more, AS and then 3 A Level subjects. Some pupils also take the Extended Project Qualification as additional study alongside their A Levels.

All Sixth Formers, who wish to, go on to university or other further education, and are encouraged to think carefully about their ultimate careers. Careers talks are given by outside speakers during the GCSE year, and the advice of specialist careers advisers and the careers teachers is available at all stages.

Activities. The School aims to develop pupils through a wide range of activities, both within the School programme and outside it.

There is a large CCF contingent, with Army, Navy and Air Force sections. Strong Service connections locally give particularly wide scope for CCF activities.

Pupils also undertake a variety of activities in Community Service and participate in the Duke of Edinburgh's Award Scheme.

Out of School there is a range of over 20 school societies in all three parts of the School, and in the holidays there is a strong tradition of annual cultural and outdoor expeditions in this country and abroad for Preparatory and Senior School pupils.

Art, Drama and Music. The School sets great store by the Arts, and uses the comparative proximity to London to take pupils to art exhibitions, concerts and the theatre. The School stages major drama productions each year, recently *Joseph and the Amazing Technicolor Dreamcoat, The Merchant of Venice, Waiting for Godot, Ruckus in the Garden* and *A Midsummer Night's Dream* have been the main presentations. There is a strong musical tradition enhanced by visiting music staff, and pupils are encouraged to learn instruments. In addition to concerts in the School and the Cathedral, the Orchestra gives a number of outside performances each year, some by invitation. The choral tradition is strengthened by the presence of the Cathedral choristers in the School who regularly undertake overseas tours. In 2011, the senior choir reached the semi-final of the BBC Songs of Praise Choir of the Year Competition.

Games. The boys' games are Rugby, Hockey, Football (Preparatory School) and Cricket and for girls' Hockey, Netball and Tennis. Other team sport options are Rowing (from our River Medway boathouse), Athletics, Cross Country, Fencing, Tennis and Swimming, and there are opportunities in addition for Squash, Badminton and Sailing. Physical Education is a regular part of the School curriculum and all pupils are required to take part in games. 80% represent the School competitively.

Religious Education and Worship. Although there is no denominational requirement for entry to the School, religious instruction is in accordance with the principles of the Church of England. All three parts of the School begin the day with an assembly or chapel service, some of which are held in the Cathedral.

Admission. Pupils can enter the School at any age from 3 to 18, although the main entry points are: 4+, 7/8+, 11+, 13+ and 16+. Entrance to the Senior School is either by Common Entrance at 13 or by the School's own examination for pupils who have not been prepared for Common Entrance.

Sixth Form entry is on the basis of interview and School report, together with satisfactory GCSE results (a minimum of 5 A*–C passes, and grade requirements for A Level courses).

Choristers. Choristerships to Rochester Cathedral (8+/9+) from Cathedral and School are awarded to boys following voice trials and a satisfactory performance in the Preparatory School Entrance Examination. Under normal circumstances, the choristership will continue until a boy transfers to the Senior School or until he leaves the choir.

Scholarships and Bursaries. *Senior School*: Up to five Major King's Scholarships (30%) and five Minor King's Scholarships (15%) may be awarded annually. At least five scholarships are for pupils from maintained sector schools. King's Scholars become members of the Cathedral Foundation.

Preparatory School: Five King's Exhibitions of 30% of tuition fees are available at 11+. Two are for pupils from maintained Primary Schools.

Music: Up to five Music Scholarships may be awarded annually with a value of up to 30% of tuition fees.

A range of Chesterfield Organ Scholarships have recently been introduced for 11+, 13+ and 16+ entry and details of these generous Scholarships are available from the Registrar on 01634 888590, admissions@kings-rochester.co.uk.

Free tuition on all instruments studied in School is given to holders of major and minor awards.

The Scholarships, available from 11+, will be awarded after an examination, usually in February, consisting of aural, sight reading and practical tests, and a viva voce. In addition, candidates at 13+ will be expected to be of Grade 5–6 standard and capable of passing Common Entrance, or a genuine A Level candidate if 15+. 11+ candidates should be at about Grade 4 level.

The Peter Rogers Scholarship of £3,000 per annum is awarded from time to time to assist an exceptionally talented musician, and a Dame Susan Morden Choral Scholarship of £2,500 is occasionally available to a Cathedral Chorister.

Boy Choristerships to Rochester Cathedral (8+/9+) from Cathedral and School.

Governors' Exhibitions are means-tested academic awards and may be of value up to 100% of fees.

To celebrate the acquisition of the new King's Rochester Sports Centre, the Principal introduced a range of Sports Scholarships for entry at 11+, 13+ and 16+.

Additional means-tested bursaries may be available.

Fee Remissions. Children of Church of England ministers are given an annually means-tested reduction in tuition fees.

Children of Service Personnel are given a 20% reduction in tuition fees.

Where parents have three or more children at the school a reduction after the second child is given, amounting to 10% of the third child's tuition fees, 20% for the fourth child and 40% for the fifth and subsequent children.

Fees per term (2014–2015). Senior School: Boarders £9,225, Day Pupils £5,680. Preparatory School: Boarders £6,425, Day Pupils £3,875–£4,400 (inc lunch). Pre-Preparatory School (Day only): £3,020–£3,240 (inc lunch).

Charitable status. King's School, Rochester is a Registered Charity, number 1084266; it is a charitable trust for the purpose of educating children.

The King's School
Worcester

5 College Green, Worcester WR1 2LL
Tel: 01905 721700 (School Office)
            01905 721721 (Bursar)
            01905 721742 (registrar)
Fax: 01905 721710
email: info@ksw.org.uk
website: www.ksw.org.uk
Twitter: @KingsWorcester
Facebook: /KingsWorcester

A Cathedral School appears to have existed at Worcester virtually continuously since the 7th century. In its present form, however, The King's School dates from its refoundation by King Henry VIII in 1541, after the suppression of the Cathedral Priory and its school. In 1884 the School was reorganised as an Independent School and in 1944 the Cathedral Choir School was amalgamated with The King's School.

Today, the King's School Worcester is a foundation comprising two junior schools and a senior school. All three schools are Co-Ed and day.

Visitor: The Lord Bishop of Worcester

The Governing Body:
Mr H B Carslake, BA, LLB (*Chairman*)
The Very Revd P G Atkinson, FRSA (*Vice-Chairman*)
Mr M Atkins, MRICS
Professor M Clarke, CBE, MA, DL
Mr D Dale, MA, FCA
Mr J W R Goulding, MA Oxon
Mr D L Green, Solicitor
Mr K D Harmer,
Mrs J H Jarvis, BA, MCIPD
Mr R S McClatchey, BA
The Hon Lady Morrison, DL
Revd Canon Dr A Pettersen, BA, PhD
Mrs P Preston, MA Oxon, DipM
Dr H Swift, MA, MSt, DPhil Oxon
Mrs I Taylor, MA Cantab, FCA
Professor J Vickerman, BSc, PhD, DSc
Mr P Walker, MBE, BSc, MPhil, CEng, MIMMM

Clerk to the Governors and Bursar: Mr J G Bartholomew, MBA, MBEng, PIIA

Headmaster: Mr M G Armstrong, MA

Senior Deputy Head: Mr J Ricketts, BSc
Second Deputy Head: Miss C Mellor, BA
Director of Studies: Mr R C Baum, MA
Academic Deputy Head: Mr D S King, BSc

Assistant Staff:
* *Head of Department*
§ *Part-time*

Art:
*Miss G Terry, MA
Mr C Haywood, BA
Miss J Hewitt, BA
§Mrs C Horacek, BA
Miss G Holden, BA

Biology:
*Dr M Parkin, MA, PhD
Mr S M Bain, BSc, MSc
§Dr C L Brown, BSc, PhD
Mrs N Essenhigh, BSc
Mr M J Newby, BEd
Mr J H Chalmers, BASc
Mrs R Worth, BSc

Careers:
*Mr S Le Marchand, BA
Mrs E Friend, BA

Chemistry:
*Mr R P Geary, BSc,
CChem, MRSC
Mrs C E Battrum, MA
Dr R J James, BSc, PhD
Mr T B Jeavons, BSc
Dr M C Poole, BSc, PhD
Mr J R Ricketts, BSc

Classics:
*Mrs S C Bradley, BA
§Miss R M Lewis, MA
§Mr P J Garland, BA
§Mr R N G Stone, BA
Miss J K Wootton, BA

Critical Thinking:
*Revd Dr M R Dorsett,
BA, MTh, PhD,
CertTheol (*Chaplain*)

Design and Technology:
*Mr C W S Wilson, BA
Mr A G Deichen, BA
Miss H Holden, BA
Mr E Lummas, BA

Drama & Theatre Studies:
*Mr S M Atkins, BA
§Ms J Price-Hutchinson,
BA

*Economics & Business
Studies*:
*Mr R P Mason, BA
§Mr G L Williams, BA
§Mrs E Friend, BA

English:
*Mr A J M Maund, MA
Miss A Briggs, BA
Mr R J Davis, BA
§Mrs R C Graff, BA
Ms L L Guy, BA
Mr D P Iddon, BA
Mr S Le Marchand, BA
Mrs S H Le Marchand, BA
§Mrs L Walmsley, BA

Geography:
*Mr S C Cuthbertson, BA
Mr W J Joyce, BSc
A W Longley, BA
Mrs C M Neville, BSc

Mrs F L Short, BA
Miss E Watts, BA

History and Politics:
*Mr P T Gwilliam, BA,
MPhil
Mr A J Ford, BA
Mrs N J Sears, BA
Mr T R Sharp, MA
Mrs S E Stuart, MA

Information Technology:
*Mrs J C Vivian, MA
Mr A G Deichen, BA
Mr E I Lummas, BA

Key Skills:
Mrs C M Neville, BSc
and various staff

Learning Skills:
*§Mrs J L Lucas, BSc,
DipSpLD
§Mrs C J Knipe, BA,
DipSpLD

Mathematics:
*Mrs A Hines, BSc
Mr O J Heydon, BSc
§Mrs K Beever, BEng
Mrs E L Darby, MA
Mr J N Gardiner, BSc
Mr J Hand, BA
Mr A A Kerley, BEng
Mrs M M Longley, BEd
§Mr M R H Mardo, BSc
§Mrs D Salkeld, BSc
§Miss A-M Simpson, BSc
Mr A R Swarbrick, BSc
§Mrs K Ahmadi Mirkani,
BSc
§Mrs D J Clarke, BSc

Modern Languages:
*Mr R A Ball, MA
Mr J L Owen, BA
(*French)
Mrs R Shearburn, BA
(*Spanish)
Miss C Mellor, BA
Mr N J Pilborough, BA
Mr E D Houghton, BA
Mrs R M Rutter, BA
Mr J Sarriegui, BA
§Mrs R Stanley, BA

Music:
*Mr S Taranczuk, MMus,
FRCO (*Director of
Music*)
Mr G M Gunter, GTCL,
LTCL
and visiting teachers

PE & Games:
Mr J Mason, BSc
(*Director of Sport*)
Mr A A D Gillgrass, BA
(**Boys' Games*)
Mrs S C Parkinson-Mills,
BSc (**Girls' Games*)
Mr J Chalmers, BASc
(*Rowing)

Mr C Atkinson, BSc
Mr S M Bain, BSc, MSc
Miss N Brennan, BSc
§Mrs J D Clark, BEd
Mr D P Iddon, BA
Mrs M M Longley, BEd
Mrs F L Short, BA
Miss L C Symonds, BSc
§Mrs K M Armitage

Physics:
*Dr D J Haddock, MA,
DPhil Oxon
Mr R C Baum, MA
Mrs L E Haddock, BSc
Mr T B Jeavons, BSc
Mr I C Robinson, BSc

Cover Supervisor:
Mrs A Sansome, BA, ACA

Headmaster's Secretary: Mrs C Swainston
Registrar: Mrs V Peckston, BA
Medical Officers:
Dr M Smith, MBChB
Dr A Woof, MBChB
Sister: Mrs C F Furber, RGN, DipN
Mrs A Odam, RGN

The King's Junior Schools

King's St Alban's
Tel: 01905 354906; email: ksa@ksw.org.uk

Head: Mr I R Griffin, BA
Deputy Head: Mrs R Duke, BA
Director of Studies: Mr D Braithwaite, BEd
Head of Pre-Prep: Miss A Roberts, BA

Mrs F Atkinson, BSc
Mr J M Bailey, BEd
Mrs K Beauchamp, BA
§Mrs N Cain, BA
Mrs K Chatterton, BSc
Mr I Fry, MA
Mrs K Hadfield
Mrs A Hind, BSc
Mrs K Kear-Wood, BSc
Mrs L Kilbey, MA, LRSM
§Mrs E Lewis, Bed

Ms L Neeves, MSc
Mrs D Page, BEd
Mrs J Pitts, BEd
§Mrs C Woodcock, BA,
CertEd
Mrs J Pitts, BEd
Mrs L Thorp, BA
Miss E Wyatt, BSc
Miss E Chadwick
Mrs V Gunter

Registrar: Mrs L Robins
Secretaries: Miss S Hurley
Matrons: Mrs K Jenkins, Mrs A Withnall
Teaching Assistants: Mrs R Amess, Mrs N Hobson, Mrs E
Monkhouse, Mrs N Mountjoy

King's Hawford
Tel: 01905 451292; Fax: 01905 756502;
email: hawford@ksw.org.uk

Head: Mr J M Turner, BEd, DipEd, ACP
Deputy Head: Mr D Peters, BMus
Assistant Head (*Academic*): Mrs C Rawnsley, BA
Assistant Head (*Pastoral*): Mrs P M Bradley, BEd
Head of Early Years: Mrs J N Willis, BA Ed

Mrs J Atkins, BA
Mrs L Baxter, BSc
Mrs J Farmer, BEd
Mrs H Fowler, BA, OCR
Cert
Mrs D Goodayle, BEd
§Mrs L Hyde, BA
§Mrs M Kavanagh, ALAM
GSA Dip

§Mrs T McCullough
Mrs A Marshall-Walker,
BA
Mr I Percival, BA
Mr R Pritchard, BSC
Mrs J Redman, BEd
Ms K Turk, BA, MA
Mr J Turvey, BA

Mrs S K Stone, BEng

Politics:
*Mr P T Gwilliam, BA,
MPhil
Mr A A D Gillgrass, BA
Mr A J Ford, BA

*Religious Studies and
PSHE*:
*Dr R Head, BA, MPhil,
PhD
Revd Dr M R Dorsett, BA,
MTh, PhD, CertTheol
(*Chaplain*)
§Miss A-M Simpson, BSc

Pre-Prep:
Head: Mrs P M Bradley, BEd

Mrs J Chambers, BA, ARCM, Dip Ed	Mrs K Farrow
	Mrs S A Gwilliam, BA
Mr R B Cook, BSc	Mrs A Jeavons, BA
Miss A Kingston, BA	Mrs E Jennings, NVQ3
Mrs C Knight, BEd	Mrs C Kennedy
Miss A Parkes, BSc	Miss J Obrey
Mrs G Riley, BSc	Mrs S Powell, BA
Mrs K Chapman, BA	Mrs R Pearman, BA
	Mrs J Simons, NNEB
Kindergarten:	Mrs S Watts, CertEd
Mrs A Catherwood	
Mrs D Field, NVQ3	

Registrar/Secretary: Mrs D Wenyon
Office Secretaries: Mrs J Cartwright, Miss G Woolley
Hawford Matron: Mrs F Geary, RGN

The School still occupies its original site south of the Cathedral. The buildings are grouped around College Green and the School Gardens. They range in date from the 14th century College Hall and Edgar Tower through the 17th and 18th century buildings surrounding College Green, to a range of modern, purpose-built accommodation, much of which has been constructed in the last twenty years. Recent additions in a continuing development programme include a library located in the heart of the school, the John Moore Theatre, a new boat house opened in 2012, a covered Swimming Pool and upgraded House accommodation. A new Sports and Performing Arts building is to be completed for September 2014. There are centres for English and Mathematics and a Music School. A Languages Computer Centre with the latest software for the teaching of French, German and Spanish has been established.

There are two Junior Schools. King's St Alban's stands in its own grounds on the edge of the main school site, offering education from age 4–11 with a purpose-built pre-prep department for girls and boys aged 4–7. King's Hawford is in a spacious rural setting just to the north of the city and offers education from age 2–11.

Numbers and Admission. The school is fully co-educational. King's St Alban's has about 250 pupils. King's Hawford has about 320 pupils. The Senior School has about 950 pupils, including 290 in the Sixth Form.

Entrance to the school is by the Junior Entrance Test at 7, 8 or 9, or by the School's Examination at 11, 12 and 13. Boys and girls also join the School at Sixth Form level; this entry is by test, interview and GCSE results.

Term of Entry. Pupils are normally admitted annually in September.

Religion. The School has an historic connection with the Cathedral. Religious education, given in accordance with the Christian faith, is non-denominational. Pupils of all denominations and faiths are welcomed.

Curriculum. Pupils are prepared for the GCSE, and A, AS and Advanced Extension papers, and for Higher Education, the Services, the professions, industry and commerce. The curriculum is designed to give all pupils a general education and to postpone specialisation for as long as possible. Further details will be found in the Prospectus.

Games. The major sports are Rugby, Netball, Hockey, Football, Rowing and Cricket. Other sports include Tennis, Athletics, Cross Country, Badminton, Rounders, Fencing, Squash, Golf, Swimming, Sailing and Canoeing. PE and games are compulsory for all; a wide choice is offered to Sixth Formers. The school has been awarded the Sportsmark Gold award.

Other Activities. The school has a Choral Society and two other Choirs, 3 Orchestras and a Wind Band; there are at least 20 concerts each year. There are more than a dozen dramatic productions each year, including two or three major School plays, one of which is usually a Musical. The School takes part in the Duke of Edinburgh's Award Scheme; there

is a CCF and a Welfare and Community Service group. Young Enterprise companies in the Sixth Form are well subscribed and highly successful. A large number of societies and groups cater for a wide variety of other out-of-school activities and interests. The School has an Outdoor Activities Centre in the Black Mountains which is widely used both during the term and in the holidays. The Himalayan Club takes about 25 pupils on expeditions each year.

Scholarships and Bursaries. Both Music and Academic Scholarships are available at 11+, 13+ and 16+ in the Senior School, value up to one third of tuition fees. Academic scholarships at 11+ and 13 + are awarded on the basis of the Entrance Test and an interview; at 16+ on the basis of an aptitude test and interview, along with a report from the candidate's school.

Means-tested bursaries up to 100% of fees are available to academically-able candidates and can be combined with a scholarship. Full details are available from the Registrar.

Fees per term (2014–2015). Senior School £4,021 Junior Schools £2,065–£3,799.

Chorister Scholarships. Entry to the Choir is by means of Voice and Academic Tests which are held at various times throughout the year. A high vocal and musical standard is naturally required and boys must also have sufficient intellectual ability to hold their own in the Choir and the School. Boys should be 7–9 years old at the time of entry.

The **Prospectus** and information about Entrance Tests, Awards and Chorister Scholarships can be obtained from the Registrar.

Charitable status. The King's School Worcester is a Registered Charity, number 1098236. It exists to provide high quality education for boys and girls.

Kingston Grammar School

London Road, Kingston-upon-Thames, Surrey KT2 6PY
Tel: 020 8546 5875
email: enquiries@kgs.org.uk
website: www.kgs.org.uk

Motto: *Bene agere ac laetari.*

A school is believed to have existed in the Lovekyn Chantry Chapel since the fourteenth century. However in 1561, Queen Elizabeth I, in response to a humble petition from the Burghers of Kingston, signed Letters Patent establishing the "Free Grammar School of Queen Elizabeth to endure for ever". In 1944 the School accepted Direct Grant Status and became fully Independent in 1976. Two years later the School went Co-educational, initially with girls in the Sixth Form, but in the following year joining in the First Year, to progress through the School. There are still close links with the Royal Borough of Kingston upon Thames, but no residential qualification for entry to the School. There are circa 820 pupils and the proportion of boys to girls is approximately 54%–46%.

Governing Body:
P Marsh, BA, LLD (*Chair*)
E A Kershaw, MA, MPhil (*Vice Chair*)
Mrs L Adam, BSc
M Annesley, BA, ACA
R W Brown, MA, ACMA
D P D Combe, BA
A D Evans, BSc, ACA
I G Galbraith, MA
Ms F C Le Grys, MA
A N McLean, BA, LLM, JP
Dr S Ofield-Kerr, BA, MA, PhD
J D Rice, LLB
Mrs K Sonnemann, Dipl-lng Architect TU Berlin RIBA
J S Tapp

Head Master: **S R Lehec**, BA

Principal Deputy Head: J M Wallace, MBA (*Mathematics*)
Deputy Head: Mrs V S Humphrey, BA (*Geography*)
Assistant Head: W Cooper, MPhil (*Religion & Philosophy*)
Assistant Head: N D Bond, BA (*English*)
Assistant Head: Mrs D M Sherwood, BSc (*Geography*)

Staff:
* *Head of Department*

Miss A M Adolphus, BSc (*Biology, Senior Tutor Fourth & Fifth Year*)
Miss L S Andrews, BSc (*Mathematics*) (*maternity leave*)
Mrs J Barkey, BA (*Art*)
A J Beard, BA (*History, Head of Fifth Year*)
M Behnoudnia, BSc (*Second in Physics, Assistant Head of Academic Scholars*)
T G Benson, MSci (*Physics, Senior Tutor First Year*)
Miss S J Boulton, MA (**Director of Drama*)
Miss K A Brackley, BA (*English*)
T A Braine, MA (*Design Technology*)
Miss A Bruce, MA (*French & German, Senior Tutor Second & Third Year*)
Mrs J Butcher, BA (*History & Politics*)
D G Buttanshaw, BEd (*PE, Mathematics, *Hockey*)
Miss S E Christie, BA (*Art*)
Mrs H L Cleaves, MA (*Librarian*) (*maternity leave*)
Ms S Clifford, BSc (*Mathematics*)
Miss L Collison, BSc (**Mathematics*)
K Connor, MEng (*Joint Second in Mathematics*)
Mrs H B Cook, BSc (*Mathematics*)
Mrs S J Corcoran, BEd (**Learning Support*)
Dr A Crampin, BSc, PhD (*Physics, Head of Second Year*)
S R Crohill, BA (*Assistant Director of Drama*)
Miss P V Crothers BA (*French, German, Head of Third Year*)
M Daly (*Assistant Director of Sport*) (*maternity cover*)
J M Davies, MA (**History*)
I Deepchand, BSc (**Physics, Senior Tutor Sixth Form*)
J A Dyson, BA (**Art*)
Mrs A L Edwards, MA (**Psychology, Joint Head of Academic Monitoring*) (*maternity leave*)
D Farr, BA (**Design Technology*)
Mrs P Fine, BA (*Geography*)
N S Forsyth, BSc (*Biology, Head of Pastoral Training & Outreach*)
O P Garner, BA (*French & Italian, Deputy Head of Sixth Form*)
Mrs P S Garside, BA, MA (**English*)
M S Grant, BA, MA (*History, Head of Fourth Year*)
Ms Y Greaves, BSc (*ICT*)
J Greggor, BA (**PE*)
Miss C M Hall, BSc (**Science*)
J Halls, BA (*Design Technology*)
Mrs E Hansford, MSc (*Biology*)
Mrs R L Hetherington, BA (*Design Technology, Head of First Year*)
Mrs N L Hempstead, L-ès-L (*French, Spanish*)
Mrs H Hunt, BA (**PSHE, Religion & Philosophy*)
Miss E M Hyde, MA (*Assistant Director of Music*)
Mrs N Jackson, BA (*History, Director of Careers & Universities*)
Miss L M Jenkins, MSc (*Geography*)
Mrs C A Jones, BSc (*Mathematics*)
Miss L Knight, BA (*English*)
H R Lawrence, BSc (*Religion & Philosophy*)
N E MacKay, BA (*French, Spanish, Director of Leadership, Outdoor Education & Trips*)
Mrs N Maclean, BSc (*Assistant Director of Sport, *Sports Studies, *Girls' Hockey*) (*maternity leave*)
Mrs J McCann, BA (*English*)
Dr R McCarthy, BSc, PhD (*Chemistry, *Football*)
J McClenaghan, BSc (*Mathematics*)

Miss B A McDonald, BA, MA (*Classics, Head of Sixth Form*)
S R Morris, BSc (**Young Enterprise, Mathematics, Careers Advisor*)
Mrs S Murphy, MA (*Librarian*) (*maternity cover*)
Miss H M Naismith, MSc (*PE*)
L W O'Brien, BA (**Director of Sport*)
Mrs E K Packer, BA (*Second in English*)
Miss R Pastore, MA (*Spanish*)
Mrs K D Pinnock, BA (*French & Italian*)
Miss A P Postgate, BA (*History, Joint Head of Academic Monitoring*)
P R C Powell, BA (*Economics*)
Mrs E Pytel, BA (**Classics, Assistant Director of Studies*)
Miss N Reynolds, BA (*Spanish*)
Mrs L Rhys, BSc (*Mathematics*)
P J Ricketts, MA (**Economics, University Admissions Tests Tutor*)
Mrs M Robinson, BSc (**Psychology*) (*maternity cover*)
M J C Rodgers, BSc, MSc (**Biology*)
Mrs T M Russell, Mag Phil (**Modern Foreign Languages*)
P Scott, BSc, MRes (**Cricket*)
Miss R J Sharp, BA (*French & Spanish, Second in Modern Foreign Languages*)
P J Simmons, BSc (**Rowing*)
J W Skeates, MA (*Joint Second in Mathematics*)
C R Smalman-Smith, BA (*Mathematics, *Junior Rowing*)
J S Smith, BA, MPhil (*Second in English*)
Miss L J C Snook, MPhil (*Classics*)
D A R Sorley, BA (**Politics, History*)
Mrs J Stapleton (**Netball*)
Mrs P W E Stones, MA (*English, Head of Academic Scholars*)
J J Tierney, BMus (*Music*)
M P Von Freyhold, PG Dip RCM, Diplom Musiklehrer Karlsruhe (**Director of Music*)
H Waddington, MPhil (**Geography*)
Mrs R Wakely, BA (*Art*) (*maternity leave*)
C G Wenham, BA (*Second in Chemistry*)
Ms A Williams, BSc (*Chemistry*)
Mrs C Williams, BA (**Religion & Philosophy, Senior Tutor Sixth Form*)
M P Williamson, BEd (*PE, Director of Coaching, Boys' Hockey Head Coach*)
Dr L H Winning, MChem, DPhil (**Chemistry*)

Bursar and Clerk to the Governors: E N Lang, BA, ACA
Facilities Manager: J Farmer
Development Director: Mrs K Moore, BA
Head Master's PA: Mrs C Pink
Registrar: Mrs C Ribolla, BA
Marketing Manager: Miss N Stops, BA

Buildings. Starting with the medieval Lovekyn Chapel, the site of Kingston Grammar School has been developed over 450 years. The refurbishment of the Fairfield Building has provided modern, energy-efficient classrooms and science laboratories. The Queen Elizabeth II building, opened by Her Majesty in 2005, has a Performing Arts Centre, a Music Technology Suite, Sixth Form Centre and classrooms. Pupils have access to an extensive networked computer system which they can access from home. The school is easily accessible by road and rail links to Kingston. The 22-acre sports ground includes an indoor training area, pavilions, 3 cricket squares, 3 netball courts, 4 tennis courts, 2 hockey pitches plus practice area, football pitches and the Boat House.

Entry to the School. Admission to the School is by examination and interview at 11+ and 13+ and GCSE grades and interview at 16+. Candidates sit the School's own examination papers; for 13+ in November prior to entry year and for 11+ in January in the year of entry. We also hold a 10+ deferred entry exam for candidates in Year 5 at primary school to enter in Year 7.

Term of Entry. Apart from occasional vacancies pupils enter in September.

Fees per term (2014–2015). £5,535; this covers all charges except examination fees and lunch.

Scholarships and Bursaries. The Governors award Scholarships (on merit) and Means Tested Bursaries to pupils entering the School at 11+ and 16+.

At age 11 there are Academic Scholarships attracting a fee remission which are awarded on the results of a scholarship examination and interviews, which is by invitation only following the Entrance Examination.

Academic Scholarships are also awarded to entrants to the Sixth Form, following a written examination, interview and successful GCSE results.

Music Scholarships, plus free tuition on one instrument, are available. Auditions are in late January for candidates who are applying for entry at either 11+ or 16+.

Art Scholarships may be awarded at 11+ and 16+ following practical test, interview and submission of a folder of work.

Sport Awards for candidates demonstrating outstanding sporting potential are available at 11+ and 16+, based on practical assessment.

Curriculum. The academic curriculum through to GCSE emphasises a proper balance between varied disciplines and range of intellectual experience, with all taking Maths, English, the three sciences and at least one modern language as part of 9 or 10 IGCSE/GCSE subjects. Maths IGCSE may be taken early by able candidates. Mandarin has been introduced for First Year pupils. There is a Learning Support Department and mentoring for pupils with specific needs. A full Careers Programme is offered with support for university entry as well. Pupils are encouraged to view academic pursuit as a desirable end in itself, using a profiling process to develop their commitment to study. In the Sixth Form, students choose at least 4 AS Level subjects in the Lower Sixth and normally continue with 3 subjects to A2 Level in the Upper Sixth. In addition, students in the Lower Sixth undertake an academic enrichment programme, designed to develop the skills necessary to learn independently and to broaden their horizons. They also engage in community service. All Sixth Form students attend a fortnightly lectures on wider social issues and international themes. Almost 100% of the Sixth Form elect to proceed to higher education, including Oxford and Cambridge Universities.

Care. A pupil's form tutor is responsible for welfare and progress. Heads of Year, supported by Senior Tutors coordinate the work of form tutors. There is a full-time qualified nurse and a School Counsellor visits two days a week to support any pupils who have concerns in and out of school. Parents' meetings are held annually and pupils receive two written reports per year, in addition to twice termly grade cards. Pastoral evenings are also held, where parents can discuss with each other and staff the difficulties and anxieties faced by young adults.

Games. The school Sports Ground is beautifully situated at Thames Ditton, by the River Thames opposite Hampton Court Palace. Kingston Grammar School prides itself on the large number of pupils who represent Great Britain in Hockey and Rowing.

Hockey (in both winter terms) and Rowing (all the year round) are main games with teams at all levels regularly competing in National Championships. The School also has representative sides in football, Athletics, Cricket, Tennis, Golf, Cross-Country and Netball, with an emphasis on sport for all and participation as well as on training for performance athletes.

Societies. The School is proud of its extensive co-curricular provision and its programme of House-based activities. A large number of School Societies provides for the interests of pupils of all ages. They range from Chess and Debating, to Natural History and Young Enterprise. The Duke of Edinburgh's Award Scheme is popular and overseas travel is

a regular feature of many activities. The Music Department has a vigorous programme of concerts and tours, and a busy and flourishing Drama Department provides a wealth of opportunity for pupils in all aspects of dramatic production.

Community Service. A large number of pupils are involved in over ten external organisations as a result of the Community Service Programme at KGS, including MENCAP, The Joel Community Project, Kingston Food Drive, local Primary schools, Kingston hospital, St Stephen's homeless shelter and Elmbridge Community Link. While older pupils are directly involved in the projects, younger pupils also support groups through activities that take place within school. Volunteering helps pupils to develop awareness and understanding of elements within society that frequently go unnoticed by young people. Although the school already offers a wide range of activities to choose from, staff are also willing to help pupils find other projects if we are unable to meet their needs. In addition, the school has a partnership with a school in Ghana; gap year students undertake periods of work experience at the school, whilst younger pupils are involved in fundraising activities and co-curricular links.

Combined Cadet Force. The CCF is divided into Army and RAF Sections with a variety of activities ranging from night exercises and flying to Outward Bound and Adventure Training. Camps are held in school holidays and pupils attend courses in a range of subjects. This is an entirely voluntary activity which pupils may take up in the Third Year.

Careers. The Careers Staff assist pupils in their choice of options at all levels, and give advice on possible future careers. They are in close touch with employers in professions, commerce and industry, and all Fifth Year pupils undertake a period of work experience after their GCSE examinations. An annual Careers Convention is held at the school. Particular attention is given to advice on entry to the Universities to which the majority of Sixth Form students go. The School is in membership of the Independent School Careers Organisation and pupils are able to take advantage of several computer assessment programs.

Parents' and Staff Association. The Association exists to further the interests of the School in the broadest possible way and does much to strengthen the links between staff, parents and students. The Sherriff Club (rowing), The Ditton Field Society (cricket, football, netball, tennis, hockey), Music Society, and Drama & Dance Society also support school activities.

KGS Friends (our Alumni Society) does much to foster a spirit of unity and cooperation. All pupils and their parents automatically join the Friends on leaving the School.

Honours. An average of 10 places are gained each year at Oxbridge.

Charitable status. Kingston Grammar School is a Registered Charity, number 1078461, and a Company Limited by Guarantee, registered in England, number 3883748. It exists to enable children to adapt their talents to meet the needs of an ever changing world, whilst holding fast to the principles of self-reliance, a sense of responsibility and a determination to seize opportunity.

Kingswood School

Lansdown, Bath, Somerset BA1 5RG

Tel:	01225 734200
Fax:	01225 734305
email:	enquiries@kingswood.bath.sch.uk
website:	www.kingswood.bath.sch.uk

Motto: *In via Recta Celeriter*

Kingswood is an independent, co-educational, Christian school represented on HMC. It was founded by John Wesley in 1748 and moved to its present 218 acre site overlooking the World Heritage City of Bath in 1851. Kingswood combines academic excellence with a concern for the development of each individual's talents. Boarders and day pupils are fully integrated within a happy and caring community environment. There are currently 713 pupils (394 boys and 319 girls) at the Senior School and 311 pupils at the Prep School.

Chairman of the Governing Body: Tim Westbrook

Clerk to the Governors & Bursar: Mr P A Sadler

Headmaster: Mr S A Morris

Deputy Head Academic: Mrs S C Dawson

Deputy Head: Mr G D Opie

Deputy Head Pastoral & Chaplain: The Revd M L Wilkinson

Director of Development & Marketing: Mrs A Dudley-Warde

Registrar: Mrs D W Patterson

Senior School Teaching Staff:

Art:
Mr S Brown (*Head of Deparment*)
Mrs L Bradbury
Miss A Nicholson (*and Design Technology*)

Biology:
Mrs J Opie (*Head of Department*)
Miss E Attwood
Mrs M Patterson
Dr N Sheffrin (*Head of Science Faculty*)

Chemistry:
Dr M Fletcher (*Head of Department*)
Mr R Garforth (*and Head of Careers*)
Miss N Sparks
Mrs J-A Wilcock

Classics:
Mrs S Dakin (*Head of Department*)
Mrs S Chilver Vaughan

Design Technology:
Mr B Brown (*Head of Department*)
Miss A Nicholson (*and Art*)
Mr S Thomas

Drama:
Mrs K Nash (*Head of Department*)
Mr D Harding
Mrs E Ward

Economics & Business:
Mr J Hills (*Head of Department*)
Mrs C Edwards
Mr M Jones
Revd M Wilkinson

English:
Mr S Campbell (*Head of Department*)
Mrs A Campbell
Mrs C Clarke
Mrs S Dawson
Mrs J Mainwaring
Mr P Smith
Miss M Telford

EAL:
Mr S Forrester (*Head of Department*)

Geography:
Mrs D Jenner (*Head of Department*)
Miss K Donovan
Mr P Hollywell
Mrs A Matthews

Mr S Smyth

History:
Mr P MacDonald (*Head of Department*)
Mr D Darwin
Mr J Davies
Mrs S Herlinger
Mr C Woodgate (*Head of Sixth Form*)

Humanities:
Mrs S Fountain

IT:
Mr G Edgell (*Head of Department*)
Mrs C Sergeant
Mr S Snowden (*Director of ICT*)
Mrs J Solomon-Gardner

Languages:
Mr R Duke (*Head of Languages Faculty and Head of German*)
Miss N Beale
Miss S Brookes (*Head of French*)
Mrs M Hutchison (*and RS*)
Mr J-M Legg
Mrs C Morris
Mrs E Pasco
Mr D Walker (*Head of Spanish*)

Learning Support:
Mrs J Cook (*Head of Department*)
Mrs J Hallett
Mrs A Hirst

Mathematics:
MrC Redman (*Head of Department*)
Mrs M Brennan
Mr S Burgon
Mr J Chua
Mrs A Knights
Mr G Musto
Mrs J Reeman
Mr R White

Music:
Mr M Haynes (*Acting Director of Music and Head of Academic Music*)
Mr J Knights (*and Musician in Residence*)
Miss R Watson

PE & Games:
Mr T Reeman (*Director of Sport*)
Mr J Brown (*Head of Boys' Games*)
Mr J Matthews
Ms M Newman
Mr G Opie
Miss U Paver
Mrs V Sim (*Head of Girls' Games*)
Miss A Wright

PSHCE:
Mrs S Marshall (*Head of Department*)

Physics:
Mr R Burton (*Head of Department*)
Mrs M Brown
Mr W Musgrove
Mr E Peerless

Psychology:
Mrs C Edwards (*Head of Department*)
Mrs A Wright

Religious Education:
Mr M Thatcher (*Head of Department*)
Mrs S Marshall
Mr M Wilkinson
Miss H Wilson

Site and Buildings. Kingswood occupies 218 acres of superb parkland overlooking the world heritage City of Bath and within easy reach of the M4 and M5 motorways, as well as rail and air links. In addition to the beautiful main Victorian buildings, there is a state-of-the-art Theatre; a spacious sixth-form centre with facilities for private study and a modern common room; a series of specialist centres for ICT, DT, Drama Studio, Art Studio and a Music School with its own recording studio. A library and resources centre was opened in September 2006 with Wi-Fi facility. All academic departments also have well-resourced areas including a new modern Language Laboratory. There are seven houses for boarding and day pupils, a beautiful Chapel and excellent sporting facilities, including a Sports Hall, indoor swimming pool, two floodlit astroturfs, and extensive playing fields. In September 2011, a new sports pavilion will also be opened with first-class sports changing facilities and excellent hospitality areas.

The School also has its own Prep School in a Georgian mansion and award-winning modern buildings in a separate section of the parkland.

Curriculum. Kingswood encourages its students to develop lively, enquiring and well-informed minds and the high standard of attainment reached by its pupils has been highly praised. From 11 to 13 pupils follow a broad and balanced curriculum. Each pupil has a tutor to supervise progress and to offer advice and encouragement. At 14 the pupils choose at least eight and up to twelve GCSE subjects to develop their particular talents whilst maintaining a broad range of skills. They are also encouraged to develop independent learning plans which they work on with their tutors. Most sixth formers specialise in at least three or four subjects and all participate in a General Studies programme. Sixteen subjects are offered at GCSE level as well as over twenty at AS/A2 Level, including Politics, Business Studies, Sports Studies, Theatre Studies, Psychology and Critical Thinking. The Extended Project Qualification is also offered.

Organisation. *Preparatory*: Pupils are drawn from a wide variety of schools, but Kingswood also has its own prep school for boarders and day pupils. Kingswood Prep School (KPS) caters for c320 boys and girls between the ages of 3 and 11, and offers a variety of activities alongside the academic curriculum. A boarding house for boys and girls aged 7–11 opened in September 1998. This "family-based" unit of 20 boarders is cared for by house-parents who also teach at the school. Children from the prep school are expected to move on to Kingswood, but parents are advised if children are felt to be academically unsuitable for entry to the Senior School at the end of Year 6. (*See Kingswood Preparatory School entry in IAPS section.*)

Westwood: A junior house operates for boys and girls aged 11–13. This is designed to settle new pupils into the school at 11+ or 12+ and provide the special environment that the younger pupils require before going into the senior houses. In effect, it means the pupils enjoy the atmosphere associated with a prep school whilst also enjoying all the facilities of a senior school. Sixth formers are especially selected to act as elder "brothers/sisters" and prefects to the younger pupils. The house is run by four resident house staff, together with house assistants.

Senior Houses: From the age of 13+ pupils are assigned to one of six houses, three for boys and three for girls, each under a resident Housemaster or Housemistress and assisted by other teaching staff. The houses ensure a good and friendly 'home from home' environment and there are also shared social areas in the centre of school. It would be normal to have c200 students in the Sixth Form, which has its own special building.

Houses. The seven houses are all very distinctive and five are set within their own grounds. Emphasis is placed on creating a family atmosphere in each house and the pastoral care provided has been judged at ISI inspection as 'excep-tional'. Tutors monitor each pupil's progress and welfare. The school has a number of houses and flats for single and married staff. Half of the staff at the senior school live on the campus which cultivates exceptionally good relationships between teachers and students.

Sports and Games. The sporting and leisure activities programmes have around 90 activities with particular emphasis on sport, drama, music, art and outdoor pursuits. Sporting activities include athletics, badminton, basketball, cricket, cross-country, fencing, golf, hockey, netball, rugby, swimming and tennis. Other activities range from the Duke of Edinburgh's Award Scheme to Computing, from Orienteering to Photography, and Bird Watching to Dance Express. Regular group activities in the instrumental field include orchestra, an award-winning jazz band, string group and wind band. There are also junior and senior choirs and a large-scale choral society and an extensive performance programme. Over 50% of the school are involved in extra music lessons. At least four dramatic productions take place each year.

Health. The well-equipped School Medical Centre is under the supervision of a fully qualified resident Sister and the School Medical Officer.

Religious Activities. Kingswood welcomes pupils from all denominations. In addition to regular morning worship, there is a wide variety of guest speakers and the Christian Fellowship organises its own events. There are regular fund-raising activities for charities and a Community Service programme. Every year a joint Methodist-Anglican Confirmation service is held and there are special services in Bath Abbey for the whole school Carol Service and for Commemoration Day.

Careers. From the earliest stage possible, students are encouraged to participate in all decisions affecting their future. Kingswood subscribes to the Independent Schools Careers Organisation and has links with local career guidance organisations. A programme of work experience is followed by all members of the Lower Sixth and is aimed at providing experience of the entire process of job application, interview and work itself. The School has established close links with local employers to make all this possible. A series of lectures and discussions with visiting employers is also organised and endorsed by the Head of Sixth Form.

Leavers. It is normal for all of our Sixth Form pupils to go on to university courses, around 94% to the place of their first choice.

Fees per term (2014–2015). £4,465 (day), £8,381–£9,624 (full boarding), £7,019–£8,695 (weekly boarding).

EAL teaching is provided for students who do not speak English as their first language – this is invoiced separately as required.

Entry Requirements. Entry is based on Kingswood's entrance examination; a report from the candidate's previous school and, where possible, a personal interview. Candidates at 13+ may also enter by Common Entrance or Scholarship papers. Entry to the Sixth Form is by a minimum of six or more GCSE passes – four at Grade B plus two at Grade C, plus school report and interview. There are some subject specific criteria, details of which are found on the school website. (Most applicants achieve considerably more than the minimum entry grades.) There are normally around 25 places available due to the extended facilities available at Sixth Form level.

Scholarships and Bursaries. Academic and Special Talent scholarships (up to a maximum of 25% of the basic fees) are available annually to day and boarding pupils entering Years 7, 9 and Lower Sixth. Special Talent scholarships are awarded for excellence in a particular field: Art, Drama, Music, Sport, Design Technology. John Wesley All-Rounder Awards are also available for boarders only.

Means-tested bursaries, worth up to 100% of fees, are available in Years 7, 9 and Lower Sixth, awarded annually at the discretion of the Headmaster and the Governors.

Very special provisions are made for the children of Methodist Ministers (up to 100% bursary assistance) and consideration may also be given to assist the sons and daughters of clergymen of other denominations, with a reduction in fees according to circumstances.

HM Forces families receive a reduction in boarding fees of up to 20% for each child, although the scheme is limited depending on demand for places within any particular year group at this rate.

Further details of scholarships and bursaries can be obtained from the Registrar or on the school website.

Charitable status. Kingswood School is a Registered Charity, number 309148. Founded by John Wesley, it maintains its Methodist tradition in providing preparatory and secondary education.

Kirkham Grammar School

Ribby Road, Kirkham, Preston, Lancashire PR4 2BH
Tel: 01772 684264
Fax: 01772 672747
email: info@kirkhamgrammar.co.uk
website: www.kirkhamgrammar.co.uk

Kirkham Grammar School, founded in 1549, is a co-educational independent School of 880 pupils aged between 3 and 18. The Senior School of 650 pupils, 65 of whom are boarders, incorporates a Sixth Form of 200, and the Junior School, for day pupils, has 230+ on roll.

Chairman of Governors: Mrs R Cartwright

Headmaster: Mr R D W Laithwaite, BA, MEd, FRSA

Deputy Head: Mrs D C Parkinson, BSc, NPQH

Deputy Head (*Operations*): Mr M J Hancock, BEd, MA, MBA

Director of Studies & Head of Sixth Form: Mr A R Long, MA Oxon

Senior Master: Mr R J Watson, BA

Heads of Year:
Sixth Form: Mr A R Long, MA Oxon
Assistant Heads of Sixth Form:
Mr M Gaddes, MA
Mrs J Stanbury, BA
Fifth Year: Mr M P Melling, BA, MA Ed
Fourth Year: Mrs A Walker, BA
Third Year: Mr D Gardner, BEng
Second Year: Mr S F Duncan, BA
First Year: Mrs K C O'Flaherty, BA

Heads of Departments:
Art: Mr S P Gardiner, BA
Biology: Mr G A Ferguson, BSc
Business Studies & Economics: Mrs L E Hargreaves, BA
Chemistry: Dr A B Rollins, BSc, PhD
Design & Technology: Mr D Gardner, BEng
Drama: Ms J E Barrie, BA
English: Mr C J Hawkes, BA, MA
Geography: Mr S R Whittle, MA
History: Mr T P Miller, BA
ICT: Mr R J Browning, BSc, ACCE
Latin: Mrs S P Long, BA
Learning Support: Mrs P Blackburn, TCert, BA, PG Dip SpLD
Librarian: Mrs G R Latham
Mathematics: Miss S R Howe, BSc
Modern Foreign Languages: Miss L E Vicquelin, BA
Director of Music: Miss J Z Crook, BMus
Physics: Mr M Gaddes, MA
Politics: Mr M P Melling, BA, MA Ed

Psychology: Mrs J Stanbury, BA
Religion, Philosophy & Ethics: Mrs L Bowles, BA
Science: Dr A C Hall, PhD, Grad RIC

Houses & Housemistresses/Housemasters:
Boarding Housemaster: Dr M A Whalley, BEd, MEd, EdD
Kirkham House: Mrs S J John, MA
Fylde House: Mr S R Whittle, MA Cantab
School House: Mr R Wu, BSc
Preston House: Mr C Wheatland, MPhys

Bursar: Mrs C E Brown

Headmaster's PA/Registrar: Mrs C M Seed

Junior School:
Headmistress of Junior School: Mrs A S Roberts, BEd
Deputy Headmaster: Mr B Edgar, BEd
Assistant Head: Mrs H Shuttleworth, GMus Hons RNCM
Head of Infant Department: Mrs P Edgar, BEd
Pre-School Manager: Mrs A Blanco-Bayo, BSc

Headmistress's PA: Miss J Stewart
School Secretary: Mrs A Giddings

Kirkham Grammar School prides itself on developing well-balanced and confident young people, the vast majority of whom go on to University. As well as excellent academic results and a good Oxbridge entry record, the School introduces pupils to as wide a range as possible of cultural, sporting and creative activities and encourages them to participate in those which appeal to them. Great emphasis is placed on preparing pupils for life beyond university.

The School has a strong Christian ethos, with an emphasis on care for the individual, traditional family values, good manners and sound discipline.

It is a friendly close-knit community where staff and pupils work closely together, fostering leadership and self-discipline, and encouraging cheerful, friendly and supportive relationships within the framework of 'one family'.

Facilities. Occupying 30 acres of its own grounds, Kirkham Grammar School boasts some excellent facilities, which include a large multi-purpose hall, a superb floodlit all-weather pitch, a Sixth Form Centre, an outstanding Technology Centre and Languages Centre, and a magnificent Dining Complex. The School has built a new Science Centre alongside a new extended classroom block incorporating interactive facilities and also a new Performing Arts Centre. The school has developed a new Music Centre and new Sports Hall.

Boarding. The School is a member of the Boarding Schools' Association. The refurbished Boarding House is pleasant and comfortable and is run by a Boarding Housemaster and his wife, whose residence is attached to the boarding wing of the School. The House also has a team of full-time support staff and Tutors.

Academic Programme. The courses lead to GCSE, A Level and AS Level. In the first three years, the basic subjects studied are English, French, Mathematics, German, Spanish, Geography, History, Physics, Chemistry, Biology, Music, Art & Design, Drama, ICT, Design and Technology, and Religious Studies. The first stage of specialisation takes place on entering the fourth form where the core subjects of English, Mathematics, Physics, Chemistry, Biology and French/German/Spanish are taught in sets, and there is a further choice of subjects from three option blocks, which include: Art & Design, Design and Technology (Product Design; Electronic Products), Drama, Economics & Business Studies, Geography, German, History, ICT, Latin, Music, Physical Education, Religious Studies, and Religion, Philosophy & Ethics.

In the Sixth Form, A and AS Level subjects are chosen from the following: English Language and Literature, Maths, Further Maths, Biology, Chemistry, Physics, French, German, Latin, Spanish, Art & Design, Music, Design Technology, Geography, History, Psychology, Philosophy, Government & Politics, Theatre Studies, Religious Studies, Economics, Business Studies, Physical Education & Electronics.

In addition all Sixth Formers follow a programme of General Studies and many voluntarily continue in the CCF and the Duke of Edinburgh's Award, Young Enterprise or Community Service. Extra tuition is provided for Oxbridge candidates. Currently a group of students are following the AQA Baccalaureate.

A comprehensive careers service is available. The School is an active member of ISCO and is also served by Careerlink.

Sport. The School has a strong sporting tradition and ranks among the very best schools in the country for rugby and girls hockey. The other main sports played are cricket, athletics, tennis, netball, cross-country, badminton, squash, swimming, rounders, volleyball and basketball.

Music. There is a very active musical life at the School, with regular Concerts both at lunchtime and in the evening, providing a platform for the Orchestra, various ensembles and Soloists.

Extra-Curricular Activities. An impressive range of extra-curricular activities is offered by a School renowned for its sporting prowess, but with strength across the board in music, art, and drama. There is a strong and popular Combined Cadet Force contingent, with Army and RAF sections, and a flourishing House System. A large number of societies cater for a wide range of interests including archery, broadcasting society, drama, debating, the very popular Duke of Edinburgh's Award scheme, chess, public speaking, badminton, climbing, magic circle, music and many others.

Admission to Senior School. Four form entry. Pupils are usually admitted at 11 years after passing the entrance examination held in January each year. Admissions to the School in other year groups, especially the Sixth Form, are possible. Day/Boarding applications should be made to the Headmaster who will be glad to provide further details.

Fees per term (2014–2015). Day (excluding lunches): Senior School £3,338; Junior School £2,505; Pre-School: £214 (full week), £44 (full day).

These Fees cover tuition, use of class, text and library books, school stationery, scientific equipment, games apparatus.

Senior School Boarding: £3,002 in addition to the Day fee. The boarding fee is discounted by 5% for children resident Monday to Friday (weekly boarders) and for children whose parents are current members of HM Forces.

Scholarships and Bursaries. The School offers an impressive number of Scholarships and Bursaries at 11+ and 16+. A detailed Scholarship Booklet is available from the Registrar.

Junior School (3–11 years). An integral part of the School under the same Board of Governors, the Junior School comprises a Pre-School, an Infant Department and a Junior Department, housed in splendid, purpose-built accommodation. The work is organised in close consultation with the Senior School to ensure that education in its broadest sense is continuous and progressive from the age of 3 to 18.

The curriculum is broadly based and balanced. The core subjects – English, Maths and Science – are given priority as set in the National Curriculum. History, Geography, RE, Music, ICT, Design and Technology, Art, PE and Games are studied as pure subjects and also as they relate to one another in a cross-curricular manner. In the Early Years we offer a fun, stimulating and caring environment, which follows the Early Years Foundation Stage Framework.

Application should be made direct to the Headmistress's PA from whom a separate prospectus may be obtained.

Old Kirkhamians Association. For further details contact the Secretary, Mr A R Long, via the School.

Charitable status. Kirkham Grammar School is a Registered Charity, number 1123869. The object of the Charity

shall be the provision in or near Kirkham of a day and boarding school for boys and girls.

Lancing College
A Woodard School

Lancing, West Sussex BN15 0RW
Tel: 01273 452213
Fax: 01273 464720
email: admissions@lancing.org.uk
website: www.lancingcollege.co.uk
Twitter: @lancingcollege
Facebook: /lancingcollege

Motto: *Beati mundo corde.*

Founded in 1848 by the Revd Nathaniel Woodard, Lancing College is the first of the schools of the Woodard Foundation.

Governing Body:
The Provost and the Directors of Lancing College Ltd

Visitor: The Rt Revd The Lord Bishop of Chichester

Governing Body:
Chairman: Dr H O Brünjes, BSc, MBBS, DRCOG, FEWI
Deputy Chair: P Bowden, LLM
Provost: The Rt Revd Lindsay Urwin, OGS, MA (*ex officio*)
Chairman of Finance Committee: M Slumbers, BSc, ACA (*OL*)
Chairman of Estates Committee: R H Stapleton, FRICS
D Austin, BSc Eng, PGCE
N A O Bennett, MA, MRICS (*OL*)
Mrs P Berry, GTCL, LTCL
Baroness Cumberlege, CBE, DL
Mrs A-M Edgell, LLB
A C V Evans, MA, MPhil, FICL, FKC
Mrs C Houston, BSc (*OL*)
H C R Lawson, MA, MBA (*OL*)
S J Moll, BEd (*OL*)
I D Parker, BSc, MBA
Major General D Rutherford-Jones, CB (*OL*)

Clerk to the Governing Body: Mrs P Bulman, FCA

***Head Master*: D T Oliver**, BA, MPhil

Bursar: M B Milling, CA
Deputy Head: Mrs H R Dugdale, MA
Deputy Head (*Academic*): J R J Herbert, BA, PhD
Assistant Head (*Academic*): S W Cornford, MA, PhD
Head of Sixth Form: S J Ward, MMath, MPhil
President of the Common Room: S R Norris, BSc, PhD
Registrar and Director of Marketing: D S Connolly, BA, FRSA
Director of Extra-Curricular Activities: C P Foster, MA (*OL*)
Acting Director of IT: A Brown
Chaplain: The Revd R K Harrison, BA, MA
Foundation Director: Catherine Reeve, BA (*OL*)

Assistant Staff:
T S Auty, BA (*Photography, Art*)
A J Betts, BA, PhD, MIL (*French, German*)
Mrs M Brookes (*German*)
N A Brookes, MSc (*Mathematics*)
Mrs E Campbell, MA (*Mathematics*)
A M Chappell, BSc (*Biology, Physics*)
A R Coakes, BA, MSc (*Design & Technology*)
D S Connolly, BA (*Head of Politics*)
S W Cornford, MA, PhD (*English*)
D N Cox, MA, FRCO, FTCL, LRAM, ARCM (*Director of Chapel Music*)

Mrs M J Creer, BA (*English*)
C P E Crowe, BEd (*Director of Sport*)
P Dale, BSc, MIBiol (*Head of Psychology, Biology*)
D G Davies, BA, ALCM (*Head of Spanish, French*)
S A Drozdov, BEd (*Head of Modern Languages, German*)
G A Drummond, BSc (*Economics*)
Mrs H R Dugdale, MA (*English, PSHE*)
J R J East, BSc (*Mathematics*)
Ms K V Edwards, BA (*Head of Girls' Games and DofE*)
Mrs P S Faulkner, BSc (*Head of Biology*)
C P Foster, MA (*Head of Geography*)
Miss L J Gaukroger, BA (*Classics*)
Miss L Gent, BA (*French, Spanish*)
J A Grime, BSc (*Geography*)
D J Harman, BA, MA (*Head of English*)
The Revd R K Harrison, BA, MA (*Religious Studies,
   History*)
Miss J J Hargrave, BA (*French, Spanish*)
D J Harvey, BSc (*Biology*)
Ms J Hayward-Voss, BA (*Head of Business Studies*)
Miss M P Howells, BA (*Learning Support*)
Dr E Keane, BA, PhD (*English, Politics*)
D A Kerney, MA, PhD (*Head of History*)
Mrs C M Krause, BA (*English, History, RS, PSHE*)
Miss R Lawrence, BA (*Art*)
Mrs S E Lawrence, BA (*Design & Technology*)
Mrs Q Liang, MA (*Chinese*)
Mrs K Lindfield, HND (*Art*)
M C J Loxton, MMath (*Mathematics*)
Ms A Maddaloni, BA (*Italian*)
D N Mann, BSSc (*Head of PE, Biology*)
Mrs S D Marchant, BA, MCLIP (*Librarian*)
R J Maru (*Director of Cricket*)
Ms A McKane, MA (*English*)
T J Meierdirk, BFA (*Head of Design & Technology*)
R P Mew, MA (*Head of Classics*)
C M Mole, BSc (*PE, PSHE*)
Mrs C R Mole, BA (*Head of Economics, Business Studies*)
I Morgan-Williams, GMus, RNCM, DPhil (*Director of
   Music*)
S R Norris, BSc, PhD (*Chemistry*)
B J O'Riordan, BSc, DPhil (*Mathematics*)
Mrs C E Palmer, MA (*History*)
M S W Palmer, BA, PhD, MIL
N L Payne, BA (*English*)
A W Pratt, MA (*Economics*)
G A Preston, BSc, PhD (*Head of Science and Physics*)
Miss C M Pringle, BA (*Head of Art*)
P C Richardson, MA (*Head of RS, Drama, History*)
Mrs H M Robinson, BSc (*Chemistry*)
W S Savage, MA (*Mathematics*)
Mrs J M Scullion, CertEd (*Learning Support Coordinator*)
J L Sherrell, MA (*Economics*)
M J H Smith, BA (*Head of Drama, Religious Studies*)
Ms H A Stevenson, BLib, MCLIP (*Assistant Librarian*)
Mrs J O Such, BA, MSc (*Head of Mathematics*)
Mrs W A Swarbrick, MSc, EdD (*Physics, Chemistry*)
G C Thomas, BEng, MInstP (*Physics*)
Miss L A Thorn, MEng (*Physics*)
Mrs A W Tritton, BSc, MA, FRGS (*Geography, PSHE*)
M E Walsh, BSc, DPhil (*Head of Chemistry*)
S J Ward, MMath, MPhil (*Mathematics*)
Mrs R M Webber, MBA, BSc (*Biology*)
D J Wilks, MA (*History*)
A P Williamson, MA (*Chemistry*)

Houses & Housemasters/mistresses:

Boys:
Head's: Mr A M Chappell
Second's: Mr D J Harvey
School: Mr C M Mole
Gibbs': Mr M J H Smith
Teme: Dr S R Norris

Girls:
Field's: Mrs M J Creer
Sankey's: Mrs E Campbell
Manor: Mrs C M Krause
Handford (*Sixth Form*): Ms A McKane

Head Master's Secretary: Mrs H L Betts, BSc
Admissions Officer: Mrs G S Prichard

Medical Officers:
Dr H Bentley, MBBS, MRCGP, DA, DRCOG
Dr I Cox, MBChB, BSc, DRCOG, MRCGP
Dr V Figuera, DM, MRCGP
Dr C Huckstep, MBBS, DRCOG, DCH
Dr E Lerner, BSc, MBBS, MRCGP

There are about 550 pupils in the school, accommodated in nine houses.

Location. The school stands on a spur of the Downs, overlooking the sea to the south and the Weald to the north, in grounds of some 550 acres, which include the College Farm.

By train, Lancing is 10 minutes from Brighton, 30 minutes from Gatwick Airport and 75 minutes from central London.

Buildings and Facilities. The main school buildings, faced with Sussex flint, are grouped around two quadrangles on the lines of an Oxford or Cambridge College.

The great Chapel, open to visitors every day, has the largest rose window built since the Middle Ages.

The College has extensive laboratories, a purpose-built Music School, a Theatre with a full-time technical manager and a modern Design and Technology Centre with computerised design and engineering facilities. Alongside this, a strikingly modern Art School provides vast studio space and a photography suite. Most recently a café has been created in the centre of the school for use by pupils and staff. There are over 330 private studies for boys and girls, many of which are study-bedrooms. There is a sports hall, indoor swimming pool and a miniature shooting range. Sporting facilities also include Squash, Tennis and Fives courts and an all-weather surface and full-sized astroturf hockey pitch.

Admission. Boys and girls are normally admitted at the beginning of the Autumn Term in their fourteenth year. Admission is made on the result of either the Entrance Scholarship, the Common Entrance Examination or by private testing. A registration fee of £100 is paid when a child's name is entered in the admission register. Entries should be made via the Registrar, who will assign a House, following as far as possible the wishes of the parents. After a pupil has joined the school, parents usually correspond with the Housemaster or Housemistress directly.

Sixth Form Entry. Applications for entry should be made to the Registrar one year prior to the year of entry. Testing takes place in November or by private arrangement.

Curriculum. Designed as far as possible to suit every pupil's potential, the curriculum provides the training required for entry to Universities and to a wide range of professions.

In a pupil's first three years the curriculum provides a broad, balanced education without premature specialisation. The total of subjects taken at GCSE is limited to about nine or ten, the object being to promote excellence in whatever is studied and to lay firm foundations for the Sixth Form years.

The following subjects are studied in the Senior School: English Language and Literature, Religious Studies, Mathematics, Physics, Chemistry, Biology, French, Spanish or German, Geography, History, Physical Education, Music, Art, Design and Technology, Latin or Classical Civilisation, Greek and Drama.

In the Sixth Form there is a choice of 25 subjects which can be studied to A or AS Level, together with a General Studies course in the Lower Sixth.

A close connection has been established with schools in Germany and Spain, with which individual and group exchanges are arranged.

Tutorial System. In addition to the Housemaster or Housemistress there are pastoral Tutors attached to each House who act as Academic Tutors to individual pupils. The Tutors' main functions are to supervise academic progress and to encourage general reading and worthwhile spare time activities. A pupil usually keeps the same Tutor until he or she moves into the Sixth Form, where this function is taken over by an Academic Tutor chosen from one of the specialist teachers.

Music and Art form an important part of the education of all pupils. There are orchestras, bands, ensembles and choirs. Organ and Choral awards to Oxford and Cambridge and Colleges of Music are frequently won. There is a full programme of extra-curricular **Drama**. The **Art School** and **Design and Technology Centre** provide for a wide range of technical and creative work.

Other Activities. Boys and girls in their first year are given the opportunity to sample the many activities on offer at the College. A well-organised extra-curricular programme is followed by pupils of all age groups and participation is strongly encouraged under the supervision of the Director of Extra-Curricular Activities.

Up to twelve plays are produced each year and pupils are able to write and perform their own plays and to learn stagecraft.

In the Advent Term the main sports are Association Football for boys and Hockey for girls; in the Lent Term Football and Hockey for boys and Netball for girls. Squash, Fives, Badminton, Basketball, Volleyball, Cross Country and Shooting (the College has an indoor range) take place during both terms for boys and girls. Some Rugby is played in the Lent Term. Cricket, Tennis, Sailing, Athletics and Rounders take place in the Summer Term, and there is Swimming all year round in the College's indoor heated pool.

The College has a CCF contingent (with Army and RAF sections) and takes part in the Duke of Edinburgh's Award scheme. There is also a flourishing Outreach group, which works in the local community. Pupils help to run a small farm (including sheep, goats, pigs, alpacas and chickens) and participate in conservation projects under the supervision of the Farm Manager.

Links have been established with local industries and pupils are involved in business experience through the Young Enterprise scheme.

Careers and Higher Education. A number of the teaching staff share responsibility for careers advice and there is a well-equipped careers section in the Gwynne Library. Over 98% of pupils go to University with about 10% gaining places at Cambridge or Oxford. All members of the Fifth Form attend the annual Careers Symposium and most enrol in the ISCO Futurewise scheme.

Scholarships and Exhibitions. Candidates for the following awards must be under 14 years of age on 1st September in the year of the examination. The age of the candidate is taken into account in making awards. A candidate may enter for more than one type of award, and account may be taken of musical or artistic proficiency in a candidate for a non-musical award; but no one may hold more than one type of award, except in an honorary capacity.

A number of Open Scholarships ranging in value from £1,000 per year to half of the annual school fee.

A number of Music Scholarships ranging in value up to half the annual school fee. Scholarships may be offered to pupils from schools where the time for Music is less than in some others, and where a candidate may have less musical experience but greater potential.

One Professor W K Stanton Music Scholarship for a Chorister from Salisbury Cathedral School, or failing that any Cathedral School. A Stanton Exhibition may also be awarded.

A number of scholarships in Art, Drama and Sport, ranging in value up to a quarter of the annual school fee.

The Peter Robinson Cricket Scholarship is awarded to an outstanding young cricketer at 13+ entry.

A number of Ken Shearwood Awards, ranging in value up to a quarter of the annual school fee, are made to pupils of all-round ability and potential who have made outstanding contributions to their present schools.

Entry Forms for Academic, Art, Music, Drama, Sport and All-Rounder (Ken Shearwood) awards are obtainable from the Admissions Officer.

Sixth Form Awards. Scholarships are available for new entrants to the Sixth Form with special proficiency in Academic subjects, Music or Art. There is also one Organ Scholarship. The candidate's general ability to contribute to the life of a boarding school community will also be taken into account. A small number of Scholarships is also available internally on the strength of GCSE results.

The value of all Entrance Scholarships may be augmented by bursaries, according to parental circumstances.

Fees per term (2014–2015). Boarding £10,650; Day £7,480.

Further details about fees, including the scheme for payment in advance of a single composition fee to cover a pupil's education during his/her time in the School, are available from the Bursar.

Charitable status. Lancing College is a Registered Charity, number 1076483. It exists to provide education for boys and girls.

Latymer Upper School

King Street, Hammersmith, London W6 9LR

Tel:	020 8629 2024
Fax:	020 8748 5212
email:	head@latymer-upper.org
website:	www.latymer-upper.org
Twitter:	@LatymerUpper

The Latymer Foundation owes its origin to the will of Edward Latymer, dated 1624. It is a Day School of 1,179 pupils, of which 350 are in the Sixth Form. The School is fully co-educational with 51% male and 49% female pupils. There are also 160 pupils in the co-educational Latymer Prep School which shares the same grounds. (*Please see entry in IAPS section.*)

Chairman of Governors: James Graham, MA, FRSA

Co-opted Governors:
Stephen Hodges, MA
Nicholas Jordan, MA
Rosemary Radcliffe, CBE, MA, MPhil, FIBC
Margaret Salmon, BA, FCIPD
Tracey Scoffield, BA
Professor Jim Smith, MA, PhD, FRS, FRSA, FMedSci
Professor Julius Weinberg, BA, BMBCh, DM, MSc, FRCP
John Wotton, MA
James Priory, MA
Ros Sweeting, LLB
Joanna Mackle, BA
Hugh Sloane, BSc, MPhil

Ex officio Governor: The Reverend Simon Downham, LLB, DipMin, MA

Clerk to the Governors: Lucinda Evans

Head: **David Goodhew**, MA Corpus Christi College Oxford

Deputy Heads:
Alex Hirst, MA Fitzwilliam College Cambridge (*Premises & Resources*)

Andrew Matthews, MA Sidney Sussex College Cambridge
(*Academic*)
Angela Tomlinson, BSc Cardiff, MA Open University
(*Staff Welfare & Development*)

Finance Director: John Tyrwhitt, MA, FCA

Director of Development: Amanda Scott, MA

Assistant Heads:
Neelam Varma, BSc, MSc Warwick (*Lower School*)
Kristan Spencer, BSc Hull, MA Cincinnati USA (*Middle School*)
Rachel Collier, MA Corpus Christi College Oxford, MA Birkbeck London (*Sixth Form*)
Richard Niblett, BA Liverpool (*Co-curriculum*)
Charlie Ben-Nathan, BA Exeter, MBA Middlesex (*Director of Studies*)

Prep School Principal: Stuart Dorrian, BA, Dip Drama, PGCE

Registrar: Catriona Sutherland-Hawes, MA

Heads of Year:
Head of Year 7: Gareth Cooper, BSc Port Elizabeth, South Africa
Head of Year 8: Katie Temple, BA Durham
Head of Year 9: Amy Sellars, BSc Cardiff
Head of Year 10: Paul Goldsmith, BA Leeds, MBA Cass Business School
Head of Year 11: Debbie Kendall, BA Leeds
Head of Lower Sixth: Sally Markowska, BA Westfield College London
Head of Upper Sixth: Mark Holmes, BA Bristol

Heads of Departments:
Academic Mentoring: Jacqueline Heywood, BSc LSE, SENCO
Art & Design: David Mumby, BA Wolverhampton, PGCE Goldsmiths
Classics: Marcel Lewis, BA Durham
Design & Technology: Edward Charlwood, BSc Aston
Director of Drama: Justin Joseph, BA London
Economics: Mark Wallace, BSc Birmingham
English: Roisin Babuta, BA King's College London, MLitt St John's College Oxford
Geography: Michael Ashby, BA Middlesex, MSc King's College, FRGS, CGeog
History: Jonathan White, MA Selwyn College Cambridge
History of Art: Ruth Bell, BA Bristol, PG Dip Art Gallery/Museum Studies Manchester
Mathematics: Patrick MacMahon, MA Emmanuel College Cambridge, MSc Open University
Modern Languages: Andrew Rees, BA Swansea, MCIL
Director of Music: Tony Henwood, MA Exeter College Oxford, ARCO, FRSA
Director of Sport: Tallan Gill, BA Manchester Metropolitan
Politics: John Gilbert, MA Wadham College Oxford
Religious Studies & Philosophy: Keith Noakes, MA Corpus Christi College Cambridge, MA Manchester
Science: Dr Brian Chaplin, BSc Portsmouth, PhD Reading

Admission. This is by competitive examination and interview at 11. The 11+ examinations are held every year in January followed by interviews for selected candidates in late January/early February. Entry to the Sixth Form is based on interview in November of the year before entry and conditional offers at GCSE.

Details of Open Days and Entry are obtainable from the Registrar.

Preparatory School. Pupils sit the 11+ Entrance Exam for the Upper School from Latymer Prep School. (*For further details see entry in IAPS section.*)

Fees per term (2014–2015). £5,770.

Bursaries. A number of means-tested bursaries are awarded every year assessed on academic merit and family circumstances. These range from 25% of fees to full fees and are available at 11+ and 16+. Currently 16% of pupils are in receipt of fee assistance.

Scholarships. *11+ Entry*: Academic Scholarships (£1,000 at time of entry) can be offered as a result of performance in the 11+ entrance examinations and interview.

Music Scholarships of varying amounts are offered, together with music awards of free tuition on two instruments.

16+ Entry: Academic Scholarships are offered, together with scholarships for Music, Drama, Art and Sport. Candidates who have satisfied the academic requirements will be invited to an interview and assessment in January.

Further details are available from the Registrar (020 3004 0478; csh@latymer-upper.org).

Curriculum. A full range of academic subjects is offered at GCSE and A Level. Languages include French, German, Spanish and Italian (European Work Experience and exchanges are run every year), Latin and Greek. Science is taught as separate subjects by subject specialists from Year 7. Form sizes in the Lower School of around 22 and smaller teaching group sizes ensure the personal attention of staff. Our own World Perspectives Course, now UCAS accredited, comprising elements of Geography, History, RS, Politics, Philosophy, and Economics is enjoyed by Years 10 and 11.

Pastoral Care. The School has a strong tradition of excellent pastoral care. There are three Divisions (Lower School, Middle School, Sixth Form) and each Division is led by an Assistant Head. A Head of Year is responsible for the pupils in each year. Teams of Form Tutors deliver a coherent PSHE programme which promotes involvement in the community, charity work, and the personal, social and academic development of the Form.

Sixth Form. The large co-educational Sixth Form offers around thirty-five A Level choices; students opt to take four subjects at A Level including the very popular Extended Project. Students have the opportunity to undertake work experience in Paris or Berlin and receive extensive Careers and Higher Education guidance. All students expect to go on to University or Art College; more than 30 went to Oxbridge last year. The Sixth Form has its own Common Room as well as a University and Careers Centre.

Music and Drama. These activities play a large part in the life of the School. The Latymer Arts Centre houses music practice rooms and a 300-seat Theatre in addition to increased facilities for Art. The Latymer Performing Arts Centre houses a 100-seat recital hall, music classrooms and more practice rooms and a dance/drama studio. There are several orchestras and bands and a number of major concerts each term, both here and in Central London venues. There are five major drama productions each year, and opportunities for all pupils to perform in events.

Science and Library. A state-of-the-art building, housing Science Laboratories, a Library, Sixth Form Study Common Room and Study Centre, opened in September 2010. All year groups have the use of these facilities.

Sport. There are excellent facilities for sport. The School has a Boat House on site with direct river access, as well as a large sports hall and an indoor swimming pool in the grounds. This is currently undergoing redevelopment and a brand new Sports Centre and Pool will be open in September 2015. There are playing fields at Wood Lane with an all-weather, floodlit playing surface. The emphasis is on involvement, participation and choice. School teams enjoy great success in the major sports of rugby, football, netball, hockey, rowing, cricket and athletics. Other sports such as karate, Judo, dance, swimming, pilates and power walking for individual interests. The School maintains excellent fixture lists for all major sports.

Extra-Curricular Activities. There is a wide range of clubs and societies at lunch time and after school. In addition, every pupil has the opportunity to have residential experience and to take part in outdoor pursuits as part of the annual Activities Week. Fundraising by a very active Parents' Gild ensures that nobody is excluded from an activity for financial reasons. The Duke of Edinburgh's Award Scheme flourishes with a number of students achieving the Gold Award each year.

Charitable status. The Latymer Foundation is a Registered Charity, number 312714. It exists to provide education for children.

The Grammar School at Leeds

Alwoodley Gates, Harrogate Road, Leeds LS17 8GS
Tel: 0113 229 1552
Fax: 0113 228 5111
email: enquiries@gsal.org.uk
website: www.gsal.org.uk
Twitter: @TheGSAL
Facebook: /grammarschoolatleeds

The Grammar School at Leeds is one of the UK's leading independent, co-educational schools. It enjoys the heritage of both Leeds Grammar School and Leeds Girls' High School with a lineage traceable back to 1552 with a long history of academic excellence. It benefits from a magnificent site on the outskirts of the north of Leeds.

We are committed to caring for our pupils as well as educating them. Our aim is to help them develop their individual abilities and talents within an ethic of teamwork, friendship and mutual respect.

We teach with pleasure and our pupils learn with enjoyment. That essentially sums up our mission. How well we accomplish it depends on much more than just excellent exam results. Our satisfaction lies in guiding children and young adults to become, quite simply, the best of their generation.

Governors:

Mr D P A Gravells, JP, MSc (*Chairman*)
Dr H Luscombe, MB BS, DA, DRCOG, MRCGP (*Joint Deputy Chairman*)
Mr P N Sparling, MBE, LLB (*Joint Deputy Chairman*)
Mrs E E Bailey, BChD, LDS, RCS, DOrthRCS
Sir Stephen Brown, KCVO
Mr J Cross, BA Oxon, ACA
Mr I Jones, MA, ACA, MBA
Mrs D Kenny, BEd
Mr A M Martin, MA, FCA
Mr K Morton, MRICS
Mr C R Obank, LLB
Mrs S A Solyom, BA, ACA
Professor D Sugden, PhD
Mr A J Walsh, ACIB
Mr J Woodward, MA
Mr E M Ziff, HonDBA

Teaching Staff:

Principal & Chief Executive: Michael Gibbons, BA, AKC

Head of Junior School: Robert Lilley
Head of Rose Court (*Pre-Prep*): Anne Pickering
Senior Deputy Head (*Pastoral Care*): Christine Bamforth
Deputy Head (*School Evaluation & Staff Development*): Paul Lunn
Senior Deputy Head (*Co-Curricular*): Neal Parker
Senior Deputy Head (*Academic*): Kevin Carson
Director of External Relations: Helen Clapham
Director of Finance: David Naylor

Director of Sixth Form: Paul Rushworth
Head of Student Development: Christine Jagger
Head of Upper Sixth: Patrick Brotherton
Head of Lower Sixth: Petra Turner
Head of Year 11: Sean Corcoran
Head of Year 10: James Veitch
Head of Year 9: Carol Heatley
Head of Year 8: Rachel Hayward
Head of Year 7: Stephen Gibbin

Heads of Department:

Art, Design & Technology: Stuart Kelly
Biology: Mark Smith
Chemistry: Ruth Boddy
Classics: Helen Morrison
Drama: Antoinette Keylock
Economics/Business Studies: Christopher Law
English: Jenny Bolton
Food Technology: Yvonne Wilson
French: Nick Hele
Geography: Simon Knowles
German: Emma Whittaker
History: Keith Milne
ICT: Tim Street
Mathematics: Orla Fitzsimons
Music: Andrew Wheeler
Physics: Tom Rogerson
Politics: Andrew Stodolny
Psychology: Alison Wilson
Religious Studies: Helen Stiles
Spanish: Rowan Reed-Purvis
Sport: Paul Morris

Admissions: Angela Boult
Headmaster's Secretary: Elaine Green

Structure. Pupils are taught using the structure that has come to be known as the 'diamond model'. Classes are fully co-educational from age three to eleven and again in the Sixth Form. Between the ages of eleven and sixteen, boys and girls are taught separately, but enjoy mixed extra-curricular and pastoral activities. Pupils therefore have both the social benefits of co-education and the academic benefits of single-sex teaching in the adolescent years.

Junior School pupils progress to Senior School, in most cases automatically. Junior School begins with Year 3, Senior School Year 7 and Sixth Form Year 11.

Religion. The School has a Chaplain and its own Chaplaincy centre which serves as a focus for worship and pastoral care. Although an Anglican foundation, the School welcomes boys and girls of all faiths and separate meetings are held for Jewish, Muslim, Hindu and Sikh pupils.

Facilities. The Grammar School at Leeds occupies a modern, purpose-built site whose facilities are unrivalled anywhere in the country. They include:

- Specialist suites of teaching rooms for all subjects with the necessary support systems for each faculty.
- Centres for each section of the School, with generous common rooms, locker and cloakroom areas.
- A large assembly hall.
- A newly extended Junior School, having its own identity, specialist resources and operating an independent timetable.
- A library incorporating multimedia facilities.
- IT centre with three interlocking suites.
- A dedicated art, design and technology unit with computer aided design suite.
- Seventeen specialist science laboratories.
- A fully resourced music school.
- Theatre with fully-equipped lighting gantry.
- A new Food Technology Suite.
- Extensive playing fields with changing facilities and hospitality areas.

- A large indoor sports complex with 2 sports halls, climbing wall, squash courts, conditioning room, a 25m swimming pool of competition standard.
- Extensive grounds with pitches, tennis courts, athletics track.
- Large play and recreation areas for each section of the School.
- Refectory for breakfast, lunch and snacks.
- Provision for a wide variety of indoor and outdoor extra-curricular pursuits.
- Conservation areas.
- A versatile Chaplaincy Centre.
- A new Sixth Form Centre with its own cafeteria, study area and IT and leisure facilities.

Curriculum. Rose Court Nursery and Pre-Prep establishes the foundation for a long and rewarding education – pursuing a broad and balanced curriculum, which builds upon the natural aptitudes, learning skills and interests of each child, whilst enabling each to develop at his/her own pace. We use our own schemes of work, broadly based upon the early years of the National Curriculum, but refined by our own expertise and experience.

In the Junior School pupils concentrate upon the core subjects of English, Mathematics and Science. History, Geography, French/German, Religious Studies, Music, Art and Technology are also taught.

Pupils follow a broad curriculum, including two foreign languages in Years 7–9.

At the end of Year 11 pupils are presented for the GCSE examination.

In the Sixth Form students choose to study up to 5 AS and 3 A2 Level subjects and are encouraged to choose a broad range of subjects.

Games. Rugby, Football, Cricket, Athletics, Swimming, Tennis, Basketball, Badminton, Cross-Country, Volleyball, Hockey, Netball, Rounders, Squash, and Golf. There is a running track, swimming pool and a sports centre, including squash courts.

Other Activities. The School's many clubs and societies offer pupils the opportunity to participate in a wide range of out-of-school activities from Mountaineering and Skiing to Choral Singing, Dancing and Drama. There are regular tours and visits abroad and there are long-established exchanges with French and German schools.

The School has an extensive Arts Programme which covers music, film, drama, debating and creative art and includes visiting groups with national reputation as well as the students' own contributions.

The School provides a contingent of the CCF (Army & RAF sections), and has a Scout Troop, with Cub Pack and Venture Scout Unit. The School participates in the Duke of Edinburgh's Award Scheme and Community Service is compulsory in the Sixth Form.

Admission. The entrance procedure takes place in the Spring term for entry the following September and is based upon an examination, an interview and school report. Very young boys and girls are assessed through a series of observed activities. The usual points of entry are 3+ for Nursery, 4+ for Reception, 7+ for Junior School and 11+ for Senior School, although applications can be made at any time for any age. Entry to the Sixth Form is based upon interview and report and the attainment of good GCSE grades.

Details of the entrance procedure together with copies of sample papers are available from the Headmaster's Secretary.

Fees per term (2014–2015). £4,038 Senior School, £3,012 Junior School, £2,763 Rose Court Nursery & Pre-Prep.

Bursaries. A number of means-tested bursaries (some full fee) are currently awarded each year to pupils entering the school at 11+ and 16+ (Sixth Form).

GSAL Alumni. This includes the Old Leodiensian Association – Leeds Grammar School and the Old Girls Club – Leeds Girls' High School. See Alumni section of school website, email: alumni@gsal.org.uk.

Charitable status. The Grammar School at Leeds is a Registered Charity, number 1048304. It exists for the advancement of education and training for boys and girls.

Leicester Grammar School

London Road, Great Glen, Leicester LE8 9FL
Tel: 0116 259 1900
Fax: 0116 259 1901
email: admissions@leicestergrammar.org.uk
website: www.leicestergrammar.org.uk

Leicester Grammar School was founded in 1981 as an independent, selective, co-educational day school to offer able children in the city and county a first-class academic education. Its founders sought to create a school which would maintain the standards and traditions of the city's former grammar schools lost through reorganisation and develop them to meet the demands of a rapidly changing environment. The School moved to a new state-of-the-art building on the south-east side of Leicester in September 2008.

Governors:
I D Patterson, LLB (*Chairman*)
Mrs E Bailey, MA Cantab
G G Bodiwala, MBBS, MS, FICS, FICA
Mrs J Burns, BA
Prof D Cartmell, BA, DPhil
Dr S M Dauncey, MRCGP
S Gasztowicz, QC
D Green, BSc, CEng, MICE, MCIWEM
Dr S E Hadley, BMedSci, BM, BS, FP Cert, DRCOG, DCM, MRCGP, PGCME
M J Holley, MA (*Vice-Chairman, Financial*)
Mr N J M Imlach, CA FCSI CF
K J Julian, MA
Dr D H Khoosal, MB, BCh, LLM RCS, FRCPsych
Prof J Saker, BSc, MSc
Dr J J A Scott, BSc, PhD (*Vice Chairman, Academic*)

Business Director: Mrs A Shakespeare, MA Fitzwilliam, Cantab, ACA, FCA

Headmaster: C P M King, MA Dunelm

Deputy Head (Academic): J W Rich, BA Cardiff (*History*)
Deputy Head (Pastoral): Mrs A Ewington, MA Nottingham, CBiol, MIBiol (*Biology*)

Assistant staff:
Dr S W Ainge, BSc, PhD Newcastle, CChem, FRSC (*Head of Chemistry*)
Miss E S Allcoat, BSc Bristol (*Physics*)
T P Allen, BA Kent (*Head of Sixth Form, History & Politics*)
J Barker, BMus, MMus (*Assistant Director of Music, Duke of Edinburgh's Award*)
Mrs A C Barre, BA Birmingham (*French*)
Mrs J A P Barrow, BEd Liverpool (*Textiles, Design & Technology*)
Dr D D Boyce, MPhys Lancaster, PhD Leicester, CPhys MinstP (*Physics*)
Miss A M Bush, BA Camberwell College of Art (*Art*)
Mrs A J Button, BA Loughborough (*Head of Physical Education*)
Mrs J R Carr, BA Roehampton (*Head of Religious Studies*)
Miss Z Carter, BSc Leicester (*Mathematics, Duke of Edinburgh's Award*)

Miss M J Clapham BA Hons, MBA Ed, PGCSE SpLD Leicester, PGC SENCO (*Head of Learning Support*)

Mrs P R E Clare, BSc Leicester, MSc Imperial College (*Biology*)

F W Clayton, BA Wolverhampton (*Religious Studies, Charities Coordinator, Head of PSD*)

P Cox, BSc UCW Bangor (*Biology, Duke of Edinburgh's Award*)

Miss L Crampton, MEng Hull (*Design and Technology, ICT, Staff Development Coordinator*)

Dr D M Crawford, MA, DPhil Jesus College Oxford, MEd Bristol, MA Ed OU, MSc OU (*Head of Mathematics*)

Mrs A J Davies, MA De Montfort (*Art*)

Mrs K R Douglas, BA Liverpool (*French*)

A N Duffield, BSc UCW Cardiff, CBiol, MSB (*Head of Biology*)

H A Ellis, BSc Loughborough (*Physical Education*)

Dr S L Ewers, BSc, PhD Bristol (*Biology*)

Mrs S M Faire, BSc Surrey (*Mathematics, Maths Learning Support*)

Dr C H Fearon, BSc Liverpool, PhD Birmingham (*Biology, AQA Baccalaureate EPQ Centre Coordinator for Enrichment Programme*)

Mrs H T Feasey, BA Stellenbosch, South Africa (*Geography, Physical Education*)

Miss N Fletcher, BA Cambridge (*MFL*)

Mrs N Franklin, BA De Montfort (*Drama*)

Dr K Fulton, BSc Durham, PhD Nottingham (*Biology, External Examinations Officer*)

Mrs P Gangar, BEd Leeds (*Music*)

Ms M Gonzalez Rodriguez, BA, MA, MA Leicester (*Classics*)

M J Gower, BA Leicester (*Head of Geography*)

Mrs E Graff-Baker, MA Queen's College Oxford (*Music*)

Mrs C Green, BSc Dunelm (*Physics*)

Mrs A L Griffin, BA Essex, MA Loughborough (*Head of Drama*)

J M Griffin, MA Fitzwilliam College Cambridge (*Deputy Head of English, Head of Learning Support*)

P M Handford, MA Queen's College Oxford (*Chemistry*)

Miss K Harrison, BSc Nottingham Trent (*Physical Education*)

A H J Harrop, MA Queen's College Oxford, Dip CG (*Head of Classics, Examinations Officer*)

Mrs W E Harvey, BA Loughborough College of Art & Design (*Design and Technology*)

Ms S Haywood, BEd Worcester College, BA OU (*Art*)

Mrs M Higginson, BEd, MA Toronto (*English, Editor of The Leicestrian*)

Mrs K Hinshelwood, BA Reading, Dip SpLD York (*English Learning Support*)

Miss L Howd, BSc East Anglia (*Mathematics*)

C W Howe, BEd CNAA Crewe & Alsager College, MISPAL (*Director of Sport*)

Miss N Hughes, BA London (*English, Staff Mentor*)

J Hunt, BA Reading (*English, AQA Bacc/Extended Project Team Leader*)

Mrs J Hutchinson, BEd Durham, MAEd OU (*Physical Education, i/c Academic PE, Mathematics*)

G Inchley, BSc Hull, MSc Bristol (*Deputy Head of Mathematics*)

R Jacobs, BSc Leeds, BA Open University (*Mathematics*)

C James, MA Girton College Cambridge (*Mathematics, Timetabler*)

Mrs C L Jess, MA Gonville & Caius College Cambridge (*French & Spanish, Head of Year 9, AQA Baccalaureate Coordinator*)

Mrs R E Kendall, BA Dunelm, MA Goldsmiths (*English*)

R W S Kidd, BA, MA Ulster (*Head of English*)

Mrs N L Laybourne, BSc, MSc Loughborough (*Physical Education*)

T Lemon, BA Bedfordshire (*Physical Education*)

R I Longson, BA UCW Aberystwyth, DipCG LGMB, Swanley MICG (*Head of Careers, History*)

D M Lupton, BA Exeter (*Deputy Head of Modern Languages*)

D W Maddock, BA Bristol Polytechnic, MA Leeds Polytechnic (*Head of Art, Assistant AQA Baccalaureate Coordinator*)

Sra I Manktelow, BSc Instituto Politécnico Nacional, Mexico (*Spanish*)

Mrs H May, BA UCW Aberystwyth (*Geography & Religious Studies*)

D McCann, BEd Leicester (*Physical Education*)

R J McLean, BA Lady Margaret Hall Oxford (*Classics*)

P Moore-Friis, BA De Montfort, CIM Dip (*Head of Economics, Young Enterprise Coordinator*)

Miss J Mould, BEd Bedford College of HE (*Head of Preparatory Department*)

N Murray, BSc Imperial, MA London, MSc Sheffield Hallam (*Mathematics*)

Mrs E Nelson, BA Northumbria (*German*)

Mrs E Nisbet, BEd Trent Polytechnic (*Food Technology*)

Mrs F Paton, DEUG and Licence Bordeaux (*French*)

Ms A M Patterson, BSc Sunderland Polytechnic (*Chemistry, Housemistress of Duke's*)

J J Peake, BSc Coventry (*Geography*)

N C Perry, MA St Catherine's College Oxford, (*Chemistry*)

A Picknell, BA Manchester, MA London (*Head of History & Politics*)

D Pilbeam, MChem Nottingham (*Chemistry, External Examinations Officer*)

Mrs K Pollard, BSc Loughborough (*Mathematics, Assistant AQA Baccalaureate Coordinator*)

L Potter (*Head of Lower School, Physical Education*)

Ms E Pottinger, MA Edinburgh (*History*)

S J R Radford, BSc Sheffield (*Mathematics*)

P T G Reeves, BSc Manchester (*Head of Physics*)

Mrs S J Sains, MA Lady Margaret Hall Oxford (*Mathematics*)

Mrs M Sian, BA Middlesex (*Head of ICT*)

P Shelley, BA Nottingham Trent, (*Head of Design & Technology*)

Mrs S Stout, BSc Aston (*Head of Modern Languages*)

T A Thacker, BEd CNAA Crewe & Alsager College (*Head of Years 10 & 11, Physical Education*)

Mrs J S Tompkins, BA Leicester, (*Religious Studies*)

Dr A Vassiliou-Abson, BA Athens, MPhil, PhD Birmingham (*Classics*)

Dr M Wheeler, BSc, PhD Bristol, CPhys, MInstP (*Physics*)

Dr D M T Whittle, BMus, PhD Nottingham (*Director of Music*)

Miss A L Williamson, BSc Loughborough (*Head of PE & Games, Geography*)

D R Willis, BSc CNAA Portsmouth Polytechnic (*Science, Housemaster of Vice Chancellors, Senior Housemaster*)

Mrs T Y Yau, BA De Montfort (*Extra-Curricular Mandarin Chinese*)

Dr S Yeomans, MA, PhD Loughborough (*Head of Politics, School Council Link Teacher*)

J R Walker, BA Warwick (*Classics*)

Headmistress, Junior School: Mrs C M Rigby, BA

There are 829 day pupils in the Senior School (391 girls, 438 boys), of whom 219 are in the Sixth Form. A further 390 pupils, aged 3–11, attend the Junior School.

Admission. An entrance examination is held in the Lent Term for boys and girls seeking to enter the Preparatory (10+) and Year 7 (11+) forms in the following September. Papers are taken in verbal reasoning, English and Mathematics. In addition admission into Years 9 and 10 takes place at ages 13 and 14 and there is provision for direct entry into the Sixth Form, offers of a place being conditional upon the GCSE grades gained. The normal entry requirement to the Sixth Form is a minimum of two A and four B grade passes at GCSE. Visitors are always welcome to make an appointment to see the school and meet the Headmaster. All applications are handled by the School Secretary, from whom all Registration forms are obtainable. Candidates at all levels may be called for an interview.

Scholarships and Bursaries. Academic, music, art and sports and all-rounder scholarships are offered to outstanding candidates on examination and assessment.

Academic scholarships (maximum 25%) are available at all ages from 11+ upwards and are given on the results of the Entrance Examination (or, at Sixth Form entrance, GCSE results).

Up to four music scholarships are offered at any age. The scholarships are given on audition in recognition of achievement and potential in musical ability and are confirmed by a pass in the Entrance Examination.

A small number of art scholarships are awarded on examination and portfolio.

Sports scholarships are available linked to ability in the school's major sports.

The School has some funds available for Bursaries. It has always been the policy of governors to try to ensure that children capable of benefiting from education at the School should not be prevented by financial considerations from entry. All awards can be supplemented by bursaries when appropriate.

Curriculum. Class sizes are about 20 to 24 in the first three years; the average size of a GCSE group is 19, of a Sixth Form group 12.

All pupils in the first three years (and those entering the preparatory form) follow a balanced curriculum covering the National Curriculum core and foundation subjects, Religious Studies and Latin (Classical Studies in the preparatory form). Classes are split into smaller groups for the creative and technological subjects, so that all pupils can gain practical experience, whether in the School's ICT suite or on its extensive range of musical instruments. From Year 8 the three science subjects, Biology, Chemistry and Physics, are taught separately. There is no streaming and setting occurs only for Mathematics and French. In Year 9 an element of choice is introduced and pupils must opt from a choice of third languages and from a list of five creative subjects.

In Years 4 and 5 pupils prepare for GCSE examinations in ten subjects, as well as doing PE/Games. All study a 'core' of five subjects: English Language and Literature, Mathematics, French and Chemistry. The range of 'options' includes Art, Biology, Chemistry, Classical Civilisation, Design and Technology, Drama, French, Geography, German, Greek, Religious Studies, History, Latin, Music, Physics, Spanish and PE.

Students in the Sixth Form normally study 4 AS levels leading to 3 or more A levels from a choice of 19 subjects, including Further Mathematics, Economics, Physical Education, Politics, Computer Studies and Theatre Studies. There is no rigid division between arts and science sides. To ensure that breadth of education does not suffer, the Sixth Form all take the AQA Baccalaureate and complete an Extended Project. The school has an excellent record of success at public examinations and university admissions, including Oxbridge. The Careers Department is very active in giving help and advice to students.

School activities. A broad range and variety of activities complements the academic curriculum. Participation rates are high.

Music, drama and sport form an integral part of life at LGS. Every pupil in the First Year learns a musical instrument and a high proportion continue afterwards with private weekly lessons. The School Orchestra gives two major concerts a year, whilst a training orchestra, a jazz band, a dance band, recorder groups and various chamber ensembles explore other avenues. The School Choir is the resident choir for the Crown Court Services and tours regularly. Links are strong with the Leicestershire School of Music

orchestras and several pupils play in national orchestras. Senior and junior drama clubs function throughout the year, a major play or musical and a junior play are staged regularly and house drama extends the opportunity to act to most pupils.

Games are seen as an important means not only of promoting health and fitness but also of inspiring self-confidence. Major winter games are hockey, netball and rugby and in summer athletics, cricket and tennis. Opportunities occur for individuals to follow their interest in badminton, basketball, squash, golf, table tennis, gymnastics, dance, sailing and cross-country running whilst swimming is an integral part of the PE programme. The School's own facilities are extensive and meet all modern standards for sport. Teams represent the School in the main games at all age groups and several students achieve recognition at county or even national level. The school is proud of the fact that it is one of only eight other schools to have been awarded the Sportsmark Gold with Distinction, for the quality of the delivery of sport within the school.

Societies and clubs complement these activities, ranging from chess to the Duke of Edinburgh's Award scheme, history and Lit Soc to model aeroplanes, debating to art, design and technology, for which the workshop and art rooms are usually open during lunchtimes and after school.

Religion. The school espouses the principles of the Church of England, teaching the Christian faith, its values and standards of personal conduct, but also prides itself on welcoming children of all faiths, who play a full part in the life of the community. Very strong links exist with Leicester Cathedral and there is a flourishing Guild of Servers and University of Leicester clergy participate in school life and prepare confirmation candidates.

Pastoral Care. Responsibility for a wide-ranging system of pastoral care and for the creation of the caring, friendly and disciplined environment, resides in four Heads of School, assisted by form teachers, personal tutors and a very active house system.

Junior School. Entry to the Junior School is by interview and, where appropriate, assessment at 3+, 4+, 7+ and into other school years, when places are available. Pupils are prepared for entry to the Senior School. A balanced curriculum is followed covering National Curriculum Key Stages 1 and 2 and beyond; French (from 5 years), classical studies and ICT are also taught. A wide range of activities complements the academic curriculum, with a strong stress on music and a rapidly growing games programme. The School is a Christian foundation and lays great emphasis upon the pastoral care of young children. (*See also Junior School entry in IAPS section.*)

Fees per term (2014–2015). Senior School £3,859; Junior School (Years 3–6) £3,233; Kinders to Year 2 £3,077.

Old Leicestrians Association. All correspondence to the OL Secretary, c/o the School.

Charitable status. Leicester Grammar School Trust is a Registered Charity, number 510809. Its aims and objectives are to promote and provide for the advancement of education and in connection therewith to conduct, carry on, acquire and develop in the United Kingdom or elsewhere a School or Schools to be run according to the principles of the Church of England for the education of students and children of either sex or both sexes.

Leighton Park School

Shinfield Road, Reading, Berkshire RG2 7ED

Tel:	0118 987 9600
Fax:	0118 987 9625
email:	admissions@leightonpark.com

website: www.leightonpark.com
Twitter: @LPSchool
Facebook: /Leighton-Park-School

Governors:
Jeff Beatty (*Chairman*)

Liz Banks	Elaine Green
Simon Best	Gill Greenfield
Paul Bowers-Isaacson	David Isherwood
Simon Clemison	Zella King
Tony Cowling	Valerie McFarlane
John Crosfield	Liza Phipps
John Flynn	Ravi Sidhu
Sarah Freeman	Catherine Wilson

Head: **Nigel Williams**, BA Bristol, MA London, PGCE

Deputy Head: Edward Falshaw, MA

Bursar: Stephen Launchbury, MA

Teaching Staff:
* *Head of Department*
§ *Part-time*
† *Housemaster*

Fawn Bartlett, BA (*Games, Dance, Beliefs & Values*)
Irene Bell, MA Cantab, BA (**Physics*)
Julian Berrow, BA (*§Modern Foreign Languages, †Reckitt House*)
Zenon Bowrey, BA (**Economics & Business Studies*)
Peter Bulteel, BA (**Boys' Games, *Middle School, †School House*)
Tom Cartmill, BA (*English as a Second Language*)
Rachel Chapman, MSc, BA (**English*)
Robert Clare, BSc (*Mathematics*)
Bridget Clarke, BSc (**Mathematics*)
John Clarke, BSc (*Physics*)
Maddie Cottam, MA (*Music*)
Harriet Custance, MA, BA (**English as a Second Language*)
Katherine Donegan, BSc (*Biology*)
§Deborah Duggan, BA (**Spanish, German*)
Jon Emerson, MA Oxon (**Science*)
Eddie Falshaw, MA (*History, Games, Educational Visits Coordinator, Deputy Head*)
§Kate Findlay, BA (**History*)
Chris Fisher, BEd (*Sports*)
§Eveline Giblin (*PE, Games*)
Pablo Gorostidi Perez, MBA (*Spanish*)
Karen Gracie-Langrick, MA, BA (*History, Deputy Head Academic Studies*)
Claire Gray (*Individual Learning Centre*)
Tim Green, BSc (*Games, †Fryer*)
Claire Gulliver, BSc, PGCE (*Psychology*)
Corin Gurr, DPhil, MSc, BSc (*Mathematics*)
Emilia Hicks, BSc (*Biology and Science*)
§Jane Ireland, BA (*Individual Learning Centre, SENCO*)
Joanne Jones, BA, PGCE (*Art and Textiles*)
Lauren Kelly, MA, BA (*Artist in Residence, Art Technician*)
Elaine King, BA (**Careers, Art, Games*)
Adél Kiss, BSc, BEd (**Mathematics*)
Lan Kuang, MA, BA (**Mandarin Chinese*)
Eithne Laird, BSc, MSc, PGCE (*Geography*)
§Bettina Lamprecht-Lieb (*German*)
Isabelle Lauzeral, MA, BA (*Modern Languages*)
§Maureen Lenehan, MA (*English*)
Ann Line, BA (*English*)
Robin Longworth, MA, BSc (**Geography*)
Jakki Marr, BEd (**PE, Games, †Field House*)
§Rachael Martin, BEd (*Individual Learning Centre, †Reckitt House*)
§Mair Mayers, BSc (*Mathematics*)
§Rachel Mayne, BSc (*Physics*)

§Chris Mitchell, BA (*Assistant Director of Music*)
Jane Mulvihill, BSc (*Mathematics*)
Myles Nash (**DT, †School House*)
Lynne Parry, BA (*Individual Learning Centre*)
Joanna Payne, BSc (**Chemistry*)
Nicola Phillips, BA, PGCE (*English, Deputy Head of Sixth Form*)
Jonathan Porter-Hughes, BA, PGCE (*English, †School House*)
Jeanne Rourke, BA, PGCE (*English as a Second Language*)
Ian Rowe, BSc (*Head of Individual Learning Centre, SENCO*)
Premnath Samyrao, MSc, MEd (*Mathematics*)
Rosemary Scales, BA, MA (**Director of Music*)
Howard Shaw, BA (*History, Government and Politics*)
Gemma Sims, MSc, BSc (*Biology*)
Mark Simmons, BEd (*PE, Games, Head of Pastoral, †Field House*)
Mark Smith, BEng, BSc (*Design Technology*)
Graham Smith, BA (*Games, Geography, †Grove House*)
Ken Sullivan, MA, BSc, PGCE (*Head of Sixth Form, Biology*)
Davina Stansfield, BSc (*Head of E-Learning, †Reckitt House*)
Adrian Stewart, BPrimEd South Africa, (*Geography, Games, †Fryer*)
Shazia Taj, BA, MA, PGCE (**Beliefs and Values*)
Michael Taylor, BA (*Economics*)
Geraint Thomas, Grad Dip (**Drama, †Field House*)
Michael Ward, BEd, MA (**Information Technology, Director of IT*)
Vicky Worrall (*Artist and Art Technician*)
§Sherilyn Wass, BSc, PhD (*Chemistry*)
Mandy Webb (*Individual Learning Centre*)
Mitch Whitehead, BA, MA (*Beliefs and Values*)
§Michael Whiteman, BA (*Music*)
Nicola Williams, BEd (*PE, Dance, *PSHE, *Pastoral Welfare and Boarding*)
Françoise Wilson, BA, MA (**French, Latin, Head of Modern Foreign Languages*)
Mark Wood (**Art*)
John Woodings, BA (**English, *Teaching and Learning*)
Vicky Worrall (*Mandarin Teaching Assistant*)
Jennifer Yabsley, DPhil, BSc (**Biology*)
§Damon Young, BA (*Drama, Theatre Studies, Senior School Enrichment Coordinator, †Grove House*)

Librarian: Chris Routh, MA, BA
Registrar: Rachael Bolding
Head's PA: Virginia Cashin

Leighton Park is a forward-looking, co-educational day and boarding school for 490 students aged 11–18. Founded in 1890 on Quaker values and set in 60 acres of beautiful parkland close to Reading town centre, Leighton Park provides a unique and inspirational learning environment, where students flourish academically and as individuals.

Students at Leighton Park experience and benefit from the provision of a holistic educational experience. The curriculum is academically rigorous, yet strives to achieve greater coherence by making connections between academic subjects and integrating the already strong pastoral and extra-curricular programme into the school day.

Students develop their intellectual curiosity while becoming independent, lifelong learners with the skills to respond positively to the challenges of a rapidly changing world. This curriculum framework affords greater opportunities for creativity, personalisation and independent learning.

Our commitment to academic excellence is balanced by our commitment to the development of every individual, deriving from our Quaker heritage. You will find at Leighton Park outstanding teaching and excellent academic results. The last ISI inspection stated, "Leighton Park is highly successful in providing an education of good quality in a strongly Quaker ethos. Pupils achieve well academically in relation to their abilities, while experiencing rich opportunities for their personal and social development". In 2014, 32% of candidates received A*/A grades, 6% higher than the national average and the average points score was 281 points per student. The 2014 cohort of International Baccalaureate students averaged 34 points against a world average of 29 points in July's results.

Curriculum. Our creative curriculum provides a distinct educational experience, where academic depth and rigour are balanced by breadth and coherence. Mandarin Chinese has been introduced in Year 7 which can be followed through to GCSE and A Level. Year 10 students are expected to follow a full GCSE course of nine or ten subjects, comprising both compulsory and optional subjects. In the Sixth Form, a wide range of academic subjects in A Level and International Baccalaureate courses is complemented by a broad extension programme, including Critical Thinking, Film Studies, European Computer Driving Licence and Dance.

Facilities. Excellent facilities and resources include a new Food Technology facility, a newly refurbished ICT Centre, a digital recording studio, a drama studio, a heated indoor swimming pool, a wonderful library and dedicated Individual Learning Centre. Oakview, the dining centre, offers a first-rate choice of meals (breakfast, lunch and tea).

Ethos and Pastoral Care. Within Leighton Park's distinctive Quaker ethos, students of many faiths and backgrounds flourish in an atmosphere of tolerance, harmony and understanding. They know they will be challenged in their work to achieve the highest standards of excellence.

Boarding and Day Boarding. We offer a highly flexible approach to boarding with full, weekly and day boarding options to suit a family and student's needs. The five houses provide a comfortable base in which all students, whether boarding or day, genuinely feel at home. Boarders and day students both have individual study facilities in the houses. Day students are welcome for breakfast and to stay for tea, prep and extra-curricular activities, included in the fees. All day boarders are given the opportunity to stay overnight at no extra charge for two nights each term.

Sport. Sport plays an important role in life at Leighton Park with many individual and team performances reaching county and national level. First rate coaching and superb facilities – which include a heated indoor swimming pool, floodlit astroturf pitch, 22 tennis courts and a cricket square – ensure that talented and enthusiastic students can develop their sporting abilities to the full.

Music. Music has for a long time been one of Leighton Park's particular strengths with around half our pupils learning instruments and performing a wide range of styles. Our facilities for practice and performance include nineteen new Yamaha pianos, a suite of ten practice rooms, a digital recording studio, a suite of Apple Macs, recital room and concert hall.

Opportunities to perform include regular concerts and foreign tours, such as The Netherlands, Sicily and Malta in 2014.

Hobbies and other activities. Pupils can participate in an enormous variety of activities both during the week and at weekends, before and after school. The Duke of Edinburgh's Award Scheme is well established and students participate in the Youth Philanthropy Initiative. In keeping with our Quaker perspective many Leighton Park students are involved in community service. Sixth Formers participate in a biennial trip to Uganda, Malawi and Tanzania lending practical support to the school's fundraising efforts in Africa.

Careers. Students have access to the well-resourced Careers Library, as well as networked computer software to help them research and evaluate their options. All Year 10 pupils complete a week of work experience and there are many other occasions when career alternatives or gap year possibilities can be explored. Thorough preparation and support for entry to university is given.

Entry. Entry to the school is by exam and interview, with an additional English test where appropriate. Pupils are normally admitted at one of three points: Year 7 (age 11); Year 9 (age 13), and the Sixth Form. Entry to the Sixth Form requires 5 GCSE passes or equivalent at Grade B or above.

Fees per term (2014–2015). Full Boarding £8,257–£10,197; Weekly Boarding £7,261–£8,777; Day £5,405–£6,548.

Scholarships and Bursaries. Several Academic, Music, Drama, Art & Design and Sports Awards are made each year for entry in Year 7, Year 9 and the Sixth Form and are also available to existing pupils. Candidates may apply for any combination of scholarships, but can only receive the financial benefits of one (in the region of 10% of Day Boarder fees). Bursaries may be available, in cases of financial hardship, to existing and prospective pupils. Bursaries are always means-tested and subject to annual review. Additional awards may be made by the David Lean Foundation.

Old Leightonians. Website: www.leightonpark.com/oldleightonians.

Charitable status. The Leighton Park Trust is a Registered Charity, number 309144. It exists to provide education for young people.

The Leys School

Cambridge CB2 7AD

Tel:	01223 508900
email:	office@theleys.net
website:	www.theleys.net

Motto: '*In Fide Fiducia.*'

The Leys is situated half a mile from the centre of the university city of Cambridge, close to the River Cam and Grantchester Meadows. The School was founded in 1875 on the initiative of a group of leading Methodists to provide a liberal Christian education, establishing a tradition which has continued unbroken to this day. The School was incorporated as a Charitable Trust in 1878. All the buildings are grouped around the Main Field and lie within the estate originally acquired for the purpose; there is a second extensive playing field nearby.

The Leys is a friendly, caring and happy community, large enough to offer many opportunities, but not so large as to lose sight of the individual. The School is fully co-educational; of a total of over 560 pupils, 200 are in the Sixth Form. Girls and boys are accommodated in separate houses. 70% of the pupils are accommodated in the boarding houses, but all, including the 160 day pupils, are able to enjoy all the opportunities offered by boarding school life.

Governors:
Chairman: Sir Tony Brenton, KCMG
N M Allen, BA
Mrs H Arthur, Cert Ed
¶R Ashby-Johnson, MA
M D Beazor, BA, FRSAHH
¶HH Judge Revd M A Bishop, MA
Mrs A M Brunner, BA
¶M A Elliott, BSc
N Hargreaves, TD, MA, MSc CEng, FIMechER
¶B Haryott, BSc, FREng, CEng, FICE, FIStructE, FRSA, CRBCCC
R B Hewitson, LLB
¶C M Kidman, ACIOB
P Lacey, MA, PGCE, FRSA
A S MacGregor BSc CertEd
Mrs M E Mackay, RGN

¶T C Moore
Mrs J Plows, BA
R C Sadler, FRICS
S H Siddall, MA
¶A V Silverton, BSc, FCSI
Revd T Swindell
¶D Unwin, MA, ACA
Dr R D H Walker, MA
R B Webster, FCA
R J Willmott, MCIOB

¶ *Old Leysian*

Headmaster: M J Priestley, MA

Deputy Headmaster: S G Wilson, BSc, LRAM (*to December 2014*)

R Adamson, BSc, PhD	R A D Hill, BA
B A Barton, BA	Mrs A Hodges, BSc, RSA
A R C Batterham, BA	Cert SpLD
Miss C E Battison, BA	Ms C C Howe, BA
D R Bell, MA	Mrs C L Howe, BSc, PhD
A Bennett-Jones, BSc	G K Howe, BSc, MSc, MA,
N R Born, MA	MEd
M A Brown, BSc	R I Kaufman, BA
Mrs R G Bryant-Davies,	Miss C A Knights, BA
MA, PhD	Mrs A Lainchbury, BA,
D Cassidy, BPhEd	MCLIP
Ms L J Clark, BA	S N Leader, BA
Miss L Corble, BA	Mrs Claire Leigh, BA,
Mrs K J Cox, BSc	MEd
P J Crosfield, BA	Mrs G L Lester, MA, BA,
Mrs E R Culshaw, MA	DipSpLD
T Dann, BSc	M P J Lindsay, MSc
P M Davies, BSc	A C R Long, BA
G J Deudney, BSc, BEd	R S McAlinden, BA
N J Dix-Pincott, BA, MA	Ms S J McEwan, BA
R J Driscoll, BA, BEd	Revd C J Meharry, BEd,
T P Dunn, BA, MSc, MEd	BTh
Cantab, CPsychol, FRSA	Mrs A P Muston, BEd
Mrs C M Earl, BSc	S A Newlove, BSc, PhD
W J Earl, BSc	D J Nye, BSc
Miss K E Eaves, MA	Ms E F Prosser, BSc
Miss H Edmondson, BA	T L Reed, MA, MSc
M A Egan, BSc	Mrs L A Reyes, MA
A S Erby, BSc	N P Robinson, BSc, MBA,
J W Fawcett, BA, MA	CEng
D K Fernandes, BSc	Mrs J A Samuel, BSc
R Francis, MA, MEd	Mrs J Schofield, BSc
Revd C I A Fraser, BA,	Mrs J Stobbart, BA
MA Ed, MCMI, PG Dip,	B R Stuttard, BA
FRSA	Miss J L Symes, BA
M C Gale, BEd	M M Taylor, MA
Miss G H Jefferies, BA	Mrs P C A Taylor, BA,
¶E M W George, BEd	MEd
Mrs J George, FIMLS	W P Unsworth, BSc, PhD
R A Hall, MA, ARCO	Miss V Waller, BMus,
S G Hancock, BA, MA	MEd
A P Harmsworth, MA,	A J Welby, BA
FRAS	P White, BEd
Ms J L Hebden, BA, MA	Mrs C E Wiedermann, MA
L D J Higgins, BA	Mrs H Williams, BA

¶ *Old Leysian*

Housemasters and Housemistresses:
Barker House: Mr G J Deudney
Barrett House: Mr M C Gale
Bisseker House: Miss E F Prosser
Dale House: Miss C E Battison
East House: Rev C J Meharry
Fen House: Mrs K J Cox
Granta House: Mrs H Williams
Moulton House: Miss A Macpherson
North A House: Mr B A Barton

School House: Mr T L Reed
West House: Mr A C R Long

Director of Studies: P J Crosfield
Director of Pastoral Care: Mrs C E Wiedermann
Senior Tutor: A S Erby
Director of Wider Curriculum: M A Brown
Chaplain: Revd C J Meharry
Director of Sport: W J Earl
Examinations Officer: Miss Anna Hunt
Head of Careers: N P Robinson
Head of Outdoor Education: R S McAlinden
Higher Education Coordinator: M A Egan
Bursar: P D McKeown, BA
Finance Bursar: Mrs M Cooksey, FCCA
Bursar's PA: Mrs K R White
Headmaster's PA: Ms R C Silcock, BA
Registrar: Mrs J A Cooper, BA
Marketing Manager: Mrs D H Goddard, MA, CIM
Medical Officers:
Dr A J Stewart, MA, MB BCh, DRCOG, DCH, MRCGP, AFOM
Dr C Lea-Cox, BSc, MB BS, MRCGP, DCH, DFFP
Nursing Staff:
Sister M A Williams, SRN, SCM
Sister V Huffman, RGN
Sister Jo Rhodes, RGN

Buildings and Facilities. There is a continuing development programme involving all areas of the School. A state-of-the-art Music School was opened in 2005. There is an excellent Humanities Building with first-class facilities for Geography, History, Classics and Divinity together with a Museum and Archives Centre, and an award-winning Design Centre, which contains workshops (metal, plastic and wood), Art School, Ceramics Studio, Electronics Workshop, Computer Centre, together with facilities for Design, Photography, Cookery and an Exhibition Centre. A Sports Hall and all-weather pitch were built in 1995. In 2008 the Sports Hall was extended to include a superb fitness suite and cricket pavilion, and a second Astroturf pitch was added. A new climbing wall was constructed in summer 2007. A major capital development has just been added, which provides a new theatre, Assembly Hall, Drama and Dance Studios, Drama Department, School Café and three new Science Laboratories. This project, known as Great Hall, was completed in summer 2013. There are 40 acres of playing fields, an indoor heated swimming pool open all the year, a boat house on the Cam for which plans have been submitted for a complete re-build, and synthetic as well as grass tennis courts. A radical re-designing and refurbishment of all boarding houses began in summer 2006, with the aim of providing the most comfortable and homely of boarding facilities. To date five of the seven Senior Boarding Houses have been refurbished. The School Library underwent a major refurbishment in 2008.

Admission. Admission for girls and boys is mainly at 11+, 13+ and 16+. Entrance tests for 11+ and 13+ entry are held in the January prior to entry. Places in the Sixth Form are available for both girls and boys who have successfully completed their GCSE or equivalent courses elsewhere. Application for admission should be made to the Admissions Office in the first instance.

Scholarships. Scholarships are available for entry at 11+, 13+ and to the Sixth Form, valued at a maximum of 5% fee remission, which can be supplemented by means-tested bursaries up to a total concession of 100%.

Academic Scholarships are available for entry at 11+, 13+ and for entry to the Sixth Form at 16+. Scholarships are also available for entry at 13+ in Music, Art, Design Technology, Sport, Drama and all-rounders, and for entry to the Sixth Form at 16+ in Music, Art, Sport and Drama.

The School also participates in the Arkwright Scholarship Scheme, which is an external examination offering

Scholarships for those wishing to take Design and Technology in the Sixth Form and who are aiming to read Engineering, Technology or other Design-related subjects in Higher Education.

The Scholarship Examinations at 11+ and 13+ take place in the Spring Term and the Sixth Form Scholarship Examination takes place in the November of the year prior to entry.

Bursary awards are made on a means-tested basis, and applications for bursaries must be made before entrance tests are taken.

Special awards for children of Methodist Ministers and members of HM Forces are available. Special consideration is given to the sons and daughters of Old Leysians.

Further particulars may be obtained from the Registrar.

Curriculum. The academic curriculum broadly conforms to the National Curriculum but is not restricted by it. Each pupil has an Academic tutor who, in conjunction with the Director of Studies and the Housemaster or Housemistress, works to tailor the pupil's programme to suit the needs of the individual wherever possible. Pupils follow a broad programme in the first three years (Years 7, 8 and 9). At the end of Year 9 they choose three from a wide range of options to add to the basic core of IGCSE English Language and Literature, separate Sciences and a Modern Foreign Language, and GCSE Mathematics and Religious Studies. The GCSE examinations are normally taken at the end of Year 11, but Religious Studies is taken by all pupils in Year 10.

In the Sixth Form, a similar option scheme operates with pupils choosing from a total of 25 subjects to take normally 4 AS Levels in the LVI and 3 at A2 in the following year.

There is considerable flexibility of combinations possible at both levels, and choices are made after consultation between parents, tutors, careers staff and subject teachers. The most able pupils are given an enrichment programme under the guidance of the Director of Academic Development, including extension projects, visits to Gifted and Talented seminars, and seminars with Cambridge undergraduate or postgraduate students. In addition, departments organise extension groups and societies and the school has a thriving Debating Society and a Model United Nations group. The school runs its own Independent Research Project to help senior pupils develop independent study skills.

About 95% of the A Level candidates proceed to degree courses. A Reading Party for potential Oxford and Cambridge candidates is held during the Summer Term.

Personal and Social Education forms an integral part of the curriculum at all levels. In the Sixth Form this is supplemented by a year-long programme that draws on the cultural resources of Cambridge University and the city as a whole.

The Chapel. The School Chapel is at the heart of the community in every sense. From the time of its Methodist foundation The Leys has been firmly based on non-sectarian Christian principles. It welcomes boys and girls of all denominations and religions, encouraging them to see the relevance of a personal faith of their own. Religious Education forms part of the curriculum. Preparation is also given for Church membership, and a combined confirmation service is held.

Physical Education. The physical education/games programme aims at introducing a wide variety of physical activities. Sports available are Rugby, Hockey, Cricket, Tennis, Athletics, Netball, Badminton, Basketball, Gymnastics, Golf, Rowing, Sailing, Dance, Shooting, Climbing, Squash, Swimming, Volleyball, Water Polo. Outdoor activities such as Camping, Orienteering, Canoeing, and Climbing are also encouraged through CCF and the Duke of Edinburgh's Award. PE is offered at GCSE and A level. The School has close links with many Cambridge University Sports Clubs, with the Sixth Form competing in University Leagues.

Careers. In the Lower School, careers guidance forms part of the PSHE programme and is carried out by tutors and

members of the Careers Department. Year 9 are supported in their option choices by tutors and Careers staff and are introduced to the Careers Library. Year 11 take the Preview Careers Selection Programme. It matches pupils' interests and abilities to appropriate career fields and is followed up by two individual interviews with career specialists. Year 11 pupils are also encouraged to participate in the Work Experience scheme. Support continues into the Sixth Form with all Lower Sixth being interviewed by Careers staff. An annual Careers Forum is organised in the Lent term, enabling pupils to investigate various career paths before embarking on their UCAS applications. Work experience is organised throughout the Sixth Form.

Societies. All are encouraged to participate in out-of-school activities of their choice. These range from Literary, Philosophical, Scientific, Mathematical, Languages, Debating, Music and Drama societies to any of the activities available in the Design Centre, which are available after School and at weekends. The life of the School is enriched by its proximity to Cambridge; distinguished visiting speakers are available, and pupils are encouraged to go to plays, concerts and lectures in the town. The programme of visiting speakers is largely run by the pupils themselves, overseen by a member of staff. A programme entitled the Cambridge Experience ensures that all Sixth Form pupils avail themselves of the cultural opportunities afforded by the school's location.

Combined Cadet Force. Except in special circumstances, pupils in Year 10 join the CCF (Army or Navy section) and also follow the Duke of Edinburgh's Award scheme. CCF camps take place annually. There is a miniature range, and a Rifle Club exists for small-bore shooting. The School is an authorised centre for the organisation of activities within the Duke of Edinburgh's Award scheme and pupils work towards the Bronze, Silver or Gold awards in the four sections: community service, expeditions, physical recreation and skills or hobbies.

Fees per term (2014–2015). Years 7 and 8: £7,000 Boarders; £4,615 Day Pupils. Years 9 to Sixth Form: £9,610 Boarders; £7,225 Home Boarders; £6,395 Day Pupils.

St Faith's Preparatory School is part of the same Foundation. It was founded in 1884 and acquired by the Governors of The Leys in 1938. There are 547 boys and girls, aged 4–13 years. The buildings, which include the Keynes Building opened in 2006 and a new Sports Hall opened in May 2011, stand in 10 acres of grounds. Full particulars may be obtained from the Headmaster of St Faith's, Mr N Helliwell, MA. (*For further details, see entry in IAPS section.*)

The Old Leysian Society. *Secretary*: J C Harding, MA, The Leys School, Cambridge CB2 7AD. Handbook and Directory, twenty-second edition, 2010.

Charitable status. The Leys and St Faith's Schools Foundation is a Registered Charity, number 1144035. It aims to enable boys and girls to develop fully their individual potential within a School community firmly based on Christian principles.

Lincoln Minster School
United Learning

The Prior Building, Upper Lindum Street, Lincoln LN2 5RW

Tel:	01522 551300
Fax:	01522 551310
email:	enquiries.lincoln@church-schools.com
website:	www.lincolnminsterschool.co.uk

Lincoln Minster School is a co-educational day and boarding school for pupils from 2½–18. The Pre-Prep, Preparatory, Senior School and boarding houses are all situated in the heart of historic Lincoln, very close to the Cathedral and Castle.

Chair of Local Governing Body: Mrs Linda Heaver

Members:
Mrs Helen Clarke
Revd Canon Gavin Kirk, MA, Precentor of Lincoln
  Cathedral
Mr Tim Overton
Professor Ieuan Owen
Mrs Annette Wood
Dr Barry Devonald
Dr Louise Dale
Mrs Sally Mundy
Mr Terry O'Halloran

Senior Leadership Team:

Principal: Mr Clive Rickart, BA Hons, PGCE

Vice Principal: Mrs C McKenzie, MA, BSc Hons, PGCE
Assistant Head Learning & Teaching: Mr R Eastham,
  MEd, BSc Hons, PGCE
Assistant Head Pupil Support & Progress: Mrs J Muir, BA
  Hons, PGCE
Director of Studies: Mr S Grocott, BSc Hons, PGCE
Director of Music: Mr A Prentice, BA Hons, MA, PGCE,
  LTCL
Director of Sport: Mr M Pickering, BSc Hons, PGCE
Head of Sixth Form: Mr P Norman, MSc, BSc Hons, PGCE
Head of Preparatory School: Mrs F Thomas, BEd Hons,
  NPQH
Head of Pre-Preparatory School: Mrs S Skinner, BMus,
  PGCE
Deputy Head of Preparatory School: Mrs S Harrod, BA
  Hons, QTS
Deputy Head of Pre-Preparatory School: Mrs P Clayton,
  CertEd
Head of Pre-Preparatory Studies: Miss J Bunker, BEd

Heads of Department:
Mrs E Barclay, BEd Hons, PGCE, Dip RSA SpLD
  (*Learning Support*)
Mr N Boot, BA Hons, DipLaw, QTS (*History*)
Mrs A Brown, BA Hons, PGCE (*English*)
Mr J Cochrane, BSc, PGCE (*Mathematics*)
Mr C Freckelton, BSc Hons, GTP (*Food Science*)
Mr A Ganfornina, BA Hons, PGCE (*Modern Foreign
  Languages*)
Mrs A Gilbert, BSc Hons (*Girls' Physical Education*)
Mrs R Gladwin, BA Hons, PGCE (*Religious Studies*)
Mrs J Glenn-Batchelor, BA Hons, GTP (*Geography*)
Mr S King, BEng Hons, PGCE (*ICT*)
Mrs H Mason, BSc Hons, PGCE (*Science*)
Mrs C Prentice, BMus Hons, PGCE, LTCL (*Senior School
  Music*)
Mrs C Servonat-Blanc, BA Hons, PGCE (*Art, Graphics &
  Photography*)
Miss A Tweedale, BA Hons, PGCE (*Business Studies*)
Mrs J Wafer, BA Hons, PGCE (*Drama*)
Mr R Wenban, BEd Hons (*Boys' Physical Education*)

Executive Assistant to the Principal: Miss C Swallow
Registrar: Mrs A Stuffins
Examinations Officer: Mrs A Pullen, BA Hons, PGCE

Structure and Organisation. Lincoln Minster School educates pupils from nursery to A Level on several delightful sites situated in the heart of historic Lincoln. In ten years the school has almost trebled its number on roll without losing the marked friendliness and responsiveness which makes it so attractive.

A new £10 million Music Centre and Sports Hall, redeveloped and extended Preparatory School and refurbished boarding accommodation have augmented the School's facilities dramatically and are bolstering the School's growing reputation for excellence. With a new strategy to open its doors worldwide, the School is seeking to build on a growing national reputation to become a school of international renown, especially in the field of Music.

Inspired teaching, individual focus and small classes create an excellent learning environment. There is excellent pastoral care and award-winning careers provision designed to equip youngsters for life beyond the classroom. The Nursery and Early Years department attained 'outstanding' status in their current Ofsted inspection report, underlining the quality of provision across all areas.

Lincoln Minster School is a member of United Learning, which owns and manages independent schools and academies across England. There is no doubt that membership of a group of this size gives Lincoln Minster School strength and breadth of contact.

Curriculum. A full range of subjects is offered and the school is proud of its excellent track record of examination success.

The curriculum is supported by a wealth of trips, visits and activities, too numerous to list, plus a comprehensive sports programme to cater for all tastes.

Pupils of all ages are encouraged to develop intellectual curiosity, resilience and self-confidence and to begin their lives within a Christian framework.

Music. As the Choir School for Lincoln Cathedral, Lincoln Minster School provides for the all-round education of boy and girl choristers. 27 music staff work in the department; approximately 70% of pupils receive individual instrument lessons. Music is a focal point of school life and opportunities for public performances abound. The strong musical and Christian ethic within the school is enhanced by daily use of the School Chapel and the Cathedral.

Boarding. Weekly and termly boarding is offered. The large family of boarders is very much at the heart of the School. In 2010, a further boarding house was acquired and superbly refurbished and this enabled the school to recruit more widely. There are 4 boarding houses, all in close proximity to the School and within the beautiful conservation area of uphill Lincoln.

Admissions. Lincoln Minster School welcomes pupils of a wide range of ability and all faiths. Admission is by interview and report, and subject to availability of a place.

Chorister Auditions, open to boys and girls 7–10 years, are held in November and March. These are worth up to 50% of boarding and tuition fees. Other dates by arrangement. For further details apply to The Registrar.

Scholarships. Academic, Music, Sport and Art Scholarships are available at 7+, 11+, 13+ and 16+. Choral Bursaries are available for members of the Cathedral Choir.

Fees per term (2014–2015). Day (including lunch): Nursery & Early Years £2,691 (all day); Pre-Prep £2,887; Prep £3,639; Seniors £4,159. Weekly Boarding: £6,567 (up to Year 6), £7,600 (Years 7–13). Termly Boarding: £7,232 (up to Year 6), £8,394 (Years 7–13), £9,952 (Overseas Boarders).

Charitable status. Lincoln Minster School is part of United Learning which comprises: UCST (a Company Limited by Guarantee, Registered in England, number 2780748, and a Registered Charity, number 1016538) and ULT (a Company Limited by Guarantee, Registered in England, number 4439859, and an Exempt Charity).

Lomond School

**10 Stafford Street, Helensburgh, Argyll and Bute
G84 9JX**
Tel: 01436 672476
Fax: 01436 678320

email: admissions@lomondschool.com
admin@lomondschool.com
website: www.lomondschool.com

Lomond is a co-educational day and boarding school for pupils aged from 3 to 18 years. The original foundations date from 1845. The current roll is 430 pupils, including 60 boarders housed in a purpose-built boarding house with en-suite study-bedrooms which was completed in March 2003. A new main building was opened in 1998 which provides excellent facilities and a conducive learning environment. 2013 saw a stunning refurbishment of the Junior School and in 2014 the school built two new departments for Drama and Health & Food Technology, resulting in the addition of an impressive Drama Studio and teaching kitchens. Strong examination results are consistently produced leading to high university uptake. New leading-edge sporting facilities, including the provision of a multi-purpose Sports Hall, opened in August 2009.

Twenty five miles from Glasgow, a thriving cosmopolitan city which is a centre for art, culture and commerce, Helensburgh is situated on the north bank of the Firth of Clyde in a quiet residential setting and with immediate access to mountain, sea and loch – ideal for outdoor activities.

Board of Governors:
Chair: Mr A J D Hope, LLB
Vice-Chair: Mr C Burnet, LLB, CA
Mr D Bowman, FNAEA
Professor R Brown, BSc Hons, PhD
Mrs M Cunningham, Dip Ed
Mr J Kemp, BA Hons
Capt P Merriman, CEng, MiMechE
Mrs L Pender, BA, PGCE
Dr T Reitano, MB ChB
Mr P Silvey, BA, PGCE
Mr F Thornton, BA, CA

Staff:

Principal: Mrs J Urquhart, BSc Hons, PGCE, MEd

Academic Depute: Mr D L Dodson, BSc Hons, Cert Ed
Pastoral Depute: Mr A B H Minnis, MA Hons, PGCE, Cert PP
Head of Junior School: Mrs S Hart, BEd Hons
Bursar: Ms A Sheehan, BA, MSc, CSBM

* *Head of Department*

Subject Teachers – Secondary:

Art & Design:
*Mrs B Croft, BA Hons, Cert Ed
Mrs L Jack, BA Hons, PGCE
Mrs D Aitken, BA Hons, Cert Ed

Business Studies:
*Mrs C McElhill, BA Hons, MSc, PGCE

Drama:
*Mr D Torbet, BA Hons, PGDE
Miss S Gibbs MA PGDE

EFL:
Mrs A Riches, BA, PGCE
Mrs J Robertson, BEd

English:
*Mr D Torbet, BA Hons, PGDE
Dr M Cotter-MacDonald, MA Hons, PhD, PGDE
Mrs M McKillop, MA Hons, MPhil, PGCE

Geography:
*Mr G M Taylor, BSc, MSc, Dip Ed Comp, Cert Ed
Mrs N McKenzie, MA Hons, PGCE

Graphic Communication:
Mr J Stewart, BSc, PGDE

Health & Food Technology:
Mrs N Harwood, BSc Hons, PGCE, MEd

History and Modern Studies:
*Mrs S Guy, MA Hons, PGCE
Mr J Forrest BA Hons PGDE
Mr A B H Minnis, MA Hons, PGCE, Cert PP

ICT:
*Mr S J Kilday, DipTechEd, DipComp

Learning Support:
*Mr H Hunter, BA Hons, PGDE
Mrs C Greaves, BSc Hons, PGCE
Mrs S Bell, BEd, PGDE

Mathematics:
*Mr G Macleod, BSc Hons, MEd, CMath, CSci, FIMA, PGCE, Adv Dip Hist Oxon
Mrs E Cameron, BSc Hons, PGCE
Mr A Laceby, BA, Dip Math, PGCE
Mrs E Stewart, BSc Hons, PGCE
*Mrs J Urquhart, BSc Hons, PGCE, MEd

Modern Languages:
*Mr A Greig, MA Hons, PGCE, PGDip
Mrs E Bruce, MA Hons, PGDE
Miss E Clarke, BA Hons, PGDE
Mrs J Robertson, BEd
Ms I Skowronski, LLCE English, PGDE

Music:
*Mr D Fleming, BMus Hons, PGCE
Miss M-C Brown, BA Hons, PGDE

Physical Education:
*Mrs M G Taylor, BEd
Mr C Dunlop, BEd Hons
Mr S Louden, BA, MEd, PGCE

RME:
Mr S J Kilday, DipTechEd, DipComp
Mrs L Jack, BA Hons, PGCE

Science:
Biology:
*Mr J Laycock, BSc Hons, PGCE
Mrs C Normand, BSc Hons, PGCE
Chemistry:
*Mr D L Dodson, BSc Hons, Cert Ed
Miss M Ward, BSc Hons, PGCE
Physics:
*Dr A MacBeath, BEng Hons, PhD, PGDE
Mr C Butler, BSc Hons, Cert Ed
General Science:
Mrs A Lawn, BSc Hons, PGCE

Careers Advisor:
Mrs J Barrett-Bunnage, MA Hons, PG Dip CG

School Nurse:
Mrs Lesley Serpell, RGN, MPH

Depute Head of Junior School:
Mrs A Lawn, BSc Hons, PGCE

Class Teachers – Junior School and Transitus:

Class Teachers – Transitus:
Mr S Fleming, BEd
Mrs C Greig, BA Jt Hons, PGCE, Dip Ed Tech
Mrs V McLatchie, DCE

Class Teachers – Clarendon
Mrs L Canero, BA, PGDE
Mrs V Cassels, MA Hons, MA, BSc, PGCE, Dip Env Dev, Cert Con Sci, Cert French
Mrs J Fullarton, BA Hons, PGCE

Mr J Grafton, BEd Hons
Mrs J Macleod, BEd Hons, MEd, Dip RSA, Dip APS, Dip
  Ed Lead, SQH
Mrs K Muggoch, MA Hons, PGDE

Nursery/Pre-School Group:
Head of Nursery: Mrs G Peace, NNEB, BA Childhood
  Practice
Ms L Lovell, HNC
Mrs J McArthur, SNNEB
Miss L Ritchie, SVQ 3 Childcare and Development
Mrs G Thomas, HNC

Aims of the School. Lomond has a proud academic tradition and nearly all of the Sixth Form will leave to attend University or College. The School aims to get the best from every pupil regardless of talent and successfully caters for the 'average' youngster as well as those with high ability. It believes strongly in developing the whole person and creating a high achievement learning environment.

Class sizes are low and there is a close monitoring of all pupils both academically and for extra-curricular input. Pupils sit Scottish Certificate of Education National 4 and 5 in Senior 4 and Higher examinations in Senior 5 before sitting Advanced Highers or further Highers in the Sixth Form. Maintaining both breadth and depth in senior years enables there to be a flexible approach to individual needs which means that a complete range of ability is successfully catered for.

Extra-curricular. The philosophy of the school looks to involvement in the extensive extra-curricular programme from every pupil. Pupils are encouraged to take part in the main sports of rugby, hockey, and athletics and in the Duke of Edinburgh's Award Scheme. There are teams for sailing, hill running, cricket and tennis and a wide variety of activities are strongly represented. Fixtures against other schools take place every weekend and there is a very extensive outdoor education programme. Music and drama are also strong and a plethora of pupils have achieved success at the highest level.

Some distinctive aspects. The extensive Duke of Edinburgh's Award Scheme programme leads to participation in such events as the Lomond Challenge Triathlon (a national event) and the Scottish Islands Peaks Race. A week long Outward Bound programme has been developed for the school which concentrates on leadership and teamwork skills. There are regular canoe and mountaineering expeditions abroad. The international dimension is significant not only with long established exchanges and work experience abroad but also due to special arrangements that have encouraged pupils from abroad to study at Lomond. This approach broadens the outlook of the school's pupils and leads to greater international understanding.

There are state-of-the-art boarding, sporting and teaching facilities together with a very supportive staff which brings out the very best in our pupils.

Each Senior School pupil at Lomond School has received an iPad. iPads are being used in the class to enhance the learning experience and get in touch with available technology.

Entry and Scholarships. Means-tested bursaries are available for entry between T2 (P7) and S6 with fee assistance ranging from 10% to 100% depending on circumstances. In addition means-tested bursaries are available for services personnel with children who board at Lomond.

Admission is by assessment in Mathematics and English for 11–13 year olds. For younger pupils placement in classes is the main requirement whilst for senior pupils reports and examination results are given due weighting.

Fees per term (2014–2015). Tuition: £571 (Nursery net of Local Authority Funding), £1,696 (Junior 1), £2,483 (Junior 2), £2,904 (Junior 3–5), £3,167 (Transitus 1), £3,362 (Transitus 2), £3,454 (Senior School).

Boarding (inc Tuition Fees): £7,670.

A levy of £50 per pupil per term is payable along with tuition fees.

Charitable status. Lomond School Ltd is a Registered Charity, number SC007957. It exists to provide education for boys and girls.

Lord Wandsworth College

Long Sutton, Hook, Hampshire RG29 1TB
Tel: 01256 862201 (Main Office)
             01256 860348 (Headmaster)
             01256 860200 (Admissions)
Fax: 01256 860363
email: info@lordwandsworth.org
website: www.lordwandsworth.org

Motto: '*Vincit Perseverantia.*'

Lord Wandsworth College is a co-educational secondary school for 550 pupils between the ages of 11 and 18. Approximately 55% of the pupils are boarders.

Chairman of Governors: R G Janaway

The Governing Body consists of 12 governors.

Headmaster: F Q Livingstone, MA

Senior Deputy Head: G D Pearson, BEng

Deputy Heads:
S L Badger, MA
Mrs J Davies, MA

Bursar: R Gammage, MA

Assistant Staff:

Mrs K Abery, BA	Miss L McNabb, BA
Mrs V Allan, BA	Miss D McPhee, BA
Miss A Asbury, BA	C Millington, BA
Mrs S Badger, MA	G J Mobbs, BA
Mrs F Byron, BA	Dr V Murtagh, BSc, PhD
Mr N Byron, BA	A Musleh, BSc
M Clinton-Baker, BA	Mrs G R Neighbour
E Coetzer, BA	A Parker, BMus
Mrs J Cooper, BA	D C Pering, MA
Ms S Dawson-Couper, BSc	C H Radmann, BA
Dr M R Eldridge, BSc, PhD	Mrs L A Radmann, BA
Mrs A-M Englebrecht, BA	M Rattray, BA
Mrs L Faulkner, MA, BSc	Mrs N Reeson, BA
Mrs A Fisher, BA	Miss R Rial Garcia
P M Gilliam, BSc	Mrs S Richardson, BA
Ms L L Griffin, BMus, MA	T R Richardson, BA Hons
A O F Hamilton, MA	Ed
C C Hicks, MA	W Richardson, BSc
J Hine, BA	T J Shedden, BA
A M Howard, MA	S Singh, MA
Miss H Hunter, BA	Mrs E Scott, BA
C Irvine, BSc	G R Smith, BA
Mrs Z Jarvis, BA	Mrs S Stevens, BA
R J Kimber, BEng	P R Summers, MA
Mrs B Lane, BA	R J Thorne, BA, MSc
A P Lay, BSc	A Turner, BSc
Miss C Liggins, BA	Mrs J Turner, BA
J K Lilley, MA	J Turney, BSc
Mrs J Loud, BSc	E Walker, BSc
A E Lumsden, BSc	I Watson, MEng
D O C Machin, BA	D L Widdowson, BSc
Miss C Mason, BA	C Wiskin
Mrs J M McKinnon, BA	

Librarian: Mrs S Brown

Director of Admissions & Marketing: Mrs M Hicks

Development Director: Mrs K Chernyshov

Headmaster's Secretary: Mrs N Grossmith

Medical Officers:

Dr R Assadourian, MB BS, BSc Hons, MRCGP, DRCOG, DFFP

Dr C Shand, MB BS, LMSSA, MRCGP, DRCOG, DFFP

Location and accessibility. The school occupies a magnificent rural setting on the North Hampshire/Surrey border just five miles from Junction 5 of the M3 and only an hour from London by road or rail.

History. Lord Wandsworth died in 1912 and left a large sum of money for the foundation of a school. The College that bears his name now occupies a 1,200 acre site. The Lord Wandsworth Foundation awards a number of places annually to children who have lost the support of one or both parents through death, divorce or separation with priority to those who have lost a parent through death.

Mission statement. LWC is a socially inclusive non-denominational boarding and day Foundation school for boys and girls. We focus on the needs of each individual, while developing in each child a concern for others and a love for and loyalty towards the school community. We ensure that each pupil shapes their values and aspirations within a stimulating and supportive environment, and strive constantly to improve the quality of teaching and learning. We aim to equip pupils with character attributes, passion, resourcefulness, independence, skills, knowledge and qualifications so they can become the best possible version of themselves and make a great contribution to a changing world. LWC should reach out and become known as a leading and opinion forming school, in principle and in practice.

The outstanding features of the school are

- that almost all academic staff live on campus allowing them to provide a high level of pastoral care;
- that Character Education is imbedded into the curriculum and co-curriculum. By promoting Character Education, we believe we will give all pupils the best chance of realising their full potentials.
- that all pupils, whether full, weekly, flexi boarding or day, belong to one of the eight houses and are fully integrated into the social life of the school;
- that the school is purpose-built with an outstanding range of facilities for both academic and extra-curricular activities;
- that the school is an unusually unpretentious, happy and caring community.

Curriculum. The aim of the curriculum is to provide a full and flexible range of subjects to fit the needs of each individual. The school's policy is to follow closely the National Curriculum.

Subjects taught to GCSE are: English (Language and Literature), French, Geography, Mathematics, History, Latin, Classical Civilisation, Drama, Physics, Chemistry, Biology, Spanish, German, Art, Music, Design & Technology, Computer Science and Religious Studies.

Most pupils continue into the Sixth Form where the subjects taught to AS and A2 Level are: English, History, Geography, Economics, Business Studies, Classical Civilisation, Critical Thinking, Music, Latin, French, Spanish, German, Physics, Chemistry, Biology, Mathematics, Further Mathematics, Art, Design, Theatre Studies, PE, Philosophy and Ethics and Psychology. We also offer the AQA Baccalaureate and EPQ.

ICT. There has been, and continues to be, significant investment into IT provision. There is a wireless networked system across the whole school.

Games. The school lays great store by its games involvement and has a local and national reputation for many of its pursuits. The main boys' games are rugby, hockey and cricket and for girls hockey, netball and tennis. In addition swimming, athletics, squash, badminton, basketball, golf, cross-country running and canoeing are all on offer.

Drama. Drama has a high profile and several shows are staged each year. There is a musical production every other year as well as showcases, reviews and workshops. Pupils are encouraged to participate in all fields of drama either acting, writing, set design, lighting, stage management, prop-making or sound.

Music. There is a large variety of instrumental ensembles, including a swing band, chamber and rock groups. Pupils sing in two choirs. Tuition is available in singing, all orchestral instruments, piano, organ, percussion and guitar. Musicians regularly perform formally and informally both within school and at local venues.

Other activities. There is an extensive extra-curricular programme. Some of the activities on offer are: Cookery, Soccer, Chess, Community Service, Pottery, Drama clubs, Mountain Biking, Dance, Photography, School newspaper, Riding, Life-saving, Self-defence, Scuba-diving, Debating and Climbing.

The Duke of Edinburgh's Award Scheme is thriving and the College has its own licence to run the scheme. There is an active CCF programme for Year 10 pupils and above which has an Army and Air Force Section.

Organisation. There is a two or three form entry at age 11. For the first two years all pupils are in the co-educational Junior House. At 13 there is another entry, mainly from children who have taken Common Entrance. All houses are in the charge of Houseparents assisted by a team of tutors and matrons.

Scholarships and Awards on offer are:

First Form (Year 7): Academic, Performing Arts (Music, Drama and Dance) and Sport;

Third Form (Year 9): Academic, Performing Arts (Music, Drama and Dance), Art, Sport and All-Rounder;

Sixth Form (Year 12): Academic, Performing Arts (Music, Drama and Dance), Art, Sport and All-Rounder.

Foundation Awards are available for children who have lost the support of one or both parents through death, divorce or separation.

Further details for all scholarships and awards may be obtained from the Admissions Office.

Fees per term (2014–15). Senior Full Boarding £9,660; Senior Weekly Boarding £9,200; Senior Flexi Boarding £7,800; Senior Day £6,840; Junior Full Boarding £8,700; Junior Weekly Boarding £8,450; Junior Flexi Boarding £7,160; Junior Day £6,370.

Charitable status. Lord Wandsworth College is a Registered Charity, number 1143359. It exists to provide education for boys and girls.

Loretto School

Linkfield Road, Musselburgh, East Lothian EH21 7RE

Tel:	School: 0131 653 4444
	Headmaster: 0131 653 4441
	Admissions: 0131 653 4455
Fax:	School: 0131 653 4445
	Admissions: 0131 653 4401
email:	admissions@loretto.com
website:	www.loretto.com

Loretto has flourished as a school since its establishment in 1827, 6 miles from Edinburgh, on the banks of the River Esk and surrounded by the beautiful countryside of East Lothian. It is a non-denominational, co-educational boarding and day school and provides for full and flexi boarders, as well as for day pupils, with a distinctive emphasis on the full development of the individual through academic, intellectual, sporting, musical, dramatic and artistic pursuits in a fine, secure environment. Loretto's distinctive ethos fosters in its pupils a quiet confidence in themselves and a spirit of readiness to succeed in the changing world beyond school.

Loretto is a small community where staff and pupils know each other personally. Classes are deliberately small so that proper individual attention is possible; recent examination results have been outstanding. Boys and girls take part in a very wide range of activities. Its pupils, from 3 to 18 years, are known and valued for themselves and are expected to respect and support each other. The School makes fullest use of its proximity to Edinburgh, enabling pupils to take advantage of the music, drama, museums and art galleries, as well as giving opportunities for sport and leisure in this capital city. To the east lie the golf courses which provide the fairway for The Golf Academy at Loretto.

Governors:

Lt Col S J M Graham (*Chairman*)
Mrs A Brobbel
K Dobson
Mrs S Geddes (*Clerk to the Board*)
F Gerstenberg
Dr P Graham
J Grant
M Hinton
Major General P C Marriott, CBE
Ms R Marshall
J Miller
M Simmers
Rt Revd B Smith
Mrs A Swanson

Headmaster: **Dr Graham Hawley**, BSc, PhD

Vicegerent: N C Bidgood, BSc, MSc, PGCE, FRGS

Deputy Head: Ms Elaine Logan, MA, PGCE

Head of Junior School: P Meadows, MA

Staff:
* *Head of Department*
† *Housemaster/mistress*

Dr D J Adamson, MA, PhD (*History and Politics, *Sixth Form*)
N Allan, BA (*Head of Hockey*)
Dr M J Baker, MA (*Physics, Mathematics*)
Mrs M Bonner, BA Hons, MA, PGCE, DIS (**Art*)
Mrs A Buchanan, MA (*Art*)
J D Burnet, MA (**Modern Languages*)
D A Burton, BEd Hons (*Director of Sport*)
Miss C Cadzow, BDes Hons (*Art, Ceramics*)
Mrs M Campbell (*Modern Languages*)
W E Coleman, MMus ARCO (*Director of Music*)
B A Cooper, MA Hons, MRes, QTS, FRSSA (*Academic Registrar; History and Politics*)
Ms A Cooper, BA Hons, PGCE (*English*)
D Coppard, BA, PGCE (*Business*)
M Crawford, MA, PGCE (*Head of English*)
Mrs C A Cursiter, MA (*Modern Languages*)
Mrs H Day, BA, PGCE (*English*)
W D Dickinson, BEd (*†Schoolhouse; Geography*)
Mrs J Dunford, BA, MA (*Head Librarian*)
P S Dunn, BSc, PGCE (*Mathematics*)
Mrs S Feria (*Modern Languages*)
Mrs J Fletcher, BSc Hons, PGCE (**Head of Girls' Games; †Balcarres*)
Dr I Fox, MSc, PhD (*Head of Physics*)
Mrs R Fox, BA Hons (*Music*)
Mrs M Galloway, MA Hons, Dip Trans (*Modern Languages, †Holm*)
D Griffiths BA, PGCE (*Director of Rugby, PE, †Hope*)
N Guise, CertEd, PGCSE (*Support for Learning*)
G Harbison, BSc Hons, MSc, PGCE (**Business Studies*)
Mrs A Horsey, BA, PGCE (*Classics*)
D A Howie, MBE (*Head of Outdoor Pursuits*)
J Idle, MSc, PhD, PGCE (*Chemistry, Head of Science, Director of Teaching and Learning*)
R Johnston, MSc PGCE (*Physics*)
J Karolyi, PGCE (*Modern Languages, Higher Education Careers and University Guidance*)
P Sutton, AKC, BD, MTh (*Chaplain*)

Mrs C Lekkas, BSc Hons, DipTEFL/TESOL (**ESL, Biology*)
Ms Z Law, MSc, PGDE (*Mathematics*)
S J M Lowe, MA Oxon, Cert Adv Studies GSMD, PGCE (*Director of Expressive Arts; Modern Languages*)
S Lucas, BA Hons, MLitt, Dip SpLD, PGCE (**Support for Learning*)
Mrs K McMillan, BA, PGCE (*Head of Geography*)
J McKenzie, BA, CELTA (*ESL, History*)
D McLean-Steel, BA Hons (**Drama; English*)
Mrs F Monk, MA (*Head of 2nd Form, Business Studies and Economics*)
D R Pierce, BSc Hons, PGCE (**Mathematics*)
M J Powell (*Director of Cricket; Assistant† Seton*)
Mrs T M Pratt, MTh, DHP, BACP, Accredited Counsellor (*PSHE*)
Ms J Prior, BA, PGDE (*English*)
Pipe Major C Pryde (*Piping*)
Mrs S Tassiker, BA Hons, PGCE (*English*)
Dr D Tidswell (*Head of History*)
Dr M G Topping, BSc Hons, PhD, PGCE (*Director of Academic Progress, *Biology*)
R I Valentine, BSc Hons, PGA (*Director of Golf*)
Mrs C Wakeford (*Chemistry*)
Mrs S Ward, BSc Hons, PGCE (**Chemistry, CCF, DofE*)
R P Whait, BSc, C Dip AF (*Head of Activities; Business Studies, Mathematics, Head of Personal Finance and Examinations Officer*)
Ms J Young, BA, Cert TESOL (*ESL*)

Houses and Housemasters/Housemistresses:

Boys Boarding:
Hope House: D Griffiths
Seton House: M Powell
Pinkie House: N Allen

Girls Boarding:
Balcarres House: Mrs S Meadows
Holm House: Mrs M Galloway
Eleanora Almond House: Mrs M Bonner

Day (Boys and Girls):
Schoolhouse: W D Dickinson

Bursar: S Howard
Director of External Affairs: J Hewat
Director of Development: R Baird

Junior School
Head: P Meadows, MA Hons, PGCE

Staff:
Mrs J Brown, SVQ3 Playwork (*After School Club Coordinator*)
Mrs K Brown (*Classroom Assistant*)
Mrs E Buchanan, MA Hons, PGCE (*Year 4*)
Mrs E Burgess, BEd Hons (*Head of Early Years / Year 2*)
C Claydon BSc Hons, PGCE (*Deputy Head, PE and Games*)
Mrs N Coleman, BMus Hons (*Early Years Music and Drama*)
Mrs N Dinwoodie, HNC Childcare and Education, BA Childhood Practice (*Nursery Nurse*)
Mrs H Fraser, SVQ2 Childcare (*After School Club*)
Mrs A Gauld, DCE, ACE (*Year 3*)
Mrs S Gold, BEd Hons (*Nursery Teacher*)
K Hutchison, DipTMus (*Director of Music – Junior School*)
J Jackman, BA Hons, PGDE (*Year 5*)
Mrs F Kelly, BA Hons, PGCE (*Support for Learning*)
Mrs F Ferguson, BSc Hons, PGDE (*Year 4*)
Mrs E Károlyi, MA Hons, PGCE (*Director of Studies – Junior School*)
Miss S A Kettlewell, BA (*Art and Drama*)
P McDouall, MA Hons, PGDE (*Year 5*)
Mrs K MacKinnon, MA Hons, PGDE (*Year 2*)

Mrs J O'Raw, HNC Childcare and Education (*Nursery Nurse*)

Mrs M Pathirana, MA Hons, PGCE (*Year 3*)

D J Pearce, BSc Hons (*Year 7*)

Mrs V Provan, MA Hons (*Year 6*)

Mrs S Scott, BEd Hons (*Nursery Teacher*)

Miss K Seabra, BEd Hons (*Year 1*)

Mrs J Selley (*Classroom Assistant*)

Mrs C Robertson, DipEd (*Nursery Teacher*)

Mrs J Robertson, SNEB (*Nursery Nurse*)

Mrs J Robertson, BEd Hons (*Year 2*)

Mrs E Shaw, BA Hons, PGCE (*Year 2*)

Miss R Wallace, SVQ3 Playwork (*After School Club*)

Miss C Ward, MEd, PGCE, BA Hons (*Year 6, French Years 6 and 7*)

Mrs K Wells, BA, PGDE (*French Nursery–Year 5*)

The Senior School consists of 431 boys and girls with almost 75% of pupils boarding.

Academic. An excellent staff/pupil ratio (1:8) ensures an environment that stimulates, supports and nurtures the potential in everyone. The academic programme aims to challenge pupils and to recognise and reward effort and attainment. A full range of curricular subjects – humanities; drama, music and art; languages and sciences; ICT and business; physical education – is offered. The depth, breadth and quality of a Loretto education encourages each pupil to achieve his or her personal best and to enjoy doing so. Pupils are prepared for success in GCSE, AS and A Level and for a choice of good university careers thereafter. The School is also running the AQA Extension Project Scheme which contributes to UCAS points. In 2012 63% of all A Levels sat were at grade A or B. 91% of GCSEs were at A–C grades. Virtually all pupils go on to higher education.

The facilities keep abreast of changing national academic demands, with modern, well-equipped specialist areas in languages, art and design, music, drama and the sciences. The Communication and Resource Centre provides a traditional library as well as a new Sixth Form Centre and computer network which can be accessed from academic departments and Houses. All pupils become familiar both with modern technology and with books, to facilitate independent learning, essential for success in Higher Education and beyond. The Support for Learning department assists the academically gifted as well as those who have a learning difficulty or those who simply want to improve essential study skills.

Pastoral Care. There are seven houses where full and flexi boarders and day pupils can relax "at home", socialise and develop their studies under the experienced supervision of dedicated resident pastoral teams. The House structure is: 6 boarding houses (4 for Sixth Form and 2 for Second, Third, Fourth and Fifth Form), and 1 day house (boy and girl). There is excellent pastoral care, nurturing an atmosphere of mutual care and support in which children mature at their own pace and older pupils are encouraged to take responsibility, not just for themselves, but for their young housemates.

Younger pupils sleep in small dormitories, while sixth formers have double or individual study-bedrooms.

The day pupils at Loretto have access to the same broad and full education provided for boarders, and are able to take full advantage of the facilities of a boarding school, while returning home to sleep.

All academic staff are involved in the boarding houses and so staff are always on hand to guide and encourage. The aim is always to ensure that the well-being and development of every pupil is closely and sympathetically monitored. An excellent programme of personal, social and health education is an integral part of the curriculum.

Health. A medical centre staffed with nurses who are qualified and registered with the NMC. The Doctors surgery is located off site. All health/medical appointments for boarding pupils are made through the Loretto School Medical Centre Staff. There is a school counsellor who visits the school twice a week.

Music, Drama and Art. Loretto is well known for the excellent quality of its Expressive Arts. Pupils are encouraged to enjoy the creative arts and to develop their individual talents. A purpose-built Music School enables a very high proportion to learn individual instruments or to take voice lessons and there is a range of concerts, recitals and performances both in School and in venues in Edinburgh and East Lothian. Loretto is Europe's first All-Steinway School. The choir and orchestra practise weekly. All pupils enjoy whole School choral singing in chapel, while performance music extends from rock, through jazz to classical music. The Loretto Pipe Band competes successfully in national competitions and has a busy schedule of appearances. A theatre is the base for much drama work, with performances – both musical and dramatic – each term involving pupils of all ages. LAMDA exams are also available. The theatre facilities have been refurbished to provide performance areas and technical facilities to the highest specifications. There is also a new campus radio station to complement the modern well-equipped studio theatre and state-of-the-art recording studio. The Art department offers drawing, painting, mixed media, ceramics, sculpture and lino-printing. The School's art gallery allows pupil work to be displayed as well as housing outside exhibitions that encourage experimentation with different techniques and styles.

Games and Activities. Pupils are encouraged to enjoy exercise and to develop their skills. The Golf Academy at Loretto is widely recognised as one of the best independent golfing schools in Britain, with on-site facilities and professional coaching. Cricket is also a major strength with the employment of former England player, Michael Powell, as Director of Cricket. Provision is also made for rugby, hockey, lacrosse, athletics, cricket, tennis, fives, badminton, swimming, shooting, and basketball, to name but a few. A well-equipped fitness centre and an astroturf pitch are also on site. Riding, sailing, skiing and snowboarding are available using excellent local facilities. Team games are important: boys play rugby, hockey and cricket; girls, hockey, lacrosse and netball. There is an extensive range of fixtures for both boys and girls at all levels. Participation in the Duke of Edinburgh's Award scheme is strong and Community Service, the Combined Cadet Force and outward bound programme offer additional experience of a range of skills and challenges. A full programme of activities, from karate to hip hop dance, operates each day and all weekend.

Sixth Form. Preparing its pupils for the world beyond school is something that Loretto takes very seriously. Loretto's Sixth Form is structured to encourage boys and girls to take responsibility for their work and organise their time. Loretto offers a wide range of academic subjects in the Sixth Form and fosters a purposeful work ethic. Academic tutors and pastoral mentors are on hand at every step to provide encouragement and guidance. A comprehensive enrichment programme has been developed which enables students to enjoy concerts, theatre trips, social evenings and outings to Edinburgh.

There is a thriving lecture society which organises visiting speakers from University and industry to enthuse and advise the Sixth Form. Additionally, the school runs a series of seminars and workshops on the humanities, literature, politics, creative writing, science and more. Pupils also volunteer to research and deliver lectures to their peers. A dedicated, experienced team of teachers are on hand to guide every pupil through their university applications, gap year choices, career paths and work-experience ventures

Beyond academic matters, Loretto furnishes each pupil with a range of leadership and teamworking opportunities. Positions of responsibility and trust are earned. Prefects are selected on the basis of a rigorous application and interview process which mirrors that of the business world. Loretto runs a range of specific leadership and teamworking exercises for Sixth Formers in the form of CCF and adventure activities. These are complemented by sessions on interview techniques, organisational skills and "CV loading". After all, in such a competitive job market, Lorettonians need to be well prepared and well informed.

Religion. Services are held in the School Chapel every week. The services are non-denominational and boys and girls are prepared for confirmation in both the Church of England and the Church of Scotland; they are confirmed at a combined service held in the Chapel. Whole School singing is a long-standing tradition at Loretto and continues to be memorable.

Developments. A Loretto Foundation has been established to provide for the mid to long-term future of the School with a particular emphasis on raising money to support scholarships and bursaries. In recent years, a major programme of development has taken place to give six science laboratories, four new classrooms, a further Art room and ICT room, a lecture theatre, and a state-of-the-art recording studio and radio station, all equipped to a very high standard. There is also an ongoing programme of refurbishment in the houses.

Uniform. The uniform is practical and comfortable. Formal dress on Sundays is the kilt for boys and girls. Ordinary School dress is charcoal trousers for boys, navy skirts for girls, with white shirts and the distinctive red jacket.

Entrance. Boys and girls are required to pass either the Common Entrance Examination or the Open Assessment Examination in English, Mathematics and Verbal Reasoning before being admitted, as well as an interview. Entrance to the Lower Sixth is based on interview and a conditional offer subject to satisfactory performance at GCSE/Standard Grade or international equivalent.

Junior School. 'The Nippers' enjoy many of the facilities of the Senior School, such as the playing fields, Theatre, Sports Hall, Music School and Chapel. The boys and girls are under closer adult supervision than in the Senior School but in other respects the system is similar. There are over 200 boys and girls aged between 3 and 12. The majority are day pupils, but occasional and flexi boarding are available. (*For further details, see entry in IAPS Section.*)

Fees per term (2014–2015). Boarding: £6,420–£9,820; Flexi Boarding (3 nights p/w): £5,420–£8,150; Overnighting £45 per night. These fees include all the expenses of board, lodging, most textbooks (though in the sixth form textbooks may have to be purchased), stationery, games material, medical attendance and medicine, CCF, transport to matches and internal school entertainments.

Day Fees (including meals): £2,630–£6,670.

Optional Expenses. These will be kept to a minimum, but include individual voice and instrumental music lessons; extra-curricular visits and expeditions.

Scholarships and Bursaries. *Junior School*: Academic and All-Rounder scholarships are available to pupils joining the Junior School at Year 6 and Year 7.

Senior School (Second–Lower Sixth Form): Means-tested Academic, Art, Drama, Golf, Music and Sports Scholarships are available. Almond Academic Scholarships (means-tested up to 100%) are also available.

Bursaries are available to support scholarship and non-scholarship award candidates who pass Loretto's entrance criteria and who the School feels would benefit from a Loretto education. Bursaries can be used to supplement a scholarship award if the financial amount of a scholarship is insufficient to allow a pupil to attend Loretto. Bursaries are means-tested and are available for prospective pupils as well as existing pupils who experience unforeseen financial difficulty. Bursary funds are limited.

Please contact the Admissions Department on 0131 653 4455 for further details.

Leaving Scholarships. A number of awards are given to assist with university education to those who have 'deserved well of Loretto' in recognition of their loyalty and service to the School.

Old Lorettonian Society. *Hon Secretary*: B G Walker, Loretto School, Musselburgh.

Charitable status. Loretto School is a Registered Charity, number SC013978. It exists in order to educate young people in mind, body and spirit.

Loughborough Grammar School

Burton Walks, Loughborough, Leicestershire LE11 2DU
Tel:　　　01509 233233/233258
Fax:　　　01509 218436
email:　　registrar@lesgrammar.org
website:　www.lesgrammar.org

Motto: *Vires acquirit eundo.*

Loughborough Grammar School was founded in 1495 by Thomas Burton, Merchant of the Staple of Calais, though it is probable that the Trustees of the Town Charity were managing a free school well before that date. The School is itself part of a larger 'family' known as the Loughborough Endowed Schools. Situated in the spacious and attractive grounds surrounding the Grammar School are Loughborough High School for Girls (*see GSA entry*) and Fairfield School, our co-educational Preparatory School (*see IAPS entry*). Links between all three are very strong.

Governing Body:
Chairman: G P Fothergill, BA
Deputy Chairman: H M Pearson, DL, DUniv Hon, BA Econ

Non-Executive Vice-Chairmen:
Mrs M Gershlick, RGN, DipNEd
Mrs C Wales

Nominative Governors:
J P T Clackson, MA, PhD Cambridge

Co-optative Governors:
Dr A M de Bono, MA, MB, FRCGP, FFOM
Dr P M Cannon, MA, BMBch, FRCS, MRCGP
Mrs E Critchley, MA
Professor A Dodson, BSc, PhD, DSc
Professor J Feather, BLitt, MA, PhD, FLA
Lady Gretton, JP, Lord-Lieutenant of Leicestershire
Dr P J B Hubner, MB, FRCP, DCH, FACC, FESC
P M Jackson, FIMI
A M Kershaw
Mrs R Limb, MA
M Mulla, BSc, MSc, MIM
Mrs P O'Neill, BA, MA
Mrs G Richards, BA Hons, MEd

Foundation Secretary & Treasurer: J Doherty

Headmaster: P B Fisher, MA Christ Church Oxford

Deputy Headmaster (Pastoral): J S Weitzel, BSc Nottingham
Deputy Headmaster (Academic): T G Willmott, BSc PhD London, MBA Leicester
Deputy Headmaster & Head of Sixth Form: C G Walker, MA Glasgow, DPhil Balliol College Oxford

Assistant Headmasters:
P S Sergeant, BEd Oxford, MPhil Nottingham
A J Dossett, BSc Loughborough

Director of Studies (Systems): R C Healey, BEng London, PhD Pembroke College Cambridge

Chaplain: The Revd D R Owen, BA Natal, HDE Natal, BA Natal, MTh Rhodes
Senior Master: B McCabe, MA Balliol College Oxford
Registrar/Marketing Director: Mrs D P Briers

Academic Departments:
* *Head of Department*

Art and Design:
*Miss E E Johnson, BA Loughborough
Miss S L Mackie, BA Nottingham Trent
Ms V Thompson, BA Loughborough

Biology:
*R B Parish, BSc MSc Bristol
Miss E S R Clingain, MSc Nottingham
Mrs M C Herring, BSc St Andrews
C S Herbert, BSc University of Sussex (*Head of Yates*)
L N Mantell, BA Oxford
J S Parton, MA Girton College Cambridge (*Head of Year 7*)
A D Waters, BSc Cambridge, PhD Bristol (*Head of Abney*)
T G Willmott, BSc PhD London, MBA Leicester

Chemistry:
*A J Haigh, MA Queens' College Cambridge
R J Ball, BSc PhD Queen's Belfast
Mrs N M A Ebden, BSc Manchester, PhD Nottingham
C B Faust, BSc Manchester, MEd Nottingham, CChem FRSC (*Head of Sixth Form Enrichment*)
P M Marlow, BSc Homerton College Cambridge
T D Morse, BSc Sheffield, MSc Dundee
P Rhodes, BSc PhD Nottingham

Classics:
*P D Bunting, MA Selwyn College Cambridge
N Lipatov-Chicherin, BA PhD University of St Petersburg
N D Pollock, BA Queens' College Cambridge
Miss H A Walters, MA Somerville College Oxford

Computing and Information Technology:
*R Statham, BSc Open
Mrs D Kaur, BA Wolverhampton (*Head of Information Technology*)
D M Starkings, BSc Nottingham, BA Open
Mrs C M Winship, BSc Reading

Design and Technology:
*P P A Jackson, BSc Nottingham Trent
R Michalak, BA Bristol
T A Moseley, BA Loughborough

Drama:
Mrs S Bruton-Lang, BA Liverpool John Moores
Miss K Eastwood, BA Liverpool Hope

Economics and Business Studies:
*R J Lightfoot, BA Birmingham, MA Warwick
Ms S A Bell, BA York
Mrs H E James, BA Durham, DipABRSM
G I Sutcliffe, BA Rhodes, South Africa

English:
*B K McCabe, MA Balliol College Oxford
Miss E Bancroft, BA Keble College Oxford
Ms K Buckley, BA Birmingham, MA Cardiff, PhD Cardiff
Mrs S Daya, BA South Africa
Miss R M Hannah, BA Lancaster, MLitt Glasgow
Mrs M E McKean, BA Sheffield Hallam, MANottingham
A J N Morris, BA Reading (*Assistant Head of Sixth Form*)
Mrs A J Quigley, BA New College Oxford
Miss A Whitehead, BA Warwick

Geography:
*M D Butcher, BSc Lancaster, MSc Lancaster
D L Evans, BSc Reading
N A Hewitt, BSc Leicester, MSc DIC Imperial, FGS
Miss L E Milner, BSc PhD Leicester
I O G Potter, BSc Southampton

Mrs D Outwin-Flinders, BEd Bristol

History and Politics:
*C W Blackman, BA Bristol
M I Dawkins, BA MA De Montfort (**Politics*)
P J Dowsett, BA Nottingham
Miss S H Jenkins, BA UCL (*Head of Year 9*)
T J McKay, BA PhD Leicester
D J Murphy, BA Oxford
C G Walker, MA Glasgow, DPhil Balliol College Oxford

Mathematics:
*C J Luke, BSc Sidney Sussex College Cambridge, PhD Manchester
Miss N Bahl, BSc Loughborough (*Head of Year 8*)
Mrs D C Barrett, BSc Nottingham, PhD Loughborough
R Bhattacharyya, BA Trinity, Cambridge
Mrs R L Cooch, BSc East Anglia
A J Dossett, BSc Loughborough
D A Happer, BSc Loughborough
C J Feakes, BSc Leicester, MSc Leicester
Mrs R French, BEd Leeds (*Head of Year 11*)
P Gacs, MSc Budapest
S D Hatfield, BEng Sheffield (*Head of Year 10*)
R C Healey, BEng London, PhD Pembroke, Cambridge
J D Jackson, BSc Nottingham (*Head of Davys*)
D M Starkings, BSc Nottingham, BA Open
J S Weitzel, BSc Nottingham

Modern Languages:
*M M Jackson, BA Leeds
R F Kerr, MA The Queen's College Oxford (*Head of German*)
Mrs H M Fisher, BA Exeter, MA Sheffield (*Head of Spanish*)
Mrs H J Coles, BA London
Mrs L E Gosling, BA Churchill College Cambridge
Mrs N V Lorente, BA Zaragoza, BA Barcelona
Miss Z Mir, LLB, Leicester, LPC, Guildford
Ms V M Perino, BA Nottingham
D Reavie, BA Hull
P Smith, BEd Manchester, MA Loughborough
R Ward, BSc Salford

Music:
*R West, BA Durham, LGSMD, LRSM, PGCertMusTech, PGCE (*Director of LES Music School*)
Miss N M Bouckley, BA Durham (*Deputy Director of LES Music*)
P J Underwood, MA Downing College Cambridge, MMus London, PhD Birmingham, FRCO CHM, FTCL, LRAM, ARCM, ADCM, FCIEA (*Head of Senior Curriculum Music*)
A Geary, GLCM (*Head of Percussion*)
Mrs A McGee, GTCL LTCL CSAT (*Head of Junior School Music*)
Miss C Revell, BMus (*KS3 Coordinator*)
D Morris, LRAM (*Head of Vocal Studies*)
Miss M Reinhard, ARCT, LPRCM (*Head of Keyboard*)

Please refer to the LES Music School website, www.lesmusic.org, for a complete list of music staff including individual teachers.

Physical Education:
*M S E Broadley, BA Leeds
C V Collington, BA Chester (*Head of Games*)
M I Gidley (*Cricket Coach*)
D J Miles, BSc Loughborough (*Senior Housemaster*)
E O Lewis, BSc UWIC (*Director of Rugby*)
J Clarke (*Hockey Coach*)
P Rhodes, BSc PhD Nottingham

Physics:
*G J Kerr, BSc Birmingham
Miss K Cartwright, BEng Birmingham
R M Green, BSc Nottingham, PhD Nottingham

N B Khan, BSc Bangladesh, MSc London
A Lloyd, BSc Leicester (*Head of Pulteney*)
R C Wright, BEd Nottingham Trent

PSHE:
*P Smith, BEd Manchester, MA Loughborough

Religion and Philosophy:
*The Revd D R Owen, BA Natal, HDE Natal, BA Natal,
   MTh Rhodes
D E Berner, BA Durham
Mrs C Livingstone, BA MA PhD Durham
M Hiebert, BA Chester College

Head of Learning Support: Mrs H L Baker, BEd Bedford,
   PG Dip Dyslexia and Literacy
Head of Careers: R J Lightfoot, BA, MA
Headmaster's PA/Office Manager: Mrs K Rajput
Librarian: Mrs V Bunn, ALA
OC CCF: Wing Commander P S Sergeant, BEd, MPhil,
   RAFVR(*T*)
CCF SSI: Fl Sgr I Foster
Medical Officer: Dr P M Cannon, MA, BMBCh, FRCS,
   MRCGP, Dip Occ Med
School Nurses: Mrs J Bryan, Mrs N Krarup

There are just over 1,000 boys in the School, including 70 boarders.

The School moved to its present site of some 27 acres in 1852 and is situated away from the centre of the town in attractive grounds containing the beautiful avenues of trees known as Burton Walks. At its centre is a handsome Victorian College quadrangle. There has been an impressive development programme in recent years – a new Music School was opened in September 2006; a new state-of-the-art Chemistry building in September 2009; a refurbished and extended Biology building in September 2011; a new Physics building in September 2012 and a new Mathematics building and boarding provision in 2013, completing the Science Park.

Admission. Entry to the School is by the school's own examination at all levels and also by Common Entrance at 13+. Sixth Form entry is dependent on GCSE results and interview with the Headmaster and other senior staff.

Boarding Arrangements. Boys are admitted to Denton House at the age of 10 or over; Sixth Form boys are in School House. Termly and Weekly boarding is available.

Fees per term (2014–2015). Day £3,682 (includes books and stationery); Full Boarding £7,969 (includes laundry, board, medical attendance).

The School offers a 25% boarding fee remission to sons of HM Forces and sons of Clergy.

Scholarships and Bursaries. A number of Scholarships are offered at 10+, 11+ and 13+/Common Entrance, based on performance in the Entrance Examination. Sixth Form scholarships are based on GCSE results. Choral and instrumental scholarships are also awarded at 10+, 11+, 13+/Common Entrance and Sixth Form. There are also a number of bursaries, dependent on parental income.

Foundation Bursaries. Free or discounted places based on financial need are offered for boys entering the school at 11+ (Year 7) and 13+ (Year 9). Such places are means-tested and an application for one requires the completion of a form declaring income, an interview with the Headmaster and, in some cases, a home visit.

Religious Teaching. The School is non-denominational though there is a strong Christian tradition. The Chaplain teaches Religion and Philosophy but is available for boys at any convenient time. On Wednesdays, Boarders attend the School Chapel and, on request, are prepared for Confirmation by the Chaplain.

Curriculum. The aim of the School is to give a broad and balanced general education to GCSE with greater specialisation afterwards. In Year 6, boys follow a curriculum similar to that of their last year of junior school; subjects included are English, Mathematics, Art, Sciences, Drama, Design and Technology, Geography, IT, History, Music, PE, RE. In Year 7, all boys study English, Mathematics, Biology, Chemistry, Physics, French, History, Geography, Latin, and Music. Additionally, all boys have lessons in RE, PE, PSHE and Games. In Year 8, Design and Technology and Classical Civilisation are introduced and, in addition to French, boys choose a second language from either German or Spanish, and the boys are taught separate sciences. In Year 9 pupils continue with both MFLs, and make some choices from their existing subjects as well as Ancient Greek and Drama.

In Years 10 and 11, for GCSE, boys study English Language and Literature, Mathematics, a modern Foreign Language, and at least two sciences. They also choose three subjects from an extensive options list. Some more able boys study a tenth subject.

The Sixth Form contains 300 boys. In Year 12, boys study 4 subjects to AS Level and in Year 13 they will take 3 or 4 of them to A2 Level. A wide range of subjects and combinations is available, along with General Studies, EPQ, Games and other activities. There are some joint teaching lessons with the Girls' High School.

Games. The School has an excellent First XI field and a junior field of over 13 acres within its precinct and within two miles are well-equipped playing fields extending to nearly 70 acres.

The School runs teams in Rugby, Soccer, Hockey, Cricket, Athletics, Tennis, Cross Country, Swimming, Badminton, Fencing and Squash. In addition there is a Sailing and Canoe Club. The School prides itself in an array of Mind Sports, with teams in Bridge, Chess, Go and Chinese Chess.

Combined Cadet Force. There is an efficient and keen CCF of about 300 boys from Year 10 onwards, run on an optional basis, with 17 Officers, an SSI and a RQMS. Boys have the choice of joining the RAF, Army or Royal Navy Sections. The CCF complex is purpose-built with excellent facilities and many varied and Adventurous Training courses are available to members.

Scouts. There is a flourishing Scout Troop of 35 boys and 1 Scouter.

Duke of Edinburgh's Award Scheme. Over 250 boys are actively involved in the scheme and each year a large number earn Gold, Silver and Bronze awards.

Music (of which most is joint with the Girls' High School): 5 Choirs, 2 Orchestras, 2 Concert Bands, Big Band, Swing Band and over twenty smaller instrumental ensembles take place in an outstanding new Music School, incorporating a recital and recording hall. The Concert Band has toured Cornwall and Geneva. The Burton Choristers (an all-boys' choir) sing services regularly at cathedrals around the UK.

Drama. The School has a fine Studio/Theatre and all boys in Years 6, 7 and 8 participate in a dramatic production. After that, there are productions for other age groups in conjunction with the Girls' High School each term.

Careers. Careers advisors are available to inform boys on options for their futures, with special regard to University or Professional careers. The School is a member of the Independent Schools Careers Organisation.

Academic Successes. An average of 15 boys per year gain admission to Oxford and Cambridge, and over 98% each year begin degree courses at Universities.

Old Loughburians. All pupils of the school become members of the Association. Correspondence should be addressed to Mr N Rowbotham at the School.

Charitable status. Loughborough Endowed Schools is a Registered Charity, number 1081765, and a Company Limited by Guarantee, registered in England, number 4038033. Registered Office: 3 Burton Walks, Loughborough, Leicestershire LE11 2DU.

Magdalen College School
Oxford

Oxford OX4 1DZ
Tel: 01865 242191
Fax: 01865 240379
email: admissions@mcsoxford.org
website: www.mcsoxford.org

Motto: *Sicut Lilium.*

Magdalen College School consists of about 750 boys aged 7–18 with girls admitted to the Sixth Form from 2010. Academic standards are amongst the highest in the country and there is a strong emphasis on study beyond the syllabus, most of all in the Waynflete Studies programme, which allows Sixth Formers to develop a personal project which is finally supervised by university academics. Almost all pupils go on to higher education with about a third each year progressing to Oxford or Cambridge. The school seeks to develop the individuality and interests of each pupil. There is a strong emphasis on extra-curricular activity, with particularly proud traditions in sport, music and drama. The school was Sunday Times Independent School of the year in 2004–5 and again in 2008–9.

Visitor: The Rt Revd The Lord Bishop of Winchester

Governors:
T P W Edwards (*Chairman*)
Dr C Benson
Sir Jonathan Baker, QC (*Deputy Chairman*)
M Bullock
Ms P Cameron Watt
Mr A James
T M Knowles
Prof Dr D Kroening
Mrs J Brooks Longworth
Dr S Mackenzie
Mrs S M McKimm
N P Record
Dr N P V Richardson
The Revd Canon K H Wilkinson
C G Young

Master: **T R Hands**, BA, AKC, DPhil

Usher: T G Beaumont, MA (*History*)

Teaching Staff:
* *Head of Department/Subject*

T W Allery, BA, Dip RCM (*Tutor to Choristers*)
Miss F J Amswych, BA (*SEN Coordinator*)
Ms S-J Arthurs, BSc (*Physics*)
Miss J C Attia, MA (*French*)
A Baker-Munton, MA (**Modern Languages*)
D S Barr, BA, MA (*English*)
D Bebbington, BSc, DPhil (**Cricket, Chemistry*)
Dr C L Bell, BSc, MPhil, DPhil (*Chemistry*)
T D Booth, MA (**Geography*)
N D Brittain, BA (*French, German*)
C J Boyle, BA (*PE, Games*)
J A Brown, MA (**Physics*)
M D Bull, BA (**Director of Sport*)
Dr J C Carter, MA, MA, MSt, DPhil (**Theology*)
B W Cole, MA (**Classics*)
A C Cooper, MSc, BA (*Professional Tutor, Mathematics*)
T P Cooper, BSc (*Head of Middle School, Mathematics*)
Dr A K Cotton, BA, MSt, DPhil (*Head of Upper School, Classics*)
J B Craven, BA (*Economics*)
J D Cullen, MA (**Director of Music*)
P A J De Freitas (*Cricket Professional*)
A C W Dixon, BA (**Learning Support, Geography*)

E Dupee, BSc (*PE, Games*)
D Dyer, BA (*Head of Junior School Sport*)
Mrs L D Earnshaw, MA (**Mathematics*)
Mrs B A Eldridge, BA, MBA (**Economics*)
Miss J A Ellis, GRSM, LRAM, MTC (*Head of Junior School Music*)
T J Elton, MMath (*Mathematics*)
A England, MA (*Deputy Head of Middle School, U4th, Mathematics*)
J N Eve, MA (**English*)
Ms N C C Ferguson, MA (*Deputy Head of Sixth Form, Pastoral, Modern Languages*)
Dr S Floate, BSc (*Chemistry*)
N J Fraser, MA (*Deputy Head, Academic, French*)
Mrs M-J Gago, BA (**Spanish*)
S Goggin, BSc (*Strength & Conditioning*)
Dr R Hamer, BA, DPhil (*Biology*)
Miss R Harding-Smith, BSc (*Waynflete Trainee, Biology*)
R Hemingway, BA (*Deputy Head of Middle School, *History*)
N J Hinze, BA (**Chemistry*)
Mrs A C S Kenyon, MA (*Classics*)
A I Kostyanovsky, BA (*Deputy Head of Sixth Form, Theology*)
Revd Dr Tess Kuin-Lawton, BA, MPhil, DPhil (*Chaplain, Theology*)
Mrs R E Lambert, BSc (*Head of Lower School, Biology*)
Miss S J Lapper, BSc (*PE*)
Mrs C A C Lewis, BA, MEng (*Mathematics*)
J A Lowe, BA (*Waynflete Trainee, English*)
P J McDonald, MA (*Deputy Head of Sixth Form, Classics*)
Dr K A McKee, BSc, PhD (*PSHCE Coordinator, Biology*)
Dr J Methven, DPhil (*Deputy Head of English*)
St J E J Mitchard, BA, MA (*Special Educational Needs*)
E Monaghan, BA (*Deputy Head of Sixth Form Monitoring, English*)
C E Newbury, BA (*Junior School Director of Studies*)
Y W Ooi, BA, BMBCh (*Medical Admissions Advisor*)
J C Otley, BA (**Art*)
S Pahl, BSc (*Physical Conditioning, Games*)
J K Panton, MSc, MPhil, DPhil (*History, *Politics*)
Mrs H C Parry, BSc (*Chemistry*)
L A Pearce, MA (*Mathematics*)
C Pearson, BSc, DPhil (**Biology*)
M Penton, BA (*Surmaster*)
Dr J C Petersen, BSc, PhD (*Physics*)
J F Place, BA (*Junior School*)
Mrs F J Pritchard, BA (*Deputy Head of Sixth Form Admissions, Art*)
R Pygott, MA (*Geography*)
Miss J A Reid, BSc (*Geography*)
Dr M H Rigby, MPhys, DPhil (*Physics*)
A Rush, BA (*Design and Technology*)
G L Seely, BA (**Rugby*)
B J Semmens, BSc (*Mathematics*)
D W Short, BA, MA (*Art*)
Miss S Shortland, BA (*Music*)
P A Shrimpton, MA, MEd, PhD (*Mathematics*)
T E Skipwith, BSc (*Head of Junior School*)
P D Smith, MA, LTCL (*Music*)
Mrs J A Soave, BA (*Junior School*)
S A Spowart, BA (*Classics*)
Mrs A Stammers, BA (*Junior School*)
Mrs H R Stammers, BA (*Theology*)
Mrs E Stapleton, BHum (*Deputy Head of Junior School*)
A D Thomas, BA (**Drama, History*)
J Unwin, BA (**Philosophy*)
T J M Vallance, BA (*Classics*)
Mrs J M Wade, BA (*Junior School*)
P S Walter, MPhil (*Mathematics*)
A Watts, BSc (**Hockey, *PE*)
J A Watts, BA (**Head of Examinations, *French*)
B White, BA (*Director of Studies, Mathematics*)

T R Williams, BA (*Head of Coach Education*)
Mrs C E Winstone, BA (*Junior School*)
M P Wood, BA (*Deputy Head of Sixth Form L6th, History, Politics*)

Assistant Music Staff:

Miss M Ackrill (*Flute*)	M R Jones (*Piano*)
Ms K Bailey (*Saxophone*)	P D Judge (*Trombone, Tuba*)
Dr E M Baird (*Violin*)	
Ms A Bendy (*Guitar*)	P Manhood (*Guitar*)
Mr C Britton (*Recorder*)	Miss E Mantle (*Singing*)
Ms E H Churcher (*Piano*)	D C McNaughton (*Trumpet*)
A Cole (*Trombone and Tuba*)	Ms V Murby (*Viola*)
R Cutting (*Trumpet*)	J Newell (*Organ*)
P B Davidson (*Drumkit*)	Ms H Parker (*Singing*)
B G Davies (*Singing*)	Mrs O Payne (*Piano*)
T Dawes (*Double Bass, Bass Guitar, Drums*)	T Payne (*Clarinet*)
R Edwards (*Piano*)	Mrs S Perkins (*Piano, Bassoon*)
Miss J A Ellis (*Violin*)	M Pickett (*Piano*)
K Fairbairn (*Percussion, Drums*)	W Purefoy (*Singing*)
Dr J Faultless (*Horn*)	B P Skipp (*Oboe*)
Miss S Goss (*Harp*)	B Twyford (*Drumkit*)
B J Hall (*Piano*)	Dr J P Whitworth (*Guitar*)
Ms E Harre (*Double Bass*)	S J Wilson (*Cello*)
	Mrs D J Wyatt (*Violin*)

Clerk to the Governors and Bursar: A J Pitchers

Master's PA: Mrs L D Beaumont

Registrar: Mrs S L Langdale, BA

History. William of Waynflete, born in 1398, rose from unexceptional social origins to become Bishop of Winchester and Lord Chancellor. Having been Headmaster of Winchester, school of the church, and Provost of Eton, school of the court, he determined to use his wealth to repay his debt to the transformative power of education. He determined to found something altogether new, a school of that exciting and rapidly expanding proposition – the university. This school would link primary, secondary and tertiary education in a novel way, and be named after his patron saint, Mary Magdalen.

Magdalen College School opened in 1480, and rapidly acquired an international reputation as a pioneer of new renaissance methods of learning. Early Masters included Thomas Wolsey, early pupils Richard Hooker, John Foxe, Thomas More and William Tyndale. The school, which from an early stage provided choristers for the College choir, was accommodated entirely in College until the late 19th century, when expanding numbers led to the acquisition and erection of buildings on the other side of the Cherwell, opposite the University Botanical Gardens and adjacent to St Hilda's College. Today's school still occupies this picturesque and privileged site.

Buildings. The school buildings include a Chapel and theatre, library, classrooms, science laboratories, Music School and art department. New science laboratories were opened in 1991 and totally refurbished in 2001. The expanded Junior School was opened in 1993, and new changing rooms and English department in 1996. New classrooms, lecture theatre, Careers Centre and a Sixth Form Centre were opened in September 1998. In June 2001, a £2m sports complex was opened. In 2002, additional science laboratories were provided as well as a new ICT centre. In 2005, the school opened its new Sir Basil Blackwell library. In Autumn 2008 a new building was opened which houses a modern refectory, Art and Design, Senior Common Room and reception. In 2010 a redesigned and enlarged Sixth Form Common Room was opened, to accommodate and welcome the first intake of Sixth Form girls. In 2012 the Sports Hall was extended to incorporate a studio and additional classrooms. A climbing wall has also been added.

Pastoral. From 7–11, boys are in form groups. Their form teacher is responsible for day-to-day care, pastoral welfare and academic progress. Boys from age 11 and Sixth Form girls are allocated to one of the six Houses. Houses are divided into seven Houserooms. A Housemaster or Tutor in charge of each section is responsible for the pastoral and academic welfare of pupils in his or her Houseroom. The Heads of Departments, SENCO, Chaplain and Matron also play their part in the pastoral organisation.

Organisation and Curriculum. All boys study a core of subjects to GCSE level, consisting of English, French, Maths and Science. In addition, there is a wide variety of options taken by pupils in their GCSE years including Latin and Greek, Geography, German, Spanish, History, Computing and Art. There is no streaming and very little setting.

Most pupils in the Sixth Form take 4 AS and 3 A2s, but a significant proportion take 4 or even 5 AS and A2 subjects.

Careers. There is a well-equipped Careers Room, and there is a team of Careers Staff. Careers Aptitude Tests are offered to all boys in the Fifth Form, and there is a weekly lecture in the Sixth Form.

Games and Societies. In addition to Physical Education which is taught in the curriculum, games play a major part in the School. Major sports are rugby in the Michaelmas Term, hockey and rowing in Hilary, and cricket, rowing and tennis in the Trinity Term. Other sports include basketball, football, fencing, cross-country, sailing and athletics. There are Army, Navy and Air Force sections of the CCF and a Community Service Organisation. Many pupils participate in the Duke of Edinburgh's Award Scheme. Girls from Oxford High School participate in the CCF.

The main playing field, surrounded by the River Cherwell, adjoins the grounds of School House and covers 11 acres. In addition, the school enjoys the daily use of the adjacent Christ Church playing fields, and also uses regularly a number of other university sporting and cultural facilities. An additional field of 13 acres with its own pavilion and changing rooms has been developed at Sandford-on-Thames, three miles from the school. The school also has use of the Magdalen College sports fields one mile from the School.

Music is extremely important in the school and there is a large Choral Society, a Madrigal Group, Senior and Junior Orchestras, a Jazz Band and other ensembles. Many pupils are involved in drama and there are several productions in the year. There are many other societies and clubs covering cultural and recreational activities. The main school concert is held annually in The Sheldonian Theatre. A summer Arts Festival began in 2009.

Admission. The main entry points are at 7, 9, 11, 13 and 16. Up to 20 boys are taken at 7, a further 20 or so at 9, and about 70 at the age of 11. Up to 25 boys are taken at 13. Around 30 boys and girls join the school directly into the Sixth Form.

Admission at ages 7, 9 and 11 is by a School Entrance Examination held in January or February each year.

Admission at age 13 is by the Common Entrance Examination for candidates at preparatory schools and by a School Entrance Examination held in March each year for candidates at maintained schools.

Offers of Sixth Form places are made after interview, and are conditional on good GCSE grades.

Candidates can be registered at any age. Full particulars can be obtained from the Registrar.

Term of Entry. Pupils enter the school in September. Exceptionally, for example if parents move into the Oxford area, other arrangements can be made.

Fees per term (2014–2015). Day pupils: £5,140 (aged 9–18); £4,950 (7 and 8 year olds). They are payable in advance and are inclusive of textbooks and stationery. The Registration Fee (non-returnable) is currently £75.

Scholarships, Exhibitions and Bursaries. Scholarships, Exhibitions and Governors' Presentation Awards are awarded at all points of entry.

A limited number of bursaries is available to boys of 7, 9, 11 and 13, awarded on a combination of academic merit and financial need. Ogden Trust Sixth Form Scholarships are available to candidates of sufficient merit from state schools.

At age 13, up to 16 Scholarships of up to £300, but capable of increase up to half fees in cases of need, are awarded each year on the results of a two-day scholarship examination in March. Candidates should be under 14 on the subsequent 1 September. Closing date for entries: 1 February.

Music, Art and Sports Scholarships are awarded each year on the results of assessments held in February (Music) or March (Art and Sports). Music award holders also receive free tuition in one instrument.

Further information can be obtained from the Registrar.

Choristerships. There are 16 Choristerships. Entry is by Voice Trial and candidates should normally be between the ages of 7 and 9. For a Chorister two-thirds of the tuition fee is remitted. All enquiries about Choristerships should be addressed to the *Informator Choristarum, Magdalen College, Oxford OX1 4AU.* Choristers normally continue at the school after their voices have broken. In deserving cases, further financial help may be available.

Honours. Almost all pupils go on to higher education when they leave. In the five years 2006–2010 inclusive 120 places have been gained at Oxford and Cambridge universities, and 277 places at other universities, from an average Sixth Form year group of 80.

Old Waynfletes. Representative Old Waynfletes of the 20th century include Olympic athlete and soldier, Noel Chavasse, VC and bar; bookseller Sir Basil Blackwell; Nobel Prize winner Sir Tim Hunt; composer Ivor Novello; educationalist Tom Wheare; theatre directors George Caird and Sam Mendes, and sports commentators Nigel Starmer Smith and Jim Rosenthal.

Secretary: M. Richardson, 110a Crescent Road, Temple Cowley, Oxford, OX4 2PD.

Charitable status. Magdalen College School Oxford Limited is a Registered Charity, number 295785. Its aims and objectives are to promote and provide for the education of children.

Malvern College

College Road, Malvern, Worcestershire WR14 3DF
Tel: 01684 581 500
Fax: 01684 581 617
email: enquiries@malverncollege.org.uk
website: www.malverncollege.org.uk

Motto: *Sapiens qui prospicit.* Wise is the one who looks ahead.

Malvern College was founded in 1865 and incorporated by Royal Charter in 1929. The College offers co-education from the age of 13 to 18. There are five girls' Houses and six boys' Houses, each of which takes boarding and day pupils. Malvern is a proper boarding school with the majority of its pupils in residence at weekends. It is associated with The Downs Malvern, a co-educational preparatory school for pupils aged 3 to 13 (*for further details, see IAPS entry*).

Ten members of the Council may be nominated, one each by the Lords-Lieutenant of the Counties of Gloucestershire, Herefordshire and Worcestershire, by the Vice-Chancellors of the Universities of Oxford, Cambridge and Birmingham, by the Service Boards of the Navy, Army and Air Force, and by the Headmaster and Teaching Staff. Ten members

are elected by the Governors, and between six and ten are appointed by the Council.

Council:
The Lord MacLaurin of Knebworth, DL (*Chairman*)
Mr G E Jones (*Vice Chairman*)
Mr R K Black (*Treasurer*)

Dr N Bampos	Ms J M Hampson
Mr S P Bennett	Mr J M J Havard
Mr P G Brough	Mr S M Hill
Mr W J Burke III	Professor P Jackson, FRSA
Mr P J Cartwright	Reverend K U Madden
Professor K J Davey, OBE	Mr D G Robertson
Mrs R Dawes, JP	Major General A Salmon,
Mrs M Edwards-Clark,	CMG, OBE, FRSA
MVO	Dr C W O Stoecker
Mr N Engert	Mr T D Straker, QC
Ms C Fairchild	Mrs J Thompstone
Mr F Francis	Mr R T H Wilson
Professor L Gullifer	

Clerk to the Council & Bursar: Mr G R H Ralphs

Headmaster: Mr A R Clark, MA Cantab

Senior Deputy Head: Dr R A Lister, BA, MTS, PhD
Deputy Head: Pastoral: Mrs S G Angus, MA
Deputy Head: Logistics: Mr P Godsland, MA
Deputy Head: Academic: Mr J A Gauci, BA

Heads of Department:
Art: Mr T M Newsholme, BA
Science, Biology: Mr C Hall, BSc, CBiol, MIBiol
Science, Chemistry: Dr N V Watson, BA, PhD
Drama: Mr K R C Packham, BA
Economics, Politics and Business Studies: Mr S C Holroyd, BA
English: Mr M Henderson, BA
Geography: Mrs J L Major, BSc
History: Mr J C Herod, MA
Life Skills and e-Safety Coordinator: Mrs S Godsland, BA
Mathematics: Mr C Thomas, BEng
Modern Languages: Mr P Godsland, MA
Music: Mr J M Brown, BMus
Sports (boys): Mr J D Cox, BSc
Sports (girls): Miss C A West, BSc
Science, Physics: Mr R N Willatt, MSc

Boarding Houses:
Mr J A O Russell, BSc, BA (*School House*)
Mr A J Wharton, BTh (*No.1*)
Mr J J W E Major, BA (*No.2*)
Mrs F C Packham, BSc (*No.3*)
Mrs A I Sharp, BA (*No.4*)
Mr T P Newman, BSc (*No.5*)
Mrs V E Young, BA (*No.6*)
Mr D J Eglin, BSc (*No.7*)
Mrs R Grundy, BMus (*No.8*)
Mr P Wickes, BSc (*No.9*)
Mrs E Brown, BA (*Ellerslie*)

Chaplain: The Revd A P Law, DipTh
Registrar: G Vosper-Brown

Malvern College is particularly fortunate in its location. Situated on the lower slopes of the Malvern Hills and close to the centre of Great Malvern, the main College campus commands striking eastward views across the Severn Valley towards the Cotswolds.

The school is justly proud of its high academic standards and the high level of pastoral care it provides. The College was rated 'Outstanding' by Ofsted in its 2010–11 report. In the Sixth Form about half study for the International Baccalaureate and half for A Levels, which gives pupils a real choice of subjects in each course of study.

Curriculum. In the Foundation Year (Year 9), pupils study a wide variety of subjects. In addition to English, Mathematics, all three Sciences, French, History, Religious Studies, Geography, Art, Drama, Design Technology and Music, nearly all are introduced to a second modern foreign language and most study Latin. All pupils study debating and creative ICT as well as Physical Education. The object of this year (as in co-curricular activities) is to show pupils as much as possible of what the College has to offer. On entering the Remove (Year 10), pupils choose their GCSE or IGCSE subjects, to be taken at the end of the Hundred (Year 11). The compulsory subjects are English, Mathematics and Double Award Science. Most pupils take French. The majority of the Remove (Year 10) take a short course GCSE in Religious Studies. Pupils also choose optional subjects from Art and Design, Design Technology, Drama, Geography, German, History, Latin, Music, Physical Education and Spanish. Greek is available for those who began it in the Foundation Year (Year 9). A Separate Sciences option enables pupils to extend the core Double Award Science to the three separate science IGCSEs. Pupils choose either three or four options, according to their academic ability. Pupils decide on their choices in consultation with their Tutors, Housemasters/Housemistresses, Heads of Year and parents.

In the Sixth Form, pupils can choose to study either A Levels or the International Baccalaureate. In the IB, combinations of the following subjects are offered: Visual Art, Biology, Chemistry, Economics, English, Environmental Systems and Societies, French, German, Geography, Greek, History, Italian, Latin, Mathematics, Further Mathematics, Music, Physics, Spanish, Technology, Theatre, Philosophy and Sport & Exercise Science. All pupils take the valuable Theory of Knowledge (ToK) Course. A Levels are available in all of the subjects listed above for the IB (except Environmental Systems and Societies and Italian) and also in Classical Civilisation, Photography, Politics and Physical Education. Pupils take four AS subjects in the Lower Sixth and most continue three subjects to A2 Level in the Upper Sixth. Level three BTEC Diploma in Sport is also available. Pupils studying AS Levels also choose, in addition, one option from the Enrichment Programme, which includes the Extended Project, an introduction to Psychology, GCSE Italian and History of Art.

Sport. Pupils are offered a range of sports throughout their time at Malvern College. Each term there is a focus on priority sports; for girls these are Hockey in the Autumn term, Netball in the Lent term and Tennis and Athletics in the summer. In addition to these, regular fixtures are offered for girls in Football, Cricket, Badminton, Golf, Fives and Cross Country. The boys' priority sports are Rugby in the Autumn term, Football in the Lent term, and Cricket in the summer. In addition to these, regular fixtures are offered for boys in Hockey, Tennis, Badminton, Golf, Cross Country, Athletics, Squash, Rackets, Basketball and Fives.

The co-curricular activity programme provides an extensive range of physical activity for pupils to engage in to develop their health, fitness, confidence and social skills.

Exceptionally talented pupils are invited to join the Elite Performer Programme, which comprises specialist strength and conditioning sessions and offers support with lifestyle management and progression through their sport performance pathway. We foster strong club links with clubs such as Worcestershire County Cricket Club, Worcester Warriors Rugby Club, Stourport Hockey Club and Challengers Netball Club.

A state-of-the-art Sports Complex includes a 25m swimming pool, a double sports hall (eight badminton courts), a shooting range, squash courts, fitness studio, climbing wall and fitness suite. The Sports Complex has a Cricket Centre which is the official training venue for Worcestershire County Cricket Club. The College has recently refurbished its two Rackets courts, which now offer Rackets facilities at equal tournament standard. In addition there are 10 hard court Tennis/Netball courts and Fives courts. In our extensive playing fields there is a Grandstand overlooking the athletics track, six football/rugby pitches and an all weather astro turf which hosts regular local club fixtures including the England Hockey Junior Development Centre. The Malvern Hills and Peachfield Common offer marvellously challenging terrain for the College's cross-country runners and mountain bikers.

Co-Curricular Activities. Pupils have the opportunity to take part in a range of additional activities such as sailing, trampolining, jewellery-making, volleyball, fencing, photography, golf, cookery, speech & drama, mountain-biking, canoeing, mixed martial arts, silversmithing, archery, and Zumba.

The College has a strong tradition of expedition training and outdoor pursuits, including rock-climbing, kayaking, paragliding and mountaineering (summer and winter, UK and abroad). Opportunities exist for the use of the College's cottage in the Brecon Beacons. Expeditions annually go to Scotland and have also recently been to Iceland, the Alps, Malta, Namibia and Costa Rica in the school holidays. Many of these activities are an integral part of the voluntary CCF (which has RM, Army and RAF sections) and The Duke of Edinburgh's Award Scheme. There is also a flourishing Community Service Volunteering Organisation.

Music is strong at Malvern. Over 35% of pupils learn a musical instrument and there are 9 musical ensembles including orchestras, concert band, jazz band and choirs. The well-equipped Music School (22 practice rooms, 3 large rehearsal rooms) includes a soundproofed practice pod for percussion and an IT suite. Attached to the Music School is St Edmund's Hall, a 150-seat recital hall with a fine Steinway piano. Pupils of all standards are encouraged both instrumentally and vocally, and regularly give performances (internal, locally and further afield). The Music Department works closely with the Drama Department and produces musicals, the most recent being *The Sound of Music* and *Oh What a Lovely War.*

Drama is a thriving creative force within the community of the school. Pupils are encouraged to play a full part in all aspects of theatre, whether as actor, stage manager, costume assistant or technician. This might be through academic study at GCSE, A Level or IB, participation in the annual House Drama Competition or the many co-curricular productions staged each year. Recent productions staged in the College's versatile and well-resourced 300-seat Theatre include *The Sound of Music, Oh What a Lovely War, Holes, The Government Inspector, A Midsummer Night's Dream, South Pacific, The Life and Adventures of Nicholas Nickleby, Les Misérables School Edition, Private Peaceful* and *Much Ado About Nothing.* Pupils have recently participated in the Shakespeare Schools Festival and are encouraged to audition for the National Youth Theatre in London. Speech and Drama tuition is a popular option for many, with pupils receiving preparation for LAMDA examinations or local public speaking festivals. Regular attendance at the Malvern Theatres in town is complemented by visits to Stratford, London and Bristol.

Art. The modern, purpose-built and spacious Arts Centre has outstanding facilities for Painting, Drawing, Printmaking (including Etching), Ceramics, Photography and 3-Dimensional Design. The standard of work produced is exceptionally high and work is displayed throughout the College.

Design and Technology. The well-equipped Design & Technology Centre ensures that pupils have the opportunity to develop their knowledge and skills through project work in this exciting subject. Facilities include Textiles Technology, Resistant Materials, Computer Aided Design and Manufacture including 3D Printing, Product Design, Architectural Design and Engineering.

Careers. In their GCSE year pupils take the ISCO/Futurewise New Generation on-line Morrisby careers guidance tests which assess ability, personality, aptitude and interests. An in-depth interview with an experienced ISCO careers advisor helps pupils to make sensible and informed choices about their future. A Careers Forum, organised jointly by the Careers Department and Parents' Society, takes place in January every year. All pupils in the Lower Sixth are encouraged to spend at least one week in the holidays on work experience. Pupils are given advice on choice of course at University (both UK and international) and help with their application by teachers in the Careers and Higher Education Department, and by their Sixth Form Tutor and Housemaster/Housemistress. Malvern College is a member of the Independent Schools Careers Organisation (ISCO).

Pastoral Care. In addition to their Housemaster/Housemistress and House Tutors, all pupils have a Form Tutor who shares the responsibility for their overall personal development and well-being. Members of the Sixth Form choose their own Tutor. There is also a full-time Chaplain (who is a member of the pastoral team in addition to the Senior Deputy Head, Deputy Head: Pastoral and Safeguarding Officer) and two Independent Listeners available by phone or email. In addition, pupils have access to school counsellors. Chapel Prefects and Peer Mentors also provide support.

Health Care. There is a modern and well-equipped Medical Centre staffed 24 hours a day by Registered Nurses.

Coaches. During the school year there are three half-term holidays and about five leave-out weekends. On these occasions, school coaches are run to Guildford, London Paddington and Birmingham airport, according to demand. A coach service to Heathrow airport runs at the start of half term and the end of term.

Admission. Most pupils are admitted between their thirteenth and fourteenth birthdays and may qualify for admission to the school by a satisfactory performance in the Common Entrance Examination or the annual Scholarship Examination. Pupils who wish to enter from schools which do not prepare pupils for Common Entrance are required to sit internal entrance tests in Maths, English and Science.

Pupils are also admitted to the Sixth Form at 16 on the basis of GCSEs/IGCSEs, interviews and entrance tests.

Application for admission should be made to the Registrar.

Scholarships. Malvern College offers a generous number of Scholarships and Exhibitions at 13+ each year, varying in value according to merit and financial circumstances up to 50% of the current fees. Candidates for all 13+ Scholarships must be under 14 years of age on 1st September in the year entry, but there is no age limit for Exhibitions. Scholarships and Exhibitions are offered for Academic potential, Art, Drama, Music, Sport and Design and Technology, as well as the Malvernian Society All-Rounder Award. Entries must be received three weeks before the examination. Entry forms are available from the Preparatory School or the Registrar at Malvern College. For academic scholarships, Malvern College offers the Common Academic Scholarship. Details and entry dates are available from the ISEB, the Preparatory School or Malvern College. Three Academic Scholarships are also awarded for the Sixth Form: an all-rounder academic award; a science award and an all-rounder award for a pupil from the state sector.

Further particulars may be obtained from the Registrar, Tel: 01684 581515, or email: registrar@malverncollege.org.uk.

Fees per term (2014–2015). Senior School: Boarding: £11,402–£11,801; Day £7,558.

An acceptance fee is payable 20 months before entry and is refunded as a deduction from the final account.

The Malvernian Society. On leaving, Malvernians retain contact with the College by joining the Malvernian Society. They also become members of the OM Club which organises various teams and a number of social functions. Secretary of the Malvernian Society: Syd Hill (Tel: 01684 581517).

Charitable status. Malvern College is a Registered Charity, number 527578. It is a charity established for the purpose of educating children.

The Manchester Grammar School

Old Hall Lane, Manchester M13 0XT
Tel: 0161 224 7201
Fax: 0161 257 2446
email: general@mgs.org
website: www.mgs.org
Twitter: @MGSMagic

Motto: *sapere aude* (*dare to be wise*)

The Manchester Grammar School was founded in 1515 to promote 'godliness and good learning' and it has endeavoured throughout its history to remain true to these principles, while adapting to changing times. It is now an independent boys' day school with around 1,500 pupils. Almost all leavers go on to university, about a third of them going to Oxford, Cambridge, London and US Ivy League Institutions. Over 150 qualified teaching staff provide all pupils with a broad, traditional curriculum and rich co-curricular opportunities.

The tradition of offering places to clever pupils regardless of their background is maintained by MGS bursaries. Over 250 pupils in the school are fee-assisted. Our pupils come both from primary and preparatory schools and represent a wide variety of cultural, ethnic and religious backgrounds.

Co-optative Governors:

J A Claughton	Mrs J Luca
J B Diggines (*Treasurer*)	Mrs C Bolton
B Dixon, CBE	J P Wainwright
P Geiger	E M Watkins, CBE
Professor T A Hinchliffe	(*Chairman*)
Ms J Kingsley	

Ex officio Governors:
The Dean of Manchester
The President of Corpus Christi College, Oxford
The Lord Mayor of Manchester

Representative Governors:
Manchester University: Dr T Westlake
Cambridge University: Professor D A Cardwell
Oxford University: Dr J R W Prag

Bursar and Clerk to the Governors: Mrs G M Batchelor, BSc

High Master: M A Boulton, BEng, PhD

Deputy High Master: P A M Thompson, BA, DPhil, MA Ed
Academic Deputy Head: N D Smith BA
Pastoral Deputy Head: A N Smith, BA
Surmaster & Head of Co-Curriculum: J W Mangnall, MA
Head of Junior School: Mrs L A Hamilton, BEd
Head of Lower School: Mrs S C James, BA
Head of Middle School: D Noble, BA
Head of Sixth Form: C P Thom, MA
Director of Development: S P Jones, BA
Assistant Head: S Foster, BA, MA
Proctor: S J Burch, BSc, PhD, MIBiol
Director of Admissions: M Strother, MA, MPhil
Director of Studies: D Jeys, BSc, MA

Academic Staff:
* *Head of Department/Subject*

[1] *Language Assistant*
[2] *Teaching Assistant*

Art & Design:
Mrs J Dobbs, BA, MA Ed
J Hargreaves, BA
[*Mrs L J Murphy, BA, MA]
Mrs J R M Shaw, BA
*Miss S Taylor, BA
M Tollitt, BA

Biology:
J Blair, BSc
Dr S J Burch, BSc, PhD, MSB
Dr S G Crawshaw, BSc, PhD
P W Freeman, BSc, MSc
Dr E Loh, BSc, MSc, PhD
Mrs N A Loughlin, BSc
Mrs C Morgan, BSc
M J Smedley, BSc, PhD
Miss B Taylor, BSc
*Miss A Wicking, BA

Chemistry:
T Ahmed, BSc
I Airth, BSc
*C Buckley, BSc
M Facchini, BSc, MSc
Dr S Graham, MSci, PhD
Mrs H M Hughes, BSc
Mrs T C James, BSc
Miss E J Lees, MChem, BSc
D Moss, MA
Miss F C Roberts, MChem
G M Tinker, MEng

Classics:
*Miss H L Eckhardt, MA
B S Edwards, MA
Miss F A Forsyth, MA
Dr P A M Thompson, BA, MA Ed, DPhil
Miss S J Whitehouse, BA
N G Williams, BA
Dr R G Williams, BA, DPhil

Computing:
*S J Duffy, BSc, MSB, CBiol

Drama:
S Abbs, BA
P N A Baylis, BA
Mrs K Hellier, BA
*M J Nichols, BA
Mrs J Sherratt, BA

Economics:
M G Coop, BSc, MSc
Miss H L Jones, BA
G J McSherry, BSc
*S R Molyneux, BA, MA, MBA
D Wilson, BA

Electronics:
*M S R Hesketh, BSc, MSc

English:
Mrs R E Adams, BA
R J L Geldard, BA, MA, MA

J C Gibb, MA
Mrs V E Horsfield, BA
Mrs S C James, BA
Miss A Lloyd-Hughes, BA
Miss L E Nelson, BA, MA
Miss C Shephard, BA, MA
B Townsend, BA
J N Tucker, BA, MA
*N Warrack, MA, MA
Miss J Welsh, BA, MA

General Science:
*D L Virr, BSc

Geography:
M D Corbett, BSc
Mrs A Curry, BSc
Miss P J Higgins, BSc
S P Jones, BA, MBA
J W Mangnall, MA
D Preston, MA, MSc
S P G Spratling, BA
Miss H Wallen, BSc
*P J Wheeler, BSc

History:
*Mrs E Carter, MA
G W H Harrison, BA, MA
R J M Hensman, BA, MA
A R T Hern, BA, MPhil, MPhil
D O Lacey, BA, MEd
Ms M A S Lowe, BA, MPhil
Dr S Orth, BA, MA, PhD
W B Pye, BA
A M Smith, MA
N D Smith, BA
M G P Strother, MA, MPhil
D M Taylor, BA

Junior School:
D Aden
Miss K V Atty, BA
Mrs D R Barnett, BEd
[2]Mrs C Burke, BSc, MSc
Mrs S M Callaghan, BA
[2]Dr T Campbell-Green, BA, MA, PhD
G Clayton, BSc
M Crewe-Read, BSc
Mrs S Gilmour, BSc
T Glennie, BA
*Mrs L A Hamilton, BEd
B A Hanson, BA
[2]R Hedley, BA
[2]Dr R Hockenhull, BSc, PhD
Mrs N Humphreys, BA
[2]Miss N Laajam, MEng
[2]Miss A Y Leigh, BEd
C B McAlister, BSc
[2]Miss L McNaught, BSc
Mrs H Mortimer, BSc, MEd
Mrs T C Neild, BA
[2]Mrs S Reed, BA
[2]Miss N Reynolds BSoc-Si
Mrs V Shingler, BA
[2]Mrs V J Tierney
Mrs J M Ward, BA
Mrs Z L Ward LLB

Miss J T Yuen, BA

Learning Support:
[2]Miss A Batchelor, BSc
*Mrs H Butchart, BA, LTCL
Mrs L Merlo, BA, MA
[2]Miss S Cocker
[2]Miss L I Ware, BA
[2]Miss R Williams, BA

Mathematics:
Mrs J Allinson, BA, MA
N T Burin, BSc, AFIMA
Dr J J Burke, BSc, PhD
Dr A P Burrows, BSc, PhD
Mrs A E Carolan, BSc
A R Davies, BSc, MSc
O P Glass, BSc
Dr A C Hunter, BSc, MSc, PhD
D Jeys, BSc, MA
I Z Khan, BSc
O W J Llewelyn-Smith, BSc
N J Matthews, BSc
G J Morris, BSc
D V Naughton MM
D Noble, BA
*T J Pattison, BSc, MIMA, CMath
Dr H G Read, BSc, PhD
Miss R L Sharkey, BA, MA
Mrs N M Williams, BSc, FRGS

Modern Languages:
E C F Cittanova, L-ès-L, M-ès-L, DEA
[1]Miss H Closa, MA
Mrs E R Dalton, L-ès-L
[1]Miss A Dietz
A P Dobson, BA, MA (*German)
[1]Miss S Fragagnano
Miss E A Garnett, BA
[1]Mrs I Kovtunenko, BA
*Mrs A V Hemsworth, BA (*Italian)
Miss A Jacinto, BA
C M Jarrett, BA, MA
Mrs O Kelly-Saltaleggio, BA
Mrs R Lan, BA, MA
Mrs D Minguito-Pantoja, BA
Mrs S J Paulson, BA
J C Reilly, BA MSt
[1]Miss M Robert
N J Sharples, BA, MA (*Spanish)

R W Simpson, BA (*French)
Mrs L Speed, Mosc Dipl
C P Thom, MA
Miss K J Tinslay, BA
[1]Miss S Vellisco
[1]Dr Y Zhang, PhD

Music:
G Blackwell
Mrs F A Bradley, BMus
Mrs H Butchart, BA, LTCL
*R M Carey, MA (*Director of Music*)
D E Francis, MusB, GRNCM, ARNCM, LRAM, LTCL, ATCL
Miss E M Shercliff, BA (*Junior School Music*)

Physical Education:
T A Grainger, BSc
G Heagerty, BSc
J L Leggett, BA
M J Roe, BSc
J H Shoard, MA
S Swindells
G Wilson
*M A Walmsley, BSc
S R Walsh

Physics:
Dr M A Boulton BEng, PhD
Ms S M Hewett, BSc
Dr P Holt, BSc, DPhil
*S J F Hunt, MA
R N Massey, BA
Dr D G McCormick, BSc, PhD
Mrs K S Michael, BSc
Dr D P Smith, MEng, PhD
Miss L Thewles, BSc

Politics:
S Foster, BA, MA
*R N Kelly, BA, MA, MPhil
Miss E C Kilheeney, BA, MA
D O Lacey, BA, MEd

Religion & Philosophy:
Mrs L J Anderson, BA
Mrs E L Bellieu, BA
*D Brown, BD, STM, MLitt
M P A Coffey, MA
D Farr, MA
A Greggs, BA
A N Smith, BA
Mrs J A Whittell, BA

Medical Officer: Dr J L Burn, FRCP, FRCPCH
PA to the High Master: Lorraine Coen
Admissions Office Manager: Kath Heathcote

Registration and Entry. Entry to the Junior School is considered at age 7, 8, 9 and 10, subject to availability at any stage during the academic year. Junior School pupils progress automatically to the Senior School. Entry for most other boys joining the School is at age 11, although entry at other ages is considered, subject to availability and applicants for Sixth Form entry are particularly welcomed. At all levels the normal assessment for entry involves prospective pupils spending a day in School, being taught and assessed in small groups. Alongside these assessment days, there is an entrance exam for entry at age 11. Sixth Form entrants have to meet GCSE grade requirements. Further details are available from the Admissions Office.

Fees per term (2014–2015). Tuition: £3,800.

Bursaries. The School offers means-tested bursaries of up to 100%. There are currently over 250 boys in receipt of financial support from the School and the majority receive full-fee support (the average fee support is currently 87%). The School does not offer academic scholarships.

Junior School. The Junior School opened in September 2008 in award-winning accommodation. It admits boys from age 7 and currently has 243 pupils. There is a strong focus in its curriculum on creativity, academic enrichment and skills-based learning. Specialist teachers from the Senior School contribute to the academic enrichment in Years 5 and 6.

Senior School Organisation and Curriculum. During the first two years the boys will study English, Mathematics, a modern foreign language (French, German, Spanish and Mandarin Chinese are offered), Classics (including Latin) History, Geography, General Science, Religious Studies, PSHE, Computing, Music, Art & Design, Drama, PE, Swimming and Games. Greek, Italian, Russian and Electronics are introduced as options in Year 9 and Classical Civilisation in Year 10. In Year 10 pupils may opt to study for an AS Extended Project Qualification. Pupils then proceed to make IGCSE/GCSE choices, typically taking ten subjects, including Mathematics, English, English Literature, a language and at least one science subject.

In the Sixth Form boys have a choice of studying either standalone subjects (A Levels, Pre-Us or International A Levels) or the International Baccalaureate; in addition, all students participate in the School's own non-examined enrichment programme, which includes a philosophical and critical thinking course (Perspectives).

Pastoral Care. Each form in the school is looked after by a Tutor, who is responsible, with the appropriate senior members of staff, for the academic and general progress of each pupil. In the Senior School Tutors work with no more than 12 boys. Regular written reports are supplemented by Parents' Evenings. The School Medical Room is staffed by a part-time doctor and two full-time Nursing staff. The older pupils selected as prefects are encouraged to help younger pupils in running societies and other co-curricular activities.

Creative Arts. All pupils experience Music, Art & Design and Drama within the curriculum; in addition, each of these areas offers activities to large numbers of pupils during the lunch-hour and after school. There are choirs, orchestras and instrumental tuition; plays, drama workshops and musicals; clubs for art, pottery, and computer design. There are regular exhibitions and public performances both in school and in public venues. A drama development including a new Theatre and studio opened in summer 2010.

Sport. All boys take part in timetabled games and the school produces successful teams in most sports. There is a gymnasium and an indoor swimming pool. A new sports hall will open in 2015. The choice of sport increases with age to include rowing, climbing and golf in addition to mainstream sports.

Outdoor Pursuits. The school has a long tradition of camping and trekking and there are numerous weekend and holiday excursions. The school is the largest centre for the Duke of Edinburgh's Award in the North West. Four annual camps cater for the full age range and offer a wide choice of activities. In recent years expeditions have visited the Alps, the Pyrenees, Morocco and Scandinavia. The school has two centres in Cumbria and one in Derbyshire.

Foreign Visits. Many trips abroad are organised each year, providing enjoyable holidays of broad educational value. Destinations include France, Germany, Spain, Russia, Italy, Greece, Mexico, Argentina, Peru, Mexico, Egypt, Tunisia, South Africa, India and China.

Societies and Activities. There are over 200 clubs, societies and activities catering for a variety of interests, including Chess and Bridge Clubs, and a school newspaper produced by pupils. The school is active in charitable fundraising and has a very extensive community action programme, including projects in Manchester and Salford as well as in Uganda.

Prizes and Scholarships. In addition to bursaries, funds are provided for grants to help deserving pupils with the expense of a range of co-curricular activities. Prizes are awarded in all subjects in the curriculum.

Old Mancunians' Association and MGS Parents' Society. The Old Boys' Association has many regional sections. There is an annual Old Boys' Dinner in Manchester. The Development Office Secretary is Mrs Jane Graham who can be reached at the School.

The MGS Parents' Society has a membership of parents and friends and exists to support school activities and promote a programme of social events.

Charitable status. The Manchester Grammar School is a Registered Charity which provides Public Benefit. The aim of the School is to prepare able boys from the Manchester area, regardless of their financial background, to proceed to university and make a positive contribution to society in their adult life.

Marlborough College

Marlborough, Wiltshire SN8 1PA

Tel:	Main Switchboard: 01672 892200
	The Master's Office: 01672 892400
	The Bursary: 01672 892390
	Admissions: 01672 892300
Fax:	Main No: 01672 892207
	The Master's Office: 01672 892407
email:	master@marlboroughcollege.org
	admissions@marlboroughcollege.org
website:	www.marlboroughcollege.org
Twitter:	@marlboroughcol

Founded 1843. Incorporated by Royal Charter.

Visitor: The Most Revd The Lord Archbishop of Canterbury

Council:
President: The Rt Revd The Lord Bishop of Salisbury
The Right Hon The Lord Malloch-Brown, KCMG, PC (*Chairman*)
Major General A S Ritchie, CBE
I D Coull
J P Hornby
A C V Evans
P J Manser, CBE, DL
The Revd Rachel Weir
Ms S Hamilton-Fairley
J K Baker (*Chairman, Finance Committee*)
T D P Kirkwood
C H Pymont, QC
Dr T E Long
S M W Bishop

Master: J Leigh, MA Corpus Christi College Cambridge, FRSA

Second Master: Dr C C Stevens, MA, DPhil
Deputy Master & Director of Corporate Resources: P N Bryan, BA, ACA
Deputy Head (Academic): J M Barot, MA, MSc
Director of Co-curricular Activities: Mrs D J Harris, MA
Senior Admissions Tutor: Dr N G Hamilton, BA, PhD
Head of Boarding: Lady Cayley, MA
Director of Development: J N Copp, BEd

Assistant Staff:

* *Head of Department*
† *Housemasters/Housemistresses*

P R Adams, BEd (**Design and Technology*)
D Allen, MA
Miss N L Allen, BSc
N M Allott, BSc
D I Andrew, MA, Msci (**Economics & Business Studies*)
A J Arkwright, BA
D R Armitage, MA
M Baldrey, BMus, FTCL
C E Barclay, BSc, FRAS, FRSA (*Director of the Observatory, Director of EPQ*)
Miss K M Bennett, MSc (**Director of Sport*)
T A Birkill, BSc
M B Blossom, MA (*Medawar Centre)
N E Briers, BEd
A J Brown, MA (*Modern Languages)
Mrs R L T Bruce, BA
M P L Bush, BA
Miss A H Cairns, MSt
Mrs B L Callender, BEd
J P Carroll, BEd (†*B House*)
Mrs M E Clarke, MA
S C Clayton, BA (*Form Coordinator*)
R A Cockett, MA (**German, Director of Cultural & Global Awareness*)
M Conlen, BSc (†*Cotton House*)
Mrs H A M Cox, BSc (†*Elmhurst*)
D P T Curry, BSc
Mr M E Dalzell, BSc
Miss J Darby, BA, GMus
Miss V G M Delalleau, BA
S M D Dempster, BA (†*C3*)
S J Dennis, MBE, MSc
Revd J G W Dickie, MA, BLitt (**Acting Religious Studies*)
J P W Dixon, MA (*History)
Dr G A Doyle, BSc, MSc, PhD, DIC, CChem, MRSC (*Science)
P T Dukes, FGSM, ARAM (**Artistic Director*)
Mr J J Duplock, MA
A S Eales, BMus
S J Ellis, BSc
P A Finn, BA
Mrs S A, Finn, BA
Mrs A J Finn, MSc (* *Mathematics*)
Dr S D Flatres, MSci, PhD
P G M Ford, MA
Mrs L F W Ford, MA (*English)
Mrs J L Fruci, BA
T J Gibbon, MA (*Spanish)
B W Giles, MA
A Gist, MA (*IB Coordinator*)
N O P Gordon, MA
M A Gow, BA (*Politics)
Mrs C E Green, MA Ed
C L Harrison, BSc
P A J Hodgkinson, BA (*Choirmaster*)
Mrs J Hodgson, BA (†*Morris House*)
J A Hodgson, BSc
Mrs R F Horton, MA (†*Mill Mead*)
Mrs V R Jhakal, MA
H E B Jones, BA
P N Keighley, BEng
Mrs A L Keighley, BA (†*Ivy House*)
D Kenworthy, BA, MFA (*Drama)
T A Kiggell, MA
Mrs K J Kiggell, MA
G D M Lane, BSc
Mrs J E Lane, BSc
Miss A C Langdale, MSc
T C M Lauze, BA (*Director of Teaching & Learning*)

Mrs D L Lilley, MA
J F Lloyd, BA, MPhil (*Classics)
Dr G M Longley, MA, MSt, DPhil
J J Lyon Taylor, BSc (†*Littlefield*)
Miss E K Mackintosh, MA
G I Macmillan, BA, (†*Turner House*)
D J Madden, BEng
G F Mavor, BA
T G R Marvin, MA (†*Preshute*)
Mrs J McClean, BA
Mrs J McFarland, BSc
Dr F S McKeown, BA, PhD (*History of Art)
M McNally, BSc
G J McSkimming, BSc
B H Miller, BSc (†*C1*)
W J Molyneux, BA
N J L Moore, MA (†*Barton Hill*)
Mrs R D Moore, BSc
Ms L M Morey, MA
P N Morley-Fletcher, BA (*French)
N Nelson-Piercy, BA (*Russian)
W D L Nicholas, BEng, MSc (†*Summerfield*)
E G Nobes, MA (*Careers)
P J O'Sullivan, BA
Mrs C E Page, MA (**Learning Support & Study Skills*)
J H Parnham, MA (*Art)
Mrs A E Paterson, MA
A S Pembleton, BSc
Mrs C N Pembroke, BA
G R Playfair, MA (†*C2*)
Dr M J Ponsford, BA, PhD
S G Quinn, BSc
Miss R L Randle, MGeog, FRGS
K J D Richards, MA (*Geography)
Dr L J Richards, BSc, PhD (*Biology)
Dr D G Roberts, MSc, PhD (*Physics)
Mrs E J Ross, MA
Dr E Ryder, BSc, PhD
R A Sandall, BCom, BA
Mrs R Scott, MA
Miss H M Scott, BSc, ICAS
G B Shearn, BSc (*ICT)
Mrs S Shearn, BEd († *New Court*)
C S Smith, BEng, MSc
Mrs E C Smith, BA
K G A Smith, BA
Miss L K Smith, BSc
C O Stewart, MA
V J Stokes, BA
Dr J P Swift, BSc, PhD
Mrs E J V Thomas, BA
H L R Tilney, BA
R Tong (*OA Coordinator*)
Miss C Toomer, GGSM
Miss M C von Weissenberg, BA
Mrs C A Walsh, BSc (*Chemistry)
I A Wilkins, MFA
R D Willmett, BA
Mrs B S Wingfield-Digby, BA
Mrs A T Woodford, BA (**Italian,* **Oxbridge Coordinator*)
M A Worsley, LLB
Mrs A Worsley, BSc
Mr J Wright, BSc

Senior Chaplain: The Revd Dr D Campbell, MTh
Medical Officers:
Dr R W Hook, MB BS, MRCGP, DRCOG
Dr S Hanson, MB BS, MRCGP, DCH
Librarian: Mrs L Pilkington, MSc
Master's Assistant: Mrs S Nicholas

The College is fully co-educational and there are 927 boys and girls in the 15 Houses of whom 892 board. The normal age of entry is either 13 or 16.

Registration. For entry to the College at 13+ registrations are accepted no earlier than four years before entry. Registrations for entry at 16+ are accepted at any time. The College assesses all applicants 20 months ahead of entry and offers places accordingly. After this date a small number of able candidates may still win a place in the College by being accepted onto the Master's List. All applicants to the College must meet our entry criteria and take either the Academic Scholarship or the Common Entrance examination. Please see our website for details of this policy: www.marlboroughcollege.org. The 13+ Scholarship examination is in March of the year of entry and the Sixth Form Scholarship examination is in the November before entry.

Scholarships. All Awards enable those with a financial need to receive bursarial assistance with the fees. The degree of support given will be subject to a means test. Candidates for entry in the Shell (Year 9) must be under 14 on 1st September. The closing date for entries is late January of Year 8. There are up to 16 academic scholarships at 13+ and a further 22 Awards in Music, Art, Design and Sport. There are also William Morris All Rounder Awards based upon strengths in academic work, sport, art, drama or music. Up to twenty awards are made at Sixth Form entry. From time to time there are a number of other special categories of scholarship based upon parental occupation and particular abilities. The College offers a limited number of Foundation (Clergy) places and Armed Services closed scholarships.

A Scholarship Prospectus and copies of past papers may be obtained from the Admissions Office. Applications and enquiries about entries and scholarships should be addressed to The Senior Admissions Tutor, tel: 01672 892300; email: admissions@marlboroughcollege.org.

Academic. The College's curriculum follows and extends the National Curriculum to allow for a proper combination of breadth and specialisation. It is designed to stimulate, challenge and support all pupils and to ensure that they maximise their potential. There is a clear focus placed upon success in public examinations, where standards are very high, but the College also takes seriously its responsibility in preparing pupils to succeed at university and in their subsequent career.

Almost all pupils go on to study at university either in the United Kingdom (currently 85% annually to Russell Group universities) or, increasingly, overseas with destinations ranging from North America to Europe and the Middle East.

In the Lower School a wide-ranging curriculum is followed with choices made at the end of the Shell (year 9) leading to ten or more (I)GCSEs. In the Sixth Form, pupils have the ability to choose amongst subjects offered by twenty-nine different departments, following either the British Curriculum (with a mixture of A levels and Pre-U courses) or the International Baccalaureate Diploma Programme.

The curriculum is supported by a wide-range of academic extension and enrichment activities through societies, lectures, theatre trips, museum and gallery visits, debates, poetry readings, conference and concerts, creating a full co-curriculum which recognises that qualifications alone do not produce an educated person.

Universities & Careers. Nearly all pupils who come to Marlborough go on into the Sixth Form and virtually all proceed to degree courses. The well-resourced Guidance Department is located at the heart of the College and assists Housemasters and Housemistresses in advising boys and girls and their parents about Sixth Form subject selection, higher education options, gap year projects, work experience and careers.

Co-Curricular. Sports facilities are outstanding. There are two brand new floodlit astro-turf pitches, acres of sports pitches, a tartan athletics track and numerous tennis and netball courts. The main sports for boys are rugby, hockey, cricket, football, athletics and tennis and for girls are hockey, netball, tennis, lacrosse and athletics. Alternative sports include aerobics, badminton, basketball, beagling, clay pigeon shooting, fencing, yoga, zumba, rackets, rugby sevens, fives (Rugby & Eton), shooting, squash, swimming and water-polo.

There is a strong Outdoor Activities Department which offers the Duke of Edinburgh's Award (Bronze & Gold), canoeing, climbing, kayaking, mountain biking and sub-aqua. The annual Devizes to Westminster kayak race has become a feature of the Lent Term for up to 10 Upper School crews. There are numerous OA physical and social activities each Sunday in term-time in House groups and more adventurous trips further afield in the school holidays. Recent destinations include the Brecon Beacons, Snowdonia, The Swiss Alps and Peru.

The College's Combined Cadet Force is thriving. It is compulsory in Year 10 and optional thereafter. It provides excellent leadership training and there is a strong record of College pupils winning Sixth Form Army Scholarships. All year-groups take part in Field Days or CCF Camps both in the UK and abroad.

The College also offers a comprehensive Outreach Programme in the local community. The mantra "with privilege comes responsibility" is the underlying philosophy. Many of the pupils are involved with local primary schools, a special school and care homes for the elderly. The College has a link with Swindon Academy which involves College staff and pupils providing academic support. Swindon Academy pupils also attend some themed residential weekends at the College. There is also a burgeoning partnership with Pewsey Vale School.

The College has a huge array of thriving academic and intellectual societies which complement and support the academic programme. The College attracts an impressive array of speakers each term.

Music. Music at Marlborough plays an essential part in the cultural life of the College.

Based in the state-of-the art, purpose-built Henry Hony Centre, the Department is home to some 40 music scholars and with over 55% of pupils taking instrumental lessons. The major groups are Chapel and Chamber Choir, Symphony Orchestra, Chamber Orchestra and Senior Wind Orchestra. Unique to Marlborough is the College's professional orchestra in partnership, London's Southbank Sinfonia.

Drama. Drama at Marlborough is all about collaboration, creative debate, experimentation and excellence. With an average of sixteen productions a year diversity of style is at the heart of what we offer; from contemporary productions of classical tragedy to musicals and farcical comedy. Independent productions give the opportunity for pupils to write, direct and produce, working alongside visiting practitioners and influenced by the wide range of touring productions that visit our three well-equipped theatres. Drama is offered as an option in the Shell (Year 9) and is popular at GCSE, A level and IB.

Art and Design. The Art Department is a vibrant, inspirational and engaging creative environment, where every pupil's individuality, visual literacy and potential to fully realize their artistic ambitions is highly valued. All pupils study Art in their first year and many go on to take the subject at GCSE, A level or the IB. Pupils may specialize in Fine Art or Photography at A level.

The purpose-built Art School houses painting, drawing, relief and intaglio printmaking studios, a photography darkroom, lecture room and an IT suite within the main building. In addition, there is a well-resourced art library. Two annex buildings accommodate ceramic workshops, the Mount House Gallery and an Apple Mac digital editing and animation suite.

There is also a purpose-built Design and Technology Centre.

Fees per term (2014–2015). £11,030 Boarding; £9,375 Day Pupils.

The Marlburian Club. www.marlburianclub.org

Charitable status. Marlborough College is a Registered Charity, number 309486 incorporated by Royal Charter to provide education.

Merchant Taylors' Boys' School Crosby

186 Liverpool Road, Crosby, Liverpool L23 0QP
Tel: 0151 928 3308 (General Enquiries)
           0151 949 9323 (Headmaster)
           0151 949 9326 (Bursar)
           0151 949 9333 (Admissions Office)
Fax: 0151 949 9300
email: infomtbs@merchanttaylors.com
website: www.merchanttaylors.com
Twitter: @MerchantsCrosby
Facebook: /merchanttaylorscrosby

Motto: *Concordia parvae res crescunt – Small things grow in harmony*

The Boys' School was founded in 1620 by John Harrison, Citizen and Merchant Taylor of London. In 1878 the School was transferred to its present site where it is now housed beneath the iconic red brick clock tower.

Governors:
Chairman: Prof P W J Batey, BSc, MCD, PhD, CGeog, FRTPI, FRSA, AcSS
P G Magill, MSc, FCIPD
Mr R J Walker, CEng, MIMechE
Miss A Dobie, BA Hons
Mr S Wilkinson, BA Hons, FCA
Mr D S Evans, MA Oxon
Mrs J L Hawkins, RGN, SCM
Ms L Martin Wright
Dr J Fox, MBCh Birm, DRCOG, MRCGP
Mr J Sutcliffe, BEng Hons, CEng, MICE, MRICS, MCIOB
Mrs B Bell, LLB Hons, FCILT, FRSA

Bursar and Clerk to the Governors: Mrs A Pope, BA Hons, FCMA, ACIS, MCSI

Headmaster: David Cook, BA, MA

Deputy Headmasters:
R A Simpson, MA
D Williams, BSc

Head of Sixth Form: J P Farrell, BSc, MA
Head of Middle School: S G Fletcher, BSc, MSc
Head of Lower School: N A Hunt, BA
Assistant Headmaster Operations: J B Green, BA
Head of Pastoral Care: J E Turner, BA, MA
Director of Music: D Holroyd, GMus RNCM, PPRNCM, ARCO
Emeritus Chaplain: Revd D A Smith, BA

Teachers:
* *Head of Department*

Art:
Miss B Baker, BA Hons
*P R Spears, BA Hons

Biology:
*G Bonfante, BSc
Miss J M Whitehead, BSc
Mrs R J Wright, BSc
R Yates, BSc

Careers:
Mrs V Mee, BA Hons

Chemistry:
*Dr I M Buschmann, DipChem, MSc, PhD
Mrs A C Byrne, BSc
Dr C M Clay, MChem, PhD
Dr S J Hardy, BSc, PhD

Classics:
Dr J Dixon, BA Hons, MA, PhD
P A Lally, BA Hons
*Mrs S Rohrer, BA Hons

Cookery:
Mrs M Molloy

Design Technology:
Miss A Evans, BA Hons
P A Irvine, BEd
*I Taylor, BEd, MA

Economics:
J P Farrell, BSc Hons, MA
*S J Kay, BSc Hons

English and Drama:
Mrs M Casaus, MA
*Dr J S Gill, BA Hons, MPhil, PhD
R A Simpson, BA Hons, MA
M Stanley, BA Hons, MA
Mrs K E Plummer, BA Hons

Geography:
*Miss R Clint, BA Hons
J Green, BA Hons
N A Hunt, BA Hons
J E Turner, BA, MA, DipC

History:
*J C Heap, BA Hons
Dr N Myers, BA Hons, PhD
S P Sutcliffe, BA Hons, MA
Miss C Thomas, BA Hons

ICT:
*Mrs S Rowell, BSc Hons

Learning Support:
Mrs A O'Brien, BA Hons
Mrs A Edwards, BA Hons
*Mrs P Lewinska, BA Hons

Library:
Mrs E Rea, BA Hons, MCLIP

Duke of Edinburgh's Award Manager:
M Slemen, BEd, Dip PE

Junior School:
Head: Mrs J E Thomas, BEd, MEd, NPQH
Deputy Head, Pastoral: D K J Youngson, BA Hons
Deputy Head, Academic: Mrs Y Bonfante, BEd
PA to the Headmistress: Mrs A Hodson

N Benbow, BA Hons
Mrs Y Bonfante, BEd
Miss C Fraser, BA Hons
Mrs P Graham, Dip Tch Asst
Miss R Hargreaves

D I Lyon, MA
J O'Shaughnessy, BA Hons
Mrs L Rogers, BEd
P A Wardle, BEd
Mrs H White, BA Hons
Mrs A Wynne, BEd

Admissions: Mrs P Saffer
PA to the Headmaster: Mrs M Delaney / Mrs S Maitland

Mathematics:
A G Heap, BSc, MSc
Mrs C Hobbs, BA Hons
Mrs C Hunt, BSc
Mrs J R Marshall, BA Hons
W K Miles, BSc
J O'Brien, BSc
*Mrs E C Peacock, BA Hons

Modern Foreign Languages:
Mrs S A Dunning, BA Hons
F J Rubia Castro, BA Hons
S G Fletcher, BSc, MSc
*P E Howard, BSc
Miss A Nielsen, BEd
A Scott, BA Hons
T Strack, BA Hons

Music:
*D Holroyd, GMus Hons RNCM, PPRNCM, ARCO
R Richardson, BA Hons

Physical Education:
J Carew, Level 2 in Coaching Rowing
S Cooke, BSc
D W King, BA Hons
*I D McKie, CertEd
G T Stiff, BA Hons
M Whalley, ASA CC L3, ASA Swimming L2, NRTSTC

Physics:
*P J Cooper, BSc
M Toney, BSc
Dr A J Patchett, BSc, PhD
Miss M Liang, BSc

Religious Studies:
*R M Fawcett, BEd

The Senior Boys' School is attended by over 550 boys aged eleven to eighteen, 158 of whom are in the Sixth Form. There is also a Junior Boys' School with 145 boys aged between seven and eleven.

The school has a reputation for academic excellence and the majority of our leavers go on to study at Russell Group universities including Oxford and Cambridge. The emphasis throughout is very much on developing learners who are able to work independently and who have a genuine curiosity in their studies.

Curriculum. In the first three years of the Lower School boys study a wide variety of national curriculum subjects including separate sciences as well as the opportunity to pick up extra modern and ancient languages. They gradually specialise in the Middle School where there is the flexibility to study between 8 and 11 GCSEs including an accelerated IGCSE mathematics course. There is an additional timetabled Friday afternoon in Years 7–9 for enrichment activities. The Gifted and Talented extension programme offers practical lessons in beekeeping, skateboard design, shooting, fencing, ceramics, journalism and many others.

In the Sixth Form the following subjects are available at A Level: Mathematics, Further Mathematics, Physics, Chemistry, Biology, Latin, Greek, Classical Civilisation, English Language, English Literature, History, Geography, Economics, French, German, Spanish, Design and Technology, Art & Design, Music, Theatre Studies and Physical Education. In addition, students in the Sixth Form will have an opportunity to follow a course in General Studies.

Games. Facilities include a brand new sports centre with climbing wall, fitness suite, sports hall and dance studio. There is a heated indoor swimming pool on site, extensive playing fields, cricket nets, a share of Northern Club's facilities and three tennis courts.

Games played are Rugby, Hockey, Cricket, Athletics, Rowing, Football, Swimming, Tennis and Cross-Country. All boys are encouraged to try at least one of the many games options available during their time at school.

School Societies. A wide range of activities and interests is covered by School Societies.

Music and Drama. About 200 boys receive weekly instrumental tuition and there is a subsidised scheme for beginners on orchestral instruments. There is a School Choral Society, Junior School Choir, Concert Band, Swing Band, a Chamber Orchestra along with various woodwind and brass ensembles. Boys regularly perform both in and out of School at a variety of events and are given many opportunities to perform publicly.

There are two full-time teachers, plus a team of visiting specialist instrument teachers. There are links in Music with our sister school, Merchant Taylors' Girls' School. There are also close links with the Girls' School in Drama, which now forms an integral part of the Senior School curriculum as well as being a major extra-curricular activity.

Combined Cadet Force. The School has a voluntary contingent of the Combined Cadet Force with Royal Navy, Army and Royal Air Force Sections. Activities include mountaineering, camping, sailing, flying and shooting, and there is the opportunity to attend a variety of camps and courses, both in Great Britain and overseas. There are around 250 members of the CCF, many of whom are girls from our sister school.

Admission. Boys are admitted to the Junior School at age 7 and to the Senior School at 11, 13 or at Sixth Form. Some Assisted Places are available at 11.

Fees per term (2014–2015). Tuition: Senior School £3,508, Junior School £2,623.

Old Boys. There is an active Old Boys' Association (The Old Crosbeians) whose Secretary may be contacted via the School and from whom a handbook/register may be obtained (please email Miss Kate Thomas in our Development Office if you wish to get in contact: k.thomas@merchanttaylors.com). The OBA is a lively and sociable association which organises events up and down the country throughout the year.

Charitable status. The Merchant Taylors' Schools Crosby is a Registered Charity, number 1125485, and a Company Limited by Guarantee, registered in England, number 6654276. Registered Office: Liverpool Road, Crosby, Liverpool L23 0QP.

Merchant Taylors' School

Sandy Lodge, Northwood, Middlesex HA6 2HT

Tel: Head Master's PA: 01923 821850
Reception: 01923 820644
Admissions Officer: 01923 845514
Bursar: 01923 825669
Fax: 01923 845522
email: info@mtsn.org.uk
website: www.mtsn.org.uk
Twitter: @MerchantTaylors
Facebook: /MerchantTaylors
LinkedIn: Thomas White

Motto: *Concordia parvae res crescunt*

The Governors of the School:
Chairman: C P Hare

R J Brooman	Mrs S Morgan
M C Clarke	A J Moss
Dr J M Cox	D J Shah
D G M Eggar	Dr J H S Sichel
Ms L Gadd	R-J Temmink
R C G Gillott	Sir M Tomlinson
D Haria	

Head Master: S J Everson, MA

Second Master: Dr T R Stubbs, BSc, PhD, CBiol, MSB
Senior Master: C R Evans-Evans, BA, MEd, NPQH
Director of Studies: B J C Horan, MA
Deputy Head, Communications: C E Roseblade, BA
Deputy Head, Information Services: Dr A R H Clarke, MA, DPhil, CPhys, MInstP
Registrar: J G Taylor, MA
Bursar: I D Williams, MBA, CMgr, FCMI, MAPM, MCIL
Development Director: N J Latham, LLB Law

Head of Upper School: M C Husbands, MA
Head of Middle School: T W Jenkin, MA
Head of Lower School: T C H Greenaway, BSc
Chaplain: The Reverend D M Bond, BA, BTh

Assistant Staff:

Art & Design:
Ms I Lumsden, BA (*Head of Art and Design*)
Miss H C Blowes, BA (*Head of Community Service and Charities*)
S N Leech, BA
J T Ramsay, MA (*Head of White House*)

Biology:
Dr J H Cocker, MA, PhD (*Head of Biology*)
C W Gray, BSc
T C H Greenaway, BSc (*Head of Lower School*)
Mrs L Pruden-Lawson, MA (*Head of Mulcaster House*)
Dr B J Stallwood, PhD
Dr T R Stubbs, BSc, PhD, CBiol, MSB (*Second Master*)

Chemistry:
T J Hingston, MChem (*Head of Chemistry*)
R I M Alexander, BSc (*Head of Hockey and teacher of Academic PE and Chemistry*)
J E L Coote, MA
A J W Horrox, MA (*Pastoral/Activities Auditor*)
Dr M Lomas, PhD
M P Powell, MA (*Assistant Head of Upper School*)
Mrs F A Rashid, BSc (*Head of Science*)

Classics:
P D Harrison, MA (*Head of Classics, SCR Representative – Governing Body*)
M F Drury, MA
J A Eales, BA

Mrs C D Fielding, BA (*Staff Tutor*)
M C Husbands, MA (*Head of Upper School*)

Computing:
G N Macleod, BA (*Head of Academic Computing*)
C P Hirst, BSc, MA (*Head of IT Development, SCR President*)
S J Coles, BSc (*and Mathematics*)

Design & Technology:
G M Stephenson, BSc (*Head of Design and Technology*)
A S Bannister, BSc
J B Coleman, CertEd, MA (*Head of External Relations*)
N J Kyriacou, BEd (*Assistant Head of Middle School*)

Drama and Theatre Studies:
D D Garnett, BA (*Director of Drama*)
Mrs K Shockley, BA (*Second in English*)
J D Manley, MA
C E Roseblade, BA (*Deputy Head, Communications*)

Economics & Politics:
C Chong, MA, MPhil (*Head of Economics & Politics*)
M I Beacham, BA, MSc
Mrs H V Butland, MA (*Joint Oxbridge/Enrichment Coordinator, subject leader for Politics*)
E P James, BA
Miss A C Thornton, MA

English:
D A Lawrence, MA (*Head of English*)
Mrs H L Barnes, BA
P M Capel, BA (*Learning Support Coordinator*)
Mrs J M Cox, BA
S J Everson, MA (*Head Master*)
T W Jenkin, MA (*Head of Middle School*)
J D Manley, MA
I J Mitchell, BA, BSc (*Head of Psychology*)
S J Morris, BA (*Independent Study Coordinator*)
C E Roseblade, BA (*Deputy Head, Communications*)
Mrs K Shockley, BA (*Second in English*)
Ms L V Smith, MA
J H Tyler, MA (*Head of Spenser*)

Geography:
Mrs S A Riddleston, BA (*Head of Geography*)
Miss M J Clarke, BA (*Head of Hilles House*)
J D Innes, BA (*Head of CCF Army Section*)
H B Phillips, BSc (*Head of Andrewes House*)
B A Rigby, BSc
M J Shaw, BSc (*Head of PSHCE*)
D L L Vanstone, BA

History:
R J Try, BA (*Head of History*)
M Flower, BA (*and Religion and Philosophy*)
M W Hale, BA (*Head of Walter House*)
B J C Horan, MA (*Director of Studies*)
H G Mackridge, MA (*Second in Oxbridge/Enrichment Coordinator*)
Ms F E Pace, BA (*Enrichment Coordinator*)
J G Taylor, MA (*Registrar*)

Information Systems:
Dr A R H Clarke, MA, DPhil, CPhys, MInstP (*Deputy Head, Information Services, Physics*)
P Gregory, HND (*Technical Services Manager*)
J P Beck (*Senior Network Engineer*)
J R Cho-Yee, BA (*Network Engineer*)
P A J G Gregory (*Network Engineer*)
L M Lindsay (*IT Technician*)
I Rudling (*Webmaster*)

Learning Support:
P M Capel, BA (*Learning Support Coordinator*)
Mrs G M Kantor, BA Hons, OCR Dip SpLD
J Hibbert, BA (*Teaching Assistant*)

Library:
Ms J A Howse, MA (*Senior Librarian*)
Mrs A J South, BSc, DipLib (*Second Librarian*)
Mrs P J Jones, BA, PGDip (*Assistant Librarian*)

Mathematics:
J D G Slator, MA (*Head of Mathematics*)
Dr F R Andrews, BSc, MEng, PhD
W J Beaumont, MA (*Head of DofE*)
S J Coles, BSc (*and Computing*)
M A Fothergill, BSc
Mrs D C Gedalla, BA
S F Hardman, BSc
M F Illing, MA
A S Miller, BSc (*Second in Mathematics and Head of Clive House*)
Miss S M Peers, BSc (*Tracking Manager and Team Leader DofE*)
S L Rowlands, BA (*Head Manor House*)

Modern Languages:
R P Bailey, BA (*Head of Modern Foreign Languages*)
Ms M E Broncano, MA (*Subject Leader for Spanish*)
Mrs M C R Castro, BA (*Spanish*)
Miss R G Haye, Licence LCE (*French & Spanish*)
Ms V M Kotsuba BA, MA (*French*)
Mrs J Li, MA (*Mandarin – part time*)
Miss H E McCullough, BA (*German & French*)
Mrs K Okamura, School Business Diploma (*Japanese – part time*)
M W Pacey, BEd, Grad Cert Arts (*Subject Leader for German*)
J M S Rippier, BA (*French and Director of Publications*)
T P Rocher, L-ès-L (*French*)
Mrs C E Udell, MA (*German & French*)
F R Vignal, DipHE (*Second in Modern Languages, and Subject Leader for French*)

Music:
H R Jones, MA, FRCO, ACA (*Director of Music*)
S J Couldridge, DipTCL (*Head of Instrumental Studies*)
Mrs J H Stubbs, MusB, ARCO, ALCM

Physical Education:
L D Foot, BSc (*Director of Sport*)
R I M Alexander, BSc (*Head of Hockey and teacher of Academic PE and Chemistry*)
J C Barnwell, BA (*Head of Academic PE*)
C R Evans-Evans, BA, MEd, NPQH (*Senior Master*)
A J Mills, BSc (*Head of Rugby*)
T Webley, BSc (*Head of Cricket and Assistant Head of Lower School*)

Physics:
Mrs A Mayadeen, MPhys (*Head of Physics*)
E J Gillett, MSci (*Team Leader DofE*)
Dr A R H Clarke, MA, DPhil (*Deputy Head, Information Services*)
N J D Hillier, BA, MSc (*Commanding Officer, CCF*)
Ms L A Slator, BSc (*Examinations Officer*)
D J Spikings, BA, MEng (*Assistant Director of Studies*)

Psychology:
I J Mitchell, BA, BSc (*Head of Psychology*)

Religion and Philosophy:
Miss K H Balnaves, BA, MA (*Head of Religion and Philosophy*)
The Reverend D M Bond, BA, BTh (*School Chaplain and Head of Phab*)
M Flower, BA (*and History*)

School Counsellor: A J C Dickinson, BA, MEd, ALCP

Visiting Teachers:
J Atkins, DipRAM (*Trumpet*)
G Boyd, DipMus (*Double Bass*)
S Byron, BMus Hons RCM (*Trombone*)

Miss S Clark, MA, LRSM, ARCM, PG Dip RCM, CT, ABRSM, LRSM (*Piano*)
Mrs N S Coleman, CertEd (*Flute*)
Miss K Cormican, GTCL, PDOT (*Violin*)
G Cracknell, LRAM (*Violin*)
A Francis, LRAM (*Clarinet*)
J Francis (*Saxophone & Clarinet*)
A Gathercole, GGSM (*Trumpet*)
R Halford (*Guitar*)
Ms N Hawkins, GLCM, FLCM (*Guitar*)
D Hester, LTCL, DipTCL (*Bassoon*)
C Hooker, LRAM, ARAM (*Oboe*)
J Lawrence, BA (*Percussion*)
D Lewis, LRAM (*Brass*)
Mrs N Manington, BMus LGSM (*Piano*)
N Martin (*Drums*)
Ms P O'Sullivan, BA (*Recorder*)
D Rowland, MMus perf (*Harp*)
D Saunderson, GGSM (*Singing*)
Mrs M Stone, MMus (*Piano*)
Mrs N Tait, LRAM Hons (*Cello*)

Sports:

P Cladd (*Tennis*)	N Lambert (*Rugby*)
C Connerrlly (*Rugby*)	F Lombard (*Rugby*)
S Dokic (*Athletics*)	P Loudon (*Hockey*)
D Emms (*Tennis*)	I McGowan (*Cricket*)
L Fazekas (*Fencing*)	M Mclellan (*Yoga*)
A French (*Watersports*)	G Price (*Fives/Wallball*)
G Furber (*Cricket*)	R Powell (*Rugby*)
J Jones (*Judo*)	U Urban (*Table Tennis*)
T Kadar (*Table Tennis*)	R Willmouth (*Chess*)
M Khalifa (*Squash*)	L Wooldridge (*Cricket*)

Head Master's PA: Mrs C Herbert
Admissions Officer: G McCann
Bursar's Secretary: Mrs S Enright

The school has enjoyed a distinguished history since its foundation by the Merchant Taylors' Company in 1561. It was one of the nine original "Clarendon" public schools and its pupils have achieved distinction throughout its history. The school enjoys close links with the Company, which, to this day, constitutes its Governing Body. In 1933 the school moved from central London to its present superb, rural setting of 250 acres at Sandy Lodge, Northwood. We are within easy reach of parents in Buckinghamshire, Hertfordshire, Middlesex and North-West London by car, train or school coach service, as well as a mere half hour by tube from Baker Street.

There are 890 boys in the school.

All pupils have an individual tutor who looks after them throughout their school career in small House tutor groups. They are encouraged to cultivate activities at which they can excel, to have confidence in their abilities and to gain self-knowledge as well as knowledge. The academic achievements of the school are first-rate and are achieved in an humane, civilised and unpressured atmosphere. We place a great emphasis on encouraging boys to organise many activities themselves and to take responsibility for others.

Admission. Entry to the school at 11+, 13+ and 16+ is by the school's own Entrance Examinations, together with an interview.

Scholarships and Bursaries. There are no separate scholarship papers in the entrance examinations. We make awards to boys who perform exceptionally well in these examinations and at a separate interview; we take into account information received from the boy's current school.

11+ entry: Up to 5 major academic scholarships each to the value of 10% of the school fee. Up to 5 minor academic scholarships each to the value of £200 per annum (the initial award will be in the form of book tokens). Up to 2 all-rounder scholarships, each to the value of 10% of the school

fee. Up to 6 scholarships for sport, art & drama (up to 2 in each subject).

13+ entry: Up to 5 major academic scholarships each to the value of 10% of the school fee. Up to 12 minor academic scholarships each to the value of £200 per annum (the initial award will be in the form of book tokens). Up to 2 all-rounder scholarships each to the value of 10% of the school fee. Up to 6 scholarships for sport, art & drama (up to 2 in each subject).

16+ entry: Up to 6 scholarships: sport (1), art (2) and drama (2), all-rounder (1). One bursary up to the value of the full school fee is available. Lower Sixth internal Exhibitions: 4 Exhibitions may be awarded to boys proceeding to the Lower Sixth.

Music Scholarships: Four Music Scholarships (one of up to 25% of the school fees; one of up to 15% and two of up to 10%) awarded across 11+, 13+ and 16+. A scholarship includes free instrumental and/or singing tuition on two instruments (or instrument and voice). Additional awards of free tuition may be made if there are boys of sufficient merit.

All Scholarships can be supplemented by means-tested bursaries should there be a proven need.

Bursaries: The school welcomes applications from parents whose sons would benefit from attending Merchant Taylors' School, and who contribute strongly to the life of the community, but who require financial assistance. Means-tested bursarial support is available up to the value of 100% fees; further details can be obtained from the Admissions Secretary.

Other Awards: There is a generous variety of awards open to Sixth Formers for travel, Outward Bound and Sail Training, as well as leaving scholarships to assist at University.

Scholarships at Oxford and Cambridge Universities. At the end of their first undergraduate year, Old Boys are eligible for election to a maximum of three Sir Thomas White Scholarships at St John's College, Oxford, a Matthew Hale Scholarship at Queen's College, Oxford and a Parkin & Stuart Scholarship for Science or Mathematics at Pembroke College, Cambridge.

Curriculum and Organisation. The curriculum in years 7, 8 and 9 (Thirds, Upper Thirds and Fourths) is a broad one: Art and Design, Biology, Chemistry, Computing, Design Technology, Drama, English, French, Geography, History, Latin, Mathematics, Music, Physical Education, Physics, PSHCE, and Religious Studies. Greek, German, or Spanish are started when 13+ boys enter the school. All boys take nine or ten GCSEs, chosen from a wide range of subjects, including Music, Drama, PE, and Computing. Boys are entered for the IGCSE in English, mathematics, modern languages and the sciences. A student entering the Lower Sixth embarks upon a two-year course in which all boys study four subjects to AS Level, followed by three subjects at A2 for most (some continue with four). An extensive choice of super-curricular options is available, including the EPQ, General Studies, Critical Thinking, career management, and courses in Japanese, and Mandarin.

Music. All orchestral and band instruments, piano, organ, percussion and guitar are taught to boys throughout the school. Choirs, orchestras, bands and chamber groups give frequent concerts throughout the year.

Free tuition for one year is available for selected boys who wish to start learning an orchestral instrument.

Games and Physical Education. Magnificent playing fields over 55 acres are dedicated to the playing of Rugby, Cricket, Soccer, Hockey, Cross-Country and Golf. There are Fives, Squash and Tennis Courts; also, an athletics track and two floodlit, all-weather pitches. The Sports Hall accommodates four badminton courts, a multi-gym, a climbing wall, a fencing piste and indoor cricket nets. The school's lakes provide a marvellous facility for our Sailing Club, canoeing and windsurfing. Physical Education is compulsory for all pupils, and all pupils learn to swim. There is an indoor swimming pool and Water Polo is offered. Coaching in Fencing, Basketball, Judo and Karate is excellent and boys enjoy national success in these sports. The school is the UK Centre of Excellence for Handball.

Service Sections. The school has a Contingent of the Combined Cadet Force with RN, Army, and RAF Sections. The CCF includes girls from St Helen's School, Northwood. There is a Rifle Range for the use of the Contingent, and we send a team to Bisley every year. The Duke of Edinburgh's Award Scheme allows boys to achieve Bronze, Silver and Gold Awards, and the Community Service programme provides an opportunity for a wide range of activities in the local area. All boys in Years 10 and 11 take part in the CCF, The Duke of Edinburgh's Award Scheme or Community Service teams.

The school places great emphasis on charitable endeavour and the boys run a great many societies to support good causes. A special feature of the school's charity work is Phab, a week-long residential holiday for handicapped children held every Easter and organised by Sixth Form boys together with the girls of St Helen's School. The school also has a charitable partnership with two schools in India.

School Societies. A large number of societies cover a wide field of interests and activities.

Careers. There is a strong Careers Advisory Service, which organises annual Careers and Higher Education Conventions at the school and a range of work experience.

House and Tutorial Systems. The school is divided into eight Houses. Each House is under the care of a Head of House and a team of tutors, which is responsible for the pastoral care of boys in that House.

Fees per term (2014–2015). £7,220 (Autumn Term), £5,415 (both Spring Term & Summer Term); these cover not only tuition, games, and lunch but also a lifetime alumnus subscription (OMT). There is a non-refundable registration fee of £100; separate admission fee deposits are charged later.

Term of entry. September unless there are very special circumstances.

Charitable status. Merchant Taylors' School Charitable Trust is a Registered Charity, number 1063740. It exists to provide a first-class all-round education for boys, irrespective of their background.

Merchiston Castle School

Colinton, Edinburgh EH13 0PU
Tel: 0131 312 2200
           Headmaster: 0131 312 2203
           Registrar: 0131 312 2201
Fax: 0131 441 6060
email: headmaster@merchiston.co.uk
website: www.merchiston.co.uk

Motto: *Ready Ay Ready.*

The School was established in 1833 and moved in 1930 from the centre of the city out to its present spacious and attractive site, bordered by the Water of Leith and close to the Pentland Hills.

Governors:
Chairman: J M Gourlay, BCom, CA

Members of the Board:
C M A Lugton, MA
H P G Maule, MA
G R T Baird
Prof L Waterhouse, BA, MSW
Mrs S Kuenssberg, CBE, BA, DipAdEd, FRSA
R M Ridley, MA
S P Abram
J L Broadfoot, BA, MEd

B M McCorkell, BA, MA Cantab
I McAteer, LLB
R W Nutton, MB BS, MD, FRCS
D R Whiteford, OBE, BSc, FRSA, ARAgs
R S Elliot
P W Yellowlees
D C M Moore BSC, MPhil, PhD
G T G Baird, FRAS

In Attendance: Mrs P Marshall, MA

Secretary to the Governors and Bursar: A G Clayton, BA University of North Wales, MBA Warwick

President of the Merchistonian Club: W A McDonald, BA

Headmaster: **A R Hunter**, BA Manchester

Senior Deputy Head: P K Hall, MA Oxford
Deputy Head Academic: Mrs M Muetzelfeldt, BSc London (*Mathematics*)
Deputy Head Co-Curricular: R A Charman, BA Canterbury

* *Head of Department*
† *Housemaster*

Ms N G Waldron, BA Kent (*Head of Merchiston Juniors*, †*Pringle*)
J C O Vaughan, BSc Edinburgh (*Mathematics*)
P S Williams, BA Leicester (*English**, *Classical Civilization*)
Mrs M V Prini-Garcia, L-ès-L Madrid (*Spanish, Careers*)
D M Turner, MA Oxford, ARCO (*ICT, Music*)
S J Horrocks, MA Cambridge (*French, Spanish, ESOL*)
P Corbett, MA St Andrews (*French, ESOL Coordinator*)
Miss F M Blakeman, Dip Des Napier (*Art & Design*)
Revd K J A Anderson, MTh St Andrews (*PSE, Religious Studies, Dean of Sixth Form*)
S Campbell, BSc Glasgow (*Mathematics**, *Assistant Head Academic*)
R C Lucas, MEng Aston, MA Sheffield (*Mathematics*)
Mrs J M Williams, BA Leicester (*Librarian*)
J M V Cordingley, MA London (*Art & Design**, †*Chalmers East*)
F Geisler, LA S11/1 Bochum (*German*)
Mrs M B Watson, BSc Glasgow (*Mathematics, ICT**)
F P J Main, BEd Edinburgh (*Design & Technology**)
R P Nicholls, BSc Durham (*Physics, Electronics**, *Science**)
K G Pettigrew, BSc, PhD Edinburgh (*Chemistry**)
Miss S M Twyford, BSc Glasgow, MSc Strathclyde, PhD Glasgow (*Physics*)
Revd N G D Blair, BA, MA Edinburgh (*Religious Studies, PSHE*)
M S King, BSc Bristol (*Biology**)
Mrs S J Binnie, MA Edinburgh (*English, Classical Civilization*)
J B Bisset, MA, MSc Aberdeen (*Director of ICT Services*)
D D J Cartwright, BSc, PhD Edinburgh (*Junior Science, Chemistry, Head of Careers and Monitoring and Progression*)
Mrs M Hsu-McWilliam, BA Tamkang, MSc Edinburgh (*Mandarin*)
Miss J R Vaughan, BA Newcastle (*Director of Studies & Head of Support for Learning – Merchiston Juniors, Mathematics*)
I H Mitchell, BSc Strathclyde, PhD Imperial (*Physics*, †*Evans*)
D M George, BSc Edinburgh (*Biology*)
W J J Clayton, MA Edinburgh (*Economics**, *Careers*)
M R Hillier, MA Cambridge (*Classics, Classical Civilization*, †*Laidlaw*)
Mrs M H Gray, MA Lyon (*Languages**, *French*)
Mrs I Stewart, BEd Glasgow (*Faculty of Support for Learning**)
Ms F Vian, PhD Parma (*Mathematics*)

S R Thompson, MA Edinburgh (*History & Politics**)
Miss K A Tully, BSc, MPhil Edinburgh (*Biology, PSHE**)
Ms G Cunningham, BA Stirling (*English*)
S M Dennis, BMus Edinburgh (*Music**)
A M Roache, BSc St Andrews (*Physics**)
C R Harrison, BSc Napier (*PE**)
J Timms, MA Edinburgh (*English, †Chalmers East*)
Mrs R J Fawthrop, BA Oxford (*Classics**)
Mrs T Bower, BA London, MSc Toronto, DPhil Oxford
  (*Geography*, Biology*)
M R Boyd, BEd Stranmills (*J4 Teacher*)
Mrs H L Bruce, MA Glasgow (*Spanish*)
B J Hall, BSc Strathclyde (*Geography*)
R McCann, BSc Ulster (*Assistant Director of Sport,
  Geography*)
R L McCorkell, BSc Edinburgh (*Mathematics*)
Ms F E Miller, BSc Glasgow, MBA Edinburgh
  (*Mathematics, ICT*)
R C Deans, BSc Abertay (*PE*)
Mrs K K Gill, BSc Leeds (*Biology, Chemistry*)
J D Loftus, BSc Robert Gordon's (*Design & Technology*)
Mrs L K McDiarmid, BA Warwick (*History, Politics*)
R A Moffat, BEd Jordanhill (*Director of Rugby, PE*)
F E Newham, MA Oxford (*History, Politics*)
R Pyper, BSc Leeds (*PE, †Chalmers West*)
Mrs K S Mitchell, BA, Keele (*Primary Teacher, Support
  for Learning*)
S R Belding, MChem, DPhil Oxford (*Chemistry*)
Ms J Bowman, MA Aberdeen (*Spanish*)
Ms N Chadwick, MChem, PhD Edinburgh (*Chemistry*)
J D Ferguson, MA Edinburgh (*Economics*)
M Harkins, BA Stirling (*Upper Primary Teacher*)
L Hayes, MA Edinburgh (*History*)
G P Jones, BA, MSc, PhD Edinburgh, MA Aberdeen
  (*Physics*)
M S Kemp, MA Aberdeen (*Geography, †Rogerson*)
M R Monteith, MSc Belfast (*Maths*)
Ms L R Pollard, BA Oxford, MA Southampton (*ESOL**)
M K Raikes, MA Manchester (*Director of Junior Sport*)
Mrs C R Smith, BA Cambridge (*Classics*)
Ms N M Steen, MSc, PhD Belfast (*Maths*)
Mrs C Thomson, BSc Heriot-Watt (*Design and
  Technology*)

Examinations Officer: T J Lawson, BA Sheffield, PhD
  Edinburgh, FSA Scot

Accounts:
A G Clayton, BA University of North Wales, MBA
  Warwick (*Bursar*)
Miss H A Jones, BA Napier, FCAA (*Finance Manager*)
Mrs C McIntosh (*Assistant Bursar*)
Mrs K M Morrison (*Purchase Ledger*)
Mrs E Walker (*HR Manager*)

Administration:
Mrs S M Dow (*Headmaster's PA*)
Mrs E Firoozi (*AMT Secretary*)
Ms C L Hall (*Deputy Head's Secretary*)
Mrs G B Gibson (*Receptionist*)
Mrs H McIntosh (*Admin Assistant*)
Mrs L Campion (*Admin Assistant*)

Development:
D Rider, MIoF (*Development Director*)
Miss J Tennant, BSc St Andrews (*Development Officer*)
Ms A L McGoldrick, BA Kent (*Development Officer*)
Ms J Khan (*Admin Assistant*)

Registrar's Office:
P K Rossiter, MA Oxford (*Registrar*)
Mrs K Wilson (*Admissions Manager*)
Mrs T I Gray, BA Napier, ChDipM (*External Relations
  Manager*)
Mrs L Melo da Silva, BA Strathclyde (*External Relations
  Assistant*)

Miss C F Nutton, BA Newcastle, MSc Heriot-Watt
  (*External Relations Assistant*)
Miss H Aitken (*Admin Assistant*)

Departmental Technical Assistants:
Mrs M Carnie (*Chief Laboratory Technician*)
A R Ross (*Laboratory Technician*)
Ms K Ryan, BSc Abertay (*Lab Technician*)
A C MacNeill (*IT Network Manager*)
C A Brown, BSc Heriot-Watt (*IT Support Officer*)
N P Burt (*Design & Technology Technician*)

Medical Staff:
Dr T McMillan, MB, ChB, MRCGP, DRCOG (*Medical
  Officer*)
Dr D A Reid, BSc, MB, ChB, MRCGP, DipSEM (*Medical
  Officer*)
Mrs K J Jones, RGN, RM, HV (*Director of Health
  Services*)
Mrs J N Fisher, RGN (*Nursing Sister*)
Mrs N Fallowfield, RGN (*School Nurse*)
Mrs D Marshall, NQ (*Health Assistant*)

Specialist Sports Coaches:
M du Coudray (*Tennis Academy Coach*)
N Lundy, BA USA (*Tennis Academy Coach*)
S Gilmour, MSc Edinburgh (*Director of Cricket*)
A Murdoch (*Golf Academy*)
S Capaldi (*Basketball*)
J Hay (*Squash*)
Mrs S Legget (*Swimming*)

Support Staff:
Major A D Ewing (*School Staff Instructor*)
G Campbell, MA Aberdeen (*Master in Charge of Pipe
  Bands*)
Mrs M Lucas, BA (*Masterchef*)
Mrs F Blair, BA, BSc, MBACP (*School Counsellor*)
Mrs J A Ghazal (*Pringle Centre Assistant*)
Mrs P Wearmouth, BEd (*Pringle Assistant*)
Mrs A McGregor, BA (*Chalmers East and Rogerson
  Housemother*)
Mrs R Pyper, BMus (*Chalmers West Housemother*)
N McWilliam, MSc Napier, BA Dundee (*School
  Assisstant*)
Mrs M T Cordingley, BA (*Exchange Shop Manager*)
Mrs F Horrocks BA (*School Shop*)
Mrs L Millard (*Bookstore Manager*)
T Catlin (*Master in Charge of Transport*)

Visiting Instrumental Music Teachers:
Mrs E Beeston (*Violin*)
Ms M C Bell (*Oboe, Clarinet*)
Ms E Roche (*Flute*)
Ms S Sahyouni (*Singing*)
A McGrattan (*Brass*)
A Mitchell (*Guitar, Bass Guitar*)
Mrs K M Nicholls (*Piano*)
J Walker (*Drumming*)
B Davidson (*Piano*)
B Donaldson (*Piping*)
Mrs K M Nicholls (*Piano*)
Mrs R Pyper (*Singing*)
Mr G McDiarmid (*Guitar*)

Visiting Language Teachers:
Mrs J L McKinlay, MA Birmingham (*ESOL Consultant*)
Mrs R Nazipova-Petherick, Omsk (*Russian*)
Mrs K Kelly (*Japanese*)
Miss C Gaudiana (*Italian*)
Mrs J Millard (*Mandarin*)
Mrs C Van Wengen (*Dutch*)
Mrs S Abdo (*Arabic*)
Mrs X Pang (*Mandarin*)
Dr M Breatnach (*French*)
Mrs N Davidson (*Japanese*)

J France (*German*)
Miss L Wylie (*French*)

Chaplaincy Team:
N G D Blair (*Leader of the Chaplaincy Team*)
K J A Anderson (*Assistant Chaplain*)
P K Rossiter
S M Dennis

There are 470 boys in the School, of whom 300 are boarders.

Admission. The normal ages of entry are 7–14 and 16, though from time to time there may be vacancies at other ages. Entry at 7–12 is by entrance assessment, interview and current school report; entry at 13 by the Common Entrance or Merchiston entrance examinations and current school report. Entry at 14 is by Merchiston entrance examinations. Entry to the Sixth Form at 16 depends on a successful showing in GCSE or National 4 and National 5 examinations as well as on interview and a school report. There are approximately 160 pupils in the Sixth Form. Entry is possible in all three terms where vacancies permit.

A prospectus and further details may be obtained from the Registrar. Prospective parents are encouraged to visit the School. Information may be also found on our website: www.merchiston.co.uk.

Courses of study. In the Juniors the curriculum comprises English, English Literature, Mathematics, Biology, Chemistry, Physics, History, French, Latin, German, Spanish, Mandarin, Geography, Religious Studies, Art and Design, Music, PE, Electronics, Design and Technology, and Information Technology.

In the Middle School a 2-year course leading to GCSEs is followed, consisting of a core curriculum: English, English Literature, Mathematics, a foreign language (French, German, Spanish, Mandarin), IGCSE Biology, Chemistry and Physics, and a wide range of optional subjects, including History, a second foreign language, Electronics, Information Technology, Geography, Latin, Religious Studies (Philosophy and Ethics), Art and Design, Design and Technology, and Music. Many boys take 10 subjects.

In the Lower Sixth, most boys study 4 subjects at AS Level. In the Upper Sixth, boys study generally 3 subjects to A2. A Level options include English Literature, Mathematics, Further Mathematics, Biology, Chemistry, Physics, French, German, Spanish, History, Geography, Economics, Government and Politics, Classical Civilisation, Religious Studies, PE, Information Technology, Latin, Design and Technology, Electronics (AS only) and Art. Other languages at A Level (including Classical Greek, Italian and Russian) are available on request and at additional charge. In addition to his main subjects, each boy follows a General Studies course offering Moral and Social Studies and Careers Guidance. Classes are small throughout the School, and all subjects are set by ability. The School prepares boys for entry to Oxford and Cambridge.

The School makes provision for specialist ESOL teaching for International students, including an opportunity to study GCSE English in the Upper Sixth year.

In 2014, the A Level A*–B pass rate was 80% with 78% of pupils gaining entry to their first choice and 95% gaining entry to their first or second choice of University.

Support for Learning Provision. Able boys with learning difficulties, including dyslexia, enjoy successful careers at Merchiston. Our aim is to enhance self-esteem through genuine praise. We encourage each pupil to find success in his area of strength, whether inside or outside the classroom. The objective is that all pupils have access to a wide and varied curriculum, and that, as a result, each discovers his own personal strengths and talents, and enjoys the resulting success. All are expected to follow mainstream GCSE courses.

Houses. Each of the boarding houses caters for a particular age group and the atmosphere and activities are tailored

accordingly. The purpose-built Sixth Form boarding house opened in 2009 offering 126 en-suite bedrooms, with modern kitchens, a multi-gym and open plan social spaces with stunning views of Edinburgh and Fife. The Housemaster and his House Tutors pay special attention to the care of the individual and to the development of both his studies and interests.

Day boys. The life of day boys is fully integrated with that of the boarders.

Games. The principal games are rugby, played in the Autumn and Lent Terms, and in the Summer Term cricket and athletics. In 2011 Merchiston launched The Golf Academy at Merchiston, which is based both at the School's 100-acre campus and also at nearby Kings Acre Golf Course, where coaching, practice and tutorial work take place. Launched in 2007, The Tennis Academy provides specialised coaching and a full training and sports science programme. There is a large indoor heated swimming pool and a sports hall, and there are good facilities for other sports including tennis, football, squash, fives, shooting, sailing, skiing, basketball, fencing, golf, badminton, hockey and curling.

Music. Music plays an important part in the life of the School. Tuition is available in all keyboard and orchestral instruments; currently about fifty per cent of the School are learning a musical instrument, and two choirs flourish. There is also a School orchestra, a close harmony group, a jazz band and two pipe bands. The choir and instrumentalists frequently go on tour, eg to the USA, the Far East, and Europe.

Drama. There is at least one major drama production a term, jointly staged with our sister school, as well as frequent House plays or drama workshop productions in a well-equipped, purpose-built theatre.

Art, Craft, Design and Technology, and Ceramics. The Art and Design Centre offers scope both within the curriculum and in the pupils' free time for painting, pottery, metalwork, woodwork and design work. Courses in Computing and Electronics are also available both within the curriculum or in free time.

Societies. There is a wide variety of clubs, including chess, debating and electronics. Visits to theatres, concerts and exhibitions are a frequent part of a boy's life at Merchiston. The Enlightened Curriculum uses Edinburgh as a prime resource for cultural experiences for all age groups.

CCF. All boys join the CCF for a period of three terms, after which point participation is voluntary. This includes outward bound activities such as climbing, hillwalking, canoeing and camping. All senior boys at Merchiston also undertake a Bronze Duke of Edinburgh's Award expedition, with participation at Silver and Gold level on a purely voluntary basis.

The School is also very active in community service work.

Girls. The School does not take girls but has a special relationship as brother/sister school with St George's School for Girls, Edinburgh and Kilgraston School in Perthshire. This includes joint expeditions, concerts, tours, seminars, debating, drama, social events and study courses. Merchiston operates a joint fees scheme with St George's School for Girls; Kilgraston School and Queen Margaret's School, York.

Careers advice. An expert careers adviser supplements the advice of the Academic Management Team, Housemasters and Academic Tutors. In the LVI year, pupils attend timetabled lessons in Careers as part of the General Studies Programme of the Sixth Form, where they are also encouraged to take a Work Experience placement and to visit local universities in the month of June. When pupils start in the Shell, they undertake Cambridge Occupational Analysts (COA) Preview and Profile assessments. These assess each individual's interests and abilities in several key cognitive areas. In the Fifth Form each individual has a discussion with the Head of Careers, during which interests are explored and feedback from the COA assessments is given. The discussion is focused on career areas of interest – as identified by the individual and the COA feedback – and identifying areas to be investigated, as well as touching on potential A Level programmes. There is an annual HE & Careers Fair to which other local schools are invited. A designated careers hub is being developed in the new Laidlaw House.

Links with parents. There are regular parent/staff meetings and parents are fully briefed and consulted with regard to all academic and career decisions. There is also a parents' forum, which holds regular meetings.

Health. There is a medical centre in the charge of the School Nursing Sisters and the School Doctor visits regularly.

Fees per term (2014–2015). Junior School: Boarders £6,100, Day boys £4,350; Forms 2 and 3: Boarders £7,090, Day boys £4,920. Senior School (Forms 4 and above): Boarders £9,520, Day boys £7,015.

Sibling, Forces and Teaching Profession (means–tested) fee reductions are available.

Scholarships and Bursaries. Scholarships are offered for competition from 10+ up to 16, with an emphasis on 13+ entry from Prep Schools.

Junior (10+-12+): Academic, Music (including a Piping Exhibition), All-Rounder.

Senior & Sixth Form (13+, 14+, 16+): Academic, Music (including a Piping Exhibition), Sports, All-Rounder, Art & Design, Design & Technology.

Scholarships no longer carry an automatic fee concession.

Means-tested financial assistance: where parental income is not sufficient to allow the pupil to attend Merchiston, parents may apply for means-tested financial assistance, which may be up to 100% of the day or boarding fees.

International Scholarships include European, Kenyan and Hong Kong. Merchiston also supports the HMC Projects in Eastern and Central Europe Scholarship scheme.

Forces: 10% fee remission is available to the sons of serving members of HM Forces.

Trust Applications: The School can apply to charities on behalf of prospective candidates who can demonstrate financial need.

Old boys. The Secretary of The Merchistonian Club, c/o the School. Former pupils include: The Rt Hon Lord John MacGregor, MP; Sir Peter Burt, former Chief Executive, Bank of Scotland; John Jeffrey, OBE (ex Scotland XV and British Lions); The Rt Hon Lord Kenneth Osborne PC, longest-serving judge of the current Scottish bench; Air Marshal Sir John Baird, Surgeon General of the British Armed Forces between 1997 and 2000.

Charitable status. Merchiston Castle School is a Registered Charity, number SC016580. It aims to give each boy in his way the capacity and confidence to live in an uncertain world and to make that life as rich as possible; more specifically, to encourage him to work hard and to take pride in achievement, to think independently, to face up to challenges, to accept responsibility, to show concern for others and the environment, and to develop wider skills and interests.

Mill Hill School

The Ridgeway, Mill Hill, London NW7 1QS

Tel: 020 8959 1221 (Admissions)
Fax: 020 8906 2614
email: registrations@millhill.org.uk
website: www.millhill.org.uk

Court of Governors:

Chairman: Dr R G Chapman, BSc, MB BS, FRCGP

A L Brooke, BA, MBA
Dr A P Craig, MBBS, DRCOG
D J Dickinson, DipQS, MRICS
R A Eliott Lockhart, MA Cantab, MPhil
Mrs S Freestone, MEd, GRSM, LRAM, ARCM, FRSA
D Harris, BSc, FCA
Miss R E Jackson, LLB Hons, AKC, QC
E Lipton, MBA, BSc Hons, ACGI, DIC, FRSA
Mrs S J Miller, BA Hons
G Nosworthy
Mrs M Patel, MBA, BCS, BFSS
R L Tray, BA Hons, MA Cantab, MBA
A W Welch, BA, MA Oxon
Mrs P H Wilkes, BEd, FRSA
M T Wilson, BSc Hons

Clerk to the Court: Dr R L Axworthy, BA, PhD

Headmaster: Dr D A Luckett, BA, DPhil, FRSA, FHA

† *Housemaster/Housemistress*

Principal Deputy Head: Mrs J Sanchez, BSc (*also Geography*)
Deputy Head (Academic): A T W Frazer, MA (*also French & German*)
Deputy Head (Pastoral): N J Gregory, BA (*also French & Spanish*)
Deputy Head (External Relations): A J Binns (*also English*)
Assistant Head (Pastoral): N J Gregory, BA (*also French & Spanish*)
Assistant Head (Academic): Mrs M Atkins, BSc (*also Biology*)
Director of Boarding: †Miss L J Farrant, BA (*also English*)

Bursar: B D Fraser, BsBA, MBA

Chaplain: Revd Dr R J Warden, BA, MTh, DMin

Assistant Teachers:

Art & Design:
A D Ross, MA (*Head of Art*)
N G Cheeseman, BA
Miss V C Dempster, MA

Business Education:
Miss L H Sharples, BA (*Head of Business Education, Director of Sixth Form and Sixth Form Gifted & Talented Coordinator*)
Mrs V G Miner, MSc
M S Sherry, BA
M S Smith, BA

Classics:
A R Homer, BA (*Head of Classics*)
†S T Plummer, BA

Design Technology:
Ms B D Banks, BEd (*Head of Design Technology*)
M C McKay, BA

English & Drama:
R W Searby, BA (*Head of English*)
D S Proudlock, BA (*Head of Drama*)
Ms E M Coyle, MA (*Head of EAL*)
Ms K E Ferson, MA (*Head of EAL*) (*maternity cover*)
†D T Bingham, BA
Mrs S Isaacs, BEd
Mrs E Kaplan, BA
J M Lewis, MA (*Director of Academic Administration*)
Miss S Martinez, BA, MEd
Mrs A Murphy, BA
Mrs S Stagg, LLB
Mrs N Stimler, BA

Miss T T Wijesinghe, BA (*Lower School Gifted & Talented Coordinator*)
Mrs P Wright, Dip ACT

Geography:
Ms S J Bull, BSc (*Head of Geography*)
†N R Hodgson, MA
D R Woodrow, BA (*Coordinator of Activities*)

History & Politics:
M Dickinson, MA (*Head of History & Politics*)
Mrs C E Adams, BA
Mrs R E Bradley, BA
F C B Evans, BA
D W Hine, MA

Information Technology:
M J Northen, BA (*Head of IT*)
Ms P A Newsome, BSc

Mathematics:
K P Bulman, BSc (*Head of Mathematics*)
Miss W Ashraf, MEng, MBA
M J Carruthers, BEng
P J Kwok, BEng
Ms O Logan, BSc
A H Slade, BA
Ms E Stewart, BA
T Trhlik, BSc (*Second in Department*)

Modern Languages:
M S V Bardou, BA, (*Head of Modern Foreign Languages & Spanish*)
C S Lowe, BA, MEd (*Head of French*)
Mrs B K Hazeldine, MA (*Head of German*)
Miss V S S David, Maîtrise d'Anglais
Miss A C Ellerington, BA
†P R Lawson, MA
Mr A B Mansilla, BA

Music:
H E Brink, BA (*Director of Academic Music*)
K Kyle, BMus Hons, LRAM, PGDip RAM (*Director of Musical Performance*)
M P Kemp, BMus, ARCO

Visiting Instrumental Teachers:
J Bradford, BA, BMus, LGSM, LLCM, ALCM, PGCE, AdvDip, Cert Berklee (*guitars*)
A Cucchiara, GRNCM (*violin*)
Mrs C Emananuel, Dip Perf RCM, Dip RAC (*violin*)
J Fleeman, GCLCM, AdvCert GSMD (*percussion*)
O Gledhill, MA Mtpp, ARCM (*violoncello*)
D Grant, LAMI (*guitar*)
P Jaekel, GRSM, LRAM, ARCO (*piano*)
Mrs H Kearns, BA, LTCL (*pianoforte*)
L Kelly, ALCM, LTCL (*trumpet*)
Mrs H Kyle, BMus, LRAM (*voice*)
A Martin, AGSM (*percussion*)
A R McAfee, BA, PGCE (*flute*)
Mrs M L Payne, BMus TCM, LTC (*saxophone*)
A Poole, BSc (*double bass, guitar*)
Mrs A Starr, MMus, BMus (*pianoforte*)
Miss J Tate, BA Mus, Grad RNCM (*voice*)

Physical Education:
Miss A J Baird, MSc (*Head of PE*)
†J D Cuff, BA, MSc
D M Halford, PGA (*Director of Golf*)
S Hendy, BSc (*Gifted & Talented Coordinator for Sport*)
Miss R L Jakeman, MEd (*Head of Girls Games & Head of PHSRE*)
†A T Morton, BSc, MEd
T J Vercoe, BSc, MA (*Director of Sport, Rugby*)

Religious Education:
Revd Dr R J Warden, BA MTh, DMin (*Head of RE*)
Miss N F Anders, MA

Sciences:
Miss A Bignell, BSc, MA (*Head of Science & Biology*)
G N Saint, BSc (*Head of Chemistry*)
L J Stubbles, MSci (*Head of Physics*)
J A Barron, BSc, MA (*Coordinator of Sixth Form Chemistry*)
Dr K R Damberg, BSc, MD
†D S Hughes, BSc
M E Jennings, BSc
J M Murphy, BSc
Dr S Radojevic, BSc, PhD
G C Stead, BSc
P H Thonemann, MA, MPhil
†G M Turner, BSc
J G W Watson, BSc
C M G Watterson, BEng, MSci

Learning Support:
Miss L N Silverman, BA, Dip SpLD (*Head of Learning Support*)
N J Alexander-Passe, BA (*Head of Learning Support*) (*maternity cover*)
Mrs A Fryatt, BEd, MA, Dip Counsel APC
Mrs J R Herbert, BA

Head of Careers:
L J Stubbles, MSci

Officer Commanding CCF: Dr D A Luckett, BA, DPhil, FRSA, FHA

Medical Officer: Dr J Peter

Nurse:
Miss A Watford, RGN (*Nurse Manager*)
Mrs V Bennett, RGN
Mrs Jane Simpson, RGN

Belmont, Mill Hill Preparatory School
The Ridgeway, Mill Hill, London NW7 4ED
Tel: 020 8906 7270; Fax: 020 8906 3519
email: office@belmontschool.com
website: www.belmontschool.com

Head: Mrs L C Duncan, BSc, PGCE

Deputy Head (*Academic*): L Roberts, MA, PGCE
Deputy Head (*Academic*): Mrs R Alford, BEd
Acting Deputy Head (*Pastoral*): J Pym, MA, PGCE
Acting Deputy Head (*Operations*): Mr J Fleet, BSc, PGSE
Head of Lower School: Mrs J Rowe, BEd
Acting Head of Upper School: P Symes, BSc, PGCE

Heads of Department:
J McNulty, BA, PGCE (*Art*)
J Clement, BA, PGCE (*Classics*)
A Warden, BEd (*Design Technology*)
Miss L Olsson BA, PGCE (*English*)
Mrs C McRill, BA, PGCE (*French*)
A Hayward, BSc, PGCE (*Geography*)
R S Pace, MA, MAT (*History*)
Mrs A Gritz, BSc, QTS (*ICT*)
Mrs G Perrin, BA, PGCE (*Music*)
Miss C Neill, MA, PGCE (*Mathematics*) (*Acting*)
Miss J Southam, BSc, PGCE (*Girls Games*)
Mrs H Lawson, BA, PGCE (*RE, PSHE*)
Mrs J Fisher, BSc, PGCE (*Science*)
Miss K Hockley, BA, PGCE (*PE*)
Mrs L Russo, BA, PGCE (*Learning Support, Drama*)
Miss P Southall, MA, BSc (*EAL*)

Subject Teachers:
Ms Y Aslam, BA, (*Mathematics*)
Mrs T Bridge, BA, PGCE (*French*)
Miss G Conroy, BEd (*PE/Games*)
D Cook, BSc, PGCE (*PE/Games*)
A Haigh, BSc, PGCE (*Science, Games*)
Mrs S Falconer, BA, PGCE (*Mathematics*)

J Ince, BA, PGCE (*English/Classical*)
Miss M Jentgen, BA, PGCE (*French*)
Mrs E Semp, BA, PGCE (*English*)
Mrs A Passer BA, PGCE (*RE, Classical Studies*)
Miss J Swailes, BA MuEd (*English, Games*)
Mrs L Pym, BA,(*Mathematics, Girls Games*)
Miss V Risanovia, BA (*DT, Games*)
T Spink, BSc, PGCE (*Mathematics, Games*)
A Warren, GTCL (*Music, RE*)

Lower School Tutors:
R Baker, BEd
Mrs N Harris, BSc, PGCE, Dip IT
Mrs N Sawdaye, BA, PGCE
Mrs E Pendred, BA, PGCE
Miss M Sevani, MA
Mrs M Slade, BEd
Ms R Sutherns, MA, SESI
A Wright, BEd
Miss H Ennett, BEd, PGCE
Mr J Norbury, MA, PGCE
Mrs P Marshall, BEd
Miss L Moses, BA, PGCE
Mr R O'Sullivan BA, PGCE
Mrs A Caldwell BSc (*Learning Support*)
Mrs K Pople, BA, PGCE (*Learning Support*)
Mrs S Lewin, RSA Dip SpLD (*Learning Support*)
Mrs M Munro BA, PGCE (*Learning Support*)
Mrs K Pople, BA, PGCE (*Learning Support*)
Ms N Khan, BA (*Learning Support*)
Mrs S Sulkin (*Learning Support*)
Mrs S Wiltshire (*Learning Support*)
Mrs H Hardy, BA, PGCE (*Learning Support*)
Mrs S Roberts, BA, PGCE (*Learning Support*)
Mrs M Corcoran, BEd, PGCPSE (*Learning Support*)

Support Staff:
Head's PA: Mrs G Ellen
Registrar & Marketing Assistant: Mrs I Manfredi
School Secretary: Miss L Thomson
School Secretary: Mrs N McDavid
Librarian: Mrs L Mason, BA, MCLIP
School Nurse: Mrs J Reehal, BA
School Counsellor: S Kohon, BA
Network Administrator: Dr J White, PhD, BSc
Science & DT: *Technician*: Mrs P Daly

Grimsdell, Mill Hill Pre-Preparatory School
Winterstoke House, Wills Grove, Mill Hill,
London NW7 1QR
Tel: 020 8959 6884; Fax: 020 8959 4626
email: office@grimsdell.org.uk
website: www.grimsdell.org.uk

Head: Mrs K Simon, BA, PGCE

Deputy Head: K Dobson, BA Hons (*also Safeguarding,
Health & Safety and Assessment Coordinator*)
Director of Studies: Mrs T Weeks, BA Hons, PGCE (*Year
2 Coordinator; English Coordinator*)

Assistant Staff:
Mrs J Baddick, BSc Hons, PGCE (*Part-time Learning
Support Teacher, RE Coordinator*)
Mrs J Barnett, BA Hons, PGCE (*Part-time Learning
Support Teacher, RE Coordinator*)
Mrs S Broom, HNC Early Childhood Studies (*Nursery
Instructor*)
Mrs F Ellis, Diplôme d'Études (*Part-time French Teacher*)
Mrs M Gold, DCE Primary Education, Dip Support for
Learning (*SENCO Head of Learning Support, Part-time*)
Mrs J Golden, BMus Hons, PGCE (*Part-time ICT Teacher*)
Mrs E Jenner, BA Hons, PGCE (*Reception Class Teacher,
PSHE Coordinator*)
Miss N Kyriacou, BA Hons QTS (*Year 1 Class Teacher,
DT Coordinator*)

Mrs A Moir, BSc Hons QTS (*Reception Class Teacher,
Computing Coordinator*)
Mrs B Myburgh, BPrimEd SA (*Class Teacher, Science
Coordinator*)
Mrs T Patel, BA Hons (*Reception Class Teacher,
Geography Coordinator*)
Miss V Platts, BA Hons QTS (*Year 2 Teacher, Art &
Display Coordinator*)
Mrs F Smith, BSc Hons, PGCE (*Year 1 Class Teacher,
Maths Coordinator*)
Mrs R Stein, Montessori Dip (*Part-time Learning Support*)
Ms V Suarez Rivas, BA Hons (*PE Specialist*)
A Wodley, BEd Hons QTS
Mrs C Cox, MA (*Music Specialist*)

School Administrator: Mrs J Clarke
Assistant Administrator: Mrs S Webb

Mill Hill was founded by Samuel Favell (1760–1830)
and Revd John Pye Smith (1774–1851) as a grammar school
for the sons of Protestant dissenters and opened in 1807. The
School's motto, *et virtulem et musas* ('both virtue and learning') continues to characterise the aims of the School.
Indeed in September 1997 the School became fully co-educational.

Location. The School is part of Mill Hill village and is
situated in a conservation area, on the borders of Hertfordshire and Middlesex, approximately 12 miles from the centre of London. Set in 120 acres of parkland originally
formed by the famous botanist Peter Collinson, the grounds
provide a spacious setting for the academic buildings,
boarding and day houses and offer extensive facilities for
sports and activities.

Buildings. Mill Hill combines a rich traditional heritage
with modern educational facilities. The present School was
designed by Sir William Tite, architect of the Royal
Exchange and opened in 1826. Since the late 19th century
numerous buildings have been added, including the Chapel,
Library, Assembly Hall, Music School and Science Block.
Other additions include the Art and Design Technology
Centre, a modern Sports Hall, a Sixth Form Centre, the
Piper library and learning resources centre, a multimedia
language centre, two networked IT suites, a music technol-
ogy centre including a hard disk recording studio, a theatre,
a studio theatre, an indoor swimming pool and 3 Eton Fives
Courts.

As well as these facilities, a brand new academic teaching
block, The Favell Building, was opened in 2007. This
houses 25 new classrooms with libraries, seminar rooms,
and departmental offices for the Geography, History, Business Education, Classics, Religious Education and the Modern Foreign Languages departments.

Houses. There are 660 pupils in the School (450 boys,
210 girls) of whom around 140 are boarders. Weekly boarding was introduced in September 2012. There are currently
50 weekly boarders. There are three boarding Houses and
seven day Houses. Day pupils take a full part in the activities of the School. Full boarders have a full range of activities and workshops on Saturday mornings. These sessions
are optional to day and weekly boarding pupils.

Admission. Application may be made as early as parents
wish. The majority of boys and girls enter at the age of 13.
Candidates are selected on the basis of interviews, examination (Maths, English, Science, French and Latin as an
optional paper) and a Head's confidential reference. Scholarship candidates are identified through the entrance tests
and are called back for interviews on the basis of their
scores. Single subject awards may be made. Awards are also
made for Music, Drama, Sports and Design Technology.
The School also offers pre-testing in Year 7 (Year 6 for girls)
for unconditional places at 13+.

There are two other methods of entry:

(a) A limited number of places are available at 14+. Candidates are selected on the basis of interview, performance

in the 14+ Entrance Examinations (English, Maths, Science and French) and a Head's confidential reference.

(b) Sixth Form Entry: Admission to the Sixth Form is open to both boys and girls, from the UK and abroad. Entry requirements are 5 GCSE passes, at least 2 at Grade A plus 3 at Grade B, together with at least C grades in Mathematics and English, or equivalent qualifications for overseas pupils. More detailed entry requirements for specific AS courses are given in the School's Sixth Form Curriculum Guide. Candidates unable to offer the number of subjects required (e.g. some overseas candidates) will be considered on their individual academic merit.

Selection is by interview at the School (there are no examinations) and by reference from the candidate's present school. Offers made are conditional on meeting the entry requirements detailed above. International candidates may be asked to complete entry tests in the subjects they wish to study in the Sixth Form. All students with English as a second language will be asked to sit an EAL paper. Scholarships are awarded on the basis of examinations and interviews in January.

Pastoral Care. Pastoral care is organised by House and individual House identities are a significant feature of Mill Hill. All of the Houses (including day houses) have their own designated space including recreational facilities and areas for relaxation and/or study. In the School's most recent full ISI Inspection in 2012, the overall quality of pastoral care was rated as *Outstanding* and genuine pride is taken in maintaining and developing this aspect as a real strength of the School as a whole.

The report also portrayed *teachers and tutors as knowing their pupils very well* and described *pupils' behaviour as showing a high degree of maturity.* The provision of boarding too was rated as '*Excellent*' and the School received particular praise for providing *a lively supportive and caring environment that allows boarders to grow in confidence, independence and sensitivity to the needs of others, in line with its aims.*

One of the principal features of the Mill Hill approach to pastoral care is the continuity of support and involvement offered by Housemasters/Housemistresses throughout a pupil's five years at Mill Hill, aided by Tutors who work within a House dealing with day-to-day matters for specific year groups.

Another particularly notable element of Mill Hill's pastoral care is the wide range of dynamic pupil councils which meet regularly covering areas as diverse as anti-bullying and mentoring, boarding, charity, environmental issues, food, Fourth Form (new Year 9 pupils), inter-faith and Sixth Form-specific issues. In addition there is a Full School Council which offers an opportunity for the pupils' voices to be heard on key whole-School issues.

Curriculum. The School's academic curriculum is broad, flexible and forward-looking and is designed to encourage among pupils intellectual curiosity, sound learning and a spirit of enquiry in the pursuit of academic excellence. It seeks to enable pupils to acquire core knowledge and skills in English, Mathematics, Science and a modern language and, in addition, to develop their own particular academic interests. It also incorporates a full programme of personal, social and health education, appropriate guidance and information for pupils on subject choices, higher education and careers. Detailed information on the curriculum for each Key Stage is set out in a series of three curriculum guides, which are available on the School website and from the Admissions Office.

Organisation of the Curriculum. Pupils normally enter the School at 13+ (Year 9). There are normally 7 sets in each of Years 9, 10 and 11. The Year 9 curriculum aims to consolidate what has been learned in the previous two years, to enable pupils to experience a comprehensive range of subjects and to maintain pace and progression as they prepare for their GCSE courses.

When choosing their GCSE option subjects pupils are encouraged to select a combination of subjects which maintain a sensible breadth of study. This will vary between pupils and is balanced against each pupil's relative strengths in his/her subjects. Greater emphasis is given to each pupil choosing option subjects which they enjoy and in which they are likely to do well, than mere breadth for its own sake. In Years 10 and 11 English Language, English Literature, Mathematics, three separate Sciences or Dual Award Science and a modern language (either French or Spanish) are core examination courses, in addition to PE and Games; pupils also choose three GCSE option subjects from Art, Classical Civilisation, Computer Science, Design Technology, Drama, Geography, German, History, Information and Communication Technology, Latin, Music, Physical Education, Religious Studies and Spanish. Statistics is offered to the ablest mathematicians, and there are opportunities to take Ancient Greek outside the regular timetable.

The **Sixth Form Curriculum** offers a wide and flexible choice of A Level courses. It aims to encourage and develop personal skills of study, research and thought and to encourage pupils to consider and discuss issues relevant to them as they move towards adulthood and participation in the full range in rights and responsibilities as citizens.

In the **Lower Sixth** pupils traditionally take four AS courses. In addition they follow a course in Personal, Social, Health and Religious Education. The most able mathematicians take Mathematics and Further Mathematics together as one of their courses. For a small number of pupils, a programme of three, rather than, four courses is appropriate. Guidance is given to pupils and their parents about making AS subject choices; this includes an external academic/careers guidance test report and interview and discussions with tutors, Housemasters/mistresses and senior members of staff.

For the **academic year 2015–16**, Lower Sixth Formers will continue to take four subjects and, for most, these will be a mixture of reformed and unreformed courses. In the unreformed subjects, pupils will sit AS examinations, as now. In the reformed subjects, there will be a rigorous School examination in the Summer term as a halfway stage to linear A Level papers at the end of the Upper Sixth year in 2017.

In the **Upper Sixth** most pupils take three subjects plus a weekly timetabled session of Personal, Social, Health and Religious Education. In the Upper Sixth year private study lessons are unsupervised, and pupils may work in House, in the Piper Library or in departmental study areas.

Provision for Pupils with Special Educational Needs (SEN) and Learning Difficulties and/or Disabilities (LDD). The School provides those pupils who have a statement of educational need or a learning difficulty or disability support to meet their requirements and a suitably adapted curriculum, where this is appropriate. The Learning Support Department plays a key role in this work, seeking to identify, through screening and ongoing monitoring, the particular needs of individual pupils and putting in place strategies (and, where necessary, additional assistance) designed to help them fulfil their potential. Pupils who have a Special Educational Need or Learning Difficulty and/or Disability may have their curriculum modified to take account of their particular needs, as appropriate. Where a pupil has a statement of Special Educational Needs, the requirements of the statement are closely followed in order to ensure that the School provides an effective and accessible educational experience. The progress of all pupils on the School's Learning Support Register is regularly reviewed and support is amended as appropriate.

Academic and Careers Guidance. Through the tutor system, presentations and information evenings, pupils are helped to make the best possible choices of GCSE and Sixth Form courses and to make well-informed and appropriate higher education choices. In the Sixth Form the School arranges visits to universities as well as presentations, workshops and information evenings. The School has an active Careers Department which provides information and advice on possible future careers paths. Careers Education is included within the School's Personal, Social, Health and Religious Education programme and careers interviews are arranged for pupils in the Fifth Form and in the Lower Sixth, and also on request for other pupils. Careers guidance was rated as 'excellent' in the 2012 ISI inspection.

Support for pupils with English as an Additional Language. For pupils whose first language is not English, class or individual tuition in EAL is provided as appropriate, to enable them to maximise their academic opportunities and to enjoy all of the social and cultural aspects of life at the School. Some EAL pupils follow a modified curriculum in order to accommodate their needs, where this is appropriate. EAL pupils are prepared for IGCSE English as a Second Language, ideally in Year 10, and IELTS in Year 11 or the Lower Sixth, depending on the point at which they enter the School. Extra, individual, EAL tuition in addition to class lessons can be arranged if required.

Modern Languages. Mill Hill places emphasis on proficiency in the use of Modern Languages in a vocational context. Full use is made of ICT resources including two state-of-the-art digital language laboratories. Irrespective of Sixth Form specialisation, many choose to take AS levels in French, German and Spanish. Thus a good number of pupils, including Mathematicians and Scientists are competent in their use of a foreign language by the time they leave school. All pupils studying French, German or Spanish are encouraged and helped to spend extended study time abroad under the European Initiative. Pupils are also encouraged to improve their debating skills by taking part in inter-school competitions hosted at Mill Hill.

The European Dimension. One of the distinctive features of the Mill Hill School Foundation is that it provides pupils with an education that is firmly set within a contemporary European context. Over the last 40 years the School has pioneered a number of initiatives, such as seminars, exchange visits, work and GAP year placements in Europe. The range of exchange visits is well established: first year pupils have the opportunity to visit France on the Rouen exchange (which has been unbroken for over 40 years), Germany or Spain for a five-day stay in Leipzig and Granada respectively. Older pupils travel to Nice, Paris and Madrid.

Up to 25 students from the European Continent spend one or two years at Mill Hill. The School also participates in an annual residential seminar week, where pupils and staff from European schools live and learn with Millhillians. Pupils can expect therefore to have first-hand experience of living and working with Europeans together with opportunities to gain qualifications which will enhance a European-based career.

Art, Drama and Music. The Creative Arts have a long and successful tradition at Mill Hill and have increasing become part of the academic curriculum as well as the extra-curricular programme. In addition to achieving excellent results in public examinations, there is a substantial and varied programme of extra-curricular activities in these subjects. The Art Department offers facilities and expertise for pupils to develop their interest and skills in painting and drawing, alternative media, film, illustration, multimedia, photography (including digital photography), printmaking, sculpture, textiles, theatre design and video.

In addition to the very extensive range and number of drama performances relating to examination courses there is a biennial inter-House Drama festival, which alternates with the biennial inter-House Music Festival), both of which attract a high level of pupil participation. There is also a biannual programme of non-exam related Drama performances, ranging from Shakespeare to musicals. The School's musical ensembles include an orchestra, wind band, string ensemble, jazz group, full choir, Chapel choir, girls' choir, boys' a capella ensemble, and numerous ad hoc pupil bands and chamber ensembles. Individual tuition in most instruments and in singing is available from high quality specialist teachers. There is an extensive programme of concerts and recitals throughout the year, some of which include recitals by professional performers.

Tours have included drama performances at the Edinburgh Festival and choir tours to New York and to Paris and more recently to perform Evensong at Canterbury Cathedral.

Sport. Every pupil, regardless of physical ability, is encouraged to participate in both individual sports and team games. The major sports for boys are Rugby, Hockey and Cricket and for girls are Hockey, Netball, Rounders and Tennis. Other opportunities include Athletics, Basketball, Cross-country, Eton Fives, Golf, Horse Riding, Sailing, Skiing, Soccer, Swimming and use of the recently refurbished Fitness Suite. Competition and excellence are valued and the level of professional coaching skills is exceptional. The school has a 25-metre indoor swimming pool, 3 Eton Fives Courts, shooting range, all-weather pitch and Sports Hall, with a range of indoor sports facilities. Mill Hill is the home to the London Golf Academy. In 2011 new golf facilities including a short course facility and new indoor golf coaching facilities were opened. There are strong links with Saracens RFC and special bursaries are available in the Sixth Form for gifted rugby and hockey players. Pupils are given the opportunity of participating in overseas sports tours which have included countries, such as Barbados, Australia, Fiji, New Zealand, Argentina, Chile, Italy, Canada, India, South Africa, Sri Lanka and Spain for Rugby, Netball, Cricket and Hockey. The tennis and cricket teams also run training camps at the renowned La Manga Complex in Southern Spain. Junior sports teams regularly make less ambitious, but equally valuable tours within the UK and Europe.

Extra-Curricular Activities. First year pupils are introduced to the range of minor sports (as above) and aspects of adventure training. All pupils are also offered a range of other activities such as debating, drama, chess, jewellery making and computing. In Year 10 pupils choose between the CCF (Army, Navy and RAF), a Sports Leaders programme, Young Enterprise and Community Action. In addition, many Societies exist to cater for a variety of out-of-school interests.

Fees per term (2014–2015). Boarding £9,609, Weekly Boarding £8,168, Day (including lunch) £6,082. Fees include the games fee and the cost of most textbooks and stationery.

Scholarships and Bursaries. Scholarships, which attract a maximum of 10% fee remission, are available to pupils showing exceptional talent in a variety of areas both in the classroom and on the sports field. Academic, Music, Drama, Art and Design, and Sports Awards are available at 13+ and Academic Scholarships are available to candidates entering the Sixth Form. In addition to major Awards, there are a number of minor Awards or Exhibitions also on offer. The Headmaster, Deputy Headmaster (External Relations) or the Assistant Registrar are happy to advise parents and feeder schools about any of these Awards.

Bursaries are available for those entrants able to demonstrate a financial need. Parents will be asked to complete a detailed statement of their financial circumstances. Applicants for Bursaries will be selected in the normal way. There is provision for the award of full-fee Bursaries for entrants at all levels. It is possible for bursary funds to be used to top up Scholarship Awards. As with scholarship queries, the Headmaster, Deputy Headmaster (External) or the Assistant Registrar are happy to offer advice.

There are also a number of special scholarships and bursaries available, further information of which is available on the school's website www.millhill.org.uk.

The Mount, Mill Hill International is a new co-educational boarding and day school for international pupils. Opening in September 2015 in North West London, The Mount, Mill Hill International will be an important part of the Mill Hill School Foundation, a family of four co-educational schools for pupils aged 3 to 18. It will offer a traditional British educational experience and an academic curriculum up to GCSE/IGCSE and specialist EAL teaching. Pupils for whom English is not their first language will receive English language tuition while at the same time studying an appropriate range of other subjects in order to equip them for further study whether at Mill Hill School or elsewhere. Suitable for British pupils returning to the UK after a period abroad, The Mount, Mill Hill International offers an intensive one year GCSE/IGCSE course for pupils entering Year 11. For further information visit the website – millhillinternational.org.uk.

Charitable status. The Mill Hill School Foundation is a Registered Charity, number 1064758. It exists for the education of boys and girls.

Millfield

Street, Somerset BA16 0YD

Tel: 01458 442291
Fax: 01458 447276
email: admissions@millfieldschool.com
website: millfieldschool.com
Twitter: @millfieldsenior
Facebook: /MillfieldSchool

The school was founded in 1935 by R J O Meyer with the philanthropic aim of using its resources to generate places for boys who were gifted but not wealthy. The school became co-educational in 1939. In 1945 Edgarley Hall was acquired and the junior pupils were transferred there. This is now Millfield Prep School. The school expanded through the 50s and 60s offering a more orthodox curriculum, although it was never a 'normal' public school. C R M Atkinson became Headmaster in 1971, and carried out a major building programme that established modern purpose-built facilities throughout the academic and recreational areas of the school, including a prize-winning Library and Resource Centre and a large Fine Arts Centre, completed in 1992, a year after his death. Further improvements to the campus include a purpose-built Mathematics Centre, and 500-seat Theatre and Dining Hall. Nine new boarding houses have been opened since 2003. A Design & Technology building with high-tech equipment was completed in 2005 and a Music School complex housing the 350-seat Johnson Concert Hall was completed in September 2006. New Science laboratories and a Science lecture theatre were completed in September 2009. The main part of the school is surrounded by over 100 acres, which includes an equestrian centre, stabling for 64 horses, a 50m Olympic Swimming Pool, a golf course and an indoor Tennis Centre.

Governors:

Chair of Governors: Sir J G Reith, KCB, CBE

W J Bushell	Mrs A Sexton
R J R Clark	M A L Simon
Mrs C Cripps	R Speed
R Exley	O R Tant
Mrs C V Flood	T M Taylor
C H Hirst	R P Thornton
J Lever	R S Trafford
A A Patel	D S Williamson
M W Roulston, MBE	

Clerk to the Governors: Mrs R Summerhayes

Headmaster: **Craig Considine**, MEd, BAppSc, DipEd, MACE

Bursar: M Suddaby, MA Hons, PGCE, ACA
Deputy Head (Academic): F J Clough, BSc Hons, PhD, QTS
Deputy Head (Pastoral): C P Seal, BA Joint Hons, PGCE
Assistant Head (Teaching and Learning): Dr C Fiddes, BA Oxon, PhD
Assistant Head (Housing): A Collins, BA, Dip, QTS
Assistant Head (Co-Curriculum): E Jones, BSc
Assistant Head (Pupil Leadership and Head of Games): Mrs S Woods, BSc
Director of Sport: D Faulkner, Olympic Gold Medallist
Registrar: J Postle, BA Hons, PGCE, FRSA
Head of Marketing: Ms T Denbigh, BA Hons

Heads of Department:
Art, Design & Technology: P Maxfield, BA Hons, PGCE
Biology: S J Whittle, BSc
Business, Computing and IT: N E Williams, BA, MPhil
Chemistry: C Middleton, BSc Hons, MRSC, PGCE
English as an Additional Language (EAL): H Winkley, MA
Economics: J M Andrews, BA Hons
English, Drama and Media: J C Baddock, BA Hons
Equine Studies: D Anholt BHSI HT
Geography: C Lane, MA
History: Mrs T J Crouch, BA
Home Economics: Mrs J Moore, BSc Hons, PGCE
Languages: Ms C Coutand-Moore, L-ès-L, PGCE
Learning Support Centre: Mrs J H Clarke, BEd
Library: D Trevis, BA, MEd
Mathematics: R Bradshaw, BSc
Music: J Jensen, BMus Hons, PGCE, Dip RAM
Physical Education: S Maddock, BA Hons, MEd
Physics: S P Houghton, BA
Religious Studies: Mrs F Thomson, BA, MA
Sciences: Mrs R Landrigan, BA Hons, MA Oxon, PGCE

Houses and Houseparents:

Boarding Houses:
Abbey House: Mr and Mrs K Shelver
Acacia House: Mr and Mrs B J McEwen
Butleigh: Mr and Mrs B C Boyd
Etonhurst: Mr and Mrs T P Akhurst
Holmcroft: Dr and Mrs C J Skinner
Joan's Kitchen: Mr and Mrs M A Speyers
Keen's Elm: Mr and Mrs T Sawrey-Cookson
Kernick: Mr and Mrs D H Landrock
Kingweston: Mr and Mrs T J Greenhill
Martins: Mr and Mrs M Bone
Millfield: Mr and Mrs R J Owlett
Orchards: Mr and Mrs M J Cole-Edwardes
Portway: Mr & Mrs Trainor
St Anne's: Mr & Mrs N A Eatough
Shapwick: Mr and Mrs J A Mallett
Southfield: Mr R Baxter and Ms T Allen
The Grange: Mr and Mrs C Gange
Walton: Mr & Mrs A J Whatling
Warner: Mr and Mrs C J Middleton

Day Houses, Boys:
Great: Mr J A Bishop
Mill: Mr B McEwen

Day Houses, Girls:
Overleigh: Mrs A E S Brade
The Lakes: Miss E A Dando
Day House Year 9 Girls & Boys:
Ivythorn: Mr S Robertson

Heads of Sport:

Athletics: G Jennings
Tutor i/c Badminton: M Milton
Tutor i/c Basketball: C Seeley

Tutor i/c Chess: M Turner, MA, Grand Master
Master i/c Cricket: R Ellison, ECB Level 3
Cross Country: J Allen
Tutor i/c Dance: J Boyd
Director of Fencing: T Parris, BAF Advanced Coach
Football: T Akhurst, UEFA A
Director of Golf: K Nicholls, PGA/LET member
Director of Hockey: R Keates, HA Coach Level 2
Martial Arts: T Cheung
Modern Pentathlon: T Parris, BAF Advanced Coach
Netball: C Mitchell, UKCC Level 3
Outdoor Activities: P Bond, MLA
Polo: R Horne, HPA Instructor
Director of Riding: D O Anholt, BHSI, HT
Rowing: E Grey
Director of Rugby: J A Mallett, RFU Level 4
Skiing: R W Smith, BASI Coach Level 1
Squash: I Thomas
Director of Swimming: J Finck, Australia Gold Licence Coach
Director of Tennis: Ms K Warne-Holland
Trampolining: Mrs C Mitchell, Level 4
Triathlon: M J Brown, BCF Level 2

The school is fully co-educational with 751 boys and 490 girls; there are 934 boarders.

Housing. There are 16 single-sex, Year 10 to Upper Sixth, boarding houses. Most Sixth Formers have their own rooms whilst younger pupils share either in pairs or fours. Since the launch of Nine at Millfield dedicated Year 9 houses have been introduced for boarding and day. All Year 9 houses lie in the heart of the campus and have a higher staff to pupil ratio to oversee every aspect of each pupil's well-being and academic progress. There are four day houses for Year 10 to Upper Sixth; they have their own base on site and may stay in the evenings to do supervised prep.

The Curriculum. The academic programme is consistent with the broad principles laid down in the National Curriculum pre-16. Thus those moving to Millfield from a wide range of independent preparatory and maintained secondary schools should find both common academic ground and unrivalled choice for GCSE, Vocational Courses and AS/A2 Level. A five-year course in Personal and Social Education is also included within the curriculum.

All pupils entering Year 9 (at age 13), regardless of ability, study English, Mathematics, three Sciences, at least one language, Art, Design and Technology, ICT, Food and Nutrition, Geography, History, Religious Studies, Physical Education and Music. The pupil : teacher ratio is 6.5:1. Pupils have a structured co-curricular programme.

In Years 10 and 11 pupils follow courses leading to GCSEs in the core subjects of English, Mathematics, Science and a Modern Language. In addition, there is a wide choice of options: Art & Design, Business Studies, Business & Communications Systems, Chinese, Computing, Drama, Economics, Food & Nutrition, French, Geography, German, Greek, History, ICT, Italian, Latin, Music, Music (BTEC), Physical Education, Product Design, Religious Studies and Spanish. The Learning Support Centre provides individual support for all pupils in need of this.

At Sixth Form level, a wide range of subjects is on offer leading to AS and A2 qualifications. These include Accounting, Art & Design, Biology, Business Studies, Chemistry, Classical Languages, Computing, Drama and Theatre Studies, Economics, English Literature, French, Further Mathematics, Geography, German, Government & Politics, History, ICT, Italian, Mathematics, Media Studies, Music, Philosophy, Physical Education, Physics, Product Design, Psychology, Religious Studies, Spanish, and World Development. Also on offer are the vocational courses of BTEC Business Studies (equivalent to a two A Level course), BTEC National Diploma in Art & Design (equivalent to a three A Level course), BTEC Sport Performance

and Excellence (equivalent to 2 A Level courses), BTEC Music Technology, the Leith Cookery Course and the British Horse Society Preliminary Instructor Certificate (BHSPI). Most pupils choose four AS Level subjects in the Lower Sixth and then take three of these to the full A Level in the Upper Sixth. Wider enrichment opportunities are available to all Sixth Formers. The curriculum offers breadth, depth and flexibility in course choice. Pupils are also prepared for STEP papers and Scholastic Aptitude tests for American Universities. English as an additional language (EAL) and Learning Support is available at all levels.

Every pupil is guided through his or her school career by a Group Tutor. Each Tutor cares for between 10 and 14 pupils within a House, taking a close personal interest in each and maintaining regular contact with parents on academic matters.

Sport and Activities. Millfield runs an unparalleled range of sports and activities to engage all pupils. Pupils in Years 9, 10 and 11 generally choose from one of the core games of the term, including athletics, basketball, cricket, dance, football, hockey, netball, riding, rugby and tennis depending on term and gender. In Sixth Form, the range extends to include all of the above plus archery, badminton, canoeing, chess, clay shooting, climbing, karate, sailing, skiing, squash, trampolining, triathlon, volleyball, and various fitness activities such as aerobics, pilates and yoga. Throughout the School, pupils may also specialise in one of our performance academies in athletics, cricket, fencing, golf, modern pentathlon, squash, swimming and tennis.

In addition, pupils in Years 9, 10 and Lower Sixth take part in the school's Activities Programme where they can further broaden their experiences through a choice of more than 80 activities, ranging from athletics to street dance, building a Caterham car or guitar, film clubs, photography, scuba diving and growing greens along the way.

Fees per term (2014–2015). Boarding £11,150, Day £7,500.

Scholarships and Bursaries. Scholarships of up to 15% are awarded for exceptional talent in academic, art, drama, music, sport and chess. A limited number of Headmaster's Awards of up to 50% are also available. Where parental resources are limited, these may be augmented by means-tested bursaries of up to 100%.

Charitable status. Millfield is a Registered Charity, number 310283. Its aim is to provide independent boarding and day education for boys and girls, and to maintain an extensive system of bursary aid to gifted pupils or those in financial need.

Monkton Combe School

Monkton Combe, Bath, Somerset BA2 7HG
Tel: 01225 721102
Fax: 01225 721181
email: admissions@monkton.org.uk
website: www.monktoncombeschool.com
Twitter: @monkton
Facebook: /monktoncombeschool

Monkton Combe School, just a mile from the World Heritage City of Bath, is an independent, co-educational boarding and day school for pupils aged 2–19. We pride ourselves on our lively Christian ethos, excellent exam results and our strong pastoral care. At Monkton, we are setting standards for life; giving young people the qualities of character they need to become trusted employees, inspiring leaders, valued friends and loving parents.

Patrons and Ambassadors:
Prof R J Berry, MA, DSc, FIBiol, FRSE
G Coates

The Baroness Cox of Queensbury, SRN, BSc Soc, BSc
  Econ, FRCN, PhD
L E Ellis, MA, AFIMA
The Lord Hastings of Scarisbrick, CBE
Canon Dr Ann Holt, OBE
The Rt Revd T Dudley-Smith, OBE, MA, MLitt
P W Lee, CBE, MA, DL
The Rt Revd J F Perry, MPhil, LTh
R D Spear, JP, MA
Lady Stanley, BSc, MSW

Governors:
Chair: R S Baldock, MA Cantab
C J Alexander, MA Oxon
Mrs R Coates, BA
T R Johns, BA, PGCE, FRGS
Prof M R B Keighley, MB BS, MS, FRCS, FEWI
Prof H Langton, RGN, RSCN, ACNT, RNT, BA Hons,
  MSc
J G W Matthews, MB, BAO, MCh, FRCS
J R Myers, BEng
Mrs J Perry, BPharm, RPharms, DipClinPharm
Mrs J Thompson, BA, DipSocSi, CQSW
Mrs M K Townsend, BSc
M R A Womersley, MA Cantab

Leadership Team:

Principal: Mr R P Backhouse, MA Cantab

Prep School Headmaster: Mr A Marshall-Taylor, MA,
  PGCE
Head of Pre-Prep: Mrs K G Morrell, BEd
Director of Development: (*to be appointed*)
Company Secretary, Bursar and Clerk to the Governors:
  Mrs A L Cracknell, BSc, ACA

Senior School Staff:
† *Houseparent*

Deputy Head (*Pastoral*): J B Morley, BA Durham
Deputy Head (*Academic*):, J E J Sidders, MA, PGCE
Director of Welfare: Mrs R H Garrod, BEd Chelsea
  College
Director of Co-Curricular: Mrs L M Vaughan, BA
  Leicester
Director of Learning: Miss V Armand-Smith, BSc London

M B Abington, BSc Brighton
Ms K Alderson
Ms R Allsop
Ms E M-L L Arnaudet, Lic DEA Sorbonne
Ms W Bedeman, BSc Hons, BA, PGCE
Ms M C Bensted, BA London
Mrs C Bevan (†*Nutfield House*)
G Bevan, MMus RCM, ARCO HMD (†*Nutfield House*)
Ms R Burnett
Mr D Bowden, BA Surrey (†*Hill House*)
Mrs A Bowden BEng Liverpool (†*Hill House*)
Mrs A Bryson, MMus Cardiff
S J Call, BSc Bath
R C F Campbell, MSc London
P Carter, BA Open University
Miss N Charania, BSc Exeter
S L Chillcott, MEng Oxford, MSc Cranfield (*Officer
  Commanding CCF*, †*Clarendon House*)
Mrs R S Chillcott, MA Oxford, PGCE Surrey (†*Clarendon
  House*)
Miss D W Clark, RGN
D Coulson, BEng Swansea (†*School House*)
T J Dewes, MA Exhibitioner of St John's College
  Cambridge, BA Open University
Mrs M Egan, BA Portsmouth
Miss A Fox, BA Oxford
J F Fuller, BA Bournemouth
M C Garrod, BSc King's College London (*Senior Master/
  Exams*)

S Gent, BSc Nottingham Trent
Mrs E Gibson, BA Portsmouth
A W R Glasgow, BA Exeter
Mrs R M Glasgow, BA Wales
J Goodman, MA Oxon, PGCE
T F Hardisty, BA Falmouth
Mrs J A Hildreth, MDes RCA
Ms J Hunnisett
Ms T A King – Dip Arts Italia Conti
Revd T Ling, BA, Exeter, Cert Theol Cambridge (†*Farm
  House, SMT*)
P Wilson-Lambert,BA, PGCE
R Mainwaring, MMus, BA Hons, ALCM, PGCE
P Marais, BSc, MEd, Stellenbosch
A D McPhee, BA Sheffield, Dip TEFL
Mrs C S Morley BEd Avery Hill College of Education
S Palmer, BA Exeter
M Parfitt, BA UWE
R Pethwick
Mrs K Pethwick
Mrs J Pring, BA Portsmouth
J Rouan, BSc University of Wales
J P C Sertin, BA Loughborough (†*Eddystone*)
A Straiton, BA Nottingham
Mrs J A Stuart, BA Camb, Cert Ed Bristol
D P J Tobias, BA Goldsmiths, Dip Act Drama Centre,
  London
Mrs S Vercher, Lic Valencia
David Sixsmith, BA Hons Cantab, MSc, PhD
Mrs H K Wilkinson, BA Huddersfield (†*Grove Grange
  House*)
S Wilkinson, BSc Keele (†*Grove Grange House*)
M Wells, BSc St Mary's Twickenham, MSc Brunel
Ms S Yuan, BA London

Support Staff:
Principal's PA: Mrs Clare Slawson
Deputy Heads' PA: Mrs T Coulson
Registrar: Mrs I Hartnell
Receptionist: Mrs J Davies
Matron: Miss D W Clark, RGN
Catering Manager: Mr S Brown
Librarian: Mrs L Webb, BSc Newcastle
Data Manager: Ms G Newnham

Situation. The geographical situation is delightful; the
Senior School faces south across the Valley, or Combe, from
which the place takes its name, about 200 feet above sea
level, while the Preparatory School is at the top of the hill
above, some 400 feet higher, with magnificent views over
Avon and Wiltshire.

Organisation. The Pre-Prep, Prep and Senior Schools
each have their own Heads and the Principal of the Senior
School has overall responsibility for the three schools. However, they share the same Board of Governors and there are
close links between them. About half of the Senior School
pupils come from the Preparatory School; the rest from Preparatory Schools all over the country, State Maintained
Schools or from abroad. The Senior School went fully co-
educational and merged with Clarendon School, Bedford, in
September 1992. The Preparatory School went co-educational in September 1993.

(*For further details see Monkton Preparatory entry in
IAPS section.*)

Numbers. *Preparatory School*: There are 331 pupils of
whom 35 board and 92 are in the Pre-Prep.

Senior School: There are 391 pupils (252 boys, 138 girls),
of whom 215 are boarders. The Sixth Form numbers 141.

Admission. *Preparatory School*. For those entering the
Prep at age 7 years through to 13 years, admission is by tests
in English and Mathematics, a Reasoning Test, a reference
from the candidate's current school and an interview.

Senior School. (a) For pupils entering the Senior School
from a preparatory school, the usual means is via the Com-

mon Entrance Pre-Test at age 11 years, taken in the Lent Term of Year 7. Arrangements for sitting the examination are usually made by the Head of the candidate's prep school. A school reference and report will also be sought. Results of the Pre-Test will be conveyed to the candidate's parents by Monkton Senior School. Offers will be conditional upon the candidate completing the Common Entrance courses at his/her school from whom a reference would be sought.

(b) For those entering the Senior School at age 14 admission is by tests in English and Mathematics and a Reasoning test, a reference from the candidate's current school and an interview.

(c) Year 12 entry: For entry into Year 12, candidates will usually sit a Reasoning Test and attend an interview, where possible. A school reference will be sought and any place then offered is subject to pupils obtaining a minimum of at least five GCSE grades A*-C, together with an average score of at least 6.0 in all of the GCSE subjects taken. At GCSE, an A* grade scores 8, an A – 7, a B – 6, C – 5, D – 4 and so on. A pupil whose score is just below 6.0, but who is admitted into the Year 12, will, in the first instance, be offered a one-year course to AS level. Progression to A2 will depend upon a satisfactory performance throughout the year and in the AS examinations in June. Please note that to study certain AS subjects, a minimum grade at GCSE in that subject may be a prerequisite. Pupils are normally expected to attain at least 2 D grades at AS level for entry into Year 13, and at least D grades in subjects they wish to pursue to A2.

Buildings. The Senior School's buildings are of Bath or Cotswold Dale stone. They have been steadily extended and modernised to meet the changing needs of the School. In recent years two new girls' Houses have been built and the boys' Houses have undergone major upgrading and refurbishing.

A new Information Technology Centre, a Sixth Form Centre, a Sports Centre, a Swimming Centre, and a Drama Studio have recently been opened. The Library has been extensively refurbished to provide a modern Learning Resource Centre and a state-of-the-art Maths & Science Centre has just been opened. A new, modern, state-of-the-art Music Centre opened in May 2012. September 2014 saw the opening of Monkton's new elite rowing centre at nearby Saltford.

The School has extensive playing fields, a newly refurbished Astroturf all-weather playing area for Hockey and Tennis, Boathouses on the River Avon, 3 Netball Courts, 14 Tennis Courts, a covered Rifle Range, a Rowing Tank, a heated outdoor Swimming Pool, 2 Squash Courts, a Sports Centre and a 25m indoor Swimming Centre and Fitness Centre.

The Monkton Campaign was launched during 1995 to assist in the further development of the School over the next few years. During the last 8 years it has raised £12 million which is part of an exciting £34 million development plan.

Chapel. There is a full-time resident Anglican Chaplain. The Chapel itself stands in the centre of the School and has recently been extended and completely refurbished. A short service or assembly is held every morning and a School Service, at which parents are welcome, each Sunday. There is a Confirmation Service each year. Pupils of other than Anglican tradition are welcomed to Communion Services.

Houses. The four boys' Houses, the two girls' Houses and the Junior House for 11 and 12 year olds are all under the care of Houseparents, who together with their tutorial teams of colleagues are responsible for the boys' and girls' general welfare.

Day Pupils are fully integrated into the boarding houses and the total life of the School and are encouraged but not obliged to stay until the end of evening prep. Senior pupils are given opportunities for responsibility as School or House Prefects during their sixth-form careers.

Tutor System. Each pupil has a Tutor, normally a member of staff of his or her own choice, who keeps in touch with parents and provides guidance and advice over every aspect of School life and over making choices for the future.

Curriculum. Our aim is to provide a broadly based curriculum in the years leading to GCSE. The curriculum reflects the spirit and fundamental goals of the National Curriculum. Those who show particular ability in French or Mathematics may proceed to work more advanced than GCSE before the end of Year 11. Personal, Social and Health Education and Physical Education are included.

In Years 7, 8 and 9 all pupils study English, Mathematics and the Sciences with a foundation course comprising at least one Foreign Language, Art, the Classics, Design Technology, Geography, History, Information Technology, Music, PE and Religious Studies. In Years 10 and 11 all pupils take IGCSE English, Mathematics, and Coordinated Dual Award Science (Biology, Chemistry and Physics). English Literature is taught alongside English to the top three sets. Pupils choose four other subjects from Art, Business Studies with IT, Classical Civilisation, Design Technology, Drama, French, Geography, History, Latin, Music, Religious Studies, Spanish and Sports Studies. Extra English is available as an option for those with particular needs in this subject.

Most pupils stay on for two years in the Sixth Form. The subjects at present offered at AS/A2 Level are: Art, Biology, Business Studies, Chemistry, Critical Thinking, Design Technology, English Literature, English Language, French, Further Mathematics, Geography, History, Mathematics, Music, Photography, Physics, Psychology, Religious Studies, Spanish, Sports Studies and Theatre Studies. Most pupils entering Year 12 study four subjects for one year to AS and continue with three to full A Level. Pupils also attend courses on world religions, the family, personal finance, self-presentation and interview technique. A notable feature of the Sixth Form programme is the wide variety of lectures and presentations delivered by visiting speakers prominent in their field.

Careers Advice and Staff/Parent Meetings. An experienced Careers Teacher works closely with Tutors in advising pupils. There is also a member of staff responsible for advice on higher education. Parents, Old Monktonians and local people are invited to help pupils in their thinking about careers. The School belongs to the Independent Schools Careers Organisation which arranges Aptitude and Interest tests. Annual staff/parent meetings are held at the School to discuss pupils' progress. Parents are of course always welcome at other times.

University Entrance. The great majority of leavers go on to degree courses at Universities and Colleges of Higher Education. Last year 96% of leavers went to their first-choice university.

Games. Those with particular abilities are encouraged to aim for excellence, but we also believe that regular games and exercise are important for all, helping to build a healthy lifestyle for the future and fostering leadership, teamwork and cooperation.

The major sports for boys are: in the Michaelmas Term, Rugby; in the Lent Term, Hockey or Rowing; in the Summer Term, Cricket, Rowing or Tennis. Boys choose either to row or to play Hockey and Cricket, but are allowed to alter their choice during their time at the School. Younger boys are normally required to play the major game of each term but as they become more senior they are allowed a greater degree of choice.

The major sports for girls are: in the Michaelmas Term, Hockey; in the Lent Term, Netball or Rowing; in the Summer Term, Tennis or Rowing. Representative teams are fielded in all these sports. As with the boys, the choice becomes more extended as girls become more senior.

There are also School teams in Athletics, Basketball, Cross-Country, Football, Judo, Squash and Shooting.

CCF and Community Service. There are sections for all three Services, besides various specialist activities such as Venture Section (through which the Duke of Edinburgh's Award scheme is offered) and car maintenance. There is also an active Community Service group.

Leisure Activities. Monkton encourages as many worthwhile leisure pursuits as possible. Between 35 and 40 different activities are offered; up to the age of 15 pupils are expected to be involved in at least one. All the facilities of the School, including the Art and DT Departments, Music Rooms and ICT Centre are available to pupils during their free time. The Choir, Orchestra, Big Band and other less formal music groups play an important part in the School's life and tuition is available in all orchestral instruments. About 45% of the members of the School take music lessons. There is a major School dramatic production in the Michaelmas Term. The School is conveniently close to Bath and Bristol for taking parties to concerts and theatres. Some 30 clubs and societies figure on the School List, ranging from the Bridge Club to the Literary Society and the Christian Union. Bible Study groups meet weekly.

Health. The School Medical Officer visits regularly and all boarders are required to register with him. The Medical Centre is under the care of a fully qualified Sister and Assistant who provide a 24-hour service.

Catering. All pupils take their meals in the Dining Hall, with cafeteria service.

Dress. The Clothes List is kept as simple as possible. All required items can be purchased in the School Shop.

Scholarships and Bursaries. Scholarships are awarded on entry to the School for candidates at Year 9 and Year 12. The Principal reserves the right to award up to two Year 10 Scholarships at his discretion; no application for this award is required. Scholarships recognise the contribution to School life which is made by exceptional performers by raising the aspirations of other pupils, by stimulating greater achievement in their peers and by enabling higher levels of performance in collaborative activities such as music, drama and sport. All scholarships awarded are conditional on this continued contribution to the area of School life which is recognized in the award. In addition, all scholarships are awarded for the duration of the pupil's time at the School. Moreover, candidates for all awards are expected to achieve satisfactory standards in Common Entrance, GCSE exams or other entry tests.

Monkton Senior School seeks to give bursaries to pupils who would otherwise not be able to come to the School. Such bursaries are available for 5–100% of fees, and special consideration is given to the children of clergy and missionaries, in accordance with the School's charitable objectives. Where a bursary and a scholarship are awarded to the same pupil, the scholarship is subsumed into the bursary (assuming this is the larger of the two); the bursary will never be reduced below the level of the original scholarship. Where a bursary has already been awarded, the scholarship will not increase the bursary unless it is greater than the bursary.

Where two scholarships are won by the same pupil, the second scholarship will have a percentage value against the remainder of the fee, rather than the total (gross fee). If the first was 20% and the second 10%, the second scholarship would be worth 10% of the remaining 80% of fees (i.e. 8% of full fees). Internal scholarships are offered for pupils moving from Y8 to Y9 at the Senior School, and for those moving from Y11 to 12, who intend to board in the Sixth Form.

Details of all awards can be obtained from the Registrar.

Fees per term (2014–2015). Senior: £7,420–£9,772 (boarders); £5,198–£6,312 (day pupils). Preparatory: £6,885–£7,420 (boarders); £3,565–£5,198 (day pupils). Pre-Prep: £2,838–£3,040.

Old Monktonian Club. The Monkton Combe School Register has been fully revised and updated. Details from the Development Office at the School.

Charitable status. Monkton Combe School is a Registered Charity, number 1057185, and a Company Limited by Guarantee, registered in England, number 3228456. Its aims and objectives are to provide education for girls and boys combined with sound religious training on Protestant and Evangelical principles in accordance with the doctrines of The Church of England.

Monmouth School

Almshouse Street, Monmouth, Monmouthshire NP25 3XP

Tel:	01600 713143
Fax:	01600 772701
email:	enquiries@monmouthschool.org
website:	www.habs-monmouth.org
Twitter:	@habsmonmouth
Facebook:	/Habsmonmouth

Motto: *Serve and Obey.*

The School was founded in 1614, by William Jones, a merchant of the City of London and a Liveryman of the Worshipful Company of Haberdashers, who was born near Monmouth and bequeathed a large sum of money to found a school and almshouses in the town. The School has derived immense advantage from this unusual association with the City of London.

The School is controlled by a Board of Governors appointed variously by the Haberdashers' Company, the Universities of Oxford, Cambridge and Wales, and local representative bodies.

Chairman of the Governors: J B S Swallow, MA, FCA

Ex officio: The Master of the Worshipful Company of Haberdashers

P M Alderman	[1]Canon E J S Hiscocks
M H C Anderson	[1]D J Hitchcock
(*Chairman,*	Miss H Hutton (*Child*
Haberdashers'	*Protection Governor*)
Monmouth School for	[1]Dr J Kelly
Girls Committee)	A M Kerr (*Chairman,*
Dr M G Archer	*Monmouth School*
Dr P E G Baird	*Committee*)
Mrs S Clayton	*A G Nicholas
[1]M E Davidson	[1]Mrs T Pike (*Grange*
Mrs C J Davis	*Governor*)
Professor S P Denyer	Mrs R F Rose
[1]C R S Hardie	Councillor S White
Mrs M K Henderson	

[1] *Member of the Monmouth School Committee*

Headmaster: S G Connors, BA, PhD

Second Master: S H Dorman, MA, MPhil
Director of Studies: A J Winter, BSc, PhD
Head of Sixth Form: H F Tatham, MA

Assistant Staff:
* *Head of Department*
† *Housemaster/Housemistress*

Mrs E R Arrand, BA (†*Severn House*)
Mrs S G Atherton, BA
Dr L M Bakker, BTech, PhD
Miss E K Barson, BSc, MSc (**Biology*)
J C Bevan, CertEd (†*Buchanan House*)
J Boiling, BA (†*Town House*)
R C Boyle, BSc (†*School House*)
M D Clarke, BSc, PhD
J P Danks, BSc, DPhil (**Chemistry,* †*Dean House*)
Miss E R Davies, BSc

Mrs S Davies, L-ès-L
Dr M T Davis, BSc
A J Dawson, BSc, MSc
J Despontin, BSc, MSc
Mrs P G Dollins, BMus
S H Dorman, MA, MPhil
G Dunn, BSc, MSc
Dr E Evans, BSc, PhD
Dr H B Evans, MSc, PhD (*Mathematics*)
Miss S L Fowler, BSc
J F Geraghty, BA
N J R Goodson, BSc
P M Griffin, BA (*Drama*)
J D Griffiths, BSc
Mrs J R Gunn, BA
J M Harrison, BA, PhD (*History*)
A Hawley, BA
D G Hope, BA (†*Weirhead House*)
Mrs L A Hope (*ICT*)
R Howe, BA (†*Monmouth House*)
P C Hunt, GRNCM, LLCM (†*Wye House*)
P D Jefferies, BSc
Mrs J A Johnston, MA
A J Jones, BA (†*Chapel House*)
D K Jones, BSc (*Head of Boarding*)
I J Lawrence, BSc, MSc
D F Lawson, BA (*Director of Music and Organist*)
Mrs L E Lewis, BA
M Lewis, BA
Mrs L R Livingston, BA
K J Madsen, BA (*Economics,* †*Glendower House*)
Mrs R J Marsh, BSc
Ms S M Mone, BA
K A Moseley, BSc, PhD, FRAS (*Physics*)
T W H Murgatroyd, BA, MPhil, PhD (*Classics*)
Mrs L C Parr, BEng, BSc
Mrs L Parsons, BA (*Modern Languages*)
A K Peace (†*Severn House*)
Mrs G S Peace, BA, MA (*English*)
M Peake, BA (*Art*)
D J Pearson, BSc
Mrs S E Phillips, BEd, MA, Dip SpLD
R D Picken, BA
Mrs T L Matthews, BA
J E Rudge, BSc
A E Shakeshaft, BA
G F Stentiford, MSc (*Geography*)
M J Tamplin, BSc (†*Hereford House*)
H F Tatham, MA
O P Thicknesse, BA
K A Tiebosch, BA
P Vaughan-Smith, BA
D M Vickers, BEd (*Director of Physical Education,*
†*Tudor House*)
A J White, BA (*Design Technology*)
Mrs R Widdicks, BA (*Study Support*)
O T R Williams, BSc, MA
P R Williams, BA
Miss S E L Williams, BA, MA
A J Winter, BSc, PhD
Mrs R L Wynne Lord, MA (*Religious Education*)

Chaplain: Revd. D J Ibbotson

The Grange (Preparatory Department)

Head: Mrs E G Thomas, BA
Deputy Head: Mrs S L Wilderspin, CertEd

Mrs L Davies, BA	Miss I L Kershaw-Naylor,
T Dixon, BEng	BA
D G Hayden, MA	Mrs K E Kirman, BSc
Mrs S M Holmes, BEd	P N Morris, BEd
S C Huson, BA, BA, MA	D G Murray, MA
	Mrs K Noel, BSc

K J Shepherd, BA
J D Walton, BMus

Bursar: D A Chowns, BEng, MA

Medical Officer: Dr J Knowles

There are approximately 580 boys in the Senior School, of whom 160 are boarders. The Grange, the School's Preparatory Department, caters for 130 dayboys aged 7 to 11, with boarding available at age 9. (*For further details see entry in IAPS section.*)

Situation and Buildings. The School was founded in 1614 by William Jones and is one of the schools of the Worshipful Company of Haberdashers. A generous endowment enables the School to provide superb facilities and an excellent academic education whilst keeping fees at a reasonable level. There are many scholarships and bursaries and the Haberdashers' Assisted Places Scheme, which replaced the Government scheme in 1998, ensures that an education at Monmouth School can be available to boys who will benefit from it, irrespective of their parents' income.

The School is enriched by close cooperation with Haberdashers' Monmouth School for Girls in many areas of school life, especially at Sixth Form level.

The School is set in the delightful landscape of the Wye Valley and much use is made of the surrounding countryside for expeditions and other outward-bound activities. There is a strong tradition of music and drama as well as of excellence in sport. A new sports complex was opened in Autumn 1999, a studio theatre in January 2001 and additional outdoor facilities, including an all-weather pitch, in Autumn 2001. The Blake Theatre (500 seats) was completed in Summer 2004. Other recent developments have included greatly expanded ICT facilities and refurbished boarding houses and classroom blocks. The Sixth Form has a dedicated Sixth Form Centre. A superb new Sports Pavilion opened in 2008 and the Prep School, The Grange, moved to an innovatively designed and exciting new building in February 2009. An ambitious development, *The Heart* Project, saw its completion in October 2013. The William Jones Building provides state-of-the-art facilities in classrooms for three departments as well as a completely new reception and administration area. This move has allowed the School to release space to expand and further enhance the boarding accommodation.

Boarding. The boarding community forms the core of the School. Junior boarders (9–12 year olds) are accommodated in Chapel House for their first few years and benefit from the care of a dedicated house team who also provide an ambitious and popular programme of extra-curricular activities, tailored to the interests of the age group.

There are three senior boarding houses for boys between 13 and 18. The School has a flexible boarding policy which provides a considerable degree of freedom for families to make boarding arrangements which fit in with their lives, but which encourages boys to take full advantage of the many sporting, cultural and extra-curricular activities for which the School is renowned.

September 2011 saw the opening of Buchanan House, a sixth form boarding house with single study-bedrooms and en-suite facilities.

Admission. The main admission points are 7, 10, 11, 13 and 16, but other stages will be considered if places are available. Candidates aged 7 and 11 sit the School's own entrance tests. At 13, candidates take the Common Entrance Examination, the School's own Foundation Scholarship Examination or its 13+ examination. Entrants to the Sixth Form are accepted either after sitting the Sixth Form Scholarship Examination or on the basis of GCSE results (or equivalent).

Candidates from overseas are welcome. Those whose first language is not English take a preliminary test of proficiency in English before proceeding to the appropriate entrance test.

The School accepts pupils with Dyslexia or similar specific learning difficulties. They are taught in mainstream lessons and additional study support is available.

Curriculum. The curriculum is designed to provide both flexibility and breadth and to be in step with the National Curriculum without being constrained by it. Those in Forms I and II (Years 7 and 8) study a wide range of subjects including Latin, French and combined Science. In Form III (Year 9) the three Sciences are taught separately and pupils have the option of starting Greek.

Pupils normally take nine or ten GCSE subjects, four of which are of their own choosing. There is a cross-curricular ICT scheme to enable pupils to make full use of the School's extensive facilities.

In the Sixth Form a range of approximately 30 AS subjects is offered along with an enrichment programme. This programme and many of the AS subjects are offered in cooperation with Haberdashers' Monmouth School for Girls.

A particular feature of the curriculum is the extensive range of Modern Languages. French is taught at all levels and Spanish and German are available from Form III. Welsh is available as an after-school conversational class and Russian is available at AS/A Level.

The Chapel. The School is an Anglican foundation and the Chapel plays an important part in its life. All pupils attend Chapel at least once each week and there is a weekly service for boarders. A varied programme of preachers is organised, including clergy and lay people of many denominations. The Bishop of Monmouth officiates at the annual Confirmation Service.

Games. The main sports are rugby, rowing, cricket and soccer. Many other sports are also available at a highly competitive level including athletics, cross-country running, golf, softball, squash and swimming. Several members of staff have international sporting honours and pupils regularly gain places to represent Wales in a variety of sports.

Activities. There is an extensive programme of activities throughout the School. Pupils in Form IV and above may join the CCF (Army and RAF sections) which enjoy excellent links with locally based regular and territorial forces. Community Service is a popular option and many boys participate in the Duke of Edinburgh's Award Scheme. There is a very strong musical tradition with many pupils taking part in choirs, orchestras and bands which achieve high levels of success in competitions, and play to appreciative audiences locally and on the regular overseas tours which take place. Drama is also strong and good opportunities are provided for participation at all levels. A wide range of School clubs and Societies further enriches the life of the School.

Fees per term (2014–2015). Day £4,729, Boarding £8,570–£9,085; The Grange: Day £3,317, Boarding £6,239.

Scholarships and Bursaries. A generous number of Entrance Scholarships are awarded to dayboys or boarders on the basis of performance in the Year 7 Entry Assessments (11+) held in February, on the Foundation Scholarship Examination (13+) held in February/March, and the Sixth Form Scholarship Examination (16+) held in February. In cases of need, Scholarships may be augmented by a Bursary.

Music Scholarships and Exhibitions may be awarded at 11, 13 and 16 up to the value of half of the fees and carrying free instrumental tuition. Sixth Form organ or instrumental scholarships also available.

Sports Awards are available to suitable candidates at 11, 13 and Sixth Form entry.

Old Monmothian and Mountjoy Awards are available for candidates who show all-round ability and potential.

The E F Bulmer Award is available to suitable Sixth Form candidates living in Herefordshire; awards range in value from 50% to 100% of the fees. A new Sixth Form Boarding Scholarship is available, which is means-tested and can cover up to 75% of the fees.

Bursaries and the Haberdashers' Assisted Places Scheme can also provide up to 100% remission of fees, in certain circumstances.

Service Bursaries are available for the sons of serving members of HM Armed Forces, thus guaranteeing no more than the minimum 10% of fees is payable by parents.

Old Monmothians. Past members of the School are eligible to join the Old Monmothian Club which enjoys a close relationship with the School. The Membership Secretary is Roger Atkins, c/o Old Monmothians, Monmouth School, Almshouse Street, Monmouth NP25 3XP.

Charitable status. William Jones's Schools Foundation is a Registered Charity, number 525616. Its aims and objectives are to provide an all-round education for boys and girls at reasonable fees; also to carry out the Founder's intention that local boys qualifying for entry should not be prevented from attending the School by lack of funds.

Morrison's Academy

Ferntower Road, Crieff, Perthshire PH7 3AN
Tel: 01764 653885
Fax: 01764 655411
email: principal@morrisonsacademy.org
website: www.morrisonsacademy.org
Twitter: @macmorrisons
Facebook: /morrisonsacademy

Motto: *Ad summa tendendum* : *Striving for the highest*
Morrison's Academy Boys' School was opened in 1860 with a Girls' Department in 1861, an arrangement which continued until 1889 when a separate school for Girls was opened within the ten acres of the original site. In 1979 these two schools were brought together to become the one Morrison's Academy. The original foundation was possible through the generosity of Thomas Mo(r)rison, a native of Muthill who became a builder in Edinburgh and who in 1813 executed a Trust Deed directing that the fee of the reversion of his estate should be used to found and erect 'an institution calculated to promote the interests of mankind, having particular regard to the Education of Youth and the diffusion of useful knowledge ...a new institution which may bear my name and preserve the remembrance of my good intentions for the welfare and happiness of my fellow men'.

Board of Governors:
Chairman: Mr L C Johnston
Mr P J Brodie, MA, MA Ed, PGCE
Mrs J Brown, BSc, MSc, MBA
Mr E Cameron, MA Hons
Mr H Campbell, BSc, CEng, MICE, MIStructE
Mr A E Christmas, FCIBS, Chartered Banker
Mr P J H Cook, BSc Hons, PG Dip
Mrs K M Elwis, BA Hons
Mr G Ferguson, BEng Hons, MSc, CEng, MCIBSE, CBIFM
Mr A P Godfrey, BSc, CA
Professor W S Hanson, BA, PhD, FSA Scot
Mr M A Johnson, MTheol, PGCE
Councillor M Lyle
Mrs J F Morrow, MA, PG Dip

Clerk to Governors: Mr J C Andrew, LLB Hons, Dip LP, NP

Staff:

***Rector*: Mr G S H Pengelley**, BA

Depute Rector: Mr D Johnston, BA
Assistant Rector: Mr P J Lovegrove, MA
Assistant Rector: Miss A McCluskey, MA

Bursar: Mr A U Beaton, MSc, Chartered FCIPD, MCMI
Head of Primary: Mr A R Robertson, Dip CE
Depute Head of Primary: Mrs L S Anderson, BEd
Director of Development and Alumni Relations: Ms N A
  Latte
Head of Nursery: Mrs B Thomson, BSc

Teaching Staff:

Art & Design:
Ms P M O'Neill, MA,
  MFA
Mr S Jewell, BDes, MDes

Business Studies:
Mrs M Stirling, MA
Miss C McGookin, MA

CDT:
Mr R G McDermott, MEd,
  BEd

Computing & IT:
Mr D Hamilton, BSc, MSc
  (*Director of IT*)
Mrs P Boal, BSc, MBCS
  (*Head of Year S1*)

English:
Mr P G O'Kane, MA
Mrs T Lafferty, BEd
Mrs D Riddell, MA (*Head
  of Year S4*)
Mrs N Greener, BA

Geography:
Mr A Wylie, BA
Mr R S Anderson, MA

History:
Mr P J Lovegrove, MA
Mr M J Clayton, MA
Mr D Johnston, BA

Home Economics:
Mrs M Neilson, BA

Mathematics:
Mr I K O Barnett, BSc
Mr A M Jack, BSc
Mrs M T O'Kane, BSc
  (*Head of Year S3*)
Mrs J McConville, BEng

Modern Languages:
Mr E Coffey, MA
Miss A McCluskey, MA
Mr R Millon, BA
Mrs J White, MA
Mrs H A Yellowley BA

Music:
Miss S Herbert, BMus
  (*Director of Music*)
Mrs S Smart, BA, LRAM

Physical Education:
Mr S G Weston, BSc
  (*Director of Sport*)
Mr L Howell, MEd,
  Chartered Teacher (*Head
  of Year S5*)
Mrs J C Lee, BEd
Miss E McCormick, BEd
Mrs D J McMillan, BEd
  (*Head of Year S6*)

Science:
Mr J B Beedie, BSc
Mr R S Armstrong, BEng
Mr F Black, BSc
Mrs A S Harper, BSc
Mr M McKeever, BSc
Mrs S Steven, BSc

Primary:
Mr A R Robertson, DipCE
Mrs L S Anderson, BEd
Ms M Anderson, BEd
Mr I Barr, MA
Mr G Chater, BA
Mrs A Jenkins, BA
Mrs G M Lauchlan, MA
Mrs J A Longmuir, DipEd
Mrs K Foote, BDes
Mrs C Marchbank, BA

Nursery:
Mrs B Thomson, BSc
  (*Head of Nursery*)
Mrs C Senior, BEd
Mrs G Thomson

Learning Support:
Mrs G Wilkie, MA
Mrs S M Keating, BSc

Early Years Assistant:
Mrs M Thomson

The School. Morrison's Academy is an integral part of the community in Crieff and comprises a 10-acre main campus supplemented by 45 acres of sports fields, main hall, after-school/holiday club and nursery: a new purpose-built Nursery has opened to accommodate 42 children adjacent to the Primary School. The school provides education for 540 boys and girls from 3 to 18 years. The Nursery was recently inspected by HMIE and the Care Commission and received an outstanding report, where all areas received 'excellent' or 'very good' indicators. The Nursery and After-School/Holiday Club together offer care from 8.00 am to 6.00 pm for 50 weeks each year.

The Primary School, housed in a separate building on the main campus, educates 160 pupils in small classes. Transfer between primary and secondary is helped by our Transitional Year (P7), which provides teaching in the primary school by a class teacher supplemented by lessons in the secondary school taught by subject specialists.

The Secondary School has 350 pupils studying towards Scottish Qualifications and entry to universities in Scotland, the rest of the UK and abroad. Academic expectations and achievements are high and small groups encourage individual learning and development. Over ninety-seven percent of our S6 go on to university.

Staff and pupils mix easily and the scale of the school allows for every individual to be known and valued by all.

Situation. Morrison's Academy is situated in the market town of Crieff on the edge of the Scottish Highlands in Perthshire. Strathearn is a beautiful area of mountains, rivers, lochs and rich agricultural land. Pupils attend from the local area and travel from Perth, Pitlochry, Dunkeld, Auchterarder, Stirling and Dunblane.

Curriculum. Pupils in Primary and lower Secondary follow broadly the Scottish 5–14 programme of study, leading in upper Secondary to Intermediate and then to Higher and Advanced Higher National Qualifications. Emphasis is placed upon academic achievement, while the pupils are also always encouraged to develop broad skills and interests outside the classroom. Co-curricular activities are extensive and Morrison's Academy makes good use of its glorious location.

Houses. All pupils are placed in one of the four houses named after local families: Campbells, Drummonds, Grahams and Murrays. There is healthy, competitive rivalry between the houses and senior pupils are encouraged to take charge of teams for sporting, music, debating and other events.

Games and Activities. Morrison's Academy encourages pupils to participate in a wide range of co-curricular activities and sports. All pupils use the playing fields and facilities on the main campus or walk to the 45 acres of playing fields and pavilions at Dallerie. Main sports are rugby, hockey, cricket, tennis and athletics. From upper primary fixtures against other schools take place, generally on Saturday mornings. Other sporting activities include soccer, basketball, netball, swimming, golf, weight training, sailing, short tennis, skiing, climbing, karate and more. To complement the sporting activities, pupils are active in The Duke of Edinburgh's Award Scheme, the Combined Cadet Force, drama, music, debating, chess, Pipe and Drum Band, environment group, Young Enterprise, charity fundraising, Christian groups, highland dancing and more. Pupils are challenged to make the most of their time and all within the wonderful environment of Perthshire.

Fees per term (2014–2015). Day: Primary £2,504–£3,567, Secondary £3,790.

The fees include tuition, textbooks, stationery, external examination fees, sports and curriculum-related travel.

Admission Procedure. Admission to the school is by entrance test and school report and/or exam results and entrance interview. The school's main entrance testing/interview days are at the beginning of February and beginning of May, for entry to the academic year commencing the following August.

For a prospectus pack and any queries please contact the Admissions Registrar.

Scholarships and Bursaries. A number of Sixth Form Scholarships are awarded after examination and interview in May. The awards, which carry a nominal financial value, recognise both achievement and potential. Means-tested Bursaries are also available.

The *Thomas Morrison Scholarship* provides means-tested assistance with tuition fees and is available to both existing pupils and new applicants, the main awards being made at entry to Form 1 in the Secondary School.

A limited number of awards are granted at other stages of the Secondary School but these are determined by the availability of funds at the time. Many of these awards are intended to assist existing pupils where there has been a significant change in financial circumstances, such as loss of income, which threatens the pupil's continued attendance at

Morrison's Academy. Further details are available from The Rector.

Charitable status. Morrison's Academy is a Registered Charity, number SC000458. The school is a recognised charity providing education.

Mount Kelly

Tavistock, Devon PL19 0HZ
Tel: 01822 813193
Fax: 01822 612050
email: admissions@mountkelly.com
website: www.mountkelly.com
Twitter: @Mount_Kelly

Kelly College was founded in 1877 by Admiral Benedictus Marwood Kelly. In 2014 Kelly College and Prep merged with Mount House (founded in 1881) to form Mount Kelly a boarding and day school for boys and girls aged 3–18.

Governors:
Chairman: Rear Admiral Chris Snow, CBE, DL
Vice-Chairman and Chair of Prep School Committee: Mr Julian Trahair
Chair of the Education Standards Committee: Mr Simon Carder
Chair of the Finance, General Purposes and Strategy Committee: Mr Alistair Grove, FCA
Chair of Mount Kelly Enterprises Ltd: Mr David Parlby
Chair of the Safeguarding Committee: Mr Michael Tanner
The Reverend Prebendary Roger Carlton (*nominated*)
Director of Mount Kelly Enterprises Ltd: Mr Keith Hollinshead
Mr James Kitson
Dr Howard J Ball
Sir Charles Lawson
Mrs Philippa Sale
Mrs Wendy Davis
Mr William May-Somerville
Ms Stephanie Walshe
Mrs Kerstin Lewis
Dr Peter Murphy
Mr Neil O'Neill

Head Master and Principal of the Mount Kelly Foundation: Mr Mark Semmence, BA Durham, MA Warwick, MBA Durham, PGCE

* *Head of Department*

Principal Deputy Headmaster: Mr Duncan Page, BA, MA (*History*)
Assistant Head (*Pastoral*): Mr Drew Bott, BA (*History)
Deputy Head (*Academic*): Mrs Margaret Duffy, BEd (*Mathematics*)
Assistant Head (*Co-Curriculum*): Mr Luke Francis, BA (*Geography)
Head of Prep: Mr Matthew Foale, BEd, MSc
Bursar: Mrs Marilyn Sena
Director of Admissions and Marketing: Mrs Vanessa Bowles, MSc
Director of Swimming and Performance Sport: Mr Robin Brew, MSc
Business Manager, Mount Kelly Enterprises: Mr Paul Birchell, BSc

Housemasters/mistresses:
Newton House: Mrs Susan Page
Courtenay House: Mr Richard Stanyer, BSc, BEd (*ICT)
Marwood House: Mrs Rachel Morel, BA (*French*)
Conway House: Mrs Emma Birchell, BSc
School House: Mrs Sarah Baldock, BSc (*Chemistry*)

Assistant Staff:
Revd Richard Bache, BA, PGCE (*Chaplain*)
Mr Jeremy Balfour, BA (*Drama)
Mrs Louise Bott, BA, PGCE (*French and Drama*)
Mr Nicholas Bottrell, RLC, GCGI (*School Staff Instructor*)
Mrs Joanna Boulton (*Learning Support Assistant*)
Mrs Susan Brassil, BSc (*Learning Support Assistant*)
Mrs Trudie Bratt, BA, MA, PGCE (*English and New Staff Induction Coordinator*)
Mrs Mary Bridger, BA, PGCE (*English*)
Mrs Julia Brown, IL (*Coordinator of Spanish*)
Miss Rebecca Callard, BSc (*Head of Sixth Form; Geography*)
Mr Paul Clark, BSc, PGCE (*Head of Mathematics*)
Mrs Debbie Collard, BEd (*DT*)
Mr Gary Collard, BEd (*DT)
Mrs Maria Collier, BA, LGSM, PGCE (*Director of Music*)
Mrs Vanni Cook, BA, PGCE (*English as a Second Language*)
Mr Benjamin Donnelly, BSc, PGCE (*Biology)
Mrs Samantha Donnelly, BSc, PGCE, MPhil Eng (*Biology*)
Mr Ben Edge, BSc, PGCE (*Head of Physical Education*)
Mrs Sally Fletcher, BEng (*Mathematics*)
Mr Luke Francis, BA (*Geography)
Mrs Susan Gray, BSc, PGCE (**Chemistry, PSHE, Coordinator of Science*)
Mrs Annette Holwill, BA (*Art*)
Mr Tom Honey, BSc (*Physical Education*)
Mrs Katherine Kelly, BSc, PGCE (*Mathematics, Physical Education, Director of Outdoor Education*)
Mr Ian Leaman, BSc, PGCE (**BTEC National Diploma in Sport*)
Mr Chris Limb, BA, PGCE (*English)
Mr Steve Martin (*Geography*)
Mr Alex McCarthy, BA (*Artist in Residence*)
Mrs Vanessa McCarty, BA, ALAM (*Speech and Drama*)
Miss Rosalyn Plumptre, BA, LTCL (*ESL)
Mr Maurice Quinlan, BSc (*Physics)
Mrs Susan Roberts-Key, BSc (*Mathematics*)
Mr Nigel Rogerson, MA (*Economics & Business*)
Revd Michael Sneary, BA (*Classics*)
Miss Gemma Spooner, BA (*Art)
Mrs Jacqueline Stockman, BA, PGCE (*Learning Support*)
Mr Dale Sutcliffe, BA, PGCE (*Science*)
Mr Mark Tailyour, BEd (**Religious Studies*)
Mr David Turnbull, BA (*Design & Technology*)
Mr Paul Williams, BSc (*Physics, *Careers*)

Prep Staff:
Mr Matthew Foale, BEd, MSc (*Head of Prep*)
Mr Patrick Savage, BA (*Director of Common Entrance*)
Mrs Judith Unwin, BSc (*Deputy Head Academic*)
Miss Michelle Pole, BEd (*Head of Pre-Prep*)

Miss Laura Armstrong, BA, PGCE (*Junior Subjects*)
Mrs Clare Balm, BSc (*Reception*)
Mr Jonathan Banyard, BA, PGCE (**Religious Studies, *PSHE*)
Mr Malcolm Bassett, BEd (**Mathematics Years 6–8*)
Mr David Briggs, BAEd (*DT)
Mrs Esse Buckett, BSc PGCE (*Geography)
Mrs Sue Buckley, BEd (*Mathematics)
Mr Steve Buckley, BSc (*Science)
Mr Graham Bush (*Learning Support*)
Mrs Sally Butcher, BA, PGCE (**English, *Latin*)
Mrs Amanda Edwards, BSc (*PE and Girls' Games*)
Miss Chloe Grubb, BA Hons, PGCE (*Junior Subjects*)
Mr Andrew Lamb, BEd (**Geography Years 6–8, Prep Housemaster*)
Mrs Becky Lamb, BA, PGCE (*History, Prep Housemistress*)
Mrs Donna Lindsey, BA, PGCE (**Art Years 2–5*)
Mrs Mary Lowther, BA, PGCE (*French)
Mrs Katie MacEacharn, BEd (*Foundation Stage Manager*)

Mrs Rebecca Martin, BA (*English*)
Mr Earl Newton, BEd (*ICT, *DT*)
Miss Alison Parker, BEd (*Year 1*)
Mr Phil Stephens, BEd (*Boys Games, General Subjects*)
Mrs Helen Shere, BEd (*RSA Learning Development Coordinator*)
Miss Jo Tribe, BA (*Art Years 5–8*)
Mrs Liz Twyman, BMus (*Drama, Assistant Head of Music*)
Mr Martin Weaver, BEd (*Junior Subjects*)
Mrs Caroline Wilson, BA (*English*)
Mrs Rosalind Russell (*Supply*)

Marketing and Development Manager: Mr Tom Godwin
Marketing Manager: Mrs Amanda Goodison
Medical Officer: Dr Mark Eggleton
Headmaster's Secretary: Ms Nikki Murton

Mount Kelly, set in over 100 acres of green fields and woodland on the edge of Dartmoor National Park, combines academic excellence with an outstanding range of opportunities beyond the classroom and exceptional pastoral care. The School, for girls and boys aged between 3 and 18, offers day, weekly and full boarding places, currently for over 550 pupils (339 are in Year 7 and above; over 50% of whom are boarders). Boarding is available from the age of 7 and most of our younger pupils take advantage of boarding at some stage in their school career.

Children at Mount Kelly are nurtured, guided and inspired to develop their own skills and interests. Each pupil joins one of the School's Houses, which serves as a boarder's 'home from home' and a day pupil's working base. Boarders and day pupils are integrated throughout the School with small class sizes offering exceptional levels of individual focus. Each pupil is cared for by a Housemaster or Housemistress and assigned a dedicated tutor who oversees their academic, pastoral and co-curricular progress. This comprehensive tutoring system produces happy pupils who are confident, well-rounded and ambitious.

Site and Buildings. Mount Kelly occupies over 100 acres of beautiful hillside in the Tavy Valley overlooking Dartmoor National Park on the edge of the historic town of Tavistock, Devon. The buildings comprise the School Chapel, Assembly Hall, Performing Arts Centre, Central Dining Hall, Library and ICT Centre, Art and Design Studios, Technology workshops, Science Laboratories, a heated indoor Swimming Pool, Indoor Sports Hall, Gymnasium, covered Fives and Squash Courts, floodlit all-weather surface for Hockey and Tennis, Armoury and Miniature Rifle Range. There is also a residential Adventure Training Centre, including a high-ropes course and trapeze jump. The School has its own Trout and Salmon fishing.

School Structure and Admission Procedures. Admission at age 11 (Year 7) is by school examination in the preceding February. Admission at age 13 (Year 9) is by the Common Entrance Examination. Entrance to the Sixth Form is on the basis of GCSE predictions. A report from the present school is required and all candidates for entry have a formal interview with the Head Master.

Term of Entry. Pupils may be accepted at any stage in the school year.

Scholarships are awarded on entry to the school at 11+, 13+ and 16+. They are competitive on entry and based on merit. For more information please contact the Director of Admissions.

At 11+ academic awards are based on the performance in the 11+ Entrance Examination and candidates for 'performance' awards are assessed as part of the routine admissions process. 13+ academic scholarship candidates will sit Mount Kelly Scholarship entrance papers in March and are assessed for 'performance' awards on an individual visit to the school. Sixth Form Scholarships are awarded on the basis of interview and predicted GCSE results.

Awards of 10% fees discount are available to sons and daughters of old pupils and to sons and daughters of members of the HM Forces (10% up to Year 8, 20% in Years 9 to 13).

Curriculum. The Lower School curriculum (Years 7–9) introduces pupils to a broad range of subjects within the Common Entrance Curriculum. In Year 7, pupils will study two modern languages (French and Spanish). All pupils study for the International/European Computer Driving Licence, which they may complete as early as the end of the fourth year in the school.

The GCSE curriculum at Mount Kelly is flexible and aims to stretch each pupil appropriately. The core subjects are Mathematics, English, Biology, Chemistry, Physics, ICT (ECDL qualification) and a Language. The range of option subjects includes Art, Design & Technology, Drama, French, Geography, German, History, Music, Physical Education, Religious Studies and Spanish.

Pupils entering the Sixth Form need to possess 6 GCSE passes and at least a B grade in their selected A Level subjects. Mount Kelly pupils study for 3 A Levels and 1 AS Level. A Level option subjects include Fine Art, Art Photography, Biology, Chemistry, Classical Civilisation, Drama & Theatre Studies, Economics, English Literature, French, German, Geography, History, ICT, Mathematics, Further Mathematics, Music Physical Education, Physics, Product Design, Psychology, Religious Studies and Spanish. All pupils in the Lower Sixth year receive tuition in Public Speaking. The Extended Project Qualification (EPQ) is also offered. All years benefit from access to the Outdoor Learning Curriculum which includes a range of opportunities to learn outside the classroom across a broad range of subjects and includes a variety of field trips and residentials across all year groups.

Combined Cadet Force. From Year 10 pupils can join the Royal Naval, Royal Air Force or the Army Section of the CCF. The CCF has a strong emphasis on Adventure Training and there are opportunities for sailing, kayaking, sub-aqua diving, orienteering, small-bore shooting and abseiling; many of which are available on site or nearby on Dartmoor. The College, originally founded as it was for the 'sons of Naval Officers and other Gentlemen', enjoys strong links with the Royal Navy at Dartmouth and pupils have the opportunity to visit the affiliated ship, HMS Argyll, when she is in port. The Duke of Edinburgh's Award Scheme is offered from Year 10 and most pupils will complete their Bronze Award and many will achieve their Gold as well.

Cultural and Academic Societies and Activities. All boys and girls are encouraged to explore new interests and to make the most of their spare time. Societies and Activities include Literary and Debating, Current Affairs, Drama, Choral, Music, Football, Computing, Photography, Robotics, Chess, Bridge, Fine Arts, Surfing and Textiles.

Mount Kelly has a strong music department. Mount Kelleians can learn a broad range of musical instruments from the Organ to the Electric Guitar. The School hosts a Concert Society which is open to pupils and members of the local community alike; and the Senior Orchestra and Senior Choir join with the local Choral Society and Orchestra to put on major concerts. There is also a Junior Choir and Junior Orchestra, plus a number of music ensembles.

There is a strong tradition of Public Speaking and debating and many of the pupils study for LAMDA qualifications at the School which is one of the largest coaching and exam centres in the country. In addition to a purpose-built Performing Arts Centre, the School Hall is fully equipped for theatrical productions – there are a number of House and School plays each year as well as informal concerts, debates, English Speaking Competitions et al.

Sport. Mount Kelly has a strong sporting tradition, particularly known for its elite international swimming programme, and has produced more Olympians and Internationals than any other school of its size. The major sports for girls are Hockey, Netball, Rounders, Tennis, Athletics and Swimming; and for boys are Rugby, Hockey, Cricket, Tennis, Athletics and Swimming. Many other sports are available in the School: Climbing, Cross Country, Golf, Riding, Rugby and Winchester Fives, Squash, Basketball, Sailing, Surfing, Tennis, Soccer and Yoga.

Dress. The school uniform for girls consists of a school kilt, white blouse and school blazer. Boys wear a blue shirt, grey flannel trousers and school blazer.

Fees per term (2014–2015). Full boarding: £6,944–£9,310; Weekly boarding: £6,880–£8,689; Day Pupils: £4,200–£5,330. Music lessons are among the voluntary extras, which are kept to a minimum.

Application. A prospectus and further details are available from the Director of Admissions, who will be pleased to arrange visits to the School.

Charitable status. The Mount Kelly Foundation is a Registered Charity, number 306716. It is a day and boarding school for boys and girls, which also grants maintenance allowances and the provision of assistance for higher education by means of Scholarships, Exhibitions and means-tested Bursaries.

Mount St Mary's College

College Road, Spinkhill, Nr Sheffield, Derbyshire S21 3YL
Tel:　　　01246 433388
Fax:　　　01246 435511
email:　　headmaster@msmcollege.com
website:　www.msmcollege.com
Twitter:　@MountSpinkhill

Motto: *Sine Macula.*

Mount St Mary's College was founded in 1842 by the Society of Jesus in order to provide an education for the country's growing Catholic population. The manor of Spinkhill in North East Derbyshire was the first home of the College, forming the nucleus of the present school. The Elizabethan manor of Barlborough Hall, 1¼ miles away, is the home of the Preparatory School to the College.

Numbers: College 270; Preparatory School (3–11 years) 177. Boarders, Weekly Boarders and Day Pupils (girls and boys) are accepted at the College.

Governing Body:
Chairman: Fr A Porter SJ
Vice Chairman: R Gilbert
Mrs L Merrick
Mrs M Bolton
M O'Hara
J McNally, MBA
Trustees:
Fr M Beattie SJ
Fr John Twist SJ
Mr J Ridley

Executive Team:
Headmaster: N Cuddihy, EdD Dublin, BRelSc, MSc

Head Teacher, Barlborough Hall School: N Boys, BA Australia
Bursar: H Ewins, Accountancy Hons Degree Liverpool
Deputy Headmaster: A Hutchings
Assistant Head – Prefect of Studies: C McAllister, BA Leeds
Assistant Head – Head of Higher Line, Sixth Form: J Murphy, BA York, FRSA

Jesuit Community:
Fr Michael Beattie SJ, STL Rome, MA London (*Resident Jesuit Priest*)

Fr Peter Knott SJ (*Resident Jesuit Priest, Barlborough Hall Chaplain*)

Academic Teaching Staff:
Mr J Brownlow, BSc Hons Cardiff, MA (*Academic Subject Leader – Physics*)
Mr M Burnett, BSc Hons, PGCE (*Head of Line – Figures, Games & PE*)
Mrs A Carberry, BSc Manchester (*Chemistry*)
Mr R Carey, BA Teeside (*Head of Line Rudiments, English as an Additional Language Coordinator*)
Mrs R Carey, BA Lancaster MA York (*Learning Support Coordinator*)
Ms R Craggs, BSc Liverpool (*Co-Curricular Coordinator, Games & PE*)
Mrs K Dawson, BSc Sheffield Hallam (*Mathematics*) (*maternity leave*)
S Dewar-Watson, BA Hons Cambridge (*English*)
Dr D Dibden, BSc, PhD Sheffield (*Biology*)
Fr S Ellis, BTh Oxon MA Bristol (*Director of Chaplaincy*)
Mr P Forbes-Jones, BTh Southampton MA Sheffield (*Academic Subject Leader – Religious Studies*)
Ms H Hallas, BSc Leeds (*Academic Subject Leader – Biology*)
Mrs G Hazlehurst, BSc Loughborough (*Academic Subject Leader – Humanities, Geography & History*)
Ms R Hodder, BA London (*History & Politics*)
Ms A Hoskin, BSc South Bank (*Head of Line – Upper Elements, Games & PE*)
Mr S Howes, BA York (*Academic Subject Leader – English & Drama, Politics*)
Mrs L Kitchener, BMus MA Sheffield (*Academic Subject Leader – Music*)
Mr M Krlic, BSc Bath (*Academic Subject Leader – Politics, Business & Economics*)
Mrs L A Lovatt-Jones, BA MA N Staffordshire Polytechnic (*Art and Design Technology*)
J Mitchell, BA Sheffield Polytechnic (*Academic Subject Leader – Chemistry*)
Ms V Perronne, Masters Sorbonne-Paris (*Academic Subject Leader – Modern Languages*)
Mrs R Powell, BEd De Montfort (*Head of Line – Syntax, Games & PE*)
Mr D Sankey, BA Notts (*Academic Subject Leader – Mathematics*)
Mrs P Saoulidou, BA Athens & Greece (*Classics & English*)
Mr S Simpson, BEd Glasgow (*Academic Subject Leader – Games & PE*)
Mr S Steed, BEd Sheffield Polytechnic (*Head of Line – Grammar, Mathematics*)
Mr M Wilson, BEng Oxford Polytechnic (*Mathematics*)
Mrs P Woodhouse, BA De Montfort (*Academic Subject Leader – Art & Design Technology*)

Part-Time Teaching Staff:
Mr D Harris, BA Sheffield (*Design Technology*)
Mr J Humphries, BA Sheffield (*Music*)
Mr S Jenkins, BEd Nottingham, MEd, MA Nottingham, FRSA (*Fencing*)
Mrs S Johnson, BA Birmingham (*Modern Languages*)
Mrs H Madigan, BA Surrey (*English & Drama*)
Ms V Taber, BA Cumbria (*Religious Studies*)
Mrs B D Wigg, BA Sheffield, MIL Dusseldorf (*Modern Languages & EAL*)
Mr A Wareham, BA Sheffield (*Modern Languages*)
Mr G Wilks, BSc London (*Accounting & Business Studies*)
Mrs C Woodward, BSc Nottingham (*Biology*)

Sports Staff:
Ms S Davies (*Girls' Games & PE*)
Mr T Rogers (*Boys' Games & PE*)

Support Staff:
Executive PA & Clerk to the Governors: Mrs S Badger

Whole School Administration Support/School Office: Mrs S Birks

Human Resources Manager & Marketing Manager: Mrs D Burn

Finance: Mr T Cadman

Senior IT Technician: Mr A Court

Finance: Mrs S Cousins

Housekeeping & Residential Manager: Mrs G Dodsworth

Estates Manager: Mr P Foster

Whole School Administration Support/HM Office: Mrs B Gates

Foundation Officer: Mrs P Gray

Catering Manager: Mr M Greveson

Art and Design Technician: Mr R Harley

Pupil/iSAMS/Admissions Assistant: Mrs D Higham

Non-Residential School Nurse: Mrs S Hirst

PA: Mrs S Jenkins

Facilities Manager: Mr M Lucas

Acting IT Manager: Mr J McGowan

Science Technician, O/C RAF Section MSM CCF: Mrs K Mullins

Assistant Director of Chaplaincy: Mrs M Neal

Exams Officer: Mrs R Nelson

Transport Manager: Ms M Platts

Athletics Coach, Facility Manager (Mount Stadium): Mr K Newton

Librarian: Mrs M Newton

Contingent Commander CCF: Mr G Powell

Senior Boarding Tutor: Mr M Powell

Residential School Nurse: Mrs A-M Reid

Science Technician: Ms E Scobbie

Learning Support: Mrs V Wake

Assistant Staff:

Mr T Drewe (*Gap Student*)

Mr L Roberts (*Gap Student*)

Mr S Ruiz Velasco (*Gap Student*)

R Sanchez (*Spanish Language Assistant*)

M Torres (*Gap Student*)

C Tronche (*French Language Assistant*)

Mount St Mary's is a co-educational independent boarding and day school and is a member of HMC, BSA, CISC and AGBIS. Entry to the College is at age 11 and to Barlborough Hall at age 3+. Pupils at Mount St Mary's are prepared for GCSEs, AS and A Levels, and University entry. Entry into the Sixth Form is based upon school reports and GCSE results.

Aims. Mount St Mary's College is a Jesuit Catholic school inspired by the ideals of St Ignatius of Loyola. The College seeks to develop the whole person and encourages an appreciation of the needs of others both in the College community and the world at large. Mount St Mary's prepares its pupils for an active life commitment through the development of 'a faith that promotes justice'. The College seeks to produce young men and women for others. Pupils of other religious denominations are welcomed.

Special Features. Mount St Mary's College is well known for its family atmosphere. Pupils benefit from the close interest and encouragement which they receive throughout their time at the College and parental involvement is particularly encouraged. The strong emphasis on extra-curricular activities illustrates the Jesuit commitment to developing each pupil's individual talents in all areas – academic, spiritual, cultural and physical.

Situation. The College lies in an extensive estate of playing fields and parkland and is easily reached from the M1 motorway, junction 30, or from Chesterfield and Sheffield, both of which are about 8 miles away. School minibuses run throughout the region.

Organisation. Each pupil is guided by a tutor and Heads of Line, who is responsible for overseeing academic progress, pastoral care, recreation and discipline. Heads of Line

work closely with the Academic Subject Leaders, Prefect of Studies and the School Pastoral Leader.

Boarders live in the boys' or girls' houses, under the care of a Resident Boarding Pastoral Leader and Senior Boarding Tutor, assisted by resident House Tutors. The majority of rooms are en-suite, with either 2–3 sharing or in single rooms.

Curriculum. The curriculum for the first three years (ages 11–13) broadly follows National Curriculum at KS3 with opportunity to pursue a second foreign language and a range of creative arts subjects. The standard GCSE package is 9 GCSEs, although more or less is negotiable according to ability; this includes a core of English, Mathematics, a foreign language and between one and three separate Sciences. Several subjects follow the IGCSE curriculum. Other subjects are chosen from a range of options. In the Sixth Form pupils follow AS Levels (usually four) in the Lower Sixth. The most able pupils can continue with four A Levels in the Upper Sixth, although many pupils will choose to focus on three subjects. The College also runs an "A Level Plus" programme to stretch the more able students. In keeping with the school's Ignatian ethos, all pupils follow a Religious Studies course at every stage in addition to a full programme of Games and Physical Education at every level. Specialist tuition is available in a variety of musical instruments and in speech and drama training. Assessment and monitoring of work is built into the tutorial system and there is a regular timetable of reports, pupil progress interviews and communication with parents. Academic excellence and breadth of knowledge are characteristics of Jesuit education and the curriculum is constantly reviewed to ensure that the widest opportunities are available to each pupil.

Religion. Mount St Mary's College is a distinctively Jesuit school, that welcomes children of all denominations to share its ethos. Ignatian principles inform the College's work in fostering a realistic knowledge, love and acceptance of self and of the world in which we live and this underpins our main objective: the formation of young men and young women for others. There are school masses, year masses and other liturgical celebrations regularly throughout the school year, as well as retreats and pilgrimages. The College enjoys close links with the Hallam Diocese and participates in the diocesan pilgrimage to Lourdes. Religious Education is a part of the curriculum to GCSE and as an examination or non-examination option in the Sixth Form. The Arrupe programme provides opportunities for Sixth Formers to give service to the local community. The College maintains a strong link with Jesuit missions in different parts of the world, finding ways to further the work of the Society in this area. Pupils have the opportunity to be involved in gap year projects supported by the Jesuits. Pupils and their parents are expected to recognise and endorse the religious commitment of the College.

Sports. The College has extensive playing fields for rugby, hockey, cricket and football. Rugby, for which the College has a strong regional and national reputation, is the major boys' sport. Cricket facilities are excellent with all-weather practice wickets and indoor practice nets. The main girls' sport in the winter term is hockey, for which there is a floodlit all-weather hockey pitch. There is a full-time Level 4 Athletics Coach. Other sports include swimming, tennis, basketball, volleyball, badminton, shooting, netball, fencing, and football.

Art, Drama and Music. There are many opportunities to be involved in the Arts within the school, both within the curriculum and as part of the extra-curricular activities. Within the Art and Design department pupils can study fine art, textiles, resistant materials within the workshop, and photography. On Saturday mornings activities are run involving sculpture, textiles, art and photography.

Music is particularly strong, and popular at all levels. Pupils are encouraged to take up a musical instrument, and can participate in a wide number of musical activities, ranging from three choirs and a barber shop group to symphony orchestra, concert band, jazz band and many ensembles. Drama is also strong in the College, and several Senior and Junior productions are put on every year. The music and drama departments collaborate to produce a whole-school musical.

Combined Cadet Force and other Extra-Curricular Activities. All pupils in Year 10 participate in the Combined Cadet Force, in the Army or RAF section. They can continue to be a member, if they choose, in Year 11 and the Sixth Form. The CCF gives opportunities for external leadership courses and adventure training and fulfilling Duke of Edinburgh's Award options. There are extensive opportunities for extra-curricular activities at lunchtime, after school and on Saturday mornings. Pupils can pursue interests in drama, music, sports, the Duke of Edinburgh's Award and many other clubs and societies.

Facilities. Facilities include a Sixth Form Centre, a Drama Studio, ICT suite of three fully-equipped rooms, Music School with practice rooms, Recital Hall and Music Studio, College Theatre, Library with ICT facilities, various pupil common rooms, Fitness Centre, heated indoor swimming pool, Sports Hall, Rifle Range, Outdoor Pursuits Centre, all-weather tennis courts and 30 acres of games fields. A grade A accredited athletics track was opened in 2007.

Admissions. At 11+ pupils enter via the College's entrance examination, taken early in the Spring term at the College. Pupils at the College's preparatory school, Barlborough Hall, make a seamless transition into the College following sitting a transfer test. At 13+, pupils either sit the College entrance examination or Common Entrance exam through their prep schools. At other ages, pupils are accepted on the basis of school reports, with College entry tests as appropriate and in the Sixth Form, pupils are accepted on the basis of GCSE results, or their equivalent.

Fees per term (2014–2015). Full Boarders: £8,704 (Years 9–13), £6,534 (Years 7 and 8). Weekly Boarders: £7,007 (Years 9–13), £5,444 (Years 7 and 8).

Day Pupils: £4,009 (Years 9–13), £3,490 (Years 7 and 8). Barlborough Hall: £3,086 (Upper School), £2,315 (Pre-Prep).

Scholarships. Academic scholarships are awarded at 11+, 13+ and Sixth Form on the basis of the College's Scholarship Examination papers. GCSE results also form an aspect of Scholarship awards at Sixth Form. Music and sports scholarships are also available and the College will be happy to provide further information on these. In keeping with the College's ethos, bursaries are awarded in cases of demonstrable need. The Old Mountaineers offer post-graduate scholarships to former pupils of the College and applications are considered annually for these. All scholarships take place early in the Spring Term at the College.

Prospectus. This may be obtained by contacting the Admissions Officer (01246 432872) at the College and parents are always encouraged to visit Mount St Mary's College or its Preparatory School. (*See also Barlborough Hall entry in IAPS section.*)

Charitable status. Mount St Mary's is a Registered Charity, number 1117998. The College was founded in 1842 to provide an education for children.

New Hall School

The Avenue, Boreham, Chelmsford, Essex CM3 3HS
Tel:	01245 467588
Fax:	01245 464348
email:	registrar@newhallschool.co.uk
website:	www.newhallschool.co.uk
Twitter:	@NewHallSchool
Facebook:	/newhallschool

Chair of Governors: Mrs Clare Kershaw, LLB Hons, MCMI

Senior Leadership Team:

Principal: Mrs K Jeffrey, MA Oxon, PGCE Surrey, BA Div PUM, MA EdMg OU, NPQH

Deputy Principal: Mrs J Storey, BSc Loughborough, ILTM, FHEA

Vice Principal (Academic): Mr D Johnson, MA Cantab, PGCE Cantab

Vice Principal (Admissions and Co-Curriculum): Mr J Sidwell, BSc Loughborough, PGCE London

Head of Sixth Form: Mr J Alderson, BA Manchester, PGCE Cantab

Director of Boarding: Mrs E Searle, BA ARU

Finance Director: Mrs J Croom, BSc Bristol, FCA, CIOT

Preparatory School Headteacher: Mrs S Conrad, BA, PGCE Dunelm, NPQH

Heads of Academic Departments:

Art:
Mr G Hughes, BA Coventry, MFA Reading

Classics:
Mrs S Marshall, Licence-ès-Lettres Grenoble, PGCE

Critical Thinking:
Mr D Yates, BA, PGCE Lancaster

Dance:
Mrs S Molina, AISTD

Design Technology & Food:
Mrs L Curtis, BA Oxford Brookes

Drama:
Mr D Rutter, BA Middlesex, PGCE Middlesex, LCM Dip

Economics & Business Studies:
Mr S Levey, BSc Aston, PGCE Cantab

English:
Dr S Foster, BA PhD Loughborough, PGCE Anglia Ruskin

English as an Additional Language (EAL):
Mrs C Edmunds, BA Soton, PGCE Soton

Geography:
Mrs J Lewis, MA Cantab, PGCE Cantab

Gifted & Talented Coordinator:
Mr D Yates, BA, PGCE Lancaster

History:
Dr L Shaw, MA Cantab, PhD, GTP

Information & Communication Technology:
Mrs L Fletcher, BSc Surrey

Learning Development:
Mrs J Fawdry, BSc Hull, PGCE London, PG Dip SpLD, AMBDA

Library:
Ms J Tait, BSc Otago, CertLibSt Wellington, Dip Tchg Dunedin

Mathematics:
Mr I Tanner, BSc UEA, PGCE UEA

Modern Languages:
Mrs S Reid, BA Bristol, PGCE Homerton, MFLE

Music:
Mr A Fardell, BA Kent, LRAM (*Director of Music*)

Physical Education:
Mr G Kirkham, BSc Lough (*Director of Girls' Sport*)
Mr O Cobbe, BA QTS St Mary's (*Director of Boys' Sport*)

Politics:
Mr A Bowman, BA Lancaster

Theology:
Mr P Bray, BA, MA Dunelm, GTP

Science:
Mrs L Willson, BSc Roehampton, GTP (*Head of Biology*)

Examinations Officer:
Mrs G Newton

Careers:
Mrs S Haddrell

Housemasters/Housemistresses:
Earle House: Miss S Kay, BA Leeds, PGCE Leeds
Magdalen House: Mrs R Mackay, MSc Loughborough, BSc Reading
Petre House: Mr J Marriott, BA Leeds, PGCE Lancaster
Hawley House: Miss J Palmer, MA Northumbria, PGCE Northumbria, BA Cumbria
Dennett House: Mrs L Price, BLIB Aberystwyth
Campion House: Mr G James, BSc ARU, PGCE Exon

Registrar: Ms H Rogers

Pupil numbers. Senior School (11–18): 868 (Day 616, Boarding 252). Preparatory School (3–11): 343.

Location. New Hall benefits from a magnificent campus and stunning heritage setting, with a Grade I listed main building that occupies a former Tudor palace built by King Henry VIII. The school is conveniently situated 35 miles north east of London and close to the town centre of Chelmsford, just off junction 19 of the A12. There is a network of coaches and minibuses for travel to school.

The school is also easily accessible for boarders, being close to London airports; the 19-mile drive to Stansted Airport takes about 40 minutes. There are frequent trains between Chelmsford and central London; the train journey takes 35 minutes. Cambridge is less than an hour's journey by car and the school organises a number of trips to this historic university city.

Our Ethos. New Hall has a distinctive Catholic foundation and Christian ethos and welcomes all who support that ethos. Students of many faiths and traditions belong to our community and we believe that everyone benefits from the universal values of love, trust, respect and fellowship that are central to our school life. In particular, a sense of community is fostered through the award-winning and nationally recognised organisation, New Hall Voluntary Service (NHVS). NHVS activities include 8 weekly Action Groups, supporting people in need in the local community through student volunteers and adult volunteer supporters.

Organisation. The 'diamond model' structure provides the optimal combination of co-educational and single-sex teaching. Children progress from the co-educational Preparatory School to the Boys' Division or Girls' Division and then to the co-educational Sixth Form in preparation for university life and future careers. The benefits of single-sex teaching for the first five years of Senior School derive from the ability to tailor pastoral and academic provision more sensitively, gender-specifically and expertly to the needs of young people going through the physical, emotional and social upheaval of adolescence.

Pastoral Care. Our emphasis on pastoral care is a reflection of our core values and ethos and is a real strength of the school. A peer-led group, Willow, provides students with a further support network, run by senior student volunteers, who offer help and guidance.

Building confidence and teaching respect for the self and others is a priority. Through the vertical house system, we foster social integration between boys and girls across the age range, developing team spirit, good humour and creativity.

Boarding. The six boarding houses offer their members a strong sense of identity and opportunities to forge new friendships. There are dedicated boarding houses for younger boarders (ages 7–11), for students in the senior division (ages 11–15) and for Sixth Form (ages 16–18), allowing each student to thrive in a boarding house shared with others of their own age and interests, All boarding houses have their own kitchen, well-equipped common rooms, internet access and a selection of books and DVDs.

Curriculum. The New Hall curriculum is distinctive in its breadth and academic rigour. An imaginatively taught and well-balanced curriculum is appropriately tailored to the needs of the individual. Students enjoy a rich and varied range of options at GCSE and A Level. There is also an Oxbridge programme and additional options including Critical Thinking and Academic Projects. The school has its own Gifted & Talented programme, which is proven to bring exceptional value added at GCSE and A Level. We believe that giftedness can be created and that students' academic skills can be developed at ever higher levels if they are given intellectual challenges and opportunities to 'think outside the box'.

Music. Music has a long and fine tradition at New Hall. Students may take individual lessons in orchestral instruments, piano, singing, drums and electric guitar. There is a host of performing groups, including: infant, junior and senior choirs; chamber choirs; a chapel choir; a junior and senior orchestra; a strings academy; wind bands; recorder consorts and chamber groups. Students are also encouraged to form jazz and pop bands, for which specialist support facilities are available.

Regular performances are given by students in assemblies, lunchtime recitals and formal concerts. Students take part in regional and national musical festivals and competitions, and groups tour regularly to perform in major venues in Europe.

Performing Arts. The Walkfares Performing Arts Centre is the home of thriving Music, Dance and Drama Departments. Performances, from Shakespeare to modern plays and musicals, give students the opportunity to develop their confidence and creative talents. There is also an annual dance show, with a cast of up to 300 girls and boys aged 4–18.

Students are encouraged to participate in the English Speaking Board (ESB) or London Academy of Music and Dramatic Arts (LAMDA) programmes.

Sport. Team spirit, physical development and good health are promoted through our emphasis on sport throughout the school. New Hall balances elite training for those with particular sporting talent, with an inclusive approach that allows students of all abilities to find at least one sport that they can enjoy. Students compete at county, regional, national and international level in a wide range of sports.

The first-class provision includes: a 25m 6-lane indoor swimming pool; a national standard athletics track and floodlit Astroturf; ten floodlit tennis/netball courts; two sports halls; dance studio; junior and senior cricket wickets and indoor training nets; hockey, rugby and football pitches; and a fitness centre. New Hall also has well-established links with a local riding school, golf and sailing clubs.

Co-Curricular Activities. Educational opportunities extend far beyond the classroom. The school's educational philosophy is reflected in the variety of extra-curricular activities through which the personal development of each individual is nurtured. Activities available include a multitude of sports teams, music groups and orchestras, the Duke of Edinburgh's Award, art & craft clubs including photography and pottery, language clubs, Young Enterprise Club and World Challenge.

Inspection. The school was last inspected by ISI and Ofsted in 2010. The Ofsted Inspection rated New Hall's Boarding provision as 'Outstanding'. The full inspection reports can be viewed on the school website.

Fees per term (2014–2015). Senior School: Day £5,360–£5,739; Weekly Boarding £7,075–£8,211; Full Boarding £7,826–£8,811.

Preparatory School: £1,665.60–£4,203; Boarding (from age 7): £5,620 (weekly), £6,209 (full).

There is a Prompt Payment Discount of £100 per term (not included in the Fees shown).

Entry requirements. Entrance examination, school report, and interview.

Scholarships and Bursaries. Scholarship candidates follow the normal entrance procedure and, dependent on the type of scholarship, a further assessment. All candidates for Year 7 entry are entered for the Academic Scholarship, which is awarded to the highest achieving student from the entrance examination results. Other scholarships at Year 7 entry 2013 are available in Drama, Music and Sport. There are also scholarships available for Catholic students. Similar scholarships are available for Year 9 entry. For Sixth Form entry, there are scholarship awards available based on GCSE examination results as well as an Open (all rounder) scholarship, Boarding scholarship and Special Talent Award.

Means-tested Bursaries (up to 100% remission of fees) are available to new and current students.

Further information on Admissions, Scholarships and Bursaries is available from the Registrar and on the school website.

Charitable status. New Hall School Trust is a Registered Charity, number 1110286. Its aim is the education of children within a Christian environment.

Newcastle-under-Lyme School

Mount Pleasant, Newcastle-under-Lyme, Staffordshire ST5 1DB

Tel:	01782 631197
Fax:	01782 632582
email:	info@nuls.org.uk
website:	www.nuls.org.uk

Newcastle-under-Lyme School, which attracts pupils from a large area of North Staffordshire, South Cheshire and North Shropshire, is a co-educational day school for 900 pupils aged 3–18. The present School was formed in 1981 through the amalgamation of Newcastle High School and the Orme Girls' School, two schools which were endowed as a single foundation in 1872 under an educational charity scheme for children in Newcastle-under-Lyme which has its roots in the 1600s. The two schools enjoyed a reputation for scholarship and for service to the community throughout North Staffordshire, a reputation which has continued with the formation of Newcastle-under-Lyme School. The School is also well known for its high standards in sport, music and drama, which play a major part in the extra-curricular life of the School. The Junior School is adjacent to the Senior School and has some 325 pupils aged 3–11.

Governing Body:

Chair of Governors: Mrs R E Evans, LLB
B C Carnes, MBE, BSc, DUniv
M Caulkin, Cert CIB
D H Cook, MA
Mrs E Gillow, BA
Professor P W Jones, BSc, MSc, PhD, CStat
Mrs K A Miller, BSc, ACA
J S Rushton, BSc, FCA, CISA
Professor G I Russell, MB, ChB, MD, FRCP
D P Wallbank, BA
M R Warren, BA, MArch

Bursar: J P Longdon, MCGI

Headmaster: N A Rugg, MA

Deputy Heads:
Mrs J A Simms, BA, MSc (*Pastoral*)
M S Snell, BSc, MA (*Academic*)

Director of External Relations: I J Cartwright, BEd, MA

Head of Sixth Form: Mrs B A Godridge, BA

English:
*Mrs A A Keay, MA
Mrs J Betts-Nicholson, BA
Mrs B Joughin, BA
R Lench, BA
Mrs L Marrable-Griffiths, BA

Mrs M Barnes
Mrs S Graham, MA
Mrs M Isherwood, BA
D G Murtagh, BA
Mrs K H Tan, BA
Mrs D A Woodcock, BA

History:
*D Dunlop, BA, PhD
D A Cawdron, BA
Mrs S J Stockdale, BSc

Mathematics:
*Miss J M Griffiths, BSc
Mrs C M Barber, BSc
D T Buckley, BSc
Mrs J C Cliff, BSc
Mrs J A Cryer, BSc
Mrs O Exley, BSc, PhD
Mrs S Goodwin, BSc
E J Griffiths, BA

ICT:
*S Luck, BSc

Chemistry:
*P Thomson, BSc, PhD
M S Lunt, BSc
G J Moore, BSc, PhD

Physics:
*N P Migallo, BSc
A Fishburne, MEng
Mrs K Rigby, BSc

Biology:
*N J Simms, BSc
N C Carter, BSc
Miss J Galvin, BSc
Mrs R Moon, BSc
D R Pepper, BSc, PhD
    (*Assistant Head of Sixth Form*)

Geography:
*T P Jowitt, BSc
Miss N J MacKintosh, BSc
Mrs F P E Williams, BA

Modern Languages:
*D L Brayford, MA, MEd

Learning Support Coordinator: Mrs J A Cryer, BSc

Librarian: Miss W F Butler, BA, MA, DipLib, MCLIP

Religious Studies:
*A Poole, BA
J S Preston, BA

Latin:
*Ms T A Thomas, BA

Economics:
*Miss L Barton, BA
Mrs M L Clutterbuck, BEd

Art and Design:
*Mrs S Parkinson, BA
Miss L Herian, BA
Mrs B W Jones, CertEd
Mrs F Jones

Design and Technology:
*D Patrick, BA
P Finney, BA

Home Economics:
*Mrs J Machin
Mrs N G Swindells, BEd

Physical Education:
*G M Chesterman, BSocSc
Miss R E Bradley
G M Breen, BSc
P J Butler, FISTC, AIST LS
Mrs D Glenn, BEd
Mrs J Pointon, BEd
S A Robson, BEd
Mrs P Smith, BEd

Music:
*T Sagar, MA
Mrs C Hughes, BA, MusEd
Mrs M Potter, GGSM, ARCM, PGCE

Careers:
Mrs B Joughin, BA

Newcastle-under-Lyme Junior School:

Head: N J Vernon, BSc, MA

Deputy Head: M J Erian, BA, MA
Head of Pre-Prep: Mrs A M Burgess, BA
Nursery Manager: Mrs A Smith, NNEB, NEBS

Mrs C Deakes, BA
Mrs N Erian
Mrs A Farnsworth
Mrs J Grisdale, BEd
Miss P D Knighton, BEd
G Lewis, BEd
Mrs L Moss, BA

Mrs S Quinn, BEd
Mrs R B L Rugg, BA
Miss F Scott, LLB
Miss C K M Shipton, BA
Miss J Stanton, BEd
Mrs K Tapp, BA

Buildings and Grounds. Set in 30 acres of grounds, the School is pleasantly situated on high ground in a quiet conservation area close to the centre of Newcastle-under-Lyme. The original buildings still form part of the School and extensions have been added from time to time. A fine dining hall was opened in one of the wings of the original building, part of the continuing programme of development and refurbishment which was begun when the School reverted to full independence in 1981. The Millennium Sixth Form Centre opened in March 2000 affording spacious new accommodation for senior students. In addition to the well equipped classrooms and Science laboratories, the School has Language laboratories, workshops, a Music School, an Art and Design Centre, two libraries, a gymnasium, and a Sports Centre which includes a sports hall, a weights room and an indoor swimming pool. Computers are accessible in subject areas and in four modern laboratories, where machines are linked on a network basis. There are also tennis and netball courts and extensive playing fields, providing pitches for cricket, rugby and hockey, adjacent to the School. An all-weather pitch with floodlighting was opened in March 2002.

Organisation. The School is organised in two sections: the Junior School – nursery (2004), pre-preparatory (2004) and preparatory (1982) – which has 300+ pupils in the age range 3 to 11 and the Senior School, with approximately 400 boys and 400 girls. The Sixth Form numbers more than 200 students.

Form Tutors and Heads of Year have particular responsibility for the pastoral welfare of the pupils in their charge.

In Year 7 and Year 8 boys and girls have their own interform and inter-house competitions, with separate Lower School assemblies. This structure gives to the Lower School forms a separate identity within the Senior School. The Senior House structure, which extends from Year 9 upwards, consists of four co-educational houses.

Curriculum. A broad curriculum in the first five years has English (Language and Literature), Mathematics, Biology, Chemistry, and Physics as core subjects. All pupils also take a Modern Foreign Language, selected from French, German and Spanish, Latin, History, Geography, Religious Education, Music, Art, Home Economics, Design and Technology, ICT, PE, Swimming and Games. Pupils have the option of taking Biology, Chemistry and Physics as a dual-award GCSE or as three separate GCSEs in Year 10 and Year 11.

Pupils take nine GCSEs and the great majority will proceed to take between three and five AS subjects in the Lower Sixth Form. There may also be the possibility of taking the Extended Project Qualification. Three or four of these subjects will be continued in the Upper Sixth as A2 qualifications.

Optional choices in the Sixth Form include A Level Business Studies, Economics, British Government and Politics and Physical Education in addition to AS Levels in the subjects available at GCSE. Pupils are also prepared for Oxford and Cambridge Entrance.

Extra-Curricular Activities. The main school games are Rugby, Cricket, Hockey, Athletics, Tennis and Cross-Country for the boys and Hockey, Athletics, Netball, Tennis and Rounders for the girls. Swimming, Water Polo, Life Saving and Synchronised Swimming, Water Polo and Life Saving also feature strongly and there are usually opportunities for Shooting, Squash, Aerobics, Basketball, Badminton, Golf and other physical activities in the Sixth Form.

There are also strong traditions in both Music and Drama and standards are very high. More than 200 pupils receive instrumental tuition and there are a number of concerts in each year with major performances being given in local churches and in the Victoria Concert Hall in Hanley. There are several major drama productions each year including one each at Senior and Lower School levels.

The flourishing Combined Cadet Force has naval, army and airforce sections and there is also a large Scout troop, which enrols both boys and girls. Pupils also participate in the Duke of Edinburgh's Award Scheme.

Clubs and Societies meet during the lunch hour and after school.

Careers. The School places much emphasis on the importance of careers guidance, both in the GCSE years and in the preparation for higher education. The School is an all-in member of the ISCO Careers Guidance Scheme, through which all pupils in Year 11 receive a careers report based on tests of ability, personality and aptitude. Pupils receive full advice on applications to Universities and other Institutes of Higher Education.

Honours. Between 1987 and 2013 278 of our students gained places at Oxford and Cambridge, while in 2013 some 95% of all Upper Sixth leavers gained entry to degree courses in Higher Education.

Admissions. Entry to the Nursery is on a first-come first-served basis. Entry to the Junior School and Years 7, 8 and 9 of the Senior School is by examination/assessment only, normally at the ages of 4, 11 and 13. A few candidates are also admitted at 8, 9, 10, 12 and 14. The entrance examinations for these age groups are usually held in January and February for entry in the following September but pupils moving into the area may be considered at other times.

Entry at Sixth Form level is by interview and GCSE qualifications.

Registration forms, and copies of the Prospectus, are available on request.

Scholarships and Bursaries. The following Scholarships and Bursaries are available:

Governors' Scholarships: Scholarships of up to £2,000 per annum for five years following entry to be awarded on the results of the 11+ and 13+ Entrance Examinations.

Sports Scholarships: A number of Sports Scholarships may be awarded to candidates at 13+ entry offering particular sporting prowess. These will be of value up to £1,000 per annum for one year following entry.

The Robert S Woodward Scholarships: One or Two Scholarships, of value up to £1,000 per annum, to be awarded annually to pupils entering, or in, the Sixth Form, for outstanding performance in the field of Mathematical Sciences.

The JCB Sixth Form Scholarship: One Scholarship, of value up to £1,000 per annum, to be awarded annually to pupils entering, or in, the Sixth Form, for outstanding performance in Physics.

Music Scholarships: A number of Music Scholarships may be awarded to candidates entering the Sixth Form at 16+ and on entry at 11+, to cover the cost of music tuition throughout the student's school career.

Bursaries: The Governors have established a Bursary Scheme to assist parents with school fees.

Further details may be obtained from the Registrar.

Fees per term (2014–2015). Senior School £3,626; Junior School: Preparatory £2,962; Pre-Preparatory £2,639; Nursery £39.50 per day (£24.50 per morning, £22.00 per afternoon session).

Charitable status. Newcastle-under-Lyme School is a Registered Charity, number 1124463. The object of the Charity shall be the provision and conduct in or near Newcastle-under-Lyme of a day or a day and boarding school or schools for boys and girls.

Norwich School

70 The Close, Norwich NR1 4DD
Tel: 01603 728430
email: enquiries@norwich-school.org.uk
website: www.norwich-school.org.uk

Motto: '*Praemia virtutis honores*'

Norwich School is a co-educational day school for pupils aged seven to eighteen. Set in the Cathedral Close, the School is an historic place. The exact date at which it came into being is unknown, but its origins can be traced back to the foundation of the Cathedral in 1096. In 1547 it was re-founded by Edward VI.

In 2014–15 there are 1045 pupils: 865 in the Senior School (age 11–18) and 180 in the Lower School (age 7–11) (*see Norwich School, Lower School IAPS entry*).

Cathedral Choristers are members of the school.

Council of Management:

Co-optative Governors:
P J E Smith, MA, FIA (*Chairman*)
T J Gould, MA (*Vice-Chairman*)

Dr S C Bamber	Ms M Jarrold, MA Cantab
Mrs A Fry, MA	A D Jeakings, FCMA
A R Grant, MA, FRSA	I Reid, BSc, MRICS
E J H Gould, MA	D W Talbot, ACA
Mrs A J C Green, BSc	J W Walker, BEd Cantab
C W Hoffman, ACIB	Miss T Yates, BA
J A E Hustler	

Representative Governors:
Professor C Andrew, MA, University of Cambridge
A R Burdon-Cooper, MA, LLB, Worshipful Company of Dyers
J R Chambers, FCA, Worshipful Company of Dyers
The Revd Canon J M Haselock, BA, BPhil, MA, Dean & Chapter
R A Leuchars, BSc, Worshipful Company of Dyers
P N Mirfield, BCL, MA, BA, University of Oxford
Dr Kay Yeoman, University of East Anglia

Senior Management Team:

Head Master: S D A Griffiths, MA Oxon

Principal Deputy Head: Miss L E Péchard, BA, MA
Deputy Head (Director of Studies): Dr D N Farr, BA, PhD, FRHS
Deputy Head (Co-Curriculum): N M Plater, MA Oxon
Assistant Head (Fifth Form and Marketing): M D Barber, BA
Assistant Head (Compliance and Outreach/Child Protection): P D Goddard, BEd
Assistant Head (Fourth Form and Admissions): Mrs N J Hill, BSc
Assistant Head (Head of Sixth Form): C Hooper, BA
Assistant Head (Teaching & Learning); Head of General Studies: P A Todd, MA Cantab
Bursar: Mrs M W T Cherry, BEng

Teaching Staff, Senior School:
Miss K E Adams, BA (*Head of Dance*)
R P Allain, BMus, FTCL (*Director of Music*)
J Ashton, BSc, MSc (*Head of Mathematics*)
Mrs C L Barber, BA (*Head of Spanish*)
D Barlow, LRSM, BA, MEd Cantab, ARCO (*Head of Academic Music, Head of Common Room*)
D P Bateman, BSc (*Head of Politics; Housemaster, Valpy*)
R H Bedford-Payne, BA (*Housemaster, Nelson*)
T D Berwick, BSc
Mrs R M Bolton, BSc (*part-time*)
Miss C Borrass (*part-time*)
Dr L S M Boutemy, MSc, PhD
Miss A E Boyt, BA (*Head of Classical Civilisation*)
Miss N Bruce, MA (*Head of Latin*)
R A Bunting (*Head of Boys' Games*)
Miss S-A Burt, BA
Miss S Calabuig Garrido, Dip Valencia (*part-time*)
A Campbell, BA, MA
E Cann, BA
C Child, BA, MA (*School Chaplain*)
C J Cole (*Head of Lower School Sport, Head of Football*)

J Cowan, BSc (*Director of Sport*)
W H J Croston, BA (*Head of Careers and Higher Education*)
A P Curtis, BA (*Housemaster, Seagrim*)
Mrs K E Curtis, BA (*part-time*)
Mrs F L Ellington, BA (*part-time*)
Miss R Figgitt, BA (*Head of Minor Games*)
Miss V L Fincham, BA, MA (*Deputy Head – Sixth Form, Head of German*)
A L Fisher, BA (*Housemaster, Parker*)
J C Fisher, BSc (*Housemaster, Repton*)
J C Gent, BSc (*Head of Biology*)
Miss C Gillham, BA
A Grant, BA, MA (*Head of History*)
T M Grieves, BA
I M Grisewood, BA (*Housemaster, School House*)
Ms J Gutierrez (*part-time*)
G A Hanlon, BSc (*Housemaster, Coke*)
I C Hayward, MSc (*Group Scout Leader*)
R Hazard, BSc
T J Hill, BSc (*Head of ICT*)
Dr A P Hinsley, BSc, PhD
E L Hodgson, BSc
M D Hopgood, BA (*Head of Geography*)
E D Hopkins, BA (*Head of Cricket, Coordinator of Curricular PE*)
J Hudson, MMath
Miss C Ibbetson-Price, BA
Miss L Ipser (*part-time*)
S A Kettley, MA
S Kirby, BSc, PhD
Ms V Konstantinidi, BA
J Large, BSc (*Deputy Head of Fifth Form*)
Mrs G L Lawton, BSc
Mme C Le Floch, Licence Bordeaux lll
Miss M E Ling, BSc
B W Mack, BSc
F J McIvor, MA (*Senior Tutor, Oxbridge Coordinator*)
M Mulligan, BA, MPhil (*Head of Philosophy*)
A Murray, MA (*Head of English*)
Mrs J Nagel, MA (*part-time*)
Mrs T M Newstead, BA (*Housemaster, Brooke*)
Mrs C Norton, BSc (*Head of Sports Science, Head of Girls' Games*)
Mrs E Ollivier, BA, NUCA, MA Royal Academy of Art Schools (*part-time*)
T Ollivier, BA
Mrs L E D Parkhouse, MA (*Head of French*)
Mrs G Parsons, MA (*Head of Work Experience*)
I R Passam, BA (*Head of Design*)
Ms K Playfair, MA (*Head of Classics*)
R W Peters, BA
Mrs C M Pywell, BSc (*part-time*)
M Ramshaw, BA
Ms N J Ravenscroft, MA (*part-time*)
Mrs E Reed, BA (*part-time*)
Dr G Richardson, BSc, PhD
Ms A Roper, BA (*Head of Learning Support*)
Miss V Rousvoal (*part-time*)
A M Rowlandson, BA
Mrs D Saywack, MA, MA (*Head of Religious Studies*)
C Shannon, BA
R Sims (*Head of Rugby, Head of Sports Academy*)
Mrs L Slade, BA
R Slade, BA, PhD, RCA (*part-time*)
Ms K Smith, BA
Mrs M Smith (*part-time*)
R E Sorrell, BSc (*Head of Hockey*)
Mrs P R Staufenberg, MA (*part-time*)
Miss E L Stone, BSc
M W Strickland, BA (*Head of History*)
R Suffling (*part-time*)
Dr S Treavett, BSc, MSc, PhD

Miss V J Turner, MA

Dr M Venables, MA, PhD (*Head of Science, Head of Physics*)

Mrs S Ward, MA (*Head of Greek*)

Mrs C O Warren, BA

Miss E L Wasserberg, BA

T J Watts, LLB (*Head of Community Service*)

A E Weeks, BA

Ms M Whalan, BA

D Whatley, BSc (*Head of Chemistry*)

T P White, BA (*Head of Economics*)

C J Williams, BSc (*Head of Rowing*)

Miss H Williams, BA

Mrs C Wood, BA (*Librarian*)

Mrs S Wortley, AGSM, GGSM, CertEd (*Coordinator of Instrumental Studies*)

Mrs C Wyndham, BA

Lower School:
Master of the Lower School: J K Ingham, BA

Teaching Staff, Lower School:

I K Blaxall, BEd

T J Brook, MSc

Miss F N R Brugger, BA

Miss C Copson, BA

C G Cordy, BA (*Second Master*)

Mrs N B Dunnett, BA

Mrs J T Farrow, BA

Mrs P Green

Mrs I R G Grote, 1st & 2nd Staatsexamen (*part-time*)

Mrs M Ingham

R A Love, BSc (*Director of Co-Curricular*)

C M W Parsons, BSc (*Director of Studies*)

Mrs G S Riche

J S G Worton, BSc

Mrs G E Wright, BEd (*part-time*)

Development Office:

Ms J Dyer, MSc, CIM (*Director of Development & Alumni Relations*)

D V Jones, BA

Mrs B Gammage, BA (*Communications & Marketing Manager*)

Mrs R M Lightfoot (*Alumni Relations Manager*)

Head Master's PA: Mrs J Grapes, BA
Assistant to the Head's PA: Mrs H Reynolds
Bursar's PA: Ms R Peters
Principal Deputy Head's PA: Mrs K Smith
Registrar: Mrs V A Gaskin, BSc
Admissions Secretary: Miss G Bailey
Data Manager: Ms J Algar
Lower School Secretary: Mrs J Bell
School Secretary: Mrs N Rodwell
Common Room Secretary: Mrs J M Raath
Secretary to Head of Sixth Form: Mrs E Reed, BA
Chief Examinations Officer: Mrs J L Powell, BA
Deputy to the Examinations Officer: Mrs S L Meader

School Nurses:

Mrs C Bennett, RGN, ONC

Miss C Castle, RGN

Mrs A Bodmer

Archivists: J W Walker, J C Fisher

Learning and scholarship are at the heart of the broad education that Norwich School provides. Christian values – notably love and compassion for one another – underpin our activities and relationships.

Norwich School is committed to:

- producing scholarly, reflective young people who are capable of handling difficult concepts and expressing profound thought;

- providing a rich, varied and broad education that develops the diverse talents of the boys and girls;
- equipping pupils for leadership and service.

Admission. The main points of entry are at ages 7, 11, 13 and 16. There may be small numbers of places available at other ages. Application for admission should be made to the Head Master on the form obtainable from the Registrar.

Fees per term (2014–2015). Senior School £4,565; Lower School £4,159.

Faith and Worship. Members of the Senior School meet in the Cathedral every morning. Services and assemblies provide precious opportunities for corporate gathering and worship. The Christian tradition of the School provides a framework for its spiritual life. Pupils of all faiths are welcomed and it is not the School's intention to proselytize or indoctrinate. It is felt right, however, that all pupils should receive grounding in the liturgy and traditions of Christian worship so that they are acquainted with the faith heritage of the School and the Cathedral that it regularly visits. Familiarity with prayers, hymns and Biblical texts provides pupils with a spiritual vocabulary and a vehicle through which to encounter important ethical and spiritual questions. The School aims to provide pupils with a secure basis from which they can embark upon their own journeys into faith.

Teaching and Learning. Good scholarship is held in high regard at Norwich School. Those pupils who exhibit strong academic ability and the desire to read, learn and express their opinions are at the heart of school activity. Inspirational teaching using imaginative methods and content is fostered throughout the School. Fundamental to all teaching and learning at Norwich School is the shared belief that a well-educated person who loves to learn and is able to think critically and creatively is more likely to lead a fulfilling and positive life. Education is perceived as a worthwhile end in itself.

Pastoral Care and Discipline. The School aims to sustain a friendly atmosphere with genuine trust and respectful camaraderie between pupils and staff. There is firm discipline within that caring environment, enabling pupils to feel secure within clearly defined parameters.

In practical terms, each pupil's welfare is the responsibility of their tutor in whom the parents have a main point of contact for pastoral matters.

The Senior School (age 11–16). There is a distinctive curriculum for the 11 to 14 age group, elements of which are sustained throughout the GCSE years. Alongside the traditional range of subjects is the Meno Programme: approximately six periods per week that incorporate unusual languages – such as Russian, Japanese and Hungarian – as well as the 'philosophy for children methodology', thinking, relaxation skills and practical elements such as engineering and photography. There are practical elements where learning takes place outdoors – to learn, for example, about ecology and food production by experience on school land. Site visits to the North Norfolk coast and other areas of the county are programmed into the year so that different academic subjects such as Art, Biology, Geography and History can combine resources on project work. The aim is to aid learning through varied experiences and stimuli and to excite the pupils about the learning process.

The Sixth Form. Almost all Sixth Form pupils go to university upon leaving Norwich School. There is a long track record of success in large numbers gaining entrance to Oxford, Cambridge and the other top academic institutions. All boys and girls are encouraged to excel in their A Level studies and to be committed to sporting, cultural and extracurricular activity.

The Advice Team, led by the Head of Sixth Form, tailors a programme of University and career preparation for each pupil and monitors their success from Lower Sixth to A Level results day – and beyond where necessary.

Creative and Performing Arts. The music department is very popular with pupils, welcoming and encouraging boys and girls of all levels of ability to explore their musical creativity. Over 65% of all pupils make music regularly. There are more than twenty-eight specialist teachers and various orchestras, ensembles, bands, choirs and groups. Performances at all levels and ages regularly take place within the School, the Cathedral and in the wider community.

Drama facilities include the purpose-designed Blake Studio. Pupils also have the privilege of performing at some of the finest venues in Norwich: the Senior Play traditionally is performed in the Maddermarket Theatre; other productions take place in the Puppet Theatre, the Lower School and the Cathedral; major musicals (*West Side Story* in November 2014) are staged at the Playhouse.

Art and Design are well-resourced and, in recent years, several talented artists and designers from the School have gained places at the top Art Colleges.

Sport. Norwich School is unusual among day schools in providing two games afternoons each week and fixtures on many Saturdays. Games and sport are perceived as vital aspects of the curriculum.

The major games for boys are rugby, cricket and hockey; and for girls, netball, hockey and rounders. There are strong fixture lists in each of these sports. Boys and girls are able to take up a broad range of other sports including swimming, netball, cross-country running, fencing, lacrosse, rowing, sailing, self-defence, soccer, shooting and badminton – among others.

Activities and Trips. The intellectual life is enhanced by an array of stimulating activities. There is a Debating Society, a Politics Forum and the Thomas Browne Society for the presentation of philosophical papers and intellectual discussion. Many academic departments run clubs to allow pupils to gain a wider experience of their subjects. The School Consultative Committee allows elected pupils to discuss school issues directly with the Head Master.

The variety of clubs and societies is continually changing as new teachers and pupils bring their own particular interests to the School. Debating, creative writing, philosophy, Amnesty International, yoga, the Duke of Edinburgh's Award, conservation, chess, cookery and film clubs are on the list at the time of writing. Music, drama and the practical arts all provide further extra-curricular opportunities.

Overseas visits broaden the experience of many pupils. The Modern Languages Department runs exchanges to France, Germany and Liechtenstein. Recent cultural, sporting or adventurous trips have gone to Austria, Canada, China, Ecuador, Egypt, Greece, Holland, Iceland, India, Israel, Russia and Turkey.

Scholarships and Bursaries. Scholarships are awarded to pupils with outstanding ability and flair, which the school assesses by examination, interview or audition. The financial value of a scholarship will be up to 10% of the annual tuition fee – irrespective of parental means. Scholarships are awarded in six categories: Academic; Music; Sport; Art, Design and Drama.

Academic, Sport and Music scholarships are awarded at 11+, 13+ and Sixth Form entry. Art, Design and Drama scholarships are awarded only at Sixth Form entry. Pupils may apply for more than one scholarship, although the maximum financial benefit that can be cumulated is 20% of the school fees.

We set aside generous bursarial funds to enable boys and girls to come to Norwich School who would not be able to do so without financial help. All bursaries are means-tested and can result in a reduction in fees of up to 100%; there is a sliding scale dependent on family income and finances.

As a general rule, it is unlikely that a bursary will be awarded when family income is greater than four and a half times the school fees. It is possible, indeed not unusual, for a bursary holder to have a scholarship. In such circumstances, up to 10% of the fees would be covered by the scholarship;

any bursary funding further to this would, of course, be means-tested.

To supplement the School's bursary provision, the Worshipful Company of Dyers, through its charitable trust, is able to give financial support to a pupil with all-round talent in L4. The criteria for the Dyers' Bursary Scheme are similar to those outlined above and potential applicants should simply register interest in bursarial assistance on the application form.

In addition to the above arrangements, the school has an association with the Ogden Trust which is able to give financial support to selected Sixth Form pupils who join us from the state sector with primary academic strengths in mathematics or the applied sciences. The Trust's financial criteria are similar to our own.

Cathedral Choristers hold Chorister Bursaries to the value of 50% of fees. Further assistance in cases of need is possible.

Lower School. *For further details, see entry for Norwich School, The Lower School in the IAPS section.*

Old Norvicensians. All enquiries should be made to Mrs R Lightfoot, Norwich School, 71a The Close, Norwich NR1 4DD.

Charitable status. Norwich School is a Registered Charity, number 311280. It exists solely to provide education.

Nottingham High School

Waverley Mount, Nottingham NG7 4ED
Tel:	0115 978 6056
Fax:	0115 979 2202
email:	info@nottinghamhigh.co.uk
	enquiries@nottinghamhigh.co.uk
website:	www.nottinghamhigh.co.uk

Motto: '*Lauda Finem*'

This School was founded in 1513 by Dame Agnes Mellers, widow of Richard Mellers, sometime Mayor of Nottingham. The first Charter was given by Henry VIII, and supplementary Charters were given by Philip and Mary, and by Queen Elizabeth. The School, which remains independent, is now administered under the terms of a scheme issued by the Charity Commissioners.

Governing Body:
The Lord Lieutenant of Nottinghamshire
The Lord Mayor of Nottingham
Two Representatives of the City Council
One Representative of the Nottinghamshire County Council
Four Representatives of the Universities
Eleven Co-optative Members

Chairman of the Governors: P Balen

Director of Finance and Estates: R J Dunmore, BA, ACA

Headmaster: K D Fear, BA Southampton

Deputy Headmaster (Pastoral): I P Spedding, BSc
Deputy Headmaster (Academic): D M Williamson, BA, MA, FRGS
Assistant Head (Head of Sixth Form): Mrs W M Robinson, MA
Assistant Head (Pastoral): Miss L Gritti, MSci
Assistant Head (Co-curricular): Mr K Heath, BSc
Assistant Head (Director of Studies): Ms S C Peacock, BSc Nottingham
Director of Finance and Estates: R Dunmore, BA, ACA

Academic Staff:
* *Head of Department*

Mrs K J Turner, BA, HDip (*ICT*)
N C Brown, BSc (*Geography*)

G Douglas, LTCL (*Music*)
P G Morris, BA (*Physics*)
A D Holding, BA (**General Studies, Modern Languages*)
S AW Hiebert, BA (**English*)
Mrs J V Day, BSc (**Biology*)
I C Adshead, MSc (**Chemistry*),
Mrs T Ford, BA (**Religious Studies*)
A Miller, MChem (*Chemistry*)
A S Winter, BA (*French*)
T A Smith, MA (*Mathematics*)
C P Sedgewick, MA (*Geography, Head of Sixth Form*)
Miss N S Giddens, BMus (*Music*)
J T Swain, MA, PhD, FRHistS (*History*)
S L Williams, BA, MA (*History*)
Dr A Bingham, BSc, PhD (*Biology*)
S P Robinson, BSc MRes (*Biology*)
Dr J C Packer, BA (*Classics*)
M D Smith, BEd (**Physical Education*)
A V Martin, BA, Dip Psych (**Psychology*)
M I Saperia, BSc (*Biology*)
D B Thomas, BEd (*Design Technology*)
G Whitehead, MA (**German*)
S J Reid, MA, MMus (**Music*)
P J Cramp, BA (**Economics & Politics*)
Mrs A Griffin, BA (*German*)
I F Thorpe, BEd (*Design Technology*)
J G Allen, MA, MSc (*Mathematics*)
Mrs K M Costante, MA (*Chemistry*)
R E Mellows, BEng (*Physics*)
Mrs B Kruger, BA (*German Assistant*)
P J Dowsett, BA (**History*)
Mrs A R G Lemon, BA (*Geography*)
Mrs C O'Brien, BA, OCR Cert SpLD (**Learning Support Coordinator*)
S A Barr-Smith, BSc (*Mathematics*)
R S C Grant, BA (**Classics*)
Miss M J Kirbyshire, BA (*Art*)
Mrs C J Howat, BSc (*Mathematics*)
Miss M L Green, BA (*English*)
S D Whitehead, BEd (*Physical Education*)
R M A Batchelor, BSc (*Mathematics*)
F A Rosas (*Spanish Assistant*)
Mrs J Poole, BSc (*Biology*)
Mrs H E Mattews, BSc (*Chemistry*)
K Heath, BSc (**Chemistry*)
Mrs H Wood, MSci (*Chemistry*)
Mrs M Hubbard, BSc (*Psychology*)
D J Allerton, BA (*Modern Languages*)
B J Harrison, BA (*Classics*)
Mrs R E Wheeler, BA (*English*)
Mrs E S Nicolson, BA, MA (*Religious Studies*)
C M Brown, BA (*Modern Languages*)
P B Gray, BSc (**Design Technology*)
Dr R Pearson, BA, MA, PhD (*English*)
C S Colman, PhD (*History*)
Miss S McCabe, MA (*Modern Languages*)
C S Farman, BSc (*Physical Education*)
Mrs R C Adams, BA (*Mathematics*)
Mrs R J Northedge, BA (*Mathematics*)
M Baker, BSc (*PE and Games*)
E B Hayton, BSc (*Physics*)
Mrs V J Pidgeon, BA (**French*)
Mrs G C Riley, BA, BArch (*Art*)
S P Robinson, BSc (*Biology*)
Miss C V Webster, BA (**Drama*)
A P Fullerton, BA (*Drama*)
D G Williams, BA (*Music*)
A Miller, MChem (*Chemistry*)
Dr B P Burton, MA (*English*)
Mrs L Woolliscroft, BSocSci (*Economics*)
S D Mitchell, BSc (*Geography*)
R Cotton, BSc (*Physics*)
Mrs S M Cooke (*Music*)

Miss J Johnson, BA (*Classics*)
Mrs S Radford, BA (*Art*)
D P Brumby, BSc (**Mathematics*)
P A Allison, MSc (*Physical Education*)

School Nurse: Ms S Jacob, RGN
Headmaster's PA: Mrs H E Bowen
Librarian: Ms Y Gunther

Infant and Junior School

Head: Mrs C Bruce, MA
Deputy Head: E Jones, BA

Junior School Staff:
Mrs H Whittamore, BA
Miss J Abell, BA
Mrs G K Sethi, BA, MA
Mrs L M Sedgewick, BEd
Mrs K B George, CertEd (*Learning Support*)
A A Simpson, BEd
T Caldwell, BSc, MSc
Miss V Walster, BA
Mrs R Slater, BA
R J Shaw, BA
Mrs L Kawalec, BEd

Lovell House Infant School Staff:
Mrs C Farman, BA
Mrs A Williams
Mrs E Baker, BEd
Mr R Miller, BA
Mrs A Barker, BA
Miss L McCluskey, BEd
Miss J Higgins, BA

Miss A Clarke (*Teaching Assistant*)
Ms J Faulkner (*Teaching Assistant*)
Mrs J Cox (*Teaching Assistant*)
Mrs J Ockleford (*Teaching Assistant*)
Mrs J Robinson (*Teaching Assistant*)

Organisation. There are 987 day boys, of whom 250 are in the Infant and Junior School and 215 in the Sixth Form. Nearly all Junior School boys go on to complete their education in the Senior School. (*For further details about the Infant and Junior School, see entry in IAPS section.*) From 2015 the school will become co-educational in the Sixth Form, followed by the other year groups from 2016.

Curriculum. The Senior School curriculum leads to examinations at GCSE in the normal range of subjects. The Sixth Form are prepared for AS and A Levels. The range of subjects is wide: Latin, Classical Civilisation, Drama, Modern Languages, English, History, Economics, Politics, Design Technology, Geography, Mathematics, Physics, Chemistry, Biology, Music, Art, Philosophy, Psychology, RS, Classical Greek, Music Technology.

Admission. Entrance Examinations and assessments are held in January each year. Applicants for the Infant School should be between the ages of 4 and 7 years, for the Junior School between the ages of 7 and 11 years, and for the Senior School between 11 and 12 years on 1 September of the year of entry. Entry is also possible higher up the School, subject to places being available and a successful interview (entry to Sixth Form is also dependent upon a minimum of 5 As at GCSE).

Fees per term (2014–2015). Tuition: Senior School £4,281, Junior School £3,410, Lovell House Infant School £2,931.

Entrance Scholarships and Bursaries. The Entrance Examination for the Senior School is held in January each year for the award of Entrance Scholarships. Part-Scholarships of a fixed sum may be awarded. They are not linked to parental finances and will normally continue throughout a boy's school career. Application does not have to be made for part-scholarships as these are awarded at the discretion of the Headmaster, subject to entrance examination performance and interview.

Following the ending of the Government Assisted Places Scheme, Nottingham High School has introduced its own means-tested Bursaries to be awarded to boys entering the Senior School at age eleven. All Bursaries will be awarded at the Headmaster's discretion and will normally continue until a pupil leaves the School.

Games. The Playing Fields, covering 20 acres, are situated about a mile and a half from the School with excellent pavilion facilities. There are also indoor cricket nets at the school. The School games, in which all boys are expected to take part unless medically exempted, are Rugby Football (together with Association Football in the Junior School) in the winter, and Cricket or Tennis and Athletics in the summer. Other alternatives provided for senior boys include Cross Country, Squash, Hockey, Association Football (Sixth Form), Badminton, Golf, Shooting and Basketball. Swimming (the School has its own 25m pool) forms part of the Physical Education programme.

Combined Cadet Force. The School maintains a contingent of the CCF based on voluntary recruitment and consisting of Navy, Army and Air Force sections. There is a small bore range, and the School enters teams for various national competitions.

Societies. Individual interests and hobbies are catered for by a wide range of Societies which meet in the lunch break or at the end of afternoon school. These include Drama, Modern Languages, Mathematics, Chemistry, Biology, English, Politics, Arts, Music and Debating Societies, the Chess Club, the Bridge Club, Christian Union, and the Scout Troop. Over 120 boys a year participate in the Duke of Edinburgh's Award Scheme. The Community Action Group, the Explorer Scouts and other Societies meet jointly with the neighbouring Nottingham Girls' High School.

Music. Apart from elementary instruction in Music in the lower forms, and more advanced studies for GCSE and A Level, tuition is offered by 3 full-time and 18 part-time teachers in the full range of orchestral instruments. There are 2 School orchestras of 50 and 30 players, 2 Choirs, a concert band (wind) of 50, a Training Band and Big Band and choral and orchestral concerts are given each year. Four instrumental bursaries, covering fee tuition on one instrument, are available to boys entering Year 7.

Honours. 13 Places at Oxford and Cambridge in 2014.

Charitable status. Nottingham High School is a Registered Charity, number 1104251. It exists to provide education for boys between the ages of 4 and 18 years.

Oakham School

Chapel Close, Oakham, Rutland LE15 6DT
Tel: 01572 758500
            Admissions: 01572 758758
Fax: 01572 758595
email: admissions@oakham.rutland.sch.uk
website: www.oakham.rutland.sch.uk
Twitter: @OakhamSch

Motto: '*Quasi Cursores Vitai Lampada Tradunt*'

Trustees:
Chairman: P O Lawson, DL, BSc, CITP, MBCS, DipMus
Deputy Chairman: T F Hart, DL, MA

Ex officio:
The Rt Revd D Allister, MA, Bishop of Peterborough
Dr L Howard, OBE, Hon LLD, JP, Lord-Lieutenant of Rutland
The Very Revd C Taylor, MA, Hon FGCM, Dean of Peterborough

Co-optative:
Mrs K S Blank, LLM, LLB
J Czarnota, MBA
P S Douty
F Foulkes
R C Gainher, BSc
Mrs J Gibson, MA, BEd
Professor N T Gorman, DL, BVSc, PhD, DVSc, DVMS, DVM, DACVIM, Dip-ECVIM, FRCVS, FRSA
Mrs J Grundy
N D G Jones, BSc
A R M Little, MA
Mrs J Lucas
Mrs J Osborne, BA, LLM
G J Schanschieff, MBE, BA Hons
M G Wilson, BA, Dipl Arch RIBA
S Woolfe

Bursar and Clerk to the Trustees: Mrs A Hedrich-Wiggans, MA Cantab, MSt Oxon, ACA

Headmaster: N M Lashbrook, BA

Deputy Head: Mrs L M North, BA
Deputy Head (*Pastoral and Co-curricular*): Mrs S J Gomm, BSc
Deputy Head (*Academic*): D A Harrow, MA

Senior Members of Staff:
Director Teaching and Learning: R Gale, MA Cantab
Head of Upper School: J Lockwood, BA
Head of Middle School: J H Robinson, BA
Master of the Lower School 'Jerwoods': V J Harvey, BSc
Director of IB: Mrs S Lorenz-Weir, MA
Senior Housemaster: A B Speers, BSc
Registrar: N S Paddock, BSocSc
Marketing Director: Mrs S Rowntree
Foundation Director: Mrs J Creighton, BA, MBA

Heads of Department:
Activities: Dr A G Headley, BSc, PhD
Careers: Mrs P C Gibbs, BSc, MBA
Computer Science: N J F Neve, BSc
Creative Arts: S L Poppy, BA
English: M M Fairweather, MA
Geography: H A Collison, BSc, MPhil
History: J N J Roberts, MA
Languages: Dr S T Glynn, MA
Learning Support: Mrs C D Hill, MA, DipSpLD
Mathematics: Miss C J Darwin, BSc
Music: P Davis, MA, ARCO
Religion and Philosophy: Dr D J Sheppard, MA
Social Sciences: P Nutter, BA
Science: Dr J A Chilton
Sport: I Simpson, BSc

Chaplain: The Revd A C V Aldous, BA

Housemasters/mistresses:

Lower School:
Ancaster: Mrs S A Wragg, BSc
Lincoln: Mrs H M Foster, BA, DipLA
Peterborough: S B Foster, GRSM
Sargants: M Durose, BSc

Middle School:
Barrow: M Boud-Self, BSc, MSc, MA Ed, FRGS
Buchanans: Mrs C L Latham, BEd
Chapmans: D W Bonanno, PGCE
Clipsham: A B Speers, BSc
Gunthorpe: Mrs K M Hegarty, MA
Hambleton: Mrs S M Healey, BSc
Haywoods: D M Taylor, BA
Rushebrookes: Mrs T Drummond, GRSM, LRAM
Stevens: Mrs A M Lear, BA, MCLIP
Wharflands: J J Cure, BA

Upper School:
Round House: Mrs E L Durston, BSc
School House: C J Foster, BSc

History. In 1584 Archdeacon Robert Johnson of Leicester founded "as many free schools in Rutland as there are market towns therein; one at Oakham, another at Uppingham". With eyes firmly fixed on the demands faced by the young of the 21st century, Oakham both respects traditions and seeks innovative solutions to contemporary challenges.

Today, Oakham School is fully co-educational with 1,046 pupils (521 Boys, 525 Girls) aged 10–18 and a 50:50 ratio of boarders to day pupils. The overall staff : pupil ratio is 1:7. Sixth formers can choose to study either the International Baccalaureate or A Levels.

Facilities. Oakham's facilities include one of the best school libraries in the country, new science laboratories, an information and communication technology centre, a state-of-the-art school of design which complements the art and design centre, a theatre and a music school. Sports facilities are extensive with superbly maintained fields, two all-weather pitches and a sports complex with an indoor swimming pool, squash courts, fives courts and fitness centre.

Organisation and Curriculum. There are four Lower School houses (age 10–12) and ten for the Middle/Upper School (age 13–17), whilst separate houses for final year girls and boys enable them to lead a freer life and to organise their own commitments to a greater degree. The Housemaster or Housemistress is responsible for pastoral support. Each pupil has a Tutor, who is responsible for pupils' personal and academic development, and for keeping a balance between academic, creative and social activities.

Lower School pupils are given a solid grounding in English, French, Geography, History, ICT, Mathematics, Religious Education, Science, Latin (most pupils) and Creative and Performing Arts. In Form 2 they add Spanish and German, selecting one during the year for further study. We also use these years to develop essential core academic skills and habits: we work to ensure that they are effective learners in their own right. Our innovative approach encourages links between different subjects, showing learners how to see beyond the narrow requirements of a particular exam and transfer their learning skills to new situations.

GCSE: all pupils follow the IGCSE syllabus in English Language, English Literature, Dual-Award Science (which comprises Physics, Chemistry and Biology), a choice of Modern Languages (French, Spanish, German) and Mathematics, together with a choice from GCSE History, Geography, Religion and Philosophy, academic Drama or Music and a variety of Creative Arts subjects (Fine Art – Painting and Mixed Media, Textile Design or Sculpture, or Design Technology focusing on Electronics Products, Resistant Materials or Graphics Products). Other academic options include Citizenship, Classical Civilisation, Computer Science, Creative iMedia, Greek, Latin and Physical Education. We expose pupils to a rich cultural environment, providing an exciting programme of projects and visits to enhance learning beyond the classroom and the exam syllabus.

Upper School pupils may opt either for the AS/A2 course or the International Baccalaureate. Subjects available are Art and Design, Biology, Business, Chemistry, Classical Civilisation, Critical and Contextual Studies, Design and Technology, Economics, English Language, English Literature, French, Geography, German, Greek, History, Italian (AS Level only), Latin, Mathematics, Further Mathematics, Music (Cambridge Pre-U course), PE and Sport Science, Philosophy, Physics, Politics, Spanish and Theatre Studies. The International Baccalaureate programme offers a similar range, but students study six subjects: three subjects are studied at Higher Level and three at Standard Level. Additionally, all students take the three Core Elements of the diploma: Theory of Knowledge, the Extended Essay and a programme of Creativity, Action and Service.

Music. Over 40% of pupils learn a musical instrument and almost half the school is involved in practical music making through participation in choirs, bands, orchestras, and music theatre productions. Nearly 80 concerts each year present a wide variety of performing opportunities both in and out of school as well as international tours. Pupils are regularly selected for national youth ensembles and the school Chamber Choir has been acclaimed in major competitions.

Drama plays an important part in the life of the School with several productions each year. A majority of pupils at all levels takes part in at least one dramatic production a year.

Art, Design and Technology. The Richard Bull Centre and the state-of-the-art Jerwood School of Design together offer an extensive array of creative and design technology opportunities, including painting, pottery, sculpture, textiles, print-making, photography, computer aided design and electronics, working in wood, metal and plastics.

Sport and Activities. Our major sports are rugby, hockey, cricket, athletics, netball and tennis. Some 30 other sports options are also offered. In 2013–14 twenty pupils represented the country in seven different sports. Oakham is proud to be a well-recognised training ground for national squads.

Each week pupils follow an Activity (or hobby) and, from the Middle School upwards, a Service Option. They can try something new or pursue an existing passion. Our Service Options develop skills and values for life. Pupils may choose from an extensive volunteering programme, the Combined Cadet Force or the Duke of Edinburgh's Award.

Entry. Normal entry points are 10+, 11+, 13+ and 16+. Pupils are accepted mainly in September at the start of the academic year. Full admissions information is available from the Registrar.

Scholarships and Bursaries. The following scholarships are available: Academic (11+, 13+, 16+), All-rounder (13+), Art (13+, 16+), Design and Technology (13+, 16+), Drama (16+), Music (11+, 13+, 16+), Science and Engineering (16+), Sport (13+, 16+). The basic value of a scholarship is 10% (academic 20%) and top-up means-tested support may be available. For further information including bursaries please visit the school website or request an information booklet from the Registrar, Tel: 01572 758758.

Fees per term (2014–2015). Lower School (age 10–12): £8,145 (full boarding), £6,410–£7,410 (transitional boarding: 2 to 4 nights), £5,310 (day).

Middle and Upper Schools (age 13+): £9,980 (full boarding), £8,985 (day boarding: 3 nights), £5,990 (day).

Honours 2014. With a 100% A Level pass rate, 40% of students gained A*/A grades and 71% were awarded A*–B grades. Of the 58 International Baccalaureate candidates 35% scored 38 or more points out of a possible 45; this calibre of student will apply for Oxbridge or other top universities. The average points score was 35.1 against a worldwide average of 30. In an excellent GCSE year 65% of pupils achieved A*/A grades, 30% gained straight A*/As and 87% A*–Bs. Nearly all leavers go to University or College; 5 pupils received Oxbridge offers; 11 gained places at Medical and Veterinary schools.

Charitable status. Oakham School is a Registered Charity, number 1131425, and a Company Limited by Guarantee, registered in England and Wales, number 06924216. Registered Office: Chapel Close, Market Place, Oakham, Rutland LE15 6DT. It exists for the purpose of education.

Oldham Hulme Grammar School

Chamber Road, Oldham, Lancs OL8 4BX
Tel: 0161 624 4497
email: admin@ohgs.co.uk

website: www.ohgs.co.uk

Motto: *Fide sed cui Vide.*
   The school, founded in 1611, was reconstituted in the 19th century under the Endowed Schools Act. The main buildings of The Oldham Hulme Grammar Schools were opened in 1895 on a commanding south-west facing site overlooking the city of Manchester.

Patron: The Lord Clitheroe of Downham

Governors:
Chairman: Mr D J Illingworth, BA, FCA
Vice Chairman: Mr V A K Srivastava, LLB Hons
Hon Treasurer: Mr J E Halliwell

Elected Governors:
Dr K Buckley
Mr P M Buckley, BSc, ACG1
Mr S A Corns, MA, FRSA
Mr R S Illingworth, BSc
Mr R Lobley, MRICS
Mr A Milnes, BA Hons
Mrs A Richards, BSc
Mr K Sanders
Mrs V Stocker, LLB
Mr J Sutcliffe
Mr A P Wild, BA

Representative Governor, Metropolitan Borough of Oldham:
Mr Z Chauhan

Bursar and Clerk to the Governors: I Martin, BSc, FCA, FCMA

Principal: C J D Mairs, MA Edinburgh

Deputy Principal – Pastoral: J C Budding, BEd Sheffield Hallam
Deputy Principal – Registrar: Miss S E Shepherd, BA London
Deputy Principal – Sixth Form: D J Dalziel, BSc London, PG Dip Leeds
Deputy Principal – Preps: Mrs C A Wilkinson, BSc Liverpool
Deputy Principal – Academic: N G H James, MA York

S P Adamson, MA Manchester (*English, Duke of Edinburgh's Award Scheme, Careers*)
W L M Atkins, BSc Keele (*Head of Biology, CCF*)
Dr P M Beagon, MA, DPhil Oxford (*Head of Classics*)
Mrs N Bibi, BSc Manchester (*Mathematics*)
Mrs K Boswell, BA Leeds (*Head of Psychology*)
Miss J C Brown, BA Liverpool (*Physical Education, Head of Year 7*)
Miss L E Bowden, BSc Manchester (*Biology*)
N P Buckley, BA Sheffield (*Business Studies and Economics*)
Mrs H Chaplain, MA Oxford (*English and Drama*)
N J Chesterton, BA Leeds (*Physical Education and Games, Head of Assheton House*)
G W Conroy, CertEd Leeds (*Physical Education and Games*)
T M J Cotton, BEd MMU (*Design Technology*)
Ms L J Cowan, MA Dundee (*History, Duke of Edinburgh's Award Scheme*)
A J Coyle, BEng Brighton (*Physics, Technology*)
Mrs N L Cross, BSc Manchester (*Mathematics*)
Mrs C Davies, BA Kent (*Head of Drama, Careers*)
M N Dowthwaite, BA Manchester (*Head of History and Politics, School Functions Officer*)
Miss C W Duffy, BA, MPhil Aberystwyth (*History*)
Mrs C A Eliot, BA Heriot-Watt (*Head of Textiles, PSHE Coordinator*)
O M Gandolfi, BSc Bangor (*Biology, Head of Year 10*)
Mrs H Garside, BA North Wales (*Modern Languages*)

Ms R M Glover, MA Sussex (*Head of English*)
M C Goodwin, MA Edgehill (*Modern Languages, i/c Spanish, Head of Booth/Platt House*)
Miss J V Graystock, BA Liverpool (*Head of Art*)
Mrs K L Gregson, BSc Lancaster (*Head of General Studies, Psychology, Biology, Deputy Head of Sixth Form*)
J J W Gumpert, MA Cambridge (*Head of Religious Studies*)
Mrs E Harris, BA Liverpool (*Physical Education*)
Mrs C Headdock, BA London (*Modern Languages, English, Learning Support*)
J R Hesten, BA Manchester (*Physics*)
Mrs A H Howarth, BEd, Manchester Metropolitan, PG Dip, Dip SEN, PG Cert SpLD (*Head of Learning Support*)
Mrs D Howarth, BSc Manchester Metropolitan (*Head of Home Economics*)
G Hulme, ARCO, LTCL (*Director of Music*)
A H B Hurst, BA Manchester Metropolitan (*Head of Physical Education*)
M C Jones, MPhys Manchester (*Head of Physics*)
G L Jones, BSc UMIST (*Chemistry*)
Mrs F J Kenney, BSc Manchester (*Home Economics*)
Mrs T A Kershaw, BA Salford (*Head of Modern Languages*)
Miss J P Knighton, BEd Leeds Metropolitan (*Head of Physical Education*)
M F Kostecky, BSc Manchester (*ICT*)
Mrs J A Lamb, BSc Liverpool (*Head of Mathematics*)
P Langdon, BEd Manchester Metropolitan (*Head of Information Technology*)
Miss L Lavin, BSc Manchester Metropolitan (*Biology*)
Mrs J Leach, BA Hull (*English*)
T A Leng, BA Leeds (*History, Teacher i/c Politics*)
Mrs A Longley, MA Manchester (*Head of Economics, Business Studies, Head of Year 11*)
Mrs D Maders, BSc Leeds, MRSC (*Head of Chemistry*)
Miss L J Malcolm, BA Liverpool John Moores (*Physical Education*)
A H Marshall, BSc Hull (*Geography, Director of Pastoral Care*)
Mrs J McCarthy, MA, PG Dip Liverpool (*Art, Design Technology, Head of Year 8*)
Ms E Mills, BA Manchester (*English*)
S McRoyall, BA Sunderland (*Art*)
Mrs H M North, BSc Liverpool (*Chemistry*)
A Peacocke, BA Glamorgan (*Geography, Head of Year 9*)
Miss H R Plews, BA Liverpool, MPhil Cantab (*Classics, Head of Lees House*)
S G Rawlings, BEng Aston (*Mathematics, Physics*)
D R A Rees, BSc Bradford (*Head of Business Studies, Economics, Head of Year 11*)
M Richmond, BSc Leeds (*Mathematics, Master i/c Football*)
D G Robertson, BMus Aberdeen, ALCM (*Music*)
Mrs A G Robinson, BSc Romania, MSc Manchester (*Physics*)
Mrs R S Shapey, BMus Birmingham, LRSM (*Music*)
A D Smith, BSc Salford (*Mathematics, Head of Hulme House*)
Dr P J Sutherland, BA Hull, PhD Bradford (*Head of Geography, Induction Coordinator*)
C R Sykes, MA Manchester (*Classics*)
C J Travis, BEd Crewe and Alsager (*Head of Design Technology*)
Mrs J Travis, DipM (*Head of Careers, Food Technology*)
Miss R L Turner, BSc Loughborough (*Mathematics*)
Miss C F P G Wéry, AESI Haute Ecole de Bruxelles – Defre Belgium (*Modern Foreign Languages*)
Mrs D Y Wheldrick, BA Preston Polytechnic (*Information Technology, Peer Mentoring Coordinator*)
Mrs J C Wood, BA Leeds (*Religious Studies, Director of Pastoral Care*)

P F Wood, CertEd St John's College, York (*Physical Education*)

Miss R L Wood, BSc Manchester Metropolitan (*Chemistry*)

Hulme Preparatory Schools:

Deputy Principal: Mrs C A Wilkinson, BSc Liverpool
Head of Kindergarten: Miss E A White, BA Durham
Director of Studies: Mrs R Knott, BA Surrey

Miss C Barnett, BA Edge Hill (*Early Years Coordinator*)
A Booth, BA Central England (*Upper Juniors Pastoral Coordinator*)
Mrs E Brocklehurst, BA Exeter, ABRSM
M P Bumford, BSc Chester
Mrs R L Christo, BEd Birmingham (*Literacy Coordinator*)
P S Coulson, BSc Edge Hill College
M G Cowley, BSc Stirling (*Lower Juniors Pastoral Coordinator*)
S Davies, BA Edge Hill University (*PSHE Coordinator*)
Miss A A Done, BA Manchester Metropolitan (*Science Coordinator, Pastoral Coordinator KS1*)
Miss G A Fulford-Brown, BA Manchester Metropolitan
Miss C Goodwin, BA Manchester Metropolitan
A J Halliwell, BEd Manchester, CertEd Manchester
Mrs B Humphreys, NNEB, HNC
Mrs W Maitland, BSc Sheffield (*Mathematics Coordinator, Induction Coordinator*)
Miss S E Oates, LTCL, LGSM, CertEd Reading
A K D Taylor, LLB Birmingham, MA Bradford
Miss H A Whitwam, BA Bradford College (*PSHE Coordinator*)

Visiting Music Teachers:
D Browne, GRNCM (*Cello*)
Miss A Cooper, GGSM (*Oboe*)
Mrs V Eastham, MA, FTCL, LRSM (*Piano*)
Dr R Gibbon, GMus RNCM, ATCL, PhD (*Clarinet & Piano*)
Ms S Gibbon, GRNCM (*Violin*)
K Heggie, GRNCM (*Guitar*)
Mrs A Holmes, GRNCM (*Singing*)
C Holmes, BMus, GRSM, ARMCM (*Piano*)
Mrs M Hulme, BSc, LTCL (*Violin*)
Mrs J Kent, CT ABRSM (*Brass*)
Miss P McMillan, BMus RNCM, ALCM (*Percussion*)
Mrs K Ord, BMus, PG Dip RNCM (*Violin*)
Miss J Puckey, BMus (*Clarinet & Saxophone*)
Mrs S Walker, GRSM, PPRCM (*Flute*)

The Oldham Hulme family of schools is renowned for delivering outstanding levels of education at each stage of a child's development. With unbeatable standards and outstanding achievements, the schools cater for boys and girls aged three to 18 and offer a caring, orderly and academically stimulating environment.

At the age of 3 school life begins in the surroundings of the Kindergarten which has recently moved into new modern premises. Confidence is then built throughout the junior and secondary years and great care is taken in the sixth form to create extremely capable, well-balanced young adults.

The schools' primary aim is to provide a caring, friendly and lively school environment that fosters a desire to learn and at all times, pupils are encouraged to think and work independently. With a reputation for academic excellence and outstanding extra-curricular activities, pupils benefit from the right environment which enables them to achieve their full potential in life so that they go on to become successful, happy and confident young men and women.

The Hulme family of schools value academic achievement and standards are high. Consequently there is an excellent record of examination success at GCSE and A Level. Pupils are taught within small classes by a team of dedicated, well-qualified staff.

The schools also offer an excellent pastoral care system which guides and supports pupils, promoting their personal development within the wider school community.

The comprehensive careers education programme on offer widens each pupil's understanding of the opportunities available in the changing world of work, while equipping them with the skills to manage their future career.

A stimulating range of extra-curricular activities provides opportunities for fun, challenge, initiative, leadership and service, while activities within the wider community encourage active involvement and promote a genuine concern for the needs for others.

Fees per term (2014–2015). Hulme Kindergarten £2,445, Preparatory Schools £2,445, Senior Schools £3,345.

A number of bursaries are awarded annually to pupils entering at the ages of 11 and 16. These awards are based on parental income and academic ability and will remain in place for the time in school subject to satisfactory progress by the pupil.

Charitable status. The Oldham Hulme Grammar School is a Registered Charity, number 526636. It exists to provide a balanced academic education for pupils aged 3 to 18.

The Oratory School

Woodcote, Reading, South Oxfordshire RG8 0PJ
Tel: 01491 683500
Fax: 01491 680020
email: enquiries@oratory.co.uk
website: www.oratory.co.uk

Motto: '*Cor ad cor loquitur*'
The Oratory School was founded in 1859, by Blessed John Henry Newman, at the request of a group of eminent Catholic laymen. The Chaplain apart, the School is administered and staffed entirely by laymen.

President: The Rt Hon Lord Judge

Vice-Presidents:
His Eminence Cardinal William W Baum
J J Eyston, MA, FRICS, KSG
Archbishop Vincent Nichols, MA, STL, PhL, MEd

Chairman: M H R Hasslacher
Vice-Chairman: C J Sehmer, FCA

The Governors:
M J Berkeley JP BSc BA IMC MCSI
B F H Bettesworth, FRICS, ACIArb
The Very Revd R Byrne, BD, AKC, Cong Orat
Mrs M Cochrane
Mrs M Edwards
Professor P W Evans, MA, PhD
F J Fitzherbert-Brockholes, MA
C J French, FRAgS
Dr C B T Hill Williams, DL, MA, FRGS, FRSA
H H Judge K A D Hornby, BA
Mrs J Moulder MA
N R Purnell, MA, QC
The Revd J N Saward, MA, MLitt
M W Stilwell
T A H Tyler, OBE, B

Clerk to the Governors & Bursar: A F Bradshaw, DMS, MCIM, FInstLM

Head Master: C I Dytor, MC, KHS, MA Cantab, MA Oxon

Second Master: T J Hennessy, BSc
Senior Master: P L Tomlinson, MFA
Lower Master: M H Green, MBE, MEd, FRSA, MRAeS
Chaplain: Rt Revd P Gee

Academic Staff:
* Head of Department
† Housemaster
§ Part-time

Mrs E K Aldington, Dip AD (§*Art*)
J Aldridge, BSc (*Mathematics*)
Mrs J H Barr, BEd, MA (*Mathematics*)
J Berkley, BA, MA (*French, Italian,* †*Norris*)
Mrs S Bevan, BA (**Biology*)
S Bosher, BSc, DipDes (*Design and Technology, CCF*)
S A Bowles, BSc, PhD (*Chemistry*)
J A Brooke, BA, MA (**English*)
P W Brown, BSc (*Physics*)
S P S Burrows, BA (**Director of Music*)
I A N Campbell, BSc (**Physics*)
P J Chaundy, BA (*Art*)
T N Danks, BSc, PhD (**Chemistry*)
A P Dulston, BA (*Religious Education*)
P J Easton, BSc (*Biology*)
Revd D J Elliot, MA (**Theology*)
M G Farnan, BSc (§*Curriculum Support, CCF, Shooting*)
M R Fec, BA (**History*)
D Forster, MA, MSc (*Director of Studies, Mathematics, Philosophy*)
C W Fothergill, BA, MA Ed (*Classical Civilisation, History*)
O C Godfrey, BA (**Drama*)
M H Green, MEd, MBE, FRSA, MRAES (**Design and Technology, Lower Master*)
Mrs S Green, BA (*Curriculum Support*)
Mrs L Haddock, BVSc, MRCVS (*Mathematics*)
T J Hennessy, BSc (*Mathematics, Second Master*)
M D Hennessy, BA (*History*)
V B A Holden, BSc, PGCE (*Science, Mathematics,* †*St John*)
N C Jones, BA, ARCO (**Academic Music, Examinations Officer*)
I P Jordan, BEd (*Physical Education, Mathematics,* †*FitzAlan*)
Mrs K S Lambert, BA (*English*)
K Laughton, BA, AIL (**Modern Languages*)
Revd K E MacNab, BA, MA (*Religious Education*)
R A O'Sullivan, BA (*English*)
Mrs S O'Sullivan, BA (*English*)
P E Poynter, BA (**Geography*)
C J Redfern (*Graduate Music Assistant*)
J A Ryan, BA, MFA (*Artist in Residence*)
C J Sudding, BEng Hons (**Mathematics*)
M P Syddall, MA (*Classics, Head of Sixth Form*)
C W Sykes, MA, MBA, PGCE (*Business Studies & Geography*)
P A Thomas, BA, MA Ed (**Economics*)
P L Tomlinson, MFA (**Director of Art & Design, Senior Master*)
S C B Tomlinson, BSc (**Director of Games*)
N E Topham (*Physical Education, CCF Admin Officer*)
Mrs A D T Tuite-Dalton (§*French*)
D O D Watkins, MSc (*Geography, Philosophy*)
C Watson, BA (*Junior Humanities, St Philip House*)
Mrs V Watson, BA (§*PE*)
Miss S E Wethey, BA (*English*)
R B Womersley, BEd (*Classical Civilisation, History;* †*Faber*)

Music Staff:
C Caiger (*Guitar*)
T D Carleston (*Singing*)
J Donnelly (*Drums, Percussion*)
Mrs S Ellison, BA, LRAM (*Oboe and Piano*)
Mrs S L Dytor, ARCM (*Violin*)
G Howarth, BSc, MA (*Brass*)
C C King, FRICS (*Drums & Percussion*)
M Knowles, AGSM (*Brass*)
Miss E V Krivenko, MMus Dip (*Piano*)
Mrs C Lancaster, BMus, MMus, PGDip (*Cello*)
Mrs K E Laughton, BA (*Saxophone, Flute*)
Miss E L Mallett, BA (*Singing*)
J P B McNamara, MA, FRCO (*Organ*)
S Nisbett, LTCL (*Guitar*)
G Williams, FTCL, FLCM, LRAM, ARCM (*Bassoon*)

School Health Centre:
Dr A Goode (*Medical Officer*)
Mrs P Codner, MSc, RGN, RM (*Health Centre Sister*)
§Mrs M Gates, RGN
Mrs C McSoley, RGN
§Mrs A R Bean, RGN, BSc
§Mrs C Thompson, RGN, BA

Non-Teaching Staff:
Miss C Bleimschein (*Bursar's Secretary*)
A F Bradshaw, DMS, MCIM, FInstLM (*Bursar*)
T R Brittan, MCSA, CEH (*Network Manager*)
Mrs N Brouard (§*Reception*)
Mrs L Coupland (*Marketing & Public Relations*)
Miss P Cunningham (*Front of House*)
Mrs L Kisiel (*Catering Manager*)
Mrs M Lee (*School Secretary*)
Mrs C Macnab (*Librarian*)
Mrs J Martin (*School Secretary*)
J K Mitchell, ACIOB (*Estates Manager*)
Mrs G Munoz (§*Reception*)
Mrs D Nash, MA (§*Archivist & Society Officer*)
A Rajan (*Finance Manager*)
M Sixsmith, BSc, MPhil (§*Computer Services*)
Mrs J Stoner, Assoc CIPD (*Human Resources Manager*)
Mrs S A Waghorn (*Head Master's PA*)
Mrs K Warren (§*Secretary*)

Sports Centre Staff:
Mrs R Moffatt, BSc (*Sports Centre Manager*)
C B Keegan (*Cricket Professional*)
L Taylor (*Assistant Professional Real Tennis*)
D Rook (*Sports Centre Assistant*)

Number in School. There are 420 boys: 220 boarding and 200 day boys.

The School is situated in an area of outstanding natural beauty in grounds of 400 acres, in South Oxfordshire. There are four Senior Houses (13–18) and one Junior House called St Philip House (11–13). Each House is run by a married Housemaster and staffed by a House team, which includes a Housemother. There is at least one other adult in each Boarding House and over three-quarters of the staff live on-site or in the local village.

The Head Master has completed a ten-year development programme. Two new boarding Houses have been constructed along with new Art & Design, DT, English, History, Maths, and Theology Departments. A new Performing Arts facility, the Hilaire Belloc Theatre, opened in 2013 and a major Sports Centre redevelopment is due for completion Autumn 2014.

Organisation. Four Senior Houses and St Philip House offer living facilities for 420 boys, both day and boarding. Particular care is taken to provide an environment which facilitates the assimilation of new boys.

Health. The School Medical Centre is under the supervision of a fully qualified resident Sister and the School Medical Officer visits once a week.

Admission. Boys enter at age 13 through the Scholarship or Common Entrance Examinations, or at 11 by informal interview and exam. A small number of boys are received directly into the Sixth Form.

Religious Education. Catholic spirituality pervades the school in an unobtrusive way. It is at the heart of the school and to be an Oratorian is something special. Respect for the individual within the larger framework of this society is the hallmark of this Oratorian ethos. There is a Resident Chaplain who looks after the needs of both boys and staff. All boys study religions.

Studies. Boys are prepared for A Levels and GCSE. A wide range of subjects is offered in the Sixth Form. There is no rigid division into Arts and Science subjects; almost any combination of subjects can be taken. Pre-U is offered in some subjects.

Games. In addition to the main games – Rugby Football, Soccer, Cricket, Shooting and Rowing – boys take part in Cross-Country Running, Swimming, Tennis, Badminton, Basketball, Squash, Golf, and Real Tennis. There is a nine-hole golf course on the 400-acre site and a four-lane indoor shooting range. National awards have been won for sport. The huge new Sports Centre will be ready for use in Autumn 2014.

CCF. There is a flourishing contingent of the CCF which, in addition to the Army section, includes the following sub-sections: RN, RAF, REME, Signals, and Adventure Training. The Duke of Edinburgh's Award Scheme is popular with the gold expedition going to Morocco. The school ranks in the top five shooting schools in the country with some team members shooting for Great Britain.

Extra-curricular activities. There are frequent theatre outings, visits to museums and art galleries, careers visits, as well as talks and lectures given in the School by visiting speakers. There is a wide range of clubs and societies.

Optional Extras. Instrumental Music, coaching in Real Tennis, Lawn Tennis, Squash and Golf.

Careers Guidance. The Head of Sixth Form provides guidance for boys in their choice of future occupation. There is also a Careers Master who organises speakers.

The School is a member of ISCO.

Fees per term (2014–2015). Boarders: £10,245 (Junior House £7,180); Day Boys: £7,450 (Junior House £5,350).

The fees include board, tuition, consolidated extras, and games. An optional insurance scheme is in operation which covers remission of fees in the event of a boy's absence through illness. A full term's notice of withdrawal is required; failing such notice a term's fees are payable. There may be a reduction for younger brothers and sons of old boys.

Scholarships. A number of Academic Scholarships and Exhibitions, and Awards in Music, Art and Sport, are offered. Awards are of varying values. Music awards include free music tuition in two disciplines. All-rounder awards are made on the recommendation and reports from Prep School Heads.

The Preparatory School is at 'Great Oaks', a property situated in grounds of 45 acres on the same ridge of the Chilterns, about 2 miles from the Main School, between Cray's Pond and Pangbourne. This is co-educational. (*For further details, see entry in IAPS section.*)

The Oratory School Society. *Chairman and Correspondent:* Mr R A Cox, 38 Home Park Road, Wimbledon Park, London SW19 7HN.

Charitable status. The Oratory Schools Association is a Registered Charity, number 309112. It is a charitable trust dedicated to continuing the aims of its Founder, Blessed John Henry Newman.

Oundle School

Oundle, Peterborough PE8 4GH

Tel:	01832 277122 (Reception)
	01832 277142 (Headmaster's Office)
	01832 277125 (Admissions Office)
	01832 277116 (Undermaster's Office)
Fax:	01832 273564
email:	admissions@oundleschool.org.uk
website:	www.oundleschool.org.uk

Motto: '*God Grant Grace*'

Oundle School was established by the Grocers' Company with the object of providing a liberal education in accordance with the principles of the Church of England. The aims of the School are: to promote excellence and allow pupils to reach their full academic and intellectual potential; to develop independence and team players who will contribute to the community; to develop strong values, encourage involvement and an understanding of adult life, and prepare pupils for life beyond Oundle; to provide a full-boarding programme such that its excellence is recognised worldwide.

Governing Body:
[1]J G Tregoning (*Chairman*)
¶D C L Miller (*Vice-Chairman*)
[1]P M Bostelmann
[1]¶J H Cartwright
The Countess Howe, DL
¶ D Hutchinson
Mrs J Kibbey
[1]¶R H Ringrose
Dr P J Rogerson
[1]J P H S Scott
M Spens
Lady Stringer
[1]J Whitmore

Ex officio:
[1]J Roundell (*Master*)
[1]C G McAndrew (*Second Warden*)
[1]O Wise (*Third Warden*)
J H O'Hare, OBE, MBA, BSc (*Bursar and Secretary*)

[1] *Member of the Court of The Grocers' Company*
¶ *Old Oundelian*

Headmaster: C M P Bush, MA
Head from September 2015: Mrs S Kerr-Dineen, MA

Deputy Head and Director of Pastoral Care: Mrs D L Watt, MA
Senior Master: P S C King, BSc, MSc
Undermaster: A B Burrows, MAEd, BSc
Director of Studies: B J Evans, BSc, FRSC
Bursar: J H O'Hare, OBE, MBA, BSc
Senior Chaplain: Revd B J Cunningham, MA
Director of Professional Development: Mrs J T Coles, BA
Director of Co-Curricular Activities: T P Hipperson, MA
Director of IT: Mrs L Waide
Registrar: G Phillips, BA
Director of Marketing and External Relations: Miss R J Vicary, BA
Director of Development: M J Dear, BTh, GDL, FInstPa
Deputy Bursar (Finance): Ms J Jones, BSc, FCA, DChA
Deputy Bursar (Estates): R M C Tremellen, BSc, AIMBM

Houses and Housemasters/Housemistresses:
Bramston: A J Sherwin
Crosby: H Roberts
Dryden: Ms K A Francis
Fisher: N J T Wood
Grafton: W W Gough
Kirkeby: Mrs A E Meisner
Laundimer: J R Hammond-Chambers
Laxton: Mrs N S Guise
New House: Mrs M L Smith
Sanderson: Mrs S L Ratchford
School House: A E Langsdale
Sidney: Dr C J Quiddington
St Anthony: P J Kemp
Wyatt: Dr N M Mola
The Berrystead: Mme S Fonteneau

Medical Officers:
Dr D Clayton, MBChB, DRCOG, DCH

Dr K Newell, MBChB, MRCGP, DRCOG

* *Head of Department*

Art:
*J D Oddie, BA
M A Case, BA
Miss G C Pontifex, BA, MA
Ms K A Hannant, MA

Biology:
J Hunt, BSc, PhD
P S C King, BSc, MSc (*Senior Master*)
W F Holmström, BSc, PhD
Mrs M A Holmström, BSc, MSc
A E Langsdale, BSc, MSc
*Dr P J Rowe, DPhil
W W Gough, BSc
O E A Peck, BSc (*Head of Science*)
S K Burman-Roy, MA
A Searle, BSc

Chemistry:
R J McKim, PhD, CChem, MRS, FRAS
R F Hammond, BSc (*Proctor*)
M J Bessent, MChem, PhD, AMRSC (*Sanderson Fellow*)
Dr C J Quiddington, MChem, PhD
B J Evans, BSc, FRSC (*Director of Studies*)
Miss T A Dorman, MChem
*J Peverley, MA
C Davison, MSc

Classics:
Mrs M P R James, MA
Mrs D L Watt, MA (*Deputy Head and Director of Pastoral Care*)
N J Aubury, MA
*T J Morrison, BA
Ms C L Westran, BA (*The Academic Assistant*)
P A Liston, MA
Miss C McDonnell, MA
Miss L Davies-Evitt, BA
Miss R L Hodgson, BA

Computing:
*R J Cunniffe, BSc (*Head of Academic Computing*)
D S Barnes (*Director of Digital Strategy*)

Design and Technology:
*C D Humphreys, BA (*Freeman of the City of London*)
D A Vincent, CAPET, MEd
R H Lowndes, BSc, MEng
Mrs R L Lowndes, BSc

Drama:
A D Martens, BA
Ms K A Francis, BA
M Burlington, BA
*Miss N M Jones, MA (*Director of the Stahl Theatre*)

Economics:
A P Ireson, MA (*Examinations Officer*)
J Röhrborn, MA
Mrs F L Quiddington, BEcon, MT
*M Tanweer, MA
Mrs J A Barnes, MSc, MA

Educational Support:
Mrs C M Redding, BA, MA
Mrs I Chamen, MA
Mrs G T Nacef, BA
Mrs C M Nolan, BA
*Mrs A M J Taylor, MA

English:
Ms M K Smedley, BA
N J T Wood, MA
Mrs J T Coles, BA (*Director of Professional Development*)
A D Martens, BA

T P Hipperson, MA (*Director of Co-Curricular Activities*)
B Raudnitz, MA (*Child Protection Officer*)
A J Sherwin, MA
Mrs H M Wells, BA
*Mrs H K Hopper, BA
R S Harry, BA
Miss A Gillham, BA

Geography:
J R Wake, CertEd
Mrs M S Turner, BA
J R Hammond-Chambers, BA
*Mrs J L L Banerjee, BSc, MEd
A C Mansergh, MA
Mrs M T Chapman, MEd
P G Pitcher, BSc

Government and Politics:
*M J G King, LLB
Mrs J A Barnes, MSc, MA

History:
C R Pendrill, MA
P J Pedley, BA
I D Clark, BA
*M P H von Habsburg-Lothringen, MA, PLD
A J Brighton, BA
P J Kemp, BA
Mrs T E Harris, BA
M R Parry, BA, MPhil, PhD
J M Allard, BA

Library:
Mrs L Guirlando, BA, MSc, MCLIP
Mrs K Stidston, BA

Mathematics:
A P Ireson, MA, DipFM (*Examinations Officer*)
D A Turner, BSc
R Atkins, BSc
N D Turnbull, BA
D B Meisner, BA, MSc, PhD (*Assistant Director of Studies*)
D P Raftery, BSc
*S G Dale, MEng, MA
Mrs N S Guise, BSc (*Head of Laxton*)
Mrs J A Allsop, BSc
A G D Furnival, BA
M A Blessett, MA
M M Sanderson, BSc
S D Coates, BSc
Miss E C Matthews, BSc
R G Montgomery, MSc
Miss A M Strachan, BSc

Modern Languages:
Dr N M Mola, BA
B Béjoint, L-ès-L
J Röhrborn, MA
Mlle G M Skinner, L-ès-FLE, L-ès-LCE
Mlle S Fonteneau, L-ès-L
T D Watson, MA (*Head of Italian*)
*Mrs S J Davidson (*Head of Modern Languages*)
Mrs L M Brighton, MEd (*Head of Girls' Games*)
S Jessop, BA (*Head of French*)
H Yan, BA (*Head of Chinese*)
Miss C A L Thompson, BA
R F Charters, MA
Miss A J Drake, BA (*Head of Russian*)
Miss K Paone, LDML
Miss B K Gannon, MA
W D Gunson, MPhil
Miss S Naga, DUEL (*Head of Arabic*)
Miss M Viruete Navarro, MA (*Head of Spanish*)
Miss E J Wagstaffe, MEd (*Head of German*)

Music:
Director of Music: Q P Thomas, BA
Organist: J C Arkell, MA, FRCO, FTCL, FLCM, FRSA
Head of Woodwind: D P Milsted, BA, LTCL
Head of Brass: Mrs A S Hudson, GRNCM, PPRNCM
Head of Keyboard: A Hone, BMus, ARCM, ARCO
Head of Strings: A P Gibbon, GRNCM
Academic Music: Mrs S L Ratchford, BA
Choirmaster: A C Eadon, BA

and 44 peripatetic teachers

Physical Education and Games:
*C J Olver, WLIHE
Mrs M L Smith, MA, CertEd
Miss R S Goatly, BA
G Terrett, BA (*Head of Boys' Games*)
G P A Maitre, BSc, MSc (*Head of Rowing*)
Mrs L M Brighton, MEd (*Head of Girls' Games*)

Physics:
*M N Wells, MA
A B Burrows, MA Ed, BSc (*Undermaster*)
Mrs L E Kirk, BSc
Mrs T E Raftery, BSc
M J Meatyard, BSc
H Roberts, BSc
D J Talbot, MPhys
B A Letts, BSc
Miss C A Rees, MSc

Psychology:
S R Heath, BA, MSc
*R Banerjee, BSc

Religious Studies:
Mrs V Gascoine, BEd
Mrs A E Meisner, BA
*B T Deane, BA
Revd B J Cunningham, MA
Mrs C A Deane, BA
Miss H A Dawes, BA

Yale Fellows:
Miss C H Ormseth, BA
Miss M E Sanford, BSc

Introduction. Oundle School originated from the bequest of Sir William Laxton, a native of Oundle, to the Grocers' Company in 1556 and became fully co-educational in September 1990. Its buildings, dating from the 17th to the 21st centuries, are dispersed throughout the attractive market town of Oundle, giving the School a distinctive and unique charm. Oundle is the third largest independent boarding and day school in England, with boarders coming from 120 feeder schools all over the UK.

Number of pupils (2014–2015). 850 boarders and 250 day pupils.

Admission. Main entry is at 11+, 13+ and 16+ with a small number of places available at other stages, including boarding places at 12+. Most pupils sit the June Common Entrance Examination or the Oundle Scholarship Examination at thirteen before joining in September. Those joining the School at eleven sit a written examination in January before entry in September, with papers in English, Mathematics, Science and Ability tests.

Facilities. Academic departments are situated in the Cloisters, the Needham building, the Adamson Centre building, the Gascoigne building, Old Dryden and SciTec, Oundle's ambitious and spectacular science building, with its extensive 'green' credentials. The teaching areas are very well equipped; the Information Technology Centre includes two fully-equipped computer rooms and there are 'cluster networks' around the School. Thin Client terminals are located for each boarder in the Houses. Electronic whiteboards and computer-driven projectors feature in most teaching rooms. The Adamson Centre for Modern Languages opened in September 2013, equipped with two state-of-the-art language laboratories, six language assistant pods, fourteen teaching rooms and an International Suite.

Art, Music, Drama and Design Technology are all very strong and are well provided for. The Art Studios are large, airy and well equipped and the department includes the Yarrow Gallery. Facilities in Music include the Frobenius Organ and an electronic Music Studio. The Drama Department is centred on the Rudolph Stahl Theatre, a cleverly converted chapel in the middle of the town, where numerous productions of both the School and visiting companies take place. The long tradition of the Oundle Workshops continues, incorporating courses and projects in Engineering and Industrial Technology with pupils building cars, off-road buggies and boats in the exceptionally spacious Patrick Centre.

The Chapel was built as a memorial shortly after the Great War and its East windows, designed by John Piper, were installed in 1956. Thirty-two stained glass windows by Mark Angus, added in 2005, compliment Piper's original vision. Religious instruction accords with the Church of England, but other faiths are welcomed.

The Sports Centre complex includes two sports halls, a forty-three metre long swimming pool, five squash courts, a large and extensively equipped fitness suite, Physical Education classrooms and four fives courts.

Oundle has fifteen houses: eight boys' boarding houses, five girls' houses, a junior boarding house and a day house. A continuous cycle of renovation and refurbishment is in operation; the most recent work has involved extensions to School and Grafton Houses. Each house has its own distinct community, with in-house dining a hallmark of the School's character.

Academic Curriculum. Third Formers (Year 9) take a general course consisting of English, Mathematics, French, Latin, Physics, Chemistry, Biology, History, Geography, Religious Studies, Art, Design and Technology, PE, Music, Drama, ICT, and German or Spanish or Chinese or Greek. A unique 'Trivium' course introduces pupils to ideas, culture and pursuit of knowledge outside a prescribed syllabus. The First and Second Form curriculum is similar.

The traditional importance of Science and Technology is still maintained, with all pupils being taught the three Sciences to IGCSE level (both Triple Award and Dual Award on offer) and all Third Formers spending time in both the Art and the Design and Technology Departments. Computing and Microelectronics are available at all levels.

Pupils take English, Mathematics and the three Sciences as the core of their GCSE/iGCSE curriculum and choose a further five subjects from Art, Chinese, Computing, Design Technology, Drama, Electronics, French, Geography, German, Greek, History, Latin, Music, Religious Studies, Spanish, Arabic, Italian and Sports Science. Almost every pupil studies at least one modern foreign language (seven are timetabled), many study two or more.

In the Sixth Form A Levels are offered in Art, Biology, Chemistry, Classical Civilisation, Computing Design and Technology, Economics, Electronics, French, Geography, Greek, Latin, Mathematics, Further Mathematics, Music, Physics, Psychology, Religious Studies, Spanish, Sports Science and Theatre Studies. The majority of these are assessed as A Levels, though Chemistry, Chinese, Economics, English Literature, German, History, History of Art, Italian and Physics can be assessed by the linear Cambridge International Examinations Pre-U qualification, with some of these subjects offering a choice between Pre-U and A Level. Pupils have the option of taking one of their four subjects to AS Level only. Studies in the Sixth Form are enhanced by pupils opting for one or two of a range of non-examined extension courses, which include Arabic, Beginners Italian, Russian, Free thinking, Further History, Modern European Literature, Music Performance, Music

Technology, Origins of Western Thought, Performance Perspectives and Theology and Philosophy through Film and Text. The most popular extension course is the AQA Extended Project Qualification, taken by almost half of the Lower Sixth. In the Upper Sixth they take a General Studies course which is based around invited speakers.

Honours. 99% of Upper Sixth Former pupils go on to higher education at good universities; in 2014 fourteen of the School's pupils secured places at Oxford and Cambridge.

Sport. The main school sports are Rugby, Hockey, Cricket, Rowing, Netball and Tennis, but others available include Aerobics, Athletics, Badminton, Clay Shooting, Cross-Country, Cycling, Fencing, Fives, Golf, Horse Riding, Sailing, Shooting, Soccer, Squash, Swimming and Volleyball. There are currently two Astroturf hockey pitches, which are also used for tennis in the summer, and more pitches are planned to be built to maintain the School's excellent standard of sporting facilities. A new cricket pavilion is due to open in the spring of 2015.

Activities. A full range of activities take place which are an integral part of the wider school curriculum. Events in Drama and Music feature prominently in the School calendar, and Art Exhibitions are held regularly in the Yarrow Gallery. A large number of Societies meet on a regular basis. Links have been established with schools in France, Germany, Spain, Hungary, the Czech Republic, Russia, China, America and Australia, with annual Exchanges taking place. Pupils are able to participate in the very large number of expeditions and trips in the UK and abroad. There is a flourishing CCF comprising Army, Navy, RAF, Fire and Adventure Training sections and a thriving Duke of Edinburgh's Award scheme is in operation. Community Action plays an important part in school life and contributes significantly to the wider community. Much time and energy are devoted to fundraising activities in support of national charities, international aid programmes and holidays run at Oundle for MENCAP and inner-city children.

Entrance Scholarships. An extensive series of entrance scholarships is offered each year.

Scholarships at 13+:

Fifteen Academic scholarships at 10% of fees. A qualifying examination takes place in January, with final papers in May.

Twelve General (All-Rounder) scholarships at 10% of fees. Assessment in March.

Ten Music scholarships at up to 30% of fees, including One Junior Organ Scholarship. Audition and interview in January.

One Drama scholarship at 10% of fees. Audition and interview in March.

Two Art scholarships at 10% of fees. Assessment and interview in May.

Two Technology scholarships at 10% of fees. Examination and interview in May.

Five Sports scholarships at 10% of fees. Assessment and interview in November.

Scholarships at 11+:

Four Junior Academic scholarships for entry to The Berrystead or Laxton at 10% of fees. Examination in January.

Two Junior Music scholarships at up to 20% of fees. Audition and interview in January.

Scholarships at 16+:

Two Academic scholarships at 10% of fees. Examination in November.

One Music scholarship at 10% of fees. Audition and interview in November.

One Art scholarship at 10% of fees. Examination and interview in November.

One Technology scholarship at 10% of fees. Examination and interview in November.

Three Sport awards at 10% of fees. Examination and interview in November.

Further details of all awards may be obtained from the Registrar (Tel: 01832 277125, email: admisssions@oundleschool.org.uk) or the Undermaster's Assistant (Tel: 01832 277116, email: hev@oundleschool.org.uk).

Bursaries. Financial help towards the payment of fees in cases of proven need is available in some instances. This assistance is available in the form of bursaries which vary in size according to circumstance; some may be as high as 100%. Bursaries are not dependent on scholastic merit but are awarded to pupils who are likely to gain most from an Oundle education and who will contribute fully to the life of the School. The pupils in question must satisfy the School's academic entry requirements and continue to work to capacity as they progress through the School. Parents who feel that they may need the support of a bursary are encouraged to discuss the matter with the School well in advance of the child's due date of entry. Decisions regarding bursary assistance are made approximately two years ahead of entry. Judgements are dependent on a supporting reference from a candidate's previous school, an informal interview and on scrutiny of the family's financial circumstances.

Further details may be obtained as above.

Fees per term (2014–2015). Boarders: Berrystead Year 1 £8,155; Berrystead Year 2 £9,460; Years 3–7 £10,720.

Day Pupils: Year 1 £5,225; Year 2 £6,065, Years 3–7 £6,875.

Details of extras are given in the School prospectus. The registration fee is £125.

Laxton Junior caters for 4 to 11 year old boys and girls. It moved to a new purpose-built facility in September 2002, increasing in size to have a two-form intake. (*For further details, see entry in IAPS section.*)

Charitable status. Oundle School is a Registered Charity, number 309921.

Pangbourne College

Pangbourne, Reading, Berkshire RG8 8LA
Tel: 0118 984 2101
Fax: 0118 984 1239
email: registrar@pangcoll.co.uk
website: www.pangbournecollege.com

Motto: '*Fortiter ac Fideliter*'

Pangbourne College was founded in 1917 by Sir Thomas Devitt of the Devitt & Moore Company to train boys for a career at sea. It is now a modern, friendly, boarding and day school for about 400 girls and boys aged 11 to 18, offering sound academic results, first-class sports coaching and an excellent pastoral structure prioritising the happiness and well being of the individual.

Governing Body:
Chairman: R Lane-Nott
Chairman Finance Committee: D O Herbert

Headmaster: T J C Garnier, BSc Bristol, PGCE

Deputy Head, Academic: W Williams

Deputy Head, Pastoral: C Bond
Deputy Head, Co-Curriculum: R Bancroft

Bursar: R Obbard

Location and Facilities. Set in fine grounds of 240 acres and a mile from Pangbourne village, neighbouring the town of Reading, the College combines a rural environment with easy access to London and Heathrow. The extensive school facilities include the Falkland Islands Memorial Chapel opened March 2000, two new girls' boarding houses, a new drama studio, ICT suite and new Music School equipped exclusively with Steinway pianos which opened in 2012.

The fully-equipped sports hall, Astroturf hockey pitch, spacious playing fields, and boathouses on the River Thames provide excellent sporting facilities. Boarding and day pupils are integrated across the seven fully-refurbished or new boarding houses. Senior pupils share study-bedrooms and have single rooms in the Sixth Form. Meals are taken in a central dining hall although the boarding houses contain kitchens for the making of snacks. Most academic staff live on the campus in College houses and there is an extremely strong community spirit.

Admission. Children normally enter the Junior House (Dunbar) at 11+ through an interview and the College entrance examination. They are joined by more boys and girls at age 13 through the Common Entrance or Scholarship Examinations. Sixth Form entry is based on interview, a satisfactory report from the previous school and good examination results. A Prospectus and Registration Form may be obtained from the Registrar who is always pleased to arrange visits to the College.

Scholarships and Bursaries. Scholarships and Awards of up to 20% of fees are mainly offered at 13, when entering Form III, and at 16, when entering the Sixth Form, but some are occasionally offered at the age of 11, when entering Form I.

Academic Scholarship papers for entry at 13+ are set and held at the College.

Music, Art, Drama and Sport Scholarships, All-rounder Awards, Sixth Form Scholarships and means-tested Bursaries are also available.

Music: Several Music Scholarships of up to the value of 20% of College fees are offered annually. All awards carry free tuition on two instruments.

Candidates should be approximately Grade V standard or above on their main instrument. A second instrument, or experience as a chorister is an advantage. String players will be given special consideration for an award even if the standard is below Grade V provided that sufficient potential is shown.

Candidates should be under fourteen on September 1 in the year of entry. The exact date of the Scholarship Examination, which is in early March, may be obtained on application. Music Scholarships are also available for entrance to the Junior School at the age of eleven.

Drama awards are available at 11+, 13+ and 16+. Candidates are invited to attend an audition in the Lent term with the Director of Drama.

Art scholarships of up to 20% of fees are available at 13+ and 16+. Candidates must present a folio of work completed over the previous two years and attend an interview in the Lent term. Successful candidates are likely to be those who have worked in a variety of media and can show depth of thought on individual pieces.

As an *Arkwright Engineering Scholarship* centre, Pangbourne may nominate outstanding students at 16+ for this prestigious award. The College also offers one Design Technology scholarship every year.

All-Rounder Awards are given to pupils of outstanding all-round talent, in academic work and a number of other areas of College life, such as sport, music and drama.

Candidates come to Pangbourne on the first Monday of the scholarship week in May and undertake a variety of academic and practical tasks relevant to their talents. Their current Headteacher's report carries considerable weight.

The College offers a small number of *Sports* Scholarships to candidates who are gifted in one or more sports. Candidates will be asked to demonstrate academic potential to achieve at least B grades at GCSE or C grade at A Level and sporting potential to be a significant member of our first teams in one or more major games, and the ability to compete at county or higher representative level.

Please contact the Registrar for more information (registrar@pangcoll.co.uk).

Junior House. The Junior House, Dunbar, offers excellent, purpose-built accommodation and common room areas for 11 and 12 year old pupils in the heart of the College. Fully integrated into the academic, cultural and social life, these pupils enjoy full use of all the Senior School's facilities and its specialist teaching. Pupils transfer automatically to the Senior School without further examination.

Academic Study. Pupils aged 11–16 years study the National Curriculum ideal of a broad and balanced education, although we do not enter pupils for the Standard Assessment Tests at 14, using instead our own assessment and reporting system. The majority follow a mainstream curriculum covering all the core and foundation subjects of the National Curriculum: English, Mathematics, the Sciences, Design Technology, French, German, History, Geography, Art, Drama, Music, Religious Studies, Physical Education, and ICT. A Learning Support Unit, staffed by specialist teachers, is available to help.

At Sixth Form level pupils follow the A Level programme with 23 subject options on offer. The College is proud of the quality of its academic and pastoral support system, and each child is guided by a Tutor, a Housemaster/Housemistress and the Director of Studies.

The College recruits across a broad spectrum of academic ability, and pupils are given considerable opportunity to discover and develop additional skills and talents through the extensive music, art, sport, drama and leadership programmes.

Careers. The Director of Sixth Form Studies and the Careers Adviser work closely with the individual's Tutor to ensure that wise, informed choices are made in the well-equipped Careers Room. The result is that, while some students will go on to Oxford or Cambridge, the majority proceed to degree courses at other fine universities, prior to taking up a wide variety of exciting careers.

Games. For a small school Pangbourne has an outstanding reputation for sport, particularly at National levels in several games. The College has won Henley Regatta four times making it one of the top rowing schools in the world. In the recent past it has dominated independent school judo, there is a strong tradition of successful rugby and the girls enjoy county championship success in hockey. Sports offered include athletics, basketball, cricket, cross-country, golf, hockey, judo, netball, riding, rounders, rowing, rugby, sailing, shooting, soccer, squash, swimming, tennis, orienteering and fencing.

Adventure Training. The College has always placed great emphasis on teamwork, leadership and the development of communication skills. There is a full programme of adventure training built into the curriculum from the First Form, with weekend and holiday expeditions. Every two years a major expedition abroad is organised. Boys and girls can join the CCF which has Army, Royal Navy and Royal Marine Sections. The College has won the prestigious Pringle Cup on many occasions. A comprehensive high and low Ropes Course is used for leadership training. Third Form pupils are entered for the bronze Duke of Edinburgh's Award.

Music and Drama. Pangbourne has a long tradition of excellence in Music and Drama. The new Music School has its own Recital Hall, adding further performance space to the existing Chapel and school Hall. The College is now a recognised Steinway School. The College Choirs, Choral Society, Orchestra, Swing Band and Marching Band perform regularly within and outside the College. Drama has an exciting and flourishing tradition and we have a fine theatre fully equipped with computerised lighting and sound systems. School productions run throughout the year at every level.

Activities. There is a full programme of activities on those afternoons when pupils are not involved in school sport.

Fees per term (2014–2015). At age 11 and 12: Boarders £7,188; Part Boarders £6,406; Day Pupils £5,104. At 13 and above: Boarders £10,172; Part Boarders £9,050; Day Pupils £7,193. These fees are inclusive of medical attendance, games and most textbooks.

Charitable status. Pangbourne College Limited is a Registered Charity, number 309096. The objective is to provide an excellent all-round education for boys and girls between the ages of 11 and 18.

The Perse Upper School

Hills Road, Cambridge CB2 8QF
Tel: 01223 403800
Fax: 01223 403810
email: office@perse.co.uk
website: www.perse.co.uk

The Perse School is Cambridge's oldest secondary school, founded in 1615 by Dr Stephen Perse, a Fellow of Gonville and Caius College. The school still maintains close links with both Gonville and Caius and with Cambridge University.

The Perse Upper School is a co-educational independent day school for pupils aged 11–18.

Governing Body:

Representing the University of Cambridge:
R J P Dennis, BSc, MA
Sir David Wright, GCMG, LVO, MA, LLD (*Chairman*)

Representing Gonville & Caius College:
Dr A M Bunyan, BA, PhD
Dr E M Harper, BA, MA Cantab, PhD

Representing Trinity College:
Dr M T J Webber, MA, DPhil, FRHistS, FSA

Co-opted:
J C Aston, OBE, MA, ACA
C J Dell
S Dorrian
K J Durham, MA
Dr C J Edmonds, BSc, PhD
I G Galbraith, MA
R G Gardiner, MA, FCA
S W Graves, BSc, MBA
Dr R C St H Mason
M P H Pooles, QC, LLB
D M Shave, MA, MBACP
B P Smith, MA, CPFA, FCIHT
C J Stenner, LLB (*Vice Chairman*)
Dr V J Warren, MA, MD, FFPH

Bursar & Clerk to the Governors: G A Ellison, MA

Head: E C Elliott

Deputy Head (Staff): D R Cross

Deputy Head (Pupils): E W Wiseman

Deputy Head (Curriculum): P D Baker

Assistant Head (Extra-curricular): S A Richardson

Ethos. A Perse education is an adventure, full of curiosity, discovery and challenge. Students come from a wide range of social and economic backgrounds thanks to the School's significant bursary programme, a commitment to keeping fee rises low, and the selection process, which puts academic ability and potential above all else. The result is an unpretentious school where children can confidently be themselves.

History. The Perse is Cambridge's oldest secondary school, founded in 1615 by Dr Stephen Perse, a fellow of Gonville and Caius College. Dr Perse left a considerable sum to establish a 'free grammar school' for talented boys from all backgrounds that would bring town and gown closer together. The School remains true to its historic roots, with close links to the University of Cambridge and a £1 million per annum means-tested bursary programme that supports more than 120 pupils.

Admission. There are approximately 1,088 students in the Upper, including 336 in the Sixth Form. The main entry points are Year 7, Year 9 and the Lower Sixth. For Years 7 and 9 candidates are examined in maths, English, verbal reasoning and undertake a short humanities video/questions exercise; Lower Sixth offers are conditional on GCSE results. All candidates are interviewed and references are sought from their current school.

Facilities. The Perse has invested more than £30 million in new facilities over the last decade. The Upper occupies an attractive 27 acre green field site with extensive playing fields and recreational areas. Yet at just over two miles from the centre of Cambridge, and adjacent to the University's biomedical campus, it benefits from easy access to world-class facilities. Pupils enjoy high specification science labs and classrooms; a purpose built sports centre; on-site sports fields and all weather surfaces; a music centre including a rehearsal hall; art studios and a gallery; a lecture theatre; and an outdoor pursuits centre, climbing wall and shooting range. There is a 20,000 volume library and high-speed wired and wireless systems to ensure ready access to online learning resources.

Academic excellence. Perse pupils learn in a purposeful and supportive environment where they are taught to think independently and to make sense of a diverse and complex world. The School achieves some of the best A Level and Pre-U results of any co-educational school in the country, regularly appearing in the top 20 schools nationally. In 2014 more than three quarters of A Level entries were graded at A or A*. Around 90% of students' GCSE and IGCSE results are A* or A. Students are encouraged to go beyond the curriculum to extend their learning and pit their wits against their peers elsewhere in the UK and overseas. They regularly excel in science and maths olympiads, economics and business challenges, drama and poetry contests, and essay and fiction writing competitions.

Rounded education. There is a buzz about daily life at The Perse. Each year there are more than 60 clubs and societies on offer. In 2013 the School was awarded the Pro Corda Special Award for Schools for outstanding contribution to chamber music making; there are more than 70 coached or directed ensembles and a typical year will see around 50–60 separate performance opportunities. The School has a fully-equipped theatre and stages productions in external venues; there are at least eight productions each year and the Perse Players drama group performs at the Edinburgh Fringe. The main sports are cricket, hockey, netball, rugby, tennis, athletics and rounders. There is an extensive fixtures list; the School fields more than 130 teams in 14 different sports and regularly enjoys regional and national success. More than 350 pupils are involved in the Perse Exploration Society, learning outdoor skills as well as life skills such as team working and resilience. Other popular outdoor pursuits include adventure racing, shooting, the Combined Cadet Force and the Duke of Edinburgh's Award programme.

Supportive community. The Upper is a happy school where pupils feel safe, secure and supported. The School works hard to strike the right balance of work and play, comfort and challenge, instruction and discovery, rules and common sense, and guidance and independence. The eight Houses provide opportunities to make friends across the School and participate in activities. Each student has a pastoral tutor who monitors their progress and ensures their well-being, and there are peer listeners, form prefects and a system of heads of year, heads of section, senior tutors and a school counsellor. The learning support department works with children diagnosed with mild specific learning needs or uneven skills profiles. The Perse has a very active programme of charitable fundraising, and pupils have the chance to become involved in the wider community, from sharing their expertise with maintained sector primary schools or teaching the older generation digital skills, to working in deprived areas overseas.

Global perspective. The Perse has strong international links including foreign language and cultural exchanges, a partnership with Christel House (a charity that educates some of the world's poorest children) and membership of the SAGE global alliance of leading schools. Pupils regularly travel overseas and increasingly collaborate remotely through the latest technology.

Moving on. The School has a seven-strong team of dedicated specialist advisers headed by the Director of Qualifications and Progression. The team provides intensive advice and guidance on all aspects of applications, including personal statements, practice interviews and preparation for additional university entrance tests such as STEP and BMAT. In 2013 students received 564 offers; 30 students were accepted at Oxbridge and 11 at medical schools. In the last two years seven students have received offers from elite overseas universities.

Fees per term (2014–2015). £4,970.

Bursaries and scholarships. Means-tested bursaries are available for families of limited means, ranging from 5% to 100% of annual tuition fees. At Year 7 and Year 9 the School offers a small number of academic and music scholarships to pupils of exceptional merit. Sixth formers are able to apply for a maximum of two scholarships from: academic, art, drama, general, music and art. Scholarships are not means tested but are limited in value, generally worth around 5% of the annual fees.

The Perse Prep is a co-educational preparatory school for pupils aged between 7 and 11. Tel: 01223 403920; email: prephm@perse.co.uk. (*See The Perse Prep School entry in IAPS section.*)

The Perse Pelican Nursery and Pre-Prep is for children aged 3 to 7. Tel: 01223 403940; email: pelicanschoolsec@perse.co.uk. (*See The Perse Pelican Nursery and Pre-Prep entry in IAPS section.*)

Alumni. Tel: 01223 403 836; email: development@perse.co.uk.

Charitable status. The Perse School is a charitable company limited by guarantee (company number 5977683, registered charity number 1120654) registered in England and Wales whose registered office is situated at The Perse School, Hills Road, Cambridge CB2 8QF.

Plymouth College

Ford Park, Plymouth, Devon PL4 6RN

Tel:	01752 505100 (School Office)
	01752 505104 (Headmaster)
	01752 505107 (Bursar)
	01752 505115 (Registrar)
Fax:	01752 203246
email:	mail@plymouthcollege.com
	slambie@plymouthcollege.com
website:	www.plymouthcollege.com
Twitter:	@plymouthcolleg1
Facebook:	/PlymouthCollege

The School was formed by the amalgamation in 1896 of Mannamead School, Plymouth, founded in 1854, and Plymouth College, founded in 1877. It is now a co-educational school. In 2004 the school merged with St Dunstan's Abbey to form one school, Plymouth College.

Governing Body:
Chairman: C J Robinson, MA
Vice Chairman: D R Woodgate, BSc, MBA
Dr P Atkinson
T J Burke
D Chapman, BA Dunelm, FCollO, FRSA
S Elford
Mrs C Evans
Miss V Harman
Mrs R Hattersley, BA
Professor D A Huntley, BA, MA, PhD
Professor M Kirkup, BA, MSc, PhD
Dr L Lloyd, PhD
P H Lowson, FCA
Mrs C Magill, BSc Econ
Mrs A Mills, ACIS, MCIPD
Dr S Peach, PhD
I Penrose
Professor P Shears, BA, LLB, LLM
Mrs L P Stevenson, BVetMed, MRCVS
C P Thomson, BSc, FCA

Bursar and Clerk to the Governors: D W J Baylis, OBE, MA, MSc, MCIM (*Senior & Preparatory School*)

Headmaster: Dr S J Wormleighton, BEd Southampton, PhD Exeter

Deputy Head: Miss S J Dunn, BSc Exeter

Director of Studies: D Rhodes, BSc London

Assistant Staff:
K C Boots, BA Wales, MEd Exeter, AMBDA
J P Gregory, BA Birmingham (*Head of Economics & Business Studies*)
R Chapman, BEd College of St Mark & St John
Dr S Jordan, PhD Dundee (*Head of Biology*)
C J Hambly, BSc Manchester (*Head of Chemistry*)
Mrs Z P Thurston, BSc Exeter
Miss A C Blunden, BA Exeter
Mrs L E S Clark, BA Open
M P Tippetts, BA Exeter (*Head of Boarding*)
Mrs H J Owen, BA College of St Mark & St John
Miss E D Tremaine, BEd De Montfort (*Head of PE*)
J Shields, BSc Hull (*Director of Personalised Learning & IB Coordinator*)
R J Prichard, MA London (*Head of English*)
A N Longden, BSc Plymouth
Mrs P M Brockbank, CertEd (*Head of EAL*)
R G Palmer, BA College of St Mark & St John (*Head of Design Technology*)
Dr A Hawker, BSc Plymouth, PhD
Dr A Miller, BSc, PhD Bristol, CChem, MRSC, CPhys, MInstP (*Head of ICT*)
Miss E Williams, BA Greenwich
Mrs E Wright, BA University College London
P J Grey, BSc Open, AMInstP (*Head of Physics*)
R L Edwards, BA Wales (*Director of Rugby*)
D A Jones, BSc Birmingham (*Head of Mathematics*)
D J Whiteley, BSc Imperial College
P J Randall, BA Oxford Brookes (*Head of French & Spanish*)
Miss S Kerr, BEng Brunel
D J Roberts, MA Northumbria, BA Leeds
Mrs V J Willden, BA Plymouth
Miss L M Odendaal, BA Stellenbosch
A R Carr, MA St Andrews (*Head of German*)
D J Martin, BA Warwick (*Head of Religious Studies*)
Miss L M Russo, MSci Imperial College
Dr A Norris, BSc Liverpool, PhD
Mrs A-L Chubb, BA Wolverhampton

D Green, BA Dartington College of Arts (*Head of Music & Performing Arts*)

Miss S Currie, BA Stirling

R P Wilson, BEng University College London

Miss A E Starling, BA Exeter (*Head of Geography*)

E J Beavington, BSc Wales, MA Birkbeck College London (*Head of Sixth Form & Head of History*)

Dr C Taylor, BSc Bath, PhD Bath

Miss M Labrousse, Maîtrise d'Anglais Université de Bretagne Occidentale

A G Summons, BSc MSc Exeter

P M Mutlow, BA Durham

Mrs L E Smith, BSc Exeter

Miss C P Sherratt, BSc Plymouth

Miss N E Turvey, BA Aberystwyth

Dr J L Burns, BSc Oxford Brookes, DPhil Oxford

D P Prideaux, BSc Bristol

Mrs R L Connor, BA Nottingham

Mrs F J Murphy, MA Edinburgh

Miss N S L Husband, BA Queen Margaret

Mrs A Savage, BSc Exeter (*Head of Psychology*)

G J Llewellyn-Rees, BEng Brunel, MEng Heriot-Watt, MBA Imperial College

D R Hawken, BA University of Wales

M P Wesley, BSc Nottingham Trent

Miss N K Baker, BA Exeter, MA Exeter

Mr M Byrne, BSc Loughborough (*Head of Cricket*)

Part-time Staff:

Miss P J Anderson, MA Emmanuel College Cambridge (*Head of Classics*)

S J A Terry, BA Magdalene College Cambridge

Mrs T K Shields, MSc Leeds

Mrs J Ashenbury, BEd Reading

Miss F Venon, Licence d'Anglais Université de St Étienne, Maîtrise

C G Nicol, Diploma Duncan of Jordanstone College of Art (*Head of Art*)

Miss A Green, BA Exeter

Mrs P M Martin, BA Southampton

Ms J Herod, BA Nottingham, MSc East London (*Head of SEN, Educational Psychologist*)

Mrs S Sullivan BA Glasgow School of Art

School Nurse: Mrs J Brookshaw, RGN

Headmaster's Secretary: Mrs S L Lambie

Examinations Officer: Mrs R Harvey

Registrar: Mrs E Aubrey-Fletcher

Preparatory School:

Plymouth College Preparatory School
St Dunstan's Abbey
The Millfields
Plymouth PL1 3JL

Headmaster: C D M Gatherer, BA

Numbers. Currently there are 515 pupils in the school (180 in the Sixth Form) and of these 212 are girls.

Buildings. The Senior School stands on high ground in Plymouth. The buildings include Science Laboratories, Art and Craft rooms including extensive facilities for pottery, photography and print-making, the Dining Hall, an Assembly Hall in which concerts and plays are performed. A well-equipped Design and Technology Block was opened in 1979. The grounds in Ford Park include a rifle range and an indoor, heated swimming pool. Playing fields at Ford Park are supplemented by two other fields close by. The Sports Hall was opened in 1986 and a new library was opened in 1996. An astro surface was built in 1999 and upgraded in 2012 and the school has use of a full-size astro for Hockey. In 2004 a new hospitality suite and Music School opened. In 2005 a dedicated Sixth Form Centre was opened. In 2011 two new boarding houses were established. There is also an outdoor education centre located on Dartmoor.

The Preparatory School at The Millfields is approximately half a mile from the Senior School and has its own playing field and sports hall.

Organisation. Below the Sixth Form there is some setting so that pupils may proceed at a pace best suited to their abilities. Pupils are organised in 4 Houses. Each pupil is under the supervision of a Tutor and Head of Year who report to the Senior Tutor and ultimately the Deputy Head. In Years 7–10 Form Prefects are appointed. There is a Chaplaincy team which also has a pastoral responsibility for all pupils. Every pupil is expected to play a full part in games and other school activities outside the classroom.

English (Language and Literature), French, Mathematics, Physics, Chemistry and Biology are taken by all to GCSE. Normally three more are chosen by the pupils.

Sixth Form. The Sixth Form is based on tutor groups with about twelve in each group. Pupils study usually four AS Levels leading to 3 or 4 A Levels and most prepare for General Studies as well. The tutor keeps a pastoral and academic watch on the pupils' performance. Most standard A Levels are available. The International Baccalaureate Diploma is also offered as an alternative to traditional A Levels. In 2012 the Sports Baccalaureate was also introduced.

Sixth Formers are prepared for Universities both in the UK and overseas, the Services and the Professions; help is given by the Careers Teacher for almost any career.

Games. Rugby, Cricket, Hockey, Netball and Swimming are the major sports. There is also Athletics, Badminton, Basketball, Cross-country Running, Sailing, Shooting, Squash and Tennis. Games are compulsory but more senior pupils have a wide range of options available to them.

School Activities. Pupils take part in a very good range of activities. There is a contingent of the CCF with Navy, Army and Air Force Sections. There is also The Duke of Edinburgh's Award Scheme and Adventure Training as well as Ten Tors. Pupils in Year 10 participate in a JSLA scheme with local primary schools. A number of overseas expeditions are also organised each year. School Societies cover a range of activities from Archery to Young Enterprise. A School Yearbook is published annually.

Music & Performing Arts. There is an excellent school choir that sings at all major school events, concerts, and church services throughout the school year. The school orchestra, like the choir, provides music at school events and concerts. Both the choir and the orchestra receive invitations to support large-scale events in and around Plymouth. In addition to these groups the school has various small ensembles that are run by the visiting specialist instrumental teachers. The school has a thriving house drama and music competition that attracts whole school support. As well as the formal/organized music making there are innumerable student-led bands that help to ensure that the music department is a vibrant environment. Tuition is provided on all orchestral instruments, including percussion. Voice, piano, organ and all types of guitar lessons are also available. Speech and drama lessons (LAMDA) are offered to all students. The music and drama departments work together on large-scale productions. The drama department offers drama clubs to all year groups. The lower school clubs focus on all aspects of stage technique and improvisation while the upper school groups tie their work in with current productions. A sound and lighting club runs which trains students in all aspects of the technical side of theatre. Both departments work with a number of visiting performers/practitioners throughout the year; these are usually focused on specific year groups or examination groups.

There are annual music and drama scholarships and instrumental exhibitions.

Boarders. In the Senior School there are 7 Boarding Houses. Six of these are situated at Ford Park: one for boys, one for girls (45 in each) and four smaller Sixth Form houses. They are situated close to the school field and are equipped with small dormitories, sickroom, common rooms and games rooms. Meals are taken in the Dining Hall, supplied by a modern, well-equipped kitchen. The seventh house, based at The Millfields site, is a dedicated boarding house for the elite swimmers.

Admission. Admission to the Senior School is normally based on the College Entrance Examination for boys and girls over 10½ and under 12 on 31 August of the year of entry, but it is also possible to enter at 13 via the Common Entrance Examination or a Year 9 Scholarship/Entrance test. Occasional vacancies are available at other ages. Application forms may be obtained from the Registrar.

Admission to the Preparatory School is from the age of 3+. Application should be made direct to the Secretary to the Headmaster of the Preparatory School.

Scholarships and Bursaries. For pupils entering at 11 there are 2 Major Scholarships (50% of fees pa) and 3 Ordinary Scholarships (one-third of the fees pa). Two of these awards are restricted to pupils coming from Plymouth College Preparatory School. There are also smaller awards for Art, Music, Performing Arts, Drama and Sport and on occasion All-Round awards are given. Awards are made on the basis of the Entrance Examination.

At 13+ there is one Major and one Ordinary Scholarship and these are awarded on a Scholarship Examination.

For those entering the Sixth Form two further awards are made based on interview and GCSE results.

There are 8 Scholarships and Awards for Art, Music, Drama and Sport. Four of these are awarded at 13 and four to Sixth Form entrants. The value of these awards is up to one-third of the fees.

Bursaries of up to half fees are available.

Further information from the Registrar.

Fees per term (2014–2015). Preparatory School: Infant Department: Kindergarten £2,360, Reception £2,470, Years 1 & 2 £2,860. Junior Department: Years 3–4 £3,050, Years 5–6 £3,200.

Senior School: Day: Years 7–8 £4,170, Years 9–11 £4,660, Sixth Form £4,920. Boarding: Years 7–8 £8,285, Years 9–11 £9,020, Sixth Form £9,420. Weekly and occasional boarding are also available.

These fees include books, stationery and games. Music lessons and lunches are extra.

Forces and sibling discounts are available.

Charitable status. Plymouth College is a Registered Charity, number 1105544. Its aim is to provide private education for boys and girls.

Pocklington School

West Green, Pocklington, York, East Riding of Yorkshire YO42 2NJ

Tel: 01759 321200
Fax: 01759 306366
email: enquiry@pocklingtonschool.com
website: www.pocklingtonschool.com
Twitter: @PockSchool

Inspired for Life

2014 is the 500th anniversary of the foundation of Pocklington School in 1514.

Our ultimate aim is to give our pupils the support and freedom they need to flourish into balanced, fully-rounded and confident adults who are inspired for life.

Pocklington School is a supportive and caring community that has been thriving in the heart of rural Yorkshire for almost 500 years.

Rooted in the values of truth, trust and courage our approach to learning and development is shaped around the spiritual and physical well-being of each child we educate.

We believe that unlocking individual potential means fostering a culture that encourages successful learning and creative thinking while rewarding initiative and independence.

It also means creating an environment in which pursuing personal passions outside lesson time complements the achievements of academic success.

Governors:
C M Oughtred, MA, DL (*Chairman*)
T A Stephenson, MA, FCA (*Vice-Chairman*)
Mrs J Atkinson
Mrs E Bryers
J L Burley, BSc, MRICS
D G Buttery, BA, DL
Father C G Everitt, OSB, MA, DPhil
J A Farmer, FCA
The Rt Hon The Earl of Halifax, JP, DL
Canon J Harrison, MA
Revd G Hollingsworth, MA
Mrs N Jennings
Rt Hon Sir Greg Knight, MP
Mr K B Morrow, BA, NPQH
Professor R C Nolan, MA
Ms D A Nott, BA, MA, Dip SocAdmin
Mrs S M Oughtred, BSc
Cllr G Perry, CEng, MIMechE, FIHEEM
The Reverend L Slow, BSc
Mr G C Stuart, MP
Mrs F C Sweeting, BSc, MSc, MIPD, AKC
Dr A J Warren, MA, DPhil Oxon, FRHS

Life Patrons:
Mrs J S Carver, DL
The Rt Hon D M Davis, MP
B Fenwick-Smith, MA
R E Haynes, MA
J L Mackinlay, DL, FCA, FCMA
D V Southwell
Major General H G Woods, CB, MVO, MBE, MC, DL, MA, DLitt Hon, FRSA, FBIM

Clerk to the Governors & Bursar: P S Bennett, BSc, FLS

Management Group:

Headmaster: M E Ronan, MA Cantab

Deputy Headmaster, Head of Boarding, Deputy Designated Safeguarding Lead: A M Dawes, BSc
Assistant Head (Academic): Miss C L Bracken, MSc
Bursar: P S Bennett, BSc, FLS
Head of Academic Administration: P J Donaldson, BA
Senior Master, Head of Chemistry: M R Evans, BSc
Head of Lower School, Head of History: G J Hughes, MA
Director of Co-Curriculum, Director of Music: M Kettlewell, BA, ACTL
Head of Sixth Form: Dr S McNamee, PhD, BSc
Director of Curriculum: Miss L J Powell, MA
Head of Middle School, Designated Safeguarding Lead: Mrs C M W Swann, BA

* *Head of Department*

English and Drama:	Mrs G F Hudson, BA
English:	Mr S Ryan (*Technical*
*I Hashim, BA	*Manager*)
Mrs A J Bond, BEd	Mrs C White (*i/c*
Mrs A K V Hallam, BA	*Wardrobe*)
Miss L A Lamb, BA	
Miss L J Powell, MA	Mathematics:
Miss A L Sargeant, BA	*J F Cullen, BSc
	Mrs V J Bell, BSc
Drama:	Miss C L Bracken, MSc
*A W J Heaven, BHum,	Mrs L Deadman, BEd
MA, CFPS SpLD	Miss L J Gray
Mrs E J Cunningham, BA	T M Loten, BA

Miss M Thompson, BSc
Mrs H V Towner, BSc

Modern Languages:
*D A Galloway, MA
Mrs C Baines, BA
Miss L E Clarke, BA
P M H L Dare, BA, MA,
  RSA Dip TEFL
Mrs C J Davies, BA
Mrs J E Haldane, BA
S C Nesom, BA
Mrs M R Peel, BA
Mrs N C Scott-Somers, BA

Science:
Biology:
*M J Butcher, BSc
Miss S J Cheadle, BSc
Mrs S A Chiverton, BSc
Dr K J Clow, PhD, BSc
A M Dawes, BSc
Mrs S Davies, BA
  (*Technician*)
Mrs C Miles Findlay
  (*Technician*)

Chemistry:
*M R Evans, BSc
Dr D B Dyson, BSc, PhD,
  GRSC (*Boarding &
  Pastoral Coordinator*)
P R Horne, BEd
Mrs S J Pratt, BSc
Mrs J R McDowell, BSc

Physics:
*G Binks, BSc
D W Hutchings, BSc,
  MInstP
S D Ward, BSc

Psychology:
*Dr S McNamee, BSc, PhD
Mrs R Anderton, BSc,
  MCIEA
Mrs L L Hutchinson, BSc

Classics:
*Mr M J Adams, MPhil,
  BA
I J Andrews, BA

Art:
*D A Cimmermann, BA
Miss G M Boiangiu, BA
Mrs S M Green
Mrs O Morris, BA
Mrs C M W Swann, BA
Mrs C Castle (*Technician*)

Cookery:
Mrs A-M Salmon, BSc

Design:
*S D Ellis, BA
Miss J Chalkley, BA
Mr P Dawson (*Technician*)

Careers & University Advice:
Dr R Farrar, PhD, BSc, PG Dip CG

Child Protection:
Mrs C M W Swann, BA (*Designated Safeguarding Lead*)

English as an Additional Language:
Mrs W J Wright, MA (*Overseas Student Coordinator*)
Mrs S R Cockerill, MA
Mrs A J Chenery, BA

ICT:
*Mrs H T Alexander, BA
S Spruyt, BA
Mrs M S Wilson, BA, MSc

Music:
*M Kettlewell, BA, ATCL
Mrs H J Kneeshaw, MMus
T E W Taylor, MA
Mrs D E Blood, GMus, PG
  Dip
Mr M A Currey, BA,
  ATCL
J Diver, BSc LRSM
D J Hardy
Mrs Harrison-Ledger
Mrs K E Hart, GRNCM,
  ARMCM
K Holbrough, GLCM
Miss C M Jowett, BA
P Judge, MA, PGTC
Mrs J Ledger, MA, PGTC
Mr D Manning
I C Sharp, BMus, GRSM,
  ARMCM
M G Smith, BA
M E Stier, LRAM, Dip
  LCM
Mr C Thornton-Holmes,
  GRNCM

*Economics and Business
  Studies and Politics*:
*N A J Tomaszewski, BA
P J Donaldson, BA
D Watton, BA

History:
*G J Hughes, MA
C Braidwood-Smith, BA
A W Hall, BA
E G Long, MA

Geography:
*Miss V J Ellis, BSc
R P Bond, BEd
Mrs A L G Cosby, BSc

Games, Sport and PE:
*D Byas (*Director of
  Sport*)
A E Towner, BA (*PE*)
Mrs J E Danby, CertEd
S A Houltham, BPhEd,
  BTchg
G M Kilsby, BSc
Mrs J S Kilsby
Miss C E O'Brien, BSc
Miss A R Brant, BSc
Miss L Cairns, BA
Mr C J Mitchell, BA Hons

Religious Studies:
*M J Davies, BA
Revd J Roberts, BA
Miss H M Young, BA

Mrs E Rutherford, BA, MA, TEFL, CELTA, TESOL

Learning Support:
Miss H Young, MA, PG Cert SpLD Dyslexia, AMBDA
Mrs R Anderton, BSc, MA

Library:
Mrs A J Edwards, BA
Mrs N Ward

Chaplain: The Revd J Roberts, BA

Boarding Houses:
Fenwick-Smith: P M H L Dare, BA, MA, RSA Dip TEFL
Dolman: Mrs W J Wright, MA
Faircote: Mrs J E Midwinter
Orchard: Mrs L Scrowston

Day Houses:
Dolman:
I J Andrews, BA (*Lower School*)
S D Ward, BSc (*Middle School*)
M Adams, MPhil BA (*Sixth Form*)
Gruggen:
Mrs C J Davies, BA (*Lower School*)
Miss S A Metcalfe, BSc (*Middle School*)
Mrs H S Biggin, BA (*Sixth Form*)
Hutton:
Miss S J Cheadle, BSc (*Lower School*)
Mr T M Loten, BA (*Middle School*)
D W Hutchings, BSc, MInstP (*Sixth Form*)
Wilberforce:
Mrs M S Wilson, BA, MSc (*Lower School*)
G Binks, BSc (*Middle School*)
R P Bond, BEd (*Sixth Form*)

Support Staff:
Bursar's Secretary: Mrs C Haselock
Deputy Bursar: Mrs J L Knott
Premises Manager: M G Partis
Domestic Bursar: A D'Arcy, MIH, CertEd
OP Liaison Officer: Mrs R J Dare, BA, MBA
Marketing Officer: Mrs M Stefanini, BA, DipM, ACIM
Personnel Services Manager: Mrs S Readhead, PG Dip,
  DSBM, AlnstAM, Chartered MCIPD
PA to Headmaster: Mrs A C Ward
Admissions Secretary: Mrs F A Lambert

Prep School:
Headmaster: I D Wright, BSc Hons, PGCE, NPQH

Deputy Head: R W Stewart, BEd
Head of Pre Prep and Designated Safeguarding Lead: Mrs
  S A Cobb, BSc
Director of Activities: J R Parker, BA
Director of Teaching and Learning: Mrs V Peart, BA

Teaching Staff:

Mrs Afford	P Haldane, BA Hons
P Allen, MA	Mrs C L Hall, BA
Mrs J Bousfield, BA	Mrs A Hughes, BA
Miss E Carless, BA	Mrs J Kay, BEd
Mrs L Cooke, BSc	J Ott, BA
Mrs C J Dance, BA	Mrs Sweeting
Mrs K J Foster, BA	P Taylor, BAS, BEd
Mrs S M Green	D G Tyrrell, BEd

Learning Support: Mrs S E Lyon, Cert Ed SpLD
  (*Dyslexia*), AMBDA

Classroom Assistants:
Mrs C V Adamson
Miss M D'Arcy

Support Staff:
Matron: Miss W Gilmour
After School Care: Mrs J M Dicker (*Prep*)
School Secretary: Miss N A S Milsom
Office Assistant: Mrs G Briggs

Number of Pupils (2014–15). There are 610 pupils (329 boys, 281 girls) at Pocklington School (ages 11–18) and 186 pupils (101 boys and 85 girls) at Pocklington Prep School (ages 4–11). These numbers include 90 boarders aged 8–18.

Pocklington Prep School is on the same site as the Senior School. (*For further details, see entry in IAPS section.*)

Curriculum. Pocklington's curriculum has been developed to motivate and stretch pupils. Following foundations at Pocklington Prep School and in the Lower School at Pocklington, there are wide-ranging options in Year 9 and GCSE. Sixth Form AS and A2 subjects offer a diverse selection of subjects and combinations. There is excellent careers and university advice. Music, drama and art thrive, as do sport, outdoor education, community service, the CCF and other extra-curricular activities. The main sports are athletics, badminton, basketball, cricket, cross-country, football, hockey, netball, rounders, rugby, squash, swimming and tennis.

Location, Campus and Development. The school is set in extensive grounds on the edge of Pocklington, a market town 12 miles east of York. Emphasis is given to the importance of personal achievement in an attractive, high-quality learning environment with very good facilities.

Admission in Years 7–9 is subject to vacancy and to a satisfactory entry exam result and school report. Interviews may also be held. Year 9 applicants sit either a Senior School entry exam or Common Entrance. There is no entry test for Sixth Form applicants who are expected to have a minimum of 4 B grades and 2 C grades at GCSE. Subject to these entry criteria, the school seeks to admit candidates who will benefit from what it has to offer and whom it will be able to support. Children with mild learning difficulties can be supported, as can those who will in due course seek entry to the most demanding university courses.

Scholarships and Bursaries. Eight academic scholarships up to the value of 10% of the annual day fee and eight exhibitions up to the value of 5% of the annual day fee are offered to entrants to the First Year and Third Year. Two academic scholarships up to 10% of the annual day fee and two exhibitions up to the value of 5% of the annual day fee are offered to Sixth Form entrants. Means-tested Sixth Form bursaries providing up to 100% of annual day fees are also available.

Awards are available to internal and external candidates. Tenure of all awards is for the duration of the pupil's time at Pocklington School subject to satisfactory performance and behaviour.

Fees per term (2014–2015). Day £4,296, Boarding £8,099, 5-Day Boarding £7,450, Extended Day Pupil (1–5 nights per week) £167–£788.

Charitable status. The Pocklington School Foundation is a Registered Charity, number 529834.

The Portsmouth Grammar School

High Street, Portsmouth, Hants PO1 2LN
Tel: 023 9236 0036
Fax: 023 9236 4256
email: admissions@pgs.org.uk
website: www.pgs.org.uk

Motto: *Praemia Virtutis Honores*

The Portsmouth Grammar School is a happy and vibrant independent school located in the historic heart of Portsmouth and only a few minutes' walk from the Solent.

The support our pupils experience at PGS and the challenges they encounter have a shared purpose: that each individual should be happy and successful, in that order. In the spirit of our founder, Dr William Smith, we seek to provide excellence in all areas of school life and encourage our girls and boys to think not only about where they will be at 18 but where they aspire to be at 25. Portsmouth is, after all, a city concerned with destinations.

Governing Body:
Chairman: Mr B S Larkman, BSc, ACIB
Vice-Chairman: Mrs M Scott, BSc
Mrs K Bishop, BA
Mrs F Boulton, BSc, MA
The Very Revd D Brindley, BD, MTh, MPhil, AKC, Dean of Portsmouth
Mr W J B Cha, BA
Mr M R Coffin, BA Econ, FCA
Mrs R Duff
Dr M Grossel, BSc, PhD, MA
Mr N D Latham, CBE, MSc, CEng, FIMarEST, MIMechE
Mr P Lodder, QC, LLB
Mr P Parkinson, BA
Professor C B R Pelling, MA, DPhil
Mr M J Pipes, MA, MBA, FInstP
Mrs S Quail, BA
Mrs S Resouly, BSc, MRPharmS
Commodore Jeremy Rigby RN, MA
Mrs A Stanford

Governors Emeritus:
Mr D K Bawtree, CB, DL, BSc Eng, CEng, FIEE, FIMechE
Mrs J Cockroft, RGN, FPC, CertEd
Mr I A Carruthers
Mr C J L Evans, FCA
Mr B N Gauntlett, Dip Surv, FRICS
Air Chief Marshal Sir Richard Johns, GCB, KCVO, CBE, FRAeS, RAF
Mr F S K Privett, LLB
Mr D W Russell
Mr P F J Tobin, MA, FRSA

Clerk to the Governors and Bursar: Mr D J Kent

Headmaster: Mr J E Priory, MA

Second Master: Mr S W Lockyer, BSc
Deputy Head (*Academic*): Mr B C T Goad, BSc
Deputy Head (*Communications and Co-Curricular*): Mr B P H Charles, BA, FRSA
Assistant Head (*Head of Sixth Form*): Mr N D Gallop BA, MSc

Academic Staff:
§ *Part-time*
¹ *Senior Teacher*

Mr D P Ager, BSc, MSc (*Mathematics, Timetabler*)
§Mrs N S Alexander-Digby, BA (*Modern Languages*)
Mr L A Ansell, BSc, MA (*Head of Design and Technology*)
Mrs L C Ashdown, MSc (*Mathematics*)
Mr J D Baker, BSc (*Mathematics*)
Mr J P Baker, TD, BSc, MA Ed, FRGS, FGS (*Geography and Geology*)
Mrs M G Bates, BSc (*Biology*)
Mrs E E Bell, BA (*English*)
Ms A E Bolton, BA, MA (*Classics*) (*maternity cover*)
Miss L V Burden, BA, MA (*Head of English*)
Mr J E Burkinshaw, BA (*English, Head of Careers and Universities*)
Revd A K Burtt, BA, MA, LTh (*Philosophy and Religious Studies, School Chaplain*)
Miss F E A Bush, BA (*History, Head of Whitcombe House*)
Mrs A S Casillas-Cross, BA (*History, CAS Coordinator, Deputy Head of Smith House*)
Mr L S Chalk, BA (*Head of Computing*)
Miss H J Chipman, BA (*Economics and Business Studies*)
Mrs A M L Clarke, MA (*Classics*)
Mrs R H Clay, BA (*History*)
Mr T B Clayton-Shepherd, BA (*Head of Rugby*)

Mrs B Clifford, BA London, BA Wales (*Classics*)

Miss R L Close, BSc (*Economics and Business Studies, Head of Summers House*)

Miss C L Coward, BA (*Head of German*)

Miss E J Cox, MSc, CPhys, MInstP (*Physics*)

Miss K I Cox, BSc (*PE and Games, Coordinator of House Sport*)

Mr W J Crénel, LLCE (*Modern Languages*)

Mrs A Cross, BTh, MA (*Philosophy and Religious Studies, Deputy Head of Careers and Universities, Assistant Timetabler*)

Miss A A Cunningham, BSc (*Mathematics*)

Mr S J Curwood, BEd (*Head of Cricket, Deputy Head of Latter House*)

Mrs A J Day, BEd (*Head of Athletics*)

Mr S J Dean, BEd (*Mathematics, Deputy Head of Sixth Form*)

Mr S G Disley, BSc (*Physics*)

Mr C J Dossett, BSc, MSc (*Director of Sport*)

Mr D T Doyle, BA (*Modern Languages, Head of Latter House*)

Mrs M G Dray, BA, HDipEd (*Learning Support*)

Mr J Dunne, MA (*English*)

Mr M W Earley (*PE and Games*)

Mr J J Elphick-Smith, MA, PG Cert SpLD (*English, Classics, Head of Smith House*)

Mr T M Fairman, BA (*Mathematics*)

Miss S J Farmer, BA (*Head of Physical Education*)

Mrs S L Filho, BA, MA (*Director of Drama*)

Miss M C Flack, BA (*Design and Technology*)

Mr D J Frampton, BA (*History*) (*maternity cover*)

Dr P W Galliver, MA, MPhil, EdD (*History*)

Mr P M Gamble, BA (*Head of French*)

Dr J H Gilbert, PhD, MA, BSc (*Mathematics*)

Mrs C Giles, BSc (*Geography and Geology*)

Mr J R C Gillies, BSc (*Mathematics, Head of Grant House*)

Mrs J L Gladstone, MSc (*Biology, Bronze DofE Coordinator, Deputy Head of Yrs 9–11*)

Mr S J Gladstone, BA (*Director of Music*)

Mrs C A Gozalbez-Guerola, BA (*Modern Languages*)

Mrs R J Hammal, MA (*History and Politics*)

Mr O G A Hancock, BA, MMus, FRCO (*School Organist*)

Mrs H Harris, BSc (*Chemistry, Head of Eastwood House*)

Mr S J Harris, MA (*Chemistry, Surmaster, CCF Contingent Commander, DofE Coordinator*)

Miss B C Hart, MA (*English*)

Mr S D Hawkswell, BA (*PE and Games, Head of Barton House*)

Miss S Heath, BMus (*Head of Academic Music*)

Mr J K Herbert, BSc (*Physics, Yr 9 Activities Coordinator*)

Dr M R Howson, BSc, PhD, CChem, MRSC (*Head of Chemistry*)

Mr C L Ives, BA (*Modern Languages*)

Mrs J Jackson, BSc (*Mathematics, Head of Middle School*)

Mr A C Johnson, BA (*Music*)

Miss K Kingsley GRSM, LRAM (*Music*)

Mrs E M Kirby, MA (*English*)

Mr M J Kirby, BSc (*Design and Technology*)

Mrs P I Langtry, BA (*Modern Languages*)

Mr A D Leach, BSc (*PE and Games, Head of Hawkey House*)

Mr D D Lee, BSc (*Mathematics*)

Mr S Lemieux, MA (*Head of History and Politics*)

Miss H V Linnett, BSc (*PE and Games, Deputy Head of Sixth Form*)

Mr B P Lister, BA (*Head of Classics*)

Mrs F E Lyon, MChem (*Physics*)

Mr J-P G McCrohon, CertEd (*Director in Residence*)

Miss G Meadows, BEd (*Drama, English*)

Mrs J L K Morgan, BA (*Philosophy and Religious Studies, Head of Pastoral Curriculum*)

Mrs R L Nash, BSc (*Mathematics, Deputy Head of Yrs 9–11, Silver DofE Coordinator*)

Ms F J Nicholson, BSc, MPH (*Geography*)

Mrs L Nogueira-Pache, LicSc, MA (*Modern Languages*)

Mrs J M Okell, BSc, DipSpLD, AMBDA (*Head of Learning Support*)

Dr P A O'Neil, BSc, PhD (*Chemistry*)

Mr S Page, BA (*Modern Languages*)

Mrs S E Palmer, BA, Dip SpLD (*Learning Support*)

Mr R A Peebles, BA (*Head of Art*)

Mrs H E Prentice, BA (*PE and Games, Head of Girls' Tennis*)

Mrs S R Pye, BSc, MSc (*Psychology, Head of Aspirant Medics*)

Miss J J Read, BSc (*Mathematics, Head of Examinations*)

Mrs K C Rees, BSc (*Design and Technology*)

Mr L F Rees, BA (*Head of Economics and Business Studies*)

Mr M P Richardson, BA, MA (*English*)

Dr R J I Richmond, MA, PhD (*Head of Philosophy and Religious Studies*)

Miss L C Rickard, BA (*History and Politics, General Studies Coordinator*)

Mr J F Robinson, LLB (*Drama*)

Mr P J Robinson, BSc (*Head of Mathematics*)

Mr D F Rutherford, (*Head of Hockey*)

Mrs H E Sands, BSc (*Geography and Geology*)

Mr A J Seddon, BSc (*PE and Games*)

Ms L A M Smith, LLB (*Philosophy and Religious Studies*)

Dr M J Smith, MSc, DPhil (*Chemistry*)

Mrs S Smith, BSc, MA (*Mathematics*)

Mrs K Sparkes, BSc (*Biology, Deputy Head of Middle School*)

Ms A C Stephenson, BSc (*Biology*)

Dr P G Stephenson, PhD (*Head of Biology*)

Miss S L Stewart, BSc (*Head of Geography and Geology*)

Mr O G Stone, BA (*Head of Modern Languages*)

Mr S C Taylor, MA (*Classics, Director of IB*)

Dr N Thomas, PhD BSc (*Biology*)

Mr J P Thomas, MSc (*Head of Physics*)

Mr G T de Trafford, BA, MA (*Physics, Deputy Head of Whitcombe House*)

Mrs J L Tweddle, BSc (*Head of Netball*)

Mrs J M H Tyldesley, BSc (*Biology*)

Mr N G Waters, BA (*Modern Languages, Head of Yrs 9–11*)

Dr A D Webb, PhD, MChem (*Chemistry, Gold DofE Coordinator, Ten Tors Coordinator*)

Mrs W Whitaker, CertEd (*Design and Technology*)

Mrs D J Willcocks, BA, AKC (*Modern Languages*)

Mr S P H Willcocks, BA (*Art*)

Mrs L A Williams, BA (*Art*)

Mr C M Williamson, BA, MSc (*Chemistry, Deputy Head of Grant House*)

Ms A J Wood, BA (*Head of Psychology*)

Mrs M J Worley, BA, MSc (*Economics and Business Studies*)

Personal Assistant to Headmaster: Mrs J E Caldow, BA
Senior School Registrar: Mrs J Hunt

Junior School and Nursery:
Headmaster: Mr P S Hopkinson, BA, PGCE
Deputy Head: Mr J Ashcroft, BSc, PGCE
Assistant Head: Mrs P Giles, BA, PGCE (*Head of Years 5 & 6*)
Head of Nursery: Mrs L Johnson, BEd, PG Dip Ed (*Early Years*)

Academic Staff:
Mrs J M Albuery, BEd (*RS Leader*)
Mrs L Budd, BEd (*Food & Nutrition, KS2*)
Mrs J Budgen, BSc, PGCE (*E-Learning Leader; Year 3 Leader*)
Mrs S Carlin, BA, PGCE (*DT & Food & Nutrition Leader, KS1*)

Miss E Carter, BA QTS (*History & Geography Leader, KS1*)

Mr A Chappell, BA QTS (*Head of Boys' Games*)

Mrs J Crossley, Cert. Ed (*PE & Games*)

Mrs L Dean, BA, PGCE (*English Leader, KS2; Year 6 Leader*)

Mrs J Dossett, BA, Cert Ed (*Games*)

Mrs J Ellis, BEd, Cert Ed, Cert Ed Early Years (*Reception Leader*)

Mrs A Evans, BPE, MEd (*Director of Sport & Physical Education*)

Mr G Evans, BA, PGCE (*Acting Head of Lower Juniors; Director of Drama*)

Mrs R Evans, BA, QTS, (*Acting House Leader; Geography Leader, KS2; Upper Junior School Librarian*)

Mrs V Francis, BA, QTS

Miss A Gall, BA, PGCE (*ICT Leader, KS1*)

Mr O Griffin, BSc, PGCE (*PSHE Leader, KS2*)

Mrs J Hardy, BA, MA, PGCE (*Senior Teacher, Head of Infants; Mathematics Leader, KS1*)

Mrs J E Ingamells, ARCM (*Head of Strings*)

Miss D H Jennings, BA, MA, ALCM, LTCL, Mus Ed, Dip Class St Open, PGCE (*History Leader, KS2; Junior School Archivist*)

Mr M LeClercq (*Games*)

Mrs J L Millward, BEd (*Acting Head of Infants, English Leader, KS1*)

Mrs F Nash, BEd (*Assistant Director of Music; Year 4 Leader*)

Mrs K Park, BA, PGCE

Mr G D Payne, (*Games*)

Mrs J Pereira, BA, BSc, MA, PGCE

Mrs L Peskett, GGSM, PGDip, RNCM (*violin*)

Mrs A Porter, BEd, Cert SpLD (*SEN*)

Mrs S Powlesland, BA, PGCE (*French Leader, KS2*)

Mrs M Price, Cert Ed (*PSHE Leader, KS1*)

Mrs A Reader, BA, QTS (*Mathematics Leader, KS2*)

Mrs C S Sayers, BEd (*Senior Teacher, Head of Lower Juniors; House Leader*)

Mr E J P Sharkey, BA, PGCE (*Senior Teacher, Director of Studies*)

Mrs E G Sharrock, BMus Perf, LRAM (*'cello, String Scheme*)

Mr B W Sheldrick, BA (*Senior Teacher, Resources; ICT Leader, KS2*)

Mrs S J Sheldrick, BEd (*Assistant Director of Music*)

Mrs V Shoebridge, BA, PGCE

Mrs M Smith, BSc, Cert Ed (*Science Leader, KS2*)

Mrs P Spodzieja, MMus, PGDip

Mrs T Squire, BA, PGCE, SpLD (*SENCo*)

Mrs L Summerskill, BEd, (*Mathematics*)

Mrs B E Tilling, BSc, PGCE (*Art & Design Technology Leader, KS2; Display Leader, KS2*)

Mrs N R Townsend, BA, QTS Dance and Education (*Dance Leader, KS2; Charities Coordinator; Year 5 Leader*)

Mrs S P Tyacke, BEd (*Art Leader, KS1; Display Coordinator, KS1*)

Miss P Watkins, BA, QTS (*Acting Year 1 Leader, Mathematics Leader, KS1, Science Leader, KS1*)

Mr I Webber, BA/Ed (*Director of Music*)

Mrs L Younger, BSc, PGCE (*Design Technology & Science*)

PA to the Junior School Headmaster: Mrs A Stutter
Junior School Registrar: Mrs K G Bull, BA, PGCE

The Portsmouth Grammar School is a fully co-educational school which assumed full independent status in 1976. There are 1,142 pupils in the Senior School and 366 pupils in the Junior School. There are no boarders.

The Nursery School opened in 2001 and offers outstanding provision for boys and girls from 2½ years old. Currently there are 60 children in the Nursery.

The Junior School for boys and girls aged 4–11, is a thriving, dynamic and popular school, committed to giving pupils the best possible start to their educational lives. The main ages of entry are 4 and 7 however there are places available for intermediate entry. (*For further details see entry in IAPS section.*)

Although moving on to the Senior School is not automatic, most of the pupils do graduate to there when they are 11.

Senior School. Admission is by the School's Entrance Assessment at 11 and at 13. Entrants at 13 are usually pre-tested at 11 to accommodate high demand for places. Pupils are admitted at other ages, should vacancies occur, subject to assessments and satisfactory reports from previous schools. Admission to the Sixth Form, which numbers 312, is subject to satisfactory standard at GCSE and interview.

Curriculum. Pupils are educated for life as well as for academic achievements through initiatives such as The Portsmouth Curriculum in Year 7 and the wide-ranging General Studies Programme in the Sixth Form. After GCSE, pupils enter the Sixth Form, which seeks to prepare pupils for the challenges of university education and subsequent competitive employment. Pupils have the choice of either studying for the International Baccalaureate Diploma or A Levels. A Level subjects include: Art, Biology, Business Studies, Chemistry, Classical Civilisation, Design and Technology, Drama, Economics, Electronics, English Literature, French, Geography, German, Government and Politics, Greek, History, Italian, Latin, Mathematics, Further Mathematics, Music, Physical Education, Psychology, Religious Studies and Spanish. The General Studies Programme is mainly taught by outside professionals and is aimed at widening personal and academic horizons as well as offering some further academic opportunities, such as AS Critical Thinking. The Sixth Form prepares candidates for entry to Higher Education, and the Careers Department provides close relations with various forms of employment.

Religion. The Portsmouth Grammar is the Cathedral school. However, Religious Instruction, given in accordance with the principles of the Christian faith, remains, in accordance with a long tradition of latitudinarianism, non-denominational. The School has a Chaplain.

Pastoral Care. Pastoral Care is of paramount importance. On entry to the school pupils are allocated to one of four Houses. Heads of House and their House Tutors are responsible for the pastoral and academic welfare of all pupils, supported by Heads of Year, and provide a focal point for communication between teaching staff and parents. Particular emphasis is placed on the triangular relationship between pupil, parents and teaching staff, including a programme of telephone calls from tutors to new parents in which all senior staff and the Headmaster have a monitoring role.

Games. Rugby football, netball and hockey are the main games in Winter and Spring, cricket, tennis, athletics and rounders in the Summer. Cross-country running, squash, judo, badminton, gymnastics, basketball, aerobics, swimming and sailing are also available. The School has enjoyed national success in recent years in sports such as football, hockey, netball, athletics, cricket and rounders.

The Co-Curriculum. There are significant opportunities for co-curricular involvement at the school. Music, Sport, Drama, CCF and Outdoor Pursuits including Ten Tors and participation in the Duke of Edinburgh's Award Scheme, play a huge role in the development of our pupils and provide them with a diverse and popular range of activities. Service to the local community and charity work is also an important feature of the school's ethos. Many clubs and societies cater for a considerable range of co-curricular interests from the Model United Nations to Wildlife Club. Numerous expeditions, holiday activities and trips are actively encouraged and include many foreign tours for sports teams and music ensembles. The School has a flourishing exchange scheme with French, German and Spanish schools. Sports teams have recently gone on tour to Singapore, Malaysia and South Africa. Recent expeditions have seen pupils travel to Borneo, Uganda, Cambodia, Argentina and Cuba.

Fees per term (2014–15). Senior School: £4,567. Junior School: £2,930–£3,249. (Fees quoted include direct debit discount.)

Scholarships and Bursaries. Scholarships are chiefly available for entry at 11, 13 and Sixth Form.

A small number of Scholarships, each amounting to no more than 10% of full fees, are awarded to outstanding candidates in the 11+ Entrance Assessments. All candidates are automatically considered for Scholarships. No application is required.

Peter Ogden Scholarships, worth up to full fees, are offered at 11+ to outstanding candidates with parents of limited income from state primary schools. Additional assistance up to 100% of fees is available through the award of means-tested Foundation Bursaries.

Scholarships from the A D Nock Trust are offered to 13+ candidates and existing pupils.

Academic Scholarships and Bursaries are awarded for entry to the Sixth Form. Art Scholarships are also available at Sixth Form level.

A variable number of Music Scholarships are available at 13+ and 16+, depending upon the quality of applicants. A Sixth Form Choral Scholarship is available up to 50% of fees. Candidates are obliged to attend for tests, interview and audition on two musical instruments.

Full details of all scholarships and bursaries are available on the School's website.

Buildings. The School is located within the historic quarter of Portsmouth. The Grade II listed buildings of the Junior and Senior School sit comfortably next to modern developments such as the Bristow-Clavell Science Centre which opened in 2010, and the new Sixth Form Centre which opened in September 2014. The School sports facilities are located at the Hilsea Playing Fields and include an all-weather pitch and Sports Pavilion.

Honours. In 2014 eleven pupils took up places at Oxbridge, with 65% going to Russell Group universities, and a further 26% going to universities within the 1994 Group. The vast majority of Sixth Formers gained a place at their first-choice University. Sportsmen include England Cricket Captain Wally Hammond, Athletics International Roger Black, and Paralympian Ross Morrison. Military distinction in abundance, including 3 VCs (one the first VC submariner), several Admirals, Generals and Air Marshals. Medicine is also a continuing theme – from pioneer ophthalmologist James Ware to Viagra researcher Ian Osterloh. Arts are well and diversely represented: dramatist Simon Gray, poet Christopher Logue, novelist James Clavell, film director James Bobin, Sky News entertainment reporter Joe Michalczuk, cathedral organist Christopher Walsh, and pop singer Paul Jones. Civil Servants, Judges and barristers galore, plus entrepreneur industrialist Alan Bristow.

Old Portmuthian Club. This maintains links with former pupils not least by holding reunions in Portsmouth, London and Oxford, and is enhanced by its relationship with the School's Development Office.

Charitable status. The Portsmouth Grammar School is a Registered Charity, number 1063732. It exists to provide education for boys and girls.

Princethorpe College

Princethorpe, Rugby, Warwickshire CV23 9PX
Tel: 01926 634200
Fax: 01926 633365
email: post@princethorpe.co.uk

website: www.princethorpe.co.uk
Twitter: @PrincethorpeCol
Facebook: /princethorpecollege

The school, which has a Catholic foundation, was founded as a boys' school in 1957 in Leamington Spa by the congregation of the Missionaries of the Sacred Heart (MSC), moving to its present site, a former Benedictine monastery, in 1966. The College became co-educational in 1996, and in September 2001 formed a partnership with Crackley Hall School in Kenilworth in order to provide continuous education from 2 to 18 years. Both schools are members of an independent trust – The Princethorpe Foundation.

Chair of Trustees: Mrs Mary O'Farrell, BEd, QTS, CTC

Headmaster: **Ed Hester**, MA Oxon, PGCE (*Mathematics*)

Deputy Head – Pastoral: Mrs Sue Millest, BSc, PGCE, NPQH (*Biology*)

Deputy Head – Staffing and Assessment: Dr Digby Carrington-Howell, BSc, MA Ed, EdD, PGCE, NPQH (*Biology*)

Assistant Head – Co-curricular: Greg Hunter, BE, Grad Dip Ed (*Physics*)

Assistant Head – Director of Studies: John Gallagher, MA Oxon, PGCE (*English*)

Assistant Head – Marketing and Operations: ¶Alex Darkes, BEd (*Photography*)

Foundation Bursar, Company Secretary and Clerk to the Trustees: ¶Eddie Tolcher, BA, ACIB, MCMI

¶ *Old Princethorpian*
* *Head of Department/Subject*

Art:
¶*Paul Hubball, BA, PGCE (*also *Photography*)
Mrs Rebecca Blunsom-Washbrook, BA, GTP (*also Photography*)
Mrs Susan Harris, BA, PGCE (*Head of Year 7*)

Careers:
*Mrs Margaret Robinson (*also Head of Sixth Form; French and CORE Programme*)
Mrs Kerry Low (*Careers Adviser*)
Dr Simon Peaple, BA, PhD, CGTC (**History and Politics; also Competitive Universities Programme Coordinator*)
Mike Taylor, BA, PGCE (**Geography; Work Experience, also Games*)

Classics:
Mrs Rachel Taylor, BA, QTS (*Classics Subject Leader*)
Dr Melinda Palmer, BA, QTS

CORE Programme:
Mrs Anne Allen, BSc, PGCE (*Assistant Head of Sixth Form; also Geography*)
Roderick Isaacs, MA Cantab, MA, CertEd (*Assistant Head of Sixth Form; also Religious Studies*)
Mrs Helen Pascoe-Williams, BA, PGCE (*Coordinator of Provision for the Most Able; also English*)
Mrs Anila Patel, BA, PGCE (**Psychology and Sociology*)
Adam Rickart, BSc (*also Psychology*)
Mrs Margaret Robinson, BEd (*Head of Sixth Form; also *Careers and French*)
David Smith, LLB, C&GAA, C&GIVA (*ICT Services Manager; also Information & Communications Technology and Computing*)

Design and Technology:
*Paul Scopes, BEd, AST
Ms Angie Ash, BA, PGCE
¶Matt Parsons, BA (*also Games*)
Mrs Sarah Sellars, BA, QTS

Drama and Theatre Studies:
Ms Aileen Cefaliello, BA PGCE (*Joint *Drama and Theatre Studies; also English*)

Miss Vicky Roberts, BA, PGCE (*Joint *Drama and Theatre Studies*)

Visiting Drama Staff:
Ms Katherine Crawshaw, LAMDA
Mrs Mary McDonald, LAMDA

Economics and Business Studies:
*Kenny Owen, BSc (*also Head of Year 8 [Maternity Cover] and Games*)
Stewart Dear, BSc, QTS (*also Geography and Games*)
Peter Griffin, BA, PGCE

English:
*Chris Kerrigan, BA, MA, PGCE
Ms Michelle Baker, BA Oxon, PGCE (*Joint Second in Department*)
Mrs Lisa Challinor, BA, PGCE
Patrick Durkin, BA, MA, HDip in Ed (*also History; Joint Second in Department*)
John Gallagher, MA Oxon, PGCE (*Assistant Head – Director of Studies*)
David Hare, BEd, Clait (*Director of Ethos*)
Ms Emma Litterick, BA, PGCE, TESOL (*Staff Development Coordinator; also Foundation Cross Phase Coordinator*)
Mrs Helen Pascoe-Williams, BA, PGCE (*Coordinator of Provision for the Most Able; also CORE Programme*)

Geography:
*Mike Taylor, BA, PGCE (*also Careers – Work Experience and Games*)
Mrs Anne Allen, BSc, PGCE (*Assistant Head of Sixth Form; also CORE Programme*)
Stewart Dear, BSc, QTS (*also Business Studies and Games*)
Mrs Sarah Evans, BSc, PGCE (*Head of Year 9*)

History and Politics:
*Dr Simon Peaple, BA, PhD, CGTC (*also Competitive Universities Programme Coordinator*)
Peter Bucknall, BA, MA (*History; also Games*)
Mrs Felicity Coulson, GMus, PGCE (*Peripatetic and Exam Coordinator for Music; History*)
Ms Katherine Darwood, BSc (*also Games*)
Patrick Durkin, BA, MA, HDip Ed (*History; also English*)
Ms Stephanie Hawkins, BA, MA, PGCE (*History*)
Mrs Tracey Hester, BA Oxon, PGCE (*History*)

Information and Communications Technology (ICT) and Computing:
*Adam Depledge, BSc
David Smith, LLB, C&GAA, C&GIVA (*ICT Services Manager; also CORE Programme*)

Mathematics:
*Mrs Sarah McKeever, BEng, PG Cert, QTS
Mrs Karen Bannister, BSc, PGCE (*KS3 Mathematics Coordinator*)
Mrs Tanya Cowan, BSc, PGCE (*Maternity leave*)
Ed Hester, MA Oxon, PGCE (*Headmaster*)
Ms Helen Lewis, BA
Mrs Sharon McBride, BSc, PGCE (*KS5 Mathematics Coordinator*)
Chris Maltby, MEng, PGCE (*Maternity cover*)
Ms Davinya Munford, BSc, PGCE
William Uglow, BSc, MA, DipABRSM
Mrs Fenola Whittle, BEd

Modern Languages:
*Mrs Stella Keenan, MA, PGCE (*Spanish Subject Leader and French*)
Ms Katherine Boothroyd, BA, PGCE (*Spanish and French*)
Ms Marion Cognac, Licence LLCE Anglaise (*French Assistant*)
Mrs Finola Coy, BA, City and Guilds Teacher Cert (*German*)

Mrs Suzanne Ellis, BA, PGCE, Cert TESOL (*German Subject Leader; also Second in Department; French*)
Ms Daniella Garnica (*Spanish Assistant*)
Mrs Caroline Perry, BA, PGCE, DEUG (*French*)
Mrs Margaret Robinson, BEd (*Head of Sixth Form; also Head of Careers; French and CORE Programme*)
Mrs Sarah Stewart, BA, PGCE, Cert TESOL (*French*)
Mrs Brigitte Wood, Cert Ed (*French*)

Music:
*Gil Cowlishaw, BMus (*Director of Music*)
Mrs Alison Wakeley, BMus, MMus, PGCE

Visiting Music Staff:
Mrs Felicity Coulson, GMus PGCE (*Peripatetic and Exam Coordinator for Music; also History; Flute, Oboe, Clarinet and Saxophone*)
Tom Abela, BMus (*Classical Guitar*)
Tom Durham, BMus (*Guitar*)
¶Miss Jodie Fisher, ATCL (*Brass; also PE and Games*)
Andrew Hughes, ABSM (*Violin and Viola*)
Mrs Joanna Kunda-Jedynak, MA (*Vocal Studies*)
Adrian Moore, BA, ARCO (*Organ and Piano*)
Mrs Abigail Rhodes, MA Oxon, LLCM, FLCM, ADPA (*Vocal Studies*)
Mrs Clare Rothwell, BMus (*Flute*)
Mrs Susan Shepherd, MA, ARCM, ARCO, LRAM, CertEd (*Piano, Harpsichord and Keyboard*)
Mrs Penny Turnbull, BA, LTCL (*Vocal Studies*)
Alan Wickett (*Drum Kit and Percussion*)

Photography:
¶*Paul Hubball, BA, PGCE (*also *Art*)
Mrs Rebecca Blunsom-Washbrook, BA, GTP (*also Art*)
¶Alex Darkes, BEd (*Assistant Head – Marketing and Operations*)

Physical Education and Games:
Neil McCollin, BA, QTS (*Foundation Director of Sport; also Coordinator of Elite Sports Programme*)
Will Bower, BSc, PG Dip QTS (*Head of Outdoor Education*)
Mrs Deborah Brookes, BA, QTS (*Head of Girls' Games*)
Peter Bucknall, BA, MA (*also History*)
Ms Katherine Darwood, BSc (*also History*)
Stewart Dear, BSc, QTS (*also Geography and Business Studies*)
Colin Dexter, MAAT (*Hockey Coach*)
Philip Duckworth, BA, MA, PGCE (*also Physics*)
Marc Edwards, BSc (*Head of Hockey*)
Mrs Sarah Evans, BSc, PGCE (*Head of Year 9*)
¶Ms Jodie Fisher, ATCL (*Teaching Assistant; also Peripatetic Music – Brass*)
Jon Fitt, BSc, PGCE (*Head of Rugby*)
Stuart Friswell (*Rugby Coach*)
Mrs Louise Harrison, BSc, PGCE (*Head of Academic PE*) (*Maternity leave*)
Ms Sarah Higgins (*Dance Coach*)
Roderick Isaacs, MA Cantab, MA, CertEd (*Assistant Head of Sixth Form; also CORE Programme*)
Mrs Chris McCullough, BA, QTS (*Head of Year 11; also KS4 Coordinator*)
Kieran McCullough, BA, PGCE (*Head of Religious Studies*)
Ms Rachael Mack, BA (*Hockey Coach*)
Ms Danette Matthews (*Netball Coach*)
Miss Laura Miller, BA, PGCE (*House Coordinator; also Religious Studies*)
Kenny Owen, BSc (*Head of Year 8 [Maternity cover]; also * Economics and Business Studies*)
¶Matt Parsons, BA (*also Design and Technology*)
Simon Robertson, BSc, PGCE (*Head of Year 10; also Biology and Chemistry*)
Mike Taylor, BA, PGCE (*Head of Geography; also Careers – Work Experience*)

Cyprian Vella, BA, MA, PGCE (*Primary School Liaison Teacher; also Religious Studies*)
Paul Whitehead (*Hockey Coach*)

Psychology and Sociology:
*Ms Anila Patel, BA, PGCE (*also CORE Programme*)
Adam Rickart, BSc, PGCE (*Psychology; also CORE Programme*)
Ms Louise Vaughan, BSc, PGCE (*also Special Educational Needs*)
Mrs Clare White, BSc, PGCE (*Head of Year 8; also Biology*) (*Maternity leave*)

Religious Studies:
*Kieran McCullough, BA, PGCE (*also Games*)
Roderick Isaacs, MA Cantab, MA, CertEd (*Assistant Head of Sixth Form; also CORE Programme*)
Ian Lane, BA, PGCE
Miss Laura Miller, BA, PGCE (*House Coordinator; also Games*)
Cyprian Vella, BA, MA, PGCE (*Primary School Liaison Teacher; also Games*)

Special Educational Needs Department:
Ms Lorna Prestage, BSc, PGCE (*Special Educational Needs Coordinator*)
Ms Kat Brittain (*Learning Support Teaching Assistant*)
Mrs Meryl Lovatt, BA, MA Cantab, PGCE, TEFL
Mrs Lee O'Gorman (*Learning Support Teaching Assistant*)
Ms Louise Vaughan, BSc, PGCE (*also Psychology and Sociology*)

The Sciences:
*Mrs Gill Smith, BSc, PGCE (*Chemistry*)
Dr Digby Carrington-Howell, BSc, MA Ed, Ed D, PGCE, NPQH (*Deputy Head – Staffing and Assessment; Biology*)
Phil Duckworth, BA, MA, PGCE (*Physics, also Games*)
Dr Emma Godfrey, BA Cantab, MPhil Cantab, PGDip (*Chemistry*)
Greg Hunter, BE, Grad Dip Education (*Assistant Head – Co-curricular; Physics*)
Mrs Sarah Lane, BSc, PGCE (*Physics*)
Mrs Sue Millest, HNC, BSc, PGCE, NPQH (*Deputy Head – Pastoral; Biology*)
Dr Stuart Rimmington, M Chem, PhD, PGCE (*Chemistry*)
Miss Faye Roberts, BSc, MSc, PGCE (*Biology*)
Simon Robertson, BSc, PGCE (*Head of Year 10; Biology; Chemistry; also Games*)
Mrs Sophie Rose, BSc, PGCE (*Physics*)
Mrs Joanne Smith, MChem, PGCE (*Chemistry*)
Mrs Catherine Warne, BSc, PGCE (*Biology*)
Mrs Clare White, BSc, PGCE (*Head of Year 8; Biology; also Psychology and Sociology*) (*Maternity leave*)

Non Teaching Staff:
Ms Shirley Allen (*Secretary/Receptionist*)
Dr Nick Baker, BA, MA, PhD, PGDipHerInt, DipEurHum, FRSA, MAHI (*Archivist*)
Will Bayley, MEng, PhD (*Senior Science Technician*)
Mrs Mary Benham, BA, CertEd (*Chaplaincy Coordinator*)
Tom Biddle (*Grounds*)
Miss Liz Brown, MAAT (*Management Accountant*)
Mrs Adele Bull, MInstAM, AdvDip (*Deputy Bursar*)
Mrs Melanie Butler, BA (*Marketing Manager and OPs Secretary*)
Mrs Cynthia Carpenter (*Estates*)
Mrs Loretta Curtis (*Registrar*)
Mrs Helen Cutter (*Assistant Matron*)
Mrs Shellagh Dodds (*Examinations Officer*)
Mrs Claire Fletcher, BA (*Shop Manager*)
Dean George IT (*Intern*)
Lester Gibson (*Estates*)
Andy Hadley (*Estates*)
¶Toby Harper-Lawrence (*Teaching Assistant*)

Mrs Ruth Hedderwick, BA (*Marketing Assistant/Sports Administrator*)
Mrs Charlotte Hetherington, BEng (*Design and Technology Technician; also Textiles*)
Mrs Carmel Hopkins (*Headmaster's Personal Assistant and Office Manager*)
Mark Johnson Foundation (*Estates Manager*)
Ms Rhianydd Jones, BA (*Reprographics Assistant*)
¶Bof Kefalas, LLB (*Assistant Estates Manager*)
Mrs Ann Kettlewell, BA (*Sixth Form Administrator*)
Tom Knowles (*Estates*)
Mrs Maria Lawless, SEN (*Senior Matron*)
Ms Ruth Laband, MA, CPCAB (*Counsellor*)
Miss Barbara Lewandowski (*Finance Assistant*)
Gerry Lovely (*Estates*)
Mrs Kerry Low, BA (*Careers Adviser*)
Mrs Gina Malin (*Finance Assistant*)
Mrs Denise Morgan (*PA to Foundation Bursar*)
Miss Helen Morgan, BA (*Secretary/Receptionist*) (*Maternity leave*)
Mrs Angela Morris, CertEd (*Laboratory Technician*)
Mrs Karen O'Connor (*Library Assistant*)
Mrs Elena Pope (*Purchase Ledger Clerk*)
Mrs Gill Price, BSc (*Special Projects Officer and Parent Portal*)
¶John Price (*Teaching Assistant*)
Tom Probert (*Grounds*)
Clive Randle (*Grounds*)
Ed Robertson (*Foundation Grounds Manager*)
¶Alex Rooney (*Teaching Assistant*)
¶Rory Rooney (*Estates*)
Mrs Vanessa Rooney (*Secretary/Receptionist*) (*Maternity cover*)
Jonathan Sant (*ICT Technician*)
Mrs Julie Satchwell (*Student Support Officer*)
Mrs Celia Scott, BA, ALA (*Associate Librarian*)
Tom Secher (*Estates*)
David Smith, LLB, C&GAA, C&GIVA (*ICT Services Manager; also CORE Programme and Information & Communications Technology and Computing*)
¶Oscar Thornton (*Teaching Assistant*)
Dr Michael Tideswell, BSc, PhD, QTS (*Curriculum Coordinator*)
Mrs Heather Tocher, MBACP Dip (*Counsellor*)
Ms Lesley Topham (*Catering Manager*)
Robert Van Spelde (*ICT Manager*)
John Vasquez (*Estates Supervisor*)
Mrs Judy Vick (*Estates*)
Mrs Elaine Warwick (*Assistant to the Registrar*)
Fr Alan Whelan, MSC, BA (*Chaplaincy*)
Paul Whitehead (*Estates*)
Ms Claire Wong (*Laboratory Technician*)

Number in School. The school has about 850 day pupils from 11 to 18 years with 200 in the Sixth Form. An extensive network of private coaches transports pupils from a wide area.

Aims. The College provides a caring, Christian environment for children where their needs can be met and their talents, confidence and self-esteem developed. There is a healthy balance between freedom and structure and an emphasis on self-discipline through responsibility and trust, which develops confidence and independence.

The College draws on a rich tradition of Catholic teaching and the spirituality of the Missionaries of the Sacred Heart, whose ethos is central to its character and disciplinary system. In welcoming families of a variety of faiths, the school community is a living example of ecumenism. The College motto, *Christus Regnet* – let Christ reign – is a reminder of Christ's love, service, forgiveness and generosity of spirit.

Academic. A broad-based, stimulating curriculum satisfies a wide range of ability and fosters a love of learning. A favourable pupil-teacher ratio, permitting personal attention, contributes to impressive value-added achievements. High fliers are stretched and provided with intellectually challenging assignments through our da Vinci Programme, ensuring that they achieve at the highest possible levels. The curriculum is well supported by a magnificent library and ICT. Qualified specialists give tuition to dyslexic pupils.

Pupils in Years 7 to 9 have a broad-based curriculum which avoids early specialisation and usually go on to take nine or ten GCSEs.

Supervised homework and free extended day are offered until 6.00 pm.

The Sixth Form. A new £2.5m Sixth Form Centre opened at the end of 2007. Students in the Sixth Form are prepared for AS Level and A2 Level examinations after which the vast majority proceed to university. The Head of Sixth Form and the team of tutors monitor the academic progress of Sixth Formers through regular discussions with the students and their teachers. Visits to university Open Days, together with professional careers advice enables students to make the best choices about their next stage of education.

There is a strong emphasis on the acquisition of key skills and the education of the whole person. Sixth Formers are offered residential outward bound courses, training programmes and retreats which provide an opportunity for reflection and exploration, to develop a mature and balanced perspective. Guest lecturers, debates and theatre outings all enhance Sixth Form life.

All Sixth Formers enjoy privileges and have the responsibilities of leadership and example; certain members are elected to perform prefectorial duties. Prefects attend a leadership course and learn valuable management skills. They organise activities for younger pupils and chair the School Council, which offers a forum for lively discussion and gives the students an influential voice in the running of the College. Sixth Formers also act as Form Patrons, mentoring younger pupils and arranging outings for them. The House Captains have a pivotal role in the organisation of inter-house events.

Princethorpe Diploma. Open to all Sixth Form students the innovative Princethorpe Diploma brings together five components (work experience, community and ethos, service to others, extra-curricular and academic studies) that we believe are critical in today's world, helping our students leave us as mature, confident, resilient, well-rounded young people, with a strong set of moral values to guide them through adult life

Careers. The Careers Advice Programme commences in Year 9 and regular tutorials are held concentrating on option subject choices and developing careers awareness. Interview technique is developed and students are assisted with work experience placements which are undertaken at the end of Year 10 and Lower Sixth. The College also holds a biennial Careers Fair for pupils in Year 10 to Sixth Form and their parents.

Art & Design. A feature which immediately strikes all visitors to the College is the outstanding display of canvases. Superb examination results and successes in national competitions are commonplace. The study of drawing, painting, graphics and ceramics are central and they are enhanced by using the work of great artists as stimulus material.

Technology includes Food, Graphics, Resistant Materials, Information and Communications Technology, Textiles and Electronics. Pupils can work with a variety of materials, realising their technical designs in the well-resourced workshops, which include CAD/CAM facilities.

Music and Drama. Music is studied by all pupils in their first three years and as an option at GCSE and A Level. The College gives regular performances and tours extensively overseas. Many pupils learn instruments and are encouraged to join the orchestra. Peripatetic staff offer tui-

tion in most instruments. There is a state-of-the-art studio with digital recording facilities for Music Technology and there is an acclaimed Binns organ in the magnificent Chapel built by Peter Paul Pugin.

The College has a well-equipped theatre and regular productions are staged including pantomimes and revues. Productions involve a large number of pupils and staff and provide an excellent way for pupils of different years to get to know each other. There are thriving Dance and Drama Clubs. Theatre Studies is offered in the Sixth Form.

Physical Education. All pupils participate in games and Physical Education classes. Physical Education can also be studied as an examination subject at GCSE and A Level. The major sports are rugby, netball, hockey, cricket, rounders, tennis and athletics; they are run in tandem with badminton, soccer, squash, basketball and trampolining.

The Sports Centre has a sports hall, fitness gym and squash courts; a floodlit all-weather surface was laid in 2003. Extensive outdoor facilities include an internationally recognised cross-country course, tennis courts and over sixty acres of games pitches.

Extra-Curricular Activities. There is always a wide range of clubs, societies and activities such as art, board games, chemistry clinic, choir, computing, cookery, debating, drama, flight, history, jazz band, mathematics workshop, meditation, music workshop, orchestra, photography, Spanish, technology and textiles. The Duke of Edinburgh's Award Scheme, World Challenge, Camps International and Outward Bound courses are also offered. The Arts Society provides a cultural programme of lectures, poetry evenings, music recitals and play readings.

Admission. Admission is by examination, usually towards the end of January, generally at 11 and 13 and at other ages as space allows. Students from other schools join the Sixth Form after their GCSE courses.

Scholarships. There is a variety of Scholarships available for particularly able or talented candidates ranging from Academic, Art and Music to All-Rounder. Additionally for the Sixth Form there are Academic, Organ and Sports Scholarships available. Scholarships to a maximum reduction of 50% of tuition fees are on offer.

Academic Scholarships: Candidates applying for entry in Years 7, 8, 9 and 10 will be considered automatically for an academic scholarship when taking the Entrance Examination. Pupils to be considered for major Academic Scholarships of between 25% to 50% will be invited for interview by the Headmaster following the Entrance Examination.

All Rounder Scholarships: Sometimes there are students who are both academically able and gifted in a variety of areas and the most outstanding of these can be awarded an All Rounder Scholarship. Supportive evidence is required, such as references from team coaches or activity leaders.

Art Scholarships: Candidates must submit a portfolio and attend an Art Scholarship day, usually in early January. Further details and an Art Scholarship application form are available from the Registrar.

Music Scholarships – Instrumental and Choral: Candidates must attend an audition. The timing of auditions is usually staggered over a week in early January. Further details and a Music Scholarship application form are available from the Registrar.

Sixth Form Academic Scholarships: Sixth Form Academic Scholarships are open to all external candidates who are expected achieve A and A* grades at GCSE. The candidates will sit a Verbal Reasoning examination and will have an interview with the Headmaster. They will also be expected to submit a personal portfolio of achievements to support the application.

Sixth Form Sport Scholarships: Senior Sport Scholarships may be awarded to internal or external candidates entering the Sixth Form. Full details are available from the Registrar.

Sixth Form Organ Scholarship: A Sixth Form Organ Scholarship of up to 50% of tuition fees is available to candidates who have a high level of ability and are committed and enthusiastic performers. Full details are available from the Registrar.

Fees per term (2014–2015). £3,536 excluding transport and meals. Instrumental tuition, external examinations and some targeted support for those with learning needs are charged as extras.

Charitable status. The Princethorpe Foundation is a Registered Charity, number 1087124. It exists solely for the education of children.

Prior Park College

Ralph Allen Drive, Bath BA2 5AH
Tel: 01225 835353
email: info@thepriorfoundation.com
website: www.thepriorfoundation.com

Motto: '*Deo Duce, Deo Luce*'

Prior Park College is a fully co-educational Catholic Boarding and Day School. Founded in 1830 by Bishop Baines, it was under the control of the Bishops of Clifton until 1924, when it passed to the Congregation of Christian Brothers. Since 1981, Prior Park has been under lay management and has more than doubled in size. Prior Park is a friendly, thriving community of around 580 pupils, with a strong boarding community, excellent academic standards and a strong devotion to educating the whole person.

The College is housed in magnificent Palladian architecture, built by John Wood for Ralph Allen, with glorious views of the World Heritage City of Bath. The 57-acre site combines an elegant setting for boarding and day education with access to Bath and its numerous cultural attractions. Proximity to the M4 and M5 motorways places the College within easy reach of London, the Midlands, the South-West and Wales. Good rail links and proximity to Bristol, Heathrow and Gatwick international airports allow easy transfer for our international students.

Patrons:
His Eminence Cardinal C Murphy-O'Connor, STL, PhL
The Rt Revd D R Lang, BA, Bishop of Clifton
Miss J Bisgood, CBE
Mr C J B Davy, CB
Mr D R Hayes
Sister J Livesey, CJ, MA
Mr F J F Lyons, KSG
Sir Cameron Mackintosh
The Rt Hon the Lord Patten of Barnes, CH, PC
The Revd Monsignor Canon R J Twomey, VF

Governors:
Mr A M H King (*Chair of Governors*)
Mr A Bury, MBA, BSc Hons
Mr S Eliot, MA Cantab
Mrs N Freeman, BA Hons, MA, PGCE
Mrs A Lloyd, MA Ed, Cert Ed, LGSM
Mr D F Lyons, BA, CTA (*Fellow*)
Fr W M McLoughlin, PhL, BD, MTh, OSM
Mr P S J O'Donoghue, MA, FCA
Mrs N Pearson, BA Hons, PGCE
Rear Admiral N J Raby, OBE, MSc
Mrs M Rae, MSc PH, Dip Ed, FFPH, FRIPH
Ms A Shepherd, MBE, BA Hons
Mr J Shinkwin, MA Oxon, PGCE
Mr P Vaughan Fowler, BA Hons
Mr J Webster, BA, BArch, MCD, RIBA, MRTPI

Headmaster: Mr James Murphy-O'Connor, MA Oxon

Foundation Business Director: Mr A McNiff, LLB FCA

Deputy Bursar: Mrs J Barr
Deputy Headmaster: Mr D G Clarke, BSc Hons (*History*)
Academic Deputy Head: Mr T J Simons, BSc, BA Hons (*Mathematics*)
Director of Communications: Mrs J Kearney, BA, DipSp
Assistant Head Co-Curriculum: Mrs L Blake, BA Hons (*Geography*)
Assistant Head Student Development: Mrs S Forshaw, BSc Hons (*Chemistry*)

Assistant Staff:
Mr R Anderson, BMedSci (*Chemistry*)
Ms K Ashby, BSc Hons (*Physics*)
Mr M Blaikley, MA (*Mathematics*)
Ms L Blake, BA Hons (*Geography*)
Mrs K Bond, BA Hons (*Design & Technology*)
Mr M Bond, BSc Hons (*PE & Sport*)
Miss V Brandwood, MusB Hons (*Music*)
Mr S Burt, BSc Hons (*Head of Geography*)
Mrs C Byron, BSc Hons (*Mathematics; Housemistress, English House*)
Mr K Chard, BSc Hons (*Head of Chemistry*)
Mrs L Collinson, BSc Hons (*Head of History*)
Mrs A Colquhoun, MA (*Theology*)
Mrs W Cornish, BEd, AMBDA (*Head of Learning Development Programme*)
Ms H Cox, BA Hons Dip, RSA (*Learning Development Programme; Geography*)
Miss C Cummins, BA (*Theology; Head of Sixth Form Academic; Oxbridge Coordinator*)
Miss A Davidson, BSc Hons, MSc (*PE & Girls' Games; Learning Development Programme*)
Miss L Dawson, BA (*History*)
Mr D Devine, BSc Hons (*History; PE*)
Mrs J Devine, BA, MMus (*Music; Housemistress, St Mary's*)
Mr S Dorey, BSc (*Physics; OC CCF Royal Navy Section; Gold DofE*)
Ms C Duque Medina, BA, MA (*Language Assistant, Spanish*)
Mrs J C Eatwell, BSc (*Economics/Business Studies*)
Mrs J Farrant, MA (*Head of Modern Languages*)
Mr R Faulkner, BSC Hons (*Head of Design & Technology*)
Mr M Fisher, MA (*Classics*)
Mrs C Ford, BA Hons, Dip CG (*Head of Careers; Housemistress, Arundell*)
Mrs S Forshaw, BSc Hons (*Chemistry*)
Mrs R Fox, BA Hons, MPh (*Dance*)
Mr R Francis, BA Hons (*Mathematics*)
Mr M French, MSci, PhD (*Head of Physics*)
Mr J Fry, BA Hons (*Business Studies; PSHCE Coordinator*)
Mrs E Garside, BA Hons (*English*)
Mrs C Giles, BA Hons, MA (*English as an Additional Language*)
Mr R Gwilliam, BA Hons (*Director of Sport*)
Mrs H Goodman, BA Hons (*Theology*)
Mr A Haines, BA Hons (*ICT Manager; Music*)
Mr A Hall, BEd Hons (*Hockey*)
Miss F Haynes, BSc Hons (*Biolog; Head of Junior Science*)
Mrs S Hearn, MA (*Head of Classics*)
Mr P Hull (*Director of Rugby*)
Ms M Huntley, BA Hons (*English*)
Mrs J Jones, BSc Hons (*Head of Mathematics*)
Miss L Justine, BA (*Language Assistant, French*)
Mrs E Knetchli, MSc (*Science; Head of ICT*)
Mr M Knights (*Rugby Coach; Housemaster, St Paul's*)
Mrs S Lane, BSc Hons (*Head of Economics and Business Studies*)
Mr D Langley, BA Hons (*Director of Drama*)
Mr D Lee, BA Hons (*Philosophy*)
Mrs A Mallon, MA (*French; Housemistress, Fielding*)
Ms C Mapes, BA, MEd (*Classics*)

Mr T Maxwell, BA Hons (*Head of Theology*)
Miss V McConaghie, BA Hons (*Geography*)
Dr K McGowran, BA Hons, MA, PhD (*Head of English*)
Mrs M Mudie, BSc Hons (*Biology; ITT Coordinator*)
Mrs E Parker, BSc Hons (*Mathematics*)
Mrs K Parker, BA Hons (*Design & Technology*)
Mr J Penrose, BA Hons (*Spanish; French*)
Mrs C Pepler, BA Hons (*French*)
Mrs H Prynne, MA (*Classics*)
Mrs L Redman, BA Hons (*PE; Girls' Games; i/c Tennis*)
Dr C Roberts, BA Hons, PhD (*German*)
Mr R Robertson, MA, ARCO (*Director of Music*)
Mr D Sackett, BA Hons (*Music; Music Technology*)
Mrs C Saunders-Prouse, BA Hons (*English; Housemistress, Baines*)
Mr B Scott, BA Hons (*Art; Photography*)
Mr V Shannon, BSc Hons (*Physics; Housemaster, Burton*)
Dr G Smith, BSc Hons, PhD (*Chemistry; Housemaster, Clifford*)
Ms L Smith, BA Hons, MA (*Librarian*)
Mrs A Spelman, BA, BSc Hons (*English*)
Mr P Stroud, BA Hons (*Head of English as an Additional Language*)
Ms N Thomas, BA Hons (*Learning Development Programme*)
Mrs K Trott, BSc Hons (*Biology; Games*)
Dr R Trott, BSc Hons, PhD (*Head of Biology; O/C CCF Army Section*)
Mrs P Vowles, BA Hons (*Modern Languages*)
Miss E West, BA, MA (*Art; Design & Technology; Learning Development Programme*)
Miss C Williams, BSc Hons (*Head of Girls' Games; Sports Science*)
Mr D Wood, BA Hons (*Head of Art*)
Ms L Young, BSc Hons (*Mathematics; Head of Sixth Form Pastoral*)

Music Staff:
Mr P Badley, PPRNCM (*Voice*)
Miss A Carroll, MA (*Voice*)
Mr T Worley, MMus, BMus (*Piano*)
Mrs J Finch, ALCM, LTCL (*Oboe*)
Miss C Gainford, BMus, GRNCM (*Bassoon, Woodwind*)
Mr A Haines, BA (*Bass Guitar*)
Mr G Harrup, BA Hons, LGSM (*Acoustic/Electric Guitar*)
Mrs A Hickmore (*Voice*)
Mrs J Mason-Smith, BA, ABSM, ALCM (*Flute*)
Mr D Pagett, GRNCM, PG Dip RNCM (*Clarinet, Saxophone*)
Ms S Power, BEd (*Cello*)
Mr S Skews, LTCL (*Piano*)
Ms A Townley, AGSM (*Violin, Viola*)
Mr R Webb, BMus, PGCE (*Trumpet*)
Mrs I Windsor, LRSM, LTCL, BA Hons (*Piano*)
Mr P Woodburn (*Drums, Percussion*)
Mrs J Devine, BA, MA (*Junior Music, Lower Brass*)
Mrs C Paterson, BMus (*Music Secretary*)

Houses and Housemasters/mistresses:
Baines (*Junior House*): Charis Saunders-Prouse
Burton (*Senior day boys*): Vincent Shannon
Clifford (*Senior day boys*): Graham Smith
English (*Senior day girls*): Colette Byron
Fielding (*Senior day girls*): Anne Mallon
St Mary's (*Senior boarding girls*): Jo Devine
St Paul's (*Senior boarding boys*): Martin Knights

Foundation Executive Personal Assistant: Ms D Miller (dmiller@thepriorfoundation.com)
Registrar: Mrs V Quinn
Chaplain: Father Malcolm Smeaton, BSc
Director of Development: Ms M Ball
Medical Officer: Dr I Batterham, MB BS, MRCGP, DRCOG
Nursing Staff:

Mrs F Whittington, RGN (*Resident Medical Sister*)
Ms S Josiah, RGN (*Medical Sister*)

Structure of the School. Prior Park is a friendly, thriving community of approximately 580 pupils. The annual three-form entry of day pupils aged 11–13 makes up our co-educational Baines Junior House. A further forty enter the school at 13, when we admit both boarders and day pupils. Each boy and girl between 13 and 18 is a member of a boarding or day single-sex Senior House. Year groups also meet regularly for assemblies. Weekly and full boarding is available.

Objects of the College. The College provides an outstanding education, within the framework of a caring, Catholic community which warmly welcomes members of other denominations. Our A Level and GCSE results are consistently excellent, with our EPQ (Extended Project Qualification) results among the best in the country. Our resident Chaplain serves the needs of the whole community and great importance is attached to the commitment of all staff to the ethos of the school. Pastoral care is perceived by the current parent body to be outstanding and great efforts are made to ensure that all pupils are nurtured and supported. A Personal Development Programme aims to equip all our pupils with information and guidance specifically addressing contemporary moral issues and problems. The College makes great efforts to developing the full potential of all its pupils, according to their individual abilities. Through all aspects of College life, through community service, and through shared experiences in sport, music and drama, we engender self-respect and respect for others. We strive to equip our young people with vitally important communication skills, as well as other skills which will allow them to leave the College as confident young adults, ready to negotiate successfully the next stage of their lives.

Buildings and Grounds. The Houses, Administration and College Chapel are to be found in the fine 18th century architecture grouped around Ralph Allen's celebrated Palladian Mansion. A major programme of modernisation has enhanced the accommodation for residential staff and their families, and added to the attractive environment for the residential community. A major refurbishment programme of boys' and girls' boarding accommodation has provided comfortable study-bedrooms, quiet areas and recreational rooms. A rolling programme of refurbishment continues, including the opening of a new Art & Design Faculty in September 2014 and the building of a new Sports Centre due for completion in February 2015.

Academic teaching is provided in modern classrooms. Eight renovated Science laboratories and a well-equipped Design Technology Centre provide a stimulating environment for practical work. ICT provision includes an ICT Centre, several suites of computers in the library, Design Technology Department and the Houses. ICT provision is also made within departments. A Dance Studio and purpose-built Theatre are excellent venues for Performing Arts.

An elegant library, with over 11,000 volumes and a full-time librarian, enhances private research and independent learning.

Curriculum. The academic curriculum conforms to and goes beyond the requirements of the National Curriculum. Core subjects to GCSE are Mathematics, English, the Sciences, a Modern Language and Religious Studies. The curriculum in Year 7–9 is broad. Great care is taken to ensure that careful guidance is given to pupils in Year 9 and Year 11 when GCSE and AS/A2 choices are being made. The Academic Deputy, his assistant and the House staff work with pupils and their parents to tailor a programme which reflects the strength and interests of the individual. The majority of pupils will study ten to eleven GCSE subjects, four AS/A2 subjects in the Lower Sixth, and drop to three A2 in the Upper Sixth.

We currently offer twenty-three AS/A2 courses and there is considerable flexibility of combinations at both GCSE and A Level. The Extended Project Qualification (EPQ) is also offered in the Sixth Form. We are delighted to have added Psychology to the A Level curriculum due to popular demand.

Virtually all Sixth Form students proceed to study Degree courses at Universities, Medical Schools or other Higher Education Institutions, with the majority gaining places at their first-choice university.

A Sixth Form Enrichment programme of visiting lecturers, assistance with UCAS applications and Oxbridge preparation ensures a broad education at Sixth Form level. MEDSOC lectures are organised by the Biology Department to allow students who are considering a degree and a career in Medicine the opportunity to meet guest speakers who are specialists within their own chosen fields.

Music. The College has a highly-deserved reputation for musical excellence. Two chapel choirs provide high quality music for the weekly sung Mass in the glorious surroundings of the Chapel of Our Lady of the Snows. The John Wood Chapel, within Prior Park Mansion, offers a further concert and rehearsal venue for the many musicians in the school.

The Music Department, also in the Mansion, houses a recording studio and teaching and practice rooms. Around half the pupils learn a musical instrument and there are several thriving orchestras, chamber groups and bands, as well as a large and ambitious Choral Society, annual competitions and festivals. Many Prior Park musicians have gone on to Oxbridge and a graduate from the class of 2014 was awarded the Trinity Choral Scholarship to Cambridge. Other graduates go to major conservatoires and play in NYO, NCO, etc.

Performing Arts. The students stage around twenty drama productions a year, Dance, Inter-House Music Competitions, Band Nights and charity events all feature prominently in the life of the school. The Julian Slade Theatre is a wonderful setting for this extensive and diverse performing arts programme. It has been extended to provide a Dance Studio and further teaching and technical support areas. There is also a full-time theatre technician.

Physical Education and Games. Physical Education is included in the curriculum. Games are an important part of school life. Main school games are Rugby, Hockey, Cricket and Tennis for boys; with Hockey, Netball and Tennis for girls. Provision is made for Swimming, Badminton, Cross-Country, Football, Volleyball, Basketball, Table Tennis, Fencing, Athletics and Rounders.

Sports facilities include a Gymnasium and fitness centre. Construction of a new Sports Centre at the College began in 2014 and we are looking forward to the work being completed by the Spring Term 2015. An astroturf, a refurbished pavilion, netball and tennis courts, as well as extensive rugby, hockey and cricket pitches are all on site. An entirely renovated and extended swimming pool and changing room complex opened in 2005.

Activities Programme. The voluntary Combined Cadet Force includes Navy and Army Sections. Adventure training takes place both in the UK and overseas. Cadets are encouraged to participate in the Service and Contingent Camps and Courses.

The Duke of Edinburgh's Award Scheme operates at Bronze and Gold Award level. Participants work on the four sections: volunteering, skills, physical, and expeditions; plus a residential project section at Gold Award level.

Boarders and day pupils alike participate in a wide range of activities after school, including arts and crafts, sports, electronics, Radio Club, chess, golf, aerobics, Scrabble, cross-country running, model engineering, dance and a whole host of challenging events. Poetry and literary groups have won national awards. Public speaking and debating thrive. All full-time boarders in Years 9 to 12 take part in Saturday Active, which takes place on a Saturday morning. Courses include Leith Cookery, archery, pony-trekking, climbing, mountain-biking, swimming, tennis and textiles. Some courses are free and in others certificates can be awarded. Over 135 pupils and parents take part in Saturday Active each term, including many day pupils.

The College operates its own Community Service Programme involving extensive work in the local community, which includes a Soup Run to the city centre. Charity work is strongly encouraged, both in the form of fundraising and visits to homes, hospitals and schools. A biennial charity week raises thousands of pounds and Sixth Formers enjoy an annual pilgrimage to Lourdes.

Careers. Our careers guidance programme combines the traditional strength of the House system with the benefits of a specialised central careers department. Every pupil receives individual guidance through the five years from Form 4 (Year 9) to Upper Sixth, with particular support at the three critical stages of choice for GCSE, A Level, and university entrance. At the same time, professional careers advice is available from the Head of Careers, who provides objective information and guidance via a programme of interviews, supported by psychometric testing and on line guidance tools.

The Careers Education input begins as earlier as Years 7/8, as part of the school's PSHCE programme and continues through year 9 with decision making skills and options choices. In Years 10/11, the world of work is explored more fully through Business Dynamics Days and work experience. In the Sixth Form, a comprehensive programme exploring the full range of post 18 options is delivered together with mock interviews, the production of CVs and the transition skills needed for successful university applications. The pastoral and general studies programmes also support the College's aim of "creating an outward looking ethos… enabling our leavers to be confident, capable, compassionate and independent minded".

Our Careers Fair brings together over fifty different occupations and is attended by pupils and their parents from Year 9 upwards.

Admission. Main points of admission are at 11+, 13+ and 16+ but pupils may transfer into the College at 12 and 14 if places are available. Early registrations are encouraged. Prospective families are encouraged to visit the College on Open Days or on an individual visit.

Entrance and scholarship examinations for 11+ and 13+ take place in January and February prior to entry in September. 16+ scholarship examinations and interviews take place in November. Please contact the Registrar, admissions@ thepriorfoundation.com, for the relevant entrance/scholarship admission booklet.

Scholarships and Bursaries. Academic Scholarships are available at 11+, 13+ and 16+. Art, All-Rounder, Drama, Music and Sporting Excellence awards are available at 11+, 13+ and 16+. Dance awards are available at 13+ and 16+. All awards carry with them a fee remission.

Academic Scholarships at 11+ are awarded following results of the general entrance examination. No further scholarship examinations are set at 11+. Scholarships are awarded annually to external candidates for 13+ entry and the examination is held in January/February. Sixth Form Scholarships are held in November.

Music awards are available at three levels of entry: a Junior Exhibition or Scholarship (for entry at age 11), a Scholarship (for entry at age of 13), and Sixth Form Scholarships. Drama Exhibitions are available at 11+, and Drama Scholarships at 13+ and 16+. All awards are worth up to 50% of fee remission. Dance Scholarships are available at 13+ and 16+.

Art Scholarships are available to exceptionally able applicants at ages 13+ and 16+. An Art Exhibition (minor scholarship) is available to exceptionally able applicants at age 11+, who may then become eligible for the 13+ Scholarship when they reach the appropriate age.

Sporting Exhibitions are available at 11+. These can be converted to full scholarships at 13+ following further assessments in the major team sports. Sporting Excellence scholarships are available at 11+, 13+ and 16+ for suitable candidates who have already achieved national recognition in their sports, which may not be one of our major team sports.

Bursaries are available, including HM Forces Bursaries of up to 20% of fees. The Bursar is pleased to discuss individual cases. Sibling discounts apply.

Fees per term (2014–2015). Boarding: £9,210 (full), £7,595 (weekly); Day 13+ £4,975; Day 11+ £4,510.

Prior Park Preparatory School. The Preparatory School is situated at Cricklade, Wiltshire, 35 miles from Prior Park and within easy reach of Swindon train station, Cirencester and the M4. It has ample boarding and recreational facilities for 180 boys and girls aged 7–13+. In addition, the adjacent nursery and pre-prep offer a wonderful educational environment for day children up to the age of six. Extra-curricular activity is an important element and the school has excellent standards in Music, Drama and Sport.

Headmaster: Mr Mark Pearce, BA Hons, QTS
For further details, see entry in IAPS section.

The Paragon School, Bath – Junior School of Prior Park College. The Paragon School is now part of Prior Park Educational Trust. Housed in an impressive Georgian mansion, the co-educational school for 3–11 years is set in beautiful wooded grounds, only a few minutes drive from Prior Park College. A broad and balanced curriculum is delivered within a happy, caring environment.

Headmaster: Mr Andrew Harvey, BA Hons
For further details, see entry in IAPS section.

Charitable status. Prior Park Educational Trust is a Registered Charity, number 281242.

Queen Anne's School

6 Henley Road, Caversham, Berkshire RG4 6DX
Tel: 0118 918 7300
Fax: 0118 918 7310
email: office@qas.org.uk
website: www.qas.org.uk
Twitter: @QASCaversham
Facebook: /Queen-Annes-School-Caversham

Queen Anne's is an independent boarding and day school for girls with over 450 pupils aged 11 to 18 years. High aspirations combined with a positive approach to learning creates an environment where girls can grow into motivated, decisive and self-assured individuals. We are renowned for academic success alongside a rich programme of extra-curricular opportunities and excellence in the arts, drama, music and sport.

We are a Church of England School and part of The Grey Coat Hospital Foundation, Westminster, London. Located in Caversham, Berkshire, the school is situated to the north of Reading near Henley-on-Thames and is just over 40 minutes from London. School transport is available throughout the local area; a coach service runs every Friday and Sunday to London.

The best way to find out about Queen Anne's is to talk to those at the heart of our community – our pupils! Our website www.qas.org.uk contains images, videos and narratives drawn from their experiences. We look forward to welcoming you to Queen Anne's!

Governing Body: The Grey Coat Hospital Foundation

Chairman: Vice-Admiral P Dunt, CB, DL
Vice-Chairman: Mr J M Noakes, MA

Mrs C Gray, BA
The Venerable Dr J Hedges, BA
Ms A Kiem, MA, BMath, DipEd
Lady Laws, BLitt, MA
Mr R F Penfold, MBE
Mrs T Rowe, BA
Mr J Slater, ACA
Mr D Taylor, MA, FRSA
Ms S A Thewlis
Mrs L Troake, BA
Miss A Wiscarson, BSc

Clerk: Mr R W Blackwell, MA

Headmistress: **Mrs J Harrington**, BA Exeter, PGCE, NPQH, Dip Counselling

Deputy Head (*Pastoral*): Ms M Chodak, BA Birmingham, PGCE
Deputy Head (*Academic*): Mr M Richards, BMus, MMus, Research Fellowship
Director of Sixth Form: Dr V Vincent, BSc, DPhil, CertEd

Registrar: Mrs J Gallie

Pastoral organisation. Queen Anne's has an excellent reputation for pastoral care. Girls can attend Queen Anne's daily or on a full, weekly, flexi- or occasional boarding basis according to individual family needs. Each girl, whether day or boarding, belongs to a House and the House system is integral to our academic and pastoral care.

The staff believe that students perform best when they are happy and secure, and Queen Anne's has effective pastoral systems in place to ensure this. The support network includes Housemistresses and the House Pastoral Team, Academic Staff and Tutors, and Heads of Year.

Curriculum. All girls follow a broad and varied curriculum up to GCSE. Separate subject sciences are taught, as well as Dual Award; mathematics and music follow IGCSE; Spanish or German may be taken from Year 9; Latin is studied from Year 7. Music, art and drama form part of the girls' timetable until the end of Year 9. Information technology is taught throughout the school. A wide range of A Level subjects is offered. A programme of personal, social and health education is followed by all girls.

Careers. All girls go on to Higher Education, many to top universities in the UK and overseas.

Extra-curricular activities. Queen Anne's is reputed for many of its achievements. It offers a full extra-curricular programme and excellent opportunities for sport, including tennis, lacrosse (National Champions on many occasions), 'rock' climbing and rowing on the nearby Thames. Music, drama and art are very strong. The Duke of Edinburgh's Award, WOHAA, public speaking and debating (National and International finalists), photography, dance, riding, socials and many more activities are available. A full programme of optional activities is available on Saturday mornings.

Admission. Girls are admitted at 11+, 13+ and at Sixth Form by Queen Anne's Entrance Examination or by Common Entrance. Sixth Form places are offered on the basis of GCSE results. For further information please contact the Registrar.

Scholarships are offered for entry at 11+, 13+ and 16+ and are awarded for excellence in one or more fields of the life of the school. Awards may be made in respect of Academic Excellence, All-Round Contribution, Art, Drama, Music or Sport.

Fees per term (2014–2015). Full Boarding £9,975; Flexi Boarding £9,480; Day pupils £6,770.

Charitable status. Queen Anne's School is part of The Grey Coat Hospital Foundation, which is a Registered Charity, number 312700.

Queen Elizabeth's Hospital (QEH)

Berkeley Place, Clifton, Bristol BS8 1JX
Tel: 0117 930 3040
Fax: 0117 929 3106
email: headmaster@qehbristol.co.uk
           office@qehbristol.co.uk
website: www.qehbristol.co.uk

Motto: '*Dum tempus habemus operemur bonum.*'
Patron: Her Majesty The Queen
By his Will dated 10 April 1586, John Carr, a Bristol merchant, founded Queen Elizabeth's Hospital, a bluecoat school in Bristol on the lines of Christ's Hospital which was already flourishing in London. The Charter was granted to the School by Queen Elizabeth I in 1590. Originally composed entirely of boarders, the School continued so until 1920 when foundation day boys were admitted. Direct Grant status was accorded in 1945. The School is now independent and day only.

Governing Body:
N Tyrrell, BA (*Chairman*)
D A Smart, BSc, FCA (*Vice-Chairman*)

G Bird, FCII
Ms S Blanks, MSc
Mrs S Cosgrove, BSc
T Davis, BSc, MRICS
J Eyles, BEd, RSA
P N Gibson, MA, FCA
R J Hill, LLB Hons, TEP
P A Keen, SCIB

P J Kilmartin, BSc
N A Mitchell, MSc, CEng, FRAeS
A J Morsley, BSc
C Russell-Smith, BSc, FRICS
Mrs J Scarrow, BA
S Speirs, MA

Bursar: R N Cook, FCA

Headmaster: **S W Holliday**, MA

Deputy Head (*Pastoral*): D M Bateson, MA
Deputy Head (*Academic*): J G Sykes, BSc
Assistant Head (*Staff Development*): C Brotherton, BA
Assistant Head (*Operations*): W R Ellis, BSc
Assistant Head (*Sixth Form*): Miss J Sharrock, BA
Director of Marketing & Development: A G Lewis-Barned, BEd

S Albon, BSc
Mrs S K Allen, BSc
P M Amor, BA
A A Berry, BSc
A E Calder, BA
Ms P Cawte, BA
Mrs E Cheetham, BA
C B Conquest, BEd
S M Cook, MSc
P A Davies, BSc
Mrs M M Dimes, BSc
R Dixon, BSc
T J Dunn, BSc
M Dutton, BEd, MA, EdD
Miss N Dyer, BA
Miss L Fenner, BA
N Folland, BA, MSc
C Gamble, BSc
E M Gent, BA
Mrs D Guthrie, BSc
R J Harris, BA
S A Harris, BSc
D T Hawkes, BSc
Mrs M Holdsworth, MA
Miss N Holcombe, BA
G A R Huband, BSc
A R Hughes, BA

Mrs N Hunter, BSc
P M Jones, BA
Dr J Jönsson, MSc, PhD
P E Joslin, BEd
J Kelly, BSc
Mrs B Kenchington, BEd
Mrs S J King, MA
P J Kirby, BA
H L Kyle, BSc, PhD
Mrs H Lung, BA
Ms S Maltin, BA
J E Martin BA
R Martineau, MEng
J R Matthews, BEd
Mrs M McGowan, BA
C Miller, BSc
P C Moore, BEd
Mrs S Moritz, BSc
S J Munnion, BA
W G Plowden, BA
Miss S Pobjoy, BMus
Mrs S Pole, BA
N Pursall, BA
Mrs A J Revill, BA, MA
Ms K Ryan, BA
Mrs L Shaw, BA
Mrs R Steven, BA

Mrs L Stotesbury, BA
A W H Swithinbank, BA
Z Verry, BA
Mrs F Waite-Taylor, BA
Mrs A Ward, BA

Mrs B Williams, BA
Mrs C J Winchester-Snell, BA
P Wright, BSc, PhD

Junior School:
Headteacher: M J Morris, BA

Visiting Teachers:
J Bacon, MMus
P Barrett, BA, PG Dip
Mrs D Dickerson, DipLCM, DipABRSM, DipESA
K Figes, LGSM, PG Dip
S Hofkes, BMus, Conducting GSMD
Mrs A Howell, BMus, FRCO, LGSM, BA
C Khajavi, BA Mus
Miss C Lindley, BA
C McCann, Dip Mus MoD
B Mullan, BMus
G Robinson, BMus
T Shevlin, BMus, PG Dip
N Shipman, BMus, LGSMD
A Stewart, BMus
Miss L Tanner, BMus, MMus, PG Dip
J Whitfield, BMus

Chaplain: The Revd S B Taylor, BA
Headmaster's Secretary: Mrs E Davies
Admissions Registrar: Mrs C Matthews
Librarian: Mrs A Robbins

Admission. There are 575 boys in the Senior School, ranging in age from 11 to 18. Entrance examinations for both Year 7 and Year 9 applicants are held in January each year; Sixth Form and other Years by arrangement.
Term of Entry. Usually September.
Entrance Scholarships. A significant number of scholarships are offered at Year 7, Year 9 and Sixth Form. These are awarded purely on academic merit for outstanding achievement in the entrance procedures and may also carry with them generous assistance for applicants whose parents' means are limited.
Music and Sports scholarships are available at Year 7 and Year 9.
Assisted Places. There are many School assisted places available. The School has a substantial foundation income and is able to give generous support to parents whose means are limited.
Buildings. The School was originally close by the City Centre but moved to new premises on Brandon Hill in 1847. A major building and improvement programme has included the building of the QEH Theatre (1990), refurbishment of the Art School (2000), new Mathematics rooms and heavy investment in ICT (2004). An 80-strong Junior School opened in 2007 (increasing to over 100 in 2012) along with a new Sixth Form Centre. In 2008 a multi-million pound development programme, in conjunction with Bristol City Football Club, saw new football pitches on 23 acres at the Sports Ground at Failand. Science facilities were extensively refurbished in 2009 and plans have been approved for a new Science building in 2015. These plans include improvements to Music and Art facilities and other areas of the school.
Curriculum. Boys are prepared for the GCSE (IGCSE in Mathematics and English) and GCE A Level, and for university entrance. The usual school subjects are offered at GCSE Level, and the AS/A2 Level subjects are: English Literature, English Language, Drama, Economics, Latin, Greek, History, Geography, French, German, Spanish, Art, Music, Mathematics, Further Mathematics, Music Technology, Physics, Chemistry, Biology, PE and Sport, Business Studies, ICT, Ethics and Philosophy, Politics and Psychology.

Music & Drama. There is a School Orchestra, Choir, Jazz Band, Brass Group, and Wind Band. Music is included in the timetable for all the junior forms. GCSE and A Level music is part of the School curriculum, and tuition is arranged for a wide range of instruments. The Choir and Instrumentalists perform regularly and also undertake joint ventures with the independent girls' schools in Bristol. Drama flourishes and the school has its own high-tech purpose-built theatre which seats 220.

Art. The Department is well equipped and offers ceramics, screen printing, photography and computer imaging.

Religious Studies. The School is a Christian one which welcomes boys of all faiths, or none. Religious Studies is part of the curriculum and boys attend two services a year in Bristol Cathedral.

Games. Rugby, Football, Athletics, Cricket, Swimming, Tennis, Badminton, Sailing, Squash, Fencing, Judo, Climbing and Mountain Biking. A large number of boys also participate in The Duke of Edinburgh's Award and Ten Tors.

Dress. Boys wear either grey trousers and a blazer or a plain dark suit. Traditional bluecoat uniform is worn by some for special occasions.

General. All parents are encouraged to join the Friends of Queen Elizabeth's Hospital, a society whose aim is to promote a close relationship between parents and staff and to further the welfare of the School. There is a flourishing Old Boys' Society, which holds regular meetings and circulates a newsletter. A panel of Old Boys, formed from all professions, and working with the Head of Careers, is available to give advice on careers to boys.

The School has long been known in Bristol as 'The City School' and its links with the Lord Mayor and Corporation are strong. Boys read the lessons and sing in the Lord Mayor's Chapel, and groups are in attendance for such occasions as Mayor-making and Council Prayers.

The central position of the School, close to the University, the Art Gallery and Museum, the Central Library, the Bristol Old Vic and the Colston Hall, affords ready access to a wide range of cultural facilities which boys are encouraged to use.

Junior School. 100 Boys aged 7–11. (*For further details see QEH Junior School entry in IAPS section.*)

Fees per term (2014–2015). Senior School £4,231, Junior School £2,765. Fees include text and exercise books, and essential educational trips but do not include public examination fees or lunches (which are £3.40 per day).

Charitable status. Queen Elizabeth's Hospital is a Registered Charity, number 1104871, and a Company Limited by Guarantee, number 5164477. Queen Elizabeth's Hospital has existed since 1590 to provide an education for boys.

Queen's College
Taunton

Trull Road, Taunton, Somerset TA1 4QS
Tel: 01823 340830 Admissions
Fax: 01823 338430
email: admissions@queenscollege.org.uk
website: www.queenscollege.org.uk
Twitter: @QueensTaunton
Facebook: /queenstaunton

Motto: '*Non scholae sed vitae discimus*' (*We learn not for school but for life*)

Visitor: The President of the Methodist Conference

Governors:
Chairman: Mr Stephen Lawson
Mrs Helen Broderick
Mrs Jenny Clough, MA Hons, PGCE

Mrs Rachel Davies, MA, BSc Hons, BA Hons, PGCE
Mr Mark Edwards
Mrs Kate Gardner, LLB
Sir Nick Harvey, MP
Mr Paul Hughes, BSc Hons, ACIB
Brigadeer Tom Lang, QVRM RD*, DL
Dr Katherine Lloyd Clark
Mr Pradeep Madhavan, Dip NB Surg, FRCS, Ed Tr and Orth
Revd Stephen Mares
Mr Ian McIntyre
Mrs Deberah Perreau
Mr Michael Powell, BSc Hons, FRICS, FAAV
Mr Peter Rigby
Mr David Savill, LLB, FCA
Mr Brian Tanner, BA Hons, CIPFA, CBE, DL
Revd Canon Graham Thompson
Mr David Turner, LLB, FCCI

Senior Leadership Group:

Headmaster: **Mr Christopher J Alcock**, BSc Durham, FRGS, FRSA (*Geography*)

Chaplain: Revd Robert Blackhall, BSc, BA (*Religious Studies*)
Business Director: Mr Graham Taylor, MBA, BA, Dip MRS
Director of Marketing and Development: Mr Nick Leiper, BSc, MSc (*Economics*)
Deputy Head – Academic: Dr Lorraine Earps, PhD, MSc (*Chemistry*)
Deputy Head – Pastoral: Mrs Gill Watson, BEd Hons (*Chemistry and Science Education*)
Assistant Head – Sixth Form and Progression: Mrs Jane Evans, BA (*Performance Studies*)
Assistant Head: Mr Andrew Free, BA Ed Hons (**Physical Education*)

Senior School Teaching Staff:
† *House Parent*
* *Head of Department*

Mr Richard Appleby (*Performing Arts*)
Miss Donna Ashman, BA (*History and Examinations Officer*)
Mrs Claire Barker, MEd, BSc (*Assistant Head of Sixth Form*, **Psychology*)
Mr Jon Bird, BA (*EAL*)
Mr Geoffrey Bisson, BA (*History*)
Mrs Kay Bloxham, BEd, MA, Learning Development BDA Level 1 & 3 (*Dance and Physical Education*)
Mr Roger Bowden, BEd (*Mathematics*)
Mrs Jennifer Brierley, BA (**English*)
Mrs Helen Brunt (*Physical Education*)
Miss Sarah Brown, BA (*Business*)
Miss Laura Burgoyne, BA (*Art*)
Mrs Alison Brothwood (*Learning Development*)
Mr Peter Burrows, BA, MSc (*Physical Education*)
Miss Rebecca Cade, BA (*Art*)
Mr Hugh Childs, BA (*Art*)
†Mrs Rebecca Cole, BSc (**Food and Design Technology*)
Mr Dave Cooke, BSc, MEd (*Biology*)
Mr Simon Copeland, BSc Hons Sports Studies (*Director of Sport*)
Mr Paul De Jaeger, BSc (*Geography*)
Mrs Henrietta Drummond, BSc (*Mathematics, Assistant Head of Sixth Form/UCAS Coordinator*)
Mrs Joanna Elliott, RAD RTS (*Performing Arts*)
Mr Stephen Eaton Evans, BA (**Theatre Studies*)
Mr Andrew Exley, BSc (*Mathematics*)
Mrs Terri Fisher, BA, PGCE (*Modern Languages*)
Mrs Amanda Free, BA, Dip Sp Ed, AMBDA (**Learning Development*)
Mr Andrew Garton, BA (*ICT*)
Mr Paul Gibson, BSc (*Mathematics*)

Miss Helen Goodall, BSc (*EAL*)
Mrs Donna Greenow, BSc (*Modern Languages*)
Dr Darren Haggerston, BSc, PhD (*Chemistry*)
Mr Ian Haley, BSc Hons (*Physical Education*)
†Mr Angus Hamilton, BA Hons (**Religious Studies*)
†Miss Claire Harrison, BSc (*Biology*)
Miss Julie Harrison, BEd (**Girls' Physical Education and Games*)
Miss Oona Hazell, BEd (*Business*)
Mr David Hedges, BA (*Music*)
Mr Ian Henden, BSc (*Chemistry*)
Mrs Lisa Henden, ACIEA, BSc Hons (**Biology*)
Mrs Terri Hicks, BA, Dip SpLD & AMBDA (*Learning Development*)
Miss Jennifer Hill, BSc (*Mathematics*)
Mr Ed Jenkins, BA Hons, ARCO, PGCE (**Music*)
Mr Timothy Jolliff, MA Cantab, MRSC (**Chemistry*)
Mrs Caroline Lewis, BH (*Physical Education and Games*)
Mrs Grace Mainstone, BA, LRSM, LTCL (*EAL*)
Miss Sarah Male, BA, PGCE (*Modern Languages*)
Mr Philip Mann, MNASC (*Physical Education and Games*)
Mr John Marston, BA (*English and Drama*)
†Mrs Carole Mason BEd (*Mathematics*) AST
Mrs Mary Mason, MRSC (*Chemistry*)
Miss Karen McIntyre, BA (*EAL*)
†Mr Christopher Monks, BSc (*Mathematics*)
Mr Scott Morrison, BMus (*Music*)
Mrs Virginia Murray, BA (*French*)
Mark Neenan, BEd (*Geography*)
Mrs Kate Newsome, BSc (*Mathematics*)
Mr Nicholas O'Donnell, BEng (**Physics*)
Ms Valerie Orme-Dawson, BA Hons, PGCE (**EAL*)
†Mr Adrian Palmer, MEd, BA, CChem, MRSC
Mrs Pamela Pawley, MA (**Mathematics*)
Mrs Sheila Platt (*Mathematics*)
Mr Roger Priest, BA (*Latin*)
Mrs Nikki Ross, BA (*Manager, Resource Centre*)
Mr Simon Ross, BA (**Geography*)
Mr Ben Rowe, BA (*Physical Education*)
Mrs Laura Schofield, MA Hons, MA, PGCE (*Modern Languages*)
†Mr Jon Shepherd, BSc (*Biology*)
Mr Roger Simon, BEd, MA (*Physical Education*)
Miss Melissa Smith, BSc (**History*)
Miss Siân Smith, BA Hons, MA Cantab (*English*)
Miss Sandra Spall, BA (*Art*)
Mr Leslie Stevens, BSc, BSc, MBCS (*Physics and Computing*)
Mr David Stockton, BEd (*Physics*)
Mr Arul Suppiah, BA (*Director of Cricket, Business*)
Dr Duncan Taylor, MA Oxon, MA, PhD (*Economics, Politics and Extended Project Qualification*)
Mr Peter Vicary, BSc (**Economics, Politics, Business*)
Mrs Anne Wade, BA, PGCE
Mr Michael Wager, BA, PGCE (**Modern Languages*)
Mr Chris Widdows, MA Cantab (*Politics*)
Mrs Kirsten Webber, BSc (*EAL*)
Mrs Sue Wedge-Thomas, BEd Hons (*Biology*)
Mrs Claire Western, BA (**Art*)
Miss Sarah Whitehouse, BSc (*Physics*)
Mrs Sharon Wilde, BA (*Physical Education and English*)
Mr Luke Wildgoose, BA (*Religious Studies*)
Mr Gareth Wilson, BSc (*Design & Technology*)
Mrs Sue Wylie, Dip Acting and Theatre Studies

PA to the Headmaster: Mrs Pam Chapman
Admissions Registrar: Mrs Sarah Frost
Academic Administrator: Miss Judith Poole
Sixth Form Administrator: Miss Rosina Cross

Junior School Teaching Staff:

Headmistress of Junior, Pre-Prep and Nursery: Mrs Tracey J Khodabandehloo, BEd, MEd, PG Dip

Deputy Head: Mr Dick Wilde, BEd Hons

Mrs Linda Alcock, BA
Mr Douglas Baker, BA
Mrs Sarah Beats, BA
Miss Nicola Cavanagh, BSc, PGCE
Mr Andrew Clark, BA,PGCE
Mr Philip Dudman BA, PGCE
Mrs Joanne Elsmore, BSc Hons, PGCE
Mrs Belinda Hoskins, BEd
Mrs Sue Marston, BA, LAMDA (*Gold Medallist*)
Mrs Vicky Miller, Dip Ed
Mrs Shirley Neale, Cert Ed, RSA Dip SpLD, AMBDA
Mr Andrew Owen, BA, PGCE
Mrs Nicola Painter, BA
Miss Sarah Scutt, BA, MA,PGCE
Mrs Candice Thompson-Gardiner, BA Hons, PGCE
Mrs Abigail Thresher, RGN
Mrs Teresa Underwood, BSc Hons,PGCE
Mrs Anne Wade, BA, PGCE
Mrs Penny Walker, BSc Hons,PGCE
Mrs Anthea Watkins, Cert Ed, RSA Dip SpLD
Mrs Kirsten Webber, BSc (*EAL*)

Secretary to Headmistress: Ms Julie Cameron
Assistant Secretary: Mrs Sarah Musgrave

Pre-Prep and Nursery Staff:

Head of Pre-Prep and Nursery: Mrs Janet Williams, BEd, CertEd, NNEB

Head of Nursery: Miss Elizabeth Hayes, EYPS, BA Teaching and Learning, Early Childhood, DPQS, NNEB

Mrs Charlotte Baker, BA
Mrs Jane Brown, NVQ3 Early Learning and Childcare
Miss Carrine Coles, Foundation Degree
Mrs Dawn Coram, NVQ3
Mrs Peta Dayus-Jones, NVQ3
Mrs Jill Fear, BEd
Mrs Kirsty Goss, Foundation Degree Childhood Studies Level 3
Forest School,,BTec Dip Childhood Studies
Mrs Clare Hammond, NNEB
Miss Christina Hardwick, BA Early Childhood Studies Level 3
Forest School, BTec Dip Childhood Studies
Mrs Gill Harrison, BEd, RSA Dip SpLD
Mrs Anne Higgins
Mrs Helen Hitchin, BA,PGCE
Mrs Clare Hood, BEd
Miss Samantha Horner, BEd
Mrs Rebecca Milby, BSc
*Mrs Vanessa Monks, BA
Mrs Diane Thompson

Medical Staff:
Dr David Downs, BSc, MBChB, DRCOG, MRCGP
Dr Gabrielle de Cothi, MBChB, DRCOG, MRCGP
Mrs Lynn Dimery, SRN, SCN
Mrs Lidia Carp, RGN
Mrs Susan Parratt, RGN
Mrs Rachael Wilson, RGN, BSc Specialist Practice
Mrs Jane Whitefield, RGN
Miss Rebecca Morgan (*Resident Matron, Junior School*)

Introduction. Queen's College is one of the South West's leading independent day and boarding co-educational schools. Queen's is very strong in sport, in particular hockey, athletics and swimming. It also has an outstanding reputation for the visual and performing arts and the School currently has some outstanding musicians in the National Youth Orchestra.

Queen's has a well-deserved reputation for the quality of its teaching and all pupils are cared for in small tutor groups. Pastoral care is outstanding. The staff work tirelessly to encourage students to develop their personal skills and abilities. Class sizes are small and the atmosphere is friendly and supportive – students are happy and motivated here.

The boarding community is strong with excellent houseparents, full activities programme and lots of support. Communication and relationships with parents are valued and all are included in the wider Queen's family.

Queen's operates a strong co-curricular programme including a wide variety of performing arts, sports, arts and outdoor pursuits and considerable emphasis is placed on participation in the Duke of Edinburgh's Award Scheme. All students take Bronze, many go on to Silver and to date, over 300 Sixth Form students have achieved their Gold Awards. Queen's hosts its own Model United Nations conference and is a centre of excellence in the South West.

Number of Pupils. The Queen's College Pre-Prep, Junior and Senior schools are based on the same site with some facilities shared: continuity of education is assured. The Senior school (11 to 18 years) has 555 pupils of whom 206 are boarders. The Junior school and Pre-Prep (3 to 11 years) has 207 pupils, with a junior boarding house. The full College complement is an excellent size of 762 meaning that there are enough pupils for good friendship groups, team sports and school plays but it is still personal enough so that the Headmaster knows every pupil. A happy, friendly, family school which doesn't stand on ceremony.

Situation and Buildings. Queen's College was founded in 1843 within Taunton's Castle walls but was relocated to the south western outskirts of Taunton three years later when the present main school buildings were constructed. It is in an excellent situation with fine views of the Quantock and Blackdown Hills, within easy reach of Exmoor and Dartmoor, just a mile and a half from Taunton town centre, easily accessible by road or rail, junction 25 of M5 is 2 miles away and serviced by Heathrow, Bristol International and Exeter Airports.

The 1846 original Grade II* listed building contained a School House, the School Hall and a Dining Room. Later a Junior School was added, an indoor heated Swimming Pool and a Music Department. Over the last twenty years there has been an extensive building programme which has included: nine classrooms for the Junior school, applied science, technology centre, new changing rooms, day girl and day boy accommodation, enlargement and modernisation of girl and boy boarding houses, school hall for the Junior school, new music school, concert/assembly hall for the Senior school, and a sixth form centre. Latest additions are a new Art & Drama building; Leisure and Performing Arts Centres; a new Science Block and major expansion of Pre-Prep facilities. Last year a new Design and Technology provision and a new hockey academy was launched with a second international-size astro pitch. This year, 2013, a state-of-the-art Sixth Form Centre provides an excellent interim between school and university equipped with multimedia, social spaces, collaborative and quiet study areas, a new Medical Centre, new Languages Centre and new boarding wing with top quality boarding accommodation. Definitely a school on the up that is modern in its outlook and does not rest on its laurels.

Organisation. There are two day boy houses and two day girl houses and each has a House Parent and Tutor for each year group. The boarding set-up is superb with some really committed House Parents who offer a combination of stability and fun. There are two boys' boarding houses and one large girls' boarding houses and each is in the care of House Parents, together with a resident assistant House Master/ Mistress. Tutors are attached to each house and are responsible for academic progress. They guide each student through GCSE and A Level choices, in conjunction with the Head, Deputy Head Academic and Head of Sixth Form. In the Sixth Form students are able to choose their tutor, who will advise them on university selection and choices of career and the academic, careers and social programmes are excel-

lent. All who want to go on to university, with 75% going on to Russell Group universities.

Curriculum. Pupils in the first three years of Senior School follow the national curriculum providing them with a sound base in the arts, sciences, humanities and technology based subjects as well as games and PSHME. They are streamed and taught as a form for most subjects and are set for mathematics, English and French. At GCSE there is a common core of English language and literature, mathematics, three sciences and a modern foreign language. Pupils then choose three option subjects.

In the Lower Sixth pupils choose 4 AS Level subjects and in the Upper Sixth the majority take three subjects to A2 Level. Throughout the Sixth Form some periods of curriculum time are devoted to a general studies course that includes RE, PSHME and key skills and significant emphasis is placed on gaining good leadership, organisation and communication skills.

Co-Curriculum. In addition to games, music and drama, pupils are encouraged to participate in a range of activities including Model United Nations – a real strength at Queen's, debating, public speaking, general knowledge quizzes, ICT, chess, photography, robotic design, electronics and cookery. There are also a number of academic societies. Outdoor pursuits such as canoeing, mountain bike riding and rock climbing are popular and participation in the Duke of Edinburgh's Award Scheme is a particular feature with a stunning 300 Queen's College pupils having now achieved their Gold Award.

Music. The music staff provides teaching for keyboard, strings, brass, woodwind, percussion and singing amongst others. The purpose-built Music Department comprises:

- classroom
- 6 large teaching rooms
- 5 practice rooms
- electronic studio for keyboard studies
- audio studio for computer-based composition (GCSE and A Level)
- The Music Department also uses the beautiful Old Music Room and Performing Arts Centre in the main building for rehearsals and small concerts as well as the stunning Queen's Hall with its 500 seater multi-purpose auditorium, two-manual pipe organ and Steinway Concert Grand Piano.

Musical organisations:

- A variety of choirs including Chapel Choir, girls musical choir, boys barbershop and younger youth choirs
- First Orchestra, Chamber Orchestra and Middle School Orchestra
- Wind Band
- Swing Band
- Sound School
- Open Mic Nights and bands

Also a wide variety of small ensembles and chamber groups for strings, brass, woodwind with or without piano. A number of concerts are staged each year. Opportunities to help prepare for the National Youth Orchestra, Somerset Orchestra and Guildhall.

Drama. The provision for performing arts at Queen's is outstanding. The programme is extremely active throughout the college with the Senior school Drama department providing courses from Year 7 to Year 13, the department aims to involve all those wishing to develop their co-curricular and academic interests and sends many students on to drama school. This year four attended the National Musical Youth Theatre over the summer. Over seven different types of dance are studied ranging from ballet and tap to hip hop and jazz with a large scale dance production and professional dancers coming in to give workshops. The school also runs a 10-day professional arts festival with performers and artists from all over the UK also open to the general public.

In the Senior school, productions take place once a term. There is both Senior and Pre-Prep productions at the end of the Autumn term, a major Dance Show at the end of the Spring term and Middle school and Junior plays at the end of the Summer term. Major productions and concerts take place in the Queen's Hall, intimate drama and comedy in the Drama Studio and the Performing Arts Centre and Old Music Room stages smaller scale concerts and readings.

Students are offered Performance Studies courses at GCSE, AS and A2 Level and there is an opportunity to study AS Level Dance. Theatre visits are arranged on a regular basis and for those studying the subject at GCSE and A Level the visits form part of their course. A whole range of dance classes is offered to pupils.

PE/Games. The 30-acre playing fields of Queen's are both extensive and adaptable and sport is strong at the school – in particular hockey, swimming, cross country, athletics and riding. However all abilities are welcomed and there are opportunities for C and D teams for those who enjoy playing for their school.

In the Autumn term the grass area provides 7 rugby pitches which are also used for sevens in the Spring term.

In the Summer there are 5 cricket squares, a 400-metre athletics track and numerous rounders pitches.

The three Astroturf pitches are used very frequently – daily for hockey in the Autumn and Spring terms – and are of such quality that Queen's has often been called upon to host County hockey tournaments. This September a new hockey academy was launched with Olympic coaches. The pitches are converted to tennis courts in the Summer, giving a total of 30 tennis courts.

The hard court surface in the middle of the field is used for netball in the Spring term and for tennis in the Autumn and Summer terms. Alongside this area are cricket nets for use in the Summer term.

The Sports Hall is used for the following activities: gymnastics, basketball, badminton, volleyball, indoor hockey, football and indoor tennis. There is a squash court and a fully-equipped fitness centre adjoining the Sports Hall. Within the complex is an indoor heated pool that is used at various times for swimming from Pre-Prep through to Sixth Form lessons. Team swimming, canoeing, canoe polo and sub aqua are regular activities throughout the year.

Admission. Education at Queen's can start at 3 years on entry to the Nursery. The majority of pupils join the Pre-Preparatory school from the age of 4 years. Junior school pupils start at age 7. Entrance to the Senior School is by examination and those who are successful in gaining places to the Junior school make satisfactory transfer to the Senior school at the age of 11. There are places for boys and girls from primary schools at the age of 11 based on entry tests in Maths, English and verbal reasoning. There are places for boys and girls at the age of 13 from Preparatory schools also with entrance examinations and a number enter the Sixth Form direct on GCSE Level results.

Scholarships. *Queen's College Scholarships*: 11+ scholarships are awarded in January, 13+ in February and Sixth Form in November.

Academic Scholarships: Up to 50% of fees for students of proven academic ability aged 11+ and 13+ on 1 September in year of entry and 16+ for the Sixth Form.

Music Scholarships: Worth up to 50% of fees for the most gifted musicians aged 11+ and 13+ at the time of entry to the College. Sixth Form entry scholarships are also available plus an Organ award.

Performing Arts Scholarships: Worth up to 50% of fees for the students of best ability aged 11+, 13+ and 16+. Queen's College offers scholarships for talented students with proven ability – Sixth Form scholarships included.

Art Scholarships: Worth up to 50% of fees for the most talented scholars. Scholarships are for talented students with an existing standard and potential for considerable development. Candidates to be aged 11+ or 13+ at projected time of entry to the college. Sixth Form scholarships included. Art scholarships are based on portfolio and interview.

Sport Scholarships: Worth up to 50% of fees for the students of best ability. Queen's College offers scholarships for talented students with proven sports ability aged 11+ and 13+ at the projected time of entry to the college. Sixth Form scholarships included.

Fees per term (2014–2015). Pre-Prep £1,895–£1,955 (day pupils only); Junior Day Pupils £2,325–£3,840; Junior Boarders £4,100–£6,200; Junior Overseas Boarders £5,100–£7,200; Senior Day Pupils £4,650–£5,470; Senior Boarders £7,320–£9,050; Senior Overseas Boarders £8,320–£10,050. The fees are inclusive of most books and stationery, but exclude external examination charges.

Charitable status. Queen's College, Taunton is a Registered Charity, number 310208. The College is a leading Charitable Trust in the field of Junior and Secondary education.

Radley College

Abingdon, Oxfordshire OX14 2HR
Tel: 01235 543127 (Warden)
            01235 543122 (Bursar)
            01235 543174 (Admissions)
            01235 543000 (General Enquiries)
Fax: 01235 543106
email: warden@radley.org.uk
website: www.radley.org.uk

Motto: '*Sicut Serpentes, sicut Columbae*'

St Peter's College, Radley, was founded by the Reverend William Sewell, Fellow of Exeter College, Oxford, to provide an independent school education on the principles of the Church of England. It was opened on 9 June 1847 and incorporated by Royal Charter in 1890. It stands in a park of some 700 acres.

Visitor: The Rt Revd The Lord Bishop of Oxford

Council:
Chairman: M E Hodgson, MA, FRICS
Vice-Chairman: S W B Whitworth, MA

T O Seymour, MA	T M Durie, BA, ACA, FSI
M J W Rushton, MA	J C Bridcut, MA
N J Henderson, MA, FRCS	R H Warner, MA, ACA
D C S Smellie, MA	A C Mayfield, MBA
A P G Holmes, MA	Sir John Holmes
Mrs D J Pluck, FCA	R N L Huntingford
G A Kaye, BSc	P E F Watson, FRGS
Mrs E McKendrick, BA	Mrs E J Martineau, FRGS
W S H Laidlaw, MA	H J R Willis, MA

Warden: J S Moule, MA

Sub Warden: B J Holden, MA, BTech
Academic Director: S R Rathbone, MA, MA

Senior Masters:
H D Hammond, BSc
R D Shaw, MA

Teaching Staff:

G Wiseman, BA	†R M C Greed, BSc (*B Social*)
J C Nye, MA	
P W Gamble, MA	W O C Matthews, BA
I P Ellis, BA, DipRASchls	†T R G Ryder, BA, MFA (*A Social*)
S Barlass, BA	
†A J McChesney, BSc (*F Social*)	D C K Edwards, MA
	R A King, BSc, MRSC, CChem
C M Bedford, BA, PhD	†J M Sparks, BSc (*C Social*)
†N Murphy, MA (*K Social*)	
I S Yorston, MA	S A Hall, BA, MPhil, PhD

N L Haggett, MBE, BEd
Mrs B L M Haggett, ATD, DipSLD
M R Jewell, BA
R Johnson, BSc
J R W Beasley, MA
I K Campbell, BA
Mrs M C Hart, BA
B R Knox, BEd
P M Fernandez, MA
D W S Roques, MA
K A Mosedale, MA, MSc
Mrs K J Knox, BA
†H Crump, LLB, BA (*D Social*)
S H Dalrymple, BA
K Halliday, BSc, PhD
R M Lowe, BA
†G H S May, MA (*H Social*)
G R King, BA
D J Pullen, BSc
R K McMahon, MA, MPhil, DPhil
C J Ellott, BA, LLB
J E Gearing, BA
D S Borthwick, DPhil, MChem
Mrs G C Porter, MA, MSc
†O H Langton, MA (*J Social*)
Mrs T Scammell Jackson, BA, MPhil
Mrs N J King, BA
Ms E E N Danis, BA
S R Giddens, BSc, MSc, PhD
†T C Lawson, BA (*E Social*)
†A C Jackson, BA (*G Social*)
C J Lee, BA
C E Scott-Malden, BA, MA
P R Wallace, BSc, MPhil, DPhil
Mrs C de Bono, BA

Dr G J A Hughes BA, MSc, MPhil, PhD
A D Cunningham, MA, PhD
P J Miron, BSc, DPhil
M P Hills, MMath
E J Tolputt, MEng
J C Wheeler, BSc
E O Holt, BA
C A San Jose, BA
D J Cresswell, BA
M J Pringle, BA
J W Schofield, BA, MSc
D L Cox, MMath
Mrs K C Ison, BA
Ms P E Henderson, BA
J M Ambrose, BA, DPhil
Ms L E Nott, BA
A M H Hakimi, BSc, MPhil, DPhil
K J Reid, MSc
M G Noone, MA
R D Woodling, MChem
T A Barfield, MSt
S J Perkins, BSc
M B Spivey, BASc
J M Sumner, BA
M E Walker, BA, MA, PhD
Mrs R E Murphy, BA
Ms M M Rodriguez
M C F Brown, BA
Miss L P Gregory, BA
R E P Hughes, BSc
T C H Norton, MA
Miss C P Oh, BA, MPhil
Dr A R Rhodes, BA, MA, DPhil
Mrs L R I Smart, BA
Mrs C E Piller
Mrs A McChesney
N M Martin, BA
M G D Glendon-Doyle, BA
Mrs A K M Coulton, BA
J P J Dodd, BA
K W S Willis-Stovold, BSc
Miss M Hurley, BA
Mrs G M Maybank, BA

Chaplain: The Revd D Wilson, BSc, BA, MLitt, PhD
Assistant Chaplain: The Revd T J E Fernyhough, BA
Librarian: Ms A K Muhlberg

Music:
Precentor: S D J Clarke, MA, ARCO
A J A Williams, MMus, DipRAM, GRSM, LRAM
Miss S-L Naylor, MA
T M Morris, MA, DPhil, FRCO

There are 36 peripatetic music staff.

Bursar and Secretary: A Ashton, MA, ACIB
Medical Officer: Dr J N B Moore, BSc, MB BS, DRCOG, MRCGP
Development Director: A L Robinson
Registrar: Mrs V M G Hammond

General Arrangements. There are 688 boys in the school, all of whom board. On admission, boys enter one of the 10 houses known as Socials. All are close together within the grounds. All meals are served in Hall on a cafeteria system. There is a daily Chapel Service for all boys.

Admission to the School. Boys are admitted between the ages of 13 and 14 in the Michaelmas Term, and qualify by taking either the Common Entrance Examination, our own entrance exam, or the Entrance Scholarship Examination.

Registration starts at birth and registration forms can be obtained from the Registrar. All entries are made centrally. A non-returnable registration fee of £100 is payable when a boy's name is entered. Registration does not guarantee a place in the school. Three years before a boy is due to come, a Final Acceptance Form will be sent to parents at which point a boy's place is guaranteed subject to passing CE. These forms are sent out in date order of registration. A Final Acceptance Fee of £1,000 (fully refundable up until the end of February in the year of entry and partly refundable against the last term's account) is payable on acceptance. Around thirty Warden's List places are reserved for those who have registered too late, or have not registered. Selection will be at the Warden's discretion on performance at interview and current school reports. Applications for these places are accepted two years before entry.

Sixth Form: A few places are sometimes available for entry: details are available on our website.

Scholarships and Bursaries. Up to twelve Academic Scholarships and Exhibitions are awarded each year. In addition All-Rounder, Music, Drama and Art Awards are offered. All awards may be supplemented by a means-tested bursary. Details of all awards are available from our website or the Registrar. Further means-tested bursaries are available for boys who would otherwise be unable to come to Radley.

Music: On average five Instrumental Scholarships and several Exhibitions are offered annually with free tuition.

Drama: Around two awards will be offered annually.

Art: Around two Art Scholarships and an Art Exhibition will be offered annually.

All-Rounder: On average six to eight All-Rounder Scholarships will be awarded annually.

Work. In the Shells, Removes and Fifth Form a broad curriculum is followed. There is some choice at GCSE with boys generally taking nine or ten subjects.

In the Sixth Form a boy can specialise in a combination of Classics, French, Spanish, German, Theatre Studies, English, History, Religious Studies, Geography, Geology, Biology, Chemistry, Physics, Mathematics, Economics, Politics, Economics and Business, Music, Art or Design, leading to AS/A2 examinations.

Careers. Advice and assistance is available to all boys on a wide range of career possibilities through the Director of Careers. The School is a member of ISCO (The Independent Schools Careers Organisation) and close connections are maintained with the professions, with firms, with the services and with Old Radleians. Visits and talks by experts in these fields are a special feature.

Games. In the Michaelmas Term rugby football is the major school game. In the other two terms the 'wet-bobs' row; the 'dry-bobs' play hockey (the major game) and soccer in the Lent Term, cricket (the major game), athletics and tennis in the Summer. There are also numerous minor sports which involve boys in competition with other schools. The playing fields are close to the main buildings.

The College has its own boathouse, and the use of a stretch of the River Thames between Sandford and Abingdon. The VIIIs compete in regattas and Head of the River races.

There are two all-weather hockey pitches, an athletics track, five squash courts, a Real Tennis court, a rackets court, two covered Fives courts, 20 hard tennis courts and a 9-hole golf course. There is a large, well-equipped gymnasium and an indoor, heated swimming pool attached to a multi-purpose sports hall. A rowing tank is under construction.

CCF and Duke of Edinburgh's Award. All boys, in their fourth term, join the Radley College Contingent, Combined Cadet Force (Army, Navy and Air Sections). They work for the Proficiency examination, which takes three terms. When they have passed Proficiency and done a week's Corps Camp in the holidays they either stay on in a special section for further training or join one of the many

Community Action Projects on offer. There is a thriving Duke of Edinburgh's Award scheme.

Fees per term (2014–2015). £11,075 (inclusive of medical attendance). There is available a system of insurance against loss of fees caused by illness, accident, or infection. Particulars can be obtained from the Bursar.

Charitable status. St Peter's College, Radley is a Registered Charity, number 309243. It exists for the purpose of the education of youth in general knowledge and literature and particularly and especially in the doctrines and principles of the Church of England.

Ratcliffe College

Fosse Way, Ratcliffe on the Wreake, Leicester, Leicestershire LE7 4SG

Tel:	01509 817000 School Office
	01509 817072/817031 Registrar
Fax:	01509 817004
email:	registrar@ratcliffe.leics.sch.uk
website:	www.ratcliffe-college.co.uk

Motto: '*Legis Plenitudo Charitas*'

Ratcliffe College is a co-educational Catholic day and boarding school. The School was founded in 1844 and opened in 1847; the original buildings by A W Pugin were erected with funds provided by Lady Mary Arundel of Wardour, who also bequeathed money for subsequent extensions.

Governing Body:
Consists of two members of the Board of Directors of the Company Limited by Guarantee which owns the College (Ratcliffe College Ltd), together with up to 10 additional governors, appointed by the Directors, who hold office for a period.

Present Governors:
Mr Richard Gamble (*Chairman and Director*)
Mr Andrew Monaghan
Judge Michael Stokes
Mr Abe Mee
Mrs Mary Goldstraw
Mr Vincenzo Lallo
Mrs Louise Marsden
Mr Louis Massarella (*Vice Chairman*)
Mr Paul Rudd
Fr Phillip Sainter (*Director*)
Mrs Margaret Smidowicz
Mr Martin Traynor

Headmaster: Mr G P Lloyd, BA Hons, MSc, FMusTCL

Senior Deputy Head: Mr J Reddin, BSc, MSc
Deputy Head Academic: Mr K Ryce, BA, MSc
Assistant Head: Mr G J Sharpe, BA, MBA
Director of Finance: Mr D Robson, BCom Accounting, ACA
Head of Preparatory School: Fr C Cann, MA St Andrews, MA Oxon, Cert Theol
Head of Nursery: Mrs S Rankine, BEd
Father President: Fr T Mullen IC

Teaching Staff:
* *Head of Department*

Mrs L Arnold, BSc, MPhil (*ICT*)
Mr M Ballard, BSc, MA (*Chemistry**)
Mr M Balmbra, BSc (*Physical Education, Geography, OC CCF*)
Miss S Beddoes, BA (*Spanish*)
Mr M Benjamin, BSc (*English*)
Mrs B Bennett, BA (*English and Drama*)
Mrs C Bennett, BA (*Media Studies*, English*)

Mr D Berry, BA Hons (*Art and Design Technology**)
Dr M Brown, BSc, PhD (*Biology**)
Mrs K Burton, BA (*Food Technology**)
Mr J Cantrill, BA (*History**)
Miss M Casas-Ojeda, BA, MA (*Spanish*)
Mrs C Caven-Henrys, AISTD (*Drama, Dance**)
Mr A Chorley, MSc (*Head of Year, Physics**)
Mrs S Clarke, BA (*Mathematics*)
Mrs J Cluley, BEd, CertEd (*SENCO**)
Mrs C Cole, BSc, MA (*Mathematics*)
Mr A Cooke, BA (*Senior Housemaster, ICT, PE*)
Mrs S Costerton, BA (*Preparatory School*)
Mrs A Crebbin, DEUG (*French, Spanish*)
Mrs S Cushing, BA (*Languages**)
Mrs D Darlington, BSc (*Science*)
Mr M Darlington, BSc (*Curriculum Director, Physics*)
Miss D Dempsey, BA (*Preparatory School*)
Mrs A Dungey, BSc (*Science, Food Technology*)
Mr A Dziemianko, BSc (*Head of Year, Geography*)
Miss D Dzierbicka (*Boarding Assistant*)
Mrs L Eccles, BA (*Latin*)
Mr P Enoux, BA (*Preparatory School*)
Mrs L Evans, BSc (*Mathematics*)
Mr W Faulconbridge, BSc (*Head of Preparatory School Sport*)
Mrs M Finning (*Spanish Language Assistant*)
Mr W Garnett (*Graduate Sports Assistant*)
Mrs N Gilchrist, BEd (*Preparatory School*)
Mr P Gilchrist, BSc (*Director of Sport*)
Miss R Green, BSc (*Preparatory School*)
Mr A Grewcock (*Graduate Sports Assistant*)
Mrs G Hadley, BA, DipEd SEN (*Learning Support, Careers Coordinator**)
Mrs L Harland, BSc (*Specialist Teaching Assistant, Mathematics*)
Mr G Higham, BSc (*Mathematics**)
Miss C Jeyes, NNEB (*Early Years Practitioner*)
Mr D Jones, BMus (*Assistant Director of Music*)
Mr M Jones, BSc (*Information and Communication Technology**) (*from Jan 2014*)
Mr K Kaye, BA (*Physical Education*)
Miss J Kearns, BA (*Deputy Head Preparatory School*)
Mr A Kellinghan, BA, MA (*Religious Studies*)
Miss K Kulisa (*Graduate Music Assistant*)
Mr M Lambert, BSc (*Geography**)
Miss N Langton, BA (*Early Years Practitioner*)
Dr C Latham, BSc, MSc, PhD (*Learning Support*)
Mrs J Leite, BA (*Learning Support – Preparatory School, Senior Housemistress – Girls' Boarding*)
Miss C Llewelyn, BA (*Preparatory School*)
Mrs F Lodder, BA, MA (*History*)
Mrs M Markham, BA (*Preparatory School*)
Mr E McCall, BMus, MMus (*Director of Music**)
Mr P McCrindell, BA (*Head of Year 10, German*)
Mr P Michel, BA (*Lay Chaplain*)
Miss J Monk, BA (*Drama*)
Miss J Mudge (*Graduate Sports Assistant*)
Mrs S Neuberg, BA (*Nursery School*)
Mr M Newman BA (*History*)
Mrs Y O'Connor, BA, MEd (*Religious Studies*)
Miss C Papadopoulou, BSc, MSc (*Geography, Sports Coach, Boarding Assistant, Careers Coordinator*)
Miss L Prentice (*Graduate Sports Assistant*)
Mrs J Reddin, BA (*French*)
Mrs M Reeves, BA, MSc (*EAL, English*)
Mr A Seth, BSc (*Design and Technology**)
Mr M Simon (*German Language Assistant*)
Mr M Sleath, BSc (*Head of Year 13, Mathematics*)
Mrs H Smith, BSc (*Mathematics*)
Mrs P Smith, BA (*Religious Studies*)
Mr P Spencer, ACIB (*Business/Economics**)
Miss T Spencer, BA (*Business/Economics*)
Miss A Stafford, BSc (*Girls' PE and Games*)

Dr L Stannard, BA, MA, PhD (*English*)
Dr S Standen, BSc, PhD (*Head of Year 8, Science*)
Mr A Suplice (*French Language Assistant*)
Mrs A Taylor, BEd (*PSHCE*, Academic PE**)
Mr L Taylor, BA, MA (*History*)
Mr N Taylor, BEd (*Head of Year 12, Physical Education, History*)
Miss E Thompson, BA (*English*)
Mr S Thorpe, BSc (*Head of Year 7, Science*)
Mr P Trotter, CChem, MRSC (*Science*)
Mr D Turner, BEd (*Preparatory School, Assistant Boys' Housemaster*)
Mrs E Walker, BA (*Preparatory School*)
Mr N Walsh, LLB (*Religious Studies**)
Mr T Walsh, BA, MPhil (*Classics**)
Mrs E Waters, BEd (*Learning Support*)
Miss F Watson, BA (*Preparatory School*)
Mrs L Whieldon, BA (*English*)
Mrs H Wilde, BA (*Design Technology*)
Mrs M Williams, BA (*Librarian*)
Mr E Woodcock, BA, MSc (*Head of Year 9, Physical Education*)
Mrs S Worsnop, BSc (*Mathematics*)
Mrs E Worthington, BA (*English**)
Miss A Wright, BA (*Art & Design*)

Medical Officer: Dr T Jennings

Senior Nursing Sisters:
Mrs D Warburton, RGN
Miss S Plant, RGN

Age Range. 3–18.

Number of Pupils. 770: 354 girls, 416 boys. Sixth Form 143; Boarders 93.

Aims. The vision of the College is to educate young people in the spirit of the Gospel and the traditions of the Catholic Church, seeking to nurture the God-given talents and potential of each individual, so that each one may become a confident, responsible and useful member of society. Whilst Ratcliffe is a Catholic school, it welcomes children of other denominations and faiths, whose parents feel they can share in and benefit from the School's ideals and environment.

Location. Ratcliffe College is set in over 200 acres of rolling parkland on the A46, seven miles north of Leicester. It is easily accessible by road and benefits from being free of congestion at peak times. The M1/M6 motorways, main line railway stations and airports of Birmingham and East Midlands are all within easy travelling distance. For day pupils, school buses operate daily from Leicester, Loughborough and Nottingham.

Site and Buildings. The main Senior School buildings surround a quadrangle and contain the Administration offices, Church, Refectory, Library, Medical Centre, Computer Rooms and Common Rooms, together with a number of subject departmental areas. In addition, there is a Music Department with Concert Hall; a fully-appointed Theatre; and a Science Centre with additional classrooms for Food Technology. Sporting facilities include extensive playing fields and a floodlit all-weather hockey pitch; the state-of-the-art Sports Centre comprises sports changing rooms, swimming pool and sports hall with a modern fitness suite. A complex of recently refurbished buildings nearby provides departmental bases for Geography, Modern Languages and Mathematics. Modernised Boys' and Girls' boarding accommodation is situated on the upper floor of the main building, in separate wings, with individual study bedrooms for older students.

The Rosmini Sixth Form Centre, named after Blessed Antonio Rosmini, the founder of the Rosminian Order, opened for use by students and staff in January 2007. With an upper floor wholly dedicated to independent academic study with full IT accessibility, and ground floor areas providing for social and extra-curricular usage, the Centre provides a flagship modern setting for Sixth Formers.

In September 2014, the College invested £4.5 million opening a brand new purpose-built Preparatory School building on the school site. The new Preparatory School has twelve classrooms located over two floors, as well as a dedicated technology and languages centre, science and food technology laboratory, library, central assembly hall and music room for the young pupils. It has been developed to be sympathetic to the original school building, opened in 1847, which itself was designed by the famous architect of the Houses of Parliament, Augustus Pugin.

The Nursery is located nearby in purpose-built accommodation also on the campus.

Organisation. The College is divided into 2 sections: Senior School (11–18 year olds) and Preparatory School (3–11 year olds including the Nursery for 3–5 year olds). The sections are closely integrated, allowing continuity of education from 3 to 18. Boarding girls and boys are accommodated in separate wings within the main Senior School building, under the supervision of the resident Senior Housemistress and Housemaster, together with their Assistants. There is a strong emphasis on pastoral care for all pupils. The teacher:pupil ratio in the Senior School is 1:10 (the ratio in the Sixth Form is much lower).

Curriculum. In the Nursery, the emphasis is on early Literacy, Numeracy and the development of personal and social skills, all of which contribute to a child's knowledge, understanding and skills in other areas of learning. Programmes of study are based on the Early Years Foundation Stage Curriculum, but extend well beyond these guidelines to develop a child's interests, talents, outlook and general knowledge and understanding of the world.

The Preparatory School offers small class sizes, well-resourced classrooms, a clear focus on the National Curriculum, an extended school day and a varied extra-curricular activities programme. The curriculum is broad and balanced including extensive provision for Drama, Music, Modern Foreign Languages, Physical Education and Latin, taught by specialist teachers. Each classroom has the most up-to-date teaching and learning resources, with specialist classrooms for Art, Music, Science, Food Technology, ICT and Performing Arts. As the children move into Year 6, approximately half their timetable is taught by Senior specialists. This enables the highest academic standards at the end of Key Stage 2, which means that all pupils move very happily into Year 7.

In the Senior School a broad and balanced curriculum is followed, which aims to identify and provide for individual needs. Most students take at least nine GCSEs. All students study a core of subjects consisting of English (Language and Literature), Mathematics, Religious Studies, a Modern Foreign Language and Science (Core and Additional or Triple Award). This is augmented by up to three further option subjects. In the Sixth Form, most students choose 4 AS Levels in Year 12 and 3 A2 Levels in Year 13. In addition to A Level work, students take a complementary studies course, which incorporates a general studies programme including preparation for university and careers guidance, study skills and moral and ethical studies.

Games. The playing fields, which surround the College buildings, cover over 200 acres. All pupils participate in Games, including Cricket, Hockey, Rugby, Football, Tennis and Athletics for boys, and Hockey, Netball, Rounders, Tennis and Athletics for girls.

Extra-Curricular Activities. Pupils' talents and interests are developed through an extensive programme of activities on weekdays and at weekends. As well as many sporting opportunities, 25% of pupils learn a musical instrument; there are many musical groups, including brass ensemble, orchestra and choirs; all Year 4 pupils have free year-round orchestral instrumental tuition. Many pupils are involved in school productions and film-making, and other media activities are popular. The Combined Cadet Force and the Duke of Edinburgh's Award Scheme both flourish. Pupils are encouraged to be caring and to have consideration for others through Chaplaincy groups and Voluntary Service activities.

Admissions.

Nursery: Entry is by school report (if applicable) and informal assessment.

Preparatory School: Entry is by school report and entrance examinations (papers in English and Mathematics) for entry to all years. The entrance examination to Years 5 and 6 also has a Non-Verbal Reasoning paper.

Senior School: Entry is normally at 11+, 12+, 13+ and 14+. Entry is normally by school report and successful performance in the entrance examinations (papers in English, Mathematics and Non-Verbal Reasoning).

Sixth Form: Entrance examinations may be set, depending on the applicant's educational background and the A Level subjects he/she wishes to study in the Sixth Form. Overseas applicants are usually required to take an English test. In general, applicants will be interviewed and entry will also be based on successful performance in GCSE (or equivalent examinations). Applicants should obtain at least six GCSE passes at B grade or better including English and Mathematics. For any subject to be studied in the Sixth Form, the student should have at least GCSE grade B in that subject (or, for subjects not taken at GCSE, at least grade B in related GCSE subjects). However, a GCSE grade A or above is required in order to study English, the Sciences, Languages or Mathematics.

Scholarships and Bursaries. Ratcliffe College offers a wide range of scholarships to recognise academic, sporting, musical, dramatic and artistic talent amongst applicants for the Senior School.

Each scholarship is worth £1,000. Points at which scholarships are offered are Years 7, 9 and 12.

Academic scholarships are retained until the end of Year 11, providing the student continues to show the attributes of a scholar. All students wishing to hold scholarships in the Sixth Form must meet the criteria for Sixth Form Academic Scholarships, based on their GCSE performance.

Talent scholarships (sport, music, drama, art & design), with associated auditions and tests held in the January prior to the year of entry (just after the academic entrance examinations), are conditional upon meeting our academic expectations for entry into the School and are retained until the end of Year 13, providing the student continues to show the attributes of a scholar in the relevant discipline.

Year 7 Scholarships: Three Academic; One boys' Sports; One girls' Sports; One Music (The Henry Goldstraw / Gerald Yell Scholarship); One Art & Design.

Year 9 Scholarships: Three Academic; One boys' Sports; One girls' Sports; One Music (The Henry Goldstraw / Gerald Yell); One Drama.

Year 12 Scholarships: 10 Academic linked to strong performance at GCSE; One boys' Sports; One girls' Sports.

A small number of additional awards are available at the Headmaster's discretion.

A limited number of Bursaries are available, generally on entry to Year 7. Sixth Form Talent Bursaries are also available in Sport, Music, Drama, Art and Design.

For further details, please contact the Registrar.

Fees per term (2014–2015). UK Students: Full Boarding (Years 6–13) £7,730; Weekly Boarding (Years 9–13) £6,891; Weekly Boarding (Years 6–8) £6,157. Boarding fees include the full cost of the programme of boarding weekend trips throughout the year.

Overseas Students: Full Boarding £8,748. Boarding fees include the full cost of the programme of boarding weekend trips throughout the year. Boarding fees include the cost of additional teaching of English as a Foreign Language with a minimum of 10 one-hour sessions per term.

Day: £2,742–£3,080 (Nursery aged 3–5); £3,094–£3,562 (Years 1–5); £4,033–£4,955 (Years 6–13).

Fees are subject to such termly increase as may prove necessary. Additional charges are made for: private Music lessons at £210 per term for 10 half-hour sessions (for individual tuition for each instrument); Where additional teaching of Learning Skills is required and agreed with parents, this will be charged at £40 per lesson. There is a non-refundable registration fee of £75 (£100 overseas) and a deposit (refundable on leaving school) of £500 for UK students and £1,000 for students from overseas.

Charitable status. Ratcliffe College is a Registered Charity, number 1115975, for the education of children.

Reading Blue Coat School

Holme Park, Sonning, Berks RG4 6SU
Tel: 0118 944 1005
Fax: 0118 944 2690
email: reception@rbcs.org.uk
website: www.rbcs.org.uk

The School was founded in 1646 by Richard Aldworth, a merchant of London and Reading, and a Governor of Christ's Hospital. There are 742 pupils (aged 11–18) including a co-educational Sixth Form.

Chairman of Governors: P Bertram

Headmaster: M J Windsor, BA Hons, MA, PGCE (*German*)

Second Master: R S Slatford, MA, CertEd, BSc Hons (*Geology*)

Deputy Head, Staff: Mrs A J Bawden, BA Hons, PGCE (*Geography*)

Deputy Head, Academic: P C K Rowe, MEd, MA, PGCE (*History, Government & Politics*)

Deputy Head, Pastoral: P D Wise, BSc Hons, PGCE (*Geography*)

Bursar: S A Jackson, BSc, MBA

* *Head of Department*

J C Allen, BA Hons, PGCE (**English*)
Mrs K M Anderson, BA, PGCE (*English*)
M J Baker, BA Hons, PGCE (**Geography*)
Mrs C E Bamforth, MA, PGCE (*Biology*)
Mrs K E Bayliss, BA (**Economics*)
Mrs L J Bennett, BEd Hons (*Religious Studies*)
Mrs S E Berry, BA, PGCE, Dip SpLD, AMBDA (**Learning Support, French*)
J Bowler, BA Hons, PGCE, LTCL, ARCM (**Director of Music, Performance Studies/Drama*)
J P Brown, BSc, PGCE (*Chemistry*)
M Brownsell, BSc, MBA (*Physics*)
Mrs N E Bruce-Lockhart, BA Hons, PGCE (*English*)
Dr A Burns, MEd, BA Hons, PGCE, MSc, PhD (**Government and Politics, History*)
Miss E Burrowes, BA Hons (*English, Music, Performance Studies/Drama*)
Mrs M A Clews, BA, PGCE, PG Cert (**Psychology*)
Mrs J A Coates, BSc, PGCE (*Chemistry*)
S J Cook, CertEd, BA (**Physical Education*)
D N Cottrell, CertEd (*Geography, Sport & Physical Education*)
Mrs R L Crossland, MESci, PGCE (*Geology*)
M Crouchman, BSc (*Psychology*)
Mrs C Dance, BA Ed Hons (*Girls' Games*)
Mrs A M Dewar, BA Hons, PGCE (*French, German, Spanish*)
Dr S M Dimmick, BSc, DipEd, MSc, PhD (**Biology*)
R G Edmondson, BSc, BSc (*Geography*)

R N Ennis, BA, PGCE (*Art*)
Miss N Evans, BA Hons, PGCE (**Classics*)
J M Fenton, BA, PGCE (**Religious Studies*)
Mrs J L Forward, BSc (*Mathematics, Physics*)
R W Gallimore, MA, BA, PGCE (*History*)
Mrs S A Head, MA (**Modern Foreign Languages, German, French*)
Miss C A Holliday, BA, PGCE (*German, French*)
Miss J Hope, BSc Hons, PGCE (**Geology*)
M J Jerstice, BSc, PGCE (**Integrated Science, Chemistry*)
Mrs G M Kelly, BA Hons, PGCE (*Religious Studies*)
Mrs R Kennedy-George, MA, MPhil, PGCE (*English*)
J Leigh, BA, MA (*History*)
A J Maddocks, BA (**French, German*)
Mrs A W Magee, BA, BA, PGCE (*English*)
Dr K J Magill, MPhil, BA, PGCE, PhD (*Religious Studies*)
N T P Matenga, BPhysEd, PG Dip Teaching (*Sport & Physical Education*)
Ms R L McAuley, BA Hons (*Psychology*)
S McCluskey, BSc Hons, PGCE (*Biology*)
Mrs T A McConalogue, BEd (*Mathematics*)
S R McFaul, MEng (*Mathematics, Physics*)
H J McGough, BSc Hons (**Design Technology*)
Mrs I A McGough, BA, PGCE (*Design Technology*)
A G McMahon, BMus, LTCL (*Music Technology*)
W E Mitchell, BA, PGCE (*Geography*)
G E Morton, BA Hons, PGCE (*English*)
Mrs C J Munro, MA, PGCE (*History*)
S W Nichol, BS, BEd (*Mathematics*)
Mrs H J Oliver, BA Hons, PGCE (*French*)
Mrs H E Rancombe, BSc Hons, PGCE (**Psychology, Biology*)
S R Roberts, BSc, PGCE (*Mathematics*)
Mrs C Rule, BA Hons, OCR SpLD Diploma (*Learning Support*)
S W Sadler, BA Hons (*English, *Drama*)
D L Salmon, MA, Computing Dip, PGCE (**Physics*)
Dr F B Santos, BSc, MSc, PhD (*Chemistry*)
D H R Selvester, BA, PGCE (*Design Technology*)
R I Shuttleworth, BSc Hons, PGCE (**Mathematics*)
J R Slack, BSc, PGCE (*Mathematics, *Careers*)
Mrs J P Smith, BSc, PGCE (*Physics*)
R P Starr, BA Hons, PGCE (*Spanish, French*)
Miss B A Truman, BA, PGCE (*English, French*)
G C Turner, BSc Hons, PGCE (*Sport & Physical Education*)
Mrs J M Turton, BSc, PGCE (**Chemistry*)
Miss T van der Werff, MA, PGCE (**History*)
W Voice, BA Hons, PGCE (*Information Technology, *Sport*)
T C Walford, BSc, PGCE (*Information Technology*)
R J Wallis, BA, PGCE (**Art*)
N J Warde, BSc, PGCE (*Biology*)
Mrs N Watmough-Starkie, BMus Hons, PGCE (*Assistant Director of Music*)
S Yates, BSc Hons, PGCE (**Information Technology*)
R W Yue, MSc, BSc, PGCE (*Mathematics*)
Mrs J F Zambon, BA Hons, PGCE (**Spanish*)

Headmaster's Secretary: Mrs L A Bell
Director of Admissions and Marketing: Mrs J Jarrett
School Nurse: Mrs G F Montgomery, RGN
Sports Centre Manager: C Bate
Archivist: P J van Went, MA, CertEd

Aims. The School aims to provide a stimulating and friendly atmosphere in which each pupil can realise his or her full intellectual, physical and creative potential. Pupils are encouraged to be self-reliant and adaptable and we hope that they will learn the basis of good citizenship founded on honesty, fairness and understanding of the needs of others.

Our School is a Church of England Foundation, and emphasis is placed on Christian values and standards.

Buildings. The School is set in an attractive 46-acre site by the banks of the Thames in the village of Sonning. School House, originally built in the eighteenth century and extensively remodelled in the Victorian era, stands at the heart of the School. The School's facilities have undergone a continuous programme of improvement over the last decade, including the construction of a new Science Centre and a Sports Hall complex, including a dining hall and kitchens. Recent developments include a new geology and psychology block, a new 23-classroom teaching facility, a new cricket pavilion, improvements to the swimming pool and a new boathouse on the banks of the Thames. The School has recently expanded its facilities for the Sixth Form and has ambitious plans for further development.

Curriculum. In Years 7 to 9, pupils study a broad range of subjects, including Classics, two modern foreign languages and Religious Studies. In Years 10 and 11, pupils follow IGCSE courses in Mathematics and Science and also opt to complete four further courses in a wide range of additional subjects, such as History, Geography (IGCSE), Geology and Physical Education, with a modern foreign language being compulsory. A wide range of subjects is offered at AS and A2 Level, including subjects such as Psychology, Government and Politics, and Performance Studies, with nearly every pupil going on to university, including Oxford and Cambridge.

Sixth Form. The co-educational Sixth Form Centre accommodates more than 250 students. Girls are fully integrated into all activities. In addition to A Level courses, all Sixth Formers follow a compulsory enrichment programme.

Games and Activities. A wide range of sports and activities is offered within the curriculum and regular school fixtures for all year groups are arranged. Full advantage is taken of the River Thames and rowing is a popular sport for both boys and girls. The main boys' games are Rugby in the Autumn Term, Football in the Spring Term, and Cricket and Athletics in the Summer Term. Girls play Netball, Rounders and Hockey. Other sporting activities include Squash, Basketball, Tennis, Golf, Table Tennis, Climbing, Swimming, Scuba Diving, Lacrosse, American Football and Sailing.

The Cadet Force is voluntary with Army, RAF and RN Sections. Camping and adventure training activities take place during holidays and at weekends. There is a wide range in the Activities Programme, which includes the Duke of Edinburgh's Award, overseas expeditions, community service and sports leadership.

Music and Drama enjoy a high profile in the life of the School. Well over a third of the pupils receive individual instrumental lessons and pupils are encouraged to join in activities such as the Choir, Orchestra, Wind Band, Brass Group, Jazz and Swing Bands. Concerts, plays and musicals are presented regularly.

Admissions. The two main points of entry in September are at 11+ and 16+. 11+ entry is by entrance examination taken the previous January. Entry at other levels is by examination and interview and is subject to vacancies. Entry to the Sixth Form for girls and boys is by assessment, interview and GCSE results.

The Foundation makes provision for awards of scholarships and bursaries, including academic, music and art awards, based on merit and need. Foundation Scholarships up to 100% of fees are available according to financial need.

Fees per term (2014–2015). £4,860.

Charitable status. The Reading Blue Coat School is a Registered Charity, number 1087839. Its aim is the provision of secondary education for pupils aged 11 to 18.

Reed's School

Cobham, Surrey KT11 2ES
Tel: 01932 869001
Fax: 01932 869046
email: admissions@reeds.surrey.sch.uk
website: www.reeds.surrey.sch.uk

Reed's is a boarding and day school for boys with girls in the Sixth Form, founded by Andrew Reed in 1813 and incorporated by Act of Parliament in 1845 under the presidency of the Archbishop of Canterbury, the Duke of Wellington and the Marquis of Salisbury. When the School was founded, its facilities were reserved for boys whose fathers had died. In 1958 the School expanded and all boys became eligible for entrance. Sixth Form girls became eligible for entrance in the 1980s. Foundation awards are still granted each year to boys and Sixth Form girls who have lost the support of one or both parents.

Patron: Her Majesty The Queen

Presidents:
Viscount Bridgeman
P B Mitford-Slade, OBE
G M Nissen, CBE

Governors:
I Plenderleith, CBE (*Chairman*)

Mrs I M Barker
U D Barnett
D R Blomfield, BSc
D H A C Caddy, FCA
M A Grenier, MA
Dr A M McLean, MB, BChir, FRCP, FRCR
Mrs L F Napier, FSI
Mrs A F Noakes
Ms B O'Brien-Twohig, MA
T D Page, MA
S T Poole, MSc
H M Priestley, MA Oxon
P D Reed
Miss K Richardson, MA
M Robinson, BA Arch, Grad Dip RIBA
Prof P Sellin, BSc, PhD, MInSEP, CPhys, IEEE
R Stewart, FCIB
N D Taunt, FCA
P H H Verstage, BCom Hons
M Wheeler, BCom, FCA

Bursar & Secretary to the Governors: Mrs L Hurford, BSc, ACMA

Headmaster: M W Hoskins, BA, MA

Deputy Headmaster: G D Spawforth, MA
Senior Master: P R Kemp, BA
Development Director: R M Garrett, BA
Director of Studies: D J Atkins, BA
Senior Housemaster: †A R Balls, BEd
Director of Sport & Activities: I A Clapp, BEd
Senior Mistress: Mrs J G Hart, BA (*Psychology*)
Director of Teaching and Learning: Ms C F St Gallay, BA
Head of Sixth Form: †L G Michael, BA (*Media Studies*)
Chaplain: The Revd A J Clarke, MA

Assistant Staff:
* *Head of Department*
† *Housemaster*

J Allison, BSc
Ms L Ashby, BA (*Spanish*)
Dr L B Askew, PhD
Mrs L Balls, BA (*Girls' Sport*)
†A J Blackman, MA
S M Bramwell, BA (*Modern Languages*)
Ms J A Brewster, BSc (*Chemistry*)
Mrs S E Butler, MA (*Academic Music*)
I B Carnegie, MA (*Director of Music*)
J E Clatworthy, MA
C E Cole, BA (*Printing*)

Mrs C C Cook, BA
A J Davey, BA
P P Davies, MA
A P Doyle, BSc
Miss Z Davison, BA
J K Ditchburn, BA
J B Douthwaite, BA
M R Dunn, HND
B J Edwards, BA (*Physical Education*)
Ms M Fitzgerald, BA (*Librarian*)
Mrs M Francis, BA
Mrs E Goswell, BEd
†B J Haining, BSc
R A Harper, BSc
Mrs R F Harris, MA
T A Harrison, MSc (*Mathematics*)
†G S Hart, HEd
Dr J D Hartley, EdD
Ms S M Hashmi-Lewis, BSc
C J Hawley, BA
W J Howell, BA
P Jenkins, LRCM
Miss A M Jiménez, BA
Miss A N Johnson, MA (*Art*)
W A Jolly, BSc
Mrs D L Kane, BSc
Mrs C A Kemp, BA
Mrs K A Lambert, BSc
Mrs J A Lawrence, BA
Mrs S L Leslie, BA
Ms E McGhee, BA (*Learning Support*)
K T Medlycott
P L Millington, BSc (*Design Technology*)
Mrs T A Millington, BEd (*Religious Studies*)
Miss K Morland, MA (*Classics*)
†J W Norman, BA
C J Osgood, MA
A R Pascoots
Mrs L Paterson, BSc (*Biology*)
Mrs E Peyton, BSc
†L Pytel, BA
Miss M K Rai, BSc
T J Rimmer, BSc
J S Ross, MA (*Geography*)
T C Rushbrooke, BA (*Computing*)
Mrs H T Salford, BA (*French*)
C Sandison-Smith, MA (*German*)
T P Silk, BA (*Media Studies, *Drama*)
Mrs R L Sullivan, BA
A R Talbot, BEd
Mrs Z Tan, BA
D Thompson, BSc (*Physics, *Science*)
C S Thomson, BA
Mrs A Trehearn, BA (*English*)
M C Vernon, BSc
D W R Wakefield, BSc
Mrs V Wakefield, BSc
A J Waller, BA (*History*)
J M Wallis, MEng
Miss H J Watson, BA
T A Webb, BA
S D Whiteley, BA (*Economics & Business Studies*)
R D Willey, GLCM
Ms L Woods, BA
J Wright, BSc

Visiting Music Teachers:

J Dalgleish (*Piano*)
G Duggar (*Cello*)
J Dunning (*Guitar*)
K Garrett (*Jazz Piano*)
D Hawkins (*Guitar*)
J Jaggard (*Oboe*)
H Morgan (*Clarinet, Saxophone*)
E Spevok (*Drums*)
J Fryer (*Saxophone*)
P Von Wielligh (*Flute*)
D Deam (*Singing*)

G Sutton (*Violin, Viola*)
A Marshallsay (*Percussion*)
P Tebb (*Singing*)
H Salmon (*Violin*)
S Rommer (*Double Bass*)

C Marroni (*Bassoon*)
S James (*Guitar*)
R Willey (*Trombone*)
C Osgood (*Piano, Organ*)
C Todd (*Trumpet*)

Headmaster's Secretary: Mrs A Gregg
Registrar: R M Gilliat, MA
Admissions Secretary: Mrs P F Gilliat
Medical Officer: R Draper, MBChB, DCH, DRCOG, DA, MRCGP

The School is situated near Esher in 40 acres of heath and woodland. It can be reached in 30 minutes by train from Waterloo and is within half an hour's drive of both Heathrow and Gatwick Airports.

To the original buildings have been added in the last 15 years a Sixth Form House; Chemistry laboratories; four Computer suites; two artificial turf hockey pitches; a new library; a new teaching block for the Physics and Mathematics departments; a Music School; an Indoor Tennis Centre; new Biology, Geography and History departments; extensions to the Day Pupil Centre and an extension to the Sixth Form House which incorporates a lecture theatre; a new Language laboratory and new Language and English classrooms; a new Design and Technology building (FutureTech).

There are 658 pupils, just under 20% of whom are boarders, divided among 5 senior houses, Blathwayt, Bristowe, Capel, Mullens and School House, and one junior house, the Close, for those under 13. There is also a separate Sixth Form House. Admission at the age of 13 is normally by the Common Entrance examination, with a pre-test in Year 6; admission at the age of 11 or 12 is by means of the School's own examination, normally taken at the School. There is admission into the Sixth Form for boys and girls.

Pupils are prepared for GCSE and GCE, AS and A Levels, and virtually 100% of Upper Sixth leavers go on to good universities. The games are Rugby, Cricket, Hockey, Athletics, Tennis, Swimming, Skiing, Squash, Golf, Netball and Basketball. The School has its own Combined Cadet Force with RAF and Army sections. The Duke of Edinburgh's Award can also be undertaken at Bronze, Silver and Gold levels. Special scholarships may be awarded for tennis, skiing and golf.

Pupils are all involved in a wide-ranging Activities Curriculum. There is also a broad range of Inter-House competitions. There is a School Choral Society, a Chapel Choir, an Orchestra, a Jazz Orchestra and various ensembles.

Religious instruction, which promotes religious tolerance, is in accordance with the principles of the Church of England. An annual Confirmation Service is held in the School Chapel for which pupils are prepared by the Chaplain. Pupils of all denominations are accepted into the School and are expected to attend chapel.

The National Curriculum is broadly followed in Years 7 to 9 and early specialisation is avoided. There is a Careers Team which advises pupils and arranges suitable visits and interviews and gives advice on University degree courses. The main responsibility for each pupil is undertaken by his or her Housemaster, supported by a Tutor. The health of the pupils is in the care of the School Doctor, and a State Registered Nurse is in charge of the Medical Centre.

Fees per term (2014–2015). Day Pupils (including meals): £5,850 (Years 7 & 8), £7,315 (Years 9–13). Boarders: £7,800 (Years 7 & 8), £9,680 (Years 9–13). All boarders may exercise a weekly boarding option. There are no compulsory extras.

Scholarships and Bursaries. Academic Scholarships are offered each year at age 11, 13 and 16. The maximum value of any award given for exceptional performance is half fees per annum.

Scholarships may be awarded for Music, Drama, Art and Sport at age 11, 13 or 16. Design & Technology scholarships are available at age 13 or 16. All-Rounder scholarships are available to applicants who offer a high performance in more than one area.

A large number of Foundation awards are made each year to boys and girls who have lost one or both parents, or whose parents are divorced or separated or whose home life is for some special reason either unhappy or unsatisfactory. The awards, which are means tested, vary according to circumstances.

All applications should be made to the Registrar.

Charitable status. The London Orphan Asylum (Reed's School) is a Registered Charity, number 312008. Its aims and objectives are to provide an education for pupils who have lost the support of one or both parents.

Reigate Grammar School

Reigate Road, Reigate, Surrey RH2 0QS
Tel: 01737 222231
Fax: 01737 224201
email: info@reigategrammar.org
            admissions@reigategrammar.org
website: www.reigategrammar.org
Twitter: @ReigateGrammar
Facebook: /ReigateGrammarSchool

Governing Body:
Chairman: Mr A Walker
Vice-Chairmen: Sir Colin Chandler, Mrs J Langham

Mr D Adams
Mr C Cobain
Mr J Dean
Mr W Dunnet
Mr E Elsey
Mrs E Fieldhouse

Mrs J Forbat
Mr L Herbert
Dr K Knapp
Mr T Morgan
Mrs J Oliphant
Professor S Sayce

Headmaster: S A Fenton, MA Oxford, MEd Oxford

Senior Deputy Head: Mrs M A Collins, BEng Bristol (*Physics*)
Deputy Head: Miss S J Arthur, BA Durham (*History*)
Assistant Head: Miss V Godbold, BA Hull (*Geography*)
Assistant Head: S J Rushby, BMus Surrey (*Director of Music*)
Head of Sixth Form: H T Jones, BA Durham, MSt Oxford (*History*)
Head of Upper School: P G Stephens, BSc Aberystwyth (*Biology*)
Head of Lower School: Mrs C Lawson, BA Liverpool (*Classics*)
Head of Upper Sixth: H T Jones, BA Durham, MSt Oxford (*History*)
Head of Lower Sixth: R T James, BSc Bristol (*Geography*)
Head of Fifth Form: N M Buchanan, BSc Edinburgh (*Chemistry*)
Head of Fourth Form: Mrs K Scaglione, BA Keele (*English*)
Head of Third Form: N J Lobb, BA Bretton Hall (*Music*)
Head of Second Form: Mrs E Bader, BEd Worcester College (*Food Technology*)
Head of First Form: M H Hetherington, BA Nottingham (*Mathematics*)
Chaplain: P J R Chesterton, BA OU, CertEd St Luke's
Bursar & Clerk to the Governors: S P Douty, FCMA
Development Director: S Davey, BSc, MA, MInstF Cert

Heads of House:
Bird: J M Aiken, BA Leeds (*History*)
Cranston: M S Russell, BEd Bulmershe (*Mathematics*)
Hodgson: Dr L Goldsmith, MA, PhD Royal Holloway (*History, Politics*)

Williamson: †Mrs C L Cline, BSc St Mary's College (*Geography, Girls' PE & Games*)

Assistant Staff:
* *Head of Department*
§ *Part-time*

Miss R J Aczel, BA Cambridge, MLitt Aberdeen (*Classics*)
J M Aiken, BA Leeds (*History*)
R D Appleton, BA Durham (*Spanish*)
Miss K L Attwood, MA St Andrews (*English*)
D G Bader, BSc Bath(*Mathematics*)
Miss S Branston, BA Wales (*Drama)
N Buchanan, BSc Edinburgh (*Chemistry*)
Mrs E Burns, BA Canterbury (**Art & Design*)
M J Buzzacott, BA Durham (*Classics, *Careers*)
Mr W Byfield, BSc Bath (*Biology, Chemistry*)
Dr T J Carter, MPhys Oxford, PhD London (*Physics*)
†Mrs B Channon, Dip Foreign Languages for Business (*Learning Support Assistant*)
Mrs L Charlesworth, MA Oxford (*Teaching Assistant*)
Mme F Chartrain, MA Nantes (**French, *Modern Languages*)
S T Chevalier, MA Oxford (*English)
Ms S Clarke, MA Sussex (*English, *Learning Support*)
Mrs C L Cline, BSc St Mary's College (*Girls' Games, Geography*)
M G Cline, BA Southampton (*Geography)
Mrs B F Collett, MA Universite d'Aix-en-Provence (*French, Spanish*)
S A Collins, BA Durham (**Outdoor Training, Geography*)
D Cooper, BA Exeter (**PE, Sport Studies*)
Miss G Cooper, BSc Exeter (*Physics*)
Mrs A Crook, BSc Edinburgh MSc Bristol (*Mathematics)
R S Crook, BSc Southampton (*Chemistry)
T S Dare, MA, MSc Cambridge, Sussex (*Biology)
†Mrs A J Davies, BEd Brighton Polytechnic (*Girls' PE & Games*)
A R Davies, BSc Bristol (*Mathematics*)
Mrs G C Dexter, BA Queen's Belfast, Cert SpLD (*Geography, Learning Support*)
Mrs R S Ellen, BA Brighton (*Art, Design & Technology*)
W H Edwards, BA Staffordshire Polytechnic (*Art & Design*)
Mrs A R Fenton, BA Leicester Polytechnic (*Food Technology*)
†J Fielder, BEd Sussex (*Music*)
Mrs S M Garcia, BSc Queen's Ontario, BEd Kingston (*Physics*)
Mrs E L Gatzanis, Educare N6 Cape College
Mrs S J T Genillard, ATC Goldsmiths (*Art & Design*)
†Mrs T J Glynne-Jones, GRRNCM RNCM (*Choral Music*)
Dr L Goldsmith, MA, PhD Royal Holloway (*History, Politics*)
Mrs F Grant, BEd Bulmershe College (*Mathematics*)
Miss C Green, BA East Anglia (*History, Politics*)
Mrs F A Gunning, MA Oxford (**History, *Politics*)
M D Hallpike, CertEd Crewe & Alsager (*Design & Technology*)
Miss K S Hancock, BSc Bath, MEd OU (*Mathematics*)
Miss M G Hare, BA Guildford School of Acting (*Drama*)
R Hare, BMus Royal Academy of Music (*Music*)
P W Harrison, BSc Loughborough (*Geography*)
E R Hogarth, BA Lancaster, MA Exeter (*Religion & Philosophy*)
M H Hetherington, BA Nottingham (*Mathematics*)
Mrs K Holbrook-Wilson, BA Rand Afrikaans, South Africa (*English*)
Mrs C M Hosegood, BSc Bristol (*Biology*)
Mrs M E Hurriaga, MEd Cambridge (**Spanish, German*)
H G Ingham, BA, MA Oxford (*Classics*)
D A Jackson, BA Middlesex (*Drama*)
A N Johnston, BA Bristol (*Chemistry*)
Mrs C J Jones, BA Durham (*English, *Academic PE*)

P C Klein, BSc Cheltenham & Gloucester College (*Geography*)
†Dr S L Lawson, BSc, PhD Plymouth (*Biology*)
A Lewis, BA Aberystwyth (*ICT, Business Studies*)
N Lobb, BA Bretton Hall (*Music*)
P Mann, BSc Loughborough (*Director of Sport*)
Miss R L Mansfield, BA Southampton Institute (*Art & Design*)
Mrs K Mason, BA York (*Business Studies, Economics*)
Mrs A McConnell, BSc Durham (*Biology & Chemistry*)
Mrs E J Mitchell, BEd Exeter (*Head of Academic PE*)
L W Morgan, BA MA Cardiff (*History, Communications & E-Learning*)
N Newman, BA Newcastle (**Business Studies, *Economics*)
Mrs S M Newton, BA Royal Holloway (*Drama*)
C S Nicholson, BSc Loughborough (*Head of Boys Hockey*)
†Mrs C J Peats, BA Nottingham (*History, Economics*)
Miss K Penman, BA Leeds, MA Durham (**Religion & Philosophy*)
Miss M L Pope, BA MSc Cambridge, MA Sussex (*Biology & Chemistry*)
A A Powell, BD, AKC London (*Religion & Philosophy*)
Mrs D Pricopie, BA, BSc Romania (*Physics*)
Miss L Purvis, BA Newcastle (*English*)
†Mrs V Ramsden, MSc Nottingham (*Geography, Religion & Philosophy*)
A G Reid, BSc London (*Physics, Project Coordinator*)
†A K Reid, BEd St Luke's College, Exeter (*Boys' Games*)
H Robinson, BA Manchester (*English*)
P I Rollitt, BSc, MSc London (*Mathematics*)
S J Rushby, BMus Surrey (*Music)
M R Russell, BEd Bulmershe (*Mathematics*)
P A Saunders, BEng Southampton (**Physics, Electronics*)
Mrs K Scaglione, BA Keele (*English*)
J M Sergeant, BSc King's College London (*Chemistry, *Examinations*)
†Mrs A Sharp, BSc Sussex (*Mathematics*)
R P Shaughnessy, BA Leeds (*English*)
†Mrs L Sileo (*Teaching Assistant*)
Mrs P S Smithson, BA Exeter, MA Sydney (*English*)
Miss M A Sowa, BA Kent (**German, French*)
Mrs J Spencer Ellis, BA Hull (*French, 6plus Coordinator*)
Dr M J Stenning, BA MA DPhil East Anglia, Sussex (*English*)
Mrs L J Stephens, BEd Cambridge (*Mathematics, Examinations*)
N Stokes, BSc, MA Surrey (*ICT)
B Stones, BSc PhD Edinburgh (*Mathematics, Curriculum & Data*)
†Mrs S Sullivan, BEd Exeter (*Girls' PE & Games*)
Mrs C S Tate, BA Oxford (*Classics, Mathematics*)
J L Tate, BA Oxford (*Classics, Mathematics*)
Mrs D S L Trewinnard, BA Chichester (*Girls' PE & Games*)
Dr C Turk, BA Bristol, MSc LSE, PhD LSE (*Mathematics, Science*)
Miss A-M Vaughan, BA Durham (*Spanish, French*)
Miss N Veronese, MA Bologna (*Spanish, French*)
A Welch, BA Cambridge (*Chemistry*)
J G White, BA Bristol (*History*)
A J Whiteley, BEd Loughborough (**Sport Studies, Director of Activities*)
†Mrs R J Wickham, BA Ed Exeter (*Girls' PE & Games*)
P J Williams, BSc Plymouth (**Design & Technology*)
Miss T R Williams, BA Royal Holloway (*Spanish*)
Mrs N Wintle, MA Oxford (*Economics*)
Mrs J Wright, BA Wales (*Spanish, French*)
Miss K E Wylie, BSc Imperial (*Chemistry*)

PA to the Headmaster: Mrs B G Eustace

Reigate Grammar School is a co-educational day school for pupils aged 11 to 18.

The school was founded in 1675 as a free school for boys. It became an independent Grammar School during the nineteenth century, but after the 1944 Education Act it came under the control of Surrey County Council. On the abolition of the direct grant in 1976, Reigate Grammar School reverted to independent status. At the same time girls were admitted for the first time, initially in the Sixth Form only, but throughout the school from 1993. The school now numbers 890 pupils, of whom 245 are in the Sixth Form. In September 2003, the school merged with Reigate St Mary's Preparatory and Choir School (*see entry in IAPS section*), which provides education to 330 boys and girls aged from rising 3 to 11.

The school is situated in the historic market town of Reigate, just outside the M25 yet with easy transport links into London, Surrey and Sussex. Pupils come from a wide geographical area and from across the social spectrum, thanks to the school's own bursary system, and to the generous support of the Peter Harrison Foundation which provides substantial financial support each year. Around 50% of pupils come from primary schools, the remainder coming from the preparatory sector.

The Governors have invested considerable sums in new buildings in recent years; a new science and humanities building opened in 2011, a new indoor swimming pool opened in January 2009; and new science laboratories and classrooms were completed in 2011. A new centre of learning incorporating a new library and Sixth Form Centre is due for completion in summer 2016. In addition to the main school site, the sports ground at Hartswood, two miles from the school, provides some 32 acres of playing fields and two floodlit all-weather pitches.

Organisation. The school is divided into thee sections: Lower School (First and Second Forms), Upper School (Third, Fourth and Fifth Forms), and Sixth Form. The welfare of pupils is overseen by the Heads of Sections and Heads of Year. Recently the school has reintroduced a House system with the four houses taking the names of previous Headmasters of the school.

Curriculum. The range of subjects on offer is traditional in the early years, but allowing for a broadening of options in the Sixth Form. Prior to GCSE (the courses for which start in the Third Form) all pupils study a core curriculum of Mathematics, English, Science, one or two Modern Languages (French, German or Spanish), Latin, History, Geography, Religious Studies, ICT, Art, Design Technology, Food Technology, Music, Drama, PE and Games. Most pupils take ten GCSEs or IGCSEs, chosen from the above, with the added options of Sports Studies and Greek. Both Dual Award Science and the separate sciences are offered.

Most pupils stay on into the Sixth Form and take four subjects to A2 level. No modules are set in the Lower Sixth. Subjects available include all of the above, with the added options of Business Studies, Economics, Politics and Philosophy and Ethics. Further details are available on the website.

Extra-curricular activities. Reigate Grammar School has a strong tradition of excellence in a wide variety of extra-curricular activities, including an enviable reputation in sport, music and drama; large numbers of pupils participate in the CCF and in the Duke of Edinburgh's Award Scheme and the school has raised up to £45,000 for charities in the course of a year. The main sports are rugby, hockey and cricket for boys, and hockey, netball and rounders for girls, but other sports on offer include athletics, badminton, basketball, gymnastics, football, squash, swimming and tennis. There is a plethora of musical groups which rehearse regularly, including two orchestras, a Swing Band and three choirs, and there are frequent concerts both inside and outside the school, including tours overseas. The Drama department presents at least one major production each term, sometimes in collaboration with the music department.

Admissions. Pupils are normally admitted to the School at 11+, 13+ or 16+, although vacancies occasionally occur at other ages. There is a registration fee of £60. All candidates are required to sit an entrance examination and attend an interview (normally in January or November) details of which are available from the Admissions Secretary. All enquiries concerning admission to the school should, in the first instance, be addressed to the Admissions Secretary.

Fees per term (2014–2015). £5,330. Sibling discounts are available.

Scholarships and Bursaries. The school offers a wide range of scholarships and bursaries, aimed at enabling parents who might not normally be able to consider an independent school to send their child to Reigate Grammar School. Discretionary Headmaster's Awards in addition to Academic, Music and Sports Scholarships are awarded at 11+, 13+ and 16+. Applicants should contact the Admissions Secretary for further details.

Bursaries may also be available, dependent on parental income and assets. Candidates living in the Borough of Reigate and Banstead may be eligible for a Harrison Scholarship, which is also means-tested and made available through the generosity of the Peter Harrison Foundation. Further details are available from the Bursar.

Junior School. Reigate St Mary's Preparatory and Choir School (*see entry in IAPS section*) is the junior and nursery school of Reigate Grammar School. It numbers approximately 300 pupils aged 3 to 11 and is one of the few choir schools in the country not attached to a cathedral or college.

Charitable status. Reigate Grammar School is a Registered Charity, number 1081898. Its aim is to provide high-quality education for boys and girls.

Rendcomb College

Cirencester, Gloucestershire GL7 7HA
Tel: 01285 832306
Fax: 01285 831331
email: info@rendcomb.gloucs.sch.uk
website: www.rendcombcollege.org.uk
Twitter: @Rendcomb

Rendcomb College was founded in 1920 by Noel Wills. The Board of Governors is a member of AGBIS (Association of Governing Bodies of Independent Schools) and the Headmaster is a member of HMC and The Society of Heads.

The Governors:
Mr R Lane (*Chairman*)
Mrs P Hornby (*Vice-Chairman*)

Mrs S Arkle	The Ven H S Ringrose
Mr E Daniels	Mr H C W Robinson
Mrs J Gunner	Mrs L Singer
Mr R Levinge	Major-General P G
Mr A R Marchand	Williams
Mrs I Ormerod	Major M T N H Wills, DL
Mr S D E Parsons	Mr R H Wills
Sir F Richards	

Headmaster: **Mr R J Martin**, BA Hons

Headmaster (Juniors): Mr M Watson, MA, BEd Hons
Second Master: Mr D C Baker, BSc (*Mathematics*)
Deputy Head (Personnel): Mrs D R Dodd, BA (*English; Theatre Studies*)
Deputy Head (Academic): Mr D C Illingworth, BSc (*Geography*)
Deputy Head (Juniors): Mr G Roberts BA Hons, PGCE
Bursar: Mrs E L Sharman, BSc
Head of Sixth Form: Mrs M A Kinson, BA Hons, PGCE
Head of Tutoring, Careers and PHSEE: Miss M Lucas-Halliwell, BSc Hons, PGCE
Head of Middle School: Mr J W Torbitt, BSc Hons, PGCE
Head of Lower School: Mrs S Read, BA Hons, PGCE

* Head of Department

Art:
*Miss A Mobbs, BA Hons, PGCE
Miss E J Roffe, BA Hons

Business Studies:
Mr B Sangster BA, Cert Ed

Design:
*Ms A B Hughes, BA Hons, PGCE

Drama:
*Mrs D R Dodd, BA Hons, Dip Tchg
Ms A Zorab, BA, PGCE

Economics:
*Mr B Sangster, BA, Cert Ed

English:
*Mr N Hopton, MA Hons, MEd Cantab, PGCE
Miss M Harries, BA Hons, MA, PGCE
Mr R J Martin, BA Hons
Miss S E Read, BA Hons, PGCE,CTE

Director of International Students:
Mrs J D Stutchbury, BA Hons, TEFL Cert

English as an Additional Language:
*Miss O L Hughes, BA Hons, CELTA
Mrs J L Collishaw, BA Hons, TESOL
Mrs A M Davis, BA Hons (*Department/Tier 4
    Administrator*)
Mrs J D Stutchbury, BA Hons, TEFL Cert

Geography:
*Miss M Lucas-Halliwell, BSc Hons, PGCE
Mr A St J Brealy, BSc Hons, PGCE
Mr D C Illingworth, BSc Hons, PGCE, MEd

History:
*Mr M H Graham, MA, PGCE
Mrs M A Kinson, BA Hons, PGCE

ICT:
*Mr J W Torbitt, BSc Hons, PGCE

Latin:
Mrs E Noble, BA

Learning Support:
*Mrs A J Bevans, BA Hons, PGCE, SpLD Adv Dip
Mrs C N Hossle BA, AMBDA, MEd, PGCE, PGC SpLD,
    APC

Mathematics:
*Mr S W Clark, BSc Hons, PGCE
Mr D C Baker, BSc Hons, PGCE
Ms S H Corkett, BSc Hons, PGCE, MSc
Mrs L A Gregory, BSc Hons, PGCE
Mr C McGuire, BEng, MSc, PGCE, ESOL, EELTA
Mr A Wilkes, BSc Hons

Modern Languages:
French:
*Mrs S I White, BA Hons, PGCE
Miss J S Longbourne, BA, PGCE
German:
*Mrs R E Fielding, BA Hons, PGCE
Miss J S Longbourne, BA, PGCE
Spanish:
Mrs R Romero Palomino, PGCE

Music:
*Mr D A Franks, MMus, LGSM, PGCE
Miss P R Crisp, BMus
Mr D J Ashman, BA Hons, PGCE

Physical Education:
Mr A H Marsden, BA Hons, PGCE

Psychology:
*Mrs G Harford, BSc Hons, PGCE

Religious Education:
Mrs A J Bevans, BA Hons, PGC SpLD Adv Dip

Head of Science: Miss S K E O'Sullivan, MA, PGDip,
    PGCE, MSc
Biology:
*Mr J H Stutchbury, BSc Hons, PGCE, MIBiol, CBiol
Mrs A Salt-Forster, BSc Hons, PGCE
Chemistry:
*Miss S K E O'Sullivan, MA, PGDip, PGCE, MSc
Mrs A E Wyndow, BSc Hons, PGCE
Physics:
*Mr P Bevan, BSc Hons, PGCE, MPhil
Mr F Whitham, BSc Hons, PGCE

Examinations Officer:
Mrs L A Gregory, BSc Hons, PGCE

Games:
*Mr W Mbanga (*Director of Sport*)
Miss S C Bell
Mrs K Coups, TDip, PGCE
Mr J Gilchriest, BSc Hons
Miss R Farrell, BA
Miss A Kelly
Mr E C Thomason

Houseparents:
Old Rectory:
Mr A St J Brealy, BSc Hons, PGCE
Mrs A Brealy, BA Hons, PGCE
Godman House:
Ms J Bond
Lawn House:
Mr P Bevans, BSc Hons, MPhil, PGCE
Mrs A Bevans, BA Hons, PGCE, SpLD Adv Dip
Stable House:
Mrs C Hossle, BA, AMBDA, MEd, PGCE
Mr T Hossle, MA Oxon
Park House:
Mr M J Coups
Mrs K Coups, TDip

Library:
Mr M H Graham, MA, PGCE (*Librarian*)
Mrs P Baker (*Library Assistant*)

Juniors' Teaching Staff:
Mr J Arnold, BEd Hons
Mrs F Auster, BSc Hons, Cert Learning Support
Mrs A Barker, BA Hons, PGCE
Mrs M Bleaken, BSc Hons, PGCE
Mrs A Brealy, BA Hons, PGCE
Mrs C Breare, BSc Hons, PGCE
Mr P Colls, MA, BMus, ARCM, LTCL, CertEd
Miss C Hayden, BA Hons, Primary Ed QTS
Mrs J Hill, BEd Hons
Mrs K Hockey, BEd Hons
Mrs C N Hossle, BA, AMBDA, MEd, PGCE, PGC SpLD,
    APC
Miss J Kitchen, BSc, PGCE
Mrs B Lee, BA Hons, PGCE, Hornsby Diploma SLD
Mrs J Lee-Browne, LDAD, BS Dip, PGCE
Mr A Lawrence, BEd Hons
Mrs L Louisson, BA, PGCE
Miss P Morrow Brown, BA Hons, PGCE
Miss C Rayner, BEd Hons
Mr E C Thomason
Mrs D Walton-Smith, Cert Ed
Mrs L Watson, BEd
Mr M Watson, MA, BEd Hons
Mrs A Whichelo, BEd Hons

Nursery Staff:
*Mrs K Hardie, NVQ3, A1, V1
Mrs V Bartlett, NVQ Level 3
Mrs K Hockey, BEd Hons

Learning Support:
Mrs S Bischoff, BEd, BPhil Ed Hons

Teaching Assistants:
Mrs S Liebenberg, BMus Dance, TCert RAD, Associate
  Ballet IDTA
Mrs J Major
Mrs N McKenna
Mrs V Bartlett, NVQ Level 3
Mrs K Burnip, BA Hons, CACHE Level 2

Music Staff – Individual Lessons:
Mr J Agg (*Cello, Double Bass, Jazz Piano*)
Mr P Anderson, MA, BMus (*Brass*)
Mr R Baggs, MA, BMus, ARCO, ARCM (*Piano
  accompanist*)
Miss E Bains (*Recorder*)
Mrs S Blewett (*Flute*)
Mr J Carter, Dip RAM (*Head of Keyboard Studies, Piano*)
Mr M Coldrick (*Percussion*)
Mr P Cordell (*Electric Guitar*)
Ms J Curnow (*Voice*)
Mrs H L Evans, CT ABRSM (*Piano*)
Mrs C de Burgh, BMus Hons (*Oboe, Bassoon*)
Mr S Kennedy, ATCL (*Acoustic Guitar*)
Mr A MacLean (*Accompanist*)
Mr J Morgan (*Clarinet and Saxophone*)
Miss J Orsman, ABSM, GBSM (*Upper Strings*)
Mrs N Phillips, GRNCM, LRAM (*Voice*)
Miss S Steele (*Piano*)
Mrs A Whichelo, BEd Hons
Mr J Wright, MA, FRCO, CHM (*Organ and Piano*)

Non-Teaching Staff:

Accountants:
Miss S Watkins
Mrs S Thomson
Admission Registrars:
Mrs C Laycock
Mrs E Stanley
Bursar's Secretary: Mrs C Endersby
Commercial Operations Manager: Mr M Naylor
Headmaster's PA: Mrs C Y Johnson
Juniors' Headmaster's Secretary: Mrs J Nichols
Development Officer: Mrs H Boydell
Network Manager: Mr M Harrison
Marketing Director: Mrs S Gilling, BA Hons
Medical Officers:
Dr S Whittles, BM, MRCGP, DCH
Receptionists:
Mrs D Baker
Miss A Hardy
Sisters:
Mrs J Rogers, RGN
Mrs F Stanford, RGN, Dip HE
Mrs J Church, SRN, BSc
Works Manager: Mr P Cairns

Situation and Buildings. The 200-acre Rendcomb estate lies in the heart of the Cotswolds, five miles from Cirencester and ten miles from Cheltenham. It is easily accessible from the M4 (J15), A40 and M5.

Numbers. There are 264 boys girls from 11 to 18 years, who either fully board, weekly board or are day pupils. Flexible boarding is available. There are 146 Juniors.

Admission. Pupils normally join at 11, 13 or 16 to enter the Sixth Form. The entrance examination for entry at 11 is taken at Rendcomb and comprises three papers: English, Mathematics and Verbal Reasoning. At 13, pupils are admitted by Common Entrance or Rendcomb Examination and at 16 by interview, school reports and GCSE results.

Character. Good Schools are exciting places to live, study and work.

Schools are first and foremost places of learning. Throughout the School, we hope to encourage our pupils to think independently, to challenge and to engage. Ultimately, we want the young people in our care to develop a genuine interest both in the world around them and in their place in it through their study.

Rendcomb aims to provide a holistic education for its pupils and encourages young people to embrace as many experiences as possible during their time in the School. The academic, sport, music, drama and outdoor co-curricular opportunities open to our students at Rendcomb are central to our idea of curriculum. It is from new experiences and new challenges that young people grow, become independent and learn to lead.

Pastoral care is also central to the School. Young people need to feel safe in their School environment and must be nurtured. The word 'family' is often associated with Rendcomb and there is a reason for that. From our youngest to our oldest pupils, we encourage pupils to build positive relationships both within their year groups and beyond them.

Curriculum. Education in the 21st Century cannot be viewed simply as achieving exam qualifications, but must extend to providing young people with the flexible and independent skills they will need to face future challenges and developments. We our rightly proud of the academic progress our students make, assisted by small class sizes (typically 15–18 in the Lower School, fewer in A Level classes). This enables the teachers to get to know the students as individuals and, working in partnership with parents, helps us to ensure our students realise their full potential.

However, the Rendcomb curriculum extends well beyond the confines of the classroom and the core teaching day. Our small size enables all students to participate in a number of sports two afternoons a week, in addition to a wide range of activities which begin after the end of formal lessons each day. Our philosophy is to consider these to be co-curricular, aimed at combining with the academic elements to genuinely develop the whole person and ensure that we provide a fully-rounded education.

University Entrance. The Leavers of 2013 at Rendcomb did particularly well in securing University places. Of the students waiting to confirm offers in further education over the summer, 100% of them secured places. 74% of students secured their first choices and 95% secured their first and second choice establishments.

High-flying Russell and 1994 Group Universities figured strongly, accounting for 70% of students' destinations.

Careers. There is a Careers Section in our Library and our Sixth Form House which offer comprehensive current information on both careers and higher education and experienced staff are available for further information, consultation and advice.

Religious Education. Church Services take place on selected Sundays and during the week in the fine 16th Century Parish Church, which also serves as the church for the small village of Rendcomb. Pupils are required to attend a short service on two days in the week and boarders attend a Morning Service on Sunday. There is an annual Confirmation and the Chaplain is available as a listening ear to all members of the school.

Co-Curricular. Education is not only what happens in the classroom but also in a variety of other environments. Staff and pupils at Rendcomb acknowledge and embrace the fact that co-curricular means exactly what it says – other areas of school life shape and benefit our pupils in a wide variety of areas. Sport, Art, Music, Drama and our Activity programme give students choice and a wide range of experiences which may lead to a lifetime's interest, participation and, in some cases, to a career.

Exam results matter and so does discovering a joy or a talent. Representing your peer group's views on our vibrant School Council; learning courage on the sports field; joining with others in singing in Choir or Chamber Choir help our students find out what they can do. We believe in giving all of our students those opportunities – not just the few stars who might dominate in other schools.

Our size means that every pupil will represent the College at sport and learn the importance of team work alongside the highs and lows of success and failure. Everyone is welcome to sing in the College Choir no matter what their level of expertise in sight reading and/or singing. Success in passing an audition and getting into the cast for a play or musical is almost always a given.

Our Art Department thrives in encouraging pupils from a wide range of artistic and cultural backgrounds to express themselves on paper, in clay, with hard materials and with photography. No one house style dominates, which so often is the case in larger schools.

Sports teams at Rendcomb are fortunate to be coached by an experienced team of coaches – some with international experience. As all pupils will represent the College in Forms 1–5 (Years 7 to 11) care is taken with both the very able and the less naturally gifted in coaching the sports which we offer. Each term we concentrate on a major sport and in the Sixth Form students have the opportunity to play that sport or to enjoy a range of other sports in our Minor Games programme. Many outsiders have commented on the remarkable results that our College teams achieve, considering the number of players available to us. We regularly win fixtures against schools that have twice the number of students from which to select a team. This is clear evidence of our belief in team work.

Our Duke of Edinburgh's Award scheme is extremely popular and encourages our students to learn not only outdoor navigation and survival skills but also service and community work required by the various elements of the award. Our Activities programme runs from 3.50 to 4.50 pm each day and pupils must participate daily from Forms 1–5. Sixth Formers sign up voluntarily. This slot in the day is when play rehearsals occur alongside a large range of choices: Chocolate Creations; Art Club; Duke of Edinburgh's Award; Cooking; Modern Dance; Horse Riding are only a few of the many possibilities.

Once again we hope to expose our student body to a variety of areas that may not be covered in the classroom. The activities change each term, so over a pupil's lifetime in the college they have the opportunity to try a huge range of possible interests.

Living Accommodation. Rendcomb has excellent accommodation for both boarders and day pupils. Most pupils in the Fourth Form and above have a comfortable single study bedroom and there are spacious Common Rooms and excellent social facilities. Sixth formers enjoy their own centre, with TV, Satellite TV, video, games room, dance area and supervised bar.

Bursaries and Scholarships. Rendcomb offers a limited number of bursaries (age 4–18) and scholarships (age 11–18) for candidates demonstrating potential, talent and who would flourish and benefit from the ethos and life at the school.

Scholarships may or may not be means tested.

Rendcomb College has always had extremely strong links with forces families and is able to offer generous bursary support for families who are with HM Armed Forces or Diplomatic Services. Rendcomb is pleased to accept payments under the CEA scheme in respect of pupils from Forces families. This can be either the Boarding or the Day CEA, depending on personal circumstance. Where applicable under the rules of the scheme, Rendcomb will make additional bursary support available.

Details of Rendcomb Scholarships and Bursaries are on the school website www.rendcombcollege.org.uk.

Fees per term (2014–2015). Senior School: Boarding £7,190–£9,505, Day £5,030–£6,910.

Junior School: Day £2,200–£3,515; Year 6 Boarding Fee £1,250.

Fees are payable termly in advance, by the first day of term. The Governors reserve the right to charge interest at up to 2% per month on fees not paid by this date. For information on monthly and other payment schemes please contact the Bursar.

The premium for a pupil's personal accident insurance scheme is included.

Rendcomb Juniors. Rendcomb Juniors takes children on an important journey from their early years to the brink of Senior School. Starting in the Nursery, the children are nurtured within a secure and safe environment that provides each individual with the independence and confidence to move with ease into the Otters (Reception to J2). During their time in The Otters, the children experience a broadly based curriculum including extensive outdoor opportunities that establish a firm foundation in preparation for their move into the Juniors.

All pupils have the opportunity to represent the school in a variety of sporting fixtures and to participate in Music and Drama productions.

Each pupil's development is closely monitored and reports, grade cards and teacher meetings provide regular feedback to parents.

After-school clubs run Monday to Thursday, from Judo to Band, Nature Club to Computer Club. The use of College facilities by the Junior School, from the Astroturf to the Multimedia Suite, raises the standard of activities. The Junior School also has its own facilities including an adventure playground.

Enquiries should be directed to the Admissions Registrar on 01285 832306.

Charitable status. Rendcomb College is a Registered Charity, number 1115884. The aims and objectives of the Charity are the provision of boarding and day independent education.

Repton School

Repton, Derbyshire DE65 6FH

Tel:	01283 559221 (Headmaster)
	01283 559200 (School)
Fax:	01283 559223 (Headmaster)
email:	registrar@repton.org.uk
website:	www.repton.org.uk

Situated in the heart of England, Repton School has been home to a spiritual community for over 800 years and the inspiring buildings of the 12th century Priory remain at the centre of our life together today.

Over its 450 years Repton has established a strong tradition of distinguished alumni in public life, sport and the arts including Roald Dahl, Archbishop Michael Ramsey, C B Fry, Graeme Garden and Jeremy Clarkson.

The 21st century Repton is a fully co-educational school with a strong boarding ethos and is home to 650 pupils. Individuality flourishes within the context of a real community and every Reptonian is encouraged to discover those areas in which he or she can excel, and to prepare for the world of possibilities that lie beyond the Arch.

Chairman of Governors: Sir Henry Every Bt

Acting Head: **Mrs S A B Tennant**, MA late Scholar of Somerville College Oxford

Deputy Head (Academic): T C Owen, MA late Exhibitioner of St Edmund Hall Oxford

Chaplain: The Revd A J Watkinson, MA Keble College Oxford

Heads of Department:
Classics: R G Embery, BA Durham
Modern Languages: Ms S J Lees, BA Leeds
English: J D Wilton, MA Lady Margaret Hall Oxford
Drama: J M G Levesley, BA Hull
History & Politics: Dr N F Pitts, BA, PhD Leeds
Geography: Miss A H McKenzie, MA London
Economics: C M Keep, MA Queen's College Cambridge
Mathematics: P V Goodhead, MA late Scholar of Pembroke College Oxford
Ethical & Religious Studies: D T Clark, MTheol St Andrews
Physics: J S Mitchell, BSc Sunderland
Biology: Dr S M Ingleston-Orme, BSc, PhD Nottingham
Chemistry: F E J Wawn, MA St Hugh's College Oxford
Director of Music: A J R Bowley, MA King's College Cambridge, ARCM
Director of Art: J H Bournon, BA Wimbledon School of Art
Design and Technology: I Setterington, BEd Loughborough
Physical Education: S J Clague, BSc Crewe and Alsager College of HE

Boys' Boarding Houses:
School House: T H Naylor
The Priory: N F Pitts
The Orchard: A J Smith
Latham House: S O Merlin
The Cross: S Earwicker
New House: W G Odell

Girls' Boarding Houses:
The Abbey: Mrs L E Wilbraham
The Garden: Mrs J P Mitchell
Field House: P J Griffiths & Mrs J Griffiths
The Mitre: Mrs A F Parish

Bursar: C P Bilson, MA, MBA Jesus College Cambridge
Registrar: Mrs C Hanneford-Smith
Headmaster's Secretary: Miss J J Taylor

Admission. Pupils are admitted at 13+ (Year 9) and 16+ (Year 12) but exceptions may be made in other years. Application for admission should be made to the Headmaster. There is a registration fee of £100. Candidates will normally have passed Common Entrance at their preparatory schools, but there is also an entrance examination for candidates not being prepared for CE.

Fees per term (2014–2015). Boarders £10,547; Day pupils £7,825. Some additional expenses (for books, stationery, pocket money, etc) will be incurred.

There is a Bursary Fund from which grants in the form of remissions from full fees may in certain circumstances be made. No remission of fees can be made on account of absence.

Scholarships and Bursaries. A number of scholarships and exhibitions are offered annually, generally at 13+ and 16+, though in exceptional circumstances candidates may be considered for awards at other entry points. The value of any award may be increased where need is shown.

Entrance Scholarships at 13+: The examination for non-academic awards is held at Repton in January for entry the following September, and the examination for academic awards is held at Repton in May for entry the following September. Candidates must be under 14 on 1 September in the year of the examination.

16+ Scholarships: The examination for both academic and non-academic awards takes place in November for entry the following September. A number of awards are available for pupils joining Repton from both the maintained and independent sectors.

Music Scholarships and Exhibitions are awarded, usually at 13+ and 16+. Examinations take place in November (16+) and January (13+). An open day for potential music scholars is held in October.

Drama Scholarships are also offered, usually at 13+ with auditions and interviews taking place in January.

Art Scholarships and Exhibitions are offered, usually at 13+ and 16+. Examinations take place in November (16+) and January (13+). Candidates will be assessed by examination, interview and an assessment of their portfolio.

Design and Technology (DT) and Information and Communication Technology (ICT) Scholarships and Exhibitions are offered, usually at 13+. Examinations take place in January. Candidates will be asked to complete a practical session and interview and to provide a folder of work for assessment.

Sports Scholarships are offered, usually at 13+ and 16+, to pupils of exceptional talent. Assessments are held by arrangement with the Director of Sport, during the Lent Term.

C B Fry All Rounder Award: awards worth up to 20% of the Repton boarding fee may be offered at 13+ to candidates exhibiting outstanding all-round leadership potential. Assessments take place in March or April when candidates are in Year 7.

Bursaries may be available to those who would not otherwise be able to attend an independent school. These may, in appropriate circumstances, be used to supplement Academic or non-academic awards. Means-tested bursaries are also available to Forces families.

Curriculum. The curriculum in Year 9 is broad to enable pupils to make an informed choice of GCSE subjects at the beginning of Year 10.

In Years 10 and 11, pupils study a combination of core and optional subjects. All pupils study English, Mathematics, Biology, Chemistry and Physics (leading either to two GCSEs in Science and Additional Science or three GCSEs in separate sciences for the more able students). The vast majority of pupils also take English Literature and French as core GCSEs. Pupils choose three subjects as optional GCSE subjects from: Art, Business Studies, Classical Civilisation, Classical Greek with Latin ("Gratin"), Design and Technology, Drama, Geography, German, History, Latin, Music, Physical Education, Religious Studies, Spanish and Three Dimensional Studies. Art and Music may also be taken "off the timetable" to provide pupils with the choice of a fourth optional subject. In Year 10, all pupils also receive one lesson in ICT and one lesson in PSHCE per week.

Most pupils study four subjects in the Lower Sixth at AS Level, though Further Mathematics can be taken as a fifth option. In the Upper Sixth many pupils choose to take three of these subjects to the full A Level; some opt to continue with all four or indeed five. The following are available as full A Levels over two years or as AS Levels over one year: Art, Biology, Business Studies, Chemistry, Classical Civilisation, Classical Greek, Design and Technology, Drama and Theatre Studies, Economics, English, French, Geography, German, Government and Politics, History, Latin, Mathematics, Further Mathematics, Music, Physical Education, Physics, Religious Studies, Spanish and Textiles. In the Lower Sixth, most pupils take "Civics", a course designed by the School to consolidate and extend their AS Level studies. In the Upper Sixth, there is a timetabled lecture programme where pupils have the opportunity to hear distinguished speakers talk on a wide variety of subjects.

Potential Oxbridge candidates are identified by the end of their second term in the Sixth Form and prepared for interview.

Chapel services are those of the Church of England and boarders are expected to attend a service every Sunday unless specially excused. A Confirmation is held each year.

Other activities. Every opportunity and encouragement is given to pupils to develop their creative interests in Art,

Music, Drama and Design Technology. Facilities include dedicated Art, Drama and Music Schools, newly renovated Theatre, Studio Theatre and Textiles Studio. There are numerous School societies, covering a wide variety of interests.

Games and sports. Football, hockey (three astroturf pitches – 2 water-based, 1 sand), cricket, netball, rugby, fives, squash, tennis (2 indoor courts and 14 hard courts), cross-country, athletics, sailing, climbing, canoeing, swimming, fencing, golf and horse riding. Superb facilities are provided for physical education including a sports hall, fitness suite, gymnasium and indoor swimming pool.

Combined Cadet Force. The School maintains a contingent of the Combined Cadet Force and every pupil is a member in Year 10. Subsequently pupils may remain in the CCF to take part in The Duke of Edinburgh's Award scheme or specialise as instructors. Sixth Formers have the additional choice of Community Service.

Houses. All pupils belong to a House, which is their home in the School, where they eat all meals, and is at the heart of their life at Repton. The Housemaster or Housemistress, who has overall responsibility for an individual pupil's work and development, lives in the House with his/her own family and is supported by a resident Matron and team of Tutors.

Repton Preparatory School and Pre-Preparatory School at Foremarke Hall are approximately 1½ miles from the main school and house 63 boarders, 273 day boys and girls and 110 pre-prep day boys and girls. Pupils are taken from age 3 and prepared for entrance to Repton and other schools. Academic Scholarship examinations take place in January.

Further information may be obtained from The Headmaster, Foremarke Hall, Milton, Derbyshire DE65 6EJ. (*See Foremarke Hall's entry in IAPS section.*)

Charitable status. Repton School is a Registered Charity, number 1093166. It exists to provide high quality education for boys and girls.

Robert Gordon's College

Schoolhill, Aberdeen AB10 1FE
Tel: 01224 646346
Fax: 01224 630301
email: enquiries@rgc.aberdeen.sch.uk
website: www.rgc.aberdeen.sch.uk
Twitter: @robertgordons
Facebook: /robertgordonscollege
LinkedIn: /robertgordonscollege

Motto: '*Omni nunc arte magistra*'
Robert Gordon was a merchant from Aberdeen who spent much of his life based in Poland. On retiring to Aberdeen, he left his fortune to found a 'Hospital' for boys' accommodation and education. The school opened in 1750. In 1881, the 'Hospital' was reconstituted as a day school under the name of 'Robert Gordon's College'. It continued to attract support from benefactors. In 1909 its charitable constitution changed to allow the development of adult education, a move which developed in the course of time into the Robert Gordon University. The next major change in the nature of the school was in 1989 when girls were admitted. Robert Gordon's College is now a co-educational day school in the Scottish tradition, which remains true to the charitable and educational principles on which it was founded by Robert Gordon over 250 years ago.

Board of Governors:
Chairman: Professor James Hutchison, Nominated by University of Aberdeen
Mrs Elizabeth Clark, Nominated by University of Aberdeen

Councillor Bill Cormie, Nominated by Aberdeen City Council
Councillor Jean Morrison MBE, Nominated by Aberdeen City Council
Councillor Ross Thomson, Nominated by Aberdeen City Council
Councillor Ian Yuill, Nominated by Aberdeen City Council
Revd B Stephen C Taylor, Nominated by Presbytery of Aberdeen
Revd Marian Cowie, Nominated by Presbytery of Aberdeen
Mr Mike Fraser, Nominated by Gordonian Association
Mr Robin Whyte, Nominated by Gordonian Association
Dr George S Stevenson, Nominated by Seven Incorporated Trades of Aberdeen
Mr Alfred Cordiner, Nominated by Aberdeen Endowments Trust
Mr Victor Beamish, Nominated by Aberdeen Endowments Trust
Mr David Rennie, Nominated by Aberdeen and Grampian Chamber of Commerce

Co-opted Governors:
Mr Paul de Leeuw (*Vice Chairman*)
Dr Tracey J H Menzies
Mr William Rattray
Mr Kevin Reynard
Mr Christopher Shepherd
Mr Alistair Hector

Head of College: **Simon Mills**, MA, PGCE, BA

Head of Senior School: Andrea Angus, BSc, PGCE
Director of Finance: Andrew W Lowden, MA, CA

Deputy Heads (Secondary):
Robin Fish, MA, PGCE
Phyllis Thomson, MA, PGCE
Colin Gambles, BSc, PGCE
Michael Elder, MA, PGCE
Stefan Horsman, MA, BA, PGCE (*Digital Systems & ELearning*)

Departments:
* *Head of Department*
‡ *Principal Teacher (Learning)*

Art:
*Andrew L Hopps, BA
Susan Blue, BA, PGCE (*Maternity Leave*)
Louise Charlton, BA, PGCE (*Maternity Leave*)
Lorna Reid, BA, PGDE
Giles Rencontre, BA
David Robertson, DA, PGCE

Biology:
*David Strang, BSc
‡Wendy MacGregor, BSc, PGDE
Gail Clark, BSc, PGCE
Alexandra Hendry, BA, MSc, PGCE
Colin Gambles, BSc, PGCE
Jessica Power, MAs, FRAS, BSc, BEd
Tracy Reid, BSc, FCCA
Peter Shand, BSc, PhD
Lydia Willetts, BSc, PGCE

Economics and Business Studies:
*Jackie Farquhar, BA, PGCE
Claire Braid, BA, PGDE

Alison Campbell, MA, PGDE
Kirsty Chalmers, BA, PGDE
Alan Smith, BEd

Chemistry:
*Jane Kennedy, BSc, PhD
‡Stephanie Rigby, BSc, PhD
Sarah Coates, MSc, PGCE
Kevin S Cowie, BSc
Kanola Anderson, BSc, PhD
John Duncan, BSc
Michelle Molyneux, BSc, PGDE

Classics:
*Allan M Bicket, MA, MLitt
‡Craig Galbraith, MA, MLitt, PhD
Rachel Carter, MSt, BA
Veronique Oldham, Licence en Philologie Classique

Computing Studies:
*Mark Hay, BSc, PGDE

Ian Simpson, BSc, PGDE
Lorna Hawthorn, BSc, PGCE
Sarah Johnson, BSc, PGDE

Drama:
*Andrew Milarvie, BA, DipDA
Laura Fyvie, BA, PGDE
Niall Hunter, BA, PGDE

English:
*Claire Cowie, MA, MLitt, PGCE
‡Marion Waters, MA, MSc, PGDE
Catherine Bannatyne, MA, PGDE
Shona Bruce, MA, MEd
Natalie Crosby, MA, PGDE
Michael Elder, MA, PGCE
Faye Hendry, MA, MLitt, PGDE
Arlene Knudsen, MA, PGDE
Amy MacBrayne, MA, PGCE
Kate Macleod, MA, PGDE
Marie Mancellon, MA, PGCE
Hannah Lincoln, BA, PGCE
Shona Rencontre, MA, PGDE
Helen Rees, BA, PGCE (*Maternity Leave*)
Elizabeth Templeton, MA, PGCE (*Maternity Leave*)
Patrick Toal, PhD, MA, PGCE

Geography:
*Jennifer Gray, MA, PhD
Stefan Horsman, MA, BA, PGCE
Louisa Maddox, MA, PGDE
Anna Nicoll, BSc, PGDE
Keith Paul, BSc, PGDE
Fiona Stone, BSc, MSc, PGCE

History and Modern Studies:
*Noel Shearer, MA, PGCE
‡Margaret Wood, BA, PGDE (*Maternity Leave*)
Kirsten Cunningham, BA, PGDE (*Maternity Leave*)
Anna Cordey, MA, MSc, PGCE
Robin Fish, MA, PGCE
Callum Francis, MA, PGDE
Stewart Hardie, MA, PGDE
Laura McCurley, MA, PGDE

Mathematics:
*Victoria Fletcher, BSc, MA Ed
‡Donna Ellis, BSc, PGCE
‡Lorna Taylor, MA, PGCE
Rebecca Drummond, MA, PGDE
John Gibb, MA, PGDE

Laura Jackson, MA, BSc, PGCE
Arthur Jamieson, BSc
Shirley MacKenzie, MA, PGDE
Abram McCormick, BA
Shilpa Pathakji, BA, PGCE
Andrew Prentice, BSc, PGCE
Eileen Smith, MA, PGCE
Gemma West, BSc, PGDE

Modern Languages:
*Nadine Clark, MA, PGDip, PGDE
‡Graeme Campbell, MA, PGDE
Amelie Caritey, MA, PGDE
Susan Chalmers, MSc, BA, PGCE
Gregor Duncan, MA
Daniel Montgomery, MA, PGDE
Judit Moscoso, MA, PGCE
Ulrike Plasberg, BA, PGDE
Katherine Tack, MA, PGDE
Phyllis Thomson, MA, PGCE
Anne Watson, BA, PGDE
Nathalie Capderou (*French Language Assistante*)
Susanna Weir (*German Language Assistant*)
Elizabeth Webster (*Spanish Language Assistant*) (*Maternity Leave*)
Cristina Sanchez Robledo (*Spanish Language Assistant*)
Simonetta Quarta (*Italian Language Assistant*)

Music:
*Kevin Haggart, BMus, MMus, PGCE
Laura Ferguson, BMusEd, DipLCM
Christopher Pearson, BMusEd
Instructors:
Kevin Cormack
Jonathan Kightley, BMusGrad, RNCM, PGCE
Julian Maunder, BA, LRAM
Lydia Thom, LTCL, Grad Dip Jazz

Physical Education:
*Stacey Stewart, BEd
*Richard Anderson, BA, PGCE
‡Carolyn Armstrong, BEd
‡Craig Harper, BEd, BSc, PGDE
‡Wendy Smith, BEd
Christopher Allan, BSc, PGDE
Stuart Axten, BSc, PGCE
Colin B Filer, BEd
Steph Ker, BEd

Jocelyn Roberts, BSc, PGCE
Lauren Robertson, BEd
Nicola Stephen, BEd

Instructors:
Sarah Baxter
Gregor McMillan
Robert Currie
Scott Donald
Susan Proctor
Mark Ramage
Stuart Scorgie
Howard Smith

Physics:
*Stuart Farmer, BSc, MBA, CSciTeach, FInstP, PGCE
‡Tim Browett, BSc, RSci, PGDE
Christopher Beaton, BSc, PGDE
David Clark, BSc, PGDE
Andrew Kirkwood, BSc

Guidance (*Principal Teachers*):
Gail Clark, BSc, PGCE
Sarah Coates, MSc, PGCE
Kevin S Cowie, BSc
Anne Watson, BA, PGDE
Colin B Filer, BEd
Tracy Reid, BSc, FCCA
Arthur Jamieson, BSc
Louisa Maddox, MA, PGDE

Principal Teacher Guidance/Careers: Dawn Pirie, BSc, MRes, RSci, PGDE
Principal Teacher Guidance/Universities: Daniel Montgomery, MA, PGDE
Principal Teacher Guidance/SFL: Sheila B Sanderson, BA, PGCE
Principal Teacher Numeracy: Donna Ellis, BSc, PGCE
Principal Teacher Literacy: Craig Galbraith, MA, MLitt, PhD
Principal Teacher Health & Wellbeing: Gemma West, BSc, PGDE
Principal Teacher Transition: Margaret Wood, BA, PGDE (*maternity leave*)
Principal Teacher Transition: Laura Fyvie, BA, PGDE (*Acting*)

Support For Learning (*Principal Teacher*): Sheila B Sanderson, BA, PGCE
Support For Learning: Ulrike Plasberg, BA, PGDE
Support For Learning: Lorna Hawthorn, BSc, PGCE

ELearning Coordinator: Ian Simpson, BSc, PGDE
International Coordinator: Gregor Duncan, MA

Combined Cadet Force:
Contingent Commander: Daniel Montgomery, MA, PGDE
Army Officer: John Gibb, MA, PGDE
OIC Pipe Band: Michael Maitland
RAF Commander: Calum Race, HND
School Staff Instructor and Piping Instructor: Jason Sumner, PDQB

Duke of Edinburgh:
Duke of Edinburgh Awards Manager: Craig McEwan, BEng, RSci, PGDE
Duke of Edinburgh Assistant Manager: Laura Jackson, MA, BSc, PGCE
Duke of Edinburgh Assistant Manager: Keith Paul, BSc, PGDE

Craig McEwan, BEng, RSci, PGDE
Dawn Pirie, BSc, MRes, RSci, PGDE
Sheila B Sanderson, BA, PGCE

Psychology:
Andrea Vlaar, MA, TQ
Samantha Wylde, BEd, BSc

Religious Education:
*Kenneth Primrose, MA, MTh, PGCE
Fiona McWilliam, MA, PGCE
Lesley Ross, MA, PGCE

Technology:
*David McLaren, DipTechEd
‡Roy Wakeford, BSc
Joseph Leiper, BEng
Lyndsey MacLean, BA, PGDE

SQA:
SQA Coordinator: Shona Bruce, MA, MEd
Assistant SQA & Exam Coordinator: Sarah Johnson, BSc, PGDE

House Staff:
House Events Coordinator: Andrew Prentice, BSc, PGCE
Blackfriars: Kate Macleod, MA, PGDE
Collyhill: Steph Ker, BEd (*Acting*)
Sillerton: Kanola Anderson, BSc, PhD
Straloch: Nicola Stephen, BEd

Support Staff:
PA to Head of College: Ann Gannon
PA to Head of Senior School: Joy Cahill, HNC
PA to Director of Finance: Pamela Cowling
School Secretary: Lynda Cunningham
Receptionist: Fiona McKay
Administration Assistant: Pam Ritchie
Admissions Officer: Philip J Skingley, BA, MEd
Finance Manager: Sam Walker, CIMA, CIOBS
Accountant: Susan Smith, NC, HND
Accounts Assistant: Joan Platt
Cashier: Linda McKenzie
Payroll Officer: Elizabeth McRobbie Smith, BSc
Head Groundsman: Donovan Reid
Deputy Head Groundsman: Luke Blackman
Groundsman: Ryan Young
Trainee Groundsman: Simon Stockford
Facilities Supervisor: Gordon Grant
Development Director: Laura Presslie, BA
Assistant Director (Alumni Relations): Laura Pike
Development Executive: Isabel Mitchell, Associate of CIOBS
Development Assistant: Lindsay Ackers, BA
Design Manager: Fiona Reid, BA
Design & Marketing Assistant: Aimee Brown, BA
Press & Communications Officer: Shelley Lee, MCIPR, LCCI Dip Marketing
Facilities Manager: Michael Maitland
Handyman/Joiner: Dennis Maule
Technical Specialist: Mike Duguid
Technical Resources Technician: George Jamieson
Phase 2 Clerk of Works: Ron Brodie
Human Resources Manager: Frances Winter, MA
Human Resources Assistant: Caitlin McQueen, BA
IT Manager: Gordon Crosher, DCR [R]
Assistant Network Manager: Brian Bruce, BSc
IT Systems Administrator: Calum Race, HND
IT Systems Administrator: Martyn Keith, BSc
IT Service Desk Operative: Dorota Wojciechowska, ITIL v3
IT Technician (Student Placement): Henry Thom, MA
Head Janitor: Kevin Burnett
Deputy Head Janitor: Stephen Noble
Janitor: David Bain
Janitor: James McAllister
Janitor: Craig Stephen
Cleaning Manager: Carolanne Bain
Day Janitor/Cleaning Chargehand: Claire Wetherly
Cleaning Chargehand: Kim Burnett
Cleaning Chargehand: Linda McCafferty
Gatekeeper: Susan Burnett
MIS Supervisor: Gina Rathbone
MIS Senior Assistant: Sarah Walker
School Nurse: Deborah Kennedy, BN
Reprographics Technician: Janet Lyon
Art Technician: Suzy Watson, BA
Biology Technician: Mary Shepherd
Biology Technician: Jill Povey, PhD, BSc
Chemistry Technician: Vicky Clarkson
Chemistry Technician: Lisa Cole, PhD, BSc
Physics Technician & Phase 2 Support: Claire Harkins, MRes, BSc

Technology Technician: Richard Lamplugh, BSc, MSc
Librarian: Elaine Brazendale, MA, ALA
Library Assistant: Jenny Strang, BSc, MSc
Archivist: Penny Hartley, BA
Archives Assistant: Tom Cumming, MA, Dip.Ed
Breakfast Playground Assistant: Mairi Anderson
Breakfast Playground Assistant: Nadia Helmy
Breakfast Playground Assistant: Leah McGill
Breakfast Playground Assistant: Ruby Stephen
Breakfast Playground Assistant: Amy Smith

Junior School:
Head of Junior School: Mollie Mennie, MBA, PGDE
Deputy Heads:
Sally-Ann Johnson, BEd, MEd
Varie Macleod, BEd

Principal Teachers Learning and Teaching:
Jenny Anderson, MA, PGDE
Susan Jamieson, MEd, MA (*Health and Wellbeing*)
Claire Rae, BSc, PGCE
Tracy Geddes, MA, PGCE
Susie Robertson, MA, PGCE

Class Teachers:

Maureen Drummond, BEd	Ashley Sutherland, MA, PGDE
Sophie Main, BEd	
Karen Miller, BEd	Jenni Little, BEd
Helen Crichton, BEd	Jackie Milne, BEd
Anne McDonald, DipEd	Katie Scott, MA, PGDE
Lorraine Wright, BA, PGCE	Ben Traynor, BEd
	Margaret Johnstone, BEd
Joanne Curran, BA, PGDE	Matt Northcroft, BEd
Sally Kinsey, BA	Heather Park, BEd
Kirsten Lochead, BEd	Ashleigh Cameron, LLB
Ciara Gallagher, BEd	Vivien Scott, BEd
Susan Jamieson, MEd, MA	Laura Allen, MBChB, PGDE (*Maternity Leave*)
Ingrid Stanyer, BA	
Jenny Anderson, MA, PGDE	

Support for Learning: Hilary Esson, MA, PGCE
Art: Joanna Holdsworth, MA, BA, PGCE; Giles Rencontre, BA
Drama: Elizabeth Rose, BA, PGDE
French: Morag Ryan, MA; Katherine Smith, MA
ICT: Caireen McDonald, BA, PGCE
Music: Amanda Watt, BMusEd; Eileen Pike
PE/Games: Carolyn Armstrong, BEd
Swimming: Sarah Baxter
Science: Tracy Geddes, MA, PGCE
Nursery Teacher: Ailsa Reid, BEd

Classroom Assistants:

Moira Murray, BA	Jane Inglis
Elisabeth MacDougall	Fiona Coull, BSc, RGN
Fiona Montgomery	

Nursery Team:
Michelle Duguid, HNC

Pauline Greenhalgh, PDA	*Playground Assistants*:
Jilly McIntyre, HNC	Julie Dinan
Hannah Muir, HNC	Sharon Douglas
Kylie Tallieu, HNC	Philip Hutchison
Jan Whyte, SVQ3	Jayne Kirkpatrick
	Madeleine Ledingham
After Nursery Club Assistants:	Linda Lynch
	Michele Peter
Michelle Duguid, HNC	Carrie Scott
Diane Legg	Fiona Wilson
Jilly McIntyre, HNC	
Hannah Muir, HNC	

After School Club:
Out of School Care Manager: Sarah Baxter, BA, BSc
Supervisor: Holly Porter

Claire Alexander
Mairi Anderson
Nachida Djedouani
Nadia Helmy
Leah McGill
Rosel Ramos

Abigail Smit
Amy Smith
Ruby Stephen
Erin Walmsley (*maternity leave*)

Breakfast Club Assistants:
Mairi Anderson
Nachida Djedouani
Holly Porter

Junior School Administrator/Secretary: Olivia More, HND
Junior School Administrator: Sarah-Jane Beaton
Junior School Receptionists: Julie Adams, Coleen Manson
Personal Assistant to Head of Junior School: Elaine Stewart
Librarian: Alison Lloyd-Wiggins, BA, CILIP

Admission. The College is divided into two sections: the Junior School (Primary Classes 1–7) 519 pupils and the Senior School (Secondary Forms 1–6) 1,112 pupils. The normal stages of entry are to Primary 1, Primary 6 and Secondary 1.

Entry to Primary 1 (age 4½–5½ years) is by interview held in January/February, and to Primary 6 (age 9½–10½ years) by Entrance Test held in January/February.

Entry to Secondary 1 is by an Entrance Examination held in January.

Entry at other stages depends upon vacancies arising, and the offer of a place is subject to satisfactory performance in an Entrance Test and interview.

There is also a Nursery for some 40 children (age 3–5).

Fees per annum (2014–2015). Nursery: £4,635 (half day inc lunch), £8,880 (full day inc lunch). Junior School (incl lunch): £7,905 (P1), £7,925 (P2), £10,600 (P3), £10,725 (P4–7). Senior School (exc lunch): £11,610. These fees are inclusive and cover Games. Pupils provide their own books.

Bursaries. Robert Gordon's College offers free places and reduced fee places to between 10 and 18 pupils every year for entry in to Secondary 1. The Burnett Scholarships offer up to half fee discounts to pupils of outstanding talent in academic subjects, in music, or in sport. Burnett Scholarships are available to pupils currently in Fifth Year at other schools who are expected to achieve excellent results in their Higher exams.

Buildings. The centre block was erected in 1732, but there have been many modern additions. The College is fully equipped with Assembly Hall, Library, Laboratories, Art Rooms, Computing areas and Workshops. There are two Gymnasia and a Swimming Pool onsite at the School. Countesswells Sports Field was opened in 1992 on a 40-acre site 3 miles from the school incorporating first-class accommodation and facilities, including a water-based hockey pitch and an astroturf all-weather sports surface. A five-storey teaching block, incorporating a Dining Hall, was opened in 1994, and a new Library and Information Centre in 2000. A new Junior School building opened in Spring 2009, with newly located and renovated Senior classrooms following in Summer 2009. A New Science and Technology Centre, and Performing Arts Centre will open in 2015.

Curriculum. In the Junior School the usual subjects of the primary curriculum are covered, with specialist teachers in Art, Drama, French, ICT, Music, Physical Education and Science. In the Senior School S1–S2 builds on the primary curriculum and as a foundation to the S3–S4 curriculum based on CfE principles. S3–S4 study National 5; S5–S6 Higher Grade and Advanced Higher. S6 pupils have Higher courses particular to them and specifically designed Enhancement courses.

The tradition of academic success continues at Robert Gordon's College with the vast majority of pupils annually going on to University.

Games. Rugby, Hockey (boys and girls), Cricket, Netball, Tennis, Athletics, Cross-Country Running. A wide range of other sports is offered, including Badminton, Basketball, Volleyball, Golf, Squash, Skiing, Swimming, Orienteering, Hillwalking and Kayaking.

Extra-Curricular Activities. There is a Contingent of the Combined Cadet Force (Army and RAF sections) and a Pipe Band. The Choirs, Concert Band and Orchestras play a prominent part in the life of the School, as do Literary and Debating Societies, which meet weekly, and dramatic societies, which present a variety of performances. Many other clubs and societies flourish, making over 100 in all. A very large proportion of pupils undertake The Duke of Edinburgh's Award.

Charitable status. Robert Gordon's College is a Registered Charity, number SC000123. It exists to provide education for boys and girls.

Roedean School

Roedean Way, Brighton BN2 5RQ
Tel: 01273 667500; Admissions: 01273 667626
Fax: 01273 676722
email: info@roedean.co.uk
website: www.roedean.co.uk
Twitter: @RoedeanSchool

Founded 1885.
Incorporated by Royal Charter 1938.

President:
Lady Patten of Barnes, BA (*OR*)

Vice-Presidents:
Mrs S M Fowler-Watt, RGN (*OR*)
Dr J M Peacey, MB BS, MRCGP (*OR*)

Chairman of Council:
Mr S Rothon, MA, MPhil

Vice-Chairman of Council:
Mrs M S Chaundler, OBE, BA (*OR*)

Council:
Ms J Barnard-Langston, BA, MA, DipCouns, JP
Ms J M Briggs, BA, MA, PGCE, Adv Dip BFM CIPFA
Mr M R Buchanan, BSc, NPQH
Mr H Fajemirokun, PhD
Ms F Cook, BSc (*OR*)
Ms S Glynn, BSc, LLB (*OR*)
Mr R S H Illingworth, BA
Ms D Patman, FRICS
Mr R Sanders OBE
Ms A Whitaker, MA, ACA
Mrs M Winckler, MA

Clerk: Mr R Poffley, BA, FCCA

ORA President: Mrs A Sheaf

Staff:

Headmaster: Mr O Blond, BA Essex

Deputy Head, Strategy: Miss T Keller, BSc Manchester, PGCE, NPQH
Deputy Head, Pastoral: Miss H Semple, MA Edinburgh
Director, Finance and Administration: Mr R Poffley, BA Sussex, FCCA
Director, Teaching and Learning: Ms V Del Federico, MA Sussex, BA Sussex, PGCE
Assistant Head for Holistic Care: Mr G Rainey, BA Durham, MA Reading
Director of External Relations & Sixth Form: Dr R Barrand, BA Durham, PhD Leeds, PGCE

Head of Sixth Form Language Pathway: Miss C Carragher, BSc Southampton, PGCE

Head of Key Stage 4: Mrs S Ellis, BA Brighton, PGCE Brighton

Head of Key Stage 3: Mrs S Bakhtiari, BA QTS, MA Brighton

Heads of Department:

Art: Mrs S Stanway, Chelsea School of Art, DipAD, ATC London

Classics: Ms J Jones, BA London, PG Dip

Dance: Miss S Stidston, LISTD Dip, RAD Teaching Dip

Design Technology: Miss E Griffiths-Moore, BA Edinburgh, PGCE Brighton

Drama: Mr J Green, BA East Anglia, QTS

Economics, Government & Politics: Mr K Thomson, BA Sheffield, PGCE Sussex

English: Mr D Woodhouse, BA Anglia, MA Sussex, PGCE Brighton (*Acting Faculty Lead*)

Geography: Mr J Maxwell, MA Cambridge, MEd Institute of Education, PGCE Cambridge

History/History of Art: Mr J M Davis, BA Lancaster, MA, MSc London, ARHistS, PGCE

ICT & Business Studies: Ms S Bakhtiari, BA, MA Brighton

Learning Support: Miss S Maguire. BA Essex, MA Open, PGCE Chichester, RSA Dip TEFL

Mathematics: Mr P Tarbet, BSc Durham, Dip Ed London, FRAS

Modern Languages: Ms A Fafalios, BA London

Music: Miss V Fewkes, BA Bath, PGCE

Personal & Social Education (*PSHE*): Ms L Harknett, BA Warwick, PGCE Oxford

Philosophy & Religious Studies: Miss K Balnaves, BA Birmingham, MA UCL, PGCE Liverpool Hope

Physical Education: Miss K Andrew, BA De Montfort, PGCE Cheltenham

Psychology: Ms F Thompson, BA Durham, PGCE Brighton

Science & Chemistry: Mr A England, MA Cantab, PGCE

Biology: Miss A Fraser, BSc London

Physics: Mrs J MacGregor, BA Dalhousie, PGCE Sussex

Registrar: Mrs D Banham

Introduction. Roedean is a day, flexi, weekly and full boarding school for 430 girls aged 11–18. The school has grown by about ten percent since last year, and, due to increased demand from UK parents, it now has a three-form entry for Year 7.

The three Lawrence sisters founded Roedean in Brighton in 1885. Their original aims were to give due emphasis to physical and outdoor education, to encourage independence and self-reliance, 'to give as much liberty as can be granted with safety' and to supply a sound intellectual training.

Today the school community is made up of 40 different nationalities and remains committed to the founders' emphasis on independent learning and the development of self-confidence in readiness for professional life. The school buildings are set on a spacious, yet safe, 45-acre site surrounded by a further 70 acres of farmland. The campus commands enchanting views of the English Channel.

Philosophy. The Roedean philosophy is for pupils to challenge themselves and everything around them. They are encouraged to be self-reliant, to explore their talents, to strive for excellence, to develop their intellectual curiosity, to lead as well as to be part of a team, and to appreciate cultural diversity. A girl educated at Roedean will have respect for herself and others, be qualified to enjoy a fulfilling career and feel confident she has the skills to balance her personal and professional life – she will grow up at her own pace within a warm, supportive, and enabling community.

The boarding approach is ideally suited to the school's 'whole life' philosophy as it provides a rich and balanced programme of learning and activities in a structured yet informal environment. Day girls benefit from this ethos as they are well integrated into the House system. The single-sex environment has particular advantages for girls: it prevents stereotyping, raises expectations and develops self-confidence by offering ample opportunities for leadership and responsibility.

Curriculum. Girls are given a structured grounding in basic skills and offered a very broad programme of knowledge and experience. Subject specialists work together in a coordinated approach to achieve maximum reinforcement and continuity across 30 subjects. The benefits of traditional subjects, including Latin, are balanced by Psychology, Design and Technology and Critical Thinking. Girls in KS3 take part in an academic enrichment programme called HHH (Heads, Hands, and Hearts), which includes Russian, cookery, Sign Language, among others. Class-sizes are consistently small, ranging between 14 and 20 girls in the Lower School, with smaller groups in the sixth form.

Each girl's GCSE programme is individually tailored to provide a broad, balanced education and to ensure that requirements for higher education are met.

The strong sixth form offers an extensive range and combination of A and AS Levels covering 25 subjects. Over time, the school has developed a strong link with the University of Sussex, enabling the most able sixth form mathematicians to study undergraduate geometry alongside their AS and A Level courses. There is also a weekly lecture programme for all girls in the Sixth Form with external speakers, covering diverse topics, such as living with AIDS, body-image, and gambling, as well as more academic topics.

Results in public examinations were the best they have been at GCSE in 2014, with 95% A*–B and 40% A*, and Roedean has a consistent success-rate, with 52.4% A*–A over the last five years.

Co-curricular Activities and Physical Education. The range of music, art and design, speech, debating, drama and dance opportunities within the curriculum are further supported by optional private tuition and club activities. The school is particularly strong in the performing arts: music (choirs and orchestras), drama and dance.

The school has an excellent record in the Duke of Edinburgh's Award and Young Enterprise Business Scheme which offer girls opportunities to develop a spirit of discovery and independence and encourage links with the wider community.

Netball, hockey, tennis, swimming, athletics, cricket and rounders are the principal sports with sailing, lacrosse, badminton, basketball, volleyball, squash, trampoline, gymnastics, fencing, golf, scuba diving and karate also available. Inter-school fixtures are part of all the major sport programmes and girls are encouraged to enter local, county and national tournaments.

Boarding. The House system provides the supportive and caring environment necessary for each girl, boarder or day, to flourish as an individual and a member of the community.

The four main Houses (for girls 11 to 17) and the separate sixth form House, Keswick, each have a dedicated team of staff in close contact with parents. Facilities range from bedrooms shared by 3 or 4 younger girls to university-style study-bedrooms for sixth formers. The girls in the four main houses are composed of a mixture of boarding and day students from each of the six year-groups.

Continuity of individual guidance and care is ensured by the school's tutorial system. Tutors monitor each girl's academic progress and involvement in extra-curricular activities and liaise with House staff on a regular basis to maintain a balanced, realistic timetable which meets each individual's needs and abilities.

Health. The School Health Centre is run by a Registered General Nurse who is assisted by a team of similarly qualified nurses. Two doctors visit the School and hold clinics regularly each week. They are "on call" in case of an emergency. There is also a Counsellor who runs sessions in school each week.

Religion. The School welcomes students of all faiths, or none. Arrangements are made for Anglicans to be prepared for Confirmation, for Roman Catholics to attend Sunday Mass locally and for Jewish girls to receive instruction.

Facilities. All subjects are taught in specialist rooms, and students have Wi-Fi access throughout the school to support their studies. There is a main library and resources' centre to support individual study. There are two art studios adjacent to a Design & Technology Centre, a multimedia Language Centre, a Performing Arts complex (including a theatre which seats 320 people, dance studios, music suite) and a Science wing with nine laboratories for biology, chemistry and physics. A multi-purpose sports hall with gym, heated indoor pool, 13 newly-refurbished hard tennis and netball courts, squash courts, ample playing fields and the use of two astroturf pitches close by support the PE/Sports programme.

School Year and Leave Out. There are three terms, beginning in September, January and April. The summer holidays last eight weeks and Christmas/Easter up to four weeks each. Girls go home for half term and there are two weekend exeats each term. All boarders are free to go home at weekends and those doing weekly boarding are escorted back to London on the train. The school provides a full boarding programme, but there is considerable flexibility to accommodate the individual needs of families.

Admission. Entry at 11+, 12+, 13+ and 16+ is through Roedean Entrance Examination papers in English, Maths, and Non-Verbal Reasoning, which can be taken at any time up to two terms before entry. A good number of suitably qualified girls are admitted each year to the sixth form.

Scholarships and Bursaries. Academic, Art, Dance, Drama, Music, and Sport scholarships (worth 10% of fees) and exhibitions (worth 5% of fees) are available for girls entering Year 7, Year 9, and the Sixth Form.

Junior Scholarship examinations are held in January; Sixth Form Scholarship examinations are held in November.

Means-tested Bursaries are available.

Details of scholarships and bursaries may be obtained from the Registrar.

Fees per term (2014–2015). Full Boarders £9,980–£11,200; Weekly Boarders (5 days) £8,650–£9,650; Flexi Boarders (3 days) £7,630–£8,450; Day Girls £5,460–£6,300. For girls entering the Sixth Form from other schools, there is an additional supplement of £1,200 per term (boarding). Parents who wish to pay a single composition fee should apply to the Director, Finance and Administration.

Extra fees are charged for individual tuition in musical instruments, speech training, ballet and some athletic activities.

For further details please contact the Registrar.

Charitable status. Roedean School is a Registered Charity, number 307063. It exists to provide quality education for girls.

Rossall School

Fleetwood, Lancs FY7 8JW

Tel:	01253 774201
Fax:	01253 772052
email:	enquiries@rossall.org.uk
website:	www.rossallschool.org.uk
Twitter:	@RossallSchool
Facebook:	/RossallSchoolUK

Motto: '*Mens agitat molem*'

Rossall School was founded in 1844 on the coast of Lancashire. It is incorporated by Royal Charter, granted in 1890, and is under the management of a Council.

"For many, a childhood by the sea is a dream; at Rossall, that dream becomes a reality. Rossall is an exceptional school, rooted in its heritage yet innately dynamic, brimming with personality and excited about the future."

Life Governors:
The Earl of Derby, President of Corporation
Mrs H N Trapnell
Mr A N Stephenson, MA

Governors:
Chairman: Mr Chris Holt, BSc, MBA, ACMA
Vice Chair: Mr S J Fisher, MA
Secretary of the Corporation and Clerk to the Council: Mr
 B E Clark, MBE
Mr M J Reece, MA
The Rt Revd R Ladds, SSc, BEd, LRSC, FCS
Mr J F Parr
Mrs C M Preston, BSc, ARICS
Mr M Craven, MA
Dr R W F Oakley
Mr J A R Prestwich, FCA
The Revd Canon P K Warren, MA
Dr H O Fajemirokun
Mr D O Winterbottom, MA, BPhil
Mr H H Aird, MA
Mr M R Mosley, MA
Prof J P Davis, BSc, CEng, FIMechE, FIoD
Mr S J Fisher, MA
Mr N K Ward, BSc
Mrs B Booth, MEd, PGCE, ALCM
Dr D M Elliott, BSc, MBChB
Mrs L Croston, BSc, PGCE, ALCM
Mrs M Smith, MSc, FFA, MinstF Dip, JP
Mrs K Thomas, MIFST, BSc, RSci

Secretary to the Corporation and Council: Mr B E Clark,
 MBE

Head: Ms Elaine Purves, BA Hons, PGCE

Deputy Head: Mr Robert Robinson, BA Hons, PGCE, MA
Bursar: Mrs Emma Sanderson
Deputy Head (Academic): Mrs Gillian Pryor, BSc Hons,
 PGCE
Head of Junior Schools: Mrs Katie Lee, MA, CPP, Cert Ed
Head of ISC: Mr Martin Gray, BA Hons TEFL
Deputy of ISC: Mr Iggi Moore, BA Hons, Cert TESOL,
 PGCE
Head of Sixth Form: Mr Mark Bradley, BSc Hons, PGCE
Senior Master: Mr Mark Pryor, BSc Hons, PGCE

Heads of Departments:

Art: Mrs Sarah Holder-Williams, MA, RSA Dip PA
Business Studies & Economics: Mr Sean Hoffman, BA,
 PGCE
English: Mrs Sheila J Cross, BA, PGCE
Mathematics: Mr P Butterworth, BSc Hons
Modern Foreign Languages: Mrs I Wallace
EAL: Mrs C Wolstencroft, MEd TESOL, BA Hons
Director of Music: Miss Margaret Young, BA Hons,
 LTCL, LRSM
Science:
Chemistry: Mrs Kathryn Griffiths, BSc, PGCE
Physics: Miss Jane Mercer, BSc, PGCE
Biology: Mr Martin Metcalfe, BSc Hons, PGCE
Geography: Mr Anthony Fairhurst, BA Hons, PGCE
History: Miss J Shillaw, BA Hons, PGCE
Physical Education:
Director of Sport: Mr Ian Cameron, BA, PGCE & Mr Nick
 James
Design & Technology: Mr Lee Hodgetts, BA Hons

Religious Studies, Philosophy and Ethics inc Psychology:
Mr Peter Jurczak, BA, MTh
Psychology: Miss K N Allen
Learning Support: Ms S Edge

Houses/Houseparents:
Anchor House: Mr Mike Kelly & Ms Kate Evans
Dolphin House: Ms Jocelyn Merris
Lugard House: Mr Tim Fletcher
Mitre Fleur de Lys House: Mr Stuart Corrie
Pelican House: Mr Mike Park
Puffin House: Ms Jane Mercer
Rose House: Ms Roz Bendelow
Spread Eagle House: Mr Ian McCleary
Wren House: Mrs Emma Williams
Maltese Cross House: Mr Martin & Mrs Michele Metcalfe

Instrumental Music Teachers for:
Brass, Flute, Guitar, Composition, Piano, Organ, Clarinet,
Saxophone, Violin, Voice, Percussion

Registrar: Mrs Michele Metcalfe
Careers: Mr J Holland
IB Coordinator: Dr Doris Dohmen, DPhil, PGCE
Examinations Officer: Mr Ron Asher, BSc, PGCE
Librarian: Mrs Beth Simmons, BA Hons
Marketing Manager: Mrs N Fielden
Medical Officer: Dr P G Carpenter, MBChB, MRCGP,
DRCOG, FPA

Academic Curriculum. All entrants are expected to take
a broad based curriculum prior to GCSE. At this stage pupils
study English Language, English Literature, Maths, Sciences and a Modern Foreign Language (French, German
and Spanish: SEN students possibly excepted); there is then
a choice of three options taken from History, Geography,
Psychology, Business Studies, Religious Studies, Art, DT,
PE, Music, Drama and ICT.

In the Sixth Form the International Baccalaureate and A
Levels are offered. At AS/A2 all the subjects at GCSE are
on the curriculum, with separate sciences, Economics,
Graphic Communications, Photography, Geology, Law and
Philosophy also on offer. There is a similar wide range of
subjects offered within the IB, where Psychology, Philosophy and Business Management are also taught. Much
emphasis in the IB is also placed upon the 'Core', the teaching of the Theory of Knowledge, the Extended Essay and
the Creativity, Action, Service component.

Some 95% of the Upper Sixth follow on into Higher Education both at home and abroad. Special arrangements are
made for those seeking entry to Oxbridge and specialist
institutions abroad.

The Arts, Science and Technology. The Music Department provides the basis for individual instrumental tuition.
The Chapel Choir sings choral services in the magnificent
Chapel of St John the Baptist. There are other choral groups,
a junior and senior orchestra and a jazz band.

The Art and Design Technology departments offer extensive art and design facilities within purpose-built art and
design workshops containing state-of-the-art tooling image
making machinery.

The School's Astronomy and Space Science Centre
incorporates an observatory, permanent planetarium, lecture
theatre and classroom suite. This is not only used within the
school for curriculum teaching but is also available for outside use. The Science Department is well used with some
50%+ of students following science at 16+. Within the
school grounds there are 3 Sites of Scientific Interest, which
are maintained by staff and students. The sea, beach and
dunes in front of the school are similar sources for study.

The IT provision is also housed primarily within the Science area with 300+ machines available through the working day and beyond both in the IT suite and in departments
around the campus. The machines are part of a secure cabled

network. The Junior School and International Study Centre
have their own provision.

The House System. All pupils are members of a House.
At age 13 there are five boys' day and boarding houses and
four girls' day and boarding houses. All boarding boys and
girls entering at 7+ are in Anchor House, which has its own
residential unit. Houseparents have responsibility for each
pupil's welfare and are supported by deputies, tutors, medical, careers staff, etc.

Religious Instruction. Rossall was founded as 'the
Northern Church of England School' and Chapel remains
central to the well-being of the community. Pupils of all
faiths are encouraged to share in this community, and the
School has its own Chaplaincy with resident Chaplain.

Games. 45 acres of playing field and a gymnasium,
floodlit Astroturf and indoor 25-metre swimming pool,
along with squash, tennis, and fives courts allow all pupils to
pursue a sporting interest. The boys mainly play rugby,
hockey, cricket, football and basketball, with the girls playing hockey, netball, rounders and tennis. All pupils are
taught to play the unique game of RossHockey on the sandy
beach owned by the School. There are full programmes of
competitive fixtures against other schools and clubs. House
matches occur in all major games, including football, cross-
country in the Lent Term. Archery, athletics, shooting, golf,
horse riding and many other activities are offered.

The CCF. Rossall proudly lays claim to having the oldest
CCF in the country. Currently most of Years 9–11 are in
either the Army, Navy or Air Force contingents. In Year 9 all
cadets will follow the Bronze Duke of Edinburgh's Award,
progress to Silver and Gold is optional. All cadets also have
the chance to follow the BTEC Service award within the
corps, the equivalent to 4 GCSEs this is completed entirely
within CCF time. The school has a shooting range, keeps
boats on the Wyre and there is opportunity to fly at RAF
Woodvale.

Activities and Clubs. Time is set aside after school 4
days a week and at weekends for activities and clubs which
operate over the 3 terms. Clubs and activities include but are
not limited to: The Literary Society, Choir, Sports, and bi-
half termly excursions.

Admission. Any term in the year for boys and girls aged
11+ and 13+, September preferably at 16+ or 17+. All applications for entrance should be made to the Registrar. On registration a fee of £50 will be charged to day applicants and
£175 to boarding applicants. Applicants will be put in touch
with a Housemaster or Housemistress as soon as appropriate.

Fees per term (2014–2015). Day £2,520–£4,060; Full
Boarding   £6,140–£11,500;   Weekly   Boarding
£4,360–£6,980.

Scholarships and Bursaries. Scholarships are offered
for academic, music, art, drama, sport and all-round
achievement. Scholarships are awarded solely on merit and
range in value. In exceptional circumstances the special
Trapnell Scholarship for excellence in Maths and Science
may award up to 100% fee remission.

Instrumental or vocal Music Scholarships are offered.
Awards can include free tuition in two instruments.

A number of clerical bursaries are awarded on a means
test to sons of Clergy who can sustain a proportion of the
Fees themselves but who need extra help. Bursaries are also
available to families from the British Armed Forces.

All enquiries about Scholarships and Bursaries and other
awards should be addressed to the Registrar.

Rossall Junior School. Rossall has its own Junior
School for children aged 7–11 situated within the same
grounds. There is also a Nursery and Infants School for day
boys and girls aged 2–7.

Access. Motorway: 15 minutes from M55 (spur off M6).
Railway: Blackpool North (6 miles). Air: Manchester International Airport (55 miles by road).

Alumni. A network of Old Rossallians is managed by Sharon Potts, Alumni Officer at the school.

The Rossallian Club. This club for former pupils keeps a record of more than 5,000 members and coordinates the activities of eight Branches. A Newsletter is published twice each year.

Charitable Status. The Corporation of Rossall School is a Registered Charity, number 526685.

Rougemont School

Llantarnam Hall, Malpas Road, Newport, South Wales NP20 6QB
Tel: 01633 820800
Fax: 01633 855598
email: registrar@rsch.co.uk
website: www.rougemontschool.co.uk
Twitter: @rougemontschool
Facebook: Rougemont-School

President: Mr I S Burge

Governors:
Chairman: Mr I G Short
Vice-Chairman: Mrs A C Thomas, JP, SRN, SCM
Mrs J Clark, BA, PGCE
Mr R Pugsley, MSc, FCCA
Dr R M Reynolds, BSc, DipEd
Mrs S Desai, BPharm, MRPharmS
Miss J Sollis, BA, AKC
Mr M Tebbutt
Prof D Fone, MB BS, MD, FFPH, FRGS, MRCGP, DCH, DRCOG
Mr I Hoppe
Mr H Clark
Mr R Green

Headmaster: Mr R Carnevale, MA Ed, BSc, PGCE

* *Head of Department*
§ *Part-time*

Head of Preparatory School: Mrs L Pritchard, BA, PGCE
Deputy Head: Mrs S Archer, BSc, PGCE (*Biology*)
Director of Staffing: Mrs S Roberts, BSc, PGCE (*Head of Mathematics*)
Director of Studies: Mrs P Rogers, MA Ed, BSc, PGCE (*Head of Geography, ICT Coordinator*)
Director of Co-Curriculum: Mr A Rees, BA, PGCE (*Physical Education, Head of Years 10 and 11, Duke of Edinburgh's Award*)
Academic Registrar: Mr M James, MA Ed, BEd, BA, BSc, CBiol, MIBiol, Cert Maths Open (*Biology*)
Finance Manager: Mrs H Perry, FCCA
Operations Manager: Mr M Baldwin

Senior School:
Miss S Ashton, BA, PGCE (*Spanish, House Tutor*)
Mr K Bell, BA, PGCE (**Physical Education*)
Mrs K Benson-Dugdale, BMus, MA, QTS, PGEM (*Higher Education Advisor, *Music*)
Mr M Bowman, BSc, PGCE (*Mathematics*)
Ms A Clason-Thomas, BA, MA, PGCE (*Learning Resources Manager, French*)
Mr D Cobb, BSc, PGCE, Cert Maths Open (**Biology*)
Miss C Dugdale, BA, PGCE (*§PE, Religious Studies*)
Mrs S Eley, BA, PGCE (*§Learning Development Centre*)
Mrs S Elson, LLB (*§Latin*)
Mrs E Ferrand, BEd (**Extra-Mural Programme, Mathematics*)
Mrs H Garratt, BSc, PGCE (*§Physical Education*)
Mrs R Garrod, BA, PGCE (*§History, Editor of School Magazine*)
Mr L Godfrey, BSc, PGCE (*Mathematics, *PHSE*)

Mrs J Goodwin, BSc (**Physics, Pupil Performance Coordinator*)
Mr J Hardwick, BSc, PGCE (*Biology, Careers*)
Mrs J Harris, CertEd, Dip Theol (**Religious Studies*)
Mrs K Hughes, BSc, PGCE, (*Geography*)
Miss R Hayes, BA, PGCE (*Design & Technology, ICT, Head of Year 12*)
Miss J Jones, BA, PGCE (**English*)
Mrs A Jenkins, BSc (*Chemistry, Physics*)
Mr M Jenkins, MA Cantab, PGCE (**History*)
Mrs C Langford, BSc, PGCE (*Chemistry*)
Mr P McMahon, MSc, BSc, QTS (*Mathematics*)
Miss A Mintowt-Czyz, BA, PGCE (*English*)
Mr L Mintowt-Czyz, BA, BTec, PGCE (**Art*)
Mrs D Moore, BA, PGCE (**Drama*)
Mrs D Morgan, BA, PGCE (**Modern Languages*)
Mrs S Morgan, MSc, BSc, PGCE, Cert Lit/Dyslexia (*Learning Development Centre, Mathematics*)
Mrs S Munro, DEUG, Licence, PGCE (*French*)
Miss C Owen, BA, PGCE (*Business Studies and Economics, Mathematics*)
Miss K Page, BSc, PGCE (*Physical Education, House Tutor*)
Miss L Parr, BA, PGCE (*Art, ICT, House Tutor*)
Mr F Pearce, BSc, PGCE, DipComp (**ICT, Physics*)
Mr A Richards, BSc, PGCE (*Mathematics, ICT, Head of Year 13*)
Mrs A Robst-Cross, BA, PGCE (*English, Media Studies*)
Mrs C Sims, BA, PGCE, AMBDA, CCET (**Learning Development Centre, Latin*)
Mr H Singer, MA Ed, BA, PGCE (*Head of Y8–9, *Design & Technology*)
Mrs L Singer, BSc, PGCE (*§Physical Education*)
Mrs R Taylor, BA, PGCE, AMBDA (*§Learning Development Centre*)
Mrs L Thickins, BA, PGCE (*English, Media Studies*)
Mrs T van der Linde, MA Ed, BSc, PGCE (*Head of Y7, *Chemistry*)

Preparatory School, Junior Department:
Mrs R Carroll, BA, PGCE (*Class Teacher, Able and Talented Coordinator*)
Mr C Dobbins, BMus, DipMus, LRSM, PGCE (*Music and Games*)
Mrs S Elson, LLB (*History and Religious Studies*)
Mrs K Galloway, KS2 (*Teaching and Learning Assistant*)
Mrs J Greenaway, CertEd (*Class Teacher*)
Miss L Hallas, BA, PGCE (*Deputy Head, English, History*)
Mrs A Jenkins, BSc (*Science*)
Mr P McMahon, BSc, MSc, QTS (*Mathematics & ICT*)
Mrs S Morgan, MSc, BSc, PGCE, DipLit/Dyslexia (*Science, Learning Development Centre*)
Mrs R Payne, NNEB (*Teaching and Learning Assistant*)
Mrs C Poore, BEd (*Science, Geography, Curriculum Director*)
Mr S Rowlands, BA, QTS (*Class Teacher, House Tutor*)
Mrs K Williams, BEd (*Class Teacher*)

Preparatory School, Infant Department:
Mrs H Ashill, NNEB (*Teaching and Learning Assistant*)
Mr A Bevan, BA, PGCE (*Class Teacher*)
Mrs A Burridge, BSc, PGCE (*Class Teacher*)
Mr C Dobbins, BMus, DipMus, LRSM, PGCE (*Music*)
Mrs S Hotchkiss, BA, QTS (*Deputy Head, Class Teacher*)
Miss C Leaves, BA, QTS (*Class Teacher*)
Mrs L McLoughlin, NVQ3 (*Teaching and Learning Assistant*)
Mrs T Mountford, BEd (*Class Teacher*)
Mrs N Noor, BA, PGCE (*Class Teacher, Curriculum Director, Infants*)
Mrs C Townsend, NVQ (*Class Teacher*)

Preparatory School, Rougemont Rainbows Nursery:
Mrs J Forouzan, NNEB (*Nursery Supervisor*)
Mrs A Exley (*Teaching and Learning Assistant*)

Mrs E Mian, NNEB (*Teaching and Learning Assistant*)
Miss Z Rees, NNEB (*Teaching and Learning Assistant*)

Registrar: Mrs N Bates

Rougemont was founded in a house of that name immediately after the First World War as a co-educational day school taking children through to grammar school entrance at 11. It moved to Nant Coch House just after the Second World War and grew to about 200 pupils.

In 1974 the school was re-founded as a Charitable Trust. Since then it has bought extensive new buildings and has approximately 600 pupils on roll in the Preparatory School (Infant Department – Nursery to Year 2 and Junior Department – Years 3–8) and Senior School (Years 9–13).

The Preparatory Junior Department and Senior School moved to a new site at Llantarnam Hall, a large Victorian mansion set in 50 acres of grounds, between 1992 and 1995, with the Infant Department joining them in April 2004. The grounds have been landscaped to provide playing fields and an extensive building programme has taken place on the site. During 1998 a Liberal Arts area including Sports Hall, Music suite and Drama Studio was completed. In 1999 a new classroom block and library was completed and in 2000 additional classrooms together with Art studio were built.

Admission to the Preparatory and Senior Schools is by interview and examination. Entry to the Sixth Form is dependent on GCSE results.

The following paragraphs refer to the Senior School although peripatetic specialists work in both and there is some interchange of teachers.

Curriculum. Pupils follow a wide syllabus to age 14. For the two years to GCSE pupils normally study nine subjects of which English Language and Literature, Mathematics, a language, science and a humanities subject are normally compulsory. 18 subjects are available.

Sixth Form. 19 AS/A2 Levels are available. Sixth Form pupils have their own common room and study area. Sixth Form pupils can also study AS Level Critical Thinking and take part in a range of extra-curricular activities and games.

Religion. Rougemont School has no direct affiliation to a Christian Church or denomination. However, the religious instruction, corporate worship and moral value system of the School is based on that of the broad tradition of the mainstream Christian Churches.

Careers. The School belongs to the Independent Schools Careers Organisation. The Senior teachers advise on all aspects of further education and careers.

Music. In addition to specialist teachers of music a large number of peripatetic teachers cover the range of orchestral instruments. There are choirs and instrumental ensembles for all ages.

Drama. In addition to the Infant Department's Spring Festival and the Senior School Eisteddfod, two major plays and two musical events take place each year.

Elocution and Dance. Visiting staff hold weekly classes for LADA courses, ballet and modern dance.

Sport. The School has developed a high standard of performance in most major sports. There is a wide fixtures programme for both boys and girls, as well as the opportunity to participate in numerous coaching courses.

Clubs. A wide variety of extra-curricular activities and clubs is available at lunch time and after school, as is supervised prep.

Duke of Edinburgh's Award Scheme. This is a very successful activity within the school and over 60 pupils have gained the Gold Award in the last twenty years.

Fees per term (2014–2015). Preparatory School: Infant Department £2,508–£2,692, Junior Department £3,072; Senior School: £3,552–£3,996.

Scholarships. An annual scholarship examination is held for entry to Year 7. A limited number of means-tested bursaries is offered from Year 7 upwards, with a separate scheme for Sixth Form entry.

Further information. A prospectus and other details are available from the Registrar (Tel: 01633 820800, email: registrar@rsch.co.uk).

Charitable status. Rougemont School is a Registered Charity, number 532341. It exists to provide education for boys and girls.

Royal Grammar School
Guildford

High Street, Guildford, Surrey GU1 3BB
Tel: Headmaster: 01483 880608
              School Office: 01483 880600
Fax: 01483 306127
email: office@rgs-guildford.co.uk
website: www.rgs-guildford.co.uk
Twitter: @RGSGuildford

Located in the centre of the historic town of Guildford, the RGS is an independent day school for around 900 boys aged 11 to 18, some 270 of whom are in the Sixth Form. As a flagship for boys' education, the School has a national reputation for academic excellence but also prides itself on its traditional values of decency and respect, supported by outstanding pastoral care. RGS boys have the opportunity to experience the widest range of enriching activities providing them with a broad and balanced education. Academic excellence is at the very heart of the School's philosophy. The RGS aims to encourage the growth of intellectual curiosity and creativity and to inculcate a life-long love of learning in the boys. The RGS is consistently one of the top five boys' schools in the country at both A Level and GCSE, and is extremely proud of its Oxbridge record; in the last decade 326 offers have been made including 28 offers in the recent round of admissions.

Governing Body:
Chairman: Cllr Mrs S K Creedy, MA
Vice-Chairman: His Honour Judge C Critchlow, LLB, DL
Mr C D Barnett, MA
Cllr M Brett-Warburton, MA RCA, MA UCB, RIBA
Mrs C F Cobley, MCIPD
The Revd Canon RL Cotton, MA, DipTh
¶Mr D J Counsell, FCA
Mr B J Creese, BA, MA
The Earl of Onslow
Mr J D Fairley, BA
Mr B Hartop, BSc
Cllr Mrs J Jordan, BA
Dr L S K Linton, MA, MB ChB, MRCP
The Mayor of Guildford
Dr H J Pearson, OBE, MA, PhD, CMath, FIMA
Mr P G Peel, FCA
Ms P S Powell, BA
Professor S Price, MSc, PhD, FBTS, ERT, FHEA
Mr C T Shorter, CEng, MIStructE, FConsE, FFB
Mr J A Smith, CEng, FCIBSE
¶Mr N E J Vineall, QC, MA

¶ *Old Guildfordian*

Bursar and Clerk to the Governors: Mr R A Ukiah, MA

Headmaster: Dr J M Cox, BSc, PhD (*Biology*)

Deputy Head (Staff): Mr G T Williams, MA (*History*)
Deputy Head (Pupils): Mr A U Woodman, BSc, MA (*Biology*)

Assistant Head (Teaching and Learning): Mr P J Bridges, BSc (*Economics*)
Assistant Head (Curriculum): Mr P J Dunscombe, BSc (*Mathematics, *Careers*)

Assistant Head (*Marketing and Communications*): Mr J W
  Pressley, MA (*Classics*)
Head of Upper School and Head of Sixth Form: Mr T W
  Shimell, MChem (*Chemistry*)
Head of Lower School and Head of Third Form: Mr N E
  Wild, BA (*Religion and Philosophy*)

* Head of Department

Art:
*Mr A M J Curtis, MA
Miss K E Price, BA, MA
Mr A N Rozier, BA

Biology:
*Dr E J Hudson, MA, MSc,
  PhD
Mr E J Badham, ARCS,
  BSc, CBiol, MSB
Mr P A Bagley, MA, FCA
Mr A H Dubois, BSc
Mrs K Walker, BSc
Dr L A Whall, BA, PhD

Chemistry:
*Mr W-S Lau, MChem
Mr S W Armstrong, MA
Dr E T Batchelar, MChem,
  DPhil
Dr J S Braithwaite, BSc,
  PhD
Dr J L Bodmer, BSc, PhD,
  MBA
Mrs S F Hudson, BSc, MSc

Classics:
*Mr E K D Bush, MA
Mrs S E Besly-Quick, BA
Mrs S Cooper, BA
Miss N S Goul-Wheeker,
  MA
Mr P G Nathan, BA
Mr D J Woolcott, BA

Design & Technology:
*Mr J B Kelly, BA, MA,
  MA RCA
Mr D M Hoyle, BEng
Mr K J Knight, BSc, MSc

Drama:
*Ms N C McClean, BA,
  MA

Economics:
*Mr D S J Wright, BA
Miss S K H Blair, BSc,
  MSc
Mrs P A Brooks, MBA
Mr N W Gough, BSc, MSc

English:
*Mr A F Smith, BA, MA,
  MA
Dr A H S Barras, BA, MA,
  PhD
Mr E J P Bradnock, BA
Mrs H M Curtis, BA
Mr A F Kettle, BA
Mr P M Leamon, BA
Miss E J Newton, BA, MA
Miss L Simpson, BA
The Revd J P Whittaker,
  MA

Geography:
*Mrs R G Waters, MA
Mr W D Cowx, BSc, MSc

Mr R E J Seymour, BEd,
  FRGS
Mrs P A Thomas, BSc,
  MSc, FRGS, MSB, Dip
  Counselling
Mr J C Witts, BSc
Mr S J H Yetman, BSc

History:
*Mr H R Wiggins, MA
¶Mr A C Dodd, BA, MA
Mr T J J Owens, BA
  (*Politics)
Mr J R Saxton, MA
Mr A J Shakeri, BA

Information Technology:
*Mr O C Lawson, BSc

Mathematics:
*Mr S G Black, MMath
Mrs L Z Banerji, BSc
Mrs M C Booth, BEd
Mr J A Casale, BSc, MBA
Mr C George, BSc
Mrs K Handley, BSc
Mrs F A Hobbs, BSc
Mr M R Jenkins, BSc
Mr M J Jennings, BA
Miss S Kendell, BSc
Mrs S J Perrett, BA
Mr N C Pinhey, BSc
Miss K E Sullivan, BSc
Mr A J W Thorn, MA

Modern Languages:
*Ms A V E Tournier, Lic
Mr S J Baker, BA
Mr C J Grace, BA, MA,
  LTCL, AMusLCM
Mr P J Hosier, BA, MEd
Mr G M Knight, BA
Mr A R Lowe, BA
Mr J Marchiafava, Lic
Miss M-L McCarter, Lic,
  MA
Mrs R J Rathmell, BA
Mrs C E Smith, BA
Mrs N Wilson, Dip HE

Music:
*Mr P H White, MA
  (*Director of Music*)
Mr D H Chambers, BMus,
  PCASS
Mr J C McHardy, BMus,
  LRAM, PG Dip, ARCO,
  ARAM
Miss J Newman, AGSM,
  CRD
Mr S J Orchard, BMus,
  MMus

Physical Education:
*Mr I Wilkes, BEd
  (*Director of Sport*)
Mr M F Baggs, BA
  (*Hockey*)

¶Mr M O Macfarlane, BSc,
  MSc (*Athletics*)
Mr T P Rogers, BSc
  (*Rugby*)
Mr C J L Sandbach, BA
  (*Cricket*)
Mr S B R Shore, BEd

Physics:
*Mr M R F Royds, BEng
Mr C S Bradford, MPhys
Mr M A Burbidge, BSc,
  BA
Mr L M Holland, BSc

Mr J P Hood, MA, MSci
Dr D Patel, BSc, PhD
Dr S G Thornhill, MA,
  DPhil
Mrs D Whitehead, BTech

Religion and Philosophy:
*Mr R B Meadowcroft,
  BA, MA
¶Mr M C Bird, BA
Mrs L Griffiths, BA
Mrs H K Suenson-Taylor,
  BA
Mr C J White, BA

Admissions Registrar: Mrs K L Sweet, BA, MCIPD

Buildings and Facilities. The Tudor buildings in Guildford's High Street have been at the very heart of the RGS for
over five centuries. The School was founded by Robert
Beckingham in 1509 and established by King Edward VI's
Charter of 1552, which decreed that there should be "…one
Grammar School in Guildford …for the Education, Institution and Instruction of Boys and Youths in Grammar at all
future times for ever to endure". Among the first in the
country to be purpose-built, the original buildings contain a
remarkable Chained Library, which is now the Headmaster's Study. The School enjoys facilities appropriate to education in the 21st century, including a state-of-the-art Music
School, Art School, purpose-built Sixth Form Centre and
Sports Hall. The Sports Ground at Bradstone Brook provides twenty acres of pitches, tennis courts and a recently
refurbished pavilion. The School also benefits from the use
of nationally renowned sports facilities in the immediate
proximity, including Surrey Sports Park.

Curriculum. The school day is from 8.45 am to 4.00 pm;
there are no lessons on Saturdays. Many extra-curricular
activities and clubs take place after school, however. In the
first three years (Years 7, 8 and 9 nationally), all boys follow
a common curriculum embodying the programmes of study
for Key Stage 3 of the National Curriculum. The subjects
studied are English, French or Spanish, Geography, History,
Latin, Maths, Information Technology, RE, PE, Art, Music,
Design and Technology, and Science. In the second year, the
boys study the separate sciences and in the third year (Year
9) all boys choose between Spanish, German and Greek as
an additional language.

GCSEs and IGCSEs are offered with boys taking ten subjects out of the 17 available. At GCSE there is a range of
ancient and modern languages including Ancient Greek and
Latin, as well as French, Spanish and German. There is the
opportunity to study Arabic, Mandarin, Japanese and Russian off timetable.

All Sixth Form boys take four subjects at AS Level and
then three or four at A Level; over twenty AS and A Level
subjects are offered. A broad curriculum also includes the
Independent Learning Assignment, the Extended Project
Qualification and a General Studies programme organised in
conjunction with Guildford High School.

Religion. The ethos of the RGS is firmly based on traditional Christian principles and the School has strong links
with Holy Trinity Church in the centre of the town and
Guildford Cathedral; however, as a non-denominational
school, boys from all faiths are welcomed. A diverse, stimulating assembly programme provides the opportunity for
collective worship and broadens the boys' horizons while
establishing a tolerant set of values. Religious Education
lessons, which are an integral part of the School's curriculum, further contribute to developing each individual's
moral compass.

Pastoral Care. Respect, tolerance and understanding of
others characterise daily life at the RGS and the very strong
rapport between boys and teachers makes for a vibrant environment. The boys establish lasting relationships within the

year group; in addition, the house system, mentoring, and role of all senior boys as prefects ensure friendships are forged throughout the School. The outstanding pastoral care on offer from dedicated form tutors, heads of year and personal tutors, all overseen by the Deputy Head (Pupils), enables the boys to thrive in a mutually supportive environment where every boy can flourish as an individual.

Extra-Curricular Activities. The exceptional range of extra-curricular activities offered is one of the greatest strengths of the School; there are currently over sixty societies at the RGS. These range from air rifle, chess, christian union, computer aided design, drama, golf, Model United Nations, music, philosophy to the West End social club. Boys have the opportunity to take Bronze, Silver and Gold Duke of Edinburgh's Award through the Combined Cadet Force, Scouts or Outdoor Pursuits. Over 30% of pupils learn a musical instrument and they can join a variety of instrumental groups including Big Band, School Orchestra, Choir and a strong Choral Society. There are many opportunities for boys throughout the School to get involved in drama productions, both for the School and their house.

Games. The School's principal games are rugby, hockey and cricket, although as boys move up the School their sporting options widen considerably. Sports available include athletics, badminton, basketball, cross-country running, fencing, football, golf, sailing, shooting, swimming and tennis. Professional coaching and outstanding facilities develop the skill levels of boys of all abilities; the School takes pride in providing competitive sport and opportunities for all while also nurturing the very best of sporting talent. The School currently has a significant number of boys who are competing for county, national and international honours.

Admission. Boys may be considered for entry to the RGS at any age between 11 and 18. The usual ages of entry, however, are at 11, 13 and 16 into the Sixth Form. Applicants at 11 take the School's entrance examination in the January before the year of entry; those for 13+ entry take the Common Entrance examination or Scholarship papers after 11+ assessment. New boys are admitted in September of each year. The Headmaster is pleased to meet parents, arrange for them to see the School, and discuss the possibility of their son's entry to the School. Appointments may be made through the Registrar, who can supply a hard copy of the School's prospectus; it is also available on the RGS website.

Fees per term (2014–2015). £5,100 (plus £250 for lunches, which are compulsory for First and Second Forms) inclusive of all tuition, stationery and loan of necessary books.

Scholarships. Scholarships of up to 20% fee remission are awarded in recognition of outstanding academic merit. For boys entering the First Form at 11 there is a competitive examination in English and Mathematics, held in January. For boys entering the Third Form at 13 there is a two-day examination covering all Common Entrance subjects, held in March. The top scholar of a year group is designated the King's Scholar.

Music scholarships of up to 20% fee remission are available at 11 and 13. It is hoped that a King's Scholarship can be awarded each year to a boy of outstanding musical potential.

One Art Scholarship and one Sports Scholarship of 10% fee remission at 13+ is available annually.

Full details of Scholarships and Bursaries are available from the Registrar.

Old Boys. The Membership Secretary of the Old Guildfordians' Association is M Granshaw, who can be contacted via the School.

Charitable status. The King Edward VI Royal Grammar School, Guildford is Registered Charity, number 312028.

Royal Grammar School
Newcastle upon Tyne

Eskdale Terrace, Newcastle-upon-Tyne NE2 4DX
Tel: 0191 281 5711
Fax: 0191 212 0392
email: admissions@rgs.newcastle.sch.uk
website: www.rgs.newcastle.sch.uk

The Royal Grammar School was founded and endowed in 1545 by Thomas Horsley, and by virtue of a Charter granted in 1600 by Queen Elizabeth it became 'the Free Grammar School of Queen Elizabeth in Newcastle upon Tyne'. For over 450 years and on six different sites the School has been of major educational importance in Newcastle and in the North East as a whole. It has valued its close links with the city and region, and its Governing Body consists largely of representatives of important companies, Local Authorities and Universities.

The School benefits from its central position, being within easy walking distance of the Civic and City Centres and of Newcastle's two Universities, and linked with the whole region by easily accessible rail, bus and metro services.

The School is a Day School and moved towards full co-education in 2006 with places being allocated to boys and girls at all entry points (7+, 9+, 11+, 16+). There are about 1300 students, including 1047 in the Senior School (age 11–18) and 258 in the Junior School (age 7–11).

Governing Body:

Co-opted Governors:
Chairman: P A Walker, BA
Vice-Chairman: Professor A C Hurlbert, BA, MA, PhD, MD
A J Applegarth, BA
P A Campbell, MA
Ms N C D'Cruz, LLB Hons
I Evbuomwan, MBBS, MD, MRCOG
N A H Fenwick, MA
P A Kramer, LLB, FCIArb
C S E Murphy, BSc
I R Simpson, ACIB

Nominated Governors:
Dr S Ali, PhD
Professor E W N Glover, MA, PhD, CPhys, FInstP, ILTM
Dr J G Holland
Councillor T Robson

Clerk to the Governors and Bursar: R J Metcalfe, MA, FBIFM

Headmaster: B St J Trafford, MA, MEd, PhD, FRSA

Deputy Head: A A Bird, BMus, MEd, LRAM

Assistant Staff:
* *Head of Department*

Art:
*G P Mason, BA
P Edwards, BA
Mrs C Egan-Fowler, BEd
Mrs K Nowicki, BA
§Miss H Bray, BA

Biology:
*P J Heath, BSc
Dr M H Bell, BSc, PhD
Mrs J A Malpas, BSc
    (*Assistant Head of Lower School*)

Dr C J Murgatroyd, BSc, DPhil
L Shepherd, BA
C J H Wancke, BSc
§Mrs S F Hutchinson, BSc

Chemistry:
Dr A J Pulham, BA, DPhil
    (*Science*)
*R W Wiggins, BSc
Dr J L Greenhalgh, BSc, PhD
T Kelso, BSc
Dr E A Smith, BSc, PhD

Mrs N Wright, BSc
§Dr R Campbell, BSc, PhD
§Miss S L Richardson,
  MSc
§Mrs M C Slack, BSc

Classics:
*Mrs V C Mee, BA
T C Clark, BA (*Head of
  Lower School*)
Mrs P R Coningham, BA,
  MA
Miss S V Tucker, BA
Miss P L Whitworth, BA
§Mrs S M Balmer, CertEd

Economics/Politics:
P Shelley, BA, MSc
Mrs S J Baillie, BA
  (*Pastoral Director*)
R C M Loxley, BSc, MEd
  (*Director of Studies*)
Y Moreno, MEcon
*J D Neil, MPhil
M J Smalley, BA, QTS

English:
*Dr S J Barker, BA, PhD
Miss S G Davison, BA
L J Gilbert, BA
Dr C Goulding, BA, MLitt,
  PhD
Mrs K J Keown, BA
A R D King, BA, MA
S C Masters, BA, MA
  (*Film Studies*)

Geography:
*D A Wilson, BSc
M G Downie, BA (*Head of
  Careers*)
Miss K E Jarvis, BA
  (*PSHE*)
Mrs R J L Laws, MA
  (*Assistant Head of
  Careers*)
Miss S J Longville, BA
  (*Head of Year 11*)
Miss Z C Morrow, BSc,
  MA

History:
*S E Tilbrook, BA
A S W Davies, BA, MSt
O L Edwards, BA
D C Greenhalgh, BA, MA
Dr E S Matthews, MA,
  PhD
§Mrs A J Palmer, MA

Mathematics:
*J A Smith, BSc
Dr J Argyle, BSc, MSc,
  PhD
Ms L Atkinson, BA, MA
A Delvin, BSc, MSc
G D Dunn, BSc
P M Heptinstall, BSc, PhD
D A Jardine, BSc
T E Keenan, BSc, MSc
  (*Head of Sixth Form*)

Junior School:
R J Craig, BEd (*Headmaster*)
J N Miller, BA (*Deputy Head*)
Dr A J Spencer, BSc, PhD (*Deputy Head*)

Miss C Pridmore, BSc
H Rashid, BSc, MSc
A Snedden, BSc
S D Watkins, BSc (*Head of
  Middle School*)
§W Gibson, MA

Modern Languages:
*Miss K E Sykes, BA
M S Bailie, BA, MA
  (**Spanish*)
Miss S Demoulin, DEUG
  (**French*)
Mrs C L Diaz-Crossley, BA
  (**German*)
Miss J Budd, BA
Miss E L Hayes, BA
M Metcalf, BA, MPhil
M E J Nicholson, BA
Mrs C Towns,
  Staatsexamen
§Mrs C A M O'Hanlon,
  BA

Music & Performing Arts:
*Z Fazlic, BA (*Director*)
Mrs G M Blazey, BMus,
  MA (*Head of Junior
  School Music*)
D M Key, MMus, BA
N A Smith, BMus
T Walters, BA
§Mrs R A Shaw-Kew, BA

Philosophy:
(*See Physics below*)

Physical Education:
*Mrs A J Ponton, BSc
M R Davidson, BSc
  (*Deputy Director*)
A G Brown, BSc
F Dickinson, BEd
Miss S N Harding, BA
Miss J Harrison, BSc
Miss K Smith, BSc
A E Watt, BA
J A Wood, BA
§R V MacKay, BSc

Physics:
*E T Rispin, BSc
J L Camm, BSc
Dr R M Houchin, MSci,
  PhD
Mrs N C McGough, MSci
Dr M B A Read, MA,
  MPhil, PhD (*Philosophy
  and Religion*)
P Wilson, BSc, MSc
§Mrs P M Gill, BEng

Psychology:
*Mrs C M Bone, BSc
Mrs A Robinson, BA

Design & Technology:
*I Goldsborough, BEd,
  MSc
Mrs C A Pipes, BA
P M Warne, MEng

Miss K L Barnes, BA
Ms C Bolam, BA
Mrs C M Cree, BSc
Miss S J Dunn, BA
Miss C Gardiner, BA
T G Lloyd, BA
Miss M A Noble, BA

J A Pollock, CertEd
Miss R S Scott, BA
Mrs L M Stairmand, BA
Mrs R S Towers, MEd
Mrs K Wall, BA
Ms A J Whitney, BA
§G Scrafton, BA

School Medical Officer: Dr C J Dias, MBBS, MRCGP
Admissions Officer: Mrs A Perry

Curriculum. The aim of the curriculum up to Year 11 is
to offer a general education, culminating in GCSE in a wide
range of subjects. All students study English (Language and
Literature), a Modern Language (French, German or Spanish), Mathematics, Biology, Physics and Chemistry to this
level and three further examination subjects are taken at
GCSE level from Art, Classical Studies, Economics, Geography, German, Greek, History, Latin, Music, Spanish,
Design & Technology and Drama. Additionally there is a
programme of Art, Drama, Music and Technology for all in
Years 7 to 9. In exceptional circumstances, students can opt
to take Dual Award Science, allowing them an opportunity
to study a fourth option from those listed above.

Sixth Formers will normally choose 4 subjects for study
to AS Level in the Lower Sixth, and in the Upper Sixth 3
subjects to A Level, most combinations from the following
list being possible: Art, Biology, Chemistry, Classical Civil-
isation, Economics, English, French, Geography, German,
Greek, History, Latin, Mathematics, Further Mathematics,
Music, Physics, Politics, Psychology, Spanish, Technology.
Philosophy, Physical Education, Theatre Studies and Film
Studies. There is a substantial course of General Studies/
Enrichment available.

Almost all sixth-formers go on to University, and success
in gaining entry at Oxford and Cambridge, and medical
schools, has been an outstanding feature of the school's
record.

Physical Education. All students are required to take
part in a Physical Education programme which, up to Year
10, includes Rugby, Football, Cross-Country, Cricket, Athletics, Gymnastics, Hockey, Netball, Tennis, Rounders,
Swimming. At the upper end of the School a wider range of
activities is offered: in addition to the above students may
opt for Badminton, Basketball, Climbing, Fencing, Fitness
training, Karate, Orienteering, Squash, Tennis, Table Tennis,
Volleyball and Dance. A wide range of activities is available
to all through voluntary membership of various Sports
Clubs.

Activities. Art, Drama and Music are strong features in
the life of the School, all of them overflowing from scheduled lessons into spare-time activity. There is a large number
of wide-ranging music groups and ensembles from choirs
and orchestras to bands, jazz ensembles and rock groups.
There are several productions in the theatre each term.
Numerous societies meet in the lunch-break or after school,
some linked with school work but many developing from
private enthusiasms. There is a thriving Duke of Edinburgh's Award scheme. There is an entirely voluntary Combined Cadet Force Contingent. Annual overseas visits
include ski-parties, sporting tours, Classics trips, visits to art
galleries and to the battlefields of World War I.

Supervision and Pastoral Care. Each student is within
the care of (a) Form Supervisor and (b) Tutor. The latter will
normally be associated with the student throughout their
school career, and the aim is to forge a personal link with
students and their families.

The Careers programme begins in Year 9; in Year 11 and
the Sixth Form every possible care is taken to advise each
student individually about Careers and Higher Education.

The School's Medical Officers are available regularly for
consultation; there are also male and female School Counsellors.

Buildings. Some of the School's buildings date from 1907 and are described by Pevsner as "friendly neo-Early-Georgian". Recent years have seen many developments and improvements, including the rebuilding of the indoor swimming pool in 1990, the opening in February 1996 of a new Sports Centre, a new Science and Technology Centre which opened in 1997, and new Maths and ICT departments in 1998. A new Junior School extension opened in 2005 and a Performing Arts Centre opened in 2006. A new 6-lane, 25m swimming pool is currently being constructed as part of an additional sports complex which will include a second sports hall, a dance and fitness suite and new indoor and outdoor changing facilities. This is due for completion in spring 2015.

Junior School. Years 3 and 4 of the Junior School are separately housed in Lambton Road opposite the Senior School playing fields. Years 5 and 6 are housed in a new extension on the main school site. Junior School students use the Sports Centre, Swimming Pool, games fields and dining hall. English and Mathematics are taught by Form Teachers, while History, Geography, French, Science, Religious Education, Music, Art and Physical Activities are taken by specialists.

Entrance. Entry is by examination. Application forms are available from the Admissions Secretary.

Junior School at 7+ and 9+. Prospective students attend Assessment Days held in November (9+) and January (7+) when they take part in a number of activities and sit a number of short tests. A reference is sought from previous/current school.

Senior School at 11+. The Senior School examination is held each January for prospective students who will be 11 on 1 September of the year in which entry is desired. Applications by 15 December (later application at School's discretion). A reference is sought from previous/current school.

Sixth Form at 16+. Applicants are considered for direct entry to the Sixth Form if their GCSE results are likely to form an adequate basis. All external candidates are interviewed and a reference is sought from the previous/current school.

Each year a small number of places may be available at entry points other than the main ones listed. Please contact the Admissions Secretary for details.

Term of Entry. Autumn, although a small number of places may become available throughout the year.

Fees per term (2014–2015). Senior School £3,731, Junior School £3,144.

Bursaries. Some bursaries, awarded on the basis of parental income, are offered. They include those awarded by the Ogden Trust, which may cover all fees and expenses depending on parental income. Details are available from the Bursar.

Charitable status. The Newcastle upon Tyne Royal Grammar School is a Registered Charity, number 1114424.

RGS Worcester

Upper Tything, Worcester WR1 1HP
Tel: 01905 613391
Fax: 01905 726892
email: office@rgsw.org.uk
website: www.rgsw.org.uk
Twitter: @RGSWorcester

The Royal Grammar School Worcester was founded ante 1291, received its Elizabethan Charter in 1561 and was granted its 'Royal' title by Queen Victoria in 1869. The Alice Ottley School was founded in 1883 as Worcester High School for Girls. The two schools merged to form RGS Worcester & The Alice Ottley School in September 2007 and was renamed RGS Worcester in September 2009.

Board of Governors:
Chairman: Mrs R F Ham
Vice-Chairman: J Q S Poole

I L Carmichael	Ms K Meredith
Mrs L Cook	J G Peters
Mr N Fairlie	Mrs J Preedy
Sir R G Fry	B W Radford
H Kimberley	Dr E Robinson

Bursar & Clerk to the Governors: I T Roberts, OBE, MA

Headmaster: J D C Pitt, MA

Deputy Head : Mrs C S Smee, BSc, MA

Assistant Heads:
Dr L J Andrew BSc, PhD (*Pastoral*)
J S Barker, BA (*Co-curricular*)
R J Houchin, BA (*Academic*)

Heads of Section:
P J Ehlers, MA, PhD (*Sixth Form*)
H Sykes, BSc (*Middle School*)
Miss A J Freeman, BA (*Lower School*)

Teaching Staff:

M Adlington, BA	R Hawking, BA
S N Alexander, BA	R A Holt, BA
Mrs E M Amos, BSc	R J Houchin, BA
A Baker, MA	Mrs S Houchin, BA
Dr D Beer, PhD	M A Howard, BTech
Miss L Bennett, NVQ3	A J H Howe, BA
R N Berry, BSc	Mrs C P Howe, BA
Miss E R Binner, BA	Mrs J Hunt, BA
Mrs J Bishop, BA	Mrs C A Hunter, BA
S Blincoe-Deval, BSc, MSc	Mrs V C James, MA
Dr M Bowdrey, MChem, DPhil	Mrs S John, BSc
	S P Johnson, MA
Miss R S Briggs, BSc	Mrs E V Jordan, MA
P J Carter, BSc	Mrs L Kent, BSc
Mrs G Cartwright, BSc	Mrs L Kettle, MA, MSocSci, BEd
P Chesworth, BA	
A E Clemit, MA	Mrs E Kilburn, BA
D V Coetzee, PhD	Mrs S A King, BA
Mrs S C Coggins, BSc	Mrs T Kosar, BA
Mrs S Cooper, BD	Miss J E Marsh, BA
D J Cotterill, BEd	Mrs C Matthews, BA
Mrs P E Cross, BSc	D A Morgan, MA, BA
Miss S C Cull, BSc	P J Newport, BA
T S Curtis, BA	G Nicholas, BEng
Mrs N J Davis, MA	Mrs S Nicholls, BA
S C Davis, BSc	P J O'Sullivan, BSc
Miss C Deval-Reed, BSc	Mrs A Park, BA
Mrs A Dimond, MA (*SEN*)	N Phillips, MA
Mrs D Drew, BA	Miss E L Pollard, BA
Miss C Duckworth, BSc	M D Ralfe, MA
Mrs N A Estaun, MA	A J Rattenbury, BA
P Evans, BSc	J A Roebuck, BSc
M Evetts, BSc	Dr S Sangster, PhD
Mrs E Faulkner, BSc	J M Shorrocks, BSc, BA
Mrs C Flannigan, BA	Dr H S Smith, PhD
Miss A J Freeman, BA	B Tanner, BA
J C Friend, BSc	B D Taylor, BSc
R Gaston, BA	Mrs L F Taylor, BSc
R T Gibson, MA	M H Vetch, MA
R Gilbert, MFA	Miss J R Waller, MA
Mrs H E Gunn, BA, MA	Mrs D Warman, BA
T J B Hallett, BA, MPhil	M D Wilkinson, BSc
M Hamilton, BA	R Willis, MPhys
Mrs D Harkness, BA	Mrs J Witcomb, BA

Preparatory School: RGS The Grange

Headmaster: G W Hughes, BEd Hons

Deputy Head (Pastoral): S Howkins, BA

Head of Pre-Prep (Academic): Mrs S Atkinson, BEd

Teaching Staff:

Miss K Arr, BA QTS	R Millard, BA
Mrs L Bebb, BA QTS	Mrs A E Parish, BEd
D Bousfield, BA	R Scase, PhD
Mrs S Coleman, BA	Miss K Singleton, BSc
Mrs M J Corrie, GTCL,	Mrs G Southwell, BSc
LTCL, ALCM	Mrs C Sykes, MEd
Mrs J Davies, BSc	Mrs T A Turner, BA
Mrs A Dimond	J Uren, BA
Mrs M C Egginton, BSc	Mrs L Walsh, BSc
Miss N Evans, BA	Mrs E Walker, BA
Mrs P Fletcher, BA QTS	Mrs P White, BEd
Mrs E Hadley, BA QTS	Miss S Wilding, BA
Miss P Hill, BA	Miss L Willis, BA
J Hodgkins, BSc	Mrs W Wreghitt, BA
T MCCallion, BA	

Preparatory School: RGS Springfield

Headmistress: Mrs L Brown, BA

Deputy Head: Mrs A Webster, BEd

Teaching Staff:

Mrs P M Arr, CertEd	Miss R Morgan, BA
Mrs D Bennett, NVQ3	Mrs S Salisbury, BEd
Mrs L Bennett, BSc	Mrs R Whittaker, BA
Mrs C Carr, CertEd	Mrs J Walker, BEd
Mrs K Kelleher, BA	Mrs E Williams, BSc
Mrs E McCabe, BA	R Wintle, MA, MBA
Mrs A Myers, BSc	

Situation and Buildings. The Senior School is situated a few minutes' walk from the centre of the City and is convenient for rail and bus stations. The Headmaster's office is housed in the Grade II* listed Britannia House, and there are several other historic buildings on the site, including the RGS Main Block, dating from 1868. Educational facilities are outstanding: there are two Sports Halls, specialist Art, IT, Technology and Textiles rooms, a Theatre, Library, Science Block, Music Technology room, and a Lecture Theatre, as well as several assembly halls. The playing fields and boathouse are close by and the School has good use of the local swimming pool. A full-size, floodlit all-weather pitch was opened in 2007 and a state-of-the-art fitness centre in 2008. A new Dance Studio plus changing facilities, two new Science Laboratories and a Digital Language Laboratory were also completed in 2008.

There are two co-educational Preparatory Schools. RGS The Grange (*see IAPS entry*) is set in 48 acres of grounds to the north of the city and has a 16-classroom, £4.5 million extension to complement the original Victorian building that houses the Pre-Prep. RGS Springfield (*see IAPS entry*) is housed in a beautiful Georgian building in the centre of the nearby Britannia Square, close to the city centre. It is secluded and secure, and benefits from its close proximity to the Senior School.

Organisation. The Senior School population is c800 (370 girls and 430 boys). The Senior School is divided into three sections – Lower (Years 7 and 8), Middle (Years 9, 10 and 11) and Sixth Form – with an Assistant Head responsible for each. The basic unit is the form, and the form tutor, under the Head of Year, is responsible for all day to day matters relating to the pupils in their charge. In addition all pupils are placed in Houses which exist mainly for internal competitive purposes, but which do provide an important element of continuity throughout a pupil's career at the School. Both Preparatory Schools admit pupils from the age of two, and most proceed to the Senior School at the age of eleven, into Year 7. RGS The Grange and RGS Springfield are both well known for the high standard of their pastoral care and for stretching the brightest children. Learning Support is particularly well organized.

Aims. A high level of academic achievement is sought within a caring and civilised society. By placing emphasis on a wide range of sporting, artistic and co-curricular activities, we aim to extend our pupils in as many ways as possible. A balanced and challenging education is offered which stands pupils in good stead for their future careers and within the community at large.

Curriculum. Pupils follow a common curriculum for the first three years in the Senior School which includes the usual academic subjects, plus IT, Design Technology, Music, Drama and PE. The GCSE option arrangements (Years 10 and 11) allow a wide choice, subject to final selection, giving a balanced curriculum which does not prejudice subsequent career decisions. Normally 9–10 subjects are studied: IGCSE English, Mathematics, a Modern Foreign Language and Sciences being setted and compulsory, plus three from French, German, Latin, Spanish, Geography, History, RE, Drama, Art, Music, Textiles, Design Technology. Most members of the Sixth Form study four subjects to AS Level and at least three to A2 Level. In addition to those subjects studied at GCSE Level, PE, Classical Civilisation, Business Studies, Economics and Politics may be taken up. The Digital Learning Programme was launched in September 2014, which saw iPads become an integral part of the teaching and learning experience.

Careers. The School is a member of ISCO; the well-equipped Careers Room is readily available and the Head of Careers is responsible for ensuring that all pupils receive basic careers education, and subsequently, access to all the necessary information and experience on which a sound decision may be made regarding future career and Further or Higher Education.

Physical Activities. The School aims to satisfy a wide range of sporting interests and abilities. For boys, Rugby Football, Association Football, Cricket and Athletics are the main activities. Girls take Netball and Hockey in the winter and spring, and Athletics, Tennis and Rounders during the summer Term. Cross-Country Running and Rowing have a full programme of fixtures. A wide range of other activities share priority in the Sports Halls throughout the year, and high-quality cricket coaching is given throughout the winter months.

Outdoor Pursuits. Combined Cadet Force and The Duke of Edinburgh's Award Scheme: all pupils may choose to join one or the other at the end of Year 9. The strong CCF comprises Royal Navy, Army and Air Force sections. Good opportunities exist for attachments to regular units in UK and abroad, for flying training, for leadership training and for Adventure Training. Those who choose The Duke of Edinburgh's Award Scheme may work for the Bronze, Silver and Gold Awards, and undertake adventure training and community service.

Other Activities. There is a wide range of clubs and societies. All Lower School pupils receive drama lessons as part of the curriculum and school productions take place each term. School music is also strong: in particular, there is a fine organ, a Big Band, several brass ensembles, two choirs, several smaller vocal ensembles and a very popular Jazz Band. The School fosters a range of international links including regular exchanges with schools in France, Germany, Spain, China and the USA. The School has strong links with schools in the developing world via the World Challenge Organisation, and the school community raises large sums for a range of local, national and international charities every year.

September Admission. This is by examination held in January, mainly at 11+ but also at 12+ and 13+. Pupils are also admitted into the Sixth Form on the basis of a test, interview and GCSE results. Exceptionally, pupils may also be examined and admitted at any time of the year. Admission to the Preparatory Schools is by assessment from age 6+ and by classroom visit before this age.

Fees per term (2014–2015). £3,620.

Scholarships and Bursaries. Scholarships are offered for academic achievement as well as for music, art, design, textiles, drama and sport of up to 50% remission of fees. Bursaries of up to 100% are also available according to parental means and academic potential. Further details can be obtained from the Registrars at the schools.

Charitable status. RGS Worcester is a Registered Charity, number 1120644. The aim of the charity is the education of boys and girls.

The Royal Hospital School

Holbrook, Ipswich, Suffolk IP9 2RX
Tel: 01473 326200
Fax: 01473 326213
email: admissions@royalhospitalschool.org
           reception@royalhospitalschool.org
website: www.royalhospitalschool.org
Twitter: @RHSSuffolk
Facebook: /RoyalHospitalSchool

The Royal Hospital School is a co-educational HMC boarding and day school with 700 pupils aged 11 to 18. Founded in Greenwich in 1712 by the Crown Charity, Greenwich Hospital, it moved to its present magnificent 200-acre estate in rural Suffolk in 1933.

Director of Greenwich Hospital: Mr H Player

Governors:
Chairman: Mr H Strutt

Brig K Beaton, OBE, QHP	Mr J Lynas
Mrs V Bidwell	Dr P Marshall
Mr J Gamp	Mr P Smith
Mr T P J Hill, QC	Capt A Tate, RN Retd
Dr H Jones	Mrs E Todd
Mr A Kerr	Mr H T Wykes-Sneyd

Senior Management Team:

Headmaster: Mr J A Lockwood, MA

Director of Finance and Operations (*Bursar*): Mr P Church, BA Oxon
Deputy Headmaster: Mr S J Dixon, MA
Assistant Head (*Academic*): Mr M R Christmas, MA
Assistant Head (*Pastoral*): Mrs S E M Godfrey, BA
Assistant Head (*Co-Curricular*): Mr C A Rennison, BSc
Director of Information and Academic Systems: Dr J Allday, MA, ALCM
Director of Communications: Mrs S Braybrooke, BA

Chaplain: Revd J W P McConnell, BEd, MA, BD, DASE

Head of Sixth Form & Careers: Mr C Graham, BSc
Head of Middle School: Mr A Wynn, BSc
Head of Lower School and Transition: Mrs J M Fox, BA
Head of Teaching and Learning: Ms M Brennan, BA
Higher Education Coordinator: Mr C J White, MA, PGDL

Heads of Department:
Art: Mr G D Ravenhall, BA, ATD
Biology: Mrs C A Stevens, BSc (*Head of Science*)
Business Studies: Mr L Thompson, BEd, BA
Chemistry: Ms M Egan-Smith, BSc
Classics: Mr M Routledge, BA
Design Technology: Mr J R Dugdale, BEd
Drama: Mr D Kerr, BA
Economics: Mr C Terry, BA
English: Ms J L Stone, BA
English as an Additional Language: Mr D P Coleman, BA
Film & Media Studies: Mr M Vickers, BA
French: Mrs J Routledge, BA
Geography: Mr L G Frost, MA, BSc, BEd

German: Mrs N J Mann, MA
History: Ms S L Nicholls, BA
Information & Communication Technology: Mr P C Du Toit, BComm, HDE
Learning Support: Mrs E Burge, MA
Librarian: Miss R Gitsham, BA
Mathematics: Mr G Mears, BA
Director of Music: Mr W Saunders, BMus
Bandmaster: Mr R B Jones, ARCM
Head of Singing: Mr D Peckham, BMus
PSHE: Mr D W Hawkley, BA
Director of Sport: Mr D P Hardman, BA
Head of Academic PE: Mrs S J Williams, MA, BEd
Physics: Mr P A Surzyn, BSc
Politics: Mr M H Godfrey, BSc
Psychology: Mrs B J Jennings, MA, BSc
Religious Studies: Mr C J White, MA, PGDL
Sailing: Mr A Nutton
Spanish: Mr R G Encinas
Thinking Skills: Mr J F Pooley, BSc

Health Centre Sister: Mrs A Thompson, RGN
CCF School Staff Instructor: WO1 [RSM] K Weaver
Duke of Edinburgh's Award and Head of Ceremonial: Lt Cdr N Griffiths
Admissions Officers: Mrs S Lewis and Mrs K Evers, BA
Development Manager: Mrs L Pembroke

Aims. The School provides a values-driven education enriched by a strong naval heritage and its aims are:
- To promote academic excellence and realise the full potential of every pupil.
- To foster creativity and imagination.
- To encourage leadership, adventure and self-discovery.
- To endorse the values of service, loyalty and commitment and uphold the School's unique and rich heritage.
- To cultivate a global outlook and environmental responsibility.
- To nurture pastoral excellence and a strong sense of community.
- To develop fitness, well-being and healthy competition.

House System. With 65% of pupils boarding full time there is a strong House System and the recently completed programme of refurbishment and development provides superb facilities and accommodation.

Pupils joining the School at 11+ are accommodated in Junior Houses purpose-built to accommodate 11 to 13 year olds in 4/6-bedded rooms, with facilities, routines and pastoral care that assist the transition between junior and senior school. Weekly boarding and the opportunity to stay overnight on an ad hoc basis are available.

At Year 9 (13+) all pupils, whether joining the School at this stage or moving up from the Junior Houses, join a Senior House. One is a co-educational Day House created specifically for pupils who routinely go home at 6.00 pm and, in many cases, use the daily school transport services. There are 3 boys' and 3 girls' Senior Boarding Houses which are each home to approximately 58 full and weekly boarders as well as day boarders. Day boarders can choose to go home at around 9 pm, after completing their prep and any evening activities, and they may stay overnight in the House on an ad hoc basis if space is available. Boarders in Years 9 and 10 share rooms with up to four other pupils and older pupils have double or single studies with en-suite facilities.

In the Upper Sixth both boarding and day boys and girls join Nelson House, where they learn to live more independently in preparation for university.

Curriculum and Academic Development. The School's curriculum shadows the National Curriculum Key Stages 3 and 4. On joining the School, pupils are placed in forms on the basis of assessed ability from entrance testing or at 13+ the results of Common Entrance examinations. The School subscribes to the Durham University Value

Added Measuring Scheme at all levels, allowing tutors to map pupil progress. In core subjects setting takes place from the outset and at GCSE level setting occurs in all core curriculum subjects. There are 66 x 55min periods over a two weekly timetable.

Lower School (Years 7–8): The subjects studied are English, mathematics, science (biology, physics and chemistry), modern foreign languages (French, Spanish and German), Latin, geography, history, design technology, art, drama, IT (Information Technology), music, religious studies, PHSE (Personal, Social and Health Education) and PE. There are four forms in Years 7 and 8 and the average class size is 18 pupils. Homework is set daily and completed within supervised sessions during the working day by both boarders and day pupils. All junior pupils must take part in three co-curricular activities after lessons.

Middle School (Years 9–11): The subjects studied in Year 9 are the same as in the Lower School and a further intake of pupils from prep schools means that there is an additional class. GCSE courses start in Year 10 and most pupils will study 10 subjects including English language and literature, mathematics, a modern foreign language, physics, chemistry, biology (either as three separate sciences or as the dual award) as the core subjects and four options from science (if taking separate sciences), history, geography, PE (Physical Education and Sports Science), French, German, Spanish, media studies, religious studies, art, music, theatre studies, design technology and business studies.

Sixth Form (Years 12 and 13): Pupils choose four options from 27 subjects. Subject choice depends upon average point scores at GCSE and grades gained in specific subjects. Pupils also follow the Sixth Form Enrichment Programme which may include GCSE Russian or Greek, AS Law, Sociology, Community Action, Model United Nations, public speaking and debating, music and culture, Sports Leadership and other activities and interests useful for University applications and personal statements. Around 97% of pupils go to the University or Higher Education institution of their choice and approximately 50% to Russell Group and other top-class universities.

Pupil progress is formally monitored by means of at least two assessments or reports per term which grade the academic performance of the pupil against their target or challenge grades. Every pupil has a personal tutor and weekly tutorial meetings are an opportunity to deal with any problems and check on progress.

All pupils have access to iPads, a suite of mobile learning apps and Wi-Fi throughout the site. Additional networked computers are available in Boarding or Day Houses as well as in computer suites around the school. Mobile learning is embraced by the teaching staff with the aim of enhancing teaching and learning.

Through high quality, enthusiastic teaching, excellent resources and dedicated tutorial support, every pupil is encouraged to aim high and achieve his or her personal best. The most able pupils' potential is realised through the mentoring of scholars, a gifted and talented scheme and Oxbridge preparation.

Sport and Leisure. Facilities include ninety-six acres of playing fields, a golf course, shooting range, assault course, sports hall, fitness suite, gym, large heated indoor swimming pool, squash courts, tennis and netball courts and an all-weather sports surface. The School has a strong sailing tradition and all pupils joining in Year 7 receive sailing instruction to RYA Level 2. Through the School's RYA-accredited Sailing Academy, pupils have access to a fleet of 60 racing dinghies on adjacent Alton Water Reservoir, as well as traditional Cornish Shrimpers on the River Stour and Orwell. The School is widely known as one of the top in the country for both fleet and team sailing and offers an elite training programme for those wishing to follow Olympic pathway. The other main sports are rugby, hockey, netball, cricket, kayaking, athletics, cross-country, rounders, basket-

ball, football, tennis, riding and swimming. The swimming pool also offers opportunities for kayak-polo, life-saving training and sub-aqua.

Music and Drama. The School has a particularly strong musical tradition and the state-of-the-art Music School provides a recital hall, specialist rooms, technical suite and "rock room". Almost half the pupils in the School are involved in music on a regular basis. The Chapel is of cathedral proportions and has one of the finest organs in Europe, much used by pupils as well as professional performers. Peripatetic teachers offer tuition in a wide range of instruments and the choir and chamber choir perform both nationally and internationally. As well as drama in the curriculum and LAMDA classes, productions are often combined with the music department for whole school performances and there is a full programme of plays, competitions and festivals each year.

CCF and Community Service. All pupils participate in the Combined Cadet Force in Years 9 and 10 and are able to choose between Army, Navy, RAF and Royal Marine sections. The emphasis is on adventure training and personal development. More than 300 pupils take part in The Duke of Edinburgh's Award Scheme and 100 of these to Gold Award. The Community Action Team promotes the School's social responsibility and is actively involved in a wide range of charitable activities in the local community.

Religion. The core values of the School are based on the Christian faith but pupils from a variety of religions and cultural backgrounds attend the School and all beliefs are respected. The magnificent Chapel, that holds over 1,000 people, is the spiritual hub of school life and the whole community gathers there most mornings for worship.

Admission. Entry to the School is normally at 11, 13 and 16 years. Pupils are asked to sit an entrance examination, comprising papers in English, mathematics and verbal reasoning, in the January prior to the September of the year of entry unless following Common Entrance for entry in Year 9. Entry into the Sixth Form is subject to a minimum average GCSE point score and specific grades in chosen AS subjects. Entry is also subject to an interview and satisfactory reference from the pupil's current school.

Fees per term (2014–2015). Full/Weekly Boarding: £7,208 (Years 7 and 8), £8,903 (Years 9–13). Non-EEA Boarders: £7,375 (Years 7 and 8), £9,070 (Years 9–13). Day: £4,324 (Years 7 and 8), £4,730 (Years 9–13). Day Boarders: £5,870 (Years 9–13). Discounts are available for services families eligible for the MOD Continuity of Education Allowance (CEA) and siblings where three or more children are in the School at any time.

Scholarships are awarded annually for academic excellence, musical talent, drama, art, sport and sailing. All scholarship candidates are required to sit the School entrance examination (unless taking Common Entrance or GCSE examinations), have an interview and undergo an assessment in their relevant field. Full details from the Admissions Office, Tel: 01473 326136 or email: admissions@royalhospitalschool.org.

Bursaries. Pupils in receipt of a scholarship award are eligible to apply for additional assistance by way of a means-tested bursary, should the financial circumstances of the family necessitate it. The School's parent charity, Greenwich Hospital, can award generous means-tested bursaries to the children of seafarers, particularly serving or retired Naval or Royal Marines personnel.

Charitable status. The Royal Hospital School is owned by Greenwich Hospital which is a Crown Charity. The School exists to provide education for boys and girls aged from 11 to 18.

The Royal Masonic School for Girls

Rickmansworth Park, Rickmansworth, Herts WD3 4HF
Tel: 01923 773168
Fax: 01923 896729
email: enquiries@royalmasonic.herts.sch.uk
website: www.royalmasonic.herts.sch.uk

Board of Governors:
Mr J Gould (*Chairman & Trustee*)
Mr K S Carmichael, CBE (*Honorary Life President*)

Mr J Clappison, MP	Mrs H Porter
Mr D Ellis, OBE	Mr R Smith (*Trustee*)
Mr K Emmerson	Mrs C Stephens
Mr J Flecker	Mr K Surry
Mrs D Gardiner	Mr M Woodcock (*Trustee*)
Ms A Gray	Mr D Yeaman

Bursar: Mrs D Robinson, BSc Hons Bristol, ACA

Headmistress: Mrs D Rose, MA Cantab

Director of Studies: Mrs E Couldridge, MA London

Assistant Heads:
Mr D Cox, BEng Brunel
Mrs K Young, BSc Notts

Head of Sixth Form: Ms N Weatherston, BSc Newcastle,
   PGCE Durham

Senior Teachers:
Mrs R L C Bloomfield-Proud, MA London, BA Leeds,
   PGCE
Mrs C Bomford, MA Greenwich, BA Manchester, PGCE
Ms V Gunn, MA York, BA Hons Cape Town, HDE Cape
   Town, PGCE

Housemistresses:
Connaught: Miss K Batty (*Head of Boarding*)
Harris House: Mrs D Dwyer
Weybridge House: Mrs N Roughley
Zetland House: Miss K J Lord
Alexandra House: Miss K Davies

Heads of Year:
Miss H S Stanley, BEd Liverpool (*Year 7*)
Miss K Cook, BSc Reading, PGCE (*Year 8*)
Mrs S Elder, BA Durham, PGCE (*Year 9*)
Mrs D E Heaffey, BA Middlesex, PGCE (*Year 10*)
Miss J Simmonite, BA Loughborough, PGCE (*Year 11*)
Ms N Weatherston, BSc Newcastle, PGCE Durham (*Sixth
   Form*)

Heads of Departments:
Art: Mrs L Kingston, BA De Montfort, PGCE
Business Studies and Economics: Mrs V Bannister, BCom
   Dublin, MBA
Computing: Mr D Buddie, BSc Dundee
Design Technology: Miss M Dines, BA Bucks
English: Mrs C Gardner, BA LLB Leicester, MA Open
Geography: Mrs C E Freeman, BSc Durham
History: Mr F Grogan, BA York
Home Economics: Mrs L Passmore, BA Kent
Latin & Classical Civilisation: Mr N M Young, MA Oxon,
   MCIBS
Learning Support: Mrs A Ralph, BSc Lancaster
Mathematics: Mr D Cox, BEng Brunel
Modern Languages: Mrs E Boast, MA, BA, Licence
   d'Anglais
Music: Mrs J Whitbread, MA Trinity, LRAM, CertRAM
Performing Arts: Mr D Hyde, BMus Birmingham, ALCM
Photography: Mr D Spain
Physical Education: Mrs E Spendiff, BSc Staffordshire
Psychology: Mrs S Reeve, MSc London
Religious Studies: Mrs S Elder, BA Durham

Science: Mrs N Timoney, MSc Warwick, PGCE
Textiles: Mrs R Bloomfield-Proud, MA London, BA Leeds

Cadogan House:
Head: Mr I Connors, BA Hons, NPQH
Deputy Head: Mrs A Brown, BA Reading

Ruspini House:
Head: Mrs K Woodhead, BA

Visiting Music Teachers for bassoon, brass, cello, clarinet,
drum kit, flute, guitar, oboe, organ, percussion, piano, saxophone, singing, steel pans, viola, violin.

Peripatetic Staff for Dance, Learning Support, Speech and
   Drama, EAL.

Estates Bursar: Mrs J Heaven
School Doctors: Dr C Orsi, Dr C Quinn
Personal Assistant to the Headmistress: Mrs J Beal
Admissions Manager: Mrs G Braiden

There are 961 pupils in school, of whom 235 are in Cadogan House (Pre-Prep and Prep Department) and 62 are in
Ruspini House, our co-ed Pre-School. There are 191 girls in
the Sixth Form. 121 of the current school population are
boarders and day girls and boarders are fully integrated
through the Houses.

Premises and Facilities. Founded in 1788, the School
came to Rickmansworth in 1934. It stands in 300 acres of
parkland on an attractive site overlooking the valley of the
River Chess. The buildings are spacious and well-appointed.
They include excellent ICT facilities, a well-equipped Science building, a Planetarium, a Chapel and Resource Centre
of exceptional beauty. A new Sixth Form Centre opened in
2012.

The Sports Hall is equipped to the highest international
standards. There is a heated indoor swimming pool, 12 tennis courts, four squash courts and superb playing fields. The
School has been awarded Sportsmark status.

Location. Central London is 15 miles to the south and
Amersham is just north of the town. The M25 is one mile
from the school and links it to London (Heathrow) – 30 minutes, London (Gatwick) – 50 minutes, and Luton Airport –
30 minutes. London Underground services (Metropolitan
Line) and British Rail from Marylebone enable Central London to be reached by train in 30 minutes.

General Curriculum and Aims. The first three years of
Senior School provide a broad general education which ful-
fils the requirements of the National Curriculum and reaches
beyond it. As well as the traditional academic subjects of
English, Mathematics, Science, History, Geography and
Religious Studies, girls study Design Technology, Informa-
tion Technology, Home Economics, Art & Textiles, Per-
forming Arts, Physical Education and PSHCE. Language
Studies begin with French or Spanish and Latin. In Year 8
German and Mandarin are also offered.

GCSE options are chosen from among all the subjects
taught in Years 7 to 9 and new possibilities, such as Child
Development, Performing Arts, Drama and Business are
introduced at this stage. Most pupils take nine or ten GCSE
subjects and girls are guided in their choices by subject
teachers, in full consultation with parents. Triple Science is
available.

The Sixth Form. The School offers a wide range of A
Level subjects in flexible combinations. Politics, Economics, Performance Studies, Classical Civilisation, Photography, Music Technology and Psychology are all new
additions to the curriculum at this stage. There are also practical and vocational courses leading to qualifications in
Business and Health and Social Care. Virtually all sixth
formers go on to higher education.

Religion. Girls of all faiths and none are welcome.
School assemblies are traditional and inclusive in nature and
Chapel Services for boarders are held according to the rites
of the Church of England.

Health. The School Doctor attends the Medical Centre regularly. There are two Nursing Sisters and a Medical Assistant.

Admission. Applications should be made to the Admissions Manager. The School sets its own entrance examinations at all levels. New boarding and day pupils are accepted into the Sixth Form where there are wide-ranging opportunities for girls of all abilities.

Scholarships and Bursaries. Scholarships are offered by the School to encourage and reward excellence. Scholarships are awarded in recognition of outstanding achievement, or promise in a particular sphere, and involve financial support, not exceeding 25% of the annual fee.

A number of scholarships are available at 11+, 13+ and 16+, and some means-tested bursaries. The former are for open competition; the latter are restricted to certain categories of pupils in need. A scholarship and bursary could run concurrently in the case of a scholar who needed financial assistance.

At 11+: Awards are given in recognition of excellence with regard to academic achievement in the entrance examination, Sport, All-Rounder potential and Music.

At 16+: Awards are given for academic excellence, Music, Art, Sport and Performing Arts.

Bursaries enable suitable girls whose parents could not otherwise afford the fees to benefit from an education at The Royal Masonic School for Girls. Bursaries are awards made to girls who reach the School's required standards but who require financial assistance to take up a place. These awards are subject to means testing, under a standard formula widely used within the independent sector, at the time the offer is made and biennially thereafter. The number of awards made in any one year will vary according to the quality and circumstances of candidates and the availability of funds.

Fees per term (2014–2015). Senior School: Boarders £8,540 (Sixth Form new students £8,600); Weekly Boarders £7,930 (Sixth Form new students £8,000); Day Pupils £4,850 (Sixth Form new students £4,970).

Cadogan House: Boarders: £5,720 (Years 3–6); Weekly Boarders: £5,510 (Years 3–6); Day Pupils: £3,120 (Reception, Years 1 and 2), £3,620 (Years 3–6). Ruspini House Pre-School (boys and girls aged 2–4): please visit our website for range of fees.

Charitable status. The Royal Masonic School Limited is a Registered Charity, number 276784. Its aims are the advancement of education.

Royal Russell School

Coombe Lane, Croydon, Surrey CR9 5BX
Tel: 020 8657 4433
Fax: 020 8657 0207
email: headmaster@royalrussell.co.uk
website: www.royalrussell.co.uk
Twitter: @Royal_Russell

Motto: *Non Sibi Sed Omnibus*

Royal Russell School is an exceptional co-educational boarding and day school, for children aged 3 to 18 years, founded in 1853. Set in 110 acres of woodland, it enjoys excellent access to London, the South, and the airports at Gatwick and Heathrow.

Patron: Her Majesty The Queen
Board of Governors and Trustees:

Chairman: Mr K Young
Deputy Chairman: Mr P J McCombie

Mrs A D Greenwood   Mrs P Hornby
Mr C T Shorter   Dr D J Begley

Mr S Kolesar   Mr J Penny
Mr A Merriman   Mrs A Martin
Dr A Fernandes   The Hon Sir Philip Moor
Mrs E Brown

Senior School:

Headmaster: Mr Christopher Hutchinson, BMet, FRSA

Deputy Head (*Curriculum*): Mr Graham Moseley, BEd Hons, MA
Deputy Head (*Academic*): Mr David Selby, BA Hons
Deputy Head (*Pastoral*): Mrs Susanne Thomas-Webb, BA Hons, MA
Head of Sixth Form: Mrs Sandra Culbert, BEd Hons, MA, MA Ed Man, Dip M, ACCEG (**Careers*)

Assistant Staff:
Ms Cathi Allison, BEd Hons, MA, NPQH, NCSL, CIEA (*Head of English*)
Mrs Nicky Archer (*Administrator – Music*)
Ms Deborah Baldwin, BA Hons, QTC (*Art*)
Miss Rachael Bainbridge, MA (*Mathematics*)
Mr John Baron, BSc Hons (*Admin and Activities Manager*)
Mr Simon Bird, MA Hons CELTA TEFL (*Head of German*)
Mr Jose Bueno, BSc Hons (*Modern Languages*)
Mr Michael Callow, MA Cantab (*Mathematics*)
Miss Sandrine Calvet, BA, MA FLE (*French*) (*Modern Languages*)
Miss Sarah Clarke, BEng (*Physics*)
Mrs Margaret Clower, BA Hons, Dip Lib, MCLIP (*Librarian*)
Mrs Mary Colyer (*Library Assistant*)
Miss Alba Conde del Rio, BA Hons, MA (*Modern Languages*)
Mrs Alex Cook, BA Hons (*Science Technician*)
Mr Peter Cook, BSc Hons (*Mathematics*)
Mrs Victoria Corcoran, Cert Ed, MA (*Food Technology*)
Ms Elayine Cripps, Cert Ed (*Head of Drama*)
Miss Sarah Culliford, BSc Hons (*PE*)
Mrs Melanie Davies, BA Hons (*Drama*)
Mr John Davies, BSc Hons (*Head of Boys' PE*)
Mrs Saira Dean, BSc Hons (*Mathematics*)
Mr Colin Dear, BA Hons (*Head of Media Studies*)
Mrs Regine Demuynck-Mandinga, BTec, HND, BTS, BA Hons (*Modern Languages*)
Mrs Kate El-Asmar, BA Hons (*English and Literacy Support*)
Mr Paul Endersby, BSc Hons (*Head of Science*)
Mrs Lynn Faulkner, BA Hons (*Business Studies & IT*)
Mr Martin Finch, BEd Hons (*Head of Design and Technology*)
Mr Steve Greaves, BSc Hons (*Mathematics*)
Miss Lydia Green, BA Hons (*English*)
Mrs Helen Hadjam, BCom Hons (*Head of Economics*)
Mrs Katharine Hanna, BSc Hons (*Geography*)
Ms Sophia Hewett, BA Hons (*Head of Art and Design*)
Mrs Lorraine Hicks, BA Hons (*Head of Girls' PE*)
Mr Ed Hutchinson, BA Hons (*Head of History*)
Mrs Marion Januszewski (*Senior Science Technician*)
Mr David Jewiss, BEd Hons (*PE*)
Mrs Beth Johnsson, BA Hons (*English*)
Mr Simon Keable-Elliott, BA Hons (*Politics & Business Studies*)
Revd Henry Kirk, BA, BD Hons, MA, Dip Hist Art (*Head of Religious Studies*)
Miss Maria Latessa, DLing, RSA Cert, TEFLA (*Head of EFL*)
Mr Colin Leggatt, RAF VR T (*Contingent Commander CCF*)
Ms Simone Lok, BA Hons (*Geography*)
Mrs Susan Lower, BA Hons, MSC (*Head of Support for Learning*)
Mr Jordi Major, BA Hons (*Head of Food Technology*)

Mr Neil Marshall, BEd Hons (*Head of Biology*)
Mrs Anne Mawer, MA, BA Hons (*Head of Modern Languages*)
Mr Alan McKenna, BSc Hons (*Head of Chemistry*)
Mrs Stephanie Milton-Thompson, BSc Hons (*Science*)
Mr Philip Millward, MA Hons, FRCO (*Head of Music*)
Miss Geeta Missan, BSc Hons, BA Hons (*Head of Spanish*)
Mr Martin Muchall, MA, BA Hons (*Religious Studies*)
Mr Jonathan Muir, BA Hons (*English*)
Mrs Karen Muldoon (*Drama Support Assistant*)
Miss Claire O'Sullivan, BA, MSc (*Science*)
Miss Karen Palenski, BA Hons, MA (*Modern Languages*)
Mr Martin Parham, BSc, PhD (*Head of Geography*)
Mr Gunvantrai Parmar, Cert Ed/Dip Ed CDT & IT (*Design and Technology*)
Miss Lisa Parish, BA Hons (*Music*)
Mrs Donna Pepperdine, BA Hons (*English*)
Mr Nigel Rocca, BA Hons (*Head of Business Studies*)
Miss Celia Roe, BSc Hons, RSA Dip, TEFL (*EFL & Spanish*)
Mrs Michelle Saunders (*Food Technology/Art & Design Technician*)
Miss Olesia Sava, BA, MA (*English, EFL & Modern Languages*)
Mrs Lindsay Smith, BSc Hons, MA (*Mathematics*)
Mr Michael Stanley, BA Hons, MBA (*Head of Mathematics*)
Mr Alexander Stathopoulos, BSc Hons (*Head of Computing*)
Mrs Susan Strutt, BSc Hons (*Biology*)
Mr Martin Tanner, BSc Hons, MA (*Head of Geology*)
Mr Adam Tansley, BSc Hons (*Mathematics*)
Mr Kieran Taylor (*Drama Technician*)
Mrs Fiona Taylor, BSc Hons (*Science*)
Mr Greg Thurstans, BSc Hons (*Director of Sport*)
Mrs Maria Wade, BA Hons (*Modern Languages*)
Miss Michele Worsfold, MSc, MA Hons (*History*)

School Counsellor:
§Ms J Bovingdon, BA Surrey, Dip HE, MBACP Accred, UKRCP Registered

Houses and House staff:

Boarding:
Cambridge: Mr S Bird
Oxford: Mr S Greaves
Queen's: Miss M Davenport

Day:
Buchanan: Mrs D Pepperdine
Keable: Mr E Hutchinson
Madden: Mr M J Tanner
Reade: Miss K Palenski
St Andrews: Mr A Tansley
Hollenden: Mrs S Strutt

Junior School:
Headmaster: Mr James Thompson, BA QTS
Head of Lower Juniors: Mrs Amanda Flynn, BA QTS, MA Ed
Head of Upper Juniors: Miss Sarah Hamlin, BSc, PGCE, MA Ed Mgt

Mrs Jan Bennett, BA Hons, PGCE
Mrs Fabienne Bird, MA (*Modern Languages*)
Mrs Fran Blount, BA, PGCE (*Learning Support*)
Miss Emma Bodenham, BA Hons
Mrs Rosie Coker, BEd (*Head of Science*)
Mr James Davis, BSc
Miss Siobhan Fox, GTCL, LTCL (*Head of Music*)
Mrs Judy Houlden, BA (*Modern Languages*)
Mr John Janowski, BSc Hons
Mrs Amanda King, BEd Hons
Mrs Jennette Lingley, BA Hons, PGCE
Mrs Laura Lloyd, BA (*Girls' PE*)

Mrs Sue Lower, BA, PGCE, MSc (*Head of Learning Support*)
Mrs Judy Moseley, CertEd
Mrs Alys Netherway, BSc, PGCE
Mrs Laura Pasquel, BA Hons, QTS
Mrs Jozie Quinn, BEd Hons
Mrs Fizza Rizvi, MA, PGCE
Miss Natasha Rogers, BA Hons
Mrs Louise Taylor, BSc
Mrs Christine Trim, NNEB, CertEd
Mr Steve Urie, BA, PGCE, QTS
Mr Phil Venier, BEd Hons (*Boys' PE*)
Mrs Hilary Walsh, CertEd
Mrs Sue Wilson, BEd, MA
Ms Lisa Woolfe, BEd Hons
Mrs Jane Wragg, BA, PGCE

Teaching Assistants:
Mrs Teresa Bridgewater, CACHE Level 3 Dip Pre-School Practice
Mrs Lynne Bruce, NNEB, CCE
Mrs Adele Cane, Level 3 Dip
Mrs Susan Haig, NVQ Teaching & Learning L3
Mrs Yayoi Ikeda, Level 3 Dip, Adv Level Apprenticeship
Mrs Nicola Jordan, OCR Level 3 NVQ
Mrs Christine Marangone, BEd
Mrs Sharmaine Nemar, NVQ Early Years L2, Level 3 Dip, Adv Level Apprenticeship
Mrs Karen Parsons, NNEB
Mrs Kelly Payne, CACHE Level 2 NVQ
Mrs Janette Vallance, Level 3 Dip
Miss Emilie Webber, Early Years Foundation Degree
Mrs Anne Willis, CACHE Level 3 Dip Pre-School Practice

Operations Director & Clerk to the Governors: Mr D Neely
Admissions Registrar: Mrs Mary King
Marketing Manager: Mrs Ciara Campbell

Number in School. There are 909 pupils in the school: 601 pupils in the Senior School, of whom 158 are in the Sixth Form, and 308 in the Junior School. In the Senior School there are 130 boarders and 471 day pupils; of these 346 are boys and 255 are girls. In the Junior School there are 174 boys and 134 girls, all day pupils.

Admission. Most pupils enter the school in the Autumn term at the age of 3+, 11 or 13. Space permitting pupils may be considered and admitted at other ages, and there is a direct entry into the Sixth Form for eligible students.

Religion. The school's religious affiliation is to the Church of England but pupils of all persuasions are welcome. Our approach to daily life is founded on Christian principles and we maintain an atmosphere of mutual respect and understanding.

The resident Chaplain is responsible for the conduct of all services and the teaching of Religious Education throughout the school. Weekly Chapel assemblies allow a brief act of worship and an opportunity to share ideas and concerns. The Sunday service is compulsory for those boarding at school, and the voluntary Eucharist is specifically for those with a Christian commitment. Enquiries regarding Confirmation to the Church of England are encouraged.

Curriculum. The keynote of curriculum organisation is flexibility and there is close alignment with the requirements of the National Curriculum. All pupils follow a curriculum designed to provide a sound foundation across a broad range of subjects. Equipped with this experience, pupils are helped in selecting their GCSE examination subjects from a wide range. Great care is taken to achieve balance in each pupil's timetable and to ensure that an appropriate number of subjects is studied.

A high proportion of pupils continue to the Sixth Form where, typically, four subjects are studied in Year 12 with three continuing into Year 13. At present A Level courses are available in Mathematics, Further Mathematics, Computing, History, Geography, Geology, Physics, Chemistry, Biology, English, Business Studies, Economics, Politics, French, Spanish, German, Drama and Theatre Arts, Media Studies, Art and Design, Photography, Design and Technology, Music, Food Science and Physical Education.

It is our expectation that all pupils will leave the Sixth Form to go on to higher education and we regularly secure places at Oxford and Cambridge for our strongest students.

Facilities. The School lies in 110 acres of stunning private grounds providing excellent academic and sporting facilities for all age groups.

There are 3 Boarding/Day Houses and six Day Houses, a well-resourced School Library and Sixth Form Study Centre. Recent refurbishment has provided new, spacious areas for Art, Design Technology, Food Science and Photography along with a new Media Studies Suite. A new Sport Pitch development has further enhanced our impressive sports facilities, providing a floodlit all-weather pitch, multi-use games area, new natural turf areas for cricket, athletics and football and re-surfaced and extended netball courts. These are in addition to our Sports Hall and indoor swimming pool.

A detached Science building contains seven modern and very well-equipped laboratories.

An outstanding purpose-built Music and Performing Arts building was opened in December 2010 along with new dining rooms, kitchen, servery and Sixth Form Café facility.

Careers. The Head of Careers coordinates Careers advice, giving individual counselling and helping with all University applications. The School is a member of the Career Development Institute whose services are available to all pupils. Towards the end of the Summer Term work experience placements are organised for those who have completed GCSE examinations, and members of the Lower Sixth participate in organised visits to Universities and Colleges.

Organisation. The Senior School is divided into nine Houses, 2 boarding and 3 day for boys, 1 boarding and 3 day for girls. Each House has its own premises, Housemaster or Housemistress and assistant House Tutors. It is expected that all pupils should be able and encouraged to participate as fully as possible in the co-curricular life of the school, becoming involved in evening and weekend activities irrespective of their status as a Boarder or Day pupil. Supervised homework sessions and drop-in subject clinics are provided for day pupils participating in evening activities and they attend supper with the boarders. Tutors play a vital pastoral and academic role, monitoring overall progress and development.

Games. Popular sports are hockey, cricket, soccer, netball, tennis and athletics. Badminton, basketball, table tennis, trampolining and volleyball are also played.

Music, Drama and Art. Music in the Senior School is in the hands of the Director of Music whilst the Assistant Director of Music concentrates on the Junior School. They are assisted by a large number of visiting teachers. There is a Senior School Orchestra and wind, brass, jazz, swing and string ensembles. Choral Society, Chapel Choir, Barbershop and Junior School Choir and Orchestra meet and perform regularly.

Drama is taught as part of the Creative Studies programme in the lower school and is available at GCSE and A Level where pupils make use of our Drama Studio, Auditorium and Technical Room.

In Art and Design, instruction is offered in a wide range of Artistic techniques using a variety of materials – paint, ink, screen printing, ceramics and pottery.

Clubs and Activities. Senior School pupils choose from a programme of over 60 regular activities, with a participation rate of over 98%. Many activities are open to pupils in both Senior and Junior Schools, and the annual House Activities Cup is keenly contested by pupils in all year groups. The school's involvement in the Model United Nations programme is unique in this country, with our annual IMUN conference each October attracting over 500 student delegates from all over the world. There is a flourishing voluntary Combined Cadet Force unit and Duke of Edinburgh's Award Scheme, the Theatre Society takes advantage of the school's proximity to London's West End, and the annual ski trip is always over-subscribed.

Junior School. The aim in the Junior School is to instil a lifelong love of learning with a strong academic focus and extensive range of clubs and activities. A Breakfast Club and After-School Care is available. The majority of children progress to the Senior School. The Junior and Early Years Section provides a happy, secure and purposeful environment. (*For full details please see our entry in the IAPS section.*)

Scholarships. A number of scholarships are available each year to pupils aged 11+ to 13+ who show particular academic, musical or drama promise and talent. Sixth Form scholarships are also awarded annually.

For further details or an appointment to visit the school apply to the Headmaster.

Fees per term (2014–2015). Senior School: Boarders £10,475 (Years 9–13), £7,750 (Years 7 & 8); Day £5,295 (inclusive of lunch and supper). Junior School: Years 3–6 £3,915 (inclusive of lunch, after-school clubs and supper), Reception–Year 2 £3,200 (inclusive of lunch), Nursery £1,795–£3,200.

Charitable status. Russell School Trust is a Registered Charity, number 271907. It exists solely for the education of boys and girls.

The Royal School Dungannon

2 Ranfurly Road, Dungannon BT71 6EG, Northern Ireland

Tel:	028 8772 2710
Fax:	028 8775 2845 Headmaster
	028 8775 2506 Bursar
email:	info@rsd.dungannon.ni.sch.uk
website:	www.royaldungannon.com
Twitter:	@RoyalDungannon

Motto: *Perseverando* (*Excellence through Perseverance*)
Founded 1608.

Board of Governors:
Chairman: H McLean, LLB, MBA
Vice Chairman: Dr D Jones, BSc Hons, PhD, DSc, CEng, CChem, FIMMM, FRSS, MRSC, MIEI, MPSNI

Members:
Mrs J Anderson, BA Hons, MCIPD
Mrs J Archer
F Bain, BSc, MCOptom
D N Browne, MIB, MIMgt
Dr C Cassidy, MB BCh, FRCPsych
G A Cooper, OBE, BSc, CEng, FICE, FCIWEM, FIEI, MConsE
J C M Eddie
R Eitel
Mrs R Emerson
Revd A J Forster, BA, BTh
Mrs E Harkness, BL
Mrs I T Holmes, MBE, BSc, DASE
The Revd K R Kingston, MA
Mrs G Leonard
P McAlister, BA, DipArch
Lord Maginnis of Drumglass, PC
Dr D Maguire, BDS
J C McCarter, BA, DipArch, RIBA
Dr H G McNeill, BA, MB, FFARCSW

Mr P G Moore, MA, PGE, GC, TEFL, DELE Int
Mrs P L Matthews, BD, PGCE
Mrs E V Stitt, BA, PGCE, DELE Sup
Revd A S Thompson, MA, BD
Dr G Walsh, BEd, PhD, ALCH, FHEA
Mrs L Watt
Mrs J Williamson

Secretary to the Governors: The Headmaster

Headmaster: Dr D A Burnett, BA, PhD, NPQH

Teaching Staff:
* *Head of Department*
¹ *Head of Year*
² *Head of House*

Deputy Head: Miss V S J Garvin, BA, PGCE, MEd
Deputy Head: R J Clingan, BSc, MEd, PGCE

Senior Teacher: *G R Black, BSc, PGCE
Senior Teacher: *¹Miss A E Chestnutt, BSc, MEd, PGCE

Head of Boarding: Mrs C J Mawhinney, BEd

Mrs A Best, BA, PGCE
A D Boyd, BMus Hons, PGCE, ALCM
Miss J Caldwell, BSc Hons, PGCE, DIS
*N J Canning, BEng, PGCE
*R E Chambers, BSc, PGCE
*Mrs W Y Chambers, BSc, PGCE
*¹Mrs M E Clingan, BA, ATD
Miss S A Colgan, BSc, PGCE
*S J Cuddy, BMus, PGCE
Mrs G S Glenn, BSc, PGCE
¹J R Graham, BA, MSc, PGCE
*Mrs R L Hampton, BSc, PGCE
*J W Hunniford, BA, MA, PGCE
*Mrs S J Jackson, BA, PGCE
Mrs P L Johnston, BSc, PGCE
¹Mrs C L Kerr, BA, PGCE
*P S Kerr, BA, PGCE
¹G S R Lucas, BSc, PGCE
²Mrs P L Matthews, BEd, PGCE
*²G W McClintock, BSc, PGCE
Miss D McCombe, BSc, PGCE
Mrs C E McMcCormick, BA, PGCE
Mrs S J McCullough, BA, PGCE
M McDowell, BA, MA, PGCE
*K McGuinness, BSc, PGCE
*¹Mrs P McMullan, BEd, PGCTEd
*Miss H Montgomery, BSc, PGCE
*P G Moore, MA, PGCE, GC, TEFL
*Ms A M Prescott, BEd, MEd
*²A S Ritchie, BSc, PGCE
*²Mrs D Robb, BSc, PGCE
Miss L Robinson, BSc, PGCE
Mrs E V Stitt, BA, PGCE
*Mrs A R Straghan, BSc Econ, PGCE
A T Turner, BSc, PGCE
¹G T Watterson, MSc, PGCE
J W Willis, BEd
I A Wilson, BSc, PGCE

Chaplain: Revd A J Forster, BA, BTh

Administrative Staff:
Bursar: Mr D Wheeler, BSc Econ, FCA
Headmaster's Secretary: Mrs A Cullen
Reception Office Supervisor: Mrs P Williamson

Matrons:
Mrs M Willis, SRN (*Day*)
Mrs M McNeill (*Evening*)
Miss R Nelson (*Evening*)

In 1608 James I made an order in Privy Council establishing six Royal Schools in Ulster of which Dungannon became, in 1614, the first to admit pupils. In 1983 plans were first drawn up to incorporate the neighbouring girls' grammar school and to use both campuses' excellent facilities for co-educational purposes. This development came to fruition in 1986. A £9 million building and refurbishment programme began in 2000 and was completed in 2003, providing very high-tech specialist accommodation in science, technology and IT. In 2007 an international standard Astroturf hockey pitch was completed with flood lighting and four new all-weather tennis courts were opened. Annual investment by Governors in the school's infrastructure has continued allowing RSD staff and pupils to enjoy excellent facilities.

For nearly four centuries the Royal School has aimed at providing an education which enables its pupils to achieve the highest possible standards of academic excellence and at developing each pupil into a mature, well-balanced and responsible adult, well-equipped for the demands of a highly complex and technological world.

There are four Houses which foster the competitive instincts and idiosyncrasies of young people. Pastorally, each year is supervised by a Head of Year who guides his/her pupils throughout the child's career in a caring school environment.

The Boarding Department provides accommodation for 52 Boarders with the Girls and Boys housed in separate wings of the modernised Old School building dating from 1789. The recently refurbished facilities include a new kitchen/dining area, recreation area with flat screen TV and games console, new furniture in all dormitories and fully regulated wireless internet throughout. There are a number of staff who assist in the Boarding Department, including a Head of Boarding, a team of seven resident teaching staff, a team of 5 day and evening matrons, and a large number of support staff. These staff all work together to ensure that high standards of care and support are maintained. The School is also serviced by a team of local doctors and dentists who support the Boarders. A major hospital is less than 30 minutes from the campus.

The extensive buildings are a mixture of ancient and modern, with recently opened technology and science accommodation. Eight well-equipped Science Laboratories, Audio/Visual Room, two Libraries, Sixth Form Centre and Study Rooms, Technology, two Music and Art Studios and two Information Technology Suites are supplemented by a Boarding Department housed in well-appointed accommodation which has been completely renovated in the recent times. Boarders are able to make use of a wide range of facilities such as Sports Hall, Computer Laboratory, Multigym, Badminton Courts, Television Lounges, satellite TV, high-speed broadband (including Skype) and nearby facilities such as the local swimming pool and extensive parkland walks. Situated in its own spacious grounds in a quiet residential area of this rural town, the School is linked directly by motorway to Belfast (40 minutes), two airports, cross-Channel ferries and railway stations.

The establishment of good study skills and practices is considered to be of crucial importance. The size of the School ensures that no child is overlooked in any way.

At A Level new subjects are offered such as Economics and, in collaboration with partner schools, Media Studies, Politics, Psychology and Business Studies.

Pupils are prepared for GCSE and A Levels under all the major UK Examination Boards and there is a tradition of Oxbridge successes as well as a high rate of entry to the University of Ulster, Queen's University Belfast and other leading British Universities. In most years around 95% of the Upper Sixth Form proceed to Higher Education. The School's overseas students typically choose to enrol both at UK universities and universities in their home country.

Many co-curricular pursuits are encouraged during lunchtime or after school, such as Choir, Orchestra, Duke of

Edinburgh's Award Scheme, Chess, Charities, Debating, Public Speaking and many more.

Alongside the School's academic achievements in both Arts and Sciences may be placed its record in the sporting world: in Rugby, Hockey, Cricket, Badminton, Shooting, Table Tennis and Tennis.

Fees per annum (2014–2015). Day: £150. 7-Day Boarding: £15,350 (non-EU passport holders), £8,850 (EU passport holders). 5-Day Boarding: £13,350 (non-EU passport holders), £8,850 (EU passport holders).

Charitable status. The Royal School Dungannon is a Registered Charity, number XN46588 A. It was established by Royal Charter in 1608 for the purpose of education.

Rugby School

Rugby, Warwickshire CV22 5EH
Tel:	01788 556216 (Head Master)
	01788 556260 (Bursar)
	01788 556274 (Admissions Registrar)
Fax:	01788 556277 (Admissions Registrar)
email:	head@rugbyschool.net (Head Master)
	bursar@rugbyschool.net (Bursar)
	admissions@rugbyschool.net (Admissions Registrar)
website:	www.rugbyschool.net

Motto: '*Orando Laborando*'

Rugby School was founded in the year 1567 by Lawrence Sheriff, native of Rugby, one of the Gentlemen of the Princess Elizabeth, a Grocer and Second Warden of the Grocers' Company. The School was endowed with estates in the neighbourhood of Rugby and in London. In 1750 the School moved to its present site on the edge of Rugby town. Between 1809 and 1814 the Head Master's House, School House and the Old Quad were built. Under Dr Arnold and subsequent Head Masters, including two later Archbishops of Canterbury, Rugby was influential in establishing the pattern of independent education throughout the country.

There are currently 794 pupils in the School (45% girls : 55% boys) of whom around 20% are day pupils.

Rugby values scholarship, team work in games, music and drama, and qualities of leadership and self-reliance in the pupils. Rugby prides itself on a sharp edge of academic excellence but its aim, as a fully co-educational school, is to encourage cooperation, seeing a wide range of enterprises through to their conclusion, an awareness of the wider world and a lively approach to a very broad range of opportunity. The boys and girls who come to Rugby are expected to have a go at a variety of things. As they leave they should feel ready for (almost) anything; that they have stretched themselves and have been asked to do a great deal; and finally that along the way life at Rugby has been fun.

Governing Body:
Mrs L Holmes, BA Hons (*Chairman*)
R Hingley, Esq, MA (*Deputy Chairman*)
Prof C H E Imray, Esq, PhD, FRCS, FRCP
The Rt Revd the Lord Bishop of Birmingham, D A Urquhart
Dr E Wood, OBE, DL, MSc, EdD, Hon LLD
P Bennett-Jones, CBE, MA.
D J Bennett, Esq, MA
Prof C Howe, Esq, ScD
S Lebus, Esq, MA
C J Edwards, Esq, MA
B J O'Brien, Esq, LLB
S R T Penniston
HM Lord-Lieutenant of Warwickshire, T B Cox
Mrs P M Stafford, BA Hons
P Smulders, BA, MBA

Ms C J Marten, MA

Bursar and Clerk to the Governing Body: G Lydiatt, BSc, FCCA

Medical Officer: Dr R Marchant, MRCGP, MBChB, DRCOG, DCH, BSc Hons

Head Master: P R A Green, MA Hons, PGCE

Deputy Head: Mrs S A Rosser, BEd

Deputy Heads:
Dr N G Hampton, MA, PhD, PGCE (*Pastoral*)
G Parker-Jones, MA, PGCE (*Academic*)

Assistant Head (*Upper School*): Dr J D Muston, MA, MPhil, DPhil

Admissions Registrar: H G Steele-Bodger, MA

Assistant Teaching Staff:

Chaplaincy:
The Revd R M Horner, BSc (*Chaplain*)
Miss L Greatwood, BSc, DipMin, PGCE

Classics:
A P Walker, MA, PGCE (*Head of Department*)
T J Day, BA
Ms A Dordevic, BA, MPhil
Miss S H D Stuckey, BA
A E L Thomson, BA

Design:
P A Byrne, BA (*Director of Design Faculty [Acting], Head of D&T*)
A D Bradbury, BA, ARPS (*Head of Photography & Graphics*)
Miss J Rayner, BA, MA, PGCE (*Head of History of Art*)
Mrs P Warford, MA (*Head of Art*)
Mrs A Bradbury, Dip AD (*Art/Graphics*)
Mrs A K Farrelly, BSc
Mrs S E Phillips, BA (*Art/Ceramics*)
B J Welch, BEng Hons, PGCE

Director of Academic ICT: B J Rigg, MA, ACA

Drama and Theatre Studies
A K Chessell, BA, MSc (*Director of Drama*)
Dr S L Hancox, BA, MA, PhD

Economics and Business Studies:
P J Bryant, BA (*Head of Department*)
A J Darby, BA
C J Fisher, BA
P J Rosser, BA
H G Steele-Bodger, MA, PGCE
J D Walker, BSc, PGCE

English:
A Fletcher, MA (*Head of Department*)
R J Smith, MA (*Second in Department*)
Mrs E M Beesley, MA
J B Cunningham-Batt, BA
S A Demetriou, BA
Miss I C Marks, BA, MA, PGCE
A J Naylor, BA
Miss J Rayner, MA, BA, PGCE
J A Sutcliffe, PhD

Geography:
J M Pitt, BA (*Head of Department*)
J C Evans, BA
Ms M H Pink, MA, GDL, LPC, PGCE
Mrs S A Rosser, BEd
A E Smith, BSc, MPhil, PhD, FRMetS, FRGS, PGCE
Mrs A D Tooke, BSc, PGCE

History:
Dr T D Guard, MA, MSt, DPhil, PGCE (*Head of Department*)

E A Beesley, BA, PhD
F J Hemming-Allen, BEd, MEd
Miss K Hollings, BA
Dr J D Muston, MA, MPhil, DPhil
Mrs A Naylor, BA, LTCL
G Parker-Jones, MA, PGCE
Ms M H Pink, MA, GDL, LPC, PGCE
W S Robinson, BA, MPhil
E E Trelinski, MA

Information Technology:
T E Rennoldson, BSc, PGCE (*Head of Department*)
Mrs L A Bell, BEng

Learning Development
Mrs L J E Stevenson, LLB, Dip SpLD (*Head of Learning
   Development*)
Mrs A L Cunningham-Batt, MA, OCR Cert SpLD
Mrs F J Fleming, MA, Cert TESOL
Mrs H Lawson, BEd, FRSA

Mathematics:
M R Baker, BA (*Head of Department*)
M A Hennings, BA, DPhil (*Second in Department*)
R J Baker, BA
P K Bell, MA, Msc, PGCE
Miss G L Dixon, BA, GTP, Dip, ABRSM
Miss R J Force, BSc
Miss H E Grant, BSc, GTP
J E Ingram, MMath
L P Rao, MA
B Rigg, MA, ACA
A J Siggers, BSc

Modern Languages:
D Gillett, BA (*Head of Department*)
Mrs J M Jordan, BA (*Head of Italian & Additional
   Languages*)
Miss S Perkins, BA, MEd, PGCE (*Head of French*)
Mrs C A M O'Mahoney, BA (*Head of Spanish*)
Mrs W J Corvi, BEd, PGCE
R M Horner, BSc
N D Jarvis, BA, MA, PGCE
Mrs R P Kayada, BA, PGCE
Dr A C Leamon, BA, MA, PhD
A M Maguire, BA, MA, PGCE
Dr J C Smith, MA, DPhil, PGCE

Music:
R J Tanner, MA, FRCO, ARAM, FGCM (*Director of
   Music*)
N H Bevan, GRSM, LRAM (*Head of Singing*)
T W Bentham, BA (*Head of Brass*)
Mrs A Brogaard, DipRDAM (*Head of Strings*)
R F Colley, MA, DipRAM, LRAM, ARCM, DipRAM,
   PGCE (*Head of Piano*)
A R Davey (*Head of Woodwind*)
J A Williams, MA, BA, DipABRSM, PGCE (*Head of
   Academic Music*)

Philosophy
Dr J L Taylor, MA, BPhil, DPhil, MInstP, PGCE
A Fletcher, MA
Dr E L Williams, BA, MA, MRes, PhD

Physical Education:
F J Hemming-Allen, BEd, MEd (*Head of PE*)
Mrs L Hampton, MSc, BEd
Miss H E Grant, BSc, GTP

Politics:
P Teeton, BA (*Head of Department*)
E Trelinski, MA

Science:
M A Thompson, BSc, PhD, PGCE (*Head of Science*)
Mrs C Shelley, BEd, MA (*Head of Biology*)
T M White, BSc, PGCE (*Head of Chemistry*)

A G Davies, BSc, PhD, PGCE (*Head of Physics*)
J S Bendall, MChem, PhD
P A Berry, BSc, PGCE
R Dhanda, BSc
O Gardner, MSci, MA, PGCE
Miss L J Greatwood, BSc, DipMin, PGCE
Mrs L M Hampton, BEd, MSc
Dr N G Hampton, MA, PhD, PGCE
Dr G C E Joyce, BSc
Miss R J Lambert, BSc, PGCE
R B McGuirk, BSc, MSc, PGCE
M A Monteith, BSc, PGCE
Dr N J Morse, BSc, PhD, CChem, FRSC
Mrs E L Sale, BSc, PGCE
E G Taylor, PhD, MPhys, PGCE
Dr J L Taylor, BA, BPhil, DPhil, MInstP, PGCE (*Director
   of Critical Skills*)
Miss E A Tilley, BSc, PGDip, PGCE

Careers and Higher Education:
Mrs D J Horner, BA (*Head of Department*)
Ms L Waweru, BPhilEd, PQCG
Mrs J A HIggins
M A Hennings, MA, DPhil

PSHE Education
Miss J Rayner, MA, BA, PGCE (*Head of Department*)

Sport
S J Brown, BSc (*Director of Sport*)
H F Beavan (*Polo Professional*)
Miss D Black, BSc (*Sports Development Officer*)
Miss L Blair (*Netball Development Officer*)
M J Powell (*Cricket Professional*)
P J Rosser, BA (*Rackets Professional*)
J Taylor, BSc (*Tennis Development Officer*)
M Taylor (*Hockey Development Officer*)
Sports Centre: H D P Bennett (*Manager*)

Houses and Housemasters/mistresses:

Boarding Houses (boys):
Cotton: Mr Ed Trelinski
Kilbracken: Mr James Walker
Michell: Mr Tim Day
School Field: Mr Mindy Dhanda
School House: Mr Peter Bell
Sheriff: Mr Maurice Monteith
Whitelaw: Mr Chris Evans

Day Boy House:
Town: Mr Tony Darby

Boarding Houses (girls):
Bradley: Mrs Liz Sale
Dean: Mrs Amy Farrelly
Griffin: Mrs Anne Naylor
Rupert Brooke: Mrs Colette O'Mahoney
Stanley (Sixth Form only): Mrs Lara Hampton
Tudor: Mrs Debbie Horner

Day Girl House:
Southfield: Mrs Lizzie Beesley

Junior Day House (boys and girls):
Marshall: Mr Barrie Cunningham-Batt

Director of Development: Mrs K Wilson, BA

Situation. Rugby is situated near the junction of the M1
and M6 motorways and is not far from the M40. It is just one
hour by hourly rail service from London (Euston) and is
close to Birmingham International Airport as well as being
within easy reach of Heathrow. Though the School is close
to the countryside and has a 150-acre campus with a full
range of facilities and games fields, it is essentially a town
school and has the practical advantages of links with indus-

try and opportunities for experience and service in the wider world.

Facilities. The main classroom block, the Macready Theatre, the Chapel, the Temple Reading Room and Gymnasium were designed by William Butterfield and to these have been added further buildings of architectural distinction, among them the Temple Speech Room and the Science Schools.

Since then there have followed a Multimedia Language Laboratory, IT Centre, a state-of-the-art Design Centre, housing Art, Design and Technology, History of Art, Photography and a professional standard TV studio for Media.

Other developments include a Sports Centre, opened by HRH The Duchess of Kent in 1990, and recently extended to include a new cafeteria, seminar room and fitness suite. There are extensive floodlit astroturf pitches and hard courts for hockey, tennis and netball. The Lewis Gallery, a new art and design exhibition space was opened in 2006 and is proving very popular with professional artists. In October 2008 HRH the Earl of Wessex opened the refurbished Science School and in April 2009 Lord Coe unveiled a plaque celebrating the link between Thomas Arnold, Pierre de Coubertin and the Modern Olympic Movement.

The School is fully networked. All pupils have a laptop computer for use in the classroom and all classrooms are equipped with Promethean Boards.

Boarding Houses. All boarding houses undergo a continuous programme of improvement. Houses provide small dormitories of 4 to 6 in the first one or two years and study-bedrooms thereafter. Meals are eaten in House Dining Halls.

GCSE. All the usual subjects are offered as well as German, Spanish, Latin, Greek, Design, Art and Music.

AS/A2. A2 Level is offered in all the GCSE subjects as well as in Economics, Business Studies, English Language, PE, Media, Theatre Studies, History of Art and Politics. AS Level is offered in Graphics, Music Technology, Italian and Religious Studies. Increasingly popular are the newly accredited Extended Projects which include Perspectives on Science, Culture and Identity. Other EPs include Culture and Identity, Digital Innovation, The Global Environment, Performance, Engineering Technology, Chemistry Investigation and People, Power and Wealth. All boys and girls go on to Higher Education and about 10% receive Oxbridge offers.

There are several learned societies and each academic department invites distinguished speakers to the School. Recent speakers include Lord Hurd, Lord Falconer, Anthony Seldon, Lord Carey and Giles Clarke.

Spiritual life. The experience of holiness, an understanding of right and wrong, and respect for the worth of each human being are the bonds of community. These values are learned in every part of our lives, but the School Chapel and the activities connected with it are a particular focus.

There are two full-time chaplains, one male and one female, who involve themselves with all the School's activities. On Mondays, Wednesdays and Fridays the School day begins with a ten-minute service in Chapel. On Sundays there is usually a morning service for the majority of the pupils, often with a guest preacher.

There is an active Christian Union, and a weekly service of meditation with Holy Communion, both of which are optional for the pupils. Members of faiths other than Christian are encouraged to attend worship and instruction within their own faith.

Sport. Sports include Athletics, Badminton, Basketball, Cricket, Cross-country, Fencing, Football, Golf, Gymnastics, Hockey, Judo, Netball, Polo, Rackets, Riding, Rugby, Sailing, Squash, Sub Aqua, Swimming and Tennis.

Activities. All boys and girls are encouraged to undertake a full programme of extra-curricular activities. The School aims to ensure that music touches the lives of all pupils as well as catering for outstanding musicians. With School, House and visiting productions and a very well-equipped

theatre, drama is well to the fore. Other activities include Ballet, Canoeing, Camping, CCF, Choirs, Climbing, Duke of Edinburgh's Award, First Aid, Orienteering, Pottery, Sculpture, Target and Clay-pigeon shooting, Silversmithing, Social Service, Television Production and School Journalism. The aim is to give all boys and girls a wide variety of experience so that they can excel in a few things but understand and develop some appreciation of most areas.

Entry. Offers of boarding places for Year 9 on the basis of previous school's report and interviews during Year 7, subject to CE at average 55% at least, or school's own maths and English tests, or scholarship entry.

Offers of day places for Year 9 on the basis of previous school's report, interview and computer based entrance test during Year 6, subject to CE at 55% at least, or school's own maths and English tests, or scholarship entry.

Offers of places for boarders and day pupils for Year 12 on the basis of previous school's report, interview and written entrance tests during Year 11, subject to at least six Bs at GCSE.

The Junior Department. At age 11 boys and girls enter Marshall House as day pupils by taking a computerised test. Foundation Scholarships and Music Scholarships are available at this stage. There is one class of 11-year-olds and one of 12-year-olds. Classes run from 8.45 am to 4.00 pm. A full programme of extra-curricular activities is offered, most of it based on the Senior School's extensive facilities. All of the teaching is done by staff from the Senior School but Marshall House has its own Head.

Scholarships. Approximately 10% of the School's annual income is currently expended in Scholarships, Foundationerships, Bursaries and other awards. Scholarships are intended to open access to talented boys and girls irrespective of parental means. All scholarships therefore carry a nominal reduction of 10% of the fee; all may be augmented to 100% of the fees subject to means testing.

Academic Scholarships at 13+: Boys and girls who are 12 or over and under 14 at midnight on August 31st in the year the examination is taken may sit. Candidates who were previously registered for entry and who do not obtain awards are normally admitted to the school on the result of the Scholarship examination. The examination is held at Rugby in early May for entry in September of the same year. A generous number of scholarships are usually awarded.

Academic Scholarships at 16+: Boys and girls aiming to enter the School after GCSE may compete for a number of 16+ Scholarships. The Scholarship interviews are held at Rugby in mid-November in the year preceding the pupil's entry to the School. Candidates must first take the Sixth Form Entrance Examination and those showing scholarship potential will be called for Scholarship interviews with the relevant Heads of Department.

Music Scholarships: Several Scholarships are awarded each year at 11+, 13+ and 16+. At 16+ the examination audition is held at Rugby in November, at 11+ in early January, and at 13+ in late January or early February of the year of entry.

Art Scholarships: At 16+ potential Art Scholarship candidates are interviewed and present their portfolios as part of the 16+ Academic Scholarship in November and at 13+ in the May of the year of entry.

Design and Technology Bursary/Scholarship: Awards are offered at 13+ and 16+. The examinations are held in conjunction with the Academic Scholarships. At 13+, candidates can, but need not, take the Academic Scholarship as well.

Sports Scholarships: A number of Scholarships are awarded each year at 13+ and 16+ to candidates with outstanding ability in team games. At 13+ applicants should be nominated by their Head Teacher to attend an initial assessment at Rugby. Shortlisted candidates will then be observed in match conditions. At 16+ candidates will be interviewed as part of the sixth form entrance examination in November and will be observed in match conditions or be invited to participate in a training session at Rugby. Shortlisted candidates will subsequently be observed in match conditions.

The Arnold Foundation: The Arnold Foundation aims to raise funds through charitable donations to support the education of talented boys and girls whose families would not be able to fund boarding school fees. Funds are available for several awards for entry to the sixth form and at 13+. Pupils offered a place through this scheme may be awarded up to 100% of the full boarding fee plus extras. The final selection is through interviews. Candidates are expected to pass the School's normal entrance requirements. Initial enquiries should be made via the Registry.

Foundationerships: In 1567 Lawrence Sheriff in his Will bequeathed money to establish a school in perpetuity in Rugby 'to serve chiefly for the children of Rugby and Brownsover'. It is in the execution of the terms of this Will that Foundation Scholarships are offered. Several awards are made each year to day boy and day girl candidates of 11+ and 13+. Awards are 10% of the fees but may be augmented up to 100% (subject to means testing) of the day pupil fee. All candidates for Foundation Scholarships must reside within a radius of 10 miles from the Rugby Clock Tower.

For further information and details of all scholarships please contact the Admissions Registrar, email: admissions@rugbyschool.net.

Fees per term (2014–2015). The consolidated termly fee for boys and girls: £10,675 (boarding), £6,698 (day). Junior Department: £3,945 (Marshall House).

Optional charge for instrumental or singing tuition: £295.

Further Information. Full information about the School's aims, its academic curriculum, facilities and activities will be found in the School's prospectus (available on the School website: www.rugbyschool.net). Enquiries and applications should be made in the first instance to the Registrar who will be pleased to arrange for parents to visit the School and to meet members of the staff and the Head Master.

'**The freedom, sophistication and civilisation of Rugby struck me as absolutely miraculous. I just loved my time there.**' (Robert Hardy, actor).

Charitable status. The Governing Body of Rugby School is a Registered Charity, number 528752. It exists to provide education for young people.

Rydal Penrhos School

Pwllycrochan Avenue, Colwyn Bay, North Wales LL29 7BT

Tel:	01492 530155
Fax:	01492 531872
email:	info@rydalpenrhos.com
website:	www.rydalpenrhos.com
Twitter:	@RydalPenrhos

Penrhos College was founded by Thomas Payne in 1880 as a Methodist girls' school; its neighbour, Rydal School, was founded five years later by Thomas Osborn, also as a Methodist boarding school. In 1999, after just over a century of co-existence, the Schools merged under the name of Rydal Penrhos; now Rydal Penrhos School. A second merger took place in 2003 when Rydal Penrhos Preparatory School merged with another local prep school, Lyndon School. The school is fully co-educational from 2½ to 18, with a total roll of 547 pupils.

The Governors:
Chairman: The Revd J P Atkinson
Vice-Chairman: Mr J I Morris

Mrs A M Watson
Revd P Barnett
Mr P D Slater
Mr R W Dransfield
Dr Revd S Wigley
Mr J P Burgess
Mr J M A Wilford
Mr J Payne
Mrs D A Draper
Dr N Bickerton
Mr I M Williams
Mr J Barnes
Dr D Fazey
Mr J Waszek
Mrs N Rutherford
Mr P Rigby

Honorary Governors:
Mr A J Hollis
Mrs E P Jones

Headmaster: Mr P A Lee-Browne, MA

Head of Preparatory School: Mr R McDuff, BEd Hons, MA
Chaplain: The Revd N Sissons, MA
Director of Finance: Miss K Baines
Deputy Head: Mr T Cashell, BEd
Head of Sixth Form: Mr P Lavery, BA
Head of Lower School: Miss F Lloyd, BA
Head of Middle School: Ms S Ashworth, BA
Director of Studies: Mrs S Harding, BA

Assistant staff:
* *Head of Department*
† *Housemaster/Housemistress*

Mr D Baker, BSc (†*Asst Housemaster*)
Mr P Baxter, BEd
Mrs A Beaumont, BA (†*Asst Housemistress*)
Mrs S Boxleitner, MA
Dr M F Brown, BSc, PhD (†*Walshaw*)
Dr S Brown, BA, MSc, PhD (†*Matron*)
Mrs A Cashell, BEd (*Learning Support*)
Mrs N J Cosgrove, BA (*Girls' Games*)
Mrs L Crimes, MA (*English & Drama*; †*Asst Housemistress*)
Mr M Cunningham, BEd
Ms F Earle, BA (†*Edwards*)
Mr M J Farnell, BA (*Economics, Business Studies & ICT*)
Mrs S A Harding, BA (*Humanities*, *Geography*)
Mr E Hughes
Miss S James (†*Asst Housemistress*)
Mr B Jones, BEd (*Design & Technology*)
Miss P Jones, BSc
Mrs C Lavery, BSc
Mr P Lavery, BA (*MFL*, †*Asst Housemaster*)
Mr M T Leach, BSc (*PE and Games*)
Mrs S Leach (†*Matron*)
Miss S Leach, BA (†*Assistant Housemistress*)
Dr J Lewis, BSc
Mrs D MacLennan, BEd
Ms A Margerison, BSc (*Biology*)
Mr P J Mather, BEd (*Boys' Games and Activities*; †*Hathaway*)
Mrs K Mather (†*Matron*)
Ms D Molinari, MA
Mrs S Morris, BA
Mrs G Murphy, BA
Mr J B Murphy, BA (*Senior Housemaster*, †*Netherton*)
Mrs W Murphy (†*Matron*)
Mr E Parri, BA
Mrs M Pearce, BA, MSc
Mr M Pender, BSc (*Chemistry, UCAS & Careers*)
Mr A Price, MA (*History*)
Mr I Richardson, BSc, MSc (†*Beecholme*)
Mrs M Richardson, BA (*Religious Education and PSHE*; †*Beecholme*)
Mr P Richmond, BSc (*Mathematics*)
Ms D Riley (†*Matron*)
Dr G Roberts, BSc, PhD
Mr D Robson, BSc, BEng (*Science*)
Mr PW Russell, BA
Mr P Sanders, BA

Mr M Sherrington, BA (*Art*)
Miss J K Simpkins, BA (*EFL*)
Mr R Tickner MA
Mr C Underwood, BA
Ms C Vallée Licence, LLCE
Dr A Warrington, BSc, MSc, PhD
Mr J Whittaker, BA, BEd, MA (*Music*)
Mrs L Williams, BSc (*Home Economics*)
Mr P Williams, Mus Dip
Mrs R Williams, BA
Ms N Wynne-Jones, BA

Admissions Officer: Mrs J Marsden

Preparatory School:
* *Coordinators*

Headmaster: Mr R McDuff, BEd Hons, MA

Deputy Head: Mrs A Hind (*Year 6 tutor, *English*)
Head of Pre-Prep: Mrs G Davies (*Year 2 tutor*)

Prep Department:
Mr J McLeod (*Year 6 tutor*)
Mr A Camp (*Year 5 tutor, *Science*)
Mrs J Pyves (*Year 5 tutor*)
Mrs C Culver (*Year 4 tutor, *Geography & History*)
Mrs J Woodthorpe (*Year 3 tutor*)

Pre Prep & Early Years Departments:
Mrs C Chamberlain (*Year 1 tutor*)
Mrs N Merrick (*Year 1 tutor*)
Mrs L Devilleforte (*Reception tutor*)
Mrs L Roberts (*EYD Supervisor*)

Specialist teaching staff:
Mrs L M Lewis (*i/c SEN*)
Mrs E McDuff (*Science & PSHE*)
Mrs S Morris (*Art*)
Ms H Rushton (*Gym*)
Ms H W Rushton (*Gym*)
Ms S Simpson (*Learning Support*)
Mme C Vallée (*French*)
Mr J Whittaker (*Director of Music*)
Mr P I Williams (*Music*)

Teaching Assistants:

Mrs R Curle	Ms N J Shilton
Mrs E Hutin	Miss N Taylor
Miss B Murtagh	Ms C Tebbits
Miss D L Roberts	Mrs C Williams
Mrs H Roberts	Mrs C E Williams
Mrs R J Roberts	Miss R Williams
Mrs Z Roberts	

Preparatory School Admissions: Mrs S Williams

Situation and Buildings. Rydal Penrhos School is within 45 minutes drive of Chester, and only one hour away from Manchester and Liverpool and their large airports that have easy access to Europe and beyond. There are also excellent rail links to London and the Midlands. The school is located in Colwyn Bay and is close to the Snowdonia National Park. It is therefore ideally placed to combine a broad academic curriculum with a rich variety of outdoor activities that make the most of the sea and the mountains. The Preparatory School (Rydal Penrhos Preparatory School), which takes pupils from 2½ years, overlooks Colwyn Bay and is adjacent to Rydal Penrhos School.

Teaching facilities include nine science laboratories, dedicated study areas for senior pupils, specialist art, music and design technology centres, a lecture theatre and a drama studio. There are also information technology suites, a well-stocked library and a recently built Sixth Form centre. A sports hall, swimming pool, fitness suite, dance studio and Astroturf pitch complement the outdoor sporting facilities.

Many of the boarding houses started their existence as large Victorian or Edwardian residences in the fashionable seaside resort of Colwyn Bay. As a result, each has a very distinctive character, and a strong sense of being a 'home-from-home'. There are four boys' houses and one girls' house. Each boarding house is supervised by resident housemaster or housemistress, with the assistance of a team of tutors and matrons.

Numbers and Organisation. There are currently 377 pupils in the senior school (221 boys and 156 girls) of which 144 are boarders. There are 170 pupils in Rydal Penrhos Preparatory School, comprising 93 boys and 77 girls.

The Prep School is divided into Early Years (age 2½–4), Pre-Prep (Reception to Year 2) and Prep (Year 3 to Year 6) departments, with separate and distinct curricula and routines. The senior school is arranged into the Lower School (Years 7–8), Middle School (Years 9–10 and pre-Sixth) and Sixth Form (IB and A Levels), each with its own Head of School. Pupils in the Prep and senior schools are also allocated to competitive Houses for academic, sporting and cultural events. The well-being and academic life of the school is driven by a tutorial structure that creates a strong framework bringing pupils, teaching staff and parents together in an effective partnership.

Religious aims. Rydal Penrhos School is a Christian school in the Methodist tradition, but welcomes pupils from all faiths or none. Prayers are held daily in St John's Church, ownership of which has now been transferred to the school. Special services are held to mark key festivals and occasions in the Church year, and there is an annual confirmation service for members of the School community.

Curriculum. The National Curriculum is shadowed and supplemented to afford the best opportunities and choices for the pupils.

In Years 7 to 9 (KS3), pupils study English, Mathematics, the three sciences, Religious Studies, French, German, Geography, History, Drama, Art & Design, Home Economics, Design & Technology, Music, ICT, Physical Education, and PSHE. Pupils have a choice of language options into Years 8 and 9.

In Year 10, the core GCSE subjects are English and English Literature, Mathematics, Science (either separate sciences or Dual Award), a modern foreign language and Religious Studies. Pupils will choose two further subjects to complete their GCSE options, and all pupils participate fully in both Physical Education and the PSHE programme. GCSEs in other languages (notably Welsh and Latin) are also available by request. EFL and Learning Support are provided to support pupils at the appropriate level and allow them to take full advantage of the academic programme.

The School welcomes new entrants into the Sixth Form, which offers both the International Baccalaureate Diploma programme and A Levels in a full range of subjects. Pupils are expected to have Grade C or above in at least 5 subjects at GCSE before entering the Sixth Form. With a wide range of options available, pupils are able to choose courses that reflect their own particular strengths and interests.

Sports and Activities. All pupils undertake a balanced programme of extra-curricular activities, with the aim of acquiring a range of physical and social skills, and developing the pupils' innate talent. The importance of competitive sport is recognised, and the School has a strong fixture list in rugby (it is a partner and host of the WRU North Wales Rugby Academy), cricket, netball, hockey (its teams are regular National champions at various age levels), athletics and tennis. The skiing and swimming teams also enjoy considerable success and School teams compete and win at regional and national level in the full range of sports available at Rydal Penrhos.

The school's coastal location within a few miles of the Snowdonia National Park offers unrivalled opportunities for a full programme of adventurous activities including mountaineering, climbing, hillwalking and kayaking. The Duke of

Edinburgh's Award is very well supported by pupils. The school runs its own RYA sailing training centre and hosts the annual Rydal Penrhos School Laser Pico Challenge; sailing is an integral part of the core activities programme.

The Arts. The school has a fine tradition in both music and drama, and pupils are actively encouraged to develop an enthusiasm for the performing arts. The Music department presents two full school concerts at Christmas and in early Summer, with many other performance opportunities on offer. Pupils also perform regularly in chapel and at other whole-school occasions. The Drama department has enjoyed real academic success for many years, and this is reflected in the high standard of performance in school plays, musicals and other performances throughout the year.

Careers. The school prides itself on the quality of its advice on careers and higher education, and the library has a well-equipped careers centre to support this function. All pupils in Year 11 are expected to arrange work experience in collaboration with the Careers department, and the School holds an annual careers convention and industrial conference. In the Spring term of Year 11, pupils are given an individual interview to discuss their Sixth Form programme to ensure that they are fully informed about their options. In preparation for university mock interviews are arranged with local businesses and the professional community. Sixth Form pupils are expected to move on to university, and the vast majority do so.

Admission. Pupils can be admitted at the beginning of any term after their 11th birthday; the largest entry is in September. Entry is normally via the school's entrance examination, held in February, or equivalent tests.

Scholarships and Bursaries. Academic, Art, Drama, Music and Sport Scholarships worth up to 50% of school fees are available for Year 7, Year 9 and Sixth Form entry. An award may be increased through a means-tested bursary up to 70% of the school fees.

There are 2 fully-funded (means-tested) day places for Year 7 entry reserved for candidates residing in North Wales.

Children of Methodist and Anglican ministers are admitted at substantially reduced fees. Bursaries for children of serving members of the Armed Forces are also available. Forces families may also be eligible for the North Wales Day Allowance.

For full details of all awards, please apply to Mrs Jenny Marsden, Admissions.

Fees per term (2014–2015). Boarding £8,200–£10,105, Weekly Boarding £7,380–£9,100, Day £4,210–£5,070.

Rydal Penrhos Preparatory School. Co-educational Day School for children aged 2½–11. (*For further details see entry in IAPS section.*)

Charitable status. Rydal Penrhos Limited is a Registered Charity, number 1063489, and a Company Limited by Guarantee. The object of the charity is the advancement of education in accordance with Christian principles.

Ryde School with Upper Chine

Queen's Road, Ryde, Isle of Wight PO33 3BE
Tel: 01983 562229
Fax: 01983 564714
email: school.office@rydeschool.net
website: www.rydeschool.org.uk
Twitter: @rydeschool
Facebook: /rydeschool2013

Motto: '*Ut Prosim*'

Ryde School with Upper Chine is a day and boarding school which provides education for boys and girls aged three to eighteen. It is situated on the Isle of Wight. Ryde School was founded in 1921 to provide a Christian educa-tion for boys. In 1992 the School opened Fiveways, which caters for pupils in the Nursery, Reception and Years 1 and 2. Upper Chine was founded as a Girls' School in Shanklin on the Isle of Wight in 1914. The two schools merged in 1994 to form Ryde School with Upper Chine and in 1996 the School took over Bembridge School. As a result of these acquisitions and mergers the School is now fully co-educational. Boarding provision is situated on a coastal site of 117 acres in nearby Bembridge.

Governors:
Chairman: Dr C J Martin, BSc, DPhil, MBA, FIChemE, CEng
Vice-Chairman: Mrs N Beckett
Hereditary Governor: A McIsaac, MA, DPhil

Ms C R Clark MA	Dr M Legg, BSc, MBBS
J H Fisher, MBE, DL	Mrs E Millett, BA
Mrs L Dennis, BEd	Mrs J V Minchin
Mrs A Harvey	The Revd Canon G Morris
C Lees, MB, BS, BSc, MD, MRCOG	N J Wakefield, MA

Clerk to the Governors: P C Taylor, JP, FCA, FRSA

Headmaster: M A Waldron, MA, MEd

Senior Deputy Head: A Shaw, BA

Deputy Head (*Academic*): P R Moore, MA, BSc

Bursar: M M Davies

Chaplain: Revd J Leggett

Senior Teachers:
S R Baxter, BA, PGCE (*Careers, Skills and Lifelong Learning*)
K J Dubbins, BEd (*OC CCF*)
Mrs S E Evans, BA (*Alumni, External Relations and Events*)
B W Penn, BSc, CBiol, PGCE (*Director of Studies*)
A M Graham, BA, HNTD (*Director of Studies, Sixth Form*)

Senior School:
M G P Alderton, MPhys PGCE (*Head of Year 8*)
Mrs M Armstrong, BA, PGCE (*Head of Year 7*)
Mrs J Barclay, BA, PGCE
Mrs S L Bayley, BSc, PGCE
Ms K Bishop, BSc, PGCE (*Head of Psychology*)
G Bowen, BEd
N Brady, BA, PGCE (*Head of Economics & Business Studies*)
K G Bridgeman, MA
Miss S Broyé, BA, MA, PGCE
Mrs J M Bryant, BEd
T Bull, BA
Mrs M E Burgess, BSc, PGCE (*Head of Geography*)
Mrs C A Carleton, BEd, PGCE (*Head of Learning Support*)
M G Chalmers, BSc, PGCE (*Head of Chemistry*)
J C Comben, BA, PGCE
Miss O C Crean, MA, PGCE (*Head of Art*)
Miss J Drabble, BA
Miss A Drinkwater, BEd, MA (*Head of Girls' Games & PE*)
Ms J A Dyer, BA, PGCE (*Head of Spanish*)
M A Eysele, BSc
Mrs K Gavin, BA, PGCE
M J Glasbey, BSc, PGCE (*Head of Year 11; Head of CDT*)
P K Griffiths, BA, MA, PGCE
A Grubb, BMus, PGCE (*Director of Music*)
Mrs T A Hall, BA, PGCE (*Head of Modern Languages*)
Mrs R A Hamar, BA (*Librarian*)
R Hoare, BA, QTS (*Head of PD*)
Miss C Hughes, BMus
P A Johnson, BSc, BA, PGCE (*Head of Mathematics*)
A Johnston, BA (*Head of ICT*)

Miss E C Jones, BA, PGCE
K Long, BEd (*Director of Sport*)
J R P MacArthur, BA (*Head of Careers*)
Ms H McComb, BA, PGCE (*Head of RE*)
S M Mead, BEd (*Head of Year 10*)
J H Mitchell, BHum, PGCE (*Head of Academic PE*)
A P Munn, BEd, MA, CertEd
Ms A J Newman, BA, PGCE (*Head of Year 9*)
Mrs M L Newte, MEng (*Head of Physics*)
Mrs L E O'Sullivan, BSc Ed
C M Ody, BA, PGCE
Dr M Postelnyak, MA, DPhil
Mrs J Ratcliff, BA, PGCE
Mrs A Selby
Mrs K J Snow, BA PGCE
Dr G R Speller, BSc, MPhil, PhD, PGCE (*Head of Science*)
P J Stott, BA, PGCE (*Head of History and Politics*)
Miss A Sutton (*Head of Boarding*)
G Taylor, MA, PGCE (*Head of English*)
C G S Trevallion, BSc, PGCE (*Head of Biology*)
Mrs R Tweddle, GTCL, LTCL (*Choral Director*)
Miss C Vince, BA, PGCE (*Head of Sixth Form*)
Mrs L L Waldron, BA, PGCE
Mrs J J Whillier, BSc QTS
M J Windsor, BSc, PGCE

Junior School
Head: H Edwards, BSc, PGCE
Director of Studies: P Dickinson, BEd (*Director of Sport*)

Mrs S Burgess, BA	Miss S Lewis, BA, PGCE
Mrs A Bull	J Mathrick, BSc, PGCE
Mrs L J Dickinson, BEd	J McGouran, BA, PGCE
Mrs J Edwards, BSc, PGCE	Mrs A Selby
A Gallerwood, BA	Mrs D Shepherd, CertEd
Mrs G Gallerwood, BA	Mrs H Vann, BA

'FIVEWAYS' Nursery and Pre-Prep:
Head: Mrs S A Davies, BEd

Miss K Clarke, NNEB	Miss V Lovell, BEd
Mrs F Curtis, BA, PGCE	Miss N Noott, BA
Mrs G Elsom, BEd	Mrs P Ong, DipPP
Miss S Glover, NNEB	Mrs T Simons, BEd
Mrs S Griffiths, BTech, NN	Mrs N Thurston, NNEB
Mrs D Grubb, BA, PGCE	HLTA
Mrs S Lea, NTD	Miss A Townson, NVQ3

Situation and Buildings. The School stands in its own grounds of 17 acres in Ryde with stunning views over the Solent and is easily accessible from all parts of the Island and the near mainland. It is within walking distance of the terminals which link Ryde to Portsmouth by hovercraft (10 minutes) or catamaran (15 minutes) and a number of pupils travel daily from the mainland. In recent years there have been many additions to the School buildings. The School now enjoys up-to-date and extensive facilities. New Art and CDT departments opened in 2011, alongside a new dining hall, in the award-winning Bembridge Building.

Organisation and Curriculum. The School aims to provide a secure and nurturing environment from which pupils gain the ambition, courage and values to face the world. It enjoys an enviable reputation on the Island for high standards both inside and outside the classroom.

In the Junior School strong emphasis is laid on core skills and on proficiency in reading, writing and number work. Pupils are prepared in this way for entry into the Senior School, and, following a recommendation from the Head of the Junior School, they are offered places in the Senior School at the age of 11.

The programme of work in the Senior School is designed to provide a broad but challenging education up to the end of Year 11. The subjects taught to IGCSE/GCSE level are English, English Literature, Mathematics, Physics, Chemistry, Biology, French, Spanish, Latin, Geography, History,

Religious Education, Business Studies, Art, Music, Physical Education, Drama and Craft, Design and Technology. All pupils also follow a programme of Personal Development (PD) and Games.

In the Sixth Form pupils may choose between the IB Diploma and three or four subjects at AS/A2 level from a wide choice. In addition, pupils are encouraged to take the Extended Project Qualification, designed to add breadth to their academic studies. Courses lead to entrance to universities, the Services, industry and the professions. The Careers Department provides advice and guidance to all pupils who go to a variety of universities and careers, over half to Russell Group universities in 2013.

Tutorial System. Each pupil has a tutor who is responsible for his or her academic and personal progress and general pastoral welfare. The tutorial system encourages close contact with parents, which is further reinforced by parents' meetings which are held at regular intervals and a parent portal. The School aims to maintain sound discipline and good manners within a traditionally friendly atmosphere and encourages pupils to live up to the School motto "Ut Prosim".

Games. The main games in the Senior School are rugby football, hockey, cricket and athletics for the boys, and netball, hockey and athletics for the girls. In the Junior School, Association football is also played. Other games include basketball, squash, golf, swimming and tennis. Regular matches are arranged at all levels against teams both on the Island and the mainland. There are growing opportunities for sailing and the School keeps some sailing dinghies at Seaview Yacht Club.

Music and Drama. The Music School incorporates practice and teaching facilities and a well-equipped recording studio. The School has a flourishing choral tradition, with opportunities for participation in a variety of choirs and instrumental groups. Concerts and musical plays are performed in both Senior and Junior Schools, and concert tours abroad have taken place in recent years. Full-length plays are produced each year by both Senior and Junior Schools, and special attention is given in the English lessons of the younger forms to speaking, lecturing and acting. Musical Theatre is a particular strength. The School has its own theatre and studio theatre.

Activities. There are many societies which cater for a wide range of individual interests. The School has a contingent of the Combined Cadet Force with Royal Navy and Royal Air Force sections. Sailing, canoeing, gliding, and other forms of venture training are strongly encouraged. There is a flourishing Duke of Edinburgh's Award scheme; last year around a quarter of the Upper Sixth achieved their Gold Award. Holiday visits and expeditions are regularly arranged, and there are opportunities for exchange visits with schools on the continent.

Boarding. Boarding for both boys and girls is available for pupils on the Bembridge campus which offers approximately one hundred acres of playing fields and woodland in a beautiful setting overlooking Whitecliff Bay and Culver Cliff, some six miles from Ryde. Transport is provided to and from Ryde for the school day.

Fees per term (from January 2015). Tuition: Foundation Stage: £1,998–£2,218 (full day), £1,010 (half day); Pre-Prep £2,408–£3,068; Junior School £3,725; Senior School £3,850.

Boarding (excluding tuition): Senior School: £4,255 (full), £3,720 (weekly).

Rates for payment by Direct Debit.

Scholarships and Bursaries. Some Scholarships worth 10% of fees may be awarded on merit to external or internal candidates for entry at 11+, 13+ and 16+. Scholarships may be supplemented by bursaries, which are means tested.

The School offers a number of Ryde Assisted Places. These are awarded to suitable candidates from outside the school. These places are means tested. Means-tested bursaries are also available to suitably qualified candidates who are already attending the school.

Charitable status. Ryde School is a Registered Charity, number 307409. The aims and objectives of the Charity are the education of boys and girls.

St Albans High School for Girls

3 Townsend Avenue, St Albans, Hertfordshire AL1 3SJ
Tel: 01727 853800
Fax: 01727 792516
email: admissions@stahs.org.uk
website: www.stahs.org.uk
Twitter: @STAHS
Facebook: /stalbanshighschoolforgirls

Motto: *The fear of the Lord is the beginning of wisdom*

Visitor: The Right Reverend The Lord Bishop of St Albans

Council:
Mr R Allnutt, LLB
Mr D Alterman, MA
Dr P Barrison, MBBS
Mrs C Callegari, BA, CertEd
Mr G Follows, BEng, FCA, DChA
Mrs H Greatrex, BA, ACA
Miss D Henderson, MA (*Chairman*)
The Very Revd Dr Jeffrey John, MA, DPhil, The Dean of St Albans
Mr B Kettle, FRICS, MCIArb, MAE
Miss R Musgrave, MA, MA, FRSA
Mr D Roe, BSc, MRICS
Mrs J Ross, BA Hons, NPQH
Mrs J Stroud, MA
Mr J Thomson, CA
Mr R Ward
Mrs M Wellens, BSc, PGCE, MA Ed
Mrs J Woolley

‡ *Holder of Teacher's Diploma or Certificate*

Headmistress: **Mrs Jenny Brown**, MA Oxon

Bursar: Mr F Campbell, BSc Glasgow, FCMA

Head of Wheathampstead House: Ms G M Bradnam, BEd WSIHE, MA Ed Mgmt De Montfort, NPQH

Deputy Head Pastoral: ‡Mrs J Taylor, MA Cantab

Deputy Head Teaching and Learning: ‡Ms J Healy, BA Oxon, MPhil Trinity College Dublin

Acting Assistant Head – Curriculum: ‡Mrs K Gorman, MEd Cambridge, BA Birmingham

Chaplain: The Revd Diane Fitzgerald Clark, BA Rhode Island, MDiv GTS, NYC

* *Head of Department*
§ *Part-time*

Senior School:
‡Dr G Alderton, PhD Leeds
‡Mr R Bailey, BSc Bath
§‡Mrs C Boothroyd, BSc Hertfordshire
‡Mr D Bowker, MA Cantab
‡Miss J Broman, BA Birmingham
‡Mrs S Brown, MA Manchester
‡Mrs A Bullen, BA Aberystwyth
‡Miss A Burgess, MA Cantab
§‡Mr N Chandler, BA Gothenburg
‡Mrs A Chapman, BA Exeter (*Classics)
‡Miss N Collins, BSc Brunel
‡Mrs S Cooper, BA Exeter
§‡Mrs E Crowther, BA UCL

‡Mrs G Davies, MSc Wales (**Design Technology*)
‡Miss S Day, MChem Oxon
‡Mrs J Douglas, BA Durham (*Senior Housemistress*)
‡Mr P Duddles, BEng Warwick
§Miss S Dumbrill, BMus, PGDip RNCM
‡Mrs W Emes, BA Bath, MSc Reading
‡Miss C Foster, BA Manchester
‡Miss A Fox, BA Oxon
‡Mrs R Frost, BA Open, BEd Dundee, MA Ed Open (*Senior Teacher*)
Mrs M Galea, BEd Exeter (**Physical Education*)
‡Mrs F Gee, BSc Cardiff
‡Mrs S Gillman, BSc Exeter
‡Mrs C Gissane, BSc Edinburgh
‡Mrs K Guille, MA Bath, BA Birmingham (*Modern Languages)
‡Mrs M Harcourt, BEd Cantab
Miss A Hedley, BEd Edinburgh
‡Mr R Hillebrand, BA Oxon
‡Dr S Hutton, PhD, MSci Durham
§‡Mrs A Jallport, BSc Hertfordshire
§‡Mrs C Johns, BA Wales, MA Open
‡Miss S Jost, MA University of Lausanne
§‡Mr E Kay, Cert Ed Lancaster, RSA SpLD
‡Mrs R Key, BA Oxon
‡Dr S Legg, BSc Birmingham, DPhil Oxon (*Science)
§Mrs D Lewis, MA Oxon, MPhil Cantab
Mr A Lunn, BEd Limerick
‡Miss R Marsh, BA Southampton
‡Miss S MacCarron, BSc Leeds
§‡Mrs R L McDermott, MSc Bristol
‡Mr S McGuinness, BA Manchester Polytechnic (*Art)
‡Mrs H McSherry, BSc Plymouth
‡Mr S R Mew, MA Essex, BA Essex (*History)
Miss M Millburn-Fryer, BA Durham
‡Mrs H Monighan, BA Durham
‡Miss H O'Neill, BA Leeds
Mrs K Osborne, BEd London
‡Mrs V Parton, BSc York, MA Hertfordshire
‡Mrs M Patel, BA Wales (**Religious Studies*)
Mrs J Powell, BA Durham
‡Miss E Pritchard, BA York (**PSHEE/eSafety*)
‡Mr S Ramsbottom, BSc Reading (**Geography/Director of eLearning*)
‡Mrs P Ray, BA Leeds
§‡Mrs L Ryan, MA Cantab
‡Mrs G Sapsford, BA Anglia Ruskin
‡Mrs E Schaffer, BA Nottingham
‡Dr N Springthorpe, PhD BMus, Surrey, FLCM, PG CertRCM Surrey (*Music)
‡Mr J Stanford, BA York (*Economics)
‡Mrs S Stewart, BSc Leicester
‡Miss K Sumner, BSc Warwick (*Mathematics)
Miss N Taylor-Imrie, BSc Hertfordshire, Dip SpLD Hornsby
‡Mr I Thomson, BA London, AKC (*Sixth Form)
‡Mrs K Thomson, BSc London
‡Mr A Tickner, MSci Durham, MA, East Anglia
Mrs C Turkington, BMusEd Cape Town
§‡Miss E Wadey, BA Winchester
‡Mr C White, BSc London (*Examinations Officer*)
§‡Mrs D Whiting, BSc De Montfort
‡Miss H Whymark, BA Hull (*Drama)
‡Miss P I Willmott, BA London
‡Mrs C A Wright, BA Ulster (*ICT Coordinator/Director of eLearning*)

Library Senior School:
Mrs J Foster, BA North London (*Senior Librarian*)
Mrs C Brailsford, BA Leicester, MA Loughborough (*Sixth Form Librarian*)

Preparatory School – Wheathampstead House:
Head: Ms G M Bradnam, BEd WSIHE, MA Ed Mgmt De
 Montfort, NPQH
Deputy Head: ‡Mr J Wadge, BA Durham
Director of Studies: Mrs J Jeavons, BA QTS Leeds
Acting Director of Studies: ‡Mrs H Barsham, BA London
Head of Infants: ‡Miss L Fidgeon, BSc Royal Holloway

§‡Miss C M Allin, Licence LLCE Poitiers, France
‡Miss C Atherton, BA East Anglia
§Mrs J Bowskill, BSc Loughborough
Mrs A Brady, BEd Leeds
Mrs J Byron, BA Wales, MSc City Univ London, Dip
 Literacy Difficulty Oxford Brookes
Mrs E Courtney-Magee, BEd Reading
Mrs N Davies, BA London
‡Mrs S Edwards, GRSM, ARCM
‡Mrs M Garton, BA Surrey
‡Miss L Hill, LLB Hertfordshire
Mrs C Hilton, BEd Hertfordshire
‡Mrs L Hughes, BA Canterbury Christ Church
‡Mrs W Job, BEd Brighton
§Mrs J Julians, MSc Loughborough
Mrs M McClean, BEd Hertfordshire
Mrs S Millac, BSc University College London
‡Mrs L Perry, BSc Liverpool
‡Mrs C Petronella-Thakera, BA Royal Holloway
‡Mrs S E Rose, BA Leeds
‡Miss T Skuse, BSc Manchester
Mrs L Still, BA Ed Exeter

Teaching Assistants, Wheathampstead House:
Mrs P Bate, BA St Martins
§Mrs L Davies
Mrs A di-Lieto, BA Hull
Mrs A Gibbs, CertEd Sussex
Mrs S Holmwood, BA Manchester Polytechnic
Mrs S Millac, BSc University College
‡Mrs E Osborne, BA Open
Mrs S Smith
Mrs C Strang

Librarian, Wheathampstead House:
§Mrs D Chopping, BSc Open

School Medical Officer: Dr A E Margereson, MMBS
 London

Visiting Staff:
Music:
Mrs J Blinko, GRSM, Dip RCM, PG Cert RCM (*Flute*)
Mrs K Bradley, LRAM (*Violin*)
Ms C Charlesworth, BMus (*Flute*)
Mr D Coleman, PG Dip RCM, BMus Birmingham (*Brass*)
Miss S Dumbrill, BMus, PG Dip RNCM (*Flute*)
Mrs L Hayter, BMus, PG Dip (*Oboe*)
Mrs C Heller-Jones, BMus, PGCE, PG Cert GSM (*Singing*)
Mr J Holling, Dip TCL, LTCL (*Percussion*)
Miss P Jeppesen, PG Dip GSM (*Violin*)
Mr S Jones, GTCL, LTCL, MTC (*Singing*)
Mr F Kerntiff, ALCM, PGCMT (*Guitar*)
Mrs M Miller, LLB, CT ABRSM, LRSM, FRSM, ATCL
 (*Piano*)
Mr K Milton, AMusA AMB, Dip T&P Sydney, Kunstl Dip
 Luebeck, MSc (*Violin*)
Mrs R Molins, BA Hons, LRAM, Dip RAM, PG Dip
 (*Brass*)
Miss C Morris Jones, AGSM, LRAM (*Harp*)
Miss F Nisbett (*Cello, Piano, Double Bass*)
Mr M Onissi, LTCL (*Saxophone and Clarinet*)
Miss G Pevy, LTCL, FTCL (*Recorder*)
Mrs H Shabetai, BMus (*Piano*)
Mr W Smith, BMus Trinity, PG Dip (*Trumpet*)
Mrs H Templeton, BA York (*Singing*)
Miss A Tysall, BMus (*Piano*)
Mrs B Valdar, AGSM (*Clarinet*)

Mrs H Wild, BMus, LRAM

Physical Education:
Ms E Carder (*Netball*)
§Mrs E Davies, BA Warwick (*Games*)
Ms J Hoare (*Swimming*)
Miss D Horton (*Netball*)
Miss N Ilkrow (*Tennis*)
‡Mrs P Moxham (*Trampolining*)
Mrs C Peers (*Yoga*)
Mr H Shah (*Badminton*)
Ms S Stephens (*Swimming*)
Mrs D Szokolovics (*Fencing*)

Speech & Drama:
Mrs L Ashton
Mrs E Elliott, Cert Ed Birmingham, LGSM, P Cert LAM

Association Officer:
Mrs L Lord LLB Law, Durham

Marketing and Admissions Office:
Communications Officer i/c ICT: Miss J Evans, BA
 Leicester, PGCE
Marketing Coordinator: Mrs A Gavin, CertEd Roehampton
Registrar: Miss S Nicholls, BEd Cantab
Admissions Liaison Officer: Mrs J Wrigglesworth

Technicians:
Mr P Abbott (*IT*)
§Mrs C Ametrano (*IT*)
§Mrs K Burchmore (*Physics*)
Mrs A Hodsden (*CDT*)
§Mrs A Kellard, BA Hertfordshire (*Art*)
§Mr A Morris (*CDT*)
§Mrs N Phillips, BA Surrey (*Art*)
§Miss R Randall (*Biology*)
§Mrs L Vardon (*Chemistry*)

Administration:
Head of IT Service: Mr B Tavakoli, BA Liverpool Hope,
 MBA Edinburgh Napier
Network Manager: Mr L Miles, BSc Glamorgan
Assistant Network Manager/VLE Technical Coordinator:
 Mr L Tobiasiewicz, BA Lancaster
Account Manager: Mr M Langley
Fees Administrator: Mrs C Anderson
Domestic Bursar: Mrs H Stopps, MIH
Headmistress's PA: Mrs R Simpson
Receptionist/School Secretary: Mrs L Jennings
School Secretary, Wheathampstead House: Mrs D Pope

St Albans High School for Girls is a day school for 950
girls aged 4 to 18. Since its foundation in 1889, it has been
closely linked with the Cathedral and Abbey Church of St
Alban and the Christian ethos is very important in the life of
the school. Services are held regularly in school or at the
Abbey. The Senior School is only a few minutes' walk from
the town centre.

The Preparatory School is a very popular, academically
selective school with a welcoming family atmosphere, offering outstanding pastoral care. It is set in 18 acres of grounds
within the village of Wheathampstead. The extensive site
includes play areas, an adventure playground, woods and an
outdoor learning classroom. (*See entry in IAPS section.*)

St Albans High School is uniquely placed in being able to
offer all the advantages of a continuous education in two
very different settings. From the ages of 4 to 11, the girls
have the freedom to grow and develop in an attractive rural
environment, before moving on to the more urban setting of
the Senior School, close to the heart of the City of St Albans.

The Senior School has facilities for the teaching of a wide
range of subjects including laboratories, specialist rooms for
IT and Modern Languages, as well as excellent provision for
all the usual academic subjects. The Jubilee Centre provides
excellent facilities and opportunities for pupils to develop

their skills in a wide range of fields including Music, Drama, Art, Food Technology, Resistant Materials and Textile Design. The curriculum, which is kept under review, includes all the subjects of the national curriculum plus Latin, a Modern Language and Drama. There are two well-stocked libraries, which include a Sixth Form library and a Sixth Form Centre to accommodate some 170 girls.

Girls are encouraged to participate in a wide range of extra-curricular activities, among which Sport and Music feature strongly, as well as the Duke of Edinburgh's Award Scheme, Young Enterprise and Community Service. Pastoral care is important at all levels of the school and girls are encouraged to feel that they are valued for their contributions to the life of the school community.

In the grounds of the Senior School there is a modern Sports Hall with adjoining leisure complex comprising indoor pool, fitness suite and dance studio. The main games field is ten minutes' walk from the school and there are eight hard tennis courts, two lacrosse pitches and a sports pavilion.

Pupils are prepared for GCSE and IGCSE examinations at the age of 16, for A Level examinations, for Oxford and Cambridge entrance and for the examinations of the Associated Board of the Royal Schools of Music.

Fees per term (2014–2015). Reception (age 4) £3,795 (inc Lunch), Years 1 and 2 (age 5–6) £4,005 (inc Lunch); Years 3–6 (age 7–11) £4,005 (exc Lunch); Senior School (age 11–16) £4,825 (exc Lunch); Sixth Form (age 16–18) £4,825 (exc Lunch).

Private music lessons, special tennis coaching, school lunch (from Year 3) and daily school coaches are all optional extras.

Scholarships. Academic Scholarships are awarded annually at ages 11+ and 16+. There are fees assistance awards available for cases of hardship. Further 16+ Scholarships in Art/DT, Drama & Theatre Studies and Sports are awarded (candidates may be external or internal).

A number of Music Scholarships are offered annually at 11+ entry. Candidates who have first reached the required standard in the entrance examinations are asked to attend the Music School for auditions.

Admission. Pupils are normally admitted in September at the age of 4, 5 and 7 for entry to the Preparatory School, 11 for the Senior School and 16 for the Sixth Form. Offers of places in the Sixth Form are provisional until the results of the GCSE examinations are known: girls are required to have a minimum of 5 subjects at grade A, including A grades in the subjects to be taken at A Level. Entrance examinations are held in the Lent Term for admission in the following September.

Open Days. Preparatory School: Friday 10 October 2014; Saturday 15 November 2014; Friday 5 June 2015. Senior School: Saturday 4 October 2014; Saturday 8 November 2014. Sixth Form: Monday 13 October 2014.

Charitable status. St Albans High School for Girls is a Registered Charity, number 311065. It exists to provide an education for girls "in accordance with the principles of the Church of England".

St Albans School

Abbey Gateway, St Albans, Herts AL3 4HB
Tel: 01727 855521
Fax: 01727 843447
email: hm@st-albans-school.org.uk
website: www.st-albans.herts.sch.uk

The origins of the School date back, according to tradition, to the monastic foundation of 948, and there is firm evidence of an established and flourishing school soon after the Conquest. Following the Dissolution, the last abbot,

Richard Boreman, sought a private Act of Parliament to establish a Free School. Charters, granted to the Town Corporation by Edward VI and Elizabeth I, together with endowments by Sir Nicholas Bacon from the sale of wine licences, secured the School's continuance.

Visitor: The Rt Revd The Lord Bishop of St Albans

Governors:
Chairman: S P Eames
Vice Chairman: Prof R J C Munton, BA, PhD, ACSS
R B Blossom, BSc, CertEd
P G Brown
A L Dalwood, BSc, BA Cantab, UKSIP
Mrs C Leach, BSc, FCA, DChA
S Majumdar, BA
Mrs J M Mark, BA
C McIntyre, BA
Dr M Pegg, MB BS, BSc
Mrs R Phillips, BSc
Dr P A V Sarris
A Woodgate, BA, Dip Land Admin, MRICS

Advisory Council:
The Mayor of St Albans
The Dean of St Albans
The President of the Old Albanian Club
Miss L M Ainsworth, MA Oxon
G R Dale, MA, MCIPD, FRSA
Mrs A Fletcher, MA
Sir Roy Gardner
D S Mercer, BSc, FCSI
P M Rattle, BA
Mrs J F Tasker, FCCA

Bursar and Clerk to the Governors: D Todd, MA, FCA

Headmaster: **J W J Gillespie**, MA Cantab, FRSA

Second Master: Ms M Jones, BSc
Director of Studies: M E Davies, MA
Heads of Sixth Form:
R G Hacksley, BA, PhD
G J Walker, MA, FRSA
Head of Middle School: P R Byrom, MSc
Head of Lower School: D Swanson, Dip RADA
Senior Master: P W Taylor, BEd

Assistant staff:

Miss L H Andrews, BSc	Mrs E W Davies, BA
Ms E Aquilina, MSc	J P Dray, MA, DPhil
T D Asch, BA	T O Eames-Jones, BA
B S Balden, MA	C J Ellegard, BSc, DipEng
A J Bateman, BA	D Forbes-Whitehead, BA
Miss R J Baxter, BA	Mrs V L Ginsburg, BA
Miss L J Benson, MA	C P A Gould, BSc
I J Black, MA	Mrs T J Gott, ARCS, BSc
Mrs T M Black, BA	Miss J M Grieveson, MA
J Blaxill, BA	M J Guy, MSc, PhD
Mrs L Bonner, BSc	R E Hagon, BA
C D Bradnam, BEng	Miss J Higgins, BA,
Miss M C Brereton, MA,	ARCM
DPhil	C C Hudson, BSc
A J Brien, HNC, BEd, MSc	J D Hughes, BA
Miss M L Bruton, BA	S A Hughes, BSc, PhD
Mrs A Butcher, Lda en	T N Jenkins, BA, MFA
Filosofía	C C Johnston, BA
G J Calvert, BEd	A K Jolly, BA
N J Cassidy, BA	Miss K Kaur-Lillian, MA
Ms S Charalambous, BA	M J Langston, BSc
I Charlesworth, MA	R J Lockhart, BA
Mrs C E Coudert, BA	Mrs C A Malacrida, MA
N S Cragg, BSc	T J Martin, BA
P F G Craig, BA	Mrs V C McClafferty, BA
Mrs J C Crouch, BSc	Mrs D McGorrian, BA
R D Daurge, BSc	P M McGrath, BA

Miss G Mendes da Costa, BA
Mrs P M Mills, MA
G D Nichols, BA
Mrs S J Offord, BSc
V Pappert, MA
Mrs D Patel, BSc
D M L Payne, MA
M A Pedroz, MA
Mrs D S Percival, MA, MIL
D J Phillips, BA
Ms A Puranik, BA, MPhil
Mrs G Renz, MA, MPhil
Mrs M L Rennie, BA
D C Richards, BCom, MBA
C A Roberts, BEng
Mrs H J Robertson, BEng
T L Robinson, BSc
Mrs C R Rogers, BSc

T N Ross, BSc
D M Rowland, MA
J R Russ, BA
D S Russell, MSc
Ms V L Sandell, BSc
J H Saunders, BA, PhD
B C Scott, BSc
I M Shillcock, BSc, PhD
G L Smithson, BSc
M J Smyth, BSc
G Spencer, BSc
D J Stone, BA
M R Stout, BMus
Mrs J H Swain, MA
R E Tanner, DPhil, BSc
Mrs R E Taylor, MSc
A C R Thompson, BA
J F M Walmsley, BSc
T H Young, MA
Mrs H Zaver, BSc

Chaplain: The Revd Dr C D Pines, MB BS, MA
Medical Officer: Dr M Bevis, BSc, MRCGP, DCH, DRCOG
Dr T Jollyman, MB ChB, MRCGP, DCH, DRCOG
OC CCF: Major K J Everitt
CCF SSI: WO1 W J Wilson

Visiting Staff:

Poet-in-Residence: J D Mole, MA

Music:
P A Bainbridge, DipRCM, ARCM
D Bentley, GGSM
T Gill, BA Hons Cantab, FRAM
Ms L Hayter, BMus
Ms C Ireland, BMus Hons
S Jones, GTCL, LTCL, MTC
Ms J Koos, MA Hons Cantab, Dip RAM
Mrs V Parker, GRSM, ARCM
R Patterson, BMus
D Richard, BMus
O Roberts, BA
Miss J E Simmons, BMus, GGSM
Mrs Z Smith, BMus Hons, GRNCM, PPRCNM
Ms J Trentham, GLCM, LLCM, TD
N Woodhouse, FLCM, LTCL, LLCM, ALCM
M Woodward, BMus
Ms C Wright, LLCM, GLCM, LRAM, Cert Adv Studies RAM

St Albans is a day school of about 830 pupils which, after being for many years part of the Direct Grant System, reverted to full independence. Girls were admitted into the Sixth Form in September 1991. Its atmosphere and ethos derive from its long tradition and its geographical position near the city centre of St Albans in close proximity to the Abbey and overlooking the site of the Roman City of Verulamium. Whilst maintaining a high standard of academic achievement, it offers wide opportunities for development in other fields, and a strong emphasis is laid upon the responsible use of individual talents in the service of the community.

Buildings. For more than 3 centuries the School was in the Lady Chapel of the Abbey. It moved in 1871 into the Monastery Gatehouse, a building of considerable historic and architectural interest, where teaching still continues. Since 1900, extensive additions include a new Sports Centre with swimming pool, sports hall, fitness centre, dance studio and climbing wall. The School campus has recently been extended significantly by the purchase of a very large building on an adjacent site and its conversion to a superb Art school, Sixth Form Centre and a suite of classrooms.

The School has close historical and musical ties with the Cathedral and Abbey Church of St Alban. By permission of the Dean, morning prayers take place twice weekly in the nave, where the School Choir sings regularly and an annual oratorio is performed in collaboration with St Albans High School for Girls.

Admission. The majority of boys enter at the age of 11 or 13 but there are also entries at 16, when girls are also admitted; candidates are accepted occasionally at other ages. For the main entry at 11 an examination in basic subjects is held at the School each year, normally in January, and parents of interested candidates should write to the School for a prospectus and application form. Candidates at 13 enter through the Common Entrance examination, and conditional offers of places are normally made about one year before entry, following a preliminary assessment. Ideally parents should apply to the School at least 2 years in advance for entry at 13.

Pupils are admitted only at the start of the Autumn Term unless there are exceptional circumstances.

Enquiries about entry should be addressed to the Registrar.

Fees per term (2014–2015). £5,292.

Bursaries and Scholarships. Some assistance with tuition fees may be available in cases of proven need from the School's own endowments. Such Bursaries are conditional upon an annual means test and will be awarded according to a balance of merit and need.

Numerous scholarships are awarded on academic merit at each age of entry. Scholarships in Art and Music are offered to existing pupils or new entrants at 13+ who show exceptional talent. Choral Scholarships are offered only at 11+.

Curriculum. The curriculum for the first three years is largely a common one and covers a wide range. All boys study three sciences and two languages, and devote some part of their timetable to Art, Drama, Music, ICT and CDT. Mathematics IGCSE is taken at the end of the fourth form (Y10), and in the fourth and fifth forms a system of compulsory subjects and options leads in most cases to the taking of at least a further nine GCSEs or IGCSEs. In the Sixth Form most pupils study four subjects at AS Level in the Lower Sixth Form and three or four A2s in the Upper Sixth. In addition, all pupils take General Studies either as an AS or a full A Level and are prepared for an AS in Critical Thinking. The choice is wide, and the flexibility of the timetable makes it possible for almost any combination of available subjects to be offered.

Virtually all Sixth Form leavers go on to universities or other forms of higher education, a good proportion to Oxford or Cambridge.

Out-of-school activities cover a wide range, and there are clubs and societies to cater for most interests. Several of these are run in conjunction with other schools. Musical activities are many and varied and include regular concerts and recitals by the School Choir, Choral Society and ensembles and by professional artists. Plays are produced 3 or 4 times a year either in the New Hall, the Drama Centre Studio, the English Centre Studio Theatre or in the Open-air Theatre, and there is ample opportunity for creative work in the Art school and the Design Technology Centre. There is a strong contingent of the CCF with sections representing the Army and RAF. Other groups train under the Duke of Edinburgh's Award Scheme and do various forms of social service and conservation work in and around the city of St Albans. The School owns a Field Centre in Wales which is used for research and recreation in holidays, as part of the Lower School curriculum and as a base for field studies and reading parties. The School also owns a working 400-acre farm within 3 miles of the school where the Woollam Playing Fields, extending to 45 acres, were opened in 2002 by HRH The Duke of Gloucester. The grounds include an Astroturf all-weather pitch and a superb state-of-the-art pavilion. There are good links with Saracens RUFC, whose training is based at the Woollam Grounds.

Games. The School competes at a high level in Rugby Football, Hockey, Cross-country, Cricket, Tennis, Athletics, Netball and Lacrosse, in addition to a range of other sports including Association Football, Squash, Shooting, Sailing, Swimming, Orienteering, Basketball, Golf and Table Tennis. The playing fields are within easy reach of the School, and the spacious and pleasant lawns on the School site, stretching down to the River Ver, give access to the open-air theatre, Tennis Courts and Shooting Range.

Old Albanian Club and the St Albans School Foundation. Information may be obtained from the Development Director: Mrs Kate Gray at the School address or at: development@st-albans.herts.sch.uk.

Charitable status. St Albans School is Registered Charity, number 1092932, and a Company Limited by Guarantee, number 4400125. The aims and objectives are to provide an excellent education whereby pupils can achieve the highest standard of academic success, according to ability, and develop their character and personality so as to become caring and self-disciplined adults.

St Aloysius' College

45 Hill Street, Glasgow G3 6RJ
Tel: 0141 332 3190
Fax: 0141 353 0426
email: mail@staloysius.org
website: www.staloysius.org

Motto: *ad majora natus sum* (I was born for greater things).

Board of Governors:
Chairman: Mr John Hylands
Rev Dermot Preston, SJ (*Jesuit Provincial*)
Rev Michael Smith, SJ
Rev James Crampsey, SJ
Sir Harry Burns
Mr Greg Hannah
Mr Nigel Kelly
Dr Amy Kerr
Prof Eileen A Millar
Mr Matthew Reilly
Mr Mike Smith
Mrs Donalda MacKinnon
Mr Joseph Hughes
Ms Jane Stuart-Smith
Sir Jim McDonald

Bursar and Clerk to the Board: Mrs Kathleen Sweeney, FCCA

Head Master: Mr John Browne, BA

Head of Senior School: Mr Frank Reilly, BSc

Senior School Depute Head: Mrs Isabelle Erskine, BSc

Assistant Head Christian Formation: Mrs Kirsty Devlin, BSc Hons

Head of Admissions and Communications: Miss Laura McLachlan, LLB Hons, MLitt

Head of Junior School: Dr Aileen Brady, BSc Hons

Head of Early Years: Mrs Marie Forbes, DipEd

PA to the Head Master: Mrs Monica Harper

Founded in 1859, St Aloysius' College is a Catholic School for boys and girls aged 3 to 18. The school is fully co-educational at all stages (Kindergarten to S6) with a total roll of over 1,100, drawn from a wide catchment area.

As a Jesuit school, it shares in a tradition of educational excellence which is almost 500 years old and it is part of a worldwide network of schools and universities whose mission is the "*Improvement in living and learning for the greater glory of God and the common good*". *St Ignatius Loyola*.

The College creates an environment which is underpinned by mutual respect, friendship and care for others. It prides itself on upholding a clear set of religious, moral and spiritual values.

Great stress is placed upon educating the whole person, with pupils encouraged to develop confidence, leadership and teamwork through sport, outdoor activity, music, drama, and many other activities.

Entrance. Pupils from P7–S2 will sit an entrance exam. In the Junior School, children are assessed according to the current curriculum. Informal meetings with parents at all stages are also part of the application process.

Buildings. St Aloysius' College is located in the historic Garnethill area of central Glasgow with additional facilities in Millerston.

The College's main Garnethill campus is made up of a number of school buildings and is well-served by public transport.

The College campus is varied, providing examples of both award-winning modern architecture and construction, as well as historic listed buildings. The original Jesuit residence, now part of the school, is a listed building, as is The Mount where Art and Music are taught, and the magnificent St Aloysius' Church which the College uses regularly.

Two further additions to the St Aloysius' College campus, The Junior School and The Clavius Building used for Maths, Science and Computing, have attracted widespread critical acclaim. Not only have the buildings been the subject of great praise, but they have won many architectural awards, including the Best New Building in Scotland 2004.

In addition to the aforementioned buildings, the College acquired the Convent of Mercy on Hill Street in 2009. The sports pavilion and playing fields are located at Millerston, and provide an excellent range of outdoor facilities.

The new Kindergarten building is the most recent addition to the College buildings. This purpose-built facility is located beside the Junior School and is the ideal place for younger pupils to learn and play.

Curriculum. The Junior School and lower years of the Senior School follow internally devised courses which are suitable for academically able children. All Junior School pupils study French and science from Kindergarten and P1. National 5 is taken at the end of S4 and pupils take five Highers in S5. A wide range of Advanced Highers and other courses are available in S6.

Co-Curricular Activities. The main sports are Rugby, Hockey, Athletics and Cross Country. Pupils are extensively involved in community service and charity work. The College has now established a choral music programme which continues to go from strength to strength. In 2013 the Junior Schola performed on stage with world-famous tenor Andrea Bocelli.

Fees per annum (2014–2015). £7,398–£10,314.

Bursaries are available on consideration of parents' income.

Charitable status. St Aloysius' College is a Registered Charity, number SCO42545.

St Bede's College

Alexandra Park, Manchester M16 8HX
Tel: 0161 226 3323 (Senior School)
             0161 226 7156 (Preparatory School)
Fax: 0161 226 3813 (Senior School)
             0161 227 0487 (Preparatory School)

email: head@stbedescollege.co.uk
enquiries@stbedescollege.co.uk
prep@stbedescollege.co.uk
website: www.stbedescollege.co.uk
Twitter: @stbedescollege

Motto: '*Nunquam otio torpebat*'

St Bede's was founded in 1876 by Bishop Herbert Vaughan, who later, as Cardinal Archbishop of Westminster, went on to found Westminster Cathedral. From small beginnings the College has grown and changed whilst remaining faithful to Bishop Vaughan's ideals. Over 500 priests have received their early training at the College; although the number of priests on the staff has been reduced in recent years our religious faith remains central to the life of the College.

Throughout the many changes that have taken place since its formation the College has remained true to its founder's intention: to provide a thorough academic education for Catholic children, in an atmosphere of stability, care and concern.

We therefore seek the highest standards of performance so that pupils are stretched to, but never beyond, their personal limit. The provision of this education within a Catholic environment remains one of the chief characteristics of the College. High expectations of personal behaviour and discipline are rooted in our faith.

The Governors introduced co-education in 1984, so that they could offer girls from Greater Manchester and beyond the benefits of a Catholic Grammar School education.

Governors:
Chair: Revd P Daly, PhB, STL
Joint Vice-Chair: Mrs R Kennedy, MA
Joint Vice-Chair: Mr D Coffey, Cert Ed London
Mr J Ainscough, BSc Hons
Rt Revd T J Brain, Bishop of Salford
Mr J Byrne, BA, MEd
Mr P Lanigan, BA, FCA, ATII
Revd P McMahon
Revd S Parkinson, MA, BA, PGCE
Mr T Richards, BSc Hons
Mr T Walsh
Mrs H West

Clerk to Governors: Mr J L Fletcher, FCA

Head: Mr R Robson, MA

Senior Deputy Head: Mrs S Pike, BSc
Deputy Head: Mr D Grierson, MA
Director of Studies: Dr A Dando, BSc, PhD
Bursar: Mr J L Fletcher, FCA
Head of Sixth Form: Miss M Curry, BSc

Heads of Faculty:
Mr P Glancy, MSc (*Augustine*)
Mrs J Hudson, BA (*Aquinas*)
Mr P McDaid, BSc (*Anselm*)

Sixth Form Pastoral Team:
Miss M Curry, BSc (*Head of Sixth Form & Transition*)
Mr M Gallagher, BBus, BEd (*Assistant Head of Sixth Form, Pastoral*)
Mrs R Lockett, BA (*Assistant Head of Sixth Form, UCAS & Careers*)

Assistant Staff:
* Subject Leader

Art:
*Mrs S Dittman, BA
Mrs J Hudson, BA
Mr H Peers, BA

Business Studies/Economics:
Mrs J Hatton, BA

Mr M Gallagher, BBus, BEd (*Director of Co-Curricular & College Sports*)
Mr P Glancy, MSc (*Head of Augustine Faculty*)
Mr D Grierson, MA (*Deputy Head*)

Classics:
*Mr J Gibson, MA
Mr G Yates, BA, MA

Drama:
*Mrs N Alderson, BA

English:
*Miss F Cochran, BA
Mrs N Alderson, BA (*Head of Drama*)
Mrs C Boylan, BA (*Assistant Head of Siena House*)
Mrs J Johnson, BA
Dr A McMonagle, PhD
Mr B Peden, MA (*Senior Head of Siena House*)
Mrs A Vyce, MA (*Assistant Head of Bosco House*)

Geography:
Mr D Stuart, BSc
Mr K Rafferty, BEd
Mrs C Smith, BA
Mrs M Vidouris, BA

Geology:
*Mr M Parker, BSc

History:
Mr J Bowden, BA
Mr A Power, BA
Mr T Fisher, Cert Ed

ICT:
*Mr P McDaid, BSc (*Head of Anselm Faculty*)
Mrs C Earles (*Network Manager*)
Mr S Fallon, BEd (*Marketing, Publications & Development*)

Mathematics:
*Mr S Bargery, BSc (*Assistant Head of Campion House*)
Mrs C Brewer, BA
Dr A Dando, BSc, PhD (*Director of Studies*)
Mr D McCotter, BSc
Mr J Parkinson-Jones, MMath
Mr K Wardell, BSc
Mr C Wright, BSc (*Internal Assessments*)

Modern Languages:
*Mrs M Reid, MA
Miss H Benson, BA
Mrs M B Girolami, BA (*Head of Campion House*)
Miss C Gray, BA
Miss S Jaen Gil, BA
Mr P Lee, MA (*Examinations Officer*)
Mrs N Perry, BEd
Mrs A Welch, BA

Music:
*Mr A Davies, BMus

PE:
*Mr K Rafferty, BEd (*Boys' PE*)
*Mrs N McCormick, BEd (*Girls' PE*)
Mrs N Lavorini, BEd
Mr L Mitchell, BA
Miss C Whitney

Politics:
*Mrs R Lockett, BA (*UCAS & Careers*)

Religion:
*Mrs E Meakin, BA
Mrs M Andrews, Cert Ed
Miss M Curry, BSc (*Head of Sixth Form*)

Science:
Physics:

*Mrs C Aspinall, BSc
Mr N O'Hagan, BSc (*Assistant Head of Bosco House*)
Mr P McDaid, BSc (*Head of Anselm Faculty*)
Chemistry:
*Mr S Hepburn, BSc
Mrs S Ball, BSc
Mrs S Pike, BSc (*Senior Deputy Head*)
Mrs S Quirk, MSc
Miss R Parkinson, BSc (*Assistant Head of Siena House*)
Biology:
*Miss C Hennity, BSc
Miss C McGregor, BSc
Mrs S Powell, BSc, PhD

Technology:
*Mr A Hennigan, BEd
Mrs M Collins, BEd
Mr S Fallon, BEd (*Marketing, Publications & Development*)

EAL:
Mrs S Alexopoulou, BEd, TEFL

Preparatory School:
Headteacher: Mrs C Hunt

Examinations Officer: Mrs M Tierney
Examinations Officer: Mr P Lee, MA
Medical Officer: Dr M Cunningham, BA, BM, BCh, MRCGP, DCM, DRCOG
College Nurse: Mrs K Taylor, RSCN
Headmaster's PA: Mrs B McGoff

Admission. Most pupils enter St Bede's at 11+ by taking the College Entrance Examination. There are occasional vacancies in other age groups, and there is an additional intake of students from outside the College into the Sixth Form each year.

The College Entrance Examination takes place in January and is open to Catholic boys and girls who will not have reached the age of 12 by 31st August in the year of the examination. Christians of other denominations are also welcomed. Details of the examination and copies of past papers may be obtained from the College Administrator. Occasional vacancies occur in other years. There is also direct entry to the Sixth Form for boys and girls who expect to obtain good GCSE results. Interviews are held from the beginning of the Easter Term.

Curriculum. Curriculum provision is constantly monitored to ensure the best possible educational provision for all students.

A common Lower School curriculum offers all expected subjects together with Latin, ICT, Technology, ample PE/ Games and pastoral time. In the Middle School four subjects are chosen from French, German, Spanish, Latin, Classical Civilisation, Economics, Business Studies, ICT, Design & Technology, Art and Music for a one year course to further enhance GCSE options.

At GCSE/IGCSE, 9 or 10 subjects are taken from a wide choice of 23 and these are available in almost any combination. Our latest additions at GCSE level are Classical Civilisation and PE.

Students must usually achieve 7 GCSE passes (grades A*–C) to be admitted to the Sixth Form where the most common model is to take four subjects to AS Level in the Lower Sixth and then three A2 subjects in the Upper Sixth. The 25 subjects available can be combined in any way and no group exceeds 12 students for A Level. All Sixth Form students in addition have pastoral time, General Religion lessons and Supplementary Studies (which amongst many other things offers opportunities to take the ECDL and EPQ).

Co-Curriculum. Our co-curricular programme allows students of St Bede's an exciting opportunity to experience a range of cultures, arts, activities and sports, outside of their formal academic lessons, that cater to their individuality and allow them to exercise their potential to become multi-talented. Our programme is designed so that it fits in with our continued endeavour to develop a well-rounded student who has had the opportunity to experience a broad range of activities that; inspire, motivate and heighten interests.

All activities have, at their core, value that links in with the College ethos found within the mission statement; being education, family, community and spiritual development. Our goal is to develop wider skills for life-long learning as well as helping to prepare students for the major ideas, innovations and challenges that they face in a rapidly changing society.

The autumn programme sees over 60 clubs, sports and societies taking place, with hundreds of students participating daily. These activities occur whenever there is time outside the classroom: lunch times, weekday afternoons and evenings, at weekends and during the holidays. The clubs are diverse in nature and include: charity, chess, cooking, debating, drama, photograph and science clubs along with forums for aspiring business, medical and law students and the introduction of new languages such as Portuguese and Italian which are proving quite popular. In the sporting arena traditional sports such as rugby, football, hockey and netball have been joined by badminton, basketball, volleyball, indoor cricket, rock climbing and table tennis with fencing, skiing and scuba diving to be offered in the near future.

Fees per term (2014–2015). Senior School £3,300, Preparatory School £2,220.

Preparatory School. St Bede's College Preparatory School, a co-educational day school for pupils aged 3–11, was founded in 1985. The school has the same Governing Body as the College and the Prep School is situated within the main College campus and has full use of College facilities.

Charitable status. St Bede's College Limited is a Registered Charity, number 700808. Its aims and objectives are the advancement and provision of education on behalf of St Bede's College.

St Benedict's School

54 Eaton Rise, Ealing, London W5 2ES
Tel:　　　020 8862 2000 (School Office)
　　　　　020 8862 2010 (Headmaster's Office)
　　　　　020 8862 2254 (Admissions)
　　　　　020 8862 2183 (Bursar)
Fax:　　　020 8862 2199
email:　　headmaster@stbenedicts.org.uk
　　　　　enquiries@stbenedicts.org.uk (Admissions)
website:　www.stbenedicts.org.uk
Twitter:　@stbenedicts
Facebook: /StBenedictsSchool
LinkedIn: /st-benedicts-school

Motto: *A minimis incipe*

St Benedict's is a co-educational school with a proud academic record. Its Mission of 'Teaching a way of living' is at the core of the holistic Catholic education that is provided to boys and girls throughout the School from Nursery to Sixth Form. The school nurtures their growth and prepares them for future challenges in an increasingly secular world. St Benedict's is committed to supporting all children to develop their full potential.

The School occupies a lovely site in West London, with outstanding sports facilities a mile away. The total number of pupils on roll is 1084 of which 804 are in the Senior School (218 in Sixth Form), 267 in the Junior School and 13 in the Nursery. Boarders are not accepted.

The recent Diocesan Inspection (September 2013) rated the school as outstanding in every respect. The ISI Inspection Report (November 2012) praised many aspects of the school's work. The academic curriculum, the programme of extra-curricular activities and the pupils' personal development were all described as excellent.

Governing Body: The Governing Board of St Benedict's School

Headmaster: Mr C J Cleugh, BSc, MSc

Deputy Heads:
Mr P W Allott, MPhil, MA, BA, BA
Mrs P Lightfoot, BSc

Bursar: Mrs C de Cintra, BA, ACA

Headmaster's PA: Mrs R Wynne

Registrar: Mrs M Moore

Old Priorian Association: M Keal, President, c/o The School

Admission to the School is in September at the age of 11, by interview and special examination. Admission to the Sixth Form is subject to good GCSE results. Application for admission should be made to the Headmaster. Registration Fee: £75.

Religion. A specifically Christian and Catholic atmosphere with a Benedictine ethos is the hallmark of the School. There are regular periods for liturgy, both formal in the Abbey Church and informal in small groups. However the School welcomes pupils of other denominations and faiths.

Curriculum. In the Senior School, for the first year all pupils follow a common curriculum including ADT, French and Music. In the second year additional languages are offered: German or Spanish. Religious Studies is undertaken by all in every year. Pupils normally take between 9 and 11 GCSE subjects. A wide choice of subjects is available at AS and A Level. The Sixth Form is large, over 200, and almost all proceed to University or further education. Pupils are also prepared for Oxford and Cambridge entrance, where there is an impressive record.

Sport. St Benedict's is renowned for its sporting tradition. Whilst promoting the highest sporting aspirations, the school is committed to sport for all. Physical Education and Games are part of the curriculum throughout the School. Rugby, hockey and cricket are the principal games for boys and netball, hockey and athletics for girls. Fencing is available for both boys and girls. Other sports are also promoted, including tennis, swimming, volleyball and table tennis. The School has 15 acres of playing fields nearby at Perivale, with a state-of-the-art Pavilion and changing rooms. St Benedict's has a national reputation for rugby.

Facilities. In the past ten years there has been huge investment in computer technology, new classrooms, the award-winning £6.2 million Cloisters complex, and a full-size all-weather facility at the playing fields. Most recently, in September 2012, a new servery adjacent to the dining hall and a conference room were opened and the library was enlarged and refurbished.

Activities. There are nearly 90 lunchtime or after-school clubs and societies including Combined Cadet Force, the Duke of Edinburgh's Award Scheme, music, drama and opportunities for Christian service. There are two major Drama productions each year. Provision for Music is extensive and almost any instrument can be learnt. Activities include choirs, a wind band, a samba band and two orchestras. Public concerts are held several times each term. Art is outstanding, with a large number of pupils passing from the Sixth Form to Art Colleges each year. Considerable use is made of opportunities available in London for visits to concerts, theatres, museums and art galleries.

Careers. Careers advice and guidance on university choice and application is available throughout the upper

years and particularly in the Sixth Form. This is delivered through seminars, a dedicated and well-resourced Careers Room and individual tutorials.

Fees per term (2014–2015). Tuition fees: Senior School £4,620, Junior School £4,070, Pre-Prep £3,660.

In the nature of a wholly day school, contact with parents is frequent and regular.

Charitable status. St Benedict's School Ealing is a Registered Charity, number 1148512, and a Charitable Company Limited by Guarantee, number 8093330. Its aim is to promote the Christian and Catholic education of young people.

St Columba's College

Whitechurch, Dublin 16, Ireland
Tel: 00 353 1 490 6791 (Warden's Office)
              00 353 1 493 2860 (Bursar's Office)
Fax: 00 353 1 493 6655
email: admin@stcolumbas.ie
website: www.stcolumbas.ie

Motto: '*Prudentes Sicut Serpentes et Simplices Sicut Columbae*'

St Columba's College was founded in 1843 by the Revd William Sewell, the Lord Primate, the Earl of Dunraven and others. The College was incorporated by Royal Charter in 1913.

Visitor: The Most Revd Dr Richard Clarke, Archbishop of Armagh and Primate of All Ireland

Fellows:
Mrs A C Kennedy
J N White, FIAVI
C D S Shiell, BSc, MSc, FCIS
Mrs K M Erwin, MA
Dr M O'Moore, MA, PhD, FTCD
P Myerscough
G D Crampton, MA, BBS
J Bailey, MA
I Roberts, BA, BAI, CEng, FIEI, FIStructE, FICE
  (*Chairman*)
G Caldwell, BBS
Ms T Banotti, MA
M Gleeson, MA, MSc
Ms D Gray, BSc, MBA
The Most Revd M Jackson, MA, PhD, Archbishop of Dublin
J R P Wardell, MA, ACA
Mrs R Johnson

Warden: Dr L J Haslett, BA, DPhil, PGCE

Sub-Warden: J M Girdham, BA, HDipEd

Bursar: Mrs S Gibbs, MA, MSc, HDipEd

Assistant Staff:
* *Head of Department*
† *Housemaster/mistress*

F H Morris, BA, HDipEd (*Senior Master*)
P J Jackson, BSc, HDipEd, MIBI (**Science, Director of Boys' Boarding, Liaison for Child Protection*)
J R Brett, MA, MSt, HDipEd (**Classics, *Latin, Senior Tutor, Librarian*)
P R Watts, DipArt, HDipADE (**Art*)
Mrs A Morris, BA, HDipEd (*Director of Girls' Boarding*)
B A Redmond, BTech, HDipSGC, DipID (**Technical Graphics and *Construction Studies*)
G R Bannister, MA, PhD, HDipEd (**Irish*)
L Canning, BA, HDipEd (*Director of Sport, English,* †*Stackallan*)

Miss A Maybury, BA, HDipEd (*Irish, *SPHE*)
Dr M Singleton, MSc, PhD, HDipEd (*Registrar, Director of Studies, *Physics, †Hollypark*)
P G McCarthy, MA, HDipEd (**Business Studies, *Classical Studies, Transition Year Coordinator*)
Mrs D Sherwood (*Learning Support, †Iona*)
Ms S McEneaney, BA, PGCE (*Learning Support*)
Mrs F G Heffernan, PGCert (*SLD*), CertEd, ACLD, ILSA, AMBDA (**Learning Support*)
Miss D Cullen, BEd (*Art, †Beresford*)
D Higgins, MA, HDipEd (*Mathematics, †Glen*)
Mrs G Malone-Brady, MA, LRAM, ARCM, LRSM (*Director of Music*)
P Cron, MA, NDip (**Boys' Games, †Gwynn*)
Mrs M D Haslett, BA, MPhil, PGCE (**History*)
Mrs S-J Johnson, BEd (**Girls' Games*)
Ms K Hennessey, BSc (*Science*)
R Swift, BA, HDipEd (**CSPE, *Drama*)
N Coldrick, BSc (*Mathematics*)
S Crombie, BSc (*Director of ICT*)
Ms R Howell, BA, HDipEd (**Economics*)
H Jones, BScEd, PGDipGC (**Agricultural Science, Guidance and Careers*)
Ms A Kilfeather, BA, HDipEd (*Modern Languages*)
M Patterson, MSc, PGCE (**Mathematics, Director Extra-Curricular Activities, †Tibradden*)
M O'Shaughnessy, MA (**Modern Languages*)
B Finn, MA, HDipEd (*History*)
E Jameson, MA, HDipEd (*English*)
Ms J Robinson, BA, HDipEd (*Mathematics*)
Ms K Smith, BA, PGDipEd (*English*)
T Clarke, BA, PGDipEd (*French, Music, Irish*)
The Revd N Crossey, MA, MTh, PDipTheol, Chaplain (**Religious Education*)
Ms E McNelis, BSc, PGDipEd (*Biology*)
T de Brit, BSc, PhD, HDipEd (**Geology, IT Administrator*)
S Duffy, BSc, PGCE (**Geography*)
W E Gibbs (*Asst †Tibradden*)
Mrs Y Crossey (*Asst †Beresford*)
Mrs T Girdham, BA (*House Tutor Iona*)
Mrs H Kavanagh (*Learning Support*)
Ms J Pyz, MA (*Asst †Iona*)
Miss K Haslett, BA (*House Tutor Beresford*)
G Dean (*House Tutor Stackallan*)
T McConville, BA (*Librarian*)

Mr A Grundy, MA Mus, HonVCM, FTCL, LRSM, ALCM (*Guitar*)
Ms S Taylor, MBA, BA, LTCL (*Piano & Theory*)
Ms K Snowe, BA, LRSM, ALCM (*Piano*)
Ms A Murnaghan, BA Mus, LRAM (*Cello, Piano, Theory*)
Ms T Lawlor, ALCM, LLCM (*Guitar*)
Ms M Comiskey, MA Mus (*Flute*)
Mr D Hatch (*Clarinet/Saxophone*)
Mr F Moran (*Percussion*)
Ms C Meehan, LRAM (*Violin, Viola*)
Ms E Shannon, MA Mus (*Singing*)
Mr E McDonald (*Singing*)
Ms A Brady, BMus (*Singing, Piano*)
Ms M Buicke, BA Mus (*Singing*)

Warden's Secretary: Ms E Bainton
Admissions Secretary: Ms N Crisp
Accountant: Mr N Grannell, FCA
Assistant Account: Ms C McLerie
Medical Officer: Dr A Khourie
Infirmary Sister: Mrs L Hanna, RGN

The College is a co-educational boarding school, with a number of day pupils, of about 300 pupils. It is situated on the slopes of the Dublin Mountains about 7 miles south of the city overlooking Dublin Bay in an estate of 138 acres. Much of this comprises playing fields, a 9-hole golf course and a deer park.

Having occupied its present site for almost 170 years, the College combines the best of architecture old and new. Recent additions include a new Library and Reading Room, a Sports Hall, a Computer Centre, a Careers Library and an Arts Centre. Two completely new boarding houses and four classrooms opened in 2004. A new Music School was opened in 2008. A second astroturf hockey pitch and an additional dining hall were also added in recent years.

Admission. Application for admission should be made to the Warden. There is a registration fee of €100. There are two junior Houses for entrants between the ages of 11 and 13 years. An assessment day is held for 11/12 year old entrants in October prior to the year of entry. Entry is determined by a number of factors, including family association, geographical spread (including Northern Ireland, the UK and overseas), date of registration and an understanding of the values which underpin the College. Entrants from Preparatory Schools take the Common Entrance Examination. Admission may also be made at 16–17 years.

Curriculum. In the Upper School, a wide choice of subjects and a large number of courses are available for the Irish Leaving Certificate. This examination keeps many options open for third-level colleges. It is the qualifying examination for entry to Irish universities and is acceptable (with requisite grades) to the faculties of all British universities. The Irish Junior Certificate is taken in the third form. A compulsory Transition Year programme follows the Junior Certificate.

Religious Teaching. Chapel services and religious instruction are based upon the liturgy and doctrine of the Church of Ireland. Boys and girls of other denominations and faiths are included and welcome.

Other Activities. Music, Art, Pottery and Technical Graphics (which are part of the curriculum in the Lower School) and Drama, Debating, Photography, Computers and various other clubs and societies function at all levels.

Games and Pursuits. Rugby Football, Hockey, Cricket, Athletics, Cross-country Running, Tennis, Badminton, Basketball, Golf, Swimming, Hillwalking, Horse Riding, Polocrosse, Sailing, Archery and Aerobics.

Fees per term (2014–2015). Day Pupils €3,452–€4,142, Day Boarding €4,126–€4,944, Full Boarding €6,207–€7,450.

The above fees are expressed in Euros. Fees may be paid in the Sterling equivalent.

Entrance Scholarships. Junior and senior awards are made at age 12 (entry to Form I), 15 (entry to Form IV) and 16 (entry to Form V). Entrance exhibitions are often awarded to candidates for entry to Form II through the Common Entrance Examination. Generous discounts are available for the sons and daughters of the Clergy of the Church of Ireland. Old Columban and sibling discounts are also available. Details on request.

Leaving Scholarship. Norman Scholarships, for three years or more at all university colleges in Britain, Ireland and elsewhere are open to the sons and daughters of Clergy of the Church of Ireland.

St Columba's Former Pupils' Society. Old Columban Society. *Hon Secretary*: G Symes, St Columba's College.

Charitable status. St Columba's College is a Registered Charity, number 4024. Its aims and objectives are the provision of Secondary Education facilities.

St Columba's College

King Harry Lane, St Albans, Hertfordshire AL3 4AW
Tel: 01727 855185
Fax: 01727 892024
email: admissions@stcolumbascollege.org
website: www.stcolumbascollege.org

Motto: '*Cor ad Cor Loquitur*'

St Columba's College was founded in 1939, and has been a school in the tradition of the Brothers of the Sacred Heart (New England Province) since 1955. It is a Catholic, selective boys' school, with a little over half of its pupils coming from other denominations and faiths. The predominantly lay staff works together with pupils and parents to provide a Christian education based on traditional values, balancing a friendly community with sound discipline and academic rigour.

St Columba's College stands in its own grounds overlooking the picturesque vale of St Albans and the Roman settlement of Verulamium. In the last few years extensive improvements have been made to Science, English and Drama, Sixth Form and Preparatory facilities, and a major building development at the heart of the College was completed in September 2013.

Governors:
Chairman: Mrs J Harrison, BEd
Vice-Chairman: Mrs J Carolan, BSc, MRICS

Trustee and Dean of the College: Brother Daniel St Jacques SC, BA, PGF HG Dip Counselling, MBACP

Bursar and Clerk to the Governors: Neville De Lord, BSc

Headmaster: David Buxton, BA, MTh, MA

Deputy Headmaster: D Shannon-Little, CertEd, BA
Academic Deputy Head: I Devereux, BEd
Head of Sixth Form: R McCann, BA
Assistant Head: Mrs C Powlesland, BA
Assistant Head: Dr S Jones, PhD
Assistant Deputy Head: S Leadbetter, MA
Head of Preparatory School: Mrs R Loveman, BSc
Prep Pastoral Deputy: M Ioannou, BEd
Prep Academic Deputy: Mrs M Shannon-Little, BEd

Heads of House:
Charles: S Murphy, BSc
Guertin: Miss C Treacy, BA
Joseph: J Tatham, BA
Martin: M Connor, BA
McClancy: K Boland, BA
Stanislaus: R Byrne, BSc

Heads of Department/Subject Leaders:
Art: W Gurney, MA
Biology: Mrs M Mester, BSc
Careers: A McDonald, BA
Chemistry: Ms R Tuckwell, BSc
Classics: S Graves, BA Cantab
Design Technology: B Barnett, BA
Economics & Business Studies: Mrs K Healer, MA Cantab, LLB
English & Drama: E Waters, BA
Geography: D Hughes, BSc
History: K Roberts, MA
Information & Communications Technology: S Leadbetter, MA
Learning Support: A Nevard, BSc, OCR Dip SpLD
Library/Media: Mrs S Mathieson, Dip Lib
Mathematics: Mrs K Parsons, BSc
Modern Foreign Languages: R Childs, BA
French: Ms S Jasieczek, BA
Spanish: R Childs, BA
Music: Mrs P MacKenzie, MA Oxon (*Director of Music*)
Director of Sport: E Lowe, BSc
Politics: R McKenzie, BA
Religious Education: Ms L Cronin, MA Cantab
Science & Physics: Dr R Osborne, PhD
Sociology: N Hogan, BA

Administration:
Registrar: Brother Denis Bessette, SC, BA

Headmaster's PA: Mrs R Coakley
Head of Prep's PA: Mrs C Tominey

Entry. St Columba's College admits boys from 4–18. Currently there are 255 boys in the Preparatory School, aged 4–11, and 625 boys in the Senior School, aged 11–18. The main entry for the Senior School is at 11, by Entrance Test and interview, with a smaller group being offered deferred entry at 13+.

Scholarships. Academic Scholarships are awarded at 11, 13 and for the Sixth Form. Additionally, the College offers two Music Scholarships each year and means-tested Coin-dre Bursaries.

The Curriculum. This is kept as broad as possible up to GCSE, pupils usually taking 9/11 subjects from the traditional range of Arts and Science options. There are 21 A Level (A2) subjects for pupils to choose from, all of which are also available as a fourth option up to AS. Sixth Form education is complemented by an enrichment course which prepares students for extra qualifications including the Extended Project, ICT and Personal Finance. Almost all of the Sixth Form go on to universities, including Oxford and Cambridge.

Careers. A full-time Head of Careers and Higher Education works from a fully-equipped Careers Centre to ensure that all students receive high-quality guidance in order to make informed decisions about subject choices and university courses with subsequent career options in mind.

Pastoral Care. St Columba's is a Catholic foundation welcoming students from all traditions. The spiritual and moral well-being of our pupils is a matter of primary importance for all of our staff, the majority being tutors. The six Housemasters and their teams are supported by a Ministry Team. Relations between the College and parents are open – a strength of the Foundation – and they are in regular contact with each other in monitoring the progress of the boys. The College seeks to nurture the academic and personal talents of each individual.

Sport. All boys participate, and the College has a strong sporting reputation. A rich variety of sports is available, including Rugby, Basketball, Football, Tennis, Cricket, Athletics, Swimming and Cross Country. For Sixth Form boys, not selected for the major sports, an even wider range of activities is available. Facilities include a large gymnasium and sports field on site. The Sports Department makes extensive use of soccer and rugby pitches, an athletics track, swimming pool and a golf course which are all immediately adjacent to the College site.

Extended and Extra-Curricular Activities. The College offers a mix of activities both at lunch-time and after school. These include sports clubs, such as archery and lacrosse, drama, art, chess, computing, Young Enterprise and many others, as well as a variety of academic and social clubs. There is a number of music ensembles, including a choir, orchestra and jazz band and four choirs of handbell ringers.

CCF. The Combined Cadet Force includes an Army and an RAF section. A full-time SSI (School Staff Instructor) is employed and the sections now include girls from The Princess Helena College, Hitchin and Loreto College, St Albans. The Duke of Edinburgh's Award Scheme comes under the same management.

Preparatory School. The Preparatory School is on the same site as the Senior School and shares many of its facilities. The College has a strong family atmosphere, providing a secure and purposeful environment in which expectations are high. It admits boys only, by assessment, into the Lower Prep and Upper Prep phases. In their final year, most Preparatory School pupils are offered unconditional places at St Columba's College Senior School, following recommendations by Prep School staff.

(*See also St Columba's College Preparatory School entry in IAPS section.*)

Fees per term (2014–2015). Senior School £4,390; Prep 4–6 £3,855, Prep 3 £3,495, Reception–Prep 2 £3,095.

Charitable status. St Columba's College is a Registered Charity, number 1088480. It exists to provide a well-rounded Catholic education for pupils from 4–18 years of age.

St Columba's School

Duchal Road, Kilmacolm, Inverclyde PA13 4AU
Tel: 01505 872238
Fax: 01505 873995
email: secretary@st-columbas.org
Junior School:
Knockbuckle Road, Kilmacolm, Inverclyde PA13 4EQ
Tel: 01505 872768
email: juniorsecretary@st-columbas.org

website: www.st-columbas.org

Motto: *Orare Laborare Literisque Studere*
Founded in 1897, St Columba's School is a non-denominational, co-educational day school for pupils aged 3–18. The School currently has just under 730 pupils with around 346 at Senior School. It is situated in the small rural community of Kilmacolm, surrounded by delightful countryside and located only 7 miles from Glasgow Airport.

Governing Body:

Honorary President: Mr Guy Clark, Lord Lieutenant of Renfrewshire

Honorary Vice-Presidents:
John C Ritchie
Dr Helen M Laird, OBE, MA, PhD, DL
Ron M Kennedy, TD, FCCII, FLIA

Board of Directors:
Colin McClatchie, BSc Econ (*Chairman*)
Dr Aileen Findlay, BSc, MBChB Ed, MRCGP (*Deputy Chairman*)
John Broadfoot, BA, MEd
Lawrie Campbell, BA, MBA
Hugh M Currie, BSc, CEng, MICE
Rob Guyler, BSc, ACMA
Katharine Hardie, LLB Hons, DLP
Helen M MacConnacher
Calum Paterson, BA, MBA, FRSE, CA
Kenneth Wilson, MA, CA
Paul Yacoubian, BAcc, CA
Colin Taylor, BSc, MRICS

Rector: **Mr D G Girdwood**, DL, BSc St Andrews, MEd Stirling, SQH

Head of Junior School: Mrs A Duncan, MA St Andrews, Dip EdMan, SQH

Depute Rector: Mrs J E Stevens, BEd Aberdeen

Depute Rector: Mr M J McLaughlin, MA Greenwich, BA Thames

Depute Rector: Mrs V Reilly, MA Edinburgh

Depute Head of Junior School: Mrs J Andrews, BA King Alfred's, MA Ed Open

Senior Master: Mr C S Clark, BEd Glasgow

Registrar: Mr B A Manson, DipPE Jordanhill

Bursar: Mr G Brewster, BSc Napier, MBA Heriot-Watt, CEng, MIET, FRSA

Rector's PA: Mrs Moira McWhirter

Heads of House:
Strathgryffe: Mrs N Smith, MA Glasgow
Kilallan: Mr G Robertson, MA Glasgow
Craigmarloch: Mrs J Scott, BA Edinburgh, DipSL
Duchal: Mr A Tait, BA Stirling, BEd Edinburgh

Senior School Teaching Staff:
* *Head of Faculty*
‡ *Chartered Teacher*

Ancient & Modern Languages:
*Ms L Rodger, MA Edinburgh
Mrs V Reilly, MA Edinburgh
Mrs N Smith, MA Glasgow
Mrs P Kennedy, MA Glasgow
Mrs K A Ingham, MA St Andrews
Mr C McCay, MA, LLB Glasgow, MLitt St Andrews
Mrs M Planchon, Université Paul Valery
Mr S Branford, MA Glasgow
Mrs D Staber, MA Munich

Design:
*Mrs H Mathie, BA Reading
Mrs M R Robinson, BA Glasgow School of Art
Mrs H Macdonald, Dip DomSc Glasgow and West of Scotland Coll, Dip SecEd Jordanhill
Mr A Morrison, BEd Strathclyde
Mr T Boag, Dip TechEd Jordanhill

English:
*Mr G McNicol, BA Hertfordshire
Mrs K Brash, MPhil Queensland
Mrs V Kennedy, BA Stirling
Mrs J E Stevens, BEd Aberdeen
Mrs A Moran, MA Glasgow
‡Mr G Smith, MA Glasgow, MEd West of Scotland
Mr M J McLaughlin, MA Greenwich, BA Thames

Humanities:
*‡Mr R Arbuckle, MA Dundee
Ms F Fowler, BSc Glasgow
Mr G Robertson, MA Glasgow
Mrs J Scott, BA Edinburgh, Dip SL
Dr C Gilmour, BA, PhD Stirling
Mrs A Gillen, MA Glasgow
Mrs R Kerr, MA Glasgow
Ms Shaw, BA Glasgow Caledonian

Mathematics & ICT:
*Mrs F I Bruce, BSc Glasgow
Mrs E Brunton, MA Glasgow
Mr C S Clark, BEd Glasgow
Mr A Walkey, BSc, MSc Glasgow
Mrs N Gardner, BA, MPA Indiana
Mrs B Mackenzie, MA Glasgow
Miss F Chisholm, BSc Strathclyde

Music:
*Ms Y Carey, Dip MusEd Glasgow
Miss C Patterson, BEd RSAMD

Physical Education:
*Mr E Milligan, BEd Edinburgh
Mrs L Carlton, BEd Edinburgh
Mr B A Manson, Dip PE Jordanhill
Mrs J Bellew, BEd Dunfermline
Mrs L Urie, BEd Dunfermline
Mr A Tait, BA Stirling, BEd Edinburgh
Miss F Ramsay, BSc Stirling

Science:

Biology:
*Mrs E Wilson, BSc Paisley
Mrs P Nicoll, BEd St Andrews Coll
Dr L Hay, BSc Aberdeen, PhD Strathclyde
Chemistry:

*Mrs T Munro, BSc Paisley, PG Dip Comp Jordanhill, SQH
Ms L Robertson, BSc Strathclyde, PG Dip IT Paisley
Physics:
*Mr I Weir, BSc Paisley, MBA Strathclyde
Miss J Boyle, MSci Glasgow

Junior School Teaching Staff:
*Mr A MacKay, BEd Strathclyde
Mrs G Maxwell, BEd Dundee
Mrs G Annetts, BA RSAMD
Mrs N Brisci, MA Edinburgh
Mrs E Corbett, BEd Jordanhill
Mrs G Henderson, BA Paisley
Miss S MacLean, MA Glasgow
Mrs H Manceau, MA Glasgow
Mrs G Hall, BA Cantab
Mrs J Wolfe, DipEd Jordanhill
Mrs S Campbell, DCE Jordanhill
Mr F Campbell, BA Strathclyde
Miss L Eadie, BEd Edinburgh
Mrs K Leighton, MA Glasgow
Mrs F MacFarlane, BEd Strathclyde
Mrs K Fleming, BA RSAMD
Mrs L Reid, BSc Caledonian, DipASN Edinburgh
Miss A Kelly, BEd Strathclyde
Mrs A Moore, DCE Craigie
Mrs J Worrall, BEd Strathclyde

With a roll of just under 730 across both the Junior and Senior Schools, teachers know each child by name. Considerable effort is made to create an environment which encourages each pupil to realise their potential, and nurtures polite, articulate and informed young people. The School consistently achieves excellent academic results, regularly placing it as one of the highest-achieving schools nationally. St Columba's was awarded Gold Investor in People status in 2013.

Facilities. The School buildings and sports facilities are located within a quarter of a mile radius of each other. A major extension to the Senior School is planned for the immediate future.

Sports facilities include: gym area for gymnastics and dance, large purpose-built sports hall including fitness suite, all-weather floodlit hockey/tennis ground, access to three rugby pitches and a large playing field used for athletics and cross-country running.

The School has a dedicated transport service and an after-school care facility.

Curriculum. St Columba's School follows the Scottish Curriculum at all stages. Junior School pupils are taught French, music and PE by specialist staff. Transitus (P7) is a transitional year with core curriculum taught by the class teacher and science, languages, art, music and PE delivered by specialist secondary teachers. Pupils in SIV are presented for Standard Grade/Intermediate 2 examinations followed by Higher Grade and Advanced Higher Grade examinations in SV and SVI.

Games. Rugby, hockey, tennis, athletics, badminton, gymnastics, swimming, volleyball, basketball, soccer, dance (girls), orienteering. Optional: netball, squash, cricket, golf, skiing/snowboarding, curling, street dance, weight-training.

Extra-Curricular. The importance of extra-curricular activities is emphasised at both Junior and Senior School level. The School offers over 20 clubs including The Duke of Edinburgh's Award, debating, sport, chess, drama and music (choirs, orchestras, ensembles, pipe band, jazz band). Individual tuition in a wide range of instruments and in Diction is available. Public performances and school shows are arranged on a regular basis.

From SIII upwards, The Duke of Edinburgh's Award Scheme attracts very large numbers with its emphasis on skills, service, sport and the expedition section at bronze, silver and gold level.

There is a very strong tradition of fundraising for charity and community service within the School.

St Columba's has strong links with schools in Australia and Canada and has annual exchanges between students for periods of time.

Organisation. The school is organised into four Houses for both pastoral and competitive purposes. Each house has a Head of House as well as pupil Captain and Vice-Captain. Career guidance is supported by ISCO.

Admission. Entry to St Columba's is by a combination of entry test, interview and, where applicable, a report from the applicant's previous school. An open week is held in November and entrance tests are held in January. The main entry points are Junior 1 and Transitus however pupils are taken in at other stages as places become available.

Fees per annum (2014–2015). Nursery £1,850, Prep £3,450, J1 & J2 £7,750, J3 £8,485, J4 £9,010, J5 & J6 £9,460, Trans & SI £10,540, SII £10,900, SIII–SV £10,540, SVI £10,600.

A number of bursary places, ranging from 10–100% of fees, are available for new applicants entering Transitus (P7), SV to study Highers and SVI to study Advanced Highers.

Charitable status. St Columba's School is a Registered Charity, number SC012598. It exists to provide education for pupils.

St Dunstan's College

Stanstead Road, London SE6 4TY

Tel:　　020 8516 7200
Fax:　　020 8516 7300
email:　info@sdmail.org.uk
　　　　admissions@sdmail.org.uk
website:　www.stdunstans.org.uk

Motto: '*Albam Exorna*'

The College was founded in the 15th Century in the Parish of St Dunstan-in-the-East, part of the Tower Ward of the City of London. In 1888 the school was re-founded in Catford, South East London. It became co-educational in 1994.

Governors:
Chairman: ¶Alderman & Sheriff Sir Paul Judge, MA, MBA, LLD Hon
Deputy Chairman: P L Coling, Esq, FRICS
Miss S Ahmed, BSc
Mrs V Alexander
C R Berry, Esq, CR
¶P W France, Esq
Mrs L Kiernan, MA, DipEd
K L Marshall, Esq, RD, FICS, ACII
Revd B Olivier
Mrs C Price, MA, FRSA
Miss D Robertshaw, BSc

¶ *Old Dunstonian*

Clerk to the Governors and Bursar: Colonel N Wallace

Senior School Academic Staff:

Headmaster: Mr Nicholas Hewlett, BSc

Deputy Head: T Kirk, MA
Head of Key Stage 5: P A Glavin, BA
Head of Key Stage 4: N M Adriano, BA
Head of Key Stage 3: B Harrild, BA

* *Head of Faculty*

Mrs S E Algeo, BA, MA　　　Mrs J Atkinson, GRSM, NCOS

R Austin, BSc	W J Holroyd, BA
G Bailey, BSc	Dr S L Ibendahl, PhD
Mrs H S Baptiste, BSc	*A W Johnston, MA
Miss R Biggs, BSc	Miss G Joyce, BA
*R R D Bodenham, BSc	Miss S Kervella, MA
Miss L Bok, MA	R W Lea, BA, BEd
Miss L Boquet, BA	Mrs D S Malpart, BSc
Ms R E Butryn, MA	Mrs R J May, BSc
Ms M M Callaghan, BA	Ms D K Mitchell, MA
Miss S Carraro, BA	*Mrs K Molteni, BA
Mrs S Cheeseman	Mrs L Morrell, BA
Mrs J Cohen, BSc	J M Newman, BA
Miss A Coleman-Smith, BA	Mrs K O'Callaghan, MA
D Connolly, BA	*Mrs S Otley, BA
Ms H L Davidson, BSc	Miss T Pearson, BA
Mrs G L Davies, BSc	G S Phillips, BSc, MSc
R W Davies, BA	R Pitman, BA
Miss F Du Sauzay, BA	D Read, BSc
Ms S Elliott, BA	D Sharples, BA
J P H Elmes, MA	P J Stobart, BA
Ms K Evans, MA	X Tan, BSc
J Folwell, BA	Miss E Vile, MA
Miss A Gilmour, BSc	*Miss D M Warren, BEng
Ms A Gomez-Ramos, BA	D J Webb, BA
Mrs L Hartwell, BSc	Mrs J V Williams, BEd
Mrs S Hearn, BSc	M Wood, BA
R Hill, BSc	M Woodward, BA
	Miss L E Zatloukal, BA

PA to the Headmaster: Mrs P Phillips
Marketing & Admissions Officer: Miss S Stammers
Assistant Admissions Officer: Mrs A Adriano
Junior School Secretary/Registrar: Mrs R Scard
College Doctor: Dr C Gonzalez-Prieto

Buildings. The College is located in mainly Victorian buildings on a 15-acre site three minutes' walk from Catford and Catford Bridge railway stations. Facilities include an imposing Great Hall, a well-equipped Learning Resource Centre, a drama studio, three state-of-the-art ICT suites and refurbished chemistry laboratories. To complement extensive playing fields on site, St Dunstan's has a sports hall, fully-equipped fitness rooms, floodlit netball/tennis courts, rugby fives courts and an indoor swimming pool, recently modernised to a very high standard. In addition to the on-site acreage, the College has bought the Private Banks Sports Ground which is in Catford on Canadian Avenue. This 20-acre property doubles the land available to St Dunstan's College and further enhances the sporting and other facilities available to all of its pupils.

Organisation and Curriculum. The College educates boys and girls from the ages of 3 to 18. The Junior School comprises a nursery class for 20 children (3+), a Pre-Prep Department for 120 children aged 4–7 and a Prep Department of 160 children aged 7–11.

In the Junior School great emphasis is placed on letting children learn in a friendly, caring and stimulating environment. Pupils study a broad curriculum and participate in a wide variety of extra-curricular activities. The Head of the Junior School is a member of IAPS (*see entry in IAPS section*).

The Senior School, with a total of 570 pupils, comprises Key Stage 3 (Years 7–9), Key Stage 4 (Years 10 and 11) and Key Stage 5 (Years 12 and 13). A considerable choice of subjects is on offer – English, Drama, French, German, Spanish, Italian, Latin, History, Geography, Religious Studies, Economics, Business Studies, Mathematics, Physics, Chemistry, Biology, Environmental Systems & Societies, Design & Technology, ICT, Physical Education, Music, Art & Design, and Personal, Social and Health Education (PSHE).

In the Sixth Form students can choose whether to study for the International Baccalaureate (IB) Diploma, or for AS/ A2 Levels. The College received accreditation from the IBO in 2004. Virtually all students proceed to Higher Education.

The College is a vibrant, academic community with a friendly atmosphere. It values cultural diversity and has a reputation for high academic standards and excellent pastoral care.

Pupils have the opportunity to join a wide range of extra-curricular activities to develop their special interests and personal strengths, for example:

- A thriving Combined Cadet Force
- The Duke of Edinburgh's Award Scheme – among London schools, the College has very strong numbers of pupils involved at all Award levels
- Community service – every year the College supports a range of British and overseas charities and local organisations
- The Armstrong Society (Science)
- Modern Languages Society
- The Stanford Tuck (History) Society
- Debating Society
- Christian Forum
- Literary Society
- Puzzle Club
- Drama Club
- Chess Club
- Electronic Workshop
- Visual Arts Society

Music. Pupils from all parts of the school participate in a variety of choirs, orchestras and instrumental ensembles. There is an annual Choral & Orchestral Concert for the whole College at St John's Smith Square.

Sport. The chief sports are cricket, hockey, netball, rounders, rugby, soccer and swimming. Students also have opportunities to take part in cross-country running, fives, tennis, basketball, badminton, sailing, golf and fitness training.

Entrance. The main entrance points are at the age of 3, 4, 7, 11 or 16. Admission to the College is competitive in all years with the exception of the Nursery, and depends on academic ability and the demonstration of potential. At 11+ an Entrance Examination is held annually in January.

Entrance Scholarships. Scholarships are offered for academic merit and also for excellence in Music, Sport, Art and Design and Drama. Means-tested bursaries are available.

Fees per term (2014–2015). The consolidated fees (including lunch) are: Nursery £2,957; Junior School £3,769–£4,749; Senior School £5,020.

Old Dunstonian Association. The ODA has 4,000 members. All pupils subscribe to the ODA while at school and automatically become life members when they leave.

St Dunstan's College Family Society. This parent-run fundraising body works to support the educational, social and extra-curricular activities of the school for the benefit of all pupils. All parents are automatically members of the Family Society.

Charitable status. St Dunstan's Educational Foundation is a Registered Charity, number 312747.

St Edmund's College

Old Hall Green, Ware, Herts SG11 1DS
Tel: 01920 824247
Fax: 01920 823011
email: admissions@stedmundscollege.org
website: www.stedmundscollege.org
Twitter: @stedmundsware

Motto: '*Avita pro Fide*'

St Edmund's College, England's oldest Catholic school, is a leading Independent day and boarding, co-educational

Catholic School for boys and girls aged 3–18. From the Nursery to the Sixth Form St Edmund's College offers an education that challenges and stimulates, developing the whole person in the intellectual, physical, emotional and spiritual areas of life; the richness of our extra-curricular provision and our high academic standards are testament to the College's success and popularity.

Located on a beautiful site in rural East Hertfordshire, only 40 minutes to London by train, St Edmund's has outstanding transport links to the surrounding area and makes full use of the excellent facilities on its 450-acre site including floodlit astroturf pitches and and indoor swimming pool.

Scholarships are available at 7+, 11+, 16+ and we welcome applications for entry to all years if places are available. St Edmund's welcomes students from all faiths who support our ethos.

President & Patron: His Eminence Cardinal Vincent Nichols, Archbishop of Westminster

Governors:
Chairman: Mr Patrick J Mitton, MSc
Deputy Chairman and Chair of PR and Marketing Sub-Committee: Dr Frances MacIntosh, MA, MRCP, MFPM
Members:
Monsignor James Paul Curry, STB
Mr N Ransley, MA, MEd (*Chair of Academic Sub-Committee*)
Sister Jean Sinclair, SHCJ, BSc
Revd Dr James Sweeney, CP, BD, BA, MTh, PhD, MA
Mr John Bryant, BA
Fr Alban McCoy, OFM Conv, BA, MLitt
Mrs Madeline Roberts, FCA

Senior Leadership Team:

Headmaster, DSM Child Protection: Mr P Durán, BA MA London

Deputy Head, DSL Child Protection: Mr M Barber, BA Oxon, MSc Manchester, MA Oxon

Director of Finance and Administration: Mr B Tomlinson, BA Hons London, ACMA

Head of Prep School: Mr S Cartwright, BSc Surrey

Assistant Head Director of Studies: Mrs K MacDonald, BA Hons, PGCE PQH NI Belfast

Assistant Head Pastoral, Deputy DSL Child Protection, Registrar: Mr A D Petty, BA Wales, FRSA

Priest in Residence: Revd Father P H Lyness, MA Rhodes

Senior Teacher in Charge of Religious Life, Charities Coordinator: Mrs P Peirce, BD AKC London

Director of Activities, Educational Visits Coordinator, CAS Coordinator, Head of Boarding, Head of Girls Boarding & DofE Coordinator: Miss E Cobb, BSc Liverpool

Head of Estates: Mr K Coleman, MBIFM

Human Resources Directors:
Mrs H Duffy, LLB Hull, PGDL
Mrs L Nice, BA Hons Herts

Director of the International Department: Miss C M Hugo, Cert Ed Newcastle, Dip RSA

Deputy Head of St Edmund's Prep, DSL Child Protection, Head of Academics: Dr F J F McLauchlan, MA PhD Cantab (*Director of Music and Performing Arts*)

Head of Music Department Performance: Mrs K L Salter-Kay, GTCL, LTCL, ALCM

St Edmund's College Teaching Staff:
* *Head of Department*

Art and Design:
*Mrs J Elliott, BA Hons Bristol, PGCE Cantab
Mrs J Morley, BA London, HHD

Business Studies and Economics:
*Miss C McShane, BEd Business Studies Belfast
Mr D R Davies, BSc Plymouth, Cert Prof Practice Boarding Education (*Head of Douglass House*)
Mr C McCauley, BEd Belfast (*Head of Elements*)
Miss C Santos Carro, BA Hons Glamorgan, PGCE Bristol

Design and Technology:
*Miss A M Healy, BA Luton
Mrs J Daly, BSc Strathclyde MFC (*Careers Adviser*)

Drama:
Mr J Bonnett, BA Hons Hull

English:
*Mrs P Ager, BA Hons Middlesex, PGCE Anglia
Mrs E Cartwright, MA Oxon, PGCE Oxon (*Head of Rhetoric & TOK Coordinator*)
Mr J Hayes, MA Oxon
Mrs M McCann, BA London, MA Birkbeck
Miss J McCarthy, BA Hons Lancaster, PGCE Westminster
Mrs P O'Neill, BA Roehampton
Mr A Simmonds, BA MA Keele, PGCE King's

Geography:
*Mr J W Morley, BA London
Mrs C McNiece, BA Hons Belfast, PGCE Dunelm
Mr R M Lewis, BEd Liverpool
Mrs N Pitman, BA Hons Wales, PGCE Bath (*Maternity Leave*)
Mrs T York, BSc Hons Wales, MA Canterbury, PGCE IOE

History:
*Mr J R Stypinski, BA York
Mr D Brett, MA Hons St Andrews, PGCE Leeds
Mrs C McNiece, BA Hons Belfast, PGCE Dunelm
Mr A D Petty, BA Wales FRSA (*Assistant Head Pastoral, Deputy DSL Child Protection, Registrar*)
Miss C Regan, MA Glasgow, PGCE Glasgow

IB Coordinator: Mr R Dexter, BSc Hons, PGCE London

Information Technology:
Director of ICT, Computing and E-learning: Mr K R Fry, BSc Brunel, MSc Herts, PGCE Exeter
Mr B Kovacevic, BSc Middlesex, BSc Croatia

International Department:
Director: Miss C M Hugo, Cert Ed Newcastle, Dip RSA
Mrs E Hawkes, MA Cantab
Mr L Hawkes, MEd Open, BA Hons Open, PGCFSE Open

Languages:
*Mrs V L Jefferies, BA MA Bucharest, MA Sussex
Mrs R Carter, BA Oxon, PGCE Oxon, MA London
Miss A Dunning, BA Bath (*Head of Talbot House*)
Mrs E Franco, MA Leon
Mrs K MacDonald, BA Hons, PGCE PQH NI Belfast (*Assistant Head Director of Studies*)
Ms L Nye, BA Sussex, PGCE Reading
Miss S Rinaldi
Miss M C Simon Licence Bordeaux (*Second in Department*)
Mrs S Theroulde-O'Neill, MA Toulouse
Mrs S Zhivanovich, BA Hons Exeter, PGCE King's (*German Literature IB*)

Language Assistants:
French Assistant: Sira Keita
German Assistant: Brigitte Webster
Italian Assistant: Francesca Camporese
Spanish Assistant: Yuly Gonzalez

Mathematics:
*Mrs R A K West, BEd Exeter

Dr L Banahan, BSc PhD PGD Dublin

Mr M Barber, BA Oxon, MSc Manchester, MA Oxon (*Deputy Head, DSL Child Protection*)

Mrs G A Burrows, BA Essex

Miss L Dunhill, BSc Hons, PGCE Nottingham (*Head of Poynter House*)

Mrs H Fraser, BSc PGCE East Anglia (*Assistant to Director of Studies – Tracking in Bounds*)

Mr N Harding, BA Hons Middlesex, PGCE Bath (*Maths Support/Permanent Supply*)

Mr J Hounsell, BSc BCA Wellington, NZ (*Head of Challoner House*)

Mr S Mohana, BEd MSc Bangalore

Mr G Perkins, MA Cantab, PGCE Greenwich

Mr G West, BSc East Anglia (*Head of Pole House*)

Media Studies:
*Mr L Woodward, BA Hons Bournemouth

Music:
Head of Music Performance: Mrs K L Salter-Kay, GTCL, LTCL, ALCM
Head of Music Academic: Mrs C Noble, BA Hons Exeter, PGCE Canterbury (*Deputy Head of Rhetoric*)
Mr C Benham, BA Colchester

Physical Education:
Miss A Hebdon, BA Hons Brunel (*Acting Head of Girls' PE and Games*)
Mr K D Jones, BA Greenwich (*Head of Boys' PE and Acting Head of Academic PE*)
Mr N J Cattermole, BEd North Staffs
Miss E Cobb, BSc Liverpool (*Director of Activities, Educational Visits Coordinator, CAS Coordinator, Head of Boarding, Head of Girls Boarding & DofE Coordinator*)
Mr A Cunnah, BA Brighton (*Head of Lower School Sport*)
Miss E Wilkins (*Graduate Teacher Trainee*)
Graduate GAP Assistants: Alexandra Heslby, Gurjort Cheema, Mark Irwin, Alex Burgess

Psychology:
*Mrs M Inglessis, BA Dunelm, MA Kent, PGCE London (*Teacher in charge of Staff Development*)
Mr C Hack, BA Hons Dunelm
Miss J-A Maguire, BA Hons Liverpool (*PSHE Coordinator and NQT/GTP Mentor*)

Religious Studies:
*Mr D D'Cruz, BA India, BA Middlesex, PGCE Surrey
Mr G Devine, BEd Belfast (*PSHE Coordinator*)
Mr C Hack, BA Hons Dunelm
Mrs M Inglessis, BA Dunelm, MA Kent, PGCE London (*Head of Psychology, Teacher in charge of Staff Development*)
Miss J-A Maguire, BA Hons Liverpool (*PSHE Coordinator and NQT/GTP Mentor*)
Mrs P Peirce, BD, AKC London (*Senior Teacher in Charge of Religious Life & Charities Coordinator*)
Mr A J D Robinson, BEd Exeter (*Head of Boys' Boarding – Allen Hall*)

Science:
*Miss M Towns, BSc West of England
Miss S Barber, BSc Liverpool, PGCE Manchester
Miss E Baxter, MA Leeds (*Director of Key Stage 4*)
Dr N Cairns, MSc Dunelm
Mr R Dexter, BSc Hons, PGCE London (*IB Coordinator*)
Dr J Eves, BSc Berkeley USA, MSc PhD Dublin (*Gifted and Talented Coordinator*)
Mrs D Mallabone BSc, PGCE Southampton (*Director of Key Stage 3*)
Ms J Marrinan, MA Open, BSc Hons London
Ms A Price, MEng Southampton, PGCE Greenwich
Mr D Webster, BEng, PGCE Science (*Director of Key Stage 5*)

Cardinal Hume Centre, Learning Support:
*Mrs S Nicholson, BA Hons Manchester, PGCE Lancaster
Mrs L Barley (*SEN Assistant*)
Mrs M Sargent, NVQ3 (*SEN Assistant*)
Mrs N Wells (*SEN Assistant*)

Careers:
Mrs J Daly, BSc Strathclyde, MFC
Mrs E Cartwright, MA Oxon, PGCE Oxon (*Head of Rhetoric & TOK Coordinator*)

Librarian:
Mrs J Tyne, BA Newcastle-Upon-Tyne, MCLIP

St Edmund's Prep School:

Head of St Edmund's Prep:
Mr S Cartwright, BSc Hons Surrey

Deputy Head of St Edmund's Prep/DSL Child Protection:
Dr F J F McLauchlan, MA, PhD Cantab

Head of EYFS/Deputy DSL Child Protection:
Mrs V Penfold, BA London Metropolitan (*Maternity Leave*)
Mrs M Murphy, BEd Hons Surrey (*Nursery Teacher*) (*Maternity Cover*)

St Edmund's Prep School Teaching Staff:

Nursery & Reception:
Mrs K Purves, BA Birmingham, EYFS Hertfordshire (*Reception Teacher*)
Mrs M Murphy, BEd Hons Surrey (*Nursery Teacher, Acting Head of EYFS, Deputy DSL*)
Mrs V Penfold, BA London Metropolitan (*Head of EYFS*) (*Maternity Leave*)

Years 1–6:
Mr M Bibby, BA Hons Sunderland, PGCE Liverpool
Mrs G Boulter, Diplôme Universitaire de Technologie France (*French & Humanities*)
Mrs A Chick, BA Hons Bristol, PGCE Bristol (*Prep Learning Support Manager*)
Ms E Christen, BA Hons London, Cert Ed London (*Year 5, Maths*)
Mrs N Crick, BA Twickenham
Mrs A Cutler, BA Leeds (*Year 4, Library*)
Mr G Duddy, BEd Wales (*Year 5, RE, Activities*)
Mr G Goodfellow, BA Northampton (*Year 4, PE/Games, Sports Manager*)
Ms S Harvey, BEd Hons Hertfordshire (*Year 3, Science*)
Mrs R Hunt, BA Lancaster (*Year 1, History*)
Mrs B Frizell, BEd Leicester
Mrs Z Kirton, BSc Hons Derby, MSc London, QTS Herts (*Year 2, Pre-Prep Coordinator*)
Mrs C Mitton, BEd Cantab (*Years 2, 4 & 5*)
Mrs E Roper, BA Surrey (*Art*)
Miss K Simpson, BA Bradford (*Year 6, ICT*)
Miss J Warnes, BA Cantab (*Year 3, English*)

Nursery and Teaching Assistants:
Mrs S Brown
Miss C Dee (*Art, Tea-timers Club Worker*)
Mrs A Drabwell (*Swiss Level 2, NVQ Level 3 and ASA Level 1 Swim Coach*)
Mrs S Goodfellow, NNEB
Miss L Hyde, BA Hons Herts
Miss L Ingrao, NVQ3 (*Nursery Nurse & Tea-timers Leader*)
Miss C Jacklin, BA Hons Nottingham
Miss S Piacquadio (*Tea-timers Supervisor*)
Mrs S Smith
Mrs V Wilkinson (*Midday Supervisor*)

Technician: Mr C Hull

Swimming Coach: Mrs L Short, Royal Life Saving Society UK – National Rescue Award for Swimming Teachers and Coaches

Admission. Pupils are mainly admitted at the ages of 11, 13 and 16, although entry is always considered at other ages if there are spaces available.

Scholarships. The College offers the following scholarships:

St Edmund's College 11+ Scholarships:

Douay Academic Scholarships are decided by the mark in the 11+ Entrance Exam, the school report, the confidential school report and the interview with the Headmaster.

Old Hall Academic Scholarships are restricted to Catholic students who are in a catholic school (and have been for the last two years). As above, this award is decided by the mark in the 11+ entrance exam, the school report, the confidential school report and the interview with the Headmaster or Registrar.

All Rounder Scholarships are decided by interview, school report, confidential report and mark in the Entrance Exam. For this award, the child will be competent academically and also be able to make a substantial contribution to other areas of life at St Edmund's. This will be as agreed with the Headmaster but contributions might be to one or more aspects, such as drama, music, technology, the Catholic life of the College, specialised sports or outdoor pursuits.

Art Scholarships are decided by examination of a portfolio and a test. Scholars are required to make a significant contribution to the artistic life of the College.

Music Scholarships are decided by audition and include the provision of free tuition in two instruments. Scholars will normally be required to play two instruments with at least one to a high standard (voice can be counted as one instrument).

Music Exhibitions may also be awarded which give free tuition in either one or two instruments. Those in receipt of Music Scholarships and Exhibitions are required to make a significant and sustained contribution to the musical life of the College.

Sport Scholarships are decided by open competition and references from sport clubs or teachers where the child is already involved in sport at a very high level for example County level. Scholars will be expected to play a full and sustained role in the sporting life of the College.

The closing date for Year 7 scholarship applications is in November for entry the following September.

St Edmund's College 13+ Scholarships:

Students will sit an examination in English and Mathematics with an assessment in the relevant field if the application is for Music, Art or Sport.

Academic Scholarships are decided by the mark in the 13+ Entrance Exam, the school report, the confidential school report and the interview with the Headmaster.

Music Scholarships are decided by audition and include the provision of free tuition in two instruments. Scholars will normally be required to play two instruments with at least one to a high standard (voice can be counted as one instrument).

Art Scholarships are decided by examination of a portfolio and a test. Scholars are required to make a significant contribution to the artistic life of the College.

Sport Scholarships are decided by open competition and references from sport clubs or teachers where the child is already involved in sport at a very high level for example County level. Scholars will be expected to play a full and sustained role in the sporting life of the College.

The closing date for Year 9 scholarship applications is in December for entry the following September.

Sixth Form Scholarships:

At 16+, the Cardinal Allen Academic Scholarships are decided by open competition using the results of specially set scholarship examinations, interview and previous school reports. Candidates for these scholarships would be expected to achieve all A/A* grades in their GCSEs. Music, Sport and Art scholarships may also be offered through competitive test.

The closing date for Year 12 scholarship applications is in October for entry the following September.

Bursaries. We also offer a limited number of means-tested Bursaries at 11+, of up to 100% of fees. The closing date is in November.

Further details are available from the Admissions Office on 01920 824247.

Fees per term (2014–2015). College: Day Pupils: £4,876–£5,238; Weekly Boarders: £6,944–£7,905; Full Boarders: £7,728–£8,836.

There are reductions for siblings and for sons and daughters of serving members of the Armed Forces.

Curriculum. All pupils follow the National Curriculum. At the end of NC Year 11, pupils take GCSE examinations in all courses that they have followed, usually more than is required by the National Curriculum.

In Rhetoric (Sixth Form) students will study four AS Levels in the Lower Sixth and 3 or 4 A2s in the Upper Sixth. Tuition is provided for entry to Oxford, Cambridge and other Universities.

Religious Instruction. St Edmund's is a College for all those who appreciate the values of a Catholic Education. All students receive instruction in Christian doctrine and practice from lay teachers. Importance is attached to the liturgical life of the College and the practical expression of faith. All faiths and denominations are welcomed.

Sport. Great importance is attached to sport and physical education throughout the College. All pupils are required to participate in a variety of sports. The major sports for boys are rugby, football, cricket and athletics, while for girls they are hockey, netball, rounders and athletics. The other sports available are cross-country, tennis, swimming, basketball and badminton. A floodlit Astroturf pitch, large sports hall, indoor swimming pool, tennis courts, fitness room, together with 450 acres of grounds provide excellent facilities.

Extra-Curricular Activities. At St Edmund's we believe our responsibility reaches far beyond the academic success of our students. We have a commitment to the whole person, which is reflected in the broad range of activities on offer to everyone and we wish to encourage the notion that success can be achieved in many ways, not just in the classroom.

Each day between 3.30–4.30 pm, time is set aside for students to pursue an interest or activity. Wednesday afternoons are also dedicated to our activities programme.

The CCF (RAF and Army sections), Community Service and The Duke of Edinburgh's Award Scheme play a prominent part in developing a self-reliant and confident individual.

Careers. There is a Careers teacher and Careers Library. Careers advice is available to pupils from the age of 13. There are regular careers lectures and visits to industry and Universities.

Prep School. St Edmund's also includes a Prep situated on the same estate. It consists of a Nursery, Infants and Junior School for pupils from age 3 to 11, which feeds into the Senior School at 11. The pupils are able to make use of many of the amenities of the Senior School such as the Refectory, Chapel, Swimming Pool and Sports Hall. There is no boarding at the Prep School.

(*For further details, see entry in IAPS section.*)

Charitable status. St Edmund's College is a Registered Charity, number 311073. It aims to provide a Catholic Education for students of all faiths between the ages of 3 and 18.

St Edmund's School
Canterbury

Canterbury, Kent CT2 8HU
Tel: 01227 475601 (Admissions)
          01227 475600 (General Enquiries)
Fax: 01227 471083
email: admissions@stedmunds.org.uk
website: www.stedmunds.org.uk

Motto: '*Fungar Vice Cotis*'

St Edmund's is an independent, co-educational day and boarding school for pupils aged between 3 and 18 years, comprising the Pre-Prep, Junior and Senior Schools. Its aim is to provide varied opportunities for academic, sporting, artistic, musical and dramatic achievement. The school has excellent teaching facilities and numerous options for extra-curricular activities.

First established in 1749 as the Clergy Orphan School in Yorkshire, the School later moved to London and settled in its present location in 1855. The School's commitment to its origins endures, as does its Christian ethos. However, the School welcomes pupils from all backgrounds and places a particularly strong emphasis on pastoral care.

St Edmund's is situated on a beautiful site at the top of St Thomas Hill, adjacent to the University of Kent and over-looking the historic city of Canterbury. It is within easy reach of the towns of East Kent, and is just over an hour from London. The proximity to London's airports, the Channel ports and Eurostar stations at Ashford and Ebbsfleet gives international pupils convenient access to the School.

The school is owned by St Edmund's School Canterbury, a charitable company limited by guarantee, registered in England and Wales.

Patron: The Lord Archbishop of Canterbury

Governors:
Chairman: Mr M C W Terry, FCA
Mr J P W Coleman, LLB
Dr P Eichorn, MD
Mr C Harbridge, FRICS, FCIA, ISVA
The Revd Canon C Irvine, MA, BTh
Mrs M L Lacamp, CertEd London, DipRSA
Mrs N Leatherbarrow, BSc, MBA
Dr L Naylor, BSc, PhD
Mr M Punt, MA, MSc
Mr S M Sutton, BA, FCA
Councillor P A Todd
Col P R M Whittington, FCMI
Mrs S J Winning, BA Hons, FCA

Head: Mrs L J Moelwyn-Hughes, MA Cantab, MEd

Master of the Junior School: Mr R G Bacon, BA Hons Dunelm
From September 2015: Mr M Jelley, BA Hons UEA, PGCE

Head of the Pre-Prep School: Mrs J E P Exley, BEd Hons CCCU

Chaplain: The Revd M S Bennett, MusB Hons Canterbury NZ, BA Hons CCCU

Bursar and Clerk to the Governors: Mr R S Smith

Deputy Head Curriculum: Mr E G O'Connor, BA Cantab, MPhil Oxon, MEd Cantab

Assistant Head Pastoral: Mr L A Millard, BSc Loughborough, PGCE

Assistant Director of Studies: Mrs J J Mitchard, BSc Hons London

Head of Departments:
[1] Department serving both Senior & Junior Schools

[1]*Art*:
Mrs A A Slater-Williams, BA Hons Glasgow School of Art, PGCE

Business Studies and Economics:
Mr R N Comfort, BSc Hons Wales

Curriculum Support:
Mrs A E Bensberg, BSc LSE, MA UCL, CELTA Cantab

Drama and Theatre Studies:
Mr M Sell, NCDT Acc Diploma ALRA, PGCE (*Director of Drama*)

English:
Mr J P Dagley, MA, PGCE Oxon, MA Kent

EAL:
Mrs H E Copland, TESOL Trinity College

Film Studies:
Dr M G Caiazza, BA MSMC, MA Kent, PGCE, PhD Kent

[1]*Geography*:
Miss D T Burren, BSc Hons Middlesex, PGCE

History/Politics:
Mr D J Morrissey, BA Hons, MSc Keele, PGCE

IT Coordinator:
Mrs J J Mitchard, BSc Hons London

Latin:
Mrs A I Heavens, MA Hons St Andrews, PGCE

[1]*Mathematics*:
Dr E R Jones, BSc Wales, MSc Liverpool, PhD Wales

Modern Languages:
Mrs D F Micheloud, BA Hons Kent, MA Fribourg, Dip MG (*Head of French*)

[1]*Music*:
Mr F G Murton, BMus, LRAM, LTCL, ARCO (*Director of Music*)

Personal, Social and Health Education:
Mrs D F Micheloud, BA Hons Kent, MA Fribourg, DipMG

Physical Education:
Mr A R Jones, BSc Sheffield

Psychology:
Dr C F Sotillo, MA, PhD Edinburgh

Religious Studies:
Mrs V A Gunn, BA OU, BA Kent, MA Kent

[1]*Science*:
*Dr L J Ashby, BSc, PhD London

Biology:
Dr G Jones, MBChB Hons Birmingham, PGCE Warwick

Chemistry:
Dr L J Ashby, BSc, PhD London

Physics:
Dr J C Horn, BSc Hons, PhD Leeds

[1]*Technology Design, Graphics, Food*:
Ms K Lloyd, MSc CCCU

Junior School:
Second Master: Mr R A Austen, BEd Hons Bulmershe
Director of Studies: Mrs E A Swallow, MA, BEd Dunelm
Senior Master: Mr T Hooley, MA Cantab
Head of Lower School: Mrs M Yearsley, BA Hons London, PGCE

Support Staff:
Senior School Librarian: Ms L Toogood
Medical Officer: Dr G Manson

Head's PA: Ms E Ottaway, BA
Junior School Master's Secretary: Mrs Y King
Head of Admissions: Mrs A Selmon

(*Please refer to the school website for full staff list*)

St Edmund's is a distinctive and historic boarding and day co-educational school where a family atmosphere is fostered, individuals are valued, the spiritual element is explored, and pupils enjoy a rich academic and cultural experience. We are committed to producing happy and successful pupils who can access a high quality education, while enjoying a wealth of stimulating and exciting extra-curricular activity. Set within a beautiful and extensive green field site affording spectacular views of the city and Cathedral of Canterbury, St Edmund's not only enjoys a stunning location, but also offers a happy, vibrant and creative environment within a supportive community.

The school offers a nurturing, yet challenging, environment where an emphasis is placed upon academic rigour and extra-curricular involvement. Its extra-curricular provision is broad, but also encourages excellence in each individual area. Its tradition of housing and educating the Choristers of Canterbury Cathedral brings much to the richness and diversity of our community.

Academic standards are set high. Its dedicated and talented teaching and support staff work alongside pupils to encourage them to develop into caring, resourceful and confident young men and women who are well equipped to tackle the demands of the modern world.

Organisation. The Pre-Prep, Junior and Senior Schools are on the same site and are closely integrated, using the same Chapel, music and art facilities, theatre, dining hall, science laboratories, sports facilities, and so on. However, for practical day-to-day purposes the Junior School is under the control of the Master of the Junior School and the Pre-Prep under the Head of Pre-Prep. St Edmund's derives much of its strength and its capacity to work efficiently and economically from its close-knit structure.

The Senior School is divided into four Houses: Baker, Wagner, Warneford and Watson, the respective Housemasters each being assisted by a team of Deputies and Tutors.

The Chapel. All pupils attend at least two of the morning services a week. Confirmation is conducted annually by the Archbishop of Canterbury (as Patron of the School) or by the Bishop of Dover acting on his behalf; the candidates are prepared by the School Chaplain. The School Carol Service is held in Canterbury Cathedral, by kind permission of the Dean and Chapter.

Buildings and Facilities. Over the past twenty years there have been extensive additions to and modernisation of the school's buildings and facilities: a new Junior School building, a new Sixth Form Centre, the main hall with tiered auditorium and exhibition area, the sports hall, the technology department, additional classrooms and major extensions to the science, art, information technology, and the Pre-Prep School, as well as the conversion of all Senior School boarding accommodation to study-bedrooms and refurbishment of Junior boarding premises. Recent additions include a purpose-built music school, new recreational facilities for Senior School boarders, Gorsefield boarding house and a refurbished library. In September 2013 additions included an Astroturf pitch, new medical centre, upgrading of classrooms, boarding and House facilities.

Academic Organisation. At St Edmund's, the academic expectations are high. The breadth and balance of the academic programme exceeds the requirements of the National Curriculum and pupils begin to be grouped by ability while they are in Junior School. This approach encourages children to apply their talents and aptitudes with diligence and perseverance. Comprehensive reports are sent regularly throughout the school year. A system of interim reports, as well as regular parents' meetings, ensures close communication with parents.

Pre-Prep School: The Pre-Prep School has its own classroom buildings and playground, creating a warm, secure and friendly learning environment in which pupils can develop to the full. The happy and purposeful atmosphere helps pupils develop their confidence.

The School has a wide range of excellent activities and teaches a broad-based curriculum that emphasises academic development as well as art, music, drama and sport. The teachers have many years' experience of working with Early Years' children and the small classes allow staff to focus on the needs of every pupil.

Junior School: The aim of the Junior School is to produce independent learners who are confident and motivated. In Forms 3 to 5, the National Curriculum is broadly followed and, while placing particular emphasis on English, Maths and Science, there is also focus on subjects such as Art, French, Geography, History, Information Technology, Latin and Music. Subject specialists teach Forms 6 to 8, helping to prepare pupils for Senior School. Music (from Form 3), Technology and Art (from Form 6) and Science (from Form 7) is taught in specialist facilities.

The House system gives older pupils the opportunity to experience the skills of organisation, cooperation and leadership, by helping and encouraging younger members of their Houses and assisting with the organisation of House teams and events. Taking on more responsibility and developing greater initiative is valuable in smoothing their passage to Senior School.

Choristers: The 25 choristers of Canterbury Cathedral are all members of the Junior School. They board in the Choir House (in the Cathedral Precincts) in the care of Houseparents appointed by the school. All their choral training is undertaken in the Cathedral by the Master of Choristers and Cathedral Organist; the remainder of their education takes place at St Edmund's.

Senior School: In the first year of the Senior School (Year 9) pupils follow a core curriculum in English, Mathematics, French, Physics, Chemistry, Biology, History, Geography, Art, Music, Information Technology, Religious Education, PSHE, Physical Education, and Technology. Drama, Spanish and Latin are options.

GCSE core subjects are: English, English Literature, French, Mathematics and the three (separate) Sciences. Options include Latin, Spanish, Arabic, Greek, History, Geography, Art (Ceramics), Art (Drawing and Painting), Technology: Resistant Materials, Food Technology, Graphic Products, ICT, Music, Drama and Religious Studies.

The following subjects are offered for AS/A2 Level examinations: Art, Biology, Business Studies, Ceramics, Chemistry, Classical Civilisation, Design and Technology, Economics, English Literature, Film Studies, French, Geography, Government and Politics, History, Mathematics and Further Mathematics, Music, Music Technology, Photography, Physics, Psychology and Theatre Studies. Pupils in the Lower Sixth are expected to study four AS Levels, most then proceeding to three A2 subjects in the Upper Sixth. In addition to their A Level choices, Lower Sixth pupils also attend Study Skills and General Studies classes and have the option to undertake an EPQ (Extended Project Qualification).

Careers and Higher Education. The School is affiliated to the Independent Schools Careers Organisation and the Careers Research and Advisory Centre. Pupils have the opportunity to undergo careers aptitude testing in the GCSE year, and all pupils are assisted in finding a placement for a week or more of work experience in the GCSE year. The careers and higher education staff give all possible help in the finding of suitable careers and in selecting appropriate universities and colleges of further education. Most A Level candidates go on to degree courses after leaving school; others join Art or Music conservatoires.

Music. Music is woven into the fabric of school life at St Edmund's, reinforced by the presence of the Canterbury

Cathedral Choristers. In the purpose-built Music School, specialist teachers give lessons to pupils from Form 1 through to the Sixth Form. Pupils of all ages participate in numerous musical ensembles which cater for a range of vocal and instrumental abilities. As a result, there is an exceptional practical examination record, with more than 80% of entrants achieving Distinction or Merit. Over twenty-five concerts and performances take place each year, from the Pre-Prep's 'Little Voices' festival and small lunch-time recitals in the Recital Hall to large gala concerts in Canterbury Cathedral. The school acts as a focus for musical excellence for children throughout East Kent and enjoys a creative partnership with the English Chamber Orchestra.

Performing Arts. Dramatic performance is included in the curriculum from the earliest years. Every term, the Pre-Prep School holds thematic drama workshops. Pupils in Junior and Senior Schools participate in school plays and other performances with vitality and enthusiasm, as an outlet for expressing their talents in acting, dancing, singing, music, choreography and technical production. The consistently outstanding GCSE and A Level results are testament to the emphasis placed on drama within the curriculum and school life in general.

Art. The emphasis St Edmund's places on creative subjects means that art is embedded in the curriculum across the three Schools. Pupils studying Art and Design enjoy excellent facilities and teaching. Drawing, painting, print-making, photography (traditional and digital), sculpture and ceramics are offered to pupils in the Junior and Senior Schools.

Sport. Association football, hockey, cricket, athletics, tennis, squash and (for girls) netball and rounders are the principal sports but there are opportunities for many other forms of exercise, including cross-country running, indoor rowing, golf, badminton, basketball, volleyball, swimming and gym-based fitness training. There is an astroturf pitch and large playing fields that adjoin the school buildings. There is an open-air heated swimming pool. The sports hall is well-equipped. There are eight tennis courts (both hard and grass), a compact golf course and a rifle range.

Activities. For those in the first four years of Senior School one afternoon a week is given over specifically to a broad range of activities. A number involve helping the local community, while other pupils learn new skills, eg archaeology, broadcasting, Eco-Schools, Japanese language and culture, kite making, literary and debating societies, photography, Rotary Interact and yoga.

In the second year all Senior School pupils join the Combined Cadet Force, a highly successful unit commanded by a member of the teaching staff and administered by an ex-soldier. There is an annual camp in the summer and an adventurous training camp at Easter, attendance at which is voluntary. Cadets may remain in the CCF for the duration of their school career if they wish, and are encouraged to do so if contemplating a career in the armed forces.

Pupils may also participate in The Duke of Edinburgh's Award Scheme and the British Association of Young Scientists. There are regular field trips, choir and music tours, sports tours and many other one-off trips.

In Junior School, too, there is a diverse range of extra-curricular activities, many of which draw on the school's excellent facilities for sport, music and drama. There is a Year 8 outdoor activities week in Spain and an annual sports tour and skiing trip.

Health. The School Medical Centre is staffed by state registered nurses and provides medical care at all times. The health of the pupils is supervised by a senior local general practitioner under the NHS. A counselling service is available.

Admission. *Pre-Prep School*: Entry at any age from 3–7. Once registered, children are invited to visit the School for informal assessment.

Junior School: Entry at any age from 7–12. Candidates will sit entrance tests and all prospective pupils will be interviewed or attend an assessment day.

Choristers: St Edmund's is the school of the Canterbury Cathedral choristers. For details of the voice trials please contact the Master's Secretary.

Senior School: Entry at 13 from preparatory schools is through the Common Entrance Examination. Candidates from other schools will be tested appropriately or sit the School's own entrance tests. There is also a large entry of pupils into the Sixth Form, usually on the basis of interview and GCSE grade estimates from their present school.

Fees per term (2014–2015). Senior School: Boarders £9,927; Weekly Boarders £9,254; Day pupils £6,217.

Junior School: Boarders £6,939, Weekly Boarders £6,323, Choristers £6,651, Day pupils £4,655–£4,737. Pre-Prep: £2,853–£3,298, Nursery £2,323.

Music fees: £232 per term. Extras have been kept to the minimum.

Entrance Scholarships. Competitive scholarships of up to 50% of tuition fees are offered in academic achievement, music, drama and sport at 11+, 13+ and 16+. In addition, art scholarships are available at 13+ and 16+. At the discretion of the Head and the Master, an All-Rounder scholarship may be made to a candidate whose combination of talents merits an award. Such a candidate will have sat the academic scholarship paper and been assessed for a scholarship in at least one other discipline.

Bursaries and Fee Concessions. Originally founded to provide a free education for the fatherless sons of the clergy of the Church of England and the Church of Wales, St Edmund's now accepts applications from boys and girls for Foundationer status. Bursaries to provide a temporary (no more than 12 months) cushion are granted on a means-tested basis to existing pupils. Fee concessions, also means-tested, can be provided to the children of the clergy, members of the armed forces and to the third and subsequent children of the same family in the school at the same time.

The St Edmund's Society (for former pupils). President: Mr E Vant.

Charitable status. St Edmund's School Canterbury is a Registered Charity, number 1056382. It exists to educate the children in its care.

St Edward's, Oxford

Oxford OX2 7NN
Tel: Warden: 01865 319323
            Bursar: 01865 319321
            Registrar: 01865 319200
Fax: 01865 319242
email: wardensec@stedwardsoxford.org
website: www.stedwardsoxford.org

Motto: '*Pietas Parentum*'

St Edward's, Oxford was founded in 1863 by the Revd Thomas Chamberlain. Originally the school buildings were in New Inn Hall Street, Oxford. In 1873 it was removed to Summertown, and the present school was built by the Revd A B Simeon.

Visitor:
The Rt Revd The Lord Bishop of Oxford

Governing Body:
Mike Stanfield (*OSE*) (*Chairman*)
Georgina Dennis, BA, MA (*OSE*)
Louise Fawcett-Posada, MA, DPhil
George Fenton (*OSE*)
Alexandra Holloway, BM, MRCGP
David Jackson, LLB
Chris Jones, MA, FRSA (*OSE*)

Kenneth MacRitchie, MA, BD, LLB
Peter Oppenheimer, MA
Jo Peach, MA, DPhil
Sir Bob Reid, MA
Michael Roulston, MBE, MEd
Charlotte Weston, BA

***Warden*: Stephen C I Jones**, BA, MSc, MLitt, FRSA

Sub-Warden: Thomas A James, BSc, MSc

Deputy Head Pastoral: James E B Cope, BA, MA

Deputy Head Academic: Matthew J Albrighton, BA, MA

Assistant Head Academic: Nicola F Hunter, BA

Chaplain: Revd E Charles Kerr, MA, MTh

Director of Sports and Activities: Andrew Dalgleish, BSc, MSc

Director of Cultural Activities: Neville C Creed, MA

Teaching Staff:

Art:
*Tova Dalgleish, BFA
Jane Bowen, BA
Adam Hahn, BA
Thomas Hunter, MA
Philip Jolley, BA, BEd
Peter Lloyd-Jones, Dip FA
Lorraine Turley, BA
Instructor: Richard Siddons
Technician: Sharon Keen

Classics:
*Mark Taylor, BA
Edmund Hunt, BA, MA
George Macpherson, BA, MA
Jonathan Nelmes, BA
Matthew Parker, MA, MSc
Abbie Stephenson, MA

Design & Technology:
*Ben Pyper, Dip AD
Oliver Barstow, MEng
Laura Marriott, BSc
Sally Spencer, BTEC
Technicians:
Stuart Giles
Susannah Baldwin
Lucian Taylor

Drama:
*Katrina Eden, BA, MA
Rebecca Clark, BA
Simon Roche, BA

Co-Curricular Drama:
*Lucy Maycock, BA, Dip RADA

Economics:
*Jeremy Mather, BA, MSc
Camilla Bacon, BA
Sam Egerton, BA
David Finamore, BSc

English:
*Jason Clapham, MA, MSc
Rachel Bellamy, BA, MA
Ewan Gault, BA, MLitt
Lucinda Gallagher, MA, PhD
John Gidney, MA, Lic Phil
Rose Glendon-Doyle, MA
Nicola Hunter, BA
Zoe Organ, MA, MPhil

Finola Picknett, MA
Millie Pumfrey, BA, MA
Simon Roche, BA

Geography:
*Gavin Turner, BSc, MSc
Matt Albrighton, BA, MA
James Cope, BA, MA
Andrew Dalgleish, BSc, MSc
Richard Howitt, BSc
Garrett Nagle, MA, DPhil
Sue Webb, MA, MA

History:
*Jonathan Lambe
Elizabeth Boast, BA
Alastair Cook, BA, MA
Anna Fielding, BA
Peter Rudge, BA, BA
Fiona Wickens, BA

History of Art:
*Nicola Hunter, BA
Charlotte Schofield, MA

Learning Support:
*Debra Clayphan, BA, MSc
Edmund Edwards, BEd
Joanna Sephton, BA

Mathematics:
*Margaret Lloyd, BSc
Andrea Antoniazzi, MSc, DPhil
Camilla Bacon, BA
Dom Barker, MMath
Henry Chitsenga, BSc
Ashley Currie, MPhys
Andrew Grounds, BA, MSc
Stephen Jones, BA, MSc, MLitt, FRSA
John Simpson, BEng
John Wiggins, MA

Modern Languages:
*Marie-Laure Delvallée, Licence d'Anglais (*French*)
Susan Norton, BA (*German*)
Barry Doherty, BA (*Spanish*)
Stuart Bartholomew, MA

Mary Bradley, BA
Nick Coram-Wright, MA
Jamie Davies, BA
Paula Diaz Rogado, BA
Trevor Hunt, BA, MA
Denise Kohlhepp, MA
Catherine Phillips, BA, MA
Ian Rowley, MA, ALCM
Nicoletta Simborowski, MA
Technician: Robert Warburton
Assistants:
French: Etienne Chaigne-Antoine
German: Michel Santana Rivero
Spanish: Ana Hernandez Botija

Music:
*Alex Tester, MA (*Director of Music*)
Neville Creed, MA
Gabriele Damiani, BMus, ARCO
Richard Powell, GRSM, LRAM, ARCM
Mark Sellen, BA, MMus, ARCM
Assistant: Tomos Watkins

Philosophy:
*Robert Fletcher, BA, MA MLitt
Philip Mallaband, BA, MA, PhD
Jonathan Thomson, BA

Psychology:
Alastair Summers, BSc
Nicholas Gardner, BSc

Politics:
*Robert Fletcher, BA, MA, MLitt
Alastair Cook, BA, MA
Jonathan Thomson, BA

Religious Studies:
*Philip Mallaband, BA, MA, PhD
Charlie Kerr, MA, MTh (*Chaplain*)
Tom Shaw, BA, MA (*Assistant Chaplain*)
Bethany Steer, BA
Jonathan Thomson, BA

Sciences:
*Kendall Williams, BSc, PhD (*Head of Science*)

Biology:
*Richard Storey, BSc
Lucy Baddeley, MA
Louise Bowen, BSc, PhD
Andrew Davis, BSc, PhD, FRGS
Lewis Faulkner, MA, MA
Nicholas Gardner, BSc
Tom James, BSc, MSc
Alastair Summers, BSc
Kendall Williams, BSc, PhD
Technicians:
Beata Kolodziej
Gail Benson

Chemistry:
*Anthony Bullard, BSc, PhD
Louise Bowen, BSc, PhD
Phaedra Gowen, BSc
David Moore, BSc, PhD, AKC, CChem, MRSC
Sophie Pollard, BSc, MRSC
Oliver Richards, MA
Alastair Summers, BSc
Mark Woodward, BSc, PhD
Technician: Judy Roberts

Environmental Science:
*Andrew Davis, BSc, PhD, FRGS
Garrett Nagle, MA, DPhil

Physics:
*Katherine Richard, MPhys, DPhil
Louise Bowen, BSc, PhD
Tanima Choudhury-Fieret, BSc, PhD
Heather Digby, BSc
Natalie McDaid, MSc
Philip Waghorn, BSc, MSc
Judy Young, BSc
Technician: Paul Taylor

Sports Science:
*Becky Bowyer, BSc
Rachel Bellamy, BA, MA
Mark Hanslip, BEd

Houses and Housemasters/Housemistresses:
Cowell's: Nicholas H Coram-Wright, MA
Sing's: Matthew Parker, MA, MSc
Field House: Mark Hanslip, BEd
Macnamara's: Debra Clayphan, BA, MSc
Apsley: Oliver L Richards, MA
Tilly's: Lewis Faulkner, MA, MA
Segar's: Simon J Roche, BA
Kendall: Philip R Waghorn, BSc, MSc
Oakthorpe: Judy Young, BSc
Corfe: Eve Singfield
Avenue: Rachel Bellamy, BA, MA
Jubilee: Phaedra Gowen, BSc

Administrative Officers:
Bursar: Stephen Withers Green, MA, ACA
Registrar: Sarah K Munden, BEd

Examinations Officer: Dr David Moore, BSc, PhD, AKC, CChem, MRSC
Librarian: Marian O Oyedoh, MSc, BSc
Head of Careers: James Vaughan-Fowler

Medical Officers:
Dr Roisin McCloskey, MBChB, MRCGP
Dr Matthew Cheetham, MB, MS
Dr Bridget Geer, MBChB, MRCGP, DRCOG

Ethos. The St Edward's ethos is underpinned by a firm emphasis on the far-reaching benefits of participation and engagement. We ask each of our pupils to engage in their academic work with real belief – in themselves and in their ability to achieve – and we encourage all pupils to take advantage of the many opportunities on offer to them at Teddies. An important touchstone for the St Edward's educational ethos is the conviction that those pupils who derive joy and satisfaction from a wide range of activities outside the classroom are those who go on to perform exceptionally well in their academic work.

History and Development. Founded in 1863, St Edward's moved to its present site of over 100 acres in North Oxford in 1873. The School roll is c680 boys and girls, of whom roughly eighty five percent are full-time boarders. Pupils live in one of 12 houses (five for girls, seven for boys), and in addition to having the run of extensive playing fields, benefit from access to an elegant quad, the Oxfordshire Health and Racquets Club (owned by the school but managed by Virgin Active), the North Wall Arts Centre, the riverside boat house, the golf course and all the amenities of a lively international city. The school has just begun work on a world-class Music School to open in 2016.

Pastoral Care. The comprehensive pastoral care system at St Edward's has long been regarded as one of the school's great strengths – a point highlighted by successive ISI reports. The system is underpinned by a highly-effective network of relationships offering distinct but interwoven levels of care. Each pupil sits at the centre of his or her network, surrounded by a range of people who can offer guidance and support. The Housemaster or Housemistress is a vital member of this web of care and in this role they are supported by an Assistant HM and a Matron. Also key are Tutors who monitor the academic and pastoral life of six to 10 pupils, meeting with them regularly to offer advice as necessary. Within the school community, Sixth Formers are trained to offer a peer listening service and the Head Boy and Girl meet regularly with senior staff to raise any areas of concern.

Academic Work. Academically, it would be hard to overstate the importance to St Edward's of being in Oxford, within easy reach of the rich academic life of the university. Academic endeavour lies at the heart of the school; pupils are expected to work consistently hard, to take responsibility for their own learning and to engage actively in the myriad opportunities open to them for broadening their intellectual horizons. The school offers GCSE (IGCSE in most subjects), A Level with the Extended Project and the IB Diploma. Alongside these qualifications, the school offers its own bespoke courses: the Shell Curriculum in the first year teaches the skills necessary for successful study, the Warden's Project in the Fourth Form introduces the idea of an independent research project and the Taught Skills Course in the Lower Sixth teaches such vital topics as critical thinking, presentation and precis-writing. Learning support is available for pupils who are mildly dyslexic or dyscalculic.

In 2014, 52% of pupils achieved the highest grades in their Sixth Form exams (A*/A at A Level, Levels 6/7 in the IB). 71% of A Level results were awarded within the A* to B grades with 62% of GCSE results graded at A* or A. In the IB Diploma, our average point score was 37.1. On average, some 75% of sixth form leavers take up places at Russell Group universities, including Oxford and Cambridge, and increasingly, pupils look to study overseas. In recent years, pupils have gone on to study at US and Canadian universities, including Georgetown, Washington; Berkeley, California; and McGill, Montreal. Pupils have also been successful in their applications to universities in Hong Kong and Japan, Trinity College Dublin and other European cities.

Higher Education and Careers. The new Careers Department is firmly rooted in the real world of work. Our Head of Careers, a former Head Hunter with first-hand knowledge of a wide range of industries, runs a structured programme. Every Fifth Former benefits from a termly, compulsory careers session to help them identify and secure the most relevant work experience placements. Some 12 or so informal careers receptions are organised each year covering everything from financial services, law, engineering and fashion to marketing services, manufacturing and design.

Higher Education advice is highly personalised and quite exceptional. The new Shell Curriculum is designed to feed directly into their career planning by explicitly teaching the skills required for today's workplace: research, self-regulation, innovative thinking, presentation, collaboration and teamwork. Pupils are given every assistance in choosing the right course of further study and in preparing a strong application, including visits by representatives of UK and US universities, mock interviews and personal statement workshops. Tailored advice is given to Oxbridge and Ivy League candidates, to those aiming for highly competitive courses such as medicine or veterinary science and to those looking to study overseas.

Music, Drama and the Arts. The arts are highly valued at St Edward's. The Music Department delivers about 450 lessons every week, taught by a team of 40 visiting specialists. The main school groups include the Orchestra, Chamber Orchestra, Chapel Choir, Chamber Choir, St Edward's Singers, Concert Band, Big Band, Jazz Band and various Chamber Music groups. There are around 60 concerts a year, with regular foreign tours. The Drama department is flourishing: main school productions, including musicals, are complemented by devised pieces, House plays, Shell plays and a Speech and Drama programme. The Art Department is strong and vibrant, benefiting from recently enhanced facilities and the stream of visiting exhibitions to The North Wall. The Dance programme is extensive, with over 30 classes every week – covering styles from ballet to cheerleading – generating a range of material for the dance shows. In addition, the cutting-edge programming of the award-winning North Wall Performing Arts Centre enriches the cultural life of both the school and the wider community, placing St Edward's at the forefront of development in arts education.

Sport, Games and Activities. A wide variety of sports, games and activities is on offer. We compete at the highest level in several sports and can boast of county and national representatives. We also encourage all our pupils to participate and to enjoy playing at more modest levels. We have fielded as many as 27 teams on one day – over 400 children representing the school. These sports, games and activities include rugby, football, hockey, cricket, rowing, athletics, netball, squash, tennis, swimming, cross-country running, sailing, golf, football, canoeing, ceramics, theatre crew, textiles, cycle maintenance and Community Service. We operate a Combined Cadet Force with Navy, Army and RAF sections, and offer all levels of the Duke of Edinburgh's Award.

Admission to the School. Registration forms can be obtained from the Registrar. There is a registration fee of £75. Places in the School, conditional upon performance in the entrance exam, are offered 18 months before entry at 13+. Boys and girls are expected to take the Common Entrance Examination or Scholarship in their last Summer term at their Preparatory School. Separate assessment arrangements can be made for applicants from schools not preparing candidates for the Common Entrance Examination. Lower Sixth scholarship and entrance examinations are held in November prior to entry; offers of places in the sixth form are subject to good performance at GCSE (at least six B grades and above) and a satisfactory report from the previous school.

Scholarships. Academic, Music, Art, Dance, Drama and Sports Scholarships are available at both 13+ and 16+ entry. In addition All-Rounder Awards are available at 13+.

Academic, Music, Sports and All-Rounder Scholarships, both for entrants at 13+ (into Year 9) and 16+ (into Year 12), can be increased on means testing up to a total of 100% fee reduction. There is no means-tested increase available for Dance, Drama or Art Scholarships.

Academic: Up to fifteen scholarships and exhibitions are available each year. 16+ academic scholarships take place in the November prior to entry in the September, 13+ academic scholarships take place in the March prior to entry.

Music scholarships: Normally candidates will be expected to perform on two instruments and all are encouraged to offer singing. Candidates are also encouraged to offer original compositions.

Dance and Drama scholarships: Candidates for both these awards will be expected to demonstrate considerable natural ability and also confirm that they have begun to reach high standards on the stage.

Music, Dance and Drama 13+ scholarships take place in the January/February prior to entry, 16+ in the November prior to entry.

Art scholarships: Candidates must submit a portfolio of work prior to the assessment. On the day of the award they will be asked to draw from observation and take a simple test to assess colour sense. 13+ scholarships take place in the January/February prior to entry, 16+ in the November prior to entry.

Sport scholarships for both 13+ and 16+ entry take place in the November prior to entry. Candidates will show considerable natural ability in at least one sport. We are particularly looking for players of rugby, cricket, hockey, netball, tennis and rowing.

All-Rounder awards are available at 13+ only. Candidates must be academically sound, expecting to obtain over 65% at Common Entrance, show strong leadership qualities and be able to demonstrate considerable talent in two of the following areas: art, design technology, music, dance, sport or drama. The All-Rounder Award takes place in the February prior to entry.

Bursaries. The School may offer bursaries for children of clergy and university dons at the Warden's discretion.

Fees per term (2014–2015). Boarding £11,111; Day £8,891

Charitable status. St Edward's, Oxford is a Registered Charity, number 309681. The aims and objectives of the school are to provide an outstanding education to pupils between the ages of 13–18 in order to prepare them for happy, fulfilled and productive adult lives.

St George's College

Weybridge Road, Weybridge, Surrey KT15 2QS
Tel: 01932 839300
Fax: 01932 839301
email: contact@stgeorgesweybridge.com
website: www.stgeorgesweybridge.com
Twitter: @sgweybridge
Facebook: stgeorgescollegeuk

Motto: *Amore et Labore*

Founded by the Josephite Community in 1869 in Croydon, the College moved in 1884 to its present attractive grounds of 100 acres on Woburn Hill, Weybridge. Within its particular family orientated ethos, the College seeks to encourage a wide, balanced Christian education in the Catholic tradition encouraging excellence and achievement across a broad spectrum of academic, sporting and extra-curricular activities. Almost all pupils move on to higher education, gaining places at a wide range of institutions including Oxford and Cambridge. The College is co-educational throughout the school.

Governing Body:
Chairman: Mr M Davie

Governors:

Mrs S Bell	Mr J Lewin
Mr D Bicarregui	Mr P Morgan
Mrs L Burrell	Rev W M Muir, CJ
Rev A Cadwallader, CJ	Mrs J Ranson
Mrs D Ewart	Mr J F Rourke
Mr C Jansen	Mrs S Wood

Clerk to the Governors and Bursar: Mr G Cole

Headmaster: Mr J A Peake, MA Oxon, PGCE

Deputy Headmaster: Mr M A Saxon, BA, MA, PGCE (*History*)
Director of Studies: Ms F M May, MA, BA, PGCE (*English*)
Curriculum Coordinator: Mr A M Gunning, BA, PGCE (*Geography*)

Mrs J A Andrew, MA Oxon, PGCE (*Physics*)
Miss S Arif, BSc Hons, MEd, PGCE (*Head of Mathematics*)
Fr Martin Ashcroft, CJ, MA, MA, STB, BPhil, BA, CertEd (*College Chaplain*)
Mr M J Barham, BA Hons, PGCE (*Head of U6th, History*)
Mr A Barton, BA Hons, PGCE (*Music*)
Mrs L Y Batten, BA Hons, PGCE (*Languages*)
Mrs M Bigwood, BSc, HDE (*Mathematics*)
Mr D J Bradford, BHum, PGCE (*Mathematics, i/c Examinations*)
Mr G A Bowman, BSc (*Mathematics*)
Mr M Bryant, BSc Hons, PGCE (*Biology*)
Mr L R Buckingham, BSc, PGCE (*Geography*)
Ms C A Butler, BA, PGCE (*Art*)
Ms A Byrne, BSc, PGCE (*Sport; i/c Girls' Hockey & Girls' Games*) (*to Jan 2015*)
Miss T V Castledine, MA, MMus, FRCO (*Director of Music*)
Mr O J Clayson (*PE/Games; Head of Cricket*)
Miss F D Cormican, BSc Hons, PGCE (*Geography*)
Mrs M Corry, BA Hons, QTS (*English*)
Mr J M Cunningham, BA, PGCE (*Religious Studies, PSE Coordinator, i/c D of E*)
Mr D P Danaher, MTL, BA Hons, PGCE (*Head of Economics & Business Studies*)
Mrs J Davies, CertEd, PG Diploma, AMBDA (*Academic Support*)
Mr J E Davies, BA, PGCE (*Head of Geography*)
Mr T Deive, BA, PGCE (*Head of Languages*)
Miss L L Dowds, BA Hons, PGCE (*Drama*)
Miss E M Duke-Gill, BA Hons, PGCE (*Head of 1st Year, Languages*)
Miss K A Edwards, BA Hons, PGCE (*Drama*)
Mr I C Facey, BSc Hons, QTS (*Technology*)
Miss A Fincher-Jones, BA Hons (*Head of 2nd Year, Girls' Games/PE*)
Mr I Findlay-Palmer, BSc, PGCE (*Head of Physics*)
Mr N J Galanis (*Languages, i/c French*)
Ms P L George, BEd, BA, MA (*Religious Studies*)
Ms S E Goodfellow, MA Oxon, BA Hons, PGCE (*Head of Chemistry*)
Mr A J Graham, BSc Hons, PGCE (*Chemistry/Science*)
Dr F Grant, PhD, BSc, MA, PGCE (*Mathematics*)

Mr P J Graves, BSc, PGCE (*Languages, Head of Activities*)
Mr D A Green, BSc Hons, GTP (*Biology, Acting Head of 4th Year*)
Mrs E Grigsby-Smith, BSc Hons, PGCE (*Mathematics*)
Mr R P Grimmer, BSc, PGCE (*Physics*)
Mr A M Gunning, BA, PGCE (*Curriculum Coordinator, Geography*)
Mrs G Hale, Deug LL France (*Languages*)
Miss S L Hall, BSc, PGCE (*Geography, Head of Lower Section*)
Mrs T A Hall, BSc, MSc, PGCE (*PE/Games, Head of Middle Section*)
Mrs L C Hanlan BA, PGCE (*Languages*)
Mr J J Haskins, BSc Hons, BA Psychology, GTP (*Chemistry*)
Mr G B Hobern, BA Hons, PGCE (*Languages, i/c Latin*)
Mr M D Holland, BA Hons, MEd, PGCE (*English*)
Mr J M Hope, BSc Hons, MPhil, PGCE (*Mathematics, Asst Management of Information Systems*)
Miss N I Houston, BA Hons, PGCE (*Religious Studies, Head of 3rd Year*)
Mr M S Hughes, MA, BA (*Head of Hockey*)
Miss C Hulf, BA Hons, MA, GTP Cert Ed (*Rowing Coach*)
Mrs A S Huysamen, BA Hons, PGCE (*Art*)
Miss S A Kent, MA, PGCE (*History*)
Miss K Kumanan, BSc Hons, PGCE (*Mathematics*)
Mrs S M Knights, BSc, PGCE (*Geography, Head of Careers*)
Mr M P Lakin, MA, BA, PGCE (*English*)
Mrs T M Lambie, BA Hons, PGCE (*Business Studies, Economics*)
Mr F P Laughton, BSc Hons, PGCE (*Biology, Head of L6th*)
Mr R J Lawrence, BA, PGCE (*English*)
Mr J S Mann, BA Music Hons, PGCE (*Head of Strings, Music*)
Miss E M Marshall, BA Hons, PGCE (*History*)
Mr J G Martin, BA, PGCE (*Economics & Business Studies*)
Ms F M May, MA, BA, PGCE (*Director of Studies, English*)
Mr T A McIlwaine, BA Hons, PGCE (*Acting Head of Art*)
Miss S L Morris, BSc Hons, PGCE (*ICT Coordinator, Asst DoS i/c Options*)
Miss S J Napier, BA, PGCE (*Geography*)
Mr M Parnham, BEd Hons, CertEd (*Head of Technology*)
Mr B J Peake, BSc, PGCE (*Physics*)
Miss R A Potter, BSc Hons, PGCE (*Biology*)
Mr A J Reynolds, BA, PGCE (*Director of Sport*)
Mrs H L Robertson, BSc Hons, PGCE (*PE/Games*)
Mr P J Robinson, BEng Hons, PGCE (*Mathematics*)
Mrs S Rowlatt, BA Hons, MA, PGCE, DipLE (*Head of English*)
Mr M A Saxon, BA, MA, PGCE (*Deputy Head, History*)
Mr M A Schofield, MA (*Director of Drama*)
Mrs J M Sciortino Nowlan, BA Hons, PGCE, MPhil (*Head of Religious Studies*)
Mrs I A Seymour, BSc, MSc, GTP (*Mathematics*)
Mrs M D Smith, BA Hons, PGCE (*Head of Sixth Form, History*)
Miss K E Snowden, MA, DMP, CBTS, ARAD Hons (*Assistant Chaplain*)
Mr M T Stather, BSc Hons, PGCE (*Head of Biology*)
Mrs M Strachan, BSc Hons, PGCE (*Mathematics*)
Mr W M Stride, BSc Hons, PGCE (*Mathematics*)
Mr C Tapscott, BA Hons, PGCE (*History*)
Mrs C A Taylor, PhD, MSs, BSc, PGCE (*Science, Mathematics*)
Mrs L K Thomas (*Learning Support Assistant*)
Mr M F Tierney, MChem, PGCE (*Chemistry*)
Mr M P Tiley, MA (*Head of History*)
Miss K E Troisi, BA, MA (*English*)
Mrs S H Turner, MA, BA, PGCE (*Religious Studies, Extension Programme Coordinator*)

Mr N Waight, BA Hons, PGCE (*English, Head of Southcote House*)
Mr G P Walters, BSc (*Biology, i/c Rowing, Head of Petre House*)
Mr J T Ward (*Head Tennis Coach*)
Mr A P Waring, BSc, PGCE (*Biology, Head of Stirling House*)
Mr A B Watters, BA, Dip BA, PGCE (*Politics*)
Mrs J B Weaver, BA Hons, PGCE (*Food Technology*)
Mr I W White, BSc Hons, GTP (*Head of Rugby*)
Mrs K Wilkinson, BSc, PGCE (*Physics*)
Mrs E L Williams, BA Hons, PGCE, GTP Art (*Art*)
Miss L M Willis, BA, PGCE (*Languages*)
Miss C J Wilde, BSc Hons, PGCE (*Chemistry, Head of Kilmorey House*)
Mr A Wingfield-Digby, MA, BA, PGCE (*Head of 5th Year, Geography*)
Mr N Wingrove, BA Hons, PGCE (*Languages*)
Mr O Yanez Vila, BA Hons, PGCE (*Religious Studies*)
Miss C N Yeoman, BA (*PE/Games, Acting Head of Netball*)

Librarian: Mrs I Monem
Head of Marketing and Admissions: Mr R Morris
Headmaster's PA: Miss P Bell
Admissions Manager: Mrs A Welford
Matron: Mrs C Jones

There are approximately 900+ boys and girls in the school.

Admission. Entry is normally at age 11 (First Year), 13 (Third Year) or 16 (Sixth Form). Students are accepted in September each year. Entry is also possible during an academic year if a place is available.

Admissions details may be obtained from the Admissions Department.

Entrance Scholarships. Academic Scholarships are awarded at 11, 13 and for the Sixth Form. Additionally, at age 11 Music and Sports scholarships are offered and at 13 and 16 Music, Drama, Sport and Art Scholarships are offered.

Details of the number of scholarships at each year group, process for application and guidance on expected standards are to be found on our website under the Admissions section. Scholarships are awarded equally to boys and girls and a certain number are allocated to Junior School candidates each year.

Details may be obtained from the website and the Admissions Department.

Bursaries. The College provides short-term financial assistance for existing families who find themselves in difficult financial circumstances. Further information is available from the Bursar.

Assisted Places Scheme. St George's offers financial assistance of up to 100% relief on fees via its means-tested Assisted Places Scheme. The scheme allows families, who would not normally be able to consider the independent sector, to seek a St George's education for their academically able son or daughter. Places are awarded from the age of seven at the Junior School and eleven at the College. As with all applications, children will need to reach the academic entry standards required at both schools. Further information is available from the Admissions Secretary.

Facilities. The Henderson Centre was opened in September 2010. Our new state-of-the-art building provides Sixth Form group and silent study rooms, social space, five History and five Geography classrooms, staff offices and meeting areas. Refurbishment over the past three years has provided modern facilities for Music, Languages, English, Mathematics, Theatre and Technology. There is an extensive Arts Centre, an impressive Library and a large indoor Sports Hall with an adjacent fitness training room. The College has 19 tennis courts, including three international standard grass courts, clay courts and an impressive four-court Indoor Tennis Centre. In addition there are floodlit netball courts, an all-weather athletics track and two astroturf hockey pitches. The College Boat Club is situated nearby on the Thames.

The Curriculum. This is kept as broad as possible up to GCSE, with a balance between Arts and Science subjects. Students usually take a maximum of 10 GCSEs, A level candidates may choose from over 20 subjects. The vast majority of the Sixth Form go on to Russell Group universities including Oxford and Cambridge.

Careers. Guidance is given throughout a student's career but particularly in making GCSE, A level and university choices. The Careers Coordinator has a modern well stocked Careers Room and makes effective use of COA testing, portfolios, work experience, trial interviews, Challenge of Industry days and computer software.

Art. The Art Department attracts large numbers of students at GCSE and A level who achieve consistently high results in public examinations. A large proportion of A level candidates successfully apply to Art Colleges, often each receiving several offers in this highly competitive field.

Music. Music plays a vital part in school life. There is a wide range of music-making encompassing early music, madrigal groups, jazz, rock, African Drumming as well as more traditional ensembles, orchestras and wind bands. The choir and orchestra give regular performances (including radio broadcasts), and tour Europe annually. Tuition is available on all orchestral instruments from a team of 36 visiting specialists who teach over 400 students each week. Students play in youth orchestras including the NYO and have gained scholarships to the major conservatoires.

Responsibility and Service. Many boys and girls are engaged in the care for the elderly at home or in old people's homes, as well as the mentally and physically handicapped. Each Easter and Summer groups of Sixth Formers accompany handicapped people on visits to Lourdes. Students find these activities a rewarding exercise in Christian service. The Prefect system and the mentor system offer positions of responsibility to the oldest students. The Duke of Edinburgh's Award Scheme is encouraged and there is a flourishing College Council.

Pastoral Care. The spiritual, moral and academic wellbeing of the students is the concern of every member of staff at the College. Nearly all staff act as Group Tutors with particular responsibility for the daily care of their students and for forging links with parents. Each Year Group is led by a Head of Year, and the Chaplain has a general pastoral role. All groups have a day of retreat away each year. The College also has four Houses to which the students are affiliated and all students have one period per week as part of their PSE programme.

Extra-Curricular Activities. There is a very wide range of clubs and societies taking place both at lunchtime and after school. In addition to music and sport, a broad range of interests is catered for such as the Science Club, Cookery, Young Enterprise, Philosophy and Model Clubs.

Sport. All students participate and there is a variety of sports: rugby, hockey, netball, cricket, tennis, rowing, and rounders, plus a wide range of other activities such as golf, athletics, badminton, basketball and cross-country. Each student has the opportunity to develop his or her own talents in small coaching groups. The College has its own boat house on the Thames, nineteen tennis courts (including four indoor), two floodlit artificial pitches with viewing stand, floodlit netball courts, six artificial cricket nets, one main pavilion and two smaller cricket pavilions, eight rugby pitches. The College has access to the Junior School heated swimming pool. All facilities are of a very high standard in an attractive setting. Overseas tours to Holland and Malta have been completed recently by hockey and cricket teams. Attendance at national hockey finals is an annual event and the College hosts a very popular U18 Hockey Sixes every year. International honours have recently been gained in hockey, cricket, rowing and tennis.

Junior School. St George's Junior School is located nearby in Thames Street, Weybridge, and is co-educational, catering for boys and girls from 3 to 11.

(*For further details, please see Junior School entry in IAPS section.*)

Fees per term (2014–2015). First and Second Forms £4,870; Third–Sixth Forms £5,550. Lunches £280.

Charitable status. St George's College Weybridge is a Registered Charity, number 1017853, and a Company Limited by Guarantee. The aims and objectives of the Charity are the Christian education of young people.

St John's School

Epsom Road, Leatherhead, Surrey KT22 8SP

Tel:	01372 373000 Switchboard
	01372 385441 Headmaster
	01372 385447 Finance Director
Fax:	01372 353372
email:	school@stjohns.surrey.sch.uk
website:	www.stjohnsleatherhead.co.uk
Twitter:	@StJohnsSurrey
Facebook:	/stjohnsleatherhead

Motto: '*Quae sursum sunt quaerite*' – 'Seek those things which are above'

Founded 1851. Royal Charter, 1922.

St John's School was founded in North London in 1851 for the education of the sons of Anglican clergy. The move to Leatherhead was made in 1872 and a Royal Charter was granted in 1922. St John's School is a co-educational independent School with day, weekly and flexi boarding for boys and girls aged 13 – 18 (11+ from 2016) and now has 659 pupils, including Foundationers (the sons and daughters of clergy).

Patron: HRH The Duchess of Gloucester, GCVO

Visitor: The Most Revd & Rt Hon The Lord Archbishop of Canterbury, DD

The Council:
Chairman: J D Willis, BA
Vice Chairman: P H Thorne, BA (*OJ*)
A M Airey, LLB (*OJ*)
Mrs M A Arnal, BA, MSc, FRSA
T Beckh, MA
The Rt Revd the Bishop of Dorking, I Brackley
P A Crossley, BA, BArch, RIBA (*OJ*)
Mrs S Dickinson, BA
J R Gravett (*OJ*)
Mrs J Harris, BA
H J Malins, CBE (*OJ*)
A J L Peake, FCA (*OJ*)
B Shaw, BSc, MRICS
L F Speller, FCA
N Teunon, MA, ACA
S A Westley, MA, MIMgt
S H L Williams, MA

Finance Director and Secretary to the Council: Mrs Y Dunne, MA, FCA

Headmaster: Martin A R Collier, MA Oxon

Deputy Headmaster: A N J Tate, MA

Director of Education: M W Clarke, BSc

Assistant Head (Co-Curricular): S Y Eales, HDE
Assistant Head (Admissions): Mrs D J Burgess, BSc
Deputy Head (Academic): Mrs E L Pattison, BA
Assistant Head (Academic): A J Lawrence, BA

Academic Departments:
* *Head of Department*
† *Housemaster/mistress*

Art:
*N J Evans, MA
A Crane (*Fellow*)

Classics:
*L D Bastin, BA
Miss J V Glanfield, BA

Design & Technology:
*J Ward, BSc
A Bass, BEd,
   (†*Montgomery*)
A D Mooney, BEd

Drama:
*J R Garbett, BA
Ms K M Hurst, BA
Miss S C Jones, BA
L R Mortell, BA

*Economics and Business
   Studies*:
*R L Davidson, BA
J B Kidd, BA, MA
R G Jones, BA (†*Churchill*)
Mrs L Pedret, BA
Miss L E Moors, BA

English:
*T Smith
N Johnston-Jones, BA
   (†*Surrey*)
J M A Ashton, BA
Miss C E Hughes, MA
Mrs H E Hunter, BA
A P King, BA, FSA Scot

Geography:
*Miss H C A Glass, BSc
Miss A D Rawlings, BSc
R W L Allan, BA, BEd,
   MA (†*North*)
H R Jones, MSci (†*West*)
P C Noble, BSc

Graphics:
*J Ward, BSc
Miss J A Belfrage, BA, MA
P A Simkins, BA
P Thomas, BSc

History:
Martin A R Collier, MA
   Oxon
*N T Whitmore, BA, MA
Miss S D Dixon, BA
M A Sartorius, BA
G Spreng, MA
A N J Tate, MA

ICT:
*A D Mooney, BEd
P Thomas, BSc

Mathematics:
*Mrs R E P Evans, BSc
Mrs L J Parker, BA
   (†*Gloucester*)
M W Bawden, MA
Mrs D J Burgess, BSc
S Blatch, BSc
M W Clarke, BSc
Miss J Fowler, BSc,
   RHBNC

J Nuttall, BSc, PhD, MSc,
   BPhil
Miss C E Reeves, BSc
Miss Z Wang, MBioChem
   (*Fellow*)

Modern Languages:
*G Hicks, BA (*MFL,
   French)
Mrs G White, BA
A C M Vargas, BA (†*East*)
Mrs N Byrne, MA
Miss J C Michael, BA
Mrs E L Pattison, BA
Miss R Serrano Ramirez,
   BA
Miss T Waheed, MA
   (*Fellow*)
G R White

Music:
*N Smith, BA
S B Bland, BA
C Mortlock, MPhil, BA
   (*Fellow*)
J-P G Sutcliffe, BMus

PE:
*C M B Roberts, BA
Miss A M Littlejohns, BA,
   MSc (†*Haslewood*)
S Hughes, BA
Miss L E Moors, BA
N S Platt, BA Ed

Politics:
*J A Thomas, BA, MSc
A N J Tate, MA
N T Whitmore, BA, MA

Psychology:
*Miss J M Day, BSc
Miss C S Finnegan, BSc

Religious Studies:
*G Wade, MA
Miss C L Byfield-
   Densham, BA
S B Bland, BA

Science:
*P Reilly, BSc, MA, PhD

Biology:
*P Reilly, BSc, MA, PhD
Miss C S Finnegan, BSc
O R Cross, BSc
J K M Fulton-Peebles, BSc
Mrs J R Kirk, BSc
M D Lotsu, BSc

Chemistry:
*J H Davies, BSc, MSc
Miss J M Day, BSc
R J Gregory, BSc
T R Leonard, MSc, PhD
Mrs P J Platt, BSc (†*South*)

Physics:
*M Rogers, BSc
D C Atkinson, BSc, MSc
A B Gale, BSc, CPhys,
   MInstP

Dr K L Turnbull, MSc,
   DPhil

Special Educational Needs:
*Mrs L S Culm, MA, BEd,
   RSA Dip SpLD,
   AMBDA
Mrs J H Chaddock, BA

Mrs A C Collier, MA
Mrs B Davies, BSc, MA,
   AMBDA

Library:
Librarian & Archivist: Mrs
   S Todd, BA, MA Ed,
   MCLIP

Admissions Registrar: Mrs S Stuart
HR Manager: Mrs C J Robinson, Chartered MCIPD
Medical Officer: Dr W S R Barr, MBBS, FRCS, MRCGP

Buildings. St John's School occupies a 50-acre site in Leatherhead within easy reach of the M25. The original 19th Century buildings form an open cloistered quadrangle, comprising the boarding and day houses, the Dining Hall, and the Chapel. The School has a Multimedia Studio, a Sixth Form Study Centre, a Performing Arts Centre and Sixth Form Social Centre. The Henry Dawes Centre and the Hamilton Building accommodate classrooms as well as purpose-built design & technology workshops, library, art studios, IT suites and classrooms. The Old Chapel, which was the original chapel located at the front of the School, is a very significant building in the history of St John's and its beautiful refurbishment was completed Spring 2014. It is now used as a multi-purpose venue by the School and the local community. Looking further ahead, a major new science complex is scheduled for completion in September 2015 and the School also has plans for a day house refurbishment and a Junior Social Club in September 2017, with further long-term plans for new indoor sports facilities. From September 2016, the new Lower School will be an integral part of St John's and is to be housed in the refurbished east wing. The purpose-designed and attractive Lower School will include common rooms, work areas, multimedia spaces, changing rooms and an outside recreational area. These current developments are exciting and stand as testament to our ambition.

Houses. The School has three girls houses: South, Gloucester and Haslewood. South and Gloucester offer flexi and weekly boarding options, while Haslewood serves day pupils only. The six boys houses comprise two boarding houses (West and East) and four day houses (North, Surrey, Montgomery and Churchill),

Religion. As a Church of England Foundation, St John's has always had a special place for worship in the life of the School and benefits from a modern chapel on site.

Curriculum. From September 2016 St John's will be opening a Lower School for Year 7 entry. Pupils will follow an imaginative and dynamic curriculum which will allow choice and breadth of opportunity. Pupils will be encouraged to explore their own talents. The core elements of English, mathematics and sciences will be balanced with humanities subjects and modern languages. An emphasis will be placed on the creative disciplines. On entry into the Fourth Form (Year 9), all pupils study English, mathematics, religious education, French, physics, chemistry, biology, geography, history, information and communication technology, art, design and technology, music, Latin or classical civilisation, and Spanish or German.

In Lower Fifth (Year 10), pupils will study English (including literature), mathematics, a modern foreign language (French Spanish or German), science (physics, chemistry and biology) and three other subjects to GCSE. The other subjects studied to GCSE include a second modern language, history, geography, religious studies, Latin, information and communication technology, physical education, design and technology, drama, art, graphic communication and music.

In the Lower Sixth, pupils will begin their AS course, generally choosing four subjects. A wide range of choices is possible from the following subjects: art, biology, business studies, chemistry, design and technology, drama and theatre studies, economics, English literature, French, geography,

German, government and politics, history, information and communication technology, Latin, mathematics, further mathematics, music, music technology, physics, psychology, religious studies, Spanish and sport and physical education. Please check the website for the vast range of current subjects offered since these are regularly reviewed and reflect the demand for specific subjects.

In the Upper Sixth, pupils will generally continue three of their subjects to A Level.

Music. St John's has a strong musical tradition. The Chapel Choir effectively complements worship in Chapel. Many boys and girls study musical instruments and are encouraged to participate in the School orchestra, wind band, string quartets, choral society, chamber choir, jazz band and rock groups. There are regular informal concerts to encourage informal performance.

Art and Design and Technology. As well as providing the facilities for pursuing the academic curriculum, the art and design facilities and the technology workshops are used extensively in co-curricular activities.

Drama. Drama plays an important part in the life of the School, with most boys and girls taking to the stage at some point, in both House Drama competitions and a variety of School productions during the year.

Information and Communication Technology. There is a school-wide network of computers and other ICT resources that support many activities and areas of school life. Interactive whiteboards in every classroom provide an invaluable resource for curricular and co-curricular activities of all descriptions. Computers are available for use throughout the School both during and outside the School day. Pupils and staff have widespread access to the internet for research and preparation.

Debating. The School competes in national and regional competitions and other inter-school events. There are inter-house competitions at junior and senior level each year.

Careers. All boys and girls are advised on their Advanced Level and Higher Education courses. ISCO careers aptitude tests are offered, as are regular careers evenings and visits. There is a work experience programme, business enterprise opportunities and regular careers events for pupils.

Sport. Rugby, football, hockey, cricket, tennis and athletics are the major sports for boys, with hockey, netball, tennis and athletics for girls. The pupils also compete in biathlon, cross-country and shooting and many other sports flourish, including fives, rounders, squash, swimming, sailing, skiing and badminton.

Combined Cadet Force. The contingent comprises RN, Army and RAF sections. Cadets train for the Services Proficiency Certificates and the various stages of the Duke of Edinburgh's Award Scheme. Field Days, Adventure Training expeditions, annual camps and courses are an integral feature of CCF training.

Community Service Programme. The School is rooted in the local community, and as part of their education pupils learn about the value of community and of helping others less fortunate than themselves. At Sixth Form they can be part of the Community Service Unit visiting and helping local able and disabled children on a weekly basis, the elderly and those in less fortunate circumstances than themselves.

Admission. For entry into the Fourth Form (Year 9), each boy and girl applying to St John's will be required to register by 1 November of Year 6, following which candidates will have a pre-assessment the following January. A report and recommendation from the respective feeder school will then be requested. Based on this information a conditional offer may be made. The offer of a confirmed place is subject to achieving 55% at Common Entrance in each subject (or the required standard in St John's own tests for those pupils attending a school that does not offer CE) and also continued positive recommendation from the respective feeder school.

There are also a number of day and boarding places available for boys and girls who wish to enter the School in the Lower Sixth (Year 12). Boys and girls will have an academic assessment and are interviewed in the November before their entry into the Sixth Form to determine whether a conditional place is offered. They will be required to satisfy the School's minimum academic entry requirement.

Foundationers. In accordance with the Foundation of St John's, places are available for sons and daughters of Anglican clergy who are resident in any Diocese of the Church of England or the Church in Wales and who are engaged in the Ministry of the Church.

Scholarships and Bursaries. Scholarships are awarded to pupils at 11+, 13+ and 16+ who demonstrate excellence in academic ability and their particular discipline. Means-tested financial support towards day fees is available for low-income families and in some cases may provide a free place (Albany Award). All applications are subject to annual means-testing and are assessed via completion of a confidential statement of financial circumstances.

Academic:

11+ (from 2016): Assessment of mathematics, English and abilities assessment plus informal interview.

13+: Pre-assessment (maths, English and abilities) in the January of Year 6 along with an interview and report from current school. Co-curricular strengths are taken into account. Common Entrance at Year 8 for those at prep schools where this is taken.

16+: Assessment on predicted GCSE results, interview and references with entry assessments held in early November

All-Rounder: Assessed by general character, academic ability, leadership qualities and a level of excellence in two or more areas of art, design & technology, drama/dance, music, sport, public speaking/debating.

Art, Drama, Design and Technology, Music and Sport: Assessed by audition/assessment and interview together with supporting references.

Scholarship assessments take place in February prior to entry for 13+ and November for 16+.

Means-tested bursaries are available. The value of a scholarship may be supplemented by a means-tested bursary.

Two Albany Awards are available each year. These are free places funded by The St John's Foundation.

Fees per term (2014–2015). Day £7,155 Weekly boarding £9,035.

Charitable status. St John's School is a Registered Charity, number 312064.

St Lawrence College

Ramsgate, Kent CT11 7AE
Tel: 01843 572900 (Principal)
          01843 572912 (Junior School)
          01843 587666 (Bursar and General Office)
          01843 572931 (Registrar)
Fax: 01843 572901 (Principal)
          01843 572913 (Junior School)
          01843 572915 (Bursar and General Office)
          01843 572901 (Registrar)
email: principal@slcuk.com (Principal)
          jsoffice@slcuk.com (Junior School)
          bursar@slcuk.com (Bursar and General Office)
          admissions@slcuk.com (Registrar)
website: www.slcuk.com

Co-educational, Day: age 3–18 years, Boarding: age 7–18 years.

The Council:

President: C Laing

Vice-Presidents:
The Baroness Cox, BSc, MSc, FRCN
¶Sir Martin Laing, CBE, MA, FRICS
G H Mungeam, MA, DPhil
S Webley, MA
The Revd Canon Nigel M Walker
A T Emby, FCA
¶B J W Isaac
M G Macdonald, MA, LLM

Chairman: D W Taylor, MA Oxon, PGCE, FRSA

Members:
¶M Iliff, MSc
G E Page
J B Guyatt, MA
A G Burgess, TCNFF, ACP
J H Tapp, BSc
¶N G Marchant
¶T L Townsend, LLB
C Lawson
A Truphet
M J Bolton, MBE, BA

¶ *Old Lawrentian*

Clerk to the Governors and Bursar: J A Connelly, MA, MBA, BEng, CEng, MIET

Principal: **A Spencer**, MA Oxon, ACA

Deputy Head: D Jackson, BA Durham
Deputy Head (Registrar): S Heard, BA Exeter
Director of Studies: I D Dawbarn, BA York, MSc Oxon (*Head of Careers, Mathematics*)
Chaplain: Revd P R Russell, BA, Dip Theo Min, PG Dip OM, CCCU (*Religious Studies*)

Heads of Department:
A E Bailey, BEd London, MA Sussex (*Head of PSHE, Games, English*)
E Barrs, BA West of England (*Head of Drama*)
C Brown, BA Exeter (*Head of Economics and Business Studies*)
G Burson-Thomas, BSc Nottingham (*Head of Biology*)
M F Ebden, MSc Bristol (*Head of Science, Chemistry*)
A J Fletcher, BEd Bristol, Cert Ed Bristol, Dip Marketing, Dip TEFLA (*Head of EAL*)
S Fraczek, BA Cambridge, MA Durham (*Head of English*)
J Gale, BA Oxon, MA Oxon (*Head of Modern Languages*)
S J Glynn-Brooks, BSc CCCU (*Head of Academic PE*)
J Good, BA Manchester Metropolitan (*Head of Design Technology*)
A J Izzard, BA Chichester (*Director of Sport*)
E Kouthouri, BSc N&C Univ, Athens (*Head of Physics*)
D P Lewis, BA KIAD (*Head of Art*)
T Moulton, BA Leeds (*Head of History, Universities*)
E L Pegden, BSc Greenwich (*Head of Chemistry*)
¶J M Rawbone, BA Leeds, PG Dip Aspergers Sheffield Hallam (*Head of AEN*)
J Van der Byl, BMus Goldsmiths (*Director of Music*)
J E Van-Ebo, BA CCCU, MA CCCU (*Head of Religious Studies*)
N Watts, BA Hons Brighton, QTS (*Head of Geography*)
¶R B Wilkening, BA London, MA Kent (*Head of ICT*)
Mrs W J Wilkening, BSc York (*Head of Mathematics*)

Houses and Housemasters/mistresses:
Lodge: N O S Jones, BA OU (*Examinations Coordinator; PGCE, GTP & NQT Coordinator*)
Tower: G Davies, BSc Hons Cheltenham, PGCE (*Geography*)
Newlands: N Watts, BA Hons Brighton, QTS (*Head of Geography*)

Bellerby: A Izzard (*Pastoral*)
Laing: A E Coe, BA Hons Hull, PGCE (*History, English, PSHE*)
Kirby House (*Middle School*): R E Muncey, BEd Soton (*History, Geography*)
Kirby House Boarding (*Middle School*): D D Spencer, BSc Hons Southampton, PGCE (*Mathematics, Games*)

Junior School
Head: S J E Whittle, BA Hons, PGCE

Number of Pupils. Senior School: 365: 215 boys (122 boarders, 93 day), 150 girls (71 boarders, 79 day).

Junior School: 14 boarders, 180 day pupils (of whom 33 attend the Nursery).

Educating children from the age of 3 to 18 years, this safe and caring school is set in over 40 acres of spacious, stunning grounds which house beautiful old architecture combined with new modern builds and facilities. Founded in 1879, it is home to 550 day and boarding pupils from local, UK and international families and welcomes boarders from 7 years of age.

A medium-sized school – small enough to ensure that individual pupils receive the attention and care they require, but large enough to provide outstanding facilities – and with something of a reputation for punching well above its weight in school competitions!

Academic. St Lawrence has a long record of providing an excellent academic education within a supportive community, but is also modern in its outlook and very well suited to preparing pupils for a rapidly changing world. Class sizes are small and pastoral support is strong. Academic standards are high and impressive results are achieved across all years in the school. An extensive choice of GCSEs and A Levels are offered, with an excellent success rate of pupils going on to their first-choice university.

Boarding. Boarding pupils enjoy a 'home from home' experience, both in terms of comfort and atmosphere. In recent years, a massive programme of investment has created some truly remarkable facilities for boarders, including the opening of a new girls' boarding house in September 2012, and a modern purpose-built home for junior boarders. All senior boarders are housed in single or double rooms with en-suite facilities and younger boarders are placed in rooms of between two and five pupils with modern streamlined en-suite bathrooms.

Facilities & Extra-curricular. Sporting facilities are exceptional and expert coaching is provided at all levels in a variety of disciplines including rugby, netball, hockey, cricket and swimming. The magnificent Sports Centre houses a fitness suite, squash courts, climbing wall, dance studio and a large sports hall for badminton, basketball, etc. Music and drama flourish, enhanced by the new 500-seat Theatre. Alongside the traditional chapel and library sits the school's modern coffee shop and boarders are able to use all of the facilities in the evenings and at weekends. All pupils benefit from an extensive activities programme which includes the CCF (Combined Cadet Force) and the Duke of Edinburgh's Award Scheme, as well as chess, archery, golf, fencing, horse riding, table tennis, musical theatre, and many more activities.

Location. The school is set in a safe, self-contained campus situated within easy walking distance of the historic seaside town of Ramsgate. It has excellent transport links to the continent, being near both Dover and the Channel Tunnel. London is only 75 minutes away by high-speed rail link to St Pancras International. Both Gatwick and Heathrow are under 2 hours away.

Exam Results. Outstanding results are achieved by the most academic students who progress to top universities. The school is also regarded as a centre of excellence for 'value added'; students who need additional support perform well beyond expectation.

2014 GCSE results: 5+ A*-C grades including English and Maths: 72%; A*/A grades: 41%

2014 A Level results: A*/B grades: 48%; A*/A grades: 19%

Admissions. At 11+ admissions are based on an Interview with the Principal. A copy of a recent school report will also be required. Testing will be carried out where appropriate.

At 13+ the offer of a place will be dependent on the Common Entrance Examination, GCSE predictions and/or an assessment of a recent school report.

At 16+ the offer of a place will be dependent on a minimum of 5 GCSEs passes.

EU and Overseas Students will be admitted on the basis of current performance, references and a short language test as interviews are not always possible. Our special EFL centre will assess and integrate overseas pupils into the curriculum by offering a range of English teaching options, including an intensive English course.

Fees per term (2014–2015). Boarders £9,985, Day £5,090–£5,643. Fees are due and payable before the commencement of the relevant school term. St Lawrence College offers generous sibling allowances.

Individual Private Tuition: £49.70 per hour. Individual Instrumental Music: £37.10 per hour.

Bursaries. Parents in HM Forces pay the MOD CEA (Continuity of Education Allowance) plus 10% of our main boarding and tuition fees. Bursaries are awarded annually to pupils in need of financial assistance and who are likely to make a positive contribution to the life of the school. Bursaries may be awarded to new or existing pupils of the College and pupils who have been awarded a scholarship which requires supplementing. Parents may apply to the Governors' Bursary Committee for assistance and will be required to complete a confidential grant application form. Bursaries are means tested.

Scholarships. Academic, Music, Sports and All-Rounder Scholarships are offered to candidates at 11+, 13+ and 16+ for entry into Years 7, 9, and 12. The value of Scholarships ranges from 10% to 50% of the fees.

Charitable status. The Corporation of St Lawrence College is a Registered Charity, number 307921. It exists to provide education for children.

St Leonards School

St Andrews, Fife KY16 9QJ
Tel: 01334 472126
Fax: 01334 476152
email: info@stleonards-fife.org
website: www.stleonards-fife.org

Motto: *Ad Vitam*

Situated in the heart of idyllic St Andrews, St Leonards offers day and boarding education for 5–18 year old boys and girls, combining academic achievement and opportunity with an inspirational atmosphere.

Members of Council:
Chairman: Mr James Murray, MA, LLB, DL
Mr Ian Adam, CA
Mr Hamish Alldridge, MA, DipEd, CertEd
Lord Balniel, BA
Mrs Victoria Collison-Owen, MA
Mr Alan Constable, BSc
Col Martin Passmore, MA, GCGI, FRSA
Mr David Pattullo, MA
Mrs Rosaleen Rentoul
Prof Louise Richardson, BA, MA, MA, MA, PhD
Mr Graeme Simmers, CBE, CA
Mr Aubyn Stewart-Wilson, BSc

Mrs Clare Wade

Academic Staff:

Headmaster: Michael Carslaw, BSc Hons Newcastle, MBA Nottingham, PhD London

Deputy Headmaster & Deputy Head Pastoral: Geoffrey Jackson-Hutt, BSc Hons, PhD Southampton
Deputy Head Academic: Dawn Pemberton-Hislop, BA Hons Sheffield, MBA Keele (*Maternity Leave*)
Deputy Head Academic Acting: John Lambert, MA Hons Dundee
Head of Sixth Form: Karen Wowk, MA Hons St Andrews
Head of Year 10 & Pre IB: Andrew Durward, BEd Hons Edinburgh
Head of Years 8 & 9: Dan Barlow, MA Hons St Andrews

Art & Design:
Donna Rae, MA Glasgow, BFA Chicago
Margaret Behrens, BA Hons Edinburgh, Dip PG Edinburgh
Lisa Ann Donald, BEd Manchester
Linda Jackson, BA Hons DJCA Dundee
Willliam Clark, MA Winchester, BA Hons Dundee

Classics:
Andrew Laing, MA Hons St Andrews
Roseanna Bochenek, MA Hons St Andrews
Maria Franzoni, BA Bolonga, MSc Edinburgh

Economics:
John Lambert, MA Hons Dundee
Paula Prudencio-Aponte, BSc Boliviana, MSc Manchester, MSc St Andrews

English:
Rupert Crisswell, BA York, MEd Cambridge
Jasmine Cortazzi, MA Nottingham, MA Leeds, BA Leeds
Katherine Gilbertson, MA Hons St Andrews – maternity leave
Denise Johnston, BA Hons Cardiff
Mick Kitson, BA Hons Newcastle
Vanessa Samuel, BA Hons Cantab

Geography:
Ben Seymour, BSc Hons UEA Norwich
Shaun Oakey, BSc Hons Plymouth, MSc London
Amy Henderson, MA Hons Dundee

History & Politics:
Mark Dunkerley, BA Oxford
Lorna Greenwood, MA Hons Edinburgh
Susannah Adrain, MA Hons Dundee

ICT:
Christian Hoehn, Dip Ing Dresden
Marcia Julius, BA Maryland, BSc Maryland, MAS Johns Hopkins

Learning Support:
Rona Wishart, MA Hons Edinburgh
Jim Boyle, BA Hons OU, BSc Paisley, MA OU
Lisa Ann Donald, BEd Manchester
Gillian Greenwood, MA Hons Cambridge
Ann Stephens, BEd Dundee

Mathematics:
Graeme Baxter, BSc Hons Aberdeen
Jonathan Edwards, BEd Hons Wales
Paul McDonald, BSc OU, MSc Napier
Louise Toye, BSc Hons St Andrews
Kristina Struck, State Exam MA Berlin
Ann Stephens, BEd Dundee

Modern Languages:
Annabelle Bossard, BA Tours
Rie Adya, BA MA Rissho, MPhil PhD Delhi
Susana Aranzana-Gonzalez, BA, MA, CAP Valladolid
Dan Barlow, MA Hons St Andrews
Anne Bavaj, MA Hons St Andrews

Anna Beck, BA Columbia MBA Cornell
Barbara Beedham, BSc Hons Salford
Sofia Dogan
Irene Kretschmann, BA Bonn
Nora Grannon, Masters History of Law Aix-Marseille
Kathryn McGregor, BA Hons Southampton
Christina Steele, MA Hons St Andrews
Haiyan Wang, BA, MA Sichuan, Chengdu, MSc Dundee
Mario Prisco, MA Hons Napoli
Anouk Vermeulen, BA MPhil Radboud, Nijmegen
Tadeusz Wojtych

Music:
Glynn Jenkins, BA Hons, PhD Mus Exeter
Marjorie Cleghorn, LGSM
Aisling Agnew, BMus Hons, MMus
Robin Bell, BMus Glasgow
Douglas Clark, Dip Mus Ed RSAMD
Martin Dibbs, MA, MLitt St Andrews, DMS
Marie Downes, BA Hons Sussex
Winston Emmerson, BSc Hons Rhodes, MSc, PhD UPE
Andrew Foden, BMus Hons RSAMD
Stuart Foggo
Janice Gibson, ALCM, Dip ABRSM
Simon Graham, BMus Hons, PGDipRNCM, PGDE
Kyle Howie, RSAMD
Kenneth Irons, SADJ
Fiona Love, BMus Hons Glasgow
Dorothy McCabe, GRSM, ARCM, ATCL, CertEd London
Marie McCabe, BMus Hons Napier
Louise Major, BMus, BSc Hons Victoria, PhD Otago
Matthew McAllister, BMus Hons RSAMD
Simon Milton, BSc Reading, MMus Sheffield
Melanie O'Brien, Dip TCL TCM London, ALCM, LLCM
  Napier
Rachel Pettican, BA Applied Music Hons Strathclyde
Lynne Ruark, DRSAM, LRAM Glasgow, CertEd
  Edinburgh
Toni Russell, BA Hons Applied Music Strathclyde

Physical Education:
Isabel Myles, BEd Edinburgh
Mark Baxter, Bed Hons Edinburgh
Rosie Dawson, BA Hons Bangor
Elizabeth Dunsmuir, Dip PE
Andrew Durward, BEd Hons Edinburgh
Neil Ronaldson Dip PE Jordanhill
Harry Scott, BA Hons Birmingham, PGA
ANdrew Turnbull, BSc Napier

Religious Studies:
Gillian Greenwood, MA Hons Cantab

Science:
Catherine Dunn, BSc Hons, PhD St Andrews
Carla Grilli, BSc Hons St Andrews
Charlotte Kirby, BSc Hons St Andrews
Diane Lindsay, BSc Hons Aberdeen
Marlene Lloyd-Evans, MSc, BSc Hons Rhodes SA
Anna Radons-Harris, BSc Hons Lancaster
Aileen Rees, MA Hons Cambridge
Rebecca Cornwell, BSc Durham, MRes St Andrews, CPhys
Alison Hill, MSc Glasgow, BSc Hons Aberdeen PhD
  Belfast
Leanne Hunter Cert HE Open
Elaine Nolan, BSc Hons Liverpool
Gillian Wilson, BSc Glasgow

Theatre:
Nichola Ledger, BEd Hons London
Elizabeth Dunsmuir, DipPE
Laura Stewart, Cert HE Open

St Leonards Junior School:

Headmaster: Andrew Donald, BSc Aberdeen

Deputy Heads:
Julianne Pennycook, BEd Hons Jordanhill
Dianne Cormack, BSc Hons St Andrews
Alison Turnbull, BEd Jordanhill

Lisa Adair-Brown, BA Hons Stirling
Nicola Arkwright, BEd Hons Coventry
Marina Barclay, PDA (*Classroom Assistant*)
Claire Boissiere, MA Hons Dundee
Valerie Donald, MA Hons St Andrews
Anna Fisher, MA Hons Dundee
Charlotte Jackson-Hutt, MA Hons St Andrews
Billie Paterson-Herd, NC Childcare & Education
Kenny McDonald, BEd Dundee
Kathleen McKimmon, BCom Edinburgh
Karen Napier, BSc Abertay
Nicola Nejman, MA Hons St Andrews
Julianne Pennycook, BEd Hons Jordanhill
Theresa Sherrat, MA Hons Edinburgh
Caroline Soutar
Laura Stewart, MA Hons Kent

Bursar: Gerald Brown
Registrar: Caroline Routledge, BSc, PhD

There are approximately 550 pupils in the School with an equal number of boys and girls and more than 130 boarders.

Ethos. Founded in 1877, St Leonards aims to prepare young people for the challenges of life ahead and to provide them with the skills and abilities that will enable them to step into the world with confidence and integrity. We offer a broad, rigorous education and exceptional opportunities, while instilling confidence, responsibility and independence.

Location and Campus. St Leonards combines a beautiful, historic campus with the inspirational buzz that comes from being in the heart of the university town of St Andrews.

The School is situated in a picturesque and secure, self contained campus within the medieval walls of the former St Andrews Abbey. Our campus has served as a place of learning since the 16th century and contains several buildings of historical significance, including our library, a building once used by Mary Queen of Scots as lodgings.

On their doorstep our pupils have golden sandy beaches, historic landmarks, world famous golf courses and the friendly town of St Andrews itself, in which our pupils are made to feel very much part of the community.

St Andrews is only 45 minutes from the cultural highlights and international airport of Edinburgh and just 20 minutes from Dundee (a one-hour flight from London).

Curriculum. The Sixth Form at St Leonards prepares pupils for the International Baccalaureate Diploma and the School is the only in Scotland to have an all IB Diploma Sixth Form.

The Senior School (Years 8–11) prepares boys and girls for GCSEs – typically around ten.

The Junior School (Years 1–7) follows the Curriculum for Excellence 'plus', delivering a seamless and coherent transition into the Senior School.

University Link. The School has close links with the University of St Andrews and each year appoints an Associate Researcher, a postgraduate student who provides a link for the pupils to the research community at the University. St Leonards students also have access to the University Library and regularly attend special lectures.

Sport, Drama, Art and Music. Opportunities in sport, music, drama and art abound. Our pupils regularly enjoy success on the sports field, earning team success and individual recognition in sports including rugby, lacrosse, hockey, tennis and football. They are also encouraged to make the most of living just a few hundred yards from the most famous golf links in the world. The School has close links with SALJGA (St Andrews Links Junior Golf Association).

All pupils have the opportunity to learn a wide variety of musical instruments, leading to ABRSM recognition.

Drama students have the chance to take part in a number of professional quality productions which are staged both within School and in the wider local community. Our Art students show off their inspiring work every year in an exhibition that is open to the public.

Co-Curricular. There is a wide range of activities in which pupils can take part, including Duke of Edinburgh's Award expeditions, falconry classes, rock climbing, skiing and debating. Foreign trips are also regularly organised with recent destinations including New York, Rome, the Italian Alps and Dresden. Community awareness is important at St Leonards and in the past few years our pupils have raised over £30,000 for charity.

Boarding. The School excels in its boarding provision, our boarding houses offering friendly and welcoming 'home from homes'. According to a Care Commission inspection report, St Leonards offers its boarding pupils, "an outstanding, Scottish, boarding experience", with the quality of care and support and the quality of the environment rated as "excellent". Both weekly and full boarding options are available.

Fees per term (2014–2015). Junior School: £2,929 (Years 1–5), £3,283 (Years 6–7). Senior School and Sixth Form: Day £3,999; Boarding £9,753.

Admission. The main ages for intake are Years 1, 4, 7, 8 and 9 and the Sixth Form though applications can be considered at any time during the School year. Bursary support may be given, based on need. Full details are available from the Registrar.

Charitable status. St Leonards School is a Registered Charity, number SC010904.

St Mary's Calne

Curzon Street, Calne, Wiltshire SN11 0DF
Tel: 01249 857200
Fax: 01249 857207
email: admissions@stmaryscalne.org
website: www.stmaryscalne.org
Twitter: @StMarysCalne
Facebook: /stmaryscalne
LinkedIn: www.cgacalne.org/linkedin

Chairman of Governors: Mr S Knight, FRICS

Headmistress: Dr Felicia Kirk, BA University of Maryland, MA Brown University, PhD Brown University

Deputy Head: Mrs D Harrison, MA Cantab

Senior Mistress: Mrs A Davies-Potter, BSc Hertfordshire, MEd Bristol, PGCE

Senior Master: Mr J Rothwell, MA Oxon

Director of Development: Mrs C Depla, MA St Andrews

School Chaplain: The Reverend J Beach, BSc Essex, BA Bristol, MTh Cardiff

Bursar: Mr R Gordon, MA Aberdeen, MBA Edinburgh

St Mary's Calne is a boarding and day school of around 350 girls aged 11–18. Around 80% of the girls board and it is a rich boarding life with all girls taking part in the full curriculum and extra-curricular activities on offer. Situated two hours west of London, escorted travel is provided to and from London and airports at all holidays and exeats.

St Mary's is committed to providing a broad and fulfilling education that will challenge and inspire its pupils, as well as helping them to achieve fantastic public examination results. All girls go on to higher education; the overwhelming majority are awarded places at their first-choice university and approximately 15% go on to Oxbridge every year. A new, purpose-built Sixth Form Centre, a tailor-made lecture programme, a Women in Corporate Culture Conference, debating competitions, careers advice, leadership roles and much more prepare the girls for university and beyond.

Pastoral Care. The school, which has a strong Sixth Form (100+ girls) is renowned for its outstanding pastoral care. Every girl is known and cared for as an individual and has a Tutor to support and guide her through every aspect of school life, from organisational skills and subject choices through to university application. St Mary's organises boarding specifically on the criteria of age. Within the seven residential Houses girls live with their own age group. This offers the maximum opportunity to establish firm friendships and fellowship across the year group which will last throughout school and beyond. Girls are therefore cared for by Housemistresses who are particularly aware of the needs of their charges' own individual age group.

Extra-Curricular Activities. Outside the classroom, there is a wide range of extra-curricular activities. Sport at St Mary's is very successful and there have been many individual and team successes. Large numbers of girls play lacrosse at County level, with many going on to play for the South West, English and Welsh Academy squads and National Teams. Girls compete in Athletics at County, Area and National level and we have a number of International Equestrians. Our cold water specialist has swum the English Channel twice as part of a relay team and raised a significant amount for her chosen charity.

All girls work for the Bronze Duke of Edinburgh's Award with large numbers going on to higher levels. 80% of girls play musical instruments and take part in a wide variety of ensembles, including the award-winning Chamber Choir. Drama productions transfer to the London stage and the Edinburgh Festival Fringe and the department boasts a unique relationship with RADA.

St Mary's offers a holistic education and the girls benefit from trips which enrich this experience. Recent expeditions have included a Chamber Choir trip to Paris, a Classics trip to Sicily, a cultural trip to Nepal, a language trip to Rouen and a Geography trip to Poland. The girls are also involved in an ongoing project working with a charity to help to build a school in Zambia.

St Mary's girls play an important part in the local community; a number of our Sixth Form take part in a mentoring programme with the local Springfields Academy. The girls have also worked together with pupils from Springfields Academy and The John Bentley School, in conjunction with the Calne Music and Arts Festival and Calne Heritage Centre, on a project reflecting on the centenary of the First World War.

Fees per term (2014–2015). Boarding £11,300, Day £8,450.

Scholarships and Bursaries. Scholarships available at main entry points include Academic and All-Rounder, which are means-tested and could be worth up to 40% of the fees; Music and Choral, which receive free musical tuition, and Art, Drama and Sport which are worth £1,000 per annum. Exhibitions may also be available to pupils showing outstanding ability in a single subject. Foundation Scholarships are means-tested and could be worth up to 100% of the fees.

All awards are retained to the end of Sixth Form and are reviewed at regular intervals. Candidates who are successful in gaining an award, but require greater remission in fees in order to be able to take up their place may apply for a means-tested Bursary. HM Forces discounts are available.

Charitable status. St Mary's School (Calne) is a Registered Charity, number 309482 and exists for the education of children.

St Mary's College

Everest Road, Crosby, Merseyside L23 5TW
Tel: 0151 924 3926
Fax: 0151 932 0363
email: office@stmarys.lpool.sch.uk
website: www.stmarys.ac
Twitter: @stmarys_college
Facebook: /stmaryscollegecrosby

Motto: '*Fidem Vita Fateri*'

St Mary's College is an Independent Catholic School for boys and girls of all faiths aged 0–18. We are a thriving community which places a high value on outstanding academic achievement and all-round personal development. Our school is built on strong values which emphasise the importance of caring for others and striving for excellence in all we do. Boys and girls can start at our Bright Sparks & Early Years department (0–4 years) soon after birth and progress to our Preparatory School The Mount (4–11 years) before moving on to the College (11–18 years), where typically they achieve up to 100% pass rates at both GCSE and A Level. Our rich programme of extra-curricular activities equips our pupils with the skills and values which will guide and support them throughout their lives. Scholarships and bursaries are available.

Governors:
Mrs S Ward, FCMA, BSc (*Chair*)

Mr J Dilworth	Mr W Lloyd
Mr C Allmark	Mr D Magill
Mrs M Burrows	Mrs L Martindale
Mr R Burrows	Mr M McKenna
Mr M Campbell	Mrs P Old
Mrs A Daniels	Councillor Mr P Papworth
Mr A Duncan	Mrs H Thompson
Mr J Dutton	Mr M Thompson
Mr B Hicks	Mr C Wright
Councillor Mr J Kelly	

Principal: **Mr M Kennedy**, BSc, MA, NPQH, CChem, MRSC

Deputy Head: Mr F Connolly, BSc

Senior Teachers:
Mrs C Killen, BEd (*Head of Sixth Form*)
Mrs J Thomas, BSc (*Assistant Principal & Head of Middle School*)
Mrs K Lane, BEd (*Head of Lower School*)
Mr N Rothnie, MA (*Extended Learning Coordinator*) (**History*)

Assistant Teachers:
* *Head of Department*

Miss N Addy, BSc (**Biology*)
Mr J Armstrong, BA
Mrs S Bartolo, BEd
Mr A Byers, BA (**Music*)
Mrs C Cahill, BSc
Mrs L Clark, BSc (**Chemistry*)
Mr P Duffy, MPhil (**Religious Studies*)
Mrs K Fallon, BA
Mrs E Ford, BA
Dr A Giafis, PhD (**Mathematics*)
Mr T Hammersley, MSc
Mrs C Hearty, BEd
M Ireland, BEng, MSc (**Design & Technology*)
Mr D Linley, MA
Mrs N Moore (**Classics & Latin*)
Mrs A Nichols, BA
Miss H Orrett, BA
Mr D Rasores-Parry, BA (**Art*)

Mr I Rhead, BSc
Mrs J Sargison, BA (**Geography*)
Miss J Simpson, BA (**Business Studies*)
Mrs A Smith, BA
Mr A Stagogiannis, BA (**Modern Foreign Languages*)
Miss N Sykes, BSc, BA (**Physics*)
Dr J Thorne, PhD
Mrs S Townsley, BSc (**Girls' PE*)
Mr N Vagianos, BSc, MBA (**Information Technology*)
Mr D Williams, BA (**Boys' PE*)

Preparatory Department:
Head: Mr M Collins, CertEd, DipMgt
Deputy Head: Mr J Webster, BA

Assistant Teachers:

Miss J Batisti, BSc	*Claremont House*:
Miss K Blackburn, BA	*Head of Early Years*: Mrs
Mrs J Booth, BEd	A Haigh, BEd
Mr D Cooke, BA	Mrs A Fielding, NNEB
Miss V Johnson, BA	Mrs S Alldritt, NNEB
Mrs V Mason, BA	Mrs S Seiffert, NNEB
Miss S Moran, BA	
Mrs P Macleod, BA	

Numbers. There are 418 pupils in the Senior School and 264 in the Preparatory School. There are no boarders.

Preparatory School. Open to boys and girls up to the age of 11. There is an Early Years Unit (0–4) comprising baby unit and kindergarten. Pupils are admitted to the Preparatory School after an interview at 4, 5 and 6 years of age and by informal assessment during a day visit.

The Mount has a strong family atmosphere, providing a secure and lively environment in which expectations are high. The school takes what is best from the National Curriculum and follows an enhanced programme with greater emphasis on the 3 Rs and fostering self-discipline.

Sciences play an important part in the curriculum. Sport and Music are particularly strong. Tutoring in a wide range of musical instruments is provided. French and Spanish are taught in small groups from Reception.

The Head of the Preparatory School, Mr M Collins, will be pleased to meet you and show you round.

Senior School. Fully co-educational, the Senior School admits pupils at 11 both from The Mount and from primary schools over a wide area. An Entrance Examination is held in January each year. Generally speaking, pupils must be between the ages of 10½ and 12 on 1 September of the year in which they wish to enter the School. Sixth Form entry and entry into other year groups is also possible if places are available. A Registration Fee of £40 is payable with the form of application for admission.

The **Curriculum in the Senior School** includes English Language and Literature, French, German, Spanish, History, Geography, Classical Studies, Latin, Physics, Chemistry, Biology, Mathematics, Information Technology, Art, Music, Drama, Design and Technology and Physical Education. A broad curriculum of 14 subjects is followed for the first 3 years. In the Fourth and Fifth Years, pupils normally take 10 subjects at GCSE, including either single Sciences or Core plus Additional Science, and all pupils study for GCSE Religious Studies and an OCR National qualification in Information Technology. In the Sixth Form there are Advanced courses in all the subjects mentioned above. Business Studies, Psychology, and Theology may also be taken to A Level and all Sixth Formers take A Level General Studies. The Sixth Form options system is flexible allowing combinations of 3 or 4 A Levels.

St Mary's is a pioneer school on Merseyside in the inclusion of **orchestral music** as a normal feature of the School curriculum. All pupils are given the opportunity to play an orchestral instrument. The School Band and Orchestra give an annual Concert in the Liverpool Philharmonic Hall, win regional contests and undertake tours abroad.

Religious Education. Religious Education is a core subject through to GCSE. In the Sixth Form there is the option of Christian Theology A Level. General Religious Education in the Sixth Form is integrated through Outreach Work in the community.

Careers. The College works in partnership with the Independent Schools Careers Organisation. Arrangements are made each year for interviews for Fifth Formers to which parents are invited. Sixth Formers are interviewed several times to help them choose appropriate courses at University or in Higher Education. Advice is given to Third Year pupils in choosing options.

Games. Games periods provide opportunities for Rugby, Cricket, Football, Hockey, Netball, Squash, Golf, Cross-Country, Tennis and Basketball. The main games for girls are Netball and Hockey. There is an adjacent modern Sports Centre.

Activities. Some 40 extra-curricular activities and societies are available, including the Duke of Edinburgh's Award Scheme.

Combined Cadet Force. There is a very active Combined Cadet Force which contains Army and Air Force sections. Membership of the Combined Cadet Force is voluntary.

Fees per term (2014–2015). Senior School £3,338; Preparatory School £2,273.

Open Academic Scholarships. There are up to six Open Scholarships based on performance in the College Entrance Examination, worth up to half fees. The awards are based on academic merit alone and are currently irrespective of income. There is also a small number of Art, Music and Sports Scholarships.

There are also School Assisted Places, known as Edmund Rice Junior Scholarships, at 11+. These are income-related and are open to pupils whose parents' joint income would have brought them within the Government scheme.

Sixth Form Scholarships. Edmund Rice Scholarships (worth approximately 10% of fees) are available on merit, and are awarded on the basis of a Scholarship Examination in January.

Charitable status. St Mary's College Crosby Trust Limited is a Registered Charity, number 1110311. The aims and objectives of the Charity are to advance religious and other charitable works.

St Mary's School Ascot

St Mary's Road, Ascot, Berks SL5 9JF
Tel: 01344 296600 (Main Switchboard)
            01344 296614 (Admissions)
email: admissions@st-marys-ascot.co.uk
website: www.st-marys-ascot.co.uk

Board of Governors:
Chairman: The Lord Hemphill
Mrs A Ayton
Mrs O Berry
Mrs C Colacicchi
Dr A Gailey
Mr P Gaynor
Mr M Hunt
Mr G Jerjian
Professor R Parish
The Revd Dr D Power, BA, BDSTL
Sr M Robinson
Mr V Thompson

Trustees:
Chairman: Mr G van Cutsem, FRICS
Mr M Armour
Mr N Davidson
Baroness S Hogg, MA

Sr C Kenworthy-Browne CJ, BA
Mrs P Mathias
Mr M Milbourn
The Hon Mrs O Polizzi
Mr B Stevens

Senior Management Team:

Headmistress: Mrs Mary Breen, BSc Exeter, MSc Manchester

Deputy Headmistress: Mrs V Barker, BSc Reading, PGCE
Deputy Headmistress Boarding: Mrs E Hewer, MA Cantab, PGCE
Director of Studies: Mrs J McPherson, BA Western Australia, DipEd Edith Cowan, MA Sydney
Head of Sixth Form: Dr G Williams, BA Camb, MA Camb, DEd Cardiff
Bursar: Mr G Brand, BA Leeds

Support Staff:
Mr C Atkinson (*Catering Manager*)
Mrs M Atkinson (*Housekeeper*)
Mrs S Austin (*Weekend Receptionist*)
Miss L Bates (*Weekend Receptionist*)
Mrs R Brand (*Chapel Housekeeper/Resources Assistant*)
Mr T Clark (*Estate Manager*)
Mrs P Dewes, BA Leeds (*Headmistress's PA*)
Mrs F Green (*School Secretary*)
Mrs S Hickmott (*Receptionist*)
Mrs C Holland (*Assistant Registrar*)
Mrs A Hoolan (*Weekend Receptionist*)
Mrs R Johnson (*Estate Manager's Administrator*)
Mrs C Leneghan (*Administrative Assistant to the Development and Alumnae Director*)
Mr R Liles (*Reprographics/Resources*)
Mrs E Mari Sanmillan (*Account's Assistant*)
Ms C Morgan-Tolworthy (*Accountant's Assistant*)
Mrs N MacRobbie, LLB Southampton (*Recruitment Administrator*)
Mrs W Nash, BA London, MEd Cantab (*Development and Alumnae Director*)
Mrs J Osborne (*PA to the Bursar*)
The Revd Dr D Power, BA, BDSTL
Mrs C Roberts, BA Chichester (*Evening Receptionist*)
Mrs C Scott, Lic Phil I Zürich (*Deputy Head's Administrator*)
Mrs S Young (*Registrar*)

Heads of House:
Mary Ward: Mrs K Jenkinson, BSc Nottingham, MA London, PGCE
Babthorpe: Mrs H West, BA Surrey, PGCE
Bedingfeld: Mr T Parsons, MA York and Mrs K Parsons, BA York, MA Warwick
Poyntz: Ms R Toner, BA Cantab, MA London, PGCE
Rookwood: Mrs H Jansen, BEd Central School of Speech & Drama
Wigmore: Mrs V Hutchinson, BA Cork, Dip CompSc, DipEd HDGC and Mr N Hutchinson, GBSM, ARCO, ARCM, LTCL

Pastoral and Residential Staff:
Mrs C Marchant, BA CCAT, PGCE (*Senior Boarding Mistress*)
Mrs M Jemmett, HE Dip Counselling (*Independent Listener*)
Mrs M McGeown, RGN SCM (*Nursing Sister*)
Mrs P Perera, RGN RM (*Nursing Sister*)
Mrs L Steele-Perkins, RGN RM (*Nurse*)
Dr G Tasker, MBRBS, DRCOG, MRCGP, DHC (*School Doctor*)
Mrs E Albery (*p/t*)
Miss J Bennett aka Miss Jane
Mrs C Candappa (*p/t*)
Mrs A Curtis, BA OU, BSc Anglia, PGCE CELTA

Mrs J Furneaux (*p/t*)
Mrs T Geraghty (*p/t*)
Miss K Horwood, BA Plymouth, FRGS
Mrs J Hunt (*p/t*)
Mrs B Lister
Mrs S Malyon, CertEd, MA Ed
Mrs P McKane (*p/t*)
Mrs K Rabey (*p/t*)
Miss V Shipley
Mrs J Shrimpton (*p/t*)
Miss S Strongman
Mrs L Swan (*p/t*)
Miss V Swire
Mrs R Webb (*p/t*)

Graduate Assistants:
Miss E Carlstedt-Duke, BSc UWE
Miss K Chalkley, BA Southampton
Miss F Latham, BA Cantab, MPhil Cantab
Miss S MacGregor, BA Bristol
Miss K White, BSc Cornell

Cover Staff:
Miss K Clements, BSc Brunel (*Cover Supervisor*)
Mrs A Heath
Mrs S McLachlan

Academic Departments:

Art and Design:
Mr M Mitchell, BA Bristol Polytechnic, PGCE (*Head of Department*)
Miss L Clarke
Miss A Czajkowskyj, BA Cardiff, PGCE
Miss L Green, BA De Montfort, Reigate College of Art & Design, PGCE (*Art and Design*)
Mrs X Harrison, BA Wales, PGCE (*Ceramics*)
Mrs G Neville, BA Coventry, MA Edinburgh (*Photography*)
Miss H Oakden, BA Manchester, MA Courtauld (*History of Art*)
Mr T Parsons, MA York (*History of Art*)

Classics:
Mrs L Povey, BA Nottingham, MPhil London (*Head of Department*)
Miss M Fisher, BA Wales, BA OU, ACCEG, PGCE
Mrs A Golding, BA Bristol, PGCE
Miss E Hyde, BA Oxford
Ms I Inskip, BA Oxford, PGCE

Drama:
Ms J Brayton, BA Lancaster (*Director of Drama*)
Mr M Barker (*Assistant Drama Technician*)
Miss B Carr, BA Southampton
Mr C Dexter (*Assistant Drama Technician*) DIP ALRA
Mrs H Jansen, BEd Central School of Speech & Drama
Mrs A McNamara, BA Manchester, MA Ed
Mr I Warboys (*Rose Theatre Manager*)

Economics & Politics:
Mr J Powell, BA Leeds, MSc London, PGCE
Mr D Hillman, BA Oxon, MSc London
Mr P Smith, BA Wales, MA Warwick, PGCE
Dr G Williams, BA Cambridge, MA Cambridge, EdD Cardiff

English:
Mrs H Trapani, BA Leicester, MA Hong Kong, PGCE (*Head of Department*)
Mrs R McGeoch, MA Glasgow, MLitt Bristol, PGCE
Mrs J McPherson BA Western Australia, DipEd Edith Cowan, MA Sydney
Mr T Parsons, MA York (*History of Art*)
Dr D Richards, BA King's College London, MA King's College London, PhD King's College London, PGCE
Ms S Rockell, BEd Bath

Miss D Staunton, BA York, MA York, PGCE
Mrs L Waltho, BA, MLitt Newcastle
Mrs S Whiteside, BA OU

Food Technology:
Ms J Sherrard-Smith, BSc Westminster, PGCE
Mrs S Malyon, Cert Ed, MA Ed

Geography:
Mr J Barker, BA Durham, PGCE
Mrs A Flamson, BSc Manchester Metropolitan, PGCE
Mrs E Veale, BA Stellenbosch, Dip SecEd CapeTown
Mrs E Hewer, MA Cantab, PGCE

History:
Mr P Smith, BA Swansea, MA Warwick, PGCE
Mr D Hillman, BA Oxon, MSc London, PGCE
Miss R Evans, BA Durham, PGCE
Miss H Rider, BA Bath, PGCE
Dr G Williams, BA Camb, MA Camb, DEd Cardiff

ICT & Networking Services:
Ms B Hudson-Reed, BA Natal Univ, HDE, FDE (*Head of Department*)
Mrs V Hutchinson, BA Cork, DipComSc, DipEd, HDGC
Miss V Parsons, BSc Portsmouth
Mr R Wakeford
Mr A West, BA UWE Bristol (*Network Services Manager*)
Mr K Delaney, BSc Wales
Mr P Rai

Mathematics:
Mrs B Breedon, BEd Queen's Belfast, MSc Ulster (*Head of Department*)
Mrs V Barker, BSc Reading, PGCE
Mrs W Dutton, BSc Southampton, PGCE
Mrs K Jenkinson, BSc Nottingham, MA London, PGCE
Mrs J Love, BA Sussex, PGCE
Mrs L Matthews, BEd London
Mrs G Miles, BSc London, PGCE
Mrs S Mwanje, BSc Makerere, MSc Hertfordshire, PGCE
Mr A Mughal, BA Kingston, PGCE

Modern Languages:
Mme E Cook, DEUG Licence Toulouse, AdvDip English Studies, PGCE (*Head of Department, French*)
Mrs R Cabrera, Lic en traducción Granada and GTP, Cilt and Leeds Univ (*Spanish*)
Miss E Caretti, MA Milan, PGCE (*Italian*)
Mrs S Chasemore (*German Assistant*)
Ms T Correa-Sanchez, BA Salamanca (*Spanish*)
Miss S Doyotte, DEUG Nancy, PGCE (*French*)
Mlle V Feuillet, DEUG Licence Maîtrise Sorbonne, PGCE (*French*)
Mrs L Harrison, BA Oxford, MA Oxon, PGCE (*French*)
Mlle M Hervi, Licence Maîtrise Rennes, PGCE (*French*)
Mrs C Marchant, BA CCAT, PGCE (*French & Italian*)
Mlle C Schwaller, BA Lorraine
Mrs S Webb, BA Cantab, PGCE (*German*)

Music:
Mrs A Rees, BA Surrey, MMus Royal Holloway, PGCE (*Director of Music*)
Miss J Green (*Music Assistant*)
Mr N Hutchinson, ARCO, ARCM, GBSM, LTCL
Miss S Jubert, BMus Surrey, PGCE
Mrs L Flockhart (*Secretary*)

Physical Education:
Miss G Eamer, BSc Coventry, PGCE (*Head of Department*)
Mr A Flamson, BTEC Loughborough, CCA Exmouth (*Head of Tennis*)
Mr B Challenger
Miss M Cordoba (*Lifeguard*)
Mrs J Freeme, BEd Johannesburg, PGCE
Miss A Haylett, Dip Sports Psychology Newcastle College

Mr R Huysamen, BSc Stellenbosch, PGCE
Mrs L Lock, BSc Worcester, PGCE
Mrs J Obertell, (*Sports Assistant*)
Miss A Stollery, BSc Birmingham
Miss S Windle, BSc, PGCE De Montfort
Mrs A Wright, BA OU, CertEd Chelsea College
Mrs H Williams, BA Cambridge (*Administrator*)

Religious Studies:
Mr J Ware, BA Oxford, MA Oxford, PGCE (*Head of Department*)
Mr P Golden, BA Stirling, MA London, PGCE
Mrs M-T Slater, BA London, PGCE, DPSE
Ms R Toner, BA Cantab, MA London, PGCE
Mrs H West, BA Surrey, PGCE
Mrs M Vandenberg, BA London, PGCE

Science:
Mrs P Shaw, BSc Leeds, PGCE (*Head of Biology*)
Mrs L Carlsson, BSc London (*Biology*)
Mrs A Curtis, BA OU, BSc Anglia, PGCE CELTA (*Biology*)
Mrs A Finlay, BSc Anglia Ruskin, PGCE (*Biology*)
Mr N Jones, BSc Wales, MSc Wales, PGCE (*Biology*)
Dr D Lampus, MSci Cagliari, PhD Nottingham. PGCE (*Chemistry*)
Mr D Marsh, MChem Surrey, PGCE (*Chemistry*)
Mr D May, BA Manchester, PGCE (*Physics*)
Mr D Riding, MPhys Sheffield, PGCE (*Physics*)
Miss C Roberts, MA Oxon, PGCE (*Chemistry*)
Mrs S Senior, BSc Durham, PGCE (*Physics*)
Mrs J Ford, ONC and HNC Med Lab Sciences (*Senior Technician*)
Mrs S Howard, BSc UMIST, MSc UMIST (*Technician*)
Mrs K Sidhu, BSc Wolverhampton (*Technician*)

Special Needs:
Mrs M Vandenberg, BA London, PGCE
Mrs E Hewer, MA Cantab, PGCE
Dr G Williams, BA Cambridge, MA Cambridge, EdD Cardiff (*Academies & Most Able Coordinator*)

Careers:
Mrs C Norvill, BA Lib, CCEG

Duke of Edinburgh's Award Scheme:
Mrs A Wright, BA OU, CertEd Chelsea College (*Coordinator*)
Mr P Edmunds, CertEd, MA Oxford Brookes
Mrs A Grigg
Ms L Guthrie
Mr N Jones, BSc Wales, MSc Wales, PGCE
Mrs Fran Kenden, CertEd ML
Mrs M Vandenberg, BA London, PGCE
Mr D Wright ML

Exam Office:
Ms A Siddiqui (*Examinations Officer*)
Mlle V Feuillet, DEUG Licence Maîtrise Sorbonne, PGCE
Mr E Smith (*Invigilator*)
Mrs J Stone (*Invigilator*)

Library:
Mrs C Norvill, BA Lib, CCEG

Skills for Life:
Mrs S Malyon, CertEd Gloucs, MA OU

Curriculum Coordinator:
Mrs G Miles, BSc London, PGCE

St Mary's School Ascot is a Roman Catholic boarding school founded by the Religious of the Institute of the Blessed Virgin Mary. St Mary's today is a self-governing, self-financing school.

Founded in 1885, the school is set in 55 acres within easy reach of London and Heathrow and close to the M4, M3 and M25 motorways.

Numbers on roll. Boarders 374, Day pupils 13.

Age range. 11–18.

Method of Entry. 11+ and 13+ School's own examination and interview. There is a small entry at Sixth Form.

Scholarships and Bursaries. At 11+ and 13+ there are three Academic Scholarships available worth 5% of the fees.

At 16+ there is one Academic Scholarship available worth 5% of the fees and the Sixth Form Science Scholarship worth up to 5% of the fees.

One Music Scholarship worth up to 5% of the fees and free tuition on two instruments is awarded annually to a pupil entering the School at 11+ or 13+. Candidates must have qualified to at least Grade V on the first study instrument at the time of application.

One Art Scholarship worth 5% of the fees is awarded annually to a pupil entering the School at 11+, 13+ or 16+.

One All-Rounder Scholarship is is awarded annually to a pupil entering the School at 11+ and another at 13+.

One Sports Scholarship worth up to 5% of the fees is awarded annually to a pupil entering the School at 13+.

Means-tested Bursaries are available. The Sixth Form Ascot Alumnae Association Bursary (means-tested) is awarded annually to a daughter of an Old Girl entering the Sixth Form and is worth 30% of the fees.

Fees per term (2014–2015). Boarders £10,950, Day pupils £7,800.

Curriculum. All pupils follow a broad curriculum to GCSE including Religious Education, English, History, Geography, Maths, Biology, Physics, Chemistry, French, German, Italian, Spanish, Latin, Music, Drama, Art and Design, Information Technology and Physical Education. Tuition is also available in Piano, most String and Wind Instruments, Ballet, Tap Dancing, Speech and Drama, Ceramics and Craft activities, Tennis, Photography.

All pupils are prepared for GCSE at 16+ and typically take 10 subjects.

Sixth Formers have a choice of 25 AS/A2 Level subjects and normally study 4 AS subjects in the lower sixth year and continue with three (or sometimes four) subjects to A2 Level in the upper sixth year. Interview, CV and course choice preparation is offered to all Upper Sixth including Oxbridge candidates. They are encouraged to undertake some of the many extra activities on offer and develop skills outside their A Level curriculum. Sixth Formers also have their own tutor who liaises closely with the Careers Specialist. Careers advice forms an integral part of the curriculum. This is supported by work experience, work shadowing placements and talks from external speakers, including Ascot Old Girls. The majority of Sixth Formers go on to university, and preparation is offered to Oxbridge candidates.

The School is a member of ISCO (Independent Schools Careers Organisation).

Religious Education is an integral part of the curriculum and the chapel holds a central position in the life of the school.

Sport. A varied programme is offered depending on age group. It includes Netball, Hockey, Gym, Swimming, Rounders, Tennis, Squash, Badminton and Athletics.

Purpose-built sports complex with sports hall, dance studio, squash courts and fitness suite. A floodlit 400m athletics track and hockey pitch provides a year-round, all-weather sports facility.

Drama. Performing Arts Centre which includes a flexible auditorium with lighting catwalks and control room with teaching facilities, fully-equipped drama studio and make-up and dressing rooms.

Art, Drama, Music, Science, Modern Languages and English. Specialist buildings are provided for all of these subjects and all pupils are encouraged to develop their musical, artistic, scientific and linguistic skills.

Libraries. The senior and junior libraries form the academic heart of the school. The senior library was built to meet the specific needs of Year 11 and Sixth Form girls and includes seminar rooms, which are used for teaching and careers advice.

Other Activities. Senior pupils are encouraged to participate in Community Service Projects, and those interested may enter the Duke of Edinburgh's Award Scheme. There is a wide range of club activities for all ages, and, as a termly boarding school, generous provision is made for evening and weekend activities.

Charitable status. St Mary's School Ascot is a Registered Charity, number 290286. Its aim is to provide an excellent education in a Christian atmosphere.

St Paul's Girls' School

Brook Green, Hammersmith, London W6 7BS
Tel: School Office: 020 7603 2288
            Admissions: 020 7605 4882
            Business Director: 020 7605 4881
Fax: 020 7602 9932
email: admissions@spgs.org
website: www.spgs.org

Founded in 1904 as one of the first purpose-built schools for girls, St Paul's is a piquant mixture of tradition and innovation. The emphasis on liberal learning established by the first High Mistress, Frances Grey, and Director of Music, Gustav Holst, finds expression today in an academically challenging curriculum, which emphasises intellectual freedom and discovery.

Governors:
Chairman: The Hon Timothy Palmer
Deputy Chairman: Dame Helen Alexander DBE
Mr Mark Aspinall
Ms Kate Bingham
Mr Nicolas Chisholm MBE
Mrs Pauline Davies
Mr Daniel Hodson
Ms Alice Hohler
Mrs Dervilla Mitchell
Miss Cally Palmer CBE
Miss Judith Portrait
Dr Julia Riley
Professor Charlotte Roueché

Clerk to the Governors: Mrs Nicola Goodfellow

High Mistress: Ms Clarissa Farr, MA Exeter

Deputy Head, Director of School:
Mr Paul Vanni, MA London (*Modern Languages*)

Assistant Head, Director of Studies:
Mr Andrew Ellams, MA Oxon (*Economics*)

Assistant Head, Director of Senior School:
Mr Will le Fleming, BA Cantab (*English*)

Assistant Head, Director of Pastoral Care:
Mrs Su Wijeratna, BA Birmingham (*Geography*)

Ms Kathryn Arblaster, BA Oxon, MSc MPhil Imperial (*Biology*)
Miss Elizabeth Armstrong, BSc Exeter, MRes Lancaster (*Geography*)
Mr Tim Askew, BA Oxon (*History*)
Dr Howard Bailes, BA Adelaide, PhD London (*History*)
Miss Helen Barff, BA Goldsmiths College, MA Camberwell (*Art and Design*)
Revd Vanessa Baron, MA Cantab, BSc City (*Religious Studies*)

Dr Julia Barron, BA, MA, PhD University of Wales (*Modern Languages*)
Mr Wayne Barron, BA Cantab (*Classics*)
Miss Sandra Barth, BA Martin-Luther-Universität Halle-Wittenberg (*Modern Languages*)
Mrs Lydia Bartlett, BA Durham (*English*)
Miss Mekhla Barua, BSc Warwick (*Mathematics*)
Miss Jessica Basch, BA Eastern MA Eastern (*Physical Education*)
Mr David Benefer, BA Norwich School of Art (*Art and Design*)
Miss Hannah Betteridge, BA Edinburgh (*Religious Studies*)
Mrs Paola Bianchi, MEng Cagliari (*Mathematics*)
Miss Laurelle Borck, BSport Waikato, NZ (*Physical Education*)
Miss Clare Brashaw, MA Leeds (*Art and Design*)
Mr Jonathan Bromley, BA Oxon (*History*)
Mr Spencer Buksh, BSc London (*Mathematics*)
Mrs Birgit Cassens, MA Christian Albrechts Universitaet Kiel (*Modern Languages*)
Mrs Rachel Chamberlin, BSc Durham (*Geography*)
Ms Mathilde Ciais, BA Toulouse (*Modern Languages*)
Miss Sophie Corthine, BA Durham (*Physical Education*)
Ms Liza Coutts, MA Oxon (*History*)
Mr Ian Crane, BSc Durham (*Mathematics*)
Miss Gill D'Lima, BSc St Andrews (*Mathematics*)
Mr Alexander Daglish, BA Plymouth (*Art and Design*)
Ms Ana Davidoff, MA Kiev (*Modern Languages*)
Ms Suzanne Debney, BA Rose Bruford (*Drama*)
Ms Phoebe Dickerson, BA, MPhil Cantab (*English*)
Mrs Marianna Doria, MChem Oxon, MSc Imperial (*Chemistry*)
Ms Alice Dvorakova (*Modern Languages*)
Dr Beth Eliott Lockhart, BA Texas, MPhil Cantab MPhil, PhD Columbia (*English*)
Mr Anthony Ellison, BSc Nottingham (*Chemistry*)
Miss Katherine Evans, BA London (*History of Art*)
Mrs Danu Fenton, BA Oxon, MA Courtauld (*History*)
Miss Gillian Fisher, MA St Andrews (*Geography*)
Dr Billy Fleming, BSc Dublin, PhD Dublin (*Chemistry*)
Miss Isabel Foley, BA London (*Drama*)
Miss Daniela Footerman, MA Oxon (*Mathematics*)
Miss Kate Frank, BA London, MA London (*Modern Languages*)
Mrs Hannah Fussner, BA Oxon, MA Stanford, USA (*Learning Support*)
Miss Penelope Garcia-Rodriguez, BA Oviedo, Spain, MA London (*Modern Languages*)
Miss Anna Gibbs, BA Oxon (*Economics*)
Ms Blanche Girouard, BA Oxon (*Religious Studies*)
Mr Roger Green, MA Kent (*Mathematics*)
Mr Chris Hack, MSci Cantab (*Physics*)
Mr Martin Hanak-Hammerl, BSc Graz, Austria (*Mathematics*)
Miss Emily Hardy, BA Cantab (*English*)
Miss Elizabeth Hodges, BA Wolverhampton Polytechnic, MA Royal College of Art (*Art and Design*)
Dr Anna Holland, BA Oxon, DPhil (*Classics*)
Ms Susan Joyce, BSc Galway (*Biology*)
Mrs Amy Kember, MChem Oxon (*Chemistry*)
Mrs Manuela Knight, BA Milan (*Modern Languages*)
Dr Kingston Koo, BSc Warwick, PhD London (*Physics*)
Mrs Nina Lau, BSc London (*Biology*)
Mr John Lee, BA Oxon, BA London (*Mathematics*)
Dr Kate Lee, BSc Witwatersrand, MSc Cape Town, PhD London (*Physics*)
Miss Hsiang-Ju Lin, BA Soochow, MA London (*Modern Languages*)
Miss Gill MacMillan, BSc Nottingham Trent (*Physical Education*)
Ms Paula Mahoney-Velez, MA Cordoba (*Modern Languages*)
Mr Rory Malone, BA Harvard (*Economics*)

Ms Silvana Marconini, BA Turin (*Modern Languages*)
Miss Daniella Mardell, MA Cantab, MEd Cantab (*Modern Languages*)
Mrs Hélène May, MA aggregation Sorbonne (*Modern Languages*)
Mr Paul McDonald, BA Oxon, MSc LSE (*Mathematics*)
Mr Richard Michell, BA Bristol, MA Chelsea School of Art (*Art and Design*)
Mrs Jo Moran, BA London (*Information Technology*)
Dr Joanna Moriarty, BSc Birmingham, PhD Reading (*Biology*)
Dr Joshua Newton, BA Reed, PhD Cantab (*History*)
Mrs Irina Ninnis, BA Moscow and London (*Modern Languages*)
Miss Narelle O'Byrne, BPhysEd Otago, NZ (*Physical Education*)
Miss Sarah O'Connor, BA Cantab (*Chemistry*)
Dr Jonathan Patrick, BA, DPhil Oxon (*English*)
Mr Roger Paul, BA Norwich, ARCO (*Music*)
Miss Emma Payler, BSc London (*Biology*)
Mr Tom Peck, BA Manchester (*History and Politics*)
Dr Alexandra Randolph, MA Oxon, PhD Nottingham (*Mathematics*)
Mrs Jocelyne Rapinac, MA Aix-Marseille (*Modern Languages*)
Mr Matthew Reeve, BSc Newcastle (*Biology*)
Miss Jessamy Reynolds, MA St Andrews (*Classics*)
Ms Leonie Rushforth, BA Cantab (*English*)
Ms Carolin Salmon, MA Mainz (*Modern Languages*)
Ms Kaarin Scanlan, BA Bristol (*Physical Education*)
Miss Eliza Scoba, BA Vermont (*Physical Education*)
Mrs Alexandra Shamloll, MA Cantab (*Mathematics*)
Mrs Holly Shao, BSc Hunan, China (*Modern Languages*)
Dr Clare Sharp, MA, DPhil Oxon (*Classics*)
Dr Marcin Slaski, BSc Krakow, PhD Krakow (*Physics*)
Mrs Kate Snook, MA, MPhil St Andrews (*History*)
Ms Claire Suthren, BA Cantab (*Classics*)
Miss Faith Turner, BA York (*English and Drama*)
Dr Damon Vosper Singleton, MMath Oxon, PhD London (*Mathematics*)
Dr Sarah Wah, MA Leeds, DPhil Cantab (*English*)
Mrs Victoria Watkins, BA Lancaster (*Drama*)
Miss Mary Wenham, BA Oxon (*Modern Languages*)
Miss Sydne Wick, BA Queen's University of Charlotte (*Physical Education*)
Mr Gregory Wilsdon, MA Oxon, MBA Stanford (*Classics*)
Ms Kirsten Wilson, BA Oxon (*Geography*)
Ms Jane Zeng, BSc Guangzhan, China (*Modern Languages*)

Director of Music:
Mr Leigh O'Hara, BA York, MMus London
Deputy Director of Music and Head of Singing:
Miss Heidi Pegler, BA Cardiff, LTCL
Head of Keyboard:
Miss Alexis White, BMus RNCM, MMus Eastman School of Music, NY
Head of Strings:
Miss Hilary Sturt, AGSM, ARCM (*Viola and Violin*)
Head of Wind & Brass:
Mr Angus Meryon, BMus, ARCM (*Woodwind*)
Music Department Manager:
Miss Helen Cocks, BMus London

Miss Rose Andresier, LLCM, FRSA (*Guitar*)
Miss Charlotte Ansbergs, LRAM, Dip RAM (*Violin*)
Mr Edward Barry, Dip Mus, LTCL (*Violin*)
Mrs Emily Bates, BA, MSTAT (*Alexander Technique*)
Ms Lisa Beckley, MA Oxon (*Singing*)
Ms Anna Boucher, BA Durham (*Singing*)
Ms Emma Brain-Gabbott, BA Cantab (*Singing*)
Mr Andrew Brownell, DMusA Guildhall, FRCO (*Piano*)
Ms Alexia Cammish, MA Cantab, MA GSMD, LGSMDT (*Horn*)

Mrs Jane Clark-Maxwell, BMus London, AKC, LTCL (*Singing*)
Miss Gillian Cracknell, LRAM (*Piano, Aural*)
Mr Adam Cooke, MusB Manchester, MMus GSMD (*Brass*)
Mr Matthew Dickinson, BA, GGSM (*Percussion, Drum Kit*)
Miss Jane Fisher, LTCL, PGCE (*Flute*)
Mr John Flinders, BA York, LGSM (*Piano*)
Miss Carolyn Foulkes, GRSM, LRAM, ARAM, Dip Adv Studies (*Singing*)
Ms Gill Hopkin, GRNCM, ARNCM, PGCE (*Violin*)
Miss Nicola-Jane Kemp, MA Cantab, MMus Opera RSAMD (*Singing*)
Mr John Langley, BA (*Theory*)
Mr Mornington Lockett, BA (*Saxophone*)
Miss Naadia Manington, BMus, LGSM (*Jazz Piano, Piano*)
Mr Alexander Mobbs, BMus (*Double Bass*)
Miss Amanda Morrison, BA (*Singing*)
Miss Helen Neilson, BSc, PG Dip Adv RCM, MMus (*Cello*)
Ms Jessica O'Leary, BMus, Dip CSM, LTCL, LRAM (*Violin, Viola*)
Ms Emma Ramsdale, GRSM, LRAM, Dip RAM, ARAM (*Harp*)
Mr Daniel Roberts (*Strings*)
Mr Neil Roxburgh, Dip RCM, ARCM, ARCT (*Piano*)
Miss Julie Ryan, ARCM (*Trumpet*)
Miss Rachel Shannon, MA Cantab, RAM (*Singing*)
Miss Erica Simpson, ARAM, ARCM (*Cello*)
Mr James Sleigh, ARCM, Hon ARAM (*Viola*)
Ms Louise Strickland, BMus, MMus, LGSMD (*Recorder*)
Mrs Sarah Stroh, BMus, Dip Dist RAM, LRAM (*Singing*)
Ms Shelagh Sutherland, ARAM, LRAM, STAT (*Piano, Alexander Technique*)
Ms Sarah Thurlow, MMus, Dip RCM (*Clarinet*)
Miss Emma Tingey, LWCMD, ACC PG Dip (*Harp*)
Mr Daniel Tong, BMus, LGSM (*Piano*)
Ms Seaming To, BMus RNCM (*Singing*)
Miss Judith Treggor, BMus Connecticut (*Flute*)
Ms Joanne Turner, Dip RCM, ARCM (*Bassoon, Flute*)
Miss Enloc Wu, ARCM, LRSM (*Piano*)
Ms Masumi Yamamoto, MMus QCGU Brisbane, PG Dip RAM, PG Dip TCM, LRAM (*Harpsichord*)
Mrs Fiona York, AGSM (*Piano*)

Business Director:
Mr Arnold Flanagan, Adv Dip BFM CIPFA

Assistant to the High Mistress: Mrs Lindy Hayward, BA Open

Admissions Officer: Miss Claire Richardson, BA Cantab

Librarian: Mrs Linda Kelley, BA Manchester, MSc UCE

St Paul's is committed to providing an outstanding academic education within a highly supportive environment. Girls regularly achieve exceptional results (over 55% A* in 2014), but the school aims to teach far beyond the prescribed curriculum, endowing girls with a lifelong love of learning and the necessary tools of scholarship and enterprise. It is also the opportunities outside the classroom which make a St Paul's education distinctive. Most of the 100+ clubs and societies are run by pupils – for pupils – and new ones are created every year to reflect passion and demand. Girls are given leadership opportunities and an environment in which to experiment, innovate and push boundaries. Girls follow a traditional liberal education and are prepared for GCSE and IGCSE in Year 11; alternative school-directed courses in art, drama and music are also offered for this age group. Sixth form students study for A Levels and are prepared for university entrance by our specialist higher education and careers advisory team. Virtually all students go on to study at major universities in the UK and the USA, with about 40 per cent going to Oxbridge annually. The creative and performing arts are at the heart of school life. Since its foundation music has always been a particularly strong feature with well over half the student body taking instrumental lessons; there are also multiple orchestras, choirs and ensembles on offer. Art and design benefit from studio and workshop facilities and there are several major exhibitions of students' work every year. Drama enjoys a purpose-built theatre and drama studio and any girl can direct her own production. Indeed, facilities are some of the best offered by a central London school with extensive sporting facilities on site. All girls from Year 7 are placed in small tutor groups of no more than 12 girls to ensure the highest standards of pastoral care. The main ages of admission are 11 and 16. There are currently 740 girls on the roll. The school is committed to making a St Paul's education available to the brightest girls whatever their means and has an active development campaign dedicated to raising funds for that purpose.

Scholarships. *Junior Academic Scholarships* (11+) of a value of £250 per annum are offered to up to four candidates who perform exceptionally well in the 11+ Entrance Examination.

Senior Academic Scholarships and Exhibitions are offered to present students on the basis of academic distinction demonstrated in a project completed at the end of the first year of A Level study.

The Ogden Trust Science Scholarship (16+) is a means-tested award which may be available to a successful senior candidate who is entering the school and who wishes to study Physics and Mathematics. The Ogden Trust has specific criteria and applications for the scholarship are made via the school.

Junior Music Scholarships (11+) of the value of £100 per annum and free tuition in one instrument are awarded to up to four candidates on the basis of practical examination and interview.

Senior Music Scholarships (16+) of the value of £250 per annum and free tuition in two instruments are awarded on the basis of written and practical examinations and interview to up to two internal candidates and two external candidates. External candidates must be successful in the Senior School Entrance Examination.

Senior Art Scholarships (16+) of the value of £250 per annum are offered to up to two internal and two external candidates who are currently in their final GCSE year and who, if applying from another school, have previously been successful in the Senior School Entrance Examination. Candidates take part in a workshop and are also required to submit a portfolio.

Bursaries. *Junior Bursaries* (11+) to a value of up to full fee remission based on proven financial need subject to annual review are available. Candidates must be successful in the 11+ Entrance Examination. The number of Junior Bursaries available each year will vary.

Senior Bursaries (16+) to a value of up to full fee remission based on proven financial need subject to annual review are available for candidates who have been successful in the Senior School Entrance Examination and who are currently in their final GCSE year at another school.

Fees per term (2014–2015). £6,958, including lunches and personal accident insurance, and excluding textbooks. The fees per term for new entrants entering at 16+ are £7,479.

Registration & Examination Fee £125.

Charitable status. St Paul's Girls' School is a Registered Charity, number 1119613, and a Company Limited by Guarantee, registered in England, number 6142007 and is governed by its Memorandum and Articles of Association. It exists to promote the education of girls in Greater London. The sole member of the charitable company is the Mercers' Company.

St Paul's School

Lonsdale Road, Barnes, London SW13 9JT
Tel: 020 8748 9162
Fax: 020 8746 5353
email: reception@stpaulsschool.org.uk
website: www.stpaulsschool.org.uk

Motto: '*Fide et literis*'

St Paul's School was founded in AD 1509, by John Colet, DD, Dean of St Paul's. An ancient Grammar School had previously existed for many centuries in connection with St Paul's Cathedral, and was probably absorbed by Colet into his new foundation. Colet laid down in the original statutes, still preserved at Mercers' Hall, that there should be 'taught in the scole children of all Nacions and Countres indifferently to the Noumber of a CLIII', the number of the Miraculous Draught of Fishes. There are still 153 Foundation Scholars, in a school of 850 pupils, in addition to about 440 pupils in the Preparatory School. Colet appointed 'the most honest and faithfull fellowshipp of the Mercers of London' as Governors of his School. The Governing Body has been extended to include University Governors and other nominees. The School was moved from its original site adjoining the Cathedral to West Kensington in 1884 and to its present position on the River Thames at Barnes in 1968. A history of the school entitled 'A miraculous draught of fishes' by A H Mead was published in 1990.

Governors:
Chairman: J M Robertson, BSc
Deputy Chairman: A Summers, BSc, MSc

Appointed by the Mercers' Company:
L Dorfman, CBE
N A H Fenwick, MA
P Higgins, MA
Professor R Luckin, BA, DPhil
Ms A Macleod, BSc, MA
The Earl St Aldwyn, MA
B Thomas, MA
C J Vermont, MA

Clerk to the Governors: T C Owens, LLB, MSc, ACIS

High Master: Professor M Bailey, PhD, FRHistS

Surmaster: B R Girvan, BA, MEng

Director of Studies: P Woodruff, MA, MSc

Director of Admissions: A J Mayfield, BSc, MSc, DPhil

Director of Learning: S N Hollands, MA

Undermasters:
G L Boss, BA, PGCE, MRes
M G Howat, BA Cantab
P J King, MA
P W Motion, BSc, DipEd
A G Wilson, BA

Housemaster: N G D Watkins, BA

St Paul's School Academic Staff:

Art:
T P M E Flint, MA
Mrs P C Holmes, BA, UED
*N W Hunter, BA Hons, MEd
§Miss E Stravoravdi, MA
I J Tiley, MA, ATC

Classics:
D J Cairns, MA
J T Harrison, BA (*PSHE/Citizenship*)
P J King, MA
*S A May, MA

H Mervis, BA
M O McCullagh, BA, MPhil, PhD
R J Taylor, MA, MLitt
A G Wilson, BA

Drama:
C P Anthony, BA, MA (*also English*)
A J Kerr, MA
*E J T Williams, MA

Economics and Politics:
G L Boss, BA
R A Edwards, MA, MSc
A C G Hibbert, BA, MA
Miss A R M O'Dwyer, BA (*Politics*)
T J Passmore, BA
J P A Pick, BA
*S P Schmitt, BSc
D E Spengler, MSc
A J Sykes, MSc, MA

English:
C P Anthony, BA, MA
A J Broughton, MA
M T Gardner, MA
*T G Hager, MA
P R J Hudson, MA, PhD
Miss J McLaren, MA
B J O'Keeffe, MA
A C Shouler, BA

Geography:
*A P D Isaac, BSc, MSc
P S Littlewood, BSc, MSc, FRGS (*General Studies*)
V J Light, BA
S J Madden, BA, MA
N P Troen, MA, MSc

History:
R A Edwards, MA, MSc
M G Howat, BA
P G P Joy, BA, GDL
A J Kerr, MA, PGCE
Mrs S Mackenzie, BSc, MA
Miss A R M O'Dwyer, BA
N J Sanderson, MA
*G E Seel, MA
N G D Watkins, BA

Learning Support Coordinator:
H J Howard, MA

Mathematics:
R A Barker, BA, PGCE
R J Baxter, BA, PhD
R J Breslin, BA
L Cereceda, MPhys, MSc, PhD
P J Charlton, BEng
H L Croft, BSc
B R Girvan, BA, MEng
C A Harrison, MSc, PhD
T N R Killick, MA, PhD
T H Lyster, BA, MSc
A J Mayfield, BSc, MSc, DPhil
T C I Morland, MA, CMath, MIMA
P W Motion, BSc Massey
J M Ramsden, BSc
D J R Rowland, BA, MMath
M Sheehan, MMath, PhD
M J R Slay, BA, MSc
*O L C Toller, MA
P Woodruff, MA, MSc

Modern Languages:
†P A Collinson, MA
P J C Davies, MA (*Spanish*)
D J M Hempstead, BA, MPhil (*French*)

A F Grogan, BA, PGCE
*S N Hollands, BA, MA
Miss E J James, BA (*German*)
R K Kemal-Ur-Rahim, BA, PGCE
Miss L Lapaire, BA
G C Larlham, BA
D E B Perrin, BA
A T L Tofts, BA
E J T Williams, MA
R A Williams, BA, PGCE

Music:
C M T Greene, BA, MPerf
T Evans, BA, MPhil, PhD
*M D Wilderspin, MA

Physical Education:
S Bill
J R Blurton, BSc
A G J Fraser
W T D Hanson, BA
*R G Harrison, BSc
A Maguire
B J D Rogers, BSc
O Rowat
S Tulley

Religious Studies:
Revd Dr J C Blackstone, BA, PhD
*R A Duits, BA, MPhil, PhD

Sciences:
J R Bennett, DPhil (*Biology*)
Dr F M Burke, BA, PhD
B R Burrows, BSc, MSc
S J Clarke, MChem
P G Deakin, BA, MEng
J A R Gilks, PhD
M O Fitzpatrick, BSc, PhD
S Holmes, MPhys, DPhil (*Physics*)
M L H Jacoby, BSc, MA
B Kremeyer, Dip-Biol
T Lowes, MChem
B C B Martin, BA
T R Orr, MChem
J M Perkins, MPhys, PhD
M P Powell, BSc, PhD
S J Roberts, MA
C N Y A Shammas, BSc, PhD
M J P Smith, MChem (*Chemistry*)
S R Squire, MSc
T N Thomas, BSc, PhD
T E Weller, MSci, PhD
K P Zetie, MA, DPhil, MSc, MInstP, CPhys (*Science*)

Engineering & Technology:
O V Avni, BSc, ARCS (*Electronics*)
R A Barker, BA, MA (*Computing*)
B A J Clark, BA
Miss K N R Douglass, BA
D A Emery
*A Gardam, MSc, PhD, CEng, FIMechE
S W Patterson, MSc, PhD
O J Rokison, MEng

ICT:
D R Smith, MA (*Director of ICT*)
M H Loosemore, MA

Chaplain: Revd Dr J C Blackstone
Finance Director: Ms H Richardson, BCompt UNISA
Chief Operating Officer: E J Flute, MBA, PGCE
Medical Officer: Dr O G Evans, BSc, MBBS, MRCP
Counsellor: Dr R Bor, CPsychol, AFBPsS, UKCP
Librarian and Archivist: Mrs A M Aslett, BA, ALA

Colet Court

The Preparatory School adjoins St Paul's School.
(*For further details see Colet Court entry in IAPS section.*)

Colet Court Academic Staff:

Headmaster: T A Meunier, MA, CChem, FRSC

Deputy Headmaster: C G Howes, MA
Senior Tutor: J Barlow, BSc
Director of Studies: Miss A J Gordon, BA
Head of Juniors: P J Kershaw, BA

Mrs A L Baker, BA	M McRill, BTech, PhD,
Mrs J R Baldock, CertEd	CBiol, MIBiol, NPQH
Ms A Bartlett, BEd	Mrs I E Mitchell, BSc, MA
P J Berg, ARCM, FRCO	Mrs R Moore, BA
Mrs A C Bodley, BSc,	S T Motz, BA
PGDip Law	Mme V C M Nolk, L-ès-L
Miss G M R Christie, BA	J A J Renshaw, MA
Miss A L Cuthbertson, BA,	P H Reutenauer, L-ès-L
MSc	A E R Roberts, BSc
D M Edwards, BEd	Miss S L Sammons, BSc
Miss R Flanagan, BSc	Mr J P Simpson, BA
V C A Fonte, LLCE	T B Taylor, BSc
T W Foster, BA, Dip	G C Tsaknakis, BSc
Acting	Mr G Waterson, BMus
N W Groom, BFA, DipT	Mrs C A B Waterworth,
S J Hamma, BSc	BA
Mrs E L Howe, BA	M J Weeks, BSc
N E L Howe, BEd	Mrs J Waller, MA, PG Dip
R L Humphrey, BA	Law
Miss J P Kinrade, BSc	Mrs J J M Wielebinska, BA
T Laessing, BEng	M J C Young, BA
Miss B Leeney, BA	T S Young, BA

Admission. Application for Admission to St Paul's is to be made via an Application form to be obtained via the School's website. 13+ candidates can register from four years before entry. In the autumn term, three years before entry, they must take the ISEB Common Online Pre-Test. The results of this, together with a detailed report from their current school will be used to select candidates for interview. Boys offered conditional places on the Main List must achieve 70% at Common Entrance Examination in June prior to entry in September. For 16+ applications should be made one year in advance. Further details can be found on the School's website.

There is a registration fee of £175.

A Deposit of one third of the termly day fee is required when a parent accepts the offer of a place for his son after interview. The Deposit will be returnable only if the boy fails to reach the necessary standard in the entrance examination or when the final account has been cleared after the boy leaves St Paul's.

Fees per term (2014–2015). The Basic Fee for St Paul's is £7,264. This covers Tuition, Games, Loan Books, Stationery, Libraries, Medical Inspection, a careers aptitude test in the GCSE year, certain School publications and Lunch, which all boys are required to attend. Charges are made for the purchase of some books (which become the personal property of boys) and Public Examination Fees.

There are facilities for up to 50 boarders (ages 13 to 18) and boarding is flexible allowing boys to go home at weekends as they wish. The Boarding Fee is £10,880 per term.

Bursaries. St Paul's takes pride in giving the best possible education to talented boys, irrespective of their family's financial circumstances. Each year there are funds available for free and subsidised places. Bursaries are means-tested each year and may change as a family's financial situation improves or deteriorates. More information can be obtained from the School's website.

Scholarships. *Foundation Scholarships*: A few Foundation Scholarships may be awarded to 11 year old boys at Colet Court on the basis of examinations. The Scholarship Examination for St Paul's is held in May. Candidates must be under 14 on 1 September. There are 153 Scholars at any given time and about 30 vacancies arise each year. All new Academic Scholarships are honorary, and carry an award of £60 per annum.

Music: A number of Music Scholarships and Exhibitions may be awarded at St Paul's each year. Auditions take place at the beginning of February. Candidates must be under 14 on 1st September following the audition and all boys must be registered for entry to St Paul's to apply for music awards. Candidates are expected to have attained at least Grade 6 standard on their principal instrument.

The Sharp Music Exhibition Award and the Dennis Brain Memorial Exhibition are awarded from time to time to a boy entering St Paul's for his A Level years.

Several South Square Choral Scholarships are awarded to senior boys each year who show full commitment to school choral activities.

Full particulars available from the Director of Music.

Art: One or more South Square Art Scholarships are available each year to boys who have taken GCSE to assist them in following a career in practical art. These scholarships can be awarded for the candidate's A Level course at St Paul's.

Arkwright Scholarships: The School is a member of the Arkwright Scholarship Scheme which offers financial assistance to sixth-formers who intend to pursue a career in Engineering, Technology, or other Design-related subjects.

Leaving Scholarships or Awards. A number of Prize Grants and Exhibitions (including the Lord Campden's exhibitions, founded in 1625 by Baptist Hicks, Viscount Campden) are given by the Governors every year to boys proceeding to Oxford or Cambridge or to any other place of further education.

Curriculum. All boys follow a broadly based course up to GCSE. Thereafter in the Eighth Form, AS and A Level subjects are so arranged that boys can combine a wide range of Arts and Science subjects if they so wish. Boys take four or five AS Level subjects, including the possibility of an Extended Project, followed by three or four A Level subjects.

Games. Games offered include: Athletics, Cricket, Fencing, Fives, Golf, Judo, Rackets, Rowing, Rugby, Sailing, Soccer, Squash, Swimming and Tennis (hard and grass).

The School has its own Swimming Pool, Fencing Salle, Tennis, Squash, Fives and Rackets Courts, and its own Boat House. The Games Centre also comprises a Sports Hall and Gymnasium. The Sports Hall is equipped for Tennis, Badminton, Basketball and indoor Cricket nets. There are Cricket and Rackets Professionals.

Music. All boys are taught music in the classroom in the first year. In subsequent years, GCSE is taught as a two-year course, and AS and A2 Levels are taught in the final two years. Additional tuition is available in piano, organ, all the standard orchestral instruments, and jazz. There are a wide range of ensemble activities – chamber music, jazz and big band, full orchestra, wind/brass/string training orchestras, several choirs and barbershop groups. The music school contains a top quality concert venue, the Wathen Hall, several rehearsal rooms, two large teaching rooms and a music technology suite. There are regular concerts and recitals, as well as music competitions, musicals and cross-curricular opportunities with the drama department.

School Societies. There is a wide choice of more than 30 Societies, including Musical, Artistic and Dramatic activities, Debating, Historical and Scientific Societies, Politics and Economics, Bridge, Chess, Natural History, Photography, European Society, a Christian Union and Social Service.

Colet Court, the Preparatory School to St Paul's adjoins the School. (*For details see entry in IAPS section.*)

Charitable status. St Paul's School is a Registered Charity, number 1119619. The object of the charity is to promote the education of boys in Greater London.

St Peter's School, York

Clifton, York YO30 6AB
Tel: 01904 527300
Fax: 01904 527302
email: enquiries@stpetersyork.org.uk
website: www.stpetersyork.org.uk
Twitter: @stpetersyork
Facebook: /stpetersschoolyork

Motto: '*Super antiquas vias*'

Founded in 627AD, St Peter's is one of the world's oldest schools. It provides outstanding boarding and day education for boys and girls from 13 to 18. Pupils at St Peter's School achieve some of the best grades in the North of England at GCSE and A Level. Its Prep School, St Olave's, admits boarding and day boys and girls from 8 to 13 and Clifton School and Nursery admits day girls and boys from 3 to 8.

Visitor: The Rt Honorable the Lord Archbishop of York

Board of Governors:
Chairman: Mr W Woolley
Vice Chair: Dr D M Hayward
Vice Chair: Mr P B Hilling

Members of the Board

Mr J E B Burdass	Mr J C Morris
Mr J R Coles	Miss S L Palmer
Mr R D Harding	Mr D Salter
Ms P Kaur	Mr A Taylor
Dr A Lees	Mr S Town
Professor M D Matravers	

Clerk to the Board: Mrs K Hodge

Head: **Mr L Winkley**, MA Oxon, MEd OU

Deputy Head: Mrs J R Wright, BA, PGCE

Academic Deputy: Mr D H Gillies, BA, MSc

Heads of Departments:
Art: Mr J Darmody, BA
Biology: Mrs S E Mckie, BSc, PGCE
Careers: Mrs P Bollands, BA, PGDip LSE, MBA, CertEd, MCIPD
Chemistry: Mr G Smith, BSc
Classics: Mr Ed Noy-Scott, BA, PGCE
Design and Technology: Mr J Whitehouse, BEd
Drama: Miss H K Lindley, BA, PGCE
Economics/Business Studies: Mr B D White, BA, PGCE
English: Mrs J D Lawrence, MA
Geography: Miss E C Ullstein, BSc
Government & Politics: Mr B Fuller, BA, PGCE
History: Mr R J Trevett, MA
Mathematics: Mr D J Spencer, BSc
Modern Languages: Mr M J Duffy, BA
Director of Music: Mr P Miles-Kingston, MA, LRAM, QTS
Physical Education & Games: Mr S J Williams, BEd
Physics: Mr M Edwards, MA Ed, BSc, MInstP
Religious Studies: Mr C D Bembridge, BTh, PGCE
Science: Mr D K Morris, BSc

All other St Peter's academic staff are listed on the school website.

Administrative Staff:
Bursar: Mr R M Schofield, FCA

Director of Marketing & Communications: Miss H E M Hamilton, MA, ACIM
Head Master's PA: Mrs S V Emson
Admissions Officer: Mrs G Daniells

The Prep School – St Olave's
Master: Mr A I Falconer, BA, MBA
Master's Secretary: Mrs C Murgatroyd

Deputy Head: Mr M C Ferguson, HDE
Senior Master: Mr C W R Lawrence, BEd, MIBiol
Director of Teaching & Learning: Mrs C Lees, BEd
Chaplain: Mr J Dodsworth, BA, MA

All other St Olave's academic staff are listed on the school website.

Clifton School and Nursery
Head: Mr P C Hardy, BA, PGCE
Head's Secretary: Mrs J Sunderland

Deputy Head: Mr C Tidswell, BEd
All other Clifton School and Nursery academic staff are listed on the school website.

St Peter's is a co-educational boarding and day school with 553 boys and girls aged 13–18. There are 145 boarders housed in four boarding houses, and all day pupils are assigned to a day house, all of which are on the campus. St Peter's offers full boarding.

Buildings & Facilities. The School occupies an impressive 47-acre site just a few minutes' walk from the historic centre of York. Playing fields stretch down to the River Ouse and the School boat house, and the sports facilities are further supplemented by three sports halls, a fitness suite, an astro pitch and a 25m 6-lane swimming pool.

Recent developments have seen the introduction of Harkness tables in some rooms, the refurbishment of the Memorial Hall and a new entrance for the Senior School. There are three performance spaces of varying capacities, a music school, an outstanding art school with its own exhibition gallery and a superb library.

Entrance. Pupils are admitted through the School's entrance examinations held at the end of January for 13+ and in mid-November for 16+. The School is oversubscribed and application before the entrance exam is strongly recommended.

Scholarships and Bursaries. Honorary scholarships are awarded to those performing extremely well in the entrance examination.

Various music awards covering a proportion of the fees and free tuition on up to three musical instruments are available for entrants at 13+ or Sixth Form. Interviews and auditions for these awards are held in January or February.

Means-tested Bursaries are available at 13+ and 16+.

Full particulars on bursaries and scholarships are available from the Admissions Officer, Mrs Gillian Daniells; Tel: 01904 527305.

Curriculum. St Peter's offers a very broad middle school curriculum including Music, PE, Art, Design & Technology, Community Action and courses in personal and social education, among many others.

Nearly all pupils proceed into the Sixth Form, and A Level courses are available in all subjects studied for IGCSE/GCSE, and in Economics, Politics, Business Studies, Further Mathematics and PE. Global Perspectives is an extension course for Upper Sixth and a similar programme, called Horizons, is in place for younger pupils.

Academic and pastoral care. A comprehensive house and tutorial system with interim assessments and reports during the term ensure the close scrutiny by all the teaching staff of pupils' academic and general development.

Religious education and worship. Religious Studies are part of the curriculum, and Chapel is seen as an opportunity for pupils to be made aware of the School's Christian heritage.

Careers and university entrance. The School is an 'all-in' member of the Independent Schools Careers Organisation. Careers staff are available for consultation, maintaining an extensive library relating to careers and higher education and organising a full programme of events for the Sixth Form.

Games and Physical Education. Physical education is a significant part of the curriculum. There is an extensive games programme and excellent sports facilities. Rugby, netball, hockey, cricket and rowing are major sports, and many other options including swimming, athletics, cross country, basketball, squash, badminton, tennis, fencing, golf, mountain biking, trampoline, fitness and weight training are available.

Combined Cadet Force. A flourishing and voluntary CCF contingent of over 120, with army and air sections, allows the pursuit of many activities including a full programme of camps, expeditions and courses.

The Duke of Edinburgh's Award is also on offer with expedition training for all levels as part of the activities programme and 150 pupils are currently participating.

Music. Musical ability is encouraged throughout the School. There is an orchestra, bands, choirs, choral society, Barbershop and Barbieshop groups and numerous smaller activities. Concerts and tours abroad are a regular feature of the school year. Tuition in all instruments is provided, and music is offered at GCSE and A Level.

Art. Drawing, painting, print-making, ceramics and sculpture may all be taken up both in and out of school hours in an outstanding department.

Drama. The School has three performance spaces: the main school hall, the Shepherd Hall and the smaller, more flexible Drama Centre. There are various productions through the year giving opportunities for acting and backstage skills.

Clubs and societies. Many societies flourish including chess, debating, Radio 627 and numerous others. The Community Action programme has over 100 regular participants.

Travel and expeditions. Recent opportunities for trips and tours have included skiing trips, Classics trips to Greece, trekking in Morocco, a CCF trip to Cyprus and sports tours abroad, among many others.

The Friends of St Peter's. Parents are encouraged to join the Friends, a society whose aim is to promote a close relationship between parents and staff.

Fees per term (2014–2015). Full Boarding £8,770, Day £5,310. Tuition fees include the costs of stationery and textbooks. There are no compulsory extras except for examination fees. Lunches are included in day fees.

Further information. Prospectuses are available on request: tel: 01904 527305, email: enquiries@stpetersyork.org.uk, or via the website: www.stpetersyork.org.uk.

(*See also entries for St Olave's School and Clifton School and Nursery in IAPS section.*)

Charitable status. St Peter's School, York, is a Registered Charity, number 1141329.

Seaford College

Lavington Park, Petworth, West Sussex GU28 0NB

Tel: 01798 867392
Fax: 01798 867606
email: jmackay@seaford.org
website: www.seaford.org

Motto: *Ad Alta – To The Heights*

The College was founded in 1884 at Seaford in East Sussex and moved to Lavington Park at the foot of the South Downs in 1946. The grounds cover some 400 acres and include extensive sports facilities and scope for future developments. The campus includes a newly-opened Prep School for pupils aged 6–13 (*see IAPS entry*), a superb Art and Design department, a Sixth Form Centre, purpose-built boarding houses, a state-of-the-art Maths and Science block, and a Music School, with its own performance arena, rehearsal rooms and recording suite.

Seaford College is controlled by an independent non-profit making Charitable Trust approved by the Department for Education and the Charity Commissioners and is administered by the College Board of Governors.

Governing Body:
R Venables Kyrke (*Chairman*)
Mrs S Sayer, CBE (*Vice Chair*)

J H Crosland	N Karonias
A G Mason, MBE	S B Baldwin
N Lacey	J R Hall
Dr S Gilroy	Mrs S Kowszun
Mrs E Lawrence	H A Phillips

Headmaster: **J P Green**, BA Hons, PGCE

Academic Deputy Head: Mrs B Jinks, BA Jt Hons, MA, NPQH
Deputy Head (*Middle School*): J A Passam, BA, FRSA
Deputy Head (*Sixth Form*): W Yates, BSc Ed

Teaching Staff:
* *Head of Department*

Art & Design:
*A G Grantham-Smith, BA, PG Dip ArtEd
Mrs K Grantham-Smith, BA (*Photography*)
Miss H Higgin, BA (*Ceramics*)
A Kirkton, BA Hons

Business Studies:
M Pitteway, BComm Hons

Classics:
T Farmer, BA, PGCE

Design Technology:
*D Shaw, BEd
W Etherington, BSc
Miss A Prince-Iles, BA Hons, PGCE

Drama:
*Dr J Askew, BA Hons

EAL:
Ms Y Clarke, CELTA, BA Hons

Economics:
E Bowden, BSc Hons
E Reynolds

English:
*J Doy, BA Oxford, PGCE
Mrs S Roberts, BA Hons, PGCE
Mrs P White, BA, PG DipSpLD
Mrs J Gargon, BA Hons
Mrs A Doy, BA, PGCE
D Pilgrim, BA, PGCE (*Media Studies*)

Food Technology:
Mrs A Wilkins Shaw, BSc Hons, PGCE

Geography:
*N Q Angier, BSc, MA
J Hart, BA, PGCE
J Follows, BA Hons, PGCE

History:
*P Griffin, BA, PGCE
T D Phillips, BA
R Stather, BA

Information Technology:
*D Crook, BA
P Bain, BA

Learning Support:
*N Foster, BA, Hornsby Dip SpLD
Mrs M Gilbert, BA Hons, PGCE, OCR SpLD
Ms A Jensen, Dip SpLD
Miss J Lorimer-Green, Dip SpLD
Mrs E Barden, BA, PGCE
Mrs P A Angier, BA, Dip CG, Dip SpLD
Mrs S Dallyn, BEd
Mrs L Ferris, OCR SpLD
Mrs H Russell, BA, OCR Cert SpLD

Mathematics:
*S Kettlewell, BA
Mrs B Jinks, MA, BA, NPQH
Mrs K Miliam, BSc, PGCE
M Hawes, PGCE
J Percival
Mrs J Percival, BSc, PGCE

Modern Languages:
*N Kyte, BA Hons (*Spanish*)
Mrs S Weekes, BA Hons, PGCE
Ms H Martin, PGCE (*French*)
C Thorpe, PGCE, BEd, MA
S Rees, BA Hons, PGCE, NPQH (*Head of Prep School*)
Mrs J Lingford, BA Hons, PGCE
Miss M Molinero Quiralte
Miss J Stroudley, BA, PGCE

Music:
*J Weaver (*Acting Director of Music & Performing Arts*)
Mrs J Hawkins, PGCE, BMus (*Asst Dir of Music*)
Mrs S Reynolds, BA Hons (*Choirmaster*)

Physical Education:
*A Cook, BA, PGCE
J Thompson, BA Hons, PGCE
Miss E Teague, BA Hons QTS
T W Gregory, BEd
W Cuthbertson (*Coach*)
Mrs D Strange (*Coach*)
N McFarlane (*Golf Professional*)
D Barnes, BA, PGCE
Miss G Sims, BA Ed, PGCE
Miss L Bryant, BA Hons
D Joseph (*Head of Cricket*)
S Paxton (*Coach*)

Psychology:
Mrs A Yates, BS, PGCE

Religious Studies:
Revd M Barter, BA

Science:
*J Rollinson, BSc, PGCE, RSA CTEFLA
Mrs G Pasteiner, BSc (*Biology*)
Miss C Haestier, BSc, PGCE
Miss S Clapton, BSc, QTS (*Biology*)
S D'Agar, BS Hons, PGCE (*Biology*)
C Telfer, BS Hons, PGCE (*Physics*)
P Nazir, BSc, PGCE (*Physics*)

KS2 Teachers:
Mrs A Hobbs, BA
Mrs S Lewis, BEd Hons
Mrs H Stevens, BA Hons
Mrs F Jones, CertEd
Mrs S Page, GRSM, LRAM, PGCE (*KS2 Music/PSE*)
Mrs M Mitchinson, BA, PGCE

Exams:
Mrs T Pickup

CCF:
WO2 S Gerrard
Mrs J Kyte

Chaplain: Revd M Barter

Finance Manager: A Golding
Facilities Manager: G Burt
Headmaster's Secretary: Mrs A Thornley
Admissions Secretary: Mrs J Mackay-Smith

Pupils. Seaford College offers options of Full Boarding, Weekly and Day facilities to girls and boys aged 6 to 18. There are over 660 pupils at the College with over 100 in the Sixth Form. There are two boys houses and two girls houses and a junior house for both girls and boys aged 10–13.

Aims. Seaford College's aim is to provide an all-round education that equips students with the skills needed to function in the commercial world after leaving their academic studies. The College takes students with a range of abilities and aims to provide the greatest possible 'value-added' for their given abilities. Streaming children in core subjects allows them to work at their own speed and makes them aware of others skills and shortcomings.

Academic. The Preparatory School (incorporating Years 2–8) offers a wide ranging curriculum which includes core subjects of English, Mathematics, Science, Spanish, French, Information Technology and extra English, as well as all the topics of Geography, History, Art, Music, DT, Sport, Forest School and PSHCE.

Years 10 and 11 lead up to the GCSE examinations. Students study the core subjects of English Literature, English Language, Mathematics and Double Science and then choose four other syllabuses to follow from a comprehensive list of subjects which include: Art, Business Studies, Ceramics, Drama, Design and Technology, Geography, French, History, Music, Physical Education, Spanish.

All students in these forms also study Information Technology and Religious Studies and take part in the College sports.

The A Level subject list is comprehensive with new subjects, such as Textiles and Graphics. In the Lower Sixth students follow a College set curriculum and choose four subjects to study for the first year at the end of which pupils sit AS examinations. They usually then choose to continue with three subjects through to A Level. Over and above this in their first year students will undertake to achieve the Duke of Edinburgh's Silver Award. In the Upper Sixth year students will concentrate on their three A Level subjects. The school has also been piloting the Cambridge Pre-U.

Music is an important part of Seaford's life and the new Music School offers the latest in recording and performing facilities. The College boasts an internationally renowned College Chapel Choir who have been requested to visit countries such as Ecuador, America and Russia to sing at Ambassadors' Christmas parties or raise money for underprivileged children; they have recorded several CDs. The College also has an orchestra and offers lessons for all instruments. Music can be studied at GCSE and AS Level.

Sports. With superb facilities available in the grounds, and staff that have coached and played at international level, the College has a reputation for sporting excellence. Facilities include: six rugby pitches, eight tennis courts, squash courts, pool, a water based all-weather hockey pitch, a large indoor sports hall that allows tennis and hockey to be played all year round, and a 9-hole golf course and driving range.

Art. The College has an excellent Art department which allows students to exercise their talents to the fullest extent in every aspect of art and design, whether it is ceramics, textiles, fine art or any other medium they wish to use. Many pupils from Seaford go on to study at design school and work for design and fashion houses or advertising companies. Students are encouraged to display their work throughout the year in the department's gallery.

Combined Cadet Force. The College has strong ties with the Military and has a very well supported Combined Cadet Force, with each wing of the armed forces well represented. Weekend exercises and training are a regular feature in the College calendar and include adventure training, canoeing, climbing, sailing and camping.

Admission. Entry at age 7 consists of a trial day only. Entry at age 10, 11 and 13 is determined on cognitive ability testing and a trial day at the school. 13+ pupils will still be expected to take the Common Entrance Examination. Sixth Form entry is dependent upon GCSE results, Trial Day and interview. Pupils are required to have at least 45 points at GCSE (=9 C grades) and these should include English and Mathematics. Pupils may enter the school without one of these subjects on condition they retake. Overseas students are required to take an oral and written examination to determine level of comprehension in English.

Scholarships and Bursaries. Academic, Music, Art, Design Technology and Sports scholarships may be awarded to boys and girls entering the prep and senior school at 11+, 13+ and 16+. These scholarships are worth a fixed value of £500 per annum. Scholarship examinations take place in February of the year of entry.

Bursaries are available on a means-tested basis. A potential scholarship recipient in need of further financial assistance may apply for a means-tested bursary.

Sibling and Forces discounts are also available. Please contact the Admissions Secretary for more details.

Fees per term (2014–2015). Years 9–13: £9,690 (Full Boarding), £8,290 (Weekly Boarding), £6,150 (Day). Years 7 & 8: £6,550 (Weekly Boarding), £4,950 (Day). £6,130 (Year 6 Weekly Boarding), £2,950–£4,490 (Years 2–6 Day).

Extras. Drama, Clay Pigeon Shooting, Fencing, Duke of Edinburgh's Award, Golf, Kayaking, Museum & Theatre trips, Creative Writing, Model Railway, Debating Club, Rock Climbing, etc.

Charitable status. Seaford College is a Registered Charity, number 277439. It exists to provide education for children.

Sevenoaks School

High Street, Sevenoaks, Kent TN13 1HU
Tel: 01732 455133
Fax: 01732 456143
email: regist@sevenoaksschool.org
          admin@sevenoaksschool.org
website: www.sevenoaksschool.org
Twitter: @SevenoaksSchool
Facebook: /SevenoaksSchoolUK
LinkedIn: Old Sennockians Sevenoaks

Motto: Servire Deo Regnari Est
Founded in 1432, Sevenoaks School is a co-educational, day and boarding school for pupils aged 11–18.

Governing Body:
Chairman: R N H Gould, BA
Vice-Chairman: Ms C Pimlott, BA

Governors:
Ms A Beckett, MBA, MA
A Boulton, MA
Mrs S Carr, BA
I Doherty, MA
Mrs S Dunnett, BA
Mrs E Ecclestone, LLb, Dip LP
Dr C Goh, MA, MB, BChir, MRCP
A R M Little, MA
J London, LLM
N May, MA, MSc
D M Phillips, BA, ACA
P Shirke, MBA
J Warde, DL, MA
Prof M J Waring, ScD, FRSC
M Whittow, PhD

Bursar and Clerk to the Governors: Air Vice-Marshal A J Burton, OBE, BSc Econ, FCIS, Chartered FCIPD

Academic Staff:

Head: Mrs C L Ricks, MA, DPhil

Senior Deputy Head: Miss T M Homewood, BSc, MA
Deputy Head (Pastoral): Miss H P Tebay, MA
Deputy Head (Academic): T R Jones, BA, MA
Deputy Head (Co-curriculum): G E Stanford, MA, MBA
Director of Admissions and Communications: Mrs A M Stuart, BA, MEd
Director of Higher Education and Careers: Mrs R A Greenhalgh, BA
Director of Information Systems: Mrs S J Williamson, BA, MSc
Director of Innovation: G A Lawrie, BSc
Director of International Baccalaureate: J T Sprague, BA, MA
Director of Administration: Miss A A Franks, MA
Sixth Form Registrar: A T Patton, BA, MA
Head of Boarding: Mrs N J Haworth, MA
Head of Sixth Form: M T Edwards, BA, MPhil, PhD

Assistant Teachers:
* *Head of Department*
† *Housemaster/mistress*

Miss N L Atkinson, BSc (*Technology*)
†Mrs E M Bassett, BA (*Chemistry*)
P R Bassett, MA (*Mathematics*)
C P Bates, BSc (*Biology*)
Miss C S Berment, BA (*French*)
M P Beverley, BA, MA (**Middle School Curriculum, *Literature & Performance, English*)
Miss F J Bolton, BSc, MSc (*Mathematics*)
Miss H M Bonsall, BSc (*Biology*)
Mrs L D Boulianne, BA, MSci, PhD (*Physics*)
Mrs V Boyd, BSc (*Mathematics*)
I C Campbell, BSc (*Psychology)
Mrs R Campbell, BA (*English*)
M R Capelo, BSc (*Spanish)
T J Carden, BA, MA (**Instrumental and Vocal Studies*)
S Carr, MA (*Classics*)
Mrs C H Collier, BA (*Classics*)
Miss M T Connolly, BSc (*Physics*)
M S Cook, MA (*Music*)
†S A J Coquelin, MA (*French*)
J D Cullen, BSc, MSc (*Physical Education*)
A G Day, MA (*Economics*)
Miss E B Delpech, BA (*Art*)
J H Dickinson, MPhys (*Physics*)
Ms L A Dolan, BA (*English*)
J Drury, MA (*Russian)
Miss A M Durnford, BA (*English*)
†Mrs C E Dyer, BA (*French, German, LS*)
C H J Dyer, BA (*Music)
Mrs T G Edwards, MChem (*Chemistry*)
J C Emmitt, BA (**Physical Education*)
P L Eversfield, MA (*Economics)
Miss N M Fayaud, MA (*French)
T J K Findley, MSc, PhD (*Chemistry*)
Mrs V J FitzGerald, BA (*History*)
I A Fletcher, BSc (*Chemistry*)
Ms M Gago Pesado, BA, MA (*Spanish*)
Miss C E Gilliat-Smith, BA (*Physical Education*)
J W Grant, BA (*Drama, Literature & Performance*)
D C Hall, MA, MPhil (*History*)
S A Hall, BSc (*Psychology*)
C M Harbinson, BA, MA (*English*)
Mrs P O Hargreaves, BA (**PSD, Drama*)
P Harrison, MA (*English*)
N T Haworth, BA (*IB Diploma Coordinator, History*)
G E Henry, BA, MA (*Director of Drama*)
Mrs C J Henshaw, BA (*English)

Mrs W J Heydorn, MA (*Religious Studies*)
Miss A Hill, BSc (*Mathematics*)
P T Hill, BEd (*Physical Education*)
S Holden, BEd (*Physical Education*)
G Howden, BSc, MA (*Mathematics*)
P J Hulston, BSc (*Economics*)
R M Jones, BSc (*Technology*)
Mrs E A Joseph, BA (*Physical Education*)
L C Kiggell, MBA (*Economics*)
E Kirby, BSc (*Biology*)
N Kunaratnam, BA (*Additional Languages, French*)
Miss S S Levine, BA, PhD (*Mathematics*)
†Mrs K Lewis, BSc
P C Lilley, BA, MA (*Geography*)
R D Lyle, BA, MA (*English*)
Mrs A Mack, BA, MA (*History*)
Miss R V Macgregor, BA (*French, Russian*)
C R Martin, MA, PhD (*Chemistry, *Science*)
P G de May, BA (*Classics*)
Mrs A J Maynard, BA (*Head of Learning Support, French*)
Miss R L McQuillin, MA (*History*)
D W Mott, BA (*Modern Languages*)
Mrs K A Mylod, BSc (*Biology*)
Miss A E Nairn, BHPE (*Physical Education*)
Mrs D Orme, BSc, MSc, PhD (*Mathematics*)
C W Openshaw, BA (*Art*)
†S M Owen, MA, PhD (*Chemistry*)
G P Parker-Jones, BA, MA (*History*)
M Parsons, BA, PhD (*Chemistry*)
R D Patterson, BSc, PhD (*Mathematics*)
Miss C M Pearson, BSc (*Physical Education*)
Miss S Pestell Jury, BA (*Chemistry*)
Mrs K L Pitcher, BSc (*Biology*)
Miss O C Power, BA (*Religious Studies, Theory of Knowlege, Philosophy*)
R Rands-Webb, MA (*Spanish, French*)
Miss N A Redstone, BSc (*Mathematics*)
S Reid, BA, MA (*History*)
Mrs H E Roff, BSc, DPhil (*Physics*)
Miss A K Russell, MA (*French*)
O J Russell, BA, MPhil (*Geography*)
Mrs J L Sands, BA, MA (*German*)
Miss A Schmaller, BA (*German*)
Ms L U Seetharaman, BA, MA (*English*)
Miss S A Shah, BA (*Art*)
S J Sharp, BSc, PhD (*Physics*)
A C Smith, BComm (*Economics*)
C P Taylor, MA (*Classics*)
C J Tavaré, MA (*Biology, Physical Education*)
P R Thompson, BA, MA (*Geography*)
Mrs A J Turner, BSc, MRes (*Biology*)
P J Turner, BSc (*Geography*)
Miss S C Ventress, BA (*English*)
D R Whiffin, BSc (*Mathematics*)
Mrs G P Williams, BSc, PhD (*Mathematics*)
†G J Willis, BA (*Geography*)
A G Wilson, MA (*English*)
Miss Y Yin, BS, MSc (*Mandarin*)
Ms S R Yu, BA, PhD (*Chemistry*)

Part-time Staff:
Mrs K Agarwal (*Hindi*)
Ms A Ashwell, MusB, MMus (*Instrumental and Vocal Studies*)
O C Barratt, BA (*Art*)
Mrs R L Brown, BA (*Design Technology*)
J N Burger, MA (*Mathematics*)
A J Cornah, LLB, MSc (*Sailing*)
Mrs C Duran-Oreiro, DegEd (*Spanish*)
Mrs J R Estop, MA (*English*)
Miss A Harmer, BA, MA (*Classics*)
Mrs S K Harvey, MA (*Higher Education*)
Mrs J Hendry, Dip RSAM, ARCM (*Music*)

Mrs A M Hulston, BA (*English as an Additional Language*)
Mrs K S Jay, BA (*Swedish*)
Mrs E Kelly (*Russian*)
Mrs J L Kiggell, MA, ARCM, AMus, TCL (*Music*)
Mrs H de May, BA (*Classics*)
Mrs S J MacLeay, MA (*Geography*)
D Merewether (*Photography*)
A C Mitchell, BA (*Film, Video*)
M J O'Reilly, BA (*Artist-in-residence*)
Miss S Rahman, BA (*English*)
Mrs A E Rochdi, BA (*French, Spanish*)
Mrs H Smith, BA (*Learning Support*)
T J Soudain, BA (*Technology*)
T D Stuart, BA (*Biology*)
Mrs A Symons, MSc (*Italian*)
T T Wey, MA (*Keyboard*)
Mrs A Williams-Walker, BSc (*Mathematics*)
R C Woodward, BSc, MA, ARCS (*Chemistry*)

Head of Library: Ms C Woodhouse
Head's PA: Mrs M Thomas

Sevenoaks School is situated on an attractive 100-acre campus adjoining Knole Park and on the edge of the town. Sevenoaks is in Kent, just 30 minutes from central London, and is conveniently close to Gatwick and Heathrow airports, the Channel Tunnel and continental Europe. The school, while set firmly in its local community, has a strong international dimension – not only in its student body, but also in its ethos, its culture and its curriculum.

In 2013 the Independent Schools Inspectorate (ISI) awarded Sevenoaks School the rare accolade of 'Exceptional' for its students' achievement. Sevenoaks topped the Department for Education's KS4 performance tables in 2012, with the highest percentage of pupils achieving all subjects of the English Baccalaureate. It was listed as the Top Independent School at A Level or equivalent in the *Independent* in 2012, and the top co-educational independent secondary school (IB) in the Sunday Times Schools Guide 2011. It was the top UK co-educational IB school 2011 and 2010 in the Education Advisers Ltd rankings (www.baccalaureate.eu.com). The school was described as 'outstanding' in the Ofsted Boarding Inspection 2009.

There are seven boarding houses: a co-educational junior house (11–13), two boys' houses (13–18), two girls' houses (13–18) and two single-sex Sixth Form houses (16–18). All of these welcome students from the UK and from around the world. Accommodation ranges from a charming Queen Anne house to modern, purpose-built facilities. There are lessons and sport for all pupils on Saturdays and a full programme of activities for boarders on Sundays.

Sevenoaks has a reputation for exploring new ideas. The school has taught the International Baccalaureate since 1978 and was the first HMC school to offer the IB Diploma Programme exclusively. More recently, Sevenoaks was among the first schools in the UK to devise its own externally accredited qualification, the Sevenoaks School Certificate (SSC), which is fully recognised by UCAS. A wide range of subjects is offered at GCSE, IGCSE and SSC, with setting in core subjects. In the Sixth Form all pupils study the International Baccalaureate Diploma Programme – a rigorous two-year diploma designed to provide a broad and balanced education. It is a well respected qualification for UK, US and other leading universities worldwide. Academic results in the school are excellent, with an average IB Diploma score of 39.1 points (world average around 30 points) and some 30 students achieving a score of 45 or 44 points. Around 40 students receive offers from Oxford or Cambridge each year, in both the arts and sciences. An increasing number of students choose to go to Ivy League and other top American universities.

There is also a strong emphasis on the co-curriculum, from sport to music, drama and art. Pupils regularly achieve representative honours at rugby, football, cricket, hockey, netball, cross-country, athletics, tennis, badminton, shooting and sailing, and there is a wide range of concerts, plays and exhibitions for pupils of all ages. A variety of clubs and societies provide opportunities for all pupils to find and develop their interests. The school has a voluntary Combined Cadet Force and is also proud of its strong tradition of community service and involvement in The Duke of Edinburgh's Award scheme.

The facilities are first class: The Space, a performing arts centre with a world-class concert hall, opened in 2010. The Sennocke Centre, a major new sports centre, was completed in 2005, and a dining hall, Sixth Form centre, language centre and athletics track have been built in recent years.

Admission. The main points of entry to the school are at 11, 13 and 16 years. A small number are admitted at other levels. At 11+, pupils are admitted on the basis of a competitive examination held in January, an interview and Head's report. At 13+, a pre-assessment day in October is followed by those in prep schools taking the ISEB Common Entrance Examination in June or, for others, the school's own Year 9 Entrance Examination in February. Alternatively, pupils can take the Year 9 Scholarship examinations in May. At 16+ students are admitted into the Sixth Form based on their performance in interview and academic entrance tests, and on the strength of their current school reports. There are boarding and day places for boys and girls at all ages. All applications for entry should be addressed to the Director of Admissions (regist@sevenoaksschool.org).

Fees per term (2014–2015). Boarders £10,626; Day Pupils £6,654 (including lunch). Fees for pupils entering directly into the Sixth Form are £11,526 (boarding) and £7,554 (day).

Scholarships and Bursaries. Up to 50 awards are available at 11+, 13+ and 16+ for outstanding academic ability or promise, as well as outstanding ability in music, sport, art and drama (at 13+ and 16+ only).

Scholarships are awarded to the value of 10% of the day fee.

Applicants are invited to apply for 11+ scholarships on the basis of performance in entrance tests and interviews, and for music scholarships when confirming their application. For 13+ awards, application should be made to the Director of Admissions by 1 January in the year of entry.

Sixth Form academic scholarships are offered on the basis of performance in entrance tests and interviews. Applications for Sixth Form Art, Music, Drama and Sport scholarships should be made by expressing an interest during the application procedure.

Means-tested bursaries are available for pupils who could not otherwise afford the fees. Priority is given to local candidates. Scholarships may be augmented by bursaries in cases of financial need.

Charitable status. Sevenoaks School is a Registered Charity, number 1101358. Its aims and objectives are the education of school children.

Sherborne Girls

Bradford Road, Sherborne, Dorset DT9 3QN

Tel:	Admissions: 01935 818224
	School: 01935 812245
	Bursar: 01935 818206
Fax:	01935 389445
email:	registrar@sherborne.com
website:	www.sherborne.com
Twitter:	@sherbornegirls
Facebook:	/sherbornegirls
LinkedIn:	/Sherborne Girls

Sherborne Girls, founded in 1899, provides an outstanding education for 11 to 18 year olds in the beautiful county of Dorset, and is proud of its extra-curricular programme and exceptional pastoral care. Girls are admitted at 11+, 12+, 13+ and into the Sixth Form. There are 450 girls, 424 Boarders, 26 Day girls. The International Baccalaureate Diploma is offered in addition to A Levels, which provides education tailored to each girl's needs. A close relationship with Sherborne School allows co-ed opportunities including some joint lessons in the Sixth Form, music, drama, activities, clubs and societies and social occasions. The schools have the same term dates. Scholarships and Bursaries are available.

Council:
Chairman: Mr S H Wingfield Digby
Vice Chairman: Mr R Strang

Lady Plaxy Arthur	Mr R A L Leach
Mrs G M Blenkinsop	Mr P Pilkington
Mrs K Brock	Mr R H Robson
Mrs I Burke	Mrs A L M Simon
Mr I Davenport	Mr O Stanley
Lt Gen Sir Robert Fry	The Hon Mrs C Townshend
Mr W J A Gordon	Mr P Ward
Mrs L Hall	

Clerk to the Council: Mr S D Miller

Senior and Pastoral Staff:

Headmistress: Mrs Jenny Dwyer, BEd Hons Cantab

Bursar: Mr S D Miller,
Deputy Head External Affairs: Mrs Fiona Clapp, BSc Hon London PGCE
Deputy Head Teaching and Learning Mrs Louise Orton, BSc Hons Swansea, PGCE
Deputy Head Pastoral Mrs Violaine Ludwick, BA Hons Dunelm
Director of Sixth Form: Mr Rowan MacNeary, BA Hons Cardiff, MA Winchester

Chaplain: Revd Rebecca Ayers-Harris, BA Nottingham, Dip Theology, PGCE

Housemistresses of Boarding Houses:
Aldhelmsted East: Mrs E Poraj-Wilczynska, MSc Leicester, CertEd London (*PE*)
Aldhelmsted West: Mrs H Vanstone
Dun Holme: Mr R Garnsworthy, BA Australia
Wingfield Digby: Mrs H Bajorat, BA Manchester, PGCE Brighton
Reader Harris: Mr J Hammond, BEd Hons Gloucester & Mrs S Hammond, BEd Wellington NZ
Kenelm: Miss K Pinsent, BA Dunelm, MSc Roehampton, PGCE
Mulliner: Miss R Brown, BSc London, PGCE Bath Spa

Staff:
* *Head of Department*

Art and Design:
*Miss J Newman, BA Norwich, ATC London
Mrs A D Heron Watkins, BA Southampton
Miss T Farris, Leiths, BSc Texas
Mr I McCarthy, BEng Leeds, PGCE
Ms P Ellis, MA London, BA Courtauld Institute, London
Mr R MacNeary, BA Hons Cardiff, MA Winchester
   (*Director of Sixth Form*)
Mr J Casely, BA Hons, MPhil Birmingham
Miss F Bugg, BA Hons, PGCE Bath

Classics:
*Miss S Jones, BA Toronto
Mrs R M Allen, BA Birmingham (*Head of Middle Fifth*)
Miss S Haslam, MA Cantab, PGCE

Drama and Theatre Studies:
*Miss E Nurse, BA Manchester, PGCE
Mr M Freestone, BA Natal
Ms J Moore, MA Warwick, BA Leicester, PGCE, DipEd
   Brighton

English:
*Mr P R Cantrell, BA Nottingham
Mrs N Alper, BA Birmingham, PGCE (*CAS Coordinator*)
Ms K Chapman, BEd Southampton
Mr J Hammond, BEd Hons Gloucester
Miss K Pinsent, BA Dunelm, MSc Roehampton, PGCE
Mrs J Ward, BA OU, Dip SpLD, TESL Toronto, AMI
   Toronto, PGCE
Mr S P Wood, BA Oxon
Mrs J Trew, BSc Bath, Dip Hornsby Int Dyslexia Centre
   (*Head of Learning Support*)

Geography, Economics and Business Studies:
*Mrs E Morray-Jones, BSc Surrey
Miss B Jones, BA Hons Durham
Mrs C Morgan, BSc Wales
Revd Rebecca Ayers-Harris, BA Nottingham, Dip
   Theology, PGCE
Mr D Banks, BSc Cardiff, PGCE UWE
Mrs K Cresswell, MA Edinburgh

History:
*Mrs S Elliot, BA Hons Reading
Mrs R Allen
Mr J Casely
Mrs S Francis, MA Oxon
Ms S Haslam
Mrs K Scorer, MA Oxon, PGCE

Mathematics:
*Mrs D Kirby, BSc, BA Leicester
Miss R Curtis, BSc Hons, PGCE Swansea
Mrs L Orton, BSc Hons Swansea, PGCE
Miss J Davidson, BSc UMIST, PGCE
Mr R Lavender, BSc Dunelm, PGCE
Dr A Moore, BEng, PhD Bristol, MA Nottingham
Mr S Payne, BSc Kent, PGCE

Modern Languages:
*Mr M Felstead, MA Cantab
Mme M-D B Bonelli-Bean, Licence LLCE Paris
Mrs G Carvia-Ruiz
Mrs P J Fieldhouse, MA London, BA Rhodes, PGCE
Mrs D Goldsack
Mrs G Henderson, BA Exeter, PGC
Mrs C Le Sueur
Mrs V Ludwick, BA Hons Dunelm
Dr G Oliver BA Cantab, PhD London
Mrs R Rogerson, Zurich
Mr D Bajorat
Miss M Jeanniard du Dot
Miss I Lorenzo Garcia

Music:
*Mr J M Jenkins, BA Dunelm, ARCO
Mr S Clarkson, BMus Edinburgh, FRCO, ARCM (*Head of
   Academic Music*)
Miss C Morgan, BMus Hons, LRAM, DipRAM
Miss A Manero, BMus, PGDip, MMus
Mrs J Nelson, Dip Ram, LRAM, RAM
Miss L Warwick
Miss C Morgan
30 visiting teachers

Musical tuition in:
Flute, Double Bass, Clarinet, Saxophone, Percussion, Sing-
ing, Alexander Technique, Oboe, Cor Anglais, Bassoon,
Bass, Electric Guitar, Baroque Recorder, Classical Guitar,
Brass, Viola, Cello, Percussion, Piano and Harp.

Physical Education:
*Mrs N Matthias, BEd St Peter & St Mary, Cheltenham
Mr J Brooker, BA London, PGCE
Mr J Brooker
Mr R Garnsworthy, BE Australia
Mrs K Stringer, BEd Crewe & Alsager College of PE
Miss D Hackett, BSc Loughborough
Mrs G Kemp
Mrs H Vanstone
Mr M Rawle

Religious Studies:
*Mr S D Loxton, PhD Seattle, BEd Sussex, MPhil Hull
Revd Rebecca Ayers-Harris, BA Nottingham, Dip
   Theology, PGCE
Mrs S Hammond, BEd Wellington, NZ
Mrs H Bajorat, BA Manchester, PGCE Brighton
Revd P Woolway, BA Oxon, PGCE

Sciences:
*Dr J Ivimey-Cook, PhD Exeter
Mr A Angelosanto, BSC York
Mrs K Smith, BSc Manchester, PGCE
Miss P Abbott, BSc, Southampton
Mr D Buck, BSc London
Mr P M Crabtree, BSc Leeds
Mrs F Clapp, BSc London, PGCE
Miss B Brown, BSc London, PGCE
Mrs A Cochrane, BSc Nottingham
Dr J Gammon, MChem, PhD, PGCE
Dr J Hopper, BSc Birmingham, PhD London, PGCE

Sanatorium Sister: Mrs A Watson
Director of Admissions: Mrs F Clapp, BSc London, PGCE
   Oxon
Librarian: Miss R Knight, BA Hons Exeter, PG Dip Aber
Marketing Manager: Mrs L Flahant, BA Hons
   Gloucestershire

Terms. Three terms of approximately 12 weeks each.
Christmas holidays 4 weeks; Easter holidays 4 weeks; Summer holidays 8 weeks. Term dates are in common with those
of Sherborne School.

Admission. Common Entrance Examination to Independent Schools. Scholarship Examinations and interviews.
The School's own entrance examinations where Common
Entrance is not possible. Girls should be registered in
advance and reports will be requested from their current
school. Pre-assessment for 13+ entry takes place 18 months
before entry. For entry into the Sixth Form girls are required
to gain 5 good passes in relevant subjects.

Registration fee £100. A deposit of £1,000 is required
before entry (a term's fees for overseas pupils) and credited
to the last term's bill.

Scholarships and Bursaries. Academic Scholarships are
offered at 11+, 13+ and 16+ annually as a result of examination and interview. There are also scholarships offered for
outstanding promise in Music, Art and Sport. All examinations are held in January and February apart from Sixth
Form in November. Scholarship awards are made on merit
with a maximum merit award of 15% of the fees. Scholarships may be combined with means-tested Bursaries which
can raise considerably the effective amount of an award.
Bursarial support (up to 100%) may be available in cases of
demonstrable need.

Music Awards (Junior and 16+): Scholarships of up to
10% of the current fees with free music tuition for up to
three lessons per week. Music Exhibitions offer free music
tuition for up to three lessons per week.

Art Scholarships (Junior and 16+): Awards of up to 10%
of the current fees. Candidates will be required to bring a
portfolio with them and would be asked to do some work in
the Art Department whilst they are here.

Sport Scholarships (Junior and 16+): Awards of up to 10% of the current fees. Candidates will offer one or more sports, preferably reaching county standard or higher.

All-Rounder Award (Junior): Awards of up to 15% of the current fees. All-Rounder Awards take into account ability in two areas of activity outside of the classroom (art, drama, music and sport) as well as academic potential. Candidates will sit papers in English, Mathematics and Science.

Fees per term (2014–2015). 13+: Boarders £10,330 Day Girls £7,505 11+: Boarders £8,335 Day Girls £6,100.

Houses. There are five Houses for 13–17 year olds and one Upper Sixth House. 11 and 12 year old girls spend their first years together in a Aldhelmsted West House.

Religion. The School has a Church of England foundation, but it values the presence and contribution of members of all the Christian traditions and of other faiths. Regular services are held in the Abbey, some jointly with Sherborne School.

Examinations. Girls are prepared for GCSE, AS/A Levels and the International Baccalaureate Diploma. There is a wide choice of subjects to be studied. Some subjects at AS/A Level are studied jointly with Sherborne School.

Games. Hockey and Lacrosse/Netball are played in the Michaelmas and Lent terms and Tennis, Rounders and Athletics during the Trinity term. Oxley Sports Centre in partnership with Sherborne Girls contains a 25m pool and state-of-the-art fitness suite. There are Squash Courts, floodlit Astroturf, Sports Hall, Dance Studio and Climbing Wall. Riding, Badminton, Cross-Country Running, Golf, Aerobics, Judo, Sailing, Trampolining are some of the alternative games.

Sherborne Old Girls. All enquiries should be made to Ms Laura Windsor at the School, Tel: 01935 818329.

Prospective parents and their daughters are invited to the School for Open Mornings in the Spring and Autumn, or private visits by appointment. Please visit the school's website or telephone Admissions on 01935 818224 for further details.

Charitable status. Sherborne School for Girls is a Registered Charity, number 307427. It exists to provide education for girls in a boarding environment.

Sherborne School

Abbey Road, Sherborne, Dorset DT9 3AP
Tel: 01935 812249
Fax: 01935 810426
email: admissions@sherborne.org
website: www.sherborne.org

The origins of Sherborne School date back to the eighth century, when a tradition of education at Sherborne was begun by St Aldhelm. The School was linked with the Benedictine Abbey, the earliest known Master was Thomas Copeland in 1437. Edward VI refounded the School in 1550. The present School stands on land which once belonged to the Monastery. The Library, Chapel, and Headmaster's offices which adjoin the Abbey Church, are modifications of the original buildings of the Abbey.

Royal Arms of Edward VI: *Dieu et mon droit*.

Governors of the School:

Chairman: Revd G M W Parry, MA
Vice-Chairman: Major General P A J Cordingley, DSO

Ex officio:
The Representative of Her Majesty's Lord Lieutenant for the County of Dorset
The Representative of the Lord Bishop of Salisbury
The Vicar of Sherborne, The Revd Canon E J Woods, MA, FRSA

Co-optative:
Dr S Ball, BM, MRCPsych
Mrs I Burke, MB BS, MRCGP
A Charlton Esq, CMG, CVO
Mrs V Cotter, LLB Hons, LLM
R S Fidgen Esq, FRICS
M L French Esq, BSc, FCA

Prof R Hodder-Williams, MA, FRSA
G A Hudson Esq
R A L Leach, MA
G Marsh Esq, MA, Cert Ed
R Robson Esq
Revd Canon K Willkinson, BA, FRSA

Staff Nominated: M Whittell, Esq

Bursar and Clerk to the Governors: Mrs L Robins, BSc, MRCIS

Headmaster: R A Barlow, BSc, FRSA, FIMA

Deputy Head (Academic): T W Filtness, BA, MA, PhD
Deputy Head (Pastoral): P J Watts, BSc, CPhys, MInstP

Housemasters:
Abbey House: M J McGinty, AKC, BA, MSc (Tel: 01935 812087)
Abbeylands: S J Clayton, CertEd & Mrs VA Clayton, BA, MCLIP (Tel: 01935 812082)
The Digby: M J Brooke, MA (Tel: 01935 810170)
The Green: A M Hatch, BA (Tel: 01935 810440)
Harper House: J J B Wadham, BSc, PhD (Tel: 01935 812128)
Lyon House: B P Sunderland, BEng (Tel: 01935 812079)
School House: K Jackson, BA (Tel: 01935 813248)
Wallace House: G T W Robinson, BA (Tel: 01935 813334)

Staff:
* *Head of Department/Subject*

Art:
*R A Cuerden, MA
J Clark, BA
Mrs E M A Cuerden, MA
J E Wright, BA, MA

J Donnelly
Mrs L A Gillott, BA
G T W Robinson, BA

Economics and Business Studies:
*R T B Harris, BA, MBA
A R Duncan, BA
M C Ewart-Smith, MBA, CEng
D Muckalt, BSc
C M O'Donnell, BA
Mrs S Salmon, BA, MA

Biology:
*D J Ridgway, BSc
T W Filtness, BA, MA, PhD
G R Harwood, BSc
J P A Manning, BSc, PhD, MEd
E L Southall, BSc, MSc
J J B Wadham, BSc, PhD

English:
*Mrs R E C de Pelet, MA
M J Brooke, MA
Mrs L A Gillott, BA
S P H Haigh, MA
M P O'Connor, BA, Cert SpLD
T W Payne, BA
G T W Robinson, BA
J L Winter, MA

Chemistry:
*W E Buckley, BSc
S L Cummings, BSc, MSc, BA
C G B Hamon, PhD, CCSci, CChem, MRSC
N C Scorer, MChem
D A Watson, BSc

Classics:
*S A Heath, BA
M A Jones, BA, MA
J J Kimber, BA
P Rogerson, MA (*Head of Careers*)
S L Tremewan, BA, PhD

Geography:
*T R J Mason, BSc
T O Flowers, BSc
A M Hatch, BA
Miss K L Millar, BA
P J Stiff, BA, PhD
C J Wake, BSc
J P A Wilson, BSc

Design and Technology:
*P R Chillingworth, BA
J Salisbury, BEd

History and Politics:
*G D R Reynolds, MA
J P Crouch, BA
P S Francis, MA
R C Le Poidevin, MA, MA, MSc

Drama:
*I C C Reade, BA
Mrs V A Clayton, BA, MCLIP
Ms B Darnley, BA

M J McGinty, AKC, BA, MSc
R M Warren, BA
B L Wild, MA, PhD

Learning Support:
*Mrs P M Barnes, BSc, MA
Mrs E J H Ashton, BBA
Mrs L J McMillan, BSc
M P O'Connor, BA, CertSpLD
M S Peters, BA
Mrs S M L Reade, BSc

Mathematics:
*N G Bradshaw, BSc, PhD
Miss A E R Civardi, BSc
T A J Dawson, BSc, Dip Stats, MA
N A Henderson, BSc, MBA
Mrs L J McMillan, BSc
S K Mertens, BA, MA, MSc, PhD
A C Morgan, BSc, MSc, FRSA
Mrs L B Phippard, BSc
Miss C M Standen, MA, ACA
B P Sunderland, BEng

Modern Languages:
*Mrs J R Thurman, BA
Miss A Bailon Artal, MA Hons
S K Byrne, BA
D B Cameron, MA
G H G Carey, BA
W E Chadwick, BA, DipLaw
R Dillow, BA, MA
Mrs C E Greenrod, BA, Cert TEFL
A D Nurton, BA
A R Oates, BA, MLitt (*French*)

Medical Officers:
C P Cleaver, MB, ChB, MRCGP
K Dixon, MB BS, MRCGP, DFFP
I A Latham, MB BS, MRCP, DFFP

Sister: Mrs C Ellwood, RGN
Sports and Uniform Shop: Mrs S Eldor (Tel: 01935 810506)
Registrar: J R O Massey, BSc (Tel: 01935 810402; email: jmassey@sherborne.org)

Situation. The School lies in the attractive Abbey town of Sherborne. By train, Salisbury is forty minutes away, London and Heathrow two hours.

Organisation. There are about 520 boarders and 40 day boys, accommodated in eight houses, all of which are within easy walking distance of the main school.

Admission. Entry is either at 13+ through the Common Entrance, Scholarship examinations, or special entrance papers or at 16+ after GCSE.

Parents, who would like to enter their sons for the School, or have any queries, should contact the Registrar.

Boys can be entered either for a particular House or placed on the general list.

Visits. Visits can be arranged at any time of the year by ringing the Admissions Office on 01935 810403.

Scholarships and Exhibitions. Sherborne offers a wide range of scholarships and exhibitions at 13+ entry: Academic (March); Music (February); Art, Design & Technol-

T J Scott, BA
Mrs J M Slade, BA

Music:
*J E C Henderson, MA
B J Davey, GRSM, LRAM
Miss S J Drury, GRSM, ARCM
M Lehnert, BA, MMus

Physical Education:
*R P McGuire, BA, MPhil, PhD
S J Clayton, Cert Ed PE, Dip Sp Psy
D A R Guy, BA (*Director of Sport*)
D N Muckalt, BSc (*Deputy Director of Sport*)
C Roberts
C Smith, BA

Physics:
*M C Thurman, BSc
J J Kimber, BSc
J S Mitchell, BSc
B A Ryder, BEng
H Straughan, BSc, MSc
P J Watts, BSc, CPhys, MInstP
J G Willetts, BA, CPhys, MInstP, MBCS

PSHE:
*Miss S L Cummings, BSc, MSc, BA

Theology:
*A C Gillott, BA
Revd L R F Collins, BD, AKC, MTh (*Chaplain*)
J A Crawford, MA
K G Jackson, BA
Revd N J Mercer, BD, MTh
S T Rowntree, BEd

ogy, Sport (March), All Rounder (March). Sixth Form Academic and Music Scholarships and Sports Exhibitions are also offered annually (November).

Open Scholarships: up to six Scholarships of up to 20% of fees (the top scholarship being the Alexander Ross Wallace Scholarship) and up to eight Exhibitions of up to 15% of fees may be awarded. In awarding one of these Exhibitions regard will be paid to special proficiency in a particular subject.

In addition Awards are available to those who are able to demonstrate outstanding ability in one of the following areas: Art, Design & Technology, Music and Sport.

A number of Music Awards are available at 13+. In addition one Marion Packer Scholarship of £600 pa for an outstanding performance on the piano may be offered. Those given Awards receive free instrumental tuition.

Up to four all-rounder awards are available for pupils showing talent and passion across a range of disciplines.

Closed Awards: Raban Exhibition of 10% of fees for the sons of serving or ex-service officers; a Nutting Exhibition of 10% of fees for sons of RN Officers.

The maximum value of any award is 20% of the fees but this may be supplemented in cases of financial need.

Further details of all awards are available from the Registrar.

Sixth Form Entry. Places are available for boys who wish to join the Sixth Form to study A Levels for two years. Scholarship examinations take place in November and entrance exams by arrangement with the Registrar. There are up to two scholarships offered annually. Also available, for good A Level candidates, is the Arkwright Scholarship for Technology.

Curriculum. All pupils follow a broadly based curriculum for their first three years to GCSE. In the Sixth Form boys study at least three A Levels and one AS Level drawn from 27 A Level and 30 AS courses. Opportunities for research projects are available to broaden the scope of their studies. Some of the courses for A Level are run jointly with Sherborne Girls.

Careers and Universities. The Careers Department has an enviable reputation. Boys experience work shadowing programmes in the fifth and lower sixth forms – these are followed by careers conventions, university visits, parents' forums and lessons in interview techniques. There is an encyclopaedic, fully computerised Careers' Room with regularly updated contacts with those at university and at work. The department has visited all universities and places of higher education. Virtually all leavers go on to university.

Pastoral Care. The boys in each house are in the care of a Housemaster and his wife, a resident tutor and a resident matron. In addition a team of tutors assists the Housemaster in the running of the House and boys have many avenues of support and advice available to them. The School Chaplain also plays a major role and will talk with a boy whenever required. A School Counsellor is available.

Tutor. Each boy has a personal Tutor who not only monitors his academic progress but provides a useful contact point for parents.

Religion. The weekly pattern of Christian services in the school Chapel or Sherborne Abbey underpin the spiritual rhythm of the school. There is a wide variety of voluntary Christian groups and services including a Friday night candlelit Eucharist which is well attended. Boys can be prepared for Confirmation into the Church of England and the Roman Catholic Church. Theology is taught throughout the school and boys can opt for a GCSE Religious Studies course and a Philosophy and Ethics A Level course.

Community Service. Boys take part in a busy programme aimed at encouraging a sense of responsibility towards the local community. Entertainment, fundraising, clubs and assistance are organised for the young and elderly in and around Sherborne.

Art. The Art School is a dynamic and highly successful department achieving outstanding academic results at all levels. The core disciplines are based around the study of Fine Art, which enables students to approach a broad curriculum encompassing an eclectic mix of approaches such as painting, photography, 3D, digital media, printing and performance.

Design and Technology. In recent years the Design and Technology Department has been through a program of complete refurbishment. The subject is taught from year nine right through to A Level and pupils can go on to higher education courses in Product and Aeronautical Design, Architecture and Engineering. The department has developed links with local industries where pupils can see CAD/CAM production, commercial furniture design and precision casting in process. It runs afternoon activities and is open on both Saturdays and Sundays.

Music. There is a strong music tradition in the School – over 400 music lessons take place every week. There are two full orchestras, various chamber music groups, many different types of jazz band, a brass group, a swing band, Chapel choir and a choral society, not to mention rock bands. Many of these groups tour both home and abroad. Numerous concerts, recitals and musical productions are held throughout the year. Lunch time concerts take place every Friday. Regular subscription concerts are given by visiting professional musicians.

Drama. Drama productions of all kinds are a major feature of school life, from large scale musicals to classical drama, substantial modern works and fringe performances, many staged with Sherborne Girls. The sophisticated technical resources of the Powell Theatre attract programmes from professional touring companies. The newly instated, state-of-the-art drama studios underpin the school's ambition for this important part of the pupils' learning.

Information Technology. The school has a fast wireless network that is available throughout the school, including in boarding houses. Safe filtering systems and time restrictions are in place to protect pupils. Pupils are encouraged to connect their own devices to the network, but there are also a large number of fixed terminal computers, including six major computer suites around the school. The school is embracing new technologies and runs a sophisticated Virtual Learning Environment to support pupils' learning away from the classroom.

Sports. There are over fifty acres of sports fields, where, at any one time, seventeen various games or matches can take place. Other facilities include two astroturf pitches, twenty tennis courts, Rugby fives courts and a shooting range. Within the School's sports centre there is a sports hall, a twenty-five metre swimming pool, a fitness suite and squash courts. A wide variety of sports and activities are offered including athletics, badminton, basketball, canoeing, cricket, cross-country, fencing, fives, golf, hockey, polo, riding, rugby, sailing, shooting, soccer, sub-aqua, swimming and tennis.

Societies and Activities. In addition to a full sporting, music and drama programme, numerous academic societies meet regularly throughout the term. Other activities and clubs take place on Wednesday afternoons and whenever time allows. They include: bridge, chess, computing, debating, photography, dining, life drawing, cooking for university, film making, community service, speech and drama and United Nations.

The school has a strong tradition of outdoor education and, in addition to The Duke of Edinburgh's Award Scheme, there are walking, climbing, kayaking and sailing trips. These are local or further afield in Scotland, the Lake District, Wales, Exmoor, Dartmoor and occasionally abroad. Boys also take part in the annual 'Ten Tors Challenge'.

Membership of the Combined Cadet Force is voluntary and the Army, Royal Navy and Royal Marine sections attract about 150 boys each year. A large number of trips and camps are arranged during the term time and the holidays.

Old Shirburnian Society. Mr John Harden, Secretary, tel: 01935 810557, email: OSS@sherborne.org.

Girls' Schools. There is close liaison with the neighbouring girls' schools, which allows us to offer many of the real benefits of co-education with all the advantages of a single-sex secondary education. As well as the Joint Sixth Form academic courses with Sherborne Girls, drama, music and social activities are arranged throughout the year.

Fees per term (2014–2015). Boarders: £10,950; Day Boys: £8,865.

Charitable status. Sherborne School is a Registered Charity, number 1081228, and a Company Limited by Guarantee, registered in England and Wales, number 4002575. Its aim and objectives are to supply a liberal education in accordance with the principles of the Church of England.

Shiplake College

Henley-on-Thames, Oxon RG9 4BW
Tel: 0118 940 2455
email: registrar@shiplake.org.uk
website: www.shiplake.org.uk

Motto: '*Exemplum docet*' (Example teaches)

Founded by Alexander Everett in 1959, Shiplake College is an independent school for day boys aged 11–18 and boarding boys from 13–18. Day and boarding girls join the Sixth Form.

Governing Body:
Chairman: The Rt Hon T J C Eggar, LLB
A Ashton, MA
R Dempster, BSc
Mrs M Carey-Elms, BA, PGCE, MA
J Dunston, MA
C Eve
J S Gordon, LLB
J R B Hobbs, BA
I Howell
R C Lester
M G E Mackenzie-Charrington
The Hon Sir William McAlpine, Bart
Lady Phillimore
Mrs S J Ryan, BSc
D W Tanner, CBE, BA, FRSA

Headmaster: **A G S Davies**, BSc, Cert Mgmt

Senior Staff:
Deputy Headmaster: R Jones, BA, PGCE
Bursar and Clerk to the Governors: J N Walne, BSc, MBA
Director of Studies: I H Munro, BSc, PGCE, FSB
Assistant Head (Co-Curricular): N J Brown, BA, PGCE

Housemasters:
Miss S G Andrew, BSc, PGCE (*Gilson*)
T M Armstrong, BA, BT (*Everett*)
R Curtis, BEd (*College*)
A D Dix, BSc, PGCE (*Senior Housemaster and Burr*)
A P R Duncan, BSc, PGCE (*Skipwith*)
J Howorth, BSc, PGCE (*Welsh*)
P S Jones, BA (*Lower School*)
A Mallins, BSc (*Orchard*)

Chaplain: The Revd S Cousins

Heads of Department:
Art: Mrs H Gillings, BA, PGCE
Biology: R Snellgrove, BSc, PhD CNAA
Business: A White, BA, PGCE, QTS
Chemistry: A Khare, BSc, MSc, PhD, DTLLS, PTLLS, MBA

Design Technology: A Hunt, BEd
Economics: D Bluck, BA, MA, PGCE
English: D Sharkey, BA, PGCE
Geography: R Johnstone, BSc, PGCE
History: L B Morgan, BA, MA, GTP
ICT: Mrs L Adamson, BSc, PGCE
Learning Development: Mrs A Higgins, BEd, MSc, Dip Law
Mathematics: Miss J Golding, BSc, PGCE
Media Studies: M Milburn, BA, PCGE
Modern Foreign Languages: Mrs J L Parrott, BA, PCGE
Music: P S Jones, BA
Physics: L Cottrell, BSc, PGCE
Psychology: R Ebbage, BSc, MSc
Sport: J Gaunt, BSc, MSc, GTP/QTS
Theology and Philosophy: J Brownley, BA, PGCE

Support Staff:
Director of Marketing and External Relations: Mrs K S F Green, BA
HR Manager and Headmaster's PA: Mrs M Flynn, BA
Registrar: Mrs J Thomas
Catering and Events Manager: B Shepherd
Estate Manager: D Greer, Dip SM, MIIRSM

Ethos. Whilst Shiplake College has evolved and moved forward since its founding in 1959, many principles remain the same. We ensure that every pupil is challenged and supported according to their need and ability, providing an education that is tailored to the individual. We firmly believe that in addition to a solid academic grounding, sporting, social and cultural achievement is vital to a pupil's long-term development. Shiplake offers a wide range of challenging enrichment activities to ensure an all-round education.

Academic. We aim to admit a well-balanced intake of pupils with a variety of skills and talents. Pupils are selected on his or her potential to make the most of the opportunities that Shiplake can offer and the value we can add to their education. We are proud of our superb value-added results. At Shiplake, teaching and learning concentrates on delivering excellent teaching through small classes and individual attention with a supportive but stimulating environment. Our teaching is delivered through a mixture of conventional teaching and inspirational multi-sensory methods to provide for a range of learning styles.

Pastoral Care. Boys joining at 11+ enter the Lower School which houses Year 7 and 8. From Year 9 all pupils become a member of one of the five houses: Burr, Skipwith, Welsh, Everett or Orchard. Both day and boarding girls join Gilson House, the purpose-built girls' house, but are attached to one of the boys' houses for social purposes, duties and inter-house competitions. The Upper Sixth boys enjoy the separate facilities of College House which helps establish independence before the move to university or a career.

Each house is run by a Housemaster who is supported by a strong team of staff including the House Matron, House Tutor, Visiting Tutors, the Medical Staff and the Chaplain. The houses provide excellent support for the pupils in addition to ensuring a comfortable, homely environment for pupils to study or relax. There is a strong house spirit in evidence with competitions organised for arts, games and academic progress.

Knowing our pupils well enables us to ensure that they get the best from their education at Shiplake. We know that every pupil is different and we aim to tailor the support and guidance they receive to suit their individual needs.

As a Christian School there is an extensive programme of worship, very often provided in the neighbouring Parish Church. The Chaplain, whose role is purely pastoral, is always available to any member of the College community. Shiplake also welcomes pupils of other faiths.

Location. The College enjoys a beautiful riverside site of 45 acres including an island in the River Thames. It sits overlooking the river, two miles upstream of Henley-on-Thames.

Although pupils love the acres of sports pitches and the country trails, parents appreciate the fact that Shiplake is conveniently placed for access to the M4 and M40 and the railway stations at Henley and Reading. This idyllic countryside location is just an hour from London and within easy reach of Heathrow and Gatwick airports.

Facilities. Shiplake House, built in 1889 as a family home, is at the heart of the school. Pupils and staff take their main meals in the wood-panelled Great Hall. The College is fortunate to have the use of the twelfth-century Parish Church for assemblies and worship.

In addition to the main school buildings, Shiplake boasts a range of facilities including the Tithe Barn Theatre, Sports Hall and Fitness Suite. The boathouses are a short walk from the main buildings, allowing direct access to the Thames. The College has state-of-the-art ICT and computing facilities, including site-wide Wi-Fi, available to all pupils.

Developments. The day and boarding house for girls opened in September 2009 as did the new Lower School. A new Arts, Music and 'Thinking Space' opened in September 2014.

Academic Structure. Boys entering the College in Year 7 follow the specially designed curriculum for Years 7 and 8 before moving on to the Upper School. In the Upper School they will enjoy the broad and balanced Year 9 curriculum which provides a strong foundation for GCSE. In the Sixth Form, pupils select up to four subjects from a choice of twenty-two.

Learning Development. Shiplake has a dedicated Learning Development Department to provide additional help for both those who are academically gifted and those who find certain subject areas difficult to access. The Department provides either a structured programme to support the curriculum, or help on an ad hoc basis, to improve pupils' confidence and self-esteem and equip them with the necessary skills. We are a school with small class sizes and our teachers are committed to providing individual attention for all abilities. Pupils are able to approach their subject teachers for additional support whenever necessary.

Sport. Our extensive site on the banks of the River Thames makes Shiplake an ideal location for pupils who love sport. The College has an excellent sporting reputation and most pupils take part in a sporting activity every day. The College enjoys direct access to the river and boathouses, hockey, cricket and rugby pitches, tennis courts, squash courts and an outdoor swimming pool. The sports hall offers a variety of indoor sports, a weight-training gym and a fitness room.

Almost all boys play rugby in the autumn term. In the spring term boys play hockey, football or row, and in the summer term there is the choice of cricket, tennis or rowing. The girls enjoy a mixed programme of sports and activities using the sporting facilities available. Basketball, badminton, squash, judo, cross-country running and athletics provide additional activities to develop skills and fitness.

For a small school, Shiplake has a remarkable number of crews and teams taking part in events and competitions with national success. There have been a number of overseas tours involving the rugby, cricket, hockey and rowing clubs.

Music, Art and Drama. The College has a thriving mixture of Arts activities and performances and all pupils are encouraged to enjoy the Arts. The annual House Music Competition ensures that every pupil in the school is involved in preparing for a performance and every term there is at least one concert for pupils to demonstrate the progress they have made. The Drama Department provides opportunities for the theatrically inclined.

Activities. Pupils choose from a wide range of activities including art, ballroom dancing, cookery, debating, football, golf, log-chopping and canoeing. The College has a thriving Combined Cadet Force with Air Force, Army and Navy sections. Pupils take part in community service activities and the school has links to a Kenyan School for which fundraising activities are regularly undertaken. The College also runs a Duke of Edinburgh's Award Scheme with a number of pupils each year collecting Gold Awards. In addition there are drama productions, debates and music recitals.

Careers. There is an experienced Careers Adviser and particular attention is paid to the choice of university and career from Year 11 onwards. The School is a member of ISCO.

Admission. The Registrar is the first point of contact for all admissions and admissions enquiries. Boys are admitted at 11+ into Year 7 and at 13+ into Year 9. There is an intake into the Sixth Form for boys and girls. Places are offered following an assessment day. Please contact the Registrar for further details. Occasional places arise in other years.

Scholarships. Means-tested scholarships and bursaries are offered for academic excellence and to outstanding sportsmen, artists or musicians at Year 7, Year 9 and in the Sixth Form.

Fees per term (2014–2015). Boarders £9,560; Day Pupils: Years 7 & 8, £5,170, Years 9–13 £6,450.

Alumni. The Old Viking Society has an annual programme of events including sports fixtures and a formal dinner. The Society produces an annual newsletter for Old Vikings.

Charitable status. Shiplake College is a Registered Charity, number 309651. It exists to provide education for children.

Shrewsbury School

The Schools, Shrewsbury, Shropshire SY3 7BA
Tel: 01743 280500 (Switchboard)
           01743 280525 (Headmaster)
           01743 280820 (Bursar)
           01743 280552 (Director of Admissions)
Fax: 01743 243107 (Reception)
           01743 280559 (Director of Admissions)
email: admissions@shrewsbury.org.uk
website: www.shrewsbury.org.uk

Motto: '*Intus si recte, ne labora*'
Shrewsbury School was founded by King Edward VI in 1552 and augmented by Queen Elizabeth in 1571. In 1882 it moved from the centre of the town to its present site overlooking the town and the River Severn.

Governing Body:

Chairman: M H Collins
Vice-Chair: Ms Lyndsey Pollard, LLB
S R Baker, BSc, FCA, CF
R Burbidge, OBE, BA, DL
T H Biggins, MA
J R Clark, MA
Prof C Dobson, FRS
Mrs D Flint, DL
Dr Fiona Hay, MA, BM, BCh, DRCOG, MRCGP, DFFP
T H P Haynes, MA
Mrs C Howarth, LLB
W R O Hunter, QC
Prof E W Jones, OBE, BSc Hons, PhD, FRAgS
R J Kendall, BSc
Prof A J McCarthy, BSc, PhD
Prof M R E Proctor, FRS, FIMA
Alderman D W L Roberts
H P Trevor-Jones, BSc, DL
P StJ Worth, FCA

Headmaster: M Turner, MA

Bursar and Clerk to the Governors: M J Ware, MA, ACA

Second Master: M J Tonks, BA
Deputy Head (Pastoral): P R Vicars, MA
Deputy Head (Academic): M J Cropper, MA
Deputy Head (Staffing): Mrs S L Hankin, BA
Director of Admissions: Mrs K Campbell, BA
Director of Shrewsbury School Foundation: J G E Rolfe

Assistant Masters/Mistresses:
* *Head of Faculty*
† *Housemaster/Housemistress*

Mrs R W Adams, BEc, BEd
S F Adams, MA, MSc (*Science)
A J Allott, MA (*Biology)
J C Armstrong, BA (*Mathematics)
Miss E L Arthur, BA
J Balcombe, BSc
Mrs K H Balcombe, BEd, OCR Cert SpLD (*Learning Support)
A S Barnard, BA (†*Port Hill – day boys*)
M W D Barrett, BSc
G StJ F Bell, BA
H R D Besterman, MA (†*School House*)
S J Biggins (*Master i/c Football*)
Mrs N J Bradburne, BA (*Head of Girls' Games*)
A D Briggs, BSc, PhD (*Chemistry)
Miss H R Brown, MA (**Director of Drama*)
Miss N M Buckley, BA
Miss J M M Burge, BSc
J R Burke, BSc
R A J Case, BSc, PhD (†*Radbrook – day boys*)
M D H Clark, MA
M J Clark, MPhil, PhD
Miss K C Collins, BA
C E Cook, MA
S K P Cooley, MEng
T A C Corbett, BSc
S H Cowper, MA (*Spanish)
Mrs A J Crump, BSc
A Dalton, BA (**Philosophy & Theology*)
N P David, BSc
The Revd G W Dobbie, MA (*Chaplain*)
Mrs L J Drew, BA
M S Elliot, MA, PhD
R T Fitton, MEng
P G Fitzgerald, MA (*Classics)
T R Foulger, BSc, PhD (*Geography)
S A A Fox, BA
J R Fraser-Andrews, MA, MMus
J Gabbitas, MA
S W Gunnell, BA
M H Hansen, BSc
M J Harding, BA
I P Haworth, MA
S Hellier, BA
R T Hudson, MA (†*Churchill's Hall*)
W A Hughes, BA (†*Ridgemount*)
A T Hundermark, BSc
M D B Johnson, BSc, BA (†*Oldham's Hall*)
D M Joyce, Dip RCM, ARCM
P A Kaye, BEng (*Educational ICT)
C W Kealy, BComm (*Business Studies)
M A Kirk, BSc (*Physics)
Mrs V L Kirk, BSc
D Kirkby, BSc
P H Lapage, BA
Mrs S G Latcham, BA
D A Law, BA, MA, PhD
Mrs J Lees, BSc
Mrs K Leslie, BA (*English)
K M Lloyd, BA (*DT)
J V Lucas, LLB
A E Mason, BA, MMus
Mrs J A Matthews, BSc

P A Merricks-Murgatroyd, BA (*Economics*)
P J Middleton, BA (†*Rigg's Hall*)
Miss S I Milanova, BA
C J Minns, MA, PhD (*German*)
J F Moore, BA, LRAM (*Music*)
T S Morgan, BSc, PhD
R H Morris, BEd
A J Murfin, BSc (*Director of Sport*)
D A G Nicholas, BA (†*Severn Hill*)
Mrs D B Nightingale, BMus, LTCL, ACCEG (*Higher Education Adviser*)
C W Oakley, MMath, DPhil
J L Pattenden, MA, DPhil
P Pattenden, MA, DPhil, CPhys, MInstP (†*Moser's Hall*)
H R W Peach, BA
Ms A R Peak, BA (†*Mary Sidney Hall*)
T P Percival, MA
D Portier, BA, MA
A P Pridgeon
F O L Reid, MA
W R Reynolds, BSc
Miss C E Rule, BSc
C M Samworth, BSc, PhD
M Schofield, BSc
M A Schutzer-Weissmann, MA
A P Scrimshaw, MEng
Mrs S L M Shantry, BSc
Mrs R Shawe-Taylor, BA, MA (*Art*)
J A Sheppe, MPhil
W M Simper, BSc
Mrs L R Temple, BA
M F Wade, MA, PhD
T D J Warburg, MA
Miss R B Weatherstone, BA
Mrs K M Weston, MSc (†*Emma Darwin Hall*)
T C Whitehead, BA (*French*)
Miss L J Whittle, BA (*History*)
Mrs C H L Wilson, BA (†*The Grove*)
R M Wilson, MEng Hons
Miss R Witcombe, BSc
Miss G Y Y Woo, MSc
M P J Wright, BA (†*Ingram's Hall*)
Mrs P A Wright, BA, BEd

Careers Fellow: Dr K S Daubney, BSc, MSc, PhD, PCLTHE University of Leeds and University of York

Harvard Fellow: Miss N A Paine, AB Harvard College, Cambridge, Massachusetts, USA

Visiting French Fellow: Miss C Piquard, MA Université de Montesquieu, Bordeaux IV

Visiting Hispanic Fellow: Miss A M Martinez, BEd San Bartolome, Rosario, Argentina

School Doctors:
The General Practitioner Team, Mytton Oak Surgery, Racecourse Lane, Shrewsbury

Dental Adviser: R J Gatenby, BDS, DGDP, RCS

Headmaster's Personal Assistant: Mrs E J Gibbs

Number in School. There are 769 pupils in the School (629 boarding and 140 day).

Admission. Most admissions are in September. Girls and boys are admitted at 13 or (direct to the Sixth Form) at 16. Registration forms and other information can be obtained from the Admissions Office. The registration fee, which is non-returnable, is £100.

Entry at 13: Pupils usually take the Common Entrance Examination or the Scholarship Examination in the term preceding that in which they wish to come. The School has its own entrance test for pupils who have not followed the Common Entrance syllabus. A Secured Places Scheme operates whereby girls and boys aged 11 can take an examination set by the School and may receive an offer of a place, subject to a satisfactory school report in the final year of preparatory school at 13.

Sixth Form Entry: Direct entry into the Sixth Form depends on an interview, examination at Shrewsbury and a favourable report from the applicant's present school.

Scholarships. At 13+ entry, the Governors currently offer 4 Academic Scholarships up to the value of 30% of fees, 6 up to the value of 20% of fees and 7 worth at least £2,000 per annum. The Academic Scholarship examination is held during the Summer term.

In addition, there are a number of Music Scholarships, up to the value of 30% of fees, Art Scholarships up to the value of 20% of fees, Design and Technology Scholarships up to the value of 20% of the fees, Drama Scholarships up to the value of 20%, Sports Scholarships up to the value of 20% of fees, All-Rounder Scholarships up to the value of 20% of fees and 10 House Foundation Awards, worth up to the value of 50% of fees, which are available for designed to provide financial support for talented pupils under 14 years of age, whose parents would otherwise be unable to afford the full fees.

At Sixth Form entry, there are 8 Academic Scholarships and six Specialist Awards, which are offered for excellence in Music, Art, Drama and Sport.

There is one Sir Martin Rees Scholarship for excellence in Physics, worth up to 100% of the fees and subject to means testing, one Sixth Form Margaret Cassidy Sports Scholarship, worth up to 100% of fees and subject to means testing, for candidates (currently at a state school) with a record of outstanding sporting ability in football, cricket or rowing, and one Alex Wilson Dayboy Scholarship, worth up to the value of 100% of the day fee, for sporting and academic excellence, also subject to means testing.

Buildings. The school operates a rolling programme of refurbishment for all boarding houses. Similarly, large-scale refurbishment of the teaching accommodation is currently under way. All classrooms are professionally equipped to a very high standard. A Music School, including an auditorium and a large ensemble room, was opened in February 2001, a cricket academy and a new house (now accommodating day and boarding girls) opened in 2006, a new swimming pool opened in 2007, a new sixth form centre was completed in 2008, and two further houses for girls opened in September 2011 and September 2014 respectively.

The Moser Library houses The School Library, the Moser collection of watercolours, and the Ancient Library, which contains medieval manuscripts and early printed books.

Courses of Study. All pupils follow a general course as far as the GCSE Level Examinations. In the Sixth Form it is usual to study 4 subjects to AS Level and 3 to A2 Level. The number of combinations of subjects for which it is possible to opt is very large. Recent additions are PE and Theatre Studies AS and A2, and Cambridge Pre-U courses in French and Physics.

Games. Rowing, Cricket, Association Football, Swimming, Lacrosse, Hockey, Netball, Cross-Country, Eton Fives and Rugby. The School has its own indoor Swimming Pool, Gymnasium, Multi-gym, Miniature Rifle Range, all-weather playing surface, Tennis Courts, Squash Courts and Fives Courts. The River Severn flows just below the Main School Building and the Boat House is within the School grounds.

Activities. Pupils are offered a considerable range of outdoor activities via the Combined Cadet Force, leadership courses and the Duke of Edinburgh's Award Scheme. The programme of activities and opportunities continues to broaden as a pupil moves up the School.

Art and Design. Art and Design are taught to all pupils in their first year. For those not doing GCSE or A Level courses they subsequently become activities followed mainly, but not exclusively, out of school hours. The Art and

CDT centres are available 7 days a week. The CDT department offers the chance of advanced design work and of creative work in a variety of materials. AS and A2 and GCSE Level design are also offered, as are AS and A2 ceramics and photography.

Societies. These range from Literary, Political, Debating, Drama and Language societies to those catering for practical skills. Hillwalkers and Mountaineers make use of the unspoilt country on the doorstep and of the Welsh hills.

Music. Teaching is available in any orchestral instrument, as well as the Piano and Organ. The charge for this is £22.38 per 40 minute lesson for all instruments. Regular Choral, Orchestral and Chamber Concerts both at the school and elsewhere (St John's, Smith Square; CBSO Birmingham) are given by the pupils. In addition concerts are given during the winter months by distinguished visiting artists.

Drama. Drama is a major feature of school life, with two school plays and up to nine house plays per year, together with regular accolades at the Edinburgh Fringe.

Field Study Centre. Shrewsbury owns a farmhouse in Snowdonia, which is used at weekends throughout the year as a base for expeditions.

Careers. There is a full-time Careers Fellow and a Higher Education Adviser. Pupils are offered the Morrisby Aptitude Tests and the services of the Independent Schools Careers Organization.

Community Service. In association with other schools in the town, pupils play an active part in caring for the old and needy in the Shrewsbury area.

Shrewsbury House. Founded in Liverpool as a Club for boys in 1903, it was re-built as a Community Centre in association with the Local Authority and the Diocese in 1974. There is residential accommodation in the Centre and groups of pupils from the School have the opportunity to go there on study courses.

Shrewsbury International School. The school has close links with Shrewsbury International School in Bangkok. Teaching and pupil exchanges take place between the two schools, and Governors of Shrewsbury School serve on the board of management of the International School.

Fees per term (2014–2015). Boarders: £10,545, including tuition, board and ordinary School expenses. There are no other obligatory extras, apart from stationery. Day Pupils: £7,385.

Application for reduced fees may be made to the Governors through the Headmaster.

Old Pupils' Society. Most pupils leaving the school join the Salopian Club, The Schools, Shrewsbury SY3 7BA; email: oldsalopian@shrewsbury.org.uk.

Charitable status. Shrewsbury School is a Registered Charity, number 528413. It exists to provide secondary education.

Sidcot School

Winscombe, North Somerset BS25 1PD
Tel: 01934 843102
Fax: 01934 844181
email: admissions@sidcot.org.uk
website: www.sidcot.org.uk

Originally established in 1699 to teach boys of Quaker families, Sidcot opened to girls in 1808 and is one of the oldest co-educational boarding schools in the UK. Today we have a vibrant community of around 560 pupils aged 3–18 years, from nearly 30 different countries. Sidcot welcomes pupils and staff of all faiths or none. About one-third of our students are boarders. Boarding has a key role in Sidcot life that enriches the friendly, family orientated atmosphere and provides opportunities for our students to engage with each other and the facilities, beyond the normal confines of the school day.

Chairman of the Committee: Paul Whitehouse

Headmaster: Iain Kilpatrick, BA Hons, MEd, FRSA

Deputy Head (Pastoral): Matt Williams, BA, MA, PGCE

Deputy Head (Academic): Russell Spooner, BA Hons, MA, Cert Ed

Director of Operations: Hilary Atkin, BSc Hons

Head of Junior School: Claire Lilley, BEd Hons

Boarding House Staff:
Head of Boarding: Matt Williams, BA, MA, PGCE
School House Girls and School House Boys: Amandine Smilevich, Licence LLCE Anglais Lyon, CELTA
Wing House: Paul Coates, Cert Ed
Combe House: Philip Lovett, BSc Hons, PGCE
Newcombe House: Charlotte Resuggan, BA Hons, PGCE

Finance Manager: Steve Harris

Admissions Registrar: Valerie Kennedy

Situation and Accommodation. Established in 160 acres of beautiful countryside in the rolling Mendip Hills, Sidcot's secure campus also benefits from being close to the cities of Bristol and Bath. We have excellent transport links and run private buses each day to Bristol, Weston-super-Mare and surrounding villages. London is only 2 hours away and Bristol International Airport is about 20 minutes door to door by car.

Sidcot has over two hundred years' experience in co-educational boarding and this philosophy has very much been woven into the fabric of the boarding houses and approach at the school.

Students may board from age 11. Flexi boarding is available and can be an attractive option for those who live just beyond an easy daily commute.

Sidcot has some outstanding facilities to inspire our students. The latest development is a Creative Arts Centre that bridges the traditional genres with modern technology. Professional, state-of-the-art facilities for fine art, music and drama include studios for painting; sculpture; photography and a digital media suite; a music school with a dedicated performance hall; practice rooms; recording studio and music technology suite; a drama department providing a studio for performances that can become a theatre for film.

To meet other interests, there is a Sports Centre with a superb 25-metre indoor heated pool, multi-gym, sports hall, squash court and a BHS approved Equestrian Centre. Students of all ages can learn to ride or join the Pony Club to work towards their badges. The centre also provides tuition in dressage, riding our cross-country course and jumping. Students are very welcome to bring their horses to Sidcot and a full livery service is available.

Aims. Sidcot excels in building children's self-esteem by encouraging all their abilities and not just focusing on academic excellence. We believe that, by enabling children to be adventurous in thought and free from negative peer pressure, they will develop self-assurance and reach their full potential as rounded individuals. We challenge our students to think with greater depth to reach a better understanding of themselves and the world they live in. We believe that this in turn leads to academic excellence – Sidcot's examination results are amongst the best in the South West.

Learning Ethos. The School has always been forward-looking and has promoted experimentation, original thinking and the nurturing of individual talent. This ethos is just as relevant today as it has been throughout the School's history – there is a deep-rooted conviction to provide a creative and stretching education that inspires children to want to learn. To achieve this, our curriculum is shaped to meet government requirements but without an exam-obsessed and prescriptive syllabus. As a school that accepts children with wide-ranging strengths and abilities, we are very proud that we achieve some of the strongest results in the South West, ranking consistently with some of the best selective schools in the region for results at GCSE, A Level and the International Baccalaureate Diploma.

Our curriculum and teaching methods are designed to harness our children's natural intellectual curiosity and encourage independent thinking and creativity. We want to educate rather than train to pass tests, to foster self-motivation and enable our students to take responsibility for their learning. This will prepare them with the skills and knowledge they will need for further education and foster a love for lifelong learning. Reflecting Sidcot's aim of providing a stimulating and creative curriculum, we offer students the opportunity to follow either the International Baccalaureate Diploma or A Levels in the Sixth Form. We believe the ethos of the International Baccalaureate, with its broad curriculum and emphasis on study skills, community service and internationalism, fits perfectly with our Quaker values. Sidcot has recently appointed a founding director of peace and global studies who will be influencing every area of the curriculum and school life, encouraging students to seek peaceful means of resolving conflict, to value others, to live simply, to care for the environment and to speak up for their beliefs.

Admissions. Sidcot School does not use Common Entrance for admitting pupils. We accept children with a wide range of strengths and abilities. Our community includes students who are gifted and talented and those with mild to moderate learning support needs. We are not selective, beyond our expectation that the student will cope with mainstream curriculum. Students can be accepted throughout the year from Nursery to Year 9.

Scholarships. For outstanding students, a wide range of talent and academic scholarships is offered to students entering Year 1 through to Year 6 in the Junior School and students entering Year 7, Year 9, Year 10 and Year 12 in the Senior School.

Fees per term (2014–2015). Day: Junior School £2,320–£3,460, Senior School £4,730–£5,200. Boarding £7,800–£9,340.

Charitable status. Sidcot School is a Registered Charity, number 296491. The aim of the school is to become a pioneer, and a world-class centre of excellence, for inspirational education that is as much about nurturing the spirit as it is about outstanding academic success.

Silcoates School

Wrenthorpe, Wakefield, West Yorkshire WF2 0PD
Tel: 01924 291614
Fax: 01924 368693
email: head@silcoates.org.uk
website: www.silcoates.org.uk

Motto: '*Clarior ex ignibus*'

Founded in 1820 and retaining its links to the United Reformed Church, Silcoates School is made up of three separate, but closely linked, sections: the Senior School, for boys and girls aged 11 to 18 (Year 7 to the Upper Sixth Form); the Junior School, for boys and girls aged 5 to 11 (Year 1 to Year 6); and Sunny Hill, for boys and girls aged 2 to 5 (Nursery, Foundation and Reception).

The Senior School and Junior School share a self-contained site in Wrenthorpe, near Wakefield, and Sunny Hill has its own site just down the road. With this structure the School offers an all-through, fully co-educational experience for children from 2 to 18. It seeks to provide an all-round education with an academic edge.

Board of Governors:

Chairman: Mrs Mary Chippendale, BSc
Vice-Chairman: Mr John Lane, LLB, AKC, TEP

Mr Tony Briggs, FCA
Mrs Rachel Copley
Dr Moira Gallagher, MBE
Mrs Jan Healey, ATCL
Ms Alison Ketchell, MSc
Revd Steven Knapton, MA
Mrs Sue Lee, BPharm, MRPharmS
Revd Janet Lees, PhD, MPhil, MTh, MRCSLT
Mr David Payling, MA, ACA
Mrs Debbie Procter, BA
Mr Craig Shannon, MA, MBA

Clerk to the Governors: Mr David Dinmore, MBE, DL, MCIPD, MCMI

Staff:

Headmaster: Darryl Wideman, MA (*History*)

Deputy Heads:
Steve Fox, MA (*Modern Languages, Latin*)
Dan Coll, BEd (*Psychology*)

Assistant Head (*Academic*): Rebecca Dews, BEng (*Mathematics*)

Head of Middle School: Richard Fenn, BEd (*Geography*)

Head of Upper School: Carol Marsh, BEd (*Religious Studies*)

Head of Sixth Form: Anand Mistry, BA (*Design & Technology*)

Head of Junior School: Adrian Boyer, BEd (*Junior Subjects*)

Chaplain: Revd Janet Lees, PhD, MPhil, MTh, MRCSLT

Assistant Staff:

* *Head of Department or Year*
† *Head of House*

Malcolm Affleck, BA (**Religious Studies*)
Wendy Affleck, BA (*English*)
Scott Benton (*Physical Education*)
Caroline Boardman, BA, MA, PhD (*English*)
Naomi Chambers, BA (*Junior Subjects*)
Sandra Coll, BA (*Modern Languages,* *Latin)
Julia Conlon, BA (*English*)
John Cooling, BSc, MMedSci, PhD (*Biology*)
David Coulson, BSc (*Biology,* *PSHCE)
Helen Crompton, BMus, MMus, LTCL (*Music)
Rachel Dix, BA (*Junior Subjects*)
Angela Eckersley, MA, BSc (*ICT)
Helen Emmett, BSc (*Geography*)
Jenny Everingham, BA, MA (*History)
Laura Featherstone, BA (*Art)
Wendy Forge, BA (*Junior Subjects*)
Gill Gibson, Cert Ed (*Music*)
Chris Green, BA, MA, PhD
Paul Grooby, BSc, PhD (*Chemistry*)
Sami Harder, BSc (*Physics*)
Marilyn Hayes, DipAD, SIAD (*Art*)
Nicki Hoare, BA (*Music*)
Laura Hoyland, BA (*Design & Technology,* †*Yonge's House*)
Cale Hugill, BSc (*Mathematics*)
Nigel Jackson, BSc (**Outdoor Pursuits, Biology*)
Mark Jeanes, BSc (*Mathematics,* †*Evans' House*)
Kurt Johnson, BA, MA, PhD (*English*)
Amy Knowles, BA (*Physical Education,* †*Spencer's House*)
Alex Lewry, BSc, MEd (*Geography)
Joanne McManus, BA (*Modern Languages, PSHCE*)

Kathy March, BEd (*Physical Education*)
Amanda Matheson, BA (*Junior Subjects*)
Jonathan Newell, BSc, CPhys, MInstP (**Physics, *Science*)
Liz Nuttall, BA (*Physical Education*)
Steve Ogden, BSc (*Physics, Chemistry*)
Sue O'Leary-Hall, BA, MA (**English*)
Liz Olumegbon, BSc (*Junior Subjects*)
Beatriz Pelaez, BA (*Modern Languages*)
Alex Paling, BSc (*ICT*)
Hilary Peach, BA (**Physical Education, †Moore's House*)
Jo Piggott, BSc (*Junior Subjects*)
Rachel Platt, BA, LTCL (*Music*)
Andy Potter, BEd (*Physical Education, *Games*)
Cathryn Powell, BA (*Junior Subjects*)
Brian Pye, BEd (*Design & Technology, *Year 11*)
David Raggett, BSc (*Mathematics*)
Patricia Richards, BA (*Economics, Business Studies*)
Glenn Roberts, BEd (*Physical Education*)
Tim Roberts, MA (**Theatre Studies, English*)
Chris Rowe, BA (**Design & Technology*)
Simon Scholfield, BA (*Physical Education*)
Barbara Shaw, BA (**Modern Languages*)
Susan Snow, BA (*Economics, *Business Studies*)
Tom Sprott, BSc (**Psychology*)
Helen Stalker, BA (*Modern Languages*)
Lorrie Sugden, BSc, MSc (*Learning Support*)
Diane Townsend, BSc (*Mathematics*)
Tom Verinder, BA (**Politics, History*)
Margaret Ward, CertEd, Cert Dyslexia & Literacy
    (**Learning Support*)
Simon Wardle, BA, MSt (*English*)
Pat Watkin, BSc (**Biology*)
Nigel Wears, GCLCM (*Music*)
Graham Wickstead, BSc (**Mathematics*)
Victoria Wilkinson, BA (*Junior Subjects*)
Fiona Wideman, MA (*History*)
Joanne Worboys-Hodgson, LTCL, ALCM (*Music*)
Peter Wright, MSci, PhD (**Chemistry*)

School Nurse: Jan Alkadi, RGN
Teaching Assistant: Lisa Boyer
Accounts Assistant: Sarah Chason
Teaching Assistant: Michelle Claven
Chemistry Technician: Michael Cole
ICT Systems Manager: Michael Collinson
Clerk to the Governors: David Dinmore, MBE, DL,
    MCIPD, MCMI
Junior School Secretary: Alison Dix
Teaching Assistant: Nicola Ferry
Catering Manager: Gary Ferguson
Head Groundsman: Dave Forrester
Design Technician: Simon Gibson
ICT Support Assistant/Assistant Exams Officer: Alyson
    Harris
Bursar: Matthew Johnson
Marketing Officer: Louise Leach
Librarian: Karen Lingard
Teaching Assistant: Cheryl Milnes
Biology Technician: John Nelmes
Head Porter: Phil Noble
School Secretary: Amanda Obridge
Accounts Assistant: Jane O'Brien
Physics Technician: George Pearson
Operations Manager: Fiona Reed
Accounts Office Supervisor: Sharron Taylor
Projects Manager: Kath Thackray
SIMS Data Manager: Rebecca Thompson
Examinations Officer: Eileen Varley
Sixth Form Supervisor: Teresa Watkin
ICT Technician: Paul Webb
Headmaster's PA/Admissions: Carol Woodhead

Admission. There are 670 pupils at Silcoates. Boys and girls are admitted to the Junior School from the age of 5 and to the Senior School from the age of 11. Places are available for girls and boys wishing to study for A Level in the Sixth Form.

Entrance Examinations take place in January for admission the following September.

The School also provides a pre-preparatory education for boys and girls from 2 to 5 years at Sunny Hill House School, just down the road from Silcoates. (*See entry for Sunny Hill House School in ISA section.*)

Curriculum. Recent inspection reports have been highly complimentary about the school's academic performance. Nearly all pupils sit a minimum of 9 GCSEs, 4 AS and 3 A2 Levels, and the vast majority go on to degree courses. There is great flexibility of subject choice at GCSE and A Level. Small class sizes and excellent facilities create a positive atmosphere for learning. Value added scores are very strong.

Games and Activities. Drama, art, music and sport all flourish at Silcoates. The school has an excellent record of individual and collective achievement in all of its extra-curricular activities. The outstanding sports facilities include an indoor pool, a new astroturf, new netball and tennis courts, and extensive sports pitches. There is a well-equipped Music School. Our very successful Duke of Edinburgh's Award programme makes extensive use of various venues in the north of England.

Pastoral Care and Careers Guidance. With a generous pupil : personal tutor ratio, the quality of pastoral care is first class. We provide a full programme of careers advice and guidance for university entrance.

Fees per term (2014–2015). Senior School: £4,210; Junior School: £2,200–£3,320.

Scholarships and Bursaries. Academic Scholarships are offered at 11+ and above; Sixth Form entrants are eligible for these awards.

Bursaries are available for the sons and daughters of Ministers and Missionaries of the United Reformed Church or of the Congregational Church, and of other recognised Christian denominations and to other parents subject to a financial assessment.

Charitable status. The Silcoates School Foundation is a Registered Charity, number 529281.

Solihull School

Warwick Road, Solihull, West Midlands B91 3DJ

Tel:	0121 705 0958 (Headmaster)
	0121 705 4273 (Admissions)
	0121 705 0883 (Bursar)
Fax:	0121 711 4439
email:	admin@solsch.org.uk
website:	www.solsch.org.uk
Twitter:	@solsch1560
Facebook:	/SolihullSchool

Motto: '*Perseverantia*'

Chairman of the Governors: M T Hopton, FCA

Bursar and Clerk to the Governors: R Bate, MA Cantab,
    ACMA

Headmaster: D E J J Lloyd, BSc

Senior Deputy Headmaster: S A Morgan, BA
Deputy Headmaster (Academic): D G Morgan, BA, MA
    Cantab
Assistant Headteacher (Pastoral Care): Mrs L A Fair, BA,
    MA
Assistant Headteacher (Co-Curricular): M J Garner, BSc
Assistant Headteacher (Academic): Ms D Harford, BA
    Oxon
Assistant Headteacher (ICT): D Reardon, BSc

Head of Sixth Form: B Sandford-Smith, BSc
Head of the Middle School: Mrs R Lancaster, BSc
Head of the Lower School: O W H Bate, BSc
Head of the Junior School: M P Penney, BA

Assistant Staff:
* *Head of Department*

G J Affleck, BA (*History*)
Miss R E Airdrie, BA
O R Anderton, BSc
Mrs N J Atkins, BEd
Dr R A Atkinson, BA, DPhil Oxon
M P Babb, BSc
Miss K Berns, BSc
M R Bishop, MSc (*Mathematics*)
Mrs C Black, BA
D J Brough, BSc
Mrs J S Brown, BA, MA
Miss T J Bryan, BA
Mrs D L Buckle, BSc
A Bussey, BA (*Economics & Business*)
Miss E A M Campbell, BA
Mrs N A Cheetham, BA
Miss S L S Compton, BSc
N E Corbett, BA (*Design Technology*)
M J Covill, BSc
Mrs P Cramb, BA (*German*)
Miss S A Crowther, BEd
G J Cureton, BSc
Mrs N Dickerson BA
Ms H Dolby, AGSM, ATCL
A J Dowsett, BA
T Emmet, BSc (*Psychology*)
Miss N Evans, BA
Mrs H M Fair, BA
D A Farrington BSc
Miss E Ford, BSc
Dr S Foster, MA Cantab, MPhil Oxon, DPhil Oxon, MBA
M Gledhill, BA, LLB
Mrs C Goodman, BSc
Miss C M Greswold, GLCM, AMus LCM, ALCM
Miss S J Gummery, BSc
R Gunchala, BSc
G Gunning, BA
Mrs H Hallworth, BSc
Miss J Hanlon, BSc
S A Hart, BA (*English*)
S R Hifle, QTS
P M Higley, BA, CertEd
Mrs J Humphreys, BEd Cantab
Mrs E Hurst, BA, Cert SpLD (*Learning Support*)
Revd Canon A C Hutchinson, BA, MEd
P J Irving, BA, ARCM, FRCO (*ICT*)
P R Jackson, BSc
D W Jenkinson, MEd
Mrs E Johnson, BA (*PE*)
Mrs J Johnson, BA, MPhil (*Classics*)
A Jones, BSc (*Science*)
M D Jones, MA, BA
A T Kermode, MA (*Director of Music*)
N W S Leonard, BEd
Miss L J Lynch, BSc
D L Maddy
Mrs J Mander, BA
P May, BSc
C I Mayer
Mrs W L Meigh, BEd
Miss L Mesrie, BA
Mrs H Middleton, BEng, BCom
S G Mitchell, BSc
Mrs C Mollison, BA
P L Morgan, BA (*MFL*)
Mrs R Morgan, BEd

Mrs U Mynette, MA
Dr M Partridge, BA Oxon, MA, PhD
Mrs D E Penney, BSc
S J Perrins, MA Cantab, FRCO (*Director of Music Emeritus*)
Mrs S J Phillips, BSc
S R Phillips, BA
Miss H E Pike, MA, BA
Dr K A Powell, PhD, MBA
Miss S C Roberts, MA, BA
Mrs A C Roll, BA (*Geography*)
Mrs B M E Rossay-Gilson (*French*)
Miss L Rutherford, MA Cantab, MEd (*Religious Studies*)
Dr S Sawicki, BA Cantab, MSc, PhD
Mrs H Smith
M K Smith, BSc (*Physics*)
Miss R Smith, BSc
P F Spratley, BA, MA
Mrs K Sykes, BA
C Thomas, BSc
Miss L Thomas, BA
Mrs S Thomas, BSc
S J Thompson, BSc (*Director of Sport*)
Miss D L Trim, BA (*Art*)
J Troth, PhD, BSc (*Chemistry*)
O M Walker, BA Oxon
Mr H Walsh, Licence d'Anglais
Miss S Walton, BSc
Miss D Wilcox, BA (*Girls Games*)
Mrs D H Wild, BSc (*Biology*)
Mrs J Wilde, BA (*Theatre Studies*)
M Worrall, MA
L K Worth, MA

Careers: Mrs J Skan, BA

Director of Development and Alumni Relations: Mrs A Bond, BA
Head of Marketing: Mrs R R Hadley-Leonard, BEd, Dip SM

OC CCF: Major N W S Leonard
SSI: WO2 P G Dean, MBE

Medical Officer: Dr S Kotecha, MBChB, FRCGP, MSc
Senior Nurse: Mrs S Serle, RGN
School Nurse: Mrs H King, RGN

Headmaster's PA: Miss L Else
Admissions Secretary: Mrs J Edwards
Bursar's PA: Ms S K Baldwin
Librarian: Mrs A M Vaughan

Solihull School was founded in 1560 with the income from the chantry chapels of the parish of Solihull. The School is particularly proud of the richness and diversity of the education that it provides. The School has always been closely involved with the community, making its sporting and theatrical facilities available, forming links with local schools.

Organisation. The School now provides education for approximately 1,030 day pupils aged between 7 and 18. The Junior School, which occupies its own separate building on the site and has its own Headmaster, has more than 220 pupils aged from 7 to 11. In the Senior School there are approximately 560 pupils from Year 7 to Year 11 and around 250 pupils in the Sixth Form. In 1973 girls were accepted into the Sixth Form. From September 2005 the School became fully co-educational.

Site and Facilities. The School moved to its present site in 1882 and the original school building, School House, survives. The site now comprises over 50 acres of buildings and playing fields, which enable all teaching, games and activities to take place on the one site. In the last decade there has been a very substantial building programme. This programme originally involved the extension of the Science

Department and Design and Technology Centre, the laying of an Astroturf pitch and three squash courts, and the substantial redevelopment of School House. In 2002 a new hall/theatre, the Bushell Hall, was built. This hall can accommodate a theatre audience of 600 and an assembly for 1000. At the same time the old hall was transformed into a library and IT rooms. In 2003, a new pavilion, the Alan Lee Pavilion, was completed. In September 2005 a new teaching area, the George Hill Building, was unveiled to provide 16 new classrooms and extensive social space. The Junior School, which has grown considerably in recent years, has been extended and entirely refurbished. A new music school was unveiled in September 2009 – The David Turnbull Music School. September 2015 will see the opening of a new four-floor, state-of-the-art Sixth Form Centre, designed to transform teaching and learning and incorporating the latest multimedia technology. Throughout the School there are excellent IT facilities for staff and pupils.

Curriculum. In the Junior School particular emphasis is placed on establishing high standards in core subjects and key skills that permeate the children's learning across the curriculum. The Junior School has specialist teaching rooms for Art, Design and Technology, Science and Music and benefits from the additional facilities it shares with the Senior School on the same 55-acre campus.

At the beginning of the Senior School, all pupils have at least one year of Latin and French. In the second year Spanish and German are option subjects. English Language and Literature, Mathematics, a Modern Foreign Language, Physics, Chemistry and Biology remain compulsory subjects to GCSE. Three other subjects are chosen from a wide range of options.

The size of the Sixth Form enables the school to offer a very wide range of subjects and combinations. These subjects are Art and Design, Biology, Business Studies, Chemistry, Classical Civilisation, Design & Technology, Drama & Theatre Studies, Economics, English Literature, French, Geography, German, History, Latin, Mathematics (and Further Mathematics), Music, Photography, Physical Education, Physics, Politics, Psychology, Religious Studies (Philosophy and Ethics) and Spanish. There is also a substantial programme of Enrichment for all pupils in the Sixth Form, ranging from Mandarin Chinese to Cookery.

Academic Success. In 2014 11 pupils received offers from Oxford or Cambridge. In 2014 more than 84% of A Levels were passed at A*, A or B grade, and 73% of GCSEs were passed at A* or A grade.

Games. Games are an integral part of the school curriculum and all pupils in the School are involved. PE is compulsory until Year 11 and all pupils in the School have a games afternoon. The School has a very strong tradition in the major team games for both boys and girls, but also offers a very wide range of other options. The principal team games are rugby, cricket, hockey (for both boys and girls) and netball. The Junior School pupils play football in addition to these sports. The School also has teams in tennis, athletics, swimming, clay-pigeon shooting, cross-country, badminton, basketball and fencing to name but a few. In recent years the School has organised very extensive tours for pupils of differing ages: in the summer of 2010 our senior rugby players toured South Africa, and our girls hockey teams visited Singapore and Malaysia. In 2012 the Rugby teams went to Canada with Netball and Hockey teams visiting Trinidad and Saint Lucia. 2013 saw a Cricket tour to Barbados and in 2014 the girls Netball and Hockey teams and the boys Rugby teams toured South Africa. Individual and team national success is a regular feature of Solihull sporting life.

Music and Drama. The School has a very strong tradition in music and drama, which has been enhanced since the building of the Bushell Hall and the David Turnbull Music School. Over one third of all pupils learn a musical instrument and there are over 25 different musical groups in the Senior School, ranging from orchestras, bands and choirs to chamber music and a percussion group. Several of these groups are very successful in competition at local festivals. There are many opportunities for pupils to perform at concerts, both formal and informal, throughout the year. There is also an excellent Chapel Choir that performs during the school week and at the chapel services each Sunday. In 2013/14 the choir also performed at St Paul's Cathedral, with Gary Barlow in Birmingham's LG Arena and on BBC Radio 4's Daily Service.

There are two major dramatic performances each year: a school musical (*South Pacific* 2010; *Grease* 2011, *Fiddler on the Roof* 2012, *Phantom of the Opera* 2013, *Spamalot* 2014) and a school play (*Oh What a Lovely War* 2009, *Blood Brothers* 2010, *An Evening of Greek Tragedy* 2011, *Ash Girl* 2012, *Macbeth* 2013, *Blood Wedding* 2014). In addition, there are several smaller productions in the course of the year.

Outdoor Pursuits. Outdoor pursuits play a major part in the School's life. In the Third Form pupils take part in an outdoor activities programme called Terriers. In the Shell Form every pupil spends a week at the School's mountain cottage in Snowdonia. From the Shell Form pupils are able to participate in the CCF, which has an Army and an RAF section, and from the end of the Fourth Form, the Duke of Edinburgh's Award Scheme. There are approximately 100 pupils in the CCF and 150 are involved at different stages of the Duke of Edinburgh's Award scheme, with 25 Gold Awards achieved in 2014. The School has a popular Mountain Club and organises biennial major expeditions: Chile in 2009, Alaska in 2011, Cambodia in 2013, and Ladakh India in 2015.

Admissions. Pupils are accepted into the Junior School through examination at 7+, 8+, 9+ and 10+, although the majority of pupils enter at 7+. Pupils joining the Junior School in Years 3, 4 or 5 (in most cases) have their places in the Senior School confirmed at the end of Year 5. The major point of entry is at 11+ (Year 7). Places are awarded on the basis of written exams in English and Mathematics and, in some cases, an interview. Some pupils are also accepted to enter the School at 12+, 13+ and 14+. A substantial number of pupils, about 60 on average, enter the School at Sixth Form level. Offers for admission to the Sixth Form are made on the basis of an interview, predicted GCSE grades and a personal profile. Such offers are conditional on achieving a minimum of 2 A grades and 4 B grades at GCSE. This should include B grades in Mathematics and English, except in certain circumstances and at the Headmaster's discretion.

The dates for entrance examinations and the Sixth Form scholarship examinations are available on the school website.

Fees per term (2014–2015). Tuition: Senior School £3,741, Junior School £3,054–£3,165. Lunch charges per day: £3.10 Junior School, £3.50 Main School. There are few obligatory extras.

Scholarships and Assisted Places. The School offers approximately 25 academic scholarship awards at 11+ and 13+ and around 30 at Sixth Form. The number of awards and their value is at the discretion of the Headmaster. There are also Sport, Art and Music, Choral and Organ Scholarships which are awarded at 11+, 13+ and Sixth Form. These are awarded based on a musical, art or sporting assessment. Sixth Form Academic scholarships are available in all A Level subjects on the basis of examination and interview.

In addition to scholarships, means-tested Assisted Places are available to offer opportunities to able pupils with financial needs. Applicants for such assistance are considered at Senior School and Sixth Form entry.

Children of the clergy are offered a 50% fee remission.

Old Silhillians Association. *Secretary*: Mr P Davies, Memorial Clubhouse, Warwick Road, Knowle, Solihull. The aim of the Old Silhillians is to support and maintain links with the School. They also have their own clubhouse and extensive sports facilities.

Charitable status. Solihull School is a Registered Charity, number 1120597. It exists to provide high-quality education for pupils between 7 and 18 years old.

Stamford School

Southfields House, St Paul's Street, Stamford, Lincolnshire PE9 2BQ
Tel: 01780 750300
Fax: 01780 750336
email: headss@ses.lincs.sch.uk
website: www.ses.lincs.sch.uk

Motto: *'Christe me spede'*
Founded by William Radcliffe, of Stamford, 1532.

Chairman of the Governing Body: Malcolm Desforges, Esq

***Principal of the Stamford Endowed Schools*: S C Roberts**, MA

Vice-Principal, Head: W Phelan, MBA

Director of Staff & Student Development: W C Chadwick, MA
Director of Teaching and Learning: H P Hewlett, BSc
Head of Sixth Form: G P Brown, MA
Head of Middle School: K J Mills, BA
Head of Lower School: K J Chapman, BEd
SES Chaplain: The Revd M Goodman, BA, BTh, MTh
Director of ICT: N A Faux, MA

Assistant Staff:
† *Boarding Housemaster*

B D Bates, BSc
Mrs L Blissett, BA
M J Blissett, BA
E J Board, BA
C W Brace, BSc, MSc
P Braud, Baccalaureate
R A Brewster, BSc
Miss E L Calvert, BSc
M C Caseley, MA
Mrs A Chauvaux, Staatsexamen
Ms H M Chew, BA, MPhil
Mrs S L Child, BA
Mrs A L Colley, MA (†*Byard House*)
Mr J F Cropper, BA, MA
D Colley, BEd (†*Byard House*)
Ms A Davies, BA
N S Davies, BA
J W Dawson, MA
Miss A R Dewey, BA
R G A Dexter, BA
Dr R Fielden, MA, DPhil
C D Fox, BA
Mrs J C Fox, BA
Miss A B Halliday, BA, PGCE
Ms F Harrison, BA
Mrs F L Haunch, BSc
Miss K M Hawkswell, BSc
R J B Henry, BEd
Mrs E J Herdale, MA, MSc
D Hodder, BSc
J P Hodgson, BSc
M V Holdsworth, BA
Mrs A J M Holland, MA
D N Jackson, BSc

Mrs K Jones
T P Jones, BEd
S M Jordan, MBA, BEng
Mr A T Kersey, BSc, PGCE
D J Laventure, BA
G S Lee, CertEd
Mrs K Leetch, MA
D Lennie, BA
J M Livingstone, BA
Mrs S Manning, BSc
Dr S Marsh, Bsc, PhD
Mrs E M McInerney, MSc Ed
Mrs F I McClarty, BA
M K Milner, BSc
G Mitchell, BSc
K G Nally, BEng, MBA
A N Pike, BA
Mrs C Pike, BA
N J Porteus, BSc
A Ramsey, BSc
Mrs M Rigg, BSc
B J Russell
P J Scargill, MSc
M P Scriven, BA
Miss C Scott, BA
Dr B E Smart, BSc, PGCE
D L R Stamp, BA
Mrs A Steven, BSc
Miss R L Tomlinson, BA
Mrs C A Walklin, DipEd
L H Ware, BSc (†*Browne House*)
G J Whitehouse, BEd
D F Williams, CertEd
R S Williams, Bsc, Med

Miss K Woodward, BSc
Mrs C A Wray, BA

SES Music Department:
G E Turner, BA (*Director of Music*)
D McIlrae, BMus, HED (*Assistant Director of Music*)
S Chandley, CT ABRSM (*Head of Brass*)
D Leetch, MA, GRSM, LRAM (*Head of Strings*)
Mrs J E Roberts, GRSM, LRM, ARCM
N S Taylor, BA

Visiting Music Staff:
S Andrews (*Kit Drum/Percussion*)
F Applewhite (*Violin, Viola*)
J Aughton (*Flute*)
S Barber (*Organ*)
C Bell, BSc, LRAM, ARCM (*Guitar*)
Mrs M Bennett, LRAM, LTCL (*Singing*)
Mrs S Bond, GLCM, LLCM TD, FLCM (*Singing*)
Mrs K Bentley, GTCL, LTCL (*Cello, Double Bass*)
F Black (*Singing*)
G Brown, BMus (*Oboe, Pianoforte*)
Mrs H Brown, BA (*Clarinet*)
P J Casson (*Saxophone, Clarinet*)
Revd Mrs J Dumat, ARCM (*Clarinet*)
Mrs J Dustan (*Flute*)
J Furrow (*Classical Guitar*)
M Duthie, BSc, ARCO (*Organ*)
N Gray (*Electric Guitar*)
Mrs E Hanlon, ARMCM (*Pianoforte*)
Mrs J Lamb (*Pianoforte, Accordion/Keyboards*)
Mrs S Latham (*Violin, Viola*)
Mrs C Lee, LRAM (*Violin*)
Miss F Maclennan (*Pianoforte*)
Mrs M Maclennan, LRAM, ARCM (*Pianoforte*)
Mrs A McCrae (*Bassoon, Pianoforte*)
Mrs E Murphy, GTCL, LTLL, PGCE (*Violin, Pianoforte*)
D Price, LRAM (*Brass*)
Mrs G Spencer, CertEd, ACRM (*Pianoforte*)
Mrs A Sumner, CertEd, ARCM (*Pianoforte*)
Mrs E A Taylor, BA (*Violin, Viola*)
Mrs L Williamson, LTCC (*Pianoforte*)

Medical Officer: C S Mann, MBChB, BSc

Introduction. Stamford School is one of three schools within the overall Stamford Endowed Schools Educational Charity, along with Stamford High School (girls) and Stamford Junior School, the co-educational junior school.

Buildings and Grounds. Stamford School dates its foundation to 1532. The grounds include the site of the Hall occupied by secessionists from Brasenose Hall, Oxford, in the early 14th century. The oldest surviving building is the School Chapel, which was formerly part of St Paul's Church, but which from 1548 until restoration in 1929 was used as a schoolroom. Extensive additions to the School continued to be made throughout the nineteenth and twentieth centuries. In 1956 the Old Stamfordians gave the School a swimming pool as a war memorial. The science school was built in 1957 and extended in 1973 when a new dining hall and kitchens also came into use. These were subsequently completely redesigned and upgraded in 2003. A music school was built in 1977 and extended in 1984. A further extensive development programme was begun in 1980 and included the building of one new senior boarding house (Browne), opened in 1981, and extensive and comparable provision in the other (Byard). Development works in 2009 saw the creation of a new Research and Learning Centre in the School House building, providing a library, study space and additional IT facilities. The Sixth Form Common Room is now located in a newly-renovated section of Brazenose House, containing quiet study areas, IT and recreation facilities. A glass atrium linking School House and the Hall has been erected, providing a new focal point for the School in a unique architectural style. The Science rooms were also upgraded. A new Sports Centre, which includes a fitness suite, gymnasium and 25m swimming pool, has recently been completed and forms a central part of the curricular and extra-curricular sports provision. The old gymnasium will now be renovated to become a state-of-the-art Performing Arts Centre.

School Structure and Curriculum. The school consists of around 680 boys divided into Lower School (11–14), Middle School (14–16) and Sixth Form. The Heads of each section, with their assistants and Form Tutors monitor the academic progress of each boy and manage the pastoral arrangements.

The National Curriculum is broadly followed but much more is added to the curriculum to make it stimulating and rewarding. Information Technology, Art & Design and Design Technology form an integral part of the curriculum and from Year 8 boys may begin German, Spanish or Russian. All boys are prepared for a complete range of GCSE examination; the great majority of them continue into the Sixth Form and then onto higher education.

In the Sixth Form of about 190 boys (and 190 girls) the timetable is so arranged that a wide range of combinations of subjects is possible. In partnership with Stamford High School all Sixth Form students can choose from the full range of 27 subjects available across the two schools.

Activities. Art, Music, Drama, Games and Physical Education form part of the normal curriculum. There is a choral society, an orchestra, a band and a jazz band, and a chapel choir. The musical activities of the school are combined with those of the High School under the overall responsibility of the Director of Music for the Endowed Schools. The school maintains RN, Army and RAF sections of the CCF and there is a rifle club. A large number of boys are engaged at all levels of the Duke of Edinburgh's Award Scheme.

The school plays rugby, football, hockey, cricket, tennis, golf. The athletics and swimming sports and matches are held in the summer term. In winter there is also badminton, cross-country running and basketball. There are squash courts and a full-sized, floodlit Astroturf hockey pitch.

There are many school clubs and societies and a thriving weekend activity programme.

Close links are maintained with the local community. The school welcomes performances in the hall by the music societies of the town and uses the excellent local theatre in Stamford Arts Centre for some of its plays.

Careers. The school is a member of ISCO and has a team of careers staff. There is an extensive new careers library, computer room and interview rooms.

House Structure. Boarding: Byard House (11–15) Mr & Mrs Colley; Browne House (15–18) Mr L H Ware.

Weekly and three-night boarding are available, as well as full boarding.

Competition in games, music and other activities are organised within a house system. Housemasters with their assistants monitor boys' commitments to the wider curriculum and act as counsellors when boys need to turn to someone outside the formal pastoral and disciplinary system.

Admission. Registration Fee £50; Acceptance Fee £250.

The main point of entry is at age 11, but boys are considered at any age. A number join at age 13 or directly into the sixth form. Application forms for admission may be obtained from the school office. The school's entrance examinations take place in late January, but arrangements may be made to test applicants at other times. Entry into the sixth form is considered at any time. Boys who enter through the Stamford Junior School progress automatically on to Stamford School at age 11 without having to take further entrance tests.

Fees per term (2014–2015). Day £4,482; Full Boarding £8,303; Weekly Boarding £7,239; 3 Night Boarding £6,291.

These fees include stationery, textbooks and games. School lunches for day boys are at additional charge.

Scholarships and Bursaries. The Schools offer a range of scholarships for pupils entering into years 7, 9 and 12 (Sixth Form). Scholarships are less common for pupils entering into other years but may at times be available. There are scholarships for Academic, Music, Art, Sports and All-Rounder performance. Means-tested bursaries can be applied for by families of pupils who would otherwise not be able to benefit from a Stamford education. Please see our website for full details.

Charitable status. As part of the Stamford Endowed Schools, Stamford School is a Registered Charity, number 527618.

The Stephen Perse Foundation

Union Road, Cambridge CB2 1HF

Tel:	01223 454700
email:	office@stephenperse.com
website:	www.stephenperse.com
Twitter:	@SPFSchools

Founded 1881.

The Stephen Perse Foundation comprises Stephen Perse Pre-Prep, Dame Bradbury's School (*see entry in IAPS section*), the Stephen Perse Foundation Junior and Senior Schools, and the Stephen Perse Sixth Form College.

We are now welcoming boys throughout our family of schools, from kindergarten through to university entrance. Boys can start at our Junior School in Cambridge from September 2014 and at the Senior School from 2018. From Year 5 through to Year 11, there will be parallel, single-sex classes for boys and girls (a structure known as the diamond formation).

In September 2013, Dame Bradbury's in Saffron Walden joined our family, making the benefits of a Stephen Perse Foundation education available outside Cambridge for the first time. This non-selective school for boys and girls aged three to 11 shares our ethos of learning for life rather than exams, helping children to become confident, happy and eager to tackle every challenge.

Governors:
Dr G Sutherland (*Chairman*)

Dr H Allen	Mr S Galbraith
Dr C Barlow	Dr G Johnson
Mrs S Barlow	Mr R Lee
Mrs J Brook (*Vice-Chairman*)	Mrs A Powell
	Mrs K Ollerenshaw
Dr J Burch (*Vice-Chairman*)	Dr F Salmon
	Mr B Schwieger
Dr M Calaresu	Dr A Thomas
Mr A Crouch	Mr D Walker
Mr J Dix (*Vice-Chairman*)	Dr C Watkins
Prof R Foale	

Bursar: Mrs J Neild

Principal: **Miss P M Kelleher**, MA Oxon, MA Sussex

Vice-Principal (*Curriculum*): Dr H M Stringer, BA Hons Bristol, MA, DPhil Sussex

Vice-Principal (*Pastoral*): Miss A Kilby, BA Hons, MA Cantab

Director of Sixth Form: Mr S Jack, MA Cantab

Director of Communications: Mr S D Armitage, BA Hons Oxon, MPhil Cantab

Head of Pre-Prep: Mrs S Holyoake, BA Hons Cantab

Head of Junior School: Miss K Milne, BEd Hons Cantab

Director of Learning & Innovation: Mr D Edwards, BSc Hons Loughborough

Head Elect of Dame Bradbury's: Mrs T Handford, MA

The Stephen Perse Foundation is different. We achieve exceptional exam results without sticking blindly to the syllabus or cramming facts and figures – but what you learn in class is only half the story. What happens on the sports field, in our art and music department, on the stage or in our clubs and societies is just as important.

We applaud success but nurture a diverse, inclusive community in each of our schools and our Sixth Form college, where friendship and support are just as important as doing well (probably more so). We're small enough to know each other but large enough to provide challenges and stimulate debate. As you would expect, we have great facilities and offer one-to-one attention but the key is brilliant teaching in an unusually warm, relaxed atmosphere and the way we encourage our pupils and students to think – independently, analytically, logically, creatively and imaginatively.

Admissions. For those interested in attending the Stephen Perse Foundation, we hold our own entrance tests and interviews; these are held annually for applicants at 7+, 8+, 9+, 10+, 11+ and 13+. We also offer regular entry at Sixth Form, based on an interview and GCSE results. Entry is available outside of these testing dates if places allow; please contact the Admissions Team if you would like more information.

Cambridge is our campus. Located in the heart of Cambridge, we consider this historic University City to be our campus; it offers our students access to a wide range of museums, sporting facilities and a host of additional places that can help our students expand their learning and encourage critical thinking – supplementing the outstanding facilities available at each of the schools within the Foundation.

Across the Foundation we offer a superb range of facilities, including a dedicated sports facility complete with all-weather pitch and tennis courts, high-spec science laboratories, a dedicated music block with 18 individual teaching rooms and performance area, a superb visual arts centre complete with mac suite, print room, textiles room and ceramics room, and multiple learning resource centres.

Education. At the Stephen Perse Foundation, we are always pushing at the frontiers of educational innovation. We recognise that students are individuals, each of them learning in a slightly different way. Therefore, we place students at the centre of our curriculum and make it work to their strengths, rather than trying to fit 'round pegs in square holes'. Exams are naturally an important part of education, and we are very proud of the outstanding results that our students achieve year-on-year but equally important is our students' ability to think outside an individual topic or subject. We work hard to embrace inter-disciplinary activity where it is relevant not only to enhance learning but also to create an enjoyable atmosphere that engages students.

We provide our students with a first-class, broad, well-balanced curriculum in a supportive environment that provides opportunities and challenges for students to discover their talents and reach their full potential. We celebrate achievement in all aspects of school life, from academic and sporting, to musical and personal successes.

We believe that technology can be a transformative tool in learning and teaching and, hence we have introduced iPads for our students and staff – we are iPad 1:1. It has provided our teachers with another method of transferring knowledge to students and also enabled the students themselves to change the way they research, collate, analyse and consume information.

We offer the International Baccalaureate as well as A Levels at Sixth Form and have an enriched curriculum. Whether we're introducing the small boys and girls in our pre-preps to the world beyond their families, helping the students in our junior and senior schools to grow in confidence and courage as they grow up or encouraging the young adults in our Sixth Form College to broaden their intellectual, personal and social horizons, we celebrate individuality and curiosity.

Together, we explore around ideas, find out where a concept might lead, come up with unusual answers to questions and learn how to sift what's relevant from what's simply clutter (a particularly useful skill in the internet age). We know that, in order to succeed, you have to lose your fear of failure, because nobody gets everything right first time. Have a go – you'll discover something useful about yourself anyway. It's an exciting journey, wherever you start. You don't have to be a genius to come here and you don't have to come from a privileged family. Our pupils and students are as mixed as any group of young people – but they all have bright, enquiring minds, whether they're artistic or academic, sporty or in need of educational support. Currently, we teach pupils and students from more than 350 schools, in both the maintained and private sectors, and from every kind of background.

All schools tell you they're wonderful but the only way to know if they're right for you is to see for yourself. At the Stephen Perse Foundation you'll find pupils and students who bubble with enthusiasm, teachers who love what they do and a place where young people blossom – and have amazingly good fun. They'll be delighted to show you what being here is really like.

Results. Our results, and our students, speak for themselves. In 2013, 94% of GCSE grades were A* or A, with 63% of our students securing 9 or more A* grades. At A Level, 75% of grades achieved were A* or A and 96% of all results were graded A*–B. At IB, 83% secured 40 points or more, and our average was 42.2 points per student, which was the highest average in the UK and joint-highest in the world. The school was awarded Sunday Times IB School of the Year. For 2014 university entry, almost a quarter of our Upper Sixth received offers from OxBridge across a broad range of subjects, including Medicine, English, History, Engineering, Economics, Archaeology and Anthropology, Natural Sciences and Veterinary Science.

Fees per term (2014–2015). Pre-Prep £3,495; Junior School £4,385; Senior School £5,135; Sixth Form College £4,970. Extras: Individual music lessons in most instruments, speech and drama.

Scholarships, Exhibitions and Bursaries. Academic Scholarships and Music awards are available in the Senior School. Sixth Form Scholarships are awarded on academic merit based on written papers and interviews. Sixth Form Music and Art Scholarships are also offered. Bursaries are available for pupils throughout the Foundation. Information about these may be obtained from the Bursary.

Pastoral Care. We place a great emphasis on pastoral care and the well-being of all our students / pupils. Established pastoral structures support the students and foster personal development, responsibility and informed choices. Subject teachers and year staff care for the academic progress and individual welfare of each student.

Charitable status. The Stephen Perse Foundation is a Registered Charity, number 1120608, and a Company Limited by Guarantee, number 6113565.

Stewart's Melville College

Queensferry Road, Edinburgh EH4 3EZ

Tel:	0131 311 1000
Fax:	0131 311 1099
email:	admissions@esms.org.uk
website:	www.esms.org.uk
Twitter:	@esmsedinburgh
Facebook:	/esmsedinburgh
LinkedIn:	/erskine-stewart's-melville-schools

Governing Council:
Chairman: Mr M Sims

Clerk to the Governors: Mr D Wright, LLB

Principal: Mr J N D Gray, BA

Bursar: Mr J B Molloy, MA Hons

Deputy Headmaster: Mr N G Clark, MA
Director of Studies: Mr G Johnston, MPhys
Head of Upper School: Mr M R Kane, MA
Director of Sixth Form: Dr I Scott, MA, PhD, FRSA
Assistant Head Teacher, Regent: Mrs M Elswood, BA, Dip TESL
Assistant Head Teacher, Guidance: Mr G F W Park, BD
Director of Administration: Mr G J Brown, BEd
Director of ICT: Dr K Hussain

* *Head of Department*
† *Head of House*

Art:
*Mr M Crichton, BA
Mr C A Nasmyth, BA

Biology:
*Mr D Lloyd, BSc, MEd
Mrs L A Lim, BSc
Mr R D Miller, BSc, CBiol, MIBiol
Mr S W Primrose, BSc

Chemistry:
*Mr P Johnson, BSc
Mr C P Kerr, BSc
Mr G Mitchell, BSc

Classics:
*Mr I Crosbie, MA
Mr M T Garden, BA

Computer Studies:
*Mr A Thomson, BA

Design & Technology:
*Mrs L Burt, BSc, FRSA
Mr S Longair, BEd Des Tech
Mr A Scott, BEng (†*Kintyre*)

Drama:
*Mrs D Sobolewska, BA

Economics:
*Ms S Burns, MA
Mr R Alexander, BA

English:
*Mr David Higgins, BA, MA
Mr J C Allan, BA (†*Appin*)
Mrs G Bakewell, MA
Mrs M Bryce, MA
Mr N G Clark, MA
Mrs S Frost, BA, MPhil
Mr S Hart, MA
Mr M R Kane, MA
Mr I A Major, BA
Mr I McNally, BA, MA

Geography:
*Mr K Turnbull, MA
Mr D Foulds, BSc, LLB
Mr N Williamson, BSc, ACA, PGCE

History:
*Mr M Longmuir, BA, CAM

Mrs J D Bennett, MA (†*Ettrick*)
Mr T J M Spowart, MA, PGDE
Mr D C Clarke, MA Hons, PGDE

Mathematics:
*Mr A J T Dunsmore, BEng, MSc
Mr S Ashforth, MA, DipCT
Mr R I Canter, BSc, HDE
Dr G Henderson, BA, BSc
Mr G Johnston, MPhys
Mr S Love, BA, MA, CEng, MBCS
Mr J J Robertson, BSc (†*Galloway*)
Mr G Smith, BSc
Mr C Kerr, MA Hons, MSc

Media Studies:
*Mr D A Orem, MA, MPhil, Cert Media Ed, DipEd

Modern Languages:
*Mr M Z Hamid, MA
*Mrs C R Siljehag, MA
Mrs N Alexander, MA
Mrs V Chittleburgh, BA, MA
Mr N A C Connet, MA
Mr M Constable, BA
Mrs M Elswood, BA, Dip TESL
Mr J F Marsh, BA
Mrs I Richardson, MA

Music:
*Mr J Orringe, BA Hons, MA
Mr A J Samson, Dip RSAMD
Mr J Skuse, BA Hons, PGCE
Mr J Matthews, BMus, GRNCM
Mrs J Wilson, BA, PGCE
Mr R Burns (*Pipe Major*)

Physical Education:
*Mr C S Spence, BEd
Mr M R Burgess, BA Ed
Mr H Lingard, BSpLS
Mr B G Lockie, BEd

Mr J Moran, BA, BEd
Mr S T Edwards, BEd Hons
Ms Pippa Johnston, BEd Hons
Mr D Roxburgh, BEd Hons

Physics:
*Miss J Macdonald, BSc
Mr J Balfour, BSc
Dr C Broughton, BSc, Phd
Mr S D Jackson, MSc, BSc, BEd

Product Design:
*Mrs L Burt, BSc, FRSA
Mr S Longair, BEd Des Tech
Mr A Scott, BEng (†*Kintyre*)

Junior School:
Head Master: Mr B D Lewis, BA Hons, H DipEd Hons
Senior Deputy Head (*Primary 4–7*): Mrs G Lyon, DCE, DipRSA
Deputy Head (*Early Education*): Miss S Mackay, ALCM, LLCM, BMus Hons, PGCE
Assistant Head (*Primary 4–7*): Mr D McLeish, DCE
Assistant Head (*Primary 4–7*): Mrs J Hewitt
Assistant Head (*Early Education*): Ms C Macpherson, BEd

Religious, Moral and Philosophical Studies:
*Mr L H F Woolley, MA Hons, PGDE
Mrs L E Crichton, MA
Mr G Innes, BD (†*Lochaber*)
Mr D S Chalmers, BA, PGDE
Mr G Park, BD Hons, PGCE, PG Dip

Support for Learning:
*Mrs C G C Maxwell, BA
Miss R Meredith, BSc, PGDip
Mrs M Nimmo, BEd

'Daniel Stewart's Hospital' was founded (1855) by Daniel Stewart and has been administered since its inception by the Company of Merchants of the City of Edinburgh. Melville College, formerly The Edinburgh Institution, was founded in 1832 by the Reverend Robert Cunningham. The two schools combined in 1972 to form Daniel Stewart's and Melville College (now Stewart's Melville College). Since 1989 management of the School has been delegated by the Merchant Company Education Board to the Erskine Stewart's Melville Governing Council.

The School enjoys a commanding position on Queensferry Road, a mile from the City Centre. The original College building is occupied by the Senior School while the Junior School is in a modern building. There are a number of excellent facilities including a Sixth Form Centre, Games Hall, Swimming Pool and The Tom Fleming Centre for Performing Arts.

Since 1978 the school has been twinned with The Mary Erskine School (*see entry in GSA section*). This includes a fully co-educational Junior School for children between the ages of 3 and 11, single-sex but very closely twinned secondary schools between the ages of 12 and 17 and a fully co-educational pre-university Sixth Form which provides the ideal bridge between school and university. Boys and Girls from Stewart's Melville College and The Mary Erskine School come together in the Combined Cadet Force, in orchestras, choirs, drama and musicals and in numerous outdoor education projects.

The Senior School (744 boys). S1 and S2 follow a broad curriculum, whereby boys are equipped to pursue all routes to National 5. In S3 boys commence eight courses, including English, mathematics, at least one modern language, at least one science, and a social or creative subject. In S5 boys are expected to take 5 subjects at Higher level. A majority will continue their studies for a Sixth Year, usually three Advanced Highers to provide a firm foundation for degree courses in Scotland and England. Most boys proceed to such courses.

The School has a sophisticated system of guidance. Boys in the first year are with a Form Tutor, under the overall direction of an Assistant Head Teacher. The next four years are spent in Houses of approximately 90 boys, each with its own Head of House and House Tutors. The Sixth Form is a co-educational year, as the girls from The Mary Erskine

School join with the boys of Stewart's Melville College in a completely 'twinned' Sixth Form. There is a well-established Careers department. The Support for Learning Department helps boys with specific learning difficulties.

Games. Rugby and Cricket are played on the school playing fields at Inverleith, while Hockey and Tennis are played at Ravelston. There are also opportunities for Athletics, Curling, Golf, Swimming, Squash, Sailing and Shooting as well as the many sports played in the Games Hall. Boys from the school are frequently selected for national teams in many sports.

Music is much-valued and flourishes within the school. Approximately 500 instrumental lessons are given each week by an enthusiastic staff of 25 visiting teachers. Most orchestral activity is combined with The Mary Erskine School, including junior and senior orchestras, two concert bands, a jazz band and numerous chamber groups. Choral singing is also very strong, from large junior choirs to more specialised groups for madrigals and close harmony. A full programme of public performances includes two major musicals every year and large choral and orchestral concerts in which our musicians combine with an active parents' choir.

Activities. The School encourages boys to take part in The Combined Cadet Force which comprises Army and RAF sections or in The Duke of Edinburgh's Award Scheme. Each week the School offers approximately 70 clubs and societies to suit the appetites of all boys. In sport the school has particular strengths in rugby, swimming, sailing, basketball, hockey, athletics and skiing with representation at district or national level.

Boarding. Dean Park House, adjoining the school grounds, serves as the Boarding House for up to 25 boys. They share dining and recreational facilities with The Mary Erskine boarders next door in Erskine House.

Fees per term (2014–2015). Day: Primary Start to Primary 7 £2,202–£2,852 (lunches included for Primary 2–7); Secondary £3,355 (plus £170 for optional lunches). Full Boarding: Primary 4–6 £5,986; Primary 7 £6,058; Secondary £6,731. Weekly Boarding: Primary 4–6 £5,818; Primary 7 £5,890; Secondary £6,563.

Scholarships and Bursaries. Means-tested Bursaries worth up to 100% of the tuition fee may be available to parents of children entering any year group in the Senior Schools and at P7 in the Junior School. Academic scholarships worth £250 annually are offered to boys applying to enter S1, following a competitive selection process. These are known as Merchant Company Scholarships. The top scholarship holder at Stewart's Melville College receives the Cunningham Scholarship, worth £1,000 annually. Scholarships are paid to the pupil and are held in trust by the school until completion of their Sixth Form year. Music Scholarships of £250 per annum are offered from S3.

ESMS Junior School. In The Junior School (1,248 pupils), girls and boys are educated together from age 3 to 11. Children in Nursery to Primary 3 are based on The Mary Erskine School site at Ravelston, while boys and girls in Primary 4–7 are taught on the Stewart's Melville College site. Normal entry points are Nursery (age 3 or 4), Primary 1, Primary 4, Primary 6 and Primary 7. The school is remarkable for the breadth of its educational programme and the quality of its sporting and cultural activities, in particular the professional standards attained in Music and Drama.

Daniel Stewart's & Melville College Former Pupils' Club. Sec: Bobby Clark, Tel: 0131 551 2331.

Charitable status. The Merchant Company Education Board is a Registered Charity, number SC009747. It is a leading charitable School in the field of Junior and Secondary education.

Stockport Grammar School

Buxton Road, Stockport, Cheshire SK2 7AF
Tel: 0161 456 9000 Senior School
           0161 419 2405 Junior School
Fax: 0161 419 2407
email: sgs@stockportgrammar.co.uk
website: www.stockportgrammar.co.uk

Motto: *Vincit qui patitur*

Founded in 1487, Stockport Grammar School is one of England's oldest schools. The founder, Sir Edmond Shaa, was a goldsmith, 200th Lord Mayor of London and Court Jeweller to three Kings of England. The School's rich history and traditions are celebrated in the annual Founder's Day Service in Stockport.

A co-educational day school, Stockport Grammar School is non-denominational and welcomes pupils from all faiths and cultures. Almost all leavers go on into Higher Education, including many to Oxbridge. Although academic performance is formidable, it is not the be-all and end-all of life at Stockport Grammar School.

Patron: The Prime Warden of the Worshipful Company of Goldsmiths

Governing Body:
C Dunn, MA (*Chairman*)
P A Cuddy, BA (*Vice-Chairman*)
D Bills, BA, ACA
F A Booth, FCA
P J Britton, MBE, MA
A P Carr, MA
Miss S E Carroll, BA
Professor J Dainton, MA, DPhil
P L Giblin, MA, MEd (*Teaching Staff*)
Mrs S Lansbury, LLB
K Lansdale, MRICS
P H Locke, BVSc, MRCVS
P Milner, BA
Dr E M Morris, MBChB, DCH
Dr R Shah, MBE, DL, JP, BSc, PhD
Miss L Wolfe, BA (*Old Stopfordians' Association*)
R P Yates, FIMI

Clerk to the Governors and Bursar: C J Watson, MA

Headmaster: A H Chicken, BA, MEd, FRSA

Senior Deputy Headmaster: D W Howson, MA
Deputy Headmistress – Academic: Mrs D L Harris, BSc
Assistant Headmaster – Operations & Admissions: R W Wallington, BSc
Head of Lower School: Mrs H R Lawson, MA
Head of Middle School: Mrs J L Smith, BA
Head of Sixth Form: Mrs J White, BA

Assistant Masters and Mistresses:
* Head of Department

Art:
*R A Davies, BA, MA
Miss R J Upton, BA

Biology:
*P J Grant, BSc
Mrs E Niven, BSc
Mrs A R Reid, BSc
Miss C R Sutton, BA, MSc
Mrs J White, BA
Mrs M Whitton, BSc
Mrs L J Withers, BA

Chemistry:
K Airey, BSc, PhD

Mrs K L Britton, BSc
*Mrs A L Glarvey, MChem, PhD
R D Heyes, BSc
Miss R F Hindley, MChem
W Krywonos, BSc, MSc, PhD
Mrs L Pitts, BSc, PhD

Classics:
J P Bird, BA
*A C Thorley, BA
P A Urwin, BA
Mrs E Zanda, BA, PhD

Drama:
Mrs A K Moffatt, BA
Economics:
*R Parker, MA
R Young, BEd

English:
Mr T Byrne
Miss R Clarke
*Mrs G A Cope, BA
D W Howson, MA
Mrs R G Johnson, BA, MA
Mrs H R Lawson, MA
Miss E MacDonald, BA, MA
Mrs S L Moore, BA
Mrs E E Suttle, BA, MEd

French:
Mrs S L Belshaw, BA
*Miss S M Gibson, BA
D Lorentz, BA, MA, DEA
Miss C L Stevenson, BA
J D Wilson, BA

Geography:
A Cooke, BSc
Mrs A C Hicks, BA, FRGS
*R Howarth, BA
D S Martin, MA, FRGS
Mrs G N Miles, BA
Mrs J L Smith, BA

German:
Mrs T Kampelmann, MA, PhD
Mrs L M Morgan, BA

History:
Mrs H R Ashton, BA
Mrs K J Chesterton, BA, MA
A H Chicken, BA, MEd, FRSA
S A Moore, BA
J P Russell, BA, MA
*S J D Smith, BA, PhD

Information Technology:
N S Clarke, BA
*M J Flaherty, BSc

Life Studies:
Mrs C M Bartlett, CEd, DipEd, MBA
*A G Ehegartner, BA

Mathematics:
A B Cheslett, BSc, MSc
Mrs M Evans, BA

*G D Frankland, BSc
M Hamilton, MSc, PhD
Mrs D L Harris, BSc
Miss M E Higgins, BSc
Mrs L Lammas, BA
Mrs A S Larkin, BSc
Mrs C L Marshall, BSc, MSc
Mrs R C Taylor, BSc
R W Wallington, BSc

Music:
*M G Dow, MA, ALCM
Mrs J Matthews, BA
Mrs E N Short, MA, LLCM
Mrs E Taylor, BMus

Philosophy/RS:
D Breffit, BA
Rev L E Leaver, MA, BTh
*J Swann, BA, MA

Physics:
Miss A Curtis, MEng
Mrs Z Dawson, MSc
M Ellis, BSc, DPhil
*Mrs H M Fenton, BSc
Mrs C M Hird, BSc
I Killey, BSc, BEng
C Shaw, BSc

Physical Education:
R Bowden, BA
E H Corbett, BA
A S Hanson, BEd
Mrs J Maskery, BEd
Miss L E Topping, BSc
Mrs K Wilkinson, BA
Miss S Withington, BEd
*C J Wright, BA

Psychology:
Mrs S J Braude, BA
*N I Browne, MA

Spanish:
Miss K A M Psaila, BA
Mrs K Christmann, MA

Technology:
Mrs R E Groves, BA
Mrs T H Samways, BSc
Mrs H Tadman, BEng
Mrs Z A Vernon, BEd
G M Whitby, BSc
*N Young, MA

Learning Support:
Mrs D H Meers, BA, MEd
Mrs D M Flint, CEd

School Chaplain: Revd L E Leaver, MA, BTh
Director of Music: M G Dow, BA, MA
Director of External Relations: Mrs R M Horsford, BA
Headmaster's Secretary and Admissions: Mrs J E Baker
Librarian: Ms J Pazos Galindo, BA, MA
School Nurse: Mrs P Ward, RGN, DipHE

Junior School

Headmaster: T Wheeler, BA, MA

Assistant Masters and Mistresses:

Miss H Baker, BEd
Mrs H Carroll, BEd
Mrs L Carr, BA
Mrs R Cole, BA
Mrs S Coombes, BSc
Mrs C Hampson, BA

Mrs N Hurst, BEd
Mrs V Hutchinson, BA
Miss C Jeans, BA
Mr M Johnson, BSc
D Makinson, HNC Eng
Mrs J Mercer, BA

S Milnes, BA
Mrs C M Nichols, BEd
Miss E Ripley, BA
Mrs K Roberts, BEd, MA
Mrs H Shanks, CertEd
Mrs C Smith, BA

Mrs A Sullivan, BEd
Mrs J Swales, BA
A Taylor, BSc
Mrs R Torz, BA
Mrs L Turner, BEd
Mrs K Wells, BA

Nursery Manager: Miss C Peake, BTEC, HND Ed
Headmaster's Secretary: Mrs B Cheyne

Stockport Grammar School aims to provide the best all round education to enable pupils to fulfil their potential in a friendly and supportive atmosphere. The backbone of the school is academic excellence, with a clear framework of discipline within which every activity is pursued to the highest level. Entry is at 3, 4, 7, 11 and 16, but vacancies may occur at other stages. There are over 1,400 pupils aged 3–18 years, with 350+ in the Junior School and over 250 in the Sixth Form.

The Senior School. Admission at age 11 is by competitive entrance examination. This is held in January, for admission in the following September. There are several open events: see website for details. Occasional vacancies are considered on an individual basis and a few places are available in the Sixth Form each year. Visitors are always welcome to make an appointment to see the school.

Curriculum. The emphasis is on how to learn. The GCSE philosophies are introduced in the first three years as part of a broad general education. The sciences are taught as separate subjects and all pupils study Latin, French and German.

On entering the fourth year, at the age of 14, pupils retain a core of subjects but also make choices, so that individual aptitudes can be fully developed. GCSE examinations are taken in the fifth year; the percentage pass rate has not been less than 97%. In 2014, 66% of entries gained an A* or A. On entering the Sixth Form, pupils take four AS Level courses. The pass rate at A Level was 100% in 2014, with 83% of all entries gaining A* to B.

Art. A high standard is set and achieved. There are facilities for all aspects of two-dimensional work and textiles, plus a fully equipped ceramics area and a sculpture court. There are regular exhibitions in School and pupils' work is displayed annually at The Lowry.

Music. The curriculum provides a well-structured musical education for all pupils for the first three years. GCSE and Advanced Level are offered for those who aspire to a musical career as well as for proficient amateurs. Three main areas of musical ensemble – choirs, orchestras and wind bands – are at the centre of activities with opportunities open from First Year to Sixth Form. Emphasis is on determination, commitment and a sense of team work. All ensembles are encouraged to reach the highest standards.

Drama. A particularly strong tradition has been fostered over many years and regular productions involve all year groups. There are drama clubs, trips to local theatre groups and workshops in school.

Physical Education. The Physical Education curriculum is diverse, with activities including aerobics, ball skills, badminton, basketball, dance, gymnastics, health-related fitness, squash, swimming and volleyball. The main winter games for boys are rugby and football, and for the girls hockey and netball. In the summer, boys concentrate on cricket and athletics, whilst the girls focus their attention on tennis, athletics and rounders. Extra-curricular clubs provide further sporting opportunities including archery, climbing and fencing. Up to 400 pupils represent the school at Saturday fixtures and the teams have an excellent reputation, gaining success in regional and national competitions. Almost fifty pupils have represented their country, region or county in the last year.

Information Technology. Dedicated Computer Suites accommodate full classes. All pupils have their own password and email address, and are able to use the Internet for research. The rooms are available to everyone as a computer resource at lunchtimes and after school. Information Technology skills are taught as part of the curriculum and academic departments incorporate the use of computers and interactive whiteboards into their everyday lessons. The subject is also available as a GCSE option.

Houses. Every pupil is a member of one of the four Houses, each led by two Heads of House staff assisted by a team of senior pupils. The Houses organise and compete in a wide range of sporting and non-sporting activities.

Clubs and Societies. The School has many active clubs and societies covering a wide variety of extra-curricular interests, for example, debating, where Fifth and Sixth Formers have the opportunity to participate in up to four Model United Nations Assemblies around the world each year.

Development. In the summer of 2012 the School completed a major project providing new classroom accommodation on the Woodsmoor site for History, Classics, English, Economics, Business Studies and Psychology.

Visits. Well-established language exchange visits are made every year to France, Germany and Spain in addition to hillwalking, camping, mountaineering, skiing, sailing and cultural trips.

Assembly. Formal morning assemblies are held for all pupils; there are separate Jewish, Hindu and Muslim assemblies. House assemblies, which sometimes include Junior School pupils, are on Wednesdays; the Sixth Form have an additional weekly assembly.

Pastoral Care. Form Tutors get to know each pupil in the form individually, and are supported by Year Heads, by the Head of Lower School (years 1 to 3), the Head of Middle School (years 4 and 5), the Head of Sixth Form and the Deputy Head (Pastoral).

Discipline. This is positive and enabling. Much importance is attached to appearance and to uniform, which is worn throughout the school.

Fees per term (2014–2015). Senior School £3,450; Junior School £2,661.

Bursary Scheme. The School's own Bursary Scheme aims to provide financial assistance on a means-tested basis to families who have chosen a Stockport Grammar School education for their children. Details available from the Bursar.

Stockport Grammar Junior School. (*See also entry in IAPS section.*) With its own Headmaster and Staff it has separate buildings and a playing field on the same site. The Junior School has boys and girls between the ages of 3 and 11 years.

Boys and girls join the Nursery when they are three. In its own building and with a designated play area, the Nursery is very well resourced. The children are looked after by qualified and experienced staff.

Entrance is by observed play at the age of 4 years into two Reception forms, and by assessment in February for an additional form at the age of 7. All pupils are prepared for the Entrance Examination to the Senior School at the age of 11.

The Junior School buildings provide special facilities for Art, Technology, Music and Computing. The winter games are soccer, rugby, hockey and netball, with cricket and rounders in the summer. There are swimming lessons every week; other activities include the gym club, life saving, athletics and chess. There are clubs running each lunchtime and after school for both infants and juniors. Matches are played every Saturday against other schools in the major sports. Many pupils have instrumental music lessons and there is an orchestra, band, recorder group and a choir. The musical, held in May each year, is a very popular event in which all pupils participate. Visits are made annually to the Lake District in May. Short annual residential visits, are introduced from age 7.

Charitable status. Stockport Grammar School is a Registered Charity, number 1120199. It exists to advance education by the provision and conduct, in or near Stockport, of a school for boys and girls.

Stonyhurst College

Stonyhurst, Clitheroe, Lancashire BB7 9PZ

Tel:	01254 826345; 01254 827073 (Admissions)
Fax:	01254 827135 (Admissions)
email:	admissions@stonyhurst.ac.uk
website:	www.stonyhurst.ac.uk

Motto: '*Quant je puis*'

Stonyhurst College is a co-educational Catholic boarding and day school. We are a Jesuit school, which means that we attach particular importance to emotional and spiritual development as well as academic excellence. Founded in 1593, it stands in its own estate of 2,500 acres in the beautiful Ribble Valley on the slope of Longridge Fell, ten miles from the M6 motorway, and just over 1 hour by car from Manchester International Airport. We are 2 hours away from London by train.

The College houses a remarkable collection of items relating to the history of the Church in England. These are used as a learning resource. The College has a full-time curator.

Governors:
Chairman: Mr J Cowdall

Miss B Banks	Fr P Nicholson SJ
Mr M J Belderbos	Fr M Power SJ
Mr R Brumby	Mr M Riley
Mr A Chitnis	Mr A C F Verity
Mr M I Davis	Sr M Walsh CJ
Dr M Guzkowska	Mr C Whitehead

Headmaster: **Mr A R Johnson**, BA

College Chaplain: Fr J Twist SJ
Deputy Headmaster: Mr M Mostyn, BA, MA Ed
Deputy Head Pastoral: Mr J D Hopkins, BA
Director of Studies: Mr V Sharples, BA
Deputy Head (Higher Line): Mrs L North, BA
Deputy Head (IB & Co-curricular): Dr P Ellis, MA, PhD

Assistant Staff:
Mrs H Addy, BA (*Hispanic Studies*)
Mr E Allanson, BA (*Head of Religious Studies*)
Mrs M Allanson, BA (*Assistant Director of Music*)
Mr P R Ansell, BA (*Head of Modern Languages*)
Lt Col A Barber (*OC CCF*)
Mr R Barrett, BSc (*graduate gap student*)
Mr J Bickerstaff, BSc (*Physics*)
Mr C Brady, BSc (*Biology*)
Mr A J Callinicos, BA, MA (*Classics*)
Miss R Carter, BSc (*Mathematics*)
Dr A Chadwick, BSc, PhD (*Chemistry; Science*)
Mr S J Charles, MSc, BA (*Head of Games & PE*)
Mr S Clark, BSc (*Graduate Assistant, Games*)
Mr W Clarke, BSc (*Mathematics*)
Ms J Cockle, BA (*Art*)
Ms L Copley, BSc (*Mathematics*)
Miss E Corns, MAG Phil (*German*)
Mrs R Crossley, BA (*Head of Geography*)
Mr I Cunliffe, BSc, MBA (*Biology; Chemistry*)
Miss C Desonis (*French Assistant*)
Mrs A Deane, BA (*Higher Line Girls' Housemistress; Spanish*)
Miss L Dixon, BA (*Head of Drama and Theatre Studies*)
Mr D A Eachus, BTech (*Grammar-Year 10-Playroom Master; Head of Design & Technology*)

Mrs J Eachus (*Non-Teaching Assistant, Registration*)
Mrs E Ellis, MA (*English*)
Mr M Evans, BSc (*Head of PE*)
Mrs L Fisher, BSc (*Head of Science; Head of Physics*)
Mrs H L Flatley, BSc, MSc (*Biology*)
Mr P Garlington, BEd (*History*)
Miss L Gentle, BA (*Graduate assistant*)
Mr D Gibbons, BA, MA (*English*)
Mrs A Goodall, BA, MEd (*PSHE, HL Day Girls*)
Miss J Greenwood, MA (*Religious Studies*)
Miss S Grix, BA (*French*)
Dr D Hallam, BDS, BSc, DMS (*Biology; Chemistry*)
Mrs H Harris, BSc, MA (*Geography*)
Mrs L Heaven, BSc (*Mathematics*)
Mr M Heaven (*Design & Technology and Syntax – Year 11
   Playroom Master*)
Mrs J Hines, BA (*Art*)
Mr N Hodgson, BSc (*Business Studies and Mathematics,
   Poetry -Yr 12 – Playroom Master*)
Mr P E Hodkinson, BSc, MSc (*Mathematics*)
Mr J D Hopkins, BA (*English*)
Mrs D Hornby, BSc (*Girls' Games*)
Mrs R Hughes, BA, PGThp, HE3 (*English*)
Ms E Kay, BEd (*Head of Physical Education*)
Mrs D J Kirkby, BSc (*Economics; Business Studies; Head
   of Enterprise*)
Miss M Lane, BA (*Religious Studies*)
Mr P Lea, BA, MSc (*Director of ICT*)
Mr L Loveridge, BSc (*Graduate assistant*)
Mr A Loney, BSc (*Games*)
Mrs Y Luker, BEd (*Physical Education*)
Ms J Lynch, BSc, MPhil (*Chemistry*)
Mr D G Mann, BA (*Director of Music*)
Mrs C M Markarian, BSc, MSc (*Mathematics*)
Mrs K Marshall, BA (*Head of Art*)
Mrs P Massey, BA (*English Literature; Latin*)
Mrs S McCavana, BA (*Spanish*)
Mr J McGarvey, BA (*ICT*)
Miss K Mitchell, BA (*English as an Additional Language*)
Dr K Morgan, BA, FRCO, LRAM, LTCL (*College
   Organist, Head of Keyboard and Master in charge of
   Music Scholars*)
Mr D Morley, BA (*German*)
Mrs S Morley (*English*)
Mrs L Morris, BSocSc (*Learning Mentor and i/c Higher
   Line Day Boys*)
Mr B J P O'Connor, BSc (*Physics*)
Mr F J O'Reilly, MA, CertObsAst (*Classics; Astronomy*)
Dr J C Roberts, MA, MPhil, DPhil (*History*)
Miss J M Parkinson, MPhil, MA, BA (*Head of Classics*)
Mr D N Rawkins, BSc (*Head of Mathematics; Prefect of
   Studies*)
Mr D C Ridout, BA (*Head of Politics*)
Mrs J Robinson, BEd (*Art*)
Mr J M B Sharples, BA (*Modern Languages*)
Mrs J Shelley, MChem (*Head of Chemistry*)
Mr J Smith, BA (*Head of English*)
Miss A Southward, BA, RAD, AISTD, CDE, ISTD
   (*Dance*)
Mrs M Strain, BA (*SEN/EAL*)
Mr T Strain, BEd (*Economics & Business Studies*)
Ms C Tanner, MMath (*Mathematics*)
Mr G Thomas (*Games*)
Mr A Thompson, MA, BSc (*Head of Biology*)
Mrs L W Timmins, BA (*Head of Economics*)
Mr M J Turner, MA (*Head of History; Religious Studies*)
Mrs G Warrilow (*Teaching Assistant*)
Mr P A Warrilow, BD (*Religious Studies; Assistant
   Chaplain*)
Mrs E Whalley, BSc (*Geography*)
Mr A Williams, BA (*Graduate assistant*)
Mrs I M Williams, BEd (*Geography*)
Mrs E Winstanley, BA (*Head of Learning Support*)

Mrs J Wood, BA (*Lower Line Girls' Housemistress,
   Pastoral Coordinator, CAS Coordinator*)
Mrs K Wright, BA (*Head of Business Studies*)
Ms L Wright, BA (*Modern Languages*)
Miss S Young, BA, MA (*Lay Chaplain*)

Visiting Music Staff:
Mr G Banks, BA (*Brass*)
Mrs J Barlow (*Clarinet*)
Mr D Hessian (*Saxophone*)
Miss A Cooper (*Oboe, Bassoon*)
Mr P Greenhalgh, BMus, ARCM, ALCM (*Piano*)
Mrs J Howarth (*Singing*)
Mrs E Hudson (*Harp*)
Mr D Lewis (*Percussion*)
Mr G Lister (*Drum Kit*)
Mrs C Lorriman (*Flute*)
Mr C Marks (*Guitar*)
Mrs J Moon, BA, ALCM (*Singing*)
Miss M Molin-Rose (*Harp*)
Mr K Parry (*Guitar*)
Ms F Prince (*Singing*)
Mrs M Rigby, GRSM, ARMCM (*Violin*)
Mrs M Turner (*Cello*)
Mr R Waldock, GMus (*Double Bass*)
Mrs S White (*Head of Strings*)
Mrs S Buttler (*Piano*)

Bursar: Mr J Ridley, BA, MA, FCMA
Development Director: Mrs R Hindle
Director of Admissions and CPD: Mrs R Hughes, BA,
   PGThp, HE3 (*English*)
Registrar: Mrs L Carr
Admissions Secretary: Mrs T Erskine
Careers Coordinator: Mrs C Anderton
Domestic Bursar: Miss F V Ahearne
Headmaster's PA: Mrs R Taylor

College Doctors:
Dr J Saunders, MBChB, MRCGP, DRCOG, DSM SA
Dr S Owen, MBChB, BA Hons, MRCGP, DRCOG, DFFP

Senior Nurse: Mrs N Fogden, RGN
Assistant Nurses:
Mrs A Bell, RGN, RSCN, DipFN, DN
Mrs G Kellet, RGN

Stonyhurst St Mary's Hall
Stonyhurst Preparatory School
Boys and Girls aged 3–13
(*see entry in IAPS section*)

Headmaster: Mr Ian Murphy, BA, PGCE

Aims. The School curriculum is intended to reflect the
ideals of the founder of the Jesuits, St Ignatius Loyola: the
importance of trying to find God in all things; the development to the full of each individual's talents whatever his or
her gifts; the need for thoroughness and breadth in learning,
helping pupils to think for themselves and to communicate
well; above all an awareness of the needs of others. We
aspire for our pupils to be men and women of competence,
conscience and compassion.

Religion. The College is Roman Catholic and strives to
educate its pupils in the principles and practice of their
Faith. Pupils of other denominations are welcomed and
encouraged to be active in the school's worship and spiritual
life.

Organisation. There are 480 pupils in the College, with
220 in the adjacent preparatory school, Stonyhurst, St
Mary's Hall, which admits boys and girls from 3 to 13 (*see
Stonyhurst St Mary's Hall entry in IAPS section*). About a
fifth of the Prep school pupils and about two-thirds of the
College students are boarders. The school is fully co-educational from 13 to 18. The pastoral care is based on 5 year
groups called 'Playrooms' or horizontal houses, each of

which is in the care of married Playroom staff assisted by others including a Jesuit priest acting as Chaplain and a Lay Chaplain. The younger girls are in the care of a resident Housemistress, and occupy their own designated area of the College. A resident Housemistress takes particular responsibility for the boarding and day girls in the Sixth Form. The Health Centre is self contained but within the main building; medical care is available on a 24 hour basis.

Academic organisation. A broad curriculum is offered up to GCSE in an attempt to avoid undue specialisation at an early age. Approximately 50% of pupils achieve A and A* grades. There are 26 AS/A2 Level subjects available and we offer the IB diploma alongside A Levels. Approximately 70% of pupils achieve A* to B grades, with 43% achieving A and A*. All Sixth Formers must follow a course in General Theology. Academic progress at all ages is monitored on a regular basis by Tutors and progress reports are sent to parents throughout the term. There are five central ICT resource centres with Video Conferencing facilities. Sixth Formers have their own ICT resource centre and networked computers in their rooms with email and controlled internet facilities. Recent developments have created the highest quality teaching areas across the whole curriculum, with a particularly impressive Science Department and provision for the Performing Arts. There is also a splendid Library/Learning and Resource Centre. Staff from the Special Needs Department are available to give help and support where required and EAL classes are held on either an individual or group basis without extra charge.

Music, Art, Design and Technology. These subjects form an integral part of the curriculum. The opportunities for both formal and informal music are extensive: there are several orchestras, a Concert Band, small string ensembles, several Choirs and other groups. Design and Technology is taught to all first year pupils along with Art, prior to the choice of GCSE subjects; the facilities for both these subjects are outstanding thanks to recent developments. Drama is strong and there are opportunities for taking part in a wide range of dramatic productions throughout the year either in our own Theatre or in the nearby Centenaries Theatre at Stonyhurst St Mary's Hall.

Games. The main games are Rugby Football, Cricket, Hockey, Netball and Athletics, but it is our aim to offer the widest possible range of sporting and recreational opportunity to all pupils. In addition to playing on our own golf course, pupils can take part in Soccer, Tennis, Badminton, Squash, Fencing, Basketball, Netball, Shooting, Sub Aqua and Cross Country. Our indoor six-lane swimming pool offers first-class opportunities for both competitive and recreational swimming, and the Sports Hall provides the usual range of indoor activities. An aqueous-based all-weather pitch is available for Hockey and other sports.

Cadet Corps and Other Extra-Curricular Activities. In Year 10 all pupils are members of the Cadet Corps, which introduces pupils to a number of activities such as canoeing, orienteering, climbing, trekking and shooting, in addition to an extensive programme of Army-based training. After the second year, membership of the Cadet Corps is by selection; it is invariably over-subscribed. An active Outdoor Pursuits Department offers opportunities for climbing, sailing, fell-walking and caving; the Duke of Edinburgh's Award Scheme is very popular with boys and girls at all ages.

Voluntary Service. Active work in the Community is a hallmark of Stonyhurst's commitment to others. Weekly programmes of community work are arranged and thousands of pounds a year are raised for charitable causes, in particular the College's own annual holiday for children with disabilities.

Higher Education and Careers. Up to 98% of our leavers go on to higher education either in the UK or abroad, with 10% to Oxbridge. We also send a number of students to medical schools each year. An average of 50% of our leavers have entered The Russell Group of Universities in the last few years. Our Careers department, based in a well-stocked Careers library with extensive research facilities, enables pupils to be fully informed about university choices and Tutors are actively involved at all stages in the decision making. Careers conferences are regularly organised.

Fees per term (2014–2015). Boarding £10,111, Weekly Boarding £8,423, Day £5,628.

Scholarships and Bursaries. A large number of scholarships are awarded each year at 11+, 13+ and the Sixth Form. A number of bursaries up to half fees are awarded annually to pupils whose parents are in need of financial assistance and who are likely to benefit from a Stonyhurst education and make a positive contribution to the life of the school.

Open Major and Minor Scholarships are awarded annually at 13+ on the basis of academic achievement or potential after competitive examinations in May. These vary in value up to a maximum of half fees. Sixth Form Academic scholarships are available. Music, Art and All-Rounder scholarships are awarded each year at 13+ and 16+. Our SFX scholarship award offers up to 70% off fees for ten boarding pupils who, in the opinion of the selection panel, are most likely to benefit from and contribute to life at Stonyhurst.

Open Major and Minor Music scholarships are also awarded annually in February on a generous scale related to parents' income and pupils' talent.

Applicants for Art scholarships are invited to submit portfolios of their work, personal as well as set pieces, which demonstrate a lively interest in and enthusiasm for the subject(s). There should also be evidence of proven ability through a variety of media and approaches. Portfolios should be sent or brought by the applicant early in May.

Admission. Enquiries about admission should be addressed to the Registrar, Tel: 01254 827073 or 827093. Candidates entering at 13+ are normally required to pass the Common Entrance Examination, but alternative Tests are available for candidates from maintained schools or from abroad. Applications for Sixth Form boarding and day places for girls and boys are particularly encouraged.

Charitable status. Stonyhurst College is a Registered Charity, number 230165. The Charity for RC Purposes exists to provide a quality boarding and day education for boys and girls.

Stowe School

Stowe, Buckingham, Bucks MK18 5EH

Tel:	01280 818000
Fax:	01280 818181
email:	enquiries@stowe.co.uk
website:	www.stowe.co.uk
Twitter:	@stowemail
Facebook:	/stoweschool

Motto: '*Persto et Praesto*'

Stowe provides an all-round education of the highest standard, supporting Stoics in their passage to adulthood by developing individual talents, intellectual curiosity and a lasting sense of moral, social and spiritual responsibility. Confidence and tolerance of others flourish in a close community. The School provides a caring environment which promotes academic excellence, sporting prowess and artistic and musical creativity. Through teaching of the highest calibre, Stoics are encouraged to think for themselves, challenge conventional orthodoxies and pursue their own enthusiasms. Stoics acquire skills that enable them to live happily, work successfully and thrive in their future lives.

Visitor: The Rt Revd The Lord Bishop of Oxford

Governing Body:
C Honeyman Brown, FCA (*Chairman*)
The Revd Peter Ackroyd
J R C Arkwright, FRICS
J M A Bewes, BA, ACA
Ms J C Brunskill, BSc
Admiral Sir James Burnell-Nugent, KCB, CBE, MA
D W Cheyne
Ms J Colman, BA, Dip Arch, RIBA (*Vice Chair*)
S C Creedy Smith, BA, ACA
Professor Sarah Gurr, BSc, ARCS, DIC, PhD, MA
Mrs J E Hastie-Smith
D Hudson, MA Cantab
Mrs A Johnson, BSc
R A Lankester, MA
Lord Magan of Castletown, FCA
Mrs E Phillips, OBE, BA, MA, AKC
Lady Stringer
C J Tate, BA, MIMC
Ex officio: S Shneerson (*Chairman of Old Stoic Society*)

Secretary to the Governors: M B M Porter, BA, MSc
Administrator to the Governors: D J Critchley, MA

Headmaster: A K Wallersteiner, MA, PhD

Deputy Headmaster: C C Robinson, MA, MPhil
Assistant Head – Director of Studies: Mrs J Potter, MPhil, BA
Assistant Head – Senior Housemaster: P A Last, BA
Assistant Head – Senior Master: M D G Wellington, BSc
Registrar: D Fletcher, BEd

Assistant Staff:
* *Head of Department*

Art:
*Mrs A Jorgensen, BA, MA
Ms A Cammish, BSc
C J Grimble, BA
Mrs S U Harmon, BA, MA
B L Johnson, MA

Biology:
*Mrs L M Carter, BSc
R R Akam, BSc, MEd
Miss A S Davies, BSc, MSc
Mrs J M Gracie, BSc
A D D Murphy, BSc
M A Righton, MA

Business Studies:
*P John, BSc
Mrs G L Bonner, BA

Chemistry:
*D S Jeffreys, BSc
R G Johnson, BSc, MA
Mrs K M McMahon, BSc
J Peverley, MChem
J M Tearle, BA
C J Warde, BSc, MSc

Classics:
*M J Bevington, MA, MEd
J A Smith, BA

Computing:
T D Higham, BSc
N J Mellor, BA, MSc

Design & Technology:
*M Smith, BSc
S Grimble, CertEd
C T McGhee, BA
C Peratopoullos, BEd

M D G Wellington, BSc

Drama & Theatre Studies:
*N D Bayley, Dip Acting & Theatre
C D Walters, BEd

EAL:
*Mrs J Y Johnson, BA, MA
Mrs P J S Kitchen, BSc

Economics:
*R B Corthine, MA
Mrs J L Hamblett-Jahn, LLB
Ms A C A Hobrow, BSc
P M Thomas BSc

English:
*W Goldsmith, MA
Mrs E J Ackroyd, BA
P S Miller, MA, PhD
J W H Peppiatt, MA
D A Roberts, MA
Ms E Sheard, BA, Cert SpLD

Games Coaching:
*I Michael, BEd
K Bennett (*Track and Field, Cross Country*)
S A Cowie, FIST (*Swimming*)
Mrs J M Duckett, BEd (*Lacrosse*)
A Hughes (*Rugby*)
J A Knott (*Cricket, Hockey*)
J S Skinner (*Tennis*)

Geography:
*Mrs S A Murnane, MA
Mrs S L Akam, BA

L Copley, BA
Mrs A J Dawson, BA
P J Deakin, BSc
P A Last, BA, Adv DipEd
A K Murray, BSc
M D Perriss, MA

History:
*J W Hayden, BA
S G Aston, BSc, MA
H J Hoare, BA
J R H Sayers, BA
C T Standley, BA
H J L Swayne, BA

History of Art:
*I O Young, MA
C C Robinson, MA, MPhil

Library:
*Mrs C M Miller, BA, Dip Lib Stud

Mathematics:
*D P C Blewitt, BSc
Mrs P A Bennett, BSc, MS
M P Dawson, BA, CertEd
Ms V A Green, BSc, CertEd
Mrs F C James, BEng
R D Knight, BSc
A McDaid, BEd
M B Møller, BA
Z Sherwood, AB (*Harvard Fellow*)
Mrs R E Trace, BA, Dip Spec Ed

Modern Languages:
*Mrs T L Jones, BA
Mrs H Browne, BA
A H de Trafford, MA
Mrs C Dickson, MA, Dip ETI
S G Dobson, MA
G D Jones, BA
G R Moffat, BA
Mrs M L D Peña, BA
Mrs A P A Savage, BA
Miss C Stirzaker, BA
Mrs A R G Tearle, MA

Music:
*S P Dearsley, MA, MMus (*Director of Music*)

B C Andrew, BMus
L A P Brito-Babapulle, BA, MSt
N C Gibbon, BSc
M R H Nottage
C Windass, ABSM, GBSM

Philosophy and Religion:
*C S Bray, BA, BPhil
The Revd C M B Huxtable, BA (*Chaplain*)
A A Macpherson, BA, MA
M P Rickner, BA

Physics:
*R J Carpenter, BSc
B Hart, BEng
S H Malling, MSc, CPhys, MInstP
T C O'Toole, BSc
P A Thompson, BSc

PSHE:
*Miss K J McLintock, BA, MA

Politics:
*C Barker, BA
J P Floyd, MA

Skills Development:
*Mrs S Carter, BA, MA, MEd
Mrs F E Atherton, BA, AMBDA
Mrs E A Birks, MA
Mrs E N Hughes, BA
Ms L C Powell
Mrs S Rawlins, HLTA, Dip ADHD
Mrs S D Rookley, BA HLTA
Ms E A Sheard, BA, Cert SpLD
Mrs R E Trace, BA, Dip Spec Ed

Sports Science:
*P R Arnold, BSc
Mrs J M Duckett, BEd
I Michael, BEd
R S Pickersgill, BA
R C Sutton, BA
Mrs S E Sutton, BA

Houses and Housemasters/mistresses:

Boys' Houses:
Bruce House: R C Sutton
Temple House: A A Macpherson
Grenville House: A D D Murphy
Chandos House: P J Deakin
Cobham House: J W H Peppiatt
Chatham House: L Copley
Grafton House: G R Moffat
Walpole House: P A Last

Girls' Houses:
Nugent House: Mrs J M Duckett
Lyttelton House: Ms V Green
Queen's House: Mrs J L Hamblett-Jahn
Stanhope House: Mrs S U Harmon

Sixth Form House:
West House: Mr R Johnson & Mrs J Johnson

Medical Officer: Dr R D Pryse, MB BS, DCH, DRCOG, DFSRH

Director of Finance: Mrs J L Hill, MA, FCA
Director of Operations: N Morris, BA, MSc, FRSA, FCILT, MIL

Stowe is a country boarding school with boys and girls from 13 to 18. The School roll is 780, comprising 665 boarders and 115 day pupils. Pupils are also accepted each year for 2-year A Level courses.

Houses. There are eight Boys' and four Girls' Houses, six of which are within the main building or attached to it and six at a short distance from it. In 2014 a new Sixth Form House, West, will be opened for boys and girls.

The Curriculum allows pupils to enjoy a wide variety of subjects before they settle down to work for their (nine or ten) GCSEs taken in the Fifth Form. A flexible Options system operates at this stage. Most boys and girls will go on to take 4 AS and 3 A Levels. Throughout the School, boys and girls have a Tutor to look after their academic welfare and advise them on higher education. A course in Visual Education was introduced in 1996 for boys and girls in their first year at Stowe. It promotes an understanding of Stowe's architecture and landscape gardens in particular and the built environment in general.

Art, Design and Information Technology. All pupils are introduced to these subjects in their first year at Stowe. Art and Design are popular both for those pursuing hobbies and for those studying for formal examinations. Traditional skills are covered alongside more modern techniques such as computer-aided design and desktop publishing.

Music and Drama flourish as important and integral parts of the School's activities both within and outside the formal curriculum. There is plenty of scope to get involved in the School Orchestras, Jazz Band, Clarinet Quartet, Choirs, School plays, House plays and House entertainments. The timetable is sufficiently flexible to allow special arrangements to be made for outstanding musicians to study outside school. Drama Clubs and Theatre Studies groups have a fully-equipped theatre at their disposal. The refurbishment of the Theatre and classrooms, alongside a brand new Music School, allows these creative arts to flourish.

Careers Guidance. Pupils are provided with a variety of opportunities which allows them to make sound career decisions. Seminars, Gap Year advice and an interview training programme are all offered. The Careers Centre is extremely well-resourced, with a suite of computers and appropriate software, DVD facilities and a wealth of literature. Every encouragement is given to pupils to make regular visits to the Centre at Stowe and parents are always welcome to attend Careers events and to spend time using the available resources.

Religion. The School's foundation is to provide education in accordance with the principles of the Church of England and this is reflected in its chapel services on Sundays. Pupils of other faiths and other Christian Churches are welcomed and in some cases separate arrangements are made for them on Sundays. Every pupil attends the chapel services on weekdays.

Games. The key sports for boys are rugby, hockey and cricket, and for girls, hockey, lacrosse and tennis. The other main sports range from badminton, basketball, cross country, football, Eton Fives, fencing, golf, netball, squash, swimming and water polo in the winter to athletics, golf, polo, rowing, sailing and swimming in the summer; there are inter-school fixtures in most of these sports.

The School enters national competitions in many sports and encourages pupils to challenge for representative honours. The School has a heated 6-lane 25m indoor swimming pool with electronic timing system, a sports hall, squash courts, Eton Fives courts, a weight training/fitness room and two floodlit Astroturf pitches which also provide 24 tennis courts in the summer. There are also hard tennis courts available all the year round, plus outdoor netball and basketball facilities, an 8-lane sandwich surface athletics track, an indoor shooting range, a clay-pigeon shooting tower, a nine-hole golf course where the National Prep Schools (IAPS) annual tournament is played, and extensive playing fields for rugby, hockey, football, cricket and lacrosse. Sculling, canoeing, sailing and fishing take place on a lake within the Landscape Gardens as well as at Northampton Rowing Club and Glebe Lake, Calvert. The School opened its Equestrian Centre in 2012 and enters local and regional competitions.

Other Activities. Pupils complement their games programme with a broad variety of extra-curricular activities, including clubs and societies. There is a full weekend programme of events and activities. Stowe's grounds lend themselves to outdoor pursuits such as fishing and clay pigeon shooting, and the School has its own pack of beagles. On Mondays a special activities programme is based on Service at Stowe and at the heart of this is the Combined Cadet Force with all three service arms, the Duke of Edinburgh's Award Scheme, Community Service (in the neighbourhood) and Leadership skills.

Fees per term (2014–2015). Boarders £10,700, Day Pupils £7,770 payable before the commencement of the School term to which they relate. A deposit is payable when Parents accept the offer of a place. This deposit is repaid by means of a credit to the final payment of fees or other sums due to the school on leaving.

Scholarships and Bursaries. A range of Scholarships and Exhibitions, up to the value of 25% of the School fees, is awarded annually. Scholarships may be supplemented by means-tested bursaries, with a limited number of fully-funded places, where there is proven financial need.

Academic Scholarships up to the value of 25% of the School fees are available for pupils at age 13+ entering Stowe's Third Form, and are awarded to gifted children already following the ISEB Common Academic Scholarship syllabus at their Preparatory School.

Stephan Scholarships are awarded to academically bright pupils from independent or state schools which do not follow the ISEB Common Academic Scholarship syllabus.

Academic Scholarships are also available to pupils wishing to join the School in the Lower Sixth Form after GCSE at 16+. Competitive Entry Examinations are held in the November of the candidate's GCSE year consisting of a Verbal Reasoning paper, two subject papers related to their AS Level choices, and an interview. Successful Scholarship candidates would normally be expected to gain A* and A grades in all their subjects at GCSE.

Music Scholarships: Candidates at age 13 should be at least Grade Five standard on at least one instrument and preferably nearer Grade Six. An Exhibitioner may be around Grade Four standard. Candidates at age 16 should be the equivalent standard of Grade Six or above on one instrument and be of a good standard on a second instrument or voice. A candidate gaining a Minor Scholarship of up to 10% or an Exhibition may be around Grade Five standard.

Some *Art and Design & Technology Scholarships* are available for pupils entering Stowe at age 13 or 16, and are offered to candidates who submit evidence of outstanding ability and a strong interest in these areas.

Sixth Form Arkwright Scholarships: Stowe is affiliated to the Arkwright Scholarships Trust which provides a number of scholarships available to students, both internal and external, who will be studying Maths and Design and Technology in the Sixth Form and intend to read Engineering, Technology or another Design-related subject at university.

Sports Scholarships may be awarded to exceptional candidates at 13+ and 16+ showing outstanding potential in at least one of Stowe's key sports: hockey, lacrosse, netball or tennis for girls and rugby, hockey or cricket for boys.

Roxburgh (All-Rounder) Scholarships at 13+ and 16+ are intended to enable any boy or girl of outstanding all-round ability and leadership potential to benefit from Stowe's unrivalled environment to develop fully his or her talents. In addition to strong academic potential, which will be demonstrated in Stowe's Entry Examinations, candidates would be expected to demonstrate a high level of ability in at least one of the following: sport, music, art and drama.

Full details may be obtained from The Registrar.

Admissions. Boys and girls can be registered at any age. Full details can be obtained from the Admissions Department, who will supply entry forms. The School is always prepared to consider applications from pupils to enter the School at 14 if they have been educated overseas or in the maintained sector. The date of birth should be stated and it should be noted that boys and girls are normally admitted between their 13th and 14th birthdays.

The Old Stoic Society. Director: Anna Semler. Old Stoic Society Office: Tel 01280 818252, email oldstoic@stowe.co.uk.

Charitable status. Stowe School Limited is a Registered Charity, number 310639. The primary objects of the charity, as set out in its Memorandum and Articles of Association, are to acquire Stowe House, which was achieved in 1923, and to provide education in accordance with the principles of the Church of England.

Strathallan School

Forgandenny, Perth, Perthshire PH2 9EG
Tel: 01738 812546
Fax: 01738 812549
email: secretary@strathallan.co.uk
website: www.strathallan.co.uk

Motto: '*Labor Omnia Vincit*'

Strathallan School was founded by Harry Riley in 1913 and moved to its present site in Forgandenny, Perthshire in 1920. The School is fully co-educational and numbers 565 pupils, of whom 208 are day pupils and 357 are boarders.

Board of Governors:

Chairman: D L Young, BArch, Dip Arch
Deputy Chairman: R K Linton, LLB, NP
J G Barrack
A Brown, BSc
Professor J S Cachia, BSc, MBChB, MD, FRCGP, DRCOG, FRCPE
Professor J A Cleland, BSc, MSc, PhD, DClinPsychol, FHEA, AFBPsS
J A R Coleman, Dip EstMan, MRICS
K C Dinsmore, BA, LLB, Dip LP
Mrs K J Dunn, LLB
R G A Hall, BArch, Dip Arch, RIAS, RIBA
S J Hay, BA, MBA, MSc
Professor T Hoey, MA, PhD, Hon FRSGS
N Houston, MA, Dip MusEd, PG Dip EdTech CNAA, PG Dip Couns, MScR Mus, FHEA
Professor R E Leake, MA, DPhil
J A Leiper, CA, BA
Mrs E Lister, BSc, Dip Ed
Dr P M Lockhart, MBChB, MPH, MRCGP, DCH, DRCOG, DFPSH
R S Mackenzie, BSc, LLB, Dip LP
J G Maguire, Dip BS, MRICS
I R McLean
Mrs P A Milne, BA, MBA, MCIPD
R Sandison, MCIM
A M D Wilkinson, MBA, MA, FSI
Mrs G M Wilson, MA, PGCE

Headmaster: **B K Thompson**, MA Oxon

Assistant Staff:
Mrs T Ailinger, Staatsexamen, Cert TESOL
Y Banda, BSc, PGCE

D J Barnes, BSc, PGCE, PGCG, FRGS (*Deputy Head Pastoral*)
G J Batterham, BSc, PGCE (*Simpson House*)
M Bergin, BSc, PGCE
D E Billing, MA, PGCE (*Nicol House*)
Mrs D Billing, MA, PGCE
Dr K E M Blackie, PhD, PGDE, BSc
Miss C Brownbridge, BA, PG Dip, PGDE
P W W Bush, Dip IAPS (*Riley House*)
Miss E de Celis Lucas, BA, CAP
W Christiansen, BSc
Dr A N Collins, BSc, BA, PhD
Dr B Cooper, BSc, PhD, PGCE
Mrs M-L Crane, BA, PGCE
S Dick, BEd
Dr S B Downhill, BA, MSc, PhD, PGCE, FRGS
S Drover, BSc, PGCE
Miss S Dunbar, BSc, MSc, PGDE
Mrs E C Duncan, MA, PGCE
A L M Dunn, MA, PGCE
Dr S R Ferguson, MA, PhD, MSc, PGCE
J R Fleming, BEd
Mrs S E Fleming, BEd
N P Gallier, MBE, MA, MSc, PGCE
G N Gardiner, BSc, PGCE
D R Giles, BA QTS, Cert PP
S Glass, BSc
J Goddard, BSc, PGCE
S Hamill, BA (*Deputy Head Academic*)
N A Hamilton, BMus
B A Heaney, BSc, Dip Ed (*Freeland House*)
Miss L Helyer, BA, PGDE
A D Henderson, UKCC
D M Higginbottom, MA, PGCE
Mrs J Higginbottom, MA, PGCE
Mrs C G Howett, BA, Dip Ed
Mrs D S Hunter, DA, Dip Ed
Mrs A Ingram-Forde, BA
Mrs L E Joy, BA, PGCE
E Kalman, BSc, MPhil
P J S Keir, BEd, Cert SpLD
L Kent, BSc, PGCE (*Thornbank House*)
E G Kennedy, BA, PGCE
G C Kitson, BSc, PGCE
Mrs E C Lalani, BEd, Dip Man
Miss C Laurie, BSc, PGCE
E Lee, MA, PGCE
Mrs F MacBain, MA (*Glenbrae House*)
Miss M J Mackie, BSc, PGDE
Miss S Mackay, BA, MSc, PGCE
J A MacLean, MA, PGDE
Mrs I I M McFarlane, MA, Cert SpLD, LLAM
Miss G McLean, BA, PGCE
Miss J L Morrison, BTechEd
C Muirhead, BA
M R Price, BEng, PGCE
Mrs D L Raeside, BSc, HDE PG
G S R Robertson, BA, DMS
S W Robertson, MA, BSc, PGCE
Miss S E Robertson, BSc, PGDE
Mrs M C Robertson-Barnett, MA, PGCE
Revd D Rutherford, BA, PGCE
Dr J D Salisbury, MA, PhD, PGCE
Mrs L Salisbury, BA, Dip Ed, PGCE, ALCM
Mrs C A Sim Sayce, BMus, PGCE
Miss A Sime, BEd (*Director of Sport*)
A C W Streatfeild-James, MA, PGCE (*Director of Studies*)
Mrs K L Streatfeild-James, BA, PGCE, Dip SpLD
Mrs R C W Stuart, MA, PGDE
Mrs J A Summersgill, BSc, PGCE
P R Summersgill, MA, PGCE
Mrs A J Tod, MA, PGCE (*Woodlands House*)
M R A J B Tod, BSc, PG Dip (*Woodlands House*)

P M Vallot, BSc
R C A Walmsley, MA (*Director of Music*)
A Watt, BComm, HDE (*Ruthven House*)
T Zhou, MSc, PhD

Bursar and Clerk to the Governors: Mr A C Glasgow,
MBE, BEng, MSc, CEng

Director of Marketing & Development: Mrs T C Howard-Vyse
Marketing Executive: Mrs L Leslie
Alumni Coordinator: Mrs A Wilson

Medical Officers:
Dr A M Lewis, MBChB, MRCGP
Dr L D Burnett, MBChB, BSc, DRCOG, MRCGP

Situation. Strathallan School is located 6 miles south of Perth in the village of Forgandenny. It occupies a glorious rural location, situated in 150 acres of richly wooded estate on the northern slopes of the Ochils and overlooks the Earn valley. At the same time, Strathallan is within easy reach of the international airports – Edinburgh (35 minutes) and Glasgow (1 hour) – and Perth (10 minutes).

At the centre of the School is the main building which dates from the 18th century and was formerly a country house and home of the Ruthven family. The School continues to invest in outstanding facilities. These include modern laboratories, a Theatre, Computer Centre, Library, Design Technology Centre, Sports Hall, Fitness and Weight Training Room, 2 Floodlit Synthetic Hockey pitches, Medical Centre, Art School and newly refurbished Boarding Houses. All boarding houses have been built within the last thirty years with modern facilities and a single study-bedroom for every boarder in the last four years.

Aims. At the heart of the School's philosophy is the commitment to provide opportunities for all to excel, to help pupils to make the most of their abilities within the framework of a caring environment.

Organisation. The School is primarily a boarding school yet also takes day pupils who are integrated into the boarding houses. There are four Senior Boys' houses (Ruthven, Nicol, Freeland and Simpson). There are three Girls' houses (Woodlands, Thornbank and Glenbrae). All boarding houses have their own resident Housemaster or Housemistress, assisted by House Tutors and a Matron. Boys have single study-bedrooms from the Fourth Form and Girls have single study-bedrooms from the Third Form.

The Junior House, Riley, is designed to cater for boys and girls wishing to enter the School at 9+. Riley is run by a resident Housemaster and his wife, assisted by tutors, two of whom are resident, and a resident Matron. After Riley, pupils move directly to one of the Senior houses. Riley is situated within its own campus, yet also enjoys the facilities of the main School. It has its own Common Room, Library, dormitories and music practice rooms.

The whole School dines centrally and there is a wide choice of hot and cold meals as well as vegetarian options. All boarding houses have "brew rooms" for the preparation of light snacks.

Religion. Strathallan has a Chapel and a resident Chaplain who is responsible for religious studies throughout the School.

Curriculum. Pupils entering the School before the age of 13 are placed in Forms IJJ, 1J, I, or II, while those who join at 13 are placed in the Third Form where they are setted by ability for their core subjects. Up until the Fourth Form, all follow the same broad curriculum which comprises English, Mathematics, French, German/Spanish, Latin, Physics, Chemistry and Biology, History, Geography, Computing, Art, Design Technology, together with Divinity, Personal and Social Education, Music and Physical Education. Instruction in French and Latin begins in Form 1.

In the Fourth and Fifth Forms, pupils take nine subjects for GCSE and Computing at Standard Grade. All the above subjects (plus Business Studies) are available at this level.

A satisfactory performance at GCSE (a minimum of five passes at C grade or equivalent) qualifies a pupil for entry to the Sixth Form where he/she prepares for AS and A2 examinations or Scottish Higher. Scottish Higher examinations are generally taken at the end of the Upper Sixth year. AS and A2 examinations are taken in the Lower and Upper Sixth.

In the Sixth Form, there is greater flexibility in the range of courses available and full details of these are issued to parents in advance. Potential Oxbridge candidates are identified in the Lower Sixth Form and additional tuition is provided. On average, more than 95% of senior pupils go on to University.

Each pupil is allocated a tutor who is a member of the academic staff and one of the duty staff of the boarding house. The tutor monitors pupils' academic and social progress and is responsible for discussing their regular reports with them. Teacher : Pupil ratio 1:7.

Games. The main School games are rugby, cricket, hockey, netball, athletics and tennis, and standards are high. Other sports include skiing, squash, rounders, football, fencing, judo, badminton, table tennis, basketball, swimming, golf, horse riding and cross-country running in all of which national and regional success have been achieved in recent years.

Strathallan has 2 squash courts, 15 hard tennis courts, 3 netball courts, 2 floodlit synthetic pitches, a heated indoor swimming pool, sports hall, gymnasium and a fitness and weight training room. The sports hall comprises a basketball court, three badminton courts, a rock climbing wall as well as facilities for six-a-side hockey and indoor cricket coaching. Sailing, canoeing and skiing are recognised pastimes, and pupils participate in School ski days in the Spring term. Strathallan also has its own nine-hole golf course as well as Tennis and Shooting Academies.

Activities. All pupils are encouraged to take part in a range of activities for which time is set aside each day. There are over 50 weekly activities to choose from including dance, drama, pottery, chess, photography, first aid, lifeguarding, judo, horse riding, shooting (both clay pigeon and small bore) and fishing. There are also many societies and a programme of external speakers who visit the School. Pupils also work towards awards under The Duke of Edinburgh's Award scheme. They are also encouraged to take part in Community Service.

Music. The Music department has its own concert room, keyboard room and classrooms, together with a number of individual practice rooms. Music may be taken at GCSE, Higher and AS/A2 Level. There are choirs, traditional music ensembles, jazz band, wind band, an orchestra, folk bands and rock bands. A house music competition takes place annually and there are regular concerts throughout the term. Individual tuition is available for virtually all instruments. Recitals and visits to concerts in Edinburgh, Perth and the environs are arranged. The School has a Pipe Band and a full-time Piping Instructor. There is also a specialist Choral Scholarship programme.

Art. Art is recognised as an important part of the School's activities and there are opportunities to study the subject at GCSE and AS/A2 Level. Pupils benefit from regular art trips abroad and have the opportunity to exhibit their work both locally and further afield. A purpose-built Art School features facilities for ceramics, sculpture and printmaking. National awards reflect pupils' achievements in this area.

Drama. Drama thrives throughout the School and the department makes full use of the theatre. There are junior and senior performances each year and pupils are encouraged to become involved in all aspects of production. The School also provides tuition in public and verse speaking and pupils regularly win trophies at the local festivals. There is also an annual Musical and pupils enter musical theatre exams.

Combined Cadet Force. There is a large voluntary contingent of the Combined Cadet Force with Navy, Army and Marines Sections.

Careers. Careers guidance begins in the Third Form. The Careers Adviser maintains close links with universities and colleges and regularly visits industrial firms. We have exchange programmes with schools in Australia, New Zealand and South Africa. There is a dedicated Careers Library, well-stocked with prospectuses, reference books and in-house magazines. Strathallan is a member of the Independent Schools Careers Organisation, a representative of which visits regularly and of the Scottish Council for Development and Industry.

All pupils have the opportunities to gain work experience in the Fifth Form, after their GCSEs. There is also a GAP year programme which provides placements for pupils to work overseas prior to going to university. Strathallan is developing particular links with Charities in Kenya.

Pastoral Care. There is a strong emphasis on pastoral care. The School has drawn up its own welfare guidelines in consultation with parents, governors and Perth and Kinross Social Work Department.

Medical Centre. Strathallan has its own purpose-built Medical Centre with consulting and treatment rooms. There are nursing staff at the Centre and the School's Medical Officers visit four times a week. Physiotherapy, chiropody, and relaxation also take place in the Centre during term time.

Entrance. Junior Entrance – Boys and girls are admitted to the Junior School (Riley House) at either age 9, 10, 11 or 12. An Entrance Day (including those sitting scholarship examinations in January) is held in early Spring each year for those who are available. Entry is based on a satisfactory school report and assessments in Maths and English.

Entry to the Senior School – Candidates for entry into the Senior School at 13 may enter via the Open Scholarship examination in February, Common Entrance or a satisfactory school report.

Sixth Form – Boys and girls may also enter at Sixth Form level, either via the Sixth Form scholarship examination in November or on the basis of a satisfactory school report and GCSE/Standard Grade results.

Scholarships. Awards are made on the basis of competitive examination/assessment. Bursary help is available to supplement awards for outstanding candidates on a financial need basis.

Awards are available in the following categories to candidates entering the school at three levels:

Junior School: Academic and Music/Choral/Performing Arts/Piping/Drumming, Drama and Sport. Candidates should be under 13 on 1 September in the year of entry. Scholarship Examination: January.

Third Form: Academic, Music/Choral/Piping/Drumming, Art, Design Technology, Drama and Sports. Candidates should be under 14 on 1 September in the year of entry. Scholarship Examination: February.

Sixth Form: Academic, Music/Choral/Piping/Drumming, Art, Design Technology/Arkwright, Drama and Sports. Candidates should be under 17 on 1 September in the year of entry. Scholarship Examination: November.

Further information is available on the School's website, www.strathallan.co.uk, or from The Admissions Office, Tel: 01738 815003, email: admissions@strathallan.co.uk.

Bursaries. Bursaries are awarded dependent on financial circumstances and are available to pupils who have qualified for entry through exam or school report or both. It is not necessary for successful candidates for bursaries to have achieved scholarship standard but it may be possible to add a bursary award to a scholarship to enable a pupil to come to Strathallan.

Fees per term (2014–2015). Junior School (Riley House): £6,906 (boarding), £4,310 (day). Senior School: £9,682 (boarding), £6,570 (day).

Prospectus. Up-to-date information is included in the prospectus which can be obtained by contacting the Admissions Office or via the School's website.

Charitable status. Strathallan School is a Registered Charity, number SC008903, dedicated to Education.

Surbiton High School
United Learning

Surbiton High Senior School:
Surbiton Crescent, Kingston-upon-Thames KT1 2JT
Tel: 020 8546 5245
Fax: 020 8547 0026
email: office@surbitonhigh.com

Surbiton High Boys' Preparatory School:
3 Avenue Elmers, Surbiton KT6 4SP
Tel: 020 8390 6640
Fax: 020 8255 3049
email: boysprep@surbitonhigh.com

Surbiton High Junior Girls' School:
95–97 Surbiton Road, Kingston-upon-Thames KT1 2HW
Tel: 020 8546 9756
Fax: 020 8974 6293
email: juniorgirls@surbitonhigh.com

website: www.surbitonhigh.com
Twitter: @SurbitonHigh
Facebook: /SurbitonHigh

Local Governing Body:
Chair: Mr Eggie Kock
Deputy Chair: Mr Ruairidh Hogg, BA
Mr Dan Bloxham
Mrs Karen Bowles, FCCA
Mrs Eileen Carroll
Mrs Sophie Cornish
Mr Gordon Faultless, BSc
Ms Ann Haydon, BSc, NPQH
Mrs Kathleen Hayes
Mr Andrew Hodge, MBE, MSc
Mr Jonathan Wilkes

Senior Leadership Team:

Principal: **Ms Ann Haydon**, BSc, NPQH

Head of Senior School: Mr Silas Edmonds, MA, NPQH
Head of Educational Development: Mrs Helen Morgan, BA
Vice Principal – Pupil Enterprise, Leadership, Community: Mr Ian Smith, MA, NPQH
Vice Principal – Pupil and Staff Development & Wellbeing: Mr Matthew Close, BA, MSc
Director of Marketing: Mrs Alex Kearney, BA
Business Director: Miss Marinke Overwater
Head of Junior Girls' and Boys' Preparatory: Ms Cath Bufton, BA
Deputy Head of Junior Girls' and Boys' Preparatory: Mrs Sally Ralph, BEd
Assistant Principal – Teaching & Learning: Mr Stuart Bachelor, MA
Deputy Head of Junior Girls' School: Mr Leigh Hardie, BA
Assistant Principal – Teaching & Learning: Mrs Hannah Horwood, BSc
Deputy Head of Boys' Preparatory School: Ms Anisa Lewis, BEd
Assistant Principal – Co-Curricular: Mr Jeremy Martin, BA

Assistant Principal – Director of Sixth Form: Mr Jonathan Owen, BSc
Assistant Principal – Digital Strategy: Mr Jose Picardo, MA
Assistant Principal – Staff Development: §Mrs Caroline Stewart, BA

Principal's Office:
Executive Assistant to the Principal: Mrs Rosie Sleeman, BA
Personal Assistant to the Principal: Mrs Caroline Blight
Personal Assistant to the Principal: Mrs Josie O'Reilly, BA
Personal Assistant to the ELT: Mrs Nicola Davies, BA

School Staff:
* *Head of Department/Subject*
§ *Part-time*

Art :
*Mrs Kate Ross, BA (*Director of Art*)
Mrs Cheryl Furlong, BEd (*Assistant Director of Art, Head of Curie House*)
Miss Daisy Chandler, BA
Miss Catherine Havas, BA
§Miss Rachel Pedder-Smith, MA, BA
Miss Hayley Rowe, BA
Miss Laura Taverner, BSc
Mrs Francesca George (*Art Technician*)
Mrs Hayley Harman (*Artist in Residence*)

Biology:
Dr Andy Keaney, PhD (*Head of Science*)
*Mrs Kavita Patel, BSc (*NQT, Trainee Teacher Coordinator*)
Mrs Hannah Horwood, BSc (*Teacher Leader to Gifted and Talented Pupils, EPQ Supervisor*)
Mrs Emily Libbey, BSc
Mrs Tamlyn Looms, BSc (*Assistant Head of Year Eight*)
Miss Charlotte Nisbet, BSc
Mr Jonathan Owen, BSc (*Director of Sixth Form*)
Miss Hannah Taylor, BSc
Miss Anna Woollen, BSc
Mrs Jennifer Zacharias, BSc
Mrs Marian Bailey, BSc (*Science Technician*)

Critical Thinking:
Miss Lucinda Gilchrist, BA
Mrs Joanna McIsaac, MA

Chemistry:
Dr Andy Keaney, PhD (*Head of Science*)
*Mr Keith Salisbury, BSc (*Oxbridge Mentor*)
Mr Simon Dodd, BSc (*Head of House and Social Enterprise*)
Miss Jessica Robinson, BSc
Miss Hannah Parker, BSc (*GTP*)
Dr Sarah Pinniger, PhD (*Assistant DoE Coordinator*)
§Mrs Hazel Breeze, BA (*Science Technician*)
§Mrs Shirley Moore, BEng (*Science Technician and Demonstrator*)

Classics:
*Miss Joanna Deeks, BA
§Mr Graham Davidson, BA, MPhil
Mrs Olivia Adams, BA
Miss Gayle Smith, BA (*NQT*)

Design and Technology:
Mr Alex Kew, BSc
Mrs Natalie Jones, BA (*Head of Textiles*)
§Mrs Christine Geard, BA, CNAA, NEBOSH (*Director of Health, Safety and Facilities*)
§Mrs Dorita Morito, BA
Miss Katherine Hartley, BA
§Mr Graham Swindells, CertEd (*Design Technology Technician*)

Drama:
*Miss Elaine Mulhern, MA (*Director of Drama*)
Mrs Chris Griffin (*Assistant Director of Drama*)
§Mrs Annalisa Hamilton, MA
Miss Kathryn McRink, BA (*Head of Year Eight*)
Mrs Lynne Tupper, BA

Economics and Business Studies:
*§Ms Zoe Brass, BSc (*EPQ Coordinator*)
Mr Colin Monks, BA
Mr Ian Smith, MA

English:
*Mrs Sharon Stead, BA
Mrs Alison Carter, MA
Miss Robyn Gladwyn (*Deputy Head of English*)
Miss Suzanne Pett, BA (*Deputy Head of English, Akenkan Charity Coordinator, Assistant Oxbridge Coordinator*)
Miss Rachel Bezant, BA (*Head of Year Nine*)
Mrs Tristania Currie, MA
Mr Ian Cushing BA, MSc, MPhil (*Assistant Head of Year Seven*)
Mr Silas Edmonds, BA, NPQH
Miss Lucinda Gilchrist, BA (*Deputy Head of English*)
Ms Bee Huntley, BA (*Oxbridge Mentor*)
Miss Ellen Phillips, MA
Mrs Sarah Rendle-Short, BA
§Mrs Lorna Syred, BA (*Chair of School Council for Years 10 and 11*)
§Mr Stuart Bird (*Writer in Residence*)

Geography:
*Mr Andy Pinks, BA
Mrs Lucy Clarke, MA (*Oxbridge Mentor*)
Mr Matthew Close, BA, MSc
§Mrs Rebecca Francis, BA
§Mrs Anna Godbold, BA
Ms Ann Haydon, BSc, NPQH
Mrs Karen Potts, BA

History:
*Miss Stella Forrester, BA
Mrs Jacqueline Bennett, BA (*Head of Year Seven, EPQ Supervisor*)
Miss Kjersti Hansell, BA (*Head of Pankhurst House*)
Miss Anja Ludgrove
Mrs Joanna McIsaac, MA (*Head of Year Eleven and Deputy Safeguarding Designated Person*)
Mrs Helen Morgan, BA
§Mrs Caroline Stewart, BA (*Staff Development Teacher Leader*)
§Mrs Geraldine Walker, BA

Information Technology:
*Mr Ian Richardson, BSc (*Assistant Head of Year Ten, Expeditions Coordinator*)
§Mr Gary Ekins, BSc (*Manager of Information Systems*)
§Ms Madeleine King, BA
§Mr Robert Skinner, BA (*DoE Coordinator, Head of Nightingale House*)

Mathematics:
*Mr John Bennett, MA
Mrs Eva Joly, BSc (*Deputy Head of Mathematics*)
Dr Antonia Castelluccio, PhD
§Mrs Azita Dara, BSc
Mrs Claire Emmerton, BA
Mr Mike Gibbons, MA
§Miss Cristina Hulea
§Mrs Alison Keeling, BSc
§Mrs Anne King, BSc
Mrs Kusum Mair, MA
§Mrs Gillian Newton, BSc
Mrs Julie Paynter, BSc
§Mrs Sarah Rawlinson, BSc
Mrs Karina Sutherland, BSc

Miss Lynsey Williams, BSc (*Assistant Head of Year Eleven*)

Mrs Emily Woodall (*Assistant Head of Year Nine*)

Modern Foreign Languages:
*§Ms Charlotte Demetz, BA
Miss Angela Fabregat, BEd (**Spanish*)
Mrs Geillis Paul, BA (**French*)
Miss Anke Reckermann, MA (**German*)
Ms Jane Daniels, BA
Mrs Dura Haroon, BA
§Mrs Carol Holmes, BA
Miss Cherry Jeffries, BA (*Head of Austen House*)
Miss Lisa Keers, BA (*Head of Year Ten*)
Mr Jose Picardo, MA
Miss Eugenie Puchois, BA
Mrs Jana Smith, MA
§Mrs Julie Stoker, MA
§Mrs Monica Vazquez, BA
Mrs Claire Carazzo, BA

Language Assistants:
§Mrs Nadia Jaffery (*French*)
§Miss Grace Martinez Centeno (*Spanish*)
§Mrs Ines Pengilly (*German*)

Music:
Mr Matthew O'Malley, BA (*Director of Music*)
§Mr Patrick Martin, BA (*Head of Academic Music*)
Mrs Anne Reece, MA (*Head of Instrumental Music*)
Mr Jeremy Martin, BA
Mrs Daisy Sunda, BA (*Assistant Head of Year Seven*)
§Miss Anna Huber, BMus (*String Coordinator*)
§Miss Eleni Mavromoustaki, BMus (*Principle Accompanist*)
§Mrs Abigail Briggs (*Music Administrator*)

Music Tutors (part-time):
Miss Katy Ayling, BMus (*Clarinet*)
Ms Elizabeth Barker, BMus (*Percussion*)
Mr Paul Brunner, Dip RAM, LRAM (*Cello*)
Mr Andre Canniere, BA (*Brass*)
Miss Lindsay Dubery (*Bassoon*)
Mrs Marta Encinas de Paredes, ARCM (*Piano*)
Ms Candice Hamel (*Flute*)
Ms Pippa Harrison (*Piano*)
Mr Andrew Harper (*Clarinet*)
Ms Lydia Hepworth (*Guitar*)
Ms Alice Hyde, BMus (*Voice*)
Mr Nicholas Ireson, BMus (*French Horn*)
Ms Sian Jones, Dip PG Perf (*Voice*)
Miss Helen Massey, BMus (*Voice*)
Mr Gerry McDonald, BMus (*Flute, Oboe, Recorder*)
Ms Francesca Moore-Bridger, Dip PG Perf (*French Horn*)
Ms Lisa Robinson, BMus (*Voice*)
Ms Sarah Stuart (*Percussion*)
Ms Wei Wei Tan (*Violin*)
Miss Cheryl Taylor-Francis, BMus (*Clarinet, Saxophone*)
Mr Andrew Vickers, BMus (*Double Bass*)
Mrs Kate Warshaw, BMus (*Voice*)
Mr Rupert Whitehead (*Trombone*)
Mr Jose Zalba-Smith, BMus (*Flute*)

Philosophy and Religious Studies:
*Miss Christina Davis, BA
Mr Stuart Bachelor, MA (*Oxbridge Coordinator, Chair of School Council*)
Mrs Fiona Etherington, MA
§Mrs Virginia Foster, BA
§Miss Kelly Hockey, BA (*Head of Fonteyn House*)

Physical Education:
Mrs Sally Beere, BSc (*Director of Sport*)
Mrs Helen Chesterton, BA (*Director of Sport, Gifted and Talented Sports Coordinator*)

Miss Sunita Pottay, BA (*Director of Sport, Compliance Officer*)
Mrs Jacky Wilkey, CertEd (*Head of Sport Operations*)
Miss Lucy Roberts, MA (*Head of Academic PE, Head of Year Twelve*)
Mr James Culnane, MSc (*Head of Hockey*)
Mrs Avelline Deighton, BEd (*Head of Athletics*)
Mr Gregg Kovic, RPT (*Head of Tennis*)
Mrs Natalie Swift (*Head of Netball*)
Mrs Kara Vass, BA (*Head of Netball*)
Mr Stewart Walker (*Head of Rowing*)
Miss Nicola Yellop, BA (*Head of Gymnastics*)
Mr Zac Elbekri (*Assistant Tennis Coach*)
Mr Paul Fordham, BA
Miss Leila Fox (*GTP, Cover for Housemistress*)
Miss Ashleigh McKeown, BSc
Mr Ben Newton, BA
§Miss Sarah Wilkey (*Ski Club Manager*)
Miss Emma Rickards, BSc (*PE Teaching Assistant*)

Sports Coaches (part-time):
Mrs Zoe Bennett (*Aerobics*)
Mrs Fiona Benzies, BA (*Hockey*)
Mr Stephen Cooper (*Skiing*)
Mrs Natalie Crosland (*Gymnastics*)
Mr Roger Everington (*Rowing*)
Ms Jennifer Fields (*Netball*)
Mr Douglas Fordyce (*Gymnastics*)
Miss Sasheana Gordon (*Athletics*)
Mr James Greenwood (*Skiing*)
Mrs Tracey Greig (*Netball*)
Mr Phillip Gunner (*Basketball*)
Mr Nicholas Illingworth (*Gymnastics*)
Ms Daisy Jones (*Glee club*)
Mr Samuel Lee-Gill (*Rowing*)
Mr William Lucas (*Rowing*)
Mrs Kim Nash (*Trampoline*)
Mrs Elisapeta Neilson (*Netball*)
Ms Georgia Osborne-Davies (*Cheerleading*)
Mr Kenneth Roberts (*Rowing*)
Mr Lee Shinkin (*Judo*)
Mr Tom Short (*Football*)
Ms Tina Smith (*Netball*)
Mrs Deborah Sutton (*Yoga*)
Ms Rebecca Thompson (*Rowing*)
Mr Alasdair Toyn (*Rowing*)
Ms Sophie Walker (*Rowing*)
Miss Elizabeth Walne (*Rowing*)
Ms Julia Weltman (*Yoga*)
Ms Kelly White (*Boot camp*)
Ms Tracy Woods (*Swimming*)

Physics:
Dr Andy Keaney, PhD (*Head of Science*)
*Dr Robert Bastin, PhD
§Dr Linda Hansen, PhD (*KS5 Physics Coordinator, Oxbridge Mentor*)
Ms Victoria Hill, BSc (*NQT*)
§Mrs Hema Mehra, BSc
Mrs Ann Pudney, BSc
§Mrs Sue Millington (*Science Technician*)

Psychology:
*Mrs Helen Cowie, BA
Mrs Garnette Watts, MA (*Head of Year Thirteen*)
§Mrs Stephanie Williams

Learning Support:
*Mrs Kathryn Slaughter, BA
§Mrs Sarah Canby, BA (*Learning Support*)
§Mrs Beate Davies, BSc (*Learning Support*)
§Mrs Valerie Humphreys, BA (*EAL*)
§Mrs Maria O'Connor, BA (*EAL*)
§Ms Lorraine Marrison, Level 3 NVQ (*Teaching Assistant*)
§Mrs Tyra Paik (*Korean Mentor*)

Director of Careers and Guidance: §Mr Terry McDermott
Examinations Officer: §Mrs Katherine Sharp, BTEC
Librarian: §Mr Joseph Humphreys, MA
Head of Admissions: Mrs Adrienne Forster, BA
Junior Schools Registrar: §Mrs Rachel Karan, LLB
International Registrar: §Mrs Sue Morris, BA

Surbiton High School is an independent academic HMC School for girls aged 4–18 years and boys aged 4–11 years which caters for the individual and believes that an education full of opportunity is a vital cornerstone of a pupil's transition and future. Surbiton High is an enthusiastic, lively and successful community with a long tradition of excellence in pastoral care. Every pupil is valued and inspired to be the best they can be and challenged to aim high, think creatively and develop enquiring, critical minds. Every success and achievement is celebrated.

Ann Haydon is the Principal of Surbiton High School, a position she took up in January 2008. Previously, Ann was Deputy Headmistress at Guildford High School, Surbiton's sister school in United Learning. Ann is committed to bringing out the 'best in everyone' and values links with the commercial sector as Surbiton prepares the pupils with the skills, knowledge and enterprising attitude that they need to prepare them for work in the global market. Ann believes that pupils should have the freedom to grow and learn at their own pace whilst being given excellent opportunities to realise their ambitions. They are encouraged to be independent thinkers who love to learn and whose learning is enriched by varied educational and exciting trips and visits to museums, art galleries, theatre performances and exhibitions, as well as residential trips abroad to countries as far as Iceland and Mongolia.

Surbiton High School remains at the forefront of learning technology with interactive whiteboards in every classroom and superb facilities for the teaching of ICT. The Sixth Form Centre has enhanced the post-16 provision helping to ensure that the girls secure places at their first choice university. In 2005 completion of a major redevelopment of the main school site took place to provide additional purpose built classrooms, Science and Modern Languages laboratories and an open plan Art Studio. The extensive sports grounds at Hinchley Wood and Oaken Lane include a pavilion, all-weather tennis and netball courts and two all-weather hockey pitches and a multi-use games area. The school is well served by school buses and public transport to enable children from a wide catchment area to attend the school.

At Surbiton High School we know that choosing the right school for your child is one of the most important decisions you will make. Just like you, we believe the happiness and success of your child are key foundations upon which their future is built. That is why we are a school which genuinely delights in the individual. We are a place where every child is valued; every child is encouraged to give of their very best; and every child has the chance to grow in confidence by participating in a wide range of inspirational learning experiences.

We pride ourselves on being an extraordinary community where people matter, results count and where a passion for excellence drives everything we do. We are committed to looking beyond A*s to offer real breadth of education. We feed our pupils' minds, but we also care passionately about their character development and happiness.

Our inspirational staff are dedicated to delivering a rich curriculum and programme of activities which challenge your child to explore ideas for themselves. Whether engaged in learning in the classroom, or through musical, artistic, sporting, enterprise or charitable activities, our pupils are constantly encouraged to connect with the wider world and embrace new experiences to build their confidence – a confidence built not on arrogance, but on self-belief and a 'can do' attitude.

Our approach to education means that Surbiton High School pupils achieve the very best exam results and are also compassionate, authentic young people with strong values, keen to make a positive difference in the world.

Fees per term (2014–2015). Junior Girls and Boys' Preparatory: £3,007 (Reception, Years 1–2); £4,021 (Years 3–6). Senior School: £4,931. Lunch: £229 (compulsory from Reception to Year 9). Fee rates apply to payment by termly direct debit.

When two or more children of the same family attend the School, a reduction in fees will be given. Reductions are also made for daughters of members of the Clergy.

Scholarships and Bursaries. Scholarships are offered at 11+ and 16+.

11+/Year 7: Academic Scholarships offering up to 50% fee reduction are available. All-Rounder, Art, Drama, Music and Sport Scholarships offer up to 50% fee reduction.

Sixth Form: All-rounder, Academic, Art, Drama, Music and Sport Scholarships and Awards, worth up to 50% of fees, are available. Also available are The Dame Angela Rumbold Science Scholarship and The Gillman & Soame Photography Scholarship.

Bursaries are awarded to girls whose families may have difficulty in meeting the cost of private education, and are means-tested.

For further particulars apply to the Admissions Registrar.

Assisted Places. United Learning offers a limited number of Assisted Places at 11+.

Surbiton High Boys' Preparatory School. Day school for boys aged 4–11.

The main age of entry is at 4 by assessment and examination, with occasional places in other year groups.

Surbiton High Boys' Preparatory School follows an enhanced National Curriculum combining traditional values with the best of modern methods. French, music and physical education are taught by specialist teachers throughout the school and information technology is a particular strength. The School has contact with some 20 senior schools in south-west London and north Surrey. Regularly the children's success in entrance examinations allows the opportunity to choose between three or more senior schools and many pupils gain scholarship awards.

(*For further details, see entry in IAPS section.*)

Surbiton High Junior Girls' School. The Junior Girls' School opened in January 1994 and provides a caring, happy and secure education for girls aged 4 to 11. The main age of entry is at 4 and 7 by assessment and examination, with occasional places in other year groups.

Surbiton High Junior Girls' School is a vibrant school which balances excellent academic achievement and learning with a broad co-curricular programme. It is a warm and welcoming school where staff inspire, encourage and empower pupils to achieve their very best both inside and outside the classroom.

Surbiton girls become independent learners and decision-makers from the earliest age. We encourage them to think for themselves and to recognise their own styles of work and learning. We also understand the importance of strong foundations in numeracy and literacy. From mental arithmetic to grammar and punctuation, our girls are exceptionally well-prepared for the demands of modern education.

There is a natural progression to the Senior School and the Junior School prepares girls well for the next stage in learning at our Senior School.

(*For further details, see entry in IAPS section.*)

Charitable status. Surbiton High School is part of United Learning which comprises: UCST (a Company Limited by Guarantee, Registered in England, number 2780748, and a Registered Charity, number 1016538) and ULT (a Company Limited by Guarantee, Registered in England, number 4439859, and an Exempt Charity).

Sutton Valence School

Sutton Valence, Maidstone, Kent ME17 3HL
Tel: 01622 845200
Fax: 01622 844103
email: enquiries@svs.org.uk
website: www.svs.org.uk

Motto: *My Trust is in God alone*
   Founded in 1576 by William Lambe, Sutton Valence School has over 425 years of proud history. Today the School is co-educational and includes a preparatory school on a neighbouring site. Both schools are situated on the slopes of a high ridge with unequalled views over the Weald of Kent in the historic, beautiful and safe village of Sutton Valence.
   Our greatest strength is our community. The relationships we enjoy between staff, pupils and parents allow us to craft an educational journey that is individually-suited to every pupil. During a family's association with the School we hope they will feel involved, listened to and informed.
   Through the high expectations and standards we set, all our young people are encouraged and helped to go further than they had thought possible in their academic, co-curricular, community and leadership journeys. We want them to become confident, civilised, tolerant and open-minded individuals who possess a love of learning and a strong sense of self-discipline along with a set of values reflecting our principles as a Christian Foundation.

Visitor: The Lord Archbishop of Canterbury

Foundation: United Westminster Schools

Director/Clerk: R W Blackwell, MA

Governing Body:
B F W Baughan, FSI (*Chairman*)
Major General David Burden, CB, CVO, CBE
The Very Revd Dr J R Hall, BA, Hon DD, HonDTheol, FRSA
A J Hutchinson, MA Cantab
T D Page
Mrs D Perry, MA, DMS, FRSA
Mrs G Swaine, BSc Hons, MEd
D W Taylor, MA, FRSA
C H Tongue, MA
Lady Vallance, JP, MA, MSc, PhD, FRSA, FCGI
M Walker, PhD, MA, FRSA
E Watts, OBE, BA, FRSA

Headmaster: **B C W Grindlay**, MA Cantab, MusB, FRCO CHM

Senior Deputy Head: J J Farrell, MA Cantab (*History*)
Deputy Head – Academic: A J Wyles, BSc London, MEd, FRGS (*Geography*)
Director of Studies: D E Clarke, BSc, CBiol, MSB Bristol (*Biology*)
Director of Co-Curricular Activities: Mrs M T Hall, BEd Southampton (*Child Protection Officer*)

Academic Staff:
† *Boarding Housemaster or Housemistress*
‡ *Day Housemaster or Housemistress*

†G N Alderman, BEd Avery Hill College (*Director of Sport*)
‡Mrs K L Andersen, CertEd Elizabeth Gaskell College (*Head of Home Economics, Head of Sixth Form Section, Director of Professional Development*)
Mrs R C Ball, BA University of Wales Lampeter (*Head of Media Studies*)
‡A R Bee, BSc Manchester (*Head of Geography*)
Dr M Brown, BSc Kent (*Physics, Chemistry, Astronomy*)

R H Carr, BA St John's College Durham (*History, Games*)
Miss E J Clement-Walker, BA Loughborough (*DT and Art*)
T P Cope, MEng Loughborough (*Mathematics*)
R F D Cottrell, BA Southampton (*MFL*)
Miss P H M Cunningham, BSc Nottingham (*Science*)
C M Davenport, BA Keele (*Head of English*)
Miss E R Davies, BA Coventry (*Drama*)
G A Davies, BA University of Wales Lampeter (*Religious Studies*)
Mrs S H de Castro Franco, BA Manchester (*Head of French*)
Ms S V Easter, BA Exeter (*Art, Editor of 'The Suttonian' magazine*)
Miss C Fordham, BA Exeter (*Acting Head of Drama*)
L Fuentes Olea, BA Granada (*Head of MFL*)
†P N Gorman, BA Edinburgh (*Head of Art*)
Mrs S Gorman, BEd University of Alcada de Henares Madrid (*MFL*)
Mrs F M Gosden, BA Rhodes (*English*)
Miss G L Gray, BA Bangor (*Religious Studies*)
Dr L Grindlay, MA Cantab (*English*)
Miss M A Halleron, BSc Leeds (*Head of Physics*)
Miss P L Hallett, BA Brighton (*Head of Academic PE and Girls' Games*)
A P Hammersley, BSc York (*Biology*)
G Harris, BA King's College (*Mathematics*)
Mrs E Head, MA Dundee (*English*)
*S J Head, MSc Bristol (*Chemistry and Head of Boarding*)
Mrs H Heurtevent, BA Caen, Normandy, DEUG I and II Université Catholique, Angers (*French*)
S P Hiscocks, BSc Essex, PhD, CChem, MRSC (*Head of Science, Chemistry*)
D W Holmes, LRAM (*Head of Strings*)
P J Horley, BA, ARCO, ALCM, College of Ripon and York St John (*Director of Music, CCF*)
M D Howell, BSc University College Worcester (*Geography and Head of Rugby*)
Mrs A Hurst, MA Dundee (*SEN*)
M B James, MEd Macquire University Sydney (*Business Studies and Economics*)
Mrs A M Kane, BA Canterbury Christ Church (*SEN*)
D J J Keep, MA Greenwich, BEd Avery Hill College (*Head of Design and Technology, CCF*)
D R Kennedy, BSc Leeds, CBiol, MIBiol (*Head of Biology, Games*)
Mrs C J Kitchen, BEng Bradford, MSc Birmingham, BSc Open (*Head of Mathematics, Asst D of E*)
Mrs K W J Luxford, BA Hull (*Head of Second Form, English*)
Miss J A Manning, BA Kent, PG Cert Dyslexia and Literacy York (*SEN*)
†Mrs A Mathews, BA Sports Science and Art (*Dance*)
D R Mathews, BSc Brunel (*Academic PE, Games, i/c Hockey*)
Miss K J McConnachie, BSc Birmingham (*ICT, Games, i/c Netball*)
G J Millbery, BA Lampeter (*Director of ICT, DofE Coordinator, CCF*)
Miss L A Mitchell-Nanson, BA Kent (*Mathematics*)
Miss N E Moore, BA Exeter (*Geography*)
A Penfold, BA Surrey (*Head of Religious Studies, Head of Teaching and Learning*)
R W J E Plowden, MA Wales, BA Newcastle (*History, Government and Politics*)
Mrs F H Porter, BA Leeds (*English*)
Miss S Pritchard, BA (*Business Studies, i/c Social Enterprise Group*)
Mrs S Rose, BEd Bishops Otter College (*Asst Head of Juniors, English, Games*)
‡D R L Sansom, BSc University College of Wales, Swansea (*Geography, Head of Juniors*)
J D Soman, BA Oxford (*Assistant Director of Music*)

Mrs A J Sunde, BA Sheffield (*Head of History, Head of Academic Scholars*)

J L van Vuuren, Port Elizabeth Technikon and University of South Africa (*Business Studies and Games*)

A P Webster, MA Oxon (*Modern Foreign Languages*)

†K R Webster, MEd Crewe & Alsager College (*Mathematics*)

V Wells (*i/c Cricket, Games*)

Mrs C Westlake, BA Sussex (*English*)

C J Westlake, BSc (*Mathematics*)

‡Mrs A F F Wilkinson, Cert Ed Calder College, Liverpool (*Home Economics, OC CCF, Head of Fourth Form*)

Mrs H M Wood, MSc, BSc Hull (*Chemistry*)

Bursar: S Fowle
Assistant Bursar: Mrs D van Leeuwen

Headmaster's PA: Mrs S O'Connell
Admissions Officer: Mrs K Webster
Development Manager: Mrs H Knott, BSc

Sports Hall Manager: J van Vuuren

Preparatory School

Head: M Gough, BA, LLB, LLM, PGCE
Deputy Head: Miss C L Corkran, MEd, BEd Hons Cantab
Head of Pre-Prep: Miss P McCarmick, MA, BSc QTS, AMBDA
Director of Studies: Mrs R Harrison, BEd Hons

Head's Secretary and Admissions: Mrs A Leckie

Ethos. The School is a supportive and inclusive community where each cares for all and where individuality is cherished.

Sutton Valence is an educational community whose philosophy embraces a breadth of challenges. Through a diverse curriculum and a wide range of activities we cultivate an appreciation of academic excellence, responsibility, leadership, kindness and friendship amongst our pupils. All members of the School develop a sense of spiritual, moral and ethical awareness and, in so doing, come to appreciate their own place in the world.

At Sutton Valence every person is valued as an individual with their own distinct sense of worth and potential. Each member of the community has abilities, talents and skills unique to them. Our School strives to provide the seedbed to allow these gifts and talents to grow, develop and ultimately flourish.

Our community is founded on the principles of trust, tolerance and openness. As such, we expect all at Sutton Valence to treat each other with respect, humanity and care. Individuals therefore are obliged to recognise that the differences between us make us collectively stronger. It is essential that we understand, appreciate and celebrate the diversity of backgrounds, world views and attitudes expressed by those in our community.

At the foundation of our community is the expectation that every student will achieve their potential. Our commitment is to strive for excellence as pupils and teachers. To achieve this it is essential that every member of the School strives to give of their very best in all that they do.

Results. Sutton Valence School has an inclusive intake, however, our academic strength lies in enabling our students to achieve beyond their benchmarked potential, whatever their ability. As recognised by our recent ISI inspection, 'GCSE results have shown a steady improvement over the last four years'.

On average, our students will gain results at A Level that outperform their predicted grade on entry to the School by 0.5 of a grade. As measured by Durham University, which has a thirty-year history of computing these statistics, this year Sutton Valence is in the top 15% of schools for adding value (amongst those participating). That means that chil-

dren at Sutton Valence do better in their exams than they would do in 85% of other schools, nationally.

It is the combination of outstanding teaching and consistent effort by our students that brings these enviable results. For example, this year our top set students (many of whom did not pass the 11+) achieved 89% A* and A grades at GCSE and 99% A* to B grades at A Level. Overall, our A Level results in recent years are similar to, or better than, those of the Kent grammar schools.

Curriculum. The academic curriculum is innovative and aims to achieve a balance between the needs of the individual and demands of society, industry, the universities and the professions. Classes are small and the ratio of graduate teaching staff is 1:9.

In First and Second Forms (Years 7 and 8) the National Curriculum is broadly followed, covering English, Mathematics, Chemistry, Physics, Biology, French, Spanish, History, Geography, Religious Studies, Design Technology, Home Economics, ICT, Art, Music, Physical Education and Drama.

The National Curriculum is again broadly followed in Third Form (Year 9) where subjects offered are the same as in First and Second Form. However, the syllabi are designed to cater for not only those who enter Third Form via First and Second Form, but also the large number of pupils who join the school at 13+.

In Fourth and Fifth Form (Years 10 and 11) pupils usually study nine or ten subjects to GCSE level. These are divided between the core – English and English Literature, Mathematics, a Modern Language (French, Spanish, German), Science, Religious Studies, PSHE and ICT – and option groups. Each group contains a number of subjects, offering a choice which allows every pupil to achieve a balanced education whilst, at the same time, providing the opportunity to concentrate on his or her strengths. Subjects on offer are History, Geography, Drama, Business Studies, a second Language, DT, Home Economics, Art, Music, iMedia and PE.

In the two years covered by the Lower and Upper Sixth (Years 12 and 13) pupils usually study four subjects at AS Level. Pupils continue with three, or occasionally, four subjects in their final year to A Level and are well positioned to meet the entrance requirements of the universities and professions. Psychology, Government and Politics, Photography, Media Studies, Theatre Studies and BTec Public Services are included in this programme.

Potential Oxbridge candidates are identified in the Lower Sixth year and suitable tuition is arranged.

Choice of Subjects: Separate booklets on GCSE and A Level options are available.

Setting, Promotion, Reporting. In First to Fifth Form Mathematics and French are setted. In First to Third Form a top group is selected.

The minimum qualification for entry into the Sixth Form is normally considered to be five B grade passes at GCSE Level, or the equivalent for overseas students.

Academic progress is monitored by tutors and at regular intervals throughout the term every pupil is graded for achievement and effort in every subject for their classwork and for effort in their prep. Parents are invited to a 'monitoring morning' at every half term to discuss their child's progress and to set targets for improvement next half term, if required. At the end of term full subject reports are written on all pupils. Promotion between sets is always possible.

ICT (iMedia). In addition to well-equipped computer suites the School has developed a sophisticated campus-wide network with its own intranet and online systems of communication with parents.

The school network serves the whole site providing open access for pupils in the computer rooms and throughout the school via a Microsoft Windows-based system working on industry-standard software. The library stocks many CD ROMs and there is a CAD system in Design and Technology. Access to the network is available to pupils in their own rooms in boarding houses.

Higher Education and Careers. Sutton Valence has a modern and well-equipped Sixth Form Centre which incorporates a careers library and the latest technologies to help in degree and career selection.

Every pupil sits a series of aptitude and ability tests during the two years prior to GCSE. This is followed by a thorough interview with trained members of staff in conjunction with the Kent Careers Service, when suggestions are made for Sixth Form academic courses and possible degrees or careers are explored.

In the Sixth Form further interviews are conducted, the Higher Education Coordinator gives advice on university and college applications and a range of career lectures and visits are laid on, including trips to Oxford and Cambridge universities.

Music. Music plays a very important part in the life of the school, and we have a deservedly fine reputation for the quality and range of our music-making. The music school contains a concert hall, five teaching rooms, ten practice rooms and an ensemble room.

Approximately 40% of the pupils learn a musical instrument or have singing lessons; there are four choirs, an orchestra, wind band, string group, jazz band, and a very full programme of concerts. Music tours to Europe are arranged, and the Music Society organises a programme of distinguished visiting performers every year.

Drama. As with Music, Drama is central to the life of the school and the creative expression of our students. Every year there will be a number of productions, in addition to theatre workshops and reviews. Drama scholars and others also receive one-to-one drama coaching lessons in preparation for LAMDA exams. The Baughan Theatre provides an adaptable venue seating up to 250 for drama, music and lectures, along with rehearsal rooms, technical gantry and scene dock.

Sport and Physical Education. Sutton Valence has a deserved reputation as a strong sporting school, competing in seventeen sports. On average, forty pupils will have representative honours at County, Regional and National levels in the main sports as well as in other disciplines. On a typical Saturday afternoon, half the school will be engaged in matches.

The Talented Athlete Group (TAG), which includes sports scholars, helps those students, both inside and outside of Sutton Valence, who are performing at a very high level (county and beyond). Once identified, the student will have regular meetings with their coach, either as a group or individually, where aims and objectives will be set and a variety of subjects will be covered. Individual strength and conditioning programmes and sessions are offered for all senior teams and are monitored by professionally qualified staff.

Our 100-acre site has one of the best cricket squares in Kent, two floodlit Astroturf pitches for hockey, a six-lane indoor swimming pool, tennis, netball and squash courts, a sports hall encompassing a full-size indoor hockey pitch, sprung-floor cricket nets and fitness suite, six golf practice holes and a floodlit all-weather running track. In all, there is a tremendous range of choice for both boys and girls, all of whom will have timetabled sport on at least two days every week and could be involved in a sporting activity every day, if they wished. Additional sports, such as football, judo, dance, horse riding, badminton, basketball, fives and fencing are offered through our activities programme.

Pastoral System. The School is arranged vertically in houses, with the Juniors (Years 7 and 8) in a separate house. Each House has a Housemaster or Housemistress and is divided into Tutor Groups containing pupils from each year and from day and boarding. Pupils meet with their Tutor every day and this allows their progress to be monitored, as well as giving pupils an opportunity to seek guidance. In addition to monitoring academic progress, tutors help pupils

develop their potential through the Personal, Social and Health Education (PSHE) programme.

The School is a Christian foundation, however, our values are very much based on openness, tolerance and inclusivity. As such, we welcome students from all faith backgrounds, as well as those families who have no faith commitment.

Community Service, CCF and Duke of Edinburgh's Award Scheme. The CCF provides an organisation within Sutton Valence School which enables boys and girls to develop self-discipline, responsibility, self-reliance, resourcefulness, endurance, perseverance, a sense of service to the community and leadership. It complements the academic and other co-curricular aims of the School in preparing our pupils for adult life. All the three service elements of Army, Navy and RAF are offered. Pupils may join in the Third Form (Year 9) and CCF is also one of the option choices in the Fourth Form (Year 10). Cadets are encouraged to join the Duke of Edinburgh's Award Scheme where there is the opportunity for planning and undertaking expeditions. Sutton Valence School CCF is affiliated to the Princess of Wales's Royal Regiment.

The Duke of Edinburgh's Award Scheme is, similarly, well supported with, on average, 18 Gold Awards being achieved each year. Others participate in Community Service activities whereby pupils visit local primary schools, old people's homes, hospitals, undertake charity work and help out with local conservation projects.

Clubs and Activities. Time is specifically set aside each week for clubs and activities. Every pupil spends time pursuing his or her own special interests, and with up to forty clubs or activities from which to choose, the range and scope is very wide. In addition, various school societies and some other activities take place out of school hours, for example the Kingdon Society for Academic Scholars.

Scholarships and Bursaries. Academic, Art, Design Technology, Music, Sport and Drama Scholarships are awarded at 11+, 13+ and Sixth Form entry. Candidates may apply for a maximum of two non-academic scholarships.

The Westminster Scholarship supports well-motivated and able pupils who enter Sutton Valence School at Sixth Form level and who are expected to achieve 5 A* grade passes at GCSE.

Bursaries are awarded according to financial need at the discretion of the Scholarship and Bursaries Committee, and are reviewed annually. Forces bursaries are available.

Further details may be obtained from the Admissions Officer.

Fees per term (2014–2015). Senior Boarding (in addition to Tuition): £3,450 (Full), £2,840 (5 nights pw), £2,340 (4 nights pw), £1,820 (3 nights pw). Junior Boarding (in addition to Tuition): £2,810 (Full), £2,455 (5 nights pw), £2,100 (4 nights pw), £1,630 (3 nights pw). Tuition: Junior £4,925–£5,600, Senior £6,435. Lunch for Day pupils and occasional boarders: £258.

Instrumental Music: £238 per term (10 lessons).

Extras: Books, stationery and clothing are charged for as supplied. A small charge is also made for entry at each stage to The Duke of Edinburgh's Award Scheme. Any other extras are those expenses personal to the individual. We have a series of bus routes available to families from areas across Kent costing up to £300 per term. Further details of routes can be obtained on request.

Charitable status. United Westminster Schools Foundation is a Registered Charity, number 309267. Its aims are to promote education through its two independent schools and one state comprehensive school.

Taunton School

Taunton, Somerset TA2 6AD
Tel: 01823 703703
       01823 703603 Headmaster
       01823 703700 Admissions
Fax: 01823 703704
email: enquiries@tauntonschool.co.uk
website: www.tauntonschool.co.uk

The School's aim is: '...to prepare young people to shape the world in the 21st century'. A friendly and purposeful institution, it upholds all the values of a good boarding school: pastoral care, value added academic achievements, fine exam results and a full extra-curricular programme. It has a sense of the modern global challenge. It offers the International Baccalaureate, Mandarin, extensive visits abroad, a welcome to pupils from all cultures and a number of exciting initiatives such as the visit to Shenzhen in China.

Governors:

Chairman: Mrs Jane E Barrie, OBE, BSc, ARCS, FCSI, DL
Deputy Chairman: Mr Henry C V Keeling
Treasurer: Mr Christopher C Butters, FCA
Mr Clive N G Arding, FRICS
Vice Admiral Sir Tom Blackburn, KCVO, CB
Mr Phil Cooper, BA Hons, MSc (*Elect*)
Ms Joan Deslandes, BEd Hons, MA
Major General Jonathan Hall, CB, OBE, FCMI, DL
Mr Tim G Hayden, LLB
Mr Mark R Hobbs, MA
Mrs Kate M-L James, BA Hons, PG Dip Law, LPC
Mr Richard I Kennedy, LLB, FCA
Mr Robert D Sandry, FCA
Mr Mark Saxton, CDir, BA, MSc
Mrs Marilyn P Trask, BEd, MA
Mrs Elaine M Waymouth
Reverend Ruth Whitehead, BSc, MA
Mr Geoffrey A Matthews, BA, LLD Hons (*Governors' Advisor*)

Honorary Life Vice Presidents:
Mr Brian P Bissell, MBE, MA, BD
Mr Michael H N Button, FCA
Miss Alannah E Hunt, FCIPD (*Elect*)
Major General Barry M Lane, CB, OBE
Mr Alan M Large, LLB (*Elect*)
Mr Geoffrey A Matthews, BA, LLD Hons (*Elect*)
Mr David T Watson, MA, FCA
Mrs Joan Williams, LLB
Bursar & Clerk to the Governors: Mr David J A Taylor, ACIS

Headmaster: Mr Lee C Glaser, MA

Deputy Headmaster: Mr Neil Mason, BSc (*Biology*)
Senior Mistress: Mrs Carol A Manley (*PSHE*)
Head of Sixth Form: Mr Mike J Cook, BSc (*Biology*)
Head of Middle School: Mrs Katherine M Walters, MA (*Head of Academic Development*)
Head of Boarding: Mrs Ruth Coomber, BSc (*Geography, †Woodyer*)
Chaplain: Reverend Matthew Dietz, MA, BA

Assistant Staff:
† *House Staff*

Mr Rob E Abell, BSc (*Head of Economics and Business Studies*)
Mrs Fiona L Baker, BMus (*Assistant Director of Music*)
Mr Jon M Baker, BA (*Head of Design & Technology*)
Miss Barbara Battaglino (*Modern Languages*)
Mrs Annegret K Beere (*Modern Languages*)

Mr Martin A Bluemel, MA (*Head of Chemistry & IB Coordinator*)
Mrs Louise M Bolland, BA (*Modern Languages, †Besley*)
Mrs Barbara Boylan, CertEd (*Academic Development*)
Miss Laura Brayley, BA (*History, i/c Debating, †Weirfield*)
Mr David J Bridges, GRSM (*Chapel Organist & Choirmaster*)
Mr James A Brodie, BA (*Head of English*)
Mr A John M Brown, MA (*Archivist*)
Miss Carey Burton, MSc (*Science*)
Mr John R Cameron, MA (*Design and Technology*)
Mr T Mark Chatterton, MA (*Assistant Director of Studies, Head of History, i/c Oxbridge*)
Mr Pierre-Alex Clarke, BA (*Languages*)
Mrs Laura A Cooke, MPhil (*Science*)
Miss Susannah L Commings, MPhil (*English*)
Mr Mark Cracknell, BA (*Director of Music*)
Dr Aidan Cruttenden, PhD (*Head of Classics*)
Mrs Lisa Davey, BA (*Economics*)
Mr Adam Dewbery, MA (*Assistant Head of Mathematics, Master i/c Rowing*)
Mr Greg Durston (*Hockey Development Coach*)
Mr Philip Edwards, BEd (*Mathematics*)
Mrs Anne Ellard (*Exams Officer*)
Mrs Joanna L Evans, BCom (*Business Studies & Economics*)
M. Greg R Fabre, Maîtrise, LLCE (*Modern Languages*)
Mrs Jane Fletcher, BA (*Geography, Head of Psychology*)
Mrs Gill Foster, BA (*English, †Bevan*)
Dr Alison S Franklin (*Assistant Head of Chemistry, Mistress i/c Tennis*)
Miss Lin Gao, MA (*Modern Languages*)
Mr Richard Godfrey, MEng (*Physics*)
Mr Thomas E Grant, BA (*Art*)
Mr Neil Gush, BA (*Design & Technology*)
Mrs Lindsay Hale, BA (*English*)
Mrs Sally Hale, BA (*Academic Development & Mathematics*)
Mrs Tracy M Hallows, BSc (*Academic Development*)
Mr A Hallows (*Biology*)
Dr Lotte Hammer, BA (*Head of Art*)
Miss Geraldine E Harris, BA (*Assistant Head of Sixth Form, Art, Photography, Mistress i/c Swimming*)
Mrs Jane E Harris, BA (*Head of Drama and Theatre Studies*)
Ms Clare M Harvie, BSc (*PE, i/c Girls' Hockey, †Jenkin*)
Mr Simon T Hogg (*Mathematics, †Evans*)
Mrs Tamsyn Hopkins, BA (*Religious Studies*)
Miss Judy F Iredale, BA (*Modern Languages & Head of German*)
Mr David Jessep, BEd (*Master i/c Cricket*)
Mr Richard J Judd, MTh (*Head of Politics, Careers*)
Mr Cyril F Kelly, BA (*PE*)
Mrs Nicola Kirby, BA (*Spanish*)
Mr Clive D Large, MA (*Mathematics*)
Mrs Jeanne J Leader, BSc (*Head of Geology*)
Miss Amanda Lockwood, MA, BA (*Learning Resource Centre Manager*)
Mr David F MacLean, BSc (*Physics*)
Miss Lisa J Manley, BA (*PE, Mistress i/c Netball*)
Miss Emma Mannings, BA (*Dance*)
Mrs Carrie L Marsden, BA (*Philosophy and Religion, History, †Wills West*)
Mr Ben Marsden, BA (*History, †Wills West*)
Miss Pauline A McKay, MSc (*Mathematics*)
Miss Rebecca L Miller, BA (*English*)
Miss Hayley Mortimer, BA (*Head of PE, Director of Sport*)
Mr Christopher A F Moule, MA (*History*)
Mrs Tracey Newns, MEng (*Physics, †Marshall*)
Mr David H Parvin, MA (*Head of ICT*)
Mrs Natalia Paul, BA (*Spanish*)
Mr Ian W Payne, MA (*Head of Mathematics*)

Dr James H J Penny, BSc (*Head of Science*)
Mrs Sally Phillips, BA (*EAL*)
Mr Ian D Piper, BSc (*Chemistry*)
Mr Andrew W Pring, BSc (*Chemistry*)
Mr Stephen E Pugh, BSc (*Economics and Business Studies*)
Mrs Lynda Rixon, BSc (*Economics & Business Studies*)
Mr Adrian Roberts, BSc (*Head of Geography*)
Mr Declan C Rogers, MA (*English, Registrar*)
Mr Nicolas Sestaret (*Director of Rugby*)
Mr Simon N J Smith, BEng (*Physics, †Fairwater*)
Mrs Carla St Louis, BA (*Drama and Theatre Studies*)
Mrs Kate M Stent, BA (*Head of Modern Languages, CAS Coordinator*)
Mr David H Tarr, BSc (*Head of Boys' PE, Master i/c Hockey & Tennis, †Wills East*)
Mrs Susan E Taylor, Cert Ed (*PSHE*)
Mr Francis Tickner, BA (*English*)
Mrs Lucy Turner, BA (*Head of Leisure Studies*)
Mr Luke Waller, BSc (*Head of Physics*)
Mr Tim E Waller, MA (*Head of Instrumental Studies*)
Miss Caroline P Wedgwood, BSc (*Head of Biology*)
Mrs Jayne Whaley, BEd (*Geography*)
Mrs Annabel White, MA (*Head of Religious Studies*)
Miss Jennie Windsor, BSc (*Psychology*)
Mr James Wood, BA (*Classics*)
Mr Tony Workman, BSc (*Mathematics*)
Mrs Suzette Youngs, BA (*Head of EAL*)

Headmaster's Secretary: Mrs Soraya Murtiza
Registrar: Mr Declan Rogers, MA
Bursar's Secretary: Mrs Jean Eales
Foundation Director: Mr Neil Longstreet, BA
Deputy Headmaster's Secretary and IB Administrator: Mrs Nell Rosser
School Secretary: Mrs Clare Wilcox
Director of Studies Secretary: Mrs Lisa Smith
Medical Officers: Dr Tim Howes and Dr Hilda Gormley

Situation. The School stands in its own grounds of over 50 acres on the Northern outskirts of Taunton, within easy reach of some of the most attractive countryside in England. Taunton is exceptionally well placed on the M5 and the Paddington to Penzance main line with easy access to all parts of the British Isles and Bristol and Heathrow airports.

Facilities. The School moved to its present site in 1870 to a fine range of buildings, purpose built in the Gothic style. The original house, Fairwater, dating from 18th century is a boys' boarding house. The Wills family, notably Lord Winterstoke, made a series of munificent gifts including the Chapel (completed in 1907), a Library, and two boys' boarding houses, Wills East and Wills West.

A separate Science Building was added as a War Memorial after the Great War, and subsequently extended. Building has proceeded continually as a result of good housekeeping and appeals, adding specialist teaching facilities, including a Drama Studio, and a purpose-built girls' boarding house. A policy of continuous modernisation has seen additions to the Houses, and in 1998 further accommodation for boarding girls. There have also been improvements to the Science laboratories and other teaching facilities. A new Arts Centre was built in 1995. An extension to the Music School opened in Sept 2008. DT and Art facilities have seen significant recent investment and extension. The astroturf pitch and eight hard tennis courts have been renewed in the last 5 years. A new girls' boarding house opened in 2011. The Preparatory School (*see separate entry in IAPS section*) was rebuilt in 1994/95.

Worship. The Chapel plays a central role in the life of the community. The School is no longer denominational and welcomes members of all Christian beliefs, or other faiths. There is a daily service and a service on Sundays for all boarders in residence. The Chapel Choir plays a major role in the enhancement of worship on special occasions. There are also instrumental music items, as part of chapel services,

each week. The present Chaplain prepares candidates for confirmation and membership of all Protestant denominations and celebrates Holy Communion for all who are in good standing with their church. Preparation for Roman Catholic First Communion and Confirmation can be arranged.

Curriculum. In the first year of the Senior School the timetable sets out to give a wide experience of subjects; these include a choice from French, German, Spanish and Mandarin in Modern Foreign Languages. Biology, Physics and Chemistry are taught as separate subjects and there is a wide range of options available, including subjects such as Business Studies, Drama, Classical Civilisation and Greek.

In Years 10 and 11 most pupils study 10 or 11 GCSEs. These include English (Language and Literature), Mathematics, a choice of Modern Foreign Language (from French, Spanish, German, Mandarin), Biology, Physics and Chemistry as a core. The optional subjects are chosen from Art, Business Studies, Classical Civilisation, Design & Technology, Drama, Economics, French, Geography, German, Greek, History, ICT, Latin, Music, PE, Religious Studies and Spanish. All Year 10 pupils take a Religious Studies short course. Study Skills and Extra Lessons in Maths and English are available for various pupils who need additional help.

Thirty-two subjects are offered at AS and A2 Level, the latest additions being Geology, History of Art, Psychology, Music Technology, Photography and Politics, with the majority of Sixth Formers aiming at university or college entry.

The School also offers the International Baccalaureate Diploma course to Sixth Form students. Subjects available include English, German, French, Italian, Spanish, Mandarin, History, Geography, Economics, Philosophy, Biology, Chemistry, Physics, Maths, Further Maths and Visual Arts.

Careers. Careers advice is an important part of school life with work experience for all in the Lower Sixth. The Head of Careers and Director of Studies advise on applications for Higher Education.

Music. Music plays a vital part in the life of the School: about half of the pupils take lessons in a great variety of instruments, and there are choral groups, orchestra, windband, ensembles, and a jazz band.

School Societies. Everyone is encouraged to participate in extra-curricular activities and a wide range is offered including debating, drama, the Duke of Edinburgh's Award Scheme, Combined Cadet Forces, community service and Greenpower. The School has a distinguished international debating record.

Games. The School has an outstanding record in games and has strong fixture lists. The principal games are rugby, hockey, netball, cricket, swimming, athletics and tennis, with excellent facilities also for squash, badminton and basketball. The School has two Astroturf pitches, with a modern Olympic blue Astro pitch opened in 2013. The school has 8 netball courts, which are also used for tennis to complement the twenty four astro courts used in the Summer term. There are two indoor heated swimming pools and the Sports Hall complex is equipped with an up-to-date Fitness Suite, climbing wall and is used for a wide range of indoor games. Pupils can also take part in: rowing, cross-country, zumba, dance, volleyball, sailing, horse riding and golf. There is also an indoor rifle range. The School's philosophy is to encourage athletic excellence as well as giving opportunities for all to enjoy physical activity.

Medical. The School Medical Centre provides the medical service for the whole School community, and is staffed by qualified nurses under the supervision of the School Medical Officer who visits daily.

Admission. The main ages of admission to the Senior School are 13 (Year 9) and 16 (Year 12), but entry into other year groups is also possible. Prospectuses and registration forms are available from the Registrar, who will also be pleased to arrange visits (01823 703700; registrar@tauntonschool.co.uk).

The Admissions Secretary at the Preparatory School (01823 703303) will be pleased to assist with enquiries for children up to the age of 13 (Nursery, Pre-Prep and Preparatory).

Entry at 13: The admission process usually requires the pupil to attend for interview and to submit recent school reports and a school reference. In some cases, the candidate may be required to sit assessment tests. Candidates attending Preparatory Schools may apply by sitting Common Entrance Examinations in June. Taunton Preparatory School pupils proceed to the Senior School on the basis of a Record of Progress.

Entry to the Sixth Form: Entry to the A Level course and the International Baccalaureate Diploma will normally be conditional on a minimum of 5 GCSE passes at grade A* to C, but interview and report play an important part in determining the offer of places. Candidates not taking GCSE examinations may be required to sit assessment tests.

Scholarships and Bursaries. A number of Scholarships are awarded at the ages of 13 and 16.

13+ Scholarships: 13+ Open Scholarships take place in the Spring term and are open to all candidates, entering Year 9, who are under the age of 14 on 1st September in the year of entry. Academic and All-Rounder Scholarships are available with examinations taking place in February/March. Scholarships and Awards in Sport, Art, Music (including an Organ Scholarship), ICT and Drama are also available. Candidates for Sport, Art, Music, ICT and Drama are not required to sit the Open Scholarship examinations but will be required to attend for interview and audition or assessment in January/February/March.

The Open Scholarship examinations (for Academic and All-Rounder candidates) are held at Taunton School in the Spring term. (In special circumstances, papers may be taken at a candidate's Preparatory School.) Compulsory subjects are English, Mathematics, a Modern Language (French, German or Spanish), Science, History, Geography, Religious Studies and a General Paper, with optional papers in Latin, French, Spanish, German and Design & Technology.

Sixth Form Scholarships: These are awarded annually in November preceding the year of entry to the Sixth Form. Awards are made to outstanding boys or girls who will be taking GCSE examinations, or equivalent, in the current year and who are regarded as strong University candidates. Academic and All-Rounder examinations are taken in November. Applicants for Sport, Music, Art or Drama Scholarships are not required to sit these examinations, but will be asked to attend for interview and audition or assessment during November.

For further information and details on 13+ and 16+ scholarships please contact the Registrar (01823 703700; registrar@tauntonschool.co.uk).

11+ Scholarships: A number of Scholarships are awarded to boys and girls, entering Year 7, who are under the age of 12 on 1st September in the year of entry. The examinations are held at Taunton Preparatory School in January and awards continue into the Senior School. Please call the Admissions Secretary (01823 703303) for more information.

Bursaries: Ministerial Bursaries may be offered to the sons and daughters of Ministers of all recognised denominations, from the age of 11, on condition that the candidates satisfy the academic requirements of the School. Service Bursaries are available for the children of Service families. Other bursarial support is offered; applicants would be required to fill in a financial circumstances form.

Fees per term (2014–2015). Senior School: Boarders £9,600 (£10,600 Sixth Form new entrants); Day £5,675.

Taunton Preparatory School: Boarders £4,150–£7,520; Day £2,450–£4,610 Pre-Preparatory & Nursery (full-time) £2,130.

Charitable status. Taunton School is a Registered Charity, number 1081420. It exists to provide education for boys and girls.

Tonbridge School

Tonbridge, Kent TN9 1JP
Tel: 01732 365555
Fax: 01732 363424
email: hmsec@tonbridge-school.org
website: www.tonbridge-school.co.uk

Motto: '*Deus dat incrementum*'

Tonbridge School was founded in 1553 by Sir Andrew Judde, under Letters Patent of King Edward VI.

Tonbridge is an all-boys, 13–18, boarding and day school. 780 boys from a variety of backgrounds are offered an education remarkable both for its breadth of opportunity and the exceptional standards routinely achieved in all areas of school life.

The school aims to provide a caring and enlightened environment in which the talents of each individual flourish. We encourage boys to be creative, tolerant and to strive for academic, sporting and cultural excellence. Respect for tradition and an openness to innovation are equally valued. A well-established house system at the heart of the school fosters a strong sense of belonging. We want boys to enjoy their time here, but also to be made aware of their social and moral responsibilities. Ideally, Tonbridgians should enter into the adult world with the knowledge and self-belief to fulfil their own potential and, in many cases, to become leaders in their chosen field. Equally, we hope to foster a life-long empathy for the needs and views of others.

Tonbridge boys are extremely successful at obtaining places at leading universities. 24 leavers in the summer of 2014 have so far gone to Oxford or Cambridge, with more applying post A level. Other popular destinations include Durham, Bristol and Imperial.

Visitors to Tonbridge are always welcome and full information about the school is available on our website: www.tonbridge-school.co.uk.

Governors:
J L Cohen, QC (*Chairman*)

D P Devitt	Mrs S Price
M Dobbs	G M Rochussen
R J Elliott	Professor C J Rudge, CBE
C J D Emms	Professor S Stallebrass
A Mayer	C A Stuart-Clark
Mrs J Naismith	Mrs K Wheadon
R Nottidge	The Earl of Woolton

Clerk to the Governors: B Plummer, CBE

Headmaster: T H P Haynes, BA

Second Master: C W Jones, MA
Director of Studies: J C Pearson, MA
Director of Teaching and Learning: R M Brookes, MChem, DPhil
Director of Admissions and Marketing: A J Leale, BA
Bursar: A C Moore, MA, MBA, INSEAD
Upper Master: A J Edwards, MA
Development Director: M S Lindo, BA, MA, MSc

Assistant Staff:
* *Head of Department/Subject*

Art:	Mrs B L Waugh, BA
*Mrs C H Chisholm, BA	*Artist-in-Residence*: Mrs J
T W Duncan, BA	Gilby
Mrs E R Glass, MA	

Art Librarian: Mrs M P
 Dennington
Art Technician: Mrs J M
 Brent

Classics:
*J A Burbidge, BA, MSt,
 DPhil
J A Nicholls, MA
P W G Parker, MA
A P Schweitzer, MA
Miss K E I Waterfield, BA

*Design Technology and
 Engineering*:
*D Dixon, BA
W D F Biddle, BSc
A O Cooke, MEng, DPhil
J M Woodrow, BA
Engineering Advisor: D L
 Faithfull, BTech, MSc,
 CEng
Technology Technicians: R
 Davies; O Longson
Teaching Assistant: C
 Martin

Digital Creativity:
*A R Whittall, MA
P J Huxley, BSc
Technology Tutors: D P
 Love MIET, C D Walker

Divinity:
*J C F Dobson, MA
R Burnett, MA
The Revd D A Peters, MA
The Revd C M Moloney,
 MA
H J M Swales, BA

Drama:
*G D Bruce, MA
R J Hartley, BA
L Thornbury, DipDrama

Modern Languages:
*L S McDonald, MA
Mrs E Saurel, BA, MA (*French*)
S Kerr (*German*)
R Lokier, BA (*Spanish*)
X J Wu, MA (*Mandarin Chinese*)
Mrs C Clugston, MA (*EAL*)
A E Bissill, MA
Mrs T Coomber, L-ès-L
Mrs C Cordero, Lda en Fil
R D Hoare, MA (*International Coordinator*)
Miss D M McDermot, MA
J A Nicholls, MA
P W G Parker, MA
T W Richards, BA
Mrs R Thomson, BA, DipHE, TESOL
S M Wainde, MA
C E Wright, BA
Mrs X Yu, BA

Music:
*M A Forkgen, MA, ARCO (*Director of Music*)
J R P Thomas, MA, FRCO (*Head of Academic Music &
 Choirmaster*)
A E L Pearson, BMus, ARCM, LRAM (*Strings*)
D L Williams, GRSM, ARCM, LRAM (*Piano*)
S J Hargreaves, MA, MEd
Miss E M Jones, BA

Physical Education:
Director of Sport and Head of PE: C D Morgan, BSc

English:
*N J Waywell, BA
J P Arscott, MA
J R Bleakley, BA
P S D Carpenter, MA
A J Edwards, MA
R H Evans, MA
Mrs D M Hulse, MA,
 DipModDrama
J Johnson, BA, MPhil
Mrs A T Phillips, MA

Geography:
*C M Battarbee, BA
C M Henshall, BA
G P Gales, BEd
J E Perriss, BA
M G Rowan, MA, FRGS

History:
*C D Thompson, BA,
 MPhil, PhD
D Cooper, MA
Mrs F C Dix Perkin, MA
J C Harber, MA
C W Jones, MA
R W G Oliver, MA
Miss M L Robinson, MA

Mathematics:
*I R H Jackson, MA, PhD
S Burns, BSc
T G Fewster, BSc
R J Freeman, MA
K A Froggatt, MA
J D King, MA, PhD
M J Lawson, BA
N J Lord, MA
V Myslov, BA
A A Reid, MChem, PhD
A P Schweitzer, MA
S J Seldon, MA, MEng
A R Whittall, MA

Science:
*W J Burnett, BSc, PhD
M J Weatheritt, BSc, MA (*Physics*)
G M Barnes, BSc
S Chalk, BSc, PhD
A O Cooke, MEng, DPhil
R L Fleming, MA, MInstP
A G McGilchrist, MA
D S Pinker, PhD, MSci
J A Fisher, BSc (*Chemistry*)
R M Brookes, MChem, DPhil
M J Clugston, MA, DPhil
D A Cruse, MA, PhD, CChem, MRSC, MRI
G C Fisher, BSc, MA
C R Lawrence, MA
A V Nagar, BSc, ARCS
J C Pearson, MA
D P Robinson, MEarthSci, DPhil
H M Grant, MA (*Biology*)
M R Ackroyd, BSc, PhD
W J Burnett, BSc, PhD
P M Ridd, MA
A T Sampson, BSc
C J C Swainson, MA

Social Science:
P J North, BA (*Economics*)
Miss K E Moxon, MA (*Politics*)
J Blake, BA, MSc (*Business Studies*)
Ms H M Harris, BA, MSc
A J Leale, BA
N R V Rendall, BA
J D W Richards, MA, PhD
A J Sixsmith, BA

Director of ICT Services:
I N Lucas, BSc

University Entrance and Careers:
Mrs A Rogers, BA

Learning Support:
J D C Lewis, BSc
Dr C M Dillow, BA, MA, PhD

Houses & Housemasters:

Boarding:
School House: R Burnett
Judde House: G P Gales
Park House: A E Bissill
Hill Side: J Johnson
Parkside: J E Perriss
Ferox Hall: A R Whittall
Manor House: C J C Swainson

Day:
Welldon House: R H Evans
Smythe House: C M Henshall
Whitworth House: W D F Biddle
Cowdrey House: R W G Oliver (*J C Harber from Jan
 2015*)
Oakeshott House: J R Bleakley

Administration:
Librarian: Mrs B Matthews, MCLIP
Headmaster's PA: Mrs L R O'Neill
Admissions Secretaries:
Miss R G Hearnden (*Senior Admissions Officer*)
Mrs V C Larmour (*Admissions Officer Lower Sixth Entry*)
Mrs R Griffiths (*Admissions Officer Pre-testing*)
Examinations Officer: Miss C E Moorcroft, BA
PA to the Second Master: Miss E J Day
Music Dept Administrator: Mrs J Marsh

Location. Tonbridge School is just off the M25, on the
edge of the Kent / Surrey / Sussex borders and attracts fami-

lies from all over southern England and beyond. It lies in about 150 acres of land on the edge of the town of Tonbridge, and thus provides a good balance between town and country living.

Admissions. The majority of boys join the school at the age of 13, having gained admission through the Common Entrance Examination or the school's own Scholarship Examination (held in early May). About 140 boys are admitted at the age of 13 each year. An additional 20 places are available for entry to the Sixth Form at the age of 16. We also have up to 6 places for boys aged 14 (Year 10).

Registration for a boy at 13+ entry should be made as early as possible, and preferably not later than three years before the date of intended entry. Boys will then be asked to come to Tonbridge to sit a short computer-based cognitive test. The results of this test, in conjunction with the current school Head's report, will determine whether the offer of a place may be made, conditional upon either Common Entrance or Scholarship entry at 13 years old. Applications for 14+ and Sixth Form entry are best made by September a year before entry, but may be considered later. Admission at 14+ (and at 13+ from schools who do not prepare boys for common entrance) is gained via our own Maths and English exams. Boys sitting for entry at 16+ will take papers in the 4 subjects they wish to study for A Level.

Parents wishing to send their sons to Tonbridge should apply to the Director of Admissions for a copy of the Prospectus, which gives full details of the registration procedure. Information is also available on the website: www.tonbridge-school.co.uk.

Scholarships and Bursaries. About 45 scholarships are offered each year: up to 21 Academic Scholarships (awarded by examination in early May); 10 or more Music Scholarships (examination in early February); up to 10 Art, Drama or Technology Scholarships (examination in early February); up to 4 Cowdrey Scholarships, for sporting ability and sportsmanship (assessment in early February); Choral Boarding Awards, for Choristers of Cathedral or other Choir Schools. 3 or 4 Sixth Form Academic or Music Scholarships are also awarded.

The value of a Scholarship may be increased by any amount up to the full school fee, if assessment of the parents' means indicates a need.

For boys over 10 and under 11 on 1st September, two Junior Foundation Scholarships are awarded, tenable at a Preparatory school. Candidates must be attending a State Primary School. Junior academic and music awards may also be made to 10 or 11 year old sons of parents requiring financial help in fee-paying Prep Schools. They are awarded as 'advance' Scholarships by competitive examination in November two-three years before entry to Tonbridge.

Foundation Awards provide means-tested support (up to 100% of the full school fee) for a Tonbridge education to boys who can clearly and substantially benefit from what the school has to offer. Awards may be made at three ages: in Year 6 (for entry to Tonbridge in Year 9), in Year 8 (for entry to Tonbridge in Year 9) and in Year 11 (for entry to Tonbridge in Year 12). Boys from the State sector who earn an Award in Year 6 will receive means-tested support through preparatory school (for Years 7 and 8); this should put them in a position to sit the Tonbridge School Scholarship Examination in Year 8 (although the place at Tonbridge is guaranteed from Year 6).

Forces bursaries are available for children of serving members of the armed forces.

Entry forms and full particulars of all Scholarships and Foundation Awards may be obtained from the Admissions Secretary; Tel: 01732 304297; email: admissions@tonbridge-school.org.

Fees per term (2014–2015). Boarders £11,721; Day Boys £8,790.

Charitable status. Tonbridge School is a Registered Charity, number 1097977. It exists solely to provide education for boys.

Trinity School
Croydon

Shirley Park, Croydon CR9 7AT
Tel: 020 8656 9541
Fax: 020 8655 0522
email: admissions@trinity.croydon.sch.uk
website: www.trinity-school.org

Motto: '*Vincit qui Patitur*'
The School was founded by Archbishop John Whitgift in 1596. The full title of the school is Trinity School of John Whitgift.

Visitor: His Grace The Archbishop of Canterbury

Governing Body:
Chairman: I Harley, MA, FCA, FCIB
His Honour William Barnett, QC, MA Oxon
The Revd Canon C J L Boswell, The Vicar of Croydon
C J Houlding
Mrs R A Jones, MA
Cllr T Letts, OBE
P J Squire, MA
G H Wright, TD, DL, FCIOB
G Barwell, MP
Cllr D Mead, FCCA, FCMA, FCIS, MBE
Ms N Clarke, MA
D C Hudson, MA
Mrs P Davies, BSc, MEd
Cllr M Mead, JP
The Rt Revd Jonathan Clark, The Bishop of Croydon
M A Proudfoot, MA, MLitt
D C Q Sutton, JP, FRICS

Clerk to the Governors: M Corney

Headmaster: M J Bishop, MA Oxford, MBA

Deputy Head and Head of Upper School: Miss S L Ward, BSc Birmingham
Head of Lower School: G Du Toit, BEd Pretoria
Director of Studies: N H Denman, MA Oxford
Director of Extra-Curricular: R Brookman, BSc London
Bursar: J Stanley, BA, CCAT, ACA

Assistant Staff:
* *Head of Department*
§ *part-time*

Miss A M Abad, BA Murcia, MA London (*Spanish**)
P G Abbott, BSc Cardiff (*Economics & Business Studies*)
M I Aldridge, BEd London (*Design Technology, Deputy Head of Sixth Form*)
S R Allison, BA Bath (*Spanish*)
Mrs J L Anderson, BSc Bath (*Biology*)
M Asbury, BSc Bath (*Mathematics, Internal Exams**)
M S Asquith, BA, MA, PhD London (*English*)
D Bastyan, BSc Warwick (*Mathematics*)
Ms N M Beaumont, BSc Oxford (*Mathematics*)
L D Benedict, BA Bristol (*English*)
Miss H A Benzinski, BSc London (*Mathematics*)
G C Beresford-Miller, BA Rhodes (*PE*)
J Bird, BSc Kent (*Biology*)
Mrs N Blamire-Marin, BA Granada (*Lektora*)
N A Bowling, BA Oxford (*Classics*)
M E Brennan, BA Oxford (*History*)
C R Burke, Port Elizabeth (*Physical Education, English*)
S I Cater, BA King's, MPhil Queensland (*English, Drama, Assistant Head of Year*)

C D Carter, BSc Imperial College London (*Chemistry**)
C D Cesar, BA Oxford (*Religious Studies*)
T W Chesters, BSc Strathclyde (*Design Technology*)
S W Christian, BA Liverpool (*French, Spanish, Language Awareness*)
Mrs M A Chitty, CertEd, Dip SpLD
A J Codling, BA Portsmouth (*Director of Sport**)
A Cornick, BA Southampton Institute (*Physical Education*)
R L Day, BSc Loughborough (*Design Technology**)
T Deakin, BSc Brunel (*Hockey*, Physical Education*)
T J Desbos, LCE Lille (*French, Language Awareness*)
A B Doyle, MA, MA Glasgow, Open (*English**)
Dr T E Durno, MA, MPhil, PhD Cambridge (*English*)
R Earl, BSc UCL (*Economics & Business Studies**)
R G Evans, BSc Aston (*Electronics, Design Technology*)
L M Flanagan, BSc Cambridge (*Physics*)
Mrs A A Fulker, BA Oxford Brookes (*Art, French*)
L J Giles, BA Bath (*Religious Studies*)
A M Godfrey, BA Bretton Hall College (*Drama Productions**)
M E Holiday, BA Oxford (*Head of Academic Music, Assistant Director of Music*)
J P Holmes, BA Oxford, BA Cambridge (*Religious Studies, Spanish, Oxbridge Coordinator*)
J Janda, BA, ATC London (*Artist in Residence*)
Mrs C S Jennings, BSc London (*Biology, ICT*)
M V Johnson, BSc London (*Biology, Careers*)
Ms R Kanji, BSc, MEd Auckland (*Chemistry*)
I Kench, BSc Loughborough, MSc Oxford (*Geography, Physical Education*)
Mrs G C Kitchen, BA Durham (*Music*)
D A Lawson, BEd Exeter (*Geography, Physical Education*)
Mrs J M Layden, MA Edinburgh (*English*)
R E Lee, MA Oxford (*Religious Studies*, CCF**)
A Liffchak, BA Hertfordshire (*Head of Rugby, Physical Education, Psychology*)
PS Lin, BA National Taiwan University (*Chinese**)
M Mariani, BSc Kent, PhD UCL (*Physics*)
P Mazur, BA Wales, MA London (*Classroom Drama*, English, PSE Coordinator*)
Mrs S J McDonald, MA St Andrews (*English*)
Miss C-J McPherson, BSc Glasgow (*Biology*)
S A McIntosh, MA Oxford (*German**)
Miss S T Melvin, BA Oxford (*Classics*)
R H Moralee, BSc Johannesburg (*Biology*)
D Moran, BSc, MA Dublin (*Chemistry, Biology*)
S Morley, BA Cambridge (*English, Head of Junior Year*)
Mrs C Morgan, BA Exeter (*Economics & Business Studies*)
Mrs H C Murray, MEng (*Mathematics*)
S Orungbamade, BEd Nigeria (*Economics & Business Studies*)
B J Patel, MA Cambridge (*Mathematics*)
B Patel, MSc UCL (*Mathematics*)
C P Persinaru, DipRAM, LRAM London (*Music*)
Mrs R J Petty, MA Oxford (*English*)
Mrs X L Phasey, MA Schiller International (*Chinese*)
E Pike, BA King's, London (*Classics*)
D J Preece, BSc Oxford, PhD UCL (*Geography*)
D K Price, 3D Design Wimbledon College of Art (*Design Technology*)
G V Pritchard, BSc Durham (*Chemistry*)
Mrs S J Rapoport, BEd Twickenham (*Academic Mentor*)
Mrs E Regan, BMus RAM, LRAM (*Music*)
M D Richbell, BSc Liverpool (*PE**)
Miss F A Ring, BA Cambridge (*History*)
R J Risebro, BSc Manchester Met (*PE*)
A J Rogers, BA Plymouth (*Art and Photography*)
K R Rogers, BSc Cardiff, PhD London (*Chemistry*)
P H Rule, BSc Leicester, CBiol, MIBiol (*Biology**)
Mrs V G Salin, MA Northumbria (*French**)
R M Salmanpour, BSc London (*Chemistry*)
Dr J J Samuel, BSc Leeds (*Mathematics*)
Mrs M R Sanders, BEd London (*Drama, English*)

J A Short, BA UCL (*History*)
A C Smith, BA, MA Kingston (*Art**)
A E Smith, BA York, MA London (*Religious Studies*)
M D Smith, BEng Bath (*Mathematics*)
J J Snelling, BSc Swansea (*Geography**)
J E Stone, BA Cambridge (*Classics**)
Miss C S Story, BA Durham (*English*)
Ms T Stevens-Lewis, BA Goldsmiths (*Art*)
Miss E E Stewart, MPhys Oxford, MSc Leeds (*Physics*)
EM Suarez, BA Juan Carlos 1 (*Spanish Assistant*)
A Sukiennick, BA, MA Paris X (*French Assistant*)
P Swainson, BA Exeter (*History*)
D J Swinson, MA, FRCO, ARCM, LRAM Cambridge (*Music**)
Mrs S Taylor, BSc Exeter (*Mathematics*)
J G Timm, BA Cambridge (*History*)
W S Tucker, BSc Exeter (*Physics**)
S Van Straten, BA King's London (*Digital Literacy**)
R J Venables, MEng Durham (*Mathematics*)
Mrs R E Wallace, MA Oxford (*Geography*)
Miss H C Whiteford, BSc Durham (*Religious Studies*)
R J Wickes, BSc Warwick (*Mathematics**)
Ms J C Wiskow, MA Berlin (*German*)

Admissions Registrar: Mrs P S Meyer
Sixth Form Admissions: Ms S Redican
Headmaster's Secretary: Mrs K Carr

The School, one of the three governed by the Whitgift Foundation, is an Independent Day School for boys aged 10–18 with a co-educational Sixth Form since September 2011. The School aims to give a wide education to students of academic promise, irrespective of their parents' income.

Buildings and Grounds. Trinity School has been in its present position since 1965, when it moved out from the middle of Croydon (its old site is now the Whitgift Centre) to a completely new complex of buildings and playing fields on the site of the Shirley Park Hotel. The grounds are some 27 acres in extent, and a feeling of openness is increased by the surrounding Shirley Park Golf Club and the extensive views to the south up to the Addington Hills. There are additional playing fields in Sandilands, ten minutes' walk from the School.

The resources of the Whitgift Foundation enable the School to provide outstanding facilities. All departments have excellent and fully equipped teaching areas.

Admission. The main ages of admission are at 10, 11 and 13. Entry is by competitive examination and interview. A reference from the feeder school will also be required. The School attracts applications from over 150 schools, with approximately 60% entering from state primaries. Entries of boys and girls into the Sixth Form are also welcomed.

Fees per term (2014–2015). £4,820 covering tuition, books, stationery and games.

Bursaries. Whitgift Foundation Bursaries (means-tested) are available providing exceptionally generous help with fees.

Scholarships. Academic, Art, Design Technology, Drama, Music and Sport Scholarships are available annually to boys applying for entry at 10+, 11+ or 13+. Boys must be the relevant age on 1 September of the year of entry. Awards are based on the results of the Entrance Examination, interview and current school reference. They are awarded without regard to parental income and are worth a percentage (maximum 50%) of the school fees throughout a pupil's career.

Academic, Art, Music and Sport Scholarships are also available for entry to the Sixth Form, based on GCSE results.

Scholarships may be supplemented up to the value of full fees if there is financial need.

Music Scholarships of up to 50% fee remission include free tuition in two instruments. Applicants are required to play two pieces on principal instrument and show academic potential in the Entrance Examination. Awards are available for all instruments and singing ability can be taken into consideration. Further details from the Director of Music.

Organisation and Counselling. The School is divided into the Lower School (National Curriculum Years 6–9) and the Upper School (Years 10–13). The Pastoral Leader in charge of each section works with the team of Form Tutors to encourage the academic and personal development of each boy. There is frequent formal and informal contact with parents.

There is a structured and thorough Careers service, which advises boys at all levels of the School and arranges work experience and work shadowing.

While the academic curriculum is taught from Monday to Friday, there is a very active programme of sports fixtures and other activities at the weekend, and all boys are expected to put their commitment to the School before other activities.

Curriculum and Staffing. The School is generously staffed with well qualified specialists. The organisation of the teaching programme is traditionally departmental based. The syllabus is designed to reflect the general spirit of the National Curriculum while allowing a suitable degree of specialisation in the Upper School.

The normal pattern is for pupils to take 9 or 10 GCSE subjects, and to proceed to the Sixth Form to study an appropriate mixture of AS and A2 level subjects, complemented by a wide-ranging General Studies programme, before proceeding to university.

Games and Activities. The main school games are Rugby, Football, Hockey, Cricket and Athletics, with the addition of Netball for girls in the Sixth Form. Many other sports become options as a boy progresses up the School. Games are timetabled, each pupil having one games afternoon a week.

At the appropriate stage, most boys take part in one or more of the following activities: Community Service, CCF, Duke of Edinburgh's Award Scheme, Outdoor Activities. There are many organised expeditions during the holidays.

Music. Music at Trinity has an international reputation, and every year Trinity Boys Choir is involved in a varied programme of demanding professional work. The Choir has performed at the BBC Proms for the past seven years and sings at the Royal Opera House, the English National Opera, Glyndebourne or Garsington 3–4 times each year. Recently the choristers have travelled to Vienna, Brussels, Venice, Dusseldorf and Wachock Abbey, Poland. They also appear regularly on radio and television. Trinity Choristers, who specialise in religious music, hold an annual residential Easter Course at a British cathedral. Choral Scholarships are awarded annually and enable boys to receive additional professional voice training without charge.

Many boys learn at least one musical instrument, and a large visiting music staff teach all orchestral instruments, piano, organ and classical guitar. There are numerous orchestras, bands and other instrumental groups for which boys are selected according to their ability. Musicians recently travelled to Dubai and instrumentalists are regular finalists in the Pro Corda National Chamber Music competition.

Drama. There are two excellently equipped stages in the school and a lively and developing programme of formal and informal productions directed by pupils, staff and members of the Old Boys Theatre Company. Drama forms part of the formal curriculum in Years 6–9 and can be studied for GCSE and A Level.

Art and Design Technology. As well as the formal curriculum, which has led to 70% of the School taking a GCSE in art or design technology, pupils are encouraged to make use of the excellent facilities to develop their own interests.

Charitable status. The Whitgift Foundation is a Registered Charity, number 312612. The Foundation now comprises the Whitgift Almshouse Charity for the care of the elderly and the Education Charity which administers three schools.

Truro School

Trennick Lane, Truro, Cornwall TR1 1TH
Tel: 01872 272763
email: enquiries@truroschool.com
website: www.truroschool.com

Motto: *Esse quam videri*

Truro School was founded in 1880 by Cornish Methodists. In 1904 it came under the control of the Methodist Independent Schools Trust (MIST) and is now administered by a Board of Governors appointed by the Methodist Conference. Although pupils come from all parts of the country and abroad, the roots of the school are firmly in Cornwall and it is the only HMC school in the county.

The religious instruction and worship are undenominational though the school is conscious of its Methodist origins.

There are 750 pupils (446 boys, 304 girls; 681 day, 69 boarders) in the Senior School (age 11+ and above). There are another 270 pupils in the Preparatory School, where boys and girls may start in the pre-prep section at the age of 3.

The school is fully co-educational throughout and there is a strong Sixth Form of some 200+ pupils.

Visitor: The President of the Methodist Conference

Administrative Governors:
Chairman: R R Cowie, FCA
Mrs C Arter, BA Hons, RN, RNT, PGCE, FHEA, JP
N Ashcroft, MBE
T Daffern, BEng Hons, CEng, MBA, FIoMMM, FAusIMM
Dr S Evans, BSc, MB, ChB, PhD, FRCP
R S Funnell, MA
Mrs E Garner, BA Hons, MEd
C N Harding, BSc, FCMA, MIMgt
Revd Dr J Harrod, BSc, MA, PhD, FHEA
Mrs C Hogg, BSc, MBA
P Kerkin, BSc Hons, FIFS
Dr R Kirby, PhD
P Rigby
R Spencer
P Stethridge, CEng, FICE, FIHT
R Thomas, BSc, MRICS
Revd S Wild, MA

Headmaster: **A Gordon-Brown**, BCom Hons, MSc, QTS

Deputy Heads:
N A Fisher, BSc, MSc, MA
P N Brewer, BA

Chaplain: A de Gruchy, MTheol

Boarding House Staff:
Mrs C Murphy, BA (*Malvern*)
J K Austin, BA (*Trennick*)
M A Nicholas, BEd (*Pentreve*)
Mrs N Kenward, BA (*Poltisco*)

Heads of Year:
Miss V J Gould, BA (*Co-Head of Sixth Form*)
Mrs J P Rainbow, MA (*Co-Head of Sixth Form*)
G D Hooper, PGCE (*5th Year*)
Mrs C McCabe, BSc (*4th Year*)
S J Latarche, BEd, ARCM (*3rd Year*)
A J Pomery, BSc (*2nd Year*)
S A Collinge, BSc (*1st Year*)

Heads of Department:
D Meads, BA (*Art*)

Miss S E Finnegan, BSc (*Biology*)
Dr A Brogden, MChem, PhD (*Chemistry*)
Miss J R Egar, BA (*Drama*)
C Baker, BSc (*Design and Technology*)
Miss H F Thompson, MA, MSc (*Economics, Business Studies and Politics*)
Mrs A L Selvey BA, MA (*English*)
Mrs J Wormald, BSc (*Geography*)
I G Kenyon, BSc (*Geology*)
Dr M H Spring, MA, PhD (*History*)
S J McCabe, MA (*Mathematics*)
Mrs I Quaife, BA (*Modern Languages*)
M D Palmer, BMus, FRCO, LRAM (*Music*)
G C Whitmore, BEd (*PE and Games*)
A L Laity, BSc (*Physics*)
M Huckle, BA, MA, CertRE (*Religious Education*)

Truro School Preparatory School
(*see entry in IAPS section*)

Headmaster: M Lovett, BA Ed
Deputy Head: A MacQuarrie, BEd
Head of Pre-Prep Unit: Mrs S Hudson, BEd, MA

Bursar and Clerk to the Governors: R G Burdell

Boarding. At the Senior School girl boarders live in Malvern and the newly refurbished Poltisco; boy boarders (5th–U6th) live in Trennick House; boy boarders (1st–4th) live in Pentreve House. All are supervised by resident teaching staff and families. Pupils eat in the central dining room with a cafeteria system. There is a School Medical Centre on site.

Campus and Buildings. The *Prep School* campus is built around a country house acquired by the school in the 30s. It has an indoor heated swimming pool, a large assembly hall and extensive areas for science, modern languages, computing, art and crafts, as well as a modern sports hall. A new Dining Hall was opened in 2013. The Pre-Prep is housed in a purpose-built unit, with a new extension opened in September 2009.

The *Senior School* occupies an outstanding site overlooking the Cathedral city and the Fal Estuary; it is only five minutes from the centre of the city but the playing fields reach into the open countryside. The school is excellently equipped. There is a first-class Library, extended and refurbished in 2010, extensive science laboratories, excellent Technology and Art facilities, a computer centre, music school, Sixth Form centre, a Sixth Form cafeteria and a range of classroom blocks. The fine block containing the Burrell Theatre, six classrooms and a drama centre has been extended to provide a Modern Languages Centre in The Wilkes Building. An attractive and newly-refurbished chapel provides a focus for the life of the school. A new Dining Hall and social area opened in November 2009. The Sir Ben Ainslie Sports Centre, completed for September 2013, provides an eight-court multi-use sports hall, two county standard glass-backed squash courts with viewing gallery, large fitness suite with a range of aerobic, strength and conditioning equipment, a multi-purpose dance and exercise studio with a sprung wooden floor, adding to the existing excellent facilities of 25m swimming pool, cricket nets, tennis courts, 40 acres of pitches and cricket pavilion.

Organisation and Curriculum. Our academic programme up to GCSE provides a balance between the three Sciences, Humanities, Creative Arts and Modern Languages. In the 1st to 3rd Year, pupils study English, Mathematics, Biology, Chemistry and Physics, French and German, Geography, History, Religious Studies, Art, Design & Technology and Music. All pupils have PE as well as Games each week. In the 1st to 3rd Year, pupils are taught in their tutor groups; exceptions are in Mathematics and Modern Languages where they are in ability sets from the 2nd Year, and in Art, Design Technology, ICT, Music, PE and Games where they are split into smaller classes. Every pupil

in the 1st Year is taught touch typing, and ICT lessons culminate in a City & Guilds certified qualification by the end of the 3rd Year.

At GCSE the norm is to study ten subjects at full GCSE, with all pupils also studying a short course in Religious Studies (equivalent to a half GCSE). Compulsory subjects are English Language, English Literature, Mathematics, Biology, Chemistry, and Physics, and Religious Studies (short course); the options we offer ensure that pupils study at least one language (French, German and Spanish) and one humanity subject. GCSEs in Geology, PE (single and double award) and Drama are also introduced as GCSE options in the 4th Year.

Sixth Formers usually study for four AS Levels in the Lower Sixth and these include the same subjects as at GCSE, but with the introduction of Further Mathematics, Religious Studies (with Philosophy and Ethics), Economics, Business Studies, Psychology, Classical Civilisation and the Extended Project Qualification. Our Extension Studies programme includes modules on Photography, Philosophy and Film Studies. As part of this we provide advice on careers and university applications, with a specialised programme for potential Medics, Dentists and Vets. The Community Sports Leadership Award is a popular option for the Upper Sixth. Three subjects will be most commonly continued into the Upper Sixth at A Level and the vast majority of Sixth Formers go on to further education when they leave.

Out-of-School Activities. Extra-curricular life is rich and varied. There is a choir, school orchestra, a jazz group, a brass band and many other ensembles. Facilities such as the ceramics room, the art room and the technical block are available to pupils in their spare time. A huge variety of activities includes fencing, climbing (2 indoor walls), squash, sailing, golf, basketball, debating, surfing, and many others. Many boys and girls take part in the Ten Tors Expedition, an exceptional number are engaged in the Duke of Edinburgh's Award Scheme, as well as local Community Service. The School has an outdoor activities centre on Bodmin Moor and pupils have a chance to spend time there during the course of their education at the school. The school is linked with Truro Fencing Club and their Fencing Salle is now on site.

Games. All the major team games are played. Badminton, cross-country, hockey, netball, squash and tennis are available throughout most of the year. Rugby and Girls Hockey are played in the Winter Term and Soccer and Netball in the Spring Term. In the summer, cricket, athletics and tennis are the major sports. The covered pool is heated.

Admissions. Truro School was once a Direct Grant Grammar School and most pupils join at the age of 11. There are vacancies for entry at other ages, particularly at 13 and 16.

Scholarships and Bursaries. Scholarships are available and the School offers a small number of means-tested bursaries up to the value of full fees. Truro School has recently linked with Truro Cathedral to offer scholarships for their new girl choristers from September 2015.

Fees per term (2014–2015). Senior School: Boarders £7,900; Weekly Boarders £6,985; Day Pupils: £4,190 (1st–5th Year including lunch), £4,075 (Sixth Form not including lunch). Prep (including lunch): £3,740 (Years 3–4), £3,885 (Years 5–6). Pre-Prep (including lunch): £2,850 (Nursery and Reception), £2,965 (Years 1 and 2).

Academic results. A number of pupils proceed to Oxbridge every year (6 received offers for September 2013) and 97% of the Sixth Form to other degree courses. The 2014 A Level pass rate was 99%, with 73% at A* to B grades. At GCSE the 2014 pass rate was 93% with over 50% at grades A* and A.

Former Pupils' Association. There is a strong Former Pupils' Association with centres locally and in London and it has its own webalumnus. The "Friends of Truro School" involves parents, staff, old pupils and friends of the school in social events and fundraising.

Charitable status. Truro School is a Registered Charity, number 306576. It is a charitable foundation established for the purpose of education.

University College School

Frognal, Hampstead, London NW3 6XH
Tel: 020 7435 2215
Fax: 020 7433 2111
email: seniorschool@ucs.org.uk
website: www.ucs.org.uk
Twitter: @UCSHampstead

University College School is a day school providing places for 500 boys aged 11–16, with a co-educational Sixth Form of 300 places. UCS admitted its first cohort of girls into the Sixth Form in September 2008. 30 girls will join UCS each year.

Established in 1830 as part of University College, London, the School moved to its present site in Hampstead in 1907. Though now independently governed, UCS has sustained by continuous reinterpretation many of the ideals of its founders. Its basis remains the provision of the widest opportunities for learning and development without the imposition of tests of doctrinal conformity, but within a balanced and coherent view of educational needs and obligations. This in turn rests on the recognition that care for a pupil's social, moral and spiritual upbringing is a shared responsibility between home and school, an understanding fostered by mutual trust and regular communication. Thirdly, the distinctive ethos of the School stems from the conviction that a positive, lively and humane community, both within and beyond the School, can only be created by the liberal encouragement and disciplined fulfilment of the diversity of gifts among its individual members.

It is in this spirit that the School day begins with a short Assembly.

Chairman: The Rt Hon Sir Brian Leveson MA, LLD Hon
Honorary Treasurer: Mr L Bard, MA FCA CTA
Dr Y Amin, BSc, MB, ChB, DA, FRCA
Ms L Bingham, MIPA, MABRP, DBA
¶Mr R Bondy
Ms S Bora BSc, MBA
Sir Stanley Burnton
Mrs J Dangoor, BSc, DIC, PhD
Mr E Fordham, BA
Mr W H Frankel, OBE, MA, FRSSSAf
Mr R Gullifer, MA
Ms J Hall, OBE, MA
¶Mr A G Hillier, MA, MBA
¶Mr A S Jacobs, MA
Mr S D Lewis, OBE, MA
¶Professor P Sands, QC
Councillor G Spinella
Dr C Tyerman, MA, DPhil Oxford, FRHistS

¶ *Old Gower*

Senior School:

Headmaster: Mr M J Beard, MA Corpus Christi College Oxford, MA King's College London

Vice Master: Mr C M Reynolds, BSc Durham, MSc Sheffield Hallam, FSS
Deputy Head (*Pastoral*): Dr D J Colwell, BA PhD Royal Holloway London
Deputy Head (*Academic*): Mr M T English, BA Magdalen College Oxford, MA Liverpool

Deme Wardens:
Baxters: Mr S A P FitzGerald, BA University College London
Black Hawkins: Mr S Hawley, BSc Sheffield
Evans: Mr T J Allen, BA Worcester College Oxford
Flooks: Dr G A Plow, MA King's College Cambridge, MA Birkbeck College London, PhD Lancaster
Olders: Miss M Hudson, BSc Bristol
Underwoods: Mr A R Wilkes, BA Reading

Sixth Form
Assistant Head, Head of Sixth Form: Mr R H Chapman, BSc Hull
Deputy Head of Sixth Form:
Mrs L M Jenkins, BA UEA, MA Institute of Education, London
Ms J Kung, BA University of Sydney, BA Macquarie University

Lower School Wardens
Lower School Warden: Mr E A Barnish, BA Sheffield, MA London
Lower School Year Warden (*Entry*): Miss E Lodato, BA Trinity College Cambridge
Lower School Year Warden (*Shell*): Mr I C Gibson, MA St Catharine's College Cambridge

Heads of Departments:
Art & Design: Mr N Price, BA Coventry, MA Wales
Art History: Mr A M Mee, MA King's College London
Biology: Mrs F Allen, MSc, CPsychol, AFBPsS Western Australia & London Guildhall
Chemistry: Mr I A Barr, MA Lincoln College Oxford
Classics: Mr D J Woodhead, BA Durham
Design & Technology: Mr R A K Hawkins, BTech Brunel, AMIMechE
Drama: Ms R Baxter, BA Homerton College Cambridge
Economics & Business Studies: Mr D G Hall, BA York
English: Mr J L Hartley, BA Emmanuel College Cambridge
Geography: Mr M B Murphy, BA Durham
History: Mr A G Vaughan, BA Peterhouse College Cambridge
ICT: Mr A Davis, BSc Sussex
Learning Support: Ms S K Thale, BA Southampton, MA Reading
Mathematics: Dr D A Robb, BSc Edinburgh, PhD Strathclyde
Modern Languages: Mr T P Underwood, BA Bath
Director of Music: Mr C R Dawe, BA, MA, MMus St John's College Cambridge, King's College London
Philosophy: Mr A Atkinson, BA, MA Nottingham
Physics: Mr A R M Sandford, BSc Loughborough
Politics: Ms J L Heaton, BA, MA University College London
PSHE: Ms T O'Neil, BEd London
Director of Sport: Mr J P Cooke, BA, QTS Brunel

Director of Operations: Mr N Stock, BSc Reading, MRICS
Admissions: Mrs L Quantick, BA Nottingham Trent
PA to the Headmaster: Mrs J A Scott

Junior Branch:

Headmaster: Mr L Hayward, BA New College Oxford, MA Ed Open University
Deputy Head (*Curriculum*): Mr M A Albini, MA BSc Birmingham
Deputy Head (*Pastoral*): Mr D J Edwards, BA Lancaster

Headmaster's Secretary: Miss D Campbell

Entry. Entry is in September only.
Admission. Boys are normally admitted to the Senior School at either 11+, 13+ or 16+. Admission at 11+ is either by promotion from the Junior Branch or by examination held in January of the year of entry. Admission at 13+ is by

the Common Entrance following the UCS Preliminary Assessment, and interviews. These are held two years prior to entry.

Applications for entry should be made to the School Admissions Secretary at any time up to mid-September two years prior to admission (13+), or by the end of November preceding the proposed year of entry (11+). There is a registration fee of £100. A substantial deposit is required when a place is accepted which will be credited against the first term's account. Fee assistance is available through a means-tested application process. Applicants of sufficient academic standing who lack financial resources are encouraged to apply to the Foundation's generous bursary programme.

Applications for 16+ entry for boys and girls should be made to the School Administrator by October one year prior to admission. Assessment for Sixth Form is by examination and interview.

The Lower and Middle Schools. The Curriculum is designed to provide a broad range of knowledge and experience for all boys over 5 years from ages 11 to 16. In the first 2 years boys take English, French, Geography, History, Mathematics, Biology, Physics, Chemistry, Latin, Art, Design Technology, Drama, Music, Information Technology and Personal and Social Education. At 13+ they add a further subject choosing two from Latin, Greek, German and Spanish. Some modifications are made one year later according to aptitude and ability and most boys offer 10 subjects at GCSE.

The Sixth Form. All boys and girls take 4 subjects to AS Level in the Lower Sixth, with the option of narrowing to 3 in the following year.

AS Level subjects may be chosen from: Art, Biology, Chemistry, Design & Technology, Economics, English, French, Further Mathematics, Geography, German, Greek History (Early Modern or Late Modern), Information Technology, Latin, Mathematics, Music, Philosophy, Physics, Politics, Spanish, Theatre Arts, and History of Art.

Boys and girls in the Sixth Form have their own spacious study and social areas in the Sixth Form Centre, opened in 1974 and remodelled in 2008, and have the major responsibility for its use and upkeep. Senior Tutors, in collaboration with the Careers Team, provide detailed advice for each pupil about the selection of courses at Universities and other further education opportunities as well as ensuring that a student's course in the Sixth Form meets the entrance requirements of his/her intended future course and professional career. The enormous majority of leavers go on to degree courses.

Students are prepared for entrance to Oxford and Cambridge. Tuition is on a seminar basis.

Pastoral Care. In the Lower School (Years 7 and 8) boys are cared for by form teachers and Lower School Wardens (Heads of Year). The Middle and Senior Schools are divided into six Demes (Houses), each under the supervision of a Deme Warden. Many activities outside the classroom are organised by Demes, but the primary responsibility of the Deme Warden is to maintain a personal relationship with each member of his/her Deme, constant throughout a student's school career. Consequently, in all important pastoral and disciplinary matters he/she deals directly with the student in consultation with parents and other teachers and is answerable to the Headmaster for the general welfare of his/her Deme.

In addition to parents' evenings, parents are encouraged to consult informally with teachers about any issues that arise with their child. A Parents' Guild exists to promote the general welfare of the School.

Careers. Pupils are guided by means of interviews and tests towards careers appropriate to their gifts and personalities. Pupils are given opportunities to attend holiday courses directed towards specific careers. Also, visiting speakers are invited to the School and there are frequent Careers events. There is a full Careers Library and a comprehensive programme of Work Experience. The Parents' Guild and Old Gowers' Club (alumni organisation) also provide advice and support.

Physical Education and Games. The State-of-the-Art Sir Roger Bannister sports complex opened in December 2006. The pupils have periods of Physical Education within their normal timetable in the sports complex.

The School playing fields cover 27 acres and are situated a mile away in West Hampstead. In addition to grass surfaces, there is a large all-weather pitch and two pavilions. The major sports for Lower and Middle school boys are Rugby, Football, Hockey and Cricket with increased choices from Year 9. The School has its own Tennis and Fives courts at Frognal, together with an indoor heated Swimming Pool. Other sports include Fencing, Athletics, Squash, Badminton, Basketball, Fives and outdoor pursuits. For sixth form boys and girls there is a wide choice of indoor and outdoor sports.

Music and Drama. There is a strong musical tradition at UCS and many pupils play in the Orchestras, Wind Band and a great variety of groups and ensembles. Choral music is equally strong and Jazz is a particular feature. Instrumental tuition is given in the Music School, opened in 1995, and this and Ensemble Groups are arranged by the Director of Music.

The School's Lund Theatre, opened in 1974, is the venue for a range of Drama from major productions to experimental plays, mime and revue. An open-air theatre was completed in 1994. A regular programme of evening events is arranged for the Autumn and Spring terms.

Other School Societies. These cover a wide range of academic interests and leisure pursuits, including the Duke of Edinburgh's Award Scheme. There is a very active Community Action Programme, which works in the local community and there are regular fundraising initiatives for both local and national charities.

Development Programme. The Foundation completed the final phase of an ambitious programme of redevelopment in 2008. A state-of-the-art Indoor Sports Centre opened in late 2006, comprising Sports Hall, Swimming Pool, Fitness Centre and Health Club. The new Jeremy Bentham Building houses Modern Languages and Art & Design Technology and opened in October 2007. There was extensive refurbishment and reorganisation of classrooms, indoor and outdoor play spaces, administrative areas of the School and Sixth Form Centre. A fundraising appeal helped to achieve these improvements and enabled the School to double the provision of fee assistance.

At the same time, three educational initiatives are under way: a learning strategy initiative is focusing on the learning experience of the pupils and the teaching styles that best promote good learning and work habits; an intellectual enrichment programme to complement the academic curriculum; and the development of pupil, staff and parent portals to enable efficient communication and e-learning opportunities.

Fees per term (2014–2015). Senior School: £5,945; Junior Branch: £5,495. Excludes fees payable in respect of music and other private lessons, and books.

Scholarships and Bursaries. Fee assistance is available through a means-tested application process. Applicants of sufficient academic standing who lack financial resources are encouraged to apply to the Foundation's generous bursary programme.

Academic Scholarships do not entitle the holder to a reduction in the school tuition fee. However, UCS is keen to recognise the ability and achievement of the candidates who sit our admissions tests and is proud to offer prizes to those candidates whose performance is exemplary. These prizes take the form of generous book tokens, with book plates inscribed to commemorate the candidate's achievement. The books will be presented at a private occasion for the pupil and his/her family, when he/she joins the school.

A Standard Music Award at UCS will entitle the holder to a reduction in the annual school tuition fee of between 10% and 25%. In cases of need, Supplementary Awards may increase the value of a Music Award up to 100% of the annual tuition fee. Details of these special awards and their values are available from the Director of Music or www.ucs.org.

Music Awards involve competitive auditions. Applicants will be required to play two contrasting pieces of their own choice on a main instrument or voice. Competition is often quite strong. We expect a minimum of Grade V at 11+, Grade VI at age 12–13 years, and Grade VIII at 16+. The age of younger candidates will be taken into consideration. There will be ear tests, sight reading and an interview. Demonstration of ability on a second instrument, or as a singer, will be welcomed.

The Junior Branch. (*See entry in IAPS section.*) The Junior Branch is housed in separate buildings at Holly Hill, a few minutes' walk from Frognal. Like the Senior School, its main purpose is to provide full scope for the steady maturing of a boy's personality and capacity and for the preparation of boys for the Senior School in order to ensure a continuity of care, stimulation and reasoned discipline. It has its own Library, Computer Room and Laboratory and shares with the main School the playing fields and sports complex. A specialist building accommodates Art, Cookery and Design Technology.

Boys are admitted at the age of 7+. As of 2010, the Junior Branch no longer operates an 8+ entry point for boys. Admission is by preliminary examination and interview. Applications should be made to the Headmaster's Secretary, The Junior Branch, 11 Holly Hill, Hampstead, at least a year in advance. There is a registration fee of £100.

History. A new History of the School was published in June 2007.

Old Pupils' Society (Old Gowers). The School maintains an active register of former pupils and plans events throughout the year.

Charitable status. University College School, Hampstead is a Registered Charity, number 312748. Its aims and objectives are the provision of the widest opportunities for learning and development of students without the imposition of tests and doctrinal conformity but within a balanced and coherent view of educational needs and obligations.

Uppingham School

Uppingham, Rutland LE15 9QE
Tel: 01572 822216
Fax: 01572 822332 (Headmaster)
           01572 821872 (Bursar)
email: admissions@uppingham.co.uk
website: www.uppingham.co.uk

Uppingham School was founded in 1584 by Robert Johnson who obtained a grant by Letters Patent from Queen Elizabeth I. The transition to one of the foremost public schools of its time from an unremarkable local Grammar School took place with the arrival of the great educationalist and headmaster, Edward Thring, in 1853. His pioneering beliefs in the values of an all-round education still mark the School strongly today and have determined many of its distinguishing characteristics: that Houses should be small and family-like; that boys (and now girls) should have privacy; that an all-round education should be offered to a broad range of pupils and that children are happier and learn better in inspiring surroundings.

The Governing Body:

Chairman: ¶The Rt Hon Stephen J Dorrell, MP
Vice-Chairmen:

Dr P Chadwick, MA, MA, FRSA
W J A Timpson Esq, CBE

The Rt Revd D Allister, MA, Bishop of Peterborough
The Very Revd C Taylor, MA, Dean of Peterborough
Dr L Howard, BSc, OBE, JP, Lord Lieutenant of Rutland
¶M C Allen Esq
J C Hanson-Smith Esq
A G Hancock Esq, MA
R Peel Esq, BSc, FRSA
¶D P J Ross Esq
Mrs R J N Morris, BA
¶A J D Locke Esq, MA
Dr S Goss, MA, DPhil
Dr D Hill, Hon DMus, MA, Hon RAM, FRCO, Hon FGCM
R Landman Esq, MA
C J Cazalet Esq, MA, FCA
Professor D Greenaway
¶Mrs S H Mason
¶R J S Tice Esq, BSc
¶A E P Smith Esq
Professor Dame Carol Black, DBE, FRCP, FMedSci
R N J S Price Esq

¶ *Old Uppinghamian*

Bursar/Finance Director, Clerk to the Trustees: S C Taylor, MA, ACA

Headmaster: **Richard S Harman**, MA

Deputy Head: K M Wilding, BA
Director of Studies: B Cooper, MA
Senior Mistress: Mrs W F McLachlan, BSc, CBiol
Registrar: C S Bostock, MA, MSc
Chaplain: The Revd Dr J B J Saunders, BA, PhD

Assistant Staff:
* *Head of Department*
† *Housemaster/mistress*
§ *Part time*

Art, Design & Technology:
*A Parker, MA
*C P Simmons, BSc
J A Davison, BA, MEd
Miss K L Hallam
Miss E K Rieveley, MA
C I Silvester
A Wilson, BA, FRPS
Miss A J Cook, MA
†S G Dewhurst, BA
S J M Foster, BA
§†Mrs A M Howe, MA, MPhil
†G S Tetlow, MA

Biology:
§P L Bodily, BSc, MEd, CBiol, MIBiol, AIB
†N K de Wet, BSc, CBiol, MIBiol
B P Fell, MA
Miss L E Hourston, BSc
Mrs W F McLachlan, BSc, CBiol
* Dr C L Pemberton, BSc, PhD
Miss A S Roebuck, BSc
J A D Wilson, MChem

Chemistry:
*L G Bartlett, MA (*Science*)
C R Birch, BSc
Dr L F Dudin, MSc, PhD
C L Howe, HDE
A Kowhan, BSc
J A D Wilson, MChem

Classics:
S P Broadbent, BA
†W A M Chuter, BA

Economics & Business Studies:
*A C Hunting, DMS
D Beggs, BSc
T G Howe, MA
D P Lovering, BSc
T G MacCarthy, BA

English:
*Mrs C A Miller, BA
†A C Boyd-Williams, BA
§Mrs J S Broughton, MA, Dip RSA SpLD
R S Harman, MA
Miss C Hayne, MA
Mrs M N L Hunting, MA
§D A McLachlan, MA
Mrs N L Reihill, MA
R E Young, BA

Geography:
*T P Davies, BSc
A N Huxter BSc
§Mrs S J Kowhan, BA
R J O'Donoghue, BA
M B Stevens, BA
K M Wilding, BA

History:
*T P Prior, BA, MA
J S Birch, MA
M R J Burton, MA
S J Hosking, BA
J Leang, BA, MA
Miss K E Price, BA
†J A Reddy, BA

History of Art:
*D S R Kirk, BA
C I Silvester, BA

Information Technology:
*Miss S E L Webster, BSc
†Mrs L J Allen, BSc, MBCS

Learning Support:
*Mrs N C Halliday-Pegg, BEd, NDT
§Mrs J S Broughton, MA, DipRSA SpLD
Mrs M Cuccio, DipSLD
§Mrs L Howe, BA
§Mrs A M Merrett, BA
§Mrs K L Tetlow, BA

Life Skills:
*Mrs M N L Hunting, MA

Mathematics:
*P G Logan, BSc
R J S G Clark, BA
†Mrs L J Allen, BSc, MBCS
P Gomm, BSc
Mrs K F Hanrahan, BSc
Dr S T Jones, BEng
†J C E Lee, MA
Mrs M J Melville-Coman, BSc
P J Nicholls, BSc
Q H Sayed, MPhys

Modern Languages:
*Miss M A Barefoot, BA (*Spanish*)
K Labbé (*French*)
§Mrs C Laquintana-Fordham (*Italian*)
Miss E S Semper, MA (*German*)
M R Broughton, MA
†Ms F C Buckley, BA, MA
†Mrs H M Johnstone, BA
Mrs J E Newcombe, BEd

Visiting Music Staff:
Miss I Adams, GRSM (*Viola*)
S Andrews (*Drums*)
M Ashford, GRSM (*Guitar*)
A Ashwin, BMus, LRSM (*Singing*)
S Baker, BMus (*Trombone*)
T Birchnall, BMus, LGSM (*Violin*)
Mrs J Burgess, BMus, LGSM (*Oboe*)
Dr J T Byron, BA, MA, PhD (*Piano*)
Mrs L Clements, BA (*Flute*)
Mrs J A Dawson, GRSM, LRAM (*Piano*)
M Fatichenti, LRAM (*Piano*)
Mrs L H Ffrench, GRSM, LRAM (*Piano*)
N M France, GMus (*Drums*)
Mrs N J Gibbons, MMus, MPhil, LRAM, LRSM (*Piano*)
A J Gourlay, BSc (*Creative Music Production*)
Mrs C A Griffiths, GMus RNCM (*Singing*)
Mrs C J Gunningham, BA, MSTAT (*Alexander Technique*)
I Hildreth (*Bagpipes*)

R Salvador Noguera
P A Westgate, BA, MA
†R M B Wilkinson, MA
T R Worthington, BA

Music:
*S J Williams, BA
*P M Clements, MA, FRCO
§Miss E M Chatterton, BA
A A Ffrench, MA, AGSM, PGDip GSMD
A G Laing, BA, DipPSMP
§O N Parker, MMus, BMus, FGMS, FASC
S A Smith, BA, PPRNCM
Miss J Stevens, GGSM, MA
A P Webster, GGSM, PDOT

Philosophy and Religious Studies:
*R C Hegarty, BA
B Cooper, MA
I J Knight, BA
P J Martin, BSc, MA
Revd Dr J B J Saunders, BA, PhD
P M Shacklady, BA

Physical Education:
*Mrs S M Singlehurst, BEd, MSc
Miss K L Smith, BSc
K G Johnstone, BEd
§J M Baker, BSc

Physics:
*J D Hoult, BSc
W S Allen, BEd
B P Fell, MA
C L Howe, HDE
G S Wright, BSc

Political Studies:
*T Makhzangi, BA
†T G Howe, MA, MSt, MBA
†K M Seecharan, BSocSci

Theatre Studies:
*Miss C J Rayner, BA
*A C Boyd-Williams, BA
J Holroyd, BA
D A McLachlan, MA

R O Hutchinson BMus Ed, MMus (*Jazz Bass*)
K Learmouth, ALCM, FRSA (*Classic Guitar*)
Ms R R E Leyton-Smith, MA, Adv PG Dip RCM (*Cello*)
Mrs C Li, BMus, LRAM(*Flute*)
G K Lumbers, BMus (*Saxophone*)
Miss J A Moffat, DipRCM (*Singing*)
S P Morris, BMus (*Clarinet, Saxophone*)
Mrs V F Morris, AGSM, LRAM (*Clarinet & Saxophone*)
Miss A Osman, BMus (*Double Bass*)
D N Price, LRAM (*Trumpet*)
Mrs A M Reynolds, MusB, GRNCM (*Piano*)
S Roberts, BMus (*Tuba*)
C Rutherford (*Horn*)
Mrs Y S Sandison, PPRNCM (*Singing*)
N Scott-Burt, BA, MMus, PhD, LRAM, ARCO (*Piano, Organ & Composition*)
Miss S E Stuart, BMus, GRNCM, PG Dip RNCM (*Percussion*)
Miss C Tanner (*Bassoon*)
Mrs E Turner (*Harp*)
J P Turville, MA, MMus, LLCM (*Piano*)
Ms P Waterfield, ARCM, MSTAT (*Alexander Technique*)
B J Weston, BA (*Music Technology*)
T J Williams, MA (*Singing*)
Mrs V D Williamson, GMus, RNCM, PPRNCM, LRAM (*Singing*)

Houses and Housemasters/mistresses:
Brooklands: Nick de Wet
Constables (*Girls*): Tyrone and Alex Howe
Fairfield (*Girls*): Mrs S M Singlehurst
Farleigh: James Birch
Fircroft: Jim Reddy
Highfield: Richard Wilkinson
Johnson's (*Girls*): Lesley Allen
The Lodge (*Girls*): Alex and Kate Boyd-Williams
Lorne House: Kurt Seecharan
Meadhurst: Sam Dewhurst
New House (*Girls*): Fiona Buckley
Samworths' (*Girls*): Helen Johnstone
School House: Simon Tetlow
West Bank: Jonathan Lee
West Deyne: Will Chuter

General Information. Uppingham School is a fully boarding school for boys and girls aged 13–18.

There are around 790 pupils in the School, of which some 350 are in the Sixth Form. More than 98% of the School's pupils are full boarders. Girls have been accepted into the Sixth Form since 1975 and make up 47% of the Sixth Form numbers. Girls were first admitted at 13+ in September 2001 and 41% of all pupils are girls. Around 15% of the School's pupils are foreign nationals, mainly from the European Union, Eastern Europe and South East Asia.

Uppingham is a Christian Foundation. Some Uppinghamians are members of other faiths and every consideration is given to their needs. The whole School meets in the Chapel five days a week; on Sunday there is a morning service usually with a visiting speaker. Pupils are prepared for Confirmation every year.

Situation and Facilities. Uppingham is a small market town set in beautiful countryside in Rutland. It is about 100 miles north of London and midway between Leicester and Peterborough on the A47. It is roughly equidistant from the M1 and A1/M11, and the A14 link road makes connections with the Midlands and East Anglia easier and faster. It is served by Kettering, Oakham, Corby, Peterborough and Leicester train stations, and by Stansted, Luton, Birmingham and East Midlands airports.

At the heart of the School is a traditional campus with investment in innovative and award-winning recent additions, including a new science centre, sports centre, music school, drama studio and workshop, sports pavilions and two Astroturf pitches reflecting the importance of the all-round education on offer.

The facilities within the central area of the School include the Victorian School Room and Chapel (designed by George Edmund Street, who designed the Law Courts in the Strand), the Memorial Hall, a well-stocked Library (housed in a beautiful building dating back to 1592), Music Schools including a third music school with state-of-the-art facilities, Language Centre and classrooms and the Humanities Departments. Nearby there is also a dedicated sixth form social centre, which also houses the Higher Education, Careers and Gap Year Departments.

At the western end of the town is the School's 'second heart' – known as the Western Quad. Recent developments have been focused on this area and it has been regenerated into a coherent and inspiring environment. The campus houses the magnificent new Science Centre which is based around a landscaped open space, creating the Western Quad itself, and includes 17 laboratories (including an environmental studies lab and outdoor classroom, and a project room), lecture theatre, departmental offices and meeting rooms. The centre also has a second library and second buttery to draw non-scientists into the building. The expansive Sports Centre, the recently refurbished Leonardo Centre (purpose built for Art and DT), Theatre and Drama Studios, and the Maths and IT Centre complete the picture.

Ranged around all these facilities, like a university campus, are the fifteen boarding houses each with its own garden, recreational facilities and dining room.

Academic Matters. Whilst the School is noted for its strong commitment to all-round education, its superb pastoral care and magnificent facilities, the pupils' academic studies are the priority. In 2014, 55.2% of all A Levels and 66.9% of all GCSEs were A*/A grades; 85.3% of A Levels were A*–B. One in three A Level candidates achieved straight A*/A grades. At GCSE 43% of the year group gained at least 8 A*/A grades and the A*–C pass rate was 96.5%. In 2014, ten pupils received Oxbridge offers. With a staff : pupil ratio of almost 1:7 all subjects enjoy the benefits of small class sizes and a wide range may be taught. 28 different A Level subjects and 20 GCSE subjects are offered.

Until GCSE, specialisation is minimal and pupils are taught in sets for most subjects. Most take a minimum of nine GCSE subjects. All members of the Sixth Form study four or five AS Levels in the Lower Sixth and three or four A Levels in the Upper Sixth which are complemented by a lecture programme and a wide variety of extra-curricular activities. Extended Project Qualifications (EPQ) are offered in addition to the A Level subjects.

The progress of all pupils is monitored by an assigned Tutor and their Housemaster or Housemistress, as well as by a system of regular reviews and reports from subject teachers. Parents and pupils may also call on the School's Higher Education and Careers advisers; visiting speakers from universities and careers are featured throughout the year. The School uses the professional careers services of Cambridge Occupational Analysts. At all stages of a pupil's career, the Housemaster/Housemistress keeps in touch with parents regularly. Parent-teacher meetings take place annually for all year groups and additional meetings are held to discuss options and higher education.

Nearly all pupils go on to further education. The School offers advice on planning GAP years. Pupils have access to a beautiful, well-stocked central Library, as well as extensive, more specialist libraries for most subject departments.

For those with learning difficulties the School has trained staff to help with special education needs and any pupil may use the services of a professional psychologist or the School's trained counsellor.

Extra-Curricular Activities. Around 40 clubs and societies flourish within the School with a further 30 areas of activity on offer. Pupils can take bronze, silver and gold Duke of Edinburgh's Award. After the first year pupils can opt to join CCF for 2–3 years or community service (visiting the elderly, assisting in primary schools, Riding for the Disabled etc).

Boarding. There are fifteen boarding houses, which are dotted around the town and School estate: nine for boys, one for Sixth Form girls and five for 13–18 year old girls. Houses are kept small and are usually home to around 50–60 children, 45 in the case of the Sixth Form girls' house. All pupils eat their meals in their own house dining room and are joined at lunch by teaching and non-teaching staff.

Almost all boys have their own private study upon arrival and, by the time they reach the Sixth Form have their own study-bedroom. All girls entering at 13 share a room with up to 3 other girls and also have their own study area. This arrangement changes in the Lower Fifth and Upper Fifth when girls have bed-sit rooms, usually shared with one other. Sixth Form girls almost all have their own single study-bedrooms.

Much of the non-teaching life of the School is organised around the houses and they engender strong loyalties. In addition to excursions and social events, there exists a long-standing tradition of house drama productions, music concerts, artistic displays, as well as inter-house debating and sports competitions.

The resident Housemasters and Housemistresses are helped by a team of at least five tutors who are assigned to particular pupils. They assist with monitoring academic progress and social development.

Music. Uppingham has always had a very distinguished reputation for music since being the first school to put music on its curriculum for all pupils. In 2006 the School opened its third music school. This inspirational music facility offers a unique environment in which to rehearse, cutting-edge music technology, and a 120-seat recital room. The School has an outstanding Chapel Choir, numerous orchestras and chamber groups, wind bands, a professional concert series as well as many thriving musical societies and rock groups. A busy programme of weekly recitals, house and year-group concerts, and larger public performances in the UK and abroad offer pupils of all abilities regular chances to perform. More than 50% of pupils learn an instrument. 42 visiting staff and 9 full-time staff enable pupils to receive conservatoire-style tuition at the school.

The School has produced several Oxbridge organ scholars and numerous choral scholars in recent years and the distinguished results also extend to Conservatoires.

Further enquiries may be made directly to the Director of Music (01572 820696).

Sports and Games. Uppingham has a strong tradition of sporting excellence and often has pupils gaining international honours in a variety of sports. All students participate in sports or games three times a week. The major sports are Rugby, Hockey, Cricket, Tennis, Cross-Country and Athletics for boys, and Hockey, Netball, Tennis, Cross-Country and Athletics for girls. Many other sports are available from Aerobics through to Sailing.

There is a full programme of formal house matches across all sports, providing an opportunity for all pupils to contribute within a team environment. The able are stretched and the very able are offered a high level of coaching from experienced coaches/professionals in all major sports, often going on to represent club, academy, county, regional or national teams. Success at first team level against rival schools is an expectation.

A magnificent Sports Centre opened in September 2010. The building includes a sports hall, six-lane 25m swimming pool, fitness studio, gym, squash courts and dance studios. The new centre houses the School's PE department and has a hospitality suite for match-day entertaining. In addition, there are more than 65 acres of playing fields including the Upper (dedicated to First XI cricket), three Astroturf surfaces (one is floodlit), Tennis, Netball and Fives courts, shooting range and climbing wall.

All these facilities are open seven days a week under the guidance of the Sports Centre manager and appointed staff.

The Leonardo Centre. The Art, Design and Technology Centre is a glass-fronted structure which allows a broad range of creative activities to take place in a single open-plan space and thereby stimulate each other. The Leonardo Centre houses a Fine Art and Printing space (which has the facility for 3D printing), studios for Design (including CAD design), Ceramics, Sculpture, Photography, Sound and Video Engineering, workshops primarily for wood, metal and plastic and teaching rooms. History of Art has expanded in to an adjacent building. The Warwick Metcalfe Gallery is used to display the work of pupils, staff and other visiting artists. The Centre is manned and open seven days a week, and is open to all pupils, whatever their public examination options.

Drama. Theatre and Drama flourish at the School and the subject is taught at GCSE and A Level. There is a well-established 300-seat theatre and in 2006 the facilities were extended to include a new foyer, two drama classrooms, a workshop space and a state-of-the-art drama studio. Major school productions are staged annually and range from big musicals, such as *Guys and Dolls* and most recently *Miss Saigon* and *Calamity Jane*, to more classic productions, like Shakespeare's *A Midsummer Night's Dream*. The theatre also hosts a wide variety of visiting professional companies and as such it plays a significant role in the cultural life of both the school and the wider community.

Technological Environment. Uppingham prides itself on providing the very best technology facilities for pupils in both academic and boarding areas delivering a very modern perspective of the School's more traditional values of 'all-round education'.

In each academic department the right technology is employed to complement the teaching and learning with teaching staff and pupils having a wide variety of tools at their disposal: from the language lab (for teaching modern foreign languages) to the suite of computers used for creating digital music (in the music technology department). Online resources supplement the more traditional research materials available in the School and department libraries. Pupils can access the online Encyclopedia Britannica as well as JSTOR, an online collection of over one thousand academic journals and one of the most trusted sources of academic content on the world wide web. The School also generates an immense variety of course specific online media which pupils can easily access from the 'Virtual Learning Environment'.

In the boarding houses, each pupil is given his or her own computer which provides a vast array of educational software as well as email and filtered internet access to complement their academic studies and ensure a fruitful but safe participation in Cyberspace.

The infrastructure to enable this high level of technology is immense with more than 1400 computers, miles of fibre optic cable, fast internet access (100 Mbps) and an enormous variety of educational resources all supported by an in-house team of eight dedicated IT experts.

Admission. Most pupils are admitted to Uppingham in the September following their thirteenth birthday. Usually prospective pupils and their parents visit the School at least three years prior to entry. Prospective pupils should be registered at this time, if not already. Two years before entry, at 11+, all registered pupils are invited to tests and interview at Uppingham. All applications must be supported by a satisfactory reference from the present school. The Headmaster offers places to the successful candidates after this process has concluded. Parents then complete and return an Acceptance Form together with an entrance deposit. Receipt of the entrance deposit guarantees a place in the School subject to the prospective pupil qualifying for admission. In completing the Acceptance Form parents also confirm that Uppingham is their first choice of school.

An offer of a place in the School is conditional upon the pupil qualifying academically (see below), and on his or her record of conduct.

There are three possible ways of qualifying academically:

- via the Common Entrance Examination (for which the qualifying standard is an average of 55% in the compulsory papers);
- via the Common Academic Scholarship Examination;
- in the case of pupils who have not been prepared for the Common Entrance Examination, by means of a report from the Head Teacher of their present school and tests and interviews at Uppingham.

To continue into the Sixth Form pupils are expected to achieve six passes of grade B or above in academic subjects at GCSE, excluding short-course GCSEs.

There are a limited number of places available for boys and girls for entry into the Sixth Form. Pupils may register an interest in Sixth Form entry to Uppingham at any time and formal registration should be completed by the end of September, eleven months prior to entry. The test, interview and offer procedures take place in November. Admission at this level is dependent on tests and interviews at Uppingham, and achieving six passes of grade B or above in academic subjects at GCSE (or equivalent), excluding short course GCSEs.

Enquiries and requests for information about admissions should be addressed to the Assistant Registrar (01572 820611).

Scholarships and Bursaries. At 13, boys and girls may apply for Academic (ISEB Common Scholarship), Art/ Design & Technology, Music, Sport and Thring (All-Rounder) Scholarships. Scholarship exams for 13+ entry are held in February/March preceding entry.

At 16, Academic, Science, Art/Design & Technology, Sport and Music Scholarships are awarded in November preceding entry.

A number of music exhibitions granting free tuition on all instruments may also be awarded.

Where a family's financial means leaves them unable to afford a place at Uppingham they may be eligible to receive support via a means-tested bursary. All candidates seeking a bursary should be registered with the School and need to fulfil the same entrance criteria as described.

Details of all scholarships and bursaries may be obtained from the Admissions Office (01572 820611).

Fees per term (2014–2015). Boarding £10,950; Day £7,665. There is a scheme for paying fees in advance; further details may be obtained from the Deputy Bursar (01572 820627).

Former Pupils. The Uppingham Association was founded in 1911 to maintain the link between OUs and the School. All pupils may become life members when they leave and a database of their names, addresses, school and career details is maintained at the School by the OU Administrator. In addition to a range of OU events that are organised each year for members, a magazine is published annually, which contains news about OUs and activities at the School, and all members are encouraged to make full use of the OU Website. Enquiries may be made directly to the Secretary to the Uppingham Association (01572 820616).

Charitable status. Uppingham School is a charitable company limited by guarantee registered in England and Wales. Company Number 8013826. Registered Charity Number 1147280. Registered Office: High Street West, Uppingham, Rutland LE15 9QD.

Victoria College
Jersey

Jersey, Channel Islands JE1 4HT
Tel: 01534 638200
Fax: 01534 727448
email: admin@vcj.sch.je
website: www.victoriacollege.je

Motto: *Amat Victoria Curam*
The College was founded in commemoration of a visit of Her Majesty Queen Victoria to the Island and opened in 1852. It bears the Arms of Jersey.

Visitor: Her Majesty The Queen

Governing Body:
Chairman: C Barton

Vice Chairman: J Giles	T Morgan
P Le Brocq	P Gray
J Laity	M Godel
C Scholefield	M Robins
N Cawley	A Hossard

Headmaster: Alun D Watkins, BEd Hons, MEd Oxon

Assistant Staff:
Miss M Adams, BA Hons

K L Akers, BA Hons	Miss A Matthews, BSc
C Baughan, BA Hons	Hons
Miss H Bell, BSc Hons	D M McNally, BSc Hons
G C Bloor, BD, MA	Ms D B Montgomery, BA
Mrs H R Bougeard, BA	Hons
Hons	Mrs E L O'Prey, BEd Hons
Miss J Bryan, BA Hons	T E Palfreyman, MA, BA
G Burton, BEd Hons	Ms M Perestrelo, BA Hons
B F Carolan, BA Hons	R J Picot, BSc
S Coe, BSc Hons	J Randles, BA Hons
S Cooke, PhD, BEng	S Roberts, BA Hons, MA,
D M Cox, BA, BEd Hons	PhD
J S Craik, BSc Hons, MA	Miss A F Robinson, BA
J Crill, BSc Hons	Hons
P J Davis, GWCMD,	D J Rotherham, BEd,
CertEd	FRGS
Miss L Douglas, BA Hons,	Mrs J A Roussel, BA Hons,
LTCC	M-ès-Lettres
A Du Feu, BSc Hons	Ms H Ryan, BSc Hons, BA
J Franco, BA Hons	Hons
W Gorman, BA Hons	I Simpson, BSc Hons
M Gosling, BA Hons	M D Smith, BA
P J Gray, BSc Hons	Mrs R O Smith, BA Hons
S Habin, BA Hons	T Smith, BEng Hons
J Hale, MPharmacol	M R Taylor, CertEd
A R Hamel, MA	Mrs M Taylor, BSc, MSc
Mrs C Herrera-Martin, BA	Ms D Twomey, BSc
Hons	Ms V G Videt, Lic-ès-
I A Hickling, BSc, MSc	Lettres
Miss S Humphries, BMus	Mrs S Watkins, BEd Hons
Hons	Mrs F Watteau, BSc Hons
Mrs G Johnson, BA Hons	R Webbe, MPhys
Oxon	M C Widdop, MChem
A C Lau, BSc Hons	Oxon, MRSC

Preparatory School
Headmaster: Russell Price, BSc, MPhil

There are currently 701 boys in College, 287 in the Preparatory School and 90 in the Pre-Prep.

The College is situated in extensive grounds above St Helier and looks south over the Bay of St Malo.

The fine building of 1852 with its Great Hall, libraries and administrative areas is set at the centre of new teaching accommodation including classrooms, a music centre, an extensive Science suite opened by Her Royal Highness The Princess Royal, a Sixth Form centre, Art and Design Technology suite, five computer suites and the Howard Davis Theatre refurbished in 1996. Building work is currently proceeding on a new Classroom block which will be finished in 2014 along with a new modern Sixth Form Centre. In September 2014 the building of new Houserooms will be complete.

College Field is adjacent to the main buildings and includes an all-weather hockey pitch.

Located in the grounds is a 25-yard shooting range, Squash courts and CCF Headquarters. A multimillion pound sports complex with swimming pool was opened in 2003.

Education. There is an emphasis on academic success; nearly all boys go on to University in the UK. The curriculum conforms to the requirements of the National Curriculum. In the Junior School boys study Religious Education, English, Mathematics, French, Spanish, History, Drama, Geography, Biology, Chemistry, Physics, Music, Art and ICT.

Thereafter the basic curriculum includes Religious Education, English, Mathematics, a language, Sciences and ICT. In addition, boys select from optional subjects those which best suit their natural talents, the choice being guided by teaching staff in consultation with students and parents.

Boys may study four or five A Level subjects suited to their objectives and abilities. Enrichment skills are developed through the CCF, Duke of Edinburgh's Award and wide-ranging co-curricular programmes.

At all Key Stages there is opportunity for voluntary work, Music and the Arts, and these, with other subjects, are also encouraged by numerous School Societies.

Prizes. Her Majesty The Queen gives three Gold Medals annually for Science, Modern Languages and Mathematics as well as two Prizes for English History. The States of Jersey offers a Gold Medal and a Silver Medal annually for French. There is an award given to the boy achieving the top score in Year 7 Entrance Examination called the St Mannelier et St Anastase Gold Medal.

Physical Education and Games. The College places strong emphasis on sport and each year there are sports tours to different countries, and to the United Kingdom. in 2012 the College was runner up in the Aviva Independent Sports School of the Year Award.

Winter games include Association Football, Rugby, Hockey, Squash; and in the summer Cricket, Swimming, Shooting, Tennis and Athletics.

Matches are played against Elizabeth College, Guernsey and College sides visit the mainland for matches against English Independent Senior Schools.

The College has an excellent CCF Contingent with an authorised establishment of 105 in the Army Section, 75 in the RAF Section and 75 in the RN Section. It is commanded by Wing Commander David Rotherham.

Admission. The age of admission is 11 years though boys are considered for entry at all ages. Entrants must pass the College Entrance Examination.

Fees per term (2014–2015). £1,612. A grant is payable by the States of Jersey to supplement fees.

Preparatory School. The College has its own Preparatory School which stands in the College grounds. Boys, on passing the Entrance procedure, progress to the College at the age of 11. (*For further details see entry in IAPS section.*)

Leaving Scholarships. There are a number of Scholarships (of varying amount). The Queen's Exhibition is tenable for three years at University; the Wimble Scholarship, the Sayers Scholarships and the Baron Dr Ver Heyden de Lancey Scholarship each of up to £750 a year, tenable at British Universities and the Rayner Exhibitions are recent additions to the rich endowment of Scholarships enjoyed by the College for its students.

Warminster School

Church Street, Warminster, Wiltshire BA12 8PJ
Tel: 01985 210100 (Senior School)
             01985 224800 (Preparatory School)
email: admin@warminsterschool.org.uk
website: www.warminsterschool.org.uk
Facebook: /WarminsterSchool
LinkedIn: /WarminsterSchool

The original boys' school was founded in 1707 by the first Viscount Weymouth, an ancestor of the present Marquess of Bath. It became an Independent Educational Trust in 1973 formed by the amalgamation of the Lord Weymouth School with the long-established local girls' school, St Monica's, founded in 1874. The School is a Limited Company whose Directors are Trustees elected by and from within the Board of Governors which is in membership of the Association of Governing Bodies of Independent Schools. The Headmaster is a member of both HMC (Headmasters' and Headmistresses' Conference) and The Society of Heads.

Patrons:
The Revd Canon E J Townroe
Mrs D P Goodger
Mr R C Southwell, QC
The Rt Revd the Bishop of Salisbury
The Marquess of Bath

Chairman of Governors: The Right Hon Sir David Latham, QC

Staff:

Headmaster: Mark Mortimer, MBA, BA

Deputy Head (Academic): Mrs Olivia Bourne, BEd
Deputy Head & Head of Pastoral Care: Rick Clarke, BA Hons, PGCE
Head of Co-Curricular: Mrs Terri Wilcox, CertEd
Head of Sixth Form: Graeme McQueen, MA, PGCE
Head of Middle School: Ms Nia Davies, BSc Hons, PGCE
Head of Lower School: Mrs Nicola Curtis, BA, PGCE
Senior Tutor: Mark Sully, BSc, PGCE
Examinations Officer: Dr Mark Martin, BSc Hons, PhD, PGCE, MIBiol

Heads of Department:
Art: Mrs Louisa Clayton, MA, PGCE
Business Studies & Economics: Alex Forbes, MA, BSc
D&T: Simon Rossiter, MSc, PGCE, CCRS
Drama: Miss Annabel Hooper, BA, PGCE
EFL: Mrs Sarah Shanks, BA Hons, PGCE, RSA Dip TEFL
English: Mrs Cristina George, BA PGCE
Geography: Miss Sarah Matthews, BA, PGCE
History: Mrs Juliette Walker, BA, QTS
Learning Support: Mrs Teri Durrell, MA (*SENCO*)
Mathematics: Mark Sully, BSc, PGCE
Modern Languages: Mrs Nicola Rogers, BA PGCE
Director of Music: Derek Harris, GRSM, Dip RCM, PGCE
Psychology: Mrs Felicity Beck, BSc Hons, PGCE
RS: Matthew Harris, MA Oxon, MPhil, MEd, PGCE
Science: Dr David Hankey, BSc, PhD, MRSC
Director of Sports: Christopher Knight, BEd Hons

There are 30 other full-time and part-time staff.

House Staff:
Mr and Mrs Jon Bonnell (*St Boniface*)
Mr and Mrs Geoffrey Knapman (*Stratton House*)
Mr and Mrs Malcolm Miller (*St Denys*)
Mr and Mrs Christopher Knight (*Old Vicarage*)
Mr and Mrs Damien Crinion (*Northdown*)
Mrs Hayley Arter, RGN (*School Nursing Sister*)

Bursar & Clerk to the Governors: Mrs Alison C Martin, MBA, FMAAT
Head of Admissions: Mrs Gayle Webb

General. Founded in 1707, the School is a co-educational boarding and day school numbering some 550 pupils (140 in the Sixth Form) from 3 to 18, of whom around 200 are boarders. The Preparatory School of 140 pupils works in close cooperation with the Senior School and enjoys many of the same facilities. (*For further details see Warminster Preparatory School entry in IAPS section.*)

The School is situated along the western periphery of the town, looking out over open countryside, while its buildings are linked by extensive gardens and playing fields.

It is easily accessible by rail (via Warminster or Westbury) from London, Heathrow, the South Coast and the West, and by road (via the M3, M4 and M5).

Aims and Philosophy. The Warminster education aims to encourage each boy and girl to fulfil their academic potential and to promote intellectual curiosity and a love of learning. In addition, the School provides a secure and supportive pastoral environment, with an emphasis on character, values, leadership and service. The School believes in an all-round education and offers a wide range of co-curricular opportunities and experiences; it fosters a culture of enthusiasm, optimism and participation. A Warminster education prepares the pupils for life beyond school, at university and in the world of work. We are a community in which each boy and girl is valued and nurtured on the basis of who they are, whatever their year group, gender, natural gifts or background. *It is a preparation for life.*

Buildings. As befits a school with a long history, there is a wide variety of historic buildings. The History department, for example, teaches in the School's oldest building, School House, which was founded by Viscount Weymouth in 1707. The school boasts one of the oldest working Fives courts in England.

A multimillion pound development programme has taken place in recent years and has included completion of the Thomas Arnold Hall – a fantastic new multi-purpose space, a state-of-the-art science centre, new library, design technology centre as well as additional boarding facilities. Existing boarding accommodation has been extensively refurbished.

Boarders are cared for by Housemasters or Housemistresses, Resident Tutors and Matrons. Pupils typically enjoy single study-bedrooms in the Sixth Form.

Curriculum. In the first three years of the Senior School, all pupils follow a broad curriculum and GCSE pupils study a full and varied range of subjects. All pupils are involved in PE and Games, and Health and Social Education, as well as a comprehensive programme of Careers advice.

In the Sixth Form greater individual freedom and responsibility are encouraged. Sixth Formers are offered a choice between studying A Levels (more than twenty different subjects are offered) and the International Baccalaureate Diploma, which is an increasingly popular choice for many of our pupils with others joining the Sixth Form from elsewhere to follow our successful IB programme. The first school in the South-West to offer the IB Diploma, our IB results have placed us each year within the top thirty UK IB schools. Although the vast majority of pupils will be aiming for University, with over 95% winning places at leading institutions including Oxford and Cambridge, some will pursue gap years or enter business or the Armed Services directly. The overall pupil : staff ratio is under 10:1. Pupils receive an exceptional amount of individual attention and are encouraged to realise their full potential in as many areas as possible. There is an extensive tutorial system and a strong sense of the importance of the individual within the community. The school is at the forefront of developing 'personal, learning and thinking skills' both through the tutorial system but also via its academic and its rich co-curricular programme. A small learning support unit is staffed by expert and dedicated specialists.

Activities. A very wide range of activities is on offer, and pupils are encouraged to involve themselves fully. The School has a strong tradition of drama, and musical activities, including choir, orchestra and jazz band, are a real strength. There are currently over 40 hobby activities available.

The School enjoys close links with the Armed Services, and the CCF, though voluntary, is traditionally strong. There is also a large involvement in the Duke of Edinburgh's Award Scheme, whilst a number of pupils are actively engaged in Community Service in Warminster and the local area.

Games. Sports offered include Rugby, Hockey, Cricket, Tennis, Athletics, Netball, Rounders, Swimming, Cross-Country running, Basketball, Squash, Badminton, and Volleyball.

There is a spacious Sports Hall with recently renovated squash courts, hard tennis courts, heated swimming pool, an Astroturf all-weather pitch and an indoor shooting range. Pupils have access to the local Golf Club and Riding Stables.

Admission. Pupils are admitted to the Preparatory School from the age of 3. Boarders are admitted from the age of 7. Pupils who enter after the age of 8 will be required to sit the Warminster School entrance examinations relative to the proposed year of entry. A report from the Head of a pupil's present school will always be requested. Older pupils who qualify by good GCSE results and school report may be admitted directly to the Sixth Form. Scholarships are available for entry at 7+, 9+, 11+, 13+ and 16+. Examinations for Scholarships are held annually. Details may be obtained from the Head of Admissions.

Progress throughout the School, including the transfer from the Preparatory to the Senior School, is not automatic but will be based on the School's assessment of each student's ability at key points and will always be dependent on the pupil's continued commitment and progress in all areas of activity.

Great care is taken to consider individual needs and circumstances. The School provides a Special Support Facility for pupils who are mildly dyslexic, or who have other similar needs. Parents of such pupils should ask to meet Mrs Durrell, who is the SENCO.

Please telephone the School (01985 210160) to arrange a visit, and to meet the Headmaster or the Head of the Preparatory School.

A Registration Fee of £100 is payable and, upon the acceptance of a place, a guarantee fee of £500 for UK based parents and £1,000 for overseas based parents, credited to the final account, will be payable.

Fees per term (2014–2015). Day: Preparatory School £2,320–£3,710; Year 7 to Sixth Form £4,650. Boarding: Preparatory School £6,560; Years 7 to Sixth Form £8,875.

Fees are as inclusive as possible, covering meals, stationery and textbooks. The Bursar welcomes consultation with parents over fees, insurance and capital payment schemes. As the School is an Independent Educational Trust, any financial surplus is used exclusively for the further improvement of the School. Fees are kept to the minimum required to run the School effectively, employ first-rate staff and keep the facilities and resources up to the level expected by parents.

Charitable status. Warminster School is a Registered Charity, number 1042204. It exists to promote the education of boys and girls.

Warwick School

Myton Road, Warwick CV34 6PP
Tel: 01926 776400
Fax: 01926 401259
email: enquiries@warwickschool.org
website: www.warwickschool.org

Motto: '*Altiora Peto*'

Warwick School is the oldest boys' school in the country and can produce documentary evidence that suggests its existence in the days of King Edward the Confessor; it probably dates from 914. In 1123 the School was granted to the Church of St Mary of Warwick. In 1545 King Henry VIII increased and re-organised the endowments. The School subsequently moved to the Lord Leycester Hospital. In 1571 it moved to another site within the boundaries of Warwick, and in 1879 to its present site south of the town on the banks of the Avon.

Governing Body:
A N Bell
[1] J P Cavanagh
Dr A D Cocker
T Cox (*ex officio*)
[1] R M Dancey (*Chairman*)
[1] A C Firth (*Vice-Chairman*)
C R Gibbons
[1] Mrs P A Goddard
Cllr Mrs M-A Grainger
[1] Prof D Grammatopoulos
[1] R M B Griffiths
N F Keegan
Mrs S E Lampitt
Mrs E L Lillyman
[1] Mrs J Marshall (*Chair – King's High School*)
[1] Miss K A Parr (*Chair – Warwick Preparatory School*)
Mrs C A I Sawdon
Mrs P A Snape
[1] D B Stevens (*Chairman – Warwick Independent Schools Foundation*)

[1] *Warwick School Committee*

Foundation Secretary: S T Jones

Head Master: A R Lock, MA

Deputy Headmaster: D J Wickes, MA

Deputy Head, Academic: S R Chapman, BA, PhD
Deputy Head, Staff: C G McNee, BA

Head of Sixth Form: J N Jefferies, MA
Head of Upper School: B L Davies, BSc
Head of Middle School: K C Davenport, BEng
Head of Lower Fourth: T D Pierce, BSc

* *Head of Department*

Art:
*R Flintoff, BA
Mrs G K Odling, BA
D Snatt, BA

Careers:
*Mrs C Oates, BA

Classics:
*D A Stephenson, MA, BA
M G L Cooley, MA, MSt
R Hudson, MA
Miss K Lathan, BA
Mrs R E Morgan, MA, BA
E P O'Neill, MA, BA

Computing:
*M J Colliver, BSc, MA
P Nield, MBA, BSc
D Seal, BSc

Design and Technology:
*B V N Schalch, BA
M J Alton, BA
C Riman, BA
J D Stone, BSc

Drama:
*M C Perry, MA
Miss J E Gurnett

Economics:
*D A Williams, MA, BA, MBA, EdD
W A C Deacon, BSc
Mrs G C Dolphin, BSc, MBA

English:
*Mrs K J Wyatt, MA, BA
C M Bond, MA
Mrs L M Haines, BA
Mrs L Hodge, BA
Miss G E Pearce, BA
Mrs A S Quinn, BA
Mrs W D Saville, BA
Dr T Shaw, PhD, MA, BA

Geography:
*Dr A Hodskinson, BSc, PhD
Miss H J Bowie, BSc
S R Chapman, BA, PhD
Miss J C Lewis, BSc
R M H Thomson, BA
Mrs E Thornton, BA

History and Politics:
C G J Gibbs, BA (*History*)
J N Jefferies, MA (*Politics*)
J E Delaney, MA, BA
E Hadley, MA
O R O'Brien, BA
J A Sutherland, BA, MSt
P M Walker, BA
D J Wickes, MA

Mathematics:
*Mrs J D'Arcy, MSc
Mrs V Bell, BSc
K C Davenport, BEng
B L Davies, BSc
G Giudici, MA
E N Leaf, BSc
W S Macro, MSc, BSc
N A Martlew, BSc
G O Milsom, BSc
P J O'Grady, MA
D J Shield, CertEd
P M Titmas. BSc

Modern Languages:
*Mrs L A Slack, MA, BA
Mrs J R Estill, BA (*German*)
Miss J A Wiltsher, BA (*Spanish*)
Mrs E R Allin, BA, MA
Mrs H V Brebner, MA
Mrs J E Goodbourn, BA
Mrs D Hammond, MA, BA
Mrs K Ingram, BA
C G McNee, BA
Mrs C Morel-Bedford, BA
Dr L M Syme, BSc, MSc, DPhil
Mrs O P M M Thomas, Lic d'Anglais

Junior School

Headmaster: G R G Canning, BA

Deputy Headmaster: T C Lewis, CertEd

Music:
*Mrs E J Green, BMus, ARCM (*Director of Music – Academic & Choral*)
*S Hogg, ARAM, LRAM, GRSM, ARCM, Dip RAM, PGCE (*Director of Music – Performance*)
R G Appleyard, GBSM
C Druce, ABSM, GBSM, ARCM, ARCO, FRCO
K D Johnson, BMus
J P B McNamara, MA, PG Dip Perf, FRCO
P Montero, BMus
J J Sampson, BMus, ARCM

Physical Education:
*G A Tedstone, BEd (*Director of Sport*)
S R G Francis, BA
A M Jarvis (*Graduate Assistant*)
E Martin
M A Nasey, BEd, Masters SpL (*Director of Rugby*)
T D Pierce, BSc
H Venter
G M F Wade

Psychology:
*Miss N L Boyd, BSc

Religious & Philosophy:
*Revd A W Gough, BA
Revd M D Hewitt, BSc, BA
L D Eaton, MA, BA

Science:
G B Callan, BSc (*Chemistry*)
I S Dee, BSc (*Biology*)
A D Millington, BSc (*Physics*)
S J Cook, MSc, BSc
G J Field, MA
G N Frykman, MA
Dr C Gane, PhD, MPhys
C J Grant, BSc
Mrs P L Hughes, BSc
M E Lucas, MSc, BEng
H S N Moore, BSc
Dr C M L Nuttall, BSc, PhD
P A Snell, BSc
Dr D J Tchakhotine, BSc, PhD
Dr K Tudge, BSc
Dr B M Twohig-Howell, BSc, MSc, PhD
Mrs M Yates, BSc

Curriculum Support:
*Mrs L E Allan, MBA
Mrs K J Birch, BA
Mrs J Downes, BA
Mrs C M Fellows, MEd, BA
Ms M Harper, BA, MA

Mrs A J Appleyard, MA
Mrs C J Askwith, BA, MA
Mrs K Bull, BEd
Mrs R J Cowie, BEd
T W Hancock, BSc
Mrs O Hartwell, BA
O R Herringshaw, BA
Mrs H J Jackson, BEd
Mrs J P Jobburn, BA, PGCE

B M Kruze, BA
K Marshall, BEd
Dr S E Marshall, BSc, PhD
Miss H N Mellor, BA
Miss J Needham, BSc
Ms H D Sayers, MA Ed, BEd
Mrs J E Schalch, MA
Miss L C Sharp, BA
J Williamson, MSc, CertEd

Librarian: Ms A Best
Medical Officer: Dr H Mulder
Headmaster's PA: Mrs C Dixon
Admissions Registrar: Mrs V Tomblin
Marketing Manager: Mrs A Hartin
Alumni Relations Officer: Mrs A Douglas

Warwick School is an independent day and boarding school for boys. There is a Senior School (approx 988 boys), age range 11 to 18 years, and a Junior School (approx 250 boys), age range 7 to 11 (*see also Junior School entry in IAPS section*). There is boarding accommodation for about 60 boys.

The School Buildings and Grounds. The school is situated on the outskirts of Warwick town with fine views over the River Avon and Warwick Castle. In 1879 the school moved into its present buildings designed in a rococo Tudor style with 50 acres of playing fields attached to the school. Many buildings have been built over the years. There is a programme of continuous development. In the last few years this has improved and extended the boarding, indoor sports facilities, music, drama and teaching facilities, an ICT and Library Building, a Performing Arts Centre, Music Department and a state-of-the-art Science Centre. A new classroom block was completed in September 2008 and most recently The Halse Sports Pavilion was completed in March 2013. The Guy Nelson Hall is due to be completely renovated, beginning Spring 2015.

Admission is by entrance examination set by the School. Entry to Junior School is at the ages of 7, 8, 9 and 10. Entry to Senior School is at 11, 12, 13 and 16. The assessment at 11+ includes Non-Verbal Reasoning, English and Mathematics. The assessment at 13+ includes English, Maths, MFL, Science and VR. Sixth Form entry requires a minimum of 5 B grades at GCSE.

Curriculum. The aim of the school is to provide a broadly based education which allows pupils to achieve academic excellence. All pupils are encouraged to develop their individual talents to the full and to accept responsibility for themselves and others.

In the Junior School the curriculum aims to give a firm grounding in the National Curriculum foundation subjects English, Mathematics and Science. A range of other subjects such as History, Geography, Technology, French, IT and Religious Education are taught throughout the school by specialist subject teachers. French is taught throughout as is Art, Music and Physical Education.

In the Senior School the curriculum offers a range of options but there is a core curriculum of English, Mathematics, French and Science (including Physics, Chemistry and Biology as separate subjects) up to GCSE which all boys take in their fifth year. Virtually all boys continue into the Sixth Form where AS Levels are taken after one year and full A Levels after a further year. The curriculum is designed to give all boys a broad general education and to postpone any specialisation for as long as possible.

Games and other activities. Active interest in out of school activities is much encouraged. Winter games are rugby, hockey, cross-country and swimming. These are played in the Michaelmas and Lent Terms and our national reputation is strong throughout. Summer games are cricket, tennis and athletics. Badminton, basketball, clay pigeon shooting, golf, squash and volleyball are played throughout the year. There are fine sporting facilities in the Halse Sports Pavilion, including a 25m 6-lane pool, squash courts, state-of-the-art rock climbing wall, fitness suite and sports hall.

There are usually some 80 different clubs and societies active in school life. There is a CCF contingent (with Army and RAF sections) an outdoor activities group and a Voluntary Service Group linked with the local community. Other activities include drama, music, debating, and fencing.

Religious teaching. The Chapel Services and teaching are according to the Church of England, but there are always pupils of other denominations and race and for these other arrangements may be made. Pupils attend services during the week, and boarders and some day pupils the service on Sunday. The Chaplain prepares members of the school for Confirmation each year, the Confirmation Service taking place in the Lent Term.

Boarding. Senior School boys may be weekly or full boarders. Boarding can sometimes be arranged for day boys to accommodate short term parental requirements. There is also an opportunity for an extended day facility.

Fees per term (2014–2015). Senior School Tuition: £3,791; Boarding (in addition to Tuition): £4,299 (full); £3,791 (weekly). Junior School Tuition: £2,948–£3,749.

Scholarships. *Governors Scholarships* (11+, 12+, 13+, 16+) are available to reward academic excellence and talent. Scholarships are awarded up to the value of 20% of fees based on the results of the entrance examination and interview. For existing Sixth Formers, the scholarships are awarded based on GCSE results and school reports.

Sixth Form Science Scholarship: The Ogden Trust sponsors pupils of outstanding scientific ability to attend Warwick School in the Sixth Form. Awarded up to 100% of fees, funded jointly by Ogden Trust and Warwick School. For pupils educated entirely in a non-selective state school, achieving a minimum of 6 GCSEs at Grade A, including Physics and Mathematics. The successful candidate must study Mathematics and Physics at A Level and intend to read a Physics degree at university. Joint parental income should be less than £50K.

Governors Music Scholarships at 11+, 13+ and 16+ are awarded up to the value of 20% of fees based on musical ability and potential with a high level of achievement in the entrance examination.

Two *J M A Marshall Music Scholarships* are available to be awarded to boys entering Year 5 in the Junior School – 50% of the music tuition fees for two years for one instrument.

Two *Choral Scholarships*, each to the value of £1,500 per annum, may be awarded each year to boys aged between 7 and 11 years on 1st September, who are either entering or who are in attendance at Warwick Junior School and the Choir of St Mary's Church, Warwick.

Further details from the Admissions Registrar, Tel: 01926 776400, email: admissions@warwickschool.org.

Charitable status. Warwick Independent Schools Foundation is a Registered Charity, number 1088057. It exists to provide quality education for boys.

Wellingborough School

London Road, Wellingborough, Northamptonshire NN8 2BX

Tel: 01933 222427
Fax: 01933 271986
email: headmaster@wellingboroughschool.org
website: www.wellingboroughschool.org

Motto: *Salus in Arduis*

The endowment of this School was first set aside for charitable purposes in the year 1478. Further land, purchased from the Crown, was granted by Letters Patent in the reigns of Edward VI and Elizabeth I. The endowment was confirmed as being for educational purposes by an Order of the Lord Keeper of the Great Seal in 1595. The School moved to its present site in 1881 upon which new and improved buildings have from time to time been added.

The School offers day co-education for boys and girls from the age of 3 to 18. The School is firmly wedded to Christian principles, to equality of opportunity and the enrichment of individuals in the community. The School is divided into a Pre-Preparatory School (age 3–8: 169 pupils), the Preparatory School (age 8–13: 295 pupils) (*see also entry in IAPS section*), and the Senior School (age 13–18: 408 pupils).

Governors:
Dr J K Cox, MA, MB BChir, BA Hons (*Chairman*)
Mrs A Coles, MA (*Deputy Chairman*)
A W Bailey
T Baldry, FCA
D K Exham, MA, PGCE
J J H Higgins
Mrs D A Line, BA Hons, CA
N B Lyon, MA
S M Marriott (*Representative of the Old Wellingburian Club*)
Mrs P Perkins, OBE
P S Phillips, MA, FCA
A H Robbs
D A Waller, MA
C A Westley
P R Tyldesley

Bursar & Clerk to the Governors: C J P Evans

Headmaster: G R Bowe, BA Kent

Senior Deputy Heads:
Mrs S M Barnhurst, BSc Salford, MA Northampton (*Physics*)
Q Wiseman, BA Newcastle, PGCE London, BSA Roehampton

Master i/c Sixth Form Academic Progress: J R Gray, BSc Bangor (*Biology*)

Assistant Staff:
§ *Part-time*
[1] *Also teaches in the Preparatory School*

Miss J H Austin (*PGCE Trainee*)
M A Baddeley, BSc York (*Mathematics*)
Mrs S J Baxby, BA Northampton (*Head of Business Studies*)
Miss L Belford, BSc Lincoln (*Biology*)
[1]Mrs F J Burgess, BEd Exeter (*PE/Games, Head of PSHCE*)
Mrs L Burton, BSc Lincoln (*Biology*)
Ms R Burn, BA Hons Durham (*Head of Learning Support*)
§Mrs F Carlisle, BSc Warwick (*Psychology*)
[1]§Mrs R E Cowley, BA Manchester Metropolitan (*Design Technology*)
[1]Miss S M Curley, BA De Montfort (*English, Latin*)
[1]S L Egan, BEng Leicester (*Head of Design Technology*)
[1]§Mrs C Y Elwyn, Dip LIC (*French, Latin*)
P J Farley, BA York, MA Liverpool (*History, Politics*)
[1]Mrs S E Fellows, BA Birmingham (*French, Spanish*)
J M Furness-Gibbon, MA London, BA Worcester (*English*)
A R Gamble, BA St Edmund Hall Oxford (*Head of English*)
Mrs J C Hennessy, BA Leicester Polytechnic (*Head of Art*)
Dr A L Higginson, BSc, MPhil Essex, PhD UMIST (*Head of Science & Physics*)
S T Hill (*Chaplaincy Youth Worker*)
[1]L M Hilton, BSc Loughborough (*Director of Sport*)
Mrs H L Hodgson, BEng Liverpool (*Head of Mathematics*)
[1]Mrs A S Holley, BA Birmingham (*Head of Classics*)

Miss C E M Horry, BA Kent (*Art*)

Mrs K R Kenney, BA Hons Birmingham (*English*)

Miss S Kielty, BA Wales, MA Warwick (*Head of History*)

Miss B Lavin Campo, Licenciado en Filosofia y Letras Valladolid, Spain (*Spanish*)

Mrs B Lawson, BSc Loughborough (*Mathematics*)

Dr K M Loak-Chrisp, BSc, PhD Aston (*Chemistry*)

P J Lowe, BA Southampton (*Head of Geography*)

[1]P R Marshall, BA Wales, LRAM (*Director of Music*)

O J Marriott (*PGCE Trainee*)

C Martin-Sims, BSc Sussex, MSc Reading, BA Open University (*Head of Drama & Psychology*)

[1]§Ms J A Mason, BA Teesside (*Design Technology*)

§Mrs J Matthews (*Careers Coordinator*)

Mrs L J McAuley, BSc Glasgow (*Mathematics*)

Dr A S Monaghan, BSc Dundee, PhD Cambridge (*Chemistry, Physics, Biology*)

A G Peacock, BA Hons Trinity College Oxford, MA Lancaster (*History, RS*)

§Mrs L Peters (*PE & Games*)

Dr P J Phillips, BSc Portsmouth Polytechnic, PhD Warwick (*Physics*)

Miss L M Pickering, BA Warwick (*Politics, History*)

Mrs G M Rodgers, MA Newnham College Cambridge (*English*)

[1]§I Runnells, BA University College Northampton (*Assistant Director of Music*)

[1]Mrs C Stroud, Licence ès Lettres Université Sorbonne Nouvelle Paris (*Head of Modern Languages*)

M S C Sudra, MSc Leicester, BSc, Nottingham Trent (*Chemistry, Biology*)

Miss C T H Thomas, BA Leicester (*French*)

[1]Revd M J Walker, BA Lincoln College Oxford, Dip ES St John's College Durham (*Chaplain, Head of Religious Studies*)

P B Waugh, BEd Manchester Metropolitan (*IT Manager*)

A D Woodward, BSc City University (*Head of Economics*)

Mrs C L Woodward, BA Surrey Institute of Art & Design (*Art*)

Housemasters/Housemistresses:

Garne's House: D A Coombes, BA Liverpool John Moores

Platt's House: T J Fourie, MSc Port Elizabeth SA (*Mathematics*)

Fryer's House: R T Campbell, BA Auckland NZ (*Geography & Business Studies*)

Cripps' House: [1]K C M Hargreaves, Rose Bruford College of Speech & Drama (*Drama*)

Parker Steyne's: [1]G E Houghton, BA Durham (*PE/Games*)

Marsh House: Miss C S Irvin, BSc Loughborough (*PE/ Games, Head of Academic PE*)

Nevill House: Miss J M Livingstone, BA Queen's Belfast (*Geography*)

Weymouth House: Mrs H M Pattison, BSc King's College London (*Head of Biology*)

Headmaster's PA: Mrs J Freer

Senior School Registrar: Mrs Y Pullen

Music Department Administrator: Mrs E A Burleigh

PA to Deputy Heads: Mrs D Barrett

Officer Commanding CCF: Major S Garfirth

School Nurses:

Mrs D Barclay, RGN

Mrs P Bowden

Preparatory School:

Headmaster:

R J Mitchell, BEd College of St Paul's & St Mary's (*Life Skills PSHE, Games*)

(*prep-head@wellingboroughschool.org*)

Preparatory School Registrar: Mrs J Roberts

Deputy Headmaster: T J Gray, BEd London, Dip Ed (*Mathematics, Life Skills PSHE*)

Assistant Head – Pupils' Academic Development: Mrs A J White, BEd Leeds (*English, Life Skills PSHE, Games*)

Assistant Head – Pastoral Care: Mrs C Petrie, BSc Loughborough (*Games, Life Skills*)

Assistant Head – Teaching and Learning: Mrs K A Owen BSc Exeter

Club Presidents:

Jaguars: Mrs C L Whitaker, BA Brighton (*Games, Geography, PE, Drama*)

Panthers: C W Pickett, BCS Auckland University of Technology, PGCE Buckingham (*History, Games*)

Bears: P W Dennis, BA Oxford Brookes (*English, Spanish, History, Games*)

Tigers: Miss S C Allan, MA Cardiff (*English, Games, RS*)

Wolves: Mrs J Rowley-Burns, BSc Greenwich (*Head of Mathematics*)

Lions: S J Whitby, BEng Kingston, PGCE Leicester

Teaching Staff:

Mrs C Allen, SpLD Cert (*Learning Support*)

Mrs L A Barltrop, BA Hons, Dip RSA, NASENCo Northampton

Miss H J Clark, BA Hons Chester, PGCE Worcester

Mrs F J Drye, BA Wales (*Head of English, Editor of the Chronicle*)

A I Fordham, BSc Hons, Oxford Brookes, MRes, Open University, PhD, Open University

K B Gray, BSc Bangor (*Science, Games*)

S Groom, BA Northampton (*ICT, Games*)

N R Grove, MA Liverpool (*Scholarships and Enrichment, English, History*)

Miss A S Kingstone, BA University College Northampton (*Year 4 Teacher, History, Games*)

Mrs C L McDougall, BSc Leeds Polytechnic

Mrs L McMillan BSc Leeds Polytechnic (*Science*)

Mrs H F Lane, BA King's College, London

W Richardson, BEd Hons Leicester

Mrs R Roberts, BEd Hons Chester (*Head of Art*)

B J Russell, Fd BSc Northampton

Miss R J Sanders, MA Durham (*Year 4 Teacher, Religious Studies, English*)

Mrs A M Simmons, BA Stirling (*Mathematics, Life Skills PSHE*)

Mrs A J Staughton, BA Leeds Polytechnic

G Sutcliffe, BA Leicester, MPhil Birmingham

L Williams, MSc Brunel (*Head of PE, Geography, Games*)

Librarian: Mrs K Cooper, BA Aberystwyth

Preparatory School Headmaster's PA: Mrs T Billington

Preparatory School Registrar: Mrs J Roberts

Assistant to Assistant Heads: Mrs K Wesley

Pre-Preparatory School:

Headmistress: Miss J M Everett, BEd Froebel Institute, MA Heriot-Watt

Assistant Head (Curriculum): D C Popplewell, BA Warwick

Assistant Head (Pastoral): Mrs R M Girling, BEd Cambridge

Teaching Staff:

Mrs J C Bradford, BEd St John's College, York

Mrs J E M Espin, BA New Hall Cambridge

S Garfirth, DipRCM, ALCM

Mrs L Gillard, BA QTS Northampton

Mrs E Jakeman, BEd Worcester College

Mrs S A Jamieson, BA University College Northampton

Mrs J Mellor, BEd Kingston

Miss K Moody, BA UEA

Mrs L C Potter, BA Leeds

Mrs C H Waite, BEd Ripon and York St John

Nursery:

Mrs S M Sandall, Adv Dip Early Years Ed & NNEB Solihull Technical College

Mrs M Gutteridge, NNEB Southfields College

Mrs H Cockbill, West Bridgford College of FE

Miss D Herbert, NVQ Early Years Care & Education Level 3

Teaching Assistants:

Mrs M E Campbell, BTEC Art Diploma Tresham College

Miss B Gosling, NNEB Northampton College

Mrs K Harris, NNEB Tresham Institute

Mrs A Martin, NNEB Stoke on Trent College

Mrs K Robson, NNEB CACHE

Mrs C Ward, NNEB Northampton College

Miss A M Ystenes, NNEB Nene College

Sports Coach: Miss S Peters

IT Coordinator: Ms M Mannion

PA to Headmistress: Miss M Riches

Wellingborough is situated 63 miles from London, 10 miles east of Northampton. Close to the main railway line from St Pancras to Leicester and Sheffield, it is served by an excellent network of motorways and dual carriageways connecting the A1, A14 and the M1.

Buildings and Organisation. The School occupies a fine site on the south of the town, and stands in its own grounds of 45 acres. In the Senior School there are five boys' houses and three girls' houses, organised on boarding house lines. Each house has about 45 pupils. The Sixth Form numbers around 140 pupils, 90% of whom go directly to higher education.

Admission at 13+ for boys and girls is by means of entry tests and interview or the Common Entrance Examination from preparatory schools. Direct entry into the Sixth Form is on the basis of an interview, school report and likely GCSE results confirmed before entry. Please note that A Level courses begin in June after GCSE examinations.

The Preparatory School, while sharing some of the facilities of the Senior School, has its own buildings and classrooms on the east side of the campus. In recent years work has been completed on a large new library, incorporating a computer research area, fiction and non-fiction working areas, classroom and science laboratory, with up-to-date facilities and IT throughout. The Pre-Preparatory School occupies its own modern purpose-built buildings which have been substantially refurbished and extended.

The main school buildings include an ICT study centre, a library, assembly hall, careers room, chapel, and three classroom blocks including seven newly refurbished science laboratories and the information technology department. There is a design technology centre, music school, modern languages centre, sports hall, 2 art buildings and central dining hall.

Religion. Religious teaching is according to the Church of England. Pupils attend a mixture of morning prayers and longer services on weekdays, and a morning service on some Sundays during term. The Chaplain prepares members of the School for confirmation each year, the confirmation service taking place in the Lent Term.

Curriculum. In the Pre-Preparatory School and the Preparatory School the curriculum is an enriched version of the National Curriculum. French, Latin and Spanish are also taught in the Preparatory School.

In the first year of the Senior School, pupils follow a core curriculum in English, Mathematics, French, Physics, Chemistry, Biology, History, Geography, Design Technology, Art, Music, RE, Information Technology and PE. Spanish and Latin are both options in this year. GCSE courses are offered in English, English Literature, French, Mathematics and dual award sciences. Options include separate Sciences, Latin, Spanish, History, Geography, Art, Design Technology, Music, Drama, PE and Religious Studies.

The following subjects are offered for A Level examination: Art and Design, Biology, Business Studies, Chemistry, Design Technology, Economics, English Literature, French,

Spanish, Geography, History, Mathematics and Further Mathematics, Music, PE, Physics, Politics and Psychology. Information Technology, Drama, English Language and Religious Studies are offered as freestanding AS Levels.

Music, Drama, Art, Design. The Music School contains a central teaching hall, a second newly refurbished teaching room and several practice rooms. Professional tuition is given on all instruments and there are chapel and concert choirs, junior and senior bands and a school orchestra.

Concerts, school and house drama productions and lectures are held in the School Hall, which has well-equipped stage facilities. The Richard Gent Design Centre offers workshops and studies for design technology and ceramics. The highly successful Two-Dimensional Art Department has its own dedicated building. Pupils are encouraged to make full use of these facilities in their spare time.

Sport. The playing fields, over 40 acres in extent, are used for the main boys' sports of rugby, soccer and cricket and hockey and netball for girls; cross country, athletics, and tennis are also highly popular. The school site also boasts a nine-hole golf course, astroturf pitch, five all-weather tennis courts, two squash courts, shooting range, gymnasium and sports hall. The latter has four badminton courts, indoor cricket nets and facilities for fencing, table tennis, basketball and dedicated fitness suite.

Other Activities. After their first term in the Senior School pupils join the Combined Cadet Force (RN, Army, Commando or RAF Section) until the end of Year 10 at least. Training is given in first aid, map reading and orienteering, and camping expeditions take place at weekends. There is an annual CCF camp and there are opportunities for band training, open range shooting, REME work, canoeing and sailing. The Duke of Edinburgh's Award Scheme is also a very popular option for older pupils.

A wide range of extra-curricular interests is available through various societies and clubs. Pupils may also take part in local community service work.

Careers. Guidance is available to all pupils on further education and careers prospects through the Head of Careers and other members of staff. The School is a member of the Independent Schools Careers Organisation.

Scholarships and Bursaries. Foundation scholarships are offered to external candidates for entry to the Preparatory School at 11+. The examination is held in January and entries are required by the end of December.

At 13+ entrance scholarships are offered to pupils entering the Senior School. The examination is held in January.

At 16+ Sixth Form academic scholarships are offered.

Music, Drama, Art and Sports scholarships are available at 13+ and 16+. An All-Rounder Scholarship is also available at 13+.

The Nevill Trust Sixth Form Bursary is awarded to pupils currently attending a Northamptonshire state school.

Bursaries are available, on a means-tested basis (subject to annual review), to support those pupils who would benefit from a Wellingborough education but whose families are unable to afford the full fees. Means-tested Bursaries may also be available to augment Scholarships.

Further details and application forms for all the above awards may be obtained from the Registrar.

Fees per term (2014–2015). Senior School: £4,473 (Years 12–13), £4,599 (Years 9–11); Preparatory School: £4,293 (Years 7–8), £4,188 (Years 4–6); Pre-Preparatory School: £2,586–£2,705 (reduced rates are offered for children in Nursery Class not attending all sessions and children from age 3–5 are eligible for the Government's Early Years Funding). Fees include most extras apart from instrumental lessons (termly payment), public examination fees and books.

Admission. Applications should be made to the Registrar for entry of boys and girls at 13+ and for direct entry into the Sixth Form. Enquiries concerning entries between the ages of 3 and 7 should be addressed to the Pre-Prep School Registrar, and entries between the ages of 8 and 12 to the Registrar of the Preparatory School.

Term of Entry. New pupils are accepted at the beginning of any term. The largest entry is in September each year.

Old Wellingburian Club. All former pupils who have spent at least one year in the School are eligible for membership. Correspondence should be addressed to the OW Club Secretary at the School.

Charitable status. Wellingborough School is a Registered Charity, number 1101485. It exists to provide education for boys and girls from the age of 3 to 18.

Wellington College

Duke's Ride, Crowthorne, Berkshire RG45 7PU
Tel: The Master: 01344 444101
        Director of Admissions: 01344 444013
        Group Finance Director & Bursar: 01344 444020
        Reception: 01344 444000
Fax: 01344 444002
email: info@wellingtoncollege.org.uk
website: www.wellingtoncollege.org.uk
Twitter: @WellingtonUK
Facebook: /WellingtonCollege

The College was founded by public subscription as a memorial to the Great Duke. It was granted its Royal Charter in 1853 and took its first pupils in 1859. The school is set in a woodland estate of 400 acres.

Visitor: Her Majesty The Queen

President: HRH The Duke of Kent, KG, GCMG, GCVO, ADC, DL

Vice-President & Chairman of Governors: Sir Michael Rake

Ex officio Governors:
The Archbishop of Canterbury, FBA, DD, DPhil, MA
The Duke of Wellington, KG, LVO, OBE, MC, DL

Governors:
P G C Mallinson, BA, MBA
Mrs O Deighton
Dr R Groves, BA, PhD
Dr P J A Frankopan, MA, DPhil, FRSA
Dr E M Sidwell, CBE, BSc Hons, PhD, FRSA, FRGS
T B Bunting, MA
R Perrins, BSc Hons, ACA
H W Veary, BA, FCA
Mrs M Chaundler, OBE
The Rt Hon The Lord Strathclyde, CH
Ron Dennis, CBE
T Cookson, MA
E Chaplin, CMG, OBE
Air Chief Marshall the Lord Stirrup, KG, GCB, AFC
R Rudd
D Ritchie, FCA
N Howard-Jones

Master: **A F Seldon**, MA, PhD, MBA, FRSA, FRHistS

Second Master: R I H B Dyer, BA
Director of Admissions: J E L Dahl, MA
Deputy (Academic): M J Oakman, BA
Deputy (Organisation): Dr A J Dunn, MA, DPhil
Deputy (Pastoral & Well-being): Mrs D A Lynch, BSc
Deputy (Performance): D Walker, BSc
Assistant Head (Co-curricular): Mrs C J Henderson, BA
Assistant Head (Alumni): I M Henderson, BA
Assistant Head (Eagle House): N C Lunnon, BSc

Assistant Staff:
* *Head of Department/Year*
† *Housemaster/mistress*

J D Oakes, ARCM
J J Breen, MA
T J Head, BA
A R Dewes, MA
M Farrington, BSc, MSc, PhD
Dr E M Hood, BSc, PhD
*J C Rawlinson, BSc
†C M Oliphant-Callum, MA
*S R J Williamson, MA, FRCO
Ms S A Lang, BA
S D Laverack, BSc, PhD
*Mrs C J Blunden-Lee, BA
Mrs D E Cook, BA
*M J D Ellwood, BEd
†J S White, BA
B A Bayman, BA
I Frayne, BSc
G I Woodrow, MA
*S C D Gutteridge, MA
*C B Ewart, MA
D Wilson, MA
*I R Morris, BA
Mrs K J Hamilton, BA
*S J Allcock, BA
Mrs B C Carr, BA
Mrs Y Tang, MA
Dr W Heathcote, MPhys, DPhil
*Dr D A James, MA, PhD
*G J Williams, MA
Mrs K E Granville-Chapman, BA
Mrs S J Henwood, GRSM Hons
S A S Owen, BA
*Mrs J M Grillo, BEd
Dr R S Kirkham, MA, PhD
*Dr J L Chapman, PhD, BSc
†Miss H Johnson, BA
Miss K Murphy, BSc
†Mrs S Y N Jobson, Lic d'Anglais, Dip d'Étude IFI
*S Shortland, BEd, MSc
†Mrs R E Loaring, BSc
*Dr R J Cromarty, MA, PhD
†E B R Venables, BA
†J Giannikas, BA
B P Lewsley, BA
Miss C L Edwards, BA
†K J Brennan, BA
†G D Franklin, BA
X Iles, BA
Dr J O Seldon, MA, DPhil
G D Carr
D Quinlivan-Brewer, BMus Hons, PGDip RCM
S J Kirkham, BA
†T C Hicks, BA
*H Macgregor, BA
*J R Heal, BA
B T Attenborough, BA
Mrs P P Gutteridge, MA
*Dr D Rosen, MSc, DPhil

*Dr J O'Loughlin, MSc, PhD
*A J Sproat, BA
M E Denhart, BA
*Mrs G E Elliott, BA
D M Townley, MChem
†I J Sutcliffe, MA, MBA
†P W Thistlethwaite, BA, MSt
Miss A E Brown, BEd
S A Farrell, BA
†A M Wilkinson, BA
*R H Atherton, BSc, MPhil
†Mrs M V Ogilvie, Lic d'Anglais
Mrs A J E Campion, MA
C R Mitchell, BEng
*Mrs G Vonchek, BEd, Cert TEFL, Cert IELTS
†R I Clarke, BA
*D Zeqiri, BA, MSc
†Miss J C Baldwin, BA
Miss E J Beardmore, BA
Mrs E J Bidston, BA
G A Bough, BSc
D M G Clements
R Drummond, BA
Mrs D Hathaway, BSc
N R Carpenter, BSc
*R J A Macpherson, MSc
*Miss H-J Stubbings, BA
K Tkachuk, BA, MSc
*Miss R R Trafford, MA
R S Tulley, BA, BSc
*T F C Wayman, MPhil
†Mrs J C Wayman, BA
Mrs N Ma, MA
Miss A A Carlisle, BA
D Clarke, BA, MSc
C N E Hendrick, MA
*Dr J M Hobbs, BA, PhD
*J C Kinniburgh, BA, MSc
Dr E Lambert, BSc, PhD
*E A S Lewis, BA
Mrs K A Mitchell, MSc
*A P Mogford, MA
Miss A Omell, BSc
Miss A E Wilson, BA
I Kurgansky, BA
*E Twohig, BEd, MA
†D R Edwards, BA
W Abdulla, BMath
J K Bough, MA
Mrs N J R Davison, BA
F J Edmunds, BSc
Mrs E R Farrell
Mrs V Giannikas, BSc
*Mrs C I Goldsmith, MSc
S C J Hitchings, BA
S R Laing, MSc
Dr R S Lexton, BA, MPhil
Miss E F Morley, BA
R A B Murphy, BA
S E Quintavalle, BA
E A C Rattray, BA
J P F Richards, BA, MFA
Miss A T Rubin, BA
G Wells, BA

Dr H W Y Wright, BSc, PhD
Ms A Gomez, BA
Mrs A A Jennings-Heal, BA, MEd
M L Pattie, MA
*Mrs J Sutcliffe, BA
Ms D J Barron, BA
W H Bickford-Smith, BA
Ms E C Bradley, BA
Miss H A Burn, BSc
Ms S L F Candappa, BSc
N M Casasanto, BA
Ms S L Culkin, BA
G R F de Voil, BA
C B H Dell, BSc
†Mrs E A Fisher, BA
Miss S B Forster, BSc
Dr V E M Gardner, BA, MLitt, DPhil
Miss R A Haycox, BSc
Miss E N Hellegouarch, Dip d'Etudes, LLCE, Bretagne Sud

Ms R C Hewes, BA
Miss J W H Ho, BA
Miss R V Humphries, BA
E D Jones, BA, MSc
Miss C L Keep, BA
T C Kirby, BA, MSt
S E Larsen, BSc, MEd
Miss C E Le Bihan, Double Licence, Provence
N D Light, MA
K J Lomax, BA
Mrs V E M Macgregor, MA
T R Macleod, BA
J K R McDonald, BSc
Ms A E R Morse, BA
K Mtindi
O J Peat, BA
K G Reesby, BSc
S F Roundell, MA
P H Williams, BSc
Ms C A Willis, BA

plus 50 visiting instrumental teachers

Senior Chaplain: The Revd T W G Novis, BA, MDiv

Houses and Housemasters/mistresses:
Anglesey: Mrs R E Loaring
Apsley: Miss H Johnson and P W Thistlethwaite
Apsley Junior: Mrs S Y N Jobson
Benson: T C Hicks
Beresford: G D Franklin
Blücher: K J Brennan
Combermere: Mrs E A Fisher
Hardinge: C M Oliphant-Callum
Hill: J Giannikas
Hopetoun: Mrs M V Ogilvie
Lynedoch: D R Edwards
Murray: I J Sutcliffe
Orange: Mrs J C Wayman
Picton: R I Clarke
Raglan: A M Wilkinson
Stanley: E B R Venables
Talbot: J S White
Wellesley: Miss J C Baldwin

CC CCF: I Frayne, BSc
Group Finance Director & Bursar: S J Crouch, BA Oxon, ACA
Director of Finance: P F Thompson, MA, ACMA
Works & Estates Bursar: G Burbidge, FCIOB, MCIOSH
Operations Bursar: S J Blosse
Development Director: E J Schneider
Medical Officer: A Sachdev, MB ChB, CFP, D Pall Med
Health Centre Sister: Mrs B J Gilbert
Registrar: Mrs L Peate, BSc
EA to the Master: Mrs A Reed
PA to the Second Master: Miss S Taylor
Bursary Assistant: Mrs L J Thompson

Wellington College, which was founded as a memorial to the Duke of Wellington more than 150 years ago, builds upon its honourable past while adapting its values and traditions for the Twenty-First Century in a dynamic and sustainable way. Our fusion of originality and innovation with tradition and history produces a uniquely inspiring education. We seek to open the hearts and minds of all at Wellington thereby making it one of Britain's and the world's most inspiring co-educational schools for boarding and day pupils. We want each and every one of our pupils to learn, to achieve and to be happy. To become, in fact, the very best versions of themselves.

We do this by providing a transformative educational experience, developing to the full each student's "eight aptitudes": (logical, linguistic, cultural, physical, social, personal, spiritual and moral). Our curriculum is challenging, ambitious and global. We offer the IB Diploma alongside A Level and GCSE.

Wellington has a Christian foundation, which celebrates and respects children from all religious faiths and backgrounds. A commitment to leadership, service and an international outlook lie at the heart of Wellington which has, at its core, values chosen by the whole community: *Courage – Integrity – Respect – Kindness – Responsibility*.

Organisation. There are approximately 1,045 pupils, with 635 boys and 410 girls, spread across all age groups.

All pupils belong to one of seventeen Houses, seven of which are located in the main College buildings and ten in the grounds. Fifteen of the Houses accommodate the 80%+ who board at Wellington as well as a handful of day pupils. There are also two specific day Houses, one each for girls and for boys. 13+ boarders share rooms in their first year, and may do so in a second or third year, but then move on to their own room. There is a central dining hall with modern kitchens and serveries. Meals are taken here on a cafeteria basis by most of the pupils although some Houses outside the main buildings have their own dining facilities. The V&A café is also open during school hours for drinks and snacks. The school has its own Medical Officer and a 9-bed Health Centre constantly staffed by fully-qualified nurses. All Houses have their own tutors, House Matrons and domestic team, which are led by the Housemaster or Housemistress.

Academic Work. Academic standards are higher than they have ever been in the College's history. In 2014, 95% of A Level grades were A*–B and over 53% of GCSE grades were A*, both College records. Wellington was also the top large IB school in the UK for its stunning IB Diploma results with the average score being 40 and with 10% of candidates securing a perfect 45 points. Almost fifty Wellingtonians have taken up places at Oxford and Cambridge in the past three years and, on average, between 15–20 leavers now enter Ivy League universities in the US each year.

Wellington's curriculum is firmly grounded in the school's commitment to developing the full range of every pupil's inherent aptitudes. The academic curriculum is designed to give pupils a broad and rounded education while allowing them maximum opportunity to develop their individual interests and strengths through their chosen fields of specialist study.

Pupils in the Third Form from September 2015 will take a Wellington designed programme offering both breadth and depth in eight key learning areas: Mathematics, Science, English, Modern and Classical Languages, Humanities, the Arts, Technology and Physical Education. The curriculum accentuates personal enquiry, independent study, internationalism and social responsibility, with all courses emphasising the links between subjects and between school and the outside world. The curriculum, tailored by Wellington College's staff to meet the aspirations of an academically-gifted intake, is varied and stimulating, offering rich breadth and depth. It provides an excellent transition between prep schools and the middle years at Wellington, whilst developing strong cross-curricular links and study skills. All Third Form pupils also pursue a super-curriculum, designed to develop their intellectual curiosity and explore subjects like Philosophy, Ethics, Politics, Economics and History of Art, which are not found on the conventional curriculum at this age. Following their initial experience of Wellington, pupils entering the Fourth Form from September 2016 will choose a single curriculum combining the more traditional programme of GCSEs and IGCSEs with a number of bespoke Wellington designed courses. This integrated curriculum will ensure both breadth and rigour in the middle school curriculum.

In the Sixth Form, pupils have the option to study the International Baccalaureate Diploma Programme, an increasingly popular choice, or a wide range of AS and A2 Level choices is available. These include all the usual combinations but at least one-third of our pupils do a combined Arts/Science grouping.

Facilities. Most work takes place in modern specialist blocks near to the main buildings. The Queen's Court building also contains a theatre. The Science laboratories are numerous and the Kent Building houses well-equipped Design & Technology and Information Technology centres. A new Art School and Physics laboratories have been built. A new Modern Languages block is now open with the Mandarin Centre across the road. The old Art School in the main buildings has been converted into a new lecture and conference room. A brand new, state-of-the-art, digital library was opened in September 2012 and this is complemented by the learning and social areas of the Water Library and Selangor Court. The College's sporting facilities include two swimming pools; two plans are in place to build a STEM building (science, technology, engineering, maths) and a new Performing Arts Centre.

Enrichment Activities. Personal enrichment is an imperative at Wellington and each student takes part in a range of activities that broaden and refine their education. Such Enrichment is structured within the eight aptitudes of learning with dedicated time on a Monday, Wednesday and Friday. There are some fifty-two clubs, societies and other Enrichment activities which include Archery, Ancient Hebrew, Mandarin, Meditation, Mountain Biking, Noble Rot (wine-tasting), Photography, Model United Nations, Petrol Heads, Food for Thought, Bush Craft, Law Society, Dance Classes, Bardophile, Film Society, Creative Writing and Understanding Disability. All pupils on arrival join the Junior Society which introduces them to a wide variety of activities. A Creative Writing Group meets regularly; two literary magazines are produced by pupils: The Wellingtonian and South Front and there are a number of other pupil-led magazines specific to particular subject areas.

Art, Music, Dance and Drama are outstanding. There are regular visiting lecturers on a variety of topics, an Artist in Residence, and masterclasses in Art, Music/Drama and Literature. The range of performance, the ambition and the comprehensive nature of Wellington's artistic programme are particular features. Wellington is particularly proud of its all-male Physical Theatre team – who perform a mixture of Street and acrobatic inspired dance, its excellent Chapel choir and its newly-established musical improvisation group: "Waiting for the Call" who were a runaway success in the annual Wellington Edinburgh Fringe run.

The school has built upon its historic legacy of leadership, dating back to the First Duke of Wellington, and has established programmes to offer each pupil training and opportunities in leadership throughout their time at the College. The College runs several annual inter-schools conferences on leadership and is currently working with the Government to develop a nationwide character-building, leadership training programme. This emphasis on building character and leadership skills is complemented by Wellington's well-being curriculum which teaches pupils how to flourish. In this, as in so many areas, Wellington is pioneering. Wellington has been a Round Square school since 1995; membership of the Round Square organisation is a fundamental part of Wellington's holistic approach to education. Partnership with over seventy schools worldwide allows us to pursue our aim to produce compassionate global citizens of the future.

Sport. At Wellington our aim is to provide a sports programme based on enjoyment, learning and performance. We believe in the development of the whole child, the fostering of an 'active life' philosophy and the promotion of a lifetime

investment in sport and physical activity. We seek to establish a sporting ethos that is linked to the College's well-being and leadership programmes and the 'eight aptitudes'.

Wellington's sporting reputation continues to thrive. The school has a national reputation for prowess in a number of sports, particularly in rugby, hockey, cricket, netball, shooting, swimming, athletics, rackets, triathlon, squash, golf, riding and polo. There are numerous opportunities for pupils to represent the College in teams across a wide range of competitive sports as well as recreational activities, all of which are supported by the outstanding College facilities. These include over 80 acres of playing fields, two all-weather pitches for hockey and all-weather tennis courts. There is a sports complex which incorporates a rackets court, five squash courts, an indoor pool, a large sports hall and a spectacular sports pavilion. The main sports centre caters for a wide variety of indoor games as well as specialist weight training and conditioning rooms, dance studios and a rock climbing area. An outstanding nine-hole golf course was opened in September 2001 and is enjoyed by many in the community. The traditional pattern of boys' sport is rugby (we regularly field up to 20 XVs) in the Michaelmas Term, hockey, football and cross country in the Lent Term and cricket, athletics, tennis and swimming in the Summer. For the girls, hockey has been the main sport in the Michaelmas Term, with netball in the Lent and cricket, rounders, athletics, tennis and swimming in the Summer. There is also the opportunity for girls to play lacrosse competitively. Recently sporting options throughout the school have been expanded and many other sports have been made available as a first or second choice option for pupils which include squash, basketball, tennis, sailing, football, rugby 7s, triathlon, fencing, karate, badminton, swimming, cross-country and a variety of fitness and health-related activities. Wellington College's coaching philosophy is continuously evolving; however, it is based around some core principles that our staff firmly believe in. We aim to provide pupils with a transformative experience, using a variety of methods to help individuals to achieve their personal sporting aspirations. Our vision is to create the best possible "safe, friendly and challenging" environment for our pupils, which in turn promotes enjoyment, learning and performance. We believe in a player-centred approach to coaching which encourages pupils to think for themselves and helps to raise the individual's self-awareness. All of our staff are regarded as high quality "people coaches".

Admission to the School. Most pupils enter the school in September when they are between 13 and 14 years of age. There are occasionally places available for pupils at 14+. Around 40 pupils also join the College for the Sixth Form. Registrations (with £200 fee) should be addressed to the Registrar, or in the case of Foundationers, to the Bursar. Those registered for 13+ entry (by 31st December of Year 6) sit the ISEB Common Pre-Test and, if sufficiently strong academically or in other areas (e.g. sport, music), are invited for an assessment day (usually in the first term of Year 7). Those who are successful are then offered a conditional place subject to satisfactory results in Scholarship, Common Entrance or other entry exams. A Waiting List also operates. Where appropriate, an overseas deposit is also payable.

Scholarships. There is a wide range of 13+ Scholarships and Exhibitions offered – Academic, Music, Art, DT, Drama, Dance and Sports. Details are shown on the website and in a separate booklet available from Admissions. Candidates for non-academic awards must satisfy our general entry requirements. Scholarships may be complemented by a means-tested bursary where the financial situation of the parents makes this appropriate. Candidates must be under 14 on 1st September in the calendar year in which they sit the examination.

For pupils entering at 16+ there is a similar range of awards across the disciplines.

Bursaries. Foundation places are available to applicants who are sons or daughters of deceased military servicemen and servicewomen and of others who have died in acts of selfless bravery. The Prince Albert Society, launched in April 2012, also provides means-tested bursary places, up to 100% of fees. More details can be obtained from the Development Office.

Fees per term (2014–2015). Boarders £11,375, Day (in boarding House) £9,600, Day £8,350. Separate charges totalling £257.50 per instrument are made for musical tuition (10 lessons). The school runs an attractive fees in advance scheme for parents with capital sums available.

Old Wellingtonian Society. The Society's primary role is to provide career networking and mentoring support for sixth formers and alumni of all ages through Career Opportunity Groups in 19 sectors of employment. In addition, the Society has 26 branches in 19 countries, clubs representing 13 different sports, around 8,500 members (with an increasing proportion of girls) and a Secretary based at College (Tel: 01344 444127; email: gros@wellingtoncollege.org.uk; website: www.owsociety.co.uk).

The Wellington Group. A significant feature of Wellington is its outward-looking, expansive approach to education. Wellington College Tianjin, Wellington College Shanghai, the Wellington Academy in Wiltshire and Eagle House prep school all offer our pupils numerous opportunities to learn with others and to engage in partnership activities. This, combined with our extensive lectures and conference programme which culminates in the annual Sunday Times/Wellington College Education Festival, reflects our commitment to lifelong learning and to leading educational debate in the country.

Charitable status. Wellington College is a Registered Charity, number 309093. It exists to provide education for boys and girls aged 13–18.

Wellington School

Wellington, Somerset TA21 8NT
Tel: 01823 668800
Fax: 01823 668844
email: admissions@wellingtonschool.org.uk
website: www.wellington-school.org.uk

Motto: *Nisi dominus frustra*

Founded in 1837, Wellington School is a co-educational, academically selective school providing a friendly, disciplined environment and a wide range of co-curricular opportunities.

Governing Body:

Chairman: P H Nunnerley, BA, FCIB
Deputy Chairman: J Knowles

Miss S Adams	B McDowell
L Dodds	K Phillips
J P Elder	J Richards
Mrs A Govey	Cllr V Stock-Williams
Mrs T Humphreys	Mrs S Vigus-Hollingsworth
Prof L la Velle	Mrs L Wyeth
Dr D Lungley	Mrs A Wilson

Headmaster: **H W F Price**, MA

Senior Deputy Head: Dr A J Daniel, BSc, MA, PhD, PGCE
Deputy Head (*Pastoral*): J Hallows, BSc, PGCE

Academic Staff:

A Anderson, BA	Mrs A E Bazley, BEd
G J W Arnold, BSc	J F Bird, BA
C A Askew, BA	P J Buckingham, BA, MA
D Bareham	Mrs L Burton, BA

Miss H Byrne	J Leonard, BA
A R Carson, BSc	Mrs L E Leonard, BA
Mr J Caulfield, BA	Miss R L Marsden, BA
Mr M Charlton, MA	R Marsh, BA
D A Colclough, BSc	Miss S Middleton, BA
Miss M Collins, BA, MA	D Millington, BA, MSc
Mrs R Davies, BA	Mrs A D Musgrove, MA,
Mrs S C Davis	MBA
Mrs S A Dean, BA	A Phillips, BSc
M E Downes, BSc	N Renyard, MSc
Mrs S D'Rozario	M H Richards, BEd
T Fasham	Mrs V K Richardson, BSc
Dr P T Galley, BSc, PhD	N Ridgway, BSc
Mrs J Gannon, BSc	Miss L A Rowe, BSc
A Garcia, CertEd	Mrs H J Salter, BA
W Garrett, BA	A C Shaw, BA, MSc
Mr C Hamilton, MChem	Mrs R Shaw, LTCL
Mrs C Harris, BA	J P W Shepherd, MA
The Revd J P Hellier, BD,	N S Smith, BSc
AKC, DipRE, CF	R E Stevens, BSocSc
T J Hill, BA	A W Stevenson, MA
Miss F E Hobday, MA	Mrs L Tabb, BSc
Dr K A Hodson, BA, MA	Mrs C Thorpe, LLB
Mrs M Jago, BA	Miss S F L Toase, BSc,
S W James, BA	MIBiol
Dr A R Jolliffe, BA, MA,	A J Trewhella, BA, ARCO
DPhil	Dr W Vacani, BA, PhD
Miss A Jones	Mrs F Vyse, BSc
C G D Jones, BSc, CChem,	N H Vyse, MA
MRCS	A Wilson, BA
S Jones, BSc	M Wilson, BA
Mrs T Kaya, BA, TESOL	Mrs F Wreford, BA

Bursar: T D Williams, BA, FCCA
Registrar: Mrs R Langdon, BSc
Medical Officer: Dr R Yates

Situation. Located on the southern edge of Wellington, at the foot of the Blackdown Hills, this fully co-educational School is equidistant from Tiverton Parkway and Taunton Railway Stations. The M5 approach road (Junction 26) is within a mile. Currently there are 700 pupils in the Lower and Senior Schools (11–18 years), of whom 20% board.

Buildings. The School has witnessed an extensive building programme over the last twenty years, the new buildings having been carefully and tastefully blended in with existing architecture.

Most recent buildings include the John Kendall-Carpenter Science Centre with its state-of-the-art laboratories and lecture theatre, a multimillion pound sports complex which opened in 2002, a purpose-built Junior School and a new classroom block and examination hall. Major improvements to Performing Arts facilities, including a new foyer and theatre space, were completed in 2010.

Grounds. There are 29 acres of playing fields as well as a floodlit all-weather hockey pitch, squash courts, an indoor swimming pool and a climbing wall.

Houses. There are separate Houses for boys and girls, and for Seniors and Lowers. All Houses have their own changing, work and recreational facilities.

There is a central Dining Hall and all meals are served on a cafeteria basis. The School also has its own well equipped laundry.

There is a fully equipped Health Centre, with a trained staff under the direction of the School Medical Officer.

Academic Organisation. The School is divided into the Upper School (Year 9–Sixth Form) and the Lower School (Years 7 and 8). The Junior School (Nursery–Year 6) is on a separate, adjoining campus.

Most pupils enter the School at Year 7 or 9. The curriculum in Years 7, 8 and 9 is designed to allow pupils to develop the skills needed to succeed at GCSE and features a good range of practical and more academic subjects including Latin. At GCSE all pupils study English, English Literature, Mathematics and a Short Course in Religious Education as well as a Modern Foreign Language and a further five or six subjects. Pupils have a free choice of studying three sciences separately or as Dual Award Science. The Mathematics and Science courses lead to IGCSE qualifications. The most able mathematicians take IGCSE at the end of Year 10 before taking Additional Mathematics in Year 11. Students have a free choice from a wide range of subjects in the Sixth Form: most start on 4 AS Levels before reducing to 3 A2 courses. A system of grades every four weeks and tutor groups ensure that academic monitoring of pupils is supportive and effective.

Religious Education is part of the curriculum throughout the School. The School is Christian in tradition and there is a short Act of Worship in the School Chapel on each weekday with a longer Sunday service. The content and form of these services are based on contemporary Anglican procedures. Attendance is expected although sensitivity is shown towards pupils of other faiths for whom alternative provision can be made.

Music. Tuition is available on all orchestral instruments, as well as piano, organ, drum kit and percussion, classical and electric guitars and voice. The department consists of 3 full-time, 2 part-time and 25 specialist instrumental staff. Facilities include a fine Steinway model D Concert Grand Piano and there is a large Rodgers Digital Organ in the Chapel. Some 30 ensembles rehearse each week, giving plentiful opportunities to performers of all ages and all instruments. The department currently runs 7 choirs of various kinds and styles from the renowned Chapel Choir to the lighter sounds of Girlforce9. Concerts of all kinds take place throughout each term and the Wellington Professional Concerts Series bring world class musicians to the School to give recitals and masterclasses. The 'Full Circle' series invites former pupils who have pursued Music to return and perform at the School. Pupils are entered for ABRSM, Trinity Guildhall and Rockschool exams each term.

Physical Education and Games. All pupils play games regularly, unless exempt for medical reasons. Physical Education, which is also part of the curriculum for Years 7 to 11, takes place in the Sports Complex. All pupils learn to swim and are given the opportunity to take part in as many sports as possible. In the winter term, rugby and hockey are the main sports; in the spring term hockey, netball and cross-country running; in the summer term athletics, cricket, tennis, swimming and rounders. Team practices take place throughout the week with matches on Saturday afternoons. The school has a specialist fencing teacher and the Sports Complex houses a purpose-built fencing salle.

Out of School and CCF Activities. All pupils from the Year 10 upwards either join the large CCF contingent, with army, naval and RAF sections, or are engaged in other activities on a weekly basis, ranging from community services and conservation, to gardening and stage crew. Outward Bound Activities, both within the CCF and as part of the flourishing Duke of Edinburgh's Award Scheme, are very popular, with many trips organised. The CCF also has a highly respected Corps of Drums, which frequently features in local ceremonial events. Societies, in addition to the above, include art, chess and drama at various levels, cookery, computing and others.

Careers. A complete careers guidance service is offered in a well-equipped suite of Careers Rooms.

Admission. Entrance exam for Year 7. Interviews for Year 8 and above. There is a registration fee of £50 for all pupils and a refundable deposit of £500.

Scholarships and Bursaries. A significant number of academic and sport, drama and art and design scholarships are offered each year for entry at 11+ and 13+. Music scholarships are awarded for entry at 11+, 13+ and above. Most awards are means-tested and may be increased by an income-related bursary. A small number of awards are offered for the Sixth Form.

Academic Grants. A number of reduced-fee places are given annually to those academically able pupils whose parents would not otherwise be able to meet the fees.

Fees per term (2014–2015). Boarders £8,556–£9,395, Weekly Boarders £6,852–£7,612, International Boarders £8,803–£9,395. Fees include tuition, board, laundry, medical attention and Health Centre, stationery and games. Day pupils £4,153–£4,553.

Extras. Apart from purely personal expenses, the termly extras are private music lessons from £200 to £275; EAL lessons at various rates depending on need.

Charitable status. Wellington School is a Registered Charity, number 310268. It aims to provide a happy, caring co-educational day and boarding community, where pupils are provided with the opportunity of making best use of their academic experience and the School enrichment activities, in order to enhance their overall preparation for life after the age of eighteen.

Wells Cathedral School

The Liberty, Wells, Somerset BA5 2ST
Tel: 01749 834200
Fax: 01749 834201
email: admissions@wells-cathedral-school.com
website: www.wells-cathedral-school.com

In 909AD there was a Cathedral School in Wells providing education for choir boys. Today, Wells Cathedral School is fully co-educational. Its spirit is a passion for learning and life; its dream an inspiring education set in a musically alive and beautiful environment as a brilliant foundation for life; and its focus, inspiring success.

Patron: HRH The Prince of Wales

Governors:
Chairman: The Very Revd John Clarke, MA, BD (*Dean of Wells*)
The Revd Canon Andrew Featherstone, MA
The Revd Canon Patrick Woodhouse, MA
Prebendary Barbara Bates, BA, MA, FRSA
Peter McIlwraith, FCA
Prebendary Helen Ball, OBE
Robert Sommers, BA
Prebendary Elsa van der Zee, BA, ALAMDA
Martin Smout, BSc, CEng, MICE

Consultant to the Governing Body:
Prof David Strange, FRAM
Prof Colin Lawson, MA, PhD, DMus, FRCM, FLCM
Jonathan Vaughan, Dip RCM Perf, Dip RCM Teach

Head: Elizabeth Cairncross, BA

Deputy Head: A Kemp, BA, MA, PGCE
Assistant Head (Teaching & Learning): A Battison, BSc, MSc Oxon
Assistant Head (Pastoral & Co-curricular): A Mayhew, BSc
Director of Music: Mrs D Nancekievill, BA, BMus, PGCE, Hon ARAM

Senior School

Teaching Staff:
Mrs A M Armstrong, BMus, LRAM, PGCE
M J Ashton, BA, PGCE
J Barnard, BSc Hons, PGCE
Mrs H Bennett, BA Hons
Prof J Berry, BSc, PhD, FIMA, CMath
J Boot, BA, FRGS
N Bowen, BA, PGCE
J Byrne, Dip Moscow Cons, GRNCM

A Clements, BSc Hons, PGCE
Mrs N A M Connock, BSc, PGCE
Mrs S Cowell, BA Hons, CTEFLA
A Davies, BA, PGCE
Mrs S Deans, MA
P Denegri, FTCL, LTCL, Hon ARAM
Ms J Desmarchelier, PGCE
Mrs R Edwards, BSc, PGCE
Mrs M C Fielding, BSc, PGCE, Cert SEN, Dip SpLD
C Finch, MA, BMus Hons, LRSM, Dip ABRSM
Mrs K Finch, BA
Mrs P J Garty, BSc, PGCE
Ms J Gearon, BA, MA, PGCE
M Grogan, MA, DipTEFL
D C Hansom, BMus, LRSM, ARCM
Revd J Hulme, BEd Hons, Cert Theo & Min, Dip Christian
    Spirituality
K H Humphreys, BSc, PGCE
Mrs M Humphreys, BA, PGCE, AMBDA
Ms S Jameson, BSc, PGCE, CSci, FIMA, FCIEA
Mrs T Jarman, BA, QTS
M A Laing, MA, PGCE
Miss C Lord, ARCM, Juilliard Diploma
Ms J Martin, MA, PGCE
M Meally, MA, BA, BEng, PGCE, Dip HSWW
R Murdoch, BA, MA, PGCE
Dr H Murphy, MA, BMus, LRAM, PhD, PGCE
Mrs E Nelson, BA Hons, QTS, CertEd
Mrs J Obradovic, LTCL
K Orchard, BSc
K Padgett, BSc
Ms L Panes, BA
L Plum, BA Hons, AKC, PGCE
Ms G Pritchard, BSc, PGCE
Ms R Redman
D Rowley, BSc, PGCE
Mrs S G Rowley, BA Hons, PGCE
Mrs J Shepherd, BSc, PhD
M Souter, AGSM, Hon ARAM
Mrs L J Stockdale-Bridson, BA, PGCS
M Swarfield, BA, PGCE, PGC
Mrs J S Tapner, BA, ADT, PGCE
S Tapner, BSc, CertEd
B Taylor, MA, PGCE
Mrs L E Walkey, CertEd
L Whitehead, BA, MA, GGSMD, PGCE
J Williams, BA Hons, PGCE

Junior School

Head of Junior School: Mrs J Barrow, BEd
Head of Early Years and Foundation Stage: Mrs J Bennett,
    BA
Director of Studies: Miss A Clark, BEd

Miss R Allen, BSc, QTS
S Bratt, BEd
Mrs J Burns, TDip CSSD, LUD Drama
Mrs K Dennis, BEd
Mrs J Edmonds, BSc, ALCM
Mrs K Fairey, BEd
K Gibson, Dip Teach, BEd
Mrs E Morley, BEd
Miss N Randy, BEd
Mrs J Tucker, DipEd
J Ward, BSc, PGCE
Ms R Warner, BA, QTS

Bursar and Clerk to the Governors: P Knell
Assistant Clerk to the Governors: D Shortland-Ball
Admissions Registrar: A Deacon, BSc, ACIB, FRSA
Head's PA: Mrs C Edwards
Communications Technology Director: J Peace
Development Director: M Coote, BA, MA Ed
Publicity Manager: Mrs K Chantrey, BSc Hons

School Doctor: Dr C Bridson, MB BS, MRCGP, DipOCC,
    MED
School Sister: Mrs A Press

There is a senior and junior school with 660 boys and
girls aged from 3 to 18. Boarders number 270, whilst the
remainder are day pupils. Once accepted, a child normally
remains in the school without further Entrance Examination
until the age of 18+.

Fees per term (2014–2015). Sixth Form (Years 12–13):
Boarders £9,283, Day £5,547. Upper School (Years 10–11):
Boarders £9,219, Day £5,506. Lower School (Years 7–9):
Boarders £8,876, Day £5,321. Junior School (Years 3–6):
Boarders £7,514; Day £4,320; Pre-Prep £2,333. Nursery:
Morning with lunch £19; Afternoon with lunch £23; After-
noon £19; All day with lunch £33.

Scholarships and Bursaries. Scholarships and academic
awards are made at 11+, 13+ and 14+ to those who show
outstanding ability in the Entrance Assessment Tests held in
late January at the school. Specialist gifts or aptitudes (e.g.
sport, drama, dance, art) are also considered. Sixth form academic awards are made following the scholarship assessment day in November. Awards are given on the basis of
performance in the assessment, rigorous interview, predicted GCSE results and a confidential reference from the
applicant's current school. The value of the awards will
depend on individual financial circumstances.

Means-tested specialist mathematics awards are available
at 11+ for outstandingly gifted mathematicians.

A number of music awards are available depending upon
the standard and quality of applicants and individual financial circumstances. Pre-auditions are held from September
to December and successful candidates are invited to the
main auditions held in January.

In addition, the school is one of only four in England designated by the Department for Education providing specialist musical education. The DfE therefore provides generous
assistance (up to 100% of fees) with tuition, boarding and
music fees for up to 78 gifted musicians, grants being linked
to parental income, under the DfE Music & Dance Scheme.

Cathedral choristerships and bursaries, which can provide up to 25% of boarding and tuition fees, are awarded
annually to boys between the ages of 8 and 10. Choral trials
and academic entrance tests take place in January. Special
arrangements can be made for children from overseas.
School bursaries to the value of 10% of tuition fees are
available for girl choristers. Supplementary means-tested
bursaries are also available.

Ex-chorister bursaries: On ceasing to be a chorister, boys
and girls are eligible for an ex-chorister bursary up to the
value of 8% of tuition or boarding fees.

For further details of awards contact the Admissions
Registrar, Tel: 01749 834213, email: admissions@wells-
cathedral-school.com.

Situations and Buildings. The mediaeval city of Wells,
with its famous Cathedral and a population of only 10,500,
is the smallest city in England. It is just over 20 miles from
Bath and Bristol where there is a good rail service, and easily accessed from the M4 and M5 motorways. Bristol International Airport is a 40-minute drive away. The school
occupies all but one of the canonical houses in The Liberty.
This fine group is planned to keep its mediaeval and 18th
century atmosphere while providing for the needs of modern
boarding education. There are modern classrooms and science laboratories built amongst walled gardens. A sports
hall provides indoor facilities for tennis, badminton, cricket,
basketball, volleyball, hockey, five-a-side football, climbing
and multi-gym. There are theatrical and concert facilities, a
music technology centre, a computer studies centre, art,
design and technology department, drama studio, library,
sixth form centre, 25-metre covered swimming pool, tennis
and netball courts, astroTurf pitch, three sports fields and an
all-weather hard play area.

There are two boarding Houses in the junior and lower school and a further seven in the senior school, three for boys and four for girls, the most senior pupils having study-bedrooms. The aim is to give security to the younger and to develop a sense of responsibility in the older.

Organisation and Curriculum. Despite its national and international reputation, the school has retained close links with the local community, and its fundamental aim is to provide all its pupils with an education consistent with the broad principles of Christianity. More specifically, the school aims to be a well-regulated community in which pupils may learn to live in harmony and mutual respect with each other and with the adults who care for them. The curriculum has been designed to enable all children who gain entry to the school to develop fully all their abilities, and to take their place in due course in tertiary education and the adult community of work and leisure. Forms are limited to a maximum of 25; average class sizes are typically less than this. Two years before GCSE a tutorial system is introduced whereby some ten boys and girls are the responsibility of one member of staff for academic progress to GCSE. Pupils then choose a subject faculty for sixth form tutoring in similar groups.

The emphasis is on setting by ability in particular subjects rather than streaming. There is every attempt to avoid early specialisation. All take IGCSE mathematics and English, as well as double science, plus a foreign language to GCSE. There is a sixth form of some 200 taking A Level courses in all major academic subjects.

The majority of pupils take up places at Russell Group Universities, with about 5–6 places regularly offered by Oxford and Cambridge; whilst musicians are regularly awarded scholarships to the top music colleges each year.

Societies. There is a wide range of indoor and outdoor activities in which pupils must participate, although the choice is theirs. Outdoor education is an important part of the curriculum. Besides a Combined Cadet Force with Army and RAF sections and a Duke of Edinburgh's Award scheme, activities as diverse as chess and kite making, photography, sailing and golf are also on offer. Ballet and riding lessons are also arranged.

Music. The school is one of four in England designated and grant-aided by the Department for Education (DfE) to provide special education for gifted young musicians, who are given substantial financial assistance. Wells is unique in that both specialist and non-specialist musicians are able to develop their aptitudes within a normal school environment. These talents are widely acknowledged by audiences at concerts given by pupils from Wells throughout the world.

There are over 200 talented pupils following specially devised timetables which combine advanced instrumental tuition and ensemble work with academic opportunity. More than half of the school learns at least one musical instrument. Violin and cello is taught to all children in the pre-prep as part of the curriculum. Pupils receive the highest quality teaching, often leading to music conservatoires and a career in music. Central to specialist music training are the opportunities to perform in public and there is a full concert diary. There are also regular concerts by the many ensembles in the school.

The Wellensian Association. Old Wellensians, Wells Cathedral School, Wells, Somerset BA5 2ST.

Charitable status. Wells Cathedral School Limited is a Registered Charity, number 310212. It is a charitable trust for the purpose of promoting the cause of education in accordance with the doctrine of the Church of England.

West Buckland School

Barnstaple, Devon EX32 0SX
Tel: 01598 760281
Fax: 01598 760546
email: headmaster@westbuckland.com
website: www.westbuckland.devon.com

Motto: '*Read and Reap*'

West Buckland School is an independent day and boarding school set in 90 acres of beautiful North Devon countryside in the South West of England. Founded in 1858, the school has always stressed the importance of all-round character development alongside good academic achievement. Our size allows pupils to receive plenty of individual care and attention to their needs and talents.

West Buckland Preparatory School educates children between the ages of three and eleven. There is strong cooperation and support between the schools which share the same grounds, so making the transition as easy as possible.

West Buckland is fully co-educational.

President: P D Orchard-Lisle, CBE, TD, DL LLD hc, DSc hc, MA, FRICS

The Governing Body:

Chairman: J M H Light, LLB

Vice-Chairmen:
Ms L Cairns, BA Joint Hons
S D Fox, BA

Governors:

The Countess of Arran, MBE, DL	R A Ingram, MA
A G Boggis, BA, PGCE	C D Phillips, BSc, FRICS, ACI, Arb, MEWI
A C B Browne, FCA, BSc Hons, ARCS	Mrs M A Read, BA Hons
Dr R Fisher-Smith, BA, MA, PGCE, PhD	Mrs S C E Salvidant, BEd Hons
The Venerable D A Gunn-Johnson, MA, STH	P R T Stucley, BA Hons, PG Dip Surv, MRICS
G G Harrison, BSc, FRICS	R J Wakefield

Headmaster: J F Vick, MA St John's College Cambridge

Deputy Head: D M Hymer, BSc University College London

Director of Studies: C J Burrows, MA Exeter College Oxford

Pastoral Deputy: A N Calder, BA/BSc Hons Brunel

Headmaster, Preparatory School: A D Moore, BEd

Chaplain: A Watkinson-Trim, BA Hons

Houses & Housemasters/mistresses:
Brereton House: Miss D J Sharman, BSc University College Cardiff
Courtenay House: C J Allin, BA Leicester
Fortescue House: Mrs A L Pugsley, BA University College Chester
Grenville House: Mrs R L Thompson, BEd Hons Carnegie College Leeds

Teaching Staff:

M J Adams, BSc Hons	Mrs P Cartmell, BA Hons
C J Allin, BA	Miss N R Cordon
Mrs T Anderson	R D Clarke, BA, BEd
Mrs J Beech	Mrs H C Clements, BA Hons
M Bohl, BA Hons	
P J Brand, BSc Hons	P H Davies, BSc
M T Brimson, BA	C H Dawson, BSc
Mrs J F Bunclark, MA	Miss H T Dixon

Miss A Episkopos, BSc
D R Ford, BA Hons
J E Freeman, BEng
Dr E N D Grew, PhD
Miss L Gomar Chapa
A E Hayes
Mrs S P Hartnoll, BEd
Mrs Y Helicon, BA
Mrs Tracy Hill, MSc
Mrs B Joly-Bloodworth
Mrs J Keech
Mrs E M Kent, BMus
A M Kimberley, BSc Hons
T M Lutley, BA Hons
C Main, BA Hons
J K McKerrow
W D Minns, BEng
G J Monk
K P Morris
Mrs K Moore, BA Hons

Mrs L Napier, BEd
T O'Brien, BSc
Miss A-S Prian
S J Prior, BSc
D Price, Ed Ord
J A Ralph, BA
Miss E Rushe, BSc
Miss O Shafikova, MMus
Miss D J Sharman, BSc
N T Shawcross, BSc
R Simpson, MA
M Smith
Mrs R C Tibble
M J Tucker, CertEd
Miss K Venner, BSc Hons
D Vickery
A Watkinson-Trim, BA Hons
Dr M Wells, PhD
Mrs A J Willmott, BEd

Visiting Music Staff:
Ms J Buckingham (*Clarinet*)
C Bundy (*Saxophone*)
Mrs L Byrt (*Oboe, Bassoon, Flute*)
Ms E Collingham (*Cello*)
Mrs L Cooper (*Piano and Flute*)
Mrs A Hammond (*Violin and Keyboard*)
P Moulton (*Trumpet, Brass, Piano*)
Mrs J Norris (*Violin, Viola*)
R Norris (*Jazz Piano*)
T Parker (*Guitar*)
Mrs A Prior (*Piano and theory*)
Ms S Sherratt (*Harp, Clarinet and Recorder*)
Mrs S Steele (*Flute, Piano*)
Mrs S Topp (*Clarinet, Saxophone*)
Mrs E Tonkins (*Singing*)
B Waring (*Percussion*)

Bursar: Cdr A R Jackson, MILT, MInstAM
Assistant Bursar: M Newby
Finance Officer: Mrs J Ramsey
Domestic Bursar: Mrs T Widlake
Bursar's Secretary: Miss A Smith
Fees Secretary: D Foster
Headmaster's Secretary: Mrs S Harris
Secretary/Admin Assistant: Miss K Edwards
Receptionist/Admin Assistant: Mrs P C Hymer
Registration Secretary/Admin Assistant: Mrs C Smalley
Medical Officer: Dr C A Gibb, BMed, BM, DA, MRCGP, DRCOG, DPD
School Sisters: Mrs C E Pouncey, RGN; Mrs G M Davies, RGN

Head of Boarding:
D R Ford
Houseparents:
M J Tucker
Mrs L Morris
Mrs N Smith
Mrs A Booker
Mrs L Grew
Mrs V Ford
Mrs A Melchior

Marketing Office:
A G Conibear (*Marketing Manager*)
Mrs L A Millar (*Admissions and Marketing Assistant*)

Development Office:
Miss V Bishop (*Manager*)
Mrs L C Lancaster (*Administration and Relationship Officer*)

Librarian: Miss L Warrillow
Uniform Shop: Mrs C Cawsey

Situation. The School stands in 90 acres of beautiful North Devon countryside on the edge of Exmoor. Barnstaple is 10 miles away and the M5 motorway can be reached in 35 minutes. Boarders arriving by train at Exeter station are met by coaches.

Buildings and Grounds. The central range of buildings, dating from 1861, still forms the focus of the school, and now includes a performing arts centre. Other developments include a Sixth Form Centre, Mathematics and Physics Centre, boarding houses for boys and girls, a Preparatory School classroom block and the ICT Centre. The campus offers outstanding sports facilities, including a 9-hole golf course, an indoor heated 25-metre swimming pool, and an Astroturf hockey pitch. The Jonathan Edwards Sports Centre opened in 2008 and the award-winning 150 Building for Art, Design Technology and a Theatre opened in 2010. We are currently in a very exciting phase of the school's development and are building a new study centre for all senior school pupils along with a Sixth Form boarding house. This development will be open for students in the Autumn Term 2015.

Admission. Boys and girls are admitted as boarders or day pupils. The present number of pupils is: 96 boarding, 513 day.

Entrance to the Preparatory School is by interview and assessment. Entry to the Senior School is by assessment at 11+ or to the Sixth Form upon interview and school report. Entry at other ages is usually possible and assessment arrangements are made to suit individual circumstances.

Fees per term (2014–2015). Senior: Boarding £7,040–£8,200; Day £4,420. Preparatory: Day £2,380–£3,610. Nursery: Government-funded places under Early Years Entitlement are available up to 15 hours per week during term time. £4.00 per hour thereafter.

Scholarships and Bursaries. A number of scholarships are awarded for entry at 11+, 13+ or 16+ (up to a value of 10% of the tuition fees). Candidates must be under 12, 14, or 17 years of age on 1st September following the examination, which will take place in late January or early February.

Music scholarships are available for entry at 13+ and Sports scholarships at 11+, 13+ and 16+.

With the support of the West Buckland School Foundation, means-tested bursaries are available for boarders and day students at all ages.

Curriculum. In the Preparatory School the main emphasis is upon well-founded confidence in English and Mathematics, within a broad balance of subjects that adds modern languages to the national curriculum. Particular attention is given to the development of sporting, artistic and musical talents.

In the Senior School breadth is complemented by specialisation. All students study the three separate sciences from Year 7, while both French and Spanish are the principal languages offered from Year 7. Our flexible options arrangements at GCSE respond to students' individual strengths and preferences. A wide range of A Level subjects is offered to sixth formers whose results uphold the high academic standards of the School.

Careers. The Careers Staff advise all pupils upon the openings and requirements for different careers. They make full use of the facilities offered by Connexions.

Games, The Performing Arts and other activities. One of the most impressive features of life at West Buckland is the quality and range of extra-curricular activities, with a high level of involvement from pupils and staff.

The school has a strong sporting tradition. Rugby, hockey, cricket, netball, tennis, athletics, swimming, cross-country, squash, golf, shooting and many other sports offer opportunities for inter-school and inter-house competition and for recreation.

About a third of all pupils receive instrumental and singing tuition from specialist teachers. The wide range of choirs and instrumental groups give concerts at least once a week throughout the year. Drama is strength of the school with productions of many kinds throughout the year. The Performing Arts are complemented by the exceptional facilities provided by the school's award-winning 150 Building which houses an impressive studio theatre.

Music. Over 120 members of the school receive instrumental tuition on all instruments. They are encouraged to perform in concerts, in choirs and instrumental groups. Music Technology is also a strong feature of the department's work.

Outdoor Education. Much use is made of the proximity of Exmoor and the coast for climbing, kayaking, mountain biking, surfing and other adventurous activities. All pupils receive instruction in camp craft, first aid and map reading. The Combined Cadet Force has Army and Royal Air Force sections, and offers a range of challenging pursuits. Our students succeed at all levels in the Duke of Edinburgh's Award Scheme each year, and there is a regular programme of expeditions in this country and overseas.

Religion. The tradition is Anglican but the school welcomes children from all denominations and faiths – or none. Services of worship are held throughout the week including many Sundays. A number of services are held at East Buckland Church. The Chaplain prepares boys and girls for confirmation every year.

Attitudes and values. The School sets out to be a friendly and purposeful community in which happiness and a sense of security are the foundation on which young lives are built. At all levels members of the school are asked to lead a disciplined way of life, to show consideration for others, to be willing to be challenged and to recognise that the success of the individual and the success of the group are inextricably linked.

Charitable status. West Buckland School is a Registered Charity, number 306710. Its purpose is the education of boys and girls from 3 to 18.

Westminster School

17 Dean's Yard, Westminster, London SW1P 3PB
Tel:　020 7963 1042 (Head Master)
　　　020 7963 1003 (Registrar)
　　　020 7963 1000 (Other enquiries)
　　　020 7821 5788 (Westminster Under School)
Fax:　020 7963 1002
email:　registrar@westminster.org.uk
website:　www.westminster.org.uk

Motto: '*Dat Deus Incrementum*'

Westminster School is a Boarding and Day School which is co-educational in the Sixth Form. The present number of boys and girls is 746.

The School traces its origins to the school that was attached to the Benedictine Abbey at Westminster. Queen Elizabeth I re-founded the School in 1560 as part of the College of St Peter at Westminster.

Visitor: Her Majesty The Queen

Governing Body:
Chairman: The Dean of Westminster, The Very Reverend Dr John Hall
The Dean of Christ Church, The Very Reverend Professor Martyn Percy
The Master of Trinity, Sir Gregory Winter, CBE, FRS
The Venerable Canon Andrew Tremlett
The Reverend Canon David Stanton
Dr Sarah Mortimer, MA, DPhil
Professor Stephen Elliott
Lord Julian Hunt of Chesterton, CB, FRS (*OW*)
Mr Michael Baughan (*OW*)
Mr Christopher Foster, FCA (*OW*)
Dr Priscilla Chadwick, MA, FRSA

Professor Sir Christopher Edwards, MD, FRCP, FRCPEd, FRSE, FMedSci, HonDSc
Dr Alan Borg, CBE, FSA (*OW*)
Mr Alex Segal
Mr Tony Willoughby (*OW*)
Sir Peter Ogden
Mr Tim Young, MA
Mr Richard Neville-Rolfe, MA (*OW*)
Dame Judith Mayhew Jonas, DBE
Mr Mark Batten
Ms Joanna Reesby

(OW) *Old Westminster*
* *Head of Department/Subject*

Secretary to the Governing Body and Bursar: C A J Silcock

Head Master: P S J Derham, MA (*History*)

Under Master: D A Smith, MA, PhD (*Mathematics*)

Director of Studies: R R Harris, MA (*Geography*)

Senior Master: K E Clanchy, MA, MBA (*French and Russian*)

Senior Tutor: J J Kemball, BSc (*Biology*)

Assistant Staff:
R Agyare-Kwabi, MSc, PhD (**Electronics*)
E Alaluusua, MA (*Art*)
H A Aplin, BA, PhD (**Russian*)
K Y Au, MMath (*Mathematics*)
S T Bailey, MA (*Theology and Philosophy*)
S Baldock, BA (**Biology*)
Mrs S M Barry, ARCM, LRAM (**Instrumental Studies; Violin*)
C J Barton, BA (*Drama*)
Miss H L Barton, BA (*History*)
S J Berg, BA (**Spanish*)
S G Blache, PhD (**French*)
P A Botton, BSc (*Chemistry*)
M R Bradshaw, MA (*Chemistry*)
G P A Brown, MA, DPhil (*History*)
Ms C M Buchanan, BA, MA, PhD (*History*)
I T Butler, BA (*Mathematics*)
Miss L Cappenberg (*German Assistant*)
P J Chequer, DipPA (** Director of Drama*)
Miss J L Chidgey, BA, MA (**Product Design*)
Miss B Choraria, MPhys (*Physics*)
Mrs J L Cockburn, MA, PhD (*History of Art*)
N L Cole, BA (*Mathematics*)
T R Cousins, BA, MMath (*Mathematics*)
E T A Coward, BA, MSci (*Chemistry*)
A M L Crole, BA, MA (*English*)
S Crow, BA (**Art*)
S N Curran, BA (*English*)
J M Curtis, MA (*Registrar; History*)
M C Davies, MA (**Mathematics*)
D East, MA, PhD (*Bookbinding*)
T P Edlin, MA (*History*) (*OW*)
D L Edwards, MA (*English*)
Miss R J Evans, PhD (*Biology*)
N A Fair, MA (*Economics*)
Ms A E Farr, MA (**English*)
M H Feltham, MA (*Master of The Queen's Scholars; Mathematics*)
Miss G M French, MSc, MRSC, LTCL, FRSA (*Chemistry*)
W D Galton, BA (*Mathematics*)
Miss A P Gandon, BA (*Classics*)
T D Garrard, BA (**Director of Music*)
Mrs R-E G Gibbons-Lejeune, BA, MA (*History of Art*)
B E J Gravell, BA (*Classics*)
Mrs A K Griffiths, BA, MA (*German and French*)
Miss V Guichard, BA, MA, PhD (*French Assistante*)
J Harding, MA (*Arabic*)
P A Hartley, BSc, PhD (*Biology*)

S C Hawken, MA (*Economics)
G D Hayter, MMath (Mathematics)
D R Hemsley-Brown, BSc, MIEE (Electronics and Product Design)
U Hennig, BA (*German)
R J Hindley, MA, CMath (Director of IT)
J N Hooper, BA (Mathematics)
G StJ Hopkins, BA (Music)
R M Huscroft, MA, PhD (History)
J A Ireland, MA (Classics)
Mrs A M Jackman (*Study Skills Coordinator)
D A Jones, BA (Classics)
G K Jones, MA (*Modern Languages; French, Russian and German)
N G Kalivas, BSc, DPhil (Mathematics)
Miss A Kebaier (French Assistant)
J D Kershen, BA, MA (*Sport and PE) (OW)
Miss E Kettleborough, BA (Physics)
C M C Kingcombe, BSc (Biology and Chemistry)
R A Kowenicki, MA, MSci, PhD (*Chemistry)
R W Landy (Ceramics)
A J Law, BA (*Keyboard; Piano)
Miss C M Leech, MA (Spanish)
Dr A E Leonard, MA (Geography)
Miss S E Leonard, BSc (Head of Girls; *Geography)
Mrs F Lofts (Italian)
L A Lorimer, BA, MA (Mathematics)
C R L Low, MA (Classics) (OW)
Mrs L D MacMahon, BA (German and French)
G D Mann, BA, MSt (*History)
Ms A Marquez, BA (Spanish Assistant)
Miss N C McCartney, MMath (Mathematics)
S McGregor, DipRCM, ARCO, ARCM (School Organist)
J Moore, BA (Biology)
Ms L C M Murphy, MA, LLM (English)
A E A Mylne, MA (Classics)
Mrs L J Newton, BSc (Economics)
Miss S Page, BA, MSc (IT; *PSHE)
T D Page, MA (Religious Studies)
Miss B L J Pannell, BA (Economics)
B W Parker-Wright, BA (Mathematics)
Miss H J Prentice, MSci, MA, PhD (Physics)
R J Pyatt, MA (English)
Miss K E Radice, BA (*Classics)
Mrs S A Ragaz, PhD (English)
C D Riches, BEd, MSc (*PE; Rowing; History)
M N Robinson, BA (Chemistry)
Mrs J Rogers (Japanese)
Miss G V Rutherford, MA (Spanish and French)
S C Savaskan, BA, MMus, DPhil (Deputy Director of Music)
P Sharp, MA, MSc (Physics)
Mrs E D Shortland, BA (Deputy Head of Sixth Form; Religious Studies)
N J Simons, MMath, DPhil (Head of Sixth Form; Mathematics)
G J A Simpson, BSc (Economics)
B J Smith, MA (French)
K W Smith, BA, MA (Study Skills)
M J A Sugden, MA (French and German)
L Tattersall, BSc, MA (Mathematics)
A Theodosiou, BA (Modern Greek)
A C Tolley, BA (Mathematics)
K D Tompkins, BA (English)
C J R Ullathorne, MA, MSci (*Physics)
R C Wagner, BA, PhD (Mathematics)
K A P Walsh, BSc, PhD (*Science and Technology; Physics)
B D Walton, BA (History of Art)
Ms H Wang, BSc, MA (Chinese)
Miss G D Ward-Smith, MA, PhD (History)
The Revd G J Williams, MA (Chaplain)
P H Williams, BSc, PhD (Biology)

J C Witney, MA, MIL (*Modern Languages)
J G Woodman, BA (Art)
T D W Woodrooffe, BA, BTh, MA (*Religious Studies)
Ms A C Wrege, BA, MA (Art)
S D Wurr, BA (Geography)

Houses and Housemasters:

Boarding House for Queen's Scholars and Girls' Day House:
College: M H Feltham

Boys' Boarding and Mixed Day Houses
Grant's, 2 Little Dean's Yard: N A Fair
Rigaud's, 1 Little Dean's Yard: Dr P H Williams

Mixed Boarding and Mixed Day Houses:
Liddell's, 19 Dean's Yard: T D Page
Busby's, 26 Great College Street: P A Botton

Girls' Boarding and Mixed Day House:
Purcell's, 22 Great College Street: Dr G D Ward-Smith

Day Houses:
Ashburnham, 6 Dean's Yard: Dr S A Ragaz
Dryden's, 4 Little Dean's Yard: D R Hemsley-Brown
Hakluyt's, 19 Deans' Yard: G StJ Hopkins
Milne's, 5A Dean's Yard: Dr P A Hartley
Wren's, 4 Little Dean's Yard: S D Wurr

Librarian: Mrs C Goetzee
Archivist: Miss E Wells

Westminster Under School

Master: Mrs E A Hill, MA
Deputy Master: P Fahy, BA (English)
Assistant Master: D S C Bratt, BA (Mathematics & Games) [On Sabbatical]

Mrs E-L Allison, BA, MA (English)
Mrs A C Apaloo, MA (Religious Studies & History, 8A Form Teacher)
Mrs J Bacon (Classroom Assistant)
I Baillie, ACTC, MBA, PG Dip Adv Net Open (ICT Consultant)
A J P Busk, Dip Fine Art (Art & 5B Form Teacher)
O T Campbell Smith, MA, MSc (Geography, Games & Head of Year 8)
C R Candy, MA (Head of Years 3 & 4, 3C Form Teacher & English)
Mrs L R Chacksfield, BA, MA (English, Enterprise Coordinator & 7C Form Teacher)
Ms R Collins, BA (Study Skills Coordinator)
Miss S E K Corps, BSc (Science)
J Cox, BSc (Laboratory Technician)
R J Dilks, BSc (Science, Games & 6D Form Teacher)
A J Downey, BA, MA (Senior Master, Latin, Greek, Games & 7D Form Teacher)
Miss M E Ellis, BEd (Mathematics, Games & 8E Form Teacher)
P J E V Evans, MA (Director of Studies, French, Games & Chess)
Miss H L Gifford, BSc (Mathematics & Head of Year 7)
G Gougay, BA (French & 6G Form Teacher)
I D Hepburn, BA, MA (Director or Sport)
C H W Hill, MA (Drama, English & 8H Form Teacher)
Ms F M Illingworth, BA (Art and 3D Design)
S R H James, BA (Latin, Greek, Games & Assistant Director of Studies)
Mrs V James, BEd (Librarian & Art)
Miss J Lawrence, BA (Art Technician)
E Matthews, MEng (Mathematics, Games & 5M Form Teacher)
P A Rosenthal, BA (English, Games & 8R Form Teacher)
Miss A Simpson, BA (Art Technician)
S M Spurvey, MA (Computer Science)
S Thébaud, BSc, MA (French, Games & 7T Form Teacher)

Mrs R Thorn, BMus, MMus (*Assistant Director of Music*)
Miss H Verney, BSc (*English & 4V Form Teacher*)
Mrs A Villari, MA (*School Counsellor*)
J S Walker, BEd, LRAM (*Director of Music*)
Miss C Wheeler-Bennett, BSc (*Geography & 4W Form Teacher*)
Miss S Wollam, BSc (*Science & 7W Form Teacher*)
M J Woodside, BSc (*Head of Years 5 & 6, English, Science, Geography & History*)

Administration Staff
Master's PA: Miss S Bueno, MA
Registrar: Ms A-M McCarthy
School Administrator: Miss A Stewart-Cox
Financial Secretary: Mrs M Waggett

The Queen's Scholars. An examination (The Challenge) is held annually to elect The Queen's Scholars. There are 40 Queen's Scholars who board in College, one of our 6 boarding houses. 8 Queen's Scholarships, worth 50% of the boarding fee, are awarded annually. Boys who do not wish to board may be candidates for the title of Honorary Scholar. Up to 5 exhibitions may be awarded each year to those who narrowly miss being offered a scholarship. Boys, who must be under 14 on 1 September of their year of entry, sit The Challenge at Westminster School in late April or early May. The examination consists of papers in Mathematics, English, French, Science, Latin, History, Geography and an optional Greek paper. A scholarship, which is not means-tested, is normally tenable for 5 years.

Application forms and past papers may be obtained from The Admissions Administrator (13+ Entry) (tel: 020 7963 1003, email: registrar@westminster.org.uk).

The value of a scholarship may be supplemented by a bursary (remission of the fees) up to a maximum of 100% if there is proven financial need. Parents who wish to apply for financial assistance should request a Bursary Application Form from the Registrar.

Music Scholarships. Up to 6 Music Scholarships worth 25% of the boarding or day fee and free tuition on three instruments are awarded annually. These may be supplemented by additional means-tested bursaries to a maximum of the full fees. There are also several Music Exhibitions which provide for free music tuition on two instruments. Applications close in early January and the auditions take place in early February. Candidates, who must be under 14 years of age on the following 1st September, must subsequently take either the Common Entrance or gain admission through the Scholarship Examination, The Challenge. The Director of Music is happy to give informal advice to potential candidates and it is recommended that an informal audition is arranged before submitting an application. Please contact the Music Administrator on 020 7963 1017.

Music Scholarships are also available at Westminster Under School at 11+.

For further information on all Scholarships, please contact the Registrar.

Bursaries. Westminster School has made it possible, since its first foundation, for academically able pupils to attend the School who would not otherwise have been able to do so without financial support. Bursaries (remission of fees) up to a maximum of 100% are available and are awarded according to individual need following a full financial assessment, which may include a home visit, to pupils who gain a place on academic merit. Bursaries are awarded at 13 + and 16+ entry to Westminster School and at 11+ entry to Westminster Under School. All bursaries continue until a pupil leaves the School at 18, although they may be adjusted up or down if financial circumstances change.

Parents who wish to apply for financial assistance should request a Bursary Application Form from the Registrar at Westminster School (tel: 020 7963 1003) or Westminster Under School (tel: 020 7821 5788).

Admission. The two main points of admission are 13+ (boys only) and 16+ (girls and boys). Parents should register their sons for 13+ entry by the start of Year 6 – the academic year of a child's 11th birthday. In the Autumn Term of Year 6, the boy will take the ISEB Common Pre-Tests in Mathematics, English and Verbal and Non-Verbal Reasoning. Selected boys will be invited to Westminster School for interview during the Spring Term. On the basis of the candidate's test results, the interview and a report from his present school a decision will be made whether to offer a conditional place. Boys with conditional places must still qualify for entry to the School by sitting the Common Entrance examinations or The Challenge (scholarship examinations) when they are 13, but failure at this stage is rare. Candidates who are not offered a conditional place may be placed on a waiting list and they may sometimes be invited to sit further tests at the start of Year 8. Registration for 16+ entry opens in the summer a year before entry. Entry is by competitive examination and interview at the School in November. Candidates choose four entry examination subjects, usually the four subjects they plan to take for A Level. For further information about entry at 13+ or 16+ or to arrange a visit to the School please telephone 020 7963 1003. Please see the school's website www.westminster.org.uk for details of open days.

Fees per term (2014–2015). Boarding: £11,264, £5,632 (Queen's Scholars). Day Pupils (inclusive of lunch): £7,800, £8,456 (entry at Sixth Form). Under School: £5,460.

Preparatory Department (Day Boys only). The Under School has 260 pupils; entry is at 7, 8 and 11. All enquiries should be addressed to the Master (Mrs E A Hill), Westminster Under School, Adrian House, 27 Vincent Square, London SW1P 2NN (tel: 020 7821 5788).

(*For further details, see entry in IAPS section.*)

Charitable status. St Peter's College (otherwise known as Westminster School) is a Registered Charity, number 312728. The school was established under Royal Charter for the provision of education.

Whitgift School

Haling Park, South Croydon CR2 6YT
Tel: 020 8633 9935
Fax: 020 8760 0682
email: admissions@whitgift.co.uk
website: www.whitgift.co.uk
Twitter: @WhitgiftSchool1
Facebook: /Whitgift-School-South-Croydon

Motto: *Vincit qui patitur*

Whitgift School is an independent day and boarding school for boys aged between 10–18. Full, weekly and flexi boarding is available for students aged 13–18.

A Whitgift education is unique and exceptionally tailor-made, which mark the School out as truly first-class.

Whitgift is friendly, challenging and inclusive. Situated in beautiful and historic parkland, it enjoys splendid facilities and a proud record of commitment to the highest standards.

The Whitgift Foundation:
Visitor: His Grace The Lord Archbishop of Canterbury

Five members are appointed by the Archbishop of Canterbury, two by the London Borough of Croydon and four by co-optation. The Bishop of Croydon and the Vicar of Croydon are appointed ex officio.

Chairman of the Court of The Whitgift Foundation: I Harley, MA, FCA, FCIB

Whitgift School:
Patron: HRH The Duke of York, KG

Chairman of the Whitgift School Governors: Mr G H
Wright, TD, DL, PPCIOB

Whitgift School Governors:
The Headmaster
His Honour W Barnett, QC, MA
The Revd Canon C J Luke Boswell, Vicar of Croydon
D C Hudson, MA
Cllr D S Mead, FCCA, FCMA, FCIS
R J A I Catto, MA, DPhil
N L Platts, MA, FCA
M A Proudfoot, MA, MLitt
J A Kerr, BSc
Mrs P Davies, BSc, MEd
B P Wordsworth, MA, MB BS, FRCP
J D G Ufton, MA, MPhil, MRICS (*WA Representative*)
Representative of the Whitgift School Association
The Second Master
The Deputy Headmaster
The President of the Common Room
The Bursar
The Chief Executive of the Foundation
The Finance Officer (*Whitgift Foundation*)

Headmaster: **Dr C A Barnett**, MA, DPhil Oriel College
Oxford

Second Master: Mr P J R Ellis, BSc Durham
Deputy Headmaster: Mr P J Yeo, BA Durham
Assistant Head (*Proctor*): Mr D E C Elvin, BSc Surrey,
MSc
Deputy Proctor: Mr R F Martin, MA Christ Church Oxford
Assistant Head (*Pastoral*): Mr S D Cook, BA Keele, MPhil
Assistant Head (*Academic*): Mr D W Munks, MA Jesus
College Cambridge, MSc, LRAM, ARCO
Head of Upper School: Mr M J Brown, BA York
Head of Lower School and Boarding: Mr A Norris, BA St
Mary's Twickenham
Head of Sixth Form: Miss J F Lowson, MA Pembroke
College Cambridge
Head of Admissions: Mr E G Lance, BSc Durham
Head of Fifth Form: Mr W E R Collinson, BA St Peter's
College Oxford, MPhil
Head of Third Form: Mr A J Marlow, BSc Bath
Head of First Form: Mrs F E Carter, BA Warwick
(*maternity leave*)
Senior Housemaster & Housemaster Mason's: Mr D J
Edwards, BA Sheffield
Head of Co-Curricular Activities & Director of Sport: Mr
A G Osborne, BA Exeter
Registrar & Deputy Head of Lower School: Mr S A Beck,
BEd West London Inst of HE

Teaching Staff:
Mr F J Allen, BA Hertford College Oxford
Mr M J Baron, MSc Saskatchewan, Canada
Mr L S Beecham, MA, MEd Homerton College Cambridge
(*Director of Drama*)
Mr T A Biddle, BA Queens' College Cambridge, MA
(*Head of English*)
Mrs D Binacchi, BA Central St Martin's College of Art and
Design
Mr C J Bowen, MSc Johannesburg, South Africa
Miss S H Brook, BA University of the Arts London
Mr W H Chaloner, BSc Loughborough (*Deputy Boarding
Housemaster*)
Miss D Chan, BSc Port Elizabeth, South Africa
Mr J J Chang, BSc Warwick
Miss A M Channing, BA Exeter
Mr C Cheng, MSci London
Mr W J Church, BA Magdalen College Oxford
Mr G G Clark, BSc Edinburgh
Miss K J Coffin, BA Jesus College Cambridge (*Head of
Mathematics*)
Mrs J Collinson, MChem Surrey (*Head of Fifth Form*)

Mr A J Cotton, BA St Hugh's College Oxford
Mr N J Croker, MSc Exeter
Mrs F J Daniels, BA Oriel College Oxford
Mr T J Davies, BA Nottingham
Mr R J Dinnage, BA Wadham College Oxford
Mr P T Dinnen, MA Edinburgh (*Head of IB*)
Mrs C S Dowdall, MMathPhys Warwick
Dr D Duo, MSc, PhD Turin, Italy
Mr P W Elliott, BSc Durham
Miss V R Ellwood, BA Durham
Mrs P R Evans, MA Edinburgh
Mrs F L Exley, BSc Brighton
Dr L Faux-Newman, BSc, PhD London
Mr O M Fernie, BA Durham (*Head of Economics*)
Miss A J Gaster, BA Regent's Park College Oxford (*Head
of Theology & Philosophy*)
Mrs E A Gell, MA Durham
Miss C Giordano, MA Udine, Italy
Ms K A Goldberg, MA Columbia, USA
Miss L Gomersall, BA Bath (*Head of Modern Pentathlon,
Head of Cross Country*)
Mr S D Goudge, BA Nottingham
Mr B Gouttenoire, BA Université Lumière Lyon II, France
Mr B Graoui, BSc London
Mr J B Green, BSc East Anglia
Miss C B Griffin, BA Camberwell College of Art
Mr J M Griffith, BA Nottingham
Mr K Gross, MA Karl-Franzens Universität Graz, Austria
(*Head of International Project Development*)
Miss S L Gush, BSc Bangor
Mr I P Hanley, BSc York
Mrs C C Hann, BA University College Oxford
Mr M Hardy, BA Brighton (*Head of Physical Education*)
Dr N P Harries, MPhys New College Oxford, DPhil (*Head
of Physics*)
Miss A C Harris, MA Wales, BA
Mr C J Harwood, BSc Bristol (*Head of ICT*)
Mr T B Hayward, BA Magdalen College Oxford, MA
Mr A P Hedges, BSc Durham
Miss S E Herring, BSc Collingwood College Durham
Mrs S M Hooker, MA Newnham College Cambridge
Miss M K Hughes, BA Queensland, Australia
Mr J S E Humphrey, BA Royal Welsh College of Music &
Drama
Ms A S Huk, MSt University College London, BA (*Head
of German*)
Mr A J Hunt, MA St Anne's College Oxford, MPhil
Mr B J Jarvis, BSc University College London
Mr R B Johnstone, BEd Warwick (*Head of Design &
Technology*)
Mr N M Kendrick, ECB Coach (*Head of Cricket, Head of
Golf*)
Mr C J Kibble, BEd Loughborough College (*Director of
Sports Facilities*)
Mrs S E Korvin, BA Leeds (*Head of Japanese*)
Mr R J H Krippner, MA Exeter (*Director of Choral Music*)
Dr M Lakin, MA Durham, DPhil Oriel College Oxford
Mrs C L Letchford, BA Brighton
Mrs P Liberti, MA Università degli Studi di Udine, Italy
(*Head of Italian*)
Mr J W Lines, MSc Durham, BA
Mr S W Litchfield, BEd College of St Mark & St John,
Plymouth
Mr L Ma, BA Bedfordshire, MSc (*Head of Mandarin
Chinese*)
Miss J E Maciak, BA University of the Arts, London
Miss M L Mackay BA Newcastle, MA
Mr W D Marginson, MA Durham
Miss L A Martin, BA Hertford College Oxford
Mr N A Martin, BSc St Mary's Twickenham
Mr S F Michael, BA York (*Acting Head of First Form*)
Mr B C Miller, MA St Anne's College Oxford (*Deputy
Boarding Housemaster*)

Miss J J Morgan, MA Sidney Sussex College Cambridge (*Head of French*)
Mr N P Morgan, BA London
Mr B R H Morris, BA Leeds, MA
Mr P J Morrison, BSc Nottingham Trent
Mrs C A Mulley, BSc London
Mrs K G Mund, BA Rheinische Friedrich Wilhelms Universität, Bonn, Germany
Mr P Muñoz-Pardo, BA Pontificia Universidad Católica, Santiago, Chile (*Head of Spanish*)
Mr R I Munro, BSc Exeter (*Head of Strength & Conditioning*)
Mr R G Murray, BSc Leeds (*Senior Boarding Housemaster*)
Miss S L Mynott, BA Trinity College Cambridge
Mrs L M-L Nelson, MA Amiens, France
Mr G O Oberti Oddi, BA Jaén, Spain, MA
Dr M Ofner, Karl-Franzens Universität Graz, Austria, PhD
Dr J A Owen, BSc PhD Manchester
Mrs A Palomo Lopez, MA Malaga, Spain
Mr C Pates, UEFA Licence
Mr A J Pearson, BSc London
Miss E A Poole, BA St John's College Oxford, MA
Mr B N Prestney, BA St Edmund Hall Oxford
Mr S C B Ratnayake, BSc London
Mr C J Reed, BA Brighton
Mrs L C Reeves, BA Durham
Mrs K Richardson, BA Anglia Polytechnic University
Miss S A Richardson, MSc Jesus College Cambridge
Mrs A M C Rigard-Asquith, BA Université de Loire Atlantique, France, MA
Mr P Rynes, MA Charles Univ, Prague, Czech Republic (*Head of Fencing*)
Mr A D Seal, BEng Nottingham
Miss R O Seal, MEng Girton College Cambridge
Mrs F L Simmons, MSci Nottingham
Mr H G Sleath, BSc Durham
Miss C A Smith, MA, MPhil Clare College Cambridge
Mr C P Smith, BA Birmingham
Mr K A Smith, BA Birmingham (*Head of History*)
Dr K M Stagno, BSc, PhD Kingston (*Head of Hockey*)
Mr D J Stanley, MSc Leeds (*Head of Geography*)
Mr N J R Stebbings, BEng Birmingham
Mrs F M Stedman, BA Leeds, MA (*Head of PSHE*)
Mr T W Stradwick, BSc Bournemouth
Mrs V A Taylor-Medhurst, BSc Birmingham
Ms L F Temple, LRAM, ARCM (*Head of Brass*)
Mr J G Thomas, BSc Durham
Mr M C Thompson, BA Bristol
Mrs T A Thompson, BSc London, MRCS
Mr D Tredger, BSc London School of Economics
Mr H R Trimble, BA New College Oxford
Miss P C Tsai, BA Shen-Te Christian Univ Taiwan, MA
Mr B C M Turner, MA London
Mr T J Unwin, MPhil Trinity Hall Cambridge
Dr H L Wallis, BSc PhD London
Mr D M Ward, ECB Coach (*Head of Cricket*)
Mrs N Watts, BA Seinan Gakuin Univ, Japan
Mr A E Weakley, MA King's College Cambridge (*Head of Academic Music*)
Mr D C Webb, BEd Manchester Metropolitan (*Head of Swimming & Athletics*)
Mrs R C Whitfield, Dip Royal College of Music (*Director of Music Development*)
Miss R S Whitmore, BA St Catharine's College Cambridge
Mr C J Wilkins, RFU Coach (*Director of Rugby*)
Mr D G Williams, BA Manchester
Mr D R Williams, BTech Brunel
Mr A T Wilson, BSc Durham
Mr P S Wilson, MA Jesus College Oxford (*Head of Performing Arts*)
Mr P Winter, GBSM, Dip NCOS (*Director of Orchestral Music*)

Mr S J Woodward, BSc Canterbury Christ Church (*Head of Academic PE & Games*)
Miss N J Wright, BA Leeds

Bursar: Mr J T Stremes, BA
School Medical Officer: Dr C J Wilcock, MBBS
Headmaster's Executive Assistant: Mrs T Lisoire, BA

Numbers. There are 1,458 boys on roll.

Buildings and Grounds. Whitgift enjoys some of the finest facilities for academic departments, co-curricular work and individual study, of any British school, all set within attractive spacious grounds.

The Performing Arts Centre incorporates a Concert Hall, Song School and music practice rooms, together with a theatre and exhibition space.

There are exceptional library and resource areas, as well as a dedicated Sixth Form Centre, with excellent facilities for group and individual study, and high-quality social space.

The Sports and Conference Centre provides some of the finest integrated indoor facilities of any school, accommodating a large number of sports to national standards. The Centre also provides conference facilities, teaching rooms, and an auditorium for music and drama.

Whitgift has modern ICT facilities, which support teaching and learning throughout the School.

The School's new Boarding House, opened in 2013, is superbly equipped and offers full, weekly and flexi boarding to boys aged 13–18. Boarders have cutting-edge ICT facilities, private study areas, en suite bathrooms, and spacious, communal social areas with kitchen facilities.

Aims. The School offers a challenging and balanced education. It aims to combine high academic achievement with the all-round development of the individual, through games and co-curricular activities, and a strong encouragement of the pursuit of excellence.

Admission. Entry for boys aged 10, 11, 12, 13 and 16 is by competitive examination and interview. Admission is based on performance in the School's entrance tests and an assessment of a boy's potential to contribute to, and benefit from, the co-curricular programme and the wider life of the School. The majority of boys enter at 10 or 11. Application forms may be obtained from the Admissions Office, or from the School website.

Fees per term (2014–2015). Day: £5,780 covering tuition, books, stationery, and games. Weekly Boarding £9,308; Full Boarding £11,132.

Scholarships and Bursaries. A number of academic scholarships are awarded at ages 10, 11, 12, 13 and 16, carrying partial remission of fees, to candidates of outstanding merit in the Entrance Examination. Scholarships for art, design technology, drama, music, sport, and all-round ability are also available.

A substantial number of fee remissions, up to the value of the full fees, are available each year for pupils who may not otherwise be able to attend the School. The fee payable is related to parental income.

Please note that bursary funding is not available for boarding places at the School.

Please apply to the Admissions Office for further information.

Curriculum. In the first three year groups, a general preparation is given. With a few exceptions, boys take all of their GCSE examinations in the Upper Fifth Form. There is no early specialisation, but various options are available, with a particularly wide range of languages, including Japanese and Mandarin Chinese, available. There is a Section Française available for native speakers. PSHE is taught to all boys throughout the School. A Learning Support department assists boys with specific learning difficulties.

In the Sixth Form, AS and A Level subjects can be taken in a wide range of combinations. The International Baccalaureate is also offered, and there are vocational BTEC courses for Sports Science, Music Technology and Business Studies. Pupils are also prepared for the Oxbridge entrance process.

Organisation. The academic progress of boys in the First and Third Forms is under the supervision of the Head of Lower School, and that of the Fifth and Sixth Forms is under the supervision of the Head of Upper School. Pastoral matters are dealt with by the respective Heads of Year and their assistants. Boys are allocated to one of eight Houses, which have Upper and Lower School sections, and Housemasters have general responsibility for supervising pupils' development in co-curricular activities. Boys in the Upper Fifth and Sixth Forms have a personal tutor to whom they can turn for help and advice if required.

Religious Education. Every attempt is made to stress the relevance of religious thought to modern living. Although the School has a close link with the Anglican Church, teaching is given in an ecumenical spirit.

Physical Education. Whitgift's sport is at the forefront of achievement, with over 130 national titles won in the past five years. More than 40 sports are available, including modern pentathlon, golf, judo and cycling. Many boys represent their country in a wide variety of sports, or go on to pursue a career at the highest level.

Music. All 10 and 11-year-old entrants have the opportunity to learn a musical instrument for their first term, free of charge.

Boys perform in various choral and instrumental ensembles. The School enjoys close links with the Royal Philharmonic Orchestra, enabling pupils to learn side-by-side with professional musicians. Orchestras and choirs tour internationally and perform at the Royal Albert Hall, the Royal Festival Hall, Cadogan Hall, Goodwood House, and the Royal Pavilion, Brighton.

Other activities. There is a Combined Cadet Force, with specialist Royal Navy, Army and RAF sections, and a Duke of Edinburgh's Award scheme. There is a large number of plays and productions, and boys are encouraged to join some of the many school societies. Field courses and foreign exchange visits are held regularly during the holidays, and there is a very large number of link schools in many parts of the world.

Careers Advice. There is a well-equipped Careers Room, and a full service of guidance is offered regarding choice of career and courses in higher education. The vast majority of pupils go on to universities and colleges after leaving Whitgift.

Charitable status. Whitgift School is part of the Whitgift Foundation, which is a Registered Charity, number 312612. The Foundation exists to provide education for boys and girls.

Winchester College

College Street, Winchester, Hampshire SO23 9NA

Tel:	01962 621100 (Headmaster and Office)
	01962 621200 (Bursar)
	01962 621247 (Admissions)
Fax:	01962 621106
email:	admissions@wincoll.ac.uk
website:	www.winchestercollege.org

Motto: '*Manners Makyth Man*'

Winchester College – 'the College of the Blessed Virgin Mary of Winchester near Winchester' – was founded in 1382 by William of Wykeham, Bishop of Winchester. Wykeham planned and created a double foundation consisting of two Colleges, one at Winchester and the other (New College) at Oxford. The two Colleges are still closely associated.

Visitor: The Bishop of Winchester

Warden: C J F Sinclair, CBE, BA, FCA

Sub-Warden: R H Sutton, BA

Fellows:
J B W Nightingale, MA, DPhil
The Rt Hon Sir Andrew Longmore, PC, MA
R B Woods, CBE, MA
Ms J H Ritchie, QC, LLM
Professor Sir Curtis Price, KBE, AM, PhD, Hon RAM, FKC, FRNCM, Hon FASC (*Warden of New College*)
Professor C T C Sachrajda, FRS, PhD, FInstP, CPhys
P Frith, MD, FRCP, FRCOphth
Major-General J D Shaw, CB, CBE, MA
C M Farr, MA
A N Joy, MA
N E H Ferguson CBE, BSc, MBA

Bursar and Secretary: A S Little, MA, FCA

Headmaster: R D Townsend, MA, DPhil

Second Master: R J Wyke, MA

Director of Studies: J G Webster, MA, DPhil

Registrar: A C Shedden, BEd

Deputy Registrar: Mrs P C McComb

Assistant Masters:
C J Tolley, MA, DPhil, FRCO
S P Anderson, MA (*Senior Tutor*)
A P Wolters, BSc, PhD, CChem, MRSC
L C Wolff, MA, FRSA (*Head of History of Art*)
C H J Hill, MA
M D Wallis, MA
A S Leigh, MA
N I P MacKinnon, BA
W E Billington, MA, MICE
P G Cornish, BA, MMus, FTCL, ARCM, PhD (*Head of Mathematics*)
D J Ceiriog-Hughes, MA, PhD, FRSA
Miss C J Ovenden, MA
A P McMaster, BSc
I E Fraser, BSc (*Master in College*)
L N Taylor, BA Ed (*Senior Housemaster*)
S K Woolley, MA
M D Hebron, BA, DPhil (*Director of Drama*)
P J M Cramer, MA, PhD
C Cai, BA, MA, PhD
C J Good, BEd
J E Hodgins, BSc, PhD
G J Watson, BA (*Head of Economics*)
C G Yates, BA (*Head of Careers and Higher Education*)
J P Cullerne, BSc, DPhil (*Under Master*)
C S McCaw, BSc, DPhil, DES, CChem, MRSC (*Head of Science*)
A D Adlam, Dip Mus
A P Dakin, BA
M Romans, BA, MA, PhD
Mrs L J Quinault, MA
J McManus, MChem, PhD
N A Salwey, MA, MSc, DPhil, ARCM, LGSM (*Deputy Master of Music*)
P M Herring, MA
D E Pounds, BSc (*Head of Geography*)
Mrs A M Lombardo, MA, BA (*Head of French*)
J J L Douglas, BA, MSc (*Head of Physics*)
D I Follows, MChem, MSc, DPhil (*Head of Chemistry*)
N P Wilks, MA, ARAM (*Master of Music*)
D E Yeomans, BA
M G Crossland, MPhys
M J Winter, MA
G E Munn, MSci

M D Archer, MA, FRCO, FGCM, FNMSM, ARCM
  (*Director of Chapel Music*)
S E Hart, MEng (*Head of Sport*)
S A Tarrant, MEng (*Head of Design Technology*)
J P Spencer, MA (*Head of Classics*)
J M Burridge, BA (*Head of PE*)
T E Giddings, BA, MSt
P E Hepworth, BSc, PhD
S D Rich, BA (*Head of MFL and Russian*)
A P Savory, BSc, PhD (*Head of Biology*)
Mrs C L Talks, MA
A Vieilleville, BA
C N Berry, MA, PhD
L M Guymer, MA PhD (*Head of History*)
Mrs E C Macey, BA, BDes (*Head of Art*)
A P Jaffe, BSc
J J C Wright, BSc
J J Sutton, BA, BMus, ARCO
E J Donovan, MSc
Miss S Atwill, BA
Dr A French, MA, MPhil, MSc, PhD
D J Leigh, MA (*Head of PSHE*)
S D Macey
Miss R Poole, MBioCHem, MSc
M J Rogers, BSc
O Tarney, BMus, MMus
C J Palm, BSc, MCMI
Mrs C Crowther, MA
A W E Artley, BA
Miss C Cadoret, BA
R E J Foster, MA, MSt, DPhil
R S Stillman, BA, MA (*Head of English*)
R J Topley, MSc, PhD
Mrs M Zampeta, BA, MSc, MA
R S Moore, BA
J A A Barron, BA, MSci, PhD,
C P Barnes, BSc
H B Cullen, BA
J E de Bono, BA
L P F Dunne, MA, BPhil
J R Fox, BSc, ARCS
J M Greenwood, BA
S J Harden, MA, MSt, DPhil
L J Ronaldson, MA, PhD
C Schofield, BA (*Head of Learning Support*)
T D Shaw, BSc
O O'Neill, BA
M P Bruzon, BA
M L Dedynski, BA
P P Elliott, BA
A M Humphreys, MMath
J J Pinnells, BA
E K M Thomas, BA
O L Welsford, BA

In Junior Part (Year 9) all boys study Biology, Chemistry, English, French or German, Geography, History, Latin, Mathematics, Physics and PE. A third foreign language is taken from Chinese, French or German, Ancient Greek, Russian and Spanish. Art, Design Technology and Music are studied by all boys on a rotating basis. At the end of Junior Part, boys make GCSE choices. Mathematics, English Language, Latin and French or German are mandatory subjects. Boys must additionally chose at least two sciences (Biology, Chemistry, Physics). They may take up to two further modern foreign languages and up to two creative subjects (Art, DT, Music). Ancient Greek and Geography are also options. Boys will normally take nine subjects to GCSE in V Book (Year 11). In VI Book (Years 12 and 13), almost any combination of arts and sciences can be studied. The School teaches the Cambridge Pre-U syllabus in all VI Book subjects. Division – a daily lesson encompassing many aspects of culture and civilisation – plays a central role throughout the curriculum at all levels.

Scholarships and Exhibitions. The Scholarship examination (Election) is held in May each year, and about 14 scholarships are awarded. All scholarships are means-tested. Bursaries are available. Scholars live together in College.

Based on performance in the Scholarship Examination, about six Exhibitions may also be awarded which ensure a place in a Commoner House. Applications for bursaries are encouraged.

Candidates must be over 12 and under 14 on 1st September following the examination.

Further particulars and copies of specimen papers can be obtained from *The Master in College, Winchester College, College Street, Winchester, Hampshire SO23 9NA.*

Music Awards. Music scholarships are available annually; they are subject to means-testing and carry free instrumental tuition for up to two instruments and singing. There are also Music Exhibitions, which offer free tuition for one or more specified instruments. In cases of financial need additional bursary grants will be awarded. One or more awards may be reserved for Winchester College Quiristers and for Sixth Form entrants. Successful candidates are generally at the level of Grade VI–VIII distinction. Music award tests take place in late January/early February each year. Music can also be offered as an option in the academic scholarship examinations in May.

The award of all Music Scholarships is conditional upon candidates satisfying the academic requirements for entry into the School. Music Award candidates who are not taking the Scholarship Examination will be required to take the Entrance Examination. For 13+ entry, candidates must be under 14 on 1 September of the year they come into the School.

The Master of Music is pleased to answer queries and to see prospective candidates at any time. Full details available from *The Master of Music, Winchester College Music School, Culver Road, Winchester, Hampshire SO23 9JF.*

Bursaries. In cases of financial hardship bursaries are available to support boys entering the school. All bursaries are awarded on a means-tested basis. Particulars of bursaries may be obtained from the Bursar. Please contact Mrs C P Hann (cph@wincoll.ac.uk).

Sixth Form entry. A number of places is offered each year to boys joining the Sixth Form from other schools. Examinations and interviews take place in Winchester in late January each year. Enquiries should be sent to the Deputy Registrar (admissions@wincoll.ac.uk).

Fees per term (2014–2015). Boarders £11,580 (£34,740 pa). There is an entrance fee of £500.

Commoners. There are about 60 Commoners in each House. The Housemasters are:
Chernocke House (A): J R Fox
Moberly's (B): P M Herring
Du Boulay's (C): L N Taylor
Fearon's (D): M J Winter
Morshead's (E): Dr J McManus
Hawkins' (F): Dr J E Hodgins
Sergeant's (G): D E Yeomans
Bramston's (H): Dr J P Cullerne
Turner's (I): C J Good
Kingsgate House (K): Dr M Romans

Boys should be registered any time after their eighth birthday and before the end of Year 5 (9+ to 10+). They are usually at least 13, but under 14, on 31 August in the year of entry to the School but exceptions may be considered in special circumstances. Places are offered after tests and an interview in Year 6. The Registrar holds a Reserve List, which includes the names of late applicants, but it is essential to have a place at another school until a firm place at Winchester has been confirmed.

The entrance examination covers the normal subjects; particulars and copies of recent papers may be obtained from the Deputy Registrar.

Term of entry. Usually September.

Old Boys' Society, Wykehamist Society. *Secretary*: A F J Roe, 17 College Street, Winchester SO23 9LX.

Charitable status. Winchester College is a Registered Charity, number 1139000. The objects of the charity are the advancement of education and activities connected therewith.

Wisbech Grammar School

North Brink, Wisbech, Cambs PE13 1JX

Tel: 01945 583631 Senior School
        01945 586780 Magdalene House
Fax: 01945 476746 Senior School
        01945 586781 Magdalene House
email: Office@WisbechGrammar.com
website: WisbechGrammar.com
Twitter: @WisbechGrammar
Facebook: /WisbechGrammar

Founded during the turbulent reign of Richard II in 1379, Wisbech Grammar School was established by a society of local merchants, the Guild of the Holy Trinity, to provide education for poor boys of the town. Now a fully co-educational day school, it draws its 544 pupils aged 4 to 18 from the three counties of Cambridgeshire, Norfolk and Lincolnshire.

Occupying a prime site on North Brink, one of England's most handsome Georgian streets and a magnet for film makers, the school – the finest in Fenland – is set in 33 acres of magnificent grounds in a conservation area. Open, friendly and welcoming, the school is small enough for staff to know all the pupils individually, but large enough to provide an impressive range of opportunities. The traditional emphasis on the pursuit of academic success is complemented by a sensitive and highly effective pastoral care system. All members of the senior school and Magdalene House Preparatory School are encouraged to develop their confidence and unlock their true potential, both inside and outside the classroom, as well as engaging with the wider community.

Governing Body:

Chairman: Dr D Barter, MB BS, FRCP, FRCPCH, DCH
Vice Chairman: J E Warren
R Calleja
C Goad, ACA
S King
The Venerable Hugh McCurdy, Archdeacon of Huntingdon and Wisbech
I MacLachlan
Mrs C Mair
Mrs S Meekins
Mrs E Morris, LLB
Dr F Sconce, MBChB, DFFP
Dr F P Treasure, MA, MSc, PhD, CStat

Nominated by the Master of Magdalene College, Cambridge:
Prof J Raven
The Revd P Hobday, Chaplain of Magdalene College

Bursar and Clerk to the Governors: S Halls, DMS, ACMA, MCMI

Teaching Staff:
* *Head of Department*
† *Head of House*
§ *Part-time*

¶ *Old Pupil*

Headmaster: C N Staley, BA, MBA

Deputy Head: Miss C M Noxon, BA (*German*)
Director of Studies: M L Forrest, MA (*Chemistry, *General Studies*)
Head of Middle School: K J Mann, BA, PhD (*History*)
Head of Upper School: M P Stump, BA (**Art & Design, Head of Upper School*)
Head of Sixth Form: Miss L Kemp, BA (*English*)

T D Chapman, MA (*History, *Government & Politics*)
S L Clarke, BSc (**ICT, Computing*)
§T W Claydon, BSc (*PE and Games*)
Miss A M Clayton, BA (*English*)
C Cole, BSc (*Physics*)
¶Miss D C Cook, BSc (*Girls' PE and Games*)
Mrs S D Cooper, BA (**Textiles, Art & Design, Deputy Head of Middle School*)
M S Davies, MSci (*Mathematics*)
Miss A Dunnet, BA (*Girls' PE and Games*)
S Emmerson, BA (*History)
Mrs E M Farr, BA (*English*)
§Mrs C A Fear, BA (*English*)
¶Mrs L Feaviour, BA (*Textiles, Art & Design*)
J G Fitzsimmons, BMus (*Director of Music*)
Mrs S C Fox, BA (**Lower School Science*, †*Holmes*)
R D Frost, BEd (**Design Technology*)
¶D S Garfoot, BSc (*PE & Games, Geography*, †*Sparks*)
S V Ghosh, BA, MA (*German)
¶Miss J M Gomm, BSc (**Psychology, Girls' PE and Games*)
Mrs S M Goodier, BSc (*Girls' PE and Games*, †*Peckover*)
Mrs C Green, BSc (*Physics)
Mrs C Harding, PG Dip, AMBDA (*SENCO*)
Miss S E Harris, BEd (*Academic PE and Special Projects Coordinator, EVC*)
P J Harrison, BA (*Art*, †*Clarkson*)
G E Howes, BSc (*Mathematics)
A P Jarvis, MA, MEd, PhD (*English)
M A Jarvis (*Hockey, Design & Technology*)
T Jestin, MA (*French*)
R D Killick, BSc (*Geography)
P J King, MA (*English, Media Relations*)
Miss J Lasouska, BSc (*Biology*)
A C Laybourne, MSc (*PE & Sport*)
A J McGarry, MA (*German, Director of Holiday Activities*)
S J Miller, BSc, PhD (**Science, *Biology, Deputy Head of Sixth Form & Higher Education Adviser*)
Mrs J M Missin, BA (*Assistant Director of Music, Deputy Head of 6th Form*)
§A Moores, BA (*Spanish*)
R W Morgan, BSc (*Chemistry)
Mrs N Neighbour MA (*French)
G H Nunnerley, BSc (**Careers, Geography*)
Mrs A Ogston, BSc (*Mathematics, Deputy Head of Upper School*)
G Paine, BSc, PhD (*Chemistry*)
§Mrs J T Reavell, BEd (*PE and Sport*)
§Mrs A Sanders (*Mathematics – classroom support*)
M G Sansom, BA (**Economics, *Business Studies*)
Mrs M Skinner, BA (*German*)
¶Mrs A L Sloan, BSc, MA (**Food & Nutrition*)
Miss K Taylor, BA (*Geography*)
C Thursby, BA, MA (*Mathematics, Director of Examinations*)
¶Mrs M Tooke, BSc (*Food and Nutrition*)
P J A Webb, BA (**Director of Sport, History*)
¶J D Williams (*Sports Coach*)

Chaplain: Father P West
Headmaster's Secretary: Mrs K Massen/Mrs T Gambell
Admissions Secretary: Mrs S Davies
Marketing Director: J Macdonald

Magdalene House Preparatory School
Headmaster: C E Moxon, BA
Deputy Head: Mrs G D Reinbold, MA

Development. The ongoing development programme has included a 6th Form centre and a floodlit, all-weather Astroturf pitch, as well as the refurbishment of the science laboratories and an upgrade of the information technology infrastructure. A new refectory is set to open in 2015 and a major expansion of the on-site playing field provision has recently been completed. Two more classrooms and a new hall have been constructed for the rapidly expanding preparatory school, which takes its name from Magdalene College. The Cambridge college has enjoyed a close connection with the Grammar School for over 350 years and the Master and Fellows appoint two of their number to the governing body. Magdalene House Preparatory School pupils also enjoy the extensive benefits of the senior school facilities and teaching expertise.

Senior school admission. The main entry is at age 11 by a competitive entrance examination in January. The test, which consists of mathematics, English and verbal reasoning, is designed to discover potential. Pupils can also enter at 2nd, 3rd and 4th Form levels. Offers of 6th Form places are made on the basis of interview and a report from a pupil's current school.

Fees per term (2014–2015). Senior school £3,885; Magdalene House Preparatory School £2,733.33. Means-tested bursaries are available at Key Stages 3, 4 and 5. These are known as Governors' Assisted Places and are reviewed annually. Currently, 104 pupils receive support from the scheme. Application forms for Governors' Assisted Places are available from the Bursar.

Travel to school. The school's catchment area embraces King's Lynn, Hunstanton, Downham Market, March, Whittlesey, Peterborough and Long Sutton. School buses run from a number of these places, visiting villages en route, and there is a late bus for pupils involved in after-school activities. The school is also well served by local buses.

Teaching and learning. The school aims to foster a love of learning and to provide an environment which nurtures talent and breeds success. In recent years the expansion of the teaching staff has helped to reduce class size and foster more individual learning. There is a high regard for the traditional disciplines, but the school is also ready to open up exciting new fields of study. An extensive academic curriculum in the first three years of the senior school includes opportunities to sample a number of technology subjects, and Spanish is offered from the third form for pupils who have shown aptitude. One pupil has recently reached the national finals of the Foreign Language Spelling Bee competition. The option system at GCSE ensures a broad-based curriculum as well as allowing pupils to play to their strengths. In the 6th Form, 25 subjects are provided and pupils have their first chance to take business studies, economics, government and politics, music technology and graphics. The school also provides support which allows bright pupils with learning difficulties and disabilities to rise to the challenge of a rigorous academic education.

The 6th Form experience. The school has a first-class track record in enabling pupils to realize their university and career aspirations. Entrusted with a greater degree of independence, sixth formers are encouraged to make their mark and develop leadership qualities, both within the house system and at a wider level. The 6th Form centre provides a fine facility for the school's most senior pupils.

Creative and performing arts. The flourishing music department provides practical opportunities for pupils to develop their creative talents. Nine visiting instrumental and vocal tutors give individual tuition to nearly a fifth of the pupils, and there are numerous opportunities to join in choirs, wind and steel bands and perform in the annual concerts and community charity events.

A dynamic tradition of drama allows pupils to build their confidence and hone their acting skills, both in major productions on the main stage and in more intimate performances in the studio. Audiences have sampled everything from Renaissance drama to experimental twentieth century works, and ambitious recent productions have included *Amadeus, Oh what a lovely war* and *Twelfth night*.

The art and design department is a highly visible presence in the school, mounting exhibitions on-site and at the Reed Barn at the neighbouring National Trust property, Peckover House, and talented artists and designers regularly win places at the top art colleges.

A competitive spirit. The Director of Sport ensures that teams enjoy the challenge of a competitive fixture list against schools across the eastern counties and in the midlands, and Wisbech Grammar School takes pride in punching above its weight. An extensive inter-house programme also allows pupils of all abilities to develop their competitive spirit. The main games for boys are rugby in the Michaelmas term and hockey and rugby sevens in the Lent term, together with cricket, athletics and tennis in the Trinity term. Girls play hockey in the Michaelmas term and netball and rugby sevens in the Lent term and rounders, tennis and athletics in the Trinity term. For pupils above the 3rd Form who are not involved in a major team game, the options range from badminton and basketball to archery and spinning. The facilities include a recently refurbished, full-sized sports hall, a fitness suite and the extensive on-site floodlit Astroturf pitch, together with generous playing field provision. Pupils also enjoy access to a covered swimming pool, a sports hall, a dance studio and a fitness centre at a neighbouring leisure centre.

Beyond the classroom. Wisbech Grammar School believes in learning on location. The biology department has recently run a field class in Galapagos, and expeditions to Borneo and Madagascar are in the pipeline. Geographers have explored the west coast of the United States and there are frequent art trips to New York. There is a flourishing exchange with the Willibrord Gymnasium in Emmerich, and the French department has added a GCSE study trip to Normandy and an A Level cross-curricular visit to Paris to the annual chateau trip. Pupils also criss-cross the country for hands-on learning, and excursions such as the 3rd Form trip to Shakespeare's Globe or the Royal Shakespeare Theatre run regularly. A sports tour to Barbados provides a chance to compete in the Caribbean sun, while 130 pupils participate in the Duke of Edinburgh's Award, with those at the highest level mounting expeditions to the Lake District, Snowdonia and Mont Blanc. The senior school adventure begins with an outdoor activity week for the first form in rural Shropshire.

Closer to home, sixth formers hone their business skills in the Young Enterprise scheme, regularly reaching the regional finals. Clubs such as language leaders, riding and grow, cook, eat help to stretch the mind and develop life skills. Members of Caritas, the charity and community service team, reach out to those in need, both on their doorstep and across the globe, and the school hosts an annual party for local pensioners.

Magdalene House Preparatory School caters for pupils from Reception to Prep 6. (*For further details see entry in IAPS section.*)

Old Wisbechians Society. Further information about the society can be obtained from the Admissions Secretary at the school, to whom requests for the school magazine, *Riverline*, should be sent. News of past pupils is published on the school website, WisbechGrammar.com.

Charitable status. The Wisbech Grammar School Foundation is a Registered Charity, number 1087799. It exists to promote the education of boys and girls.

Withington Girls' School

Wellington Road, Fallowfield, Manchester M14 6BL
Tel: 0161 224 1077
Fax: 0161 248 5377
email: office@wgs.org
website: www.wgs.org
Twitter: @WGSManchester

Motto: *Ad Lucem*
Independent (formerly Direct Grant)
Founded 1890.

Board of Governors:
Chair: Mrs E Lee, LLB
Mr D Illingworth, BA, FCA (*Hon Treasurer*)
Mr M Adlestone
Dr J Allred, MB ChB, MRCGP, DRCOG, DFFP
Mrs C H Evans, BA
Professor S B Furber, CBE, FRS, FREng, FBCS, CEng, MA, PhD
Miss S Johnson-Manning, GRSM, LRAM, ARCM
Mrs J Kinney, FdSc, LLB
Dr A Kirkham, BSc, BA, MA, PhD, ACA
Mrs M McVeigh, MSc
Mr A Pathak, BSc
Mr M Pike, LLB
Mrs L Sabbagh, BA

Headmistress: Mrs S E Marks, MA Oxon, AdvCertEdMan Leicester, CertTh Exeter

Deputy Head: Mrs S J Haslam, BA Lancaster (*English*)

Director of Studies: Mr I McKenna, BA Manchester (*Religious Studies*)

Bursar: Mrs S Senn, BSc ACA

Full-time Staff:
Mrs J M Baylis, BA Leeds (*Drama & Theatre Studies*)
Mr S Boddy, BA Oxon, MA London (*Economics*)
Mrs J W Bowie, MA Dundee (*English*)
Mrs L Bradshaw, MA Cantab (*Physics*)
Miss K L Browning, BA London (*Geography*)
Mrs J Buckley, BA Durham (*Geography*)
Miss M Cahill, BA Leeds (*History*)
Mrs A Collard, BSc Durham (*Mathematics*)
Mrs N Cottam, BSc Durham (*Biology, Careers*)
Ms C J Davies, BA Hull, MA Open University (*English*)
Mrs K Day, BA Manchester (*Religious Studies*)
Mr K Eckersall, BSc Leicester, MA Durham (*Education*)
Miss J E Ellis, BA Bath (*German*)
Mrs M Ferrol, BEd Dunfermline College (*Physical Education*)
Mrs S E Fletcher, BEd Brighton (*Mathematics*)
Mr C Forrest, MPhys Manchester (*Physics*)
Ms A Godwin, BA Oxon (*Spanish*)
Mrs S E Hamilton, MA Aberdeen (*Geography*)
Miss H Hardwick, MChem Manchester (*Chemistry*)
Mrs J Healey, BSc Newcastle (*FTT*)
Miss A R H Holland, BMus Birmingham (*Music*)
Mrs J C Howling, MA Cantab (*Classics*)
Dr S E Madden, PhD Newcastle (*Biology*)
Ms J C Maher, BA Sheffield (*History*)
Dr E A Maisey, PhD London (*Chemistry*)
Mrs Y T Menzies, MA Salford (*French, German*)
Ms C Morton, MA Sheffield (*Spanish*)
Mrs S I Mounteney, BSc London (*Mathematics*)
Miss B O'Neal, MSc MMU (*Psychology*)
Mrs C Ositelu, DEA-ès-L Nantes (*French*)
Mr A Parry, BSc Manchester (*Mathematics*)
Miss J Richards, BA Liverpool John Moores (*PE & Games*)

Mrs E K Robinson, MA Cantab (*Classics*)
Mrs G E Sargent, BMus London (*Music*)
Mrs G A Smith, BSc Nottingham (*Biology, Chemistry*)
Mr A Snowden, BSc Warwick (*ICT*)
Dr D Verity, PhD Hull (*Physics*)
Dr C P G Vilela, PhD Lisbon (*Biology, Chemistry*)
Ms N A West, BA Manchester (*English*)

Junior School:
Mrs E S K Burrows, MA St Andrews (*Year 6*)
Mrs S J Rigby, BA Nottingham (*Year 5*)
Mrs K Williams, BA Victoria, Canada (*Year 5*)
Mrs H Stallard, BA Newcastle-upon-Tyne (*Year 4*)
Mrs B Lowe, BSc Northumbria (*Year 3*)
Mrs D Odeyinde, BSc Queen's Belfast (*Year 3*)

Part-time Staff:
Mrs C Air, BA Oxon (*History*)
Mrs U Asim, BSc UMIST (*Science*)
Mrs S Birch, BEd Lancaster (*FTT*)
Mrs F Cotton, BA Heriot-Watt (*Design & Technology*)
Miss S Deadman, BEd De Montfort (*PE & Games*)
Mrs C E Edge, MA Leeds (*English*)
Mrs R Fildes, MA MMU (*Art*)
Mrs P M Gavan, BA Open (*Mathematics*)
Ms L Holden, BA Edinburgh (*Classics*)
Mrs A Humblet, BA University of Dijon (*French, Spanish*)
Mrs J Johnston, BA MMU (*Art*)
Dr Z Kenny, PhD Edinburgh (*Biology*)
Mrs V Kochhar, BSc Exeter (*Mathematics*)
Ms M Lopez, BSc Pennsylvania (*Spanish*)
Miss M McLaren, BA Cantab (*Classics*)
Mrs K Orme, BSc Northumbria (*PE & Games*)
Dr R Pavey, PhD Liverpool (*Science*)
Mrs V Scott, BSc Liverpool (*Mathematics*)
Mrs J Stockton, BA Leeds (*English*)
Mrs Z Taylor, BA MMU (*Art*)
Dr E L Terrill, DPhil Oxon (*Mathematics*)
Mrs J C Wallis, BA Leeds (*Politics*)
Mrs N Watson, BA Leeds (*FTT, Careers*)

Librarians: Mrs D Sutton, MA MMU; Mrs H Brackenbury, MA Sheffield
Network Manager: Mr A Lockett, BSc Bradford
School Nurses: Mrs J Lees, RGN; Mrs V Proudley, PgDip Clinical Nursing
Examinations Officer: Mrs H Coubrough
Assistant Examinations Officer: Dr S E Madden PhD Newcastle
Development Director: Mrs T Leden, BSc Surrey
DofE Award Scheme Coordinator: Mrs R Lindsay-Dunn, MSc Manchester

Administration:
PA to Headmistress: Mrs A L Adams BA Sheffield Hallam
School Secretary: Mrs A Easton MSc Birmingham
Assistant Bursar: Mrs L Quinn Matthews BA MMU, ACMA

Since its foundation in 1890, Withington has remained relatively small, with about 650 pupils, 90 of whom are in the Junior Department and 160 in the Sixth Form. This size allows a friendly, intimate environment together with a broad and balanced curriculum. Withington provides a wide range of opportunities for girls, helping them to achieve their potential, academically, socially and personally. Withington attracts pupils from a wide geographical area and from many different social and cultural backgrounds, producing a diversity in which the school rejoices.

The School's A Level and GCSE results have been consistently outstanding. Girls who gain a place as a result of the entrance examination take at least 10 GCSE/IGCSE subjects, followed by 4 AS Levels, 3 or 4 A2 Levels. In addition, they have the option to take AS or A Level General Studies. Studies are directed towards developing learning for its own sake as well as towards the ultimate goal of University entrance, including Oxford and Cambridge. All the girls go on to Higher Education.

The School enjoys excellent facilities and has an ongoing programme of major developments. Recent projects have included a new classroom wing, new Science Laboratories, enhanced Language and Music facilities and a new Sixth Form Centre (2009). A new, expanded Junior School Building and a central, enclosed "Hub" at the heart of the senior school are due for completion by September 2015.

Withington fosters all-round development and the girls' academic studies are complemented by an extensive range of extra-curricular activities. Music is strong and very popular; there is a comprehensive range of choirs and orchestras, involving all age groups. Drama also thrives with regular productions including original works. Girls play a variety of sports, including hockey, lacrosse, netball, tennis, athletics, cricket and football. Pupils are regularly selected for county and national squads and there are regular sports tours within Europe and further afield, such as to Australia and South Africa. In addition to fixtures with other schools, games players compete within the school's House system. The four Houses, named after Withington's founders, also provide a focus for dramatic, musical and other activities.

The Duke of Edinburgh's Award and Young Enterprise Schemes, Model United Nations Conferences, voluntary work in the local community, Science and Mathematics Olympiads, residential activity weekends, foreign trips and local fieldwork all feature prominently in the School's provision. Numerous extra-curricular clubs and societies include Italian, photography, bridge, literature, debating, mosaics, robotics, chess, board games and dance. Awareness of the wider world is encouraged, girls participate in many fundraising activities and the School has special links with a hospital and two schools in Kenya. Each year parties of girls give up their holiday time to participate in community projects in Uganda and The Gambia; in 2015 a World Challenge expedition will also depart to Thailand and Cambodia. Preparation for life after school starts early and involves a programme of careers advice, work experience and UCAS application guidance.

Visitors are warmly welcomed at any time. Open Days are held in November. A substantial number of means-tested Bursaries are awarded annually together with awards from various outside Trusts. Entrance at age 7–11 is by Entrance Examination, held in January, together with interview and report from current school. Admission to the Sixth Form is by interview and is conditional upon GCSE results.

The School engages in a number of projects with local State schools and has strong links with the local community. Withington was The Sunday Times Parent Power Top Independent Secondary School of the Year 2009/10 and the Financial Times Best Value Independent Day School in 2012.

Fees per term (2014–2015). Senior School £3,600, Junior School £2,675. LAMDA and individual instrumental music lessons are charged separately.

Charitable status. Withington Girls' School is a Registered Charity, number 526632. It aims to provide an exceptional quality of opportunity, to encourage independence of mind and high aspirations for girls from seven to eighteen.

Wolverhampton Grammar School

Compton Road, Wolverhampton WV3 9RB
Tel: 01902 421326
Fax: 01902 421819
email: wgs@wgs.org.uk
website: www.wgs.org.uk
Twitter: @WGS1512
Facebook: /Wolverhampton-Grammar-School-Official

Wolverhampton Grammar School was founded in 1512 by Sir Stephen Jenyns – a Wolverhampton man who achieved success as a wool merchant, became a member of The Merchant Taylors' Company then Lord Mayor of London. He decided to benefit his home town by founding a school "for the instruction of youth in good manners and learning". The school retains close links with the Company.

Wolverhampton Grammar School is now an independent, selective day school for boys and girls aged 11–18 from a wide catchment area throughout the West Midlands, Staffordshire and Shropshire.

In 2011 the school opened a junior school (Wolverhampton Grammar Junior School) for students aged 7–11.

The school's mission is to provide education as individual as your child. The school delivers a personalised curriculum to provide an education and learning experience that is unique. Students achieve excellent GCSE and A Level exam results alongside an experience that includes the largest range of extra-curricular activities available in the area.

The school was inspected in April 2011 and was judged to be excellent in all areas. The report can be read on the ISI website: www.isi.net.

Council Members:
Chairman: Mr Philip Sims, ACIB
The Mayor of Wolverhampton (*ex officio*)
Mrs Anne-Marie Brennan
Mr Mervyn Brooker, BA
Revd Sarah Cawdell
Mr Robin Cooper (*OW*) (*ex officio USA*)
Mrs Mina Crisp
Dr Stephen Gower, MA, PhD (*OW*) (*Appointed by the University of Birmingham*)
Mr Peter Hawthorne, CBE, MA (*OW*)
Ms Kate Lawrence
Professor Keith Madelin, OBE, MSc, CEng, FICE, FIHT
Mr Peter Magill (*Appointed by the Merchant Taylors' Company*)
Dr Mark Nicholls, BA, MA, PhD (*Appointed by St John's College Cambridge*)
Mr Tony Phillips (*OW*) (*Appointed by the Old Wulfrunians Association*)
Mr Jay Patel
Mr Robert Purshouse, LLB (*OW*)
Mr James Sage, BSc Hons
Mr Sathnam Sanghera, MA (*OW*)
Mr Eddie Sergeant, BSc, BTh (*OW*)
Mr Carl Tatton, BA, ACMA

(OW) *Old Wulfrunian*

Head: Mrs Kathy Crewe-Read, BSc Aberystwyth

Deputy Heads:
Mr Peter Hills, BA Nottingham
Mr Nic Anderson, BSc Leeds

Head of Junior School:
Mr Andrew Hymer, BA Sheffield, DipEd, MA Birmingham City, NPQH

Staff:
Mrs Kate Baker, BA Swansea (*Head of Big Six and Year 5*)
Mr Tom Baker, BSc Edinburgh (*Head of Geography*)
Mrs Linda Barnett, Cert Ed Dartford College (*Girls' Games*)
Mr Mark Benfield, BA Leeds, GCD Birmingham (*Assistant Head, Head of English & Assessment*)
Miss Emma Bowater, BA Birmingham City (*Art*)
Dr Neil Bradley, BSc, PhD Nottingham (*Maths*)
Miss Dawn Bradley-Buxton, BA Hons Birmingham Conservatoire (*Music*)
Mrs Sarah Brentnall, BA Birmingham (§*Modern Languages*)

Mrs Kathryn Burden, BA Worcester College Oxford (§*Music*)

Mr Nathan Burden, BSc Reading (*Physics*)

Dr Jean-Pierre Camm, BSc, PhD Sheffield (*Biology, Work Experience*)

Mr Andrew Carey, BSc London (*Head of Chemistry*)

Mr Russell Charlesworth, BA Lady Margaret Hall Oxford (*Head of History*)

Mr Steven Clancy, BSc Loughborough (*Boys' PE & Games, English*)

Mrs Clare Cooper, BA Royal Holloway London (*Year 5 Teacher (NQT)*)

Mrs Victoria Corbett, BA Ripon and York St John (*Big Six Teacher*)

Mr Truan Cothey, BSc Lancaster (*Big Six Teacher*)

Mr Nigel Crust, BA Bangor (*Deputy Head of Sixth Form, Head of Boys' Games*)

Mrs Anna Dalton, BA Nottingham Trent (*Year 5 Teacher*)

Mr Joe David, BA Newcastle-upon-Tyne (*History*)

Mr Owen Davies, BSc Birmingham (*Chemistry & Physics*)

Mrs Katherine Dyer, BSc Gloucestershire (*Head of Year 9, Psychology, Girls' games*)

Mrs Katherine Finn, BA Manchester (*Head of Theology & Philosophy*)

Dr Karen Flavell, BSc, PhD Wolverhampton (*Biology*)

Mrs Diana Gibbs, BA Bristol (*Year 4 Teacher*)

Mrs Petra Grigat-Bradley, Erstes und Zweites Staatsexamen, Ruhr-Universität Bochum (§*Modern Languages*)

Ms Nikki Guidotti, BA Anglia Ruskin (§*Music, Music Technology*)

Mr Jonathan Hall, BA Newcastle upon Tyne (*Head of Year 11, English*)

Mr Edward Hamill, BSc Glasgow (*Science*)

Mrs Elizabeth Harris, BA Southampton (*Head of German*)

Mrs Helen Hills, BSc Nottingham (*Head of Biology*)

Mrs Mary Howard, BA Leicester, Dip RSA (§*OpAL*)

Mr Toby Hughes, MA, MPhil Queens' College Cambridge, PGCE Homerton College Cambridge (*Assistant Head, Head of Sixth Form*)

Mr Stephen Jackson-Turnbull, BA, MA Huddersfield (*Head of Year 8, Design & Technology*)

Mr John Johnson, BSc Aston (*Chemistry, Marketing, Games*)

Mr Peter Johnstone, BA Hull (*Head of Psychology*)

Miss Claudine Jones, BA Nottingham Trent, Dip RSA (*Head of Year 7, OpAL*)

Mr Theo King, ICC, Senior Coach (*Games Coach i/c cricket*)

Ms Alison Kingshott, BA, MA Royal Holloway & Bedford New College London (*Head of Classics*)

Mrs R Maria Laurino-Ryan, Cert Ed London (§*Theology & Philosophy, French, Italian*)

Mrs Pav Mahey, BA Central England (§*Head of ICT, Economics, Business Studies*)

Mrs Patrizia Manzai, BA Turin (*Head of Italian*)

Mr Robert Mason, BA Nottingham (*German*)

Miss Alison McAllister, BSc Birmingham, MA Wolverhampton (*Head of Girls' Games, Psychology*)

Mr Duncan McAllister, Tripos Christ's College Cambridge (§*Latin, Classics*)

Mr James Millichamp, BA, MA Wolverhampton (*Head of Art*)

Mr Nick Munson, BSc Birmingham (*Head of Physics*)

Mrs Rachel Munson, BA Leeds (§*Modern Languages*)

Mr Sam Neville-Young, BA University College London (*Maths*)

Dr Chris O'Brien, BSc, PhD Imperial College London (*Head of Maths*)

Mr Simon O'Malley, BA Wolverhampton (*Head of Design & Technology*)

Mr Simon Palmer, Senior Coach (§*Girls' Hockey Coach*)

Mrs Jill Pawluk, Prof Cert RAM, Dip RAM, LRAM (*Year 3 Teacher*)

Mr Mark Payne, BA Warwick (*English*)

Miss Rhiannon Platt, BA Birmingham (*English*)

Mrs Christine Preston, BSc Sheffield (*Deputy Head of Sixth Form, Maths*)

Mr Vince Raymond-Barker, BA Kent (*Head of French*)

Mr Jim Ryan, BEd Crewe & Alsager College, MEd, Adv Dip SNE Open University, AMBDA, SpLD APC (*Head of Year 10, OpAL*)

Miss Arti Shukla, BA Wolverhampton (*Year 4 Teacher*)

Mr Gordon Smith, BEd Loughborough (§*Design & Technology*)

Mr Tom Smith, BA Strathclyde (*Head of Economics & Business Studies*)

Mr Liam Taylor, BA Reading (*History*)

Miss Jill Trevor, BSc Wales (*Year 5 Teacher*)

Mr Ian Tyler, BA Saskatchewan, MEd Birmingham, Dip DA RADA (*Assistant Head, Head of Teaching & Learning, Director of OpAL, SENCO, English, Theatre Studies*)

Mr Kartar Uppal, BA Wadham College Oxford, MPhil Birmingham (*Maths*)

Mrs Diana Ward, BA, MA Birmingham (*Art*)

Miss Emily Watson, BSc Manchester (*Physics*)

Miss Helen Whittaker, MChem York (*Chemistry*)

Miss Victoria Wiseman, BA Cambridge (*Geography*)

Mr Jonathan Wood, BA Royal Holloway London (*Big Six Teacher, OpAL, Peer Support*)

Bursar: Mrs P Rudge
Head's PA: Mrs Nicola Murphy

Buildings. The stunning 23-acre site includes a purpose-built Sixth Form Centre and a £3.8 million Arts & Drama Centre home to the Viner Gallery and Hutton Theatre. A new Junior School was opened in September 2011, whilst at the same time a former art centre was transformed into the new Modern Languages suite. A Sports Centre and floodlit Astroturf pitches provide some of the best sporting facilities in the area, with a new Sports Pavilion unveiled in October 2012 providing panoramic views of the sports fields. The early 20th century Merridale and Caldicott buildings house laboratories that have been refurbished to the highest modern standards. State-of-the-art ICT facilities provide broadband internet access to all parts of the school.

Admission. The School accepts applications to the Junior, Senior and Sixth Form (boys and girls from Years 3 to 13) throughout the year, although new students usually join the school in September. The school's own entrance tests are held in the preceding November. For the Sixth Form: offers of places are made subject to GCSE results and interview.

Fees per term (2014–2015). Junior School £3,268, Senior School £4,085.

Entrance Scholarships. There are a number of options available which offer support with fees, including a range of Bursaries and Scholarships. The awards vary according to the level of family income and are reviewed annually so please contact Jane Morris, Admissions Registrar on 01902 421326 for further details.

Assistance with Fees. The School offers a number of means-tested bursaries to children from less affluent families who can demonstrate academically and personally that they will benefit from the opportunity of an education with Wolverhampton Grammar School. Bursaries are reviewed annually so please contact Jane Morris, Admissions Registrar on 01902 421326 for further details.

Curriculum. In the first three years students study a broad curriculum of English, Mathematics, three Sciences, History, Geography, Art, Information Communication Technology, Design Technology, Theology & Philosophy, PE & Games and Music, in addition to French, German and Latin or Italian. In Year 10 students pursue a core of English Language and Literature, three separate Sciences, Mathematics and at least one Modern Language. There is a wide range of additional optional subjects, and most students take ten GCSEs. 90% of students proceed to the Sixth Form to take three or four subjects at AS/A2 Level and almost all continue in Higher Education, including a number of students who go to Oxford or Cambridge and other leading Russell Group universities. Over 80% of students go on to their first choice university.

Games and Outdoor Activities. Wolverhampton Grammar School offers the largest range of extra-curricular activities, clubs, societies, trips, international expeditions and sport tours of any independent school in the area. Sport has a long tradition at the school and students compete at city, regional and national level. The 23-acre site includes rugby, cricket, hockey and football pitches, netball courts, an all-weather Astroturf and athletics track as well as a fully equipped sports centre with multi-gym and indoor courts for badminton, squash and nets. A 'sport for all' attitude exists in games and PE, where the staff endeavour to match the student to a sport or activity in which they can succeed. There is a commitment to the highest standards of skill and sportsmanship but the emphasis is also placed on enjoyment. The school participates in The Duke of Edinburgh's Award scheme and there are opportunities to undertake field trips and foreign exchanges. There is a vigorous outdoor education programme. The School also boasts Fives Courts as well as a purpose-built climbing wall and sports pavilion offering panoramic views of our large outdoor sports fields.

Dyslexia. The School's OpAL (Opportunities through Assisted Learning) programme, which started in September 1998, is designed to allow bright children with Specific Learning Difficulties (Dyslexia) to enjoy the challenge of a first-rate academic education. OpAL students have consistently achieved 100% A*–C grades at GCSE, and all A Level students have been offered university places.

Arts and Other Activities. Purpose-built facilities for art, music and drama provide the best venues possible for exhibitions and school productions. The location of the music department at the heart of the school ensures the sound of singing, ensemble and band music is always heard on campus. There is a wide variety of extra-curricular clubs and activities giving students the opportunity to discover and cultivate new interests, both inside and outside the classroom. A Community Service programme and an active student Charity Fundraising Committee ensure that all students are involved in working for the good of others.

Pastoral Care. The school is proud of the pastoral care and support it offers to its students. In the Junior and Middle Schools care is provided by a form tutor under the overall responsibility of the appropriate Heads of Schools. Regular consultations are held with parents supported by full and frequent reports. An important forum is the Student Parliament which consists of elected representatives from all year groups who are encouraged to voice concerns and suggest improvements to the running and organisation of the school. The weekly meetings, with the Head plus one other member of staff in attendance, are run by an elected Chair and Secretary.

Charitable status. Wolverhampton Grammar School Limited is a Registered Charity, number 1125268.

Woodbridge School

Burkitt Road, Woodbridge, Suffolk IP12 4JH
Tel: 01394 615000
Fax: 01394 380944
email: admissions@woodbridge.suffolk.sch.uk
website: www.woodbridge.suffolk.sch.uk

Motto: '*Pro Deo Rege Patria*'

Governing Body: The Trustees of The Seckford Foundation

Chairman: R Finbow, MA Oxon

Headmaster: N P Tetley, MA

Deputy Head: M R Streat, MA, PGCE
Director of Studies: G B Bruce, MA, CertEd
Senior Master: R F Broaderwick, BA, PhD
Senior Mistress: Miss H V Richardson, BA, PGCE
Chaplain: The Revd I A Wilson, BTh

Assistant Staff:
J R Penny, MA, CertEd
S E Cottrell, BEd, CSci, CPhys, MInstP
R E Fernley, BA, PGCE
A P Jackson, BSc, PGCE
Miss J A Gill, BEd, MA Ed
J A Hillman, BSc, CertEd
J H Stafford, ARCM
Mrs A McGlennon, BA, PGCE
Mrs A P Willett, CertEd, AdDipEd SEN
R A Carr, BA, ATC
B T Edwards, BA
P A Trett, BSc, CertEd
Mrs C V E Johnson, BA, PGCE
N E Smith, BA, CertEd
Mrs L R Chandler, MA, PGCSE
K J Stollery
L V Rickard, BSc, PhD, CertEd
M Davis, MA, BA
Mrs W E McNally, BSc, CertEd
J A Wharam, BSc, PhD, PGCE, CBiol, MIBiol
J M Percival, BA
Mrs T H Knowles, BEd
A G Lubbock, BSc, CertEd
Mrs C E Brown, CSci, CPhys, MInstP
Mrs A Hillman, BSc, CertEd
Miss S E Norman, BA, PGCE
C Eager, BA, CertEd
P M Lawrence, BA, MA, CertEd
D J Neuhoff, BA, UED
Mrs J A Hill, BSc, CertEd
A C Hunt, BSc
Mrs C F Neuhoff, DipEd
Mrs M M Barclay, CertEd, TEFL
D A Brous, BSc, CertEd, MA Ed
S D Richardson, BA, CertEd, CertTEFL
Mrs E R Green, BA, PGCE
H J Tebbutt, BA
J P Chandler, MA
Mrs C R Parker, BSc, CertEd
J M C Allen, BSc, MSt, PGCE
Mrs M G V Pilkington, BA, CertEd
Mrs H Guan, BA, CertEd
Mrs I Brown, BMedSci, MEd
Dr A E Renshaw, BA, MA, PhD, CertEd
J R Hill, BSc, PhD, QTS
Miss N L Sanders, BA
R N Bradshaw, BA, CertEd
Mrs J M Wright, BA, QTS
R S Willis, MA, CertEd
Mrs R Oldfield, BSc
M R Fernley, BA
Mrs M L Verona, BA, MSc, QTS
Ms N S Carter, BA, QTS
A C Garvie
Ms G L Mayes, BA, QTS
Mrs C F Davis, BA, CertEd
Mrs M K Carlson, DipRAM
Mrs M Wynn-Higgins
Miss C Weston, BA
J Williams, BA, QTS
Miss A Bealings
Miss S L Cousins, BSc, PGCE

Mrs L K Rogers, BSc
Dr G Gilbert, MA, PhD
Ms E George, BSc, MSc
Mrs A Kuribayashi-Coleman

Bursar: G E Watson, ACIS
School Medical Officer: Dr J P W Lynch, MBChB,
    MRCGP, FPCert
Headmaster's Secretary: Miss C Shaw, BA

The Abbey – Woodbridge Junior School
Tel: 01394 382673

Master: N J Garrett, BA, PGCE
Second Master: Mrs C M T Clubb, BEd
Head of Pre-Prep: Mrs J King, BEd

Assistant Staff:

C J S French, BA, CertEd	Miss A J King, MA, PGCE
D A Graham, BEd	Mrs C R Parker, BSc,
R D O Earl, BA, CertEd	CertEd
Mrs L B Ford, DipEd	Mrs H C Forrest, BA
Mrs S K Cox-Olliff, BA	Miss J Duncan, BA
Mrs R C Walker, BEd	Mrs K Spalding
Mrs H Norman, BEd	Mrs M Kiley
C C Smith, BSc, CertEd	Mrs S Jarvis
Mrs J Chamberlain, MA	Mrs S Clench
Mrs J Lawrence, BSc,	M Fernley
CertEd	Mrs M Huxley
Mrs R M Copestake,	Mrs P Martin
CertEd	Mrs M Williams
Miss K C Theobald, BEd	

Situation. Woodbridge is an attractive market town on the River Deben, opposite the site of the famous royal Saxon ship burial at Sutton Hoo. Timber-framed buildings dating from the Middle Ages, and Georgian facades draw many visitors to the town throughout the year as does the Aldeburgh Festival at the nearby international Snape Maltings Concert Hall. Excellent sailing facilities are available on the River Deben. Woodbridge is seven miles from the Suffolk coast and close to the continental ports of Felixstowe and Harwich. The rail journey to London takes a little over an hour.

History and Buildings. Woodbridge School was originally founded in 1662. The scholars were to be taught "both Latin and Greek until thereby they be made fit for the University (if it be desired), but in case of any of them be unapt to learn those languages …they should be taught only Arithmetic, and to Write, to be fitted for Trades or to go to Sea". They were also to be "instructed in the principles of the Christian Religion according to the Doctrine of the Church of England".

For 200 years, the School existed in cramped quarters in the town until its incorporation with the Seckford Trust. Endowment income then enabled it to move to its present undulating site overlooking the town and the River Deben and to begin the steady expansion and development which have accelerated over the last 25 years. The School has been fully co-educational for nearly four decades. The latest additions are the new state-of-the-art 350-seat Seckford Theatre and refurbished Britten-Pears Music School.

Woodbridge has had close links with the local community and, through its outstanding Music and Science, with Finland, France, Spain, The Netherlands, Hungary and Germany. Woodbridge has a British Council International School Award for its international links, pupils are able to go on cultural exchange to countries as diverse as Australia, Oman, South Africa, India and China.

The Abbey prep school is centred in a beautiful house dating from the 16th Century in the town, adjacent to which two large new buildings have been added. Taking pupils from 7–11, it has full use of the Senior School swimming pool, sports hall, tennis courts, etc. (*For further details, see entry in IAPS section*.) There are currently 160 pupils in the Abbey prep school.

Queen's House, the pre-prep department for 85 pupils aged 4–6, opened in 1993 in its own building on the Woodbridge School site.

Organisation. There are approximately 850 pupils. The Senior School (11–18) numbers 305 boys and 296 girls, with a Sixth Form of about 200. There is a co-educational Boarding House for pupils aged 13+. A Day House system exists with a Junior House for 11 year old entrants and four other Day Houses for those aged 12–16. All Sixth Form day pupils are based in the Sixth Form Centre.

Music, Games and Activities. Music is at the heart of much of the life of the School. Over 60 concerts every year, large and small, offer pupils opportunities to perform at all levels. Some 45% of pupils study at least one instrument. In recent years Woodbridge School has had more members of the National Youth Choirs of Great Britain than any other school in the UK.

Woodbridge is a chess centre of excellence, representing England at the world chess championships.

Sailing, riding, shooting and hockey are real strengths. Other main games are rugby and netball in the winter; cricket, also tennis, athletics, swimming and rounders in the summer. The Sports Hall has facilities for most indoor sports.

The first-class Combined Cadet Force embraces Army, RAF, and Royal Navy Sections. The large variety of clubs and societies includes the Duke of Edinburgh's Award Scheme. All 11 and 12 year olds follow the Seckford Scheme which paves the way for these, and many other, activities.

Careers. The School offers comprehensive careers advice and there are close links with county and university careers departments.

Chapel and Religious Education. The School has a strong Christian ethos and pupils attend Chapel every week. There is an annual Confirmation Service.

Admission. The majority enter the Senior School at 11 through the School's own examination, interview and report. At age 13, entry is through the School's own or the Common Entrance examination. Entry to the Sixth Form is based on interview and GCSE results. Admission to The Abbey is at any stage from the age of four.

Registration Fee: £50 (day), £100 (boarding). Acceptance Fee: £300 (day), £500 (UK boarding), £9,167 (overseas boarding).

Fees per term (2014–2015). Day: Pre-Prep (Queen's House) £2,647; Prep (The Abbey) £4,802; Senior School: Years 7–9 £4,568; Years 10–13 £4,944. Boarding: £9,167.

Scholarships and Bursaries. Due to its generous endowment, the School is able to offer remission of up to 100% of fees to pupils whose parents have incomes in the lower and middle ranges through Awards and/or Means-Tested Bursaries.

Academic Scholarships, worth up to 50% of tuition fees, are available for entry at 11, 13 and 16. These are awarded on the results of the annual entrance examinations at 11+ and 13+ and on the basis of interview and GCSE results at 16+.

Music scholarships are available, worth up to 50% of fees plus free music tuition. Instrumental or Choral Awards, entitling pupils to free music tuition, may be offered.

Drama scholarships are available worth up 25% of fees including a free weekly LAMDA lesson.

Art scholarships, worth up to 10% of fees at 11+ and up to 25% of fees at 13+ and 16+, are available annually.

Sport scholarships are available annually, worth up to 10% of fees at 11+ and up to 25% of fees at 13+ and 16+.

All-round Awards can be offered at 11+, 13+ and 16+ to those who have good overall talent, but who have not reached the standard of Award in any specific area.

Chess Awards are available worth up to 10% of tuition fees and include free tuition for one chess lesson each week.

Charitable status. The Seckford Foundation is a Registered Charity, number 1110964. Its aims are to give education for "poor children" by the provision of scholarships and fee remissions out of charity funds, and to maintain "the elderly poor" by providing a subsidy out of the charity for the Almshouses and Jubilee House.

Woodhouse Grove School

Apperley Bridge, West Yorkshire BD10 0NR
Tel: 0113 250 2477
Fax: 0113 250 5290
email: enquiries@woodhousegrove.co.uk
website: www.woodhousegrove.co.uk

Motto: '*Bone et fidelis*'

Woodhouse Grove enjoys a lovely rural setting. Screened by woods, its extensive grounds are spacious, yet the school is conveniently located close to major airports, rail and motorway networks.

The School was founded by the Methodist Conference (now known as the Methodist Independent Schools Trust) in 1812 for the education of the sons of ministers, but now welcomes members of all denominations and none, both as pupils and as staff. It is fully co-educational, taking pupils from the age of 3–18.

Visitor: The President of the Methodist Conference

Governors:
A Wintersgill, FCA (*Chairman*)
S Burnhill, BSc
Mrs E E Cleland, BA, Dpe PE, CertEd, FRSA
R S Drake, LLB Hons, ACIArb
A Ekoku, BA
Mrs P M Essler, BSc
Dr G H Haslam, MBChB
R C Hemsley, FCA, MA
A S P Kassapian
M D Leigh, BA, MA, DipEd
F J McAleer, BA Arch, Dip Arch, RIBA
T Mulryne, MA, BEd, FRSA
P W Rigby, BA Econ Hons, ACA
I M Small, BA, DipEd
Mrs V Snowden, BEd, MEd, FRSA
Revd Dr R L Walton
J Weaving, BA, ACA
Revd P Whittaker, BA

Staff:

Headmaster: D C Humphreys, BA

Deputy Headmaster: D N Wood, BA
Second Master: J K Jones, CertEd
Director of Studies: E Wright, BSc
Head of Year 7 and Head of Lower School: A M Cadman, BA
Head of Year 8: A Sweeney, BA
Head of Year 9: P Moffat , BA
Head of Year 10: P L Watson,MA
Head of Year 11 and Head of Upper School : K D Eaglestone, BSc
Head of Year 12: Mrs R Vernon, BA
Head of Year 13 and Head of Sixth Form : Mrs E Ainscoe, MA

Chaplain: Revd D H Bonny, BA, BD
Clerk to the Governors & Finance Director: D Ainsworth, BA, ACA
Operations Director: P Thompson

* *Head of Department*
† *Head of House*

Mrs E Ainscoe, MA (*Biology*)
Miss F Alimundo, BSc (*Geography*)
J Allison, BA (**Design Technology*, †*Vinter*)
S Archdale (*Speech and Drama*)
Miss A Barron, BA (*German*)
E Bean, BSc (*Physics)
A Cadman, BA (*PE*)
J Carter, BA (**History & Politics, RE*)
Mrs P N Charlton, MA (*Art & Design*)
J C Cockshott, CertEd (*Design Technology*)
A J Copping, MA (**Languages, English*)
Mrs C J Couzens, BA (*PE and Games*)
A N Crawford, BA, ARCO (*Music, Mathematics,* †*Findlay*)
Miss C Couper, BA (**Drama and Theatre Studies*)
Mrs K Curtis, BSc (*PE and Games*)
T Davis, BA (*Chemistry)
S Dillon, BA (*Mathematics*)
K Eaglestone, BSc (*Mathematics*)
Mrs J L Edger, BSc (*Physics*)
Mrs E Farley, BA (*English & Media Studies*)
Mrs H Fisher, MA (*Psychology*)
R I Frost, BEd (*PE and Games)
Mrs C Gibson, BA (*Business Studies and Economics,* †*Towlson*)
Mrs K L Goodwin-Bates, MA (*English & Media Studies*)
C K Henderson, BSc (*Chemistry, Biology,* †*Southerns*)
D Hole, BSc (*Chemistry*)
Mrs A Howard, BA (*PSE, Physics*)
E R Howard, BA, BEd (**Sport & History*)
Mrs F L Hughes, BEd (*French*)
A Jarvis, BA (*Modern Languages*)
Miss C D Jemmett, BA (*English*)
A Jennings, BA (*Religious Studies*)
Mrs K Jennings, BEd (*PE)
R Johnson, BA (*English*)
J K Jones, CertEd (*PE and Games*)
Miss A Kerr, BSc (*Mathematics*)
P Lambert, BA (*Modern Foreign Languages*)
Miss E Landy, BSc (*Chemistry, Biology*)
P W Lodge, BA (**Modern Foreign Languages*)
O Mantle, BA (*IT,* **Business Studies and Economics,* †*Atkinson*)
J M McCabe, BSc (*Chemistry*)
Mrs H Mitchell, BA (*Modern Foreign Languages*)
P J Moffat, BA (*Geography*)
Miss B Monk, BA (**ESOL,* *Learning Support)
M F Munday, BA (*Geography*)
Mrs C Nott, MA (**Mathematics, IT*)
Miss L Oakley, BA (*English)
Miss C Pearce, BA (*PE and Games, Geography*)
A J Pickles, BA (**Art & Design*)
Mrs H Priestley (*Drama and Dance)
J B Robb, BA (**Religious Studies*)
Miss J Russell, BA (*IT*)
Mrs R Sharpe, BA (*English and Media Studies*)
Mrs D L Shoesmith-Evans, BA (*Humanities)
N Smith, BSc (*Biology)
Miss J Stevens, BDes (*Design Technology*)
D Sugden, BSc (*Mathematics*)
A Sweeney, BA (*History*)
J P A Tedd, MA (*Music)
Miss M Thompson, BA (*Art & Design*)
Miss R V Thompson, BA (*Geography)
Mrs R Vernon, BA (*PE*)
S Vernon, BA (*PE,* †*Stephenson*)
Mrs R Ward, BA (*English*)
Mrs R Warner, BA (*Politics, History*)
Mrs R Wickens, BA (*Geography)
Mrs P L Watson, MA (*Business Studies, IT*)
G Williams, BSc (*Science)

D N Wood, BA (*English and Media Studies*)
E Wright, BSc (*Mathematics*)

Headmaster's Secretary & Registrar: Mrs T Gilks

Brontë House
Headmaster: S Dunn, BEd
Deputy Head: J Peacock, BEd
Director of Studies: Mrs N Woodman, MPhil
KS1 Coordinator: Mrs H J Simpson, BA
Foundation Stage Coordinator: Mrs A Hinchliffe, BA

Numbers. There are 700 pupils in the Senior School including 92 boarders and 211 students in the Sixth Form. Brontë House (2½–11) has 304 pupils.

Buildings. Our buildings include a purpose built sports centre with a multi-functional sports hall, a fitness suite, a new 25m 6-lane swimming pool, squash courts, floodlit outdoor courts, floodlit all-weather pitch, Performing Arts Centre and recently added climbing wall. We have good science laboratories, a new state-of-the-art DT and Art centre, a spacious Music and Drama block, language suite and fully-equipped IT rooms. We have recently relocated and modernised our Sixth Form Centre and refurbished one of the Boarding houses to provide sixth form accommodation.

Sport and Music. Playing fields adjoining the School cover about 40 acres. Cricket, Netball, Rugby, Football, Squash, Basketball, Athletics, Swimming, Tennis and Rounders are the main games, and there are several all-weather Tennis Courts and a floodlit outdoor court for netball and tennis and a new floodlit all-weather pitch. The Sports Centre includes a large multi-functional hall, a fitness suite and an aerobics studio.

There are 3 Orchestras, many ensembles, several Choirs and a Concert Band. Many pupils take extra instrumental lessons.

Curriculum. Boys and girls enter the Senior School at the age of 11, 13 or 16 and the curriculum is arranged to provide a continuous course through Brontë House and upwards through the Sixth Form to University entrance. Special support is available for pupils with learning or language difficulties. For GCSE, all pupils take the following core subjects, (English, French, Maths, Science–Dual Award, IT), together with three others chosen from German, Geography, RS, History, Art, CDT, PE, Spanish, Drama, Music. In the Sixth Form each pupil selects 4 subjects from 23 possible options for study at AS and A2 level. In addition, all Sixth formers can take a two-year course in General Studies.

A school-wide IT network, full-time IT Manager and IT Technician, and state-of-the-art PCs ensure that all pupils enjoy access to excellent IT facilities and full-site Wi-Fi.

Sixth Form Entry. Places are available for students who want to come into the School at the Sixth Form stage.

Scholarships and Bursaries. Academic scholarships are awarded at 11+ and 13+ on the basis of examination performance, interview and school report. Awards at 16+ are made based on GCSE results. Music scholarships are awarded to promising musicians. Awards generally contribute to or cover tuition fees on one or two instruments. Sports scholarships are awarded in the Sixth Form.

Parents may apply for financial assistance via our Bursary Scheme. Bursaries are means-tested. Special assistance is given to the children of Methodist ministers (boarders and day pupils) and to boarders who are sons and daughters of serving members of HM Forces.

Term of Entry. Pupils are usually accepted in September, though arrangements may be made for entry at other times. All admissions are subject to selection criteria and available places. We are happy to welcome pupils mid-year.

Brontë House is the Preparatory School and takes boys and girls rising three. Ashdown Lodge Nursery & Reception takes pupils on a day or part-day basis, all year round. (*See Brontë House entry in IAPS section.*)

Fees per term (2014–2015). Main School: £7,980–£8,020 (boarders), £7,450–£7,550 (weekly boarders), £3,830–£3,940 (day). Brontë House: £2,875–£3,450 (day). Ashdown Lodge Nursery and Reception: £2,620 (full day), £1,620 (half day). Fees include meals, books, stationery, examination fees and careers tests.

Extra Subjects. There is a wide range of extra subjects available including: Piano, Violin, Viola, Violoncello, Organ, Flute, Clarinet, Oboe, Trumpet, Trombone, Horn, Saxophone, Bassoon, Guitar, Percussion, Singing, Speech and Drama Training, Dancing, extra sports coaching, debating, Duke of Edinburgh's Award, photography and fencing.

Old Grovians Association. *Secretary*: Mrs Heather Garner.

Charitable status. Woodhouse Grove School is a Registered Charity, number 529205. It exists to provide education for children.

Worksop College
A Woodard School

Worksop, Nottinghamshire S80 3AP
Tel: 01909 537100
            Headmaster: 01909 537127
Fax: 01909 537102
email: headmaster@wsnl.co.uk
website: www.wsnl.co.uk
Twitter: @worksopcollege

Motto: '*Semper ad Coelestia*'

Foundation. Worksop College is the last of the Woodard (Church of England) Schools to be founded personally by the 19th Century educationist Canon Nathaniel Woodard, who died between the School's foundation in 1890 and its opening in 1895.

Governing Body:
The Board of Woodard Schools (*Nottinghamshire*) Limited

Visitor: The Rt Revd The Bishop of Chichester

Board Members:
The Revd Canon B Clover, MA, LTCL (*Provost*)
C J D Anderson, MA (*Chairman and Custos*)
T D Fremantle, MBA, DL
R P H McFerran, FRICS, CAAV
Mrs J C Richardson, MBE, BA, JP (*Vice-Custos*)
M A Chapman, MLIA Dip
M E Hartley, BSc, FCA
Mrs P A Rouse (*Vice-Custos*)
Mrs M F T Critchley, BA
K S Jones, BSc, FRICS, FAAV
Ms J H Smith
Mrs E Lee
R R Steel, BSc
G A R Cormack, BA
P Spillane, BA
D Wilson, FCA, CTA
J Palmer, BA
Mrs S Cundy, BSc, ACA

Headmaster: G W Horgan, BA Exeter College Oxford

Deputy Head: J Anderson, BA (*Geography*)

Assistant Deputy Heads:
Mrs E A Warner, CertEd (*Physical Education*)
T J Halsall, MEd, BA (*English and Theatre Studies*)

Chaplain: Revd P Finlinson, MA, BA (*Head of Spiritual and Moral Studies*)

Teaching Staff:
Mr A Appleton, BSc (*Physical Education*)

Mr A J Axelby, MA (*History*)
Mrs W H Bain, BA (*English, Head of Drama*)
Mr R S Baker, BEd (*Head of Physical Education*)
Mrs S M Baker, BA (*Head of Business Studies and Economics*)
Mr J Bayston, BA (*Business Studies and Economics and General Studies*)
Mrs C M Beckett, BA (*Learning Support*)
Ms E F Bennett, BA (*EAL*)
Mr S D Breheney, BSc (*Physics*)
Mrs G Burton, CertEd (*Food & Nutrition*)
Mrs M J Christodoulou, BEd (*Head of Food and Nutrition*)
Mr C D Cook, BA (*Design Technology*)
Miss S J Dalby, BSc (*Head of Science*)
Mr G R Duckering, BEd (*Head of Design Technology*)
Mr M Fagan, BEd (*Mathematics*)
Mr T J Franse, BA (*Chemistry and Physical Education*)
Mr A D Futter, BSc (*Director of Sport*)
Mrs C E Futter, BA (*Modern Languages*)
Miss J O Gatley, BA (*Religious Studies & PSHE*)
Mrs A A Gray, BEd (*Learning Support*)
Mrs S Halsall, BA (*Art*)
Mrs S P Harris, MA (*ICT*)
Mr N S Hill, BSc (*Science*)
Mr R James, BSc (*Head of Geography*)
Miss E L Kelvey, MA (*English*)
Mr A B B Kenrick, MA, BA (*Director of Art*)
Mr N A K Kitchen, MA (*Head of History, Head of Sixth Form*)
Dr K A Koon (*Classics and Latin*)
Dr S N Koon, PhD, MA (*Head of Classics*)
Mr T P Larkman, BSc (*Geography*)
Mr N J Longhurst, BA (*Maths*)
Mr S P Madigan, BSc (*Head of Physics*)
Mr R J Marks, BEd, BPhil (*Learning Support*)
Ms A J Marriott, BSc (*Psychology*)
Mr P R Murray, BA (*History*)
Mr I C Parkin, BSc (*Head of Cricket*)
Mrs P S Parkinson, BA (*Head of Modern Languages*)
Mr C G Paton, BA (*Modern Languages*)
Miss C C Phillips, BA (*Assistant Director of Music*)
Mrs H Platt-Hawkins, MA (*Art*)
Mrs S Powell, BSc (*Games*)
Mrs A J Price, BA (*Head of Careers*)
Mr W G Robinson, BSc (*Head of Activities and Outdoor Education, Mathematics*)
Mrs G J Robson-Bayley, BA (*English*)
Mr P D Scott, MChem (*Chemistry*)
Ms B D Sims, MA (*English, Theatre Studies*)
Mrs M L Smith, MA (*Head of English*)
Mr G R Tattersall, BSc (*Mathematics*)
Mrs C E Tilley, BEd (*Physical Education*)
Mr K D Topham, MSc, BSc (*Biology*)
Mr J D Turner, BSc (*Head of Mathematics*)
Mr T J Uglow, MA, ARCO (*Director of Music*)
Ms A L Varney, BSc (*Biology*)

Houses and Housemasters/mistresses:
Head of Boarding: Mrs C E Tilley

Boys:
Mason: P R Murray
Pelham: T P Larkman
Portland: T J Franse
Shirley: G R Duckering
Talbot: I C Parkin

Girls:
Derry: Mrs S Powell
Gibbs: Mrs C E Tilley
School House: Mrs P S Parkinson

School Doctor: Dr K Fairholme
Admissions Registrar: Mrs D Shaw
Old Worksopian Society Secretary: Mrs W Marks

Worksop College Preparatory School, Ranby House:
Headmaster: C S J Pritchard, MA, BA Hons QTS

There are 364 pupils in the College of whom about 41% are girls.

Worksop College is a safe, supportive and a caring environment in which we educate, enrich and encourage high-quality education. Pupils from as early as age 3 and up to age 18 are inspired to reach for success academically and to develop their personal potential beyond the classroom. We provide a happy learning framework for children at Nursery age to young adults for Sixth Form. The Worksop College community is committed to preparing pupils to grow in self-confidence, interdependence and be adaptable for the diverse and ever-changing society.

Worksop College is set across two beautiful campuses, the College site (ages 13 to 18) and the Prep School, Ranby House site (ages 3 to 13), offering a seamless education from 3 to 18 years. (*See entry for Worksop College Preparatory School, Ranby House in IAPS section.*)

The two campuses are set close to each other in North Nottinghamshire and are extremely well-situated for access, being close to the A1 and A57/A614. Extensive daily bus routes operate from a wide area. Before and after school care is also available to suit your needs.

Worksop College has outstanding facilities for all ages and high academic expectations and super sporting, art, music, design technology and extra-curricular activities, we provide our pupils with the opportunity of a lifetime.

The College is situated in over 300 acres of magnificent countryside in North Nottinghamshire. The facilities are outstanding: 2 Computer Centres, computer-equipped Art and Design Technology Departments, modern science laboratories, a music school, theatre and drama studio, Modern Languages department with new computer language laboratory, lecture theatre, central library, extensive playing fields, indoor heated swimming pool, two floodlit astro pitches, an 18-hole golf course and sports hall. The College has a magnificent Chapel that acts as a focus for the spiritual and moral well-being of the community. Whilst the majority of pupils are Anglican, pupils of other faiths and of no faith are equally welcome.

We are non-selective and believe that education is for life, so whether joining the school in the dedicated Nursery School at the Worksop College Preparatory School, Ranby House, with its forest learning, or at the start of the Sixth Form for AS and A Levels including an extensive academic enrichment programme, or at any stage in between, your child will be given the chance to flourish as they gain confidence and maturity and the opportunity to take on positions of responsibility.

Houses. There are 8 Houses. 4 boys' Boarding Houses, a boys' Day House and a girls' House are all in the main College. The girls' Boarding House and a girls' Day House are in separate buildings. Excellent pastoral care is provided by the Housemasters/Housemistresses and the House Tutors. At the same time the compactness of the buildings makes it easy for boys or girls to seek advice from other members of staff, in particular the Chaplain, and to make friendships with boys or girls in other houses as well as their own.

Curriculum. Because the College enjoys the ratio of 1 teacher to fewer than 10 pupils, close attention can be given to individual needs at every level. The Curriculum is designed to give pupils as wide an education as possible in the first three years, leading to the GCSE examinations. In the Sixth Form, a broad range of A and AS Level examinations is available including English, History, Geography, French, Spanish, Latin, Classical Civilisation, Mathematics, Physics, Chemistry, Biology, Further Mathematics, Economics & Business Studies, Music, Art, Design Technology, Physical Education, Psychology, Theatre Studies and General Studies. Additionally, Applied Business, Leiths Basic

Certificate in Food & Wine and AS Home Economics are offered.

Music. A large Music School containing a recital and rehearsal room with a capacity of 150, 12 teaching and practice rooms with pianos and a Music Library is the focal point for the Director of Music and a large visiting staff.

Art. The Director of Art has at his disposal 2 large studios for painting and drawing, a room for graphics and digital photography, textiles and sculpture areas and a library and teaching room.

Design and Technology. A purpose-built Technology Centre has facilities for design, the use of computers and areas for work in metal, wood and plastic, as well as CAD-CAM facilities.

Drama. There is a fully-equipped theatre as well as a Drama Studio, and plays involving boys and girls are put on 3 or 4 times a year.

Physical Education and Games. Physical Education is an integral part of the curriculum for a pupil's 5 years. The major games for boys are Rugby (Autumn Term), Hockey and Cross-Country (Spring Term), and Cricket, Athletics, and Swimming (Summer Term). For girls, they are Hockey (Autumn Term), Netball (Spring Term) and Tennis, Athletics and Swimming (Summer Term). Pupils are also encouraged to play other sports (Badminton, Basketball, Golf, Sailing, Soccer, Squash, Sub-Aqua, Tennis, Trampolining, Volleyball, Water Polo, Weight Lifting) and, as they become more senior, are permitted to specialise in them rather than in the main games if they choose. The Sports Hall has facilities for many sports and additional features for cricket as well as a fully-equipped fitness suite.

Activities. In their first year all pupils are taught life-saving, first-aid and other basic skills. There is then the choice of joining a section of the CCF and later doing voluntary community service. There is training in camping, orienteering, climbing, canoeing, motor engineering, shooting (the school has its own 25-yard range), signalling, and survival swimming. Boys and girls have all these options as well as the chance to take part in the Duke of Edinburgh's Award Scheme.

There are various Societies and Hobbies which include: Archery, Art, Badminton, Boat Maintenance, Car Maintenance, Chess, Canoeing/Kayaking, Climbing, Cookery, Dance, Drama, Duke of Edinburgh's Award, Fencing, Golf Coaching, Judo, Kick-Boxing, Mountain Bikes, Music, Pop Lacrosse, Soccer, Sub-Aqua, Squash, Table Tennis, Trampolining, Weight Training/Fitness Suite and Yoga.

Fees per term (2014–2015). Full & Weekly Boarders £8,650; Day Pupils £5,410. Flexi Boarders £6,600*.

*Parents may choose the defined status of Flexi boarding for which a termly fee is payable in advance and entitles the pupil to stay in a boarding house up to a maximum of two nights per week.

Scholarships, Exhibitions and Bursaries. Academic Scholarships (up to 25% of fees pa) and Exhibitions (up to 15% of fees pa) may be awarded annually for 13+ (Year 9) entry by examination in February. Candidates must be over 12 and under 14 on 1 Sept in the year of entry. Several Sixth Form Academic Scholarships (up to 25% of fees pa) are available each year, for which there is an interview with the Headmaster for external candidates.

Music and Art Scholarships (up to 25% of fees pa) and Exhibitions (up to 15% of fees pa) are available for entry to Year 9 and Sixth Form. Sports and Golf Scholarships (both up to 25% of fees pa) are also available for entry to Year 9, Year 10 and Sixth Form. All-Rounder Scholarships: up to 3 awards for all-round ability and leadership potential may be made to pupils entering Year 9.

For further information about all scholarships, please contact the Admissions Registrar.

Bursaries may be given in addition to Awards if the financial circumstances of the parents make this necessary. A wide range of bursaries is offered to enable talented pupils to enter the school who would not otherwise be able to do so.

A number of Bursaries are awarded to the children of Clergy and to children of members of Her Majesty's Armed Services (up to 15%) on the basis of financial need.

Admission. The main intake is in September each year, but pupils do join at other times. Pupils for September from preparatory schools will join through either the Entrance Scholarship or the Common Entrance Examination. Other Entry Tests are held at the College throughout the year for 13+ applicants from the maintained sector. Increasingly boys and girls are joining the College after GCSE to study in the Sixth Form.

Charitable status. Woodard Schools (Nottinghamshire) Limited is a Registered Charity, number 1103326. It exists for the purpose of educating children.

Worth School

Turners Hill, West Sussex RH10 4SD
Tel: 01342 710200
Fax: 01342 710230
email: registry@worth.org.uk
website: www.worthschool.co.uk

Worth is a Catholic Benedictine boarding and day school for boys and girls aged 11–18. It is a truly distinctive school, known for its strong community values, friendly atmosphere and the excellence of its all-round education.

Our magnificent school is in the heart of the Sussex countryside, about halfway between London and Brighton, and only 15 minutes from Gatwick airport. We are ideally placed to allow students to sample some of the cultural highlights that Britain has to offer, while providing a beautiful environment in which to learn.

In January 2011 we had a full Ofsted inspection on provision for Boarders at Worth. The school was found to be 'Outstanding' and no recommendations were made. In the words of one pupil quoted by Ofsted, "This school grows happy pupils, organically".

The school offers a broad curriculum, where students can opt for the International Baccalaureate Diploma or A Levels. The School has offered the IB since 2002 and is a UK top 10 IB School, achieving an average of 38 points per student in the summer 2014 examinations. A Level results are also excellent and pupils enter the best universities in the UK and abroad, including Harvard, Oxford, Cambridge and leading Russell Group universities.

The wider curriculum is rich and varied with a huge range of activities, societies, lectures and trips from which to choose. There is also a lively sporting programme which has produced students of national and county standard, and the school's reputation for performing arts is outstanding.

The Abbot's Board of Governors, comprising both monks and laity.

President: Dom Luke Jolly, BA

Chairman: Mrs Alda Andreotti, FCILT

Revd Dom Mark Barrett, MA Cantab, MA London, PhD
Sir David Bell BA, MA, KBE
Mr David Buxton BA, MTh, MA
Fr James Cutts OSB
Mr Nick Deeming, BA, MBA
Mr Benedict Elwes, BSc
Mr Gerry Fletcher, BA
Mrs Christina Fitzsimons, BSc
Mrs Minette Fudakowski
Mr Peter Green, MA, Cert RE
Mr John Guyatt, BA
Mr Gordon Moore, BA Econ, CA

Dom Aidan Murray, BSc, BA, PhD, PGCE
Mrs Fiona Newton, BA, PGCE

Head Master: **Mr Gino Carminati**, BA, MA

Second Master: Mr André Gushurst-Moore, MA
Deputy Head Academic: Mrs Anne Lynch, BA
Deputy Head Pastoral: Mr Gordon Pearce, MA
Senior School Chaplain: Dom Peter Williams
Director of Finance and Operations: Mr Mark Sweeting
Assistant Head, Director of ICT: Mr Simon Fisher, BA

Teaching Staff:
* *Head of Department*

Miss Siobhan Aherne, BA (*Girls' Games*)
Mr Paul Ambridge, BA (*Physics, Austin Housemaster*)
Mrs Frances Baily, MSc (*Physics*)
Miss Jo Barnes (*Girls' Games*)
Dr Sheena Bartlett, BSc, PhD (*Chemistry*)
Mr Jonathan Bindloss, BA (**Christian Theology and Philosophy, Theory of Knowledge*)
Mr Richard Bingham, MA (*English*)
Mlle Anouck Brenot, BA, Maître Lettres Modernes (**French*)
Mrs Judith Bridge, BSc (*Learning Support*)
Mr Andrew Brinkley, BA (*History*)
Ms Amanda Brookfield, BA (*Head of Sixth Form*)
Mrs Caroline A Brown, MA (*Christian Theology*)
Mr Nathan Brown, BA, Dip EFL (*English*)
Ms Sophie Burton (*French Language Assistant*)
Mrs Lucinda Button, BA (*Art*)
Mrs Anne Carminati, BA (*EAL*)
Ms Louise Chamberlain, BSc (**Biology*)
Mr Raj Chaudhuri, BCom (*Cricket Coach*)
Mrs Minakshi Chaudhuri, BA (*Activities*)
Mr Philip Chorley, BA, MA (**English*)
Ms Samantha Clark, BEd (**Girls' Games and Academic Physical Education*)
Mr Damian Cummins, BA (*Physical Education, Rutherford Housemaster*)
Mr Simeon Dann, BA, MA (*Christian Theology*)
Mrs Jayne Dempster, BSc (**Mathematics*)
Mr Stephen Doerr, BA, CertEd (*Learning Support*)
Dr Brian Doggett, BSc, PhD (**Sciences*)
Mr Matthew Doggett, MA, MSci (*Mathematics*)
Mr Clement Donegan, BSc, MA (*Chemistry, Butler Housemaster*)
Mr Sebastien Donjon, Deg Maths (*Mathematics, Timetable*)
Mr Jeremy Dowling, BEd (*Mathematics*)
Mrs Ursula Evans (*Spanish Language Assistant*)
Mr John Everest, BA (*Art/Photography*)
Mrs Andrea Fullalove, BA (**Learning Support*)
Mrs Theresa Gartland-Jones, MA (*Art*)
Ms Joanne Geraghty, BA, MA, DELE (**Spanish*)
Mr Kevan Goddard, BA (*Mathematics*)
Mrs Joanna Gray, BA (*Assistant Director of Music*)
Mrs Sheila Gupta, BA, Dip ELICS (*EAL Subject Leader*)
Mrs Joanna Hall-Palmer, BA (*Physical Education & Games*)
Miss Juley Hudson, BA, MA (**Art*)
Mrs Kate Huxley, MA (*Mathematics*)
Mr Henning Kaaber, BSc (*Director of Sport*)
Mrs Sandi Kaaber (*St Anne's Housemistress*)
Mrs Andrea Kirpalani, BSc (*Chemistry*)
Mr Andrew Lavis, BA (**Geography*)
Mrs Daniele Lloyd, Lic ès Lang (*Modern Languages*)
Mr Mark Macdonald, BSc (*Geography*)
Mr Alick Macleod, BA, MSc (*Geography*)
Mr Eamon Manning, BA (*Christian Theology and Philosophy*)
Mr Mike Matthews, BA (*Music, St Bede's Housemaster*)
Mr Alan Mitchell, BSc (*Games and Physical Education*)

Mr Bruce Morrison, BEd (*Physical Education, Head of Core PE*)
Ms Ainhoa Novillo Cruces, BA (*Spanish*)
Mr Michael Oakley, BA, MA, MMus (*Director of Music*)
Mr Robert Outen, GNVQ (*Rugby Development Officer*)
Mr Andrew Oxley, BSc (*Sciences*)
Mr James Phillips, BA (**Academic ICT*)
Mr Richard Phillips, BSc (**Economics and Business Studies*)
Mr Tom Phillips, BA, MA (**History*)
Ms Alessandra Pittoni, Laurea in Lingue (*Italian*)
Dr Duncan Pring, MA, PhD (*Economics and Business Studies, *Careers, Farwell Housemaster*)
Ms Linda Rice, BA, MA (*Learning Support*)
Mr Philip Robinson, MA (*Classics*)
Ms Victoria Sadler, MA (*Geography*)
Dr Peter Scott, MA, PhD (*Biology*)
Mr Christopher Smith, MPhys (*Sciences, *Physics*)
Mrs Sarah Smith, BA (*English, Drama*)
Mr Stefan Steinebach, Staatsexamen (*German, *Modern Languages, Director of IB*)
Mrs Rebecca Steinebach, BA (*Modern Languages*)
Mr Andrew Taylor, BA (*History*)
Mrs Louise Taylor, BA, MA (**Drama [Acting HoD], Deputy Head of Sixth Form*)
Mrs Tricia Taylor, BA (*French*)
Mr Guy Teasdale, BEd (*Economics and Business Studies*)
Mr Philip Towler, MA (**Classics*)
Mr Giles Watson, BA (*History, Gervase Housemaster*)
Mrs Samantha Webster, MA (*Christian Theology and Drama*)
Mr James Williams, BSc (*Physics, Chapman Housemaster*)
Mr Julian Williams, MA, BSocSc, PG Dip LTCL, TESOL (*History, Director of the Wider Curriculum*)
Mrs Naomi Williams, BSc (**Psychology*)
Mr Michael Yardley, BA (*Economics*)
Mrs Maria Young, BA, MA (*Music, St Mary's Housemistress*)

Registrar: Ms Yvonne Lorraine
Head Master's Secretary: Mrs Samantha Braund

Medical Officers: Dr N Mohabir, Dr B Bartman
Senior Nursing Sister: Cheryl Cheeseman, SRN, Paediatric Dipl
Nursing Sisters:
J Doyle, RN
L Lindo, RN
H Paine, SRN

History. Worth School is situated in the midst of the beautiful Worth Abbey estate where a monastery was founded in 1933 by a group of monks from the Benedictine community at Downside in Somerset. The monks bought a large country house called Paddockhurst and its 500-acre estate situated on a ridge of the Sussex Weald which had formerly been the property of the first Lord Cowdray and opened a prep school for boys. In 1957, the monastery became independent and Worth admitted the first boys to its own senior school in 1959.

Worth welcomed girls into Years 7 and 9 in September 2010. They joined other girls in an already thriving co-educational Sixth Form, and the School has been fully co-educational since 2012 with girls integrated into all aspects of school life.

Courses of study. At GCSE level, students usually take between nine and eleven subjects at GCSE. The compulsory core is: English, Mathematics, Religious Studies, Sciences, French or Spanish or German, and ICT (plus PE and SMSC). Two or three options are chosen from: Art, Drama, Economics & Business Studies, English Literature, French or Spanish as a second language, Geography, History, Latin, Music and Physical Education. Tuition is available (for an additional fee) in Greek, Italian and Chinese to GCSE and A Level.

There is a wide choice of subjects at A Level: Art, Biology, Business Studies, Chemistry, Drama, Economics, English, French, Geography, German, History, ICT, Maths and Further Maths, Music, Music Technology, Physics, Physical Education, Photography, Psychology and Spanish. There is also the opportunity to take the Extended Project Qualification (EPQ).

Alternatively, Sixth Form students may study the International Baccalaureate. This involves the study of six subjects, three at Higher Level and three at Standard Level. Students study one subject from each of the following groups:

Group 1: English, German, Italian

Group 2: English, French, German, Greek, Italian (ab initio), Latin, Spanish (also ab initio)

Group 3: Economics, Geography, History, Philosophy, Psychology

Group 4: Biology, Physics

Group 5: Mathematics (HL), Mathematics (SL), Mathematical Studies (SL)

Group 6: Music, Theatre Arts, Visual Arts, Chemistry, French, History, Economics, Greek

Virtually all students go on to university. Sixth Form students may also choose to study for Oxbridge entrance and a significant number gain places at either Oxford or Cambridge.

A Benedictine school. Worth believes that each person is on a spiritual journey and that the school should support them wherever they are on that journey, and try to encourage a faith which will sustain pupils in later life. Over half of the 580 students at Worth are from Roman Catholic families, and there are a significant number of Christians from other denominations. Equal members of the community in every way, non-Catholic pupils have no difficulty integrating in the school and bring a different perspective which is most welcome. The School Chaplaincy team includes a part-time Anglican Chaplain, as well as Catholic Chaplains and lay members. Everyone is expected to subscribe to the School's Benedictine values which include Hospitality, Service, Worship and Community amongst others.

There are prayers each day in Houses, whole school worship each Thursday and Mass every Sunday for those boarding over the weekend and for local families.

Pastoral Care. Care of each student is of central importance throughout the School, as evidenced by our 'Outstanding' Ofsted grading for Boarder provision. Each pupil is a member of a House and has a personal tutor who monitors work progress and assists the Housemaster/Housemistress with overall care. The House support structure also includes a Chaplain and, for boarding houses, a matron. There is a counsellor who is available should pupils need him. The Benedictine tradition of community life underpins everything. Many staff families live on-site and parents are welcomed as integral to the school. There are regular points of contact, with parent-teacher consultations, meetings, social events and active support from the Friends of Worth (the parents' association).

Sport. Worth loves its sports. The main sports are: rugby, football, hockey, netball, cricket, tennis and athletics. Other sports played at competitive level include fencing, squash, golf and basketball and sports are also available through school clubs and activities (see below). There is a floodlit Astropitch, an eight-hole golf course, squash courts, tennis courts, fencing salle, dance studio and fitness suite. The school also makes use of the excellent athletics facility and 50m swimming pool at the new multi-sports centre nearby.

Music is important at Worth. There is a flourishing choir that is involved in tours and recordings as well as regular appearances in the Abbey Church. Parents, local friends and students join the Choral Society for at least two concerts each year (performing such works as Requiems by Fauré and Duruflé). The School orchestra performs regularly, as does the Jazz Band. The annual House Music, Battle of the Bands and Worth Unplugged competitions provide all pupils with an opportunity to perform and encourage an interest in music.

Drama also flourishes with regular productions at all levels and the standard of performance is exceptional. Major recent productions included the Senior School students in an excellent version of *Arcadia*, while Junior pupils have captivated with the musical *Oliver!* and pupils in the Middle School performed a haunting version of *A Picture of Dorian Gray*. Performances take place in our purpose-built Performing Arts Centre which comprises a 250-seater theatre, box office, drama office and workshop, dressing rooms, recording studio, a sound-proofed 'rock room', rehearsal rooms, a recital room and music classrooms.

Extra-curricular activity. On Wednesday afternoons every pupil participates in one or more activities, ranging from Age Concern and photography to sailing, clay pigeon shooting, and polo. Worth is also a centre of excellence for the Duke of Edinburgh's Award Scheme. There are lectures by external speakers who last year included journalists, an MP, professors and members of the British Army, amongst others.

Continuous investment. Worth has invested in its facilities and will continue to do so as part of its vision for the next ten years. The School has embarked on a 'Heart of Campus' development programme as part of its vision for the next 10 years. The demolition of the Old Rutherford building has created space and light at the heart of the campus and this will be enhanced next year with the opening of a second girls' day house, a joint house for boys and girls in Years 7 and 8, extra classrooms, an exciting art facility, building and gallery, and a move of the chaplaincy to a new central location.

The most striking and important 'new' building since 1933 is the modern Abbey Church which underwent an extensive refurbishment during 2010–11. It continues to be an inspiring place of prayer and retreat as well as an iconic building in its own right.

Admissions Policy. *Entry at 11+:* Entrance tests in English, Maths and Non-Verbal Reasoning are held in January each year. Offers are based on test results, a report from the student's current school and an interview with the Head Master.

Entry at 13+: Entrance tests in English, Maths and Non-Verbal Reasoning are held in January each year. Worth now also offers the entrance process one year earlier for those seeking entry into Year 9. Offers are based on test results, a report from the student's current school and an interview with the Head Master. Common Entrance examination results will be used for setting purposes only.

Entry at 16+: Entrance into the Sixth Form depends on the student's GCSE results or equivalent, an interview with the Head Master and a satisfactory reference from their current school. The normal requirement for students entering the Sixth Form at Worth is six GCSE passes at grades A to C, with at least three at grade B or above.

For further information on Admissions please contact the Registrar on 01342 710231.

Scholarships and Bursaries. Academic, Music and All-Rounder scholarships are awarded annually, varying in value up to 40% of the annual fees.

Academic scholarships are available to candidates at 13+ demonstrating academic excellence in the Common Scholarship examinations held in February and on the basis of scholarship interviews and references from their current school. Academic scholarships are also available for entry at 11+ based on the entrance tests in English, Maths and Non-Verbal Reasoning and an interview, held at Worth in January. Sixth Form Scholarships are awarded to students aged 16, based on scholarship examinations in November, a good school report, good GCSE results and an interview.

Music and All-Rounder Scholarships are available for entry at 11+, 13+ and 16+. Music Exhibitions are also offered giving free instrumental/vocal tuition. Candidates for All-Rounder Scholarships will demonstrate excellence in one or more of the areas: Art, Drama, Music or Sport. Auditions/trials and interviews are held in the Lent Term for 11+ and 13+ and in November for 16+.

Scholarships may be supplemented by a means-tested bursary up to a maximum combined value of 50% of the annual fees.

St Benedict's Scholarships enable local Catholic children of real ability, whose parents' financial circumstances would normally preclude attendance at Worth, to benefit from the opportunities offered by the school. One day place is available for Year 7 and two day places for Year 12 are available each year.

Fees per term (2014–2015). Years 9–13: Boarding £9,990, Day £7,085; Years 7 & 8: Boarding £6,560, Day £5,810, Flexi (boys only) £6,260.

Friends of Worth. The parents of children at Worth run their own programme of social events to which all parents are invited. Typical events are coffee mornings, drinks receptions and a bi-annual ball.

Worth Society. All Worthians are entitled to join the alumni society. Contact Mary Lou Burge at Worth School.

Charitable status. Worth School is a Registered Charity, number 1093914. Its aims and objectives are to promote religion and education. If Worth had a motto it would be: *The glory of God is a person fully alive.*

Wrekin College

Wellington, Shropshire TF1 3BH

Tel:	Main: 01952 265600
	Headmaster's Office: 01952 265601
	Admissions: 01952 265603
Fax:	01952 415068
email:	admissions@wrekincollege.com
website:	www.wrekincollege.com
Twitter:	@wrekincol

Motto: '*Aut vincere aut mori*'

Wrekin College was founded in 1880 by Sir John Bayley and in 1923 became one of the Allied Schools, a group of six independent schools including Canford, Harrogate Ladies' College, Stowe and Westonbirt.

Visitor: The Rt Revd The Lord Bishop of Lichfield

Governors:
¶H W Campion, ACA, ATII (*Chairman*)
R D Bubbers, MA Oxon
A J Dixon, LLB
¶M Halewood, BEng, CEng, MICE, MAPM
P A T Hunt, BA
V L Hughes-Hines
¶A B Huxley
A F Lock, MA Oxon, PGCE
J T S Peacock
R J Pearson, BSc
¶T Shaw, BSc, MRICS
¶N A Wilkie, MA Cantab, MSc, FRSA

¶ *Old Wrekinian*

Headmaster: Dr H P Griffiths, BSc, PhD

Senior Deputy Head: Mrs S E Clarke, BA, FRGS

Deputy Head (*Teaching and Learning*): Mrs A Wright, BSc

Director of Planning: Dr G Roberts, BSc, PhD

Head of Sixth Form: T Southall, BSc

Chaplain: Revd M Horton, MA, MA, CertTh, DipTh

Assistant Staff:
† *Housemaster/mistress*

J Ballard, BSc	Miss L F Jones, BA
Mrs H E Berry, CertEd	†Mrs J D Kotas, BA
P J Berry, BA	K B Livingstone, BA
†A J I Brennan, BA	D McLagan, BA
†H S R Brown, BA	Dr A Whitton, BA, MA,
Miss A H Calloway, BA	PhD
Miss B Camargo Castillo,	R B Nayman, BA
FyL	Mrs E M Perry, BSc
Mrs F Coffey, BSc	J G Phillips, BA
Mrs G Cordingly, BSc	Mrs C A Ritchie-Morgan
†Mrs M Crone, BA	T A Southall, BSc
Dr K Cusack, BSc, MSc,	P M Stanway, BSc
DIC, PhD	Mrs C Thust, BSc
†Mrs K Davies, BSc	C J Tolley, BSc
A Francis-Jones, BSc	A J Ware, BSc
J C Frodsham, CertEd, Adv	Mrs M N J Warner, BSc
DipEd	Mrs A E Wedge, BSc
Miss A V Gardener, BA	Ms G T Whitehead, BA
H R Gray, BSc	†I Williamson, BA
Miss J Harris, BSc	†D J Winterton, BA
S J Hield, BSc	M M Winzor, BSc, MAEd
A R Hurd, BSc	

Support for Learning:
Mrs J M Lloyd, BSc, MEd, DupELS, AMBDA, TEFL, APC SpLD Patoss, TPC SpLD Patoss
Mrs A H Livingstone, MA, RSA CELTA
French Assistante: Mrs F Kennedy

Visiting Music Staff:
Miss K Burningham, MA, Dip ABRSM (*Piano & Organ*)
Ms N J Clifton-Griffith, BMus, PgDip (*Singing*)
Miss S Croxon, BMus (*Brass*)
M M Davy, MA, FRCO, LRAM, ARCM (*Organ*)
C Hickman, BMus (*Trombone & Lower Brass*)
C J Jones, BMus (*Piano, Clarinet and Saxophone*)
L Jones, BA, RNCM (*Violin*)
Miss Y Kagajo, MMus PGDip (*Piano*)
Miss S A Lane, ARCM (*Flute*)
Ms J Magee, MA, GRSM, LRAM, ARCM, ABSM (*'Cello*)
T Mvula, BMus (*Singing*)
P Parker (*Guitar*)
G Santry (*Drums*)
Mrs F Stubbs, MA, GCLM (*Bassoon*)
M Svensson, BMus (*Head of Strings*)
Ms R Theobald (*Piano, Oboe & Singing*)

Games:
M Winzor (*Head of Boys' Games*)
Mrs C A Ritchie-Morgan (*Head of Girls' Games*)

Sports Coaches:
Mrs K Bennett (*Girls' Games*)
S Blount (*Boys' Games*)
D Clarke (*Swimming*)
G Davies (*Cricket*)
B Gleeson (*Cricket Umpire*)
K Holding (*Fencing*)
S Jenkins (*Basketball*)
R Oliver (*Cricket*)
Mrs R Reilly (*Swimming*)
A C Sammons (*Rugby*)
C J Sheperd (*Cricket*)
G Singh (*Cricket*)
Mrs C Still (*Gymnastics*)
M de Weymarn (*Cricket Umpire*)

Medical Officers: Dr J Middleton & Dr E Williams

CCF:
SSI & Outward Bound Activities Instructor: RQMS, E J Fanneran, late RA

Secretary OWA: M Joyner, BSc

Bursar: Mrs Y K Thomas, MBA, FCA

Deputy Bursars:
Facilities: B C Crone
Operations: P Rowles

Foundation Manager: Mrs S Kyle
Marketing Manager: Mrs A Nicoll
Admissions Registrar: Mrs K Guest
Headmaster's Personal Assistant: Mrs P Bottomley

The College is situated in an estate of 100 acres on the outskirts of the market town of Wellington. We pride ourselves on the excellent quality of our people, as well as the excellent quality of our facilities, and we measure our achievements not only by our outstanding examination results, but also by the whole development of individuals within the school. Being a relatively small school, about 400 pupils, the quality of relationships is good and enables a purposeful atmosphere to prevail in which pupils can achieve their potential, both in academic and extra-curricular activities. We are splendidly equipped with many modern facilities including a purpose-built Theatre, a double Sports Hall, Astroturf and 25m indoor swimming pool, together with all the expected classrooms, ICT facilities and a Sixth Form Centre. Teaching is expert and disciplined. Co-educational since 1975, there are 7 Houses, which cater for both day and boarding pupils, and these include dedicated junior Houses for the 11 to 13 intake. Everyone eats together in a central dining room and a Medical Centre is available to all pupils. The Chapel is central to the school both geographically and in the impact it makes on the ethos of the school.

Admission. Boarders and day pupils are admitted at 11+ or 13+ after passing the Entry Examination or Common Entrance. There is also a Sixth Form entry based on GCSE achievement. Entry into other years is dependant on places being available.

Term of entry. The normal term of entry is the Autumn Term but pupils may be accepted at other times of the academic year in special circumstances.

Academic Matters. The core purpose of the school is teaching and learning to support each child in reaching their academic potential. Wrekin is proud of its strong academic record, based on stimulating intellectual curiosity, providing excellent and inspiring teaching, and making learning exciting. Our guiding principle is to help every child achieve the most they are capable of, to prepare them for the competitive world they will enter, and to give them a lasting sense of the pleasure and value of learning that will enrich their future lives.

Classes are small, typically no more than twenty for the younger pupils and between eight and fifteen at A Level. Our teachers are experienced, expert and approachable, and give a great deal of time to pupils both inside and outside the classroom. Our tutoring system means each pupil has personalised academic support throughout the year. Our Support for Learning staff can help those with additional needs, and our enrichment programme stimulates and stretches our more able students.

Our curriculum is constantly reviewed in the light of changes in educational policy and philosophy, but we are committed to offering our pupils a solid and broad academic foundation. We offer a wide range of subjects for GCSE, AS and A2 exams, and guide pupils in choosing subjects that suit their interests, abilities and future plans. Our Head of Careers advises pupils throughout their time at school, and the Head of Sixth Form offers expert advice on university applications.

Sport. For a small school, our sporting prowess is remarkable. We aim for very high standards in our core sports and a very wide range of options – up to twelve different sports in any term. Our sporting philosophy is based on a pyramid, with elite athletes at the top (including our

national level gymnasts, swimmers, athletes and cross-country runners) and minor sports to appeal to all at the base. We believe in excellence but also in participation – sport for all, and for life.

Educating the Whole Person. The outdoors is one of Wrekin's most valuable classrooms. The skills learned and adventures experienced during pupils' participation in the Combined Cadet Force and the Duke of Edinburgh's Award Scheme stay with them for life. Both are enthusiastically supported by highly dedicated staff, and the take up among our middle year pupils is impressive. We are very proud that Wrekin's 'completion rate' at all levels of the scheme is substantially above the national average.

What happens on the sports pitch and in the music rooms, the theatre and the art studios is just as important a part of a Wrekin education. The range and quality of activities available to every pupil is outstanding, especially for a school of this size. Our pupils' development and achievements in these areas are supported by wonderful facilities and highly dedicated staff.

Scholarships and Bursaries. *Academic Scholarships* are awarded at our normal entry points of 11, 13 and 16. Candidates should be under 12, under 14 or under 17 on September 1st of the year in which they will enter the school. Age may be taken into account when comparing candidates, so that those who are young for their year are not disadvantaged.

Music and Art Scholarships take place in November (11+/16+) and February (13+). As for all other scholarships, Music and Art Awards will not exceed twenty five per cent of the fees. However, Music Scholarships carry with them a specified amount of free instrumental and/or vocal tuition. Candidates must also satisfy the school's normal academic entry requirements.

Sports Awards: Sports Scholarships may be awarded to candidates with outstanding ability in Sport. Applicants must attend a sports assessment day and satisfy the school's normal academic entry requirements. Candidates should be capable of a very significant contribution to the sporting success of Wrekin College. Typically candidates will have representative success at regional or National level.

Pendle Awards may be offered to all-rounders who have high academic standards and excellence in other areas such as sport, music or art. Those seeking a Pendle Award must sit the academic Scholarship Examination, either at 11+, 13+ or 16+ level and meet scholarship standard in at least one other area.

Bursaries may be awarded on entry and can be awarded in addition to a scholarship. All bursaries are means tested and could in some circumstances cover the whole school fee.

For further information please visit our website www.wrekincollege.com.

Fees per term (2014–2015). First and Second Forms: £4,475 (day); £6,430 (weekly boarding); £7,981 (full boarding). Third-Sixth Forms: £5,420 (day); £7,620 (weekly boarding); £9,260 (full boarding).

Music lessons £21.70 per 35 minute session; Extra Tuition £21.70 per 35 minute session.

We offer a 10% discount to serving members of the Armed Forces; to children of Old Wrekinians; and for a second boarder from the same family. When three siblings are enrolled in Wrekin College/The Old Hall School each child attracts a 20% remission in fees.

Old Wrekinian Association. A flourishing Wrekinian Association of over 3,500 members exists to make possible continuous contact between the School and its old pupils, for the benefit of both and to support the ideals and aims of the school. It is expected that pupils will become members of the Old Wrekinian Association when they leave Wrekin.

Charitable status. Wrekin Old Hall Trust Limited is a Registered Charity, number 528417. It exists to provide independent boarding and day co-education in accordance with the Articles of Association of Wrekin College.

Wycliffe College

Bath Road, Stonehouse, Gloucestershire GL10 2JQ
Tel: 01453 822432
Fax: 01453 827634
email: senior@wycliffe.co.uk
website: www.wycliffe.co.uk

The School was founded in 1882 by G W Sibly and placed on a permanent foundation under a Council of Governors in 1931.

President: S P Etheridge, MBE, TD, JP, MBA, FIFP, CFP, FCII, ACIArb

Chair of Governors: Brigadier R J Bacon, MBA, Chartered FCIPD, FCMI, CMILT

Vice Presidents:
Major General G B Fawcus CB, MA, MInstRE
Air Chief Marshal Sir Michael Graydon, GCB, CBE, FRAeS

Vice Chairman: A J P Clayton, BSc, ACA

S K Collingridge
Mrs C Duckworth, MA
Mrs K R Fife, BA, BSc
T G Hale, MSc, MBA
M H Jones, BSc, MCIMA
Mrs S J Lacey, MEng, BA
S F Lloyd, BSc Hons Est Man, MRICS
I H Paling, BMet, MMet
J C H Pritchard, DipM, FIMC, MCIM, MIMI
Group Captain G Reid, MB ChB, FRCPsych, RAF
J Slater, FRICS
J R E Williams, FCA

Financial Director and Company Secretary: A C Golding, ACA

Head: **Mrs M E Burnet Ward**, MA Hons, PGCE

Senior Deputy Head: P Woolley, BA, PGCE (*Politics*)
Deputy Head (Academic): S V Dunne, BA, PGDipJ, PGCE (*Media Studies*)
Deputy Head (Pastoral): Mrs E A Buckley, BSc, PGCE (*Physical Education*)
Head of Sixth Form, Head of Higher Education and Careers: J M Hardaker, BA, PGCE (*Economics & Business Studies*)
Director of Quality Assurance and Head of Lower School: S Callister, BA, MA, PGCE (*Art*)
Director of ICT: B Ittyavirah, BSc, MSc, PGCE (*ICT*)
Chaplain: The Reverend J M McHale, BTh, BA, PGCE (*RS*)

House Staff:
Collingwood House: Mr K Patrick, BA Hons, PGCE (*History*)
Haywardsend: Mrs S L Trainor, H DipEd, PGCE (*Biology*)
Haywardsfield: I Russell, BSc, PGCE (*Mathematics*)
Ivy Grove: Mrs E J Lunch, BSc, PGCE (*Mathematics*)
Lampeter House: Mrs L Knighton-Callister, BSc, PGCE (*Head of Applied Science*)
Loosley Halls: G P Buckley, BA, M Inst SRM Dip, MILAM PGCE (*Head of Physical Education*)
Robinson House: J S Mace, BSc, PGCE (*Head of Biology*)
Ward's House: A M Golightly, BA, MA, PGCE (*Head of Drama*)

Teaching Staff:
M J Archer, BSc (*Curriculum Leader Science*)

R O Beamish, BA, PGCE (*Head of Media & Film Studies*)
J A S Beltrami, BA, PGCE (*Mathematics*)
G C Brown, BSc, PGSE (*Computer Science*)
Miss C E Browne, BA, PGCE (*English*)
B D Cadenhead, BSc, PGCE (*Physics, Careers Advisor*)
Mrs E C Chadwick, BA Hons, TEAL (*SEN*)
J P Clements, BEng, PGCE (*Head of Physics*)
Mrs A K Cobbs, BA, PGCE (*Head of Mathematics*)
Mrs S V Collinson, BA, PGCE (*Business Studies*)
G P Constable, BA, QTS (*Business Studies & Economics*)
Mrs C R L Conway, BA, MA, QTS (*History*)
Mrs B Cook, BA, PGCE (*ICT & Coaching, Mentoring Coordinator*)
Mrs J Cottrell, BA, PGCE (*SEN*)
E M Crownshaw, BA, PGCE (*Physics*)
W H Day-Lewis, BA DiELTA, PGCE (*Head of Development Year*)
M V Dennis, BA, PGCE (*Mathematics*)
Mrs S M Dudley, BSc, PGCE (*Head of Girls' Games*)
Miss K F Elliott, BA, PGCE (*Head of ESOL*)
A J Finebaum, BEng, PGCE (*Mathematics*)
G G Flower, Cert Higher Ed Sports Coaching (*Head of Rowing*)
Mrs S Flye, BSc, PGCE (*Mathematics*)
B W Gannon, BSc, Level 3 Cert Cricket Coaching QCF (*Sport*)
S R Garley, BAF (*Fencing Coach*)
Mrs N Golightly, BEd (*Drama*)
Miss N Green, BA, PGCE (*Head of Art*)
Mr C J Hancock, BA, PGCE (*RS and Life Skills*)
Mrs M Hardwick, MA, PGCE (*French & Spanish*)
J C Harford, Level 3 Coach Award Squash (*Director of Squash*)
W H Helsby, BA, RSA DipTEFL, PGCE (*ESOL*)
Mrs R Honeywill, BA, Cert Ed (*French & German*)
Miss J Howard, BA, PGCE (*PE, Games & Head of BTEC*)
S J Hubbard, BA (*Art*)
Mrs E J Hughes, BSc, PGCE (*Mathematics*)
Ms B A Imrie, MA, PGCE, CFBT (*English*)
M J Kimber, New Zealand Coaching Cert, ECB Level 1, RFU Levels I & II (*Head of Boys' Games*)
Mrs T Kinnison, MA, BSc, PG Dip Computing, PGCE (*Chemistry & Physics*)
Ms S Knight, MChem, PGCE (*Chemistry*)
Mrs E S Lambert, BA, PGCE (*English*)
D Lester, BA Hons, MEd Applied Linguistics (*French Assistant*)
J Lunch, BSc Hons, PGCE (*Head of Boys training*)
Miss S L Madden, BA Hons, PGCE (*English*)
M Martinez, PGCE (*Spanish*)
Mrs S M Matthews, BSc, PGCE (*Head of Psychology and Social Sciences*)
Miss N Mikesch, PGCE (*Head of German*)
Mrs C Moran, BA, Celta (*ESOL*)
A C Naish, BSc, PGCE (*Director of Sport*)
Mrs L Newton, BA, PGCE (*Head of Business Studies & Economics*)
Mrs L Nicholls, BA, PGCE (*Geography*)
J J O'Sullivan, PGCE (*Economics*)
R Pender, BSc, PGCE (*Head of Geography*)
Mrs H S Phelps, BA, BSc, MSc (*Psychology and Sociology*)
Mrs V Ralph, BSc, PGCE (*Biology & Chemistry*)
Miss S K Revie, BA, PGCE (*Head of Japanese*)
Dr R K Rose, MA, MSc, PhD, PGCE (*Chemistry*)
Lt Col P N Rothwell (*OC CCF*)
Mrs G L Russell, BA, PGCE (*Director of Music*)
Mrs N J H Scott, BA, PGCE (*Head of History*)
P D Scott, MBioChem, PGCE (*Mathematics*)
Miss H Sherwood, Level 2 Cert Hockey Coaching QCF, Level 1 Cert Teaching Swimming (*Sport*)
Mrs J Smith, BA, PGCE (*Curriculum Leader Modern Languages, Head of French*)

Mrs S Suzui, BEd (*Head of Japanese*)
J E Thomas, BSc, PGCE (*Mathematics*)
W A Weaver, BMus, MMus, PGDE (*Assistant Director of Music*)
Mrs E A Wentzel, BA, MA TESOL (*ESOL and US University Admissions*)
G J Wheeler, BEd (*Head of Design & Technology*)
Mrs J A White BSc Hons, PG Dip SpLD, APC 0414/361; PG Cert Boarding Management; PG RSA DELTA (*Head of Learning Support & SEND*)
Mrs H P Williams, BA, PGCE (*Head of English*)
I L Williams, BSc, PGCE (*Science*)
Miss J Wilson, BA, PGCE (*English*)
Mrs L Wisbey, BA, PGCE (*Head of Spanish*)
Mrs L A Wong, BSc, RSADipTEFLA, PGCE (*ESOL*)
Mrs R A S Wordsworth, BA (*Art & Photography*)

Teaching Support Staff:
Mrs M Bray (*Teaching Assistant*)
T Dyer, BSc Eng (*Engineering Projects*)
R Feather, BA, PGCE (*Data & Exams Manager*)
Mrs S A Hodgkins (*Librarian*)
Mrs P M Rhymes, BSc (*Careers Education Manager*)

Visiting Music Staff:
Mrs S Blewett, FTCL, LTCL, LWCMD (*Flute*)
Mr M Bucher, Dip Perc (*Percussion*)
Mrs M Cope, GMus, LTCL, Cert ABRSM (*Piano*)
Mr I Dollins, BMus, ARCM (*Voice & Piano*)
Mrs V Green, GRSM, ARCM, LRAM (*Piano & Double Bass*)
Mr N Nash (*Saxophone & Clarinet*)
Miss J Orsman, GBSM (*Violin & Viola*)
Mr G Rees, Dip Trpt (*Brass*)
Mr P Reynolds, BA Hons (*Guitar*)
Mr D Thompson, MA, BA Hons (*Piano*)
Mrs L Thompson, BMus Hons, ARCM, CertEd (*Cello*)

Medical Officers and Staff:
Dr J Sivyer, MBChB, DRCOG, & Partners
Mrs J Lewis (*School Nurse*)
Mrs P Norman (*School Nurse*)

Administration:
Director of Operations: Mrs A Bromley
Director of Marketing: Mrs M Gray
HR Manager: Mrs W Jenkins
Alumni Relations Manager: Mrs C Roberts
Registrar: Miss C H Phillips
Head's PA: Mrs C J Philp

Preparatory School:
(*see also entry in IAPS section*)

Headmaster: A Palmer, MA, BEd, MA
Headmaster's Wife: Mrs J Palmer, Cert Ed (*KS1 SENCO, General Subjects Teacher*)
Deputy Head: Mrs V Jackson, BA, PGCE, TEFL (*Languages Teacher*)
Director of Pastoral Care: Mrs L Askew, LAMDA (*Head of Drama*)

Teaching Staff:
S J Arman, BEd (*Chaplain, Head of Shaftesbury, Head of Humanities*)
Mrs B Bate, BSc, PGCE (*Head of Sciences*)
Mrs J Baylis, NVQ3 (*Year 1 Assistant*)
Mr T Bloodworth, BSc, PGCE (*Year 4 Teacher*)
Mrs S Bond, BEd (*Reception Teacher*)
Miss H Boswell, BA Hons, PGCE (*Head of Swimming and Girls' Games*)
D Broadhead, BA, PGCE (*Languages Teacher*)
Mrs C Brown, BA, PGCE, TESOL (*Head of Lincoln, Head of Modern Foreign Languages*)
Mrs A Cleere, BEd, ASA Level 2 (*Art, DT & Swimming Teacher*)
P Duffy, BMus, GBSM, ABSM, PGCE (*Director of Music*)

Miss J Florio, BSc, PGCE (*General Subjects Teacher*)
Mrs N Gaunt, BEd, OCR Level 5 (*SEN Teacher*)
R Gaunt, BA QTS (*Head of Mathematics*)
Mrs C Graham, BSc, PGCE, Cert SpLD (*SEN Teacher*)
Mrs S Green, BA (*Middle Prep Classroom Assistant*)
C Guest, BSc, PGCE (*Head of Scott, Head of SEN*)
Mrs R Hanson, BA, PGCE (*Head of Grenfell, English and Humanities Teacher*)
T Holroyde, BSc, PGCE (*Science*)
R Irwin, BSc, PGCE (*Middle Prep Director of Studies, Gifted and Talented Pupils Coordinator*)
Miss C Lewis, BA (*Year 2 Teacher*)
Mrs Y Martin, BEd (*Year 1 Teacher*)
Mrs E Muszasty, BA (*Head of English*)
C Norman, NVQ3 (*Reception Assistant*)
Mrs A Oliver, BEd (*Head of Lower Prep, Year 2 Teacher*)
Mrs S Poccard, TEFL, CELT (*ESOL Teacher*)
Miss M Potts, BA (*Head of ICT, Data Manager*)
Mme N Robinson, BA Hons (*Lower Prep French Teacher*)
Ms S Sabin, BEd (*Year 2 Assistant*)
Mrs E Shearer, BEd (*PPA Teacher*)
Mrs L Sherwood, SENAC Special Support Assistant, ASA Cert Assistant Teacher of Swimming (*Year 2 Assistant*)
A Sinclair, BA, PGCE (*Year 3 Teacher*)
Mrs C Stanley, BA, PGCE, SpLD (*SEN Teacher*)
M Stopforth, BA, PGCE (*Head of Art & DT*)
Miss E Upadhyay, BEd (*Upper Prep Director of Studies, Year 3 Teacher*)
Mrs N C Warden, BEd (*Year 5 Teacher*)
Mrs S Warren, BEd (*Games Teacher*)
S Wainwright, BA (*Head of PE and Boys' Games*)
Miss C Williford, BA (*Year 1 Teacher*)
Mrs C Young, BEd Year 4 Teacher)

Boarding House Staff:
Mr M Lewis (*Assistant Housemaster*)
Miss V Hearle (*Assistant Housemistress*)
Mrs L Field (*Housemistress*)
Mrs J Porter (*Matron*)
Mrs J Swirski Matron)
Mrs K Yates (*Matron*)

Day Matrons:
Mrs S Phillips, British Red Cross First Aid at Work Cert, GCS Foundation to Counselling
Mrs N Murray

Administration Staff:
School Secretary: Mrs J Fisk
Registrar: Mrs W Robertson
Headmaster's PA: Mrs S Rogers

Nursery:
Mrs C Marsh, NNEB, C&G Child Care 0–7, Supervisory Management Educare Plus Cert, NVQ4, FDEY Foundation Degree in Early Years (*Nursery Manager*)
Mrs A Hawes, BA Early Childhood Studies, EY Professional Status, Designated Child Protection Officer Early Years (*Deputy Nursery Manager, Upper Nursery Teacher*)
Mrs B Overs, NVQ3 (*Lower Nursery Teacher, SENCO*)
Miss S Wadley, NVQ3 (*Upper Nursery Teacher*)
Miss D Bullivant, NVQ3 (*Nursery Assistant*)
Miss L Chapman, NVQ3 (*Nursery Assistant*)
Miss A Chivers, NVQ2 (*Nursery Assistant*)
Miss C Holmes, NVQ3 (*Nursery Assistant*)
Miss C Woollard, NVQ3 (*Nursery Assistant*)

Out of School Care:
Mrs R Sampson, NVQ3
Mrs L Summers, NVQ3

Location. Wycliffe College is a thriving day and boarding school set in a stunning 54-acre campus for over 730 girls and boys, including around 300 boarders across the

Prep and Senior Schools. The elegant main house is surrounded by first-class teaching facilities, extensive sports pitches, state-of-the-art boarding accommodation and extensive social areas such as a Costa café available for all pupils at the senior school.

The Preparatory School (under its own Headmaster) is on a separate, adjacent campus with extensive facilities including a new classroom block for Years 7 and 8. The £3 million university-style centre features high-tech teaching resources and new spacious classrooms.

The art block and the science centres have been upgraded during the summer, as well as extensive work in the prep boys' boarding house.

Conveniently located in the South West of England midway between the famous cities of Bath and Cheltenham, Wycliffe is within easy reach of international airports such as Heathrow, Bristol and Birmingham as well as major road and rail connections. The school is under two hours from London by car (M4 motorway) or train (direct line to the local station).

Organisation. Senior School 13–18: 230 Boys, 175 Girls, 230 Boarders, Sixth Form 170. Class sizes vary from 3–15 pupils. Preparatory School 2–13: 166 Boys, 156 Girls.

Admission. Pupils are admitted at key entry points following interview and assessment, via Common Entrance or Scholarship examinations at 13+ and via GCSE or Scholarship examinations into the Sixth Form. Application should be made to the Head who is whole-hearted in her desire for all pupils to achieve their full potential in every sphere of education and undertakes to be readily available to parents.

Religion. Christian interdenominational, all faiths welcome. Confirmation classes, Christian Fellowship group and daily worship in keeping with this generation are an integral part of College life.

Houses. Wycliffe's House system promotes a strong sense of community, building staunch friendships and promoting healthy competition, and ensuring high levels of personal and pastoral care. There are eight Houses with dedicated study areas for day pupils and three Sixth Form Halls of Residence, each with study-bedrooms and en-suite facilities. All boarding houses are refurbished on a rolling programme. Main meals are taken in Wycliffe Hall.

Tutors. Each pupil has a House-based tutor in the Lower School and a specialist tutor in the Sixth Form. Supported by a Housemaster/Housemistress, Tutor, Chaplain and Head of Year, each pupil gains maximum advantage towards personal fulfilment in a community noted for its friendly and caring support.

Medical Centre. 24-hour attendance is provided by qualified staff in a state-of-the-art Centre. The Health Centre is nearby. Special dietary requirements for health or faith are met by first-class catering facilities.

Development Year. Some international pupils choose to join the Development Year (DY) at Wycliffe before embarking on the full two year A Level programme. This is because they wish to improve their English and experience a range of subjects while living and working in a traditional British boarding school.

DY pupils study a broad range of subjects including English, Maths and the Sciences and many can take up to six GCSEs as well as a range of ESOL exams. During the year they also receive an introduction to some A Level subjects, in preparation for Sixth Form. The DY students are part of all the house, sports, and social activities in which they can build friendships and improve their language skills. Included in the timetable, students benefit from expert tuition in English as a Second Language.

A Levels. As a general rule students choose four, or occasionally five, AS subjects to study in the Lower Sixth or one of two available BTEC courses. Most students then continue to study three subjects in the second year to A2 Level. Apart from the traditional subjects, the following are also on offer to A2 Level: Art and Design, Design and Technology, Japa-

nese, Psychology, Business Studies, Media Studies, Government and Politics, Theatre Studies, Music Technology, Sociology and Physical Education.

GCSEs are usually taken three years after 13+ entry. The School offers a wide range of subjects supported by outstanding tutorial practices. Four modern languages and four sciences are among those on offer to students who may make a free choice at age 14.

Scholarships and Bursaries. Thanks to the generosity of Trustees, Old Wycliffians and Friends of Wycliffe, awards are available offering a reduction of up to 40% of the fees. These may be supplemented in cases of financial need up to a maximum of 90%.

For 13+ entry a candidate must be under 14 on 1 September of year of entry and sit the examination in the Spring Term.

For 16+ entry, examinations are held in the Autumn prior to arrival or by arrangement.

At other ages, applications to be made to the Registrar.

Awards are made to candidates with academic talent or potential and also specifically in music, art, design technology, drama and sport including pupils highly talented in cricket, rugby, football, girls' hockey, netball, squash, rowing and fencing.

Special awards are also available to (a) those with all round merit, (b) children of serving members of the Services school fees fixed at CEA + 10% of school fees, (c) vegetarians.

Physical Education. Our sports and physical education programme gives opportunities to develop talents and skills and to enjoy sport as a team member, individual or for recreation. We recognise and support gifted sports players and have the facilities to offer a wide range of sports such as rowing, rugby, hockey, fencing, soccer, netball, squash, badminton, basketball, swimming, cricket, tennis, athletics, health and fitness, yoga, shooting, and cross country.

Training for Service is available via the Combined Cadet Force, Duke of Edinburgh's Award Scheme, Leadership Courses, and the Wycliffe Charitable Organisation.

International Travel is regularly organised for varied groups; trips can enhance academic study, provide exchanges with our sister schools in Chicago and Osaka, be part of the Comenius partnership with schools in Europe or specific sporting or musical tours. Pupil trips and exchanges are arranged for those studying foreign languages.

School Societies. Among those available are Drama Workshops, Stage Management, Philosophy, Language, Debating, Archaeology, Pottery, Craft, Computing, Electronics, Astronomy, Shooting, Choral, Instrumental Music, First Aid, Cookery, Dance and a Sixth Form Club.

Sunday Specials. Brunch is a highlight of Sunday morning and a variety of activities, both at the College and locally, are organised for boarders.

Music. A purpose-built music school including a dedicated Music Technology suite with enthusiastic staff enables high standards to be achieved. Music is taken at GCSE and A Level with Music Technology also offered at A Level; several pupils each year continue their music studies at the Conservatoires and universities. There are two choirs, numerous large ensembles and bespoke chamber ensembles developing a high level of performance in all styles of music. Associated Board Examinations are taken every term as well as Trinity and Rock school exams. The School hosts professional concerts and dramatic productions annually as well as the School's own artistic output.

Careers Guidance forms a vital department which is recognised as a centre of excellence. The College has its own experienced Careers Manager who is available to advise and support students throughout the school day. The Careers Library is well-equipped with information on careers and entrance to Higher Education. The school offers SAT preparation for American Universities.

Teacher Training. Wycliffe has been selected as a training centre for teachers, reflecting the high esteem in which the College is held.

Fees per term (2014–2015). Senior School: Boarders £9,395–£9,460, new Sixth Form entrants £9,850, Development Year £10,655; Day pupils £5,480–£5,995. Preparatory School: Boarders £5,610–£7,180, Foundation Year £7,900, Residential Short English Course £680 per week; Day pupils: £2,005–£4,155.

It is the College's aim to keep extras to a minimum but may include expeditions, exam fees and certain Society subscriptions.

Alumni. The Old Wycliffian Society supports OWs through its website, mailings, reunions, OW Carol Service, and a termly issue of the Wycliffe Times. Visit the OWS website: www.wycliffe.co.uk or contact the OW Registrar tel: 01453 820439, email: ow@wycliffe.co.uk for further details.

Charitable status. Wycliffe College Incorporated is a Registered Charity, number 311714. It exists to provide education for boys and girls.

Wycombe Abbey

High Wycombe, Buckinghamshire HP11 1PE
Tel: 01494 897008
email: registrar@wycombeabbey.com
website: www.wycombeabbey.com

Motto: *In Fide Vade*
   Founded in 1896.

Governing Council:

President: The Rt Hon The Lord Carrington, KG, GCMG, CH, MC, JP, PC

Vice Presidents:
Mr A K Stewart-Roberts, MA
Mr A M D Willis, LLB, FCIArb
Mrs C M Archer, MA

Chairman:
Mr P P Sherrington, LLB, LLM, FCIArb

Council Members:
Lady Sassoon, MA
Mr Keith Oates, MSc, BSc Econ, LLD, DSc
The Rt Hon Sir Anthony May
Dr C A Seville, MA, BMus, LLM, PhD
Air Vice-Marshal T B Sherrington, CB, OBE
Mrs Sue Singer, BA
Ms C Riley, MB, BA, MA, DBA
The Hon Mrs Justice Carr, DBE
Dr S V M Hordern, MBBS, BSc, MRCP, MD
Mr D P Lillycrop, LLB, FCMI
The Rt Revd Dr Alan Wilson, MA, DPhil, Bishop of Buckingham
Mrs Diana Rose, MA
Dr Louise Fawcett, MA, DPhil
Mr Richard Ashby, MSc, BSc Eng, ARSM, FRICS
Mr Richard Winter, BA, FCA
Mr J W Bailey, ACA
Mr Patrick Lewis, MA, MBA

Staff:

Senior Leadership Team:

Headmistress: **Mrs R Wilkinson**, MA Oxon, PGCE, MEd, Dip SpLD

Bursar and Clerk to the Council: Mrs A Bolton, MA Cantab, MBA

Deputy Headmistress: Mrs A Hems, MA Oxon, PGCE Cambridge
Director of Studies: Miss E Boswell, MA Oxon, PGCE Roehampton
Director of Operations and Co-Curriculum: Miss R A Keens, BEd Liverpool
Director of External Relations: Miss K Fox, MA Cantab
Director of Higher Education and Careers: Mr J Franks, MA Cantab, GTP e-Qualitas

Head of Boarding: Mrs A Spillman, BA Open, BSc Exeter, PGCE Greenwich (*Mathematics, Psychology*)
Assistant Director of Studies: Mr M Welch, MEng, BA Cantab, PGCE Nottingham
Head of Learning Support: Mrs K J Kuhlmey BA AKC London, PGCE Cantab

Housemistresses (Pastoral):
Airlie: Mrs S McGeehan, BSc Glasgow, PGCE Jordanhill College (*Physics*)
Barry: Mrs A Spillman, BA Open, BSc Exeter, PGCE Greenwich (*Mathematics, Psychology*)
Butler: Mrs A Buxadé del Tronco, BA Southampton, PGCE Belfast, CPP Roehampton (*English, French, Spanish*)
Campbell: Dr A Yuasa, BA Oxon, PhD Reading, PGCE Cantab (*Music*)
Cloister: Mrs A Clee, BA Central England, QTS Wolverhampton (*ICT*)
Pitt: Miss H Allen, BA Hons, Cert Ed Brunel (*DT*)
Rubens: Miss C Perri, Licence de Litterature Université Aix-Marseille, PGCE Cambridge
Shelburne: Mrs S Jenkins, CertEd West Midlands, DipEd Reading, CPP Roehampton (*Physical Education*)
Wendover: Miss S B Lafford, BSc Bristol, PGCE London (*Biology*)
Junior House: Miss V Marks, BA Swansea, GTP Reading (*History*)
Head of Clarence: Mrs A Clee, BA Central England, QTS Wolverhampton (*ICT*)

Clarence Senior Academic Tutors:
Miss R Harris, BA Durham, PGCE Bristol (*Geography*)
Dr J Ryder, MPhys Oxon, DPhil Oxon (*Mathematics*)

Chaplain: The Revd J Chaffey, MA Oxon, BA Dunelm

Heads of Department:
English: Mr S Winchester, BA Hons Leeds, PGCE Institute of Education London
Mathematics: Mr R Tidbury, MPhys Warwick, PGCE Oxon
Science & Physics: Mrs S Jones, BSc Dunelm, PGCE Oxon
Chemistry: Mrs Z Edwards, BSc St Andrews, PGCE Dunelm
Biology: Mr M Whiteley, BA Cantab, PGCE Canterbury
Modern Languages and French: Miss S Landsmann, Licence d'anglais La Sorbonne Nouvelle, PGCE Reading
German: Mrs M Dworkin, MA Cantab, PGCE King's College London
Spanish: Ms E Piqué, MA Langues Etrangères et Appliquées Droit et Commerce Montpellier, PGCE Cardiff
Classics: Mrs J Tidbury, MA Cantab, PGCE Cantab
Geography: Mr T Bennett, MA Cantab, PGCE Oxford Brookes
History: Dr S Tullis, BA DPhil PGCE Oxon, MLitt St Andrews
History of Art: Miss E Bowen, BA Oxon
Religious Studies: Mrs A Khan, MA, PGCE Oxon
Economics: Miss L Peden, BSc Queen's Belfast, PGCE Manchester
Information Technology: Mr A Porter, BSc, PGCE East Anglia, MA Reading, MBCS
Art, Design and Technology: Miss F Clark, BA Goldsmiths London, PGCE London

Drama: Miss C Livesey, BEd Cantab, AGSM Guildhall
Director of Music: Mr L Tubb, BA Oxon, ABRSM
Director of Sport: Miss L Taylor, BSc Hons Bath, PGCE
  Chichester
*Personal, Social, Health and Citizenship Education
  Coordinator*: Mrs J Wright, BA Thames Valley, PGCE
  KCL, MA Brunel

For a full staff list, please visit our website.

Numbers on roll. 551 Girls: 518 Boarding; 33 Day Girls.
Age range. 11–18.

Aims. Wycombe Abbey aims to provide an education in
the widest sense and our pursuit of academic excellence
goes hand in hand with our commitment to pastoral care. We
believe the welfare and happiness of every girl to be paramount. Each individual is encouraged to achieve her full
potential; she receives first-class academic teaching and has
the opportunity to discover and develop her talents – artistic,
creative, musical, sporting. She also learns to take responsibility for herself and to have respect for others. It is an
intrinsic part of the School ethos that girls care for each
other and offer service to the community.

Location. Near the centre of High Wycombe, five minutes' drive from the M40.

Buildings. The School buildings are all within the extensive grounds of 160 acres which include playing fields,
woods, gardens and a lake.

Boarding Houses. There is a Junior House for UIII. At
LIV, girls move to one of nine Houses where they remain
until the end of the Lower Sixth. In the final year all girls
move to the Upper Sixth House where they are encouraged
to prepare for university life.

Religion. Wycombe Abbey is a Church of England foundation with its own Chapel. All girls attend morning prayers
and a Sunday Service. (Roman Catholic girls can attend
Mass and Jewish girls may receive instruction from a
Rabbi.) Christian principles inform the whole ethos of the
School and a resident Chaplain oversees spiritual matters
and plays a central role in pastoral care.

Curriculum. The Lower School curriculum includes the
study of English, English Literature, History, Geography,
Religious Studies, French, German, Spanish, Latin, Greek,
Mathematics, Biology, Chemistry, Physics, Information
Technology, Design and Technology, Art, Cookery, Drama,
Music, Singing, Personal, Social and Health Education and
PE. In the Sixth Form, Economics, History of Art, Classical
Civilisation, Government and Politics, Psychology and
Physical Education are also available. Critical Thinking AS
is compulsory. Girls are prepared for the IGCSE, GCSE, AS
and A2 Level examinations, Pre-U and for university
entrance. Girls proceed to leading universities in the UK
with about 35–40% going to Oxbridge and a handful to
America.

Teaching facilities are very good and have been extended
and upgraded over recent years.

Physical Education. The School has excellent outdoor
facilities, including five lacrosse pitches, a full-size multi-
purpose floodlit Astroturf pitch, an athletics track and
twenty tennis courts which can be used for netball in the
winter. The Davies Sports Centre is a state-of-the-art sports
complex including a six-lane 25m swimming pool, well-
equipped fitness suite and four glass-backed squash courts.
Girls are taught lacrosse, netball, tennis, athletics, swimming, gymnastics and dance. A huge range of extra-curricular sports and activities is also available.

Music. There is a strong tradition of music-making with
outstanding facilities for tuition and for recitals. About
three-quarters of the girls study at least one musical instrument and are taught by a large team of visiting specialists
who provide tuition in a wide range of instruments, including voice. There are many opportunities for performing in
orchestras and ensembles. In addition, there is a strong tradi-

tion of singing; the Chapel choir plays a central role in
Chapel worship and undertakes biennial overseas tours.

Drama. As well as class Drama, GCSE and A Level
Drama, extra-curricular Speech and Drama lessons are also
available from Year 8 in groups of approximately six girls
and from Year 10 in pairs or solo. LAMDA examinations
take place in the fully-equipped 436-seater proscenium arch
theatre and generally culminate in a Grade 8 Gold Medal in
the final year. There are extra-curricular production opportunities at various points throughout the year, several girls
annually get into the National Youth Theatre and alumnae
include Naomi Frederick, Rachel Stirling and Polly Sten-
ham.

Art, Craft, Design & Technology. Girls can pursue their
interests in these subjects at weekends when the studios are
open, as well as in curriculum time. Visiting artists provide
workshops at weekends to give girls a broad experience in
the subject.

Other Activities. A wide range of clubs and societies,
usually led by girls, are very popular as are the numerous
social events with leading boys' schools.

Fees per term (2014–2015). The fees for boarders are
£11,525 (£8,645 for day boarders). They are inclusive and
cover, in addition to the subjects and activities already mentioned, lectures, concerts, most textbooks and stationery.

Admission. Girls are admitted at the age of 11 or 13.
Application should be made well in advance. The suggested
procedure is given in the prospectus information booklet.

Sixth Form Entry: Competitive entry by examination for
a limited number of places. Application must be received at
least fifteen months prior to the proposed date of entry.

Scholarships and Bursaries. Lower School Entry: A
variety of Scholarship and Exhibition awards are available
for candidates under 12 and under 14 on 1 September of the
proposed year of entry.

Some awards are also available for candidates entering
the Sixth Form.

Music Scholarships and Exhibitions of varying value are
available to candidates under the age of 14 on 1 September
of the proposed year of entry. A Music Scholarship is also
available to girls entering the Sixth Form.

Art: One Art Scholarship for 11+ entrants and one for 13+
entrants, each worth up to 5% of the annual fee, are available. Candidates must be recommended for Scholarship by
the Headteacher of their current school.

Bursaries: A number of means-tested bursaries are available. Bursaries are held subject to the satisfactory conduct
and progress of the recipient.

For further information, please contact the Director of
Admissions.

Charitable status. The Girls' Education Company Limited is a Registered Charity, number 310638. Its aim is the
provision of first class education for girls.

Yarm School

The Friarage, Yarm, Stockton-on-Tees TS15 9EJ
Tel: 01642 786023
Fax: 01642 789216
email: dmd@yarmschool.org
website: www.yarmschool.org

Yarm School, a co-educational day school, was founded in
1978. It has its own separate Preparatory School for pupils
from 4 to 11 years of age and a nursery for 3 year olds.
There are about 1,100 pupils in the School including 330
pupils in the Preparatory School (*see entry in IAPS section*).
There are about 200 in the Sixth Form.

Governing Body:
Chair: Ms C Evans, MA, MBA, ARCM

Vice-Chairman: C G Edmundson, MA, FRCO, CHM, ADCM, ARCM, FRSA
Mrs F Ajekigbe, BSc, PGCE, MEd, NPQH
Mrs S H Anderson, FCA, BSc
Mr S R Davidson, BSc, PGCE
L D Gamble, MA, VetMB, MRCVS
J M James, BA, FCA, CTA
Mrs R M Langford, BDS
Dr R S Sagoo, MB ChB
M Thompson, BA, ACMA
A P Thomson, LLB, FCCA, FIDM
Dr A M Turner, BSc, MB, ChB, MRCS Eng, MRCS Ed, PhD
A Waite, FCCA

Headmaster: **D M Dunn**, BA

Deputy Headmaster: D G Woodward, BSc, CBiol, MIBiol
Director of Studies: D K Morton, MA
Head of Sixth Form: Dr A M Goodall, MA, PhD
Head of Middle School: Mrs K A Gratton, BEd
Head of Learning and Achievement: D Boddy, BA, MSc, FCIEA, FCollT, FRSA

Senior Master: §Dr P M Chapman, MA, PhD

Headmaster's PA: Mrs J L Herbert, BSc, MIL

* *Head of Department*
† *Housemaster/mistress*
§ *Part-time*

G Addison, BSc (*Head of Fifth Year*)
Mrs J C Ankers, BA
*Miss E L Backhouse, MA, MA, MSc
*Mrs K L Baines, BSc
§Miss Z Bellamy, ARAD Dip TCL BA
Ms H Blakemore, BA, MA
§G C Booth, MA
Ms R L Bownas, BSc
§Dr R A Brinham, BSc, PhD
*I H Burns, BSc
§Mrs P Clarke, BSc
*P J Connery, MA, BA
Miss S J L Cottrell, BEd
S H A Crabtree, BSc (*Head of Careers*)
*E M Craig, BA
§Mrs R M Crookes, BA
T J Day, CertEd
§Mrs S Dugdale, BA
Mrs F C Dunn, BEd (*Deputy Head of Sixth Form*)
*D V G Dunn, MA, BA
S Edwards, BA, MPhil
G Emerson, BA
*T E Fellows, MA, MSt
§Mrs S Fletcher, BMedSc, CertEd
T L Foggett, MSc, BA, BSc, CertEd F
Miss H Gamble, MSci
T C Grimwood, BA
*A I Guest, BEd
Mrs J L Guest, BEd (*Head of Fourth Year*)
*J S Hall, MA
S P Hardy, BEd
*Mrs E L Harrison, MA
§Mrs S M Heavers, BA
§Frau J Heinen, MA
Miss E M Howell, BTEC, BSc
§J G Hulme, BSc
Mrs A Jackson, BSc (†*Oswald*)
§Miss M Johnson, BSc
Miss E C Jones, BA
*A D Law, MA
Mrs G A Leary, BA (*Head of Second Year*)
Mrs H J McCormack, BA
W T E Macaulay, BA
§Mrs J R Menzies, BA

§P Menzies, MA
A J Monk, BSc
A J Morrison, BA (*Head of Third Year*)
C P Mulligan, BSc (*Head of First Year*)
*Mrs J H Nickson, BA, CPE Law
*Ms M J Pallister, BSc
T J Parker, BA (†*Cuthbert*)
*T D J Pender, BA
*Dr K W Perry, BSc, PhD
§M J Pointon, MA, MBA, BSc
Dr P D Prideaux, BSc, PhD (†*Bede*)
§Mrs S J Pyke, MA (†*Aidan*)
*S R Ravenhall, BA, MPhil
Miss N E Redhead, BEd
Miss C E Rhodes, BSc
§Mrs D E Ruston, BA, BA, MA
M C Rye, BA
§Mrs H C Salvage, BSc, MBA
P C Skerratt, BA
*§Mrs S Snape, BA, PG Dip SpLD
*Mrs K E L Staggs, MA
*Ms E Stebbings, BA
C I Taylor, MMath, MRes
P N Telfer, BA
C Thomas, BEd
§Mrs G Thompson, CertEd
S M Thompson, BSc
§Dr A A D Tulloch, MChem, PhD
Miss J M Turner, BA, Dip ABRSM
*Miss B Walker, BA
§Mrs E A Walker, BSc, MSc, PG Dip
C A C Webb, BA
Dr K E Woodhead, MSci, PhD
D J Yates, MA

School Manager: Mrs N L Brown, LLM

Preparatory School

Headmaster: W E C Sawyer, BA, PGCE

Deputy Headmaster: G N Stone, BEd, MA
Director of Studies: S G Pearce, BA, BEd, ADEE
Pre-Prep Coordinator: Mrs J Speight, BA Ed, QTS

Mrs A Arrol, BA, PGCE
Mrs F E H Barton, BA, PGCE, QTS
Mrs J J Catterall, CertEd
§Mrs F A Cook, LGSM, ALCM
Mrs H Craven, BA, QTS
Miss S Darbar, MA, BA, PGCE
C R Davis, BEd
§Mrs B A Desmond, BEd
Mrs A J Gray, BEd
J Grundmann, BSc, PGCE
Miss R Hall, BEd, QTS
K J L Harandon, MA, PGCE, QTS
§Mrs S M Heavers, BA
Mrs K E Jennings, BA, PGCE
Mrs H N Jones, BEd
Mrs H Lofthouse-Hill, LLB, QTS
Mrs K Mavin, BSc, QTS
Mrs H J McCormack, BA, PGCE
Miss K J Moran, BA
Mrs C A Pearce, BA, Cert TESOL
§Mrs J E Pratt
Mrs S M Pugsley, BEd
Miss L H Rowlands, BMus, QTS
M Sellers, BSc
§Mrs S Snape, BA, PGCE, PG Dip SpLD
Mrs A White, BEd

Teaching Assistants:
Ms K Bell, NVQ Level 3
§Mrs S P Carling Still, NVQ Level 3
Mrs J Jones, NNEB

Mrs R Mulligan, BTEC Nat Dip
§Mrs L J North, BA, NVQ Level 3
Mrs R Parker, BA
Miss K L Phillips
Mrs G Selby, PPA Cert
§Mrs D M Symington
§Mrs S Thomas, NCFE St2

Situation and Buildings. Yarm School is situated in the attractive and historic town of Yarm on a beautiful site with the River Tees running through it.

The Senior School is set around The Friarage (an impressive eighteenth century mansion). There are outstanding facilities, including a first-rate science and design technology building, Sixth Form Centre, sports hall, fitness suite and two all-weather, floodlit pitches. A performing arts centre for music, dance and drama was added in 2012 which includes the stunning 800-seat Princess Alexandra Auditorium which has won several national design awards.

The Preparatory School, opened in 1991 in response to public demand for traditional preparatory school education, occupies an adjacent site and also has a range of first-class facilities, including a purpose-built Pre-Prep which was opened in 2012.

Admission. Pupils are admitted to the Senior School at 11 and 16 by means of the School's own Entrance Examination. The Preparatory School has its own entrance procedures.

Curriculum. The School's academic reputation in the area is high and virtually all leavers go on to take university degrees. In 2013 over 13% of the leavers went to Medical School and a further 5% to Oxbridge.

In the Preparatory School the curriculum is both wide ranging and demanding. Whilst the basics in English and Mathematics are given great emphasis, the Sciences, Technology and Modern Languages also form an important part of the timetable.

In Year 7 all pupils study the following subjects: English, Mathematics, Physics, Chemistry, Biology, Technology, French, German, Latin, History, Geography, Information Technology, Art, RS and Music. Setting by ability takes place in Mathematics, English and Modern Languages. In Year 8 there is also setting in the Sciences. IGCSE is taken as a two-year course comprising seven compulsory core subjects (English, English Literature, Mathematics, German or French, Physics, Chemistry and Biology) and 3 or more options. Options can usually be selected from French, German, Spanish, Latin, Classical Studies, Greek, History, Geography, Information Technology, Technology, Design and Realisation, Art, PE, Music and Religious Studies. The more able pupils (perhaps a third or more of a year group) will take IGCSE Mathematics and Classics a year early enabling them to take these subjects to levels beyond GCSE whilst still in Year 11.

In the Sixth Form A Levels are selected from about twenty options. All Lower Sixth students take 4 AS Levels and 3 or 4 A2s in the Upper Sixth. General Studies is also taught in the Upper Sixth.

Modern languages are enhanced by means of regular exchanges with twin schools in France, Germany and Spain. Teams entered for nationwide Mathematics and Science/Technology competitions have won several awards in the last three or four years.

Organisation. Pastoral care is based on both a year group and a House system. Every pupil belongs to one of four Houses for his/her whole school career. Houses exist to promote competitions, sports events, charity fundraising etc. Each pupil also has a personal Tutor and Head of Year whose task it is to look after all the pupils within a given year group. Sixth-formers have the opportunity to serve as House Officers, School Prefects and as Peer Support Mentors.

Games and Activities. The school believes firmly in "education for life" and has more sport and activities within its timetable than is offered in most day schools. Its sporting reputation is enviable, with success being achieved right up to national level (London 2012 Olympic gold medallist, Kat Copeland, learned to row at Yarm) and the wide range of sports offered caters for most tastes and both genders. Rugby, hockey, rowing, football and netball are the School's main winter games and there are representative teams in these sports for all age levels. In the summer, rowing, cricket, tennis and athletics become the major sports. In addition canoeing, squash, orienteering and cross-country are also pursued at inter-school level throughout the year. Several other games are available as options.

There are many school societies. A great deal of extra-curricular activity is centred on the Duke of Edinburgh's Award Scheme. Rock climbing, canoeing and other aspects of outdoor education are given some prominence and residential weekends at an outdoor pursuits centre are a fixed part of the curriculum. There is a flourishing CCF contingent (membership, though popular, is entirely voluntary). School excursions are frequent and very varied. Expeditions in recent years have travelled as far as India, America and Guyana. Drama (at least three major productions a year) and Music (several choir and orchestral concerts are given each year) are given every encouragement and have a strong following. Activities which are an extension of Art or Technology or Biology also flourish particularly well.

Religion. The School is an interdenominational community comprising pupils of both Christian and non-Christian backgrounds. There are regular assemblies and occasional services held in the local Parish Church.

Fees per term (2014–2015). Senior School £3,867; Preparatory School £2,917–£3,227; Pre-Prep and Nursery £2,291–£2,331; Pre-Prep and Nursery (with Nursery Grant): £1,568. Lunches are extra.

Scholarships and Bursaries. A range of scholarships and bursaries is available.

Several (usually six each year) Academic Scholarships, up to the value of 10% of the full fee, are awarded as a result of performance in the 11+ Entrance Examination (held late January).

Ogden Trust Sixth Form Science Scholarships are available and awarded on academic merit (subject to other criteria being met) based on the January scholarship examination.

The school is affiliated to the Arkwright Scholarships Trust and offers Sixth Form Design and Technology Scholarships.

The school also offers Music Scholarships which provide for fee remission of up to 20%. Free instrumental tuition is usually included. Candidates for major awards are normally expected to offer a minimum of two instruments or one instrument plus voice. Music Scholarships can be awarded at any stage in the pupil's school career and modest awards can be upgraded in the light of further outstanding progress.

Means-tested bursaries are available to allow children who satisfy the entry criteria to be educated at Yarm School.

Please contact the School for further details.

Former Pupils. Past members of the School are eligible to join the Former Pupils' Society whose Hon Secretary may be contacted via the School Office.

Charitable status. Yarm School is a Registered Charity, number 1093434. It exists to provide quality education for boys and girls.

Entrance Scholarships

Academic Scholarships

Abingdon School (p. 7)
Ackworth School (p. 9)
AKS (p. 10)
Aldenham School (p. 11)
Alleyn's School (p. 13)
Ampleforth College (p. 15)
Ardingly College (p. 17)
Ashford School (p. 18)
Ashville College (p. 19)
Bablake School (p. 21)
Bancroft's School (p. 22)
Barnard Castle School (p. 25)
Bedales School (p. 27)
Bede's Senior School (p. 29)
Bedford Modern School (p. 30)
Bedford School (p. 33)
Benenden School (p. 37)
Berkhamsted School (p. 41)
Birkdale School (p. 44)
Birkenhead School (p. 46)
Bishop's Stortford College (p. 47)
Bloxham School (p. 50)
Blundell's School (p. 52)
Bootham School (p. 55)
Bradfield College (p. 57)
Brentwood School (p. 62)
Brighton College (p. 64)
Bristol Grammar School (p. 66)
Bromsgrove School (p. 68)
Bryanston School (p. 72)
Campbell College (p. 75)
Canford School (p. 77)
Caterham School (p. 80)
Charterhouse (p. 83)
Cheltenham College (p. 86)
Chigwell School (p. 91)
Christ College (p. 93)
Christ's Hospital (p. 95)
Churcher's College (p. 96)
City of London Freemen's School (p. 98)
City of London School (p. 101)
Clayesmore School (p. 104)
Clifton College (p. 106)
Cokethorpe School (p. 109)
Colfe's School (p. 110)
Colston's School (p. 112)
Cranleigh (p. 113)
Culford School (p. 116)
Dame Allan's Boys' School (p. 119)
Dauntsey's School (p. 120)
Dean Close School (p. 121)
Denstone College (p. 123)
Dulwich College (p. 129)
Durham School (p. 132)
Eastbourne College (p. 134)
The Edinburgh Academy (p. 136)
Elizabeth College (p. 138)
Ellesmere College (p. 139)
Eltham College (p. 141)
Emanuel School (p. 143)

Epsom College (p. 145)
Eton College (p. 149)
Exeter School (p. 151)
Felsted School (p. 154)
Fettes College (p. 156)
Forest School (p. 159)
Framlingham College (p. 162)
Francis Holland School (p. 163)
Frensham Heights (p. 164)
George Heriot's School (p. 167)
Giggleswick School (p. 169)
Glenalmond College (p. 174)
The Godolphin School (p. 179)
The Grange School (p. 180)
Gresham's School (p. 183)
Guildford High School (p. 186)
The Haberdashers' Aske's Boys' School (p. 188)
Haileybury (p. 191)
Halliford School (p. 194)
Hampton School (p. 196)
Harrow School (p. 200)
Hereford Cathedral School (p. 202)
Highgate School (p. 203)
Hurstpierpoint College (p. 207)
Immanuel College (p. 212)
Ipswich School (p. 214)
The John Lyon School (p. 218)
Kent College (p. 220)
Kent College Pembury (p. 222)
Kimbolton School (p. 225)
King Edward VI School (p. 227)
King Edward's School (p. 228)
King Edward's School (p. 231)
King Edward's (p. 232)
King Henry VIII School (p. 234)
King William's College (p. 235)
King's College School (p. 237)
King's College (p. 241)
King's School (p. 243)
The King's School (p. 245)
The King's School (p. 248)
King's Ely (p. 249)
The King's School (p. 252)
The King's School (p. 255)
King's Rochester (p. 256)
The King's School (p. 258)
Kingston Grammar School (p. 260)
Kingswood School (p. 262)
Kirkham Grammar School (p. 265)
Lancing College (p. 266)
Latymer Upper School (p. 268)
Leicester Grammar School (p. 271)
Leighton Park School (p. 273)
The Leys School (p. 275)
Lincoln Minster School (p. 277)
Lord Wandsworth College (p. 280)
Loretto School (p. 281)
Loughborough Grammar School (p. 284)
Magdalen College School (p. 287)
Malvern College (p. 289)

Marlborough College (p. 293)
Merchant Taylors' School (p. 297)
Merchiston Castle School (p. 300)
Mill Hill School (p. 303)
Millfield (p. 308)
Monkton Combe School (p. 309)
Monmouth School (p. 312)
Morrison's Academy (p. 314)
Mount Kelly (p. 316)
Mount St Mary's College (p. 318)
New Hall School (p. 320)
Newcastle-under-Lyme School (p. 322)
Norwich School (p. 323)
Nottingham High School (p. 326)
Oakham School (p. 328)
The Oratory School (p. 331)
Oundle School (p. 333)
Pangbourne College (p. 336)
The Perse Upper School (p. 338)
Plymouth College (p. 339)
Pocklington School (p. 341)
The Portsmouth Grammar School (p. 343)
Princethorpe College (p. 346)
Prior Park College (p. 350)
Queen Elizabeth's Hospital (QEH) (p. 354)
Queen's College (p. 355)
Radley College (p. 358)
Ratcliffe College (p. 360)
Reed's School (p. 364)
Reigate Grammar School (p. 365)
Rendcomb College (p. 367)
Repton School (p. 370)
Roedean School (p. 375)
Rossall School (p. 377)
Rougemont School (p. 379)
Royal Grammar School (p. 380)
RGS Worcester (p. 384)
The Royal Hospital School (p. 386)
The Royal Masonic School for Girls (p. 388)
Royal Russell School (p. 389)
Rugby School (p. 393)
Rydal Penrhos School (p. 396)
Ryde School with Upper Chine (p. 398)
St Albans School (p. 402)
St Benedict's School (p. 406)
St Columba's College (p. 407)
St Columba's College (p. 408)

St Dunstan's College (p. 411)
St Edmund's College (p. 412)
St Edmund's School (p. 416)
St Edward's, Oxford (p. 418)
St George's College (p. 421)
St John's School (p. 423)
St Lawrence College (p. 425)
St Mary's School Ascot (p. 431)
St Paul's School (p. 436)
St Peter's School, York (p. 439)
Seaford College (p. 440)
Sevenoaks School (p. 442)
Sherborne School (p. 446)
Shrewsbury School (p. 450)
Sidcot School (p. 452)
Silcoates School (p. 453)
Solihull School (p. 454)
Stamford School (p. 457)
The Stephen Perse Foundation (p. 458)
Stonyhurst College (p. 463)
Stowe School (p. 465)
Strathallan School (p. 468)
Surbiton High School (p. 470)
Sutton Valence School (p. 474)
Taunton School (p. 477)
Tonbridge School (p. 479)
Trinity School (p. 481)
Truro School (p. 483)
University College School (p. 485)
Uppingham School (p. 487)
Warwick School (p. 493)
Wellingborough School (p. 495)
Wellington College (p. 498)
Wellington School (p. 501)
Wells Cathedral School (p. 502)
West Buckland School (p. 504)
Westminster School (p. 506)
Whitgift School (p. 508)
Winchester College (p. 511)
Wolverhampton Grammar School (p. 516)
Woodbridge School (p. 518)
Woodhouse Grove School (p. 520)
Worksop College (p. 521)
Worth School (p. 523)
Wrekin College (p. 526)
Wycliffe College (p. 528)
Yarm School (p. 532)

All-Rounder Scholarships

Abingdon School (p. 7)
Ampleforth College (p. 15)
Ardingly College (p. 17)
Bloxham School (p. 50)
Blundell's School (p. 52)
Bradfield College (p. 57)
Brighton College (p. 64)
Bryanston School (p. 72)
Caterham School (p. 80)
Charterhouse (p. 83)
Cheltenham College (p. 86)
Christ College (p. 93)
Claysmore School (p. 104)
Cokethorpe School (p. 109)
Cranleigh (p. 113)

Culford School (p. 116)
Dauntsey's School (p. 120)
Dean Close School (p. 121)
Denstone College (p. 123)
Ellesmere College (p. 139)
Epsom College (p. 145)
Felsted School (p. 154)
Fettes College (p. 156)
Forest School (p. 159)
Framlingham College (p. 162)
Giggleswick School (p. 169)
Glenalmond College (p. 174)
Gresham's School (p. 183)
Haileybury (p. 191)
Hampton School (p. 196)

Hereford Cathedral School (p. 202)
Hurstpierpoint College (p. 207)
Ipswich School (p. 214)
The John Lyon School (p. 218)
King Edward's (p. 232)
King's School (p. 243)
The King's School (p. 258)
Kingswood School (p. 262)
Lancing College (p. 266)
Leicester Grammar School (p. 271)
The Leys School (p. 275)
Lord Wandsworth College (p. 280)
Loretto School (p. 281)
Malvern College (p. 289)
Marlborough College (p. 293)
Merchant Taylors' School (p. 297)
Merchiston Castle School (p. 300)
Monmouth School (p. 312)
Mount Kelly (p. 316)
Mount St Mary's College (p. 318)
Oakham School (p. 328)
The Oratory School (p. 331)
Oundle School (p. 333)
Pangbourne College (p. 336)
Plymouth College (p. 339)
Princethorpe College (p. 346)
Prior Park College (p. 350)
Queen's College (p. 355)
Radley College (p. 358)

Ratcliffe College (p. 360)
Reed's School (p. 364)
Repton School (p. 370)
Roedean School (p. 375)
Rossall School (p. 377)
The Royal Masonic School for Girls (p. 388)
St Edmund's College (p. 412)
St Edmund's School (p. 416)
St Edward's, Oxford (p. 418)
St John's School (p. 423)
St Lawrence College (p. 425)
St Mary's School Ascot (p. 431)
Seaford College (p. 440)
Shrewsbury School (p. 450)
Stamford School (p. 457)
Stonyhurst College (p. 463)
Stowe School (p. 465)
Surbiton High School (p. 470)
Taunton School (p. 477)
Uppingham School (p. 487)
Wellingborough School (p. 495)
Wells Cathedral School (p. 502)
Whitgift School (p. 508)
Wolverhampton Grammar School (p. 516)
Woodbridge School (p. 518)
Worksop College (p. 521)
Wycliffe College (p. 528)

Art Scholarships

Abingdon School (p. 7)
Ackworth School (p. 9)
AKS (p. 10)
Aldenham School (p. 11)
Alleyn's School (p. 13)
Ardingly College (p. 17)
Ashford School (p. 18)
Ashville College (p. 19)
Bablake School (p. 21)
Barnard Castle School (p. 25)
Bedales School (p. 27)
Bede's Senior School (p. 29)
Bedford Modern School (p. 30)
Benenden School (p. 37)
Berkhamsted School (p. 41)
Bishop's Stortford College (p. 47)
Bloxham School (p. 50)
Blundell's School (p. 52)
Bradfield College (p. 57)
Brentwood School (p. 62)
Brighton College (p. 64)
Bristol Grammar School (p. 66)
Bromsgrove School (p. 68)
Bryanston School (p. 72)
Campbell College (p. 75)
Canford School (p. 77)
Caterham School (p. 80)
Charterhouse (p. 83)
Cheltenham College (p. 86)
Chigwell School (p. 91)
Christ College (p. 93)
Christ's Hospital (p. 95)
City of London School for Girls (p. 103)

Clayesmore School (p. 104)
Clifton College (p. 106)
Cokethorpe School (p. 109)
Colston's School (p. 112)
Cranleigh (p. 113)
Culford School (p. 116)
Dauntsey's School (p. 120)
Dean Close School (p. 121)
Denstone College (p. 123)
Dulwich College (p. 129)
Durham School (p. 132)
Eastbourne College (p. 134)
The Edinburgh Academy (p. 136)
Ellesmere College (p. 139)
Eltham College (p. 141)
Emanuel School (p. 143)
Epsom College (p. 145)
Felsted School (p. 154)
Fettes College (p. 156)
Forest School (p. 159)
Framlingham College (p. 162)
Francis Holland School (p. 163)
Frensham Heights (p. 164)
Giggleswick School (p. 169)
Glenalmond College (p. 174)
The Godolphin and Latymer School (p. 176)
The Godolphin School (p. 179)
Gresham's School (p. 183)
Haileybury (p. 191)
Halliford School (p. 194)
Hampton School (p. 196)
Harrow School (p. 200)
Hereford Cathedral School (p. 202)

Hurstpierpoint College (p. 207)
Immanuel College (p. 212)
Ipswich School (p. 214)
The John Lyon School (p. 218)
Kent College (p. 220)
Kent College Pembury (p. 222)
Kimbolton School (p. 225)
King Edward VI School (p. 227)
King Edward's School (p. 228)
King Edward's (p. 232)
King Henry VIII School (p. 234)
King's College School (p. 237)
King's College (p. 241)
King's School (p. 243)
The King's School (p. 245)
King's Ely (p. 249)
The King's School (p. 252)
Kingston Grammar School (p. 260)
Kingswood School (p. 262)
Lancing College (p. 266)
Latymer Upper School (p. 268)
Leicester Grammar School (p. 271)
Leighton Park School (p. 273)
The Leys School (p. 275)
Lincoln Minster School (p. 277)
Lord Wandsworth College (p. 280)
Loretto School (p. 281)
Magdalen College School (p. 287)
Malvern College (p. 289)
Marlborough College (p. 293)
Merchant Taylors' School (p. 297)
Merchiston Castle School (p. 300)
Mill Hill School (p. 303)
Millfield (p. 308)
Monkton Combe School (p. 309)
Mount Kelly (p. 316)
Norwich School (p. 323)
Oakham School (p. 328)
The Oratory School (p. 331)
Oundle School (p. 333)
Pangbourne College (p. 336)
Plymouth College (p. 339)
The Portsmouth Grammar School (p. 343)
Princethorpe College (p. 346)
Prior Park College (p. 350)
Queen's College (p. 355)
Radley College (p. 358)
Ratcliffe College (p. 360)
Reed's School (p. 364)
Reigate Grammar School (p. 365)

Rendcomb College (p. 367)
Repton School (p. 370)
Roedean School (p. 375)
Rossall School (p. 377)
Royal Grammar School (p. 380)
RGS Worcester (p. 384)
The Royal Hospital School (p. 386)
The Royal Masonic School for Girls (p. 388)
Royal Russell School (p. 389)
Rugby School (p. 393)
Rydal Penrhos School (p. 396)
St Albans School (p. 402)
St Dunstan's College (p. 411)
St Edmund's College (p. 412)
St Edmund's School (p. 416)
St Edward's, Oxford (p. 418)
St George's College (p. 421)
St John's School (p. 423)
St Mary's School Ascot (p. 431)
St Paul's School (p. 436)
Seaford College (p. 440)
Sevenoaks School (p. 442)
Sherborne School (p. 446)
Shrewsbury School (p. 450)
Solihull School (p. 454)
Stamford School (p. 457)
The Stephen Perse Foundation (p. 458)
Stonyhurst College (p. 463)
Stowe School (p. 465)
Strathallan School (p. 468)
Surbiton High School (p. 470)
Sutton Valence School (p. 474)
Taunton School (p. 477)
Tonbridge School (p. 479)
Trinity School (p. 481)
Truro School (p. 483)
Uppingham School (p. 487)
Wellingborough School (p. 495)
Wellington College (p. 498)
Wellington School (p. 501)
Whitgift School (p. 508)
Woodbridge School (p. 518)
Woodhouse Grove School (p. 520)
Worksop College (p. 521)
Worth School (p. 523)
Wrekin College (p. 526)
Wycliffe College (p. 528)

Dance Scholarships

Bede's Senior School (p. 29)
Brighton College (p. 64)
Bristol Grammar School (p. 66)
Dauntsey's School (p. 120)
Epsom College (p. 145)
Frensham Heights (p. 164)
Lord Wandsworth College (p. 280)

Prior Park College (p. 350)
Queen's College (p. 355)
Reigate Grammar School (p. 365)
Roedean School (p. 375)
St Edward's, Oxford (p. 418)
Wellington College (p. 498)
Wells Cathedral School (p. 502)

Design Technology Scholarships

Abingdon School (p. 7)
Aldenham School (p. 11)
Ardingly College (p. 17)
Bedford Modern School (p. 30)
Benenden School (p. 37)
Bloxham School (p. 50)
Brighton College (p. 64)
Bryanston School (p. 72)
Canford School (p. 77)
Cheltenham College (p. 86)
Clayesmore School (p. 104)
Culford School (p. 116)
Dauntsey's School (p. 120)
Dean Close School (p. 121)
Denstone College (p. 123)
Durham School (p. 132)
Eastbourne College (p. 134)
Epsom College (p. 145)
Felsted School (p. 154)
Framlingham College (p. 162)
Giggleswick School (p. 169)
Haileybury (p. 191)
Harrow School (p. 200)
King's College (p. 241)
King's School (p. 243)
King's Ely (p. 249)
Kingswood School (p. 262)

The Leys School (p. 275)
Malvern College (p. 289)
Merchiston Castle School (p. 300)
Mill Hill School (p. 303)
Mount Kelly (p. 316)
Oakham School (p. 328)
Oundle School (p. 333)
Pangbourne College (p. 336)
Reed's School (p. 364)
Reigate Grammar School (p. 365)
Repton School (p. 370)
RGS Worcester (p. 384)
Rugby School (p. 393)
Seaford College (p. 440)
Sherborne School (p. 446)
Solihull School (p. 454)
Stowe School (p. 465)
Strathallan School (p. 468)
Sutton Valence School (p. 474)
Tonbridge School (p. 479)
Trinity School (p. 481)
Uppingham School (p. 487)
Wellington College (p. 498)
Wellington School (p. 501)
Whitgift School (p. 508)
Wycliffe College (p. 528)

Drama Scholarships

Abingdon School (p. 7)
Ackworth School (p. 9)
AKS (p. 10)
Ardingly College (p. 17)
Ashford School (p. 18)
Ashville College (p. 19)
Barnard Castle School (p. 25)
Bede's Senior School (p. 29)
Benenden School (p. 37)
Berkhamsted School (p. 41)
Bloxham School (p. 50)
Blundell's School (p. 52)
Bradfield College (p. 57)
Brentwood School (p. 62)
Brighton College (p. 64)
Bristol Grammar School (p. 66)
Canford School (p. 77)
Caterham School (p. 80)
Cheltenham College (p. 86)
Chigwell School (p. 91)
Christ College (p. 93)
Christ's Hospital (p. 95)
City of London School for Girls (p. 103)
Cokethorpe School (p. 109)
Colfe's School (p. 110)
Colston's School (p. 112)
Culford School (p. 116)
Dauntsey's School (p. 120)
Dean Close School (p. 121)
Denstone College (p. 123)
Durham School (p. 132)
Eastbourne College (p. 134)
Ellesmere College (p. 139)

Eltham College (p. 141)
Emanuel School (p. 143)
Epsom College (p. 145)
Eton College (p. 149)
Felsted School (p. 154)
Forest School (p. 159)
Framlingham College (p. 162)
Frensham Heights (p. 164)
Giggleswick School (p. 169)
The Godolphin School (p. 179)
Gresham's School (p. 183)
Halliford School (p. 194)
Hereford Cathedral School (p. 202)
Hurstpierpoint College (p. 207)
The John Lyon School (p. 218)
Kent College (p. 220)
Kent College Pembury (p. 222)
King Edward VI School (p. 227)
King Edward's School (p. 228)
King Edward's (p. 232)
King William's College (p. 235)
King's College School (p. 237)
King's College (p. 241)
King's School (p. 243)
The King's School (p. 245)
King's Ely (p. 249)
The King's School (p. 252)
Kingswood School (p. 262)
Lancing College (p. 266)
Latymer Upper School (p. 268)
Leighton Park School (p. 273)
The Leys School (p. 275)
Lord Wandsworth College (p. 280)

Loretto School (p. 281)
Malvern College (p. 289)
Merchant Taylors' School (p. 297)
Mill Hill School (p. 303)
Millfield (p. 308)
Monkton Combe School (p. 309)
Mount Kelly (p. 316)
New Hall School (p. 320)
Norwich School (p. 323)
Oakham School (p. 328)
Oundle School (p. 333)
Pangbourne College (p. 336)
The Perse Upper School (p. 338)
Plymouth College (p. 339)
Prior Park College (p. 350)
Queen's College (p. 355)
Radley College (p. 358)
Ratcliffe College (p. 360)
Reed's School (p. 364)
Reigate Grammar School (p. 365)
Rendcomb College (p. 367)
Repton School (p. 370)
Roedean School (p. 375)
Rossall School (p. 377)
RGS Worcester (p. 384)
The Royal Hospital School (p. 386)

Royal Russell School (p. 389)
Rydal Penrhos School (p. 396)
St Dunstan's College (p. 411)
St Edmund's College (p. 412)
St Edmund's School (p. 416)
St Edward's, Oxford (p. 418)
St George's College (p. 421)
St John's School (p. 423)
Seaford College (p. 440)
Sevenoaks School (p. 442)
Shrewsbury School (p. 450)
Stowe School (p. 465)
Strathallan School (p. 468)
Surbiton High School (p. 470)
Sutton Valence School (p. 474)
Taunton School (p. 477)
Tonbridge School (p. 479)
Trinity School (p. 481)
Wellingborough School (p. 495)
Wellington College (p. 498)
Wellington School (p. 501)
Whitgift School (p. 508)
Woodbridge School (p. 518)
Worth School (p. 523)
Wycliffe College (p. 528)

Music Scholarships

Abingdon School (p. 7)
Ackworth School (p. 9)
AKS (p. 10)
Aldenham School (p. 11)
Alleyn's School (p. 13)
Ampleforth College (p. 15)
Ardingly College (p. 17)
Ashford School (p. 18)
Ashville College (p. 19)
Bablake School (p. 21)
Bancroft's School (p. 22)
Barnard Castle School (p. 25)
Bedales School (p. 27)
Bede's Senior School (p. 29)
Bedford Modern School (p. 30)
Bedford School (p. 33)
Benenden School (p. 37)
Berkhamsted School (p. 41)
Birkdale School (p. 44)
Birkenhead School (p. 46)
Bishop's Stortford College (p. 47)
Bloxham School (p. 50)
Blundell's School (p. 52)
Bootham School (p. 55)
Bradfield College (p. 57)
Bradford Grammar School (p. 59)
Brentwood School (p. 62)
Brighton College (p. 64)
Bristol Grammar School (p. 66)
Bromsgrove School (p. 68)
Bryanston School (p. 72)
Campbell College (p. 75)
Canford School (p. 77)
Caterham School (p. 80)
Charterhouse (p. 83)

Cheadle Hulme School (p. 85)
Cheltenham College (p. 86)
Chetham's School of Music (p. 89)
Chigwell School (p. 91)
Christ College (p. 93)
Christ's Hospital (p. 95)
Churcher's College (p. 96)
City of London Freemen's School (p. 98)
City of London School (p. 101)
City of London School for Girls (p. 103)
Clayesmore School (p. 104)
Clifton College (p. 106)
Cokethorpe School (p. 109)
Colfe's School (p. 110)
Colston's School (p. 112)
Cranleigh (p. 113)
Culford School (p. 116)
Dauntsey's School (p. 120)
Dean Close School (p. 121)
Denstone College (p. 123)
Dulwich College (p. 129)
Durham School (p. 132)
Eastbourne College (p. 134)
The Edinburgh Academy (p. 136)
Elizabeth College (p. 138)
Ellesmere College (p. 139)
Eltham College (p. 141)
Emanuel School (p. 143)
Epsom College (p. 145)
Eton College (p. 149)
Exeter School (p. 151)
Felsted School (p. 154)
Fettes College (p. 156)
Forest School (p. 159)
Framlingham College (p. 162)

Francis Holland School (p. 163)
Frensham Heights (p. 164)
Giggleswick School (p. 169)
Glenalmond College (p. 174)
The Godolphin and Latymer School (p. 176)
The Godolphin School (p. 179)
The Grange School (p. 180)
Gresham's School (p. 183)
Guildford High School (p. 186)
The Haberdashers' Aske's Boys' School (p. 188)
Haileybury (p. 191)
Halliford School (p. 194)
Hampton School (p. 196)
Harrow School (p. 200)
Hereford Cathedral School (p. 202)
Highgate School (p. 203)
Hurstpierpoint College (p. 207)
Ipswich School (p. 214)
The John Lyon School (p. 218)
Kent College (p. 220)
Kent College Pembury (p. 222)
Kimbolton School (p. 225)
King Edward VI School (p. 227)
King Edward's School (p. 228)
King Edward's School (p. 231)
King Edward's (p. 232)
King Henry VIII School (p. 234)
King William's College (p. 235)
King's College School (p. 237)
King's College (p. 241)
King's School (p. 243)
The King's School (p. 245)
King's Ely (p. 249)
The King's School (p. 252)
The King's School (p. 255)
King's Rochester (p. 256)
The King's School (p. 258)
Kingston Grammar School (p. 260)
Kingswood School (p. 262)
Kirkham Grammar School (p. 265)
Lancing College (p. 266)
Latymer Upper School (p. 268)
Leicester Grammar School (p. 271)
Leighton Park School (p. 273)
The Leys School (p. 275)
Lincoln Minster School (p. 277)
Lord Wandsworth College (p. 280)
Loretto School (p. 281)
Loughborough Grammar School (p. 284)
Magdalen College School (p. 287)
Malvern College (p. 289)
Marlborough College (p. 293)
Merchant Taylors' School (p. 297)
Merchiston Castle School (p. 300)
Mill Hill School (p. 303)
Millfield (p. 308)
Monkton Combe School (p. 309)
Monmouth School (p. 312)
Mount Kelly (p. 316)
Mount St Mary's College (p. 318)
New Hall School (p. 320)
Newcastle-under-Lyme School (p. 322)
Norwich School (p. 323)
Oakham School (p. 328)
The Oratory School (p. 331)

Oundle School (p. 333)
Pangbourne College (p. 336)
The Perse Upper School (p. 338)
Plymouth College (p. 339)
The Portsmouth Grammar School (p. 343)
Princethorpe College (p. 346)
Prior Park College (p. 350)
Queen Elizabeth's Hospital (QEH) (p. 354)
Queen's College (p. 355)
Radley College (p. 358)
Ratcliffe College (p. 360)
Reed's School (p. 364)
Reigate Grammar School (p. 365)
Rendcomb College (p. 367)
Repton School (p. 370)
Roedean School (p. 375)
Rossall School (p. 377)
Royal Grammar School (p. 380)
RGS Worcester (p. 384)
The Royal Hospital School (p. 386)
The Royal Masonic School for Girls (p. 388)
Royal Russell School (p. 389)
Rugby School (p. 393)
Rydal Penrhos School (p. 396)
St Albans School (p. 402)
St Benedict's School (p. 406)
St Columba's College (p. 408)
St Dunstan's College (p. 411)
St Edmund's College (p. 412)
St Edmund's School (p. 416)
St Edward's, Oxford (p. 418)
St George's College (p. 421)
St John's School (p. 423)
St Lawrence College (p. 425)
St Mary's School Ascot (p. 431)
St Paul's School (p. 436)
St Peter's School, York (p. 439)
Seaford College (p. 440)
Sevenoaks School (p. 442)
Sherborne School (p. 446)
Shrewsbury School (p. 450)
Solihull School (p. 454)
Stamford School (p. 457)
The Stephen Perse Foundation (p. 458)
Stonyhurst College (p. 463)
Stowe School (p. 465)
Strathallan School (p. 468)
Surbiton High School (p. 470)
Sutton Valence School (p. 474)
Taunton School (p. 477)
Tonbridge School (p. 479)
Trinity School (p. 481)
Truro School (p. 483)
University College School (p. 485)
Uppingham School (p. 487)
Warwick School (p. 493)
Wellingborough School (p. 495)
Wellington College (p. 498)
Wellington School (p. 501)
Wells Cathedral School (p. 502)
West Buckland School (p. 504)
Westminster School (p. 506)
Whitgift School (p. 508)
Winchester College (p. 511)
Wolverhampton Grammar School (p. 516)

Woodbridge School (p. 518)
Woodhouse Grove School (p. 520)
Worksop College (p. 521)
Worth School (p. 523)

Wrekin College (p. 526)
Wycliffe College (p. 528)
Yarm School (p. 532)

Sport Scholarships

Abingdon School (p. 7)
Ackworth School (p. 9)
AKS (p. 10)
Aldenham School (p. 11)
Alleyn's School (p. 13)
Ardingly College (p. 17)
Ashford School (p. 18)
Ashville College (p. 19)
Bablake School (p. 21)
Barnard Castle School (p. 25)
Bede's Senior School (p. 29)
Bedford Modern School (p. 30)
Bedford School (p. 33)
Benenden School (p. 37)
Berkhamsted School (p. 41)
Birkenhead School (p. 46)
Bishop's Stortford College (p. 47)
Bloxham School (p. 50)
Blundell's School (p. 52)
Bradfield College (p. 57)
Brentwood School (p. 62)
Brighton College (p. 64)
Bristol Grammar School (p. 66)
Bromsgrove School (p. 68)
Bryanston School (p. 72)
Campbell College (p. 75)
Canford School (p. 77)
Caterham School (p. 80)
Charterhouse (p. 83)
Cheadle Hulme School (p. 85)
Cheltenham College (p. 86)
Christ College (p. 93)
Christ's Hospital (p. 95)
City of London School (p. 101)
Clayesmore School (p. 104)
Clifton College (p. 106)
Cokethorpe School (p. 109)
Colfe's School (p. 110)
Colston's School (p. 112)
Culford School (p. 116)
Dauntsey's School (p. 120)
Dean Close School (p. 121)
Denstone College (p. 123)
Dulwich College (p. 129)
Durham School (p. 132)
Eastbourne College (p. 134)
The Edinburgh Academy (p. 136)
Ellesmere College (p. 139)
Eltham College (p. 141)
Emanuel School (p. 143)
Epsom College (p. 145)
Felsted School (p. 154)
Fettes College (p. 156)
Forest School (p. 159)
Framlingham College (p. 162)
Frensham Heights (p. 164)
Giggleswick School (p. 169)

Glenalmond College (p. 174)
The Godolphin School (p. 179)
Gresham's School (p. 183)
Haileybury (p. 191)
Halliford School (p. 194)
Harrow School (p. 200)
Hereford Cathedral School (p. 202)
Hurstpierpoint College (p. 207)
Ipswich School (p. 214)
The John Lyon School (p. 218)
Kent College (p. 220)
Kent College Pembury (p. 222)
Kimbolton School (p. 225)
King Edward's School (p. 228)
King Edward's (p. 232)
King William's College (p. 235)
King's College School (p. 237)
King's College (p. 241)
King's School (p. 243)
The King's School (p. 245)
King's Ely (p. 249)
The King's School (p. 252)
King's Rochester (p. 256)
Kingston Grammar School (p. 260)
Kingswood School (p. 262)
Kirkham Grammar School (p. 265)
Lancing College (p. 266)
Latymer Upper School (p. 268)
Leicester Grammar School (p. 271)
Leighton Park School (p. 273)
The Leys School (p. 275)
Lincoln Minster School (p. 277)
Lord Wandsworth College (p. 280)
Loretto School (p. 281)
Magdalen College School (p. 287)
Malvern College (p. 289)
Marlborough College (p. 293)
Merchant Taylors' School (p. 297)
Merchiston Castle School (p. 300)
Mill Hill School (p. 303)
Millfield (p. 308)
Monkton Combe School (p. 309)
Monmouth School (p. 312)
Mount Kelly (p. 316)
Mount St Mary's College (p. 318)
New Hall School (p. 320)
Newcastle-under-Lyme School (p. 322)
Norwich School (p. 323)
Oakham School (p. 328)
The Oratory School (p. 331)
Oundle School (p. 333)
Pangbourne College (p. 336)
The Perse Upper School (p. 338)
Plymouth College (p. 339)
Princethorpe College (p. 346)
Prior Park College (p. 350)
Queen Elizabeth's Hospital (QEH) (p. 354)

Queen's College (p. 355)
Ratcliffe College (p. 360)
Reed's School (p. 364)
Reigate Grammar School (p. 365)
Rendcomb College (p. 367)
Repton School (p. 370)
Roedean School (p. 375)
Rossall School (p. 377)
Royal Grammar School (p. 380)
RGS Worcester (p. 384)
Royal Russell School (p. 389)
Rugby School (p. 393)
Rydal Penrhos School (p. 396)
St Dunstan's College (p. 411)
St Edmund's College (p. 412)
St Edmund's School (p. 416)
St Edward's, Oxford (p. 418)
St George's College (p. 421)
St John's School (p. 423)
St Lawrence College (p. 425)
St Mary's School Ascot (p. 431)
Seaford College (p. 440)
Sevenoaks School (p. 442)
Sherborne School (p. 446)
Shrewsbury School (p. 450)

Solihull School (p. 454)
Stamford School (p. 457)
Stowe School (p. 465)
Strathallan School (p. 468)
Surbiton High School (p. 470)
Sutton Valence School (p. 474)
Taunton School (p. 477)
Tonbridge School (p. 479)
Trinity School (p. 481)
Truro School (p. 483)
Uppingham School (p. 487)
Wellingborough School (p. 495)
Wellington College (p. 498)
Wellington School (p. 501)
Wells Cathedral School (p. 502)
West Buckland School (p. 504)
Whitgift School (p. 508)
Wolverhampton Grammar School (p. 516)
Woodbridge School (p. 518)
Woodhouse Grove School (p. 520)
Worksop College (p. 521)
Worth School (p. 523)
Wrekin College (p. 526)
Wycliffe College (p. 528)

Other Scholarships

Arkwright Engineering
Birkdale School (p. 44)
Bradfield College (p. 57)
Bristol Grammar School (p. 66)
Hereford Cathedral School (p. 202)
Ipswich School (p. 214)
Oakham School (p. 328)
St Paul's School (p. 436)
Stowe School (p. 465)
Strathallan School (p. 468)
Yarm School (p. 532)

Boarding
Caterham School (p. 80)
Rydal Penrhos School (p. 396)

Chess
Millfield (p. 308)
Reigate Grammar School (p. 365)
Woodbridge School (p. 518)

Choral
Aldenham School (p. 11)
Brentwood School (p. 62)
Brighton College (p. 64)
City of London School (p. 101)
Dean Close School (p. 121)
Denstone College (p. 123)
Elizabeth College (p. 138)
Hereford Cathedral School (p. 202)
King's Ely (p. 249)
The King's School (p. 252)
King's Rochester (p. 256)
Lincoln Minster School (p. 277)
Loughborough Grammar School (p. 284)
Norwich School (p. 323)
The Portsmouth Grammar School (p. 343)

Princethorpe College (p. 346)
St Albans School (p. 402)
St Edmund's School (p. 416)
St Paul's School (p. 436)
Strathallan School (p. 468)
Tonbridge School (p. 479)
Warwick School (p. 493)
Wells Cathedral School (p. 502)

Classics
Charterhouse (p. 83)
Ellesmere College (p. 139)

Design
Norwich School (p. 323)
St Dunstan's College (p. 411)

Expressive Arts
George Heriot's School (p. 167)

Golf
Ellesmere College (p. 139)
Loretto School (p. 281)
Worksop College (p. 521)

Hockey
Culford School (p. 116)

ICT
Repton School (p. 370)
Taunton School (p. 477)

IT
Bedford Modern School (p. 30)

Mathematics
Bristol Grammar School (p. 66)
Wells Cathedral School (p. 502)

Modern Languages

Bristol Grammar School (p. 66)
Wells Cathedral School (p. 502)

Ogden Trust Science

Birkdale School (p. 44)
Bootham School (p. 55)
Bristol Grammar School (p. 66)
Exeter School (p. 151)
Hereford Cathedral School (p. 202)
Ipswich School (p. 214)
Norwich School (p. 323)
Oakham School (p. 328)
Warwick School (p. 493)
Yarm School (p. 532)

Organ

Charterhouse (p. 83)
Cheltenham College (p. 86)
Clifton College (p. 106)
Dean Close School (p. 121)
Durham School (p. 132)
Ellesmere College (p. 139)
Glenalmond College (p. 174)
King's Ely (p. 249)
The King's School (p. 255)
King's Rochester (p. 256)
Lancing College (p. 266)
Princethorpe College (p. 346)
Queen's College (p. 355)
St Edmund's School (p. 416)
Solihull School (p. 454)
Taunton School (p. 477)

Performing Arts

Bedford Modern School (p. 30)
Bradfield College (p. 57)
Caterham School (p. 80)
Ellesmere College (p. 139)
Lord Wandsworth College (p. 280)
Plymouth College (p. 339)
Queen's College (p. 355)
Strathallan School (p. 468)
Wells Cathedral School (p. 502)

Photography

Frensham Heights (p. 164)
Surbiton High School (p. 470)

Piping

Fettes College (p. 156)
Glenalmond College (p. 174)
Merchiston Castle School (p. 300)
Strathallan School (p. 468)

Rugby

Culford School (p. 116)
Ellesmere College (p. 139)
Plymouth College (p. 339)

Sailing

The Royal Hospital School (p. 386)

Science

Bedales School (p. 27)
Bristol Grammar School (p. 66)
Caterham School (p. 80)
Dauntsey's School (p. 120)
Eastbourne College (p. 134)
Ellesmere College (p. 139)
Framlingham College (p. 162)
Kirkham Grammar School (p. 265)
Oakham School (p. 328)
Surbiton High School (p. 470)
Uppingham School (p. 487)

Swimming

Culford School (p. 116)
Ellesmere College (p. 139)
Mount Kelly (p. 316)
Plymouth College (p. 339)

Tennis

Culford School (p. 116)
Ellesmere College (p. 139)

Textiles

RGS Worcester (p. 384)

Bursaries

Abingdon School (p. 7)
Ackworth School (p. 9)
AKS (p. 10)
Aldenham School (p. 11)
Alleyn's School (p. 13)
Ampleforth College (p. 15)
Ardingly College (p. 17)
Ashville College (p. 19)
Bablake School (p. 21)
Barnard Castle School (p. 25)
Bedales School (p. 27)
Benenden School (p. 37)
Berkhamsted School (p. 41)
Birkdale School (p. 44)
Birkenhead School (p. 46)
Bishop's Stortford College (p. 47)
Bloxham School (p. 50)
Blundell's School (p. 52)
Bolton School Boys' Division (p. 54)
Bootham School (p. 55)
Bradfield College (p. 57)
Bradford Grammar School (p. 59)
Brentwood School (p. 62)
Brighton College (p. 64)
Bristol Grammar School (p. 66)
Bromsgrove School (p. 68)
Bryanston School (p. 72)
Bury Grammar School Boys (p. 74)
Campbell College (p. 75)
Canford School (p. 77)
Caterham School (p. 80)
Charterhouse (p. 83)
Cheadle Hulme School (p. 85)
Cheltenham College (p. 86)
Chetham's School of Music (p. 89)
Chigwell School (p. 91)
Christ College (p. 93)
Christ's Hospital (p. 95)
Churcher's College (p. 96)
City of London Freemen's School (p. 98)
City of London School (p. 101)
City of London School for Girls (p. 103)
Clayesmore School (p. 104)
Clifton College (p. 106)
Cokethorpe School (p. 109)
Colfe's School (p. 110)
Culford School (p. 116)
Dame Allan's Boys' School (p. 119)
Dauntsey's School (p. 120)
Dean Close School (p. 121)
Denstone College (p. 123)
Dollar Academy (p. 125)
Dulwich College (p. 129)
The High School of Dundee (p. 131)
Durham School (p. 132)
Eastbourne College (p. 134)
The Edinburgh Academy (p. 136)
Ellesmere College (p. 139)
Eltham College (p. 141)
Emanuel School (p. 143)
Epsom College (p. 145)
Eton College (p. 149)
Exeter School (p. 151)

Felsted School (p. 154)
Fettes College (p. 156)
Forest School (p. 159)
Framlingham College (p. 162)
Francis Holland School (p. 163)
Frensham Heights (p. 164)
George Heriot's School (p. 167)
Giggleswick School (p. 169)
The High School of Glasgow (p. 172)
Glenalmond College (p. 174)
The Godolphin School (p. 179)
The Grange School (p. 180)
Gresham's School (p. 183)
Guildford High School (p. 186)
The Haberdashers' Aske's Boys' School (p. 188)
Haileybury (p. 191)
Halliford School (p. 194)
Hampton School (p. 196)
Harrow School (p. 200)
Hereford Cathedral School (p. 202)
Highgate School (p. 203)
Hurstpierpoint College (p. 207)
Hutchesons' Grammar School (p. 209)
Hymers College (p. 211)
Immanuel College (p. 212)
Ipswich School (p. 214)
Kelvinside Academy (p. 219)
Kent College (p. 220)
Kent College Pembury (p. 222)
Kimbolton School (p. 225)
King Edward VI School (p. 227)
King Edward's School (p. 228)
King Edward's School (p. 231)
King Edward's (p. 232)
King Henry VIII School (p. 234)
King William's College (p. 235)
King's College School (p. 237)
King's School (p. 243)
The King's School (p. 245)
The King's School (p. 248)
King's Ely (p. 249)
The King's School (p. 255)
King's Rochester (p. 256)
The King's School (p. 258)
Kingswood School (p. 262)
Kirkham Grammar School (p. 265)
Lancing College (p. 266)
Latymer Upper School (p. 268)
The Grammar School at Leeds (p. 270)
Leicester Grammar School (p. 271)
Leighton Park School (p. 273)
The Leys School (p. 275)
Lomond School (p. 278)
Loretto School (p. 281)
Loughborough Grammar School (p. 284)
Magdalen College School (p. 287)
The Manchester Grammar School (p. 291)
Marlborough College (p. 293)
Merchant Taylors' School (p. 297)
Merchiston Castle School (p. 300)
Mill Hill School (p. 303)
Millfield (p. 308)
Monkton Combe School (p. 309)
Monmouth School (p. 312)
Morrison's Academy (p. 314)

Mount St Mary's College (p. 318)
New Hall School (p. 320)
Newcastle-under-Lyme School (p. 322)
Norwich School (p. 323)
Nottingham High School (p. 326)
Oakham School (p. 328)
Oundle School (p. 333)
Pangbourne College (p. 336)
The Perse Upper School (p. 338)
Plymouth College (p. 339)
Pocklington School (p. 341)
The Portsmouth Grammar School (p. 343)
Princethorpe College (p. 346)
Prior Park College (p. 350)
Queen Elizabeth's Hospital (QEH) (p. 354)
Queen's College (p. 355)
Radley College (p. 358)
Ratcliffe College (p. 360)
Reed's School (p. 364)
Reigate Grammar School (p. 365)
Rendcomb College (p. 367)
Repton School (p. 370)
Robert Gordon's College (p. 372)
Roedean School (p. 375)
Rossall School (p. 377)
Rougemont School (p. 379)
Royal Grammar School (p. 380)
RGS Worcester (p. 384)
The Royal Masonic School for Girls (p. 388)
Royal Russell School (p. 389)
Rugby School (p. 393)
Rydal Penrhos School (p. 396)
Ryde School with Upper Chine (p. 398)
St Albans School (p. 402)
St Aloysius' College (p. 404)
St Benedict's School (p. 406)
St Columba's College (p. 407)
St Columba's College (p. 408)
St Dunstan's College (p. 411)
St Edmund's College (p. 412)
St Edmund's School (p. 416)
St Edward's, Oxford (p. 418)
St George's College (p. 421)
St John's School (p. 423)

St Lawrence College (p. 425)
St Mary's School Ascot (p. 431)
St Paul's School (p. 436)
St Peter's School, York (p. 439)
Seaford College (p. 440)
Sevenoaks School (p. 442)
Sherborne School (p. 446)
Sidcot School (p. 452)
Silcoates School (p. 453)
Solihull School (p. 454)
Stamford School (p. 457)
The Stephen Perse Foundation (p. 458)
Stockport Grammar School (p. 461)
Stonyhurst College (p. 463)
Stowe School (p. 465)
Strathallan School (p. 468)
Surbiton High School (p. 470)
Sutton Valence School (p. 474)
Taunton School (p. 477)
Tonbridge School (p. 479)
Trinity School (p. 481)
Truro School (p. 483)
University College School (p. 485)
Uppingham School (p. 487)
Wellingborough School (p. 495)
Wellington College (p. 498)
Wellington School (p. 501)
Wells Cathedral School (p. 502)
West Buckland School (p. 504)
Westminster School (p. 506)
Whitgift School (p. 508)
Winchester College (p. 511)
Wisbech Grammar School (p. 513)
Wolverhampton Grammar School (p. 516)
Woodbridge School (p. 518)
Woodhouse Grove School (p. 520)
Worksop College (p. 521)
Worth School (p. 523)
Wrekin College (p. 526)
Wycliffe College (p. 528)
Yarm School (p. 532)

Headmasters' and Headmistresses' Conference International Members

PAGE

Aiglon College, Switzerland 555
Anglican Church Grammar School, Australia 553

Beijing Dulwich International School, China 552
The British School of Barcelona, Spain 555
The British School of Brussels, Belgium 548
The British School of Milan, Italy 555
The British School in The Netherlands, Netherlands . 549
The British School, New Delhi, India 552
The British School of Paris, France 550

Camberwell Grammar School, Australia 553
Campion School, Greece 555
The Cathedral & John Connon School, India 552
Christ Church Grammar School, Australia 553
Christ's College, New Zealand 554

Doha College, Qatar 555
The Doon School, India 552
Dubai College, United Arab Emirates 555

The English College in Prague, Czech Republic . . . 555
The English School, Cyprus 554

Geelong Grammar School, Australia 553
The Grange School, Chile 554

Haileybury, Australia 553
Hillcrest International Schools, Kenya 552

The International School Bangalore, India 552

Jerudong International School, Brunei Darussalam . . 552
Jumeirah English Speaking School,
    United Arab Emirates 555

Kincoppal-Rose Bay School of the Sacred Heart,
    Australia 553
King's College, New Zealand 554
King's College, Spain 550
The King's School, Australia 553
Knox Grammar School, Australia 553

PAGE

Kolej Tuanku Ja'afar, Malaysia 553

The Lawrence School, India 552

Melbourne Grammar School, Australia 553
Mentone Grammar School, Australia 553
Methodist Ladies' College, Australia 553
Michaelhouse, South Africa 552

Oporto British School, Portugal 555

Peponi School, Kenya 552
Peterhouse, Zimbabwe 552
The Prague British School, Czech Republic 555

Ridley College, Canada 554

St Andrew's Scots School, Argentina 554
St Catherine's British School, Greece 555
St Christopher's School, Bahrain 555
St George's British International School, Italy 555
St George's College, Zimbabwe 552
St George's College North, Argentina 554
St George's College Quilmes, Argentina 554
St Julian's School, Portugal 555
St Leonard's College, Australia 553
St Paul's School, Brazil 554
Scotch College, Australia 553
The Scots College, Australia 553
Shawnigan Lake School, Canada 554
Shore School, Australia 554
Shrewsbury International School, Thailand 553
Sydney Grammar School, Australia 554

Tanglin Trust School, Singapore 553
Trinity Grammar School, Australia 554

Upper Canada College, Canada 554

Wesley College, Australia 554
Woodstock School, India 552

Schools in Europe

The British School of Brussels

Pater Dupierreuxlaan 1, 3080 Tervuren, Belgium
Tel: 00 32 2 766 04 30
Fax: 00 32 2 767 80 70
email: admissions@britishschool.be
website: www.britishschool.be
Twitter: @BSB_Brussels
Facebook: britishschoolbrussels
LinkedIn: /company/the-british-school-of-brussels

Patron:
Her Excellency the British Ambassador to the King of the
  Belgians

Chairman of the Board: Mr Ian Backhouse

Principal: **Mrs Sue Woodroofe**, BA Hons, NPQH

Creation. The British School of Brussels (BSB) was founded in 1969 as a non-profit making organisation in Belgium and was opened in 1970 by HRH The Duke of Edinburgh. It is run by a Board of Governors, comprising distinguished British and Belgian citizens from both the professional and business worlds, together with parent and staff representatives.

Site. The school occupies a beautiful site of ten hectares, surrounded by woodlands and lakes near the Royal Museum of Central Africa in Tervuren, which is 20–25 minutes by car from the centre of Brussels. The site belongs to the Donation Royale, the Foundation which manages the estates left to the Belgian people at the beginning of the 20th century by King Leopold II.

Facilities. The school has excellent modern facilities, including a science and maths centre, networked IT suites, all with internet access and Wi-Fi and an Apple Mac suite. Students in a number of year groups have their own iPads and there is a current initiative to provide Secondary School students with their own laptop computer. The school has dance and drama studios as well as nine science laboratories, four art studies and three technology workshops, including a state-of-the-art design & technology workshop and food & nutrition rooms, comprehensive modern languages and humanities suites and a self-service cafeteria. The Early Learning & Development Centre for children of 1–3 years is situated in a separate Villa next to the school. The school is developing its sporting facilities extensively and will be the only international school in Belgium to have its own swimming pool by 2016.

Organisation. The British School of Brussels is an independent, fee-paying, non profit-making international school. The School is a co-educational, non-selective day school for students from 1 to 18 years of age, with over 1,350 currently on roll. Approximately 40% of the students are British and there are 70 other nationalities represented. Our curriculum, both in the Primary and Secondary Schools, is a British-based curriculum, adapted to suit the needs of our European context and international students. In the Secondary School, students sit GCSE/IGCSE examinations at the end of Year 11 (aged 16). Senior students then have the choice of three pre-university qualifications: the International Baccalaureate (IB) Diploma (with English/French or English/Dutch bilingual options), GCE A Levels or vocational courses in BTEC business, sports and hospitality prior to moving on to Higher Education in the UK, Belgium or beyond. Provision is also made for Oxbridge tuition. Our examination results, year on year, are very impressive for a non-selective school.

In 2014 our students achieved 100% pass rate in all three pre-university courses.

BSB has an established French/English bilingual programme for children aged 4–14 years to complement its English-medium teaching. We introduce the teaching of Spanish, German or Dutch as optional additional languages in the Secondary School. We have developed programmes to help students with learning differences and to help students who join us with little or no English skills. The school also employs a counsellor.

Sports and Extra-Curricular Activities. Use of the extensive sports facilities (two gymnasia, all-weather artificial pitches, grass pitches, floodlit training area, four outdoor tennis courts, indoor sports hall and the 240-seat Brel Theatre), together with programmes for children over the summer, make the school a focal point for the local and international community. In addition to curricular sport, a wide range of competitive sports is offered: athletics, cricket, cross-country, gymnastics, hockey, rugby, football, swimming and tennis, as well as recreational activities such as basketball and golf. The school participates very successfully in the International Schools Sports Tournaments (ISST) and GISGA. In 2016 BSB will be the only international school in Belgium to have its own swimming pool.

Music and Drama. The Music Department houses an extremely well-equipped music technology studio, a recording studio and a rehearsal studio for the School's orchestras, concert bands and instrumental ensembles. Individual instrument lessons are available from visiting specialist teachers, and take place in the suite of music practice rooms. The school is the largest Associated Board centre in Europe. Each year up to fifteen drama productions –including student-directed performances –are presented across the full student age range. The Theatre has its own workshop and Green Room, as well as a more intimate studio space that seats 80.

Careers. The school has the highest expectations of its student population and advice on careers, as well as higher and further education opportunities, is of vital importance to the further development of the students. The school takes part in many careers conventions and has its own international higher education and careers team. In 2014 94% of students were accepted on their first-choice university destination.

Fees per annum (2014–2015). From €23,950 (Reception) to €30,650 (Years 10–13). Some assistance is offered as part of the school's Assisted Places Scheme.

Past Students' Association. The school has a growing association of Alumni and has its own official BSB Alumni Facebook page. Please visit the Alumni section of the school website: www.britishschool.be to see how to subscribe to the alumni newsletter and follow the school on Twitter and LinkedIn.

The British School in The Netherlands

BSN Junior School Leidschenveen (3–11 years)
Vrouw Avenweg 640, 2493 WZ, The Hague,
Tel: 00 31 (0)70 315 4077
Fax: 00 31 (0)70 444 7861

BSN Junior School Diamanthorst (3–11 years)
Diamanthorst 16, 2592 GH, The Hague
Tel: 00 31 (0)70 315 7620
Fax: 00 31 (0)70 444 7621

BSN Junior School Vlaskamp (3–11 years)
Vlaskamp 19, 2592 AA, The Hague
Tel: 00 31 (0)70 333 8111
Fax: 00 31 (0)70 333 8100

BSN Senior School (11–18 years)
Jan van Hooflaan 3, 2252 BG, Voorschoten
Tel: 00 31 (0)71 560 2222
Fax: 00 31 (0)71 560 2200

email: admissions@britishschool.nl
website: www.britishschool.nl
Twitter: @BSN_Netherlands
Facebook: /BSNofficial
LinkedIn: /the-british-school-in-the-netherlands

Principal: **Mr Martin Coles**
Principal's Office: Boerderij Rosenburgh,
   Rosenburgherlaan 2, 2252 BA, Voorschoten
Tel: 00 31 (*0*)71 560 2251
Fax: 00 31 (*0*)71 560 2290

The British School in The Netherlands (BSN) was founded in 1931 as an independent, non-denominational school. Since then, it has grown into a school of around 2,000 students from Foundation 1 (age 3) to Year 13 (age 18). Although around 25% of the students are of British origin, the school truly serves the international community, with children on roll from over 80 nations. The BSN has four sites in The Hague.

Aims. The School aims to develop the potential of its students by providing a caring environment, in which they are offered the greatest possible educational opportunities. Students are helped to develop their powers of reasoning, increase their knowledge and become aware of the importance of their individual contribution and responsibility to society. All are encouraged to aim for excellence and to respect one another. These aims are achieved in a happy school whose students join with high expectations and where they are encouraged in the belief of their fulfilment.

The School was inspected by The Independent Schools Inspectorate (ISI) in 2009. The Inspection report concluded that *"The British School in The Netherlands is highly successful in fulfilling its aims"* and that *"The school has no significant areas of weakness"*.

Junior School Diamanthorst. JSD opened in September 2003 and currently offers places around 380 children. The site boasts excellent resources including a new dance/drama studio, as well as a recently fully landscaped brand new outdoor learning/play area.

Junior School Leidschenveen. JSL opened in 2010 and can provide around 570 places for children. Within its landscaped grounds, the campus includes dedicated facilities for Out of School Care, a Day Care Centre for 0 to 3 year olds as well as a Sports and Community Centre.

Junior School Vlaskamp. JSV can accommodate approximately 760 children. This award-winning building was opened in 1997 and provides a range of excellent resources, including notably extensive outside play and environmental areas.

Senior School. The Senior School is located in Voorschoten (a small town just north of The Hague). A huge building project was completed in 2003 offering enviable state-of-the-art facilities, including new science laboratories, information technology stations, library resources and much more. The school building is also undergoing major renovation due for completion in early 2015, which will include a brand new events foyer, improved fitness facilities, as well as a remodelled Sixth Form area and Student Café. This investment represents a commitment to providing a modern and stimulating learning environment, to support the comprehensive educational programme.

Staff. Each school has a Headteacher, supported by a Deputy Headteacher. The Principal has overall responsibility for all schools in the BSN group. All teachers (192 full-time, 97 part-time) are fully qualified and are mostly recruited from the United Kingdom.

Transport. An independent school bus service links the schools and covers most of The Hague, Voorburg, Leidschendam, Wassenaar, Voorschoten, as well as parts of Rotterdam, Rijswijk, Leiden, Amsterdam and Zoetermeer.

Curriculum. Students follow challenging programmes of study based on the National Curriculum for England and Wales but with an added international dimension. All students study English, mathematics, science, technology, history, geography, music, art and physical education from the age of five years. Dutch is taught from the age of five and French from the age of ten. In the Senior School, Spanish and German are also taught from Year 7 at age 11. Students prepare for the GCSE (at 16+) and IB Diploma Programme or AS/A2 Level examinations at 17/18 years. The School has a long and proud record of success with the majority of students entering universities and other higher education institutions all over the world.

Sport. Facilities are available for indoor and outdoor games, including rugby, hockey, aerobics, tennis, athletics, judo, football, basketball, volleyball and gymnastics. At Senior School level, fixtures are arranged with local clubs and other schools, including annual tours and tournaments in the United Kingdom and elsewhere in Europe.

Activities and Trips. The School takes pride in its regular participation in the annual Model United Nations Conference in The Hague. It also operates a full programme of field and activity trips in The Netherlands, the United Kingdom, France, Switzerland, Spain and Germany, capitalising on its central location in Europe.

Pastoral System. To ensure that each pupil is known individually, and cared for, there is a pastoral system which begins with the form teacher, who is responsible to a year group leader. Together they work to care, support and guide the individual in all aspects of school life. Success is achieved only through close cooperation between home and school, a positive learning environment and high standards of discipline.

Special Needs & EAL. Special provision is made for students with learning difficulties. Any child with Special Needs will be considered according to the School's policy on Special Needs Provision, which is available on request. Specialist help is provided throughout the School for students requiring individual tuition in English as an Additional Language.

Admission. Admission is granted at any time in the school year, depending on availability and the School's ability to meet the academic needs of the child. Great care is taken to ensure the academic and social integration of each child.

Fees per annum (2014–2015). Foundation Stage Full Time €13,260, Years 1–2 €13,560, Years 3–6 €13,740, Years 7–9 €17,820, Years 10–11 €18,360, Years 12–13 €18,720.

Charitable status. The British School in The Netherlands is a Registered Charity, number V409055. It aims to offer a British education to international children living temporarily or permanently in The Netherlands.

The British School of Paris

38 quai de l'Ecluse, 78290 Croissy sur Seine, France
Tel: 00 33 1 34 80 45 90
Fax: 00 33 1 39 76 12 69
email: info@britishschool.fr
website: www.britishschool.fr

Chairman of Governors: Mr P Kett

Headmaster: **Mr N Hammond**

Head of Senior School: Dr J Batters

Head of the Junior School: Ms K Tuckwell

Registrar: Mrs V Joynes

Age Range. 3–18.
Number of Pupils. 780 (Boys and Girls)
Fees per annum (2014–2015). Senior School €24,130–€26,231; Junior School €15,080–€22,007.

The BSP provides, in a caring environment, a high-quality British-style education for international students, to enable them to become caring citizens and to lead fulfilling lives.

Located just 15 kilometres from Paris, the School caters for English-speaking children of over 70 nationalities (about 30% are British) from ages 3–18. It is a not-for-profit association in France and is presided over by a governing body under the patronage of His Excellency the British Ambassador to France.

The **Junior School** provides education for primary aged children from 3–11 years. The purpose-built Junior School is located very close to the Senior School along the leafy banks of the river Seine. There are 35 classrooms accommodating up to 500 pupils, as well as 4 bespoke classrooms and 2 activity areas that are dedicated to our foundation stage/nursery section. Studies are based on the English National Curriculum with emphasis on English, Maths and Science, and of course, the French language. Being a holistic educator the BSP has a strong extra-curricular base with a special focus on music and drama as well as a large variety of sports. (*For further information about the Junior School, see entry in IAPS section*).

The **Senior School**, which caters for pupils aged from 11–18 years, is situated beside a beautiful stretch of the Seine in Croissy sur Seine. The buildings, with the exception of two nineteenth century houses, have been built since 1990. The Science and Technology block provides excellent facilities for Science, Information Technology, Electronics and Design. There are six large, well equipped science laboratories. The other classroom blocks house Humanities, Art, Business Studies, Modern Languages, Music, English and Mathematics. Other facilities include a generously staffed and resourced student career guidance programme, a library, IT labs, a refectory, a large sports hall and fitness centre. Students enter at the age of 11 and for the first three years, a broad general education is maintained in line with the National Curriculum. Pupils are prepared for the GCSE and AS/A Level examinations in a comprehensive range of subjects.

Music and drama are an integral part of school life; the music centre includes teaching and practice facilities as well as a well-equipped electronic studio. Specialist teachers visit the School to provide individual lessons in a wide range of instruments. Children take the Associated Board exams at regular intervals.

The School has had considerable sporting success over the years, winning the International Schools' Sports Tournament competition in girls' field hockey, and boys' rugby. Our international fixture lists provide an incentive to gain a place in school teams. As well as local matches our teams travel regularly to Belgium, Holland and the UK.

Small overall numbers, modest class sizes and a supportive pastoral system all help new pupils integrate quickly. Our examination results are outstanding. At A Level over 40% of all grades were A* and A and 91.6% of all grades at GCSE were between A* and C in 2014. These results compare very favourably with high-calibre schools in the UK. Most students continue their education at prestigious universities in the UK, USA, France and worldwide. BSP students have been successfully admitted to the Universities of Cambridge and Oxford, London School of Economics, University of Pennsylvania, Stanford University, McGill University, Universidad de Madrid, Seoul National University, L'Université de la Sorbonne, to mention but a few.

King's College
The British School of Madrid

Paseo de los Andes 35, Soto de Viñuelas, Madrid 28761, Spain
Tel: 00 34 918 034 800
Fax: 00 34 918 036 557
email: info@kingscollege.es
website: www.kingscollegeschools.org
Twitter: @Kings_Soto
LinkedIn   /King's College Soto

King's College is a British co-educational day and boarding school founded in 1969. It is the largest British curriculum school in Spain and the first school to have had full UK accreditation through the Independent Schools Inspectorate. The Headteacher is an international member of HMC, while the school is a member of COBIS, NABSS and BSA.

The school is governed by the Board of Directors and School Council which is composed of distinguished members from the business and academic communities.

Headteacher: **Andrew Rattue**, MA Oxon, MA London, PGCE London

Deputy Headteacher: Charles Ellison, BA Hons Warwick, Dip Psych Newcastle

Head of Secondary Department: Christopher T Parkinson, BEd Hons Crewe and Alsager

Director of Studies: James Slocombe, BSc Hons Bath, PGCE Bristol, MA OU

Head of Primary Department: Paula Parkinson, BA Hons Newcastle, PGCE Manchester

Deputy Head of Primary: Kirsty Sharp, BA Hons Hull

Head of Spanish Studies: Fernando Lage, Lic Filosofía UAM

Head of Boarding: Hanan Nazha, BA QTS London

Head of Admissions: Rebecca Conlon, BSc Hons Kent, MSc London Metropolitan University

There are three separate schools in Madrid which cater for children of approximately 48 nationalities between the ages of 2 and 18 years. Pupil enrolment in 2013–14 was 2,125 –including 44 boarders. There are over 140 fully-qualified staff, most of whom are British.

The Vision of King's College, is "to be at the forefront of British education internationally" as well as to provide students with an excellent all-round education while fostering tolerance and understanding between young people of different nationalities and backgrounds.

King's College, Soto de Viñuelas caters for nearly 1,500 pupils between the ages of 2 and 18 years (Pre-Nursery –Year 13) and stands on a 12-acre site in a residential area about 25 km from the centre of Madrid near the Guadarrama mountains and surrounded by open countryside. It is well connected to the city centre by motorway and rail. There is an optional comprehensive bus service to the city of Madrid and its outlying residential areas and all routes are supervised by a bus monitor.

Facilities. There are extensive, purpose-built facilities which include 7 science laboratories, 2 libraries, an art studio, 3 computer centres with multimedia stations, and 2 music rooms. All classrooms are fitted with interactive whiteboards and there are computers in all Primary classrooms. The school offers a purpose-built Early Learning Centre, an Auditorium with seating for over 350 people and a Music School with 6 rooms for individual or small group tuition. The sports facilities include a 25-metre indoor heated swimming pool, a floodlit multi-purpose sports area, football pitches, basketball and tennis courts, a gymnasium with fitness centre and a horse riding school. Future development includes plans for a covered sports hall.

Tenbury House, the school boarding residence, opened in September 2011 and offers brand new purpose-built accommodation for up to 44 boarders. The residence is located in the school grounds and offers pupils a breakfast room, kitchen, laundry, work room, lounge, TV room, storage and easy access to the new AstroTurf pitch and sports facilities.

King's College School, La Moraleja. The school caters for more than 500 pupils aged 3 to 14 (Nursery to Year 9) and is located in a residential area just 16 kilometres from the centre of the city. The modern on-site facilities include a library, ICT centre, laboratory, music room, multi-purpose sports surface and gymnasium.

At the age of fourteen, at the end of National Curriculum Year 9, pupils transfer to King's College, Soto de Viñuelas to complete their final four years of study.

King's Infant School, Chamartín. Conveniently located in the Chamartín area of central Madrid, the school offers purpose-built facilities for boys and girls between the ages of 3 and 6 (Nursery to Year 2) and has a capacity of approximately 200 pupils. There are air-conditioned, spacious and well-equipped classrooms, complete with independent bathrooms for the Nursery pupils, a library and computer room and a playground area. At the age of seven, at the end of National Curriculum Year 2, pupils from King's Infant School automatically transfer either to King's College, Soto de Viñuelas or King's College School, La Moraleja.

Curriculum. Pupils at all three King's College schools in Madrid follow the English National Curriculum leading to (I)GCSE, GCSE, AS and A Level examinations. A wide range of subjects is available. All pupils learn Spanish. The school has a reputation for high academic standards and excellent examination results with students going on to top universities in Britain, USA and Spain amongst others.

An Oxbridge preparatory group works with the most able students to prepare university applications. There is a very experienced Careers and University Entrance Advisory Department for all students.

Activities. King's College has choirs, musical ensembles and drama groups, which participate in numerous events throughout the year. Pupils are encouraged to explore their capabilities in the areas of music and the arts from a very early age.

Sports play an important role at the school and pupils are encouraged to take part in tournaments and local competitive events, in addition to their normal PE classes. King's College currently has football, basketball and swimming teams participating in local leagues, and also takes part in inter-school championships in athletics and cross-country.

There is a programme of optional classes which includes horse riding, ballet, judo, Spanish dancing, swimming, tennis, tuition in various musical instruments, performing arts and craft workshops.

Admission. Pupils entering the school at the age of 7 or above are required to sit entrance tests in English and Math-

ematics and possibly other subjects, while younger candidates are offered a review by the Head of Admissions in each school. For those applying to the Sixth Form, admission depends on the results of the (I)GCSE examinations, or equivalent.

Fees per term (2014–2015). Tuition: €1,978–€3,798 excluding lunch and transport. Boarding (including tuition): Full €7,333–€8,000.

Scholarships. The school offers a small number of scholarships to Sixth Formers selected on academic merit.

Further information may be obtained from The Director of Admissions at the School: Rebecca Conlon, rebecca.conlon@kingsgroup.org.

Other International Schools

Africa

Kenya

Hillcrest International Schools
PO Box 24819, Karen 00502, Nairobi, Kenya
email: admin@hillcrest.ac.ke
website: www.hillcrest.ac.ke

Principal & CEO: **Mr Chris Wheeler**

Headteacher, Secondary School: Mr Leon Bareham

Headteacher, Preparatory School: Mr Ian Rosario-Hopkins

Peponi School
PO Box 236, Ruiru 00232, Kenya
email: info@peponischool.org
website: www.peponischool.org

Headmaster: **Mark Durston**

South Africa

Michaelhouse
Balgowan 3275, Kwazulu-Natal, South Africa
email: info@michaelhouse.org
website: www.michaelhouse.org

Rector: **Greg Theron**

Zimbabwe

Peterhouse
Private Bag 3741, Marondera, Zimbabwe
email: rector@peterhouse.co.zw
website: www.peterhousegroup.com

Rector: **Howard W Blackett**

St George's College
Private Bag 7727, Causeway, Harare, Zimbabwe
email: headsec@stgeorges.co.zw
website: www.stgeorges.co.zw

Headmaster: **G Kevin Atkinson**

Asia

Brunei Darussalam

Jerudong International School
PO Box 1408, Bandar Seri Begawan BS8672, Negara
Brunei Darussalam
email: enrol@jis.edu.bn
website: www.jis.edu.bn

Principal: **Barnaby Sandow**, BSc Eng Durham, PGCE
Exeter

(See entry in IAPS section)

China

Beijing Dulwich International School
89 Capital Airport Road, Shunyi District, Beijing
101300 PRC, China
email: info@dulwich-beijing.cn
website: www.dulwich-beijing.cn

Headmaster: **Mr David J Mansfield**

India

The British School, New Delhi
Dr Jose P Rizal Marg, Chanakyapuri, New Delhi 110021,
India
email: britishschool@british-school.org
website: www.british-school.org

Director: **Dr Nick Argent**, BA Hons, PGCE, PhD

The Cathedral & John Connon School
6 Purshottamdas Thakurdas Marg, Fort Mumbai 400
001, India
email: cajcs@mtnl.net.in
website: www.cathedral-school.com

Principal: **Mrs Meera Isaacs**

The Doon School
The Mall, Dehradun 248001, Uttaranchal, India
email: hm@doonschool.com
website: www.doonschool.com

Headmaster: **Dr Peter McLaughlin**

The International School Bangalore
NAFL Valley, Whitefield-Sarajapur Road, Near
Dommasandra Circle, Bangalore –562 125, Karnataka
State, India
email: school@tisb.ac.in
website: www.tisb.org

Principal: **Mr Peter Armstrong**

The Lawrence School
Sanawar 173202, District Solan, Himachal Pradesh,
India
email: snaoffice@yahoo.com
website: www.sanawar.edu.in

Headmaster: **Praveen Vasisht**

Woodstock School
Tehri Road, Mussoorie, Uttarakhand 248179, India
email: communications@woodstockschool.ac.in
website: www.woodstockschool.in

Principal: **Dr Jonathan Long**

Malaysia

Kolej Tuanku Ja'afar
Mantin, 71700 Negeri Sembilan, West Malaysia
email: principal@ktj.edu.my
website: www.ktj.edu.my

Principal: Dr Simon Watson

Singapore

Tanglin Trust School
95 Portsdown Road, Singapore 139299
email: admissions@tts.edu.sg
website: www.tts.edu.sg

Chief Executive Officer: Peter J Derby-Crook

Head of Junior School: David Ingram

(*See Junior School entry in IAPS section*)

Head of Infant School: Paula Craigie

Thailand

Shrewsbury International School
1922 Charoen Krung Road, Wat Prayakrai, Bang
Kholame, Bangkok 10120, Thailand
email: enquiries@shrewsbury.ac.th
website: www.shrewsbury.ac.th

Principal: Stephen Holroyd

Australia and New Zealand

Australia

Anglican Church Grammar School
Oaklands Parade, East Brisbane, Queensland
QLD 4169, Australia
email: reception@churchie.com.au
website: www.churchie.com.au

Headmaster: Dr Alan Campbell

Camberwell Grammar School
PO Box 151, Balwyn, VIC 3103, Australia
email: headmaster@cgs.vic.edu.au
website: www.cgs.vic.edu.au

Headmaster: Dr Paul Hicks

Christ Church Grammar School
Queenslea Drive, Claremont, WA 6010, Australia
email: info@ccgs.wa.edu.au
website: www.ccgs.wa.edu.au

Headmaster: Garth E Wynne

Geelong Grammar School
50 Biddlecombe Avenue, Corio, VIC 3214, Australia
email: principal@ggs.vic.edu.au
website: www.ggs.vic.edu.au

Principal: Stephen Meek

Haileybury
855 Springvale Road, Keysborough, VIC 3173, Australia
email: admissions@haileybury.vic.edu.au
website: www.haileybury.com.au

Principal: Derek Scott

Kincoppal-Rose Bay School of the Sacred Heart
New South Head Road, Rose Bay NSW 2029, Australia
email: reception@krb.nsw.edu.au
website: www.krb.nsw.edu.au

Principal: Mrs Hilary Johnston-Croke

The King's School
PO Box 1, Parramatta, NSW 2124, Australia
email: headmaster@kings.edu.au
website: www.kings.edu.au

Headmaster: Dr Tim F Hawkes

Knox Grammar School
7 Woodville Avenue, Wahroonga, NSW 2076, Australia
email: contact@knox.nsw.edu.au
website: www.knox.nsw.edu.au

Headmaster: John Weeks

Melbourne Grammar School
Domain Road, South Yarra, Melbourne, VIC 3004,
Australia
email: mgs@mgs.vic.edu.au
website: www.mgs.vic.edu.au

Headmaster: Roy Kelley

Mentone Grammar School
63 Venice Street, Mentone, VIC 3194, Australia
email: enquiry@mentonegrammar.net
website: www.mentonegrammar.net

Principal: Malcolm Cater

Methodist Ladies' College
207 Barker Road, Kew, Victoria 3101, Australia
email: college@mlc.vic.edu.au
website: www.mlc.vic.edu.au

Principal: Miss Diana Vernon, BA, PGCE, MACE,
MACEL

St Leonard's College
163 South Road, Brighton East, VIC 3187, Australia
email: stleonards@stleonards.vic.edu.au
website: www.stleonards.vic.edu.au

Principal: Mr Stuart Davis

Scotch College
1 Morrison Street, Hawthorn, VIC 3122, Australia
email: scotch@scotch.vic.edu.au
website: www.scotch.vic.edu.au

Principal: I Tom Batty

The Scots College
Victoria Road, Bellevue Hill, NSW 2023, Australia
email: reception@tsc.nsw.edu.au
website: www.tsc.nsw.edu.au

Principal: Dr Ian P M Lambert

Shore School

PO Box 1221, Blue Street, North Sydney, NSW 2059, Australia

email: headmaster@shore.nsw.edu.au
website: www.shore.nsw.edu.au

Head: Dr Timothy Wright

Sydney Grammar School

College Street, Darlinghurst, NSW 2010, Australia

email: kmr@sydgram.nsw.edu.au
website: www.sydgram.nsw.edu.au

Head: Dr John T Vallance

Trinity Grammar School

PO Box 174, 119 Prospect Road, Summer Hill, NSW 2130, Australia

email: mcujes@trinity.nsw.edu.au
website: www.trinity.nsw.edu.au

Head Master: G Milton Cujes

Wesley College

577 St Kilda Road, Melbourne, VIC 3004, Australia

email: principal@wesleycollege.net
website: www.wesleycollege.net

Principal: Dr Helen Drennan

New Zealand

Christ's College

Rolleston Avenue, Private Bag 4900, Christchurch, New Zealand

email: headmaster@christscollege.com
website: www.christscollege.com

Headmaster: Simon Leese

King's College

PO Box 22012, Otahuhu, Auckland 1640, New Zealand

email: reception@kingscollege.school.nz
website: www.kingscollege.school.nz

Headmaster: Mr Michael Leach

Central, North and South America

Argentina

St Andrew's Scots School

Roque Saenz Peña 654, 1636 Olivos, Buenos Aires, Argentina

email: administration@sanandres.esc.edu.ar
website: www.sanandres.esc.edu.ar

Head: Gabriel Rshaid

St George's College North

C. Rivadavia y Don Bosco, Los Polvorines 1613, Buenos Aires, Argentina

email: informes@stgeorges.org.ar
website: www.stgeorges.edu.ar

Headmaster: Ian D Tate

St George's College Quilmes

Guido 800, CC2 (1878), Quilmes, Buenos Aires, Argentina

email: infoquilmes@stgeorges.edu.ar
website: www.stgeorges.edu.ar

Headmaster: Derek Pringle

Brazil

St Paul's School

Rua Juquiá 166, Jardim Paulistano, São Paulo SP 01440-903, Brazil

email: spshead@stpauls.br
website: www.stpauls.br

Head: Ms Louise Simpson

(*See entry in IAPS section*)

Canada

Ridley College

PO Box 3013, 2 Ridley Road, St Catharine's, Ontario L2R 7C3, Canada

email: headmaster@ridleycollege.com
website: www.ridleycollege.com

Headmaster: J Edward Kidd, BA, BEd, MSc

Shawnigan Lake School

1975 Renfrew Road, Shawnigan Lake, BC V0R 2W1, Canada

email: rtaylor@shawnigan.ca
website: www.shawnigan.ca

Head: David Robertson, MA, PGCE

Upper Canada College

200 Lonsdale Road, Toronto, Ontario M4V 1W6, Canada

email: admin@ucc.on.ca
website: www.ucc.on.ca

Principal: Dr James Power

Chile

The Grange School

Av Principe de Gales 6154, La Reina, 687067, Santiago, Chile

email: rectoria@grange.cl
website: www.grange.cl

Rector: Rachid R Benammar

(*See Grange Preparatory School entry in IAPS section.*)

Europe

Cyprus

The English School

PO Box 23575, 1684 Nicosia, Cyprus

email: head@englishschool.ac.cy
website: www.englishschool.ac.cy

Headmaster: Graeme Garrett

Czech Republic

The English College in Prague
Sokolovska 320, 190-00 Praha 9, Czech Republic
email: office@englishcollege.cz
website: www.englishcollege.cz

Headmaster: Mr Simon Marshall, MA, MA, MPhil

The Prague British School
K Lesu 558/2, 142 00 Praha 4, Czech Republic
email: info@pbschool.cz
website: www.pbschool.cz

Head of Senior School: Tim Roberts

Head of Primary Schools: John Bagust

Greece

Campion School
PO Box 67484, Pallini, Athens 153 02, Greece
email: satherton@campion.edu.gr
website: www.campion.edu.gr

Headmaster: Stephen W Atherton

St Catherine's British School
PO Box 51019, Kifissia GR 145 10, Greece
email: headmaster@stcatherines.gr
website: www.stcatherines.gr

Headmaster: Mr Stuart Smith

Italy

The British School of Milan
Via Pisani Dossi 16, 20134 Milan, Italy
email: info@sjhschool.com
website: www.sjhschool.com

Principal: Dr Carlo Ferrario

St George's British International School
Via Cassia, La Storta, 00123 Rome, Italy
email: secretary@stgeorge.school.it
website: www.stgeorge.school.it

Principal: Martyn J Hales, BSc

Portugal

Oporto British School
Rua da Cerca 326/350, 4150-201 Porto, Portugal
email: school@obs.edu.pt
website: www.obs.edu.pt

Head Master: Mr Tom McGrath

St Julian's School
Quinta Nova, 2776–601 Carcavelos Codex, Portugal
email: ccoelho@stjulians.com
website: www.stjulians.com

Headmaster: Craig Monaghan

Spain

The British School of Barcelona
Cognita Schools Group
Carrer de la Ginesta 26, 08860 Castelldefels, Barcelona, Spain
email: school@bsb.edu.es
website: www.britishschoolbarcelona.com

Headmaster: Dr Josep Lluís González

Switzerland

Aiglon College
CH-1885 Chesières-Villars, Switzerland
email: info@aiglon.ch
website: www.aiglon.ch

Head Master: Mr Richard McDonald, MA Oxon, PGCE

Middle East

Bahrain

St Christopher's School
PO Box 32052, Isa Town, Kingdom of Bahrain
email: office.principal@st-chris.net
website: www.st-chris.net

Principal: Mr Ed Goodwin, BA, MA, MBA

(See entry in IAPS section)

Qatar

Doha College
PO Box 7506, Doha, State of Qatar
email: seniorexec@dohacollege.com
website: www.dohacollege.com

Principal: Mark Leppard

United Arab Emirates

Dubai College
PO Box 837, Dubai, United Arab Emirates
email: dcadmin@dubaicollege.org
website: www.dubaicollege.org

Headmaster: Mr Peter Hill

Jumeirah English Speaking School
PO Box 24942, Dubai, United Arab Emirates
email: jess@jess.sch.ae
website: www.jess.sch.ae

Director: Mr R D Stokoe

Headmasters' and Headmistresses' Conference

Associates

In addition to Full membership (open to Heads of independent schools in the UK and Ireland) and International membership (open to Heads of independent schools overseas), HMC also elects a small number of Associates each year.

HMC Associates are either heads of high-performing maintained sector schools proposed and supported by HMC divisions or influential individuals in the world of education, including university vice-chancellors and academics, who endorse and support the work of HMC.

The following is a list of current HMC Associates:

BRIDGET TULLIE
Batley Grammar School, Batley, West Yorkshire
website: www.batleygrammar.co.uk

DR STUART D SMALLWOOD
Bishop Wordsworth's Grammar School, Salisbury, Wiltshire
website: www.bws.wilts.sch.uk

DR MARK FENTON
Dr Challoner's Grammar School, Amersham, Bucks
website: www.challoners.com

ROBERT J MASTERS
The Judd School, Tonbridge, Kent
website: www.judd.kent.sch.uk

RUSSEL ELLICOTT
Pate's Grammar School, Cheltenham, Gloucestershire
website: www.pates.gloucs.sch.uk

SIMON CORNS
Queen Elizabeth's Grammar School, Blackburn, Lancashire
website: www.qegsblackburn.com

PAUL D SPENCER ELLIS
Royal Alexandra and Albert School, Reigate, Surrey
website: www.raa-school.co.uk

PETER MIDDLETON
Welbeck – The Defence Sixth Form College, Loughborough, Leicestershire
website: www.dsfc.ac.uk

JILL BERRY
Educational Consultant

BRENDA DESPONTIN
Former Head

TOBY MULLINS
Executive Principal, David Ross Education Trust

PART II
Schools whose Heads are members of the Girls' Schools Association

ALPHABETICAL LIST OF SCHOOLS

PAGE

	PAGE
The Abbey School, Berks	561
Abbots Bromley School, Staffs	562
Abbot's Hill School, Herts.	563
Adcote School, Shropshire.	564
Alderley Edge School for Girls, Cheshire	566
Badminton School, Bristol.	567
Bedford Girls' School, Beds.	569
Blackheath High School, London	569
Bolton School Girls' Division, Lancs	570
Brighton & Hove High School, E Sussex	572
Bromley High School, Kent	572
Bruton School for Girls, Somerset.	574
Burgess Hill School for Girls, W Sussex	575
Bury Grammar School Girls, Lancs	576
Channing School, London	577
Cheltenham Ladies' College, Glos	579
Cobham Hall, Kent.	580
Cranford House School, Oxon.	582
Croydon High School, Surrey	583
Dame Allan's Girls' School, Tyne and Wear	584
Derby High School, Derbyshire	585
Dodderhill School, Worcs	587
Durham High School for Girls, Durham.	588
Edgbaston High School, W Midlands	589
Farlington School, W Sussex	592
Farnborough Hill, Hants.	593
Francis Holland School, London.	594
Gateways School, W Yorks	596
Greenacre School for Girls, Surrey	598
Haberdashers' Aske's School for Girls, Herts.	599
Haberdashers' Monmouth School for Girls, Wales	601
Harrogate Ladies' College, N Yorks.	603
Headington School, Oxon	605
Heathfield School, Berks	607
Hethersett Old Hall School, Norfolk.	609
Howell's School Llandaff, Wales	610
Ipswich High School, Suffolk	611
Kilgraston, Scotland	612
King Edward VI High School for Girls, W Midlands.	613
King's High School, Warwicks	615
The Kingsley School, Warwicks.	617
The Lady Eleanor Holles School, Middx	618
Lavant House, W Sussex.	621
Leicester High School for Girls, Leics.	623
Leweston School, Dorset	624

	PAGE
Loughborough High School, Leics	626
Luckley House School, Berks	628
Manchester High School for Girls, Greater Manchester	629
Manor House School, Surrey	630
The Marist Senior School, Berks	631
The Mary Erskine School, Scotland	632
Marymount International School, Surrey	634
The Maynard School, Devon	636
Merchant Taylors' Girls' School, Merseyside.	638
Moira House Girls School, E Sussex	639
More House School, London	642
Moreton Hall, Shropshire	644
The Mount School, N Yorks.	646
Newcastle High School for Girls, Tyne and Wear	648
North London Collegiate School, Middx	649
Northampton High School, Northants	650
Northwood College for Girls, Middx	652
Norwich High School, Norfolk	653
Notre Dame School, Surrey	654
Notting Hill and Ealing High School, London	657
Nottingham Girls' High School, Notts	658
Oxford High School, Oxon	659
Palmers Green High School, London	659
Pipers Corner School, Bucks	661
Portsmouth High School, Hants	661
Princess Helena College, Herts	662
Prior's Field, Surrey	664
Putney High School, London	665
Queen Margaret's School, N Yorks	668
Queen Mary's School, N Yorks	671
Queen's College, London, London	672
Queen's Gate School, London.	673
Queenswood School, Herts	675
The Red Maids' School, Bristol	676
Redland High School for Girls, Bristol	678
The Royal High School Bath, Somerset.	680
Rye St Antony, Oxon	682
St Augustine's Priory School, London.	684
St Catherine's School, Surrey	687
St Catherine's School, Middx	689
St Dominic's Brewood, Staffs	690
St Dominic's Priory School, Staffs	691
St Gabriel's, Berks.	692
St George's, Ascot, Berks	694
St Helen & St Katharine, Oxon	696
St Helen's School, Middx	698
St James Senior Girls' School, London	701

	PAGE
St Leonards-Mayfield School, E Sussex	702
St Margaret's School for Girls, Scotland	704
St Margaret's School, Herts	706
St Margaret's School, London	707
St Martha's, Herts	707
Saint Martin's, W Midlands	709
St Mary's School, Cambs	710
St Mary's School, Essex	713
St Mary's School, Bucks	714
St Mary's School, Dorset	715
St Nicholas' School, Hants	717
St Swithun's School, Hants	719
Sheffield High School, S Yorks	723
Shrewsbury High School, Shropshire	723
South Hampstead High School, London	725
Stamford High School, Lincs	726
Stonar, Wilts	728

	PAGE
Streatham & Clapham High School, London	729
Sutton High School, Surrey	731
Sydenham High School, London	733
Talbot Heath, Dorset	734
Tormead School, Surrey	734
Truro High School for Girls, Cornwall	736
Tudor Hall, Oxon	737
Walthamstow Hall, Kent	739
Westfield School, Tyne and Wear	741
Westholme School, Lancs	743
Westonbirt School, Glos	743
Wimbledon High School, London	745
Woldingham School, Surrey	746
Wychwood School, Oxon	748
Wykeham House School, Hants	749

The following schools, whose Heads are members of both GSA and HMC, can be found in the HMC section:

Benenden School
Berkhamsted School
City of London School for Girls
Downe House
Francis Holland School, Regent's Park
The Godolphin and Latymer School
The Godolphin School
James Allen's Girls' School (JAGS)
Kent College Pembury
New Hall School
Queen Anne's School
Roedean School
St Albans High School for Girls
St Mary's Calne
St Mary's School Ascot
St Paul's Girls' School
Sherborne Girls
Withington Girls' School
Wycombe Abbey

GEOGRAPHICAL LIST OF GSA SCHOOLS

PAGE   PAGE

ENGLAND

Bedfordshire
Bedford Girls' School. 569

Berkshire
The Abbey School 561
Heathfield School. 607
Luckley House School 628
The Marist Senior School. 631
St Gabriel's 692
St George's, Ascot 694

Bristol
Badminton School 567
The Red Maids' School. 676
Redland High School for Girls 678

Buckinghamshire
Pipers Corner School 661
St Mary's School 714

Cambridgeshire
St Mary's School 710

Cheshire
Alderley Edge School for Girls 566

Cornwall
Truro High School for Girls. 736

Derbyshire
Derby High School 585

Devon
The Maynard School 636

Dorset
Leweston School 624
St Mary's School 715
Talbot Heath. 734

Durham
Durham High School for Girls 588

Essex
St Mary's School 713

Gloucestershire
Cheltenham Ladies' College 579
Westonbirt School. 743

Greater Manchester
Manchester High School for Girls 629

Hampshire
Farnborough Hill 593
Portsmouth High School 661
St Nicholas' School. 717
St Swithun's School. 719
Wykeham House School 749

Hertfordshire
Abbot's Hill School. 563
Haberdashers' Aske's School for Girls 599

Princess Helena College 662
Queenswood School 675
St Margaret's School 706
St Martha's 707

Kent
Bromley High School. 572
Cobham Hall 580
Walthamstow Hall 739

Lancashire
Bolton School Girls' Division 570
Bury Grammar School Girls 576
Westholme School 743

Leicestershire
Leicester High School for Girls. 623
Loughborough High School 626

Lincolnshire
Stamford High School 726

London (see also Essex, Middlesex, Surrey)
Blackheath High School 569
Channing School 577
Francis Holland School. 594
More House School. 642
Notting Hill and Ealing High School 657
Palmers Green High School 659
Putney High School. 665
Queen's College, London. 672
Queen's Gate School 673
St Augustine's Priory School 684
St James Senior Girls' School 701
St Margaret's School 707
South Hampstead High School 725
Streatham & Clapham High School 729
Sydenham High School. 733
Wimbledon High School 745

Merseyside
Merchant Taylors' Girls' School 638

Middlesex
The Lady Eleanor Holles School 618
North London Collegiate School 649
Northwood College for Girls 652
St Catherine's School. 689
St Helen's School. 698

Norfolk
Hethersett Old Hall School 609
Norwich High School. 653

Northamptonshire
Northampton High School 650

Nottinghamshire
Nottingham Girls' High School. 658

Oxfordshire
Cranford House School 582
Headington School 605

	PAGE
Oxford High School.	659
Rye St Antony.	682
St Helen & St Katharine	696
Tudor Hall.	737
Wychwood School	748

Shropshire
Adcote School.	564
Moreton Hall	644
Shrewsbury High School	723

Somerset
| Bruton School for Girls. | 574 |
| The Royal High School Bath | 680 |

Staffordshire (see also West Midlands)
Abbots Bromley School.	562
St Dominic's Brewood	690
St Dominic's Priory School.	691

Suffolk
| Ipswich High School | 611 |

Surrey
Croydon High School.	583
Greenacre School for Girls	598
Manor House School	630
Marymount International School	634
Notre Dame School.	654
Prior's Field.	664
St Catherine's School	687
Sutton High School	731
Tormead School.	734
Woldingham School.	746

Sussex (East)
Brighton & Hove High School	572
Moira House Girls School	639
St Leonards-Mayfield School.	702

Sussex (West)
| Burgess Hill School for Girls | 575 |

	PAGE
Farlington School.	592
Lavant House.	621

Tyne and Wear
Dame Allan's Girls' School	584
Newcastle High School for Girls	648
Westfield School	741

Warwickshire
| King's High School. | 615 |
| The Kingsley School | 617 |

West Midlands
Edgbaston High School.	589
King Edward VI High School for Girls.	613
Saint Martin's.	709

Wiltshire
| Stonar. | 728 |

Worcestershire
| Dodderhill School. | 587 |

Yorkshire (North)
Harrogate Ladies' College	603
The Mount School	646
Queen Margaret's School.	668
Queen Mary's School.	671

Yorkshire (South)
| Sheffield High School | 723 |

Yorkshire (West)
| Gateways School | 596 |

SCOTLAND
Kilgraston.	612
The Mary Erskine School.	632
St Margaret's School for Girls	704

WALES
| Haberdashers' Monmouth School for Girls. | 601 |
| Howell's School Llandaff. | 610 |

Individual School Entries

The Abbey School

Kendrick Road, Reading RG1 5DZ
Tel: 0118 987 2256
Fax: 0118 987 1478
email: schooloffice@theabbey.co.uk
website: www.theabbey.co.uk
Twitter: @theabbeyschool
Facebook: /The-Abbey-School

Founded 1887. Incorporated 1914. Church of England Foundation.

Board of Governors:
Chairman: Dr Debby Reynolds, CB BVSc Bristol, PhD, DSc, MRCVS
Dr C F Print, DBA, ACMA, ADipC
Mrs J Cornell, BA
Dr I Kemp, MB BS, FRCP, MRCGP, DCH, DRCOG
Mrs M Cottingham, BA
Mr M Emmanuel
The Revd Ann Templeman
Dr Russell Hampshire
Mrs B McDiarmid, CertEd, DipSEN, DipSpLD
Mr P Smith
Mr S Dimmick, LLB
Mrs M Edwards
Mrs C Lane, DPSE SEN
Mrs H Rennie, ACA
Mrs S Colebrook
Mr S Smith, BSc Est Man, FRICS, FCIArb, FBEng
Mr P Uppal
Mrs J Anderson
Lady Louise Bell
Mrs F Rutland

Head: **Mrs Rachel Dent**, BA Southampton, QTS/QTP Reading

Deputy Head – Operations and Communications: Mrs K Macaulay, BEd Newcastle

Director of Sixth Form: Mr B Fanning, BA, MSc, PGCE Oxon

Acting Head of Junior School: Mrs N Dick-Cleland, BA Oxon, QTP/QTS Reading

Heads of Department:
Art: Mrs E Harvey, BA Reading, PGCE
Biology: Dr M Spencer, BSc, MSc, PhD Cairo, PGCE
Chemistry: Mrs J Harrison, BSc Warwick, PGCE
Classics: Mrs E Sutcliffe
Drama: Miss C V Bellman, MA Oxon, PGCE
Economics: Mrs M A'Bear
English: Mrs J Turkington, BA Lancs, BA Open, MA Lancaster
Food Technology: Mrs K Macaulay, BEd Newcastle
French: Mrs I Berrow, Lic-ès-Lettres, PGCE
Geography: Mrs J Gray, BSc, PGCE
German: Mrs D Oldfield, BA Sheffield, PGCE Reading
History: Mrs R McGee, BA Oxford, PGCE
ICT: Mrs K Macaulay, BEd Newcastle
Mathematics: Miss E Cook, BA, MA Oxford, PGCE
Modern Foreign Languages: Mrs U Byrne, IPTS Kiel, QTS
Music: Mr S Willis, BA, MA Cambridge, PGCE
Instrumental Music: Mrs B Salisbury, ARCM, LRAM (*also Assistant Head – Pastoral Support*)

Physics: Mrs M Robinson, BSc Liverpool, PGCE (*also Head of Careers*)
Physical Education (*acting*): Mrs J Gray, BSc, PGCE
Psychology: Miss A Davies, BA Sussex, PGCE
Religious Studies: Miss A Hadwin, MA Oxon, PGCE Cantab
Science: Mrs R Johnson, BSc, ARCS London
Spanish: Mrs I Fanning, MA London
Textiles: Mrs J Lesbirel, BEd Cardiff

Junior School:
Science: Ms L Wild, BA Open, QTS
IT: Mrs N Kaura, BDS London, BSc Surrey, DMS, PMP, PMI
Music: Mrs R Adams, BA Ed Music Exeter
PE: Mrs N Orr, BA Birmingham

There are 20 Visiting Music Staff and a School Nurse.

Bursar: Mr C King
Admissions: Mrs A Buckley & Mrs S Radford

Number of Girls. 1,105 aged 3–18.

School Ethos. The Abbey School has a reputation for academic excellence that is achieved through strong pastoral care and the particularly broad curricular and extra-curricular programme. A Church of England School that warmly welcomes girls of all faiths and of none.

Facilities. International-standard all-weather sports surface opened September 2013. Purpose-built arts and humanities wing with state-of-the-art classrooms for Years 8 and 9, Art Studios and an additional ICT Suite. A 12-lab science block, a separate sixth form centre, six computer rooms, an extensive modern library, a music centre with rooms for class teaching and individual instrumental teaching, and two large assembly halls. There is a language laboratory, indoor heated swimming pool, gym, dance studio and sports field.

The Junior School has its own buildings, including science lab, music facilities (for group and peripatetic lessons), computer room and a fine assembly hall. 2013 saw the opening of a new site for Reception and Year 1 girls offering bright, spacious classrooms, superb outdoor space and an all-weather pitch that is used by all Junior School girls. The Nursery is housed in a self-contained house with a secluded garden, so that outdoor education is incorporated into the curriculum.

Education. The Abbey School provides an enriched education from Nursery to Sixth Form. Younger girls thrive in the happy, stimulating environment of the Nursery and Junior School, where academic, physical and social skills are developed. They easily make the transition to the Senior School, where girls enjoy an excellent education. A very broad range and flexible timetabling enables girls to choose from a wide range of academic subjects. The International Baccalaureate is offered as an alternative to A Levels in the Sixth Form and results in both are excellent. Many girls go on to top universities including Oxbridge.

Standards of Music, Sport and Art are very high and Inspectors described extra-curricular provision as outstanding, with many varied clubs and trips on offer. Level of participation in Duke of Edinburgh's Award at Silver and Gold Level is impressive.

Optional Extra Subjects. Music and Speech and Drama lessons are available to children from the age of 7. Tuition is available in a wide variety of musical instruments and singing.

Admission is by assessment for the youngest girls and examination and interviews from Key Stage 1 upwards.

Fees per term (2014–2015). Nursery (3+ years) £2,990, Reception (4+ years) £3,500. Junior School (Years 1–6): £3,680–£4,230. Senior School (Years 7–13): £4,830.

Scholarships and Bursaries. Academic scholarships are available at point of entry to Senior School to top performers in the entrance exam at 11 or 13 and special Sixth Form Scholarship exam. Music (giving free tuition on up to two instruments), Drama, Art & Design, and Sport scholarships (giving access to an advanced programme in each subject) are also offered.

A means-tested bursary scheme (up to 100%) is in place to enable families who could not otherwise afford the fees to send their daughters to The Abbey School.

Charitable status. The Abbey School is a Registered Charity, number 309115. The School exists to educate academically able girls.

Abbots Bromley School
A Woodard School

High Street, Abbots Bromley, Staffordshire WS15 3BW
Tel: 01283 840232 (24 hrs)
email: head@abbotsbromley.net
website: www.abbotsbromley.net
Twitter: @AbbotsBromley
Facebook: /abbotsbromleyschool

Founded in 1874, the school is part of the Woodard Schools Corporation (Midland Division).

Visitor: The Rt Revd The Bishop of Lichfield

Council:
Custos: Mrs P Norvall
Vice Custos: Mr R Mansell, ACIB
Mr S Bourne, LLB
Revd S Davis, MA, MIET
Mrs S Goff
Mrs H Graham
Mr M Hedges, MA, FCA, FRSA
Mr S James, ICAEW
Mr R Knight, FRICS
Major R Wilson, BMus Hons

Clerk to the Council and Bursar: Mr D King, BSc Hons, MAAT

Executive Head: **Mrs V Musgrave**, BA Hons, MEd Mgt, FRSA

Deputy Head: Mrs A Johnson, Hon BA, CertEd, Cert Prof St Ed

Head of Preparatory School: Mrs A Johnson, Hon BA, CertEd, Cert Prof St Ed

Senior School Leadership Team:
Executive Head: Mrs V Musgrave, BA Hons, MEd Mgt, FRSA
Deputy Head: Mrs A Johnson, Hon BA, CertEd, Cert Prof St Ed
Director of Academic Studies: Mrs K Rowlands, BA Hons, PGCE
Director of Learning and Training: Mr R Udy, BSc Hons, PGCE
Bursar: Mr D King, BSc Hons, MAAT

Senior Staff:
Director of Sixth Form & External Liaison: Mrs V Hawley, BA Hons
Sixth Form Tutor Academic: Ms E Godwin BA Hons, PGCE, MA
Senior Tutor Scholars/Gifted & Talented: Mrs V Standing MEng, PGCE

Senior School House Coordinator: Mrs B Coulthard, BA Hons, PGCE

Heads of Faculty:
STEM: Mrs E Ellis, BSc Hons, PGCE
Languages: Mrs M Steer, BA Hons, PGCE, Dip SEN
Physical & Creative Arts: Mrs A Moore, BA Hons, PGCE
Humanities: Mr R Udy, BSc Hons, PGCE

Subject Leaders:
Art: Mrs D Crispin, CertEd
Business Studies: Mr R Armour, BA Hons
English: Mrs M Steer, BA Hons, PGCE, Dip SEN
English as a Foreign Language: Mrs E Lampard, BA Hons, PGCE, CELTA OU Dip (*Mandarin, German*)
Geography: Mr R Udy, BSc Hons, PGCE
History: Mrs S Towell, BA Hons, PGCE
Information Technology: Mr R Armour, BA Hons
Learning Enrichment:
Mrs U Griffiths, BA Hons, ELS Dip SpLD, AMBDA Dip Hyp CS, Dip CP
Mrs J Turnbull, FdA DPP NVQ3 IPM
Mathematics: Mrs S Booth, BSc Hons, PGCE
Modern Languages: Mrs B Coulthard, BA Hons, PGCE
Music: Mr J Rayfield, BMus Hons, PGCE
Visiting Specialist Instrumental Staff: Bassoon, Brass, Cello, Clarinet, Flute, Guitar, Oboe, Organ, Percussion, Piano, Piccolo, Saxophone, Violin, Viola, Voice
Physical Education: Miss S Sheldrick, BA Hons
Visiting Specialist Coaches: Swimming, Tennis, Netball, Fencing, Akido, Trampoline, Hockey
Religious Studies: Mrs K Rowlands, BA Hons, PGCE
Sciences: Mrs E Ellis, BSc Hons, PGCE
Social Sciences: Mrs V Hawley, BA Hons

Key Stage Coordinators:
KS4 Years 10–11: Mrs S Booth, BSc Hons, PGCE
KS3 Years 7–9: Mrs S Towell, BA Hons, PGCE

Abbots Bromley Preparatory School:
Head of Preparatory School: Mrs A Johnson, Hon BA, CertEd, Cert Prof St Ed
Deputy Head: Mrs W Gordon, BEd Hons

Kindergarten Leader: Mrs A Dunmore, NVQ3
Learning Enrichment & Support/Pastoral Leader: Mrs M Swinnerton, BA Hons, PGCE, Cert SpLD

Form Teachers:
Mrs W Gordon, BEd Hons
Mrs S Crout, DipEd
Mrs J Spiby BA Hons Early Years, PGCE
Mrs M Swinnerton, BA Hons, PGCE, Cert SpLD

Extra-Curricular Departments:
Dance:
Artistic Directors: Mr R Alkins, RAD Cert TC Dist
Mrs M Alkins, RAD Cert
Visiting Specialist Dance Staff: Ballet, Modern & Tap, Musical Theatre, BTEC

Riding (Abbots Bromley Equestrian Centre):
Director of Equitation: Miss S Vickers, BSI Snr BHS Assessor, Cert Ed, NVQ4, NVQ Assessor

Speech & Drama: Mrs A-M Morrell, LLAM, FRSA, HND Theatre Design, Dip Fashion & Design

Registrar/Admissions Coordinator: Miss T Forbes-Owen
PA to Headmistress, Senior School: Mrs K Addy

Abbots Bromley School encourages individualism and girls from 3–18 are nurtured and encouraged to learn the skills they need for life, whilst been given limitless opportunities to develop and succeed. Founded in 1874, Abbots Bromley School was the very first Woodard School for girls and since then we have continued to evolve and develop to become one of the leading girls' school whilst still retaining many traditional values. From September 2015 the Sixth Form will become co-ed and the school will be offering students the opportunity to study in the newly opened AB International College for 1 year courses in Y11 for GCSEs and intensive English.

Our fantastic 52-acre site allows our students to flourish in beautiful natural surroundings. Our Christian ethos makes for a secure and happy atmosphere where pupils thrive and the impressive Chapel, which is a key feature of the School, remains at the heart of all that we do.

Young minds. Our Preparatory School is happy, busy place; here we educate boys and girls from Kindergarten to Year 6. This co-educational school offers its own dedicated range of facilities including ICT suite, dance studio, science laboratory and new outdoor play area. We offer a warm, welcoming and wonderfully nurturing environment for our younger pupils to grow and develop. Our impressive enrichment programme has been developed specifically for pupils both in and outside the classroom.

Our Preparatory School pupils are encouraged to be a part of the senior school and a gradual change of pace throughout Key Stage two prepares girls for a smooth transition to the senior school, which is a crucial time in their education.

All pupils who attend Abbots Bromley need to be prepared to get involved in the all-round nature of the School, to engage with the wide array of activities and opportunities that makes the School distinctive. We expect high academic standards with girls needing to demonstrate appropriate intellectual ability and independence that will allow them to flourish in the classroom and beyond – to become women leaders of the future.

In addition, our pupils are encouraged to challenge themselves at every opportunity beyond the classroom and enjoy a well rounded curriculum packed with opportunity, challenge and enrichment activities that enables them to discover their true potential. Abbots Bromley girls go on to study a variety of exciting courses at many prestigious universities across the country/globe, having enjoyed all that school life has to offer.

Beyond the curriculum. We offer an extensive, interesting and exciting range of activities for pupils to take advantage of and enjoy outside the classroom whether it is dance, music, sport or equestrian.

Our internationally respected dance school 'Alkins School of Dance' offers dance and musical theatre classes for all levels. The Vocational Dance Course allows students to extend their studies to a professional level, unusually alongside an academic programme. Our experienced staff includes former international ballerinas and a Director of Dance with many years' experience as an examiner with the Royal Academy of Dance.

The Equestrian Centre boasts superb facilities with our floodlit outdoor manège, indoor school and stabling offering opportunities for both the beginner and the experienced rider. On-site facilities mean girls can either bring their own pony or ride one of the school's own and study for the BHS qualifications under the tutelage of our highly-qualified instructors.

Music is also a key feature within the School and the opportunities for musicians are enhanced with overseas choral tours. Pupils sing in Chapel each week and everyone is encouraged to participate. On an individual level pupils can join our highly acclaimed junior and senior choirs, orchestra and band or learn an individual instrument. Our experienced and specialist team of musicians ensure pupils varied talents are explored and encouraged.

With specially trained teachers, high academic standards and an extensive range of modern facilities within the preparatory and senior school, we offer an unrivalled range of opportunities to inspire and enjoy.

Home from home. As a full boarding school, our boarding house affords a high degree of pastoral care and we know that girls learn better and thrive in our friendly, family environment. Boarding offers advantages for girls to develop their independence and gain confidence in their own abilities whilst being supported by understanding staff. We have a variety of options for girls: full boarding, weekly, flexi and occasional packages are available to suit every parent's requirements.

Our ambition is to offer more and ensure our girls become poised, articulate, confident, and self assured in order to learn, live and lead our global society of the future.

Fees per term (2014–2015). Full Boarding: £6,968–£8,575; Weekly Boarding £5,680–£7,184; Day: £1,506–£5,119.

Scholarships. Abbots Bromley is delighted to offer a variety of scholarships for entry into years 7, 8, 9, 10 and 12. Awards are available for academic, art, dance, music, equestrian and sport for our more able girls enabling them to further challenge themselves at every opportunity. The value of scholarships ranges from 10–20% of gross fees.

Charitable status. Abbots Bromley School for Girls Ltd is a Registered Charity, number 1103321.

Abbot's Hill School

Bunkers Lane, Hemel Hempstead, Herts HP3 8RP
Tel: 01442 240333 (both Prep and Senior Schools)
Fax: 01442 269981
email: registrar@abbotshill.herts.sch.uk
website: www.abbotshill.herts.sch.uk

Motto: *Vi et Virtute*
Founded 1912.

Chairman of the Governing Body: Mrs J Mark, BA Hons, QTS

Headmistress: Mrs E Thomas, BA Hons, PGCE, NPQH

Head of Prep School: Miss K Twinn, BA Hons with QTS

Head of Senior School: Miss P Maynard, MA, BEd Hons, JP

Bursar: Mr J Woods, BA Hons, MA

Registrar: Ms A Cooper

Abbot's Hill School is an Independent Day School for girls aged 3–16 years and boys aged 3–5 years. There is a total of 440 pupils in the School from Nursery through to Year 11. The School is situated in 76 acres of parkland on the edge of Hemel Hempstead.

A great emphasis is placed on providing a complete and balanced education. Class sizes are deliberately kept small, which helps to ensure that pupils are well motivated and eager to learn, and allows individual attention from staff members. Each pupil is actively encouraged to achieve their potential, and parent-teacher relationships are excellent in this warm and enabling environment. The excellent results achieved at GCSE can be seen as a reflection of the School's success.

With small classes and a high teacher-pupil ratio, the school aims to develop the academic and creative talents, social skills and confidence of each pupil. Every pupil benefits from being known personally by the Headmistress and teaching staff who seek to create a happy and caring environment.

Senior Department. The Senior Department is based in a spacious and comfortable 19th Century house, which, combined with purpose-built teaching blocks, Science, Sport, Performing Arts and ICT suites, provides our pupils with first-class facilities.

Curriculum. During the first three years, a broad programme based on the National Curriculum is followed, encompassing both academic and creative subjects. Each girl's potential and progress is carefully monitored by both teaching staff and a personal tutor. Subjects studied include English, Maths, Science, French, Spanish, Geography, History, Media Studies, Information and Communication Technology, Religious Studies, Music, Personal, Social, Health, Economic and Citizenship Education, Art and Design, Drama, Food Technology and Physical Education.

In Years 10 and 11 a core GCSE curriculum of up to 8 subjects is followed with girls choosing up to three further subjects.

Music and Performing Arts. The School has very strong Music and Performing Arts Departments with excellent facilities. The Performing Arts building includes studios for dance, drama and music as well as a theatre. The School Choirs and Orchestra perform regularly in concerts, recitals, plays, musicals and various functions throughout the year and there is a school production each year.

Sports. The School has a strong sporting tradition. There is a well-equipped Sports Hall, lacrosse pitches, grass and hard tennis courts, and a heated outdoor swimming pool. The main sports played are Lacrosse, Netball, Athletics, Tennis, Rounders and Swimming. All girls are encouraged to participate in the sporting opportunities at Abbot's Hill and currently there are a number of girls who have reached County and National standard in selected sports.

Extra-Curricular Activities. Many activities and clubs are held outside of School and these vary in range from Dance, Art, Duke of Edinburgh's Award Scheme, Music, Speech and Drama and all sports.

Sixth Form and Beyond. Baird House girls are encouraged to consider their future prospects and are very well prepared to choose from a wide range of A Level courses when they leave. Leavers are highly sought after by sixth forms and colleges and many achieve scholarships. There is a comprehensive careers programme available to further enhance their decisions including an annual Sixth Form Forum where many schools exhibit their Sixth Form Courses.

Religion. Abbot's Hill is a Church of England foundation. Children of all faiths are welcome at the School and all religious observations are respected.

Admission. Admission to Abbot's Hill is by Entrance Examination, interview, and a report from the previous school. Girls are admitted to the Senior Department at 11. There may be occasional vacancies at 12 and 13.

Scholarships and Bursaries. Academic, Art, Drama, Music and Sport scholarships are available giving 5–10% reduction in fees. Means-tested Bursaries are also available.

Fees per term (2014–2015). Senior School: £5,444 (Years 7–11); Prep School: £3,053–£3,798 (Reception to Year 6); Nursery: £305 (per morning session per term), £207 (per afternoon session per term).

Prep School. Abbot's Hill Prep is situated in the same grounds as the Senior School. The Prep School provides Nursery, Pre-Preparatory and Preparatory education for girls aged 3–11 and boys aged 3–5. The Prep mixes the formal setting of the classroom with the wealth of opportunity provided by our physical surroundings. Children are given the freedom in which to grow, learn and play. Classrooms and corridors are bright and well decorated with children's work reflecting the diversity of the curriculum.

The Prep School plays a very important role within our school community and is an integral part of the school as a whole. It is our aim at Abbot's Hill to nurture the whole child, thus enabling our pupils to develop their talents whether they be academic, artistic or sporting. Specialist teaching is introduced from a child's earliest days; French, Music and PE are introduced in the pre-school year. This is added to as a child progresses to include Drama, Games, ICT and Geography. By the time a girl reaches Year 5 she is being completely subject taught and is able to adapt to moving around whilst being supported by a class teacher.

The small class sizes at Abbot's Hill Prep enable individual needs to be recognised and met early with the minimum disruption. For those who need extra support this is offered within the classroom setting or one-to-one as appropriate. Gifts or talents for a particular area of learning can be extended and developed to their potential.

The wider curriculum plays a key role. Educational visits are an integral part of the teaching programme and children are regularly taken on visits to galleries and museums to enhance their learning experience. Outside visitors lead workshops at school for year groups or the whole school as appropriate. The extra-curricular programme is wide ranging and ever changing. It currently includes such wide-ranging pursuits as languages, trampolining, gardening and board games as well as a wealth of musical and sports clubs.

Further information. Abbot's Hill welcomes visits from prospective parents and pupils. If you would like to visit the School, please contact the Registrar for an appointment on 01442 240333 or email registrar@abbotshill.herts.sch.uk.

Charitable status. Abbot's Hill Charitable Trust is a Registered Charity, number 311053, which exists to provide high quality education for children.

Adcote School

Little Ness, Shrewsbury, Shropshire SY4 2JY
Tel: 01939 260202
Fax: 01939 261300
email: admissions@adcoteschool.co.uk
            hwakefield@adcoteschool.co.uk
website: www.adcoteschool.co.uk
Twitter: @AdcoteSchool
LinkedIn: /Adcote School for Girls

Board of Governors:
President: Mr T Morris, BSc
Chairman: Lt Col [Retd] J Moody, OBE
Chairman of Finance: Mr I Galliers
Secretary: Miss J Hughes, BA Hons

Members:
Mr J Leighton, BSc Hons, Dip Ed
Mrs C Brown, BA Hons
Mrs A Jones, Cert Ed Bristol
Mrs C Bright, MA, PG Dip EB Bristol, CIMA

Headmaster: Mr G Wright, BA Hons Warwick, MA London, PGCE Oxford Brookes, NPQH

Senior Deputy Head: Miss E Stephenson, BSc Hons City, PGCE London

Director of Studies: Mrs N Pritchard, BA Hons Bristol, PGCE Bristol, PG DIP Int Bristol

Deputy Head Pastoral: Miss L Hudson, BEd Hons Bedford

Head of Junior School: Mrs A Ravenscroft-Jones, BEd Hons Birmingham

Chaplain: Revd L Burns, BA Birmingham

Bursar: Mr R Walker

Academic Staff:
Mr D Barker, BSc Hons Manchester, Cert Ed Wolverhampton (*Physics*)
Mrs E Barnett, BSC Hons Glasgow, PGCE Bristol (*Science*)
Mrs C Besterman, BA Hons Cambridge, MA Hons Cambridge (*Classics*)
Miss N Bignall, BEng Hons Liverpool, PGCE Wolverhampton (*Science*)
Mrs A Brown, BSc Hons Nottingham, PGCE Lancaster, Dip SpLD OCR APC (*Learning Support*)

Mrs N Candler, BA Hons Birmingham, PGCE
Wolverhampton (*Junior School*)

Mr G Carter, BA Hons Leeds, PGCE Leeds (*EAL*)

Mrs R Clayton-Wright, BSocSc Hons Birmingham, PGCE
Birmingham (*Junior School*)

Mrs M Cooke, BPhil Hons Durham, PGCert Canterbury
(*Drama, Child Development, Dance*)

Mrs J Crawford, CertEd Birmingham, TEFL (*EAL*)

Miss S Dale, BA Oxford Brookes, PGCE Edge Hill
(*English*)

Mr J Davies (*Drama, English*)

Mr C Farmer, BEng Hons Coventry, PGCE, (*Head of ICT,
ICT Manager*)

Mr T Harries, TEFL Trinity (*EAL*)

Mrs G Heawood, BA Hons Wolverhampton, PGCE Glos
(*Junior School*)

Mrs S Hernandez, BA Hons OU, Cert Ed Wolverhampton
(*French, Spanish*)

Mrs J Hill, BSc Hons Loughborough, PGCE,
Loughborough (*EAL, Sport*)

Mr K Knight, BA Hons Birmingham, PGCE Exeter
(*Mathematics*)

Mrs J Magee, MA Open, GRSM, ARCM, LGSM, ABSM,
PGCE, Birmingham (*Head of Music*)

Ms L Nixson (*Assistant Director of Sport*)

Mr I Phillips, BSc Hons Leeds, PGCE Aberystwyth (*Head
of Science, Head of Sixth Form*)

Mrs J Phillips, BSc Hons Leeds, PGCE Chester (*Science*)

Miss A Pugh, BSc Hons Loughborough, PGCE
Birmingham (*Director of Sport*)

Mrs L Richards, BSc Hons Leicester, PGCE Leicester
(*Mathematics*)

Mrs K Rink, BA Oxford (*English*)

Mrs R Roberts, BSc Hons Bath, PGCE Staffordshire (*Food
Technology*)

Miss S Roberts, BA Hons Chester, PGCE Aberystwyth
(*History*)

Miss S Sahota, BSc Hons Aston, PGCE Keele (*Physics,
Chemistry*)

Miss M Warner, BSc Hons Huddersfield, PGCE
Birmingham (*Textiles*)

Mrs C Wemyss, BA Hons Cardiff, PGCE Cardiff (*Junior
School*)

Mrs P Wilson, BA Hons Durham, PGCE Wolverhampton,
Cert ICP Derby (*RE, Psychology, Child Development*)

Mrs H Wrobel, BA Hons NE Wales, PGCE Chester (*Art*)

Director of Admissions: Mrs H Wakefield

Age Range. 4–18.
Number in School. 300 Girls.

Adcote School is a thriving boarding and day school for
around 300 girls currently. Despite its imposing exterior, we
are proud of our welcoming, friendly and unpretentious reputation. The School's size means that the children, staff and
parents really get to know each other. We are fortunate to be
located in a beautiful and safe rural setting with a magnificent Grade I listed building, with 30 acres of beautifully
landscaped parkland surrounding the school. These wonderful gardens provide an incredibly safe, secure and idyllic
backdrop to this historic school. Adcote has begun a multimillion pound project of modernisation and investment in
the school – the most significant development in Adcote's
107 year history. New facilities are planned including new
classrooms, science labs, catering facilities and boarding
accommodation.

Perhaps Adcote's greatest achievement is the variety and
breadth of education that it provides for its pupils. Both day
girls and boarders benefit from excellent tuition in a range of
activities including tennis, horse riding, gymnastics and
swimming as well as plenty of healthy competition with
local schools in netball, hockey and other sports. Every year,
as the GCSE and A Level examination results come in, we
are proud of the achievements of each girl and of our school.

The excellent results and high league table ranking reflect
the hard work of the girls, excellent teaching and the support
of parents and families.

Every girl at Adcote, when she leaves the school, should
feel she has achieved all she can both academically and
intellectually.

Curriculum. Adcote is committed to fostering the
achievement of all our girls, without undue pressure. Self-
confidence and poise distinguish our pupils whose teachers
are dedicated to cultivating the strengths of each girl.
Adcote produces confident, enquiring and well-rounded
girls who are equipped to play full and constructive roles in
an ever-changing society.

Years 7, 8, and 9 follow a broad curriculum which
ensures that there is continuity and progression together
with sufficient flexibility to respond to individual needs and
interests.

The GCSE and IGCSE programme taught in Years 10
and 11, includes the core subjects of English Language,
English Literature, Mathematics, ICT (Cambridge Nationals), PE (non-examined) and PSHE (non-examined), plus at
least one Science and 7 other subjects from a range of 16
options choices. IGCSE qualifications are internationally
recognised by schools, universities and employers as equivalent to, or even slightly more challenging than, UK GCSEs.
They are an excellent preparation for A/AS Level courses.

Adcote's outstanding academic results at A Level,
Oxbridge success, and entry to other top Universities,
accounts for the recent and growing number of pupils in the
Sixth Form. The Sixth Form requires each girl to follow her
specialist subjects in depth. In Lower Sixth (Year 12), most
girls choose to take four A Level subjects from a list of 21
options, in addition to PSHE and PE, which are compulsory
but non-examined. In the Upper Sixth (Year 13) three subjects are usually continued to full A Level (A2). As part of
ongoing investment in buildings and facilities, the School
has recently created a dedicated Sixth Form Centre.

Performing Arts. The School places great emphasis on
Music, Dance, and Drama as well as a range of other activities. All the performing arts are included in the core curriculum to age 14, and thereafter voluntarily. Instrumental
playing is much encouraged, there are several choirs in the
school which practice regularly and there are extra-curricular workshops in dance and drama, and performances several times a year.

Activities. All girls participate in a wide range of activities, including rowing, fencing, Chinese, Russian, Yoga,
gardening and horse riding. Sport plays an important part in
the life of the school. The school regularly plays hockey,
netball, rounders and tennis, with gymnastics being particularly strong. Outward bound programmes also play an
important part of life at Adcote, as do interesting weekend
activities, and trips away from school. There is an interesting programme of weekly activities for boarding students.
The school has built a new sports hall in 2014 for use by all
pupils.

Pastoral Care. The school's size means that the children,
staff and parents really get to know each other. There is a
tangible sense of community, creating a warm and enabling
family atmosphere. Boarders are looked after by Housemistresses and the resident staff, and all girls have a personal
tutor, responsible for individual welfare and academic progress. Great importance is attached to understanding the individual and developing personal abilities so that girls meet
the demands of the modern world with confidence and good
judgement. There is a range of full and weekly boarding
options.

Fees per term (2014–2015). UK/Domestic Students:
Day Girls £1,592–£4,573; Weekly Boarders £5,320–£7,629;
Full Boarders £6,046–£8,351.

Reductions are made in fees of second and subsequent
sisters. Bursaries are available for children from the clergy
or from Forces families. There are scholarships for aca-

demic excellence. The School welcomes applications from girls whose parents cannot afford the fees in full or in part. In line with our aim as a Charity to provide public benefit the school offers means-tested bursaries to outstanding pupils who would not otherwise be able to benefit from the education we provide. The School offers a wide range of discretionary and means-tested bursaries each year to pupils.

A prospectus and further details may be obtained from the Admissions Assistant: admissions@adcoteschool.co.uk.

Charitable status. Adcote School Educational Trust Limited is a Registered Charity, number 528407.

Alderley Edge School for Girls

Wilmslow Road, Alderley Edge, Cheshire SK9 7QE

Tel:	01625 583028
Fax:	01625 590271
email:	jbedigan@aesg.co.uk
website:	www.aesg.co.uk
Twitter:	@schoolforgirls

Chair of Governors: Mrs S Herring

Headmistress: Mrs Sue Goff, BA Hons Durham, PGCE Oxford

Deputy Headmistress: Mrs C Wood, BA Hons, PGCE Leicester

Director of Studies: Mrs J Hodson, MA Cantab, PGCE Nottingham

Director of Pastoral Care: Mrs J Waterhouse, BA Manchester, PGCE Leeds

Head of Junior School: Ms B Howard, BEd Hons Exeter

Head of Lower School (Years 7–8): Mrs J Barker

Head of Year 9: Miss M Moss

Head of Upper School (Years 9–11): Mrs J Waterhouse

Head of Sixth Form: Mrs C Cheetham

Bursar: Mrs P McGill

Registrar: Mrs J Bedigan

Heads of Department:

Art: Mrs C Latimer
Business Studies: Mrs C Rule
Chemistry: Dr D Hughes
Classics: Mr P Tandler
Design Technology: Mrs K Boyland
Drama: Mrs C Foster
English: Ms L Telford
Food Technology: Mrs C Leigh
Geography: Miss N Johal
History: Miss K Mawdsley
ICT: Mr J Chadwick
Mathematics: Mr S Cunliffe
Modern Foreign Languages: Mrs I Jones
Music: Mrs A Pattrick
Physical Education: Mrs S Waite
Physics: Mrs K Torr
Psychology: Mrs A Raval
Religious Education: Ms A Laing
Science: Dr D Hughes

Age Range. 2–18.

Number in School. Nursery, Pre-School and Reception 44; Junior School 139; Senior School 259; Sixth Form 95.

Fees per term (2014–2015). Nursery £2,235; Pre-School £1,890; Key Stage 1 £2,271; Key Stage 2 £2,727; Senior £3,426.

Background. For many years the village of Alderley Edge was the location for two of the finest Independent Girls' Schools in the North West of England. In September 1999 the two schools became one. An independent, all girls, ecumenical school is unique in England and the merger of the two schools was welcomed and supported by the Angli-

can and Roman Catholic clergy and the founders of both schools.

The Sisters of St Joseph, a Roman Catholic Order, founded Mount Carmel School in 1945. St Hilary's was founded in 1817 and became part of the Woodard Corporation, a Church of England foundation, in 1955. Alderley Edge School for Girls is linked to the Woodard Corporation, the largest group of schools in England. Among them are independent and maintained schools in England, the United States and Australia.

General. This forward-looking girls' school offers a high level of personal attention. Respect for hard work, the development of the whole person and good discipline are the traditional principles on which our creative and innovative educational philosophy is based. We aim to provide a well-balanced education which celebrates achievement in all aspects of school life from Nursery to Sixth Form.

Location. The school is situated in a semi-rural area of Alderley Edge in Cheshire, 15 miles south of Manchester, with easy access to the motorway network and only minutes from Manchester Airport and two Intercity mainline stations. Transport is readily available throughout the area.

Admissions. The Nursery School caters for girls from 2 years. Admission for girls to the Junior School is at 4/5 years old. Admission to the Senior School is at 11 years by Entrance Examination and interview.

Curriculum. *Senior School*: Students follow a broad and balanced curriculum based on the National Curriculum but with many additions. Subjects include: Mathematics, English Language, English Literature, Computer Science, Biology, Chemistry, Physics, French, German, Spanish, Latin, History, Geography, Music, Drama, Religious Studies, Food Technology, Art, Design Technology, Business Studies, PPE (Philosophy, Politics, Economics), PSHE (Personal, Social, Health Education) and Physical Education. At A Level the following subjects are offered in addition those listed above: Further Mathematics, Philosophy & Ethics, Economics, Psychology and Theatre Studies.

In addition to their normal academic studies, all Lower Sixth pupils study AS General Studies and high fliers are encouraged to do the Extended Project Qualification (EPQ).

Academic excellence is the school's main aim and attention is paid to meeting the individual needs and abilities of the students. Small classes and continuous assessment ensure high levels of pupil achievement.

Junior School: Creative and academic learning are at the heart of the Junior School. The work is based on the National Curriculum with English, Mathematics and Science providing the foundations for learning with History, Geography, RE, Art, Design, Computing, Music, PE, French, Dance/Drama and Spanish completing the curriculum. Latin is also taught from Year 5. There is considerable input into the specialist teaching from the Senior School staff.

Examination Results 2014. Junior school pupils undertake InCAS (Interactive Computerised Assessment System) assessments.

GCSE results: Overall pass rate (A*–C) 97%; over a quarter of all passes at A*.

A Level results: Pass rate 100%; 90% of all grades at A*–C.

The Arts. *Music*: A very large percentage of pupils learn a musical instrument and examinations may be taken. The school runs 4 choirs, 2 orchestras, a jazz band and numerous smaller instrumental ensembles including string groups, a brass group and 5 different woodwind groups. Many cups have been won in local festivals and pupils perform in local youth orchestras.

Drama and Dance: Both are offered. The majority of pupils are involved in school productions and all pupils participate in House and other productions. There are four dance squads which rehearse weekly and holiday courses in Dance and Drama are also on offer.

Sports and Clubs. *Sports*: tennis, rounders, hockey, athletics, netball, gymnastics, football, swimming, dance, cross-country, badminton, volleyball, squash, fitness, self-defence. In the Sixth Form a huge variety of options are available for the girls including golf and aerobics.

Senior Clubs: language club, Biology/Chemistry/Physics workshops, Maths clinics, French club, book club, DT and Art clubs, magazine committee, dance, drama, poetry, public speaking, hockey, netball, tennis, rounders, athletics, Duke of Edinburgh's Award, Games, Comenius European Educational Project, Model United Nations, Young Enterprise, Youth Speaks and Mock Trial.

Junior Clubs: Contemporary Dance, Drama, Judo, Short Tennis, Brownies, Gardening, French, Netball, Spanish, Library, Cycling Proficiency and many more.

Facilities. In creating a new school we achieved our objective to remain small enough to care for every child's needs and yet the school enjoys all the benefits and resources of a much larger school. A multi-million pound investment programme has provided a new Senior School, and a completely refurbished Junior School. Facilities include six superbly equipped science laboratories, four ICT suites with online facilities throughout the school, Language Suite with language laboratory, Humanities block with Business Studies centre, competition-size Sports Hall, Gymnasium, Performing Arts Centre, Chapel and a Library with breathtaking views over the Cheshire Plain. In addition there is a modern and well-appointed Sixth Form centre – including a dedicated ICT suite – to accommodate the increasing number of girls in our Sixth Form.

Scholarships and Bursaries. Several Academic scholarships and scholarships for Music are awarded at 11+, 13+ and 16+. Art and Sport scholarships are available at 11+. Bursaries are also available (income linked).

Charitable status. Alderley Edge School for Girls is a Registered Charity, number 1006726. It exists to provide education for children.

Badminton School

Westbury-on-Trym, Bristol BS9 3BA

Tel: 0117 905 5200
Fax: 0117 962 3049
email: admissions@badmintonschool.co.uk
website: www.badmintonschool.co.uk

Motto: *Pro Omnibus Quisque Pro Deo Omnes*
Founded 1858. Non denominational.

Chairman of Governors: Mrs A Bernays, DLL Hons, FRSA

Clerk to the Governors, Secretary and Bursar: Mr T Synge, BA Exeter, FCA

Vice-President: Professor Richard Hodder-Williams

Headmistress: Mrs R Tear, BSc Hons Exeter, MA London, PGCE London

Deputy Head: Mrs A Chapman, BA Hons Birmingham, PGCE Birmingham

Director of Studies: Mr S Dalley, BA Hons Exeter, MA Bristol

Head of Junior School: Ms E Davies, BA Hons Cardiff, PGCE

Director of Boarding: Mrs J Scarfe, BA Wales

Heads of Department:

Head of Creative Arts Section and Head of English: Mrs L Griffith, BA Oxon

Drama: Mr S Gentry, BA Hons Leicester, DIP, PGCE

Music: Mrs D Lee, BA Cambridge, MA Cambridge, PGCE

Art: Miss F Creber, BA Hons Wales

Head of STEM Section and Head of Biology: Mrs N Warden, BSc Exeter, BA Oxon

Chemistry: Mr B Wharton, BA Hons Bristol

Physics: Mr P Foster, BSc London

Food and Nutrition: Mrs F Williamson, BEd Wales

Mathematics: Mr D Cook, BA Oxon

Head of Languages Section and Head of French: Mrs N Walton, BA Durham

German: Miss S J Whyatt, BA London, PGCE

Spanish: Mrs K Gilbert, BA Hull

Classics: Miss S McNee, BA Cantab, PGCert

Head of Humanities and Head of Geography: Miss C Morgan, BA Hons Durham

Head of History and Politics: Mr R Hambly, BA Southampton, PGCE Kingston

Economics: Mrs D Betterton, BA Exeter

Religious Education: Ms R Harris, MA London, BA Hons London, PGCE

History of Art: Mrs K Dodd, MA Essex

Head of Sixth Form: Mrs K Dodd, MA Essex

Executive Assistant to the Headmistress: Mrs S Brown

Admissions Officer: Miss K Balmforth

Badminton is an independent girls' boarding, weekly boarding and day school situated in a 15-acre site in Westbury-on-Trym on the outskirts of the university city of Bristol.

Age Range of Pupils. 3 to 18.

Number of Pupils. 450: Boarding 187; Day 263.

Number of Staff. Full-time teaching 37, Part-time teaching 16. Teacher Pupil ratio is currently 1:7.

Educational Philosophy. Whilst the school retains an outstanding academic record, its focus continues to be on nurturing the girls' natural curiosity and fuelling their passion for learning. The enduring excellence that Badminton girls achieve, stems from the positive atmosphere in the School and the holistic approach to education, as well as the exceptional relationships between staff and pupils, which are mature, friendly and based on principles of courtesy and mutual respect. Teachers are highly-qualified specialists in their field and encourage girls to develop academic confidence and to become independent learners by taking responsibility for their work and progress. The most important feature of academic life at Badminton is the resounding philosophy that it is the norm to ask questions, to seek help and, above all, to enjoy learning.

It is a characteristic of Badminton girls that they are thoughtful individuals, able to evaluate information and decide for themselves. This approach extends beyond their studies and into the day-to-day life of the School, where girls are given a wide range of opportunities to grow, develop and express themselves in an enormous range of activities. Staff also enjoy sharing their enthusiasm for their subject and often involve girls in projects and competitions in the local community and nationally.

The Badminton community gives girls a chance to develop an understanding of the viewpoints of others and to think about contributing to the world around them. Girls leave Badminton ready to face the changing and challenging wider world and, when they do, they take with them a strong network of lifelong friends developed through a wealth of shared experiences.

Boarding. The size of the campus and community at Badminton gives a homely and vibrant feel to the School. This, coupled with excellent pastoral care, leaves no scope for anonymity, but rather lends itself to strong mutually supportive relationships between girls as well as between girls and staff.

The boarding accommodation is split into three areas (junior, middle and Sixth Form) so girls get a good sense of progression and development as they move up through the school. Full-time, weekly or flexi boarding are offered and day girls are welcome to flexi board, allowing girls to easily combine their academic schedules with the many activities that are on offer after school and at weekends.

Bartlett House offers cosy bedrooms for boarders in Years 5–8 and easy access to gardens and play areas. Sanderson House, a modern boarding house opened in 2008, accommodates boarders in Years 9, 10 and 11. The Sixth Form Centre provides Years 12 and 13 with a more independent environment in double or single study-bedrooms. In each House, boarders have the support of a resident Housemistress, assistant Housemistresses and Resident Tutors and there is a broad range of clubs and activities on offer every day as well as a full weekend programme.

The School's enrichment programme is extremely important in the overall development of the pupils and girls participate in many activities and are encouraged to do so. The activities offered vary depending on the interests of the girls; some have an academic bias, others let the girls explore their creative interests. Girls are very much encouraged to enjoy and value their own and their peers' successes and triumphs in every area of life.

Curriculum. The School's broad curriculum provides a rich and varied experience for the girls. Through Art, Drama and Music programmes, each girl has many opportunities to express her individuality and develop her own unique identity. In an increasingly global society, the importance of languages has never been greater and girls have the opportunity to study Mandarin and Greek in addition to more traditional languages such as French and Latin.

Small classes ensure that all the girls receive individual help and attention from their teachers. Badminton girls are proactive and independent learners; they are not afraid to take intellectual risks and are always happy to ask questions. The emphasis at Badminton is on a holistic education, not narrowly academic, and both the curriculum and the timetable are constructed to create a balance between academic achievement, personal development, life skills and other enterprising activity.

Academic Record. Badminton has a fine academic record at GCSE, AS and A Level. The GCSE and A Level pass rate is 100%. Sixth Form leavers go on to study at some of the top universities and Music Conservatories in the UK, including Oxford, Cambridge and the Royal Academy of Music and further afield.

Facilities. All the facilities of the school are on site and include a 25m indoor swimming pool, international-sized astro pitch, 7 tennis and 4 netball courts, gymnasium and fitness suite as well as a fully-equipped Science Centre, Creative Arts Centre and self-contained Sixth Form Centre. There are extensive fiction, careers, music and art libraries as well as a Music School.

Music, Drama and Creative Arts. All girls are involved in the Arts, both within the curriculum and as extra-curricular activities, and the School attaches great importance to the development of musical and artistic talent.

Music is extremely popular at Badminton with over 85% of all pupils studying at least one musical instrument. There is a wide range of choral and instrumental groups to join including Junior and Senior Choir, Schola (choral group), orchestra, swing band, string ensembles, woodwind ensembles and other mixed musical groups. With visiting peripatetic teachers, all of whom are professional musicians, the students can study any instrument of their choice. There are a wide variety of performance opportunities including informal concerts and concerts for the local community.

There are several drama productions every year including plays directed and produced by the girls. Many girls take optional Speech and Drama lessons and LAMDA examinations.

There is an excellent Creative Arts department, with a wide choice of subjects for the girls to pursue including Fine Art, Pottery and Sculpture, Textiles, Printmaking, Design, Jewellery-making and Photography.

Clubs and Societies. A wide range is offered including: The Duke of Edinburgh's Award, Modern Languages, Debating, Drama, Musical Theatre, Mandarin, Cookery, Christian Union, Art and Crafts, Science Outreach and The Prince's Trust.

Games and Activities. Specialist PE teachers and coaches offer timetabled and optional sport including Hockey, Tennis, Netball, Swimming, Athletics, Rounders, Gymnastics, Badminton, Basketball, Self-Defence and Judo.

Optional extras. All girls participate in activities which include the full choice of Games, Creative Arts and Clubs as above and boarders have the opportunity of additional activities at weekends. There are regular trips abroad as well as annual exchanges with schools in South Africa and Australia.

Badminton is fortunate in being sited on the outskirts of the university city of Bristol; regular visits are arranged to concerts, lectures and theatres and there is considerable contact with Bristol University. Community and voluntary work is strongly encouraged, with girls assisting with Science Outreach and reading in local primary schools, volunteering in local hospitals and charity shops.

Admission. Girls sit the Senior School entrance assessments in the January prior to year of entry. Entrance assessments are taken in English, Mathematics as well as an online adaptive test. Girls are also interviewed by a senior member of staff and the girl's current school is asked to provide a reference.

Girls sit Sixth Form entrance papers in the November in the year prior to joining. They choose two academic subjects they are intending to study for A Level and also sit a General Paper. They too will be interviewed by a senior member of staff and the girl's current school is asked to provide a reference.

Prospective Junior School pupils are assessed by spending a day in the school during which they are observed and assessed informally by staff and the Junior School Headmistress, Mrs Emma Davies. This also helps them to make initial relationships with their prospective peers and gives them a real taste for life at Badminton. From Years 3–6 the tests are more formal and written papers in English, Maths, Reading and a Reasoning test are completed during the assessment day. Entry for Little Acorns (our pre-reception class) is by appointment with the Junior School Headmistress, Mrs Emma Davies, and girls will also have a short assessment session in our Little Acorns class.

Prospective parents are encouraged to visit the school individually or attend one of our Open Mornings. To obtain a prospectus and arrange a visit, please contact the Admissions Department via email at admissions@badmintonschool.co.uk or call 0117 905 5271.

Scholarships. Academic, Music and All-Rounder scholarships are available for girls entering Badminton in Years 7, 9 and 12. From time to time, scholarships for entry into the upper end of the Junior School are also available. Parents of girls who are awarded scholarships are also eligible to apply for a means-tested Bursary.

Scholarship application forms and more information can be obtained by emailing our Admissions Department at admissions@badmintonschool.co.uk.

Bursaries. Bursaries are means-tested and awarded on the basis of parents' financial circumstances. Application forms may be obtained by emailing admissions@badmintonschool.co.uk.

Fees per term (2014–2015). Day: Juniors £2,760–£3,720, Seniors £5,330–£5,810. Boarding: Juniors £6,930–£7,290, Seniors £10,250–£11,010.

Forces families in receipt of CEA or an equivalent civilian allowance receive 20% remission of fees.

Charitable status. Badminton School Limited is a Registered Charity, number 311738. It exists for the purpose of educating children.

Bedford Girls' School

Cardington Road, Bedford MK42 0BX
Tel: 01234 361918
email: admissions@bedfordgirlsschool.co.uk
website: www.bedfordgirlsschool.co.uk
Twitter: @BedfordGirlsSch

Foundation – The Harpur Trust.
"Let me keep an open mind so I understand as much as I can in my lifetime and not reach the limits of my imagination."

Chair of Governors: Ms T Beddoes

Head: Miss J MacKenzie

Deputy Head: Mr T Hill

Assistant Head: Mrs K Jones
Assistant Head: Mrs N Keeler
Assistant Head: Mrs S Mason-Patel
Assistant Head: Mrs S Willis
Director of Sixth Form: Dr J Walters

Head of Bedford Girls' School Junior School: Mrs C Howe

Bedford Girls' School is a dynamic, forward-thinking selective independent day school for girls aged 7–18. As an exceptional school, we value creativity and innovation highly. From Year 3 to Sixth Form, it is our belief that learning should be exciting and life-long, so that girls leave us fully equipped academically, personally, emotionally and morally fulfilled individuals capable of achieving their full potential in every aspect and at every stage of their lives.

Part of the Harpur Trust, we are one of the few girls' schools in the UK to offer both the International Baccalaureate and A Level to Sixth Formers. Whichever course of study our pupils elect to take post-16 our philosophy lies in equipping them with critical thinking skills and the attributes of the IB learner profile from the moment they join us, whether in the Junior or Senior Schools. As such, we are one of a very small number of UK schools to offer Thinking Skills as a timetabled subject and creativity is valued across the curriculum and beyond. As a result, we find that the natural curiosity of the girls is heightened and sharpened and they are extremely engaged with their own learning. In consequence, not only do they excel academically but also as well-rounded, capable young women equipped for compassionate leadership in the 21st century.

The atmosphere of our school is unique and exciting. Classrooms fizz with energy and enthusiasm and each day brings forth new discoveries and achievements. We would be delighted to welcome you to visit, either for one of our Open House events or a private tour, to experience at first hand a true flavour of life at Bedford Girls' School. Please visit www.bedfordgirlsschool.co.uk for further information or call our Admissions Team on: 01234 361918.

Admissions. Entry to the Junior School is on the basis of informal assessment and written tests in Mathematics, Reading and Writing. Entry to the Senior School is on the basis of interview, written tests in Mathematics, English and Verbal Reasoning, school report and reference. Sixth Form entry is on the basis of interviews, Verbal Reasoning, GCSE results, school report and reference.

Fees per term (2014–2015). Junior School (7–11 years) £2,818; Senior School (11–16 years) £3,960; Sixth Form (16–18 years) £3,960.

Bursaries. The Harpur Trust welcomes bursary applications from families of girls in the Senior School and Sixth Form who require financial assistance. All awards are means tested and subject to annual reassessment. Bursaries can be awarded from a value of 25% of fees up to a full bursary place at the discretion of the School and the Harpur Trust.

Charitable status. Bedford Girls' School is part of the Harpur Trust which is a Registered Charity, number 1066861.

Blackheath High School
GDST

Vanbrugh Park, London SE3 7AG
Tel: 020 8853 2929
Fax: 020 8853 3663
email: info@bla.gdst.net

Junior Department:
Wemyss Road, London SE3 0TF
Tel: 020 8852 1537
Fax: 020 8463 0040
email: info@blj.gdst.net

website : www.blackheathhighschool.gdst.net

Founded 1880.
Blackheath High School is part of the GDST (Girls' Day School Trust). The GDST is the leading network of independent girls' schools in the UK. As a charity that owns and runs 24 schools and two academies, it reinvests all its income in its schools. For further information about the Trust, visit www.gdst.net.

Additional information about the school may be found on the school's website and a detailed prospectus is available from the school.

Chairman of Local Governors: Mr J Vennis, BSc, PGCE

Headteacher: **Mrs C Chandler-Thompson**, BA Exeter, PGCE

Deputy Head: Dr H Pascoe, PhD Reading, MSc, PGCE

Assistant Head: Mrs C Maddison, BA Staffordshire, MSc Leicester, PGCE

Assistant Head: Mr S Parsons, BA Lancaster, PGCE, MA King's College London

Head of Junior School: Mrs S Skevington, LLB Hons Sheffield, PGCE EYP

Head of Sixth Form: Mrs K Elliott, BSc Cardiff, PGCE

Admissions Secretary: Mrs F Nichols, BA London

School Business Manager: Mr A W L Sutherland, MBE

We believe that the key to success for girls is confidence, and the confidence, resilience and leadership skills developed through taking on challenges spills over into all areas of their life, including the academic. All students are encouraged to participate in activities that challenge them physically, emotionally and socially, such as sport, performing arts, debating, outward bound courses and the Duke of Edinburgh's Award Scheme.

The Junior School is housed in the original 19th Century premises in Blackheath Village and includes a purpose-built nursery with its own entrance, playground and forest area. The Senior School is just across the Heath, near to Greenwich Park, and combines historic buildings with modern purpose-built facilities, including a state-of-the-art Theatre, Digital Radio Station and a Language laboratory. The school's five-acre sports field includes a sports pavilion, an all-weather pitch and 13 tennis courts.

Many of our students live in the local area whilst others travel from further afield. The area is well served by public transport but we also provide school transport to East London, Docklands & Surrey Quays, destinations in South East London and Chislehurst, Kent.

Admission to the school is by examination and interview; scholarships and bursaries are available. Regular Open Days are held in the autumn and spring terms, but visitors are always welcome and the Headteacher likes to discuss each girl's particular needs individually with pupils and parents. Please telephone our Admissions Secretary on 020 8557 8409 for a prospectus and to arrange a visit.

Curriculum. We offer a broad choice of subjects at GCSE and an even wider choice at AS and A Level. We offer all the traditional A Level subjects plus other newer but popular ones, such as Psychology, Business Studies, Mandarin, Photography, Music Technology and Theatre Studies.

Fees per term (2014–2015). Senior School £4,693, Junior Department £3,861, Nursery £3,005.

The fees cover the regular curriculum, school books, stationery and other materials, choral music, and games, but not optional extra subjects, school visits or lunch.

Bursaries. The GDST makes available to the school a number of scholarships and bursaries. The bursaries are means tested and are intended to ensure that the school remains accessible to bright girls who would profit from our education but who would be unable to enter the school without financial assistance.

Scholarships. A number of Scholarships are available to internal or external candidates for entry at 11+ or to the Sixth Form.

Several Academic scholarships are offered every year, awarded on academic merit as measured by the entrance examination. Particulars of the examination are available from the Admissions Secretary.

Up to 2 Music Scholarships may be offered annually. Auditions are held following the entrance examination.

One Art Scholarship may be offered annually. Art assessments are held following the entrance examination.

Charitable status. Blackheath High School is part of The Girls' Day School Trust, which is a Registered Charity, number 306983.

Bolton School Girls' Division

Chorley New Road, Bolton, Lancs BL1 4PB

Tel: 01204 840201
Fax: 01204 434710
email: seniorgirls@boltonschool.org
website: www.boltonschool.org/seniorgirls
Twitter: @BoltonSchool
Facebook: /boltonschool.org
LinkedIn: /bolton-school

Bolton School Girls' Division was founded in 1877 as the High School for Girls and quickly gained a reputation for excellence. In 1913 the first Viscount Leverhulme gave a generous endowment to the High School for Girls and the Bolton Grammar School for Boys on condition that the two schools should be equal partners known as Bolton School (Girls' and Boys' Divisions).

Bolton School is a family of schools, where children can enjoy an all-through education, joining our co-educational Nursery for 3 and 4 year olds or Infant School before moving up to our single-sex Junior and Senior Schools with Sixth Forms. We are strong believers that girls and boys from 7+ perform best in a single-sex environment, but one

where there are co-educational activities – the best of both worlds.

Chairman of Governors: M T Griffiths, BA, FCA

Headmistress: Miss S E Hincks, MA

Deputy Head: Mrs L D Kyle, BSc
Assistant Head: P Linfitt, BSc, MEng
Assistant Head: Ms H Bradford-Keegan, MA

Head of Sixth Form: Mrs C Winder, MA
Head of Upper School: Mrs I Smalley, BSc
Head of Middle School: Mrs J Head, BA

Senior School:

Heads of Departments:

Art, Design & Technology: Miss J A Fazackerley, BA
Careers and Higher Education: Mrs E Lowe, BA
Classics: Mrs J Hone, BA
Economics & Business Studies: Miss L Jones, BA
English: Mrs R Worthington, BA
Food Technology: Mrs I M H Smalley, BSc
Geography: Ms S Noot, BA
History: C Owen, MA
ICT: Mrs S Brace, BSc
Learning Support Coordinator: Mrs A Elkin, BA
Mathematics: G Heppleston, BSc
Modern Languages: Mrs A Shafiq, BA
French: C Fico
German: Mrs P Sheaff, BA
Spanish: Mrs A Shafiq, BA
Music: Mrs A Price, MA
Physical Education: Mrs K A Heatherington, BA
Religion and Philosophy: Mrs K E Porter, BA
Resistant Materials: Miss R Langley
Science: Dr A Fielder, BA
Biology: Mrs A D Furey, BSc
Chemistry: Miss S Gorner, BSc
Physics: Mr R Ball, BSc
Psychology: Mrs J Sanders, BSc

Instrumental Music Staff:
Brass, Cello, Clarinet, Flute, Guitar, Oboe, Organ, Percussion, Piano, Saxophone, Singing, Violin.

Lower Schools:

Junior Department (Age 7–11):
Head: Mrs R Brierley, CertEd
Deputy Head: Mrs H Holt, BEd

Beech House (Age 4–7):
Head: Mrs D Northin, BEd
Deputy Head: Mrs L Procter, BEd

The School occupies a stunning 32-acre site and the Girls' Division Senior School contains over 750 day pupils. The co-educational infants' school, Beech House, offers an education for 225 pupils aged 4–7 and up to a further 200 girls are educated in the Girls' Division Junior School (age 7–11). In the Senior School over 200 girls are in the Sixth Form. The School also has its own nursery.

Bolton School Girls' Division seeks to realise the potential of each pupil. We provide challenge, encourage initiative, promote teamwork and develop leadership capabilities. It is our aim that students leave the School as self-confident young people equipped with the knowledge, skills and attributes that will allow them to lead happy and fulfilled lives and to make a difference for good in the wider community.

We do this through offering a rich and stimulating educational experience which encompasses academic, extra-curricular and social activities. We provide a supportive and industrious learning environment for pupils selected on academic potential, irrespective of means and background.

Facilities. Housed in an attractive Grade II listed building the school has an impressive Great Hall which seats 900 people, spacious corridors, a theatre, two Resistant Materials workshops, two Textile studios, two Food Technology rooms, four computer rooms, seven laboratories, three Art studios and two fine libraries staffed by two qualified librarians and their staff. As of September 2013, the Sixth Form moved into the purpose-built £7m Riley Sixth Form Centre, where girls and boys share a Common Room, cafe and learning areas equipped with the very latest technology.

Besides having its own fully-equipped gym, the Girls' Division shares the award-winning Careers' Department, the Arts Complex and Sports Hall, a 25-metre swimming pool, extensive playing fields, the Leverhulme Sports Pavilion and an outdoor pursuits facility at Patterdale Hall in the Lake District. Pupils also have the option of spending a week undertaking sailing lessons in the Irish Sea on the School's boat, Tenacity of Bolton.

Beech House Infants' School. The curriculum, though based on the National Curriculum, extends far beyond it. Specialist teaching is provided for older pupils in Physical Education and Music and all children are taught French. The school has recently moved to purpose-built state-of-the-art premises and in addition to its own resources, Beech House benefits from the use of Senior School facilities such as the swimming pool, playing fields and Arts Centre.

The Girls' Junior School. There are 2 classes in each of Years 3–6. In September 2010, the junior girls moved into their new £5m school which has its own hall, laboratory, art and design facility, IT suite and library, as well as large classrooms. Besides following the National Curriculum with Senior School specialists teaching PE, Music and French, pupils have additional opportunities. The many clubs and wide range of extra-curricular activities ensure a full and well-balanced programme.

The Senior School. The curriculum encompasses all the National Curriculum but also offers the study of two modern languages, the classics and a wide range of modules in Technology. At age 11 all girls follow a similar weekly timetable. The twelve subjects offered are: Art, English, French, Geography, History, Classical Studies, Mathematics, Music, PE, Religion and Philosophy, Science and Technology. All pupils in Year 9 begin to study GCSE Biology, Chemistry and Physics. The above list does not fully show the great variety of opportunities available which also include: Athletics, Biology, Chemistry, Computer Graphics, Dance, Drama, Earth Science, Electronics, Food Technology, Gymnastics, Information Technology, Lacrosse, Netball, Physics, PSHE, Resistant Materials Technology, Rounders, Swimming, Tennis and Textiles Technology. This breadth is maintained to GCSE with a second language, German, Latin or Spanish, being offered in Year 8. In Years 10 and 11 we also offer Archery, Badminton, Basketball, Climbing, Fitness/Gym sessions, Football, Rounders, Unihoc and Volleyball.

GCSE. There is extensive choice at GCSE. All follow a common curriculum of English, English Literature, Mathematics, Biology, Chemistry and Physics (with an option to consolidate down to Dual Award Science at the end of Year 10) together with non-examined courses in Information Technology, PE, and Religion and Philosophy. Personal aptitude and inclination are fostered by allowing a maximum of 11 GCSEs: the core subjects plus options chosen from Art, Biology, Business and Communication Systems, Chemistry, Food Technology, French, Geography, German, Greek, History, Information Technology, Latin, Music, Physics, Religious Studies, Resistant Materials Technology, Spanish and Textile Technology. Essential balance is maintained by requiring all to include one Humanity and one Modern Language, but the choice is otherwise entirely free.

The Sixth Form. Flexibility is a key feature of the Sixth Form. Teaching in the Sixth Form is in smaller groups and single-sex teaching remains the norm, although in a very few subjects co-educational arrangements are in operation.

Students choose from a list of approximately 30 AS courses. Breadth is promoted further by our complementary Curriculum Enrichment Programme. All students have the opportunity to follow a range of non-examined courses as well as Physical Education (sports include golf, football, life-saving, rugby, self-defence, tennis and yoga). Links beyond school include the Community Action Programme and Young Enterprise scheme, as well as opportunities with Business Awareness and Work Experience.

Students in the Sixth Form have greater freedom which includes wearing their own smart clothes, exeat periods and having their own Sixth Form Centre away from the Senior School. Joint social and extra-curricular events are regularly organised with the Boys' Division. There are opportunities for students to assume a variety of responsibilities both within the school and in the wider community. Increasing personal freedom within a highly supportive environment helps students to make the transition to the independence of the adult world. Some students stretch themselves by taking the AQA Baccalaureate qualification.

Almost all students (95%) go on to Higher Education (10% to Oxford and Cambridge).

Music and Drama are popular and students achieve the highest standards in informal and public performances. The wide variety of concerts and productions may take place in the Arts Centre, the Great Hall or the fully-equipped Theatre, all of which make excellent venues for joint and Girls' Division performances. The School regularly performs at Manchester's Bridgewater Hall.

Personal, Social and Health Education, and Citizenship. PSHE and Citizenship are targeted in a variety of ways and coordinated centrally. Some issues may be covered within departmental schemes of work while others will be discussed in the informal atmosphere of form groups led by the form tutor. Those areas which require specialist input are fitted into longer sessions run by experts from outside school.

Careers. The Careers Department helps prepare students for adult life. It is staffed by two experienced assistants and has a resource centre giving access to all the latest information. The extensive programme starts at age 11 and includes communication skills, work sampling, and support in making choices at all stages of schooling. In addition, girls prepare their CVs and applications to Higher Education with the individual help of a trained tutor.

Extra-Curricular Activities. Patterdale Hall, our outdoor pursuits centre in the Lake District, offers many activities including abseiling, gorge walking, orienteering and sailing, both on Lake Ullswater and in the Irish Sea on the ketch, Tenacity of Bolton. Awards are regularly made to enable individuals to undertake a variety of challenging activities both at home and abroad while every year over 50 pupils embark on the Duke of Edinburgh's Award Scheme. In addition to the annual exchanges for Modern Languages students, we also offer a wide range of educational and recreational trips both at home and abroad. All have the opportunity to follow a wide range of non-examined courses of their choice, including Physical Education.

Admission. Entrance to the school is by Headteacher's report, written examination and interview in the Spring term for girls aged 7 and 11. New girls are also welcomed into the Sixth Form. Applications to other year groups are welcomed and spaces may be available depending upon migration.

One in five Senior School pupils receives assistance with their fees through the School's own bursaries.

Fees per term (2014–2015). Senior School and Sixth Form £3,632; Infant and Junior Schools £2,905. Fees include lunches.

Charitable status. The Bolton School is a Registered Charity, number 1110703. Under the terms of the Charity it is administered as two separate Divisions providing for boys and girls under a separate Headmaster and Headmistress.

Brighton & Hove High School
GDST

The Temple, Montpelier Road, Brighton, East Sussex
BN1 3AT
Tel: 01273 280280
Fax: 01273 280281
email: enquiries@bhhs.gdst.net
website: www.bhhs.gdst.net
Twitter: @BHHSGDST
Facebook: /BrightonHoveHighSchool

Founded 1876.

Brighton & Hove High School is part of the GDST
(Girls' Day School Trust). The GDST is the leading network
of independent girls' schools in the UK. As a charity that
owns and runs 24 schools and two academies, it reinvests all
its income in its schools. For further information about the
Trust, see p. xxi or visit www.gdst.net.

Additional information about the school may be found on
the school's website and a detailed prospectus is available
from the school.

*See also Brighton & Hove High School Junior School
entry in IAPS section.*

Chair of Local Governors: Mrs J Smith

Head: Jennifer Smith, MA Glasgow, MEd

Deputy Head: Mrs S Mashford, BSc Manchester

Head of Junior School: Mrs S Cattaneo, BA, Cert Ed
Sussex

Head of Sixth Form: Miss H Boyes, BSc King's College
London, PGCE Hull

(*Full staff list available on the school's website.*)

Number of Pupils. 400 Girls in the Senior School (age
11–18), including 50 in the Sixth Form; 230 in the Junior
School (age 3–11).

Location. The school stands in its own grounds in the
centre of the city of Brighton and Hove. It is about half-a-
mile from Brighton Railway Station and pupils come in
from Lewes, Haywards Heath and Lancing by train. It is
easily reached by bus from all parts of Brighton and Hove.

The Junior School is housed in premises in Radinden
Manor Road. The Senior School is in the Temple, a gentle-
man's residence built by Thomas Kemp in 1819 which has
been considerably altered and enlarged to offer all modern
amenities, most recent of which is a Sports Hall and Dance
Studio. There is a self-contained Sixth Form Centre and the
school owns a Field Centre on the River Wye in mid-Wales.

Curriculum. The school course is planned to provide a
wide general education. Girls are prepared for GCSEs and in
the Sixth Form a wide choice of A Level subjects is offered
in preparation for universities and other forms of professional training.

The school has an all-weather hockey pitch at the Junior
School site with facilities for hockey, rounders, netball and
tennis. Gymnastics and dance are also taught with swimming for junior forms, and senior forms choose from activities including badminton, cricket, netball, aerobics and self-
defence.

Fees per term (2014–2015). Senior School £4,035–
£4,155, Junior School £2,495–£2,960, Nursery £2,055.

The tuition fees cover the regular curriculum, school
books, stationery and other materials, choral music and
sport, but not optional subjects. There is compulsory catering in Years 7, 8, 9 and 10, invoiced termly.

The fees for extra subjects (instrumental music and
speech and drama) are shown in the prospectus.

Admission at all ages is by interview and test/entrance
examination, except at 16+ where GCSE qualifications are
essential. The main entry points are 3+, 4+, 11+ and 16+,
though occasional vacancies occur at all ages.

Scholarships and Bursaries. The GDST has made available to the school a number of scholarships and bursaries.
The bursaries are means tested and are intended to ensure
that the school remains accessible to bright girls who would
profit from our education but who would be unable to enter
the school without financial assistance.

Trust Scholarships are available on merit, irrespective of
income, to internal or external candidates for entry at 11+ or
to the Sixth Form.

Charitable status. Brighton & Hove High School is part
of The Girls' Day School Trust, which is a Registered Charity, number 306983.

Bromley High School
GDST

Blackbrook Lane, Bickley, Bromley, Kent BR1 2TW
Tel: 020 8781 7000
Fax: 020 8781 7002
email: bhs@bro.gdst.net
website: www.bromleyhigh.gdst.net
Twitter: @bromleyhs
Facebook: /bromleyhighschoolGDST

Founded 1883.

Bromley High School is a selective school offering an
exceptional education to girls 4–18 years. The school is part
of the GDST (Girls' Day School Trust). The GDST is the
leading network of independent girls' schools in the UK. As
a charity that owns and runs 24 schools and two academies,
it reinvests all its income in its schools. For further information about the Trust, see p. xxi or visit www.gdst.net.

Additional information about the school may be found on
the school's website and a detailed prospectus is available
from the school.

Chairman of the Local Governors: Mrs P Emburey, BA,
ACA

Headmistress: Angela Drew, BA, MBA Dunelm

Head of Junior School: Mrs C Dickerson, BA Anglia

Deputy Head Pastoral: Mrs H Elkins, BA King's College
London

Director of Finance & Operations: Mr K Ringmo, BA,
MIH, FNASBM

Assistant Head (Head of Sixth Form): P Isted, BA Bristol

Assistant Head (Co-curricular): A Morter-Laing, BSc
Swansea

Admissions Manager: Ms H Knowles

Marketing Manager: Ms D Woodfield, MCIM

Bromley High School was originally situated in the centre of Bromley. In 1981 it moved to Bickley to occupy new
buildings set in 24 acres of beautiful grounds.

Pupil Numbers. Senior School (ages 11–18): 600
(including the Sixth Form). Junior School (ages 4–11): 312.

Sharing the same site, the buildings of both departments
provide excellent facilities.

The Junior School. Our two-form entry Junior School is
housed in separate purpose-built accommodation on the
same site as the Senior School.

We provide a stimulating and happy environment in
which our pupils are encouraged to strive for excellence in
all they do and to derive satisfaction from their achieve-

ments both great and small. From the earliest years we offer a broad curriculum which encourages, challenges and excites the young mind. Our aim is to foster a love of learning, develop independent thinking and promote a spirit of enquiry. In our approach to teaching and learning we blend the traditional with progressive insights into learning styles and the particular needs of young girls as learners in a modern world. We teach the full range of the National Curriculum, including French, Spanish, German and also Latin and accord sports and the creative arts a significant place in the timetable whilst ensuring that the foundations of the core subjects are well established. Class lessons are differentiated and we offer extension and support where appropriate and specialist teaching, sometimes from Senior School staff, in a number of subjects. Our girls achieve high standards and we are proud of our excellent results in public examinations.

Bromley High believes in preparing girls for the challenges beyond school and values the importance of a holistic approach. The school provides many varied opportunities within a vibrant co-curricular programme including sporting, musical, dramatic and other creative activities. We make the most of our beautiful school grounds to provide opportunities for outdoor learning, in which our Forest School is a vital part.

Forest School is a planned programme that takes place in a woodland environment with the aim of developing opportunities for the learner to encounter the beauty, joy, awe and wonder of the natural environment. The approach is 'hands on' and seeks to promote the holistic development of the unique child, including physical, spatial, linguistic, emotional and spiritual aspects. Self-confidence and independence are increased through freedom, time and space to learn. A safe and secure environment allows the girls to extend their learning beyond their comfort zone; to challenge their existing boundaries and ideas and to tackle investigations and tasks which in the classroom may not be possible. Collaboration and cooperation between the learners, their peers and the forest school leader is at the core of the Forest School programme. Social skills develop through risk-taking and an understanding of the consequences of your own actions, whilst self-awareness, self-regulation and empathy for others are also developed. Forest School enables children to be active participants in their own education and development.

In the delivery of our curriculum we are well served by outstanding facilities which, in addition to comprehensively equipped classrooms, include a music wing, a library, ICT suite, a science room, and an art and technology room, a sensory garden and outdoor 'classrooms'. We share many other facilities with the Senior School including a swimming pool, gymnasium, sports hall, tennis courts and an all-weather pitch. Our pupils have their lunch in the main school dining room where a wide variety of hot dishes or sandwiches are served.

The Senior School. The school provides an environment in which girls of all ages work hard to develop their abilities. Academic studies are of paramount importance and standards are high with a curriculum making equal provisions for arts, sciences, practical and creative subjects The school also provides for a wide range of extra-curricular activities and has a reputation for excellent pastoral care, delivered by teams of tutors overseen by year heads and the pastoral deputy. The school community focuses on the individual and strives to encourage girls to believe that anything is possible. An environment of supportive encouragement and a staff of teachers who are experienced in teaching girls allows our young women to develop skills and interests in all curriculum areas.

The senior school building is a purpose-built, largely refurbished building built in the 1980s. New science facilities, library, sixth form centre, drama studio, and specialist teaching rooms for the creative arts enable departments to have their own dedicated spaces for teaching and extra-cur-

ricular activities. Recent sixth form common room and major sports refurbishment; in the summer of 2013 £1m development improved the dining room facilities and completely refurbished the changing room and swimming pool with floodlights recently installed in the astroturf hockey courts. Constant improvement to the buildings keeps them smart and fresh. The visual and creative arts are well supported and their work is very present throughout the school. Art work is of a very high standard, some talented GCSE students do really well, textiles and photography recently introduced as A Level choices for budding artists. Dance GCSE introduced in 2011 to supplement and extend the co-curricular dance offer. Every year girls go on post A Levels to study dance, drama, music and art at the highest level. In Key Stage 3 girls study a wide and well-balanced curriculum which includes two modern languages (3 are offered), Latin, the humanities, creative arts, ICT, Computer Science, and sport (including cricket and dance) as well as the core subjects. Most teaching rooms are equipped with Smart Boards and all have Wi-Fi and digital projector facilities which allow pupils to use their own mobile computer devices. Teachers are encouraged to teach lively, challenging lessons and the annual enrichment activities in the summer are a key part of the curriculum provision to support and extend girls' learning in preparation for GCSE study. Myriad trips and activities, including music tours abroad for Year 7, residential field work for Y8 geographers and Y9 art trips to European cities mean that girls are confident and independent learners by the time GCSE choices are made in Year 9. All KS3 girls study ICT GCSE, leading to the public examination qualification in June of Year 9. The modern foreign languages department has links with France, Germany and Spain and arranges exchanges, visits and work experience placements. The school was recently awarded the British Council's full International School Award.

At KS4 girls study 9 or 10 GCSE subjects. Beyond the core subjects, modern languages, including a thriving French, Spanish and German department, are very strong, Theatre Studies GCSE is a popular option subject and the vast majority of girls opt to study history or geography. In 2012 87% of pupils qualified for the English Baccalaureate, despite a free choice option system which builds the timetable around the girls own selections (both at GCSE and A Level). Alongside the other option subjects Latin and Classical Civilisation is available at GCSE, as is Computer Science.

Sport. Sports facilities include a large, well-equipped Sports Hall, a gymnasium, a 400-metre athletics track, two grass hockey pitches, netball and tennis courts, a fine indoor heated swimming pool, and an Astroturf pitch, which was opened in 2000. Sport is both integral to the curriculum and an important part of the extra-curricular life of the school. Individuals and teams compete regularly at county and regional level in sports ranging from swimming to skiing, gymnastics, hockey and netball.

Sixth Form. The large Sixth Form enjoys a wide A Level and AS Level curriculum, with sciences and modern languages retaining a high profile alongside the arts and humanities. Recent additions to the A Level programme include photography, textiles and classical civilisation. There is a broad provision for minority studies, opportunities for taking responsibility and for work experience and travel to Europe and beyond. In addition to the many sports available in the Senior School, Sixth Formers are able to participate in a range of sports including rowing. Almost all students go on to higher education and each year girls maintain the school's "Oxbridge" tradition. Applications for Sixth Form entry are welcome. Careers education has a high profile throughout all key stages and the school is a member of ISCO. In the Sixth Form the benefits of GDST-wide initiatives, such as leadership conferences and Oxbridge preparation residential visits, are especially relevant and beneficial to both staff and pupils.

Extra-Curricular Activities. A great emphasis is put on an enthusiastic involvement in music, art, sport, drama and community activities. The school has a high local reputation for its annual dance production and holds several sports championships. Major school concerts are organised at venues such as Westminster Abbey and Southwark Cathedral. To celebrate the School's 125th anniversary, an extravaganza 'Flying High', a bespoke expression of Music, Drama and Dance, was held at the Royal Albert Hall.

All extra-curricular activities flourish in this lively community where Young Enterprise, work experience, work shadowing, Neighbourhood Engineer and Challenge to Industry schemes have considerable support. The Bromley High Parents' Association supports the school most generously. Girls enjoy contributing to local, national and international charities and to community service. They are prepared for the Duke of Edinburgh's Award Scheme and there is a keen interest in environmental issues. There are many clubs in which girls of all ages take a share of responsibility, including a recently-formed guide and brownie unit. There are regular exchanges to France, Germany and Spain as well as annual Geography and Biology field trips. World challenge expeditions have visited Laos, Malaysia, Ecuador, Thailand, Guyana, Namibia and Vietnam, Zambia, Guatemala, Belize, Mexico and Mongolia. The Annual Music Tours have travelled to Australia, Venice, Malta, South Africa, Malawi, Slovenia, Catalonia, the United States, China, Estonia and Germany. The Year 6 and 7 Music Tours have visited Paris, Brussels, Normandy and Bruges.

Fees per term (2014–2015). Senior School £4,896, Junior School £3,948.

Fees cover tuition, stationery, textbooks and scientific and games materials as well as entry fees for GCSE and GCE Advanced Level examinations. Extra tuition in Music and Speech and Drama is available at recognised rates.

Bursaries. The newly-introduced scheme of Founders' Awards is seeking to actively increase levels of fees assistance to pupils who would otherwise not have access to independent education. These are means-tested awards which provide, for successful applicants, a minimum of 50% of fees and may also include uniform and trips allowances for those on very high awards.

Scholarships. There are Academic scholarships for the most successful candidates in the 11+ examinations and for entry into the Sixth Form. There are also Music and Sports scholarships at 11+ and Music, Arts, Sports and Drama scholarships are awarded in the Sixth Form. A small number of scholarships are awarded at 13+ for entry into Year 9. These are awarded for excellence in sport, the creative arts (music/dance/drama or art) and for academic excellence.

Admission and Entrance Examination. Admission into the school is at 4+ (Reception) and 7+ (Year 3) by assessment and testing. Pupils from the Junior School progress automatically to the Senior School but external applicants, or those wishing to be considered for scholarship or bursary are assessed at 11+. This covers verbal and quantitative assessments as well as creative writing. Entry into the Sixth Form is dependent on results at GCSE (please contact admissions for further information). Common Entrance (Year 9) and entry for GCSE (Year 10) may be available on occasion.

Charitable status. Bromley High School is part of The Girls' Day School Trust, which is a Registered Charity, number 306983.

Bruton School for Girls

Sunny Hill, Bruton, Somerset BA10 0NT
Tel: 01749 814400
Fax: 01749 812537
email: info@brutonschool.co.uk
website: www.brutonschool.co.uk
Twitter: @BrutonSchool
Facebook: /Bruton-School-for-Girls

Governors:
Chairman: Mr D H C Batten

Headmistress: Mrs Nicola Botterill, BSc, MA, PGCE, NPQH, FRGS, FRSA

Deputy Head: Mrs Rachel Robbins, BA, PGCE

Head of Preparatory School: Mrs Helen Snow, BEd

Bursar: Mr A H D Harvey-Kelly

Director of Admissions: Mrs Carrie Crook

Established in 1900 and set in beautiful English countryside in Somerset, overlooking Glastonbury Tor, Bruton School for Girls is a day school for girls and boys aged 2–7 and a day and boarding school for girls aged 7–18. It is a small school with approximately 250 pupils, of whom roughly 80 board. Full, weekly and flexi boarding options are available. The teaching week is Monday to Friday with no Saturday lessons.

Sunny Hill Preparatory School comprises the Nursery School, Pre-Prep and Prep School. Boarding is available for girls from the age of 7 years old. Reception, Year 1 and Year 2 classes are co-educational until the age of 7. A low pupil-teacher ratio and good relationships enable creative and dedicated teachers to make the most of the inquisitive childhood years and ensures that every pupil receives quality individual attention. Pupils develop strong learning habits. In a broad curriculum, they explore the exciting world of science, information technology, humanities, French, music, design technology and creative arts. Mathematics and English programmes build firm foundations for purposeful learning. The Early Years Foundation (Nursery to Reception) has an 'Outstanding' Ofsted rating. (*See also entry in IAPS section.*)

The **Senior School** is a thriving community of girls age 11–16 years who are taught in separate year groups 1–5. Girls joining the Senior School come from a wide variety of local, national and international schools, as well as from Sunny Hill Prep School. At GCSE, 18 subjects are offered with an A* to C pass rate well above the national average, most girls taking 9 or 10 subjects. Pupils are set for Mathematics, English, Modern Languages and Sciences to maximise individual achievement. The curriculum offers three separate sciences and three foreign languages. Additional learning support is available from specialist Skills Development teachers where appropriate.

The **Sixth Form** offers excellent preparation for university, with tutorial support and individual study programmes. The school has a considerable reputation for academic achievement, "Oxbridge" and university entrance. Cultural and social skills are developed to enhance independence and career ambitions. An extensive range of A Levels is complemented by cultural activities, extension studies and extra-curricular activities which include public speaking and the Leiths Certificate in Food and Wine. Career and Higher Education advice feature prominently at this stage. Many girls entering the Sixth Form transfer from the Senior School but are joined by students from other schools.

Why choose BSG? We are passionate about, and experts in, girls' education. We believe in offering every girl a well-rounded education in an environment with the space to inspire, challenge, encourage and support her to develop her full potential to become the amazing person she can be in this fast-changing world. We want your child to grow with us, learn with us, make friends for life and enjoy her time with us. We encourage her to develop intellectual curiosity, self-esteem, respect and care for others, independence and excellence in all she does, with a real love for life.

Academic and Personal Expectations. Academically, the school has high expectations and many girls gain places at prestigious universities. The girls are encouraged to have self-belief, to set challenging goals, display independence of thought and enjoy learning for its own sake.

There are many opportunities for leadership and the development of personal and social skills, particularly in the Sixth Form, where students may take up the role of prefect or hall captain.

Location. Set on a 40-acre campus in beautiful countryside, the school is close to the Somerset, Wiltshire and Dorset borders, and has easy access to the M3/A303 corridor between London and the South West. Bristol, Bath, Salisbury and the south coast are all within approximately one hour's travel. Castle Cary station, served by London Paddington-Exeter express trains, is 4 miles away and Templecombe on the line to London Waterloo is 10 miles; the school offers minibus connections. Students are collected from London Heathrow, Bristol International and other airports. A network of daily buses serves the school from surrounding areas.

Boarding. Three boarding houses provide comfortable and well-appointed accommodation appropriate to the different age ranges of pupils. Facilities include common rooms, games rooms, kitchens and dining areas as well as access to computer facilities and telephones. Younger girls share dormitories while Fourth, Fifth and Sixth Form students have their own study-bedrooms or, in Form 4, may share with one other girl. Sixth formers enjoy an increased degree of independence that aims to bridge school and university. The boarding houses are situated on the school campus and girls are cared for by experienced Housemistresses and assistant house staff. A variety of activities is offered each weekend.

The school has its own medical centre with a qualified nursing Sister on duty every weekday during term time and comprehensive medical care available at Bruton Surgery.

A high standard of catering is provided, with a wide variety of choice. Specific dietary needs are catered for.

Extra-Curricular Activities. Art, Drama, Music and Sport feature strongly. The outstanding success of the Art department is reflected in work displayed around the school. The Hobhouse Studio Theatre provides a professional-standard performance space for productions and 'speech and drama' presentations. There is a wide range of opportunities for both instrumental and choral performance, with four choirs performing music across a range of styles and numerous instrumental groups, including two school orchestras and a wind band. The sports department offers a wide range of activities in which every girl can participate either competitively or for her own enjoyment. There is a full fixture list of competitive matches in the traditional sports of hockey, netball, rounders, swimming, athletics and tennis. Tennis coaching, horse riding, judo, trampolining, modern and classical dance, yoga and individual exercise regimes are available. There is also the popular Duke of Edinburgh's Award programme. Having been awarded the Eco-Schools Green Flag, many girls participate in the Eco Club and assist with the schools recycling programme. In the Preparatory School, all pupils from Reception to Prep 6 participate in Forest School.

Entry. There is open entry into the pre-prep and preparatory school from which pupils normally progress seamlessly into the senior school. The senior school entry process includes the school's own diagnostic assessments or Common Entrance. Entry into the Sixth Form is by interview and GCSE or equivalent qualifications.

Fees per term (2014–2015). Day: £4,850 (Senior School and Sixth Form), £3,480–£3,580 (Preparatory School), £1,740–£2,319 (Pre-Preparatory School), £20 per session (Nursery).

Boarding: £6,348–£8,858 (full), £5,755–£7,662 (weekly boarding), £53.50 per day (casual boarding).

Scholarships and Bursaries. Bruton School for Girls has a range of scholarships, which are offered on entry to the Senior School at 11+, 13+ and Sixth Form on the basis of aptitude and achievement in particular areas, including academic studies, music, art, sport and drama.

11+: Foundation Scholarships (Academic), Besly Music Scholarship.

13+: Chappell Scholarship (Sport), Golledge Scholarship (Art, Humanities or Languages), Knight Scholarship (Sciences or Mathematics), Hobhouse Scholarship (All-Rounder), Palmer Music Scholarship.

Sixth Form: Edith Radford Scholarship (Academic), Howard Music Scholarship, Zhou Guang-Ren Scholarship (Piano), Cumberlege Scholarships (Art, Drama or Sport).

Governors' Exhibitions (means-tested) exist to support those pupils whose families would find difficulty in meeting the full fees and are awarded on entry to the Senior School and Sixth Form.

Charitable status. Bruton School for Girls is a Registered Charity, number 1085577, and a Company Limited by Guarantee. It exists to provide education.

Burgess Hill School for Girls

Keymer Road, Burgess Hill, West Sussex RH15 0EG
Tel: 01444 241050
Fax: 01444 870314
email: registrar@burgesshill-school.com
website: www.burgesshill-school.com
Twitter: @BHSfG
Facebook: /BurgessHillSchoolforGirls
LinkedIn: /burgess-hill-school-for-girls

An independent day and boarding school or girls age 2½ to 18 years, founded in 1906 by Miss Beatrice Goode. Our school has a Nursery (Nursery 51 accept boys), Junior School, Senior School and Sixth Form. To fully appreciate our school come for a visit and talk to the students, they will be delighted to show you around.

Chairman of Governors: Mr C Cooper, BSc, MEd, MBPsS

Headmistress: Mrs Kathryn Bell, BSc Hons, PGCE

Deputy Headmistress: Mrs E Laybourn, BEd Hons
Director of Academic Development: Mr R Tapping, BSc Hons, PGCE, NPQH, CGeog, FRGS
ICT Development Director: Mr S Trask, BA Hons, MSc Dip, PGCE
Head of Sixth Form: Mr N Dyson, BA Hons, PGCE
Head of Junior School: Mrs H Miller, BA Hons
Deputy Head of Junior School: Mrs T Pearson-Rujas, BSc Hons, PGCE, QTS, Cert Mgmt
Head of Upper School: Mr T Clarke, BA Hons, PGCE
Head of Lower School: Miss M Bramley, BSc Hons, PGCE

Heads of Faculty:
English: Ms S Trivière, BA Hons, MA, PGCE
French: Mrs I Martin, Licence Maîtrise, DDT
German: Mrs J Edey, MA Hons, PGCE
Spanish: Mr J Montesinos, BA Hons, PGCE
Classics & Latin: Mrs B Johns, BA Hons, PGCE
Mathematics: Mr R Stanway, BSc Hons, PGCE
Biology: Miss M Bramley, BSc Hons, PGCE
Chemistry: Mrs S Lympany, BSc Hons, MSc, PGCE
Physics: Mrs S Marsh, BSc Hons, MSc, PGCE
Business Studies & Economics: Mrs J King, BEd
Information Technology: Mr S Trask, BA Hons, MSc Dip, PGCE
Geography: Mr T Lucas, MA, PGCE
History: Mr T Clarke, BA Hons, PGCE
Religious Studies: Miss S Cull, BA Hons, PGCE
Psychology: Mrs G Humphrey, BSc Hons, PGCE, MBPsS

Art: Mrs M Carruthers, Dip AD, ATC, PGCPD
Speech & Drama: Mrs E Cassim, BA Hons, PGCE
Music: Mr P Newbold, BMus Hons, MMus, PGCE
Physical Education & Games: Miss S Clapp, BA Hons QTS
Design & Technology: Mrs B Bradley, BEd Hons C&G

Bursar: Mr G Bond
Head of Admissions & Marketing: Mrs Y Irvine, DipM ACIM
Senior Housemistress: Ms C Trevor, BA Hons
Housemistresses:
Mrs L Bussell
Miss M Buckley
Mrs D Scott
School Nurse: Mrs S Ramanan, RGN
Careers Adviser: Mrs J Edey, MA Hons, PGCE

General. The ethos of the School is to provide a caring, challenging and supportive atmosphere which encourages young people to use their initiative, be inquisitive and creative and develop responsibility and independence. Boys are welcome in the nursery. Our school is a community in which girls flourish; from age 4 the focus is firmly on girls and the way they learn. They develop self-esteem and confidence and go on to make a positive contribution in their chosen professions. We have small classes with fully qualified, professional staff dedicated to catering for the needs of each individual child. The School has established a reputation for excellence in Music, Sport, Art, Textiles and Drama and achieves impressive academic results. We are consistently highly ranked nationally and regularly lead the field in Sussex. We believe that education for life involves much more than academic success alone. Girls can, and do, strive for excellence wherever their talents lie.

School Facilities. The Senior School offers specialist teaching rooms including: a state-of-the-art language suite equipped with computers and specialist software for personalised listening and speaking; a Music room equipped with the latest Apple Mac composition software; Music practice rooms; two Art studios with an exhibition area, Art library and a kiln area; a Drama studio; a fully-equipped Media suite; two modern Chemistry labs; a specialist Textiles room and Technology workshop; a Learning Resource Centre and enhanced outdoor PE facilities with tennis courts and an Astroturf training area. The Performing Arts facilities have been extended with a glazed, curved entrance foyer.

The Junior School's facilities include a Learning Hub which incorporates a library, large learning space and access to iPads and interactive electronic screen. The Junior School also offers fully-equipped subject-specific classrooms for Music, ICT, Art, Science and Technology and access to all the sports facilities on the main school campus. The Infants are based in a building with bright, open classrooms and have their own hall and library. The Infants and Juniors have an exciting playground with a wooden adventure trail and outdoor classroom.

The Sixth Form centre includes a seminar room, contemporary classrooms, a study room with ICT facilities, a higher education library, a music practice room, two common rooms and a new student kitchen. All curriculum areas are well served with appropriate specialist accommodation, either in the Sixth Form Centre or in the Senior School complex for Art, Drama, Music, Media, PE, Science, Technology and Textiles. All classrooms are equipped with interactive whiteboards, and suites of laptop computers ensure that technology is available when and where needed.

The school has two Edwardian boarding houses with bedrooms and common rooms which are spacious, light and pleasantly furnished.

Curriculum. The curriculum is broad and challenging and relevant to the needs of young people. There is a wide choice of subjects both at GCSE and A Level with many extra-curricular activities.

ISI Inspection. The 2009 inspection reports clearly confirm that the School has a great many strengths in all aspects of its provision. The Early Years provision was judged to be outstanding. Moving through into the Junior School the inspectors commented that, "*The highly effective teaching and excellence of the whole educational experience inspire a love of learning and exceptional motivation to achieve the highest possible standards in academic work, sport, drama and music*".

The Junior School was also delighted to note that the inspectors picked up on the happy atmosphere of the School commenting that, "*The quality of relations between staff and pupils is excellent. Respect and courtesy are evident and so is humour; relations are clearly warm and relaxed and there is an air of happiness and purpose*".

The Senior School report concludes that, "*The educational experience enables pupils of all abilities and interests to find success and personal achievement. The quality of pastoral care is outstanding. The support for and nurturing of individuals are key elements in shaping the outstanding personal development of pupils*".

Inspection reports can be viewed on www.isi.net.

Entrance Procedures. Entrance to either the Junior or Senior School is by examination and school reference. Senior girls are also interviewed by the Headmistress. Scholarships are awarded each year for academic and/or musical excellence into Years 3–6 inclusive, 7, 9 and the Lower Sixth. Sport/Creative scholarships are available for students entering Year 7, 9 and the Lower Sixth. The Margaret Morris All-Rounder Scholarship is available to girls entering Year 9.

Fees per term (2014–2015). Senior School: £4,840–£5,100 (day girls); £8,740–£9,000 (boarding). Junior School: £2,340–£4,130 (day girls).

Old Girls' Association. The Old Girls' Association is an association run by former students and the school. It helps everyone to keep in touch with each other and what is happening at the School. Chairman: Mrs K Ruff.

Charitable status. Burgess Hill School for Girls is a Registered Charity, number 307001.

Bury Grammar School Girls

Bridge Road, Bury, Lancs BL9 0HH
Tel: 0161 797 2808
Fax: 0161 763 4658
email: info@bgsg.bury.sch.uk
website: www.bgsg.bury.sch.uk
Twitter: @BuryGrammarSch
Facebook: /BuryGrammarSchoolGirls

Motto: *Sanctas Clavis Fores Aperit*

Acting Chair of Governors: Mr L A Goldberg

Bursar and Clerk to the Governors: Mrs J Stevens

Headmistress: Mrs R Georghiou, BA Manchester, MEd Liverpool

Deputy Headmistress: Mrs J A Buttery, BA Lancaster

Assistant Heads:
Mrs S Fielden, BSc London
Mrs H Ward, BA Leicester

Senior Teachers:
Mrs Y Hanham, BSc Salford
Mr J Southworth, BA Liverpool

Heads of Departments:
Mrs J Southworth, BA Liverpool (*Art and Design*)
Mrs S Taylor, BSc Manchester (*Careers*)
Dr J Yates, BSc Durham, PhD Bristol (*Chemistry*)

Mrs C Kilshaw Walster, BA London, MA Manchester
(*Classics*)
Mrs M Whitlow, BA York (*Economics and Business
Studies*)
Miss V White, BA MA Manchester (*English*)
Mrs V Leaver, BSc Hull (*Geography*)
Mrs C Bevis, BA Bolton (*History*)
Mr D Ashworth, BA Manchester Metropolitan (*ICT*)
Mrs Y G Hanham, BSc Salford (*Mathematics*)
Mrs R Melia, BA Oxon (*Modern Languages*)
Miss R Britton, BMus Manchester (*Music*)
Mrs J Slade, BSc Loughborough (*PE*)
Mr D Lehan, BEng Liverpool, BA Oxon (*Physics*)
Mrs S Thorpe, BA Salford (*Politics*)
Ms C McDermott, BA Sheffield (*Psychology*)
Mrs L C A Kerr, BA Manchester (*RS*)
Mrs S Fielden, BSc London (*Science and Biology*)
Mrs H Hammond, BA Liverpool (*Theatre Studies*)

Head of Sixth Form: Mrs H Ward, BA Leicester
Head of Upper School: Mrs R Newbold, BSc
Loughborough
Head of Middle School: Mrs J Haworth, BA Keele
Head of Year 7: Mrs S C Banfield, BA Bangor

Co-educational Infant and Girls' Junior School:
Mrs V Hall, BSc Cardiff

Registrar: Mrs B Wrigley

The Girls' School was founded in 1884 as the Bury High
School for Girls and amalgamated, a few years later, with
the Bury Grammar School (Boys). The school maintains
high academic standards and traditional grammar school
values whilst encouraging each girl to develop her individual
talents and abilities as far as she can in a lively environment
which responds to the challenge of change.

The numbers at present are 39 in the Pre-School, 146 in
the Co-educational Infant Department, 150 in the Junior
School and 431 in the Senior School.

The **Senior School** is housed in a distinctive Edwardian
building which dates from 1906. The school is conveniently
situated near the centre of the town and the bus-tram interchange.
Facilities are regularly improved and updated; a
major building project has recently led to the creation of an
Arts Centre containing a modern library and work facility in
the heart of the school surrounded by new classrooms for
English, Art, Design and Technology, Textiles and Food
Technology. The final stage of the project, due for completion
in September 2014, is the creation of a dedicated sixth
form pre-university centre which will be used jointly by
girls and boys. This will contain seminar rooms with full
access to interactive learning, private study areas which will
allow students to complement their lessons with independent
learning and access to the library and internet and a
Cafetorium with a central sixth form entrance and landscaped
gardens.

The curriculum is broad and balanced in the first five
years of the Senior School. At Key Stage Three all girls follow
a core curriculum of Mathematics, English, the three
Sciences, PE, RS, History and Geography which is
enhanced by courses in Art, ICT, Design Technology, Food
and Nutrition, Latin, Classical Civilisation, Business Studies
and two Modern Languages from a choice of French, German
and Spanish. Traditional teaching methods are combined
with pupil-centred learning work, group work,
investigative work and a problem-solving approach. In a
variety of cross curricular projects, pupils seek solutions to
problems and take an ever-increasing responsibility for their
own learning.

PE and Music are well established; in recent years the
School has been represented in National Netball, Tennis and
Swimming Championships and on County Netball, Hockey,
Cross-Country, Swimming, Tennis, Athletics and Badminton
teams. Each year the Festival Choir gives concerts inter-

nationally and in the UK. There are also two orchestras,
string quartets, a flute choir and a jazz band.

The School works closely with Bury Grammar School
(Boys) for dramatic and musical productions, and other
extra-curricular activities. The Sixth Form common rooms
are open to both boys and girls.

Public examinations are taken in Years 10, 11, 12 and 13,
according to the requirements of individual pupils. There is
a wide choice of subjects in the Sixth Form and each year all
or virtually all students proceed to degree courses at prestigious
universities, including Oxford and Cambridge. The
School achieves high pass rates in public examinations.

These successes and initiatives, along with PSE, careers
advice and extra-curricular activities, clubs, visits, holidays
in England and abroad, charity work and school productions,
offer wide educational opportunities and encourage
links to be forged with industry and commerce and with the
community in Bury and beyond.

The **Junior School** has its own purpose-built premises on
the Senior School site, has shared use of the Roger Kay Hall,
Gymnasium, Sports Hall, and Swimming Pool. The eight
large and attractive classrooms, Music Room and large
Library/Computer suite provide a comfortable and very
pleasant environment in which the girls aged 7–11 learn and
work.

The Junior School curriculum is based on the National
Curriculum but with enhancements. The curriculum
includes the three core subjects and Design/Technology,
ICT, History, Geography, Religious Education, Art and
Craft, Music and Physical Education. Particular emphasis is
placed on the teaching of skills in reading, writing and mathematics.
The aim is to provide a broad and balanced education
and to give each girl the opportunity to develop her full
potential. The combination of a dedicated staff and excellent
facilities allows girls to maintain the high academic standard
enriched by many extra-curricular activities with particular
strengths in music and sport.

The School has a purpose-built **Co-educational Infant
School** situated on the school campus which includes a pre-school
taking pupils who will become 3 during the academic
year. In lively and stimulating surroundings the children
progress rapidly in all six areas of learning. They make use
of the Senior School pool and have specialist PE instruction,
their own dedicated gymnasium and tuition in music in a
specially designed music room. The focal point of the new
building is the central octagonal hall used for assemblies and
performances. Pupils also have access to a unique and exciting
rooftop play area and a Learning Resource Area with
supervised computer access. There is a Breakfast Club
before school and an After-School Club.

Bursaries. At 11+ the Governors offer a number of
means-tested bursaries.

Fees per term (2014–2015). Pre-School, Infant and
Junior School £2,427; Senior School £3,266.

Charitable status. Bury Grammar Schools Charity is a
Registered Charity, number 526622.

Channing School

The Bank, Highgate, London N6 5HF
Tel: 020 8340 2328 (School Office)
             020 8340 2719 (Bursar)
Fax: 020 8341 5698
email: info@channing.co.uk
website: www.channing.co.uk
Twitter: @ChanningSchool
Facebook: /ChanningSchool

Governors:
Ms C Leslie, LLB (*Chair*)

Mr J Alexander, FCA

Mr A Appleyard, BSc (*Vice Chair*)
Mrs J Burns, BA
Revd D Costley, BA
Mrs J De Swiet, MA
Ms M Jayaweera, MA
¶Mrs J Otterburn-Hall, BSc
Miss D Patman, FRICS, ACIArb
Ms B Rentoul, MA Yale
Mrs C Richards, BSc
Mr W Spears, MBA
Mrs C Stephenson, Cert Ed
Dr A Sutton, MRCGP

¶ *Former Pupil*

Bursar & Clerk to the Governors: Mr R Hill

Headmistress: Mrs B M Elliott, MA Cantab Modern & Medieval Languages

Deputy Head: Mr A J Underwood, MEd Cantab Theology

Director of Studies: Mrs K Thonemann, MA Oxon Mathematics

Ms S Beenstock, BA Leeds (*English*)
Mrs G Bhamra Burgess, BA London (*Economics, Assistant Head of Middle School Year 9*)
Mr T Bigglestone, BA Durham (*Head of Religious Education, Humanities*)
Mr A Boardman, BA Durham (*Geography, Assistant Director of Studies*)
Mr P Boxall, GRSM, ARCO Royal Academy of Music (*Director of Music*)
Miss J Bramhall, BA Oxon (*Head of Geography*)
Dr M Bremser, DPhil Oxon (*English & Critical Thinking, Oxbridge Programme Coordinator part-time*)
Miss E Burns, MA Cantab (*History of Art part-time*)
Mr D Carr, BA Southampton (*Head of French*)
Mr D Coram, BA Dunelm, MA London (*Classics*)
Mr P Daurat, BEd Huddersfield (*Mathematics*)
Ms S Della-Porta, BEd Australia (*Head of Physical Education*)
Ms A Derbyshire, MA Goldsmiths (*Art part-time*)
Mrs W Devine, BA Reading (*Head of Politics, Publications Manager*)
Dr N Devlin, MA, DPhil Oxon (*Classics part-time*)
Mrs S Elliot, BA Cantab (*Head of Classics*)
Miss P Evernden, MA Cantab (*Head of English*)
Miss L Feilden, BA Brighton College of Art (*Art part-time*)
Mr S Frank, BSc Birmingham (*Head of Biology*)
Miss S-L Fung, BSc Coventry (*Physics*)
Ms A Gill Carey, BA Canterbury (*Head of Drama*)
Mr P Gittins, BA Wolverhampton (*Art, Head of PSHE, Assistant Head of Middle School*)
Mrs S Gorrie, MA Glasgow (*Spanish, French*)
Mrs G Hannan, MA Cantab, MTeach London (*Head of History, Gifted & Talented Coordinator*)
Mrs R Harper, BA Kent, ALAM (*English, Head of Middle School*)
Mr A Haworth, MA RCA (*Head of Art*)
Mrs B Hernandez, BA Alicante (*Spanish, French*)
Mr M Holmes, BSc City of London Polytechnic (*Head of Information and Communication Technology*)
Miss A Hosseini, BSc London (*Head of Chemistry*)
Mr R Jacobs, BA Oxon (*Head of Physics, Head of Science*)
Mrs H Kanmwaa, BA Oxon (*English*)
Mrs A Kennedy, MSc London (*Chemistry*)
Miss C Long, MA London (*French*)
Ms T MacCarthy, BSc Edinburgh (*Mathematics part-time*)
Mrs S Mahmood, BSc Alberta (*Chemistry part-time*)
Mrs L Marshall, BSc Edinburgh (*Chemistry*)
Ms J Newman, BA Leicester (*Head of Economics, Head of Sixth Form*)
Mrs H Nissinen-Lee, BSc London (*Geography part-time*)
Mrs J Ogidan, BSc Liverpool (*Biology, Head of Careers, Head of Upper School*)
Miss H O'Sullivan, BSc Birmingham (*Physical Education*)
Miss V Penglase, BA London (*Drama and Theatre Studies part-time*)

Ms Y Rabet, BA UHB France (*Head of Modern Foreign Languages, Head of Spanish*)
Mr D Riggs-Long, BSc London (*Mathematics part-time*)
Miss S Salmon, MA London (*Geography*)
Ms M Sharma-Yun, BSc London (*Mathematics part-time*)
Mrs D Shoham, BSc Birmingham (*Biology part-time*)
Dr C Spinks, PhD Manchester (*Chemistry*)
Miss H Stacey, BA Nottingham (*English part-time*)
Ms A Stöckmann, MA Westfaelische Wilhelms (*Head of German*)
Mr P Thompson, MA Oxon (*History and RE part-time*)
Miss M Wilkes, BA London (*Spanish and French*)
Miss A Wilkinson, MA London (*History*)
Ms K Wilkinson, BA East Anglia (*English, Assistant Head of Upper School*)
Mrs R Williams, BSc London (*Mathematics part-time*)
Mr P Williamson, BEd Huddersfield (*Head of Mathematics*)
Miss A Yasamee, MA Manchester (*Librarian*)
Miss L Zanardo, BA Mus Australia (*Assistant Director of Music*)
Ms N Zekan, BEd Australia (*Physical Education*)
Mrs D Zuluaga de la Cruz, MA France (*French part-time*)

Junior School:

Head: Mrs L Lawrance, BPrimEd Hons Port Elizabeth, South Africa

Deputy Head: Mrs C Constant, MA Greenwich (*Year 6*)

Mrs P Gibson, MEd London (*Classroom Teacher*)
Miss E Glennon, BA Manchester (*Classroom Teacher Year 1*)
Miss K Goldstein, BA Birmingham (*Classroom Teacher Year 2*)
Mrs I Hawkins, BEd London (*Classroom Teacher Year 3 part-time*)
Mrs T Luxford, BA Middlesex (*Classroom Teacher Year 3 part-time*)
Ms R McGinnety, BA Cantab (*Classroom Teacher Year 4*)
Miss A McLennan, BA Leeds (*Classroom Teacher Reception*)
Ms M Mort, BSc Sydney (*PE Teacher*)
Miss L Panton, BA Southampton (*DT & Drama, Art, ICT*)
Miss M Pepper, LTCL (*Head of Music – Junior School*)
Miss A Phipps, BEd Middx Polytechnic (*Classroom Teacher Year 2*)
Mrs C Rand, CertEd (*Classroom Teacher part-time*)
Mrs B Rayner, BA Twickenham (*Classroom Teacher Reception*)
Miss S Snowdowne, BEd Plymouth (*Classroom Teacher Year 5*)
Ms S Unsworth, BA Bath Spa (*Classroom Teacher Year 1*)
Ms H Younger, BA Oxon (*Director of Studies – Junior School & Classroom Teacher Year 6*)
Mrs S Ahmed (*Teaching Assistant Year 3 part-time*)
Ms A Beasley (*Teaching Assistant Years 4–5 part-time*)
Mrs C Brierley (*Teaching Assistant Year 2*)
Mrs A Done (*Teaching Assistant Year 2 part-time*)
Mrs D Galli (*Teaching Assistant Year 2 part-time*)
Mrs K Hadjipateras (*Teaching Assistant Reception part-time*)
Miss Z Hira (*Teaching Assistant Reception*)
Miss M Holmes (*Teaching Assistant Year 6 part-time*)
Miss J Hudson (*Teaching Assistant Year 1*)
Ms S Ibrekic (*Teaching Assistant Reception part-time*)
Miss E Krajewski (*Teaching Assistant Year 1*)
Miss S Litiu (*Teaching Assistant Reception*)
Mrs R Pieri (*Teaching Assistant Year 3 part-time*)

Visiting Music Teachers:
Mr S Allen, ARCM (*Clarinet*)
Miss J Bacon, BA, PG Dip (*Voice*)
Mrs H Bennett, BMus Hons (*Trumpet*)
Miss S Bircumshaw, GRSM Hons (*Violin Junior*)

Mrs M Bradbury-Rance, MA (*Voice*)
Mr A Brown, Dip TCL (*Percussion*)
Mrs P Capone, AGSM (*Piano*)
Miss M Carroll, BMus (*Double Bass*)
Mr N Harrison, GRSM, SRCM (*Bassoon*)
Miss J Herbert, BA (*Cello*)
Mrs H Jolly, GRSM (*Flute*)
Ms M Keogh, ARAM (*Harp*)
Mr A Khan, LTCL (*Guitar*)
Mrs L Knight, MA (*Singing*)
Mrs P Malloy, LRAM, ABRSM (*Violin/Viola*)
Miss N Myerscough, ARAM (*Violin*)
Miss C Philpot, LRAM (*Oboe*)
Miss J Rayner, BA (*LAMDA*)
Miss E Rossiter, PG Dip, MMus (*Piano*)
Miss L Seddon, Dip ABRSM, BMus Hons (*Cello*)
Miss H Shimizu, BMus (*Piano*)
Miss A Szreter, BA (*Singing*)
Ms A Thomas, BMus (*Flute*)
Miss C Thompson, LRAM (*Violin*)
Mr T Travis, BMus (*Saxophone*)
Miss S Vivian, LTCL, Dip (*Singing*)
Miss J Watts, FRCO, GRSM, LRAM (*Piano*)
Mr A White, MMus, MA (*Lower Brass*)

Assistant to Bursar & Clerk to the Governors: Miss E
  Lismore-Burns
Headmistress's Secretary: Ms L Carreras
Development Director: Ms H Tranter
Director of Marketing: Mrs H Gething
Registrar: Mrs M McHarg
Senior School Secretary: Mrs E Ingram
Junior School Secretary: Mrs L McInerney
Development Assistant: Miss G Greco
School Counsellor: Miss W Jones (*part-time*)
SENCO: Ms C Dodsworth (*part-time*)
Nurses: Mrs C Cooper & Mrs T Franklin

At Channing everything is possible!

Channing School values the individuality of every girl and their unique system of Personalised Education ensures that girls will be understood, respected, supported and empowered.

Founded in 1885, Channing is a day school for girls aged 4 to 18, with 561 in the Senior School including the Sixth Form and 240 in the Junior School. The School has been a centre of academic excellence in North London for more than 130 years and its results consistently place it in the top 50 schools in the country. The stimulating and vibrant educational experience nurtures and sustains independent thinking, confidence and creativity. Channing upholds its Unitarian heritage and encourage girls to develop respect, tolerance and understanding of all faiths as well as individual and social responsibility.

The School is situated in Highgate Village, in attractive grounds, and offers a balanced education combining a traditional academic curriculum with modern educational developments. The complex of old and new buildings has been constantly adapted to provide up-to-date facilities, and there are strong links with the local community and local schools.

Girls usually take nine or ten subjects to GCSE and there is a wide range of A Level choices, including Ancient Greek, Further Maths, Government and Politics and Theatre Studies. The Junior School has its own building – the elegant family home of Sir Sydney Waterlow, one-time Lord Mayor of London – set in spacious gardens, and is notable for its happy and secure atmosphere.

Most girls learn at least one musical instrument and there are frequent concerts and theatrical productions. The school is fortunate in its gardens, open space and its facilities. The school is currently further investing in new facilities including a Sixth Form Centre with bespoke study facilities, which opened in December 2014, and a modern Performing Arts Theatre and Sports Centre.

Entry is by assessment at 4+, an examination and interview at 11+ and predicted GCSE results and interview at 16+. In addition, entry is subject to a satisfactory report from the applicant's current school. Entry assessments for occasional vacancies that arise for other years are age appropriate.

Further information can be obtained from the School prospectus and the Sixth Form prospectus available from the Registrar and the school website (www.channing.co.uk).

Scholarships and Bursaries. Academic Scholarships are offered at 11+. Academic awards are also offered to Sixth Form entrants, based on predicted GCSE grades and contribution to the school or as a result of interview and predicted GCSE grades for external candidates. Music Scholarships are offered at 11+ and 16+. These cover up to 50% of the tuition fees and lessons in school on one instrument for a year (renewable). Art Scholarships are offered to Sixth Form entrants based on submission of a portfolio of work. Bursaries are offered at 11+ and 16+. Please see the school website for further details.

Fees per term (2014–2015). Junior School (Reception to Year 6) £4,910; Senior School (Years 7–13) £5,340.

Charitable status. Channing House Incorporated is a Registered Charity, number 312766.

Cheltenham Ladies' College

Bayshill Road, Cheltenham, Glos GL50 3EP
Tel: 01242 520691
Fax: 01242 227882
email: enquiries@cheltladiescollege.org
website: www.cheltladiescollege.org

Chairman of the Council: Ms Libby Bassett, MA, ACA

Principal: Ms Eve Jardine-Young, MA

Vice-Principal: Mr Richard Dodds, BSc
Vice-Principal (*Academic*): Miss Jackie Adams, BSc

Director of Admissions: Dr Hilary Laver, BSc
Finance Director: Mr Jeffrey Speke, BSc, MPhil, ACA
Development Director: Ms Samantha Bagchi, BSc
Curriculum Director: Mr James Pothecary, MSci
Head of Pastoral Care: Miss Caroline Ralph, BEd
Head of Sixth Form College: Mr Jonathan Marchant, BA, MA
Head of Upper College: Dr David Gamblin, MChem, MRSC
Head of Lower College: Mrs Caroline Pellereau, BSc, MA

A College education gives girls the best possible opportunities to achieve their potential in both the academic and personal spheres.

Academic excellence forms the basis of College life, but just as important is the formation of character. We are committed to making our girls ready for their lives well beyond College. We recognise also that an education in the 21st century needs to inspire, prepare and equip children to sustain a lifetime of independently sought learning, and to give them the flexibility and resourcefulness to flourish in our rapidly changing world.

Girls are encouraged to embrace a broad range of co-curricular activities to suit their passions and interests, from the sporting to the intellectual and cultural. Added to this, a global outlook encourages girls to play a part in the wider world, creating young women who value the communities to which they belong. The curriculum promotes the values of mutual respect, integrity and courage, while nurturing intellectual curiosity, creativity, confidence and an enduring sense of belonging.

Girls are at the heart of all College does; we are ambitious for their futures, collectively and individually.

Numbers. Approximately 200 day and 650 boarding.

Fees per term (2014–2015). Day £7,069, Boarding £10,530. New Entrants to Sixth Form: Day £8,039, Boarding £11,862. Some extras are charged, e.g. music, riding.

Admission. Entry at 11+, 12+, 13+ and 16+ via the College's own examinations. An interview is also required for some entry points.

Pastoral Care. As a large school, College is able to offer extraordinary advantages in resources and choices, but we are also divided into small groups too, through the three academic Divisions (LC, UC & SFC), the Tutor groups and the House system. These create interlocking layers of pastoral care which enable every girl, the reserved as well as the extrovert, to find opportunities to lead a confident, fulfilled and enjoyable life at College. This network is backed up by an experienced and well-resourced Medical Centre based in College, an informed and skilled Catering department and the support of the College Chaplain.

Buildings. College is set in a 23-acre dispersed estate in the centre of Cheltenham. The single teaching site is built in a Gothic revival style which is complemented by more recent additions such as an Art and Technology block and the Parabola Arts Centre, which houses a 325-seat theatre. The day and boarding houses and a large sports complex are located in nearby residential areas within walking distance of the main site.

Houses. There are six Junior Boarding Houses and three Day Houses. All girls move into one of six houses at Sixth Form, which is an excellent stepping stone to university life. Day girls are fully integrated into all College activities, regularly joining boarders on weekend trips and expeditions.

Music, Drama and Dance. More than 800 individual music lessons take place each week, and there are generally five choirs and five orchestras running at any time during the academic year. Around 450 girls have individual drama lessons. In addition to the six productions put on each year, Sixth Form girls also take a piece to Edinburgh Fringe Festival. Dance and gymnastics are also available and very popular.

Sport and Extra-Curricular. College aims to encourage all girls to enjoy physical exercise and to take up an interest which will last throughout their lives. The main sports are hockey, lacrosse, netball, swimming, athletics and tennis, but College aims to provide what girls enjoy and about 40 different sports are offered, including rowing, cricket, football, squash and golf. There is a large and superbly equipped sports centre, including fitness suites, indoor swimming pool, tennis courts, netball pitches and synthetic astroturf pitches. More than 80 clubs and activities are on offer including art and design, chess, computer programming, dance, debating, drama, fencing, golf, journalism, keep fit and martial arts, model UN, music, natural science, philosophy, street dance, young engineers, young enterprise, environmental clubs and international clubs.

Scholarships and Bursaries. A number of Academic, Art, Day Girl, Drama, Music and Sport Scholarships and other awards are made annually for girls of all ages.

Applications for bursaries are welcome from girls whose parents require financial assistance in order to help their daughter join College.

Former Pupils (Guild). There are approximately 9,000 Guild members throughout the world, and they are a valued source of help to current girls, particularly in providing work experience and careers advice.

Charitable status. The Cheltenham Ladies' College is a Registered Charity, number 311722. It exists to provide a high standard of education for girls.

Cobham Hall

Brewers Road, Cobham, Kent DA12 3BL

Tel:	01474 823371
Fax:	01474 825906
email:	enquiries@cobhamhall.com
website:	www.cobhamhall.com
Twitter:	@CobhamHall

Founded 1962, Cobham Hall is the only all-girls Round Square school with both boarding and day pupils in the United Kingdom.

Governing Body:
Mr C Sykes (*Chairman*)

Mr A Tuckwell	Mr M Pennell
Mr C Balch	Mrs P Tebbitt
Mr M Frost	Mrs S McRitchie
Mrs L Ellis	Dr K O'Neill-Byrne
Mr J Dick	

Staff:

Headmaster: Mr P Mitchell, BSc Newcastle

Deputy Headmistress, Director of Studies: Dr S Coates-Smith, BSc, PhD London
Bursar: Mr D Standen, BSc Bradford
Assistant Headmistress and Head of Boarding & Sixth Form: Mrs W Barrett, BSc London
Assistant Head of Sixth Form: Miss A L Quinn, BA Durham
Senior Tutor for Middle School: Mrs S Carney, BEd Exeter
Senior Tutor for Lower School: Miss A Williams, BA Brasenose College Oxford

* *Head of Faculty*

English:
*Miss J Stevens, BA Hull
Miss F West, BA Reading
Miss J West, BA Oxford, MA Oxford

Mathematics:
*Mr P Gilchrist, BSc Leeds
Mrs W Barrett, BSc London
Mrs M Martin, BSc Loughborough
Mr M Pattison, BSc NE London, MA London

Science:
*Mr J Fryer, BSc Leicester, MA Kent (*Biology*)
Dr S Coates-Smith, BSc, PhD London (*Physics*)
Mr I Geldard, BSc Durham (*Chemistry*)
Mrs M Thompson, BSc London (*Biology*)
Mr P Hosford, BSc Thames Polytechnic (*Physics*)

Art:
*Mrs K Walsh, BA Kent Institute of Art & Design
Mrs A Lockheart, BA Illinois State University, PGCE London

Classics:
Miss A L Quinn, BA Hons Durham, PGCE King's College London

Drama:
Miss K Martin, BEd Queensland, MA RADA and King's College London
Mrs P Gough, BEd London

Economics:
Mr M Pattison, BSc NE London, MA London

Film Studies:
Miss F West, BA Reading

Geography:
Mrs R-M Turner, BSc Exeter

Mrs S Carney, BEd Exeter
Miss K Lambert, BSc Gloucestershire

History:
*Miss A Williams, BA Brasenose College Oxford
Mr N Bushell, BA York

IB Coordinator:
Ms P Clements, BA London

ICT:
Mr K Eyers, Teaching Diploma Canterbury Christ Church

Modern Foreign Languages:
Mrs B Tismer, BA London
Mrs E Wilkinson, BA London
Miss J Caro Quintana, Licenciada en Filologica Inglesa, Valencia, Spain
Mrs M Gutierrez, Licenciada en Lenguas Extranjeras Columbia, GTP Christ Church
Mrs X-W McArthur, BA China, PGCE Canterbury
Mrs T Russell, BA La Sorbonne, PGCE Lancaster

Music:
Ms P Clements, BA London
Mr M Haas, BA Michigan, MMus London

Physical Education:
Mrs K Hooper, BA Greenwich
Mrs S Carney, BEd Exeter
Miss K Lambert, BSc Gloucestershire

Religious Studies:
Miss A Williams, BA Brasenose College Oxford

PSHE:
Mrs D Rabot, BA Lancaster, OCR Dip SpLD
Mrs M Thompson, BSc London
Miss K Lambert, BSc Gloucestershire
Mrs R Hillier, BA Exeter
Mrs B Tismer, BA London
Mrs E Wilkinson, BA London

Psychology:
Mrs K-A Hickmott, BSc Middlesex

Theory of Knowledge:
Mrs P Gough, BEd London
Miss K Lambert, BSc Gloucestershire

EFL:
*Mrs C M von Bredow, BA Hons Birmingham, MA Exeter, PGCE Open University, RSA Dip TEFL

Student Support Department:
*Mrs D Rabot, BA Lancaster, OCR Dip SpLD
Mrs J Balson, BTEC Level 3 (*Teaching Assistant*)
Mrs R Hillier, BA Exeter

Careers:
Sixth Form: Mrs W Barrett, BSc London
Middle School: Mrs S Carney, BEd Exeter
Lower School: Miss A Williams, BA Brasenose College Oxford

Librarian:
Mrs A Jakso, BA Perth, BEd Tasmania

Laboratory Technicians:
Mrs B Reed
Mrs D Weaver

Art Technician:
Mrs L Hunt

Computer Support:
Mr D Wright (*Network Manager*)

Boarding Staff:
Mrs W Barrett, BSc London (*Head of Boarding*)
Mrs D Didzinskiene, BA Šiauliai Univ Lithuania, MS Vytautas Magnus Univ Lithuania (*Day Housemistress*)

Mrs M Gardner, RGN/RSCN (*Resident Nurse/ Housemistress*)
Miss L-E Paine, BA Loughborough (*Assistant Housemistress*)
Mrs D Jackson (*Housemistress*)
Mrs C Fenice (*Housemistress*)
Miss A Forte, LLB, MLitt Edinburgh (*Graduate Housemistress*)
Miss P Bates, BA Exeter (*Graduate Housemistress*)
Miss B Largier, BComm RMIT Univ, Melbourne, Australia (*Support Housemistress*)

Visiting Staff:
There are visiting staff for Cello, Clarinet, Double Bass, Drums, Flute, French Horn, Guitar, Keyboard, Oboe, Percussion, Piano, Recorder, Saxophone, Trombone, Trumpet, Tuba, Viola, Violin, Drama, Voice and Communication, Ballet, Self Defence and Tennis.

Administration:
Registrar: Mrs A Strong (*maternity leave*)
Assistant Registrar: Mrs J Shelley (*Acting Registrar*)
Marketing Assistant: Mrs J Booth
Marketing Assistant: Miss B Largier, BComm RMIT Univ, Melbourne, Australia
Receptionists: Mrs C Cheney, Mrs C Coster
Headmaster's PA: Mrs C Blackwell
Deputy & Assistant Heads PA: Mrs K Theobald
School Secretary: Mrs J Webster
Bursar's Secretary: Mrs J Brace
Accountant: Mr B Jelley, CPFA
Accounts Administrator: Mrs K Pinder, MAAT
Accounts Assistant: Mrs P Gambell
Estates Manager: Mr T Curran, ARICS
Maintenance Foreman: Mr J Best
Grounds Foreman: Mr T Gilbert

Cobham Hall is an international boarding and day school for 200 girls aged between 11 and 18. It is an IBO World School and offers International Baccalaureate Diploma or International Baccalaureate Diploma Courses in the Sixth Form.

Situation. The school is set in 150 acres of parkland. Situated in North Kent, close to the M25 and adjacent to the M2/A2. Thirty minutes from London, 60 minutes Heathrow, 45 minutes Gatwick and Stansted, 60 minutes Dover and Channel Tunnel, 10 minutes Ebbsfleet International Eurostar Railway Station (17 minutes St Pancras, 2 hours Paris).

School Buildings. This beautiful 16th century historic house was the former home of the Earls of Darnley. There are many modern buildings providing comfortable accommodation for study and relaxation. Brooke and Bligh Houses are separate buildings within the school grounds offering Sixth Form accommodation in single or twin study-bedrooms, many with en-suite facilities. Both Houses have common rooms with a kitchen and computer room.

Curriculum. An IBO World School, Cobham Hall offers the IB Diploma or IB Diploma Courses in the Sixth Form, with a wide range of subjects across Languages, Social and Experimental Sciences, Mathematics and the Arts.

Sixth Form. The Sixth Form numbers 60–70 students. Academic tutorial groups are spread across the two years and facilitate interaction between students. There are exceptional leadership opportunities, including election to the Student Leadership Team which plays a significant part in the management of the school. University destinations include University College London, Leeds, Manchester and Nottingham Trent, as well as Oxford and Cambridge.

Sporting and other activities. The school's main sports are Tennis, Swimming, Hockey, Athletics and Netball. There are seven hard tennis courts, six netball courts, a large, indoor multi-sports complex, including fitness centre, dance studio and a heated indoor swimming pool, which is in use throughout the year. Horse riding and golf may be taken as 'extras'. A wide variety of extra-curricular activities is available.

Careers. High-quality Careers Guidance and personal support is offered across Lower and Middle School and in the Sixth Form by school staff. Activities in partnership with external providers include Futurewise Profiling, Interview Training and an annual "Dragons Den" Day.

Round Square. The school is a member of this international group of schools, which subscribes to the philosophy of educationalist Dr Kurt Hahn. Annual conferences are attended by a school delegation including Sixth Formers. In recent years these have been held in Australia, America, India, South Africa and Germany. Younger students attend Round Square conferences in the UK and Europe. Students have the opportunity to visit other member schools on an exchange programme as well as visit other countries by taking part in service projects and relief work organised by the Round Square.

Health. Residential trained nursing staff providing 24-hour medical care.

All Terms. Girls have two Exeat Weekends and a Half Term holiday.

Admission. Admission is by the School's own entrance assessments which can be taken on Entrance Assessment Days in October (Lower/Middle School) and November (Sixth Form) or at a girl's own school. Girls normally enter the school between the ages of 11+ and 13+ and follow a course leading to GCSE level at the end of the fifth year and to the International Baccalaureate Diploma at the end of the seventh. Girls wishing to enter the Sixth Form should achieve at least five GCSE or equivalent examination passes at Grade C or above.

Scholarships. Scholarships are available for 11+, 13+ and Sixth Form entry.

11+: Academic, Art, Drama, Music and Sport.

Candidates for Academic Scholarships who demonstrate outstanding potential at Entrance Assessment Day will be invited back to sit a General Scholarship paper. Candidates for other scholarships will have an audition/assessment on Entrance Assessment Day.

13+: Academic, Art, Drama, Music and Sport.

Candidates for Academic Scholarships who demonstrate outstanding potential at Entrance Assessment Day will be invited back to sit scholarship papers in the Spring term. Candidates for other scholarships will have an audition/assessment on Entrance Assessment Day.

Sixth Form: Academic, Art, Music, Theatre and Physical Education.

Scholarship examinations and interviews usually take place in the second half of the Autumn term. Candidates sit entrance papers in English, Mathematics, and a scholarship paper in one other subject, which must be one which the candidate intends to study as part of her IB Diploma Programme. Candidates for other scholarships will have an audition/assessment.

All Scholarships are subject to annual review by the Headmaster.

For further information contact Admissions on 01474 823371.

Bursaries. Special bursaries are available for boarders from British Services families, diplomats and those families working for UK Charitable Trusts overseas and charitable bursaries for very able children from certain areas. For further information, contact Admissions.

Fees per term (2014–2015). Day girls: £5,156–£6,526. Boarders: £7,789–£9,817.

Old Girls' Association. Known as Elders. There is a representative committee which meets regularly in London or at the School. The Chairman is Mrs Tracey Balch, email: tracey.balch@virgin.net or elders@cobhamhall.com.

Charitable status. Cobham Hall is a Registered Charity, number 313650. It exists to provide high quality education for girls aged 11–18 years.

Cranford House School

Moulsford, Wallingford, Oxfordshire OX10 9HT

Tel:	01491 651218
Fax:	01491 652557
email:	office@cranfordhouse.net
website:	www.cranfordhouse.net
Twitter:	@CHSMoulsford

Board of Governors:
Mrs N Scott-Ely (*Chair*)
Mr G Cole (*Chair Finance Committee*)
Mrs H Gittins (*Education Committee, SEN*)
Mrs G Moody (*Chair of Bursaries Committee*)
Mrs L Kilroy (*Bursaries & Scholarships Committee, Legal*)
Mr Ml Windsor (*Education Committee*)
Mrs M FLower (*Safeguarding*)
Mr R Fisher
Mr P Tollett

Head: Dr James Raymond

Deputy Head: Mrs L Lawson, BA Hons, PGCE
Assistant Head (Academic): Mr C Corr, MA Cantab, PGCE
Assistant Head (Pastoral): Mrs P Hawson, CertEd
Head of Key Stage 1: Mrs N I'Anson, BEd Hons
Head of Key Stage 2: Miss H Stanley BA Hons; Mrs L Morris, MSc, BA Hons
Head of EYFS: Mrs K Knight, BA Hons, EYPS
Bursar: Mrs E Taylor, MA
Director of Admissions: Mrs J Simmons, NNEB

Senior School Teaching Staff:
Mr R Barker, BSc Hons, PGCE
Mrs N Butler, BA Hons, CAPES
Dr N Carr, MA, PhD, PGCE
Mrs D Carter, BA Hons, PGCE
Miss C Chaplin, BEd
Ms J Cirillo, MEd
Mr H Cooke, Cert Ed
Mr S Cowley, BA Hons, PGCE
Mrs S Eccles, BA
Mrs C Ellis, MA, MEd
Mrs L Gifford-Guy, BMus Hons
Mrs K Heard, BA Hons, PGCE
Miss A Holbrook, BSc Hons
Miss G Joyce, MA, PGCE
Mrs S Kirkwood, HDipEd
Mrs R Lanyon, MSc, PGCE
Mrs A Macmillan, PGCE MFL
Mrs J McCallum, MA, PGCE
Mrs E Mean, BA, PGCE
Mrs J Powell, BA Hons, Dip Adv Studies RAM
Mrs C Smythe, BA Hons, DipEd
Mrs S Stegeman, BSc, PGCE
Mrs F Stone, BA Hons, PGCE
Mrs A Tamblin, MA, PGCE
Mrs J Turner, BA Hons, PGCE
Mrs N Tiedeman, BA Hons, PGCE
Mrs A Watkins-Cooke, BEd
Miss D Whitbread, BA Hons, PGCE

Junior School Teaching Staff:
Miss V de Trense, BA Hons, PGCE
Mrs A Diamond, BEd Hons
Mrs B Graham, BSc Hons, PGCE
Mrs Y Goodier, MSc
Mrs A Greedy, BEd Hons
Mrs A Howell, BEd Hons
Mrs J Morris, BA Hons, PGCE
Miss C Oliver, BA Hons, PGCE
Mrs N O'Loughlin, BA Hons, PGCE

EYFS Staff:
Mrs S Pritchard, Montessori

Mrs C Bennett, BA Hons, EYPS
Mrs L Burrows, NVQ3
Miss R Carpenter, BA Hons, PGCE
Miss S Carrington, BA Hons, PGCE
Mrs E Davies
Mrs A John, NVQ3
Ms B Kwidzinska
Mrs Z Levy, NVQ3
Mrs M Longden, NVQ3
Mrs L Stockford, GNVQ3
Miss S Swift, NVQ3

Centre for Individual Development:
Miss D Smale, BA Hons, BSc Hons
Mrs A Wise, OCR Level 7 SpLD
Mrs V Little, BEd, RSA Dip SpLD
Mrs J Redley, BA Hons, PGCE

Support Staff:

Mrs K McKenzie	Mrs M Stoker
Mrs J Plant	Mrs S Sulley
Mrs W Rant	Mrs K Wynn
Mrs J Ryde	

Administrative Staff:
Mrs S Andresen-Guimaraes (*Music Department*)
Miss P Athorne (*ICT*)
Mrs K Chang (*Senior School*)
Mrs S Crowe (*Matron*)
Mrs J Cuffe (*Facilities*)
Ms K Frederick (*Bursar's Assistant*)
Mrs K French (*HR Assistant*)
Mrs J Goddard (*PA to the Headmistress*)
Mrs E Hayward (*Human Resources*)
Mrs M Parfitt (*Matron*)
Miss H Parkinson (*Receptionist*)
Mrs J Patel (*Receptionist/Office Administrator*)
Mr M Patrick (*Network Director*)
Miss S Treadwell (*Office Administrator/Compliance Officer*)
Mrs A Young (*Marketing Manager*)

Cranford House is a non-selective independent day school for girls aged 3–16 years and boys 3–7 years. It has an excellent reputation for providing its 400 pupils with a balanced, all-round education within a warmly nurturing environment. Set in over 14 acres of rural South Oxfordshire the small class sizes, close community and committed staff ensure each pupil is ably supported and challenged to achieve their full potential. The school was rated as 'Excellent' in all categories in its ISI Inspection of November 2014. The Early Years Foundation Stage was rated as 'Outstanding'.

The Early Years Foundation Stage (EYFS) encompasses Nursery and Reception, catering for boys and girls aged 3–5 years. Pupils benefit from a large, off-site Nursery School in a beautiful setting with plenty of green space for free-flow activities and learning. There are many links to the main school site for integration with Reception, swimming lessons and whole-school productions and activities.

The Junior School comprises Reception to Year 6. Juniors benefit from Senior School facilities and specialist subject teachers are increasingly used in a variety of disciplines. All pupils play competitive sports matches from Year 3 upwards. Lesson content is based on the National Curriculum, but supplemented to ensure pupils develop their own collaborative, reflective and reasoning skills and abilities. Results are excellent. Responsibility is offered at a young age through posts such as Junior Head Girl and team captains.

In the Senior School girls follow a common core curriculum and in Years 10 and 11 they study their chosen GCSE subjects, with the majority of girls sitting between nine and eleven subjects. The 2014 Sunday Times league tables rated Cranford House as sixth best school nationally for GCSE results within the small schools, no sixth form category. Girls belong to a House system and, on reaching Year 11, enjoy further positions of responsibility and privilege. The school has extensive recreational and games fields. In winter, hockey and netball are played, and in summer, tennis, rounders and athletics. Swimming takes place on site. Dramatic, musical and dance productions are an important aspect of school life.

In addition to the extensive range of enrichment activities offered throughout the school, all pupils have the opportunity to join educational trips and excursions. For Senior pupils, the Duke of Edinburgh's Award Scheme at Bronze and Silver level is offered in addition to The World Challenge. There are opportunities for overseas travel with the Senior Choir and through exchanges and the bi-annual ski and sports trips. School transport operates over a wide area.

Scholarships are offered for entry into the Senior School: Academic, Sport, Drama, Art and Music.

Our aim is to encourage pupils to achieve their full potential, becoming motivated, confident and happy individuals, recognising the importance of respect and support for others, but ready to seize life's opportunities.

Fees per term (2014–2015). £3,470–£5,020.

Charitable status. Cranford House School Trust Limited is a Registered Charity, number 280883.

Croydon High School
GDST

Old Farleigh Road, Selsdon, South Croydon, Surrey CR2 8YB

Tel:	020 8260 7500
Fax:	020 8657 5413
email:	info2@cry.gdst.net
	admissions@cry.gdst.net
website:	www.croydonhigh.gdst.net
Twitter:	@croydonhigh
Facebook:	/Croydon-High-School/125631170874682

Founded in 1874, the school's original site was in Wellesley Road Croydon but is now situated in the leafy suburb of Selsdon.

Croydon High School is part of the GDST (Girls' Day School Trust). The GDST is the leading network of independent girls' schools in the UK. As a charity that owns and runs 24 schools and two academies, it reinvests all its income in its schools. For further information about the Trust, see p. xxi or visit www.gdst.net.

Additional information about the school may be found on the school's website and a detailed prospectus is available from the school.

Chairman of Local Governors: Mr A Spiro

Head: Mrs D Leonard, BEd, MEd Birmingham

Deputy Head: Mrs P Clark, MA London

Assistant Head, Enrichment: Mrs I Bennett, BEd Leeds Met

Assistant Head, Sixth Form: Mrs H Mester, BA Nottingham

Assistant Head, Curriculum: Mr M Pickering, BA, MSc Manchester

Head of Junior School: Mrs S Bradshaw, BA Bristol

School Business Manager: Mrs A Hinkson, MBA Kingston

For over 140 years, Croydon High School has provided a superb all-round education for girls, around the Croydon area and further afield. The school combines tradition with a forward-looking, supportive and nurturing atmosphere where every girl is encouraged and supported to achieve her personal best. The school welcomes girls from a wide range of backgrounds; excellent pastoral care ensures that each girl is known as an individual.

Croydon High offers girls a wide range of extra-curricular opportunities ensuring that each can find something she enjoys. The school regularly achieves local, regional and national success in Sport; its Arts are also outstanding, with a vibrant Music department offering opportunities to musicians at varying ability levels to develop their talents in all musical genres. Termly productions involve students across all year groups and young artists are motivated and inspired to develop their creative talents in different media.

The school aims to develop confident young women with wide ranging interests and abilities who have also achieved excellent academic results. Emphasis is placed on ensuring that girls are happy and fulfilled in whatever career path they choose for the future, be this as a business high flyer or a contented homemaker.

Number of Pupils. Senior School (aged 11–18): 380 girls (including 110 in the Sixth Form). Junior School (aged 3–11): 215 girls (including 17 in the Nursery).

Facilities. The purpose-built school has outstanding facilities; including specialist music rooms, a drama studio, a language laboratory, 5 computer suites, 10 science laboratories, design technology room and a recently refurbished sports block incorporating sports hall, gym, indoor swimming pool, fitness room and dance studio. The school is surrounded by spacious playing fields with netball/tennis courts, athletics track and an all-weather hockey pitch.

The Junior School, which has its own Nursery, is in an adjacent building on the same site, sharing many of the excellent facilities.

The Sixth Form have their own suite of rooms, including a common room and quiet study area, adjacent to the school library.

Curriculum. Most girls take 10 GCSE subjects with the aim of providing a broad and balanced core curriculum which keeps career choices open. Over 23 subjects are offered at AS and A Level including Government & Politics, Economics, Latin and Physical Education. Almost all girls proceed to University, and, each year, a number are offered places at Oxbridge.

Admission. A whole school Open Day is held annually in October and a Sixth Form Open Evening in November. An Open Evening is held in the Summer Term. Tours and private visits are welcome and can be arranged at any time through the Admissions Registrar.

The school admits girls to the Junior School on the basis of either individual assessment (younger girls) or written tests (girls of 7+ and above). Selection procedures are held early in January for Juniors and assessments for Infants are held during the Autumn and Spring Terms for entry in the following September.

For entrance to the Senior School in Year 7, the school holds Entrance Tests in November for entry in the following September. All applicants are interviewed by the Headmistress and references are taken up.

Entrance Tests are held in January for Year 9 entry in the following September.

For the Sixth Form, the school interviews applicants and requests reports from the present school. A Sixth Form Open Evening is held in November and Scholarship and Bursary applicants sit an examination later that month.

Further details on the admissions process are available on the website or via the Registrar, admissions@cry.gdst.net.

Fees per term (2014–2015). Senior School £4,633–£4,818, Junior School £3,785, Nursery £2,923.

Scholarships and Bursaries. Following the ending of the Government Assisted Places Scheme, the GDST has made available to the school a number of scholarships and bursaries.

Academic scholarships are available for entry at 11+ or to the Sixth Form. Music, art & design, drama and sports scholarships are also available at 11+ and 16+.

For entrance at Year 9, the school offers two Academic Plus scholarships to applicants joining from other schools, who have chosen to be assessed academically and in one of the following subjects; art, music, drama or sport.

Bursaries are means tested and are intended to ensure that the school remains accessible to bright girls who could not otherwise benefit from the education we offer. These are available to Senior School girls only.

The school has a vibrant and active Old Girls Network – The Ivy Link – which supports the school in numerous ways, including offering careers and mentoring connections.

Charitable status. Croydon High School is part of The Girls' Day School Trust, which is a Registered Charity, number 306983.

Dame Allan's Girls' School

Fenham, Newcastle-upon-Tyne NE4 9YJ

Tel:	0191 275 1500 (School); 0191 274 5910 (Bursar)
Fax:	0191 275 1502 (School); 0191 275 1501 (Bursar)
email:	enquiries@dameallans.co.uk
website:	www.dameallans.co.uk
Twitter:	@dameallans
Facebook:	/Dame-Allans-Schools

The School was founded in 1705 by Dame Eleanor Allan and in 1935 was moved to Fenham on a site of 13 acres.

Governors:
Chairman: Mr E Ward
Vice-Chairman: Mr B W Adcock

Dr D Bevitt	Prof R Plummer
Mrs K Bruce	Mrs P Robinson
Prof E Cross	Mrs M E Slater
Mr M Davison	Mr A M Stanley
Mrs M Nicholson	Mr D Tait Walker

Ex officio:
The Lord Mayor of Newcastle upon Tyne
The Dean of Newcastle
The Vicar of the Parish of St John

Clerk to the Governors and Bursar: Mrs M Lant

Principal: **J R Hind**, MA Downing College Cambridge, MEd Newcastle, PhD Durham

Vice-Principal (Pastoral): N Shaw, BSc Liverpool
Vice Principal (Academic): A Hopper, BA Merton College Oxford
Head of Girls (Years 7–11): E C Fiddaman, BA Hertford College Oxford
Head of Sixth Form: D C Henry, BSc Heriot-Watt, FIMLS

Z Allonby, BA Glasgow School of Art
L M Bell, BA Sunderland
A Brown, BA Newcastle
C Cedeyn, CertEd
C Charlton, BA Newcastle
L Clough, CertEd IM Marsh College of PEd
H Dresser, BA Liverpool
S J Dunne, MSc Sunderland
S Dutton, CertEd Leeds
K Fraser, BSc, PhD Newcastle
A H Gillis, BSc, MSc, PhD Durham
D Gillott, BSc Hull

J Golding, BA Northumbria
B Green, LLB Warwick
P Halliwell, BEd Liverpool
K F Heatherington, BA Newcastle
M Hill, BSc Leicester
A Lill, BSc Northumbria
S McDougall, BSc Sheffield Hallam
C McFall, BSc Hull
G M Maughan, BEd Homerton College Cambridge
C E D Morgan, BA Newcastle
G S Mundy, MA Newnham College Cambridge
R Ogg, BA Durham
C Parker, MBA Sunderland
P Pulford, BA Newcastle
M Pyburn, BSc Manchester
J M Raines, BA Lancashire
H Ratter, BA Northumbria
F Ripley, BSc Newcastle
J Strong, MA Queens' College Cambridge
K Tew, BSc Northumbria
R Waters, BA Leeds
V Waugh, BA Durham, MA Durham
S A Winton de Lezcano, BSc Nottingham, MSc Imperial
   College London

Junior School:
Head: A J Edge, MA St Andrews
Deputy Head: D M Farren, BA Warwick
A Bodfield, BTEC
A Brown, BSc Northumbria
K Carruthers, BSc Loughborough
J Dennis, BTEC
K Ellis, BA Liverpool
T E Fox, Cert Early Years
A L Jackson, LLB Sheffield
C Henderson, BA Manchester
J Loraine, BEd Newcastle
B Metcalf, BSc York
J Needham, BA Durham
R Johnson, BA Northumbria
C Peacock, BA York St John
P Pollock, CertEd Leeds
B Shaw, BA Newcastle
R Watson, BA Leeds
G Williams, BA Ripon & York St John

There are approximately 350 girls in the School which has a three-form entry at 11+. With the Boys' School, which is in the same building, it shares a mixed Sixth Form and a mixed Junior School for pupils aged 3–11.

The Main School follows the normal range of subjects, leading to examination at GCSE. German is introduced in Year 8 and Spanish is offered in Year 9.

Most girls stay on into the Sixth Form and from there normally go on to Higher Education.

Buildings. In recent years, developments have included additional classrooms, a new Library, Computer Resource Centre, Technology Centre, ICT network, a new Sixth Form Centre, and a Drama and Dance Studio. The Schools opened a new, state-of-the-art junior school in September 2012.

School Societies. The current list includes: outdoor pursuits (including Duke of Edinburgh's Award scheme and our own in-house expedition award for younger pupils), choirs, Ceilidh Band, drama, computing, art, Christian Fellowship, chess, Cookery Club, history, science, electronics, mathematics, dance, public speaking and debating.

Pastoral. Each girl is placed in the care of a Form teacher who oversees her progress and development. In the Sixth Form she has a Tutor who is responsible for both academic and pastoral care.

Careers. There is a structured programme, beginning in Year 9, with a contribution from Connexions.

Sixth Form. In 1989 the Sixth Form was merged with that of our brother School, giving both Schools the rare con-

stitution of single-sex education (11–16) with a co-educational Sixth Form. The Head of Sixth Form is Mr D C Henry who will welcome enquiries concerning admission.

Physical Education. Hockey, netball, tennis, gymnastics, athletics, squash, swimming, trampolining and volleyball. The playing fields adjoin the school. Instruction in swimming is given at a local pool. Dance is particularly popular.

Admission. Governors' Entrance Scholarships are awarded on the results of the Entrance Examinations held annually in the Spring Term at all ages from 11+ to 13+. Bursaries are available to pupils aged 8 and over on entry. Assessments for entry to the junior school take place throughout the year.

Fees per term (2014–2015). Senior School £3,756; Junior School £2,309–£3,025.

Dame Allan's Allanians Society. President: Mr B Sanderson, c/o Dame Allan's Schools.

Charitable status. Dame Allan's Schools is a Registered Charity, number 1084965. It exists to provide education for children.

Derby High School

Hillsway, Littleover, Derby DE23 3DT
Tel: 01332 514267
Fax: 01332 516085
email: headsecretary@derbyhigh.derby.sch.uk
website: www.derbyhigh.derby.sch.uk
Twitter: @derbyhighschool

Derby High School is an independent day school conveniently situated in the Derby suburb of Littleover which educates boys and girls aged 3 to 11 and girls only from 11 to 18.

Academically, the school regularly achieves the best results in the county, however a Derby High education is about much more than academic results. Whether your child is musical, creative, analytical or sporty, at Derby High each student's individual strengths are identified to help them achieve their potential in a fun, friendly and supportive atmosphere.

Governors and Foundation Governors:
Chairman: Dr R Faleiro
Mr B Bailey
Ms H Barton
Mrs J Bullivant
Dr V Churchhouse
Mrs S Clover
[1]Mr M R Hall, DL, Hon D Univ, FCA, FCMA, FCT
Mrs R Hughes, BA, ACIB
[1]Mr H M L Jenkins, DM, FRCOG
Mrs F Lazenby
[1]Mrs M Moore
Mr T Ousley
Mrs R Williams

[1] *Foundation Governor*

Head: Mrs D Gould, BA Comb Hons Birmingham, PGCE Birmingham, NPQH

Deputy Head: Mrs J Sample, BSc Hons Durham, PGCE Cambridge

Head of Sixth Form & Assistant Head: Mr A Lee, BA Hons Salford, PGCE Leicester

Assistant Head: Miss A Jordan, BA Hons Wolverhampton, PGCE Newcastle

Assistant Head: Mr A Maddox, MMath Oxford, PGCE Oxford, PGDES Oxford

Chaplain: The Reverend R Barrett, MA Exeter, BA Hons Exeter, PGCE Exeter

Bursar: Mrs M Mitchell

* *Head of Department*

Miss A Allum, BSc Hons Brunel, PGCE Brunel (*Physical Education*)

Mrs A Arthey, BA Comb Hons Birmingham, PGCE Nottingham (*French, *Careers*)

Mrs M Aspinall, BA Hons Durham, PGCE Durham (**Modern Languages*)

Mrs K Aydi, BSc Aberdeen, PGCE Bath (**Biology*)

Mrs J Bennion, BA Sheffield Hallam (*Art*)

Miss K Bishop, BA Hons Manchester Metropolitan (*Physical Education*)

Mrs A Bodycombe, BA Hons Central St Martin's College of Art & Design, MA Coventry, PGCE OU (*Art, Design Technology*)

Mrs A Brown, BA NSW, BEd Adelaide, DipEd Adelaide, CGeog (**Geography*)

Mrs S Bussey, BSc Econ Hons Aberystwyth (*Information Resources Manager*)

Mrs C M Cleave, BSc Exeter, PGCE Cambridge (**Physics*)

Mr D Connell, MBA Derby, PGCE Staffordshire, ACIB (*Economics and Business and *Careers*)

Mr R Dodson, MEng Hons Bristol (**Mathematics*)

Mrs N Driver, BEd Hons Lancaster (**Religious Education, PSHE, Head of Years 7–9*)

Mrs C Eales, CertEd Birmingham (*Mathematics*)

Mrs J Fraser, BSc Hons Derby, PGCE Nottingham Trent (*Psychology*)

Mrs S Goodman, BSc Hons Sheffield, PGCE Sheffield (*Physical Education, Deputy Head Sixth Form*)

Dr H Gould, BSc UMIST, MSc Warwick, PhD Warwick, PGCE Manchester (*Physics*)

Mrs L Hamblett, BSc London, PGCE Derby (*Mathematics and DofE Award*)

Mrs J Hancock, BEd Hons Manchester Metropolitan (**Physical Education*)

Mrs K Hewitt, BSc Hons Birmingham, PGCE Leeds (*Biology, SENCO*)

Mrs S Hilton, BA Hons Brighton, PGCE Brighton (**Business & *ICT*)

Mrs L Hough, BSc Hons Brunel, CertEd (**Design Technology, Young Enterprise*)

Mrs R Johnson, BSc Hons Derby, PGCE Manchester Metropolitan (*Geography*)

Miss A Jordan, BA Hons Wolverhampton, PGCE Newcastle (*History, Assistant Head*)

Mrs S Jukes, BA Hons, PGCE (*Drama*)

Miss S Kelliher, BA Hons Dublin, PGCE Birmingham (*German*)

Mrs R Lesley, BMus Hons Birmingham, PGCE Birmingham, LTCL

Miss Z Livingstone, BA Hons Portsmouth, PGCE Liverpool (*Spanish*)

Mr A Maddox, MMath Oxford, PGCE Oxford, PGDES Oxford (*Mathematics, Assistant Head*)

Mrs M Martinez Hernandez, BA Salamanca, PGCE Madrid (*Spanish*)

Mrs S Martin-Smith, HND Swansea, BA Hons Swansea, PGCE Swansea (**Art*)

Dr S Mathews, BA Hons Sheffield Hallam, MSc Manchester, PhD Manchester (**History*)

Mrs C McDonald, BSc Manchester, PGCE Manchester (**Home Economics*)

Dr J Myers, BSc York, PGCE Leics, PhD Edinburgh (*Chemistry*)

Dr J A Nelmes, BSc Hons London, PGCE Nottingham, PhD Loughborough (*Physics and Chemistry*)

Mrs J A Priestnall, BSc Hons Hatfield, PGCE Leicester (*Biology*)

Mrs C E Read, BA Hons Reading, PGCE London (*English, *General Studies*)

Miss M Render, BA Hons Hull, PGCE Hull (*English*)

Miss C V Riley, BSc Hons Leeds, PGCE Leeds (**Chemistry, Head of Years 10 & 11, DofE Award*)

Mrs M Roe, BA Hons Nottingham (*Geography, DofE Award*)

Mrs L Seymour, BA Hons, PGCE Notts (*German*)

Mrs D G Stringer, BEd Hons Cardiff, DipEdMan Nottingham (*Home Economics*)

Mrs F Supran, BA Hons Manchester, PGCE Oxford, Cert TEFLA Oxford Brookes (*English and *Drama*)

Mr E Temple, MusB Hons Manchester, PGCE Manchester (**Director of Music*)

Mrs J Webster, MA Hons Cambridge (**English & Psychology*)

Mr S Williams, BSc Hons Birmingham, PGCE Nottingham (*Mathematics*)

Music:

Mr R Abraham MMus Birmingham Conservatoire (*Drums and Percussion*)

Mrs C A Barker, CertEd Manchester, CT ABRSM, Dip ABRSM (*Flute and Fife*)

Mrs V Cunningham, BA Hons (*Oboe and Clarinet*)

Mrs G Feeney, BSc Hons, CT ABRSM (*Piano*)

Mr A Gatford (*Guitar*)

Mrs D Gould, CertEd (*Violin, Viola*)

Mrs A Hardy, GBSM, ABSM, Dip Orchestral Studies Goldsmiths (*Flute*)

Mrs M Marubbi, MA, BA Hons, ALCMTD (*Piano*)

Mr A Rutter, BMus Huddersfield, MA Huddersfield (*Brass*)

Miss S Watts, BMus Hons, LRAM (*Clarinet and Saxophone*)

Primary School:

Head of Primary: Mrs M Hannaford, BEd Hons Derby, MA Ed OU, NPQH

Mrs K Hopkinson, BEd Hons Derby (*Primary Assistant Head*)

Miss L Pitt, BA PrimEd Birmingham (*Primary Assistant Head*)

Mrs K M E Carey, BEd Liverpool Chester College (*Primary Pastoral Coordinator*)

Miss L Baker, BA Hons Derby, PGCE Derby

Mr T De Vies, BA Hons Leicester, PGCE Nottingham Trent

Mrs S Evans-Bolger, BA Hons QTS, MA Ed BG University College Lincoln

Mr C Horne, BEd Primary Hons Derby

Miss H Law, BA Hons Nottingham

Mrs L Soutar, BA Hons Nottingham, PGCE Music Leeds

Mrs J Swainston, BEd Hons Sheffield

Dr A Worthington, PhD Nottingham, BSc Hons Lancaster, PGCE Nottingham Trent

Miss M Allen, BA Hons Primary Ed Birmingham City

Mrs M Blount, BEd Hons Derby

Mrs J Bowden, BA Ed Primary Reading

Mrs C Courtney-Hale, BA Ed Hons Wales, MA Ed Loughborough

Mrs A Dowell, BSc Hons, QTS Newman Coll of HE

Miss D Hyland, BA Hons Birmingham, PGCE Birmingham

Miss R Ford, BA Hons Leeds, PGCE Primary Bradford

Mrs J Foster, BEd Hons Derby

Miss L Pitt, BA PrimEd Birmingham

Mrs A Trindell, BSc Hons QTS BG University College Lincoln

Primary Admissions: Mrs K Tudor

Senior Admissions: Miss S Callaghan, BA Hons Warwick

There are 542 pupils in school of whom 299 are in the Senior School, which is for girls only, and 243 are in the Juniors and Kindergarten which are both co-educational.

The Primary Department follows an enhanced national curriculum course. KS1 and KS2 take internal assessments. ASPECTS are used for pre-school and INCAS for Year 5. There is considerable enrichment in the curriculum with a wide variety of sports, music, drama and other activities available both within the curriculum and at club time.

The Senior School offers courses in Art and Design, Biology, Chemistry, Design Technology, Drama, Economics & Business, English Language and Literature, French, General Studies, Geography, German, History, Home Economics, ICT, Mathematics, Further Maths, Music, Physical Education, Psychology, Physics, Religious Studies, Spanish and Theatre Studies. The curriculum is enhanced by activities such as Young Enterprise, The Duke of Edinburgh's Award Scheme, World Challenge and the charitable work undertaken in Ethiopia. Sports, drama and music are also strengths, with pupils gaining recognition at county and national level.

The main points of entrance are at 11+ and 16+ where Scholarships and Assisted Places are available. Entrance is by examination and interview. Entrance at other ages is by assessment and takes place by arrangement.

The school has an active Christian ethos and broadly follows the teaching of the Church of England, but pupils of all faiths are welcomed and valued.

Examinations. Pupils are entered for ASPECTS, INCAS, GCSE and GCE AS and A Level examinations, some Sixth Form pupils take the EPQ. The school takes part in INCAS and MidYIS testing. Short course GCSE ICT is taken by all pupils. Many pupils have individual music lessons and take music examinations through the Associated Board of the RCM. LAMDA is offered in the Junior School, leading to examinations. The Young Enterprise examination may be taken by Company members.

Games. Hockey, Netball, Rounders, Tennis, Swimming, Athletics, Short Tennis, Tag Rugby, Football and Trampolining are major sports.

Fees per term (2014–2015). £2,550–£3,760.

Charitable status. Derby High School Trust Limited is a Registered Charity, number 1007348. It exists to provide education for children.

Dodderhill School

Droitwich Spa, Worcestershire WR9 0BE

Tel: 01905 778290
Fax: 01905 790623
email: enquiries@dodderhill.co.uk
website: www.dodderhill.co.uk

Founded in 1945, Dodderhill School is an independent day school for girls from 3–16 years and boys from 3–7 years.

Governors:

Mr D Allchin
Mrs L Grimer
Mrs W Haines
Mrs J Hardy
Mrs J E Lowe

Mr P Martin
Mr A Robinson (*Chairman*)
Mrs R J Shearburn
Mrs K Wormington

Headmistress: Mrs C Mawston, BA Hons

Academic Staff:

Mrs J Allen Griffiths, BA Hons
Mrs J Askew, BEd Hons
Mrs E R Barnett, BA Hons

Mrs A Benigno-Thomas, BA Hons
Miss S Berwick, BA Hons
Mrs R Bradley, BA Hons

Mrs A Cartwright, BSc Hons
Miss L Crane, BA Hons
Mr P D Cross, BSc
Mrs M Finnikin, BA Hons
Mrs H R Forecast, BEd Hons
Mrs C German, BA Hons
Mrs R Hatfield, BA Hons
Mrs S C Johnson, MEng Hons

Mrs S G R Loveday-Fuller, BEd Hons
Mrs A L Macrae, BA Hons
Mrs T Palmeri, BEd Hons
Mrs C E Radcliffe, BSc Hons
Mrs J Randell, BA Hons
Mrs S Richards, BSc Hons
Mr J Rudge, BSc Hons
Mrs C A Salter, BSc Hons
Mrs C Vinson, BMus Hons
Miss C Williams, BA Hons

Administrative Staff:
Bursar: Mrs P A Lewis
Headmistress's PA: Mrs Y Wood
Junior and Bursar's Secretary: Mrs A Lane
School Secretary: Mrs R Brown
ICT Technician: Mr C A Payne
Matron: Mrs J Cameron-Price

Introduction. Dodderhill School is a non-denominational day school administered by a Board of Governors. The school provides a seamless education for girls aged 3 to 16 years and welcomes boys from 3 to 7 years. Small classes and experienced, motivated staff mean that pupils can achieve their academic and personal potential. Excellent pastoral care and a friendly, family atmosphere help pupils to build the confidence, self-esteem and maturity that will help them to continue to achieve in the world of post-16 and higher education.

Location. The school is set in its own grounds on the outskirts of Droitwich Spa and only minutes from the M5/M42 interchange. It serves families from Droitwich Spa, Bromsgrove and a wide area of North Worcestershire. Minibus transport is provided between school and Droitwich Spa station and many pupils take advantage of the excellent local rail network.

Facilities. A superbly designed foundation stage and junior block incorporating a spacious multi-purpose school hall complements the newly refurbished original Georgian buildings. An ongoing development programme instituted by the governors in 1998, included in March 2004 an exciting new Nursery providing babies and toddlers (6 weeks to 3 years) with the same warm, happy, caring and family friendly atmosphere enjoyed throughout the school. In 2008 a new building was opened providing further classroom accommodation and a new food technology room. During 2009 a second ICT room for use by teaching staff was completed and in October the redesigned and enlarged outside area for the Early Years Foundation Stage was opened. In 2009 and 2010 science laboratories were refurbished to provide the latest up-to-date facilities for girls in Years 4–11. In 2013 the old gymnasium was converted to a Performing Arts Centre.

Curriculum and Teaching. From the Early Years until Year 3 emphasis is on literacy and numeracy and children are class taught with specialist input in ICT, French, Music, PE and, from Year 3, DT. From Year 4 all subjects are specialist taught and in Years 5 and 6 increasing use is made of senior facilities to ease transition and enhance learning opportunities. In Years 7, 8 and 9 in addition to the core subjects of English, mathematics, science, RE and PE, all girls learn French, German, Spanish, geography, history, classic civilisation, philosophy, art, catering, ICT, music and textiles. For GCSE all girls take English, mathematics, science, RE, a modern foreign language, history or geography and two additional subjects from a choice of a second foreign language, a second humanity and the creative subjects. Class sizes are small, expectations are high, teachers are well qualified and experienced and the individual is paramount. Results are excellent. Dodderhill is regularly at or near the top of the Government GCSE performance tables for Worcestershire. In 2011 the School topped the tables for the third successive year.

Extra-Curricular Activities. The school offers a stimulating and diverse range of extra-curricular opportunities. Creative arts, music, outdoor activities, including the Duke of Edinburgh's Award and sport are all catered for. Pre-school care is available at no charge from 8.00 am. There is an after-school club until 6 pm and a Holiday Club in the long holidays – a charge is made for these services.

Admissions and Scholarships. Formal entrance examinations are held in January each year for entry at 9+, 11+ and 13+. Two 11+ academic scholarships and an 11+ music scholarship are available at this time. Children may transfer from other schools at any time during the year and admission is then by taster day, examination and school reference. Entrance for younger children is by taster day and individual assessment.

Bursaries. The Board of Governors has set up a Bursarial Fund to widen access to Dodderhill by providing assistance to girls entering the school at Year 5 or later.

Fees per term (2014–2015). Tuition fees are from £2,420 in Kindergarten to £3,350 in the senior school, inclusive of lunches and textbooks. There is a 5% reduction for siblings.

Charitable status. Dodderhill School is a Registered Charity, number 527599. It exists to provide education for girls and boys.

Durham High School for Girls

Farewell Hall, Durham DH1 3TB
Tel: 0191 384 3226
Fax: 0191 386 7381
email: enquiries@dhsfg.org.uk
website: www.dhsfg.org.uk

Governors:
Mrs M Cummings, BA (*Chairman*)
Mr S Cheffings (*Vice Chairman*)
Miss L Clark, BEd, MA
Revd Dr H Cleugh
Mr K Delanoy, FCCA
Dr C English
Miss M Green
Mrs D Hedley, MB BS, MRCP, MRCGP, DCH
Captain M Hill
Revd P Kashouris
Mr A Lake
Mrs G Prescott, BVM&S, MRCVS
Mr A Richchester, MBE, FCA

Headmistress: Mrs L Renwick, BEd, NPQH

First Deputy Head: Mrs I Woodland, MA Cantab (*Geography*)

Deputy Head: Miss A Richmond, BSc, MA, NPQH (*Mathematics*)

Assistant Head: Mrs L Ibbott, BA Cardiff (*English; Marketing and Development*)

Head of Junior House: Mrs K Anderson, BEd Neville's Cross

Bursar: Mr D Payne, BSc London, ACA

Senior House:
Mrs C Ackerley, BA Dunelm (*Psychology*)
Dr N Alvey, MPhys, PhD Kent (*Physics*)
Mrs T S Bickerdike, BSc Dunelm (*Mathematics*)
Mrs M I Brown, BA Hull, MSc LSE (*History*)
Mrs P G Clarke, BSc Cork (*Physics, PSHE, Citizenship*)
Miss G Colon, BA Hons London (*Modern Languages*)
Mrs J Coxon, BEd Liverpool (*Physical Education*)

Mrs C I Creasey, BA Dunelm (*Geography*)
Mrs V M Dyson, BA Dunelm (*LTCL, Music*)
Mrs S A Egglestone, BEd Dunelm (*ICT*)
Mrs D L Elliott, BSc Dunelm (*Biology*)
Mrs J Flavell, MA Cambridge (*Chemistry*)
Mrs C Gamble, BA, MA Cambridge (*Mathematics*)
Mrs E Gentry, BSc St Andrews (*Science*)
Dr S Grant, BSc Newcastle (*Chemistry*)
Dr L Hardy, BA, PhD, PGCE, LTCL (*Flute*)
Mrs S Harrison, BA Hons Dunelm (*Geography*)
Mrs A Hawkins, BA London (*English, Sociology*)
Mr P Hitchcock, BA Sunderland (*Art*)
Mrs M Kenyon, BSc York (*Chemistry*)
Mrs A Lee, BA Manchester (*Learning Support*)
Mrs J Lonsdale, BA, MA Leeds (*Drama*)
Mr T Lonsdale, BA Leicester (*French, German*)
Mrs S May, BEd Cheltenham and Gloucester (*Physical Education*)
Mrs L Middleton, BA Dunelm (*Religious Studies*)
Mr J Neeson, MA Manchester (*Art*)
Mrs J Newby, BSc Warwick (*Biology*)
Mrs H O'Neill, BA Hons Dunelm (*Modern Languages*)
Mr J Priest, MSc Bath (*Mathematics*)
Mrs D Rabot, MA Ed Sunderland (*ICT*)
Mr A Randall, BA Dunelm, classics
Mrs K Ridley, BSc Liverpool, Careers Coordinator
Mrs J V Slane, BSc Surrey (*Physical Education*)
Mr D Smith, MA Oxon, CertTh York (*History*)
Miss J Sneddon, BA Hons, MA Edinburgh (*Art Textiles*)
Mrs R Stephenson, BA Newcastle (*English*)
Mrs M Thomas, MA St Andrews (*French, German*)
Miss L Thompson, MA Newcastle, Physical Education
Ms D Todd, BA Hons Sunderland (*English*)
Mrs J Tomlinson, BSc Newcastle (*Biology*)
Mrs V Turnbull, BA Newcastle (*Business Studies and Economics*)
Revd B Vallis, BA Cambridge, BA Theology Dunelm (*Chaplain and Religious Studies*)
Mrs D Woodman, BA Newcastle (*Classics*)

Junior House:
Mr P Allaker, BA Hons Dunelm
Mrs E Brothers, BSc Sheffield (*Deputy Head*)
Mr R Dellar, MSc Birmingham
Mrs J Dilley, CertEd Sussex
Mrs P Everett, BEd Hons Cambridge
Mrs K A Hall, BA Central Lancashire
Mrs C M Hopper, BA Nottingham
Mrs L Mock, BA Dunelm
Miss L Pickering, BA Dunelm
Miss S Rose, BSc Wales, MSc London, MA Durham
Mr G Wright, BA Hons Sunderland

Junior House Support Staff:
Mrs A Maddison, NNEB Durham
Mrs C Gorman
Mrs M Harrison
Mrs J Tipple (*After School Care*)

Visiting Staff:
Miss V Bojkova, Diplomas in Conducting & Piano Performance (*Singing and Piano*)
Mr Bovill (*Drum Kit and Percussion*)
Miss S Innes, BMus, LRAM (*Violin & Viola*)
Mr P Judson (*Bassoon*)
Mrs R Barton-Gray (*Cello*)
Mrs J Rousseau (*Oboe*)
Mr G Ritson, GRNCM, PPRNCM (*Brass*)
Miss R J Shuttler, BA, MMus, LTCL (*Piano*)
Miss C Smith, BA, FRSA (*Clarinet & Saxophone*)
Miss B Walker (*Violin*)
Mrs E Walker, BSc Newcastle, MSc Sheffield (*Educational Psychologist*)
Mrs D Meki-smith, LAMDA
Ms H Saunders (*School Counsellor*)

Administrative Staff:
Head's PA: Mrs A Thompson
Administrator:
Marketing/Publicity Secretary: Mrs A Wright
Librarian: Mrs J Durcan, ALA
Assistant Bursar: Mr B Craig
Accountant: Mrs K Atkinson
ICT Systems Manager: Mr J Kerton
ICT Technician: Mr P Cass
Reception: Mrs P Steele, Mrs C Gillham
Catering Manager: Mrs A Hibbart
Laboratory Manager: Mrs M A Bartley, BSc Open
University
Laboratory Technician: Mrs Gemski, BA Robert Gordon
Laboratory Assistants: Miss J Cummings, Mrs L Deveaux-
Robinson, Miss L Tinnion
Performing Arts/Art Technician: Mr N Raine, BSc
Newcastle, BEd Sunderland
Caretaker: Mr K Riding
Assistant Caretakers: Mr D Wilson, Mr P Tennant, Mr P
Davis

Durham High School for Girls aims to create, within
the context of a Christian ethos, a secure, happy and friendly
environment within which pupils can develop personal and
social skills, strive for excellence in academic work and
achieve their full potential in all aspects of school life.

- Highly qualified, specialist staff.
- Excellent examination results.
- Continuity of education from 3 to 18 years.
- Entry at 3, 4, 7, 10, 11 and 16.
- Superb modern facilities include state-of-the-art Science/
ICT/Library Block and Performing Arts Suite.
- Academic, Music, Performing Arts, Art, Drama and
Sports Scholarships.
- Financial assistance available at all stages.

Number on roll. 486 day pupils.

Age range. Seniors 11–18; Juniors 7–11; Infants 4–7;
Nursery from age 3.

Entry requirements. Assessment, formal testing and
interview if age is applicable. Sixth form entry is dependent
on the level of achievement at GCSE.

Junior House (age range 3–11). A purpose-built Nursery provides a stimulating environment for children aged
3–4 years. Children may start the day after their 3rd birthday. Early Years Funding available. Superb Outdoor Learning environment.

Junior House follows a topic-based curriculum linked to
the National Curriculum which enables girls to enjoy every
aspect of learning and discovery. Form teachers encourage
and support a high standard of achievement in all areas of
the curriculum and promote a feeling of warmth and security.

Extra-curricular activities include: Choirs, Instrumental
Tuition, Young Textiles Group, Drama, Gymnastics,
Hockey, Rounders, Netball, Tennis, Ballet, Chess, Karate,
Dance and Drama. A range of sports fixtures are made with
other schools.

The immediate environment plays an important role in
stimulating learning and regular visits are made to the theatre, museums and places of educational interest.

Senior House Curriculum. The curriculum is designed
to be enjoyable, stimulating and exciting, providing breadth
and depth in learning.

- Wide choice of options at GCSE and Advanced Levels.
- Languages: French, German, Spanish, Latin and Classical
Greek.
- Separate Sciences.
- Personal and Social Awareness programme.
- Careers Education and Guidance.

Extra-curricular activities include regular visits abroad,
foreign exchanges, visits to the theatre, art galleries, museums and concerts. There is also a thriving programme of
Music, Drama and Sport, as well as a flourishing Duke of
Edinburgh's Award scheme.

The Sixth Form. The Sixth Form of 81 girls takes a full
and responsible part in the life and organisation of the
school. A wide range of A and AS Level subjects is available. Girls take 4 or 5 subjects in L6, 3 or 4 in U6.

Fees per term (2014–2015). Nursery £2,370, Infants
(Reception–Year 2) £2,535, Juniors (Years 3–6) £2,800,
Seniors (Years 7–13) £3,750.

Extra subjects. Greek, Speech and Drama, and Music
(piano, strings, brass, woodwind, singing).

Scholarships and Bursaries. Means-tested Scholarships
are available at 7–9+.

At 11+ a number of academic Open Scholarships are
offered and bursaries are available in cases of financial need.
There is also the Barbara Priestman award of £600 per
annum for daughters of practising Christians. Scholarships
(Academic, Performing Arts, Sport and Music) are awarded
at 11+ and financial help is available at all stages from age
11.

At 13+ Academic, Music, Performing Arts and Sport
Scholarships are available.

At 16+ there are a number of academic scholarships
available to external and internal candidates. Music scholarships are also available at 16+, as well as Performing Arts,
Sports and an Art Scholarship.

Transport. Transport is available from most local areas
and the school is also accessible by public transport.

After School Care. After School Care is available until
5.30 pm and is free of charge (there is a charge for Nursery
children).

Further information. The Head is always pleased to
welcome parents who wish to visit the school. For further
information and a full prospectus please contact the School
on: tel: 0191 384 3226; fax: 0191 386 7381; website:
www.dhsfg.org.uk; email: enquiries@dhsfg.org.uk.

Charitable status. Durham High School for Girls is a
Registered Charity, number 1119995. Its aim is to create a
friendly, caring community based on Christian values and to
encourage academic excellence.

Edgbaston High School

Westbourne Road, Birmingham B15 3TS
Tel: 0121 454 5831
Fax: 0121 454 2363
email: admissions@edgbastonhigh.co.uk
website: www.edgbastonhigh.co.uk

President: Sir Dominic Cadbury, BA, MBA

Vice-Presidents:
Mr Duncan Cadbury, MSc
Her Honour Judge Sybil Thomas, LLB

Council:
Chairman: Mr J D Payne, MRICS
Deputy Chairman: Mrs C Fatah, RGN

Ms H J Arnold, BSc Hons
Lord Bhattacharyya, KB, CBE
Mrs S A England Kerr
Mrs A E Howarth, CertEd, DipEd
Dr J Leadbetter, PhD, PGCE, BSc Hons, MEd Ed Psych,
AFBPsS, CPsychol
Mrs V Nicholls, Chartered MCIPD
Mr G I Scott, MA Oxon
Mr G H Tonks, BSc, FCA

Representing the Old Girls' Association:
Mrs A Stanley

Clerk to the Governors: Mrs M Osborn

School Staff:

Headmistress: Dr Ruth A Weeks, BSc, PhD Birmingham

Deputy Head Academic: Miss S-E Easton, MA Oxford
Deputy Head Pastoral: Mrs J Coley, BA Reading
Director of Studies: Miss J Rance, BSc Manchester, MEd Birmingham

Ms G Ajmal, BA Wolverhampton (*English*)
Miss Maria Aznar-López, BA Birmingham (*Spanish, French*)
Miss M Barbet, Licence d'Anglais Université de Clermont-Ferrand, France (*French, Spanish*)
Mrs L Batchelor, BSc Birmingham (*PE*)
Mr G Bateman, BMus Sunderland, DipABRSM (*Music*)
Mr D Berman, MA Oxford (*Science*)
Miss A G Bosc, BSc Birmingham (*Biology*)
Mrs A Brookes, BSc Brunel (*Science*)
Mrs C Cardellino, BA Leicester (*German*)
Mrs J Chalmers, BA York (*Mathematics*)
Mrs A Cirillo-Campbell, BA UCE Birmingham (*ICT*)
Mrs R Coldrick, BEng Aston (*Physics*)
Dr E Cruice, BSc Sussex, PhD Birmingham (*Science*)
Miss A Cummings, BA Northampton (*Food & Nutrition and Textiles*)
Mr N Day, BA Huddersfield (*History*)
Mr M D Dukes, BA Wolverhampton (*Art*)
Mrs Z Ehiogu, BA University East London (*PE*)
Mrs C A Evans, CertEd Anstey (*PE*)
Mrs S Flitter, MA Oxford (*Classics*)
Mr A Flox-Nievo, BA Castilla, Spain (*Spanish*)
Mrs J Forrest, BSc Open University (*Biology*)
Ms D Graham, BSocSc Birmingham, Grad Dip Psych Aston (*Sociology & Extended Project*)
Miss J P Harrison, BA Southampton, MA Birmingham (*English*)
Miss M Hayday, BA Hull (*Religious Studies*)
Mrs J Hayward, BSc Newcastle upon Tyne (*Mathematics*)
Mrs S Hewison, BA Ed Exeter (*PE*)
Mrs H Howell, GBSM, ABSM Birmingham (*Music*)
Miss K Jacks, BA Durham (*PE*)
Mrs J Johnson, BA Aberystwyth (*French & Spanish*)
Miss N Jones-Owen, BA Manchester Metropolitan (*English, Media Studies*)
Miss N Khodabukus, MBiochem Oxford (*Chemistry & Science*)
Ms M Khuttan, BSc Keele (*Mathematics*)
Mrs A Lacey, BSc University of East Anglia (*Biology*)
Mrs P M Lampard, CertEd Bath College of HE (*Food & Nutrition and Textiles*)
Mr S Lane, BA Theatre Plymouth (*Drama*)
Mrs A Lee, BSc Birmingham (*Mathematics*)
Mrs S Lynch, BSc Sheffield, MA Sheffield (*Science*)
Mr P Malone, BA Sheffield (*ICT, Business Studies*)
Miss K Massey, BSc Reading (*Geography*)
Mrs R J Matthews, BSc Aberystwyth (*Science, Biology*)
Miss M P Monet-Rossetti, BA Open University (*French, German*)
Mrs L Mooney, BA Wolverhampton (*Food & Nutrition and Textiles*)
Miss S Mullett, BA Nottingham (*Art*)
Mrs K E Newling, Birmingham (*Mathematics*)
Mrs R Norman, BSc Liverpool (*Mathematics*)
Miss S O'Hare, MA St Andrews (*English*)
Mrs S Park, BA Cardiff, MPhil Cardiff (*English*)
Mr C J Proctor, BA Swansea (*English*)
Miss F Richards, BSc Bristol, BA Birmingham (*Art*)
Miss R Richardson, BA Reading (*History*)
Miss R Richardson, LLAM, ALAM, Dip BSSD (*Drama*)
Mr K Robson, BMus Birmingham, MA Huddersfield (*Music*)
Miss K Rowley, BA Durham (*Geography*)
Mrs J Ruisi, BEd Sussex (*Psychology*)
Mr J Sabotig, BSc Birmingham (*Physics*)

Dr Y Shang, BSc Peking, China, MSc Beijing, China, PhD Loughborough (*Mandarin*)
Mrs J Shutt, BA Keele (*Business & Economics*)
Mr B Smith, BA Birmingham, MPhil Birmingham (*History*)
Mr P Smith, BA Staffordshire (*Religious Studies*)
Mrs K J Stocks, BMus Birmingham, ARCM (*Music*)
Miss G Suter, BSc Cardiff (*PE*)
Dr J Tepe III, BA Pennsylvania, USA, MA Arkansas, USA, PhD Birmingham (*English*)
Mr M Tomaszewicz, BSc Birmingham (*Chemistry*)
Miss S E Vann, BEd De Montfort (*PE*)
Mrs C Whitney, BA Leicester (*Classics*)
Mr M Wiggins, BA Birmingham (*Religious Studies*)

Librarian: Mrs S E Sansom, BA Bangor, MCLIP
Library Assistant/Examinations Officer: Mrs J Hall, BSc Surrey

Language Assistants:
French: Ms M Romero
German: Miss N Heitz
Spanish: Mrs C Nickson

Technicians:
Mr J Coley, BSc Northampton
Mrs C Harris
Mrs A Duvnjak, BSc Coventry, MSc Birmingham
Miss V Gutzmore, BSc OU, HND
Mrs S Griffiths
Mr A Ijaz
Miss C Phipps, BA Leeds

Network Manager: Mrs S Srinivas, MSc

Preparatory School:

Head: Mrs S Hartley, BEd Bristol

Deputy Heads:
Mrs S Alderson, CertEd City of Birmingham College of Education
Mrs K Gater, BA Manchester Metropolitan

Miss O Ash, BEd Wolverhampton
Mrs A Aston, BSc, PGCE Birmingham
Mrs A M Collins, BEd Birmingham, TCert Dudley College of Education
Miss S Dawes, BSc Leeds
Mrs S Draper, BSc Swansea
Mrs S Dudley, CertEd Northumberland College of Education
Mrs Z Ehiogu, BA University East London
Mrs A Ferguson, MA Ed London
Mrs J Goodyear, BA Ed Worcester College of Higher Education
Miss L Hannabuss, BSc Birmingham
Miss S Howarth, BSc Worcester College of Higher Education
Miss L Jones, BA Swansea
Mrs J Knott, BA, PGCE Birmingham
Ms K McKee, BA Sussex, PGCE Warwick
Mrs M Poade, BA Reading
Miss C Robinson, BA Exeter
Miss L Sansom, BSc Bangor
Mrs F Scott Dickins, BA London
Miss A Smith, BSc Cardiff
Miss V Walker, BA Warwick
Mrs K Waterworth, BSc Aston
Mrs F Watson, BA Leeds, PGCE Worcester
Mrs V Woodfield, BEd Birmingham

Librarian/Swimming Coach:
Mrs N Ash

Teaching Assistants:
Mrs D Audley
Mrs J Russon

Mrs M Bracey
Mrs H Coulson
Mrs C Mills

Technician: Mr R Sejic
Secretary: Mrs L Barton

After-School Supervisors:
Mrs J Eyres
Mrs K Hancox
Mrs M Rees
Mrs C Mills

Pre-Preparatory Department:
Mrs L Bowler, BA Leicester
Mrs V Brockbank, BA Lancaster
Mrs A Hartland, BEd Birmingham, CertEd Dudley
Mrs D A Kennedy, BEd West Midlands College of HE
Mrs H Robinson, BEd University of Wales
Mrs H Skidmore, BA Trinity College Carmarthen

Teaching Assistants:

Mrs R Aulak
Mrs E Barnsley
Mrs J Corbett
Miss E Cornelius
Mrs D Deakin

Mrs F Green
Mrs A Knight
Mrs A de Salis
Mrs K Thomas
Mrs P Varma

Visiting Staff:
Ballet: Miss D Todd

Before School Care Supervisor: Mrs C Harris
After School Care Supervisor: Mrs M Henry

Special Subjects:

Head of Music Department: Mr K Robson, BMus
  Birmingham, MA Huddersfield
Pianoforte:
Ms E Cockbill, MA, LLCM, ALCM
Mrs H Howell, GBSM, ABSM
Mrs L Kitto, GBSM, ABSM, LTCL
Miss M Morris, MMus, LRSM
Mrs C J Purkis, GBSM, ABSM, LRAM
Flute:
Miss H Jones, BA
Mrs S Wilson, BA
Oboe/Recorder:
Mrs K J Stocks, BMus, ARCM
Clarinet/Saxophone:
Miss M Harper, GRNCM, ARMCM
Mr J Meadows, BA, ABRSM
Bassoon:
Mr P Brookes, GBSM, ARCM, DipOrchStudies
Horn:
Mrs C Butler, BMus
Violin/Viola:
Miss A Chippendale, BMus
Mr M Owen, LRAM
Cello:
Miss J Carey, GRSM, ARCM
Guitar:
Miss F Griffin, LGSM, LTCL
Miss L Larner, BMus
Singing:
Mrs S Allsop, ARCM, ABRSM
Miss S Purkis, BMus
Miss S Vango, BMus
Brass:
Mrs M Brookes, DRSAMD
Percussion:
Mr J Huxtable, BMus
Theory:
Mrs K Stocks, BMus, ARCM
Miss M Harper, GRNCM, ARMCM

Fencing: Professor P Northam, BAF

LAMDA:
Mrs C Fidler, BA, LRAM, FETC, IPA
Mrs T Bolt
Life Saving: Rose Link
Gym Club: Mrs S Hewison

Facilities Manager: Mr S Watson, MHCIMA
Nurses:
Mrs J Irving, RGN, SCM
Mrs M Al-Ani
Mrs V Jones

Headmistress's PA: Ms G Franchi
Head of Marketing & Development: Mrs A Rowlands, BSc

This independent day school, founded in 1876, attracts girls both from the immediate neighbourhood and all over the West Midlands. They come for the academic curriculum, the lively programme of sporting, creative and cultural activities, and for the individual attention and flexibility of approach.

Personal relationships at EHS are of paramount importance. Parents, both individually and through their association, give generously of their time to support our activities; while staff, through their hard work and good relationship with the girls, create an atmosphere at once orderly and friendly.

Organisation and Curriculum. There are three departments working together on one site which caters for over 950 day girls aged two and a half to eighteen. One of the features of EHS is the continuity of education it offers. However, girls can be admitted at most stages. Staff take special care to help girls settle quickly and easily. Pupils enjoy a broadly based programme which substantially fulfils the requirements of the National Curriculum and much more.

The Pre-Preparatory Department, known as Westbourne, offers facilities for about 100 girls aged two and a half to five in a spacious, purpose-built, detached house. The staff aim to create an environment in which they can promote every aspect of a girl's development. A brand new Nursery (part of the £4 million Octagon building) was opened in February 2005.

The Preparatory School accommodates over 350 girls from 5+ to 11 in up-to-date facilities, among them a new IT suite, Science Laboratory, Library and Design Technology Centre. A full curriculum, including English, Mathematics, Science and Technology, is taught throughout the department.

The Senior School caters for about 500 girls aged 11+ to 18. Girls follow a well-balanced curriculum which prepares them for a wide range of subjects at GCSE and Advanced Level.

Examination results are very good with high grades distributed across both Arts and Science subjects. The vast majority of girls in the Sixth Form of over 100 proceed to Higher Education. Every year girls obtain places at Oxbridge and Russell Group Universities.

Extra Curricular Activities. Girls can take part in a broad range of activities including art, ceramics, Mandarin, drama, Duke of Edinburgh's Award, music, sport and Young Enterprise. There are clubs during the lunch hour and after school. Instrumental music lessons are available. There is a strong music tradition in the school. Girls go on visits, expeditions and work experience in this country and abroad. We encourage girls to think of the needs of others.

Accommodation. There is a regular programme of improvements to the buildings. An exciting new multi-purpose hall, The Octagon, was opened in February 2005. A floodlit all-weather surface was opened in Summer 2006. The school has its own indoor swimming pool, 12 tennis courts and 8 acres of playing fields. Work on extended Sixth Form accommodation, a new library and fitness suite, at a cost of £3.5m, was completed in January 2011.

Location. The school is pleasantly situated next to the Botanical Gardens in a residential area, 1½ miles south-west of the city centre. It is easily accessible by public transport and also has its own privately run coaches.

Fees per term (2014–2015). Pre-Prep £1,532 (mornings to 11.45 am), £1,659 (mornings to 1.00 pm), £2,423 (5 days); Prep £2,508–£3,523; Senior £3,729.

Scholarships and Bursaries. Academic Scholarships are available at 11+, awarded on the basis of performance in the entrance examination. Sixth Form Academic Scholarships are awarded based on examination and interview.

Two external scholarships of up to 20% are offered to suitable candidates for entry into Year 3, following assessments in Mathematics, Reading Skills and Creative Writing. Assessments take place in January.

Two Music Scholarships are also offered annually: one at 11+ and one at 16+. 11+ candidates must sit the main entrance examination in January and then have written, aural and practical tests. Candidates at 16+ attend an audition and interview in January.

At 16+ there are further scholarships for Art, Performing Arts and Sport awarded to girls of outstanding ability. Assessments take place in January.

A Bursary fund exists to help girls of good academic ability in financial need to enter at 11+ and the Sixth Form and to assist those whose financial circumstances have changed since they entered the Senior School. Bursaries may cover part or full fees. All scholarships can be combined with means-tested bursaries in cases of need.

Further information. Full details may be obtained from the school. Parents and girls are welcome to visit the school by appointment.

Charitable status. Edgbaston High School for Girls is a Registered Charity, number 504011. Founded in 1876, it exists to provide an education for girls.

Farlington School

Strood Park, Horsham, West Sussex RH12 3PN

Tel:	01403 254967
Fax:	01403 272258
email:	office@farlingtonschool.net
website:	www.farlingtonschool.net
Twitter:	@Farlington_Sch
Facebook:	FarlingtonSchool

Motto: *Vive ut Vivas*
   Founded 1896.

Governing Body:
Council of twelve members
Chairman: Mrs S Mitchell, BA, MA, PGCE

Headmistress: Miss L Higson, BSc, PGCE

Assistant Head (*Academic*): Mrs A Binns, BA, PGCE

Assistant Head (*Pastoral*): Mrs A Higgs, BEd

Head of Prep School: Mrs Frances Mwale, BSc, PGCE

Deputy Head of Prep School: Mrs S E Povey, BEd, CertEd

Bursar: Mr R Bosshardt, FCIPD, BSc, MSc

Registrar: Mrs J Coveney, BEng

Boarding Staff:
Mrs D Roberts-Barter
Mrs V Kelly, BA
Mrs Y Crook
Mrs J Humphreys

Nurses:
Mrs C Parsons, RGN
Mrs A Walker, RGN

The School. The official foundation of Farlington School (then Farlington House) was in 1896 at Haywards Heath. The School moved to its present site in 1955. It is situated in 33 acres of beautiful parkland on the Sussex-Surrey border. It has two lakes, sports and recreational facilities.

Farlington has approximately 350 girls aged from 3 to 18. Girls can board from the age of 8, on a full, weekly and occasional basis, or attend as day girls. All are equally important members of the School community. In September 2008 the Courtyard Building opened, designed to complement the existing Prep School building which opened in 1997. This offers facilities for our co-educational Nursery Class for children aged 3–4 years. The building also includes further classrooms, a multi-purpose hall, a kitchen, a library and administration offices. Girls at Farlington also enjoy a purpose-built Science Building, a Sports Hall with facilities for badminton, volleyball, netball and basketball, a floodlit all-weather hockey pitch, and a modern Sixth Form Centre.

See also Farlington Preparatory School entry in IAPS section.

Farlington was last inspected by the Independent Schools Inspectorate in 2010. Farlington was rated excellent/outstanding in every standard. The report included the following two quotes: "*An overall excellent curriculum and outstanding teaching enable preparatory and senior school pupils to achieve excellent all-round standards.*" "*As a result of excellent guidance pupils exhibit outstanding personal development. The school is successful in fostering individuality, pupils are happy, succeed and flourish, and relationships are very positive. It is a very friendly, welcoming school.*"

Curriculum. We aim to provide a broad and balanced curriculum for all age groups. Our academic standards are high, and we encourage girls to raise their own expectations of achievement. Our approach involves good teaching practice coupled with clearly set targets and positive encouragement throughout every girl's school life. The rewards are excellent examination results: in 2014 a 95.5% pass rate at A Level with 75.8% at grades A*–C, and 96.5% overall pass rate at grades A*–C at GCSE. 100% of our sixth formers go on to study the subject of their choice.

Important though academic standards are, Farlington is about more than examination results: we aim to educate the whole child.

Spiritual awareness, care for others, tolerance and compassion are the basis of our religious education. We are a Church of England foundation, but we welcome all faiths. There is an assembly most weekday mornings, and boarders are given the opportunity to attend a service at a church of their choice on Sundays. Work for charity and service to the community are part of the ethos at Farlington.

Farlington's emphasis on care and guidance in personal development is underlined in our tutorial system. Each girl is placed in a tutor group where she is given individual attention. Tutors liaise with other members of the teaching staff, boarding staff (where appropriate) and parents. They monitor academic progress and extra-curricular activities. Each week a tutor period is devoted to the discussion of a wide range of topics within our Life Skills programme, including moral issues, personal relationships, health education and study skills.

Extra-Curricular Activities. Opportunities for pursuing activities of all sorts exist after school and during lunch hours. Some are physical activities, such as The Duke of Edinburgh's Award Scheme, trampolining, fencing; others are more creative like Art or Drama club. Musical activities are popular with numerous choirs, ensembles, orchestras and bands on offer. There is a strong drama and music tradition within the School, and three major productions are staged each year. A wide range of sporting activities is available and the School enjoys considerable success at county and national level in many sports. Other activities include

Debating, Chess Club and Ballet. All girls are encouraged to take at least one activity, and there is also supervised prep until 5.45pm.

Admission. Admission is by the School's own entrance examination and interview. *Entrance Examination Day in 2015*: Tuesday 6th January.

Scholarships are awarded on merit. Scholarships will be held for the duration of the girl's time at Farlington, subject to annual review. This year we are launching our new Vive Scholarship for Year 7 entry in 2015.

There will be an enrichment programme for, and public recognition of, Scholars, and all girls who maintain their scholarships until they leave after A Levels will be further acknowledged at their final Prize Giving.

Scholarships are available at three points of entry in the Senior School:

Entry into Year 7: Examination in January.

Academic, Music, Sport, Drama and Art Scholarships are available. Both internal and external candidates need to apply for all subject Scholarships. Candidates should be registered and entered by the last Friday in the preceding November. All girls who sit the Entrance Examination in January will automatically be considered for Academic Scholarships so there is no need to apply for these.

The new Vive Scholarship offers a 50% reduction to the annual tuition fee to girls entering Year 7 in 2015 who can demonstrate academic excellence and expertise in at least one other extra-curricular area. Closing date for applications is 21st November 2014.

Entry into Year 9: Examination in January.

Academic, Music, Drama, Sport and Art Scholarships are available to both internal and external candidates who will need to apply in all cases. Candidates should be registered and entered by the last Friday in the preceding November.

Entry into the Sixth Form: Examination in November.

Academic, Music, Drama, Sport and Art Scholarships are available to both internal and external candidates who will need to apply in all cases. Candidates should be registered and entered by the first Monday in the November of Year 11 as the assessment will take place later that month.

Scholarship application forms may be obtained from the Registrar.

Bursaries. The School offers means-tested Bursaries up to 90% of tuition fees for all prospective and current pupils from Year 5 upwards. A maximum of two bursaries in excess of 50% are awarded per year. Bursaries are not available when one or more parent is resident outside of the UK, with the exception of serving members of the UK Armed Forces and members of the UK Diplomatic Corps.

The main bursary award process is carried out in the first half of the Spring Term and applications, therefore, should be made in the second half of the preceding autumn term.

Subject to available funds, applications for bursaries will be considered at other times of the year, on a half-termly basis if parental circumstances change unexpectedly.

Fees per term (2014–2015). Tuition: Prep School £2,350–£4,515, Senior School £5,385. Boarding (in addition to Tuition fees): £3,150 (weekly), £3,505 (full).

Charitable status. Farlington School is a Registered Charity, number 307048. It exists to provide education for girls.

Farnborough Hill

Farnborough Road, Farnborough, Hampshire GU14 8AT

Tel:	01252 545197/529811
Fax:	01252 513037
email:	admissions@farnborough-hill.org.uk
website:	www.farnborough-hill.org.uk

Twitter:	@FarnboroughHill
Facebook:	/Farnborough-Hill

Motto: *In Domino Labor Vester Non Est Inanis*
Founded 1889.

Board of Governors:
Mr J Hull (*Chairman*)
Mrs C E Hamilton (*Deputy Chair*)
Dr C Chadwick
Mr T J Flesher
Mr M D Hoad
Miss M Holt
Mrs D O'Leary
Mr S Nelson
Mrs G Rivers
Mrs J Windeatt

Headmistress: **Mrs S Buckle**, BSc Exeter, MA, PGCE Reading, NPQH

Deputy Head: Mrs A Griffiths, BEd Roehampton, MA Surrey, NPQH

Assistant Head Teachers:
Mrs C Dales, BA Sussex, PGCE Reading
Mr J Hoar, BA Hull, PGCE Soton

Teaching Staff:
Miss D Andrews, BSc Cardiff, PGCE Homerton (*Biology, Chemistry*)
Mrs A Barker, BSc Bath, PGCE Kingston (*Mathematics*)
Miss P Bartlett, BA, PGCE Oxon (*Mathematics*)
Mrs S Batt, BSc Glasgow, QTS GTP (*Computing and ICT*)
Mrs S Bond, BA Soton, CertEd Sheffield Hallam (*Art and Design*)
Mrs J Brereton, BA Soton, PGCE Reading (*Geography*)
Dr M Bright, BSc Sierra Leone, MSc PhD Birmingham (*Chemistry*)
Mrs G Brocklehurst, BSc UWIST, PGCE OU (*Mathematics*)
Mr M Brown, BSc, PGCE Exeter (*Computing and ICT*)
Mr P Butler, BA, PGCE Reading (*French, Classics*)
Mrs R Byrne, BA South Glamorgan Inst, Art TCert Goldsmiths College (*Art and Design*)
Mrs S Campbell, BA Dunelm, PGCE Oxon (*English*)
Mrs S Camprubi-Reches, BA Barcelona, MEd Cardiff, PGCE Barcelona (*Spanish*)
Mrs C Cantor, BA Bath, PGCE Oxon (*German*)
Mrs K Cappleman, BSc Exeter, QTS GTP (*Mathematics*)
Miss E Casey, BA Exeter, PGCE Roehampton (*French, Spanish*)
Mrs K Clarke, MA Cardiff, PGCE Bath Spa (*English*)
Miss H Clutterbuck, BSc, PGCE Warwick (*Biology, Chemistry, Physics*)
Mrs H de Mattos, BA, PGCE Roehampton, MA Royal Central School of Speech and Drama (*Drama*)
Mrs B Dunnage, BA Birmingham, PGCE Southampton (*Geography*)
Miss V Ellender, BSc St Mary's Twickenham, PGCE Brunel (*Physical Education*)
Mrs L J Evans-Jones, BA Royal Holloway, PGCE Roehampton (*English*)
Miss C Ferguson, BEd St Mary's Belfast (*Religious Education*)
Mr P Forrest-Biggs, MA London, QTS CfBT (*Classics*)
Mrs L Fowles, MA UCL, PGCE Institute of Education (*Classics, History*)
Mr P Gillingham, BA Reading, PGCE Bath (*History, Government and Politics*)
Mrs A Goddard, BEd Bath (*Design and Technology*)
Mrs S-E Godde, BEd Sydney, QTS Cowes Enterprise College (*Physical Education*)
Mrs C Goldsmith, BA W Surrey College of Art and Design (*Art and Design*)

Mrs S Gregory, MA Cantab, PGCE Moray House (*French, Spanish, Italian*)

Mr S Haddock, BSc UEA, PGCE Institute of Education (*Psychology*)

Mrs E-J Harrison, BA QTS Brighton (*Physical Education*)

Mrs S Hayes, BSc Leicester, PGCE Ripon and York St John (*Biology*)

Mrs S Haynes, BSc Imperial College, PGCE Reading (*Chemistry, Physics*)

Mrs J Hollis, BA Luton, PGCE Manchester Met (*Spanish, German and French*)

Mrs L Hooper, BSc Liverpool, GTP Reading (*Mathematics*)

Mrs K Jackson, BEd Bedford (*Physical Education*)

Mr A Johnson, BA UCA (*Graphics*)

Mr K Johnson, MA Cantab, DipEd Oxon (*Greek*)

Mrs H Jones, BA, PGCE Roehampton (*RE*)

Miss F Kelsey, BA QTS St Mary's Twickenham (*Physical Education*)

Miss V Lee, BA UCC, PGCE Oxon (*RE, Philosophy and Ethics, History*)

Mrs S Macey, BSc UMIST, PGCE Cantab (*Chemistry*)

Mr S McSweeney, BA Liverpool, PGCE Liverpool Hope (*Music*)

Miss L Miller, BA Reading, PGCE UWE (*Economics*)

Mrs E Nelson, BSc St Andrews, CertEd Dundee (*Mathematics*)

Mrs J Nix, BEd Winchester (*Design & Technology, Information Technology*)

Miss D O'Laoire, MA Nottingham, PGCE King's College (*Classics*)

Mrs A Payne, BSc BCHE, PGCE Bristol (*Geography*)

Miss K Pengelley, BA Nottingham, MA, PGCE Institute of Education (*Classics and History*)

Mrs K Phillips, BA Reading, ALCM (*Music*)

Miss K Price, BA Bristol, PGCE Southampton (*History*)

Mr J Quinnell, BA Winchester, MA Durham, PGCE Lancaster (*English*)

Dr S Rawle, MA, DPhil Oxon (*Physics*)

Mrs H Rix, BATh Maynooth, HDipEd Trinity College Dublin (*Religious Education*)

Mrs D Robinson, BEd Central School of Speech & Drama (*Drama*)

Mrs A Smith, MA Cantab, PGCE Cantab (*Mathematics and ICT*)

Mrs L Storrie, BSc Salford, PGCE Manchester (*Biology*)

Dr I Taylor, BA, MSt, DPhil Oxon (*Music and Music Technology*)

Miss R Taylor, BA Cantab, PGCE Exeter (*Geography*)

Miss L Turner, MSc Oxon, GTP Herts (*Biology and Chemistry*)

Dr A Tytko, BSc, PhD Leeds, MBA Dunelm, PGCE Kingston (*Economics and Business Studies*)

Mr R Wellington, BA Exeter, PGCE Birmingham (*Theology*)

Miss P White, BA UCL, PGCE King's College London (*French and Spanish*)

Mrs L Winch-Johnson, BA Hertfordshire, MSc, PGCE Surrey, CCRS Dip Perf Coach Newcastle (*English, Drama, Learning Support Coordinator*)

Librarian and Website Manager: Mrs J Wood, MA Cantab, DipLIS London

Matron: Mrs C Wilding, RGN

Bursar: Cmdr A Woolston, CDipAF

Director of Admissions: Mrs C Duffin, BA Hons, FCIM Chartered Marketer

Chaplain: Miss S Farmer, BA Hons, Dip Counselling UEA, MBACP, Spiritual Director, Dip Spiritual Accompaniment

ICT Coordinator: Mr A Labuschagné

Examinations Officer: Mrs S Cahalane, BSc Hons

Farnborough Hill is a leading independent Roman Catholic day school for 550 girls aged 11 to 18. The school was established in Farnborough in 1889 by The Religious of Christian Education and is now an educational trust. It welcomes girls of all Christian denominations, other faiths or no faith, who are supportive of the ethos. Farnborough Hill is committed to the education of the whole person in a happy, caring Christian community in which each individual is valued.

Academic standards are high with students usually taking ten GCSE subjects. In the Sixth Form most students take four AS subjects in the Lower Sixth and three A Levels in the Upper Sixth. The vast majority then go on to Higher Education. The school is a member of ISCO and there is a well-equipped Careers department and a specialist Careers teacher.

Farnborough Hill offers a wide range of extra-curricular activities and is especially renowned for its reputation in music, sport, drama and art.

The school's impressive main house, once the home of Empress Eugenie, has had modern purpose-built facilities added. These include a sports hall, indoor swimming pool, newly refurbished laboratories, drama studio, IT suites, art and design technology centre, a music suite, a chapel and extensive playing fields.

Although within a few minutes' walk of both Farnborough Main and Farnborough North railway stations, the school is situated in 68 acres of parkland and woodland with magnificent views over the Hampshire countryside. Girls come from Hampshire, Surrey and Berkshire with many travelling by train or by school coach.

Admission. Entry is by examination taken in January for the following September.

Scholarships and Bursaries. The school offers academic, music and sports scholarships and also bursaries for parents who are in need of financial assistance. Six Academic scholarships are offered for entry at 11+. One of these is reserved for a Roman Catholic student. In addition one Music scholarship, one Sports scholarship and one Art scholarship are awarded at 11+. Sixth Form scholarships are awarded for academic achievement, excellence in the performing arts, the creative arts and sports. An additional scholarship is awarded by Farnborough Hill Old Girls' Association.

Fees per term (2014–2015). Tuition: £4,230.

Further information. The prospectus is available from the Director of Admissions. The Headmistress is pleased to meet prospective parents by appointment.

Charitable status. The Farnborough Hill Trust is a Registered Charity, number 1039443.

Francis Holland School
Sloane Square

39 Graham Terrace, London SW1W 8JF
Tel: 020 7730 2971
Fax: 020 7823 4066
email: office@fhs-sw1.org.uk
website: www.francisholland.org.uk

Founded 1881.

Patron: The Right Revd and Right Hon The Lord Bishop of London

Council:
Chairman: Mrs M Winckler, MA
Vice Chairman: Mrs A Edelshain, BA, MBA, MCIPD
Mr P Ashton, BSc, ACA
Mr A Beevor, BA, MBE
Miss E Buchanan, CVO, LLD, ARAgS

The Revd J Cave Bergquist, BA
Mr D Dowley, MA, QC
Mr J Dunston, MA, ACIL, FRSA
Mrs S Graham-Campbell
Dr M Harrison, BA
Mrs S Honey, BA
Mrs C Longworth, BA
Mrs B Mathews, BA, FCA
Professor J Parry, MA, PhD
Mr S Pitchford, MA
Miss S Ross, BSc, FInstP (*Safeguarding Children – Child Protection*)
Dr H Spoudeas, MBBS, DRCOG, FRCPCH, FRCP, MD
Professor J Yeomans, MA, DPhil

Secretary to the Council & Bursar: Mr G Wilmot, BA, ACA
Clerk to the Governors: Mrs G Shaw, BSc

Senior Leadership Team:

Headmistress: Mrs L Elphinstone, MA Cantab, FRSA (*English*)

Deputy Head Academic: Mr P Williams, MA Oxon (*Mathematics*)
Deputy Head Pastoral: Mrs C Remy-Miller, BSc, MSc France (*French*)
Director of Sixth Form & HE: Miss A Stevenson, BA Durham, BA Open, MA Open (*Spanish*)
Director of Operations: Mrs A Margetson, PE Cert Australian CPE (*Physical Education*)
Head of Juniors: Miss S J Styles, BA Surrey, MA London
Deputy Head of Juniors: Mrs C Spencer-Kruger, BSc Leeds, MSc Sheffield

Senior School – Full time:
* Head of Department
Miss D Adams, BA Wellesley College USA (*History*)
Miss J Arlington, BA Surrey (*Animation*)
Mr C Bartram, BA Portsmouth (*Biology*)
Dr P Bennett, BSc Durham, PhD Bristol (*Mathematics*)
Ms M Bonnaud, Licence Montpellier (*French and Spanish*)
Miss E Boon, MA Oxon (*History*)
Mr F Calvet, MPhil Grenoble, MA Perpignan, Diploma Toulouse (*French*)
Mrs K Cronan, BA York, BSc Open (*English, Head of Upper School Years 10–11*)
Mr L Dare, BA Cantab (*Physics/Science*)
Miss H Davidson, BA Newcastle (*Music*)
Mr D Edes, BA Exeter (*Art*)
Miss H Ford, BA Cantab (*Mathematics*)
Miss C Graham, MA Oxon (*Religious Studies*)
Miss R Halfacree, BA Chichester (*Physical Education*)
Mrs G Hammond, BA Sheffield (*Psychology*)
Miss N Hogg, BA Bath (*Physical Education*)
Mrs S Hyde, BA London, PGC London (*Economics*)
Miss D Kaleja, I and II Staatsexamen Hanover, BA London (*German*)
Father M Kenny, BA Leeds, MA London (*Religious Studies*)
Mme A Lenec'h, Licence Rouen, MA Connecticut USA (*French, Head of Lower School Years 7–9*)
Mr T-S Li, BA London, MPhil Cantab, MTeach London (*English*)
Dr T Marshall, BA Cantab, PhD Edinburgh (*Biology and Chemistry*)
Miss M McLaren, BSc Glasgow (*Science*)
Mrs S Moore, BSc Newcastle (*Mathematics*)
Miss G Newsome, BA Bath (*Physical Education*)
Mr D Nickerson, BA Oxon (*ICT*)
Miss D Ortega, MA London (*Spanish*)
Miss O Partington, BA Nottingham (*PE*)
Ms M Pryce, MA Sydney (*English, *Drama*)

Miss A Rinck, BA Cantab, MEd Manchester (*Biology/Science*)
Mrs C Santry, BSc Newcastle (*Mathematics*) (*maternity leave*)
Miss H Silvester, BA Durham, MA London (*English*)
Mrs R Smith, MA Cantab (*Classics*)
Mr H Stone, BA Birmingham (*Religious Studies*)
Miss R Townend, BSc Birmingham (*Geography*)
Dr N Upcott, BSc, PhD Leeds (*Physics*)
Miss H Vickery, MA Cantab, LRAM, Dip RAM (*Music*)

Junior Staff – Full time:
Miss J Anand, BPA Northern School of Contemporary Dance
Miss J Cameron, MA Edinburgh
Ms L French, BA Oxford, MEd Cantab
Mrs D Greig, BA SOAS London
Miss N Hackett, BSc Oxford Brookes
Miss Y Jeevanjee, Adv Montessori Dip
Miss V Kay, BA Sheffield
Mrs H Kernot, BA London
Ms N Mikac
Miss H Poyer, BSc Bath
Miss E Scatchard, BA London
Miss C Smith, BA Oxford Brookes
Miss N Van Kamp, MA Central Saint Martins
Miss R Walker, BEd Macquarie
Ms M Whitfeld, MA Edinburgh
Miss A Wilson, BA AI

Staff – Part time:
Mrs M Arnaud, MA Grenoble (*French*)
Mrs J Banks BA Durham, MA London (*English*)
Dr L Bourne, BA Oxon, MRCPath (*Chemistry/Science*)
Ms S Carr-Gomm, BA UEA, MA London (*History of Art*)
Mr C Chisnall, BSc Aberystwyth (*Mathematics*)
Miss J de Rome, BEd London, Cert Ed Homerton (*Art*)
Ms P Edgeley, MA London (*Art*)
Mrs K Francis, BEd Hertfordshire College (*Learning Support*)
Ms W Grimshaw, BA Manchester (*History*)
Mr B Howard, BA Sheffield (*Economics*)
Dr M Ifode, MA St Andrews, MPhil Cantab, PhD Cantab, FHEA
Ms H Lambert, BA London (*Classics*)
Ms M Leaf, BA London (*Speech & Drama*)
Mr D Mathews, BSc York (*Music Technology*)
Mrs J Mesrie, BSc Leeds (*Art*)
Miss S Pope, BSc City University
Miss D Powell, BA York (*Biology/Science*)
Ms P Scott, BSc Thames Valley (*Learning Support*)
Dr P Severn, BA Durham, PhD London (*Mathematics*)
Mrs N Tawil, BA London (*Geography*)
Ms J Zhang, MSc Nanjing
Mrs J van Zwanenberg, BA Cantab (*Music*)

Visiting Staff:
Mrs G Bailey-Smith (*Jazz Dance*)
Ms L Barry, BA, MMus Canterbury (*Singing*)
Mrs S Ben-Haim (*Art*)
Ms J Benson, BA (*Singing*)
Miss C Constable, MMus, BMus, PG Perf, Cert RCM, ABSM (*Cello and Piano*)
Miss B Corsi, LTCL, FTCL (*Clarinet, Recorder, Piano*)
Miss A Cviic, BA, PG Dip RCM (*Singing*)
Mr P Dalle (*French Club*)
Mr J Godfrey, BMus, PG Dip RCM (*Percussion*)
Miss K Grandi, MA RCSSD (*Speech & Drama*)
Ms D Halpin, BMus, PG Dip (*Singing*)
Mrs J Harris, LRAD, ARAD (*Ballet*)
Mrs V Hitchen, RBS, TTC Dip, Children's Examiner RAD (*Ballet*)
Miss S Jones (*Yoga*)
Mr H Lamb (*Tennis*)
Ms M Leaf, BA London (*Drama*)

Miss A LeBruin (*Zumba*)
Ms J Lin (*Mandarin*)
Miss E Svensson, MA (*Pottery*)
Mr S Mantas (*Chess*)
Mr M Mason (*Cricket*)
Miss E Mazzon, MA Trieste (*Italian*)
Ms A Moore, ARCM, Dip RCM (*Harp*)
Mr P Moore, BMus, LRAM, LGSMD (*Piano*)
Mrs Y Parrott (*Mandarin*)
Miss V Puttock, BMus (*Saxophone*)
Mr D Schroyens, FTCL (*Piano*)
Mrs S Shaub, LRAM, GRSM (*Piano*)
Mrs S Shepherd, ARAD (*Ballet*)
Miss V Smith, BMus RCM (*Violin*)
Mrs L Sparks, MMus RAM (*Flute*)
Mr J Sparks, BA, MA FCCM (*Guitar*)
Mrs S Stewart, BMus, LRSM, PG Dip RCM (*Singing*)
Mr C Weale, BMus, PG Dip RCM (*Piano*)
Mrs J Wilson (*Ballet*)
Mrs S Wykeham, MMus (*Violin*)

Ms A Barnett (*Admin Assistant & Resources*)
Mrs C Bradshaw (*Lab Technician*)
Mr P da Costa, BSc (*Information Systems Manager*)
Miss E Devane (*Receptionist*)
Miss L Ellwood, BA (*Marketing Assistant*)
Miss H Fathers, MA (*Learning Support Assistant*)
Mr C Hannan (*Office Administrator*)
Mrs F Holland (*Registrar*)
Miss L Ivison, BA (*Librarian*)
Mrs V McKinley, BA (*Communications Director*)
Miss V Phillips (*Headmistress's PA*)
Dr S Rankine, MB BS, DCH, DRCOG, DFFP, MRCGP
   (*School Doctor*)
Miss G Sorrell, BA (*School Secretary*)
Ms J Zhang, MSc (*Lab Technician*)

Numbers and age of entry. There are 490 Day Girls in the School and entry by the School's own examination is at 4+ for the Junior School (ages 4–11), 11+ for the Senior School (ages 11–18) (member of The North London Independent Girls Schools' Consortium) and 16+ for Sixth Form.

Curriculum and Aims. Excellent academic standards are achieved through the provision of a challenging academic curriculum and talented staff who encourage an enthusiasm for learning, intellectual curiosity and creativity. This allows our girls to thrive in a relaxed and happy environment where they are respected as individuals and able to fulfil their unique potential.

Junior School. There is a Junior Department attached to the school.

Religious Education. The school's foundation is Anglican but girls of other faiths are welcomed.

Physical Education. Hockey, Netball, Volleyball, Rounders, Health-related Fitness, Gymnastics, Athletics, Tennis and Swimming are taken. Senior girls have a choice of other activities as well including Squash, Step Aerobics, Boot Camp Fitness, Golf, Pilates, Yoga and Rowing.

Fees per term (2014–2015). £5,095–£5,790.

Scholarships and Bursaries. There are the following competitive awards each year:

11+: 4 Academic scholarships and 1 Music scholarship, both up to the value of 25% of fees. 1 Art award is also available.

Sixth Form: 3 Academic scholarships (internal and external) up to the value of 50% of fees, 1 Music scholarship up to the value of 25% of fees, 1 Drama scholarship up to the value of 25% of fees.

We will consider awarding a bursary to girls who demonstrate the ability to succeed at Francis Holland, but whose parents might not have sufficient financial resources. The level of assistance provided will depend on individual circumstances, which will be reviewed annually. The number of bursaries awarded each year is at the discretion of the Governors and may vary.

Remission of a third of the fees is available for places offered to daughters of the clergy.

Charitable status. The Francis Holland (Church of England) Schools Trust Limited is a Registered Charity, number 312745. It exists to provide high quality education for girls.

Gateways School

Harewood, Leeds LS17 9LE
Tel: 0113 288 6345
Fax: 0113 288 6148
email: gateways@gatewaysschool.co.uk
           head@gatewaysschool.co.uk
website: www.gatewaysschool.co.uk

Governing Body:
Chairman: Mr R Barr
Revd Canon A F Bundock
Mrs L Croston, BSc Hons, PGCE, ALCM
Professor D Hogg, BSc Hons, MSc Hons, DPhil
Mr M Shaw LLB
Professor D Shorrocks-Taylor
Dr R H Taylor, BEd, MA, PhD
Mr S Watson
Mr R Webster, BSc

Staff:

Headmistress: Dr Tracy Johnson, BSc, PhD, PGCE

Assistant Head: Mrs K Titman, BEng, PGCE (*ICT*)

Head of Preparatory School: Mrs S A Wilcox, BEd Hons

Miss J Ansbro-Westmoreland, BA Hons, NNEB (*Nursery Nurse*)
Dr E Anscombe, MSc Hons, DPhil, PGCE (*Science*)
Miss K Ashurst, BSc Hons, PGCE (*Head of Science, Physics*)
Mrs C Bartle, NNEB (*Head of Early Years*)
Miss E Blenkin, BA Hons, PGCE (*Prep*)
Mrs L Blundell, BA Hons, PGCE (*Prep School*)
Miss L Boyd, BA Hons, PGCE (*Subject Leader of PE*)
Mrs G A Brennan, BA Hons, PGCE (*French and Spanish*)
Mrs K Brown, BEd Hons (*Prep School*)
Mrs L Brown, BA Hons, PGCE (*Head of German*)
Mrs R Burton, BSc Hons, PGCE (*Chemistry*)
Mrs M Burns, BA Hons, PGCE (*Head of English*)
Mr A Copeland, BA Hons (*Head of Prep Games & PE*)
Mrs S Crawshaw, BA Hons, PGCE (*Subject Leader of Art*)
Mr J Crosby, MA, BA Hons, PGCE (*Latin and History*)
Mr M Danes, BA Hons, PGCE (*Business Studies*)
Mrs A Davies, BMus Hons, LTCL, Cert Dalcroze (*Prep Music*)
Mr M Davison, BA Hons, PGCE (*Head of Sixth Form, English, Media Studies*)
Mrs S Drake (*Nursery Practitioner*)
Mr J Dunford, BA Hons, LTCL, ARCO, AMusTCL, ALCM (*Director of Music*)
Miss S Ellison, BTEC, FdA in Early Years (*Foundation Stage*)
Mrs J Emerick, BA Hons, Dip Dramatic Art (*LAMDA*)
Miss F Feeney, BA Hons, PGCE (*Prep School*)
Mrs L Fleming, BA Hons, PGCE (*Drama*)
Mrs P Garbutt, BA Hons, PGCE (*History*)
Mrs M Gilliver, BA Hons, PGCE (*Prep School*)
Miss E M Green, CertEd, DPSE (*Learning Support*)
Mrs H Grogan, BA Hons, QTS (*Prep School*)
Mrs E Hayward, BSc Hons, PGCE (*Geography, Psychology*)
Mrs S Holmes, BA Hons, QTS (*Technology*)

Mrs A Ingham, BA Hons, MPhil, CertEd (*Subject Leader of Religious Studies*)
Mrs N Kelly, BSc Hons, PGCE (*Mathematics*)
Mrs D Kennedy, BSc, PGCE (*Head of Mathematics, Mathematics*)
Mrs J Lascelles (*After School Care Assistant*)
Mrs A McKeefry, BA Hons, PGCE (*English*)
Dr S Newton, BSc, PhD, PGCE (*Physics, Biology*)
Mrs T Richmond, BSc Hons, PGCE (*Mathematics*)
Mrs J Rooney, FdA in Early Years, NNEB (*Foundation Stage*)
Mrs S Roth, NVQIII (*Nursery Nurse*)
Mrs R Schofield, BSc Hons, PGCE (*Prep School*)
Ms J Smith, CACHE 3, MAKTON 4 (*Early Years Practitioner*)
Mrs B Smith, NNEB (*Early Years Practitioner*)
Mr P Walker, BA Hons, PGCE (*Business Studies*)
Mrs H Wallis, BA Hons QTS (*Prep School*)
Mrs F Wilson, BA Hons, PGCE (*Head of MFL, Spanish & French*)
Mrs K Wood (*Nursery Practitioner*)
Mrs L Wood, BSc Hons, PGCE (*Head of Pupil Development, Science*)

Associate Staff:
Mr J Halliday, ACA, (*Finance Director*)
Mr S Bartle (*Maintenance Supervisor*)
Miss K Bland (*Teaching Assistant*)
Mrs L Brydon (*After School Supervisor*)
Mrs J Chennells, BA Hons, MHSM, DipHS (*Finance Administrator*)
Mr S Clark (*Laboratory Technician*)
Mrs D Dixon (*Registrar*)
Mrs J Foster, MA (*Community Outreach and House Coordinator*)
Mrs N Harris (*PA to the Headmistress*)
Mrs A Hill, BEd, CertEd (*Homework Club Supervisor*)
Mr N Holloway, BA Hons (*IT Systems Manager*)
Mrs N Matharoo, LLB Hons (*Learning Support Assistant*)
Mrs M Sharrock, BA Hons, MCLIP (*School Librarian, Careers Coordinator*)
Mrs D White, RGN (*School Nurse*)
Mrs S Wood (*Finance Assistant*)

Visiting Teachers:
Miss W Crawford, LTCL (*Classical Guitar*)
Mr D Champken (*Guitar*)
Dr G Cloke (*Brass*)
Mr D Darling, BA Hons, QTC (*Voice and Piano*)
Mr T Foster (*Violin*)
Mrs J Jennings (*Voice*)
Mrs S Robertson, DipMusEd, LTCL (*Piano*)

Gateways School is an independent school, founded in 1941, located in a delightful rural area on a 20-acre site in Harewood village between Leeds and Harrogate. It currently welcomes girls from age 2 to 18 and boys aged 2 to 11.

The school has international status in recognition of its work in promoting multiculturalism, global issues and internationalism. The school has an active Community Outreach programme which organises several events throughout the year to raise funds for charities supported by the school, while the proactive Environment club, and its commitment to green issues, has contributed to Gateways' ongoing status as a Green Flag school.

The ethos and objectives of Gateways School are to provide, within a structured framework, the opportunities and encouragement for every pupil to achieve his or her personal best. The environment is safe and caring, with outstanding pastoral care. Pupils develop self-confidence, self-discipline and a breadth of interests.

Teaching and Learning. Gateways consistently achieves excellent academic results – 100% achieved A* to C grades at GCSE including Maths and English in 2014; at A Level 50% achieved A* and A and 83% were awarded A* to B grades. The Telegraph listed Gateways as the third best small independent school in the country. All this while encouraging students to make the most of the wide range of extra-curricular and enrichment activities on offer. Smaller class sizes allow pupils to develop academically through high-quality teaching from dedicated staff in a supportive environment.

The curriculum at Gateways is broad and challenging and pupils are always encouraged to think for themselves, and to become inquiring and independent learners. A wide range of subjects is offered at AS and A2 Level.

The Stella programme ensures that the most able pupils are challenged and support is available to help individuals with specific learning needs.

Pupils participate in a variety of extra-curricular activities including Drama, Music, Sport, the Duke of Edinburgh's Award Scheme, Leeds Young Enterprise and Community Outreach.

Facilities. The school has an ongoing programme of development to renew and enhance its facilities. Recent projects include The Terrace Music Suite with recording studio. There is a state-of-the-art Performing Arts Centre, extensive playing fields, tennis courts, well-equipped Sports Hall and Fitness Suite, the Cox-Simpson Library and specialist facilities for Science, Mathematics, Languages and Business Studies.

The Gateways Community. The Friends of Gateways (PTA) and The Old Gatewegians Association both play an active role within the school community.

Location and Transport. Gateways School is set in beautiful parkland in the village of Harewood, just north of Leeds. The former Dower House of the Harewood Estate forms the heart of the School. Gateways is within easy reach of Harrogate, Wetherby, Leeds, Ilkley, Otley and the surrounding villages. A comprehensive school transport service is available. The school also has a mini-bus.

Scholarships and Bursaries. The school has a programme of Scholarships which are awarded through examination or assessment and interview depending on the type of scholarship applied for. Academic, Sports and Arts (including Music, Drama, Dance and Art and Design) Scholarships are awarded to pupils who demonstrate exceptional ability. In addition, an Exhibition Scholarship is awarded for all-round contribution to school life, high standards across the curriculum and in extra-curricular areas. A Foundation Scholarship is awarded to a candidate who performs at a high academic level but who could not otherwise access education in an independent school. It holds up to 100% fee remission. The value of the Scholarships will be up to a maximum of 25% of the tuition fee.

The school operates a means-tested bursary scheme.

Fees per term (2014–2015). Sixth Form £3,940; High School (Years 7–11) £3,940; Prep School (Lower 2–Lower 3) £3,040, (Upper 1) £2,925, (Lower 1, Transition and Reception) £2,470; (Pre-Reception) £2,370 (school day), £2,960 (extended day); Nursery: £23.30 (morning/afternoon), £45.00 (extended day). Lunch: Reception to Lower 1 £230 per term, Upper 1 to Sixth Form £245 per term.

Charitable status. Gateways Educational Trust Limited is a Registered Charity, number 529206. It exists to offer a broad education to girls aged 2–18 and boys aged 2–11, where they are encouraged to strive for excellence to the best of their ability.

Greenacre School for Girls

Sutton Lane, Banstead, Surrey SM7 3RA
Tel: 01737 352114
Fax: 01737 373485
email: admin@greenacre.surrey.sch.uk
website: www.greenacre.surrey.sch.uk

Motto: *Fides et opera*

Council:
Chair: Colonel Paul Davis CBE
Mrs S Banton
Mr M Boxall
Mrs S Gilbert
Mrs N Perricone
Miss L Thompson
Mr P Watts
Mr B Williams
Mr A Winyard

Bursar and Clerk to the Council: Mrs K A Maltby, AIAM Dip

Headmistress: **Mrs L E Redding**, BSc Hons

Deputy Head : Mr A Weston, BA Hons

Teaching Staff:
* *Head of Department*

Miss C Black, BA Hons (*Head of Year 10, PE*)
Mrs B Bradley, BEd (**Business Studies*)
Mrs K Bramley, BTEC Dip, BA Hons (*Head of Senior School, *Textiles*)
Mrs S Burge, BSc (**Geography*)
Mrs C Carter, NVQ3 (*Learning Support*)
Mrs L Chambers, BSc Hons (*i/c Biology*)
Mrs L Chessell, BSc Hons (**Mathematics*)
Ms L Cooper, BA (*Head of Year 8, Biology, House Coordinator*)
Miss S Davis, BA Hons (*Juniors*)
Mrs N Durward, BA Hons (**Drama*)
Mrs M Y Emery, BA Hons (**Spanish, Head of Sixth Form*)
Mrs M Epperlein (*Junior French*)
Mr T Finch, MA (**Humanities, *RS*)
Miss R Freeman, BA Hons (*Juniors*)
Mrs M George (*Learning Support*)
Mr P Griffiths, MA (*Latin*)
Mrs M Guinan, BEng Hons (*Head of Year 9, Mathematics*)
Mrs P Hanham, BSc Hons (**Psychology*)
Mrs R Hart, BA Hons (*Head of Infants*)
Mr S Hume, BEd, MA (**ICT*)
Mr M Huxley, BSc Hons (**Photography*)
Miss L Jakes, BA Hons (*English, Performing Arts*)
Mrs M-J Jeanes, MA (**Science, *Chemistry*)
Mr C Lester, BSc Hons, PG Dip (*Teacher i/c Physics*)
Mrs S Maundrell, DEUG (*French*)
Mrs T Milbourn, BA Hons (*Junior PE*)
Mrs F Miles, BEd Hons (*Learning Support Co-ordinator*)
Mr G Miller, BA Hons (*Head of Music*)
Mrs R Murphy, CertEd (*Juniors*)
Mrs E Nissan, BA Hons, PhD (*Juniors*)
Mr M Norris, BA Hons (*English, Duke of Edinburgh's Award Coordinator*)
Miss H O'Hare, BA Hons (*Textiles*)
Mrs C Paine, BEd (*Head of Year 7, History, RS, Science*)
Mrs R M Pedrick, BA Hons (**Modern Foreign Languages, Head of Year 11*)
Mrs S Potter (*Learning Support*)
Mrs J Robson (*Learning Support*)
Mrs C Schembri (*Swimming*)
Mrs S Sheehan BSc, HDipEd (*Mathematics*)
Mrs A Smith, BEd Hons (**Physical Education*)
Mrs H Smith, BA Hons (*Nursery Teacher*)
Mrs I Smith, MA (**English*)
Mrs A Stubbings, BA Hons (*Modern Foreign Languages*)
Mrs A Tharp, BA Hons (**PE*)
Dr C Thompson, DPhil (*Head Technician, Physics*)
Mr I Tunnell, BA Hons (*Juniors, Music*)
Dr R Waller, DPhil Oxford (**History & Politics*)
Mrs L Wigley, BSc Hons (*Geography*)
Mrs J Windett, BEd Hons (*Head of Juniors*)
Mrs M Wraith, CertEd (**Creative Arts*)

Head's PA and Office Manager: Mrs F Skinner
Assistant to the Bursar: Mrs S Ball
Admissions Registrar: Mrs L Armstrong
Careers and Examinations Officer: Mrs J Rawlins

A local school at the heart of the community.

Greenacre School was established in 1933 by two exceptional young women: Miss Sabine Pasley and fellow teacher, Mrs Patricia Wagstaffe. Both had a deep flair for teaching and a vision for a school that would provide not only excellent academic standards, but also an education tailored specifically to the needs of girls and young women. That vision is still central to the school today.

Greenacre is a thriving and vibrant school, large enough to offer variety, challenge and opportunities for all talents and interests, but small enough for each girl to be known as a unique individual, enabling her to realise her full potential. Staff are highly qualified and committed to instilling the very best work habits in the girls and preparing them for an active role in the world. Academic standards are high and the school offers a very broad curriculum at all levels, with class sizes that allow teachers to respond to individual girls and their preferred learning styles. This results in the girls reaching the very best of their academic ability, as our exam results demonstrate.

Greenacre is also a human and sociable school in which girls of all ages, from 3 to 18, have the opportunity to develop fully, with all its resulting freedom and happiness. Pastoral care is exceptional and all girls are known and treated as individuals. Staff and parents work in partnership to support and develop each girl. There is a discernible atmosphere of consideration, friendliness and compassion throughout the school.

It is a very happy community that values its links with the wider world, both locally and globally. Girls are encouraged to develop as responsible citizens and rounded individuals through many varied activities. Many girls are involved in sport, music, drama and the Duke of Edinburgh Award scheme; fundraising events for nominated charities are imaginative and well supported; varied and exciting overseas trips are on offer as well as opportunities to develop skills in public speaking, leadership and team work.

The original ethos of the school is still in place today and is shared by the Headmistress, Mrs Redding. She says "I am delighted that Greenacre School continues to uphold and further these principals. Greenacre girls flourish in the school's wonderful environment and atmosphere where an innovative and outward looking approach is aligned with a respect for traditional values. They emerge as articulate, confident and inquisitive, accomplished, yet considerate young women of whom we are rightly proud."

Fees per term (2014–2015). £2,966–£5,094. Lunches are included from Nursery (full day) through to Sixth Form.

Scholarships. Academic Scholarships, including the Founders' Scholarship, are awarded to girls on entry to the Senior School. Sports, Performing Arts and Creative Arts Scholarships are also awarded at 11+ and Sixth Form. Academic Scholarships are awarded at 16+.

Charitable status. Greenacre School for Girls Ltd is a Registered Charity, number 312034. It exists to provide education for girls.

Haberdashers' Aske's School for Girls

Aldenham Road, Elstree, Herts WD6 3BT
Tel: 020 8266 2300
Fax: 020 8266 2303
email: theschool@habsgirls.org.uk
website: www.habsgirls.org.uk

Motto: *Serve and Obey*
 This School forms part of the ancient foundation of Robert Aske and is governed by members of the Worshipful Company of Haberdashers, together with certain representatives of other bodies.

Clerk to the School Governors: Mr C M Bremner

Headmistress: Miss B A O'Connor, MA Oxon

Personal Assistant to the Headmistress: Mrs B Cohen

Senior Deputy Head: Mr R James-Robbins, BA London
Deputy Head (Academic): Dr S Lindfield, BSc Liverpool
Deputy Head (Pastoral): Miss G Mellor, BA Exeter

Bursar: Mr D Thompson, BA Manchester, ACIB

Teaching Staff:
* *Head of Department*

Art:
*Mrs P White, BA Sheffield School of Art & Design
Mrs S Deamer, BA Manchester
Mrs D Hobbs, BA Lancaster
Miss K Shaw, BA Manchester Met
Mrs S Wiseman, MA London

Careers and Higher Education:
*Mrs R Davies, BA Cardiff

Classics:
*Mr A Doe, BA Oxon
Miss A Dugdale, MA Oxon
Mrs C Jessop, MA Cantab
Miss E Tesh, BA Cantab

Design and Technology:
*Mr M Squire, BSc South Bank
Mrs S Deamer, BA Manchester
Mr J Oliver, BA Warwick
Mr S Turner, BSc Brunel

Drama:
*Ms L Wallace, BA London
Ms E Bridgeman-Williams, BA Middlesex

Economics:
*Mr M Catley, BSc LSE
Mrs S K Hender, BA Leeds
Mrs K Sobczyk, BSc London (*Deputy Head of Sixth Form*)

English:
*Miss I Condon, BA Manchester
Mr J Benjamin, MA Cantab
Miss K Humpage, BA Leeds
Mr R James-Robbins, BA London
Mrs A Leifer, BA Birmingham
Dr F Miles, BA Cantab (*Head of Upper School*)
Mrs K Nash, MA Cantab
Mrs J Seddon, BA Manchester
Mr D Thakerar, BA London
Mrs L Winton, BA Manchester (*Head of Middle School*)

Geography:
*Mrs S Ashton, BSc Keele
Ms A Bowen, BSc Manchester, MSc London, FRGS
Mrs C Gilbert, BA, PGCE Nottingham

Mrs C Needham, BSc Loughborough
Miss H Wakefield, MSc Lougborough

History:
*Mrs A Pearson, BA Dunelm
Mr K Davies, MA London
Mrs R Davies, BA Cardiff
Mrs C De Groot, BSc Loughborough
Mr P Harper, MA Oxon
Mr D Sabato, BA Nottingham
Mrs C Wilding, BA Bristol (*Government and Politics*)

Individual Educational Needs:
Ms A Baker, BA Oxford Brookes (*Senior School*)
Mrs S Stringer, BEd Exeter (*Junior School*)

Information Technology:
Mrs N Verma, BSc Westminster

Library:
Mrs A Fynes-Clinton, BA Canterbury, New Zealand

Mathematics:
*Mrs C Godfrey, BSc Leicester
Miss L Chelliah, BSc Kent
Mrs N Gohil, BEng Aston
Mr C Howlett, BSc Dunelm
Mr J Kinoulty, MSc Dublin
Mrs S Lee, BSc Manchester
Mrs R Patel, BSc LSE
Mrs S Patel, BSc City
Mrs K Roantree, BA York
Mrs L Woodville, BSc York

Modern Languages:
*Sr J Carbonell, MA London (*Spanish*)
Mrs A Bass, MA Le Mans, France
Miss J Bouchard, Licence, Lyon
Miss A Conti, MPhil Cantab
Mrs E Green, BA Oxon
Miss G Mellor, BA Exeter
Miss K Osmond, BA Bristol
Mrs F Ray, L-ès-L Maître, CAPES (*French*)
Miss H Robinson, BA Cantab
Ms M Salvatierra-Romero, Eng and Phil Seville
Mr M Smeaton, BA Leeds
Mrs M Tamura, BA Yokohama, Japan
Miss A Tebb, BA Oxon (*German*)
Ms K Ting, BA Taiwan
Ms A Villarejo-Carrion, BA Portsmouth
and 5 visiting oral teachers

Music:
*Mr A Phillips, MMus London
Miss O Clarke, BA Oxon
Mr D Davies, BA Keele
Mr T Scott, MA Cantab (*Assistant Director of Music*)
Ms A Turnbull, LRAM
and 25 visiting teachers

Physical Education:
*Miss C Hill, BSc Birmingham
Miss N Burns, BSc Exeter
Miss E Daly, BEd Plymouth
Miss N Haw, BA Leeds
Mrs C Prendergast, BA Brighton
Miss K Roberts, BSc Loughborough

Politics:
*Mrs C Wilding, BA Bristol

Religion and Philosophy:
*Mrs K Opie, MA London
Ms L Childs, BA Manchester
Mrs S Evans, MA Oxon

Science:
*Mrs V Leigh, BSc London (*Biology*)
Mr B Anderson, BSc Birmingham

Dr C Badger, MA Cantab (*Chemistry*)
Mrs B Bhatti, BSc London
Dr H Burgess, MA Cantab
Dr R Catchpole, MSc London, MBBS
Mrs J Dabby-Joory, BSc Southampton
Miss E Dinsey, BSc London
Mrs N Ghinn, BSc Nottingham
Dr J Harvey-Barrett, BSc Newcastle
Dr S Harnett, MA Oxon (*Head of Sixth Form*)
Mr G Jervis, MA London
Miss R Lane, BA Cantab
Dr S Lindfield, BSc Liverpool
Mrs Z Makepeace-Welsh, MA Oxon
Miss N Percy, BSc Leeds (*Physics*)
Dr C Ruddick, BSc Exeter
Mrs A Sharif, BSc London
Mr C Shaw, BSc London
Mr R Shopland, BA Exeter
Mr E Stock, MPhys Oxon

Junior School:
Interim Head: Mr R James-Robbins, BA London
Deputy Head: Mrs A Latimer, BA Hull
Head of Infants: Mrs B Mayho, New Zealand
Miss E Burman, BA Surrey
Miss C Chapman, BA East Anglia
Mrs S Collins, MA Kingston (*ICT Specialist*)
Mrs P Dear, BSc Wales
Mrs M Demetriou, BEd Hertfordshire
Mrs R Desbois, BSc London
Miss E Galvin, BA Warwick
Mrs C Gibson, BSc Worcester
Ms M Hirsch, BMus London
Mr N Hobley, BSc Oxford Brookes
Dr J Hogg, BSc North Wales (*Curriculum Coordinator*)
Miss K Keith, BA Bournemouth
Mrs L Liddelow, BEd Exeter
Mrs A Mack, BEd Brighton
Mrs E Miller, BA Hertfordshire
Mrs J Millman, BEd Leeds
Mrs J Nicholas, BA Newcastle
Miss L Ryan, BA Brighton
Mrs C Sawkins, BA Surrey
Mr I Stroud, BSc London
Mrs M Tatman, BA Hertfordshire
Ms S Tersigni, BA Middlesex

Haberdashers' Aske's School for Girls is situated on a site of over 50 acres, and has an excellent reputation for academic, sporting and musical achievements. Entry to the Junior School is at 4+, 5+ or at 7+; at the Senior School, it is at 11+ and Sixth Form. The academic results are outstanding, the reflection of able pupils who enjoy learning and thrive on a full and challenging curriculum.

First-class facilities, with work in progress on a brand new Dining Room and Learning Resources Centre, and a very wide range of extra-curricular activities, are provided within the school. Sport, music, drama, art and debating thrive and there are many other opportunities for leadership within the school community including the Duke of Edinburgh's Award Scheme, the Community Sports Leadership Award and a very active community service programme. Life at Habs is busy and challenging, embracing new technology, for example, digital language labs, touchscreen interactive whiteboards and remote access to all electronic work areas via the intranet, alongside old traditions, which include the celebration of St Catherine's Day as patron of the Haberdashers' Company.

Over 110 coach routes, shared with the Haberdashers' Aske's Boys' School next door, bring pupils to school from a thirty-mile radius covering north London, Hertfordshire and Middlesex. The provision of a late coach service ensures that pupils can take part safely in the wide range of the many clubs and societies organised after school. The St Catherine Parents' Guild, the school's parents' association, provides enormous support to the school through fundraising and social events.

Junior School. There are approximately 300 day girls aged 4–11 in the Junior School, with one reception class and two parallel classes of equal ability from Years 1–6.

Pastoral Care: Class teachers and teaching assistants maintain close contact with girls and their parents. It is very important that the girls feel happy and comfortable. Every adult has a responsibility for the girls' welfare and security and there are many layers of care in place. From the outset, through the behaviour code, girls are encouraged to be friendly and polite to everyone else in the community, adults and children. There are two nurses, a counsellor and an individual needs specialist as well as the teaching and assistant staff available for pastoral care. Where appropriate, older girls have responsibility for younger ones and Senior School Sixth Formers regularly help Juniors in the classroom. A programme of PSHCE (personal, social, health & citizenship education lessons) covers important issues of self-development. Many parents are involved in the classroom, clubs and outings.

Spiritual and Moral Education: Haberdashers' is a school with a Christian tradition which welcomes the rich diversity of faiths within the community. Assemblies are held for the whole school once a week and on other days are separate for Infants and Juniors. Themes, stories and prayers are drawn from a range of cultures and faiths. Once a year, each class performs an assembly to which their parents are invited. Parents are also invited to attend Harvest Festival, the St Catherine's Day assembly and the Carol Service. Girls take part in many charitable ventures throughout the year, raising money and enhancing their awareness of lives in the wider world.

Enrichment: There is a wide range of over 30 clubs covering the girls' interests in sport, music, arts and crafts, languages, science, maths, creative writing, reading, games and puzzles, cookery and gardening. Termly visits linked to the curriculum are arranged for every class and there are regular visitors to school such as theatre companies, historical recreations, authors, illustrators, musicians and scientists.

The curriculum provides a core of gymnastics, dance, swimming, netball, tennis, athletics and rounders. Teams in netball, cricket, football, gymnastics, rounders and pop lacrosse compete against other schools. There are two major drama productions annually: an Infant production for all girls in Reception and Key Stage One, and a dramatic production for Year 6. The annual Spring Concert showcases all the musical groups and ensembles as well as a massed choir of all Key Stage Two girls. The summer Chamber Concert features ensembles of girls who learn a musical instrument. Informal lunchtime concerts occur at least once a term for Year 4 to 6 soloists or duets. Art and design work is displayed around the school.

Curriculum: There is a broad and challenging curriculum with the provision of opportunities for active and independent learning, with plenty of practical tasks and problem solving, to enable girls to develop their bright young minds. Fun is a vital ingredient. There are curriculum evenings for parents to learn about the school's approach to particular subject areas and how they can best support the girls at home and work in true partnership with the school.

The Early Learning Goals of the Foundation Stage are met through a balance of child-initiated opportunities and teacher-led activities. There is a daily range of stimulating, play-based activities which prompts girls to ask questions, to discover, to wonder and to learn new skills. No homework is set in Reception or Year 1 so that girls can enjoy the precious childhood pleasures of imaginative play and being read to by a parent when they get home. Music and daily PE lessons are taught by specialist teachers. Phonics teaching enables girls to make rapid progress with reading and to gain an easy independence in their writing while the foundations of mathematical thinking are laid through carefully selected practical tasks. Girls spend time in the ICT suite mastering computing skills. Creativity is fostered in music and dance, in art, design technology, literacy activities, drama and role play. The school grounds provide a rich environment for building knowledge about the world of nature as well as space to develop physical skills.

At Key Stage One, curriculum subjects are English, mathematics, science, history, geography, religious studies, French, ICT, art, design technology, music, PSHCE and physical education, including swimming. Fostering a love of reading is paramount. A little homework is introduced in Year 2.

As girls progress through Key Stage Two they encounter more subject specialists. Science lessons, which are taught in the well equipped laboratory, strongly feature practical and investigative work. The Art Room is a magnificent space for the creation of stunning works of art while girls can feel transported to another culture as soon as they step into the Languages Room.

Senior School. There are approximately 890 day girls aged 11–18 in the Senior School.

Pastoral Care: In such a big and busy school, care for each individual girl is deeply important so that all girls flourish and fulfil themselves in every way. Looking after them is a pastoral team consisting of the Deputy Head, Heads of Section, Form Tutors, a School Nurse, a Counsellor and an Individual Needs Specialist. The provision of pastoral care is designed to help girls make decisions and to care about others within the framework of a very diverse community. There is an outstanding range of opportunities for the girls' personal development and to help them consolidate a system of spiritual beliefs and a moral code. The welfare of the girls is of paramount importance and it is the responsibility of all members of staff, teaching and support staff, to safeguard and promote it. From the moment a girl joins the school, emphasis is placed on the partnership with parents so that, hand-in-hand, school and parents can support each child, operating on a basis of trust and with people she knows from the start.

Spiritual and Moral Education: Haberdashers' is a school with a Christian tradition which welcomes the rich diversity of faiths within the community. Every day begins with a whole school or Section assembly, often led by the girls themselves. Once a week there are separate Christian, Hindu, Jain and Sikh, Humanist, Jewish and Muslim assemblies. Girls can choose which one they attend. Holy Communion takes place twice a term. Roman Catholic Mass is celebrated each half term, either in the Girls' or the Boys' School. Muslim girls may pray at lunchtime in a room set aside for them to do so. Girls organize and run many charitable events throughout the year. This enhances their awareness of the wider world as well as raising funds for charities small and large, at home and abroad.

Enrichment: There is a wide range of clubs on offer in the Senior School, including art, creative writing, cricket, dance, debating, design technology, drama, football, Japanese, maths, philosophy, science, and swimming; there are also campaigning groups such as Amnesty International and the Animal Welfare Society. Trips and visits include a Year 7 adventure holiday and various trips abroad, with language exchanges, work experience, and study visits. Subject specific trips in the UK and abroad include field trips, theatre visits, trips to sites of historical importance, museums and art galleries, music and sports tours.

The core curriculum includes gymnastics, dance, swimming, lacrosse, netball, tennis, athletics and rounders. For older girls, there are additional options in self defence, basketball, volleyball, football, step-aerobics, trampolining, badminton, weight-training, judo, life-saving, synchronised swimming, water polo, golf and squash. There are clubs in a range of sports for recreational enjoyment as well as for the teams. There are major drama productions in all sections of

the school and symphonic concerts showcasing a variety of ensembles including three orchestras, wind and jazz bands, percussion groups, flute choirs, and rock bands as well as recitals and chamber concerts. There are annual Drama and Music Festivals; occasionally, there are joint productions and orchestral concerts with the Boys' School. Girls' painting, sculpture and design installations are displayed around the school.

Opportunities for leadership and challenge are valued and encouraged. Activities include: The Duke of Edinburgh's Award; Tall Ships; Community Service; Community Sports Leader's Award; European Youth Parliament; Model United Nations; English Speaking Union; and the Oxford Union.

Curriculum: The school follows its own wide-ranging academic curriculum tailored to the needs of its very able pupils. It preserves the best of a traditional education whilst responding positively to curricular developments. Much emphasis is placed on developing the girls' ability to think and learn independently, nurturing an intellectual resilience and self confidence which will prepare them for the world beyond school. In all subjects, the curriculum aims to be something that inspires the girls and stimulates discussion and ideas. A high value is placed upon creativity, imagination and the opportunity to pursue topics beyond the confines of the exam specifications. The school is not required to follow the National Curriculum but draws upon the best practice of what is happening nationally and in other schools. In the first three years of the Senior School, girls follow a set curriculum, choosing either Spanish or German as their second modern language. As they progress through the school they are given greater choice and the opportunity to personalise their curriculum to suit their needs and interests. Thus the GCSE curriculum has space for up to four optional subjects. In the Sixth Form the girls have a free choice of subjects from the 23 subjects on offer. At each level, the curriculum is designed to prepare them for the opportunities, responsibilities and experiences of the next stage of their education and their lives.

Fees per term (2014–2015). Senior School £4,834; Junior School £4,173. A number of scholarships are awarded annually and means-tested financial assistance (up to full fees) is also available.

Charitable status. The Haberdashers' Aske's Charity is a Registered Charity, number 313996. It exists to promote education.

Haberdashers' Monmouth School for Girls

Hereford Road, Monmouth NP25 5XT

Tel:	01600 711100
Fax:	01600 711233
email:	admissions@hmsg.co.uk
website:	www.habs-monmouth.org

Motto: *Serve and Obey*

Trustees: The Worshipful Company of Haberdashers

Governing Body:
Chairman: Mr J B S Swallow, MA, FCA

The Master of the Worshipful Company of Haberdashers (*ex officio*)

Miss H Hutton
Dr J Kelly
Mr A M Kerr
Mr A G Nicholas

Mrs T Pike
Mrs R F Rose
Councillor Mrs S White

Clerk to the Governors: Mrs F Creasey, BCom, ACMA

Bursar: Mrs T Norgrove

Headmistress: Mrs C A Pascoe, BSc Hons Bristol, MSc Leicester, PGCE Roehampton

Deputy Head: Mr T Arrand, MA Oxon, PGCE Cantab
Director of Studies: Mrs O E Davis, BSc Joint Hons Salford, MA Ed, PGCE York
Academic Registrar: Mr D R Evans, BA Hons Coventry, MA Wales, PGCE Wales
Head of Sixth Form: Mrs J A Poyner BSc Hons Exeter, PGCE Wales, MBA Education Keele
Head of Boarding: Mrs P J Mills, BA Hons Sheffield, PGCE Cambridge
Chaplain: Reverend D P Ibbotson, BSc Manchester, FDA Winchester

* *Head of Department*

Art:
*Mrs V E Reynolds, BA Hons Oxford Brookes, MA Brighton, PGCE Wales
Mr C Beer, BA Hons, PGCE UWIC
Miss L Porritt, BA Hons Wales, PGCE Wales
Mr J Kavanagh, BEd Bristol, LRPS (*Photography*)

Business Studies:
*Mr D R Evans, BA Hons Coventry, MA Wales, PGCE Wales
Ms M C Attrill, BTEC Dip Bus Studies, CertEd UWCN

Careers:
*Mrs A Jervis, BSc Hons Wales, MA UWCN, PGCE Wales

Classics:
*Mrs L Beech, BA Hons Birmingham, PGCE Cambridge
Dr C H Geisz, Licence BA France, MA Paris IV, DPhil Oxon

Dance:
Director of Dance: * Ms R V Parry, BA Hons, PGCE Bedford
Ms Z Pritchard, TCert RAD, Teaching Associate ISTD, Dip Dance Ed
Mrs C Thomas, LRAD, ARAD, AISTD, ALAM, BA Open

Drama & Theatre Studies:
* Ms H Wragg, BA Hons Leeds

Economics:
*Mr D R Evans, BA Hons Coventry, MA Wales, PGCE Wales

English:
*Mrs Z Harvey, BA Hons Wales, PGCE London
Mr J A Edwards, BA Hons, MA Warwick, PGCE Wales
Mrs C Gunter, BA Hons Swansea
Mrs J Hastings, BA Hons London, MSc Westfield, LSE, BA Hons, Open Univ PhD, LSE
Ms J Knight, BA Hons Cardiff, MA Cardiff, PGCE UWE

Geography:
*Mr N Meek, BA Hons Middlesex, MA Leicester, PGCE Wales, MEd Birmingham
Mr L Jones, BSc Hons Reading, PGCE Swansea, MA Worcester
Mr M Seaton, BA Hons, PGCE Swansea
Mrs J E Harper, BSc Hons, PGCE Aberystwyth

History:
*Mr D Griffiths, BA Hons Wales, PGCE Wales
Mrs R Griffiths, BA Hons Wales, MA Wales, PGCE Wales
Mr M Seaton, BA Hons, PGCE Swansea

ICT:
*Mrs C Jones, BSc Hons, PGCE Wales

Mathematics:
*Mrs C L McGladdery, BSc Hons, PGCE Manchester
Mrs B M Keyton, BSc Hons Wales, PGCE Wales
Dr S Lawlor, BSc Hons Dublin, PhD Leeds, PGCE UWIC
Mrs J E Morris, BSc Hons, PGCE Wales
Mrs J A Poyner, BSc Hons Exeter, PGCE Wales, MBA Education Keele
Mrs V R Price, BSc Ed UWCN

Modern Languages:
* Mrs H K Smail, MA Reading, PGCE Birmingham (*French, *German)
Mrs K Wellings, BA Hons Hull, PGCE London (*French*, *Spanish)
Mrs O E Davis, BSc Jt Hons Salford, MA, PGCE York (*Spanish*)
Mrs C A Griffiths, BA Hons London, PGCE Reading (*German, French*)
Mrs A Hutchings, BA Hons Bath, PGCE UWIC (*French, German*)
Mrs P Mills, BA Hons Sheffield, PGCE Cambridge (*French, Spanish*)
Mrs R Rees, BA Hons Manchester, PGCE Bristol (*French, German*)
Miss F Froment (*French Foreign Language Assistant*)
Miss M Karner (*German Foreign Language Assistant*)

Music:
Director of Music: *Mr M Conway, BMus Hons, MA, PGCE Wales, LTCL, ARCM
Mrs A Clouter, BA Hons Bristol, MA Cardiff, PGCE UWIC
Mrs R Friend, LRAM, LRAM TD

Personal and Social Education (*Confidence 4 Life*):
Miss J Johnson, BSc Hons OU, PGCE Carmarthen

Physical Education and Sport:
Director of Sport: *Miss K Marshall, BSc Hons Sports Coaching Wales
Head of Physical Education: Mrs C F Crawford, BA Hons UWIC, PGCE UWIC
Mrs R Harris, BSc Hons Sport and Physical Ed UWIC, PGCE Exeter
Mrs C E Jones, BSc Hons Wolverhampton, MSc Wales, PGCE
Mrs S J Rossiter, BSc Hons South Bank, PGCE Wales
Miss L Scott, BA Hons QTS PE Chichester

Psychology:
*Mrs A E Jervis, BSc, Hons Wales MA UWCN, PGCE Wales
Mrs K Smith, BSc Hons Bath Spa, Dip Teaching

Religious Studies:
*Mr J M Lewis, BDiv MTh, PGCE Wales, MPhil
Mr T Arrand, MA Oxon, PGCE Cantab
Miss J Johnson, BSc OU, PGCE Carmarthen

Rowing:
*Mrs K A Callaghan, BA Hons Surrey
Mr K Williams, Rowing Coach and Boatman
Miss P Thomas, Assistant Rowing Coach

Science:
* Mrs D E Clarke, BSc Hons Newcastle, PGCE Durham (*Chemistry)
Miss L J Woodburn, BSc Hons, PGCE Glasgow (*Biology)
Mrs A B Kavanagh, BEd Hons Cheltenham (*Physics)
Mrs L C Arnold, BA Hons Oxford
Mrs C Avila-Jones, BSc Hons Wales, PGCE UWIC (*Physics*)
Mrs D L Davies, BSc Hons, PGCE Wales (*Physics*)
Miss R J Higgins, BSc Hons Physiotherapy Cardiff (*Biology*)

Mrs V Lyons, BSc Hons Cardiff, PGCE (*Biology*)
Mrs S P Marks, BSc Hons OU, PGCE Wales (*Chemistry*)
Mrs C Natt, BSc Hons Swansea, PGCE Worcester, MA Ed OU (*Biology*)
Dr I Wallace, BSc Hons Newcastle, PhD Cantab, PGCE OU (*Chemistry*)

Speech & Drama
* Mrs M Hill, BA Belfast, Cert Ed, LGSM
Ms H Wragg, BS Hons Leeds

Technology:
* Mr S McCluskey, BSc Hons Wales, PGCE Wales
Mrs N Clayton, BA Hons Central England, PGCE UWCN
Mrs J Vickers, CertEd Wales

Learning Support:
Mrs J Jefferies, BEd Liverpool, PGCE Gloucestershire
Mrs J Hendry, BA Hons Hull, PG East Anglia

Duke of Edinburgh's Award Coordinator
* Miss L Scott, BA Hons QTS PE Chichester

Inglefield House (*Preparatory Department*):
Headmistress: Mrs H J Phillips, BA, BEd Exeter
Deputy Head: Mr T Evans, BA Hons Aberystwyth, PGCE Cardiff
Mrs P M Champion, Dip Prim Ed Moray House
Mrs M E Dummett, BSc OU
Mrs H D Edmunds, BEd Liverpool
Mrs A Griffiths, BA Hons Bristol
Mrs J A Jones, BA Hons Surrey, PGCE Kingston
Mrs S Latheron, BSc Hons Brighton, BSc OU, PGCE Bristol
Miss C Pledger, BA English Plymouth, PGCE UWIC
Miss N C Price, BEd Hons UWE
Mrs H Rees, BA Joint Hons Cardiff, PGCE Wales
Miss A Roskilly, BA Hons Kent, PGCE Brighton

Learning Support for Inglefield House
Mrs A Copley, BHEd Kingston Polytechnic

Haberdashers' Monmouth School for Girls is one of the three schools of the Jones's Monmouth Foundation, arising from a bequest of William Jones, Merchant, in 1614, and administered by the Worshipful Company of Haberdashers. The School stands high on the outskirts of the town of Monmouth, in the beautiful countryside of the Wye Valley.

There are 461 girls in the Main School including a Sixth Form of 136. Pupils aged from 7 to 11 years have their own preparatory school, Inglefield House, of 111 girls on site. A thriving Boarding Community with accommodation on the school site, includes a Junior House and modern Senior House with study-bedrooms and Augusta House, the newly opened Sixth Form Boarding House with 45 en-suite bedrooms.

Classrooms and laboratories are extensive, with special Sixth Form provision. Specialist workshops are provided for DT and Drama. Full use is made of the ample sports facilities: spacious playing fields, all-weather pitch, tennis courts, sports hall, indoor swimming pool and gymnasium. All are adjacent to the School. A new classroom extension, including 4 new ICT suites, opened in September 2006, an updated Sixth Form block and Library in 2010 and a new Sixth Form Boarding House in 2012.

The School has its own Chaplain and is a Christian foundation. Girls are encouraged to attend the places of worship of their own denomination.

A large and fully qualified staff of graduates teaches a modern curriculum, which aims to achieve high academic results within a broader education, acknowledging our cultural inheritance and technological and social needs.

Classics is taught throughout the School. At examination level, Latin GCSE, Latin AS/A Level, and Classical Civilisation AS/A Level are offered. Classical Greek is offered by request as an extra-curricular activity.

Almost all pupils progress to Higher Education. With excellent careers advice, girls are aware of the scope of degree subjects. A number annually enter Oxford and Cambridge.

Every encouragement is given to creative and practical work, especially Music and Drama. Girls frequently attend concerts, plays and exhibitions, and an active interest is taken in industry and management. Local businesses lend support to the School's Young Enterprise schemes.

Girls participate in the Duke of Edinburgh's Award scheme, CCF at Monmouth School, help in the community and many also belong to local voluntary organisations.

Main sporting activities include lacrosse, netball, tennis, rowing, fencing, hockey and dance, many played at County, National and International level.

Fees per term (2014–2015). Day £4,419, Boarding £8,570–£9,085. Inglefield House: Day £3,317, Boarding £6,239.

Entry is usually at 7, 11, 13 or post GCSE, although occasionally other vacancies occur. Informal assessments for entry at 7+ to Inglefield House are held in the Lent Term. Entry to the Senior School is by examination, interview and report from the current school. The interviews and entrance examinations are held for 11+ in January, 13+ in February/March (or Common Entrance in June), and for 16+ in November.

Further information and a Prospectus is available from the Admissions Registrar, Tel: 01600 711104, email: admissions@hmsg.co.uk.

Scholarships and Bursaries. A number of academic scholarships are awarded at 11+, 13+ and 16+ to the best candidates on the basis of the school's entrance examination, interview and report from the current school. Music scholarships, also available at 11+, 13+ and 16+, are awarded on the basis of audition and interview held in the Lent Term for 11+ and 13+ and the Michaelmas Term for 16+.

At 13+ and 16+ entry, there are also Sports (including dance) and Creative Arts (art and drama) scholarships, which are awarded following an assessment day held at HMSG in the Lent Term for 13+ and the Michaelmas Term for 16+. New for entry in 2015 is an 11+ Sports scholarship (to include dance) with assessments in January 2015.

Means-tested Bursaries and Assisted Places of up to 100% of fees are also available at all entry points.

Further information may be obtained from the Admissions Registrar (as above).

Old Girls' Association. *Secretary*: Mrs S Rossiter, c/o Haberdashers' Monmouth School for Girls, Monmouth. The OGA Annual General Meeting is held at the school on the second Saturday in November.

Charitable status. William Jones's Schools Foundation is a Registered Charity, number 525616. The object of the Foundation shall be the provision and conduct in or near Monmouth of a day and boarding school for boys and a day and boarding school for girls.

Harrogate Ladies' College

Clarence Drive, Harrogate, North Yorkshire HG1 2QG
Tel: 01423 504543
email: enquire@hlc.org.uk
website: www.hlc.org.uk

Board of Governors:

Mrs R Bletcher	Dr A Fahy
Mrs R Bradby	Mrs S Gosling
Mrs L Byrne	Mrs S Jackson
Mr R Court	Mrs P Jones
Mr C Davies	Mrs C Peasgood
Mrs V Davies	Mr J Poskitt

Mrs S Pullan (*Chairman*)   Mr J Skinner
                                Mrs R Tunnicliffe

Secretary to the Governors and General Manager of Allied Schools: Mr M Porter, BA, MSc

Principal: Mrs Sylvia Brett, BA Dunelm, MA London

Deputy Head, Academic: Miss C Preece, BSc Manchester, MA OU

Deputy Head, Organisation: Mrs H Stansfield, BEd Bedford

Assistant Head, Head of Lower School: Mrs J Grazier, BEd Warwick, ACA

Assistant Head, Head of Middle School: Mrs F Irvine, BEd Bedford

Assistant Head, Head of Sixth Form: Mr R Tillett, MA Cantab

Assistant Head, Head of Boarding: Mr J Welham, BSc Durham

Director of Finance: Mrs R Henricksen, MA Edinburgh, ACA

Director of IT: Mr M Denby, BSc Royal Holloway

Head of Domestic Admissions: Mrs L Withy

International Registrar: Mrs S Downham

Heads of Departments:

Dr R Ashcroft, BA, PhD Huddersfield (*Head of History and Politics, Deputy Head of Sixth Form*)

Miss N Butters, BA Leeds, MMedSci Sheffield (*Director of Physical Education*)

Miss H Clothier, BA Salford (*Head of Geography*)

Mr M Cook, Dip NCDT, MA King's College, CELTA (*Head of Drama*)

Mrs R Donegan-Cross, BA Durham (*Chaplain*)

Mr P C Gill, BA Leeds, MA Leeds (*Head of Religious Studies*)

Mr R Hartley, MEng Cambridge (*Head of Physics*)

Mrs J List, BA York (*Head of Science and Biology*)

Mrs E Livesey, BA Central Lancashire (*Director of Technology*)

Mrs B Lumber, BSc Manchester (*Head of Mathematics*)

Mrs C M Martin, BA Leeds Polytechnic, AIL (*Head of Modern Languages*)

Mrs K Morgan, BMus, MusM Manc, PG Dip Music Therapy (*Director of Music*)

Mrs S Parker, BA Oxon (*Head of English*)

Mrs C Whelan, BA UCL (*Head of Classics*)

Miss K Williams, BEd Leeds (*Head of Art*)

Harrogate Ladies' College is a Boarding and Day school for 342 girls aged 11–18. Situated within the College campus, Bankfield Pre-Prep is a Day Pre-Prep for over 70 boys and girls between the ages of 2–4. Highfield Prep School, which opened in 1999, is a Day Prep school for over 214 boys and girls between the ages of 4–11.

Location. The College is situated in a quiet residential area on the Duchy Estate about 10 minutes' walk from the town centre and is easily accessible by road and rail networks. Leeds/Bradford airport is 20 minutes' drive away. Harrogate itself is surrounded by areas of natural interest and beauty.

Accommodation. Approximately half of the pupils are full or weekly boarders. Houses are arranged vertically from Upper Three (Year 7) to Lower Sixth. Upper Sixth Formers enjoy a greater sense of freedom in their own accommodation called 'Tower House'. This contains a large, modern kitchen, comfortable lounges and relaxation areas and girls have individual study-bedrooms. Each house has a Housemistress and Assistant Housemistress who are responsible for the well-being of the girls. There is a well-equipped Health Centre with qualified nurses.

Curriculum and Examinations. The College aims to provide a broad-based curriculum for the first three years in line with National Curriculum requirements. This leads to a choice of over 28 subjects at GCSE, IGCSE, Applied, AS and A Level mainly using syllabuses of the Northern Examination and Assessment Board (AQA). Each girl has a form tutor who continuously monitors and assesses her development.

Facilities. The central building contains the principal classrooms, hall, library, and dining rooms, and a VI Form Centre with studies, seminar rooms, kitchens and leisure facilities. The College Chapel is nearby. An extension provides 8 laboratories for Physics, Chemistry, Biology and Computer Studies. Three dedicated computer suites, provision in the boarding houses and throughout the school, form a computer network of 235 computers running Windows XP. Sixth formers have network access using their own laptops from studies and bedrooms. Additional facilities for specialised teaching include studies for Art, Pottery, Design and Technology, Drama and also for Home Economics and Textiles.

Our award winning HLC Business School is where girls are able to enjoy the academic study of Economics, Accounting, Business Studies and Psychology in a state-of-the-art business-like environment which helps prepare young women of today for the global world of tomorrow.

Sport. The College has its own sports hall, a full size indoor swimming pool, gymnasium, fitness centre, playing field, 9 tennis courts and 2 squash courts. Girls are taught a wide range of sports and may participate in sporting activities outside the school day. Lacrosse and netball are played in winter, and tennis, swimming and athletics are the main summer physical activities. Extra-curricular sports include badminton, sub-aqua, skiing, self-defence, judo, sailing and canoeing.

Sixth Form. The College has a thriving Sixth Form Community of 153 pupils. Girls have a choice of 26 courses at AS/A Level. There is a broad range of general cultural study. In preparation for adult life, Sixth Formers are expected to make a mature contribution to the running of the school and many hold formal positions of responsibility. Personal guidance is given to each girl with regard to her future plans and most pupils choose to continue their education at University.

Religious Affiliation. The College is Anglican although pupils of other religious denominations are welcomed. Religious teaching is in accordance with Christian principles and all girls attend Chapel services. A school confirmation is held each year in the chapel and girls may be prepared for acceptance into membership of churches of other denominations.

Music. A special feature is the interest given to music and choral work both in concerts and in the College Chapel, and the girls attend frequent concerts and dramatic performances in Harrogate. There are Junior and Senior choirs, orchestra, string, wind and brass groups.

Scholarships. Scholarships for music, art, drama and sport as well as some bursaries are awarded annually on the results of an examination held each Spring term and there are also several awards to girls already in the School.

Fees per term (2014–2015). Boarding from £8,500–£10,695; Day £4,935. There is a reduction for a girl joining her sister in the School. The fees cover most normal school charges. Individual tuition in a musical instrument, Dance (Ballet/Tap/Modern), Riding or Diction is an extra charge.

Entry. Entry is usually at age 11, 13 or at Sixth Form level. Entry is based on the College's own entrance examination and a school report. Sixth Form entry is conditional upon GCSE achievement and an interview with the Principal.

Charitable status. Harrogate Ladies' College Limited is a Registered Charity, number 529579. It exists to provide high-quality education for girls.

Headington School

Oxford OX3 7TD
Tel: 01865 759100
        Admissions: 01865 759113
Fax: 01865 760268
email: admissions@headington.org
website: www.headington.org

Governing Council:
Chair of Governors: Mrs Helen Batchelor, BSc
Vice Chair of Governors: Professor Adrian Banning, MB
   BS, FRCP, MD, FESC
Mrs Caroline Bevan, BSc, ACA, CTA
Dr Susan Burge, OBE, BSc, BM, DM, FRCP
Professor Katya Drummond, MA Oxon, PhD
Mr Christopher Harris
Mr Steven Harris, BSc, ACA
Lady Nancy Kenny, BA, PGCE
Mrs Penelope Lenon, BA Hons
Miss Bryony Moore, MBA
Mrs Sandra Phipkin, ACA
Miss Margaret Rudland, BSc
Mr Stephen Shipperley
Mrs Kate Simon, BA Hons, PGCE

Company Secretary: Mr John Clarke, BA of Stone King
   LLP

Clerk to the Council: Mr Richard Couzens, MBE, MA
   Cranfield

Headmistress: Mrs C Jordan, MA Oxon

Executive Committee:
Mrs C Jordan, MA Oxon
First Deputy Head (Academic): Dr J Jefferies, BSc, PhD
   Exeter
Deputy Head (Pastoral): Mr R Smith, MA Aberdeen
Bursar: Mr R Couzens, MBE, MA Cranfield
Mrs J Crouch, BA Keele, MA London

Senior Leadership Team:
First Deputy Head (Academic): Dr J Jefferies, BSc, PhD
   Exeter
Second Deputy Head (Staff & Systems): Mrs C Knight, BSc
   Strathclyde
Deputy Head (Pastoral): Mr R Smith, MEd Buckingham,
   MA Aberdeen
Deputy Head (Co-curricular): Mr S Hawkes, BA Brunel
Bursar: Mr R Couzens, MBE, MA Cranfield

Senior Management Group:
Assistant Bursar (Finance): Mrs K Hoy, BSc Birmingham
Assistant Head (EVEC): Mrs L Gregory, BA Exeter
Assistant Head (IB): Mr J Stephenson, BSc Nottingham
Assistant Head (Pupil Development): Mr J Kelly, MChem
   Oxon
Assistant Head (Staff): Mrs V Sinclair, Cert Ed London,
   CELTA
Assistant Head (Systems): Mrs R Bowen, MA Oxon
Academic Director of Sixth Form: Mrs J Partridge, BA MA
   Cantab
Pastoral Director of Sixth Form: Mrs C Ellott, BA Oxon,
   MA London
Head of Lower School: Mrs E Bedford, BA Durham, MA
   Oxford Brookes
Head of Middle School: Ms B Dyer, BEd Central School of
   Speech & Drama
Admissions Registrar: Mrs S Sowden, BSc London
Director of Development: Mr T Edge, BA London
Estates Manager (Clerk of Works): Mr P Mulvany, CIOB
HR Manager: Mrs J Seetaram, CIPD Oxford Brookes
Marketing Manager: Ms N O'Shea, MA Cantab, CIM
Head of Boarding: Mrs K Olliver, BA Dublin

Chaplain: Mr T Howell, MBiochem Oxford

Heads of Year:
Head of U6: Miss S Patterson BSc Edinburgh
Head of L6: Dr T Waite, BSc, PhD Oxford Brookes
Head of U5: Mrs M Clarke, BSc Portsmouth
Head of L5: Mr S Drew, BA Lancaster, MA Lancaster
Head of U4: Mrs A Struele, MSci Imperial
Head of L4: Mrs D Bates-Brownsword, BEd South
   Australian College
Head of U3: Miss N Bromley, BSc Brunel

Boarding:
Head of Boarding: Mrs K Olliver BA Dublin
Celia Marsh Housemistress: Mrs M Rahmatallah LLB
   Durham
Davenport Housemistress: Miss R Collings, BA Sussex,
   MA Durham
Hillstow Housemistress: Mme C Preston, Licence Orléans
MacGregor Housemistress: Miss C Brown, BSc
   Manchester, MSc Cranfield
Napier Housemistress: Miss L Holloway, BA Oxon

IB Team:
Director of IB: Mr J Stephenson, BSc Nottingham
Creativity Action Service Coordinator: Mrs V Sinclair, Cert
   Ed London, CELTA
Theory of Knowledge Coordinator: Mr M Wilson, MusB
   Manchester

Heads of Departments:
Art and Design and Art History: Mr M Taylor, BA
   Coventry
Classics: Mrs A Barrett, BA Oxon
Drama and Theatre Studies: Mrs C Rigby, BA, MA Rose
   Bruford College of Speech & Drama
Economics and Business Studies: Mrs H Waywell, BSc
   Loughborough
English: Dr S Burley, BA UCL, MPhil Oxon, PhD London
English as an Additional Language: Mrs V Sinclair, Cert
   Ed London, CELTA
Environmental Science: Mrs J Quirk, BSc Birmingham
Geography: Mr D Cunningham, BSc Glasgow
History: Mrs S Wilkinson, BA Newcastle
Home Economics: Mrs M Colquhoun, BEd Bath
Information and Communication Technology: Mr M Howe,
   BA East Anglia
Law: Mrs C Shepherd, LLB
Learning Development: Dr J Leadbeater, BA, PhD Durham
Mathematics: Mrs H Spencer, BA Oxon
Modern Languages: Mrs R Pike, BA Exeter
French: Mme V Crépeau, Licence Caen
German: Mr R Kendall, BA London
Spanish: Mrs R Pike, BA Exeter
Music: Mr J Hutchings, BMus London
Philosophy and Religious Studies: Mr C Fox, BA Sheffield,
   MA Warwick
Physical Education:
Director of Sport & Rowing: Mr R Demaine, BA Rhodes
   University
Head of Curriculum PE and Head of Netball: Miss P
   Thomas, BEd De Montfort
Head of Games and Head of Hockey: Mr D Bridle
Politics: Mr M Edwards, BA, MA Exeter
PSHE: Miss L Allen-Mirehouse, BEng Plymouth
Psychology: Mrs K Pigott, BA Cape Town, MA Oxford
   Brookes
Science: Mr J Morris
Biology: Mrs J Quirk, BSc Birmingham
Chemistry: Dr E Regardsoe, BSc UCL, MPhil and DPhil
   Oxford
Physics: Mr A Bacon, BSc London

Admissions Registrar: Mrs S Sowden, BSc KCL

Headington is a highly successful day and boarding school in Oxford for 800 girls aged 11–18 with a Preparatory School for 280 girls aged 3–11 occupying its own site just across the road. (*See Headington Preparatory School entry in IAPS section.*)

The school offers girls from Nursery to Sixth Form an unrivalled opportunity to pursue academic, sporting and artistic excellence in a caring and nurturing environment.

Founded in 1915 and set in 23 acres of playing fields and gardens, our superb facilities provide the perfect backdrop for teaching and learning that extends way beyond the classroom and curriculum. We encourage participation in all aspects of sport and culture, teamwork and leadership, challenging girls to discover and explore their own potential and achieve more than they thought possible.

Consistently in the premier league of academic schools in the UK, life at Headington is about much more than exam results. Through the sheer breadth of subjects and activities at Headington – and the option to study for the International Baccalaureate – we aim to educate the complete individual, giving girls the confidence and self-awareness to compete, contribute and succeed at school, university and in their adult lives.

Facilities. Headington offers a superb range of facilities to day girls and boarders to support and enhance their learning. Our state-of-the-art Music School is a worthy addition to the school's arts complex and has superb acoustics that inspire musicians of all abilities. As well as its teaching rooms it includes a recording studio and electronics studio. The 240-seat Theatre, run by a professional team who provide expertise in set design, lighting and sound design, is home to the school's drama department. The Art School provides a fitting environment to display our students' work, complemented by four art studios and a photography darkroom. Our sports facilities include a floodlit all-weather pitch, sports hall and light and airy 25m indoor swimming pool.

Curriculum. In Years U3 and L4 in the Lower School girls are taught in four classes of around 20 each, which increases to six slightly smaller classes in U4 after 13+ entry. They learn English Language and Literature, Mathematics, three sciences, French, Latin, Geography, History and Religious Studies, with a choice of German or Spanish added in L4. The inclusion of Art, DT, Textiles, Food and Nutrition, Drama, Music, ICT and PE in the timetable from U3 means all girls can benefit from the widest possible curriculum. Girls choose their GCSE options in U4, usually taking a maximum 10 subjects in years L5 and U5. We offer a mix of IGCSE and GCSE, with seven core subjects and a free choice from a further 14 subjects. The majority of students move into the Sixth Form from the Middle School and many new girls, both day and boarders, also join us at this stage. Headington offers both A Levels and the International Baccalaureate Diploma in the Sixth Form (our Diamond Jubilee building, opened in 2012, has 13 full-size classrooms and includes two Sixth Form teaching rooms fitted out as IT suites).

Physical Education. From Olympic rowers to recreational dancers, Headington offers a genuinely inclusive approach to PE and extra-curricular sport and encourages each girl to enjoy sport at the level that suits her. PE is taught throughout the school and many girls choose to study PE to GCSE. They can choose from more than 30 different sporting activities, from dance and fencing to equestrian and trampolining. Games such as hockey, netball and athletics are played competitively against other schools and girls have the chance to represent the school across a range of abilities. More than 70 girls currently compete at county level and beyond and the school enjoys national success in a wide range of sports including swimming, cheerleading and rowing. Our rowers compete at the very highest level, with the school consistently triumphing at the National Schools' Regatta and earning its spot at the top of the sport. More than 150 of our girls row and regularly go on to represent Great Britain at international competitions.

Music. At Headington every girl has the opportunity to enjoy music at the level that is right for her, both within the curriculum and beyond. Musical opportunities in our state-of-the-art Music School are impressive. Five hundred individual music lessons take place each week and 28 visiting teachers offer girls the opportunity to learn a wide range of instruments. The Senior School has three orchestras and three choirs, varying in style from the Second Orchestra and Third and Fourth Form Choir, for which there are no auditions, to the exceptional Chamber Choir, which has made numerous recordings and toured overseas.

Drama. The 240-seat Theatre is home to a thriving drama department. There is a busy programme of productions each year and girls of all ages become involved in all aspects of theatre, from writing and producing their own plays, to lighting, costume and make-up. Girls progress from a weekly class in the Lower School to choosing drama at GCSE and A Level, or as part of the International Baccalaureate. Many girls also elect to take private Guildhall Speech and Drama exams in school.

Extra-curricular activities. More than 50 extra-curricular activities take place every week during lunchtime, before and after school. A wide choice of subjects, sports, interests and hobbies ranges from the Duke of Edinburgh's Award and Drama to Astronomy and Run Your Own Company and includes such diverse pastimes as debating and fencing, cheerleading and quilting. Headington has a very successful Combined Cadet Force, with around 60 cadets from L5 and above in our Army detachment. Success at CCF and the Duke of Edinburgh's Award gives girls a huge sense of personal achievement, increased confidence, leadership and teamwork.

Higher Education and Careers. Whether they have chosen to study for A Levels or the International Baccalaureate Diploma, all girls continue to higher education, heading to leading universities in the UK and abroad. A significant number of girls choose Oxbridge each year; some head for medical or veterinary college and others take up Art Foundation courses. Girls graduate from a wide range of arts and science degrees in subjects as diverse as civil engineering, architecture, classics and natural sciences. Detailed assistance on choice of universities is given in the Sixth Form through specialist computer programmes and careers tutors. A careers programme is in place throughout the school, with plenty of individual help as girls reach their GCSE years.

Boarding. Headington has always been a boarding school and almost a third of the school – around 250 girls – board with us today. The four boarding houses provide the girls with a 'home from home' where, supported by a team of highly experienced staff, they learn to develop into mature and independent young people. Many of our boarders come from the UK and we are also very proud of our international boarding community, made up of more than 30 nationalities from all over the world. Girls can choose between full boarding or weekly boarding.

Uniform. The blue-checked skirt, pale blue shirt, jumper and blazer are smart, comfortable and easy to care for. Girls in the Sixth Form wear their own smart-casual clothes.

Entrance. Entry to the Prep School is in order of application from nursery to 6+, with priority given to girls with siblings already at Headington, and by examination from 7+. The main entry points to the Senior School are at 11+, 13+ or, for the Sixth Form, 16+. Girls are occasionally able to join at other ages if places become available. Girls enter the school at 11+ via our own examination day and interview in December and, at 13+, through the spring Common Entrance Examination. Sixth Form entrance examinations and interviews are held in the November before the proposed year of entry.

Our registration fees for the Prep School are £95 (UK) and £150 (overseas based families) and for the Senior School are £125 (UK) and £250 (overseas based families). For information about admissions, please check our website, www.headington.org, or contact our friendly admissions team who will be happy to help.

Fees per term (2014–2015). Senior School: Full Boarders: £9,200–£10,700; Weekly Boarders: £8,370–£9,550; Day Girls: £4,960–£5,480.

Scholarships and Bursaries. Scholarships are awarded for academic achievement, art, drama, music and sport. These awards recognise talent and achievement and carry only a nominal financial benefit – our scholars are highly respected and enjoy a special status in the school. The Headington Access Programme (HAP) supports talented girls who would benefit from all that the school has to offer but who may not be able to access a Headington education without some form of financial assistance. Means-tested bursaries of up to 100 per cent of fees are available for local day girls who achieve high marks in our entrance examinations and are awarded at 11+, 13+ and in the Sixth Form.

Charitable status. Headington School Oxford Limited is a Registered Charity, number 309678. It exists to provide quality education for girls.

Heathfield School
Ascot

London Road, Ascot, Berkshire SL5 8BQ
Tel:	01344 898343
Fax:	01344 890689
email:	registrar@heathfieldschool.net
website:	www.heathfieldschool.net
Twitter:	@HeathfieldAscot
Facebook:	/HeathfieldSchool
LinkedIn:	/HeathfieldSchool

Board of Governors:

Chairman: Mr Steven Bishop, BA Oxon
The Rt Revd Dr Jonathan Baker, Bishop of Fulham, MA Oxon, MPhil, Dip Theol
Mrs Sally-Anne Barrett
Mrs Penny Bristow, BSc Hons London, FRSA
Mr Charlie Caminada
Mr Tom Cross Brown, MA Oxon, MBA Insead
Mr Guy Egerton-Smith, FRICS
Mr Robert Gregory, BSc Hons Sussex
Miss Caroline Slettengren, BSc Hons Southampton, CPE/ Grad Dip in Law, LPC College of Law
Mrs Sally Tulk-Hart
The Revd Canon Dr Philip Ursell, BA Wales, MA Oxon

Senior Leadership Team:

Headmistress: Mrs J Heywood, BSc Hons Kingston, PGCE Kingston

Bursar: Mr J Bueno, FAIA, MCMI
Director of Studies: Mrs M Gardiner Legge, MA Oxon, PGCE Hong Kong
Director of Pastoral and Co-Curricular Activities: Mrs K de Ferrer, MA Leeds, BA Hons USA, PGCE London
Director of Sixth Form: Mr Jeremy Hart, MA London, BA Hons London
Director of Boarding: Mrs L Curtis
Director of IT: Mr M Taylor, BSc Eng London, PGCE Greenwich, MBCS, CITP

+ *Head of Faculty*
* *Teacher in Charge/Subject Leader/Coordinator*

Head of Mathematics & Sciences Faculty: Miss C Wells, BSc Hons Bath, PGCE Exeter

Business Studies, Accounting & Economics:
*Mrs G Kendall, BA Hons Reading, PGCE London, D&B Dip Credit and Financial Analysis, Business Studies, Economics & Accounting

Mathematics:
*Mrs Z Benjamin, BSc Hons Reading, PGCE Bath
Mr J Doyle, BA Canberra, DipEd Canberra
Miss J McSweeney, BSc Hons Newcastle, PGCE Sheffield
Miss E Fagan, BSc Hons Galway, DipEd Galway
Mrs G Kendall, BA Hons Reading, PGCE London, D&B Dip Credit and Financial Analysis, Business Studies, Economics & Accounting

Psychology:
*Mrs R Oakley, MSc Bristol, BA Hons Swansea, PGCE West England

Science:
Miss E Fagan, BSc Hons Galway, Dip. Ed Galway
*Dr N Harden, PhD Bristol, BSc Hons, PGCE Bristol
Mrs J Kemp, BSc Hons London, PGCE London
*Mr S Moore, BSc Manchester, MEng Manchester, PGCE Reading
+*Miss C Wells, BSc Hons Bath, PGCE Exeter
Mrs A Milner, HND Ulster, BSc Ulster (*Senior Science Technician*)
Mr I Whitehurst, BA Surrey (*Science Technician*)

Head of Creative Arts Faculty: Miss K Sass, BA Hons Middlesex, PGCE Exeter

Art:
Mrs M Butler, BA Hons TVU
Miss H Eldridge, BA Hons London College of Fashion
*Mrs J Leibovici, BA Hons Winchester, PGCE Reading
Ms A Rutili, BA Hons Fine Arts Academy Italy, PGCE Greenwich

Cookery:
Mrs M Blackburn, BEd Cardiff
*Miss P Fairclough, BA Hons Oxford Brookes, Adv Cert Leiths Food & Wine

Dance:
Mrs N Shaw, BA West Sussex, ALAM, RAD. TC, AISTD

Drama:
Mrs K de Ferrer, MA Leeds, BA Hons USA, PGCE London
*Ms S O'Connor, MA Ed Chichester, PGCE Reading, QTS, NPQH
Mrs N Shaw, BA West Sussex, ALAM, RAD. TC, AISTD

Music:
*Mrs J Dance, BA Hons Birmingham, PGCE Birmingham, LRAM
Miss S M Kong, MA Birmingham City, BA Hons UCSI University Malaysia, Adv Piano Studies Franz Liszt Academy of Music, FTCL
(*plus visiting peripatetic staff*)

Photography:
Mrs M Butler, BA Hons TVU
*Miss K White, BA Hons Oxford Brookes, ABIPP

Head of Humanities & Languages Faculty: Mrs B Mason, BA Hons Nottingham, PGCE London, Cert SpLD Level 5

English
Mrs M Gardiner Legge, MA Oxon, PGCE Hong Kong
*Mr A Grey, MA Oxon, PGCE Ambleside
Ms S O'Connor, MA Ed Chichester, PGCE Reading, QTS, NPQH
Mr T Pithers, BA Hons Exeter, PGCE Newcastle

EFL:
*Mrs R Colley, BA Hons Oxford Brookes, PGCE London, Dip SpLD, TEFL

Mr M Snow, MPhil London, MA Aberdeen, MSc Robert Gordon

Geography:
+*Mrs B Mason, BA Hons Nottingham, PGCE London, Cert SpLD Level 5
Mrs L Worrall, BSc Hons Kingston, PGCE Kingston

History & Politics:
*Mrs N Holsgrove-Jones, BA Hons East Anglia, PGCE East Anglia
Mr J Hart, MA London, BA Hons London
Mrs L Worrall, BA Hons Kingston, PGCE Kingston

History of Art:
*Ms J Meeson, BA Hons East Anglia

Latin & Classical Civilisation:
Mrs C Green, BA Hons Bristol, PGCE Cambridge
Fr T Tregunno, MTheol St Andrews, PGCE Buckingham
*Mr A Valner, MA Nottingham, BA Nottingham, PGCE London

Librarian & Head of Careers:
Mrs K Bramley, MA Wales, Dip Lib

Modern Foreign Languages:
Mrs A Diaz, BA Hons Open, CertEd Cambridge (*French and Spanish*)
Miss J Menon, MA France, PGCE (*Oxford Brooks*)
Mrs A Pullen, BA Hons Cordoba (*Spanish*)
*Mrs F Rayner, MA Strasbourg, PGCE Oxford Brookes (*French & Spanish*)
Miss J Roubieu

Religious Studies:
Miss R Rothwell, MA Edinburgh, PGCE Roehampton
*Miss K Sass, BA Hons Middlesex, PGCE Exeter
Fr T Tregunno, MTheol St Andrews, PGCE Buckingham

Spectrum Learning Development:
Mrs M Battleday, HLTA Maths, NOCN Speech and Language, ADHD, Dyspraxia, Dyslexia
Mrs A Jones, Diplome de Langues Paris
*Mrs R Colley, BA Hons Oxford Brookes, PGCE London, Dip SpLD, TEFL
+Mrs B Mason, BA Hons Nottingham, PGCE London, Cert SpLD
Mrs S Simpson BEd Birmingham, PG Cert Dyslexia & Literacy York

Physical Education:
Miss D Adlington, BSc Adelaide, BEd Adelaide
Mrs S Bettison, DipEd London
Miss S Kay, BA Hons Manchester Metropolitan, PGCE Buckingham
*Miss W Reynolds, BEd Hons Liverpool
Miss J Talbot, BPhysEd Otago
(*plus visiting coaches*)

Equestrian Coordinator:
*Mrs G Glimmerveen

Duke of Edinburgh's Award Coordinator:
*Mrs D Hunt

PSHE Coordinator:
*Mrs A Diaz, BA Hons Open, CertEd Cambridge

Pastoral:
Director of Boarding: Mrs L Curtis
Chaplain: Fr T Tregunno, MTheol St Andrews, PGCE Buckingham
Director of Sixth Form: Mr Jeremy Hart, MA London, BA Hons London
Head of House, Austen: Mr A Valner, MA Nottingham, BA Nottingham, PGCE London
Deputy Head of House, Austen: Miss K White, BA Hons Oxford Brookes, ABIPP
Head of House, De Valois: Miss J Talbot, BPhysEd Otago

Deputy Head of House, De Valois: Miss J McSweeney, BSc Hons Newcastle, PGCE Sheffield
Head of House, Seacole: Mrs J Kemp, BSc Hons London, PGCE London
Deputy Head of House, Seacole: Miss E Fagan, BSc Hons Galway, Dip Ed Galway
Head of House, Somerville: Mr J Doyle, BA Canberra, Dip Ed Canberra
Deputy Head of House, Somerville: Mr T Pithers, BA Hons Exeter, PGCE Newcastle

Head of Lower School: Miss R Rothwell, MA Edinburgh, PGCE Roehampton
Housemistress, Form I: Mrs C Beresford
Housemistress, Form II: Miss S Crafer, NNEB, RSH
Housemistress, Form III: Miss L Champion, BA Hons Derby
Housemistress, Form III&IV: Mrs A Diaz, Cert Ed Cambridge, BA Hons Open
Housemistress, Form IV: Ms A Brooks
Housemistress, Form V: Mrs J Liepa, BA Hons London, PGCE Middlesex
Housemistress, LVI Form: Miss S Broomfield
Housemistress, UVI Form: Mrs P Munro, BSA Boarding Dip and Mrs P Kerley

Senior Nursing Sister: Sister E Hill, SRN, DN Cert
Nursing Sister: Sister M Couzens, RGN
Nursing Sister: Sister L Brazel, BSc Hons London, RGN

Administration:
Registrar: Mrs R Farha
Headmistress's PA & Marketing & PR Coordinator: Ms P Lavender, BA Hons Open
Director of IT: Mr M Taylor, BSc Eng London, PGCE Greenwich, MBCS
Director of Communications: Miss E Ivens, BA Hons Oxon, NCTJ
Deputy Bursar: Mrs L Farrin
Marketing Manager: Mrs S Frost, MSc Hull, BA Hons Hull
Administration Supervisor: Mrs C Bradberry

Introduction. Heathfield School in Ascot, Berkshire, is a renowned boarding school for girls aged 11 to 18. The school offers full boarding and, from September 2015, a small number of day boarding places. It is set in 36 acres of stunning grounds, just 45 minutes from central London, and within easy reach of major airports, motorways and rail networks.

As a small school of around 200 pupils, Heathfield focuses on the individual with an unrivalled emphasis on nurturing each girl so that she achieves the best she possibly can. The school was recently recognised by both the ISI (Independent Schools Inspectorate) and the national media for its outstanding pastoral care. Each pupil is a key part of an exciting community: Heathfield believes time spent outside the classroom is just as important as the time spent in it. Academically, each girl is guided by a personal tutor in a system which constantly monitors and analyses her work. Heathfield also has a varied and exciting extra-curricular programme, offering continuous opportunities for personal growth and development, seven days a week.

Evenings and weekends are filled with a diverse range of activities, from clubs and sports to the Duke of Edinburgh's Award and overseas trips.

Atmosphere and Ethos. The school's aim is to help every student get the most out of life by providing the very best intellectual stimulation, physical challenges and pastoral care. The school is founded on Church of England principles but welcomes all faiths.

Pastoral Care. Heathfield's strength is in its size meaning each girl is supported throughout her school career and can never slip under the radar. Pupils are overseen by a team of academic staff, Housemistresses, Heads of House and prefects. They work together to provide the highest level of pastoral care. Teachers will meet with your daughter regularly to discuss her particular needs and to ensure she is achieving her maximum potential.

Curriculum. Heathfield offers variety in terms of the subjects on offer as well as fundamental excellence in all the traditional subjects. At AS and A Level, girls can choose from over twenty subjects. Academic results are consistently impressive and all girls go on to higher education. Extras such as the Leiths Basic Certificate in Food and Wine are also offered. The school is famous for its excellence in the creative arts and launched a unique progression partnership with the University of the Arts, London, in September 2014.

Activities. The St Mary's Theatre and the Sports Hall are always hives of activity and there are many other extra-curricular activities: frequent museum and theatre trips, field trips and overseas visits.

Sport. Heathfield's outstanding facilities include a large multi-purpose gym, two squash courts, a dance studio, five lacrosse pitches, tennis courts and an indoor swimming pool. The school competes successfully at lacrosse, netball, swimming, rounders, athletics, polo, and show jumping. Girls have represented the school regionally, nationally and internationally in a variety of sports.

Boarding Accommodation. Boarding accommodation is first-class. From Form IV onwards, all girls have single rooms. For more freedom and independence, the Upper Sixth live in the Sixth Form Bungalow which contains two fully-equipped kitchens and areas in which to study and socialise.

Medical Welfare. Three nursing sisters and the school doctor are in charge of the girls' medical welfare, supported by Heads of House, Housemistresses and Tutors. The Heads of House or Housemistresses are available at all times for any parental concerns.

New Facilities. A state-of-the-art STEM (Science, Technology, Engineering and Maths) block is currently under construction for completion by Summer 2015.

Admission. Entry for the majority of pupils is at eleven. Girls also join at twelve or thirteen. Girls are also invited to apply for Sixth Form entry for A Level studies. Junior entrants are assessed at the school on 'invitation days' which involve examinations, workshops and interviews and to which girls are invited to bring work that they are proud of. Common Entrance examinations are also used as a guide if they are taken. Entry into the Lower Sixth Form is via predicted GCSE grades and interview.

Scholarships and Bursaries are awarded. Scholarships are worth £750 per annum. Bursaries are available varying between 10% and 40% reduction in fees. Bursaries are awarded at the Headmistress's discretion and are financially means tested.

Fees per term (2014–2015). Forms I and II: £10,437. Forms III–UVI: £10,750. Day boarding fees at 70% of boarding fees.

Charitable status. Heathfield School is a Registered Charity, number 309086. It exists to provide a caring boarding education leading to higher education for girls aged between 11 and 18.

Hethersett Old Hall School

Norwich Road, Hethersett, Norwich, Norfolk NR9 3DW
Tel: 01603 810390
Fax: 01603 812094
email: enquiries@hohs.co.uk
website: www.hohs.co.uk
Twitter: @HOHS_tweets
Facebook: /HethersettOldHallSchool

Chairman of Governors: Mr Martin Matthews

Headmaster: **Mr S G Crump**, MA

Deputy Headmistress: Mrs J Collin

Senior Housemistress: Mrs A Wright

Financial Administrator: Mrs H Eastwood

Head's Secretary: Mrs S Brown

Registrar: Mrs L Jones

Hethersett Old Hall School, founded in 1938, is located in 16 acres of beautiful Norfolk countryside in the heart of East Anglia, just minutes from Norwich city centre.

The school is a charitable trust administered by a Board of Governors, which is in membership of AGBIS. The Headmaster is a member of GSA and the school is also in membership of BSA.

The school provides education for around 200 pupils aged between 3 and 18 years old. The school is co-educational from age 3–11 and girls only from age 11 (Year 7). Full, weekly and flexi boarding is available for girls from age 9 (Year 5). The school welcomes international students. Younger boarders live in the historic main house and sixth formers have their own separate building. All girls are cared for by resident house staff that organise an exciting programme of evening and weekend activities.

Aims. Hethersett offers a friendly, supportive community in which each child is encouraged to develop their academic, creative and practical skills and to become self-reliant, tolerant and concerned for others.

Curriculum. Classes are small and teaching staff are well qualified, well informed and enthusiastic.

The Preparatory School is situated in modern, purpose-built accommodation with a dedicated play area. In Lower Prep (pupils age 3–7) the key skills of reading, writing and numeracy are developed in a stimulating atmosphere that builds on children's natural inquisitiveness and enthusiasm for learning.

The Upper Prep department (pupils age 7–11) provides a thorough grounding in the core curriculum. Sport, drama and music feature strongly in each year's programme of study. There are many opportunities for pupils to compete against other schools in swimming galas and games fixtures.

Pupils in the Senior School are offered a broad range of academic, technological and creative subjects. Their achievements at GCSE are consistently high and in 2014, the school achieved a 100% pass rate and 94% achieved 5+ grades A*–C. Support, advice and individual care throughout the senior school enables pupils to be confident in planning their future education and careers.

Sixth Form. Over 20 AS and A Level subjects are offered, from the unusually creative combination of art, photography and art textiles to a range of highly academic subjects; Maths, Biology, Chemistry and Physics. The majority of sixth formers choose to go on to university after benefiting from dedicated personal guidance from staff in choosing courses, completing their UCAS form and composing their personal statement. Since 2007, 100% of applicants have gained entry to their first-choice university, including Oxford and St Andrews to study medicine, Liverpool to study veterinary science and London College of Fashion to study art and design.

Buildings and Facilities. The school has excellent teaching facilities with bright, modern, purpose-built teaching blocks. The senior school teaching blocks feature an ICT suite, science laboratories, an art and technology suite with photography dark room, design technology and food and nutrition rooms. Pupils also benefit from the dedicated music rooms, 'The Barn' for drama, an indoor heated swimming pool, tennis courts, sports fields, gardens, woodland and an orchard. Sixth formers have their own common room, kitchen, study room and careers library. The boarding facilities include bright, attractive accommodation for younger girls with en-suite bathrooms. Older girls move onto single study-rooms and sixth formers are housed in their own separate building.

Recreational Activities. The school offers a wide range of recreational activities and optional extras which includes drama, dance, choir, orchestra, rock band and individual musical instrument tuition, sport clubs – swimming, tennis, football, rugby, badminton, tae kwon do, trampolining, kayaking, shooting, rounders, hockey and netball. The majority of senior school girls successfully take part in The Duke of Edinburgh's Award scheme, achieving their Bronze, Silver and Gold awards. There is also a Public Speaking Club, Book Club, Science Club, Art Club, Drama Club, Bird Club and Green Club,

Entrance. Entry is by the school's own assessment designed to give staff an indication of the child's stage of development, and to ensure they are able to meet the demands of the curriculum. The assessment focuses on maths, English and a reasoning test. Entry to the Sixth Form is by interview, school record and assessment. For further information or to obtain a prospectus please contact the Registrar.

Scholarships are open to internal or external candidates.

Year 7 and Year 9 Scholarships. Three types available: academic – day and boarding, creative and sporting. Academic Scholarships are awarded on the basis of examination and interview. Creative Scholarships are awarded on the basis of audition or practical test plus interview with the head of subject and the Headmaster. They can be taken in art, music or drama. Sporting Scholarships are awarded on the basis of ability trials held by the PE Department plus interview with the Head of PE and Headmaster. Applications and assessments are made in the January preceding September entry.

Years 8 and 10 Scholarships. Up to two Academic Boarding Scholarships are available for girls entering the school in Years 8 or 10. They are awarded on the basis of examination and an interview exploring the contribution the candidate could make to school life. Applications and assessments are made in the January preceding September entry.

Sixth Form Scholarships. Two types are available: academic – day and boarding and citizenship – day and boarding. Academic Scholarships are awarded on the basis of examination and interview with a panel of senior staff and the Headmaster. Citizenship Scholarships are awarded on the basis of a letter outlining the contribution a candidate could make to school life and an interview with a panel of senior staff and the Headmaster. Applications and assessments are made in the November preceding September entry.

Bursaries. Means-tested bursaries are available to enable pupils to attend the school who meet the entry criteria but who cannot afford the fees. These awards may be up to 100% of fees. They are limited in number and their award is discretionary.

Fees per term (2014–2015). Nursery fees (age 3–4) vary according to the length of the term and are charged at £39.50 for a full day, £25.25 for a morning session and £19.95 for an afternoon session, charged per term in advance and with cooked lunch included in full day and morning sessions. Lower Prep Department £2,740; Upper Prep Department (age 7–11): £3,225 (day), £5,565 (weekly boarding); £7,025 (full boarding); Senior School: £4,300 (day), £6,640 (weekly boarding); £8,100 (full boarding).

Charitable status. Hethersett Old Hall School is a Registered Charity, number 311273. It exists to provide a high quality education.

Howell's School Llandaff
GDST

Cardiff Road, Llandaff, Cardiff CF5 2YD

Tel:	029 2056 2019
Fax:	029 2057 8879
email:	admissions@how.gdst.net
website:	www.howells-cardiff.gdst.net
Twitter:	@HowellsSchool

Founded in 1860 as a school for girls, the school was built by the Drapers' Company from the endowment left in 1537 by Thomas Howell, son of a Welshman, merchant of London, Bristol and Seville and a Draper.

Howell's School Llandaff is part of the Girls' Day School Trust (GDST). The GDST is the leading network of independent girls' schools in the UK. As a charity that owns and runs 24 schools and two academies, it reinvests all its income in its schools. For further information about the Trust, see p. xxi or visit www.gdst.net.

Additional information about the school may be found on the school's website.

Chairman of Governors: Miss K Powell

Principal: Mrs S Davis, BSc London

Deputy Principal: Mrs N Chyba, BA London

Deputy Principal: Dr S Southern, BSc PhD Durham

Deputy Principal: Mrs J Ashill, BEd Swansea

Director of Finance and Operations: Mr R C Read, OBE, CDir

Director of Development and Communications: Mrs V Yilmaz, BA

Student numbers. 830: Nursery 40; Junior School 240; Senior School 310; Co-Educational College 240.

Howell's School, Llandaff is Wales's leading nondenominational, school for girls aged 3–18 and boys aged 16–18, and has a proven track record of success in public examinations. Howell's offers so much more than an education. Its extensive Enrichment Programmes together with its impressive Well-being and Laureate Programmes make Howell's a special place to learn and develop in an exciting, creative and thriving environment. The School's strong Leadership Team, talented and dedicated teaching and support staff, wonderful young people, and committed and interested parents make Howell's distinctive.

From the moment you enter Howell's gates you are greeted by glorious grounds; beautiful buildings; friendly staff; and a happy and positive environment. The excellent facilities include an indoor swimming pool, an outdoor classroom in the Junior School; and most recently an extensive refurbishment of the Art department. Modern Science laboratories provide our students with the best teaching laboratories in the area.

The Nursery @ Howell's, which is aptly situated in Roald Dahl's childhood home takes influence from its famous former occupant. Girls who enter the nursery experience a safe, family atmosphere, making the transition from home to nursery a relaxed and happy one. The Junior School invokes an atmosphere in which every child is valued and nurtured. Great emphasis is placed on developing the self-identity, self-esteem and self-confidence of every girl.

When entering the Senior School girls are encouraged to develop skills of self-analysis and reflection, and choose the learning methods that suit them best, whilst teachers challenge and motivate them towards an appetite for lifelong learning. Howell's aims to help students acquire skills essential to tackling a competitive and rapidly changing world.

The established co-educational college has a proven track record and offers students an exceptional learning experience designed to manage the transition between school and university. Combining academic excellence with flexible teaching styles geared to the individual, the college ably prepares its students for higher education and beyond.

Curriculum. All National Curriculum subjects including Welsh are taught at Key Stages 1, 2 and 3. In Year 7 French, Spanish and Welsh are on offer. Latin is introduced in Year 8. First language Welsh (throughout) and Greek (A Level) are taught on demand. A broad range of AS and A2 subjects is available in the College. Examinations in all AS subjects are taken at the end of Year 12. Active learning styles are an essential part of the classroom experience. The curriculum is made more diverse by:

- Educational visits, locally and abroad;
- Visiting authors, poets, musicians, artists and lecturers;
- Special activity weeks focusing on particular areas of the curriculum.

Extra-curricular activities. Howell's aim is to fulfil the potential of all the students in all areas, which it achieves through a rich extra-curricular programme of activities:

- Orchestras, choirs, chamber and jazz groups;
- Reading and reviewing, green, science, maths, history, geography, language and religious and cultural clubs;
- Concerts, plays, drama festival and eisteddfodau;
- Tennis, hockey, rounders, lacrosse, swimming, athletics, cross-country, netball, rugby and football teams;
- The Duke of Edinburgh's Award, Envision and Interact;
- Quiz, public speaking and debating teams;
- Community service and fundraising for charities.

The school seeks to support the widest range of students' needs through specialist dyslexia teaching at our on-site Dyslexia Institute satellite, and through an extensive and comprehensive careers programme.

Admission. A selection process operates for all points of entry. Contact Admissions for further details.

Fees per term (2014–2015). Sixth Form College: £4,169; Senior School (Year 11): £3,943; Senior School (Years 7–10): £4,125; (Years 3–6): £3,172; Junior School: (Rec–Year 2): £3,114; Nursery: £2,441.

Scholarships and Bursaries. Bursaries, which are means-tested, are available in the Senior School and in the Sixth Form College; these are intended to ensure that the school remains accessible to bright students who would benefit from our education, but who would be unable to enter the school without financial assistance.

Details of scholarships and bursaries are available, on request, from the school.

Charitable status. Howell's School Llandaff is part of The Girls' Day School Trust, which is a Registered Charity, number 306983.

Ipswich High School
GDST

Woolverstone, Ipswich 1P9 1AZ
Tel: 01473 780201
Fax: 01473 780985
email: admissions@ihs.gdst.net
website: www.ipswichhighschool.co.uk

Founded in 1878.

Ipswich High School is part of the GDST (Girls' Day School Trust). The GDST is the leading network of independent girls' schools in the UK. As a charity that owns and runs 24 schools and two academies, it reinvests all its income in its schools. For further information about the Trust, see p. xxi or visit www.gdst.net.

Additional information about the school may be found on the school's website and a detailed prospectus is available from the school.

Chairman of Local Governors: Annie Reid

Headmistress: **Ms Oona Carlin**, BSc Imperial

Head of Junior School: Mrs Eileen Fisher, BEd

Registrar: Mrs Bernadette Ross-Smith

A pioneering heritage
Ipswich High School's early pupils were among the first women to obtain university degrees and to enter professional work. Today, although the school has grown and changed immeasurably, the pioneering spirit and commitment to education for young women remain.

An inspiring choice
Our philosophy is to create an environment in which our girls are inspired to reach new heights.

Outstanding results
We provide an extraordinary breadth of education and as a single-sex school there is no gender stereotyping in the choice and enjoyment of subjects. It is not considered unusual to excel in Maths, Science or Design & Technology any more than in Languages, Arts or Humanities. We have high standards and expectations of all our pupils in every subject and that is reflected in our outstanding exam results at all age ranges.

Developing the whole girl
We spend time with our pupils in extra-curricular activities such as sport, music and drama to enhance their personal development. This helps them develop not just academic skills, but social skills as well.

An enriching environment
We are privileged to have the magnificent Woolverstone Hall as our home with 80 acres of beautiful parkland, splendid buildings and an incredible array of facilities – a huge sports hall, theatre, spacious suites, design technology workshop, language laboratory, IT suites, a 25m indoor swimming pool and an all-weather pitch for hockey and tennis.

The support of the GDST
As part of the GDST, Ipswich High School has a strong and secure future. The GDST gives each of the schools autonomy to identify its own needs and determine its own development, but then gives guidance, helps planning and supports financially to realise projects. Visit the GDST website at www.gdst.net for more information on the full extent of the GDST network of schools.

Prepared for the future
Our girls act as inspirational role models for each other. They are ambitious, enthusiastic and have a real zest for learning and life. When the time comes for them to leave us, all our girls go forward with the confidence and courage not to be held back by social stereotypes, but to take themselves to new levels of success.

Ipswich High School has a proven track record and a bright future ahead – we hope you will choose to be part of it.

Admissions. Admission to the Nursery School is on the basis of informal assessment in a play situation. Entry to the Junior School is on the basis of informal assessment or written test. Entry to the Senior School is on the basis of interviews, written tests and school report. Sixth Form entry is on the basis of interviews, GCSE results and school report.

Fees per term (2014–2015). Senior School: Years 10–13 £4,107, Year 7–9 £4,050; Junior School: Years 3–6 £2,935, Years 1 & 2 £2,768, Woodland Pre-Prep £613.

Scholarships. Our Scholarships are highly sought after and are reserved for those candidates we believe to be of an exceptional standard. We look to our Scholars to continuously raise the standard in their chosen field and to provide inspiration to others. For entry at 11+ (Senior School) and

16+ (Sixth Form) we offer Academic, Art, Drama, Music and Sports Scholarships.

Bursaries. The GDST provides the school with a number of bursaries for entry at 11+ and Sixth Form. These are means tested and ensure that the school remains accessible to bright girls who would profit from the education provided but who would be unable to enter the school without financial assistance.

Charitable status. Ipswich High School is part of The Girls' Day School Trust, which is a Registered Charity, number 306983.

Kilgraston

Bridge of Earn, Perthshire PH2 9BQ
Tel: 01738 812257
Fax: 01738 813410
email: headoffice@kilgraston.com
website: www.kilgraston.com
Twitter: @kilgraston

Kilgraston is an independent boarding and day school, for girls aged 2½ to 18 years and boys aged 2½ to 5 years. The Independent School Awards named Kilgraston UK Independent School of the Year in 2011, making it Scotland's first school to be awarded this accolade. Kilgraston is an all-through school comprising Nursery, Prep, Senior School and Sixth Form with 116 pupils in the Prep School and 208 in the Senior School and Sixth Form.

Chairman of Board of Governors: Mr Timothy Hall

***Acting Principal*: Mrs C A Lund**, BA Hons, MA, MA Ed Man, PGCE
Principal from April 2015: Mrs D MacGinty, BEd, NPQH

Bursar and Secretary to the Board: Mr B Farrell, BCom, FIDE, ACIS
Acting Deputy Head – Academic and Head of Sixth Form: Mrs E Prentice, BSc Hons, PGCE
Head of Pastoral Care and Boarding : Mrs G McFadden
Head of the Preparatory School: Mrs K Ebrahim, BSc Hons, PGCE
Chaplain: Miss C Laidlaw

Academic & Pastoral Staff:
Ms C Austin, BSc Hons, PGCE (*Residential Mistress, Mater*)
Mrs J Baird (*Classroom Asst/Playground Supervisor*)
Mrs L Baxter, BEd PE Hons (*Head of Curriculum Physical Education, Moncreiffe Housemistress*)
Miss C Beveridge, MA, PGDE (*Head of Geography*)
Ms C Blackler, BSc (*Science Technician*)
Mrs A Bluett, BA Hons, PGCE (*French, Latin*)
Miss A Brennan, PGDE (*Swinton Assistant Residential Mistress and Evening & Weekend Coordinator*)
Mrs A Caldwell, BSc Hons, PGDE (*Mathematics*)
Mr C Campbell, MA, PGDE (*Head of History and Modern Studies*)
Mrs J Carmichael, LLB, PGCE (*Form Teacher, Prep Coordinator*)
Mrs C Clarke, BSc (*Home Economics*)
Dr M Comrie, BSc Hons, PhD, PGDE (*Science*)
Mr E Connolly, BSc Hons, PGDE (*Director of Science*)
Mrs P Corral, HNC (*Early Years Practitioner*)
Mlle I Dépreux, BA Hons, Maîtrise, PGCE (*French*)
Mrs L Easton, BA, MA (*Nursery Manager*)
Mrs C Farrell, Dip Ed (*Butterstone Assistant Residential Mistress*)
Mrs B Ferguson, MTheol, PGCE (*Religious Studies*)
Mrs P Ferguson, MA Hons, PGCE (*Form Teacher, Early Years Coordinator*)

Mr A Fynn, MA Hons, PGDE (*Head of Modern Languages*)
Miss L Gardner, BSc Hons, PGCE, PGCA (*Learning Support*)
Mrs S Hewett, MSc, BSc, PGCE (*Physics*)
Mrs S Hewitt (*Swimming Pool Manager*)
Miss S Howett, BA Hons (*Assistant Residential Mistress, Mater*)
Mr S Johnston, MA, BA, PGDE (*Religious Studies*)
Mr T Kearns, MA Ed, Dip Lit, PGCE, BA Hons (*Head of English*)
Miss A Kelly, BA (*Residential Mistress, Butterstone*)
Mrs C Kirkpatrick, BEd, MEd (*Learning Support, Form Teacher*)
Miss H Lindsay, BA Hons, PG Celta (*ESOL*)
Miss G MacLeod, BA Hons (*Art*)
Miss R Masson, MA Hons, MLitt (*Classics and Assistant Residential Mistress*)
Mrs M McCabe, MA, PGCE (*Spanish, RE, Inchcolm Housemistress*)
Mrs D McCormick, BSc Ed Hons (*Science Teacher, Kinnoull Housemistress*)
Mr A McGarva, BA, PGCE (*Director of Music, Deputy Head of Prep*)
Miss B McKell (*Residential Assistant*)
Mr K McKinney, BEd (*Mathematics, Arran Housemaster*)
Miss R McLean (*Riding Instructor*)
Mrs M Malloch (*Prep Learning Assistant*)
Ms P Martin, BA Hons (*Art*)
Mrs K Megahy, NVQ Early Years Care and Education (*Early Years Practitioner*)
Mrs M Morton, MA Hons, Dip Ed (*Modern Languages*)
Mr G Muirhead, BSc Hons (*ICT Manager*)
Mrs L A Murray, RGN, SCM (*Matron*)
Mrs P Murray (*Assistant Residential Mistress*)
Mrs A Ness, BA (*Theatre Studies, LAMDA, Drama Teacher*)
Mrs D Neville, MA Hons, PGDE (*ESOL*)
Mrs J Newton, BSc, PGSE (*Science*)
Mrs A O'Hear, BSc Hons, PGCE (*Biology, Teaching & Learning Coordinator*)
Mrs L Oswald, BEd Hons (*History, Mathematics, Senior Prep Coordinator, Form Tutor*)
Mrs R Reid, MA, BEd (*Learning Support & ESOL, Form Teacher*)
Mrs E Rodger, BEd Hons (*Physical Education, Form Teacher*)
Mrs M Saunders, BA Hons (*English*)
Mrs L Scott, BA (*Drama*)
Mrs K Scott (*Groom/Stable Manager*)
Miss K Seatter, BEd Hons (*Physical Education*)
Mrs S Speed, BSc Hons, PGCE (*Head of Mathematics*)
Miss B Spurgin, MA Hons (*Librarian*)
Mr A Stewart, MTheol, PG Dip OEd, PGDE (*Form Teacher*)
Mrs S Stewart, BA Hons, PG Dip, PGDE (*Business Studies*)
Mrs E Stewart, Dip Ed (*Form Teacher*)
Mrs P Stott (*Director of Sport*)
Miss M Strupitis-Haddrick (*Residential Assistant*)
Miss M Timm (*Residential Assistant*)
Miss L Watt (*Equestrian Assistant*)
Mrs H Whitaker, BA Hons, PGCE, Form Teacher
Mrs E Young, BHSAI, (*Chief Riding Instructor*)

Language and Activities Manager: Ms S Littlejohn, BA Hons
Marketing Manager: Mrs K Welch, BA Hons

Administration Staff:
Miss E Forsyth (*Finance Assistant*)
Mrs S Harrison (*School Secretary*)
Mrs A McHugh (*Receptionist*)
Mrs J Kennedy (*Receptionist*)

Mrs B McGarva (*Admissions Secretary*)
Mrs L Osborne-Moore, BA Hons (*Principal's PA and Admissions Coordinator*)
Mrs A Roger (*Assistant Bursar*)
Miss T Stack (*School Secretary*)

Kilgraston is a Georgian mansion house and the campus is set in 54 acres of stunning parkland three miles from the centre of Perth with Edinburgh and Glasgow only an hour away. The school has benefited from extensive recent investment in facilities including a state-of-the-art science centre, a brand new sixth form study centre, a 25m indoor swimming pool complex, and floodlit all-weather hockey pitch and tennis courts. Kilgraston is also the only school in Scotland with an on-site equestrian centre incorporating a 60m x 40m floodlit arena with show jumps.

Visitors to Kilgraston are struck by its warm and welcoming atmosphere, and the sense of community and friendship across the year groups. Staff know each pupil individually, and are proud of the well-rounded girls who thrive in a range of curricular and co-curricular activities. Kilgraston's Sacred Heart ethos is central to school life, providing a firm foundation for personal growth and individual contribution, whilst welcoming girls of all faiths and none.

The Curriculum. Kilgraston follows the Scottish educational system with all the girls studying a broad curriculum before selecting subjects to continue at Intermediate 2 (GCSE equivalent). Over 18 subjects are offered at Higher/ Advanced Higher (A Level equivalent). Kilgraston has a record of high academic achievement and the girls gain entrance to top UK and international universities including Oxbridge.

Music, Art and Drama play an important part of life at Kilgraston. The Music Department alone has 14 individual teaching rooms, a new recording studio and two large music rooms designed to suit all needs. There are also many opportunities for pupils to perform throughout the year by participating in orchestra, string orchestra, fiddle, woodwind and brass groups or one of several choirs.

The Art Department is housed in the top of the mansion with superb views across the Ochil Hills and the school boasts an impressive number of past pupils who are practising artists.

Sports and recreation are catered for within a superb sports hall including a climbing wall and fitness gym. The extensive grounds incorporate the indoor 25m swimming pool, nine floodlit all-weather courts, playing fields and athletics track. Whilst the main sports are hockey, netball, tennis, rounders, swimming and athletics other sports include football, touch rugby, skiing, cricket, badminton, yoga, karate, fencing, aerobics, ballet, modern dance and highland dancing. Fixtures and competitions are also arranged against other schools throughout the year. Kilgraston also hosts the Scottish Schools' Equestrian Championships every Spring.

Kilgraston is divided into houses which compete against each other in games, music and debating. The girls can also take part in the Duke of Edinburgh's Award Scheme and are encouraged to use all the facilities not only for curriculum lessons but also for leisure activities.

Kilgraston Preparatory School and Nursery is co-educational up to the age of five. The boarders live in the newly refurbished Butterstone House. All of the pupils benefit from the many facilities of the Senior School. (*See separate entry in IAPS section.*)

Admission is normally interview and school report. Entry to the Prep School is by interview and assessment.

Means-tested bursaries are available on application. Scholarship Examinations are held in early February and awards are also offered each year as a result of outstanding performance in the Academic Scholarship Examinations. Scholarships are also offered in Art, Music, Drama and Sport.

Fees per term (2014–2015). Senior: Day £5,225, Boarding £8,925, Prep: Day £2,995–£4,850, Boarding £7,095.

Charitable status. Kilgraston School Trust is a Registered Charity, number SC029664.

King Edward VI High School for Girls
Birmingham

Edgbaston Park Road, Birmingham B15 2UB
Tel: 0121 472 1834
Fax: 0121 471 3808
email: enquiries@kehs.co.uk
website: www.kehs.org.uk

Independent, formerly Direct Grant.

Governing Body: The Governors of the Schools of King Edward VI in Birmingham

Principal: Mrs A Clark, MA Cantab, PGCE

Vice Principal: Miss A C Warne, BA Birmingham, PGCE
Vice Principal: Miss S Pallister, MA Birmingham, PGCE
Assistant Head: Mrs K Sangha, BA De Montfort, MBA, PGCE Warwick

Teaching Staff:
Mrs R M Arnold, MA Cambridge, PGCE
Dr B Ashfield, BA Oxon, PhD Birmingham, PGCE
Mrs M Atkins, MA Reading
Mrs N Azmat, BA London, ACCA, PGCE
Mrs J L Bagnall, BSc Sheffield, PGCE
Miss L J Baker, BA London, QTS
Mrs S Bhagi, BSc Birmingham, PGCE
Miss S A Blanks, BA Birmingham, GTP
Mrs M C Britton, BA London, PGCE
Miss C A Brown, MA Cambridge, PGCE
Miss A L Buckley, BA Oxon, GTP
Ms H Chambers, MA Cambridge, PGCE
Mrs G K Chapman, BEd Brighton
Mrs R M Coetzee, MA Cambridge, PGCE
Mr T O Cooper, BA Bristol, PGCE
Mrs F M Corran, MPhil Oxon
Mrs K Cowan, BSc Glasgow, PGCE
Mrs R D'Aquila, BA Italy
Mr R Devey, BSc Derby, PGCE
Mr A E Duncombe, MA Cambridge, PGCE
Miss H Dyke, BA Nottingham, GTP
Miss E M Edwards, BEd Bristol
Mme L D Franco, Maîtrise LLCE, France PGCE
Dr V L Gray, BSc, PhD Cardiff
Dr C E Gruzelier, MA Auckland, DPhil Oxon, PGCE
Mrs F Hall, MA Oxon, PGCE
Dr S Hayton, BSc, PhD Newcastle, PGCE
Mr R M Hopkinson, BSc Hull, MSc London, PGCE
Mrs C M Hosty, BA York, PGCE
Mrs S A Huxley, BEd Bradford
Ms S Huxley-Edwards, BA Birmingham, PGCE
Mrs R M Jackson-Royal, MA London, PGCE
Mr T Jarvis, MusB Manchester
Mr H J Kavanagh, BA Cantab, PGCE
Mrs H D Kavanagh, BA Bristol, PGCE
Miss R Laurent, Diplome Haute Alsace, PGCE
Mrs V J Law, BA Hons Oxford, PGCE
Mr F Mackinnon, BA Strathclyde, PGCE
Mrs J K Mahon, BSc London, PGCE
Mrs A Marquette, BA, MA France, PGCE
Mrs S M May, BSocSci Birmingham, PGCE
Mr K A Merrall, BA Oxon, PGCE
Mrs S J Merrall, BA Oxon, PGCE

Mrs J E Moule, BA Durham, PGCE
Miss J Oldfield, BSc Durham, PGCE
Miss H Plant, BA Cambridge, GTP
Miss S Platt, BSc Manchester, PGCE
Mrs C M Pollard, BSc Nottingham, PGCE
Dr M Popat-Szabries, BSc London, MA Warwick, PhD Warwick, PGCE
Miss H Proops, BA Central School of Speech & Drama, GTP
Ms M N Sanders, GRSM, ARCM Birmingham, PGCE
Mr R T Sheppard, BEng Manchester, PGCE
Mrs S K E Shore-Nye, BA Swansea, PGCE
Dr M Simpson, BSc Birmingham, PhD Birmingham, PGCE
Mrs J C Smith, CertEd Bedford College of PE
Dr B L Tedd, BSc London, PhD Leicester, PGCE
Mrs B Thompson, BSc Sheffield Hallam, PGCE
Mr A Wager, BA Birmingham, PGCE
Mrs J Whitehead, BSc Birmingham, PGCE
Miss C E Woods, BA Warwick, QTS
Mrs A Young, BA Birmingham, PGCE

Librarian: Miss S Alan
Principal's PA: Mrs C L Tovey
Admissions Registrar: Mrs C Oakes
Matron: Miss T Norman

Founded in 1883, the School moved in 1940 to its present buildings and extensive grounds adjacent to King Edward's School for Boys. There are 540 girls from 11 to 18 years of age, all day pupils.

Curriculum. The curriculum is distinctive in its strong academic emphasis and aims to inspire a love of learning. The purpose of the curriculum is to help girls realise their full potential. Excellence is sought in aesthetic, practical and physical activities as well as in academic study. Our aim is to achieve a balance of breadth and depth, with dropping of subjects postponed as long as possible so that girls may make informed choices and have access to a wide range of possible careers.

In **Year One** all girls take English, Mathematics, separate Sciences, Religious Studies, French, History, Geography, Music, Art and Design, Drama, Information Technology, Games, Swimming, Dance and Creative Skills.

In **Years Two and Three** all girls take English, Mathematics, separate Sciences, Religious Studies, French, Latin, History, Geography, Music, Art and Design, Information Technology, Physical Education, Creative Skills.

Core subjects in **Years Four and Five** are English Language, English Literature, Mathematics, Biology, Chemistry, Physics, Latin, French. Girls then choose from 3 option blocks their other GCSE subjects. Another modern language can be taken as a two-year GCSE course.

In the **Sixth Form** girls choose for AS and A2 from a wide range of subjects, all Arts, or all Sciences or a mixture of the two. Some subjects are taken jointly with King Edward's School. Stress is placed on breadth at this level. All girls take General Studies at A Level (normally as their fifth subject) with courses for all in Critical Thinking. Various philosophical, scientific and practical topics are explored in short courses.

All girls follow a course in personal decision-making in which they explore and discuss a wide range of issues which call for personal choice and which helps develop life skills.

Religious and moral education are considered important. Academic study of them is designed to enable girls to be informed and questioning. In the last two years, courses (apart from the choice of Religious Studies at A Level) are designed as part of the General Studies programme. There is no denominational teaching in the school in lessons or morning assembly. Girls of all faiths or of none are equally welcome.

Girls take part in Physical Education, until the Upper Sixth Form where it is voluntary, with increasing choice from gymnastics, hockey, netball, tennis, rounders, dance, fencing, badminton, squash, fives, swimming, athletics, basketball, volleyball, self-defence, aerobics, archery, health related fitness. We have our own swimming pool, sports hall and extensive pitches, including two artificial hockey areas.

In addition to the music in the curriculum, there are choirs and orchestras which reach a high standard. These are mostly joint with King Edward's School. Individual (or shared) instrumental lessons, at an extra fee, are arranged in school in a great variety of instruments. Some instruments can be hired. Individual singing lessons can also be arranged.

A large number of clubs (many joint with King Edward's School) are run by pupils themselves with help and encouragement from staff. Others (eg Drama, Music, Sport) are directed by staff. Help is given with activities relating to the Duke of Edinburgh's Award scheme. Some activities take place in lunch hours, others after school and at weekends.

As part of the school's commitment to developing an awareness of the needs of society and a sense of duty towards meeting those needs, girls are encouraged to plan and take part in various community service projects as well as organising activities in school to raise money to support causes of their choice.

A spacious careers room is well stocked with up-to-date information. Individual advice and aptitude testing is given at stages where choices have to be made. One member of staff has overall responsibility but many others are involved with various aspects. Girls are encouraged to attend conferences, gain work experience, make personal visits and enquiries. Old Edwardians and others visit school to talk about their careers. There is good liaison with universities and colleges of all kinds. Virtually all girls go on to higher education. A wide range of courses is being taken by Old Edwardians.

Admission of Pupils. Entry is normally for girls of 11 into the first year of the school in September. Applications must be made by January for entry in September. Girls should have reached the age of 11 years by 31st August following the examination. Girls up to 1 year younger than this can be considered in some circumstances; parents of such girls should communicate with the Principal in the previous autumn term. Girls are examined at the school in English, Mathematics and Reasoning. The syllabus is such as would be normally covered by girls of good ability and no special preparation is advised.

Girls from 12 to 15 are normally considered only if they move from another part of the country, or in some special circumstances. Applications should be made to the Principal in writing as soon as the move is planned. Such girls can be admitted at any time if there is a vacancy.

There is an entry into the Sixth Form for girls wishing to study four main A Level subjects and General Studies. Application should be made to the Principal as early as possible in the preceding academic year.

Fees per term (2014–2015). £3,750.

Scholarships and Bursaries. The equivalent of up to a total of two full-fee scholarships may be awarded on the results of the Governors' Admission Examination to girls entering the first year, with a maximum of 50% for any individual scholarship. These are independent of parental income and are normally tenable for 7 years.

Means-tested Bursaries are available for girls entering the school at 11+ and 16+.

Charitable status. The Schools of King Edward VI in Birmingham is a Registered Charity, number 529051. The purpose of the Foundation is to educate children and young persons living in or around the city of Birmingham mainly by provision of, or assistance to its schools.

King's High School

Smith Street, Warwick CV34 4HJ
Tel: 01926 494485
Fax: 01926 403089
email: enquiries@kingshighwarwick.co.uk
website: www.kingshighwarwick.co.uk

*Chairman of Governors of Warwick Independent Schools
   Foundation*:
Mr D B Stevens, BA

Chairman of King's High School Committee:
Mrs J Marshall, BA

Members of the King's High School Committee:
Dr A D Cocker, BA, DPhil, MBA
Mr N Keegan, MA Oxon, FCA
Mrs S Lampitt, BA, DipEd (*Vice-Chairman*)
Mrs C Sawdon, BSc, JP
Mrs P Snape

Foundation Secretary: Mr S Jones

Staff:
Head Mistress: Mrs E Surber, BA, MA Exeter

Deputy Head (Academic): Mr S Bethel, BSc Birmingham
Deputy Head (Pastoral): Mrs C Renton, BSc Leicester,
   MSc London

Head of Sixth Form: Mr J W Wood, BA Nottingham, MSc
   Leicester
Head of Key Stage 4: Mrs K Hewitt, BA Bristol
Head of Key Stage 3: Dr R Cheetham, BSc London, PhD
Head of Careers: Mrs J A Coplestone-Crow, BA Durham
Head of Science: Mrs R Chapman, MA Oxon
Examinations Secretary: Mrs L Y Sherren, BSc Sheffield

* *Head of Department*
§ *Part-time*

Art, Design and Food Technology:
*Mr S Jarvis, BA Nottingham Trent
Mrs E Ashby, BA Kent
§Dr M J Barwell, PhD, MA, BEd Warwick
Mrs S Didlick, BEd, CNAA (*Teacher in Charge of Food
   Technology & Voluntary Service Coordinator*)
§Mrs J Knight, BA Portsmouth (*maternity leave*)
§Mrs J Porter, BEd Sheffield
Mr N C Walker, BSc Brunel (*Teacher in Charge of Design
   Technology & DofE Award Coordinator*)

Business Studies:
§Mrs E A Thornton, BA Nottingham (*Teacher in Charge*)
§Mrs A E Browning, BA London

Careers:
*Mrs J A Coplestone-Crow, BA Durham
Miss R Bradbury, BA York, MA Leeds (*Oxbridge
   Coordinator*)
§Mrs A E Browning, BA London (*Work Experience
   Coordinator*)
Dr G Gifford, PhD, MSc, MA Edinburgh (*Careers Advisor*)
Dr R Lidgett, BA, PhD Birmingham (*Careers Advisor*)

Classics:
*Mrs J A Coplestone-Crow, BA Durham
§Mrs R Morgan, BA Bristol, MA UCL

Drama:
*Miss C Price, BA Manchester
§Mr P Atkins, MA Leeds
§Mr M Cosgrif, BA Open University, MA Lancaster
Mrs S Marshall, BA Schol Guildhall
§Mr J Partridge, BA Birmingham

English:
*Miss R Bradbury, BA York, MA Leeds

§Mrs R Barton, BA University College London
Miss P James, MA Warwick
Miss J Mimms, MA Glasgow
§Mrs C Richards, BA Exeter
Mrs L Shaw, BA Warwick, MA University of the West of
   England

Economics:
Mr J W Wood, BA Nottingham, MSc Leicester (*Teacher in
   Charge*)

Geography:
*Mrs S Watson, MA Oxon
§Mrs A E Browning, BA London
Mrs R Cresswell, BA Georgia
Mrs C Renton, BSc Leicester, MSc London
§Mrs E A Thornton, BA Nottingham
§Mrs C Walker, BEd Chelsea School of Movement
Mrs K White, BA Exeter, MEd Cantab (*maternity leave*)

History & Politics:
*Miss E Carney, BA Manchester
Dr G Gifford, PhD, MSc, MA Edinburgh
§Mrs I Gillett, German teaching degree Johann Wolfgang
   Goethe, Frankfurt
Mrs C Wellman, BA Warwick (*Teacher in Charge of
   Politics*)

Information Technology:
*Mrs E Powell, BSc Anglia Ruskin
§Mrs N Russell, BSc Loughborough

Mathematics:
*Mr A Wild, BSc Wales
Mr H Ashby, BEng CNAA
Mr S Bethel, BSc Birmingham
Miss U Birbeck, BA Warwick
Miss R M Court, BSc London
Mr T Larkin, BSc Manchester, MA Warwick
Mr R Sharpe, BEd Bristol Polytechnic, Dip DA New
   College of Speech and Drama
Mrs L Y Sherren, BSc Sheffield
§Mrs C Topping, BSc Wales, MSc Warwick

Modern Languages:
*Mrs A Dickinson, BA London (*Teacher in Charge of
   Spanish*)
§Ms K Gibson, BA Salford
Mr L J Herrera, Law Degree Madrid, MA London
   Metropolitan
Mrs L King, BA Warwick (*Teacher in Charge of French*)
   (*maternity leave*)
§Mrs V McRoberts, Licence MA Saint-Étienne
§Mrs E Montiel, Licenciatura en Educación
Mrs C Murphy, BA Royal Holloway (*Acting Teacher in
   Charge of French*)
§Mrs R Wickes, MA Cantab (*Teacher in Charge of
   German*)
§Mrs K Bartel (*German Assistant*)
§Mrs M Esteban-Stephenson (*Spanish Assistant*)
§Mrs M H Quinney, DEUG Nantes & Chartres (*French
   Assistant*)

Music:
*Mr M Smallwood, BA Mus Anglia Polytechnic University
Mrs D Wallace, BMus, LRAM, LTCL, LTCL

PSHE:
Mrs C Renton, BSc Leicester, MSc London
Dr R Cheetham, BSc, PhD London
Mrs J Day, BA, MA Oxon
Mrs K Hewitt, BA Bristol
Mrs E Surber, BA, MA Exeter
Mrs S Watson, MA Oxon

Physical Education:
*Miss C E A Gilbert, BA Liverpool John Moores
Mrs K Bryce, BSc Brunel (*maternity leave*)

Miss D A Ellis, BSc Cumbria
Mrs L Steinhaus, BSc Sheffield Hallam
Mrs C Walker, BEd Chelsea School of Movement

Psychology:
Miss N Wright, BSc Aston (*Teacher in Charge*)

Religious Education:
*Dr R Lidgett, BA, PhD Birmingham
Mrs J Day, BA, MA Oxon
Dr G Gifford, PhD, MSc, MA Edinburgh
Mrs K Hewitt, BA Bristol

Science:
*Mrs R Chapman, MA Oxon
Biology:
§Mrs A Sims, MA Cantab (*Teacher in Charge*)
Dr K Bier, Diplom Martin Luther, DPhil Oxford
§Dr P M Boulton, BSc London, PhD Birmingham
§Dr C M Pickup, BSc Manchester, DPhil Oxon, AMBDA
§Mrs B Pirie, BSc Liverpool, MSc UMIST
§Mrs K Pitchford, BSc Southampton
Chemistry:
Dr A Grist, BSc, PhD Leicester (*Teacher in Charge*)
Dr K Bier, Diplom Martin Luther, DPhil Oxford
Mrs R Chapman, MA Oxon
Dr R Cheetham, BSc, PhD London
Miss D Deegan, BSc Limerick
§Mrs K Pitchford, BSc Southampton
Physics:
Dr A Chamberlain, BSc, PhD Warwick (*Teacher in Charge*)
§Mrs K Clarke, BSc, MSc Birmingham
Mr T Larkin, BSc Manchester, MA Warwick

Special Educational Needs Coordinator:
§Mrs A Thomas, Dip Ed Strathclyde Jordanhill, Dip SpLD Dyslexia Warwick, PG Cert ASD Worcester

Gifted & Talented Coordinator:
Dr A Chamberlain, BSc, PhD Warwick

Visiting Music Staff:
Mrs L Braithwaite, BMus LTCL, PGRNCM (*Oboe*)
Mrs C Herbert, BMus (*Clarinet*)
Mrs S M Irving, BEd Cantab, MMus (*Piano/Violin*)
Mrs R Jefferies, BA, MMus, ARCM (*Piano*)
Mr N Jones (*Drum Kit*)
Mr P Luckhurst, ATCL, TDip (*Guitar*)
Miss D Mason, BA, LTCL, ABRSM (*Flute*)
Mr C E Matthews, BA, MA (*Piano*)
Mr R B Meteyard, AGSM (*Violin*)
Mrs S Meteyard, GBSM, ABSM (*Violin/Viola*)
Ms C Mills, BMus, LTCL, ABRSM, LRSM, ARCM
Miss B Morley, BA Coll (*Bass/Singing*)
Mrs M Todd, Diploma Lucerne Conservatoire (*Cello*)
Miss A H Whelan, DRSAMD (*Brass*)
Mrs A Williams, LRAM, ARCM (*Singing*)

Visiting Coaches/Teachers for Activities:
Miss P Barlow (*Martial Arts*)
Mr M Beckett (*Duke of Edinburgh's Award*)
Mr D Bryce (*Hockey*)
Mrs C Callaghan (*Yoga*)
Mrs S Cartwright-Randle (*Badminton*)
Miss V Carvell, Warwick Prep (*Swimming*)
Mr N Chapman, Warwick School (*Fencing*)
Mrs A Cooke (*First Aid*)
Mrs J Curry (*Gymnastics*)
Mrs L England (*Dance*)
Ms H Godfrey (*Mandarin*)
Mr S Haig-McMahon (*Clay Pigeon Shooting*)
Mr P Helps, Warwick School (*Clay Pigeon Shooting*)
Mr G Henderson (*Tennis*)
Miss S Higgins (*Ballet*)
Miss H Lound (*Contemporary Dance*)
Mr A Millington, Warwick School (*Climbing Club*)

Mrs D Monnington (*Badminton*)
Mr P Nield, Warwick School (*Swimming*)
Mr C Osborne (*Badminton*)
Mr P Pardoe (*Clay Pigeon Shooting*)
Mrs A Stanley (*Zumba*)
Mr A Wilson (*Duke of Edinburgh's Award*)
Mrs C Wilson (*Duke of Edinburgh's Award*)
Mrs M Yeates, Warwick School (*Lifesaving*)

Marketing/Communications Manager: Mrs J Horton
Marketing Assistant: Mrs H Cartwright
Registrar: Mrs G Worrall
Head's Secretary: Mrs D Ralphs
Administration Manager: Miss H Shawcross
Office Receptionist/Administrator: Mrs F Eddy
Office Receptionist/Administrator: Miss K Lewis
Data Administrator: Mr A Sherren
Matron: Mrs T Rutter
Administrative Assistant, Music Dept: Mrs A Williams
Librarian: Mrs A Falconer Hall
Alumnae Relations Manager: Mr R Gellert-Binnie
Database and Administration Assistant: Mrs E Guest
Head Caretaker: Mrs R Cox
Secretary of Old Girls' Association: Mrs P Beidas

King's High School is an independent day school for girls aged 11 to 18. From our beginning in 1879, our expertise has been girls; providing an exceptional educational environment tailored to their needs in which they may thrive and become well-rounded, well-educated and compassionate young women. The school is part of the Warwick Independent Schools Foundation, alongside Warwick School and Warwick Preparatory School, and we enjoy our strong links with our Prep and brother schools. Located in the heart of Warwick, the listed 18th century Landor House is complemented by superb ultra-modern additions: the Sixth Form Centre and St Mary's Building opened by Dame Judi Dench, DBE in 2006, the Creative Arts Centre opened by Miss Catherine Bott in 2009 and the Dining Room opened by Miss Prue Leith in 2011.

The curriculum aims to give pupils as broad, engaging and rigorous an education as possible. All pupils study two modern languages and Latin and may choose three separate sciences for the IGCSE. There is an exceptionally wide choice of A Level subjects.

Our pupils' outstanding success at GCSE and A Level and in gaining places at prestigious universities of their first choice was remarked on in our 2011 Inspection Report, which especially noted that our A Level exam performance exceeded that of pupils in selective maintained schools. This success continues today with our 2013 and 2014 A Level A*–B results having been the best across Warwickshire.

Extra-curricular and community activity flourish. Most girls achieve the Duke of Edinburgh's Bronze Award and many continue to Silver and Gold. Girls distinguish themselves in sport, music, drama and the countless other activities on offer. The school organises many day, evening and residential trips to destinations at home and abroad and invites prestigious women, such as Dame Judi Dench, DBE and Professor Germaine Greer, to visit and speak.

King's High provides an enjoyable, safe and stimulating experience in which girls can grow into confident and secure young women, equipped to make choices as they progress through their education and enter the world, prepared for change and able to make a positive and generous contribution to society.

Admission. Girls are required to take an entrance examination and attend an interview.

Fees per term (2014–2015). Tuition £3,623. Music: Brass, Pianoforte, Strings, Woodwind, Guitar, Drums, Singing £231 for 10 lessons.

Financial Assistance. Academic and subject scholarships in Art, Drama, Music and Sport are available on entry at age 11. Performance Awards are available for girls in

Years 7–11. Application for Academic Scholarships and Performance Awards is open to internal and external candidates for the Sixth Form. Means-tested Warwick Foundation Awards, up to the value of full fees, are also available on entry at 11+ and at Sixth Form.

Charitable status. King's High School is a part of the Warwick Independent Schools Foundation which is a Registered Charity, number 1088057. The aim of the charity is "to provide for children (3–18) of parents of all financial means – a high proportion of whom shall come from Warwick and its immediate surroundings, but subject to satisfying academic standards where required – education of academic, cultural and sporting standards which are the highest within their peer groups".

The Kingsley School

Beauchamp Hall, Beauchamp Avenue, Royal Leamington Spa, Warwickshire CV32 5RD
Tel: 01926 425127
Fax: 01926 831691
email: schooloffice@kingsleyschool.co.uk
website: www.thekingsleyschool.com

Independent Day School for Girls aged 3 to 18, and boys up to 7 years, founded in 1884.

Council:
President: Mr A Noble

Joint Chairs:
Mrs A Darling
Mrs J White, BSc Eng, FCA

Governors:

Mrs L Bartlett
Mr T Baumfield
Mrs J Burns
Mr R N Button
Mr A Bye

Mr D Cleary
Mrs M P Hicks, CertEd
Mrs E Smith
Dame Y Buckland

Head: Ms H Owens, BA, PGCE, NPQH

Deputy Head (Pastoral): Mrs J Bailey, BA, CertEd

Assistant Headteacher (Curriculum & Administration): Ms R Dyson, BA, PGCE

Head of Preparatory School: Miss A Hornsby, MSc, CertEd

Head of Sixth Form: Mrs D Morgan, BA, PGCE

Staff:
* *Head of Department*

Art:
*Mr E Lax, BA Hons Fine Art, PGCE

Classics:
*Ms I Peace, BA, PGCE

Design & Technology:
*Mrs C Dempsey, BEd
Mrs K Hughes O'Sullivan, MA, BEd
Mrs L Lepoidevin, BEd

Economics & Business Studies:
*Mrs M Bennett, BEd, MA

English:
*Mrs A Hamilton, BA, PGCE

Mrs P Doubleday, BA Phil, BA, CertEd
Mrs D Morgan, BA, PGCE
Miss J Roche, BA, PGCE, MA

Geography:
*Mrs R Rogers, BSc, PGCE
Mrs J Bailey, BA, CertEd
Mrs D Frydman, BSc, CertEd

History:
*Mrs S Waterson, BA, PGCE
Ms R Dyson, BA, PGCE
Mrs A Warren, BA, PGCE

Information Technology:
*Mrs M Bennett, BEd, MA
Mrs C Dempsey, BEd
Mrs S Mace, BA, PGCE
Mrs M Roberts, BEd, MA

Mathematics:
*Miss K Davis, BSc, PGCE
Mrs L Laubscher, HE Dip SA, QTS
Dr A Smith, BA, PhD, PGCE
Mr A Edwards, BSc, PGCE

Modern Languages:
*Mr I Stickels, BA, PGCE
Miss M Mahé
Mrs C Cocksworth, BA
Mrs H Foulerton, BA, PGCE

Performing Arts:
*Mrs J Walton, BEd
.Mr J Smith, BMus, PGCE
Mrs A Vallance, BA QTS

Preparatory School:
Head: Miss A Hornsby, MSc, CertEd

Mrs G Adair, BN, PGCE
Mrs C Hall, BEd
Mrs Y Hargreaves, NNEB
Mrs R Harrold, PGCE
Mrs S Holmes BA, PGCE
Mrs C Machin, BA, PGCE
Miss C Harris, BSc, PGCE

Miss M Knight-Adams, BSc, PGCE
Miss L Miller, BA
Mrs C Divers, BA
Mrs C Lopez, BA, MA
Miss J Wish, BA, PGCE

Careers:
Mrs J Marriott

Learning Support:
*Mrs S Smith, BA, PGCE
Ms J Harper, BA
Mrs Y Raja, Cert Learning Support
Mrs C Cocksworth, BA

Learning Resources Centre:
Mrs D Blumberg

Finance Office:
Mr B Cheney, ACMA (*Senior Finance Manager*)

Administration:
Mrs J Bostock (*PA to Headteacher*)
Mr A Savage (*Premises Manager*)
Mrs J Dudley (*Exam Secretary/Cover Administrator*)

Marketing:
Mrs C Watson (*School Registrar*)
Mrs A Radley, MIPR (*Marketing and PR Coordinator*)

Duke of Edinburgh's Award Scheme:
Mrs K Hughes-O'Sullivan, MA, BEd

Speech and Drama:
Mrs V Comer, LAMDA

Dance:
Ms N Shurvinton (*Modern Dance Tutor*)
Mrs A Vallance, BA, QTS

School Nurse: Mrs T Ball, SRN, BSc

Physical Education:
*Miss S Windsor, BEd
Mrs S Bates, BA, CertEd
Mrs K Close
Miss S Jones, BA QTS

Psychology:
*Mrs S Mace, BA, PGCE
Mrs K MacLeod, BSc

Religious Studies:
*Mrs E Mackenzie, BPhil, MEd, CertEd
Mrs L LePoidevin, BEd
Mr J Smith, BMus, PGCE

Science:
*Mr A Edwards, BSc, PGCE
Dr C Robertson, BSc, PhD, PGCE
Mrs C Duke, BSc, PGCE
Mrs A Hawthorn, BEng, MSc, PGCE
Mrs S Bains, MSc, PGCE

The Kingsley School has a long history of success in every area of the curriculum and its traditions and ethos combine to make it a happy and secure environment for its pupils. The school is a Christian foundation but welcomes pupils of different faiths. Since 1884, Kingsley has upheld traditional values in a happy, purposeful and well-disciplined environment. It enjoys an enviable teacher: pupil ratio of 1:9 and the talents of each individual are recognised and nurtured academically and socially.

Kingsley **Preparatory School** offers a rich, vibrant and extensive curriculum which goes way beyond the National Curriculum, with pupils achieving excellent results. There are specialist teachers in the key areas of French, music, drama, PE, games and swimming.

Throughout their junior years, children thrive in a caring, homely and academically stimulating setting that prepares them well for entry to the Senior School.

The **Senior School** provides a wide range of GCSE subjects including 3 separate sciences, astronomy, 2 modern languages, Latin, business and communication studies, physical education, drama, dance and music. Academic standards are high, with the 2014 GCSE results showing a 95% pass rate at grades A* to C in at least 5 subjects, of which 80% of passes were at grades A* to B.

The **Sixth Form** at Kingsley combines the desire for academic success with the creation of confident, self-motivated and independent young women. Curriculum provision and choice is broad as the School offers traditional A Level subjects as well as economics, politics, psychology and business studies. In the 2014 A Level exams there was a 100% pass rate with 30% A* to A grades. Most girls go on to their first-choice university, including Oxbridge.

Extra-curricular Activities. The diverse selection of clubs and activities on offer include: astronomy, art, badminton, Bookworm Club, child development, Chinese, cross stitch, classics, Food Club, hockey, orchestra, public speaking, swimming, swing band, tennis, quiz club and the Kingsley Riding Squad.

From a young age, pupils are encouraged to explore their creative abilities through a rich programme of expressive arts including speech and drama, singing, dance and music. A high proportion of girls take LAMDA and ABRSM exams as well as work towards the Arts Award.

Older girls can take part in Young Enterprise, World Challenge and a thriving Duke of Edinburgh's Award scheme, with many girls achieving their gold award.

Many cultural and sporting trips are organised every year to enrich the taught curriculum and learning: recent examples include visits to local businesses, museums and theatres as well as destinations further afield such as Barbados, India, Pompeii and Ypres.

Fees per term (2014–2015). Preparatory School: £3,045 (Reception to Year 2), £3,550 (Years 3–6). Senior School: £3,820.

Scholarships and Bursaries. Academic, art, music, drama, sport and performing arts scholarships are available at 7+, 11+, 13+ and 16+.

Up to 100% bursaries are available.

Private transport serves a wide area and before and after-school care is available.

Charitable status. The Kingsley School is a Registered Charity, number 528774. It exists to provide high quality education for girls aged 3 to 18 and boys up to 7 years.

The Lady Eleanor Holles School

Hanworth Road, Hampton, Middlesex TW12 3HF
Tel: 020 8979 1601
Fax: 020 8941 8291
email: office@lehs.org.uk
website: www.lehs.org.uk

This Independent Girls' School derives its endowment from a Trust established in 1710 under the will of Lady Eleanor Holles. The Cripplegate Schools Foundation administered the Trust from 1711, when the original school for girls was founded in Cripplegate in the City of London, until 1 November 2009 when a new charitable company limited by guarantee (named 'The Lady Eleanor Holles School' with company registration number 06871042 and registered charity number 1130254) became active, and the Memorandum and Articles of Association of the company now form the constitution of the School. The School is therefore now established as a new legal entity with a distinct and separate legal personality from that of the Foundation. The Foundation continues to exist as an unincorporated charity and to own the buildings and land in which the School operates. The Governors are now the directors and charity trustees of the incorporated School. The present school in Hampton accommodates about 890 girls, aged from 7 to 18 years.

The Cripplegate Schools Foundation

Chairman of the Foundation: Mr C S Stokes

Governors:
Mr G Cox, ACE, CA SA
Mrs E de Vise, BA
Mr P Gray, ACA, CA SA
Mr N D Lewis, LLB
Dr S McCormick, MA Oxon, PhD, CBiol, FIBiol
Ms A Meyric Hughes, BA, PGCE, MA
Mr R T Welch, FCA
Mrs W J Wildman, BA, PGCE

Clerk to the Governors: Mr G Stokes

Head Mistress: Mrs Heather G Hanbury, MA Edinburgh, MSc Wolfson College Cambridge

Deputy Head: Mr R J J Nicholson, MA Pembroke College Oxford, ARCO, PG Cert Ed Man

Senior Assistant Head: Miss A Proctor, BA Jesus College Oxford, MSc Durham

Senior Assistant Head: Mr M J Williams, BA City of London Polytechnic

Assistant Head (Pastoral): Mr M Tompsett, MA Selwyn College Cambridge

Assistant Head (Pastoral): Miss M J Waters, BEd Bedford College of HE

Assistant Head (Director of Studies): Mr A P McCleave, BA Manchester, MA Institute of Education

Assistant Staff:

Senior School

Art and Craft:
Miss S Pauffley, BA Goldsmiths University of London
Mr L Curtis, BA Slade School of Art, MA Royal College of Art
Ms K Jeffery, BA Leicester (*History of Art*)
Mrs E Knight, BA Wimbledon School of Art
Miss H Peat, BA Loughborough College of Art and Design (*Deputy Head of Middle School*)
Ms A E Seaborn, BA Winchester School of Art
Miss Susanna White, BA (*University of the Arts*)

Classics:
Mr D Piper, BA King's College London
Mrs R Brown, BA Durham
Ms V Clark, BA Wadham College Oxford
Miss K C Eltis, BA Balliol College Oxford
Miss M Hart, BA Exeter

Design Technology including Home Economics:
Miss A M Travers, BEd Surrey
Mrs A M Angliss, BEd Trinity College Dublin
Mr S G Bicknell, BSc Brunel, PG Dip

Drama:
Dr B J Tait, BA CSSD, PhD Royal Holloway University of London

Mrs S E Campbell, BA Royal Holloway University of London

Visiting Drama Staff:
Mrs M Ford-Johansen, BA Wilson College, Pennsylvania, MA Royal Holloway University of London (*Speech & Drama*)
Mrs J Oxborrow, BA
Ms S Torrent, BA

Economics:
Miss A J Matthews, BA Leicester
Miss D A Self, BSc Brunel

English:
Mrs H M Ndongong, BA St Edmund Hall Oxford
Miss H Barnett, BA Durham
Miss E Evans, MA Durham
Mrs V Griffin, BA Homerton College Cambridge
Mrs U Renton, MA Aberdeen
Mrs C Richardson, BA Reading
Miss A-M Wright, MA Aberdeen

Geography:
Mr C Tracey, BSc Lancaster
Mrs A R Lloyds, BSc Exeter (*maternity leave*)
Mrs J M Mackay, BSc Southampton, MA London
Mr A P McCleave, BA Manchester, MA Institute of Education (*Director of Studies*)
Miss A Proctor, BA Jesus College Oxford, MSc Durham (*Senior Assistant Head*)
Miss A Spelman, BA King's College London
Mr L M Tresserras, BA Southampton (*Examinations Officer*)

History:
Miss R Hillsdon, BA Sidney Sussex College Cambridge
Mrs A M Bradshaw, MA St Andrews
Mr T J Hurst, BA Queen Mary University of London, MA King's College London
Miss S E Stowe, BA Warwick

Information Technology:
Mr M Britland, BSc Gloucestershire (*Director of ICT*)
Mrs P M Stewart, BSc Bath

Mathematics:
Mrs F M Wimblett, BSc Royal Holloway University of London (*Deputy Head of Sixth Form*)
Mrs N Banerjee, BA Delhi
Mrs A Hornsby, BSc Manchester
Mrs S Leigh, BSc Edinburgh
Mr S Maloney, BA York, MSc Open
Mrs M Najjar, BSc University College London
Mrs M Read, BSc Durham
Mrs K Sinnett, BA Peterhouse Cambridge
Miss C Swainston, BSc Surrey
Mr M J Williams, BA City of London Polytechnic (*Senior Assistant Head*)

Modern Languages:
Mrs Y Wiggins, BA Staatsexamen Universität Würzburg (*Head of Modern Languages and German*)
Mrs A Buck, Licenciada en Filología Anglogermanica Universidad de Valencia (*Spanish and German*)
Mrs I M Colclough, BA Royal Holloway University of London (*German*)
Mrs R A M Johnson, BA Cologne (*German*)
Mrs V M Kean, BA Leeds (*Head of French*)
Ms N Murray, BA Leeds, MA Leeds
Miss U Peña-Lekue, BA Deusto, Bilbao (*Head of Spanish*)
Mrs N J Rees, MA New Hall Cambridge (*Spanish and Special Educational Needs*)
Mrs K Reid, MA University of Trier, Germany
Miss D L Robbins, MA St Andrews (*French*)
Mrs A Rowe, BA Nottingham

Mr M Tompsett, MA Selwyn College Cambridge (*German; Assistant Head (Pastoral)*)

Music:
Director of Music: Mrs M Ashe, MA St Catherine's College Oxford
Mr B G Ashe, BA York, PGCE, LRAM (*Piano, Choir Accompanist*)
Dr B L Hughes, MA St Catherine's College Oxford, MMus Goldsmiths University of London, PhD London, QTS (*Composer-in-Residence*)
Mr R J J Nicholson, MA Pembroke College Oxford, ARCO, PG Cert Ed Man (*Deputy Head*)
Miss N Redman, BMus Manchester, MMus GSMD
Mr J Akers, BMus RCM, MMus, PGADip RCM (*Classical Guitar*)
Miss A Arnopp, BA, Post Grad, LRAM (*Musical Theatre Singing*)
Miss S Bodsworth, BMus, PGDip RCM, GradDip (*Voice*)
Miss E Bradley, MMus SOAS, GRNCM (*Double Bass*)
Miss F Chesterman, BMus, Dip Perf (*Violin*)
Miss J Clark, MA, PGDip (*Voice*)
Ms A Cohen, DRASM, ARCM, LRAM (*Piano*)
Mrs M Cooper, BMus, MMus, PGDip (*Flute*)
Mr N Fletcher, BMus, MA (*Piano*)
Miss L H Goddard, MA Girton College Cambridge (*Violin*)
Mr G Hobbs, BMus, PGDipMus (*Bassoon*)
Mrs D L Hume, DSCM (*Violin*)
Miss I Jones, BMus, Dip RCM, Advanced RCM (*Oboe*)
Ms D Kemp, MA, ARCM PG, Dip RCM (*Viola*)
Mr J Kennedy, MMus (*Voice, Music Theatre*)
Mrs P A Kent, GRSM, LRAM (*Piano*)
Mr N McGovern, MMus (*Saxophone*)
Mr R Millett, Dip RCM (*Music Technology, Percussion, Percussion Group*)
Ms A Moore, Dip RCM, ARCM (*Harp*)
Ms C Overbury, BMus Oxon, PGDip Mus (*Flute*)
Miss A Prowse, BA Girton College Cambridge (*Voice*)
Mr S Ridley, BMus, PGDip RCM, ARCM (*Piano*)
Mrs H Roberts, MMus, GTCL, LTCL, FTCL (*Voice*)
Ms J Routledge, BMus, MA, (*Bassoon and Piano*)
Mr M Schofield, BMus, PGDip (*Viola and Violin*)
Mr T Sharp BSc, MSc, LGSM (*Piano, Jazz Piano*)
Ms E Sheridan, BMus Hons, RCM, PG Dip RCM (*Clarinet*)
Dr S-W Tseng, MMus, LRAM (*Cello*), LRAM (*Piano*), DMA
Mr T Varrell, BMus (*Rock Guitar, Bass Guitar, Rock Band*)
Mr D Ward, AGSM Grad GSMD (*Brass*)

Mrs P Tate (*Music and Drama Administrator*)

Natural Sciences:
Mrs A Jeffery, BSc Southampton (*Chemistry, Head of Science*)
Mrs L J Anstey, MA New Hall Cambridge (*Psychology and Biology*)
Mrs J Barwise, BSc Manchester, MA London (*Physics*)
Mrs P R Bond, BSc Leeds (*Biology*)
Mr J R Bossé, BSc, BEd Université de Moncton, Canada (*Head of Biology*)
Mrs N C Camilleri, BSc Manchester (*Physics*)
Mrs J Crook, BSc Nottingham (*Chemistry*)
Mrs P Earl, BSc Swansea (*Biology*)
Mrs K M Ellis, BSc Durham (*Physics*)
Mr A Hayter, BSc Durham (*Head of Chemistry*)
Ms H Humbles, BSc University College London (*Biology*)
Mr R Ives, BSc Sheffield Hallam (*Head of Physics*)
Mrs S Jansz, BSc Bangor (*Chemistry*)
Mrs J Monteil, BSc Swansea, MSc London (*Head of Psychology, Biology*)
Mrs C R Nicholls, BSc Cardiff (*Biology*)
Miss S S Ostrander, BSc Bristol (*Psychology and Biology*)
Ms C Packer, BSc University College London (*Chemistry*)

Miss R Parker, BSc Manchester (*Chemistry*)

Physical Education:
Director of Sport and Outward Bound Activities: Mrs N
    Budd, BSc Brighton
Mrs L J Brennan, BEd University of Sydney, Australia
    (*Deputy Head of Lower School*) (*maternity leave*)
Mr J Cheesman (*Head of Rowing*)
Mrs R Crane, BA St Mary's Twickenham
Miss A Cutteridge, BA Durham
Miss C Gaunt, BSc Birmingham, MSc Loughborough
Miss K Walsh, BA Oxford Brookes
Miss M J Waters, BEd Bedford College of HE (*Assistant
    Head Pastoral*)
Miss E Morris, BSc St Mary's Twickenham (*Duke of
    Edinburgh's Award Coordinator*)

Religious Education:
Dr P Gibbons, BA Surrey, MA Surrey, DPhil Regent's
    Park College Oxford
Miss L Prothero, BA Harvest Bible College, Melbourne,
    Australia, MA University College London

Careers Advice:
Miss A J Matthews, BA Leicester Polytechnic (*Economics*)
Mrs L J Anstey, MA New Hall Cambridge (*Psychology
    and Biology*)
Miss M Hart, BA Exeter (*Classics*)
Mr A Hayter, BSc Durham (*Chemistry*)
Ms H Humbles, BSc University College London (*Biology*)
Mrs R A M Johnson, BA Cologne (*German*)
Mrs H M Ndongong, BA St Edmund Hall Oxford (*English*)
Mrs C R Nicholls, BSc Cardiff (*Biology*)
Miss S S Ostrander, BSc Bristol (*Psychology and Biology*)
Miss R E Parker, BSc Manchester (*Chemistry*)
Mr M Tompsett, MA Selwyn College Cambridge (*German,
    Assistant Head Pastoral*)

Learning Support:
Miss M Christodoulou, BA Middlesex, MA Durham,
    PGCert Dyslexia and Literacy (*Head of Learning
    Support*)
Ms J Davies Cert Ed Gloucestershire, OCR Cert Helen
    Arkell, Dip Dyslexia Inst
Mrs N Rees, MA New Hall Cambridge

Manager LRC: Mrs L Payne, BA University of California
    (Davis), MA California State University San Francisco,
    MCLIP

Junior Department

Head of Department: Mrs F Robinson, BA Cardiff, MA
    King's College London

Assistant Staff:
Mrs J E Allden, BSc London, MSc Kingston
Miss V M Barnes, BA Kingston
Mrs M M Bass, BEd Natal
Mrs J Deverson, BEd Oxford Brookes
Mrs J Dilworth, BSc UCL, MPhil Cambridge
Miss L Evans, BA Kingston
Mrs M Frampton, BEd Exeter
Miss S L Gain, BSc St Mary's Twickenham
Mrs S Grant-Sturgis, BA Exeter
Mrs S Harding, BEd De Montfort
Mrs K Hide, BEd La Sainte Union College of Education
Mrs C Lyne, Dartford College of Physical Education, BA
    OU
Miss J Mackay, BEd Westminster College, Oxford (*Deputy
    Head of Junior Department*)
Mrs V M Moran, BA Durham
Mrs M Walker, BA Canterbury Christchurch
Mrs V Wood, BEd College of St Mark & St John,
    Plymouth
Mrs L Cowin (*Teaching Assistant*)
Mrs L Hovsepian (*Teaching Assistant*)

Administration:
Director of Finance: Mr M Berkowitch, BSc, JD
Estates Manager: Mr M Walburn, BSc
Marketing & Development Coordinator: Ms S Newton
Personal Assistant to the Head Mistress: Mrs C E Dinsdale
*Personal Assistant to the Deputy Head and Head of Junior
    Dept*: Miss J Chudleigh
School Secretary (*Senior Department*): Mrs S Austyn
Registrar: Mrs A Stark
School Nurse: Sister S Brew, RGN
School Secretary (*Junior Department*): Mrs J Rees

The school dates from 1710 and is named after its bene-
factress The Lady Eleanor Holles who directed that the surplus from her Will should be used to establish a school for
young girls. Originally in the Cripplegate Ward of the City
of London, it moved in the nineteenth century to Hackney
and then in 1937 to Hampton. The present, purpose-built,
school was opened by Princess Alice, Duchess of Gloucester and accommodated 350 pupils. Numerous additions to
the building and the acquisition of more land have enabled
the school to increase in size to some 700 girls who enjoy a
wealth of specialist facilities and the use of 24 acres of playing fields and gardens. Nine science laboratories, Learning
Resources Centre, Sixth Form Library, a Design and Technology suite, extensive IT and multimedia language facilities and a dedicated Careers area are complemented by grass
and hard tennis courts, netball courts, 5 lacrosse pitches,
track and field areas and a full-sized, indoor heated swimming pool. A Boat House, shared with Hampton School,
was opened in October 2000 and a large Sports Hall, adjacent to the swimming pool, in September 2001.

September 2012 saw the opening of a new Arts Centre
consisting of a 300-seat theatre, new Music and Art Departments, Sixth Form Common Rooms, followed in September
2013 by a new dining room, a new suite of classrooms, two
dedicated Drama Studios, a Conference Room which also
serves as the school's chapel, and The Friends' Courtyard.

Both the Junior and Senior Departments are equipped
with a lift for the disabled.

The School's Statement of Purpose embodies the original aim, to encourage every girl to develop her personality
to the full so that she may become a woman of integrity and
a responsible member of society. It also emphasises the
value of a broad, balanced education which gives due
importance to sport, music and the creative arts in general
whilst providing the opportunities for girls to achieve high
academic standards within a framework of disciplined, independent study.

The Curriculum. In Years 7–9, girls experience two
modern foreign languages, Latin, separate sciences, dedicated ICT lessons and a PSHE programme which continues
throughout the school. Selection rather than specialisation
for GCSE allows girls to respond to individual abilities and
attributes whilst the School's scheme ensures that every girl
continues to experience a broad education in which as few
doors as possible are closed. A large sixth form of about
190–200 girls enables a wide choice of Advanced and
Advanced Subsidiary subjects to be offered by the School.
Most girls will study four or five subjects at Advanced Subsidiary Level, proceeding to A Level with three or four. The
girls have the option of entering for the AQA Baccalaureate,
which embraces their A Levels, General Studies AS, an
Extended Project and extra-curricular activities. All sixth
form students move on to further training, the majority to
universities, and there is a sizeable Oxbridge contingent
annually. The formal Careers programme which begins in
Year 9, continues throughout the school and uses external
specialists, parents and past pupils, ECCTIS and other computer programmes as well as the School's own, trained staff.

Extra-Curricular Activity. A key strength of the school
is the range and diversity of its flourishing extra-curricular
provision. Some 120 clubs run each week ranging from

Music, Drama and PE to Outward Bound and subject clubs, all aiming to stimulate further and inculcate a love of learning outside the classroom: 'The Other Half'. Sixth Formers lead a number of groups which focus on various political, environmental and ethical issues, including 'Model United Nations', 'Amnesty' and 'Make Poverty History'. Girls are encouraged to take the initiative to form their own clubs with a Medic Group, Law Society and Book Club formed in the recent past. The school is very much at the heart of the educational community and has developed a wide range of activities to ensure that students are aware of their social responsibilities, including Service Volunteers which works with disadvantaged students and the elderly, and running numerous activities in local primary schools, including language and drama clubs. Pupils are strongly encouraged to participate in extra-curricular activities.

The Junior Department (190 pupils aged 7–11) is accommodated in a separate building in the grounds, which was very extensively renovated and refurbished in 2003. It is an integral part of the whole school community and uses some specialist facilities.

(*See entry in the IAPS section for more details.*)

Entrance. The majority of girls in the Junior Department are offered guaranteed places in the Senior Department based on an assessment of their performance and attitude. Those that are not may sit the Senior Department entrance examinations if they wish. Pupils may enter the Junior Department from the age of 7, and the Senior School at 11 years. Girls with good academic ability may apply for direct entry to the Sixth Form. All external applicants must sit the School's competitive entrance examinations, which are held in November for Sixth Form entry and January (7+ and 11+) each year for admission in the following September.

Registration and Entrance Examination Fee: £100.

Scholarships and Bursaries. *11+ Entry Academic Scholarships*: On average ten awards are offered each year. These are expressed as percentages of the full fee and will thus keep pace with any increases. Awards are likely to be for 10%. The awards are based on performance in the school's own Entrance Examinations and subsequent interview.

Sixth Form Academic Scholarships: A maximum of ten Scholarships worth 10% of fees over the two years of Sixth Form study are offered to internal and external candidates who sit the Sixth Form Entrance and Scholarship Examination in November before the year of proposed entry.

Music Scholarships: Both Major and Minor Awards for Music are available at 11+ and 16+. These are likely to be for 10% and 7.5% respectively of fees and free tuition on one instrument. Candidates must satisfy academic requirements in entrance papers before being invited to a music audition. Full details are available from the school.

Governors' Bursaries: Candidates who sit entrance papers at any stage may be considered for a bursary award. These are means tested and subject to annual review.

Fees per term (2014–2015). £4,750 in the Junior Department; £5,800 in the Senior School. Fees are inclusive of Books, Stationery, Games and exclusive of Public Examination fees.

Former Pupils' Association. The Holly Club address for communications: Alumnae Administrator c/o The Lady Eleanor Holles School; email: nnolan@lehs.org.uk.

Lavant House

West Lavant, Chichester, West Sussex PO18 9AB

Tel: 01243 527211
Fax: 01243 530490
email: office@lavanthouse.org.uk
website: www.lavanthouse.org.uk
Twitter: @Lavant_House

Governors:

Mrs M Scott (*F & GP*) (*Chairman*)

Mrs J Buckley, BA, PGCE (*Education*)

Mrs L Butt, MEd

Mr R Carlylse, BA Hons London, MBA Leicester, PGCE London, Cert Dysl & Lit York, AKC King's College London, ATS BDA (*Communications/F & GP*)

Mrs H Herson, CertEd Bedford (*Health & Safety, Child Protection Safeguarding*)

Mr R J Hoare, OBE, MA Oxon (*Bursary/F & GP*)

Mrs R Kamaryc, BA, MSc, PGCE (*Education*)

Mr A Malcolm Green

Mr R H Malcolm-Green, CEng, BSc London (*F & GP*) (*Deputy Chairman*)

Mr C Maultby

Mr J Pressdee, FCA (*F & GP*)

Mr M Sullivan, LLB Bristol (*F & GP*)

Mrs H Todd

Clerk to the Governors: Mr M Chapman, MA Cantab, MBA

Headmistress: Mrs C Horton, BSc Hons London, MEd Exeter

Senior Staff:

Deputy Head & Head of Lower School: Mrs D van Beek, BEd Exeter, Dip Ed Southampton (*Child Protection Officer*)

Director of Studies: Mrs J Martin, BEd Hons Chichester

Head of Junior Lavant: Mrs K Wade, BSc Hons London, PGCE West Sussex Institute

Senior Housemistress: Mrs C Costello

Deputy Housemistress: Mrs S Zanger, BEd Hons West Sussex Institute

School Nurses:

Mrs J Dawes RGN

Mrs F Moore RGN

Administration:

Bursar: Mr M Chapman, MA Cantab, MBA

Bursar's Assistant: Mr A Ennor, BA Hons Portsmouth

Registrar: Mrs L Cranfield, BA Hons Brighton

Secretary/Receptionist: Mrs L Norland

IT Consultant: Mr J Platt, LRAM

Librarian & Old Girls' Coordinator: Mrs T Grayston-James

Domestic Bursar: Mrs E Darvill

Catering: Mr P Allaway, Mrs K Staples

Teaching Staff:

English:

Mrs M Mack, BA Durham, PGCE London (*Form V Tutor, Debating, Public Speaking*)

Mrs P Furmidge, BEd Hons, MA Sussex, BA OU

Mrs S Jones, BA Hons OU, CertEd Gloucester College, Dip SpLD Kingston (*Forms I & II Assistant Tutor*)

Mathematics:

Mrs D van Beek, BEd Exeter, Dip Ed Southampton (*Deputy Head, Form III Tutor*)

Mrs J Martin, BEd Hons Chichester (*Director of Studies, Form IV Assistant Tutor*)

Mrs C Horton, BSc Hons London MEd Exeter

Biology:

Mrs E Marks, BSc Hons Warwick, SRN, RM, PGCE Leicester, MSc OU (*Form VI Tutor, PSHE Coordinator, D of E*)

Chemistry:

Mrs C Jones, BSc Warwick, PGCE Portsmouth (*Form V Assistant Tutor*)

Mrs J Sharp, MA Hons Cambridge, PGCE Reading

Physics:
Mrs K Labedz, BSc Hons London, PGCE Liverpool

Science Technician: Mrs L Richardson, C&G HNC

Computer Studies:
Mrs S Davis, BA Hons Exeter, MSc Bath
Communication Studies: Mrs S Jones, BA Hons OU, Cert Ed Gloucester College, Dip SpLD Kingston

History & RE:
Mrs L Ayling, BA Hons, PGCE Chichester (*Forms I & II Tutor*)

Geography:
Mrs J Adams, BA Hons Hull, PGCE King's College (*Assistant Form III Tutor*)

French:
Mrs E Bracey, BA Hons Warwick, PGCE Sheffield (*Form IV Tutor*)

Spanish:
Mrs G Rosado, BA Ciudad Real, PGCE Granada

Classics/Latin:
Miss H Claxton-Roper, BA Hons Reading, PGCE London

Drama: Miss C Boyd-Wallis, BA Hons, PGCE Chichester

Business Studies, Lower School English & EAL: Mrs P Furmidge, BEd Hons, MA Sussex, BA OU

Media Studies: Miss A Gordon, BA Hons Portsmouth, PGCE Portsmouth

Music:
Director of Music: Mrs S Howell Evans, GTCL Trinity, ARCM, LTCL, PGCE London, ARSCM, FGMS (*Choir & Coordinator of Peripatetic Music Staff*)

Art:
Mrs S Stone, BA 3D Design Hons Ravensbourne College, Master of Art Hons Royal College of Art, PGCE Dist Greenwich (*Art Club*)

PE:
Mrs C Cobden, BSc Glos, PGCE Southampton (*Form VI Tutor*)
Mrs S Zanger, BA Hons West Sussex Institute

SENCO:
Mrs S Jones, BA Hons OU, CertEd Gloucester College, Dip SpLD Kingston

Learning Support:
Mrs C Skewis, BA Hons, PGCE Roehampton Dip SpLD
Mrs L Metcalfe, BSc Hons London, PG Cert York, PG Dip York
Mrs J Eden, CertEd Exeter, Dip SpLD London

Speech & Drama:
Mrs J Pressdee, LGSM, ANEA Stage Technique

Tennis:
Mrs E Ellicott, LTA registered

Counsellor:
Mrs L Kyffin, BA Hons Chichester, Dip Humanistic Counselling Chichester

Junior Lavant House:
Head of Junior Lavant: Mrs K Wade, BSc Hons London, PGCE West Sussex Institute (*Years 5 & 6 Tutor, Maths & History*)
Miss H Frampton, BA QTS Canterbury (*English, Science, Music & PSHE*)
Miss G Baker, BEd Hons Cambridge, CertEd, Adv Dip Lang Ed (*Years 3 & 4 Tutor, French & Science*)
Mrs S Zanger, BA Hons West Sussex Institute (*Geography, PE & Games*)
Teaching Assistant: Mrs E Taws

Lavant House is a forward-looking independent school. It aims to provide girls with a challenging and positive academic education within a caring community, to enable each individual to develop her abilities to the full whilst acquiring a strong set of personal values. The school is small with about 100 pupils throughout the age range from 4 to 18. The intimate size of its classes creates an opportunity for personalised learning within an atmosphere of trust and cooperation, bringing out the best in every pupil and resulting in confident, happy, sociable and successful young women ready to meet the challenges of the future.

Boarding. The school has a mix of day and boarding pupils, with both full and flexible boarding arrangements. There is an informal family atmosphere in the House, and Sixth form boarders have a considerable degree of independence in their own adjacent accommodation, "The Cottage".

Situation and Facilities. The school is situated between the South Downs and the sea, just north of the historic cathedral city of Chichester, in the heart of glorious Sussex countryside. The lovely eighteenth century flint buildings and well-tended gardens and grounds contribute to a secure and tranquil environment, with excellent facilities for Science, ICT, Drama and Sport. An impressive Art Studio opened in 2006 and a new Learning Centre and Food Technology Department opened in 2012. 2015 will see a new Physics lab and the refurbishment of the school's outdoor swimming pool. All main teaching rooms have computers with Internet access, and the majority of classrooms have interactive whiteboards. In addition there are suites of networked PCs in the school's Computing department as well as in the Junior School, library and the Learning Centre.

Curriculum. A traditionally broad academic curriculum is taught through to GCSE and a full range of subjects is offered at AS and A Level in the small, lively Sixth Form. The school boasts strong Art and Drama departments which regularly run exhibitions and major productions, and there is an accomplished Senior Choir, Strings and Flutes groups and Chamber Orchestra. Regular Chamber Concerts give young musicians a chance to perform.

Specialist help for dyslexic pupils is available, and English as an Additional Language for overseas students is offered.

Sport. Games provision includes a large playing field, three superbly surfaced netball and tennis courts, and an outdoor heated swimming pool, as well as the gymnasium. The main curriculum sports are netball and hockey in winter, and rounders, tennis, athletics and swimming in the summer, but girls also do football, badminton, volleyball, aerobics, dance, gymnastics and table tennis. Many matches are organised for girls of all age groups, and the teams are very successful in area competitions. The senior netball team has been West Sussex West Area and League Champions for the last four years.

Lavant House Stables are next to the school and many girls ride. There are two floodlit all-weather arenas in addition to fifty acres of pasture and woodland.

There is an active Duke of Edinburgh's Award scheme, with expeditions organised during the summer.

Transport. The school operates three minibus routes over a twenty mile radius for day girls. From Chichester there are rail links along the South Coast and up to London; Heathrow and Gatwick airports are about one and a half hour's drive away.

Admission. Admission is by interview and informal testing. There is an assessment day in the Spring Term for entry at 11+. Academic scholarships are available for the Senior School and the Sixth Form. Scholarships are also offered at 11+, 13+ and Sixth Form entry for exceptional talent in Art, Music and Sport and at 11+ the school offers one Riding scholarship.

Fees per term (2014–2015). Junior Day: £2,250–£2,980 (Reception – Year 4), £3,810 (Years 5 and 6). Senior Day: £4,500. Boarding: £5,900 (Junior), £7,100 (Senior). A returnable deposit of one term's boarding fees is charged for overseas pupils.

Charitable status. Lavant House School Educational Trust Limited is a Registered Charity, number 307372.

Leicester High School for Girls

454 London Road, Leicester LE2 2PP
Tel: 0116 270 5338
Fax: 0116 270 2493
email: enquiries@leicesterhigh.co.uk
website: www.leicesterhigh.co.uk
Twitter: @LeicesterHigh
LinkedIn: Leicester High School for Girls Limited

The school is a Trust with a Board of Governors in membership of AGBIS and the Headmaster belongs to the GSA.

Board of Governors:
Chairman: Mrs M Bowler, JP, BA Hons
Vice-Chairman: Mr J Jethwa, BSc
Mr J Allen, FCA
Mr M Dunkley, LLB, TEP
Mr A Jarvis, FCA
Mrs M Neilson, BEd
Mrs J Prescott, BSc, NPQH
Revd K Magee
Mr T Leah, BA, NPQH

Clerk to the Governors: Mrs E Mackay, AAT

Headmaster: Mr A R Whelpdale, BA, NPQH

Deputy Head: Miss D E J Wassell, BA

Head of Sixth Form: Mrs A Lancini, BA (*English*)

Senior School:

* *Head of Department*
§ *Part-time*

Assistant Staff:
Mrs E Bott, BA (*Art and Design*)
§Mr P Bott, DipHE
Miss J Brice, BA
§Mrs E Brookes, BA
§Mrs M Buxton-Thomas, BA
Mr A Chappell, BSc (*Science*)
Mrs J Davison, BEd (*Physical Education*)
Mrs C Dwyer, BA
Miss S Enderby, BA
§Mrs P Formoy, BA (*Modern Languages*)
§Mrs P Gascoigne, BA (*Dance*)
Mrs K Haresign, BA (*Geography/Economics*)
Dr S Hills, BSc, MSc, PhD (*Mathematics*)
Mr P Hoyle, BSc
§Mrs E Martin, BEd
Mrs D A Morgan, BSc (*PSHCE*)
Mr S Norbury, BSc (*Information Technology*)
Miss N Parveen, BSc (*Psychology/Sociology*)
Miss A Paul, BA (*History*)
§Mrs N Pulham, BA
Mrs H Rai, BSc, MSc (*Biology*)
Mrs H Rees, BA
Mrs J Rose, BA (*Drama*)
§Frau D Sauer, MA
Dr N Singleton, BSc, PhD (*Chemistry*)
Mr A Stewart, BSc
§Mr J Stoeter, BSc
Mr A Tang, BA (*Music*)
Mr J Taylor, MEng
Miss C Teal, B Theol (*Religious Studies*)
Miss E Tyler, BSc (*Careers*)
§Mrs K Kennedy, BA

§Mrs J Whalley, BSc (*Food Studies*)

School Business Manager: Mrs E J Mackay, AAT
Finance: Mrs J Gardiner, Mrs K Allen
Registrar: Mrs J Harbage
PA to the Headmaster: Ms S Davies
Academic Administrator: Mrs K Lock
Examinations Officer: Mrs P Gascoigne, BA
Receptionist: Mrs K Clark
Librarian: Miss A Adams, MA
Marketing & Media: Mrs A Whitlock, BSc
Art Technician: Mr P Bott
Assistant Librarian: Mrs L M Humrich, BA, DipLib
IT Systems Manager: Mr A Collins
Laboratory Technicians: Mrs M Cupac, Mrs M Atter
School Nurse: Mrs A Cox, HE RN
Caretakers: Mr M Hopkins, Mr G Neary

Visiting Staff:
Mrs G Bater (*Voice/Cello*)
Mr C Beadling (*Fencing*)
Mr N Bott, BA (*Percussion*)
Mrs J Bound, GBSM (*Piano*)
Ms A Donnelly, BA (*Piano*)
Mrs C Lee, LRAM (*Violin*)
Mrs K Loomes, FIDTA (*Ballet*)
Mrs A Mitchell, LTCL (*Clarinet, Flute, Saxophone*)
Mr J Pagett (*Guitar*)
Mrs R Pells, GSMD, LAMDA, EMPA, IDTA (*Speech and Drama*)
Miss C Sullivan, BA (*Speech & Drama*)

Junior Department:

Head of Department: Mrs L Fowler, BA Ed
Assistant Head: Mrs S J Davies, BA Ed
Foundation Stage Coordinator: Miss C Pow, BA
Administrator: Mrs M Singh, NVQ

Mrs S Hague, BA	Mrs S Wayman, BEd
Mrs E Hawtree, BSc	§Mrs V Williams BEd
Miss E Stell, BA	§Mrs J Woodcock, BEd
§Mr J-L Scherrer	

Ancillary Staff:

Mrs L Boyer	Mrs N Sturmey, NNEB
Mrs L Dunn	Mrs J Jethwa, Early Years
Miss S Gray, NNEB	Practitioner
Mrs J Hunter, NNEB	Mrs A Cobley
Mrs P Jackson, NNEB	

Leicester High School is a well established day school for girls situated in lovely grounds on the south side of the city. Founded in 1906 as Portland House School, it now comprises a Junior Department of 110 girls (3–9 years) and a Senior School of 375 girls (10–18) sited on the same campus.

The school offers an academic education of a high standard, and the Sixth Formers almost invariably go on to Higher Education. It is a friendly community where an emphasis is placed on honesty, integrity and respect for the views of others. Class size is kept small so that there is every opportunity for each girl to achieve her full potential whilst developing the self-confidence and self-discipline to help in her future.

The Headmaster is responsible for both the Junior Department and Senior School. The staff are well-qualified specialists and the school is renowned for both its academic excellence and extra-curricular programme. At present 17 subjects are offered at GCSE Level and 21 subjects at A Level.

Facilities. The premises are a combination of modern purpose-built units and the original Victorian house, skilfully adapted to its present purpose. The facilities of the school have been systematically improved. A purpose-built library and resource centre and new sixth form centre was opened in September 2001. The Junior Department benefited from new buildings opened in January 2002. The extension and improvement includes a computer suite and new library, enlarged hall, dining facilities and new classrooms. The EYFU was extensively redesigned in 2009. In September 2010, the school completed new facilities for Science, Art & Design and Modern Languages, and in 2014, a new Drama Studio was opened.

Religion. The school has a Christian foundation but welcomes girls of other faiths or of none.

Admission. All candidates over the age of 7 are required to pass an entrance examination for admission into the Junior and Senior sections. Entry into the Senior School would normally be at Year 6 or Year 7, but entry at other ages is considered. There is also direct entry into the Sixth Form dependent on GCSE results. Entrance into the Foundation Unit is by assessment. A registration fee of £50 is payable for all applicants.

Fees per term (2014–2015). £2,630–£3,625.

Extras. Individual Music lessons, Speech and Drama, and Ballet are offered.

Scholarships and Bursaries. Bishop Williams Scholarships for outstanding academic ability are awarded annually to girls entering Year 7 on the basis of performance in the January Entrance Examination. In 2014 a Maud Elkington Scholarship and a Sir Thomas White Scholarship and in 2015 The Headmaster's Scholarship were also introduced for Year 7 pupils. Music scholarships are also available throughout the school, and Bursaries are available from Year 6 onwards. The Ogden Trust sponsors a fully-funded scholarship covering 100% of the fees, subject to a means test, which is on offer to any Sixth Form candidate who is planning to study Physics and Maths at A Level.

The Headmaster is always pleased to meet parents of prospective pupils and to show them around the school. All communications should be addressed to the Registrar from whom prospectuses, application forms and details of fees may be obtained.

Charitable status. Leicester High School Charitable Trust Limited is a Registered Charity, number 503982. The Trust exists to promote and provide for the advancement of education based on Christian principles according to the doctrines of the Church of England.

Leweston School

Sherborne, Dorset DT9 6EN

Tel: 01963 210691
Fax: 01963 210786
email: admin@leweston.dorset.sch.uk
website: www.leweston.co.uk
Twitter: @LewestonSchool
Facebook: /Leweston

Independent Boarding (full, weekly and flexi) and Day School for Girls aged 11–18 with a separate, purpose-built, co-educational Junior Department for girls and boys aged 3 months – 11 years on the same campus. Roman Catholic foundation but all denominations welcome. Excellent academic reputation and strong Sixth Form.

Governing Body:
Mrs M Head (*Chair*)
Mrs B Wingfield Digby (*Deputy Chair*)

Mr N Bathurst	Fr R Meyer
Mr C Comyn	Mr E Newton
Mr C Fenton	Mrs E Treichl
Mrs S Gordon Wild	Mr K Newton (*Advisor for*
Mr M J F Hudson	*the Board*)

Head: **Mr A J F Aylward**, MA Oxon

Deputy Head: Mrs J Miles, MA Oxon, PGCE (*Modern Foreign Languages*)

Head of Sixth Form: Mrs E Massey, BSc Hons Oxford Brookes, PGCE Chichester (*Mathematics, Geography, Coordinator of Global Perspectives*)

Director of Studies, Head of Careers: Mr G Smith, BSc Hons Open University, PGCE (*Mathematics*)

Director of Boarding: Miss L Fielding, BA Hons Newcastle, PGCE Lancaster (*Art*)

Bursar: Mr J Fogarty, BA Hons

Visiting Chaplain: Fr Jean-Patrice Coulon
Chaplaincy Coordinator: Dr Genevieve Cox, PhD

Teaching Staff:

Classics:
Miss L Flannery, BA Hons Warwick (*Head of Classics*)
Miss V Baba, MA (*Classics, History*)

English and Drama:
Miss S Evans, BA Hons Sheffield, PGCE London (*Head of English*)
Mrs C Nash, BA Hons Southampton, PGCE Southampton, MEd Gloucestershire (*English*)
Mrs K Reynolds, LLB Bristol, PGCE Bath (*English, Head of EAL*)
Mr A Irvine, MA Oxon, PGCE, Adv Cert Royal Welsh College of Music & Drama (*Head of Drama*)
Mrs C Dempsey, Gold Medal Verse & Prose LAMDA, BA Hons Graphic Design (*Drama*)
Mrs K Pankhurst, HND Theatre and Performing Arts, PGCE (*Speech and Drama*)
Mrs J A Miller, MEd Bristol, BA Hons Southampton, PGCE Keele, DipSpLD Hornsby Int (*Head of Individual Needs*)
Mrs J Ogilvie, PG Dip Dyslexia & Literacy York (*Individual Needs Literacy*)
Mrs A Croy, BA Hons Newcastle, PGCE Edinburgh (*Individual Needs Teacher*)

Modern Languages:
Mrs L Bryson, BSc Hons Bournemouth, CertEd Exeter (*Head of Modern Languages, Spanish*)
Mrs S O'Connor, BEd Hons London (*German, French, Head of Years 10 and 11*)
Mrs C Cot, MA Aberdeen, PGCE Edinburgh (*French*)
Mrs L Maynard, MA Hons University of Liberec (*French*)
Mrs J Miles, MA Oxon, PGCE (*Spanish, French, Deputy Head*)

Geography:
Mr D Barlow, BSc Hons Nottingham, MSc London, PGCE Birmingham (*Head of Geography, Physical Education*)
Mrs E Massey, BSc Hons Oxford Brookes, PGCE Chichester (*Geography, Mathematics, Coordinator of Global Perspectives, Head of Sixth Form*)

Home Economics, Health & Social Care:
Mrs S Larkin, Dip Naturopathy, Sydney, PGCE Exeter

Mathematics:
Mr K Whitehead, BEng Hons, MSc (*Head of Mathematics, Outdoor Pursuits*)
Mr J Cross, BSc Hons London (*Mathematics, Careers*)
Mr G Smith, BSc Hons Open University, PGCE (*Mathematics, Director of Studies*)
Mr N Mackay, CertEd Rhodesia (*Mathematics*)

Religious Studies:
Mr D Kearney, BA Hons Manchester (*Head of Religious Studies*)
Ms C O'Toole, BA Hons London, PGCE, Catholic TCert Liverpool (*Religious Studies, PSHE Coordinator, Head of Years 8 & 9*)

Psychology:
Mrs S Hunt, BA Hons Bournemouth, PGCE Exeter (*Head of Year 7*)

Science:
Mrs A Harwood, BSc Hons London, PGCE Oxon (*Head of Science & Biology*)
Mr P Ainsworth, BSc Hons, PGCE (*Physics*)
Mrs R Dawson, BSc Hons Bristol, PGCE Cambridge (*Biology*)
Dr O Kemal, BSc Hons, PhD London, PGCE Surrey, MRSC (*Head of Chemistry*)
Dr C Maunder, BSc Hons London, PhD Bristol, PGCE Open University (*Chemistry, Biology*)
Mrs A Valentine, BSc Hons Swansea, PGCE London (*Head of Physics*)
Dr R Whale, BSc, PhD Birmingham, PGCE Exeter, CChem, MRSC (*Chemistry*)

Economics and Business Studies:
Mrs S Antill, BA Hons Kingston-upon-Thames, PGCE Brighton (*Economics and Business, Academic Administrator*)
Mrs L Rondeau-Robinson, MBA Rivier College, Nashua, NH, USA, BA Cum Laude University of Lowell, MA, USA, C&G TCert Yeovil College (*IT Coordinator, UCAS Administrator, Business and Communication Systems*)

History:
Mr M Hayward, BA Hons Oxon (*Head of History, History of Art*)
Mrs J Gregory, BA Hons Worcester, MA Hons Exeter, PGCE (*Head of Government and Politics, History*)

Art, Design and Technology:
Mrs E C Williams, BA Hons London, PGCE Manchester (*Head of Art & Design*)
Mr F Bush, BTEC Nat Dip Plymouth, BA Hons St Martins (*Art*)
Miss J Lacey, BA Hons Winchester School of Art (*Art Textiles*)

English as an Additional Language:
Mrs K Reynolds, LLB Bristol, PGCE Bath (*Head of EAL, English*)
Mrs K M Walker, MA Birmingham, BA Hons Bristol, Dip TEFSL

Physical Education:
Mr P Miles, BA Ed Hons Exeter (*Director of Sport and Activities*)
Miss K Mullen, BEd Hons Sussex, CertEd Chelsea (*Head of Physical Education, Head of Sports Studies*)
Mrs K Evans, BEd Hons
Miss S Millard, BA Hons Chichester, QTS
Miss K Persey, BSc Hons UWIC, PGCE Exeter
Miss G Phipps, CertEd Chelsea (*Housemistress – Years 9, 10 and 11*)
Mr M Long, LTA Coach (*Tennis*)
Mr T Prideaux-Brun (*Tennis*)
Mr S Wilson, DCA, BTCA (*Tennis*)

Music:
Mrs C Hawkes, BMus Hons Royal College of Music, ATCL, FSRCM (*Director of Music*)
Mrs W Bednall, BA Hons Southampton, ALCM (*Pianoforte*)
Miss C Bentley, GTCL, ARCM, LTCL (*Flute*)
Mrs A Heaton, BMus, MMus (*Singing*)
Mr M Hewitt, BA Hons, LGSM (*French Horn*)
Mr P Huddleston, BTech (*Percussion*)
Dr R Milestone, PhD (*Singing*)
Mr D Price, LRAM (*Violin, Viola*)
Mrs N Price, GRSM Hons, ARCM, LRAM (*Pianoforte, Bassoon*)
Mr A Serna (*Violoncello*)

Mrs A Slogrove, BA Hons, LRSM, PGCE (*Piano*)
Ms K Whatley (*Harp*)
Ms A Whittlesea (*Recorder*)

Marketing & Admissions Manager: Miss L Cox
Senior Registrar: Mrs M Liddle
Registrar: Mrs C Damant
Librarian: Mrs A King
Headmaster's Secretary: Mrs S Chant
Domestic Bursar: Miss S Fudge

Leweston School welcomes girls aged 11–18 as full, weekly and flexi boarders or as day pupils.

Situated in 46 acres of beautiful Dorset parkland, 3 miles south of Sherborne, the school offers all the advantages of both the traditional and modern in education with excellent facilities, particularly in the Sciences, Design & Technology and Sport.

Founded by the Sisters of Christian Instruction in 1891, the school is a Catholic School but has a large percentage of pupils from other denominations. There are approximately 230 girls in the School of whom around 130 are boarders. The ethos of the school is based on a wide social mix with a spread of talents, firm but friendly discipline and a keen sense of Christian and moral values. The Head is forward looking with a strong sense of leadership and vision. The school has a Visiting Chaplain and girls are expected to attend Chapel once a week. Preparation for confirmation is available for both Catholic and Anglican pupils.

The academic standard of the school is high. At both GCSE and A Level pass rates are consistently over 95% and the school's reputation for excellence in Music and Drama runs parallel with academic achievement in Sciences and The Arts. The real success of the school, however, is achieved by realising the full potential of each individual girl, whether they are high fliers or not. Each year girls gain places at leading universities and go on to read a wide range of degrees.

Teachers are dedicated and imaginative, including specialist teachers for Dyslexia and EAL. The school's special quality is its ability to encourage in each pupil a sense of her own worth and ability. Girls are outgoing, well-mannered and unstuffy. While Leweston has a high proportion of day girls, the school is fully committed to boarding offering a wide programme of activities in the evenings and at the weekends. Riding is especially popular.

The school has close links with Sherborne School and there are many combined social, recreational, musical and cultural activities between the schools. Milton Abbey join in with many of our music activities and in recent years the Sixth Form has visited Italy with Winchester School. Sherborne is an attractive historic abbey town with few of the distractions of a large city but at the same time is served by regular Network Express trains to and from London and good road links to Salisbury, Exeter and Bath. The school's facilities are among the best in the West Country. There is a fine floodlit all-weather sports pitch, Art and Design Centre, modern Senior Science Centre, Health Centre, Home Economics and Cookery Suite, large Library, heated indoor swimming pool, sports hall, multi-gym, squash courts, tennis courts and extensive well-maintained grounds and playing fields.

Leweston Junior Department (IAPS) for girls and boys aged 3 months–11 years, with boarding provision for girls from age 7, is situated on the same campus, thus offering continuity of education for girls to age 18. Excellent early years provision including French from 3 years, beautifully situated Nursery and weekly Parent and Toddler Group. (*For further details, see entry in IAPS section.*)

Scholarships are awarded at 11+, 12+, 13+ and Sixth Form entry. Academic scholarships are available as well as Music, Art, Drama, Sport and a limited number of all-rounder awards. Dates of examinations: Late November for Sixth Form scholarships, early February for others. Further details and entry forms can be obtained from the Registrar or found on the school website.

Fees per term (2014–2015). Full Boarding £7,450–£9,576; Weekly Boarding £6,515–£7,777; Day £5,520–£5,928. Flexi Boarding (including supper) £38–£46 per night.

Charitable status. Leweston School Trust is a Registered Charity, number 295175. It is a charitable foundation set up for educational purposes.

Loughborough High School

Burton Walks, Loughborough, Leicestershire LE11 2DU
Tel: 01509 212348
Fax: 01509 215720
email: admin@leshigh.org
website: www.leshigh.org

Loughborough High School is part of Loughborough Endowed Schools. Loughborough Grammar School (*see HMC entry*) is the brother school and the co-educational junior school is known as Fairfield (*see IAPS entry*). We enjoy a very old foundation, established in 1850 as one of the oldest girls' grammar schools in England. The High School is located on a delightful 46-acre site close to the town centre with many first-rate facilities, which are being added to and improved continuously.

Loughborough High School is an 11 to 18 school of approximately 600 day girls with a large Sixth Form numbering above 170. At the High School we aim to provide an excellent academic education in a caring atmosphere. Since we are a comparatively small school, we are able to know our pupils as individuals and this leads to a strong community spirit. In providing a strong academic education in a disciplined atmosphere we hope to enable each girl ultimately to enter the career of her choice. The school offers a wide range of cultural, recreational and sporting activities and there are clubs and societies for virtually all tastes and interests (many in the senior school are run jointly with Loughborough Grammar School). We believe that our academic curriculum and extra-curricular activities nurture our pupils and encourage them to become active citizens of a modern world.

Further details about the school can be obtained by contacting the school's Registrar.

Governing Body:
Chairman: Mr G P Fothergill, BA
Deputy Chairman: Mr H M Pearson, DL, DUniv Hon, BA Econ

Vice-Chairs:
Mrs M Gershlick
Mrs C Wales
Professor J Feather, MA, PhD, FRSA

Co-optative Governors:
Dr A de Bono, MA, MB, FRCGP, FFOM
Dr P Cannon, MA Cantab, BM BCh Oxon, FRCS, MRCGP
Mrs E K Critchley, MA Oxon
Professor A Dodson, BSc Hons, PhD, DSc
The Lady Gretton, JP, Lord-Lieutenant of Leicestershire, LLD Hon, DUniv Hon, Hon DLitt
Dr P J B Hubner, MB, FRCP, DCH, FACC, FESC
Mr P M Jackson, FIMI
Mrs R J E Limb, MA Cantab
M Mulla, BSc, MSc, MIM
Mrs P O'Neill, MA Cantab
Mrs G Richards, BA Hons, MEd, Hon EdD

Foundation Secretary & Treasurer: J Doherty

Senior Leadership Team:

Headmistress: Mrs G M Byrom, BSc Manchester, MA Ed Open

Deputy Head: Mrs W Kempster, BSc Reading

Director of Studies: Dr S Jackson, BSc PhD UMIST, CChem, MRSC

Heads of Key Stage:
Head of Key Stage 3: Miss C E Nelson, BSc Manchester
Head of Key Stage 4: Mrs K M Snelling, BSc Stirling
Head of Key Stage 5: Miss C Todd, BSc Manchester

Assistant Head of KS3: Miss V Standring, BSc MSc Chester
Assistant Head of KS4: Mrs J A Lewis, BA Nottingham
Assistant Head of KS5: Mrs M A Reilly, BSc Surrey

Art and Design:
Mrs S R O Henson, BA Loughborough
Miss S Budzik, BA Leeds, MA Surrey

Artist in Residence (*Textiles*):
Miss E Notman, BA Cumbria

Careers:
Dr C Burnett, BEng, EngD Swansea
Mrs L Beasley, BA Reading
Mrs R E F Burn, MA Cambridge
Dr D Cladingboel, BSc, PhD Southampton
Mrs K M Snelling, BSc Stirling

Classics:
Mrs R E F Burn, MA Cambridge
Miss L Dickinson, BA Birmingham
Mr G C Stevens, BA Liverpool

Drama:
Ms S E Boon, BA Plymouth – Dartington
Miss K Eastwood, BA Liverpool Hope

Economics and Business:
Mr R J L Needs, BA Nottingham, IMS Cert, ACCA, Dip Ed Mgmt Leicester
Mrs L J Beasley BA Reading

English:
Mrs N J Young, BA UEA
Mrs L Harrison, BA Leeds Met
Mrs H Jones, BA King's College London
Mr D Lockhart, BA Sunderland
Miss A Wright, BA Chester

Food:
Mrs M A Reilly, BSc Surrey
Mrs J A Squire, CertEd Nottingham

Geography:
Mr A Moreton, BA Manchester
Mrs J Day, BSc Manchester
Miss H Kugele, MSc Loughborough
Miss V Standring, BSc MSc Chester

History:
Dr E C Eadie, BA Birmingham, DPhil Oxford
Miss A E Chambers, BA London, MA Nottingham
Mrs J Leader, BA, MA DMU
Mrs B Lewis, MA Loughborough

Information & Communications Technology:
Mr J Singh, BA Coventry
Mrs C Winship, BSc Reading

Mathematics:
Miss C Hitchen, MEng Newcastle
Mrs J Beardsley, BEng Surrey
Mrs L J Beasley, BA Reading
Mrs W Kempster, BSc Reading
Miss R Mistry, BSc Warwick
Miss S Mann, Post Grad Dip Lincoln

Miss C I Shawcross, BSc Loughborough
Mrs A Smith, BA Oxford
Mrs C Urwin, BSc Warwick

Modern Languages:
Mr R W Tomblin, MA Oxford
Miss J Anguiano Gomez, BSc, MRes MEd, Granada
Mr D Gough, BA Sheffield
Mrs A Lee, BA Nottingham
Mrs C C Mackie, MA Cambridge
Mrs E Raouf, BA Salford
Mrs M West, MA Swansea

Language Assistants:
Miss M Cadet (*French Assistant*)
Miss, C Metz (*German Assistant*)
Miss L Ruiz Gago (*Spanish Assistant*)

LES Music School:
Mr R J West, BA Durham, MSc Herts, LGSMD, LRSM
Miss N Bouckley, BA Durham
Miss E R Jennings, BA Bishop Grosseteste, Lincoln
Miss C Revell, BMus Huddersfield
Dr P J Underwood, MA Cambridge, MMus London, PhD
    Birmingham

Personal, Social, Health & Citizenship Education:
Mrs J Conway, BA, MA Ulster

Physical Education:
Miss S Cockayne, BA Birmingham
Miss S Griffin, BSc Loughborough
Miss G McAndrew, BA Manchester Metropolitan
Mrs F Moore, BEd De Montfort Bedford
Miss V Standring, BSc MSc Chester

Psychology:
Mrs A Kenyon, BA Hull
Miss E Rees, BSc Leeds

Religious Studies:
Mrs J A Lewis, BA Nottingham
Mrs A Justice, BEd Warwick
Miss G McAndrew, BA Manchester Metropolitan
Miss R Pain, MA Nottingham

Science:
Mrs J E Stubbs, BSc Nottingham
Mrs M Ghaly, BSc Teesside
Mrs J Pellereau, MA Cambridge
Dr D Cladingboel, BSc PhD Southampton
Dr J Downing, BSc, PhD Bristol
Mrs A Gibbon, BA Loughborough
Dr S Jackson, BSc, PhD UMIST CChem, MRSC
Miss S Jogee, BSc Leicester
Miss C E Nelson, BSc Manchester
Mrs G Nightingale, BSc Sheffield
Mrs J Peart, Grad Dip Phys Guy's
Miss H Perridge, BSc Aston
Mrs K Snelling, BSc Stirling
Miss C E Todd, BSc Manchester
Dr A Williamson, BSc, PhD Imperial College London

Learning Support: Ms E Johanson, BA Bradford

Librarian: Mrs G Burton, BLS Loughborough
Matrons: Mrs A Cannon, RGN; Mrs S Chad-Smith, RGN
Examinations Officer: Mrs S English, Level 4 Prof Cert
    Managing Examinations
E-Learning Coordinator: Mrs C Winship, BSc Reading
PR, Communications & Events Manager: Ms L E Shipman
PA to the Headmistress: Miss C Hughes, BA Leicester
Registrar and Data Manager: Mrs A M Brackstone, BSc
    Aston
School Secretary: Mrs A Cox
Receptionist: Ms J Calow
Administrative Assistant and Reprographics Technician:
    Miss A Burrows, MA Bangor

Charity Coordinator: Ms L E Shipman
Voluntary Service Unit Coordinator: Miss L Dickinson,
    BA Birmingham
ICT Support: Miss E Rees, BSc Leeds; Mr T Simpson
Art / Food Technician: Mrs J Pheby
Modern Languages & Humanities Technician: Mrs T Hicks

Laboratory Technicians:
Mrs J F Owens, BA Keele, MPhil Loughborough
Mrs K Bedwell, BSc De Montfort, MSc Loughborough
Mrs L Deamer, BSc Loughborough
Mrs E Fraser, BSc DMU

LHS Duke of Edinburgh's Award Scheme Coordinator:
Mr M House, BSc Ambleside

Bursary:
Foundation Secretary and Treasurer: Mr J Doherty, ISBA
Foundation and Schools' Accountant: Mr R Harker, BA
    Coventry, FCA
Estates Manager: Mr T Allardice, MCIOB, MBEng
Compliance Officer: Mr G Leeson, BA Northumbria
Commercial Manager: Mrs G Collicutt, BA, Nottingham

Development Office:
Mrs J Harker (*Head of Development and External
    Relations*)
Mrs E Parry (*Marketing Manager MCIPR*)

Catering:
Mrs J L Johnstone (*Operations Manager – Catering &
    Events*)
Mrs F Coltman (*Catering Manager Fairfield Kitchen*)

School Curriculum. Art and Design, Biology, Business, Chemistry, Classical Civilisation, Computer Studies, Drama, Economics, English, French, Games (hockey, netball, tennis, rounders and athletics), Geography, German, Greek, Gymnastics, History, Latin, Mathematics, Modern Dance, Music, Physical Education, Physics, Politics, Religious Studies, Spanish, Food, Nutrition and Health, ICT, Psychology and Theatre Studies. Careful note is taken of the National Curriculum with additional subjects included within the curriculum to provide breadth and depth.

Fees per term (2014–2015). £3,553. Music (individual instrumental lessons): £211.50 (for 10 lessons).

Scholarships and Bursaries

Academic Awards

The Governors offer a number of scholarships at 11+ which are awarded on academic merit. All candidates are considered for these awards without the need for any further application.

Music Awards

Music Scholarships are available to musically promising and talented pupils who are successful in the Entrance Examinations. Auditions are held around the time of the Entrance Examinations.

Bursaries

Means tested Foundation Bursaries of up to 100% remission of tuition fees are available. These awards are normally made only to those entering at 11+ and 16+.

Further details of all these awards are available from the School.

Charitable status. Loughborough Endowed Schools is a Registered Charity, number 1081765, and a Company Limited by Guarantee, registered in England, number 4038033. Registered Office: 3 Burton Walks, Loughborough, Leics LE11 2DU.

Luckley House School

Luckley Road, Wokingham, Berkshire RG40 3EU
Tel: 0118 978 4175
Fax: 0118 977 0305
email: registrar@luckleyhouseschool.org
website: www.luckleyhouseschool.org
Twitter: @LuckleyHouse
Facebook: LuckleyHouseSchool
LinkedIn: Luckley House School

Governing Body:
Ms L Moor (*Chair*)
Reverend G Curry
The Lady Farmer
Mrs V Houghton
Mr B Gardiner
Dr J Ledger
Mr A Imlay
Mr R Scurlock
Mrs C Tao

Head: Mrs J Tudor, BSc Hons UCL, MA Ed Open University

Bursar: Mr N Patterson, MSc
Deputy Head: Mrs K McGonnell, BEd Hons Exeter
Director of Teaching & Learning: Mrs J Morelli, Licence Université de Nantes
Assistant Head, Academic Development: Mrs S Hills, MSc London, BEd Hons Leeds
Head of Sixth Form: Miss C Edgerley, BA Brighton

Staff:
* *Head of Department/Subject*

English:
*Mrs C Rees, BA Hons Queen's Belfast, MA York, PGCE Bristol, MEd Bath
Mrs M Kempton, MA, BA Hons Reading, BEd Hons London, Cert TESOL, Dip RSA (*also EAL*)
Mrs E Simpson, BA Hons Portsmouth, PGCE Sussex
Mrs E Kermode, BA Hons University of South Africa

Mathematics:
*Miss R Duncan, BSc Hons Surrey
Mrs M Sherwood, MA Canterbury
Mrs E Mallett, British Bachelor Hons Univ of Seoul
Mrs N Dawson, Higher Diploma Univ of Natal, South Africa

Science:
Mr R Everatt, BSc Hons York (*Chemistry, *Science*)
Mr S Bond, MA Oxon (*Physics*)
Dr R Jones, PhD Aberdeen (*Biology*)
Mrs J Tudor, BSc Hons UCL, MA Ed Open University
Mrs H Buck, BSc Hons York
Dr W Ross, PhD Imperial College London

Modern Languages:
Mrs J J Morelli, Licence, Université de Nantes (*MFL*)
Mrs S Berns, BA Hons Reading
Mrs K McGonnell, BEd Hons Exeter
Mrs E Samnée-O'Brien, BA Cologne University, Germany

Business Studies:
*Ms L Stephens, BA Hons York

Classics:
*Mrs D Gummery, BA Hons Southampton

Geography:
*Mr G Cromb, BSc Hons London
Miss A Caldwell, BSc Hons Hull, MSc London (*also Religious Studies & Careers*)

History:
Mr P Maynard, BA Hons Portsmouth

Mrs B Gathercole, BA Hons, Nottingham (*Religious Studies*)

Psychology:
Mrs E Kermode, BA Hons University of South Africa

Religious Studies:
*Mrs B Gathercole, BA Hons Nottingham
Miss A Caldwell, BSc Hons Hull, MSc London

Information Technology:
Mrs C Bennett, BEd Hons Plymouth

Design & Technology (*Food Technology & Textiles Technology*):
*Mrs S Gibson, BSc Home Economics
Mrs C McCafferty, HND CertEd MlfL QTLS

Art:
Miss J Simmonds, BA Hons London

Drama & Theatre Studies:
*Mrs J Cordery, Dip Musical Theatre
Mrs E Clay, BA Hons Winchester

Music:
Mrs E Bull, GRSM ARCM

Physical Education:
*Miss K Dobney, BA Hons Brighton
Miss C Edgerley, BA Brighton
Mrs S Hills, MSc London, BEd Hons Leeds Polytechnic (*also SEN*)
Miss J Cumming, BA Hons Carmathen

Finance Bursar: Mrs R Stevens, BA Hons, ACA
Registrar: Mrs Claire Bell
School Secretary: Mrs J Leatherby
Headmistress's PA: Mrs N Hall
School Nursing Sister: Mrs J Craven
Marketing Manager: Mrs M Fahey, Dip CIM
ICT Manager: Mr B Clarke

Luckley House School has high expectations for all its students, achieves excellent academic results and is proud of its exceptional added-value record. Luckley was founded on its present site in 1918. In 1959 it amalgamated with Oakfield School, established in 1895 in the Lake District. Initially the school was administered by the Church Society but in 1969 it became an independent educational trust. A gracious Grade II listed Edwardian country house forms the centre of the school, which is on a 14-acre site with views of the countryside and woodlands.

Luckley boasts fantastic facilities: the school is set in beautiful, safe and secure grounds, with modern classrooms, new science laboratories, contemporary boarding accommodation, a state-of-the-art music centre, well-equipped art studios and a large Sports Centre with extensive playing fields, tennis courts, fitness suite, climbing wall and fully-sprung dance floor. A new state-of-the-art Performing Arts Centre is now under construction and is due for completion by Christmas 2015. The Centre will house a 179-seat auditorium, a dance and drama studio, a workshop, classrooms and offices.

The school is now co-educational and will be accepting boys from September 2015. The current numbers are 206 girls aged 11 to 18. The majority are day pupils, but approximately 30 girls are either full or weekly boarders. Pupils are selected on the basis of an entrance examination and interview. The main age of entry is at 11 years, 13 years and into the Sixth Form. Our in-house transport service covers a wide area, with late drop-offs for students wishing to stay for pre- or after-class activities.

Curriculum. The curriculum is broad and challenging with pupils taking 9.5 subjects for GCSE. A wide variety of AS and A2 courses is offered and almost every student goes on to higher education as a preparation for careers in, for example, languages, medicine, engineering, law, business and design.

The school has a well-deserved reputation for Art, Drama, Music and Sport and offers a range of other activities including computing, debating, riding, polo, The Duke of Edinburgh's Award Scheme, Combined Cadet Force and Young Enterprise. Boarders and Day students are encouraged to join in this extensive programme of extra-curricular activities during the extended day slot from 4.30–5.30 pm. Instrumental lessons, Singing, Speech and Drama and Latin are offered as additional subjects.

Boarding. Weekly and flexi boarding offer the opportunity to experience the fun of boarding while keeping close links with home and avoiding long daily journeys. Full boarding, with an extensive weekend activity programme, can provide a stable and secure education for pupils whose schooling would otherwise be interrupted. Year 7–13 boarders live in the Main House, however, sixth form boarders have their own dedicated study areas within the Sixth Form Centre.

Ethos. Luckley House School is built on the Christian foundations of love and service. We enable our students to thrive in a secure and encouraging environment, thereby equipping each pupil to be resourceful and resilient, and ready to take on the challenges and opportunities that lie ahead.

Fees per term (2014–2015). Full Boarders £8,801; Weekly Boarders £8,156; Day Girls £5,029.

Scholarships and Bursaries. Scholarships are awarded at 11+ on the results of the Entrance Examination and on entry to the Sixth Form. Music, Drama, Art and Sports scholarships are also available.

Means-tested Bursaries offering a reduction of up to 80% of fees are offered at Year 7 and Sixth Form entry. Forces Bursaries are also available.

Charitable status. Luckley House School Limited is a Registered Charity, number 309099. It offers day and boarding education for girls on the basis of Christian values.

Manchester High School for Girls

Grangethorpe Road, Manchester M14 6HS
Tel: 0161 224 0447
Fax: 0161 224 6192
email: administration@mhsg.manchester.sch.uk
website: www.manchesterhigh.co.uk

Board of Governors:
Chairman: Mrs C Walker, BA
Dr A Ahmed, DCH, DRCOG, DFFP, MRCGP
Mrs S Beales, MA
Mr A Clarke, FCA
Lady R Cooper, OBE
Dr J Dwek, CBE, BSc, BA, DSc
Mrs M Grant, Cert Ed
Mrs S Klass, MA Oxon
Mrs D Kloss, MBE, LLB, LLM, Hon FFOM
Her Honour Judge L Kushner, LLB, QC
Professor R W Munn, PhD, DSc, FRSC
Mr S Ruia, BSc
Mrs C V F Sargent, BSc
Mr C J Saunders, OBE, MA, FSI
Mr F R Shackleton, MA, LLM
Mrs S E Spence, BA
Mr K S Yeung, MBE

Hon Treasurer: Mr A Clarke, FCA

Head Mistress: Mrs A C Hewitt, BSc, NPQH

Deputy Heads:
Mrs H Jeys, BA Durham (*Religion & Philosophy*)

Mrs S M Smith, BSc Leeds, MEd Bristol, NPQH (*Mathematics*)

Assistant Heads:
Mr W Perry, BSc Warwick, PG Cert Educational Leadership, Leicester (*Director of Co-Curriculum, Physics*)
Mrs S Norton, BA UC Berkeley USA, MA Mills College USA (*Director of Sixth Form Studies, English*)

Staff:
* *Head of Department*
§ *Part-time*

§Mrs P Bell, BA Leeds Polytechnic (*Art & Design Technology*)
Mrs C Bennett, BSc Staffordshire (*Physics*)
Mr A Bradley, BMus Birmingham (*Music)
Ms J Burley, BA Liverpool (*English*)
Mrs A G T Chambers, BA West Surrey College of Art & Design, ATC (**Art & Design Technology*)
Mr J Clarke, BA, MPhil Manchester (*History)
§ Miss E Compton, BSc Nottingham (*Psychology*)
Miss L Cooke, BSc Wales (**Careers, Biology*)
Mrs E S Counsell, BA Leeds, MSc Birmingham (*French, German*)
§Mrs R E Crowley, BSc Manchester (*Mathematics*)
§Mrs T Davey, BA University of Wales (*English*)
Mrs E A Diamond, BA Birmingham (*Religion & Philosophy*)
Mr B Eaton, BSc Manchester (*Physics*)
Mrs J L Fordham, Cert Ed Manchester (*Art & Design Technology*)
§Mr K Gilkes, BSc Bolton (*ICT*)
Miss S Hadley, BA Liverpool (*Psychology*)
§Miss C Hannan, MA Cantab (*Classics*)
§Mrs J Haves, BA De Montfort Leicester, PGCE (*Drama*)
Mrs J R Heydecker, BA Leicester (*History*)
Mr F Heywood, BSc Nottingham, MSc UMIST (*Mathematics*)
§Mr C Hilton, BA, MA Cambridge, Dip TEO QTS Manchester (*Mandarin*)
Dr R E Hoban, BSc, PhD Newcastle (*Chemistry)
Mr S P Holmes, BSc Nottingham (*Mathematics*)
Ms E Hudson, BA Hull (*English*)
Mrs P Inglis, BSc Manchester (*Chemistry*)
Mr D L Jones, BSc Manchester (*Mathematics*)
Miss K Large, BSc Leeds (*Chemistry*)
Dr M Leach, BA Oxford, PhD Durham (*Physics)
Miss C Livesey, BA King's College London (*Spanish, French*)
Mrs K Loughrey-Davies, BA Warwick (*English*)
§Miss K Martin, BA Birmingham, MPhil Birmingham (*History*)
Dr F Menon, MSc Padova, PhD Manchester (*Biology*)
§Mrs C Mills, MChem Oxford, PGCE (*Chemistry*)
Dr L Moore, BSc Lebanon, MSc UMIST, PhD (*Chemistry*)
Mrs S A Moores, BA Cardiff (*Modern Languages*)
Mrs N Morgan, BMus Lancaster (*Music*)
Mrs S Newman, BEd Leeds Metropolitan (**Physical Education*)
Mr P J O'Brien, BA Hull (*German, *Modern Foreign Languages*)
§Mrs E Othen, MA, MPhil, Cambridge (*Classics*)
§Mrs C J Ousey, BA Southampton (*English*)
§Miss J Parker, BSc Imperial College London (*Biology*)
Mrs C Pattison, BSc Newcastle (*Mathematics*)
Dr C M Poucher, BSc, PhD Leeds (*Biology*)
Mrs M Price, BA Manchester (*English*)
Ms A N Protheroe, BSc Swansea (*Mathematics)
§Mrs C Purvis, BA Lancaster (**Religious Studies*)
Mr M Randall, BA CNAA, MA Leicester (**Business Economics IT*)
Miss C Rennox, BSc Leeds Metropolitan (*Physical Education*)

§Mrs S Reynolds, BA UCL, MSc Kingston (*Geography*)
Miss D Robinson (*Dance & PE*)
Mr D Rose, BA, MA Kent (*English*)
Miss S C Rowley, BA Staffordshire (*Physical Education*)
Mrs P Scott, BA Duncan of Jordanstone College of Art (*Art & Design Technology*)
§Mrs T Slack, BA Manchester (*Modern Languages*)
Dr R Smither, BSc Bath, MPhil, PhD Cambridge (*Biology*)
Mr N M Tattersall, MPhys Oxford (*Mathematics*)
Mrs J Taylor, BA Manchester (*Philosophy & Literary Studies*)
Mrs R Thompson, BA, MPhil Birmingham (**Spanish*)
§Mrs D E Troth, BA Exeter (*History*)
Miss R Tyler, BA Durham (**Geography*)
§Mrs C M Tynan, BA York (*Physics*)
Mr S R F Vance, BA Manchester (*Art & Design Technology*)
Dr A Walker-Taylor, MSc Warwick, PhD UCL (**Biology*)
Miss L Warwick, BSc Manchester Metropolitan (*Physical Education*)
§Mrs J Watson, BSc Newcastle-upon-Tyne (*Geography*)
§Mrs A T Wells, BA Essex (*English*)
Miss J Welsby, BA Manchester (**Classics*)
Mrs K A Whelan, BSc Bradford (*Business Economics and IT*)
Mrs C Wilkes, BA Sorbonne, MA Rennes (*Modern Languages*)

Preparatory Department Staff:

Head of Preparatory Department: Mrs R H Edwards, BEd

Mrs K Adam, BSc Sheffield Hallam
Mrs R A Anderson, BEd Glasgow
Mrs V Baird, BSc Lancaster
Mrs C Callanan, BA MMU
Miss S Diamond, BEd Cantab
Mrs S Edale, BA Derby
Miss J H Floyd, BA Charlotte Mason College
Mrs M R Heggie, BMus, BEd New South Wales
§Mrs R James, Cert Ed, PG Dip SpLD, CCET
Mrs E Mason, BA Nottingham
Mrs R Mason, Cert Ed Leicester, Dip Ed Manchester
Mrs J Newton, BA UMIST
Mrs J C Philip, BA Manchester
Miss F Sanderson, BA Manchester Metropolitan
Miss C Taylor, BSc UMIST
Mrs C Westall, BA Huddersfield

Bursar: Mr J P Moran, FCCA
Registrar: Mrs K Joynes
PA to Head Mistress: Mrs S Bowker
Librarian: Miss Z Hawker, BA Liverpool, MSc Northumbria
Archivist: Dr C Joy, BA, PhD Leeds
School Medical Officer: Dr J Herd, BM BS, DFFP, DRCOG, MRCGP

Manchester High School for Girls (MHSG) offers students a vibrant atmosphere and a strong sense of community. In such a supportive environment, each girl feels happy, cared for and valued as an individual. Its academic record is outstanding; in GCSE, A Level and the IB Diploma girls are taught not just how to achieve excellent examination results, but are encouraged to enjoy learning.

MHSG was founded in 1874 and has a long and successful history. The School offers a seamless education from age 4 to 18 and has extensive experience of helping girls to achieve their best. All members of the school community have a strong sense of the School's traditions, but MHSG is forward looking and keen to embrace new educational developments. Since September 2010, girls entering the Sixth Form have been able to choose to study the International Baccalaureate (IB) Diploma.

At MHSG, artistic and sporting talents are nurtured and students enjoy a diverse range of extra-curricular activities. These are complemented by superb modern facilities which include a state-of-the-art Sixth Form Centre with lecture theatre, common room and study area, a sports complex, a fitness suite, a dance studio, all-weather sports pitches, a multi-purpose auditorium, a drama studio and a purpose-built Music House. Instrumental and Speech & Drama lessons are optional extras.

Students at Manchester High come from a wide range of backgrounds and this rich social and cultural mix gives the School a warm and friendly feel. The girls learn about the importance of social responsibility with charity, voluntary and community work strongly encouraged.

Highly skilled and committed staff strive to ensure that every MHSG student leaves the School a well-educated young woman, with highly-developed interpersonal skills and a broad range of interests. Our girls are confident in their own worth, prepared for an independent life and capable of making a positive contribution to society. It is from this cornerstone that they go on to pursue varied and fulfilling careers.

Entry to the Reception class is by assessment while an entrance examination is set for the Juniors and Year 7. From time to time vacancies in other year groups can become available, but the main entry levels are at ages 4, 11 and 16. Sixth Form assessment is by interview and GCSE qualifications.

MHSG is committed to providing education to academically gifted girls regardless of circumstance. In the Senior School financial assistance is offered through a limited number of part or full means-tested bursaries. One or more scholarships may be awarded for excellence in performance in the entrance tests taken at the age of 10 or 11 for admission to the Senior School in September. Such scholarships will be awarded on merit only, not on the basis of parental income, and will provide part remission of fees. Music, Sports and Dance scholarships are also available.

Further details and a prospectus are available from the Registrar.

The Report of the ISI Inspection in October 2010 can be viewed on the School's website.

Fees per term (2014–2015). Seniors £3,546, Juniors £2,591, Infants £2,550.

Charitable status. Manchester High School for Girls Foundation is a Registered Charity, number 532295. The aim of the charity is the provision and conduct in Manchester of a day school for girls.

Manor House School

Manor House Lane, Little Bookham, Leatherhead, Surrey KT23 4EN
Tel: 01372 457077
Fax: 01372 450514
email: admin@manorhouseschool.org
           admissions@manorhouseschool.org
website: www.manorhouseschool.org
Twitter: @MHSDeputy
Facebook: /manorhousesch

Motto: *To Love is to Live*

Governors:
Chairman: Mr P Barlow, FIA
Miss Z Axton, BSc Hons, PGCE
Dr J Baldwin
Mr J Compton, LLB Hons, LLM
Father A Mackenzie
Mr M Parkhouse, BA Hons, MA, MSc
Mr M Ruscoe

Mrs G Sims-Brassett
Mrs C Turnbull, BA Hons

Headmistress: **Miss Z Axton**, BSc Hons, PGCE

Deputy Head: Mr M Gates, BMedSc Hons, MEd

Subject Staff:
Mrs T Banfield, BEd Hons (*Physical Education*)
Mrs A Beacock, BSc, PGCE (*Biology*)
Mr K Boyd, MA Hons, PGCE (*English*)
Mrs S Brodie, BSc Hons, PGCE (*Science*)
Mrs S Buck, BSc Hons, PGCE (*Physical Education*)
Mr J Conway, BSc Hons, PGCE (*ICT*)
Mrs V Diprose, BA Hons, PGCE (*French*)
Mr A Edmeades (*Drama*)
Mrs T Evans, BSc Hons, MSc, PGCE (*Science*)
Mrs K Gall, BE, PGCE (*Mathematics*)
Miss C Grindrod, BSc Hons, PGCE (*Geography*)
Ms L Holloway, AISTD (*Drama*)
Mrs V Homewood, BA, PGCE (*Religious Studies*)
Mrs S Howes, NPQH, BSc Hons, PGCE (*Learning Support*)
Mrs J Lewis, BA Hons, PGCE (*Music*)
Mrs E Mayes, BA Hons (*English*)
Mrs H McClure, BA, Cert Ed (*Spanish*)
Mrs C Parish, Cert Ed (*English*)
Mrs S Parsons, BA Hons, PGCE (*Art*)
Mrs C Peel, MA, PGCE (*MFL*)
Mr D Pelham, BSc Eng Hons, CEng, MBCS, CITP (*Mathematics*)
Mrs L Pillar, BEd Hons (*Religious Studies*)
Miss C Poultney, BEd Hons (*Physical Education*)
Mrs R St Johnston, MA Hons, PGCE (*History*)
Mrs S Rickerd, BA QTS (*Learning Support*)
Ms A Van Dyk, BA, DipHE (*Mathematics*)
Mrs L Stephens, BA Hons, PGCE (*Latin*)
Mrs K Tercan, BEd Hons (*Home Economics*)
Ms A Walker, RAD Reg, RAD TCert, AISTD Ass Dips (*Dance*)
Miss J Ward, BA Hons, PGCE (*Music*)
Mrs T Williams, BA Hons, PGCE (*Art and Drama*)

Prep and Junior Departments:
Miss J Anderson, BA Hons, PGCE
Mr D Ayling, MA Cantab, PGCE
Miss C Brazil, Cache Diploma
Mrs S Chatrath, MSc Hons, QTS (*Head of Early Years and Preps*)
Mrs R Darlington, BEd Hons Cantab
Mrs A Doughty, Cache Level 3
Mrs A Harvey, NNEB
Mrs T Hilleard, MA, BEd Hons (*Head of Juniors*)
Mrs D Horrocks, HDip PrimEd
Mrs S Legg, MTeach Hons, QTD
Mrs J Morrison, BA Hons, Cache Diploma
Mrs H Redward, BA, PGCE
Mrs J Roy, BA Hons, Dip Montessori Dist
Mrs J Smith, BA Hons, PGCE

Also Peripatetic, Teaching and Learning Support Assistants.

Admissions and Marketing, Ms M Fowell, Higher Dip
Bursar, Finance: Mrs C Miller, MBA
Bursar, Admin: Mrs V Allcott

Manor House School is a selective independent day school for girls aged 2 through to 16 years in Surrey. We provide a supportive and nurturing educational environment delivering strong academic performance in a smaller setting. Our individualised teaching ethos is renowned for building confidence and achieving academic success for our pupils. Founded in 1920, the school is a charitable trust located partly in a Georgian building and set in seventeen acres of parkland within easy distance of London in the Surrey commuter belt. Our own minibuses meet the trains at Effingham Junction station morning and evening and we provide a range of minibus routes from other areas before school each day. Our day boarding system operates from 8 am to 6 pm.

Our excellent facilities include a purpose-built spacious Art/Textiles studio, Music and Drama room and Home Economics facility, a recently refurbished ICT suite, language laboratory, fit-for-purpose Science block, and Sports/Theatre/Assembly Hall in addition to our Main Arcot Hall in the Manor House itself. The School has excellent sports facilities which include an open-air heated swimming pool, five floodlit tennis and netball courts, hockey and rounders pitches, and an athletics track.

Manor House girls follow a wide curriculum throughout their school career and generally take 9.5 or 10.5 GCSE subjects achieving consistently strong academic results and being highly sought after by sixth form and college destinations. Pupils are expected to partake fully in the life of the school, and develop their individual talents in Art, Drama, Music and Sport where applicable. Manor House School provides a plethora of extra-curricular clubs and activities in addition to the school curriculum and these are an important part of school life.

The aim of the school is to create a happy, secure and disciplined environment where each girl can achieve her individual academic potential. Pastoral care is a particular strength of the school. Senior girls are caring role models for younger pupils and we have a flourishing peer support group. Manor House is a Christian non-denominational school but has close links with the Church of England. A Manor House girl is academically successful, confident and outgoing with a strong sense of values and the ability to succeed in her chosen career. Girls are encouraged to be independent and to take responsibility for themselves and others. Our motto 'To Love is to Live' covers the essential human virtues of integrity, honesty and loyalty towards each other and is embodied by our pupils.

Admission to the Senior Department at 11+ and 13+ is by the school's own Entrance Examination, which is held in the January prior to the September of entry. Entry at other ages is subject to availability of places and the selection criteria is determined by a visit to the school followed by an invitation to a taster and assessment day. Offers are made following the outcome of this process.

Scholarships and Bursaries. Academic scholarships are offered each year for entry to Years 7 and 9. The awards are based on performance in the Entrance Examination and an interview with the Headmistress. Art, Drama, Music and Sports Awards may be awarded to girls who show outstanding talent in these areas.

Means-tested bursaries up to 100% of fees may also be applied for.

Further details are available from the Marketing & Admissions Office.

Fees per term (2014–2015). Tuition: £1,220–£5,060.

Charitable status. Manor House School is a Registered Charity, number 312063. It exists for the promotion of children's education according to their academic, social, sporting and musical abilities.

The Marist Senior School

Kings Road, Sunninghill, Ascot, Berkshire SL5 7PS
Tel: 01344 624291
Fax: 01344 874963
email: officesenior@themaristschools.com
website: www.themaristschools.com

Independent Catholic Day School for Girls aged 11–18 founded in 1870 by the Marist Sisters. The school has been at the current site since 1947 and is set in 55 acres of attractive woodland in the village of Sunninghill near Ascot.

Chair of Governors: Mrs M Cairns

Headteacher: Mr K McCloskey, BA Hons, PGCE, MA

Senior Assistant Headteacher: Mrs W Reed, BA Hons, PGCE

Heads of Department:
Art: Mrs R Ellwood, BA Hons, PGCE
Classics: Mrs A Osmond, BA Hons
Drama: Miss J May, BA, PGCE, MA
Economics/Business Studies: Mr J Bennett, BSc Hons, PGCE & Mrs P Elstone, BA Hons, PGCE
English: Mrs L Lutton, MA Hons, PGCE
Food Science: Mrs G White, CertEd
Geography: Mr E de Grande, BA Hons, PGCE
History: Mrs D Bishop, BA Hons, PGCE
ICT: Mrs J Shill, CertEd, CertSpLD, DipWp
Mathematics: Mrs A Hynds, BSc Hons, PGCE
Modern Foreign Languages: Mrs M Halksworth, L-ès-L, PGCE
Music: Miss J Slocombe, BA Hons, MMus, ARCM, PGCE
Psychology: Mrs J Cope, BA, HDipEd
Physical Education: Mrs J Bishopp, BA Ed Hons
Religious Education: Miss L Vaughan Neil, LLB, BA, PGCE
Science: Mrs A Royston, BSc Hons, PGCE
Textiles: Miss M Tooman, BSc, PGDipEd

Head of Sixth Form: Ms D Player, Cert Ed, BEd, MSc

Number of Pupils. 320 girls.
Mission Statement. The Marist is a community where Christian values inspire all aspects of learning and where the potential of each individual is recognised, valued and affirmed.
Strengths.
- Strong reputation for academic excellence as well as sport, drama, music and creative arts.
- Able to offer a wide range of both academic and extra-curricular activities.
- Strong emphasis on pastoral care, spiritual and personal development; care and consideration for others.
- Small class sizes to enhance individual progression and recognition.
- The school is renowned for its high standards regarding moral values, community spirit, respect and care. This is in line with the overall ethos of the Marist order which has a worldwide presence, providing a truly international dimension to a girl's education.

Facilities. Indoor swimming pool, dedicated Sixth Form suite, comprehensive ICT suite, Music and Drama block, Language Laboratory, Ceramics Studio & Darkroom, Astro-turf Multi-Sports Surface and Library.
Academic Curriculum. Art, Biology, Business Studies, Classical Civilisation, Chemistry, Drama/Theatre Studies, Economics, English, French, Geography, German, History, ICT, Italian, Latin, Mathematics (also Pure & Mechanics, Pure, Statistics, Pure & Statistics), Music, Personal, Social & Health Education, PE, RE, Religious Studies: Philosophy & Ethics, Science, Spanish, Sports Studies, Textiles, Food Science, Psychology, Photography and Government & Politics.
Sixth Form. The school offers a total of 26 subjects at AS/A2 Level. Year 12 students will study 4 subjects at AS Level in their first year (in certain circumstances some students can take 5). After AS Levels, girls will decide which 3/4 subjects they wish to continue on to A2 Level.
Extra-Curricular Activities. Art, Athletics, Choir, Clarinet & Saxophone Ensemble, Drama Club, Duke of Edinburgh's Award, Flute Group, French Films, Greek (Ancient), Guitar Group, History Films, Hockey, Human

Rights, ICT, Latin, Library Club, Literacy, Netball, Orchestra, Prayer Group, Public Speaking/Debating, Rock Band, Science, Strategy/Numeracy, Swimming, Swing Band, Textiles, Tennis, Young Enterprise.
Results. 2014: 79% of all grades were A*–B. 75% of students went to Russell Group Universities and all Marist university applicants secured a place for undergraduate study. GCSE students achieved 51% A* against the national average context where 25% of students attained A* and A grades. Each student averaged 11 GCSEs A* to C.
Admission. Entrance examination tests in (1) English, (2) Mathematics and (3) cognitive abilities, (4) Portfolio, (5) Compulsory Interview with the Headteacher and (6) Reference from Primary/Preparatory Headteacher.
Sixth Form Entry. General requirements for 3 or 4 AS subjects: a minimum of 7 GCSEs A*-C grade or above, preferably B grade in subjects to be studied.
General requirements for 5 AS subjects: most grades at GCSE should be A*.
Note: there are recommended subjects and grades at GCSE for each AS subject available in the Sixth Form Prospectus and on the school's website.
Fees per term (2014–2015). £4,200. Extra benefits: Generous sibling discount scheme (4th and any subsequent children free), after school care provided.
Scholarships. Year 7 and Sixth Form Academic, Art, Drama, Music and Sport scholarships are available.
Preparatory School. We also have a Preparatory school on the same campus which is for girls aged 2½–11. This allows girls to continue their education with their friends in the happy and secure environment they are used to. (*For further details, see the Marist Preparatory School entry in the IAPS section.*)
Affiliations. Girls' Schools Association (GSA), Catholic Independent Schools Conference (CISC), Silver Artsmark, Eco-Schools award and Healthy School.
Charitable status. The Marist Schools is a Registered Charity, number 225485. The principal aims and activities of the Marist Schools are religious and charitable and specifically to provide education by way of an independent day school for girls between the ages of 3 and 18.

The Mary Erskine School

Ravelston, Edinburgh EH4 3NT
Tel: 0131 347 5700
Fax: 0131 347 5799
email: admissions@esms.org.uk
website: www.esms.org.uk
Twitter: @esmsedinburgh
Facebook: /esmsedinburgh
LinkedIn: /erskine-stewart's-melville-schools

Governing Council:
Chairman: Mr Mike Sims

Clerk to the Governors: Mr D Wright, LLB

Principal: Mr J N D Gray, BA

Bursar: Mr J B Molloy, MA Hons

Deputy Head: Mrs L A Moule, BA Hons, PGCE
Director of Studies: Mr A P McDiarmid, BA Hons PGCE
Staff Development Coordinator: Mr N Dawson, MA Hons, MEd
Head of Upper School: Dr E A Murray, BSc Hons, MEd, PhD, PGCE
Head of S1/Admissions: Ms K S S Nicholson, MA Hons, PGCE
Director of Sixth Form: Dr I R Scott, MA Hons, PhD, FRSA, CertEd

* *Head of Department*

† *Head of House*

Art:
*Mrs F J MacGregor, BDes Hons, PGCE
Mrs C Burns, BA Hons, PGCE

Biology:
*Dr S Corbet, BSc Hons, MSc, PhD, PGCE
Miss K Davies, BSc Hons, DipEd
Mrs S Horrix, BSc, PGCE
Dr C Turnbull, BSc, MSc, PhD
Mrs M Irvine, MChem, PGCE

Business Studies:
*Mrs F K McCrudden, BA Hons, PGCE
Mrs E Proudfoot, BA Hons, PGCE, PGDip
Mrs M Thorniley-Walker, MA Hons, MCIPS, PGCE
Mrs J Walker, BA, PGCE, PGDip, PG Cert

Careers:
*Mrs P McInally, BA Hons, PGCE

Chemistry:
*Dr C J Spracklin, BSc Hons, PhD, PGCE
Mrs S Ferrington, BSc Hons, PGDE (†*Appin*)
Mrs C Murdie, BSc Hons, PGCE
Dr E A Murray, BSc Hons, MEd, PhD, PGCE (*Head of Upper School*)

Classics:
*Mr T E McBratney, MA Hons, PGCE
Mrs J R Brown, BA, MA, GTP

Drama:
*Miss J R Flockhart, BA Hons, PGCE
Mrs L Howarth, MA Hons, PGCE

English:
*Mrs K A J Yip, BA Hons, MA, PGCE
Ms D Esland, BA Hons, PGCE
Mrs N Ramirez, MA Hons, PGCE (†*Kintyre*)
Mrs R Connet, BA Hons, PGCE
Mr N Dawson, MA Hons, MEd (*Staff Development Coordinator*)
Mrs A Holt, BA Hons, PGCE, ALCM (†*Lochaber*)
Mrs C S Park, MA Hons, PGCE (†*Torridon*)
Mrs M Tetley, BA Hons, MSc, QTS

Geography:
*Dr M Davies, BA Hons, PGCE, PhD
Ms K S S Nicholson, MA Hons, PGCE (*Head of S1/ Admissions*)
Miss J F Pollitt, MA Hons, PGCE
Miss M Wilkinson, MA Hons, PGDE

History:
*Mrs A J Ferguson, MA Hons, MEd, PGCE, PGCE
Mrs L F Alexander, MA Hons, PGDE
Mrs L J Allan, MA Hons, PGCE (*Deputy Head, Sixth Form*)
Mr R Robertson, MA Hons, PGCE
Mr A P McDiarmid, BA Hons, PGCE

Home Economics:
*Mrs J Hetherington, Dip DomSc, LSSN
Mrs N L Murray, BA, PGCE, PGC

Mathematics:
*Mrs F J Houbert, BEd Hons
Dr B Duncan, MPhys, PhD, PGCE
Mr J D Hamilton, BSc Hons, MSc, PGCE
Mrs C A Morrison, BSc, DipEd
Mrs J Smart, BSc Hons, FFA, PGDE
Mrs M Grant, MA Hons, PGCE
Miss M Murphy, BSc, Hons, PGDE
Miss B Fleming, BSc Hons, PGDE

Modern Languages:
*Mr M G Chittleburgh, MA Hons, DipEd, PGCE
*Mrs S Old, MA Hons, DipEd

Dr S M Benn, MA, PhD, PGCE
Ms J H Bremner, MA Hons, PGCE
Mrs J Fitzgerald, MA Hons, PGCE
Miss L McGuinness, MA, PGCE
Mrs P McInally, BA Hons, PGCE
Miss C Watson, MA Hons, PGDE
Ms C Wolseley, MA Hons, PGCE

Modern Studies:
Mrs R Molloy, MA Hons, PGCE

Music:
*Mrs S Headden, DRSAM, DipEd
Mr J Matthews, BMus, PGDE
Mrs J Wilson, BA, PGCE

Philosophy:
*Dr I R Scott, MA Hons, PhD, FRSA, CertEd (*Director of Sixth Form*)
Mr D Kemp, MTheol, PGCE

Physical Education:
*Mrs V G Thomson, BEd Hons, BSc
Mr G Blackhall, BEd Hons
Miss C Lampard, BEd Hons (†*Appin*)
Mrs G Longmuir, BEd Hons
Mrs K Salmond, BEd Hons
Mrs J L Miller, BEd Hons
Mrs K A Mundell, BEd Hons
Miss K J Henderson, BA Hons, PGCE
Miss C MacLean, BEd Hons

Physics:
*Dr T Hely, MSc, PhD, PGCE
Mrs J McLaren, MEng Hons, PGDE
Mrs J Paterson, BSc Hons, MPhil, PGCE

Product Design:
*Mr D K Bowen, BA Hons, ATC, DipSIAD
Mrs C A Hemmati, BSc Hons, PGCE, MSc
Mr R Strachan, B Des Hons, PGDE

Religious Moral and Philosophical Studies:
*Mr D Kemp, MTheol, PGCE
Ms J Shepherd, BA Hons, PGCE

Support for Learning:
*Mrs C Maxwell, BA, DipEd
Mr S Hollins, BA Hons, PGCE
Miss R Meredith, BSc, PGCE, PGDip
Mrs J Miller, BEd Hons
Mrs L A Moule, BA Hons, PGCE (*Deputy Head*)

Junior School:
Head Master: Mr B D Lewis, BA Hons, H DipEd Hons
Senior Deputy Head: Mrs G Lyon, DCE, DipRSA
Deputy Head (Early Education): Miss S Mackay, ALCM, LLCM, BMus Hons, PGCE
Assistant Head (Primary 4–7): Mr D McLeish, DCE
Assistant Head (Primary 4–7): Mrs J Hewitt, BSc, PGCE
Assistant Head (Early Education): Ms C Macpherson, BEd

The Mary Erskine School was founded by Mary Erskine and the Company of Merchants of the City of Edinburgh in 1694. It is therefore one of the oldest schools in the UK endowed specifically for girls. Known in its early years as 'The Merchant Maiden Hospital', its aims were to educate and care for the daughters of City Burgesses who found themselves in reduced circumstances. Throughout its history, the school has been administered by the Edinburgh Merchant Company. In November 1989 this authority was devolved to the Erskine Stewart's Melville Governing Council.

The school, named The Mary Erskine School in 1944 to mark the 250th anniversary of its foundation, has been housed on various sites in the city – the Cowgate, Bristo, Lauriston and Queen Street – and the buildings are depicted on the engraved glass panels in the Sports Centre and on murals in the Assembly Hall. The current school buildings, at Ravelston, command splendid views of the nearby city and castle.

Since 1978 the school has been twinned with Stewart's Melville College (*see entry in HMC section*). This includes a fully co-educational Junior School for children between the ages of 3 and 12, single-sex but very closely twinned secondary schools between the ages of 12 and 17 and a fully co-educational pre-university Sixth Form which provides the ideal bridge between school and university. The girls and boys from The Mary Erskine School and Stewart's Melville College come together in the Combined Cadet Force, in orchestras, choirs, drama and musicals and in numerous outdoor education projects.

The Senior School (747 Girls). The school curriculum corresponds predominantly with practice in Scotland. Girls generally sit the public examinations prescribed by the Scottish Qualifications Authority.

SI and S2 follow a broad curriculum, whereby girls are equipped to pursue all routes to National 5. In S3 girls commence eight courses, including English, Mathematics, at least one modern language, at least one science, and a "humanities" subject. In S5 the majority of girls take five subjects at Higher level. Girls are expected to achieve their full potential. The majority will continue their studies for a Sixth Year, usually at Advanced Higher level, to provide a firm foundation for degree courses in Scotland and England. Most girls proceed to such courses.

The playing fields at Ravelston underpin a fine tradition in hockey and tennis. Physical Education facilities include grass hockey pitches, two floodlit astroturf hockey pitches, a running track and twelve tennis courts. A Games Hall and Fitness Suite complement the other sporting facilities. The Pavilion, which provides the Sixth Form girls and boys with a Common Room and Study area during the week, is available to parents and friends as a coffee area on Saturday mornings and other times when sports events take place.

Staff from the well-equipped Technology Centre work closely with those in the bright, modern Home Economics Department. The attractive Library is next to one of the computer rooms, forming a combined resource centre which is accessed by all departments.

In the Art Department the girls enjoy first class facilities which help them develop diverse artistic talents. There is a specially designated area for Sixth Form girls, many of whom proceed to Art colleges, as well as darkroom facilities for keen photographers.

The Music Department possesses fine facilities in Ravelston House and the school enjoys a notable reputation for the quality and range of its musical activities. The attractive School Hall and designated Studio offer good facilities for drama and there are frequent productions involving girls and boys of all ages.

The Combined Cadet Force comprises Army and RAF sections. The combined Pipe Band has an international reputation and girls in the Highland Dancing team also achieve frequent success in competition. Many girls participate in the Duke of Edinburgh's Award Scheme, as well as in hillwalking and other forms of outdoor recreation. Each week the school offers to girls a wide variety of extra-curricular clubs and societies ranging from curling to drama.

The school has a sophisticated system of Guidance. SI tutors, led by the Head of S1, help girls to make the transition from Junior School to Senior School a smooth and happy experience. During the next four years girls belong to one of six houses. The Heads of House, led by the Head of Upper School, liaise closely with colleagues on each girl's academic progress, teach the personal and social education programme in house groups and encourage each girl to derive maximum benefit from the school's extra-curricular programme.

The Sixth Form is co-educational with the Sixth Formers of Stewart's Melville College. While girls sustain their loyalty and commitment to The Mary Erskine School, they are equally at home in the Sixth Form Centre of the boys' school. We see the Sixth Form as a preparation for university, when girls and boys assume greater responsibility for their academic programme and their career aspirations. All girls in the school receive guidance and help from the staff of a well-established careers department.

Boarding. There is a boarding house (Erskine House) with accommodation for approximately 28 girls in brightly decorated study-bedrooms. The girls share dining and recreational facilities with the Stewart's Melville boarders in Dean Park House. Both Houses have a friendly, family atmosphere and provide an ideal "home from home" for brothers and sisters.

Fees per term (2014–2015). Day: Primary Start to Primary 7 £2,202–£2,852 (lunches included for Primary 2–7); Secondary £3,355 (plus £170 for optional lunches). Full Boarding: Primary 4–6 £5,986; Primary 7 £6,058; Secondary £6,731. Weekly Boarding: Primary 4–6 £5,818; Primary 7 £5,890; Secondary £6,563.

Scholarships and Bursaries. Means-tested Bursaries worth up to 100% of the tuition fee may be available to parents of children entering any year group in the Senior Schools and at P7 in the Junior School. Academic scholarships worth £250 annually are offered to girls applying to enter S1, following a competitive selection process. These are known as Merchant Company Scholarships. The top scholarship holder at The Mary Erskine School receives the Mackay Scholarship, worth £1,000 annually. Scholarships are paid to the pupil and are held in trust by the school until completion of their Sixth Form year. Music Scholarships of £250 per annum are offered from S3.

ESMS Junior School. In The Junior School (1,248 pupils), girls and boys are educated together from age 3 to 11. Children in Nursery to Primary 3 are based on The Mary Erskine School site at Ravelston, while boys and girls in Primary 4–7 are taught on the Stewart's Melville College site. Normal entry points are Nursery (age 3 or 4), Primary 1, Primary 4, Primary 6 and Primary 7. The school is remarkable for the breadth of its educational programme and the quality of its sporting and cultural activities, in particular the professional standards attained in Music and Drama.

The Mary Erskine School Former Pupils' Guild. Contact: MES Guild Office, The Mary Erskine School, Ravelston, Edinburgh, EH4 3NT. Tel: 0131 347 5722.

Charitable status. The Merchant Company Education Board is a Registered Charity, number SC009747. It is a leading charitable school in the field of Junior and Secondary education.

Marymount International School

George Road, Kingston-upon-Thames, Surrey KT2 7PE
Tel: 020 8949 0571
Fax: 020 8336 2485
email: admissions@marymountlondon.com
website: www.marymountlondon.com

An Independent boarding and day school for girls aged 11–18. A member of GSA, CIS and MSA (USA).

Headmistress: **Ms Sarah Gallagher**, BA Hons, HDipEd, MA Hons Ireland

Deputy Head, Designated Person for Child Protection: Ms Annah Langan, MA Hons Glasgow, MA St Mary's Twickenham, PGCE Roehampton
Bursar: Mr Alan Fernandes, MBA, BSc Surrey
Middle School Coordinator, Pastoral Life Coordinator: Mrs Geraldine Donnelly, BA Barry (*English*)
Director of Admissions: Mrs Cheryl Eysele, BA South Africa, Cert Further Professional Study Cambridge

Chair of Theory of Knowledge, English, College Counsellor: Mr Matthew Harvey, BA Hons Warwick, MA Hons St Mary's Twickenham, QTS Reading

IB Dip and MYP Coordinator: Mr Nicholas Marcou, BA Hons York, PGCE Roehampton (*Music*)

Head of Boarding: Ms Duveen Pierce, Dip Ed South Africa, Cert Ed Zimbabwe, TEFL UK, CELTA UK

Director of Development & Communications: Mrs Karin Purcell, BA South Africa

Senior Mistress: Miss Kahlen Spaulding

Faculty:

Miss Ella Ballinger, BA Australia, CELTA Cambridge (*ESL/English B*)

Mr João Barroca, BSc Hons Portugal, MBA Spain (*Physics*)

Mr Malcolm Blake, BSc Sheffield, PGCE Reading (*Mathematics*)

Mr Brian Brackrog, BA USA, MA USA (*Economics and Social Studies*)

Dr Eamon Byers, BA Hons Belfast, MA Hons Belfast, PhD Belfast (*English A and B, Philosophy*)

Ms Raquel Cagigas, BA Spain (*Spanish*)

Ms Ya-Ling Chien, BA Taiwan, MA Sussex (*Chinese*)

Mr Stephen Clarke, MA Hons Glasgow (*Chair of English Dept, English*)

Ms Ruth Connor, BA Hons Graz, MA Hons Salzburg, MPhil Salzburg (*German*)

Ms Amy Corrigan, BA Hons St Mary's Twickenham (*Physical Education, PSE*)

Ms Helen Cressall, BA Hons London Metropolitan (*Technology*)

Dr Alexandre Delin, BA Brittany, MA Brittany, PGCE Wales, PhD Paris (*French, Latin, MYP Community and Service Programme*)

Dr Marie-Ange Depierre, BA Paris, PhD, MLitt Montreal (*Chair of Modern Languages, French*)

Ms Katrina Dodds, BSc App HMS-ED Queensland (*Chair of Physical Education & Athletics, PE*)

Ms Sandra Forrest, BA Denison University, US, MA NYU (*Learning Resources & Enrichment Programme Coordinator, NHS*)

Ms Dolores Garcia Suarez, BA Spain, MA Kings, London (*Coordinator of Creativity, Action & Service, House Coordinator, Spanish*)

Ms Susana Gonzalez, MEng Bath, PGCE Kings, London (*Chemistry*)

Mr Jolyon Hinton, BEd, DipTEFL Cambridge (*Chair of Arts, Art, ESL*)

Ms Linda Holland, BSc Hons QMC London, MSc Birkbeck, PGCE Chelsea, CBiol MSB FRES (*Chair of Science, Science, Biology*)

Ms Linda Kelly, BA Hons Bradford, PGCE Nottingham (*ESL/English*)

Mrs Jung Soon Lee Park, MA Ed Cheon Nan University, Korea (*Korean*)

Ms Teresa Lucas, MA Oxford, MA St Mary's Twickenham (*Spiritual Life Coordinator, PSE*)

Mr Sandor Lukacs, MSc Budapest (*Mathematics*)

Ms Kate Martin, MA Cambridge, PGCE Roehampton (*Performing Arts, Music, Choral, PSE, Philosophy*)

Ms Victoria Mast, BA Hons Durham, PGCE Buckingham (*English*)

Ms Ana Maria Navarro, BA Spain, DipEd Spain (*Spanish*)

Ms Amy O'Brien, BSc Hons Cardiff, PGCE Roehampton (*Mathematics*)

Mr John O'Farrell, BRE Dublin, MMus Dublin, MA London (*Director of Music*)

Ms Ulrike Richter, BA Hons Sussex, MA Sussex (*Geography*)

Mr Jerome Ripp, BA, MA Oxford, BSc Open (*Chair of Mathematics Dept, Chair of Economics Dept, Mathematics*)

Mr Jim Robertson, BA Hons Kingston (*Acting Chair of Technology, Art/Design & Technology*)

Mrs Helena Sansome, BA Hons, H DipEd Dublin, B Phil Liverpool MLITT Oxford (*Chair of Humanities, History, Social Studies, Geography*)

Mr Mitsuo Shima, BA Meiji Gakuin, Cert Japanese as a Foreign Language (*Japanese*)

Ms Niamh Somers, BSc Hons Dublin, PGCE Bradford (*Biology*)

Ms Helen Szymczak, BA Dramatic Art Hons AFDA South Africa, ATCL, MA London (*Performing Arts, Theatre, Public Speaking & Performance, Student Council Advisor*)

Mr Alexis White, BA Hons Oxford, PGCE St Mary's Twickenham (*Religious Studies*)

Mrs Lieve Vanrusselt, BSc Belgium, MSc Belgium, MA London, PGCE Open (*Mathematics*)

Dr Alwyn Williams, BA, PhD Sydney (*Social Studies, History, MUN Coordinator*)

Residential Houseparents:

Mrs Paula Horton (*Assistant Head of Boarding*)

Ms Shara Campbell-Starreveld, BA Hons Wolverhampton, BTEC Art & Design

Ms Jolly Chou BSc, MSc Lancs

Ms Charlotte Cowderoy, BA Hons Nottingham, MSc UCL

Ms Martina Michalcova, BSc OU

Mrs Sandee Roberts

Miss Emily Smith, BSc Hons Warwick

Librarian: Ms Jennifer Beeftink, BA Newcastle

PA to Headmistress: Ms Sue Palmer-Simmons

Alumnae Coordinator: Mrs Deirdre Lee BH Hons London, PGCE London

Number of Pupils. 260, including 100 boarders.

Established in 1955 by the Sisters of the Religious of the Sacred Heart of Mary, Marymount International School is an independent day and boarding school for girls, aged 11–18 (grades 6–12), representing approximately forty different nationalities. The school is within a half-hour's drive of Heathrow Airport and conveniently located for M25/A3 road links.

The school aims to provide an intellectually stimulating and emotionally secure environment in which the academic, social and personal needs of each individual student may be met. Education is seen as a continuous process of growth in awareness and development towards maturity in preparation for participation in the world community. Small classes enable students to attain their full personal and academic potential. Each student's schedule is individually tailored to the subjects she wishes to follow. The language of tuition is English (fluency is essential) but additional languages on offer for native speakers include German, Spanish, French, Japanese, Chinese, Korean, Italian and Arabic. The overall student : teacher ratio is 6:1 and the average class size numbers 11 students.

Facilities in the beautiful seven-acre campus include a Fab Lab (the first in a UK School), newly refurbished Library, Sports Hall, Auditorium, Art Studio, Science Centre, Music Centre and tennis courts. New classrooms have been recently added and e-learning has been introduced across the entire school with Mac TVs (to be used in combination with iPads) planned for all classrooms.

Curriculum. Students are prepared for the International Baccalaureate Diploma (ages 17/18, grades 11–12) by the IB Middle Years Programme (ages 11–16, grades 6–10). Marymount was the first British school to be accepted to teach the MYP, and now offers students an IB curriculum from ages 11–18 (grades 6–12).

The School has taught the IB Diploma since 1979 and has unparalleled experience in its delivery. The IB diploma syllabus leads to UK university admission and US college credit. On average, ninety-eight percent of graduates go on to third level education in the UK and abroad. In 2014 77% of UK applicants gained places at Russell Group Universities, including Oxford. Perfect scores of 45 are not uncommon and 25% of Class of 2014 scored above 40 points, which is achieved by only 5% worldwide.

The school programme also includes the option to visit a variety of foreign locations designed as educational trips and closely aligned to the curriculum.

Admission. Previous reports, teachers' recommendations, placement testing in English and Mathematics and interview.

Fees per annum (2014–2015). Tuition: £18,090 (Grades 6–8); £20,670 (Grades 9–12). Boarding Supplement: Grades 6–12: £12,750 (5-day), £14,235 (7-day).

Charitable status. Marymount International School is a Registered Charity, number 1117786. It exists for the promotion of education.

The Maynard School
(Sir John Maynard's Foundation)

Denmark Road, Exeter, Devon EX1 1SJ
Tel: 01392 355998
Fax: 01392 355999
email: admissions@maynard.co.uk
website: www.maynard.co.uk

The Maynard is a selective independent day school in Exeter, for girls aged 7–18. We are the third oldest girls' school in the country, founded in 1658 by Sir John Maynard. Girls and boys learn differently and we are experts in educating girls; our long history is testament to our ability to bring out the best in each and every one of them.

Governors:

Appointed by the Governing Body of St John's Hospital:
Mr Simon Gregory
Mr Henry Luce
Lady Jan Stanhope
Ms Sarah Witheridge

Co-opted by the Governors:
Lady Jan Stanhope (*Chair*)
Ms Mandy Pearse
Mrs Sarah Pritchard
Mrs Lynn Turner

Appointed by Devon County Council:
Mr Peter Bowden

Appointed by Exeter City Council:
Mr Norman Shiel

Appointed by the University of Exeter:
Ms Jilly Court
Prof Robin Mason

Staff Governors:
Mrs Sian Fanous
Mrs Cathy Gabbitass

Parent Governors:
Lt Col Nick Bruce-Jones
Mr Paul Morrish

Ex officio:
The Right Worshipful, The Lord Mayor of Exeter

Headmistress: Ms B Hughes, BEd Hons, MBA, NPQH

Deputy Head: Mrs P Wilks, MA Oxford (*History*)
Head of Sixth Form: Mr T Hibberd, MA Cambridge
Director of Studies: Dr P Rudling, MA Cambridge, MSc, PhD Exeter
Head of Junior School: Mr S Smerdon, BEd Exeter

Bursar/Secretary to the Governors: Mr P Hammond, BSc Warwick

Teaching Staff:

Full-time:
Ms J Bellamy, BA Manchester (*Drama*)
Miss A Blackwell, BA, MA Durham, LTCL (*Director of Music & Performing Arts*)
Mrs A Briscoe, BA Hons Sussex (*English*)
Mrs A Cox, MA Bristol (*Classics*)
Mrs W Dersley, BSc Open University (*Mathematics*)
Mrs S Fanous, BEd Keele (*Food & Nutrition/Textiles*)
Mr I Flower, BSc Sussex (*Chemistry, Physics*)
Miss K Gwynne, MTheol St Andrews; ThM, Princeton (*Religious Studies*)
Mrs R Halse, BA University of Arizona (*Spanish*)
Mrs K Harvey, BSc Bristol, MEd Exeter (*Geography*)
Dr L Hawtree, MA, PhD Exeter, MA St Andrews (*Classics*)
Mrs A J Horton, BSc Exeter (*Mathematics*)
Mrs S Kerrane, BSc Swansea (*Biology*)
Mrs L Masson, BSc Pietermaritzberg (*Junior School*)
Dr P Merisi, MPhil, PhD Exeter (*Mathematics*)
Miss L Millar, BEd Belfast (*Physical Education*)
Mr D O'Neill, BA York (*German & French*)
Dr E Ouldridge, BSc Birmingham, PhD Leeds (*Biology/Physics/Chemistry*)
Miss S Payne, BA, MA Cambridge (*English*)
Mrs I Powell, BSc, MSc Rennes (*French*)
Mrs H Reynolds, BSc Open University (*Junior School*)
Mr C Ridler, MA Hons Warwick (*Physics*)
Mrs C Rowe, DipEd Edinburgh (*Junior School*)
Mr S Ryder, BSc Hons Birmingham, MSc London (*Information & Communication Technology*)
Mr J Tabb, BA London (*History & Geography*)
Mrs S Thorne, BSc Nottingham (*Chemistry, Biology*)
Mrs S Wood, BA Ed Exeter (*Physical Education & Mathematics*)
Mrs Z Vingoe, BA Manchester Metropolitan (*Art*)

Part-time:
Mrs C L Austin, GRSM, LRAM (*Music*)
Mrs G Cameron, BEd, Cheltenham (*Physical Education*)
Mrs C Finnegan, BA Central Saint Martins (*Food & Nutrition/Textiles*)
Mrs C Flavelle, BA, MA Cambridge (*History*)
Mrs K Fry, BEd Exeter (*Junior School*)
Mrs C M Gabbitass, BSc Loughborough (*Physical Education*)
Mr A Ganley, BA Nottingham (*Drama*)
Mrs C Gorrod, BA Surrey (*Junior School*)
Ms A M Hurley, MA London (*Art*)
Mrs E Kilkelly, BA Exeter (*Religious Studies*)
Mrs R Khreisheh, BA Oxford (*Junior School*)
Mrs B Knight, BEd Cambridge Institution of Education (*SENCO*)
Mrs D Lewis, BA Cheltenham (*Geography, Examinations Officer*)
Miss T Lothingland, MA Exeter (*EFL*)
Mrs V Martin, BA Hull (*English*)
Mr P Pienkowski, BSc London (*Economics*)
Mrs A Rowley, BA Liverpool (*English*)
Mrs C Smith, MA Tours (*French/Spanish*)
Mrs A Weeks, BSc Loughborough (*Physics*)
Mrs S Wood, BA Ed Exeter (*Physical Education & Mathematics*)
Mr T Woodford, BA Surrey (*Music*)
Mrs S Woolley, MA Oxford (*Study Skills & Learning Support*)
Mrs V Woulfe, BSc Keele (*Mathematics*)

Non-Teaching Staff:
Mrs S Arnold (*Assistant Chef*)
Mr A Ayre (*Chef Manager*)

Mrs G Baker (*Kitchen Assistant*)
Ms M Beach (*Junior School Teaching Assistant*)
Mrs E Bremner (*Marketing and Development Assistant*)
Mrs J Burston (*Kitchen Assistant*)
Mrs J Conway, BSc Southampton (*Marketing and Development Manager*)
Mrs J Crowley (*Assistant Secretary*)
Mrs M Davey (*Junior Department Support Assistant*)
Mrs D Courtney (*Assistant Secretary*)
Mr M Everhard (*Estate Dept*)
Mrs A Farndell (*Bursar's Assistant*)
Mrs S Gardner (*Senior Finance Manager*)
Mrs M Green (*Bursar's Assistant*)
Mrs H Halpin, BSc Surrey (*Resources Manager*)
Mrs W Holt, BEng Plymouth (*Science Technician*)
Mrs J Hourihan, BSc Birmingham, BA Hons Open University, PG Dip Information & Library Studies Robert Gordon University (*Assistant Librarian*)
Mrs J Jephson (*Art Technician*)
Mrs K Jones (*Kitchen Assistant*)
Miss K Kovacova (*Cleaner*)
Mrs D Lees (*Pastoral Secretary*)
Mrs M Linnen-Jones, BA Derby (*Registrar*)
Mrs L Mitchell (*Chemistry Technician*)
Mrs J Piatkowska (*Cleaner*)
Mr K Pomeroy (*Estates Manager*)
Mrs F Prior-Palmer (*School Nurse*)
Mr B Pugh (*Cleaning Supervisor*)
Mrs J Pugh (*Assistant Cleaning Supervisor*)
Mr M Reid (*Multimedia Creative Manager*)
Mrs J Ridehalgh, BA Warwick (*Marketing & Development Assistant*)
Mrs B Ripper (*Counsellor*)
Mrs K Sanders (*Resources Assistant*)
Mrs J Slade (*Kitchen Assistant*)
Mrs A Tancock (*Reception & Office*)
Mrs J Thomas (*Marketing & Development Manager*) (*maternity cover*)
Mrs J Wallis (*Kitchen Assistant*)
Mr J Wicksteed, BSc St Andrews (*IT Systems Manager*)
Mrs H Wright (*Science Technician*)

Visiting Staff:
Mrs C Austin GRSM LRAM (*Oboe*)
Mrs R Allsop, BEd (*Clarinet*)
Mr D Cottam, AGSM (*Guitar*)
Miss S Caffrey, PTCA (*Tennis Coach*)
Dr E Grier (*Harp*)
Mrs J Hannah, LGSM (*Flute*)
Mrs A Higgins, ARCM (*Piano, Bassoon*)
Ms E Highton, BA, ALCM, LTCL (*Piano, Flute*)
Mrs S Hill, BMus Hons Cardiff (*Singing and Flute*)
Miss M Hiley, Dip RCM (*Percussion*)
Mr N Lawrence (*Voice*)
Mrs P Leonard, NCSD, LUD (*Speech & Drama*)
Mrs F Maclean-Buechel (*Violin, Viola*)
Mr A Nuthall (*Brass*)
Mr T Parker (*Badminton Coach*)
Mr R Taverner, ARCM (*Piano*)

Ethos. A dynamic and supportive community, The Maynard is committed to excellence in providing learning opportunities that inspire and challenge. Students will demonstrate creativity, be socially responsible and through their shared experience, become independent and reflective learners. A wide-ranging extra-curricular programme enables students to achieve in all aspects of school life. Pastoral care is a vital ingredient to ensure every student is valued. Students achieve highly in all public examinations.

Numbers. There are approximately 370 day girls in the School, of whom 80 are in the Junior School and 80 in the Sixth Form.

School Buildings. The School is situated in an attractive conservation area five minutes from the centre of the city.

The extensive buildings include a separate Sixth Form Centre; a purpose-built block for Science, Mathematics, and Computing; well-equipped Food & Nutrition and Textiles Rooms; Music and Art Rooms, a large Gymnasium, and an impressive Sports Hall which provides full-scale indoor facilities. The Junior School is situated within the grounds and is fully equipped for the education of girls aged 7–10 years.

Curriculum. The curriculum is academically rigorous and maintains a good balance between Arts and Science subjects. English, Mathematics, the Sciences and Sport are particular strengths; full scope is given to creative and practical activities, as well as ICT skills. The School prepares all girls for University, including Oxford and Cambridge. A carefully developed programme of careers advice, begun at 11+ and continuing through to the Sixth Form, ensures that all pupils are individually guided in subject options with their long-term career interests at heart. The Maynard Aspire programme is an enrichment initiative for high achieving students in Upper 5 (Year 11) and the Sixth Form who are ready to develop their skills in a wider context as they make decisions about their future career paths.

Examinations. Candidates normally take 10 subjects at GCSE and 3 at A Level. Students are fully prepared for Oxford and Cambridge University Entrance.

Physical Education. Hockey (outdoor and indoor), Netball, Badminton, Basketball, Volleyball, Fencing, Dance and Gymnastics are offered in the winter terms; Tennis and Rounders are played in the Summer Term. Training is given in Athletics and Swimming is part of the normal timetable for all girls during the Summer Term. Besides its excellent indoor facilities and the three hard courts in its own grounds, the School has access to a playing field a short walk away and is close to three swimming pools and an Astroturf playing area. The school has an extensive fixture programme in Netball, Hockey, Indoor Hockey, Badminton, Basketball, Tennis, Swimming, Athletics and Rounders. Teams have regularly reached national standard. In addition, The Maynard has a strong extra-curricular programme of outdoor pursuits including the Ten Tors, the Duke of Edinburgh's Award and Exmoor Challenge.

Admission. All admissions, except sixth form, are subject to an Entrance Assessment graduated according to age and held in January each year for entry in the following September.

Fees per term (2014–2015). Junior School £3,123, Senior School £3,906. There is a generous Sibling Discount Scheme.

Scholarships and Bursaries. A range of Academic, Music and Sports Scholarships are available for senior school entry at 11+ and 13+. Sixth Form Scholarships are available: 2 for Art, 2 for Music and 2 for Sport, plus candidates can apply for an Academic Award, awarded to three internal and one external student(s) annually. An Ogden Trust Science Bursary (100% of fees) is also available to external girls from State School backgrounds. Up to four Governors' Leaving Exhibitions are awarded in the Upper Sixth year.

Means-tested Governors' Bursaries are available.

Further Information. The Prospectus and Governors' Bursaries information are available from the Admissions Office. Visitors are very welcome by appointment, and tours and taster days can be arranged for girls considering the school.

Old Maynardians. Email: RachaelBoard@maynard.co.uk.

Charitable status. The Maynard School is a Registered Charity, number 1099027. It exists to provide quality education for girls.

Merchant Taylors' Girls' School
Crosby

Liverpool Road, Crosby, Liverpool L23 5SP
Tel: 0151 924 3140
Fax: 0151 932 1461
email: admissionsmtgs@merchanttaylors.com
website: www.merchanttaylors.com
Twitter: @MerchantsCrosby
Facebook: /merchanttaylorscrosby

Motto: *Concordia Parvae Res Crescunt*

Governors:
Chairman: Prof P W J Batey, BSc, MCD, PhD, CGeog,
    FRTPI, FRSA, AcSS
P G Magill, MSc, FCIPD
Mr R J Walker, CEng, MIMechE
Miss A Dobie, BA Hons
Mr S Wilkinson, BA Hons, FCA
Mr D S Evans, MA Oxon
Mrs J L Hawkins, RGN, SCM
Ms L Martin Wright
Dr J Fox, MBCh Birm, DRCOG, MRCGP
Mr J Sutcliffe, BEng Hons, CEng, MICE, MRICS, MCIOB
Mrs B Bell, LLB Hons, FCILT, FRSA

Bursar & Clerk to the Governors: Mrs A P Pope, BA Hons,
    FCMA, ACIS, MCSI

Headmistress: Mrs L A Robinson, BA Hons York, PGCE,
NPQH, MEd Liverpool

First Deputy Headmistress: Miss J Tyndall, BD Hons/AKC
King's College London

Deputy Headmistress: Mrs M L Bush, MA Liverpool,
BMus Hons Wales, FRSA, NPQH

School Staff:

Art & Craft:
Mr M Gill, BA Hons Newcastle upon Tyne, MA Royal
    Academy
Miss L McWatt, BA Hons UWE Bristol

Biology:
Mrs J Johnson, MA Oxon, BSc OU
Ms N Houghton, BSc Hons
Mr J S Jones, BSc Hons Liverpool
Miss J Burns, BSc Hons

Business Studies:
Mrs A H Irwin, BA Hons UCLAN Preston
Mr F Lawell, BA Hons

Careers Coordinator:
Mrs V Mee, BA Hons

Chemistry:
Mrs B Miller, BSc Hons Bristol
Dr M McWatt, PhD Birmingham, BSc Hons Birmingham
Mrs L Syms, BSc Hons Central Lancashire
Mrs V Copley, MChem Hons Manchester

Classics:
Mr D Lamb, MA Liverpool, BA Hons Liverpool
Mrs A Wadsworth, BA Hons Durham
Mr G Evans, BA Hons
Miss J Johnson, BA Hons

Drama & Theatre Studies:
Ms S Tickle, BA Manchester

English:
Mrs J Cecil, BA Joint Hons Aberystwyth, DipEd Liverpool
Mrs M Myring, MPhil Bangor, BA Hons UCNW, MA
    SDUC

Mrs E Neophytou, BA Birmingham
Mrs A Hickey, BA Hons

Geography:
Mrs C Mason, BSc Hons Manchester
Mrs H M Peppin, BSc Hons Leeds
Mrs R Hames, BSc Hons Leeds

Gifted and Talented Coordinators:
Mrs R Hames, BSc Hons Leeds (*Years 7–10*)
Mrs S Heywood, MA Oxon (*Years 11–13*)

History & Politics:
Mrs C Grindley, BA Hons Leeds
Mr G Evans, BA Hons Hull

Home Economics:
Ms M Hutchins, BA Hons Newcastle-Upon-Tyne
Mrs B Jones, BEd Liverpool

Information Technology:
Mr J Power, BEd Hons

Librarian:
Mrs A Barry, BLib Aberystwyth, MCLIP, Dip Arc, Trinity
    Cert TESOL

LDD Coordinator:
Miss L Rimmer, BSc Hons Lancaster

Mathematics:
Mr M Wood, BSc Hons Aberystwyth, MSc Dundee
Mrs H F Hurst, BSc Joint Hons Keele
Miss E Smith, MEng Durham
Miss C Hampson, BSc Hons
Miss R Bradshaw, BSc Hons

Modern Languages:
Mrs C Y Whalley, BA Hons Leeds
Mrs J Doyle, BA Hons Nottingham
Mrs F Menzies, CLA d'Abidjan
Mme P Mistry, Licence University of Metz
Mr F Rubia, BA Hons
Mrs C Southworth, BA Hons Bristol
Mrs S M Thomson, BEd Hons Liverpool
Miss E Hutchinson, BA Hons

Music:
Mrs J Thompson, MA, BMus Hons Wales, ALCM
Mrs M L Bush, MA Liverpool, BMus Hons Wales, FRSA,
    NPQH

Visiting and Part-time Music Staff:
Miss J A Carr (*Voice*)
Miss S Hayes (*Voice*)
Mr S Lock (*Clarinet, Saxophone*)
Mr B Johnson (*Flute, Oboe*)
Mr D Bridge (*Guitar*)
Miss L Gregg (*Percussion*)
Mr D Byles (*Percussion*)
Miss D O'Hara (*Piano*)
Mrs J Richards (*Cello, Double Bass*)
Mrs L Mycock (*Violin, Viola, Flute*)
Mr C Jones (*Clarinet, Saxophone*)
Mr M Palmer (*Brass*)

Physical Education:
Miss E Jones, BEd Hons Liverpool
Miss L Taylor, BSc Hons
Miss L Hilton, BA Hons

Physics:
Mrs H Heaton, BSc Hons Durham
Mr P Price, BSc Hons Leeds
Mrs J Lynch, BSc Hons

PSHE Coordinator:
Mrs N Houghton, BSc Hons Liverpool John Moores

Psychology:
Miss S Ladbrook, BSc Hons Central Lancashire

Mr B Wilson, BA Hons

Religious Studies:
Mrs G Vaughan, BA Hons Manchester
Mr B Wilson, BA Hons St David's Lampeter
Miss J Tyndall, BD Hons, AKC London

Marketing and Admissions:
Marketing & Development Director: Miss M J Riches, BA Hons
Admissions Officer: Mrs S Barrington

Administration:
PA to Headmistress: Mrs J Baccino
School Secretary: Mrs A Regan
Receptionists: Mrs A Cave, BA Hons Liverpool, Mrs N McKie-Thomson
Examinations: Mrs J E Custard, BSc Hons Coventry
Examinations Secretary: Mrs G Hurst
Computer Network Manager: Mr S Coughlan, BSc Hons
New Media and ICT Technician: Mr A Heighway-Sephton
Central Reprographics Manager: Mrs S Nield
Central Reprographics Assistants: Mrs A Bramhall, Mr A Best, Mr D Crompton
Lab Technicians: Mrs S Childs, Mrs S Cheetham, Miss L Harrison
School Nurse: Miss A Dalton, RGN, RSCN, Dip Child Health

Merchant Taylors' Primary School, 'Stanfield':
Head of School: Miss J E Yardley, BA Hons Liverpool, PGCE, NPQH
Deputy Head: Mrs J Callaway, BA Hons QTS Prim Ed, PGC SEN Coordination

Miss V Beckerleg, BA Hons Leeds
Mrs J Birtwistle, BA Hons Loughborough
Mrs K Bonner, BA Hons London, MA Brighton
Mrs S Curwen, BEd Hons Lancaster
Mrs C Darbyshire, BTech Child Ed (*Nursery Nurse*)
Mrs A Dunne BSc Hons Coventry, MBA Open University (*Teaching Assistant*)
Mrs C Evans (*Netball Coach*)
Mrs S Garforth, BEd Hons Lancaster
Mrs L Gaskell, BA Hons Huddersfield
Mrs K Higham, BA Hons
Mrs A-L Hodkinson (*Swimming Coach*)
Miss S Ley, BA Hons John Moores, PGCE Prim Ed
Mrs R Loan, BA Hons Nottingham
Mrs S McEvoy, BA Hons
Mrs A Nagy, BEd Liverpool
Mrs C Oakes, BA Hons Manchester
Mrs J O'Mahony, BA, CertEd Lancaster
Mrs L Ramsdale, BA Hons
Mrs B Richardson, BEd London
Miss E Riding, BA Hons QTS
Mr T Roberts, BA Hons Dunelm, ATCL
Mrs S Ryan, NNEB (*Nursery Nurse*)
Mrs A Saunders, Teaching Degree (*Nursery Nurse*)
Mrs M Silverman, BA Hons Liverpool
Mrs S Taylor, BEd Leeds
Miss C Watkins, BA Hons Lancaster
Mrs D Whiteside, BA Hons (*Nursery Nurse*)

PA to Head: Mrs M Langham
Receptionist: Mrs N McKie-Thomson

ICT Coordinator: Mrs A Coughlan, HNC Computing

Visiting Music Staff:
Miss H Burgoyne (*Piano*)
Mr S Lock (*Flute, Clarinet, Saxophone, Oboe*)
Mrs J Richards (*Cello and Double Bass*)
Mrs S Rookyard (*Singing*)
Mr D Elliott (*Guitar*)

The Senior Girls' School was opened in 1888 on the site which had been occupied by the Boys' School for over 350 years. The original grey stone building, erected in 1620, is still in daily use as the Library. Extensions have been made from time to time to include a Fitness Suite, Science Laboratories and a Sixth Form Centre. The Centenary Hall provides ample accommodation for concerts, plays and sports. The School is beautifully situated approximately 8 miles from Liverpool and within 10 minutes' walk of the Sefton coastline. There are netball and tennis courts on the premises with a playing field and the joint schools' multimillion pound sports centre, opened in 2011, is situated a short distance away on the Boys' School site. The Centre incorporates a Sports Hall suitable for a variety of indoor sports, dance and fitness studios, a refreshment area and classrooms.

A new entrance was built in 2009 incorporating a new reception area and art gallery space called The Vitreum. This gallery has been used to showcase pupils' work as well as exhibitions from local, national and international artists.

Merchant Taylors' is a family of Schools. There is a separate Primary School, 'Stanfield', situated in a self-contained building near to the Main School with girls aged 4–11 and boys aged 4–7. This is currently undergoing a £5 million redevelopment scheduled to finish in December 2014. The Senior Girls' School age range is 11–18. There are at present 848 pupils at both schools.

The girls receive a broad academic education. Subjects included in the curriculum are Art, Biology, Chemistry, Classics, Drama and Theatre Studies, Economics, English Language and English Literature, French, Geography, German, Government and Politics, History, Home Economics, Information Technology, Latin, Mathematics, Music, Physical Education, Physics, Psychology, Religious Studies and Spanish.

Fees per term (2014–2015). Tuition: Senior School £3,508; Junior School £2,623, Infant School (ages 4–7) £2,596.

Examinations. Pupils are prepared for their GCSE and A Level examinations.

The Music Examinations taken are those of the Associated Board of the Royal Schools of Music, The London College of Music, Trinity Guildhall.

Parent Teachers' Association. *Chairperson:* Helen Ashton, c/o The School.

Old Girls' Association. *Hon Secretary*: Mrs S Duncan, 'Fairhaven', The Serpentine South, Liverpool L23 6UQ.

Charitable status. The Merchant Taylors' Schools Crosby is a Registered Charity, number 1125485, and a Company Limited by Guarantee, registered in England, number 6654276. Registered Office: Liverpool Road, Crosby, Liverpool L23 0QP.

Moira House Girls School

Upper Carlisle Road, Eastbourne, East Sussex BN20 7TE

Tel: 01323 644144
Fax: 01323 649720
email: admissions@moirahouse.co.uk
website: www.moirahouse.co.uk
Twitter: @moirahouse1875
Facebook: /moirahouse

Motto: *Nemo A Me Alienus*
  Established 1875.

The Council:
Chairman: Ms Jill A Jackson-Hill, BA Hons, FRSA (*Company Director and former pupil*)
Dr Debbie Davison, MBBS, DRCOG (*parent of pupil*)

Mr Peter Hawley, FIH (*Hotelier, parent of former pupil*)
Mr Patrick Henshaw, BSc Hons, MRICS, MaPS
Mrs Jenny Herold, BDS, FDSRCPS, MSc, MOrthRCS
  (*Consultant Orthodontist, parent of former pupil*)
Mr Chris Manville, BA, Mont Dip (*parent of pupil*)
Mrs Elizabeth Mullaney, Dip Res EA (*Solicitor*)
Mr Michael Ogilvie, FCA, CPC
Mr Eric Reynolds, BA Hons, PGCE

The Common Room:
Mrs Karen Best (*Active Chair of the Common Room
  Committee, Faculty Head, Head of Science and Physics*)

Senior Leadership Team:

Principal: Mr James Sheridan, MA, BSc

Deputy Principals:
Mr Kevin Ashby, MA, BA Hons QTS
Mrs Elodie Vallantine, BA Hons, PGCE

School Management Team:
Mrs Theresa Bees, BSc QTS (*Head of Pre-Prep and KS1,
  Year 2*)
Mr Adrian Cooper, BA Hons (*Digital Learning and IT
  Network Manager, Exams Officer, Staff Cover, DT*)
Mr Stephen Crum, BA Hons, PGCE (*Mathematics KS3
  Pastoral Coordinator*)
Mr James Harding (*Director of Admissions*)
Mrs Ruth Harris-Moss, BA Hons, PGCE (*Faculty Head,
  Head of Modern Foreign Languages, Head of Sixth
  Form*)
Ms Hannah Holland, CIM (*Director of Marketing,
  Communications & Development*)
Mrs Sarah Hughes, BA Hons Early Years (*Head of
  Nursery*)
Mr Graham James, MIH (*Operations Manager*)
Miss Katherine James, BA Hons PE QTS (*Faculty Head,
  Head of Physical Education, KS4 Pastoral Coordinator*)
Mrs Cecy Kemp, BSc, Dip RE (*Head of KS2, Year 6*)
Mrs Carol Richards, BA, HDE (*Director of Pastoral and
  Boarding*)
Mrs Nicola Langford (*Principal's PA & Administration
  and Personnel Manager*)

Senior School Academic Staff:

*Art, Design Technology, Food Technology, ICT and
  Special Educational Needs (SEN)*:
Mrs Emma-Jayne Haining, BA Hons, PGCE (*Faculty
  Head, Head of Art, DT & Photography, Residential
  Housemistress*)
Miss Georgina Bates, BA Hons, PGCE, BIPP
  (*Photography*)
Mr Adrian Cooper, BA Hons (*DT*)
Mr Oscar de la Torre-Martin (*CDT Technician*)
Mrs Judith Kneen, Cert Ed (*Art Technician*)
Mrs Christine Mcmahon, Cert Ed (*GCSE Food
  Technology*)
Mrs Barbara Power, PG Dip, Cert Ed (*Head of ICT*)
Mrs Moira Reid, BA Hons, PGCE (*Junior and Senior
  School Art*)
Mrs Suzanne Teear, BA Ed Hons, QTS (*SENCO*)
Mrs Karen Williames, BA Hons, PGCE (*Art*)

Drama and Music:
Mr Robert Cousins, BMus Hons, PGCE (*Faculty Head,
  Director of Music & Public Performance*)
Mrs Barbara Ashby, GGSM, PGCE (*Music, Music
  Coordinator KS4 & 5*)
Mrs Natasha Jordan, Dip Professional Acting Hons
  (*Director of Drama Junior and Senior School*)
Dr Rebecca Swingle-Putland, DMA, MM, BM, BA
  (*Director of Outreach & Assistant to the Director of
  Public Performance*)
Mr Frank Schulmeyer (*Audio Visual Technician*)

*English, Geography, History, Library, PSE and Religious
  Studies*:
Mr John Brennan, BA Hons, PGCE (*Faculty Head, Head
  of History*)
Mrs Olivia Barber, BA, BSc Hons, PGCE (*Religious
  Studies Subject Leader*)
Mrs Alison Gamester, BA Hons, PGCE (*RE, Geography &
  History*)
Mrs Ella Lewis, BA Hons (*Assistant Librarian*)
Ms Linda Rosson, MA, BA Hons, PGCE (*English*)
Mrs Alison Standen, BA Hons (*Senior Librarian*)
Ms Tamara Stevens, BSc Ed (*Head of English, Academic
  Enrichment Coordinator*)
Mrs Jacqueline Wood, BSc Hons, PGCE (*Head of
  Geography*)

*English as Additional Language (EAL) and Modern
  Foreign Languages (MFL)*:
Mrs Ruth Harris-Moss, BA Hons, PGCE (*Faculty Head,
  Head of Modern Foreign Languages, Head of Sixth
  Form*)
Miss Gabrielle Bonner, MA, BA (*Head of EAL*)
Mme Nathalie Couture, BA Hons, MBA, PGCE (*Junior
  and Senior School French*)
Ms Hong Deng, MA, PGCE (*Mandarin*)
Mrs Rosie Horsnell (*Mandarin*)
Mr Duncan Martin, BA Hons, PGCE, CELTA (*EAL*)
Mrs Bernardine Mcnamara, BA Hons, PGCE (*French*)
Mr Christopher O'Reilly, BA Hons, PGCE, TEFL
  (*Spanish, Latin*)
Miss Camilla Venditti (*Assistant Teacher*)
Mrs Lucinda Westwood, BA Hons, PGCE, CTEFLA (*EAL,
  Spanish*)

Psychology and Science:
Mrs Karen Best, BA (*Faculty Head, Head of Science and
  Physics*)
Mrs Dorinda Dodd, BSc Hons, PGCE (*Subject Leader
  Chemistry*)
Ms Cheryl Lloyd, BEd Hons (*Science Technician*)
Dr Fiona Mansfield, BSc, PhD, QTS (*Subject Leader
  Biology*)
Miss Hannah Savage, BSc (*Subject Leader Psychology,
  English*)
Miss Eleni Symeon (*Science Technician*)
Mrs Sandra Twaites, BA Hons, QTS (*Science*)

Business Studies, Economics and Mathematics:
Mrs Jane Lambert, BA Hons (*Faculty Head, Head of
  Mathematics*)
Mr Kevin Ashby, MA, BA Hons QTS (*Mathematics*)
Mr Stephen Crum, BA Hons, PGCE (*Mathematics KS3
  Pastoral Coordinator*)
Mrs Christine Hamilton, BA Hons, PGCE (*Mathematics*)
Mr Colin Mcmahon, BSc, PGCE (*Mathematics*)
Mr David, Pollard, BA Hons, QTS (*Mathematics*)
Mr Stephen Wood, MA Ed, BA Hons, PGCE, FCIEA
  (*Head of Business Studies & Economics*)

Physical Education:
Miss Katherine James, BA Hons PE QTS (*Faculty Head,
  Head of Physical Education, KS4 Pastoral Coordinator*)
Miss Dawn Cook, BEd (*Physical Education*)
Mrs Lesley Pyle, BEd Hons (*Physical Education*)
Miss Alison Rowsell, BA Hons, PE QTS, PGDPSE
  (*Physical Education*)
Mrs Wendy Pritchard, FIST Level 1 Coach (*Swimming
  Teacher*)
Ms Gillian Burt, IOS, ASA, STA (*Swimming Teacher/
  Rookie Instructor*)
Mrs Renee Harris (*Assistant Swimming Teacher*)
Ms Catherine Hook (*Swimming Teacher*)
Mr William Dodd (*Lifeguard*)
Miss Debra Miller (*Swimming Teacher*)

Teaching Assistants:
Ms Gill Burt (*Teaching Assistant*)
Mrs Helen Deane (*Teaching Assistant*)
Miss Veronica Fernandez del Villar Lledo (*Language Assistant*)
Miss Maria Gomez Berrocal (*Language Assistant*)
Miss Romy Martin, BSc Hons (*Teaching Assistant*)

Administration:
Mrs Nicola Langford (*Principal's PA & Administration and Personnel Manager*)
Miss Nicola Difrancesco (*School Office Administrator*)
Mrs Jenny Hafernik (*Junior School Office Administrator*)
Mrs Judith Langford (*School Administrator*)
Mrs Jane Mole (*Database Administrator*)
Mrs Elizabeth Powell (*School Office Receptionist/Administrator*)
Mrs Miriam Ripley (*School Office Receptionist/Administrator*)

Admissions and Marketing:
Ms Hannah Holland, CIM (*Director of Marketing, Communications & Development*)
Mr James Harding (*Director of Admissions*)
Mrs Elaine Allen (*Admissions & Marketing Administrator*)
Mr Giles Carrington (*Market Development Manager*)

Operations:
Mr Graham James, MIH (*Operations Manager*)
Mrs Jane Stutter, NVQ2 in Team Leading (*Domestic Bursar*)

Finance:
Mrs Jayne Hollister-Sheppard (*Accountant*)
Mrs Jayne Ring, MAAT (*Accountant*)

Information Technology:
Mr Adrian Cooper, BA Hons (*Digital Learning and IT Network Manager*)
Mr Ryan Dray (*IT Technician*)

Examinations Officer:
Mr Adrian Cooper, BA Hons (*Examinations Officer*)

Extra Curricular Activities:
Miss Alison Rowsell, BA Hons PE QTS, PGDPSE (*Extra-Curricular Activities Coordinator*)

Junior School Academic Staff:
Mrs Theresa Bees, BSc QTS (*Head of Pre-Prep and KS1, Year 2*)
Mr James Collins, BA Hons (*Year 4*)
Mme Nathalie Couture, BA Hons, MBA, PGCE (*Junior and Senior School French*)
Mrs Cecy Kemp, BSc, Dip RE (*Head of KS2, Year 6*)
Mr Christopher Kerswell, BA Hons QTS (*Year 3*)
Mrs Wendy Lambert, BA Hons, PGCE (*Physical Education*)
Mrs Fiona Martirossian, BA Hons, PGCE (*Year 1*)
Mr Martin Neill, Dip Mus, BMus Hons, PGCE (*Head of Junior School Music*)
Mrs Karon Pont, NVQ Level 3 (*Teaching Assistant*)
Miss Jacqueline Sheridan, BA, PGCE (*Year 5*)
Miss Gemma Wood, BA Hons, Primary EYPS (*Reception*)
Mrs Linda Whicker (*Lunch time and After-School Club Coordinator*)

Mini Nursery Moho / Baby MoHo:
Mrs Sarah Hughes, BA Hons Early Years (*Head of Nursery*)
Mrs Carly Cornford, BA Learning & Development, EYP Early Years Professional (*Deputy Nursery Manager*)
Miss Margaret Diaper, NNEB (*Nursery Nurse*)
Miss Hannah Evenden, NVQ Level 3 Childcare (*Nursery Nurse*)
Mrs Jane Keen, Dip Level 3 (*Nursery Nurse*)
Mrs Danielle Legg, Dip Level 3 Early Years Care and Ed (*Nursery Nurse*)

Miss Courtney Neate, NVQ Level 2 (*Nursery Nurse*)
Miss Lisa Tomasetti (*Nursery Nurse*)
Miss Helen Wallis, NVQ Level 3 Childcare (*Nursery Nurse*)
Miss Carly Winter, NVQ Level 3 (*Nursery Nurse, Acting Deputy*)
Mrs Loraine Worrall, NVQ Level 3 Playgroup Practice (*Nursery Nurse*)

Boarding House Staff:

Director of Pastoral Care and Boarding (*Residential*): Mrs Carol Richards (*School House*)

Senior Housemistresses (*Residential*):
Mrs Helen Deane (*Senior Housemistress, Boston House*)
Mrs Emma-Jayne Haining (*Senior Housemistress, Boston House*)
Miss Alison Rowsell (*Senior Housemistress, School House*)
Housemistresses:
Mrs Jennifer Shuman (*School House*)
Mrs Samia Slim (*Boston House*)
Mrs Christine Armstrong (*School House & Boston House – Residential*)

Graduate Assistants (*Residential*):
Miss Camilla Venditti
Miss Maria Gomez Berrocal
Miss Veronica Fernandez del Villar Lledo

Housemothers:
Mrs Judith Kneen
Ms Anna Romnaki
Mrs Lynda Sorrell-Fleet
Mrs Julie Summers
Miss Deborah Walton

Visiting Staff:
Mrs Yvonne Burrell, BA Hons Humanities with Music (*Piano*)
Miss Alison Barnard, FISTD, Imperial Ballet Grades Examiner (*Dance Teacher*)
Mr Paul Beasley, BA, EPEE L1 (*Fencing Coach*)
Mr Paul Bridge, GNAS L1 (*Archery Coach*)
Mrs Maeve Cooper, Dip RCM Perf, Dip RCM Ten (*Violin*)
Mr Dave Cottrell (*Percussion*)
Mr Peter Cousins, FRCO, ARCM (*Accompaniment*)
Mr James Cruttenden, BA Hons, ABSM (*Double Bass*)
Mr Alun Francis, Professional Cert RCM (*Clarinet, Saxophone*)
Miss Natalie Golding, Law Society
Ms Susan Gregg, BA LTCL (*Flute*)
Mrs Rachel Grimes, BA Mus (*Cello*)
Mrs Franciska Laursen, DRS (*Piano*)
Mr Ben Lucas, Youth Worker, All Saints Church
Miss Lydia Hammond, Youth Worker, All Saints Church
Mr Kevin Pallister (*LAMDA*)
Mr Marcus Plant, BA Hons, LRAM, Dip RAM, PGCE (*Brass*)
Mrs Paula Pout (*Singing*)
Mr Jeremy Taylor, OBE (*Drama*)
Mrs Claire Walker, DIP L3 (*Dance Teacher*)

Medical Centre:
Dr Alice Sharma, MB ChB (*School Doctor*)
Dr Jenny Rowe, MBBS, BSc, DFSRH, DRCOG, MRCGP (*School Doctor, Cover in Dr Sharma's absence*)
Mrs Audrey Bushnell, RGN (*Nursing Sister*)
Mrs Nicola Freeborn, RGN (*Nursing Sister*)

Foundation. Moira House was founded in 1875 in Surrey. The School moved to its present site in 1887. The founders, Mr and Mrs Charles Ingham, were regarded in their time as gifted pioneers in the field of female education. In 1947 the School became an Educational Trust.

Situation and Facilities. Situated on high ground in Eastbourne with views over the sea, the grounds open directly onto the Downs which provide magnificent walking country and offer opportunities for expedition work and field studies. There are extensive playing fields with facilities for Tennis, Cricket, Soccer, Hockey, Netball and Athletics, a 25-metre indoor heated swimming pool and an excellent all-weather sports hall. Each subject has its own resource base. Eastbourne is a thriving cultural centre containing 3 theatres, an art gallery and a concert hall.

Faith. The School is interdenominational.

Organisation. *Junior School* (IAPS): The Junior School has provision for 120 day girls. We offer Junior boarding starting from the age of 9. (*See Junior School entry in IAPS section.*) Our Nursery welcomes boys and girls and we also have a Baby Unit.

Senior School: The Senior School has provision for 140 boarders and 150 day girls.

Boarding Houses: There are two boarding houses, one of which is dedicated to Sixth Form students with single and twin study-bedrooms. Each house has a team combining resident staff and house mothers. Emphasis is placed upon a full range of extra-curricular activities, both in the evenings and at weekends.

Curriculum. *Junior School*: We offer a wide curriculum, whilst preparing for transfer to the Senior School.

Senior School: The formal academic courses follow a broad curriculum offering 22 subjects leading to GCSE, AS and A Level and University Entrance. At GCSE we offer English Language, English Literature, Mathematics, Business Studies, Biology, Chemistry, Physics, Computing, French, German, Spanish, Latin, History, Geography, Religious Studies, Music, Economics, Mandarin, Photography, Drama, Art and Design, Design/Technology, Physical Education and Food Technology.

Sixth Form: A Levels are offered in Art, Craft and Design, Biology, Business Studies, Chemistry, Theatre Studies, Economics, English Literature, Further Mathematics, Geography, History, ICT (Applied), French, German, Spanish, Latin, Mathematics, Music, Photography, Physical Education, Physics, Psychology, and Religious Studies.

Careers Counselling. We have a strong programme of Careers Counselling, led by our Careers Counsellor.

Drama and Music. Drama and Music have always been strengths of Moira House. We are aware of the part Speech and Drama play in the development of clear communication and creative expression. There are a number of School productions and concerts each year, and school choirs take part in performances throughout Sussex. We also enter the local festival of Music and Drama and proximity to Glyndebourne gives girls a chance to have their first taste of opera at an early age. As well as regular class music lessons, there is every opportunity to learn a musical instrument, and the exams of the various musical examining bodies are taken. There is also a state-of-the-art recording studio. There are also overseas tours, most recently a Paris music tour.

Physical Education and Sport. We provide excellent new facilities. The main sports are Swimming, Netball, Tennis, Athletics and Hockey, and teams represent the School in these and in cricket and football. In addition, coaching is given in Sailing, Riding, Squash, Dance, Golf and Badminton, to name a few.

Activities. Activities are considered an essential part of the curriculum. Many activities are offered, including: Drama, Music, Trampolining, Pottery, Chess, Local History, Sailing, Down-walking, Environmental Studies, Poetry/Play Reading, Table Tennis, Duke of Edinburgh's Award, Mandarin, Japanese, and Debating. Girls are also encouraged to be aware of the needs of others. Senior girls work regularly with local charities. There are annual expeditions both within this country and to Europe and the School has links with French, German and international schools of a similar nature to ours.

Health. The school doctor holds regular surgeries at the School and there are Sisters in charge of the health centre.

Entry. Entry is by interview and review of previous school reports and references. Admission to the Junior School at any age; to the Senior School usually at 11–13+ and 16+.

Scholarships and Bursaries. Academic Scholarships are awarded annually for admission to Years 3 to 12. Junior School candidates have assessments in the Junior School and are also interviewed by the Principal.

In addition, the School offers Music, Art, Drama and Sport Exhibitions to candidates who are especially gifted in these disciplines, and these are awarded on the basis of an audition or practical assessment. Where appropriate, these awards may be supplemented with a Bursary.

Fees per term (2014–2015). Senior School: £4,785–£5,110 (Day Pupils); £7,500–£8,995 (Weekly Boarders); £7,940–£9,900 (Boarders).

Junior School: £2,850–£4,000 (Day Pupils); £6,680 (Weekly Boarders); £7,180 (Boarders).

Charitable status. Moira House Girls School is a Registered Charity, number 307072. It exists to provide quality education for young women.

More House School

22–24 Pont Street, London SW1X 0AA

Tel:	020 7235 2855; Bursar: 020 7235 4162
Fax:	020 7259 6782
email:	office@morehouse.org.uk
website:	www.morehouse.org.uk

Governing Body:
Chairman: Mr J Fyfe, BA Birmingham
Mr J Davidson, BA, OBE
Mr P I Ewings, BA Belfast, Solicitor of the Supreme Court in England and Wales
Fr K J Fox, SJ, MA Oxon
Ms N Patel, BA Nottingham Trent, MCIPD, CQSW
Mrs S Shale, BA Birmingham, FCA (*Vice-Chairman*)
Mrs S Sturrock, BMus London, ARCM
Mr J W Wates, MA Oxon, BSc, FRICS

Clerk to the Governors: Mr D D A Leslie, BA London, MA London, MBE

Head: **Mrs A Leach**, BSc Liverpool

Deputy Head: Mr M R Keeley, BMus London, MSc Manchester

Director of Studies: Mr L Garwood, BA Brunel, MA Ed Hertfordshire

Senior Teachers:
Ms S Brown, BA Bristol
Ms K Devine, BA Bristol
Mr T Robertson, BSc Leeds

Bursar: Ms J Forsyth

Chaplain: Father Michael Doyle

PA to the Headmaster and Registrar: Mrs J Barnwell
Communications and Development: Ms K Atti, BSc London, MSc London

Academic Departments:
* *Head of Department*

Art:
*Ms L Beatty, BA London
Ms K Devine, BA Bristol
Ms D Rigby, MA Chelsea
Ms K Spelman, BA Oxford, MA London

Business Studies and Economics:
*Mrs P Revell, BA Wellington

Classics:
*Mrs R Gilbertson, MA St Andrews
Mrs K Spelman, BA Oxford, MA London
Mrs R Tunicliffe, BA London, MA London

English and Drama:
*Mrs J Boulter, BA London
Miss H Travers, BA Bristol
Mr P Hegarty, BA London
Mrs J Taylor, BA Bristol
Mr D Bignell, BA Dartington

Humanities:
*Ms G Collins, BA Birmingham and Santa Barbara
Mr J La Frenais, BA Leeds
Mrs P Revell, BA Wellington
Miss P Crawley, MA Oxon, MA SOAS
Mr L Garwood, BA Brunel, MA Hertfordshire

Information Technology:
Mrs A Leach, BSc Liverpool
Mr D Bignell, BA Dartington
Mr M Keeley, BMus London

Support for Learning:
Ms J Jones, Dip Theatre, Cert Ed, Cert SpLD, CELTA
Mrs A Williams, MA Cambridge
Miss A Miller, BA Cambridge

Mathematics:
*Mr M Ginever, BSc Exeter
Mrs J Mullins, MSc Cape Town
Mr T Robertson, BSc Leeds

Modern Foreign Languages:
*Ms S Brown, BA Bristol
Ms C Gremillet, BA Barcelona, BA Bristol
Mr M Caroll, BA Belfast
Mrs M Romero, BA London, MA London, MA Spain

Music:
Mr D Anstice, MA London (*Director of Music*)
Mr M Keeley, BMus London
Miss F Ho, BA Southampton

Physical Education:
*Miss S Minto, BSc Brunel, QTS Brunel
Mr L Garwood, BA Brunel, MA Ed Hertfordshire

Religious Studies:
*Mrs E Hamley, BA Durham
Miss P Crawley, MA Oxon, MA SOAS
Ms K Gulin, MA Sweden

Sciences:
*Mrs C Hextall, BSc Edinburgh
Mrs H Crowder, BSc, MAT Washington
Mrs F Gbadeyan, BSc Nigeria, MSc Nigeria
Miss S Ricci, BSc Manchester, MSc London
Ms J Seconi, BSc Massey, MSc Massey
Mrs R Sym, MEng, MA Cantab

Mr S Keeley (*Network Manager*)
Miss M Barratt (*Science Technician*)

Peripatetic staff:
Ms D Matthews Forth, RAD TC, BBO TD, IDTA T, IDTA M

(*plus various instrumental teachers*)

More House is an Independent Day School of up to 220 girls between the ages of eleven and eighteen. It occupies two adjoining houses, conveniently situated in Knightsbridge, retaining many of the original architectural features, but modernised to include four laboratories, two computer rooms, common rooms, study room and computer room for the sixth form, a chapel, a library and a newly refurbished drama and dance studio. More House is a small and happy community in which a generous teacher: pupil ratio allows the talents of each girl to flourish with all the stimulus and encouragement that she needs. The maximum class size is normally fifteen, streamed where necessary in mathematics, science and languages. All girls leaving the Sixth Form proceed to Higher Education, including Oxbridge, and then to careers in every field. Girls are given full advice about careers and Higher Education.

A Catholic Foundation, More House was opened in 1953 by the Canonesses of St Augustine; since 1969 it has been under lay management as a charitable trust and with a Board of Governors which has always included parents of present pupils. More House celebrated its Golden Jubilee in the academic year 2003–2004. The School attracts pupils from a wide area of London. More House warmly welcomes girls of all faiths.

Places at the school are usually awarded on the basis of an interview, a report from the candidate's previous school, and an examination held in January each year. Girls who join us in the Sixth Form are required to have achieved grades A–C in at least five subjects at GCSE Level.

Our level of pastoral care is very high indeed, supporting the girls in all aspects of their lives.

Instrumental tuition is available in school and in recent years the School Choir has given performances in Portugal, Spain, Paris, Rome, Malta and the USA. The most recent school choral concert featured our five choirs performing Carmina Burana. Full advantage is taken of the school's position in Central London and regular visits to lectures, galleries and exhibitions are organised. In 2008, six Year 11 Art pupils had their GCSE performance placed in the top 10 nationally.

Extra-curricular activities include Music, Drama, Sport, Dance, Art, Fencing, Photography and the Duke of Edinburgh's Award Scheme and World Challenge Expeditions. The latest school drama production was 'The Mikado' performed at the POSK Theatre in Hammersmith.

The Curriculum. The school curriculum offers a wide range of subjects at all levels. In the first two years all girls study Mathematics, Science, English, French, German, Latin, History, Geography, Religious Studies, Information Technology, Drama, Art, Physical Education and Music. Spanish is added in Year 9, giving the possibility of taking two modern languages at GCSE, where the core curriculum of Mathematics, Science, English Language and Literature and Religious Studies is supplemented by four further options.

The Advanced Level courses offered are structured around each girl's choice of subjects, new options available at this stage being History of Art, Business Studies, Classical Civilisation, Economics, Physical Education, Textiles and Theatre Studies; further breadth of study is achieved through a General Studies programme. Each subject has its own specialist rooms and for Physical Education the excellent sport and leisure facilities available in the neighbourhood are used.

Fees per term (2014–2015). £5,500 including lunch, stationery and some educational visits. Academic and Music Scholarships are available on merit.

Charitable status. More House Trust is a Registered Charity, number 312737. It exists to provide an academic education for girls aged 11 to 18 within the framework of a Catholic Day School.

Moreton Hall

Weston Rhyn, Oswestry, Shropshire SY11 3EW
Tel: 01691 773671
Fax: 01691 778552
email: admin@moretonhall.com
website: www.moretonhall.org
Twitter: @moretonhall
Facebook: /moretonhall

One of the UK's highest achieving schools, Moreton Hall was founded in 1913 by Ellen Lloyd-Williams (Aunt Lil) in Oswestry and moved to its present location in 1920. In 1964, the school became an educational trust. Although the school is predominantly boarding, a number of day pupils are admitted each year.

Member of GSA, The Society of Heads, AGBIS, ISCO.

Governing Body:
Chairman: Dr L V Boon, MB BS, LRCP, MRCS
D Edwards
P Booth
Mrs J G France-Hayhurst, LLB Hons (*Barrister-at-Law*)
E R Graham-Wood, MA, FRICS
M Heath
Mrs C M Neilson
Mrs S Tunstall
C Waters, BA Hons Law
Mrs L Yule, BSc
S Roberts, MA
S Fisher, BEd Hons
A Woolstone, LLB
J Flynn

Senior Management:

Principal: Jonathan Forster, BA, FRSA

Vice Principal: Carolyn Tilley, GRNCM, PPRNCM
Deputy Head (Academic): Sarah Hughes, MTheol
Head of Moreton First: Catherine Ford, MA, BSc
Director of Studies: Ian Fitton, BSc
Head of Academic Development: John Nanson, MA
Head of International Study Centre: Victoria Eastman, MA

* *Head of Department*

Mathematics:
*Sean Lang, BEng Cranfield, MSc Cranfield, MA King's College London, MBA Open, CEng, FIMechE
Ian Fitton, BSc Bangor
Adrian Feehan, BEng Ulster
Ian Wood, BEd Keele
Patricia Fitton, BSc Open University
Frances Cummins, BA Durham, PGCE Worcester
Helen Long, BSc Surrey, Cert SpLD
Mark Twells, MA Oxon, MSc Loughborough

English and Drama:
*Andrew Macdonald-Brown, BA Oxon (*Head of English*)
Caroline Lang, BA Warwick, MA University College London
Sarah Thomas, BA Cardiff
*Lowri Williams, BA Aberystwyth (*Head of Drama*)
Matthew Dennison, MA Oxon, MPhil Glasgow
Vivien Lewis, BA Durham, Cert SpLD (*Learning Support*)
Kate Howells, BA Hons Guildford School of Acting

Learning Support:
Alison Wray, BSc Staffordshire, CELTA, OCR Dip SpLD, APC, AMBDA (*SENCO*)
Vivien Lewis, BA Durham, Cert SpLD

Modern Languages:
*Lesley Eyre, BA Exeter (*Head of French*)
Andrea Greaney, BA, MA Sheffield (*French*)

Menir Edmunds, BA, MA Cardiff, PhD Bangor (*German*)
Susan Evans, BA Leeds (*Spanish and French*)
Shirley Lee, BA Derby (*Mandarin*)
Raymond Rhodes, BA Leeds (*Mandarin*)
Anne Simpson, BA Oxon (*Spanish*)
Gisele Slater, BA Lancaster (*French*)
Montserrat Jorge Tarrega (*Spanish*)
Alice Davies, BA Bristol (*Spanish*)

Classics:
*Judith Morton, MA Edinburgh (*Head of Subject*)
Chris Symons, BA University College London
John Godwin, MA Oxon, PhD Open University, LRAM, FRSA

Science:
*Martyn Long, BSc Durham, PGCE Birmingham (*Physics*)
Sona Champion, MSc Manchester, BSc Loughborough (*Psychology, Chemistry and Biology*)
Frances Cummins, BA Durham, PGCE Worcester (*Physics*)
Patricia Fitton, BSc Open University (*Biology*)
Tim Keeley, BSc Manchester, CBiol, MSB
David Kelly, BSc Imperial College London, PhD Glasgow, ARCS (*Chemistry*)
David Kynes, BSc York (*Chemistry*)
Sean Lang, BEng Cranfield, MSc Cranfield, MA King's College London, MBA Open, CEng, FIMechE (*Physics*)
Ian Monro, GRSC Kingston (*Junior Science*)
*Hannah Peel, MA Cantab, MSc University College London, PGCE (*Biology and Ecology*)
Raymond Rhodes, BA Leeds (*Junior Science*)
Richard Singleton, BSc London (*Physics*)

Geography:
John Nanson, MA Cantab, PGCE Leeds (**Humanities, Professional Tutor*)
Abigail Plowden, BA West of England (*Geography)
James Hindson, PhD, BA Aberystwyth
Jeremy Long, BA Natal, MA De Montfort

History:
*David Reffell, BA Royal Holloway College London
Matthew Dennison, MA Oxon, MPhil Glasgow
Grainne Dennison, BA Durham

Art and History of Art:
*Janet Miller, BA Kingston, PGCE London
Ian Edwards, BA Sussex, MA Reading
Lizzie Langford, BA Central Saint Martins London
Jane Lingard, BA Reading, MA Courtauld Institute of Art, London

Religious Studies:
*Jill Blanchard, BA Open University
Sarah Hughes, MTheol St Andrews
Chantal Swain, BA Cardiff

Business Studies and Economics:
*Catherine Ashworth, BEd Wales (*Business Studies*)
Karen Booth, HND Lancashire (*Business Studies*)
Alison Matthews, BSc Wales, MSc London (*Economics*)

Food Technology:
*Jill Field, BEd Bristol
Sheena Bayton, Dip Ed Moray House College of Education, Edinburgh
Chloe Sheffield, BSc Sheffield Hallam, PGCE Manchester Metropolitan

Computing and ICT:
Sona Champion, MSc Manchester, BSc Loughborough
Ian Monro, GRSC Kingston
David Kelly, BSc Imperial College London, PhD Glasgow, ARCS
Ben Sutcliffe, BA Glyndwr

Physical Education:
*Kate Simlett-Groves, BCom Johannesburg, MSc Loughborough
Carike Barnardo, PGCE Sports Science, Cambridge ESOL, CELTA
Charlie Dilks, BA De Montfort
Jenny Sanderson, BEd Bedford College of Higher Education
Louise Lewin, BEd Bedford College of Higher Education
Simon Taylor, BA Derby
Taryn Abbassian, BA Dickinson College, Level 2 Qualified Lacrosse Coach
Hollie Harrington, BSc Birmingham (*Lacrosse Coach*)

Music:
*Helen Rayner, BMus Hons Bangor (*Director of Music*)
Carolyn Tilley, GRNCM, PPRNCM
Catrina Lapage, BMus Cardiff, MA Cardiff, ARCO
Amy Lott, BA Hons Bangor

Moreton First:
*Catherine Ford, MA, BSc Leicester (*Head of Moreton First*)
Grainne Dennison, BA Durham
Nicola Perry, BEd Crewe and Alsager College (*EYFS Manager*)
Janet Sheppard, Cert Ed Lady Spencer Churchill College Oxford
Mary Davies, BA Glyndwr
Ben Sutcliffe, BA Glyndwr
Ian Wood, BEd Keele
Alice Davies, BA Bristol
Chantal Swain, BA Cardiff
Jenny Eaton, HLTA, STAC Open University (*Learning Support*)
Stephanie Phillips (*Teaching Assistant*)
Karen Longland (*Teaching Assistant*)
Maggie Roberts, BA Wolverhampton (*Teaching Assistant*)
Jennifer Bromage BA Sweet Briar College, MA Manhattanville
Jenny Firkins, BA Bangor
Helen Ingoldby, BA Jt Hons Nottingham
Sharon Davies (*Moreton First Administrator*)

International Study Centre:
*Victoria Eastman, MA Swansea, PGCE, CELTA
Elyse Conlon, BA Hons Liverpool, EFL Prof Grad Dip Education Applied Linguistics, CELTA
Emma Pemberton, BA Hons Lincoln, TOEIC (*Head of Pastoral Care*)
John Davies, BSc, PhD Leicester (*Mathematics, Physics and Chemistry*)
Ruth Howlett, BSc Liverpool (*Mathematics*)
Delfino Taboada, CELTA (*EFL*)
Emma Taboada, BA Hons Bristol CELTA (*EFL*)
Ann Rincon, CELTA (*EFL*)
Morag Beattie, BA Hons London (*EFL*)
Helen Ingoldby, BA Joint Hons Nottingham (*EFL*)
Jeremy Long (*Houseparent*)
Helen Long (*Houseparent*)

Spoken English:
Merriel Halsall-Williams, BA, LGSM, ALAM North West School of Speech and Drama, FESB
Mags Jones

Tennis Coaches:
Alison McDonald, BSc Hons Northumbria, UKCC Level 5 LTA Master Coach

Swimming Coach:
Laura Jones, ASA Level 2 and NPLQ Lifeguard

Careers:
Rona McKechnie, BA and MA Hull
Anne Simpson, BA Joint Hons Oxon

Librarians:
Elspeth Nolan, BA Open University
Paula Forster, BA Manchester, Dip Library & IT Studies

Science Technicians:
Joan Stonier NVQ Level 3
Stephen Ferrington, BSc Open University, Dip Geoscience

ICT Technicians:
James Ryan
Gavin Woodcock

Health Centre:
School Medical Officers:
Jane Roberts, BA, MA, BMBCH, MRCP, DRCOG, MRCGP, DFFP
Elizabeth Thompson, MB ChB
School Nursing Sisters:
Anne Davies, RM, DN, Dip N, JP (*Sister in charge*)
Pam Hughes, RGN (*Sister*)
Katrina Cox, BNursing Adult Bangor (*Sister*)

House Staff (*Resident and non-resident*):

The Stables (*Years 7 and 8*):
Grainne Dennison (*Head of Prep School Boarding*)
Elaine Mason (*Housemistress*)
Carmel Byrne (*Assistant*)
Joyce Brown (*Assistant*)

Pilkington (*Years 9 and 10*):
Isobel Parry (*Housemistress*)
Frances Cummins (*Resident Assistant*)
Stephanie Phillips (*Assistant*)
Norma Hale (*Assistant*)

Gem (*Years 9 and 10*):
Patricia Fitton (*House Parent*)
Ian Fitton (*House Parent*)
Carike Barnardo (*Assistant Housemistress*)
Carolyn Tilley (*Resident Tutor*)
Sally Penrose (*Assistant*)
Gloria Wright (*Assistant*)

Lloyd-Williams (*Year 11*):
Charlie Dilks (*Housemistress*)
Sally Cheetham (*Resident Assistant*)
Lesley Williams (*Assistant*)

Rylands (*Year 12*):
Sarah Hughes (*Housemistress*)
Karen Davenport (*Assistant*)
Ann Rincon (*Assistant*)

Charlesworth (*Year 13*):
Caroline Lang (*Housemistress*)
Sean Lang (*Resident House Tutor*)
Taryn Abbassian (*Resident House Assistant*)
Julia Hughes (*House Assistant/Matron*)
Nilou Hughes (*Weekend House Assistant*)

Mitchell House (*ISC*):
Helen Long (*Houseparent*)
Jeremy Long (*Houseparent*)
Joan King (*Assistant*)

Moreton First Boarding:
Grainne Dennison (*Houseparent*)
Matthew Dennison (*Houseparent*)

Administration:

Bursary:
Ian Davies (*Financial Controller*)
Rebecca Watkinson (*Finance Office Manager*)
Louise Cobb (*Accounts Assistant*)
Suzanne Janes (*Accounts Assistant*)
Aidan Porter (*Financial Controller's Assistant*)

School:
Ruth Brown (*Principal's PA and Admissions*)

Victoria Stearns (*School Administrator*)
Heidi Gingell (*Transport Manager, Exam Assistant*)
Pat Willis (*School Receptionist*)
Shona Macdonald (*School Administration Assistant*)

Foundation and Marketing:
Katy Tanner (*Foundation and Development Director*)
Alexandra Hankinson (*Marketing Director*)
Richard Briggs (*Communications Development Manager*)
Melissa Evans (*Marketing Assistant*)

Business Development:
Anne Griffith (*Business Development Director*)
William Taylor (*Business Development Assistant*)
Robert Watkinson (*Facilities Manager*)
Gill Leigh-Ford (*International Recruitment Consultant*)
Michael Couch (*International Recruitment Consultant*)

Admission. Moreton First is the preparatory school of Moreton Hall, sharing not only its extensive facilities but also a commitment to nurture and celebrate the talents of each child. Moreton First takes girls and boys from Transition (age 3) to Year 6 and offers a unique start to their education, ensuring academic rigour goes hand in hand with encouragement to achieve success in all creative and sporting fields.

Girls are admitted to Moreton Hall, normally in September at age 11 and 13, either by Common Entrance or by the School's entrance examination which is held at the end of January each year. This examination requires no knowledge of foreign languages and is designed to test potential ability rather than factual recall. This examination can be taken by pupils at 10+, with supplementary papers at 12 and 13. Candidates from preparatory schools may enter through Common Entrance if they so choose at ages 11, 12 and 13. Sixth Form entrance is by current school report and interview, and numbers are limited. All applications should be addressed to the Principal.

Though predominantly boarding, day girls are welcomed. Boys may board from the age of 8–11.

Scholarships and Bursaries. A number of Academic scholarships worth up to 10% of fees will be awarded to pupils at ages 11+, 12+, 13+ and 16+. Scholarships for Music, Drama, Art and for outstanding sporting talent are also available. Students may apply for more than one scholarship. Means-tested bursaries may be awarded up to the value of 100% of fees. The new Bronwen Scholarship is available to girls entering the school in Years 5–8.

Fees per term (2014–2015). Boarders: £6,560 (Moreton First), £9,560 (Years 7 and 8), £10,100 (Years 9–13). Day pupils: £2,850–£4,015 (Moreton First), £7,695 (Years 7 and 8), £8,320 (Years 9–13).

Curriculum. Going well beyond the National Curriculum, some 20 subjects are available at GCSE, varying from traditional academic subjects such as Latin and the Sciences, to practical subjects such as Drama, Dance and Physical Education. Modern Languages available include French, German, Spanish, Mandarin Chinese and Russian. A Levels in History of Art, Social Biology, Business Studies and Theatre Studies extend the range of the curriculum. Information Technology is a compulsory subject up to Sixth Form, optional thereafter.

Examinations offered. GCSE, A Level, ABRSM, ESB (English Speaking Board). Over 95% of Upper Sixth go on to University.

Religious activities. Non-denominational. Weekday service, longer service on Sunday, visiting preacher.

Academic, Sporting and Extra-Curricular facilities. Moreton Hall is engaged in an ambitious development programme and has facilities of the highest quality designed to provide the right environment for the education of girls in the twenty-first century.

Younger girls are housed in the Stables building under the supervision of resident houseparents, assistants and matrons. The building is designed to create a family atmosphere with dormitories split into smaller units, close to common rooms, washrooms and staff accommodation.

As pupils progress up the school, the dormitories are gradually replaced by double and finally single study-bedrooms. The Sixth Form Houses provide single and double en-suite facilities. Here, within the structure of a boarding school, senior girls are given the necessary freedom to prepare for the next stage in their careers.

A Centenary Science Centre was completed in 2013 with a unique Medical Science Faculty. The Science Centre, Information Technology rooms and Art and Design Centre are housed within a short distance of the central classroom, careers and library complexes.

All classrooms, libraries and boarding houses are networked and all Sixth Formers have internet access from their study-bedrooms.

An exceptionally well-equipped Sports Centre comprising a sports hall and floodlit tennis courts along with a heated indoor swimming pool, nine-hole golf course, an all-weather surface, and playing fields are set in one hundred acres of beautiful parkland at the foot of the Berwyn hills. The school offers a wide range of sporting options including Lacrosse, Netball, Hockey, Cricket, Tennis and Athletics. Sailing and Riding are also popular.

The Musgrave Theatre, Outdoor Theatre and Music School stimulate theatrical and musical activities ranging from house plays, lunchtime shows and jazz evenings through to ambitious school plays and orchestral concerts. Great emphasis is placed on girls taking part in as wide a range of extra-curricular interests as possible.

The nationally acclaimed Moreton Enterprises offers the girls real business experience. Supervised by professional advisers but all run by the girls themselves, Moreton Enterprises consists of 7 retail businesses on site with a turnover of £50,000.

Old Moretonian Association. Katy Tanner, c/o Moreton Hall.

Charitable status. Moreton Hall Educational Trust Limited is a Registered Charity, number 528409. It exists to provide a high quality education for girls.

The Mount School
York

Dalton Terrace, York, North Yorkshire YO24 4DD

Tel: 01904 667500
            01904 232326
email: registrar@mountschoolyork.co.uk
website: www.mountschoolyork.co.uk
Twitter: @MountSchoolYork

Motto: Fidelis in Parvo

"The Mount is genuinely caring and brings the most potential out of its students. It is often mentioned that the School is a 'family'; the interaction between girls, from the top of the school through to the very first years, is endearing. Personally I like everything about The Mount. My daughter always had a sunny disposition but this has magnified ten times since moving here from London. She even likes getting up in the morning to go there – amazing for a teenager!" – A Current Parent.

2015 Good Schools Guide describes The Mount's pastoral care as "an absolute strength of the school".

"The strong Quaker ethos creates an environment in which everyone appreciates and values each other, fostering both independence and equality. The pupils thrive in this atmosphere of safety, confidence and trust." – ISI Report, 2012.

Committee of Management:
Clerk: Timothy Phillips

Trina Mawer	Greg Willmott
Aileen McLeish	Andrew Gardiner
Alice Unwin	Gwenan Sykes
Fiona Waddington	Katharine Rowntree
David Gray	Joanna Mahler
Luke Murphy	

Staff:

Principal: **Julie Lodrick**, BA Hons University College, Chichester, West Sussex, NPQH National College for School Leadership, Cert Professional Practice in Boarding Mgt BSA and Roehampton, MA Ed Mgt Open University, PGCE Kingston

Deputy Principal (Academic): Joanne Hayward, MA Cantab, PGCE Leeds

Head of Junior School: Rachel Capper, BEd Hons

Heads of Departments/Subjects:
English: Louise Williams, BA Hons Lancaster, PGCE Eltham College
Mathematics: Helen Mumby, BSc London, PGCE Durham
Modern Languages: Nicola Brunger, BA, PGCE
Latin, Greek and Classical Studies: Carron Downes, MA, PGCE
Science: Anthony Welbrock, BSc Hons Edinburgh
Religious Education: Linda Moore, BEd Hons Sussex, MA College of Ripon & York St John
History: Helen Snelson, BA Hons Oxon, MSc Hull, PGCE York
Geography: Carol Cook, BA Hons London, PGCE Newcastle upon Tyne
Art & Design: Sian Gabraitis, BA Hons Bristol, PGCE Cardiff
Design Technology: Rachel Milton, BA Hons, PGCE Coll of Ripon & York St John, MSc Huddersfield
Business Studies and IT: David Blamires, BA Hons Humberside, PGCE Leeds
Music: Derek Chivers, BA Hons York, DPhil Keele, PGCE Open University
Special Needs Coordinator, Learning Support (Dyslexia): Juliet Bleasdale, BA Hons Sheffield, PGCE Bath
Sociology & Psychology: Liz Williams, BA, BSc, MSc
Physical Education: Gillian Lindsay, BSc
Careers: Wendy A Thompson, CertEd Edge Hill College, Lancaster, CFPS Cambridge
English as an Additional Language: Jo Soden, MA York, BA Hons Bristol, PGCE York

Librarian: Patricia Ratcliffe, BA, PGCE

Housemistresses:
School House: Laura Rudd, BA, BEd
College House: Jo Atkinson, BA, MA

Health Centre: Cindy Magyar, SRN
Medical Officer: Dr Hazel Brown, BM, DRCOG

Junior School Teaching Staff:
Laura Glass, BA, QTS, EYP
Jan Wilson, BEd, MA
Kate Rainbow, BA, PGCE
James Newton, BA, PGCE
Victoria Smart, BA, QTS
Cheryl Snowden, BA, PGCE
Jill Harvey, BEd

Administrative Staff:
Bursar: Graeme Oliver
Finance Officer: Helen Lambeth
Registrar: Andrew Witherspoon, BEd
Principal's PA: Sandra Houston
Maintenance Manager: Ian Long, ACIOB, IOSH

Director of Marketing: Vanessa Charters, BA, MBA Hong Kong
Director of Foundation and Development: Kath Morrill, BSc

Age Range. Senior: Girls 11–18. Junior: Girls 2–11, Boys 2–7.

Numbers. 84 Boarding, including Weekly boarding, 203 Day.

Values. The Mount is the UK's only Quaker School for girls. Our School encourages everyone to:
- respect and value every individual
- have the freedom to flourish in a calm and caring community
- strive for personal excellence
- think and live adventurously
- make a positive contribution to our changing world.

Facilities. Set in sixteen acres of magnificent grounds a convenient ten-minute walk from York's historic city centre, The Mount has exceptional purpose-built facilities for Science, Art and Design, Music, Drama and Sport. With on-site pitches, tennis courts, our own 25-metre indoor pool, multi-purpose sports hall, gymnasium and outdoor Forest School, students enjoys a wide range of sporting activities and outdoor pursuits.

Organisation. After Year 6 at The Mount Junior School girls gain automatic entry to The Mount Senior School and transfer into Year 7. A number of Senior School events, such as the Inter-Form Music Afternoon and College I Pantomime, invite Year 5 and 6 pupils, easing their transition into the Senior School community. Boarding and day pupils mix well throughout the school, and flexible boarding arrangements cater for all family situations.

Curriculum. GCSE, AS and A Levels plus AQA BACC, incorporating Extended Project Qualification (EPQ). 20 AS/A Level subjects.

Sixth Form: Most sixth formers take 4 or 5 subjects at AS Level (mix of arts and sciences), 3 at A Level; in addition, some take AS and A Level General Studies.

Vocational: Work experience is available and encouraged in Year 11.

Special provision: Specialist learning support teacher and Qualified EAL provision.

Languages: French, German and Latin offered to GCSE, AS and A Level (French or German compulsory to GCSE); also GCSE Spanish in Sixth Form and clubs in other languages, e.g. Russian and Japanese. Regular visits to Europe; classical trips to Italy biennially.

ICT: computers with internet access (at all times) in computer suites and all departments; pupils have their own school email addresses; wireless networked throughout school; OCR Nationals in ICT offered.

Extra-Curricular. Girls can participate in their choice of 50 extra-curricular activities: Crafts (e.g. ceramics, textiles, photography); Dance; Languages (e.g. Spanish, Mandarin, Russian); Music (piano, brass, strings, wind and Associated Board examinations); Speech and Drama (LAMDA examinations); individual and team Sports (e.g. fencing, hockey, netball, riding, martial arts, ultimate frisbee).

Entrance. The Mount School Scholarship Examinations for Years 7 and 9 take place in January. The School can arrange for Entrance Examinations to be taken at other times of the year. College Scholarship Examinations take place in November.

Entry at age 11 and above (into Years 7–10): Girls sit our entrance exam and take papers in English, Mathematics and Verbal Reasoning (for entry to Years 7–9 only). The English paper comprises a reading comprehension exercise and a piece of writing; the Mathematics paper (one part to be completed with the use of a calculator and one without) includes a wide variety of questions. Year 10 candidates take papers in English and Mathematics only. Girls are invited to attend a Taster Day and meet the Principal. School references and the interview are given weight alongside exam performance.

Entry at 16+ (A Level study): Prospective entrants are invited for interview. There is no examination if the entrants are studying for GCSE or IGCSE. The offer of a place will usually be conditional upon gaining at least 6 GCSEs at Grade C or above and at least Grade B in the subjects the student wishes to pursue at A Level. School references and the interview are given weight alongside exam performance. Prospective pupils who are not studying for GCSE or IGCSE will be expected to take papers in English and Mathematics.

Scholarships and Bursaries. Academic and Music scholarships are available for Year 7 entry; also Academic, Music, Drama, Art, and Sport scholarships in Year 9 and College (Sixth Form). A Scholarship is awarded for the duration of a girl's school career at The Mount up to and including College (Sixth Form). The value of awards is 5% of the current day fee, to which a means-tested bursary may be added which can be worth up to 100% of fees. The York Scholarship is a full Scholarship, offered to the leading Year 7 candidate.

Members of the Society of Friends are assessed under the Joint Bursaries Scheme for Friends' Schools and according to need may be helped by other Friends' funds in addition to School funds.

Means-tested bursaries are also available for other candidates.

Fees per term (2014–2015). Senior School: Years 9–13: Full UK Boarders £8,729; Weekly Boarders £7,770; Day Pupils £5,515; Years 7–8: Full or Weekly Boarders £6,075, Day Pupils £5,407.

Additional charges are made for private lessons, craft materials, external examination fees, outside lectures and concerts. Parents not expected to buy textbooks. Further details about registration, offers of places and Awards may be obtained from the Registrar.

Junior School: Juniors (Years 3–6) £3,316; Infants (Years 1–2) £2,498; Reception £2,451; Pre-School: £49 per extended day (7.30 am to 6 pm). Government Nursery Vouchers are accepted in part payment.

The Junior School, for day children aged 2 to 11 years, shares the ethos of the Senior School, to encourage and develop the potential of the individual. There is a creative and stimulating learning environment which promotes the exploration of skills and the development of confidence. Academic standards are high and progress is carefully observed.

See The Mount Junior School entry in IAPS section.

Composition Fees Scheme. Parents are encouraged to consider paying School Fees by lump sum in advance. This can generate considerable reductions in the overall cost. The acceptance of a Composition Fee Payment is not a guarantee that a place can be offered at the appropriate time, but such payments are normally transferable between schools. Composition Fees may be accepted at any time prior to the probable date of entry and may be supplemented by additional payments either prior to or during the child's schooling. Further particulars are available from the Bursar.

Mount Old Scholars' Association. Hon Secretary: Susan Croft, via The Mount School, York.

Charitable status. The Mount School (York) is a Registered Charity, number 513646. It exists to provide education for girls from 2 to 18 and junior boys.

Newcastle High School for Girls
GDST

Senior School:
Eskdale Terrace, Jesmond, Newcastle-upon-Tyne NE2 4DS
Tel: 0191 281 1768
email: seniorschooloffice@ncl.gdst.net

Junior School:
Chapman House, Sandyford, Newcastle-upon-Tyne NE2 1TA
Tel: 0191 285 1956

website :   www.newcastlehigh.gdst.net
Twitter: @NewcastleHigh

Newcastle High School for Girls was launched in September 2014 following the merger of Central Newcastle High School and Newcastle Upon Tyne Church High School. It builds on the unique strengths of each of its founding schools, both of which were known equally for their academic excellence, pastoral care and support.

Newcastle High School for Girls is part of the GDST (Girls' Day School Trust). The GDST is the leading network of independent girls' schools in the UK. As a charity that owns and runs 24 schools and two academies, it reinvests all its income in its schools. For further information about the Trust, see p. xxi or visit www.gdst.net.

Chair of Local Governors: Mr P Buchan, BSc Hons, Dip Arch, RIBA, FRFA

***Headmistress*: Mrs H J French**, MA Oxon, MEd Newcastle, PGCE Durham, NPQH

Executive Adviser: Mrs J Gatenby, BA Hons, PGCE Durham

Deputy Head (Development and Wellbeing): Mr M Tippett, MA Oxon, PGCE Cantab, NPQH

Deputy Head (Teaching and Learning): Miss L Cook, BA Hons Lancaster, PGCE Durham, NPQH

Director of Sixth Form: Mrs H Harrison, BA Hons Huddersfield, PGCE Newcastle

Director of Finance and Operations: Mr J Crosby, MEng Nottingham, Adv Dip Durham, FCA

Head of Junior School: Miss A Charlton, BA Hons, PGCE Newcastle, NPQH

Deputy Head of Junior School: Mrs J Brown, BEd Hons Leeds Metropolitan

Pupil Numbers. 970: Senior School 670 (aged 11–18 years) of whom 200 are in the Sixth Form; Junior School 300 (aged 3–11 years).

Launched in September 2014, Newcastle High School for Girls has quickly established itself as a leading School in the North East and among one of the best in the country; not surprisingly so with the combined 250 years of experience brought from its two founding schools.

Newcastle High was formed by the merger of Central High and Church High and is one of the 26 schools of the Girls' Day School Trust, the UK's leading network of independent schools. Its mission is to deliver an outstanding, forward looking education, rooted in traditional values.

In keeping with its proud history, Newcastle High School for Girls is exciting and innovative. The ethos, environment and curriculum have all been designed to meet the demands of the 21st Century. It aims to develop outward looking and socially responsible girls who are equipped with the confidence and ability to be the person they want to be and to embrace the opportunities and challenges of adult life. At Newcastle High, girls excel academically, develop skills, build character and participate in a wide range of co-curricular and enrichment activities.

With academic rigour and excellence at its heart, the school curriculum benefits from cross-curricular planning and a focus on deep learning that spans the subject disciplines through open ended enquiry and independent research. Creativity flourishes across the whole curriculum and the pupils at the School are motivated and full of energy. There is outstanding provision for Sport, Music, Art, Dance and Drama and the girls have the opportunity to develop many new interests and skills through the varied co curricular-curricular programme.

The School strongly believes that one of the main reasons why girls succeed is its impressive pastoral care system underpinned by strong pupil teacher relationships and a supportive and caring school community.

The facilities across the whole School are excellent and all girls are able to take full advantage of them. Situated at Chapman House, Sandyford Park, Newcastle upon Tyne, the Junior School has undergone a major refurbishment to provide the very best learning environment for girls. Set in five acres of grounds, and including a John Dobson designed mansion, Chapman House offers a piece of the countryside right in the heart of the city centre. New classrooms have been furnished with excellent resources to support teaching and learning and the Early Years have direct access to a specific open-air learning environment. There is ample indoor and outdoor space to explore ideas, discover and think creatively. The grounds have recently been landscaped to include all-weather surfaces, outdoor classrooms, a story telling area, kitchen garden and bog garden – just some of the exciting features designed to bring learning to life.

The Senior School is based at Eskdale Terrace, Jesmond. Extensive redevelopment of the site in recent years has created a school with an uplifting atmosphere and excellent facilities. Attractive classrooms, up to the minute laboratories, modern Library, generous ICT provision (including laptops and ipads) and specialist centres for Art, Music, Modern Languages, Sport and the Sixth Form all provide the perfect learning environment. As part of its mission to create a 21st Century learning environment for the older girls, Newcastle High is planning the development of a new Senior School in Jesmond which it aims to move to in September 2016.

Curriculum. The Junior School follows an innovative and creative curriculum which is focused on extending the girls' learning by allowing them to explore topics and subjects in greater depth. It is enriched with Music Art, Drama and Dance to give the girls ample opportunity to express their creativity. Outdoor leaning is an important part of the curriculum and the Junior School is an accredited Forest School.

The Senior School curriculum is designed to provide girls with the skills, knowledge and understanding that they will need in the years to come. The curriculum is rich in the Arts and strong in Humanities, Sciences and Languages. Sport is for all. Breadth and depth of intellectual challenge is a strong feature. As well as subject specific lessons, the Newcastle High curriculum promotes a cross-curricular approach that enables girls to make more sense of their learning. Knowledge and skills in one subject area are used to reinforce learning in another.

In Sixth Form, intellectual challenge and a love of learning are at the centre and the girls can choose from a wide range of A Levels. In addition to their A Level studies, the girls take part in an enrichment programme designed to extend their studies and broaden their understanding. All girls take an Extended Project Qualification on a topic of their choice.

Admissions. Junior School: by assessment and interview.

Senior School: by entrance examination, interview and school report.

Sixth Form: by GCSE results, interview and school report.

Fees per term (2014–2015). Senior School £3,896, Junior School £3,004, Nursery £2,455.

The fees cover the regular curriculum, non-residential curriculum trips, school books, games and swimming but not optional extra subjects or school meals.

Bursaries. The GDST Bursaries Fund provides financial assistance in the Senior School to suitably qualified girls whose parents could not otherwise afford the fees to enter or remain in the School.

Charitable status. Newcastle High School for Girls is part of The Girls' Day School Trust, which is a Registered Charity, number 306983.

North London Collegiate School

Canons, Canons Drive, Edgware, Middlesex HA8 7RJ

Tel: Senior School: 020 8952 0912
            Junior School: 020 8952 1276
Fax: 020 8951 1391
email: office@nlcs.org.uk
website: www.nlcs.org.uk
Twitter: @NLCS1850
Facebook: /nlcs1850

North London Collegiate School has provided an outstanding education for girls since its foundation in 1850 by Frances Mary Buss.

North London Collegiate School is a unique school, a school that combines academic excellence with a vibrant extracurricular life, an international outlook, glorious facilities and a warm community. Since its founding over 160 years ago, the School has offered girls the finest available education.

We are proud of our tradition of producing independent, often pioneering, young women with the drive and confidence to make the most of opportunities and a difference in the world. That was the vision of the founder, Frances Mary Buss, in 1850, and it remains true of the school today. The School is steeped in tradition but has always helped to pioneer women's education and constantly looks to improve the education offered. That is why we have enjoyed the accolade of being named the leading Independent Secondary School of the Year twice in the last decade.

Examination success is only part of the picture. Art, music, drama, dance, sport, community service projects and over 30 clubs and societies create a vibrant atmosphere and help girls to flourish and enjoy their time at North London. Every girl matters and the pastoral care at the school ensures pupils feel supported and valued throughout their time here.

The Governing Body:
Mr T Suter, MA (*Chairman*)
Mr M Baughan
Mr K M Breslauer, BSc, MBA
Mr N Carrington, MA, CGDHA
Mrs S Carter, BSc Hons, Associate CFA
Mrs E Davis, BA, Dip ONL
Mr A Emmanuel, BSc, MD, FRCP, FRCPE
Mr A Fox, MA, MD, MSc, MB BS, DCH, FRCPCH, FHEA, Dip Allergy
Mrs C Froomberg, MA, FCMA, FRSA (*Treasurer*)
Mr S Jaffe, BSc Hons, FCA
Mr P Linthwaite, MA
Ms J Quinn, LLB Hons, BCL
Mr L Rabinowitz, QC, BA, LLB, BCL
Mrs E A Raperport, BA, FCT
Mr D Shah, BSc, ACA (*Chairman of Finance & Estates*)

Dr S Stoddart, PhD, FSA, MIFA (*University of Cambridge nominee*)

Bursar and Clerk to the Governors: Mr G Partington

Headmistress: Mrs Bernice McCabe, BA, MBA, FRSA

Deputy Head – Academic: Mr M Shoults, MA Oxon, PGCE Cantab

Deputy Head – Pastoral: Mrs A Wilson, BA Surrey, MA London

Deputy Head – External Affairs: Mr D Lewis, BA Monash, Australia

Director of Studies and Administration: Mr M Burke, BA Newcastle, MA Durham

Head of Junior School: Mrs J M Newman, BEd Cantab

Development Director: Mrs D Sobel

Head of Sixth Form: Ms D Picton, BA Oxon

Head of Upper School: Mrs M A Fotheringham, MA Oxon

Head of Middle School: Miss A Cocksworth, MA Cantab

Director of University Admissions: Mrs K Hedges, MA Cantab

SEN Advisor: Miss F Delany, BA Cantab

Director of IB: Mr R Paler, MA London

Careers Advisor: Mr H Linscott, BA London, MA London

Academic Tutor: Mr P Langdale, MA Oxon

Heads of Academic Departments:
Art and Design: Mr T Hardy, BA Middlesex
Classics: Mrs D O'Sullivan, BA Cantab
Economics: Mr S Foster, BA Oxon, MA Warwick
English: Mr D James-Williams, BA London, MA Open
Drama: Miss D Gibbs, BA Surrey
Geography: Miss M Wheatley, BSc London
History and Government & Politics: Mrs R Brown, BA, MSt Oxon
Information Technology: Dr A P Cripps, PhD London
Mathematics: Ms M Copin, MA Cantab
Modern Languages and Spanish: Mr R Sykes, BA Manchester
French: Miss K Bonnal, Maître Avignon
Italian: Mr P Langdale, MA Oxon
Russian: Mr N Massey, MRes London, BA Cantab
German: Dr J Baughan, BA Bristol, MLitt Bristol, PhD Exeter
Music: Mr L D Haigh, BMus Edin
Physical Education: Mrs L Cooper, BSc Loughborough
Religious Studies & Philosophy: Mr J Holt, BA Durham, MA Open
Science and Biology: Mr R McMillan, BSc Southampton
Chemistry: Dr T Thomas, BSc Durham, PhD Bristol
Physics: Mrs N Timoshina, MSc Moscow

PA to the Headmistress: Mrs G Conway

The pupil teacher ratio is 11:1

North London Collegiate School enjoys the beauty, space and safety of a parkland setting within London. The school provides an ambitious education for girls from a wide range of social backgrounds. The very best of academic teaching is coupled with the widest range of extra-curricular activities to help the pupils fulfil their potential.

There are approximately 1,080 girls at North London Collegiate School: 120 in the First School aged from 4+ to 7, 190 Juniors aged 7–11, and 770 in the Senior School aged 11–18, of whom 235 are in the Sixth Form.

North London Collegiate School draws on a rich tradition. It was founded by Miss Frances Mary Buss in 1850 to provide an education for girls that would equal that of boys and produced many of the first women graduates.

The school's academic record is outstanding. It has twice been named as *The Sunday Times* "Independent School of the Year" and *The Daily Telegraph* has described it as the most consistently successful academic girls' school in the country. Results in 2014 were again consistent with the school's academic profile. Almost 98% of A Levels were A*–B grades, with 87% of students gaining straight A* or A grades in all subjects taken.

For the ninth year running the International Baccalaureate results placed our students in the top 5% of candidates worldwide. Four girls gained the maximum score of 45 points, something achieved by approximately 150 students out of 60,000 internationally. 67% of entries in Higher Level subjects were graded 7, the equivalent of an A* grade at A Level.

21 students secured places at Oxford or Cambridge Universities. This reinforces the Sutton Trust's report published in 2011, which placed North London first nationally for the proportion of students gaining places to highly selective universities.

The GCSE 2014 results were equally outstanding, with 99% of grades at A*/A.

The facilities at the school are first class, designed to offer the girls every opportunity to develop themselves both academically and socially. These facilities include lacrosse pitches, all-weather tennis courts and a Sports Centre with indoor swimming pool and fitness centre.

The Performing Arts Centre, with a 350-seat auditorium, orchestra pit, galleries and rehearsal rooms, hosts over 35 productions a year. Music and Drama are strong, with opportunity for all to take part in productions, choirs and orchestras. The music programme includes challenging pieces for the most able, with such events as the National Chamber Group competition where the school has won the Founder's Trophy as the most successful competing school on several occasions. On the campus are a Music School, Drawing School and Design Technology Block, all situated around the lake, where waterlilies in the summer make it the ideal place to relax during the long lunch interval. Alternatively, girls may visit the beautifully light and spacious four-floor library.

There is an extensive school coach scheme.

Full details of Open Days and "Taster Afternoons" are on the school's website. Midweek visits can be arranged by appointment. Please contact 020 8952 0912 to arrange a visit.

Bursaries. Enabling bright girls from all backgrounds is central to the ethos of the school. Many bursaries are offered to girls who do well in the 11+ test and those entering the Sixth Form, whose parents can demonstrate financial need.

Scholarships. A number of Academic Scholarships, up to the value of 50% fees, are awarded each year based on the results of the 11+ and 16+ entrance examinations and interviews.

A number of Music Scholarships, up to the value of 25% fees, are awarded at 11+ each year.

Fees per term (2014–2015). Senior School: £5,875; Junior School: £4,966.

Charitable status. The North London Collegiate School is a Registered Charity, number 1115843. It exists to provide an academic education for girls.

Northampton High School
GDST

Newport Pagnell Road, Hardingstone, Northampton NN4 6UU
Tel: 01604 765765
                 01604 667979 Junior School

Fax: 01604 709418
email: nhsadmin@nhs.gdst.net
website: www.northamptonhigh.gdst.net
Twitter: @NorthamptonHigh
Facebook: /NorthamptonHigh
LinkedIn: /northampton-high-school-gdst

Northampton High School is part of the GDST (Girls' Day School Trust). The GDST is the leading network of independent girls' schools in the UK. As a charity that owns and runs 24 schools and two academies, it reinvests all its income in its schools. For further information about the Trust, see p. xxi or visit www.gdst.net.

Local Governing Body:
Dr S D Gregory (*Chairman*)
Mrs D Newham (*Vice Chairman*)
Dr M Blake
Mr S Chown
Mr J Church
Mr J Griffiths-Elsden
Mr J Lane
Ms V Miles

Staff:
* *Head of Department*
‡ *Holder of Teacher's Certificate or Diploma*
§ *Part-Time*

Senior Leadership Team:

Head Mistress: ‡Mrs S A Dixon, BA Hons Warwick (*English*)

Senior Deputy Head: ‡Mrs L Davies, BA Sheffield (*German, French*)

Director of Studies: Mr J Rickman, MBA Leicester, BA Hons Kent (*French*)

Head of Junior School: Mr R Urquhart, BSc Hons Brunel, QTS

Director of Finance and Operations: Mrs A Morris, BA Hons Manchester, ACMA

Development Director: Mrs J Fitzroy-Ezzy, BA Hons Nottingham

Senior School Teaching Staff:
‡Mr R Attwood, BSc Hons Leeds (**Biology*)
‡§Mrs S Barker, BA Open University (*Chemistry*)
§Mrs S Battams, BSc Hons Nottingham (*Physics*)
‡Mrs M Beacroft, BA Hons Northumbria (**Art*)
‡Mrs J Bell, BA Hons Leeds (*French, Spanish*)
‡Miss A Buxton, BA Hons Wolverhampton, PG Dip Lib Northumbria (*Librarian*)
‡Mrs J Cantwell, BSc Hons Durham (*Science, Chemistry, Director of Sixth Form*)
‡Dr N Carr, BSc, PhD Hull (*Chemistry*)
‡Miss A Chapman, BSc York (**Psychology*)
‡Mrs K Cowell, BEd Birmingham, MBA Leicester(**Mathematics*)
‡Mrs J Davis, CertEd Bradford (*Food, Textiles & Design Technology*)
‡Mr M Dezelu, BSc Hons Coventry (*Music*)
‡Mr A Donaldson, BA Hons Warwick (**History*)
‡Mrs A Down, BSc Hons London (*Mathematics*)
‡Mrs J Drew, BA Hons Cardiff (**Music*)
‡Mr J Earp, BA Hons Nottingham (**Geography*)
‡Mrs R Fenn, BA Hons, MA Cambridge, QTS (**Chemistry*)
‡Mrs C Fieldhouse, BA Hons, PG Dip, CertEd, MA Nottingham(**Drama*)
‡Mrs E Ford, Business Studies Dip Northampton (*Physical Education*)
‡Miss S Fraser, BA Hons De Montfort (*Physical Education*)

‡§Mrs G M Gray, BA Hons, MA London (*History*)
‡Mr F Gutierrez, MA Madrid, QTS (**Spanish*)
‡Mrs A Halstead, BA Hons London (*English*)
‡§Mrs K Harrison, BA Hons Lancaster (*Mathematics*)
‡Mrs D Hill, BA Hons Leeds (**Modern Languages, French*)
‡Mrs J Hackett, BEd De Montfort (**Physical Education*)
‡Mrs L Heimfeld, BA Hons Wales (*English*)
‡Mr J Holland, BA Leicester, MA Hertford, MSc Cambridge (*Classics*)
‡Mrs C Hopley, BA Hons Liverpool (*English*)
‡Mrs S L Holland, MA Oxford (**Classics*)
‡Miss C Hurst, BA Hons Brighton, QTS (*Physical Education*)
‡Mrs J James, BA Hons Belfast (*Sapnish*)
‡Mrs J Jennings, BEd Hons De Montfort (*Physical Education*)
‡Miss R Kneen, BSc Hons Exeter (*Geography, Deputy Director of Sixth Form*)
‡Mrs S Lamb, CertEd, MA De Montfort (**Theology and Philosophy*)
‡Mrs M Langhorn, BSc Hons Coventry (**Business Studies & Economics*)
‡Mr D Laubscher, BA South Africa (*Art*)
Mrs R Laubscher, BSc South Africa (*Mathematics*)
‡Mrs D MacArthur, CertEd Bath College of HE (*Design Technology*)
‡Mrs E Morgan, BA Hons Bristol (*Spanish*)
‡Ms S Margareto, BA, DipEd Macquarie, Sydney (*Special Education Needs*)
‡Mr J Martin, MA Belfast (**Computing and eLearning*)
‡Miss K Mason, BA Hons Newcastle (*Classics*)
‡Mrs S Moss, BEd Keele (**Design Technology*)
‡Mrs J Ogilvie, MEng Leeds and Pennsylvania State (*Mathematics*)
‡Miss C Parboteeah, MA Hons Leicester (*Chemistry*)
‡§Mrs E Pearson, BSc Hons, MSc Birmingham (*Biology*)
‡Mrs L Peck, BA Hons Oxford (*Theology and Philosophy*)
‡Mr I Riley, Grad Dip Leeds (*Music*)
‡Mrs I Tansley, BA Hons Kingston (**Economics and Business*)
‡Miss L Urban, BA Leeds (*Economics and Business*)
‡Mrs A Vizor, BA Hons Cambridge (*Physics*)
‡Mrs J Webb, BA QTS De Montfort (*Physical Education*)
‡Mr J Williams, BA Hons Manchester (**English*)

Junior School:
Deputy Head: Mrs J Purvey-Tyrer, BEd Hons Leeds

‡Mrs C Bleech, BSc Bristol
Miss N Brandon-Jones, BA Hons Wales
‡Mrs S Dadge, BA Hons Warwick
‡Mrs S Dale, BA Hons Bedfordshire
§Mrs A Davis, OGCE Ripon and York St John
‡Ms F Duck, BA Hons Cardiff
‡Mrs K Farrar, BEd Hons Northampton
‡Mrs K Fordham, BA Hons Exeter
‡Mrs L Green, BA Hons Manchester Polytechnic
‡Mrs H Greenbank, BEd Hons Plymouth
Miss S Mayes, BA Hons Surrey
‡Mrs C Miller, GTCL Trinity College of Music, London
‡Mrs E Shaw, BEd Hons Newman College, Birmingham
‡Mrs S Shaw, BA Hons Northampton
‡Mrs J Stock, BEd Hons Newland Park College
‡Miss N Taylor, BSc Hons Bristol
‡Mrs E Andrew, NVQ Level 4 Northampton College
‡Mrs S Waters, BA Northampton

Headmistress's Secretary: Mrs D Brown

Peripatetic Instrumental Staff:
Miss F Brannon, BMus Hons, MA (*Flute, Recorder*)
Mrs R Clennel, BMus Hons, PG Cert (*Violin and Viola*)
Mrs D Couling, LRSM, Dip ABRSM, CT ABRSM (*Piano*)
Miss J Coventry, LGSM Hons (*Brass*)

Miss J Hooper-Roe, ARCM, GBSM, ABSM (*Singing*)
Mrs C Jones, BMus Hons MTC (*Cello and Double bass*)
Ms V Murby, ARCM (*Violin and Viola*)
Mr S O'Gorman, BMus (*Clarinet and Saxophone*)
Ms J Partridge, AGSM, LRAM (*Piano, Jazz Piano and Theory*)
Mrs K Roberts, BMus Hons (*Oboe and Basoon*)
Ms R Sherry, BA Comb Hons, MA, LRAM (*Singing*)
Mr P Slane, AGSM, DipEd, ARCM (*Singing*)
Ms A Sparks, BA Hons (*Singing*)
Mr A Turner (*Violin/Viola*)
Mrs K Warcaba, BA Hons, MA (*Piano*)
Mr M Wild (*Drum Kit*)

Our school, which opened in 1878, is an independent day school for girls. We encourage our pupils to develop values which will provide them with a constant base in an ever-changing world and aim to respond to the individual needs of every girl. In 1992 we moved to a 27-acre site on the southern edge of town. Our extensive purpose-built accommodation includes 8 well-equipped laboratories, Art, Textiles, Information Technology, Music, Design Technology, Home Economics, Modern Languages and other specialist rooms for all curriculum areas. A large library with computer facilities for independent study is also provided.

The Junior School, which takes girls from the age of three, adjoins the main buildings and has its own hall, dining facilities, library, practical room and IT suite. At the age of 11 the majority of girls transfer to the Senior School.

There are splendid sports facilities on the site. These include a 25m swimming pool, all-weather pitch, a fitness suite, badminton, squash, netball and tennis courts and hockey pitches.

Girls are prepared for GCSE and Advanced Level examinations and go on to universities and other institutions of higher education.

Scholarships are offered at 11+, 13+ and in the Sixth Form. Means-tested bursaries are available in the Senior School.

Fees per term (2014–2015). Senior School (Years 7–13): £4,335. Junior School: £3,265 (Rec–Year 3), £3,341 (Years 4–6). Fees include Lunch.

Old Girls and Associates. *Secretary*: Mrs C White, Northampton High School, Newport Pagnell Road, Hardingstone, Northampton NN4 6UU.

Charitable status. Northampton High School is part of The Girls' Day School Trust, which is a Registered Charity, number 306983.

Northwood College for Girls
GDST

Maxwell Road, Northwood, Middlesex HA6 2YE

Tel:	01923 825446
Fax:	01923 836526
email:	admissions@nwc.gdst.net
	office@nwc.gdst.net
website:	www.northwoodcollege.gdst.net

Northwood College for Girls is part of the GDST (Girls' Day School Trust). The GDST is the leading network of independent girls' schools in the UK. As a charity that owns and runs 24 schools and two academies, it reinvests all its income in its schools to create modern and innovative learning environments. For further information about the Trust, see p. xxi or visit www.gdst.net.

Combining academic excellence with strong pastoral support and a focus on moral development we inspire, challenge and support each individual girl. The education of girls lies at the heart of our vision. Academic rigour and excellent exam preparation are a given – girls deserve the opportunity to grow as individuals, assume leadership roles, develop lasting friendships, take risks and excel in an environment that caters for their needs.

Governors:
Chair: Mr Geoff Hudson
Mr Ken Wild
Mr David Tidmarsh
Mr Tony Patteson
Mrs Catherine Pain
Professor Ashley Braganza
Mr John Orchard
Mrs Thavam Sivam
Mr Dipesh Patel
Ms Ana-Mari Hough
Mr Nhamo Shire

Head Mistress: Ms Jacqualyn Pain, MA, MA, MBA, NPQH

Director of Finance & Operations: Mr Tim Brown, BA, MBA

Deputy Head Mistress (*Academic*): Ms Claire Adby, BSc Hons, PGCE

Deputy Head Mistress (*Learning Innovation, E-Learning and Staff Development*): Ms Jane Jackman, BA Hons, PGCE, MBA

Director of Marketing and Development: Ms Claudine Moyle

Deputy Head Mistress (*Pastoral Development and Well-Being*): Mrs Elizabeth Skelton, MA, DipEd, NPQH

Director of Sixth Form: Mrs Jenny Smart, BA Hons, PGCE

Head Mistress Junior School: Mrs Hina Thaker, BA Hons, PGCE

Heads of Faculty:
Performing, Creative Arts & Design: Mrs Leanne Brown, BSc Hons, PGCE
Maths, Science & IT: Miss Caroline Hinchliffe, MA, PGCE
English & Humanities: Miss Natasha Shirman, BA Hons, PGCE
Learning Outside the Classroom/Co-curriculum: Miss Jo Simpson, BA Hons
Learning Enrichment & Personal Development: Mrs Tara Smith, BA Hons, MA, PGCE

Registrars:
Mrs Jemma Davidson
Mrs Jane Smith

Foundation. An independent day school for girls, Northwood College for Girls was founded in 1878 as one of the first girls' schools in London and now educates 926 girls aged 3 to 18 years.

Ethos. Our aim is to raise young women who know their own minds and are creative and flexible thinkers, as well as being able to achieve outstanding exam results.

We are academically selective, but not narrowly exclusive. We value girls for more than simple academic performance, because our unique approach to advanced thinking skills means that we can develop, stretch and challenge every single one of them. We think that makes for an interesting and vibrant school community – and it's what makes Northwood College for Girls special.

Thinking Skills. Our approach to thinking skills is another one of our defining characteristics. It sets Northwood College for Girls apart, and gives our girls an edge in the way they approach any task or challenge. Through the programme, we ensure our girls start to understand and develop the way they think from the day they join Nursery through to the end of the Sixth Form. Over the years, they build up their reasoning skills, improve their creativity and acquire strategies for tackling complex problems and decisions. It gives them a life skill that will be as useful at university and in the workplace as it is at school.

Location. The school is 14 miles from Central London and a 5 minute walk from Northwood tube station on the Metropolitan Line. There are several good local bus services and 6 different supervised school coach routes.

Single Site. All parts of the school share a single site, divided into distinct areas. The Junior School occupies its own self-contained buildings and our youngest girls have a purpose-built Early Years Centre. (*See also Junior School entry in IAPS section.*)

Facilities. We have enviable facilities for all subject areas in both the Junior and Senior Schools. Highlights include three art rooms, ten science laboratories, four ICT Suites and specialist centres for Technology and Modern Languages. We also have a fabulous Performing Arts Centre, with sophisticated sound-recording and music technology suites.

Sports facilities include a sports hall and 25-metre six-lane indoor swimming pool, as well as three hard tennis/netball courts, a hockey/rounders pitch and an all-weather pitch.

Examinations. Pupils are prepared for the General Certificate of Secondary Education (GCSEs), for AS and A2 Levels and for University Entrance.

Curriculum. We offer all National Curriculum subjects. In addition, French is taught from Year 3, Spanish from Reception, German from Year 7, and Latin from Year 4. Drama is taught throughout the school. A very wide range of A Level subjects is available in the Sixth Form, including Psychology, Economics, Politics, and Music Technology.

Music and Drama are real strengths at Northwood College for Girls with a fantastic range of opportunities for young musicians and budding thespians. The school has a wide range of orchestras, bands and choirs and we hold concerts each term, as well as music competitions and fully staged musical productions. Instrumental tuition is extensive and girls are prepared for the Associated Board examinations.

There is one major school play or musical every year in both Junior and Senior Schools that is always a highlight in the school calendar and often elicits rave reviews in the local papers. A number of smaller productions take place year round and girls may take individual drama lessons with visiting teachers.

Physical Education. We recognise the importance of encouraging girls to stay physically fit and active. Trained staff teach a wide variety of sports such as Hockey, Netball and Gymnastics during the winter months and Tennis, Rounders, and Athletics in the summer. Swimming is taken all year round and senior girls are able to explore other sports such as Golf, Self-Defence and Fitness Training.

Entry Requirements. Entry to the College is by examination and interview, except for Nursery, which uses a play-based assessment. At 11+ we use the North London Girls Schools' Consortium exam. Entry to the Sixth Form is by GCSE results and interview.

Scholarships and Bursaries. For details, please contact the Admissions Office.

Fees per term (2014–2015). Sixth Form £4,982; Senior School: Years 7–11 £4,982–£5,022; Junior School: Years 3–6 £4,139–£4,146, Reception–Year 2 £3,469–£3,483, Nursery (full-time) £3,107. Fees include lunch, loan of text books, stationery and certain school trips.

Charitable status. Northwood College for Girls is part of The Girls' Day School Trust, which is a Registered Charity, number 306983.

Norwich High School
GDST

95 Newmarket Road, Norwich, Norfolk NR2 2HU
Tel: 01603 453265
Fax: 01603 259891
email: admissions@nor.gdst.net
website: www.norwichhigh.gdst.net

Founded 1875.

Norwich High School is part of the GDST (Girls' Day School Trust). The GDST is the leading network of independent girls' schools in the UK. As a charity that owns and runs 24 schools and two academies, it reinvests all its income in its schools. For further information about the Trust, see p. xxi or visit www.gdst.net.

Additional information about the school may be found on the school's website and a detailed prospectus is available from the school.

School Governors:
Chairman: Mrs R Randle, LLB Hons

Headmaster: **Mr J J Morrow**, MA Oxon, MA Wake Forest, North Carolina

Senior Deputy Head: Mr S D Kavanagh, BA Leicester, NPQH

Deputy Head (*Pastoral*): Mrs H P Dolding, BEd De Montfort

Director of Studies: Miss P J Dunn, MA Oxon, MA Essex

Head of Junior School: Mrs J A Green, BSocSc Cape Town, NPQH

Director of Communications and Admissions: Mrs T R Hewett, BEd Ripon & York St John

Director of Finance and Operations: Mrs J C Thompson, ADSBM

Registrar: Miss A Ready

Number of pupils. Senior School: about 500, aged 11–18 years, of whom about 140 are in the sixth form. Junior School: about 200, aged 3–10 years.

Norwich High School draws its pupils in almost equal numbers from the city of Norwich and the county of Norfolk. It stands in 13 acres of grounds on the main Newmarket Road, a mile-and-a-half from the city centre. The main buildings are attached to a distinguished Regency house, built in 1820. In addition, there is a junior school with many specialist rooms, a recently extended sixth form centre, music school, spacious sports hall, 25m indoor heated pool and a performing arts centre. All the playing fields are around the school and a wide range of indoor and outdoor physical activities is offered, including netball, hockey, lacrosse, athletics, tennis, rounders, badminton, gymnastics and dance. The school holds the International Schools' Award, the Sportsmark Gold Award for its sporting achievements and Artsmark for creative subjects.

The school is a caring community and parent-friendly. We are open early for breakfast and late for tea. Girls may use the ICT and library facilities after school in the senior school; the junior school has its own after-school club. There is a minibus service from Norwich Railway Station before and after school.

Admission. All girls are assessed prior to entry. The normal ages of admission are 3, 7, 11 and 16. Occasional vacancies may occur at other ages.

Curriculum. The school has always been proud to provide a broad and rich education, preparing girls for admission to universities, professions, commerce and industry. A wide range of subjects is available, currently 25 at A Level and 22 at GCSE.

Information systems. A computer network is shared by all departments, including the laboratories, library, all teaching rooms, two computerised language laboratories, the sixth form IT suite as well as the two senior and two junior IT suites. All girls work towards the European Computer Driving Licence qualification in Years 8–9.

Careers education and advice. A carefully planned Careers Information Education and Guidance programme commences in Year 7. Virtually all sixth formers continue on to higher education and the school ensures that they have received comprehensive guidance and preparation from their tutors, the Head of Sixth Form, the careers department and outside speakers and experts from a higher education background and the world of work.

Co-curricular Activities. These are extensive, for infants through to seniors. Music, Sport and Drama are all strong features of the school. Girls also participate in both the Duke of Edinburgh's Award and Young Enterprise schemes, rowing, equestrian, debating and chess clubs, Amnesty International, Christian Union, fencing and life saving, and over 20 other clubs and societies.

Many excellent residential and day trips are arranged each year, by various departments. These are finely tuned to the curriculum and cover a full range of activities.

Fees per term (2014–2015). Senior School £4,119, Junior School £3,101, Nursery £2,578.

The fees cover the regular curriculum, school books, stationery and other materials, games fixtures and swimming lessons, but not optional extra subjects or school meals. The fees for extra subjects, including individual music tuition, are shown in the prospectus.

Financial Assistance. The GDST has made available to the school a substantial number of scholarships and bursaries.

Bursaries are available on or after entry to the senior school and applications should be made to the Head in cases of financial need. All requests are considered in confidence. Bursaries are means tested and are intended to ensure the school remains accessible to bright girls who would profit from a GDST education, but who would be unable to enter the school without financial assistance.

Various **Scholarships**, including music scholarships, are available to internal or external candidates for entry at 11+ or to the sixth form.

Charitable status. Norwich High School is part of The Girls' Day School Trust, which is a Registered Charity, number 306983.

Notre Dame School

Burwood House, Cobham, Surrey KT11 1HA
Tel: 01932 869990
email: registrar@notredame.co.uk
website: www.notredame.co.uk
Twitter: @NotreDameCobham
Facebook: /notredamecobham

Set in 17 acres of beautiful parkland in Cobham, Notre Dame School nestles in a picturesque 18th century mansion beside the River Mole. Despite the tranquil setting Notre Dame School is a hive of activity, with approaching a thousand children and teachers working hard in the important business of education. The school has an enviable reputation for the highest academic standards underpinned by over 400 years of international educational tradition in 30 countries. In 2014 our A Level students gained the highest percentage of A*–B grades (84%) in over ten years and girls are going on to study at prestigious Russell Group universities in a wide range of disciplines. At GCSE over half the grades

awarded were A and A*. Twin aims of academic success and self-confidence create rounded, compassionate, highly qualified and wise young women. Past pupils proliferate the professional sphere, many of whom enthusiastically retain links to Notre Dame.

Governors:
Mr Gerald Russell (*Chair of Governors*)
Sr Ernestine Velarde ODN
Sr Anne Gill ODN
Fr Mervyn Williams SDB (*Chair of Finance Committee*)
Sr Inmaculada Naranjo Cruces ODN
Sr Maria Quinn ODN (*Chair of Lestonnac Committee*)
Mrs Wanda Nash (*Chair of Education Committee*)
Mrs Mary-Claire Travers (*Health & Safety Committee*)
Mrs Susan Bailes (*Education Committee*)

Executive Team:

Principal: **Mr David Plummer**, BEd Hons, Dip HE, FRSA, IAPS

Head Teacher (*Senior School*): Mrs Anna King, MEd, MA Cantab, PGCE
Head Teacher (*Prep School*): Ms Merinda D'Aprano, BEd Hons, MA, CTC, FRSA, ISI Team Inspector
Director of Finance: Mrs Tracy Jones, BComm, ACA

Senior Leadership Team:
Executive Team (*as above*)
Assistant Head – Curriculum: Ms Sarah Badger, BSc Hons, PGCE
Assistant Head – Teaching and Learning: Mr Michael Coackley, BA Hons, PGCE
Assistant Head – Sixth Form: Miss Janine Harber, BA Hons PGCE
Assistant Head – Pastoral: Mrs Jan Slade, BA Hons, PGCE
Assistant Head of Prep: Mrs Helen Evans, Cert Ed
Head of Pre-Prep: Mrs Sally Palmer, Cert Ed
Director of Studies (*Prep*): Mrs Laura Wood, BA Hons, PGCE
Estates Manager: Mr Anthony Madigan

Chaplaincy Team:
Sister Patricia Grady ODN
Miss Melanie Allen, BA Hons, PGCE
Mrs Colleen Peoples, BMusEd Hons

Pastoral:
Assistant Head – Pastoral: Mrs Jan Slade, BA Hons, PGCE
Year 7: [Miss Sophie Dudgeon, BEd Hons]
Acting Head of Year 7: Mrs Mary Turner, BA Hons, PGCE
Year 8: Mr Kim McClenaghan, BA Hons MSc
Year 9: Mrs Candice Chislett, BA, HDE
Year 10: Mrs Anita Ingram, BSc, PGCE
Year 11: Mrs Ellie Ha, BA Hons, PGCE
Sixth Form: Miss Janine Harber, BA Hons, PGCE

Senior School Teaching Staff:

Art:
Mrs Su Avizius, BA Hons
Mrs Deborah Howorth, BA, PGCE

Design and Technology:
Mrs Janine Sankey, BA, BTEC

Drama:
Miss Christina Graham, BA Hons, PGCE
Mr Matthew Rowlands-Roberts, BA Hons
Mrs Sherna Treherne, LAMDA

Economics/Business Studies:
Mrs Karen Franco, BA, PGCE

English:
Mrs Christine Johnson, BA Hons
Mrs Candice Chislett, BA, HDE
Ms Bianca Hendicott, BA Hons, MSc

Mr Kim McClenaghan, BA Hons, MSc
Mrs Mary Turner, BA Hons, PGCE, Cert Counselling
  Skills
Mrs Lex Franklin, BSc Hons, PGCE

Food and Nutrition:
Ms Ruth Macintyre, BA Hons PGCE

Geography:
Mr Brendan Conway, MA, BSc Hons, PGCE
Mrs Andrea Griffiths, BA Hons
Miss Janine Harber, BA Hons PGCE

History, Classical Civilisation, Politics, Sociology:
Mrs Ellie Ha, BA Hons, PGCE
Miss Lucy Evans, BA Joint Hons, PGCE
Mr Michael Coackley, BA Hons, PGCE
Miss Janine Harber, BA Hons PGCE
Mrs Anna King, MEd, MA, PGCE

Information Technology:
Mrs Catherine Archer, MSc, BA Hons, PGCE

MFL:
Miss Christèle Claveau, Tours University, PGCE
Mrs Marjorie Clifton, MA Hons, PGCE, Dip CIM
Mrs Juliana Costa-Veysey, BA Hons, MA, PGCE
Mrs Maria Edwards, BA Hons, TEFL
Mrs Marie-Claire McGreevy, BA Hons, MA, PGCE
  (*maternity leave*)
Mrs Anne McVay, BA Hons, PGCE
Mrs Liz Davey, BA Hons, PGCE

Mathematics:
Mrs Sarah Breame, BSc Hons, PGCE
Ms Sarah Badger, BSc Hons, PGCE
Mrs Anita Ingram, BSc, PGCE
Mrs Alison Paige, BA Hons, PGCE
Mr Ben Sin, MA Hons, PGCE
Mrs Helen Brittain, BSc Hons, PGCE

Music:
Dr Robin Fenton, MMus Hons, BMusic, PGCE, PhD
Mrs Julie Shaw, BA Hons, PGCE
Mr Paul Clifford, Dip Sound Recording Eng (*Music
  Technology*)
Mr Matthew Abrams, BMus Hons (*Music Administrator*)

Physical Education:
Mrs Heather Marsh, BA Hons, PGCE
Miss Sophie Dudgeon, BEd Hons
Mrs Clare Khan, BSc Hons, PGCE
Miss Rebecca Hooker, BSc Hons, PGCE

Psychology:
Mrs Candice Chislett, BA, HDE
Mrs Sabrina Siddiq, BSc, PGCE (*maternity leave*)
Ms Lex Franklin, BSc Hons PGCE

Science:
Miss Anushka Ponniah, MA, BSc Hons, PGCE
Mrs Rachael Bantin, BA Hons, MA, PGCE (*maternity
  leave*)
Dr Heather Prideaux-King, BSc Hons, PGCE, PhD
Mrs Ruth Levings, BSc Hons, PGCE
Ms Carmel O'Keeffe, BSc, HDipEd
Mrs Sabrina Siddiq, BSc Hons, PGCE (*maternity leave*)
Mrs Jan Slade, BA Hons, PGCE
Mr Luke Howse, MPhys Hons, PGCE

Theology:
Miss Melanie Allen, BA Hons, PGCE
Miss Lucy Evans, BA Joint Hons, PGCE
Mrs Sally Carter-Esdale, BA Hons PGCE

Technicians:
Science:
Mrs Vanessa Catalano
Mrs Judy Matkin

Art and D&T:
Ms Gillian Goldfarb
Mrs Rosie Rees

Examinations Officer: Mrs Anita Ingram, BSc, PGCE
Librarian: Mrs Pam Thomas, Chartered Librarian

Preparatory School and Nursery Teaching Staff:
Pastoral Director: Mrs Helen Evans, Cert Ed
Director of Studies: Mrs Laura Wood, BA Hons, PGCE
Head of Pre-Preparatory: Miss Sally Palmer, Cert Ed
BlueBelles Nursery Team Leader: Ms Melanie Hookway,
  BA Hons, EYPS
Art Juniors: Mrs Tracy Smith, BA Hons
Art Pre-Prep: Miss Geraldine Deen, BA Hons, QTS
Drama: Ms Lucy Fletcher
English: Mrs Clare Barber, BSc Hons, PGCE
Humanities (TASK): Mrs Carole West, BA Hons, PGCE
Information Technology: Mrs Louise Plummer, BSc Hons,
  Dip M, PGCE, Cert IT
MFL: Mrs Nerea MacDonald, BA, PGCE
Mathematics: Miss Caroline Niven, BA Hons, QTS
Music:
Mrs Julie Shaw, BA Hons PGCE
Mr Matthew Abrams, BMus Hons (*Music Administrator*)
Physical Education: Miss Terry-Lee Scholtz, BA Hons,
  QTS
Swimming: Mrs Elaine Jones, IOS, RSA
Science Juniors: Mrs Caroline Singleton, BSc, PGCE, CTC
Science Pre-Prep: Mrs Rachel Hunt, BA Hons, QTS

Form and Subject Teachers:
Ms Jenn Caverhill, BA, PGCE
Mrs Rachel Hunt, BA Hons, QTS
Mrs Irene May, BA Hons, Dip Ed, CEPC
Mrs Jane Pollard, BEd, CTC
Mr Matthew Power, BA Hons, PGCE
Mrs Caroline Singleton, BSc, PGCE, CTC
Mrs Stephanie Singleton, BA, MA, QTS
Mrs Laura Wood, BA Hons, PGCE
Mrs Christiana Wilcox, Cert Ed, CTC
Dance: Mrs Rachel Thomas, RAD
LAMDA: Mrs Collette Wighton, Dip Ed, LTCL

Teaching Assistants:
Mrs Tracy Davies, BSc Hons, Cache Level 3 Childcare and
  Education
Mrs Virginia Martin, City & Guilds TA Cert DPP
Miss Kirsty Morton, BTEC, Edexcel Level 3 Early
  Learning and Childcare

Nursery Teachers:
Mrs Celia Cheadle, NNEB
Mrs Caroline Moffatt, NNEB
Mrs Louise Roberts, NVQ3
Miss Karen Stephens, NNEB

Nursery Assistants:
Mrs Tracy Ambidge
Mrs Antonella Callari, BA Hons
Mrs Eleonora Ferguson
Miss Rachel Martin
Mrs Marzena Wajnert, NVQ6
Mrs Pauline Irving
Miss Tara Nicholls

Librarian: Mrs Anne Thompson, BSc Hons

School Support Services:
Aftercare Supervisor: Sister Maria Quinn ODN
Bursary:
Mrs Tracy Jones, BComm, ACA
Mrs Alison Angol
Finance:
Mrs Maxine Burgess
Mrs Beckie Purkiss
Mr D Munson, BSc Hons, ICAEW

Human Resources: Mrs Paula Clifton, MCIPD
Estates Department: Mr Anthony Madigan
Maintenance:
Mr A Fletcher
Mr C Green
Grounds:
Mr R Nicholls
Mr R Johnson
Caretaker: Mr L Borg
ICT Department:
Mr David Colpus, BSc, PGCE
Mr Lawrence Hepworth, BSc
Mrs Judy Gillett, LRQA
Mr Luke Howse, MPhys Hons, PGCE
Learning Support:
Mrs F Watts, BA, PGCE, RSA, OCR, Dip PS
Mrs Kate St John, BA Hons
Mrs Samantha Rice, NVQ2 LSA
Mrs Helen Brittain, BSc Hons, PGCE
Mrs Catherine Bremner, BSc Hons, OCR
Mrs Sarah English, BSc Hons, OCR
Mrs Rowan Johnson, BA Hons, PGCE, TEFL, NLP Master Practioner, MBTI Practioner Cert
Mrs Lynda Shore, BSc Hons, MSc, C&G TCert Adult Education
Mrs Sue Duckworth, Cert TESOL, Hornsby Dip SpLD, Dys Inst Mathematics Prog
Marketing: Mrs Louise Plummer, BSc Hons, Dip M, PGCE, Cert IT
Registrar: Miss Anna Morgan
School Nurse:
Mrs Helen Skinner RGN
Ms Susan Bradley
School Visits Coordinator: Mrs Carole West, BA Hons, PGCE
Support Services:
PA to Principal; Mrs C Geary
PA to Heads: Mrs M Hart
School Secretary/Administrators:
Mrs N Hallala School
Mrs J Russell
Mrs J Clay
Theatre Manager: Ms S Gilhespie, BA Hons

Notre Dame School is an independent Roman Catholic day school for approximately 700 girls aged 2–18. There are 350 girls in the Senior School, 300 girls in the Prep School and 50 girls & boys in the Nursery. Set in 17 acres of beautiful, rural parkland, our school is part of a worldwide educational organisation, founded in Bordeaux in the 17th century by Saint Jeanne de Lestonnac. The Company of Mary Our Lady is the oldest recognised educational order, devoted to the teaching of girls and a belief in the unique contribution they make to society. We welcome families, of all faiths, who wish their daughters to grow spiritually, academically and socially in a dynamic, challenging yet caring environment.

Our objective is to give every girl a balanced perspective, based on motivation, achievement, enjoyment and high personal expectations. We recognise and nurture strengths, identify and resolve weaknesses, and encourage individuality and independence.

From their first day in the Senior School, well-motivated girls are challenged by a wide-ranging curriculum, delivered by highly qualified subject specialists. Enthusiasm is the hallmark of lessons at Notre Dame, whether for science or arts subjects, technology, humanities or mathematics. Confidence is fostered by small teaching groups, so that academic rigour can be encouraged and enjoyed by all.

We give as much focus to sport, art, music, design and drama as we do to science, languages, maths, the humanities and English, and as we do to leadership opportunities, community service, supporting others and building confidence.

It is our mission to recognise and nurture individual potential in all areas of endeavour. Inherent in all we do is our ethos; that we are all important, special, and valued. We are a community, and we are, together, accompanying our young women in their efforts to build their lives for today and tomorrow.

By providing opportunities for pupils to grow intellectually, spiritually and socially, Notre Dame aims to enhance talents, develop interests and enable the fulfilment of ambitions. It is our firm belief that by respecting the best traditions of the past and meeting the rigorous requirements of the modern world through the provision of extensive, high-quality facilities and effective teaching and learning, we will prepare young women for their role as responsible citizens of the wider world.

Sixth Form. Notre Dame Sixth Form is superb: an exciting community where exam results are excellent, facilities are modern and the culture of opportunity and responsibility thrives. It is a vibrant learning environment with an exciting range of extra-curricular opportunities, all of which are designed to complement academic study.

Girls who make the decision to join Notre Dame Sixth Form can expect to leave us as independent learners, and active members of the community, confident in the pursuit of their chosen goals. Whether the girls leave us for university, further education or employment, they will be empowered with choices and will be able to fulfil any role with purpose, direction and a sense of fun.

Developments. Notre Dame has embarked on a multi-million pound investment programme in recent years, not only in attracting top-quality teaching staff, but also in capital expenditure to ensure that the school keeps well ahead of the demands of a thoroughly modern education programme. Our pupils are fully prepared to go out into the world and able to take their place in society, thanks to the opportunities and facilities they enjoyed during their treasured, formative years at Notre Dame. In recent years, this investment programme has seen the completion of:

- Fantastic Multi-Space Learning Resources Centre
- Senior School Library and Networked IT Suites
- Fully Equipped Six-lab Science Block
- Self-Contained BlueBelles Nursery
- Complete Classroom Refurbishment
- Professionally Equipped 380-Seat Theatre
- Specialist Dance and Drama Studios
- 25m Indoor Swimming Pool
- Forest School and Adventure Tree House
- Dining Hub and Coffee Bar
- Dedicated Sixth Form Centre
- All-Weather Sports Facilities

Transport: We run a comprehensive selection of coach and minibus routes covering all the local area along with routes on the A3 from/to Guildford, Wimbledon and Putney, and can offer flexible single/return journeys. Private coaches from: Barnes, Fulwell, Mortlake, Putney Bridge, Putney Heath, Richmond, Sheen, Teddington, Twickenham, Wandsworth, Wimbledon and all over Surrey.

Admission. Admission to the Senior School is normally at 11+, although girls may be admitted at other ages subject to an entrance examination and the availability of places. Academic scholarships are awarded at 11+ based on the entrance examination. Scholarships are also awarded to girls entering the Sixth Form. A number of means-tested assisted places are available on entry to the school. Short-term bursaries may be made available to assist parents in times of personal financial hardship. Approximately half our intake at 11+ comes from Notre Dame Prep.

Preparatory School. For further information about the Prep School, please see entry in IAPS section.

Fees per term (2014–2015). Senior School £4,875; Prep School £1,035–£3,995.

Charitable status. Notre Dame School Cobham is a Registered Charity, number 1081875. It exists to provide education for girls.

Notting Hill and Ealing High School

GDST

2 Cleveland Road, Ealing, London W13 8AX
Tel: 020 8799 8400
Fax: 020 8810 6891
email: enquiries@nhehs.gdst.net
website: www.nhehs.gdst.net

Founded 1873.

Notting Hill and Ealing High School is part of the GDST (Girls' Day School Trust). The GDST is the leading network of independent girls' schools in the UK. As a charity that owns and runs 24 schools and two academies, it reinvests all its income in its schools. For further information about the Trust, see p. xxi or visit www.gdst.net.

An academically selective, independent day school for girls aged 4 to 18. Separately housed and run Junior Department (ages 4+–11) and Senior Department (ages 11+–18) on the same site.

Chairman of Local Governing Board: Mr Julian Simmonds BA Hons

Head: **Ms Lucinda Hunt**, BSc Hons London, ARCS

Deputy Head – Pastoral: Ms Sarah Davies, BA Hons, PGCE
Deputy Head – Academic: Mrs Olivera Raraty, BA Hons, PGCE

Head of Junior Department: Mrs Silvana Silva, BEd Hons

History and Ethos. This is a school with a long tradition of academic excellence and creativity within an exceptionally warm and supportive environment. Notting Hill and Ealing girls are well grounded, confident and independent. They are proud of their school and value kindness and laughter, fun and friendship. This is a place where tolerance and mutual respect are nurtured; where you can be yourself. With a wide variety of activities and opportunities, and a strong emphasis on charitable giving, everyone can enjoy being part of a vibrant community and express their passion for learning, and for life.

Pupils and Location. Approximately 900 pupils. 590 in the Senior School (153 in the Sixth Form) and 310 in the Junior Department. Transport links are excellent (Ealing Broadway station is nearby and several buses stop outside the school). Girls come from Ealing and all over west London.

Pastoral Care. The system of pastoral care is overseen by the Deputy Head – Pastoral working through the Heads of Year and Form Tutors. The Head also takes a personal interest in all pupils. The result is a well structured system that is sufficiently flexible to support every girl and to ensure that she is treated as a whole person with individual strengths and needs. In the Sixth Form the tutor team is led by the Head of Sixth Form and her deputy.

Curriculum. Throughout the Junior and Senior Schools our curriculum is broad and balanced and encourages independence of learning and thought. In Years 7–9 everyone follows courses in English, History, Geography, Mathematics, Physics, Chemistry, Biology, Design Technology, ICT, Religious Studies, Art, Music, and Drama. In Year 7 all girls study Mandarin plus a second modern language (French or Spanish). In Year 8 German and Latin also become available. Girls usually take ten subjects at GCSE, including a compulsory core of English Language and Literature, Mathematics, 3 Sciences (IGCSE) and a Modern Language. 26 subjects are offered at AS and A2 Level and those who wish may also take the Extended Project Qualification which is highly regarded by university admissions tutors. Most girls take 4 or 5 subjects at AS Level and 3 or 4 at A2 Level. Each department runs a special programme to support UCAS applications and there is additional support for those applying to Oxbridge or particularly competitive universities. There are also lessons in personal health, ethical and social issues appropriate to each age and stage. Physical Education is taught throughout the school.

The Sixth Form. Our sixth formers play an important role in the school. They enjoy the independence of their own new Sixth Form Centre with common rooms, outdoor space for relaxing, café and fitness centre. They take responsibility for many extra-curricular activities such as organising clubs and act as mentors for girls in the lower years. Additional leadership opportunities are offered by the House system, and voluntary and charity work. All go on to Higher Education and, with excellent results (92% achieving grades A*, A or B in 2014, with 69% of grades being A*/A and 27% of grades being A*), successfully secure places at their choice of university (including Oxford and Cambridge).

Extra-Curricular Activities. As well as covering a wide variety of sports and activities connected with art, drama and music these range from computer animation to A Capella from Chinese to competing in the London-wide Hans Woyda Maths competition and from debating to the Duke of Edinburgh's Award Scheme.

We take full advantage of everything London offers, with visits to theatres, museums, galleries, performances, and conferences incorporated into the curriculum. Trips abroad are arranged for modern languages, history, art and art history, politics and economics. There is an annual ski trip and sixth form expedition.

Careers Advice. All girls are offered the Morrisby test free of charge in Year 10 and the school is a member of ISCO (the Independent Schools Careers Organisation) which entitles all students to careers help and advice until the age of 23. Sixth formers receive extensive support with university applications, including mock interviews. The GDST Alumnae Network, the unique resource from the GDST, offers each student access to a database of former GDST students, who will give advice and support on careers (including helping with work experience) and universities. An annual Careers Evening typically featuring senior representatives from almost 70 different professions and occupations is organised by the Parent's Guild.

Creative Arts. There are three orchestras, three choirs, and many chamber and ensemble groups. School productions offer opportunities either to perform or to work with production, lighting, sound, costume and staging. Art thrives within the curriculum and through various art clubs. It also contributes to work in design technology and various aspects of ICT, such as web design and animation projects.

Sport. Sport is taken seriously with success in local fixtures and championships, and we encourage participation and enjoyment at all standards. On site facilities include all-weather pitch, four-court sports hall, dance studio and indoor swimming pool. Gymnastics and dance are particularly popular, and there is an excellent gym squad. Lifeguard training is available for sixth formers. Fencing, aerobics, self-defence, and football are among the extra-curricular sports clubs currently available.

Fees per term (2014–2015). Senior School £5,250, Junior School £4,083.

The fees cover the regular curriculum, necessary school books, normal examination fees, membership of the FUTUREWISE scheme including the Morrisby careers aptitude test, stationery and other materials, but not optional extra subjects or school meals. Fees for extra subjects including instrumental music, speech and drama, are shown in the prospectus. Certain off-site sports are charged for separately, as are school trips.

Scholarships and Bursaries. Academic and music scholarships are available at 11+. At 16+ there are academic awards as well as awards for Physical Education, Drama, Art, and an All-Rounder scholarship.

Means tested bursaries are available in the Senior Department only. Application should be made via the school.

Admission. Usually at 4+, 7+, 11+ and 16+, by appropriate test and/or interview.

Occasionally, vacancies may become available in other year groups.

Charitable status. Notting Hill and Ealing High School is part of The Girls' Day School Trust, which is a Registered Charity, number 306983.

Nottingham Girls' High School
GDST

9 Arboretum Street, Nottingham NG1 4JB
Tel: 0115 941 7663
Fax: 0115 924 0757
email: enquiries@not.gdst.net
            admissions@not.gdst.net
website: www.nottinghamgirlshigh.gdst.net
Twitter: @NottmGirlsHigh
Facebook: /FriendsofNGHS
LinkedIn: /Friends Nottingham Girls High School

Founded 1875.

Nottingham Girls' High School is part of the GDST (Girls' Day School Trust). The GDST is the leading network of independent girls' schools in the UK. As a charity that owns and runs 24 schools and two academies, it reinvests all its income in its schools. For further information about the Trust, see p. xxi or visit www.gdst.net.

Additional information about the school may be found on the school's website and a detailed information pack may be obtained from Central Admissions at the school.

Chairman of Local Governors: Professor Jenny Saint, OBE, JP, DL

Headmistress: Mrs S M Gorham, BA, MA Ed Mgt

Deputy Head: Miss J Keller, BA

Assistant Heads:
Ms J K Davis, BA
Miss R A Lewis, BSc
Mrs L M Wharton-Howett, BA

Head of Junior School: Mrs F Potter, BA

Director of Finance and Operations: Mr J C Dunn, ACA

Central Admissions:
Mrs S M Webb-Bowen
Mrs C L Haddow

Number of Pupils. Senior School 700 (including 190 in the Sixth Form); Junior School 285.

A selective day school, NGHS is on a single site adjacent to a park in the middle of Nottingham. The original Victorian houses have been modernised and there have been extensive additions to create a well-resourced school. The Junior School is housed in separate buildings on the same campus as the Senior School, and has been extended to include a library and ICT learning resources centre as well four additional classrooms. A major programme of refurbishment in the Senior School has included refitting the science laboratories, food technology and design technology. A

state-of-the-art performing arts centre is due to be completed in 2016.

There is a self-contained Sixth Form Centre providing a large coffee shop-style common room and recreational area. The tutorial rooms are spacious and light, all fully equipped with the latest technology.

The school grounds include a large all-weather pitch, gymnasium, sports hall and fitness suite. There is also a sizeable sports field close to the school. The modern dining hall has excellent facilities for providing a wide choice of snacks and meals throughout the day.

Although examination results are among the best in the country, the school believes that education for life involves much more. Leadership, confidence, teamwork, flexibility and reliability are among the qualities increasingly demanded in today's ever changing society. Everyone is encouraged to take the opportunity to participate fully in a wide range of enrichment activities to develop skills and qualities that will lead to a happy, successful and fulfilling life.

At all ages, it is hoped that the girls will enjoy their studies. The school provides a lively, stimulating learning environment to encourage girls to discover the excitement and satisfaction of high academic achievement coupled with growing knowledge and understanding.

Curriculum. The curriculum is designed to give a broad academic education and due regard is paid to the National Curriculum. In the Junior School as well as following a pattern of work designed to help develop a confident grasp of core skills, the girls benefit from a stimulating and challenging integrated creative curriculum with enrichment experiences firmly embedded into teaching and learning. Girls take complete internal assessments in Year 6 and results are consistently very high. There is liaison with the Senior School staff, helping to ensure continuity for pupils at 11+. In the Senior School girls are prepared for GCSE, AS and A2 Levels, with almost all girls proceeding to university.

Girls at all ages follow a comprehensive programme of personal and social development including aspects of careers, citizenship, health and sex education, current affairs and environmental issues.

Throughout the school girls are encouraged to develop their physical skills and the school has an excellent sports record; teams regularly win trophies at City and County level with many being selected to compete at regional or national level.

Admissions. At 4+ entry, small groups of girls are invited to come into school and take part in a number of activities together to see if they are ready for school. Entry at 11+ is by interview and a written test which includes English, mathematics and verbal reasoning and is designed to determine potential and understanding. Most of the existing students stay on at 16+ and a number of students are admitted into the Sixth Form from other schools. The entry requirement is 8 GCSE subjects at an average of grade B, with grades A or B in any subject to be studied in the Sixth Form as specified by the department. This is supported by individual interviews and a report from the current school. The school will consider applications for admission into most year groups if there are available places.

Fees per term (2014–2015). Seniors (excluding lunch): Years 7–13 £3,932; Juniors: Rec–Year 6 (inc lunch) £3,029. The fees cover non-residential curriculum trips, school books, stationery and other materials, games and swimming, but not optional extra subjects.

Scholarships and Bursaries. The GDST makes available a substantial number of bursaries. These are means tested and intended to ensure that the school remains accessible to bright girls who would profit from our education but who would be unable to enter the school without financial assistance. Up to 100% of the tuition fee may be awarded. Bursary application forms are available through Central Admissions at the school.

A limited number of scholarships are available each year for entry to the Senior School at both 11+ and direct into the Sixth Form. The value of a scholarship is to a maximum of 10% of the current tuition fee. Scholarships are awarded solely on the basis of academic merit and no financial means test is involved. Music scholarships are available from Year 10.

Charitable status. Nottingham Girls' High School is part of The Girls' Day School Trust, which is a Registered Charity, number 306983.

Oxford High School
GDST

Belbroughton Road, Oxford OX2 6XA
Tel: 01865 559888
Fax: 01865 552343
email: oxfordhigh@oxf.gdst.net
website: www.oxfordhigh.gdst.net
Twitter: @oxfordhighsch

Motto: *Ad Lucem.*

Oxford High School is an independent day school for girls founded in 1875. It is Oxford's oldest girls' school and is located in the heart of Oxford. It is part of the Girls' Day School Trust (GDST) which is at the forefront of educational innovation, teaching over 20,000 girls across the UK in 26 schools and is the leading network of independent girls' schools in the UK. Tatler recently described OHS girls as 'fearless and independent' and with outstanding results, record numbers entering Sixth Form and a 'have a go' attitude, it remains true to its heritage of pioneering girls' education.

Chairman of School Governing Board: Mrs L Ansdell

Head: **Mrs J Carlisle**

Deputy Head – Students and Staff: Dr S Squire

Deputy Head – Academic: Dr P Secker

Assistant Head – Curriculum: Mr J Nicholl

Head of Junior School: Mrs E Stacey

Director of Finance and Operations: Ms J Hasnip

Head of Sixth Form: Miss R Pallas-Brown

Admissions Registrar: Mrs Teresa Hobbs
Admissions Secretary: Miss Harriet Gemmell

Pupil numbers. 900: Junior School 300, Senior School 600.

The school is on three sites in North Oxford. New buildings at the Senior School include the School Hall, Lecture Theatre, Dining Hall, Library, Drama Studio and Language Suite. Already extremely well resourced, the Senior School has a sports hall, indoor swimming pool, The Mary Warnock School of Music, and separate purpose-built centres for all other subjects and the Sixth Form. The school is networked with well-equipped ICT areas.

Curriculum. The broad curriculum offers a full range of subjects, incorporating ICT throughout the curriculum. Girls are prepared for GCSE and AS/A Level. Sixth-formers choose from 26 subjects and their timetable is individually tailored around their choice of subjects. Mandarin is a compulsory language for Year 7 along with French. The school offers 8 languages including Latin and Ancient Greek. Approximately 30% proceed to Oxbridge annually. Many girls take examinations in Music, and Speech and Drama, as well as belonging to the Duke of Edinburgh's Award Scheme, Young Enterprise and the Combined Cadet Force.

A strong co-curricular programme offers about 100 clubs at any one time, with everything from rock bands to gardening.

Admission. The main points of entry are at Reception, Year 3, Year 7, Year 9 and Year 12. Contact Mrs Teresa Hobbs, Admissions Registrar for details.

Fees per term (2014–2015). Reception to Year 2: £3,135 (plus lunch £200); Years 3–6: £3,236 (plus lunch £240); Senior School (Years 7–13): £4,341 (plus lunch £240 for Years 7–11). Lunch is compulsory for girls from Reception to Year 11 and optional for Sixth Form girls only.

The fees cover the regular curriculum textbooks, stationery and other materials, educational visits, choral music, games and swimming, but not optional extra subjects or school meals.

Bursaries. The GDST provides the school with a number of bursaries. These are means tested and ensure that the school remains accessible to bright girls who would profit from the education provided but who would be unable to enter the school without financial assistance. Bursaries are available before or after entry throughout the Senior School and confidential application can be made to the GDST.

Scholarships. Scholarships for Year 7 and Year 9 entry in Art, Drama, Sport, Music, Academic and the Head's Scholarship. Year 12 scholarships in Art, Academic, Drama, Music and Sports and the Head's Scholarship.

Charitable status. Oxford High School is part of The Girls' Day School Trust, which is a Registered Charity, number 306983.

Palmers Green High School

Hoppers Road, London N21 3LJ
Tel: 020 8886 1135
Fax: 020 8882 9473
email: office@palmersgreen.enfield.sch.uk
website: www.pghs.co.uk

Motto: *By Love Serve One Another*
Founded 1905.

School Council:
Chairman: Dermot Lewis, FCIB IAC, Banker
John Atkinson, FRICS, Chartered Surveyor
Anna Averkiou, International Media Consultant
Melanie Curtis, Solicitor
Dr Anita Goraya, BSc Hons, MBBS, MRCGP, Medical Practitioner
Loraine Cavanagh, Retired Headteacher
Gay Kettle MBE, Retired Dental Professional
Robert Keys, Retired
Margaret Lawrence, Retired Teacher
Kate McCann, Retired
David G Orfeur, JP, FRICS, Retired Chartered Surveyor
Jeffrey Zinkin, FEA, Accountant

Headmistress: **Mrs Christine Edmundson**, BMus London, MBA Exeter, PGCE, LRAM, ARCM

Bursar: Mr Ken Evans, BA Open, Cert Acc Open, CMgr, FCMI
Deputy Head KS4 and Head of Careers: Dr Mark Caddy, BSc, PhD Warwick, PRI
Deputy Head KS2 and Head of ICT: Mrs Karen Thompson, BA Denver, Colorado

Mrs L Aghassi, CertEd Middlesex (*Head of Computing*)
Mrs M Amankwah, BA Exeter, PGCE (*Lower School Class Teacher*)
Mrs H Bhundia, Dip Playgroup Practice (*First Aid Coordinator, Teaching Assistant*)
Mrs J Billingham, BA Nottingham (*Art*)

Mrs M Brent, MA Cantab, GTP London Institute (*Head of Geography*)

Mrs B Broad, BEd Leeds (*Head of Physical Education*)

Mrs E Christodoulou, BA Middlesex PGCE (*Lower School Class Teacher*)

Mrs K Conlon, MSc London BSc London (*Librarian*)

Mrs A Davey, BA Leeds, PGCE (*English*)

Mrs A Deans, BSc London Metropolitan, PGCE (*Lower School Class Teacher*)

Mrs T Delaney (*Lower School Teaching Assistant*)

Mr A Desai, BEng, BEd India, OTTP, PGCE (*Mathematics*)

Mrs C Doe, BA East Anglia, MA Ed Open, PGCE (*Head of English*)

Dr J English, BA Southampton, MMus London, PhD Cantab, PGCE Manchester (*Music*)

Mrs H Eve, BA Bristol, PGCE, (*Head of Drama*)

Mrs K Gil, CACHE Level 3 (*Nursery Assistant*)

Miss S Govani, BA London School of Economics, PGCE Oxford (*Head of History*)

Mrs S Hagi-Savva (*Assistant School Secretary, Teaching Assistant*)

Mrs S Harney, BEd Cantab (*Head of Nursery*)

Mrs E Hassan, NVQ3 (*Lower School Teaching Assistant*)

Ms J Henry , BA Newcastle, MA, PGCE (*Head of Art*)

Mrs S Kazim, BSc Middlesex, PGCE (*Head of Science*)

Senora M Larotonda, MA London, BEd Buenos Aires, PGCE (*Spanish*)

Mrs A Lee, BEd Birmingham (*Lower School Class Teacher*)

Miss H Lucas, BSc Sussex, MSc, PGCE (*Prep Department Coordinator, Lower School Class Teacher*)

Mrs S Mandal, BSc, MSc Visva Bharati, India, PGCE (*Science Teacher*)

Miss L Martin BA Manchester MSc London (*Individual Needs Coordinator*)

Mr J Matthews, BMus Cardiff, LTCL (*Head of Music*)

Mrs M Mehran, BSc North London (*Science Technician*)

Ms L Meltzer, MA Oxon, PGCE (*Individual Needs*)

Mrs A Michael, NNEB (*Nursery Assistant*)

Mrs G Moris, MA Oxon, PGCE, (*Lower School Class Teacher*)

Miss J Newman, BA London, PGCE (*French*)

Mrs M Nicolaou, NVQ3 (*Teaching Assistant*)

Mme K Parry-Garnaud, Licence d'Anglais Tours, France, BA Sunderland (*Head of Modern Foreign Languages*)

Mrs J Pauk, BA Aberystwyth, PGCE (*Lower School Class Teacher*)

Mr A J Pepper, BSc Loughborough, CertEd (*Head of Design and Technology*)

Miss L Selley, BA Brighton (*PE*)

Ms A Singh, BA London (*Examinations Officer & Individual Needs Teaching Assistant*)

Mrs C Shaw, BSc Warwick, PGCE (*Head of Mathematics*)

Miss M Smith, BEd Newcastle (*Lower School Class Teacher*)

Mrs M Suleyman, NVQ3, Childcare (*Reception Teaching Assistant*)

Mrs S Turanli, BSc London, PGCE (*Physical Education*)

Mr S Turner, BSc Newcastle, PGCE (*Science Teacher*)

Mrs K Woods-Shelley, BA Middlesex, PGCE, LLAM (*Drama*)

Mrs S Worringham (*ICT Systems Manager*)

Visiting Staff – Instrumental Tuition:
Clarinet/Saxophone: Mr J Matthews, BMus, LTCL
Flute: Ms K Bircher, BA, FTCL
Piano: Miss S Pope, LRAM
Singing: Miss M Taylor, AGSM, PGCE, ATCL
Violin/Viola: Miss V David, AGSM
Violin/Viola: Miss M Pound, FTCL, LTCL

Administrative Staff:
Assistant Bursar: Mrs A Monty, MAAT

Assistant to the Bursary Department: Ms M Soudah
Headmistress's PA, School Registrar/Office Manager: Mrs D Cruickshank
Assistant School Secretaries: Miss V Bennett, Mrs A Dudley, Mrs S Hagi-Savva
Marketing Officer: Mrs D Simmons, BA Bournemouth, Dip Marketing CIM
Caretaker: Mr P Vasou

Palmers Green High School is an independent day school for approximately 300 girls aged 3–16. Located in the pleasant suburb of the London Borough of Enfield, the school has good transport links by car, bus rail and tube. It is close to British Rail Stations in Winchmore Hill and Palmers Green. Southgate on the Piccadilly Line is the nearest Tube Station.

The school has a reputation for excellence and the girls flourish in its friendly and challenging environment. At secondary level average teaching group sizes are 12–14, helping the girls to achieve the very best results at GCSE. Primary age pupils enjoy subject specialists teaching them in Art, DT, Drama, Music and PE – frequently in half class groups.

A broad range of extra-curricular activities enriches the multi-cultural school community and educational visits feature regularly in the school calendar with excursions to local, national and international places of interest. These include educational visits to the nearby London museums, art galleries and theatres as well as field trips to Dorset and the Isle of Wight, outdoor pursuits and the Duke of Edinburgh's Award scheme for senior pupils. There are also optional winter ski courses and watersports activity weeks.

The School was founded by the late Alice N Hum in buildings in Green Lanes, Palmers Green and transferred to Avondale Hall on its present site in Hoppers Road, Winchmore Hill in 1918. The School's motto 'By Love Serve One Another' was carefully selected by Miss Hum to reflect her deep Christian convictions derived from her membership of the Society of Friends (Quakers). The motto epitomises the school's special ethos, where individual talent is fostered, celebrated and appreciated, and where contribution to the community is greatly valued.

Palmers Green High School continues to provide the warm and supportive environment of a small school in which both sound academic and personal development go hand in hand. The School aims to foster and maximise the individual talents of each girl while encouraging her to think independently, act in a responsible way and acquire self-discipline.

The compact site has been developed in recent years to extend the school's facilities. The games facilities used are among the best in the area, covering a wide range of sport. Outward bound courses are organised on a regular basis and this wide range of sporting activities forms the basis for the study of a GCSE in Physical Education at the age of 14.

In 2008 the school opened a new nursery for 3–4 year olds – The Alice Nursery – in Bush Hill Park which can accommodate up to 24 children. The Alice Nursery is situated approximately 10 minutes' drive from the main school and is open from 8.45 am until 3.45 pm. The day is divided into morning and afternoon sessions with a break in the middle of the day for lunch. Girls may attend Nursery for the whole day or morning with lunch only. Being an academic nursery, pupils follow a stimulating but demanding curriculum in preparation for Reception at the main school.

The curriculum, embracing the National Curriculum, is designed to give a broad education in which the active acquisition of skills, as well as knowledge is encouraged. Children are familiarised with computers from the Preparatory Department upwards. The performing arts are encouraged in the school and each term sees a large number of pupils taking part in plays, musicals and concerts. Careers education is an integral part of the timetabled curriculum from 11–16 and all pupils participate in careers lectures, exhibitions and work experience placements. Pupils are prepared for up to 10 GCSE subjects, with a view to continuing their studies to A Level and beyond.

Fees per term (2014–2015). Nursery: £2,710 (Full time), £1,605 (Part time); Reception–Year 2 £3,195; Years 3–6 £3,425; Years 7–11 £4,465.

Scholarships. Academic scholarships and bursaries of up to 100% of fees and Music awards are available to candidates aged 11+ for entry in September.

Entrance. Admission to all forms is by test and interview, the main intakes being at 3+, 4+ and 7+ and 11+.

Charitable status. Palmers Green High School Limited is a Registered Charity, number 312629. It exists for the education of girls.

Pipers Corner School
High Wycombe

Great Kingshill, High Wycombe, Bucks HP15 6LP
Tel: 01494 718255
Fax: 01494 719806
email: theschool@piperscorner.co.uk
website: www.piperscorner.co.uk

Visitor: The Rt Revd The Lord Bishop of Buckingham

Chair of Governors: Lady Allison, MA
Mr B R Callaghan, FCA
Ms E Carrighan, MBA, MA
Mr M F T Harborne, CBII
Mrs J B Ingram, BA, JD
Mr D B Jones, MPhil
Professor P B Mogford
Ms H F Morton MA, MScBA
Mr J H Phimester, AIB
Mr H B P Roberts, BSc Eng, FCA
Mrs J E Smith, BEd, MSc, DipM, MCIM, Chartered Marketer

Headmistress: **Mrs H J Ness-Gifford**, BA Hons, PGCE

Deputy Head: Mr N Walker, BSc, PGCE, MA

Deputy Head, Academic: Ms D Walmsley, BSc Hons, MSc, MPhil, CEng, MBCS, CITP

Assistant Head: Mrs E Cresswell, BA Hons, PGCE

Assistant Head: Mrs C Derbyshire, BSc Hons, PGCE

Bursar and Clerk to the Governors: Mr P R Forrester, MA, FCA

Director of Admissions & Marketing: Mrs F Knight, BA Hons

Director of Digital Strategy: Mr A Rees, BSc Hons, PGDip

Head of Preparatory Department: Mr D Leith, MBA, PGCE

Pipers Corner is an independent day school for girls aged 4–18. From Pre-Prep through to Sixth Form there is a focus on academic excellence as girls are supported and challenged to achieve their full potential. Academically successful, our girls progress to further study at Oxbridge and other top universities or specialist dance, drama and music colleges.

Set in 36 acres of beautiful Chiltern countryside, the school is less than one hour from central London (40 minute rail links to Marylebone Station in London) and 45 minutes from Heathrow airport, 4 miles north of High Wycombe and 2 miles from Great Missenden.

The standard and extent of our excellent facilities along with our commitment to a programme of continual improvement means that our girls have all the space and equipment they need to enable them to excel. Sport is popular at Pipers and from the 25 metre indoor swimming pool, to the sports hall and outdoor pitches we can accommodate a wide range of activities. Similarly those with creative interests benefit from the use of dance, drama, textiles, art, ceramics, design and technology studios, as well as a large music department.

In addition to providing a stimulating learning environment we also encourage the girls to cultivate any sporting or creative talents they have through a wide range of lunchtime and after school clubs and activities. Girls are able to develop their own interests in areas including: sport, music, dance, drama, technology, languages and outdoor pursuits. Team spirit is developed through a regular programme of sports fixtures.

The Pipers Corner environment allows girls to thrive. Whatever their strengths, the girls are challenged and supported as they pursue their own unique learning journeys. This approach enables them to fulfil their academic and personal potential and emerge as mature, confident and independent young women.

Fees per term (2014–2015). £2,625–£5,100.

Scholarships and Bursaries. Pipers Corner girls are extremely successful in many areas of achievement. In recognition of this success, the Governors are keen to encourage girls' potential and to widen access to ensure that as many talented girls as possible are able to take advantage of the excellent education that Pipers Corner can provide.

Girls from any primary school, as well as girls from Pipers Corner Prep Department may apply for an 11+ Scholarship for entry into the Senior School in any one of the following areas: Academic, Art, Drama, Music and PE.

Means-tested Bursaries are also available up to a maximum of 100% of fees (including any Scholarship award).

The Jessie Cross Award – for an all-rounder at 11+ – is a means-tested award of up to 100% of fees, available to a deserving student currently educated in a maintained primary school and who shows promise in a number of areas. Students applying for the award would need the recommendation of their Headteacher and would also need to provide supporting evidence of their achievements and involvement in their school, church or community. Girls applying for the Jessie Cross Award may not also apply for a scholarship.

Applications for Scholarships and Bursaries must be received by early December of the year preceding the intended entry to the School. Entrance Assessments are held early in January and potential scholars will be invited back shortly afterwards for further interview and assessment. Prior to this girls will also be invited in to school for an entrance interview with the Headmistress.

Sixth Form Academic Major and Minor Scholarships: Girls from any secondary school as well as girls from Pipers Corner may apply for a Sixth Form Scholarship. Girls who apply for a Scholarship may be awarded either a Major or Minor Scholarship for study in the Pipers' Sixth Form. Neither of these Awards is means-tested. The entry process is the same for both Awards. Please contact the school for further details.

Charitable status. Pipers Corner School is a Registered Charity, number 310635. It exists to provide high quality education for girls.

Portsmouth High School
GDST

25 Kent Road, Southsea, Hampshire PO5 3EQ
Tel: 023 9282 6714
Fax: 023 9281 4814
email: headsec@por.gdst.net
website: www.portsmouthhigh.co.uk

Founded 1882.

Portsmouth High School is part of the GDST (Girls' Day School Trust). The GDST is the leading network of independent girls' schools in the UK. As a charity that owns and runs 24 schools and two academies, it reinvests all its income in its schools. For further information about the Trust, see p. xxi or visit www.gdst.net.

Additional information about the school may be found on the school's website and a prospectus pack is available from the Admissions Officer at the school.

Chair of the School Governing Board: Mrs A McMeehan-Roberts, BA

Headmistress: **Mrs J Prescott**, BSc Cardiff, PGCE, NPQH

Deputy Head (*Pastoral*): Mrs H Trim, MSc Leicester, BSc Southampton

Assistant Head (*Sixth Form*): Mrs J Cresswell, BA Dunelm

Director of Studies: Mr J Paget-Tomlinson, BA Reading, MA King's College

Headmaster, Junior School: Mr P Marshallsay, BA Education

Admissions Officer, Senior School: Miss L Nunan
Admissions Officer, Junior School: Mrs G Gilbert

Number of Pupils. 320 are in the Senior School (11–18), 110 in the Junior School (rising 3–11).

Portsmouth High School is a community of learning committed to academic excellence and preparing girls to be the leaders of tomorrow. Each girl is encouraged to develop her own voice and her own views and to understand and build on her strengths. A broad based education encourages each girl's talents and potential to the full in an atmosphere of achievement and excellence. Characteristic of the GDST philosophy, Portsmouth High School has a profile of sustained academic achievement, strong relationships with the local community and outstanding pastoral care. Situated close to the sea, the school draws pupils from an extensive area of Hampshire, West Sussex and the Isle of Wight. All major transport providers serve the area.

The Senior School provides a broad and balanced education that prepares girls to specialise at A Level and the Sixth Form provides a perfect bridge to higher study. The Senior School is accommodated in the original building; a capital investment programme has seen the development of a Sport, Design Technology and Geography building on the senior school site.

A partnership with the University of Portsmouth means the school has joint use of the Langstone sports ground facilities, including a floodlit synthetic turf pitch and a multi-use games area; the site is just 2 miles from the school. In addition, the school site facilities include a Sport England standard sports hall, 4 hard tennis courts and 6 netball courts. Sixth Form students do not wear uniform, but have a 'Dress for Work' code. Sixth Formers have a recently refurbished Sixth Form Centre with a large common room, kitchen, study rooms and IT room.

The Junior School, through the provision of our innovative and challenging curriculum, develops curious, confident and collaborative learners. The Junior School is located 2 minutes' walk away in a wonderful period house with extensive gardens including 4 netball courts, and a range of indoor and outdoor facilities. Major investment in the Junior School saw the completion of an award-winning Pre-Prep building and science discovery lab. With the addition of a nursery class which, along with reception, was judged 'Outstanding' in all categories in the school's ISI inspection, the school is able to offer continuity of education throughout the Foundation Stage.

The Curriculum. The aim at Portsmouth High School is to foster in each girl the confidence to take risks and tackle new challenges within an atmosphere of ambition and enterprise, by providing appropriate teaching, advice and support. The focus on girls' learning is reflected in the design of learning spaces; the use of digital technology; a challenging and rewarding curriculum and a focus on pupils taking responsibility for their learning and having the confidence to take intellectual risks.

Extra-Curricular Activities. There is an extensive programme of extra-curricular activities in both the Junior and Senior schools. The lunchtime and after-school clubs range from dance to public speaking. There is an enthusiastic involvement in music, art, sport and drama with many performances and fixtures throughout the School calendar for Junior and Senior girls. Senior Girls have the opportunity to become involved in the Duke of Edinburgh's Award Scheme as well as a Sixth Form Seminar Group and Enrichment Programme. There are regular overseas music tours.

Admission Procedures/Entrance Examinations. At 11+ and 13+ entry the examinations in Mathematics and English are designed to test potential rather than knowledge. Prior to the 11+ examinations all girls take part in a series of team activities in school. At 13+ girls take part in a Shadowing Day and are interviewed by the Headmistress. Sixth Form entry is based on having at least 7 GCSEs at grade B or above. Most subjects will require at least grade A as a prerequisite for A Level study and applicants are invited for interview. Entry into the Junior School is based on assessments and examinations dependent on age.

Fees per term (2014–2015). Senior School £4,089, Junior School £2,963, Nursery £2,447.

The fees this year cover the regular curriculum, school books, non-residential curriculum trips, stationery and other materials, public examinations, choral music, games and swimming. The fees for extra subjects, including individual lessons in instrumental music and speech training, are shown in the Admissions Handbook.

Scholarships and Bursaries. The GDST makes available to the school a number of scholarships and bursaries. Bursaries are means tested and are intended to ensure that the school remains accessible to bright girls who would be unable to enter the school without financial assistance.

Academic and Music Scholarships are available for 11+, 13+ and Sixth Form, with Art, Drama and Sport Scholarships available in the Sixth Form. HSBC scholarships are also available for Sixth Formers.

Charitable status. Portsmouth High School is part of The Girls' Day School Trust, which is a Registered Charity, number 306983.

Princess Helena College

Preston, Hitchin, Hertfordshire SG4 7RT
Tel: 01462 432100
Fax: 01462 443871
email: head@princesshelenacollege.co.uk
website: www.princesshelenacollege.co.uk
Twitter: @PHCPreston

Motto: *Fortis qui se vincit*

Patron: Her Majesty the Queen

President: HRH The Duchess of Gloucester

Governing Body:
Chairman: Dr Susan Parkins, BPharm Hons, PhD, MRPharmS
Vice-Chairman: Mr Nicholas O'Sullivan, MA
Treasurer: Mr Ian Chambers, BSc, FCA

Clerk to the Governors and Bursar: Dr James Bentall, MA, MBA, PhD, ACII, ACMI

Headmistress: **Mrs Jo-Anne Duncan**, MA

From April 2015: Mrs Susan Wallace-Woodroffe, BSc

Deputy Head: Ms Rachel Poston, BSc, PGCE

Head's PA & Registrar: Mrs Heather Baim

Old Girls' Association Secretary: Mrs Susannah Goodbody

Princess Helena College is a dynamic school, where you will find happy, successful and confident day girls and boarders aged 11–18. We provide a vibrant, modern and challenging education whilst respecting and encouraging traditional values.

History. Founded in 1820 we are one of England's oldest academic girls' schools. We are extremely proud of our heritage and aim to maintain high academic standards and respect for traditional values. The school was founded for daughters of officers who had served in the Napoleonic Wars and daughters of Anglican priests. We now encourage this tradition by offering bursaries to daughters from families that are in the forces and the clergy.

Ethos. At Princess Helena College, we believe every girl is an individual and aim to inspire her to achieve both her academic and personal goals. We choose to remain a small school because we strongly believe this unique approach provides many benefits in academic, extra-curricular and pastoral areas. The educational benefits include a flexible curriculum and small classes. Both result in individual attention and excellent value-added attainment. A smaller school allows teachers to understand girls' individual learning styles, to recognise their particular strengths and weaknesses and to set individual learning targets. Pastoral care is strengthened by excellent relations between pupils and staff, which result in a strong family atmosphere. Knowing our girls well allows us to encourage them to take risks safe in the knowledge that we will support them. This allows every girl to be challenged, to achieve and to grow. Within a small school your daughter's chances of being selected for a team, a place in the orchestra, a part in a play or a position of responsibility are far higher. Having the opportunity to take part or perform in these activities will increase her confidence and self-belief. The value of this should not be underestimated.

Facilities. As well as an idyllic and safe learning environment, Princess Helena College has excellent educational facilities. The main building is a beautiful Queen Anne mansion that lies in fine Gertrude Jekyll gardens and 183 acres of parkland. Over the past 5 years the school has invested heavily in developing the facilities for all girls: a new fitness suite has been added, the Sixth Form boarding facilities have been improved and the school dining room has been refurbished. Other developments include a new science centre, art and design studios, and a refurbished learning resources centre.

Curriculum. We offer every girl the opportunity to excel within a varied and stimulating curriculum. Taught in small classes by highly-qualified and enthusiastic teachers who are dedicated to supporting each girl's talents and interests, our girls attain high levels of academic excellence and confidence. Girls are taught in sets that rarely exceed 18 and their potential and progress is carefully monitored.

The lower school curriculum (Years 7–9) consists of English, French, Spanish, German, Mathematics, Computing, Biology, Physics, Chemistry, History, Geography, Religious Education, Music, Drama, Physical Education, Art and Design. There are also programmes in PCC (PSHEE, Citizenship and Careers), touch typing and general studies.

In Years 10–11, girls follow their chosen GCSE subjects, following much consultation with staff and parents. On average, girls study between 8 and 10 GCSE subjects. The pass rate A*–C is 98% with nearly 60% of the GCSEs being passed at A* or A grade.

In the Sixth Form, A Level courses are available in all the traditional academic subjects, as well as Economics, Dance,

Media Studies, Psychology and Theatre Studies. Extensive career and Higher Education support and advice is provided.

The CLIMB (Considering, Linking, Interacting, Motivating, Broadening) extension programme supports girls in developing these vital academic skills. This is integrated into everyday teaching, as well as being the focus of off-timetable days, specific trips and events across the whole year.

A flexible approach to boarding. Princess Helena College is a vibrant community made up of boarders and day girls. We offer a very flexible approach to boarding and full, weekly, and flexible boarding are well established. Day girls can choose to stay into the early evening to make full use of the optional extended school day, participating in supervised prep or one of the numerous after school activities.

The Arts. Princess Helena College is particularly strong in Art & Design, Dance, Drama, Music and Speech & Drama. Girls may enter examinations in all these areas. Dance is a hugely popular activity, with girls learning jazz, modern, ballet, Irish and tap. Most of the College is involved in some form of musical activity, with many girls choosing to take part in one of the many different music groups or ensembles. Plays are staged throughout the year and there are regular joint productions with neighbouring boys' and co-educational schools.

Sport. In addition to timetabled lessons, there are sports activities on weekdays after school and on some Saturdays. Girls participate in a wide range of sports including lacrosse, netball, tennis, athletics, badminton, cross-country, rounders and swimming. Girls are given the opportunity to participate in competitive sport, recreational sport and fitness – we aim to encourage all girls to find an activity they will enjoy at school and in the future.

Co-curricular activities. Life is busy at Princess Helena College – there is an exciting array of extra-curricular activities and clubs, which form part of our exciting SCITLLE (Serve, Create, Inspire, Thrive, Lead, Learn, Explore) programme. Girls can choose to join in with these activities either during their extended lunch break or after school. From photography to public speaking, from language club to life saving and from touch typing to trampolining, there is an activity for everyone. The Duke of Edinburgh's Award Scheme is also a popular activity, with girls attaining Gold, Silver and Bronze awards each year.

Religion. Girls attend the nearby village church of St Martin's in Preston, which is also used for the school's Confirmation Services. Although the school's affiliation is to the Church of England, girls of other denominations and religions are welcomed.

Location. Set in 183 acres of rural parkland the College offers an easily accessible location within a safe and beautiful environment. The College is situated 30 minutes north of London between the A1 and the M1, just 5 minutes from the market town of Hitchin. Our excellent transport links include rail access (35 minutes to King's Cross) and proximity to several airports (Luton 15 mins, Stansted 45 mins and Heathrow 60 mins). There is an extensive network of school bus routes to Ashwell, Brookmans Park, Cottered, Cuffley, Digswell, Enfield, Gustard Wood, Hadley Wood, Harpenden, Hertford, Hitchin, Kimpton, Little Wymondley, London Colney, Luton, Potters Bar, St Albans, Stevenage, Stotfold, Welwyn and Wheathampstead.

Admission. We welcome girls aged 11–18. Most girls join the school at age 11 (Year 7), but there are also entrants at age 13 (Year 9) and the Sixth Form (Year 12). Please contact Heather Baim, Registrar (01462 443888) for a prospectus or to find out the date of our next Open Day. All girls must sit either the College's own Entrance Exam or the Common Entrance Exam. Sixth Form places are conditional on GCSE results.

Fees per term (2014–2015). Day Girls: Years 7 and 8 £4,895; Years 9–Sixth Form £5,995. Weekly Boarding or Full Boarding: Years 7 and 8 £6,985; Years 9–Sixth Form

£8,705. Fees include break, lunch, afternoon tea and supervised prep but exclude some books. Flexible boarding costs between £50 and £60 per night.

Scholarships and Bursaries. Scholarships (worth up to 15% of annual fees) are available for academically able pupils. Art, Dance, Drama, Music and Sport scholarships are also available. Bursaries of 10% of fees are available for daughters of the clergy and of members of the armed forces. Sibling bursaries are 5% of fees.

Charitable status. Princess Helena College is a Registered Charity, number 311064. It was founded in 1820 for the purposes of education.

Prior's Field

Priorsfield Road, Godalming, Surrey GU7 2RH
Tel: 01483 810551
Fax: 01483 810180
email: registrar@priorsfieldschool.com
website: www.priorsfieldschool.com
Twitter: @priors_field

Prior's Field has always been an extraordinary and exciting place in which to learn. In its most recent ISI report, the school was awarded the top rating – excellent – in all categories of inspection including quality of achievement, teaching, pastoral care, boarding and links with parents.

Its ethos is that pupils flourish in an innovative, warm environment where originality and all talents are encouraged. It's a school where you can become a radio presenter, learn from artists-in-residence, design and race cars, make your own CD in the Music Department, have supper with the Poet Laureate one evening and be coached by an Olympic Hockey Player the next. Pupils are happy and motivated by excellent teaching. Inspectors described the progress made at GCSE as exceptional.

Board of Governors:
Chairman: Mr R P Green, FCA
Mr N A Andrews, LLB
Mrs D C C Colvin
Mr I N H Davis, BA, BArch, RIBA
Mr P Grinham, MSc
Mr G J Haig, OBE
Dr I Hamerton, BSc, PhD
Mr I Hinckley, ACA, CTA
Dr A M Jacob, PhD, MBA, PGCE, DipTESOL
Mr D Long, BSc
Mr R W J Long, FRICS
Mr J R MacLeod
Mrs A Morris, BSc, PGCE
Ms I Restell, MA, ACA
Mr B Southey, BA, FCA

Headmistress: Mrs Julie A Roseblade, MA, PGCE, FCMI (*English, Drama*)

Deputy Head: Mrs Ruth Saunders, BSc, PGCE (*ICT*)
Assistant Head (*Curriculum*): Mrs Karen Wilcock, BSc, PGCE (*Mathematics, Staff Development*)
Assistant Head, Teaching and Learning: Mrs Amanda Morwood, MA (*History*)

Head of Pastoral Care: Mrs Kerry Sapseid, BA, HDE (*English*)
Head of Sixth Form: Mrs Desi Lyon, MA, QTS (*English*)
Bursar and Clerk to the Governors: Mrs Leonie Ranson, BA, DipEurHum, FCMI, MBIFM

Heads of Department:
Miss Jane Allen, BSc Hons, PGCE (*Head of Biology*)
Mrs Kate Beresford-Miller, BA, PGCE (*Head of Religious Studies, Oxbridge Coordinator*)

Miss Antonia Berry, BA, QTS (*Head of English, EPQ Coordinator*)
Mrs Jillian Buckley, MEd, DMS, CertEd, MCMI (*Head of Careers*)
Mrs Val Burnett, BA, PGCE (*Head of History and Politics*)
Mrs Pamela Edworthy, BSc, PGCE, DipSpLD (*Head of Learning Support*)
Mrs Charlotte Gomez, BA, PGCE (*Head of Languages*)
Miss Louise Gordon, BSc, PGCE (*Director of Sport, Head of Austen House*)
Mr Jeremy Hepworth, BA, MIA (*Head of ICT, Coordinator of Adventure Training*)
Mrs Penny Horton, BA, PGCE (*Head of Drama*)
Mr Geoffrey Jones, MSc, PGCE (*Head of Science*)
Mr Stephen Kinder, BA, PGCE (*Head of Creative Arts*)
Mrs Clare Lutwyche, BSc, PCGE (*Head of Business Studies and Economics, Sixth Form Enterprise*)
Mr Trevor Pratt, BA, ARCO, LTCL (*Director of Music*)
Mr Barry Rood, BSc, PGCE (*Head of Design Technology*)
Mrs Amanda Rusholme, BSc Hons, PGCE (*Head of Mathematics*)
Ms Catrin Treanor, BSc, PGCE (*Head of Geography, Exceptionally Able Coordinator*)

PA to Head: Mrs Anne Robinson
Registrar: Miss Penelope Harris, BSc Hons, MSc
Admissions Manager: Mrs Josie Cook
Alumnae Coordinator: Mrs Samantha Bushell, BSc
School Secretary and Office Manager: Mrs Sophie Irving, BA
Head of Boarding: Mrs Emma Picken
Junior Housemistress: Miss Deborah Pretty

Age Range. 11–18.
Numbers. 456 current pupils of whom 110 are boarders, on either a full, weekly or flexi basis.
Location. Prior's Field is set in 23 acres of Surrey parkland, situated between the towns of Godalming and Guildford, and is just minutes from the A3 to London and the South Coast. The nearest railway station is 5 minutes away in Godalming and the school is conveniently placed (via the A3 and M25) for both Heathrow and Gatwick Airports.

At the start and finish of term, girls may be escorted to, or met from, either airport or railway station. There is a weekly minibus to and from London and daily local school bus services.

Facilities. Facilities include a magnificent science centre and library, sports hall, tennis and netball courts, outdoor heated pool, Sixth Form gym, all-weather sports pitch and on-site Tennis Academy for pupils whose ambition is to play at national and international level.

In September 2013, a new three-storey teaching centre was opened that sites the Creative Arts in one area, provides state-of-the-art facilities for Maths and Modern Languages, additional classrooms and a new school entrance.

The original buildings were designed by Charles Voysey, a prominent member of the Arts and Crafts movement, and the gardens in consultation with Gertrude Jekyll.

Boarding. Prior's Field welcomes boarders from all over the world as well as the UK and girls board on a full, weekly or flexible basis, supported by a team of live-in boarding staff.

Younger girls share rooms, whilst those in Years 9–11 have single study-bedrooms. Sixth Form boarders reside in a separate sixth form house which incorporates 20 en-suite study-bedrooms. Here they lead more independent lives under the supervision of the resident Sixth Form Housemistress. Throughout the boarding houses, the emphasis is on working together and the creation of a warm, supportive, environment which enables the girls to achieve highly and mature into young women who think for themselves.

ISI Inspectors found that boarders are very happy together, feel well cared for and listened to. Provision of facilities and activities at the weekend and the quality of food were all highly praised.

Curriculum. Girls at KS3 follow a broad curriculum including Art, Music, ICT, Design and Technology (including digital photography), as well as all the 'core' subjects. Languages include French, Spanish and Latin. Girls in the First and Second Form follow a course in Thinking and Learning which involves philosophy, touch-typing, debating, library/research and study skills.

GCSE and A Level courses are offered at KS4 and in the Sixth Form. Girls are prepared for Oxbridge and other competitive universities by a dedicated tutor. Careers is taught across the school as part of the PSHE programme. In addition, visits are arranged to university open days and the school also organises talks by visitors from a wide range of professions. Fifth formers are encouraged to join a work experience scheme. Those studying languages at A Level are encouraged to take up work placements in Europe. The school has excellent IT provision to support all teaching and well-established programmes for its most able, and scholarship, students.

Music. Music flourishes throughout the school. A wide range of instruments is taught and 70% of the girls take individual lessons. Extra-curricular activities include 3 main choirs, an orchestra, jazz group, rock groups and many instrumental and vocal ensembles. Professional engagements include the RPO at Wembley, local festivals, the Royal Albert Hall and churches in London. Music Technology is taught in Years 9 to 11 and offered alongside Music at A Level.

Sport. Hockey, netball, tennis, athletics and rounders are the main games, but opportunities exist for many other sports and dance through after-school activities. Coaching in golf, fencing, self-defence and aerobic training is available. Prior's Field runs an on-site Tennis Academy for girls with exceptional tennis potential. Ice skating, bowling and swimming take place at the Guildford Spectrum for all pupils who are interested and the equestrian team practises locally and competes in eventing.

Extra-Curricular Activities. Girls are encouraged to involve themselves in clubs – more than 50 ranging from drama and young engineers to silversmithing, photography, golf, climbing, trampolining and art. Older girls can join the Duke of Edinburgh's Award Scheme and Young Enterprise. Throughout the year there are numerous educational visits to theatres, adventure and field centres and venues for debating and public-speaking competitions. Trips in the UK and abroad are an important part of a Prior's Field education and recent destinations have included: the Museum of Flight in Seattle, USA; Morocco, where girls trekked and wild-camped; and Malaysia.

Admission. Admission is by the School's entrance examination. Open days are held every term and individual visits are arranged at parents' convenience by the Admissions Manager.

Scholarships. Each year, a number of Prior's Field scholarships are awarded for entry at 11+, 13+ and 16+ to pupils displaying above average ability either academically or in the areas of art, drama, music or sport. Scholarships can be worth up to a 20% reduction in fees for either day or boarding pupils; exhibitions up to 10%. A scholarship or exhibition will usually be held throughout a pupil's career at Prior's Field and the continuity of the award is subject to satisfactory performance. It is expected that all scholars will make a whole-hearted contribution to the life of the school and will remain at Prior's Field for the Sixth Form.

In recent years, our academic scholars have obtained excellent public examination results, gaining places at some of the country's top universities including Oxbridge.

Bursaries. Prior's Field encourages applications from any pupil who would benefit from a place at the school, regardless of their financial situation. Means-tested bursaries are available at all points of entry, including Sixth Form

academic bursaries for day places, and may be up to 100% of fees.

In addition, there is limited funding available for bursarial help where parents experience unforeseen financial hardship.

Bursary awards are subject to annual testing of parental means and may be increased or decreased, depending on parental circumstances. Initial applications should be made through the Admissions Manager on 01483 813 402. Prior's Field uses an independent, external company to assess bursary applications.

Other Fee Reductions. Pupils who have a parent serving in the armed forces or in the Foreign and Commonwealth Office are eligible for a 20% reduction in school fees; a 10% reduction is offered to the daughter of a Prior's Field Old Girl; and a 10% reduction is offered to the eldest daughter while at least three siblings are at Prior's Field at the same time.

Fees per term (2014–2015). Boarders £8,910; Weekly Boarding £8,525; Day Girls £5,395.

Charitable status. The Prior's Field School Trust Limited is a Registered Charity, number 312038.

Putney High School
GDST

35 Putney Hill, London SW15 6BH

Tel:	020 8788 4886
Fax:	020 8789 8068
email:	putneyhigh@put.gdst.net
website:	www.putneyhigh.gdst.net

Putney High School is one of the UK's leading schools, offering the challenge of a rich and inspiring education to bright girls aged 4–18.

Founded 1893.

Putney High School is part of the GDST (Girls' Day School Trust). The GDST is the leading network of independent girls' schools in the UK. As a charity that owns and runs 24 schools and two academies, it reinvests all its income in its schools. For further information about the Trust, see p. xxi or visit www.gdst.net.

A more detailed prospectus may be obtained from the school or via the school's website.

There are just over 900 pupils, of whom about 585, including a Sixth Form of 150, are in the Senior School (ages 11–18) and 315 in the Junior School (ages 4–11).

Local Governing Body:
Mr P Wake, MSc City (*Chairman*)
Mrs C Boardman, MA Cantab, MBA City
Mr J David, BA Keele
Ms A Di Marco, MA Cantab, MBBS King's, Guy's and St Thomas', MRCS Eng, AKC
Ms C Lux, MA Oxon
Mrs M Matley, MA Oxon
Prof C Ozanne, BA, MA Oxon, DPhil
Ms A Scott-Bayfield, MA, Solicitor of the Supreme Court
Mr M Wright FCSI
Mr T Wheare, MA, DipEd, FRSA (*GDST Council*)

Headmistress: Dr Denise V Lodge, BSc, MSc, PhD London, PGCE

Senior Leadership Team:
Deputy Head (Academic): Mrs S Longstaff, BA Dunelm
Deputy Head (Pastoral): Mrs K von Malaisé, MA Cantab
Head of Junior School: Mrs J Wallace, BMus, MA Bath
Director of Sixth Form: Mr P Dwyer, BA Oxon
Director of Co-curricular Activities: Dr J Brandon, BMus, PhD London
Director of Assessment: Mr G Oliver, MA Cantab

Director of Finance and Operations: Mr A Gray, BSc Aberdeen, MA Cranfield
Director of Communications & Development: Mrs S Fearon

Senior School:

Art:
Mrs I Vickers, BA Oxon
Mr N Murray, BA Camberwell
Miss C Bluck, BA Kingston

Business Studies and Economics:
Mr A Ross, BCom Edinburgh

Classics:
Mrs A Nicoll, MA Oxon
Mrs C Christie, BA London, MPhil Cambridge
Mrs G Witty, BA Liverpool

Design Technology:
Miss S Norman, BA Brunel
Ms M Mescall, BEd Surrey
Mr S McLaughlin, MDes RCA
Miss T O'Hara, BA Loughborough

Drama:
Mrs R Pugh, BA London, PGDip Central School of Speech and Drama
Mrs E Armstrong, BA London, MA Birkbeck
Ms E Burford, BA London

English:
Miss J Sharp, BA, MLit Newcastle
Miss M Slesser, BA Reading
Mr E Artro-Morris, MA Oxon
Ms K Fereday, BA Cardiff
Ms K Jeffrey, BA Cambridge, MA Tufts USA
Mrs K von Malaisé, MA Cantab
Miss R Wait, BA Oxon

Geography:
Mr S Turner, BSc Southampton, MEd Birmingham
Mrs M Beaumont, BA Newcastle
Mrs E Matthews, BA Exeter

History/Government & Politics:
Miss B Britten, BA Sheffield
Ms S Knowles, BA London
Mr P Dwyer, BA Oxon
Mr P Coulson, BA Leeds
Miss A Martin, MA Oxon

History of Art:
Mrs I Vickers, BA Oxon
Miss C Bluck, BA Kingston

ICT:
Ms S Longstaff, BA Dunelm
Mrs G Oliver, MA Cantab

Learning Enrichment:
Mrs C Lewis, BA Ulster
Mrs D Tizzano, BA Cantab

Mathematics:
Mr M Finnemore, BSc Imperial, ARCS
Mrs A Arnold, BSc Reading
Mrs S Fairlamb, BSc Birmingham
Miss L Gill, BSc Nottingham
Mrs B Hawkins, BSc Hull
Ms S Longstaff, BA Dunelm
Miss L Speight, MMathStat Newcastle

Modern Languages:
Mr L Bambridge, BA Hull
Ms J Holl, BA Reading
Miss P Coate, MA Oxon
Mrs J Patton, MA Oxon
Miss I Huang BA Taipei, MA Warwick

Mrs T Srikanthan, MEd Munster
Mrs T Back, Licenciada en Filología Inglesa Oviedo
Miss C Donau, BA equiv Ludwig-Maximilian, Germany
Mrs W Wen, BA Overseas Chinese Institute of Technology

Music:
Mr N Robinson, BA Canterbury
Dr J Brandon, PhD London
Ms J Nicholls, BA Bristol

Physical Education:
Mrs E Fraser, BA Brighton
Miss E Merrick, BA Leeds
Miss C Halliday, BA Roger Williams University USA
Miss L Hillsley, BA Liverpool
Miss J Kapa, BDes Auckland
Ms K Scuffil, BSc Birmingham
Miss L Westcott, BSc Manchester Metropolitan

Psychology:
Miss E Keeble, BSc Cardiff

Religious Studies:
Mrs S Tyler, BD King's College
Miss J Heap, BEd Cambridge
Miss C Rudd, BA Hull

Science:
Dr W Dixon, MA, DPhil Oxon (*Head of Science*)
Biology:
Mr R Cameron, BSc Deakin
Mr M O'Brien, BA Cambridge
Chemistry:
Ms V Filsell, BSc London
Dr H Fenton, MChem, MSc, PhD
Dr D Henriques, BSc UCL
Mr J Walia, BSc London
Physics:
Mr M Ogretme, BSc Istanbul, MSc Istanbul
Mrs R Peacock, MSc Cranfield, BSc Southampton
Dr N Rolfe, MSci, PhD

Junior School:
Head of Junior School: Mrs J Wallace, BMus, MA, PGCE
Deputy Head of Junior School (*Academic*): Mrs B Matthews, BEng Wales
Deputy Head of Junior School (*Pastoral*): Mrs W Archibald, BA OU, LTCM
Miss C Bonham, BA Durham
Miss T Bodeker, BEd Durban, MA Roehampton
Miss A Brennan, BA Surrey
Mrs G Donald, BA, Cambridge
Miss H Ferguson, BA Bristol
Miss I Franks, BA Kingston
Ms S Gibson, BA Bristol
Mrs E Hooper, BA Thames
Mrs J Jones, BSc Southampton
Mrs E Kipling, BA Dunelm
Miss N Moorby, BSc Loughborough
Miss L Sinclair, SSc Roehampton
Mr J Sullivan, BSc Brunel
Mrs T Todd, BSc Birmingham
Mrs L Wakefield, BA Leeds
Mrs R Wyatt, BSc London

Visiting Staff – Instrumental Music:
Miss H Ashenden, BMus (*Cello*)
Mr M Barley, BA Oxford ARCO (*Piano, Organ*)
Ms E Bloom, BMus RCM, PGDip RAM (*Recorder*)
Mrs C Coulter-Young, BMus Royal Conservatoire of Scotland Performance (*Flute*)
Miss S Crawford, BMus Guildhall, MPerf RCM (*Bassoon*)
Mrs A Eddie, BMus (*Clarinet, Saxophone*)
Ms J Edwards, ARCM, RCM (*Violin*)
Ms J Holland, LRAM (*Clarinet*)
Ms E Hosker, ARCM, GRSM (*Violin*)
Ms G James, AGSM (*Double Bass, Flute*)

Mrs A Kendall, ARCM (*Voice*)
Mr S Keogh, GGSM, ARCM (*Trumpet*)
Ms R Lyske, Bmus
Ms R Munro, BA London (*Voice*)
Mr T Murray, MMus (*Piano*)
Ms C Philpot, ARCM (*Oboe*)
Mrs J Raeburn, BA Dunelm, ARCM (*Flute/Recorder*)
Mr P Riley, BMus Trinity London (*Saxophone*)
Mr I Stott, Dip ABRSM (*Horn*)
Mr P Taggart, ARCM Flute)
Mr S Tate, BA MMus Southampton (*Guitar*)
Mr M Wheeler, ACM (*Percussion*)
Mrs P Whinnett, GMus RNCM (*Piano*)

PA to the Headmistress: Mrs H Gordon-Smith, BA Exeter

School Doctor: Dr G Provost
School Counsellor: Ms V Walmsley

Putney High School is an independent selective girls' day school located on a green and leafy site close to the heart of Putney in London.

Putney offers a stimulating, nurturing environment where girls are supported and encouraged to make the most of their individual gifts and talents.

We are a school with a caring ethos where each girl encounters stimulating personal and intellectual challenges within a warm, supportive environment. This nurtures success.

Girls take pleasure in discovery and work together to engage in discussion, to debate and challenge the opinions of each other and those from outside.

We anticipate that each girl will contribute to our school, through her studies and many other activities including art and design, drama, music, sport and through charity and working with the local community.

Students leave here conscious of their own worth, prepared for an independent life and capable of making a positive contribution to society. It is from this basis that they go on to pursue a variety of fulfilling careers.

Established in 1893, we are well known for providing the challenge of a rich and broad education to bright girls from 4–18.

With the expertise of dedicated staff, girls develop the self-confidence they need to take intellectual risks and to think independently.

We are proud of the high academic achievements of our girls, with many accepting places at popular universities such as Oxford and Cambridge.

Indeed, we have an extensive World Class Universities programme in place to support girls in making the right choice for them, and in helping to secure places at the best universities both in the UK and abroad.

However, we place equal importance on ensuring that ours is a friendly school and recognise all girls are individuals, each making a positive and valuable contribution.

A strong network of parents and friends share our values, building upon the school's integrity and sense of community spirit.

Facilities. Our state-of-the-art Sixth Form Centre sets a new benchmark for sixth form development, with outstanding facilities such as a rooftop terrace, internet café and fitness suite, as well as latest ICT and inspiring study areas.

In the Senior School facilities include a new library with state-of-the-art audio-visual equipment, a mezzanine level with laptops and private study space. There is a language lab and a music ICT composition room as well as purpose-built classroom blocks, an impressive Music Centre, seven well-equipped Science laboratories, excellent Art studios, a Design and Technology centre, a superb Sports Hall, drama studio and extensive ICT provision. A Performing Arts Centre is set to open in 2015.

Our on-site Junior School houses a well-equipped Hall, specialist Science facilities, an Art Studio, a large ICT suite, a Music room and a well-stocked, comfortable and engaging Library.

Sport. Putney High School has earned a reputation for excellence in sport. Each term has a full extra-curricular fixture list and squads regularly compete and achieve success in regional and national level competitions. The school also promotes a 'sport for all' policy which encourages all pupils to participate for enjoyment and fun.

The school's facilities – as well as use of additional off-site grounds – enable a wide range of sports to be played.

All girls have lessons in netball, lacrosse, gymnastics, tennis and athletics. Rowing is introduced in Year 9 and is a popular extra-curricular club from Year 7. Other clubs include dance, badminton, trampolining, cross-country and fencing. Tennis, lacrosse, netball, rowing, cross-country, gymnastics, athletics and sports acrobatics teams compete successfully nationally. Girls are regularly selected to join county, South of England and national and international lacrosse teams.

Curriculum. Well-qualified, specialist staff provide continuity of education from Reception through to A Levels at 18. Girls are welcome to enter the school at 4+, 11+ and 16+ or in other years if an occasional vacancy arises.

In the Senior School, the girls follow a broad and balanced curriculum, which includes Latin with Greek, French, Chinese (Mandarin), German, Spanish and Design Technology. On entering the GCSE years, all girls study the core subjects plus Biology, Physics and Chemistry and at least one modern language. They are also able to choose from a wide list including Statistics, Textiles, ICT, Design Technology, Art, Drama, Latin, Classics, PE, Music, History, Geography and RS. At AS and A Level these subjects may be supplemented by others such as Business Studies, Economics, Government & Politics, History of Art, Further Mathematics, Psychology and Critical Thinking. In addition to their A Level studies, students can also complete an Extended Project on a topic of their choice. A carefully structured Life Skills programme broadens their interests and skills and helps prepare them for life beyond school. Indeed, in the Sixth Form, students enjoy increased academic freedom as well as a wealth of extra-curricular opportunities.

Sixth Form. Sixth Formers play an important part in school life, acting as role models for younger children. The Head Girl, Deputies, House Officials and Prefects are essential to the smooth running of the school and there is ample scope for all to become involved in School Council, the organisation of House events, debating, charity work, lunchtime clubs, drama, music and sport.

The **Junior School** provides a secure and encouraging environment where the girls grow in skills and confidence. A warm relationship is established with each family so parents and staff work together throughout the girls' years with us.

A cross-curricular approach to learning is adopted including many visits to places of interest, concerts, museums, art galleries and theatres. Wide opportunities capture the girls' unlimited enthusiasm and enable them to explore and extend their natural talents.

The Junior School has earned a reputation for success in music, netball, tennis, gymnastics, chess, and writing skills in local, county and national events in recent years. The choirs have been invited to perform for the BBC – and at the Royal Festival Hall and the Royal Albert Hall several times.

Music. Putney is renowned for its musical excellence throughout both Junior and Senior schools. A high percentage of girls learn a musical instrument; many are accomplished musicians, studying at the junior conservatoires and/or are members of nationally auditioned choirs and orchestras.

The Music suite provides spacious and well-equipped facilities for class teaching, private tuition and practice rooms. Private tuition is available in all instruments and voice. Girls have many opportunities to participate in music – three orchestras; four Senior Choirs and a Junior Choir and many smaller ensembles. There are two annual composition competitions and an Inter-House Music Festival attracting hundreds of entries.

The school has achieved success in prestigious national competitions and there have been choir tours to New Zealand, Barcelona, Venice and Lisbon.

Fees per term (2014–2015). Senior School £5,290, Junior School £4,339.

The fees cover the regular curriculum, school books, stationery and other materials, choral music, games and swimming, but not optional extra subjects or special sports. All pupils below the Sixth Form take school meals for which the charge is £174 per term (Reception–Year 2) and £206 per term (Years 3–11). The fees for instrumental tuition are shown in the Prospectus.

Financial Assistance. We are committed to offering opportunities to bright girls whose parents would not be able to afford the fees. The GDST has its own means-tested Bursary Scheme. Bursaries are available in Senior School and Sixth Form.

Scholarships. There are a number of academic, music and sports scholarships available to internal or external candidates (up to 50% of fees) for entry at 11+. At 13+ (Year 9 entry) scholarships are available in music and sports. At 16+ we provide academic, art, design, drama, music, and sports scholarships, as well as travel scholarships in modern languages and science.

Charitable status. Putney High School is part of The Girls' Day School Trust, which is a Registered Charity, number 306983.

Queen Margaret's School

Escrick Park, York YO19 6EU
Tel: 01904 727600
Fax: 01904 728150
email: enquiries@queenmargarets.com
website: www.queenmargarets.com
Twitter: queenmargarets

Motto: *Filia Regis*

Board of Governors:

Chairman: Mrs Emma Carnegie-Brown

Mrs C M Gooder	Miss E Pearson
T S Kettlewell, Esq	Mrs K Preston
N Lambert, Esq	Her Grace the Duchess of
D Maddan, Esq	Rutland
M D Oakley, Esq	F A Scott, Esq
D Parker, Esq	I M Small, Esq

Company Secretary & Clerk to the Governors: D T King, LLB Hull

School Solicitors: Messrs Addleshaw Goddard, Messrs Crombie Wilkinson
School Auditor: PricewaterhouseCoopers LLP

Acting Head: Mrs Carole Cameron, BA Reading, MA Open, PGCE, NPQH, FRGS
From April 2015: Mrs Jessica Miles, MA Oxon, PGCE

Deputy Head (*Academic Studies*): Dr Anne Buchan, BSc Hull, PhD Leeds, PGCE
Deputy Head (*Enrichment & Extension*): Mr Stuart Thompson, GRSM, ARAM, MBA London
Director of Pastoral Care & Child Protection Officer: Mrs Claire Wike-Elwers, BSc Loughborough
Bursar (*Director of Business & Finance*): Mrs Liz Raper, BSc Nottingham, ACA

Clerk (*Director of Administration & Compliance*): Mr Tom King, LLB Hull
Director of Marketing: Mrs Katherine Walker, BSc Lancaster, MA Nottingham

* *Head of Department*
§ *Part-time*

Mathematics:
*Mr Adam Taylor, BA Cantab, PGCE
Mrs Christine Herbert, BSc Leeds, PGCE
Mr David Lamb, BSc Edinburgh, MA Open, PGCE
Ms Louise McAllister, BSc Leeds, PGCE
Mrs Alicia Viant, BSc Hull, PGCE
Mrs Claire Wike-Elwers, BSc Loughborough

Physics:
*Mr David Grainger, BSc Edinburgh, PGCE
Mrs Kate Robson, MA St Andrews, DipHE Sheffield Hallam, QTS
Mrs Sian Thomas, BSc York, PGCE
Mr Neal Jackson (*Technician*)

Chemistry:
*Mrs Elizabeth Morton, BSc London, PGCE
Dr Anne Buchan, BSc Hull, PhD Leeds, PGCE
Mrs Sarah Gorton, BSc Leeds, PGCE
Mrs Eileen Rust (*Technician*)

Biology:
*Mr Joseph Hazlewood, BSc Aston, MA OU, PGCE (*Head of Science*)
Dr Katherine Mariner, BSc Nottingham, MSc, PhD, PGCE, SGM
Mrs Gerina Labonté-Hazlewood (*Technician*)

English:
*Mr Mark Payton, MA Oxon, PGCE
Mrs Carole Cameron, BA Reading, MA Open, PGCE, NPQH, FRGS
Mrs Ruth Doyle, BA, MA York, PGCE
Miss Julia Millhouse, MA Cantab, PGCE
Dr Nicola Onyett, BA, DPhil York, PGCE
Dr Sarah McLoughlin, BA Oxon, MA Toronto, PhD, PGCE York

English as an Additional Language:
*Miss Anna Stanglewicz, BA Zielona Gora, MA London, DELTA, QTS
Miss Stephanie Houlston, BA Newcastle, MA Birmingham, CELTA

Classics:
*Mr William Grant, MA St Andrews, MSt Oxon, PGCE
Mrs Rosemary Waugh, BA York, MA Hull, PGCE

Oriental Languages:
*Miss Jenny Chen, BA Sun Yat-sen, MSc Oxford

European Languages:
*Miss Estelle Leclerc, BA Leeds, PGCE (*Spanish, French*)
Mrs Maria Algobia Vila, BA, MA Madrid, PGCE (*Spanish, French*)
Mrs Amanda Debenham, BA Newcastle, PGCE (*Spanish, French*)
Mrs Agnes Goodrick, BA, MA Paris, PGCE St Martin's College (*Arabic, French, Spanish*)
Mrs Birgit Kirkham, BA Halle, PGCE (*German*)
Mrs Isabelle Leaf, BA Lyon, PGCE (*French*)
§Miss Daniela Corbitt, Dip Accountancy Pouzini, CTLLS City & Guilds (*Italian*)
§Mrs Mila Green, Cert Ed York St John (*Spanish*)
§Mrs Veronique Weller (*French*)

Religion & Philosophy:
*Revd Robert Owen, BD Wales, PGCE

History & Politics:
*Mr James Rollinson, BA Oxon, PGCE

Miss Harriet Peacock, BA Lancaster, PGCE

Geography:
*Mrs Leyla Seeney, BSc Leicester, PGCE
Miss Lauren Barker, BA, PG Dip Birmingham, PGCE
Cantab
Miss Fiona Whittle, BEd Bedford CPE, FIOS

Economics & Business Studies:
*Mrs Mary McDougall, BA Oxford Polytechnic, PGCE
Mrs Claire Nadin, BSc Hatfield, PGCE Nottingham Trent

History of Art:
Mr Thomas Cooke, BA Holloway, MA York

Art & Design:
*Mr Graham Alcock, BA Bristol Polytechnic, ATC Sussex
Mrs Paula Alpine-Eales, BTEC, BA Sunderland, PGCE
Mrs Helen Colman, BA Leeds, MA Newcastle, PGCE
Mrs Lesley Heaton, BA Trent Polytechnic, MA Leeds
Mrs Debbie Stewart, BA Wolverhampton, MA Leeds,
PGCE
Mrs Sally Wade (*Technician*)

Home Economics:
*Miss Jennifer Hardy, BSc Northumbria, PGCE
Mrs Gerina Labonté-Hazlewood (*Technician*)

Music:
*Mr Robert Duff, BEd Aberdeen (*Director of Music*)
Dr Samantha Horseman, BMus Huddersfield, MA York,
PhD Huddersfield
Mr Stuart Thompson, GRSM, ARAM, MBA London
§Mr Andrew Passmore, MA York (*Organist, Accompanist,
Piano*)
§Mr Nigel Bellamy, BA Dartington, Exeter, CELTA, Cert
RCO (*Piano, Organ, Violin*)
§Mrs Julia Brewer, BA York, PGCE (*Cello, Piano*)
§Lady Katherine Skipwith, BA York (*Singing, Piano*)
§Mrs Jillian Garside, PG Dip Mus Colchester, LTCL
London, MA York, PGCE (*Oboe*)
§Mrs Georgina Goodier, DipTCL, LRSM (*Harp*)
§Mrs Catherine Griffiths, GMus RNCM, PGCE, PDVT,
GSMD (*Singing*)
§Dr John Mackenzie, BEng UCL, PhD Leeds, FTCL,
FLCM, IGSM, LRAM (*Guitar*)
§Mr Vincent Parsonage, BSc OU, PGDipMus, LTCL, Dip
ABRSM (*Viola, Violin*)
§Mrs Dorothy Pomfret, LGSM, Dip Ed (*Piano*)
§Mr Bryan Robinson, BEd Sunderland (*Scottish Bagpipes,
Snare Drum*)
§Mr Jonathan Sage, BA York, MA York (*Clarinet,
Saxophone, Bassoon & Piano*)
§Mr Martin Scheuregger, BA York (*Percussion*)
§Mr Piotr Selwesiuk, MA Wroclaw (*Brass*)
§Mr Philip Titcombe, BA York (*Piano*)
§Mr Joel Newsome (*Singing*)
§Ms Louise Evans (*Flute*)

Drama, Theatre & Film:
*Mrs Deborah Whitcombe, BEd Central School of Speech
& Drama, London (*Director of Drama*)
Mr Quentin Sands, BEd Central School of Speech &
Drama, London (**Theatre Studies*)
Mr Ian Giles, BA Sussex, MA Leeds (**Film Studies*)
Mr Emrys Jones (*Technician*)

Dance:
*Miss Alison Leadley, RAD, AISTD CB, UABPA Dip, BA
Surrey, MA Leeds Met
§Mrs Samantha Bolsher, AISTD
§Miss Adrienne Pithers, AISTD
§Miss Rebecca Goodall, AISTD
§Miss Rhona Firth, AISTD
§Mr Anthony Croome, RAD

Sport:
*Miss Anne Davies, MEd Wales, PGCE (*Director of Sport*)

Ms Claudine Shaw, BEd Liverpool (**Lacrosse*)
Miss Jill Rastall, BSc Wales, PGCE (**Pentathlon*)
Mrs Karen Mitchell, LTA (**Racquets*)
Miss Emily Joiner, BA Leeds Metropolitan, PGCE
(**Fitness & Exercise*)
Miss Jennifer Blood, BA, QTS Bedford
Miss Annabel Hartshorne, BA Manchester Metropolitan,
PGCE Staffordshire
Miss Emily McMillan, BSc Lynchburg College
Ms Jacqueline Whay, BEd Liverpool
Miss Fiona Whittle, BEd Bedford CPE, FIOS
Mr Nigel Allison, BA Ripon & York St John (*Technician*)
§Mr Steven Eales (*Fitness Coach*)
§Mr Matthew Bridson (*SRA Squash Coach*)
§Mr Dennis Cleary (*Badminton Coach*)
§Mrs Christine Place, Cert Ed Bedford CPE (*LTA Tennis
Coach*)
§Mr Andrew Potter (*LTA Tennis Coach*)
§Ms Joanna Craven (*LTA Tennis Coach*)

Higher Education:
*Dr Nicola Onyett, BA, DPhil York, PGCE
Miss Julia Millhouse, MA Cantab, PGCE

Careers:
*Mrs Claire Nadin, BSc Hatfield, PGCE

Learning Support:
Mrs Juliet Edwards, BSc Dunelm, MA Leeds, MSc Open,
PGDip Psych OU, PGCE
Mrs Dawn Hill, BA UCRYSJ, PGCE

Examinations & Data:
*Mrs Michelle Randall

Senior Tutors:
Senior Tutor Key Stage 3: Mrs Amanda Debenham, BA
Newcastle, PGCE
Senior Tutor Key Stage 4: Mrs Claire Nadin, BSc Hatfield,
PGCE
Senior Tutor Key Stage 5: Mrs Ruth Doyle, BA, MA York,
PGCE
Senior Tutor Scholars: Miss Harriet Peacock, BA
Lancaster, PGCE

Academic Extension:
Mr Darren Ledson, BA, PGCE

Extended Project Qualification:
Dr Katherine Mariner, BSc Nottingham, MSc, PhD, PGCE,
SGM

Model United Nations: Mr David Lamb, BSc Edinburgh,
MA Open, PGCE
**Duke of Edinburgh's Award*: Miss Caroline Goddard

Heads of Houses:
Miss Alison Leadley, RAD, AISTD CB, UABPA Dip, BA
Surrey, MA Leeds Met (*School*)
Mr Ian Giles, BA Sussex, MA Leeds (*QM Hall*)
Mrs Deborah Whitcombe, BEd Central School of Speech &
Drama, London (*Garry*)
Dr Katherine Mariner, BSc Nottingham, MSc, PhD, PGCE,
SGM (*St Aidan's*)
Mr William Grant, MA St Andrews, MSt Oxon, PGCE
(*Pitlochry*)
Miss Leah Geldeard, BA Lancaster (*Duncan*)

Queen Margaret's Prince's Trust Business Challenge:
Ms Moira Richardson, BA Liverpool, CELTA

The King Society:
Miss Harriet Peacock, BA Lancaster, PGCE

School Administrator – Enrichment & Extension:
Mrs Lynsey Griggs, BA Southampton
Mrs Lena Ledson

Data & Information Administrator
Ms Fiona McHale

Pastoral:
*Chaplaincy: Revd Robert Owen, BD Wales, PGCE (*Chaplain*)

Medical Centre:
*Mrs Glenda Swinglehurst, RN (*Senior Sister*)
Mrs Amanda Bates, RN (*Sister*)
Mrs Jane Crowther, RN (*Sister*)
Mrs Anna Craven, BSc Huddersfield PGCE, RN (*Sister*)
§Mrs Sue Burton, BA Leeds (*School Counsellor*)

International Students Counsellor:
Ms Jacqueline Whay, BEd Liverpool

The Cottages (*UVI*):
Mr Darren Ledson, BA, PGCE (*Housemaster*)
Ms Moira Richardson, BA Liverpool, CELTA (*Assistant Housemistress*)
Ms Jacqueline Whay, BEd Liverpool (*Assistant Housemistress*)
Mrs Joy Jackson (*Assistant Housemistress*)

The Cloisters (*LVI*):
Miss Julia Millhouse, MA Cantab, PGCE (*Housemistress*)
Miss Caroline Goddard (*Assistant Housemistress*)
Mrs Anna Craven, BSc Huddersfield, PGCE, RN (*Assistant Housemistress*)

Winifred Holtby House (*Year V*):
Mrs Paula Alpine-Eales, BTEC, BA Sunderland, PGCE (*Housemistress*)
Miss Leah Geldeard, BA Lancaster (*Assistant Housemistress*)
Mrs Susan Willoughby (*Assistant Housemistress*)

Atholl House (*Year IV*):
Mrs Georgina Killip, BA Leeds MA, Leicester (*Housemistress*)
Miss Lauren Barker, BA, PGDip Birmingham, PGCE (*Assistant Housemistress*)

Scarborough House (*Year III*):
Mrs Lorraine Thackray, BTEC, NVQ3, NVQ4 City & Guilds (*Housemistress*)
Ms Annabel Hartshorne, BA Manchester Metropolitan, PGCE Staffordshire (*Assistant Housemistress*)
Mrs Jane Hyland (*Assistant Housemistress*)

Howard House (*Year II*):
Miss Cassandra Thackray, BA York St John (*Housemistress*)
Miss Aimee Dubiel, BSc Northumbria (*Assistant Housemistress*)
Mr Mark Elwers (*Assistant Housemaster*)

Red House (*Year I*):
Mrs Katie Hargreaves (*Housemistress*)
Mrs Julie Simpson (*Assistant Housemistress*)
Miss Abigail Weir, BA Brighton (*Assistant Housemistress*)

School Administrator – Pastoral: Mrs Sandra Speight

Administration & Development:

PA to the Acting Head: Mrs Karen Romeniuk-Horsley

Admissions & Communications:
Mrs Charlotte Cocker (*Admissions Officer*)
Mrs Sarah MacGregor (*Receptionist*)
Mrs Gina Skene (*Receptionist*)

Marketing & Events:
Mr Ian Giles, BA Sussex, MA Leeds (*Editor*)
Miss Katy McWhirter, BA Belmont, MA York (*Marketing Manager*)
Mrs Alison Ruddick (*Events Manager*)

Digital Strategy:
*Mr Jonathan Witts, BA Lincolnshire, ITIL Huddersfield, CEOP (*Director of Digital Strategy*)
Mr Granville Mark, BSc, MCSE (*Network Manager*)

Mr Gareth Howe, MSc (*System Engineer*)

Business:

Catering:
*Mr Shaun Gayton (*Catering Manager*)
Mrs Cathy Pope (*Catering Supervisor*)
Ms Amy Smith (*Catering Supervisor*)
Mr Jamie Newby (*Chef*)
Ms Lauren Shepherd (*Chef*)
Mr Paul Walker (*Chef*)

Estate:
*Mr Quinn Cardy (*Estate Manager & Health & Safety Officer*)
Miss Katie Duncan (*Estate & Health & Safety Administrative Assistant*)
Mr Stacy Bramley (*Workshop Supervisor*)

Finance:
*Mrs Elaine Ryan (*Finance Manager*)
Mrs Hazel Brown (*Bursar's Assistant*)
Mrs Lesley Walton (*Bursar's Assistant*)

Housekeeping:
*Ms Pamela Bridges (*School Housekeeper*)
Mrs Kate Smith (*Deputy School Housekeeper*)
Mr Keith Robson (*Caretaker*)

Foundation. Queen Margaret's was founded in Scarborough in 1901 by the Woodard Foundation and named in honour of Scotland's only female saint. Following eventful years which included evacuation to Pitlochry during the First World War, and Castle Howard during the Second, the school came to its current home in 1949.

In 1986, following an initiative by the parents and governors, the school was re-established under a new company, limited by guarantee and registered with the Charities Commission. At the same time the school became independent of the Woodard Foundation and began a period of dramatic expansion, investing almost £10 million in new and improved facilities to create the superb learning environment enjoyed by pupils today.

Situation. Escrick Park is an idyllic location in which to study and relax. The beautiful grounds provide a serene backdrop to the busy and purposeful life of the school. Yet the ancient city of York is just 6 miles away; home to two universities, world-class museums and the renowned Minster as well as theatres and cinemas. Our proximity to York station with its direct train services to all major cities and a number of airports makes travelling to Queen Margaret's very straightforward. London is just 2 hours away, Edinburgh 2½ and Manchester even closer.

Numbers. Boarding 300; Day 75.

Admission is by Entrance Examination at 11+, 12+ and 13+. There is also entry at 16+.

Fees per term (2014–2015). Boarders £9,530; Day Girls £6,125.

Curriculum. QM offers a wide academic curriculum. Girls usually complete 9 or 10 GCSEs and have a free choice of A Level subjects, taught by specialist graduate teachers. Class sizes are small and, from the classroom to the laboratory and from the studio to the study, we encourage girls to think for themselves.

The Sixth Form at QM offers the best possible preparation for life at University and beyond. Students have increasing independence and take on greater responsibility for their own learning. Comprehensive and highly personalised guidance on Higher Education and possible careers helps each girl to understand and realise her individual ambitions by evaluating the available options and making wise choices for the future. 29 subjects are offered for A and AS Level in a wide variety of Arts and Science subjects. Candidates are prepared for all University entrance including Oxbridge. High academic standards are achieved at all levels.

Classrooms are modern and well equipped and ICT provision is widespread and up-to-date. There are seven science laboratories. Art, Design and Food Technology are located in a purpose-built centre. Pottery, sculpture, textile and fabric design, printing, as well as drawing and painting, are on the curriculum. Notable spaces include the spectacular theatre and dance complex, competition-sized indoor swimming pool, superbly equipped Medical Centre and Languages suite as well as purpose-built senior boarding accommodation in Winifred Holtby House.

Drama is important in the curriculum and school productions are mounted regularly. In addition girls can take classes in modern, tap and ballet dancing and individual tuition is available. Music plays a major role in school life at Queen Margaret's and there are three full time and twenty specialist music teachers on the staff. There are two orchestras and two bands, smaller ensembles, rock bands, chapel choir and junior choir. The school's choir provides the music for services in Chapel as well as the Parish Church and local concerts and regularly sings in York Minster and occasionally abroad.

Sport. The school has first-class sports facilities including astroturf, sports hall and competition swimming pool. All-weather courts ensure year-round tennis of a high standard, and there are two squash courts and a nine-hole golf course. Main activities are lacrosse, hockey, netball, tennis, rounders, swimming and athletics with fixtures at all ages against schools and clubs of all types. Other clubs and societies cater for fencing, badminton, rowing, canoeing, martial arts and skiing.

The Riding School is situated within the grounds adjacent to the main school campus and offers riding to girls of all standards from beginners to Pony Club B Test level.

The School is divided into six Houses which compete in Games, Music, Drama, and other activities. Girls take part in the Duke of Edinburgh's Award Scheme at Bronze and Gold level.

Scholarships. Awards can be made at any stage and are regularly reviewed. Academic, Art, Dance, Drama, Choral, Music and Sport awards are available. In addition to their scholarship, holders of music awards usually receive free tuition on two instruments. Auditions are held in the Spring Term. For further details apply to the Admissions Office or consult the school's website.

Bursaries Means-tested bursaries are offered at all levels.

Charitable status. Queen Margaret's School, York is a Registered Charity, number 517523, which aims to provide high quality education for girls.

Queen Mary's School
A Woodard School

Baldersby Park, Topcliffe, Thirsk, North Yorkshire YO7 3BZ

Tel:	01845 575000
Fax:	01845 575001
email:	admin@queenmarys.org
website:	www.queenmarys.org
Twitter:	@QueenMarysSch
Facebook:	/Queen-Marys-School

Queen Mary's is an all-girls boarding and day school for pupils aged 7 to 16. It has a co-educational Early Years and Pre-Prep department for day pupils aged 2 to 7. The total school roll is currently 240.

Queen Mary's has a unique family atmosphere with friendliness and concern for others being an important part of the school's ethos. The country setting provides a safe haven for girls to thrive and develop self-confidence.

Chairman of Governors: Dr H R V Morgan Williams, OBE BA

Headmaster: **Mr R A McKenzie Johnston**, MA Cantab

Deputy Head: Mrs D Hannam Walpole, BEd Hons

Miss E Abrahams, Mont Dip (*Year 1*)
Mr P Bailey, BA Hons, PGCE (*Head of Mathematics*)
Mr N Carter, GRSM, ARCM, LRAM, LGSM, PGCE (*Director of Music*)
Miss V Charmer, BA Hons (*Outdoor Education*)
Mrs J Coles, BEd Hons (*Year 5, KS2 Science*)
Mrs D Coull, BA Hons, PGCE (*English*)
Mr A Cowey, BEd Hons (*Year 2, KS1 Coordinator*)
Mrs T Devenish, BEd, BA Hons (*Head of Design Technology*)
Miss F Edwards, BA Hons, PCGE (*Head of Modern Languages*)
Miss C Fitzgerald, BSc Hons, PGCE (*Head of PE*)
Mrs R Foster, BSc Hons, PGCE (*Year 4*)
Mrs C Grace, BA Hons, PGCE (*Modern Languages*)
Mrs M Grant, MA, PGCE (*Learning Support*)
Mr N Hanysz, BSc Hons, PGCE (*Science*)
Mrs E Hopkins, CertEd (*Head of Modular Science, Learning Support Coordinator*)
Mrs A Howard, BA Hons
Mrs S Hughes, BMus, MA, PGCE (*KS2 Music*)
Mrs H Kavanagh, BA Hons QTS (*Year 3*)
Miss A Kopp, BA Hons, MA, PGCE (*Art*)
Mrs E Lindsley, BSc Hons, PGCE (*Head of Physical Education*)
Mrs H McKell, BA Hons, PGCE (*English*)
Mrs J Nuttall, BEd Hons (*Year 6 KS2 English*)
Mrs L Nuttall, BSc Hons, PGCE (*Mathematics*)
Mr P Nuttall, BSc Hons, PGCE (*Head of Science*)
Miss A Pearson, BA Hons, PGCE (*Head of History*)
Mrs A Petty, CertEd (*Special Needs*)
Mrs V Potter (*Physical Education*)
Mrs M Redmond, PGCE (*German, Spanish*)
Mrs D Sheppard (*Teaching Assistant*)
Mrs V Sherwood, Dip PGCE, MA (*Latin/Classics*)
Mrs M Smerdon, BA Hons, QTS (*Head of KS3/4 and Religious Studies*)
Mrs C Sommerville, BSc, DipEd (*Head of Chemistry*)
Miss A Telford, BA Hons, MA, PGCE
Miss K Vaughan, BEd Hons, ALAM, UCPD (*Drama*)
Mr D Walker, BA Hons QTS, MEd (*KS2 Mathematics*)
Mrs L Weston (*Classroom Assistant*)
Mrs V Wild, BA Hons, PGCE (*KS2*)
Mrs C Wiggins, BSc Hons, PGCE (*Head of Geography*)
Mr A Would, BA Hons, PGCE (*KS2*)
Revd Graham Wright, DipTh, Dip Min (*Religious Studies*)

Early Years Department:
Head of Early Years: Mrs M-J Foster, BA, PGCE
Reception Assistant: Mrs J Tindall
Early Years Practitioner: Mrs L Welburn, DPP3
Early Years Practitioner: Mrs C Moore, DPP3
Early Years Practitioner: Mrs P Bruce, DPP3

Careers and Work Experience: Mrs M Smerdon, BA Hons, QTS

Head of Boarding: Mrs A Hickling
School Nurse: Mrs S Beaumont

School Chaplain: Reverend Graham Wright
Roman Catholic Chaplain: Fr Leo Chamberlain, OSB

Drama: Mrs P M Coghlan, ALCM, LAM, Gold Medal (*Speech & Drama*)
Riding: Mrs C Turner

Head's PA and School Secretary: Mrs S Lovell
Finance and Estate Manager: Mrs J Wright
Admissions: Miss M Chapman

Location. Queen Mary's is situated at Baldersby Park in a beautiful Grade 1 Palladian mansion, with 50 acres of grounds, including formal gardens, playing fields, and riding stables. Despite its idyllic surroundings, it is only 2 miles from Junction 49 of the A1 and within ten minutes of Thirsk railway station. York and Harrogate are within easy reach and so are Leeds/Bradford and Teesside airports. Six minibuses, each covering a twenty-five mile radius, transport girls to and from home on a daily basis.

The Curriculum. The National Curriculum forms the basis of what is taught, and all pupils sit Key Stage tests at the appropriate age. However, pupils are offered much more in terms of breadth and depth of learning. Generous time is given to core subjects, English, mathematics, science and modern languages, but strong emphasis is also placed on the supporting subjects – geography, history, religious education, classics, ICT, design technology, music, art and a varied programme of physical education. Classes are kept deliberately small, which means that every girl can receive plenty of support from her teachers. The school has an excellent learning support department for those pupils who have specific learning difficulties. The two years leading up to GCSE are full and focused, with most girls taking nine or ten subjects at GCSE. The public examination results are outstandingly good and the school is one of the highest achieving non-selective schools in the country.

Pastoral care. All girls in school have personal tutors who oversee the academic, social and emotional development of each of their tutees. Building self-confidence and developing the individual talents of each pupil is seen as a vital aspect of the education offered. Each girl is encouraged to be self-reliant from an early age and pupils are taught a real concern for the needs of others. Girls in their final year at Queen Mary's undertake a number of important responsibilities to help the school community function smoothly.

Boarding. Queen Mary's offers a number of boarding options to suit the needs of parents and their daughters. Those who choose to board may be weekly or full boarders. The experience of boarding is considered to be valuable for all girls and, when space permits, day girls may board on a nightly basis to fit in with extra-curricular commitments or parental need. The boarding accommodation is all within the main building and the girls find their dormitories cheerful and comfortable. The full boarders, who stay at weekends, enjoy lots of varied activities and trips, often much to the envy of those who go home. The Housemistress, together with her colleagues, looks after the general health of the girls, while the school nurse and the school doctor oversee all medical care.

Extra-Curricular Activities. An impressive range of extra-curricular activities is available to all members of the school community. Choral and orchestral music are both huge strengths of the school; sport is good too with hockey, lacrosse and netball being played in the winter terms and tennis, rounders and athletics in the summer. Facilities include a modern indoor swimming pool and astroturf pitch. Drama, debating and The Duke of Edinburgh's Award at bronze level are highly popular choices and the new, all-weather outdoor riding manège allows more than 90 girls to ride each week. All children also enjoy the weekly Adventure Club, which gives them the opportunity to climb the newly-installed Climbing Wall, canoe on the adjacent River Swale, or participate in pheasant-plucking club. For the intellectuals, there is film-making club and story club to name just a few.

Religious Affiliation. The school is part of the Woodard Corporation, an Anglican foundation which promotes Christian education and high academic and pastoral standards within all its schools. The school has its own Church of England chapel. The school Chaplain prepares girls for confirmation. Girls of other denominations are welcome.

What happens after GCSE? Queen Mary's has no Sixth Form and this is seen as a real strength of the school. Specialist careers advice is offered throughout the senior school and well informed staff support the girls as they seek to make application to their new schools and colleges. Each senior girl is able to choose a school or Sixth Form college which can offer her exactly the courses and educational environment she requires for her Sixth Form studies. A healthy proportion of the girls join their new schools as scholars. A few girls will embark on GNVQs or vocational training. Queen Mary's girls can be found in the Sixth Forms of over 30 different schools and colleges.

Scholarships. Scholarships are offered at 11+, 12+ and 13+ to those candidates who show particular academic flair or have special talent in Music, Sport or Art. Examinations are held during the Michaelmas Term.

Entrance. By interview with the Head. Entry can be at most stages, subject to availability. An up-to-date prospectus will be dispatched immediately on request. The school's website also provides useful information.

Fees per term (2014–2015). Day: Nursery £25.50 per half-day session; Reception £2,210; Years 1–2 £2,615; Year 3 £4,150; Years 4–6 £4,380; Years 7–8 £4,720; Years 9–11 £5,390.

Boarding: Years 4–6 £5,905; Years 7–8 £6,280; Years 9–11 £6,990.

Extra subjects per term. Music £205, Speech and Drama £70, Riding £200.

Charitable status. Queen Mary's School (Baldersby) Ltd is a Registered Charity, number 1098410. It exists to educate children in a Christian environment.

Queen's College, London

43–49 Harley Street, London W1G 8BT
Tel: 020 7291 7070
Fax: 020 7291 7090
email: queens@qcl.org.uk
website: www.qcl.org.uk

Queen's College was the first institution to provide an academic education and qualifications for young women. It was founded in 1848 by F D Maurice, Professor of Modern History at King's College, and was housed originally at 45 Harley Street.

Today it is a thriving school of 350 girls aged from 11–18, of whom 80 are in the Sixth Form. Queen's College Preparatory School (020 7291 0660), which opened in 2002 at 61 Portland Place, takes girls from age 4–11.

Patron: Her Majesty The Queen

Visitor: The Rt Revd and Rt Hon the Lord Bishop of London

Council:
Chairman: Michael Sharman, BSc Southampton
Vice-Chairman: Ms Jessica Pulay, MA Oxon, MCIL
Miss Gillian Adams, BSc, MBchB, FRCS Ed, FRCOphth
The Revd Charlotte Bannister-Parker, BA MA Durham
Ms Sally Cass
Mrs Susan Deans, MA Oxon, FCA
Lady Hopkins, AADip, Hon FAIA, Hon FRIAS
John Jacob, BSc Southampton
Mrs Danielle Salem, BA Farnham
Miss Sarah Shebbeare, BA London
Tim Streatfeild, MA Oxon, FCA
Professor Alison While, BSc MSc PhD London, RGN RHV

Bursar and Secretary to the Council: S N Turner

Principal: **Dr F M R Ramsey**, MA DPhil Oxon

Headmistress of Queen's College Preparatory School: Mrs A-M Dempsey, BA London

Senior Tutor: Mrs K C Woodcock, BA Bristol

Director of Studies: M J Wardrop, MChem Oxon

Admissions Secretary: Mrs R M Kershaw

Queen's College is situated in Harley Street, combining the beauty of four eighteenth century houses with modern facilities for science, languages, art, drama, music and ICT, as a well as a Hall and gymnasium. Two libraries, in the care of a graduate librarian, offer the students some 17,000 books, and we also preserve a unique archive recording the history of the College.

Curriculum. Class sizes rarely exceed twenty and the normal size of a year group is 55–60, divided into three forms. The year group is streamed for mathematics and French during the first year and at a later stage for English, Latin and science.

The curriculum is wide, including five modern languages, as well as Latin, Greek and classical civilisation. Girls usually take nine or ten subjects at GCSE, and the three sciences are taught separately. At A Level it is possible to study history of art, economics, or government and politics as well as the subjects already taken at GCSE.

There is a very full programme of sport offered, with the traditional team games taking place in Regent's Park. Girls play netball, lacrosse, rounders, and tennis; there are thriving clubs before and after school for swimming, cross-country running and other leisure pursuits. Dance and PE are offered at GCSE. Regular sports fixtures are arranged against local schools. The Duke of Edinburgh's Award is organised at bronze, silver and gold levels. Individual music lessons are offered in all instruments including voice, and the musical or dramatic productions and jazz concert are highlights of each year.

The location of the College means that theatre and other educational visits in London are an integral part of the curriculum, complemented by opportunities to travel abroad or to other parts of the country. Every summer Year 7 visit Northumberland for a week and in recent years groups of girls have visited France, Greece, Germany, Italy and Russia. There is at least one ski trip each year, usually run jointly with Queen's College Preparatory School.

Almost all girls leaving Queen's proceed to university, including Oxford or Cambridge; and several students each year choose to take an Art Foundation course at one of the London colleges. Former students are prominent in medicine, education, writing and the media; they retain contact with each other and the college through the Old Queen's Society, which also gives bursaries to families in financial need.

Pastoral Care. Queen's College prides itself on its friendly and informal atmosphere, highly valued by girls, parents and staff. Pastoral care is strong and we have a full-time nurse to support the work of form tutors and pastoral staff. A specialist in various special educational needs works individually with pupils once the need has been identified. We send reports to parents every half-term and hold regular Parents' Evenings; contact with parents benefits from the use of email by all members of staff. Parents also support the College through membership of the Parents' Association, giving practical and some financial assistance to College functions.

Admission. The College is a member of the North London Independent Girls Schools' Consortium for entry at 11+ and all candidates are interviewed individually. As well as high academic standards we value enthusiasm and creativity, and academic, music and art awards are available to 11+ entrants.

If vacancies arise we also welcome applicants at other ages, particularly after GCSE, where there is a long-standing tradition of accepting students to undertake their A Level education at Queen's. Some scholarships are available on entry at this stage. Means-tested bursaries are available at all points of entry.

Fees per term (2014–2015). £5,410.

Charitable status. Queen's College, London is a Registered Charity, number 312726. It exists to provide education for girls. It is an Anglican foundation, open to those of all faiths or none who are prepared to subscribe to its ethos.

Queen's Gate School

133 Queen's Gate, London SW7 5LE
Tel: 020 7589 3587
Fax: 020 7584 7691
email: registrar@queensgate.org.uk
website: www.queensgate.org.uk

Governors:
Mr Michael Cumming (*Chairman*)
Mrs Laura Marani (*Deputy Chairman*)
Mr William Gillen
Mr Gary Li
Dr Shirley A Radcliffe
Mrs Victoria Schild
Mr Peter Trueman
Mrs Manina Weldon

Staff:

Principal: Mrs R M Kamaryc, BA Hons, MSc, PGCE Queen's Belfast

Director of Teaching and Learning: Mr M Alter, BSc Hons, PGCE
Director of Pastoral Care: Ms C A Yates, MA, BEd
Senior Tutor: Mrs I Jones, BA Hons, PGCE
Assessment & Learning Coordinator and Head of Upper School: Mr M Crundwell, BSc, MPhil Lon, MEd Dist, QTS
Head of Sixth Form: Dr M Lee, PhD Lon, BSc
Head of Form IV: Mr R Moss, BA Hons, PGCE
Dep Head of Form IV: Miss F Sutherland, BDiv Hons, MA RADA London, PGCE, LGSM
Head of Lower School: Mr J Denchfield, BA Hons, PGCE

Art and Design:
Mr S Mataja, BA, PGCE
Mrs J Jokhoo, BFA, Dip Teaching NZ
Mrs K Bonnington, BA Hons, PGCE

Art, History of:
Ms I Cornwall-Jones, MA, PGCE

Biology:
Miss N Mia, BSc Hons, MSc, PGCE
Mrs C Mayne, BSc, PGCE
Miss L Coulton, BSc Hons, PGCE
Mr A Selkirk BSc, BComm, PG Dip Teaching Secondary

Careers Education & Guidance:
Ms I Cornwall-Jones, MA Hons, PGCE
Mrs S Sexon, BA, MA, QTS

Chemistry:
Mrs C Mayne, BSc, PGCE
Mr A Selkirk, BSc, BComm, PG Dip Teaching Secondary
Dr K Georgiou, BSc Hons, PhD

Classics:
Dr T Bell, MA
Miss C Fox, BA Hons, PGCE
Mr R Moss, BA Hons, PGCE
Mrs N J Clear, BA Hons, PGCE

Design and Technology:
Mrs C Wilkinson, BA Hons, PGCE
Mr J Francis, BA Hons, PGCE
Mrs V Thompson BSc, PGCE

Mr T Allen, MSc, BA (*Maternity Cover*)

Drama and Speech Training:
Ms L Arthur, MA Hons, MA RADA London, Dip
    Teaching NZ
Miss F Sutherland, BDiv Hons, MA RADA London,
    PGCE, LGSM
Ms J Doolan, MA

English:
Mr J Denchfield, BA Hons, PGCE
Ms C A Yates, MA, BEd
Miss R Wade, BA Hons, PGCE
Mrs V Harrison, BEd Hons
Miss F Sutherland, BDiv Hons, MA RADA London,
    PGCE, LGSM
Miss F Clarke-Williams, BA Hons, PGCE
Mrs S Sexon, BA, MA, QTS
Mrs E Burnside, MA, BA, PGCE

French:
M. A Pierrejean, BA
Mlle A Merin, Maîtrise de Littérature Afro-Américaine,
    PGCE
Mlle C Manier, MA, PGCE
Mrs J Tweedie, Licence-ès-Lettres English, PGCE Modern
    Languages

Geography:
Mr M Crundwell, BSc, MPhil Lon, MEd Dist, QTS
Miss S Scott, BSc Hons, PGCE, PCET, MEd
Dr M Lee, PhD Lon, BSc

German:
Mrs I B Atufe-Kreuth, MA, Mag Phil, CertEd

History:
Mrs J S Ditchfield, MA Hons, PGCE
Ms J FitzGerald, BA, MA, PGCE
Mrs S Sexon, BA, MA, QTS

ICT:
Mrs I Jones, BA Hons, PGCE
Mlle A Merin, Maîtrise de Littérature Afro-Américaine,
    PGCE

Italian:
Dr M Cadei, Dottoressa in Lingue e Letterature Straniere,
    Bergamo

Mathematics:
Mrs L Rose, BSc, BA Hons, MA, PGCE
Mrs R M Kamaryc, BA Hons, MSc, PGCE
Miss P Howe, BA Hons
Mr M Alter, BSc, PGCE
Mrs S Neale, BEd, ARCM, LTCL
Ms A Helm, BSc, PGCE

Music:
Mr E Liepa, BMus Guildhall
Ms L Sansun, MA, LRAM, MTC

Physical Education:
Miss B Ward, BEd Hons
Miss C Hurlbatt, BA Hons, PGCE
Miss A Owen, BSc, NQT
Miss S Clarke-Hackston, MSc, BA
Mr V Meshkov (*Fencing Master*)

Philosophy:
Mr R Stevens, BA Hons, PGCE
Mrs N J Clear, BA Hons, PGCE

Physics:
Dr J Mercer, PhD, BSc, ARCS, PGCE
Miss C Wise, MPhys, QTS

Psychology:
Miss S Palframan, BSc, PGCE

Religious Studies:
Mrs N J Clear, BA Hons, PGCE
Mr R Stevens, BA Hons, PGCE

Sociology:
Miss S Palframan, BSc, PGCE

Spanish:
Sta S Gomez, Licenciada en Filología

Laboratory Technicians:
Mr D I Swan, BSc Hons, MRSC
Mr M Sell, BSc

Art & DT Technician:
Mr K Lynn, BA Hons

Librarian: Mrs E Scott, BA, MScLIS, US Teaching
    Certificate
Assistant Librarian: Miss C Podavitte, Dottoressa in
    Archeologia, Milano

ICT Network Manager: Mr H Hirani
Assistant: Mr S Sikder

SEN Coordinator: Miss S Robertson-Glasgow, BEd Hons,
    MA Ed, Adv DipEd

Junior School:
Headmistress: Mrs C Thomson, MEd, BEd
Senior Tutor and Director of Studies: Mrs S Neale, BEd,
    ARCM, LTCL
Form Tutors:
Mrs S Neale, BEd, ARCM, LTCL
Miss E Allan, BA, BEd, PGCE
Mrs C Makhlouf, BEd Hons
Miss J Hasler, BEd Hons
Ms E Corcoran, MA, BA, PGCE
Miss G Davies, BA Hons, MEd
Miss E Smith, BA, MA, PGCE
Miss A Heale, BA, PGCE

Learning Support:
Miss S Robertson-Glasgow, BEd Hons, MA Ed, Adv
    DipEd

Teaching Assistants:
Mrs L Menez, BA
Mrs Y Meneely
Miss H Reid, BA
Miss K Jonczyk, BA, MA

French: Mrs J Tweedie, Licence-ès-Lettres English, PGCE
    Modern Languages

Music:
Ms S Hörcsög, BA Hons

Peripatetic Music Staff – Senior and Junior Schools:
Mrs G Haynes, Dip Piano ED and Accomp
Mrs A Chua, MA, FLCM, LLCM (*Piano*)
Mr L Sollory, ALCM (*Guitar*)
Miss V Evanson, BA, MMus ('*Cello*)
Mr J Stewart, BMus Hons (*Trumpet*)
Miss N Klouda, MMus, PG Dip, BMus (*Violin*)
Miss R Davies, MA, BMus, LRSM (*Clarinet/Saxophone*)
Mrs K Grace, GTCL Diploma
Miss K Stephenson, BA Hons Music (*Percussion*)
Mrs S Mailey-Smith, BMus Hons, RCM, PG Dip Dist
    Opera (*Singing*)
Ms L Sansun, MA, LRAM, MTC (*Singing*)

Bursar: Mr J Cubitt, ACCA
Financial Assistant to the Bursar: Ms M Spasova, BSc
    Hons, ACCA
Bursar's Assistant: Lady Wilkinson
Registrar: Miss J Micklewright
Principal's PA: Mrs S Evans, BA
Principal's Assistant: Mrs C Bickford
School Secretary: Miss C Crocker

*Junior School Headmistress's PA & Junior School
  Secretary*: Miss P Jackson
School Archivist: Miss C Podavitte, Dottoressa in
  Archeologia, Milano

Queen's Gate School is an independent day school for girls between the ages of 4 and 18 years. Established in 1891, the school is an Educational Trust situated in five large Victorian Houses within easy walking distance of Kensington Gardens, Hyde Park, Stanhope Gardens and the Museums of South Kensington.

The aim of the school is to create a secure and happy environment in which the girls can realise their academic potential and make full use of their individual interests and talents. The School encourages the development of self-discipline and creates an atmosphere where freedom of thought and ideas can flourish.

Close cooperation with parents is welcomed at every stage.

There is no school uniform except for PE and for the Junior girls, a top coat in winter and blazer and boater in summer. There is a dress code and girls are expected to wear clothing and footwear suitable for attending school and taking part in school activities.

Curriculum. Girls follow as wide a curriculum as possible and generally take GCSE in ten subjects that must include English, Mathematics, Science and a modern language.

An extensive range of AS/A Level subjects is offered. Four or five AS Levels are studied in the first year and three (or four) of these are taken at A2 Level.

Games. Netball, Hockey, Tennis, Swimming, Rowing, Athletics, Basketball, Horse Riding, Cross-Country, Biathlon and Dance.

Admission. By test and interview in the Junior School; by the North London Independent Girls' Schools' Consortium entrance examination at 11+; by the School's own entrance examinations for entry to other years in the Senior School. Applicants for the Sixth Form are expected to have passed a minimum of six GCSEs at A Grade with A grades required in those subjects they wish to pursue to A Level.

Registration fee: £100.

Fees per term (2014–2015). £4,950–£5,850.

Queenswood School

**Shepherd's Way, Brookmans Park, Hatfield,
Hertfordshire AL9 6NS**
Tel: 01707 602500
Fax: 01707 602597
email: admissions@queenswood.org
website: www.queenswood.org
Twitter: @QueenswoodSch
Facebook: /Queenswood-School-Hertfordshire-UK

Motto: 'In Hortis Reginæ' – 'In the Queen's Gardens'.

The School was founded in 1894 in Clapham Park, London. It moved to its current site in Hertfordshire in 1925.

Governors:
Chairman: Mr E M Sautter, MA
Vice-Chairman: Miss A M Rawlinson, MA, NPQH
Mr R Baines, BSc, CIMA, CEng, MICE
Reverend A E Brown, BSc Hons
Mr H J de Sausmarez, BA Hons, FCIS
Mr T C Garnham, BSc Hons
Mr D J Harvey
Professor Q McKellar, CBE, BVMS, PhD, FRSE, MRCVS
Mrs V R Neale (*Old Queenswoodian Representative*)
Mr A D Poppleton, BEng, AKC, FIET, FBSC
Mr R C C Saville, BSc Hons

Mrs J Sotiriou
Reverend T Swindell, BA Hons, BSc Hons, FCA
Mrs P M Wrinch

***Principal*: Mrs P C Edgar**, BA Hons London, PGCE

Bursar and Clerk to the Governors: Mr I Williams, BEng
  Hons RMCS Shrivenham, CEng
Deputy Head Academic: Mr I Sheldon, MChem Oxon,
  PGCE, MRSC
Deputy Head Pastoral & Boarding: Mrs A Wakefield,
  BMus Hons Sheffield
Deputy Head Staff: Mrs S Sanders, BA Hons London,
  PGCE
Head of Sixth Form: Mr P Merrell, BA Hons UCL, MPhil
  Birmingham, PGCE
Head of Middle School: Miss P Sex, BA Hons Swansea,
  MA Ed Hertfordshire, PGCE
Head of Lower School: Mrs M Gourd, BA Hons
  Nottingham, MA London, PGCE

Heads of Departments:
Art and Design: Mr A Wright, BA Hons Sunderland,
  PGCE
Design & Technology: Ms M Archer, BSc Hons UCL,
  PGCE
Drama: Mrs A Kelley, BA Hons Wales, MA Portsmouth
English: Miss L Morton, BA Hons Oxon, PGCE
Geography: Mrs S Sanders, BA Hons London, PGCE
History: Mr S Daughton, BA Hons Sunderland, PGCE
History of Art: Dr W Bird, BA Hons Leicester, PGCE, PhD
  Reading
ICT Life Skills: Mrs S Goodwin, RSA Teaching Cert
Languages: Mrs L Law, BA Hons Middlesex, PGCE
Mathematics: Miss H Nendick, BSc Hons Dunelm, PGCE
Music: Mr J Dobson, Prof Cert Hons RAM, LRAM
Physical Education: Mrs J Wakeley, BEd Hons London
Practical Cookery: Mrs J Lee
Religious Studies: Ms C de la Pena, MA London, PGCE
Science: Mrs M F T Davidson, BSc Hons Leicester, PGCE

Head of Marketing and Admissions: Mrs A Steiger, BSc
  Hons Manchester

Queenswood is a progressive boarding and day school for around 440 girls, aged between 11 and 18, where boarders make up half of the School. An all-round education focuses on equipping the girls with all the life skills required of women in the 21st century. Within a caring and supportive framework, the girls enjoy a dynamic academic curriculum, supported by a diverse and exciting co-curricular programme.

It is a warm and friendly community where everybody knows each other. Girls thrive within a nurturing House structure tailored to meet their needs as they progress from the Lower School, through the Middle School, and on into the Sixth Form. Day girls are fully integrated within the Houses, are able to enjoy all the facilities and opportunities available to the boarders, but choose to go home at night after a packed school day. There is a flexible approach to boarding to meet the varying needs of individual families; girls may choose to be full boarders or just to remain in School for four or five nights a week.

Queenswood is proud to be an international community with an outward-looking approach; overseas girls make up around 20% of the pupils. We welcome girls of all faiths and none, recognise and support an individual's adherence to her own faith, but expect all girls to embrace the School's broad spiritual ethos.

The girls are ambitious high achievers, winning places at the top universities both at home and abroad prior to embarking upon a range of exciting careers. The School is, however, resolutely neither an academic hothouse nor overly selective. Individual talent also flourishes in sport and the creative and performing arts. As important as individual achievement is the development of a sense of responsibility for each other and the world in which they live. Queenswood girls are thoughtful young people with a secure set of values and self-confidence.

The beautiful Queenswood estate provides the perfect educational environment. Being just 25 minutes from central London, it also has the advantage of easy access to the cultural richness of the capital. At the same time, its proximity to major international airports provides ease of travel for both our overseas girls and for those participating in the School's foreign exchange and visit programmes.

Entry. Entrance to Queenswood is by examination (CEE or Queenswood's papers), interview and a report from the pupil's current Headteacher.

Scholarships. Academic, art, dance, drama, music, sports, hockey and tennis scholarships (honorary) are available at 11+, 13+, and Sixth Form entry. Bursaries are means tested and reviewed annually.

Fees per term (2014–2015). Boarders: Sixth Form £10,750; Years 9–11 £10,400; Years 7–8 £9,650. Day: Sixth Form £8,150; Years 9–11 £7,950; Years 7–8 £6,800.

Old Queenswoodians' Association (OQA) with 4,000+ members, organised in regional branches throughout the UK and the world, contactable through the school and website.

Charitable status. Queenswood School Limited is a Registered Charity, number 311060, which exists to provide high-quality education for girls.

The Red Maids' School

Westbury Road, Westbury-on-Trym, Bristol BS9 3AW
Tel: 0117 962 2641
Fax: 0117 962 1687
email: schoolsecretary@redmaids.bristol.sch.uk
website: www.redmaids.co.uk
Twitter: @RedMaidsSchool
Facebook: /redmaidsschool

Red Maids' is the country's oldest surviving girls' school, founded in 1634 by John Whitson, former Mayor and MP for Bristol. Whitson's vision for the school – to provide for "40 poor women children" who would be "kept and maintained and taught to read English and to sew" – is remembered each year on Founder's Day. It is a proud day for students, staff, parents and governors as the school processes through the centre of Bristol to a service of thanksgiving at Bristol Cathedral. The school is fortunate to still benefit from Whitson's financial legacy, allowing the provision of generous scholarships and bursaries to girls from a wide range of backgrounds. The spirit of our founder is therefore very much alive today as the school continues to empower and equip young women to make their mark in the world.

Governing Body:
Chairman: Mrs J MacFarlane

Mrs C Culligan	Mrs T Howell
Mr M Davies	Mrs L Pollock
Mrs V Dixon	Mr S Ryan
Mr J Fox	Mrs A Taylor
Mr A Hardwick	Mr D Taylor
Mr A Hillman	Mrs J Whatmough

Senior School

Headmistress: **Mrs I Tobias**, BA Hons New Hall Cambridge (*English*)

Senior Deputy Head: Mrs K Doarks, BSc Hons Bristol (*Mathematics*)
Deputy Head Academic: Mrs L Beynon, MA Durham (*Geography*)

Director of Sixth Form: Miss K Fleming, BSc Hons Manchester (*Microbiology*)
Senior Teacher – Pastoral: Mrs J Turner, BSc Hons Aston (*Modern Languages*)
Senior Teacher – Operations: Mr T Johnston, BA Hons Bath College of Higher Education (*Design Ceramics*)
Senior Teacher – Academic: Mr H Briggs, MA Durham (*Theology*)

Full-time academic staff:
Dr Z Bell, PhD Bristol (*Chemistry*)
Mr B Bohane, BA Hons UWIC (*Business Studies & Economics*)
Mrs S Bramley-Dymond, BA Hons Anglia Ruskin (*Learning, Research and Technology*)
Mr P Brealey, MSc Birmingham (*Geography*)
Mr S Browne, GRSM, LRAM, ARCM Royal Academy of Music (*Music*)
Miss L Bullion, BA Hons Liverpool John Moores (*Home Economics*)
Mrs C Cains, BSc Hons Bath Spa (*Geography*)
Mr J Cooper, MA Hons St Andrews (*Modern History*)
Miss A Corrigan, BA Hons Durham (*French & Italian*)
Mrs E Cross, BA Hons Manchester (*History and Italian*)
Miss J Dalley, MA Winchester (*History of Dress and Textiles*)
Mrs L Davies, BA Kent (*English*)
Mr Z Dif, BSc Algiers (*Physics*)
Mrs V Domone, BSc Hons Bristol (*Psychology*)
Mr M Fielding, BSc Exeter (*Mathematics & French*)
Miss K Hames, BSc Durham (*Chemistry*)
Miss S Hannah, BA UEA (*English*)
Mrs E Jackson, MA Hons Christ's College Cambridge (*Classics*)
Mrs R Killick, BA Liverpool Hope (*Music*)
Mrs S Lansdell-Woods, MA Bristol (*Classics and Ancient History*)
Mr E Levy, MA, Exeter (*English and Drama*)
Miss C Locock, BA Hons Durham, NQT (*Modern Languages*)
Miss C Maggs, BEd Hons University College of St Mark & St John (*Physical Education*)
Ms Z Matthews, BSc Hons Durham (*Mathematics*)
Mr A Newman, BA Bradford (*German & French*)
Mrs C North, BA Exeter (*French & Spanish*)
Mr J Owen, MA Hons St Catherine's College Cambridge (*English Literature*)
Mrs E Parker, BA Queens' College Cambridge (*Theology & Religious Studies*)
Mrs H Philpott, BSc Hons Birmingham (*Sport and Exercise Science*)
Miss S Russé, BA Hons Bath Spa (*Physical Education*)
Mr D Seamark, BSc Imperial College London (*Mathematics*)
Mrs E Sims, BSc Hons Brunel (*Art with Sports Studies*)
Dr A Simms, PhD Bristol, NQT (*Chemistry*)
Mr P Slade, BSc Worcester College Oxford (*Physics*)
Mr C Stainthorp, BSc Warwick (*Mathematics*)
Miss N Stubbs, MSc Warwick (*Mathematics*)
Miss M Tomaszewski, BA Queen's College Oxford (*Modern Languages*)
Mr C Turner, BA Hons Liverpool (*Modern Languages*)
Mrs V Turner, BSc Bristol (*Biology*)
Mrs C Warrington, BSc UWIC (*History*)
Mr C Watson, BSc Leeds (*Chemistry*)
Mrs C Woodman, GBSM, ABSM, LLCM, ALCM Birmingham School of Music (*Piano*)
Mrs P Wooff, BSc Sheffield (*Biology*)

Part-time academic staff:
Mrs R Beaney, BA Hons St Mary's Twickenham (*Theology & RS*)
Mrs W Bird, BSc Hons Bath Spa (*Food Nutrition*)
Ms J Bryant, BSc Birmingham (*Sport & Exercise Science*)

Mrs M Evans, BSc Cardiff (*Spanish*)
Ms A Geeson, BA Hons UWE (*Business Studies*)
Mrs C Koenig, BSc Hons Oxford Brookes (*Psychology*)
Ms C Knight, MA Wales (*Fine Art*)
Mrs S Lear, BA UWE (*Design & Technology*)
Mrs K Lewis-Barned, MEd Bristol (*English*)
Mrs K Markwell, BA Bristol (*English and Drama*)
Mrs K Price, BEd Hons Sussex (*Physical Education*)
Mrs R Pullen, BSc Hons Cardiff (*History*)
Mrs A Ransom, BA Hons Durham (*Modern Languages* (*Russian*)
Ms J Ratcliffe, BA Hons Bristol Polytechnic (*Art & Ceramics*)
Miss M Rhind, BSc London (*Biology*)
Mrs L Sayers, BSc Hons Bristol (*Mathematics*)
Mrs A Tyler, BA Joint Hons Cardiff (*Classical Studies*)
Mrs N Weir, BEd Nottingham (*Information Technology*)
Mrs P West, BSc Bristol (*Geography*)
Dr J Whalley, BA Hons Victoria University of Wellington (*Classics*)
Mrs S Willicombe, BA Hons Norwich School of Art & Design (*Art*)

Junior School

Headteacher: Mrs L Brown, BSc Leicester
Miss S Browning, BA Manchester Metro
Mrs M Edbrooke, BEd King Alfred's College, Winchester
Ms B Fenton, BEd Bristol Polytechnic
Mrs S Hiley, BSc Lancashire
Mrs L Joslin, BEd Dunfermline College of Physical Education
Dr J Moe, PhD Bristol
Mrs A Purdy, MA UWE
Ms J Ratcliffe, BA Bristol Polytechnic
Mrs L Woodward, BSc Birmingham

Bursar: Mr P Taylor
Headmistress's PA: Mrs J Bell
Bursar's PA: Mrs S Wooldridge
Admissions Registrar: Mrs E Bamber

Character. Red Maids' is a friendly, purposeful school; intellectual curiosity, energy and enthusiasm are characteristic of students and teachers alike. Red Maids are encouraged to discover and develop their own abilities, to think for themselves and to strive for success whether this is academic, on the sports field, in the creative arts or in the practical technologies.

Facilities. Set in 12 acres of peaceful parkland, sports facilities are all on site including an international standard astroturf and two competition standard grade 1 netball courts. The award-winning extension to the Junior School opened in 2008 as part of ongoing investment that has also included refurbishment of the school's science laboratories, the re-development of the Sixth Form Centre and in 2014 the building of a two-storey library, refurbished dining hall, servery and a new visitor's reception.

Extended Day. We offer an extended day at no extra charge. Girls can buy breakfast from 7.45 am and can stay at school for supervised homework or to take part in extra-curricular activities until 5.30 pm. Clubs and societies include: Chess, Current Affairs, choirs, orchestras, The Duke of Edinburgh's Award, Film Production, Drama, Mandarin and a wide range of sports clubs, teams and societies.

School Life. The School Council and Sixth Form leadership positions encourage students to take responsibility for others. Peer support systems, clubs run by older students and staff, and charitable fundraising of all sorts demonstrate the pupils' energetic involvement in their community.

Assemblies celebrate pupils' achievements in every sphere, examine current affairs and topical issues and offer opportunities for thought, reflection and spiritual exploration.

Curriculum. For the first three years of Senior School, all Red Maids shadow Key Stage 3 of the National Curriculum. Mathematics, French and Latin are taught in sets from Year 7; separate Science subjects from Year 9. In Years 10 and 11, Red Maids study IGCSEs in English, Science, Mathematics and Modern Languages. Adopted in 2009 for their greater academic content, they are an excellent platform for IB or A Level study. GCSE subjects include Religious Studies, History, Geography, Latin, Food Technology, Textiles Technology, Art, Music, Drama, Physical Education, Business Studies, and Classical Civilisation.

Sixth Form. Red Maids' offers the choice of studying the International Baccalaureate (IB) Diploma or A Levels. At A Level, additional subjects include Economics, Further Maths, Philosophy and Ethics, Psychology and Theatre Studies. IB Diploma students select six subjects, one each from English, Mathematics, Science, Humanities, Languages and one other. These subjects, together with Theory of Knowledge, Creativity Action Service and the Extended Essay form the Diploma programme over two years.

Sixth Form students at Red Maids' enjoy excellent teacher relationships and the independence of a new, purpose-built Sixth Form Centre with dedicated teaching rooms, seminar rooms, common rooms, café, an ICT suite and a dedicated careers library. Students achieve their full academic potential through high-quality teaching and developing habits of independent study and academic rigour. Almost all students go on to study at University, including Oxbridge.

Sixth formers have many opportunities to take on leadership roles within the school and to develop a broader understanding of the wider world through the varied community service programme and the general studies course. Sixth formers also follow a Life Skills enrichment course and receive individual careers advice.

Fees per term (2014–2015). Senior School £4,090, Junior School £2,780. Curricular school trips are included in this fee. The only extras are Music lessons (piano, clarinet, flute, viola, French horn, oboe, bassoon, violin, cello, saxophone, singing, trumpet, guitar), Speech and Drama lessons and optional non-academic trips.

Admission to Senior School. All students are admitted on the basis of an entrance examination, interview and headteacher's report. Key points of entry are at Year 7, 9 and 12. The entrance exam for Years 7 and 9 is held in January for admission the following September. Entry can take place into other years, subject to availability. For full particulars about fees, scholarships and admission procedures, application should be made to the Admissions Registrar.

Scholarships and Bursaries. Scholarships are available to new entrants to the school at 11+, 13+ and in the Sixth Form. Four non-means tested academic Scholarships worth up to 25% each can be awarded annually for outstanding performance in the 11+ Entrance Examination. A Sports Scholarship and two Music Scholarships are also available.

In addition two 100% places are awarded to girls on the basis of their performance in the 11+ entrance examination and taking financial need into consideration.

Academic, music and sports scholarships can also be considered for students joining at Year 9.

Scholarships are available for A Level or IB Diploma students joining the school at Sixth Form, awarded on academic merit and interview.

A number of bursaries are available to students joining the school at Year 7. Bursaries are based on means-testing as well as the student's academic ability and awards are likely to be valued at up to a maximum of 50% of full fees.

Contact our Admissions Registrar for more information.

Junior School. *See Junior School entry in IAPS section.*

Charitable status. The Red Maids' School is a Registered Charity, number 1105017. It has existed since 1634 to provide an education for girls.

Redland High School for Girls

Redland Court, Bristol BS6 7EF
Tel: 0117 924 5796
Fax: 0117 924 1127
email: admissions@redlandhigh.com
website: www.redlandhigh.com
Twitter: @RedlandHigh
Facebook: /RedlandHighBristol

Motto: *So hateth she derknesse*
The School was founded in the year 1882, and established at Redland Court in 1884. The aim for which the School was instituted was to provide for the girls of Redland and its neighbourhood a non-denominational public school education of the highest class.

Governors:

School Council:
President: Mrs C Lear, BA
Chair of Governors: Dr T L Chambers, OBE, JP, FRCP
Deputy Chair of Governors: Mrs P Pyper, BA, MA
Mrs S Dore, BA, MA
Mrs A M Ebery, BA
Mr W Goodchild, BA, LGSM
Mr M Henry, FRICS, MCIArb
Mr S Holliday, MA Jesus College Cambridge
Dame Dr Elisabeth Hoodless, DBE, BA Dunelm, Dip App Soc Studies LSE
Ms H Lancaster, MA Oxford
Dr J S Littler, BA, BSc, MA, DPhil, MRSC
Mrs S Perry
Mr T Phillips, MSc, BSocSc, MBCS, CITP
Mr M Whife, BSc, MRICS, MAPM, ACIArb
Ms A Harrill, Grad Dip Phys Birmingham, SRP, MCSP

Bursar and Clerk to Governors: Mr N Cutland, ACIS

Headmistress: Mrs Caroline P Bateson, BA UCL, PGCE London, MA UWE

Senior School Staff:

Deputy Headmistress: Mrs P Davidson, BA, PGCE Bristol
Director of Studies: Mrs S E Barnes, BA, Dip HE Bloemfontein
Head of Sixth Form: Ms D Heywood, BSc Bristol, PGCE Cambridge
Head of Lower School: Miss H A Drew, BA Leeds, PGCE Cambridge
Head of Year 10 & 11: Mrs L McLaughlin, BSc, Grad DipEd Charles Sturt University

Heads of Houses:
Rowan: Mrs S Harrison, BA, PGCE Bristol
Maple: Miss Z Leach, BSc, PGCE Exeter
Willow: Mr M A K Sloan, BSc Bristol, PGCE Edinburgh
Chestnut: Ms E Sefer, Maître, LLCE Provence, PGCE Wales

* *Head of Department*

Art including Ceramics, Fabric Craft and History of Art:
*Ms R V Clapp, BA Middlesex
Ms L Dickson, BTEC BA Staffordshire
Mrs F Hughes Games, BA Hons PGCE London Metropolitan
Mrs C Smith, BA Essex

Biology:
*Dr M Quick, BSc Liverpool, PhD, PGCE Bristol (*also Head of Science*)
Ms D Heywood, BSc Bristol, PGCE Cambridge
Dr J Stone, PhD, BSc Swansea, PGCE UWE

Careers & Assistant Head of Sixth Form:
Ms L Jephcote, BA Reading, PGCE Wales

Chemistry:
*Mrs K Cook, BSc London, PGCE Bath
Ms A McAxup, BSc Southampton, PGCE Bristol

Classics including Latin, Greek and Classical Civilisation:
*Ms S Knights, BA, PGCE Bristol
Mrs G Holliday, MA Cambridge

Computing and ICT:
*Ms J Gale (*Director of Computing and ICT*)
*Ms Fiona Crick BSocSc Birmingham (*Head of Computing and ICT – Academic*)
Mrs J Marsden, BA OU, PGCE UWE
Mr A Chappell (*IT Support Technician*)
Ms M R Viney, BA, PGCE University of Wales, MEd Bristol

Drama and Theatre Studies:
*Ms S McCormack, BA Manchester, MA Bristol, PGCE Cambridge
Miss R Williams, BA Joint Drama & Education UWE

Speech & Drama:
Ms J Owens-Powell, BA Bristol, PGCE UWE
Miss R Williams, BA Joint Drama & Education UWE

Economics & Business Studies:
*Mr A Donald, BA Hons PGCE Lancaster

English:
* Mrs C Rodliffe, BA, PGCE Bristol
Mrs A J I Adams, MA St Andrews, PGCE Christ Church
Mrs P Davidson, BA, PGCE Bristol
Ms S McCormack, BA Manchester, PGCE Cambridge, MA Bristol
Ms J Owens-Powell, BA Bristol, PGCE UWE
Dr L White, BA Oxford, MA UWE, PhD Birmingham

French:
*Miss C M Douglas, BA Keele, PGCE Cardiff
Mr A Clark, BA, PGCE Oxford,
Mrs P M Hamilton, BA Belfast, PGCE Oxford
Ms N Mallem, BA UWE (*French Assistant*)
Ms E Sefer, Maître, LLCE Provence, PGCE Wales

Geography:
*Mrs J Neil, BSc, MSc Lancaster, PGCE Edinburgh, NPQH, CGeog(*teacher*)
Mrs S M Argent, BA Worcester College, PGCE Exeter
Mrs G Holliday, MA Cambridge

German:
*Mrs P M Hamilton, BA Belfast, PGCE Oxford
Mrs J Sommerville, BA Durham, PGCE Bristol
Ms K Ehmen (*German Assistant*)

History & Politics:
*Ms A L Earle, BA Brunel, PGCE Exeter
*Mrs M Bishop, First Degree University of Venice, MLitt Cambridge, PGCE Bath
Mrs C P Bateson, BA University College London, PGCE University of London Institute, MA
Mrs G Holliday, MA Cambridge
Mr H T Whately, MA Edinburgh, MSc Oxford, MA Berlin, PhD, PGCE London

Library:
Ms J Owens-Powell, BA Bristol, PGCE UWE

Mathematics including Mechanics and Statistics and Further Mathematics:
*Mrs S E Barnes, BA, DipHE Bloemfontein
Mr M P Ehrlich, BA Cambridge, MBA London Business School, PGCE Bristol
Mrs S Locke, BEd UWE
Mrs A Stean, BSc Leicester, PGCE Bristol Polytechnic

Music:
*Mr S M Daykin, BMus, PG Dip Royal Welsh College of Music & Drama
Mrs S Harrison, BA, PGCE Bristol

Visiting Music Staff Junior & Senior Schools:
Ms E Adams, ALCM (*Voice and Music Theatre*)
Ms C Barratt, BMus, ARCM (*Piano*)
Ms M Barrett (*Clarinet, Saxophone*)
Ms V Bremner, BA, ATCL, ALCM (*Voice and Music Theatre*)
Mr B Fitzpatrick (*Percussion*)
Miss C Hiles, MA, Dip TCM (*Piano*)
Miss V Hodges, BA, ALCM (*Clarinet, Saxophone*)
Mr A King, GBSM, ABSM, LTCL (*Oboe*)
Ms S Kirk-Harris (*Voice*)
Ms M Krawiec (*Flute*)
Ms L McCabe, BMus, DipRCM, Dip Music Therapy (*Viola*)
Ms J McCarthy, GGSM (*Cello*)
Ms E Preston (*Saxophone, Clarinet*)
Mr P Tedbury (*Guitar*)
Ms F Trezevant (*Voice*)
Mr R Webb, BMus (*Brass*)
Ms E Whitfield, BA Nottingham (*Bassoon*)
Mrs R Whitworth, BSc Bristol (*Violin*)

Physical Education:
*Miss Z L Leach, BSc, PGCE Exeter
Miss E R Harrington, BSc, PGCE Gloucestershire
Mrs L McLaughlin, BSc, Grad DipEd Charles Sturt University
Ms J Wood, BEd Sussex, MSc Leicester
Mrs S Thomas (*Tennis Coach, Junior & Senior School*)

Physics:
*Mr M A K Sloan, BSc Bristol, PGCE Edinburgh
Ms R L Nelson, BSc Montreal, PGCE Bristol

Psychology:
*Ms L Jephcote, BA Reading, PGCE Wales

Religious Studies:
*Miss H A Drew, BA Leeds, PGCE Cambridge
Mrs L Gillion, CertEd
Mr H T Whately, MA Edinburgh, MSc Oxford, MA Berlin, PhD, PGCE London

Science Curriculum Support Staff:
Mrs J Boynton
Mr J Icke
Miss K Edwards

Spanish:
*Mrs T Asiain-Escobar, MA Eastern Michigan University
Ms M E Rodriguez Dominguez, BSc Valladolid (*Spanish Assistant*)

Special Educational Needs:
Ms L Brown, BA Hons London
Mrs J R Anstee, BEd Sheffield, Prim Ed CAPSE Special Needs

Technology including Design, Food & Textiles:
Miss H A Drew, BA Leeds, PGCE Cambridge
*Mrs L M Hunt, BA Nottingham Trent, PGCE Gloucestershire
Ms M R Viney, BA, PGCE University of Wales, MEd Bristol

Junior School:

Head Teacher: Mr J P Eyles, BEd Bath Spa

Lower Foundation: Mrs E Buffham, BA, PGCE Bath Spa
Upper Foundation:
Ms Kerri Vaughan, BSc Hons
Mrs K Jones, BA UWE
Mrs V Farnham

Early Years Assistant: Miss A Tippett, NNEB Bristol
Early Years PE Games: Mrs S Falconer, BA Sussex, PGCE London
Year 1 Teachers:
Mrs K Buckley, BSc Portsmouth, PGCE UWE
Mrs J Lear, BA UWE, QTS
Year 2 Teacher: Mrs A James, BA, PGCE Bath Spa
Year 3 Teacher: Mrs K Lashley, BA, PGCE Carmarthen
Year 4 Teacher: Miss S F Rendall, BA Bristol, PGCE Bath Spa
Year 5 Teachers: Mrs L Baker, BSc, PGCE Bath Spa
Year 6 Teacher: Mrs R Hayward, CertEd Bristol
After School Care:
Ms R J Wilcox, Cache Diploma
Miss A Tippett, NNEB Bristol (*Maternity Cover*)
Ballet: Miss D Sims, ARAD, Adv TDip, LISTD, Dip RBS TTC
French: Ms E Sefer, Maîtrise, LLCE Provence, PGCE Wales
German: Mrs P M Hamilton, BA Belfast, PGCE Oxford
PE/Swimming Teacher: Mr J P Eyles, BEd Bath Spa
Director of Computing and ICT: Ms J Gale
IT Support Assistant: Mr A Chappell
Latin: Ms S Knights, BA, PGCE Bristol
Special Educational Needs: Ms L Brown, BA Hons London
Classroom Assistants:
Ms R Wilcox, Cache Diploma
Mrs C Cheek, Cache Diploma
Mrs M Crane
Mrs A Doherty
Mrs N Goguadze
Ms V Hayden
Mrs J Smith, Cache Diploma
Miss A Tippett, NNEB Bristol
Mrs J Trump, Cache Diploma, CTA3
Music:
Mrs S Harrison, BA, PGCE Bristol
Miss S F Rendall, BA Bristol, PGCE Bath Spa
Craft: Miss L Dickson, BTEC BA Staffordshire
(*Visiting Music Teachers as for Senior School*)
Physical Education:
Mr J P Eyles, BEd Bath Spa
Miss E Harrington, BSc, PGCE Gloucestershire
Miss Z L Leach, BSc, PGCE Exeter
Mrs L McLaughlin, BSc, Grad DipEd Charles Sturt University
Ms J Wood, BEd Sussex, MSc Leicester
PSHE: (*to be appointed*)
Science: Mrs K Lashley, BA, PGCE Carmarthen
Speech & Drama: Miss R Williams, BA Joint Hons Drama & Education UWE

Administration:
Bursar: Mr N Cutland, ACIS
Bursar's Secretary: Miss F Atkin, BEd Exeter
Payroll Officer: Miss A Brice, BA Portsmouth
Fees Officer: Mrs K L Gardner, FCCA
PA to Headmistress and Office Manager: Mrs D Waine
Admissions Secretary: Miss S Patch
School Secretary: Mrs J Speight
Junior School Secretaries:
Mrs L Stannard
Mrs J Trump, Cache Diploma, CTA3
Receptionist: Mrs H Kent
Marketing & Development Manager: Mrs E Down, CIM
Alumni Officer: Mrs L Spencer-Small, BSc Bristol
Resources Technician: Mrs J Walker
Head of Maintenance: Mr V Hill
Maintenance Staff:
Mr M Cox
Mr K Harris
Mr R Hutton
Mr S Pope

Catering and Cleaning: Ms H Tovey, Manager, Chartwells
Golden Hill Sports Ground: Mr and Mrs Cato

Redland High is an Independent School for girls between the ages of 3 and 18, with approximately 150 Juniors and 390 Seniors. All girls are given a broadly based education aimed at developing the ability and potential of each individual. The school is a friendly, purposeful, disciplined and caring community.

The Junior School is housed in Victorian houses close to the Senior School. We place due emphasis on ensuring that the Junior girls acquire excellent core skills but also devote time to many extras that are not part of the National Curriculum. Our extra-curricular activities programme (which includes judo, orienteering and chess club) ensures that girls throughout our age range can choose something to suit their interests whether sporting, musical, artistic, scientific or literary. We strongly encourage our pupils to try at least one activity to ensure she receives the benefit of a rounded education. Many educational trips are run through the year to enhance classroom learning. Class sizes are small to ensure each girl gets optimum attention and to enable the girls to express their individuality and know that they are special members of our close-knit community. In 2008 we opened a new Activity Hall which gives additional space for Year 5 and 6 pupils, in response to the demand for places. We also offer after-school care and our Redland Rascals Holiday club in support of working families. Visitors notice straight away that there is a buzz about this school that is to do with purposeful and innovative approaches to enhancing the girls' learning experiences. Because we are determined to 'reach' each and every pupil, we try lots of different methods so that each one of them will have the opportunity to find and develop her own learning style with enthusiasm and success. The Junior and Senior schools work very closely together enabling Junior pupils to benefit from specialist teachers for Music, Latin and Modern Languages and to use the Senior School facilities for Art, PE and Technology.

The Senior School is situated in a beautiful eighteenth-century mansion to which additional classrooms and excellently equipped laboratories have been added. There is a very impressive Art department housed in an Arts Centre, an ICT Suite, a Technology Workshop a well-equipped Home Economics unit and a gymnasium with a climbing wall and a large stage, well designed for dramatic productions. Music, which is a particular strength of the school, is housed in a dedicated Music School close by. Redland High has a fine tradition of very high examination results, effective and supportive pastoral care and a wide range of extra-curricular activities. The school's undoubted proficiency in encouraging all its pupils comes from outstanding teaching and having a school of optimum size: sufficient students to make a considerable subject choice viable but a low enough pupil to staff ratio for each individual pupil to be appreciated.

The school curriculum consists of Religious Studies, English Language and Literature, Drama, French, German, Spanish, Greek, Latin, Classical Civilisation, History, Geography, Mathematics, IT, Design Technology, Biology, Chemistry, Physics, Textiles, Art, Home Economics, Craft, Music and Physical Education which includes Gymnastics and Dancing, Hockey, Netball, Athletics, Tennis, Badminton, Squash, Orienteering, Cricket and Swimming. Additional subjects available in the Sixth Form are Economics and Business, History of Art, Government & Politics, Psychology and Theatre Studies.

Students who enter the Sixth Form have the exclusive use of the Mary Crook Study Centre which provides excellent facilities and spacious accommodation for teaching and study; there is also a large common room available where the girls can relax. Sixth Formers do not wear uniform and are encouraged to develop their independence by sharing responsibility in the running of the school. The Senior School has a well-established link with a school in Marburg,

Germany and pupils take part in the annual Bristol/Bordeaux exchange. Other educational trips are organised and girls may take part in the Duke of Edinburgh's Award and the Young Enterprise Scheme.

Girls throughout the school can learn a broad variety of musical instruments and there are Junior and Senior choirs and orchestras. Wide reading and individual work is strongly encouraged supported by generous library and computer provision in both schools.

Fees per term (2014–2015). Senior School: £3,880 (which includes stationery and books). Junior School: Lower Foundation £21.75 per half day session; Upper Foundation, Years 1 & 2 £2,400; Years 3–6 £2,750.

Scholarships and Bursaries. Scholarships are available for entry at Year 7 (11+), Year 9 (13+) and Sixth Form.

Academic, Art and Sport Scholarships are awarded annually to girls who display high academic potential at 11+, 13+ and for outstanding academic, artistic and sporting achievement at Sixth Form level. They are valued up to a maximum of half remission of fees and are awarded entirely on merit.

Music Scholarships are awarded to girls who are especially gifted in Music at Year 7 (11+), Year 9 (13+) and on entry to the Sixth Form. These are given irrespective of parental income and are valued up to a maximum of half remission of fees, or for free tuition on one or two instruments, as appropriate.

Bursaries: A number of Bursary awards are available each year from Year 5 upwards to those girls who show good academic ability and whose parents are in need of financial help to meet fees. The John James Bristol Foundation enables the school to provide annual Bursary Awards in its name to girls residing in the City of Bristol.

Charitable status. The Redland High School for Girls is a Registered Charity, number 311734.

The Royal High School Bath
GDST

Lansdown Road, Bath BA1 5SZ

Tel: 01225 313877
Fax: 01225 465446
email: royalhigh@rhsb.gdst.net
website: www.royalhighbath.gdst.net
Twitter: @royalhighbath

The Royal High School Bath is part of the GDST (Girls' Day School Trust). The GDST is the leading network of independent girls' schools in the UK. As a charity that owns and runs 24 schools and two academies, it reinvests all its income in its schools. For further information about the Trust, please visit www.gdst.net.

The Royal High School Bath is a leading independent day and boarding school of choice for girls aged 3–18 and the only school in the GDST to offer boarding in addition to day provision and the only one to offer the International Baccalaureate at Sixth Form. The school provides a happy, seamless experience that transforms and adds value at every level. This year that value added, from girls coming up through the school from Year 7 to Year 13, amounted to 0.87% at GCSE and 0.33% at A Level (independently verified), which when combined, equates to girls achieving a whole grade higher in exams. We deliver that value added because we value the individual girl.

***Acting Head*: Mrs Emma Ellison**, BSc Hons
   (*January–April 2015*)
Head: Mrs Jo Duncan, BA Hons, MA (*from April 2015*)

Senior Deputy Head – Curriculum: Mrs Emma Ellison, BSc Hons

Deputy Head – Pastoral: Mrs Debbie Dellar, BEd Hons

Director of Sixth Form College: Mr Andrew Melton, BEd Hons

Head of Junior School: Miss Heidi Hughes, BSc, PGCE, MA Ed Mgt

Senior Resident Housemistress: Mrs S Walworth, CertEd

Registrar: Miss Lynda Bevan, BA Hons

Number of Pupils. 680, including 180 in our Junior School and 190 in the Sixth Form.

Boarding. The Royal High School is unique among Trust schools in offering the enriching experience of boarding in the Junior School (from Year 5), Senior School and Sixth Form College. This gives parents the flexibility to choose the type of education best suited to their daughter's needs. If family circumstances change, so too can school arrangements. Our boarding accommodation is comfortable, spacious and well-equipped. The school enjoys a splendid location in beautiful grounds in the World Heritage City of Bath.

The School – Nursery, Junior, Senior, Sixth Form College. Laughter and a lifelong love of learning, collaboration and camaraderie, drive and determination, inspiration and involvement, aspiration and achievement – those are the qualities that that form the heart of our school. From a group of giggling, three year old girls holding hands in the playground of our 'outstanding' Ofsted rated Nursery; to a revitalised Junior School where lifelong friendships are forged and sporting and academic triumphs shared: to a passion for continued discovery and exploring new horizons at our exceptionally high-achieving Senior School and onto our dynamic Sixth Form College buzzing with mature, confident, gregarious young women, the RHS journey is a seamless one, with four life-enhancing experiences along the way.

This all-through, all-girls education is unique in Bath. We embrace all-round excellence and help every single girl to be happy and to be who she wants to be. We do this with a rich and exciting curriculum, with every opportunity for girls to focus on their strengths but also to develop their skills and talents across the broadest academic, social and personal spectrum. The school develops the confidence, capabilities and character needed to underpin success at university, throughout careers and in achieving ambitions in every aspect of life.

Our doors are always open to welcome girls from across the UK and across the world, who come here to achieve their very best academically, socially and personally, have fun, make friends, live, develop a global perspective in education, enjoy life and learn how to fly.

The Junior School. The Junior School has a new home, Cranwell House in Weston Park, a beacon of academic excellence for girls aged 3–11. The school includes an 'outstanding' Ofsted rated Nursery School in its own 11-acre grounds. With the Cranwell Curriculum, anything and everything is possible. It is a rich, diverse, unique, girl-centred and enabling curriculum that provides the girls throughout the Junior School with extraordinary opportunities to seek out irresistible challenges and support incredible learning adventures. The Cranwell Curriculum uses initial explorations to help the girls develop a sound understanding of all the subjects they are studying, develop a rich vocabulary relating to the subject and to understand it in terms of scientific, linguistic and creative possibilities. It means more traditional ways of working within the curriculum are considerably enhanced and become even more valuable.

The Royal High Junior School was the top performing independent Junior School in the area in a recent Sunday Times 'Parent Power' guide. The school recently gained the Arts Council's Artsmark Gold award for its extensive provision in the expressive and performing arts. Many girls have individual drama or music lessons. Extra-curricular activities include judo, theatre club and pottery. We have an after-

school care programme which enables pupils to stay in school until 6.00 pm and a breakfast club starting at 7.30 am. The Junior School also offers holiday clubs for girls and boys aged 3–11, which prove very popular and girls have the opportunity to excel at Modern Foreign Languages studying French, Spanish and Mandarin.

The Senior School. We are a dynamic, warm, friendly, culturally cosmopolitan school that values the special spark in each girl and gives her the confidence, character and self-esteem to explore her unique talents. We watch that spark of passion ignite into The Royal High School spirit.

Glittering exam results and outstanding statistics are one thing (and we certainly have those), but it's your daughter that matters most to us. We are happy if she is happy, liked and respected for who she is, what she is good at, what she wants to be good at, what she wants to do and where she wants to go. We are proud of our holistic approach towards developing accomplished young women and we work as a team to help each girl find her own special place in the school. Here, your daughter will find she can become the very best that she can be, in whatever fields she chooses.

Wisdom, leadership, teamwork, energy, courage, self-knowledge, confidence, compassion, courtesy, integrity and a sense of humour are part of the school's DNA and run through everything that we do and the way that we do it. They are qualities demonstrated by all our girls. In common with all GDST schools, academic standards are excellent. The broad curriculum includes a choice of four modern European languages plus Mandarin. Most students study three sciences separately at GCSE. Girls can also take Latin or Classical Greek.

GCSE Results 2014. 95% A*–C grades (36% at A*). One student achieved 11 A*, three with 10 A* and three with 9 A* plus A. A*/A grades up at 66%. Stellar performances across the broadest ever spectrum of subject disciplines from 100% A*–B in Religious Studies to 100% A*–B in Textiles. With 100% A* in Ancient Greek and Italian and 100% A*–B in Latin and in Mandarin, we also celebrate the continued resurgence of interest in both classic and modern languages and 96% A*–B in English Language and English Literature, 91 % A*–B in Physics and 85 % A*–B in Maths, anchor these results in solid academic achievement.

Sixth Form College. The Royal High Sixth Form College offers the International Baccalaureate Diploma Programme as an alternative to our extensive choice of A Level courses. We are one of a growing number of approved IB World Schools, which share a commitment to high-quality, challenging, internationally-focused education. Whether you choose the International Baccalaureate Diploma or A Levels and whether you have come up through The Royal High School or you are joining us from another school, or another country, you will be developing the academic credentials and an outlook on life that will shape your future. In addition to a choice of academic pathways, the college offers a real alternative to the traditional Sixth Form experience, with a greater measure of responsibility and a clear understanding that these two years are the preface to the next step of Higher Education and employment. All students are provided with a laptop to enhance learning. Results are excellent and the majority of students move on to Russell Group Universities and leading international institutions. Support for the UCAS process is superlative with tailored programmes to support applicants to particular disciplines, eg Medicine.

A Level and IB Results 2014. Our results have improved once again with 100% of students off to their chosen university or art foundation course.

A Level: Well over 50% of the grades this year were A*/A and 65% of students studying Mathematics achieved A*/A, with next year promising more success in this subject with 20 As from 37 entries at AS level.

IB: Notable successes include one student with an outstanding 45 points out of 45; three other girls scored 36 points or over, which puts them well above the national average; and nearly 50% of girls attained the much-coveted double A in Theory of Knowledge and the Extended Essay, which gives them full marks for these core components.

Extra-Curricular Activities. Girls are encouraged to participate in our rich extra-curricular programme, including weekend activities. We have a strong tradition in music and drama; we stage a number of major performances each year, in addition to informal lunchtime concerts. Our students regularly win prizes in the local annual performing arts festivals. We currently have record numbers of students participating in The Duke of Edinburgh's Award scheme and Ten Tors.

Sport. We believe in nurturing all sporting talent, both in individual and team sports and in recent years a number of our students have represented their country in a range of sports including swimming, diving, gymnastics, rowing, fencing and badminton. A large number of teams are fielded for weekend and evening fixtures. Girls who prefer non-competitive sport are encouraged to join in other fitness activities, such as one of our dance classes. Opportunities for sport and exercise are available every day at lunch times and after school and, as we are a boarding school, at weekends too. The school holds the prestigious Sportsmark awarded by the Sport England Foundation for its extensive provision and commitment to sport.

Our elite sportswomen also benefit from using the wonderful facilities at Bath University nearby, the training ground for world champions.

Entry Procedures. In the Junior School, admission is by informal assessment. In the Senior School, entry at Year 7 is by examination and personal interview in January. For pupils currently in our Junior School, transfer to the Senior School is automatic, unless parents have been informed in writing (by the end of Year 5) that the transfer cannot be guaranteed. We have students who join later, subject to availability of places. Admission in these years is by entrance examination. While Y11 students automatically transfer to the college, a substantial number of students also join us for the Sixth Form. All students entering the Sixth Form College are expected to have passes in at least 6 subjects at grades A*–B, with grade A/A* in any subject they intend to study, together with a minimum of a C in Maths and English.

Fees per term (2014–2015). Full Boarding £7,033–£8,499; Weekly Boarding £6,330–£7,611; Day £2,851–£4,050. 10% discount on full boarding fees for serving members of HM Forces. Flexi boarding is available.

Scholarships and Bursaries. Scholarships are awarded at entry to Years 7, 9 and 12 for the Sixth Form College for all-round academic excellence or for outstanding promise in specialist areas such as art, music, sport and drama. A Scholars' Programme ensures additional enrichment opportunities for the most able students.

Our bursary scheme ensures that the school is accessible to bright and talented students from families who require financial assistance towards the fees. Bursaries up to 100% (means-tested) are awarded at Years 7, 9 and 12 to girls who demonstrate outstanding all-round academic excellence or exceptional promise in a specialist area.

Charitable status. The Royal High School Bath is part of The Girls' Day School Trust, which is a Registered Charity, number 306983.

Rye St Antony

Pullen's Lane, Oxford OX3 0BY
Tel: 01865 762802
Fax: 01865 763611
email: info@ryestantony.co.uk
website: www.ryestantony.co.uk

Motto: *Vocatus Obedivi*

Rye St Antony is an independent Catholic Boarding and Day School, founded in 1930.

Governing Body:

Chairman: Mrs H Stafford Northcote, BA
Vice-Chairman: Mr T J Morton
Dr J Byren, MRCGP
Mr I Callaghan
Mr S Calnan
Dr T M M Czepiel, BMus, DPhil, PGDip LATHE
Mrs S Hampshire
Revd Dr J F Jackson, DPhil
Dr E Lowe, BA, PhD
Mrs S McGregor, BA
Mr P Mitchell
Mr D Parke
Mr R Potts
Mrs M Shinkwin, BA, MEd, NPQH

Clerk to the Governors: Mrs T Hudson

Headmistress: Miss A M Jones, BA York, PGCE Oxon

Deputy Head: Mrs A Neil, BA Southampton (*History and Politics*)

Senior School Staff:
Miss S Brookes, BA East London, PGCE Cantab (*Art and Design*)
Miss L Burgoine, BSc Sheffield Hallam, PGCE Sheffield Hallam (*Home Economics, Food Technology*)
Mr M Carter, BA, MA, CELTA (*Economics, History, Politics*)
Mrs R Carter, BSc, PGCE (*Mathematics*)
Mrs G Chang, MSc, CPhys, MInstP (*Physics*)
Miss J Croft, Maîtrise Strasbourg, BA QTS Westminster (*French*)
Miss S Defoe, BA Loughborough (*Art and Design*)
Miss N DeRushie, MA Waterloo, PGDE Edinburgh (*English*)
Ms J Dixon, BA Winchester, PGCE Oxon (*Art and Design*)
Mrs P D'Souza-Eva, BA Essex, PGCE London (*Mathematics*)
Miss E Eldridge, BSc Southampton (*Learning Support*)
Mrs A Evans, BA Nene University College, QTS Reading (*Drama*)
Mr M Evans, BA Durham, PGCE London, MEd Oxon (*Mathematics*)
Miss I Falcón, BA Granada, QTS Derby (*Spanish and French*)
Mr I Forrester, BSc, Leeds, MA Oxford Brookes, PGCE Hull (*Biology and General Science*)
Mrs J Ganly, BA Leeds, PGCE Bath (*French*)
Miss A Gate, BA Oxon (*Latin and Classics*)
Mr C Gill, BA, PGCE (*Director of Music*)
Mrs K Harman, BSc Cardiff, RSADipTEFLA Bournemouth (*EAL*)
Miss A Hartnell, BA Oxon (*Chemistry*)
Miss P Horlock, BA Stellenbosch, PCGE Stellenbosch (*Physical Education*)
Mrs Z Ireland, BA, PGCE (*History, Government and Politics*)
Mrs C Lau, BA Hong Kong, MA Oxford Brookes (*Chinese*)
Mrs J Lowe, BA Nottingham, MA London, PGCE Oxford (*English*)
Mrs A Lynes, BA, PGCE (*Italian*)
Miss K Mackenzie, BSc Liverpool, PGCE Exeter (*Head of Physical Education*)
Mrs V Matthews, BSc Oxford Brookes (*Home Economics, Food Technology*)
Mrs J McLuskey, BA Southampton, PGCE London (*English and Drama*)

Mr G Morran, BA, PGCE, MSc (*Business Studies and Psychology*)
Mrs F Mullaney, BSc Paisley, MSc Glasgow, PGCE Queens Belfast (*ICT*)
Mrs I Nishikawa, BA Tokyo (*Japanese*)
Mrs S Oscroft, BSc Sheffield, MSc Oxford Brookes, PGCE Sheffield (*Geography*)
Mrs J Owens, BSc Aberystwyth, CBiol, MIBiol, PGCE Lancaster (*Biology*)
Miss C Peck, BEd Leeds (*Physical Education*)
Miss F Pujos, Licence La Sorbonne Nouvelle, Paris, PGCE Oxford Brookes, Maître Angers (*French*)
Mrs E Roberts, BA York, PGCE Cantab (*English*)
Mrs M Roger, BEd Augsburg (*Mathematics*)
Ms A Selkovaja, BSc Daugavpils, Latvia, BSc Madrid, MSc Oxford, PGCE Oxford (*Mathematics*)
Miss T Simpson, BA Cambridge, MA Cambridge, PGCE (*Geography*)
Miss J Smail, BA Lancaster, MA Lancaster, PGCE Southampton (*History*)
Miss J Stevens, BA Buckinghamshire Chilterns (*Drama*)
Mrs F Stuart, MA, PGCE Oxon, ARCM (*Music*)
Miss H Tomlinson, BEd Brighton (*Physical Education*)
Mr A Vesty, BSc Manchester (*Chemistry and Physics*)
Mr D Williams, BSc Bath, Cert Ed Bath (*Chemistry and General Science*)
Mr S Willis, MA Exeter, BA Exeter, QTS Oxford Brookes (*Religion and Philosophy*)

Junior School Staff:
Head of Junior School: Ms J Reed, BEd Cambridge

Miss E Birkett-Evans, BA Open University, PGCE Bangor
Mrs S Blandy, BA Manchester
Mrs K Delacour, BA, PGCE
Miss C Eadle, BEd Oxford
Mrs C Gowler, BEd
Miss K Holland, BSc Reading, PGCE Oxford Brookes
Mrs M-E Judges, BA New York, BEd Oxford Brookes, PGCE Oxford Brookes
Dr C Kirtley, BSc Durham
Miss R Ladbrook, BA Oxford Brookes, MA Reading, MA Oxford Brookes, MPhil Oxford Brookes, PGCE Oxford Brookes
Miss S Lee, HLTA British School in Tokyo

Nursery Department Staff:
Mrs C Annells, NVQ3
Ms A Coveley, Cert Ed
Mrs T Lakani, Level 3 Dip Early Years and Education
Mrs A Strauther, Level 3 Dip Pre-School Practice

Visiting Music Staff:
Mr I Best, BA, Dip Mus, LTCL, ABRSM (*Trumpet*)
Mr D Chambers, BA, ARCO (*Organ, Piano*)
Dr E Chivers, MA, DPhil, PG Dip (*Violin, Viola*)
Mr P Foster, LTCL (*Saxophone*)
Mr R Foster, BA Oxford Brookes (*Rock Group*)
Mrs J Froomes, GradDipMus (*Violin, Viola*)
Mrs C Goodall, MA Oxford (*Clarinet and Piano*)
Mrs E Hobbs, BA, DPhil, PGCE, GRSM Hons, LRAM (*Flute*)
Miss E Hodson, MA, DPhil, PGDip (*Violin and Viola*)
Mrs M Jones, MEd, BA, PGCE (*Music*)
Mr P Manhood, ATCL (*Guitar*)
Mrs P Miller, BA, LTCL (*Clarinet*)
Mrs S Palys, LTCL Trinity College of Music (*Singing*)
Mrs A Stevens, MA, PGDip, LTCL (*Harp*)
Mrs F Stuart, MA, PGCE, ARCM (*Piano, 'Cello*)
Mrs E Walker, BA, MMus

Librarian: Mrs F Benfeghoul, MA Tours, BA Tours
Assistant Librarian: Miss C Birdseye, BA Oxford Brookes, MA Oxford Brookes

Medical Advisers: Bury Knowle Health Centre, Oxford

School Nurses:
Mrs S King, RGN

Administrative Staff:
Bursar: Mrs T Hudson, MBA MP, DMS, MAAT
Finance Officer: Mrs N Sanhotra
Bursary Assistant: Mrs J Curl
Human Resources Manager: Miss E Phelips, BA
Headmistress's Personal Assistant: Mrs E Cheeseman
School Secretary: Ms Fern Saxton
Staff Secretary: Miss I Ripper

Rye St Antony was founded in 1930 by Elizabeth Rendall and Ivy King as a lay Catholic school in Oxford, initially for day pupils – boys and girls – and eight in total. The decision to start the school was taken during a visit to Sussex and the Church of St Antony in Rye, in commemoration of which the school was named. Numbers quickly grew, and, at the end of the first year, the school moved from Hamilton Road to Woodstock Road. Here, there was room to accommodate the first boarders. Then, in 1939, came the move to Langley Lodge and its fine gardens and grounds. The neighbouring house, The Croft, with its splendid gardens and woodland, was acquired in 1945. Thus the school came to occupy its twelve acres of exceptionally beautiful grounds on a quiet lane overlooking the city about a mile from the centre of Oxford.

In 1960 Miss Rendall died, and in 1963 the school became an educational trust with a Governing Body. Miss King continued as Headmistress until 1976 and, unfailing in her interest and encouragement, spent her retirement in a house in the school grounds until her death in 1993. Miss King's younger sister, Miss Gwen, joined the school in 1939 and faithfully served the school until her death in 2000 at the age of ninety-nine. Miss King's successor as Headmistress was Patsy Sumpter who came to the school in 1959 and worked alongside Miss King in various posts before succeeding her as Headmistress from 1976 until 1990. Alison Jones, the fourth and current Headmistress, was appointed as successor to Miss Sumpter on Miss Sumpter's retirement in 1990.

A steady programme of building and refurbishment has provided the school with excellent teaching and residential facilities, all the twentieth century building being carefully harmonised with the architecture of the original handsome Victorian houses. King House was opened in 1986, the Art, Design and Technology Centre in 1989, the Information Technology suite in 1991, the eastern extension of the Rendall Building in 1993 and the Sumpter Building with its science laboratories in 1995. The Performing Arts Centre, the Janet Ward Building, was completed in 2005; the Sports Centre opened in September 2008; the refurbishment of the Chapel was completed in 2009; the Sixth Form Centre was opened in September 2010. A new library and classrooms, in extension of the Rendall Building, were completed in 2012.

Of the 400 pupils, 150 are in the Junior School (ages 3–11) and 250 are in the Senior School (ages 11–18). Of the 60 members of Sixth Form, all prepare to continue their studies at university. In recent years the average UCAS points score per candidate has been 350; two-thirds A Level grades have been A*, A or B. GCSE results each year give almost everyone grade C or above in at least five subjects, 70% + with grade C or above in at least ten subjects.

The school is highly regarded for its happy and purposeful atmosphere and its strong sense of community. The school's aim is to help each pupil develop the intellectual curiosity and skills, the emotional understanding and resources, the ability to work independently and with others, and the personal, social and spiritual values that will lead to personal fulfilment and the ability to contribute something of value to the world.

The school offers boarding and day places for girls aged 5–18, some day places for boys aged 5–8, and in the Nursery

School whole-day and half-day places for boys and girls aged 3–5. Short-stay and occasional boarding arrangements, varying in length from a single night to a whole term or more, can be made according to need.

Religious Life. The school's sacramental life is of fundamental importance, the Eucharist in particular uniting the school with Christ and his Church and giving a focus to prayer, both liturgical and private. Several Oxford priests regularly celebrate Mass for the whole school on special feast days and at the beginning and end of each term; they also celebrate the Sunday Masses, form Masses and week-day Masses. Religious Education is an integral part of the curriculum throughout the school, and all pupils are involved in the Christian life of the school community, not least its liturgical celebrations.

Senior School Curriculum. Academic standards and expectations are high, girls are offered many opportunities in music, art, drama and sport, and there is a busy programme of evening and weekend activities.

In the Senior School all girls follow a broad and balanced common course for the first three years, comprising English, Mathematics, Physics, Chemistry, Biology, Religious Education, French, History, Geography, Technology, Information and Communications Technology, Art, Music, Drama and Physical Education. Latin and Spanish are optional subjects. There is a cross-curricular Health Education programme.

Twenty plus subjects are offered as GCSE subjects. For the two-year GCSE course girls usually study 10 subjects, a mixture of options and core subjects (including Coordinated Science, a double award subject).

In the Sixth Form girls typically study four AS subjects in the first year of Sixth Form and continue with three of these subjects as A2 subjects in the second year, thus completing Sixth Form with certification in 3 A Level subjects and an additional AS subject.

Careers Guidance. The school's careers advisory service provides help and guidance for all girls, and there is a formal programme of careers advice throughout Years 9, 10 and 11 and Sixth Form. All girls go on to university and are helped to investigate thoroughly the Higher Education and careers options open to them, careful guidance being given concerning their applications and interviews. The support of the Headmistress, the Deputy Head and other senior staff is available at all stages. Work experience placements are organised, and girls are encouraged to make particular use of this option at the end of their GCSE courses. The school belongs to the Independent Schools Careers Organisation and benefits from its many services. Visiting speakers give lectures on various higher education and careers topics; visits to appropriate conferences and exhibitions are arranged; and the school organises and hosts a biennial Careers Convention. The school has two well-resourced careers libraries of printed, video and computer-accessed information.

Junior School Curriculum. The Junior School and Senior School are closely linked, and Junior School pupils are steadily introduced to the specialist teaching and facilities of the Senior School. In the early years the teaching of most subjects is undertaken by the class teachers. In Years 5 and 6 girls are taught by subject teachers, some of whom also teach in the Senior School, and this arrangement gives girls the benefit of specialist teaching and encourages them to develop a feeling of confidence and continuity when the time comes for them to move into the Senior School. Use of the Senior School facilities is particularly valuable in Science, Art, Music, Physical Education and Drama. There is a Junior Library in Langley Lodge, and older Juniors may also use the King Library in the Senior School.

Performing Arts. The school has a strong tradition of debating and public speaking, and girls have many successes to their credit in city, county and regional competitions. A major drama production each year, and various smaller presentations give girls the opportunity to develop their skills in performing, directing, lighting, sound, stage design, costume design and make-up. There are frequent visits to Stratford, London and regional theatres including the Oxford Playhouse and some girls perform at the Playhouse in the annual schools' gala. The majority of girls learn one musical instrument and some learn two or more; there are two choirs, one orchestra and several smaller ensembles, and some girls are members of the Oxford Girls' Choir, the Oxford Youth Chamber Choir, the Oxford Schools' Symphony Orchestra, the Oxfordshire Youth Orchestra and the Thames Vale Orchestra. Instruments learnt include piano, violin, viola, 'cello, flute, oboe, clarinet, trumpet, bassoon, saxophone, French horn, guitar and percussion. Through musical productions, concerts and the liturgy there are many opportunities for girls to contribute to the musical life of the school. In Drama pupils prepare for the examinations of the London Academy of Music and Dramatic Art (LAMDA), and in Music, they prepare for the examinations of the Associated Board of the Royal Schools of Music (ABRSM).

Sport. The school has an indoor sports centre, good playing fields, all-weather hard courts and an outdoor heated swimming pool. The principal winter sports are netball and hockey; the principal summer sports are tennis, swimming, athletics and rounders. Girls compete regularly in local, county and regional tournaments.

Duke of Edinburgh's Award. The school has an outstanding record in the Duke of Edinburgh's Award, each year about 35 girls achieving the Bronze Award, 20 girls or so achieving the Silver Award and 20 or more girls achieving the Gold Award. The purpose of the Award is to give challenge, responsibility and adventure to young people, thus encouraging them to develop initiative and team skills.

Visits. Fieldwork, conferences, lectures, art exhibitions, plays and concerts give girls an interesting programme of visits within the UK. Visits abroad include study courses, exchanges, sports tours and skiing holidays, and the school regularly hosts visiting groups from schools overseas.

Health. The School Nurses work closely with the School Medical Adviser who sees girls at the nearby Health Centre. Dental and orthodontic treatment can be arranged locally, and the John Radcliffe Hospital is five minutes away.

Admissions. Admission to the Junior School is by interview and the school's own entrance tests. Admission to the Senior School is by interview and entrance examination. Admission to the Sixth Form is by interview, school report and GCSE results.

Scholarships. Scholarships are available at 11+, 13+ and 16+.

Fees per term (2014–2015). Senior School: Full Boarders £7,355; Weekly Boarders £6,995; Day Pupils £4,475. Junior School: Full Boarders £6,300; Weekly Boarders £5,945; Day Pupils £2,945–£3,555.

Charitable status. Rye St Antony School Limited is a Registered Charity, number 309685. Its purpose is the furtherance of Christian education.

St Augustine's Priory School

Hillcrest Road, Ealing, London W5 2JL

Tel: 020 8997 2022
Fax: 020 8810 6501
email: admissions@saintaugustinespriory.org
website: www.saintaugustinespriory.org.uk
Twitter: @staugustinesp

Motto: *Veritas*

Board of Governors:
Mrs J Austin, BA
Mrs F Baker, MA
Professor G Bennett, MA Cantab

Mrs F Carey, BA
Deacon A Clark, BA, BD
Mrs S Collis, BA, ACA
Professor A Hemingway, BSc, MBBS, FRCR, FRCP
Mrs S Kirby, BA (*Chair of Governors*)
Mrs J Moore, BSc
Mrs C Nathan, BEd, NPQH
Mrs C Phillips, LlB (*Vice-Chair of Governors*)
Mr C Tipping, BA, MBA

Headteacher: Mrs S Raffray, MA, NPQH (*Designated Safeguarding Officer – Seniors*)

Acting Deputy Head – Seniors: Miss A Gandi, MA
Head of Preps and Pre-Preps: Miss E Keane, BA (*Designated Safeguarding Officer – Preps And Pre-Preps*)
Deputy Head – Juniors: Mrs N Tippen, BA (*Designated Safeguarding Officer – Juniors*)

Heads of Subject Departments:
Art: Ms F McTaggart, MA
Science: Mr J Barnes, BSc
Chemistry: Mr P Thomas, BSc, MEd, MCIEA (*Examinations Officer*)
Classics: Dr G Carleton, MA, PhD
Drama: Mrs F Murphy, BA, Dip LAMDA
English: Mrs D Farmer, BA
Geography: Ms M Dolan, BA
History (Acting): Mrs C Lunn, BA
IT: Miss F Sharp, BSc
Key Stage 1: Miss E Keane, BA
Key Stage 2: Miss A L Gambrill, BEd
Mathematics: Mr S Bale, BSc
Modern Languages: Mr A Alejandro, BA
Director of Music: Mr P Martin, MA Cantab, LRSM
Physical Education: Miss H Lymburn, BSc
Religious Studies & Faith Life: Mrs L Mcdermott, BA
Social Sciences: Mr P Murphy, BSc, MEd (*Director of Sixth Form – UCAS*)

Teaching Staff:
Ms F Assemat, MA (*Modern Foreign Languages*)
Dr S Atkinson, MD (*Science*)
Miss P Bani, EYPS (*Nursery*)
Mrs J Bennet, MA Oxon (*Mathematics*)
Ms C Brown, BA (*Drama*)
Mrs C Costello, BEd
Mrs L Cvetkova (*EYFS Practitioner and Teaching Assistant*)
Mrs N Drury, NNEB (*EYFS Practitioner*)
Mr N Elder, BA (*English*)
Miss C Eng, BSc (*Art & Learning Support*)
Mr P Ferguson, BA (*History*)
Dr G Gill, MA, PhD (*English & Classics*)
Mrs L Griffiths, BA (*Classics*)
Miss J Grundon, BA (*Art*)
Miss L Hales, BA (*PE*)
Miss L Halton, NNEB (*Teaching Assistant*)
Mrs L Harley, BSc (*Biology*)
Miss G Hayden, MSc (*Science*)
Mrs A Islam (*Level 3 Teaching Assistant*)
Miss E A Jackson, BA, BTEC, EYFS Practitioner, EYPS (*Nursery*)
Miss F Johnson, MA, ALCM (*Music/Senco*)
Miss M Keep, BA (*Geography*)
Ms M De Lahitte, BA (*Learning Support*)
Mrs T Lakomy, BSc (*Mathematics*)
Mrs C Lindsay (*PE*)
Ms C Macallister, ALCM, BA, ACA (*Humanities*)
Mrs J Martin, Cert Ed (*English, Learning Support*)
Dr I Maryniak, MA Cantab, PhD (*Russian*)
Mr M Maryniak, MSc, RSA Dip, ALCM (*Music*)
Mrs A Moore (*Learning Support Teacher*)

Mr P J Murphy, BSc, MEd (*Director of Sixth Form – UCAS*)
Miss C O'Brien, BA
Miss L O'Connell, BA
Mrs P O'Connell, DPP (*Teaching Assistant*)
Mrs B A Ogley, BEd (*English, Drama*)
Miss L Pfannes-Varrow, BSc, MSc (*Science*)
Mrs C Racadio, BSc (*Mathematics*)
Miss H Rai, MA (*Junior Department*)
Mrs H Round, BA (*Junior Department*)
Miss T Rutherford, BSc, BEd (*Mathematics*)
Ms G Taher, BSc (*Psychology*)
Mrs Z Thackray, BA (*Learning Support Teacher*)
Mr P Thomas, BSc, MEd, MCIEA (*Science, Examinations Officer*)
Mrs K Toynton, BA (*Modern Foreign Languages*)
Miss P Trybuchowska, MA Oxon (*History*)
Mrs C Young, Mont Cert (*Support in Learning Assistant*)

Welfare Staff:
Mrs R Good, BSc, Dip Counselling (*Counsellor*)
Ms J Roberts (*School Health Practitioner*)

Peripatetic Staff:
Ms R Aspinall, BMus TCM (*Harp*)
Mrs E Curran, MGR (*Piano*)
Mr R De Sousa, MSc (*Learning Support*)
Mrs E Ellis, Life Member RAD (*Ballet*)
Miss V Ellis, MRAD (*Ballet*)
Mrs J Fenton, Cert TEFL (*English Support*)
Miss E Ferrari, ALCM (*Singing*)
Miss E Jackson, MA, GMus, ARCM (*Violin, Viola*)
Mr I Judson, LWCMD, ALCM (*Flute*)
Mr W Lakomy, Cert Ed (*Maths Support*)
Miss L Peacock, BMus (*Woodwind*)
Miss K Pett, MMus (*Percussion*)
Miss M Mercedes (*Spanish Club*)
Mr M Rose, BMus (*Guitar*)
Mr C Smith, BMus, LRAM (*Brass*)
Mr A Storey, LLCM, ALCM (*Guitar*)
Miss E Tingey, LWCMD, ACC (*Oboe*)
Mrs J Warren, GTCL (*Cello*)

Technicians:
Miss M Cherepanova (*Gap Laboratory Assistant*)
Miss R Ghanadian (*Gap Laboratory Assistant*)
Mr J Mcauley (*ICT Technician*)
Ms P Morrison, BSc (*Laboratory Technician*)

Administration:
Ms L Cawdron, BA (*Registrar and Marketing Manager*)
Mrs A Clarke, MA Oxon (*Director of Operations*)
Mrs C Corbett (*Gap Assistant*)
Mrs C Cox, BSc Econ (*Design Manager*)
Mrs S Daly, BA, FCA (*Bursar*)
Mrs F Donovan (*PA to the Headteacher*)
Miss C Hewitt (*Admissions Assistant*)
Ms M King, BA (*Communications Administrator*)
Mrs J Lanek (*Domestic*)
Mr P Martin, BA (*ICT & Data Services Manager*)
Mrs M Mcpartlin (*Operations Assistant*)
Mrs S Nelson (*Receptionist*)
Mrs J Reilly (*Assistant Bursar*)
Mrs R Sharma (*Domestic*)
Mrs C Sumpter (*School Office Manager*)
Miss K Tarsey (*Receptionist*)

Estate Staff:
Mr C Mortimer, BSc (*Groundsman*)
Mr I Smith (*Groundsman*)

St Augustine's Priory was founded in France in 1634 by Lady Mary Tredway to provide a haven where young English women could be provided with an Independent Education. Moving to Ealing in 1914–15, at its current location, the School follows the philosophy expounded by its

Patron, St Augustine of Hippo, and known to every parent that is that children (and for that matter adults) achieve their best when they are happy. Pressurising girls yields very short term dividends. Our excellent results are achieved by stimulating the girls and passing on to them a joy in learning. This is far more effective and indeed much more fun for the teachers.

The School's success is firmly rooted in its readiness to adapt to change while retaining its unique identity and, by adhering to these ideals, we provide our girls with those skills which will enable them to face the future with confidence.

Our academic achievement is only part of our success and we firmly believe in equipping girls with a range of important skills to be effective in the workplace and beyond.

Number of Pupils. There are approximately 460 girls aged from 4–18 (63 in the Sixth Form).

Location. The School is well served by public transport, with Hanger Lane, North Ealing and Park Royal Underground stations all within a ten minute stroll and Ealing Broadway Underground and main line station approximately 20 minutes' walk away. The School sits on top of Hanger Hill in an idyllic setting of thirteen acres, with views across to the South Downs. Buses stop near the entrance.

Admission. St Augustine's Priory is a unique and vibrant community, and the best way to understand it is to come and look around the school and importantly to meet our pupils, Headteacher and staff. During the application process we invite Parents to visit us on Open Day during the Michaelmas and Lent Term and you are also warmly invited to visit the school for a private appointment at other times. Admission to the Preps is via interview in the Michaelmas Term. Girls from St Augustine's Junior School transfer automatically into the Senior School. External candidates for 11+, 13+ and 16+ sit examinations in Lent Term. We make offers based on academic performance, personality and an assessment of what the girl and her family want from the school and can offer to it. We hold an Open Evening for prospective Sixth Formers and their parents during the Michaelmas Term, which is followed up by a Taster Day. The Taster Day allows prospective Augustinians to experience a day in the life of our School and get a feel for how they would fit in. Interviews are then conducted by the appropriate Heads of Department along with the Headteacher, and offers are sent out with conditional GCSE pass requirements. Occasionally places arise in other years. Once a completed Application Form is received, your daughter's name will be placed on the Applications Register appropriate for her age, and will be considered should a vacancy arise.

Religion. St Augustine's Priory is a Catholic Independent Day School for Girls. The Chapel is at the heart of school life and is used for assemblies, weekly Masses and as a place for moments of quiet reflection and prayer. Whilst most students are Catholic, we welcome girls from other religions and faiths and learn from them.

Pastoral Care. Children from all backgrounds and all races, with a wide range of gifts, make up the vibrant community which is St Augustine's. From their first day, girls become part of a family which respects the beliefs and customs of its members and learns to work together. When problems arise and questions need to be asked, we encourage a very personal approach. The Form Teacher has a special relationship with pupils, looking after their day-to-day needs and encouraging them to get the very best out of their time at school. It is to the Form Teacher that pupils and parents can look in the first instance for help and guidance.

Curriculum. We offer an extensive and balanced curriculum including PSHE, and offer 20 subjects at GCSE and IGCSE and 23 subjects at AS and A2 Level. Girls can take a number of subjects as part of a fast-tracking programme. Girls are expected to take ten or more subjects at GCSE.

The Sixth Form and Careers. The Sixth Form facilities include a common room, kitchen and balcony overlooking

the South Downs. The Head Girl and Deputy Head girls have their own offices.

Sixth Form students have the chance to take part in a range of additional activities to try out new sports or skills and meet people from other schools.

We encourage girls to think about their next step and to make informed decisions at every stage of their development. The Sixth Form is supported by the Careers team providing advice and guidance. The team works with the students to consider their many future options, assisting with university and course selection, preparation for Oxbridge and other university applications and subsequent interviews. This process is supplemented by an annual Careers Conference with guest speakers, mentors and experts in key fields invited in to speak and to offer advice and insight.

Working with the Directors of Sixth Form, every girl is encouraged to examine her own strengths and to explore possibilities suitable for her interests and personal abilities. Talks, conferences, seminars and courses, a visit to a Careers Fair and University Open Days, career profiling, as well as a well-stocked, up-to-date Careers library and the Internet, allow all our students to keep abreast of opportunities on offer. The school is a member of ISCO.

All of this support builds on the guidance received throughout the school. When our girls leave here for university, they take with them not only impressive qualifications but also kindness, an understanding of, and the ability to adapt to, the world in which they live, the confidence to succeed in whatever they choose to do and above all, friendships which will last them through life.

Extra-Curricular Activities. Apart from Physical Education in the curriculum, the school also excels in its extremely popular after-school sports activities fielding winning teams in hockey, netball, swimming and cross country. Tennis, karate, football, ballet and gymnastics are all catered for after school.

Whilst Drama forms a part of the curriculum and is very strong here at St Augustine's we also stage an annual major production in the Spring which allows involvement by the whole Senior School.

Music is a particular strength with girls from Prep III to the Sixth Form being given the opportunity and encouragement to take any instrument they choose, from violin, cello and flute to harp, drums and guitar. If a girl is interested in a particular instrument we will try to find a teacher for her. As a result music flourishes throughout the school with girls taking part in lunchtime and after-school orchestras, music groups and choirs, and music tours abroad.

The Art is outstanding with the girls' work displayed throughout the school. An annual Art Exhibition is held each summer, and the department makes use of visits to the many theatres, museums and galleries in London.

The School is licensed as a Centre for The Duke of Edinburgh's Bronze, Silver and Gold Awards. Trips to Nepal, Borneo and China are recent examples of the girls' visits into the far-flung reaches of the world with skiing trips for Juniors and Seniors, French student visits and Husky Sledging in Norway forming the basis of our recent European travels.

Facilities. St Augustine's Priory offers superb amenities including a full-size floodlit all-weather astroturf pitch and floodlit competition-sized netball court set in stunning 13-acre grounds.

In addition to sporting facilities, our 13 acres include a dedicated Prep meadow, orchards, Sixth Form rose garden and croquet lawn. The state-of-the-art Science Wing opened in 2007 with four laboratories and dedicated Senior and Junior music and drama rooms. A new Nursery block was completed in March 2011. To complement this there are two IT suites, music practice rooms, Senior and Junior Art rooms, a Sixth Form Art studio, Modern Languages Academy, dedicated Sixth Form areas and private studies, and

Scriptorium. Kitchens are on site and the Chef and catering staff serve fresh cooked lunches daily.

Fees per term (2014–2015). Nursery Department £1,328–£2,945, Preparatory Department £3,100, Junior Department £3,500, Senior Department £4,200.

Additional information may be found on the school's website and a more detailed prospectus may be obtained from the School.

Charitable status. St Augustine's Priory School Limited is a Registered Charity, number 1097781.

St Catherine's School
Bramley

Bramley, Guildford, Surrey GU5 0DF
Tel: 01483 893363
Fax: 01483 899608
email: schooloffice@stcatherines.info
            admissions@stcatherines.info
website: www.stcatherines.info
Twitter: @stcatsbramley
LinkedIn: St Catherine's School, Bramley (Under Companies)

Founded as a Church of England School for Girls in 1885, welcoming both day girls and boarders, St Catherine's is one of the UK's premier girls' schools. The location, just three miles south of Guildford and surrounded by miles of countryside offers space and green vistas and yet is within one hour of central London and Heathrow Airport.

In a recent Sutton Trust report, St Catherine's was positioned in the top 5 schools in the country sending students to the UK's most highly selective universities. Superb examination results are testament to the quality of teaching and learning, where students are not afraid to show enthusiasm and ambition. Lessons are taught in well-appointed classrooms by subject specialists.

With extensive playing fields, superb sports facilities and an auditorium which boasts better acoustics than many London venues, it is no surprise that St Catherine's is always buzzing with life after the teaching day is over.

A well-established House system underpins the whole School, allowing new girls to feel at home very quickly, encouraging an ethos of care and concern for others as well as a friendly competitive spirit.

Governing Body:
Chairman: Mr P J Martin, BA, FRGS, FCCA
Dr Helen Bowcock, DL
A Carruthers, BCom
J Corrie, MA
Mrs P Crouch, LLB
Professor Andrea Dlaska, DPhil, Mag Phil
Mrs M Greenway, LLB, QTS
Mrs C Johnstone [Dr Clare Higgens], MRCS, LRCP, MBBS, MD, FRCP
Dr M Jordan, MA, MB BChir, FRCA
T W Kendall, FRICS
Dr Janet McGowan, MBBS, FRCA
Mrs M O'Donovan, DLitt
M Ommanney
Mrs S E Shipway
J C M Tippett, BSc, FCA, TEP
B M Way, DArch RIBA

Headmistress: Mrs Alice Phillips, MA Cantab

Business Manager:
Mrs Christine Silver, BSc Durham, PGCE
Head of Boarding:
Mrs Lorinda Munro-Faure, MA Oxon, PGCE
Director of Studies:

Mrs Jacki Deakin, BSc UCL, PGCE
Senior Housemistress:
Mrs Kirsty Meredith, BA Hons London, AKC, PGCE
Director of Staff:
Mrs Caroline Rose, BA Nottingham, PGCE
Head of Sixth Form:
Mrs Claire Wyllie, MA Durham, PGCE
School Administrator:
Mrs Sheila Kelsall, MA Open, BSc Hons Brighton, PGCE
Senior Teacher:
Mrs Heather Bryn-Thomas BSc Kent, PGCE
Head of Prep School:
Miss Naomi Bartholomew, MA London, BEd Cantab
Deputy Head – Curriculum:
Mrs Julie Micklethwaite, BEd Hons Roehampton
Deputy Head – Pre-Prep:
Mrs Jill Cochrane, BEd, CertEd Leicester, PGCPSE Open
Deputy Head – Staff:
Mrs Wendy Gibbs, BEd Hons Winchester

Marketing: Mrs Gill David, BA Manchester, PGCE
Development Director: Ms Pippa Carte, BD, MA
Association Director: Mrs Dawn Pilkington, BA

Chaplain: Revd Dr Benjamin McNair Scott, BA, MA, PGCE, CELTA

School Housemistresses:
Ashcombe: Mrs Amanda White
Merriman: Mrs Rosa McQuade
Midleton: Mrs Kirsty Meredith
Musgrave: Mrs Penny Harris
Russell-Baker: Mrs Sue Hall
Stoner: Mrs Simone Berry

Boarding Housemistresses:
Bronte: Miss Lindsey Cullen
Symes: Miss Amy Dingley-Jones
Keller: Mrs Charlotte George
Sixth Form: Mrs Nathalie Hart

Heads of Departments:
Art: Mr Alexander Perry-Adlam, BA Hons Liverpool John Moores, Cert Ed
Biology: Mrs Claerwen Patterson, MA Oxon, PGCE
Careers: Mrs Sue Weighell, BA Hons Birmingham, QTS Business Studies
Chemistry: Mrs Nicola Austin, MChem Oxon, QTS
Classics: Mrs Sophia Ridley, BA Hons Durham, PGCE
Drama: Ms Madeleine Lewis, BA Hons Kent, PGCE
Design Technology: Mr Alastair White, BA Hons Winchester
Economics/Business Studies: Mr Nigel Watson, BA Hons Ealing College of Higher Education, PGCE
English: Mr Jonathan Worthen, MA Oxon, PGCE
Examinations Coordinator: Dr Rebecca Robinson, PhD UCL
French: Mrs Lucy Strong, BA Hons Bristol, PGCE
Food and Nutrition: Mrs Nicola Genzel, BA Hons Roehampton, PGCE
Geography: Mrs Sophie Mackness, BSc Hons London, PGCE
German Ms Elodie Nevin, MA Oxon, QTS
History: Mrs Gill David, BA Hons Manchester, PGCE
History of Art: Miss Lisa Hayat, MA Reading, BA Hons, PGCE
ICT: Mrs Catherine Lamb, BA and DipE Central Queensland University, QTS
Librarian: Mrs Kathryn Bainbridge, MA Loughborough, BA Hons, CILIP
Study Skills Coordinator: Miss Caroline Cross, BA Hons, Lancaster, PGCE
Mathematics: Mr Alasdair Wright, BSc Hertfordshire, PGCE
Director of Music: Mr Geoffrey Field, GRSM Hons, DipRAM, ARCO, LRAM

Physical Education: Mrs Vic Alexander, BEd Hons
    Brighton
Physics: Mr Matthew Greenfield, MEng Oxon, QTS
Politics: Mr Carl Gladwell, BA Hons London, PGCE
Psychology: Mrs Jean Arrick, BSc Hons Liverpool, PGCE
PSHE: Mrs Amanda White, BSc Hons Wales, PGCE
Religious Studies: Mrs Cecilia Townley, MA London, BA
    Hons Sheffield, PGCE
Sixth Form General Studies: Mr Carl Gladwell, BA Hons
    London, PGCE
Spanish: Miss Kate McDowell, BA Hons Durham, PGCE
Textiles: Mrs Lorna Crispin, BA Hons Manchester
Timetable:
Mrs Heather Bryn-Thomas, BSc Kent, PGCE
Mr Matthew Greenfield, MEng Oxon, QTS

Administration:
Senior School Registrar: Mrs Judy Corben
Prep School Registrar: Mrs Sally Manhire
PA to the Business Manager: Mrs Diane Haeffele
PA to the Headmistress: Miss Toppy Wharton
Office Manager: Miss Sally Marshall

The outstanding results gained by our students in public examinations secure them places at the top universities, in competitive disciplines like medicine and veterinary science, law and languages. This success comes not only as a result of the fine quality of the teaching, but is also due to the individual attention received by every girl. St Catherine's places great emphasis on creating a happy environment where every girl is encouraged to work hard to maximise her talents. The atmosphere is friendly and one in which children can develop and grow in a very stimulating environment.

Pivotal to the life of St Catherine's are the six school Houses. The girls' loyalty and affection for their Houses is impressive with memories of inter-house plays, competitions and matches enduring long after School days have ended.

A broad and varied curriculum allows all pupils to participate in many challenging and rewarding extra-curricular activities. As a Church of England School girls are encouraged to think of others and impressive sums of money are raised for charity each year. The School has its own beautiful chapel which is used by the girls on a daily basis.

The School's flexible approach to boarding is making it increasingly attractive to busy, professional families; the ISI team picked out boarding as one of the outstanding features of St Catherine's. The School welcomes both weekly and full boarders who enjoy a busy and exciting programme.

There are exceptional on-site facilities including 3 lacrosse pitches, a multi-purpose sports hall, fitness suite and indoor pool. The auditorium provides superb acoustics for our musical and theatrical productions, better than many London venues. The Sixth Form girls have their own Library which provides a perfect study environment right at the heart of the School. These facilities i.e. the Anniversary Halls and the Speech Hall Library were officially opened by HRH the Duchess of Cornwall in February 2014. The first Baron Ashcombe, the Duchess's Great-Great Grandfather was one of the original founders and benefactors of St Catherine's.

Activities Week is held each year in the Summer Term when every girl in the School participates in a variety of programmes organised to both support the curriculum and offer challenges not normally met in the classroom. Pupils participate in outward bound ventures, an industrial heritage tour to the north and midlands, modern language courses in France, Germany and Spain, whilst Sixth Formers focus on university choices. Activities Week costs are included in the fees.

International links are also very important. St Catherine's has an exchange programme with St Catherine's Melbourne,

Australia and there are also links with schools in Kenya, South Africa and Afghanistan.

St Catherine's has an unrivalled reputation in art, music, sport and drama; photography and textiles are popular options amongst the Sixth Form, and younger girls are encouraged by an enthusiastic Art and Design department to take advantage of the superb facilities, and join many after-school clubs.

Music is an important feature of school life, with numerous choirs, orchestras and concert bands rehearsing each week and performing regularly. There are in excess of 500 individual music lessons taking place each week where over half the girls learn to play a musical instrument. There are flute choirs, string quartets, recorder groups and ensembles to cater for all levels of ability. Concerts and recitals are held regularly. An exciting venture has been the Organ Academy and the Jennifer Bate Organ Scholarship in conjunction with Guildford Cathedral. The Senior School Summer Concert was held, this year, in St John's, Smith Square, London.

Many girls go on to represent their county in netball, lacrosse, swimming, squash and athletics. Every girl is encouraged to take part in sport at school, whatever her level of expertise. The PE Department regularly fields four or five teams for lacrosse and netball, allowing every girl who wishes to play competitively the opportunity to do so.

Drama and Theatre Studies are extremely popular options and all girls are encouraged to audition for the annual middle and senior school plays. As well as acting opportunities, pupils are also offered the opportunity to help backstage and front of house and learn many valuable skills as a result. LAMDA classes are offered to all year groups. With the opening of the impressive new performance halls including state-of-the-art lighting and acoustics, facilities for Theatre are second to none. St Catherine's also has its own very popular School of Dance.

The Preparatory School: most girls join at 4 with a limited number of places available in other years. It aims to support families in helping younger pupils develop a strong sense of values, high standards of behaviour and consideration to others, as well as achieving excellent academic success. The girls benefit from specialist teaching, combining the best of traditional methods with modern technology to prepare them for the Entrance Examinations to all Senior Schools at 11+, including St Catherine's.

St Catherine's is situated in extensive grounds, in the heart of the attractive Surrey village of Bramley, three miles south of Guildford which has a main line station (Waterloo 35 minutes). The school operates a return bus service to Guildford Station Monday to Friday and there is a Friday evening bus service to London for weekly boarders. There is easy access to Heathrow and Gatwick and travel arrangements are made for overseas boarders. Close proximity to London allows frequent visits to theatres and galleries and the miles of countryside on our doorstep is an asset to the many girls who take part in the Duke of Edinburgh's Award Scheme.

Fees per term (from January 2015). Day Girls (including lunch): Pre-Prep 1 £2,720, Pre-Prep 2 £3,295, Pre-Prep 3 £3,890; Prep School £4,595; Middle and Senior School £5,535.

Boarders: Middle and Senior Boarding and Tuition £9,115.

Fees include the Activities Week programme for Senior School girls and lunches for all pupils aged 4–18.

Entry. This is by Entrance Examination held in January. The Preparatory School also holds its entrance tests in January.

Scholarships and Bursaries.

11+: There are four Academic Entrance Scholarships available for pupils at age 11. These are awarded on the results of the Entrance Examination. Two scholarships are for 20% of the fees payable and the other two are for 10% of the fees. These run through the Middle School and can be extended through the Sixth Form at the discretion of the Headmistress and in consultation with the teaching staff.

Upper 5 and Sixth Form (Year 11): The following scholarships are awarded during the Summer Term of the girls' Lower Fifth (Year 10). Selection for the awards is based on the results of the June examinations at the end of the Lower Fifth, performance throughout the Lower Five year, a Scholarship Examination paper, and an interview.

There are several internal academic Sixth Form Scholarships: these are scholarships of 20% of the fees payable to run for three years (through Upper 5 and the Sixth Form).

Sixth Form Scholarships: These are scholarships of 20% of fees. However, this group can be extended by a mix of additional 20% or 10% awards depending on the performance of the candidates and the recommendations of the awarding panel.

The Clare Gregory Memorial Sports Scholarship: This is awarded for sporting prowess and is for 20% of the day fees in the Sixth Form.

The Sixth Form Art and Textiles Scholarship: There is an Art and Textiles Scholarship to the value of 20% of the School Fees, awarded during the Autumn Term of Upper 5.

The Sixth Form Drama Scholarship: There is a Drama Scholarship to the value of 20% of the School Fees, awarded during the Autumn Term of Upper 5.

Scholarships for New Entrants to the Sixth Form: There are up to three external academic scholarships of up to 20% of fees and these are awarded at the discretion of the Headmistress, to new pupils joining the School in the Sixth Form. N.B. The Sixth Form Art and Music Scholarships may be applied for by external applicants by the end of October each year.

Music Scholarships and Awards:

An *11+ Music Scholarship* of 20% of the fees and tuition on one instrument may be awarded annually upon entry to an 11+ candidate adjudged by the Director of Music and the independent adjudicator to have strong musical talent. A second Music Scholarship of 10% of fees and tuition on one instrument can be awarded in years where the field of applicants is particularly strong. Applications should be made by November and auditions are in January. A *Sixth Form Music Scholarship* is awarded to a pupil entering the Sixth Form – from within the School or as an external applicant – to the value of 20% of the School Fees.

The Jennifer Bate Organ Scholarship, offered in conjunction with Guildford Cathedral, is awarded in alternate years to a girl who is already a good organist or shows potential. This award is typically for 20% of fees payable, but may involve means-tested bursary assistance if appropriate.

Further Music Awards which cover music tuition, exam fees and sheet music on a range of musical instruments from chapel organ to piccolo and voice are available to pupils in the Senior School. Some are specifically for those wanting to take up less 'popular' instruments. Auditions for Awards take place at the same time as Music Scholarship auditions.

Bursaries: Means-tested bursaries are available to external applicants which may cover up to 100% of the fees payable. For further details please contact the Business Manager.

Prospectus and School Visits. Please apply to the Registrar. The Headmistress will be pleased to see parents by appointment.

Charitable status. St Catherine's School Bramley is a Registered Charity, number 1070858. It exists to provide education for girls in accordance with the principles of the Church of England.

St Catherine's School
Twickenham

Cross Deep, Twickenham, Middlesex TW1 4QJ
Tel: 020 8891 2898
Fax: 020 8744 9629
email: admissions@stcatherineschool.co.uk
website: www.stcatherineschool.co.uk

Motto: '*Not Words But Deeds*'

Chair of Governors: Mr Edward Sparrow

***Headmistress*: Sister Paula Thomas**, BEd Hons, MA

Deputy Head: Ms M Fisher, BA

Bursar & Clerk to the Governors: Mr I G Stewart, BAcc, CA

Admissions Secretary: Mrs A Faulkner

Age Range. Girls 3–18 years.
Number in School. 410 Day Girls.

Founded in 1914 by the Sisters of Mercy, St Catherine's moved from its original site to its current location in 1919. Today the school is under lay management. St Catherine's is a Catholic School in the ecumenical tradition, and pupils of all denominations are welcome.

Aims. Our aim is to provide a broad and balanced education within a stimulating and supportive environment which encourages and challenges girls to strive to be the best they can be in all areas of the curriculum. Success is achieved through personal responsibility, high expectations and a close partnership between parents and school. Emphasis is placed on self-discipline, responsibility and the importance of respect for others. Since we are a relatively small school with small class sizes the staff know the pupils as individuals and there is a strong sense of community which promotes academic success.

Situation. The school enjoys an enviable position, being located next to the River Thames. It is a short distance from the centre of Twickenham and approximately 10–15 minutes' walk from Strawberry Hill and Twickenham Stations. Both have regular services to London (Waterloo), Surrey, Berkshire and Middlesex. There are also a number of local bus routes.

Entrance. Main points of entry are at 3, 5, 7, 11 and 16 but girls are accepted at any stage subject to availability. Places at the school are usually awarded on the basis of an interview, a report from the candidate's previous school and an assessment (examination in the Senior School).

Scholarships and Bursaries. Academic Scholarships, up to the value of 50% of the fees, are awarded annually at 11+ and 16+. At 11+ girls are invited to sit scholarship papers on the basis of their entrance examination results. At 16+ students are required to sit three examination papers, two in subjects that they plan to study at A Level and a third General Studies paper. Art, Drama, Music and Sport scholarships are also awarded annually following an audition/ assessment and are conditional on the applicant achieving the school's academic requirement for entry.

A limited number of means-tested Bursaries are offered depending on need and funds available.

Curriculum. In the Senior School pupils follow courses in English, Mathematics, Biology, Chemistry, Physics, Religious Studies, French, German, Spanish, History, Geography, Drama, Music, Art, Food Technology, ICT and Physical Education. All of these subjects are offered at GCSE with the addition of Economics and Psychology. Most pupils study ten subjects to GCSE level. All of the above subjects are available at A Level, with the addition of Business Studies, Classical Civilization, Government and

Politics, Graphics, History of Art, Law, Further Mathematics, Music Technology, Sociology and Textiles.

There is a strong commitment to Sport, Music, Drama and extra-curricular activities. The school has its own hockey pitch and indoor swimming pool as well as tennis and netball courts. Sports include swimming, netball, athletics, hockey, tennis, gymnastics, trampolining and rounders and our pupils achieve considerable success at county, regional and national level.

Music plays an important part in the life of the school; all pupils are encouraged to participate in choirs, orchestras and ensembles, and there is a varied programme of concerts and informal performances each term.

Drama is popular and, as well as opportunities to perform in school productions, regular theatre visits take place during the year.

Buildings. The Preparatory and Senior departments are on one site. The buildings include a large multi-purpose hall as well as a smaller assembly hall, well-stocked Prep and Senior Libraries, three ICT Suites, a spacious Art and Photography Suite and a Food Technology Room. The Music Centre has class and individual practice rooms. There are fully-equipped laboratories for Physics, Chemistry and Biology. A large programme of new building has recently added extra teaching blocks, a Sixth Form Centre, Drama Studio and Fitness Suite.

Extra-Curricular Activities. These play a significant role in the life of the school. Activities include the Duke of Edinburgh's Award scheme, Badminton, Science Club, Football, Rugby, Rowing, Cross-Country Running, Zumba, Chess and Photography. Trips, both locally and abroad, add to the extensive range of activities on offer. Pupils also take part in community service and fundraising activities.

Fees per term (2014–2015). Nursery £3,190, Reception £3,410, Years 1 and 2 £3,500, Years 3 to 6 £3,675, Years 7 to 13 £4,405 (excluding examination fees).

Charitable status. St Catherine's School, Twickenham is a Registered Charity, number 1014651. It aims to provide for children seeking education in a Christian environment.

Heads of Faculty:
Mathematics: Mrs R Cowley, BA, CertEd
Expressive Arts: Miss L Hovland, BEd Hons
Science and Technology: Mr I Henderson, BA Hons, PGCE, QTS
Communications: Mrs N Hastings-Smith, BA Hons, PGCE, NPQH
Humanities: Mrs C Morris-Smith, BSc Hons, PGCE

Head of Foundation Years and Pre-Preparatory: Mrs K Grevett, BEd Hons, NCertEd, CertEd

Head of Preparatory: Mrs S Kirwan, BA, QTS

Bursar: (*to be appointed*)

Admissions Officer: Mrs S Molloy

Teaching and Learning. Small class sizes facilitate individual attention and enable teachers to build a profile of each learner; strengths and weaknesses are diagnosed and all work is tailored to match each individual's needs both in the Preparatory School (boys and girls aged 3 to 11) and in the Senior High School (girls only aged 11 to 18).

Teachers and learners work closely together to make education challenging, interesting and fun. We believe in close partnership with parents, keeping you informed about your child's progress.

Work is differentiated to challenge and support individual learners and progress is closely tracked and monitored to ensure optimum learning opportunities.

As girls enter Year 7 they are taught by dedicated specialist subject teachers in small classes. The enhanced curriculum delivered allows some students to be fast tracked at GCSE level and gives excellent Value Added, with pupils exceeding expectations based on their initial entrance assessment.

Curriculum. We offer a broad and balanced curriculum with enhancement and enrichment. The National Curriculum is taught throughout the school and this is further enhanced with additional subjects such as performing arts, dance, drama and singing, which are integrated into the weekly timetable. We offer a comprehensive range of subjects at AS and A Level.

Expressive Arts. St Dominic's Brewood is renowned for its musical and dramatic excellence and is frequently approached by companies for our pupils to audition in local productions. Our contemporary Performing Arts Centre houses a Drama and Dance Studio, a Music Suite and a Recording Studio.

Pupils are encouraged to join the choirs, play an instrument, take up dance or singing or tread the boards. Throughout the year there are a variety of performances ranging from the Pre-Preparatory Christmas play, to the all-singing and all-dancing productions such as Oklahoma and Annie.

The pupils participate in many competitions, local, regional and national. They regularly take part in local festivals and public speaking events. Many girls do LAMDA examinations and all Year 7 girls take English Speaking Board examinations.

Sports. We offer a broad and interesting curriculum which includes netball, hockey, dance, gymnastics, aerobics, football, volleyball, basketball, badminton, rounders, tennis, golf, athletics and cross-country and some learners have represented county, regional and national sports.

Our all-inclusive extra-curricular programmes provide further sporting variety and include Zumba, gymnastics, trampolining, modern dance and ballet, with all abilities encouraged to attend.

There is a comprehensive fixtures programme, as well as our competitive inter-house events including Annual Junior and Senior Sports Days. We take part in ISA sporting events at local, regional and national level.

The facilities used to deliver this popular subject include newly resurfaced and extended netball and tennis courts and

St Dominic's Brewood

Bargate Street, Brewood, Staffordshire ST19 9BA
Tel: 01902 850248
Fax: 01902 851154
email: enquiries@stdominicsbrewood.co.uk
website: www.stdominicsbrewood.co.uk
Twitter: @StDomsBrewood

St Dominic's Brewood is one of the leading independent schools in Staffordshire, providing education for over 250 pupils – girls aged from rising 3 to 18 and boys from rising 3 to 11. Development of the 'whole person' is at the heart of our school. We believe each child has special talents and we act to develop those gifts so that they may achieve their full potential within a caring environment. Our aim is to develop the pupils academically, socially, creatively and spiritually. In the recent ISI report, the school was rated *excellent/outstanding* in every aspect – *The pupils' achievements are well supported by the quality of the teaching, throughout the school, which is excellent and often inspirational.*

We are pleased to have introduced overseas students to our Sixth Form – boarding with local 'homestay' families – from September 2013.

Chairman of the Board of Governors: Mr R Turton

Head: **Mr H Trump**, MA, NPQH

Deputy Head (*Curriculum*): Mr P McNabb, BSc Hons, PGCE

our playing fields which include a hockey pitch, athletics track, football pitch and rounders pitches. We also have an excellent fully-equipped sports hall.

Extra-Curricular Activities. Four days a week there is an all-inclusive after-school programme where the learners can undertake a broad variety of activities ranging from The Duke of Edinburgh's Award Scheme to street dancing, debating, cooking, Young Enterprise, STEM Club and gardening.

Throughout the year, pupils are encouraged to become involved in fundraising for local and national charities. These activities help each girl develop a good community spirit with respect and consideration for others.

Pastoral Care. Our outstanding pastoral care system and Christian ethos create an atmosphere which fosters trust and mutual respect between pupils and teachers. Pupils feel relaxed and secure and develop their self-respect, self-confidence, personal discipline and consideration for others.

Examination Results. Our learners achieve outstanding exam results year on year, outperforming the national averages of both comprehensive and independent schools at Key Stage 2, GCSE and A Level.

Facilities. We have a whole school state-of-the-art ICT system and a purpose-built Kindergarten and junior building, which encompasses a Junior Hall, IT room, DT and Art room, Home Economics room and a library. The Senior building has fully-equipped science laboratories, IT room and a library. All classrooms have networked computers and interactive whiteboards. Plasma information screens are installed in the foyers. The Sixth Form and Performing Arts Centre is a modern, state-of-the-art facility housing the latest technology in music, IT and the Performing Arts.

The new Sixth Form Centre has a common room with terraces and a well-equipped Library with Wi-Fi technology.

Admissions. Although selective, we draw our pupils from a wide ability range, which makes our record of results outstanding. Assessment is made during trial days at school. Entry into the Senior department is through entrance assessment in November and a place in the Sixth Form is conditional upon GCSE results.

Fees per term (2014–2015). £1,075 (Nursery, 5 mornings inc lunch), £2,005 (Reception inc lunch), £2,415 (Year 1 inc lunch), £2,630 (Year 2 inc lunch), £3,050 (Years 3–6), £3,700 (Years 7–9), £3,875 (Years 10–13). Sixth Form 'Homestay' Boarding: £21,500 per annum.

Scholarships and Bursaries. Scholarships are available for Preparatory (Y3–6) and Academic, Sport and Performing Arts scholarships are awarded for entry into Year 7. Art scholarships are awarded for entry into Year 8 with a full range of scholarships awarded in Year 12. Bursaries are available across all years and application forms can be obtained from the Bursar.

For further information please view our website which also contains a copy of our ISI Inspection report March 2011.

St Dominic's Priory School

21 Station Road, Stone, Staffordshire ST15 8EN
Tel: 01785 814181
Fax: 01785 819361
email: info@stdominicspriory.co.uk
website: www.stdominicspriory.co.uk

St Dominic's Priory School is an outstanding independent day school and Nursery, educating girls aged from 3 months to 18 years and boys to 11 years. Our beautiful Georgian boarding house is designed to a very high standard, and is a 'home from home' for 17 girls over the age of 10.

Chair of Governors: Mr Michael Hughes

Headteacher: **Mrs Rebecca Harrison**

Deputy Headteacher: Mrs Pamela Porter

General Manager: Mr Gareth Cunningham

Geography: Mr David Farrar
History: Mrs Rebecca Abbotts
History: Mr Graham Finlay
Religious Studies: Mrs Judith Cook
Sociology & Psychology: Mrs Judith Deakin
Art: Miss Jane Jovanovic
English: Miss Lucy Bartlett
English/General Studies: Mrs Rosalind Chatburn
French: Mrs Margaret Kitchener
Music: Miss Kathleen Lynch
Spanish: Mrs Elizabeth Crofts
EAL: Miss Clare Wadley
Biology: Dr Laura Hibberts
Biology: Mrs Susan Whitehouse
Chemistry: Mrs Violet Burge
ICT/Business & Communications: Mrs Judith Dunk
Mathematics: Mr Nathan Jones
Mathematics: Mrs Pamela Porter
PE: Miss Barbara Capper
Physics: Mrs Jennifer Bryant

Prep French: Mrs Tracy Gauvin
Prep Music: Mrs Susan Dickson
Prep Science: Mr Joseph Messenger
Reception Teacher: Miss Karen Davies
Primary 1: Mrs Eliza Jarvis
Primary 2: Mrs Joanna Talbot
Primary 3: Mrs Joanne Coombs
Primary 4: Mrs Victoria Banks
Primary 5: Mrs Sarah Shelton

We provide a friendly place of learning and are proud of our reputation for academic achievement. Our ethos and vision value the worth of each individual. High-quality teaching, small classes and our combination of day and boarding provision create an environment in which true potential can be maximised at all times.

Location. Centrally located within North Staffordshire, the school is situated in the picturesque canal town of Stone, Staffordshire, within easy reach of Newcastle-under-Lyme, Stoke-on-Trent, Stafford, Uttoxeter, Cheadle and the surrounding villages. We provide school transport from a number of locations and Stone Railway Station is only a 5 minute walk from school.

Aims and Ethos. Life is a journey, and every journey has a beginning. We aim to give each child the best possible start, to give them the tools to navigate their chosen path and the confidence to believe in themselves. Teachers and pupils work together with energy and imagination; they motivate and inspire each other in order to achieve their very best.

Boys and girls are co-educated from the age of 3 months within the purpose-built Nursery. The beginnings of reading, writing and number work are introduced at an early age.

The curriculum within the Preparatory Department encompasses all aspects of the National Curriculum with specialist teaching in many subjects including French, Drama and Music. Great emphasis is placed on high standards of presentation and regular homework reinforces the work undertaken at School.

Here at St Dominic's we aim to develop the capacity for independent thought through a rigorous and stimulating academic education. One of St Dominic's great strengths is taking pupils with a broad ability range and achieving outstanding A Level and GCSE results. With the benefit of small classes, teaching is geared to the needs of individual girls who are supported throughout by a strong pastoral care system. The School provides regular opportunities for pupils to take on positions of leadership and to develop a sense of their own worth and a determination to realise all their talents. Students leave St Dominic's with excellent academic grades, self-confidence and friends for life.

Religion. St Dominic's Priory is a Catholic School where children of all faiths are welcomed.

The Arts. The School excels in the Creative and Performing Arts and our busy programme of sport, cultural events, visits and activities ensures that there is something for everyone at St Dominic's. Pupils regularly take part in public speaking competitions, productions, festivals, concerts, recitals and exhibitions, both within and outside the School.

Sport. The School has a strong sporting tradition. Sports include tennis, badminton, hockey, netball, volleyball, gymnastics, athletics, football, tennis, cross-country running, climbing, sailing and tri-golf.

Extra-Curricular Activities. Numerous clubs and activities are held after school and during lunchtimes for both the Prep and Senior Schools. These include the Duke of Edinburgh's Award, fencing, musical theatre, choir, and percussion ensemble.

Sixth Form and Beyond. The School has an extensive and well-resourced careers programme which includes work experience, work shadowing, a Careers Library, and support from school careers staff.

Admission. Please contact the school directly for information on admissions or visit the website.

Scholarships and Bursaries. Academic scholarships are available in the Prep School as well as Academic, Music and Sports scholarships in the Senior School. Academic, Art and Music scholarships are available at Sixth Form level. Bursaries are available throughout the School. Details can be obtained from the Admissions Office and the school website.

Fees per term (2014–2015). Day: Reception £2,750; Primary 1–6 £3,058; Seniors £3,354; Sixth Form £3,482. Full Boarding £8,000. Nursery: we offer different fees for those parents requiring a full year or term only nursery and a variety of session times. Please refer to the Nursery section of the school website for further details.

Further Information. The School welcomes visits from prospective parents and pupils. For more information please telephone the School Office on 01785 814181.

Charitable status. St Dominic's Priory is a Registered Charity, number 271922, providing quality education for children aged 3 months to 18 years.

St Gabriel's

Sandleford Priory, Newbury, Berkshire RG20 9BD
Tel: 01635 555680
Fax: 01635 555698
email: info@stgabriels.co.uk
website: www.stgabriels.co.uk

Church of England Independent Day School for Girls, in membership of GSA and IAPS.

Governing Body:
Chairman: Mr N Garland, BSc Hons

Mr S Barrett	Mr S Ryan
Mrs S Bowen	Mr M Scholl
Mr D McAllan	Mr J Toogood
Mrs A Rowse	Mrs J Whitehead

Principal: Mr A Jones, LTCL, LWCMD

Vice-Principal: Mrs C Sams, CertEd (*Mathematics*)
Bursar & Clerk to Governors: Mrs J Bond, BSc Hons
Director of Studies: Mrs W Rumbol, BA Hons, PGCE, DMS (*French & Spanish*)
Head of Junior School: Mr P Dove, BA Hons, PGCE

Deputy Head of Junior School: Miss A Smith, BEd Hons (*Form Tutor Year 2, History & ICT*)
Sandleford Curriculum Manager: Mrs C Lawrence, BA Ed, PGCE (*Form Tutor Reception*)
Pastoral Head, Years 7 & 8: Mrs H Trevis, BSocSc Hons, PGCE (*Religion, Philosophy & Ethics*)
Pastoral Head, Years 9, 10 & 11: Mrs R Wright, BSc Hons, PGCE (*Physical Education*)
Head of Sixth Form: Mrs C Reseigh, BA Hons, PGCE (*French*)

Senior School Teaching Staff:
* *Head of Department*
Mrs N Archer, BA Hons, PGCE (*English*)
Mrs S Baxter, BEd Hons, ACSD (*Drama)
Mrs A Beake (*Science Technician*)
Mrs C Causer, MA, BA Hons, QTS (*Latin, Classics & English*)
Mrs A Chicken, BA Hons, PGCE (*Mathematics & Academic Data Manager*)
Miss J Coles, BA Hons, PGCE (*Latin & Classics*)
Mrs K Cook (*Art Technician*)
Mrs S Court (*Science Technician*)
Miss R Dadds, BSc Hons, PGCE (*Psychology*)
Miss S Ferretti, BA Hons, PGCE (**Modern Foreign Languages, Italian & French*)
Mr J Franey, BSc Hons, PGCE (*Physics*)
Mrs M Goodhead, Cert SpLD (*Individual Needs*)
Miss M Gu, MSc, BSc Hons, PGCE (*Mandarin Chinese*)
Ms M Gunn, BA Hons (*Music*)
Ms S Hall, BA Hons, PGCE (*English)
Mrs E Hammons, LLB, PGCE (*Politics*)
Mrs R Heveron, MMath Hons, PGCE (*Mathematics*)
Ms P Highton, BA Hons, PGCE (*Drama*)
Mrs R Horner, BEd Hons, DipSpLD (*Individual Needs)
Ms M Hunter, BA Hons (*Art & Photography*)
Mr M Ives, MA, BA Hons, PGCE (**Latin, Greek & Classics*)
Mrs P Joseph, MEd (*Physical Education*)
Miss A Keenleyside, BEd Hons (*Photography*)
Mrs Jennifer Knott, BSc Hons, PGCE (*Design Technology*)
Mr B Lewis, MA Cantab, PGCE (**History & *Politics*)
Miss C Linney, BA Hons, PGCE (*Art)
Mrs P Lyons, BA Hons, PGCE (*Business Studies)
Mr J Mannion, BA Hons, PGCE (**ICT Teaching & Learning & History*)
Miss T Matthews, CertEd (*Religious Studies*)
Mr G May, BA Hons, QTS (*Physical Education*)
Mrs Y Murray, BEd Hons, Cert Ed (*French*)
Mrs N Parsons, BSc Hons (*Science Technician*)
Mrs A Pasternakiewicz, BEd Hons (*Physical Education*)
Miss L Pitt, BSc Hons, PGCE (*Geography*)
Mrs H Porter, BSc Hons, PGCE (*Biology & KS3 Science Coordinator*)
Ms H Rayner, BA Hons, PGCE (*Physics*)
Mrs A Reeve-Howarth, MA, BEd Hons (*Home Economics – Food & Nutrition*)
Mrs N Rogers, BA Hons, PGCE (*French & Italian*)
Mr J Scobie, MA Ed, BSc Hons, PGCE (**Science & Technology*)
Mrs S Sim, BSc Hons, PGCE (*Mathematics)
Mrs M Smiles-Cook, BA Hons, QTS (*Physical Education*)
Dr P Tebbs, DPhil Oxon (*Music)
Mrs A Thayer, MA Cantab, BA Hons, QTS (*English*)
Mrs L Tyler, BA Hons, PGCE (*Spanish*)
Mrs V Vaughan, BSc Hons (*Mathematics*)
Mrs S Vines, BEd Hons (*Textiles Technology*)
Mr C White, BSc Hons, PGCE (*Chemistry*)
Mrs P Willetts, BA Hons, PGCE (**Geography & *Economics*)
Mr I Williamson, BSc Hons, PGCE (*Biology & Chemistry*)
Miss K Wilson, BA Hons, PGCE (*Dance)
Mrs S Yeoman (*Technology Technician*)

Junior School Teaching Staff:
* *Subject Leader*

Miss S Black, BEd Hons Cantab (*Form Tutor Year 3*)

Mrs S Bloxsom, BA Hons (*Form Tutor Year 2*)

Mrs M Davidson, BEd Hons (*Form Tutor Year 5 & *English*)

Miss M Gu, MSc, BSc Hons, PGCE (*Mandarin Chinese*)

Ms M Gunn, BA Hons (**Music*)

Mr R Havercroft, MEng (*Form Tutor Year 6, *Science*)

Ms P Highton, BA Hons, PGCE (*Drama*)

Mrs P Joseph, MEd (*Physical Education*)

Mrs J Knott, BSc Hons, PGCE (*Design Technology*)

Mr G May, BA Hons, QTS (*Physical Education*)

Mrs C Moriarty, BEd Hons, CertEd (*Form Tutor Year 5, *Modern Foreign Languages*)

Miss H Moth, BA Hons (*Form Tutor Year 4 & *Art*)

Mrs Y Murray, BEd Hons, Cert Ed (*French*)

Miss V Neal, BSc Hons, PGCE (*Form Tutor Year 5 & *Mathematics*)

Mrs A Pasternakiewicz, BEd Hons (**Physical Education*)

Miss J Pearine, BA Hons, PGCE (*Year 6 Form Tutor & *Humanities*)

Mrs A Reeve-Howarth, MA, BEd Hons (*Home Economics – Food & Nutrition*)

Miss A Smith, BEd Hons (*Form Tutor Year 2,*ICT*)

Mrs L Tyler, BA Hons, PGCE (*Spanish*)

Mrs V Vaughan, BSc Hons (*Mathematics*)

Mrs S Webb, BSc Hons, PGCE (*Form Tutor Year 1 & *PSHE*)

Miss K Wilson, BA Hons, PGCE (*Dance*)

Teaching Assistants:
Mrs H Martin
Mrs S Morris

Examinations Officer: Mrs H Corkhill, BEd Hons
Librarian: Mrs A Borzoni, BA Hons, PG Dip
Medical Officer: Mrs S Porter-Scott (*Matron*)

Visiting Music Staff:
Mr T Bott, BMus Hons, PG Dip (*Violin*)
Mr T Bryanton (*Guitar*)
Mr N Burrage, BA Hons (*Guitar, Drums*)
Mr N Cope (*Piano & Singing*)
Mrs J Frith, CT ABRSM (*Flute*)
Miss E Gregory, BMus Hons (*Voice*)
Mr M Lijinsky, CT ABRSM (*Piano*)
Mrs C Millar, BA (*Bassoon*)
Mr S Parker, ALCM, LLCM, CT ABRSM (*Clarinet & Saxophone*)
Mrs H Rawstron, BA, LTCL (*Oboe*)
Mrs S Riddex, BA Hons, PECE, LTCHM, LESMD (*Cello*)
Mr P Tarrant, ARCM, CertEd (*Brass*)
Mrs V Toll, LRAM, CertEd (*Piano*)
Mr D Wirdnam, BA Hons, LRSM (*Flute*)

Administrative Staff:
Mrs J Benney (*Registrar*)
Mrs J Goodman-Mills (*Transport Coordinator*)
Miss C Jackson (*Executive Secretary*)
Mrs A Kail (*Data Manager*)
Mrs T Robinson (*School Secretary*)
Mrs A Williams (*Bursar's Office Assistant*)
Mrs S Willson (*Assistant Bursar – Finance*)
Mrs A Morris (*HR & Operations Coordinator*)

Number of Pupils. 435.

Academic excellence, high expectation, intellectual challenge and a fulfilling extra-curricular life are all vital elements of St Gabriel's. Securing the very best possible results and university places for students is the bedrock of this successful school.

Visitors to St Gabriel's quickly recognise that this is no ordinary school. From Nursery to Sixth Form they are struck by the enthusiasm and sense of purpose of both staff and pupils. Some parents choose St Gabriel's because of its reputation for achieving exceptional academic standards; others welcome the individual attention which is given to all pupils.

Curriculum. The formal curriculum is broad and well-balanced, providing an education that is both traditional and forward-thinking. A choice of 26 subjects is offered at GCSE of which English, English Literature, Mathematics, all three sciences, a Modern Foreign Language, a Humanity and Religious Studies are compulsory. The majority of students take 10 subjects.

At Sixth Form, students choose four subjects to study to AS Level from the 29 offered, with at least three being pursued through to A Level. Students may also study for the Extended Project Qualification.

Extra-Curricular Activities. As well as offering a thorough academic education, the school provides a wide range of opportunities outside of the classroom. Numerous activities and visits extend and enrich the girls' learning experience throughout the school. The performing and creative arts, sport and a wide range of clubs and societies ensure that the girls progress to the next stage of their education with confidence. Whether it is through The Duke of Edinburgh's Award or World Challenge, the girls constantly rise to meet new challenges.

To ensure connectivity to the real world and to prepare the girls to meet the challenges of the modern workplace, the school has forged strong links with high-tech industry and multinational businesses.

Music. There are two orchestras, four choirs a wide range of ensembles including two string quartets, jazz and rock bands and several woodwind ensembles. Any orchestral instrument may be learned.

Sport. Netball, Hockey, Swimming, Rounders, Athletics, Cross-Country, Dance, Gym and Tennis.

Facilities. State-of-the-art ICT and MFL block, multi-disciplinary sports hall, digital theatre and dance studio.

Christian Community & Ethos. St Gabriel's has a Church of England foundation but girls of other faiths are welcome. A strong moral code and Christian values ensure the girls leave the school as well-balanced, unpretentious, spirited individuals with the confidence to be assertive and decisive with warmth and without arrogance. The girls are always encouraged and supported to resist pressures and to have the confidence to make the right choices.

Supervised Prep. This is provided on a daily basis between 4 pm and 6.30 pm.

Scholarships & Bursaries. Academic, Sport, Art, Dance, Drama and Music scholarships are awarded at 11+ and 13+. Sixth Form scholarships are also awarded at 16+. Full bursaries are available through the Montagu Award scheme, which aims to ensure that St Gabriel's is accessible to girls who would otherwise not be able to enjoy the unique education the school offers.

Admission. Entry to the Junior School for children aged 6–10 years is by assessment. An entrance exam is held in November for entry at 11+ and 13+ and girls are accepted in to the Sixth Form on the basis of their GCSE results and an interview.

Fees per term (2014–2015). £4,790–£4,960.

Junior School. (*See entry in IAPS section*).

Charitable status. The St Gabriel Schools Foundation is a Registered Charity, number 1062748. It exists to provide education for girls.

St George's, Ascot

St George's School, Wells Lane, Ascot, Berks SL5 7DZ
Tel: 01344 629920
Fax: 01344 629901
email: admissions@stgeorges-ascot.org.uk
website: www.stgeorges-ascot.org.uk

Member of GSA, AGBIS, BSA.

Governors:
[1]Mr E Luker, FRICS Chairman
[2]Mr G W P Barber, MA Oxon, LVO
[2]Mrs D R Brown, MBE
[2]Mrs A Hems, MA Oxon, PGCE
[1]Mrs R E S Hirst, BArch Hons, RIBA
[1]Mr P James
[1]Mrs A Laurie-Walker BSc, MSc
[1]Mr A Mackintosh
[2]Mr A Miles, BSc Hons, PGCE

[1] *Member of Finance & Marketing sub-committee*
[2] *Member of Education sub-committee*

Staff:

Headmistress: Mrs R C F Owens, MA Hons Oxon, PGCE, NPQH

Bursar and Clerk to Governors: Mrs J M Wood, JP, BA Hons, Dip FM
Deputy Head (Academic): Mr K C Harris, BSc Exeter, PGCE, FRGS, CGeog
Deputy Head (Pastoral): Mrs H L Simpson, BEd Hons Exeter (*Head of Boarding, Head of PSHE, Child Protection Officer, Physical Education*)
Head of Sixth Form: Mrs A Dourountakis, BA Hons Durban, PG HDipEd, ESL Diploma (*Religious Studies*)

Teaching Staff:
* *Head of Department*

Art, Textiles and Photography:
*Mrs C Fidler, BA Wolverhampton, PGCE
Ms E Townsend, BA East Anglia, PGCE
Mrs A Morgan, BA Dundee, PGCE
Ms K Gilbert, BA Chichester, PGCE

Classics:
*Miss L Fontes, BA Leeds, PGCE
Mrs C Phipps, BA Nottingham, PGCE

Drama:
*Mr A Carroll, BA St Mary's, PGCE
Mrs E Gregan, BA Liverpool, PGCE

Economics:
*Mr A Verma, MA Oxon, GTP

English:
*Mr N Lee, BD BA MA London, PGCE
Mrs L Jones, BEd Durham
Mrs H Dorey, BA Wales
Mrs E Gregan, BA Liverpool, PGCE
Ms M Johnston, BA East Anglia, MA London, PGCE

EAL:
*Mrs N Anderson, MA East Anglia, PGCE
Mrs S Davies, CTESOL Trinity
Mrs D Ractliffe, CertEd Homerton, CTEFLA, DTESOL Trinity

Film Studies:
*Mr I Charnock, BA Wales, MA London, PGCE
Mrs E Gregan, BA Liverpool, PGCE

Geography:
*Mrs S Johnson, BSc Exeter, PGCE

Miss E Cartlidge, BA Leeds, PGCE
Mr K Harris, BSc Exeter, PGCE, FRGS, CGeog

History and Politics:
*Mr T Sharkey, BA Exeter, PGCE
Miss L Jackson, BA Aberystwyth, MTL Canterbury, PGCE
Dr A Tieanu, PhD Babes-Bolyai, Romania
Mr A Verma, MA Oxon, GTP

History of Art:
*Mr I Charnock, BA Wales, MA London, PGCE

IT and Business Studies:
*Mrs R Belkacem, BSc London, PGCE
Mr Naeem Mohammad, MA Punjab, BSc Punjab, HDipE
Mr A Verma, MA Oxon, GTP

Languages:
*Mrs F Burrows, Maîtrise Toulouse, GTP
Miss A Figueira, Licence Paris, PGCE
Mrs R Martinez, BA Portsmouth, PGCE
Mrs S Cope, Licence Orléans, PGCE

Learning Support:
*Ms M Johnston, BA East Anglia, MA London, PGCE

Mathematics:
*Mr P Wilson, BEng Nottingham, PGCE
Mr J Cameron, MA MMath Cantab
Mrs C Lilley, BSc London, PGCE
Mr Naeem Mohammad, MA Punjab, BSc Punjab, HDipE

Music:
*Mr I G Hillier, GLCM, FLCM, FCSM, FGMS, PGCE
Miss P May, BMus Edinburgh, PGDip Trinity

Physical Education:
*Miss K Lofthouse, PTI Cert Army
Mrs K Collingwood, BSc Loughborough, PGCE
Miss K Spencer, BA Chichester

PSHE:
*Mrs H Simpson, BEd Exeter
Mrs K Collingwood, BSc Loughborough, PGCE
Miss E Cartlidge, BA Leeds, PGCE

Psychology:
*Mrs A Bushill, BSc Southampton, PGCE

Religious Studies:
*Mrs M Magill, BA Bristol, PGCE
Mrs A Dourountakis, BA Durban, PGDE, DESL

Science:
*Mr S Rhodes, BSc Canterbury, New Zealand, PGCE
Mr P Goldsbrough, BSc Nottingham, PGCE
Mrs J Smith, BEd Reading
Miss D Schmidt, MSc BEd Pretoria, South Africa
Dr C Alsop, PhD Durham, PGCE
Mrs S Hetherington, BSc Open
Mr Naeem Mohammad, MA Punjab, BSc Punjab, HDipE

Residential Staff:
Markham Housemistress: Mrs S Hetherington (*First to Fourth Years*)
Knatchbull Housemistress: Mrs H Dorey (*Fifth Year and Sixth Year*)
Loveday Housemistress: Mrs A Farmer-Mason (*Seventh Year*)
Assistant Housemistress: Dr A Tieanu, PhD Babes-Bolyai, Romania
Matron: Miss H Woodward, DipHE
Director in Residence: Miss R McCann, BA Warwick
Artist in Residence: Miss H Moore, BA UAL
Resident Lacrosse Coach: Miss I Spilde, BA Marywood, USA
Resident Lacrosse Coach: Miss K Flynn, BA Iona, USA

Extra-Curricular Staff:
Head of Alexander House: Miss L Jackson

Head of Becket House: Mrs L Jones
Head of Churchill House: Mrs C Fidler
Head of Darwin House: Mrs H Dorey
Baccalaureate: Mrs J Smith
Careers: Mr D Moran
Charities: Revd J Sistig
Debating: Mr T Sharkey
Duke of Edinburgh's Award: Mr D Moran
Magazine: Mr N Lee
Partnerships: Mr A Carroll

Visiting Staff:
Mrs A Langlois (*French*)
Mrs T Velazquez (*Spanish*)
Mrs K Baldwin (*Chinese*)
Mrs K Forrester (*Japanese*)
Mr G Galli (*Italian*)
Mrs M Strain (*Russian*)
Mrs R Baxter (*Learning Support*)
Mrs N Bolt (*Learning Support*)
Mrs J Hooper (*Learning Support*)
Mrs D Burt (*Flute*)
Mr R Smith (*Percussion*)
Mr S Perkins (*Violin*)
Mrs D Head (*Clarinet and Saxophone*)
Mr T Carleston (*Singing*)
Mrs A Watson (*Singing*)
Miss E Krivenko (*Piano*)
Mrs K Stanley (*Piano*)
Mr M Stanley (*Piano*)
Mrs M Fitzgerald (*LAMDA*)
Mr N Ingham (*Tennis*)
Ms E Haigh (*Pilates*)
Miss E Withall (*Dance*)
Mrs N Leader (*Squash*)

Support Staff:
Director of Marketing and Admissions: Mrs H Lightwood
Admissions Assistant: Miss E Bridge
Marketing Assistant: Mrs K Elliott
Deputy Bursar: Mr M Heather
Finance Manager: Miss G Plumb
Bursar's Assistant: Mrs T Barber
PA to Headmistress: Mrs J Witt
Administrator: Mrs C Reader
Secretary (Mon and Tue): Mrs N Hutchison
Secretary (Thu and Fri): Mrs D Macro
Administrative Assistant: Mrs S Berry
Data Manager: Ms A Shevills
Alumnae Officer: Mrs S van der Veen
Domestic Bursar: Mr S Cornish
Deputy Domestic Bursar: Mrs J Burns
Chef: Mr J Eddyvean
Network Manager: Mr J Skinner
IT Apprentice: Mr J Bonner
Theatre Technician: Mr R Pearn
Science Technicians:
Miss S Bale
Mrs C Grater
Mr B Nguessan
Art Technician: Mr C Esling
Nurse: Mrs S Horth, RGN
Chaplain: Revd J Sistig
Librarian: Mr D Moran
Clerk of Works: Mr R Cotterell
Groundsman: Mr P Thompson
Carpenter: Mr H Bowyer
Electrician: Mr M Collingwood
Painter: Mr D Edwards
Gardener: Mr M Kirk

St George's is a boarding and day school for girls aged 11 to 18. The school is set in 30 acres of beautiful grounds with magnificent views. We are just a stone's throw from the world-famous Ascot racecourse and Windsor Great Park, and less than 25 miles from London.

At St George's we are extremely proud of the special blend of excellence in academic and pastoral development that we offer our girls. We encourage each girl, whether a boarder or day pupil, to take advantage of every opportunity she has to learn and explore new challenges and experiences. Her happiness and moral and spiritual welfare are of paramount importance and we believe that by providing a safe and secure environment, in which she feels comfortable and happy, we enable her to focus on her strengths and abilities and to discover where her passions lie.

We are passionate advocates of girls' education. Our aim is to foster a lifelong love of learning and to give young women the confidence and skills to be the best version of themselves, in order to make a difference in the world.

At the heart of our ethos is the relationship between our dedicated staff and each individual pupil. Each girl is allocated to her own individual Tutor, who is responsible for her academic progress, discipline and pastoral care. Our boarders live in year groups with a resident housemistress, who works closely with the Tutor to ensure a consistent approach to supporting the progress and well-being of each girl. We operate a House system, which provides opportunities for entertainment and healthy competition and encourages the girls to make friends across the age groups.

We give each girl increasing independence and freedom, but also introduce a sense of responsibility as she progresses through the school, so that at the end of Sixth Form she is equipped and ready to face the challenges that university life will bring. Girls leave St George's not only with excellent qualifications, but self-confidence, fond memories of their school days and lasting friendships.

Curriculum. Our small class sizes ensure that every girl is given the right balance of academic challenge and support by our inspirational teaching staff, who deliver a wide-ranging and varied curriculum. Girls are given opportunities to excel, not only in traditional subjects but also in Art, Drama, Music and Sport. Team sports are offered in Lacrosse, Netball, Swimming, Tennis, Rounders, Athletics, Squash and Polo.

Academic results at St George's are strong, with high proportions of the girls going on to Oxbridge and other Russell Group universities. The AQA Baccalaureate and Extended Project Qualifications are offered in addition to A Levels, where typically one third of the candidates achieve three or more A grades.

Entrance. Entry at 11+ is by our own assessment comprising an Admissions Day, reference from the current school, examinations in English, Mathematics and Verbal Reasoning and a short presentation to a senior member of staff. For entry at 13+, pre-testing takes place in the February preceding entry and a place is offered. 13+ entrants can also be pre-tested when they are in Year 6 for a Year 9 place. Entrants to the Sixth Form take two subjects of their choice for entrance in the November prior to entry. They must achieve a minimum of six GCSE passes at Grades A*–C, and at least a Grade B in any subject to be studied at A Level. A wide range of scholarships are available at 11+, 13+ and 16+.

Fees per term (2014–2015). £10,375 Boarding, £6,750 Day.

Scholarships. Scholarships are available at 11+, 13+ and 16+ for outstanding potential, as evidenced by examination results. Academic, Art, Performing Arts, Sport, Music and All Round scholarships and instrumental awards are available at 11+ and Academic Art, Music, Drama, Performing Arts, All Round and Sport scholarships at 13+ and 16+.

Extra Subjects. Other languages (including Mandarin), Music (most instruments), Speech and Drama, Ballet, Modern Stage and Tap Dancing, Individual Tennis, Polo, Riding, Zumba, Pilates, and Yoga.

Charitable status. St George's School Ascot Trust Limited is a Registered Charity, number 309088. It exists to provide independent secondary girls' education.

St Helen & St Katharine

Faringdon Road, Abingdon, Oxon OX14 1BE
Tel: 01235 520173
Fax: 01235 532934
email: info@shsk.org.uk
website: www.shsk.org.uk

Founded in 1903, St Helen and St Katharine is a 700-strong day school for girls from 9–18 years, with 200 pupils in the Sixth Form.

Governors:
Miss J E Cranston (*Chairman*)

Ms A J Allden	Mrs D M May
Mrs P E Cakebread	Miss B O'Connor
Mr J Gabitass	Dr M Oppenheimer
Mrs R M Kashti	Mr G Steinsberg
Mr D J Lea	Mrs S Tinson
Mr K Leggett	Mr I Todd
Mr I Mason	Mr J J H Wormell

Clerk to the Governors: Mrs K E J Wait

Headmistress: Mrs R Dougall, MA King's College London, GTP

Bursar: Mr D Eley, BSc, ACA
Deputy Headmistress Academic: Mrs B Stubley, MA Greenwich, PGCE
Assistant Head, Director of Students: Mrs L Hughes, BA Warwick, PGCE
Assistant Head, Director of Staff: Mr J Hunt, MA St Andrews, QTS
Director of Communications & Development: Mr M Holland, MA Westminster

Chaplain: Revd K Windle, MTheol OU, PGCE
Head of Sixth Form: Mrs J Armstrong, BSc Leeds, PGCE
Head of Middle School: Mrs H Nash, BA Southampton, PGCE
Head of Lower School: Mrs K Taylor, BA Wales, PGCE

Head of Year Upper Sixth: Mrs C Canlan-Shaw, BSc Loughborough, PGCE
Head of Year Lower Sixth: Mrs S Hughes-Morgan, BA Exeter, PGCE
Deputy Head of Middle School: Mr J Earnshaw-Crofts, MA London, BA London, PGCE
Deputy Head of Lower School: Miss E Haines, BA Oxon, PGCE
Head of Junior Department (*Years 5 & 6*): Miss N Talbot, BSc Nottingham, PGCE

Art, Design and Technology:
Mrs J McDonald, MA RCA, ATC London
Mr B Drew, BA London, QTS
Mrs C Langston, BA Middlesex, PGCE
Miss H McCague, BA West of England, PGCE
Miss A Wardell, MA London

Business Studies & Economics:
Mrs C McKenna, BSc Manchester, PGCE
Mr S Grant, BA Oxon

Higher Education and Careers:
Mrs J Armstrong, BSc Leeds, PGCE, Adv Cert CEG
Mrs D Croft, Tech IOSH, MInstLM
Mrs D Laidlaw, BA London
Mrs J Bridge, BA Liverpool, Grad CIPD

Classics:
Mr D Hodgkinson, MA Oxon, MLitt Dublin
Ms L Grieve, BA Oxon, PGCE
Mrs J Twaits, MA Cantab, PGCE

Drama and Theatre Studies:
Ms J Watt, BA Durham, PGCE
Miss E Jewitt, BA London, PGCE
Miss R Pearmain, BA London
Ms S Pullen-Campbell, BA Loughborough
Mr A Verjee, BA UEA

English:
Mrs C Nash, MA Oxon, PGCE
Ms A Fogg, MA Maryland, QTS
Mrs E Haines, BA Oxon, PGCE
Mrs S Hughes-Morgan, BA Exeter, PGCE
Dr F Macdonald, BA, MSc, DPhil Oxon, PGCE
Mrs H Nash, BA Southampton, PGCE
Mrs T Surrey, MA London, PGCE
Ms F Tierney, MA Cantab, PGCE

Examinations Officer:
Mrs J Andrews

General Studies:
Ms S Hayward, BA Durham, PGCE

Geography:
Mrs C Douglas, BA London, PGCE
Ms L Snowdon, BA London, PGCE
Mrs A Tate, BA, Leeds, PGCE

Government and Politics:
Dr L Gribble, MA Münster, DPhil Oxon, PGCE
Mr J Smart, BA Exeter, PGCE
Mrs B Stubley, MA Greenwich, PGCE

History:
Miss D Smith, BA Durham, PGCE
Dr L Gribble, MA Münster, DPhil Oxon, PGCE
Mrs L Hughes, BA Warwick, PGCE
Mrs S Scott-Malden, BA London, PGCE
Mr J Smart, BA Exeter, PGCE

Home Economics:
Mrs G Grant-Ross, BEd Liverpool, CertEd

Information Technology:
Mrs W Parry, BA Brighton, QTS

Junior Department:
Miss N Talbot, BSc Nottingham, PGCE
Mrs R Green, MA Oxon, PGCE
Miss D O'Brien, BA Cantab, PGCE

Library:
Mrs D Pocock Bell, BA Wales, MA London
Mrs E Dickins, BA Birmingham
Mrs K Gray, BSc Manchester, Dip IPM

Mathematics:
Mr C Morris, MA Oxon, PGCE
Mrs S Allwright, BA Cantab, PGCE
Mrs H Hanratty, MA Oxon, PGCE
Dr A Hull, BA Nottingham, PhD Nottingham, PGCE
Mr D Ireland, BSc Leicester, QTS
Miss S Kennedy, MA Cantab, PGCE
Mrs M Moore, BSc Lancaster, PGCE
Mr P Moylan, BA Oxon, PGCE
Mrs C Russell, BSc London, PGCE
Dr R Strong, MPhys Bath, PhD Cantab, QTS

Medical:
Dr M Hughes, MBBS
Mrs J Leahy, BA Open University, PCert Reading
Nurse J Rimmer, RGN
Nurse R Byerley, RGN

Modern Languages:
Miss L Hillier, BA Exeter, PGCE
Mrs L Astbury, BA Birmingham, PGCE
Dr G Clark, MA Cantab, DPhil Oxon, PGCE
Mrs M Abbott, CFS Liège, Dip French Alliance Française, Brussels
Mr J Earnshaw-Crofts, MA London, BA London, PGCE
Mrs C Fisher, Milan, BA Milan, PGCE
Ms C Gomes, BA Lisbon, MA Kent, PGCE
Mrs I Hichens, Licence/BA, Paris La Sorbonne, PGCE
Mrs L Littlejohn, MA Cantab, PGCE
Mrs K Taylor, BA Wales, PGCE

Music:
Miss H Rakowski, BA, MA Oxon, PGCE (*Director of Music*)
Miss Lisa McAdam, BA, MA Cantab, PGCE, Dip ABRSM (*Assistant Director of Music*)
Rev Dr E Pitkethly, MLitt Oxon, BPhil Warwick, PGCE)
Mrs S Edwards, BEd Hons Sussex (*Music Department Secretary*)
Mr P Foster, LTCL (*Head of Wind and Brass*)
Miss P Grant, BA, MA Oxon (*Head of Singing*)
Ms E Hayes, Dip. RCM, CTABRSM (*Head of Keyboard*)
Mrs M Walton, PG Dip Birmingham Conservatoire, LGSM, BA York (*Head of Strings*)
Miss J Broome, MA Cantab (*Harp*)
Mr R Burley, ALCM, LLCM (*Guitar*)
Mr M Cooke, PPRNCM, GRNCM (*French Horn*)
Mrs J Craven, MA, BA, GTCL, LTCL, LRAM (*Piano*)
Mr R Cutting, RMSM Kneller Hall (*Brass*)
Mr W Dutta, BMus, LTCL (*Piano*)
Mr S Fawbert (*Percussion*)
Mrs V Findlay, LRAM, MA (*Cello*)
Miss R Gladstone, BA, MA Cantab (*Cello*)
Ms E Harré, LRAM, GRSM Hons, Dip Ex Sc (*Double Bass*)
Mrs H Haskell, ARCM (*Violin & Viola*)
Mrs L Howarth, BA Cantab, MMus (*Singing*)
Dr R Manasse, BSc London, DPhil Cantab (*Flute*)
Mr D McNaughton, BA Oxon (*Brass*)
Mrs S Mears, MA Oxon, LRAM, PGCE, Dip HSW OU (*Piano*)
Mrs A Phillips, BMus RCM, ARCM (*Singing*)
Miss J Rhind-Tutt, BA Oxford Brookes, QTS, CTABRSM (*Oboe*)
Miss C Scott, MA Oxon, MMus Perf, PPRNCM (*Clarinet*)
Miss J Thomas, BMus Birmingham, PGCE (*Singing & Class Teaching*)
Mr A Thorne, BMus Glamorgan (*Electric Guitar, Jazz Bass*)
Mr R Thorne, BMus, AMusA (*Flute*)
Miss L Tugwell, MMus Perf, BMus (*Clarinet*)
Mr G Williams, LRAM, ARCM, FTCL, FLCM, MSTAT, PGCE (*Bassoon, Clarinet, Saxophone*)
Mr S Wilson, BA Oxon (*Cello*)
Mrs S Windsor-Lewis, BMus Surrey, PG Dip, Art Dip (*Singing*)
Mr J Wood, MSc London, LRSM, Dip ABRSM (*Singing*)

Personal Development (*PD*):
Ms K Meuleman, BEd Eeklo, Belgium, PG Worcester

Physical Education:
Mrs S Wilson, MA OU, BSc Brunel, QTS
Miss E Aston, BSc Loughborough, PGCE
Mrs J Chilvers, FTI
Mrs S Keogh, BSc Birmingham, QTS
Miss N Lydall, BSc Bath, PGCE
Mrs L Trumper, BEd Liverpool
Mrs A Wilson, BEd Brunel

Psychology:
Mrs C Canlan-Shaw, BSc Loughborough, PGCE
Mrs K Collett, BSc Worcester, PGCE

Religious Studies:
Ms S Hayward, BA Durham, PGCE
Ms K Meuleman, BEd Eeklo, Belgium, PG Worcester
Revd Dr E Pitkethley, MLitt Oxon, BPhil Warwick, PGCE
Mr J Williams, MTheol St Andrews, PGCE

Science:

Biology:
Mrs R James, BSc Bristol, MSc Oxon, PGCE
Dr T Bainbridge, BSc Leeds, PhD London, PGCE
Miss A Bourne, MSc Bristol, PGCE
Mrs C Canlan-Shaw, BSc Loughborough, PGCE
Mrs K Homann, MA Cantab, PGCE
Dr M Wait, Phd Nelson Mandela Metropolitan, MSc Port Elizabeth, PGCE
Mrs K Wright, BSc London, PGCE

Chemistry:
Mrs G Lydford, BSc UEA, QTS
Mrs J Armstrong, BSc Leeds, PGCE
Mrs J Bell, BSc Bristol, MSc Oxon, CertEd
Dr C Holyoak, BSc Manchester, DPhil Manchester Metropolitan
Dr J Saba, BSc Aberdeen, DPhil Leeds, PGCE
Mrs T Lewis, BSc Reading, PGCE

Physics:
Mrs J Edwards, BSc Nottingham, PGCE
Dr Z Chater, MPhys Birmingham, PhD Birmingham, PGCE
Mrs D Jackson, MSc OU, BSc Keele, PGCE
Dr M Leigh, BSc, MSc, PhD Newcastle

Special Educational Needs Coordinator:
Mrs D Cobbing, Cert SpLD, Dip SpLD

Registrar: Miss L Johnson
Headmistress's PA: (*to be appointed*)

St Helen and St Katharine is located on the outskirts of Abingdon within easy reach of Oxford and surrounding villages. An extensive network of school buses operates to bring pupils from across Oxfordshire and Berkshire. Academic excellence, the School is consistently placed in the Top 20 in the country, is combined with a broad extra-curricular programme. Eager to learn, and motivated to do their best, pupils are encouraged to challenge themselves, both academically and beyond the classroom, to fulfil their potential and achieve success as they define it.

Buildings. The original school building dates from 1906. In recent years an extensive building programme has been undertaken. Most recent developments include a Performing Arts Centre with studio theatre, dance studio and extensive music rooms, a refurbished refectory and new Sports Centre with fitness suite. An exceptional library facility which includes ICT Suites, lecture theatre and careers library was opened in 2010 and the Sixth Form Centre was extended and refurbished in 2011. A state-of-the-art Science facility opened in September 2014.

Curriculum. The school encourages girls to maintain a broad and balanced curriculum which includes the following subjects: Art, Biology, Business Studies, Ceramics, Chemistry, Classics, Design Technology, Drama and Theatre Studies, Economics, English Language, English Literature, Food Studies, French, Geography, German, Government and Politics, Greek, History, ICT, Italian, Latin, Mathematics, Further Mathematics, Music, Physical Education, Physics, Pottery, Psychology, Religious Studies, and Spanish. A programme of community service and personal development encourages girls to be responsible for themselves and take care of others. The school has its own Chapel in which a weekly Eucharist is offered to staff and girls.

Music and Drama. The school has a very strong musical tradition with many girls learning at least one instrument.

Tuition is provided in all major instruments including the harp and organ. There are numerous orchestras, choirs and ensembles that cater for all abilities and achieve significant recognition and success in festivals and competitions. The drama department, based in the Performing Arts Centre, delivers a busy schedule of productions of the highest quality making it a popular and rewarding part of the extra-curricular programme as well as supporting significant success and GCSE and A Level.

Sports. Sport is a central part of school life. Competitive teams and clubs, at all age groups and abilities, are offered and major sports include lacrosse, netball, athletics, tennis, gymnastics and rounders. There is also a wide range of recreational sports clubs available including biathlon, tae kwon-do, badminton, dance, sailing, swimming, fencing, cross country, cricket, basketball, equestrian, trampoline and football. Over 130 girls compete at County level or above. Thirteen St Helen's girls currently compete internationally.

Societies. All pupils are encouraged to take part in the wide range of extra-curricular activities available. Over 100 clubs and societies and groups are on offer. Of particular note are Debating and Public Speaking, The Duke of Edinburgh's Award Scheme and Young Enterprise Programme, which all enjoy a strong tradition in the school.

St Helen's has strong links with Abingdon School and in the Sixth Form selected subjects are taught jointly including a joint Critical Thinking course taken by all Lower Sixth pupils The close relationship between the two schools also enables music, drama and debating as well as many social events to take place together.

Admission is at ages 9+, 10+, 11+, 13+ and 16+. An entrance examination is held in January for 9+, 10+ and 11+ and in November for 13+ for admission in the following September. Girls are accepted into the Sixth Form on the basis of their GCSE results and an interview. There may be occasional vacancies in other years of the school.

Scholarships and Bursaries. Scholarships are awarded, by the Headmistress, to recognise excellence, ability and potential. Academic, music, art, drama and sport scholarships are available. Academic scholarships are valued at 10% of fees, music scholarships provide free tuition in one/two instruments and all other scholarships are valued at £300 pa. All scholarships are open to both internal and external candidates. Further information is available from the Admissions Office.

Bursaries up to 100% of the fees are available to pupils from Year 7 and are based on a means-tested assessment of financial circumstances.

Fees per term (2014–2015). £4,510.

Charitable status. The School of St Helen and St Katharine Trust is a Registered Charity, number 286892. The Trust was established to promote and provide for the advancement of education of children in the United Kingdom and elsewhere; such education to be designed to give a sound Christian and moral basis to all pupils.

St Helen's School

Eastbury Road, Northwood, Middlesex HA6 3AS
Tel: 01923 843210
Fax: 01923 843211
email: enquiries@sthn.co.uk
            admissions@sthn.co.uk
website: www.sthn.co.uk

Independent Day School for Girls founded in 1899.

Council of Governors:

Chairman Ms S Woolfson, BSc, FCA
Vice-Chairman Mrs J Lewis, BSc Econ, FCIPD
Mrs M Bhandari, LLB, LLM, LPC

Mr N Boghani, BSc Hons, CA
Mr T Jones, BA
Mrs J Kirchheimer, BVetMed, MRCVS
Mrs A Little, MA Cantab
Ms P Mongia, MA MEng Cantab, CEng, MRAeS, MBA
   London Business School
Mrs A Phillipson, MA Cantab, MBA, PGCE
Dr S M Pitts, MSc, MA, PhD
Mr V Sapra, SFA, MBA, CEng, BEng, MICE
Mrs M Weerasekera, Mont Dip, LLB

Headmistress: **Dr M Short**, BA London, PhD Cantab

Deputy Head Development: Dr P Arnold, MA DPhil Oxon
Deputy Head Pastoral: Mrs J Parker, BA Liverpool
Deputy Head Academic: Mr P Tiley, BSc Bristol
Business Director and Clerk to the Council: Mr M
   Mackenzie Crooks, BSc, MSc, MBA
Head of Sixth Form: Mr H Dymock, BA Durham, MA
   London
Head of Upper School: Mrs D Sinclair, MA London
Head of Middle School: Mrs C Hill, BA Newcastle
Head of Junior School: Mrs K Serinturk, BEd London
Head of Little St. Helen's: Miss K Cooper, BA Canterbury
PA to the Headmistress: Mrs C Brown, BA Coventry; Miss
   D Quane
PA to the Business Director: Mrs K Campbell
Secretary to the Deputy Heads: Mrs A Bedin

Senior School Staff:
* *Head of Department*

Art:
*Mrs N Smith, BA Sunderland
Mrs J George, BA Solent
Mr V Hazeldine, BA London
Mrs J Restick, BA Guildhall (*Technician*)

Careers:
*Miss E McKinley, BA Heriot-Watt (*Deputy Head of Sixth
   Form*)
Mr H Dymock, BA Durham, MA London

Classics:
*Mr K Buck, BA Johannesburg
Dr P Arnold, MA DPhil Oxon
Dr A Berriman, BA Bristol, PhD Nottingham Trent
Mr H Dymock, BA Durham, MA London

Design & Technology:
*Mr B Gee, MA OU
Mrs K Gibbons, BSc Nottingham Trent
Mrs L Hallam, BA Middlesex
Mr R Shaikh, BA Brighton
Ms A Young, BTEC (*Technician*)

Drama:
*Mrs M Connell, BA Manchester
Mrs H Casingena, BA Oxon, LSDE Lamda
Mrs K Newby, BA Loughborough
Mrs D Sinclair, MA London
Mr T Boxall, BA Hull Events Sound & Lighting
   (*Technician*)

Economics & Business Studies:
*Mrs M Bowman, BEd Leeds
Mr M Khan, BSc Wollongong, Dubai, MSc London

English:
*Mr R Johnston, BA Liverpool
Ms S Ahmed, BA Essex, MA London
Mrs K Douglas, MA St Andrews
Mr T Gerig, BA Illinois
Mrs L Spicer, BEd Oxon
Mr M Stewart, BA UWI, Jamaica

Geography:
*Miss E Rynne, MA London
Mrs C Beake, BA London

Mr D Froggatt, BSc Cardiff
Mr R Pimlott, BA Middlesex

History, Government & Politics and History of Art:
*Mr B Nemko, BA Birmingham, MSc City, MA London
Miss L Hamilton, MA Manchester, MA St Andrews
Mrs C Hill, BA Newcastle
Mrs R Reidel-Fry, MA Courtauld, MPhil, MA Columbia, USA (*Deputy Head of Upper School*)
Mr A Reynolds, BA Birmingham
Mrs H Sinclair, MA St Andrews
Mr P Whalley, BA Portsmouth

Individual Needs:
*Ms J Halmagyi, MA Debrecen, Hungary, NASCO Middlesex
Mrs R Bird, BA London
Ms P Vine, BA Exeter

Information and Communications Technology:
*Mr M Hoffman, BA South Africa
Mr J Firestone, MA Brighton

Mathematics:
*Miss C Kerry, BEng London
Miss H Blazewicz, BSc Bristol
Dr J Donovan, MEd, MSc, PhD London
Mrs S King, BEng Bristol
Mrs S Michaels, BSc Manchester
Mr C Norris, BSc London
Mrs T Onac, BSc London
Mr D Patel, BSc Bristol
Mrs A Pateli, CertEd St Mary's

Modern Foreign Languages:
*Mrs E Serrano, Filología Inglesa Degree Madrid (*Head of Modern Foreign Languages and Spanish*)
Mrs R Chaperlin, BA Birmingham
Mrs G Chuykov, BA Yaroslavl, Russia, MA London
Mrs D Clayden, BA Leeds
*Mrs E Davis, BA Birmingham, MA Westminster (*Subject Leader for German, Deputy Head of Middle School*)
Mrs M Ishikawa, MA London
Ms J Lee, MSc Queen Mary (*Subject Leader for Mandarin*)
Mrs L Louiset, BA MA Antilles
Miss E McKinley, BA Heriot-Watt
Mrs J Orme, BA Durham
Mrs N O'Hagan, CertEd
Mrs J Parker, BA Liverpool
Mrs N Wright, BA Manchester
Mr P Vines, BA UAE (*Head of French*)
Mrs C Gauci, BA Mexico (*Spanish Assistant*)
Miss B Lee (*Mandarin Assistant*)
Miss N Müller (*German Assistant*)
Miss A Norin (*French Assistant*)

Music:
*Mr R Crowley, MSc, PGCMT Herts, BMus London, ARAM, LRAM, Dip RAM
Mrs R Yates, GRSM, LRAM, ARCM

Music – Visiting:
Ms C Barry, BA Mod Trinity College Dublin, LTCL
Miss J Chen, BMus, PGDip Royal Academy of Music
Miss E Coleman, MA, BA Chichester
Mrs D Ellin, BMus Royal Scottish Academy of Music, PGDip LRAM
Mr A Gathercole, GGSM, ALCM Guildhall School of Music and Drama
Mrs S Gregory, LRAM, LTCL
Mr D Hester, DipTCL, LTCL, PDOT Guildhall School of Music and Drama
Mr C Hooker, ARAM, LRAM, DipRAM
Miss D Kemp, MA Oxon, Dip RCM, ARCM
Miss R Krbilkova, DiS Pardubice Conservatory, Czech Republic
Mrs S Lawman, GRSM, ARCM

Mr J Little, BA Central Saint Martins, Dip TCM
Mrs J Maclean, BSc City LTCL
Mr I Marcus
Mr N Martin, Cert NLP
Mr A McAfee, BA Nottingham Trent, PG Cert Trinity College of Music
Mrs M Sebata MMus BMus Royal College of Music
Mrs N Tait, Prof Cert LRAM
Mr K Tomita, MMus BMus Royal College of Music
Mr M Vishnick, MPhil City, MSc Herts, LLCM TD, ALCM

Physical Education:
*Miss J Hurt, BA Brunel
Mrs A Arnot, BEd Bedford
Mrs J Ball, BEd Manchester Metropolitan
Mrs J Barton, BA Oxford Brookes
Mrs N Barton, BSc Loughborough
Miss S Chadburn, BSc Sheffield Hallam
Miss H Harding, PTTLS Award
Miss S Heath, BEd Bedford, MA Brunel
Miss D Hodkinson, BSc Brunel
Miss K Pickering, BA Chichester
Mrs M Wiltshire, BSc Loughborough
Miss A Borda, BA New York
Miss E Randall

Psychology:
*Mrs L Winter, BSc Plymouth
Mrs A Hussain, BSc MSc Brunel

Religious Studies, Philosophy & Ethics:
*Mr G Bezalel, MSc LSE, MA IOE
Mr H Dymock, BA Durham, MA London
Mr A Giblin, BAPhil Lancaster
Mr E McCartney, BSc London
Miss H Williams, MA Edinburgh

Science:
*Dr J Schofield, BSc PhD London (*Head of Science*)
*Mrs A Adlam, BSc Southampton, MSc Imperial MInstP (*Head of Physics*)
Mrs J Arthur, BSc Reading
Miss K Baker, BSc Southampton (*Deputy Head of Middle School*)
Mrs K Barnes, BSc Leeds
*Mrs C Jenkins, BSc Cardiff (*Head of Biology*)
Dr C Jones, BSc Nottingham Trent PhD London
Mr C Le Bas, BSc Edinburgh
*Mr M Reynish, BSc York (*Head of Chemistry*)
Mrs S Thomas, MSci London
Mr P Tiley, BSc Bristol
Mrs S Wardley, BSc Southampton
Mrs S Williams, BSc Exeter
Mrs Z Alidina, City & Guilds, Pharmacy (*Technician*)
Mrs A Ghosh, BSc Calcutta Technician
Mrs B Lee, BEng China Technician
Mrs Y O'Connor, BSc MSc PhD Japan (*Technician*)

Library:
*Ms E Howard, BA, ALA, Chartered Librarian
Mrs S Gleave
Mrs R Serbos, BA Sheffield Hallam, MA London

Junior School Staff:
*Mrs K Serinturk, BEd London
Mrs I Cane, BA Birmingham
Miss E Carey, BA Durham
Mrs A Cawthorne, BSc Surrey, MA Middlesex
Mrs G Collins, BEd Queen's University, Ontario
Mrs L Crawford
Miss S English, BA Portsmouth
Mrs A Groves, BA Brunel
Ms S Gupta, BA Roehampton
Mrs J Hunt, BEd Herts
Mrs N Lawson, BA Bath

Mrs D Morton, BA West of England
Mrs K Palamarchuk, MA Crakow, Poland
Mrs M Parry, BA Warwick, MTeach London
Mrs M Pratt, BA Griffith, PDipEd Queensland
Mrs P Prosser, BEd Durham
Mrs E Sami, MEd Herts (*Deputy Head of Junior School*)
Miss L Steerwood, BA St Mary's
Mrs J Webb Science (*Technician*)

Pre-Preparatory Staff Little St Helen's:
*Miss K Cooper, BA Canterbury
Mrs D Allsopp, MontDip London
Mrs L Baldwin, BEd Cantab
Mrs S Begley, BSc Bangor, MPhil Pontypridd (*Deputy Head of Little St Helen's*)
Miss J Collins, BA Herts
Miss R Cox, BA Ryerson, BEd Queen's University, Ontario
Mrs N Johar, BA Brunel
Miss R Kansagra, BA Leeds
Mrs J Kirk, ARCM RAM
Mrs A Lam, BA Essex
Miss H Manber, BA Birmingham
Miss D Masters, BEd Oxon
Mrs R Rajani, BSc London
Mrs D Roberts, BA Surrey
Ms D Sarnat, BA Tel Aviv
Mrs R Sirera, BA MA Manchester
Mrs D Smith, BEd Warwick (*Deputy Head of Little St Helen's*)
Mrs T Wood, BA Surrey

Administrative Staff:
Accountant: Mr D Dhrona, FCCA
Development Director: Ms Z Baines BA Birmingham, MSc LSE
Head of Admissions: Mrs L Hailey
Registrar: Miss S Heath, BEd Bedford, MA Brunel
Domestic Bursar: Mrs L Toms
Estates Manager: Ms A Steele, BA Manchester
Human Resources Manager: Mrs S Hart, BSc MIPD
IT Systems & Projects Manager: Mr D Nanton
Sports Centre Manager: Mr M Jones
Senior School Office Coordinator: Mrs S Page
Senior School Secretary: Ms C Julien
Junior School Secretary: Mrs P Robbins
Little St Helen's Secretary: Mrs F Kahan

St Helen's School has a commitment to academic excellence that has given us an enviable reputation for over 100 years. To build on this tradition, the school is also embarking on an exciting and creative long-term plan to become the 'exceptional' choice for girls' day schools in North London, including the building of a state-of-the-art new Junior School, to open in September 2016. We provide a complete academic education for able girls, developing personal integrity alongside intellectual, creative and sporting talents. The staff are highly qualified and enthusiastic, the facilities are excellent, and we pride ourselves on knowing, valuing and nurturing every pupil as an individual. Above all we encourage all the girls at St Helen's to pursue their dreams and develop the academic, social and transferable skills which will enable them to become leaders in their fields, professions and communities.

The school is divided into three departments: Little St Helen's (3+ to 7), Junior School (7+ to 11) and Senior School (11+ to 18), enabling continuity and progression in the education of every pupil. Main entry points are at 3+, 4+, 7+, 11+ and 16+.

St Helen's has an excellent academic record and girls achieve outstanding results in public examinations at all levels. In our flourishing Sixth Form there are approximately 150 girls. A Levels are offered in the Sixth Form, with girls able to choose from 30 subjects and going on to prestigious universities, including Oxford and Cambridge, after comprehensive support through the university applications and preparation process. We additionally offer a broad Enrichment programme: Sixth Form students are able to complement their A Level programme with additional qualifications such as the European Computer Driving Licence (ECDL) or the Extended Project Qualification (EPQ), take up modules offered by the Open University, acquire additional languages or study a range of additional courses including Critical Thinking. All students follow a programme in core skills to help them hone their study techniques, and participate in a lecture series which aims to broaden horizons and encourage discussion of a wide range of topics. Additionally, the St Helen's Portfolio, awarded to each Year 13 student, records and celebrates the full and impressive range of skills, qualifications and co-curricular experiences of each girl throughout her time in the Sixth Form.

The curriculum is designed to enable every girl to achieve intellectual and personal fulfilment and to develop her talents to the full. We support the aims of the National Curriculum, but offer a wider range of subjects and teach to greater depth, so enabling the girls to explore their interests and talents. The staff are subject specialists whose aim is to inspire a love of their subjects. They help the girls to learn how to study independently and develop good study habits, through stimulating and rigorous teaching. On entry to the Senior School in Year 7, all girls study two modern foreign languages together with Latin. Science subjects are popular at all levels of the Senior School. We expect the girls to study with commitment and to develop qualities of intellectual curiosity and resilience. Music, Art, Drama and Sport are all an integral part of the life of the school and involve every girl. Many also take extra Music, Ballet, Speech & Drama lessons and Sports coaching.

Girls take a full part in the broader life of the school and, through co-curricular activities, discover new interests to complement their academic achievements. Clubs and societies abound, catering for the widest possible range of interests and hobbies, and we have a flourishing programme of optional outdoor and adventurous activities. We have recently been recognised as an independent licensing authority for the Duke of Edinburgh's Award Scheme, and many girls successfully complete their Bronze, Silver and Gold Awards; in the summer of 2014 a cohort of 16 girls participated in a memorable Gold Award Expedition to Malawi. A full range of CCF activities is offered in partnership with Merchant Taylors' School. We have a thriving vertical House system which girls actively help to run, and competition between the Houses is characterised by universal participation and friendly rivalry.

St Helen's is located on a spacious 21-acre greenfield site and is easily accessible on the London Underground Metropolitan Line. Northwood Station is less than five minutes' walk from the school. The School also runs extensive and flexible coach services from the surrounding areas.

Our popular breakfast club and after-school care programme allow girls to extend their day in the safety of the school environment. Our qualified staff involve the girls in many activities, such as baking, games and paper craft, and enable them to complete their homework before they go home. Breakfast club and after-school care are housed in Longworthe House in familiar surroundings and tea and supper are provided. The Mint Café, a sixth form facility during the school day, is available to all Senior School pupils from 7.30 am and after 4 pm.

Fees per term (2014–2015). Senior School: £4,977. Junior School (including Speech & Drama): £3,910. Little St Helen's: Reception, Year 1 and Year 2 (including Lunch, Ballet, Speech & Drama) £3,735; Nursery (including Lunch, Ballet, Speech & Drama) £3,424.

Registration Fee: UK £75; Overseas £100.

Scholarships. Academic entry scholarships to Senior School are awarded annually at 11+ and 16+; Music Scholarships and Exhibitions are available at 11+ and 16+ for applicants of exceptional musical ability. Sport Scholarships are available at 11+ and 16+, and Sixth Form Drama and Art Scholarships are also awarded. Bursaries are available; an academic Scholarship is awarded each year to a pupil at 14+.

St Helen's Old Girls' Club. *Secretary*: Mrs Sally Fleming, 2 Moneyhill Road, Rickmansworth, Herts WD3 2EQ.

Charitable status. St Helen's School for Girls is a Registered Charity, number 312762. It exists to provide quality education for girls.

St James Senior Girls' School

Earsby Street, London W14 8SH
Tel: 020 7348 1777; Admissions: 020 7348 1748
Fax: 020 7348 1717
email: admissions@sjsg.org.uk
website: www.stjamesgirls.co.uk

Motto: *Speak the truth. Live generously. Aim for the best.*

Governors:
Mr Jeremy Sinclair (*Chairman*)
Mrs Koula Ansell, BA Hons
Mrs Jennie Buchanan, Mont Dip
Mr Michael Cranny, FCII, Chartered Insurer
Mr George Cselko, BA Hons
Mr Aatif Hassan, BSc Hons, CA (*Joint Deputy Chairman*)
Mrs Miranda Munden, BA Hons, PGCE
Mr Jon Pickles BA, ACMA
Mr John Story, FRICS (*Joint Deputy Chairman*)
Mr Hugh Venables, BSc, MBA
Mr Jerome Webb, MA, MRICS
Dr Fenella Willis, BSc, MBBS, MD, FRCP, FRCPath

Headmistress: Mrs Sarah Labram, BA

Deputy Heads:
Mr Bertie Cairns, MA Cantab, QTS (*Academic*)
Mr Christian Daw, BA, BPh, STB, QTS (*Pastoral*)

Director of Studies: Dr Jane MacRae, MSc, PhD, QTS

Head of Sixth Form: Mrs Katharine Bayes, BA, PGCE (*Drama*)
Head of PSHE/Lower School: Mrs Annabel Lubikowski, BA, MPhil, PGCE (*Head of Economics*)
Senior Teacher: Mr Peter Holloway, BA, PGCE (*Head of Music*)

Teaching Staff:
Mr Stephen Allen, MA Cantab, MSci, PGCE (*Chemistry*)
Mr David Bevan, MA Cantab, MSc, QTS (*English*)
Mr Nick Burrows, BSc, PGCE (*Head of Geography*)
Miss Edel-Anne Byrne, MA Cantab, QTS (*Head of English*)
Miss Hannah Capron, BA, MA, PGCE (*Art*)
Mlle Mylène Chaudagne, Licence, MA, PGCE (*Head of Modern Foreign Languages*)
Mrs Sue Cooper, BA Art & Design Assoc RSA (*Head of Art*)
Dr Josef Craven, BA, MPhil, PhD (*Head of History; Citizenship*)
Mr Nicholas de Mattos, BA, PGCE (*Classics*)
Mrs Danniella Downs, MA, DipRS, AMI, PGCE (*Head of Religious Studies*)
Miss Pauline Flannery, MA, PGCE (*Head of Drama*)
Mrs Sarah Forrester, BA (*Head of Careers, French*)
Miss Stephanie Furneaux, BSc, PGCE (*Teacher of PE, in charge of lacrosse*)
Mrs Melissa George, MA, PGCE (*English*)

Ms Ioanna Georgiou, MSc, MPhil, QTS (*Second in Mathematics Department*)
Miss Anna Holliss, BA, QTS (*Head of PE*)
Mr Alastair Horsford, BA, QTS (*Geography*)
Mrs Elena Jessup, BSc, MA (*Sanskrit*)
Mr Warwick Jessup, BA Oxon, MA, MPhil (*Head of Sanskrit*)
Mrs Sally Kuhrt, BA (*Head of Art of Hospitality*)
Mr Rudi Ölschlägel,BA, PGCE (*History, History of Art & Classics*)
Mrs Jane Mason, MA Oxon, PGCE (*Head of Classics; Academic Enrichment Coordinator*)
Mr Ben Mohammed, BSc, PGCE (*Head of Mathematics*)
Miss Annette Morgan, Sanskrit Dip EAL, Cambridge Cert (*Sanskrit*)
Mrs Sylvie Piegelin-Coles Maître, PGCE, MA, BLT (*French*)
Mr Luka Radović, BSc, PGCE, MEd Cantab (*Mathematics*)
Miss Lorraine Razzell, BA LRAD (*Dance*)
Ms Selina Shah, PGDip, PGCE (*Head of ICT & Computer Science*)
Mrs Gordana Tarundzioska, BEd, BSc (*Mathematics*)
Dr Clare van der Willigen, MSc, DPhil, PGCE (*Head of Science & Biology*)
Mrs Lynsey Walters, BA, QTS (*PE; Head of Outdoor Pursuits*)
Mrs Vivien West, BA, PGCE (*Head of Study Support, SENCO*)
Mr Tomas White, BSc, PGCE (*Head of Chemistry*)
Mrs Montserrat Wight-Rahona, BA, QTS (*Head of Spanish*)
Mr Stuart Young, BSc, QTS (*Head of Physics; Head of ICT Strategy*)

Visiting Staff:
Mrs Emily Johnston, AMI Mont Dip, ITEC Dip (*Meditation Programme Coordinator*)
Mrs Rosemary Downs (*Needlework*)
Mrs Sine Pickles (*Needlework*)

Support Staff:
Miss Katharine Barnard BA (*Librarian*) (*maternity cover*)
Mrs Anna Bhowmick (*Teaching Assistant*)
Mrs Alison Buchanan (*Examinations Officer*)
Mrs Selina Coleman (*Senior Laboratory Technician*)
Mrs Clare Featherby, RGN (*School Nurse*)
Miss Eleanor Parker, MA (*Librarian*) (*maternity leave*)

Administrative Staff:
Miss Tricia D'Sa, BSc (*PA to Headmistress*)
Miss Sarah Price, BA (*School Secretary & PA to Director of Education*)
Mrs Sue Allen (*Registrar & School Uniform*)
Miss Aimie Robinson BA (*Secretary to Deputy Heads*)
Mrs Lindsey Kavanagh, BA, ACIM (*Marketing Manager*)
Ms Leah Murray (*Events Manager*)

Bursary:
Mr William Wyatt (*Bursar*)
Mr Roy Kemp (*Assistant to Bursar*)
Ms Nanouchi Malo (*PA to Bursar*)

Property Management:
Mr Nigel Lacey (*Site Manager*)
Mr Richard Hithersay
Mr Alex Bekvalac
Mr Salah Chebiouni

Founded in 1975, St James Senior Girls' School is a day school for 330 pupils aged from 10–18. We are situated on a spacious site in Olympia, West Kensington, shared by our own Junior School. The Senior Girls' School provides an education which draws out and magnifies the unique talents innate in every individual. We provide an environment which enriches the intellectual, spiritual and physical development of our pupils in an atmosphere which supports unity and is conducive to the happiness of all. We inspire our pupils with a love for the finest aspects of human life so that they themselves develop the inner strength to live honest, dignified and magnanimous lives, employing their talents creatively for the benefit of humanity. The school has strong spiritual and moral values, which lie at the heart of the education we offer.

Girls work together, delighting in the achievement of others as well as their own. Our girls are industrious, openhearted and courageous. We encourage pupils to develop self-discipline and the capacity to hold firmly to their intelligent understanding of right principle.

Our teachers are experts in their subjects and have been chosen because they have the capacity to devote themselves to the well-being and development of their pupils.

Good care of our pupils depends upon unity of approach between school and home. The principles of the school need to be supported by parents and we consider close communication between school and home to be of paramount importance.

Whilst admission to the school is through a selective procedure, the school seeks to admit those candidates who are able and willing to make good use of the education offered. The school aims to foster creativity and intellectual curiosity, challenging its pupils to achieve excellence. Standards in public examinations are high: 95% of leavers proceed to Higher Education degree courses either at university, a specialist music college or to pursue an art foundation course.

The Curriculum offers appropriate education in PSHE, SMSC, Citizenship, Philosophy and Religious Studies. Emphasis is given to the cultivation of leadership training, public speaking and debating. Community Service runs throughout the school and is supported by a Pupil Community Service Council. Career Guidance is offered to all pupils from Years 8–13. All pupils engage in Sports, Singing and Dance. Drama, Music and ICT are also taught from Years 6–9.

Subjects available to GCSE: English (Language and Literature), Mathematics, French, Spanish, Latin, Greek, Sanskrit, History, Geography, Physics, Biology, Chemistry, Religious Studies, ICT, Art, Music, Drama. The three sciences and Set 1 Maths take IGCSE examinations. Years 6 and 7 are taught General Science prior to commencing the three separate sciences in Year 8. Years 6 and 7 also receive lessons in needlework and the Art of Hospitality.

Subjects offered at AS and A Level: English, Greek, Latin, Sanskrit, French, Spanish, Mathematics, Further Mathematics, Physics, Chemistry, Biology, History, Art & Design, Music, Geography, Economics, Drama & Theatre Studies, History of Art and Religious Studies. Students also take the Extended Project, a project which develops research and independent learning skills.

The Sixth Form. Most pupils stay on to complete their education in the Sixth Form. This is treated as a very distinct stage. Support and encouragement is given for the development of initiative and responsibility through leadership opportunities. The PSHE and SMSC programme is continued in order to provide support for personal development through a series of talks, debates and workshops. Emphasis is given to academic excellence and the cultivation of social awareness and, in particular, leadership skills are developed through assuming responsibility for younger pupils in the school. In Year 12 students are offered a community service project abroad (currently each year a group travel to Kolkata, India to help orphaned children and another group travel to South Africa to trek in the wilderness and do volunteer work in a Zulu village).

Creative Arts. Music, Drama and Dance are strong features of the school. There is a tradition of choral and solo singing, as well as instrumental music making. A fully-staged opera or musical is performed biennially in association with our brother school, St James Senior Boys' School (*Fiddler on the Roof* in 2012, performed at the Royal College of Music). There are several choirs, orchestras and instrumental ensembles and girls are strongly encouraged to take up individual instruction with one of our visiting instrumental and/or vocal teachers. Many pupils participate in extra-curricular vocal and/or instrumental lessons. The latest dramatic productions include *The Crucible* (Sixth Form), *Into the Woods* (Years 7 and 8) and Shakespeare's *Pericles* (Year 9). The Dance programme introduces pupils to a variety of dance forms: ballet, modern dance, ballroom and choreography. As well as extra-curricular lessons, pupils also have the opportunity to perform in the school's biennial Dance Festival and Music, Speech, Debating and other artistic competitions.

Physical Education. Sports and games are an important part of school life. Lacrosse, Netball, Athletics, Gymnastics, Pilates, Rounders and Tennis are all offered within the curriculum. There is an on-site gymnasium and pupils visit a sports ground in nearby Chiswick on a weekly basis.

Extra-Curricular Activities. Pupils are offered a wide range of clubs including Art, Classics, Cookery, Dance, Drama, Lacrosse, Netball, Rounders, Science, The Duke of Edinburgh's Award, ICT, Choir and Orchestra. All girls attend the annual Activity Week with their own class at a variety of locations within and outside the UK.

Admission. For entry at 11+ girls sit the North London Independent Girls' Schools Consortium Entrance examination; at Sixth Form candidates are required to sit an entrance exam and to attain the necessary GCSE grades for A Level study. For occasional vacancies in Years 6, 8 and 9 candidates will need to take an entrance examination. All candidates are interviewed individually.

Fees per term (2014–2015). £5,400.

Bursaries. There are limited funds available for Bursary assistance. Awards are discretionary and based on a full financial enquiry into parents' means by the Bursary Fund Committee. The funds are primarily to assist children already attending St James, but some help may be available to new parents in specific circumstances. Enquiries should be made in the first instance to the Bursar.

Charitable status. The Independent Educational Association Limited is a Registered Charity, number 270156. It exists to provide education for children.

St Leonards-Mayfield School

The Old Palace, Mayfield, East Sussex TN20 6PH

Tel:	01435 874623 (Headmistress and Secretary)
	01435 874600 (School)
	01435 874642 (Admissions)
Fax:	01435 872627
email:	enquiry@mayfieldgirls.org
website:	www.mayfieldgirls.org

At St Leonards-Mayfield School, girls will find the space to be themselves, within a challenging yet supportive environment. Mayfield girls learn how to combine rigorous academic study with a diverse range of activities beyond the classroom, while still finding the time to be still and know God. When they come to leave at the end of the Sixth Form, they will have matured into educated and independent young women, confident in their beliefs and prepared to make a positive difference in the world in which they find themselves, a force for good in responding to the challenges of the 21st century.

Of course, it is important to achieve the finest possible examination results, and Mayfield students do, but the best independent learners know there is much more to education than simply achieving A grades. At Mayfield, we encourage girls to educate their mind, body, heart and soul. Every pupil has unique potential and, from the day she joins us, we support each girl to develop a love of knowledge, sound working habits and a responsibility for her own learning. In this way, she will become the best that she can be, academically, socially, physically and spiritually.

The Governors:
Lady Davies of Stamford, MA Oxon, MBA (*Chairman & Chairman of Finance Committee*)
Mrs Elizabeth Byrne-Hill, BA, MA, PGCE (*Deputy Chairman & Chairman of Education Committee*)
Mrs Teresa Blaxland, BA
Miss Julia Bowden, BA PGCE MBA
Mr Chris Buxton, BA, ACA
Sister Maria Dinnendahl, SHCJ BA, MA Oxon, BA, Lic. Phil.
Mrs Karan Douglas, PGCE
Mrs Sara Hulbert-Powell, BA
Sister Judith Lancaster, SHCJ BA, MTh, MA, PGCE
Mrs Maureen Martin, BA, PGCE
Mrs Cloe Moody, BA
Sister Marie Quayle, SHCJ BA, MSc, MA Oxon, PGCE
Dr Christopher J Storr, KSG MA, PhD, FRSA (*Chairman of Governance Committee*)
Sr Paula Thomas, SHCJ BEd, MA
Mr Eddie Walshe, OBE, PhD, BSc

Society of the Holy Child Jesus (*at Mayfield*):
Sr Teresa Joseph Barrett
Sr Maria Dinnendahl
Sr Jean Sinclair

Headmistress: Miss A M Beary, MA, MPhil Cantab, PGCE

Senior Managers:
Deputy Head (*Academic*): Mr S Skehan, BA, PGCE, MA, NPQH
Deputy Head (*Pastoral & Boarding*): Mrs S Ryan, MA Oxon, MA
Bursar: Lt Col [retd] A H Bayliss, MA Cantab, CEng, MICE
Head of Lower School: Mr P Christian, BA Dunelm, MA, PGCE
Head of Middle School: Mrs S Rothero, BEd, CertEd
Head of Sixth Form: Mr J Filkin, BA Oxon, MA, PGCE
Lay Chaplain: Miss P Cronin, MA
Director of Organisation: Mrs L Varley, MA Oxon, PGCE
Director of Marketing and Development: Mr P d'Aguilar

Teaching staff:

Art:
Miss J Thackray, BA, PGCE (*Head of Department*)
Mr R Lamb, BA, MA
Mrs A Sivyour, BA, PGCE

Ceramics:
Mr T Rees-Moorlah, BA, PGCE, QTS (*Head of Department*)
Mrs Y McFadyean, BA
Miss A Simmons, BA (*Artist in Residence*)

Classics:
Mrs D Downing, BA, MA (*Head of Department*)
Mr John Arnold, BA, MA, PGCE
Mrs M Bushell, BA, PGCE
Mrs S Ryan, MA Oxon, MA

Drama & Theatre Studies:
Mrs H Halliday, Hon Dip (*Head of Department*)
Mrs S Gerstmeyer, BA, GTP, QTS
Mrs J Upton, ALAM, LLAM, CertEd, PGCE

Economics & Business Studies:
Mrs A Cox, BSc, PGCE (*Head of Department*)
Mrs C Bryan, BA, MA, PGCE

English:
Mrs N Evans, BA, PGCE (*Head of Department*)

Mrs C Cox, BA Oxon, PGCE
Mrs E Crawley, BA, PGCE, Cert SPLD, EYPS
Mr J Filkin, BA Oxon, MA, PGCE
Mrs J Foley, BA, PG Dip Ed
Mrs J Leslie, BA, PGCE
Mr S Skehan, BA, PGCE, MA, NPQH

ESOL:
Mrs J D Sandoval, MA, DipTEFLA (*Head of Department*)
Miss A Gallagher, BA, CELTA, QTS
Mrs K Kilvington, BA, MA
Miss P Kotesovska

Food & Nutrition:
Mrs S Rothero, BEd, CertEd (*Head of Department*)
Mrs C Davies, CNAA, BEd, PGCE
Mrs Y Nash, CB Dip

Geography:
Mr S Gough, BSc, PGCE (*Head of Department*)
Miss V Brown, BA, MA, MSc, PGCE, QTS
Mrs F Morris, BEd

History:
Mr D Warren, BA, PGCE (*Head of Department*)
Mrs M Bushell BA, PGCE

History of Art:
Mrs J Weddell, BA Arch, MA (*Head of Department*)

Information Technology:
Miss L Jackson-McKenna, BA, QTS, Dip RSA (*Years 7–11 Head of Department*)
Mr S Gough, BSc, PGCE (*Years 12 and 13 Head of Department*)
Mrs A Leschnikoff, CertEd

Learning Support:
Mrs J Foley, BA, PG, DipEd (*Head of Department*)
Mrs P Bryer, HLTA
Mrs D Colebeck, BA
Mrs K Daughtrey, CertEd
Mrs D Downing, BA, MA
Mrs Z Sargent, BA Oxon, PGCE

Librarian:
Mrs Julie Gabriel, BA

Mathematics:
Mrs A Pullinger, BSc, PGCE (*Head of Department*)
Mrs J Stone, BSc, MSc, PGCE
Miss A Demetriou, BSc, PGCE
Mrs L Motoc, BSc, PGCE
Mr E Reid, BSc, PGCE
Miss N Robinson, BA, MA Oxon, QTS
Miss J vanDriesen, MA, PSTC

Modern Languages:
Mrs A C von Wulffen, MA Oxon PGCE (*Head of Department*)
Mrs R E Boumediene, BA PGCE
Ms M Criado, BA, PGCE
Miss Anna Gallagher, BA, CELTA, QTS
Mlle C Richard, BA, MA, MA, PGCE
Mrs B Santini, Dip di Laurea Pisa
Miss Xiang Yu, BA

Music:
Mr P Collins, GRSM, LRAM, ARCM, PGCE (*Director of Music*)
Mr E Reid, BSc, PGCE
plus c.20 visiting music teachers

Physical Education:
Miss S Evans, BA, QTS, Dip RSA (*Head of Department*)
Mrs G Fletcher, BA, MA, PGCE
Miss E Howell
Miss S Healey, FDI, BTech
Mrs J Jones, BA, QTS, Dip RSA

Mrs H Miller, BA, PGCE
Mrs F Morris, BEd
Mrs P Whitby, BA, QTS

Politics:
Ms Catherine Bryan, BA, MA, PGCE (*Head of
    Department*)

Psychology:
Mrs D Buchner, BA, HDE, BA, CBT Diploma (*Head of
    Department*)

Religious Studies:
Mr P L Oxborrow, BA, MA, PGCE (*Head of Department*)
Mr S Cahill, BTh Oxon, PGCE
Mr P Christian, BA Dunelm, MA, PGCE
Mrs E Warnett, BA, MA, PGCE

Riding:
Miss J Barker, BEd, BHSII J, CertEd (*Director of Riding*)

Sciences:
Mr A Chan, MEng, PGCE (*Head of Physics*)
Ms R Frost (*Head of Biology*)
Mrs J Tayler, BSc, PGCE (*Head of Chemistry*)
Mr D Bullock, BSc, MA, PGCE
Mrs S Buckle, BSc, GCE
Mrs J Gradon, BA, PGCE
Miss R Jackson, BSc Dunelm, PGCE
Miss M Kedziora, BSc, PGCE
Miss T A Rakowska, BSc, PGCE
Dr D Shah-Smith, BSc, PhD, PGCE
Mrs L Varley, MA Oxon, PGCE

Textiles:
Mrs T Budden, Dip Fashion Design & Construction
Miss H Cobb

Scholarship Coordinator: (*to be appointed*)

Housemistresses, pastoral & medical staff:

Leeds House:
Mrs Elizabeth Crawley, BA, PGCE, Cert SPLD, EYPS
    (*Housemistress*)
Miss J Porter-Evans BA (*Matron*)

Connelly House:
Mrs J Roberts, HND, CertEd (*Housemistress*)
Mrs C Jones (*Matron*)

Gresham House:
Mrs S Buckle, BSc, GCE (*Housemistress*)
Miss J Staunton, BA, MPhil, DPhil (*Assistant
    Housemistress*)

St Dunstan's House:
Mrs C Davies, CNAA, BEd, PGCE (*Housemistress*)
Mrs J Mead (*Matron*)

School Doctor: Dr A Fyfe

Senior Nurses:
Mrs D Streeter, RGN
Ms A Winter, RGN, RSCN
Mrs C Slade, RCN

Head of Lower School:
Mr P Christian, BA Dunelm, MA, PGCE

Head of Middle School:
Mrs S Rothero, BEd, CertEd

Head of Sixth Form:
Mr J Filkin BA Oxon, MA, PGCE

Careers Coordinator:
Miss J vanDriesen, MA, PSTC

The vibrant and dynamic community at St Leonards-Mayfield School, where numbers are increasing, has been boosted further this year by yet more investment in the form of a brand new state-of-the-art Sixth Form Centre and an Equestrian Centre. The three boarding houses provide accommodation for girls arranged horizontally in year groups and further expansion is planned to accommodate the growing boarding numbers within the School.

Curriculum. The curriculum at Mayfield is designed to reflect the Catholic foundation of the School and is rooted in the convictions of its founder, Cornelia Connelly. As such, the curriculum aims to provide breadth and depth of opportunity: it is wide and varied, and all subjects within it are granted equal value within School.

Our curriculum meets the individual needs of each girl. It is designed to challenge all pupils and to extend the most able, but also support those with weaknesses in certain areas and those for whom English is a second language.

In Years 7, 8 and 9 (Key Stage 3) a rigorous curriculum is in place offering a breadth of subjects from languages such as Spanish, German and Mandarin, to Textiles and Ceramics encompassing Humanities and separate sciences, all taught by subject specialists. Most girls study eleven subjects at GCSE, including a compulsory core of eight subjects and three optional subjects chosen from a substantial list. Options blocks for both GCSE and A Level are structured around the choices of current students. The guiding principles of the A Level course at Mayfield (Years 12 and 13) continue to offer breadth and depth. Pupils choose up to five subjects at AS Level, three or four of which are then pursued at A2 Level, from a list of 31 possible options. This leads to students accepting offers from Oxbridge, American and European Universities as well as from the Russell Group.

Extra-Curricular Activities. All students are expected to engage in a wide range of extra-curricular activities ranging from riding, fencing and shooting to textiles, music and drama.

Admission. At 11+ via the School Entrance Examination; at 13+ via the School Scholarship Examination or Common Entrance Examination; at 14 (exceptionally) on assessment and school report; at 16+ (for Sixth Form Course) an offer is normally conditional upon the pupil achieving at least nine GCSEs at grades A* to C, with grades A* or A in the subjects she wishes to study at A Level.

Registration fee: £100 (£200 EEA, £275 non-EEA).

Fees per term (2014–2015). Full Boarders £10,000, Day girls £6,250.

Scholarships and Bursaries. Academic Scholarships and Gifted & Talented Scholarships are available for entry at 11+, 13+ and 16+. Scholars are identified through a programme of examination and assessment and are expected to show a high degree of academic aptitude, or considerable talent in one or more of Art, Choral Singing, Dance, Drama, Music and Sport (including Riding). Scholarships are offered on merit and awards of up to 100% are made subject to means tested bursaries.

Examinations and assessment for 11+, 13+ and 16+ Scholarship assessments take place in November.

Charitable status. St Leonards–Mayfield School is a Registered Charity, number 1047503. It exists to provide education for girls in keeping with its Catholic foundation.

St Margaret's School for Girls
Aberdeen

17 Albyn Place, Aberdeen AB10 1RU
Tel: 01224 584466
Fax: 01224 585600
email: info@st-margaret.aberdeen.sch.uk
website: www.st-margaret.aberdeen.sch.uk

Founded in 1846.

School Council:
Councillor J Gifford (*Chair*)
Mr J M Baillie, BSc Hons, MEng
Mr A Bannister, BA, CA
Mrs J Craik, BSc Hons, PGCE
Mr M Grattidge, BSc Hons Arch, Dip Adv Arch, ARIAS, ARB
Professor J Harper, BSc, PhD, CChem, FRSC
Dr J M House, MBBS, MRCGP
Mr D Wood
Dr A Bruce
Mrs G King
Mrs A Everest
Mrs M A M Ruddiman, LLb, Dip LP

Clerk to the Council: Squadron Leader [Ret'd] A R Mountain

Head: Miss Anna Tomlinson, MTheol Hons, PGCE

Deputy Head: Mrs S Lynch, MA Hons, PGCE (*Modern Languages*)

Senior Staff:
* *Head of Department*
§ *Part-time or Visiting*

Mr R Adair, BSc Hons, PGCE Sec (**Chemistry*)
§Miss J Aitken, BEd (*Physical Education*)
Ms S Brown, BEd, ATCL (*Music*)
§Mrs A Bryce, BSc Hons, PGCE (*Mathematics*)
Ms L Chellal, Licence d'Anglais Pau, Licence FLE Grenoble, PGCE (**Modern Languages*)
Miss K Cowie, BA Hons, PGCE (**Art and Design*)
Mrs E Crisp, BA Hons, CGeog, FRGS, PGCE (**Geography*)
Mr G Cunningham, MA Hons, PGCE Sec (**Economics and *History*)
Mrs D Dale, MA, PGCE S (*English*)
Ms P Davey, BA, DipTchg (*Geography, *Modern Studies*)
Mr P Fitzgerald, BSc, DipEd, FiDiagEng (**ICT*)
Miss S Forgie, BA Hons, PGCE (*Modern Languages*)
§Mrs K Fowler, BEd Hons (*Physical Education*)
Mrs L Goodwin, BEd (**Speech and Drama*)
Mrs L Gurney, LTCL (*Music – Woodwind*)
§Mrs L Howitt, BSc Hons, PGDE (*Biology and Chemistry*)
§Mrs H Jennings, BD, PGCE (*History, *Philosophy and *RMPE*)
§Mrs J Johnson, DipDomSc, DipSEN (**Food Technology*)
Mrs S Lynch, MA Hons, PGCE (*Modern Languages*)
Mrs S MacFadyen, BSc, PGCE (*Mathematics*)
Miss W Main, BA Hons, PGCE (**Classics*)
§Mrs A Miller, BSc Hons, PGCE (**Biology*)
Miss E Moore, BSc Hons Physics, BSc Medical Physics, PGDE (**Physics*)
§Mrs H Nehring, BA, PGCE (*Modern Languages*)
Mrs K Norval, BEd Hons (**Physical Education*)
§Miss S Orr, MA Hons, PGDE (*History*)
Mr P Parfitt, BA Hons, MMus (**Music*)
Mrs J Reid, BEd Hons (*Physical Education*)
§Mrs J Richardson, BA Hons, PGCE (*Art and Design*)
§Mrs J Robson, GRSC pt11, PGCE (*Chemistry*)
Mrs J Slater, Dip Comm (**Business Mgt, Word Processing, Guidance and PSE*)
Mrs S Smith, BA Hons, PGCE (**Mathematics*)
§Miss S Stuart, BSc Hons, PGDE (*Biology, Physics*)
§Mrs L Tapper, BSc Hons, PGCE (*Mathematics*)
§Mrs C Werb, BA Hons, PGCE (*English*)
Mr J Witte, MA Hons, PGCE (**English*)

Junior Department:
Miss F Black, BEd Hons
§Mrs C Bradbury, DPE
Miss E Bryce, BEd
Miss S Cowie, BEd Hons, PGC Autism and Learning
Ms A Dressel, BSc, PGCE

Mrs N Murray, BSc Hons PGCE (**Head of Junior School*)
§Mrs L Reilly, MA, CertEd
§Ms A Robertson, BEd Hons
Mrs M Smith, BEd PGC Inclusive Practice

Classroom Assistants:
Mrs C Duncan, HNC
Mrs D Gregory, SVQ2 in Care
§Ms A Robertson, BEd Hons

Nursery at St Margaret's:
Miss W Fraser, HNC Childcare & Education SVQ Level 3
Miss J Lumsden, HNC Early Years Education and Childcare
Miss J Minett, BA Hons Childhood and Youth Studies (**Early Years Coordinator*)
§Mrs M Paterson, HNC Childcare and Education (*maternity leave*)
Miss K Ray, HNC Early Education and Childcare, NC Early Education and Childcare SCQF Level 6
Miss K Thomson, CCLD Level 3 (*maternity leave*)

Support for Learning:
*§Mrs L Williamson, MA, DPSE, SEN
Mrs I Laing, BSAc Hons Speech and Language Therapy
§Ms A Robertson, BEd Hons
§Mrs J Robson, GRSC pt11, PGCE

Administrative Staff:
Bursar: Squadron Leader [Ret'd] A R Mountain
Assistant Bursar: Mrs M Raitt, FIAB
PA to Head: Mrs G Smith
Admissions: Mrs K Schmitz
Marketing Officer: Mrs F Littlejohn
Financial Administrator: Mrs A Robertson
School Administrator/Receptionist: Miss A Fraser
ICT Technician: Mr C Morris, BSc Hons
Laboratory Technician: Miss K Mackie, ONC, HNC, Bio Sci
Reprographic Technician: Mrs S Ingram
Sports Coordinator: Mrs S Lowe, MA Hons, PGCE

After-School Care and Playground Supervision:
Ms H Bertre, Licence Bachelor Degree in Spanish
Mrs S Crabb
Miss W Fraser, HNC Childcare & Education SVQ Level 3 (*After-School Care*)
Ms M Hussain, BA, MSc, Cert Primary Education
Mrs S Ingram (*Playground Supervisor*)
Mrs I Laing, BSAc Hons Speech and Language Therapy
Miss J Minett, BA Hons Childhood and Youth Studies (**Early Years Coordinator*)
Ms A Robertson, BEd Hons (**Holiday Club Manager*)
Miss K Thomson, CCLD Level 3 (*After-School Care*) (*maternity leave*)

There are also visiting instrumental teachers for strings, brass and percussion and three modern language assistants for French, German and Spanish.

Founded in 1846, St Margaret's School is the oldest all-through girls' school in Scotland and the Head is a member of the Girls' Schools Association, Scottish Girls' Schools Group and SLS. Education is provided for around 400 girls from Nursery to Sixth Year. The Nursery is within the main building, and boys and girls are admitted from the age of 3 years.

St Margaret's School is conveniently situated in the west end of Aberdeen. The school's excellent facilities include spacious, well-equipped science laboratories, dining room, art studio, an attractive music suite, a fine gymnasium, playing fields and a pavilion at Summerhill. The school has three computer suites, and the whole school is networked.

Aims. We aim to provide a stimulating education for girls in an all-through school where each girl is encouraged to realise her potential in a friendly, caring atmosphere. The school also aims to provide public benefit through the advancement of education. We encourage staff and girls to contribute to the development of Scottish education.

Curriculum. Girls are prepared for National 4, National 5, Intermediate 2, Higher and Advanced Higher examinations of the Scottish Qualifications Authority. National examinations can be taken for awards in music and drama.

The curriculum includes Art and Design, Biology, Business Management, Chemistry, Classical Studies, Computer Studies, Drama, Economics, English (language and literature), Food Technology, French, Geography, German, History, Information Systems, Latin, Mathematics, Modern Studies, Music, Personal and Social Education, Philosophy, Physical Education, Physics, Religious and Moral Education and Spanish.

Girls are encouraged to take part in extra-curricular activities which include dance, swimming, drama, debating, computer club, science club, Scripture Union, junior and senior orchestra, woodwind ensemble, junior, senior and chamber choir, Duke of Edinburgh Award Scheme, Young Enterprise, highland dancing, chess and Choi Kwang Do.

Admission. Girls are admitted to the School by informal or formal assessment.

Fees per term (2014–2015). Nursery (10 half day sessions) £2,582; 1 Junior £2,357; 2 Junior £2,507; 3 Junior £3,102; 4 Junior £3,178; 5, 6 and 7 Junior £3,310; I to VI Senior £3,734.

These fees include SQA examination fees and all books and materials for nursery and early years classes; they are payable termly with an option to pay monthly. A reduction is made when three or more siblings attend at the same time.

Means-tested bursaries are available for entry to 6 and 7 Junior, I Senior, V and VI Senior.

Charitable status. St Margaret's School for Girls is a Registered Charity, number SC016265. It exists to provide a high quality education for girls.

St Margaret's School
Bushey

Merry Hill Road, Bushey, Herts WD23 1DT
Tel: 020 8416 4400
Fax: 020 8416 4401
email: schooloffice@stmargarets.herts.sch.uk
website: www.stmargaretsbushey.co.uk
Twitter: @stmargsbushey
Facebook: /StMargaretsBushey
LinkedIn: /St Margaret's School, Bushey

Motto: *Sursum corda Habemus ad Dominum*
Founded 1749.

Trustees:
Chairman: Margaret Rudland
Chairman, F&GP Committee: Philip Walton

Headmistress: Mrs Rose Hardy, MA Oxon, MEd, FRSA

Academic Deputy: Mrs G Erdil, BSc Hons
Pastoral Deputy Head: Miss J Chatkiewicz, BA, PGCE
Bursar: Dr K Young, ARSM, DIC
Examinations Officer: Mr R Aniolkowski, BSc, PGCE

Heads of Departments:

Art:
Mrs L Stewart, BA Hons, PGCE

Careers:
Mrs B Blakemore, BA New York

Classics:
Mrs C Lewis, BA Hons, PGCE

Drama:
Mr T Lewis, BA Hons, PGCE

English:
Mrs P Metcalfe, BA London, TEFL Dip

Food Technology:
Ms S Letchett, BSc, PGCE

Geography:
Ms A Hulme, BA, PGCE

History:
Mrs A Harper, BA, PGCE

Information Technology:
Ms D Soulsby
Mr M A Hammond, MA Cantab, PGCE, FRCO, LRAM

Mathematics:
Mr S Moore, CEng, MA Cantab, PGCE

Modern Languages:
Ms A Corbach, MA, BA Cologne, PGCE

Music:
Mr I Hope, BMus, PGCE, LTCL

Psychology:
Dr L D'Souza, BSc Hons

Physical Education:
Mrs D Pimlott, BEd Hons

Religious Studies:
Ms K Roberts, BA, MA London, PGCE

Science:
Mr D Anderson, BSc, BEd, PGCE

Social Studies:
Mrs E Chaudhri, BA, PGCE

Learning Support:
Ms J Collier, BEd Hons

Preparatory Department:
Head: Mrs C Aisthorpe, BEd Hons, LRAM

Senior Housemistress:
Mrs J Bedborough, Cert Prof Studies Education, Foundation Degree Childhood Studies

Duke of Edinburgh's Award Scheme:
Mrs A Ribton, BA Hons

St Margaret's School in Bushey is among the oldest girls' schools in the UK. It has an excellent record of academic success, which is attributed to its emphasis upon providing the very best pastoral care, which has been a continuous hallmark of the school since it was established for the orphans of Church of England clergy in 1749. The School is set within 74 acres of stunning Hertfordshire countryside, which offers girls abundant space to grow and be inspired in safety. St Margaret's educates girls all the way through from age 4 to 18. It is predominantly a day school; however, boarding facilities are available to a limited number of 90 girls, from the age of 11.

St Margaret's has evolved into a thriving multi-cultural community, ideally located in rural surroundings, yet within easy reach of London and the country's best national and international transport links. The school's facilities boast the best of old and new. The main school building (including its chapel) was designed by the celebrated Victorian architect Sir Alfred Waterhouse, who also designed London's Natural History Museum and Manchester Town Hall. Modern buildings have been added to the campus over the past century and the School is presently in the process of a multimillion pound development which will see it become one of the best resourced schools in the UK.

St Margaret's offers a wide range of sporting and cultural activities, for example, the Duke of Edinburgh's Award and the Young Enterprise Scheme as well as charitable fundraising drives. The school has close links with fellow Comenius project partners in Germany, Hungary, Portugal, Italy, Belgium, Poland and Norway, and there are regular field trips, outings and theatre visits. Other activities include choir, orchestra, speech and drama, drama, ballet and judo.

St Margaret's has a full school open day each year, as well as a sixth form open evening and a variety of 'school at work' mornings, which allow parents to see classes in action. The School's website contains the most up-to-date information: www.stmargaretsbushey.co.uk

Fees per term (2014–2015). Senior School (Years 7–13): Day £4,910; Full Boarding £9,200; Weekly Boarding: £6,740 (up to 3 nights), £7,890 (up to 5 nights). Preparatory School: Years 4–6 £4,100, Transition (Year 3) £3,730, Reception, Years 1 & 2 £3,110.

Means-tested bursaries are available and discounts for members of the Forces and Clergy.

Scholarships. Academic and Music Scholarships are awarded at Year 7 and Sixth Form at the discretion of the Head. An Art Scholarship is also available in the Sixth Form.

St Margaret's Guild (Old Girls' Association). *Secretary*: Mrs J Wilson, 43 Chase Ridings, Enfield, Middx EN2 7QE. Guild Membership available to any old girl of St Margaret's School.

Charitable status. St Margaret's School Bushey is a Registered Charity, number 1056228.

St Margaret's School

18 Kidderpore Gardens, Hampstead, London NW3 7SR
Tel: 020 7435 2439
Fax: 020 7431 1308
email: enquiry@st-margarets.co.uk
website: www.st-margarets.co.uk

Founded 1884.

Chair of Governors: Emily Brettle

Principal: **Mr Mark Webster**, BSc, PGCE, NPQH (*Maths and Psychology*)

Deputy Principal: Ms Sarah Treagus, BA (*CPO, PE*)

Mr B Benson, CertEd, CSSD Dip Acting (*Drama, Y10 Form Tutor*)
Mrs K Broughton, BA, MA, PGCE (*Art*)
Mr M Brown, Dip T (*ICT & Maths*)
Ms R Crassweller, BA, PGCE (*French and Mathematics, Y5 Form Tutor*)
Mrs A Froggatt, BEd, BSc (*Art Teacher, Careers Advisor, Y11 Form Tutor*)
Mrs F Gonzalez, BA, TFL, PGCE (*Spanish*)
Mr R Hartley, BA, PGCE (*History & Citizenship, Y9 Form Tutor*)
Mrs J Herman, BA, MA (*Y2 Form Tutor*)
Ms C Hickey, BA, DipED (*PE*)
Mrs E Keenlyside, MA, PGCE, BA (*Music Coordinator*)
Ms K Jamieson, BA, MA, PGCE (*Y5, Y6 English, Y6 Mathematics, Learning Support*)
Mrs J Jefferys, Mont Dip, CertEd (*Y1*)
Miss H Johnson, BSc, MSc, PGCE (*Science, Y7 Form Tutor*)
Mrs R Johnson, BA QTS (*Y3 Form Tutor*)
Mrs L Livermore, BA, PGCE, TESOL (*English, Y8 Form Tutor*)
Ms F Pantelli, LLB, PGCE (*Y4, Y3*)
Mrs A Ross-Jones, BSc, PGCE
Ms J Steinberg, BA (*French*)
Mr M Urrestarazu, BSc, PGCE (*Mathematics*)
Ms C Whittle-Long, DipEd

Ms G Wilson, BA, PGCE (*Director of Studies & Geography*)

Bursar: Mrs S Beschizza
School Secretary/Admissions: Mrs L-A Scorgie

Age Range. 4–16.
Number in School. 155 Day Girls.
Fees per term (2014–2015). £3,470–£4,020. Compulsory extras: Books and outings.

St Margaret's is a small school situated in a quiet residential area of Hampstead, North London. In 2008/9 and 2009/10 the school topped the Sunday Times Small Independent School League Table.

Classes throughout the school are small, averaging 12 in the Junior School and 15 in the Senior School. Girls in Reception to Year 3 are taught mainly by their form teachers with specialist teachers for PE, French, ICT and Music. Specialist teaching increases in Years 4, 5 and 6 to include Art, Geography, History and Science. In Years 7–11 the girls are taught by specialist teachers for all subjects.

The girls enjoy a wide range of sporting activities at a number of local sites. Their after-school clubs include yoga, netball, football, tennis, cross-country, bicycle maintenance, self defence and choir. The girls play netball competitively against local schools. All girls take part in the *125 Things To Do Before You Leave St Margaret's* programme.

Girls take SATs at age 7, and in Year 11 take 9 or 10 GCSE subjects. At 16 girls are prepared for Sixth Form entry. Former pupils are currently studying at Henrietta Barnett, Highgate, Channing, and North London Collegiate amongst others.

A wide range of outings are organised to London galleries, museums and theatres. Girls in Year 10 undertake a week's work experience and trips abroad are organised to support the French and Spanish curriculum.

St Margaret's works hard to achieve high standards in work and discipline, while fostering a happy atmosphere in which girls feel involved and engaged. Their personal development is valued as highly as their academic.

Entry requirements: In class assessment to Year 3, thereafter by testing.

Charitable status. St Margaret's School (Hampstead) Ltd is a Registered Charity, number 312720. It exists as a charitable trust to provide a good education for girls with the emphasis on each girl fulfilling her own potential.

St Martha's

Camlet Way, Hadley Wood, Barnet, Hertfordshire EN4 0NJ
Tel: 020 8449 6889
Fax: 020 8441 5632
email: admissions@saint-marthas.org.uk
website: www.st-marthas.co.uk
Twitter: @stmarthas
Facebook: /St-Marthas-School

Governors and Trustees:

Chair of Governors: Mr Les Edgar

Mr Michael McCann
Mr Seamus O'Sullivan
Sr Irene Brogan
Mrs Maureen Howie
Mr Joseph Medayil
Mrs Stella Asker
Mrs Pina Griffin
Mr Sean Heaney

Mrs Jennifer Moccia

Trustees:
Sister Cécile Archer
Sister Christina O'Dwyer
Sister Janet Sinden
Sister Teresa Roseingrave

School Staff:

Headmaster: **Mr Matthew Burke**, BA Hons, PGCE, Adv DipEd

Deputy Head: Sister T Roseingrave, CertEd, CTC

Chaplin: Fr T Seasman

Bursar: Mr S Rayner

Assistant Bursar: Mrs E Boonzaier, BEd, BCom, HDE

Assistant Heads:
Dr M Wall, BSc, PhD, PGCE (*Director of Studies*)
Mrs A Orr

Head of Sixth Form:
Miss R McGonagle, BA, PGCE

Admissions and Development Director:
Mrs N Mullens

House Mistresses:
Mrs K Fallon, BA, GTP (*Avila*)
Miss C Garratt, BA (*Siena*)
Mrs D Williams, BA, MA, PGCE (*Lisieux*)

* *Head of Faculty*

Art & Design:
Miss C Garrett, BA
Ms E Somerville, BA, PGCE
Mrs M Dixon (*Teaching Assistant*)

Business Studies and Economics:
*Mr J Boonzaier, BCom, HDE

Classics:
Mrs K Fallon, BA, GTP

Drama:
*Miss R McGonagle, BA, PGCE
Miss L Taber, BA

English:
*Mrs D Williams, BA, MA, PGCE
Mr E Whitmore, BA, MLS, PGCE
Mr P Foley
Miss L Taber, BA

Geography:
*Mrs H Pestaille, BA, PGCE

History:
Miss I Saenz-Some, BA, PGCE
Mr P Foley

Home Economics:
Mrs B Rodgers, BA, GTP
Sister T Roseingrave, CertEd, CTC

Information Technology
*Mr J Boonzaier, BCom, HDE

Latin:
Mrs F Stamidou, BA, MA

Learning Resources:
Mrs A Melekis

Mathematics:
*Mr J Boonzaier, BCom, HDE
Mr L Kasza, BEng, PGCE
Mrs M Platona-Basiel, BSc, PGCE
Mr R Hugill, BSc, PGCE

Modern Languages:
French:
*Mrs A Orr, BA, PGCE
Mrs M Lazouras
Spanish:
Miss M Lourdes

Music:
Miss C Potts

Physical Education:
Miss P Smyth
MIss S Wilkins

Religious Education:
*Ms M Clancy, BA, PGCE
Mrs D Mela, GLCM, ALCM

Science:
*Mr R Odell, BSc, PGCE
Mrs R Stern
Dr M Wall, BSc, PhD, PGCE
Miss F Agrotis, Dip Med Tech (*Laboratory Technician*)

Sociology:
Mr P Foley

International Student Admissions:
Mrs A Swynnerton

Visiting Teachers:
Mr J Lee (*Drums*)
Mrs K Sherry (*LAMDA*)
Miss Tomas (*Singing*)
Ms F Hammacott (*Singing*)
Mr R Richards (*Violin*)
Mr N Barnes (*Football coach*)
Mr E Flores (*Piano*)
Ms R PIckering (*Woodwind*)

Administration:
Ms F Watts (*Headmaster's PA*)
Mrs A Fitzpatrick, BA (*Admissions Secretary*)
Mrs A Kane (*Admissions Assistant*)
Mrs F O'Regan (*Reception*)
Catering: The Brookwood Partnership
Information Technology Manager: Mo Moleiu Akbarabadi
House Keeping: Mrs P Meally
Site Manager: Mr C Heaney
Assistant Caretaker: Mr E Georgiou
General Assistant (p/t): Mr J Salman
General Assistant (p/t): Ms J Fathers
General Assistant (p/t):Ms S Rose

Age Range. 11–18 Girls.
Number in School. 220 Day Girls.
Fees per term (2014–2015). £4,345.

St Martha's is an independent Catholic school for girls welcoming all denominations and faiths into our community. Located in the leafy environs of Monken Hadley Common, we treasure our picturesque rural surroundings yet benefit from close public transport links by tube and rail to central London.

We are renowned as a warm and friendly school that believes a demanding and challenging ethos can go hand in hand with a caring and supportive atmosphere. Intellectual endeavour and hard work should be part of an exciting, stimulating and enjoyable environment that inspires achievement. St Martha's is in the top 100 independent schools for girls and places great emphasis on high academic standards, which places us in the top 5% of independent schools in the UK for added value.

With the benefit of small classes, we also have an outstanding sixth form that inspires all of our young ladies to become women of the future, where their talents are nurtured and developed by dedicated specialist teachers. Girls achieve well in exams and develop the skills and attitudes, which enable them to work and study successfully.

Pastoral care and support are fundamental to ensuring the girls achieve their best in all areas of school life. St Martha's is a close-knit community where the girls are encouraged to look after each other. We are very proud of our girls' endeavours and achievements across the curriculum.

The girls also engage in an array of extra-curricular activities, which we believe is vital to their development as a whole person and enables them to develop their self-esteem and confidence so that all their talents grow and flourish. Our clubs are designed not only to widen your daughter's experiences beyond the classroom but also to allow her to have fun with her peers.

St Martha's also provides a bus service and a shuttle service to and from local rail and underground stations. The routes available on the bus service are extensive and we are accommodating in trying to add new pick up points onto these routes.

Choosing a school for your daughter for the vital years of secondary education is an important and often difficult task, and so we want to provide you with every opportunity to visit and be welcomed by us. Please come along to see just what makes us so special and experience at first hand why so many parents are choosing St Martha's to educate their daughters.

Charitable status. Congregation of the Sisters of Saint Martha is a Registered Charity, number 233809.

Saint Martin's
Solihull

Malvern Hall, Brueton Avenue, Solihull, West Midlands B91 3EN
Tel: 0121 705 1265
Fax: 0121 711 4529
email: mail@saintmartins-school.com
website: www.saintmartins-school.com

Motto: *The Grace of God is in Courtesy*

Saint Martin's School ….. life changing! We are an exceptional independent day school for girls that has the tradition of providing the best education from Nursery to Sixth Form. We are proud of being a school that educates girls and only girls.

Board of Governors:
Patron: Baroness Joan Secombe, JP
President and Chair: Mrs P Harbour, MA
Revd D Ballard, BSc, CertD, DipD, MTh
Ms E Butler, JP
Mrs N Davis, BA
Mr V Hallan, MSc, JP
Dr N Manley
Mrs C McNidder, BSc, MG, PhC
Mrs F de Minckwitz
Mr J Shepherd, FRICS
Mrs G Tillman, BSc

Honorary Governors:
Revd J Bradford, BA, MEd, AdvCertEd, FRSA
Mrs N S Bridgewater, JP

Clerk to the Governors and Bursar: Mr S Brown, BSc Loughborough

***Head*: Miss N Edgar**, BA Hons Liverpool, PGCE, NPQH

Deputy Head: Mrs J Parker, BSc Reading, MA Nottingham, PGCE

Director of Studies: Mrs C Smith, BA Oxon, PGCE
Head of Sixth Form: Mrs R Speirs, BA Nottingham, PGCE
Head of Years 7 to 11: Mrs F Fowles, BA Dunelm, MSc Reading

Staff:

Art:
Mrs M Terry, BA University of Wales Newport, PGCE
Technician: Mr J Hands, BA Northampton

Business Studies and Economics:
Mr K Reeves, BA Lancaster, PGCE

Classics:
Mr K Carroll, BA Nottingham, PGCE
Mrs L Beaumont, BA Manchester, PGCE

Dance:
Ms J Felix

Drama:
Mrs K Stafford, BA Hull, MA Birmingham, PGCE
Mrs C Smith, BA Oxon, PGCE

English:
Mrs C Inns, BA Kent, PGCE
Mrs R Speirs, BA Nottingham, PGCE
Mrs S Watton, BA Hull, PGCE

Food and Textiles:
Mrs J Massarella, BEd Bath College

Geography:
Mrs F Fowles, BA Dunelm, MSc Reading, PGCE
Miss C Bednall, BSc Cheltenham, MSc London, PGCE

History:
Mr M van Alderwegen, BA Leeds, MA Nottingham, PGCE
Mrs C Smith, BA Oxon, PGCE

Information Technology:
Mrs C Dance, BSc Keele, PGCE
Network Manager: Mr P Carlson, BS from St Paul TVI
Technician: Mr D Johnson

Learning Support:
Mrs F Franklin, BA Trinity & All Saints

Mathematics:
Mrs E Linford, BSc Salford, MSc Southampton, PGCE
Mrs L Gunn, MEng Warwick PGCE
Mrs R Lawson, BEd Warwick
Mrs A Short, BSc London, PGCE

Modern Languages:
Mr P Delaney, BA Exeter, PGCE
Mrs C Gibney, DUT Nancy, MIL, PGCE
Ms K Harris, BA Leeds, MA Birmingham
Mrs I Jardon, DipIl, PGCE

Music:
Mr P Allen, BA Liverpool, PGCE, ALCM
Cello: Mr A Teale, BMus, PGCE
Clarinet/Saxophone: Mrs K Moore
Flute: Mrs A Thompson, BA, PGCE
Guitar: Mr M Whittaker, BMus
Piano: Mrs J Bamford, GLCM, PGCE
Piano/Keyboard: Ms L Hands
Piano: Mr O Srba
Piano/Keyboard/Singing: Mrs G Hattley, GBSM, ABSM
Violin/Viola: Mrs G Kirby, G Mus, PGCE, ALCM, LTCL

Physical Education:
Mrs H Burgess, BA Birmingham, PGCE
Mrs J Elston, CertEd Bedford College
Mrs T Gallagher, BEd Leeds
Mrs J Green, BSc Cheltenham and Gloucester, PGCE

Psychology:
Mrs M E Thompson, BSc Nottingham, PGCE

Religious Studies:
Mrs I Igoe, BEd Newman

Science:
Mrs B Ridley, BSc Wales, MA Ed, PGCE
Mrs J Parker, BSc Reading, MA Nottingham, PGCE
Mrs S Parker, BSc Leicester, PGCE
Dr R L Parkin, BSc Coventry, PhD Glasgow, PGCE
Dr F Ryland, BSc Warwick, MPhil Birmingham, PhD Birmingham, PGCE

Mrs A Short, BSc London, PGCE
Mrs R Trainor, BSc Warwick, PGCE
Mrs J Waters, BSc Birmingham, PGCE
Technician: Mrs A Flanagan, BSc Nottingham

Technology:
Mrs L Winnett, BEd Sheffield, CertEd
Technician: Mr J Hands, BA Northampton

Head of Nursery to Year 6: Mrs A Wilson, BEd Dunelm

Junior School (Years 4–6):
Deputy of Junior School: Mrs E Inglis, BEd
Mrs T Dacombe, BEd Leeds
Mrs D Griffiths, BA Open, CertEd
Mrs G Ireland, BEd Northampton, PGCE
Mrs T Marsh, BEd Bath College of Education
Miss H Winn, LLB Manchester Metropolitan, PGCE
Teaching Assistant: Mrs J Crampton

Alice House (Nursery–Year 3):
Deputy of Alice House: Mrs McArthur, BA East London,
    PGCE
Miss J Chatwin, BEd UCE
Mrs L Harper, BA Oxford Brookes
Mrs V Higley, BEd Christ's & Notre Dame
Mrs R Jenkins, BMus Birmingham, Dip Music Therapy,
    MA, GTP, ALCM
Mrs J Pendred, Cert Ed Hereford
Mrs E Pimlott, BSc Portsmouth, PGCE
Mrs E Sones, BA Warwick, MA Warwick

Teaching Assistants:
Mrs P Annandale
Mrs K Duffy
Miss W Evans
Miss M Field
Mrs J Green
Mrs M Lee
Mrs S Sargent

Location. Saint Martin's is a well-established day school for approximately 400 girls situated in a beautiful twenty-acre site in the south of Solihull. Solihull is about 8 miles from Birmingham and is on the edge of a rural district within very easy reach of Warwick, Coventry, Leamington Spa and the M42.

Buildings and Facilities. In addition to the main school buildings which are attached to the very fine Grade II listed Malvern Hall, there are separate, self-contained buildings for the Nursery, Preparatory and Junior Departments; the Sixth Form is housed in renovated and extended listed buildings near to the main school. The school has its own 25-metre indoor swimming pool and an astro pitch has recently been opened on the site. All playing fields, including tennis and netball courts, are on the premises and an exceptionally wide range of indoor and outdoor activities is offered.

The school enjoys well-resourced, specialist accommodation for teaching science, music, art, ICT and technology. A Performing Arts Building was completed in Summer 2012 and offers specialist facilities in drama and dance.

Curriculum. Girls receive a broad academic education with considerable opportunities for the development of individual interests and good academic standards are maintained. Emphasis is placed on hard work and independent learning. Courses leading to GCSE examinations are offered in all the usual subjects as well as ICT, Spanish, German, Latin, Classical Civilisation, Art and Music and all girls are required to continue with Mathematics, English Language, English Literature, a modern language and all three sciences. Classes are not streamed, but some subjects are taught in ability sets. In the Sixth Form, the majority of girls will study four Advanced Subsidiary subjects in the first year and complete three Advanced Level courses in the second year chosen from the same range as is offered at GCSE, with the addition of Economics, Business Studies and Psy-

chology. The Extended Project Qualification is offered to the Upper Sixth. Virtually all Sixth Form students go on to higher education and all senior pupils receive extensive careers education and advice and all take part in work experience in Year 11 and the Lower Sixth.

Extra-Curricular Activities. Sport, music and drama are all strong in school: plays and concerts are held throughout the year at all ages and a very large proportion of girls study at least one instrument. A large selection of other extra-curricular interests is catered for, such as Young Enterprise and the Duke of Edinburgh's Award Scheme. Clubs and societies are encouraged. There are many visits to enrich the curriculum, including regular field trips, and trips abroad to Merville, Iceland, Geneva, Italy, China and New York among others.

Admission is by assessment for girls aged 5–10 and by interview and examination for older pupils. Girls are admitted to the Sixth Form on the basis of GCSE results and interview.

Fees per term (2014–2015). Reception–Year 2 £2,726; Year 3 £2,859; Years 4–6 £3,192; Senior School and Sixth Form £3,749. Nursery: £41 per full day.

Scholarships. A number of Academic scholarships are offered each year for entry to the Senior School at 11+. Awards are made to candidates who show outstanding ability in the entrance examination and interview. Music, Performing Arts and Sports scholarships are also available at 11+.

Scholarships are also awarded annually to pupils entering the Sixth Form. Candidates are required to sit papers assessing a variety of skills and their potential for further study. Those who are shortlisted are interviewed by the Head and the Head of Sixth Form.

Charitable status. Saint Martin's (Solihull) Limited is a Registered Charity, number 528967. It exists to provide education for girls.

St Mary's School
Cambridge

Bateman Street, Cambridge CB2 1LY
Tel: 01223 353253 Headmistress and School Office
Fax: 01223 357451
email: enquiries@stmaryscambridge.co.uk
website: www.stmaryscambridge.co.uk

St Mary's School, Cambridge is a Christian school in the Catholic tradition, offering boarding and day provision for girls aged 4 to 18.

Situated in the heart of the academically and culturally vibrant city of Cambridge, the school offers a safe and secure learning environment for girls. Founded on the principles of Mary Ward, the principles of the Catholic Church underpin our approach to education. The school has a unique atmosphere which supports learning and development, and fosters self-esteem, confidence and friendship.

There are 159 girls in the Junior School, 369 girls in the Senior School and 106 in our Sixth Form. A fifth of the girls at St Mary's School, Cambridge are boarders. Reflecting the cosmopolitan community of Cambridge, 14% of pupils at the school are from overseas, from 34 countries worldwide.

Our Governing Body comprises 15 representatives from education, industry and faith organisations.

Mr F Morgan (*Chair*)	Mr C Jones
Mrs J Bates	Mr W Matthews
Ms J Clements OBE	Mrs A McAllister
Prof J Driscoll	Mr A Milne
Mr A Freeman	Mr G Minto
Mr A Grant	Fr P Leeming

Sister F Orchard

Mr C Smart
Dr N Ward

Clerk to the Governors: Mrs C Hodgskiss

Senior Leadership Team:

Headmistress: Ms Charlotte Avery

Bursar: Mr Duncan Askew
Deputy Head (*Pastoral*): Miss Aodain Fleming
Assistant Head: Mrs Sonia Gears
Assistant Head (*Teaching & Learning*): Dr Charlotte
  Goddard
Head of Juniors: Mr Chris Hald
Assistant Head (*Director of Studies & Academic
  Registrar*): Ms Emma Hall
Assistant Head (*Communications and Admissions*): Mrs
  Hannah Helliar
Director of Digital Strategy: Mr Joe Hunnable
Deputy Head (*Academic*): Mr Stephen Seidler

Ex officio:
Mr Daniel Bennett
Mrs Hélène Compain-Holt

Senior School and Sixth Form:

Heads of Year:
Mrs Karole Lewis (*Sixth Form*)
Mr Paul Mallabone (*Year 11*)
Ms Chris Klimaszewska (*Year 10*)
Mrs Ruth Beer (*Joint Year 9*)
Mrs Julia Hutchison (*Joint Year 9*)
Miss Sonia Josiffe (*Year 8*)
Mrs Helen Garrett (*Year 7*)

Heads of Department:
Art & Design: Mrs Gill Clifford
Biology: Mrs Anita Chatterjee
Business Studies & Economics: Mrs Tricia Nicholson
Chemistry/Science: Dr Cristina Alves Martins
Classics/Latin: Dr Charlotte Goddard
Drama: Miss Esther Roberts
EAL: Ms Valerie Bevan
English: Mrs Helen Garrett
French: Mrs Kate Darch
Geography: Miss Fleur Spore
German: Mrs Hélène Compain-Holt
History: Mrs Kate Latham
Language & Learning: Miss Jane Earley
Mathematics: Mr Darren Kelly
MFL: Miss Nicky Lees
Music: Miss Emma Levy
PE: Mrs Jackie Ewing
Physics: Mrs Delia Russell
Politics: Mrs Kate Latham
Psychology: Mr Reg Quirk (*maternity cover*)
Religious Education: Mr Daniel Bennett
Spanish: Miss Nicky Lees
Technology (*Food, Textiles, ICT*): Mrs Anna Ladds

Subjects & Responsibilities:
Dr Christina Alves Martins (*Head of Chemistry, Head of
  Science*)
Mr Richard Atkinson (*Outdoor Education Coordinator,
  DofE Bronze Award*)
Mrs Ruth Beer (*RE*)
Mr Daniel Bennett (*Director of Christian Life, Head of RE*)
Ms Valerie Bevan (*Head of EAL*)
Mrs Patricia Brooks (*EAL*)
Mrs Susan Brown (*Mathematics, DofE Gold Award,
  Rowing*)
Dr Alexandra Cardwell (*Chemistry, Science*)
Mr Aurélien Cassan (*French, Spanish*)
Mrs Anita Chatterjee (*Head of Biology*)
Mrs Gillian Clifford (*Head of Art & Design*)
Ms Verity Cole (*EAL*)

Miss Kimberley Cooil (*2nd in Charge PE*)
Ms Joanna Cottingham (*English*)
Mrs Heather Collison (*Maths*)
Mrs Hélène Compain-Holt (*Head of Boarding, Head of
  German, French*)
Mrs Kate Darch (*Head of French*)
Miss Rebecca Dunn (*2nd in Charge Classics*)
Miss Jane Earley (*Head of Language and Learning*)
Mr Toby Edwards (*Mathematics*)
Mrs Jackie Ewing (*Head of PE*)
Mr Pantelis Fanourakis (*Mathematics, Rowing*)
Miss Aodain Fleming (*Deputy Head Pastoral, RE*)
Mrs Lisa Fleming (*PE*)
Mr Daniel Gabbitas (*Physics, SEN Support*)
Mrs Yan Gao (*EAL, Mandarin*)
Mrs Helen Garrett (*Head of English, Individual Needs
  Specialist*)
Mrs Sonia Gears (*Assistant Head, Music*)
Dr Charlotte Goddard (*Assistant Head – Teaching &
  Learning, Head of Classics, Scholars' Officer*)
Ms Emma Hall (*Assistant Head – Director of Studies &
  Academic Registrar, Maths*)
Miss Victoria Handley (*Biology*)
Mrs Hannah Helliar (*Assistant Head* (*Communications &
  Admissions*), *History, Politics*)
Mr Michael Hemingway (*History, Geography,
  International Coordinator, Silver DofE*)
Mrs Rachel Hill (*German, French*)
Miss Anna Hughes (*English*)
Mr Joe Hunnable (*Head of Digital Strategy, Latin*)
Mrs Elizabeth Hurles (*English*)
Mrs Julia Hutchison (*Geography*)
Miss Sonia Josiffe (*Head of Year 8, PE*)
Mrs Maria Kakengi (*Textiles, Democracy Coordinator*)
Miss Rajpreet Kaur (*Economics, Business Studies*)
Mr Darren Kelly (*Head of Maths*)
Miss Surabhi Khanna (*Maths, Leadership Coordinator*)
Mrs Julie Kitson (*Spanish*)
Ms Chris Klimaszewska (*Head of Year 10, Biology*)
Mrs Anna Ladds (*Head of Technology, Food, Textiles*)
Mrs Diana Larman (*English, Library*)
Mrs Kate Latham (*Head of History and Politics*)
Miss Nicola Lees (*Head of MFL, Head of Spanish*)
Mrs Sophia Leighton-Scott (*Geography, EAL*)
Miss Emma Levy (*Head of Music, Arts Award
  Coordinator*)
Mrs Karole Lewis (*Head of Sixth Form, Psychology, EPQ,
  Visiting Boarding Tutor*)
Mr Paul Mallabone (*Head of Year 11, RE*)
Miss Karen Marinho (*Head of Computer Science and
  Digital Literacy*)
Miss Clare McEwan (*Art and Design*)
Mrs Ruth McGuiness (*Learning Technologist*)
Dr Amy McKinney (*RE*)
Dr Ailish Meadows (*Chemistry, Science*)
Mr Wade Melville (*Art & Design, Photography*)
Dr Gordon Miller (*Physics, Radiation Protection Officer*)
Ms Sarah Mitchell (*Head of Psychology*) (*maternity leave*)
Mrs Sarah Newbery (*Careers*)
Mrs Patricia Nicholson (*Head of Economics and Business
  Studies, Assistant Head of Sixth Form, Sixth Form Young
  Enterprise*)
Miss Aurelie Nivanen (*French*)
Mrs Janine Norman (*Geography*)
Mrs Cindy O'Connell (*PE*)
Ms Jane Oliver (*Drama, Induction and Professional Tutor*)
Dr Alicia Pena Calvo (*Spanish*)
Mrs Lauren Pink (*Art & Design, Textiles, Extra-curricular
  Coordinator*)
Mr Reg Quirk (*Head of Psychology*) (*maternity cover*)
Mr Alexander Reeve (*Chemistry, Biology, Physics*)
Mrs Louisa Reid (*English*)
Miss Esther Roberts (*Head of Drama*)

Mrs Delia Russell (*Head of Physics*)
Miss Helen Seabourne (*PE*)
Mr Stephen Seidler (*Deputy Head (Academic), RE*)
Mr Martin Scott (*Chemistry, Biology*)
Mrs Tessa Shercliff (*Physics, STEM Coordinator*)
Miss Fleur Spore (*Head of Geography, DofE, EVC, Visiting Boarding Tutor*)
Mr David Walker (*English, Environment Coordinator, Magnolian Editor*)
Mrs Mel Ward (*RE*)
Mrs Alison Wilson (*Examinations Officer, ICT, Food, Textiles*)

Senior School Peripatetic Teachers:
Quintus Benziger (*piano*)
Sarah Blazeby (*flute*)
Lorely Britton (*piano*)
Peter Britton (*piano*)
Anne Bury (*flute/clarinet*)
David Carter (*clarinet/guitar*)
Susanne Dymott (*Voice*)
Hilary Hymas (*oboe*)
Julian Landymore (*saxophone*)
Jessica Norton (*Musician in Residence*)
Gillian Oldham (*cello*)
Rohan Platts (*harp*)
Christian Rutherford (*brass*)
Jayne South (*piano*)
Petra Stephenson (*violin/viola*)
Julie Stevenson (*violin*)
Alison Summers (*voice*)
Gabrielle Sutcliffe (*violin*)
Andrew Vellacott (*percussion*)
Kate Weber (*speech & drama*)
Lyn Welland (*flute*)

Senior School Technicians and Support Staff:
Emma Alonso (*Chemistry*)
Monica Crammond (*Physics*)
Davinia Irvine (*SEN Teaching Assistant*)
Katharine McHugh (*Textiles*)
Kate Mead (*Music Administrator*)
Lis Miller (*Biology*)
Joe Nicholson (*Drama*)
Katharine Percival (*Food Technician*)
Emily O'Hare (*Art*)
Vijaya Rodger (*Mathematics Support SEN*)
Jennifer Scott-Villalobos (*SEN Teaching Assistant*)
Loretta Seanior (*Art*)
Robyn Sorensen (*Learning Support Assistant*)
Andrea Turpin (*Chemistry*)

Junior School:

Head of Juniors: Mr Christopher Hald

Junior School Teaching Staff:
Mrs Sarah Cliff (*Teacher Year 6, English Coordinator*)
Mrs Susan McKay (*Teacher Year 6, Science Coordinator, ICT Responsibility*)
Ms Jane Freebairn (*Teacher Year 5, Art Coordinator*)
Mr Matthew O'Reilly (*Teacher Year 5, Assistant Head – Pastoral, Humanities Coordinator*)
Mrs Samantha Duncan (*Teacher Year 4, MFL Coordinator*)
Miss Agata Wygnanska (*Teacher Year 4, Maths and RE Coordinator*)
Mrs Fiona McWilliam (*Teacher Year 3, PE Coordinator*)
Miss Ysmay Gill (*Teacher Year 3*)
Mrs Kerry Owens (*Teacher Year 2, Deputy Head and Pre-prep Coordinator*)
Mrs Carol Kew (*Teacher Year 1*)
Miss Natalie Shale (*Teacher Reception, Early Years Coordinator*)

Mrs Nathalie Hamilton (*Teacher French*)
Mrs Sophia Huang (*Teacher Mandarin*)
Mrs Carolyn Johnson (*Teacher of Religious Education*)

Dr Marie-Geraldine Lea (*Teacher French*)
Mrs Petra Stephenson (*Music Teacher*)

Junior School Peripatetic Teachers:
Patricia Birchall (*violin*)
Gillian Oldham (*cello*)
Eoin O'Mahony (*piano*)
Anne Rollings (*singing*)
Petra Stephenson (*violin*)
Alison Townend (*flute*)
Emma Heras (*Language and Learning*)
Rosemary Dickson (*Language and Learning*)

Junior School Support Staff:
Dr Beverley Degnan (*SENDA – LSA*)
Mrs Kate Fernandez (*Learning Support Assistant*)
Mrs Jackie Hey (*Learning Support Assistant*)
Mrs Judith Price (*Learning Support Assistant*)
Mrs Linda Roach (*Learning Support Assistant*)
Mrs Deborah Littlefair (*Learning Support Assistant – EYFS*)

Senior & Junior Schools Non-Teaching Staff – Duties & Responsibilities:

Mr Duncan Askew (*Bursar*)
Dr Claire Hodgskiss (*Executive Officer to the Governors*)
Mrs Melanie Brown (*School Accountant*)
Mrs Kay Simms (*Finance Officer*)
Mrs Jean Doe (*Accounts Secretary*)
Mrs Amanda Knowles (*Finance Assistant*)

Mgr Peter Leeming (*Chaplain*)
Mrs Kay Dodsworth (*Assistant Chaplain*)
Mrs Jane McCann (*School Counsellor*)
Mrs Tanya Fynn (*School Nurse*)
Mrs Fiona Myers (*School Nurse*)
Mrs Claire Green (*School Nurse*)

Mrs Janet Bauld (*School Secretary*)
Miss Jenny Boscoe (*Assistant Registrar, UK Admissions*)
Mrs Pam Down (*Staff Support Secretary*)
Mrs Sally Law (*Reprographics*)
Miss Louise Mannox (*Uniform Shop*)
Mrs Kate Martin (*HR Assistant, Exams Assistant*)
Miss Tiffany McCrea (*Admissions Officer, International*)
Mrs Kate Mead (*Music Administrator, Food Technician*)
Mrs Doris Stutely (*Receptionist/Finance*)
Mrs Carole Turner (*Receptionist*)
Mrs Penny Vallins (*PA to Headmistress*)
Mrs Kate Ross (*PA to Head of Juniors*)

Mr Damian Griffiths (*Head of Network Systems and Services*)
Mrs Abigail Earl (*Senior IT Technician*)
Mr Scott Williamson (*IT Technician*)

Mr Gary Sharp (*Domestic Bursar*)

Mr Brian Cornell (*Site Maintenance Manager*)
Mr Eric Knight (*Site Maintenance*)
Mr Trevor Simms (*Site Maintenance*)

Mr Gerry Sansom (*Health & Safety Manager*)
Mrs Helene Compain-Holt (*Head of Boarding*)
Miss Stephanie Breen (*Gap Student Assistant*)
Mrs Anne Crawford (*Assistant Housemistress*)
Miss Susan Edgar (*Housemistress, Main School*)
Ms Trish Hale (*Assistant Housemistress*)
Mrs Rose Khan (*Weekend Boarding Assistant*)
Miss Janka Skrzypek (*Housemistress, Bateman*)
Miss Sharlene Walton (*Boarding Assistant*)
Miss Joy Warner (*Housemistress, Bateman*)
Miss Pascale Whyte (*Housemistress, Main School*)

Admission. The school's main entry points are at 4+, 7+, 11+, 13+ and 16+. A few vacancies occur at other ages. For entry into Reception (4+) children will take part in age appropriate activities. For Year 3 (7+) entry pupils are assessed in Mathematics, Verbal Reasoning, Non-verbal reasoning and creative writing. For Year 7 (11+) entry students are assessed by Cognitive Ability tests. For Year 9 (13+) entry students are assessed in English, Mathematics and a Foreign Language. Sixth Form entry is by examination and interview, conditional on seven GCSE passes at A*–C, with B grade or above in those subjects to be studied at A Level.

Extra Subjects. Piano and Instrumental Music, Speech and Drama, and Dance.

Fees per term (2014–2015). Day Girls: Junior School: £2,868 (Pre-Prep), £3,613 (Years 3 & 4), £3,758 (Years 5 & 6); Senior School and Sixth Form £4,638. Weekly boarding £8,525; Full boarding £9,902.

Scholarships. Academic, Art, Creative Writing, Dance, Design and Enterprise, Drama, Mary Ward, Music, Sport and Textiles Scholarships are offered at 11+, 13+ and 16+. An Academic (STEM) scholarship is offered at 13+ and 16+. A Photography scholarship and the Ogden Trust Mathematics and Physics Scholarship are offered at 16+.

Curriculum. Within the setting of a Christian community the school provides an 'all-round' education, enabling each girl to realise her full potential. Students are prepared for GCSE, A Level, Oxbridge entrance, and for other forms of higher education and professional training in a wide variety of careers. The curriculum includes Religious Education, English, History, Geography, Latin, French, German, Spanish, Mathematics, ICT, Physics, Chemistry, Biology, Art and Design, Textiles, Theatre Studies, Music, Drama, PE. Option schemes in Year 10 are arranged in such a way that each girl has a balanced programme without premature specialisation. In the Lower Sixth, students choose four subjects to study, making their choice from a total of 20 subjects. In the Upper Sixth, students continue their study of three or four subjects to A2 Level. All Sixth Form students follow an enrichment programme.

The school stands in its own grounds, close to the centre of Cambridge and adjoining the University Botanic Gardens. The complex of buildings contains Science laboratories, assembly halls, gymnasium, library, specialist rooms for Geography, Music, IT, Art, Textiles and Cookery.

Junior School. The Junior School is housed in a stunning historic building with grounds on Chaucer Road. St Mary's Junior School, Cambridge is a welcoming, caring and dynamic environment for your daughter. The Junior School is a place where she can explore and broaden her interests, build her strengths and gain her independence while developing an enthusiasm for learning, which will stay with her for life.

Senior School. The classrooms at St Mary's Senior School, Cambridge are happy, nurturing environments, where passionate teachers inspire girls to enjoy reaching their academic potential. This is borne out by the results our girls achieve across all academic and creative subjects in their public examinations.

Sixth Form. The newly-opened Sixth Form Centre, just a short walk from the rest of the school, provides the independence which Sixth Form students crave, while also maintaining the benefits of links with the main site. The spacious and modern centre provides a social and study area to help our students prepare for life after Sixth Form.

Extra-Curricular Activities. The school provides a wide range of activities at lunch-times and after school – everything from Dance to Rowing and Arts Award, to The Duke of Edinburgh's Award Scheme and Young Enterprise Company.

After-School Clubs. Junior School: Twilight Club is available from 5–6 pm Monday to Friday. Senior School: Homework Club is available from 4–6 pm Monday to Thursday.

Boarding. We offer full as well as weekly boarding to students aged 11+. Younger boarders share comfortable bedrooms (3–4 girls per room). Our weekly boarding facility is popular with both students and their parents as it offers the best of both worlds at school and at home.

Charitable status. St Mary's School, Cambridge is a Registered Charity, number 290180. It aims to promote and provide for the advancement of the education of children of any creed but particularly of the Roman Catholic faith.

St Mary's School
Colchester

Lexden Road, Colchester, Essex CO3 3RB

Tel:	01206 572544 (Office)
	01206 216420 (Registrar)
Fax:	01206 576437
email:	info@stmaryscolchester.org.uk
website:	www.stmaryscolchester.org.uk
Twitter:	@stmaryscolch

Motto: *Scientia et Veritas*

Chair of Governors: Mr J Pendle

Principal: **Mrs H Vipond**, BSc Hons, MEd, CertEd, DipEd, NPQH

Director of Senior School: Miss A Jones, BEd, NPQH

Director of Lower School: Mrs E Stanhope, GMus, NPQH

Bursar: Mr S Cooke

Registrar: Mrs J Tierney

The only all-girls independent school in North Essex, St Mary's has more than a hundred years' experience of educating girls aged 4 to 16. However, we are always looking to the future and to the important roles our pupils will play in life. This was recognised by the Independent Schools Inspectorate in October 2014, when inspectors reported: 'Pupils develop as confident, talented and educated young women who are ready to make a difference in the world around them.'

We are very much a school for girls. We recognise that girls are different to boys in their academic, social and emotional development. We tailor our educational approach so that each girl is understood and can thrive. We also encourage every pupil to have confidence in herself and to be equipped and prepared to embrace life's challenges.

We demonstrate that 'happy girls become high achievers'. Our friendly and inclusive approach creates a happy atmosphere in which girls enjoy school and love learning. St Mary's has the best GCSE results of any independent school in North Essex and was ranked eighth of all schools in the entire county (with a 95% pass rate), according to the Government's 2014 GCSE League Tables. Our Year 6 girls' SATs results place our Lower School in the Sunday Times list of Top 100 Preparatory Schools in the UK. This success is all the more notable as St Mary's is non-selective on entry.

An all-round, value-added education. Although our girls benefit from a focused academic education, they also make the most of a wealth of opportunities designed to stretch each individual intellectually, creatively and physically and to support her as she develops into young adulthood. Our small class sizes, exceptional pastoral care and unique tutoring system allow each girl to be known, understood, challenged and developed. Art, music, textiles, home economics and sport thrive alongside more academic subjects throughout both the Lower and the Senior Schools. Charity initiatives are entered into with great enthusiasm and our girls are always keen to challenge themselves through a range of exciting activities, including the Duke of Edinburgh's Award Scheme.

St Mary's girls engage with life. Not only do we instil the important values of respect and courtesy that will stand them in good stead throughout their lives, we also encourage St Mary's girls to be active, to voice their opinions and to develop a 'have-a-go' attitude, to prepare them for success.

Our experience of educating girls – and our constant connection with the changing world of work and life's expectations – makes St Mary's well equipped to give each of our pupils a solid foundation for the life that lies ahead.

Kindergarten. Ofsted 'outstanding' provision for boys and girls aged rising 3 to 4 years in a purpose-built setting in the grounds of St Mary's Lower School. Caring, experienced staff prepare children for school in a relaxed, happy environment. As well as focusing on developing early reading and number skills, children take part in a range of activities (including dance, drama, music, art and forest school) aimed at increasing their confidence and encouraging good manners and social skills.

Lower School. Sunday Times Top 100 Preparatory School for girls aged 4 to 11 on a spacious seven-acre campus, ten minutes from central Colchester and five minutes from the A12. Small classes of girls enjoy lively academic lessons, as well as drama, dance, art, sport and forest school. Preparation for Essex selective schools 11+ examination as well as scholarships. All girls are assured of a place at the (largely over-subscribed) St Mary's senior school.

Senior School. High-quality academic teaching (best GCSE results of any independent school in North Essex in 2012, 2013 and 2014) as well as vibrant drama, music, art, textiles and sport for girls aged 11–16. Excellent pastoral care programme includes health and safety and first aid training as well as opportunities for the discussion of teenage issues and support for the individual. Many trips to museums, galleries, workplaces and to attend events relevant to the curriculum, plus a wide range of in-school workshops and visiting speakers.

Fees per term (2014–2015). Senior School: £3,810–£4,100; Lower School: £2,699–£3,444; Kindergarten: from £43.64 per day. Fees are inclusive of accident insurance, lunch and drinks (including milk in the Lower School), as well as extra tuition and learning support if required.

Charitable status. St Mary's School (Colchester) Limited is a Registered Charity, number 309266.

St Mary's School
Gerrards Cross

Gerrards Cross, Buckinghamshire SL9 8JQ
Tel: 01753 883370
Fax: 01753 890966
email: registrar@st-marys.bucks.sch.uk
website: www.stmarysschool.co.uk
Twitter: @StMarysSchoolGX
Facebook: /St-Marys-School-Gerrards-Cross

Badge: *Ecce Ancilla Domini*
    Founded by Dean Butler in 1872. Formerly at Lancaster Gate. Established in Gerrards Cross in 1937 as an Independent Day School catering for 330 day girls.

Governors:
Chairman: Mr D R Wilson, BA, FCA
Mrs C Bayliss, CertEd
Mr D Campkin, ACA, BSc Hons
Mrs C Eilerts de Haan, MSc, ChemTech Ingenieur, PGCE
Mr N Hallchurch, LLB Hons
Mrs P Hurd, NDD, ATC
Mr J Loarridge, OBE, RD, BA
Prof S Machin, MBChB, FRCP, FRCPath

Mr N Moss, MNAEA
Ms J Pain, MA, MA, MBA, NPQH
Mr A Rahman

Senior Leadership Team:

Headmistress: Mrs J A Ross, BA Hons Manchester, NPQH (*French*)

Bursar: Mrs J Wilson, MBA
Assistant Head: Ms J Ambrose, BA Hons Swansea (*English*)
Head of the Preparatory Department: Mrs M Carney, BA Hons Galway (*French*)
Director of Studies, Preparatory Department: Dr H Creber, PhD Cardiff
Assistant Head: Mrs J Kingston, MPhil Bath, BSc Hons Cardiff
Assistant Head: Mrs M Moore, BSc Hons Cambridge (*Mathematics*)
Head of Sixth Form: Mrs E Persaud, BA Hons Leicester (*History, Careers*)

Senior House:
Mr M Adams, BSc Hons London (*Physics, Chemistry*)
Mrs P Baggott, BPharm Hons Bradford, MPS (*Chemistry, Biology*)
Mrs E Beasley, BA Hons Cambridge (*Geography*)
Miss S Betteridge, BA Hons York (*French, Spanish*)
Mrs J Cannon, BA Hons Newcastle (*Spanish, French, Latin*)
Mrs J Deadman, BAEd Hons Exeter (*Physical Education*)
Mr J Dodd, BSc Hons Lancaster (*Business Studies, Economics*)
Mr A Gibb, BA Hons Queen's Belfast (*Head of English*)
Mrs Z Glenister, BA Hons Newcastle (*French, German*)
Miss R Hillier, BA Hons Sussex (*Religious Studies*)
Mrs N Lake, BSc Hons UCL (*Head of Geography*)
Mr A Lipkin, BEng and Comms Birmingham (*Physics*)
Mr P Macken, BA Hons Essex (*Teacher in Charge of Drama*)
Mrs S Moore, BEd Sussex (*Physical Education*)
Miss R Mulchrone, BSc Hons St Mary's Twickenham (*Head of Psychology*)
Mrs J Phillips, MA Beds (*Head of Music*)
Mrs E Roberts, BEd Sheffield (*Home Economics*)
Mrs B Sivaramalingam, MA London (*Mathematics*)
Miss H Snaith, MA Canterbury Christ Church (*Information Technology*)
Mrs K Stansfield, MA York (*History*)
Miss L Stewart-Thomas, BA Hons Loughborough QTS (*Art & Design*)
Mrs G Swart, BA Hons Durham (*French, Spanish*)
Mrs B Taylor, PGD Leeds, BA Hons De Montfort (*Head of Support for Learning*)
Mr C Tucker, MA Oxon (*Mathematics*)
Mrs H Williams, BA Hons Cardiff (*English, Media Studies, Year 13 Form Tutor*)
Mrs T Wingfield, MA Oxford Brookes (*Head of Science*)
Mrs L Winter, BA Hons Nottingham, MBA (*Head of Business Studies*)

Preparatory Department:
Mrs M Carney, BA Hons Galway (*Head of Department, Y6 Class Teacher, French*)
Dr H Creber, PhD Cardiff (*Y5 Class Teacher, Director of Studies, ICT, RE*)
Mrs L Louth, BA Hons Kingston (*Y1 Class Teacher*)
Miss R Rose, BA Hons Plymouth (*Y2 Class Teacher*)
Mrs S Brereton, BA Hons Leicester (*Y3 Class Teacher, Numeracy Coordinator*)
Mrs M Schwartz, BA Hons Leeds (*Y4 Class Teacher, Geography*)
Mr H Hayes, BMus RAM (*Music*)
Mrs K Hemsworth, BEd De Montfort (*Physical Education, 11+ Coordinator*)

Miss E Roche, BSc Hons Leeds (*KS2 Art/Design Technology Specialist*)
Mrs J C Stone, BSc Hons Leicester (*Science*)
Mrs C Stuart-Lee, MA Oxon (*French*)
Mrs G Batsman, NVQ Level 3 (*Classroom Assistant*)
Mrs M Keal, Level 4 Dyslexia Cert (*Classroom Assistant*)

Early Years:
Mrs H Mackinder, BA Hons Brighton Primary Educ QTS (*Early Years Coordinator*)
Miss J May, Montessori International Teaching Diploma (*Nursery Leader*)
Mrs S Kettlewell (*Teaching Assistant*)

Visiting Staff:
Mr R Corden, ARCM Kneller Hall (*Flute, Clarinet, Saxophone*)
Miss K Harding, MA Hons, MPhil Cantab, LTCL (*Cello, Double Bass*)
Miss L McClaren (*Violin*)
Mrs G Pierozynski, GRNCM, ARNCM (*Piano, Singing*)
Miss J Stevenson, AGSM (*Singing*)
Miss E Try, BA Hons Winchester (*LAMDA, Dance*)
Mrs G Tucker, BMus London (*Piano*)
Miss C Wells (*Classical Guitar*)
Mrs R Wheeler, ALCM, CTABRSM (*Piano*)

Registrar & Headmistress's PA: Mrs C Pearcey

The School is situated in the attractive residential area of Gerrards Cross which is surrounded by beautiful countryside, 20 miles from London, close to the M25 and A40/M40, on the main bus routes and 10 minutes from the Railway Station.

The aim of the School is to provide an excellent academic and rounded education leading on to University for day girls between the ages of 3 and 18 and to enable each of them to develop their own talents and personalities in a happy, caring and purposeful environment, and to become successful, fulfilled adults.

Curriculum. Subjects offered include English Language and Literature, History, Geography, RE, Drama, French, German, Spanish, Business Studies, Economics, Information Technology, Mathematics, Psychology, Chemistry, Biology, Physics, Music, Art & Design, Food & Nutrition, Gymnastics, Hockey, Netball, Tennis, Rounders, Football, Rugby, Swimming, Media, Personal, Social, Cultural and Health Care, Dancing and other sporting activities. Regular trips are made to places of educational interest, field courses are undertaken, foreign visits including a ski trip to the USA are arranged, and there is highly successful participation in The Duke of Edinburgh's Award Scheme and Young Enterprise. There is an excellent staff/pupil ratio.

Examinations: Girls are prepared for Entrance to the Universities and Colleges in all subjects; for the General Certificate of Education at AS, A2 and GCSE/IGCSE Level; Associated Board Examinations in Music and examinations in Speech and Drama (LAMDA). The School is an 11+ centre.

The Buildings are an attractive mixture of old and new and include two Libraries, Dining Hall, a Science Block with Laboratories, a Geography Room, a large open-plan Art Studio, a Home Economics Room, Textiles Room, two Computer Suites, a modern Sixth Form Centre, two Music Rooms, Drama Studio, Chapel and two Assembly Halls/Gymnasiums equipped to the highest standards. The Prep Department, in the grounds of the Senior House, comprises a Nursery and two modern purpose-built blocks, with a Science Laboratory, Hall, Gymnasium, Textiles/Art room and ICT suite. The lovely grounds include tennis and netball courts, a hockey pitch and an athletics lawn. A new Sport England full-size Sports Hall opened in 2009.

School Hours. The hours are 8.30 am – 3.40 pm. The School year is divided into 3 terms.

Reports are sent to Parents at the end of each term and there are regular Parent/Staff meetings. The School also communicates with Parents via ParentMail.

Fees per term (2014–2015). £1,285–£4,652.

Scholarships and Bursaries. Academic scholarships are available at 7+, 11+ and at 16+ in the Sixth Form. There are also two Music scholarships and one Art scholarship at 11+. A means-tested Bursary scheme is in operation.

Charitable status. St Mary's School (Gerrards Cross) Limited is a Registered Charity, number 310634. It provides education for girls from Nursery to A Level in a well-structured, academic and caring environment.

St Mary's School
Shaftesbury

Shaftesbury, Dorset SP7 9LP
Tel: 01747 852416 (General Enquiries)
       01747 857111 (Admissions)
Fax: 01747 851557
email: admin@st-marys-shaftesbury.co.uk
website: www.st-marys-shaftesbury.co.uk

Governors:
Major General Sir Sebastian Roberts (*Chair*)
Mr M Catchpole
Dr D J Ceiriog-Hughes
Mr R T Moulding
Dr K Mounde
Mrs B Quest-Ritson
Miss J Taylor
Miss V Younghusband

Senior Management Team:

Headmaster: Mr R James

Deputy Head: Miss J Walker
Bursar: Mr L Tuson
Director of Studies: Dr C Enos
Head of Boarding: Mrs A Salmon
Head of Information Services: Mr J Pearce

Chaplain: Miss A Le Guevel

Resident Priest: Father Andrew Moore

Leadership Team:
Mrs G Cork
Mr P Rigby
Mrs D Webb

Heads of School:
Mrs D Webb (*Head of Sixth Form*)
Mrs S Pugh (*Head of Senior School*)
Mrs G Cork (*Head of Middle School*)
Mrs H Key (*Head of Lower School*)

Marketing Manager & Registrar:
Mrs C Stephens

Teaching Staff:
* *Head of Department*

Art & Design:
*Mrs J A Ridgway
Mrs K Banneel (*Art Technician*)
Miss M Bridger (*Photography*)
Mrs J Hodge (*Textiles*)
Mrs D Sudlow (*Art, Design*)
Mrs J Tidbury-Coates (*Art Technician*)

Business Studies:
Mrs M Reddyhoff

Classics:
*Mr P Daley

Mrs D Clark
Mrs M Harland

Drama:
*Mr C J Sykes (*MAG&T Coordinator*)
Mrs S Holman

Duke of Edinburgh's Award Scheme:
Mrs M Reddyhoff

Economics:
Mr A Pavlou

English:
*Ms R M R Brand
Mrs S Holdaway
Mrs H Key

English for Speakers of Other Languages:
Mrs C Waddington

Examinations Officer:
Mrs M Reddyhoff
Mrs D Whitehead (*Assistant*)

Geography:
*Mr P Davies
Mrs S Bramble

History:
*Mr T Goodwin
Mrs M Andow
Mrs M Harland

History of Art:
Mrs O Karamenova

Information & Communication Technology:
Mr J Pearce (*Head of Information Services*)
Mr C Davis (*ICT Technician*)
Mr G Holdaway (*Subject Teacher*)
Mrs K Le Poidevin (*Subject Teacher*)
Mr C Norman (*Database Manager*)

Learning Support:
*Mrs R Kerby (*Coordinator*)
Mrs Y Atkinson
Mrs R Dixon
Mrs H Hayward
Mrs J Kaskow
Mrs G Phillips
Dr H Vaughan

Library:
Miss A Edmonds (*Librarian*)

Mathematics:
*Mrs J Hall
Mr G Holdaway
Mrs D Kok
Miss A McGirr
Mr J O'Hare
Mr A Rowden

Modern Languages:
*Mr J Giblin (*Spanish, French, Italian*)
Mrs S Abraham (*German Language Assistant*)
Mrs G Cardozo (*Italian*)
Mrs G Cork (*French*)
Mrs O Green (*Spanish Language Assistant*)
Mrs R Howcroft (*Spanish*)
Mrs A Lodder (*French, German*)
Miss V Raffenne (*French Language Assistant*)
Mrs A Rigby (*French*)
Mrs C Waddington (*Portuguese*)
Mrs D Webb (*French, Spanish*)

Music:
*Miss D Radford (*Director of Music, Piano, Singing*)
Mrs S Pugh (*Head of Instrumental Music, Oboe, Recorder*)
Mrs K Alder (*Piano, Aural Classes*)

Mrs J Brookfield (*Piano, Flute*)
Mrs A Caunce (*Piano*)
Mr J Gilbert (*Percussion*)
Mr R James (*Piano*)
Miss S Lockyer (*Clarinet, Saxophone*)
Mr S Lockyer (*Cello, Double Bass*)
Miss L Lowndes-Northcott (*Harp, Viola, Violin*)
Mrs J Lucas (*Violin*)
Mr C Mahon (*Pipe Organ*)
Miss M Marton (*Singing*)
Mr D Mayo (*Acoustic & Electric Guitar*)
Mr M Newman-Wren (*Brass*)
Mrs W Partridge (*Classical Guitar*)
Miss T Seligman (*Singing*)
Miss E Tolfree (*Clarinet, Bassoon, Saxophone*)
Miss S Williams (*Flute*)

Personal & Social Education:
*Miss J Walker
Mrs A Salmon

Physical Education:
*Mrs N Boyer-Castle
Mrs K Booth
Mrs C Collard
Mrs E James
Mrs B Roberts (*Pool Manager*)
Mrs A Salmon
Miss J Walker

PE Coaching:
Miss T Carter (*Cross Country, Athletics*)
Mrs E Deuxbury (*Tennis*)
Mr I Griffin (*Tennis*)
Mr I Metcalfe (*Hockey*)
Mrs V Peck (*Tennis*)

Psychology:
Miss S Williams (**Careers*)

Religious Education:
*Mrs J Bowe (**Critical Thinking*)
Mrs H Savile

Science:
*Mr P Rigby (*Physics*)
Dr G Caunt (*Biology & Chemistry*)
Mrs A Fearnley (*Chemistry*)
Miss S Flower (*Biology*)
Mrs K Le Poidevin (*Biology*)
Mrs D Kok (*Physics*)
Mrs V Rushton (*Biology*)
Mrs C Gray (*Science Technician*)
Mrs J Hill (*Assistant Lab Technician*)

Speech & Drama:
Mrs S Holman
Mrs E Brown
Mrs H Earle
Mr S Earle

Administration:
Mrs S Awdry (*Assistant to Registrar*)
Mr C Bent (*Head Groundsman*)
Miss R Bye (*Administration Assistant*)
Miss L Coffin (*School Office*)
Mrs M Drake (*Bursar's Assistant*)
Mrs M Gordon (*Accounts & Human Resources Bursar*)
Mrs L Gardiner (*Domestic Bursar*)
Mr C Hedger (*Assistant Caretaker*)
Mr A Watford (*Accounts Assistant*)
Miss K Macey (*Reception – Morning*)
Mr R A Pitman (*Caretaker*)
Mrs J Sampson (*Head's PA*)
Mrs J Waterton (*Reception – Afternoon/evenings/weekends*)
Miss D Williams (*Accounts Assistant*)

House Staff:

Head of Boarding: Mrs A Salmon

Givendale House:
Mrs A Rigby (*Housemistress*)
Mrs A Hannam (*Assistant*)
Mrs B McLeod (*Assistant*)

Harewell House:
Mrs S Holman (*Housemistress*)
Mrs S Shutler (*Assistant*)
Mrs E Samoluk (*Assistant*)

Hewarth House:
Ms E Seal-Newman (*Housemistress*)
Mrs S R Hill (*Assistant*)
Mrs M Tomlinson (*Assistant*)

Mary Ward House:
Mrs D Webb (*Housemistress*)
Mrs E Boote (*Assistant*)
Mrs T Richards (*Assistant*)

Mulwith House:
Mrs B Roberts (*Housemistress*)
Mrs E Hawkins (*Assistant*)
Mrs K Bull (*Assistant*)

Newby House:
Mrs D Whitehead (*Housemistress*)
Mrs H Sanger (*Assistant*)
Mrs D Healey (*Assistant*)

Nursing Staff:
Mrs E Crossley, Registered Nurse
Mrs L Fish, Registered Nurse
Mrs S Savage, Registered Nurse, Senior Nurse
Mrs K Webber, Registered Nurse

Founded in 1945, St Mary's School, Shaftesbury is an outstanding Independent Catholic Boarding and Day School for girls aged 11–18. Situated in the heart of the Dorset countryside, St Mary's offers a very special environment in which girls thrive academically and socially. A strong commitment to traditional values is fostered and girls are inspired to achieve a fulfilling all-round education, embracing every kind of learning.

St Mary's is a very happy and friendly school; two-thirds of the school is boarding and everyone here enjoys a real sense of community, staff and pupils alike. Girls are welcomed usually at eleven, but also at twelve and thirteen, and at sixteen into the Sixth Form.

Situated in 55 acres of park and woodland, St Mary's offers an excellent combination of the traditional and modern, with excellent facilities and a forward thinking approach. St Mary's is less than two hours by train from London; on the A30 just outside Shaftesbury, it is very accessible for visits and school trips to Salisbury, Bath and the surrounding area.

Houses. There is a junior boarding house and 4 main boarding houses with a modern Upper Sixth Form house which was extended last year. A new academic facility for English, History and Geography and Learning Support was opened in Sept 2013 and the new art building will be completed in April 2014. This will be home to Fine Art, Photography, History of Art, Textiles and Ceramics and will create an inspiring work space for the students here.

Admission. The School has its own Entrance Examination held in January for 11+ and 13+ entry. Sixth Form entry is by testimonial and interview and is then conditional on 5 GCSE passes.

Scholarships and Bursaries. 11+: Academic, Sport, Music and Catholic Local Primary School scholarships are awarded.

13+: Academic, Music, Sport and Art scholarships are awarded.

Sixth Form: Academic and Art scholarships are awarded. Additional Head's Scholarships can also be awarded at 11+, 13+ and 16+.

All Scholarships offer up to 10% remission of day or boarding fees with a further 40% available by a means-tested bursary.

Scholarship Examinations take place in January.

Fees per term (2014–2015). Year 7: Boarders £7,998, Day Girls £5,520. Year 8: Boarders £8,407, Day Girls £5,782. Years 9–13: Boarders £8,990, Day Girls £6,195.

Aims and Curriculum. The School aims to give girls as broad an education as possible, combining academic, personal, spiritual and extra-curricular, to foster independent thinking and the opportunity for each girl to realise her own strengths and potential. We are concerned with all that a girl is and could become.

During Years 7–9 all girls follow a common curriculum which includes, English, History, Geography, French, Latin, Mathematics, Information Technology, Religious Education, Science, Art, Textiles, Music, Singing, PSE and PE. From Year 10 both the core curriculum: English Language and Literature, Mathematics, One Modern Foreign Language, Religious Education and either Triple or Double Award Science; options are arranged to ensure that each girl follows a balanced course suitable to her ability and interests.

We offer a choice of 22 subjects at A Level in addition to General Studies, General RE, and PE. Girls in the Sixth Form also have the opportunity to do the Leiths Basic Certificate in Food and Wine as a professional qualification. The majority of girls gain places at Russell Group Universities, and Oxbridge success is realised. Some go on to more vocational forms of Higher Education or pursue their studies in the Creative Arts.

The School is a member of ISCO (Independent Schools Careers Organisation) and all girls receive individual careers advice from the Head of Careers and Guidance.

Music. With a thriving Music Department any orchestral instrument may be learned. In addition there are two school choirs, an orchestra and various instrumental ensembles. Bi-annual choir trips have been to Vienna, Rome, Budapest and Venice.

Sport. Winter: Hockey, netball, cross country, swimming and water polo teams with a wide range of additional activities also available such as dance, badminton, volleyball; tag-rugby and football. Summer: Swimming, tennis, rounders, athletics & water polo and also a range of other activities available to choose from. The School has its own Sports Hall, Fitness Suite, floodlit Astroturf and a 25m six-lane indoor swimming pool.

Extra subjects or activities. Speech and drama, ballet, riding, polo, tennis coaching, Duke of Edinburgh's Award, photography, and a wide range of other clubs and societies including book groups, debating, Politics, Science club and many more.

Charitable status. St Mary's School Shaftesbury Trust is a Registered Charity, number 292845. Its aims and objectives are to administer an independent Roman Catholic school for the education of children of any denomination.

St Nicholas' School

Redfields House, Redfields Lane, Church Crookham, Fleet, Hampshire GU52 0RF

Tel:	01252 850121
Fax:	01252 850718
email:	headspa@st-nicholas.hants.sch.uk
website:	www.st-nicholas.hants.sch.uk

Motto: *Confirma Domine Serviendo*

Chair of Governors: Mr G Cockayne

Headmistress: **Annette V Whatmough**, BA Hons Bristol, CertEd

Deputy Head – Pastoral: Caroline Egginton, BEd Hons London

Deputy Head – Academic: Christine Moorby, BSc Hons Southampton, CertEd

Bursar: Caroline Taylor, MA Hons Edinburgh, CA

Teaching Staff:
Josephine Allen, BA Hons QTS West of England (*Key Stage 2*)
Cherill Anderson, MA Cantab (*Modern Languages*)
Alison Audino, BEd Hons Bath (*Food Technology*)
Helen Barnes, BA Ed Hons Exeter (*Key Stage 2*)
Jenny Brackstone, BA Hons Nottingham, PGCE (*Key Stages 3 & 4*)
Nicky Brooks, BA Hons Exeter, PGCE (*Key Stage 2*)
Joanne Carr, BEd Hons Southampton (*Key Stage 2*)
Sarah Carter, BEd Hons Southampton (*Key Stage 2*)
Janet Coombe, BA Hons Manchester, PGCE (*Geography*)
Isabel Cook, BA Hons Southampton, PGCE (*Head of History*)
Josie Downer, BA Hons Leeds, MA King's (*Head of Drama*)
Barbara Edwards, BA Hons Sheffield, PGCE (*English*)
Amy Franke, BMus Hons Surrey, MMus (*Assistant Director of Music*)
Brenda Green, CertEd, CNAA (*Director of Sport*)
Edwina Grosse, BA Hons Trent (*Head of Art*)
Rosalie Hague, BA Hons Lancaster, PGCE (*Head of English*)
Valerie Helliwell, BEng Hons Liverpool, PGCE (*Head of Mathematics, Examinations Officer*)
Laura Homer, BA Hons Wales, PGCE (*Key Stage 1*)
Maureen Idowu, GRSAM Royal Scottish Academy (*Director of Music*)
Janice R King, BSc Hons London, PGCE (*Head of Biology*)
Alexandra Lawrence, MA Oxon, PGCE (*Head of Modern Languages*)
Elizabeth Madden, BA Hons Otago (*Head of Classics*)
Deborah Martin, BA Hons Surrey (*Key Stage 2*)
Julie Merker, BA OU, CertEd (*PE*)
Michelle Morgan, NNEB (*Nursery*)
Paul Nicholls, BA Hons London (*Key Stage 2*)
Virginia Pearson, Perf Cert RAM, LTCL, ARCM (*Part time music*)
Tracy Perrett, BEd Sussex (*Head of Juniors*)
Joanna Pont, BMus Hons (*String Tutor*)
Lee Render, BA Hons QTS Surrey (*Head of Infants*)
Laura Ridge, BA Hons QTS Warwick (*Key Stage 2*)
Lisa Ruffell, BA Hons QTS Surrey (*Key Stage 2*)
Paula Simpson, BSc Hons Bath, PGCE (*Textiles*)
Jane Stansbury, BEd Cambridge, PG SpLD Kingston (*Curriculum Support Teacher*)
Michelle Strevens, BEd, CNAA (*Foundation Stage*)
Joanne Taylor, BA Hons Reading (*Head of Foundation*)
Julia Tiley, BA Hons QTS Kingston (*Foundation Stage*)
Gail Tomblin, BSc Hons Loughborough, CertEd (*Mathematics*)
Jane Tomlinson, BA Hons London, PGCE (*Modern Languages*)
Frances van Heerden, BSc Natal, UED (*Science*)
Suzanne Walch, BA Hons OU (*Head of Curriculum Support*)
Catherine Williams, BA Hons Salford (*Head of IT*)
Xinsheng Zhang, MEd Johannesburg SA (*Chinese Mandarin*)

Peripatetic Music:
Jonathan Baxter (*Drums*)

Wendy Busby, BMus Hons (*Voice*)
Rebekah Duncalfe, BMus (*Violin*)
Sylvia Ellison, BA Hons, PG Dip RCM (*Oboe*)
Catherine Evans, Dip TCM (*Piano*)
Rosemary Fox, BA Hons, BSc, Dip ABRSM (*Flute*)
Susan Gillis, PG Dip Mtpp, ALCM, LLCM (*Piano*)
Amy Hosken, BMus Hons (*Violin*)
Natasha James, Batchelor Degree (*Piano*)
Valerie Mitchell, LRAM (*Piano, Cello*)
Austin Pepper, ALCM (*Brass*)
Megan Pound (*Violin*)
Sally Pryce, BMus Hons RCM (*Harp*)
Rachel Riordan, Adv Teaching RSM (*Saxophone, Clarinet*)

Administration:
Classroom Assistant: Tanya Negus
School Nurse: Sarah Watkins, RGN, NNEB
Payroll Clerk: Mary Wales
Headmistress's PA: Dawn Brown, FInstAM
Marketing & Admissions Registrar: Melissa Brown, BA Hons Hertfordshire
School Secretary: Sarah Watkins
Accounts Secretary: Deborah Davies, Cert AAT London
Laboratory Technician: Michele Axton, BA OU
Catering: Chartwells, Compass Group PLC
Maintenance: Peter Sleet, Peter White, Joseph Carrig, Stephen Turner
Caretaker: Robert Crail
Bus Driver: Timothy Hunt
Second Hand Uniform Shop: Maureen Mullins
Librarian: Sarah Stokes

The School. St Nicholas' School is a small independent day school for girls aged 3–16 and boys 3–7. Founded in 1935 in Branksomewood Road, Fleet, the school moved to Redfields House, Redfields Lane, Church Crookham in 1996. Redfields House, a Victorian Mansion, is set in 27 acres of glorious parkland and playing fields.

Branksomewood, the Nursery and Infant department, retains the original name of the road where the school was founded. Being built of natural wood with a wonderful airy atmosphere this building gives light and space to our younger children, creating a calming environment in which they thrive. With an adventure playground set in the woods, a large hall fitted with PE equipment, overlooking the grounds and our experienced teaching staff, it is no wonder the children are so happy.

St Nicholas' junior department is based in Redfields House itself which keeps the charm of the old family house with its oak panelling and the senior department is located in the newer part of the school behind. All three departments have benefited from several building projects.

December 2000 saw the opening of the Olympic-size sports hall with netball and tennis courts showers, changing rooms and a viewing gallery. This has enhanced the sports lessons and enabled even more sports competitions as well as extra-curricular activities. Badminton, tennis, netball, volleyball and basketball may be played throughout the year.

Spring 2006 saw yet another addition with the opening of the art, design technology and textiles centre, offering three spacious rooms with large work benches, and a kiln for pottery. By having this wonderful new building it opened an opportunity for the school to adapt the old art centre into several music practice rooms. Tuition in the violin, piano, guitar, harp, drums as well singing, woodwind and brass is offered.

November 2009 saw the grand opening of the performing arts centre. With raked seating for over 330, in the semi round, with an orchestra pit, concerts and plays are staged regularly. The drama department has in addition two studios.

September 2013 welcomed the opening of state-of-the-art laboratories for juniors and seniors. The new classrooms include teaching areas as well as practical learning spaces in a bright and welcoming environment.

Pupils come to St Nicholas' from Hampshire, Surrey and Berkshire. School buses operate from Farnham, Odiham, Fleet, Basingstoke, Camberley, Yateley, Aldershot and Farnborough. Situated just off the A287, Hook to Farnham road, junction 5 of the M3 is approximately 4 miles short away.

Religion. The school is a Christian foundation but children of other faiths are welcomed Assemblies are held each morning. Children are encouraged to show tolerance, compassion and care for others.

Curriculum. St Nicholas' offers an extended day, from 8 am to 6 pm. Academic standards are high and a balanced curriculum is offered. Small classes place greater emphasis on the individual and pupils are encouraged to achieve their full potential in every area of school life. The curriculum is kept as broad as possible until the age of fourteen when choices are made for GCSE. The option choices vary year by year depending upon the girls' abilities and talents. On average each girl sits ten subjects at GCSE. More than twenty subjects are offered at this level. A carefully structured personal development course incorporates a Careers programme. Our girls move confidently on to enter sixth form colleges or scholarships to senior independent schools. Choir, drama and music thrive within the school and there are frequent performances which enable the girls to develop self-confidence.

Physical Education. Pupils take part in inter-school and local district sports matches: hockey, netball and cross-country in winter; and tennis, athletics and swimming in summer. Rounders and lacrosse are also played.

Entry. Children may enter at any stage subject to interview, school report and waiting list. Scholarships and Bursaries are available. For 11+ candidates there is an entrance examination.

Fees per term (2014–2015). Infants (Reception, Years 1 and 2) £3,142; Juniors (Years 3 to 4) £3,575; Juniors (Years 5 to 6) £3,600; Senior School £4,265. Nursery: £8.50 per hour.

Further Information. The prospectus is available upon request from the Registrar. The Headmistress is pleased to meet parents by appointment.

Charitable status. St Nicholas' School is a Registered Charity, number 307341. It exists to provide high quality education for children.

St Swithun's School

Alresford Road, Winchester, Hampshire SO21 1HA

Tel:	01962 835700
Fax:	01962 835779
email:	office@stswithuns.com
website:	www.stswithuns.com
Twitter:	@st_swithuns
Facebook:	/StSwithunsSchool

St Swithun's is a modern and flourishing educational organisation. The school is set on an impressive and attractive campus of 45 acres in the South Downs National Park on the outskirts of Winchester. It offers girls excellent teaching, sporting and recreational facilities.

The school offers weekly boarding and full boarding and day options for girls aged 11–18. At present the senior school (girls aged 11–18) has 282 day girls and 227 boarders. There is an adjoining Junior School for girls aged 3–11 and boys from 3–7 years (*see Junior School entry in IAPS section*).

Visitor: The Bishop of Winchester, The Right Reverend Tim Dakin

School Council:
Chairman: Professor Natalie Lee, LLB
The Right Worshipful, the Mayor of Winchester Cllr Berry (*ex officio*)
The Dean of Winchester (*ex officio*)
The Headmaster of Winchester College (*ex officio*)
Mr Tom Bremridge
Mr Luke Meynell, MA
Dr Harry Mycock, BA, BSc, MSc, MBA, PhD, QTLS, MCIM, MNLP, MI Hort, MIfL, FHEA, Chartered Marketer
Mr Martin Reid, MA, FCA (*Treasurer, ex officio*)
Miss Rebecca Rothman, BA, ACA
Ms Margaret Rudland, BSc, PGCE
Professor Michael Whitehouse, MA, MD, FRCP, FRCP(E), FRCR, FMedSci
Mr Mike Wilson, BA
Mrs Frances Robinson, LLB Hons
Mr Jonathan Russell, BSc Hons, MSc

Headmistress: **Ms Jane Gandee**, MA Cantab

Deputy Headmistress: Mrs Alison Burns-Cox, BSc London
Director of Studies: Mr Charlie Hammel, AB Princeton, MLitt St Andrews
Bursar and Clerk to the Council: Mr Matthew Carter, FCMI
Chaplain: Revd Katrina Dykes, BA Bristol

Senior School Teaching Staff:

Art:
Mrs Kim Ross, BA Surrey
Miss Katie Lintott, BA Warwick, MA The Courtauld Institute of Art
Mrs Libby Mason-Smith, BA Reading, MA Southampton
Ms Christine Packer, BA London
Miss Charlotte Wirdnam, BA Wimbledon School of Art

Classics:
Dr Liza Martin, MA, PhD Cantab
Mrs Pippa Giles, BA Birmingham
Mrs Georgia Condell, BA King's College London
Mrs Claire Webster, MA Oxon

Design and Technology:
Mrs Hilary Mitchener, BEng Exeter

Drama and Theatre Studies:
Ms Tracy Spring, BA Hertfordshire, MA Middlesex, CertEd
Miss Tamzin Mason, BA Winchester

Dramatist in Residence:
Miss Gina Thorley, BA Winchester

Visiting Staff:
Mrs Marie Armstrong, BA Bretton Hall
Ms Judith Wilson, BA North London, MA Winchester, LRAM, LLAM
Mrs Leigh McQueen, Dip Webber Douglas Academy

Economics:
Mrs Jacqueline Campbell, BSc Plymouth State University USA

English:
Miss Alison Oliver, BA Warwick
Mrs Naomi Anson MA, Mtcg London
Miss Alana Burton, BA Southampton, MA Southampton
Miss Claire Goymour, BA London
Miss Caroline Howard, BA Leicester
Mr Sam Lenton, BA Cambridge, MA Cantab
Mrs Sophie Toland, MA Cantab
Mrs Sally Walmsley, BA Oxford

English as an additional language:
Mrs Nicola Young, BA Birmingham
Miss Nicola Thomas, BA Cantab

Food Technology and Textiles:
Mrs Nicola Sanvoisin, BSc Cardiff
Mrs Rachel Curry, BA Manchester
Miss Heather Jones, BA Liverpool

Geography:
Mr Jonathan Brown, BA Birmingham
Mrs Tansy Gill, BSc Brighton
Mrs Lisa Parson, BSc Liverpool

History and Politics:
Ms Georgina Manville, BA Bristol, MA Bristol
Mrs Kathryn Batten, BA West of England
Mrs Jenny Dixon-Clarke, BA Reading, MA London
Mr Charles Hammel, AB Princeton, MLitt St Andrews
Miss Emily Tait, BA Bedfordshire

ICT:
Mrs Anne Walker, BEd Leeds

Mathematics:
Mr Stephen Power, BA Oxon, MSc Colorado
Mrs Corinna Bolger, BEng Exeter, CEng, MIMechE
Mr Paul Debont, BSc Warwick, MSc Essex
Mrs Helen Greene, BSc London, MA OU
Mr John Gillespie, BSc Dunelm
Mrs Hannah Savory, MEng UMIST
Mrs Cindy Thompson, BSc Ed Exeter

Modern Languages:
Miss Fiona Bolton, MA Oxon
Mrs Caro Bewes, Maîtrise Université d'Artois, Pôle
    d'Arras
Mrs Laura Camba-Robinson, BA OU
Dr Catherine Dey, BA Birmingham, PhD Birmingham
Ms Jane Gandee, MA Cantab
Mrs Sandra Hayward, MA London
Mrs Manu Grice, BA Southampton
Mrs Nelly Porter, Maîtrise Strasbourg
Mrs Anne Steer, MA Ed Frankfurt
Mrs Imelda Weingart-West, MA Freiburg

Music:
Mrs YiRu Hall, MA Cantab
Miss Elizabeth Barter, BA, MA Cantab, FRCO
Ms Natasha Wright, BMus Hons, PPRNCM, MMus,
    PGDipGSMD
Mr Clive Watkiss, GRSM, LRAM

Visiting Music Staff:
Mrs Michelle Allen, BMus, Dip LRAM (*voice*)
Mrs Sally Bartholomew, BMus (*bassoon*)
Mrs Fiona Brockhurst, ARCM (*french horn*)
Mr Mark Eden, GRSM, LRAM, Dip RAM (*guitar*)
Mrs Kate L Field, PPRNCM, BMus, RNCM (*voice*)
Mr Mark Frampton (*double bass*)
Mr Simon Gallear (*voice*)
Mr Brian Gordon, LRAM, DipRAM (*voice*)
Mrs Kate Ham, BMus Hons (*harp*)
Mrs Vicki Harding, BSc (*violoncello*)
Mrs Jane Lloyd, ARCM, LGSM (*piano*)
Ms Claire Lowe, GRSM, LRAM (*voice*)
Mr Michael Mace, Dip RAM (*violoncello*)
Ms Rebecca Miles, LTCL (*recorder*)
Mr Richard Morrow (*guitar*)
Mrs Sarah Mudd, ATCL (*oboe*)
Miss Kate Murrelli, BA, MMus (*piano*)
Miss Helen Paskins, MA Cantab, Dip RCM (*clarinet*)
Mr Todor Nikolaev, MMus, BMus Hons GSMD (*violin*)
Mr Jason O'Kane, LWCMD (*guitar*)
Mr Donal O'Neill, PG Cert Perf, BA Mus (*percussion*)
Mrs Jo Paterson-Neild, BA (*saxophone*)
Mrs Angela Roberts, BA London Dundee (*flute*)
Mrs Gilly Slot, BMus, ALCM, LTCL (*piano*)
Mrs Karen Tavener, BA Hons (*piano*)
Mrs Judith Turner, MSTAT (*Alexander Technique*)
Miss Salvita Vysniauskiene, MMus, LMTA (*piano*)

Mr Alastair Warren, BMus Hons RCM, MMus RCM
    (*trombone, tuba*)
Dr Nigel Wilkinson, MMus, ARCM, Hon ARAM (*piano*)
Miss Karen Wills, GTCL, LTCL, DipRAM (*flute*)

Religious Studies:
Miss Antigone Storey BA Dunelm, MA Dunelm
Miss Jo Cox, BA Birmingham
Mrs Marie Jervis, Cert Ed

Science:
Mrs Susanna Wilkinson, BSc Southampton
Mrs Laura Bream, MSc, DipM
Mrs Penny Burley, BSc Swansea
Mrs Alison Burns-Cox, BSc London
Mrs Catherine Elkins, BSc Reading
Mrs Sarah Evans, BSc London, MA OU
Mr Bruce Hansen, BSc, MSc Canterbury New Zealand,
    Grad Dip TchLn Christchurch New Zealand
Dr Hilary Otter, BA, PhD Cantab, FSB, CBiol
Mr Ravi Shah, BSc East Anglia
Dr Jemma Savillewood, BM Southampton
Dr Susan Sturton, BA Oxon, PhD Leeds
Mr Michael Tanner, BSc Loughborough

Physical Education:
Mrs Justine Mackenzie, BSc Temple University USA
Mr Paul Boyd-Leslie
Mrs Leonie Campbell, BA Chichester
Miss Jill Durgin, BA Charlotte USA
Miss Emily Harris, BA Bedfordshire
Mrs Dot Hogg, BSc Swansea
Mrs Sara Heffernan, BA Chichester
Miss Zoe Hillyard, BSc Chichester
Miss Kate Nelson-Lee, BA Swarthmore College USA

Visiting Staff:
Mrs Natalie Potter (*aerobics*)
Mrs Fredricka Brooks (*Pilates*)
Miss Caroline Pont (*judo*)
Mr Simon Budden (*karate*)
Mr Allen Cooke (*fencing*)
Mrs Patricia Francis, BA National Teaching University,
    Colombia (*gym*)

Duke of Edinburgh's Award Coordinator:
Mr Andrew Parker, BA Newcastle, MBA Manchester

Psychology:
Dr Julia Adlam, BSc, MSc, PhD Hamburg

Higher Education & Student Guidance:
Mrs Anna Campbell, BA Dunelm, DipRE Nottingham,
    CFPS Portsmouth, RSA DipTEFLA

Learning Support:
Miss Sarah Brown, BA, MA Essex, MA SpLD/Dyslexia
    Bath Spa, PGCE Greenwich
Miss Margaret Sturton, BA, MA Southampton

IT:
Mr Adam King, BEd Warwick, MITT (*Head of IT
    Services*)
Mr Andy Healy (*IT Systems Manager*)
Mr Laurence Moon (*Data Manager*)

Boarding House Staff:
Head of boarding: Miss Jayne Webber
Finlay:
Housemistress: Miss Jo Cox
Assistant: Miss Nicola Thomas
High House:
Housemistress: Miss Hayley Gaj
Assistant: Ms Karen Butler
Hyde Abbey:
Housemistress: Miss Heather Jones
Assistant: Miss Charlotte Graham
Earlsdown:

Housemistress: Mrs Sophie Toland
Assistant: Miss Tansley Jordan
Hillcroft:
Housemistress: Mrs Tamzin Mason
Assistant: Miss Charlotte Jaques
Le Roy:
Housemistress: Mrs Marie Jervis
Assistant: Miss Jo Parsons

Day House Staff:
Caer Gwent:
Housemistress: Mrs Anna Campbell
Assistant: Mrs Nicola Sanvoisin
Venta:
Housemistress: Mrs Hilary Mitchener
Assistant: Mr Bruce Hansen
Davies:
Housemaster: Mr Ravi Shah
Assistant: Ms Tracy Spring

Library:
Mrs Alice Kelly (*librarian*)
Mrs Maggie Macdonald (*library assistant*)

Medical Staff:
Dr Lorraine Cole, MBBS, DRCOG
Mrs Paulette May, RGN
Mrs Eleanor Oakley, RGN
Ms Nicola Smith, RGN

Clinical Counselling Psychologist:
Dr Helen O'Connor, PhD London, BA Wales

Technicians:
Miss Charlotte Wirdnam (*art*)
Mrs Jennifer Dickinson, Mr Ian Newton, Mrs Annette
  Ward (*science*)
Mr Niall Burke (*technology*)

Admissions:
Registrar: Mrs Kate Cairns
Assistant Registrar: Mrs Liz Turner

Administrative Staff:
PA to the Headmistress: Mrs Rachel Nicholls
Examinations officer: Miss Sarah Stevens
School Secretary: Mrs Barbara Tyler-Smith
Assistant School Secretary: Mrs Laura Slaney-Sharpe
Music Administrative Assistant: Mrs Karis Grover
Development Director: Mr Simon Mayes
Communications Officer: Mrs Mel Kinder
Old Girls Association Manager: Mrs Hilary Turner
Performing Arts Technical Manager: Mr Simon Freakley
Swimming Pool Manager: Mr Len Stanley

Bursary:
Accountant: Mrs Jan Bollard
Domestic Bursar: Ms Sarah Draycott
Domestic Bursar's Assistant: Mrs Sandra Kelly
Bursary Supervisor: Mrs Lorna Gale
Bursary Assistant: Mrs Pam Eynon
Bursary Assistant: Mrs Sally Warden
HR Officer: Mrs Helen Wentworth
Estates Manager: Mr Jim Ewing

Junior School

Headmistress: Mrs P Grimes, BA Hons Sussex, PGCE
  King Alfred's College

Deputy Head: Mrs K Grosscurth, BSc Plymouth, PGCE

Director of Studies: Mrs K Allen, BSc Hons St Andrews,
  PGCE King Alfred's College

Teaching staff:
Miss C Albin, BA Hons Leeds, PGCE
Mrs K Brown, BSc Hons Reading
Mrs L Caldwell, BA Hons, PGCE Cardiff

Mrs J Hayden, BSc Hons Open University, NNEB, Cert
  Nat Sci
Mrs R Hay, BEd Hons Bedford College of Higher
  Education
Mrs J Heinrich, Cert Ed Oxford
Miss K Jones, BEd St Martin's College, Lancaster
Mrs J Kingsford, Cert Ed King Alfred's College
Mr R Marshall, BEd Wales
Miss V Meinel, BA Hons Kent
Mrs J Nicholson, BEd Hons London
Mrs S Romero, BEd Hons Newcastle Polytechnic
Miss C Silvester, BMus Hons RCM, PGCE Reading, Dip
  RCM, LTCL, ALCM
Miss K Sprunt, BEd Hons Homerton College Cambridge
Miss S Taylor, MA, PGCE Edinburgh, MCIL

Headmistress's PA: Mrs A Robinson
Registrar: Mrs S Mathieson

Ethos. St Swithun's is an 'appropriately academic' school which means that we celebrate intellectual curiosity and the life of the mind, but not to the exclusion of all else. We expect our pupils to develop individual passions and through them to acquire a range of skills and characteristics. These characteristics will include a willingness to take risks, to question and to debate, and to persevere in the face of difficulty. In the words of Samuel Beckett: "Ever tried. Ever failed. No matter. Try again. Fail again. Fail better." If a girl can immediately excel at everything we ask of her, we as educators must set the bar higher.

We want all girls to learn about life beyond the school gates, to appreciate the rich variety of our world, to develop an understanding of compassion and to value justice. We encourage all pupils to become involved in fundraising and community work. They should appreciate how their decisions and their actions can affect those around them.

St Swithun's was founded by Anna Bramston, daughter of the Dean of Winchester, and Christian values underpin our approach to education. We provide a civilised and caring environment in which all girls and staff are valued for their individual gifts and encouraged to develop a sense of spirituality and of kindness. We believe that kindness and tolerance are at the heart of any fully functioning community.

Location. The school is on a rural site in Winchester's 'green belt' but only a short distance from the city centre. It is easily accessible from Heathrow and Gatwick airports and is one hour from London by car (via the M3 motorway). There is a frequent train service to London Waterloo (one hour).

Curriculum. Girls at St Swithun's benefit from a broad and balanced curriculum that promotes individual choice and achievement. The timetable is designed to enable each pupil to fulfil her intellectual, physical and creative potential through a dynamic range of purposeful lessons and activities.

From their first years here girls are taught to examine social, cultural and moral issues so that they can make informed decisions about their own way of living as well as respecting the values of each individual. The PSHEE & citizenship programme is tailored for each year group and is delivered through a range of school activities and specialist speakers.

There is a weekly academic enrichment programme (Stretch) for the entire school. The girls in L4–L5 (Years 7–9) follow a compulsory programme of activities such as astronomy, thinking skills, experimental art, discovering the news and the great egg challenge while the older girls will have a choice of courses including ethics and science, Socratic discussion and UK political issues.

Games and PE are taught throughout the school so that girls can participate in a wide range of team and individual sports. Both in lessons and as recreational activities, the emphasis is on personal enjoyment and the development of a healthy, active life, but all pupils receive expert coaching and the most talented individuals and teams are entered into county, regional and national competitions.

Learning support provides bespoke support for individual girls who may be experiencing difficulties in aspects of their academic studies.

Girls take 10 GCSE exams to allow time for other interests and activities. Everyone takes English language, English literature, mathematics and physical education and then girls choose six or seven subjects from a choice of 19. There is a recommendation that at least two science subjects and a modern foreign language are included. Girls are encouraged to take at least one humanity or social science to ensure a breadth of knowledge and skills.

In the sixth form girls are offered 22 subjects from which they choose four (five if maths and further maths are chosen). One of these will normally be followed to AS Level only while the remainder are taken through as full A Levels. Advice is given about the implications for their choice of university, degree course and career to ensure sensible combinations. Some girls choose to follow courses in subjects which are not offered at GCSE. Over half the sixth form study at least one science subject at A Level. Some will continue all four AS choices to full A Levels.

In addition, all sixth-form girls follow an enrichment programme of taught short courses and lectures from visiting speakers. Areas of study include science and ethics, student survival, money matters, politics, cookery, philosophy, relationship matters, creative skills, first aid and what it means to be English. All sixth-formers may also choose to do the Extended Project Qualification (EPQ). This is worth half an A Level and is graded from A*–E. The qualification gives girls the opportunity to research an area of personal interest. Universities recognise the value of the skills required for the qualification and it attracts UCAS tariff points.

Religion. The school is a Church of England foundation. There are close ties with Winchester Cathedral, where termly services and the annual confirmation and carol services are held. A full-time chaplain prepares girls for confirmation and teaches in the school. There is a newly converted chapel at the heart of the school.

Music. From the first hymn in the morning to the final applause on concert nights every day is enriched by music and the school enjoys a fine reputation for the excellence and variety that girls achieve. Through lessons, practice, rehearsals, exams, competitions, performances and cathedral services, the girls are drawn together to make the most of a busy and ambitious musical life: 75% have instrumental lessons and there is a choice of twenty-two instruments to study. Twenty flourishing school ensembles create a wealth of music and everyone is welcome to join in. Our most accomplished musicians are also cathedral choristers or play in county and national groups. There are endless possibilities at St Swithun's whether it is Renaissance church music, African drumming or 21st century pop music that girls wish to study, listen to, compose or perform. They are taught to appreciate many different styles of music from all over the world and from different historical eras. Learning to compose enables some to express themselves through music and we encourage performing as an integral part of what we offer. Learning a musical instrument and sharing this with an audience requires a high standard of creativity, commitment, technique and courage.

Sports. All girls are encouraged to be involved in sport throughout their time at the school. Sport at St Swithun's has so much to offer, emphasising cooperation, leadership, teamwork, competition and respect. Our girls learn how to deal with success and failure, how to be self-disciplined and how to communicate with each other. We expect every girl to try her best in every area of school life and sport is no exception. Many girls represent their county, region or even country in sports as diverse as lacrosse, fencing, diving, athletics and tennis and we are naturally very proud of these individuals. However, whilst we celebrate success and our teams aspire to excellence, we value effort and sportsmanship as much as winning and we are proud to run first, second and sometimes third teams for all age groups.

Of supreme importance to us is identifying at least one sport to suit each girl so that she will acquire a lifelong enjoyment of exercise.

Facilities. The original school building contains the main teaching rooms and libraries and has been extended and developed to provide specialist areas for languages, information technology, food and textiles and careers. The science wing contains eight fully equipped modern laboratories and project rooms. In addition, there is an art, design and technology centre and a performing arts building was opened in 2003. This has a 600-seat main auditorium and two smaller performance spaces. A new library, careers and ICT facility was opened in 2007.

School Houses. There are 6 boarding houses and 3 day girl houses, each staffed by a housemistress and assistant who take pride in the high level of pastoral care offered to each girl. The junior house is for girls aged 11 who are then transferred to one of the senior houses after a year. They remain in the senior house until they have completed one year in the sixth form. The upper sixth house is for boarders and day girls together, with study-bedrooms for boarders, study facilities for day girls and common rooms and galley for all.

Careers. Most girls continue to university, including Oxford and Cambridge, and all continue to some form of higher education and training. Each girl is counselled by one of the team of careers staff in a well-resourced department. Lectures and video presentations are organised frequently and a careers fair held annually.

Leisure Activities. There is an extensive range of co-curricular activities and an organised programme of visits and activities at the weekend. Girls participate in the Duke of Edinburgh's Award Scheme, Young Enterprise and local community service work. The sixth form are able to assist with Stretch activities and this can count towards their UCAS tariff. Each year there are drama productions as well as regular drama activities. There are many overseas study and activity trips which include visits to St Katherine's, the sister school in Uganda, volunteer work, language trips, ski trips and watersports holidays.

Health. The school health centre forms part of the main buildings. It is staffed by qualified RGNs and visited by the school doctor twice a week.

Entrance. Entry is by means of a pre-test and the Common Entrance examination for Independent Schools. The majority of girls enter the senior school at the age of 11 or 13 years, but girls are accepted at other ages, including the sixth form, subject to satisfactory tests.

Scholarships and Bursaries. Academic scholarships, carrying a fee subsidy of up to 20%, are available for day girls and boarders entering the school at 11+, at 13+ and to the sixth form.

Music scholarships carry a subsidy of up to 20% and provide free tuition on two instruments; exhibitions provide free tuition on one instrument. Music scholars can apply for a means-tested award of up to 100% of school fees.

Sports scholarships may be awarded each year to suitable applicants at 11+ and 13+. These scholarships will have a maximum value of 20% fee remission.

Bursaries of up to 100% of school fees are available for girls who meet the school's entrance criteria, but are not scholars. All bursaries are subject to means-testing.

Fees per term (2014–2015). Senior School: Boarders £9,855; Day Girls £6,150. Junior School: £1,560–£4,020.

Charitable status. St Swithun's School Winchester is a Registered Charity, number 307335. It exists to provide education for girls aged 11–18 years.

Sheffield High School
GDST

10 Rutland Park, Sheffield, South Yorkshire S10 2PE
Tel: 0114 266 0324
email: enquiries@she.gdst.net
website: www.sheffieldhighschool.org.uk

Founded 1878.
Sheffield High School is part of the GDST (Girls' Day School Trust). The GDST is the leading network of independent girls' schools in the UK. As a charity that owns and runs 24 schools and two academies, it reinvests all its income in its schools. For further information about the Trust, see p. xxi or visit www.gdst.net.

Additional information about the school may be found on the school's website and a detailed prospectus is available from the school.

Chair of Local Governors: Mr M Greenshields, FCA

Headmistress: **Mrs V A Dunsford**, BA Manchester, NPQH

Deputy Head: Mrs N Gunson, BSc, Huddersfield, MA Huddersfield

Senior Teacher: Miss H Thorneloe, BEd Liverpool John Moores

Assistant Head (Examinations, Assessment and Learning): Mrs K Boulton-Pratt, MSc Leicester

Director of Sixth Form: Mr A Redfern, BSc Manchester Metropolitan

Assistant Head (Pastoral): Mrs A Reed, BA Sheffield Hallam

Head of Junior School: Mrs A Jones, BSc South Bank

Director of Finance and Operations: Mr I Kane, BSc Open

Number of Pupils. 943: 210 (Junior School), 536 (Senior School), 197 (Sixth Form).
The school was opened in 1878 and has occupied its pleasant site in the suburb of Broomhill since 1884. It draws its pupils from all parts of the city and from more distant rural and urban areas of Nottinghamshire, Derbyshire and Yorkshire, many travelling on special coaches organised by parents.

The Junior School, Senior School buildings and Sixth Form Centre are adjacent and share gardens, sports hall, hockey/rounders pitch, netball/tennis courts and a gymnasium on the site. An additional hockey and athletics field is situated a short bus ride from the school. In January 2007 the two-form entry Junior School acquired a new Infant building and ICT suite adjacent to the the main junior School building, Melbourne House.

The infants and juniors have their own purpose-built libraries, a science room and art and music studios. The Junior School also provides a breakfast club from 7.45 am and supervised after-school care is available until 5.45 pm.

Recent additions to the Senior School include a new IT suite, Science laboratories, additional Art & Design studios, Music facilities, a Drama studio, two new libraries and a language media suite. A large £1 million extension to the Sixth Form Centre was completed in 2010 and now houses refurbished common rooms, teaching rooms and tutorial bases as well as a new Learning Resource Centre which provides access to key study materials, laptop computers and a wealth of careers resources. There is a modern and bright café-diner as well as a decked outside eating areas for the students. In 2012 the School opened a Year 11 common room with kitchen facilities in the Year 11 base in the Moor

Lodge building. Further developments are scheduled for 2015–2016 and include the refurbishment of the Old Gym and School House to enhance the school's facilities for Sport and Drama and to create an area for cookery.

Curriculum. The usual Junior subjects are taught plus French, German, Spanish, Art, Computer Studies, Art/Technology, Drama, Music and PE. Most lessons are with form teachers but specialist staff teach older girls. In the Senior School, girls generally take 10 GCSE subjects from the range of usual options plus German, Greek, Latin, Drama, Spanish, Art and Design, Business Studies, Geology, Music and PE. Over 75% stay on to the Sixth Form and nearly all go on to Higher Education.

The school attaches great importance to the wide range of opportunities it offers and has received a string of prestigious national awards for the exceptional quality of its extra-curricular provision such as PE Quality Mark with Distinction, Arts Mark (Gold), GO4it, ICT Quality Mark, Eco-Schools Award and the International Schools Award. The school's sporting provision has also been commended nationally for its outstanding quality with teams regularly competing in national finals in addition to fielding national finals teams in film-making and debating. The School has almost 100 lunchtime and after school clubs, which encourage excellence in sport, music, drama and art and offers the full Duke of Edinburgh's Award Scheme. A varied programme of residential trips and expeditions at home and abroad is offered, including Sport, Music, Foreign Language and Art tours. The School has strong community links and has received Independent School Awards consecutively for the past four years for Best Independent-Maintained School Collaboration, Outstanding Community Initiative and Best Leadership Team.

Fees per term (2014–2015). Senior School £3,805, Junior Department £2,682-£2,767.
The fees cover the regular curriculum, school books, stationery and other materials, most extra-curricular activities, but not school meals for Senior girls.

Scholarships and Bursaries. The GDST makes available to the School a substantial number of scholarships and bursaries. The bursaries are means-tested and are intended to ensure that the School remains accessible to bright girls who would profit from the education offered but who would be unable to enter the School without financial assistance.

A large range of scholarships and bursary support are provided at Sheffield High School. From Year 7, a number of prestigious Academic Scholarships are provided each year with an additional four means-tested HSBC Scholarships also available. In the Sixth Form, a range of Scholarships, as well as a further four HSBC Scholarships, are also made available to suitably talented girls.

Charitable status. Sheffield High School is part of The Girls' Day School Trust, which is a Registered Charity, number 306983.

Shrewsbury High School
GDST

Senior School:
32 Town Walls, Shrewsbury SY1 1TN
Tel: 01743 494000
Fax: 01743 494039

Prep School:
Old Roman Road, Shrewsbury SY3 9AH
Tel: 01743 494200

email: enquiries@shr.gdst.net
website: www.shrewsburyhigh.gdst.net
Twitter: @ShrewsburyHigh
Facebook: /Shrewsbury High School

Shrewsbury High School is widely regarded as one of the UK's leading independent schools and is proud of the special blend of academic excellence, all-round opportunity and pastoral care offered. From our website you will gain an insight into the friendly, stimulating environment where all pupils, whatever their talents or interests, have the opportunity to reach their full potential whether this be at the junior or senior level.

Founded in 1885, Shrewsbury High School is part of the Girls' Day School Trust, the leading network of independent girls' schools in the UK. As a charity that owns and runs 24 schools and two academies the GDST reinvests all its income in its schools. For further information about the Trust visit www.gdst.net.

The school's website and prospectus contain comprehensive information about the school. Shrewsbury High School has a Prep School a few minutes' walk from the Senior School. (*See also Prep School entry in IAPS section.*)

Chairman of Local Governors: Mrs S Short, OBE, TD, RGN, RGNT

Head: Mr M Getty, BA Hons Northumbria, NPQH

Deputy Headmistress: Mrs H M Jones, BSc Liverpool

Acting Head of Prep School: Miss C James, BA Hons University of Central England

Director of Sixth Form: Mrs R Saad, BA Manchester

Heads of Departments:

Art: Mr M Warner, BA Gwent
Biology: Mr B Brown, BSc Sheffield
Chemistry: Mr D Payne, BSc Exeter
Classics: Mrs J Lashly, MA Oxford
Drama: Mr N Jones, LAMDA Birmingham
Economics & Business: Mrs M Rumble, BA Staffordshire
English: Mr R Aldridge, BA University of Wales
Geography: Mr J High, BA Liverpool
History, Government & Politics: Mr G Niblock, BA Belfast
Home Economics: Miss L Hughes, BA Liverpool
ICT: Mr T Curtis, BSc West London Inst, Brunel
Mathematics: Mrs J Mills, BSc Cardiff
Modern Languages: Miss R Smith, BA Durham
PE: Mrs L Royston, BA Stellenbosch, South Africa
PSHE: Mrs C Tonks, BA Westminster College
Physics & Science: Dr S Richards, PhD London
Psychology: Mrs M Morgan, BSc Open, MA Open
RE: Ms E J Thomas, BEd Polytechnic of Wales

Director of Finance and Operations: Mr J Harper, BSc, HFMA, ACMA
Admissions Officer: Mrs S Jones
Office Coordinator: Mrs J Humphreys
ICT Development Manager: Mrs E Gosney
Network Manager: Mr L Hodgkinson, BA
Librarian: Mrs A Hale
Marketing Officer: Mrs J Jepson, BA Hons Nottingham
School Doctor: Dr A Cameron, BSc, MBBS, DRCOG, MRCGP
School Nurse: Mrs S Livesey, RGN

Number of Pupils. 626: 426 girls in Senior School, 200 pupils in the Prep School.

Shrewsbury High is one of the highest achieving schools in the country and became the first and only school in Shropshire to win an award at the prestigious Independent School Awards in November 2014. The Award recognises outstanding excellence and at Shrewsbury High School it was the quality of sport that drew particular praise. The sporting work across the school was scrutinised by the judging panel and the judges praised sports initiatives as "long-standing and sustainable", commenting that it was "good to see sport given such a place in the school's life". In addition,

it was once again prestigiously placed in the Times and Telegraph newspapers' Top 100 schools at A Level.

However, we value our broader education with equal importance. Holistic education is where we excel; we aim to ensure that our extra-curricular provision is of the very highest of standards throughout the school, from Music and the Performing Arts through to Sport and beyond. We aim to nurture each student academically and personally through highly skilled teaching in a happy, supportive and well equipped environment.

If you are in the process of choosing a school, the best way to catch the spirit of Shrewsbury High and experience the warmth and enthusiasm of our teaching staff and pupils is to come and visit. Shrewsbury High educates girls seamlessly through from age 3 to 18 and boys from 3 to 13.

Curriculum. Alongside the academic subjects of the national curriculum, the school has excellent facilities for music, art and design, drama and sports.

The Prep boys regularly achieve scholarships to Senior Schools at 13+.

Sports in the Senior School include athletics (including an Elite Athletes Programme), gymnastics (SHS Gymnastics Academy) badminton, cricket, football, rugby, hockey, netball, rounders, swimming, tennis, rowing (Shrewsbury High Boat Club), canoeing, mountain-biking and volleyball. Opportunities exist for participation in debating, drama, Duke of Edinburgh's Award, music, public speaking, Amnesty, and Young Enterprise in the Senior School and ballet, judo, music, gym, crafts, ICT, chess and specialist speech and drama classes at the Prep.

Fees per term (2014–2015). Senior: Years 7 to 9: £4,089, Year 10 & 11: £4,136, Year 12 & 13 (Sixth Form): £4,136.

The fees cover tuition across the regular curriculum, school books, games and swimming, stationery, choral music and other materials. They also cover non-residential curriculum trips and activities. They do not cover lunches, optional extra subjects or the cost of travel to school. Lunch costs are £176 per term. Lunches are compulsory for all prep pupils and senior girls in Years 7 and 8.

Admissions Procedures. Full details are available from the Admissions Officer or on the school website.

Entrance Examinations. The 11+ Entrance Examinations are held in January. Sixth Form Scholarship Examinations are held in the Autumn Term of Year 11.

Open Days. Open Days are held from September to November each year, and also from January to March. We welcome personal visits from parents at any time of year.

Scholarships and Bursaries. The GDST provides a substantial number of scholarships and bursaries. Scholarships are available each year for entry at 11+, 13+ or in the Sixth Form. In addition to academic scholarships, specialist scholarships are available in Sport, Music, Art and Drama for those entering at 11+ or Sixth Form, and in Sport and Music for entry at 13+.

Bursaries are means tested and ensure that the school remains accessible to bright girls who would profit from private education, but who would be unable to enter the school without financial assistance. They are available for entry at 11+. In cases of financial need bursaries may be available after entry to the Senior School.

Charitable status. Shrewsbury High School is part of The Girls' Day School Trust, which is a Registered Charity, number 306983.

South Hampstead High School
GDST

3 Maresfield Gardens, London NW3 5SS
Tel: 020 7435 2899
Fax: 020 7431 8022
email: senior@shhs.gdst.net
           junior@shhs.gdst.net
website: www.shhs.gdst.net
Twitter: @SHHSforgirls
LinkedIn: South Hampstead High School

Founded 1876.
    South Hampstead High School is part of the GDST (Girls' Day School Trust). The GDST is the leading network of independent girls' schools in the UK. As a charity that owns and runs 24 schools and two academies, it reinvests all its income in its schools. For further information about the Trust, see p. xxi or visit www.gdst.net.

Local Governors:
Chairman: Mr J Rosefield, BA Oxon, MBA Harvard
Miss E Clements, BA, BArch, RIBA, FRSA
Mrs K Fear
Prof R Jackman, MA Cantab
Mrs J Solomon
Mrs H Strange
Mrs M Trehearne, MA, BEd

Headmistress: Miss Helen Pike, MA Oxon, MA Michigan, MA London (*History*)

Deputy Heads:
Mr D Bradbury, MSc Keele, MA Open, MInstP, CPhys (*Mathematics and Physics*)
Mrs V Boyarsky, BA Cantab, MPhil London (*History*)
Mrs C Wagner, BA Bristol (*History*)

Head of Sixth Form: Dr D Koch, DPhil Oxon (*History*)
Director of Marketing and Communications: Ms J Dark, LCC (*French & German*)
Director of Finance and Operations: Mr C Euden, BA

Senior School Teaching Staff:
Mrs J Arundale, BSc Lancaster (*Physics*)
Mr P Arundale, BSc Manchester (*Chemistry*)
Mr K Baker, MSc Imperial (*Mathematics*)
Miss P Baker, BA Greenwich
Mrs R J Banfield, BA Brighton (*Physical Education*)
Mrs A Bartnicka, (*German*)
Mrs S Bernstein, BSc London (*Physics*)
Miss L Billings, BSc Bristol (*Mathematics*)
Miss E Blakemore, BA Birmingham (*Geography*)
Miss L Bush, BA Oxford Brookes (*Sport*)
Mr E Cabezas, BA Seville, Spain (*Spanish*)
Mrs J Coates, BA Bristol, MA Hawaii (*History*)
Miss A Cockerill, BA Durham (*Theology and Religion*)
Ms M Cohen Christofidis, (*Philosophy*)
Dr S Collisson, MusB Manchester (*Music*)
Mrs G Cooke, BA Brighton (*Physical Education*)
Mrs O Crossley-Holland, BA Oxon (*English*)
Mr A Crockatt, BMus GSMD, BA ACM (*Music*)
Dr M Egan, BA UCL, MA Essex, PhD UCL (*Politics, History and Critical Thinking*)
Ms N Elliott, BA Manhattanville College, NY, USA (*Biology*)
Miss S Ellis, BMus Cardiff (*Music*)
Mrs S Fanning, BSc London, Dip Arch RIBA (*Design and Technology*)
Miss M Fajardo Duran, (*Spanish*)
Mrs C Finley, CAPES Toulouse (*French and Spanish*)
Miss N Fowler, BA Brighton (*Art*)
Mrs L F Frank, BA York (*Mathematics*)

Mrs C Gallagher, BHSc Leeds (*Biology, Geography and Physics*)
Miss K Garnett, BA Exeter (*Physical Education*)
Mr N Garrard, MA Cantab, MA Manchester (*English*)
Mr C Gerstrom, BA Oxford (*History*)
Miss M Greenland, BSc London (*Computing*)
Miss L Hailstone, BA Exeter (*Drama*)
Mr J Hansford, BA York (*Mathematics*)
Mr B Harkins, MA Cantab, MA London (*English*)
Miss R Helps, MChem Cantab (*Chemistry*)
Mrs D F Hugh, BA Manchester, MBA (*Modern Languages*)
Miss J Humphreys, BSc Birmingham (*Geography*)
Mr N Hunter, BA Liverpool, MA Goldsmiths London (*Art*)
Mrs A S Johnson, BA Birmingham (*Theology and Religion*)
Mr T Jones, BA Cantab (*Mathematics*)
Ms A Kennedy, BA Ulster, MA Philadelphia (*History of Art*)
Mrs E Keyte, MA Edinburgh, MSt Oxon (*English*)
Ms A Kohursheed, MA Surrey (*Arabic*)
Miss L Knowles, BA Sheffield (*History and Theology and Religion*)
Miss A Knox, MSci Durham (*Chemistry*)
Mr P Larochelle, BA Massachusetts (*Drama and English*)
Mrs A Logan, BSc Wales (*Science*)
Miss S-L Lui, BA Oxon (*Classics*)
Miss S G Lopez, BEd Edinburgh (*Physical Education*)
Mrs N Liston, MA Oxon (*Geography*)
Miss N Marchant, BA Cantab (*Classics*)
Mrs E Marriott, BA Oxon (*Classics*)
Miss J Matthews, BSc Loughborough (*Netball*)
Mr C McDonald, BSc Nottingham (*Chemistry*)
Miss H McDougall, BA Oxon (*History and Politics*)
Miss J Meyer, MA/BSc London (*German*)
Dr E Morewood, MA Cantab (*Biology*)
Mrs P Morgan, MA Cantab (*History*)
Miss S Morgan, BA Norwich (*Art*)
Mr M Morley, BA Lancaster (*French and Spanish*)
Miss A Morton, BA Bristol (*English*)
Mr W Moss, BA Cardiff (*Art*)
Mrs J Patel, BA York (*Mathematics*)
Ms P Porter, BSc UMIST (*German*)
Mrs L Raitz, MA Cantab (*French*)
Mrs E J Sanders, BSc Miami (*Geography*)
Ms V M Spawls, BSc Westminster (*Biology*)
Miss R Stern, BA London (*Drama*)
Mr D Suarez, BSc London (*Mathematics*)
Mrs A Svoboda, BSc Imperial College London (*Mathematics*)
Mr C Tanfield, MA Oxon (*Classics and Universities Officer*)
Mr M Trevisan, MA Bath (*Physics*)
Ms V Trinder, MA London (*Design Technology*)
Ms M Vasey, MA Brighton (*Art*)
Miss C Waghorn, BA Exeter (*Psychology*)
Mr J Waller, BA Oxon (*Economics*)
Mr S Waygood, MA Victoria University of Wellington, NZ (*Philosophy and Mathematics*)
Mr G Willson, BA Bath (*Design Technology*)
Ms S Wilson, MA Oxon, MA London, Solicitor [NP] (*English*)
Miss Z Wing-Davey, BA Cambridge (*Classics*)
Dr C J Woodward, BSc, PhD London (*Biology*)
Miss H Young, BA Portsmouth (*Design and Technology*)

Artist in Residence: Miss A Ongar-Perez, MA Eindhoven

Language Assistants:
Mrs B Arnold
Miss D Cobo Montes
Mrs I Rush-Canevet

Librarians:
Miss M Ravetto-Wood

Dr M Brainard, MA, PhD, MSLIS

Head of Junior School: Mrs Gabrielle Solti, BA Oxon

Deputy Head of Junior School: Miss L Szemerenyi, BSc Sussex

Junior School Teaching Staff:
Mrs C Atkinson, MA Cantab
Miss A R Benjamin, CertEd Leeds
Mrs C Bercott, BA Middlesex
Mrs H Blackford, BSc Durham
Ms J Chapman, BA London
Miss V Croly, BA Exeter
Ms L Dawson, Dip TMus Dundee
Mrs S Elian, BA Strathclyde
Miss N Evans, BSc UCL
Mrs R Kersley, BA Newcastle
Mrs L Lane, BSc Manchester
Mrs S-J Lewis, BA London
Mrs J Lowen, BSc Leeds Metropolitan
Miss C MacSwiney, BSc Sussex
Miss S Prevezer, BA Manchester
Ms K Rattenbury, BMus Manchester
Mrs A Ruffini, MA Milan
Mrs L Young, BEd Bath
Mr M Weddell, BEng Brunel

Junior School Librarian:
Ms T Volhard, BA
Mrs P Evans (*Assistant Librarian*)

Support Staff
Admissions Registrar: Ms P Karavla
Admissions (Junior School): Ms N Flack
Deputy Heads' Secretary (Senior School): Miss C Hibbert, BA
Director of IT: Mr R Bailey, BSc
Exams Officer and Music Administrator: Mrs D Greengrass, BSocSc, PG Dip
Finance Manager: Mrs B Quilantang, BSc, CPA
Headmistress's PA and Administrative and HR Manager: Mrs L Cripps, AssocCIPD
Office Manager: Mrs S Bell
Junior School Secretary: Ms S Denton
School Counsellor: Mrs R Shock
School Life Coach: Ms R Leonello
School Nurse: Mrs L Mullins
SIMS Data Manager: Mrs S Halai

The school was opened in 1876. It is situated close to the Finchley Road and Swiss Cottage underground stations and to Finchley Road and Frognal railway station. It is also easily reached by bus from central, north and north-west London.

In the Senior School there are 640 pupils, including 144 in the Sixth Form. There are 260 girls in the Junior School. Entry to the Junior School is at 4 and 7; entry to the Senior School is at 11; occasional vacancies arise at other ages and new girls are welcomed into the Sixth Form if they achieve the necessary entrance qualifications. Full details of the admission procedures are available from the school website: www.shhs.gdst.net

The Junior School occupies two large houses with gardens about 5 minutes' walk from the main Senior School site. The Senior School is in a brand new purpose-built premises which was opened in November 2014. Sixth Form students occupy the Oakwood Centre, a large house which is interconnected to the Senior School. Their common room has its own café and kitchen; they have dedicated classrooms and workspaces as well as full use of facilities in the Senior School building.

At SHHS, the curriculum is designed to provide a secure and imaginative basis for academic progress at each key stage of a pupil's development. Our intention is that all our girls will develop their own enthusiasms and initiative

within a broad educational framework. The curriculum aims to provide our pupils with a rich experience in linguistic, mathematical, scientific, technological, human and social, physical, and aesthetic and creative education. In the Junior School we have a clear focus on developing literacy and numeracy skills and have established an integrated approach to our curriculum whereby we focus the learning across several subjects around a theme. In this way girls develop real depth of knowledge, as well as confidence in key skills such as research, analysing results and interpreting and presenting information. In the Senior School our curriculum has a strong academic spine. English, Mathematics, Biology, Chemistry and Physics are studied from Year 7 to Year 11 by all students; at least one modern foreign language must be studied to GCSE level; History and Geography are studied from Year 7 and at least one of the humanities must be taken through to GCSE. Alongside these students also study Art, Drama, Music, Theology & Religion, Latin, Design Technology and Computing, all of which are available as option choices for GCSE. Most students study for 10 subjects at GCSE of which 2 are their free options. A few choose to study for 11 subjects, taking a third free option. In the Lower Sixth, pupils choose 4 subjects to study at AS level. Many will continue to A2 with four subjects into the Upper Sixth and others will drop a subject and concentrate on 3. Classical Civilisation, Economics, History of Art, Politics and Psychology are offered in the Sixth Form.

Pupils participate enthusiastically in an enormous number of extra-curricular clubs, societies and courses. Creativity in art, writing, music and drama is strongly encouraged at all stages. There are many orchestras, ensembles and choirs. Tuition in almost any instrument and singing can be arranged and girls are prepared for the examinations of the Associated Board of the Royal School of Music. Large numbers of pupils participate in the Duke of Edinburgh's Award Scheme and Young Enterprise Business Scheme.

Fees per term (2014–2015). Senior School £5,074, Junior School £4,023.

The fees cover the regular curriculum, games and swimming, but not school meals or instrumental/singing lessons. The fees for instrumental/singing lessons are detailed in the prospectus.

Scholarships and Bursaries. A number of scholarships and bursaries are available through the GDST to internal or external candidates for entry at 11+ or to the Sixth Form. The bursaries are means tested to ensure that the school remains accessible to bright girls who would benefit from our education but who would be unable to enter the school without financial assistance.

Charitable status. South Hampstead High School is part of The Girls' Day School Trust, which is a Registered Charity, number 306983.

Stamford High School

St Martin's, Stamford, Lincolnshire PE9 2LL
Tel: 01780 484200
Fax: 01780 484201
email: headshs@ses.lincs.sch.uk
website: www.ses.lincs.sch.uk

Motto: *Christe me spede*
Founded by Browne's Hospital Foundation, of Stamford, 1876.

Chairman of the Governing Body: Malcolm Desforges, Esq

***Principal of the Stamford Endowed Schools*: S C Roberts**, MA

Vice-Principal, Head: Mrs Y L Powell, BEd, NPQH

Deputy Head: Mr A D Murphy, BSc, MSc

Director of Teaching and Learning: Mrs L A Johnson, BSc
CPD & Marketing Coordinator: Mrs D E Evans, BA
Head of Careers: Mrs S Killgren, BSc
Head of Sixth Form: Mrs C A Hawkins, BSc
SES Chaplain: The Revd M Goodman, BA, BTh, MTh
Director of ICT: N A Faux, MA
Librarian: Mrs A Virgo

Teaching Staff:

Miss K Ainsworth, BA	Miss L Hornby, BA
Miss K Allen, BSc, MSc	Mrs J Husbands, BSc
Mrs D Ashley, BA	Mrs N Ingrams, GRSM
Revd G B Austen, MA,	RAM, LRAM
MPhil	Miss E L Jackson, BSc
Mrs T R Bennie, BSc	Mrs B Joint, BEd
Dr Y Birch, Bsc, PhD	Mr R Keenan BA PGCE
P A Bowden, MA	Miss E Kerbrat, BA, MA
Mrs C A S Boyfield, BA	Mrs J Lewis-Gorman, BA
Miss K Burghardt, BSc	Mrs G Moss, BSc
Mrs M L Cade, BSc	Mrs E Mount, BEd
Mrs L M Cannon, BSc	Miss H Myles, BA
N S A Clift, BA	Miss F Pace, BA
C Coles, MA	Mrs A Rackham, BA
A J Cox, BA	Miss A D Reilly, BSc
Mrs A J B Cox, BA	O Roland, BA
Dr A Crookell, BSc, PhD	Mrs E Salt, BA
Miss S J Davies, BA	Mrs V Saunders, BA
Mrs K Dexter, BA	K Sekhar, BSc
A J Elliott, BEd	Miss V A Sheriff, BA,
Mrs Y Forman, BA	PGCE
R M Gale, BA	A Skailes, BA
Mrs P A Galloway, RBTC	Mrs C Skailes, Beng,
P Galloway, BA, Drama	PGCE
Dip	Miss A Squibb
Mrs A P Gossel, BA	Mrs C Vie, BA
Mr G Gould, BEd	Mrs N J Watson, BA
Miss J Hamphlett, BSc	Mrs A Wenban, BA
Miss E A Hardy, BSc	G J Whitehouse, BEd
G C Harman, BSc	C Williamson, BA
Mrs L Harte, BSc	Mrs K Wilson, BEd
Dr T Hill, BSc, PhD	Mrs V Wilson, MA
Mrs L Holden, BSc	Mrs Y Woodings, PGCE

Music Department:

G E Turner, BA (*Director of Music*)
D McIlrae, BMus, HED (*Assistant Director of Music*)
S Chandley, CT ABRSM (*Head of Brass*)
D Leetch, MA, GRSM, LRAM (*Head of Strings*)
Mrs J E Roberts, GRSM, LRM, ARCM
N S Taylor, BA

Visiting Music Staff:

S Andrews (*Kit Drum/Percussion*)
F Applewhite (*Violin, Viola*)
J Aughton (*Flute*)
S Barber (*Organ*)
C Bell, BSc, LRAM, ARCM (*Guitar*)
Mrs M Bennett, LRAM, LTCL (*Singing*)
Mrs K Bentley, GTCL, LTCL (*Cello, Double Bass*)
F Black (*Singing*)
Mrs S Bond, GLCM, LLCM TD, FLCM (*Singing*)
G Brown, BMus (*Oboe, Pianoforte*)
Mrs H Brown, BA (*Clarinet*)
P J Casson (*Saxophone, Clarinet*)
Revd Mrs J Dumat, ARCM (*Clarinet*)
Mrs J Dustan (*Flute*)
J Forrow (*Classical Guitar*)
N Gray (*Electric Guitar*)
Mrs E Hanlon, ARMCM (*Pianoforte*)
Mrs J Lamb (*Pianoforte, Accordion/Keyboard*)
Mrs S Latham (*Violin, Viola*)
Mrs C Lee, LRAM (*Violin*)
Miss F Maclennan (*Pianoforte*)
Mrs M Maclennan, LRAM, ARCM (*Pianoforte*)

Mrs A McCrae (*Bassoon, Pianoforte*)
Mrs E Murphy, GTCL, LTLL, PGCE (*Violin, Pianoforte*)
D Price, LRAM (*Brass*)
Mrs G Spencer, CertEd, ACRM (*Pianoforte*)
Mrs A Sumner, CertEd, ARCM (*Pianoforte*)
Mrs E A Taylor, BA (*Violin, Viola*)
Mrs L Williamson, LTCC (*Pianoforte*)

Boarding:

Welland House:
Miss E Kerbrat (*Resident Housemistress*)
Mrs M Tyers (*Assistant Housemistress*)
Mrs J Rose (*Assistant Housemistress*)

Park House:
Mrs C Vié (*Resident Housemistress*)
Mrs S Johnson, Mrs W Hartley, Mrs J Rose (*Assistant Housemistresses*)
Mrs S Kavanagh (*Deputy Housemistress*)

Medical Officer: Dr J Barney, MBChB, DAvMed, DOccMED, MRCGP

Introduction. Stamford High School is one of three schools within the overall Stamford Endowed Schools Educational Charity, along with Stamford School (boys) and Stamford Junior School, the co-educational junior school.

Numbers and Boarding Houses. There are 633 girls aged 11–18 years including boarders. The main point of entry is at age 11 though applications are welcomed at any stage up to the Sixth Form. Girls who enter through the Junior School progress automatically on to the High School without further competitive entrance testing. Boarders are received from the age of 8 (in the Junior School). There are two Boarding Houses for girls including a Sixth Form Boarding House where the girls have single or shared study bedrooms. The School accepts full, weekly and three-night boarders.

Fees per term (2014–2015). Day £4,482; Full Boarding £8,303; Weekly Boarding £7,239; 3 Night Boarding £6,291.

These fees include all stationery, textbooks and games. School lunches for day girls are at additional charge.

Registration Fee £50. Acceptance Fee £250.

Extras. Individual music lessons, Speech and Drama, Dancing (Riding for boarders only).

Curriculum. The curriculum is designed to ensure all girls have a balanced educational programme up to age 16 thus avoiding premature specialisation. The National Curriculum is broadly followed but much more is added to the curriculum to make it stimulating and rewarding. Most girls are entered for at least 9 GCSE examinations and for GCE AS and A Level examinations leading to university entry. In partnership with Stamford School, all Sixth Form girls have access to the full range of A Level subjects offered across the two schools providing an exceptionally wide choice of 28 subjects.

Throughout their time in the school girls are prepared for the examinations of the Associated Board of the Royal Schools of Music in music and The London Academy of Music and Dramatic Art for speech and drama. There is much scope for creative activities in Music, Art and Drama and state-of-the-art facilities for Information & Communication Technology, including access to the Internet. The Director of Music for the Stamford Endowed Schools ensures that the Music Department works very closely with Stamford School providing access to a wide range of activities for orchestras, bands, Chapel Choir and choirs. There are joint drama productions and a Performing Arts Studio.

Sport and Physical Education include Hockey, Netball, Tennis, Swimming, Golf, Judo, Athletics, Volleyball, Basketball, Badminton, Trampoline, Gymnastics and Squash. There is a very full programme of extra-curricular activities including Olympic Gymnastics, Athletics and Taekwondo. There is a heated, indoor swimming pool, a Sports Hall and a floodlit artificial hockey pitch. The Duke of Edinburgh's Award Scheme operates at Bronze, Silver and Gold levels with a considerable number of girls taking part each year. There is a thriving, mixed CCF offering RN, Army and RAF sections. There are many school clubs and societies and a thriving weekend activity programme.

Entrance Examinations are held in January.

Scholarships and Bursaries. The Schools offer a range of scholarships for pupils entering into years 7, 9 and 12 (Sixth Form). Scholarships are less common for pupils entering into other years but may at times be available. There are scholarships for Academic, Music, Art, Sports and All-Rounder performance. Means-tested bursaries can be applied for by families of pupils who would otherwise not be able to benefit from a Stamford education. Please see our website for full details.

Charitable status. As part of the Stamford Endowed Schools, Stamford High School is a Registered Charity, number 527618.

Stonar

Cottles Park, Atworth, Wiltshire SN12 8NT
Tel: 01225 701740
Fax: 01225 790830
email: office@stonarschool.com
website: www.stonarschool.com
Twitter: @Stonarschool
Facebook: /Stonar

Day and Boarding School from Nursery to Sixth Form. Stonar currently educates girls aged 2–18 and boys aged 2–11. From September 2016, boys will be admitted into Year 7 and co-education will be extended through the Senior School.

Board of Directors:
Mr A McEwen, NACE UK Ltd (*Chairman*)
Mr P Piñán, NACE Educational Services Ltd

Head: Mr Toby Nutt, MSc, BSc Hons, PGCE, NPQH

Bursar: Mrs Sam Jadeja, ACA, BSc Hons

Deputy Head, Curriculum: Dr Sally Divall, MA, PhD, PGCE

Deputy Head, Pastoral: Mrs Nicola Hawkins, MSc, BSc Hons, PGCE

Senior Teacher: Mrs Alison Rivers, BSc Hons, PGCE

Senior Staff:
§ *Part-time*

Mrs S Aikman, BA Hons, PGCE (*Head of Modern Foreign Languages*)
Mrs C Bennett, BA Hons, PGCE (*Head of Sixth Form, Geography, RS*)
§Mrs H Brain, BA Hons, PGCE (*Learning Support*)
§Mrs T Brain, BA Ed Hons (*English*)
§Mrs J Brighouse, BA Hons, PGCE (*French, EAL*)
Mr S Butler, BA Hons, PGCE (*Head of Business Studies*)
Mrs L Carolan, BA Hons, PGCE (*Art*)
Mrs J Cross, BEd Hons (*Head of Learning Support, Art*)
Mrs R Cross, BEd (*Maths, ICT*)
Mrs S Crouch, NNEB (*Teaching Assistant*)
Mr A Curtis, MSc, BSc Hons, PhD (*Head of Careers, Psychology*)
Mrs C Deans, MA, TEFL Dip (*Head of EAL*)
Mr J Dyde, BA Hons, PGCE (*Head of English*)
§Mrs T Gates, BA Hons, PGCE, PGDip (*Learning Support*)
Mrs C Giles, MEd, BA Hons, PGCE (*EAL*)

Mr N Goodall, BA Hons, MMus, PGCE (*Director of Music, ICT*)
Miss V Gray, BSc Hons, PGCE (*PE*)
§Mrs D Harding, BEd (*Learning Support*)
Miss L Havranek, BA Hons, PGCE (*French, Spanish, Houseparent of Hart*)
Mrs J Helps, BEd, ADTS (*Head of Home Economics*)
Mrs M-P Jones, BA Hons (*French*)
Miss P Kirby, BSc Hons, PGCE (*Subject Leader of Biology*)
§Dr F Martinelli, BSc Hons, PhD, PGCE (*Science*)
§Mrs S McQueen, BA Hons PGCE (*EAL*)
§Mrs L Medworth, MA, PGCE (*Maths, Learning Support*)
Miss S Meehan, BA Hons, PGCE (*Assistant Director of Music, English*)
Mr R Miller, BA Hons (*Director of Sport and PE*)
Mrs S Moore, BSc Hons, PGCE (*Maths, Houseparent of Ganbrook*)
Ms P Nix, BSc Hons, PGCE (*Head of Chemistry*)
Mrs L Noad, BA Hons (*RS, Assistant Houseparent*)
Mr A O'Hanlon, BA Hons, PGCE, PGDip (*Head of Art & Photography*)
Mr N Proud, MA, BA Hons, PGCE (*Head of Drama*)
Mrs A Rivers, BSc Hons, PGCE (*Head of Maths*)
Mrs L Ross, BA Hons PGCE (*Head of History*)
Mrs G Sherman, BSc, MCLIP, MBCS (*Head of ICT, Latin*)
Mrs L Smith, BSc Hons, PGCE (*Head of Geography*)
Mrs T Tilley, BSc Hons, PGCE (*PE, Biology, Houseparent of Curnow*)
Mr D Wicks, MSc, BSc Hons, PGCE (*Head of Science, Physics*)
Mrs J Wigley, BLib Hons, MCLIP (*Learning Resources Supervisor*)
Mrs P Willcox, BA Hons, PGCE (*Learning Support*)
Mrs R Wood, BSc Hons (*Learning Support*)
Miss A Young, BSc Hons, PGCE (*Assistant Director of PE and Sport*)

Prep School:

Head of Prep: Mr M Brain, BA Ed Hons (*Year 6 Tutor*)
Deputy Head of Prep: Mrs A Thethy, BEd (*Year 5 Tutor*)
Mrs T Atwell, BA Ed Hons (*Reception Class Tutor*)
Mr G James, BA Hons PGCE (*Year 2 Tutor*)
Mrs E Proud, BSc Hons, PGCE, Dip M (*Year 3 Tutor*)
Mr J Shack, BA Hons, PGCE (*Year 4 Tutor*)
Mrs M Tober, MEd (*Year 1 Tutor*)
Mrs K Whittleton, Cert Ed (*Part-time Teacher*)

Head of Early Years: Mrs K Willder, BA Hons, PGCE, EYPS
Mrs D Carnie, RGN (*Nursery Assistant*)
Mrs P Corbett, BA Hons, NVQ3 (*Nursery Assistant*)
Mrs J Redsull, NNEB (*Forest School Leader*)
Mrs A Rudman, NVQ3 Nursery Assistant
Mrs A Sewell, NVQ3 (*Nursery Team Member*)
Mrs S Shellard, NVQ3 (*Nursery Leader*)
Mrs K Willder, BA Hons, PGCE, EYPS (*Upper Nursery Class Tutor*)

Equestrian Centre:
Mr D Scaife, FBHSI, BE AcCoach UKCC Level 3 (*Director of Riding*)
Miss J Chilcott, BHSII (*Senior School Instructor*)
Miss J Foster, BHSAI (*Prep School Instructor*)
Miss E Halsey, BHSII (*Prep School Instructor*)
Miss J Edge (*Centre Manager*)
Miss R Hogg (*Yard Manager*)
Mr T Passmore (*Yard Manager*)
Miss J Cockin (*Head Groom*)
Mr M Bailey (*Equestrian Apprentice*)
Miss K MacKeith (*Equestrian Apprentice*)
Miss L Evans (*Equestrian Apprentice*)
Mrs E Sowels (*Equine Secretary*)

Registrar: Mrs K Ibbott

Ethos. Stonar combines an impressive all-round education, with a wide-ranging curriculum and a wealth of extra-curricular activities. Pupils go on to achieve outstanding academic results, with 100% gaining their first choice of university course in 2014. Stonar develops the talents of every individual, enabling pupils of all abilities to achieve their potential across and beyond the formal curriculum. There is a positive work ethic and quality pastoral care. Curiosity, confidence and independence are encouraged so that pupils leave school well-equipped for the challenges of adult life and keen to contribute to the wider community.

Curriculum. A talented and committed staff offers pupils a broad and flexible curriculum, with literacy and numeracy firmly at the centre of the Prep school timetable and an individual choice from wide ranging options in addition to the core of Science, Maths, English, a foreign language and ICT at GCSE. AS and A2 courses can include Psychology, Photography, Business Studies, PE and IT. Able and Talented pupils are identified throughout school and opportunities to extend their learning exist both within the curriculum and in extra-curricular activities.

Considering the wide range of academic ability, Stonar's results are outstanding and pupils go on to university courses ranging from Medicine, Law and Accountancy to Geology, Veterinary Science and Music. Talented artists proceed to a variety of Art Foundation Courses. Young riders take up careers in eventing or go for the Equine Studies option. The BHS stage examinations are available to pupils in Year 11 and the Sixth Form.

Extra-curricular Activities. The school's internationally renowned Equestrian Centre provides tuition for all ages and abilities. Facilities include indoor and outdoor arenas, cross country training fields and a hacking track. The Equestrian Centre has the top level of BHS accreditation and is also a Pony Club centre.

The Sports Hall, indoor Swimming Pool, Astroturf, Theatre, Music, Sixth Form & Arts Centre offer first-class opportunities for sport, music and drama. A timetabled tutorial period provides a rolling programme of careers advice, health education, study skills, first aid, self-defence, citizenship and industrial awareness. An extensive programme of after-school activities includes academic, sporting and life skills options which challenge and extend pupils' development. In the Sixth Form, girls enjoy debating, dance, film studies, aerobics and the Leith's Cookery Course. The Duke of Edinburgh's Award scheme flourishes at Stonar.

Boarding. Boarders live in comfortable, family-style houses, each with internet access. Pupils of any religion and of all nationalities are welcomed and can work towards IGCSE English, if this is not their first language.

Admission. Straightforward entrance procedures via Stonar entrance examinations in early January and school report at appropriate ages.

Fees per term (2014–2015). Prep Day £2,555–£3,545; Senior Day £4,595–£4,965; Prep Boarding £6,020; Senior Boarding £8,960.

Scholarships and Bursaries. Year 7 & Year 9 Entry: Academic, Art, Drama, Sport, Music and Riding Scholarships are offered. Scholarship assessments take place in January following the Entrance Examination.

Sixth Form Entry: Academic, Art, Drama, Sport, Music, Riding and All-Rounder Scholarships are available. Scholarship examinations, assessments and interviews held in November.

Means-tested Bursaries are available. A Forces Bursary is available to Senior School boarders whose parents are current serving members of HM Forces.

Governance. Stonar is a part of NACE Educational Services Limited, Company Registration No. 8441252, Registered Address: 17 Hanover Square, London, United Kingdom W1S 1HU.

Streatham & Clapham High School

GDST

42 Abbotswood Road, Streatham, London SW16 1AW

Tel:	020 8677 8400 (Senior School)
	020 8674 6912 (Junior School & Nursery)
Fax:	020 8677 2001
email:	enquiry@schs.gdst.net
	senior@schs.gdst.net
	junior@schs.gdst.net
website:	www.schs.gdst.net

Streatham & Clapham High School is a distinguished historical foundation. It was founded, as Brixton High School, in 1887 by the Girls' Public Day School Trust as one of its earliest member schools. HRH Princess Louise, Duchess of Argyll opened its buildings in Wavertree Road, London SW2, in 1895, now the site of the Junior School. In 1994 the Senior School moved to Abbotswood Road, London SW16, into the imposing buildings of the former Battersea Grammar School.

The School offers an inspiring, enlightened and intellectually challenging education for its pupils in a lively, vibrant and warmly supportive environment. The family ethos of Streatham & Clapham High School enables its masters and mistresses to know, value and nurture each pupil as an individual. The School celebrates diversity and draws strength from its rich social and cultural mix.

The School's core belief is that all members of its community should be inspired to outperform expectations on a daily basis. The pursuit of excellence is thus the School's defining feature. It nurtures pupils to attain success across the widest spectrum of activity, extending far beyond the conventional 'academic' horizon. In so doing, they learn the beauty of reason, the allure of the aesthetic, and the vitality of the physical. The School's pupils thus learn to navigate the landscape of the human spirit and achieve beyond the realms of expectation.

The Board of Local Governors:
Mrs S Wrixon, BA, PGDip Journalism (*Chairman*)
Miss M Heggie, BSc, MSc, RN, RMW
Mrs F Smith, BA Dunelm, PGCE
Mrs J Rawnsley
P Wright, ACA, BSc

Head Master: **Dr Millan Sachania**, MA Cantab, MPhil, PhD, FRSA

Second Master: R Hinton, BSc, PGCE (*Mathematics*)

Deputy Head Mistress: Mrs A Hooper, BSc, PGCE (*Biology*)

Assistant Head Master (Sixth Form): O Hogben, BA, PGCE (*Drama*)

Director of Studies: Miss Nicola Shepherd, BSc, PGCE (*Mathematics*)

Head of Junior School: T Mylne, BA, PGCE

Director of Finance & Operations: J Gibson, Grad Inst Personnel Management, MCIPD

Senior Mistress: Mrs G Cross, BA, MA, PGCE (*English*)

Assistant Masters and Mistresses (Senior School):
* Head of Department
¹ Head of Year

Mrs S Akintunde, BSc, MSc, GTP (*Chemistry*)
Mrs A Allen, BA, PGCE (*English*)
Mrs S Aslam, BA, PGCE (*Mathematics*)
Ms R Baker, BA, PGCE (*Art*)
P Baldock, BMus, MA, PGCE (*Music)

Mrs C Barry, BA, Dip SLD (*Learning Support*)
Mrs E Basson, BA, PGCE (*Physical Education*)
¹Mrs K Birtwistle, BSc (*Biology*)
Mrs F Brent, BA, PGCE (*Art*)
¹Madame C Casset, BA, MA, PGCE (*French*)
K Chaudery, BSc, MSc, PGCE (*Mathematics*)
Dr S Choudhry, MEng, PhD, PGCE (*Science*)
A Christie, MA Oxon, PGCE (*Classics*)
Mrs J Cobain, BA, PGCE (*English*)
Mrs C Copeman, BA Cantab, PGCE (*Mathematics*)
A Doddridge, BSc, PGCE (*Geography*)
Miss M Durello, BA, PGCE (*Italian*)
Ms B Elton, BA, PG Dip D&T, PGCE (*Design and Technology*)
Mrs M Evans, BA, PGCE (*Drama*)
Miss S Fitzgibbon, BSc (*Physics*)
Mrs E Fitzsimons, BA, PGCE (*English*)
Miss C Forber, MMaths, PGCE (*Mathematics*)
P Frost, BA, ACMA, PGCE (*ICT*)
Miss C Garcia-Gomez, BA, PGCE (*Spanish*)
¹Miss H Gibbons, BA, MA, PGCE (*History*)
Miss A Gunga, BA, PGCE (*Religious Studies*)
T Heaton, BA, QTS (*Design and Technology*)
Ms F Helszajn, BA (*Spanish*)
Mrs A James, BSc, PGCE (*Biology*)
C Johnston, BA, MEd, PGCE (*Economics, Government & Politics*)
Miss G Kennedy, BSocSc, PGCE (*Geography*)
Mrs J Kirby, BA, PGCE (*Mathematics, Examinations Officer*)
Miss M McDonagh, BSc, PGCE (*Physical Education*)
Miss M Merrigan, BSc, PGCE (*Physical Education*)
W Nolan, BA, PGCE (*Classics*)
Ms J Rawstron, BMus, PGCE (*Music*)
Mrs S Sellers, BA, PGCE (*History*)
Miss A Sillitoe, BA, PGCE (*Art*)
¹Miss C Skews, BEd (*Physical Education*)
B Smith, BEd, PGCE (*Design and Technology*)
M Spooner, BSc, MA, PGCE (*Physics*)
Ms F Stone, BA, PGCE (*Mathematics*)
Dr E van Heerden, BA, BA, BEd, MSocSci, DPhil, PGCE (*Psychology/Government & Politics*)
Ms J Watts, BD, PGCE (*Religious Studies, Critical Thinking*)
Mrs A Weymes-McElderry, BA, PGCE (*Modern Foreign Languages*)
Mrs E Wheeler, BSc, PGCE (*Biology*)
Mrs K Wheeler, BEd (*Physical Education*)
G Wright, BSc, PGCE, PGDip Innovation and Educational Leadership (*Chemistry, *Science*)
Ms D Zoromba, BA, PGCE (*English*)

Head Master's PA: Mrs B Wheeler, BMus, BSc, PGDip Ed Mgmt
Registrar: Mrs P Warner

General information. Streatham & Clapham High School is an independent, academically selective school for girls aged 3–18, with just under 700 pupils on the roll. Girls aged 3–11 and boys aged 3–5 attend the Nursery and Junior School, located in spacious buildings with outstanding facilities in Wavertree Road in Streatham Hill. The Senior School inhabits a four-acre site focused on a symmetrical 1930s building designed by J E K Harrison, FRIBA in a delightfully tranquil and leafy oasis of south London, next to Tooting Bec Common, where the soundscape is dominated by birdsong.

Many girls live locally and an increasing number walk or cycle to School, encouraged by the School's commitment to sustainable travel. The Senior School is 10 minutes' walk from Streatham Hill National Rail station and twenty minutes from Balham National Rail and Underground. Other pupils come from further afield, including Battersea, Clapham, Wandsworth, Dulwich, Tooting and Brixton. The

School is also within easy reach of the theatres, museums and galleries of central London.

Facilities. The School enjoys first-class facilities for learning, providing an environment that enables girls to develop their interests and strengths both inside and outside the classroom. The School keeps up-to-date with teaching methods and innovative techniques, such as interactive online learning, and use them to engage and extend its pupils. The senior-school facilities include two ICT suites, a music suite including a dedicated music technology suite, a recital hall, two design and technology workshops, a magnificent full-size indoor sports hall, dance, art and pottery studios, and sports pitches and tennis courts. The Sixth Form is housed in the Millennium Building, which comprises several study areas, a common room, a kitchen area and a dedicated, state-of-the-art café. The Junior School and Nursery have large and well-equipped premises, including a new library and a spacious indoor and outdoor area built specifically around the needs of the Nursery children. The School is soon to embark on a £13 building development project, which will provide for a new sixth form centre, a creative arts faculty, new dining facilities, and freshly landscaped grounds.

Academic matters. The ability profile of the School is significantly above the national average, with a proportion of pupils being far above the national average. In recent years, the School has been in the top 20% of independent schools in terms of its public examination results: for instance, in 2014 over 40% of pupils achieved an A* or an A grade in at least nine GCSE subjects. Virtually all sixth-form students proceed to the most competitive Russell Group universities.

Curriculum. Pupils in the Upper Third, Lower Fourth and Upper Fourth (Years 7 to 9) study the core disciplines of English, Mathematics, and Science. Other subjects offered include Art, Classics, Computing, Design & Technology, Drama, French, Geography, History, Italian, Latin and Ancient Greek, Music, Physical Education, Religious Studies, and Spanish. All of these subjects (except Classics) are available in the Fifth Form (Years 10 and 11); pupils follow the GCSE or IGCSE courses depending on the subjects they have chosen.

The School offers a range of subjects for study at AS and A Level, including Art and Design, Biology, Chemistry, Classical Civilisation, Latin, Critical Thinking, Design and Technology, Drama and Theatre Studies, Economics, English Literature, Geography, Government and Politics, History, French, Italian, Spanish, Mathematics, Further Mathematics, Music, Physical Education, Physics, Psychology and Religious Studies. Sixth-form students also have the opportunity of pursuing the Extended Project Qualification to extend their interests and knowledge.

The timetable is organised into 80 teaching periods over a two-week cycle. Each period is of 40 minutes' duration, except for the 'Kinza' period, which is 55 minutes in length (see below).

Enrichment programme ('Kinza'). Kinza, an Arabic term meaning 'hidden treasure', is the unique enrichment programme of timetabled weekly sessions throughout the year. Every Kinza activity is designed to encourage a love and respect for learning for its own sake, utilising the interests and expertise of staff. The activities provide a wide spectrum of choice for each pupil, covering an extremely broad range of activities, including Mandarin, Forensic Science, Bee-keeping, Origami, Saints and Their Attributes in Italian Painting, Meditation, Arabic, Programming Software, and much more. Opportunities to deepen aspects of the broad knowledge acquired through Kinza are afforded through co-curricular trips, individual research, and collaborative working processes in a vertical tutoring system, with younger pupils learning side-by-side with older girls. Each participates in several different activities during the course of the year.

Activities. The School has a thriving co-curricular life, with societies and clubs in the fields of Art, Design and Technology, Classics, English, Geography, History, ICT, Mathematics, Modern Foreign Languages, Science and Religious Studies, as well as more specialised activities such as Young Enterprise. There are a very large number of performing arts activities, pupils having the opportunity to perform in a number of dramatic productions during the school year or to belong to around 15 music ensembles, including choirs and orchestras, which annually lead the School's Carol Service at Southwark Cathedral. Pupils may belong to a legion of sporting clubs and fixtures, and have the opportunity to participate in a number of outdoor educational activities, such as the Duke of Edinburgh's Award. A busy programme of trips and expeditions is scheduled, for instance Classics and Languages trips to Greece and Italy, a History trip to discover the Paris of Henri IV, and Music tours of the Continent. Pupils have recently trekked across the Atlas Mountains in Morocco and reached the Base Camp of Mount Everest. The School's proximity to central London makes possible many excursions to concerts, museums, art galleries and theatres.

Pastoral care. The School does not view outstanding pastoral care as an 'add-on' to its academic programme. Neither does it believe that a 'hothouse' atmosphere is desirable or healthy. The School's core belief is that girls achieve best if they are happy and settled in their social relationships. Hence the 'family' ethos of the School, which holds that the way in which individuals are nurtured and valued is intrinsic to the pupils' progress and success. All members of staff, up to the Head Master, are easily accessible to pupils, and to ensure that the School's social and emotional care is comprehensive and alert, the School has a Deputy Head Mistress with oversight of pastoral matters. In conjunction with the work of the Heads of Year and the sixth-form mentoring scheme, this enables the School to identify challenges or problems early and then work with pupils and where necessary their parents to overcome them. It also helps the School to encourage and celebrate real progress and achievement every day. The strong prefectorial system and school council under the leadership of the Head Girl ensure that the pupil voice has suitable influence in shaping the life and work of the School.

Admission. There are six principal admission stages: by assessment for the Nursery (3+ years), 4+ and 7+, and by competitive entrance examination at 11+ and 13+ and at Sixth Form entrance. Occasional places sometimes arise at any age; interested parents are advised to contact the Registrar. All candidates for 11+ entry are called for interview in the Michaelmas Term. Applicants for 13+ entry will have individual interviews after the 13+ entrance examination.

All senior-school applicants sit the School's entrance examination. The 11+ examination comprises papers in English and Mathematics. Applicants for 13+ entry sit papers in English, Mathematics and Science.

The transfer of a pupil from the Junior to the Senior School is not automatic but contingent on the School's assessment of the pupil's suitability for admission into the Upper Third Form (Year 7).

Fees per term (2014–2015). Senior School £5,013, Junior School £3,895, Nursery £2,968.

The fees are inclusive of non-residential trips and extras, but exclude the cost of lunch.

Academic scholarships. A number of academic scholarships, worth up to a maximum of 50% of fees, are available for 11+ entrance. They are not means-tested. Candidates who perform highly in the 11+ entrance examination are invited to a scholarship interview, and awards are made on the basis of individual candidates' performance in the entrance examination and interview. A number of sixth-form academic scholarships are also available, on the basis of a written assessment and interview.

Specialist scholarships. Specialist scholarships are awarded at 11+ in the fields of Art, Drama, Music and Sport. Further details are available on the school website.

Bursaries. A small number of means-tested bursaries are available at 11+. All requests are considered in confidence and application forms are available from the Registrar.

Charitable status. Streatham & Clapham High School is a member of The Girls' Day School Trust, which is a Registered Charity, number 306983.

Sutton High School
GDST

55 Cheam Road, Sutton, Surrey SM1 2AX
Tel: 020 8642 0594
Fax: 020 8642 2014
email: office@sut.gdst.net
            admissions@sut.gdst.net
            junioroffice@sut.gdst.net
website: www.suttonhigh.gdst.net
Twitter: @SuttonGirlsHigh
Facebook: /Sutton-High-School-GDST
LinkedIn: /SuttonHighSchoolOGA

Founded in 1884, Sutton High School is part of the GDST (Girls' Day School Trust). The GDST is the leading network of independent girls' schools in the UK. As a charity that owns and runs 24 schools and two academies, it reinvests all its income in its schools. For further information about the Trust, visit www.gdst.net.

A more detailed prospectus may be obtained from the school or downloaded at www.suttonhigh.co.uk

Chairman of The School Governing Body: Professor
   Deborah Bowman

***Headmistress*: Mrs K Crouch**, BSc Leicester, NPQH

Head of Sixth Form and Upper School: Ms E Clark, BSc
   Southampton

Head of Lower School: Mrs V O'Keeffe, BA Oxford

Head of Junior School: Mrs A Cooper, BEd Exeter

Deputy Head of Junior School: Miss A Musgrove, BA Ed
   Warwick

Director of Studies: Mrs J Ward, BSc Westminster MSB

Director of Finance & Operations: Mr M Leeson, BSc City
   University

Director of External Relations: Mrs D Young

Marketing and Communications Manager: Mrs N New, BA
   Middlesex and Reims, France

Admissions Secretary: Mrs C Filby

Sutton High School is an academically selective Independent day school for girls aged 3 to 18 which provides a broad and challenging curriculum to its pupils. Strikingly positive relationships between the girls and their teachers, both within the classroom and beyond, make a significant contribution to the quality of the girls' academic and personal development. Our girls feel safe and cared for in a warm and secure environment which gives them the space to develop a strong sense of who they are and their place in the community. The school is a member of the Girls' Day School Trust and distinguished former pupils include the novelist Susan Howatch, BBC correspondent Sue Littlemore, and Ruth Kelly, MP.

There are over 630 girls in the school: 264 aged 3–11 years in the Junior School and 368 aged 11–18 years in the Senior School. The Sixth Form is over 70 strong. Girls enter the school aged 3+, 4+, 11+, 13+ or 16 after taking the school's own entrance tests. With occasional places available throughout the school year. Open Mornings take place in the Autumn, Spring and Summer Terms when girls provide enthusiastic and informative tours of the school and the Head provides a welcoming talk and is available to answer questions. to book a place at one of the scheduled Open Mornings please visit www.suttonhigh.co.uk or for further information and personal tours during the school day please contact the Admissions department on admissions@sut.gdst.net.

Aims and Values. Sutton High is a diverse community dedicated to enabling its pupils to develop their intellect and talents and a confidence to believe that their aspirations are achievable. From an early beginning, we encourage the girls to be honest, reliable and trustworthy. Academic rigour is valued at all stages and the focus in the classroom and beyond is on challenge, engagement and enjoyment. Learning is celebrated. The school has a well qualified and highly motivated staff, both teaching and non teaching. All members of the community are valued and given the opportunity to flourish in a caring and supportive ethos.

Our vision is that Sutton High gives girls:

- A rich and diverse curriculum in which they can achieve at all levels within a creative and vibrant atmosphere.
- The self confidence to be independent learners and achieve beyond the school environment.
- An enquiring and discriminating mind and a desire for knowledge.
- Respect for others.

We value the partnership which exists between school, parents and community and the part it plays in realising this vision.

Situation. The school occupies a central position in Sutton and is reached easily by train or bus from Dorking, Leatherhead, Epsom, Carshalton, Wallington, Worcester Park, New Malden, Wimbledon and Burgh Heath. Our own school buses offer a service every morning from the Wimbledon area. The school is only 5 minutes' walk from Sutton Station. The school has developed a specific green travel plan which is supported by the London Borough of Sutton.

Facilities. The Junior and Senior Schools provide well-resourced accommodation for all major subjects. The Sports Complex is home to a Dance and Fitness studio, changing facilities, a hospitality and viewing area for parents and visiting teams, large sports hall and indoor swimming pool. Girls have access to astroturf pitches, athletic facilities, netball and tennis courts. There is a dedicated music building and well-equipped art facilities. A new Sixth Form Centre was opened in September 2013 providing the Sixth Form girls with dedicated teaching rooms, private study areas, common rooms and a Gym. The Nursery has just completed a wonderful refurbishment programme and the new Junior School Playground was opened last Spring.

Curriculum. Girls are admitted to the Junior School from 3 years of age following an informal assessment and enter our Nursery. The National Curriculum creates a framework for teaching and Key Stage 1 and 2 SATs are taken. In Junior School there are many varied opportunities for extra-curricular activities including Music, ICT, Sport, Drama, Chess and Mandarin. Girls study French from 4 years of age and there is specialist teaching in many subject areas. Pre-school and after-school care is available from 7.30 am to 6.30 pm for all Junior School girls. Girls are encouraged to show kindness towards others, which is developed in our daily Act of Worship, our teaching, work in the local community and fundraising for charity. The school recognises the need for independent learning and homework is set regularly.

In the Senior School girls follow an enriched version of the National Curriculum in preparation for entrance to university and the professions. The school regularly sends students to Oxford, Cambridge and Russell Group Universities

where girls successfully study a wide range of courses. In 2014, 2 girls gained places at Oxford to study French & Russian and Law. 58% of the girls achieved places at Russell Group Universities.

In Years 7–9 girls participate in a broad curriculum that, while encompassing Curriculum 2000, provides many extension opportunities. Two modern languages are studied and Latin from Year 7. It is a hallmark of the school that Science is taught as three distinct subjects by specialist teachers. At GCSE girls study 9 or 10 subjects including a core of English, IGCSE Mathematics, a Modern Language, Religious Studies and Sciences together with optional subjects from a wide range. Emphasis is placed on the use of ICT as a tool to enhance all aspects of education. Wherever possible, cross-curricular opportunities are exploited, such as in the French and Geography residential visit to Lille for Year 8 girls. Careers advice is given from Year 7 and all girls are able to take extra lessons in Speech and Drama and Music. Each year over 300 girls pass the Poetry Vanguard and Guildhall Speech and Drama Examinations and over 100 pass the Associated Board and Trinity College Music Examinations.

In the Sixth Form, students benefit from teaching styles that are supportive but provide opportunities for independent study. Students currently take four or five AS/A2 Levels from a wide range of disciplines and the Extended Project Qualification. In 2014, the girls achieved a 100% pass rate at A Level, 79% gained A* to B grades with 100% taking up places at University. The Extended Project Qualification is an integral part of the Sixth Form and in 2014 38% of girls achieved an A* for their EPQ project.

Extra-Curricular Activities. Each year an excellent and varied programme of concerts, musicals, plays, art exhibitions and festivals in both Junior and Senior Schools enables members of the drama groups, choirs and orchestras to perform in public.

An elected committee of girls, led by the Head Girl and her deputy, contributes to the smooth running of the school. The Sixth Form also runs societies, produces musicals and concerts in aid of charity. A House system operates throughout the Senior School culminating in the award of the House Cup at the end of the Spring Term each year.

Sport at Sutton High School is inclusive rather than exclusive and provides all abilities with an opportunity to take part in a team and represent their school. Many girls take part in swimming galas, Hockey, Netball, Gymnastics, Badminton, Rounders and Tennis matches, including all major county tournaments; several girls reach county and national squad level each year. In 2013 the Senior School has the opportunity to visit South Africa on the Hockey and Netball tour. The Junior School Gymnastics team are visiting Holland to compete in a National competition.

A wide variety of clubs and activities are provided for girls during the lunch break and after school. In addition, parents run the Otter and Centipede Clubs which offer sports and coaching sessions. Staff regularly arrange cultural visits to places as varied as New York, Paris and Yorkshire and an exchange programme is now in place with the Fachhochschule in Tübingen, Germany. The Junior School organises annual residential visits in Years 4, 5 and 6.

A number of girls take part in Mathematics and Physics challenges and competitions with an excellent record of success. The school has a good reputation for debates and public speaking. In the Sixth Form girls form their own companies and compete in the Young Enterprise competition and have won the Sutton and Merton area 'Best Company' award in previous years.

Community Links. In addition to Harvest and Christmas parcel collections for the elderly, the whole school organises fundraising activities for their chosen House charities.

The school has a thriving Friends of Sutton High Association which arranges school fairs each year and a range of social activities. Money raised by the Association has been used on many projects including the upgrading of performance facilities in both the Junior and Senior Schools and equipment for the Discovery Zone in the Junior School.

Close links with a local boys' school have resulted in such productions as *Little Shop of Horrors, The Boyfriend, Grease, West Side Story, The Wedding Singer* and in 2012 *Our House*.

Fees per term (2014–2015). Senior School £4,929, Junior School £3,835, Nursery (full-time) £2,920.

The fees cover the regular curriculum, examination entry fees, school books, stationery and other materials, games and swimming, but not optional extra subjects or lunch. Details of the fees for extra subjects, including instrumental music, and Speech and Drama, are available from the school.

Scholarships and Bursaries. Following the ending of the Government Assisted Places Scheme, the GDST has made available to the school a substantial number of scholarships and bursaries. The bursaries are means tested and are intended to ensure that the school remains accessible to bright girls who would be unable to enter the school without financial assistance. At present there are, available to internal or external candidates, part-fee scholarships for entry at 11+ and for entry at 16+ into the Sixth Form. Performance Scholarships are awarded at 11+ in Sport, Music and Drama and in the Sixth Form for Music, Drama, Sport and Art.

Charitable status. Sutton High School for Girls is part of The Girls' Day School Trust, which is a Registered Charity, number 306983.

Sydenham High School
GDST

19 Westwood Hill, London SE26 6BL
Tel: 020 8557 7000
email: info@syd.gdst.net
website: www.sydenhamhighschool.gdst.net

Founded 1887.

Sydenham High School is part of the GDST (Girls' Day School Trust). The GDST is the leading network of independent girls' schools in the UK. As a charity that owns and runs 24 schools and two academies, it reinvests all its income in its schools. For further information about the Trust, see p. xxi or visit www.gdst.net.

Additional information may be found on the School's website and a more detailed prospectus may be obtained from the School.

Chair of Local Governors: Ms G Evans

Headteacher: **Mrs K E Pullen**, BA Warwick, MA London, PGCE

Deputy Head: Dr C Laverick, BA Swansea, MEd OU, PhD Hull

Deputy Head (Student Development): Mr K Guest, MA St Mary's Twickenham, PGCE

Head of Junior School: Ms C Boyd, BA London, PGCE

Head of Sixth Form: Ms J Henderson, BA Durham, PGCE

Pupil numbers. Senior School 420, Junior School 225.

For over 125 years, Sydenham High School has been committed to the fundamental aim of providing a first-class education for girls – grounded in a tradition of academic excellence and focused on developing in our pupils the skills and confidence to face the challenges and enjoy the opportunities of life both in and beyond school.

Occupying the grounds of a Victorian mansion, we enjoy an open, leafy setting in a location that is easily accessible by public transport. Our Junior School has its own facilities with ready access to those of the Senior School. The School has a distinctive blend of Victorian buildings and purpose-built accommodation refurbished to a high standard. Our facilities are impressive and include an extensive library with online facilities, several ICT suites and a design technology centre. We have seven science laboratories, five of which have been recently refurbished and a Performing Arts Centre, featuring a Theatre and Recital Hall. New dining facilities, including a café area, are due to open at the end of 2014.

Excellent on-site sports facilities comprise a Sports Hall and all-weather pitch, supplemented by extensive sports fields close by in Lower Sydenham. We produce fine sportswomen who compete in a variety of sports at national level and our elite athlete support programme helps girls who train outside school to balance their school and sporting commitments.

Curriculum. The School offers a broad curriculum, ensuring all our pupils are stimulated and excited by learning. English and maths provide a solid foundation while languages offered include French, German, Spanish, Italian and Latin. All students study biology, chemistry and physics. Creative and practical subjects include design technology, art, PE, music and drama. Humanities include History, Geography, Religious Studies and Classical Civilisation. All pupils receive a thorough grounding in ICT, taught as a discrete subject and confidently used as a cross-curricular tool.

In the Sixth Form, further mathematics, business studies, government & politics, ICT, theatre studies, PE and sociology are offered in addition to the normal range of AS and A Level courses. Specifically-focused preparation is provided for entry to prestigious universities, including Oxford and Cambridge. Our co-curricular and careers programmes bring in speakers and take students out to visit exhibitions and industry. Huge opportunities are available for leadership across the school, including SydApprentice, Young Enterprise, sports teams, administering clubs, and an extended prefect system.

Students make informed choices of GCSE, AS and A Level subjects, supported throughout by specialist staff. Work in Careers and PSHE also informs the decision making process. Our students are offered places at top universities, while some take gap years abroad. The breadth of extra-curricular opportunities encourages all pupils to broaden their interests and develop personal skills. Drama is popular with numerous clubs and productions at the Junior and Senior Schools. A diversity of opportunity for making music is available to pupils whatever their instrument or level of expertise. Highly-qualified peripatetic staff teach instrumental lessons. Specialist music staff train school ensembles, orchestra and choirs which perform in, and beyond, the School on a regular basis. Involvement in the wider community is encouraged through our successful Duke of Edinburgh's Award Scheme and charity work.

Fees per term (2014–2015). Senior School £4,864, Junior School £3,822.

School fees include examination fees, textbooks, stationery and other materials, choral music, PE and swimming, ISCO and Careers counselling. They do not include instrumental music, speech and drama, and after-school clubs.

Scholarships and Bursaries. *Entrance Scholarships*: The Girls' Day School Trust provides a number of scholarships each year for entry to the Senior School at 11+ and directly into the Sixth Form. Scholarships are awarded on academic merit and no financial means test is involved.

Bursaries: The GDST provides bursaries which are means-tested and intended to ensure that the School remains accessible to bright girls who would benefit from our education, but who would be unable to enter the School without financial assistance. Bursaries are awarded on the basis of financial need and academic merit. Details can be obtained from the Admissions Secretary. It is recognised that occasions will arise when some form of short-term assistance is required – a small fund exists to help pupils taking public examinations in such cases.

Sydenham High School Scholarships: Art, music, drama and sports scholarships may be awarded on entry at 11+ in addition to our academic scholarships.

Charitable status. Sydenham High School is part of The Girls' Day School Trust, which is a Registered Charity, number 306983.

Talbot Heath

Rothesay Road, Bournemouth, Dorset BH4 9NJ

Tel: 01202 761881 Senior School Admissions
          01202 763360 Junior School Admissions
          01202 755410 Finance
Fax: 01202 768155
email: office@talbotheath.org
website: www.talbotheath.org

Motto: *Honour before Honours*

The School is an Independent School, founded in 1886 by private effort and transferred to Trustees in 1898 and is administered under a scheme drawn up by the Ministry of Education in 1903. It is a Church of England Foundation and pupils of all denominations are welcome. This School is committed to safeguarding and promoting the welfare of children and young people. The School is also committed to a policy of equal opportunity.

Governing Body:
Chairman: Mr G Exon
Vice Chair: Mrs C Norman
Dr T Battcock
Mrs D Leadbetter
Dr A Main
Mr R Peak
Revd Canon Dr C Rutledge
Mrs R Small
Mrs S Thomas, LLB
Mr D Townend
Mr D Whelan
Mrs C Sutcliffe

Head: **Mrs A Holloway**, MA Oxon

Deputy Head, Academic: Dr S Orchard, BSc Southampton, PhD
Deputy Head, Pastoral: Mrs C Stone, BSc Hons Royal Holloway London
Head of Junior School: Mrs K Leahy, BA Hons London
Deputy Head of Junior School: Mrs J Rook, BA Hons London

Heads of Faculty Senior School:
Mrs T Magrath, MA York (*English*)
Mrs J Hooton, BSc Hons Nottingham (*Mathematics*)
Mr A Hill, BMus Hons, FTCL (*Creative Arts & Technology*)
Mr M Gibson, BSc Hons Hull (*Science*)
Mrs H Chapleo, BSc Hons Kingston (*Humanities*)
Miss L Marks, BSc Hons Loughborough (*Physical Education*)
Miss A Klemz, PGCE Liverpool

Visiting teachers also attend for Piano, Violin, Violoncello, Double Bass, Flute, Clarinet, Oboe, Bassoon, Horn, Saxophone, Trumpet, Trombone, Tuba, Percussion, Singing, Dancing, Speech Training and Voice Production, English for foreign students, French, Spanish and German Conversation.

Director of Support Services: Mr C Evans
Medical Officer: Dr M Shaw

Director of Finance: Mrs J Cameron
Head's PA/Office Manager/HR Manager: Mrs C Snow
Head of Admissions: Mrs K Wills

There are some 327 girls in the Main School, of whom 80 are in the Sixth Forms and 40 are Boarders. There is a Junior Department for about 147 girls between the ages of 7 and 11. The Pre-Preparatory department caters for 120 girls aged 3+ to 7.

Talbot Heath is among the longest-established schools in the Bournemouth area, with over a century of success. The school enjoys an attractive wooded site and outstanding facilities for Art, Drama, Music and the Sciences (new Art and Drama studios opened in September 2000, new Science Centre opened in March 1999) together with good ICT provision and extensive modern accommodation for a wide range of sports activities.

The school follows the best practice of the National Curriculum but does not undertake Key Stage testing at levels 1, 2 and 3.

Examinations. 21 subjects are offered to GCSE (including Core Subjects) and Advanced Level, and girls gain places at a variety of universities, including Oxford and Cambridge, or go on to other forms of higher education or professional training.

Admission. Girls are admitted into the Junior School by examination at 7 and above and into the Main School by examination at 11+, 12+ and 13+. The Entrance Examination is held annually in January and girls must be capable of working with those of their own age. Entry to the Pre-preparatory Department requires no examination.

Boarding Houses. St Mary's Boarding House is located in the School grounds, Miss Scarr being in overall charge.

Fees per term (2014–2015). Tuition: Senior School: £4,113; Junior School: £1,886–£3,355; Kindergarten according to sessions.

Boarding (in addition to Tuition Fees): £3,137 (full); £2,831 (weekly).

Scholarships and bursaries are available and there is also a discount for daughters of Service families and the clergy.

Charitable status. Talbot Heath is a Registered Charity, number 283708. It exists to provide high quality education for children.

Tormead School

Cranley Road, Guildford, Surrey GU1 2JD

Tel: 01483 575101
Fax: 01483 450592
email: registrar@tormeadschool.org.uk
website: www.tormeadschool.org.uk
Twitter: @TormeadSchool

Founded 1905. Academically selective independent school for around 760 day girls from 4 to 18 years of age.

School Council:
Chairman: C W M Herbert, Esq, BSc Hons
Vice-Chairman: W T Gillen, Esq, MA

Governors:
Miss R Edbrooke, BEd
Mrs R Harris, BA Hons, ACA
Dr C Kissin, MBChB, MRCP, FRCR
Prof G Nicholls
P J O'Keefe, Esq, RIBA, MCIOB, MIMgt
R Jewkes, Esq, BEng
Dr J Page, LLM, BSc, MB BS, MRCP, FRCR, MFFLM
D M Williams, Esq, BA, FCA
Cllr J Wicks

Bursar and Clerk to the Governors: Mr M O'Donovan, BA Canterbury

Headmistress: Mrs Christina Foord, BA, MPhil, PGCE Birmingham

Deputy Headmistresses:
Pastoral: Miss T King, BA Cambridge, PGCE Oxford (*English*)
Curriculum: Mr J Coles, BA Swansea, PGCE UEA (*Geography and IT*)

Senior School Staff:
* *Head of Department*

Mrs A Arnold, BA, PGCE Keele (*French/German*)
Miss R Bayes, BSc UEA, PGCE Kingston (*Science*)
Ms A Beecher, BA, Grad DipEd Melbourne (*English*)
Miss D Bell, BA, PGCE Greenwich (*Physical Education*)
Mrs H Boczkowski, BSc Bath Spa (*Head of Food Technology*)
Mr T Breslin, BA Sussex, PGCE Buckingham (*History*)
Miss S Buchan, BA & MEng Cambridge, PGCE Oxford (*Physics*)
Mrs E A Burton, BA, PGCE Birmingham (*Mathematics, Physical Education*)
Mrs N Chaffe, MA Open University (*English*)
Mrs L A Chapple, BSc Manchester, PGCE Southampton, Dip Geosciences OU, Dip Molecular Science OU (*Science*)
Dr I Ciuca, MA Bucharest (*Head of Classics*)
Mrs S Clarke, MA Cantab, DipLib, MCLIP (*Senior Librarian*)
Mrs S Culhane, BA Washington USA, PGCE Goldsmiths London (*English*)
Mrs F Khan-Evans, BA London, MA Surrey Institute, PGCE London (*Head of Art*)
Mrs C Don, MA Oxford, PGCE Surrey (*Mathematics*)
Mrs T A Dyer, BA Swansea, PGCE London (*Spanish, French*)
Mrs S Elmes, BA King's College London, PGCE Cardiff (*Religious Studies*)
Mr R Ewbank, BA, PGCE Goldsmiths London (*Art, Technology, ICT*)
Mrs A Ferns MA Cantab (*Assistant Librarian*)
Miss K Finch (*Physical Education*)
Mrs K Fletcher, BA UCL, CTEL, PGCE Trinity College London (*Classics*)
Ms A Franchot, MA Paris (*French Language Assistante*)
Mrs S M Gibbs, BSc Bangor, PGCE Nottingham (*Science*)
Mrs C Gibson Oxley, MSt Oxford, PGCE Oxford (*Head of Sixth Form*)
Mrs J Glazier, BSc Exeter, PGCE Gloucs (*Mathematics*)
Mrs S E Haddy, BSc Surrey (*Second in Charge of Mathematics*)
Mrs S Harrod Booth, MA Kingston, PGCE Cambridge (*Head of Mathematics*)
Miss J Hansen, BA Pace University, New York, PGCE Cambridge (*Drama*)
Mr P Heap, BA Hull, PGCE Manchester Metropolitan (*Teacher in Charge of Drama*)
Ms T Hetherington, BA Westminster, MA St Martin's College, PGCE Roehampton (*Art, 3D Studies*)
Miss J Hoffmann, BSc, PGCE Nottingham (*Mathematics*)
Mr M Holford, BMus Surrey, PGCE Roehampton, ARCO, LTCL (*Assistant Director of Music*)
Mrs S Jones, BSc Surrey, PGCE St Mary's College (*Geography*)
Mr J Keey, MA St Andrews, PGCE St Mary's College (*Religious Studies*)
Mrs C Kennedy, BA Cambridge, MA Twickenham, PGCE GTC (*Head of RS*)
Mrs E Lange, MA ESCP Europe, BA North Carolina USA (*MFL*)

Miss M Langlet, MA Toulouse le Mirail, PGCE Oxon (*Teacher in Charge of French, Spanish*)
Mrs D Ledgerwood, MA Oxon, PGCE Reading (*Head of Chemistry*)
Mrs G M Mackay, BA, UED Rhodes (*English*)
Mrs M Meats, BSc Leicester, MSc Open, CertEd (*Head of Biology*)
Mr A Merryweather, BA East Anglia, PGCE Buckingham (*Director of Music*)
Mr S Millward, BSc Nottingham, PGCE Manchester (*Science*)
Mrs P Moodie, BA Manchester Metropolitan, PGCE Manchester (*Teacher in Charge of Spanish, French*)
Miss E Murray, MA St Andrews, Dip Law, Manchester, PGCE Cumbria (*Head of History*)
Mrs M O'Brien, BEd Chichester (*Director of Gymnastics*)
Mr J Parsons, BA & MA Lancaster, PGCE Reading (*Head of English*)
Miss I Painter, BA Durham (*Classics*)
Mrs K Perkins, BA Surrey (*Physical Education*)
Mr G Press, BSc, CertEd Brunel (*Teacher in Charge of Design and Technology*)
Mrs G Ralfe, BSc Aberystwyth, PGCE Exeter (*Geography*)
Mrs E Robinson, MA Oxon, PGCE York (*Spanish*)
Mrs M Soltysik, BA Lille, PGCE Cantab (*Language Assistant/French*)
Mr J South, BA & MA London, PGCE London (*History*)
Mr J E Sykes, BA Westminster, MSc LSE (*Government & Politics*)
Mrs C Tee, BA South Bank, CertEd South Bank (*Food Technology*)
Mrs L Tidy, BA Chichester (*Physical Education*)
Ms S Travis, MA, PGCE Cantab (*Chemistry*)
Miss M Uezzell, BA Southampton (*Physical Education*)
Miss E Walshe, BSc Greenwich, PGCE Surrey (*Science*)
Mrs S Wightman, (*Head of PE*)
Mr D Wilkinson, BMus Huddersfield, PGCE Durham, DipPsych Open University (*Head of Psychology*)
Mr K Wild, BA Bristol, PGCE Oxford Brookes (*Head of Modern Foreign Languages, German*)
Mrs C Williams (*Head of Careers, Head of Economics*)
Mr P Wilkinson, MA Cantab, MSc UCL, MBA Brunel, CEng, CSci, MIChemE (*Head of Physics*)
Mrs A Woodfine, MEng Oxford, PGCE Chichester (*Mathematics*)

Junior School Staff:
Head: Mrs L Salmond Smith, BA East Anglia, MMus Hull, PGCE Gloucestershire, MBA Keele
Deputy Head: Mrs K Moulder, MA Kingston, BEd Avery Hill

Mrs E Alderman, BSc Leeds (*Class Teacher*)
Mrs G Blackburn, BSc Sussex, RSA Dip Helen Arkell Dyslexia Centre (*Special Educational Needs, Dyslexia*)
Mrs C Boyd, BA UWE (*Class Teacher*)
Miss E Brailsford (*Class Teacher*)
Mrs C Broadway, BSc, PGCE Roehampton (*Design Technology Teacher*)
Miss M Colyer, BSc York, PGCE Cantab (*Class Teacher*)
Mrs S Doggett, NNEB Kingston (*Teaching Assistant*)
Mrs N Fry (*Class Teacher*)
Mrs S Heslop (*After-School Supervision*)
Miss S Insch (*Class Teacher*)
Mrs P Inskip, BSocSc, PGCE, CNAA (*Class Teacher, Mathematics Coordinator*)
Mrs J Johnson, BA Durham (*Key Stage 2*)
Mrs J L Norman, MPhil Reading, BSc Nottingham (*Teaching Assistant*)
Mrs P Oldroyd, CertEd Reading (*Teaching Assistant*)
Miss L Payne, (*Teaching Assistant*)
Mrs K Perkins, BA Surrey (*Physical Education*)
Miss H Rees, BA York, PGCE Birmingham (*Class Teacher*)

Mrs K Richards, BEd De Montfort (*Class Teacher*)
Mrs S Vega, BA, PGCE Durham (*Music*)
Miss L Warden, BEd Hons Kingston (*Pre-Prep Class Teacher*)

Registrar: Mrs C Poole
Headmistress's PA: Mrs Y Nixon
Junior School Secretary: Mrs D Adams/Mrs N Overgaard

Tormead is an academically selective independent day school for girls, aged 4 to 18. Founded in 1905, it stands in pleasant grounds, close to the centre of Guildford. The atmosphere is lively and the teaching stimulating and challenging. Standards and expectations are high and girls leave the school as confident, articulate and self-reliant young women, ready to meet the challenges of university and beyond. Almost all girls leave Tormead to read for degrees at the university of their choice. On average, 10% gain an Oxford or Cambridge place.

An extensive extra-curricular programme provides further challenge and opportunity. We believe that a breadth of interests, skills and initiative are an essential complement to academic success for the future lives of our pupils.

The school has a lively and active musical life with orchestras, various chamber groups, ensembles and choirs as well as a highly popular and talented Jazz Band which has undertaken tours to various European countries. Drama, dance, public speaking and debating, Young Enterprise, The Wings of Hope Achievement Award, and Duke of Edinburgh's Award are all very well supported and sixth form girls have the opportunity to travel to Vietnam and Zambia.

A wide range of sports is on offer and there is a busy programme of fixtures in Hockey, Netball, Rounders, Athletics and Swimming in all of which we compete with great success. Gymnastics has been a particular strength for some years with our teams competing successfully at national level.

Fees per term (2014–2015). Reception £2,330, Years 1–2 £2,575, Years 3–4 £3,830, Year 5–6 £3,890, Years 7–13 £4,550.

Scholarships and Bursaries. Academic, Music and Art Scholarships are offered at 11+ and 16+. Bursaries are available at 11+ and 16+ entry and are dependent on the level of parental income.

Tormead Old Girls' Association. Email: toga@tormeadschool.org.uk.

Charitable status. Tormead Limited is a Registered Charity, number 312057. It exists to provide education for able girls.

Truro High School for Girls

Falmouth Road, Truro, Cornwall TR1 2HU
Tel: 01872 272830
Fax: 01872 279393
email: admin@trurohigh.co.uk
website: www.trurohigh.co.uk
Twitter: @TruroHigh
Facebook: Truro High

Founded 1880. Independent, formerly Direct Grant.

Governors:
President: The Rt Revd Tim Thornton, BA, Bishop of Truro
Chairman: Mr R Hygate, FRICS
Mrs S Bennet
The Very Revd Roger Bush
Mr I Halford, MA Oxon
Mrs S Hall, BVet Med, MRCVS
Mr David Hobbs
Mr Peter Lamble

Mr J Nichols, MA Cantab, FRSA, FCollP
Mr J Sharp, MA, FCSI
Mrs H O'Shea, BA Hons
Mr N Trefusis, RN, DL
Miss K Whitford, LLB Hons
Mrs S Wilding, FCA

Headmaster: Dr G Moodie, BA, MA, Dip Arts, PhD

Deputy Head: Mrs M Smith, BA Hons
Head of Sixth Form: Mrs A Hanson, BSc Hons
Head of Preparatory School: Mrs A Miller, BSc Hons
Head of Upper School: Mr P Crump, BA Hons, NPQH
Head of Lower School: Mrs A Simmonds, MA

Assistant Staff:
* *Head of Department*

Art, Design Technology and Food:
*Mrs J Tutin, MA
Mrs L van der Lem, BSc Hons
Mrs S G Weiringa, BSc, MBA (*Textiles*)
Miss C Rowe, MA (*Art Technician*)

Business Studies/Economics:
*Mr J Brand, CertEd, BEd Hons, MA

Careers & Work Experience:
Mr P Crump, BA Hons, NPQH
Mrs K Pooley, BSc Hons

Classics:
*Mrs S J Brown, MA Oxon
Dr G Moodie, BA, MA, Dip Arts, PhD

English and Drama:
*Mrs J A Holland, BA Hons
Miss A Whitney, BA Hons
Mr I Tutin, BA Hons
Mr P Crump, BA Hons, NPQH
Mrs J Trewellard, BA Hons
Mrs S Bradbury, BA Hons, PgDip (*Speech and Drama peripatetic*)

Geography:
*Mrs J Rice, BA Hons
Miss S Morris, BA Hons

History:
*Mr G Ford, BA Hons

ICT:
Mr A Purchase, BSc Hons
Mr S Bullock, BSc Hons (*ICT Manager*)
Mrs B Clark, BSc Hons (*Data Manager*)

Mathematics:
Mrs A Hanson, BSc Hons
*Miss C Harding, BSc Hons
*Mrs C Goodright, BSc Hons
Mrs A Lamble, BSc Hons

Modern Languages:
*Mrs S Murley, BA Hons
Mrs M Smith, BA Hons
Mrs A Simmonds, MA
Mr T Wylde, BA Hons
Mrs F Ferris, BA Hons

Music:
*Mr R Norman, BA Hons
Mr M Steer, BA Hons

Peripatetic Music Staff:
Miss K Allen (*Singing*)
Mrs R Brenton (*Clarinet, Saxophone*)
Ms J Courtenay (*Piano, Theory*)
Mrs J Edwards (*Violin, Viola*)
Mr M Edwards (*Piano*)
Mr G Graham (*Guitar*)
Ms F Hooper (*Flute*)

Ms J Kershaw (*Brass*)
Mrs M Hoadley (*Singing*)
Ms H Robinson (*Cello*)
Mrs N Williams (*Guitar*)

Physical Education:
*Mrs K Barbary-Redd, BEd Hons
Mrs J Barnfield, BEd Hons
Mrs G Tregay, CertEd
MIss K Horam, BEd Hons

Psychology:
Miss K Webster, BSc Hons

Preparatory Department and Nursery:
Head: Mrs A J Miller, BSc Hons
Mrs K Griffin, BA Hons
Mrs Y Simpson, BEd Hons
Mrs K A Roberts, BEd Hons
Miss H Mills, BEd Hons, MEd
Mrs E Symons, BA Hons
Mrs R Bateson, BA Hons
Miss T Kemp, NNEB (*Nursery Manager*)
Miss S Turriff, Deputy Nursery Supervisor
Mrs L Kingdon, NNEB (*Teaching Assistant*)
Mrs J Dick

Religious Philosophy & Ethics:
*Mr P J Mothersole, BA Hons, MA
Mrs R Westley, BA Hons
Mrs J Trewellard, BA Hons
Mr I Tutin, BA Hons

Science:
*Mr J Dean, BSc Hons, NPQH
Mrs M Sharp, BSc Hons
Mr G Bennett, BSc Hons
Mrs C Hallam, BSc Hons
Mr S Loosley, BSc Hons
Miss E Bird, BSc Hons
Mrs K Haigh (*Laboratory Technician*)

Special Needs:
*Mrs K Wood, SpLD, CCET Level A
Miss S Morris, BA Hons
Mrs R Westley, BA Hons

Librarian: Mrs R Westley, BA Hons

Medical:
Dr C Newton, MB, ChB, MRCGP, DRCOG, DFFP, DCH
Mrs H Ramsay, SRN

Bursar: Mr B Login, MA, MBA, FCIS, MBIFM
Estates Supervisor: Mr G Williams
HR Manager: Mrs H Andrew, BA Hons, MCIPD
Accountant: Miss C Beacham, BA Hons, HND
Assistant Accountant: Miss K Hocking, AAT
Payroll Assistant: Mrs S Talbot
Headmaster's PA and Registrar: Mrs F Ellison
Development Officer: Mrs F Osman, BA Hons
Marketing Assistant: Miss G Kennard, BA Hons
School Secretaries: Mrs K Cameron, Mrs C Shaw
School Receptionists: Mrs F Knight, Mrs K Grose
Reprographics: Mr C Beechey-Newman, BSc Hons

Truro High School combines a Nursery and Preparatory Department of approximately 100 girls aged 3–11 (Nursery: boys and girls aged 3–5) and a Senior School of approximately 300 girls (aged 11–18). Boarding accommodation is provided from the age of 7. Entry is based on the school's own selection procedure. Academic, Music, Sport, Drama and Art Scholarships are offered on entry to Years 7 and 12. An All-Rounder Boarding Scholarship is offered on entry to Year 9. Means-tested Bursaries are available from Prep 3 up.

A broadly based curriculum is provided to GCSE including Art, Religious Philosophy & Ethics, English, History, Geography, Latin, French, German, Spanish, Mathematics, Physics, Chemistry, Biology, Music, Art, Food and Nutrition, Textiles, Theatre Studies and Physical Education. Further subjects at AS/A2 in the Sixth Form are Business Studies/Economics, Classical Civilisation, and Psychology alongside an Extended Project Qualification. A Careers Department exists to advise girls and parents on openings available over a wide field including entrance to Universities and other institutions of Higher Education. Music forms an important part of the curriculum and there are two orchestras, two strong choirs, jazz band and numerous ensembles. The school has good facilities: six well-equipped Science laboratories, a Modern Languages block with digital laboratory, a new Studio Theatre, Textiles and Cookery rooms, three Information Technology suites, indoor heated swimming pool, tennis and netball courts and an all-weather hockey/athletics pitch. Pupils in the Sixth Form have their own Sixth Form Centre with individual cubicles for private study and a wi-fi Study Zone. Two outstanding boarding houses are located in the centre of the campus.

There is a wide range of extra-curricular activities and all pupils are encouraged to participate. The school enjoys good relationships with other schools in the neighbourhood.

Fees per term (2014–2015). Tuition: Pre-Prep £1,545-£1,854; Prep £3,602; Senior School £3,851.

Boarding (in addition to Tuition fees): £3,401 (weekly), £3,487 (full), £3,587 (overseas).

Charitable status. Truro High School for Girls is a Registered Charity, number 306577.

Tudor Hall

Wykham Park, Banbury, Oxon OX16 9UR
Tel: 01295 263434
Fax: 01295 253264
email: admissions@tudorhallschool.com
         admin@tudorhallschool.com
website: www.tudorhallschool.com
Twitter: @TudorHallSchool
Facebook: /TudorHallSchool

Motto: *Habeo Ut Dem*

Board of Governors:
Mr J Gloag (*Chairman*)
Mr J W Lewis (*Chairman of Finance & General Purpose Committee*)
Mrs Kathy Figeons (*Director of THSE Ltd*)

Mr A T Brett	Miss H Holden-Brown
Mr C Dodson	Mrs L Mayne
Miss C Duncombe	Mr A Mobley
Mr B T Gamble	Mr P C R Whittle
Mrs V Harley	Mr R P Wilson
Mrs R Hayes	

Senior Management Team:

Headmistress: Wendy Griffiths, BSc Wales, PGCE London

Bursar: Helen Jackson
Deputy Head: Clare Macro, MA Oxon, PGCE Oxon
Deputy Head (*Pastoral*): Rani Tandon, BA Birmingham, PGCE Manchester Met
Assistant Head (*Sixth Form*): Ian Edwards, BSc Newcastle, PGCE UEA
Senior Teacher: Julia Thorn, BA Reading, MSt Oxon
Senior Teacher: Lucy Keyte, BA Nottingham, PGCE Warwick
Head of Teaching and Learning: John Field, MA Oxon, PGCE Oxon
Extra-Curricular Coordinator: Susie Jeffreys, BSc Plymouth, PGCE Exeter

Director of Operations: Lesley Evans

Teaching Staff:

Joani Adkins, BSc OU, CertEd Oxon (*Learning Support*)

Sarah Allitt, BSc Oxford Brookes (*Learning Support*)

Elaine Austin, BA Leicester, PGCE Cantab, TEFL, EAL (*EAL, Classics*)

Carola Beecham, BA Exeter QTS (*English*)

Jo Benlalam, BMus, AKC, PGCE London (*Head of PSHE, Music*)

Sarah Bourne, MA Cantab, PGCE (*Classics*)

Amanda Brauer, BA Kent, PGCE Bedford (*Physical Education*)

Elizabeth Buckner-Rowley, BA Portsmouth, PGCE Leeds (*Spanish*)

Paul Carine, Outdoor Leadership Lancs, PGCE Keele (*Geography, Director of Outdoor Education*)

Alan Christopher, MA Essex, BTEC Kingshurst, HND Coventry (*Drama*)

Sheila Craske, BA Oxon, PGCE Manchester Poly (*Head of Art, Photography*)

Celia Dawson, BSc London, RSA Dip SPLD Oxon, PGD PRM OU (*Head of Learning Support*)

Nicola Donson, BMus Lancaster, PGCE Nottingham Trent (*Music, PSHE*)

Gerard Duncan, PGDSST, BPE University of Otago, New Zealand (*Physical Education*)

Pip Duncan-Jones, BSc Loughborough, PGCE Leeds (*Director of Sport*)

Ian Edwards, BSc Newcastle, PGCE UEA (*Mathematics*)

John Field, MA, PGCE Oxon (*English*)

Mair Forde, BA Oxon, MA Birmingham, (*Head of Spanish*)

Sara Fordy, BA Winchester, PGCE Oxon (*Textiles*)

Jonathan Galloway, BA Middx, PGCE London (*Head of Religious Studies*)

Alison Gamble, MA London, CPE Law (*Head of Senior History & Politics*)

Marie Genot, MA Provence, France, PGCE UWE (*French, Spanish*)

Shazia Gleadell, BA Birmingham, PGCE Chester (*Religious Education*)

Harriet Granville, BA London, QTS (*History*)

Emily Gray, BA Cantab, MA, PhD Courtauld (*Head of History of Art*)

Kerri Hadfield, BA Leeds, PGCE Canterbury (*Head of Geography*)

Jane Haggarty, CertEd Bedford (*Head of Home Economics*)

Kate Hardiman, BEng Leeds, QTS (*Mathematics*)

Matthew Harper, BA Oxon (*French*)

Marilyn Harris, BA London, PGCE Bulmershe (*French*)

Kate Hart, BA Manchester Metropolitan, PGCE Birmingham (*Head of Textiles*)

Sarah Huggins, BA, PGCE Bath (*Physical Education*)

Susie Jeffreys, BSc Plymouth, PGCE Exeter (*Geography*)

Christine Jolliffe, BSc, PGCE Leicester (*Head of ICT*)

Diana Jones, BA Sussex, Dip Art & Design OU, PGCE Sussex (*Art*)

Nicola Jones, BA, MA Dunelm, MA Arts & Musical Theatre London (*RS, Drama*)

Joanna Kelly, LTA Level 2 Coach, Netball Level 2 Coach (*Physical Education*)

Matthew Kent, BA Keele, MA, PGDip.Ed Birmingham (*English*)

Lucy Keyte, BA Nottingham, PGCE Warwick (*French*)

Holly Kidman, BA Portsmouth, QTS (*Textiles*)

Julie Kissick, BA Hons Belfast, PGCE Ulster (*Music*)

Rachael Knapman, Netball Level 1 Coach UKCC (*Physical Education*)

Geoff Langer, BSc North Staffordshire, PGCE Oxon (*Physics*)

Lindsey Lea-James, BMus, LTCL, ALCM, PGCE Huddersfield (*Director of Music*)

James Long, BA, PGCE Liverpool (*Physical Education*)

Clare Macro, MA, PGCE Oxon (*Religious Studies*)

Victoria Marsh, BSc Keele, PGCE Exeter (*Mathematics*)

Sarah Malpass, BSc Sheffield, MSc Dunelm, PGCE London (*Head of Junior Science & Biology*)

Kieran McIntyre, Mathematics with Education BSc York (*Head of Mathematics*)

Liz McVey, BEd Bedford (*Physical Education*)

Richard Moody, BSc PGCE Southampton (*Mathematics*)

Bev Murphy, BA Wales, MA, PhD, PGCE UEA (*Head of Junior History*)

Pervin Özkan, Licence Tours, France, PGCE Exeter (*Head of French*)

Kitty Peat, BA London, QTS (*Duke of Edinburgh's Award*)

Ryan Pickering, NPLQ, NUCO, DEFIB TA (*Sporting Facilities & PE*)

Drew Pountney, BSc Wolverhampton (*Mathematics*)

Michaela Power, BA St Anselm College, USA (*Physical Education*)

Cherylin Preston, BSc Leicester, PGCE Exeter (*Head of Chemistry*)

Andrew Proven, PhD Cantab, BSc London (*Chemistry*)

Verity Redrup, BA London, PGCE Canterbury (*Biology*)

Bob Roberts, BA, MA, Warwick, PGCE Lancaster (*Head of English*)

Bronwen Robinson, BEd Worcs, Dip PE (*Dance*)

Ian Robinson, BEng PGCE Lancaster (*Head of Science*)

Ginny Seckerson, BA Loughborough, PGCE Brighton (*Head of CDT*)

Joan Shaw, MPhys, PGCE Bath (*Physics*)

Polly Skye, BA London MSc LSE MA Southampton, PGCE Kent (*English*)

Elizabeth Snoddon, BA Portsmouth, PGCE Portsmouth (*Photography*)

Rhea Stafford-Smith, BA York (*History, Politics*)

James Stead, BA Cumbria, PGCE Wales (*Art, Photography*)

Justine Stephens, BA London, PGCE Middx (*Head of Drama*)

Rani Tandon, BA Birmingham, PGCE Manchester Met (*History, PSHE, Politics*)

Martin Taylor, BA OU, PGCE Bedfordshire (*CDT*)

Holly Thomas, BA Bath, PGCE Coventry (*Head of Modern Languages*)

Richard Thompson, MA Oxon, PGCE London (*Head of Economics*)

Julia Thorn, BA Reading, MSt Oxon (*Head of Classics*)

Kelly Thornton, BA, QTS De Montfort (*Physical Education*) (*maternity leave*)

Nicole Thurgur, BA South Africa, MA Hertfordshire, QTS (*Textiles*)

Christine Varney, BEd Oxon (*Head of Careers & Business Studies*)

Sara Wills, HND Bath, BSc Loughborough, QTS (*Physical Education*)

Layla Williams, BA London, PGCE De Montfort (*Dance*)

James Woodward, BSc Wales, PGCE Exeter (*Head of Biology*)

Health Centre:

School Doctors: Dr Shelley Hayles & Dr Nicola Elliott

Sister in Charge: Janet Bonham, RGN

Sister: Caroline Howes, RGN

Sister: Virginia Rayner, RGN

Sister: Lindsay Pickering, RGN

Careers: Chris Varney

Registrar: Philippa Drinkwater

Admissions & Marketing Manager: Shanna Wells

Headmistress's PA: Jenny Lewis

PA to Bursar: Penny Ranken

Senior Administrative Secretary: Helen Mascall

Examinations Officer: Richard Moody

Old Tudorians: Julia Huddart

Data Manager: Laura Pountney
Financial Controller: Harriet Stapleton

Tudor Hall is an Independent Boarding School for Girls aged 11–18 years. The school was originally founded in 1850 and moved to Wykham Park in 1946. It is situated in spacious grounds 1½ miles from Banbury Station and is within easy access of London, Oxford and Stratford-upon-Avon – M40, Junction 11. This enables the girls to enjoy a wide range of cultural and educational activities.

The school accommodates approximately 258 boarders and 78 day girls. Its buildings comprise a 17th century and an 18th century manor with a modern purpose-built house for 96 Sixth Formers and extensive new facilities. These include laboratories for biology, chemistry, physics and general science; CDT workshop; 2 information technology rooms; language laboratory; modern languages and domestic science rooms; drama studio; music school; studios for art and pottery; textiles room; gym and sports hall. There are tennis and netball courts, a swimming pool, squash courts, astroturf and pitches for hockey, lacrosse and rounders. An extension to the Sixth Form block has been completed, with the original rooms undergoing extensive refurbishment. The Year 10 House has recently undergone extensive refurbishment and plans are in place to build a purpose-built drama studio and sports complex.

The curriculum includes a full range of academic subjects and, where possible, outings and fieldwork are arranged. All girls begin Latin and French with Spanish or German. Italian, Ancient Greek, Mandarin and Russian are also available. Music and Drama are strongly encouraged. Girls are prepared for GCSE and Advanced Level GCE, and appropriate certificates in optional extra subjects. Girls may also take riding and dancing lessons. There is a library and a careers room where advice is given about university entrance and further training.

Admission is by internal examinations at 11+ and internal examinations and Common Entrance at 13+. Entry may also be made to the Sixth Form where all girls pursue courses leading to higher education or vocational training and they are treated as students. Those entering at 11 are accustomed to being away from home by being housed separately in a smaller environment. Girls are divided into four competitive Houses but residence is with their own age group.

Tudor Hall places great importance on having a friendly atmosphere, a lively and united spirit and high standards. Girls are expected to take an interest in a wide range of activities as well as following a broad educational programme. Involvement in the local community through the Duke of Edinburgh's Award and social service, and participation in events with other schools are encouraged. Debating and public speaking are strong and there is keen involvement in the Young Enterprise Scheme, Model United Nations and European Youth Parliament. Tudor Hall is an Anglican school but members of other religious groups are welcomed. There is a small chapel.

Scholarships and Bursaries. *Academic* 11+/13+ and 16+. These are awarded to candidates entering at 11+ or 13+ on the basis of their performance at Common Entrance and interviews. At 16+ awards are offered on the basis of interview, school report and examination. The value of the award is up to £1,000 per annum. These awards are intended for the support of the pupil's academic interests.

Music 11+/13+ and 16+. These are awarded on the basis of ability and potential at 11+, 13+ and 16+. The value of the award is up to £1,000 per annum to entrants who show outstanding musical ability. Music awards exist in the form of free tuition in one or more instruments for the duration of the student's time at the school.

Art 13+/16+. These are awarded on the basis of ability and potential either at 13+ or 16+. The value of the award is up to £1,000 per annum. These awards are intended for the support of the pupil's Art interests.

Dance 16+. These are awarded on the basis of ability and potential at 16+. The value of the award is up to £1,000 per annum. These awards are intended for the support of the pupil's Dance interests.

Drama 13+/16+. These are awarded on the basis of ability and potential either at 13+ or 16+. The value of the award is up to £1,000 per annum. These awards are intended for the support of the pupil's Dramatic interests.

Sport 13+/16+. These are awarded on the basis of ability and potential either at 13+ or 16+. The value of the award is up to £1,000 per annum. These awards are intended for the support of the pupil's Sporting interests.

Textiles 16+. These are awarded on the basis of ability and potential at 16+. The value of the award is up to £1,000 per annum. These awards are intended for the support of the pupil's Textiles interests.

Bursaries are awarded to new and current parents who are in financial need.

Fees per term (2014–2015). £10,070 for boarders; £6,420 for day pupils.

Walthamstow Hall

Senior School:
Holly Bush Lane, Sevenoaks, Kent TN13 3UL
Tel: 01732 451334
Fax: 01732 740439

Junior School:
Bradbourne Park Road, Sevenoaks, Kent TN13 3LD

email: registrar@walthamstowhall.kent.sch.uk
website: www.walthamstow-hall.co.uk

Walthamstow Hall is an Independent girls' day school based on two separate sites in Sevenoaks. Founded in 1838, the school celebrated its 175th anniversary in 2013. The Junior School in Bradbourne Park Road takes pupils from age 3–11 years and the Senior School in Holly Bush Lane takes pupils from 11–18 years.

The school has a long established history of preparing academically-able girls for stimulating, purposeful and happy lives within and beyond school. The belief that every student given the right opportunities, encouragement and inspiring teaching can develop an incredible range of skills and talents is central to the everyday life of the school.

The Headmistress is a member of the GSA (Girls' Schools Association).

The school was judged to be 'Excellent' by the ISI in 2013, excellent being the highest category awarded.

Chairman of Governors: Ian Philip Esq, FCA

There are 14 school governors.

Headmistress: Mrs J Milner, MA Hons Oxford, PGCE Oxford

Senior Deputy Head: Mrs J Joynes, BA Hons Southampton, NPQH (*History and Politics*)
Deputy Head: P Howson Esq, BA Hons Plymouth, AST London (*English*)
Director of Studies: S Ledsham Esq, MA Oxford, PGCE Sussex (*Physics*)
Head of Junior School: Mrs D Wood, BSc Hons Durham, PGCE
Senior Teacher, Head of Sixth Form and Careers: Ms E Ancrum, MA Oxford, MPhil Hong Kong, PGCE London (*Economics/Business Studies*)

Senior School Assistant Staff:
* *Head of Department/Teacher in Charge of Subject*

Mrs F Boorman, BA Hons Kent (*Business Studies, Assistant Head of Lower School*)

Mrs V Bower-Morris, BA Hons Surrey, PGCE Goldsmiths (**Drama/Trinity Guildhall Drama*)

Mrs E Brown, BA Hons Leeds, PGCE Brighton (*Art and Textiles*)

N Buckingham Esq, BA Hons, MA Reading, PGCE London (**Classics, Examinations Officer*)

Miss K Burtenshaw, BEd Westminster College Oxford, Cert Ed (**Geography, Assistant Head of Careers*)

N Castell Esq, BMus Hons Manchester, PGCE Manchester (**Director of Music*)

Mrs J Cox, MA Cambridge, PGCE Open, ATCL (**Biology*)

T Dakin Esq, BSc Hons Bristol, PGCE Sussex (*Mathematics, Able, Gifted and Talented Coordinator*)

Dr R Davies, BSc Hons, PhD Imperial College, PGCE King's College (*Numeracy/Maths Learning Support, Mathematics*)

Mrs P Durrant, BSc Hons Southampton (*Mathematics*)

Mrs A Earnshaw-Punnett, BA Hons Sheffield Hallam, QTS Canterbury (*PE, ICT, *i/c Lacrosse*)

Mrs C Evans, BA Hons Greenwich (**Design & Technology*)

Mrs S Fitzmaurice, BSc Hons Manchester, PGCE Manchester (*Biology*)

Miss M Fournier, Licence, Masters Lille (*MFL*)

Mrs E Garcia, BA Hons Seville (*MFL*)

Mrs J Griffiths, BA Hons Reading, PGCE King's College (*Classics*)

Mrs K Hofmann, MA St Andrews, QTS (*MFL*)

Mrs H Hook, BA Hons Aberystwyth, PGCE Cambridge (*English*)

Miss L Hope, BSc Hons London (*Science*)

Mrs K Howlett, BEd Hons Sussex (*PE, Head of Lower School, *i/c Swimming*)

Mrs C Hughes, BA Hons West Surrey College of Art and Design, PGCE London (**Art and Textiles*)

Mrs R Hunt, BA Hons Exeter (**MFL*)

Mrs S Isted, BA Hons Warwick, PGCE King's College (*Classics*)

Mrs R Jennings, BSc Hons Southampton, PGCE Open, MICA (**Mathematics*)

Ms M Knight, BA Hons London, PGCE Canterbury (*English, Learning Support Coordinator*)

Dr P Le Bas, MA Cambridge, DPhil Oxford, STB/STL Rome, PGCE St Mary's College (**Physics*)

Miss S Mehaffey, MA, PGCE Edinburgh (**English, Assistant Head of Sixth Form*)

Mrs E Morgan, BA Hons Hull, PGCE London (*MFL*)

Mrs C Mulcahy, BA Hons Surrey, PGCE London (*Design & Technology, Art*)

Ms A Murphy, MA Oxford, PGCE East Anglia (*History/ Politics, Oxbridge Coordinator*)

Mrs E Peters, BSc Hons, PGCE Southampton (*Mathematics*)

Mrs A Phillips, BA Hons Bristol, QTS (*Drama, Charities Coordinator*)

Mrs C Platt, BA Hons London, QTS (*French/Spanish*)

Mrs L Rowell, BA Hons Surrey, PGCE King's College (**Computer Science and ICT*)

Mrs A Sherwen, BSc Hons London, PGCE Leeds (*Biology*)

Mrs C Solan, BA Hons London, PGCE Canterbury (*Art and Textiles, Photography*)

D Swann Esq, BSc Hons, PGCE Canterbury (*Mathematics, ICT & Computing, D of E Coordinator, Examinations Manager*)

Mrs B Tanner, BA Hons Wales, PGCE Southampton (*Spanish*)

Miss B Taylor, Teachers' Certificate Physical Education Cambridge (**PE, Head of Middle School*)

Mrs L Thomas, MA Open, BA Hons Wales, PGCE Bristol (*History, GPR Coordinator*)

Mrs L von Kaufmann, MA, BA Hons Oxford, PGCE Bristol (*RS, Geography*)

P Walker Esq, BSc Hons Loughborough, ACA, PGCE London (*Mathematics*)

Mrs S Walker, BSc Hons London, QTS Greenwich (*Chemistry*)

J Ward Esq, MMus, BMus Hons RCM, PGDip London (*Acting Head of Curriculum Music*)

Dr S Willcox, MA Cambridge, DPhil Oxford, SCITT/QTS Bromley (*Science*)

S Wilson Esq, BA Hons Sunderland, PGCE London (**i/c Sociology*)

Mrs C Winder, MA Kent, BA Hons Exeter, PGCE Oxford (*English*)

Ms O Windle, MA, BA Hons USA (**History, Politics*)

Mrs M Wood, BSc Hons Aberdeen, PGCE London (**Chemistry, *Science*)

Mrs Z Wood, MA Hons St Andrews, PGCE London (*RS*)

Junior School

Deputy Head Teacher: Mrs A Rotchell, BEd Hons Westminster College, Oxford, Dip SpLD York

Director of Studies: Mrs P Potter, BEd Southampton, Dip MEd Roehampton Institute

Head of Pre-Prep: Miss E Dargie, BEd Hons Canterbury

Mrs N Armitage, BA Hons Nottingham GTP

Mrs G Cameron, Foundation Degree

Mrs A Carr, BEd Hons Cheltenham

Mrs L Carter, BSc Hons Durham

Mrs L Everitt, Cert Ed North Worcestershire College of Education

Mrs K Fassnidge, BA Hons Cardiff

Mrs M Fewster, BSc Hons, PGCE Bath

Miss S Harris, Cert Ed Lady Spencer-Churchill College of Education, Oxford

Mrs H Malcolm, Dip Ed Aberdeen College of Education

Miss S Millington, BA Hons, Cert Ed Kent, QTS (*Head of Junior School Music*)

Miss M Murphy, BA Hons Swansea, PGCE Liverpool Institute of Higher Education

Mrs K Pattison, BA Hons Keele, MEd Open, PGCE Durham

Miss A Philip, BEd Hons Nottingham Trent, PG Dip Open

Ms R Pitt, BMus Hons Cardiff, PGCE London

Mrs L Thompson, Montessori Gold Seal Diploma

Mrs G Watts, MA Hons St Andrews, QTS, EYPS (*Maths, Classroom Assistant, Gifted & Talented Coordinator, Enrichment Coordinator*)

Administrative Staff:
Bursar: M Browning Esq, ACIB, Dip BA, FCMI, FRSPH
Registrar: Mrs A Knight
Head of Marketing: Mrs S Pelling, BA Hons Keele
Network Manager: Mrs E M Grant, BSc Hons Open University
PA to the Headmistress: Miss K Lippiatt
PA to Head of the Junior School: Mrs W Fahy

Librarians:
Ms R Boardman, Management Diploma Canada (*Assistant Librarian, Archives*)
Mrs L White, MA Brighton (*Lead Librarian, i/c School Archive*)

Medical Centre:
Mrs E Leisinger, Dip Nursing Brighton
Mrs L J Mottram, Dip Nursing Studies City University

Facilities. Walthamstow Hall is set in its own grounds within the town of Sevenoaks. Girls are taught in light and airy classrooms in buildings specifically designed for learning. The original 1882 Arts and Crafts school building still lies at the heart of the school. Recent campus developments have included: swimming pool complex opened in 2008,

Maths Suite and Drama Studio opened in 2009, Music and Design Technology rooms opened in September 2010, additional IT room and Student Entrance and Art Gallery opened in 2012. The school's Ship Theatre was refurbished in 2014 and a gym created for students in Year 10 upwards. A new Dining Hall opened at the Junior School in 2014. A new Sports Centre will open at the Senior School in September 2015.

Curriculum. Walthamstow Hall delivers an enriched curriculum which is innovative and flexible, facilitating breadth and individual choice, without sacrificing depth of study. This is brought to life with inspirational teaching.

All girls in their first three Senior School years (7, 8 and 9) follow a core curriculum of 17 subjects, with a second language being added in Year 8. As they progress through to public examinations the flexibility of the curriculum, enables girls to study a wide breadth of subjects rather than being shackled by restrictive subject blocks.

Subjects taught include: Art, Biology, Business Studies, Chemistry, Classical Civilisation, Computer Studies, Design and Technology, Drama, Economics, English, Fine Art, French, History, Geography, German, Government and Politics, ICT and Computing, Latin, Mathematics, Music, the Global Perspectives and Research Project, Photography, Physical Education, Physics, Religious Studies, Sociology, Spanish, Creative Textiles and Theatre Studies.

Girls are prepared for GCSE, IGCSE, AS, A2 Levels and Cambridge Pre-U. The record of success in public examinations is excellent. In 2014 100% of Pre-U, 89% of A Level and 95% of I/GCSEs were passed at grades A*–B.

The breadth and flexibility of the curriculum, combined with expert teaching and encouragement to be ambitious, enables students to be highly successful in their post-Sixth Form choices. In 2014 95% of leavers took up a place at their first-choice university; over 75% of these final destinations were to Russell Group universities, including Oxford and Cambridge; 17% of Upper Sixth students were offered Oxbridge places in 2014.

Religious Teaching is interdenominational.

Extra-Curricular Activities. The high profile of Drama, Music, Sports, trips, careers and study skills and personal development, together with an excellent pastoral system, provides further opportunity and support for every girl.

An active policy of 'sport for all' enables both team players and individuals to find the sporting activities that suit them best. Lacrosse, netball, swimming, athletics, judo, fencing, curling and tennis teams achieve highly at local, county and national levels. In 2013 the U15 lacrosse team were national champions and in 2014 the junior swimmers (Year 7 and 8) competed in the top 25 nationally.

A high proportion of students participate in the Duke of Edinburgh's Award scheme, Business enterprise, the school choirs and orchestra and Trinity Guildhall Drama.

Girls undertake voluntary service within the local community and abroad.

Admission. Admission to the Junior School is by interview and tests suitable to the age group. Admission to the Senior School for Year 7, 9 and Sixth Form is through the School's own entrance examinations and interview. Parents are warmly invited to visit the School at Open Mornings or on a personal visit.

Fees per term (2014–2015). Senior School and Sixth Form £5,750.

Scholarships. Academic scholarships are awarded annually to the candidates who show the greatest academic potential in the school's own Year 7, 9 and Sixth Form scholarship examinations.

Music and Sport scholarships are also available for Year 7 entry. Music, Sport, Drama and Art scholarships are offered for Year 9 entry.

Academic scholarships and Art Awards are offered in Sixth Form.

All awards are available to both internal and external candidates.

In addition, a means-tested bursary scheme in the Senior School provides financial help with school fees based on a family's financial circumstances. The scheme includes our Founders' Bursary, which pays nearly 100% of a pupil's school fees throughout their time at the school.

Charitable status. Walthamstow Hall is a Registered Charity, number 1058439. It exists to provide education for girls.

Westfield School

Oakfield Road, Gosforth, Newcastle-upon-Tyne
NE3 4HS
Tel: 0191 255 3980
email: westfield@westfield.newcastle.sch.uk
website: www.westfield.newcastle.sch.uk

Governors:
Chairman: Mrs O Forster, FCCA
Dr J Berry, MA, MBA, FCIM, FRSA, FIC
A C Coulson, FNAEA
I Greenshields, LLB
Mrs J Keep, MCSP, SRP
M Magowan, BSc Hons, FCIB, FCIM
Mrs D McGowan
Dr K Manzo, PhD
Mrs J Robson
S Simpson, BA Hons, FCA

Headmistress: **Mrs C Jawaheer**, BA Hons Liverpool, PGCE, Dip Ed, NPQH

Deputy Headteacher: Mrs D Thompson, MA Hons Cantab, PGCE

Assistant Head: S Ratcliffe, LLB Newcastle, BA Hons Wimbledon School of Art, MFA Cranbrook Academy of Art, Michigan

Assistant Head: G Wilson, BTL Canterbury NZ

Head of Sixth Form: Mrs E Wise, BA Hons Newcastle, PGCE

Art/Design:
S Ratcliffe, LLB Newcastle, BA Hons Wimbledon School of Art, MFA Cranbrook Academy of Art, Michigan
D Stone, BA Hons Kingston, PGCE

Biology: Mrs S Vallance, BSc Hons London, PGCE

Business Studies: Mr S O'Dwyer, BA Hons UCNW, PGCE
Careers: Mr S O'Dwyer, BA Hons UCNW, PGCE

Chemistry: P Russell, BSc Hons Bath, PGCE

Drama/Theatre Studies: Mrs E Forster, BA Hons Cantab, PGCE

English:
Dr A Leng, BA Hons Reading, MA Reading, PhD
Mrs E Forster, BA Hons Cantab, PGCE

Food & Nutrition:
Mrs L Hender, BA Hons Northumbria

French:
Mrs F Boyce, BA Hons Salford, PGCE
Mrs S Dodds, BA Hons Dunelm, PGCE
Mrs E Wise, BA Hons Newcastle, PGCE

Geography:
Mrs D Thompson, MA Hons Cantab, PGCE
C Dunn, MA Hons Cantab

German: Mrs E Wise, BA Hons Newcastle, PGCE

History:
Mrs J Harris, BA Hons Northumbria, PGCE

Information Communication Technology:
Mrs C Lloyd, BA Hons, PGCE Liverpool

Mathematics:
Dr C Barnett, MMATH Newcastle, PhD Dunelm
Mrs F Swift, BA Cantab, MEng Cantab, PGCE

Music:
G Wilson. BTL Canterbury NZ

Physical Education:
Mrs N Bolton, BSc Lancaster, PGCE
Miss M Lamb, BSc Sheffield, PGCE

Physics:
Dr E Corbin, BA Oxon, MSc Newcastle, PhD Newcastle

Religious Studies:
S Shieber, BA Hons Durham, PGCE, MA

Science:
Miss H Fraser, BSc Columbia, New York
Mrs J Dudley, BSc Hons Newcastle, PGCE

Spanish:
Mrs S Dodds, BA Hons Durham, PGCE

Additional Learning Support:
Mrs C Hatcher, BEd Hons Liverpool

Junior House:
Assistant Head: Mrs K Clappison, MA Hons Glasgow,
  PGCE

Teachers/Teaching Assistants:
Mrs N Alexanders, BA Hons Newcastle, PGCE
Miss J N Brown, BSc Hons Huddersfield, PGCE
Mrs F Collier, BA Hons Keele, PGCE
Mrs H Dean, BEd Hons Newcastle
Mrs S Hann, BA Hons Hull, PGCE
Mrs N Kyle, BA Hons Durham, PGCE
Mrs M Johnson, CertEd Eastbourne
Mrs K Meeson, BSc Hons Northumbria, PGCE
Miss G McKeating, BEd Hons York
Mrs L McNaught, BA Hons Staffs, NCFE2
Mrs T McQuade, NCFE Level ONC Dyslexia Level 3
Mrs A Rabey-Wilson, BA Hons London, PGCE
Mrs J Slack, BA Hons Hull, PGCE
Mrs A Winks, BEd Hons Newcastle

Visiting Staff:
Music:
B Alimohamadi, BA OU, LGSM, CertEd Newcastle
Mrs M A Huntingdon, BSc, FTCL, LRAM
Mrs P Green, BA Hons Newcastle, CT ABRSM
Mrs Alison Northey
Miss S Harrison, LTCL
J Radford
Dancing:
Mrs A Hall, MNCDTA
Tennis: Mrs F Twaddle, LTA Coach
Fencing: G Thompson, BFA County Coach
Gymnastics:
P Gleghorn, NPQH, BEd Hons, Senior Club Coach
Miss C Anderson, Assistant Coach

Bursar: Mrs K Wightman, BSc Hons, CAT, DipM, MCIM
Domestic Bursar: Mrs D Oldroyd
Headmistress's Secretary: Mrs J Jokelson
School Secretary/Marketing Coordinator: Mrs J Stead
Junior House Secretary: Mrs A Dryden, BA Northumbria
Laboratory Technician: K Wood
Examinations Officer: Miss H Fraser, BSc Columbia, New
  York
Assistant Examinations Officer: Mrs J Stead
School Librarian: Mrs J Stead

Westfield is a day school for 380 girls aged 3+ to 18, in Junior and Senior Houses situated on one campus in a very pleasant wooded site of over 6 acres. The School's aim is an uninterrupted education, a high academic standard and a wide curriculum offering scope and stimulus for individual development. There is a vast range of extra-curricular activities with particular emphasis on Sport, Outdoor Pursuits, Music, Art and Drama. The Duke of Edinburgh's Award Scheme has a high profile and all senior girls are encouraged to participate. In addition to a sound grounding in basic skills, Junior House (3–11) offers specialist teaching in Art, Craft, PE, French and Music. So that every child may be assured of individual attention class sizes are restricted to a maximum of 20. Frequently, classes are further divided into smaller units.

Senior house (11–18), has first rate classroom and laboratory facilities with excellent specialist accommodation for Home Economics and Music. A wide range of subjects is taught by specialists. Initially all girls have lessons in the traditional academic core subjects, in English, Mathematics, Geography, History, Science (taught as 3 separate subjects) and French, as well as in Music, Drama, PE, Food and Nutrition, ICT and Design. German and Spanish are introduced in the second year. Girls are encouraged to aim for breadth in their choice of subjects at GCSE. Most girls achieve 9 passes in the A–C range of the GCSE, a number with straight A and A* passes. There is a carefully structured programme of Careers and Personal and Social Education and a well developed pastoral system.

The Sixth Form occupies a cottage block in the grounds and is under the direction of the Head of the Sixth Form.

There is a full range of AS, A2 and other courses and girls are prepared for University and other Higher Education courses, including Oxbridge, as well as for other courses and for employment. The A level pass rate is always over 90%, ensuring for most girls a place in their first choice of institute of higher education.

Sixth Formers have considerable responsibility within the School in addition to their own thriving academic and cultural life.

Westfield is a member of Round Square, a worldwide association of schools which share a commitment, beyond academic excellence, to personal development and responsibility through service, challenge, adventure and international understanding. Girls from Westfield have the opportunity to attend the Annual International Conference and to participate in exchanges with member schools from all over the world, and in the Round Square International Service Projects in developing countries.

Westfield is totally committed to producing happy, self-confident, well-balanced young women who are international in their outlook and fully prepared to face life in the 21st Century.

Admission to Westfield is by interview and examination. While children of all faiths are accepted, the religious life of the school is based on Christian principles.

Fees per term (2014–2015). In Junior House fees range from £2,325–£3,095 and in Senior House are £3,915.

Scholarships are available at 11+, including Academic, Art, Music and PE. Some bursaries are also available in cases of financial need.

Charitable status. Westfield School is owned and administered by the Northumbrian Educational Trust Ltd, which is a Registered Charity, number 528143. It exists for the purpose of education.

Westholme School

Meins Road, Blackburn, Lancashire BB2 6QU
Tel: 01254 506070
Fax: 01254 506080
email: principal@westholmeschool.com
website: www.westholmeschool.com

Governing Body:
Chairman: Mr B C Marsden, FCA
Vice Chairman: Mr P Forrest, MRICS, FCIOB
Mr M Abraham, BEd
Mr K J Ainsworth, FGA
Mr D J Berry, BA, FCMA, MIBM
Mrs A Booth
Mrs J Meadows, BSc Hons, ACA
His Honour E Slinger, BA
Professor R D Taylor, MA, LLM
Mr J R Yates, BSc

Clerk to the Governors: Mr J Backhouse, LLB Hons

Principal: Mrs Lynne Horner, BA Hons, PGCE

Commercial Director: Mrs Vivienne Davenport, MA Oxon

Deputy Headteacher, Curriculum: Miss Francine Smith,
    FRSA, BSc Hons Brunel, PGCE

Deputy Headteacher, Pastoral: Mrs Jude Gough, BA Hons
    Wolverhampton, PGCE, MISTC

Assistant Headteacher: Mr James Dumbill, BA Hons
    Bristol, PGCE

Westholme School comprises: Nursery (Boys and Girls
from the age of 2), Infant School (Boys and Girls aged 3–7),
Junior School (Boys and Girls aged 7–11), Senior School
(Girls and Boys aged 11–16) and Sixth Form (Girls aged
16–18).

There are currently 800 day pupils at Westholme: 500
girls in the Senior School and Sixth Form, 370 in the Infant
and Junior Departments, and 30 boys and girls in the Nursery.

Westholme School is administered by a Board of Governors which includes three nominated Governors representing current parents. Although the school is non-
denominational, its Christian foundation is regarded as
important, the emphasis being placed on the moral aspect of
Christian teaching.

Senior School, Sixth Form. The aim of the Senior
School is to provide an atmosphere in which each pupil can
develop his or her abilities to the full and can excel in some
field of activity. There is constant effort to widen interests
and to instil a strong sense of individual responsibility. Most
students continue to the Sixth Form and then move on to
Higher Education. Most pursue degree courses, a significant
number at Oxford and Cambridge.

The Senior School offers an academic curriculum in
English Language and Literature, Mathematics, Biology,
Chemistry, Physics, Geography, History, French, German,
Mandarin, Spanish, Design Technology, Food, ICT, Tex-
tiles, Art, Business Studies, Classical Civilisation, Drama,
Latin, Music, Ethics, Philosophy & Religion (EPR), Psy-
chology, Sociology and Theatre Studies. Most of these sub-
jects can be taken for the GCSE examination and at AS and
A Levels; Oxbridge tuition is also offered.

Set in the countryside to the west of Blackburn, Westholme School offers excellent facilities. The premises have
been regularly upgraded to give purpose-built accommodation for specialist subjects such as Art, Design and Information Technology and Music; seven modern laboratories
support the three separate sciences. Sporting facilities
include a sports hall, indoor swimming pool, brand new all-
weather pitch and tennis courts and a large playing field

with running circuit. The full-sized professional theatre
opened in 1997, seats 700 and offers students outstanding
production resources. The library has open-access multimedia giving students full research facilities. The Sixth Form
wing opened in September 2003 complete with lecture theatre, common room, café and classrooms.

The Performing Arts are a special feature of the school.
There are several school choirs and girls have the opportunity to learn a string, brass or wind instrument and to play in
the school orchestras or wind ensembles. Co-curricular
drama includes the full-scale spectacular musical, in the
round productions, club and house competitions, while
make-up and costume design are popular options at GCSE.

School societies and house teams meet on most days
during midday break and girls are encouraged to participate
in a variety of activities and in their house competitions.
These provide younger girls with opportunities beyond the
curriculum and older students with the chance to assume a
leadership role.

Westholme Infant School, Westholme Junior School.
There is close cooperation between these schools and with
the Senior School. A family atmosphere allows children to
learn in a supportive and happy environment. Firm academic foundations are laid with the emphasis upon the basic
skills of literacy and numeracy. Excellent facilities afford
ample teaching space and resource areas; the Junior School
has three halls, music rooms and specialist provision for
Information Technology. Co-curricular activities include
public speaking, orchestra, choir, sports, societies and
school visits. Music and sport are taught by specialists and
all Departments use the swimming pool, sports hall, athletics track and outdoor pitches at the Senior School.

Admission. Pupils usually enter the school in September.
Entry to the Junior and Senior Schools is by examination,
and to the Infant School by interview. The normal ages of
entry are at 2, 3, 4, 7, 11 and 16.

In view of the demand for places, parents are advised to
make an early application.

The Principal is happy for prospective parents to visit the
school during normal working hours; appointments may be
arranged through the Registrar, from whom application
forms are available. Annual Open Days are held in October
and other open days are held in the spring and summer
terms.

Private coaches run from Accrington, Blackburn Boule-
vard, Bolton, Burnley, Colne, Chorley, Clitheroe, Darwen,
Leyland, Preston, Standish, Ribble Valley, South Ribble, the
Rossendale Valley and Wigan.

Fees per term (from January 2014). Senior School
£3,200; Junior School £2,515; Infant School: £2,100 (full
day), £1,065 (half day); Nursery £194 pw.

Scholarships are available at the Senior School for students who show good academic ability and various Bursaries are available (means-tested).

Charitable status. Westholme School is a Registered
Charity, number 526615. It exists for the education of children between the ages of 2 and 18.

Westonbirt School

Tetbury, Gloucestershire GL8 8QG
Tel: 01666 881301
email: admissions@westonbirt.org
            enquiries@westonbirt.org
website: www.westonbirt.org
Twitter: @westonbirtsch

Governing Body:
Chairman: Mr D McMeekin, MBA
Vice-Chairman: Miss J Greenwood, BSc, FRICS
Mr M Barrow, CBE
Mr D Battishill, BA Hons

Mrs K Broomhead
Mr T Gaffney, MBA
Mrs P Leggate, BA, MEd, PGCE
Mrs H Metters, BSc Hons, PGCE
Ms S Pennie, ACA
Mr M Pyper, OBE
Mrs S Whitfield, MA
Mr C Wyld, MA
Mr S Smith

Head: Mrs N Dangerfield, BA Brighton

Deputy Head: Mr M Gluning, BSc, PGCE Aberystwyth,
  MA Kingston

Assistant Head – Academic: Mrs D Browne, BA UC Wales,
  PGCE Exeter, MEd Gloucestershire, NPQH

Assistant Head – Admin & Extra-Curricular: Mrs J Bell,
  BEd Bath

Operations Director: Mr J Olver, MA Cantab

Director of Admissions: Mrs P Stevenson

Director of Marketing & Digital Communications: Mrs L
  Brook, BSc Hons, CIM Dip

Finance Director: Mr D Godding, LLB Bristol, FCA

Chaplain: Revd A Monaghan, BA Cambridge, MA
  Edinburgh

Heads of Department:

Art:
Mrs M Phillips, BA, FPS Photog, CertEd Liverpool, MA
  Open

Business Studies:
Mrs J Gould, BA Exeter

Classics:
Mrs G Geers, BA Southampton, DipEd Oxford

Design Technology:
Mr J Sproule, CertEd London

Drama:
Miss G Hemming, BA Exeter, PGCE Gloucestershire

ELT:
Miss C Lloyd, BA, MA Coventry, Cert TESOL London

English:
Mrs D Browne, BA UC Wales, PGCE Exeter, MEd
  Gloucestershire, NPQH

Food & Textiles Technology:
Mrs J Bell, BEd Bath

Geography:
Mrs N Gill, BA Hons Manchester, PGCE Cambridge

History:
Miss A Stredwick, MSc Leicester, BA UC Cardiff, PGCE
  Open

Information & Communication Technology:
Mr C Burkinshaw, BA Manchester Metropolitan, PGCE
  Leicester

Learning Support:
Mrs P Reuter, BA London

Mathematics:
Mrs J Barlow, BSc Birmingham, PGCE Open

Modern Languages:
Mrs C Rock, L-ès-L Université de Metz

Music:
Director of Music: Mrs E Parkes, BA Liverpool

Physical Education:
Mrs L Johnson

Psychology & Religious Education:
Mr P Bolam, BSc Bradford, MA Keele, PGCE
  Wolverhampton

Science: Miss H Rogerson, MPhys Southampton, PGCE
  Edinburgh
Physics: Dr J Stimpson, PhD Leicester, BSc Leicester,
  PGCE Leicester
Biology: Mrs S Barr, BSc, PGCE Leeds
Chemistry: Mr M Gluning, BSc, PGCE Aberystwyth, MA
  Kingston

Health & Wellbeing Centre: Mrs D Cook, BSoc
  Birmingham

Housemistresses:
Badminton House: Mrs J Price, BA Durham, PGCE
  Cambridge
Beaufort House: Miss C Crowley
Dorchester House: Miss S Gould
Holford House: Mrs V Downes, BEd Wolverhampton
Sixth Form: Mrs E Kirby, BA Cardiff

Location. Westonbirt School is a Senior all-girls Day and
Boarding School and Westonbirt Prep is a mixed Prep
School – both are set in 210 acres of magnificent parkland in
the heart of the Cotswolds, close to the cultural cities of
Bath, Bristol and Cheltenham and only 90 minutes from
London.

Philosophy. Westonbirt School encourages every girl to
achieve her full potential, instilling confidence without arrogance in a safe, secure yet stimulating environment. This is
achieved through our boarding ethos, which is shared by day
pupils, and delivered through an education which combines
tradition with modernity. We aim to balance academic, cultural and recreational activities within a strong spiritual
framework.

We are a Church of England School, with our own
Chapel and Chaplain and our Christian ethos underpins all
that we do. Whatever your religious belief or faith, you will
receive support for your personal spiritual development.
Deep friendships are formed across year groups and every
girl is guided by nurturing academic and pastoral staff.

The Curriculum. All pupils follow the national curriculum and, in addition, are offered a full sporting timetable
and a wide range of extra-curricular activities to give each
and every girl an outstanding all round education. The
exceptionally able are stretched and challenged and additional help and support is provided by specialists for those
who need learning support or English language training.

The School has performed consistently well in both
GCSE and A Level results and is in the top 5% of schools in
the UK for its 'value-added' scores (generated by the University of Durham) which measure how much pupils
improve their predicted academic performance.

Each girl has her own personal tutor who supports her
inside and outside the classroom, helps her manage her time
and acquire effective study skills from the moment she joins
until she secures her place at university. In addition, girls
follow a 'Skills for Life' programme which includes interview skills, personal finance lessons and other preparations
for life after school.

Music, Drama and Art and Design. The music department has a comprehensive range of specialist facilities. The
new Music Technology Centre boasts a rehearsal room,
technology suite fully equipped with Apple computers, midi
keyboards and a recording studio. As well as individual lessons, girls have many opportunities to perform regularly in
choirs, orchestras or ensembles.

Art and design is a key strength and has its own fully
equipped design studio, there is also the opportunity to work
with textiles. Pupils go onto study at top design and art colleges.

Drama is thriving at the school with two productions
every year. The Orangery Theatre, with adjacent Green

Room and Rehearsal Room, provides a versatile venue not only for the performing arts but also for special events such as fashion shows, charity events and socials. Individual speech and drama lessons are popular with many successfully competing in local competitions.

Sports and Leisure. We have extensive pitches, courts and tracks with wonderful facilities for sport, including lacrosse, netball, tennis, rounders, athletics, golf and polo. The £3m Sports Centre has an impressive 25m indoor swimming pool, sports hall, aerobics and dance room and fitness suite. Many girls also participate in our popular tennis programme and enjoy playing golf on our superb nine-hole golf course. Those keen on equestrian sports may take riding lessons at nearby stables, and polo at the neighbouring Beaufort Polo Club. Our sports teachers and coaches are experts in their fields and many of the girls go on to play at county level and beyond.

Extra-curricular Activities. Girls are encouraged to participate in the broad range of extra-curricular activities on offer. Drama, music and dance are particularly popular, but there are many other options, from riding and golf to knitting and fencing. There are also regular socials, debates and dances with boys' schools. Many of the older girls participate in the Duke of Edinburgh's Award scheme, World Challenge, Leiths cookery school or try out their business skills in the Young Enterprise scheme. There are planned activities every weekend including cultural, fun and shopping trips, which are open to day girls as well as boarders. Outdoor pursuits range from surfing and mountain biking to trapeze jumping, as well as overseas trips to countries including France, Italy, Spain the USA and Peru. Community and fundraising projects are strongly supported at the school and the girls often initiate projects themselves for causes which are close to them.

Learning Support. Westonbirt has an excellent specialist Learning Support department which offers support and guidance to girls with dyslexia, dyspraxia and other special needs. We assess each girl before entry to the school to ensure we can fully support her at Westonbirt.

ELT (English Language Training). Our English Language teaching department offers specialist individual and group lessons. All pupils are assessed on entry to ensure they have the requisite amount of support needed and are taught in mainstream lessons for all other subjects. International girls really appreciate the friendly and professional ELT department who work closely with all the academic staff.

Facilities. Against the wonderful historic backdrop the school offers excellent modern facilities, including an impressive £3m Sports Centre, state-of-the-art Music Technology Suite, a new Business School which opened in September 2013, Information Advice and Guidance Centre, nine-hole golf course, as well as our own Chapel.

We have a dedicated Science, Art and Design Technology block including laboratories with, three bright art rooms and two well-equipped design studios. Independent learning is supported in our suite of libraries and resource rooms. We are also improving communications to give greater accessibility to learning online and pupils will be able to bring their own technology into classroom learning.

All Year 7 and 8 girls live in a dedicated junior house with their Housemistress. This gives them two years to settle in among their peer group before joining their respective senior boarding houses. Sixth Formers enjoy the benefits of single study-bedrooms with shared common rooms, in a separate modern block, providing an excellent halfway house to university life.

Entrance Requirements. Girls normally join the school at 11, 13 or 16, though they may do so at other ages in special circumstances. At 11+ and 13+ they must sit either the Common Entrance Examination or take the school's own entrance papers, attend an interview with the Headmistress, and provide a reference from their current school. Sixth Form entrants must have a minimum of 5 GCSEs at grades A*–C, attend an interview and sit tests in the subjects they intend to study at A Level.

Fees per term (2014–2015). Boarding (full & weekly) £8,605–£10,995; Day £5,765–£7,100. The fee is inclusive of tuition, board, lodging, stationery and laundry. Day girls may stay one night per week free of charge and on additional nights for a small fee. The school is renowned for its flexible approach to boarding.

Scholarships and Bursaries. Scholarships are awarded at 11+, 13+ and 16+ entry. Scholarships may be awarded for academic prowess, or for Drama, Art, Music, Performing Arts or Sport. Means-tested bursaries may be awarded wherever financial need is proven and Armed Forces are offered between 10–20%. For daughters of Clergy there is a reduction of up to 30% in fees which is means tested. When sisters are at school together, a 5% reduction from net fees is made for the second sister and a 10% reduction from net fees for the third. Full details are available on request.

Charitable status. Westonbirt School Limited is a Registered Charity, number 311715. It exists for the education of girls in mind, body and spirit.

Wimbledon High School

GDST

Mansel Road, London SW19 4AB

Tel:	020 8971 0900 (Senior School)
	020 8971 0902 (Junior School)
Fax:	020 8971 0901 (Senior School)
	020 8971 0903 (Junior School)
email:	info@wim.gdst.net
website:	www.wimbledonhigh.gdst.net
Twitter:	@WimbledonHigh
Facebook:	/WimbledonHighSchoolGDST

Founded 1880.

Wimbledon High School is part of the GDST (Girls' Day School Trust). The GDST is the leading network of independent girls' schools in the UK. As a charity that owns and runs 24 schools and two academies, it reinvests all its income in its schools. For further information about the Trust, see p. xxi or visit www.gdst.net.

Additional information about the school may be found on the school's website. A prospectus may be obtained from the school.

Chairman of the Local Governors: Mrs B Rosewell, MSc

Head: Mrs J Lunnon, BA Bristol

Deputy Head, Academic: Mrs J Mitchell, BSc Bristol

Deputy Head, Pastoral: Miss S Ferro, MA University College London, MA Oxon

Head of Junior School: Miss K Mitchell, MA York

Director of Finance & Operations: Mrs S Lawton, AInstAM Dip

Assistant Head (Director of Sixth Form): Dr J Parsons, BMus, MA, PhD Cardiff

Assistant Head (Director of Studies): Mr B Haythorne, MA Oxon

Assistant Head (Co-curricular): Miss J Cox, BSc Brunel

Deputy Head, Junior School: Miss G Peacock, BA Nottingham Trent

Pupil numbers. Junior School: 324 aged 4–11; Senior School: 580, including 150 in the Sixth Form.

Wimbledon High School combines academic strength with a firm belief that learning should be fun. Jane Lunnon took up the Headship in September 2014 and says she has been "struck by the natural, unaffectedness of the students, their scholarship and their willingness to get involved in all aspects of school life". Results at A Level and GCSE are consistently extremely high, music and drama are a vibrant part of school life and a new Director of Sport has rejuvenated PE at the school, introducing rowing and girls' football. Activities include World Challenge, Model United Nations and the Duke of Edinburgh's Award Scheme, alongside many smaller clubs and societies, from Mah Jong to Basketball. The girls often run these themselves.

A secure framework of pastoral care supports students through what can sometimes be difficult teenage years. They increasingly gain more responsibility as they move up through the school. Sixth Formers practise leadership through the School Council and by mentoring younger girls; there is a peer counselling service and older students help with Easter revision classes at local schools.

Junior and Senior Schools share one central Wimbledon site, with excellent facilities: a swimming pool and sports hall, Performing Arts Centre and a centre for design and technology. The playing fields are ten minutes' walk away at Nursery Road (the site of the original All England Lawn Tennis and Croquet Club) providing a full-size, all-weather hockey pitch and five netball/tennis courts. The school believes in nurturing all sporting talent and a fit and active lifestyle is encouraged.

The **Junior School** provides a creative and academic education in a happy and stimulating environment – bright, purpose-built accommodation, with specialist rooms for art, ICT and science. There is a balance of class and specialist subject teaching and girls are set clear and challenging targets for their learning. An enriched and extended National Curriculum is the foundation, with the school embracing the 'creative curriculum' encompassing various areas of learning at the same time; Spanish, Italian and French are taught at various times, as well as Latin. An after-school care programme offers flexibility to working parents.

The **Senior School** curriculum runs over a two week timetable. In Key Stage 3, girls study English, Mathematics and Combined Sciences; they learn German or Spanish alongside French (Latin is added in Year 8) as well as Geography, History, Religious Studies, PE, Music, Drama, Art, Design & Technology (textiles, product design and food technology, on rotation), Computer Science, Study Skills and PSHE (Personal, Social and Health Education).

At Key Stage 4 all girls study English (Language and Literature), Mathematics and three separate sciences as well as PE, RS and PSHE (non-examined). The girls have a free choice of four other subjects, of which one must be a Modern Foreign Language, with the possibility of adding Classical Greek. A Global Perspectives course in Year 10 brings breadth beyond the curriculum, and Mind Matters is a series of thought-provoking talks held for Year 10 and above. The school also holds regular Roswell Lectures for older girls, parents and staff.

In the **Sixth Form,** students may choose from the same subjects on offer at GCSE (except PE – compulsory in Year 12 but non-examined and Critical Thinking, that is also offered), plus Further Mathematics, Economics, Psychology and Theatre Studies. The school has moved to a linear programme, with students taking 3 or 4 A Levels (not AS – with the exception of AS Mathematics). There is a high uptake of science subjects and in recent years the Extended Project Qualification has been popular. An extensive programme of enrichment (starting in Year 11 and continuing in Years 12 and 13) offers short courses in scores of subjects from dissection to Zumba, as well as the opportunity to participate in Community Service or the Young Enterprise scheme. PSHE continues and a comprehensive programme of careers and university entrance advice is offered.

Admissions. 4+ girls are assessed in groups in a nursery-style environment; indication of a girl's potential is the key at this stage, rather than evidence of what has already been learnt.

7+ girls have a small group interview following formal assessments in English including comprehension and a story, mathematics and verbal reasoning.

For 11+ entry, applicants are interviewed in the autumn term, prior to the entrance examination (in verbal and non-verbal reasoning) in January. The occasional entry examination has a Science paper.

16+ assessment comprises entrance exam and interviews. Offers of places are conditional upon GCSE A grades in candidates' chosen A Level subjects, and a minimum of nine B grades overall.

Fees per term (2014–2015). Senior School £5,250, Junior School £4,043.

The fees cover the regular curriculum, school books, choral music, games and swimming, but not optional extra subjects.

Scholarships and Bursaries. Academic scholarships are awarded to girls who do exceptionally well in the 11+ exam, worth 5% of the fees. There is also a music scholarship at 11+. At 16+, a separate academic scholarship exam can be taken and there are scholarships in Art, Drama, Music and PE, worth up to 10%. A 16+ science scholarship is worth up to 50%. Details and application forms available on request.

Bursaries take account of academic merit, but all are means tested. The maximum value is the full fee.

Charitable status. Wimbledon High School is part of The Girls' Day School Trust, which is a Registered Charity, number 306983.

Woldingham School

Marden Park, Woldingham, Surrey CR3 7YA
Tel: 01883 349431
Fax: 01883 348653
email: registrar@woldinghamschool.co.uk
website: www.woldinghamschool.co.uk
Twitter: @woldinghamsch
Facebook: /woldinghamschool.co.uk

Independent School for Girls aged 11–18.

Chairman of Governors: Mr Ian Tyler, BCom, ACA, FICE

***Headmistress*: Mrs J Triffitt**, MA Oxon

Deputy Head: Mrs A Hutchinson, MA Oxon
Director of Pastoral Care: Mrs J Brown, BEd CNAA
Director of Studies: Dr J Murphy, BA, MSc, MPhil, DPhil Oxon
Head of Marden: Mrs M Giblin, BA Maynooth
Head of Sixth Form: Miss F Kennedy, MA Oxon
Bursar: Mr N T Campbell, MBA, DEF
Marketing Director: Mr P McNulty, BA Ulster

Registrar: Mrs L Underwood

Heads of Departments:
Art: Miss C Reay, BA Manchester Metropolitan
Careers and Higher Education: Ms F Kennedy, MA Oxon (*Acting Head*)
Classics & Latin: Mrs E Williamson, BA Birmingham, MA Western Ontario, LLB London
Design & Technology: Mr D Wahab, BA Brighton
Drama: Mrs L Mann, Dip Drama Middlesex
EAL: Mrs T Carrilero, BA Spain
Economics & Business Studies: Mr R MacLean, BSc Cass, MSc Durham
English: Mrs J Vivian, BA Wales, MEd Newcastle
French: Mrs C Maillot BA equiv France

Geography: Mr S Baird, BSc Edinburgh
German: Mr V Ceska, BA Czech, MA France
Government & Politics: Mrs K Payne, BA Dunelm
History: Mr H Patterson, BA Bristol
History of Art: Mr A Cullen, BA SOAS
Information Technology: Mr A McGreevy, BSc Liverpool, MA IOE
Learning Enhancement: Mrs P Frisby, BA Keele, MA OU, Adv Dip SEN
Mathematics: Mrs C Sinclair, MA Oxon
Media Studies: Mr S Maunder, BA Sheffield
Music: Mr J Hargreaves, BA York
Personal, Social & Health Education: Miss A O'Neill, BEd London
Physical Education: Mrs S Nunes, BA North West University of South Africa (*Acting Head*)
Religious Education: Mr T Oulton, BA MSt Oxon
Science: Mr P Price, BSc UEA
Biology: Mrs S Baldwin, BSc London
Chemistry: Dr M Haywood, BSc Cardiff, PhD Cardiff
Physics: Mrs K Connor, BSc East Anglia
Psychology: Dr C Stevenson, BSc PhD Edinburgh
Spanish: Mr A Lopez, BA Oviedo

Woldingham is a leading independent Catholic boarding and day school for girls. It is a happy and successful school and develops confident and compassionate young women. Woldingham's approach to religious instruction is 'all-inclusive', welcoming girls from all faiths.

Foundation. The school was founded in 1842 by the Society of the Sacred Heart and has been sited at Woldingham since 1946. Today, under lay management, Woldingham is part of the international network of over 200 Sacred Heart schools in 44 countries.

Situation and Buildings. Woldingham is situated south east of London, just inside the M25 at Junction 6. The school is set within 700 idyllic acres in the Surrey countryside with its own train station in the grounds that offers easy access to Clapham Junction (25 minutes) and London Victoria (35 minutes). Journey times to Gatwick and Heathrow airports are 25 and 45 minutes respectively. A stunning Jacobean house is the centre piece of the idyllic setting in a designated Area of Outstanding Natural Beauty. An intensive yet sympathetic buildings programme has now furnished the school with some impressive facilities.

The Millennium Centre for the Performing Arts includes a 600-seat auditorium with orchestra pit, industry standard sound and lighting control rooms, scenery construction dock, wardrobe room for costume and prop construction and a fully-equipped studio theatre. In addition, the Centre hosts a Recital room, a Mac Suite, keyboard studio, String and Woodwind rooms, numerous practice rooms and an exceptional eight-track digital recording studio. The purpose-built Art department comprises two large 2D studios, facilities for printmaking and a superb 3D area equipped with a range of power tools and two kilns. Design Technology is taught in a fully-equipped workshop and studio, using state-of-the-art computer-controlled machinery. The Sports Centre includes a Sports Hall, 2 squash courts, fully-equipped Fitness Studio and a Dance/Gymnastics studio. In addition there are extensive outdoor playing areas, an indoor tennis dome, an indoor swimming pool and an all-weather floodlit pitch. "The grounds are stunning and sports facilities are excellent" (Tatler).

Boarding accommodation is impressive, "more like home than home" (Good Schools Guide 2014), "almost boutique-hotel standard" (Tatler). Shanley House, the Upper Sixth centre, is a modern block with en-suite accommodation. Berwick House is the Lower Sixth centre and provides single room accommodation. All girls from Year 10 have single study-bedrooms in Main House. Marden House is a small, friendly junior house with welcoming accommodation for the first two years.

Developments over the past five years include the completion of a new whole school dining area with state-of-the-art food preparation facilities and serveries. The Year 11 boarding area has been entirely refurbished to bring it up to date and in line with the newly redecorated and refurnished junior boarding house, Marden, for Years 7 and 8. Four new, airy and modern classrooms were built for the History and Politics Department within the junior boarding house development and January 2013 saw the inauguration of an entirely new building – the Examination Centre. This new centre includes spacious, contemporary testing rooms, individual examination suites and additional classroom space. In summer 2014, two new Biology laboratories were entirely refurbished and modernised in the Science block with further refurbishment planned for 2015.

Size. The school accommodates over 550 girls within the 11–18 age range, some 330 of whom are boarders. 60% of boarders are from families living in London and Home Counties and 25% come from overseas. Approximately 25% of the intake are of nationalities other than British; these students enrich the school by bringing to it an international dimension and outlook.

Pastoral Care. This is a key strength of the school and the teaching is "adorned with dollops of TLC" (Good Schools Guide 2014). In each year care of the boarding side of the school life is the responsibility of the Head of Year, who acts in loco parentis and ensures that each girl is known and cared for as an individual. The Head of Year is assisted by a team of Tutors, each of whom is responsible for the girls' individual guidance. Buddy schemes ensure that girls provide support for each other. The boarders in each year are cared for by two House Mistresses.

Curriculum. All girls take a common course for the first two years. Year 7 students take Latin and two of French, German or Spanish. In Year 9 the creative subjects and languages are optional, with the majority of girls choosing to continue with two languages (of which Latin can be one) and three creative subjects (from Art, Drama, Design Technology, ICT and Music). The more able linguists may choose three languages and only two creative subjects at this time, while others may choose to only study one language and the four creative subjects instead. Health Education is studied by all students in Years 7–9, but is not examined.

It is expected that the majority of Years 10 and 11 girls will follow a total of 10 (occasionally 9) GCSE courses. The aim is to provide a broad and balanced curriculum for all up to the age of 16. All students take GCSE courses in English Language and Literature, Mathematics, Religious Education and at least one Modern Foreign Language. Science is also compulsory; most girls take it as an IGCSE double award, although a sizeable minority sit separate papers in Biology, Chemistry and Physics. For their options, girls are recommended to choose an overall combination of subjects which includes Geography or History, plus one creative or practical subject, including ICT and Physical Education.

Students in all year groups have weekly PSHE sessions, which includes the Thrive programme, developing healthy study skills and focussing on the importance of reaching their goals through a balanced, healthy and mindful approach. In 2014 72.4% of GCSEs were A*–A grade and 89.8% were A*–B grade.

In the Sixth Form, girls study four AS Levels in the L6th and three A2 Levels in the U6th leading to three full A Levels and one AS qualification. A very small number of girls, usually those pursuing Further Mathematics, take five AS and four A2 Levels. Selected students in Sixth Form are invited to take the EPQ (Extended Project Qualification). All Sixth Formers have Physical Education lessons.

A Level pass rate is consistently 100% with 87.7% A*, A & B grades. The school bucks the national trend in uptake of Science, Economics and Mathematics. Girls also achieve outstanding results in Humanities and Languages. The School also has a Gifted and Talented Programme, a Tutor to the Scholars and an Oxbridge Coordinator in place to provide specialist support and guidance.

Careers Guidance and University Application. The School encourages students to begin thinking early in their education about their future careers and the skills and qualifications required through a variety of software programmes and career talks. A biennial careers fair is open to all year groups. In the GCSE years students participate in the ISCO Futurewise programme and receive a detailed skills analysis supported by professional careers guidance to assist in choosing A Level subjects and higher education options. Over 80% of Sixth Form leavers attend Russell Group universities and the School prides itself on the range of subjects students pursue in both the Sciences and the Arts. The School also sends several students to top USA and overseas universities and to both Art Foundation courses and Drama colleges.

Music. Woldingham is well known for its strong and lively tradition of music. Over half the students play a musical instrument; there is a full school orchestra, a string orchestra, two wind bands, a jazz band, Scholars ensemble, and three choirs. School musical productions, public concerts, international tours, and the Church's liturgical celebrations provide scope for a variety of talent and performance. A Mac suite provides for Music Technology learning, as well as composition using Sibelius and Logic.

Drama. Drama is run by dedicated professionals and is very impressive here providing high standards of both curricular and extra-curricular Drama. Girls are involved in local and professional theatre and may go on to become specialists in their chosen field of Drama.

Art. Everyone takes Art for the first two years, developing creative and imaginative powers and acquiring a visual language, with the option to specialise at GCSE or A Level. On offer are drawing, painting, sculpture, ceramics, textile design, printmaking and photography. Our students visit St Ives and this provides an excellent opportunity for working with local artists in their studios, and also the Tate and Hepworth Museums there.

Sport. The School has good sporting facilities, supporting an extensive range of team/individual games/activities to cater for a wide range of interests. It organises competitive matches in the sports of hockey, netball, swimming, cross country, rounders, tennis, and athletics. There are also fixtures for badminton, fencing, football, lacrosse and squash. Although not formally part of the curriculum, the School is able to provide girls with polo, sailing, skiing and fencing instruction. All girls are encouraged to attend extra-curricular activities and sessions are run across the ability range. Elite athletes are guided towards the county pathways for their chosen sport. Certain evenings are dedicated to sports matches and training so girls can pursue music and drama options as well.

International Exchanges. Close links exist with Sacred Heart schools abroad. There is an excellent exchange programme to France and Spain and an annual German trip.

Extra-Curricular Activities. These are not optional extras; they are considered an essential part of a girl's education at Woldingham. The programme of regular weekly activities includes a priority schedule to enable girls to make manageable choices.

The extensive programme of activities, in addition to traditional sports and clubs, offers something for everyone and includes: fencing, archery, taekwondo, polo, jazz band, close harmony singing, backstage drama, life drawing, Chinese and Russian, community service and mountain biking.

The 'Saturday Active' programme is available to girls in Years 7–10, running until noon. The girls can choose from a wide range of high-quality activities, delivered by visiting specialists in their fields.

The Duke of Edinburgh's Award scheme has become well established at Woldingham. The majority of Year 10 girls are involved at Bronze level and a large number go on in the Sixth form to achieve their Gold Award.

Community. The School is involved with many community projects, including volunteering at local nursing homes and a hospice shop, running reading groups at primary schools and helping out at a sports club for adults with learning difficulties, as well as year-round fundraising for several charities both at a local level and internationally.

Exeats. A weekly boarding arrangement is in place for Year 7 and sixth form boarding students, All boarders are allowed home most weekends from Saturday midday. There are two long weekends (from Friday evening) each term with an additional two optional exeats each term.

Health. There is an excellent Health Centre which has two resident nurses. Two doctors attend regularly. There is a Health Education programme which emphasises healthy living. Our Wellness Centre provides support and a positive approach to matters of health.

Admissions. Main entry to Woldingham is via the Woldingham School examination in the autumn prior to the year of entry for 13+, 11+ and 16+ candidates. Students wishing to join the Sixth Form should be capable of taking at least four AS and three A2 courses and should have passed eight or more subjects at GCSE, 6 of which must be at least grade B, including Maths and English (grade A in Sixth Form options).

Applicants for occasional vacant places in other year groups are also required to sit the school's own entrance examination.

Scholarships. Academic, Art, Music, Drama, Sport and All Rounder scholarships are offered at 11+, 13+ and 16+. A Science Scholarship is also offered at 16+

Fees per term (2014–2015). Boarders: £9,850–10,725; Day £6,160–6,715. Sixth Form Direct Entry carry a premium for Boarders of £500, Day £250.

Charitable status. Woldingham School is a Registered Charity, number 1125376. It exists for the education of girls.

Wychwood School

74 Banbury Road, Oxford, Oxfordshire OX2 6JR
Tel: 01865 557976
Fax: 01865 556806
email: admin@wychwoodschool.org
website: www.wychwoodschool.org
Twitter: @wychwoodschool

Staff List:

Headmistress: Mrs A Johnson, BSc Dunelm, PGCE

Deputy & Head of Wychwood Sixth: Ms B Sherlock, BA, MEd (*English*)
Senior Mistress: Mrs S Cripps, MA Cantab, PGCE (*Chemistry*)

Miss H Barnes, BSc Hons, MSc Hons, PGCE (*Physical Education*)
Mrs A Bennett-Jones, BSc, PGCE (*Mathematics*)
Miss J Bettridge, TESOLCert (*EAL*)
Ms M Bridgman, LDS (*Textiles*)
Miss V Castel, BEd Hons, OTT QTS (*Spanish, French*)
Mrs C Chalstrey, BA Hons, PGCE (*RS, SENCo*)
Mrs C Collcutt, DEUG (*French, Examinations Officer*)
Mrs E Dean, MA Oxon PGCE (*English*)
Mrs L Doughton, BSc Hons, MA (*Biology*)
Mrs S Gauden, BA Hons, PGCE
Mr P Ilott, BEng (*Physics*)
Ms A Jones, BA Hons, PGCE (*Art & Design*)
Ms S Jones, BA Hons, PGCE (*Drama*)
Mrs H Kirby, BA Hons, PGCE (*English*)
Mrs M Nash, BA Hons, PGCE (*Psychology*)
Mr M Pennington, BA Hons, MA (*Photography*)
Mrs F Roitt, BSc Hons, PGCE (*Geography*)
Mrs J Sherbrooke, BSc Hons, MSc, PGCE (*History*)
Mr G Singh, BSc Hons, PGCE (*ICT, Network*)
Mrs B Stevens, BSc Hons, PGCE (*Mathematics*)
Mrs G Troth, BSc Hons (*Economics & Business Studies*)
Mrs B Walster, BMus Hons, PGCE (*Music*)
Mrs J Williams, BA Hons, PGCE, SRN, RSCN (*History of Art*)

Reception /Office Assistant Miss M Bewsey-Lord
Head's PA: Mrs S Grainger
Marketing & Admissions: Miss N Jones, BEd Hons
Bursar: Mr I Williams
Senior Housemistress, Head of Boarding: Mrs L Henk
Junior Housemistress: Miss J Tyers
School Doctor: Dr C Hornby, MB BChir, MRCGP
School Counsellor: Mrs M Davis

Wychwood is a unique and friendly day and boarding school for girls, with excellent academic grades and outstanding pastoral care. Situated in the heart of Oxford, the school offers an exceptional education for pupils of all abilities through its small class sizes which allow for extensive individual attention without intense pressure. Established in 1897, individuality has always been more important than conformity at Wychwood and the girls have opportunities for success in many directions.

Curriculum. All girls are expected to take up to 10 subjects at GCSE; most go on to work for AS and A2 and University entrance. The lower school curriculum includes: Religious Education, English, History, Geography, Mathematics, Biology, Physics, Chemistry, French, ICT, Textiles, Singing, Art, Photography, Music, Computing, PSE, Gymnastics, Spanish (from Year 8), Drama, Swimming and Games. Visiting staff teach other optional foreign languages and musical instruments; there is a school choir and chamber groups.

School Council. Day-to-day life is largely controlled by the School Council which meets weekly and consists of staff, seniors (elected by the school) and form representatives. This is a type of cooperative government, the matured result of a long series of experiments, which trains the girls to deal with the problems of community life and gives everyone, in greater or lesser degree according to her age and status, an understanding of, and a voice in, the rules necessary for a sensibly disciplined life.

Sixth Form. Members of Wychwood Sixth have considerable freedom yet play an active part in the life of the school. The choice of subjects at AS and A2 is wide, and classes are small and stimulating. Individual help with university applications and careers is a key feature of the Sixth Form. There are regular outside speakers and girls attend a variety of lectures, conferences, exhibitions and meetings. Their participation in school plays and concerts as well as School Council is greatly valued. Sixth Form girls may spend approximately 2 hours per week on community service. Optional computer courses are run after school. Sixth Form boarders have individual study bedrooms.

Entrance. A personal interview is usually essential between the Headmistress and both a parent and the pupil, though this may be waived where circumstances make it impossible. There is an entrance test to satisfy the staff that the girl will benefit from an education of this kind; the opinion of the girl's former school is also taken into account, particularly in relation to non-academic qualities.

Scholarships and Bursaries. Scholarships are offered in creative arts, art, music, science and academic areas.

Academic: At 11+ one Scholarship worth £1,200 pa and two Scholarships worth £600 pa are offered. Academic Scholarships are awarded on the results of the general entrance paper.

Academic: At 16+ one Scholarship worth £1,800 pa and one Scholarship worth £900 pa are offered, and one Science Scholarship worth £1,800 pa.

Two Music Scholarships are offered at ages 11+ or 16+ to cover instrumental tuition on up to 3 instruments. Candidates will be expected to play two prepared pieces on their instrument(s) and to do some sight reading and aural tests.

Two Creative Arts Scholarships, each worth £1,200 pa, are offered at age 11+ to candidates with outstanding ability in Art or Creative Writing.

Creative Writing: Candidates are asked to bring six different pieces of writing, including poetry, a story and a description. These will be discussed with the Head of English. A piece of creative writing will be set on the afternoon of the test day.

Art: Candidates are asked to bring six artistic compositions or craft items which will be discussed with the Head of Art. A short unprepared task will be undertaken on the afternoon of the test day.

Bursaries: There are means-tested bursary funds available for a limited number of pupils in particular financial need.

Fees per term (2014–2015). Boarders £7,150, Weekly Boarders £6,820, Day Girls £4,550.

Charitable status. Wychwood School is a Registered Charity, number 309684. It exists for the education of girls from the ages of 11 to 18.

Wykeham House School

East Street, Fareham, Hampshire PO16 0BW
Tel: 01329 280178
Fax: 01329 823964
email: office@wykehamhouse.com
website: www.wykehamhouse.com

Motto: *Vouloir C'est Pouvoir*

A day school for girls aged 3 to 16 in the heart of Fareham and a fully separate day school for boys aged 3 to 11. This separate day school for boys was opened in September 2013 and will grow year on year until we have the complete age range from 3 to 16. The boys' school is located in a beautiful Georgian House on the High Street in Fareham, a short walk from the girls' school.

Trustees:
Chairman: Mr J Charles
Vice Chairman: Mrs S Heaysman

Mr D Arthur	Mr J B Fullarton
Mrs P Bryant	Mrs B Gudgeon
Revd S Davenport	Mr S Hocquard
Mrs C A Freemantle	Mr D Luckett

Mr W Pitt
Miss H A Tyler
Mr G Zaki

Staff:

Headmistress: Mrs L R Clarke, BSc Hons, PGCE, PG
Dip Nottingham

Deputy Headmistress: Mrs J R Caddy, BEd Hons King
Alfred's Winchester
Head of Senior School: Miss H Wilson, BEd Hons
Chichester Inst of HE
Head of Girls' Junior School: Mrs H Cuthbert, BA Hons
Leeds, QTS
Head of Boys' Junior School: Mr G Case, BEd Hons
Homerton College Cambridge, PG Dip Portsmouth
Bursar: Mr D Bryant

Full-Time Staff:
Mrs J Corrigan, BA Hons Chichester Institute of HE
Mrs J Disley, BSc Hons Aberdeen, PGCE King's College
London, RSci
Mrs C Flack, BEd Hons Westminster College, Oxford
Mr P Gago, BEd Hons Sunderland Polytechnic
Mrs A P Jones, BA Hons, PGCE Portsmouth
Mr D Jones, BMus Hons Cardiff, QTS
Mrs K Lincoln, BA Hons Sunderland, PGCE Southlands
College, Wimbledon
Mr D Robertson, BA Hons, PG Dip Duncan of Jordanstone
PGCE Strathcylde
Mr B Sillitoe, BA Hons Norwich, PGCE Chichester
Mrs J Thimbleby, BSc Hons Manchester, PGCE
Southampton

Part-Time Staff:
Mrs A Bailey, BA Hons Exeter, MA Portsmouth, PGCE
Bath
Miss C Ball, NNEB Foundation Stage Practitioner
Mrs S Beacon, BA Hons Exeter, PGCE St Mary's
Twickenham
Mrs J Bristowe, BEd Rolle College, Devon
Mrs S Cross, BA Hons PGCE Reading
Miss V Currie, BSc Hons PGCE Southampton
Mr S Dearden, BSc Leeds, PGCE Loughborough
Mrs C Edden, NVQ3 Early Years Care and Education
Mrs G Kennard, BEd Hons Sussex
Mrs M I Menendez, MA BA Oviedo, Spain, PGCE
Portsmouth
Mrs C E Noyce, BSc Hons, PGCE Bristol
Revd C R Prestidge, BEd Hons West Sussex Inst of HE,
BA Hons OU, Dip Ministry and Mission, Surrey, STETS
Mrs M Reversé-Hayes, Licence d'enseignement France,
PGCE, MA Ed Southampton
Mrs S Savage, BA Hons Portsmouth, PGCE Exeter
Mrs J Shaw, Foundation Degree, Early Years Care and
Education
Mrs A M Taylor, MA PGCE St Andrews
Miss A Todd, BSc Hons Southampton, PGCE Portsmouth
Mrs S Todd, BSc Hons Cardiff, PGCE Aberystwyth

Learning Support:
Mrs D Leighton, BA Hons Portsmouth, CertEd CertEd FE
London, SpLD APC Patoss (*Learning Support
Coordinator*)
Mrs K James (*Learning Support Coordinator*)

Visiting Staff:
Mr M Brown, PDip Composition & Music
Miss C Draycott, LLB Hons., Middlesex, FE TCert,
Chichester College, Dip ABRSM Flute Perf
Mrs J Flatman, LRSM, BA Hons, PGCE
Mrs L Heathorn (*Speech and Drama*)
Mrs F Morris, BMus Hons Hull, PGCE Cambridge
(*Singing*)
Mr G Walker (*Drums*)

Headmistress's Secretary: Mrs L J Upton

School Administrator: Mrs E Lloyd
Office Assistant: Mrs R Sandy
Boys' School Administrator: Mrs J North

Wykeham House School in Fareham celebrated its centenary in 2013 and has a fine reputation for outstanding pastoral care, excellent results and a dedication to small class
sizes and individual attention. In its 2013 Independent
Schools Inspectorate Report the School was highly praised
achieving the top grading of 'excellent' across many key
areas. The excellent care and education were well recognised throughout the report which is available in full on
the school's website. The new boys' school was recognised
in the report, which stated that 'Much care has been given to
adapting the curriculum and timetable to suit the needs of
the boys'.

The School's concept of education extends beyond the
classroom with the aim of developing self-confident, self-
disciplined and motivated pupils. The excellent facilities at
the School provide the opportunity to take part in art, music,
drama, sport and other outdoor activities and emphasis is
placed on courtesy and concern for others.

The Foundation Stage, which incorporates the Nursery
and Reception classes and is the only co-educational part of
the school, is in its own self-contained unit within the
School and provides a happy and caring environment for the
children. It has its own indoor and outdoor play areas,
including an outdoor classroom, as well as having the
advantage of being able to use the exceptional facilities at
the School.

The Junior Schools (3 to 11 years) have an individuality
of their own which contributes greatly to the School's atmosphere and the sense of community. All the usual activities,
which are taught at Primary level, are covered by the Junior
Curriculum. The teaching methods employed place an
emphasis on the acquisition of the basic skills of Literacy
and Numeracy. Full opportunities are given for creative
work, self-expression and individual development.

At the age of 9+ children are introduced to a number of
specialist teachers who teach across a wide curriculum. This
helps to ensure a smooth transition to the Senior School.

The Senior School (11–16 years). The curriculum aims
to maintain standards and yet recognizes the need to keep
apace of educational developments and modern teaching
techniques. The Curriculum is under constant review by the
Headmistress and the Staff Committee. Specialist rooms,
three well-equipped laboratories and two computer suites
are available to staff and all rooms have computers and projectors.

The subjects taught in the Senior School cover a broad
curriculum leading to GCSE.

An options system is in existence from Year 10 and all
pupils take English, Mathematics, a Modern Language, Science (either the separate subjects of Physics, Chemistry and
Biology or a Science and Additional Science). Private study
periods are included in the option groups to encourage individual study skills and full use is made of the School
Library. All pupils study PSHE, PE and a lesson a week in
RS, Philosophy and Ethics.

Visits are undertaken to theatres, museums, art galleries,
and other places of interest. Field work is an integral part of
the study of Humanities and in Science while Modern Language study involves visits to Europe. Lecturers and performers are invited to the School while the pupils are
encouraged to take part in Music, Art and Drama as well as
other leisure pursuits.

Senior girls participate in the Duke of Edinburgh's Award
Scheme. In this way they test their own initiative, discover
fresh challenging pursuits, make new friends and become
aware of the needs of others.

Many activities occur during lunch times and after school
such as the mathematics workshop, games practices, school
choirs, instrumental groups, dramatic productions, cookery,

dancing, St John Ambulance First Aid, Rotary Interact Group, Rainbows, Brownies and much more.

The Headmistress and Deputy Headmistress are together responsible for careers advice in the School and there is an extensive library of careers literature freely available. The School runs its own Careers Conference every two years, which is very well supported by parents at the School. Close contact is maintained with local sixth form colleges, further education colleges and other schools in the area.

The pastoral system is organized on a House basis: the pupils belong to four School Houses where the year groups mix socially and competitively.

Physical Education. The School supplements its Games facilities by hiring nearby local amenities. Netball, Hockey, Tennis, Rounders and Athletics form the basis of the Senior Girls' Physical Education programme. Girls also have swimming lessons at the local pool. The Boys' PE curriculum is very varied and will also be utilising the huge range of local sporting amenities.

Admission. Entry is by a Taster Day with age appropriate assessment. Entry to Year 7 in the Senior School is through the School's own Entrance Examination in January or a Taster Day at other points.

Fees per term (2014–2015). Reception–Year 2 £2,775; Years 3–6; £2,995; Years 7–9 £3,790; Years 10–11 £3,990.

Nursery Fees: Wykeham House participates in the Early Years Extended Entitlement (Pathfinder) Scheme which provides 15 free hours of childcare per week. Any additional hours between 8.30 am and 3.30 pm are charged at £5.20 per hour. Employer childcare vouchers are also accepted subject to HMRC criteria.

Scholarships and Bursaries. A number of Scholarships worth a fixed amount each year towards the cost of books, tenable for five years, are awarded each year based on good 11+ entrance results and interview.

The School also operates a means-tested Bursary Scheme.

Charitable status. Wykeham House School Trust is a Registered Charity, number 307339. It exists to provide education for girls and boys.

Entrance Scholarships

Academic Scholarships

The Abbey School (p. 561)
Abbots Bromley School (p. 562)
Abbot's Hill School (p. 563)
Alderley Edge School for Girls (p. 566)
Badminton School (p. 567)
Blackheath High School (p. 569)
Brighton & Hove High School (p. 572)
Bromley High School (p. 572)
Bruton School for Girls (p. 574)
Burgess Hill School for Girls (p. 575)
Channing School (p. 577)
Cheltenham Ladies' College (p. 579)
Cobham Hall (p. 580)
Cranford House School (p. 582)
Croydon High School (p. 583)
Dame Allan's Girls' School (p. 584)
Derby High School (p. 585)
Durham High School for Girls (p. 588)
Edgbaston High School (p. 589)
Farlington School (p. 592)
Farnborough Hill (p. 593)
Francis Holland School (p. 594)
Gateways School (p. 596)
Greenacre School for Girls (p. 598)
Haberdashers' Aske's School for Girls (p. 599)
Haberdashers' Monmouth School for Girls (p. 601)
Harrogate Ladies' College (p. 603)
Headington School (p. 605)
Heathfield School (p. 607)
Hethersett Old Hall School (p. 609)
Howell's School Llandaff (p. 610)
Ipswich High School (p. 611)
Kilgraston (p. 612)
King Edward VI High School for Girls (p. 613)
King's High School (p. 615)
The Kingsley School (p. 617)
The Lady Eleanor Holles School (p. 618)
Lavant House (p. 621)
Leicester High School for Girls (p. 623)
Leweston School (p. 624)
Loughborough High School (p. 626)
Luckley House School (p. 628)
Manchester High School for Girls (p. 629)
Manor House School (p. 630)
The Mary Erskine School (p. 632)
Marymount International School (p. 634)
The Maynard School (p. 636)
Moira House Girls School (p. 639)
More House School (p. 642)

Moreton Hall (p. 644)
The Mount School (p. 646)
North London Collegiate School (p. 649)
Northampton High School (p. 650)
Northwood College for Girls (p. 652)
Norwich High School (p. 653)
Notre Dame School (p. 654)
Notting Hill and Ealing High School (p. 657)
Nottingham Girls' High School (p. 658)
Oxford High School (p. 659)
Palmers Green High School (p. 659)
Pipers Corner School (p. 661)
Portsmouth High School (p. 661)
Princess Helena College (p. 662)
Prior's Field (p. 664)
Putney High School (p. 665)
Queen Margaret's School (p. 668)
Queen Mary's School (p. 671)
Queen's College, London (p. 672)
Queen's Gate School (p. 673)
Queenswood School (p. 675)
The Red Maids' School (p. 676)
Redland High School for Girls (p. 678)
The Royal High School Bath (p. 680)
Rye St Antony (p. 682)
St Catherine's School (p. 687)
St Catherine's School (p. 689)
St Dominic's Brewood (p. 690)
St Dominic's Priory School (p. 691)
St Gabriel's (p. 692)
St George's, Ascot (p. 694)
St Helen & St Katharine (p. 696)
St Helen's School (p. 698)
St Leonards-Mayfield School (p. 702)
St Margaret's School (p. 706)
St Martha's (p. 707)
Saint Martin's (p. 709)
St Mary's School (p. 710)
St Mary's School (p. 714)
St Mary's School (p. 715)
St Nicholas' School (p. 717)
St Swithun's School (p. 719)
Sheffield High School (p. 723)
Shrewsbury High School (p. 723)
South Hampstead High School (p. 725)
Stamford High School (p. 726)
Stonar (p. 728)
Streatham & Clapham High School (p. 729)
Sutton High School (p. 731)

Sydenham High School (p. 733)
Talbot Heath (p. 734)
Tormead School (p. 734)
Truro High School for Girls (p. 736)
Tudor Hall (p. 737)
Walthamstow Hall (p. 739)
Westfield School (p. 741)

Westholme School (p. 743)
Westonbirt School (p. 743)
Wimbledon High School (p. 745)
Woldingham School (p. 746)
Wychwood School (p. 748)
Wykeham House School (p. 749)

All-Rounder Scholarships

Badminton School (p. 567)
Bruton School for Girls (p. 574)
Burgess Hill School for Girls (p. 575)
Cobham Hall (p. 580)
Croydon High School (p. 583)
Derby High School (p. 585)
Gateways School (p. 596)
Harrogate Ladies' College (p. 603)
Leweston School (p. 624)
Marymount International School (p. 634)

Moreton Hall (p. 644)
Notting Hill and Ealing High School (p. 657)
Pipers Corner School (p. 661)
St George's, Ascot (p. 694)
Stamford High School (p. 726)
Stonar (p. 728)
Talbot Heath (p. 734)
Tudor Hall (p. 737)
Woldingham School (p. 746)

Art Scholarships

The Abbey School (p. 561)
Abbots Bromley School (p. 562)
Abbot's Hill School (p. 563)
Alderley Edge School for Girls (p. 566)
Badminton School (p. 567)
Blackheath High School (p. 569)
Brighton & Hove High School (p. 572)
Bromley High School (p. 572)
Bruton School for Girls (p. 574)
Burgess Hill School for Girls (p. 575)
Channing School (p. 577)
Cheltenham Ladies' College (p. 579)
Cobham Hall (p. 580)
Cranford House School (p. 582)
Croydon High School (p. 583)
Derby High School (p. 585)
Durham High School for Girls (p. 588)
Edgbaston High School (p. 589)
Farlington School (p. 592)
Farnborough Hill (p. 593)
Francis Holland School (p. 594)
Gateways School (p. 596)
Greenacre School for Girls (p. 598)
Haberdashers' Monmouth School for Girls (p. 601)
Harrogate Ladies' College (p. 603)
Headington School (p. 605)
Heathfield School (p. 607)
Hethersett Old Hall School (p. 609)
Ipswich High School (p. 611)
Kilgraston (p. 612)
The Kingsley School (p. 617)

Leweston School (p. 624)
Luckley House School (p. 628)
Manor House School (p. 630)
Marymount International School (p. 634)
The Maynard School (p. 636)
Moira House Girls School (p. 639)
More House School (p. 642)
Moreton Hall (p. 644)
The Mount School (p. 646)
Northampton High School (p. 650)
Northwood College for Girls (p. 652)
Notting Hill and Ealing High School (p. 657)
Oxford High School (p. 659)
Pipers Corner School (p. 661)
Portsmouth High School (p. 661)
Princess Helena College (p. 662)
Prior's Field (p. 664)
Putney High School (p. 665)
Queen Margaret's School (p. 668)
Queen Mary's School (p. 671)
Queen's College, London (p. 672)
Queenswood School (p. 675)
Redland High School for Girls (p. 678)
The Royal High School Bath (p. 680)
Rye St Antony (p. 682)
St Catherine's School (p. 687)
St Catherine's School (p. 689)
St Dominic's Brewood (p. 690)
St Dominic's Priory School (p. 691)
St Gabriel's (p. 692)
St George's, Ascot (p. 694)

St Helen & St Katharine (p. 696)
St Helen's School (p. 698)
St Leonards-Mayfield School (p. 702)
St Margaret's School (p. 706)
St Martha's (p. 707)
St Mary's School (p. 710)
St Mary's School (p. 715)
St Nicholas' School (p. 717)
Sheffield High School (p. 723)
Shrewsbury High School (p. 723)
Stamford High School (p. 726)
Stonar (p. 728)

Streatham & Clapham High School (p. 729)
Sutton High School (p. 731)
Sydenham High School (p. 733)
Tormead School (p. 734)
Truro High School for Girls (p. 736)
Tudor Hall (p. 737)
Walthamstow Hall (p. 739)
Westfield School (p. 741)
Westonbirt School (p. 743)
Wimbledon High School (p. 745)
Woldingham School (p. 746)
Wychwood School (p. 748)

Dance Scholarships

Abbots Bromley School (p. 562)
Edgbaston High School (p. 589)
Gateways School (p. 596)
Manchester High School for Girls (p. 629)
Queen Margaret's School (p. 668)

Queenswood School (p. 675)
St Gabriel's (p. 692)
St Leonards-Mayfield School (p. 702)
St Mary's School (p. 710)
Tudor Hall (p. 737)

Drama Scholarships

The Abbey School (p. 561)
Abbot's Hill School (p. 563)
Bromley High School (p. 572)
Bruton School for Girls (p. 574)
Burgess Hill School for Girls (p. 575)
Cheltenham Ladies' College (p. 579)
Cobham Hall (p. 580)
Cranford House School (p. 582)
Derby High School (p. 585)
Durham High School for Girls (p. 588)
Edgbaston High School (p. 589)
Farlington School (p. 592)
Francis Holland School (p. 594)
Gateways School (p. 596)
Haberdashers' Monmouth School for Girls (p. 601)
Harrogate Ladies' College (p. 603)
Headington School (p. 605)
Heathfield School (p. 607)
Hethersett Old Hall School (p. 609)
Ipswich High School (p. 611)
Kilgraston (p. 612)
The Kingsley School (p. 617)
Leweston School (p. 624)
Luckley House School (p. 628)
Manor House School (p. 630)
Marymount International School (p. 634)
Moira House Girls School (p. 639)
More House School (p. 642)
Moreton Hall (p. 644)
The Mount School (p. 646)

Notting Hill and Ealing High School (p. 657)
Oxford High School (p. 659)
Pipers Corner School (p. 661)
Portsmouth High School (p. 661)
Princess Helena College (p. 662)
Prior's Field (p. 664)
Putney High School (p. 665)
Queen Margaret's School (p. 668)
Queenswood School (p. 675)
The Royal High School Bath (p. 680)
Rye St Antony (p. 682)
St Dominic's Brewood (p. 690)
St Gabriel's (p. 694)
St George's, Ascot (p. 696)
St Helen & St Katharine (p. 698)
St Helen's School (p. 700)
St Leonards-Mayfield School (p. 704)
St Mary's School (p. 712)
Sheffield High School (p. 725)
Shrewsbury High School (p. 725)
Stonar (p. 730)
Streatham & Clapham High School (p. 731)
Sutton High School (p. 733)
Sydenham High School (p. 735)
Truro High School for Girls (p. 738)
Tudor Hall (p. 739)
Walthamstow Hall (p. 741)
Westonbirt School (p. 745)
Wimbledon High School (p. 747)
Woldingham School (p. 748)

Music Scholarships

The Abbey School (p. 561)

Abbots Bromley School (p. 562)

Abbot's Hill School (p. 563)

Alderley Edge School for Girls (p. 566)

Badminton School (p. 567)

Blackheath High School (p. 569)

Brighton & Hove High School (p. 572)

Bromley High School (p. 572)

Bruton School for Girls (p. 574)

Burgess Hill School for Girls (p. 575)

Channing School (p. 577)

Cheltenham Ladies' College (p. 579)

Cobham Hall (p. 580)

Cranford House School (p. 582)

Croydon High School (p. 583)

Derby High School (p. 585)

Durham High School for Girls (p. 588)

Edgbaston High School (p. 589)

Farlington School (p. 592)

Farnborough Hill (p. 593)

Francis Holland School (p. 594)

Gateways School (p. 596)

Greenacre School for Girls (p. 598)

Haberdashers' Aske's School for Girls (p. 599)

Haberdashers' Monmouth School for Girls (p. 601)

Harrogate Ladies' College (p. 603)

Headington School (p. 605)

Heathfield School (p. 607)

Hethersett Old Hall School (p. 609)

Howell's School Llandaff (p. 610)

Ipswich High School (p. 611)

Kilgraston (p. 612)

King's High School (p. 615)

The Kingsley School (p. 617)

The Lady Eleanor Holles School (p. 618)

Lavant House (p. 621)

Leicester High School for Girls (p. 623)

Leweston School (p. 624)

Loughborough High School (p. 626)

Luckley House School (p. 628)

Manchester High School for Girls (p. 629)

Manor House School (p. 630)

The Mary Erskine School (p. 632)

Marymount International School (p. 634)

The Maynard School (p. 636)

Moira House Girls School (p. 639)

More House School (p. 642)

Moreton Hall (p. 644)

The Mount School (p. 646)

North London Collegiate School (p. 649)

Northwood College for Girls (p. 652)

Norwich High School (p. 653)

Notre Dame School (p. 654)

Notting Hill and Ealing High School (p. 657)

Oxford High School (p. 659)

Palmers Green High School (p. 659)

Pipers Corner School (p. 661)

Portsmouth High School (p. 661)

Princess Helena College (p. 662)

Prior's Field (p. 664)

Putney High School (p. 665)

Queen Margaret's School (p. 668)

Queen Mary's School (p. 671)

Queen's College, London (p. 672)

Queenswood School (p. 675)

The Red Maids' School (p. 676)

Redland High School for Girls (p. 678)

The Royal High School Bath (p. 680)

Rye St Antony (p. 682)

St Catherine's School (p. 687)

St Catherine's School (p. 689)

St Dominic's Brewood (p. 690)

St Dominic's Priory School (p. 691)

St Gabriel's (p. 692)

St George's, Ascot (p. 694)

St Helen & St Katharine (p. 696)

St Helen's School (p. 698)

St Leonards-Mayfield School (p. 702)

St Margaret's School (p. 706)

St Martha's (p. 707)

Saint Martin's (p. 709)

St Mary's School (p. 710)

St Mary's School (p. 714)

St Mary's School (p. 715)

St Nicholas' School (p. 717)

St Swithun's School (p. 719)

Sheffield High School (p. 723)

Shrewsbury High School (p. 723)

South Hampstead High School (p. 725)

Stamford High School (p. 726)

Stonar (p. 728)

Streatham & Clapham High School (p. 729)

Sutton High School (p. 731)

Sydenham High School (p. 733)

Talbot Heath (p. 734)

Tormead School (p. 734)

Truro High School for Girls (p. 736)

Tudor Hall (p. 737)

Walthamstow Hall (p. 739)

Westfield School (p. 741)

Westholme School (p. 743)

Westonbirt School (p. 743)

Wimbledon High School (p. 745)

Woldingham School (p. 746)

Wychwood School (p. 748)

Sport Scholarships

The Abbey School (p. 561)

Abbots Bromley School (p. 562)

Abbot's Hill School (p. 563)

Alderley Edge School for Girls (p. 566)

Brighton & Hove High School (p. 572)

Bromley High School (p. 572)

Bruton School for Girls (p. 574)

Burgess Hill School for Girls (p. 575)

Cheltenham Ladies' College (p. 579)

Cobham Hall (p. 580)

Cranford House School (p. 582)

Croydon High School (p. 583)

Derby High School (p. 585)

Durham High School for Girls (p. 588)

Edgbaston High School (p. 589)

Farlington School (p. 592)

Farnborough Hill (p. 593)

Gateways School (p. 596)

Greenacre School for Girls (p. 598)

Haberdashers' Monmouth School for Girls (p. 601)

Harrogate Ladies' College (p. 603)

Headington School (p. 605)

Heathfield School (p. 607)

Hethersett Old Hall School (p. 609)

Ipswich High School (p. 611)

Kilgraston (p. 612)

The Kingsley School (p. 617)

Leweston School (p. 624)

Luckley House School (p. 628)

Manchester High School for Girls (p. 629)

Manor House School (p. 630)

Marymount International School (p. 634)

The Maynard School (p. 636)

Moira House Girls School (p. 639)

Moreton Hall (p. 644)

The Mount School (p. 646)

Northampton High School (p. 650)

Northwood College for Girls (p. 652)

Notre Dame School (p. 654)

Notting Hill and Ealing High School (p. 657)

Oxford High School (p. 659)

Pipers Corner School (p. 661)

Portsmouth High School (p. 661)

Princess Helena College (p. 662)

Prior's Field (p. 664)

Putney High School (p. 665)

Queen Margaret's School (p. 668)

Queen Mary's School (p. 671)

Queenswood School (p. 675)

The Red Maids' School (p. 676)

Redland High School for Girls (p. 678)

The Royal High School Bath (p. 680)

Rye St Antony (p. 682)

St Catherine's School (p. 687)

St Catherine's School (p. 689)

St Dominic's Brewood (p. 690)

St Dominic's Priory School (p. 691)

St Gabriel's (p. 692)

St George's, Ascot (p. 694)

St Helen & St Katharine (p. 696)

St Helen's School (p. 698)

St Leonards-Mayfield School (p. 702)

St Martha's (p. 707)

Saint Martin's (p. 709)

St Mary's School (p. 710)

St Mary's School (p. 715)

St Nicholas' School (p. 717)

St Swithun's School (p. 719)

Sheffield High School (p. 723)

Shrewsbury High School (p. 723)

Stamford High School (p. 726)

Stonar (p. 728)

Streatham & Clapham High School (p. 729)

Sutton High School (p. 731)

Sydenham High School (p. 733)

Talbot Heath (p. 734)

Truro High School for Girls (p. 736)

Tudor Hall (p. 737)

Walthamstow Hall (p. 739)

Westfield School (p. 741)

Westonbirt School (p. 743)

Wimbledon High School (p. 745)

Woldingham School (p. 746)

Other Scholarships

Boarding

Hethersett Old Hall School (p. 609)

Truro High School for Girls (p. 736)

Choral

Queen Margaret's School (p. 668)

St Leonards-Mayfield School (p. 702)

Westonbirt School (p. 743)

Design

Putney High School (p. 665)

Equestrian

Abbots Bromley School (p. 562)

St Leonards-Mayfield School (p. 702)

Stonar (p. 728)

Hockey

Queenswood School (p. 675)

Ogden Trust Science

The Maynard School (p. 636)

Organ

Queenswood School (p. 675)

St Catherine's School (p. 687)

Westonbirt School (p. 743)

Performing Arts

Greenacre School for Girls (p. 598)

The Kingsley School (p. 617)

St Dominic's Brewood (p. 690)

St George's, Ascot (p. 694)

Saint Martin's (p. 709)

Westonbirt School (p. 743)

Photography

St Mary's School (p. 710)

Science

Putney High School (p. 665)

Wimbledon High School (p. 745)

Woldingham School (p. 746)

Wychwood School (p. 748)

Tennis

Queenswood School (p. 675)

Textiles

Tudor Hall (p. 737)

Bursaries

The Abbey School (p. 561)
Abbots Bromley School (p. 562)
Abbot's Hill School (p. 563)
Alderley Edge School for Girls (p. 566)
Badminton School (p. 567)
Bedford Girls' School (p. 569)
Bolton School Girls' Division (p. 570)
Brighton & Hove High School (p. 572)
Bromley High School (p. 572)
Bruton School for Girls (p. 574)
Burgess Hill School for Girls (p. 575)
Bury Grammar School Girls (p. 576)
Channing School (p. 577)
Cheltenham Ladies' College (p. 579)
Croydon High School (p. 583)
Dame Allan's Girls' School (p. 584)
Derby High School (p. 585)
Durham High School for Girls (p. 588)
Edgbaston High School (p. 589)
Farlington School (p. 592)
Farnborough Hill (p. 593)
Francis Holland School (p. 594)
Gateways School (p. 596)
Greenacre School for Girls (p. 598)
Haberdashers' Aske's School for Girls (p. 599)
Harrogate Ladies' College (p. 603)
Headington School (p. 605)
Heathfield School (p. 607)
Hethersett Old Hall School (p. 609)
Howell's School Llandaff (p. 610)
Ipswich High School (p. 611)
Kilgraston (p. 612)
King Edward VI High School for Girls (p. 613)
King's High School (p. 615)
The Kingsley School (p. 617)
The Lady Eleanor Holles School (p. 618)
Lavant House (p. 621)
Leicester High School for Girls (p. 623)
Loughborough High School (p. 626)
Luckley House School (p. 628)
Manchester High School for Girls (p. 629)
Manor House School (p. 630)
The Mary Erskine School (p. 632)
Marymount International School (p. 634)
The Maynard School (p. 636)
Moira House Girls School (p. 639)
More House School (p. 642)
Moreton Hall (p. 644)
The Mount School (p. 646)
Newcastle High School for Girls (p. 648)
North London Collegiate School (p. 649)
Northampton High School (p. 650)
Northwood College for Girls (p. 652)
Norwich High School (p. 653)
Notre Dame School (p. 654)

Notting Hill and Ealing High School (p. 657)
Nottingham Girls' High School (p. 658)
Oxford High School (p. 659)
Palmers Green High School (p. 659)
Pipers Corner School (p. 661)
Portsmouth High School (p. 661)
Princess Helena College (p. 662)
Prior's Field (p. 664)
Putney High School (p. 665)
Queen Margaret's School (p. 668)
Queen Mary's School (p. 671)
Queen's College, London (p. 672)
Queen's Gate School (p. 673)
Queenswood School (p. 675)
The Red Maids' School (p. 676)
Redland High School for Girls (p. 678)
The Royal High School Bath (p. 680)
Rye St Antony (p. 682)
St Catherine's School (p. 687)
St Catherine's School (p. 689)
St Dominic's Brewood (p. 690)
St Dominic's Priory School (p. 691)
St Gabriel's (p. 692)
St Helen & St Katharine (p. 696)
St Helen's School (p. 698)
St James Senior Girls' School (p. 701)
St Leonards-Mayfield School (p. 702)
St Margaret's School for Girls (p. 704)
St Margaret's School (p. 706)
St Martha's (p. 707)
St Mary's School (p. 710)
St Mary's School (p. 714)
St Mary's School (p. 715)
St Nicholas' School (p. 717)
St Swithun's School (p. 719)
Sheffield High School (p. 723)
Shrewsbury High School (p. 723)
South Hampstead High School (p. 725)
Stamford High School (p. 726)
Stonar (p. 728)
Streatham & Clapham High School (p. 729)
Sutton High School (p. 731)
Sydenham High School (p. 733)
Talbot Heath (p. 734)
Tormead School (p. 734)
Truro High School for Girls (p. 736)
Tudor Hall (p. 737)
Walthamstow Hall (p. 739)
Westfield School (p. 741)
Westholme School (p. 743)
Westonbirt School (p. 743)
Wimbledon High School (p. 745)
Wychwood School (p. 748)
Wykeham House School (p. 749)

PART III
Schools whose Heads are members of
The Society of Heads

ALPHABETICAL LIST OF SCHOOLS

PAGE

Abbey Gate College, Cheshire. 761
Abbotsholme School, Derbyshire. 763
Austin Friars St Monica's School, Cumbria. 764

Bedstone College, Shropshire 766
Beechwood Sacred Heart School, Kent 768
Bethany School, Kent 769
Bournemouth Collegiate School, Dorset. 770
Box Hill School, Surrey 770

The Cathedral School Llandaff, Wales. 772
Claremont Fan Court School, Surrey 772
Clifton High School, Bristol 773
Concord College, Shropshire 776

Derby Grammar School, Derbyshire. 777
Dover College, Kent 778
d'Overbroeck's College, Oxon 780
Dunottar School, Surrey 782

Ewell Castle School, Surrey 783

Farringtons School, Kent 784
Friends' School, Essex. 785
Fulneck School, W Yorks 787

Hampshire Collegiate School, Hants 788
Hill House School, S Yorks 790
Hull Collegiate School, E Yorks 790

Kingham Hill School, Oxon 792
Kingsley School, Devon 793

Langley School, Norfolk. 795
Lichfield Cathedral School, Staffs 797
Longridge Towers School, Northumberland. 798
LVS Ascot (The Licensed Victuallers' School), Berks 800

Milton Abbey School, Dorset 801

Newcastle School for Boys, Tyne and Wear. 803
North Cestrian Grammar School, Cheshire 803

PAGE

Ockbrook School, Derbyshire 804
Oswestry School, Shropshire 806
Our Lady's Abingdon Senior School, Oxon. 807

The Peterborough School, Cambs 808
Pitsford School, Northants. 810
Portland Place School, London 811
The Purcell School, Herts 813

The Read School, N Yorks. 815
Reddam House Bearwood, Berks 816
Rishworth School, W Yorks 818
The Royal School, Wolverhampton, W Midlands. . . . 820
Ruthin School, Wales 822

St Bees School, Cumbria. 823
St Christopher School, Herts. 825
St Edward's School, Glos 827
Saint Felix School, Suffolk 828
St George's School, W Midlands 830
St James Senior Boys' School, Surrey. 832
St John's College, Hants. 833
St Joseph's College, Suffolk. 834
Scarborough College, N Yorks. 835
Shebbear College, Devon 837
Sibford School, Oxon 838
Stafford Grammar School, Staffs 840
Stover School, Devon 841
Sunderland High School, Tyne and Wear 843

Tettenhall College, W Midlands 844
Thetford Grammar School, Norfolk 846
Tring Park School for the Performing Arts, Herts. . . 847
Trinity School, Devon 848

Welbeck – The Defence Sixth Form College, Leics. . 849
Windermere School, Cumbria 850

The Yehudi Menuhin School, Surrey 851

The following schools, whose Heads are members of both The Society of Heads and HMC, can be found in the HMC section:

Ackworth School
Bedales School
Bristol Grammar School
Clayesmore School
Cokethorpe School
Halliford School
King's Ely
Kirkham Grammar School
Leighton Park School
Lincoln Minster School
Reading Blue Coat School

Reed's School
Rendcomb College
Rydal Penrhos School
St Columba's College, St Albans
St George's College
Seaford College
Shiplake College
Sidcot School
Silcoates School
Warminster School
Wisbech Grammar School

The following schools, whose Heads are members of both The Society of Heads and GSA, can be found in the GSA section:

Burgess Hill School for Girls
Francis Holland School, Sloane Square
King Edward VI High School for Girls
Moreton Hall

Saint Augustine's Priory School
Stonar
Westholme School

THE SOCIETY OF HEADS
GEOGRAPHICAL LIST OF SCHOOLS

PAGE   PAGE

ENGLAND

Berkshire
LVS Ascot (The Licensed Victuallers' School)... 800
Reddam House Bearwood 816

Bristol
Clifton High School................. 773

Cambridgeshire
The Peterborough School 808

Cheshire
Abbey Gate College................. 761
North Cestrian Grammar School 803

Cumbria
Austin Friars St Monica's School......... 764
St Bees School 823
Windermere School................. 850

Derbyshire
Abbotsholme School 763
Derby Grammar School.............. 777
Ockbrook School 804

Devon
Kingsley School................... 793
Shebbear College 837
Stover School 841
Trinity School................... 848

Dorset
Bournemouth Collegiate School 770
Milton Abbey School 801

Essex
Friends' School 785

Gloucestershire
St Edward's School 827

Hampshire
Hampshire Collegiate School........... 788
St John's College 833

Hertfordshire
The Purcell School 813
St Christopher School............... 825
Tring Park School for the Performing Arts 847

Kent
Beechwood Sacred Heart School 768
Bethany School 769
Dover College................... 778
Farringtons School 784

Leicestershire
Welbeck - The Defence Sixth Form College 849

London (see also Essex, Middlesex, Surrey)
Portland Place School............... 811

Norfolk
Langley School 795

Thetford Grammar School 846

Northamptonshire
Pitsford School 810

Northumberland
Longridge Towers School............. 798

Oxfordshire
d'Overbroeck's College.............. 780
Kingham Hill School 792
Our Lady's Abingdon Senior School 807
Sibford School 838

Shropshire
Bedstone College 766
Concord College 776
Oswestry School 806

Staffordshire (see also West Midlands)
Lichfield Cathedral School 797
Stafford Grammar School............. 840

Suffolk
Saint Felix School................. 828
St Joseph's College 834

Surrey
Box Hill School................... 770
Claremont Fan Court School 772
Dunottar School.................. 782
Ewell Castle School................ 783
St James Senior Boys' School 832
The Yehudi Menuhin School 851

Tyne and Wear
Newcastle School for Boys 803
Sunderland High School 843

West Midlands
The Royal School, Wolverhampton........ 820
St George's School 830
Tettenhall College................. 844

Yorkshire (East)
Hull Collegiate School 790

Yorkshire (North)
The Read School 815
Scarborough College 835

Yorkshire (South)
Hill House School................. 790

Yorkshire (West)
Fulneck School 787
Rishworth School................. 818

WALES
The Cathedral School Llandaff 772
Ruthin School................... 822

Individual School Entries

Abbey Gate College

Saighton Grange, Saighton, Chester CH3 6EN
Tel: 01244 332077
Fax: 01244 335510
email: admin@abbeygatecollege.co.uk
website: www.abbeygatecollege.co.uk

Motto: *Audentior Ito*
    Founded in 1977, Abbey Gate College is a co-educational day school for 515 boys and girls from 4–18 years of age.

Visitor: His Grace The Duke of Westminster

Chairman of Governors: Mr D Weir, CA

Head: Mrs T Pollard, BEd Hons, NPQH, MA

Deputy Heads:
D P H Meadows, BA Hons, PGCE (*History*)
G Allmand, BSc Hons, PGCE (*Geography*)

Academic Staff:
Miss C Andrews, BA Hons, PGCE (*Drama*)
A Austen, BSc Hons, PGCE (*Geography*)
S Ball, PhD, MPhys (*Physics*)
Miss K Burdon, BSc PGCE (*Mathematics*)
Mrs N Burton, MA, BA Hons PGCE (*Art*)
M Cavallini, BSc Hons, GTP (*Mathematics*)
Mrs J Connor-Webb, MA, PGCE (*Modern Foreign Languages*)
C Cutler, BSc Hons (*PE*)
Mrs S Dolan, BSc Hons, PGCE (*Biology*)
M Dickins, BA, PGCE (*History*)
Mrs R Fitzhugh, BA Hons, PGCE (*Geography*)
Mrs V Goodwin, MusB Hons, PGCE (*ICT*)
A P Green, BEd (*PE & Mathematics*)
Mrs S Hall, BA Hons, History, QTS, AMBDA, PGCE (*Learning Enrichment*)
Mrs C Houghton, BA Hons, PGCE (*History*)
Mrs K Jackson, HDE, GTP (*English*)
Miss E Jones, BA Hons, (*Physical Education*)
Mrs J Jones, CertEd (*Home Economics and Religious Studies*)
Mrs S J Kay, BSc Hons (*Mathematics*)
Mrs C Kingsley, BSc Hons, PGCE (*Mathematics*)
Mrs H Kitchin, BSc Hons, PGCE (*Economics & Business Studies*)
Dr E Leatherbarrow, PhD, BSc Hons PGCE (*Science*)
Mrs N Moses, BA Hons, PGCE (*English*)
Mrs S Parker, MSc, PGCE (*Geography*)
Mrs L Poyser, BSc, PGCE (*Chemistry*)
Mrs A Prestwich, Maître FLE, PGCE (*Modern Foreign Languages*)
D Rowett, BSc Hons, PGCE (*PE*)
Mrs C Russell, PGCE, MA (*English*)
Mrs E Sanders, BEd Hons (*PE*) (*Maternity*)
Miss Z Shaughnessy, BA Hons, PGCE (*English*)
S F Smith, BA, CertEd, ARCM, LMusLCM (*Music*)
D I Stockley, MSc, PGCE (*Design & Technology*)
Mrs S Storrar, BSc (*PE*)
M Tempest, BEng Hons, PGCE (*Physics/Chemistry*)
Mrs Z Walker BA Hons PGCE (*Art*)
Miss C Williams BA Hons, PGCE (*Modern Foreign Languages*)

Part-time Staff:
Mrs J Ashurst, BSc Hons, PGCE (*Science*)

Mrs C Ayton, BA Hons, PGCE, PGC SpLD, AMBDA, APC (*Learning Enrichment*)
Mrs K Baty, MA, PGCE (*English*)
Mrs S Campbell-Woodward, BEd (*Modern Foreign Languages*)
Mrs J Dukes, BEd (*Music*)
K Gray, BSc Hons, PGCE (*Geography*)
T L C Griffiths, BEd Hons PGCE (*History*)
Mrs A Hall, BSc Hons (*Mathematics*)
Miss J Hearty, BA Hons (*PE*)
Mrs J Heaton, BEd Hons (*Learning Support*)
Mrs F Kay, BSc Hons, PGCE (*Biology & Psychology*)
Mrs J Lewis, BA Hons, PGCE (*Modern Foreign Languages*)
Mrs M Pilkington, BA Hons, PGCE (*Art*)
Mrs N Stammers, HND, BA Hons, PGCE (*ICT*)
Mrs J Townsend, CertEd (*PE*)
Mrs J Walker, BSc, PGCE (*Mathematics*)

Junior Department:
Head of Junior Department: Mrs R Findlay, BEd Hons
Assistant Head: Dr J Gallagher, PhD, BSc Hons, PGCE
P Butcher, BEd Hons
Mrs H Courtney, BEd Hons
Mrs W Richards, BEd Hons
Mrs S Tomlins, BA Hons, PGCE
Mrs C Travis, BA Hons, PGCE
Mrs A Williams, BEd Hons
Miss E Williams, BEd Hons
Mrs K Williams, BEd Hons
Miss M Webley, BSc Hons, PGCE, MA
Teaching Assistant: Mrs C Spreyer
After School Care Coordinator: Mrs G Foulkes

Musical Instruments Teaching:
Mrs S Andrews (*Piano*)
Miss K Banerjee (*Piano*)
E Hartwell-Jones BMus (*Singing*)
A Bowen-Lewis, CT ABRSM, Adv Dip MusTech (*Brass*)
G Macey (*Woodwind*)
Miss A Makin (*Violin*)
J McCarthy, LLB (*Drums*)
Miss R Owen (*Woodwind*)
P Williams (*Guitar*)

Speech and Drama:
Mrs C Faithfull, LRAM, FNEA

Bursar: Mrs H Barnes, MEng
Finance Manager: Mrs P Rees, FCCA
Director of ICT: D Stewart
Finance Manager's Assistant: Mrs K Campion
Examination Officer: Mrs J Moulton, BA Hons
Registrar: Mrs S Boyd
PA to Head: Miss S Allen
PA to Aldford Head and Data Manager: Mrs J Rawlinson-Smith
PA to SLT & Clerk to the Governors: Mrs S Knowles
School Secretary: Mrs K Cox
School Reception: Mrs A McCleary
School Administrator: Mrs D Humphreys
School Nurse: Miss P Sheckley
Librarian: Mrs J Littler
School Helper: Mrs W Jones
After School Care Assistant: M Puaca
After School Care Assistant: Mrs R Leach
Technicians: S Huxley, J Jones, Mrs J Leach, B Shaughnessy, R Slater, J Bowles, J Harrison

Location and Facilities. The senior school is set in beautiful grounds at Saighton Grange some three miles south of the City of Chester. The history of Saighton Grange goes back long before the Norman Conquest, although most of the present building is Victorian. From 1853 the Grange was a residence of the Grosvenor family. Additional facilities include a large Sports Hall, playing fields and an Arts and Media Centre opened in March 2004 by HRH the Duchess of Gloucester. A purpose-built Art and Design & Technology Centre and new science laboratory were completed in Spring 2008 and opened by His Grace the Duke of Westminster. The completion of a modern Sixth Form Centre with purpose-built ICT, Careers, Social and Study facilities marked the culmination of the 30th Anniversary celebration in 2008. In 2013 developments included a new multi-purpose classroom and drama studio and the next scheduled developments include a learning resource centre, modern classrooms, two purpose-built science laboratories and an all-weather pitch. The Junior Department is sited at Aldford, a picturesque village only two miles from Saighton. Facilities here include excellent playing fields, an ecology and wildlife area plus a number of other outdoor learning spaces. The Juniors and Infants benefit from shared use of the senior site facilities and specialist staff that teach throughout the age range.

Aims. The College encourages its pupils to aim to achieve their academic and personal potential. Outside the world of academia our objective is also to introduce our boys and girls to a wide range of extra-curricular activities. In addition much emphasis is placed on good manners and discipline; this is a friendly, family school particularly aware of the values of moulding character in conjunction with the search for excellence in the classroom. We provide a caring environment; we are proud of the relationship between the teaching staff and their pupils; we encourage a love of learning and ensure that children feel safe, happy and eager to do their best.

Academic Programme. The College aims to provide children with a broad general education through GCSE, AS and A2 Levels, to university, or other forms of higher education. In Years 7 and 8 pupils study Art, Drama, English, French, German, Spanish, Home Economics, Geography, History, Mathematics, Music, Physical Education, PSHE, Textiles, Religious Studies, Science, Spoken English, Design & Technology, Information and Communication Technology.

In Years 10 and 11 an option scheme takes effect: within the core, all pupils study English, English Literature and Mathematics, a modern foreign language and at least two Sciences. Study skills are developed and all pupils participate in sport and a rolling PSHE programme. To support their academic curriculum, Year 10 undertake a week's work experience and participate in a Development Course designed to build teamwork, self-confidence, leadership skills and peer mentoring.

Option subjects for GCSE are taken from the following: Art, Biology, Chemistry, Design and Technology, Drama, French, Geography, German, History, Music, Physics, ICT, Spanish and PE.

In the Sixth Form AS and A2 Level subjects available (according to demand) are: Mathematics, Further Mathematics, English Literature, English Language, History, Government and Politics, Geography, Geology, Economics, Business Studies, Physics, Chemistry, Biology, French, German, Art, Music, Product Design, PE, ICT, Psychology and Theatre Studies. Sixth Form students follow a comprehensive PSHE programme, have the opportunity to study AS Citizenship, complete and EPQ (Extended Project Qualification) and participate in a range of sports, music and drama at the College.

In the Lower Sixth students may also join the Young Enterprise scheme which gives theoretical and practical knowledge of the business world. They enjoy an active community service programme. A number of outside speakers visit the school and regular trips to theatres, conferences or galleries are arranged. All the Lower Sixth students also attend a study skills and team building course in the Lake District in their first term which supports the transition from GCSE to A Level.

Music. The College is well known throughout Chester and North Wales for the outstanding quality of its music. The Chapel Choir has for several years undertaken week-long summer visits to Cathedrals in various parts of the country including Ely, Gloucester, St Albans, Ripon, Tewkesbury, Hereford, Winchester, Durham, York, Bath, Norwich and Hereford, as well as touring overseas: the USA in 2003; more recently, Italy in 2009, Belgium in 2010 and Poland in 2013. Annually, the Chapel Choir sings Evensong at St Paul's Cathedral or St George's Chapel, Windsor. The College also has a Concert Band, The Saighton Syncopators dance band, a modern Funk Band and a Barber Shop Group.

Many pupils of all ages take music lessons and with visiting staff are prepared for the Associated Board Examinations.

Drama. There are two major drama productions each year and these can be drama and musical. There is a whole-school production, a Key Stage 3 performance and GCSE and A Level plays. Pupils are also prepared for examinations in Speech and Drama and regularly enter local competitions with great success. All pupils in Years 7–9 participate in the English Speaking Board scheme within the English and Drama curriculum, helping to develop their confidence and public speaking skills. Year 6 Junior pupils also present a summer performance in their final term before moving into Year 7.

Sport. The College has extensive playing fields, tennis courts and a sports hall, with plans for a state-of-the-art all-weather surface. The Sports Hall offers four badminton courts, five-a-side soccer, volleyball, basketball, netball, indoor hockey, tennis and cricket nets.

All pupils participate in physical education and games. Boys play rugby, soccer, cricket and tennis; girls play hockey, netball, tennis and rounders. Athletics is popular for both boys and girls and all sports provide full fixture lists for the various College teams. The local swimming pool is reserved each week for sessions with a fully-qualified instructor for the younger pupils.

The College competes in both Regional and National Independent Schools sports events, and has enjoyed great success in athletics and swimming. Pupils are regularly sent for trials for Chester and District and County teams with players selected to represent Cheshire in handball, football, hockey, cricket and rugby. There have been soccer tours to Malta and recent Hockey tours to South Africa, Germany and Spain. The school's Ski Racing team trains weekly and is involved in many competitions including the annual British Championships in France where individual and team performances have been impressive. A number of pupils already train with the English Schools Ski Squad. The equestrian team has achieved national honours, with riders being selected to represent their country and the college organises a local competition and sponsors a number of pony club or equestrian competitions.

Junior Department. Our Junior Department provides excellence in education with a broad based curriculum supported by a diverse extra-curricular programme that gives children aged 4–11 a wide range of opportunities. These include choir, gymnastics, team games, Spanish, Belleplates, Ju-Jitsu, creative arts and drama to name but a few. There are frequent school trips and excursions that support the school experience, including a Year 6 residential outdoor and adventurous week at Glaramara in the Lake District.

Other activities. The College has a remarkable record of giving generously to Charities and the three Houses serve to raise money through sponsorship; Sixth Formers take a leading role in this. At weekends and during holidays many pupils take advantage of outdoor pursuits and many choose to follow the Duke of Edinburgh's Award Scheme; there are over 70 participants at all levels from Bronze to Gold Award.

Admission. *Senior School*: Most pupils enter the College at age 11 following an Entrance Examination held in the Spring Term, although where occasional places occur in other year groups, assessments can be made mid year. Each pupil is allocated to one of the Senior School Houses; the house system encourages competition, community and positive attitudes through the allocation of home points.

Junior Department: Pupils are admitted to the Junior Department at Aldford by means of short assessment and interview at ages 7, 8, 9 and 10 dependent on spaces being available. It is expected that children already in this part of the school will move directly into the College at age 11 if they pass the Entrance Examination.

Infant Department: Entry at ages 4, 5 and 6 is also available. Reception places are limited and assessments run on separate occasions throughout the year.

Sixth Form: Priority is given to existing pupils but places are offered to others and are conditional on good results at GCSE.

Scholarships. A number of academic scholarships are available following the results of the Entrance Examination. A comprehensive Bursary Scheme also operates at 11+ and Sixth Form entry offering places to pupils with proven ability or talents who would normally not be able to afford the school fees.

For musical talent awards are offered including Music Exhibitions at Year 7 and Sixth Form level and the Daphne Herbert Choral Scholarship. In addition there are sports awards available at 11+.

Fees per term (2014–2015). Tuition: Infant and Junior Departments £2,515.67; Senior School £3,676.67.

Old Saightonians. All pupils are encouraged to join the Old Saightonians' Association. Further details of the Association can be obtained from the Registrar at the College.

Charitable status. Deeside House Educational Trust is a Registered Charity. number 273586. It exists to provide co-education for children in the Cheshire, Wirral and North Wales areas.

Abbotsholme School
Derbyshire

Rocester, Uttoxeter ST14 5BS
Tel: 01889 594265 (admissions)
            01889 590217 (main number)
Fax: 01889 591001
email: admissions@abbotsholme.co.uk
website: www.abbotsholme.co.uk
Twitter: @AbbotsholmeSch
Facebook: /abbotsholmeschool
LinkedIn: /abbotsholme-school

Set in beautiful, rural surroundings in the heart of England, Abbotsholme is a leading co-educational boarding and day school for girls and boys aged 2–18. It is a school unlike any other: a wonderful place in which to learn and develop, where each child's contribution is properly valued and encouraged throughout.

President: Mr Nicholas Wilford, FRICS

Chair of Governors: Dr Paul Kirtley

Headmaster: Mr Steve Fairclough, MSc

Headmaster's PA: Mrs Julie Noon

Admissions Coordinator: Mrs Michele Archer

ISI Inspection. Following its latest inspection in May 2011 by the Independent Schools Inspectorate, Abbotsholme received another excellent report with many comments of "outstanding" and "excellent". The report stated that: "*Abbotsholme is exceptionally successful in achieving its aims. Pupils are empowered to find success …Achievement is excellent. The pupils' personal development is exemplary. Pupils embrace wholeheartedly the school's aspirations of courage, honesty, humility, integrity and respect.*"

Ethos. Abbotsholme is a small, friendly school providing a modern, progressive education based on cooperation rather than competition, a compassion for others, and a whole-hearted respect for the environment. Abbotsholme is also a wholly inclusive school, where everyone in the community is valued for the individual contribution they make. We genuinely provide opportunities for self-discovery and personal development. This approach to education gives all our young people knowledge to facilitate success and achievement, commitment to nurture and care for the environment, challenges to build strength and test courage, cultural enrichment to widen perspective and responsibility for the needs of others. From this carefully planned curriculum emerge essential skills for life.

Location. Abbotsholme is located on the Staffordshire/Derbyshire border in a beautiful estate of some 140 acres on the banks of the River Dove in rural Derbyshire, close to the magnificent Peak District, easily accessible by road and rail and less than an hour away from three international airports.

Special Characteristics. Membership of the *Round Square* organisation (www.roundsquare.org) provides a strong international perspective. A worldwide and unique association of schools committed to personal growth and responsibility through service, challenge, adventure and international understanding, members share one aim – the full and individual development of every pupil into a whole person.

Our *outdoor education* programme is both well known and well regarded. Its pioneering principles inspired such organisations as the Outward Bound Movement, the United World Colleges and the Duke of Edinburgh's Award Scheme. With adventures both close to home and internationally, it presents pupils with personal challenges, both physical and mental, and teaches them the importance of taking responsibility for themselves and others. Many pupils are involved in the Duke of Edinburgh's Award Scheme and all participate in summer camps and autumn hikes each year.

Abbotsholme is one of the very few schools in England to have a working *farm* upon which pupils are able to learn about animal husbandry and crop management and gain a healthy respect for the environment. In addition to the 70-acre farm, our British Horse Society approved *Equestrian Centre* is a popular place to be for our horse enthusiasts, who happily involve themselves in the upkeep of the stables and yard and can study for NVQ or BHS exams.

Music is a way of life at Abbotsholme. All pupils are encouraged to appreciate music in some way, either by learning to play an instrument or taking singing lessons or by simply attending some of the performances that are frequently organised. Both the orchestra and the choir comprise a mixture of staff and pupils, which fosters the special atmosphere so typical of Abbotsholme.

Drama flourishes, in and out of the classroom, with performances in the 120-seat theatre always oversubscribed. All pupils who are keen to be involved, whether on stage or behind the scenes, find regular opportunities to experience the fun and self-discipline characteristic of performance and improvised theatre.

The influence of the *Art* department is evident throughout school, where pupils' painting, drawing, pottery, ceramic, graphic design and 3D creations are permanently on display. In addition many pupils enjoy the facilities of the *Design and Technology* Department, which provides excellent opportunities for developing creative design into quality manufacture. Hours are also spent in the cutting edge *Film Studies* Unit, which enables pupils to design animation projects and create and edit film on computer, through digitisation.

We believe that the physical and mental disciplines of working together in a team are very important. *Sport* teaches the art of winning and losing with equally good grace, self-reliance and leadership, and the opportunities to compete are grasped by many of our pupils. Sports at Abbotsholme include: rugby, football, hockey, netball, tennis, swimming, athletics, squash, skiing, cross-country, horse riding, badminton and basketball.

Curriculum. Abbotsholme caters for a broad ability range. Academic standards are high with the majority of sixth formers going on to their first-choice university. Breadth and balance shape the curriculum, which aims to develop critical and creative thinking and self-discipline across a wide range of subjects at GCSE and A Level.

Activities. Abbotsholme firmly believes that a school should have a greater purpose beyond preparing students for College or University. As a result we seek not only to help all pupils realise their individual academic potential but also to develop in everyone a sense of responsibility for themselves and others through active participation within the community as well as a sense of adventure through challenges in and beyond the classroom. A comprehensive range of compulsory activities is integral to the curriculum, taking place on four afternoons a week. Each week's activities alternately include Outdoor Education and Farm/Conservation work, commitments to team sports, singers, and drama as well as a number of individual choices, including: art, bookworms, chess, debating, drama (major productions are staged every year), French for fun, music (including many concerts and recitals), Young Enterprise and Warhammer.

Home from Home. The boarding experience at Abbotsholme is a happy one, where staff and pupils know each other well and where every individual shares equal responsibility for the community's well being and progress. Small, friendly homes are run by resident houseparents as family units. Younger boarders share bright and comfortable dormitories in threes and fours whilst older pupils have single or shared study-bedrooms. A log cabin village has been added for sixth formers giving them opportunities to experience a greater degree of independence and privacy. Weekly boarding has become a popular option for families with busy lives and for our full boarders, a full programme of weekend activities provides plenty of choice and lots of fun, balancing academic work with social time. Our modern approach to boarding means that sleepover and flexi boarding are also options.

Facilities. These include: dedicated classroom areas for each subject, including specialist science laboratories, art, music, design and IT centres (two suites), a purpose-built studio theatre for drama, sixth form centre, log cabin complex, indoor climbing wall, 70-acre working farm, equestrian centre and manège, film studies and films, a modern, multi-purpose sports hall, extensive playing fields and swimming pool, and a chapel, which combines as the venue for morning assembly as well as concerts.

Fees per term (2014–2015). Day £2,760–£6,735; Weekly Boarding £5,380–£8,285; Full Boarding £7,360–£9,890; Occasional Boarding £35 per night.

The Abbotsholmians' Club. The Club currently has some 2000 members and is run by a Committee of Old Abbotsholmians, elected yearly. Members receive regular mail-outs, which give contact addresses and details of the adventures of OAs, young and old. There are also regular invitations to events, to help them keep in touch with each other and with current developments at the school. An enormous amount of networking takes place between OAs, often facilitated by the Club, ensuring that friendships are sustained and memories are relived.

The Club operates a small Bursary fund specifically aimed at helping to educate sons and daughters of OAs at Abbotsholme.

Abbotsholme Arts Society. The School is host to one of the most respected concert presenters in the country. Although embracing jazz, poetry and drama performances, its core programme of chamber music has brought a Who's Who of big-name musicians to the school over the years – Ashkenazy, Brendel, Galway, Hough, the Amadeus Quartet to name just a few. Pupils are able to attend any of the Arts Society concerts free of charge.

Abbotsholme Parents' Association. Run by parents, for the benefit of parents, children and school, the Parents' Association (APA) aims to help new families settle in and become quickly familiar with Abbotsholme and all that it has to offer. Keen to promote active parental involvement in the school, members regularly organise social activities and fundraising events.

Charitable status. Abbotsholme School is a Registered Charity, number 528612. It exists to advance education and in particular to provide for children and young persons a broad, general education in accordance with the principles, traditions and aims developed since the school's foundation in 1889 by Dr Cecil Reddie.

Austin Friars St Monica's School

Etterby Scaur, Carlisle, Cumbria CA3 9PB
Tel: 01228 528042
Fax: 01228 810327
email: office@austinfriars.cumbria.sch.uk
           admissions@austinfriars.cumbria.sch.uk
website: www.austinfriars.cumbria.sch.uk
Twitter: @AFSMSchool
Facebook: /AFSMSchool
LinkedIn: /Austin Friars St Monica's School

Austin Friars St Monica's is an independent co-educational day school, founded by members of the Order of St Augustine in 1951 and is one of the network of Augustinian schools across the world. Pupils of all denominations are welcome in the School, giving all the opportunity to embrace the Christian traditions on which the School is founded.

The School Motto is "*In Omnibus Caritas*". The word "caritas" embraces so much more than the accepted English translation "charity": it is indeed a summary of all the virtues. Christian principles hold a central place in the life of the School with a pupil's faith creating a lively and effective influence on attitudes and activities.

The Senior School provides secondary education for 330 boys and girls aged 11–18. There are 160 children aged 4–11 in the brand new state-of-the-art Junior School and the purpose-built Pre-School has places for 24 children aged 3–4. (*For further details, see Junior School entry in IAPS section.*)

Chairman of Trustees: Revd Dr Peter Tiplady, MB BS, MRCGP, FFPHM, FRIPH

Headmaster: Mr M F Harris, BSc, PGCE

Deputy Headmaster: Mr G R Barr, BA, PGCE
Director of Studies: Mr M C F Fielder, MA, PGCE
Head of Sixth Form: Mr S Parry, MEd, BSc, PGCE, Dip RSA
Head of Junior School: Mr J Slingsby, BEd
Bursar: Mr E Swinton, ACIBS
Admissions Registrar: Miss A Burns, BA

Heads of Department:
Art and Photography: Miss K Quinn, BA, PGCE
Science and Biology: Mr R Holden, BSc, PGCE

Design Technology: Mr M Turnbull, BSc, PGCE, NPQH
Chemistry: Mrs R Fielder, BSc
Classical Civilisation: Mr P Thornton, BA, PGCE
Drama: Mr M Judge, BA, PGCE
Economics: (*to be appointed*)
English: Mrs J Agnew, BA, PGCE
Geography: Mr S Parry, BSc, PGCE
History: Mr S Wright, MA, BA, PGCE
Mathematics: Mr N Barraclough, BSc, PGCE
Modern Languages: Mrs S Green, BA, PGCE
Music: Mr C W J Hattrell, MA
Physical Education: Mr J Tiffen, BA, PGCE
Physics: Mr N Edmondson, BEd
Religious Studies: Mr J Finn, BA, PGCE

The School stands in its own grounds of 25 acres overlooking the historic City of Carlisle in North Cumbria. It is within easy reach of the M6 and there is excellent access to the North West and North East of England and to South West Scotland. There are also outstanding opportunities to take advantage of the cultural heritage of the area stretching back to Roman times and Hadrian's Wall, and for outdoor activities in the Lake District, Northumberland and north of the border in Scotland.

Austin Friars St Monica's School aims to foster the personal development of its pupils spiritually, academically, socially and physically to enable them to take their place creatively in society. The School has high expectations of its pupils and encourages them to develop their potential in a disciplined, happy, positive and productive atmosphere. Consequently, Austin Friars St Monica's School has established an enviable reputation for bringing out the best in each of its pupils. This means not only attaining high academic standards but realising sound spiritual and social values, self-discipline and the development of a sense of purpose for life.

The School is justifiably proud of its academic facilities, the breadth of its curriculum and its pupils' record in public examinations, which are among the best in the North of England. The School's highly qualified staff, the close attention to the individual pupils throughout their school careers and the nurturing of a positive attitude to work, ensure consistently good results and a sound preparation for higher education.

Both staff and pupils appreciate that school extends beyond the classroom and extra-curricular activities are a strong facet of Austin Friars St Monica's. The School is an excellent centre for developing new and existing interests and talents and offers numerous opportunities for participation in cultural and leisure activities and involvement in charitable work. Each year the School produces a musical/play and termly concerts. There are regular visits to theatres, concerts and galleries and school visits abroad. Qualified and enthusiastic staff provide coaching in team sports, and the School's record in inter-school competition is acknowledged far beyond Cumbria. Awards in the Duke of Edinburgh's Scheme are gained annually by a significant number of pupils, and other outdoor pursuits include climbing, fell walking and skiing.

The School has benefited from a large capital investment in the facilities over recent years including: a Sixth Form Centre; a dedicated Learning Support unit; the installation of an all-weather pitch; a music recital, practice and classroom suite; ICT facilities across the whole School; the Mendel building, a science facility with 4 dedicated labs and technician rooms; and a state-of-the-art Junior School (*see entry in IAPS section*).

The quality of pastoral care is one of the School's greatest strengths. All pupils belong to a tutor group, and the tutor who is the first point of contact for the students and parents. The Senior School is divided in to three Houses. A key feature and strength of the school, the House is central to the strong sense of a community which older and younger pupils mix freely; kindness, self-respect and respect for others are instantly evident.

Studies. The following subjects are available to GCSE and/or A Level: English, Latin, French, Spanish, History, Geography, Economics, Mathematics, Further Mathematics, Physics, Chemistry, Biology, Art, Music, Classical Civilisation, Religious Studies, General Studies, Design Technology, ICT, PE, Drama, Philosophy and Ethics, Psychology and Photography.

The size of classes is restricted so that each pupil may receive close attention and be taught as an individual. Reports are sent to parents four times a year. Sixth Formers are expected to learn to organise their time and their work in their own way. The dedicated Sixth Form Centre has a common room, a games room and two study rooms, allowing the pupils to develop a sense of independence while still under the care of the Head of Sixth Form and the rest of the staff. Specialist help is available for dyslexic pupils in the new Learning Support Centre.

The Learning Resources Centre is well equipped and designed for serious study, access of information and relaxation. The Centre's Librarian assists pupils in developing their information-handling skills and supervises the Careers Library.

Activities. The Junior and Senior Schools Choir and the Dramatic Society's annual production provide important extra-curricular activities (a musical is performed every other year). The School Orchestra and Swing Band are also very active. Extra tuition in piano, woodwind, brass, percussion and elocution is provided by peripatetic teachers, who also run ensemble classes for groups of wind, brass, strings and guitar. All this takes place in the dedicated music department.

Some 40 extra different extra-curricular activities are available to the students including Chess, Fell Walking, Photography, Public Speaking, Duke of Edinburgh's Award Scheme, Young Enterprise, and Rock Climbing. Pupils are encouraged to attend events outside the School in connection with their studies and interests. Outings are organised annually to both abroad and to places of interest in Britain. Situated as we are in an area which is rich in Roman History, there are endless opportunities for visiting and studying historical monuments. There are also trips to the Lakes, which are on the doorstep. Other extra-curricular trips offer the opportunity to travel abroad for further study including trips to France, Iceland, Borneo and Spain.

Sport. The school has a full-sized astroturf which is utilised throughout the year. The range of sporting options available is vast: Rugby, Hockey, Netball, Cross-Country in winter; Athletics, Rounders, Cricket, Tennis in summer. Football, badminton, dance and fitness are all offered within the activities programme. The pupils regularly achieve county status in their various sports. Annual skiing trips take place in Europe and the USA.

Admissions. The Senior School adopts a three-form entry policy. The majority of places are offered at 11+ with a further entry at Sixth Form. Admissions at other ages are considered, subject to availability of places.

All pupils at 11+ sit the Senior School's entrance examination; entry to the Sixth Form is on the basis of performance at GCSE. At other levels, entry is on the basis of school reports and school-based assessment. The 11+ entrance examination takes place in January prior to entry the following September. Prospective pupils undertake an entrance examination assessing their abilities in English, mathematics and non-verbal reasoning. All prospective pupils are screened for specific learning difficulties.

Fees per term (2014–2015). £4,193 (Years 7–13). Fees are inclusive of lunches.

There is a reduction of 5% for brothers/sisters in the School at the same time. Bursaries are available at all levels.

Junior School. *For information about Austin Friars St Monica's Junior School, see entry in IAPS section.*

Travel. Carlisle is a main stopping point on the West Coast Mainline. The M6 motorway connects Carlisle with the South, the Midlands and North Wales, and there are excellent links to the east. The A74/M74 is the continuation of the M6 to Glasgow. There is easy access to International Airports. School bus services run from several of the surrounding areas.

An invitation to see the School and meet the Headmaster is extended to all those who write for information.

Charitable status. Austin Friars St Monica's School is a Registered Charity, number 516289. It exists for the purpose of educating boys and girls.

Bedstone College

Bucknell, Shropshire SY7 0BG
Tel: 01547 530303
Fax: 01547 530740
email: admissions@bedstone.org
            headmaster@bedstone.org
            reception@bedstone.org
website: www.bedstone.org
Twitter: @BedstoneCollege
Facebook: /Bedstone-College

Motto: *Caritas*

Bedstone College, founded in 1948, is a fully co-educational, independent, boarding and day school catering for children between the ages of 3 and 18 years. The school enjoys a beautiful 40-acre campus within an idyllic setting amongst the south Shropshire hills.

The school comprises the Pre-Preparatory Department (for children aged 3 to 7 years), the Junior School (for ages 8 to 11 years) and the Senior College (for ages 11 to 18 years), all integrated within one campus. Over 50% of the pupils in the senior school are full boarders.

Bedstone offers a broad and balanced curriculum with some 18 subjects available at GCSE, AS and A2 Levels. Despite being non-selective and catering to those of all ability levels, Bedstone is proud to boast that over 90% of its Upper Sixth leavers secure places at University with a large majority (80% in 2014) being at their first-choice institution.

The College aims to fulfil the potential of every child wherever that potential may lie and, with an average teacher : pupil ratio of 1:8, the smaller class sizes allow individual needs to be catered for. The well-qualified and highly-motivated staff believe that each child has a unique talent which it is their job to find and to nurture.

Bedstone is very aware of the problems that learning difficulties, such as dyslexia, can cause and the highly-regarded learning support unit, led by its full-time director with the aid of fully-qualified staff, is central to the help provided. Bedstone is one of just 37 schools (both state and independent) in the UK to be accredited by CReSTeD as a Specialist Dyslexia Unit.

The Governing Body:
Chairman: Grp Capt J Fynes, RAF [Retd]
Vice Chairman: Lt Col T Lowry

Mr J B P Jones   Mr E Dunphy
Mr D J Owens   Commander M Williams
Mrs Y Thomas BSc   Mr B Meldrum
Mr J Smith   Dr M Lawton

Headmaster: Mr D Gajadharsingh, BSc, PGCE, CPhys, MInstP, NPQH

Deputy Headmaster: Mr J Lynch, BA, PGCE, MA Ed
Director of Studies: Mr A A Whittall, BA, PGCE
Head of Prep Department: Mr J Forster, BSc, MSc
Bursar: Mr A R Gore, AFA, FIAB, AIMgt

Houseparents:

Boys Boarding:
Pearson House: Mr & Mrs A Whittall
Rutter House: Mr and Mrs J Forster

Girls Boarding:
Bedstone House: Mr & Mrs P Singh
Wilson House: Mr & Mrs M Rozée

Members of Common Room:
Mrs J Bartley, BA, PGCE (*Head of Modern Foreign Languages*)
Ms J Bird, BA, Dip TEFL (*Head of EAL*)
Mr C Braden, BEd, QTS, PG Dip Man (*Head of Design Technology, Head of UCAS & Careers*)
Mrs E Bryden, BA, PG Dip Perf RCM, MMus, PGCE (*Head of Music*)
Miss L Bullock, BA, PGCE (*Head of History & PHSE*)
Miss E Davis, BA, PGCE (*Sports Studies, Head of Girls' PE & Games*)
Mr E Olive, BSc, PGCE (*Head of Physics*)
Mr D Foreman, BSc, PhD, PGCE (*Head of Biology*)
Mr R Hillman, GTS (*Teacher of Mathematics*)
Mrs C Hunter CDMVA La Sorbonne (*Teacher of Modern Foreign Languages*)
Miss C Jenkins, BA, MPhil, PGCE, Adv Cert TEFL (*Head of English*)
Mr J Lowe MA, PGD Inclusion & SEN, PGCE (*Head of Learning Support*)
Miss A Moore, BA, PGCE (*Teacher of English*)
Mrs S Morris, BA, PGCE, Cert TEFL (*Head of Religious Education*)
Mr D P Marsh, BSc, PGCE (*Head of Geography*)
Mr D M Rawlinson, BSc, PhD, PGCE (*Head of Mathematics*)
Mr D M Rozée, BSc, PGCE, MSRC (*Head of Science*)
Mr J P Smith, BA (*Head of Art*)
Mr J R Simpson, BA, QTS (*Sports Studies, Head of Boys' PE & Games*)
Mr I Spencer, BA, PGCE (*Head of Business Studies*)
Mrs S Stevens, BSc, PGCE (*Teacher of Science*)

Preparatory Department:
Mrs J Richards, BA, PGCE, MA Ed
Mrs S Crabtree, BA, QTS
Mrs R Rawlinson, BSc, MSc, PGCE

Pre-Prep and Nursery:
Head: Mrs M Savery, Dip Montessori
Mrs J Williams, BEd
Mrs L Meredith, NNEB

Learning Support:
Mr J Lowe, PGD Inclusion & SEN, PGCE
Mrs T Chilles, BSc, PGCE, PGD SpLD Dyslexia, AMBDA

EAL:
Ms J Bird, BA, Dip TEFL
Mr C Morris, BA, CELTA
Ms G Kindermann

Lay Chaplain: Mr A C Dyball, MA Cantab, Dip Ed

School Medical Team: Mrs N Stead, RGN & Mrs T Chave, RGN

School Counsellor: Mrs C Hall

School Doctors: Dr M L Kiff & Dr A Lempert

Visiting Music Staff:
Mr D Kirk (*Drums*)
Mr D Luke (*Guitar*)
Mrs S Freeman (*Brass*)
Mr J Hymas (*Violin*)
Mrs K Norton (*Piano*)
Mr M Buxton (*Singing*)

Competitive Houses:
Hopton: Miss C Jenkins

Stokesay: Miss E Davis
Wigmore: Mr J Lowe

Headmaster's PA: Mrs Paula Davis
Accounts Administrator: Mr Paul Downes
Head of Admissions, Marketing & Enterprise: Mrs Rachel H Pritchard
Admissions Marketing & Enterprise Assistant: Ms Beckie Broadbent
IT Manager: Mr Steven Davis, BSc
Drama: Mrs E Bryden
Receptionist: Mrs Meradith Hart
Accounts Clerk: Mrs Sara Gore, BSc
Science Laboratory Technician & Librarian: Mrs Ruth Shenton
Catering & Domestic Manager: Mr J Hart
School Shop: Mrs A Forster
Transport Manager: Mr Parvinder Singh

Character of the College. Many children who join Bedstone have done so because their parents feel that the individual strengths of their child have become lost within their current school; that the challenges and opportunities for fulfilling their child's unique talents do not exist, or that they wish for greater pastoral support and guidance for their child. Every parent knows that what they want is the education of the whole child – mind, body and spirit – and Bedstone provides that with its academic and extra-curricular programme coupled with its outstanding pastoral care and boarding ethos.

Family Education. There is a guarantee that once any member of a family is accepted at Bedstone, brothers and sisters will gain automatic entry by interview only. This is of immense value to parents who wish for all their children to be educated at the same school.

Accommodation. The main house, Bedstone Court, is a listed building of fine architectural merit and accommodates the Junior and Senior boys' houses. In addition it houses the administration, library, dining hall and sixth form club. The two girls' boarding houses are on the opposite side of the campus with the senior girls accommodated within a purpose-built boarding house and the junior girls within the homely surroundings of an 18th century manor house. All boarding houses have been completely refurbished. All boarding houses have resident staff and their families as houseparents. There is seating for 300 people in the Rees Hall Theatre with full AV facilities. There is a modern well-equipped Sports Hall, Design Technology and Art Centre, Music School, a Medical Centre staffed by RGNs, Fitness Suite, Dance Studio, Learning Support and Counselling facility, a heated swimming pool and a wide range of additional facilities. There is also a social club for the Sixth Form with a weekend bar manned and carefully controlled by staff. The College has a campus-wide wireless LAN.

Religious Education. Religious teaching at Bedstone is according to the tenets of the Church of England though other denominations and children without any religious affiliation, are warmly welcomed. Children, whose parents wish it, are also prepared for Confirmation by the Chaplain. The College enjoys a strong choral tradition and the Choir enjoys an excellent reputation.

Senior College Curriculum. From the First Form (Y7) to the Third Form (Y9) (when a number join from other Preparatory Schools) the subjects taught are: Religious Education, English Language and Literature, History, Geography, French, Spanish, Mathematics, Biology, Physics, Chemistry, Design Technology, Art, Music, Physical Education and ICT.

In the Fourth and Fifth Forms, in addition to the Core Curriculum of English, English Literature, Mathematics, one modern foreign language (French or Spanish), and the three Sciences, options are: History, Geography, Art, Business Studies, Music, French, Spanish, Design Technology,

Sports Studies and ICT. Latin and German tuition are also available off timetable.

Throughout the College, in all classes, we help students achieve the very best that they are capable of and surpass their own expectations. There is no "cramming" at Bedstone and we are not an academic hothouse, but considerable effort is required from each pupil and, with the aid of close tutorial support, a well-qualified staff an excellent staff/pupil ratio, good progress and examination success are assured. AS/A2 & BTEC courses are offered in English, History, Geography, French, Business Studies, Art, Design Technology, Mathematics, Further Mathematics, Music, Physics, Chemistry, Biology, Psychology and Sports Studies. The Extended Project Qualification (EPQ) is on offer to all Sixth Form students.

The College has its own Learning Support unit. Excellent EAL provision is available for those who require it in addition to pre-sessional intensive English courses.

Careers. There are specific careers staff and a well-resourced Careers Room. Bedstone makes full use of the Independent Schools' Careers Organisation and all members of the Fifth Form take the ISCO Psychometric tests and have the opportunity to undertake work experience.

Games and Physical Education. There are 15 acres of playing fields, with an excellent Sports Hall, fitness suite, dance studio and netball & tennis courts plus an astroturf. The success of the boys and girls in physical activity at school, county and district level has been nothing short of remarkable. The school holds several ISA National Championships in various disciplines including Rugby 7s (2013), Cross Country and Hockey.

Rugby, Football, Athletics, Basketball and Cricket are the main sports for the boys and Hockey, Netball, Rounders and Athletics for the girls but they can join in many more. A rotation system ensures that all students, to a greater or lesser degree, have their share of such activities as Basketball, Cross-Country running, Swimming and Tennis. Nor are the individualists forgotten. Horse riding is popular and there are facilities for Badminton, Table Tennis and Mountain Biking, whilst the South Shropshire and Powys Hills provide excellent opportunities for Duke of Edinburgh's Award activities.

Clubs and Activities. The Duke of Edinburgh's Award scheme flourishes and there is a wide range of out of class activity, including splendid dramatic and musical productions, debating, individual music tuition and an assortment of clubs to suit most tastes. Pupils are expected to know and observe all College rules and parents to cooperate in seeing that this is done. Prefects play an important part in the pastoral system of the College. There are also a number of trips and visits that take place throughout the year, including visits to some of the most beautiful cities in Europe. Every two years there are major international sports tours for both the boys and the girls.

Bedstone Prep School & Nursery is for boys and girls aged 3 to 11 years. The school is housed in its own accommodation and yet shares all the facilities of the senior school. Science, Modern Foreign Languages, Sport and Music are all taught by senior school subject specialists within specialist areas. There is a specialist gifted and talented mathematics programme for the most able prep school pupils. The nursery school is based upon the Montessori system.

The Prep School is an integral part of the College and children find the transition to the Senior College seamless. Any child accepted within the Prep School is automatically accepted into the Senior College.

Scholarships. For entry to the Senior College, there is a scholarship examination, held at the College on a Saturday in early March. Bedstone offers Academic, Sport, Music, Art, DT and All-Rounder scholarships at 11+/13+ and 16+ with the maximum award being up to 25% remission of fees. For local children from maintained schools, who might not have realistically considered Bedstone as an option, there is also the 'Four Counties' Scholarship which is worth up to 50% remission of fees. The school is also able to provide "top-up" means-tested bursaries for exceptional pupils. Forces fees discounts available upon request.

Fees per term (2014–2015). Senior: £4,555 (day), £8,255 (boarding). Prep: £3,300 (day), £5,430 (boarding). Pre-Preparatory: £1,565.

Old Bedstonian Society. *Hon Secretary*: Ms Hannah Croft.

Charitable status. Bedstone College is a Registered Charity, number 528405. It is established for the education of young people.

Beechwood Sacred Heart School

Pembury Road, Tunbridge Wells, Kent TN2 3QD
Tel: 01892 532747
Fax: 01892 536164
email: bsh@beechwood.org.uk
website: www.beechwood.org.uk

Beechwood is an independent co-educational day and boarding school for pupils aged 3–18. Founded in 1915 by the Society of the Sacred Heart, Beechwood has been a lay school since 1973; as a Sacred Heart School, it retains sound Catholic values, whilst welcoming pupils from all nations and beliefs.

The Nursery School (age 3–5), Preparatory School (age 5–11) and Senior School (age 11–18) are located in 23 acres of landscaped grounds overlooking open countryside, close to the centre of the historic town of Royal Tunbridge Wells.

Boarding is offered for boys and girls in newly structured and modernised accommodation on site.

Governors:
Mrs Marie-France Mason (*Chairman*)
Dr David Findley, BSc, PhD (*Vice-Chairman*)
Mrs Veronica Fulton
Mr Patrick Holland, BA Oxon
Lady Hilary Newman
Sister Moira O'Sullivan
Mrs Caron Peppard
Mr Michael Southern
Mr Michael Stevens
Dr Amanda Turner

Company Secretary and Clerk to the Governors: Mr Andrew Harvey

Head: Mr Aaron Lennon, BA Hons, NPQH

Deputy Head: Mrs Helen Rowe, BA Hons, PGCE
Director of Studies: Mrs Kim Allen, BSc Hons, PGCE
Chaplain: Fr Peter Stodart; Fr Anthony Cassidy

Staff:

Heads of Division:
Mrs Mary Allen, BSc Hons (*Junior Division*)
Mrs Carol Mitchell, BA, PGCE (*Middle Division*)
Mr Michael Awdry, BA Hons, PGCE (*Senior Division*)

Heads of Department:
Mrs Olga Clarke, PGCE, Maître MA, Licence/Deug BA (*Modern Languages*)
Mr Gary Hatter, MEd, PGCE (*Art*)
Miss Louise Harvey, BSc Hons, PGCE (*Geography*)
Mrs Gwen Goodley, MBA, BA Hons, BSc Hons (*History*)
Mrs Elizabeth Grossman, BA Hons, DELTA (*EAL*)
Mrs Anne Hopper, BSc Hons, PGCE (*Science*)
Mrs Sarah Kershaw, BA Hons, PGCE (*Music*)
Mrs Virginia Letchworth, PGCE, PG Dip SpLD Dyslexia (*Learning Development*)

Mrs Carol Mitchell, BA, PGCE (*Physical Education*)
Mrs Candy Prodrick, BD, PGCE (*Religious Education, PSHE*)
Mrs Diana Ringer, BSc Hons, PGCE, MSc (*Mathematics*)
Mr Mark Thomas, BSc Hons, PGCE (*ICT*)
Mrs Nicky Phipps, BA Hons, PGCE (*English*)
Mrs Fiona Lennon, BEd Hons, MA (*Drama*)
Mr James Walters, BSc Hons, PGCE (*Design Technology*)

Preparatory School:
Head: Mrs Rachel Burton, BSc Hons, PGCE
Director of Studies: Mrs Teresa Cutts, MA Cantab, PGCE

Head of Boarding: Mrs Cecilia Rejbakoz
Head of Boys' Boarding: Mr Luke Donovan, BSc Hons, PGCE

Head's Secretary: Miss Liz Milner
Registrar: Mrs Sue Dyke

Beechwood is noted for its genuine family atmosphere. Consideration for others underpins the code of behaviour for all pupils, making Beechwood a happy school with high academic standards being achieved through expectation and challenge, rather than prescription. We are an ambitious, caring school and that sense of confidence and generosity of spirit permeates throughout the school. At Beechwood we prepare our pupils for the future but encourage them to enjoy the present.

Curriculum. In our small classes, teachers stimulate pupils to excel in what they are good at and build confidence in areas they find difficult, from the youngest child in the Preparatory School through to our oldest Senior School pupils. Our Learning Development department supports the individual needs of those pupils who require extra support.

Beechwood provides a broad education. At Key Stage 3 all pupils study a range of subjects including our innovative COGS+ (Thinking Skills) programme in Years 7 and 9. Most subjects are taught in mixed-ability classes of boys and girls. Mathematics is setted from Year 7. French is studied in Year 7, with options to study Spanish and German from Year 8. Academic standards are important and we challenge our pupils to do their best. We also encourage our boys and girls to participate in a wide range of extra-curricular activities. There is something for everyone at Beechwood from improving skill and fitness through sport, to building robots or creative writing for our budding authors.

At GCSE pupils can study from a range of over twenty subjects. Biology, Chemistry and Physics ('triple Science') are offered as single subjects for the more able pupils. Pupils participate in a diverse PE curriculum and study PHSCE as part of their personal development.

At A Level, more than twenty subjects are offered including three Sciences, Theatre Studies, Further Mathematics, Business Studies, Photography, Product Design, Psychology, Law, Media Studies, History and Textiles. The Sixth Form curriculum is enhanced by an enrichment course that includes Life Skills and comprehensive Careers and University application advice.

Sixth Formers are encouraged to show initiative and take responsibility. They have opportunities for leadership as prefects and in organising activities for younger pupils. All leavers successfully gain places at university on a wide range of courses.

Examination Results. Beechwood's record in public examinations is particularly impressive for a non-selective school, with a pass rate (A*–C) of around 90% at GCSE and 100% at A Level, and is in the top 25% of schools for value-added at A level. Beechwood regularly appears in the top 10% of schools nationwide in A Level league tables.

Sports. Pupils are encouraged to experience a wide variety of sports, the emphasis being on fun and participation. Recent successes include being Kent County Basketball Champions. Sports facilities include hockey and football pitches, netball, basketball and tennis courts, cricket nets, gymnasium, badminton and volleyball courts. We also take advantage of local all-weather pitches.

Preparatory School and Nursery. Adjacent to the Senior School, the Preparatory School and Nursery provide a sound beginning for every child in a supportive, family atmosphere. The curriculum stimulates enquiry, academic standards being maintained through regular monitoring and assessment. French is studied from Year 1 and all pupils also enjoy cookery lessons. In addition, by sharing the facilities of the Senior School, pupils participate in a wide variety of sports and can represent the school in matches. Extra-curricular activities include chess, crafts, gardening and keyboard music making, and many pupils have instrumental music lessons.

Entry Requirements. The school is non-selective academically, selection being based on interview with the Headmaster, previous school report and confidential reference. All enquiries and applications should be addressed to the Registrar.

Fees per term (2014–2015). Full boarders £8,820; Weekly boarders £7,820; Day pupils £3,020–£5,312.

Scholarships. Scholarships are available at 11+, 13+ and 16+ in Academic, Music, Art, Sport and Drama. 11+ and 13+ Entrance and Scholarship Days take place in the Spring Term and 16+ in November.

Charitable status. The Sacred Heart School Beechwood Trust Ltd is a Registered Charity, number 325104.

Bethany School

Curtisden Green, Goudhurst, Cranbrook, Kent TN17 1LB
Tel: 01580 211273
Fax: 01580 211151
email: registrar@bethanyschool.org.uk
website: www.bethanyschool.org.uk
Twitter: @bethanyschkent
Facebook: bethanyschkent
LinkedIn: Bethany School Kent

The School was founded in 1866 by the Revd J J Kendon. It is a Charitable Trust administered by a Board of Governors, a member of the Association of Governing Bodies of Independent Schools.

Governors:
Mr A Pengelly, MA, FRCS (*Chairman*)

Mrs R Bates
Mr D Boniface, MA, MSc
Mrs A Carboni, MA Cantab
Mrs A Culley, CertEd
Mr J M Fenn, LLB
Mr M L Hammerton, BSc, MBA

Dr R Hangartner, BSc, MB BS, MBA, FRCPath
Mrs W Hedges
Mr N P Kimber, BSc, FCA
Mr R J Pilbeam
Mr R J Stubbs, BSocSc, MMRS
Mr R Walden

Bursar and Clerk to the Governors: Mr S J Douglass

Staff:

Headmaster: Mr M F Healy, BSc, HDipEd, NPQH

Deputy Headmaster: Mr S Winter, BA

Assistant Head Academic: Mrs D Gale, BSc

Assistant Head Pastoral: Mr A Sturrock, BA

Lay Chaplain: Mrs C Turvey

Staff:

Miss K Berry, BA
Miss S Boyle, MDrama
Miss N Brown, BDes
Mrs D Coley, MA
Mr C Cooper, MSc
Mr C Coupland, MA

Mr S Davies, BA
Mrs J Digby, BSc
Miss H Foster, BSc, PGCE
Miss K Gee, MA Ed, PGCE
Mrs K Harper, BSc Hons, QTS, PGCE SpLD
Mr T P Hart Dyke, BA
Mrs F Healy, BA, SpLD
Mr P Hughes, BA
Mr A A Khan, BA
Miss S King, BA
Miss K Leach, BSc
Mr E Lloyd, BBA
Dr J Marks, BSc, PhD
Mrs R McGovern, BA
Miss C Mills, BEd, PG Cert SpLD
Mr G Mourey, MA
Miss N Nixon, BA

Mr P Norgrove, BEd
Mr M D G E Norman, BEd Hons
Mr M Payne, BSc
Mrs C Price, BA
Miss R Rayner, BA
Mr D Reilly, BSc
Ms C Romero, MA
Mrs C Shapland, BA
Mr D Schooledge, BSc
Miss F E Shaw, MA. PGCE
Mr G Stubberfield, BA
Mr M Thomas, BSc, PhD
Mrs K Thornton, MA
Mr G K Thorpe, BA
Mrs S Thorpe, BA
Mr J Vickerman, BSc
Mrs J Wareham, BEd Hons
Miss C Wood, BA

Medical Officer: Dr J N Watson, MBBS, MRCGP

Marketing & Admissions Manager: Mrs G Corbett

Registrar: Mrs S Martorell

Headmaster's Secretary: Mrs A Discombe

Bethany has 350 pupils, aged 11 to 18. Approximately 30% board on either a weekly or termly basis, with a varied weekend programme of activities available for termly boarders. A generous staff to pupil ratio of 1:8 ensures small classes and high quality pastoral care. Individuals are encouraged to develop their potential to the full in academic and all other respects. Most teaching takes place in modern classroom blocks, the result of an ongoing building development programme. Development in ICT has been a priority at Bethany: a wireless network enables pupils from Year 8 upwards to use laptops across the curriculum, and our Year 7 pupils are gifted an iPad by our Alumni to use for their studies.

The Sixth Form house offers single study-bedrooms with en-suite facilities for the Upper Sixth boarders, study rooms for day pupils and communal facilities for both Upper and Lower Sixth Form students. Recent additions to the School include a Science Centre, a Food Technology Centre, a new Textiles Department and Modern Language classrooms. Building work is under way for a new six-lane, 25m indoor swimming pool. A major refurbishment programme has also been completed for our girls boarding house ensuring they are able to enjoy a home-from-home environment.

Situation. The School occupies a scenic, 60-acre site in the Weald of Kent, easily accessible from most parts of South East England: an hour from Charing Cross (Marden Station) and easy access to Gatwick and Heathrow Airports, the Channel ports and Ashford and Ebbsfleet International railway stations.

Admission. The normal age of entry is at 11 or 13 by the School's Entrance Assessment and at Sixth Form level based on predicted GCSE grades, but the school welcomes students to the Bethany community at other stages if places are available.

Fees per term (2014–2015). Full Boarders £8,614–£9,246, Weekly Boarders £7,988-£8,443, Day Pupils £5,160-£5,457. Learning Support and English as an Additional Language, if required, incur an additional fee of up to £580 per term.

Scholarships and Bursaries. Academic Scholarships are awarded based on performance in the Entrance Examination. Scholarships are also available in Art, Design Technology, Drama, Music and Sport at the main points of entry: Years 7 and 9 and into the Sixth Form. The Christopher Jackson Scholarship is available for pupils who attend local state primary schools within a 14 mile radius of Bethany, are particularly able and have a capacity for academic excellence. Means-tested bursaries are also available. Children of Members of HM Forces and the Clergy receive a 10% fee discount.

Curriculum. The broad curriculum is based on the National Curriculum. The full range of subjects is taught including Information Technology from 11+ and Spanish from 13+. There are 22 GCE A Levels including Business Studies, Food Technology, Government & Politics, Music, Photography, Politics, Textiles, Theatre Studies and Media Studies. The Double A Level in Business is also very popular and successful, as are the BTEC National Awards in Sport and Music Performance. Almost all Sixth Form leavers proceed to degree courses at University.

Dyslexia. The Dyslexia and Learning Support department, which enjoys an international reputation, has been supporting pupils at Bethany for over 30 years.

Games and Activities. The School offers a wide range of sporting opportunities and enjoys an extensive fixture list, having established a long tradition of inter-school Sport. Facilities include a Sports Centre, climbing wall, fitness room, three squash courts, tennis courts, a swimming pool and a floodlit astroturf. There is a wide range of clubs and activities. The Duke of Edinburgh's Award Scheme is well established at Gold, Silver and Bronze levels.

Music. There are wide-ranging opportunities for instrumental tuition. There are sectional instrumental groups including: a Symphony Orchestra, Rock School, Jazz Band, Concert Band, Brass Consort and a Choir, all making use of the fine Music School with its recording studio and music technology area.

Careers. The School is a member of ISCO (Independent Schools Careers Organisation) and Careers Education is an important part of the Curriculum. Sixth Form pupils take part in the Coursefinder Analysis Scheme and receive detailed advice regarding Higher Education and Gap Year opportunities.

Chapel. The Chapel, built in 1878, is the focal point of School life and all pupils are expected to attend services. Confirmation classes are offered for those who wish to participate.

Charitable status. Bethany School Limited is a Registered Charity, number 307937.

Bournemouth Collegiate School
United Learning

Senior School:
College Road, Southbourne, Bournemouth, Dorset BH5 2DY
Tel: 01202 436550
Fax: 01202 434602
email: senior-admin@bournemouthcollegiateschool. co.uk
Twitter: @BCSPrincipal

Prep School:
40 St Osmund's Road, Lower Parkstone, Poole, Dorset BH14 9JY
Tel: 01202 714110
email: prep-admin@bournemouthcollegiateschool. co.uk
Twitter: @BCSPrep

website: www.bournemouthcollegiateschool.co.uk

Chair of Governing Body: Mrs N Dunne

Acting Head of Senior School: **Mrs Maria Coulter**, BSc Hons, PGCE, NPQH, Dip Ed

Acting Vice Principal – Personalised Learning: Mrs Helen Pike, BSc Hons, PGCE

Head of Prep School: Miss Kay Smith, BEd, NPQH

Assistant Principal – Pastoral and Discipline: Mrs Alison Davies, BA Hons, PGCE

Assistant Principal – Academic: Dr Stephen Pumphrey, PhD, BSc, DIC, ACGI

Business Manager: Mrs Vicky Keating

The Best in Everyone

Bournemouth Collegiate School is a popular and successful independent, non-selective, co-ed Senior School (day and boarding, 11–18), situated in an inspiring location next to Bournemouth's golden beaches, and Preparatory School (day, 3–11) in a spacious woodland setting in Lower Parkstone, Poole.

Parents and pupils are attracted by the small classes, excellent results and outstanding facilities across both sites including indoor swimming pools at both schools.

BCS is an extraordinary place to learn. We are part of a country-wide educational group, United Learning, that seeks 'the best in everyone', and we take that mission very seriously.

We offer an exhaustive extra-curricular, sporting and music programme and run a successful Sports Academy for talented athletes. BCS really believes in developing the potential of every pupil and is determined to get the best out of everyone.

The caring, supportive ethos of the school is based on a policy of mutual respect. We encourage independent learning and intellectual curiosity and enable pupils to experience a broad range of experiences which includes numerous trips, seminars, talks by guest speakers and the opportunity for fun, expression and friendship in the many school events on offer.

Fees per term (2014–2015). Prep School: £2,100–£3,300. Senior School: Day Students £4,400; Boarders £8,400.

Scholarships and Bursaries. Scholarships may be offered to pupils who join the school into Year 7 to Year 12. They are awarded to students with all-round excellence or special ability in academia, music, performing arts, art or sport.

A Sixth Form award is also available.

Assisted Places Bursaries are available for those entering into Year 7, Year 9 and Year 12.

Children of ministers and lay members of the United Reformed and Congregational Churches may be eligible for a bursary from the Milton Mount Foundation. A small number of assisted places (means-tested) may available for children entering the school in Year 7, Year 9 and Year 12. Applications for assisted places must be received in the autumn term prior to entry.

Charitable status. Bournemouth Collegiate School is part of United Learning which comprises: UCST (a Company Limited by Guarantee, Registered in England, number 2780748, and a Registered Charity, number 1016538) and ULT (a Company Limited by Guarantee, Registered in England, number 4439859, and an Exempt Charity).

Box Hill School

Mickleham, Dorking, Surrey RH5 6EA
Tel: 01372 373382
            01372 385002 (Registrar)
Fax: 01372 363942
email: enquiries@boxhillschool.com
website: www.boxhillschool.com

Affiliations: The Society of Heads, Round Square, BSA, AGBIS, ISBA, BAISC, IBO, DofE, NAGC.

Warden: Vice-Admiral Sir James Weatherall, KCVO, KBE

Chairman of Governors: Mr John Banfield

Headmaster: Mr Cory Lowde

Bursar: Mr John Pratten

Registrar: Mrs Kirstie Hammond

Headmaster's PA: Mrs Sandy Watt

Box Hill School is a co-educational school set in forty acres of grounds in the heart of the Surrey countryside, offering day and boarding places for 11–18 year olds. We have a strong educational, artistic and sporting tradition; however, what makes us stand out is that we discover and nurture the talents and abilities of every student, so that they all unlock their potential. Box Hill School is proud of its academic attainment and broad curriculum. Standards, recognised as outstanding by inspectors in the 2012 Inspection, are consistently high, and the school is always above national averages in exam performance.

The Sixth Form curriculum focuses on the IB Diploma programme and as of September 2013 A Levels have been introduced as an exciting curriculum expansion initiative. Subject combinations are flexible within the constraints of our options timetable system, and we aim to cater for as wide a range of choices as possible.

Box Hill School is a proud founder member of the Round Square, an international organization of over 90 schools united by a set of 'IDEALS': Internationalism, Democracy, Environmental concern, Adventure, Leadership and Service.

All the Houses at Box Hill School are small and friendly, and students never feel lost or overlooked. The six single-sex Boarding Houses each board around 20–35 pupils with the majority of boarders' rooms being doubles, particularly at Key Stage 4 and above. First-time Boarders are reassured by the family structure of our Houses and find them easy to settle into. To strengthen the bond between students even further, a central school dining room is provided and students are allocated to competitive group teams for school-wide competitions. Full-time Boarders also enjoy a variety of outings at the weekend. An on-site medical centre is provided, staffed by qualified nurses with two non-resident school doctors on call. Boarders may stay in school during term time, except at half terms. There are no 'exeat' weekends.

We provide strong pastoral support for each student, each one being assigned to a House, complete with common room and kitchen. The Houses are run by teaching House staff and each student is assigned to a personal tutor within their house – a member of teaching staff who supports their academic and pastoral development.

We believe that activities outside the classroom form an important part of education, and all students take part in the extensive timetabled activities programme. As well as this regular programme, younger students take part in expeditions around the UK twice a year. The Duke of Edinburgh's Award is particularly strong in the school. Students have the opportunity to participate in Round Square expeditions, carrying out community based projects in locations including Peru and South Africa. They also have the opportunity to go on an exchange to another Round Square school overseas.

The school has an active Parents Association, comprised of supportive parents and friends of the school who maintain links with the local community as well as running social functions and fundraising events. Parents are strongly encouraged to join.

Special features of the School.
- International opportunities through Round Square membership
- IB World School
- Small classes and a high level of academic support
- Outstanding pastoral care
- Weekly and termly activities for all students from an exciting and wide range of options
- International Study Centre

Courses offered. GCSE: Mathematics, English Language, English Literature, Biology, Chemistry, Physics, Geography, History, Business Studies, ICT, French, German, Spanish, Mandarin, Music, Art, Textiles, Drama, Physical Education, Design Technology.

IB: Biology, Environmental Systems, Business Management, Chemistry, Psychology, Theatre Arts, Economics, English, Visual Art, Geography, History, Mathematics, German, Russian, Japanese, Mandarin, French, Spanish, Music, Physics, Design Technology.

A Level: Art, Biology, Business Studies, CDT, Chemistry, Drama, English, Fashion and Textiles, Further Mathematics, Geography, History of Art, ICT, Mathematics, Music, Music Technology, Physics, Psychology, Spanish, Sport Studies.

Sports. Athletics, basketball, cricket, football, hockey, netball, rounders, rugby and tennis as competitive sports but many others as part of the activities programme. Horse riding, Taekwondo, pilates, golf and mountain biking are available by arrangement.

Drama, Music and Art. Art students gain excellent examination grades each year, with many going on to be accepted at major art schools. Our purpose-built Music School has greatly enhanced the already wide range of musical opportunities within school, including a choir, chamber choir, wind ensemble, string ensemble, jazz band, funk band and numerous rock/pop bands. The school stages senior and junior plays each year and has performed *The Crucible* and *Bugsy Malone* in the last academic year. LAMDA coaching is available and the school has an excellent record in these examinations.

Fees per term (2014–2015). Years 7–11: Boarders £9,650; Weekly Boarders £7,920; Day Pupils £5,200–£5,450. Sixth Form: Boarders £9,980; Weekly Boarders £8,310; Day Pupils £5,700. ISC Fee: £11,500.

A fee discount of 20% is offered to students who have a parent who is a serving member of HM Armed Forces.

Scholarships. A variety of awards are offered for entry to Box Hill School; the latest information can be found on the school's website. Scholarships are available for those entering Years 7, 9 and the Sixth Form, under the following categories: Academic, Art, Expressive/Performing Arts, and Sport.

Bursaries are available on application following registration and are subject to means testing and are offered on the basis of a formula laid out in the school's Scholarships and Bursaries Policy which is available on request from the Bursar. All bursaries are reviewed annually.

Method of Entry. Entry is based on an interview, the two most recent reports from the pupil's present school, and written tests in Maths and English. Sixth Form entry is based on report, interview and GCSE predictions. For overseas pupils a personal interview on site is desirable but we are happy to conduct a Skype interview if necessary. Main school entrance ages are 11, 13 and 16 years. Under normal circumstances, we like to meet prospective pupils and their parents or guardians – this also gives you an opportunity to have a look around our campus facilities and meet key staff and students.

Charitable status. Box Hill School Trust Limited is a Registered Charity, number 312082. It exists to promote the advancement of education.

The Cathedral School Llandaff
A Woodard School

Llandaff, Cardiff CF5 2YH
Tel: 029 2056 3179
Fax: 029 2056 7752
email: registrar@cathedral-school.co.uk
website: www.cathedral-school.co.uk
Twitter: @cslcardiff

Chairman of the Council: G C Lloyd

Senior Management Team:

Headmaster: **S W Morris**, BA, MEd, PGCE

Deputy Head Pastoral: Mr Lawrence Moon, BA, MA, GTP

Deputy Head Academic: Mrs Pam Creed, BSc

Head of Sixth Form: Mrs Catrin Ellis-Owen, BA

Deputy Head Juniors: Mr Bret Garland, CertEd, BEd

Director of Infants: Mrs Sally Walsh, BEd, NPQH

Bursar: Mr Robert Leek

Set in 15 acres of parkland and playing fields within minutes of Cardiff city centre, the Cathedral School was founded in 1880. Acknowledged by Estyn as an "excellent" school (2012), there are currently 750 pupils at the co-educational school between the ages of 3 and 18 years. The Cathedral School is a member of the Woodard Corporation and adheres to a firmly Christian ethos.

Building on Strong Foundations. Pupils at the Cathedral School receive first class academic teaching, take part in a wide co-curricular programme, develop their leadership skills and confidence and are supported through high quality pastoral care, within a Christian context. The school is small enough to ensure that everyone is known and cared for, yet large enough to offer a real breadth of challenge and opportunity. Pupils of all denominations and faiths are welcomed.

Nursery, Infants & Juniors. A positive experience of learning in our earliest years at school sets the foundations for being an engaged and successful learner later on. The classroom is a place of energy and creativity, a place of high expectations within an atmosphere of nurture and encouragement. Beyond the classroom walls there are extensive opportunities to enjoy competitive sport, especially team games which have busy and challenging fixture lists; opportunities to perform music at an excellent standard including opportunities for boys and girls to join choirs and to sing in Llandaff Cathedral, along with drama, dance and elocution; opportunities to enjoy the outdoors, wildlife, outward bound activities; opportunities to get involved in action for good causes, including environmental awareness and charity work. There are also plenty of inter-house activities to get involved with which create a vibrant atmosphere.

Nearly all pupils transfer into the Senior Section to continue their educational journey through to 18.

The Seniors. At this school we pride ourselves upon being a strong learning community. It is important that everyone feels valued and that they have a meaningful part to play. From the initial Year 7 'bonding weekend' creating new friendships, to the competitive house system, a mutually supportive environment means that every pupil's skill, interest, talent and potential are nurtured.

Regularly recognised, whether by the schools inspectorate Estyn, or in newspaper 'league tables', as one of the highest achieving schools in Wales academically, a great emphasis is also placed upon the "co-curricular". For Years 10–13 the Duke of Edinburgh's Award is followed, which is hugely popular and delivered by our own dedicated staff and for Years 7–9, the Headmaster's Award, a junior and anticipatory version of "D of E".

In September 2014, a new Senior classroom block was opened, featuring two Science laboratories, eight classrooms and study areas.

The quality of music at the Cathedral School is outstanding. It is our boys and girls who sing Llandaff Cathedral's choral services day by day, and the same excellence of musicianship rubs off in school within a wide range of genres, from the classical to rock and pop, chamber music to jazz. On the sports field a similar appetite for excellence pervades all we do. With a very high coach : player ratio and a busy, competitive fixture list, rugby, football, sevens, cricket, hockey, netball, rounders, rowing, kayaking, climbing and gym all thrive here. Equally, ambitious participation in public speaking and debating competitions, challenging drama productions and various genres of fine art all add to the opportunities for all pupils to achieve standards which help them grow in confidence.

Sixth Form. The Cathedral School Sixth Form began in September 2013, offering very small classes, highly experienced staff with close university links and a culture which is ambitious and supportive in equal measure.

The new Sixth Form Centre provides dedicated social and study space for students. Every sixth former is invited to engage in the school's professional mentoring programme, which pairs students with leading professional figures in the areas of working life which most appeal to them, for advice and guidance.

Beyond their A Level studies, students have many opportunities to broaden their interests and abilities through initiatives including outward bound expeditions, the Duke of Edinburgh's Award at Gold Level, competitive sport, outstanding musical performances, debating and public speaking and the Extended Project Qualification.

A Level Subjects: Art, Psychology, Chemistry, Computing, Economics, Biology, English Literature, Spanish, Geography, Mathematics, Further Mathematics, Philosophy & Ethics, Latin, History, Design & Technology, Physics, French, German, Music and Physical Education.

Scholarships & Bursaries. Financial support is available for bright pupils at Year 7 and Year 12 entry, with scholarships for especially gifted children – academic, music, all-rounder – and means-tested bursaries worth up to 100% of fees.

School Transport. School transport is available with bus routes from Castleton, Cowbridge, Caerphilly, Colwinston, Llantrisant and Lisvane. Working parents are helped by wrap-around care available daily from 8 am to 6 pm.

Fees per term (2014–2015). Year 7 & above £3,740, Years 5 & 6 £3,426, Years 3 & 4 £3,040, Reception, Years 1 & 2 £2,665, Nursery £2,289.

Charitable status. The Cathedral School Llandaff Limited is a Registered Charity, number 1103522. It exists to provide a high standard of education for girls and boys with a caring Christian ethos.

Claremont Fan Court School

Claremont Drive, Esher, Surrey KT10 9LY
Tel: 01372 467841
Fax: 01372 471109
email: info@claremont.surrey.sch.uk
website: www.claremont-school.co.uk

Head of Senior School: **Mr Jonathan Insall-Reid**, BSc Waikato, NZ, BArch Hons VUW, NZ, Teaching Dip

Head of Preparatory School: Mr Duncan Murphy, BA Hons Sheffield, MEd Buckingham, FRSA, FCMI, FCollT

Head of Pre-Preparatory and Nursery School: Mrs Louise Fox, BEd Hons Sussex

Situation. Claremont Estate is one of the premier historic sites in the country. The original house and the famous Landscape Garden were first laid out by Sir John Vanbrugh for the Duke of Newcastle early in the eighteenth century. Later Capability Brown built the present Palladian Mansion for Clive of India. For over a century Claremont was a royal residence and played an important part in Queen Victoria's early years. In 1930 the School acquired the Mansion and now owns 100 acres of peaceful parkland. Esher is only 16 miles from London and almost equidistant from Heathrow and Gatwick airports with access points onto the M25 within 3 miles.

General Information. Claremont Fan Court School is a co-educational school for pupils from 2½–18 years. The School consists of the Pre-Preparatory and Nursery School for pupils aged 2½–7 years, the Preparatory School for pupils aged 7–11 years and the Senior School for pupils from 11–18 years. Claremont Fan Court is a school with strong Christian values and welcomes pupils from all faiths and none

Aims. To care for and value the potential of every child. With this recognition comes the expectation of high academic achievement and participation in sporting and cultural activities.

Curriculum. The core curriculum provides all pupils with the opportunity to learn the skills and understandings required to continue learning throughout their lives. Emphasis is placed on the acquisition and development of skills in numeracy and literacy while providing a wide and varied range of subjects to stimulate the joy and wonder of learning. These curriculum ideals are delivered in a manner appropriate to the ages of the pupils throughout the Pre-Preparatory, Preparatory and Senior School.

An important element in our teaching philosophy is to understand the link between academic rigour and the value of good character. The academic curriculum ensures that all pupils attain the highest qualifications of which they are capable for entry into university or college.

Many pupils excel in the sporting arena where they develop talents through fixtures against other schools as well as in county or national school championships. Annual tours, both nationally and overseas, give an added dimension to pupils' sporting education.

Music, art and drama are also important aspects of the daily curriculum. All contributions are valued, whether they be leading, supporting or backstage roles, in order for the participants to be given every opportunity for creative thought and individual expression and to develop an awareness of self-worth.

Sixth Form. The Sixth Form is a vibrant and vital part of the School, focusing on 27 A level courses. It forms a bridge between the years of compulsory schooling and the more independent years of Higher Education. Students take on many responsibilities including leadership and organisational roles which provide an all-round experience of special value to universities, colleges and employers.

At Sixth Form, Claremont Fan Court also welcomes external students, who meet our entry requirements. The Sixth Form Centre provides recreation and study facilities and is housed in the historic surroundings of White Cottage, designed by John Vanburgh in 1715.

Careers. Pupils receive careers advice from Year 8 onwards. All sixth form students have a weekly dedicated Careers lesson, delivered by a specialist Careers teacher. This ensures that all students receive detailed personalised guidance, leading them to courses and career choices that are appropriate for their individual preferences. Interviews are organised for pupils and conducted by external advisors.

Co-Curricular Activities. Making individual choices in the learning programme and developing a wide range of interests are both necessary preparations for lifelong learning. All pupils are actively encouraged to participate in a wide variety of clubs and enrichment activities, including the Duke of Edinburgh's Award Scheme, offshore sailing and international trips.

Admissions. The main intake of pupils occurs at 2½, 3, 7+, 11+, 13+ and Sixth Form. Places are offered subject to a pupil reaching the School's entry requirements. Applications for entry at other levels are welcome subject to a place becoming available.

Fees per term (2014–2015). Pre-Preparatory and Nursery: Nursery £1,525; Reception–Year 2 £3,040. Preparatory School: Years 3–6 £3,915. Senior School: Years 7–8 £4,820; Years 9–11 & Sixth Form £5,090.

Scholarships. Academic Scholarships are offered at Year 3, to continue through to the end of Year 6, and at Year 7 and Year 9 to continue through to the end of Year 11. Offers are based on a written examination and interview. Sixth Form Academic Scholarships are also available.

All-Round Scholarships are offered at Year 7.

Music Scholarships are available for Senior School applicants. As a guide, scholarship candidates should be working at the following levels before applying: Year 7 – Grade 4, Year 9 – Grade 5, Sixth Form – Grade 6. Sixth Form Scholarships will be awarded for the two-year course. Year 7 and Year 9 Scholarships will be awarded through to the end of Year 11.

Sports Scholarships are awarded for pupils of exceptional sporting ability. Sixth Form Scholarships are awarded for the two years of the course. Year 9 Scholarships are awarded through to the end of Year 11.

Art and Drama Scholarships are available to candidates applying for a Sixth Form place and are awarded for the duration of their two-year course.

Full details about scholarships are available on the school website.

Charitable status. The School is owned and run by an educational foundation with charitable status, Registered Charity number 274664.

Clifton High School

College Road, Clifton, Bristol BS8 3JD

Tel:	0117 973 0201 (School Office)
	0117 933 9087 (Admissions)
	0117 973 3853 (Finance)
Fax:	0117 923 8962
email:	admissions@cliftonhigh.bristol.sch.uk
website:	www.cliftonhigh.bristol.sch.uk
Facebook:	/CliftonHighSchoolBristol

Clifton High School, founded in 1877, is a co-educational independent school offering a first-class education to around 500 pupils from nursery school class (rising 3s) to Sixth Form. Family boarders are accepted from the age of 16 years. Unique in Bristol, the school has adopted a Diamond Edge model where boys and girls are taught separately in core subjects in Years 7–9 before becoming fully re-integrated in Year 10 and above.

Governing Body (*School Council of Governors*):

President: Mr Hugh Stebbing, BSc, FRICS, FBIFM, FRSA, FICPD
Vice-President: Ms Lise E Seager, MBA, BA

Mr James Caddy
Prof Selena Gray, BSc, MBCLB, MD, FRCP, FFPH
Mr A David Marval, BArch Hons, Dip Arch, RIBA
Mr John Smith, MA
Mr Martin Ursell
Mrs Hilary Vaughan, BEng, CEng, MICE
Mr Richard Whitburn

Head of School: **Dr Alison M Neill**, PhD, BSc Hons UCW Aberystwyth, PGCE

Director of Operations: Mr Guy Cowper, MSc Sheffield, BA Hons Warwick

Senior School Teaching Staff:

Senior Leadership Team:
Assistant Head – Academic, Curriculum and Timetable: Mr Glenn A A Taylor, BA Hons York, PGCE
Assistant Head – Sixth Form, External Examinations: Mr Manolis Psarros, MA Bristol, BA Hons Wales, C&G Teacher Training, MEd Bristol
Assistant to Deputy Head and Head of Years 7–9: Mr Chris Collins, BA Hons UWIC, MA Bath PGCE
Assistant to Deputy Head and Head of Years 10–11: Mr Sam Goldsmith, BSc Hons Birmingham, GTP
Designate Safeguarding Lead: Ms Alison Taylor, BSc Hons Reading, MEd Bristol, PGCE
Induction Lead: Mrs Gill Malpass, BA Hons London, Labon Dance Cert PGCE

* *Head of Department*

Art and Design:
*Mr Paul Ayers, MA Falmouth, BA Hons Cornwall, PGCE
Ms Claire Jaques, BA Hons Plymouth, PG Dip Ed, PGCE

Business Studies:
*Mr Peter G Jackson, BA Hons Westminster, PGCE

Classics:
Mr Andrew McConnell, BA Hons Cambridge, PGCE
*Mr Manolis Psarros, BA Hons Wales, MA Bristol, C&G Teacher Training, MEd Bristol

Design and Technology:
Mr Andrew Cleaver, BA Hons Lincoln & Hull (*Music Technology*)
Mr Sam Goldsmith, BSc Hons Birmingham, GTP (*Food and Nutrition*)
Mrs Rachel Hindmarch, BMus Hons Manchester, PGCE (*Music Technology*)
Mr Bryan Murphy, MA Cambridge, PGCE (*Design*)
Mr Justin Noyce, BA Hons Manchester, PGCE (*Graphic Design*)
Miss Emma Warwood, BSc Hons Bolton, PGCE (*Textiles Technology*)

Drama:
Mrs Sue Johnson-Martin, BA Hons Royal Holloway College London, PGCE
*Mrs Gill Malpass, BA Hons London, Labon Dance Cert PGCE

English:
Mr Christopher Hope, BA Hons Hull, MA Birmingham, PGCE
Mrs Siobhan P Hosty, MA Kingston, Dip TEFL (*also PSE Coordinator*)
*Mrs Jill P Pritchard, BA Hons Exeter, PGCE

Futures and Skills:
*Mrs Laura Giles, BSc Hons Loughborough, PGCE
Mr Sam Goldsmith, BSc Hons Birmingham
Miss Louise Sobey, BA Hons Portsmouth, PGCE

Geography:
*Mrs Laura Giles, BSc Hons Loughborough, PGCE
Mrs Helen Ellerton, BSc Manchester, PGCE

History / Government and Politics:
Mr Alistair Baker, BA Hons Bristol, MA Bristol, PGCE
*Dr Alison McClean, PhD MA Essex, BA Hons UWIC, Cert HE TVU, PGCE
Mr Oliver Mullins, BA Hons Birmingham

Information Technology:
*Mr Justin Noyce, BA Hons Manchester, PGCE
Mr Glenn A A Taylor, BA Hons York, PGCE

Mathematics:
*Mrs Sharon Hargroves, BSc Hons King's College London, PGCE, Dip Inf Eng
Miss Grace Hogan, BSc Hons Loughborough, PGCE
Mr Richard Shelswell, MEng Hons Bath, PGCE
Ms Alison Taylor, BSc Hons Reading, MEd Bristol, PGCE
Mr Glenn A A Taylor, BA Hons York, PGCE
Mrs Kathryn Vaughan, BSc Hons Exeter, MEd, PGCE, Bristol

Modern Languages:
Mrs Tara Harris, BA Hons Newcastle upon Tyne, PGCE (*German*)
Miss Helen McKenna, BA Hons York, PGCE (*French*)
Mrs Louise Sobey, BA Hons Portsmouth/Murcia, PGCE (*Spanish*)
Miss Marianne Mitchell, BA Hons Portsmouth, PGCE (*French and Spanish*)
Mrs Kate Clarke, BA Hons Oxford, PGCE (*French*)

Language Assistants:
Ms Sara Roman de la Pena (*Spanish*)
Mrs Ev Milker (*German*)
Miss Marie Boehler (*French*)

Music:
*Mrs Rachel Hindmarch, BMus Hons Manchester, PGCE
Mrs Maria Johnson, MA, MEd, PGCE

Physical Education:
*Mr Chris Collins, BA Hons UWIC, MA Bath, PGCE, (*Head of School Games, Boys*)
*Mrs Lynne Reid, BSc Hons Cardiff, PGCE, (*Head of School Games, Girls*)
Mr James Taylor, BSc Hons Sheffield Hallam, GTP
Mrs Val Williams, CertEd, Dip PE Bristol
Miss Alice Woodyatt, BSc Hons Brunel, PGCE

Religious Studies:
*Mrs Jacinth Awolola-McNab, BEd, CertEd Birmingham

Science:
Ms Louise Brackenbury, BSc Hons University of Wales, Cardiff, PGCE (*Chemistry*)
Dr Alison Camacho, PhD Cardiff, BSc Hons Bristol, PGCE (*Physics*)
Mrs Alison Derricourt, BSc Hons Sheffield, PGCE (*Biology*)
Dr Alice England, PhD Sheffield, BSc Hons Sheffield PGCE (*Science*)
Mr Bryan Murphy, MA Cambridge, PGCE (*Physics*)
Mr Richard Storey-Walker, BSc Hons, Loughborough, PGCE, Goldsmiths (*Chemistry*)

Extra-Curricular Lead: Mr James Taylor, BSC Hons Sheffield Hallam, GTP

Early Years and Junior School Teaching Staff:

Senior Management Team:
Assistant to Deputy Head, Years 3–6: Mrs Sarah Barker, BEd Hons UWE
Assistant to Deputy Head, Nursery–Year 2 : Mrs Jane Lee, BA Hons Plymouth, PGCE
Lead Support to Assistant to Deputy Head, Years 3–6: Mrs Alice Bagnall, BSc Hons Cardiff, PGCE
Lead Support to Assistant to Deputy Head, Nursery–Year 2: Mrs Julia Sutcliffe, BA Hons Warwick, PGCE

Miss Charlotte Coe, BSc Hons Bath Spa, PGCE
Ms Claire Jaques, BA Hons Plymouth, PGCE, PG Dip Ed
Mrs Josie Knott, BEd Bristol
Mr Charles Lowe, BA/Ed Joint Hons Goldsmiths College London
Miss Hannah Phillips, BEd Hons Winchester
Miss Elizabeth Poustie, BSc Hons Gloucester, PGCE
Mr David J E Pye, BA Hons West London Inst of HE, PGCE

Mrs Helen Tabb, BA Hons QTS Surrey
Mrs Donna Andrews, BSc Hons QTS Bath, EYPS
Mrs Linda Mitchell, BSc Hons Edinburgh, PGCE
Mr Oliver Mullins, BA Hons Birmingham
Mrs Caroline Pope, BA Hons London, PGCE
Mrs Aleyna Roberts, BSc Hons Southampton, PGCE
Mrs Sarah Willerton, BA Hons Bath Spa, PGCE
Mrs Jo Denyer-Warr, BA Hons UWE

School Music Lead: Mr Andrew Cleaver, BA Hons Lincoln and Hull

Teaching Assistants:
Mrs Amanda Clancy, NNEB
Miss Dawn Clark, HNC
Miss Debbie Clements, NNEB
Mrs Jane Doubleday, Teaching Assistant Stage III
Mrs Amanda Godshaw, NNEB
Mrs Viviane Owen, CertEd Bristol
Mrs Emma Takle, NNEB

Enhanced Learning Department:
SENCO: Mrs Gabrielle Pilgrim, BA Hons Reading, PGCE, BDA ATS, SpLD APC Patoss
Miss Kate Lockwood, BA Hons Manchester, PGCE, CELTA
Miss Jenny Norris, BSc Bath, PGCE
Mrs Amanda Swannell, BA Hons Hull, PGCE, PG Cert Ed, MA UWE, PG Dip Dyslexia
Mrs Alison White, BEd Hons London, PG Dip SpLD, CAPSE
Mrs Brenda Williams, NNEB

Pupil Welfare and Business Support Staff:

School Nurses:
Mrs Emma Shaw, RGN
Mrs Kate Franklin, RGN

Counsellor:
Mrs Penny Telling, MSc Bristol, PG Dip Counselling
Mrs Jackie Brangwyn, BEd Hons Sussex, MSc Bristol

Designated Safeguarding Lead:
Ms Alison Taylor (*Y7–13*)
Mrs Aleyna Roberts (*Foundation Stage to KS2*)

Administration:
Admissions Registrar: Mrs Melanie Johnson
Host Family Boarding Coordinator: Mrs Capucine Sha'ban
PA to Head of School: Mrs Trudy Scales
Marketing: Ms Jenny Robertson
Marketing Executive: Miss Lucy Forbes
School Office Manager: Mrs Emma Hill
HR and Administration: Mrs Kate Solly
School Office Administrator and Events Coordinator: Miss Feona Horrex
Administration Assistant to the Head's Office: Miss Georgia Clark
School Office Administration Assistant: Miss Rachel Robinson
Databases Administrator and Examination Support: Mrs Emily Freire Baños

Finance:
Accountant: Mr Anthony Willford
Fee Administrator: Mrs Tracy Gajewski
Payroll and Pensions: Miss Tracey Nicholls
Finance Assistant: Mrs Sandra Furlong

Librarian: Mrs Sarah Cuthill

Science Technicians:
*Mr Michael Johnson
Mrs Heather Power

Art Technician:
Ms Sonya Nutter

IT Systems & Support:
*Mr Janos Fülöp
Mr Charlie Jones (*Apprentice*)

Maintenance:
*Mr Stephen James
Mr Adam Tayler
Mr Mark Cooper
Mr Graham Hooper

Catering:
*Mr Tim Fletcher
Ms Mel Johnson

Aims. The school is a community that places importance on knowing each and every member – students, parents, staff and old friends. High value is placed on the importance of the individual. The school aims to inspire, support and challenge the individual, enabling pupils to achieve their full potential and excel at their particular talents. The school believes that each and every student has a brilliance; within an environment of high expectations, excellent teaching, supportive staff and outstanding pastoral care the school aims to give pupils a rich and varied educational experience where they can realise that brilliance. The school believes that with the privilege of an excellent education comes responsibility, and they aim to send students out into the world who not only have a lifelong passion for learning but who are ready to make a real and positive contribution to society.

Facilities. The school occupies a splendid site in Clifton, near the Downs and Suspension Bridge. The facilities and accommodation are excellent including a science centre with seven laboratories, well stocked libraries and over 250 networked workstations with latest green technology implemented, a multimedia language laboratory, Sixth Form centre and a state-of-the-art performing arts studio and cinema. Sports facilities include a heated 25m indoor swimming pool, gymnasium and floodlit multi-games courts on site. Professional grade offsite sports facilities, in partnership with the University of Bristol, include an indoor tennis centre (four courts), ten outdoor courts, two artificial turf hockey pitches and grass pitches for football, rugby and cricket.

Curriculum. Class sizes average 15 in the Early Years and Junior School and 18 in the Senior School.

The *Nursery to Junior Schools* offer an excellent academic, social and moral foundation:

The *Early Years* follow the Foundation Stage curriculum, focusing upon: personal, social and emotional development; communication; language and literacy; problem solving, reasoning and numeracy; knowledge and understanding of the world; physical development and creative development. The children enjoy a myriad of experiences in a safe and stimulating environment. Recognition that they are "outstanding in every area" (Ofsted 2008), achievement of the Bristol Standard and accreditation by an Investors in Children quality assurance scheme, have all endorsed the splendid reputation of the Early Years Department.

Years 1 and 2, working in an informal atmosphere within a structured framework, focus on high standards of literacy and numeracy, stimulating the children's minds through creative work and challenging projects. The curriculum also includes English, Mathematics, French, IT, Science, History, Geography, Art, Music, Swimming and Games. Pupils in Years 1 and 2 enjoy regular visits to a nearby Forest School throughout the year.

The *Junior Department* gives children a strong grounding in English, Mathematics, Science, IT, History, Geography, Modern Languages, Music, Art, Drama, Design Technology, Religious Studies, Gymnastics, Athletics and Games (Netball, Hockey, Rugby, Football, Tennis, Rounders and Cricket). French, Mathematics, Science, Music, Swimming and PE are taught in the Junior Department by specialist teachers. Over 40 extra-curricular activities are on offer including Choirs, Orchestra, IT, Speech and Drama, Dance and Art and Craft, together with a wide range of sports clubs providing for individual and team sports. Visiting speakers and regular trips to the local area and further afield enhance the curriculum in all departments. Children in the Junior Department also have the opportunity to enjoy overnight visits each year.

The *Senior School* is fully co-educational throughout. Boys and girls are taught separately for Modern Languages in Year 7, for English, Mathematics, IT, Physics, Chemistry and Biology and Games in Years 7–9 and together in all other subjects before moving back into fully mixed classes for their chosen examination subjects when they reach Year 10. This is the pioneering Diamond Edge Model of education and Clifton High School is the only school in the Bristol area to adopt this approach. Year 7–9 pupils study a broad and balanced curriculum including English, Mathematics, Physics, Chemistry, Biology, IT, History, Geography, Religious Studies, modern languages (French, German, Spanish), Latin, Drama, Music, Art & Design, Design & Innovation, Food & Nutrition, Graphic Design and Textiles, PE and Personal and Social Education (PSE). In Years 10 and 11, Physical Education and PSE form part of the general programme. For study at GCSE there is a common and balanced core of English, Mathematics, separate sciences, humanities and a modern foreign language, in addition to which pupils may select subjects based on their interests and career plans. There is also a newly introduced programme of Life Skills and Competencies which runs alongside the GCSE courses and provides further opportunities for pupils to develop and identify extra skills, qualifications and interests. The school has an excellent academic record at GCSE, AS and A Level. Throughout the Senior School and Sixth Form pupils have a personal tutor who monitors their academic and social welfare.

The co-educational *Sixth Form* is a thriving centre of excellence within the school. The students play an important part in the whole school community, developing their leadership skills with the younger pupils through a peer support scheme, the House system, the Pupil Council, the Head's Team, the Eco Club Committee and many other opportunities. Students have a wide choice of A Level subjects. Almost all students progress to university; in 2014 almost 80% went to Russell Group Universities. The most able are encouraged to apply for Oxbridge entrance and the vast majority of those who apply gain the offer of a place. All Sixth Form students take part in Futures and Skills which is an enrichment programme designed to offer a range of experiences and also have individual careers guidance sessions. All students have regular one-to-one tutorials. Sixth formers holding scholarships are encouraged to manage a scholars' *Forum* by producing an annual programme of debates and current affairs discussions with other pupils and for inviting speakers in to the school to talk on specific topics of interest.

Host Family Boarding. Clifton High School offers a unique opportunity for students over 16 (especially those from overseas) to board, full-time or weekly, with families with a very close link to the school. All host families are carefully vetted by the school. The Host Family Boarding Coordinator continuously supports the student and the host family, and oversees the welfare and progress of the student during his or her stay at CHS. The 2009 Ofsted Inspection of the School's Family Boarding Facilities awarded the school "outstanding" in all areas and a very positive interim ISI inspection in 2013 confirmed compliance with all National Minimum Standards.

Physical Education is a key part of the curriculum, not only for competitive sport, but for promoting a healthy lifestyle through the enjoyment of sport and exercise. In addition to the school's traditional sports of hockey, netball, football, rugby, swimming, athletics, rounders, cricket, tennis and gymnastics, specialist staff also teach a wide variety of other activities including squash, badminton, volleyball, basketball, water polo and trampolining. Boys and girls regularly gain county and national honours and both boys and girls sports teams perform strongly in their relevant leagues and tournaments.

Music and Drama. Virtually any instrument, including voice, may be studied, with some 50 per cent of pupils having individual lessons. Associated Board examinations are taken. There are opportunities to belong to orchestras, wind bands, drama groups and choirs who perform in a variety of concerts and productions throughout the year including some of the highest profile events in the school calendar. In Speech and Drama, a large number of pupils enter LAMDA examinations.

Charitable and Extra-Curricular Activities. Pupils have a strong sense of social responsibility and are actively involved in various local and national charity fundraising events throughout their school careers. Annual collections amount to several thousand pounds. There is a lively extra-curricular activities programme throughout the school, responding to pupils' interests. There are well over 20 clubs running at any time including Science, Debating and Public Speaking, Astronomy, Mathematics, Trampolining, Craft Club, Robotics, Guitar Club, Eco Committee, Woodworking and Taekwondo. Pupils regularly take part in the Duke of Edinburgh's Award and World Challenge programmes. There is a rich programme of trips both home and overseas.

Admission and Scholarships. Entry to the Nursery class is not selective. Entry to Early Years and Junior School is by in-class assessment and taster session with the relevant class. Entry to the Senior School is dependent on the results of an entrance examination, Head's interview and school report. Pupils in Clifton High School Year 6 also sit the entrance exam to Senior School. Some academic scholarships are awarded for Year 7, 9 and Sixth Form entry level but there is sometimes flexibility. Some school-assisted places are available in the Senior School as are Music and Sports awards. Sports, performing arts and creative arts awards are also available in the Sixth Form. Further details are available from the School Admissions Registrar.

Fees per term (2014–2015). Tuition: Nursery School – details on request from the Admissions Registrar; Junior School: Years 0–2 £2,890, Years 3–6 £2,970; Senior School: Years 7–13 £4,270. Lunch: Years 0–6 £220, Years 7–13 £230. Family Boarding (exclusive of Tuition): £3,405. EAL: Nursery–Year 2 £150 per term for first year, Years 3–13 £700 per term for first year.

Reductions for siblings concurrently in the school (except where fees are paid by an authority or bursary): 2nd – 7%; 3rd – 15%; 4th – 25%.

Charitable status. Clifton High School is a Registered Charity, number 311736. It exists to provide first-class education for pupils aged 3 to 18 years.

Concord College

Acton Burnell Hall, Shrewsbury, Shropshire SY5 7PF
Tel: 01694 731631
Fax: 01694 731389
email: enquiries@concordcollege.org.uk
website: www.concordcollegeuk.com

Concord College is a highly successful international boarding college providing GCSE and A Level courses. Set in 80 acres of Shropshire parkland, the College combines outstanding facilities with first-rate academic performance. The College is regularly rated in the top 20 schools in the UK. Students are cared for by a dedicated staff in a safe and beautiful environment. UK day and boarding students are also welcome at the College. Concord is a community that celebrates national and cultural diversity while students and staff are united by the wish to set high standards. The result is a happy and open community in which students are polite, articulate and conscientious without ever losing their sense of fun.

The College dates back to 1949 and moved to its present site in 1973. In 1983 it became a charitable trust. Over the years, students from over eighty countries have attended Concord.

Chair of the Governors: Dr Iain M Bride

Clerk to the Governors and Bursar: Mrs Barbara Belfield-Dean

Principal: **Neil G Hawkins**, MA Cantab, PGCE

Vice-Principal (Academic): Tom Lawrence, BA, PGCE
Vice-Principal (Pastoral): Jeremy Kerslake, MA
Head of Lower School: Mrs Gail Denham, BA
Director of Enrichment and Examinations: Phil Outram, PhD, BSc

Principal's Personal Assistant & Admissions Registrar: Mrs Wendy Hartshorne

The College is a co-educational day and boarding school for students aged 13–19.

Number of students: 500 (approximately equal numbers of boys and girls) of whom over 440 are boarders.

Facilities. Facilities at Concord College are superb. Based around an historic Main Building, there are many new additions as well as medieval ruins within the grounds. There is a stunning Theatre and Music School, an excellent Sports complex, indoor swimming pool as well as an outstanding Science facility. Students eat their meals in the College Dining Room and select from a variety of international cuisine. Most students have individual study-bedrooms on campus, some with en-suite bathrooms. Students have a wide variety of facilities including a sports hall, social centre and student kitchen.

Education. Teaching at Concord is undertaken in groups that average 16 at GCSE and 14 at A Level. Teachers are experts in their subjects.

At GCSE Biology, Chemistry and Physics are taught as separate subjects and emphasis is placed upon laboratory experience. Other compulsory subjects are Mathematics, English, Religious Studies and Physical Education. Optional subjects include Art, Economics, Geography, History, IT, Music, Spanish, French and German.

At AS and A Level students normally study at least three A Levels and at least one further AS Level. Subjects include Art, Accounting, Biology, Chemistry, Chinese, Economics, English Language, English Literature, Geography, History, Law, Mathematics, Further Mathematics, Music, Photography, Physics and Spanish. All students who do not have GCSE English are expected to study English.

Lessons are taught in a variety of excellent classroom facilities. The new classroom block, The Jubilee Building, which opened in September 2010 houses the English and Mathematics departments in state-of-the-art classrooms.

In addition to their teachers, students have an individual tutor with whom they meet daily and who monitors their academic progress. Students also have a House Parent who is responsible for their well-being. Support is available to all students to develop their oral and discursive skills to ensure that they are able to express their ideas confidently especially at university interview.

Examination Results and University Entry. The College achieves excellent examination results with 95% A*/A/B at A Level in 2014, placing Concord within the top 10 schools in the UK according to The Times and The Daily Telegraph league tables. The College is highly successful in placing students into UK medical schools and other top UK universities. In 2014, 12 students won places at Oxford or Cambridge University, 16 at Imperial College London and 16 at the LSE. 24 students went on to read Medicine at medical schools.

Selection for Entry. The college selects applicants upon the basis of interviews, school record and entry tests. Online tests are arranged for overseas applicants. Students can be accepted for entry at all ages.

Fees per annum (2014–2015). Full Boarding £32,400, Day £12,546. (Boarding fees are payable in 2 instalments.)

Scholarships and Bursaries. A fee reduction of up to 10% of full fees may be available to students who have a particularly strong academic background. For entrants to GCSE classes, scholarship entry tests are administered. General bursaries are also available on request: indeed the College has a 'needs blind' admissions policy for its day students.

Holidays. Half term holidays involve only a long weekend. The Christmas holiday is one month and Easter is only two and a half weeks. There is a long summer vacation from the end of June until early September.

The college remains open at half term and during the Easter holiday (for students over the age of 16) and there is no additional charge for holiday accommodation and meals.

The School Day. Lessons run from 9 am to 4 pm Monday to Friday with Wednesday afternoon allocated to sport and to a trip to Shrewsbury for senior students. There is compulsory supervised study (prep) for two hours each evening Monday to Friday.

Saturday morning is used for whole-college testing. The public examination rooms are used for this purpose so that the rooms hold no fear for the students when the final public examinations are taken.

Reports to Parents. These are sent at half term in the first term and subsequently at the end of each term.

Clubs, Sports and Extra-Curricular Activities. Students at Concord can choose from a multitude of activities. Sports, music, dance and drama are all available in our own facilities. There is a Sports Hall, squash courts and gymnasium as well as outdoor facilities including football, athletics and tennis. A wealth of sporting activities is on offer ranging from archery to fencing and badminton to Taekwondo. For dancers, there is a purpose-built dance studio where ballet, modern, latin and ballroom and streetdance clubs take place. Musicians can join the orchestra, wind or string groups. Choir and singing club can develop all levels of vocal talent. Many other activities are also offered ranging from bridge and chess to horse riding and mountain-biking. Students take part in Concord's outdoor education programme and the Duke of Edinburgh's Award Scheme is also available. Whatever their talents, students are able develop them at Concord.

Charitable status. Concord College is a Registered Charity, number 326279. It exists to provide high quality education for secondary age students.

Derby Grammar School

Rykneld Road, Littleover, Derby DE23 4BX
Tel: 01332 523027
Fax: 01332 518670
email: headmaster@derbygrammar.co.uk
        admissions@derbygrammar.co.uk
website: www.derbygrammar.co.uk

Chair of Governors: Mr David Walker

Vice Chair of Governors: Mr Simon Richardson

Headmaster: **Mr Richard Paine**, BA Hons, PGCE

Deputy Headmaster: Mrs L C Reynolds, BSc Hons
Senior Master: Mr P D Hilliam, BA Hons
Head of Lower School: Mr K Clark, BA Hons
Head of Upper School: Mrs V Charnock, BAHons
Head of Sixth Form: Mrs C Bramall, BA Hons
Chaplain: Revd P Taylor, BA Hons
School Bursar: Miss J Jameson, MAAT
Registrar: Mrs L Slater Blackwall

Senior School Teaching Staff (principal subjects):

Art:
Ms E Sellors, BA Hons

Biology:
Mrs L C Reynolds, BSc Hons
Mr I Lowden, BSc Hons

Chemistry:
Mr R Edge, BSc Hons
Mrs S Burton, BSc Hons

Classics:
Mr S Fletcher, BA Hons

Design Technology:
Mr R Smith, BEd
Mr P Lakritz, BSc Hons

Economics:
Mrs K Cowgill, BSc Hons

English:
Mrs C Bramall, BA Hons
Miss J Rowe, BA Hons
Mr S Penny, MA
Mrs K Watson, BA Hons

Geography:
Mr C Critchlow, MA

History:
Mr R Paine, BA Hons
Mr J Taylor, BA Hons

Mathematics:
Mr M R Allen, BSc Hons
Miss C Bruce, BSc Hons

Junior School Staff:
Head of Junior School: Mrs P Bennett, BA Hons
Mrs K Genders, BSc Hons
Mrs D Harper, BSc Hons
Mrs E Jackson, BSc Hons
Mrs H Monk, BEd Hons
Mrs A Sly, BEd Hons (*Senior Teacher*)

Mrs V Charnock, BSc Hons
Mr C D Whitworth, BA Hons

Modern Languages:
French:
Miss K Stebbings, BA Hons
Mrs J Lathbury, BA Hons, MBA

German:
Mrs K Schwarz Caswell, MLitt, BA Hons
Mr I Watson, BA Hons

Spanish:
Miss K Stebbings, BA Hons

Music:
Miss F Davies, BMus
Mr N Coley, BA Hons

Physical Education:
Mr K Clark, BA Hons
Mr C D Whitworth, BA Hons

Physics:
Mr D Hills, BSc Hons, BEd
Mr K Lambert, BSc Hons

Religious Studies:
Mr P D Hilliam, BA Hons
Mrs K Lacey, LLb Hons

Derby Grammar School is a boys' school with a co-educational Sixth Form which was founded in 1995 to provide a high quality education for able pupils in Derbyshire, Staffordshire and Nottinghamshire. It has 270 pupils from the age of 7 (Year 3) to 18 (Year 13). Whilst pupils perform extremely well academically, the School places great emphasis on developing character and leadership skills across and beyond the curriculum. There is a full competitive sports programme and a wide ranging and flourishing music scene. There is an extremely strong tradition of charity work and fundraising, featuring ongoing links with a community in Tanzania. The School has a broad programme of outdoor education, including The Duke of Edinburgh's Award, as well as numerous trips and visits both at home and overseas.

Location and Facilities. The School is set in a superb Victorian parkland site on the edge of the city of Derby, near to the arterial A38 and A50 routes. The original manor house has been converted and extended with a purpose-built teaching block, Chemistry and Design Technology building. The buildings also house specialist Biology and Physics laboratories and Music and Music Technology rooms and a recording studio.

Curriculum. The Junior School follows an enhanced national curriculum, providing a strong grounding in all subject areas. In addition, the pupils have specialist teaching in Music, French and Latin. In the Senior School, all pupils follow a broad common curriculum at Key Stage 3 which includes teaching in each of the separate sciences and two modern foreign languages up to the end of Year 9. Pupils will study either 10 or 11 GCSEs or IGCSEs, including two

Mathematics and English subjects, at least one modern foreign language and the three separate sciences. A small number of students choose to take the Dual Award in Science in order to increase their free choice options. Pupils in the Sixth Form can choose from over twenty different A Level subjects and the options process is based around pupil choice rather than being in fixed blocks. In recent years nearly 75% of students have studied at least one science at A Level and over 25% have gone on to study biomedical, science or engineering degrees at university.

Admissions. Admission to both the Junior and Senior School is through assessment in English, Mathematics and reasoning papers. The main Entrance Examinations are held in January but are available throughout the year.

Open days are held each term, but visits and taster days are welcomed at any time by prior appointment. For further information contact Admissions Secretary, Louise Slater Blackwall, on 01332 510030 or visit the school website.

Scholarships and Bursaries. There is a full range of Scholarships and Bursaries available for entry into the Senior School. Specialist Sports, Music and Choral Scholarships are available and are awarded after successful trials or auditions.

Fees per term (2014–2015). £2,645 (Years 3–4), £3,134 (Years 5–6), £3,916 (Years 7–13).

Charitable status. Derby Grammar School is a Registered Charity, number 1015449.

Dover College

Effingham Crescent, Dover, Kent CT17 9RH
Tel: 01304 205969
email: admissions@dovercollege.org.uk
website: www.dovercollege.org.uk
Twitter: @DoverCollege
Facebook: /DoverCollege
LinkedIn: /DoverCollege

Dover College was founded in 1871 and occupies the grounds of the Priory of St Martin, a 24-acre site in the heart of Dover on the southeast coast of Kent. The site has been occupied for nearly 900 years and the College Close is surrounded by a number of impressive medieval buildings. Pupils still use the original Refectory, and the School Chapel is a fine 12th Century building. Another 20 acres of playing fields are nearby.

The College was granted a Royal Charter by His Majesty King George V in 1923 and the Patron of the College is the Lord Warden of the Cinque Ports.

We are the closest school to continental Europe, with easy access by Eurostar, Tunnel or Ferry. Dover Priory Station with its High Speed Link and good road links are within easy reach of the School making London about an hour away. London Heathrow and Gatwick airports are convenient by car.

Governors:
Members of the Council:
J T Sullivan, Esq (*Chairman*)
A Lancaster, Esq (*Vice-Chairman*)

P Chadwick, Esq	Prof G M Nicholls
G A Conlon, Esq	A Rolls, Esq
M J Dakers, Esq	J G Ryeland, Esq
J A Evans, Esq	The Rt Revd T Willmott

Other Governors:

A Barrow, Esq	J P Gatehouse, Esq
Ms S Capito	M Goodridge, Esq
S Devalia, Esq	N Harris, Esq
R D S Foxwell, Esq	J Hodge, Esq

Ms C Kirby
H J Leslie, Esq
Revd Canon N P Nicholson
Ms K Rogers
J C H H Sinclair, Esq

Ms N F Sullivan
P R Tapsell, Esq
Ms P Vanninen
W T Westwater, Esq

Headmaster: **Mr Gerry Holden**, MA St Andrews, FRSA

Deputy Head: Mr D Ellerington, BSc, BA, MA

Head of Infant & Junior School: Mrs F Donnelly, CertEd

Assistant Teaching Staff:

Mrs A Akuffo-Kelly, BA Hons, MSc
Ms S Allen
Ms S-J Ali, BA Hons
Mrs E Aylward, BA
Miss C Bean, BA Hons
Mr E. Breeze
Mr D Brooks, BSc Hons
Mr G Came, CEd
Mrs C Caskie
Mrs S Chatterjee, BSc Hons
Mr K Cox, BA Hons
Miss R Chohan, BSc
Miss E Dalliere, BA
Mrs L Dawson
Mr J Dewick, BA Hons
Ms J Dixon
Mrs F Donnelly, CertEd
Mr P A H Donnelly, BA, DipTEFL
Mrs N Dougall, BSc Hons, National Award for SEN Coordinator
Mrs S E Eberlein, MA, BEd Hons, PGC Speech, Language and Social Communication Difficulties, PGC Literacy Difficulties/ Dyslexia
Mrs J Ellerington, Adv DipEd, PGCPSE
Mr B Fairclough, BA Hons
Ms L Geddes
Ms J Green
Mrs S Groombridge, BSc
Mr C Hadler, BEng Hons

Mr G R Hill, MA Oxon
Mrs L Hodson, HND, TEFL Dip
Mr B Horton, BSc Hons
Mr K Ives
Ms S Lingden, BSc and QTS
Mr C Lockyer, BMus Hons
Mr F Macmillan, BEd Hons
Revd T Marchand
Miss C Marié
Ms S Marriott
Mr G Mees, BA, BEd Hons
Mrs T Mills, BA Hons
Mr J Payne
Mrs C R Pearson-Miles, BA Oxon
Miss Y Ramadharsingh, BSc
Mrs J Richardson, BA Hons
Ms S Richardson
Ms L Rushworth
Mrs L Salter, MA
Ms L Shefford
Miss J C Single, BA Hons
Mrs E Smith
Mr R G Spencer, MA, FRCO
Ms A Squire, Montessori TDip
Mr A Stones
Ms T Taylor, BA, Dip de Cand
Miss E Tresidder, BA Hons
Ms L Walters, BA Hons
Mr P Young, BA

Bursar and Business Manager: Mr S Bartlett
Marketing Manager: Mrs G Degrange
Admissions Registrar: Mrs V Henderson
Headmaster's Secretary: Ms K Anderson
Medical Officer: Dr Barley
Medical Centre Sisters: Mrs C Hunt, S Robinson, S May
IT Manager: Mr C Judd

Co-education. Dover College (3–18) has been fully co-educational since 1975 and the 345 boys and girls are integrated at all levels. There are 130 boarders.

Organisation. The school divides into four parts: the Infants and Juniors from age 3–11, Priory from 11–13, Lower College from 13–16, and the Sixth Form. For Lower College and the Sixth Form there are four Houses, all situated on the College Close, two for boys and two for girls, all incorporating both day pupils and boarders.

Dover College's Infant and Junior School is housed in a spacious self-contained building within the beautiful grounds of Dover College and Priory has its own House accommodation.

Catering. The catering team provides delicious, healthy, well-balanced homemade food and meals are taken in the Harry Potter style Refectory.

Curriculum. Infants and Juniors study a wide range of subjects. Great importance is placed upon literacy, numeracy, information technology, science and key skills. Pre-Reception children follow the Early Years "learn through play" curriculum. French, Spanish and Music are taught by specialist teachers. Fourth and fifth form pupils study between six and ten GCSE subjects, depending on their level of ability. The curriculum at this level is flexible, enabling pupils to have an academic curriculum designed to suit individual needs.

All pupils are given very careful guidance when making their GCSE level choices, by their Academic Tutor, Housemaster/Housemistress, the Careers Department and by the Director of Studies.

At all stages of a pupil's time at Dover College, progress is carefully monitored. Assessment periods occur regularly, during which pupils are graded for achievement and effort. A merit/demerit system operates for pupils up to 16 years. Classes at Dover College are kept as small as possible. Class size up to GCSE are generally between 15–20 and at A level 10–15. Some A level sets are smaller.

Considerable emphasis is placed upon the breadth of education offered: music, art and drama are an integral part of the curriculum. All pupils participate in a variety of sports, with stress placed upon the development of leadership skills.

Sixth Form. The Sixth Form is overseen by a Head of Sixth Form and pupils are able to choose AS and A Levels from a list of over 20 subjects. Some BTEC subjects are also available (Sports, Health and Social Care, Travel and Tourism). Traditional academic subjects are provided, as are the practical subjects of art, design and technology, textiles, photography, drama and music.

Sixth Formers wear a distinctive uniform and are given more choice and freedom than junior pupils, being expected to respond positively to their treatment as young adults. A well-equipped Sixth Form Centre is used as a meeting place and social club.

The School's Careers Adviser works in close liaison with Connexions to plan, deliver and evaluate an integrated careers' education and guidance programme. This enables pupils to gain the necessary knowledge, skills and understanding in order to make informed career plans before attending the universities of their choice.

International Study Centre (ISC). The International Department was started in 1957 and backed at the time by members of NATO, although international boarding has a far longer history than this starting point. The International Study Centre provides intensive English courses for pupils whose first language is not English. These courses vary in length and the aim is to enable all pupils to integrate fully into the life of Dover College as soon as possible after their arrival.

Individual Support. There is an Individual Needs Department in which pupils with learning difficulties (eg Dyslexia) receive 1:1 tuition. Each pupil has a member of staff as a personal tutor. The tutor supervises his/her pupils' general academic progress.

Art and Technology. The Art Department is situated in purpose-built accommodation. Fine Art, pottery, textiles and photography are all available. Examination results are always excellent both at GCSE and A Level.

The Technology Department shares the building with Art and is situated in a large, well-equipped, open-plan workshop. Pupils are encouraged to work with a range of materials (wood, plastic etc) and use CAD software. Design Technology is available at GCSE and A level. There are many opportunities for the students to use the workshop outside curriculum time. Design and Technology also thrives as an activity.

Music and Drama. Music plays a particularly important part in the life of the School. The well-equipped Music School was relocated on site in January 2011 and opened by Julian Lloyd Webber. It comprises high-tech soundproof pods of various sizes for practice, classrooms and recital room. Extra-curricular activities are numerous. The Chapel Choir meets three times a week and is the backbone of the many concerts and services, but there are weekly rehearsals for the Choral Society, String group, Windband, Jazz band, and Madrigal group. There is a concert at the end of each term, held in the Refectory, and numerous informal concerts in a variety of locations. A House Music competition takes place annually.

Drama is a very active part of the cultural life of the School, as well as part of the Lower School curriculum; there is a major school production each year together with additional House productions. Drama is offered at A Level and GCSE.

Learning Resources Centre. It provides cutting-edge facilities and resources to all pupils, including Careers information.

Sport. The School's main playing fields are a short distance away; on site are tennis courts, an astroturf, basketball court and an excellent Sports Hall with a fitness suite. Sports include Athletics, Badminton, Basketball, Cricket, Cross Country, Running, Football, Hockey, Netball, Sailing, Tennis, Volleyball and various PE activities. Swimming takes place at the indoor swimming pool in the local leisure centre. Golf may be played on local courses and riding is also offered locally.

Extra-Curricular Activities. In addition to sport, pupils have the opportunity of taking part in a wide range of over 50 activities including Adventure Training, Art, Car Mechanic, Chess, Computing, Debating, Duke of Edinburgh's Award, Dancing, Fencing, First Aid, Horse Riding, Language Clubs, Music, Photography, Wine Tasting, Stage Management and Technology. The London West End theatres are within easy reach and regular trips to a variety of productions are made.

Pastoral Care. All pupils benefit from a carefully designed system of outstanding pastoral care. Every Dover College student belongs to a House and Boarders are provided with comfortable accommodation in one of four boarding houses. All Sixth Formers have single study-bedrooms. A Housemaster or Housemistress, supported by a team of tutors, runs each House; it is their role to give pastoral support as well as supervising the pupils' academic progress.

Pupils have access to a fully equipped and professionally staffed Medical Centre, which can accommodate pupils overnight.

Religious Life. College has its own Chapel and is a Church of England school. All pupils are encouraged to respect each other's beliefs and faiths from a position of tolerance and understanding.

Entry. Pupils are typically admitted into the Senior School at 11, 13 or 16 but may come at any age. Most pupils join the College in September, but entry in January and April is possible.

Entry into the Infants and Juniors is by interview and an informal assessment carried out during a "Taster Day" at the school. The School has its own 11+ examination. 13+ pupils normally sit the Common Entrance at their own Preparatory School. Provision is made for direct entry into the Sixth Form for boys and girls. This is normally conditional upon GCSE results. Further information can be obtained from Admissions.

Fees per term (2014–2015). Junior Day £2,250–£3,300; Senior Day £3,900–£4,750; Senior Flexible Boarding (up to 12 nights per fortnight) £6,300–£7,400; Senior Part-Flexible Boarding (up to 3 nights per week) £5,350–£6,300; Full Boarding £6,900–£9,300.

Scholarships. Academic Scholarships are awarded by competitive examinations.

Scholarships for Music, Art, Sport and All-Rounder are available by competitive interview.

Scholarships are available to pupils at 11+, 13+ and 16+. Scholarships are not awarded to pupils in the Infant and Junior School.

Sibling Bursaries (10%) and Service Bursaries are automatically awarded. Members of HM Armed Forces and the Diplomatic Service who are eligible for the boarding allowance only pay a parental contribution of 10% of the full boarding fee.

Further details may be obtained on application to Admissions.

Old Dovorian Club. *Secretary*: R Upton, Esq, c/o Dover College.

Charitable status. Dover College is a Registered Charity, number 307856. The School exists to develop confidence and individual talents.

d'Overbroeck's College

The Swan Building, 111 Banbury Road, Oxford OX2 6JX

Tel:	01865 310000
Fax:	01865 552296
email:	mail@doverbroecks.com
website:	www.doverbroecks.com

Principal: **Sami Cohen**, BSc

Administrative Principal: Richard Knowles, MA, DPhil (*Philosophy**)

Bursar: Peter Talbot, BEd

Head of Lower School (*Years 7–11*): Mark Olejnik, BA, PGCE (*History*)

Academic Head of Sixth Form: Alasdair MacPherson, MA (*English**)

Director of the d'Overbroeck's International Study Centre: Helen Wood, MA, PhD, DTEFLA (*EAL*)

Academic Coordinator: Alastair Barnett, BA, PGCE (*History**)

Teaching Staff:
* *Head of Department or Departmental Coordinator*

Katie Amiri, BA, TESOL, TEFL (*EAP*)
Louise Arnould, BA, BTec (*Art*)
Rosie Astley, Froebel Dip, RSA SpLD (*Learning Support*)
Daniel Austin, BA (*EAP**)
Michelle Barton, MSc, PGCE (*Chemistry*)
Franziska Becker, MA, PGCE (*German*)
Astrid Bernasconi, BA, MA, CELTA (*Italian*)
Shanti Bharatan, MSc, PhD (*Biology*)
Marina Bogdanova, MA, PGCE (*Russian*)
Ursula Boughton, BSc, PGCE (*Mathematics*)
Christophe Brinster, M-ès-L (*French**)
Kelly Bristow, BSc, PGCE, CPsychol (*Psychology*)
John Butler, BA, PGCE (*Sociology**)
Evelyn Campbell, BA, PGCE (*Mathematics*)
Francesca Centamore, BSc, PGCE (*Physical Education*)
Jennifer Clark, BSc, PGCE (*Chemistry, Science*)
Jane Cockerill, BA, MEd, PGCE (*Music*)
Andrew Colclough, BA, MA (*Politics**)
Catherine Coldstream, BA, Dip ABRSM (*Religious Studies*)
Claire Coltellini, MA, PGCE (*French*)
Siobhan Coskeran, BA, PGCE (*History, Politics*)
Margaret Craig, BSc, FAETC (*History of Art*)
Stephen Creamer, MEng, PGCE (*Chemistry, Physics*)
Joanna Cripps, BA, PGCE (*Design Technology*)

Charles Currie, MPhys, PGCE (*Physics**)
Patricia Dass, MSc (*Psychology**)
Jon-Paul Davies, BSc, MA, PGCE (*Geography*)
Robert Dixon, BA (*Mathematics*)
Jing Ping Fan, BA, MA, PGCE (*Mandarin*)
Warrenford George, MSc (*Physics*)
Elena Germanino, BA, MA (*Italian*)
Andrew Gillespie, MA (*Business Studies**)
Laurence Goodwin, MA (*Classics*)
Anita Goriely, MS, PhD (*Mathematics*)
Matthew Graham, BSc (*Economics*)
Nick Haines, MPhil (*Mathematics*)
Keiko Harada, MA (*Japanese*)
Robert Harris, BA, MSc (*Sociology*)
Simon Harrison, BA (*Economics**)
James Holburn, MA CPE (*English*)
Christopher Holland, BA, MPhil (*English*)
Graham Hope, MA, DPhil (*Mathematics*)
Clare Horne, BSc, PhD, PGCE, PGDip (*Mathematics*)
Margaret Horton, MA, PGCE (*History*)
Fizza Hussain, BA, PGCE (*Drama*)
Anna Irvine, BA, TESOL (*EAP*)
Adam Johnstone, MA, MSt (*AQA Baccalaureate**, *Biology*)
Anne-Marie Jones, BSc, PhD (*Biology*)
Joana Kalies, BSc (*Physical Education*)
Susanne Kreitz, PhD (*German**)
Andrew Latcham, BA, DPhil (*History, Politics*)
Kate MacDonald, BA, DSpLD (*Learning Support*)
David Mackie, BA, MA, DPhil, CPE, PGDL (*Classical Civilisation, Philosophy*)
Kathryn Manning, BSc (*Mathematics*)
Christine Martelloni, MSc (*French*)
Graham Maughan, MA, PGCE (*Physics*)
Susan McKendrick, BA, PGCE (*Music**)
Andrew McNeill, BSc, PhD (*Mathematics**)
Elina Medley, BA, MA, PGCE (*Photography*)
Alan Milosevic, BSc, PGCE (*Maths, Computing**)
Sandra Monger, BA, CELTA (*EAP*)
Jane Nimmo-Smith, BA (*Classics**, *Ancient History**)
James O'Connor, BTEC HND (*Music Technology*)
Kate Palmer, BSc, PGCE, SDes (*Geography**)
Max Parsonage, BSc, PGCE (*Chemistry**)
Jill Partridge, BSc, PGCE (*Biology*)
Mark Pennington, BA, MA (*Photography*)
Guiseppe Pezzini, BA, MA, DPhil (*Italian*)
Mark Piesing, BA, PGCE (*Communication and Culture**)
Robert Pollard, BA, TESOL, PGCE (*History, Politics*)
James Popplestone, BSc, DPhil (*Biology, Science*)
Martin Procter, BA, PGCE (*Physical Education**)
Philip Purvis, BMus, MMus, PhD, PGCE (*Music*)
Wendy Rawding, BA, PGCE (*Art*)
Nick Reeves, MA, PGCE (*Art**, *History of Art**, *Photography**)
Jonathan Richards, BSc (*Physical Education**)
Angus Roberts, BA, PGCE (*Mathematics, Physics*)
Sara Roberts, MA, BA (*English*)
Ana Rodriguez Nodal, BA (*Spanish*)
Emily Saddler, BA, PGCE (*English, Drama*)
Sarah Shekleton, BA, MA, PGCE (*Mathematics**, *Leckford Place*)
Aoife Squires, BSc, MSc (*Chemistry, Science*)
Mary Stephenson, BA, PGCE (*Business Studies, ICT**)
Lee Summers, MSc, PGCE (*Physics*)
Joe Swarbrick, BA, PGCE (*Drama**)
Jaimie Tarrell, BEd (*Biology**)
Emma Tinker, BA, MA, PhD (*Communication & Culture, English, Film Studies*)
Anton Viesel, BA, MA, PGCE (*English, German*)
George Vlachonikolis, BA, MA, PGCE (*Economics*)
David Wareham, BA, MA, TESOL (*EAP*)
Natasha Wertheim, BA, PGCE (*Religious Studies and Critical Thinking*)

Louise Wheaton, BSc, PGCE (*Geography*)
Paul Wheeler, BSc, PGCE (*Geography*)
Clare Wildish, BA (*Business Studies*)
Helen Wilson, BA, PGCE (*Art*)
Nicole Wilson, BA, GDL, LPC (*Spanish*)
Henry Winney, MA, PGCE (*Chemistry, Biology*)
Sharon Wyper, BA, PGATC, MA (*Art*)
Jonathan Young, BA, BSc (*Business Studies*)

Sport & Extra-Curricular Activities:
Jo Kalies, BSc (*Physical Education*)
Jonathan Richards, BSc (*Physical Education**)

Registry:
Years 7 – 11: Rob Barker
Sixth Form:
Lynne Berry, BA
Sarah Jex, BTec

Boarding Office:
Felisa Deas, BA

College Counsellor: Catherine Bech, BA

Higher Education & Careers Coordinator: Mark Piesing, BA

Principal's PA: Tracy Roslyn, BA, DipRSA

Age Range. 11–18 (11–16: day only; 16–18: day and boarding).
Number in School. 450.
Fees per term (2014–2015). Tuition: £4,800 (Years 7–11); £6,860 (Years 12–13). Boarding: £2,200–£3,700.

d'Overbroeck's is a co-educational school in Oxford for pupils aged 11–18. We are fairly evenly divided between residential and day students in the Sixth Form; but are day only up to the age of 16.

Our academic approach is characterised by small classes (maximum of 10 students per class in the Sixth Form and 15 up to GCSE) and a highly supportive and encouraging approach that builds on each student's strengths and enables outstanding academic achievements.

Teaching is highly interactive and seeks to generate enthusiasm for the subject, sound academic skills and effective working habits – while at the same time providing a thorough preparation for public examinations and ensuring that the learning experience is motivating and fun. The environment is friendly, stimulating and engaging with staff and students working together to achieve the best possible results.

A wide range of sporting and other extra-curricular activities is available to complement the learning in the classroom. Students can take part in numerous College events and performances as well as benefit from the wide range of educational, cultural and social activities which Oxford has to offer. We believe that happiness and success go hand in hand – and throughout the College we do our utmost to ensure that every student is given new opportunities to develop and is encouraged and rewarded – whether in the classroom, on stage or on the sports field.

The Sixth Form is based on a different site from Years 7 to 11 and the value of this is that it allows us to provide a clear sense of progression as students start their A Level studies and begin to make the transition towards university. Many students from other schools also join us for direct entry into our Sixth Form.

We expect high standards of commitment and effort from our students and have a track record of strong GCSE and A Level results, both in absolute terms and on a value-added basis. Students benefit from excellent teaching and a positive approach which enables them to maximise their potential. In 2014, for example, our students achieved 71% grade A or A* at A Level. The overwhelming majority of students go on to university and we have an excellent record of success with entry including Oxford and Cambridge (usually

10% of the Upper Sixth), as well as medical, law and art schools.

Main Entry Points: at 11+, 13+ and directly into the Sixth Form, post GCSE.

Scholarships: Academic, Science, Art, Music, Drama and Environmental Awareness.

Dunottar School
United Learning

High Trees Road, Reigate, Surrey RH2 7EL
Tel: 01737 761945
Fax: 01737 779450
email: info@dunottarschool.com
website: www.dunottarschool.com
Twitter: @dunottarschool
Facebook: /Dunottar

Chair of Board of Governors: Dr R Given-Wilson

Head Teacher: **Mrs R Cole**, BSc Hons Exeter, MBA

Senior Management:
Assistant Head: Mr M Broughton, BA Hons Worcester
Director of Sixth Form: Mrs B Jackson, BA Hons
   Loughborough, Dip IL, PGCE
Assistant Head: Mrs P Smithson, BA Combined Hons
   Exeter, PGCE, MEd

* *Head of Department*

English:
*Mr A Simmons, MA Greenwich, BA Hons London,
   PGCE
Ms K Lewis, MBA De Montfort, BEd Hons Sunderland
Mrs C Turner, BA Hons London, PGCE
Mrs G Shields, BA Hons Cambridge
Mr C Watts (*Drama*)

Mathematics:
Miss E Carr, BSc Hons Edinburgh, PGCE
Mrs R McTavish, BSc Hons York, ACMA, CSBM, PGCE
Mrs J Pardoe, MA Cantab, PGCE

Science:
Mrs J O'Dwyer, BSc Hons Durham, PGCE
*Mrs R Pope, BSc Hons Nottingham, PGCE
Mrs J Prothero, BSc Hons Leeds, PGCE (*PSE Coordinator,
   Biology*)
Mrs S Sagar, MSc Coventry, BSc Hons Birmingham,
   PGCE
Dr S Sookhun, BSc Hons Mauritius, MInstP, PhD
   Nottingham, Senior Physicist

Foreign Languages:
Mrs B Jackson, BA Hons Loughborough, DipIL, PGCE
Ms S Saward, BA Hons London, LTCL, QTS, CELTA
Miss A Welsh, BA Hons Bristol, PGCE

Information and Communications Technology:
Mr J Lyne, HND Surrey, PGCE

Design and Technology:
Miss H Tekeste, BA Hons Chelsea College of Art, PGCE

Geography:
Mrs S Thorne, BA Hons Leicester, PGCE
Mrs N Jackson, BSc Hons Sheffield, PGCE

Economics and Business Studies:
Mrs N Wintle, MA Oxon, PGCE

History:
*Mrs J Boden, MA St Andrews, PGCE
Mrs R Stringer, BA Hons Warwick, PGCE

Sociology:
*Mrs J Boden, MA St Andrews, PGCE

Mrs N Wintle, MA Oxon, PGCE

Art and Design:
*Mrs S Emblem, BA Hons Wimbledon, PGCE
Mrs M Baker, BA Hons Bath Academy, PGCE

Music:
Mr D Black, MMus Newcastle, BA Hons Berkley, BEd
   Hons, FTCL, LTCL, LGSM, LRSM, QTS (*Director of
   Music*)

Physical Education:
Mr R Clarke (*Director of Sport*)
*Mrs E Pieters, BA Hons Brighton, QTS
Miss H Field (*PE Assistant*)
Mr H New (*PE Assistant*)

Religious Studies:
Mrs V Ikwuemesi, MA London, BEd Hons London

Food Technology:
Mrs J Prothero, BSc Hons Leeds, PGCE

Careers & Work Experience:
Mrs B Jackson, BA Hons Loughborough, Dip IL, PGCE
   (*Sixth Form*)
Mrs S Thorne, BA Hons Leicester, PGCE

Support Staff:
Headmistress's PA, Admissions Secretary: Mrs S Edwards
Special Needs Coordinator: Mrs A Aylwin, RSA Dip
   SpLD
Marketing Manager: Mrs P Crosthwaite, BA Hons
   Bournemouth
Marketing Officer: Mrs M Denton, BSc Hons Aston
Bursar's Secretary: Mrs L Moon
Financial Controller: Mrs S Fribbance
School Secretary: Mrs J Jones
School Nurse: Mrs C Allison
IT Systems Manager: Mrs S Ameen, BSc Hons
   Southampton, AIEE

Dunottar School is a co-educational day school for pupils between the ages of 11 and 18. The School was founded in 1926 and became an Educational Trust in 1961. It is situated in 15 acres of gardens and playing fields on the outskirts of Reigate, convenient to mainline stations and bus routes. Development over the years has provided additional classrooms, art and design & technology studios, careers room, Assembly hall, music rooms, Sixth Form common room and 25-metre heated indoor swimming pool. The school is fully networked and has three dedicated computer suites. A Science Block opened in the early 1990s, followed by a block of eight classrooms in 1997. A major development programme has also provided a sports hall, sixth form facilities, library and art studios.

Aim. The School's aim is to ensure that we provide an inspiring, happy and fulfilling place of learning for all. Pupils will be taught and encouraged to work hard, to discipline themselves, to make the most of their opportunities, while recognising and responding to the needs of others. High standards of behaviour are maintained. Parents receive detailed reports twice yearly and have regular opportunities to discuss progress with teachers. Appointments can be made at any time to see the Head. There is a flourishing Friends' organisation.

Religion. The School holds the Christian ethos paramount and welcomes children from any denomination or none.

Curriculum. Eighteen GCSE and twenty-three A Level subjects are on the curriculum, which provides a broad education and preserves a balance between arts and science subjects. Early specialisation is avoided, though some subject options become necessary from the beginning of the GCSE year. Subjects include Religious Studies, English Language and Literature, French, Spanish, History, Geography, Mathematics, Biology, Physics and Chemistry taught for Science and Additional Science examinations and also as separate subjects, Business and Economics, Design & Technology, Information & Communications Technology, Physical Education, Drama, Food & Nutrition, Music, Art & Design and Sociology. The School has strong sporting and music traditions. Teaching is given in a wide range of musical instruments and pupils are encouraged to join the School orchestras and music groups. There are a number of School choirs. Instruction is available in Speech & Drama, in Dance, and in a wide variety of musical instruments. Drama and music performances are given frequently. There are excellent on-site games facilities including a large indoor heated swimming pool and playing fields. A great number of extra-curricular activities are provided and the School participates most successfully in The Duke of Edinburgh's Award Scheme at Bronze, Silver and Gold levels.

Careers. Advice is provided at each key stage of education. Pupils are encouraged to research and discuss career plans and opportunities with staff and work experience is offered in a variety of careers.

Physical Education. Sports and games are an important part of School life, and there are excellent facilities.

Examinations taken. GCSE and A Levels, Associated Board of the Royal School of Music, London Academy of Music and Dramatic Art, Imperial School of Dancing, Royal Society of Arts.

Admissions. 11+ entrance examinations are held in January prior to entry the following September. Early application is advised.

13+ entrance examinations are held in November prior to entry the following September. Early application is advised.

Applications are also accepted directly into the Sixth Form.

Fees per term (2014–2015). £4,700 (Year 7 to Upper Sixth).

Scholarships. Academic Scholarships are awarded annually at 11+ and 13+ to those who reach the highest standard in the entrance tests. 16+ scholarships will be awarded to those who reach a high standard in the scholarship papers. The 16+ scholarship examinations take place in November.

Music Scholarships at 11+, 13+ and 16+ are offered to pupils who show exceptional promise and talent in Music.

The School offers Sports Scholarships to those who show exceptional talent and promise in at least two sports. The awards are offered at 11+, 13+ and at 16+.

Art and Design Scholarships are offered at 11 +, 13+ and 16+ to pupils who show exceptional talent and promise in either Art, or Design & Technology, or both. Assessments take place in November or January.

All scholarships are offered to both new and current pupils except for the prestigious John Zinn Scholarship, which is awarded annually to a current prospective Sixth Form student on the basis of academic performance and contribution to the life of the school.

All candidates are automatically considered for the Headteacher's Award, which is based upon the interview and potential to contribute to school life.

Further particulars may be obtained from the Head Teacher's PA who will also arrange an appointment to visit the school and meet the Head Teacher.

Charitable status. Dunottar School is part of United Learning which comprises: UCST (a Company Limited by Guarantee, Registered in England, number 2780748, and a Registered Charity, number 1016538) and ULT (a Company Limited by Guarantee, Registered in England, number 4439859, and an Exempt Charity).

Ewell Castle School

Church Street, Ewell, Surrey KT17 2AW
Tel: 020 8394 3561 (admissions)
        020 8393 1413 (main office)
Fax: 020 8786 8218
email: admissions@ewellcastle.co.uk
website: www.ewellcastle.co.uk
Twitter: @EwellCastleUK

Ewell Castle, a day school in Surrey, twenty minutes from London, was built as a castellated mansion in 1814. It is co-educational in the Junior School and the Sixth Form, and from September 2015 girls will also be welcomed into Years 7 and 9 (the usual entry points into the Senior School).

The gardens and playing fields cover some fifteen acres and were once part of Nonsuch Park. The Senior School is accommodated at The Castle. The Junior School occupies two other premises in Ewell village: Chessington Lodge, a Georgian house minutes from The Castle; and Glyn House, the former Rectory to the parish church, opposite the Senior School. The School, which was founded in 1926, is registered as an educational charity and is administered by a Board of Governors, which is in membership of AGBIS (Association of Governing Bodies of Independent Schools). The Principal is a member of The Society of Heads and the Head of the Junior School is a member of IAPS (Independent Association of Prep Schools).

Chairman of the Governing Body: Mr P Durnford-Smith, BA, MCIM

Principal: Mr P Harris, MSc, BSc, PGCE, NPQH

Head of Junior School & Vice Principal: Mrs M Phillips, BEd
Deputy Head of Senior School & Director of Studies: Mr S Bromley, BA, PGCE (*Head of Geography*)
Head of Teaching and Learning : Mr S Leigh, BA, PGCE
Head of Pre Prep and Acting Deputy Head of Junior School: Mrs S Fowler, BSc, PGCE
Bursar: Mr G Holland, BSc, ACA
Marketing, Development & Alumni Manager : Ms C Hernandez, BA, CIM Grad Dip

Heads of Department:
Art & Design & Photography: Ms D Carrick, BA, QTS
Business Studies, Economics, & Politics: Mr M Carragher, MPhil, BSc, PGCE
Design Technology: Mr D Thompson, MDes RCA, PGCE
Drama: Mr L Bader-Clynes, BA, RADA
English: Ms K Wallace, BA, PGCE
History & Classics: Mr J C W Blencowe, BA, PGCE
Information Technology: Mr J Bernardo, MEd, BSc
Learning Support, SENCo: Mrs C Buckley, BA, PGCE
Mathematics: Mr D Vijapura, BSc, PGCE
Modern Foreign Languages: Ms R Iksilara, MA TESOL, BSc, BA, PGCE
Music: Mr B Essenhigh, BA, QTS
Physical Education: Mr J Grindrod, BA, PGCE
Science: Mr K Hungsraz, BSc, QTS
PSHCE: Mr K Peto, BA, PGCE
Psychology: Mr J D'Souza, BSc, PGCE
Religious Studies: Mrs D Hillman, MA, BEd

Principal's PA: Mrs K El-Dahshan, BA
Registrar: Mrs T Wilkins

The school comprises approximately 550 pupils in total with 350 pupils in the Senior School and 200 pupils in the Junior School.

Buildings. The school is located on three sites within the village of Ewell, accommodating The Junior School (Chessington Lodge: co-educational 3–7 years; Glyn House: co-educational 7–11 years) and the Senior School (The Castle: boys 11–16 years and co-ed 16–18 years). Academic departments are well resourced and accommodated. A new classroom block on The Castle site (completed August 2011) provides six new classrooms, purpose-built kitchen and dining/assembly area, Sixth Form cafeteria, cloakrooms and office accommodation. Other recent developments include: major refurbishment of the Library (The Castle), new hard play area (Glyn House), the building of a new nursery building and establishment of new garden area (Chessington Lodge).

Aims and Values. The aim is to achieve potential and excellence over a broad field: in academic, in sport, and the arts, and in numerous other extra-curricular activities and aspects of school life. The cornerstone of this small school is the strong pastoral care system and Christian values upheld, which enable the school, not only to achieve its main purpose, but also to maintain high standards of discipline, conduct and appearance.

A highly qualified and committed staff achieve very impressive results at KS2, KS3, GCSE, AS and A Level from pupils with a range of abilities.

Classes are small, averaging fifteen at the Senior School, where setting is also adopted in core subjects, and seventeen at the Junior School.

Organisation. The Junior School is co-educational and accepts pupils from three years. Most pupils transfer to the Senior School, whilst others go to a range of Independent and selective/non-selective schools at 11+. The Sixth Form has been co-educational since September 2013 and the School will move closer towards becoming fully co-educational in September 2015 when it welcomes girls into Year 7 and Year 9 (its normal entry points).

Curriculum. National Curriculum requirements are incorporated into Senior and Junior School schemes, although the broad and flexible curriculum extends beyond such criteria. Breadth at KS3 (11–13 years) is replaced at KS4 (14–16 years) by a core of Mathematics, English, Science and Religious Studies, supplemented by a wide ranging option scheme covering the languages, arts, humanities and technologies. There is an increased range of subjects available at AS and A Level in the Sixth Form

Work experience is undertaken by pupils in Year 11. Specialist HE/Careers guidance is available from Year 9 within the Senior School.

After the Sixth Form the majority of pupils proceed to universities and colleges, with most pupils achieving their first choice of institution.

Extra-Curricular Activities. The principal sports are rugby, football, hockey and cricket. In addition there are numerous pursuits which include: athletics, badminton, basketball, table tennis, skiing, and tennis. There is an extensive music and drama programme and other activities such as the Duke of Edinburgh's Award Scheme. Regular language, sports and field trips embarked for America, Austria, Belgium, France, Germany, Iceland, Ireland, Italy and Spain in recent years.

The school benefits from an active PTA.

Admissions. Boys and girls are admitted to the Junior School at the age of three. There are no entry requirements at this stage. Older children are invited to attend the school for a day's assessment, within a class, during which time they may undertake tests in English & Mathematics.

At the Senior School the standard points of entry are at 11+, 13+ and 16+. Subject to availability, there may be places at other levels. Entry requirements include interview, report from previous school and written assessments. At 13+ and 16+ the assessments may take the form of Common Entrance or GCSE respectively.

Visitors are welcome to the school on scheduled Open Days or by appointment. Individual assessments are held by arrangement. Scholarship assessments are undertaken in January each year.

Scholarships. Scholarships are available for pupils entering the school at 11+, 13+ and 16+. At 11+ awards are made on the basis of competitive examination/assessment in the designated category. In the case of 13+ and 16+ awards are likely to be made on the basis of Common Entrance and GCSE performance respectively. Awards are made for Academic excellence and also in the categories of Art & Photography, Design & Technology, Drama, Music, and Sport.

Fees per term (2014–2015). Senior School £4,560, Junior School £1,365–£3,130.

Junior School. *For further information, see Ewell Castle Junior School entry in IAPS section.*

Charitable status. Ewell Castle School is a Registered Charity, number 312079. The aim of the charity is to achieve potential and excellence over a broad field: in academic, in sport, in the arts, and in numerous other extra-curricular activities and aspects of school life.

Farringtons School

Perry Street, Chislehurst, Kent BR7 6LR
Tel:　　　020 8467 0256
Fax:　　　020 8467 5442
email:　　fvail@farringtons.kent.sch.uk
website:　www.farringtons.org.uk

Methodist Independent Schools Trust.

Governing Body:
Chairman: Mr D Chaundler, OBE
Vice-Chairman: Mrs R L Howard, BSc, BA, LGSM

Members:
Miss M Faulkner, BSc
Mr T Harris, FRICS, FCIArb
Dr H Richardson, MA
Mr S Richardson, FRSA
Mr W Skinner
Mr M Vinales
Dr A G Williams, MB, MRCGP, DipPal Med
Mrs C York
Reverend M Youngson

Bursar and Clerk to the Governors: Mr I Condie, BSc Hons

Headmistress: **Mrs Dorothy Nancekievill**, MA, BMus, PGCE, HonARAM

Head of Junior School: Mr G Twist, CertEd, BEd, CNAA, BA, DU, NPQH
Assistant Head Senior School: Mr B Smith
Assistant Head Senior School: Mr N Young, BA Hons
Chaplain: Reverend Dr J Quarmby
Registrar: Mrs J Grima (*Day*), Mrs F Vail (*Boarding*)

* *Head of Department*

English:
*Mrs V Denman, BA Hons, PGCE
Miss S Bliss, BA Hons, PGCE
Mrs L Bowdery, BA Hons, PGCE
Mr B Coultard
Ms L Hirsh, BA Hons
Ms K MacMahon, BA Hons, PGCE
Mrs E Russell
Mrs A Wigley

Mathematics:
Mrs I Haider, PGCE

Mrs Z Hanson, BSc, PGCE
Mrs E Lovell, MSc, PGCE
Revd Dr J Quarmby
Mr M Sansom, BTech, PGCE, Adv DipEd
*Ms D Scagell
Mr C Watson, BSc Hons

Science:
*Mrs N Callaghan, BSc
Mrs J Daws
Mr C Jarvis
Miss L Maggs, BSc Hons
Mrs A Maunder, BSc Hons, PGCE
Mr M Ray

Mrs L Sriram, BEd, NIIT India

Modern Languages:
*Mlle I Mosqueron, L-ès-L, PGCE
Mr D Cooper, BA, PGCE, CELTA, DELE
Miss R Frances BA Hons, MA
Mrs H Razii-Rydall, Joint Hons
Mr P Scowen, BA Jt Hons, PGCE, Cert TESOL

Humanities:
Miss S Bradley, BA Hons, PGCE
Mr E Case, BEd, DipEd
Mr C Catling
*Mr G Curran, MA
Mr A Essex, BSc Hons, PGCE
Mrs A Harris, ICA
Mrs K Hodge, BSc Hons
Mrs M Kershaw, BA Hons, CELTA
Miss K Ootim
Mrs H Rowett, BA, PGCE
Mr K Wilson, BA Jt Hons

Technology:
Mrs G Allen, BA Hons, MA, PGCE
Miss R Azulay, BA Hons, PGCE
Mr J Gardner, BSc, MSc, PGCE
Mrs K Matthews, CertEd
Mr L Smith, BA Hons
Miss C Thorpe, BA Hons
Mrs S Watson, BA Hons, PGCE

Music
*Mr N Rayner
Mrs P White, BA Hons

Learning Support:
Mrs J Maynard, OCR Cert

Mrs J Pyle, CertEd
Mrs A Vinales

Sport:
*Mr C Doyle, BEd
Ms N Duthie, BSc Hons
Mrs G Ody, BEd Hons
Miss J Roberts
Mr B Suverkrop, BEd

Junior School:
Ms S Austin, BEd Hons
Mrs G Bastos, BA
Mrs L Benjamin, BA Hons
Mrs P Brookman, BA, JPED, BEd
Miss S Cox, BA Hons, PGCE
Ms J Cox, BEd Hons
Mrs C Crouser, BA
Mrs J Cryan, BA Hons, PGCE
Mrs V Fox
Mrs H Hill, BSc, PGCE
Mrs S Hook, BA Hons, PGCE
Mrs L Long, BEd
Ms A-M Meola, CertEd
Mr J Mole
Miss K Randall, BA Hons, PGCE
Mr T Ruffle, BEd, CertEd
Mr J Shimmin, BSc Hons, PGCE
Mr B Suverkrop, BEd
Miss J Taylor, BA Hons
Mrs N Tetley, BA
Mrs A Vinales
Mrs S Walker, BA Mus
Mrs C Williams
Miss H White, BEd Hons

Boarding Staff:
Mr S Dillow
Mrs S Medcraft
Mrs V Suverkrop
Mr K Wilson, BA Jt Hons

Farringtons School is situated in 25 acres of green belt land in Chislehurst, which provide attractive surroundings while still being within easy reach of London (25 minutes to Charing Cross), the South Coast and Gatwick (45 minutes) and Heathrow airport via the M25 (1 hour).

The School is committed to providing a first-class education for pupils of all ages in a caring community which supports all its members and helps each pupil to achieve his or her full potential both academically and personally. After school care is available until 6 pm.

The curriculum offered is that of the National Curriculum, with a wide range of GCSE and A Level subjects available. Nearly 100% of Sixth Form leavers customarily go on to degree courses at Universities or Higher Education Colleges. Academic standards are high from a comprehensive intake of pupils and in 2014 ran at 100% pass rate at A Level.

The excellent facilities include a Technology building, a large Sports Hall with Dance Studio and Fitness Suite, splendidly-equipped Science and Modern Language departments, well-stocked libraries, Careers Room, new indoor heated swimming pool and extensive playing fields, as well as a School Chapel, where the School regularly comes together.

The main sports are netball, tennis, football, rugby, swimming and athletics, but badminton, volleyball and table tennis are also undertaken and other extra-curricular activities available include the Duke of Edinburgh's Award Scheme, Business Enterprise, various choirs and instrumental ensembles, gymnastics, jazz-dance, ballet, drama club, fencing, etc.

To obtain a prospectus and further information or to arrange a visit, contact the Registrar.

Fees per term (2014–2015). Day: £2,720 (Pre-Reception full time), £3,420 (Junior), £4,390 (Senior); Weekly Boarding £8,100; Full Boarding £8,610.

Charitable status. Farringtons School is a Registered Charity, number 307916. It exists solely to provide a high-quality, caring education.

Friends' School

Mount Pleasant Road, Saffron Walden, Essex CB11 3EB
Tel: 01799 525351
Fax: 01799 523808
email: admissions@friends.org.uk
website: www.friends.org.uk

Clerk to the Board of Governors: Susan Garratt

Head: **Anna Chaudhri**, BA, MA Cantab, PGCE

Bursar: Stephen Welch, FCA
Deputy Head: Eleanor Mackenzie Lambert, MEd Cantab, BSc, Dip Env Sc

Teaching Staff:
‡ *Holder of PGCE*

Art:
‡Serena O'Connor, BA
‡Matthew Miller, BA, BTEC

Business Studies:
Carolyn White, MEd, BEd

Careers:
Julie Anderson, BEd

Critical Thinking:
§‡Brigid Vousden, BA

Design Technology – Product Design:
‡Jessica Armitage, BA
‡Richard Twinn, BA

Design Technology – Food:
§Catherine Whyte, BEd

Drama:
‡Richard Smith, BA
Shelley Dowsett, BSc, GTP

Economics:
Mark Munsen, MA

English:
‡Gillian Kinnear, BA
§Joanna Matthews, BEd
Adrian Lockwood, BA, MA

ESOL:
‡Lynda Langford Powell, MA
‡Rebecca Auty

Film Studies:
‡John Searle-Barnes, BA, MA

Geography:
‡Jonathan Slinger, BA, BEd, MEd
‡Hannah Sargent, MSc, BSc

History:
‡John Searle-Barnes, BA, MA

‡Charlotte O'Neill, BA
Jennifer Allwood, BEd

ICT:
§Carolyn White, BEd
Teresa Shepherd
Jessica Armitage, BA

Library:
Jennifer Mizen

Mathematics:
Adrian Clarke, BEd
Victoria Charlesworth, BMus, MEC
‡Geoffrey Curtis, BSc
Carolyn White, MEd, BEd

Modern Languages:
‡Peter Fasching, BA
§‡Jane Pearce, BA
‡Anna Chaudhri, MA

Music:
‡Gavin Greenaway, BA
Mary Richardson, BA

Peripatetic Music Teachers:
Mary Richardson, BA, PGCE, DipABRSM
Jason Meyrick, FTCL, LRAM, LTCL, Prof Cert
Alison Townend, BA, LLCM, LGSM, LTCL
Nicky Ogden, BA, PGCE, LRAM
Edward Dodge, MA, GRSM, ARMCM, PGCE
Steven Hynes, BTEC
Louis Thorne, BSc
Mark Townend, GRSM, LRAM, DipRAM
Sarah Clark, BTEC
Angela Lesslie, BMus, PGCE
Amy Klohr, BA, LRAM
Richard Partridge, BMus

Physical Education:
Nicholas Batcheler, BEd, DipT
Jennifer Allwood, BEd
Raymond Mordini, BPHE
Shelley Dowsett, BSc, GTP
Grant Ward, BA

Psychology:
Jonathan Slinger, BA, BEd, MEd

Religious Studies & PSHE:
§‡Helen Golden, BA
‡Brigid Vousden, BA, MPhil

Science:
Wayne Steel
‡Philip Dant, BSc
§Julie Anderson, BEd
‡Eleanor Mackenzie Lambert, MEd, BSc, Dip Env Sc
Raymond Mordini, BPHE

Speech & Drama:
Sonia Lindsey-Scripps, BA

Study Centre – Specialist Teaching:
Caryn Pepper
Heather Douglas, MSc
‡Brigid Vousden, BA, MPhil
‡Max Ford, BA
Jacqui Parnham

House Staff:
‡Matt Kiely, BSc
Grant Ward, BA
Sonia Hood, BSc

Head of Junior School: Ruth Darvill, BEd Cantab
Deputy Head: Sally Meyrick, BA

Junior Class Teachers:
‡Kate Richardson, BSc

Elizabeth Brimer, MPhil
Emily Carman
Jackie Branch
Deborah Ballingall, BEd
‡Sally Meyrick, BA
Lucy Nicholson, MA, PGCE

Infant Department & Early Years:
Sally Manser, CertEd (*Head*)
Tiffany Johnson
Nicky Morgan, BEd
Claire Milner, BSc

Learning Support:
Gillian Bunting, BEd

Nursery Coordinator:
Catherine Armstrong, NNEB
Caroline Clark, NNEB

Friends' School is a school with a difference. Small, diverse, vibrant, and located in the heart of Saffron Walden, Friends' is one of only seven Quaker schools in England. Located on a beautiful 37-acre site, with a tradition of more than three hundred years of enlightened education for both boys and girls, the school offers education for students aged 3–18 with boarding from age 11. High standards of teaching and academic attainment are enriched by a broader framework of personal development.

At Year 6, pupils finish the Junior School well prepared for their transition into the Senior School. Friends' currently delivers almost a grade higher in value added scores, improving the achievement between age 11 and GCSE. We achieve this through small teaching groups with excellent, committed staff and a focus on academic progress and achievement within a framework of all-round development. Our supportive environment results in secure, happy students who succeed academically with internationally recognised qualifications and go onto a range of good British Universities.

We are a small, family-orientated school with a strong and supportive community. Our pastoral care is excellent and our pupils receive high levels of individual attention. The school was founded in 1702 by the Religious Society of Friends (Quakers). Quakers believe that there is something of God in everyone. This belief influences all relationships within Friends' School and creates an environment where your child will be treated as an individual and integrated into the community.

We also seek to provide a broad foundation for your child's future, with a wide range of cultural and physical activities. We have a strong creative tradition in the performing arts, while our extensive playing fields, heated swimming pool and modern sports hall offer a wide range of sporting opportunities for all children.

We offer full and weekly boarding in three houses: Girls, Boys and Sixth Form. House staff provide supportive and friendly environments where boarders are encouraged to take increasing amounts of responsibility and to contribute to the life of the Boarding House.

With excellent road and rail connections to London, Cambridge and Stansted Airport, access is easy both locally and nationally.

Admissions. Open to Quaker and non Quaker, determined by interview, entrance test and school report.

Fees per term (2014–2015). Day £2,375–£5,305, Weekly boarding £6,615–£7,690, Full boarding £7,190–£8,590.

Scholarships and Bursaries. Scholarships are available to internal and external candidates.

Academic scholarships are available to applicants wishing to join Years 7, 9 and Sixth Form. In addition, there are awards made for Art, Drama, Music and Sport.

Further details are available from the Admissions Secretary.

Friends' School is able to offer some assistance with fees in some cases. No application for a child who would benefit from the education that Friends' School provides should be discouraged solely on the grounds of financial need. Please contact the Bursar for further information.

Charitable status. Friends' School Saffron Walden is a Registered Charity, number 1000981.

Fulneck School

Pudsey, Leeds, West Yorkshire LS28 8DS
Tel: 0113 257 0235
Fax: 0113 255 7316
email: enquiries@fulneckschool.co.uk
website: www.fulneckschool.co.uk

Fulneck School was established on 1 September 1994 by the merger of Fulneck Boys' School and Fulneck Girls' School, both originally founded in 1753, by the Moravian Church (a very early Protestant Church which has two schools in England and many more abroad) as part of a settlement on the slopes of a valley within the Green Belt on the outskirts of Pudsey. Leeds and Bradford are both nearby and the School has easy access to the motorway network and airports.

The School is a registered charity and the Provincial Board of the Moravian Church is the Trustee of the School. The Governing Body provides a range of professional expertise and is in membership of AGBIS (Association of Governing Bodies of Independent Schools). The Principal is a member of The Society of Heads and the Head of the Junior School is a member of IAPS (Independent Association of Prep Schools).

The Governing Body:
T R Smith (*Chairman*)
C J Stern (*Vice-Chairman*)

C Robinson	J Newman
Revd M Newman	Mrs L Sharp
L A Fairclough	Mrs A Roberts
D Scott	Mrs L Johnson

Principal: **Mrs D M Newman**, BEd Bedford

Vice-Principal, Head of Senior School: D Newman, MA Oxford, BA, PGCE

Head of Junior School: C Bouckley, BEd

Bursar: G Blackstone

Originally founded for the education of the sons and daughters of ministers and missionaries, the school nowadays provides an education for about 400 pupils from all backgrounds. Most of the pupils live in West Yorkshire and travel daily to School, but approximately 85 of them are boarders including some who board weekly and return home from Friday evening to Monday morning.

The School is co-educational and provides a modern, academic curriculum based on Christian principles. Fulneck Sixth Form offers 20 A Level subjects and the school has an outstanding record of success in public examinations. Class sizes rarely exceed 20 and most teaching groups are smaller; in the Sixth Form groups seldom exceed 10.

Buildings. The main buildings of the School are part of the original settlement, yet other buildings on the campus have been added over the years. Most recently these include a new Junior Library with ICT facilities, a new self-contained Sixth Form Centre, performing arts building and a totally refurbished teaching block. The boys' boarding accommodation was extended in the summer of 2008 with further extensions under way in 2012 involving both boarding houses. Extensive playing fields and tennis courts are

located on the site, which adjoins Fulneck Golf Club, and looks over to the Domesday village of Tong.

Pastoral Care. The staff work closely and effectively together, sharing in the duties and recreational needs of the School. A senior Pastoral Tutor and two assistants look after the pupils' welfare. The School Nurse, who is medically qualified, and other house staff take care of the boarders in conjunction with the resident teaching staff and the Principal, who also lives on the campus. Weekly and flexi boarding are offered in addition to full boarding.

Sport. Netball, Hockey, Football, Rugby, Cricket and Tennis are the main games of the School, but Athletics, Basketball, Badminton, Cross-Country running, Golf, Rounders, Swimming, Table Tennis and Martial Arts are all available to the pupils as part of a rapidly expanding programme of outdoor pursuits. Teams of various ages, in most sports, have full fixture lists with neighbouring schools. Dance classes are also run.

Activities. Music education is very strong with choirs, bands, a jazz group, a flute group, a rock band, and other orchestral groups. The Senior Choir performs often to the public. Drama is actively pursued with pupils involved in both lessons and Theatre Workshop productions.

There are a number of clubs and societies such as Art, Computer, Cooking, Golf, Orienteering, Hockey, Netball, Table Tennis, Forensic Club, Theatre Workshop, Science, Gardening, Eco Friends, Dance and Martial Arts.

The Duke of Edinburgh's Award Scheme is available to pupils over the age of 14, together with a wide range of trips and residential visits, walking and skiing. The school has regularly participated in World Challenge expeditions.

Careers. The Careers teacher is on hand to advise, and the Library stocks most of the available literature on the whole range of courses and careers. All pupils complete a period of work experience at the end of Year 10.

Foundation Stage/Key Stage 1. This is housed within the main building and caters for children from the ages of 3 to 7.

Junior School (Key Stage 2). The Junior School is self-contained and caters for pupils from the ages of 7–11. Once a pupil is admitted he or she will usually progress into the Senior School, after examination at age 11. The Junior School has access to many of its own specialist facilities for Science, Art, Technology, Music, IT and Library, as well as to the Senior School sports facilities.

Learning Support Unit. Specialist staff provide help on an individual or small group basis to children with dyslexia or other learning differences. The Unit is CReSTeD approved and has repeatedly confirmed its 'DU' status, the highest grade awarded to mainstream schools.

Parents and Friends Association. There is a flourishing organization which acts as a fundraising body, and also supports the School in a variety of other ways. This is a living example of the belief that education is a partnership between home and school.

Admission. Admission to the school is welcomed at any age depending on the availability of places, although the main intake is at the ages of 3, 7 and 11. Direct entry to the Sixth Form is also possible. Means-tested academic bursaries and other scholarships are available.

Fees per term (2014–2015). Junior School Day: Nursery (mornings only) £1,375; Foundation Stage (full day) £2,230; Years 1 & 2 £2,420; Years 3–6 £2,995; Weekly Boarding: £5,525; Full Boarding £5,955; Flexi Boarding £45 per night. Senior School: Day £3,950; Weekly Boarding £6,670; Full Boarding £7,425; Flexi Boarding £45 per night.

Fulneck Former Pupils' Association. Mr D Robbins, Fulneck School, Pudsey, West Yorkshire LS28 8DS.

Charitable status. Fulneck School is a Registered Charity, number 251211. It exists to provide a traditional, Christian education for boys and girls between the ages of 3 and 18.

Hampshire Collegiate School
United Learning

Embley Park, Romsey, Hampshire SO51 6ZE
Tel: 01794 512206 (Senior School)
           01794 515737 (Prep School)
Fax: 01794 518737
email: info@hampshirecs.org.uk
website: www.hampshirecs.org.uk
Twitter: @hampshireschool
Facebook: /hampshireschool

Hampshire Collegiate School (HCS) is a warm and welcoming independent day and boarding school for boys and girls aged 2½–18. There is a collective energy about the school's 130 acre campus which provides a beautiful space in which students can learn, play, compete and achieve. HCS continues to go from strength to strength and visitors to the school will witness a dynamic Sixth Form as well as a thriving boarding community that attracts both UK and international students.

At HCS our aim is to focus on each individual child, creating an environment where they will flourish, whatever their ability and talent. Our vision is that our students have the enthusiasm to learn and the ambition to succeed. It is important to us that they have the confidence and determination to explore their interests and that they have the opportunity to develop creatively as well as academically. We are a truly international community where a fundamental value is respect for all, regardless of nationality, interest or ability. Academic excellence continues to be a key priority and we strive to help your child achieve to the very best of their ability.

Mr D A d'Arcy Hughes (*Chairman*)
Dr S Allen
Mr R Butler
Ms C Levy
Mr R Mancey
Mrs D Moody, AILAM
Mr S Neilson
Revd T Sledge
Professor T Thomas

Principal: Mrs E-K Henry, BA

Senior School:

Deputy Head Academic: Mr G Yates, MA
Deputy Head Pastoral: Mrs M Bateman, MA
Head of Boarding Boys: Mr C Cates, BSc
Head of Boarding Girls: Mrs A James, CertEd
Head of Sixth Form: Mr J Hillier, BA
Director of Studies: Mr S Bowyer, MA

Heads of Years:
Mrs L Goodey, BA
Mr N Joisce, BA
Miss E Boutcher-West, BA
Mrs J Kennedy, MSc
Mr J Schofield, BSc

Head of Design & Technology & Art Faculty: Mr M Lambert, MA
Head of Drama: Ms S Clarke, BA
Head of English: Mrs E Driver, MA
Head of Geography: Mrs N Spurr, BA
Head of History, Government and Politics: Mr R Hay, BA
Head of Mathematics: Mrs S Cornforth, BSc
Head of Modern Language: Mrs S O'Leary, BA
Head of Music: Mr S Kent-Davies, BA
Head of Science: Mrs L Miller, BSc
Director of Sport: Mr A Egford, BSc
SENCO: Ms J Hodge, BA

Teaching Staff:
Mr A Barbor, MEng (*Mathematics, Maths Challenge Coordinator, Head of Nightingale House*)
Mrs W Bonney, CertEd (*Psychology, Mathematics*)
Miss E Boutcher-West, BA (*PE, Head of Academic PE, Professional Mentor*)
Mrs N Brown, BA (*Mathematics, i/c KS3 Maths*)
Mr C Cates, BSc (*Physics, Mathematics*)
Mr J Churchill, BSc (*Chemistry*)
Mrs B Clark, BA (*Geography*)
Miss G Cornick (*Girls' Sport, i/c Hockey, Textiles*)
Mrs A Fernandez Garcia, BA (*Spanish, French*)
Mrs L Goodey, BA (*Spanish, French*)
Mrs S Haywood Smith, BSc (*ICT, Head of eLearning*)
Mr J Hiller, BA (*English*)
Mr P Hilton, BSc (*Head of ICT, Business Studies*)
Mrs A James, CertEd (*Head of Religious Studies*)
Mrs J Johnson, BA (*French*)
Mr N Joisce, BA (*PE, Head of PSHE*)
Mrs J Kennedy, MSc (*Biology, Science*)
Mr M Laverty, BA (*Business Studies, Economics*)
Mr A Leatham, BA (*PE, Head of Core PE, Head of Palmerston House*)
Mr C Lehane-Kendrick, BSc (*Mathematics*)
Mrs B Luxton, BA (*Art*)
Mrs M Matlock, BA (*English*)
Mrs A Mole, MA (*EFL*)
Mrs L Newhall, BA (*Law, Government & Politics*)
Mr C O'Sullivan, BA (*English*)
Mrs J Penfold, BA (*French, German*)
Mrs S Platt, BA (*Spanish, French*)
Dr M Price, PhD (*Chemistry/Physics*)
Mrs M Raymond, BSc (*Head of Physics*)
Mrs S Rowe, BA (*Learning Support*)
Mr J Schofield, BSc (*Business Studies*)
Mrs M Sleigh, BA (*English*)
Mr P Stanley, MA (*Drama*)
Miss K Stewart, BTh (*Religious Studies, Able Gifted & Talented Coordinator*)
Mr I Stuart, BA (*English, Director of Activites, i/c Cricket*)
Mr R Summerson Watson, BA (*Design Technology, Head of Chichester House*)
Mr A Thickbroom, MA (*Head of Chemistry, Mathematics, Head of Austen House*)
Ms C Walker, BA (*Learning Support*)
Mrs A Wolfe, MA (*Learning Support*)

Prep School:
Head of Prep School: Mrs H Donnelly, BA, BEd
Deputy Head of Prep School: Mr P Brady, BEd (*Geography, Palmerston House Tutor*)

Teaching Staff & Learning Assistants
Mrs F Adams, BA Ed (*Head of Key Stage One, History*)
Miss R Alford, Level 3 CACHE (*Teaching Assistant*)
Miss L Barnes, BA (*Nursery Assistant*)
Mrs C Baxter, BA (*Class Teacher*)
Miss Z Boyle, BMus (*Music*)
Mr T Brittan, BSC (*Design Technology*)
Mrs K Brown, NVQ3 (*Teaching Assistant*)
Mrs L Chandler, HLTA (*Higher Level Teaching Assistant*)
Mrs T Collins, NVQ2 (*Teaching Assistant*)
Miss M Corlass, NVQ3 (*Nursery Assistant*)
Mrs M Corlass, TCert (*Teaching Assistant & Lunchtime Supervisor*)
Mrs M Coveney, BA (*Art*)
Mrs C Fletcher, BA (*English, Austen House Tutor*)
Mrs S Gordon, BEd (*Drama*)
Mrs J Hammond, BEd (*SENCO*)
Miss S Hardy, BA, EYPS (*Head of Early Years*)
Miss L Kemp, BEd (*Head of Prep School Sport*)
Mr P Meaden, BA (*Educational Visits Coordinator*)
Mr J Milligan, QTS (*KS2 Teacher*)
Mrs K Ross, MA (*Class Teacher*)

Mrs L Phillips, NVQ3 (*Nursery Assistant*)
Mrs T Sacree, NVQ3 (*Deputy Nursery Manager*)
Mr P Shuttleworth, BEd (*Mathematics & ICT, Head of Teaching & Learning, Chichester House Tutor*)
Mrs W Speirs, BEd (*Class Teacher*)
Mrs E Squires, BSc (*Science*)
Mrs S Sturgess, NVQ4 (*Nursery Manager*)
Mrs K Tibble, NNEB (*Nursery Assistant*)
Mrs F Walker, BEd (*Class Teacher, LOC*)
Mrs F Woodley, NVQ3 (*Nursery Assistant*)
Mrs V Worden, MA (*Modern Foreign Languages*)

Visiting Tutors:
Mr R Armstrong, RMSM (*Percussion*)
Mr R Garrard-Abrahams, BEd (*Piano*)
Mrs R Gao (*Chinese*)
Mrs J Gover, ATCL, LTCL (*Flute*)
Mrs G Kuznicki, ALCM, LLCM (*Singing*)
Mrs R McDonald, BMus (*Viola & Piano*)
Mrs N McKeown, BA, PGCE (*Piano*)
Mr D Phaure Dip Level 6 (*Acting and Coaching*)
Mrs M Shearer, GTCL, LCTL (*Clarinet & Piano*)
Miss C Williams, BA CertEd (*Brass*)
Miss M Williams (*Woodwind*)
Mr C Wickland, Dip Mus (*Electric Guitar*)
Mr P Wray (*Kit Percussion*)

Principal's PA: Mrs R Wells, BA
Registrar: Mrs J Baird
Prep School Head's PA: Mrs J Piper
Business Manager: Mr P Dawson, CIMA, DipM
Finance & Transport Officer: Mr A Peters
Librarian: Mrs H Cunliffe, Cert Lib Prac
Senior Matron: Mrs D Jarvis, RGNII
Assistant Matron: Mrs E Appleton, RGNII (*part-time*)
Domestic Matron: Mrs C Gray
Domestic Matron: Mrs K Lelean

Constitution. There are about 558 pupils, with approximately 90 in the Sixth Form and 181 in the Prep School. Boys and girls are admitted at 11 and 13 by examination; and into the Sixth Form, at age 16, on GCSE results.

There are boarding places available for both boys and girls (11–18), and the whole School is divided into four houses. Day pupils and boarders are members of the same houses, thus obviating any feeling of division between boarding and day.

All senior pupils attend Assembly, often with Chapel and then commence six 55-minute lessons (with a twenty-minute morning break and an hour lunch break). Following the academic routine, every afternoon and at lunchtime, games or activities are organized allowing day pupils to depart between 4.00 pm and 5.00 pm having experienced the daily routine and ethos of a boarding school. Many day pupils opt to board in their senior years.

Prep School lessons are from 8.45 am to 3.15 pm for Nursery, with staggered finishes, then to 3.35 pm for KS2, followed, again, by voluntary activities every afternoon.

Curriculum. The Prep School follows the National Curriculum in the main and as a basis but seeks to go beyond this in many areas using imaginative teaching and innovative cross-curricular projects. The use of ICT is increasingly embedded throughout the curriculum. In addition French is taught together with Spanish in the older age groups. There is a wide range of after-school clubs including sport, art, performance and music activities.

The GCSE curriculum offers a choice of many subjects (including separate subject sciences) and careful note has been taken of those elements of the National Curriculum considered vital to personal development. All pupils study Spanish in Year 7, and continue with Spanish and French from Year 8. Each pupil must study a minimum of 1 foreign language to GCSE level. There is a wide range of subjects on offer. Most pupils take a minimum of 9 GCSE examinations.

More than 20 AS and A Level subjects are available.

Careers guidance is given by tutors from the earliest days, and is backed up by professional advice. Work experience is undertaken in the summer of Year 10.

Games and Activities. Rugby, Football, Cricket, Hockey, Rounders and Netball are the main games, with Cross-Country, Basketball, Swimming, Tennis, Athletics, Lacrosse and Golf among others in a supporting role.

The School has a strong games tradition, achieving representation at County level, and beyond, a reputation for drama and art and a thriving musical life.

The School has its own practice golf course, floodlit pitch, lake, and 7,000 sq ft Sports Hall, dance studio, all-weather playing areas, tennis courts under lights and swimming pool.

All Senior School pupils are encouraged to attempt the Duke of Edinburgh's Award Scheme; there are several expeditions each year in the neighbouring New Forest National Park, or in Wales; and abroad, including two ski trips. In the Prep School Year 6 take part in a residential activity week in Normandy.

Admission Procedures. Admission to the Prep School is by informal assessment and a 'taster day' for younger pupils and, for the older pupils, interview with the Head Teacher, satisfactory reports and assessments in English and Mathematics.

An examination is set at 11 + and an interview expected, plus report from present school (often a State Primary School).

At 13+ HCS Entrance examination and an interview and report.

At 16+ an interview and report including details of GCSE success are expected.

Places are occasionally available in other age groups.

Examination and interviews may take place at any time during the twelve months preceding entry.

Details from the Registrar.

Scholarships and Assisted Places. Scholarships and Assisted Places are available to both internal and external candidates at 11+, 13+ and 16+. An assessment morning and takes place in January.

Scholarships may be awarded for Academic, Music, Art, Design Technology, Drama, Sport or All-Round ability. Assisted Places may also be awarded.

Sixth Form Scholarships are awarded to internal and external candidates on the basis of GCSE and contribution (both actual and potential) to wider school life.

Fees per term (2014–2015). Nursery: £2,590 (full time). Payment by Termly Direct Debit: Prep School £2,989–£3,373; Senior School: £4,715 (day), £7,987 (UK boarding), £8,874 (International Boarding).

There is a reduction for brother/sister and children of the Clergy, HM Forces and Teachers.

Location. Easily accessible from Southampton Airport (20 minutes), Southampton Parkway Railway Station (20 minutes) and M27 (5 minutes), HCS is 1½ miles North West of Romsey, on the Salisbury (A27) road. There is a railway station in Romsey.

Former Pupils. email: HCSSociety@hampshirecs .org.uk.

Charitable status. Hampshire Collegiate School is part of United Learning which comprises: UCST (a Company Limited by Guarantee, Registered in England, number 2780748, and a Registered Charity, number 1016538) and ULT (a Company Limited by Guarantee, Registered in England, number 4439859, and an Exempt Charity).

Hill House School

Fifth/Sixth Avenue, Auckley, Near Robin Hood Airport, Doncaster, South Yorkshire DN9 3GG
Tel: 01302 776300
Fax: 01302 776334
email: info@hillhouse.doncaster.sch.uk
website: www.hillhouse.doncaster.sch.uk

Hill House was founded in 1912 and now occupies the site of the former RAF Officers' Quarters of RAF Finningley. The school provides a seamless, fully co-educational day education from age 3 to 18, and aims to provide a top-class holistic education where extra-curricular success and personal development stand alongside academic excellence. Hill House was named Independent School of the Year 2012–13.

Governors:
Mrs E Paver (*Chair*)
R De Mulder (*Deputy Chairman*)
C Webb (*Chairman Elect*)

S Colbear   P Iqbal
Mrs V Cusworth   Mrs J Jameson
N Ebdon   R Leggott
R Fennell   J Sprenger
P Goel   Mrs H Upson
M Gutowski

Headmaster: David Holland, MA Cantab

Deputy Head: Dr Madeline Fraser, PhD
Head of Junior School: Mr Jonathan Hall, BEd Hons
Senior Master: Mr Simon Hopkinson, BA Hons
Head of Sixth Form: Mrs Caroline Rogerson, BSc Hons
Deputy Head of Junior School: Mrs Charlotte Leach, BA Ed Hons
Bursar and Clerk to the Governors: Mrs Karen Kidney, ACMA Hons

Heads of Departments:
Mr Mark Cadman, BA Hons (*Director of Music*)
Mr Richard Dorman, BA Hons (*Head of History*)
Mrs Rachel Frisby, BA Hons (*Head of Geography*)
Mr Chris Keyworth, BEd Hons (*Head of Physical Education*)
Mrs Julia Major, BEd (*Head of Modern Languages*)
Mrs Wendy Parkhurst, BA, MA (*Head of Art*)
Mrs Caroline Rogerson, BSc Hons, ARCS (*Head of Science*)
Mrs Mahjabeen Thomas, BSc Hons (*Head of Mathematics*)
Mr Martin Webdale, BSc Hons (*Director of Sport*)
Mr Andrew Wildin, MA, (*Head of English*)

Housemistress (Field House): Mrs Mahjabeen Thomas, BSc
Housemistress (Master House): Mrs Wendy Parkhurst, BA, MA
Housemaster (School House): Mrs Christine Havard, BA Hons

Number of Students. There are 640 pupils, with an equal number of boys and girls.
Education. Children enter the School at 3 years of age via Nursery where structured play and learning are the order of the day. As children progress through the School there is a gradual change to subject based teaching in specialist rooms, in preparation for GCSEs at 16 and A Levels at 18. Upon leaving the Junior School children enter a full house system for pastoral care. All main school subjects are offered, including individual Sciences, French, Spanish and Latin.

Facilities. The whole school is based in a historic building with new, purposely renovated classrooms. The site includes a large hall, dining room and theatre. In 2011 Hill House Sixth Form was launched, housed in its own new Sixth Form Centre, including classrooms, coffee shop and large common room. A new Music School contains practice rooms, a recording studio and a performing studio. 2013 saw the opening of the school's new sports grounds at Blaxton.
Extra-Curricular Activities. Music, Drama, Art and Sport play an important part in the life of the School. Throughout the year over 100 academic, recreational, musical and sporting activities per week are also offered in extra-curricular time. The major sports undertaken include rugby, soccer, netball, hockey, cricket, tennis, athletics and rounders. There is a competitive fixture list including a number of overseas tours. There are two orchestras and five choirs within the school, who enjoy the newly-built Music School. Drama productions and concerts are undertaken on a regular basis. Residential trips and sports tours are undertaken at most age levels.
The School Day. School opens at 8.00 am, with lessons from 9.00 am to 4.00 pm. Activities run from 4.00 pm, and a before and after school club operates from 7.30 am and until 6.00 pm. The school operates a five-day week, with a full games afternoon for all ages above 7. There are some activities and fixtures at weekends. Sixth Formers also have an Internship Afternoon, where they spend time at local businesses, hospitals etc.
Fees per term (2014–2015). £2,600–£3,670 according to age. Fees include lunch and most extras.
Scholarships. Scholarships are available at 11+ for Academic, Sport, Art, Music and Performing Arts, and at 16+ for Academic and Leadership.
Charitable status. Hill House School Limited is a Registered Charity, number 529420.

Hull Collegiate School
United Learning

Tranby Croft, Anlaby, East Yorkshire HU10 7EH
Tel: 01482 657016
Fax: 01482 655389
email: enquiries@hullcollegiateschool.co.uk
website: www.hullcollegiateschool.co.uk

Local Governing Body
Mr P Grimwood (*Chair*)

Prof K Bardon   Miss T Oakshott
Mr S Brett   Mrs S Swetez
Mrs A Warneken Gold   Mr R Gillingwater
Mr P Bryan   Revd S Wilcox
Mr G Rymer

Senior Leadership Team:

Headteacher: Mrs R Glover, BEd Leeds, NPQH

Deputy Headteacher (Curriculum and Assessment): Mr S F Jolly, BSc Durham, PGCE
Deputy Headteacher (Learning and Teaching): Mr A D Norburn, BMus Birmingham, PGCE, LTCL, ALCM
Assistant Headteacher (Care and Guidance): Mr C M Wainman, BA Leeds, MA, PGCE
Associate Assistant Headteacher (Curriculum and Assessment): Miss J Dyer, BA York, PGCE
Head of Preparatory School: Mrs K A Williams, BEd Cantab
Deputy Head of Preparatory School: Mrs J Plewes, BA Leeds, PGCE, NPQH
Key Stage 2 Coordinator: Mrs A Meltham, BA Sheffield, PGCE, MA Ed
Key Stage 1 Coordinator: Mrs K Dent, BEd Durham

Foundation Stage Coordinator and Nursery teacher: Mrs J Maltby, BEd Leeds
Business Services Manager: Miss S O'Brien

Senior Teaching Staff:

Art & Design (Art & Textiles):
Mrs E Wallis, BA Leeds, PGCE (*Acting Head of Department*)
Mr S Doncaster, BA Leicester, PGCE

Business Studies and Economics:
Mrs S R Kelsall, BSc Bradford, PGCE (*Head of Department and Head of Humanities*)
Mrs M J Hugill, BSc UMIST, PGCE

Design Technology:
Mr R J Chambers, BA with QTS Trinity & All Saints, Leeds (*Head of Department*)

Drama:
Mrs A Asbury, Dip LAMDA, BA Hull, PGCE (*Head of Department*)
Mrs C Ullyart, Dip AD Goldsmiths, MA Leeds, ATC

English:
Mrs H Y Binks, BA Hull, MA Lit, PGCE (*Acting Head of Department*)
Mrs K Bloomfield, BA Hull, PGCE
Miss A L G Harrison, BA Lancaster, MA Hull, PGCE
Mrs E L Larard, BA Newcastle, PGCE

Food Technology:
Mrs S East, BEd Worcester, MSc Humberside (*Joint Head of Department*)
Mrs J Holvey, BEd Sheffield (*Joint Head of Department and Head of Year*)

Geography:
Mrs R H Brennan, BA Durham, PGCE (*Head of Department*)
Mr C M Wainman, BA Leeds, MA PGCE
Mrs M Hugill, BSc UMIST, PGCE
Mr A D Norburn BMus Birmingham, PGCE, LTCL, ALCM
Mrs R Glover, BEd Leeds, NPQH

HE and Careers Guidance Coordinator: Mrs D Heads, BSc Hull, PGCE

History:
Mrs C R Atkin, BA York, MA Leeds, PGCE (*Acting Head of Department*)
Miss S McDowell, BA York, PGCE
Miss A M Wadsworth, BA Liverpool John Moores, PGCE

ICT:
Mr R Tuck, BA Keele, PGCE (*Head of Department*)
Mr S Doncaster, BA Leicester, PGCE

Languages:
Mr G Stephenson, BA Newcastle, MA, PGCE, Dip Ed (*Head of Department*)
Ms J Blencoe, BA Hull, PGCE
Mrs J Grimley, BA Hull, PGCE
Mrs N J Lough, MA Edinburgh, PGCE
Mrs V Pick, BA Wales, PGCE

Latin:
Mr B Gilles, MA Oxon, PGCE

Mathematics:
Miss J Dyer, BA York, PGCE (*Head of Department*)
Mrs G M Evans, BSc Leeds, PGCE
Mr S F Jolly, BSc Durham, PGCE
Mrs P Jolly, MA Cantab, PGCE
Mr M E Roper, BSc Bradford, PGCE
Mrs F E Wells, MSc Hull, BSc Liverpool, PGCE

Music:
Mr J A Webb, MA Cantab, ARCO PGCE (*Head of Department*)
Mrs S L Maynard, BEd Leeds
Mr A D Norburn, BMus Birmingham, PGCE, LTCL, ALCM

Physical Education:
Miss A D Davis, BSc Birmingham, MA, PGCE (*Head of Department*)
Mr F S Henderson, BSc York St John, GTP (*Head of Boys' PE/Games*)
Mr J W Windeatt, BSc Hull, GTP
Mrs A E Harvey, BA Manchester Metropolitan

Psychology:
Mr A Birtchnell, BSc UWE, PGCE

Religious Studies:
Mr J M D Mishra, BA Roehampton, PGCE

Science:
Mr S D Pearce, BSc Portsmouth, PGCE, CBiol, MIBiol (*Head of Science Department*)
Mrs S J Gibbs, BSc Leicester, PGCE
Mr A F Giraud, BSc Huddersfield PGCE
Dr E R Kebbell, BSc Warwick, PhD East Anglia, PGCE
Mrs P Jolly, MA Cantab PGCE
Mr T E Norris, BSc Nottingham, PGCE
Dr S C Turner, BSc Heriot-Watt, PhD Sheffield, GTP

Data Management:
Mr M E Kirby, BEd Ripon & York St Johns

Examinations Officer:
Miss R L Baldry

Special Educational Needs:
Mrs N Lough, MA Edinburgh, PGCE (*Head of Department*)
Mrs P J Carlisle, BEd Christchurch, Kent, Dip SpLD Dyslexia
Mrs A Manton, BSc Hull, PGCE, Dip SpLD Dyslexia
Mrs J K North, BA Trent Poly, PGCE, Dip SpLD Dyslexia

Learning Support Assistants:
Mrs S Douthwaite, NVQ2 & 3 Teaching & Learning in Schools
Mrs S Groves
Mrs C Palmer
Miss A Spacey
Ms E Witty BA Hull, GTP

Preparatory Teaching Staff:
Head of Preparatory School: Mrs K A Williams, BEd Cantab
Deputy Head of Preparatory School: Mrs J Plewes, BA Leeds, PGCE, NPQH
Foundation Stage Coordinator and Nursery Teacher: Mrs J Maltby, BEd Leeds
Key Stage 1 Coordinator: Mrs K Dent, BEd Durham
Key Stage 2 Coordinator: Mrs A Meltham, BA Sheffield, PGCE, MA Ed
Prep School Teacher: Mrs C Wood, BSc York, QTS
Reception: Mrs J Purdy, CertEd Hull, BA DME; Mrs J Hamilton BA Hull QTS
Year 1: Mr D Manners, GRSM, LRAM, ARCM, PGCE
Year 2: Mrs K Dent, BEd Durham; Mrs C Smith, BA Durham, PGCE, MBA; Mrs K Dewhirst, BSc Newcastle, PGCE
Year 3: Mrs H Silk, BA Hull, QTS
Year 4: Mrs R Hazel, MA Oxon, PhD, PGCE; Mr A North, BA St Pauls, MSc, PGCE
Year 5: Mrs A Meltham, BA Sheffield, PGCE, MA Ed
Year 6: Miss C E Barley, BA Hull, MCD, PGCE; Mrs A Nicholls, BA Lampeter, PGCE
Special Educational Needs: Mrs A Manton, BS Hull, PGCE, Dip SpLD dyslexia

Art Coordinator: Mrs H Silk, BA Hull, QTS
Music Teachers: Mr D Manners, GRSM, LRAM, ARCM,
  PGCE; Mrs S Maynard, BEd Leeds; Mr J Webb, MA
  Cantab, ARCO, PGCE

Teaching Assistants and Nursery Nurses:
Mrs A Haworth, NNEB
Mrs K Rogers, BA, NNEB
Mr P Seymour
Miss L Ballard, NNEB
Mrs D Charlton, NVQ3, Level 3 TA
Mrs J Taylor, DPP Level 3
Mrs A Fairhead, Dip Pre-School Practice Level 3
Mrs V Young, NVQ3
Mrs K. Daniel, Dip Pre-School Practice Level 3
Mrs A Broughton, Cert Learning Support Level 2, Dip Pre-
  School Practice Level 3

Morning Care:
Miss L Ballard, NNEB (*Deputy Manager*)
Mrs D Charlton, NVQ3, Level 3 TA
Mrs S Douthwaite, NVQ2 & 3 Supporting Teaching and
  Learning in Schools

After School Care:
Mrs V Young, NVQ3 Playwork (*Manager*)
Miss L Ballard, NNEB (*Deputy Manager*)
Mrs J Cooper, NVQ2 Playwork
Mrs D Hickman, NVQ2 Playwork
Mrs K Daniel, Dip Pre-School Practice Level 3

Hull Collegiate School is a co-educational day school which educates 650 pupils from nursery age (the term in which they turn 3) to Year 13 (age 18).

Location and Facilities. Set in the Victorian country house of Tranby Croft, the school benefits from nine hectares of mature, landscaped grounds and is located approximately four miles to the west of Hull and one mile north east of the Humber Bridge.

The Preparatory School is housed in a purpose-built facility which adjoins the Senior School and in 2005 a multimillion pound investment provided the school with state-of-the-art classrooms and science laboratories, an indoor sports hall built to Sport England standard, D&T workshops, a large open-plan art school and a café-style refectory.

A dedicated Sixth Form Centre housing spacious common and study rooms, a drama rehearsal room and further classrooms opened in 2007.

Inspection Report. The 2010 ISI report applauded the school's ethos, pastoral care and teaching, listing its key strengths as:

"*The reflective and encouraging culture of the school provides an environment in which pupils thrive, becoming willing, independent learners.*

The personal development of the pupils is excellent and is a significant strength of the school, meeting its aims to care for and respect pupils, and to nurture each individual.

Pupils respond to the school's high expectations of achievement, conduct and work.

The pupils are thoughtful and considerate of others, and the nurturing of these attitudes creates a happy atmosphere where they feel comfortable and secure."

Curriculum and Extra-Curricular Activities. The school has a history of consistently excellent academic results both at GCSE and A Level and boasts a very strong pastoral system, priding itself on preparing its pupils for entry to higher education. There is a wide choice of academic subjects available and the choice of extra-curricular activities is equally varied; participation in sport, music and drama is strongly encouraged, as the school plays a considerable amount of competitive sport and produces regular concerts and plays. There are many trips abroad every year, as well as numerous shorter visits to places of interest closer to home.

Admission. Hull Collegiate School welcomes pupils of a wide range of ability and all faiths. Admission is by pre-entry assessment, interview and report and subject to availability of a place. For further information please contact the Registrar.

Scholarships and Bursaries. The scholarship system rewards outstanding performance; however, the majority of the available funds are allocated to the bursary system which enables pupils, who otherwise would be unable to do so, to attend the school.

All scholarships result in a fee reduction of £100 per term and are based on academic merit or for outstanding ability in an area such as Music, Art, Drama or Sport. Scholarships are awarded at 12+, 14+ and 16+.

Fees per term (2014–2015). Reception, Years 1–2 £2,185; Years 3–4 £2,519; Years 5–6 £3,004; Years 7–13 £3,571. Lunch included in school fees for Reception to Year 13.

Full-time year-round Nursery for 3–5 year olds: EYFS and nursery vouchers accepted; full pricing structure available on the school website.

Charitable status. Hull Collegiate School is part of United Learning which comprises: UCST (a Company Limited by Guarantee, Registered in England, number 2780748, and a Registered Charity, number 1016538) and ULT (a Company Limited by Guarantee, Registered in England, number 4439859, and an Exempt Charity).

Kingham Hill School

Kingham, Chipping Norton, Oxfordshire OX7 6TH
Tel: 01608 658999
Fax: 01608 658658
email: admissions@kingham-hill.oxon.sch.uk
website: www.kingham-hill.oxon.sch.uk

Motto: *In virum perfectum.*

Kingham Hill School is a thriving boarding and day school for 285 girls and boys from 11–18 years.

Governors:
J Richardson (*Chairman*)

Mrs C Anelay	Col J Lewis
Miss D Buggs	Lt Col Stephen Renner
Revd R Cunningham	K Targett
Mrs B Goodwin-Hudson	C Townsend
Revd J Juckes	Revd S Wookey

Headmaster: Revd Nick Seward, BEng, MA

Deputy Headmaster: Andrew Evans, BA, BSc, MBA

Teaching staff:
G Abouyannis, BSc

D Ansley, BEng Hons	H Evans, BA
C Ashton, BSc Hons	M Eyles, BSc
Mrs J Balinski, BA, MA	A Ferrero, BA
D Beasant, BA Hons	J A Fowler, BEng Hons
S Birnie	N Fox
M Buckler, BA Hons	L Gill, BA
Dr P Carlin, BDS	P Greenhaugh, BSc
M Cartwright, BSc Hons	Mrs C Heath, BEd Hons
D Chambers	Miss H Hiscox, BA, MA
J Chapman, BA Hons	L Hosker
A Curwen, BA, MA Ed, MA	A Hutchings, BEd
	R Jones, BA, MA
Mrs A Curwen, BA Ed, MA Ed	A Kennedy
	G Lane, BSc Hons
N Dupont, BA	C Larner, BA
J Elliott, BA	S Lowe, CertEd, AGSM
A Evans, BA, BSc, MBA	R Lund, BA

K McFarlane, BEd, BMus
N McLachlan, BEd
M Metcalfe, BA, PGCE
S Miller, BSc
H Monro, BA
A Muirhead, BA Hons
S Petra, BSc
P Phillips
G Rees, BA Hons
D Ritchie, BA Hons
C Rogers
A Savage, BTh, BSc Hons, MSc

Mrs D Saxby, BSc Hons
E Scates, MA
N Seward, BA
H Shand
K Showler, BA
T Venables, BA
J Webb, BComm, PGCE
G Williams, BA Hons, PGCE
M Williams, BSc
J Wyer

Chaplain: Revd A Savage, BTh, BSc, MSc
Honorary Chaplain: The Revd Canon Geoffrey Shaw, MA

Administration:
Bursar: Mrs C Thompson, BEng Hons
PA to Headmaster, Admissions Officer: Mrs J Cavan
Estates Manager: A Reid

Medical Officer: Dr D R Edwards, MB BS, DRCOG
Medical Centre: Mrs E Barton

Beautifully situated, Kingham Hill has offered many generations of students the best possible opportunity to flourish, enjoying their formative years and becoming successful, responsible and well-rounded adults.

The Headmaster and his dedicated staff team ensure that the school's special qualities benefit all:

- Vibrant Christian ethos
- Superb pastoral care
- Academic excellence
- Value-added across the ability range
- Excellent extra-curricular provision

Kingham Hill is an exceptional school with an inspiring history, stunning setting and ambition for every pupil.

We excel with able and average-ability students. Our record for enabling significant improvement in grades, achievement on the sports field and stage, and growth in all-round confidence, is superb.

We run an academic society – Octagon. The seven most able pupils from each year group sit with the master in charge and are challenged with extended studies, visits to public lectures, involvement in debates, etc. These pupils are expected to achieve outstanding results and go on to top universities.

The school's sporting facilities are superb and include: a leisure complex incorporating a pool, fitness suite and dance and drama studio; huge floodlit astroturf area; tennis and netball courts; sports hall; various grass pitches and athletics track; renowned assault course.

Kingham Hill School is situated on a beautiful 96-acre site in rolling Cotswold countryside. Oxford is just 24 miles away, Stratford-upon-Avon 25 miles, and London one hour and twenty minutes by train.

Open Mornings: 11 October 2014, 7 February 2015, 9 May 2015.

Assessment Days: 27 November 2014, 6 March 2015.

Fees per term (2014–2015). Full Boarding: £7,340 (Years 7 & 8), £8,985 (Years 9–11), £9,490 (Sixth Form). Weekly Boarding: £7,075 (Years 7 & 8), £8,270 (Years 9–11), £8,695 (Sixth Form). Day: £4,965 (Years 7 & 8), £5,680 (Years 9–13).

SpLD tuition: £1,200, SpLD for Sixth Form: £748. ESOL tuition: £1,250. American Studies: £1,895.

Scholarships and Bursaries. The School is able to offer several categories of Scholarship: Art, Junior, Music, Organ, Performing Arts, Sixth Form and Sport. Generous Bursaries for sons and daughters of HM Forces personnel.

Charitable status. The Kingham Hill Trust is a Registered Charity, number 1076618, and a Company Limited by Guarantee, registered in England, number 365812. The school exists to provide education for girls and boys from 11 to 18.

Kingsley School
Methodist Independent Schools Trust

Bideford, Devon EX39 3LY
Tel: 01237 426200
Fax: 01237 425981
email: admissions@kingsleyschoolbideford.co.uk
website: www.kingsleyschoolbideford.co.uk
Facebook: /KingsleySchoolBideford

Governors:
Chairman: Mr David Pinney

Dr Mike Cracknell
Mrs Sue Fishleigh
Mrs Jane Hellier
Mr Richard Holwill
Mr Andrew Laugharne

Mr Michael Portman
Mr John Tomalin
Mrs Jane Woodhams
Mr Ian Huggett
Mt Patrick Hamilton

Ex officio:
Mr Peter Rigby, Senior Executive Officer and Director of Finance, Methodist Independent Schools Trust
The Revd Canon Graham Thompson, Chairman of Plymouth and Exeter District of the Methodist Church

Head: Mr Simon Woolcott, BSc, ARCS

Junior Head: Mrs Jane Bruce, BA, Dip SpLD

Deputy Head & Director of Studies: Dr Susan Ley, BSc, PhD

Senior School Teaching Staff:
* *Head of Department/Subject*

Mr Chris Beechey, BA, MA, ACIEA (**History*)
Mrs Michele Borsten, BA, MA (**Drama, EAL*)
Miss Gemma Braunton (*PE & Games*)
Mrs Judith Brock, MEd, BA (*Information Technology*)
Mr Leigh Crossman (*Head of Music*)
Mr Simon Cullingham, BEd, Dip SpLD, Cert TEFL (*Dyslexia Dept*)
Mrs Sally Davies, BSc (*Physics, Chemistry*)
Dr Jan Dawson, BSc PhD (*Chemistry*)
Mr Jon Dickinson, BA (**Art & Photography*)
Miss Rosaleyn Dyer, BSc Hons (*Mathematics*)
Mrs Sarah Gosai, BA (*Librarian*)
Mr Ian Holleran, BSc (**Science, *Physics*)
Revd Capt Steve Hunt, CA (*Chaplain, Outdoor Ed, *RS, PSHME, EAL*)
Mrs Sue Johnson, BSc (*Mathematics, Head of Years 7 to 9*)
Mr Andy Lane, BEd, Dip SpLD (*Head of Dyslexia Centre*)
Dr Susan Ley, BSc, PhD (*Biology, Deputy Head & Director of Studies*)
Miss Kathryn Makepeace, BA (*Head of Sixth Form, *English*)
Mr Simon Mathers, BSc (**Boys' PE & Games, Science*)
Miss Sarah Parsons, BSc (*Mathematics, Careers Coordinator, Head of Lower School*)
Ms Diana Percy, BA, MEd (**Psychology, *EAL*)
Mrs Hilary Roome, BEd (*PE & Games*)
Mrs Barbara Sochon, BEd, Adv Dip SEN (**Food Technology, PSHME, RS, EAL*)
Mrs Linda Stella, BA (**Girls' PE & Games, Head of Boarding*)
Miss Kat Timms, BA (*Art & Photography, PE*)
Mr Roger Tisdale (*Mathematics*)
Mrs Sandrine Toubin-Whale, DEUG Licence, BA (**French, EAL*)
Mrs Sue Trick, BA Hons, Dip Open, ALCM (*Music*)
Mr Simon Ward (*PE & Games*)

Mr Steve Whaley, BSc (*Geography, Head of Pastoral Care, CPO*)
Miss Caroline Williams, BA (*Spanish*)
Mrs Louise Wivell, BA (*Business Studies*)

Junior School and Pre-School Teaching Staff:
Mrs Jane Bruce, BA, Dip SpLD (*Junior Head*)
Miss Gemma Braunton (*PE and Games*)
Dr Jennie Cousins, BA, MA, PhD (*Class Teacher*)
Mrs Kim Curtis, BTEC National Dip (*Pre-School Assistant*)
Miss Emma Ford, BA (*Class Teacher*)
Mrs Jackie Guy-Owers NNEB (*Pre-School Assistant*)
Mrs Jeanette Harding-Crook (*Junior Assistant*)
Mrs Elaine Henry, Montessori Cert Teaching (*Pre-School Deputy Manager*)
Mrs Mary Lock, Montessori Cert Teaching (*Pre-School Assistant*)
Mrs Meda Maynard, Montessori Teacher (*Pre-School Manager*)
Miss Claire Moran, CACHE Dip Childcare & NVQ 4 (*Pre-School Assistant*)
Mrs Barbara Sochon, BEd, Adv Dip SEN (*Food Technology*)
Mrs Janet Minhinnett, BEd, MEd SEN (*Class Teacher*)
Miss Catherine Smith, NVQ Children's Nursing Level C (*Pre-School Assistant*)
Mrs Melanie Smithson, BA (*Class Teacher*)
Mrs Linda Stella, BA (*PE & Games*)
Miss Alison Sunman, Foundation Degree Early Childhoood Studies (*Pre-School Assistant*)
Mrs Elaine Thorne, BA (*Class Teacher*)
Miss Kat Timms, BA (*Art*)
Mrs Sandrine Toubin-Whale, DEUG Licence, BA (*French*)
Miss Sian Wade, BTEC Level 3 Childcare & Learning Dev (*Pre-School Assistant*)
Mr Frank Watson, BTec National Dip Health & Social Care L3, BTec Cert Supporting Teaching & Learning L2 (*Teaching Assistant*)
Mrs Emma Wilson, BA Ed (*Class Teacher, Head KS1 & Early Years*)
Mr Paul Wilson (*Class Teacher, Forest Schools Teacher*)
Miss Rachel Wilson, BA (*Class Teacher, Head KS2*)
Mrs Fiona Woolcott, BEd, Dip SpLD, Cert Inclusive Ed, Cert TEFL (*Class Teacher, Individual Needs Teacher*)

Nursery Staff:

Manager, CP Officer, SENCO: Mrs Andi Fletcher-Cullum [Richards], Montessori Early Years Foundation Teacher, Further Education Teaching Certificate, NVQ4 Management, Business Management in Childcare, National Day Nurseries Inspector

Miss Loren Braund, BA Early Childhood Studies
Miss Natasha Daniel, BTEC National Dip Childcare
Miss Harriet Dare, National Dip Children's Care, Learning & Development Level 3
Miss Alice Davey, National Dip Children's Care Learning & DevelopmentLevel 3
Miss Chloe Elliott, National Dip Children's Care, Learning & Development Level 3
Miss Victoria Fulford, BA Early Childhood Studies Level 6
Miss Rebecca Hill, NVQ Level 3 (*Trainee*)
Miss Jemma Hoare, Dip Children's Care, Learning & Development Level 3
Miss Samantha Loates, BTEC National Cert Children's Care, Learning & Development Level 3
Miss Eloise McPake, BTEC Childcare, Learning & Development Level 3
Mrs Naomi Russell, NVQ3 Children's Care, Learning & Development
Miss Saskia Scott, BTEC National Dip Children's Care Learning & Dev
Mrs Jenny White, Cache Dip Level 3 (*part-time*)

Marketing and Development Manager: Mrs Lucy Goaman, BA, MA
Director of Finance: Mr Andy Stevenson
Registrar: Mrs Caroline Bailey, BSc
Head's PA: Ms Sandie Hall
Junior Departments Secretary: Mrs Mel King
Logistics Administrator: Mrs Ann Neale
Exams Officer & Data Systems/Web Manager: Mrs Fo Edmonds, BA
Student Support Services & Stationery Manager: Mrs Wendy Flint
Theatre and Performance Manager: Mr Simon Smith
Food Technology Technician: Mrs Katharine Stone
Senior Science Laboratory Technician: Mrs Philippa Veillet
ICT Technician: Mr Adam Warren

Medical Centre:
Sister Karen McEndoo, BSc, RGN

Location. Kingsley School is situated in the market town of Bideford, an historic port beside the estuary of the River Torridge. The spectacular scenery of the North Devon coast is on our doorstep and there is easy access to the National Parks of Exmoor and Dartmoor. The North Devon link road, which passes close to Bideford, provides a direct route to the M5 motorway.

Organisation. Kingsley School is entirely co-educational and comprises a Senior School with approximately 252 pupils, aged 11 to 18 years, and a Junior School with approximately 128 pupils aged 2½ to 11 years, as well as 51 in our Nursery which offers wrap-around care for children from 8 weeks to 3 years old. The Grenville Dyslexia Centre, with a nationwide reputation for outstanding dyslexia provision, serves around 25% of the school's pupils.

Site and Buildings. Situated on a beautiful 25-acre site, the School has two Boarding Houses for boys and one for girls, all of which have immediate access to extensive playing fields, an all-weather hockey pitch, netball and tennis courts.

In recent years an ambitious programme of building has led to the provision of first-class facilities for science, ICT, drama, gymnastics, art and science. The Library provides an excellent environment for study, research and career guidance.

Curriculum. Senior School pupils study a core of subjects, including English, Mathematics, Biology, Chemistry, Physics, Modern Languages and Religious Studies. Subjects such as Geography, History, Art, ICT, Food & Nutrition, Design & Technology, Drama, Music, Sport and PSE complete the programme of study for Years 7–9.

For GCSE, in addition to the core subjects, other courses include Design & Technology, Food & Nutrition, ICT, Physical Education, Art, Statistics, Drama, Geography, History and Music.

In the Sixth Form there is a wide choice of AS and A Level subjects including English, Mathematics, Biology, Chemistry, Physics, Geography, History, Art, French, Spanish, Psychology, Business Studies, ICT, Further Mathematics, Performance Arts and Music Technology. In addition to these AS and A Level choices, a Cambridge Technical course in Sport is also taught.

Tuition in English for speakers of other languages is also available.

Sport and Physical Education. All pupils, girls and boys, are encouraged to participate in a large variety of sports including: rugby, hockey, netball, cross-country, athletics, cricket, gymnastics, badminton, squash, volleyball, basketball, football, rounders, tennis, judo, swimming and health-related fitness. The Judo Academy has a unique link with the elite Team Bath, and the School's gymnasts compete at a local, regional and national level.

Clubs and Activities. There is a range of 40+ extra-curricular activities which are organised and supervised by staff. Among the most popular are The Duke of Edinburgh's Award Scheme, choir, orchestra, Judo, computing, art, music, canoeing, and surfing. Numerous expeditions and field trips, both in the UK and abroad, are organised each year. Musicals, plays and concerts are regularly presented in the school's purpose-designed theatre.

Careers. From Year 9 onwards, pupils are offered a planned programme of careers education and guidance as part of the tutorial programme. This is complemented by presentations from visiting professionals, visits to careers events and close contact with Careers advisers from Connexions Cornwall and Devon. All pupils have access to the latest careers information in the School Library.

Religion and Pastoral Care. In common with every Methodist Group School, Kingsley has a Christian ethos, and welcomes children of all religious denominations, as well as those without religious affiliation. In addition to their Year Heads, all pupils have a personal Tutor who is responsible for monitoring their academic progress and personal well-being. For Boarders, care is also the responsibility of the Housemaster or Housemistress.

Admission. Boys and girls are admitted to the Nursery from the age of 3 months. Entry to the Senior School for pupils aged 11 and 12 years is by interview and taster day. Assessment for academic scholarships is made through written tests in Mathematics, English and Science, as well as a verbal reasoning test. For pupils with recognised learning difficulties entry is by interview together with an up-to-date educational psychologist's report. 13+ admission is through our own Entrance Examination or Scholarship Examination. For older pupils, an interview together with a report from their present school is required.

Prospectus. The Kingsley School prospectus is available from the Registrar, Mrs Caroline Bailey, email: admissions@kingsleyschoolbideford.co.uk, tel: 01237 426200 or online via the school's website: www. kingsleyschoolbideford.co.uk. Visitors are most welcome to tour the School by appointment.

Scholarships. Entrance Scholarships are offered annually for pupils joining Year 7 and Year 9 on the basis of the results of entrance tests held in the preceding January. A maximum of ten Academic Scholarship awards can be made each year; an exceptional candidate can receive an exceptional award. Awards are also available where candidates show outstanding ability in Music, Art, Drama, and Sport. Sixth Form Academic Scholarships are awarded on the basis of GCSE performance.

Fees per term (2014–2015). Senior School: £7,990 (full boarders), £6,630 (weekly boarders), £3,920–£4,170 (day pupils including lunch).

Junior School: Day: £1,840 (Reception), £1,940 (Years 1 and 2), £2,410 (Years 3 and 4), £3,130 (Years 5 and 6). Boarding (from Year 4): £5,330 (weekly), £6,770 (full).

Charitable status. Kingsley School, Bideford is a Registered Charity, number 306709.

Langley School

Langley Park, Loddon, Norwich, Norfolk NR14 6BJ
Tel: 01508 520210
Fax: 01508 528058
email: cmayes@langleyschool.co.uk
website: www.langleyschool.co.uk
Twitter: @Langley_School
Facebook: /LangleySchool

Langley School, formerly the Norwich High School for Boys, was founded in 1910. The School relocated from Norwich to Langley Park in 1946 and was renamed. It is the Senior School to Thorpe House Langley Preparatory School and the business affairs of both schools are managed by a Council of Management as a non-profit making educational charity.

Langley admits boys and girls between the ages of 10 and 18 years to day, weekly boarding, flexi boarding or full boarding status. There are 550 pupils in the School, of whom around 100 are boarders.

Council of Management:
Chairman: Mrs Margaret M Alston, JP

Mr D J B Coventry, CA	Mrs P Parker
Mr C E Self, FRICS, IRRV	Mr A Harmer
Mr C Townsend	Mr S Brown
Mr J Fuller	Lady Bacon
Mr R Hewitt	Mr G Barham
Mrs J Timmins	Mr M Harrowven

Headmaster: Mr Dominic Findlay, BA Ed Exeter, NPQH

Senior Deputy Head Pastoral: Mr Michael Rayner, BA Hons Leeds, PGCE Oxford
Deputy Head Academic: Mr Frank P L Butt, BEng Hons Bath, PGCE Roehampton
Assistant Head Student Welfare: Mr Jamie L McRobert, BA Joint Hons, PGCE Swansea
Head of Sixth Form: Dr Clare A Lowery, BSc, PhD Birmingham, PGCE UEA
Assistant Head Curriculum: Mr Andrew Walker, BA Hons, QTS

Teaching Staff:

Science:
Mr Jamie Clegg, BSc Hons, PGCE Hull (*Head of Science*)
Mrs Leslie McRobert, BSc Hons Applied Biology (*Science, Head of Biology, Assistant Head of Sixth Form*)
Dr Clare A Lowery, BSc, PhD Birmingham, PGCE UEA (*Chemistry*)
Dr Aysin Mason, BSc, MSc, PhD MET University, PGCE UEA (*Science, Head of Chemistry*)
Miss Louise Madeley (*Science*)
Mr Philip McComish, BSc, PGCE (*Head of Years 10/11, Academic Head of Physics, Head of Careers*)
Mr Robbie Brittain (*Gifted and Talented Coordinator and Physics*)
Mr Leigh Sitch, BSc, MEd, PGCE (*Chemistry, Academic Head of Years 8/9*)
Dr Craig Munday BSc Hons, MMedSci, PhD (*Science, Biology*)
Miss Emma Rowley (*Deputy Head Years 6 & 7, Science, Biology*)
Mrs Sarah Clegg (*Science & Mathematics*)

English, Drama and Media:
Mr Rufus Wood, BA Hons, MPhil, PGCE Liverpool (*Head of English*)
Mrs Alison Clark, MA Hons Dundee, PGCE Swansea (*Head of Psychology 2nd i/c English & KS4*)
Mr Jamie L McRobert, BA Joint Hons, PGCE Swansea (*English Head of PSHE*)
Ms Jenny Corser, BA, PGCE (*KS3 English*)
Mrs Tanya Martin, BA Hons, PGCE UEA (*Head of Years 8/9 Pastoral, English*)
Mrs Sarah Cossey, BA Hons PGCE, MA (*English/Literacy Coordinator*)
Mr Jon Aldridge (*Head of Drama*)
Mr Adrian Slack (*Drama*)
Mr Craig McAllister, BA Hons, PGCE (*Head of Media Studies*)

Mathematics:
Mr Stuart Goodhew, MEng Hons, PGCE (*Head of Mathematics*)
Mrs Sumudu Edwards (*Mathematics & KS5*)
Mr Andrew Briggs, BA Hons OU, Teachers' Cert (*Mathematics*)

Mrs Chris A Feakes, BEd Worcester (*Head of Years 10/11 Pastoral, Mathematics, Geography*)

Miss Andrea Hanzelyova, MA Preston QTS (*Duke of Edinburgh's Award Coordinator, KS3 Mathematics and ICT*)

Ms Lynne White, BSc Hons, PGCE (*2nd i/c Mathematics*)

Ms Laura Daniel, BSc, PGCE (*Gifted and Talented Coordinator and Mathematics*)

Languages:
Mr Tim J Batchelor, BA Hons Nottingham, PGCE Homerton (*Head of Modern Languages*)

Mrs Jenni L Skelton, BA Hons Oxford Brookes, PGCE Leeds (*i/c German, French*)

Mrs Laura Holmes, BA Hons, PGCE UEA (*French, Spanish*)

Mrs Diana Harrington, BA Joint Hons, PGCE, RSA Dip TEFL (*French, i/c Spanish*)

Mrs Mary Ellwood, BA Hons, PGCE (*Spanish, French*)

Mrs Abigail Yandell, BA Hons Newnham College Cambridge, PGCE, Cert TEFL (*EAL*)

Mrs Jo E Butt, BA Hons Wolverhampton, Cert TEFL (*Head of EAL*)

Mrs Angela Smith (*EAL*)

Mrs Gillian Ogden (*EAL*)

Mrs Victoria McComish (*EAL*)

Humanities:
Mr Iain Felton, BA Hons, PGCE, DPM (*Head of History*)

Mr Jon Kempton, BA Hons Bristol, PGCE Bristol (*History, Assistant Head of Sixth form*)

Mr Michael Rayner, BA Hons Leeds, PGCE Merton College, Oxford (*History*)

Mrs Angela Dain, Cert Ed, BEd Cambridge, MA, PhD UEA (*History*)

Mr Andrew Walker, BA Hons, QTS (*Head of RE*)

Ms Nikola Bodmer-Tripp (*Humanities*)

Miss Sam King, BSc Hons, PGCE (*Geography*)

Mrs Karen Lambert, BA Hons Sussex, PGCE Nottingham (*Head of Geography*)

Mr Matt Vanston, BSc Hons Sheffield, PGCE UEA (*T & L Coordinator, 2nd i/c Geography*)

Mr Tim Goodge (*Geography*)

Mr David T Madgett, BA Hons UEA, DipAcc City of London, PGCE Worc, Cert TEFL (*Head of Economics, Business Studies*)

Mr Paul Clark, BA Hons Northumbria, PGCE Sunderland (*Head of Years 6/7, Head of Business Studies, Economics*)

Mr Trevor Kirkham, BSc Hons (*Business Studies, Work Exp Coordinator*)

Mrs Helen Yates (*Business Studies*)

Miss Clare Wyatt, BSc Hons, PGCE (*Head of Psychology*)

Mr Stephen Read, LLB Cardiff (*Head of Law, Psychology, Head of Mancroft*)

Art:
Mr John N Ogden, BA Hons, PGCE Lancashire (*Head of Art*)

Miss Rebecca Robinson, BA Hons, MA (*i/c Photography, Art*)

Mrs Hannah Cole, BA Hons, PGCE (*Textiles, Art*)

Technology:
Mr John Norton, BA Hons, MA (*Head of Design Technology*)

Mr Frank Butt, BEng Hons Bath, PGCE Roehampton (*Design Technology*)

Mr Matt J Holmes, BA, Cert Ed Brunel (*Design Technology, i/c Cricket*)

Mr Stuart Hughes (*Design Technology*)

Mrs Moira Woolsey, Cert Ed Bath College of Educ (*Home Economics, PSHE*)

Mrs Anne Reynolds, BEd Hons (*Home Economics*)

ICT:
Mr David Innes, BA Hons Falmouth (*Head of ICT*)

Mr Derek Haysom (*Information Technology*)

Resident Tutor/Cover Teacher: Mr Mike Webb

Music:
Mrs Rebecca George-Broom, BA Hons Music (*Head of Music*)

Mr Rob White, ATCL (*Assistant Head of Music, Head of St Giles*)

Mr A Cronin (*Brass*)

Mr S Durant (*Guitar*)

Ms Samantha Wingham (*Piano and Voice*)

Mr C Brady (*Percussion*)

Learning Support:
Mrs Velda Rickman (*Learning Support Manager, Child Protection Officer*)

Mrs Jayne Camburn (*Special Educational Needs Coordinator*)

Learning Support Assistants:
Mr Richard Hull, Cert Ed

Mrs Rachel Hull

Mrs Karen Coulson

Mrs Caroline Goodge

Mrs Katherine Ashford

Miss Nina Hobbs

Mrs Beverly Leech

Mr Nigel Sullivan

Mrs Valerie Lund

Games:
Miss Sam Tea, BEd Hons (*Director of Physical Education, Head of Girls' Games*)

Mr Tim Malone (*Director of Sport, Head of Crome*)

Mr Chris Greenhall, BA, PGCE Wales (*Head of Beauchamp House, Teacher of Games*)

Mrs Claire Vinsen, BSc, PGCE M (*Girls' Games, Sport BTEC*)

Miss Emily Creed, BA Hons, PGCE (*Girls' Games, Girls Ambassador Coordinator*)

Combined Cadet Force:
Contingent Commander: Maj Chris J Cooper, PPC

Officer i/c Army Section: Lt Frank Butt

Officer i/c RN Section: Lt Cmdr Matt J Holmes

RN Section: Sub Lieutenant Matt Vanston

Medical Sisters:
Mrs Fiona Lambert, SRN

Mrs C Hughes

Matrons:
Miss Gemma Robinson

Mrs Wendy Kerry

Mrs Sarah Ryder

Medical Officers:
Dr P Barrie, MB ChB, DRCOG, DCH

Dr A Guy, FP Cert, MB, BA, BS

Commercial Director: Mr M Randall

Headmaster's PA: Mrs Claire Mayes

Langley School aims to provide a framework within which each pupil will develop effective learning skills and will achieve their maximum academic potential. A happy, secure and well-ordered environment is maintained in a beautiful Grade 1 listed country house setting with 110 acres of extensive grounds and playing fields, where individuals are encouraged to set their sights high. Their progress is monitored by a strong tutorial system to ensure that they follow a course of study that best suits their individual skills and needs. Langley pupils are encouraged to identify their talents and to use and develop them whilst contributing to a wide variety of new experiences that will help them acquire the values of honesty, enterprise, independence and social awareness. Small classes and a well organised House system help our children to sample these new experiences with confidence. They will learn to take personal and social responsibility and will get ample opportunities to develop leadership qualities. We hope to produce young people who will be prepared to meet the demands of a rapidly changing and demanding world which will require versatile, adaptable, receptive and confident citizens of the future.

Location and Facilities. Situated in over 100 acres of playing fields and wooded parkland south of Norwich, Langley benefits from good accessibility by road, rail, air and sea.

In recent years the school has been steadily expanding and its facilities have been substantially enhanced. Recent developments include a complete refurbishment programme for boarding facilities, a new floodlit Astroturf pitch, a new eleven-room Science Centre, an Art and Sculpture Studio, a multi-media suite for Modern Languages, a fully refurbished and extended Mathematics block and a multi-gym with fitness centre. In September 2010, a new state-of-the-art block of fifteen classrooms and four ICT rooms was opened, alongside the refurbishment of two other blocks. In September 2012 a brand new medical centre was opened and a new Sixth Form Centre and Performance Hall opened in January 2014.

Academic Curriculum. Syllabuses and schemes of work are designed to complement the National Curriculum and the Common Entrance Examination Syllabuses up to Year 9.

Lower School (10–13 years): All pupils in these years study English, Mathematics, French, German, Geography, History, Biology, Chemistry, Physics, Design and Technology, Drama, Art, Information Technology, Music, Physical Education and Religious Studies. A programme of Personal and Social Education includes study skills and careers guidance. Pupils are setted on ability in the core subjects while in other subjects streaming applies.

Middle School (14–16 years): All pupils are prepared for the GCSE examinations. The School is an examining centre for a number of Boards, and this enables staff to select those syllabuses which they believe are most appropriate to the needs of their pupils. All pupils study English, Mathematics and the Sciences. A variable number of additional subjects are selected which enables the most able pupil to study up to eleven subjects. A brochure on GCSE courses is available on request.

Most students in the Sixth Form will study 4 AS Levels in the Lower Sixth from a choice of 28 subjects and continue with three of these to A Level in the Upper Sixth. Other permutations of AS and A Levels are possible to suit students of varying ability.

Monitoring Academic Progress. High priority is given to the monitoring of each pupil's progress and is the specific responsibility of the Heads of Year with a team of tutors. A combination of complementary short, medium and long-term recording systems are in use. This permits effective communication between teachers, and between the School and the parent.

Extra-curricular Activities. The school offers a wide choice of sports, artistic, musical, dramatic, scientific, technical and literary activities to enhance students life-long learning. In total there are more than 80 such activities operating throughout the week. All staff and students are required to contribute to this programme. The major sports are rugby, football, cricket, tennis, athletics, hockey and netball. Sailing, fencing, judo, squash, basketball, climbing, shooting, polo and golf are but a few of the other options.

The School has a thriving CCF (Army, RAF and Navy sections) and encourages participation in the Duke of Edinburgh's Award Scheme.

The self-confidence which can be acquired through participation in music and drama is immeasurable. Consequently, the school promotes participation by all in dramatic and musical events at a class, house and school level. An Arts Umbrella programme offers the opportunity for pupils to experience the theatrical and musical productions in London and other centres.

Admission. Pupils will be considered for admission to Langley at 10+, 11+, 13+ and into the Sixth Form. Entry may be possible at other levels when vacancies permit and is conditional on an interview followed by detailed and satisfactory school reports. At Sixth Form level, satisfactory performance in GCSE is required.

Scholarships. Scholarships may be awarded in each of the following categories: Academic, Art, Drama, Music, Sport and Design & Technology. We also offer an All Rounder Scholarship Award for academically bright students, who also have a flair in one or more of the non-academic areas – in Years 6, 7, 9 or 12.

Further details and a Scholarships application form may be obtained from the Headmaster's PA.

Fees per term (2014–2015). Years 6–13: Boarders £8,930, Weekly Boarders £7,450, Day Pupils £4,395.

Generous family and Forces discounts are offered.

Further Information is available on the school's website. A School prospectus, Sixth Form brochure and GCSE brochure are available on application from the Headmaster's PA: 01508 522474 or cmayes@langleyschool.co.uk.

Charitable status. Langley School is a Registered Charity, number 311270. It exists to provide a sound education for boys and girls.

Lichfield Cathedral School

The Palace, The Close, Lichfield, Staffordshire WS13 7LH

Tel:	01543 306170
Fax:	01543 306176
email:	thepalace@lichfieldcathedralschool.com
website:	www.lichfieldcathedralschool.com

Governors:
Chairman: Mr C Hopkins, BA, MBA
Mrs C Abbott, BA
Mr H Bishop
The Very Revd A Dorber, BA, MTh, Dean of Lichfield
Sir B Fender, BSc, PhD
The Revd Canon P Holliday, BCom, MA, FCA
Mrs J Mason
The Revd Canon Dr A M Moore, MA, PhD Cantab
Dr A Primrose, MA Cantab, PhD, PGCE
Mr C Rickart, BA Hons, PGCE

Headmaster: Mr David Corran, MA, PGCE

Deputy Head: Mrs S E Hannam, BA Hons, MA, PGCE
Head of Junior Years: Mrs J M Churton, BSc Hons, PGCE
Head of Middle Years: Mrs C R O'Donnell, BEd Hons
Head of Senior Years: Mrs J M Hart, BA Hons, QTS
Head of Early Years Foundation Stage: Mrs A M Stevens, BEd
Director of Studies: Mrs H Ghazireh, BSc Hons, MSc, PGCE

Mrs D Rice, BA Hons, PGCE (*Acting Director of Music*)
Mr J Mather, BSc Hons, PGCE (*Director of Sport*)
Mrs J M Sedgley, BA Hons, PGCE (*Head of English*)
Mrs J Reynolds, BSc Hons, PGCE (*Head of Mathematics*)
Dr J Ewington, BSc Hons, MSc, PhD, PGCE (*Head of Science*)
Mrs C Farrell, Licence d'Anglais, PGCE (*Head of Modern Foreign Languages*)
Mrs I Johnson, BA Hons, PGCE (*Head of Religious Studies*)
Mrs B A Dunne, BA, PGCE (*Head of Drama*)
Mrs S E Whatley, BA Hons, PGCE (*Head of Art and Design*)

Mr J Gardiner, BA Hons, PGCE (*Head of Information and Communication Technology*)
Miss E Davies, BA Hons, PGCE (*Head of History*)
Mrs S Black, BSc Hons, PGCE (*Head of Geography*)
Mrs I Johnson, BA Hons, PGCE (*Head of Religious Studies*)

Residentiary Canon and School Chaplain: Canon A M Stead, MA, BA

Age Range. 3–18.
Number of Pupils. 410 including 20 Cathedral chorister boarders.
Fees per term (2014–2015). Day Pupils £2,610–£4,650; Chorister Boarders: Weekly £5,060–£5,615; Full £5,795–£6,110. Instrumental Music Tuition: £220 per instrument per term.

Our mission is to be an internationally recognised school that serves its local area by creating an inclusive school community devoted to Christian ideals of learning, raising the aspirations of each of its members and fulfilling their potential in body, mind and spirit. Founded in 1942 principally as a boarding school for the choristers of Lichfield Cathedral, the school has since grown considerably and now provides all through education for boys and girls aged 3 to 18.

The ethos of the school is that of a community where Christian values are upheld and, whilst most pupils are members of the Church of England, children of other denominations and religions are welcomed.

The school occupies two main sites: the Junior Years are located 3½ miles north of Lichfield city centre in six acres of countryside at Longdon Green, while the Middle and Senior Years occupy several buildings in the Cathedral Close, one being the magnificent 17th century Palace, the home of the Bishops of Lichfield until 1952.

The link with the Cathedral remains strong with a twice-weekly school service, as well as concerts and services throughout the year. The 20 boy choristers (aged 7–13) board at the school on scholarships provided by the Dean and Chapter, while the 20 girl choristers (aged 10–15) are all day pupils. Former choristers continue their choral training in Cantorum, the scholarship-based youth choir. Academic, art, drama, sport and music scholarships are available to internal and external students entering Year 7 (11+), Year 9 (13+) and Sixth Form.

Learning in the Early Years Foundation Stage is planned around half-termly topics and the children take part in a range of activities which are balanced between adult-led and child-initiated opportunities. Activities are carefully structured to challenge children, encouraging them to develop confidence and the skills needed to solve problems. The outdoor facilities offer children an exciting environment in which to explore and investigate, and we ensure children have the time for free play. Forest School is a popular element of the Junior Years curriculum that provides a holistic, individualised approach to outdoor learning, with a strong focus on developing self-esteem, confidence, communication skills and social and emotional awareness.

The spirit of intellectual enquiry is at the heart of teaching and learning at the school. Academic results are strong, particularly at GCSE and A Level. Throughout Key Stages 1 to 3, pupils follow a broad and balanced curriculum of English, Mathematics, Science, French, History, Geography, Religious Studies, Art, Design, Music, Drama, Physical Education and Games and Personal, Social and Health Education. ICT skills are developed across every subject.

We offer a wide range of GCSE subjects, including Art and Design, Biology, Business Studies, Chemistry, Design Technology, Drama Studies, English Literature, English Language, French, Geography, German, History, Information and Communication Technology, Mathematics, Music, Physical Education, Physics, Product Design, Religious Studies and Spanish. The same subjects are offered at A

Level with the addition of Economics, Further Mathematics, Music Technology, Philosophy and Ethics, Psychology and Theatre Studies.

Through a collaboration with nearby Abbots Bromley School, we are able to offer additional subjects at A Level and a BTEC in Performing Arts. This partnership also provides our secondary students with access to first-class sports facilities including an indoor pool, gymnasium and equestrian centre.

A co-curriculum of 'Beyond the Classroom' activities ensures students are well-rounded and gain valuable skills for higher education, employment and life outside school. Extra-curricular activities every day after school cover a wide range of subjects from chess to cooking and from Aikido to tennis. Several orchestras and ensembles are extremely active, as are the six main school choirs. All pupils have access to a rich variety of both residential and day trips as well as pupil exchanges, overseas expeditions and cultural immersion opportunities. Many are directly linked to the curriculum, but the benefits to pupils go far beyond the purely educational. The Duke of Edinburgh's Award scheme is thriving, along with Young Enterprise. The school has a long-term association with the Waterloo Schools Project in Sierra Leone; Sixth Form students lead the fundraising efforts as well as visiting the project annually to help with the restoration and rebuilding of primary and secondary schools and the improvement of facilities in the neighbouring refugee camp.

Parents are welcome to contact the school for a tour and a meeting with the Head or to attend the any of the school Open Events held throughout the year.

Charitable status. Lichfield Cathedral School is a Registered Charity, number 1137481. It exists to provide education for boys and girls.

Longridge Towers School

Longridge, Berwick-upon-Tweed, Northumberland TD15 2XQ
Tel: 01289 307584
Fax: 01289 302581
email: enquiries@lts.org.uk
website: www.lts.org.uk
Twitter: @LongridgeTowers

Motto: *Carpe Diem*

Board of Governors:
Chairman: Mr J Smithson
Vice-Chairman: (*to be appointed*)

Mr A Bell   Dr E Miller
Mr A Birkett   Mrs J McGregor
Mrs J Coats   Professor C Phillips
Mrs C Davies   Mr J Robertson
Mr J A Houston

Headmaster: Mr T M Manning, BSc, PGCE

Deputy Head: Mr P Whitcombe, BSc, PGCE

Head of Junior Department: Mrs S Maddock, BEd

Senior Teachers:
Mrs I Cheer, BA, BSc, Cert HSC, Dip HSW (*Music, Pastoral, SENCO*)
Mr I Dempster, BEd (*History, Games, Examinations*)
Mr P Dodd, BEng, DIS, PGCE (*Mathematics, Operations*)

Teaching Staff:
Mr P Brooke, BA, PGCE (*English*)
Ms D Bryden, BEd (*Junior Department*)
Mrs S Bullen, BA, HLTA, FDEYP, QTS (*Reception/EYFS*)
Mr M Caddick, BA, PGCE (*German*)

Mrs B Chynoweth, MA, PGCE (*Junior Department*)
Dr N Dalrymple, PhD, MLitt, BA, PGCE
Mr R Davie, BSc, PGCE (*Mathematics, Computing*)
Mrs A Gettins, BA (*Librarian, English*)
Mr R Glenn, BSc, PGCE (*ICT Coordinator*)
Mrs N Green, BA, PGCE (*EFL*)
Mr R Johnson, BA, MA, PGCE (*English*)
Mrs J Masey, BSc, PGCE (*Science*)
Mrs B Mayhew, BA, PGCE (*French/Spanish*)
Miss J McCalvey, BSc, PGCE (*Science*)
Mrs E McCorquodale, BA (*Art*)
Mr P McParland, BSc, MSc, PGCE (*Geography, Mathematics*)
Mrs L Monkman, BA, QTS (*Junior Department*)
Mr R Moscrop, BA (*Junior Department*)
Mrs L Peters, BEd (*Girls Games, Sports Studies*)
Mr A Phillips, BA, PGCE (*Boys Games, German, Sports Studies*)
Miss K Phillips, BA (*Drama/Speech & Drama*)
Miss J Roberts, BEd (*Careers, PSHE, Psychology*)
Mr E Roney, BSc, MSc, PGCE
Mr P Rowett, BA (*RE, History, Geography*)
Mrs E Shaw, BA, PGCE (*Girls Games, Sports Studies*)
Mr A Skeen, BA (*Economics, Games*)
Mrs G Skeen, BSc, QTS (*Junior Department*)
Mr A Skipper, BSc, PGCE (*Physics*)
Mr A Westthorp, BEng, PGCE (*CDT, Computing*)
Mrs K Westthorp, MA, PGCE (*French*)
Mrs A Young (*Teaching Assistant Sport*)

Boarding Staff:
Mr G Hattle (*House Parent*)
Mrs V Richards (*House Parent*)
Mrs M Robson (*Senior House Parent/Resident Matron*)
Mr M Short (*House Parent*)

Visiting Music Staff:
Mr D Dougall
Ms C Fish
Mrs M Humphreys
Mr F McDermid
Ms V Richards
Mrs M Rowland
Mrs C Smith
Mrs J Warren

Greek/Latin: Revd M Mountney

Matron: Mrs M Hattle, RGN

Administration:
Bursar: Mr S Bankier, BA, FCMA
Assistant: Miss L Muckle
Head's Secretary: Mrs J Higgins
Marketing: Mrs M Burns
Reception: Mrs C Jobson
Site Manager: Mr L Caldwell
Catering Manager: Mrs C Krause

The school occupies a Victorian Mansion set in 80 acres of woodland in the beautiful Tweed Valley and enjoys excellent road and rail links with England and Scotland. Daily school bus services operate within a radius of 30 miles from the school.

Longridge Towers, refounded in 1983 under its founder and President, the late Lord Home of the Hirsel, has grown from 113 pupils to nearly 300 pupils. It is probably unique in offering the close personal relationships between pupils, staff and parents which creates a genuine 'family atmosphere'. The school has a reputation for turning out well-rounded and confident young people, the vast majority of whom continue their education at university.

Alongside the excellent academic results, the school offers many opportunities through its sporting and extra-curricular enrichment activities. All of these combine to give all pupils the chance to participate and acquire a variety of skills.

Sport figures strongly in the life of the pupils and many gain representative honours at county and national level in a variety of sports, such as rugby, hockey, cross-country running, athletics, tennis and cricket. Art, Music and Drama are also very popular and successful activities.

Entry. The school caters for a wide spectrum of abilities among its pupils who are taught in small classes. Special provision is made for the needs of pupils with mild dyslexia and for the small proportion of pupils for whom English is their second language.

Assessments upon entry to the Junior and Senior Departments in Mathematics and English are diagnostic and have no fixed pass mark.

The school is divided into 2 departments, Junior and Senior, and caters for pupils throughout their school career, from three to eighteen years. Pupils may enter at any age provided that a vacancy exists. Classes are small with less than 20 pupils per teaching set, reducing to about half this in the Sixth Form.

Activities. Longridge Towers is a school where the development of the pupils outside the academic sphere is considered to be vital. Every afternoon there is an extensive Enrichment programme offering a wide range of activities including: archery, rocket making, lacrosse, football, computer construction, dance, karate, judo, drama, kick boxing, creative writing, wildlife and gardening, young engineers, science club, debating, along with many others. The major team games are rugby, hockey, tennis, cross-country running, athletics and cricket. Many senior pupils participate in the Duke of Edinburgh's Award Scheme. The musical activities within the school are varied and numerous. There are five Choirs, two Orchestras and various instrumental groups. Almost half of the pupils take private instrumental lessons and the taking of grade examinations is encouraged. No visitor to the school could fail to be aware of the variety and excellence of the artwork on display which includes clay modelling and photography.

Public Examinations. Sixteen subjects are offered at GCSE level, including Physics, Chemistry and Biology and 19, including Economics, Psychology, Sports Studies and Drama, are offered in the Sixth Form at A or AS Level.

Parents receive reports half-yearly and three-weekly Grade Cards ensure that they are kept up to date about their children's progress.

Boarding. The Boarding House and pastoral care are in the hands of resident non-teaching house parents. There is medical and dental care. Pupils have access to telephones and email and may send or receive fax messages using the facilities in the school office. Boarders may attend on a weekly or termly basis from age 8 years onwards. At weekends the boarders participate in a wide range of activities.

Scholarships and Bursaries. Academic awards at various levels are available annually to pupils aged 9–14 and 16 (into Sixth Form). Music, Sports and All-Rounder Scholarships are also available to pupils aged 11–14 and 16.

Bursaries are available to children of serving members of the Armed Forces.

Bursaries are also available to pupils; the value of these is determined after consideration of a statement of parental income.

Fees per term (2014–2015). Full Boarders: £7,706 (Junior), £8,132 (Senior). Weekly Boarders: £5,874 (Junior), £6,313 (Senior). Day pupils: Government funded Nursery with charges for extra hours, £2,555 (Junior age 4–7), £3,552 (Junior age 7–11), £3,992 (Senior age 11–18).

Charitable status. Longridge Towers School is a Registered Charity, number 513534. It exists to provide an academic education for boys and girls.

LVS Ascot (The Licensed Victuallers' School)

London Road, Ascot, Berkshire SL5 8DR
Tel: 01344 882770
email: registrar@lvs.ascot.sch.uk
website: www.lvs.ascot.sch.uk

The School was founded in 1803 and has been co-educational from the outset. It is controlled by a Board of Governors on behalf of the parent charity, The Licensed Trade Charity.

Patron: Her Majesty The Queen

Director of Education: Mr I Mullins, BEd Hons, MSc, MBIM

Head of Senior School: Mrs C Cunniffe, BA Hons, MMus, MBA

Head of Junior School: Mr N Funnell, BSc Hons, PGCE

Deputy Head/Academic: Mr C Davis, BSc Hons, PGCE

Deputy Head/Pastoral: Mr C Cunningham-Watson, BA Hons, MA, PGCE

Asst Head/Director of Studies: Dr P Hodges, PhD, BSc, MSc, PGCE

Asst Head/Head of Sixth Form: Mr C Jenkins, BA Hons, PGCE

Housemasters/mistresses:

Boarding Houses:
Housemaster of Bass: Mr J Rudkin, MEd, BA, PGCE
Assistant HM of Bass: Miss J Atkinson, BSc
Housemistress of Carlsberg: MrsC Marsh, BA Hons
Assistant HM of Carlsberg: Dr L Franklin, PhD, PGCE
Housemistress of Gilbey: Mrs R Jarrett, BA, PGCE
Assistant HM of Gilbey: Ms S Natta, BA Hons, PGCE
Housemaster of Guinness: Mr A Towse, BA Hons
Assistant HM of Guinness: Mr B Hunt, BSc Hons, PGCE

Day Houses:
Housemaster of Bell's: Mr B McMurray, BSc Hons, PGCE
Housemistress of Courage: Mrs T Bason, BA, PGCE
Housemaster of Whitbread: Mr E Dennis, BA, PGCE

Designated Safeguarding Leads:
Mr C Cunningham-Watson, BA Hons, MA, PGCE (*Senior School*)
Mr N Funnell, BSc Hons, PGCE (*Junior School*)
Mrs L Rawlinson, BEd Hons (*Junior School*)

Child Protection Officer (*Snr Sch*): Mrs R Sandford, BA Hons
Child Protection Officer (*Jnr Sch*): Mrs L Rawlinson
Deputy Child Protection Officer (*Snr Sch*): Mrs S Litherland, BA Hons, PGCE

Heads of Departments:

Art and Design: Mrs S Litherland, BA Hons, PGCE
Business Studies/Economics: Mr S Dhokia, BA Hons
Design Technology: Miss C Henderson, BA Hons, PGCE
Drama: Mrs G Windsor, BA Hons, PGCE
English and Media Studies: Ms S Quant, BA Hons, MA, PGCE
Additional Learning Needs (*ALN*): Mrs K Barnett, MSc, Dip Psych, Dip RSA, PGCE
Geography: Mrs D Finch, BA Hons
History: Mr T Jarrett, MA, PGCE
Information Technology: Mrs S Featherstone-Clark, BA Hons
Law: Mr K Towl, LLB, PGCE

Mathematics: Mr R Bignell, MBA, BSc Hons
Modern Foreign Languages: Mr J Nye, BSc, PGCE, MA
Director of Music: Mr D Gravett, BSc Hons
Director of Sport: Mr J Percy, BSc
Psychology: Mr B Stephenson, BSc, MA
Philosophy and Religion: Mr B Padrick, BA
Science: Mr G Cunningham, BSc Hons PGCE
Learning Resource Centre: Mrs S Bastone, ACLIP

Junior School:
Assistant Head of Junior School: Mrs L Rawlinson, BEd Hons

Administrative Staff:
Examinations Officer: Mrs S Chapman
Head of Senior School's PA: Mrs L Humphreys
Marketing: Mrs P Smith
Registrars: Mrs M Buttimer, Mrs H Leigh
Senior School Secretaries: Miss H Austin, Mrs L Reddy
Senior School Reception: Mrs A Davies
Head of Junior School's PA: Mrs D Pearce

LVS Ascot is a co-educational day and boarding school for young people aged 4–18.

Numbers. Junior School 175, Senior School 720 (including 188 in Sixth Form), boarding approx 180.

Organisation. Pupils aged 4 to 11 (Years R to 6) are taught in the Junior School, where they are taught in separate classes, each with a class teacher. Houses are used for sports and other competitions. Junior School pupils may board from Year 3 (age 7) and join a mixed House (Bass House), which is an integral part of the Junior School buildings.

Senior School pupils, aged 11 to 18 (Years 7 to 13), are placed in tutor groups and a school House, with a tutor who monitors their pastoral care and oversees their academic performance. Students are taught in ability groups with a maximum class size of 20. Boarders are accommodated in four separate boarding Houses, each supervised by Housemasters/mistresses: Bass (Junior House) is mixed for pupils from Year 3 to Year 7; Carlsberg (girls' House) for pupils from Year 8 to Year 11; Guinness (boys' House) for pupils from Year 8 to Year 11; Gilbey (mixed Sixth Form House) for pupils in Years 12 and 13.

Location. LVS Ascot is north of the A329, close to Ascot Racecourse and Royal Windsor. The school is easily accessible from the M3, M4 and M25 motorways as well as Heathrow and Gatwick airports. The school bus service connects with trains at Ascot Station, as well many surrounding towns within a 20 miles radius.

Facilities. LVS Ascot is a modern day and boarding school in the UK. The purpose-built facilities, set in 26 acres of landscaped grounds, include: boarding accommodation and classroom blocks, a sports centre, all-weather pitch, indoor swimming pool, fully-equipped theatre and a music technology suite. LVS Ascot hosts over five-hundred networked computer workstations, with every classroom equipped with ICT resources for digital and interactive learning. Wireless networking provides additional facilities for centrally-managed student laptops, eBooks and other devices in a secure environment. There is a dedicated Sixth Form Centre, and a Learning Resource Centre, that has an extensive range of books and journals.

Curriculum. The curriculum is broad and based on the national curriculum "plus". Pupils follow a common core curriculum of English, Mathematics, Science, one/two foreign languages, plus PE and PSHE. Science is taught as separate subjects. At GCSE, students select their choices from: Business Studies, Technology, Art & Design, Geography, History, Food Technology, Music, Drama, Media Studies, Economics, Physical Education, Computer Science, Spanish, German or French.

A wide range of A Level and vocational options are provided, including Mathematics, Physics, Chemistry, Biology,

Music, Geography, History, Economics, Business Studies, English, Art & Design, Theatre Studies, Design & Technology, Media Studies, Photography, Psychology, French, Spanish, German, ICT, Computer Studies, Engineering and Physical Education.

Sport. The school has superb indoor and outdoor facilities with a large Sports Hall, dance studio with ballet bars, a 25-metre swimming pool and a well-equipped gym as well as rugby, football and hockey pitches, tennis courts and an all-weather pitch. The school has achieved considerable success in providing County, Regional and National standard players in a wide range of sports. Whilst all pupils play team games such as Rugby, Football, Cricket, Hockey, Tennis, Netball, Basketball or Athletics in their early years, the range of options widens as pupils become older to encourage fitness for life, with opportunities such as skiing, skating, polo, fencing and playing squash.

Clubs and Activities. LVS Ascot is an accredited Duke of Edinburgh's Award training centre and runs a vibrant and popular award scheme. Alongside this there is a range of co-curricular activities such as music ensembles, newspaper club, riding, canoeing, rowing, climbing, cookery, animation and film club.

Admissions. There is no entrance examination; reports are requested from a student's current school. All students are interviewed prior to acceptance. Prospective students and their families are welcome to visit the school. Dates of the regular Open Days are listed on the school's website. Personal tours can also be arranged by appointment.

Fees per term (2014–2015). Infants £2,972; Junior: £3,558 (Day), £7,603 (Boarding); Senior: £5,049 (Day), £5,589 (Extended Day), £9,010 (Full/Weekly Boarding); Sixth Form: £5,128 (Day), £9,010 (Full/Weekly Boarding).

Scholarships and Bursaries. Academic, Music, Art, Drama, Sport Scholarships are available at Year 7 entry and various Scholarships are available for entry to the Sixth Form (Year 12).

Fee discounts and Bursaries are available to assist parents working in the Licensed Drinks Trade, MoD and British Diplomats. Third child discount is also available.

Charitable status. The Society of Licensed Victuallers is a Registered Charity, number 230011. It exists to provide education for boys and girls.

Milton Abbey School

Blandford Forum, Dorset DT11 0BZ
Tel: 01258 880484
Fax: 01258 881194
email: admissions@miltonabbey.co.uk
website: www.miltonabbey.co.uk

Visitor: Revd C W Mitchell-Innes, MA

Governors:
Chairman: J E A Barnes, BA, PGCE
K Butler, MA Hons
Col O Chamberlain
¶Maj N Hadden-Paton
¶A Harvey, BA Hons, PGCE
¶P W McGrath, MA, MW
Mrs S Russell, LLB
M Sherwin, BSc
J H Simm, MA, FCA, JP
¶P M G Stopford-Adams, FCSI, ACFA, DL
Sir Philip Williams, Bt, MA, JP, DL
S J Young, MC, JP, FRICS, DL

¶ *Old Miltonian*

Bursar and Clerk to the Governors: Julian Litchfield, FCIPD

Headmaster: Magnus Bashaarat, MA

Deputy Head: Matthew Way, BSc Hons, MEd
Assistant Head: †Simon Kibler, BA
Director of Studies: *Kate Timmis, BA, DipEd
Director of Total Curriculum: Francesca Porter
Admissions & Marketing Manager: Diana Morant, BEd

Housemasters:
Athelstan: Chris Barnes, BA
Damer: Matthew Porter, BA Hons, PGCE
Hambro: Peter Timmis, BA, PGCE
Hodgkinson: Kate Kibler and Simon Kibler, BA, PGCE
Tregonwell: Fergus Wilson, BSc, PGCE

Head of Upper School Studies, Director of UCAS & Careers: Joshua Bradbury, BA, MA, PhD, PGCE
Examinations Officer: Rachael McNulty, HND
SENCO: Ruth Dal Din, BSc
Chaplain: Jo Davis, BA Hons, MTh, PG Cert
Library Manager: Maggie Butler, BA Hons, TEFL
Director of Total Curriculum: Francesca Porter
CCF Staff School Instructor: W02 Chris Adams, Coldstream Guards

* *Head of Department*

Art:
*Sara Burton, BA Hons
Kate Clarkson, BA Hons
Sarah Church, BA Hons, PGCE (*History of Art*)
Elizabeth Barnes, BA Hons

Business Studies/Economics:
*Rebecca Barton, BSc Hons
Chris Barnes, BA Hons

Communication Studies:
Joshua Bradbury, BA, MA, PhD, PGCE

Design & Technology:
*James Ratcliffe, BA (*Director of Design*)
Michael Benjafield, BSc
Mark Warder, HND (*Technician*)

Drama:
*Al Duncan, Dip Act
Georgina Morton
Louisa Thompson (*Theatre Manager*)
Susan Duncan (*Speech and Drama*)

English:
*Kate Timmis BA, PGCE, MEd
Charlotte Peach, BA Hons, GTP (*Second in Department*)
Joshua Bradbury, BA, MA, PhD, PGCE
Will Fraser, MA

Enrichment:
Daniel Roberts, BSc (*Head of PSHCE*)

Geography:
Robin Nicholson, Cert Ed (*Subject Leader*)
Henry Stoot, BA Hons
Nick Batchelor, BSc Hons

History:
Chris Barnes, BA Hons (*Subject Leader*)
Matthew Porter, BA Hons
Matthew Way, BSc Hons, MEd

Information Technology:
Angela Giesens, BSc Hons (*Director of ICT*)

Learning Support:
*Ruth Dal Din, BSc
Sandy Spencer, BA
James Burlton, MA
Sarah Isard, HND
Sally Dean (*Learning Support Assistant*)
Ginny Catarinella (*Learning Support Assistant*)
Catherine Molland, HND

Mathematics:
*Michael Sharp, BA, MA, Cert Ed
Michael Rumbado, BA Hons
Danielle Ash, BA Hons
Andrew Watson, BA (*Extra Tuition*)

Modern Languages:
*Christophe Douchet, Maîtrise, DP, LPC, PGCE
Hugo Mieville, BA, MA, Dip EdMan
Philip Morrow, MA, CELTA (*Able, Gifted and Talented Coordinator*)
Emily Clark, BA Hons

Music:
*Shaun Pirttijarvi, BA Hons, PGCE, FMAOS
Darren Jones (*Music Technology*)
Faye Eldret
Dan Baker, BSc (*Bass Guitar, Jazz Piano*)
Paul Beavis (*Percussion*)
Ros Dawson, MEd, ARCM, CPP (*Flute, Oboe*)
Tony Hind (*Saxophone*)
Martin Ings, MA, ARCM (*Trumpet, Horn*)
Bob Walker (*Bagpipes*)
Richard Hall, BA, PhD (*Piano*)

Politics:
Matthew Porter, BA Hons

Religious Studies:
Gabriella Burchell, BA Hons
Jo Davis, BA Hons, MTh, PG Cert

Science:
*Natalie Perry, BSc Hons, MSc
Daniel Roberts, BSc (*Applied Science, Biology*)
Peter Timmis, BSc (*Applied Science, Physics, Chemistry*)
Fergus Wilson, BSc (*Biology*)
Martyn Earley, BEng Hons
Robert Pay (*Laboratory Technician*)
Janet Collins (*Laboratory Technician*)

Vocational Studies:
*Tony Stroud (*Head of Vocational Studies/Equine Management*)
Elisabeth Carr, BSc Hons, DTLLS (*Head of Countryside Management*)
Ruth Wilkins (*Countryside Management*)
Gail Marsh (*Equine and Farm Assistant*)
Kevin Hurst (*Countryside Management Technician*)
Leonie Monaghan (*Head of Hospitality*)
Elka Charlton (*Hospitality*)
Elizabeth Askew (*Hospitality Technician*)
Simon Kibler, BA (*Sport*)
Erin Clare Cassidy, BA (*Sport*)
Holly Turbill, BSc (*Sport*)
Jack Fielding (*Sport*)

Foundation. Milton Abbey was founded in 1954 and comprises 230 pupils. From September 2012 the School became fully co-educational.

It aims to provide a Christian education, to develop individual potential as fully as possible and to furnish wide opportunities for the exercise of responsibility. Milton Abbey helps to produce pupils who mature into balanced adults. Boys and girls, who may find that a larger school environment drains their confidence, can be judged by their own capabilities and encouraged to achieve their maximum potential. The school provides a framework of rigorous kindness in a safe but stimulating environment with a well-qualified and enthusiastic team of teaching and pastoral staff who know each individual well.

Situation. The School lies in a wooded valley on the site of a Benedictine Monastery (founded 1,000 years ago) and a short distance from the picturesque village of Milton Abbas. The nearest towns are Blandford and Dorchester. The cam-

pus provides ample space for playing fields and a nine-hole Golf course.

Buildings. The two remaining buildings of the Monastery are the Great Abbey, which is now the School Chapel, and the Abbot's Hall around which a Georgian mansion was built by the Earl of Dorchester in 1770. Today these great buildings form a perfect partnership to fulfil the needs of a boarding school. Outside the mansion house, the modern facilities which are on a par with those of a much larger school including contemporary boarding houses, a Music school, Art Studio, Pottery, Technology/Computer building, 370-seat theatre, IT suite, farm, rifle range, all-weather pitch, indoor heated 25-metre pool, cricket pavilion, Design Technology centre and a new Library.

Organisation. There are five boarding houses. During the first year pupils are housed in a dormitory of up to 4. From the second year onwards the majority move into study-bedrooms for up to three occupants. In the Sixth Form pupils usually have single study-bedrooms. The School takes meals in the Abbot's Hall where the cafeteria service provides an informal atmosphere, but is well-disciplined.

Curriculum. All pupils follow a broad and balanced curriculum up to GCSE. A pupil is setted separately in most subjects, enabling him or her to work towards academic goals at a comfortable pace. Most GCSE subjects are taken over years 10 and 11. New Pupils wishing to enter the sixth form must have an interview with the Headmaster. The Sixth Form offers a range of academic courses which incorporate traditional A Levels, vocational BTECs and top-up GCSEs. Subjects available are: mathematics, further mathematics, physics, chemistry, biology, history, English Literature, French, Spanish, geography, religious studies, business studies, economics, art, photography, music, music technology, design and technology, communication and culture, drama; and the following BTECs: Hospitality, Countryside Management, Sport and Exercise Science and Equine Studies.

Music. Individual tuition is available in all instruments, and in singing. A strong tradition of choral singing supports worship in the Abbey. Ensembles of all sorts perform music in a notably wide variety of styles.

Clubs and Societies. A wide range of interests and activities are encouraged in free time.

Service Afternoons. *CCF, Duke of Edinburgh's Award and Community Service*: The School's thriving CCF contingent has Royal Navy, Army and Royal Air Force sections, and enjoys close links with service establishments in the area. There are regular camps in the holidays, as well as expeditions at home and abroad. Most weekends offer an opportunity for a pupil to choose from caving, climbing, sailing, windsurfing and canoeing. In their first year in school, pupils undertake a range of activities every Wednesday afternoon, designed to broaden their spectrum of interest. Activities include: helping on the school farm, mountain biking, woodland studies, anti-bullying workshops, social education and cultural and art trips. All pupils are enrolled in the Duke of Edinburgh's Award Scheme, starting at the end of their second year in the school. Community service, with its links to local community based projects, and the expanding school farm, is the alternative to CCF. These activities positively support our aspiration to become a member of the Round Square organisation and form the pillars of the Round Square IDEALS (Internationalism, Democracy, Environment, Adventure, Leadership, Service).

Games. Michaelmas Term: Rugby, Football and Hockey. Lent Term: Hockey, Netball, Lacrosse and Cross-Country. Summer Term: Cricket, Athletics, Dinghy Sailing and Racing in Portland Harbour, Tennis and Rounders. All year round: Swimming, Squash, Rifle Shooting, Basketball, Golf, Polo, Fencing, Riding, Canoeing and Clay Pigeon Shooting.

Admission. The flexible curriculum and the small size of classes enable the school to cater effectively for a wide spread of ability. A few qualify through the Scholarship Examination held during the Lent Term. The majority sit the Common Entrance Examination in June for entry in the following Autumn Term. Those not prepared for Common Entrance sit the School's own entry papers in Maths and English. An average of 50% in the Common Entrance ensures a place but the School is also prepared to consider a few candidates who seem unlikely to reach this standard because their academic progress has been uneven. Sixth Form assessment day in Lent Term.

Fees per term (2014–2015). Boarding £10,690, Day £5,495.

Scholarships. Several Scholarships are awarded annually: Academic scholarships (held during the Lent Term); Music, Drama, Art, DT, Sailing and Sport scholarships (held during the Lent Term). Candidates must be under 14 on 1 September. Scholarships also awarded at Sixth Form entry level. Full particulars from the Admissions Office. Bursaries may also be considered in cases of need.

Charitable status. The Council of Milton Abbey School Limited is a Registered Charity, number 306318. It is a charitable Trust for secondary education.

Newcastle School for Boys

Senior School:
34 The Grove, Gosforth, Newcastle-upon-Tyne NE3 1NH
Tel: 0191 255 9300
Fax: 0191 213 0973
email: senioroffice@newcastleschool.co.uk

Junior School:
30 West Avenue, Gosforth, Newcastle-upon-Tyne NE3 4ES
Tel: 0191 255 9300
Fax: 0191 213 1105
email: junioroffice@newcastleschool.co.uk

website : www.newcastleschool.co.uk

Chairman of Governors: Dr N Lloyd-Jones, MBBS, MRCGP, LLB, LLM

Headmaster: **D J Tickner**, BA, MEd

Deputy Head: G Hallam, BSc

Deputy Head: A Newman, BA

Head of Sixth Form: Mrs S Rourke

Head of Juniors: S Asker, BA

Head of Infants: Mrs S G P Woosnam, BEd

Bursar: Mrs S Collis, ACA

Age Range. 3–18.
Number of Boys. 400.
Fees per term (2014–2015). £2,630 (Reception), £3,095 (Years 1–2), £3,190 (Years 3–6), £3,910 (Year 7 and above).

Newcastle School for Boys is now established as the only independent school in the north east providing continuous education for boys from ages 3 to 18. Situated on three sites in Gosforth, Newcastle-upon-Tyne, the Senior School site on The Grove covers 5 acres of playing fields and buildings that currently house Years 7 to 13. Our Junior School is housed on nearby sites on West Avenue (Juniors) and North Avenue (Infants). The School currently has 380 pupils on role from Nursery to Year 13.

The academic curriculum starts in the Infants and provides boys with opportunities for stretch and challenge from the outset. This leads through the Juniors to GCSE and A Level qualifications in a wide range of disciplines at the Senior School.

Pastoral care is outstanding throughout the school and boys receive plenty of individual attention so that they grow in confidence and independence.

Newcastle School for Boys believes strongly in enhancing learning beyond the classroom and runs an extensive trips and visits programme with great emphasis being placed on this in the junior and infant departments. Residential and day visits are offered to all pupils from age 5 onwards and culminate in major overseas trips and Duke of Edinburgh's Gold Award expeditions in the Sixth Form.

Senior School. The Senior School starts at Year 7 (11+) and runs through to Year 13 (18+).

We generally run two classes per year group and offer an enhanced curriculum leading up to GCSE, where most boys sit 10 subjects. The Senior School provides an extensive co-curricular programme of music, drama and a wide range of sports, including a number of major overseas trips. The School enhances its sporting provision through the use of a number of excellent local facilities including at South Northumberland Cricket Club and Northern Rugby Club.

Sixth Form. The School has established a new Sixth Form offering students a wide choice from a traditional AS and A Level structure. The Sixth Form provides the learning and support the boys need to achieve their best possible academic and personal outcomes.

Entrance and Scholarship Examinations are offered in January for boys entering Year 7 (11+), Year 9 (13+) and Year 12 (16+). Entry at other points is possible following a full academic assessment and interview.

Junior School. The well-established Nursery and Infant Department is housed in spacious accommodation to the west of Gosforth High Street and lays the foundations for everything which is to follow. A happy and safe environment is provided, where self-esteem and self-confidence are paramount. Throughout the Foundation Stage and Key Stage 1, the curriculum is a blend of the traditional and the innovative, and is designed to balance the need for adventure and fun, while maintaining progress in numeracy and literacy.

Breakfast club and after-school clubs and activities provide full 'wrap-around' care,

In the Junior Department (Years 3–6), the learning environment is tailored to the needs of the younger boys, taking into account their energy and enthusiasm for challenge and discovery. The boys are provided with opportunities to develop their individual academic talents and to pursue their creative goals. Excellence is also pursued in the sporting arena where boys have opportunities including soccer, rugby, cricket, golf and fencing.

Regular drama performances and musical productions encourage teamwork and build confidence from an early age.

Charitable status. Newcastle School for Boys is a Registered Charity, number 503975.

North Cestrian Grammar School

Dunham Road, Altrincham, Cheshire WA14 4AJ
Tel: 0161 928 1856
Fax: 0161 929 8657
email: office@ncgs.co.uk
website: www.ncgs.co.uk

North Cestrian Grammar School was founded in 1951 to provide independent grammar school education for boys aged 11–16 with a co-educational Sixth Form. Since September 2008 the School has been fully co-educational.

As befits a School of 300 pupils attention to the individual is a reality, not an empty phrase. Over the years the School has acquired an enviable reputation for developing confidence and getting the best out of each child so that today's pupils come not only from the locality but from as far afield as North Manchester, Warrington, Macclesfield and the heart of rural Cheshire.

Board of Governors:
Chairman: Mr I T Parrott

Mr N Bailey	Mr J-P Glaskie
Mr T D Brown	Mr P F Morton (*Emeritus*)
Mr R Burdge	Mr J H Moss
Mr D J Common	Dr A Pocklington
Mr P Dicker	Mr C J Smart
Mr J Finley	Mrs R Smart
Mrs S Forster	

Headmaster: **Mr L R Bergin**, BA

Deputy Head/Director of Teaching and Learning: Mr M Bell, BSc

Pastoral Director: Mr A Brown, BA

Assistant Staff:

Mrs C Cooper, BA	Mr P R Robinson BSc
Mrs H L Dempsey, MEd	Mrs E Holmes BSc
Mrs C Collins, BA	Mr P R Whittaker, BSc
Miss E Demeur, BA	Mr T E O Wilson, BSc
Miss B A Ross, BA	Mr S M Cruxton, BA
Mrs L P Cove BA	Mrs P L Patterson, BSc
Miss L Mallorie, BSc	Mr P S Stobbs, BA
Mr S A D Mills, BA	Mr A C Boswell, BA
Mr M Whittam, BA	Miss J M E Connell, BA
Mrs L Facchin, BA	Mrs G Morrison, BMus
Ms E Nixon, BA	Miss K L Allison, BSc
Mr A P Heslop, BA	Miss H Moss, BSc
Mrs E M A Klutz, BSc	

Learning Support Team:
Mrs R Clifford, BSc, MEd
Miss L Mallorie, BSc, Adv SEN, CCET
Mrs B Robson, MEd, TEFL, Dip SpLD, AMBDA

Bursar: Mrs M Ratcliffe, AAT, CIMA
Finance Officer: Mrs C Thompson
Headmaster's PA: Mrs S M Roby
Receptionist/Admin Assistant: Mrs S Williams
External Examinations Officer/Database Manager: Mrs V Rogerson
Librarian: Mrs Y Stevenson
Network/School Technicians: Mr W D Parker, Mr M Sorbie
Premises Officer: Mr P Bloomfield

Facilities. The School is housed in fine modern buildings constructed around an imposing Victorian mansion. Continuing investment in school facilities has provided excellent teaching accommodation including an imposing Library, school hall, technology wing and ICT suites. Recent additions include a six-laboratory science block opened at Easter 2010 and since then a Drama Studio, Sixth Form Common Room, Learning Support Centre and a Food Technology facility. Art has special provision for ceramics and photography and there are specialist suites for most departments. In addition to a well-equipped and spacious sports hall with dance studio and fitness centre, the 20-acre sports grounds provide pitches for soccer, hockey and cricket, alongside an athletics track and tennis courts and netball facilities.

Academic. The School aims to provide a balanced curriculum offering each pupil a broad range of subjects. High standards of academic work are expected with an emphasis on individual guidance. The majority of pupils are prepared for 9 GCSEs, but a small group are offered the chance to follow a restricted curriculum of 7 subjects within small teaching sets and with additional learning support. There is a wide range A Levels, to cater for a diverse range of interests and abilities. Most students secure places at their choice of university.

Key Stage 3 pupils are taught in parallel classes. Specialist dyslexia and support staff are available to give individual assistance by private arrangement and all new students are screened to flag up any potential for Learning Support needs. From Year 10 there is some streaming, based upon ability in Maths and English, with a view to accelerating the pace for the most able whilst providing smaller teaching groups for those who need most attention. There is also a comprehensive PSHE Programme.

North Cestrian has a reputation for individual support and personal development in both academic and social terms and "added value" is closely monitored through the use of NFER assessment. The work of the learning support team and the extensive support given to those with dyslexia and other Learning Disadvantages or Disabilities has been recognised both statistically and in the School's most recent ISI inspection report (Sept 2013).

Extra-Curricular Activity. A wide range of extra-curricular activities aims to allow each pupil to excel in some area, thus building his or her confidence and self-esteem. North Cestrian has a strong sporting tradition and there is an extensive programme of inter-school fixtures. National and county honours have been gained in hockey, athletics, swimming, football and basketball. Regular holidays are offered both in Britain and abroad, from the snowy Alpine peaks to the plains of India. The Languages Department conducts a series of annual foreign visits to strengthen European awareness. The Duke of Edinburgh's Award Scheme is well supported and there is a series of outdoor pursuit trips for younger pupils. All pupils take part in weekly enrichment activities including orienteering, "wild cooking" and farming. Public speaking, board games, music, drama and an extensive charity programme are a reflection of the care taken to oversee the development of the whole pupil in a friendly and supportive family atmosphere.

Admission. There is a competitive examination in February for entry at 11+. Applications for other years are considered at any time and Sixth Form offers are made on the basis of predicted GCSE grades.

Bursaries. Bursaries based upon family income are made at the discretion of the Governors. Significant scholarships may be available for students of exceptional ability.

Fees per term (2014–2015). £3,142 (£9,426 per annum).

Location. The School is situated conveniently close to central Altrincham and there are few Manchester or Cheshire schools so easily accessible by either public or private transport. Ideally placed for mainline trains and buses which converge on Altrincham, the Metrolink provides a rapid link and regular service from Central Manchester whilst outlying districts are served by school coaches. Travel by car is easy as the School lies close to the A56 and within two miles of Junction 7/8 on the M56.

Further Information. A School Prospectus, Sixth Form Brochure and GCSE Options Booklet are available on the website or application to the School Office. Parents and their children are welcome at a number of Open Events, but alternative arrangements for a personal interview, taster day and tour of the School at any reasonable time can be made through the Office.

Charitable status. North Cestrian Grammar School is a Registered Charity, number 525925. It exists for the purpose of educating children.

Ockbrook School
Derby

The Settlement, Ockbrook, Derbyshire DE72 3RJ

Tel:	01332 673532
Fax:	01332 665184
email:	enquiries@ockbrooksch.co.uk
website:	www.ockbrooksch.co.uk

Twitter: @ockbrooksch
Facebook: /Ockbrook-School

Motto: *In Christo Omnia Possum*
Founded in 1799.

Independent Day and Boarding School for boys and girls aged 2–18. Phasing co-education in throughout Senior Department from September 2013 with full co-education from 2020. Member of The Society of Heads, IAPS and AGBIS.

Governing Body:
Chair of Governors: Mrs A Redgate, LLB
Deputy Chair: Mr J Luke
Revd D Howarth, BA Hons
Dr G Lamming, FRCOG
Dr V Poultney, MEd
Mr C Purcell, BA Hons, MCIPR
Mrs M Ralph, MEd, MCollP
Mrs G Taylor, FCA
Ms H Waters-Marsh

Clerk to the Governors: Mrs J Buckley

Leadership Team:

Headmaster: **Mr T Brooksby**, BEd Crewe & Alsager, NPQH

Head of Primary & Music Coordinator: Mrs S Worthington, BA Exeter
Deputy Head: Mrs H Springall, BA Newcastle, MA Open, NPQH
Deputy Head of Primary & ICT Coordinator: Mr R Beach, BA Sussex
Head of Lower (Years 7–10): Mrs S Wood, BA Hull
Head of Upper [Years 11–13] & Head of Science: Mrs J Whitaker, MSc Leicester
Head of Achievement and Progress: Mr A Walsh, BA Huddersfield

Early Years:
Mrs S Taylor, BA Scarborough (*Head of Early Years, EY SpLD*)
Mrs C McBeth, BEd MSc Loughborough

Primary Department:
Mrs S Breedon, BA Nottingham (*English Coordinator*)
Mrs N Gajic, BA Loughborough
Mrs L Ireland, BEd Derby (*PSHCE Coordinator*)
Mrs M Lamell, BA Newcastle (*Drama*)
Mrs H Marsden , BEd Derby (*History, Geography & RS Coordinator*)
Mrs K Morris, BA Norwich School of Art & Design (*Art, DT Coordinator*)
Mrs J Mullineux, BEd Bedford College (*Physical Education, Dance, Humanities*)
Mrs B Thornton, BEd Derby (*Science Coordinator*)
Mrs M Watkins, BA Leeds (*French*)
Mr D Williams, BEd Bangor (*PE Coordinator*)
Mrs W Wilton, BPhil, MEd Nottingham
Mrs P Ward, CertEd Kesteven

Senior Department:
Mrs L Archibald, BA Leeds (*Food Technology & Head of Careers*)
Mrs S Barclay, BEd Bedford (*SEND*)
Mrs F Birkbeck, BA Edinburgh, MEd (*Psychology*)
Dr E Burguin, BSc Sheffield, PhD York (*Languages*)
Ms K Chetwin, BSc London, BA Nottingham (*Science & Business Studies*)
Ms K Cleland, MA Glasgow (*English*)
Mrs L Coggle, BSc Sheffield (*Mathematics & Head of Boarding*)
Mrs F Faulkner, BSc Newcastle (*ICT*)
Mrs C Fletcher-Eton, BSc Loughborough (*Religious Studies*)

Mr S Gilbert, BSc Sheffield (*Mathematics & Duke of Edinburgh's Award*)
Mr N Gupta, BSc MAPSE Leicester (*Physics & Assistant Head of Sixth Form*)
Mrs H Killip, BEd Sheffield (*Food Technology, Technology*)
Mrs J McGahey, BA Leeds (*Fine Art, Art & Design, Art Textiles*)
Mr J McNaughton, MA Cambridge (*Geography*)
Mrs E Marsh, BSc Leeds (*Physics, Sciences*)
Mr G Maskalick, BA MA Carnegie USA, CT ABRSM (*Music*)
Mrs S Mitchell, BA Hull (*English*)
Mrs K Moorhouse, BSc Loughborough (*Physical Education, Dance*)
Mrs A M Newton, BSc Essex (*Mathematics*)
Mrs R O'Reilly, BA Liverpool (*Physical Education, Dance*)
Mrs S Price, BSc York (*Chemistry/Sciences*)
Miss A Renow, BA Leicester, MEd Nottingham (*History*)
Mrs C Saunders, BEd Dartford (*Humanities*)
Mrs S West, BA Birmingham (*Drama*)

Support Staff:
Head Teacher's PA: Mrs C Derbyshire
Business Manager: Mr S Malkin
Finance Manager: Mrs E Green
Operations Manager: Mrs J Buckley
Registrar: Mrs J Sheldon
Administrator: Mrs N Brierley
Admin Apprentice: Miss L Lambord
Network Manager: Mr A Crowter

Boarding Houses Staff:

Mrs M Cooper	Mrs C Horspool
Mrs S Cooper	Miss A McComb
Mrs K Fisher	Mrs C Rigby
Mrs R Gascoigne	Miss M Truman
Nurse W Holmes, EN	

Classroom Assistants:

Mrs C Bowers	Mrs L Holmes, BTEC
Mrs S Cooper, Cert EYP	Mrs A Kenyon, NNEB
Mrs J Federici	Mrs J Leighton, NNEB
Miss K Fisher, NNEB	Mrs C Newby, BSc
Mrs J Harvey	Mrs M Shawcross
Mrs S Hawksworth, NNEB	Mrs J Sheldon
Mrs A-M Heaps	

Playground Supervisor: Mrs E Nason

Nurse: Mrs L Tanser, RN

Visiting Music Teachers:
Mrs J Ford, LGSM, BA Hons Birmingham (*Piano & Harp*)
Mrs D Hensler, MA Hons Music, BA Hons Music Manchester (*Piano*)
Mr P Marshall, ABRSM (*Voice*)
Mrs A Negus, University of Performing Arts, Stuttgart (*Woodwind*)
Mr J Rippingale, BPA Leeds (*Guitar*)
Miss L Ryder, GMus RNCM (*Woodwind*)

Grounds & Maintenance:
Mr D Bailey
Mr P Davis-Wells
Mr A White

Technicians:
Mrs S Cullen, BSc (*Combined Science*)
Mrs S Miller, BSc (*Biology and Geography*)
Miss V Betesta

Librarian: Mrs C Purcell, BSc, MSc

Situation. Situated in the heart of the Midlands, Ockbrook School lies equidistant between the historic towns of

Derby and Nottingham and is easily accessible from the motorway network, rail and air transport. The School is set in a superb rural position overlooking the Trent Valley and it is surrounded by its own estate including landscaped gardens, grounds, playing fields and farmland. This setting and the high standard of facilities within it provide an excellent environment for learning …free from urban noise and distractions.

Pupils. There are c400 pupils, girls aged 2–18 and boys aged 2–12, who are divided between the Primary Department (age 2–11) and Senior Department (age 11–18). We are currently in the process of phasing in co-education in the Senior Department which commenced with Year 7 entry in September 2013. The whole school will be fully co-educational by 2020. For the time being, female-only boarders are accepted from the age of 11 years for entry into Year 7 or above.

Ethos. We aim to develop individual potential and self worth through stimulating and positive relationships and through an understanding of Christian values so that our pupils are prepared for the changes they will face in their future lives. We believe that education should be a partnership between School, pupils and parents. To this end we provide comprehensive feedback on progress in the classroom and welcome family and friends at our extra-curricular drama productions, concerts, sports events, open door days and acts of worship.

Curriculum.

Primary Department:

Early Years (Ages 2–5). A dynamic programme of language, numeracy and scientific activities provide a secure foundation for later conceptual development.

Key Stage 1 (Years 1 & 2). The core subjects of Mathematics, Science and English are covered in addition to nine other subject areas including French and Information Communications Technology.

Key Stage 2 (Years 3–6). Study for the core of subjects continues with additional experience in nine other subjects including Dance, Drama and Gymnastics.

Teachers' assessments are carried out throughout both Key Stages and form the basis of internal assessment procedures for progression through to the Senior Department at 11+.

Senior Department:

Lower School (Years 7–9). Pupils study the core subjects and a broad range of additional subjects including ICT, French, Drama and PSHCE (Personal, Social, Health & Citizenship Education). From Year 9 students follow IGCSE courses in Mathematics, English, Music and the three sciences and can study German and Spanish in addition to French.

Upper School (Years 10–11). At GCSE level all pupils study Mathematics, English Language and English Literature, plus additional subjects; there is a wide range of options.

Sixth Form. Students usually study for 4 AS Levels in the Lower Sixth and proceed to 3 A2 subjects in the Upper Sixth. A wide range of subjects is available and students can opt to do an additional EPQ. Great emphasis is placed on the development of Life Skills which help to develop the competencies so necessary for adult life, whilst adding to the breadth of study. The vast majority of pupils leaving the Sixth Form proceed to higher education, including Oxbridge.

Sport. As well as the core PE subjects the school has a strong tradition in sport, i.e. athletics, cross-country, netball, swimming and rounders etc. A rapidly expanding programme of outdoor pursuits is also available for pupils which includes sailing, water skiing and golf. Teams of various ages, in most sports, have full fixture lists with neighbouring schools and the School is proud of its County and National representatives. We are also a member of the Sports Leaders Award Scheme.

Activities. The Duke of Edinburgh's Award Scheme is available to pupils over the age of 14, together with a wide range of trips and outdoor holidays, walking, canoeing and skiing. Other activities include Young Enterprise, Wilderness Expertise, Community service, chess, debating, and numerous other clubs or societies. A School Holiday Club also operates from the School.

Music and Drama. Many pupils learn musical instruments and a large number play to a high standard. Opportunities are provided by the Primary and Senior choirs, orchestras, chamber choir, strings group, and wind band. Performance venues include Westminster Abbey, Manchester, Derby and Barcelona Cathedrals, Ojab-Haus Aigen, Salzburg, Salzburg Cathedral, Pfarrkirche Bad Ischl Salzburg and Chatsworth House, Derbyshire. There is a wide range of dramatic productions each year providing as many pupils as possible with the chance of developing their dramatic talents.

Art and Design & Technology. Great emphasis is given to the development of creative talent both as academic subjects and interests. Out-of-class involvement is strongly encouraged.

Fees per term (2014–2015). Tuition: £2,548–£3,755. Boarding (in addition to tuition fees): Weekly £2,185, Full £3,380.

Admission. *Primary Department*: Entry is decided as a result of a combination of interview, assessment day and school report (if applicable).

Senior Department: Entry is decided as a result of a combination of interview, assessment, school report and if necessary an entrance examination held throughout the year and in January for Year 7 and Year 12.

Sixth Form: Entry is decided as a result of a combination of interview, school report, predicted GCSE grades and ultimately a good performance in the GCSE examinations.

Scholarships and Bursaries. Scholarships are available for Academia, Sport, Art, Drama and Music (including voice) for Year 7 and Sixth Form entry. A Head Teacher's Award is also available for all-round achievement. Bursary applications are considered by way of a full means test which may also include a home visit assessment. Full details are available from the Registrar, Mrs J Sheldon, email: enquiries@ockbrooksch.co.uk.

School Prospectus. A prospectus and registration details may be obtained from the Registrar, details as above, or on the school website: www.ockbrooksch.co.uk. Parents are encouraged to visit the School and appointments may be made by contacting the Registrar.

Charitable status. Ockbrook School is a Registered Charity, number 251211.

Oswestry School

Upper Brook Street, Oswestry, Shropshire SY11 2TL

Tel: 01691 655711

Fax: 01691 671194

email: enquiries@oswestryschool.org.uk

website: www.oswestryschool.org.uk

Motto: '*We learn not for school but for life.*'

Oswestry School, founded in 1407, is one of the oldest non-denominational schools in England. The School is registered as a Charitable Trust and administered by a Board of Governors which is in membership of the Association of Governing Bodies of Independent Schools.

Governing Board:

Chairman: Mr P T Wilcox-Jones

Vice-Chairman: Mr T Moore-Bridger

Mrs E Channon	Mr A Moss
Mr J Edwards	Mr M Symonds
Mr D Evison	The Revd S G Thorburn
Mr J Hancock	Mrs J Warner
Mrs E Hill-Molenaar	Mr B Welti
Miss B Y Gull	

Headmaster: Mr J P Noad, BSc

Deputy Head (Academic): Mr T Jefferis, MSc, BSc, PGCE

Deputy Head (Pastoral): Ms S Nancini, BA Manchester, PGCE, FAHE

Oswestry School is a co-educational day and boarding school for pupils aged 4 to 18. Pupils are taught on two closely situated sites. The Prep Department, Bellan House, is situated in the town centre a short walk from the Senior School. The Senior School, located on the outskirts of the town, caters for First Form to Upper Sixth, ages 11 to 18, both day and boarding. Oswestry School moved to its present site in 1776, and its beautiful grounds and playing fields now occupy a site of 50 acres.

Curriculum. The School aims to provide a broad general education up to GCSE with more specialised subjects in the Sixth Form. At present, the following subjects are taught to AS/A2 Level: Art, Biology, Business Studies, Chemistry, Design Technology, English Literature, Economics, French, Geography, History, ICT, Mathematics and Further Mathematics, Music, Physics, Psychology, Religious Studies, Spanish, Sports and Physical Education. The IGCSE programme consists of an intensive one-year course of study for both boys and girls between the ages of 15 and 17. Successful completion of the course is excellent preparation for Sixth Form study. All pupils, supported and encouraged by an excellent team of staff, are expected to make the most of their abilities. The size of the School helps Oswestry achieve its ethos and pupils are bright, energetic, confident and, above all, happy. The School is large enough to grant pupils a feeling of independence and to house many superb facilities, but small enough for each pupil to be well known and make a significant contribution to the School. A combination of the School's size and a high teacher-per-student ratio allows Oswestry to give personalised and consistent care and attention, and to monitor and motivate pupils as they make academic and personal progress. The School is extremely proud of the excellent academic results achieved given its non-selective admission process; A Levels over recent years have had a 97–100% pass rate and around 90% of GCSE grades were A*–C.

Boarders. Boarders are accommodated in three comfortable boarding houses on the School site, and are cared for by attentive and dedicated house staff. Each boarding house has a resident Houseparent and Assistant Houseparents, and every pupil benefits from a high level of pastoral care. Wi-Fi throughout the School site makes it easy for pupils to stay in touch with home. The spacious, modern dining hall provides three hot meals a day; food is served as a buffet selection and includes fresh vegetables, fruit and desserts and there is plenty of variety to ensure all diets are catered for. In addition to the academic programme, a wide range of weekend activities is arranged for the boarding pupils by members of the teaching staff.

School Chapel. The School Chapel plays an important part in the life of the School and the Chaplain is central to the pastoral structure of the School.

Games. The School has a strong tradition of participation in sports. Extensive playing fields, a new artificial pitch, gymnasium, netball/tennis courts and a twenty-metre heated indoor swimming pool are some of the sporting environments at Oswestry.

Out of School Activities. There is a wide range of extra-curricular activities and all pupils are encouraged to join at least two clubs. The clubs and extra-curricular activities on offer are designed to appeal to pupils of various ages and interests. The inclusion of such a programme serves to further personal development and leadership skills. Included are such diverse activities as sailing, chess, photography, horse riding, rock climbing, self-defence, personal fitness, badminton and mountain biking. After-School activities and clubs vary each term but there is always a wide variety of activities to choose from.

CCF and Community Service. There is an active CCF contingent, membership of which is voluntary after two years' service; pupils may also pursue the Duke of Edinburgh's Award Scheme. Both schemes offer opportunities to develop leadership skills, self-reliance and responsibility.

Admissions. Pupils from 4+ are welcome to apply for entry to the Prep Department at any time, however, as places are limited, early registration is advised. Boys and girls are accepted into the Senior School from the age of 11, although applications are always considered for entry up to Fourth Form and for Sixth Form. Scholarships are available at 9+, 11+, 13+ and 16+.

Registration fee: £50.

Fees per term (2014–2015). Day Pupils: £2,560 (Reception), £2,640 (Years 1 & 2), £2,720 (Years 3 & 4), £3,110 (Years 5 & 6), £4,340 (First and Second Form), £4,610 (Third Form–Upper Sixth). Boarding: £7,360 (First–Third Form), £8,595 (Fourth Form–Upper Sixth). IGCSE Boarding Students: £9,240 (One-year course).

Scholarships. Academic, Art, Music and Sport scholarships are available at 11+, 13+ and 16+.

Further details of all these Scholarships are available from the Headmaster.

Reductions for Services Families. Generous awards are available for children of Services personnel (when the child is in full-time education).

Charitable status. Oswestry School is a Registered Charity, number 1079822.

Our Lady's Abingdon Senior School

Radley Road, Abingdon, Oxfordshire OX14 3PS

Tel:	01235 524658
Fax:	01235 535829
email:	office@olab.org.uk
website:	www.olab.org.uk
Twitter:	@OLAabingdon
Facebook:	/OLAabingdon

Motto: Age Quod Agis – "Whatever you do, do it well"

Founded in 1860 by Sister Clare Moore of the Sisters of Mercy, Our Lady's Abingdon (OLA) is an independent, Catholic day school, for boys and girls aged 3–18.

Board of Governors:
Chairman: Mr E McCabe, MA Oxon, MBA

Governors:
Mr T Ayling MA Oxon
Mr M Barber, MA Oxon, MSc
Dr A Colbrook, BSc, PhD
Mr J Cunliffe, MA Oxon
Mrs A Freeman, BEd
Mr D Heavens
Father J McGrath, STB, MA
Mr T Prosser, BSc, MSc, MBA, FIFireE
Mrs H Ronaldson
Ms J Shillaker, MA, LIM
Mrs M Shinkwin, BA, MA Ed, NPQH
Mr A Sullivan
Mr I Yorston, MA

Bursar & Clerk to the Governors: Mr S Hughes, BA Hons

Principal: **Mr Stephen Oliver**, BA, MLitt

Vice Principal: Miss B Habayeb, MSc, PGCE

Deputy Head: Mr N Hathaway, BA Hons, PGCE, PGDipEd

Director of Studies: Mrs S Wales, BA Oxon, PGCE

Sixth Form Tutor: Mr N Hathaway, BA Hons, PGCE, PGDipEd
Year 11 Tutor: Mrs A Okeke, BSc Hons, MSc, PGCE
Year 10 Tutor: Mr R Ford, BSc, PGCE
Year 9 Tutor: Mr L Allen, BSc, PGCE
Year 8 Tutor: Mr P Hudson, BSc Hons, PGCE
Year 7 Tutor: Miss F Gunn, LLB Hons, PGCE, MA

Heads of Departments:
Art: Mrs H Holden, BA Hons, MSt, PGCE
Business Studies: Mrs J Acutt, BA Hons, PGCE
Careers: Mrs A Varney, BEd, CertEd
Classics: Miss P Smith, BA Hons Oxon
Design & Technology: Mr C Sephton, MSc, PGCE
Drama: Dr E Lawson, BA Hons, MA, PhD Loughborough
Economics: Mrs W Meigh, BEd
English: Miss M Hemingway, BA Hons, PGCE
Food Technology: Mrs H Black, BA Hons, PGCE
Geography: Mr A Jackson, BA, MSc, PGCE
History: Mrs J Mead, BA Hons, PGCE, MA
Information Technology: Miss B Habayeb, MSc, PGCE
Learning Support: Mrs L Barr, MSt, MA, BA, PGCE
Mathematics: Mr R Ford, BSc, PGCE
Modern Languages: Mrs C Friend, MA Hons Oxon, MA, PGCE
Music: Dr P Foster, BA Hons, MMus, PhD Reading, PGCE
Physical Education: Mrs M Barnett, BA Hons, QTS & Mr E Barnett, BA Hons, QTS
PSHE: Mr T Carroll, BSc, SSTQ
Psychology: Mrs A Beasley, MA Hons, PGCE
Religious Studies: Mr D Willcock, MA Oxon
Science: Mr P Hudson, BSc Hons, PGCE
Textiles: Mrs K Rowe, CertEd

Admissions Registrar: Mrs F Russell

OLA offers outstanding pastoral care and a wide range of academic and extra-curricular activities, ensuring that pupils are confident, engaged and excited about their next steps in life.

Small class sizes allow staff to get to know every single pupil, giving them the support and encouragement they need to fulfil their academic and personal potential.

The school encourages independence of thought and responsibility for one's own learning and behaviour. OLA, a Christian school in the Catholic tradition, welcomes pupils of all faiths and none, who wish to share its ideals and expectations.

The school received an excellent Inspection Report in 2010, which noted in particular that:

"*Pupils achieve excellent results in a range of extra-curricular activities, especially in sport.*

Pupils make exceptional progress in their academic studies in relation to their ability profile.

Pupils' spiritual, moral, social and cultural development is excellent.

The outstanding pastoral care does much to ensure their safeguarding, and to foster their personal development and academic achievement."

Numbers. There are 384 pupils aged 11–18 in the Senior school and 120 pupils aged 3–11 in the Junior section, which is on the same site under its own headmaster, Brendan O'Neill. (*See Junior School entry in IAPS section.*)

Facilities and Buildings. Bright, spacious classrooms and an excellent library provide a pleasant ambience conducive to study and learning. The grounds surround both buildings, an attractive setting of lawns, flowerbeds and trees in which the pupils can relax during breaks. Sports facilities include a number of tennis courts, a sports hall with fitness room, hockey and athletics provision and a 25-metre indoor swimming pool. It has benefited recently from the creation of a new Design & Technology Centre, with other recent building projects including an auditorium and library, the latest in ICT equipment, an extended Art department and additional Science laboratories. The Music department benefits from new facilities to aid composition and to support the wide variety of instruments taught in the school.

Curriculum. The school teaches a balanced range of subjects both academic and practical during the first three years. Latin is a core subject. Pupils take 9 or 10 subjects at GCSE, including English, Mathematics, Science, Religious Studies and two modern languages. Options are chosen from the Humanities to Classics and Physical Education. Four subjects are studied in the Lower Sixth at AS, continuing with three at A2. The great majority of the Sixth Form go on to Higher Education, but some have also succeeded in gaining places on highly competitive professional placement programmes. There is also support for Special Educational Needs, and for pupils for whom English is not their mother tongue.

Extra-curricular activities. The school provides a wide programme of extra-curricular activities including drama, music, art, debating and many forms of sport. Rowing and sailing are particularly popular. Buses run later on three evenings of the week to accommodate these activities and to allow for supervised homework. There is also a strong commitment to local community schemes and an impressive record in the Duke of Edinburgh's Award Scheme and Young Enterprise. In both 2011 and 2012 the OLA Young Enterprise group won the award for Best Business Plan.

In 2008 and 2011 OLA was one of only 508 schools to be accredited with the Department for Education's International School Award for the "outstanding work done by the staff and pupils". The school has gained the Eco-Schools Silver Award and is working towards the "Green Flag".

Fees per term (2014–2015). £4,348.

Admission. Through the school's own Entrance Examination at 11 and 13; Pupils require at least 5 GCSEs Grade B for entry at Sixth Form level. Pupils interested in entering the Sixth Form for whom English is a second language must in addition have achieved a minimum level of 6.5 in IELTS for each category. Pupils may join in any year if a place is available.

Pupils may apply for Scholarships for entry to Year 7, Year 9 and the Sixth Form. Candidates may also apply for Bursaries which are awarded at the discretion of the Governors.

Charitable status. Our Lady's Abingdon Trustees Limited is a Registered Charity, number 1120372, and a Company Limited by Guarantee, registered in England and Wales, number 6269288.

The Peterborough School
A Woodard School

Thorpe Road, Peterborough PE3 6AP
Tel: 01733 343357
            Bursar: 01733 355720
Fax: 01733 355710
email: admin@thepeterboroughschool.co.uk
website: www.thepeterboroughschool.co.uk
Twitter: @PeterboroughSch

The Peterborough School is the City's only independent school with Nursery for boys and girls aged from 6 weeks to 18 years. Situated in beautiful surroundings in the heart of Peterborough, the School enjoys excellent road and rail links. The School is a member of the Woodard Corporation, the largest group of Church of England Schools in England and Wales.

School Council:
Chairman: Ms L Ayres, LLB
Mrs A Arculus, MA Hons
Mr C Beard
Mrs P Dalgliesh
Mrs L Frisby
Mrs K Hart, BA Hons
The Revd R Hemingray, LLB
Prof C J Howe, MA, DPhil, FLS
Mrs J M Mark, BA Hons
Mr S G Menon, MSc, MTech
Mrs E Payne
The Revd Canon B Ruddock
Mr D Sandbach, BA, FCA, D Ch A
Mr P Southern, FRICS
Dr J S Thompson, LMSSA, MBBS, DRCOG
The Senior Provost, The Woodard Corporation
The Rt Revd Robert Ladds, Assistant Provost, The Woodard Corporation

Head: **Mr A Meadows**, BSc Hons Manchester, NPQH

Deputy Headmaster: Mr R Cameron, BA Hons Southampton
Head of the Preparatory School: Mrs A-M Elding, MA OU, BEd Hons Derby
Head of Pastoral Care: Mrs E Rivers, BSc Hons London
Chaplain: Revd I Watts, BA Hons Hull

Staff:
Miss H Adams, BSc Hons (*Mathematics*)
Mrs L Andrew, BEd Hons (*Preparatory*)
Mr P Baldwin, BA Hons (*Preparatory*)
Mrs R Bierton, BA Hons (*Head of Individual Learning*)
Mr K Bingham, BA Hons (*Preparatory*)
Mrs L Boyle, BA, Cert EYP (*Preparatory*)
Mr C Brocklesby, BA Hons (*Geography*)
Mrs K Brocklesby, BSc Nottingham (*Mathematics*)
Mrs K A Brown, MA Oxon (*Mathematics*)
Mrs L Cade-Stewart, BA Hons Oxon (*Latin*)
Miss Z Chappell, BA Hons Cantab (*Preparatory*)
Miss S M Clarkson, BA Hons Cantab (*History*)
Miss J Clifford, BSc Hons (*Dance*)
Mr G Cloke, BSc Hons (*Preparatory*)
Mrs L Coles, BA Hons (*French, Head of Sixth Form*)
Mrs C Coulson, MSc, BA Hons (*Economics, Business Studies, Careers*)
Mrs K Davis, BSc Hons (*Chemistry, Head of Key Stage 3*)
Mrs R Ditcher, BSc Hons (*Preparatory*)
Ms T Doyle, MNATD (*Director of Creative Arts*)
Mrs J Evans, Licence (*French*)
Dr L Fox-Clipsham, BSc, PhD (*Science*)
Mrs L Grinyer, BA Hons (*English*)
Mrs R Hampson, BA Hons (*Art, Textiles*)
Mr A Harwin, BA Hons (*Art*)
Mr S Holbird, BA Hons, MSc (*Graphic Products*)
Mr A Jackson, BA Hons (*German*)
Miss C Johnson, BSc Hons (*Biology*)
Mr C King, BSc Hons, CMath, MIMA (*Mathematics*)
Mr S Law, BSc Hons (*Physics*)
Miss A Loffman, BA Hons (*Religious Education*)
Miss L McChlery, BEd (*Preparatory*)
Mrs L McClarnon, BEd Hons (*Preparatory*)
Mrs H McKillop, BA Hons (*Music*)
Mr C McManus, MA Ulster (*History*)
Mr J Marsden, BSc Hons (*Physical Education*)
Mrs G Mason, OND Hotel & Catering (*Food Technology & Preparatory Classroom Assistant*)
Miss R Mayle, BA Hons (*Geography*)
Miss R Morris, BA Hons (*Drama*)
Mr D Moxon, BSc Hons, MSc (*Psychology*)
Mrs L Parkinson, BA Hons (*Preparatory*)

Ms E Potbury, BA Hons (*French*)
Mrs A Quy, BSc Hons (*Preparatory*)
Mrs J Roberts, BA Hons (*English*)
Mr S Roberts, BA Hons (*Director of Sport*)
Ms S Robinson, BEd Hons (*Preparatory*)
Mr P Samuels, LGSM (*Speech & Drama*)
Mr P Schavier, Masters Degree (*German*)
Mrs N Scott, BA Hons (*English*)
Mrs M Silvester, BSc Hons (*Mathematics*)
Mrs A Skelton, BA Hons (*Preparatory*)
Miss J Smith, BSc Hons (*Physical Education, Head of Key Stage 4*)
Miss C Steward, BA Hons (*Preparatory*)
Miss E Symns, BSc Hons (*Physical Education*)
Mrs S Ward, BSc Hons, PGCE (*Biology*)
Mr M Webb, BSc Hons (*Computing & Digital Strategy*)

Music Department:
Mr J Crackle, BMus (*Flute*)
Mr J Cranfield, BA Hons (*Guitar*)
Mr S Hamper, Army School of Music (*Percussion*)
Mr G Haynes, BA Hons (*Choral Music*)
Mr M Jewkes (*Jazz Piano & Saxophone*)
Mrs M McAuliffe, Dip ABRSM (*Violin*)
Mrs R Ochala-Greenough, BMus Hons (*Singing*)
Mrs L Reid, MA Hons Oxon (*Choral Director/Singing*)
Miss E Smith BMus Hons (*Lower Strings*)
Mr I Stafford, BEd Hons (*Choir Master*)

Administrative Officers:
Bursar: Mr C Charlton, BA Hons
Head's PA: Mrs J Farrow
Marketing Manager/Registrar: Mrs L Pengelly
Development Manager/Assistant Registrar: Mrs I Zizza
Administration/HR Assistant: Mrs Z Vickers
Administrative Assistant: Miss E Nicholson
Accounts: Mrs J House BA Hons, Mrs R Forman
Domestic Bursar: Mrs Z Clark
Estate Manager: Mr D Thornton
Laboratory Technician: Mrs A E Albon, BSc OU
Computing: Mr D Helstrip, Mr S Crier
Food Technology Technician: Mrs V Tobin
LRC Manager: Mrs C Thomson
Receptionist: Mrs R Adcock

Teaching Assistant/After Care Supervisor: Mrs E Penniston
Teaching Assistants:
Mrs S Browne
Mrs K Clatworthy
Ms E Drew, BA Hons
Miss Z House
Mr L Jacobs
Miss A Weingaertner
Mr R Westbrook

Medical Staff:
Mrs M Doust, RGN (*Senior Matron*)
Mrs F Aylmore, BSc Hons (*Matron*)
Mrs M Lay, BSc Hons (*School Counsellor*)

Situation and Buildings. The School is located in beautiful secluded grounds, near the centre of Peterborough, 50 minutes by fast train from King's Cross and easily accessible by road from the A1, A14 and A47. The elegant Victorian house is the centre of a modern purpose-built complex of classrooms, laboratories, Music School, Art Block, Sixth Form Centre, Library and a modern ICT Suite. The new Sports Facility was completed in September 2012.

The Preparatory School. Boys and girls are admitted into the Reception Class from the age of 4+. The National Tests are taken at Key Stage One and Two. The whole range of Key Stage subjects is covered in addition to a variety of other subjects and activities. Some subjects are taught by specialist staff from the Senior School. There is emphasis on academic standards, good manners, Physical Education, Music and Drama.

The Senior School. The curriculum of the Senior School is characterised by small classes and an emphasis on individual guidance and target-setting. A balanced programme leads to high achievement at GCSE. English, Mathematics, Sciences, Religious Education, Games and PE remain compulsory throughout; Languages, Computer Science, History and Geography, Art, Art Textiles and Graphic Products, Music, Drama, Latin and Physical Education form the matrix of options. Unusually, German, French and Latin are studied from Year 7.

External candidates are selected from the entrance examination and opportunities for Scholarships exist at Year 7 entry.

The School has a modern Computing suite with state-of-the-art equipment. All classrooms are networked. ICT skills are central to the work of every department, and coordinated to allow the students to build up CLAIT certification in several modules by the end of Year 11.

There are specialist laboratories for all sciences.

In the Sixth Form students usually take four subjects at Advanced Subsidiary (AS) Level and three at A Level. In addition to studies for AS and A Level, student participate in a wider programme of activities within the curriculum. The School delivers the AQA Baccalaureate, which is a portfolio-style qualification with four main elements: three A Levels at its heart, a so-called 'Breadth' AS Level in Critical Thinking or General Studies and an Extended Project Qualification on a topic of the candidate's own choosing.

As a School with pupils from Reception and children in the Nursery from 6 weeks and above, older pupils have many opportunities to develop a sense of involvement and responsibility, and carry out valuable service in the wider community of the city during the Sixth Form. Business sense is developed through the Young Enterprise scheme, in which the School is very successful.

The Nursery. The Peterborough School Nursery offers daycare for children aged from 6 weeks to 4 years. Optional lessons include French, Ballet and Key Sports.

Religion. Weekly Communion Services are held and attendance is compulsory.

Music and Drama. The music of the School, in particular its choral tradition, is renowned and the School is benefiting from its new Centre for Creative Arts. Tuition in singing, piano and all orchestral instruments is available. Major theatrical and musical productions take place several times a year, and the School enjoys its links with theatres in the city.

Games and Physical Education. The pupils achieve outstanding success in team and individual sports and athletics. Many pupils have represented the county, the region, and even England. The School estate is spacious with several pitches and all-weather courts. The many and varied sporting facilities of the city are within easy reach for swimming, rowing and athletics. The School is benefiting from the major development of its Sports Facility, including a Fitness Suite and Climbing Wall.

Extra-curricular Activities. Many clubs and societies operate in extra-curricular time, and field visits and excursions illuminate classroom work. Exchange schemes for French and German operate on an annual basis as does a Sixth Form Cultural trip. Many pupils undertake the Duke of Edinburgh's Award Scheme at both Bronze and Gold levels, with outstanding success.

Fees per term (2014–2015). Reception/Infants £3,186; Years 3–6 £3,866; Years 7–13 £4,526.

Lunches, breaktime snacks and all UK based educational trips and visits are included.

Scholarships. Academic, Art, Music and Sport are the main scholarships available to those entering Year 7. Please apply to the Registrar for more information.

Westwoodians' Association. Secretary: Mrs Ivana Zizza who is based at the School.

Charitable status. The Peterborough School Limited is a Registered Charity, number 269667. It is an independent school which exists to promote the education of children.

Pitsford School

Pitsford Hall, Pitsford, Northamptonshire NN6 9AX
Tel: 01604 880306
Fax: 01604 882212
email: office@pitsfordschool.com
website: www.pitsfordschool.com

Governing Body:

Chairman: Mr A Tait

Mr M Adams	Mr A Moodie
Mr J Brown	Lady Morton**
Mr S Frater	Mr A Ross
Mrs J Harrop	Mrs J Tice**
Mr J Lockhart	Reverend S Trott
Mrs F McGill	

** *Foundation Governor*

Headmaster: Mr N R Toone, BSc, MInstP, FRSA

Deputy Head: Mrs F M Kirk, BA, MEd

* *Head of Department*

Mr O Auckland, BA Hons (*Junior School*)
Miss T Calnan, BEd (*Junior School*)
Mrs F L Care, MA (*Mathematics*)
Mrs L A Chacksfield, BEd (*PE and Games**)
Mme M H Conroy, BA (*Junior School*)
Mrs J Cowie, BA (*Junior School*)
Mrs A Cowling, BSc Hons (*Biology*)
Mr M E Dean, BSc (*Physics**)
Mrs J M Drakeford, BSc (*Chemistry and Biology**)
Mme C R Filliol, BA (*Modern Languages**)
Mrs S E Goode, BSc Econ (*Junior School*)
Mr D A Hallowell, BEd (*History**)
Miss S M Jackson, BSc (*Head of Sixth Form, Chemistry*)
Mrs F Jeffrey, BA Hons (*Asst Head of Early Years and KS1, Junior School*)
Mrs L Jones, BA (*Junior School*)
Mr M Kefford, BA (*PE and Games*)
Mrs C King, BA (*EFL*)
Mrs F M Kirk, BA, MEd (*English, General Studies*)
Mrs J M Leeke, BSc (*Mathematics*)
Mr M J Lewis, BSc, FRGS, FRMetS, CGeog (*Geography**, Careers & Higher Education*)
Mrs L M Lyon, BEd (*Modern Languages*)
Mrs S E Matts, BSc, MA Ed, MIBiol, CBiol (*Biology*)
Ms M F McQuilkin, BA (*Art**)
Mrs M McNally, BA (*Geography and Games*)
Mrs J Middlewood, BA (*Spanish*)
Mrs G Montford, NNEB (*Nursery Nurse*)
Miss M Parker, BA, FTCL (*Junior School Class Music*)
Mr J Smorfitt, BA (*Economics**)
Mr C L Stoner, BSc (*Mathematics**, Director of Studies*)
Dr A Templeton, BSc, MSc, PhD (*Physics*)
Mr R P Tickle, BA, DipTh (*History and Religious Studies*)
Mrs E Walsh, BMus Hons (*Director of Music**)
Mr J A White, BA, DipTh (*English**)
Mrs C Whiting, MA (*ICT**)
Mrs J Willmott, BEd (*Head of Junior School*)
Dr J Wood, BA, MA, PhD (*English*)

Bursar: Mr C Bellamy
Marketing and Development: Mrs J Heaton-Harris
Registrar: Mrs K Cannon

Age Range. 3–18 Co-educational.
Number of Pupils. 315 boys and girls.
Fees per term (2014–2015). Kits (Pre-School): £1,652–£2,507; Junior School: £2,497–£4,048; Senior School: £4,333. Lunches: £245.

The School was founded in 1989 to offer a traditional Grammar School standard education to boys in Northamptonshire. Today, the School still offers the same high standards of education but to boys and girls from 3–18 years of age.

In 2012, a brand new £2 million state-of-the-art Junior School was built on the 26-acre site.

Pastoral Care. The School's academic success is complemented by effective pastoral support. By keeping class sizes small, a friendly, family atmosphere is evident, allowing pupils to grow and develop in confidence as they progress through the School.

Admissions. Nursery, Year 7 and Sixth Form are the most common years of entry to the School, although pupils may be admitted in other years when required, if space is available.

Entry to Key Stage 1: pupils are invited to spend a day with their current year group to ensure they are happy in their future surroundings.

Entry to Key Stage 2: pupils are invited in for an Assessment.

Entry to the Senior School: Prospective pupils are invited to sit the School's own entrance test.

It is expected all pupils will take 10 GCSEs before transferring to the Sixth Form at the end of Year 11.

The Sixth Form is structured to provide a stepping stone from the discipline of Senior School to the demands of Higher Education. Sixth Formers take a full part in the life of the School and have many positions of responsibility.

Sport and Extra-Curricular Activities. Rugby, netball, cricket and tennis are played throughout the School. In addition, the School's Cross Country Team enjoys ongoing success when competing against other Schools. The Pitsford Run is a well known local event.

Numerous Extra-Curricular Activities are on offer to pupils throughout the School:

Junior School activities range from School Council to English Speaking Board (ESB) and from Rugby and Netball to Art and Craft.

Senior School pupils have over 60 activities to choose from. Most Activities take place on site, however the School's excellent location means that a number of activities such as Sailing, Kayaking, Horse Riding and Fishing are available just a short distance from the School. All are extremely popular.

Music and Drama. Music and Drama are integral elements of school life at Pitsford School.

Musical Recitals are held in Pitsford Hall every Thursday lunchtime and in addition, the School holds Four Evening Concerts per year. As well as individual music lessons in a wide range of instruments, group participation and performance opportunities include woodwind, guitar, percussion, strings, sax and flute ensembles and also two choirs.

A number of Junior and Senior plays take place throughout the year, ranging from Shakespeare to Musicals.

Charitable status. Northamptonshire Independent Grammar School Charity Trust Limited is a Registered Charity, number 298910.

Portland Place School
Alpha Plus Group

56–58 Portland Place, London W1B 1NJ
Tel: 020 7307 8700
Fax: 020 7436 2676
email: admin@portland-place.co.uk
website: www.portland-place.co.uk

Portland Place School was founded in 1996 in response to demand in central London for a mixed school that provided for pupils from a broad range of backgrounds and abilities.

Headmaster: **David Hyman**, BSc Hons London, PGCE, NPQH

Deputy Head (Pastoral): Miss Elayn ONeill, MEd Edinburgh, BEd Phys Ed/Health Ed, PG Dip Counselling

Teaching Staff:
Simon Aaronson, BSc BEd Perth Australia, MInstP, PGCE (*Physics*)
Kamran Akhtar, MSc London, PGCE (*Mathematics*)
Mrs Kalliopi Alvanos, BA Ed, PGCE Middlesex, MA IoE London (*SEN*)
Miss Clare Bacon, BA Hons Leeds Metropolitan, PGCE (*Physical Education*)
Adrian Barlow, MSci Hons UCL, PGCE (*Chemistry*)
Thomas Barnes, MA Cantab, PGCE (*English*)
Leonardo Blonda, PhD Bari Italy, MA London, BA Bari Italy (*Film Studies*)
Mrs Martina Boggian, BA University of Bologna, Italy, PGCE (*MFL*)
Richard Brightwell, BA York, PGCE (*Music*)
Colin Bryce, BSc Glasgow (*Physical Education*)
Miss Charlotte Butler, BA Hons Leeds, PGCE (*History*)
Juan J Caballero, BA, CAP Seville EFL, PGCE IoE London, MA IoE London, MEd Barcelona (*ICT*)
David Chivers, BA Cumbria, PGCE (*Drama*)
Miss Lydia Coles, BA Hons Oxford Brookes, PGCE (*Teacher of Years 5 and 6*)
Miss Danielle English, MSc Queen Mary London, MRSC, PGCE (*Chemistry*)
Miss Daciana Florea, BEd Oradea Romania, PGCE (*EAL*)
Ms Kirin Gill, BA Brunel, PGCE (*English*)
Miss Elise Hartopp, BA Hons York, PGCE (*English*)
Ms Lisa Hunt, MPhil, MA London, PGCE (*History*)
Miss Hannah Johnston, BSc Hons St Andrews, PGCE (*Geography*)
Mrs Audrey Jones, BA Calvin College USA (*Teacher Assistant Years 5, 6, and 7*)
Miss Kelly Jones, BA Hons PrimEd University of Wales, PGCE (*Teacher of Years 5 and 6*)
Matthew Jones, BA London, PGCE (*Art*)
Paul Jones, BA Leeds, PGCE (*Media and Film Studies*)
Mrs Natalie Keen, BA Hons Manchester, PGCE (*English*)
Miss Khadija Khairoun, BA Hons Greenwich, PGCE (*Mathematics*)
Ms Hina Kizilbash, BSc Brunel, MSc IoE London (*Psychology*)
Dr Charlotte Knox-Williams, BA Hons Falmouth, PGCE Brighton, MA Winchester, PhD (*SEN Specialist Teacher*)
Joe Kubik, BA Hons St Marys University College, PGCE (*Physical Education*)
Thomas Lalande, BA Bordeaux, PGCE (*French and Spanish*)
Mrs Charlotte Lichman, BSc Hons Open, GTP (*Business Studies and Economics*)
Miss Christine Linton, BA Hons University of the Arts London, PGCE (*Design & Technology*)

Chad Macfarlane, BA Goldsmiths London (*Design and Technology*)
Miss Charlotte Magniez, BA and MA Boulogne-sur-Mer, GTP (*French and Spanish*)
Adrian Martjiono, BSc London, PGCE (*Chemistry*)
Jamie McLoughlin, BSc Brunel, PGCE (*Physical Education*)
Miss Caroline McMeekin, BA Lancaster, PGCE (*Drama*)
Ms Sarah Nelson, BA Cardiff, PGCE (*English*)
Miss Lauren O'Donnell, BA Hons Queen Mary London, PGCE (*English*)
Miss Teffany Osborne, BA Hons Slade (*Art*)
Miss Emma Parker, BSc Hons Manchester, PGCE (*Biology*)
Ms Ruth Picado, BA Coruna Spain, PGCE (*Spanish*)
Ms Lucy Price, MA Edinburgh, PGCE (*Classical Civilisation and History*)
Miss Sana Razvi, BSc Hons Brunel, PGCE (*Mathematics*)
Mrs Julie Rider, BSc London, GTP (*Physical Education*)
Scott Rider, BA Brunel, PGCE (*Physical Education*)
Miss Imogen Riley, BA Oxon, PGCE (*Geography*)
Richard Rodger, BA Glasgow, MA London, PGCE (*Politics and Sociology*)
Pardeep Sagoo, MSci Imperial College London, GTP (*Biology/Chemistry*)
Miss Sara Segerstrom, BEd Kalmar Sweden, PGCE (*Mathematics*)
Patrick Smullen, BSc Open, PGCE (*Biology*)
Parwez Soogund, MA London, PGCE (*Design and Technology*)
Phillip Stanway, BA Manchester Metropolitan, PGCE (*Physical Education*)
Ms Alison Stringell, PG Theatre Design Slade, PGCE Goldsmiths (*Art*)
Toni Tasic, BA Hons UCL, PGCE (*English*)
Steve Thompson, BSc Plymouth, PGCE (*Physics*)
Miss Amanda Valentine, BA Southampton, PGCE (*Music*)
Klaus Wehner, MA LCP (*Photography*)
Dr David Wellings, MSc LSE, PGCE (*Business Studies*)
Ms Virginia West, BSc Hons Sheffield, PGCE (*Mathematics*)
Dr Nader Yazdi, MSc Leeds, PhD UCL, MBA Imperial (*Computing and ICT*)

Visiting Music Teachers:
Nick Bentley (*Brass and Tech*)
Adam Blake (*Guitar*)
Miss Zrinka Bottrill (*Classical Piano*)
Dan Ezard (*Bass*)
Sam Jesson (*Drums*)
Siobhan Lavin (*Voice & Flute*)
Darren McCarthy (*Guitar*)
Mike O'Neill (*Jazz Piano*)
Miss Rosie Secker (*Voice*)
Balint Szekely (*Violin*)
Miss Naomi Thomas (*Clarinet*)

Administration/Support Staff:
Mrs Jane Monk (*Bursar/SMT*)
Miss Emmy Gaulter (*Finance Assistant to Bursar*)
Mrs Sharon Norman (*SIMS/TACO Administrator/ Examinations Officer*)
Ms Sharon Wood (*Headmaster's Secretary*)
Miss Michelle Botha (*Admissions Registrar*)
Miss Clemmie Studd (*School Secretary*)
Ms Amanda Murray (*School Buildings Manager – Harford House*)
Mrs Nihad Soogund (*Database Manager/Administrator – Great Portland Street*)
Miss Amanda Berrisford, BSc Econ (*Librarian*)
Kim Wykes (*Laboratory Technician*)
Miss Sade Williams (*SEN and Database Administration*)
Mrs Helene Latey (*Learning Support Assistant*)
Miss Laura Bateman (*Learning Support Assistant*)

Miss Dearbhaile Flynn (*Learning Support Assistant*)
Ms Alicia Mather (*Assistant to Admissions*)

Caretaking Staff:
Joseph Akyeampong (*Caretaker*)
John Himana (*Maintenance*)

Age Range. 9–18 Co-educational.
Number of Day Pupils. 263 Boys, 176 Girls.
Fees per term (2014–2015). £6,035.

Aims and Philosophy. Portland Place is an inclusive and non-elitist school. We encourage pupils to excel in the arts, sport and in their academic studies. Discipline is firm, but compassionate. Our uniform is simple and functional. Teaching is structured. All teachers are not only specialists in their subjects, but are chosen for their ability to enthuse and draw out the best in all students at all levels. The relationship between teachers and pupils is courteously informal. We teach in small classes to offer every child individual attention. While we always strive for academic excellence, we never allow this to overshadow our dedication to nurturing natural intelligence or true potential. Each child's progress is followed through tests, homework and up to six reports a year. Parents are also encouraged to meet our staff to discuss any concerns at any time, as well as at a Parents' Evening every term. We are also a school in touch with the real world. The future of the children in our care comes first in all our decisions and the education every child receives is a journey to a successful later life.

Location and Buildings. Portland Place is ideally located right in the centre of the capital, less than five minutes' walk from Regent's Park (where much of the outdoor sporting activities take place) and ten minutes' walk from Oxford Circus. The school is housed in two magnificent Grade II* listed James Adam houses in Portland Place with a separate Art, Drama and Science building and a Senior School building close by in Great Portland Street. The buildings have been refurbished to an exceptionally high standard. Classrooms are supplemented by specialist rooms for drama, photography and computing.

Curriculum. The curriculum at Portland Place is developed from the English National Curriculum and offers a flexibility that puts the pupil first. Homework is supervised until 5.00 pm for those who want or require it and each pupil has a homework diary that details the homework programme for each week. Each child takes part in a comprehensive programme of physical education. Pupils in Years 5–9 have four PE sessions per week. Full advantage is taken of its central London location and excellent local facilities available. The outdoor programme takes place in neighbouring Regent's Park and includes athletics, hockey, football, rugby, tennis and cross-country. Indoor sports include basketball and fencing. Pupils represent the school in numerous matches against other London schools and in national tournaments. Class music is a compulsory part of the curriculum in Years 5–9 and all pupils are encouraged, if they do not already play one, to take up a musical instrument and take advantage of the team of visiting instrumental teachers.

Sport and Extra-Curricular Activities. Our central London position means that we have easy access to world class facilities. All children are encouraged to participate in an interesting and varied physical education programme. Portland Place School offers a wide range of popular sport including: Athletics, Basketball, Cricket, Cross Country, Fencing, Football, Hockey, Netball, Rounders, Swimming, Tennis and Rugby. Outdoor sports such as football, netball, tennis, cricket and athletics take place in Regent's Park less than a ten minute walk from the school. Indoor activities including basketball and fencing take place at the University of Westminster gym just minutes away in Regent Street. Swimming is at the Seymour Centre, and in the summer we have nets at Lords indoor school. Optional after-school sport activities abound with senior and junior clubs for matches held with schools across London and the UK.

There is a wide and expanding range of extra-curricular activities that are offered at the end of afternoon school. Whole school productions, concerts, chamber groups and small dramatic workshops take place throughout the year and clubs ranging from politics and debating to games and Christianity all thrive throughout the year. During the last week of the summer term all pupils take part in an Activities Week that includes outdoor adventure centres and overseas trips.

Admission. Entry to the school (usually at 9+, 10+, 11+, 13+ and Sixth Form) is by examinations in English and Mathematics and interview. Interviews for September entry are held in the Autumn term prior to entry and the school's entrance examination is in January.

Governance. Portland Place School is part of the Alpha Plus Group of schools.

The Purcell School

Aldenham Road, Bushey, Hertfordshire WD23 2TS
Tel: 01923 331100
Fax: 01923 331166
email: info@purcell-school.org
website: www.purcell-school.org

The Purcell School is one of the world's leading specialist centres of excellence and has a national and international reputation in the education and training of exceptional young musicians. There are 175 pupils, boys and girls, aged from 9 to 18, with around 80 in the Sixth Form. All pupils are means-tested on entry to the School and receive Scholarships under the Government's Music and Dance Scheme or from the School's Scholarship Fund.

Royal Patron: HRH The Prince of Wales

Patrons:
Sir Simon Rattle, CBE (*President*)
Baroness Warnock, DBE (*Vice-President*)
Vladimir Ashkenazy, CBE
Sir Andrew Davis, CBE
Mrs Donatella Flick
Dr David Josefowitz, CBE
Dame Kiri Te Kanawa, DBE
Yevgeny Kissin
Dame Fanny Waterman, DBE

Governing Body:
Sir Roger Jackling, KCB, CBE (*Chairman*)
Peter van de Geest (*Deputy-Chairman*)
Jenny Agutter, OBE, FRSA, Hon DLitt
Charles Beer, MA Cantab (*Chairman of Finance and General Purposes Committee*)
Stephen Benson, BA Oxon, MA London, FIPA
Professor Timothy Blinko, MMus, BMus Hons, Dip RCM
Dr Xanthe Cross, BMed Sci, MBBS, MRCGP, DFSRH
Jonathan Eley, MA Cantab
James Fowler, MA Oxon (*Chairman of Education Committee*)
Janice Graham, ARCM, AGSMD, ACT Julliard
Professor Colin Lawson, MA Oxon, MA, PhD, DMus, FRCM, FRNCM, FLCM
Lady Jean McGregor
Julie Nicholls, BA, ACA
Mark Racz, BA, MFA, Hon FBC, Hon RAM
Joanna Van Heyningen, MA Oxon, MA Cantab

Headmaster: **David Thomas**, MA Oxon

Deputy Head (*Students & Innovation*): Christine Rayfield, BA Hons Birmingham, PGCE
Deputy Head (*Staff and Communications*): James Harding, MA Glasgow, PGCE

Bursar: Aideen McNamara, BA London

Head of Sixth Form: Elizabeth Willan, BA Hons London, PGCE

Music Department:

Head of Strings: Charles Sewart (*Violin*)
Tony Cucchiara (*Violin*)
Alda Dizdari (*Violin*)
Sadagat Mamedova-Rashidova (*Violin*)
Charles Sewart (*Violin*)
Carol Slater (*Violin*)
Nathaniel Vallois (*Violin*)
Susie Meszaros (*Violin/Viola*)
Ian Jewel (*Viola*)
Pal Banda (*Cello*)
Alexander Boyarsky (*Cello*)
Natalia Pavlutskaya (*Cello*)
Ana Cordova (*Double Bass*)
Neil Tarlton (*Double Bass*)
Francesco Mariani (*Guitar*)
Jean Mercer (*Alexander Technique*)
Paul Moore (*Alexander Technique*)

Head of Keyboard: William Fong
Lidia Amorelli (*Piano*)
Andrew Ball (*Piano*)
William Fong (*Piano*)
David Gordon (*Harpsichord & Improvisation*)
Caterina Grewe (*Piano*)
Gareth Hunt (*Piano*)
Emily Jeffrey (*Piano*)
Jianing Kong (*Piano*)
Alla Kravchenko (*Piano*)
Ching-Ching Lim (*Piano*)
Roshan Magub (*Piano*)
Pascal Nemirovski (*Piano*)
Tessa Nicholson (*Piano*)
Tatiana Sarkissova (*Piano*)
Deborah Shah (*Piano/Accompanist*)
Daniel Swain (*Accompanist*)
Valeria Szervansky (*Piano*)
John Thwaites (*Piano*)
Patsy Toh (*Piano*)

Head of Wind, Brass, Percussion, Voice & Harp: Kevin Hathway (*Percussion*)
Hannah Grayson (*Flute*)
Anna Pope (*Flute*)
Melanie Ragge (*Oboe*)
Rachel Baldock (*Oboe*)
Barbara Law (*Recorder*)
Sarah Burnett (*Bassoon*)
David Fuest (*Clarinet*)
Carlos Lopez-Real (*Saxophone*)
Tony Cross (*Trumpet*)
Rob Workman (*Trombone*)
Stephen Wick (*Tuba*)
Sue Dent (*Horn*)
Beth Randell (*Horn*)
Daphne Boden (*Harp*)
Charlotte Seale (*Harp*)
Tom Marandola (*Voice*)
Daniella Ganeva (*Percussion*)
Kevin Hathway (*Percussion*)

Head of Jazz: Simon Allen (*Jazz Saxophone*)
Ross Anderson (*Jazz Trombone*)
Steve Waterman (*Jazz Trumpet*)
Oliver Hayhurst (*Jazz Bass*)
Chris Montague (*Jazz Guitar*)
Kit Downes (*Jazz Piano*)
David Gordon (*Jazz Piano*)
Darren Altman (*Jazz Drums*)
Clark Tracey (*Jazz Drums*)

Jacqui Hicks (*Jazz Voice*)

Head of Composition: Alison Cox, GRNCM, PGCE
Joseph Phibbs, BMus, MMus
Karim Said, BMus Hons RAM
Simon Speare, MA, ARCM

Head of Academic Music: Mary Kate Gill, BA Oxon, Adv
Cert GSMD, PGCE
Alison Cox
Edward Longstaff
Christine Rayfield
Karim Said
David Thomas
Andrew Williams

Head of Music Technology: Aidan Goetzee, MSc, GRSM,
ARCM

Academic Staff:
* *Head of Department*
§ *Part-time*

Peter Banks, BSc Hons Wales, PGCE (*Chemistry*)
Catherine Burrell, BA Cheltenham, CELTA (*§EFL*)
Alison Cox OBE, GRNCM, DipAdvStdMus Comp, PGCE
(*§Academic Music, *Composition*)
Paul Elliott, MA Hons Glasgow, PGCE (**German,
Drama)
Panos Fellas, BSc Surrey, MA Sc Ed (**Science, *Physics*)
Mary-Kate Gill, BA Oxon, AdvCert, GSMD, PGCE
(**Academic Music*)
Aidan Goetzee, MSc, GRSM, ARCM (**Music Technology*)
James Harding, MA Hons Glasgow, PGCE (*Deputy Head
Staff & Communications, English*)
Derek Hayward, CertEd St Mary's, BSc Open (*§Juniors*)
Jocelyne Hazan, BA MA Paris X (*§French, Overseas
pupils Guardian Coordinator*)
Katherine Higgins, BEd Warwick, MA TEFL, MSc (**EFL*)
Sarah Irving, BSc London, PGCE (*Biology*)
Saleem Izhar, BSc Manchester, MSc UCL, PGCE
(*§Mathematics*)
Andrew Leverton, BA Tasmania, Dip Ed (**English*)
Edward Longstaff, BMus Hons, MMus London, LRSM,
PGCE (*Music*)
Monica Lowenberg, BA Hons QTS Sunderland and
Toulouse, MA Sussex (*§German*)
Darrell Pigott, BSc Bradford, PGCE (**History*)
Mary Pitkin, BSc Hons Manchester, CPhys, MInstP
(*Physics/Maths, Director of Pupil Welfare*)
Christine Rayfield, BA Birmingham, PGCE (*Deputy Head
Students & Innovation, Music*)
Nadine Sender, BA Hons Sheffield Hallam (**Art*)
Yvonne Tagoe, BA Hons, MBA, PGCE (**Mathematics*)
Sally Pearson, BA York, MA UCL (*English*)
Andrea Thomas, MA Oxon, PhD Edinburgh (*§History*)
David Thomas, MA Oxon (*Headmaster, Music*)
Martin Whitfield, BSc MSc Cranfield, PGCE
(*Mathematics*)
Sally-Ann Whitty, BA (**Learning Support*)
Elizabeth Willan, BA Hons London, PGCE (**Modern
Languages, *French*)
Andrew Williams, BA Liverpool, MA London, PCGE
(*§Academic Music*)

Boarding Houses:
Avison: Jennifer Henderson
Gardner: Mary Pitkin
Graham Smallbone: Rachel Branch
Sunley: Sally Pearson

Resident Graduate Music Assistants:
Lucy Armstrong, BA York
Lucy Caunt, BA Bristol
Harriet Rayfield, BA Bristol

Resident Graduate Sports Assistant:
James Awofisan, BSc Brunel

Administration Staff:
PA to Headmaster: Gail Remfry, AIST, RSA
Assistant Bursar: Jo Wallis
Office Administrators: Antonia Holmes, Jannice Raw,
Caroline Fletcher
Music Department Secretary & Registrar: Karen
Gumustekin
Music Timetabler: Fiona Duce, BA Hons
Librarian: Joe Duer, BA Bristol
Concerts Manager: Jane Hunt, BMus
Concerts Administrator: Sam Batchelor, BA Hons
Fundraising Manager: Ruth Blake, BSc
Development Department Assistant: Emma McGrath
Fundraising Assistant: Celia Crowne
Finance Officer: Ms Susan Pickard, MAAT
Computer Network and Telecommunications Manager:
Simon Kingsbury
Art Technician: Lucy Jay, BA Hons
Art Technician: Alison Humphrey, BA Hons
Lab Technician: Hawreen Osman
Estates: Tina Stewart
House Keeper: Tina Litte
Catering: Holroyd Howe Independent Limited
School Nurse: Hilary Austin, RGN
Pastoral Counsellor: Nikki Bennett
Physiotherapist: Sarah Upjohn, MA, MCSP

The Purcell School is an independent co-educational specialist music school of around 175 pupils aged from 9 to 18.
It is the oldest specialist music school in the UK, having
been founded as the Central Tutorial School for Young
Musicians in 1962. It moved to its current site in Bushey, on
the outskirts of London, in 1997.

The School's pupils are funded largely by the Government's Music and Dance Scheme, along with the School's
own scholarship funds. It has consistent success in national
and international competitions and has an extensive programme of outreach and community work. The majority of
pupils progress to music conservatoires although a small
number each year elect to go to University to study both
music and non-musical subjects.

The Purcell School exists to provide young musicians of
exceptional promise and talent with the best possible teaching and environment in which to fulfil their potential, irrespective of their background.

The Music Department at The Purcell School aims to
provide:

- A stimulating and challenging musical environment, at
  the heart of which is an individually tailored programme
  for every pupil. We try to ensure that both the balance of
  musical studies and the balance between musical and academic work are fine-tuned to suit each pupil.
- A flexible timetable, designed to enable pupils to practise.
  Pupils in Years 5 to 8 are able to put in up to 3 hours each
  day on their first study. In Years 9 and 10, that rises to 3–4
  hours and sixth formers are able to do 4–5 hours or even
  more depending on their academic commitments. We provide practice supervisors, themselves graduate musicians,
  who work with pupils up to Year 9 to ensure they use their
  practice time effectively. Our experienced and expert instrumental teachers set practice goals and teach practice
  strategies.
- Twice-weekly contact with the pupil's first study instrumental teacher for a total of up to 2 hours' tuition. All our
  instrumental teachers have considerable experience of
  working with motivated young musicians and have prov-
  en their ability to enable their students to succeed. Many
  of them also teach at the London conservatoires.
- An enriched musical programme that includes chamber
  music, orchestras, piano classes, choirs and aural and theory training. Frequent performing opportunities range

from daily lunchtime concerts at school and in the surrounding area to formal recitals around the UK and in the capital's leading venues. Pupils can audition for the chance to play concertos with the school's orchestras, to give solo and chamber music recitals at the Wigmore Hall, Purcell Room and other prestigious venues.

- The work of our regular teachers is enhanced by visits from the world's leading musicians for masterclasses, recitals, courses and collaborative projects.
- An academic programme which (as far as possible) is organised around each pupil's musical commitments, whilst still enabling pupils to achieve the necessary examination grades and all-round education to pursue a musical career if they choose, or to otherwise enjoy a successful future.
- Pastoral care which is provided by professionals who understand the demands on and needs of performing musicians. This includes dedicated boarding staff, a school nurse, physiotherapist and independent counsellor.
- A supportive and sympathetic peer group, keen to help each other to achieve their potential. We are well aware of the benefits of being embedded in a musical environment in which all students understand and support each other, and this is an approach which we actively foster.

Academic Studies. The school aims to achieve a balance between musical studies and an all-round general academic education. Music comprises a significant proportion of the timetabled time depending on age and needs. The remainder of time is spent studying a range of subjects including mathematics, English, sciences, modern languages and humanities.

The size of the school ensures that classes are generally small. This allows for a great deal of individual attention from an experienced and dedicated staff of teachers.

All pupils are set homework each day and time is allocated in the boarding houses each evening for this to be completed. Pupils' academic progress is closely monitored and parents receive frequent progress reports.

Boarding. The Purcell School is international in its outlook and welcomes pupils from all over Britain and from all over the world. About 70% are boarders, all of whom live on the School campus. The needs of overseas pupils are cared for by a dedicated member of staff.

The youngest pupils, aged between 9 and 12, live in Avison House. Sunley House (girls) Graham Smallbone House (girls) and Gardner House (boys) are all superb new or recently refurbished boarding facilities. Members of the Sixth Form can use their rooms for practice as well as for study. In addition to the Houseparents, resident practice supervisors help the pupils to maintain their busy musical schedules.

In each half of the term there is an Exeat weekend when all pupils go home or to their guardian or to friends. There is also an extended half-term period in each of the three terms.

Admission. Entrance is by musical audition and interview – please see the school website for further details. The Registrar, Mrs Karen Gumustekin, will be pleased to answer queries.

Fees per term (2014–2015). Day £8,259; Boarding £10,562.

Scholarship funding is available, for those pupils who meet the eligibility criteria, under the Department for Education Music and Dance Scheme, or from the school's Scholarship Funds. Parents are welcome to consult the Bursar for guidance.

Charitable status. The Purcell School is a Registered Charity, number 312855. It aims to offer specialist musical training, combined with an excellent general academic education, to children of exceptional musical ability.

The Read School
Drax

Drax, Selby, North Yorkshire YO8 8NL
Tel: 01757 618248
Fax: 01757 617432
email: enquiries@readschool.co.uk
website: www.readschool.co.uk

Chairman of Governors: R S Manock, LLM

Head: J A Sweetman, BSc, PhD

Deputy Head: M A Voisey, BA (*Head of English*)

Assistant Head (*Curriculum*): Ms C M Palmer, BSc, MSc (*Head of Mathematics*)

Teaching Staff:
Mrs R A Ainley, MA (*Modern Foreign Languages, Head of Key Stage 3*)
§Mrs S Ashworth-Lilley, BSc (*Psychology*)
§Mrs P Anderson, BEd (*Prep School*)
Miss J Bullock, BSc, MSc (*Head of Science, English Additional Language*)
§Ms S L Campbell, BSc (*Prep School*)
§Mrs S Chambonnet, BA (*Latin, French*)
Mrs J Clark (*Music, brass instruments, piano, CCF*)
Miss C Cross, BA (*English*)
Mrs L Fairhurst, BA (*Pre-Prep School*)
B Garrard, BSc (*Head of PE and Games*)
Mrs E Gilmore, BA (*Head of MFL and EAL, Spanish, German*)
D I Gisbourne, BSc (*Director of ICT, Mathematics*)
§Mrs H Hewson, BA (*English*)
Mr G Hill, BA (*Prep School*)
§Mrs K Ives, BA (*French, Spanish*)
§Mrs P Kavanagh, BA (*Business Studies*)
R S Kendrick, BA (*Mathematics, Exams officer*)
Mrs K Limbert (*Pre-School Manager*)
J L Matthews, BSc (*Housemaster, Sport & PE*)
§Mrs B J Maunsell, BA (*Drama*)
Mrs S Morrell, BEd (*Religious Studies, PSHE Coordinator*)
Mrs K E Patrick, PGDip Counselling, PGDip SEN, MA (*Head of Inclusive Learning*)
C S Patrick, BSc (*Specialist Tutor*)
Mrs S Prosser, BA (*PE and Games*)
§M Raisborough, BEd (*Mathematics*)
§Mrs S Rothwell-Wood, BEd (*Design Technology, Food*)
Mrs S Scholefield, BSc (*Head of Humanities*)
§Mrs E Stark, BSc, DipEd (*Biology, Chemistry*)
§R P Stark, BSc, DipEd (*Physics*)
§J Staves, BSc, PhD (*Chemistry*)
Mrs R M Wake, BA (*Key Stage 2 Coordinator*)
Mrs A L Watson, BA (*Key Stage 1 Coordinator*)
R C Whyley, BA (*History, Boys' Games*)
§Mrs A Wightman, BA, LLB (*Prep School*)
P Woodward, BA, MA (*Design Technology*)
Mrs C M Wynne, BEd (*Pre-Prep School*)
Ms S A Yates, BA (*Art and Design, Tutor for Girls*)

Age Range. Co-educational 2–18 (Boarding 8–18).
Number in School. Total 240: Day 200, Boarding 40; Boys 140, Girls 100.

The school is pleasantly situated in the rural village of Drax and is very convenient for main rail (Doncaster, York, Leeds) and road access (M62, M18, A1). Manchester is the nearest international airport (1½ hours distant). It is a relatively small school where children are well known to each other and to the staff.

The school has been a focal point for education in the Selby-Goole area for almost 350 years, first as Drax Grammar School, and (since 1967) as The Read School. The school is now co-educational, offering a wide range of academic studies at GCSE and A Level, together with a full programme of Sports, Drama, Music, CCF and recreational activity. There is one class in each Prep School year from Pre-School to Year 6. There are two classes in each of the Senior years (7–11). There is a small Sixth Form (40 pupils) following AS and A Level courses. High standards are expected in all aspects of endeavour, and in behaviour and manners.

Facilities. In addition to the refurbished Edwardian buildings there continued to be steady developments in the facilities and accommodation throughout the 1980s and 1990s. These include the fine Moloney Hall, Ramsker classrooms, Sports Hall, Coggrave Building for the Prep School (Years 3–6), in addition to internal developments, especially in the provision of IT. The Pre-Prep has recently moved into the Shipley building on the main school campus and enjoys more up-to-date facilities. The girls' boarding accommodation is situated on its own site in the village at Adamson House. In 2007 a Multi-Use Games Area with Astroturf pitch was provided and in 2008 complete refurbishment of Norfolk House (boys' boarding) and the chemistry lab was carried out. In 2009 a new Creative Arts Centre was provided for Art, Design Technology and Food. More recently, the biology and physics labs have been fully refurbished, as has the Memorial Library and the girls' boarding accommodation. In the summer of 2011 a stunning upgrade of the Sports Hall was implemented.

Fees per term (2014–2015). Boarders: £6,740–£8,610; Day: £2,505–£3,580.

Sibling discount is available at a fixed sum of monetary value equivalent to 5% of the basic fee on entry, applicable to 2nd or subsequent children in the school at the same time.

Admission. An offer of a place in the school is made after interview (and verbal reasoning and mathematics tests for admission to the Senior School) and satisfactory report from the pupil's current school.

Charitable status. The Read School is a Registered Charity, number 529675. It exists to provide a proper education for boys and girls aged 2–18.

Reddam House Bearwood
Formerly Bearwood College

Wokingham, Berkshire RG41 5BG
Tel: 0118 974 8300
Fax: 0118 977 3186
email: headmaster@bearwoodcollege.co.uk
               registrar@bearwoodcollege.co.uk
website: www.bearwoodcollege.co.uk
               www.reddamschools.com

Reddam House Bearwood (the former Bearwood College) is a co-educational independent day and boarding school, which inspires excellence in education for pupils from three months to 18 years old. This newly restructured throughschool, which has been divided into three sections – an Early Learning School, a Junior School and a Senior School – is set in a majestic parkland of 120 hectares comprising extensive playing fields, woodland and a lake.

While its historic buildings are situated in a beautiful and secure rural estate, the school is conveniently located between Reading and Wokingham in the royal county of Berkshire, a vibrant location with very easy access to the M3, M4, Heathrow and London.

The recent change to the school's name came about on the acquisition of Bearwood College by the Reddam House group of schools (see further below) in September 2014; and under its new banner it has been selected as the group's flagship school among its expanding network in the UK and Europe.

Bearwood has a proud history, originally as a school for children of merchant seamen. A strong culture has emerged over the years – closely aligned to the existing Reddam culture – in which pupils are acknowledged as individuals and their distinct personality traits, attributes and special strengths are celebrated and optimised.

The Reddam House philosophy and formula for success are based on the quality and depth of their schools' curricula, cultural and sporting activities and – above all – on the uncompromising selection of outstanding teaching staff, in full recognition that the rapport between teacher and pupil is the strongest influence on an individual child's development and on the overall success of a school.

The Reddam House Group has its origin in South Africa and has opened other schools in Sydney, Australia. In both countries the schools have achieved singular success – both in terms of the well-rounded quality of person introduced to the world and in academic ranking: they top the league tables in South Africa and are among the top ten schools in New South Wales. They are also extremely successful in the diversity and quality of their co-curricular activities: music, dance, drama, public speaking and a wide range of sports. They are also true to their motto 'We Shall Give Back', instilling a strong sense of civic engagement, which holds a special appeal to pupils and parents.

Patron: Her Majesty The Queen

President: HRH The Prince Philip, Duke of Edinburgh, KG, KT

Board of Governors:
Mr Graeme Robert George Crawford (*Chairman*)
Mr Graham George Able
Mr Mark William Joseph
Mr Nadim Marwan Nsouli
Dr Michael Stephen Spurr

Head: **Donald Wilkinson**, BA, MLitt Oxon
From September 2015: Toby Mullins, MBA, BA

Academic Deputy: G Penlington, BA, Dip Teach
Second Master: R P Ryall, BA, PGCE, FRGS

Faculty Heads:

Letters (*English, Drama, Film Studies*): Philippa Phillips, BA, Dip RSA, PGCE

Creative Arts (*Art, Photography, Textiles, Music*): Stephen Abery, BA, PGCE

Humanities (*History, Geography, Religious Studies, Business Studies, Economics, Psychology, Sociology, French, Spanish*): Kathryn Langford-Holt Odenwalder, BA, PGCE

Science & Mathematics (*Biology, Chemistry, Physics, Maths, ICT*): Sarah Nichol, BSc, PGCE

Sports:
Kelly Elsworth (*Head of Girls' Games*)
Jason Dance, BEd (*Head of PE and Boys' Games*)

Study Support/ESOL:
Head of Study Support: Mrs P Bell, BA, Dip RSA
Head of ESOL: Mrs J Michel, BSc, Cert TESOL

Pastoral Staff:
Housemasters:
Blake House (*Boarding, Girls and Boys*): David Leese, BSc, PGCE
Raleigh House (*Day, Boys*): Alistair Hoare, BA, PGCE
Nelson House (*Day, Boys*): Jason Dance, BEd
Cook House (*Day, Boys*): Chris Thomas, BA, PGCE
Jellicoe House (*Juniors Day*): Stephen Abery, BA, PGCE
Grenville House (*Day, Girls*): Allison Ellis, BEd

Matrons: Theresa Greenham, Marlene Simmonds

Administrative Staff:
Registrar: Louise Lawson-Hatch

Academic Structure. At Reddam House we expect each child to achieve his or her best. Each pupil works to an academic programme which is individually targeted and permanently monitored. It provides a structured, supported and demanding academic challenge appropriate to each pupil's capacity. The academic curriculum is based on and exceeds the guidelines of the National Curriculum. In the years up to GCSE, we provide a programme which offers choice, breadth of experience and the opportunity to develop particular academic skills, which are then further developed in greater depth at A Level. The individual attention and specialized teaching that continues into the Sixth Form enables an enviable success rate of entry into first-choice universities.

Pastoral and Boarding Arrangements. Day care and education is available for children from 3 months to 18 years with boarding from 11–18. Once joining the Senior School the following day/boarding arrangements are available:

- Full boarding with continuous care and involvement for seven days a week.
- Weekly boarding with the chance to go home at weekends once school commitments have been fulfilled.
- Occasional or flexible boarding for limited or irregular periods to help busy parents.

Sport and Activities. All pupils take part in a wide range of games and activities outside the classroom. They enjoy a breadth of experience as well as being expected to discover specific areas in which to excel.

Everyone takes part in physical activities on most days. Sports and games give the pupils physical fitness, personal and team skills and recreation. They offer many opportunities to find a sense of achievement. On-site sports and activities on the extensive array of playing fields and facilities include all the usual field sports together with additional opportunities for: golf, equestrian sports, cycling and mountain biking, sailing, shooting, and canoeing.

Extra-curricular activities: Outdoor pursuits are encouraged to balance the pursuit of academic excellence. The extensive grounds and lake are used for sailing, canoeing, mountain biking, camping, cross country and many other activities. Few schools can boast such a varied estate.

Combined Cadet Force: All pupils in the third and fourth forms of the Senior School join the Combined Cadet Force (CCF). Cadets learn self-reliance and teamwork, and develop their own leadership skills. The CCF also provides an unrivalled opportunity to experience outdoor pursuits. Two camps are held during holiday periods each year. The annual adventure training expedition provides boys and girls with the opportunity to experience environments that test and challenge their characters whilst under the supervision of highly qualified staff. Many cadets choose to continue their service in the cadet force during their fifth and sixth form years. At this time they take on the extra responsibilities of being senior cadets. The experience they gain from taking an active role in teaching and helping younger cadets provides a valuable insight into the qualities required from leaders.

The Duke of Edinburgh's Award Scheme: All pupils in the fourth form are encouraged to start the Duke of Edinburgh's Award at bronze level. This is organised partly in conjunction with the cadet force who help with the training for the expedition section. Senior pupils are encouraged to continue with both silver and gold awards. The scheme provides pupils with an ideal opportunity to develop their own skills, fitness and commitment to others whilst fostering self-confidence and personal esteem.

Music: Music is part of the life of every pupil, non-specialist and specialist alike. Everyone participates in music events including the House Singing Competition and the Choral Society. There are regular informal and formal concerts given by instrumentalists and singers. All pupils are encouraged to take up instrumental and vocal lessons with professional peripatetic musicians. Regular visits to concerts and other musical outings take place.

Theatre and Drama: Our Theatre represents the very best that is available for the pursuance of music and dramatic arts. A busy programme of concerts, recitals and plays ensure that this 350-seat auditorium is continually in use. All pupils are encouraged to make a contribution to these productions. Pupil performers are supported by their peers as theatre technicians, lighting and sound engineers, stage crew and scenery builders. Drama is for all, and all have their part to play in the many productions.

Specialist tuition leading to LAMDA Speech and Drama grades and awards is available. These help to develop confidence and competence in acting, public speaking and general communication.

Dance: Dance is an exciting and vibrant part of everyday life. Whether pupils decide to study GCSE or A-level Dance, or enjoy dance outside the curriculum, there is a class for everyone. A variety of dance styles are taught outside the curriculum, including, Ballet, Contemporary, Jazz and Street Dance allowing the truly passionate to share their commitment and flair through performance.

Facilities. The splendid Mansion House is the centre of the school, around which all our other buildings are located. Historic rooms house modern facilities.

The Cook Library is situated in the former drawing room, one of the most beautiful rooms in the Mansion. It has a collection of both fiction and non-fiction books for loan and reference use. The library resource is further enhanced by networked computers with internet access. Pupils are encouraged to read daily quality broad sheet newspapers to keep abreast of current affairs, politics and news. This learning resource is run by a full-time Librarian and supports all areas of the curriculum as well as providing for recreational reading.

The need for modern technology is supported by four computer resource suites. All departments in the College have networked PCs and wireless is available throughout the school, and ongoing investment in digital technology for teaching and learning is integral to the restructuring process undertaken by Reddam House.

The range of further facilities for pupils at Reddam House is extensive. A fully-equipped photographic suite, extensive sports pitches, netball courts, a swimming pool, tennis courts, weights-training room and rifle range are all found immediately adjacent to the main building.

Our grounds contain access to many additional features: two golf courses; a fifty-acre lake and a well-equipped fleet of sailing dinghies, canoes and kayaks; generous woodlands with a professionally-built obstacle course and fitness trail; a mountain bike course; and stables.

The Early Learning School and Junior Schools are located close to the main Victorian Mansion House, in a thoughtfully converted, listed Coach House. The splendid surroundings of the wider campus combined with the intimate security of the Coach House allow children safely to explore, discover and learn. The Reggio Emilia approach to teaching young children introduced by Reddam House puts the natural development of children as well as the close relationships that they share with their environment at the centre of its philosophy – something which is uniquely enabled by the school's parkland setting.

Admission. Entry is normally 0+, 3+, 5+, 11+, 13+ and the Sixth Form, but applications at other ages are accepted, subject to vacancies. Assessment is by interview, assessment and by Common Entrance where appropriate. Entry to the Sixth Form is normally conditional upon the achievement of a minimum of 5 GCSEs at B grade or above.

Fees per term (2014–2015). £50.05 (short day), £64.00 (full day); Pre-Prep: £2,995 (Reception–Year 2); Prep School: £3,519 (Years 3–6). Senior School: Day £4,985

(Years 7–8), £5,870 (Years 9–13); Boarding £8,740 (Years 7–8), £10,075 (Years 9–13).

Scholarships. A significant number of Academic, Dance, Drama, Music, Art and Sport Scholarships are offered each year for entry at 11+.

Rishworth School

Rishworth, West Yorkshire HX6 4QA
Tel: 01422 822217 (Main School)
Fax: 01422 820911
email: admissions@rishworth-school.co.uk
website: www.rishworth-school.co.uk
Twitter: @RishworthS
Facebook: /RishworthSchool

Rishworth is an exceptionally friendly, caring community, in which pupils are as strongly encouraged to rejoice in each other's achievements as to take pride in their own. The School succeeds in combining a disciplined environment with a relaxed and welcoming atmosphere.

While pupils are at Rishworth, we try to ensure that, in addition to the knowledge and skills acquired through academic study, they develop:

- A love of learning and the will to succeed.
- A sense of responsibility, self-discipline, purpose and ful-filment.
- A capacity for both self-reliance and cooperation.
- An appreciation of certain personal virtues and spiritual values, such as honesty, dependability, perseverance, commitment, humility and respect for others.

Visitor: The Most Reverend The Lord Archbishop of York

Honorary Governor: A J Morsley, Esq

The Governing Body:
Dr C A G Brooks (*Chairman*)
G C W Allan, Esq
Mrs J C Slim
J G Wheelwright, Esq
T M Wheelwright, Esq
Mrs D M Whitaker, JP
J S Whittaker, Esq
Mrs M L Ringland
Revd T L Swinhoe
W P Hodgson, Esq

Advisor to the Board: Revd Canon Hilary Barber

Bursar and Clerk to the Board of Governors: J Clague, BA Hons, FCA, CTA

Teaching Staff:
* *Head of Department*

Headmaster: A S Gloag, BA

Deputy Headmaster: P Seery, BSc, MEd (*Chemistry*)
Director of Administration: Mrs I Shelton, BA (**Art*)
Director of Marketing: Mrs S J Stamp, BSc (*Geography*)
Director of Studies: S Ogden, BSc (*Geography, Mathematics*)
Head of Heathfield: A M Wilkins, BA, MA, MA

Mrs E Allison, BSc (*EYFS Section Leader, Heathfield*)
T Anderson (*Sports Coach, Games Teacher, Heathfield*)
Mrs M T Arbelo-Dolan, BA (*Spanish*)
Mrs R Aujla, BA (**Geography*)
D Baker, BA (*KS2 Teacher, Heathfield*)
Miss C Bartlett, BA (**Drama*)
P Bell, BA, MSc (*ICT & Computing*)
Mrs H Bower, BSc (**PE & Sport, Mathematics*)
Mrs J Bradley, LTCL, GTCL, CKME (*Music Coordinator, Heathfield*)

C Brass, BSc (*Science Coordinator, KS2 Teacher, Heathfield*)
Mrs J Bridges, NVQ3 (*Nursery Manager, Heathfield*)
Ms V Callagher (*Foundations Stage Key Person, Heathfield*)
Mrs S Chatterton, BEd (*Deputy Head, KS2 Teacher, Heathfield*)
J P Chilton, BSc (*Mathematics*)
Mrs C Devney, BA, BSc (**Learning Support*)
M L Dunn, BA (**ICT & Computing, Design Technology, Assistant Boarding House Master*)
Mrs K Fraser, BA (*Art, Press Officer, Assistant Head Lower & Middle School*)
Mrs S Gaynor, BTEC (*Out of School Care Deputy Manager, Teaching Assistant, Heathfield*)
Ms N Goldthorpe (*Swimming Coach, Heathfield*)
Mrs E Gregory, BA (*History*)
Mrs C Hall, BA, DipEd (**Food Technology & Catering*)
S Haslam, PhD (*Science*)
Mrs J Higgins, NNEB (*Teaching Assistant, Learning Support, Heathfield*)
C D Holmes-Roe, BA, MA (*History, RS, Assistant Boarding House Master*)
D I Horsfall, BSc (*Mathematics*)
Miss J Houghton, BA (*Economics, Business Studies*)
Mrs J Hudson (*Learning Support Coordinator, Heathfield*)
Mrs V Hutchinson, BA (*RE Coordinator, KS2 Teacher, Heathfield*)
Mrs N I'Anson, BA (*Foundation Stage Key Person, Heathfield*)
Ms K A James, LLB (*EFL, Resident Boarding Housemistress*)
Mrs K Jones, BSc (*Mathematics*)
P W Jones, MA Cantab (*Science Advisor, Teacher i/c Biology*)
Miss R Joyce, BSc (*Science*)
Mrs A M Kellett-End, BA, PGCLD (*Learning Support*)
Mrs S Kiy, BA (*French Coordinator, KS1 Teacher, Heathfield*)
Dr J Ladds, MChem, PhD, MEd (**Science, Assistant Head Sixth Form, Careers Coordinator, Assistant Boarding House Mistress*)
A Larvin, BSc (**Mathematics*)
C Lewis, BA, LRAM, LGSM (**Music*)
Ms J Marsden, BA (*English, Drama*)
Mrs R C McGarry, BA (**English*)
S H J McGarry, BEng, MSc (*Science, Teacher i/c Physics*)
Mrs L Meredith, BA, ARCM (*Music, English, EFL, Teacher i/c Provision for Academically Most Able*)
Mrs R Millington, MA Cantab (*Science*)
Mrs S Moore, BA (*English*)
D Newby, BTech (**Design Technology, Day House Area Master for Hanson House, Years 9 & 10*)
Mrs R Ogden, BEng (*Mathematics*)
Mrs P Pritchard (*Out-of-School Care Manager, Teaching Assistant, Heathfield*)
A Rhodes (*Head of Boys' Boarding, House Master of Calder*)
Mrs C E Rhodes, BA (**Psychology, RS, Staff Mentor for Management, Teaching & Learning, EPQ Coordinator*)
Miss E P Robinson, BA (*Art – Rishworth; Art & Library Coordinator – Heathfield*)
P I M Robinson, BEd (**Business Studies, Head of Sixth Form, UCAS & HE Coordinator*)
Mrs J Roe, BA (*EFL*)
Mrs K Rose, BA (*PE Coordinator, KS2 Teacher, Heathfield*)
Ms J Sheldrick, BSc (*Science, Head of Lower & Middle School*)
Mrs S P Sheppard (*Librarian*)
M E Siggins, BA (*Acting Head of English, Coordinator of Enhanced Sixth-form Curriculum & General Studies*)
G M Smith, BA (**Modern Languages*)

Mrs M Smith, BA (*PE Coordinator, Heathfield*)
Miss H E A Stembridge, BEd (*Humanities Coordinator, KS1 Teacher, Heathfield*)
Mrs G Sunderland, S R N (*Marketing, Heathfield*)
A J Thomas, BSc (*Director of Physical Education and Sport*)
Mrs J Thompson, BA (**EFL*)
Miss L V Turner, BA, MA (*French, EFL*)
Miss D Van-Eda, BA (*Teaching Assistant, Foundation Stage Key Person, Heathfield*)
Ms L Watkins, BA, MA (*English*)
Miss H Whiteley, NVQ3 (*Part-time Foundation Stage Key Person, Heathfield*)
Mrs C L Williams, BA (*Psychology*)
J S Williams (*House Master of Goat House, Sports Coach*)
M Wilson, BA (**History*)
Mrs L E Wood, BSc (*Physical Education & Sport, PSHCE Coordinator*)

Instrumental Music Teachers:
Mrs R K Burbidge
C D Wood
Miss H Bywater
P Brown
N Darwent
Ms H Grieg
Ms C Bishop
M Wagstaff
C Pulleyn

Administrative Staff:

Bursar: J Clague, BA Hons, FCA, CTA
Assistant Bursar: Mrs V Wheeler
Admissions Officer: Mrs J Sutherland
Headmaster's PA: Mrs S Billington
Matron: Mrs D K Robinson

General organisation. Founded in 1724, Rishworth is a co-educational day and boarding school comprising a nursery for children from age 3, a Junior School, Heathfield, which has its own separate site where children are taught up to the age of 11, and the Senior School up to age 18. Rishworth is a Church of England foundation, but welcomes children of all faiths, or of none. Numbers stand at about 500 pupils, of whom over 100 are boarders.

Facilities and Location. Superbly located in 130 acres of a beautiful Pennine valley, the School has a mix of elegant older buildings and excellent modern facilities including a capacious sports hall with fitness suite, a separate, newly-redeveloped Sports Club with 25-metre indoor swimming pool and squash courts, a large expanse of games pitches, a music block, 3 modern ICT suites, wireless (and cabled) Internet and Intranet connection across the whole site, a Performing Arts Theatre, a centre dedicated to sixth-form study, freshly-refurbished boarding houses and newly-installed, state-of-the-art science laboratories.

Access to the School by road is easy, with the M62 within five minutes' drive. School buses run to the Halifax, Todmorden, Rochdale, Oldham and Huddersfield areas.

Welfare and Pastoral. The unusually high degree of attention afforded to pupils by small teaching groups, the careful monitoring of progress, coordinated pastoral support and a close working partnership with parents enables pupils to build on their strengths and allows specific needs to be addressed. Each boarding pupil is under the direct care of a Housemaster or Housemistress, who is ably supported by assistant staff in each boarding house.

Teaching. Taught by a dedicated staff of qualified specialists, the curriculum, both academic and non-academic, is broad and stimulating, and offers every pupil the chance to be challenged and to excel. A general curriculum, broadly in line with the National Curriculum, is followed until Year 9, after which pupils select GCSE options in consultation with their parents, tutors and subject teachers. AS and A2 options are also selected via consultation.

Support is given by qualified specialists for certain special needs including dyslexia and English where this is not the pupil's first language.

Broader Education. In order to help our pupils to become the confident, balanced and considerate young men and women we wish them to be, we encourage participation in a wide range of activities outside the classroom.

Sports are well appointed and well taught, and each term boys and girls enjoy excellent results. The School also has a justly high reputation in music and drama.

Other activities range from The Duke of Edinburgh's Award to golf, skiing, and many others.

Boarding. We have no dormitories. Boarders (from age 10 or 11, and sometimes age 9) are accommodated in individual study-bedrooms, almost all single or double occupancy, which allow pupils their personal space. These are located in spacious houses, overseen by house staff. The boarding houses have recently undergone major refurbishment which has ensured that the character of the historic buildings has been retained alongside the provision of top-rate modern amenities. A full programme of activities is arranged for the evenings and weekends, and there are good recreational facilities reserved for the boarders, including dedicated social areas.

Admission. Places in the Junior School, Heathfield, are given, subject to availability, on individual assessments appropriate to each applicant's age and previous education. Entrants for Rishworth at Year 7 are asked to sit the School's own entrance assessment, which also forms the basis for the award of scholarships.

Those who wish to join the School at other stages are assessed individually.

Fees per term (from April 2014). Reception to Year 2 £1,935; Years 3 to 6 £2,840; Years 7 & 8: £3,485 day, £7,485 full boarding, £6,795 weekly boarding; Years 9 to 13: £3,795 day, £8,160 full boarding, £7,435 weekly boarding. The School operates a number of schemes, including monthly payments, to ease the financial burden on parents.

Scholarships and Bursaries. Scholarships & Bursaries are available, the former on merit, the latter for demonstrable financial need. The extent to which these awards can be offered will also be determined by other factors, such as the School's own circumstances and the nature of a given cohort of applicants.

Scholarships may be awarded, up to a value of 50% of Tuition fees, for excellence in academic work, sport, music or drama. For Year 7 entry scholarships, applicants are formally assessed. For Year 12 entry, awards are made on the basis of an individual's past record (including examination results).

Most awards are made to applicants at these entry levels. However, suitable candidates at any stage will be considered.

Substantial discounts are available for siblings of pupils in the School, for children of serving members of the Armed Forces and of ordained members of the Church of England. Bursaries may also be available in cases of financial need.

The Old Rishworthian Club maintains a fund for the grant of scholarships to children of ORs.

For more information contact the Admissions Officer.

Charitable status. Rishworth School is a Registered Charity, number 1115562. It exists to provide education for boys and girls.

The Royal School, Wolverhampton

Penn Road, Wolverhampton WV3 0EG
Tel: 01902 341230
Fax: 01902 344496
email: info@royal.wolverhampton.sch.uk
website: www.theroyalschool.co.uk
Twitter: @TheRoyalSchool
Facebook: /The-Royal-School

Motto: *Nisi Dominus Frustra.*
     The School was founded in 1850 and was granted a Royal Charter by Queen Victoria in 1891. His Royal Highness The Earl of Wessex is our current Patron.

Patron:
HRH The Earl of Wessex, KG, KCVO

Vice-Patrons:
The Countess of Lichfield
The Duke of Sutherland

Board of Governors:
P Hill, FCMA, MIMC (*Chairman*)
D Swift, BEd (*Vice-Chairman*)
Mrs G Atwal
Prof S Chung, JP, FCIB, MRICS, FB Eng, FASI, MSc Dip Man
R H Etheridge
Mrs J Lawson, BA, ACIB
M Masters
A Rashid, JP, MA, MPhil
A T Sharp
Dr S Suresh, BSc Eng, ME, PhD

Headmaster: M Heywood, BA, PGCE

Deputy Head (Learning and Teaching): Mrs l Hale, BEd, Cert Ed
Deputy Head (Boarding & Pastoral): D P Ireland, BEng Hons, PGCE
Director of Finance: Ms D Parsons, FCMA
Administrator, Clerk to the Governors: Mrs S Seivewright
Lichfield House Parent: Mrs M Johanesen, BA Hons
Dartmouth Housemaster: M Taylor, BA Hons
Rogers Housemistress: Mr M White, Cert Ed
York House Parent: Mrs N Zhang
Victoria Housemaster: Mr W Duckworth, BSc Hons, PGCE

Senior School Staff:

Arts, Craft, Design & Technology:
M Allison, BA Hons, PGCE, BTec National Diploma (*Head of Art*)
Mr I Pugh (*Head of Design and Technology*)
Miss A M Atherton, BA, PGCE (*Head of Food Technology*)
Mrs L Fabre, BA Hons, PGCE

Business Studies:
C J Walker, BSc Hons, PGCE (*Head of Key Stage 3, Head of Business Studies*)
Mrs L Bostock

English:
Ms C Gardner, BA Hons, PGCE (*Head of English*)
Mrs A Nabbs, BA Hons, PGCE

Geography:
Miss C Cadwallader, MSc, BSc (*Head of Geography*)

History:
Miss S Murphy

Information Technology:
C Wilke-Zhang, BSc Hons, DIP (*Head of Information Technology*)

Mathematics:
A Long (*Head of Mathematics*)
D Ireland, BEng Hons, PGCE
W Duckworth, BSc Hons, GTTP
Miss A Maciag, MA, PGCE

Modern Languages:
Mrs A Goodlad, BA Hons, PGCE (*Head of Modern Languages*)
Mrs R Boden, BA Hons, PGCE

Physical Education:
Mrs R L Ingerfield-Lapsley, BA Hons, PGCE (*Head of PE, Head of PSCHE/Careers, Rogers Housemistress*)
Miss A M Atherton, BA, PGCE
Miss N Gardner, BA, QTS PE
M Taylor, BA Hons (*Dartmouth Housemaster*)

Psychology/Sociology:
Miss C Martin, BSc, MSc (*Head of Psychology & Sociology*)

Science:
Miss H Prosser, BSc, PGCE (*Head of Science*)
Dr W Chhabra, MPhil, BSc, MSc, BA Ed
R Beardsmore, BSc Hons, PGCE
Mrs S Tappin, CChem, MRSC (*Laboratory Assistant*)
Mrs R Nurpuri, BA Hons, PGCE

TEFL:
Miss J L Kyle, BA, PGCE

Junior School Staff:
R Alder, BA Hons, PGCE (*Year 4 Teacher*)
Mrs Cartwright, NVQ3 (*Pre-Prep Teaching Assistant*)
Miss C Galbraith, BA, PGCE (*Year 3 Teacher*)
Mrs K Harris, BA Hons, PGCE (*Reception Teacher*)
Mrs J Hocknull, BEd Hons, CertSpLd (*Special Educational Needs Coordinator*)
Mrs C Ireland, BA Hons, PGCE (*Teacher in charge of Junior School*)
Mrs E Tandy, DCE Cert EYP (*Year 1 Assistant*)
Mrs K Jefferson, BEd Hons (*Year 2 Teacher, Head of Junior Library*)
Mrs D McKenzie (*Early Years Assistant*)
Mrs K Newton, BA Hons, HBO Hons, PGCE (*Year 1 Teacher, Key Stage 1 Coordinator*)
Mrs E Tandy (*Pre-Prep Teaching Assistant*)
Miss P Walters (*Reception Teacher*)
Miss L Young (*Pre-Prep Teaching Assistant*)

Nursery:
Mrs S Lawrence, NNEB (*Head of Nursery*)
Mrs J Cooper, BTEC (*Nursery Nurse, Deputy SENCO*)
Mrs P Brannan (*Assistant*)
Mrs A Brennan, NVQ3 (*Nursery Nurse*)
Miss K Brittain, NVQ3 (*Nursery Nurse*)
Miss S Burke, NVQ3 (*Nursery Nurse*)
Miss L Butters, NVQ3 (*Nursery Nurse*)
Miss E Cash, BTEC (*Nursery Nurse*)
Miss C Chinn, BTEC (*Nursery Nurse*)
Miss S Colley, BTEC (*Nursery Nurse*)
Mrs S Edwards, BTEC, FD (*Nursery Nurse*)
Miss L Fletcher, BTEC (*Nursery Nurse*)
Ms L Franklin, NVQ3 (*Nursery Nurse*)
Miss L Glaze, NVQ3 (*Nursery Nurse*)
Miss Z Hands, CACHE Level 3, CCLD Level 4 (*Nursery Nurse*)
Mrs K Harbias, NVQ3 (*Nursery Nurse*)
Mrs E Harris, NCFE2 (*Nursery Nurse*)
Miss S Rogers, NVQ3 (*Nursery Nurse*)
Mrs A Seymour, BTEC (*Nursery Nurse*)
Miss S Shaw, NVQ2 (*Nursery Nurse*)

Miss L Webb, NNEB (*Nursery Nurse*)
Miss R Woolley, NVQ3 (*Nursery Nurse*)
Miss G Worth, NVQ3 (*Nursery Nurse*)

Music Staff:
I Hackett, BMus Hons, PGCE (*Director of Music, Head of Key Stage 4*)

Visiting Music Staff:
Miss C L Appleby, MA, BMus Hons (*Woodwind*)
Mrs J Davis, LCM Hons (*Keyboard, London College of Music Rep*)
Miss A Finch, BMus, PG Dip (*Strings*)
Miss R Lakeland, CertEd, ALCM (*Singing/Harp*)
Mrs M Morton, GRSM, ARCM, LRAM, PGCE
B Perkins, ABSM (*Guitar*)
S Read, LGSM, ARCM, CertEd (*Brass*)
S Terry (*Keyboard/Drums*)
G Walker, BA Hons, ARCO, FRSA (*Piano*)

Administrative Staff:
Registrar: Mrs M Orton
Marketing Director: Mrs J Hodgson
PA to the Headmaster: Mrs J Edwards
External Relations Officer: Mrs N Butler
Junior School Secretary: Miss R Gossage, Mrs K Patel
Academic Secretary: Ms K Hill
School Fees: Mrs M Wilkinson
Accounts Assistant: Mrs K Bastable, Mrs P Hennesey
Office Administration: Mrs R Rollason
Resource Centre Manager: G Davies, BSc Econ
Head of International Office: Mrs M Wilkinson

Medical Staff:
Dr D DeRosa, BSc, MB, CLB, MRCGP
Mrs C Dinham, RGN, RSCN
Mrs E Heath

Estates Manager: D Brittain
Catering Manager: C Cooke

The Royal School, Wolverhampton occupies a 28-acre site in a pleasant residential area to the west of Wolverhampton and provides an education for boys and girls aged 6 weeks to 19 years. The Royal Junior School, Wolverhampton and The Young Royals' Nursery has approximately 200 pupils and the Senior School 250 pupils. Pupils can attend on a daily basis or as weekly, full or flexi boarders. The School can accommodate 170 boarders, from age 10 years upwards.

Facilities. The School has been transformed since its days as an orphanage and the elegant ivy-clad main school building has been continually updated and augmented with a number of substantial modern developments. Over the past ten years, the School has spent over £10 million on improvements to the buildings and equipment. Today, it offers tradition combined with modern facilities, including a brand new swimming pool and sports complex, a new sixth form centre and internet café, an art, craft and design centre, dining room and kitchens, a library, modern boarding houses, 5 refurbished science laboratories, 3 information technology suites and a floodlit astroturf. The most recent addition is the Baby Unit, opened in September 2010, which increased the Early Years Provision to a maximum of 135 children.

The School's boarding accommodation houses boys and girls according to their age. Younger children share with 2 or 3 others of the same age and pupils in the Sixth Form either have a single study-bedroom or a twin room. All boarding houses have a lounge as well as a kitchen and a launderette. Pupils are carefully supervised by the School's residential staff at all times. In the January 2009 Ofsted Boarding Inspection Report, the boarding provision was classified as "good" overall and "outstanding" in the category "Helping children achieve well and enjoy what they do".

The School's own catering staff serves a variety of meals to suit all tastes. A cooked lunch is provided for day pupils and boarders can enjoy breakfast, lunch and dinner. Special dietary requirements, for religious or medical reasons, can be accommodated.

Religion. The Royal Wolverhampton School has its own Chapel within the School grounds. This fine building forms a focus for School life, with daily assemblies and important events in the School calendar being held there. Although the School has a religious affiliation to the Church of England, it welcomes pupils of all religions. Staff will assist pupils of other religions in pursuing their beliefs during their stay at the School.

Pastoral Care. The well-being of all pupils in the School is of prime importance and pastoral care is a universally recognised strength. Both day and boarding pupils are allocated to "houses" under the guidance of a housemaster or housemistress. All pupils have a tutor responsible for overseeing their pastoral and academic welfare, although all staff are expected to take corporate responsibility for pupil welfare and pupils are entitled to consult any member of staff regarding matters of concern.

In case of illness, the School has a fully equipped sanatorium, which provides 24 hour healthcare.

Transport Links. The Royal School, Wolverhampton is easily accessible by road, train and air. The school can arrange transfers from all major UK airports including Manchester, Birmingham, Heathrow and Gatwick. A daily school transport service is organised for pupils locally.

Curriculum. Use of IT is integral to the curriculum from Reception onwards. The School offers a broad education at all levels, which is based on the National Curriculum. Recent additions to the curriculum include: French in the Nursery; Sociology at GCSE; Psychology, Sociology and Photography at A Level; Photography and Electronics at AS Level. Pupils in Year 10 study five compulsory subjects (English and English Literature, Mathematics, ICT and the Sciences) plus four optional subjects, out of a total of sixteen. Pupils of higher ability may take separate Sciences and additional Mathematics, both taught within the standard timetable. At the end of Year 11 all pupils take GCSE examinations.

At A Level students are advised on the number and type of subjects they should choose, bearing in mind their proposed university course and career. Twenty-two different A Level courses are available. The School has strength in a variety of areas and on six recent occasions pupils have finished in the top five in the UK in one of their A Level subjects.

Sixth Form. The School prides itself on the great care it takes in advising Sixth Form students on careers and universities. The School has direct links with many universities and students have the opportunity to discuss various options with representatives from Higher and Further Education. It is common for 100% of those students who wish to go to university to secure a place at the institution of their preferred choice.

In addition to the School's other facilities, which can be used by all pupils, Sixth Form pupils have their own study area, Sixth Form Centre and Internet Café where they can meet, study and relax.

Music and Drama. The School has an excellent reputation for its musical standards and is a recognised examination centre for the London College of Music. Our active Music Department, equipped with the latest technology, provides pupils with an opportunity to learn how to play 20 different instruments. In addition, pupils are encouraged to take part in the School's choir and to perform in a wide variety of events, including at the National Indoor Arena in Birmingham.

The Music Department organises regular Performing Arts festivals at which pupils of all ages perform. One of the highlights of the School calendar is the Variety Show, which presents the best of the School's dramatic and musical talents to parents and other guests.

The School supports the Mayor of Wolverhampton by providing musical evenings in order to raise money for the Mayor's charities.

Sport and Extra-Curricular Activities. The School aims to educate well-rounded individuals and a wide variety of extra-curricular activities are enjoyed by all pupils.

Pupils can choose from fifteen different sports and matches are frequently arranged both inter-house and against local schools. The School has a strong basketball team which has achieved major successes nationally.

The School launched an Elite Swimming Programme in conjunction with West Midlands Swimming and Sport England in September 2009. The Squad has already achieved Youth Olympic, European Junior and National success in the short time it has been open.

The School has a very strong Combined Cadet Force with Army and RAF sections. The shooting team has finished in the top ten in the UK in the RAF Assegai shooting competition for seven years in succession and regularly wins trophies in Army "March and Shoot" competitions. Pupils are also given the opportunity to participate in the successful Duke of Edinburgh's Award Scheme and various other community projects.

The School ethos promotes compassion towards those less fortunate than ourselves and considerable amounts of money are raised for local and national charities.

Entrance. The Senior School holds two entrance examinations each year for entry to Year 7, one in November and one in March. The minimum entry requirement for Sixth Form is five GCSE passes at Grade C or equivalent.

Entry to the Nursery and Baby Unit is throughout the year and entry to the Junior School usually takes place each September. Limited access is available at other time during the year by assessment.

Scholarships and Bursaries. *Academic*: Merit scholarships are available each year to pupils entering Senior School from Year 7 dependant on exam performance.

Music: A limited number of Music scholarships are available to pupils entering Senior School from Year 7. Such scholarships are awarded following an assessment. Future musical potential is also assessed.

Sports: The School offers a limited number of Swimming and Sports scholarships. Candidates will be expected to have achieved distinction in at least one sport and show potential for future development.

Sixth Form: Academic scholarships at Sixth Form level are normally awarded on the basis of GCSE or equivalent grades. The amount of the award depends upon the academic ability of the pupil concerned.

In addition the School can offer support via its Bursary Scheme.

Orphan Foundation Scholarships are available to children who have lost one or both parents, whose father or mother is incapacitated through illness or who are from single or divorced families. A need for a boarding education normally has to be established. Foundation Scholarship entry forms are available from the Clerk to the Governors.

Awarding of such concessions takes full account of the Charity's requirement to deliver "public benefit".

For full details of Scholarships and Bursaries please contact The Registrar.

Fees per term (2014–2015). Senior School: Full Boarders £6,760–£9,610; Weekly Boarders £6,565–£7,600; Day Pupils £3,375–£4,410. Junior School: Boarders £6,500; Day Pupils £2,850–£3,375. A prompt payment discount of £200 per term is available. Baby Royals (age 6 weeks–2 years) £840–£3,605; Tiny Royals (age 2–3) £1,585–£2,680; Young Royals (age 3–4) £1,450–£2,460.

Day fees include: lunch, textbooks, stationery, compulsory teaching materials and personal accident insurance cover. In addition to the above, boarding fees include: full board accommodation, laundry, dry cleaning, medical attention and nursing in the Sanatorium.

Boarding Fees include all meals, medical attention and nursing in the Sanatorium, textbooks, stationery and compulsory teaching materials. The fees also include the costs of any English as a Foreign Language (EFL) tuition that takes place during the lesson timetable for all students in years 10 and 11. If the Headmaster feels an individual student may require extra EFL tuition, this will be charged at up to £375 a term for each block of additional tuition. No charges for extra tuition will be made without parental agreement.

Day Fees include all text books, stationery and compulsory teaching materials. Junior School fees include lunch. Senior School lunches are a chargeable extra. Parents may choose one of the following options: (a) pre-pay for lunch by adding the sum of £125 to their fee invoice (this works out at approximately £2.00 a day for a two-course meal); (b) pay daily for their meals. There is a minimum charge of £3.00 a day which is payable in cash at the point of service.

The children of Serving Personnel in the Armed Forces receive a Bursary of £1,500 per term. The children of Old Royals receive a reduction of 25% off the basic fees and discounts are also available for siblings.

Old Royals' Association. The Association regularly organises reunions for former pupils. Founders' Day in June and Remembrance Sunday are also popular times for Old Royals and Old Rowans to return to the School. For further information, please contact Mr Mike Masters, 139 High Street, Coleshill, Birmingham B46 3AY; Tel: 01675 463093; email: mike_masters@talk21.com.

Charitable status. The Royal Wolverhampton School is a Registered Charity, number 1092221. It exists solely to provide an education for children.

Ruthin School

Mold Road, Ruthin, Denbighshire LL15 1EE
Tel: 01824 702543
Fax: 01824 707141
email: registrar@ruthinschool.co.uk
website: www.ruthinschool.co.uk

Motto: *Dei gratia sum quod sum*

The School was originally founded in 1284. Refounded in 1574 by Gabriel Goodman, Dean of Westminster, the School was a centre of academic excellence in North Wales, and was granted a Royal Charter.

Visitor: Her Majesty The Queen

Patron: Sir William Gladstone, Bt, KG, MA

Council of Management:
Chairman: Mrs J Oldbury
A R Bale
C W Conway
Revd J S Evans
Mrs T Kerrigan
Dr G H Roberts
J E Sharples
His Honour Judge I J C Trigger

Principal: T J Belfield, MA Cantab

Vice-Principal: I Welsby, BSc, MIBiol, PGCE, DipEd
Head of Teaching & Learning: Mrs J K Higham, MA, PGCE, CPE
Head of Lower School: I M Rimmer, BSc, PGCE
Head of Sixth Form: Miss K A Goodey, MEd, TESOL, BEd, CETFLA

Assistant Staff:
N J R Blandford, BA, MA, PGCE
Mrs E T Brodzinska, LLB, MA, DELTA

Mrs E M Brown, BA, MA Ed, PGCE, TEFL, AMBDA
B Cribb, BA, PGCE, MEd
Mrs R Crowther, BA, PGCE
Dr D G Edwards, BA Hons, DPhil
Dr N Fairbank, PhD
Miss P Foster, BA, PGCE, DELTA
P J French, BSc, PGCE
Mrs S Frencham, BSc, PGCE
J P Hamer, BA, PGCE
Dr M D Hannant, PhD, PGCE
J R Henry, BA, PGCE
M H L Hewer, MA Oxon, DipEd
D J Heywood, BA, PGCE
L Hogan, BSc, PGCE
Dr A W Hughes, BEng, PhD
Mrs K Hughes, BA, PGCE
Mrs M Kenworthy, BSc, PGCE
Mrs S Morley, BEd
Prof M O'Brien, CEng, PhD, MBA, MBCS
D A Owen Booth, MGCI, BEd, DipHE
M S Robinson, BA, MA Oxon, PGCE
C Sennett, DRSAMD, PGCE
R A Wadon, BSc, PGCE
Miss J Warriner, BSc, MEng, MA, PGCE
Miss H Webb, BSc, PGCE
Miss D A Williams, BSc, PGCE
Dr M Wilton, PhD, PGCE
K Whiting, BSc, PGCE
Miss L Zhao, BA, PGCE

Registrar and PA to the Principal: Mrs S E Williams
Finance Administrator: Mrs L Evans
School Medical Officer: Dr T Kneale
School Nurse: Mrs C Bland, RGN

The School. Ruthin School is co-educational with some 270 pupils in the School comprising 180 boarders and 90 day pupils. The emphasis is on academic excellence and providing an environment to gain our students entry to the very best universities in the UK. Good manners, personal discipline and respect for others are of supreme importance, as is a thorough grounding in central subjects of the curriculum. We believe that social responsibility can be developed in a small community with a family atmosphere, comprising a wide range of academic and other talents. This is reflected in our entry policy. Ruthin School is committed to providing an education of the highest quality, endeavouring to develop the potential of all its pupils in all spheres of education. The pupils develop self-confidence through recognising and building upon their strengths as well as identifying and striving to improve their weaknesses. They are thus prepared to face the challenges of the changing world beyond school.

Organisation. Places (both day and full boarding) are offered to boys and girls from the age of 11.

The five boarding houses – Archbishop Williams, Ellis, Goodman, Russell and Wynne – have their own House system under the guidance of resident Housemasters.

Admission. The normal method of entry to the School is by interview, examination and reports.

Activities. A wide range of non-curricular activities is provided and has included fitness training, basketball, swimming, yoga, judo, Taekwondo, drama, rock climbing, sailing and canoeing, mountain biking, stage management, shooting, weight training, table tennis, badminton, conservation, gardening and tennis. Boys and girls are encouraged to participate in the Duke of Edinburgh's Award Scheme at the age of 14 until they have completed the Bronze Award; several go on to complete the Silver and a few aspire to the Gold Awards. A lively mix of traditional and contemporary musical and dramatic productions is a feature of the school year and half the pupils receive individual instrumental tuition from the professional music staff. A programme of excursions is organised for boarders in the evenings and at weekends and these are open to all pupils.

Bursaries and Awards. In addition to academic awards, remissions are available for siblings, children of members of the armed forces, and of Old Ruthinians.

Curriculum. A wide curriculum is offered and includes English, Mathematics, History, Geography, separate Biology, Physics and Chemistry, Art, Music, Information Technology, French, Mandarin and Spanish. PE and Business Studies are added at GCSE Level. Economics is added in the Sixth Form. Further Mathematics is also taught in the Sixth Form.

An option scheme operates for Form 4, but English, Mathematics, and one science subject are compulsory.

Careers. Guidance begins in the Senior School and a comprehensive programme evolves through Forms 4 and 5 and the whole of the Lower Sixth is devoted to research and visits before university applications are made. All members of the Sixth Form who wish to enter university are successful. Work experience is undertaken in Form 4 and the Lower Sixth.

Games. Rugby, basketball, football, cross-country, netball, tennis and athletics all feature in the coaching programme. A new Sports Hall was opened in January 2004.

Fees per annum (2014–2015). Day £9,000–£11,750; Boarding £24,500. Fees are payable twice yearly, at beginning of August and February. British parents have the option to pay monthly by Direct Debit.

Transport. The School provides daily transport to and from the North Wales coast, Holywell and Mold. Transport is provided for boarders from Manchester and Liverpool airports to the School, at the beginning and end of each term.

The Old Ruthinian Association fosters close links between past and present pupils of the School.

Charitable status. Ruthin School is a Registered Charity, number 525754. It exists to provide education for boys and girls.

St Bees School

St Bees, Cumbria CA27 0DS
Tel: 01946 828000
Fax: 01946 823657
email: mailbox@stbeesschool.co.uk
           admissions@stbeesschool.co.uk
website: www.stbeesschool.co.uk
Twitter: @stbeesschool
Facebook: /StBeesSchool

Motto: Ingredere ut Proficias

Founded by Edmund Grindal, Archbishop of Canterbury, in 1583. Now conducted as a co-educational independent school under a scheme approved by The Charity Commission.

Governors:
Chairman: Professor H F Woods, CBE, FRCP, FRCPE
Chairman of Executive Committee: Mrs C T McKay
The Rt Revd J W S Newcome, Bishop of Carlisle
The Revd Canon B Smith
D Davies, Esq, BSc
M P T Hart, Esq, FRICS, DipQS
W Lowther, Esq, OBE, CBE, DL
Dr K M Illsley, MBChB, MRCGP
Ms C Hensman
M G Rigby, Esq
G R Smith, Esq, BSc, CBE, DL
A J Wills, Esq

Head: J Davies, BMus, ACertCM, FASC, LGSM, PGCE

Senior Teacher: Miss J L Dyer, BSc
Senior Housemistress: Mrs J C Malan, BA (†*Lonsdale House*)

Chaplain: Revd C R Swartz, BA Cantab

Teaching Staff:
† *Housemaster/mistress*

Mrs G F Hudson, MA	J Lynch, MA
Mrs J A Bell, LLCM	Ms L Gray, BA (†*Bega*
Mrs S L Bromiley, BA	*House*)
Mrs J A Carnegie, BA	Ms E Clegg, BSc
M K Midwood, BA	Mrs J Ransom, BA
S McNee, BA	Ms M A D'Angelo, BA
M Ollis, BA	Ms N Cheers, BA
Mrs S J Evans, BEd	Mrs A Warne, BA
M J George, BA	Miss M Murphy, BSc
Mrs S G A Ollis, BA	Dr P Callow, BSc, PhD
B R Allen, BA (†*School*	Dr M Brookes, BSc, PhD
House)	Mrs F Corrigan, BA
Mrs V Smart, BSc, PhD	J R Corrigan, BA
Dr R A Young, BSc, MSc,	D Boardman, BSc
PhD (†*Grindal House*)	Mrs T Webb Rogers, BA
R B Bardsley, BA	O Rogers, BEd
Mrs C M Mauger, BEd	

Prep School:
Ms R Field, BA
Miss K J Sharman, BA
I M Pointon, BA

Medical Officers:
G J Ironside, MBChB, MRCGP, DRCOG
S E Megan, BMedSci, BM BS, MRCCP, DRCOG, DCH

Bursar: N Halfpenny, BSc, MSc, PGCE
Registrar: Mrs J Hawley
Head's Secretary: Mrs E Graham

Situation and Buildings. The School stands in 150 acres of the attractive Valley of St Bees, half a mile from a fine sandy beach and on the western edge of the Lake District National Park.

The principal older buildings, including the Chapel, Library, Art & Design Department, Gymnasium and Swimming Pool are of St Bees sandstone and are situated on a raised terrace overlooking the main playing fields. The original school-room, which dates from 1587, now forms one side of a quadrangle and is used as the dining hall.

In addition there is a self-contained music school with extensive teaching and practice facilities, together with a basement studio which houses an iMac digital composition suite, a Sixth Form Centre with a private study room and a fully-equipped kitchen, a 15-meter heated, indoor swimming pool and changing rooms, a large sports hall featuring a climbing wall, cricket nets and squash court, three Eton Fives Courts and a Golf Academy with a chipping and putting green, all centred around the School's 9-hole golf course.

Organisation. There are 300+ pupils aged 4–18, divided into a Senior School and a Prep Department. In the Senior School each pupil is the responsibility of a Housemaster or Housemistress and a personal tutor. There are two Houses for boys and two for girls. All boarders share twin or three-bedded rooms with some Sixth Form boarders having single study-bedrooms. Boys and girls who live within commuting distance of the School are accepted as day pupils and the School also admits weekly and flexi boarders. The School operates an extensive bus service.

Religion. The Chapel stands at the centre of the School buildings and there are short services on certain weekdays before morning school. The Vicar of the Parish is the Chaplain and on Thursdays the whole School attends a short service in the Parish Church, The Priory.

Aims. The purpose of the School is to provide an education based on Christian principles, which will enable each pupil to develop his or her individual talents to the full. Particular emphasis is placed on academic excellence, good personal relationships and strong pastoral care. Thriving artistic, dramatic and musical traditions coupled with a wide range of sporting facilities help to avoid any narrow specialisation.

Curriculum. In the Prep Department, the curriculum is carefully planned to meet the needs of each individual child. Literacy and numeracy objectives follow the National Framework guidelines, but look to challenge and extend the pupil as appropriate. Science covers the main programmes of study from the National Curriculum and promotes the understanding of Science through 'hands on' investigative work whenever possible. The majority of the work is topic based and during this time cross-curricular links are forged. Pupils are also given the opportunity to experience learning French and Latin under the guidance of one of the language/classics specialists employed by the School.

In the Senior School, the curriculum provides GCSE courses in English, Latin, French, Spanish, History, Geography, Mathematics, Physics, Chemistry, Biology, Information Technology, Home Economics, Art, Physical Education and Music. An option system permits pupils to select the combination of subjects best suited to their abilities. There is a dedicated Head of Sixth Form. Most members of the Sixth Form will study four subjects at AS Level and three at A2 Level together with a Key Skills and General Studies programme. Virtually all proceed to higher education. There is a highly successful CReSTeD registered Teaching and Learning Centre supporting those pupils requiring specialist support and an International Department offering support to pupils whose first language is not English.

Careers. The Senior School has developed good links with the locally-based Careers Offices. Members of the Staff are responsible for providing specialist advice on careers and higher education and for developing links with industry and commerce. The Head, Housemasters and Housemistresses are also involved in this work and there is regular contact between parents and staff so that progress, future options and career plans can be discussed.

Games. The major sports for boys are Rugby Football, Cricket and Athletics. The girls play Hockey and Rugby 7s and are given a wide choice of games, including Tennis and Athletics, during the Summer Term. The School provides many County and Regional Representatives in all major sports. A large number of other sports flourish; the School has its own Golf Course, indoor heated Swimming Pool, large multi-purpose Sports Hall, and courts for Eton Fives, Squash Rackets, Tennis and Badminton.

Other Activities. There is a wide variety of societies and clubs, for example Young Enterprise, Debating and Public Speaking, and each pupil is encouraged to develop cultural interests. The School offers an extensive and varied weekend programme for boarders. Recently these have included theatre excursions to Stratford, days out to York, Glasgow, Edinburgh and Newcastle, beside the usual cinema, ten-pin bowling etc.

Music. The School possesses a strong musical tradition and a large proportion of the pupils receive tuition in an instrument. In addition to the Orchestra and Choir there are strings, brass and woodwind ensembles. Keyboard players have access to a Willis organ and have the opportunity for private tuition in this instrument from the Headmaster. The Choir and instrumentalists perform regularly at the School and in the locality. There are close links with drama.

Drama. Drama is part of the Lower School curriculum and each year there are at least four productions involving all age groups.

Combined Cadet Force. Pupils are members of the CCF in the Third and Fourth Forms (Years 9 and 10) and may choose to extend their service while they are in the Fifth (Year 11) or Sixth Form. There are Army and RAF Sections and all cadets receive instruction in Shooting. The Duke of Edinburgh's Award scheme can be taken through to Gold whilst pupils are cadets. Advanced courses are available in

Leadership Training. Courses in flying and pilot training are also arranged.

Outdoor Activities. The School makes full use of its unique location between the Lakeland Fells and the sea and outdoor activities are encouraged for the enjoyment that they give and the valuable personal qualities which they help to develop. Adventure Training is part of the curriculum for Lower School pupils. Experts in mountaineering and watersports are employed by the School and all pupils have opportunities to receive instruction in camping, canoeing, hillwalking, orienteering and rock climbing. There are annual skiing parties to Europe.

Admission. Candidates for entry between 4 and 10 is by individual interview and submission of previous school reports. Candidates for entry at age 11 or 13 sit the Scholarship and Entrance Examination in February. Entry to the Sixth Form is dependent on interview, school report and the gaining of a minimum of five GCSE passes. The Head is prepared to give individual consideration to candidates entering at other ages.

A fee of £40 is payable at the time of registration.

Further particulars from The Registrar (01946 828010; admissions@st-bees-school.co.uk).

Scholarships and Bursaries. Academic Scholarships are available to pupils entering the First Form at age 11 and to pupils entering the Third Form at age 13. Music Scholarships are available at the ages of 11, 13 and 16. Academic Scholarships with Art and Sports Awards are available to pupils entering the Sixth Form.

The School also offers a limited number of means-tested Bursaries.

Fees per term (2014–2015). Prep Day: EU £2,355–£2,595; Non EU Day/Weekly Boarding £4,100. Senior Day/Weekly Boarding: EU £4,225–£5,450, Non EU £6,100–£8,100. Senior Full Boarding: EU £6,500–£8,995; Non EU £7,320–£9,985.

Former Pupils. The St Beghian Society Secretary, c/o the School. Handbook and Register of Members (Latest Edition 2000).

Charitable status. St Bees School is a Registered Charity, number 526858. It exists to provide high quality education for boys and girls.

St Christopher School

Barrington Road, Letchworth Garden City, Herts SG6 3JZ
Tel: 01462 650850
Fax: 01462 481578
email: school.admin@stchris.co.uk
            admissions@stchris.co.uk
website: www.stchris.co.uk

Fully co-educational from its foundation in 1915, St Christopher has always been noted for its friendly informality, breadth of educational vision, good academic standards and success in developing lifelong self-confidence. There are now some 505 pupils from rising 3 to 18. Boarders can start from age 11. Weekly Boarding is available in Years 7–11 and Full Boarding is also available for Sixth Formers. We aim for our young people to develop competence and resourcefulness, social conscience and moral courage, a capacity for friendship and a true zest for life.

When the School was founded in 1915 the Daily Herald reported that the School was based 'not on the sameness of children, their conformity to type, but on their differences'. This concept of treating children as individuals was revolutionary at the time and continues to be one of the distinctive characteristics of a St Chris education. We do things differently because they work. We allow children to decide what they wear to school because it teaches them to be self-reliant and to make informed choices. Everyone is called by their first names (pupils and teaching staff alike) because we have found that this promotes better relationships between children and teachers, based on mutual trust. Parents also tell us that the use of first names makes conversations with teachers easier and more productive.

Board of Governors:
Bertie Leigh (*Chairman*)
Peter de Voil (*Vice-Chairman*)
Peter McMeekin
Tom Routh
Julie Bolter
John Simmonds
Sarah Kilcoyne
Roy Macgregor

Head: **Richard Palmer**, BEd, FRSA

Deputy Head: Cliff Canning, BD, BA, HDipEd
Director of Pastoral System: Gavin Fraser-Williams, BA, MA
Director of Activities: Byron Lewis, BSc
Head of Upper Juniors: Bryan Anderson, BEd
Head of Lower Juniors: Sam Selkirk, BEd
Registrar: Pauline Barker

Teaching Staff:
Alison Bagg, MA (*Head of Mathematics*)
Lizzie Anstice-Brown, BA, MA (*Art, Artist in Residence*)
Sylvester Beecroft, BA, PGCE (*French, Careers, Head of Examinations*)
Anne-Marie Knight, BA, MA (*Music, PSHE*)
Rebecca Clarke, DPhil (*Physics*)
Michael Collins, BA, MA, PGCE (*History, Politics*)
Wendy Cottenden, Cert Ed (*Head of PSHE*)
Chris Drayton, BSc (*Mathematics, Outdoor Pursuits*)
Denise Eades, BA (*Head of Geography*)
Gemma Fernandez, Licence University of A Coruna (*French, Spanish*)
Gavin Fraser Williams, BA, MA (*Craft, Design & Technology*)
David Gouldstone, BA (*English*)
Janine Hall, BA (*Art, Art Technician*)
Ian Hughes, BA (*Head of PE & Games*)
David Ilott, BA, DipEd (*Head of English, Head of EFL*)
Andrew Lambie, MA, PGCE (*Chemistry*)
Charlotte Leeke, BSc (*Geography*)
Byron Lewis, BSc (*Maths, ICT, Director of Activities*)
Samantha Lloyd, BSc, PGCE (*Biology*)
Penny Main, BA, MA, PGCE (*History, English*)
Liane May, BA, MA, PGCE (*English, Media Studies*)
Mario May, BA, MA, PhD, PGCE (*Head of History & Politics, Humanities Faculty Coordinator*)
Isabelle Mills, Licence d'Anglais, PGCE (*French, Spanish*)
Helen Ogilvie, PhD, MSc, PGCE (*Chemistry*)
Angeles Ojeda, Licendiada (*Spanish, German*)
Andy Owen, BSc, PGCE (*Physics, Head of Science Faculty*)
Emma Roskilly BA, PGCE (*English, Head of Media Studies*)
Jennifer Savage, BA, MA (*Geography*)
Andy Selkirk, MBA, BSc, DipPhy, PGCE (*Second Deputy – Academic Director, Biology*)
Emma Semple, BA, MA, PGCE (*Head of Arts Faculty*)
Cyrille Simon, Maîtrise (*Head of MFL, Faculty Coordinator*)
Claire Slater, BEng (*Maths*)
Rebecca Sweeney, BA, MA (*English*)
Maria Walker, BSc (*Mathematics*)
Ben Wall, BSc, PGCE (*Head of Craft, Design & Technology*)
Sarah Waller, BSc (*Biology*)
Jeremy Wallis, BSc, MA (*Economics*)
Ian Warder, MA, MSc, PGCE (*Mathematics*)

Jenny White, BEd (*Head of Girls' PE and Games*)
Hamish Wilson, BA, MA (*Head of Drama*)
Rebecca Wilson, BA, PGCE (*English, ICT*)
Susan Woollard, BSc, MSc (*Psychology, Science*)
Jonathan Wright, BSc (*PE, Games*)
Naz Yeni, BA, MA (*Drama*)

Junior School and Early Years Centre:
Head of Upper Juniors: Bryan Anderson, BEd
Head of Lower Juniors: Sam Selkirk, BEd
Secretary: Jean Benjamin
Daniel Bartlett, BEd
Anne Holland, BA, PGCE
David Jackson, BA, PGCE
Clare McComb, BA
Lyn McGregor, BEd (*PE & Games*)
Carly Ougham, BA, PGCE
Louise Robb, BA, Dip Music
Alyson Shiel, Cert Ed
Sally Wall, BA, PGCE
Jennifer Whale, BA
Sam Selkirk, BEd
Lesley Farrell, HNC, AMI Asst Cert
Sarah Brown, Maria Montessori Diploma
Denise Sheelan
Debbie Mintz
Avril Harker, BA

Director of Music: Martin Goodchild, GRSM, LRAM,
   PGCE

Librarian: Linda Aird, BA, Dip Lib, MCLIP
Performing Arts Technician: Robert Johnson
School Doctor: Carole Brookes, MBChB, DRCOG
School Nurse: Caroline Dorrington
Assistant School Nurse: Vivien Morse

Special Needs Tutors:
Armande Fryatt, MA, BEd
Cordelia Lewis, BSc, MA
Jayne Thomas, BA
Jane Miller
Lysandra Sinclaire-Harding, MPhil
Sarah Moxey, BA
Paula Murray-Rochard, BA
Maria Overhill
Linda Moore, BSc, PGCE (*Mathematics*)

Joint Heads of Special Needs:
Karen Hoyle, BA, Cert Dyslexia and Literacy
Liz Miller, BEd

Bursar, Company Secretary & Clerk to the Governors:
   William Hawkes, MA

Boarding Staff:
Arundale: Chris and Cecilia Drayton
Arunside: Malcolm and Pippa Hodgson

The School provides for children of average to outstanding ability. All who are admitted the Junior School (for 3 to 11 year olds) may continue through the Senior School, subject to performance. Entry to the Sixth Form is dependent on GCSE results and the ability to cope with the AS/A Level programme.

Academic Programme. The Montessori has its own very particular curriculum and is part of the Early Years Centre at St Christopher. Close attention is given to the transition to the Junior School which follows a programme which includes extensive enrichment built around the core elements of the National Curriculum. The Junior School offers small classes and a wide range of opportunities, including the use of specialist teachers and use of Senior School facilities. In the Senior School a wide-ranging programme continues to the age of 16, including the study of sciences to Double Award GCSE or GCSE in all three Sciences. In Modern Languages there are exchange schools in France or

Spain. The creative and expressive arts are particularly encouraged and the School has been awarded the Arts Council Artsmark Gold award.

The Sixth Form. Although St Christopher is not a large school, the Sixth Form is a good size (generally numbering around 80+) with excellent facilities in its Sixth Form Centre. 21 AS/A Level courses are on offer with all the usual Arts and Science subjects and, in addition, Theatre Studies, Psychology, Economics, Media Studies and Design Technology. There is a lively extra-curricular programme.

Learning through experience. There is an emphasis on learning through experience both with regard to academic subjects and more generally. There are many opportunities for practical and community work and for Outdoor Pursuits. At the end of the Summer Term the timetable is suspended for all pupils to undertake an extended project, generally away from the School campus. Each year two groups of sixth formers visit development projects in the Indian desert province of Rajasthan. There are also long-standing international projects in Ladakh. As a result of these the School was awarded the International School Award by the Department for Education through the British Council. A new cookery centre is opening in September 2011.

A humane and global outlook. There is no uniform (except for games). All children and adults are called by their first names. Internationalist and green values are encouraged and the School was re-awarded the Eco-Schools Award in 2010. People of different religions and of none feel equally at home; there is a significant period of silence in every assembly.

Self-Government. The informality of the School encourages openness: children speak up for themselves – and for others. Everyone, child and adult, is represented on the School Council which is chaired by an elected senior pupil. The elected Major Officials and Committees look after different aspects of community life.

Treating children as individuals. From the outset the School has sought to treat children as individuals. In consequence, the ethos is an encouraging one and suits children who enjoy a broad education and who will thrive in a non-competitive academic environment. In our Learning Centre individual and group help is available. We also deal individually with those of very high ability and children are placed "a year ahead" or "a year behind" according to their needs.

Creative and Performing Arts. The School has an excellent tradition in these areas and has fine purpose-built facilities that reflect this. There are several productions a year in the Theatre which has tiered seating and full technical resources. Similarly there are regular concerts and recitals in the Music Centre. A Music Technology Suite opened in 2007. In the Arts Centre there are studios for fine art, for design and for ceramics, together with individual Sixth Form work areas and a lecture theatre.

Technology and Computing. The School benefits from a modern ICT Centre; internal online resources for teaching and learning have been developed.

Clubs and Societies. There are plentiful activities for pupils to join in with, taking place after School and at weekends. Staff share their enthusiasms and pupils too can take the lead in their own areas of interest.

Health, Fitness and Physical Education. The diet is broad and healthy and considerable pride is taken in the catering. There is a full-time nurse with relief staff on call. The PE programme is full and varied, making use of playing field, gym, sports hall, all-weather surface and a 25m indoor swimming pool. Matches take place against many other schools.

Full collaboration with parents. The Parents' Circle was founded in 1921 and the School has throughout valued the close involvement of parents, who are welcome in the School not just for consultation about their children but also to take part in evening classes and in sharing the many performances and information evenings. We want parents to share in the education of their children and in the School community.

Boarders. There are up to 50 boarders living in 2 boarding houses. The provision for younger pupils has a strongly domestic feeling, with each under the supervision of resident house staff. The accommodation for sixth formers in a newly refurbished Sixth Form house is along student lines with almost all in single rooms.

Day Pupils. Day pupils benefit from the residential nature of the community, sharing in the evening and weekend life and taking meals in the School when they wish. Sixth formers have their own study areas in the Sixth Form Centre.

Fees per term (2014–2015). Day Pupils £1,144–£5,615, Full Boarding £9,935, Weekly Boarding £6,135–£7,595. There are discounts for second and subsequent children, so long as they have an older sibling in the School. A range of financial assistance is available through our Bursary Scheme. Fees for International students on application.

Admission Procedure. The most usual ages of admission are "rising 3", 4, 7, 8 or 9 into the Junior School, and at 11 or 13 into the Senior School. A number also enter at Sixth Form level. Our assessment procedure includes diagnostic tests and interview. Assessment for Years 7 and 9 entry takes place in January. Art and Academic Scholarships are available for entry into Years 7, 9 and 12.

Situation and Travel. The School has an attractive 35-acre campus on the edge of the Garden City with excellent communications. The A1(M) is a mile away and London (King's Cross) is 35 minutes by train. Stansted Airport is 35 minutes and Heathrow 60 minutes by car.

Old Scholars. The Membership Secretary of the St Christopher Club is David Cursons who can be reached c/o The School. The Annual Reunion is held over a weekend each July.

Charitable status. St Christopher School is a Registered Charity, number 311062. It exists to provide education for boys and girls, aiming to treat all as individuals and to develop their proper self-confidence.

St Edward's School

Cirencester Road, Charlton Kings, Cheltenham, Glos GL53 8EY

Tel: 01242 538600
Fax: 01242 538610
email: headmistress@stedwards.co.uk
website: www.stedwards.co.uk

Motto: Quantum Potes Aude

Formed from two former Grammar Schools in 1987, St Edward's is a co-educational Catholic Day School for 11 to 18 year olds. Proud of its Roman Catholic foundation as the Carmelite Boys' School, Whitefriars, and the Girls' Convent School, Charlton Park, St Edward's is now lay-run and warmly welcomes all denominations. We have 400 pupils currently on roll, of whom over 100 are in the Sixth Form. The School is set in 17 acres of beautiful grounds on the southern outskirts of Cheltenham. The site was originally King Edward the Confessor's Hunting Lodge and the main building dates from the 18th century. Small classes enable pupils to learn at their own pace and develop excellent relationships with their peers and teachers. St Edward's is a calm and happy school in which all pupils excel.

Chairman of Trustees: Mr Peter Goatley

Headmistress: Mrs Pat Clayfield, BSc, PGCE

Organisation. On entry to the Senior School at age 11, the students are allocated to one of three Forms. They are taught in three or four teaching groups which are set by ability for the principal subjects. The pastoral system of the School is based on Sections for the different age groups, with Section Heads leading teams of Tutors. The Sixth Formers have their own Common Room, study area, Careers Centre and Café. As Prefects, they play a vital role in the life of the School.

Developments. The School recently opened the Abbott Building, comprising a spacious new Refectory, state-of-the-art Drama Studio and additional teaching rooms. Older buildings were also refurbished as extra Art studios & Photography room, and a Careers Centre. In recent years there have also been: a CCF Headquarters, an additional Science laboratory, and numerous classroom and laboratory refurbishments.

Academic Curriculum. A broad range of subjects is offered up to GCSE, with 25 at A Level. During the first two years all pupils study Art, Drama, English, French, Geography, History, Information Technology, Latin (or Classical Civilisation), Mathematics, Music, Physical Education, Religious Studies, Science, Spanish, German and Technology (including Resistant Materials, Food and Textiles). In the third year, Science is studied as separate subjects: Biology, Chemistry and Physics.

The compulsory subjects for GCSE are English Language, English Literature, Mathematics, Religious Education, at least two Sciences (from Biology, Chemistry and Physics) and at least one Modern Language. Up to three further subjects are studied from: Latin, Classical Civilisation, French, German, Spanish, History, Geography, Music, Drama, Art, Design & Technology, PE, or Food Technology.

The A Level subjects offered include: Mathematics, Further Mathematics, English, History, Geography, Religious Studies (Philosophy & Ethics), Biology, Chemistry, Physics, French, German, Spanish, Latin, Classical Civilisation, Art (including Photography and Textiles), Music, Theatre Studies, Design Technology, Business Studies, Psychology and Physical Education.

Spiritual. Whole School Masses and other liturgies are celebrated several times a term. The pupils go on spiritual 'away days' each year.

Careers. A specialist Higher Education Counsellor guides Sixth Formers through the university application process and there is a specialist Oxbridge and American University Adviser. The School has had record numbers winning Oxbridge places over the last few years. In Year 11 pupils participate in a Work Experience week, and there is a Careers guidance programme for the lower Years. The Young Enterprise scheme is popular with Year 12 pupils.

Sport. The principal sports for boys are Rugby, Hockey, Football and Cricket; for girls Hockey, Netball and Rounders. The School also competes very successfully in Swimming, Tennis, Basketball, Athletics, Badminton, Golf and Cross-Country. There are regular sports tours, most recently to Australia and South Africa.

Facilities include four rugby pitches, three hockey pitches (including one synthetic-turf), cricket square, several tennis courts, two sports halls, a fitness centre and a large indoor swimming pool.

Clubs and Activities. There is a thriving CCF Contingent with both Army and RAF sections. The Duke of Edinburgh's Award Scheme is also flourishing. There are two School Plays a year – recent productions have included: *The Wizard of Oz, Macbeth, Noughts and Crosses*, and, for the younger pupils, *Arabian Nights*. As well as the Carol Service in Tewkesbury Abbey, there is a major concert held in the Pittville Pump Room featuring the School orchestra, jazz band and ensembles. The school has a very successful Design and Technology department and pupils have built and compete with their Greenpower racing car. Other societies range from Debating and Chess to Creative Writing and Bridge. Pupils are encouraged to take full advantage of the many activities which take place both at lunch time and after school. Trips abroad are a major feature of school life, including: an annual Ski Trip; a tour of the Normandy Bat-tlefields; a French Cuisine Trip; German, Spanish and French exchanges; a residential Art Course; trips to Iceland and Costa Rica; expedition to Borneo and Ecuador.

Admission. The main entry to the Senior School is at age 11; the entry examination takes place in November. Pupils can also join the School at age 13 and into the Sixth Form. Scholarships are available for entry into Year 7, 9 and 12.

Fees per term (2014–2015). £4,050–£4,900. Discounts are offered for the third, fourth and subsequent children.

The Senior School offers means-tested Bursary-Scholar-ships for entry at age 11, scholarships for academic excel-lence, art, music, drama and sport. For entry into Year 9 scholarships are available for academic excellence, art, music, drama, sport and design and technology. Scholar-ships for entry into Sixth Form are available for academic excellence, art, music, drama and sport.

Preparatory School. St Edward's Preparatory School, with over 400 boys and girls aged 2½–11, is on a separate nearby site with its own extensive buildings and 45-acre grounds containing the main Sports Fields which are used by both the Senior and Preparatory School. It is very well equipped with its own Science laboratories, well-resourced Library, Technology room, Music rooms, Drama studio and specialist Art rooms. Admission to the Preparatory School is possible at any age depending on ability and the availability of places. With an emphasis upon sound learning of basics (French is studied from Kindergarten), yet with a broad range of opportunities, pupils are fully prepared for entry to the Senior School. Academic Scholarships are available for entry into Year 3 and 5.

The Kindergarten, in an extremely well-resourced mod-ern building, takes children from the age of 2½ and is open nearly all year round.

(*For further details, see entry in IAPS section.*)

Old Edwardians' Association. Secretary: Mrs P Hem-ming, St Edward's School, Cirencester Road, Charlton Kings, Cheltenham, Gloucestershire GL53 8EY.

Further information is available on the School's web-site www.stedwards.co.uk. A School prospectus is available on request from the Headmistress's PA & Registrar. You are warmly invited to arrange a visit to the School by telephon-ing her on 01242 538600.

Charitable status. St Edward's School is a Registered Charity, number 293360.

Saint Felix School

Southwold, Suffolk IP18 6SD
Tel: 01502 722175
Fax: 01502 722641
email: schooladmin@stfelix.co.uk
website: www.stfelix.co.uk
Twitter: @StFelixSch
Facebook: /Saint-Felix-School

Motto: *Felix Quia Fortis*
Founded 1897.

Board of Governors:
Chairman: Dr John Kelly
Vice-Chairman: Dr John Hunt
Chairman (F&G): Mr John Whyte
Mrs Hazel Anthony, BA
Mr Les Dawson, OBE
Mr Kevin Dobson
Mrs Raewyn Hope-Cobbold, BA, TCert
[1]Mr N Johnson, BA
Mrs L Rous
Revd Barrie Slatter
Mr Richard Turvill

Head: [1]**Miss M F D'Alcorn**, BA Hons Birmingham, MA UEA

[1] *PGCE/DipEd qualification*

Deputy Head: [1]Mr J Harrison, BA Hons Durham

Head of Upper School: Mrs J Harlock, BA Hons Nottingham, MA De Montfort

Head of Prep Department: Dr J Dodsworth, PhD Bath, BEd Hons Cantab

Head of Pre-Prep Department: Mrs S Duckett, NNEB, CertEd

Senior School:

Art & Design:
Mrs S Bassett, BA Hons East London
Mr G Litchfield, BA Hons Leicester Polytechnic
[1]Ms L Roberts, BA Hons Leicester
[1]Mrs S Yates, BA

Business Studies/Economics:
Mrs J Harlock, BA Hons Nottingham, MA De Montfort
[1]Mr A Williams, BA Exeter, MA Hons Keele

Design Technology:
Mr R Kay, BEd Hons, DipEd Nottingham
[1]Mr D Kirby, BSc Loughborough

Drama and Performing Arts:
Miss C Franklin, MA Hons Glamorgan
[1]Ms A Hardcastle, BA Hons Huddersfield
Mrs T Marriott, MIDA, SIPBE

English:
[1]Mr P Currie, BA Hons Bolton Institute of Higher Education
[1]Ms A Hardcastle, BA Hons Huddersfield
[1]Mr R Lynch, BA Hons Birmingham, MA London

English as an Additional Language (EAL):
[1]Mrs A Eastaugh, MA Hons Edinburgh, TEFL
[1]Mr D Rogers, BA Hons Wales, MA Cantab, CELTA

Geography:
Mrs J Anderson, BA Hons OU, CertEd Wales
[1]Mr I McLean, BSc Hons UEA

History:
Mrs J Anderson, BA Hons OU, CertEd Wales
[1]Miss M F D'Alcorn, BA Hons Birmingham, MA UEA
[1]Mr R Farrands, BA Hons Kent
[1]Mr J Harrison, BA Hons Durham

History of Art:
[1]Ms L Roberts, BA Hons Leicester, CTEF

Home Economics:
Mrs J Anderson, BA Hons OU, CertEd Wales

ICT:
Mr C Barlow
Mr M Grunnell, BEd Exeter

Latin:
Dr J Dodsworth, PhD Bath, BEd Hons Cantab
[1]Mr J Harrison, BA Hons Durham

Mathematics:
Mr J Cowan BSc Hons Sheffield Hallam
[1]Miss S Fenwick, BA Hons Warwick
Mr M Grunnell, BEd Exeter
Mr C Smith, BEd Nottingham Trent
Mrs M Westlake, BSc Hons UEA

Modern Languages:
[1]Mr S Burnett, BA Hons Oxford
[1]Mr H Morton, BA Hons Bath
[1]Mrs J Rogers, BA Hons Nottingham

Music:
¹Mr A Jenkins, BA Huddersfield
Mrs V Wise, BMus, STD, PDO, PDM, LRSM, UPLM, RCMAC, ARCM, APC Nice

Pastoral:
¹Ms A Hardcastle, BA Hons Huddersfield
Mrs J Harlock, BA Hons Nottingham, MA De Montfort
¹Mr I McLean, BSc Hons UEA

Photography:
¹Ms L Roberts, BA Hons Leicester, CTEFL

Politics:
Mr R Farrands, BA Hons Kent

PSHE:
Mrs J Anderson, BA Hons OU, CertEd Wales

Psychology:
Mr R Kearney, BSc Hons St. Andrews

Science:
¹Mrs N Cowan, BSc Hons OU
¹Mr A Hill, BSc Wales, MA OU (*Physics*)
¹Mr D Swann, BSc Hons Sheffield
Mrs M Westlake, BSc Queen Mary College London

Sports:
Mr B Collis, LTA Tennis Coach
¹Miss S Fenwick, BA Hons Warwick
Mrs T Marriott, MIDA, SIPBE
Mrs G Nash, CertEd Sussex
¹Mr T O'Connell, BSc Hons Exeter
Miss E Rushmere, BSc Hons Kingston
Miss C Savage, BA Hons De Montfort

Swimming:
Mrs J Greenacre, BEd Hons W Sussex, MA UEA
Mrs L O'Connell, ASA Swimming Assistant, BSc Hons Exeter
Ms S Purchase, ASA Swimming Coach
Mr N Thompson, Junior Swimming Coach
Miss A Watling

Technicians:
Miss B Laybourne

Careers & Sixth Form:
¹Miss M F D'Alcorn, BA Hons Birmingham, MA UEA
¹Ms A Hardcastle, BA Hons Huddersfield
Mrs J Harlock, BA Hons Nottingham, MA De Montfort

Learning Support:
Mrs K Bland, BA Hons Open, OCR Level 5 Spld (*Dyslexia*)
Mrs B Every, LSA
Mrs J Grunnell, NOCN Level 3 Dyslexia & SaLT
Mrs A Horne, NVQ3

Chaplain: Mrs H Meldrum, BA Hons London

Librarian: Mrs C Thomas, BA Hons London, PG Dip, MCLIP

House Staff:

Head of Boarding: ¹Mr T O'Connell, BSc Hons Exeter
House Parents:
Mrs L Boyce
Mrs L Barker-Harrison
Mr M Grunnell, BEd Exeter (*House Tutor, Fawcett House*)
Mrs J Grunnell, NOCN Level 3 Dyslexia & SaLT (*House Tutor, Fawcett House*)
¹Mr J Harrison, BA Hons Durham Mrs G Nash, CertEd Sussex (*Somerville House*)
¹Mr D Kirby, BSc Loughborough
Mr R Kearney, BSc Hons St. Andrews
Mrs G Nash, CertEd Sussex
Mrs L O'Connell, BSc Hons Exeter (*Fawcett House*)
¹Mr T O'Connell, BSc Hons Exeter (*Fawcett House*)

Ms G Poulter
Miss A Robb
Miss E Rushmere, BSc Hons Kingston

Medical Centre:
Sister A Carr, RGN
Sister F Canham, RGN

Medical Officer: Dr M Niemeijer

Management Support:
Office Manager: Ms G Poulter
Receptionist/School Secretaries: Mrs J Grunnell Mrs D Whittington
Headmaster's PA: Mrs E Foskett
Registrar/Database Administrator: Miss M Bridgman
Finance Assistants: Mrs L Davison, Mr D Rees, Mrs J Tracey
Marketing Coordinator: Mrs J Anderson

Pre-Prep, Prep Departments and Nursery:
Mrs K Barbrook, BA Hons (*Nursery Assistant*)
Mrs K Bland, BA Hons Open, OCR Level 5 SpLD Dyslexia (*Learning Support*)
Miss C Brindle, BA Hons Hertfordshire Campus (*Nursery Assistant*)
Mrs T Grimmer, HLTA (*Teaching Assistant*)
¹Mrs R Crane, BA Hons (*French*)
Miss K Craven, HNC, HND (*Teaching Assistant*)
Dr J Dodsworth, PhD Bath, BEd Hons Cantab (*Head of Prep Department*)
Mrs S Duckett, NNEB, CertEd (*Head of Pre-Prep Department, Year Teacher, Key Stage 1 Coordinator*)
Mrs A Evans, BA Hons (*Head of Prep Department – Curriculum, Year Teacher*)
Miss C Franklin, MA Hons Glamorgan (*Speech & Drama*)
Mrs J Greenacre, MA UEA, BEd Hons W Sussex (*Girls' Games, Swimming*)
Miss S Greenfield, BEd (*Year Teacher, English Coordinator*)
Mrs T Grimmer, HLTA (*Teaching Assistant*)
Mrs J Heal, Cert EYP Open FD Open (*Associate Teacher*)
¹Mrs P Kinsella, BA Hons (*Year Teacher*)
Miss S Knights, CCLD, NVQ2, EYP (*Nursery Assistant*)
Mrs L Laughland, CCE, DNN (*Nursery Supervisor*)
Miss A Lee, EYCE, NVQ3, EYP (*Nursery Supervisor*)
Mrs G Nash, CertEd Sussex (*Girls' Games*)
Mrs A Nunn, BA Hons (*Year Teacher, Art*)
Mrs L O'Connell, BSc Hons Exeter (*Swimming Teacher*)
¹Mr T O'Connell, BSc Hons Exeter (*Year Teacher, Geography, PE & Games*)
Miss C Oldman, Dip LCM (*Music*)
Mrs J Proctor, NVQ3 (*Learning Support Assistant*)
Mrs J Rogers, BA Hons Nottingham (*French*)
Mrs E Sayer, BTec 3 (*Learning Support Assistant*)
Mrs A Scriven, BTec Level 3 (*Teaching Assistant*)
Mrs M Westlake, BSc Hons UEA (*Science*)

Peripatetic Staff:
Mr J Bimson (*French Horn*)
Mr B Carben (*Woodwind*)
Mr M Chapman (*Guitar*)
Mrs C Cliff, DipEd Music (*Piano, Recorder, Cello*)
Miss A Evans, GRSM, ARCM, ATCL, MTC (*Piano, Singing*)
Mr M Fagg (*Double Bass*)
Mr D Friend (*Brass*)
Mr J O'Toole (*Violin*)
Mrs C Skinner, GRSM, ARCM (*Flute*)
Mr N Williamson, BMus Hons, MMus, MMA (*Piano*)

Age Range. 2–18.
Number of Pupils. 350.
Saint Felix School was founded in 1897 and is set in 75 acres overlooking the Blyth Estuary near the picturesque

town of Southwold in Suffolk. The extensive buildings are purpose built and well equipped.

As a co-educational day and boarding school Saint Felix offers boys and girls a broad and balanced curriculum from the age of 1 to 18. A through school from the Nursery, Pre-Prep & Prep Departments (ages 1–10) through to the Senior Department (ages 11–16) and then into the Sixth Form.

Academic. A well-structured timetable, and a broad and balanced curriculum, encourages children in the Pre-Prep and Prep Departments to achieve their personal best, both academically and socially. Small class sizes and specialist teaching staff ensure excellent results together with happy, well-mannered and confident pupils.

In the Senior Department, each individual child is encouraged to achieve the highest grade attainable, made possible by the expertise of committed, skilled and motivated teachers working in small class groups. A wide and distinctive range of subjects can be studied at GCSE, AS and A Level. Sixth Form students this year achieved 100% pass rate at A Level, enabling entry into many of the country's finest Art, Drama and Music colleges, and universities. In addition the school's system of pastoral care ensures that children have continuous support and mentoring throughout their time at Saint Felix.

Music. Music is popular with over half taking peripatetic lessons. There is a variety of musical groups including chapel and chamber choirs, choral societies, orchestras as well as several chamber ensembles, eg piano trio, string quartets, jazz group and a rock band with electric guitar and drums especially popular. All pupils are encouraged to learn an instrument and Pre-Prep pupils learn the recorder. A 'Music in Residence' group encourages pupils to take up instruments. Music can be studied at GCSE and A Level. The department has 18 practice rooms and a performance area.

Sport. Facilities include a 25m indoor swimming pool, sports hall complex, squash courts, fitness suite and a 25-acre equestrian cross-country course.

A wide variety of sports are on offer including tennis, rugby, cricket, football, netball, hockey and rounders. Swimming is particularly strong throughout the school resulting in pupils competing in county, regional and national championships and achieving national recognition. An extensive range of other sports is available including squash, sailing, basketball, fencing, table tennis, wall climbing and horse riding.

Arts. The school promotes the Arts with regular exhibitions and displays and eagerly-awaited school productions throughout the year. The combination of Art, Music and Drama is actively encouraged through an Arts Week. Photography and Art throughout the school is of a very high standard with excellent results at both GCSE and A Level. The Silcox Theatre with a 200-seat capacity and state-of-the-art lighting and sound system further enhances the creative arts, one of the great strengths of Saint Felix.

Extra Curricular Activities. There is an extensive list of activities available. All pupils are actively encouraged to take part in the Duke of Edinburgh's Award Scheme. A similar scheme runs in the Prep Department. The school day is extended to include activities.

Community. The school actively encourages the local community to get involved in school life and various clubs are closely linked to the school (Norwich City Football Club, Guides, Brownies, The Choral Society, Southwold Rugby, Netball and Tennis Clubs) enabling pupils to be involved in groups outside school.

Fees per term (2014–2015). Day: £2,235–£4,845; Boarding: £5,325–£6,790 (weekly), £7,000–£8,465 (full).

Forces Boarding School Allowance available.

Scholarships. Saint Felix School seeks high-calibre candidates, who will contribute very positively and proactively to the life of the school community. The maximum award

for an academic scholarship is 50% and for an exhibition 25% of the fees.

Academic awards at 11+ and 13+. All applicants will sit competitive academic examination papers. Awards will be made to high flying candidates, who demonstrate flair and the potential to excel in their academic studies. Exhibitions are awards given for candidates who show promise but do not attain the exacting standards demanded of scholars.

Examinations. Applicants for academic awards at 11+ and 13+ will sit examination papers in English, Mathematics, Science and Aptitude. Topics will be closely linked to those covered in Key Stages 2 and 3.

Music Scholarships at 9+ through to 14+. These will be awarded on the basis of an audition, voice test and interview with the Director of Music and members of the Scholarship Selection Committee. Candidates will be asked to offer two instruments, one of which should be an orchestral instrument.

Margaret Isabella Gardiner Scholarship for candidates aged 11+ and 13+. Outstanding candidates may be eligible for this highly prestigious award, worth up to 75% of the fees. This scholarship will be awarded only to a candidate of sufficiently high calibre and not necessarily on an annual basis.

Performing Arts awards at 13+ and 14+. Open to applicants who excel in at least two of the following disciplines: Drama, Dance, Music (including singing).

Sports Scholarships at 9+, 11+, 13+& 14+. Candidates should offer a range of sporting talents. Pupils at 11+ should be playing at club level in at least one sport. Pupils at 13+ should have been selected for county/regional level sport and be playing at club level in at least one sport. There should be evidence of success in competitions and events for both age groups.

Swimming Scholarships at 9+ through to 14+. These are awarded to candidates who swim at county, regional and national level and are currently dependent on the level of times gained.

Sixth Form Scholarships and Exhibitions. Scholarships and exhibitions for Academic Studies, Design & Technology (Phipps Award), Drama, Music, Sport and Visual Arts (Art & Photography) are available for talented Sixth Form applicants, as the result of a competitive examination, trial or audition.

Full details of all awards, including Founder's Scholarships, Remissions and Swimming Scholarships may be obtained from the Registrar. Further information on Bursaries (available to current parents only) are available from the Bursar.

Charitable status. Saint Felix School is a Registered Charity, number 310482. It exists to promote and advance education.

St George's School
Edgbaston

31 Calthorpe Road, Birmingham, West Midlands B15 1RX

Tel: 0121 625 0398
Fax: 0121 625 3340
email: admin@sgse.co.uk
website: www.sgse.co.uk

Chairman of Board of Trustees: Sir Robert Dowling, MEd, Dip Psych, Dip SpLD

Headmaster: Mr Gary Neal, BEd Hons

Deputy Headmaster: Mrs Jennifer Shaw, BEd Hons

Head of Sixth Form: Mr Mark Loveday, BA Hons

Upper School:

English:
Mrs Adele Waits, BA Hons
Miss Katy Perks, BA Hons
Mr Robert Jagger, BA Hons
Mrs Vanessa Johnson, BA Hons
Mrs Natalie Wright, BA Hons
Mrs Helen Taylor, Cert Ed, BEd Hons

Mathematics:
Mr Ryan Bibb, BSc Hons,
Mrs Balvinder Gill, BA Hons, GTP
Mr Geoff Thompson, BEd Hons
Mr Andrew Smith, BSc Hons

Science:
Mr David Lai, BSc Hons
Mrs Kendal Smallwood, BSc Hons
Mr Brian Duckworth, MSc Hons
Mr Brian Ducille, BSc Hons, Dip CS
Miss Sabeena Jootna, BSc Hons
Miss Sophie Duckworth, BSc Hons, MEd
Mr Andrew Norton, BSc Hons

Information Technology:
Miss Jennifer Davis, BSc Hons, PGCE
Mrs Michelle Fowler, BSc Hons, PGCE

Business Studies:
Mrs Dianne Gorning, BSc Hons

Modern Languages:
Mrs Mila Webb, BA Hons
Miss Sarah Larkin, BA Hons

Religious Studies:
Mrs Julie Glover, BA Hons

Economics & Accounts:
Mrs Helen Yare, BSc Hons

Psychology:
Mrs Wendy Copsey, BSc Hons, BA Hons

Government & Politics:
Mr Jonathan Yates, BA Hons, MA

History:
Mrs Helen Reader, BA Hons,
Mrs Eleanor Webster, BA Hons

Geography:
Mrs Ria Doak, BA Hons

Design Technology:
Mrs Michelle Harbott, BA Hons
Mr Adrian Eynon, BA Hons

Food Technology:
Mrs Corrine Roberts, BEd Hons, Dip RE/PSE

Art and Ceramics:
Miss Carla Webb, BA Hons
Miss Rachel Smith, BA Hons

Photography:
Miss Rachel Smith, BA Hons, NQT

Music:
Mrs Sarah C Russell, MA Cantab

Drama:
Mrs Adele Waites, BA Hons

Physical Education:
Miss Anne Hollman, BSc Hons QTS
Mr Joe Finn, BA Hons,
Mr Luke Nicholls, BSc Hons

EAL
Mrs Jo Dore, BEd Hons

Inclusion & Support

Mr Jason Collet, BA Hons
Miss Karen Trough, BSc Hons
Mrs Hazel Hughes, Cert Ed, BPhilEd, Dip SpLD

Lower School:

Head of Lower School: Mrs Jennifer Shaw, BEd Hons

Lower School Staff:
Mrs Claire Burrows, BSc Hons
Miss Victoria Brookes, BA Hons
Mrs Hannah Girling, BA Hons
Mr Daniel Lumley, BSc Hons
Mrs Emelia McNeil, BA Hons
Mrs Helen Murphy, BA Hons
Miss Sally Russell, BA Hons
Mrs Joanne Sadiq, BEd Hons
Mrs Lorraine Sparkes, BA Hons
Miss Josie Stinton, BA Hons

Nursery Manager:
Miss Sarah Jane Averill, BA Hons

Technical Staff:
Miss Lisa Allen, BSc
Mr Adam McCabe, MA Hons

Head's PA: Mrs Maureen Fahy
Finance Department: Ms Tracy Perry, Mrs Patricia
    Mortiboys
Marketing & Admissions: Mrs Natalie Williams
Secretarial Assistants:
Mrs Brenda Brown, Miss Rita Fergus (*Upper School*)
Miss Annette Dodd, Mrs Julie Griffiths Edwards (*Lower
    School*)

The school opened in September 1999 as the amalgamation of Edgbaston Church of England College for Girls and Edgbaston College. The School is co-educational and accepts pupils of all faiths. We pride ourselves on our warm family atmosphere where each child is known as an individual.

Entry to the upper school is selective and the majority of pupils expect and are expected to carry on their education into Sixth Form. Entry into the Lower School follows an informal interview.

The school is a listed building which has been sympathetically adapted to meet pupils educational needs.

Curriculum. The curriculum will provide each pupil with a broad education appropriate to their age and needs.

The overriding educational priority is to allow and encourage every pupil to be the best they can be.

The educational diet provides a wider range of subjects than required by the National Curriculum.

In the Sixth Form, which has its own centre, there is a wide breadth of subject choice. Sixth Form pupils provide various services to those in need in the local community.

Extra-Curricular Activities. Pupils take part in lunch-time and after-school activities. These include music, drama, and sports. Instrumental music, speech and drama, ballet and fencing lessons are provided as required.

Fees per term (2014–2015). £2,020–£3,255 (excluding lunch). Full details may be obtained on application to the School. We will be pleased to forward a copy of the prospectus and to arrange an opportunity for parents to visit the School to discuss their child's education with the Headmaster.

Charitable status. St George's School, Edgbaston is a Registered Charity, number 1079647. It exists to provide a quality education for boys and girls within the Birmingham area.

St James Senior Boys' School

Church Road, Ashford, Surrey TW15 3DZ
Tel: 01784 266 930
          01784 266 933 (Admissions)
Fax: 01784 266 938
email: admissions@stjamesboys.co.uk
website: www.stjamesboys.co.uk

St James Senior Boys' School, founded in 1975, is registered as an educational charity and is administered by a Board of Governors. The Headmaster is a member of The Society of Heads and the Independent Schools Association. The school is a member of the International Boys' Schools Coalition (IBSC). These Associations require that excellence is assured by regular inspections by the Independent Schools Inspectorate which is itself monitored by Ofsted.

The school has 380 students – all boys, aged between 11 and 18. There is a small weekly boarding option.

The school relocated from its riverside site in Twickenham in 2010 and now resides in the magnificent Victorian/Gothic building which once housed St David's School in Ashford, Surrey, set in 32 acres of grounds.

This move has provided the physical space necessary for every boy to develop his sporting, artistic and dramatic talents in addition to working in high-quality classrooms and state-of-the-art laboratories.

Chairman of Governors: Jeremy Sinclair

Headmaster: David Brazier, BA Hons, PGCE, MSc

Deputy Headmaster: Koen Claeys, BA, GLSE Belgium (*French, German*)

Deputy Headmaster Academic: Charles Neave, BA, Grad Dip Ed, Grad Dip Mus, QTS (*Head of English*)

Assistant Headmaster: David Hipshon, BA Hons, MPhil Cantab, PhD, PGCE (*History*)

Head of Sixth Form: David Beezadhur, BA Hons, MA, GTTP (*Ancient History*)

Head of Upper School (*Years 9–11*): James Johnson, BSc Hons, PGCE (*Science*)

Head of Lower School (*Years 7 & 8*): Richard Fletcher, BSc Hons, GTTP (*Maths*)

Academic Staff:
Charlotte Atkinson, BA Hons, PGCE (*English*)
Paul Bahia, BSc Hons, PGCE (*Mathematics, Economics*)
Lucy Bailes, MA (*Chief Librarian*)
Kevan Bell, MA, MSc, BEd (*Sports Performance Director*)
Gillian Bloor, MA (*English, History*)
Helen Brennan, BSc Hons, PGCE (*Head of Geography*)
Stuart Bridge, BA Hons, PGCE (*German, French*)
Anne-Helene Choimet, BA France, PGCE MFL (*French & German, G & T Coordinator*)
Marian Ciuca, BA, PhD (*Classics*)
Aine Corrigan, MSc (*Mathematics*)
Sarah Ford, BSc Hons, PGCE (*Chemistry*)
Dominique Foxton, BSc Hons (*Mathematics*)
Rishi Handa, MA, BSc Hons, awaiting PhD (*Sanskrit, Classical Greek, Religious Studies*)
Adam Hooper, BEng (*Physics*)
Emma Garner, MA Oxford (*French*)
Valentin Gerlier, MA (*English*)
Stephanie James, BA Hons, PGCE (*Drama/Music*)
David Lacey, BA Mod, HDipEd, CPhys, MInstP (*Head of Science*)
Nic Lempriere, MA, PGCE (*Head of English*)
Rosie Levick, MA (*English*) (*maternity leave*)
Neil MacKichan, BSc Hons, GTTP (*Head of ICT, Computing*)

Pardeep Marway, BSc Hons, PGCE (*Biology, Child Protection Liaison Officer*)
Craig McCready, BSc (*Head of Mathematics*)
Nicola Michael, BA Hons, PGCE (*History & Geography*)
Stevie Mitchell, BA Hons, PGCE (*Mathematics*)
Alison O'Brien, BSc (*Economics*)
Nathaniel Palmer, BA Hons, PGCE (*Geography*)
Daniel Paul, MA Oxford (*Classics*)
Caroline Pugh, BA Hons, PGCE (*Head of Drama*)
Virginie Quartier, BA, GLSE Belgium (*Head of Modern Languages, EAL Coordinator*)
Antonia Ruppel, BA, MPhil, PhD Cambridge (*Sanskrit, Classics*)
Julia Russell, BA Hons, GTTP (*Art, Art of Science Coordinator*)
Derek Saunders, BA Mus, PGCE (*Director of Music*)
Oliver Saunders, BA Hons, GTTP (*Head of History*)
Mark Saunders, BA, HND Art & Design (*Head of Art*)
Yolanda Saunders, BA Hons, PGCE (*Head of Classics*)
Lorraine Soares, MSc Hons, PGCE (*Chemistry*)
Jessica Thomas, BA Hons, PGCE (*English, History*)
Alex Wain, BA Hons (*Head of Design Technology*)
Ben Wassell, BSc Hons, GTTP (*Head of PE*)
Sandra Williams, BEd (*Head of Business Studies*)
Stuart Willis, BSc Hons (*PE*)

Learning Support:
Jayne Chandler
Christine Davies
Sarah-Jane Hipshon, BA Hons Lit Open
Billy Jeffreys
Caroline Moir, BSc Hons Psychology, Sp Lg Dip (*SENCO*)
Carola Robinson-Tait (*Learning Support Specialist Teacher*)
Clare Wassell
Cora Wren, Cert Ed, BA Hons, OCR Level 5 Dip SpLD (*SENCO*)

Boarding Staff:
Koen Claeys, BA, GLSE Belgium (*Housemaster*)
Virginie Quartier, BA, GLSE Belgium (*Housemother*)
Luke Rone (*Gap Year Student*)

Registrar and Marketing:
Patrick Lawler, BA
Lauren Hamill, BSc

Aims and Values. St James Senior Boys' School offers a distinctive education that unites a unique philosophical ethos with academic excellence and outstanding skills for life.

At St James we believe that every child is a pure and perfect being; it is our job as educators to help the pupils in our care to discover and express their individual talents and reveal their brilliance. With this room to grow and blossom each boy develops in body, mind and spirit.

Although academic potential is important to us, pupils at St James are not selected solely on their examination performance; we are also interested in strength of character, future potential and emotional intelligence. We are looking for a boy with a spark, who gives freely of themselves whether in the classroom, on the stage or the sports field.

We are known internationally for our championing of Meditation and Mindfulness, something we have been successfully practising for 40 years. Each boy has the opportunity to connect with their inner being in periods of Quiet Time each day. This makes an enormous difference to pupil development and academic achievement.

We also like to offer the pupils in our care the opportunity to push themselves beyond any self-imposed limits, and our beautiful 32-acre site certainly enables a wealth of sports, drama, music and other extra-curricular activities to flourish. Activities offered include: Cadets, The Duke of Edinburgh's Award scheme, Sailing Club, Mountain Biking, Kayaking and even Open Water swimming in our lake!

At St James we wish to produce young men who can question with sharp minds, who can contemplate in quietude, who can find their way ahead with wisdom and moral discrimination and who can meet others with open-hearted compassion.

St James is ideally located with easy access from Central London and the South West London Suburbs through to the Thames Valley.

Academic Standards and Successes. Academic standards are high, but we also measure success to the extent that boys surpass their own expectations. 2014 results were: GCSE 100% pass rate; A*AB 76%; A*ABC 92%; A Level Pass Rate 100%, A*ABC 90%.

Extra-Curricular Activities. Boys are offered an adventure pursuits programme designed to challenge the young men in terms of fitness, endurance, courage, leadership skills, service, self-esteem and confidence. Cadets (239 Para detachment), Duke of Edinburgh's Award Scheme, Skiing, Sailing Club, Climbing Club, Community Service and Task force are among the activities offered.

Educational Trips. These are fairly regular and frequent for the Lower School, but there is an Activities Week in March when Year 7 enjoy an adventure break in the UK; Year 8 go to Greece to further their studies of Classical Civilisation; Year 9 stay in Paris for a week, speaking the language and being introduced to French culture; and Year 10 spend some time in Luca in Italy for leadership training and aspects of teamworking, then move on to Florence to study Renaissance art and architecture.

Philosophy. Each class throughout the school has one period of Philosophy per week. The boys are opened up to the great ideas relating to human values and relationships. Broadly, the themes prepare boys through different stages of development – Years 7 to 8: the correct use of mind, the power of attention; Years 9 to 11: aspiring to a great vision of Man and exploring human relationships and personal mastery; Years 12 to 13: living the philosophical life, making it practical, the importance of service.

Meditation and Quiet Time. The importance of inner stillness is recognised in the school, with two 10 minute periods of Quiet Time every day. During this time, boys can meditate, pray, read something of value or just be still. Every lesson begins and ends in a quiet moment of stillness and rest.

Admissions. The standard entry is at 11+, 13+ and 16+. Boys applying for entry to Year 7 take an Entrance Exam in January and also are all interviewed by the Headmaster shortly afterwards. Boys are not judged solely on their exam results for the Headmaster favours selection by character and their ability to express themselves. At 13+, we can either accept Common Entrance or we offer our own 13+ papers. We welcome applications to our Sixth Form at 16+. Very good GCSE performance and satisfactory interviews will be the basis of selection.

Fees per term (2014–2015). £5,090. Weekly Boarding Fee: £2,170.

Open Days and Visits. Every year we hold two Open Days in early November. We also encourage parents to come and see the school in action. This takes the form of a tour, which can be booked by telephoning the admissions department.

Charitable status. The Independent Educational Association Limited is a Registered Charity, number 270156.

St John's College

Grove Road South, Southsea, Hampshire PO5 3QW

Tel: 023 9281 5118
Fax: 023 9287 3603
email: info@stjohnscollege.co.uk
website: www.stjohnscollege.co.uk

Founded in 1908 by the De La Salle Brothers, St John's seeks to provide an excellent all-round day and boarding education to boys and girls of all abilities. The school has a strong Christian ethos inspired by the teachings of St John Baptist De La Salle, the patron saint of teachers. Children of all Christian denominations, those of other faiths and those with no formal religious affiliation but who are in sympathy with the values of the school are welcome.

Chairman of Governors: Mr T Forer

Principal: Mr G Best, BA

Head of the Senior School: Mr T Bayley, BSc, MA
Head of the Junior School: Mr T Shrubsall, MA Ed, BH
Assistant Head Academic: Mr A Martin, MEng, ACGI, Fri, PGCE
Assistant Head Pastoral: Mr M Round, BSc, PGCE
Senior Master: Mr M Renahan, BA, HDE, MEd
Senior Mistress: Mrs M Maguire, BSc, PGCE
Bursar: Mr S Merriam, BSc
Estates Manager: Mr R Phillips
Head of Marketing and Development: Miss C Young, BA
Admissions Registrar: Mrs J Mengham

Heads of Department:
Art and Design: Mrs K Brown, BA
Design and Technology: Mr R Kirby, BA, QTS
Economics & Business Studies: Mrs N Maloy, BSc
English: Mr D Celestine, BA
Geography: Mr P Hyde, BSc
Government & Political Studies: Dr G D Goodlad, PhD, BA
History: Mrs K Audsley, BA, MA
ICT & Computing: Mr T Harris, BSc, QTS
Learning Support: Mrs L Gorham, BA, DipSpLD
Mathematics: Mrs M Maguire, BSc
Modern Languages: Mr G Walker, MA
Music: Mr K Ellison, BA, PGCE, LRSM, ARCM
Physical Education: Mr A Tart, BA
Religious Studies: Mrs J Turner, BA, MA
Sciences: Mr A Martin, BSc

Head's PA/Admissions: Mrs H Williams

St John's is a thriving co-educational day and boarding school for pupils aged 2 to 18 (boarding from Year 5). Number of Pupils: 382 Boys, 224 Girls, 125 Boarders.

Situation. St John's day and boarding campus is located in the heart of Southsea, an attractive and thriving seaside suburb of Portsmouth. The College's 40 acres of sports fields are located on the outskirts of the city, with transport provided to and from that site.

Approach and Ethos. Academically, St John's is a non-selective school, its aim being excellence for every pupil according to their personal potential. All children who are able and willing to benefit from the curriculum provided are welcome to join the school community. The school's academic record – by all measures – is outstanding.

The pastoral care offered to boarders and day pupils is of very high quality. The commitment of the staff to the welfare and progress of each pupil is second to none. In return, honest effort and application is expected from the children – in order to meet the challenging standards set in academic work, sporting endeavour, behaviour and self-discipline.

Nursery. The Nursery (Little St John's) is located within the Junior School. It has its own entrance and secure playground. The Nursery caters for children aged from two to four years and is open 51 weeks of the year. The children are actively involved in a carefully constructed pre-school programme. Great emphasis is placed on creative artwork, outdoor play and educational visits – as well as on acquiring foundation skills and concepts relating to numeracy and literacy.

Junior School. The Junior School is also located within the main College campus. This enables younger children to make daily use of all the College's excellent facilities and to benefit in some areas from specialist tuition by Senior School staff. The broadly-based curriculum incorporates and extends the National Curriculum. Great emphasis is placed on English, mathematics and science – which is taught in well-equipped laboratories. Musical talent is also carefully nurtured, with all pupils learning a musical instrument from the age of seven. The Junior School Choir and Orchestra provide opportunities for ensemble playing and performance.

Senior School. The Senior School curriculum again incorporates and extends the National Curriculum. All subjects are taught by appropriately qualified specialists in well-resourced subject areas. A wide range of GCSE subjects is offered alongside IGCSE Maths, English and Science. Instrumental tuition is encouraged and the Senior School Choir and Orchestra are open to all pupils. Sport – principally rugby, cricket, hockey and netball – is strong at all levels. Pupils' progress in all areas is assessed formally each half-term, with formal examinations being held twice yearly.

Sixth Form. As they progress into the Sixth Form, older students are enabled and encouraged to become independent and self-motivated learners – in preparation for Higher Education. The teaching and pastoral staff continue to work closely with parents, who are kept fully informed of progress and achievement. A wide range of AS and A2 Level subjects is offered. The College ensures a good student/teacher ratio, allowing for close and constant monitoring of the performance and effort of each student. Preparation for Oxbridge entry is available, and in 2014 three students progressed to Oxford colleges as well as many others to Imperial College London and other Russell Group universities. Students are also offered practice interviews for university and job applications and a full careers service.

Beyond the formal curriculum, a wide range of sporting, academic, dramatic, cultural and social activities is available. The Politics Society, administered predominantly by Sixth Form students, enjoys a national reputation.

Admission. Pupils are accepted and placed on the basis of a formal assessment and previous reports.

Fees per term (2014–2015). Junior School: Day £2,710–£2,895; Years 5 & 6 UK Boarding £7,690. Senior School: Day £3,550; UK Boarding £7,690; Overseas Boarding £8,240.

Occasional Boarding (including bed, breakfast, evening meal): £38 per day.

Music fees are extra.

Scholarships and Bursaries. Academic and other scholarships and bursarial awards are available.

Charitable status. St John's College is a Registered Charity, number 232632.

St Joseph's College

Belstead Road, Ipswich, Suffolk IP2 9DR
Tel: 01473 694575
Fax: 01473 602409
email: admissions@stjos.co.uk
website: www.stjos.co.uk

St Joseph's College is a vibrant day and boarding school, for girls and boys aged 3 to 18. Its Nursery, Prep, Senior and Sixth Form provision offers a broad, well-rounded and seamless education.

Located on a 60-acre parkland site near to the centre of Ipswich, the College is situated just ten minutes' walk from Ipswich train station or alternately just a five-minute drive from the A12/A14 interchange.

Traditional values are at the heart of the school community which, at the same time, is forward-thinking as it meets the challenges of an ever-changing world. Pupils are provided with every opportunity to develop their talents to the full, growing up in a happy and fulfilling Christian environment where all are valued and encouraged.

Governing Body:
Chair: Mr Paul Clement, BSc Hons, MA
Vice Chair: Mr Richard Stace, LLB

Mr John Button	Mr Perry Glading
Ms Joanna Carrick	Mr Andrew Goulborn
Mrs P Cavenagh	Mr Marc Howes
Mrs Renata Chester	Mrs Josephine Lea
Mr Joseph Cook	Mr T Newman
Mr Philip Dennis	Mr Matthew Potter
Mr Malcolm Earl	

Special Responsibilities:
Primary & EYFS: Mrs Josephine Lea
Safeguarding: Mr Richard Stace
Boarding: Mr Anthony Newman

Senior Leadership Team:

Principal: Mrs D Clarke, BA Hons, NPQH

Vice Principal and Head of the Prep School: Dr M Hine
Director of Studies: Mr S Phaup
Bursar: Mrs D Baber
Director of Marketing and Admissions: Mr J Hamp

Senior School Heads of Faculty and Pastoral Leads:
Mrs L Bloore (*Director of Music*)
Mr A Bloore (*Head of Technology*)
Miss L Cunningham (*Head of Learning Support*)
Mrs S Daley (*Head of Girls PE and Games*)
Mr M Davey (*Head of Sixth Form*)
Mrs K Drake (*Head of English*)
Mr P Duckett (*Drama*)
Miss G Fitzsimons (*Dance*)
Mrs A Hall (*Head of Upper School, English*)
Mrs V Harvey (*Head of Creative & Performing Arts*)
Miss L Hassell (*Head of Science*)
Mr C McNicholas (*Head of ICT, Geography*)
Mr M Patterson (*Director of Sport*)
Mr A Reavill (*Head of Humanities, UCAS*)
Mrs G Rowlands (*Head of MFL & Boarding*)
Mrs J Scott (*Head of PSHE, History*)
Mrs M Simmonds (*Head of Lower School, Languages, Housemistress*)
Mr N Walkinshaw (*Head of Mathematics*)

Prep School:
Mrs V Wood (*Deputy Head of the Prep School*)
Mrs C Gardiner (*Head of EYFS & Infants, Nursery to Year 2*)
Mrs M Sharp (*Head of Juniors, Years 3 to 6*)

Ethos. St Joseph's feels different. And that's the way we like it. Our unique environment is shaped by our ethos, derived from the educational philosophy and faith of St Jean Baptiste de La Salle, Patron Saint of Teachers, and the example set by St Joseph, Patron Saint of Workers. This ethos combines strong Christian values with a unique approach to individually supporting and nurturing children within a friendly, family environment. Along with the pursuit of excellence, this approach is reflected in all aspects of life at the College whether it is academic, sporting or cultural.

Developments. In September 2008, the innovative new Primary school building was formally opened. This fascinating curved building with its Maltings-style wind-catcher towers provides a highly stimulating environment for pupils between 3 and 10 years of age and is resourced with the latest technological and physical resources. In 2009, a new fitness suite and dance studio were installed, and in March 2014 a floodlit astroturf, new changing rooms, a spectators viewing facility and function suite were added to the school's facilities within its 60 acres.

ISI Inspection. In March 2013 and 2010, the College received excellent ISI inspection reports.

All areas of EYFS were judged to be outstanding. The quality of pupils' spiritual, moral, social and cultural development; pastoral care and quality of teaching; the curriculum and extra-curricular provision; and pupils' achievement was all excellent. ISI judged that 'all children make excellent progress and achieve better than age-related expectations in all areas of learning.'

The quality of boarding provision and care was found to be excellent. Arrangements for safeguarding boarders and ensuring their welfare were excellent, the leadership and management of boarding were excellent, and Boarders in both houses were very happy and thrive within a caring and supportive atmosphere.

The arrangements for pastoral care were judged to be excellent. '*A well-developed network of support, with clear lines of communication, provides the basis for pastoral care throughout the school and supports the pupils' excellent personal development. The family community is an obvious strength of the college. Pupils value the kindness and support that staff show them and enjoy positive relationships with all.*'

Judgements on achievement and teaching and learning included: '*Standards in the EYFS are high and pupils continue to make good progress towards their GCSE exams, where results are good. Pupils' personal and social development are excellent, in accordance with the Christian values which permeate the life of the college. Teachers have good subject knowledge and the most successful teaching promotes academic rigour and uses a variety of methods and resources. The pupils' performance in extra-curricular activities is frequently outstanding. They have had significant successes in sport, particularly rugby and cricket, but also in drama, music and art.*'

Boarding. Although primarily a day school, we also offer flexible, weekly and full boarding in family-run, spacious and warm boarding houses. The College has two boarding houses which provide both single and shared rooms with kitchen, study and recreational facilities.

Curriculum. The curriculum is designed to provide a broad and balanced education for all pupils from 3 to 18. Strong foundations in the core skills of reading, writing and numeracy, are laid down in the Infant Department through innovative programmes such as Read Write Inc and Singapore Mathematics. The Junior Section continues the process of preparing the children for their secondary education by concentrating further on the core skills. In addition to these subjects, Science, French, Music and PE are taught and the children are introduced to a wider curriculum, including Design and Technology, Art, History, Geography, RE, IT and Games.

The Senior School prepares pupils for entrance to universities, other forms of higher education and the professions. Pupils are set according to ability in certain subjects. In Years 7 to 9, the emphasis continues to be placed on the core subjects whilst developing knowledge, skills and experiences necessary for the GCSE courses. Languages studied at the College include French and Spanish.

GCSE studies maintain a broad and balanced curriculum but with the introduction of a degree of specialisation. Mathematics, English Language and Literature, Double Science Award, and RE are compulsory. Once again core subjects continue to be set by ability. To cater for developing interests and abilities there is a wide range of further choices from Food Technology and Photography to History, Spanish and Business Studies.

The majority of our pupils continue into the Sixth Form to complete their A Level courses before going on to university. There is a wide range of subjects available in the Sixth Form and students choose 4 AS Level subjects for examination in the Lower Sixth, reducing to 3 A2s for completion in the Upper Sixth. General Studies are an integral part of the post-16 curriculum at the College, with a wide range of sporting and other leisure and cultural opportunities.

A Learning Support department operates throughout the College to provide support individually or in small groups for students of all abilities with specific learning needs and differences.

There is comprehensive careers guidance from Year 9 and extensive help with university admission in the Sixth Form.

Extra-Curricular Activities. Sport, Art, Music, Dance and Drama are strongly encouraged, together with participation in The Duke of Edinburgh's Award scheme. A large number of extra-curricular clubs meet weekly. Regular ski trips, activity holidays and language exchanges are organised throughout the College.

Admission. Entry to the College is normally at 3+, 7+, 11+, 13+ and the Sixth Form, with applications for vacancies at other ages, subject to spaces being available. The entry process includes an interview, a Taster Day in the school, a formal assessment and a report from the applicant's previous school. For the Sixth Form, the academic assessment is replaced by GCSE results.

Fees per term (2014–2015). Nursery: £42.85 (per full session); Infants (Reception to Year 2): £2,585; Juniors (Years 3 to 6): £3,365 (day). Senior School (Year 7 to Upper Sixth): £3,975–£4,365 (day), £6,965–£7,615 (weekly boarding), £7,295–£9,420 (full boarding).

Scholarships and Bursaries. The College offers a number of Academic Scholarships each year for different points of entry, as well as Scholarships for Music, Art, Sport and Drama. A number of bursaries are also available in cases of need. Please contact the Admissions team for further information.

Charitable status. St Joseph's College is a Registered Charity, number 1051688. It exists to provide high quality education for children.

Scarborough College

Filey Road, Scarborough, North Yorkshire YO11 3BA

Tel:	01723 360620
Fax:	01723 377265
email:	admin@scarboroughcollege.co.uk
website:	www.scarboroughcollege.co.uk
Twitter:	@ScarboroughColl
Facebook:	/ScarboroughCollege

Motto: *Pensez Fort*

Governors:
Dr J Renshaw (*Chairman*)
A S Green (*Deputy Chairman*)

M Baines	J Rowlands
Mrs G Braithwaite	R Guthrie
J M Green	S Fairbank
R Marshall	Mrs F Humphries
Dr I G H Renwick	Revd T L Jones
Dr C Rhodes	

Business Manager & Clerk to the Governors: Sqn Ldr T Fenton, MBE

Senior Management Team:

Headmistress: Mrs Isobel Nixon, BA Hons York, PGCE York, MA Leeds

Deputy Head: Miss Kate Tipton, BSc Warwick (*Head of Boarding*)

Director of Studies: Mr Simon Harvey, BSc London, PGCE
(*Head of Science and Chemistry*)

Assistant Head – Academic Administration: Mr James
Fraser, MSc Liverpool, PGCE (*Head of Biology*)

Heads of Department:
Mathematics: Mr Hamish Brown, BSc Edinburgh, PGCE,
MSc Warwick, MMus RSAMD
English & Drama: Mrs Sarah Grice, BA Durham, PGCE
Physics: Mr Tom Brough, BSc Durham, PGCE
Science & Chemistry: Mr Simon Harvey, BSc London,
PGCE
Biology: Mr James Fraser, MSc Liverpool, PGCE
Modern Languages: Mrs Catherine Lucas, BA Hons Hull,
PGCE
History: Mr Richard Scott, BA Kingston Polytechnic
Geography: Mr Richard Robson, BSc, MSc Oxford
Polytechnic, PGCE
Information Technology: Miss Sarah Clyde, BSc
Loughborough, PGCE
Director of Music: Mrs Rebecca Leeson, BA Bristol, PGCE
Art: Mr Paul Sutcliffe, BA Staffordshire, PGCE
Director of Sport: Mr Chris Barker, BA, PGCE
Business: Mr John Precious, BA Trent Polytechnic, PGCE
Learning Support: Mrs Rose Lavelle, MA Hull, PGCE
SEN, PGDip York Dyslexia

Boarding House Staff:
Senior Housemaster, Weaponness House, Boys Boarding:
Mr John Precious
*Assistant Housemaster, Weaponness House, Boys
Boarding*: Mr Dan Davey
Senior Housemistress, Willersley House, Girls Boarding:
Mrs Jenny Robinson
Assistant Housemistress, Willersley House, Girls Boarding:
Miss Sarah Hammond
*Senior Housemistress, Denys Crews House, Girls
Boarding*: Mrs Sarah Grice
Senior Housemaster, Bramcote House, Boys Boarding: Mr
Paul Sutcliffe
House Duty Staff: Mrs Janet Thomas, Mr Phil Wilson, Miss
Heather Ramsay, Mr Simon Harvey, Mrs Pascale Rigley,
Mr Mike Price-Stevens, Mr Kieron Middleton

Scarborough College is a co-educational day and boarding school for children aged 3–18. The College and its
Junior School, Bramcote Junior School, share the same site.
Our beautiful campus overlooks the spectacular North Yorkshire coast and is about a mile from the centre of the popular
seaside town of Scarborough. It has fine views overlooking
the South Bay of the town and Scarborough Castle. The
boarding houses are separate from the main campus, but
within easy walking distance of the school.

Although the ethos of the College is firmly based upon
wholesome traditional principles we have a progressive
approach to education, which has led to us offering the International Baccalaureate in our Sixth Form, a qualification
that is acknowledged throughout the world.

Admission. *Junior School*: Admission is by visit to the
school and an interview with the Head of Junior School.
Taster days can be arranged.

Senior School: Admission at age 11 is following an
Entrance Assessment and Scholarship Examination in
November. Admission at all other ages is subject to recommendation from the previous school, an interview and satisfactory performance in a general assessment.

Sixth Form: Admissions are subject to the achievement of
a minimum of five GCSEs at Grades A* to C and an interview with IB staff. Students may be required to take an
entrance examination. There is a Sixth Form Scholarship
Examination in February for UK and MOD entrants.

Overseas Students are required to submit: school reports
for the previous two years; certificates, if appropriate

(GCSE or equivalent and any other exams taken); written
reference from the Head of current/previous school.

Senior School. Whilst children moving up from the
Junior school have the advantage of both continuity of care
and philosophy, they can look forward with excitement to
new faces and new subjects. For children joining us as new
students in the Senior school, they will find a happy and
welcoming family atmosphere in which they will rapidly
feel a sense of belonging.

The students will study three modern languages and three
sciences, providing them with a firm foundation for further
study. Along with English and Maths, they also study traditional subjects including history, geography, music, art, religious education, ICT, drama, Classical Studies and Design
and Technology. There is certainly something for everyone,
plus additional GCSE subject choices at Year 10.

Our Support Staff are equally skilled and committed to
ensuring our students have the best possible chance of
achieving their academic potential, be that through our Special Education Needs Coordinator or students who require
help with English as a second language.

Sport, Music, Art and Drama are also very important
parts of the College life and educational experience with the
school producing and enhancing some extremely gifted and
talented children in all of these areas in recent years.

Bramcote Junior School. The Junior School was formed
in 2012 through the merger of two fine schools: Bramcote
Preparatory School and Scarborough College Junior School.

Our educational vision is simple; the pursuit of excellence in every aspect of school life in an environment which
will develop active, questioning, confident, thinking children.

At the core of our school is a traditional academic
approach and a challenging curriculum. We provide the best
pastoral care and support for every child. We also pride ourselves on the breadth of our education within and outside of
the classroom. Art, drama and music are taught, as well as
games and outdoor pursuits, and an extensive enrichment
programme.

In addition we offer wrap around care for our busy working parents, who are investing in their child's early years
education, plus a fun and caring Holiday Club for those who
need additional child care support. The benefit of having all
of this as part of the Bramcote Junior School package is that
children are happy and confident in a known environment
with teachers and carers who know and care about them.
There is little disruption for them, with continuity from the
age of 3 all the way through to 18.

Little Owls Pre-School. Little Owls Pre-School at Scarborough College is more than just a nursery: with outstanding provision for 3 and 4 year olds, it is the perfect
preparation for a child's introduction to Reception when
they are five. Introducing structured learning as well as play,
all learning is based around the EYFS structure.

There are FREE funded places for 3 and 4 year olds for a
guaranteed 15 hours per week. What's more, we are able to
offer block bookings spread across three half days (the
equivalent of 5 hours per day, including a hot meal for those
who attend morning sessions and healthy snacks for the children who attend in the afternoon), making it a convenient
and cost effective choice for parents.

Wrap-around care from 8.00 am to 6.00 pm is included in
the pre-school fees. After school care means the children are
able to share some facilities with Infant School children and
benefit from playing with and learning from older children.

There are many advantages to being under the umbrella
of Scarborough College, not least the opportunity to share
the College's superb facilities, including a theatre, lecture
room and sports complex.

Sixth Form and the IB Diploma. The International Baccalaureate Diploma programme provides our Sixth Form
students with a stimulating and challenging post-16 curriculum. Our experience has shown that the IB encourages the

development of inquisitive, critical and reflective thinkers who engage fully in the learning process to acquire knowledge.

Within our Sixth Form, students develop a new relationship with their teachers and tutors as a university style is approached in smaller classes. They have many opportunities to show and develop their leadership skills and become very involved in the School Council, hosting and organising school, house and social events as well as Prefect duties and helping younger students in roles such as mentors and sports coaches. There is a rich programme of visiting speakers and exchange visits, and they have their own dedicated Study Centre, Café and Common Room. This is a caring, friendly and warm environment which is a great place to develop and grow into inquisitive and confident young adults.

Boarding. There are four traditional and charming boarding houses at Scarborough College, offering boarding accommodation for pupils aged 11–18 years from all around the world. These really do provide a warm family environment with a home-from-home feeling for all our students, both British and foreign.

A busy programme of weekend entertainment is planned each term to keep the students active. More spontaneous events include house barbecues, football or any sport in the gardens, trips to the beach, go karting, mountain biking and cinema trips, just to name a few.

Our boarding staff are all experienced members of staff with families of their own, so know how challenging and demanding teenagers can be from time to time, but also are very caring, understanding and sympathetic to the needs of each and every individual child.

Enrichment Programme. Education outside the classroom plays an essential part in both developing the interpersonal skills of individuals and making them into interesting people. We encourage all our students to take part in at least two activities per term, but most are involved in considerably more. This helps each child find activities in which they can excel outside of the classroom and allows them to try new skills in a safe environment. It also allows some students extra classroom tuition for various subjects if they need it, or revision sessions in the run up to GCSE and IB examinations.

Enrichment Programme Activities on offer are:

Sport: Rugby, Hockey, Netball, Cricket, Rounders, tennis, Badminton, Athletics, Running Club, Yoga and Zumba.

Languages: French Conversation, Spanish Conversation, German Bootcamp, Ab Initio Spanish Conversation (beginners) and Latin.

The Arts: Art, Choir, Musical Production, Band and Drama.

Others: Duke of Edinburgh's Award training, Fitness Bootcamp, Touch Typing, Debating Society, Maths Extension, Maths Booster, Reading Booster, Supervised Prep, Computer Games, Calligraphy, ICT Prep Club, Science Club, Wargames, Sixth Form Tutor time, Chess and Film Club.

The programme is reviewed each term and new activities are often added at the request of students via the School Council or when new staff bring new skills, hobbies and interests to the school, outside of their classroom duties.

Day Pupils. Day pupils and boarders are fully integrated in school; they share studies and use all school facilities. They have lunch at school and enrichment activities are available at lunchtime Monday to Friday and after school Monday to Thursday. The school bus service operates daily to Bridlington, Whitby, Driffield, Malton and Pickering.

For further up-to-date information on the school, please visit the College's website.

Fees per term (2014–2015). Senior School: £3,885–£4,331 (day), £6,403–£7,205 (UK and MOD boarding), £6,931–£7,672 (EU boarding), £7,326–£8,110 (Overseas boarding). Junior School: £2,207–£3,546 (day).

Charitable status. Scarborough College is a Registered Charity, number 529686.

Shebbear College

Shebbear, North Devon EX21 5HJ

Tel:	01409 282000
Fax:	01409 281784
email:	registrar@shebbearcollege.co.uk
website:	www.shebbearcollege.co.uk

Shebbear College is a day and boarding school for boys and girls between the ages of 3 to 18 years. Set in 85 acres of beautiful Devon countryside, the school, which was founded in 1841, offers superb facilities and plenty of room to run around in a very safe and healthy environment. The school is part of the Methodist Independent Schools Trust and embraces all faiths as it welcomes pupils from all over the world. The secure, happy family atmosphere at Shebbear, free from urban distractions, offers pupils full, weekly, or occasional boarding and day education. We aim to instil self-confidence in all our pupils, we teach them to be self-disciplined and they leave the College with excellent qualifications, many of our Sixth Form leavers achieving places at their chosen universities. Shebbear College offers all our pupils "A foundation for life".

Chairman of the Governors: Mr M J Saltmarsh

Headmaster: Mr S D Weale, MA

Deputy Headmistress: Mrs A Farrell, MEd, BEd

Bursar: Mr B Horn, ACMA, ACIS

Teaching Staff:
* *Head of Department or Subject Leader*

Mrs S Akers, CertEd (*Learning Support)
Miss J Aliberti
Mr L Oxenham, BA Hons, PGCE, MSc (**Business Studies & Economics*)
Mr A Barlow, BA (*Art)
Mrs E Bearpark, LLB (*Mathematics)
Mr A Bryan, CertEd
Mr I Burnett, BA
Mrs C Cardoo, BSc
Mr I Lazenbury (**Physics, *Science*)
Mr A Colville (*Biology)
Dr S Crook, BSc, PhD (*Chemistry)
Mrs C Fanet (*Modern Languages)
Miss S Ham, BSc (*Girls Games)
Mr S Bee (*History)
Mrs F Lovett, YTEFLA, CELTA
Mr M Newitt, BSc, FRGS (*Geography)
Miss M O'Shaughnessy
Mr K Parker, GRSM (*Music)
Mrs L Parker, GRSM, LRAM
Mrs K Purdew, CertEd
Mr M Rogers, MA (**Religious Studies*)
Mr J Sanders
Mr A Steel, BSc (*Boys Games)
Mrs P Thomas, BA (*IT)
Mr S Trask, BEng
Mrs J Welby, ALA (*Librarian*)
Mrs D Wahl
Mrs A Vassilaki (*ESL)
Miss L Body (*Science*)

Senior House Staff (*Boarding*):
Mrs L Quirk, BSA (*Head of Boarding & Pastoral Care*)
Mr J Sanders, BSc Hons GTP (*Pollard Houseparent*)

Junior School Teaching Staff:
Head of Junior School/Year 6: Mr M Furber, BEd Hons

Kindergarten: Mrs J Biddlecombe, MITD
Years 1 and 2: Mrs D Jones, BA Ed Hons, Cert SpLD
Year 3: Mrs T Brock, BEd
Year 4: Mrs L Parker, GRSM, LRAM, PGCE
Year 5: Mrs J Burnett, BA
Learning Support: Mrs K Clarke

Registrar: Mrs S Lindley
Marketing Manager: Mr M Charman

Medical Department:
Sister R Light, SEN, RGN Dip Part 1

Visiting Music Staff:

Ms M Orriss (*Flute*)	Mr O Marriott (*Percussion*)
Mrs S Smith (*Clarinet &*	Mrs A Morphy (*Piano*)
Saxophone)	Mrs R Cornish (*Piano*)
Mrs C Frith (*Violin*)	Ms R Slater-Lyons
Mr A Edwards (*Brass*)	(*Singing*)
Mr A Duncan (*Guitar*)	

Number in College. In the Senior School there are around 280 pupils, of whom around 80 are boarders, and around 80 pupils in our Junior (Prep) School.

Situation and Location. Shebbear College borders on Dartmoor National Park and stands in 85 acres of unspoilt countryside. It can be easily reached by main road and rail links; only 40 miles west of Exeter and 40 miles north of Plymouth. Both cities have their own regional and international airport.

Buildings. The main College buildings include Prospect House, Lake Chapel, Beckly Wing, Shebbear College Prep School, Science Department, Music School, Sixth Form Centre, Language Centre and Sports Hall. There are 2 Senior boarding houses and 1 Junior boys boarding house. (The Junior girls have a separate area within the Senior girls house.)

In recent years there has been an impressive record of school building projects. The latest work has been to build a full-size all-weather pitch and multi-gym. A new Prep School extension houses new classrooms and Assembly Hall. For completion in September 2015 we have scheduled two new buildings – a Music Department and a new Sixth Form Centre. All classrooms have interactive whiteboards.

Admission. The Kindergarten accepts children from the age of 2½ where boys and girls are admitted to the Junior School from the age of 5. Entrance to the College at 11 years from other schools is by examination in January for entry in September. Pupils are also admitted at 13 or 14 after submitting Common Entrance Examination papers, but if they wish they may sit our own entrance papers instead. Entry into the Sixth Form is conditional upon GCSE performance.

Houses. Every pupil belongs to a House – Ruddle, Thorne or Way. These Houses organise activities and games competitions throughout the year. Our boarders also belong to an additional boarding house – Pollard House for Senior boy boarders, Pyke House for Junior boy boarders and Ruddle House for girl boarders – each having a Senior Houseparent and two assistants who live in. The House Tutors watch each child's progress academically as well as their general development.

Curriculum. All pupils at Shebbear College follow the National Curriculum until the age of 14. A wide choice of subjects is available in the following two years, leading to GCSE, but everyone is obliged to take English, Mathematics, Science and, usually, a foreign language. In the Sixth Form there is not only a wide choice of A2 and AS levels, but there is particularly flexible timetabling which enables students to mix Arts and Science subjects.

Sport. With more than 25 acres of playing fields, modern sports hall with multi-gym, dance studio, cricket nets, all-weather pitch, tennis and netball courts, pupils have the security to exercise within the school grounds confidently. The main games covered for the boys are rugby, football,

hockey and cricket, in which we have fixtures with most of the major schools in the South West of England. For the girls, we have teams in netball, hockey, rounders and tennis. All pupils are also offered tennis, basketball, athletics, cross-country, badminton and table tennis. All pupils up to the 4th Form have one afternoon of games plus an additional one period of PE every week.

Music and Drama. Pupils are strongly encouraged to participate in music and drama. Our choir has over 40 members and our orchestra, which represents most instruments, also has over 40 members. Players perform regularly in concerts and instrumental ensembles. Every term candidates proudly achieve Honours and Distinctions with The Associated Board of the Royal School for Music. Also, every term, a theatrical production is performed to a very high standard.

Societies and Activities. All pupils participate in at least 4 afternoons a week of extra-curricular activities. This widens their interests and develops their self-confidence. The list of activities is endless and includes the usual and unusual. Many pupils enjoy getting involved with Ten Tors training, hillwalking, camping, sailing, canoeing, and surfing. The Army-run Ten Tors Challenge is proving to be very popular and many pupils are involved in the Duke of Edinburgh's Award scheme.

Careers. Careers advice is taken very seriously. Staff help our students prepare for their chosen career. The College is a member of ISCO. Individual attention is given at appropriate levels and a team of Old Shebbearians covering many professions visits the school regularly and helps with work experience and placement.

Scholarships and Bursaries. Scholarships up to the value of half fees are awarded as follows:

At 11+: All candidates take the Entrance and Scholarship Examination in February.

At 13+: The Scholarship Examination is held in the Spring Term. Awards are also made following Common Entrance Examination results.

For Sixth Form candidates, scholarships are awarded on the basis of interview, school report and GCSE performance. Further details may be obtained from the Registrar.

Fees per term (2014–2015). Infants £1,950. Junior School: Day £2,490–£2,890, Weekly Boarding £4,295–£4,700, Full Boarding £5,570–£5,950. Senior School: Day £3,950, Weekly Boarding £5,950, Full Boarding £7,790.

Charitable status. Shebbear College is a Registered Charity, number 306945. It exists to provide high quality education for children.

Sibford School

Sibford Ferris, Banbury, Oxon OX15 5QL
Tel: 01295 781200
Fax: 01295 781204
email: admissions@sibfordschool.co.uk
website: www.sibfordschool.co.uk
Twitter: @SibfordSchOxon
Facebook: /Sibford-School

Founded 1842. A Co-educational Independent Boarding (full/weekly) and Day School. Membership of The Society of Heads, BSA, AGBIS.

There are 392 pupils in the school aged between 3 and 18: 332 pupils in the Senior School and 60 pupils in the Junior School. There are 85 teachers plus visiting staff.

Chair of School Committee: Seren Wildwood

Head: Michael Goodwin, BA

Deputy Head: Maggie Guy, BA (*English, Child Protection, Boarding*)

Senior School:
* *Head of Department*
§ *Part-time*
† *House Parent*
LSA *Learning Support Assistant*

Simon Baker, BSc (**Geography, Enrichment Week Coordinator, EcoSchools Coordinator, SLT secondment*)
§Katie Bertie (*Dyslexia Teacher*)
§Alison Blake, BA, Cert Ed (*LSA*)
Derek Bottomley, BSc, Cert TEFL (*Mathematics)
§Angela Bovill, BEd, CertEd (*Countryside & Environmental Sciences & Horticulture*)
Laurence Caves, DPhil (*Science*)
Simon Chard, BA (*PE, Vocational Education*)
John Charlesworth MA, (*Assistant Head, Curriculum*)
Debra Collins, BSc (*Mathematics*)
Lesley Cooley, BSc (*LSA*)
Zoë Connor, BA, MA, AKC (**RS, Philosophy & Ethics*)
Hannah Copping, BSc (*Geography*)
§Emma Crocker, BA (*Design Technology,* *Home Economics)
Melanie Deans, BSc, Cert Ed (*Mathematics*)
Darren de Bruyn, B Bus Admin (**Business Studies, Head of House*)
§Christopher Dudley, BA, MEd (*Economics*)
Felicity Dyndor, BSc (*2nd in Science, Head of House*)
Frances Eason, Dip Theatre Design/Craft, Cert Ed Post 16 (*LSA*)
Debby Evans, Cert Ed PCE, Cert SpLD (**ICT, Careers Coordinator*)
†§Claire Ferley, BSc (*PE*)
†§Richard Ferley, BSc (*PE)
§Rebecca Flynn, BA, MA, CTEFL (*Psychology, ESOL*)
Andrew Foakes, BA, MA (**Media, English, Head of House*)
†Andrew Glover, Dip SpLD, BA, Dip TEFL (*Dyslexia, Activities Coordinator*)
§Alan Greenslade-Hibbert, LLB, Dip TEFL (*ESOL*)
†Victoria Hall, BA (*English, Media*)
§Cath Harding, BSc (*Science)
Susan Hirst, BA (*English, Enrichment*)
§Deborah Holroyd, BSc, MA Ed (*Science*)
Fiona Hudson, BA, Licenciate Trinity College Music (*Music)
§Gillian Hughes, BA, Cert SpLD (*LSA*)
§John James, BA (*Ceramics Teacher*)
Jane Kenehan (*LSA, Dyslexia*)
Tracy Knowles, BA Ed (*Assistant Head Pastoral, English*)
Anna Jo Lawrence, BA (*Director of Studies – Teaching and Learning, NQT Mentor, G&T, History*)
Tracey Leigh, MA (*Art)
Victoria Macaulay, MSc (*Science, Head of House*)
Neil Madden BA (*Drama)
Cate Mallalieu-Needle, MA, NPQH (*Head of Sixth Form, English/Drama*)
§Joanna Mayes, BA, Cert TEFL, Cert Ed (*ESOL*)
Andrew Newbold, BSc, PhD (*Director of Studies – Examinations, Science*)
§Ingar Noble, Dip Clinical & Pathological Psychology (*LSA*)
Dolores Papin, Licence Anglais, Maîtrise Anglais (**Modern Foreign Languages*)
Linda Phillips, BSc, MA (*Mathematics*)
Sally Pickering, BA, Dip TEFL (*ESOL)
§Matthew Platt, Grad Dip Music, LGSM Teaching Dip (*Music Performance*)
Sophie Pringle, BA (**Textiles, Home Economics*)
Jeremy Ross, MA (*Assistant Head of Sixth Form, History*)
Annie Smith, BSc, Cert Dyslexia & Literacy (*Assistant Head of Support for Learning*)
§Michael Spring, BEd (*Photography*)
Penelope Spring, BA (**English, PGCE mentor*)
Victor Stannard, BA (**Design Technology*)

§Laurence Suckling, BA, Cert TEFL (*ESOL Teacher*)
§Elizabeth Thomas, BA (*Dance*)
Allison Warrillow, BA (*Assistant Head of PE*)
§Ginette Wheeldon BA, CLAIT, NVQ (*Teaching Assistant Coordinator*)
Jayne Woolley, BA, Cert Ed (*Dyscalculia*)
§Joseph Zetter, Cert Ed (*Modern Foreign Languages*)

Sibford Junior School:
Edward Rossiter, BSc, PG Dip Social Sciences (*Assistant Head, Year 3*)
Nicola Watson, MA (*Early Years)
Margaret Allen, BA (*Year 5*)
Helen Arnold, BA (*Year 5*)
§Wendi Court (*LSA*)
Alice Goodman NVQ 3 (*Senior Early Years Assistant*)
§Kim Haddrell, BA (*LSA*)
Nicholas Hadley BA (*Year 4*)
Jason Harris (*Outdoor Environment Facilitator*)
Jane Kenehan (*LSA, Dyslexia*)
Trudy Koochitt, BA, Dip Mandarin, Dip TEFL (*Year 6*)
§Amanda Levett, BA (*Junior School Dyslexia teacher*)
§Michael Maguire, BA (*LSA*)
§Gill Newbold, Teacher's Certificate (*Dyspraxia, PE*)
Nicola Parfitt, BA Education (*Early Years Assistant*)
Alison Sayer BEd (*Year 1/2*)
Lois Self, BA (*LSA*)
§Claire Solesbury (*LSA*)
Susan Spillett, BA (*LSA*)
Hazel Sykes, BA (*Year 6, Dyslexia teacher*)
Jayne Woolley, BA, Cert Ed (*Dyscalculia*)

Business Manager: Peter Robinson
Admissions Officer: Elspeth Gregory

Curriculum. Broad and balanced curriculum which reflects our view that while some may have talent for maths or history others may be gifted in the arts or horticulture. Renowned dyslexia tuition and support for a small number of pupils with other learning difficulties.

Junior School (age 3–11): a wide-ranging curriculum with an emphasis on outdoor education is provided to children in small groups. Literacy, numeracy, science and technology skills are emphasised alongside art, music, drama and PE. Enriched Curriculum in Year 6 with Senior School Staff. Specialist teachers help individual children with specific learning difficulties.

Senior School (age 11–16): all pupils follow courses leading to GCSE, in a curriculum expanding on the National Curriculum. Information Technology is introduced at an early age and the use of laptop computers is widespread.

Dyslexic pupils have special tuition in small groups on a daily basis. Highly regarded Specific Learning Difficulties (Dyslexic) Department provides specialised support within the timetable. Personal and Social Development runs through the school.

Sixth Form (age 16–18) students take A Levels and/or BTEC Diplomas. The Sixth Form curriculum leads to higher education, and offers a particularly wide range of opportunities for further study.

Overseas pupils are welcomed into the school community. English as an additional language is taught by ESOL qualified teachers.

Entry requirements. Admission to the Junior School, Senior School and Sixth Form is by interview and internal tests. Where applicable a report from the candidate's current school is required. No religious requirements.

Examinations offered. A Level, GCSE, BTEC Diploma, Associated Board Music Examinations, Oxford and Cambridge IELTS Examinations.

Academic and leisure facilities. Exceptional Performing & Creative Arts in purpose-built facilities, multi-purpose Sports Centre, squash courts, 25m indoor swimming pool, well-equipped Library and Information Technology Centres,

Design Technology Centre, separate Sixth Form Centre, wide range of indoor and outdoor activities, 50 plus-acre campus set in beautiful North Oxfordshire countryside. Three boarding houses (for girls, boys and sixth form). Easy access to Stratford, Oxford, Cheltenham, Birmingham, London.

Religion. The School has a distinctive Quaker ethos. It welcomes pupils of all faiths, backgrounds and nationalities, encouraging in each of them genuine self-esteem in a purposeful, caring and challenging environment.

Fees per term (2014–2015). Full Boarders £8,380–£8,549, Weekly Boarders £5,496–£7,960, Flexi Boarding £55 per night, Day Pupils £4,314–£4,400.

Junior School: Day Pupils £2,741–£3,316.

The fee for a full term of learning support is £1,528.50.

Scholarships and Bursaries. The School offers general Academic scholarships and specific scholarships in Art, Music and Sport. A limited number of bursaries is offered to both Quaker and non Quaker children.

Charitable status. Sibford School is a Registered Charity, number 1068256. It is a company limited by guarantee under number 3487651. It aims to give all pupils a vehicle to educational and personal success.

Stafford Grammar School

Burton Manor, Stafford, Staffordshire ST18 9AT
Tel: 01785 249752
Fax: 01785 255005
email: headsec@staffordgrammar.co.uk
website: www.staffordgrammar.co.uk

Motto: Quod tibi hoc alteri

Patrons:
The Right Hon The Earl of Shrewsbury
The Lord Stafford
The Right Hon The Earl of Lichfield

Governing Body:
B K Hodges (*Chairman*)

J Archer, TD, FCIS, JP	R Nicholls
B Baggott	D Pearsall
Mrs C Bloxham	Mrs P Pearsall
Mrs J Colman	C Sproston
Mrs S Flatters	Mrs H Watson Jones
J Lotz, FRCS	A Wright

Headmaster: **M R Darley**, BA

Deputy Head: M P Robinson, BA, DipEd Man
Director of Studies: Dr P A Johnson, BSc, PhD
Senior Teacher: Mr R C Green, BA
Senior Teacher: Mrs A Saxon, MA, BEd

Assistant Staff:

C Anderson, BSc	Mrs K Horsley, BA
Mrs E Ayirebi, BA	A C Johnson, BSc
D R Beauchamp, BSc	M J Jones, BSc
Mrs R Beauchamp, BA	T Kirsch, BSc
G Beckett, BSc	G R Lamplough, BMus
C Cooke, BA	Miss K Lewis, BA
Dr F G Crane, BSc, PhD	Mrs A Lonsdale, BSc
Dr R Foster, BSc, PhD	Miss L McConville, BSc
S Godwin, MSc, BA	D Marshall, BEd
Mrs L J Griffiths, BA	D Mole, BA
Miss H Hackett, BSc	Mrs E M Neville, BA
J. Hamilton, BSc	Mrs P H Patrick, BSc
L J Harwood, BEd	Mrs E L Paton, BA
Mrs M M Hinton, BA	Mrs B Robson, BSc
Mrs T A Hollinshead, BSc, MSc	G Robson, BSc

Mrs F F Shakesheave, BSc, BA	Mrs S Smith, BA
	L H Thomas, BA
Mrs D Shaughnessy, BA, MA	Miss A K Wallis, BA
	Mrs A L Weetman LAES

Chaplain: Prebendary R Sargent, MA

Bursar: J Downes

Headmaster's Secretary: Mrs S M Pickavance

Number in School. There are 363 pupils (11–18 years) of whom 170 are boys and 193 girls. There is a Sixth Form of just over 100. Stafford Preparatory School has just over 100 pupils.

Stafford Grammar School is housed in a fine Victorian manor house, designed by Augustus Pugin, standing in 47 acres of grounds with sports pitches, tennis courts and extensive additional specialist accommodation. A new Science and Sixth Form Centre opened in 2007. Sixteen acres of sports land have recently been developed to further enhance outside sport provision.

Curriculum. In Year 7 and Year 8 all pupils follow a common course consisting of English, Mathematics, Science, French, German, Geography, History, Music, Art, Drama, Computing, Design, Technology, Religious Education and Physical Education. Year 9 sees Science divide into separate subjects.

Pupils in Years 10 and 11 study nine or ten subjects at GCSE: English (2), Mathematics, Science (IGCSE dual or triple award) and a language, together with three further subjects chosen from a whole range including humanities and practical subjects. Physical Education continues and Careers and Life Skills are introduced.

There is setting in Mathematics from Year 8, Science from Year 9 and English from Year 10. Other subjects are taught in mixed ability groups. Classes are kept small (maximum 20) so that pupils can receive individual attention.

In the Lower Sixth Form students study three or four A Level subjects (AS) leading to three or four A Level subjects (A2) in the Upper Sixth Form. Approximately 20 A Level subjects are available.

Creativity and the Arts. The School has an extensive Art and Design Department. Pupils' powers of observation and awareness are developed through practical skills and theoretical studies involving areas as varied as painting, printing, 3-D work, photography and textiles. There are frequent competitions and exhibitions of work as well as projects linked with other departments.

Music plays an important part in the life of the School. There is an orchestra, a concert band and choirs which perform on many occasions in musicals, church services and concerts. Ensembles, both instrumental and vocal, are encouraged. Pupils have the opportunity to learn to play a wide range of musical instruments with tuition provided by peripatetic teachers. The bi-annual music trips abroad are well supported.

Drama enables pupils to gain confidence and self-understanding. It is particularly effective in the early years in the School. Two annual School Plays are major productions on the School's excellent stage and involve a large number of pupils. Recent productions include *Beauty and the Beast* and *Les Misérables*.

Art and Drama are available at both GCSE and A Level.

Peripatetic LAMDA tuition is available from Grade 1 to Gold Medal (Grade 8). LAMDA students also attend local drama festivals.

Sport and Activities. Whilst competitive sport plays a prominent part in School life, the emphasis is also on preparation for future leisure time.

The School has outstanding sports facilities and the following sports are available: Soccer, Hockey, Rugby, Cricket, Tennis, Badminton, Basketball, Netball, Volleyball, Athletics, Gymnastics, Rounders, Table Tennis, and Health-related Fitness, as well as Swimming. The School has an extensive fitness suite.

The School plays a large number of matches against other schools, both state and independent, and is fully involved in local leagues. Individuals regularly secure places in Staffordshire and Midlands teams.

Our range of activities is deliberately wide since we believe that every child is good at something and that it is our job to discover and develop talent in any direction.

There are many Clubs and Societies of widely differing kinds and a large number of pupils are working for The Duke of Edinburgh's Award Scheme.

At present there are 15 inter-House competitions. These range from Technology to Public Speaking and from Football to Hobbies, and include some which are specifically for younger pupils.

The intention of these is not only to enable as many pupils as possible to represent their Houses, but also to stress that we value excellence in any area.

Pastoral Care. In its pastoral organisation, the School seeks to nurture the potential of every child giving both support and encouragement in an overt and practical way. The School is divided into three houses, the Head of House being the key figure in the academic and personal development of each child. Tutor groups are kept small and are based on the House to maintain continuity and to strengthen communal bonds. Tutors maintain strong links with each pupil using a programme of active tutoring which includes scheduled interviews. We place great emphasis on close contact with parents, believing that lack of progress and other problems are best addressed jointly and as early as possible.

In the Sixth Form a slightly different system operates. Although retaining the same House Tutor, the pupil will have a Form Tutor from a specialist team of Sixth Form Tutors. Additionally one of the Senior Teachers is attached to this team. Further to this is the opportunity for each pupil to choose a Personal Tutor with whom to build a special rapport.

Sixth Form. The Sixth Form is the ideal environment in which to foster confidence, responsibility, leadership, initiative and self-discipline.

The keynote of the Sixth Form is freedom with responsibility. At this stage pupils still need help in planning their time and in establishing good working habits, and the guidance of an understanding tutor can mean the difference between success and failure. There is an extensive UCAS programme which includes Oxbridge preparation.

Careers. Considerable attention is paid to career advice, and there are frequent visits by speakers from industry and the professions. From Year 10 onwards, individual advice is given by our own careers staff, and pupils are also encouraged to consult the County Careers Service.

Religion. Although we welcome pupils of all faiths, or none, the School is a Christian foundation.

The School seeks to live by the Christian ideal, in particular by being a community in which members genuinely care about each other.

Admission. Entrance is by examination and interview in order to ensure that pupils have sufficient reasoning ability to be able to attempt GCSE in a reasonable range of subjects.

Entrance to the Sixth Form is by GCSE results and interview.

Scholarships and Bursaries. The Governors have allocated funds to enable pupils of exceptional ability or limited means to join the school.

Fees per term (from January 2014) Grammar School: £3,666 excluding lunch; Preparatory School (including lunch): Years 1, 2, 3 & 4 £3,162, Years 5 & 6 £3,287.

Stafford Preparatory School opened, in purpose-built accommodation, in September 2007 admitting pupils into Year 5 and Year 6. A Year 4 class was admitted in September 2008, a Year 3 class in 2009, Years 1 and 2 in September 2012. and a Reception class in 2014. Stafford Preparatory School provides exciting opportunities for pupils to prepare for selective senior school education at Stafford Grammar School or elsewhere.

Charitable status. Stafford Independent Grammar School Limited is a Registered Charity, number 513031. It exists to provide education for children.

Stover School

Newton Abbot, South Devon TQ12 6QG
Tel: 01626 354505 (Main switchboard)
           01626 331451 (Preparatory School)
           01626 335240 (Finance Office)
Fax: 01626 361475
email: mail@stover.co.uk
website: www.stover.co.uk

Board of Governors:

Chairman: Mr S Killick, ND, ARB
Vice Chair:
Commodore B J Key, BSc, FCMI, RN
Mr D Wilson, ACIB, MBA

Members:
Ms B Atkinson, MSc, BSc, RGN, RSCN, Dip N Lond
Mrs M Batten, BSc RHC
Lt Col D Hourahane
Mrs L Jones MA
Mrs J Milstead, BSc
Mr C Oliver, LLB, MBA
Mr M Roberts, BA, MRTPI

Honorary Members:
Professor R Hawker, OBE
Dr P J Key, OBE, MB BS
Mrs C Walliker, BSc, MBA

Clerk to the Governors: Mr S J Drabble, BSc

***Executive Head Teacher*: Mr Richard Notman**, BCom Hons

Deputy Principal Senior School with responsibility for Boarding: Mrs K Veal, BEd Hons
Head of Preparatory School: Mrs C Coyle, BEd, MA
Director of Teaching & Learning: Dr J Stone, BSc, MEd Open, PhD, HDipEd
Head of Sixth Form: Mr C Baillie, BSc Hons
Director of Finance & Operations: Mr H Cummins, ACMA

Chaplain: Mrs F Wimsett, BA, PGCE
PA to the Executive Head Teacher: Miss J Warrender
Examinations Officer: Mrs H Cleaton, BSc, BTEC
Academic Secretary: Mrs S Simpkin
Registrar: Miss F White
Assistant Registrar: Mrs H Symons
Communications Manager: Miss R Littlefair
Senior School Secretary: Mrs C Ettridge
Preparatory School Administrator: Mrs F Martin
Finance Manager: Mrs G Hanbury
Finance Assistant: Miss L Lount
Finance Assistant: Mrs M Barnard

Academic Staff:
Ms P Absalom, BA (*Head of Drama*)
Dr D Allway, BSc, MSc, PhD (*Head of Science*)
Mrs M Ayela, DEUG, Licence ES (*Head of Modern Foreign Languages*)
Mr C Baillie, BSc (*Head of Sixth Form & Science*)
Mr P Barter, BA (*Head of Humanities*)
Mrs A Bradley, BA (*Philosophy & Ethics*)
Mrs L Cocker, BSc (*Head of Mathematics*)

Mrs A Coster, BA (*Learning Support, PE*)
Mrs H Coyne, BA (*Modern Languages*)
Miss T Craven, BA, QTS (*Head of Physical Education*)
Mrs E Creates, BA, MA (*Geography*)
Miss E Evans, BA, (*French*)
Mrs S Farleigh, BA (*Music*)
Mrs R Fenton, BA (*Head of English, Teacher of Media*)
Mr G Forsyth, BA, (*English*), TEFL
Mrs K Gardner, BA (*History*)
Mr D Geeves, BSc (*Physics*)
Mrs S Griffin, BEd (*Head of Years 7, 8 & 9*)
Mr J Haigh, BA, MA (*Mathematics, Sixth Form Tutor*)
Mrs C Howard, BA (*Head of Art & Photography*)
Dr L le Tissier, BA, BSc, PhD, (*Head of Psychology*)
Mrs E Machin, BA (*Director of ICT, Head of D&T
   Graphics, Head of Years 10 & 11*)
Miss A Morgan, BSc (*Science*)
Mrs A Richards, BSc Ed, (*Head of Physics*)
Mrs C Simmons, BEd (*Mathematics, Science*)
Mrs A Stone, BA (*Head of English as an Additional
   Language*)
Mr J Tizzard, BMus, Dip Ed
Mr L Turnbull, BA (*Business Studies*)
Mr D Veal, BA (*Science, Head of Senior Boys Physical
   Education*)
Mrs C Wightman, BA (*Art*)
Mrs F Wimsett, BA (*RE, Chaplain*)

Learning Support Staff (Special Educational Needs):
Mrs K Sorensen-Parkes, Dip Bus Mgt (*Head of Learning
   Support*)
Mrs T Dodd, NVQ3 Child Care
Mrs J Ford, NCFE Level 2
Mrs S Hunt, NVQ3 Child Care
Mrs L Lewis, BA, QTS
Mrs M Roberts, NVQ3 Child Care
Mrs G Thompson, NVQ3 EYCE
Mrs M Wolbold, NVQ3 EYCE

Support Staff:
Mr R Camilleri, BSc, PGCE
Mrs L Turnbull

Visiting Staff:
Mr P Adcock (*Accompanist*)
Mr J Allnatt (*Double Bass*)
Mrs F Austen (*Harp*)
Mr J Baldwin (*Keyboard, Piano*)
Mrs J Berry (*Speech & Drama*)
Mrs A Brown (*Piano, Aural Training*)
Mr P Butcher (*Tennis Coach*)
Mrs V Davies (*Latin*)
Mr S Douglas (*Drum kit*)
Mrs S Durant (*Brass*)
Mrs S Farleigh, BA (*Voice and Flute*)
Miss C Hayek (*Violin and Viola*)
Mr P Hill (*Guitar*)
Mr B Knight (*Tennis Coach*)
Mrs A O'Donovan (*Woodwind, Piano, Keyboard*)
Mr T Unwin (*Jazz Piano*)
Mrs H Wills, ALCM (*Cello, Piano*)
Mr A Yang (*Mandarin*)

Stover Preparatory School:

Head of Preparatory School: Mrs C Coyle, BEd, MA

Leadership Team:
Mr M Appleby, BEd, MA, MEd, PG Dip Psych (*Director
   of Teaching & Learning*)
Mrs R Reynolds, BSc (*Preparatory School Coordinator*)

Teachers
Mr M Ayer, BSc Ed
Mr C Brown, BA (*Head of SPS Physical Education*)
Ms D Fallshaw, BA
Mrs C Harrison, BA

Mrs J Jamin, BEd
Mrs M Pallister BEd
Mr L Ryan, BSc
Mrs F Waring, Cert Ed DELE, TEFL
Mr B Watt, BA
Mrs S Yonge, BA Ed

Assistants
Mrs K Freeman, NNEB
Mrs J Sanders, NNEB
Miss A Trapnell

Nursery:
Mrs D Battershall, City & Guilds Level 2
Miss N Carey, NVQ3 (*Nursery Group Leader*)
Mrs J Cross, NNEB (*Nursery Coordinator & Leader*)
Mrs I McIntosh, NNEB (*Nursery Coordinator & Leader*)

Residential Staff:
Mrs A Bradley, BA Hons (*Houseparent*)
Mrs H Cleaton, BSc Hons (*Houseparent*)
Mrs F Martin (*House Tutor*)
Mr C Brown, BA Hons (*Houseparent*)
Mr L Ryan (*House Tutor*)
Boarding Assistants:
Miss E O'Connell
Miss C Kirkman
Mr T Milenovic

School Medical Officer: Dr D Milburn, MB BS
School Nurses:
Miss S Edworthy, RGN
Mrs J Williams, RGN

Stover School is one of the South West's leading schools, set in 64 acres of beautiful grounds; intentionally a small, friendly day and boarding school for both boys and girls from 3 years to 18. Stover enjoys the benefits of a rural location with an excellent transport network to the A38, railway station and local airports.

Stover's aim is to provide a supportive, nurturing environment enabling pupils to acquire excellent qualifications and the confidence to achieve their aspirations, pupils are happy; they thrive and flourish. Our record of achieving outstanding results at GCSE and A Level, is a testament to the hard work of the pupils and staff.

Stover offers a full boarding package: full boarding, weekly boarding, and flexi boarding, which can be tailored to individual boarding needs. There is a wonderful ethos of providing an enriching and varied programme for the boarders, and there are now 3 boarding houses on site – two for girls and one for boys.

Stover provides a supportive, hard-working and purposeful atmosphere. The emphasis is on regular work routines, independent learning, and a sense of community. Academic results are impressive and sit alongside our sporting achievements, musical talents and moral well-being. We offer an extensive extra-curricular programme, offering circus skills, web design, chess, golf, horse riding, Duke of Edinburgh's Award, Ten Tors Training and many more. Overseas trips have included: Trek to the Annapurna Base Camp in Nepal, World Challenge Trip to Botswana and Zambia, Art Trip to New York, Language trips to Paris and Barcelona, History trip to Flanders and Geography trips to Southern Italy, Costa Rica and California, skiing and watersports trips.

Stover has a thriving musical department, with choirs, orchestras, jazz band and ensembles offering plenty of opportunities to perform at school and at local festivals and concerts. We hold our whole-school drama performance once a year and smaller productions throughout the year for younger pupils in both prep and senior schools.

Within the grounds we have a dedicated Sixth Form Centre, where students have study, recreational facilities and a kitchen. The Sixth Form is a strong, tight-knit community with a culture of hard-working independent study.

Stover has a superb Art, Media and Photography Centre, and Science Centre with four fully-resourced laboratories and Mathematics Department upstairs.

Stover is a dynamic and exciting place to be; parents can be assured that their child is receiving the best possible care enabling them to achieve their aspirations.

We look forward to welcoming you to Stover School.

Examinations. Public examinations set by all examination boards are taken at GCSE Level and at A Level. Music examinations are set by the Associated Board of the Royal Schools of Music. Speech and Drama examinations are set by LAMDA.

Physical Education. Hockey, rugby, netball, football, rounders and cricket are the core team games. Individual sports include athletics, gymnastics, golf, tennis, badminton and cross country. Other sports throughout the year include adventure development, orienteering and dance.

The school has extensive grass pitches, six tennis courts (3 floodlit), a covered sports dome, a 3-hole short golf course, cross-country tracks and cricket nets. We run a full range of in-school and after-school sports clubs and fixture lists for both Senior and Prep.

Optional subjects. In addition to a wide variety of activities organised by Stover's own staff there are specialist peripatetic staff for instrumental and voice tuition, speech and drama, riding and golf and tennis coaching.

Fees per term (2014–2015). Preparatory School: Day: Reception–Year 2 £2,462, Year 3 £2,678, Years 4–5 £3,049, Year 6 £3,327. Weekly Boarding: Year 3 £5,243, Years 4–5 £5,614, Year 6 £5,892. Full Boarding: Year 3 £6,067, Years 4–5 £6,438, Year 6 £6,716.

Senior School: Years 7–11: £3,883 (day), £6,788 (weekly boarding), £8,024 (full boarding); Years 12–13: £3,996 (day), £6,932 (weekly boarding), £8,178 (full boarding).

Entrance and Scholarships. Entrance assessments are sat by all prospective pupils from 7 years to 15 years either during a taster day or our entrance day in January. Scholarships are available at 7+, 11+, 13+ and 16+ in Academic, Art, Music and Sport. In addition means-tested Scholarships and bursaries are available, Laurus and Maurice Key Awards. Stover School in association with Plymouth University also offers the Excellence in Mathematics Scholarships to International students, which attracts a 25% remission of fees at Stover for the duration of the A Level course (2 years) and 10% remission of fees at Plymouth University for the duration of the Undergraduate Degree course (3 years).

Health. Twenty four hours a day nursing care is provided by a team of SRNs and regular visits by a local GP.

Old Stoverites. *Secretary*: Mrs M Downey, c/o Stover School.

Charitable status. Stover School Association is a Registered Charity, number 306712. Stover School is a charitable foundation for education.

Sunderland High School
United Learning

Mowbray Road, Sunderland, Tyne and Wear SR2 8HY
Tel: 0191 567 7674
Fax: 0191 510 3953

Junior School:
Tonstall House, Ashbrooke Road, Sunderland SR2 7JA
Tel: 0191 514 3278
Fax: 0191 565 6510

email: registrar@sunderlandhigh.co.uk
website: www.sunderlandhigh.co.uk

Co-educational Day School established by the United Church Schools Trust, now called United Learning, and opened in 1884.

Governing Body: The Council of United Learning

Local Committee:
M Litchfield (*Chairman*)

D K Sherwood-Smith	U Patel
V Ward	P McLachlan
J Milne	S Atkinson
R Brannigan	J May
J Lee	

***Head*: Dr A J Slater**, BA, PhD

Head of Junior School: Mr C W Bulmer, BEd, MA, NPQH

Deputy Head of Junior School: Mrs G Prior, BA, PGCE

Senior School:
Mrs A Bovill, CertEd, Dip Psych (*English, Learning Support*)
Miss H Bowerman, BSc (*Physical Education*)
Mrs C Bowmer, BA, PGCE (*Head of Science*)
Ms J Bruce, BA, PGCE (*German, French*)
Mrs J Craven, BA Eng, BA MFL (*English, Media*)
Mrs B Fitzsimmons, BA Hons, PGCE (*History*)
Mr D Gardner, BSc PGCE, MA (*Physical Education*)
Miss D Greest, BA Hons (*English, Drama*)
Dr L Hallam, BA, PGCE, MA, PhD (*German*)
Mrs B Harrett, BA, PGCE (*German*)
Mrs J Hill, BA, Hons, PGCE (*Head of ICT*)
Mr J A Hodson, BA, PGCE (*Mathematics*)
Mrs E Hope, BA, PGCE (*Religious Studies*)
Mrs A Joyce, BA, PGCE (*DT and Art*)
Mrs J Little, BSc, PGCE (*Physical Education*)
Mrs L Mason, Cert Ed (*Latin*)
Mr D Percy, BSc, PGCE (*Physics*)
Miss S Probets, BSc, PGCE (*Mathematics, Science*)
Mrs J Robson, BA, PGCE (*HE, Sociology*)
Mrs L Taylor, BEd (*Food and Nutrition*)
Mr A Temple, BSc, PGCE (*Head of Mathematics*)
Mrs J Thompson, BEd (*Head of English*)
Mrs A Wayman, BA, CertEd (*Geography*)
Mr S Wardle, BA Hons, PGCE (*Business Studies*)

Shared Staff:
Mrs C Summers, BA PGCE (*Director of Music*)

Infant & Junior School:
Mrs J Charalambous, BA, PGCE (*Key Stage 2 Coordinator*)
Mrs V Dixon, MA, PGCE (*Modern Foreign Languages*)
Miss A Eden, BSc Ed ICT (*Class Teacher*)
Mrs R Keating, BA, PGCE (*Class Teacher*)
Mr I McDonough, BSc, PGCE (*Science Coordinator*)
Mr NR Rich, BA, PGCE (*Class Teacher*)
Mr A Smith, BA Hons, PGCE (*ICT Coordinator*)

Nursery Staff:
Miss R Brown, BTec in Early Years (*Nursery Manager*)
Mrs P Bilton, CACHE L3 Childcare NVQ, Learning and Development (*Nursery Assistant*)
Mrs J Clark, CACHE L3 Childcare NVQ, Learning and Development (*Nursery Assistant*)
Mrs D Fearon, NNEB Nursery Nurse (*Senior Nursery Nurse*)
Mrs S Parker, NNEB Nursery Nurse (*Senior Nursery Nurse*)
Miss R Liptrot (*Nursery Nurse*)
Mrs J Dutton (*Lunchtime Assistant*)
Miss J Porterfield-Smith (*Lunchtime Assistant*)

Visiting Staff
Mr O Cassidy (*Drums*)
Mrs R Crossley-Tombs (*Karate*)

Dr L Hardy (*Flute*)
Mrs K Knox (*Ballet/Disco*)
Mrs V Swales (*Learning Support Assistant*)
Mrs A Foster (*Clarinet*)
Mr S Innes (*Violin*)
Mr N Pride (*Guitar*)

Support Staff:
Miss Stephanie Browning (*Senior School Teaching Assistant*)
Mrs S Critchley (*Senior School Teaching Assistant*)
Miss E Coxon (*Junior School Teaching Assistant*)
Mrs M Diaz (*Junior School Teaching Assistant*)
Mrs C Gallagher (*Senior School Housekeeper*)
Miss N Gallagher (*Senior School Secretary*)
Miss L Hughes (*Junior School Teaching Assistant*)
Mrs P Hughes (*Senior School Science Technician*)
Miss S Lindsay (*Finance Officer*)
Mrs E Martin (*Head's PA/Registrar*)
Mr G Osman (*Junior School Caretaker*)
Mrs M Brannigan (*Marketing Officer*)
Mr C Peacock (*Systems Administrator*)
Mr J Schofield (*Senior School Caretaker*)
Miss D Hall (*Senior School Administrator/Exams Clerk*)
Mr A Thompson (*Premises Manager*)
Mr M Thompson (*Senior School Groundsman*)
Mrs M Walls (*Teaching Assistant/Uniform Shop*)
Mr A Wright (*Minibus driver*)
Mrs C More (*Junior School Secretary*)

The school is situated in the centre of the town, close to the bus and railway stations. Pupils travel from Gateshead, Chester-le-Street, Washington, South Shields, Peterlee, Houghton-le-Spring and Durham. Transport services are good. School buses are organised from South Shields, Washington, Peterlee, Houghton-le-Spring and Durham.

The Junior School, for Nursery, Infant and Junior boys and girls, was opened by HRH – The Princess Royal in May 1994. The building has specialist rooms for Science, Art, Computers and Music as well as a fully equipped Sports Hall. Outdoor sports facilities include a full-sized, floodlit all-weather pitch and grass pitch. These sports facilities are shared by Junior and Secondary pupils for their games programme which includes hockey, netball, football, rugby, cricket, tennis, rounders and athletics. All boys and girls in the Junior School, including the Nursery, have swimming classes also.

The Nursery admits boys and girls on a full or part-time basis and prepares children for school through constructive educational play.

The Infant and Junior Departments provide a sound education for boys and girls. The special feature of the Infant and Junior programme is the Early Language Programme in which German is a popular core curriculum for all pupils from the age of 4+. Junior School pupils enter the Senior School on the recommendation of the Head of Junior School, and they may take a scholarship test at that point. These scholarships are awarded on academic merit. There is also a music scholarship awarded at this stage.

The Senior School (Years 7 to 11) in Mowbray Road has three sites. The Centenary building provides excellent classrooms, four science laboratories and a networked Information Technology Room. The original building includes a fifth laboratory, a second networked Computer Room, library, art room, Design and Food Technology Centre, careers room and further classrooms.

The Junior School in particular achieved 39th place in The Sunday Times Top 100 Prep Schools ranking – just 3 places below their ranking the year before.

The Curriculum. The school is small enough for all pupils to be in close contact with the staff. Classes are limited in size and allow for teachers to deal with individual needs extremely effectively.

The Curriculum is designed to provide a broad education from 4+ to 18+, in line with the requirements of the National Curriculum. Pupils are encouraged to acquire the right qualifications for further study, an independence of spirit, a self-awareness of their personal qualities and sensitivity to the needs of others.

In the Junior School, core subjects are taught in forms with specialist subjects being added as pupils get older. German is taught to pupils from the age of 4+ as part of the school's European awareness policy.

In the Senior School, there are some twenty subjects which pupils study from the age of 11. Pupils receive guidance in Year 9 to enable them to make a wise and balanced choice of subjects for the GCSE courses. In Year 11 Work Experience is organised after the GCSE examinations.

Music, drama and sport are strongly encouraged as well as extra-curricular activities, including the Duke of Edinburgh's Award Scheme. Regular ski trips, activity excursions and visits abroad are organised for both junior and senior pupils.

The Sixth Form. The Sixth Form is the only Independent Sixth Form in Sunderland. Boys and girls are admitted to the Sixth Form subject to a satisfactory standard at GCSE. Most students take four AS Level subjects in Arts and/or Science, leading to three A2 Levels. A General Studies programme is also offered. Extra courses, such as the CSLA and Young Enterprise, are part of the General Studies programme. All students are encouraged to help in the organisation of the school. Most students proceed to University and other areas of Higher Education. Scholarships are available on entry to the Sixth Form.

Admission. Entry to the school is normally at 4+, 7+, 11+, 13+ and the Sixth Form, but applications at other ages are accepted, subject to vacancies. Entrance is partially selective and may include an interview, written tests and a reference from the applicant's previous school.

Fees per term (2014–2015). Infants £2,226; Juniors £2,677; Seniors (including the Sixth Form) £3,077. The fees include textbooks and stationery. Lunches are extra.

Foundation Assisted Places are also available.

Additional Subjects. Music, Speech, Karate, Dancing (Fees on request).

Scholarships and Bursaries. Entrance Scholarships are available at 11+. These are awarded on academic ability and are worth up to 25% of the fees. Scholarships are also available to students wishing to join the School at 16+. These are awarded according to academic ability (interview and test).

A Music Scholarship worth 10% of the fees is available to pupils on entry to the School at age 11.

Foundation Assisted Places are available. A reduction in fees is also available to children of Clergy families and awarded by United Learning.

Charitable status. Sunderland High School is part of United Learning which comprises: UCST (a Company Limited by Guarantee, Registered in England, number 2780748, and a Registered Charity, number 1016538) and ULT (a Company Limited by Guarantee, Registered in England, number 4439859, and an Exempt Charity).

Tettenhall College

Wood Road, Tettenhall, Wolverhampton, West Midlands WV6 8QX

Tel: 01902 751119
Fax: 01902 793000
email: head@tettcoll.co.uk
website: www.tettenhallcollege.co.uk
Facebook: /TettenhallCollege

Motto: '*Timor Domini Initium Sapientiae*'

Tettenhall College is a co-educational school for 2 to 18 year olds set in 33 acres of stunning historical woodland grounds. The Nursery, Preparatory School and Senior School which make up Tettenhall College share wonderful on-site facilities. These incorporate modern science laboratories, dedicated art studios, the famous Towers Theatre and excellent sporting facilities which include a swimming pool. All of these combine to create a unique environment where your child can take their first steps in their educational journey and grow as individuals from Nursery right through to Sixth Form.

It is a thriving school where pupils in all years exceed expectations whether that be their reading levels in Preparatory School, GCSE examinations or A levels in Sixth Form. Leavers' destinations include some of the most prestigious names in the educational world – Oxford, Cambridge and RADA to name a few. Alongside academic achievement pupils are involved in a full programme of exciting extra-curricular activities and opportunities which we believe develops the whole individual. Our unique programme in the Sixth Form prepares pupils for their next step and they leave us as young adults ready to embrace the challenges that lie ahead.

Governors:
Chairman: J F Woolridge, CBE, DL, BSc Hons
Vice-Chairman: Revd Prebendary G Wynne, DLitt, MTh, BSc Soc, BD, AKC
P G Brough, BA
K Bruerton, BA Hons, FCCA
Mrs L Cook, BA
Mrs C Hammond, BA
Mrs H L Hawkins, FCIPD, MSc
Mrs S Isbister
S C P Maddox, AB Eng, ICIOB
Mrs D Margetts
Mrs J Parker, SRP, MCSP, JP
G D H Sower, BA

Clerk to the Governors: R Ennis

Senior Leadership Team:

Headmaster: D C Williams, BA, MSc

Bursar: C Way, BSc
Deputy Head (Academic): S Wrafter, BA
Deputy Head (Pastoral): J Shipway, BSc, MA
Head of Preparatory School: P Foley, BA, NPQH

Teaching Staff:

Miss C Belcher, BTEC, FDE	S L Lawrence, BSc Hons, Cert Ed
J Bullock, BSc	Mrs J Lawrence, Cert Ed
P J Bullough, BA	R M Leighton, BA, MA
T Clark, BEng, MSc	Mrs M Lofting, BA, MA
Mrs N Claxton, BTEC Level 3	Miss N Minaker, BSc
R Ellmore, BSc	Mrs A Nash, ACIB
P G Evans, BSc	Mrs V O'Neill, BSc Hons, PGCE
Mrs C Foley, BA	Miss N Parkes, BTEC
A T Foster, BA	Mrs S Patchett, PGCE
Ms R Gennard, HLTA	Miss N Pike, BA, BTEC
Miss J Griffin, BA, GRTP	Miss R Popplewell, BA
D Groom, BA, BEd	Mrs R Samra-Bagry, BSc Hons, PGCE
Mrs E J Gwilt, BSc	T Seston, BA, MA
Mrs L Hall, BA	Mrs D E Spencer, BEd
J Higgs, BA	Mrs J L Taylor, C in E, Dip Sp Psych
M T Jackson, BEd	Miss J Turner, NNEB
Miss S Jassal, NVQ3	Miss M D Uttley, BA, PGCE
Mrs P Jones, Cert Ed, Dip RSA SpLD	I F Wass, BEd
Dr M Lawley, BSc, MSc, PhD	

Miss Z Wise, BTEC
Mrs K Ziolkowski, BA, CACHE

Visiting Teachers:
11 staff provide Music tuition, 3 take pupils for individual learning support and 2 provide additional sports coaching.

Personal Assistant to the Headmaster: Mrs N Phelps

Medical Officers:
Dr J Bright
Dr A Williams

School Nurse: Mrs C Wagstaff

Situation and Buildings. Set in acres of 33 acres of beautiful woodland grounds, with outstanding sporting facilities, Tettenhall College is a blend of historic buildings and modern amenities where pupils thrive within a caring family atmosphere. Located in the historic village of Tettenhall, yet only 40 minutes from Birmingham International Airport, the School is one of the leading independent day and boarding schools in the region catering for girls and boys from 2 to 18 years.

Amenities include a Sixth Form Centre, a campus-wide Information Technology Network, Library and Resources Centre, Swimming Pool, Sports Hall, Sports Pavilion and floodlit courts for Netball and Tennis. There are two Cricket squares and playing fields for Rugby, Soccer, and Athletics.

The College is embarking on an ambitious development plan to bring all the facilities at the School up to the highest standard. The Boys' Boarding House is to be completely refurbished as are the classrooms and theatre in the Towers. A full-size floodlit artificial pitch is to be installed, together with two smaller floodlit artificial pitches for Tennis, Netball and 5-a-side Football. Wi-Fi will also be installed across the site.

There are also plans to further develop the Woodlands with a mountain bike trail and a high ropes course. This will enhance their use in many aspects of the Schools educational offering where its exceptional setting is often used to promote pupils' learning experience.

Religion. Services in the College Chapel are interdenominational.

Entry. The school accepts girls and boys. Entry to the Senior School (age 11–18) is normally by way of assessment in Mathematics, English and Non Verbal Reasoning. By arrangement with the Headmaster, pupils may be interviewed and tested according to their individual needs. Assessments are set by the Head of Preparatory School for pupils between the ages of 7 and 11. These can be taken in any term by appointment.

Organisation. Senior School (Years 7 to 11 and the Sixth Form) and the Preparatory School (Reception to Year 6) are divided into four Houses which compete in activities, work and games. The Nursery comprises Day Nursery and Pre-School from the age of 2 to 4.

Senior School Curriculum. GCSEs may be taken in the following subjects: Art, Biology, Business Studies, Chemistry, Drama, Electronics, English, French, Spanish, Geography, History, Information Technology, Mathematics, Music, Physics, Physical Education and Religious Studies.

In the Sixth Form numerous combinations of subjects are possible, and AS and A Level courses offered include Art, Biology, Business Studies, Chemistry, Drama and Theatre Studies, Economics, Electronics, English, French, Geography, German, History, Mathematics, Further Mathematics, Music, Photography, Physics, Physical Education and Psychology.

Careers. Extensive advice is given by the Head of Careers and Personal Tutors and this is supported by many visits and seminars throughout the year from external organisations such as universities and local companies. In addition the School is supported by Old Tettenhallians who will come in to host career talks and seminars.

Societies and Activities. All pupils are encouraged to become fully involved in the life of the community and to play a part in the social and cultural organisations.

Pupils take part in the Duke of Edinburgh's Award Scheme, working for Bronze, Silver and Gold Awards. In addition to the sporting opportunities already mentioned, there is a full range of other sports activities available at lunchtime or after school, including Archery, Badminton, Basketball, Cross Country, Table Tennis and Fencing. There are numerous clubs and societies that meet regularly, for example Chess, Cookery, Classical Civilisation, Photography, Debating, Drama, Dance, Latin, Mandarin, Spanish, Pottery and Business Enterprise. Excursions are frequently arranged by all subjects, and foreign excursions have, in recent years, regularly included music tours, science trips, sports tours, art and business studies trips, as well as foreign exchanges. School plays and musicals are produced each year; there is a house festival of Performing Arts and the Music Department has a deservedly strong reputation for its quality of performance and opportunities.

Preparatory School. The Preparatory School is housed separately in a purpose-designed building opened in 2002. It shares a number of the facilities with Senior School and Senior School Staff help with games and specialist teaching.

The curriculum goes far beyond the confines of the national curriculum. Younger pupils are taught by a form teacher with an emphasis on the acquisition of key skills in Literacy and Numeracy. As children move through the years they are introduced to teaching from subject specialists.

Athletics, Cricket, Netball, Hockey, Rounders, Rugby, Soccer, Swimming and Tennis are the main sports and all pupils have PE and two afternoons of games each week. Extra-curricular activities change regularly but include clubs in all the previously mentioned sports plus Art and Craft, Chess, Computing, Dance, Drama, Latin and Table Tennis. Drama, Music and the playing of musical instruments are strongly encouraged.

Fees per term (2014–2015). Senior School: Senior Boarders: £8,833 (Years 10–13), £6,366 (Years 7–9); Weekly Boarders: £6,833 (Years 10–13), £5,833 (Years 7–9); Day Pupils £4,200.

Preparatory School: Boarders £6,366, Weekly Boarders £5,833, Day Pupils £3,150. Pre-Prep: £2,200–£2,666.

Scholarships and Bursaries. Senior School Academic Scholarships may be offered to outstanding boys and girls from either state or independent schools. Scholarships are also awarded for Music, Art, Drama, Performing Arts and Sport.

Means-tested Bursaries are available. There is a reduction in fees for the children of the Clergy and members of HM Forces as well as children of former pupils.

The Old Tettenhallians' Club. Membership is automatic on reaching 18 years of age.

Charitable status. Tettenhall College Incorporated is a Registered Charity, number 528617. It exists to provide a quality education for boys and girls.

Thetford Grammar School

Bridge Street, Thetford, Norfolk IP24 3AF
Tel: 01842 752840
Fax: 01842 750220
email: hmsec@thetgram.norfolk.sch.uk
website: www.thetgram.norfolk.sch.uk

Refounded in the 17th century by Sir Richard Fulmerston, Thetford Grammar School can however show an unbroken roll of Headmasters from 1119 and traces its origins to the 7th century. In more recent times it was voluntarily controlled until, augmented by the adjacent girls' grammar school, it returned to independence in 1981. Today it is a two-form entry 3½–18 co-educational day school with 270 pupils drawn from a radius of 30 miles across the Norfolk/Suffolk border. We seek to combine worthwhile academic standards with a tradition of care and support for the individual and commitment to the breadth of educational experience. A member of The Society of Heads (elected 1996) and AGBIS, the school is administered by the Governors of the Thetford Grammar School Foundation, acting as Trustees on behalf of the Charity Commission.

The Governing Body:

Chairman of Governors: Mrs M Eade
Vice-Chairman: Cllr R Kybird (*Breckland District Council Representative*)
J Brown
Cllr B J Canham (*Thetford Town Council Representative*)
Mrs J Chamberlin
I M Clark
Mrs K Colborn
Mrs B Garrard, MA, BSc, Cert Ed
T J Lamb, BSc
S McGrath
Major T MacMullen, BA TCD
J Pearson, MCIWM
Dr R Scurr (*Senate of the University of Cambridge nominee*)
Mrs J M Sinclair
R Walden, BSc, FRICS

Bursar and Clerk to the Governors: Wing Cdr P J McGahan, MCMI, MInstLM

Headmaster: G J Price, MA Oxon, PGCE

Deputy Head: Mrs K Elders, MA Nottingham
Head of Sixth Form: S G Spencer, MA Ed Open University, OGCE, MCIL
Head of Junior Department: Mrs H Butler-Hand, BA, MEd Cantab

Assistant Staff:
Mrs N Absolum
Mrs A Alecock, BA Manchester
Miss E Bailey, MEd Cambridge, PGCE
Mrs T Beukes, BSc Stellenbosch SA
S Braden, BSc RMCS Shrivenham
D Bradfield, BA Bristol, PGCE
Mrs J Bull, BA Leicester, PGCE
Mrs S Collins
Mrs R Dimminger, Dip Ed Bulawayo
Miss D Dunsmore, BSc Cambridge, PGCE
A M Durling, BA UEA, MCIL
Mrs J Fifield, BA Aberystwyth
M Foreman, BEd Nottingham
Mrs J Foreman, BA Warwick
Miss F Foster, BA Warwick
M Glassbrook, BSc Northumbria, PGCE
Mrs T E Granger, BSc Wolverhampton, PGCE
M Hill, BA Bedfordshire
Miss K Humphrey, BSc Portsmouth, PGCE
Ms G Irving, MA Lancaster, PGCE
J A Law, BEd Loughborough
R Maringue, MA Grenoble, PGCE
Mrs N Peace, BA Bishop Grosseteste
Ms L Pearson, BA Oxford Brookes, Cert Ed
Mrs L Perry, BA Sussex, PGCE
Mrs H Pringle, BA Teesside Polytechnic
Mrs C Salt, BEd Exeter
Miss A Sherring, BA Camberwell School of Art
Dr A Shillings, MSci Bristol, PhD Cantab
S R Simpson, BSc Birmingham, PGCE
Dr M Stoppard, PhD UEA/City University, BA Notts, PGCE

Miss F Travers, BA Nottingham Trent
Mrs A Vant, BA Cork
A Ward, BSc London, PGCE
Mrs V S Webber, BA Open University
Miss M Wharton, BA Bristol, PGCE
Mrs L Wingham, BA London, PGCE
B Young, MA UWCC, PGCE

Teaching Assistants:
Miss J Blakemore
Miss K Fitch
Mrs M Trotter

Learning Support:
Mrs K Jones, BSc QTS, Dip SpLD, AMBDA, SpLD APC
    Patoss
Mrs P Ballard, BEd Southampton

Visiting Music Staff:
Mrs N Absolum (*Piano*)
Mrs S Brotherhood (*Woodwind*)
M B Clarke, BA Sussex, MA Illinois (*Clarinet, Saxophone*)
Ms F Levy, LLCM TD, ALCM (*Violin*)
J Rowland (*Drum Kit and Jazz Piano*)
A H Salazar, GSMD, PGC, PG Adv Dip TCM (*Voice*)
D Scragg (*Brass*)
C Ward, BA (*Guitar*)
Mrs J G Weeks, GRSM, ARMCM (*Piano*)

Administrative Staff:
Mrs E Brooks (*Headmaster's Secretary*)
Mrs I Cracknell (*Junior School Secretary*)
Mrs C Reynolds (*Senior School Secretary*)
Mrs J Settle (*Librarian*)
Miss M Templeman (*Accounts Secretary*)

Technicians:
Mrs S Grimwood (*Art*)
Mr A Jenkinson (*DT*)
Mrs A Kingsnorth, BSc London, PGCE (*Science*)
Mrs G Lloyd, MChem UEA (*Science*)
D Simpleman, BSc Southampton (*ICT*)

Buildings and Situation. Situated close to the centre of Thetford, the school occupies a well-established site graced by several buildings of architectural interest and the ruins of a medieval priory. There are extensive playing fields with a refurbished pavilion within walking distance of the main buildings, as well as an award-winning, eco-friendly Sixth Form Centre built around the original Cloisters.

Organisation. Junior School pupils are taught primarily in their own premises with independent facilities. Older juniors, however, have contact with specialist teachers in several subject areas and benefit from similar integration into many other aspects of school life. Main School education from 11 follows a two or three-form entry pattern with setting in core subjects to GCSE. Sixth Form students, who have their own Common Room, play a full part in the life of the school.

Curriculum. Junior School teaching follows National Curriculum lines with strong emphasis on the English/Mathematics core and the range of specialist subjects in support. Music and Drama are important within the Department, while a full programme of PE and Games allows for the development of team sports and individual fitness.

Main School education through to GCSE is based on a common core of English, English Literature, Mathematics, a Modern Language (French or German) and the Sciences. Options allow students to develop skills and interests in History, Geography, RS, Business Studies, Languages, the Expressive Arts, Physical Education and Technology. IT is strongly represented across the curriculum. AS and A2 courses are offered in all these subjects, with the addition of Psychology. Mathematics and Science lead a strong pattern of results at this level and sixth form students proceed to university degree courses.

Sport and Extra-Curricular Activities. The life of the school extends widely from the classroom into sport, community service, dramatic and musical presentation; the lessons taught by the pursuit of excellence through individual commitment and teamwork are greatly valued.

Winter sports are Rugby, Soccer, Hockey, Netball and Cross-Country with Cricket, Tennis, Rounders and Athletics in the Summer. Popular indoor sports such as Basketball, Aerobics, Badminton, Volleyball and Gymnastics are also followed.

A majority of pupils take part in training for the Duke of Edinburgh's Award Scheme. Musically, a lively concert programme supports individual instrumental tuition and choral rehearsal while opportunities for theatre are provided termly by House and School productions.

There is a varied programme of curricular and extra-curricular trips including expeditions and foreign visits.

Admission. Admission into the Junior School follows a day in school with the appropriate year group during which an assessment is made. Admission into Main School is by formal examination with interview and school report. Sixth Form entrance is on the basis of interview and school report, with subsequent performance at GCSE taken into consideration. The main Entrance Examination is held in January but supplementary testing continues through the year. Full details from the Headmaster's Secretary.

Fees per term (2014–2015). Reception-Year 2 £3,397, Years 3–6 £3,776, Main School £4,109 including books and tuition, but excluding uniform, lunches, transport, examination entry fees and some specialised teaching such as instrumental music lessons.

Scholarships and Bursaries. Within the limits of available funds the Governors are able to provide financial support with the fees in case of need. Such bursaries are based on a declaration of family income and can be up to 100% of the fees. They are available from Year 7 upwards. They are dependent of course on the pupil fulfilling the entrance requirements of the school. Scholarships of an honorary nature may be awarded to the top performers in the entrance examinations. Music scholarships are available on entry in Year 7 or 9 which will provide free instrumental or voice tuition. Scholarships are also available into the Sixth Form for both internal and external candidates. These can provide a reduction in fees for two years and are awarded as the result of a scholarship paper sat in November or in recognition of outstanding GCSE performance in the summer.

Details of all awards may be obtained from the Headmaster.

Charitable status. Thetford Grammar School is a Registered Charity, number 311263. It exists to provide education for boys and girls.

Tring Park School for the Performing Arts

Tring Park, Tring, Hertfordshire HP23 5LX
Tel: 01442 824255
Fax: 01442 891069
email: info@tringpark.com
website: www.tringpark.com

Board of Governors:
Chairman: Mr Michael Geddes
Mrs Mary Bonar
Ms Alice Cave
Mr Michael Harper
Mr Mark Hewitt
Mrs Juliet Murray
Mrs Angela Odell
Mr Eric Pillinger
Mrs June Taylor

Principal: **Mr Stefan Anderson**, MA Cantab, ARCM, ARCT

Deputy Principal: Mr Anselm Barker, MSt Oxon, BA Harvard

Director of Dance: Miss Rachel Rist, MA, FRSA
Deputy Director of Dance: Miss Teresa Wright, ARAD Adv, FISTD Cecchetti Branch Dip

Director of Drama: Mr Edward Applewhite, BA Hons
Deputy Director of Drama: Heather Loomes, BA Hons
Deputy Director of Drama: Dominic Yeates

Director of Music: Elizabeth Hewett, BMus Hons, PGCE, ALCM
Head of Commercial Music Course: Harmesh Gharu, MA, BMus Hons, PGCE

Director of Musical Theatre Course: Donna Hayward, FISTD
Deputy Director of Musical Theatre Course: Simon Sharp, BA Hons, PGCE

Head of Performance Foundation Course: Miss Louisa Shaw
Head of Theatre Arts: Elizabeth Odell

Director of Academic Studies: Mrs Juliet Cooke
Deputy Director of Academic Studies: Mrs Janet Allen, BSc Hons, MSc, PGCE

Director of Finance and Administration: (*to be appointed*)

Marketing Director: Miriam Juviler, ARAM, LRAM
Appeal Director: (*to be appointed*)

Head of Learning Support: Suzanne Kennedy, BA Hons, PGCE, MA, NPQH, SpLD, SENCOs

Age Range. 8–19 years.
Number in School. Boarders: Boys 37, Girls 168. Day: 64.
Fees per term (2014–2015). Prep School: Boarders £7,525, Day £4,460. Age 11–16: Boarders £9,940, Day £6,415. Sixth Form Entry: Boarders £10,640, Day £7,110. Sibling discount 10% of termly fees. Forces discount available on request.

Aided places for Dance are available under the Government's Music and Dance Scheme and Post 16 Dance and Drama Awards. School scholarships are available for Drama and Musical Theatre.

Tring Park School for the Performing Arts offers a unique opportunity for pupils from the age of 8 to 19 who show a particular talent in one or more of the Performing Arts, yet still wish to benefit from an excellent academic education to GCSE, BTEC and A Level.

Tring is a small market town situated 30 miles northwest of Central London, within easy travelling distance of the major international airports and motorways. Set in 17 acres of attractive and secluded grounds, the School is principally housed in a superb mansion, formerly the home of the Rothschild family. The school now boasts 5 superb Performance Studios.

Dance, Drama, Musical Theatre and Commercial Music are taught to the highest level and pupils perform regularly in our excellent modern theatre as well as at prestigious venues in London and the South East. Many pupils go on to enjoy successful performing careers. Academic achievements at GCSE and A Level enable many of our students to progress to Degree courses in higher education.

Whatever the career or course chosen, the fusion of natural talent, creativity and personality with sound teaching and direction produces young communicators, well-equipped to take the many opportunities that lie ahead.

Charitable status. The AES Tring Park School Trust is a Registered Charity, number 1040330. It exists to provide vocational and academic education.

Trinity School

Buckeridge Road, Teignmouth, Devon TQ14 8LY
Tel: 01626 774138
Fax: 01626 771541
email: enquiries@trinityschool.co.uk
website: www.trinityschool.co.uk

Patrons:
Rt Revd Christopher Budd, Bishop of Plymouth
Rt Revd Michael Langrish, Bishop of Exeter

Chairman of Governors: Mr Simon Brookman

Headmaster: Mr Tim Waters, MA, MSc Oxon

Senior Deputy Head (*Pastoral*): Mr Lawrence Coen, BSc Hons Aberystwyth
Deputy Head (*Academic*): Mrs Wendy Martin

Senior Department:
Mr Mark Acher, BSc Hons Sheffield (*Head of Sixth Form*)
Mr James Atkinson, BSc Hons Plymouth (*Head of House, Boys Yrs 11–13*)
Mrs Rachael Arkell, BA Hons (*Director of Music*)
Mrs Anna Brown, BA Hons Glamorgan (*Dep Head of Sixth Form*)
Mrs Julia Bryant, MEd Open, BSc Hons London (*Professional Development Coordinator – Academic Staff, Head of Psychology*)
Mr Patrick Cairns, BEd Liverpool (*Head of Art*)
Mrs Fenella Cooke, BA Hons Worcester (*Head of Drama & Performing Arts*)
Mrs Sheridan Couch, BA Ed Hons Exeter (*Head of Physical Education*)
Mrs Kathryn Crook, Dip TEFL, LTCL Trinity (*Head of the International Department*)
Mr Edward Donaldson, BTech Ireland (*Head of Design and Technology*)
Mrs Claire Entwistle, BA Hons Lancaster, MA Open (*Head of Religious Studies*)
Mrs Gerri Davis (*Head of Key Stage 3*)
Mrs Jana Fischer (*Head of House – Girls Boarding*)
Mr Matthew Fitzpatrick, BSc Hons Edinburgh (*Head of Mathematics*)
Mrs Jan Hargood, BA Open, BPhil Special Education, Cert SENCO (*Head of Learning Support*)
Mrs Sandrine Haytread, Dip Travel & Tourism Ecole Cadre Paris (*Head of Modern Languages*)
Mrs Sarah Jennings, BA Hons Portsmouth (*Head of Humanities – History & Geography*)
Mr Darrel Jones, BSc Hons Liverpool (*Head of Science*)
Mr Adam Lewis (*Head of English*)
Mr Robert Larkman, BEd Hons Plymouth (*Head of KS4*)
Mr Mike Milne, BA Hons UWE (*Head of Business Studies*)
Lt Cdr Geraldine Poulet-Bowden RN, BSc Hons Imperial College, ARCS, CSci, CPhys, MIoP (*Head of CCF*)
Revd Jonathon Ross-McNairn (*Chaplain*)
Mrs Gill Sinden, BA Hons Birmingham (*Whole School Director of Sport*)
Mrs Giulietta Swift, BA Hons Bristol (*Head of ICT*)

Preparatory Department:
Mrs Rachel Eaton-Jones, BSc Hons Bristol, NPQH (*Head of Preparatory Department*)
Mr Michael Burdett, BEd Hons Oxon (*Deputy Head of Preparatory Department, Year 6, Assessment Coordinator*)
Miss Lydnsey Elliott (*EYFS/KS1 Coordinator*)
Miss Elizabeth Parker, BA Ed Hons Exeter (*KS2 Coordinator*)
Mr Simon Fisher, BSc Hons Wales (*Head of Prep Sport & Class 5 teacher*)

Nursery Department:
Mrs Liz Saunders, NNEB (*Nursery Manager*)
Mrs Claire Savva, Montessori Dip Level 4 (*Assistant Nursery Manager*)

Administration:
Bursar: Mr Shaun Dyer, BA Portsmouth
Development Director: Mr Chris Cullen
Registrar: Ms Fleur Rogers
Headmaster's Secretary & Personal Assistant: Mrs Alison Miles
Academic Administrator: Mr John Turner
Prep Administrator: Carol Hulme

Foundation and Ethos. With a joint Anglican/Catholic foundation, Trinity School's Christian ethos and family atmosphere are complemented by a commitment to excellence in both academic and personal development. With recent inspections by both ISI and Ofsted rating the School as 'Outstanding', the School has successfully demonstrated a determination to deliver the best education possible for the pupils in its care.

Pupil Body. 470 pupils from Nursery to 19 years: 110 boarders. 295 Boys, 175 Girls. Full ability range with about 10–15% receiving targeted support through the Learning Success Department.

Location and Facilities. The School offers excellent facilities in a very attractive environment with panoramic views of Lyme Bay. The School has embarked on an ambitious building and development programme, spending in excess of £6 million in ten years. Facilities include a Design Technology building, assembly hall, IT laboratories, a Music Centre, a Science and Resources block, a Food Technology Centre, en-suite boarding accommodation for Sixth Formers, indoor tennis facilities, a 25m heated swimming pool, and an Art Centre. The School is very well connected by road and rail, with the nearest railway station being under a mile away and on the London main line.

Academic Record. At the upper end of our ability profile, we have a proven track record of sending pupils to Russell Group universities including Oxbridge, Imperial, University of London and LSE. We have gained 6 Good School Guide Awards for performance in English, Business Studies and Science. Prep pupils' performance considerably exceeds expectations at KS1 and KS2. ISI rated all aspects of EYFS provision to be 'Outstanding' (2012).

Our commitment to ensuring that all pupils, irrespective of ability, are given opportunity to succeed and to be stretched, means that many of our lower ability pupils produce results that put them on course for university. 95% of Sixth Form students in recent years have progressed to university, the majority to their first choice institution.

24 A Level subjects are taught (incl all facilitating subjects).

Pastoral Care and Welfare. The quality of the School's pastoral care is an established and considerable strength. Trinity was rated Outstanding in five out of six areas in its 2010 Ofsted Boarding Inspection that focused on pastoral issues. Our Anglican/Catholic ethos permeates all that we do. We believe that, for care to be effective, it is essential that school and family work closely together – the relationship needs to be dynamic, honest and built on mutual trust and understanding. This approach, and the fact that Trinity provides education for girls and boys of all ages, helps to generate the School's warm, 'family' atmosphere.

Personal Development. Extensive sporting, cultural, charitable and leadership opportunities are available at all ages: Rich musical life; South West Junior Choir of the Year 2011 and 2012; Highly praised National Theatre Youth Festival production 2012; One of the most active CCF sections in the country; silver medal at UK CCF sailing championships 2012; Ten Tors and DofE regulars; Lawn Tennis Association centre of excellence with one national LTA champion and 4 Independent Schools Association (ISA)

champions; ISA UK boys' hockey champions U16 (2012); over 40 pupils have won medals at ISA national sports finals (swimming, athletics, cross country, tennis – Prep and Senior); ISA South West U16 netball champions 2012; National Public Speaking finalists 2010.

Admissions. Entry to the School is by assessment and interview of the younger pupils, and entrance test and interview for the older pupils. Scholarships are by open competition at 11+, 13+ and 16+, for academic, music, art, drama, sport and all-rounder Notre Dame Awards (selection in January). Bursaries and HM Forces Bursaries.

Fees per term (2014–2015). Tuition: £2,400–£3,785. Boarding (in addition to Tuition): Preparatory: £3,065 (weekly), £3,570 (full); Senior: £3,905 (weekly), £4,555 (full). No compulsory extras.

Charitable status. Trinity School is a Registered Charity, number 276960.

Welbeck – The Defence Sixth Form College

Forest Road, Woodhouse, Loughborough, Leicestershire LE12 8WD
Tel: 01509 891700
Fax: 01509 891701
email: helpdesk@dsfc.ac.uk
website: www.dsfc.ac.uk

Welbeck Defence Sixth Form College aims to provide an environment in which young people from all backgrounds can reach the very highest academic and personal standards in pursuit of a career as a Technical Officer within the Armed Services and the Civil Service. Welbeck's history began in September 1953 at Welbeck Abbey, near Worksop in Nottinghamshire, as a Sixth Form College for potential Engineering Officers for the British Army. The Defence Training Review of 2002 resulted in the decision to expand the College across all three Armed Services as well as the Defence Engineering and Science Group (DESG), and in September 2005 Welbeck – The Defence Sixth Form College opened at its new purpose-built site in Woodhouse, Loughborough. Welbeck is the first stage of the Defence Technical Officer and Engineer Entry Scheme (DTOEES) which sponsors students to study their A Levels at Welbeck and then move on to partner Universities to study Technical or Engineering degrees. Students receive an annual bursary of £4,000 whilst at University, and once they have graduated they will enter Initial Officer Training with the service that has sponsored them through the scheme or, in the case of DESG, they will enter the Graduate Training Programme.

Chairman of Governors: Director General, Defence Academy of the United Kingdom

Principal: Mr J P Middleton, MA Oxon

Welbeck is a full boarding establishment offering a technically focused A Level education. There are approximately 170 Year 12 places available each year to students who have passed the selection for sponsorship by one of the three Armed Services or DESG. The College will also accept a limited number of applications from private students.

Situation. Welbeck College is situated on a 36-acre site in the charming rural setting of Charnwood Forest in Leicestershire. Welbeck has a spacious campus with state-of-the-art facilities and amenities.

Approach and Ethos. Our aim is to provide all students with an outstanding education that will enable them to achieve A Level results that will qualify them to continue to the next stage of the DTOEES scheme – an engineering or technical degree at a top university.

Welbeck educates its students in the broadest sense of the word; it offers a programme of intellectual, personal and physical development specifically designed to meet the needs of today's modern Armed Forces. Pupils will have innumerable opportunities to develop their understanding of leadership and of success, and in doing so will leave the College better equipped for life in the Armed Forces. As you would expect, there is a strong emphasis on core military skills and values. Additionally, sport plays a prominent role for all students with College teams regularly securing regional, and occasionally national, honours. At Welbeck, such an education is founded on moral integrity, responsibility and a genuine sense of service, which together lead to inculcating the core skills of leadership which are not only strong in our community but enduring.

Our students come from all over the United Kingdom and from a variety of backgrounds. The vast majority of them have never boarded before, but find themselves surrounded by others who are in the same position. Pastoral care at Welbeck is outstanding, and through House Staff and personal Tutors all individual students are supported throughout their time at the College. Welbexians are ambitious and motivated, and thrive in an environment with other like-minded individuals who have the same drive and determination to succeed and make the most of each and every opportunity. Students leave the College resolute, skilled in communication and with their ambitions extended, having shared excellence and involvement in the many and varied experiences offered by the College.

Admission. To apply to Welbeck, and subsequently the Armed Services, candidates should be medically fit UK, Commonwealth or Irish citizens aged between 15 and 17 years and six months on 1st September in the year of entry to the College. Commonwealth citizens are required to have 5 years residency in the UK prior to application. Certain other single-service conditions may apply and will be outlined at the time of application. To join Welbeck as a DESG Civil Service student candidates must be British citizens or hold dual nationality, one of which must be British. To join the Welbeck Private Scheme (WPS), applicants must show a strong commitment to develop themselves both personally and academically at Welbeck, and are also required to meet the academic, medical and fitness criteria of the MOD Sponsored students.

Requirements for successful candidates will include an A in Maths, B in Physics or BB in Dual Award Science and C in English Language at GCSE or the equivalent qualifications.

All MoD candidates are required to attend a Service Selection Board prior to entrance to Welbeck. Welbeck Private Scheme (WPS) candidates undergo a similar selection process at Welbeck.

Fees. *MoD students*: Tuition is paid for by the Ministry of Defence. Parents or guardians are required to make a contribution towards the cost of their child's maintenance which covers board, lodging and the value of clothing and services provided. *Welbeck Private Scheme*: Fees per term £6,000.

Windermere School

Patterdale Road, Windermere, The Lake District, Cumbria LA23 1NW

Tel: 015394 46164
           International +44 15394 46164
Fax: 015394 88414
email: admissions@windermereschool.co.uk
website: www.windermereschool.co.uk
Twitter: @windermeresc
Facebook: /Windermere-School

A small and friendly school, with an emphasis on challenge through adventure and academic excellence.

Chairman of Governors: Mr Michael Dwan

Head: Mr Ian Lavender, MA Oxford, BA Hons Oxford, NPQH

Deputy Head: Miss J Parry, MPhil, BSc Hons Liverpool, PGCE Manchester

Deputy Head Academic: Mr S King, MA Aberdeen, MSc Oxford, PGCE Northern College of Education

Administrative Staff:
School Business Manager: Mrs V Wood
Head's PA: Mrs J Jones
School Secretary: Mrs S Dougherty
Head of Admissions: Mrs J Scott

Windermere School, is an independent co-educational boarding and day school, founded in 1863, and is an Educational Trust administered by a Board of Governors. It is divided into the Senior School (ages 11 to 18) and the Preparatory School (ages 2 to 11).

Located in the heart of the English Lake District National Park, our school offers a rich environment in which pupils can achieve academic and personal excellence. It has the beauty and tranquillity of a wooded campus overlooking the mountains and lake, along with a lakefront boathouse, beach and watersports centre. The amenities of the vibrant resort of Windermere are within minutes of the school. Even with its breathtaking location, the school has easy access to the motorway network, main rail lines and major airports.

Adventure activities and watersports opportunities are provided for each pupil with nationally recognised certificates from organisations including the Royal Yachting Association and the British Canoe Union. This combined with the rich literary and cultural heritage of the Lake District provides a unique setting for academic study and self-development; thus the motto Vincit qui se Vincit, *One conquers, who conquers oneself*.

The Senior School and Sixth Form is located on a mountainside campus overlooking the lake, with the Preparatory School campus and watersports centre nearby. The school owns over 100 acres in the Lake District National Park. There is a modern Sixth Form Boarding House with single and double study-bedrooms, plus a lodge-style Boys Boarding House with magnificent views south and west over Lake Windermere and the mountains, and a traditional girls dormitory in Browhead, formerly a private estate.

Numbers. There are approximately 355 pupils in total. The Senior School has approximately 256 pupils, of whom 50% are boarders. The size of the community has the advantage of providing a friendly atmosphere of understanding and fosters good staff-pupil relationships. Many members of the teaching staff hold additional qualifications in outdoor adventure. There is a 4-house system for competitions and games.

Curriculum. The curriculum offered at Windermere School reflects the belief that students should be exposed to as many opportunities as possible and leave the school as well-rounded individuals. It is tailored to the needs of each child, with small class sizes. Each pupil is provided with a personal tutor that stays with them throughout their years at the school, to oversee work on a daily basis and act as an advocate. One year and two year GCSEs and IGCSEs are taken in Years 10 and 11. Sixth Form students undertake the internationally recognised International Baccalaureate Diploma.

There are qualified staff and programmes in place for Special Educational Needs, English as an Additional Language, and Gifted and Talented pupils.

Music, Art, and Drama play an important part in the life of the school. There are two choirs, and individual instruction leading to chamber groups and orchestra. Students are prepared for the written and practical music exams of the Associated Board of the Royal Schools of Music. The school participates in regional Music Festivals. The Central School of Speech and Drama and LAMDA's examinations are also taken in Speech and Drama. Art, Pottery and Design Technology provide considerable scope and opportunity. The Art Studios contain facilities for History of Art and an Art History Library. Drama classes are included in the curriculum, and there are several productions staged each year.

Extra-Curricular Activities. Windermere School's watersports centre, Hodge Howe with over 160 metres of lakefront on the shores of Windermere, hosts a wide range of activities during the school's timetabled curriculum, and as part of the extra-curricular activity programme. The centre has accreditation from the British Canoeing Union and the Adventure Activities Licensing Authority, as well as being a Royal Yachting Association Teaching Centre. The school has been awarded RYA Champion Club status for its race training and is the first school in the UK to receive this. There are traditional competitive sports teams in hockey, netball, tennis, athletics and more. Many students play for regional and national teams, as well as for the school.

Service. Windermere School has a strong tradition of Community Service where pupils are active participants. The most high profile is Life Change South Africa with many staff and pupils travelling to South Africa each year to contribute to projects. The school supports many other charities including local Hospices, Young Carers, NSPCC, Save The Children Fund and works with regional Rotary Clubs.

Religion. The school is Christian in outlook and welcomes other denominations.

Medical. The health of the pupils is under the care of appointed school Doctors and a School nurse. There is a regular clinic, and dispensary twice daily.

Societies. More than 40 Clubs and Societies provide a variety of interests for out-of-school hours.

Uniform. Senior School – Girls wear blue kilt and striped blazer plus light blue blouses and optional navy jumper. Boys wear dark grey trousers, navy blue blazer, white shirt and school tie with optional navy jumper. Home clothes may be worn at weekends. The Sixth Form wear dark suits and they may wear home clothes in the evenings and at weekends.

Preparatory School – Girls wear blue kilt and striped blazer plus light blue blouses in the winter. In the summer the kilt is worn with a blue and white flowered short-sleeved blouse and blue sleeveless slipover. Boys wear grey trousers, pale blue shirts and sweater, the school tie and blazer.

Boarding. There is a strong boarding tradition at Windermere School that benefits the whole school community. Each Boarding House has live-in staff supervised by a House Mistress or House Master. Each evening, academic staff oversee prep and are available for extra tuition and advice. There are weekend activities both on campus and with staff-led excursions throughout the Lake District and beyond. It is a safe and caring extended family environment where pupils can excel both academically and personally.

Round Square. The School is a member of the international Round Square group of schools. Exchanges and Overseas Service Projects are regularly arranged between the schools involved in Australia, Canada, Germany, India, Switzerland, South Africa and USA and Brunei.

Preparatory School. The nearby Preparatory School is in the care of a Headmaster, and takes boarders from age 8, along with day children up to Year 6. The Preparatory school is fully integrated with the Senior School giving continuity of teaching programmes and use of joint facilities. (*For further details, see entry in IAPS section.*)

Entry. Pupils are accepted into the Senior School from Prep and Junior schools at age 11+, or by direct entry into the Sixth Form. In other circumstances students may be accepted at other times. In the Preparatory School, pupils are taken at various stages from Nursery onwards. Visitors are welcome at anytime during the year, and Open Days are held once a term.

Fees per term (2014–2015). *Average* Day Fees (including lunch): Year 7–8 £4,767, Year 9–11 £5,282, Year 12–13 £5,378.

Average Weekly Boarding Fees: Year 7–8 £8,005, Year 9–11 £9,045, Year 12–13 £9,142.

Average Full Boarding Fees: Year 7–8 £8,455, Year 9–11 £9,530, Year 12–13 £9,632.

International Students (payable in all 3 terms): Years 7–8 £8,980, Years 9–13 £9,900.

Discounts are available for Forces families eligible for the MOD Continuity of Education Allowance (CEA).

Scholarships. Academic, Performing Arts, Visual Arts and Sport Scholarships are available. For more information please visit the school's website or contact Admissions.

Charitable status. Windermere Educational Trust Limited is a Registered Charity, number 526973, with a mission to provide education of the highest quality.

The Yehudi Menuhin School

Stoke d'Abernon, Cobham, Surrey KT11 3QQ
Tel: 01932 864739
Fax: 01932 864633
email: admin@yehudimenuhinschool.co.uk
angela.stockbridge@yehudimenuhinschool.co.uk
website: www.yehudimenuhinschool.co.uk
Twitter: @menuhinschool

The Yehudi Menuhin School was founded in 1963 by Lord Menuhin and is situated in beautiful grounds in the Surrey countryside, close to London and within easy reach of both Gatwick and Heathrow.

The School provides specialist music tuition in stringed instruments, piano and classical guitar to around 70 musically-gifted boys and girls aged between 8 and 19 and aims to enable them to pursue their love of music, develop their musical potential and achieve standards of performance at the highest level. The School also provides a broad education within a relaxed open community in which each individual can fully develop intellectual, artistic and social skills. We are proud that our pupils develop into dedicated and excellent musicians who will use their music to inspire and enrich the lives of others and into friendly, thinking individuals well equipped to contribute fully to the international community.

President: Daniel Barenboim

Vice-Presidents:
Barbara R-D Fisher, OBE
Sir Alan Traill, GBE, QSO

Governor Emeritus:
Daniel Hodson
Anne Simor

Music Patrons:
Sir András Schiff
Heinrich Schiff
Steven Isserlis, CBE
Tasmin Little, OBE

Governors:
Chairman: Richard Morris, MA Oxon, Hon FRAM, RCM, RNCM
Vice-Chairman: Peter Willan, BSc Hons, MBA, FCMA

Noël Annesley	Prof Sebastian Forbes
The Hon Zamira Menuhin Benthall	Andrew Hunter Johnston
	Oscar Lewisohn
John Everett	Stuart Mitchell

John Pagella
Alice Phillips
Geoffrey Richards

Vanessa Richards
Dr John Scadding
Veronica Wadley

Staff:

Headmaster: Dr Richard Hillier, MA Cantab, PhD, PGCE

Director of Music: Malcolm Singer, MA Cantab
Director of Studies/Mathematics: Richard Tanner, MA Oxon
Bursar: Simon Browning, BA Hons, FCMA
Development Director: Vanessa Casey, GLCM, LLCM TD, ALCM

Academic Staff:

Art & Craft: Patsy Belmonte, BA Hons
Biology & Science: Karen Lyle, BSc Hons, PGCE
Biology & Science: Jenny Dexter, BSc Hons, PGCE
English & Drama: Simon Larter-Evans, BA Hons, PGCE, FRSA
German and French: Didier Descamps, MA
German & Russian: Petra Young, MA
History: Sarah Howell, BA Hons, PGCE
Junior Subjects: Janet Poppe, BA Hons, PGCE
Mathematics: Foster Williams, BSc Hons, PGCE
EFL: Hazel Brier, CertEd, MA TESOL
Chinese: Xiang Yun Bishop, MA, TCAFL
Japanese: Akiko Kubo, BA
Spanish: Nuria Lopez-Costa (*part-time*)
Turkish: Ayla Turacli (*part-time*)

Music Staff:

Violin:
Natalia Boyarsky, Dip Solo Performance
Diana Galvydyte, MMus, RCM
Akiko Ono, Dip Mus & Perf Arts, Vienna
Viola/Violin:
Boris Kucharsky, MMus Konzertexamen Koln, MMus Yale
Violin Assistants:
Akerke Ospan
Oscar Perks, BA Hons Cantab
Gergana Raykova, BA Hons Cantab
Jenna Sherry, BMus Violin Perf, MPerf

Cello:
Thomas Carroll, Cert Munich Hochschule, ARCM
Bartholomew LaFollette, BMus Hons, MMus GSMD
Cello Assistant: Steffan Morris

Bass:
Caroline Emery, LTCL, GTCL, CertEd

Piano:
Ruth Nye, DipMusPerf Melbourne Conservatory
Marcel Baudet, Groningen Cons
Mariana Izman, BMus Conservatorium van Amsterdam
Second Study Piano:
Mariko Brown, BMus Hons LGSM (*Piano 1st Study*)
Zoe Mather, AGSM
Piano Assistant: Prach Boondiskulchok, BMus, MPerf

Harpsichord:
Carole Cerasi, Hon ARAM

Guitar:
Richard Wright, GRSM Man, ARNCM
Guitar Assistant: Laura Snowden, BMus, MPerf

Coach Accompanist:
Svitlana Kosenko, Baccalaureate Diploma
Nigel Hutchison, BMus Hons

Chamber Music:
Ioan Davies, MA Cantab
Malcolm Singer, MA Cantab

Senior Orchestra:
Malcolm Singer, MA Cantab

Junior Orchestra:
Dr Oscar Colomina i Bosch, PhD RAM, MMus, BMus Hons GSMD

General Music:
Malcolm Singer, MA Cantab
John Cooney, BMus Hons
Damian leGassick, PG Dip Surrey
Dr Oscar Colomina i Bosch, PhD RAM, MMus, BMus Hons GSMD

Choral:
Richard Hills, MA Oxon

Outreach:
Outreach Officer: Nicola Darke, BMus, MMus
Diana Galvydyte, MMus RCM
Oscar Perks, BA Hons Cantab
Chance to Play: Elliott Perks, BMus

Interpretation through Improvisation: David Dolan, BMus, MMus

Voice:
Jenevora Williams, BA Hons, ARCM

Composition:
John Cooney, BMus Hons, Cert Adv St RCM & GSMD

Alexander Technique:
Hannah Walton, NNEB, MSTAT

Pastoral Staff:
Housemother: Maria Trkulja, MA Oxon
Assistant Housemother: Gergana Raykova, BMus Hons, PG Dip Perf RCM
Housemaster: Simon Larter-Evans, BA Hons, PGCE, FRSA
School Nurse: Ann Sweeney, MSc, RN, SN, QN
Assistant Nurse: Chris Owen, RN, SN Cert

Administrative Staff:
Headmaster's PA: Angela Stockbridge, LRPS
Concert Secretary: Catharine Whitnall, MA Cantab, LTCL
Development Assistant: Sally Williams, BA Hons
Enterprise Assistant: Simon Maher
Temporary Receptionist: Jo Greenwood
Accounts:
Accountant: Mark Armstrong, ACCA, BSc Hons
Bookkeeper: Christine Feline

Menuhin Hall Staff:
Hall Manager: Ambrosine Desoutter, BA Hons, LTCL
Technical Manager: Brian Fifield
Assistant Technical Manager: Luke Brough, BSc Hons (*part-time*)
Assistant Technical Manager: Tim McKeever (*part-time*)
Box Office Manager: Penny Wright
Box Office Assistant: Wendy Gabriel

Examinations and Alumni Officer: Elaine Hillier, BA Hons
Science Lab Technician: Delphine Wellington
Teaching Assistant: Philippa Brown

Estate Manager: Brian Harris
Assistant Estate Manager: Simon Shipp
Housekeeper: Irma Barbosa
Catering Manager: Jean Labourg
Senior Chef: Jo Busby

Music. At least half of each day is devoted to musical studies. Pupils receive a minimum of two one-hour lessons each week on their first study instrument and at least half an hour on their second study instrument. Supervised practice is incorporated into the daily programme ensuring that successful habits of work are formed. All pupils receive guidance in composition and take part in regular composers' workshops and concerts. Aural training and general musicianship studies are included in the music curriculum. To awaken feeling for good posture, training in Alexander Technique is provided. GCSE and A Level Music are compulsory core subjects for all pupils.

Regular opportunity for solo performance is of central importance to the musical activity of the School, and pupils also perform chamber music and with the String Orchestra. Concerts are given several times each week within the School and at a wide variety of venues throughout the United Kingdom and overseas. The most distinguished musicians have taught at the school, including Boulanger, Perlemuter, Rostropovich and Perlman. Lord Menuhin visited the school regularly. Selection of pupils is by stringent audition which seeks to assess musical ability and identify potential. Special arrangements are made for applicants from overseas, who account for almost half of the School's pupils.

The School opened a state-of-the-art Concert Hall in 2006 seating 315 with outstanding acoustics. Concerts and outreach programmes are now presented in this new facility. An appeal is underway to raise funds for new purpose-built Music Studios (planning permission already granted).

Academic Studies and Sport. The curriculum is designed to be balanced and to do full justice to both the musical and the general education of each pupil. Academic studies including the understanding of art, literature and science are considered vital to the development of creative, intelligent and sensitive musicians. All classes are small with excellent opportunities for individual attention, and as a result GCSE and A level examination grades are high. To broaden their artistic and creative talents, all pupils work in a wide variety of artistic media including painting, ceramics, jewellery and textiles. Pupils from overseas with limited English receive an intensive course in the English Language from specialist teachers.

The extensive grounds allow plenty of scope for relaxation and sport, including tennis, dance, badminton, football, running, swimming and yoga. An indoor swimming pool was opened in 2010.

An International Family. The international reputation of the School brings pupils from all over the world who find a happy atmosphere in a large musical family. Pupils live in single or shared rooms and are cared for by the resident House Staff and Nurse, and the School Doctor. Special attention is paid to diet with the emphasis on whole and fresh food.

Fees and Bursaries. All pupils fully resident in the UK are eligible for an Aided Place through the Music and Dance Scheme which is subsidised by the Department for Education (DfE). Parents pay a means-tested contribution to the school fees based on their gross income assessed on a scale issued by the DfE. Pupils from overseas pay full fees for two full calendar years until they acquire the residence qualification needed for support through the Music and Dance Scheme. The school has some bursary funds available to assist with fees for pupils until they become eligible for the Music and Dance Scheme.

Admission. Entry to the School is by rigorous music audition, and prospective pupils are auditioned at any time during the year. Candidates may audition at any age between 7 and 16.

Charitable status. The Yehudi Menuhin School is a Registered Charity, number 312010. It exists to provide musical and academic education for boys and girls.

Entrance Scholarships

Academic Scholarships

Abbey Gate College (p. 761)
Austin Friars St Monica's School (p. 764)
Bedstone College (p. 766)
Beechwood Sacred Heart School (p. 768)
Bethany School (p. 769)
Bournemouth Collegiate School (p. 770)
Box Hill School (p. 770)
The Cathedral School Llandaff (p. 772)
Claremont Fan Court School (p. 772)
Clifton High School (p. 773)
Derby Grammar School (p. 777)
Dover College (p. 778)
d'Overbroeck's College (p. 780)
Dunottar School (p. 782)
Ewell Castle School (p. 783)
Friends' School (p. 785)
Hampshire Collegiate School (p. 788)
Hill House School (p. 790)
Hull Collegiate School (p. 790)
Kingham Hill School (p. 792)
Kingsley School (p. 793)
Langley School (p. 795)
Longridge Towers School (p. 798)
LVS Ascot (The Licensed Victuallers' School) (p. 800)
Milton Abbey School (p. 801)
Newcastle School for Boys (p. 803)
Ockbrook School (p. 804)

Oswestry School (p. 806)
Our Lady's Abingdon Senior School (p. 807)
The Peterborough School (p. 808)
Pitsford School (p. 810)
Portland Place School (p. 811)
The Purcell School (p. 813)
The Read School (p. 815)
Reddam House Bearwood (p. 816)
Rishworth School (p. 818)
The Royal School, Wolverhampton (p. 820)
Ruthin School (p. 822)
St Bees School (p. 823)
St Christopher School (p. 825)
St Edward's School (p. 827)
Saint Felix School (p. 828)
St Joseph's College (p. 834)
Scarborough College (p. 835)
Shebbear College (p. 837)
Sibford School (p. 838)
Stafford Grammar School (p. 840)
Stover School (p. 841)
Sunderland High School (p. 843)
Tettenhall College (p. 844)
Thetford Grammar School (p. 846)
Trinity School (p. 848)
Windermere School (p. 850)

All-Rounder Scholarships

Bedstone College (p. 766)
The Cathedral School Llandaff (p. 772)
Dover College (p. 778)
Dunottar School (p. 782)
Hampshire Collegiate School (p. 788)
Langley School (p. 795)

Longridge Towers School (p. 798)
Newcastle School for Boys (p. 803)
Ockbrook School (p. 804)
Saint Felix School (p. 828)
Scarborough College (p. 835)
Trinity School (p. 848)

Art Scholarships

Bedstone College (p. 766)
Beechwood Sacred Heart School (p. 768)
Bethany School (p. 769)
Bournemouth Collegiate School (p. 770)
Box Hill School (p. 770)
Claremont Fan Court School (p. 772)
Dover College (p. 778)
d'Overbroeck's College (p. 780)
Dunottar School (p. 782)
Ewell Castle School (p. 783)

Friends' School (p. 785)
Hampshire Collegiate School (p. 788)
Hill House School (p. 790)
Hull Collegiate School (p. 790)
Kingham Hill School (p. 792)
Kingsley School (p. 793)
Langley School (p. 795)
LVS Ascot (The Licensed Victuallers' School) (p. 800)
Milton Abbey School (p. 801)
Newcastle School for Boys (p. 803)

Ockbrook School (p. 804)
Oswestry School (p. 806)
Our Lady's Abingdon Senior School (p. 807)
The Peterborough School (p. 808)
Portland Place School (p. 811)
Reddam House Bearwood (p. 816)
St Bees School (p. 823)
St Christopher School (p. 825)
St Edward's School (p. 827)

Saint Felix School (p. 828)
St Joseph's College (p. 834)
Scarborough College (p. 835)
Shebbear College (p. 837)
Sibford School (p. 838)
Stover School (p. 841)
Tettenhall College (p. 844)
Trinity School (p. 848)
Windermere School (p. 850)

Dance Scholarships

Kingham Hill School (p. 792)
Ockbrook School (p. 804)

Reddam House Bearwood (p. 816)
Saint Felix School (p. 828)

Design Technology Scholarships

Bedstone College (p. 766)
Bethany School (p. 769)
Dunottar School (p. 782)
Ewell Castle School (p. 783)
Hampshire Collegiate School (p. 788)

Kingsley School (p. 793)
Langley School (p. 795)
Milton Abbey School (p. 801)
St Edward's School (p. 827)
Saint Felix School (p. 828)

Drama Scholarships

Beechwood Sacred Heart School (p. 768)
Bethany School (p. 769)
Bournemouth Collegiate School (p. 770)
Box Hill School (p. 770)
Claremont Fan Court School (p. 772)
d'Overbroeck's College (p. 780)
Ewell Castle School (p. 783)
Friends' School (p. 785)
Hampshire Collegiate School (p. 788)
Hull Collegiate School (p. 790)
Kingham Hill School (p. 792)
Kingsley School (p. 793)
Langley School (p. 795)

LVS Ascot (The Licensed Victuallers' School) (p. 800)
Milton Abbey School (p. 801)
Newcastle School for Boys (p. 803)
Ockbrook School (p. 804)
Portland Place School (p. 811)
Reddam House Bearwood (p. 816)
Rishworth School (p. 818)
St Edward's School (p. 827)
Saint Felix School (p. 828)
St Joseph's College (p. 834)
Tettenhall College (p. 844)
Trinity School (p. 848)
Windermere School (p. 850)

Music Scholarships

Abbey Gate College (p. 761)
Bedstone College (p. 766)
Beechwood Sacred Heart School (p. 768)
Bethany School (p. 769)
Bournemouth Collegiate School (p. 770)
Box Hill School (p. 770)
The Cathedral School Llandaff (p. 772)
Claremont Fan Court School (p. 772)
Clifton High School (p. 773)
Derby Grammar School (p. 777)
Dover College (p. 778)

d'Overbroeck's College (p. 780)
Dunottar School (p. 782)
Ewell Castle School (p. 783)
Friends' School (p. 785)
Hampshire Collegiate School (p. 788)
Hill House School (p. 790)
Hull Collegiate School (p. 790)
Kingham Hill School (p. 792)
Kingsley School (p. 793)
Langley School (p. 795)
Longridge Towers School (p. 798)

LVS Ascot (The Licensed Victuallers' School) (p. 800)
Milton Abbey School (p. 801)
Newcastle School for Boys (p. 803)
Ockbrook School (p. 804)
Oswestry School (p. 806)
Our Lady's Abingdon Senior School (p. 807)
The Peterborough School (p. 808)
Portland Place School (p. 811)
The Purcell School (p. 813)
The Read School (p. 815)
Reddam House Bearwood (p. 816)
Rishworth School (p. 818)
The Royal School, Wolverhampton (p. 820)
St Bees School (p. 823)

St Edward's School (p. 827)
Saint Felix School (p. 828)
St Joseph's College (p. 834)
Scarborough College (p. 835)
Shebbear College (p. 837)
Sibford School (p. 838)
Stafford Grammar School (p. 840)
Stover School (p. 841)
Sunderland High School (p. 843)
Tettenhall College (p. 844)
Thetford Grammar School (p. 846)
Trinity School (p. 848)
Windermere School (p. 850)

Sport Scholarships

Abbey Gate College (p. 761)
Bedstone College (p. 766)
Beechwood Sacred Heart School (p. 768)
Bethany School (p. 769)
Bournemouth Collegiate School (p. 770)
Box Hill School (p. 770)
Claremont Fan Court School (p. 772)
Clifton High School (p. 773)
Derby Grammar School (p. 777)
Dover College (p. 778)
Dunottar School (p. 782)
Ewell Castle School (p. 783)
Friends' School (p. 785)
Hampshire Collegiate School (p. 788)
Hill House School (p. 790)
Hull Collegiate School (p. 790)
Kingham Hill School (p. 792)
Kingsley School (p. 793)
Langley School (p. 795)
Longridge Towers School (p. 798)
LVS Ascot (The Licensed Victuallers' School) (p. 800)
Milton Abbey School (p. 801)

Newcastle School for Boys (p. 803)
Ockbrook School (p. 804)
Oswestry School (p. 806)
Our Lady's Abingdon Senior School (p. 807)
The Peterborough School (p. 808)
Portland Place School (p. 811)
The Read School (p. 815)
Reddam House Bearwood (p. 816)
Rishworth School (p. 818)
The Royal School, Wolverhampton (p. 820)
St Bees School (p. 823)
St Edward's School (p. 827)
Saint Felix School (p. 828)
St Joseph's College (p. 834)
Shebbear College (p. 837)
Sibford School (p. 838)
Stafford Grammar School (p. 840)
Stover School (p. 841)
Sunderland High School (p. 843)
Tettenhall College (p. 844)
Trinity School (p. 848)
Windermere School (p. 850)

Other Scholarships

Choral

Abbey Gate College (p. 761)

Derby Grammar School (p. 777)

Newcastle School for Boys (p. 803)

Equestrian

Saint Felix School (p. 828)

Organ

Kingham Hill School (p. 792)

Performing Arts

Hill House School (p. 790)

Saint Felix School (p. 828)

St Joseph's College (p. 834)

Tettenhall College (p. 844)

Photography

Ewell Castle School (p. 783)

Saint Felix School (p. 828)

Sailing

Milton Abbey School (p. 801)

Science

d'Overbroeck's College (p. 780)

Swimming

Saint Felix School (p. 828)

Bursaries

Abbey Gate College (p. 761)

Austin Friars St Monica's School (p. 764)

Bedstone College (p. 766)

Bethany School (p. 769)

Bournemouth Collegiate School (p. 770)

Box Hill School (p. 770)

The Cathedral School Llandaff (p. 772)

Clifton High School (p. 773)

Concord College (p. 776)

Derby Grammar School (p. 777)

Dover College (p. 778)

Dunottar School (p. 782)

Ewell Castle School (p. 783)

Friends' School (p. 785)

Fulneck School (p. 787)

Hampshire Collegiate School (p. 788)

Hull Collegiate School (p. 790)

Kingham Hill School (p. 792)

Longridge Towers School (p. 798)

LVS Ascot (The Licensed Victuallers' School) (p. 800)

Newcastle School for Boys (p. 803)

North Cestrian Grammar School (p. 803)

Ockbrook School (p. 804)

Our Lady's Abingdon Senior School (p. 807)

Pitsford School (p. 810)

The Purcell School (p. 813)

The Read School (p. 815)

Reddam House Bearwood (p. 816)

Rishworth School (p. 818)

The Royal School, Wolverhampton (p. 820)

Ruthin School (p. 822)

St Bees School (p. 823)

St Christopher School (p. 825)

St Edward's School (p. 827)

Saint Felix School (p. 828)

St James Senior Boys' School (p. 832)

St Joseph's College (p. 834)

Scarborough College (p. 835)

Sibford School (p. 838)

Stafford Grammar School (p. 840)

Stover School (p. 841)

Sunderland High School (p. 843)

Tettenhall College (p. 844)

Thetford Grammar School (p. 846)

Trinity School (p. 848)

Windermere School (p. 850)

The Yehudi Menuhin School (p. 851)

The Society of Heads

Additional Members UK

RUSSELL COLLIER
Headmaster
Chetwynde School, Barrow-in-Furness, Cumbria
email: info@chetwynde.cumbria.sch.uk
website: www.chetwynde.co.uk

JOHN WEEKS
Head Master
London Academy of Excellence, Stratford, London E15
email: office@excellencelondon.ac.uk
website: www.excellencelondon.ac.uk

Additional Members Overseas

MATTHEW FARTHING
Principal
The British International School Bratislava, Bratislava, Slovakia
email: info@bisb.sk
website: www.bisb.sk

DR WALID EL-KHOURY
Principal
Brummana High School, Brummana, Lebanon
email: info@bhs.edu.lb
website: www.bhs.edu.lb

TOBY SPENCE
Headmaster
Greensteds International School, Nakuru, Kenya
email: office@greenstedsschool.com
website: www.greenstedsschool.com

KOEN RINGOOT
Head
Leerwijzer School, Oostduinkerke, Belgium
email: info@leerwijzer.be
website: www.leerwijzer.be

MARK DURSTON
Headmaster
Peponi School, Ruiru, Kenya
email: info@peponischool.org
website: www.peponischool.org

JONATHAN HUGHES D'AETH
Headmaster
Repton School Dubai, Dubai, UAE
email: info@reptondubai.org
website: www. reptondubai.org

VALERIE MAINOO
Principal
The Roman Ridge School, Accra, Ghana
email: enquiries@theromanridgeschool.com
website: www.theromanridgeschool.com

ANDREW BOULLE
Acting Headmaster
St Andrew's Senior School, Turi, Molo, Kenya
email: officesenior@turimail.co.ke
website: www.standrews-turi.com

CHRISTIAN BARKEI
Principal
St George's International School, Luxembourg
email: info@st-georges.lu
website: www.st-georges.lu

PART IV
Schools whose Heads are members of the Independent Association of Prep Schools
ALPHABETICAL LIST OF SCHOOLS
UK

PAGE

Abberley Hall, Worcs 872
Abercorn School, London 872
Aberdour School, Surrey. 872
Abingdon Preparatory School, Oxon 873
Aldenham Preparatory School, Herts 873
Aldro, Surrey. 874
Aldwickbury School, Herts 874
All Hallows School, Somerset 875
Alleyn Court Preparatory School, Essex. 875
Alleyn's Junior School, London 876
Alpha Preparatory School, Middx 876
Altrincham Preparatory School, Cheshire 877
Amesbury, Surrey 877
Ardingly College Prep & Pre-Prep Schools, W Sussex 877
Ardvreck, Scotland. 878
Arnold House School, London. 879
Ashdell Preparatory School, S Yorks 879
Ashdown House, E Sussex. 879
Ashfold School, Bucks. 880
Ashford Prep School, Kent 880
Ashville College Junior School, N Yorks 881
Ashville College Pre-Prep School, N Yorks 881
Austin Friars St Monica's Junior School, Cumbria . . 882
Avenue House School, London 882
Avenue Nursery & Pre-Preparatory School, London . 883
Aysgarth School, N Yorks 883

Babington House School – Preparatory
   Department, Kent. 884
Bablake Junior School and Pre Prep, W Midlands . . 884
Badminton Junior School, Bristol 885
Ballard School, Hants 885
Bancroft's Preparatory School, Essex 885
Barfield School & Nursery, Surrey 886
Barlborough Hall School, Derbyshire 886
Barnard Castle Preparatory School, Durham 887
Barnardiston Hall Preparatory School, Suffolk 887
Barrow Hills School, Surrey. 888
Bassett House School, London 888
Beachborough, Northants 888
The Beacon, Bucks. 889
Beaudesert Park, Glos 889
Bede's Preparatory School, E Sussex 890
Bedford Girls' School Junior School, Beds 890
Bedford Modern Junior School, Beds 891
Bedford Preparatory School, Beds. 891
Beechwood Park, Herts 892
Beeston Hall School, Norfolk 892
Belhaven Hill, Scotland 892
Belmont, London. 893
Belmont Grosvenor School, N Yorks 894
Belmont School, Surrey. 894
Berkhampstead School, Cheltenham, Glos 895
Berkhamsted Pre-Preparatory School, Herts. 895
Berkhamsted Preparatory School, Herts 896

PAGE

Bickley Park School, Kent. 896
Bilton Grange, Warwicks 896
Birchfield School, Shropshire 897
Birkdale Prep School, S Yorks. 898
Bishop's Stortford College Prep School, Herts 898
Bishopsgate School, Surrey 898
Blackheath Preparatory School, London 899
The Blue Coat School, W Midlands 900
Blundell's Preparatory School, Devon. 900
Bootham Junior School, N Yorks 901
Boundary Oak School, Hants 901
Bradford Grammar Junior School, W Yorks. 902
Brambletye, W Sussex 902
Bramcote Junior School, N Yorks 903
Bramley School, Surrey 903
Brandeston Hall, Suffolk. 904
Brentwood Preparatory School, Essex. 904
Bricklehurst Manor, E Sussex 905
Brighton & Hove High School Junior School, E Sussex 905
Brighton College Prep School, E Sussex 906
BGS Infants and Juniors, Bristol. 906
Brockhurst School, Berks 907
Bromsgrove Preparatory & Pre-Preparatory
   School, Worcs. 907
Brontë House, W Yorks 908
Brooke Priory School, Rutland 908
Broomwood Hall, London 909
Broughton Manor Preparatory School, Bucks 909
Bruern Abbey School, Oxon. 910
The Buchan School, Isle of Man. 910
Buckingham College Preparatory School, Middx . . . 910
Burgess Hill School for Girls – Junior School,
   W Sussex 911
Bute House Preparatory School for Girls, London . . 912

Caldicott, Bucks 912
Cameron House, London 912
Cargilfield, Scotland. 913
Carrdus School, Oxon 913
Casterton, Sedbergh Preparatory School, Cumbria . . 914
Castle Court Preparatory School, Dorset 914
Caterham Preparatory School, Surrey 915
The Cavendish School, London 915
Chafyn Grove School, Wilts 915
Charlotte House Preparatory School for Girls, Herts . 916
Cheam School, Berks 916
Cheltenham College Preparatory School, Glos 917
Chesham Preparatory School, Bucks 917
Chigwell Junior School, Essex. 918
Chinthurst School, Surrey 918
The Chorister School, Durham 918
Christ Church Cathedral School, Oxon 919
Churcher's College Junior School, Hants 919
City of London Freemen's Junior School, Surrey . . . 920

PAGE

Claremont Fan Court Pre-Preparatory
 and Nursery School, Surrey. 920
Claremont Fan Court Preparatory School, Surrey . . . 920
Clayesmore Preparatory School, Dorset 921
Clevelands Preparatory School, Lancs. 921
Clifton College Pre-Preparatory School, Bristol. . . . 922
Clifton College Preparatory School, Bristol 922
Clifton School and Nursery, N Yorks 923
Cokethorpe Junior School, Oxon 923
Colet Court (St Paul's Preparatory School), London . 924
Colfe's Preparatory School, London. 924
Collingwood School, Surrey 925
Colston's Lower School, Bristol 925
Combe Bank Preparatory School, Kent 925
Copthorne School, W Sussex 926
Cottesmore School, W Sussex 926
Coworth Flexlands School, Surrey. 927
Crackley Hall School, Warwicks. 927
Craigclowan School, Scotland 928
Cranford House Junior School, Oxon 928
Cranleigh Preparatory School, Surrey 928
Cranmore School, Surrey 929
Crescent School, Warwicks 929
The Croft Preparatory School, Warwicks 930
Crosfields School, Berks 930
Culford Preparatory School, Suffolk. 931
Cumnor House School, Surrey. 931
Cumnor House School, W Sussex 931

Dair House School, Bucks 932
Dame Bradbury's School, Essex. 932
Danes Hill, Surrey 933
Daneshill School, Hants 933
Davenies School, Bucks 933
Dean Close Pre-Preparatory School, Glos 934
Dean Close Preparatory School, Glos 934
Denmead, Middx. 935
Denstone College Preparatory School at
 Smallwood Manor, Staffs. 935
Derwent Lodge, Kent 936
Devonshire House Preparatory School, London 936
Dolphin School, Berks 936
The Downs Malvern, Worcs 937
The Downs School, Bristol 938
Downsend, Surrey 938
Dragon School, Oxon 939
Duke of Kent School, Surrey 939
Dulwich Prep London, London 940
Dulwich Preparatory School, Kent. 940
Dumpton School, Dorset. 941
Dunhurst, Hants 941
Durlston Court, Hants 942
Durston House, London 942

Eagle House, Berks 943
Eaton House The Manor Girls' School, London. . . . 943
Eaton House The Manor Pre-Preparatory
 School, London. 943
Eaton House The Manor Preparatory School, London 944
Eaton Square School, London 944
Edge Grove, Herts 944
Edgeborough, Surrey. 945
Elm Green Preparatory School, Essex 945
The Elms, Worcs 946
Eton End School, Berks 946

PAGE

Eversfield Preparatory School, W Midlands. 946
Ewell Castle Junior School, Surrey 947
Exeter Cathedral School, Devon. 947
Exeter Junior School, Devon. 947

Fairfield Preparatory School, Leics 948
Fairstead House School, Suffolk. 949
The Falcons Schools, London 949
Farleigh School, Hants. 949
Farlington Preparatory School, W Sussex 950
Felsted Preparatory School, Essex 950
Feltonfleet School, Surrey 951
Fettes College Preparatory School, Scotland 952
Finton House, London 952
Foremarke Hall, Derbyshire 953
Forest Preparatory School, London 953
Forres Sandle Manor, Hants 953
Fosse Bank School, Kent 954
Friends' Junior School, Essex 955
The Froebelian School, W Yorks 955

Garden House School, London 956
Gatehouse School, London 956
Gayhurst School, Bucks 956
Giggleswick Junior School, N Yorks 957
Glebe House School, Norfolk 957
The Gleddings Preparatory School, W Yorks 958
The Godolphin Preparatory School, Wilts. 958
Godstowe Preparatory School, Bucks 958
Grace Dieu Manor School, Leics 959
The Grange, Wales. 959
Grange Park Preparatory School, London 960
The Granville School, Kent 960
Great Ballard, W Sussex 961
Great Walstead School, W Sussex 961
Greenfield, Surrey 962
Gresham's Prep School, Norfolk 962
Grimsdell, London 963
Guildford High School Junior School, Surrey. 963

The Haberdashers' Aske's Boys' Preparatory
 & Pre-Preparatory School, Herts 964
The Hall, London 964
Hall Grove, Surrey. 965
Hallfield School, W Midlands 965
Halstead Preparatory School for Girls, Surrey. . . . 965
Hampshire Collegiate Prep School, Hants. 966
Handcross Park School, W Sussex. 966
Hanford School, Dorset 967
Haslemere Preparatory School, Surrey 967
Hatherop Castle Preparatory School, Glos. 968
Hawkesdown House School, London 968
The Hawthorns, Surrey 968
Hazelwood School, Surrey. 969
Hazlegrove, Somerset 969
Headington Preparatory School, Oxon 970
Heath Mount School, Herts 970
Heatherton House School, Bucks 971
Heathfield, W Yorks 971
Hereford Cathedral Junior School, Herefordshire . . . 971
Hereward House School, London 972
Herries Preparatory School, Berks. 972
High March School, Bucks 973
Highfield & Brookham Schools, Hants 973
Highfield Prep School, Berks 973
Highgate Junior School, London. 974

	PAGE
Hilden Grange School, Kent	974
Hilden Oaks School & Nursery, Kent	974
Hoe Bridge School, Surrey	975
Holme Grange School, Berks	976
Holmwood House, Kent	976
Holmwood House Preparatory School, Essex	977
Holy Cross Preparatory School, Surrey	978
Homefield Preparatory School, Surrey	978
Hornsby House School, London	979
Horris Hill, Berks	979
Hunter Hall School, Cumbria	979
Hurlingham School, London	980
Hurstpierpoint College Preparatory School, W Sussex	980
Inglefield House, Wales	981
Ipswich Preparatory School, Suffolk	982
James Allen's Preparatory School, London	982
Keble School, London	982
Kensington Prep School, London	983
Kent College Nursery, Infant & Junior School, Kent	983
Kent College Preparatory School, Kent	984
Kew College, Surrey	984
Kew Green Preparatory School, Surrey	985
Kilgraston Preparatory School, Scotland	985
Kimbolton Preparatory School, Cambs	985
King Henry VIII Preparatory School, W Midlands	986
King's College School, Cambs	987
King's College Junior School, London	987
King's Hall School, Somerset	988
King's Hawford, Worcs	988
King's House School, Surrey	988
King's Junior School Gloucester, Glos	989
King's St Alban's School, Worcs	989
Junior King's School, Kent	990
King's Ely Junior, Cambs	990
King's Rochester Preparatory School, Kent	991
Kingshott, Herts	992
Kingsmead School, Merseyside	992
Kingswood House School, Surrey	992
Kingswood Preparatory School, Somerset	993
Knighton House, Dorset	993
The Lady Eleanor Holles School (Junior Department), Middx	994
Lambrook, Berks	994
Lancing College Preparatory School at Hove, E Sussex	995
Lanesborough School, Surrey	995
Lathallan School, Scotland	996
Latymer Prep School, London	996
Laxton Junior – Oundle School, Northants	996
Leaden Hall School, Wilts	997
Leehurst Swan School, Wilts	997
Leicester Grammar Junior School, Leics	998
Leweston Junior Department, Dorset	998
Littlegarth School, Essex	999
Lochinver House School, Herts	999
Lockers Park, Herts	1000
Longacre School, Surrey	1000
Lorenden Preparatory School, Kent	1001
Loretto Junior School, Scotland	1001
Loyola Preparatory School, Essex	1001
Lucton School, Herefordshire	1002
Ludgrove, Berks	1002
Lyndhurst House Preparatory School, London	1002

	PAGE
Magdalene House Preparatory School, Cambs	1003
Maidwell Hall, Northants	1003
Maldon Court Preparatory School, Essex	1004
The Mall School, Middx	1004
Maltman's Green, Bucks	1004
Manor Lodge School, Herts	1005
The Manor Preparatory School, Oxon	1005
The Marist Preparatory School, Berks	1006
Marlborough House School, Kent	1006
Marlston House School, Berks	1007
Mayfield Preparatory School, W Midlands	1007
Micklefield School, Surrey	1008
Millfield Prep School, Somerset	1008
Milton Keynes Preparatory School, Bucks	1009
The Minster School, N Yorks	1009
Moira House Junior School, E Sussex	1010
Monkton Prep School, Somerset	1010
Moor Park School, Shropshire	1011
Moorfield School, W Yorks	1011
Moorlands School, W Yorks	1011
Moreton Hall Preparatory School, Suffolk	1012
Moulsford Preparatory School, Oxon	1012
The Mount Junior School, N Yorks	1013
Mount Kelly Preparatory School, Devon	1013
Mylnhurst Preparatory School & Nursery, S Yorks	1014
Naima Jewish Preparatory School, London	1014
The New Beacon, Kent	1014
New College School, Oxon	1015
New Hall Preparatory School, Essex	1015
Newbridge Preparatory School, W Midlands	1016
Newcastle Preparatory School, Tyne and Wear	1016
Newland House School, Middx	1017
Newton Prep, London	1017
Norland Place School, London	1018
Northbourne Park, Kent	1018
Northcote Lodge, London	1018
Northwood College for Girls – Junior School, Middx	1019
Northwood Prep, Herts	1019
Norwich School, The Lower School, Norfolk	1020
Notre Dame School, Surrey	1020
Notting Hill Preparatory School, London	1021
Nottingham High Infant and Junior School, Notts	1022
Oakwood Preparatory School, W Sussex	1023
Oakwood School, Surrey	1023
Old Buckenham Hall School, Suffolk	1023
The Old Hall School, Shropshire	1024
The Old School Henstead, Suffolk	1024
Old Vicarage School, Surrey	1024
The Oratory Preparatory School, Oxon	1025
Orchard House School, London	1025
Orchard School, Beds	1026
Orley Farm School, Middx	1026
Orwell Park, Suffolk	1027
Our Lady's Abingdon Junior School, Oxon	1027
Packwood Haugh, Shropshire	1028
Papplewick, Berks	1029
The Paragon, Somerset	1029
Parkside, Surrey	1030
Pembridge Hall School, London	1030
Pennthorpe School, W Sussex	1030
Perrott Hill, Somerset	1031
The Perse Pelican Nursery and Pre-Preparatory School, Cambs	1032

PAGE

The Perse Preparatory School, Cambs 1032
Pilgrims Pre-Preparatory School, Beds 1033
The Pilgrims' School, Hants 1033
Pinewood, Wilts 1034
Plymouth College Preparatory School, Devon 1034
Pocklington Prep School (formerly Lyndhurst
    School), E Yorks 1034
Port Regis, Dorset 1035
The Portsmouth Grammar Junior School, Hants . . . 1036
Pownall Hall, Cheshire 1036
The Prebendal School, W Sussex 1037
Prestfelde, Shropshire 1037
Prince's Mead School, Hants 1038
Prior Park Preparatory School, Wilts 1038
Priory Preparatory School, Surrey 1038
Prospect House School, London 1039

Quainton Hall School, Middx 1039
Queen Elizabeth's Hospital (QEH) – Junior
    School, Bristol 1040
Queen's College Junior School, Somerset 1040

Ramillies Hall School, Cheshire 1041
Ravenscourt Park Preparatory School, London . . . 1041
The Red Maids' Junior School, Bristol 1041
Redcliffe School, London 1042
Reddiford School, Middx 1042
Redland High School for Girls Junior School, Bristol. 1043
Reigate St Mary's Preparatory and Choir
    School, Surrey 1043
RGS Springfield, Worcs 1044
RGS The Grange, Worcs 1044
The Richard Pate School, Glos 1045
Richmond House School, W Yorks 1045
Riddlesworth Hall Preparatory School, Norfolk . . . 1045
Ripley Court School, Surrey 1046
Rockport School, Northern Ireland 1046
Rokeby, Surrey 1047
Rose Hill School, Kent 1047
Rosemead Preparatory School, London 1047
Rowan Preparatory School, Surrey 1048
The Rowans School, London 1049
The Royal Masonic School for Girls, Herts 1049
Royal Russell Junior School, Surrey 1049
Rudston Preparatory School, S Yorks 1050
Rupert House School, Oxon 1050
Russell House, Kent 1051
Rydal Penrhos Preparatory School, Wales 1051
Ryde Junior School, Isle of Wight 1051
Rydes Hill Preparatory School, Surrey 1052
The Ryleys, Cheshire 1052

St Albans High School for Girls Preparatory
    School, Herts 1053
St Andrew's Prep, E Sussex 1053
St Andrew's School, Berks 1054
St Andrew's School, Woking, Surrey 1054
S. Anselm's, Derbyshire 1055
St Anthony's Preparatory School, London 1055
St Aubyn's School, Essex 1056
St Bede's Preparatory School, Staffs 1056
St Benedict's Junior School, London 1057
St Bernard's Preparatory School, Berks 1057
St Catherine's Preparatory School, Surrey 1057
St Cedd's School, Essex 1058
Saint Christina's RC Preparatory School, London . . 1058

PAGE

St Christopher's School, London 1058
St Christopher's School, E Sussex 1059
St Columba's College Preparatory School, Herts . . 1059
St Dunstan's College Junior School, London 1059
St Edmund's Junior School, Kent 1060
St Edmund's Prep School, Herts 1060
St Edmund's School, Surrey 1061
St Edward's Preparatory School, Glos 1061
St Edward's School, Berks 1061
St Faith's School, Cambs 1062
St Francis School, Wilts 1063
St Gabriel's, Berks 1063
St George's Junior School, Surrey 1064
St George's School, Berks 1065
St Helen's College, Middx 1065
St Hilary's School, Surrey 1065
St Hilda's School, Herts 1066
St Hugh's, Oxon 1066
St Hugh's, Lincs 1067
St Ives School, Surrey 1067
St John's Beaumont, Berks 1068
St John's College Infant and Junior School, Hants . . 1068
St John's College School, Cambs 1068
St John's International School, Devon 1069
St John's School, Middx 1070
St Joseph's In The Park School, Herts 1070
St Lawrence College Junior School, Kent 1071
St Leonards Junior School, Scotland 1071
St Margaret's Preparatory School, Wilts 1071
St Margaret's Preparatory School, Herts 1072
St Martin's Ampleforth, N Yorks 1072
St Martin's School, Middx 1073
St Mary's School, London 1073
St Mary's Preparatory School, Scotland 1074
St Michael's Preparatory School, Channel Islands . . 1074
St Michael's Preparatory School, Essex 1074
St Michael's Prep School, Kent 1075
St Neot's Preparatory School, Hants 1075
St Olave's Prep School, London 1076
St Olave's School, York, N Yorks 1076
St Paul's Cathedral School, London 1077
St Peter and St Paul School, Derbyshire 1077
St Piran's, Berks 1078
St Pius X Prep School, Lancs 1078
St Richard's, Herefordshire 1078
Saint Ronan's, Kent 1079
St Swithun's Junior School, Hants 1079
Salisbury Cathedral School, Wilts 1080
Sandroyd School, Wilts 1080
Sarum Hall School, London 1081
Seaford College Prep School, W Sussex 1081
Seaton House School, Surrey 1082
Sevenoaks Preparatory School, Kent 1082
Sherborne Preparatory School, Dorset 1083
Shrewsbury High Prep School, Shropshire 1083
Shrewsbury House, Surrey 1084
Shrewsbury Lodge School, Surrey 1084
Solefield School, Kent 1084
Sompting Abbotts, W Sussex 1085
South Lee School, Suffolk 1085
Spratton Hall, Northants 1085
Spring Grove School, Kent 1086
Staines Preparatory School, Middx 1086
Stamford Junior School, Lincs 1087

PAGE

Stockport Grammar Junior School, Cheshire 1087
Stonar Preparatory School, Wilts 1088
Stonyhurst St Mary's Hall, Lancs 1088
Stormont, Herts 1089
Stover Preparatory School, Devon. 1089
Stroud School, Hants. 1089
The Study Preparatory School, London 1090
Summer Fields, Oxon 1090
Sunningdale School, Berks 1091
Sunninghill Prep School, Dorset. 1091
Sunny Hill Preparatory School, Somerset 1091
Surbiton High Boys' Preparatory School, Surrey . . . 1092
Surbiton High Junior Girls' School, Surrey 1092
Sussex House, London. 1093
Sutton Valence Preparatory School, Kent 1094
Swanbourne House School, Bucks 1094

Talbot Heath Junior School, Dorset 1095
Taunton Preparatory School, Somerset 1095
Taverham Hall Preparatory School, Norfolk. 1096
Terra Nova School, Cheshire 1096
Terrington Hall, N Yorks. 1097
Thorngrove School, Berks 1097
Thorpe House School, Bucks 1098
Thorpe House Langley Preparatory School and
  Nursery, Norfolk 1098
Tockington Manor, Glos 1099
Tormead Junior School, Surrey 1099
Tower House School, London 1100
Town Close School, Norfolk. 1100
Truro Preparatory School, Cornwall 1101
Twickenham Preparatory School, Middx 1101
Twyford School, Hants. 1102

Unicorn School, Surrey 1102
University College School – Junior Branch, London . 1102
University College School – The Phoenix, London . . 1103
Upton House School, Berks 1103
Ursuline Preparatory School, London 1103
The Ursuline Preparatory School Ilford, Essex 1104

Victoria College Preparatory School, Channel Islands 1104
Vinehall School, E Sussex 1104

Walhampton School, Hants 1105
Walthamstow Hall Junior School, Kent 1105

PAGE

Warminster Preparatory School, Wilts. 1106
Warwick Junior School, Warwicks 1106
Warwick Preparatory School, Warwicks. 1107
Waverley School, Berks 1107
Wellesley House, Kent. 1108
Wellingborough Preparatory School, Northants. . . . 1108
Wellington Prep School, Somerset. 1109
Wellow House School, Notts 1109
Wells Cathedral Junior School, Somerset 1110
West Hill Park, Hants 1110
West House School, W Midlands 1111
Westbourne House, W Sussex 1111
Westbourne School, S Yorks. 1112
Westbrook Hay, Herts 1112
Westminster Abbey Choir School, London 1113
Westminster Cathedral Choir School, London. 1113
Westminster Under School, London 1113
Westonbirt Prep School, Glos 1114
Westville House School, W Yorks. 1114
Wetherby Pre-Preparatory School, London 1115
Wetherby Preparatory School, London 1115
Widford Lodge, Essex 1115
Willington Independent Preparatory School, London . 1116
Wilmslow Preparatory School, Cheshire 1116
Wimbledon Common Prep School, London. 1117
Winchester House School, Northants 1117
Windermere Preparatory School, Cumbria 1117
Windlesham House School, W Sussex 1118
Winterfold House, Worcs 1119
Witham Hall, Lincs 1119
Woodbridge School – The Abbey, Suffolk 1120
Woodcote House, Surrey. 1120
Woodford Green Preparatory School, Essex. 1121
Worksop College Preparatory School, Ranby
  House, Notts 1121
Wycliffe Preparatory School, Glos 1122

Yardley Court, Kent 1122
Yarlet School, Staffs 1123
Yarm Preparatory School, Cleveland 1123
Yarrells Preparatory School, Dorset 1124
Yateley Manor Preparatory School, Hants. 1124
York House School, Herts 1125

GEOGRAPHICAL LIST OF IAPS SCHOOLS

PAGE

PAGE

ENGLAND

Bedfordshire
Bedford Girls' School Junior School 890
Bedford Modern Junior School 891
Bedford Preparatory School 891
Orchard School 1026
Pilgrims Pre-Preparatory School 1033

Berkshire
Brockhurst School 907
Cheam School. 916
Crosfields School 930
Dolphin School 936
Eagle House. 943
Eton End School 946
Herries Preparatory School 972
Highfield Prep School. 973
Holme Grange School. 976
Horris Hill. 979
Lambrook 994
Ludgrove 1002
The Marist Preparatory School 1006
Marlston House School 1007
Papplewick 1029
St Andrew's School 1054
St Bernard's Preparatory School 1057
St Edward's School 1061
St Gabriel's 1063
St George's School 1065
St John's Beaumont 1068
St Piran's 1078
Sunningdale School 1091
Thorngrove School 1097
Upton House School 1103
Waverley School 1107

Bristol
Badminton Junior School 885
BGS Infants and Juniors 906
Clifton College Pre-Preparatory School 922
Clifton College Preparatory School. 922
Colston's Lower School 925
The Downs School 938
Queen Elizabeth's Hospital (QEH) – Junior School 1040
The Red Maids' Junior School 1041
Redland High School for Girls Junior School . . . 1043

Buckinghamshire
Ashfold School 880
The Beacon 889
Broughton Manor Preparatory School 909
Caldicott. 912
Chesham Preparatory School 917
Dair House School 932
Davenies School 933
Gayhurst School. 956
Godstowe Preparatory School 958
Heatherton House School 971
High March School 973
Maltman's Green 1004
Milton Keynes Preparatory School 1009
Swanbourne House School 1094
Thorpe House School 1098

Cambridgeshire
Kimbolton Preparatory School 985
King's College School 987
King's Ely Junior 990
Magdalene House Preparatory School 1003
The Perse Pelican Nursery and Pre-Preparatory
    School 1032
The Perse Preparatory School. 1032
St Faith's School 1062
St John's College School 1068

Channel Islands
St Michael's Preparatory School 1074
Victoria College Preparatory School 1104

Cheshire
Altrincham Preparatory School 877
Pownall Hall 1036
Ramillies Hall School. 1041
The Ryleys 1052
Stockport Grammar Junior School 1087
Terra Nova School 1096
Wilmslow Preparatory School 1116

Cleveland
Yarm Preparatory School 1123

Cornwall
Truro Preparatory School 1101

Cumbria
Austin Friars St Monica's Junior School 882
Casterton, Sedbergh Preparatory School 914
Hunter Hall School 979
Windermere Preparatory School 1117

Derbyshire
Barlborough Hall School 886
Foremarke Hall 953
S. Anselm's 1055
St Peter and St Paul School 1077

Devon
Blundell's Preparatory School 900
Exeter Cathedral School 947
Exeter Junior School 947
Mount Kelly Preparatory School 1013
Plymouth College Preparatory School 1034
St John's International School 1069
Stover Preparatory School 1089

Dorset
Castle Court Preparatory School 914
Clayesmore Preparatory School 921
Dumpton School 941
Hanford School 967
Knighton House. 993
Leweston Junior Department 998
Port Regis 1035
Sherborne Preparatory School 1083
Sunninghill Prep School 1091
Talbot Heath Junior School 1095
Yarrells Preparatory School. 1124

PAGE

Durham

Barnard Castle Preparatory School 887
The Chorister School 918

Essex

Alleyn Court Preparatory School 875
Bancroft's Preparatory School 885
Brentwood Preparatory School 904
Chigwell Junior School 918
Dame Bradbury's School 932
Elm Green Preparatory School 945
Felsted Preparatory School 950
Friends' Junior School 955
Holmwood House Preparatory School 977
Littlegarth School 999
Loyola Preparatory School 1001
Maldon Court Preparatory School 1004
New Hall Preparatory School 1015
St Aubyn's School 1056
St Cedd's School 1058
St Michael's Preparatory School 1074
The Ursuline Preparatory School Ilford 1104
Widford Lodge 1115
Woodford Green Preparatory School 1121

Gloucestershire

Beaudesert Park 889
Berkhampstead School, Cheltenham 895
Cheltenham College Preparatory School 917
Dean Close Pre-Preparatory School 934
Dean Close Preparatory School 934
Hatherop Castle Preparatory School 968
King's Junior School Gloucester 989
The Richard Pate School 1045
St Edward's Preparatory School 1061
Tockington Manor 1099
Westonbirt Prep School 1114
Wycliffe Preparatory School 1122

Hampshire

Boundary Oak School 901
Churcher's College Junior School 919
Daneshill School 933
Dunhurst 941
Durlston Court 942
Farleigh School 949
Forres Sandle Manor 953
Hampshire Collegiate Prep School 966
Highfield & Brookham Schools 973
The Pilgrims' School 1033
The Portsmouth Grammar Junior School 1036
Prince's Mead School 1038
St John's College Infant and Junior School 1068
St Neot's Preparatory School 1075
St Swithun's Junior School 1079
Stroud School 1089
Twyford School 1102
Walhampton School 1105
West Hill Park 1110
Yateley Manor Preparatory School 1124

Herefordshire

Hereford Cathedral Junior School 971
St Richard's 1078

Hertfordshire

Aldenham Preparatory School 873

PAGE

Aldwickbury School 874
Beechwood Park 892
Berkhamsted Pre-Preparatory School 895
Berkhamsted Preparatory School 896
Bishop's Stortford College Prep School 898
Charlotte House Preparatory School for Girls . . . 916
Edge Grove 944
The Haberdashers' Aske's Boys' Preparatory
    & Pre-Preparatory School 964
Heath Mount School 970
Kingshott 992
Lochinver House School 999
Lockers Park 1000
Manor Lodge School 1005
Northwood Prep 1019
The Royal Masonic School for Girls 1049
St Albans High School for Girls Preparatory
    School 1053
St Columba's College Preparatory School 1059
St Edmund's Prep School 1060
St Hilda's School 1066
St Joseph's In The Park School 1070
St Margaret's Preparatory School 1072
Stormont 1089
Westbrook Hay 1112
York House School 1125

Isle of Man

The Buchan School 910

Isle of Wight

Ryde Junior School 1051

Kent

Ashford Prep School 880
Babington House School – Preparatory Department 884
Bickley Park School 896
Combe Bank Preparatory School 925
Derwent Lodge 936
Dulwich Preparatory School 940
Fosse Bank School 954
The Granville School 960
Hilden Grange School 974
Hilden Oaks School & Nursery 974
Holmewood House 976
Kent College Nursery, Infant & Junior School . . . 983
Kent College Preparatory School 984
Junior King's School 990
King's Rochester Preparatory School 991
Lorenden Preparatory School 1001
Marlborough House School 1006
The New Beacon 1014
Northbourne Park 1018
Rose Hill School 1047
Russell House 1051
St Edmund's Junior School 1060
St Lawrence College Junior School 1071
St Michael's Prep School 1075
Saint Ronan's 1079
Sevenoaks Preparatory School 1082
Solefield School 1084
Spring Grove School 1086
Sutton Valence Preparatory School 1094
Walthamstow Hall Junior School 1105
Wellesley House 1108
Yardley Court 1122

PAGE

Lancashire
Clevelands Preparatory School 921
St Pius X Prep School. 1078
Stonyhurst St Mary's Hall 1088

Leicestershire
Fairfield Preparatory School 948
Grace Dieu Manor School 959
Leicester Grammar Junior School 998

Lincolnshire
St Hugh's 1067
Stamford Junior School 1087
Witham Hall. 1119

London (see also Essex, Middlesex, Surrey)
Abercorn School 872
Alleyn's Junior School 876
Arnold House School 879
Avenue House School. 882
Avenue Nursery & Pre-Preparatory School. . . . 883
Bassett House School 888
Belmont 893
Blackheath Preparatory School 899
Broomwood Hall 909
Bute House Preparatory School for Girls 912
Cameron House 912
The Cavendish School 915
Colet Court (St Paul's Preparatory School). . . . 924
Colfe's Preparatory School 924
Devonshire House Preparatory School 936
Dulwich Prep London. 940
Durston House 942
Eaton House The Manor Girls' School 943
Eaton House The Manor Pre-Preparatory School . 943
Eaton House The Manor Preparatory School. . . . 944
Eaton Square School 944
The Falcons Schools 949
Finton House 952
Forest Preparatory School. 953
Garden House School 956
Gatehouse School 956
Grange Park Preparatory School 960
Grimsdell 963
The Hall 964
Hawkesdown House School 968
Hereward House School 972
Highgate Junior School 974
Hornsby House School 979
Hurlingham School 980
James Allen's Preparatory School 982
Keble School 982
Kensington Prep School 983
King's College Junior School. 987
Latymer Prep School 996
Lyndhurst House Preparatory School. 1002
Naima Jewish Preparatory School 1014
Newton Prep 1017
Norland Place School 1018
Northcote Lodge 1018
Notting Hill Preparatory School 1021
Orchard House School 1025
Pembridge Hall School 1030
Prospect House School 1039
Ravenscourt Park Preparatory School 1041
Redcliffe School 1042
Rosemead Preparatory School 1047
The Rowans School 1049

PAGE

St Anthony's Preparatory School 1055
St Benedict's Junior School. 1057
Saint Christina's RC Preparatory School 1058
St Christopher's School 1058
St Dunstan's College Junior School 1059
St Mary's School 1073
St Olave's Prep School 1076
St Paul's Cathedral School 1077
Sarum Hall School 1081
The Study Preparatory School 1090
Sussex House 1093
Tower House School 1100
University College School – Junior Branch 1102
University College School – The Phoenix 1103
Ursuline Preparatory School 1103
Westminster Abbey Choir School 1113
Westminster Cathedral Choir School 1113
Westminster Under School 1113
Wetherby Pre-Preparatory School 1115
Wetherby Preparatory School 1115
Willington Independent Preparatory School . . . 1116
Wimbledon Common Prep School 1117

Merseyside
Kingsmead School 992

Middlesex
Alpha Preparatory School. 876
Buckingham College Preparatory School. 910
Denmead 935
The Lady Eleanor Holles School (Junior
  Department) 994
The Mall School 1004
Newland House School 1017
Northwood College for Girls – Junior School . . . 1019
Orley Farm School 1026
Quainton Hall School 1039
Reddiford School 1042
St Helen's College 1065
St John's School 1070
St Martin's School 1073
Staines Preparatory School 1086
Twickenham Preparatory School 1101

Norfolk
Beeston Hall School 892
Glebe House School 957
Gresham's Prep School 962
Norwich School, The Lower School 1020
Riddlesworth Hall Preparatory School 1045
Taverham Hall Preparatory School 1096
Thorpe House Langley Preparatory School and
  Nursery 1098
Town Close School 1100

Northamptonshire
Beachborough. 888
Laxton Junior – Oundle School. 996
Maidwell Hall. 1003
Spratton Hall 1085
Wellingborough Preparatory School 1108
Winchester House School. 1117

Nottinghamshire
Nottingham High Infant and Junior School. 1022
Wellow House School. 1109
Worksop College Preparatory School, Ranby
  House 1121

PAGE

Oxfordshire
Abingdon Preparatory School. 873
Bruern Abbey School 910
Carrdus School 913
Christ Church Cathedral School 919
Cokethorpe Junior School. 923
Cranford House Junior School 928
Dragon School 939
Headington Preparatory School. 970
The Manor Preparatory School 1005
Moulsford Preparatory School 1012
New College School 1015
The Oratory Preparatory School 1025
Our Lady's Abingdon Junior School 1027
Rupert House School 1050
St Hugh's 1066
Summer Fields 1090

Rutland
Brooke Priory School 908

Shropshire
Birchfield School 897
Moor Park School. 1011
The Old Hall School 1024
Packwood Haugh 1028
Prestfelde 1037
Shrewsbury High Prep School 1083

Somerset
All Hallows School 875
Hazlegrove 969
King's Hall School 988
Kingswood Preparatory School. 993
Millfield Prep School 1008
Monkton Prep School 1010
The Paragon 1029
Perrott Hill 1031
Queen's College Junior School 1040
Sunny Hill Preparatory School 1091
Taunton Preparatory School 1095
Wellington Prep School. 1109
Wells Cathedral Junior School 1110

Staffordshire (see also West Midlands)
Denstone College Preparatory School at Smallwood
   Manor 935
St Bede's Preparatory School. 1056
Yarlet School 1123

Suffolk
Barnardiston Hall Preparatory School 887
Brandeston Hall. 904
Culford Preparatory School. 931
Fairstead House School 949
Ipswich Preparatory School. 982
Moreton Hall Preparatory School. 1012
Old Buckenham Hall School 1023
The Old School Henstead. 1024
Orwell Park 1027
South Lee School 1085
Woodbridge School – The Abbey. 1120

Surrey
Aberdour School 872
Aldro 874
Amesbury 877
Barfield School & Nursery 886

PAGE

Barrow Hills School 888
Belmont School 894
Bishopsgate School 898
Bramley School 903
Caterham Preparatory School. 915
Chinthurst School 918
City of London Freemen's Junior School 920
Claremont Fan Court Pre-Preparatory and Nursery
   School 920
Claremont Fan Court Preparatory School 920
Collingwood School 925
Coworth Flexlands School 927
Cranleigh Preparatory School. 928
Cranmore School 929
Cumnor House School 931
Danes Hill. 933
Downsend 938
Duke of Kent School 939
Edgeborough 945
Ewell Castle Junior School 947
Feltonfleet School. 951
Greenfield. 962
Guildford High School Junior School 963
Hall Grove 965
Halstead Preparatory School for Girls 965
Haslemere Preparatory School 967
The Hawthorns 968
Hazelwood School 969
Hoe Bridge School 975
Holy Cross Preparatory School 978
Homefield Preparatory School 978
Kew College 984
Kew Green Preparatory School. 985
King's House School 988
Kingswood House School 992
Lanesborough School. 995
Longacre School 1000
Micklefield School 1008
Notre Dame School 1020
Oakwood School 1023
Old Vicarage School 1024
Parkside 1030
Priory Preparatory School 1038
Reigate St Mary's Preparatory and Choir School . 1043
Ripley Court School 1046
Rokeby 1047
Rowan Preparatory School 1048
Royal Russell Junior School 1049
Rydes Hill Preparatory School 1052
St Andrew's School, Woking 1054
St Catherine's Preparatory School 1057
St Edmund's School 1061
St George's Junior School 1064
St Hilary's School. 1065
St Ives School. 1067
Seaton House School 1082
Shrewsbury House 1084
Shrewsbury Lodge School 1084
Surbiton High Boys' Preparatory School. 1092
Surbiton High Junior Girls' School. 1092
Tormead Junior School 1099
Unicorn School 1102
Woodcote House 1120

Sussex (East)
Ashdown House. 879
Bede's Preparatory School 890
Bricklehurst Manor 905

	PAGE
Brighton & Hove High School Junior School	905
Brighton College Prep School	906
Lancing College Preparatory School at Hove	995
Moira House Junior School	1010
St Andrew's Prep	1053
St Christopher's School	1059
Vinehall School	1104

Sussex (West)

Ardingly College Prep & Pre-Prep Schools	877
Brambletye	902
Burgess Hill School for Girls – Junior School	911
Copthorne School	926
Cottesmore School	926
Cumnor House School	931
Farlington Preparatory School	950
Great Ballard	961
Great Walstead School	961
Handcross Park School	966
Hurstpierpoint College Preparatory School	980
Oakwood Preparatory School	1023
Pennthorpe School	1030
The Prebendal School	1037
Seaford College Prep School	1081
Sompting Abbotts	1085
Westbourne House	1111
Windlesham House School	1118

Tyne and Wear

Newcastle Preparatory School	1016

Warwickshire

Bilton Grange	896
Crackley Hall School	927
Crescent School	929
The Croft Preparatory School	930
Warwick Junior School	1106
Warwick Preparatory School	1107

West Midlands

Bablake Junior School and Pre Prep	884
The Blue Coat School	900
Eversfield Preparatory School	946
Hallfield School	965
King Henry VIII Preparatory School	986
Mayfield Preparatory School	1007
Newbridge Preparatory School	1016
West House School	1111

Wiltshire

Chafyn Grove School	915
The Godolphin Preparatory School	958
Leaden Hall School	997
Leehurst Swan School	997
Pinewood	1034
Prior Park Preparatory School	1038
St Francis School	1063
St Margaret's Preparatory School	1071
Salisbury Cathedral School	1080
Sandroyd School	1080
Stonar Preparatory School	1088
Warminster Preparatory School	1106

Worcestershire

Abberley Hall	872

	PAGE
Bromsgrove Preparatory & Pre-Preparatory School	907
The Downs Malvern	937
The Elms	946
King's Hawford	988
King's St Alban's School	989
RGS Springfield	1044
RGS The Grange	1044
Winterfold House	1119

Yorkshire (East)

Pocklington Prep School (formerly Lyndhurst School)	1034

Yorkshire (North)

Ashville College Junior School	881
Ashville College Pre-Prep School	881
Aysgarth School	883
Belmont Grosvenor School	894
Bootham Junior School	901
Bramcote Junior School	903
Clifton School and Nursery	923
Giggleswick Junior School	957
The Minster School	1009
The Mount Junior School	1013
St Martin's Ampleforth	1072
St Olave's School, York	1076
Terrington Hall	1097

Yorkshire (South)

Ashdell Preparatory School	879
Birkdale Prep School	898
Mylnhurst Preparatory School & Nursery	1014
Rudston Preparatory School	1050
Westbourne School	1112

Yorkshire (West)

Bradford Grammar Junior School	902
Brontë House	908
The Froebelian School	955
The Gleddings Preparatory School	958
Heathfield	971
Moorfield School	1011
Moorlands School	1011
Richmond House School	1045
Westville House School	1114

NORTHERN IRELAND

Rockport School	1046

SCOTLAND

Ardvreck	878
Belhaven Hill	892
Cargilfield	913
Craigclowan School	928
Fettes College Preparatory School	952
Kilgraston Preparatory School	985
Lathallan School	996
Loretto Junior School	1001
St Leonards Junior School	1071
St Mary's Preparatory School	1074

WALES

The Grange	959
Inglefield House	981
Rydal Penrhos Preparatory School	1051

IAPS Member Heads and Deputy Heads

	PAGE
Acheson-Gray, C J	1034
Adams, I	919
Aisher, Mrs J	1075
Aisthorpe, Mrs C	1072
Alexander, D A	1017
Arkell, N	975
Arnold, D S	1017
Aston, D W N	874
Atkinson, P C E	892
Austin, Mrs M	984
Austin, Mrs P A	965
Ayres, T	1098
Bacon, R G	1060
Bailey, Dr S J	1102
Bailey, S	881
Baker, N	1115
Balfour, E W	1018
Banks, J M	888
Banks, Miss B M	1078
Barber, S W T	1002
Barker, M	1111
Barnard, A P N	943
Barratt, Mrs D	1039
Bartholomew, Miss N	1057
Bartlett, J R	1011
Bass, Miss J R	996
Bate, Ms J H	1059
Batt, Mrs J M	1042
Baty, C	961
Baugh, J R	939
Beach, M J	1030
Beardmore-Gray, B	1012
Beardmore-Gray, F J	979
Bell, Mrs E S	908
Bell, Mrs S	1052
Berrie, Mrs C L	881
Bevington, N	1100
Bicker-Caarten, D	1002
Blom, L J	1056
Botting, Mrs T	962
Bourne, Mrs C	968
Bourne, Mrs S M	1042
Boys, N	886
Bracewell, Mrs A	1000
Bradnam, Ms G M	1053
Brain, M	1088
Bray, A	1047
Brearey, M	993
Brooks, P R	992
Brooks, W	1035
Brotherton, M S	957
Brough, J	980
Brown, A	1027
Brown, Mrs L	1044
Browning, A D J	900
Browning, A W	941
Bruce, Mrs C	1022
Buck, Mrs T	1117
Bufton, Miss C E	1092
Bufton, Miss C E	1092
Bunbury, T W	1029
Burch, C J	898
Burgess, Mrs P	903

	PAGE
Burrett, Mrs J M	950
Burton, Mrs A	1026
Calvey, C B	877
Calvey, T	1026
Cameron Ashcroft, Miss J	912
Cameron, Mrs J	1021
Camm, Mrs A B	879
Candia, C	1023
Cannell, T R	1037
Canning, G R G	1106
Canwell, Mr J	909
Capper, Miss R	1013
Carnochan, S G	914
Carroll, J	1078
Carter, A J	983
Cartwright, S	1060
Cattaneo, Mrs S	905
Cavanagh, Mrs L	910
Cawthorne, Mrs P	888
Challen, Mrs W L	956
Chanter, M	1116
Cheesman, N S	1057
Childs, Mrs A H	982
Chippendale, J T S	988
Chippington, N R	1077
Chitty, M O M	880
Clare-Hunt, P	931
Clarke, Mrs S	1048
Clarke, S	1085
Clifford, Mrs S J	973
Coakley, J T	1122
Coates, Mrs M	1016
Cobb, D	925
Cochrane, P I	1045
Collins, Mrs M I M	1103
Collins, S D	872
Connolly, M P	929
Connors, I	1049
Conrad, Mrs S	1015
Cook, A S	937
Cook, M	930
Cook, Mrs C A	923
Cook, P W	1109
Cordingley, Miss A	954
Cordon, Mrs K E	1071
Corlett, Miss R J	910
Cowell, A H	898
Coyle, Mrs C	1089
Creeth, M L	1010
Crehan, D A	1065
Crofts, J P	957
Cross, R P	895
Crossley, M A	1096
Crossley, Mrs J	1011
Crouch, Mrs J	970
Culverwell, M B	1043
D'Aprano, Miss M	1020
Darvill, Mrs R	955
Davey, D	903
David, P	940
Davies, C J	945
Davies, G R A	875
Davies, M	917
Davies, Mrs E	885

	PAGE
Dawson, T A C N	1091
Day, Mrs Y F S	918
de Falbe, F	1078
Delaney, G E F	1068
Deval-Reed, Mrs J	907
Disley, Mrs J E	1045
Doble, K A	1084
Dodds, A J L	1089
Dodgson, T W T	887
Doggart, S J G	912
Donald, A R M	1071
Donaldson, A J	1009
Donnelly, Mrs H	966
Dorrian, S P	996
Douch, S J	1085
Dove, P	1063
Draper, M	1007
Duigan, R	927
Dunbar, Mrs T R	915
Duncan, Mrs L C	893
Dunhill, B H	1035
Dunlop, W	921
Dunn, G	1005
Dunn, S W	908
Eager, Mrs J	997
Earnshaw, A R	948
Easterbrook, P	968
Ebrahim, Mrs K	985
Edmonds, Dr P A	1058
Edwards, A A	952
Edwards, D A H	1106
Edwards, H	1051
Edwards, J P	944
Entwisle, G	890
Evans, B	944
Evans, G	1100
Everson, Fr S C	949
Evitt, P G S	973
Eyles, J P	1043
Faber, D J C	1090
Falconer, A	1076
Farnish, Mrs A	1103
Fenwick, R B	969
Finlayson, Miss J	1006
Fisher, Mrs S	1016
Fisher, P	959
Fleming, D J W	907
Fleming, Mrs A E	1017
Flowers, Mrs C	905
Floyd, A E	952
Floyd, J	910
Foale, M	1013
Follett, R	1104
Ford, S	1039
Foster, R J	1118
Fox, Mrs L	920
Francis, R	956
Freeman, B C	1117
Fremont-Barnes, Mrs J	939
Fysh, Mrs M	883
Gabriel, N H	902
Gainer, D	958
Gainher, R C	892

PAGE

Garrett, N J 1120
Gatherer, C D M 1034
Gear, J 935
Gibbons, M G 992
Gibson, A 1109
Gilmour, I 992
Gocher, Mrs V 873
Goddard, C A A 883
Godwin, C 964
Goldsmith, Mrs E 1117
Goldsworthy, Miss K 1067
Gough, A J 1046
Gough, M 1094
Goulbourn, D 1036
Graham, A R 965
Gray, J P 1125
Green, Ms S 972
Greystoke, Mrs A S 872
Griffin, I R 989
Grimes, Mrs P 1079
Groome, M C 1037
Grubb, Mrs J 941
Guest, Mrs L F 1004
Gullifer, N R 1015
Gunn, M A 938

Haas, Mrs A 989
Haigh, T C 916
Hair, Mrs S 978
Hales, V W 874
Handford, Mrs T 932
Hansford, A J 1018
Hardy, P C 923
Harris, M J S 1080
Harrison, L 1082
Hart, Mrs J 1121
Hartley, M N 953
Harvey, A 1029
Harvey, R 878
Harvey, W J 1074
Hastings, H 906
Hayward, L 1102
Head, S 1012
Heinrich, C St J S 931
Helliwell, N L 1062
Hepher, S 944
Heyworth, P 1005
Hicks, J B 1112
Hill, Mrs E A 1113
Hitchings, S L 1094
Hobbs, Mrs S A B 1025
Hope, Mrs G 1084
Hopkinson, P S 1036
Hornshaw, J 896
Howard, Mrs T 1107
Howe, Mrs C 890
Howes, C G 924
Hoyland, P J 1034
Huckle, P R 906
Hudson, A J W 1064
Hughes, G W 1044
Hyde-Dunn, C 873

Ibbetson-Price, W C R 1119
Ingham, J K 1020

James, Mrs R 1114
James, S C 918
James, S M 974

PAGE

Jaspal, S 895
Jenkinson, Mrs C J M 909
Johns, T R 968
Johnson, M R 916
Johnston, R 967
Jones, C J 926
Jones, K L 1068
Jones, N 1070
Jones, P H 999
Jones, W J B 1086

Kaye, N P 1093
Keighley-Elstub, K 1030
Kendrick, N I 942
Keyte, P M 1055
Khodabandehloo, Mrs T 1040
King, A 1097
King, M 1030
Kirk, Miss P S 1038
Knight, H 1120

Lamb, A M 1077
Lankester, R A 1003
Larter, S H 1069
Laurent, A P 995
Lawson, Mrs A E 984
Layburn, J P 885
Leahy, Mrs K 1095
Leake, R N S 997
Lee, Ms A 973
Lee, T D 1019
Linthwaite, Mrs G 1024
Livingstone, D 1054
Lockett, W 872
Logue, A J 1091
Lovell, N M 986
Loveman, Mrs R 1059
Lovett, M J 1101
Lowe, Mrs H 912
Lynas, Mrs C 1050
Lynch, Mrs P J F 983
Lyttle, A M J 1111

MacAskill, I K 892
MacDonald, R A 1045
Malam, D P 1101
Malcolm, G D 1038
Marjoribanks, J D B 976
Marriott, C 1080
Marsh, Mrs S 924
Marshall, R H 929
Marshall-Taylor, A 1010
Martin, Mrs S E 1089
Mattar, P R 1018
May, H 943
McCarthy, C 1051
McCarthy, G P 982
McDade, C 1065
McDuff, R 1051
McElhone, M 1011
McGillewie, Miss J 949
McKernan, S 1061
McKinney, W J 1024
McLaughlan, N P 1113
McLaughlin, Mrs B 960
Meadows, P 1001
Mercer, Miss Y M 964
Merriman, Mrs J Y 894
Merriman, R P 953

PAGE

Meunier, T A 924
Michau, Mrs S 936
Miller, Miss J 958
Miller, Mrs H 911
Mills, T N A 1105
Milne, J E 922
Milner, Mrs A E 945
Milton, J H 1113
Mitchell, A J 977
Mitchell, M 1096
Mitchell, Miss J 916
Mitchell, R J 1108
Mockridge, M N P 931
Monk, A G 1120
Moore, H 879
Morgan, R 961
Morris, M J 1040
Morris, Mrs J M 1011
Morrison, A G 951
Morrison, Mrs D 1082
Morse, R J 1031
Mortimer, Mrs P 1058
Mottram, G 1061
Moxon, C E 1003
Mulryne, S 1097
Murdock, W D 933
Murphy, D 920
Murphy, I 1088
Murray, R 919
Mwale, Mrs F 950
Myers-Allen, M K 904
Myott, H V 897

Newman, Mrs J 922
Newton, E J 915
Nicholson, P G M 1001
Noakes, A 953
Nott, A J P 1066

O'Donnell, M F 1072
Oldroyd, P 1098
O'Malley, S T P 1108
O'Neill, B 1027
Oosthuizen, Mrs C 1124
O'Shaughnessy, Mrs K 1041
Osiatynski, A P M 896
O'Sullivan, T 1023
Outwin-Flinders, R 965
Overend, R P 991
Owton, G R 966

Palmer, A J 1122
Pardon, Mrs J R 1004
Parlane, Mrs L 921
Patterson, Miss D M 1041
Pattison, I D 980
Pauley, Mrs H A 1009
Pearce, M 1038
Peck, J R 1047
Peck, J 985
Pepper, Mrs S 1090
Perks, A K 1054
Perry, J F 994
Phillips, Mrs H 981
Phillips, Mrs M 947
Phillips, Mrs S J 963
Phillips, P 1055
Philps, D A 1084
Piercy, M R 1014

	PAGE
Piper, J.	1032
Piper, Mrs S.	936
Potter, M J.	996
Potts, A C.	877
Pratt, J W.	1014
Price, D.	1004
Price, N A.	884
Price, R.	1104
Pritchard, C S J.	1121
Proctor, Mrs G.	1023
Quick, J H W.	962
Ramsay, A P.	1110
Rawlinson, Miss A M.	1073
Raybould, I.	1123
Rees, E.	979
Rees, M.	1074
Rees, S.	1081
Reid, A J C.	1002
Reid, A J.	885
Rex, Mrs J C.	891
Rigby, Mrs C.	998
Rigby, Mrs H.	1116
Riley, Mrs C E.	1007
Roberts, L.	893
Robinson, M S.	1070
Robinson, M.	920
Robinson, Mrs C.	976
Robinson, Mrs F.	994
Robinson, N J.	987
Rogerson, T F.	926
Rose, Mrs L.	1008
Roulston, M.	940
Rowcliffe, Mrs G B.	1041
Rushforth, P H.	971
Rycroft, C F.	887
Salmond Smith, Mrs L.	1099
Sawyer, Ms S.	1086
Sawyer, W.	1123
Schofield, M.	931
Scott, Mrs C J.	960
Searle, T J.	950
Segrave, Mrs S.	943
Severino, S.	1053
Sevilla, Ms L.	1104
Shaw, Mrs M J.	969
Shaw, N.	1114
Shayler, Mrs S.	1008
Shelley, Dr C A.	934
Sheridan, J.	1010
Sherwood, Mrs C.	884
Shrubsall, R A.	1068
Sibson, D W T.	1063
Silk, I.	891
Silverlock, Dr G A.	987
Simmonds, Mrs R.	1001
Simmons, R G.	1057
Simon, Mrs K.	963
Sims, A.	956
Sinclair, D.	1095
Skrine, Mrs H C.	894
Slingsby, J.	882
Smart, S.	925
Smith, J J.	1025
Smith, Mrs C A.	1081
Smith, Mrs E.	1087
Smith, R.	967
Smith, T.	935
Smith-Langridge, C N.	1028
Snell, M W E.	1115
Snow, Mrs H E.	1091
Southall, P J.	883
Southgate, A D.	900
Spencer, S V.	933
Spinney, M W.	889
Stack, Miss F N.	982
Stafford Northcote, H B C.	1056
Stevenson, R D P.	914
Stokes, Mrs S.	946
Stott, M C.	1024
Struck, R H A.	1004
Styles, Miss S J.	1066
Sweeney, Mrs A.	927
Symonds, S R.	1099
Tait, P S.	1083
Taylor, N.	877
Taylor, R.	913
Thaker, Mrs H.	1019
Thomas, A.	946
Thomas, Mrs E G.	959
Thomas, V W P.	879
Thompson, C.	1102
Thompson, J C.	1049
Thompson, Mrs P J.	899
Thorpe, I D.	938
Tidmarsh, D T.	1073
Tilly, J.	1076
Todd, Mrs H.	901
Toleman, W J.	898
Toley, R.	996
Tollit, G F.	979
Tompkins, S.	1074
Towers, J.	978
Tranmer, J.	955
Trelawny-Vernon, W E H.	1079
Trinidad, C J W.	876
Trowell, S C.	1115
Tuckett, H W G.	915
Turnbull, Mrs C M A.	995
Turner, J M.	988
Turner, M.	988
Turner, M.	1107
Turner, Mrs A J.	947
Unsworth, M J.	888
Vance, G.	1046
Vinsome, Mrs D.	979
Waddington, Mrs S.	1032
Walker, B.	999
Walliker, A J.	1061
Wansey, D C.	942
Wansey, J P.	930
Ward, C A.	1067
Ward, M.	1006
Watson, C D J.	933
Way, E.	913
Webb, Mrs S A.	974
Webster, Mrs J.	1033
Welch, A C.	1119
Wells, P M.	990
Wells, R J.	985
Wenham, P.	896
West, Mrs S A.	1058
Westcombe, P D.	1047
Westlake, N T.	902
Wheeler, T C.	1087
Whipp, D.	1085
Whiskerd, K J.	904
Whittingham, Mrs J.	1065
Whittle, S J E.	1071
Whybrow, J F.	917
Whymark, R J.	990
Wilkins, A M.	971
Willatt, G C.	1050
Williams, D.	918
Williams, G.	949
Williams, R J.	1124
Wilson, C.	1000
Wilson, M T.	928
Wilson, Mrs P J.	958
Wingrove, Mrs S.	1049
Wintle, T.	932
Withers, J A S.	1059
Withers, J.	974
Withers, P.	1075
Womersley, J P R.	889
Wood, Mrs D.	1105
Wright, C.	971
Wright, I D.	1034
Wright, Miss E.	925
Yates, R A.	946
Yeates, R.	880
Yeo, S G.	947
Young, K D.	1112

Individual School Entries

Abberley Hall

Worcester WR6 6DD
Tel: 01299 896275
Fax: 01299 896875
email: gill.portsmouth@abberleyhall.co.uk
website: www.abberleyhall.co.uk
Twitter: @abberleyhallsch

Chairman of Governors: The Hon David Legh

Headmaster: W J Lockett, BA, PGCE

Deputy Headmasters:
N Richardson, BSc Hons
C Whitworth

Age Range. 2–13.
Number of Pupils. Prep School: 186 (114 Boys, 72 Girls; 110 Boarders, 76 Day Pupils). Pre-Prep & Nursery: 83 (47 Boys, 36 Girls).
Fees per term (2014–2015). Prep: Boarders £6,910, Day Pupils £5,195–£5,505. Pre-Prep: £1,615–£3,265.

Abberley Hall is co-educational. It is situated 12 miles north-west of Worcester, with easy access to the M5. It is a boarding school for boys and girls aged 8–13 years, and is set in 100 acres of gardens and wooded grounds amid magnificent countryside.

Pupils are prepared for all Independent Senior Schools. Although there is no entry examination, the school has a strong academic tradition with consistently good results in scholarships and Common Entrance, thanks to a highly-qualified staff, favourable teacher/pupil ratios and small classes. This also helps encourage the slower learners, for whom individual attention is available.

The school's facilities include an indoor swimming pool, chapel, library, music school and concert studio, two science laboratories, technology room, DT centre and extensively equipped computer centre, art studio and pottery rooms, multi-purpose hall with permanent stage, rifle range and climbing wall, sports hall, hard tennis courts, Ricochet court and ample playing fields for the major games and athletics, including a large Astroturf pitch. The school also owns its own French chalet where children go on three-week blocks for total immersion into the French language and way of life.

The pupils are also encouraged to take part in a wide range of hobbies and activities including archery, chess, fishing, golf, horse riding, fencing, model-making, printing, ballet, mountain-biking, woodwork and many more.

The school aims to combine a friendly atmosphere with the discipline which enables pupils to achieve their full potential and learn to feel responsibility for themselves and others.

Charitable status. Abberley Hall is a Registered Charity, number 527598. Its aim is to further good education.

Abercorn School

Early Years:
28 Abercorn Place, London NW8 9XP
Tel: 020 7286 4785
email: admin@abercornschool.com

Pre Prep:
The Old Grammar School, 248 Marylebone Road, London NW1 6JF
Tel: 020 7723 8700
email: togs@abercornschool.com

Prep:
38 Portland Place, London W1B 1LS
Tel: 020 7100 4335
email: portland@abercornschool.com

website: www.abercornschool.com

High Mistress: Mrs A Greystoke, BA Hons
Headmaster: Mr D Morse, BSc Hons, PGCE

Age Range. 2½ to 13+ Co-educational.
Number of Pupils. 400.
Fees per term (2014–2015). £2,900–£5,500. Fees include all extras, apart from lunch and school transport.

At Abercorn we take great pride in guiding both pupils and parents through the educational journey to ensure your child reaches their full potential through individualised target setting and regular self-evaluation for each child. We also communicate daily with our parents as we understand the importance of school and families working together to help achieve these targets and strive for academic excellence.

Our sister schools in New York City and Austin continue to ensure that we don't just teach with a global perspective, but are global in our philosophy. As such Abercorn has gained an enviable record of excellence and achievement in and outside the classroom, working with our families to gain places in top schools in London and further afield. In recent years pupils have gained places or scholarships to City of London Boys, UCS, Mill Hill, Francis Holland, North London Collegiate, Westminster and St Paul's/Colet Court.

So why not come and see for yourself what Abercorn can offer you and your child by either joining us on one of our Open Days or by contacting the school to book a private tour. We look forward to seeing you soon!

Aberdour School

Brighton Road, Burgh Heath, Tadworth, Surrey KT20 6AJ
Tel: 01737 354119
email: enquiries@aberdourschool.co.uk
website: www.aberdourschool.co.uk

The School is an Educational Trust run by a Board of Governors.

Chairman of the Governors: Mr R C Nicol, FCA

Headmaster: Mr S D Collins, CertEd

Deputy Headmistress: Mrs T Thomas, BEd Hons
Deputy Headmaster: Mr G Clark, BEd Hons
Head of Pre-Prep: Mrs A Terry, BA Hons

Age Range. 2–13.
Number of Pupils. 355 Day Boys and Girls.
Fees per term (2014–2015). £1,165–£4,300 fully inclusive.

Children are taken at 2 years old into the pre-preparatory department and transfer to the preparatory school at age 7. Children are prepared for all the major Senior Schools and many scholarships have been won. There is a school orchestra and a concert band as well as a large school choir. There are ample playing fields, two all-weather areas, a large sports hall and indoor heated swimming pool. There are two science laboratories and a design technology room. All the usual games are coached and the general character of the children is developed by many interests and activities. Aberdour offers a uniquely personalised education.

Charitable status. Aberdour School Educational Trust Limited is a Registered Charity, number 312033. Its aim is to promote education.

Abingdon Preparatory School

Josca's House, Kingston Road, Frilford, Abingdon, Oxon OX13 5NX
Tel: 01865 391570
Fax: 01865 391042
email: registrar@abingdonprep.org.uk
website: www.abingdon.org.uk/prep

The School was founded in 1956. In 1998 it merged with Abingdon School to become part of one charitable foundation with a single Board of Governors.

Chairman of the Governors: Adrian Burn

Headmaster: **Crispin Hyde-Dunn**, MA Oxon, PGCE, MA Ed, NPQH

Age Range. Boys 4–13.
Number of Pupils. 250 Day.
Fees per term (2014–2015). £3,360–£4,620.
Main entry points are at age four and seven. Pupils are prepared for senior school entrance examinations. A strong majority goes on to Abingdon School.

Abingdon Preparatory School is a thinking and learning school – as well as a teaching school. Pupils' needs are served by providing a happy and stimulating environment where the children are encouraged to develop self-reliance and a sense of responsibility. Considerable emphasis is placed on helping pupils to develop good working patterns together with sound organisational and learning skills.

The school enjoys extensive facilities including dedicated art, drama, ICT, music, CDT and science suites and a multipurpose sports hall. There has been substantial refurbishment of many of the existing facilities including the swimming pool, library and classrooms. The School benefits from extensive grounds with woodland, gardens, adventure play areas and acres of sports fields.

The extra-curricular activities are a major strength of the school outside the classroom. The splendid amenities enable every child to participate in a wide range of sports and activities. There are regular fixtures against local schools in the main school sports of rugby, football, cricket, tennis and athletics. All pupils swim at least once a week. There is a range of after-school clubs, which includes amongst many others, orchestra, choir, art, science, judo, golf, fencing, gardening, chess, computers and drama.

A regular number of academic, music, drama and all-rounder awards are gained every year – the majority to the senior school, Abingdon.

A large number of trips are organised for all year groups during the year and the oldest boys go abroad for a week on completing their Common Entrance examinations.

Charitable status. Abingdon School is a Registered Charity, number 1071298. It exists to provide for the education of children aged 4–18.

Aldenham Preparatory School

Aldenham Road, Elstree, Herts WD6 3AJ
Tel: 01923 851664
Fax: 01923 854410
email: prepschool@aldenham.com
website: www.aldenham.com

Chairman of Board of Governors: J S Lewis, DL, FCIS

Head of Preparatory School: **Mrs V Gocher**, MA

Age Range. 3–11.
Number of Pupils. Total 171: 103 Boys, 68 Girls.
Fees per term (2014–2015). Prep: £4,038; Pre-Prep: £3,647; Nursery: £26.06 per morning or afternoon session, £53.22 per day, £2,783 per term.

At Aldenham Preparatory School, we provide a warm, happy and nurturing environment where quality learning takes place and the needs of each individual child are fulfilled.

The Preparatory School is a co-educational day school encompassing the Nursery (3–4 years), the Pre-Prep Department (4–7 years) and the Prep Department (7–11 years). It forms an integral part of the main school which was established in 1597 and remains on the same glorious site, set in over 110 acres of countryside yet only 13 miles from the centre of London.

Our primary aim is to provide an excellent all-round education, presenting all of our pupils with exceptional opportunities. The school is dedicated to ensuring the flexibility for each child to develop their own individual abilities, whether they are academic, creative or sporting. We offer high-quality teaching from enthusiastic, motivated and caring staff.

An inspection commissioned by the Independent Schools Inspectorate (ISI) praised the school for being "*...a lively, happy community in which young children thrive. They benefit from a high standard of education and very good care in all year groups. Children's attitude to learning and their behaviour are exemplary. Relationships between children and staff are friendly and courteous.*"

Small class sizes (a maximum of 23 in the Pre-Prep and Prep) and expert teaching from an early age ensure that academic attainment is high. The requirements of the National Curriculum and preparation for 11+ entrance exams are blended into a broad based curriculum. This along with an excellent staff/pupil ratio enriches our children's learning and encourages them to work to the very best of their ability.

Extensive extra-curricular provision including Cookery, Fencing, Chess, Choir and Karate and specialist teachers in French, Drama, Music and Sport enrich the children's education.

The accommodation for both Pre-Prep and Prep Departments is first class with pupils having access to their own DT and art room, library, music and drama suite, computer room and three-acre playing field. We are also able to share the Aldenham School campus as a whole, enabling us to enjoy use of the extensive grounds and facilities, including the sports complex, artificial turf pitch, chapel, dining hall, and theatre. (For further information about the senior school, see Aldenham School entry in HMC section.)

We have high expectations of all our pupils and encourage initiative, independence and self-confidence. We also insist on good manners and consideration for others, as a result there is a strong sense of community at Aldenham.

Entry is primarily at rising 3 and 4+, although there are also a number of places available at 7+.

Our excellent established Nursery facilities provide a structured lively and stimulating introduction to Aldenham School with morning and afternoon classes or full days.

All our children find themselves well equipped and prepared for the next stage of their education with many moving on to Aldenham Senior School.

Charitable status. The Aldenham School Company is a Registered Charity, number 298140. It exists to provide high quality education and pastoral care to enable children to achieve their full potential in later life.

Aldro

Lombard Street, Shackleford, Godalming, Surrey GU8 6AS

Tel:	01483 409020 (Headmaster)
	01483 409019 (Admissions)
	01483 810266 (School Office)
email:	hmsec@aldro.org
website:	www.aldro.org

Chairman of the Governors: Philip Robinson

Headmaster: **David W N Aston**, BA, PGCE

Age Range. 7–13.
Number of Boys. 230: 50 boarders, 180 day boys.
Fees per term (2014–2015). Boarding: Form 3 £6,840, Forms 4–8 £7,415. Day: Form 3 £5,170, Forms 4–8 £5,745.

Aldro is a boys' boarding and day prep school set in a beautiful rural location yet within a mile of the A3 and 45 minutes of central London, Gatwick and Heathrow airports.

Aldro aims to offer boys an exceptional all-round education in a happy, purposeful community. It has a Christian foundation and this underpins the values and ethos of the school. Each school day starts with a short service in the lovely Chapel, beautifully converted from an eighteenth century barn.

The school is fortunate in having a spacious site including a lake and about 30 acres of playing fields. There are also four hard tennis courts, two shooting ranges and a covered games area. The facilities are excellent and there has been much investment in new buildings over the past ten years. The Centenary Building opened in 2000 and houses most of the classrooms, the ICT centre, an outstanding library and, in the basement, changing rooms and a large common room. The Crispin Hill Centre incorporates a Music School, theatre and sports hall. Two science laboratories and the Art and Design Technology Centre have been developed in eighteenth century buildings either side of the Chapel. The Argyle Building including a new dining hall and kitchen was opened in late 2003. The dormitories in the main building have recently been refurbished. The boarders enjoy high quality pastoral care and a varied programme of activities in the evenings and at weekends.

In the classroom, there is a balance between the best traditional and modern approaches, whilst firm and friendly encouragement of each individual has led to an outstanding academic record of success at Common Entrance and Scholarship level. Thirty academic awards have been won in the last four years to leading schools such as Charterhouse, Eton, Sherborne, Winchester, Radley, Shrewsbury and Wellington College.

Aldro is committed to giving boys real breadth to their education and much emphasis is placed on extra-curricular activities. There are many opportunities for the arts, with a good record of success in Art and Music scholarships – 20 awards have been won in the past four years. Many boys learn musical instruments and there are three choirs, two orchestras and numerous ensembles. Drama also features prominently with several productions each year.

The major sports are rugby, soccer and hockey in the winter, with cricket in the summer. Athletics, tennis, swimming, cross-country running, squash and shooting are secondary sports and high standards are achieved. A huge range of activities are available including badminton, dodge ball, pioneers, bottle digging, fly fishing and pétanque. The school has an enviable record for Chess with 8 teams winning National championships in the past five years.

Boys at Aldro are treated as individuals with talents to develop. They lead cheerful and purposeful lives, and are well-prepared for a wide range of leading senior schools.

'Bringing out the best in boys' is what Aldro has been achieving through the generations. There is a focus on excellence and achievement, whether that is in the classroom, music room or on the sports field. Aldro prepares boys for the rest of their lives.

Charitable status. Aldro School Educational Trust Limited is a Registered Charity, number 312072. It exists to provide education for boys.

Aldwickbury School

Wheathampstead Road, Harpenden, Herts AL5 1AD

Tel:	01582 713022
Fax:	01582 767696
email:	secretary@aldwickbury.org.uk
	registrar@aldwickbury.org.uk
website:	www.aldwickbury.org.uk

Chairman of Governors: S A Westley, MA

Headmaster: **V W Hales**, BEd Hons Exeter

Age Range. 4–13.
Number of Boys. Prep School: 220 (including up to 34 weekly boarders). Pre-Prep: 120.
Fees per term (2014–2015). Day Boys: Pre-Prep £3,818–£3,945, Years 3–8 £4,218–£4,676. Weekly Boarding Fee: £28–£35 per night.

Aldwickbury is a day and boarding school set in 20 acres on the outskirts of Harpenden. Aldwickbury is a boys' school that focuses on boys' education, their growth and development. We allow them to flourish in an environment that challenges and stimulates them whatever their interests, passions or talents. Our teaching mixes traditional approaches together with modern ideas and methods; interactive whiteboards have been installed in all departments.

The school provides an extensive extra-curricular programme for the boys. Music, art and drama are well catered for with an emphasis on involvement as well as the desire for excellence. There are plays and concerts providing performance opportunities for all age groups, both formally and informally. A games session is held every day for all boys in Years 3–8 and teams in all the major sports at every level. The school has an excellent reputation at all sports and has had national recognition in skiing, swimming, athletics, tennis and soccer in recent years.

The school has excellent facilities based around a large Victorian House. Purpose-built teaching blocks, including a modern pre-prep department, ensure that the education is of a high standard. Other facilities include an indoor swimming pool, tennis courts, gymnasium, DT workshop and playing fields. Recent additions to the buildings have been a library, dining room and changing rooms. A new hall complex including a new music department, performance space and classrooms was completed in April 2014.

The boys move onto a wide range of senior schools, both day and boarding. The recent results at Common Entrance, entry tests and scholarships have been a reflection on the good teaching that the boys receive.

The Pre-Preparatory Department is accommodated in a building opened in 2001.

Charitable status. Aldwickbury School Trust Ltd is a Registered Charity, number 311059. It exists to provide education for children.

All Hallows School

Cranmore Hall, Shepton Mallet, Somerset BA4 4SF
Tel: 01749 881600
Fax: 01749 880709
email: info@allhallowsschool.co.uk
website: www.allhallowsschool.co.uk
Twitter: @Allhallowsnews

Interim Headmaster: **Mr Trevor Richards**
Headmistress from April 2015: Ms Annie Lee, BA, PGCE, MA

Age Range. 3–13 Co-educational.
Number of Pupils. 284: 134 Boys, 150 Girls.
Fees per term (2014–2015). Boarding £6,850, Day £4,630 (over 7), £2,460 (under 7). There are no compulsory extras.

The all-round personal development of children has long been at the heart of the vision and ethos at All Hallows. The school passionately promotes an individualised and holistic approach to learning that seeks to inspire each child to fulfil their potential. The dedicated and experienced team at All Hallows works in partnership with parents to truly prepare children for the ever changing world they are growing up in and for the lives they will lead, nurturing and encouraging them to live responsibly and compassionately and to embrace with energy and enthusiasm the fantastic opportunities that lie ahead.

All Hallows pioneered Catholic boarding co-education for preparatory school age children and the school continues to be very innovative and quite distinct being rated '*Excellent*' in all areas by ISI in 2014, '*Outstanding*' in all categories by Ofsted in 2009, and in 2010 for Boarding and pastoral care – the latter finding no recommendations for improvement. In their latest report ISI recognised the school in all areas as "*of exceptionally high quality*" noting that "*children are exceptionally well cared for*".

Christian principles are integrated into daily life so that all faiths are welcomed into the life of this Roman Catholic foundation. Professionally qualified, energetic and family-orientated staff, many of whom reside in the school, provide for the academic and pastoral welfare of the children.

The school has a happy and deliberate mix of boarders and day pupils. Attractive flexibility exists between boarding and day arrangements. There is an extensive and innovative Activities Programme for all children each evening after school, with weekend and holiday highlights as well as an innovative Saturday enrichment programme for years 6, 7 and 8 comprising an ever broader range of extra-curricular activities.

The school enjoys regional and national sporting success in rugby, hockey, cricket, tennis, trampolining and athletics, as well as regular competitive fixtures for children of all abilities against local opposition in the traditional team sports. Excellence within a framework of sport for all is our aim. Our Tennis Academy carries an LTA Clubmark for excellence and is available to every child in the school as well as siblings and parents. It also has strong links with the Tennis Performance Centre in Bath.

Music and the Arts thrive, ranging from the grace of the Chapel Choir to the creativity and performance of dance and drama. Exceptional facilities throughout the campus allow the children and staff to discover talent and develop potential. A new state-of-the-art Creative Centre opened in 2014 offering the children fantastic design facilities including 2D and 3D design packages, 3D printing, laser cutting, animation, digital photography and fantastic 'making' opportunities. All Hallows also enjoys Forest School status, this fresh learning approach brings immense benefits and the outdoor environs are an integral part of the curriculum at the school, helping to foster the skills and wider perspective that truly encourage innovation, risk-judging and positive risk-taking, self-belief, ambition and a genuine sense of optimism.

All Hallows' independent status from any one particular senior school enables parents and the Head to select the most appropriate senior school to suit a particular child's needs and talents. In the last few years we have sent pupils to over forty different schools. In 2014 60% of the leavers gained an Award to their Senior School. We offer a range of scholarships and bursaries.

Charitable status. All Hallows is a Registered Charity, number 310281. The school is a Charitable Trust, the raison d'être of which is the integration of Christian principles with daily life.

Alleyn Court Preparatory School

Wakering Road, Southend-on-Sea, Essex SS3 0PW
Tel: 01702 582553
Fax: 01702 584574
email: office@alleyn-court.co.uk
           admissions@alleyn-court.co.uk
           head@alleyn-court.co.uk
website: www.alleyn-court.co.uk
Twitter: @AlleynCourt; @AlleynCourtPE

Headmaster: **Mr G R A Davies**, BA Hons, PGCE, MEd

Age Range. 2½–11.
Number of Pupils. 312 Boys and Girls.
Fees per term (from April 2014). £869–£3,627 according to age.

Alleyn Court was founded in 1904 by Theodore Wilcox and is a non-selective, family-owned, co-educational day school, for children aged 2½–11. The school is situated in beautiful grounds within the Thorpe Bay area of Southend and has an excellent reputation for its breadth of curriculum, academic achievement, sporting success, art, music, French and general all-round pastoral care. A happy and relaxed atmosphere, family ethos and strong sense of community underpin the purposeful approach to school life and activities.

The school is split into three sections: two parallel Pre-Preparatory departments, located on the main school site in Thorpe Bay and on the original school site in Westcliff, offer an education based on Montessori principles for children aged 2½–5 years in the EYFS. The Junior School offers class-based teaching and a solid academic grounding for Years 1–3 and the Senior School offers largely subject specialist teaching and preparation for entrance exams and 11+ to Years 4–6. All year groups have parallel classes, which rarely rise above 20 children. Children are accepted for entry into any year group, providing that spaces are available.

Children are prepared for 11+ entry to the local selective grammar schools and for senior independent schools, with some successfully gaining scholarships. French is taught from age 4, with specialist teaching for Art, French, Music and PE from Year 1 upwards. All lessons in Years 5 and 6 are taught by subject specialists in dedicated subject rooms.

Academic facilities on the main school site include a library, fully-equipped science laboratory, music department, modern computer suite and network with 21 workstations, an additional support unit (ASU) and an art and design technology studio. Part of the school site has recently been developed to create a Woodland School and outdoor classroom to offer more practical and skill-based learning. A lifeskills programme also encourages and develops study skills, critical and lateral thinking, problem-solving and philosophy for children. Independent learning is widely encouraged and children also use iPads for research projects and learning enrichment.

The school offers extensive provision for sport and extra-curricular activities, with a variety of clubs being offered whenever children aren't in the classroom – these occur and are well attended before and after school, as well as during morning and lunch breaks. The school offers the following sports: athletics, badminton, basketball, cricket, cross-country, dodgeball, football, gymnastics, hockey, orienteering, rounders, rugby and table tennis.

Sports facilities include: large, picturesque, on-site playing fields, sports hall, cricket nets, refurbished netball and tennis courts, a woodland cross-country course and a smart pavilion with changing rooms, kitchen and function room.

The performing arts are also well provided for with a dedicated music block which houses a classroom and music practice rooms. Additionally, an indoor and outdoor stage provide space for drama and LAMDA activities, where children prepare for productions, exams and local festivals and competitions.

Non-sporting clubs include: art, ballet, chess, debating, drama, DT, French, G&T core subjects, IT, jewellery, karate, VR.

Scholarships and means-tested bursaries are available annually for pupils with academic, sporting, musical, dramatic or artistic talent.

Alleyn's Junior School

Townley Road, Dulwich, London SE22 8SU
Tel: 020 8557 1519
Fax: 020 8693 3597
email: juniorschool@alleyns.org.uk
website: www.alleyns.org.uk

Chairman of Governors: Prof the Lord Kakkar, BSc, PhD, FRCS

Acting Head: **Mrs Alison Wright**, BSc Hons, PGCE, MA

Age Range. 4–11.
Number of Pupils. 241 boys and girls.
Fees per term (2014–2015). Reception to Year 2 £4,713; Years 3–6 £4,911 including lunches, out of school visits and one residential trip per year for Years 3–6.

The school is part of the foundation known as 'Alleyn's College of God's Gift' which was founded by Edward Alleyn, the Elizabethan actor, in 1619.

Opened in 1992 to provide a co-educational Junior School for Alleyn's School and sharing the same excellent green site, Alleyn's Junior School provides a happy and lively environment in which well-motivated boys and girls follow a broad and academic education. Boys and girls work together with their teachers in a calm and structured way to develop their potential and self-confidence as they pursue the highest standards across a curriculum which embraces many opportunities for art, MFL, drama, music, ICT and a wide range of sports. Entry to the school is at 4+, 7+ and 9+. The overwhelming majority of children move on to Alleyn's senior school at 11+.

Within small classes and with a balance of class and specialist subject teaching, children are set clear and challenging targets for their learning. Children perform at above average level in KS1 and KS2 tests. The school enjoys a strong extra-curricular life offering children varied and exciting opportunities to extend their learning beyond the classroom.

Progress is carefully monitored and individual differences appropriately met. Competition has its place in the encouragement of the highest academic, artistic and sporting standards, but it is always tempered by an emphasis on values of thoughtfulness, courtesy and tolerance. All members of the school community are expected to maintain high standards in their behaviour, manners and appearance, showing pride in themselves and their school.

The school enjoys excellent support from its parent body. Regular meetings and reports keep parents informed of academic progress and pastoral matters and The Alleyn's Junior School Association works tirelessly to promote social cohesion within the school and to support the charity, sporting, dramatic and extra-curricular programmes. It also organises an After School Care scheme through which children can be supervised at school each day during term time until 6 pm.

Charitable status. Alleyn's College of God's Gift is a Registered Charity, number 1057971. Its purpose is to provide independent education for boys and girls.

Alpha Preparatory School

Hindes Road, Harrow, Middlesex HA1 1SH
Tel: 020 8427 1471
Fax: 020 8424 9324
email: sec@alpha.harrow.sch.uk
website: www.alpha.harrow.sch.uk

Chairman of the Board of Governors: Mr I Nunn

Headmaster: **C J W Trinidad**, BSc Hons, PGCE

Age Range. 3–11.
Number of Pupils. 200 boys and girls (day only).
Fees per term (2014–2015). Inclusive of lunch, with no compulsory extras: Nursery £1,050–£2,140; Pre-Preparatory £2,980; Main school £3,300.

The School, situated in a residential area of Harrow, was founded in 1895, and in 1950 was reorganised as a non-profit-making Educational Charity, with a Board of Governors elected by members of the Company; parents of pupils in the School are eligible for membership.

The majority of children enter the Main School at the age of 4 by interview and assessment but there can also be a few vacancies for older pupils and here entry is by interview and/or written tests, dependent upon age.

There is a full-time staff of 16 experienced and qualified teachers, with additional part-time teachers in instrumental Music. The main games are Football and Cricket, with cross-country, athletics, tennis and netball. Extra-curricular activities include Piano and Violin instruction.

Religious education, which is considered important, is non-sectarian in nature, but follows upon the School's Christian foundation and tradition; children of all faiths are accepted.

Outside visits to theatres, concerts and museums form an integral part of the curriculum and during the Lent Term pupils in Year 6 visit the Isle of Wight.

Regular successes are obtained in Entrance and Scholarship examinations, with many Scholarships having been won in recent years.

The School has its own Nursery (Alphabets) for children aged 3 in the term of entry. Further details can be obtained from the Registration Secretary.

Charitable status. Alpha Preparatory School is a Registered Charity, number 312640. It exists to carry on the undertaking of a boys and/or girls preparatory school in Harrow in the County of Middlesex.

Altrincham Preparatory School

Marlborough Road, Bowdon, Altrincham, Cheshire WA14 2RR
Tel: 0161 928 3366
email: admin@altprep.co.uk
website: www.altprep.co.uk

Headmaster: **Mr A C Potts**, BSc

Age Range. 3–11.
Number in School. 320 Day Boys.
Fees per term (2014–2015). £1,871–£2,538. Altrincham Preparatory School has been well known in the Manchester area for over 75 years and has, throughout its history, held a reputation for excellent academic, music and sporting achievements as well as personal development. The school offers a broad education with its academic programme dovetailing with the entrance examination requirements for the selective grammar schools locally, particularly The Manchester and Altrincham Grammar Schools, as well as other maintained and independent schools nationally.

The school enjoys enviable examination success whilst, at the same time, maintaining a strong curriculum emphasis on sport, music, languages, information technology and art & design technology. The school was described as outstanding in the last ISI Report (January 2010), with the inspectors praising the school for the exceptional progress the boys make in their learning. Specific comment was made on the excellence of the teaching, the breadth of opportunity and the extensive involvement of all pupils.

Since the 2010 inspection, facilities have been updated and improved. In 2010–11 the school secured the Bowdon Cricket, Hockey and Squash club's sports facilities as their home ground so that the boys have access to a state-of-the-art all-weather surface, a minor counties cricket square and a large grass playing area. A property, with accompanying extensive recreational land, adjacent to the school's infant site was purchased in 2012. The building has been completely refurbished to create an EYFS centre with conference and training facilities whilst the additional land significantly enhances the school's outdoor provision.

The space released by the EYFS development means that the school shall, in 2014/15, develop its junior and infant sections to provide better facilities for the two libraries and the teaching of science, music, art and ICT.

Amesbury

Hazel Grove, Hindhead, Surrey GU26 6BL
Tel: 01428 604322
email: l.wright@amesburyschool.co.uk
website: www.amesburyschool.co.uk

Chairman of the Governors: Tarquin Henderson

Headmaster: **Nigel Taylor**, MA

Age Range. 2–13.
Number of Pupils. School roll is limited to 325 by Waverley Borough Council.
Fees per term (2014–2015). Prep School: £4,265–£4,625; Pre-Prep: £3,020; Early Years (Pre-Nursery to Reception): from £28.75 per session.

Amesbury is a co-educational day school founded in 1870 and is the only co-educational Prep school in the Hindhead/Haslemere area. The main building is unique, as the only school to be designed by Sir Edwin Lutyens, and stands in its own 34-acre estate in the heart of the Surrey countryside.

We are a family school, keen for siblings to study together and to feel equally valued irrespective of their aptitudes and abilities. There is no competitive entry. Entry is based on registration plus a visit – not a formal assessment but the opportunity for child and school to get acquainted.

Classes are small guaranteeing individual attention. Study programmes currently lead to Common Entrance or senior school scholarship examinations at 11+ and at 13+. We have a proud tradition of academic, sporting and artistic achievement. The school has excellent purpose-built facilities with a new Visual Arts Facility planned for completion in 2015.

We pride ourselves on sending children to the best senior schools in the country at both 11+ and 13+. Amesbury's academic record is excellent with an average of 20% of pupils receiving senior school scholarships. "Many a school may claim to be 'academically rigorous'. Not all would also make such a virtue out of also being 'relaxed' …this one does." (Good Schools Guide 2013).

In addition to a compelling academic record, Amesbury has a thriving Performing Arts Department: "Music embraces everything from formal chapel choir to semi-secret bands formed each year, strutting stuff at annual concert. There's plentiful dance and drama including ambitious takes on Shakespeare" (Good Schools Guide 2013). As for sport, the site is 34 acres, with an all-weather astro, indoor sports hall and an all-school tennis programme. Our Extra Curricular programme runs a whole host of activities including Mandarin Chinese, Judo, Golf, Chess, Music Technology, Drama and many more.

Amesbury understands its role as part of your family life. We believe weekends should be your time; there is no Saturday school. Prep can be done at school and our Pre-Nursery and Nursery operate 47 weeks of the year with early morning drop-off and evening pick-ups. Breakfast Club and After School Care are on offer.

Open Mornings take place in October, February and May.

Charitable status. Amesbury School is a Registered Charity, number 312058. It exists to provide education for boys and girls. It is administered by a Board of Governors.

Ardingly College Prep & Pre-Prep Schools
A Woodard School

Haywards Heath, West Sussex RH17 6SQ
Tel: 01444 893200 (Prep)
01444 893300 (Pre-Prep)
email: registrar@ardingly.com
website: www.ardingly.com

Chairman of School Council: Mr J Sloane, BSc

Headmaster: **Mr C B Calvey**, BEd Hons

Deputy Head: Mr J Castle, BEd

Head of Pre-Prep: Mrs H Nawrocka, MSc, PGCE

Age Range. Pre-Prep 2–7, Prep 7–13.
Number of Pupils. Pre-Prep 120, Prep 265.
Fees per term (2014–15). Day Pupils: Nursery & Pre-Nursery: £2,630 (5 full days), £2,015 (5 half days); Additional sessions: £21.10–£36.50 per session or £47.55 per full day; Reception, Years 1 & 2: £2,630; Years 3–4 £3,775, Years 5–6 £4,630, Years 7–8 £4,745, including meals. Weekly Boarding (in addition to Day Fees): £220–£1,100 (1–5 nights). Casual boarding: £30 per night.

Ardingly College Prep School is the Preparatory School for Ardingly College Senior School (*see entry in HMC section*).

Ardingly College Prep School is set within 250 acres of glorious Sussex countryside, which it shares with the Senior School and Pre-Prep. The School is co-educational and has over 360 pupils from Pre-Nursery to Year 8 (ages 2–13). The Prep School benefits from the College's Chapel, Music School, Dining Hall, Gymnasium, Sports Hall, Indoor Swimming Pool, Astro Pitch, Medical Centre and School Shop. The Prep School has recently moved into a refurbished teaching block which provides bright and modern classrooms in a building which has retained its original character. Girls and boys are admitted into the Pre-Prep from the age of 2, and into the Prep School from the age of 7. The Prep School offers weekly boarding to children from Year 3 with pupils taking an option of anything from one to five nights a week. There is an extensive after-school care provision which includes activities that run until 7 pm for all pupils.

The extra-curricular activities include Riding, Drama Club, Fencing, Lego Club, Dance, Swimming Clubs, Orchestra, Jazz Club, Greek Club, as well as numerous Sports Clubs.

Children are prepared for Common Entrance in the core subjects, but follow our own Humanities curriculum which links with the programmes of study in the Senior School.

Girls play hockey, netball and rounders. Boys play football, hockey and cricket. In the summer both girls and boys enjoy athletics, cross country and swimming.

Religious Education is in accordance with the teaching of the Church of England.

Details of Scholarships available may be obtained from the Registrar.

The Farmhouse Pre-Prep provides children with the perfect introduction to their education. Safely yet idyllically situated within the College estate, our Pre-Preparatory is housed within carefully restored Grade 2 listed Victorian farm buildings. We have full use of the College facilities, including the swimming pool, sports hall, playing fields, chapel and full medical on-site care. The school grounds provide us with a wealth of resources for many different purposes including Forest School.

We aim to lay the basic foundations – academic, social, physical and spiritual – upon which every child can build a sound education, all within a vibrant, caring and yet challenging atmosphere.

The Farmhouse caters for children from 2 to 3 years in our Pre-Nursery, 3 to 4 years in our Nursery and from 4 to 7 in the Pre-Preparatory classes. The Pre-Preparatory children are taught in classes of about 16 pupils, whilst the Nursery may cater for up to 25 children (full day available).

The Farmhouse has its own highly qualified staff and access to a range of specialist staff. French is taught from the age of 4 years and a wide variety of sport is included in the curriculum.

After-school activities include Hockey, Ballet, Football, Zumba, Chess, Tennis, Modern & Tap dance, ArdinGlee and Lego Clubs.

Our school is run from Monday to Friday. There are no boarding facilities at this age but a Before-School (from 8 am) and After-School (to 6 pm) Care service is available.

Charitable status. Ardingly College Limited is a Registered Charity, number 1076456. It exists to provide high quality education for boys and girls aged 2–18 in a Christian context.

Ardvreck

Crieff, Perthshire PH7 4EX
Tel: 01764 653112
Fax: 01764 654920
email: office@ardvreck.org.uk
           admissions@ardvreck.org.uk
website: www.ardvreckschool.co.uk
Twitter: @ArdvreckSchool
Facebook: /Ardvreck-School

Chairman of the Governors: A K Miller

Headmaster: **Richard Harvey**, MTh, PGCE

Age Range. Co-educational 3–13.

Number of Pupils. Main School: 80 Boarders, 40 day. Little Ardvreck 15.

Fees per term (2014–2015). Main School: £6,500 (boarders), £4,325 (day); Little Ardvreck £2,025.

Admission is by a meeting with the Headmaster and an overnight or day 'taster'. Financial assistance is available. Means-tested bursaries.

Ardvreck stands in extensive grounds on the edge of Crieff, having been purpose built and founded in 1883. The School has a long tradition of providing academic excellence as well as outstanding achievement in sport and music. There are 17 full-time and 3 part-time members of the teaching staff and classes are no larger than 16. Health and domestic arrangements are under the personal supervision of the Head of Pastoral Care who is assisted by four full-time Matrons (two resident) and one qualified school Nurse.

The School Doctor visits regularly and dental and orthodontic treatment can be arranged if necessary.

Boys and girls are prepared for senior schools throughout Britain. In recent years, all have passed the Common Entrance to their schools of first choice both North and South of the border and over 35 scholarships have been awarded in the past four years.

Rugby, Netball, Hockey, Cricket, Rounders and Athletics are the main games and on several Saturdays in the summer, pupils are provided with picnic lunches enabling them to explore the surrounding countryside, accompanied by members of staff, where they can study the wildlife, fish in one of the rivers or lochs, climb, sail or canoe. Other activities include Golf, Riding, Tennis, mountain biking and Shooting, a sport for which the School has a national reputation for excellence having won the UK Prep Schools Championship for the last fifteen years. Outdoor Pursuits are a regular fixture on the Ardvreck calendar with a range of activities on offer from munro bagging and mountain biking on offer.

A modern and well-equipped Music School provides the best possible opportunities for music-making. There is an orchestra and choir both of which regularly achieve distinction at music festivals. Visiting music specialists teach a wide range of instruments including the bagpipes. Music and Drama play an important part in the life of the School and a major production is staged annually with several smaller productions and numerous concerts taking place throughout the year. Ardvreck boasts the largest prep school pipe band in Scotland.

There is a heated, indoor swimming pool (all children are taught to swim), an Astroturf surface for hockey, tennis and netball, and a superb sports hall.

Most full-time staff live within the School grounds and a special feature of Ardvreck is that there are three houses – one for the Juniors, one for the senior girls and one for the senior boys. The senior houses are where pupils gain a little more independence and are encouraged to show greater personal responsibility in readiness for the transition to senior schools.

Many boarders live overseas (forces and expat) and they are escorted to and from Scottish Airports; all necessary documentation can be handled by the School if required. Overseas pupils are required to have a guardian in the UK with whom they can stay during exeats.

Charitable status. Ardvreck School is a Registered Charity, number SC009886. Its aim is to provide education for boys and girls.

Arnold House School

1 Loudoun Road, St John's Wood, London NW8 0LH
Tel: 020 7266 4840
email: office@arnoldhouse.co.uk
website: www.arnoldhouse.co.uk

Chairman of the Board of Governors: B O'Brien Esq

Headmaster: **V W P Thomas**, BEd, MA

Age Range. 5–13.
Number of Boys. 260 (Day Boys only).
Fees per term (2014–2015). £5,650 including Lunch.
Arnold House is an independent day school for boys founded in 1905.

Most boys join the school after their fifth birthday. A few join at other ages.

The Arnold House website gives full details of recent developments in the school's curriculum and facilities. These include the complete refurbishment and extension of the main teaching facilities at Loudoun Road. At the school's 7 acres of playing fields at Canons Park, Edgware, the existing pavilion hall has been adapted to become an auditorium seating 150 with a fully-equipped stage and associated facilities. The Canons Park Activity Centre has become an important addition to the excellent facilities at Loudoun Road.

Boys transfer to their chosen independent senior schools at the age of 13. Arnold House has an enviable record of success in placing each boy in the school that is right for him. More than half of the boys move on to the most sought-after London day schools: City of London, Highgate, Mill Hill, St Paul's, UCS and Westminster. Others transfer to renowned boarding schools: Bradfield, Charterhouse, Eton, Harrow, Marlborough, Rugby and Winchester have been popular destinations in recent years. Arnold House takes a long view of a boy's education. Academic breadth, a balance between study, sport, music, the arts and activities together with excellent pastoral care constitute the foundations of the school's philosophy and success.

Charitable status. Arnold House School is a Registered Charity, number 312725. It exists to provide education for boys in preparation for transfer to senior independent schools at 13.

Ashdell Preparatory School

266 Fulwood Road, Sheffield S10 3BL
Tel: 0114 266 3835
email: office@ashdellprep.co.uk
website: www.ashdellprep.co.uk
Twitter: #ashdellprep

Girls Day Preparatory.

Chairman of Council of Management: Ian Walker

Headmistress: **Mrs A B Camm**, BEd

Deputy Head: Mrs R Leslie, MA, BA Hons QTS

Age Range. 4–11 years.
Number of Pupils. 122 (including boys and girls in pre-school).
Fees per term (2014–2015). £3,105–£3,320.
At Ashdell we take great pride in maintaining our traditions but eagerly embrace modern life. Our classrooms are fitted with interactive whiteboards; the girls use laptops, pcs and iPads on a daily basis, encouraging our girls to grow to meet the challenges of the 21st Century. Traditions like our

smart uniform create a sense of belonging and pride amongst our girls. Ashdell recognizes that every girl is unique and has different needs and expectations and because of this girls are allowed to develop at their own pace. We provide a rich curriculum where Music, Art, Sport and Humanities are nurtured and given full weighting with Maths, English and Science. Ashdell has an excellent reputation for academic success and for providing its pupils with a friendly, caring environment in which to flourish. We aim to develop each girls unique potential and are able to achieve this through small class sizes (average 14) and our careful attention to the basics. The school maintains a high pupil : teacher ratio and the cosy atmosphere ensures that all children are well known and individual needs are catered for. We have programmes to support learning and to develop the talented or gifted child. Girls are prepared for entrance examinations to Independent Senior Schools at the age of 11. Girls study a broad range of subjects including English, Mathematics, Science, French, Spanish, ICT, Music, Swimming, Tennis, Drama, PE, Ballet, Judo, Cookery and Woodwork. The School has an excellent music programme with a choir, orchestra, flute and clarinet choir, string group and brass group. Individual lessons are offered in a variety of instruments and there are many opportunities for pupils to perform. The Prep School boasts excellent ICT, music and practice rooms, a science lab, art room and large gym. A rich Physical Education programme makes good use of local university sports facilities for swimming, netball, hockey and tennis. We recognize that the working day of a parent is longer than their daughter's school day, so even when the bell has gone, the learning goes on with an extensive range of after-school clubs to further the enrichment of our girls. Accommodated in a beautiful Victorian building our Pre-Preparatory Department caters for the 4–7 year olds. It has its own Art and Design Technology room, ICT facilities and a safe outdoor play area. Our Pre-School, 'Snowdrops' is for boys and girls aged 3–5. Three-course lunches are cooked in house and pupils eat lunch in family-style groupings. We offer a breakfast club which starts at 7.30 am and after-school care runs until 6.00 pm to cater for working parents. Our fee schedule reflects our all-inclusive policy but excludes individual music tuition and the many extra-curricular clubs such as gym, tennis, cookery and art.

Charitable status. Ashdell Schools Trust Limited is a Registered Charity, number 529380. It was founded for the education of girls.

Ashdown House

Forest Row, East Sussex RH18 5JY
Tel: 01342 822574
Fax: 01342 824380
email: secretary@ashdownhouse.com
website: www.ashdownhouse.co.uk

The School is part of The Cothill Educational Trust.

Headmaster: **Haydon J S Moore**, BTh Oxon, PGCE

Age Range. 4–13 Co-educational.
Number of Pupils. 125.
Fees per term (2014–2015). Boarding: £8,230 (Years 3–8); Day: £6,100 (Years 7–8), £5,570 (Years 5–6), £4,500 (Years 3–4), £2,570 (Years 1–2).
The School (mainly full boarding with most day pupils begging to board by Year 5 or 6) is a Latrobe house situated in its own grounds of 40 acres, on the edge of the Ashdown Forest. We have an indoor sports hall, theatre and music centre, new Science Block and well-equipped ICT provision. There is an indoor swimming pool, three tennis courts,

a golf course and open countryside surrounding us for field studies and adventure.

An escorted train to London and back on exeat weekends and easy access to Gatwick & Heathrow airports make us a popular choice for London parents and families living abroad.

Every child in Year 7 spends a full term in the Château de Sauveterre and there are numerous other residential trips, such as La Chaumière and the Old Malthouse, both owned by the Trust.

There are 26 full-time members of teaching staff, most of whom live within the grounds. Music of all kinds is studied under resident and peripatetic teachers and Art, DT and ICT are part of every child's curriculum. Scholarships are regularly won in all disciplines.

Games. Major sports for boys are cricket, soccer, rugby; the girls play netball and rounders, and hockey and athletics are played by both girls and boys. In addition there are huge numbers of other sporting opportunities, including swimming, tennis, riding, golf, squash, archery and cross-country.

The Headmaster and his wife, supported by houseparents, matrons and a State Registered Nurse look after all pastoral and domestic arrangements.

Charitable status. The Cothill Educational Trust is a Registered Charity, number 309639.

Ashfold School

Dorton House, Dorton, Bucks HP18 9NG
Tel: 01844 238237
Fax: 01844 238505
email: registrar@ashfoldschool.co.uk
website: www.ashfoldschool.co.uk

Chairman of Governors: Mr H Taylor

Headmaster: **M O M Chitty**, BSc

Age Range. 3–13 Co-educational.
Number of Pupils. 169 boys, 100 girls (day pupils and weekly boarders).
Fees per term (2014–2015). Weekly boarders £6,025; Day £4,815–£4,960; Pre-Prep £1,260–£3,515.

Ashfold is an independent day, weekly and flexi boarding school for boys and girls aged three to thirteen years. Set in thirty acres of beautiful grounds in rural Buckinghamshire, the School is located within easy reach of Thame, Princes Risborough, Oxford, Bicester and Aylesbury. The nearest mainline station with regular connections to London Marylebone and Birmingham is just 15 minutes away. Ashfold is a busy and vibrant place with a reputation as a friendly, family-orientated school.

Founded in 1927, Ashfold is a country prep school offering the very best in both traditional and innovative teaching. The School's extensive facilities include a purpose-built Pre-Prep Building, sports hall, full-sized astroturf and a heated outdoor pool. Plans for future investment in facilities include a new, purpose-built Art & Technology Building due for completion in 2015.

Most children join the School in the Pre-Prep Department and move on to top independent senior schools at 13+. Ashfold has a strong academic record with more than forty per cent of the Sixth Form achieving scholarships or awards to their chosen schools in recent years.

The School offers an excellent all-round education with outstanding opportunities for sport, art, music and drama as well as a wide-ranging programme of extra-curricular activities.

Pastoral care is rated 'excellent' by the Independent Schools Inspectorate (ISI) which noted that '*the strength of the natural relationships and warm atmosphere created by*

the head, deputy and staff mean that pupils thrive at Ashfold.'

Charitable status. Ashfold School Trust is a Registered Charity, number 272663. It exists to provide a quality preparatory school education, academically and in other respects, for all the children entrusted to its care.

Ashford Prep School
United Learning

Great Chart, Ashford, Kent TN23 3DJ
Tel: 01233 620493
Fax: 01233 636579
email: ashfordprepschool@ashfordschool.co.uk
website: www.ashfordschool.co.uk
Twitter: @AshfordSchool
Facebook: /ASA.AshfordSchoolAssociation

Co-educational Day School with Boarding from Year 6.

Chairman of School Council: Mr P Massey, MA

Head: **Mr R Yeates**, BA Hons

Age Range. 3–11.
Number of Pupils. 326: 175 Boys, 151 Girls.
Fees per term (2014–2015). Day: Nursery: £530 (one full day per week), £2,650 (full-time); Reception £2,600, Years 1 and 2 £2,850, Years 3–6 £4,150.

Ashford Prep School is part of United Learning and as such has benefited from significant recent investment, including extensive refurbishment and new facilities. The school believes in the importance of focusing on the development of the individual through a broad education in which every child can find success whilst developing confidence, motivation, self-esteem and emotional intelligence.

A focus on pastoral care and the pursuit of excellence go together with high standards of discipline and a strong Christian ethos.

Situated in a rural setting, Ashford Prep School lies in some 25 very attractive acres. The School enjoys both classroom-based and excellent specialist teaching with well-designed facilities for science, art, music, PE, ICT and design technology and has recently undergone a large investment development. These new buildings provide 18 new classrooms, new kitchens, reception area, library facilities and a new hall. The School is fully networked and has exceptional provision for ICT with ACTIVboards in all classrooms, a computer room capable of accommodating entire classes and broadband access to the Internet throughout.

The thriving Nursery operates on a flexible basis and the school offers full, wrap-around care from 7.30 am to 6.00 pm for all our children. The school operates Mondays to Fridays. Holiday Clubs operate during school breaks.

Throughout the school, team sports include rugby, hockey, netball, football, rounders, athletics and cricket. Regular fixtures are held with other local schools. Children also participate in PE and swimming as part of their curricular programme.

An extensive range of co-curricular activities is provided, both at lunchtime and after school. Individual music tuition with a wide range of instruments is available. Music, drama, dance and public speaking are all important opportunities; productions and presentations are performed by all age groups to a high standard and take place throughout the year. The choir and orchestra meet regularly.

A programme of educational trips and visits provides a stimulating and important addition to the all-round education and development of the 'whole' child and the costs of these are included in the fees.

An inspection by the Independent Schools Inspectorate in March 2014 declared the whole school 'outstanding' or 'excellent' in every category.

Children normally progress to Ashford Senior School (*see HMC entry*) without the need to take an entrance test unless they wish to sit scholarship exams. The Prep School has had considerable success in preparing children for scholarships to leading independent schools as well as other entrance tests including the 11+.

Charitable status. Ashford Prep School is part of United Learning which comprises: UCST (a Company Limited by Guarantee, Registered in England, number 2780748, and a Registered Charity, number 1016538) and ULT (a Company Limited by Guarantee, Registered in England, number 4439859, and an Exempt Charity).

Ashville College Junior School

Green Lane, Harrogate, North Yorkshire HG2 9JP
Tel: 01423 724800
Fax: 01423 505142
email: ashville@ashville.co.uk
website: www.ashville.co.uk
Twitter: @AshvilleCollege
Facebook: /AshvilleCollegeHarrogate

Chairman of Governors: Mr P Whiteley, BSc, FCA

Headmaster: Mr S Bailey, BA

Age Range. 7–11 Co-educational.
Number of Pupils. 150.
Fees per term (2014–2015). Tuition: £2,970–£3,590. Boarding (in addition to tuition fees) £2,400 (full), £2,200 (weekly). Lunch for Day Pupils: £250.

Ashville College Junior School, located on the South side of Harrogate, has gone from strength to strength in recent years and can now legitimately claim to be one of the leading Independent Junior Schools in the North. In 2011 the ISI (Independent Schools Inspectorate) rated the Junior School "outstanding" in all areas. The majority of pupils are day pupils, however a number of pupils board in a thriving, newly refurbished co-educational boarding house.

Academically, children are taught in form groups of no more than 22 pupils and additional learning support is available for those who need it. Pupils have excellent attitudes towards learning and are proud of their achievements. Academic standards are high and the most able children are well catered for through an excellent Gifted & Talented programme. Consequently, national test results are well above average.

Sporting facilities are outstanding, with all children using the full size swimming pool weekly for lessons. Recently in competitive sport the school has had some notable successes. In Rugby, the U11 boys recently won the Westville Festival and Lyndhurst Invitational Sevens. In Cricket, the U11 team reached the National Finals, the U10 Netball were runners up in the HMC North East Tournament and the Swimming team are ranked 8th nationally.

Music is a strong feature of the school. There are two choirs, an orchestra, and over 100 children taking individual exams. Concerts are performed throughout the year. Drama also features, with an annual full-scale production in addition to individual speech and drama lessons for children working towards their LAMDA exams.

There are over fifty extra-curricular clubs and activities available to the children to ensure that pupils find their niche, whatever it may be. Ashville College Junior School Pupils are confident and caring with a purposeful approach to school life.

Charitable status. Ashville College is a Registered Charity, number 529577.

Ashville College Pre-Prep School

Green Lane, Harrogate, North Yorkshire HG2 9JP
Tel: 01423 724815
Fax: 01423 505142
email: ashville@ashville.co.uk
website: www.ashville.co.uk
Twitter: @AshvilleCollege
Facebook: /AshvilleCollegeHarrogate

Chairman of Governors: Mr P Whiteley, BSc, FCA

Headteacher: Mrs C Berrie, BEd Hull

Age Range. 4–7 (Reception to Year 2) Co-educational.
Number of Pupils. 100.
Fees per term (2014–2015). Tuition: £2,475. Lunch: £225.

Ashville Pre-Prep School is part of Ashville College. It is a warm and friendly school which focuses on the individual child, with class sizes of no more than sixteen in Reception and eighteen in Year 2. The school is housed in a modern, purpose-built building which benefits from a library, a spacious school hall, a baking and technology area and a well equipped playground and garden. The children also have access to the facilities of the Senior School; for example all children partake in weekly swimming lessons in the College pool, and also have use of the Sports Hall where the children in Year 2 have their Games lesson. These children also benefit from the expertise of a tennis coach who comes in to teach them on a weekly basis. The extra-curricular opportunities are outstanding; during the school day children all participate in a dance lesson and many also have Speech and Drama lessons; they are encouraged to play a musical instrument and many learn the violin or cello and have piano lessons, whilst all the children in Year 2 learn to play the recorder. Spanish is also taught throughout the Pre-Prep School. After-school activities include ballet, tap, street dancing, ICT and judo and the Pre-Prep School also has its own Rainbow pack.

Learning to read and all aspects of Literacy are a priority in the Pre-Prep School and attainment in reading is high. A love of books is fostered from the very beginning and consequently the children's enthusiasm for reading and their thirst for knowledge permeate the rest of the curriculum. They read aloud willingly and confidently and are keen to participate in class and school assemblies and concerts. These skills acquired at such an early age equip the children to move through the school with confidence.

The small class sizes enable the teachers to differentiate in numeracy also, ensuring all children are challenged and reaching their full potential. There are dedicated teachers in charge of all the foundation subjects, which are taught around topic work. This creative curriculum is organised on a three year cycle so that the topics are always new and exciting, indeed they are inspirational In addition specialist teachers from Senior School also contribute to the curriculum programme, particularly with MFL, PE, music and RE.

The children display good relationships with each other and also with their teachers. This enables them to ask for assistance and explore new ideas confidently. Motivation is high in lessons; they are keen to answer questions and share their ideas, which mean they make considerable progress. Learning is promoted by the children's willingness, eagerness and enthusiasm to cooperate and focus on their work.

The Pre-Prep provides children with the best start in life, offering a safe environment where they are encouraged to enjoy all aspects of life, from helping in the garden, to learning Spanish, to taking part in the annual school play. In addition there is a wide range of trips which link with their topic work, an annual highlight being the Year Two trip in the summer term, which last year took the children to Edinburgh; the previous year the children had travelled to London. Children leave with a strong sense of community and respect, which enables them to move on to Junior School as happy confident children who have enjoyed a rich and varied programme in their early years of schooling.

Charitable status. Ashville College is a Registered Charity, number 529577.

Austin Friars St Monica's Junior School

Etterby Scaur, Carlisle, Cumbria CA3 9PB
Tel: 01228 528042
Fax: 01228 810327
email: office@austinfriars.cumbria.sch.uk
            admissions@austinfriars.cumbria.sch.uk
website: www.austinfriars.cumbria.sch.uk
Twitter: @AFSMSchool

Chairman of Trustees: Revd Dr Peter Tiplady, MB BS, MRCGP, FFPHM, FRIPH

Headmaster: Mr M F Harris, BSc, PGCE

Head of Junior School: Mr J Slingsby

Age Range. 3–11.
Number of Pupils. Junior School: 132; Pre-School: 28.
Fees per term (2014–2015). Junior School: £2,034 (R–Year 2), £2,359 (Years 3–4), £2,760 (Years 5–6). Pre-School: £5.30 per hour, plus £1.75 for lunch.

Austin Friars St Monica's Junior School offers a wide and varied curriculum, which encourages academic achievement alongside sporting, musical, cultural and creative development, thus allowing each child's talents and potential to be fully pursued.

The importance of good primary education cannot be over emphasised and the Junior School commits itself to this purpose.

The teaching staff form a capable and highly motivated team totally dedicated to the aims and ethos of the School.

Pupils benefit from specialist teaching in subjects such as ICT, music, drama, modern languages and sports and games. Learning support is an integral part of the curriculum for those who will benefit.

Academically, the school has a fine reputation within the City of Carlisle and beyond, with a record of many scholarship successes at age 11.

Music, speech and drama have a high profile.

Annually Junior 1 (Year 3) pupils are given a musical instrument to learn and enjoy specialist tuition.

Juniors take LAMDA Verse and Prose Speaking Examination achieving consistently high grades.

Good use is made of the extensive grounds surrounding the school, including Astroturf, providing ample scope for PE lessons as well as hosting matches against local school teams.

A wide range of extra-curricular activities is offered from 4.00–6.00 pm, including history, chess, hockey, art, science, computing, young engineers, French, football and netball.

Due to the expansion of pupil numbers, a £3.1 million state-of-the-art Junior School was completed in February 2008.

The Junior School is an Ofsted registered provider of Free Nursery Education Entitlement for three and four year olds. Reception follows the Early Years Foundation Stage curriculum.

The Early Years Foundation Stage Pre-School occupies a spacious detached two-storey house, adjacent to the main School.

Set within its own grounds and bordered by a mature garden, the Pre-School provides pupils with excellent facilities, including an interesting garden bordered by mature trees and all-weather safe play area. The secure building and grounds offer parents an opportunity to educate children within a natural and comfortable setting.

The main aim of the Pre-School is to provide a caring and stimulating environment, endowing children with a positive attitude to learning which will serve them through their formative years. The Early Years Foundation Stage curriculum covers the six areas of learning. Through carefully-structured and well-planned, play-based activities pupils are encouraged to develop their own ideas and to learn sound spiritual and social values by being cooperative and aware of others. Pre-School pupils are taught to listen carefully, to make friends, share, take turns and be polite and to use good manners.

Admission. Children are admitted into the Pre-School in the three to four age range. 24 places are available per session.

Entry into the Junior School at all levels, except Kindergarten, is by formal assessment of English, mathematics and non-verbal reasoning; prospective pupils spend a taster day in School. All prospective pupils are screened for specific learning difficulties. Entry into Kindergarten is by interview and a taster afternoon.

Senior School. *For information about Austin Friars St Monica's Senior School, see entry in The Society of Heads section.*

Charitable status. Austin Friars St Monica's School is a Registered Charity, number 516289.

Avenue House School

70 The Avenue, Ealing, London W13 8LS
Tel: 020 8998 9981
Fax: 020 8991 1533
email: school@avenuehouse.org
website: www.avenuehouse.org

Co-educational Day School.

Proprietor: Mr David Immanuel

Headteacher: Mr Justin Sheppard, BA Hons, PGCE

Age Range. 3–11.
Number of Pupils. 140.
Fees per term (2014–2015). £1,920–£3,400.

Avenue House School provides a small, caring environment where children gain the confidence to flourish in all areas of the curriculum. Good manners, mutual respect and a caring community are prevalent at all times.

Children are taught in small classes conducive to the development of an excellent work ethos and achieve high standards in academic subjects as well as an appreciation and understanding of Drama, Art, Music and Sport.

Avenue House School does not test children on entry to Reception as we feel that each child develops at their own individual rate. All pupils are monitored and assessed individually throughout the year and meetings between parents and school are frequent as we believe a positive approach leads to excellence.

Children have access to our own small library and small hall for the younger children. The school has laptop computers with wireless broadband internet connection and whiteboards are installed throughout.

Pupils are prepared for the competitive entrance examinations to the London Independent Day Schools.

Avenue House School is proud of the many high standard musical and drama productions that are performed throughout the year from Nursery children to Year 6.

Physical Education is an important part of our curriculum and all pupils go swimming every week. Children in the Nursery, Reception and Year 1 have Physical Education in our Gymnasium and small playground. From Year 2 the children have weekly sports lessons at Trailfinders Sports and Leisure Club. The traditional annual sports day for the whole school is also held. The children are also involved in inter-House matches.

Extra curriculum activities form a valuable and key part of our education. Apart from the daily homework club other activities include football, drama, guitar, Junior & Senior choir, Junior & Senior ICT, art, ballet, Mad Science, French and gardening (Summer Term). For Years 5 & 6 we also have lunch-time clubs which include Debating, School Magazine and Mathematics Club.

Educational visits play an important role in helping children relate their class work to the real world. For this reason pupils are taken on outings each term where they can benefit from having first-hand knowledge of London and its surrounding areas. Children have the opportunity to go on residential trips which include Dorchester, France, the Isle of Wight and Black Mountain in Wales.

Avenue Nursery & Pre-Preparatory School

2 Highgate Avenue, Highgate, London N6 5RX
Tel: 020 8348 6815
Fax: 020 8348 8123
email: info@avenuenursery.com
website: www.avenuenursery.com

Joint Principals: **Mrs Mary Fysh & Mrs Sarah Tapp**

Age Range. 3–7 Co-educational.
Number of Pupils. 75.
Fees per term (2014–2015). £2,250–£4,100.

The ethos of the School is the happiness of every child through a secure, friendly and exciting environment. The provision of a wide and different extra-curricular programme of activities from pottery to ice skating contributes considerably towards achieving this aim. The high staff/child ratios enable children to learn and achieve in small groups thus progressing successfully throughout the curriculum. External assessments (PIPS) are introduced in the Nursery and continued through Reception, Year 1 and 2. The results are collated and provide a useful means of tracking the progress of each child: it also aids the planning and learning needs of different children. The School is non-denominational and children of all denominations or none are welcome. Children are made aware of major religious festivals including Christmas.

Pre-Nursery children enter the School when rising 3. The staff ratio is 1:6 and the children enjoy participating in many different activities designed to promote speech and language skills, hand/eye coordination and learning to interact with peers and adults. The large garden provides many opportunities for physical activities, role play and social interaction.

The Nursery takes children from the age of 3+ for five mornings a week and the staff ratio remains at 1:6. The children build on the skills they have learned in Pre-Nursery and are also introduced to letters and numbers. Pottery is added to the curriculum plus visits off site to places of interest.

The Reception Class is divided into two groups according to age. These groups are taught Literacy and Maths in groups of 9 and the work is differentiated so that each child is able to achieve at the level appropriate to them. French and trampolining are added to the curriculum. Children remain at school until 3 pm and bring a packed lunch.

The Year 1 and 2 children's respective class teacher remains with them throughout Key Stage 1 to ensure a seamless transition from Year 1 to 2 greatly benefiting the children's preparations for their future 7+ assessments. The classes follow a curriculum based on the National Curriculum but designed to enable each child to progress towards a successful outcome at 7+. Ice skating is added to the extra-curricular timetable.

Children leave the School at varying stages. Some of the girls leave at 4+ and others at 7+. Boys generally stay until 7+. We have built up good relationships with other schools in the area and as members of the IAPS (since November 2009) enjoy meeting and visiting member schools.

Aysgarth School

Bedale, North Yorkshire DL8 1TF
Tel: 01677 450240
Fax: 01677 450736
email: enquiries@aysgarthschool.co.uk
website: www.aysgarthschool.com

Chairman of Governors: J M P D Stroyan

Headmaster: **C A A Goddard**, MA Emmanuel College Cambridge

Assistant Headmaster: P J Southall, BA Hull, PGCE St Mary's Twickenham

Age Range. 3–13.
Number of Pupils. 220. Pre-Prep Department: 70 boys and girls aged 3–8. Prep School: 150 boys aged 8–13.
Fees per term (2014–2015). Boarders (full and weekly) £7,340, Day £5,640, Pre-Prep £2,190–£2,905.

The Prep School is a boarding school for boys set in 50 acres of grounds in Wensleydale about 6 miles from the A1. It attracts boys from all over the UK, and boys go on to the country's leading independent senior schools, many of them in southern England. Some boys start as day boys or weekly boarders to enable them to adjust to boarding gently. For exeats, boys are escorted on trains from Darlington to the north and south and there are coaches to and from Cumbria and Lancashire.

Boys of all abilities are welcomed and academic standards are high. All boys are prepared for Common Entrance and several gain scholarships. Before entry, each boy is assessed to ensure that any special needs are identified early and given fully integrated specialist help where necessary. Class sizes are typically around 12. There is a newly equipped computer centre and every teacher has a laptop to link to digital projectors and interactive whiteboards in most classrooms.

The activities in which boys can participate are enormously varied. The facilities include a new heated indoor swimming pool, a modern sports hall, tennis, fives and squash courts, 17 acres of excellent playing fields and a floodlit all-weather pitch. Cricket, Soccer and Rugby Football are the main school sports, and there are opportunities to participate in a wide range of other sports. Music is one of the strengths of the school with more than 75% of boys playing a musical instrument and several boys have been awarded music scholarships. There are three choirs and the school musicians have regular opportunities to perform both in the school and locally. Each term different year groups produce a play or musical. Art and Craft and Design & Technology are taught by specialist teachers.

The school has a fine Victorian chapel, and boys are encouraged to develop Christian faith and values in a positive, caring environment. Pastoral care is the first priority for all staff. The headmaster and his wife, a housemaster and his wife and three matrons, are all resident in the main building.

A wide range of exciting activities in the evenings and at weekends ensure that boys are keen to board, and they are encouraged to do so particularly in their last two years as preparation for their next schools.

The school aims to encourage boys to be well mannered and courteous with a cheerful enthusiasm for learning and for life and a determination to make the most of their abilities.

There is also a flourishing Pre-Prep Department including a Nursery for day boys and girls aged 3 to 8.

Charitable status. Aysgarth School Trust Limited is a Registered Charity, number 529538. Its purpose is to provide a high standard of boarding and day education.

Babington House School – Preparatory Department

Grange Drive, Chislehurst, Kent BR7 5ES
Tel: 020 8467 5537
Fax: 020 8295 1175
email: enquiries@babingtonhouse.com
website: www.babingtonhouse.com

Chairman of Governors: Mr C Turner

Headmaster: **Mr T Lello**, MA, PGCE, NPQH, FRSA

Head of Preparatory Department: **Mrs C Sherwood**, BA Hons, PGCE

Age Range. 3–11 Co-educational.
Number of Pupils. 233: 147 Girls, 86 Boys.
Fees per term (2014–2015). £3,774 (Reception to Year 6); £2,760 (Full-time Nursery including Early Years Funding).

At Babington House Preparatory we provide a happy, family atmosphere, where children can flourish, develop their academic potential and enjoy success in a wide range of other activities.

We believe that children learn best in a caring, friendly environment, where they feel valued as individuals and confident in themselves.

Our expectations are high, encouraging good behaviour, a strong work ethic and an awareness of the wider community. Pupils engage with each other with respect and an appreciation of diversity, following a curriculum designed to promote curiosity and stimulate a desire to learn about the world in which they live.

High-quality teaching effectively supports pupils to become creative and critical thinkers, who can employ different learning styles to improve their understanding.

We recognise that every child is unique and we greatly value the contribution they each have to make to our school. Babington House School pupils have a reputation for being articulate, enthusiastic and well-mannered.

The Preparatory Department is housed in new purpose-built accommodation linked to the Senior School, thus ensuring close liaison and smooth transition between the two. We are proud of the exciting series of developments providing facilities to enhance the impressive standards for which our pupils have become known.

At each Key Stage our pupils achieve results for above the National Standards and are well prepared for the next stage of their education.

Charitable status. Babington House School is a Registered Charity, number 307914.

Bablake Junior School and Pre Prep

Junior School:
Coundon Road, Coventry, West Midlands CV1 4AU
Tel: 024 7627 1260
Fax: 024 7627 1294
email: jhmsec@bablakejs.co.uk

Pre Prep:
8 Park Road, Coventry, West Midlands CV1 2LH
Tel: 024 7622 1677
Fax: 024 7623 1630
email: preprep@bablakejs.co.uk

website: www.bablakejuniorschool.co.uk

Chairman of Governors: Mr R Atkins, QC

Headmaster: **N A Price**, BA Hons, PGCE

Age Range. 3–11.
Number of Pupils. 330 Day Pupils.
Fees per term (2014–2015). £2,060-£2,580.

Bablake Junior School offers an outstanding educational experience that allows young people to thrive. Pupils enjoy coming to school and are given broad opportunities to develop and learn. They acquire skills and interests that will equip them for life and their future learning.

We are a school where children are nurtured as individuals. This helps them to achieve all that they are capable of academically, creatively and on the games field. Excellent learning support is offered to those failing to achieve their potential. Most of our pupils continue their education at Bablake until they complete their A Levels. (*See Bablake School entry in HMC section.*) Throughout the school we help our pupils make the most of their abilities and the outstanding opportunities that exist here for them.

We follow a broad and balanced curriculum – lessons are interesting and our academic results excellent. Our teachers' commitment to helping everyone achieve their potential is reflected in the support of our parents and the hard work our pupils put into their studies. All achievement – academic, creative or sporting – is recognised and celebrated. The support and respect of the community helps all children achieve their best.

Pupils receive expert coaching in a wide variety of sports and have the opportunity to take part in many activities. We believe in participation and the pursuit of excellence and all children have the opportunity to represent the school on the games field. We share the swimming pool, fields, sports hall and astroturf with our Senior School and make use of Bablake's fantastic theatre and other specialist facilities. Taking part in a wide variety of activities builds confidence and reinforces positive child development.

Children may join Bablake Pre Prep in the September after they turn 3. The Pre Prep offers a happy, homely and stimulating environment where thorough and considered preparation takes place for the challenges ahead. Admission to the Junior School is usually at age seven although children may join Bablake Junior and Pre Prep at other times if places are available. An assessment of a pupil's potential takes place before entry.

Charitable status. Coventry School Foundation is a Registered Charity, number 528961. It exists to provide education for boys and girls.

Badminton Junior School

Westbury-on-Trym, Bristol BS9 3BA
Tel: 0117 905 5271
Fax: 0117 962 3049
email: admissions@badmintonschool.co.uk
website: www.badmintonschool.co.uk

Chairman of Governors: Mrs Alison Bernays

Headmistress: **Mrs Emma Davies**, BA, PGCE

Age Range. 3–11.
Number of Girls. 132.
Fees per term (2014–2015). Day: £2,760–£3,720 inclusive of lunch and extended day. Boarding (from Year 5): £6,930–£7,290.

Educational Philosophy. Children learn best when they are interested, happy and supported in their work. Our girls thrive in a stimulating environment where high standards of work and behaviour are expected. All subjects in the Junior School are taught by enthusiastic subject specialists in classes of up to seventeen pupils. We provide a welcoming and friendly atmosphere so that all of our girls feel emotionally secure and we encourage them to develop their own particular talents and interests. Key notes in our philosophy are the development of self-confidence, a healthy respect for one another and the nurturing of inquiring and critical minds.

We believe children enjoy being kept busy and acquiring new skills and so we try to create a balance between academic work in the classroom, plenty of physical exercise, a range of extra-curricular activities and opportunities for recreational and creative play. The girls are given the opportunity to explore and develop their language skills and study French, Latin, German and Spanish whilst additional languages, such as Mandarin and Italian, are offered in afterschool clubs.

Facilities. The Junior School is well appointed with light airy classrooms, dedicated rooms for Art and Music, a Science laboratory, and an ICT suite. We have a well-stocked library and an Assembly Hall in which various activities including ballet, drama and musical concerts take place. There is a wonderful, secure adventure playground which the girls make the most of during break and lunch times.

Being on the same campus as the Senior School, the girls make use of all the facilities on site which include the 25m indoor swimming pool, gymnasium and the all-purpose sports pitch. There are excellent facilities for music, which plays an important part both inside and outside the curriculum.

With our extended day facilities we aim to provide a warm and caring environment to suit the needs of all our pupils and their parents. Every day clubs, such as gardening, chess, drama, art or playground games take place after school and girls are welcome to stay on for prep or late stay until 5:45 pm, at no additional cost

For further information on Badminton School, see entry in GSA section. A prospectus is available on request from Miss Karen Balmforth (admissions@badmintonschool. co.uk).

Charitable status. Badminton School Limited is a Registered Charity, number 311738. It exists to provide education for children.

Ballard School

Fernhill Lane, New Milton, Hampshire BH25 5SU
Tel: 01425 626900
Fax: 01425 638847

email: admissions@ballardschool.co.uk
website: www.ballardschool.co.uk

The School is a non-profit making Educational Trust under a Board of Governors. It is a co-educational school through to GCSE level and provides a family friendly all-round education. The school is non-selective and boasts a strong examination success record which enables students to achieve their first choice of school for the next stage of their education.

Chairman of the Board of Governors: Mr C Ford

Headmaster: **Mr Alastair J Reid**, MA Cantab, PGCE, NPQH

Age Range. 18 months 16 Co-educational.
Number of Children. 500 day children.
Fees per term (2014–2015). Years 9–11 £4,395, Years 6–8 £4,225, Years 3–5 £4,145. Reception–Year 2 £2,440. Fees include the cost of school lunches.

The School is situated 2 miles from the sea and on the borders of the New Forest in 32 acres of grounds and woodlands. A good network of school buses covers the surrounding area.

Ballard School is a through school divided into four integrated areas, each catering for the specific needs of the pupils at each age range. The whole school has recently received an excellent ISI inspection report.

There are over 60 qualified teaching staff plus a dedicated Learning Support Unit. Academic results are consistently excellent at all stages (7+, 11+, 13+ and GCSE) with many pupils gaining scholarships and all reaching their first choice of further education. The School offers a broad curriculum with further strengths in music, visual arts, performing arts, dance and sport. More than 60 extra-curricular activities are offered.

Facilities are excellent, including brand new International Standard Astro pitch, 5 science laboratories, large art department, 4 computer suites, 3 libraries, large music block including a recording studio, technology laboratory, dance studio, home economics laboratory, large sports hall, extensive playing fields, with tennis courts, netball courts, heated outdoor swimming pool, outdoor basketball court, and Performing Arts Centre seating audiences of 200.

The School has a Christian foundation and the aim of the School is to provide an all-round education where traditional values and standards are valued combined with facilities to prepare children for the 21st century.

Charitable status. Ballard School Ltd is a Registered Charity, number 307328. It exists for the education of children.

Bancroft's Preparatory School

High Road, Woodford Green, Essex IG8 0RF
Tel: 020 8506 6751
           020 8506 6774 (Admissions)
Fax: 020 8506 6752
email: prep.office@bancrofts.org
website: www.bancrofts.org

Chairman of the Governors: Prof P Ogden, BA, DPhil, AcSS

Head: **J P Layburn**, MA

Assistant Head: M Piper, BA
Director of Studies: N Thomas, BCom, MA

Age Range. 7–11.
Number of Pupils. 141 girls, 119 boys.
Fees per term (2014–2015). £4,085.

Bancroft's Preparatory School was established in September 1990 in the attractive grounds of Bancroft's School in Woodford Green (*see entry in HMC section*) and became a member of IAPS in 2000. Academic results are excellent and places are much sought after – the school is heavily oversubscribed with numbers of registrations rising year by year.

The Prep School has its own distinct character within the Bancroft's community and has the advantage of being able to use the excellent Senior School facilities including the sports hall, music facilities, Chapel, catering facility and hard play area. The School has recently expanded with an impressive new wing providing a further three classrooms, a performing arts studio for drama, music and dance, a science/design & technology room, a new front entrance and reception area as well as a children's adventure play area. This expansion has enabled the school to reduce its class sizes; the School now has three forms in each of its four year groups.

The school seeks to provide an education enriched by a vibrant, multicultural environment. Pastoral care is seen as key and the happiness of all the children is fundamental. Assemblies link with PSHE and focus on key values – such as treating others as you would like to be treated and going "the extra mile". The school constantly seeks to encourage children to feel part of a happy and caring community.

Regular charity work is seen as very important and through it children gain an appreciation of the advantages on offer to them and so develop a sense of compassion for the world beyond Bancroft's.

The class teacher has a central role to play and there is an emphasis on specialised teaching in the top two years, so that staff can pursue their subject passions to the benefit of the children. Academic standards are high with a broad, structured curriculum including French, Humanities, Creative Thinking, PSHE, Drama, Music, Games, Swimming, PE and Art. The Prep School wants its bright pupils to have fun and "to sparkle" while they learn so that they will derive a lifelong love of learning.

As well as establishing a strong academic base, the school is very much concerned with an holistic approach for each child – encouraging good manners, respect for others and a keen sense of humour. Children take part in a great variety of extra-curricular activities at lunch times, after school and at weekends. Older children are given the opportunity to take on responsibilities around the school – every child becomes a Monitor at some stage in their final year. The school hopes that the children will in time become successful adults who will make a difference in the 21st century.

Children are assessed for entry at the age of six/seven, visiting the school in small groups and testing by the Head and Head of Transition is friendly and low key. Once accepted, pupils have guaranteed transfer to Bancroft's Senior School (on the same site) at the age of eleven. Bancroft's Prep School offers up to two Francis Bancroft's means-tested awards for pupils entering the School at the age of 7 each year. These are awarded based on disclosure of family finances and performance in the entrance tests; these only cover Prep School fees.

The administration of the Prep School and Senior School are closely linked and the Head and Assistant Head of the Prep School are members of the Senior Management Team of Bancroft's School.

In 2010 the Prep School was inspected and the school was delighted with the excellent report in which they were awarded the top grade in most areas. The full report can be read by visiting the ISI website: www.isi.net.

Charitable status. Bancroft's School is a Registered Charity, number 1068532. It exists to provide a rounded academic education for able children.

Barfield School & Nursery

Guildford Road, Farnham, Surrey GU10 1PB
Tel: 01252 782271
Fax: 01252 781480
email: admin@barfieldschool.com
website: www.barfieldschool.com

The School is an Educational Trust, administered by a Board of Governors.

Chairman of Governors: Ms Denise Le Gal

Acting Head: **Mr James Reid**, BEd Hons

Age Range. 2+–13 Co-educational.
Number of Children. 220.
Fees per term (2014–2015). Prep £4,210–£4,340, Pre-Prep £2,920–£3,080, Nursery £1,685–£2,920.

Barfield, set in 12 acres of beautiful grounds, is a first-class IAPS Day Preparatory School for girls and boys. The Pre-Prep Department has an excellent reputation for high academic standards and caring staff. It enjoys all the facilities of the Prep School, which are based on one site, and include a Cook House, Library, Auditorium, Music and Music practice rooms, ICT suite, Art and DT rooms.

The school has a flourishing PE and Outdoor Pursuits Department, with most major and minor sports covered. There is a magnificent indoor heated swimming pool. Children are encouraged to participate in a wide range of extra-curricular activities from Synchronised Swimming to Adventure Training. Activity courses are run throughout most of the school holidays and children aged 4 and above are eligible to attend.

Children, taught in small classes, are prepared for Common Entrance and Scholarship examinations, and for Grammar School entry. Visitors are always welcome – please contact the school.

Charitable status. Barfield is a Registered Charity, number 312085. It exists to provide a quality education for boys and girls.

Barlborough Hall School
Preparatory School to Mount St Mary's College

Barlborough, Chesterfield, Derbyshire S43 4TJ
Tel: 01246 810511
Fax: 01246 570605
email: headteacher@barlboroughhallschool.com
website: www.barlboroughhallschool.com

Chair of Governors: J Kelly, KSG

Headteacher: **N Boys**, BA

Age Range. 3–11 Co-educational.
Number of Pupils. 177.
Fees per term (2014–2015). £2,315–£3,086.

Barlborough Hall School is a co-educational preparatory school in the Jesuit Catholic tradition, welcoming pupils aged 3–11 of all denominations. The preparatory school to nearby Mount St Mary's College (11–18), Barlborough is set in over 300 acres of parkland.

Barlborough became a school in 1939 and is built around an Elizabethan manor house which now houses many of the teaching rooms. The school encourages children to develop their talents in many different areas: academic, social, spiritual and physical with a strong focus on the individual. Academically, pupils achieve success through small classes, low pupil to teacher ratios and setting from Year 3 onwards. Teaching facilities ensure that children receive a traditional preparatory school education and include a science laboratory, technology lab and ICT suite. Pupils learn French from Nursery and most pupils learn Latin in Years 5 and 6.

All pupils receive pastoral care and academic tutoring through their form teachers, under the leadership of the Key Stage Coordinators. There is a clear sense of progression from Pre-Prep, situated in its own distinct area with its own playground, to the Upper School, which allows pupils to develop greater independence but still within a nurturing environment. There is a Jesuit chaplain who works closely with the teachers on the Chaplaincy team.

Emphasis is placed on developing the whole person, and the school enjoys an impressive reputation for its sport and music. There is an indoor heated swimming pool, dance studio and extensive games fields, and pupils enjoy a wide range of sports. Barlborough Hall is well-established on the rugby, football, hockey and netball circuit and plays regularly against other schools. Many pupils learn instruments from skilled peripatetic teachers and the school's music teacher leads prize-winning choirs and an orchestra. Drama also flourishes, with a major production every year in the school's theatre.

There are many extra-curricular activities, allowing pupils to develop their interests in a wide range of fields. Pupils are encouraged to take part in at least two activities a week and have the option to attend Saturday school, where they are able to enjoy hobbies in a more relaxed environment or practise for team sports. The wide range of activities available includes Chess, Ballroom Dancing, Art, Drama and Touch Typing. Pupils can also stay after school every evening to do homework under teacher supervision.

Admission to Barlborough Hall is by interview. Further details and a prospectus can be obtained from the Headteacher's Secretary.

Barlborough Hall pupils can automatically transfer at age 11 to Mount St Mary's College (*see entry HMC section*).

Charitable status. Mount St Mary's is a Registered Charity, number 1117998.

Barnard Castle Preparatory School

Westwick Road, Barnard Castle, County Durham DL12 8UW
Tel: 01833 696032
Fax: 01833 696034
email: prep@barneyschool.org.uk
website: www.barnardcastleschool.org.uk

Chairman of Governors: Mr A Fielder

Headmaster: **Mr C F Rycroft**, BEd Hons

Age Range. 4–11 years.
Number of Pupils. 201 girls and boys, including 20 boarders.
Fees per term (2014–2015). Prep: £5,561 (Boarders), £2,875 (Day). Pre-Prep: £1,893.

Barnard Castle Preparatory School is the junior school of Barnard Castle School and offers an all round, high quality education for boys and girls aged between 4 and 11 years. The School offers both day and boarding places and is situated in a beautiful setting on the edge of a traditional English market town.

The campuses of the two schools are adjoining, allowing shared use of many excellent facilities. At the same time the Preparatory School is able to provide a separate, stimulating environment, with small classes, a wide range of extra-curricular activities and an exciting school excursion programme. The school has recently benefited from an

extensive building and refurbishment programme. This has included the construction of a new hall and greatly improved art, design, IT, teaching and library facilities.

The School is well served by a bus network system and a breakfast club and after school supervision is readily available. The boarders reside in a newly developed boarding house, which creates a warm and friendly environment supported by a full range of facilities including the School's medical centre.

Our Director of Studies oversees a carefully designed, broad and balanced curriculum. Sport, drama and music occupy important places in the life of the School. All children have numerous opportunities to participate in each of these, as well as in an extensive co-curricular programme. The School also offers a qualified learning support service to those children who require further assistance.

Charitable status. Barnard Castle School is a Registered Charity, number 1125375. Its aim is the education of boys and girls.

Barnardiston Hall Preparatory School

Barnardiston, Nr Haverhill, Suffolk CB9 7TG
Tel: 01440 786316
Fax: 01440 786355
email: registrar@barnardiston-hall.co.uk
website: www.barnardiston-hall.co.uk

Principal: K A Boulter, MA Cantab, PGCE

Headmaster: **T W T Dodgson**, BA Hons, PGCE

Registrar: Mrs L P Gundersen

Bursar: Mrs A Gregory

Age Range. Co-educational 6 months – 13 years.
Number of Pupils. Day 204, Boarding (full and weekly) 50.
Fees per term (2014–2015). Day Pupils £1,292–£4,120; Weekly Boarders £5,700; Full Boarders £6,180.

Barnardiston Hall, set in 29 acres of grounds on the borders of Suffolk, Essex and Cambridge, offers an individual all-round education for boys and girls, both day and boarding. High standards are achieved by small classes taught by graduate and teacher-trained staff, a caring approach and close liaison with parents.

The School has good facilities, including a Pre-Preparatory Block and Art Room / CDT complex, a very modern and well-equipped computer room, assembly hall, music room, science laboratory, library, tennis/netball courts, astroturf and extensive sports fields. For the boarders, the dormitories are bright, uncluttered and home-like.

The curriculum is designed to allow pupils to reach Common Entrance standards in the appropriate subjects. The best of traditional methods are mixed with modern ideas to provide an enjoyable and productive learning environment. French and computers are taught from the age of 3; Latin from age 7. The School is CReSTeD registered. It has received outstanding gradings in recent ISI reports for both welfare and education. Pupils go on to a wide range of secondary schools.

Sports in the Michaelmas and Lent Terms are hockey, swimming (Pre-Prep only) and cross-country/orienteering for all pupils, rugby for the boys and netball for the girls. During the Summer, all do athletics, cricket/rounders, and tennis/short tennis. The School has won the National Orienteering Championships for the last six years.

There is a wide range of clubs and societies including 3 choirs, an orchestra, recorders, chess, painting, drama, carpentry, air rifle, cookery and pottery. Ballet, speech and drama, piano, guitar, woodwind, violin, brass, string and singing lessons are also offered.

Throughout the term, there are weekend activities for boarders (optional for day pupils) which include mountain walking. Derbyshire Dales at 6, Ben Nevis at 8, camping, visits to museums/historic buildings and other places of interest and theatre trips. There is an annual trip to Europe. Some pupils aged 7+ have reached Everest Base Camp.

Barrow Hills School

Roke Lane, Witley, Godalming, Surrey GU8 5NY
Tel: 01428 683639/682634
email: info@barrowhills.org
website: www.barrowhills.org.uk
Twitter: @BarrowHills
Facebook: /BarrowHillsSchool

Chairman of the Governors: Mrs Justine Voisin

Headmaster: **Mr Matthew Unsworth**, BEng Hons, PGCE

Age Range. 3–13.
Number of Pupils. 250.
Fees per term (2014–2015). Tuition: £3,152–£4,867 (including meals). Kindergarten according to sessions.

Barrow Hills is a prep school that believes having a long and happy childhood is integral to being a successful person in later life. This demands the highest standards of pastoral care and academics, underpinned by core values. Our ethos is the Catholic ethos of education: educate the whole child, find out what they are good at and celebrate this in the school community. To achieve this aim we have a broad and deep curriculum, increasingly specialist taught, as children progress through the school. Ability in specific subject areas is identified and supported. There is a Hebrew proverb, 'Do not confine children to your own learning for they were born in another time'. Embracing this, we are a 'totally connected' school and have provided Samsung tablets with digital s-pens for each and every child from Year 3 upwards. Access to tablet devices is also provided for younger pupils along with Wi-Fi, large screen digital displays and air printers across the entire school. Resources are cloud based and we have our own encrypted site on Google, running Google apps for education. You also need to know that our children have a full childhood; they are encouraged to be themselves and take risks with their learning. All we do is underpinned by our values of kindness, honesty, empathy, fortitude and charitable works. Music and theatre is in our DNA and our children are part of a culture that sees everyone, every year, perform. Sport matters too, and by Year 3 all children have five hours of sport a week including, whenever possible, competitive matches against rival schools. The major team sports are: hockey, netball, rounders, tennis and some lacrosse for girls; football, rugby, hockey and cricket for boys. We have strong links with excellent senior schools and many of our children are awarded scholarships. We are proud of our 100% success at Common Entrance with all children gaining entry to their chosen senior school at 13+. We offer broad range of extra-curricular activities and a comprehensive programme of educational and residential visits.

Barrow Hills School is an independent co-educational Catholic day school for children of all denominations aged 3 to 13 years. Our main building is an attractive Arts and Crafts house, and we have 33 acres of beautiful gardens, playing fields and woods in the Surrey Hills countryside. We are close to Guildford, Godalming and Haslemere. Key entry points: Kindy, Reception, Year 3 and Year 7.

Charitable status. Barrow Hills School Witley is a Registered Charity, number 1000190.

Bassett House School

60 Bassett Road, London W10 6JP
Tel: 020 8969 0313
Fax: 020 8960 9624
email: info@bassetths.org.uk
website: www.bassetths.org.uk

Motto: *Quisque pro sua parte* (From each to the best of his or her ability).

Chairman of Governors: Mr Anthony Rentoul

Head: **Mrs Philippa Cawthorne**

Age Range. 3–11 Co-educational.
Number of Pupils. 195.
Fees per term (2014–2015). Nursery (5 mornings) £2,510, Pre-Prep £5,020, Prep £5,240.

Bassett House School was founded in 1947. As a member school of the House Schools Group, it has two sister schools, Orchard House School in Chiswick and Prospect House School in Putney, both of which, like Bassett House School, take both boys and girls from the age of 3 or 4 until the time they leave for their next senior or, in some cases, intermediate preparatory schools. Bassett House takes children from age 3 to age 11. Entry is, in the younger years, non-selective. Aspects of the Montessori method are used in the Early Years. The school has some 195 pupils in twelve classes.

The school was built towards the end of the 19th century and what was originally designed as a large family house now provides classrooms that are spacious, brightly lit and well heated and ventilated. The entire building was substantially rebuilt in 2001 to a very high standard. The school premises include the church hall at St Helen's Church, just around the corner from 60 Bassett Road, providing an assembly hall with a stage and gymnasium, three classrooms, a kitchen and a garden. The main school building has a playground which doubles as a basketball or netball court.

Bassett House provides a thorough grounding in the usual educational subjects and the children are prepared for the entrance examinations to leading day and boarding preparatory schools. In recent years the entrance examination results to these schools have been excellent. The reason this school has enjoyed such a long track record of success is mainly due to its happy yet purposeful atmosphere …indeed, this is a hallmark of Bassett House: the school believes that only if a child is happy and actively wants to come to school will his or her potential in the widest sense be maximised. The school does not stint to obtain the very best staff and to support them with the best in resources. Within a friendly but nevertheless structured and disciplined academic environment, the school aims to bring out the best in every one of its children.

Beachborough

Westbury, Nr Brackley, Northants NN13 5LB
Tel: 01280 700071
Fax: 01280 704839
email: office@beachborough.com
website: www.beachborough.com

The School is administered as a non-profit-making Educational Trust by a Board of Governors.

Chairman of Governors: C Dudgeon, BA Oxon

Headmaster: **J M Banks**, BA, MEd Buckingham

Age Range. 2½–13.
Number of Children. Main School 200 (40% flexi boarding), Pre-Prep 100.
Fees per term (2014–2015). Prep School: Forms III–VI £5,056, Forms I & II £4,637, Reception, Pre-Prep 1 & 2 £3,219. Nursery £271 per session per term. Flexi boarding £28 per night.

Beachborough is a friendly and energetic Independent Prep School ideally situated on the borders of Buckinghamshire, Oxfordshire and Northamptonshire. We provide an outstanding all-round education for around 300 boys and girls, a quarter of whom take advantage of our flexible boarding provision. We are large enough to have a diverse and lively community, yet small enough for each individual to be known and nurtured.

We believe that a good prep school education will give children opportunities that will equip them intellectually, physically, culturally and emotionally for the challenges of the twenty-first century. At whatever stage your child joins us, be it Early Years (pupils aged 2½ to 5), Pre-Prep (pupils aged 6 to 7) or Prep School (pupils aged 8 to 13) they will be warmly welcomed into the school. We are not obsessed with reflecting on past glories or the latest headline-grabbing news, but have an active desire to find each child's individual talent and help them surpass their personal best. Our parents use words such as inclusive, nurturing and rounded to define our school, so if you share in our belief that happy children thrive, please come and visit.

Charitable status. Beachborough is a Registered Charity, number 309910.

The Beacon

Chesham Bois, Amersham, Bucks HP6 5PF
Tel: 01494 433654
Fax: 01494 727849
email: office@beaconschool.co.uk
website: www.beaconschool.co.uk
Twitter: @Beacon_School
Facebook: /beaconschoolamersham

Chairman of the Governors: D M Hollander, Esq

Headmaster: **Michael Spinney**, BEd, CertEd Reading

Age Range. 4–13.
Number of Boys. 500.
Fees per term (2014–2015). Upper School (Years 5–8) £4,800–£5,100, Middle School (Years 3 & 4) £4,650 Lower School (Years 1 & 2) £3,500, Reception £3,150.

The Beacon is an independent day school for boys aged 4 to 13 years. The Beacon prepares boys for secondary education through a curriculum that offers both richness and diversity of opportunity. From the earliest steps in initial learning, to independent success in competitive examinations; the priority is to ensure sound academic development, within a happy and stimulating environment.

The ethos of The Beacon is encapsulated in the words: *Traditional Values, Contemporary Education.* Over 490 boys are educated in extremely well-resourced buildings; a blend of old: 17th century farmstead and barns; and new: including a Design and Technology Suite, Food Technology room, Drama Studio, Modern Language Laboratory, Music Technology Suite, two Libraries, a large Sports Hall and an astroturf, set in attractive surroundings, with sixteen acres of playing fields.

There are three Reception classes with a maximum of 18 boys in each. Each class teacher has an assistant.

There is a second entry point in Year 3 at age 7 when boys join the Middle School. Class sizes are a maximum of 18. Boys study a broad range of subjects, including international studies from Year 2 to Year 5. They look at nine of the most

spoken languages in the world examining their cultures, practices and languages, including Mandarin as well as Spanish and French.

The school's attitude to sport is all-inclusive and exemplifies teamwork, emphasising the school ethos that everybody matters. Boys regularly compete at County level in cricket, hockey, tennis, swimming and rugby. The Beacon have an excellent record of success in the many national and regional competitions.

The music department has twelve instrumental ensembles, five choirs, individual music scholarship mentoring, music technology work on Cubase and a 'Rock Band' Club. There are 24 visiting music teachers with 300 weekly music lessons taking place. Beacon choirs compete and tour.

The third entry point is in Year 7 at age 11 where boys are prepared for the Beacon Certificate of Achievement, Common Entrance or Scholarship examinations to many leading independent senior schools. Year 8 presents an opportunity to take on leadership roles and boys are given greater responsibility and independence.

The School's examination record is excellent, both at 11+ into Buckinghamshire Grammar Schools and at 13+ to senior independent day and boarding schools, with a variety of academic, music, art and sports scholarships being won each year.

Charitable status. The Beacon Educational Trust Limited is a Registered Charity, number 309911. It exists to provide education for boys.

Beaudesert Park

Minchinhampton, Stroud, Gloucestershire GL6 9AF
Tel: 01453 832072
Fax: 01453 836040
email: office@beaudesert.gloucs.sch.uk
website: www.beaudesert.gloucs.sch.uk

Chairman of Governors: R S Trafford, MA

Headmaster: **J P R Womersley**, BA, PGCE

Age Range. 3–13.
Number of Pupils. Weekly and Flexi Boarders 158, Day Boys and Girls 155, Pre-Prep Department 113.
Fees per term (2014–2015). Nursery from £1,595 (5 mornings or 3 days); Reception £2,600; Years 1 & 2: £2,710; Year 3 £3,570; Year 4 £4,285; Years 5–8 £5,150. Boarders (Years 5–8) £6,700.

The School was founded in 1908 and became an educational trust in 1968.

Beaudesert Park is a preparatory school for boys and girls from 3–13. There is a strong academic tradition and all pupils are encouraged to work to the best of their ability. There is great emphasis on effort and all children are praised for their individual performance. Pupils are prepared for Common Entrance and Scholarship examinations. They are given individual attention in classes which are mostly setted not streamed. Over the last five years an average of 16 scholarships a year – academic, art, music, sport and technology – have been awarded to leading independent senior schools. The staff consists of 44 full time teaching staff and 12 music teachers, all of whom take a personal interest in the children's welfare.

Good manners and consideration for others are a priority. Beaudesert strives to create a happy and purposeful atmosphere, providing for the talents of each child in a wide range of activities – cultural, sporting and recreational. There are thriving drama, art, pottery and music departments. Sporting activities include cricket, soccer, rugby, hockey, netball, rounders, tennis, swimming, athletics, golf, badminton, fencing, dance, judo, riding and sailing. A wide number of societies and clubs meet each week.

The school is very well equipped with indoor and outdoor swimming pools, sports hall, art centre, design technology and music departments. There are also astroturf tennis courts and hard courts which are situated in beautiful wooded grounds. The school stands high up in the Cotswolds adjoining 500 acres of common land and golf course. Despite its rural location, the school is within half an hour of the M4 and M5 motorways and within easy reach of the surrounding towns of Gloucester, Cheltenham, Cirencester, Swindon, Bath and Bristol.

Charitable status. Beaudesert Park is a Registered Charity, number 311711. It exists to provide education for boys and girls in a caring atmosphere.

Bede's Preparatory School

Duke's Drive, Eastbourne, East Sussex BN20 7XL
Tel: 01323 734222
email: prep.school@bedes.org
website: www.bedes.org

Co-educational day and boarding school with Nursery and Pre-Prep departments.

Chairman of Governors: Anthony Meier, CB, OBE

Headmaster: **Giles Entwisle**, BA Hons

Deputy Head: Diane Lindop

Age Range. 3 months–13 years Co-educational.
Number of Pupils. 364: Prep 239 (160 boys, 79 girls), Pre-Prep 46, Nursery 71. Boarders: 20 with many more pupils flexi boarding.
Fees per term (2014–2015). Boarding £2,425 (in addition to Tuition); Tuition: Prep £4,210–£5,220, Pre-Prep £3,070. Nursery Prices per session.

Bede's Prep School, founded in 1895, is situated in Eastbourne, on the South Coast with spectacular views of the sea. It takes a couple of minutes to reach the beach from the school and the principal playing fields are in a wide natural hollow nestling in the South Downs.

Boarders sleep in cosy bedrooms in a house that has a real family feel and are looked after by dedicated and caring staff. Both winter and summer weekends are filled with an exciting variety of activities and special celebrations take place on the children's birthdays.

Pupils are prepared for Common Entrance and the more able are tutored to sit scholarships to independent senior schools. Approximately 74% of pupils choose to continue their education at Bede's Senior School (*see HMC section entry*).

Bede's offers academic, sport, music, dance, art and drama scholarships and bursaries for children from the ages of 7 to 12 years.

Pupils from the age of 4 are given Information Technology lessons at least once a week in a Computer Centre which is constantly updated to keep at the forefront of educational technology. French and Music, Short Tennis and other Sports are also introduced to children in this age group.

New science laboratories and classrooms were opened four years ago. In September 2009 a beautiful new building overlooking the sea and housing new kitchens and dining room and eight new classrooms opened.

February 2010 saw the Nursery and Pre-Prep moving into bespoke accommodation and since September 2009 the Nursery has operated for 51 weeks a year with a holiday club for Pre-Prep pupils operating outside of term time. Babies from three months old can join the Nursery.

The Art and Design and Technology Departments are both very strong, opening for after-school activities to encourage young talent. Music also plays an important role at Bede's. There is a thriving orchestra and the majority of pupils learn one or more instruments, with children as young as six playing in recorder groups. Informal concerts take place during the school year and there are also several choirs.

Drama forms an integral part of the school. The Pre-Prep produces a Christmas play and there are frequent productions throughout the year for older children to take part in.

Sport at Bede's is taken seriously. Boys play soccer, rugby, hockey, cricket, tennis and athletics and the major sports for girls are netball, hockey, rounders, athletics, cricket and tennis. All the pupils use the indoor 20-metre swimming pool. The fixture list is very comprehensive and, whilst the top teams enjoy a high standard of coaching and performance, special emphasis is placed on ensuring that the other teams also have the opportunity to play matches against other schools. The Matt Sports Hall covers two indoor tennis courts and is used to house a huge variety of sports. Wet weather activities include badminton, basketball and table tennis.

There is a Learning Enhancement department staffed by qualified learning support staff which can cater for pupils who require additional or particular support. The school also has an EAL centre which is run by highly trained and experienced staff. Gifted children are placed on a Curriculum Enhancement Programme to maximise their potential.

On Monday and Thursday afternoons and every evening after school the pupils are encouraged to participate in an extensive range of activities. In all there are over fifty activities on offer each week which range from fencing to cookery and basketball to art masterclasses. Day pupils who stay late for activities enjoy supper with the boarders and often flexi-board a few nights each week.

The school runs a comprehensive coach and minibus service locally and transport to and from Gatwick and Heathrow airports is arranged by the transport department.

Entry to Bede's Prep School is by interview.

Charitable status. St Bede's School Trust Sussex is a Registered Charity, number 278950. It exists to provide education for boys and girls.

Bedford Girls' School Junior School

Cardington Road, Bedford MK42 0BX
Tel: 01234 361918
email: admissions@bedfordgirlsschool.co.uk
website: www.bedfordgirlsschool.co.uk
Twitter: @BedfordGirlsSch

Foundation – The Harpur Trust.

"Let me keep an open mind so I understand as much as I can in my lifetime and not reach the limits of my imagination."

Chair of Governors: Ms T Beddoes

Head of Bedford Girls' School: Miss J MacKenzie, MSc, BSc

Head of Bedford Girls' School Junior School: **Mrs C Howe**, BA

Age Range. 7–11.
Number of Pupils. 250 Girls.
Fees per term (2014–2015). £2,818.
Bedford Girls' School is a dynamic, forward thinking selective independent day school for girls aged 7–18. As an exceptional school, we value creativity and innovation highly. It is our belief that learning should be exciting and

lifelong, so that girls flourish academically, personally, emotionally and morally fulfilled individuals capable of achieving their full potential in every aspect and at every stage of their lives.

This journey begins in the Junior School where our expert teachers recognise and ignite the curiosity of each individual girl, harnessing her natural curiosity and fuelling her confidence to develop her own thoughts, opinions and talents. In consequence, pupils not only excel academically but also as well-rounded, insightful, caring girls with a joy and passion for life and learning.

The atmosphere of our school is unique and exciting. Classrooms fizz with energy and enthusiasm and each day brings forth new discoveries and achievements. We would be delighted to welcome you to visit, either for one of our Open House events or a private tour, to experience at first hand a true flavour of life at Bedford Girls' School Junior School. Please visit www.bedfordgirlsschool.co.uk for further information or call our Admissions Team on: 01234 361918.

Admissions. Entry to the Junior School is on the basis of informal assessment and written tests in Mathematics, Reading and Writing.

Charitable status. Bedford Girls' School is part of the Harpur Trust which is a Registered Charity, number 1066861.

Bedford Modern Junior School

Manton Lane, Bedford, Bedfordshire MK41 7NT
Tel: 01234 332513
Fax: 01234 332617
email: info@bedmod.co.uk
website: www.bedmod.co.uk

Chairman of the School Committee: I McEwen, BPhil, MA, DPhil

Head of Junior School: **Mrs J C Rex**, BA Hons, PGCE

Age Range. 7–11 Co-educational.
Number of Pupils. 145 Boys, 111 Girls.
Fees per term (2014–2015). £2,903.

The Junior School is housed in its own separate buildings adjacent to the Senior School. Facilities include specialist rooms for Art and Science, ICT, Design Technology and a newly refurbished Library, with designated Year 3 classrooms and play area and a superb state-of-the-art School Hall.

The whole site overlooks the School playing fields and the Junior School has extensive views over the Ouse Valley. Many of the Senior School facilities are available to the Junior School, including full use of the playing fields, Sports Hall, Gymnasium, covered and heated Swimming Pool and all-weather pitches. The Howard Hall provides facilities for full-scale drama productions and use is made of the Music School.

There is a strong musical, dramatic and sporting tradition. Pupils are admitted to the Junior School at ages 7, 8, 9 and 10, after taking tests in English, Maths and non-verbal reasoning, some of them on computer, in January each year. Pupils proceed automatically to the Senior School at 11, unless special circumstances prevent this.

(See Bedford Modern School entry in HMC section.)

Charitable status. Bedford Modern School is part of the Harpur Trust which is a Registered Charity, number 1066861. It includes in its aims the provision of high quality education for boys and girls.

Bedford Preparatory School

De Parys Avenue, Bedford MK40 2TU
Tel: 01234 362216
Fax: 01234 362283
email: prepadmissions@bedfordschool.org.uk
website: www.bedfordschool.org.uk
Twitter: @bedfordschool
Facebook: /Bedford-School

Chairman of Governors: Professor Stephen Mayson, LLB, LLM, PhD, Barrister, FRSA

Headmaster: **I Silk**

Deputy Head: G J Wickens, MA

Age Range. 7–13.
Number of Boys. Dayboys 366, Boarders 18, Weekly Boarders 8.
Fees per term (2014–2015). Day £3,699–£4,847, Full Boarding £6,583–£7,818, Weekly Boarding £6,275–£7,509.

Bedford Preparatory School combines the two schools formerly known as the Preparatory School and the Bedford Lower School. Their extensive campus offers excellent facilities: three purpose-built and well-equipped Science Laboratories, an Art Studio, excellent computing resources, specialist teaching rooms, a library and a spacious Assembly Hall.

Curriculum. Boys are prepared for the Bedford School 13+ Entrance Examination, which is allied to Common Entrance, but under normal circumstances boys transfer automatically. The curriculum is otherwise carefully tailored to match and prepare for the curriculum followed in the Upper School, and includes in addition to the usual subjects: French, Information Technology and Design/Technology from the age of 7 and Latin, Spanish and French from the age of 11.

The boys enjoy full use of the facilities available to Upper School pupils: the Recreation Centre, incorporating an excellent theatre, an indoor swimming pool and a large sports hall; the Technology Centre; superb playing fields, all-weather pitch and tennis courts. All the usual games are played to a high standard and boys are often selected to play in county or national teams.

Many boys play musical instruments, and orchestra and bands perform frequently. There are good School Choirs and selected boys sing alongside Upper School pupils in the Chapel Choir trained in the English Cathedral tradition. There are several theatrical productions each year in the theatre or hall, often in conjunction with girls from sister Harpur Trust School, Bedford Girls' School.

Boarding. Full boarders and a small number of weekly boarders live in the purpose-built Boarding House in the grounds of the Preparatory School. Boys are cared for by the Housemaster and his wife, two resident house-tutors and a full-time matron.

Pastoral Care. The progress and well-being of pupils is carefully monitored, and parental involvement and contact are maintained through reports and Parents Evenings and other formal and informal meetings. A competitive House system is in use.

Financial Assistance and Scholarships. Bedford seeks to identify boys of outstanding talent and give them access to a Bedford School education regardless of background. The school offers Scholarships and Bursaries to boys who excel academically, or show outstanding talent in Drama, Music or Sport.

Awards are available for boys joining the Upper School at 13+. For more information, please visit www. bedfordschool.org.uk.

Charitable status. Bedford School is part of the Harpur Trust which is a Registered Charity, number 1066861. It aims to provide high quality education for boys.

Beechwood Park

Markyate, St Albans, Hertfordshire AL3 8AW
Tel: 01582 840333
Fax: 01582 842372
email: hmsecretary@beechwoodpark.herts.sch.uk
website: www.beechwoodpark.herts.sch.uk

Chairman of Governors: G Freer, Esq

Headmaster: **Patrick C E Atkinson**, BSc, MIBiol, PGCE

Age Range. 3–13.
Number of Pupils. 485: 55 boarders (aged 9–13),250 day boys and 180 day girls (aged 4–13). In addition there are 35 pre-school children at the Montessori Nursery which is at a separate location less than one mile from the main school.
Fees per term (2014–2015). Day pupils: Senior £4,693, Middle £3,802, Junior £3,748, Reception £3,200. Boarders (up to 4 nights per week in addition to day fees) £1,115. No compulsory extras.

Beechwood Park occupies a large mansion, with a fine Regency Library and Great Hall, in 38 acres of surrounding grounds. Modernisation has added kitchens, changing rooms, Science laboratories, language rooms, Design Technology workshop, comfortable dormitories with modern facilities and spacious common rooms, gymnasium and sports facilities, including a large sports hall and two squash courts, hard tennis courts and two heated indoor swimming pools. Three purpose-built classroom blocks house the Middle Department, Junior Forms and Reception classes. A Music Department has a music chamber, 14 practice rooms and a new Music Technology Suite. More recently a Performance Hall and an all-weather pitch have been added.

Day pupils use private buses serving Harpenden, St Albans, Dunstable and the surrounding villages. Many subsequently convert to boarding under the care of the Houseparents, Mr and Mrs R Humphreys.

Class size is 20; major subjects are setted. Qualified class teachers teach the Juniors; older children are taught by subject specialist graduates. There is a resident Chaplain. The Director of Music has a staff of visiting instrumentalists.

The number of scholarships gained each year and Common Entrance results affirm a high standard of work, against a background of every kind of worthwhile out-of-class activity. Music is distinguished.

Soccer, Rugby, Cricket, Golf, Hockey, Netball, Swimming, Athletics and a Sport for All programme, which includes an unusually wide range of minor sports, are all coached by well-qualified PE Staff.

Beechwood Park is a non-profit-making trust administered by governors of wide professional and educational experience.

Charitable status. Beechwood Park School is a Registered Charity, number 311068. It exists to provide education for boys and girls from 3–13.

Beeston Hall School

West Runton, Cromer, Norfolk NR27 9NQ
Tel: 01263 837324
Fax: 01263 838177
email: office@beestonhall.co.uk
website: www.beestonhall.co.uk

Chairman of Governors: D D Marris
Headmaster: **R C Gainher**, BSc Hons
Business Manager: S Watts

Age Range. Co-educational 7–13 years.
Number of Pupils. 132: 71 Boarding, 61 Day Pupils. 78 Boys, 54 Girls.
Fees per term (2014–2015). Boarding: £5,942 (Year 3), £7,325 (Years 4–8); Day Pupils: £3,714 (Year 3), £5,423 (Years 4–8).

Beeston Hall was established in 1948 in a Regency house set in 30 acres in North Norfolk, close to the sea and surrounded by 700 acres of National Trust land. Beeston's reputation for being a happy, caring family school is in no small part due to the real sense of community which pervades throughout. The strength of the Pastoral Care system ensures that every child is closely watched over and cared for. Beeston is a Boarding and Day School offering Full, Weekly and Flexi boarding; most of the children experience boarding before they leave, the majority moving on to boarding schools such as Ampleforth, Eton, Gresham's, Harrow, Oakham, Oundle, Queen Margaret's York, Radley, Repton, Rugby, Stowe, Tudor Hall and Uppingham. In addition to the usual examinable subjects, Art, Music, DT, Computing and Theatre Studies are all timetabled, providing the children with a wide curriculum and the opportunity to find an activity in which they can excel. The school enjoys great success at scholarship level, with over 50 scholarships won in the last 5 years. Extra help is given on a one-to-one basis in English, Mathematics and French; a dedicated, professionally run Learning Support department emphasises the importance of the learning support work being carried into the classroom. There is a positive emphasis on values such as courtesy, kindness, hard work and awareness of others, and at every stage of their education the children are encouraged to maximise their potential and think and act for themselves. Drama and Music are considered important for every child: each takes part in at least one play production each year. Three choirs and ten different music groups meet every week and over 90% of the school learn a musical instrument. The school is equally proud of its record on the sports field where all children are coached regardless of ability by a dedicated team of staff, and where all are, at some stage, given the opportunity to represent the school. In addition to the usual major sports, others offered include Cross Country, Athletics, Swimming, Tennis and Shooting, whilst a comprehensive activities programme provides opportunities to suit all tastes: Modern Martial Arts, Fencing, Sailing, Golf, Chess and Cooking, to name but a few.

The 2010 ISI Inspection Report comments on: "*the rich educational experience provided ...the excellent pastoral care and support ...the excellent relationships between staff and pupils ...and the overall excellent curricular and extra-curricular provision.*"

Religious denomination: Mainly Church of England; 15% Roman Catholic.

Charitable status. Beeston Hall School Trust Limited is a Registered Charity, number 311274. It exists to provide preparatory education for boarding and day boys and girls.

Belhaven Hill

Dunbar, East Lothian EH42 1NN
Tel: 01368 862785
Fax: 01368 865225
email: secretary@belhavenhill.com
website: www.belhavenhill.com

Chairman of Governors: Mrs M G Clough
Head Master: **I K MacAskill**, BEd Hons

Age Range. 7–13 Co-educational.

Number of Pupils. 67 boys, 54 girls. Boarders 80, Day 41.

Fees per term (2014–2015). Boarding £6,885. Day: £4,775 (Form 6: £3,375).

Religion. Non-denominational.

Overlooking the sea in an idyllic East Lothian parkland setting, Belhaven is an independent boarding and day school for boys and girls from 7 to 13 years. Since its establishment in 1923, the school has focused on developing well-rounded, happy, confident children through a rigorous academic curriculum, lots of sport and a broad extra-curricular programme. Ideally placed just off the A1, it is close to both a mainline London-Edinburgh railway station and less than an hour to Edinburgh airport.

A full boarding and day school, Belhaven Hill has a long tradition of providing a first class all-round education before sending its pupils far and wide to all the leading public schools in both England and Scotland. These include Ampleforth, Downe House, Eton, Fettes, Glenalmond, Harrow, Loretto, Merchiston, Oundle, Queen Margaret's York, Radley, Rugby, Shrewsbury, Stowe and Uppingham. Committed and enthusiastic members of staff work with small classes of between 10–16 pupils. There is ample opportunity for scholarship and extended work, resulting in an excellent number of awards being gained every year. A strong learning support department with two dedicated, trained staff provides one-to-one and small group tuition.

Belhaven Hill pupils are renowned for being happy children and this is in no small part due to the excellent pastoral care provided. The majority of staff live on site and the policy of the governors has been to keep the school comparatively small in order to retain a family atmosphere. The boys are housed in the original main building and the girls in a newly-refurbished purpose-built house. The pastoral system revolves around the six patrols, with each pupil being looked after by their form teacher in the junior years and a personal tutor, higher up the school. Six matrons take care of the children's health.

The school has an excellent reputation for sport with rugby, netball, hockey, cricket, rounders, tennis and athletics, making up the main part of the sporting programme. Swimming takes place all year round either in the school's heated outdoor pool or at a local indoor pool. In addition many opportunities abound for a wide variety of other recreational activities: skiing, surfing, horse riding, fencing, golf on the adjacent links course, carpentry at a local renowned furniture makers and gardening for those who want to grow their own produce in the school's walled garden. An extensive Activity Programme offers something for everyone to discover and enjoy such as bridge, debating, 'mastermind', fly-tying, model-making, computer programming, cookery, crafts, chess, Mandarin, fencing, modern dance and reeling to name but a few.

Music and Drama flourish at Belhaven and every child has ample opportunity to perform in regular concerts and productions throughout the year. A new state-of-the-art music building houses a vibrant department which caters for a wide range of instrumental ensembles and choirs. Over 90% of the children play one or more instruments, with specialist tuition provided by a team of peripatetic music staff.

The school is well resourced with purpose-built facilities, including a swimming pool, floodlit all-weather pitch, playing fields, sports hall, specialist music and art schools, attractive teaching rooms, two ICT suites and a new library.

Belhaven begins with the belief that every child is an individual who has a talent and that it is their mission to foster both their individuality and abilities. To achieve these aims it places the child at the core of everything it does. By providing an environment that promotes enjoyment, exploration and nurturing of curiosity, each child grows to understand that they too are responsible for their learning, alongside staff and parents. As a result they grow to value

and respect those around them, delighting in the achievements of others as well as their own. Qualities such as courtesy, tolerance, honesty and perseverance are all encouraged and celebrated, with the children understanding that it is better to have had a go and fail, than never to have tried at all. Whether they are day pupils or boarders, all our children benefit from a boarding school ethos of community and friendship, where challenges are plenty, but where a sense of fun and enjoyment pervades all school life.

The school now welcomes a seven year-old entry and has introduced an outdoor education element into its junior curriculum where children can learn more about their environment through practical, hands-on learning experiences.

Means-tested bursary support is available. Fee concessions are available for children of members of the armed forces, as well as third and fourth sibling concessions. For a prospectus and more information please see our website www.belhavenhill.com or contact Tessa Coleman at secretary@belhavenhill.com.

Charitable status. Belhaven Hill School Trust Ltd is a Registered Charity, number SC007118. Its aim is to educate children in the full sense of the word.

Belmont
Mill Hill Preparatory School

The Ridgeway, Mill Hill, London NW7 4ED

Tel:	020 8906 7270
Fax:	020 8906 3519
email:	office@belmontschool.com
website:	www.belmontschool.com

Chairman of the Court of Governors: Dr R G Chapman, BSc, MB BS, FRCGP

Head: Mrs L C Duncan, BSc, PGCE

Deputy Head (Academic): L Roberts, MA, PGCE
[Deputy Head (Academic): Mrs R Alford, BEd]
Acting Deputy Head (Pastoral): J Pym, MA, PGCE
Acting Deputy Head (Operations): Mr J Fleet, BSc, PGSE
Head of Lower School: Mrs J Rowe, BEd
Acting Head of Upper School: P Symes, BSc, PGCE

Age Range. 7–13.

Number of Pupils. Day: 240 Boys, 213 Girls.

Fees per term (2014–2015). £5,207 including lunch.

Belmont is situated in the Green Belt on the borders of Hertfordshire and Middlesex, yet is only ten miles from central London. It stands in about 35 acres of its own woods and parkland and enjoys the advantages of a truly rural environment, but at the same time the capital's cultural facilities are easily accessible.

Belmont is part of the Mill Hill School Foundation; the Pre-Prep Grimsdell and Mill Hill School are situated less than a quarter of a mile away. Opened in 1912, Belmont takes its name from the original mansion built on the Ridgeway about the middle of the eighteenth century. Successive alterations and additions have provided a chapel, a gymnasium, music-rooms, science laboratories and a fully resourced ICT room, ample games fields, five all-weather cricket nets, two all-weather cricket pitches, and six hard tennis courts. A major building and refurbishment programme has recently been undertaken and provides a large new multi-purpose hall, junior classroom block, extra science labs, a new resources centre, design technology room, additional music teaching space and catering facilities.

Use is made of the Fives courts and the indoor heated swimming pool at Mill Hill School.

The School became co-educational in 1995 and 48% of the pupils are girls.

The usual age of entry is at 7 or 11 years, but 8, 9 and 10-year-olds are considered as vacancies occur. It is expected that most children will pass to Mill Hill at the end of Year 8, but some may be prepared for entry to other senior schools.

There is a permanent teaching staff of 40, with 20 visiting teachers for Instrumental Music, supportive English and Mathematics, Ballet and Fencing. There is a full-time Matron and a visiting counsellor while the school's catering is all in-house.

The main games are Rugby, Soccer, Cricket, Hockey, Netball and Rounders, but minor sports also flourish, as do instrumental and choral music, drama, and many out-of-school activities. There are French exchanges with Belmont's 'twin' school in Rouen, and all the children take part in the Summer Activities Programme, which includes for senior children a Geography field trip and an outward bound week.

Charitable status. The Mill Hill School Foundation is a Registered Charity, number 1064758. It exists to provide education for boys and girls.

Belmont Grosvenor School

Swarcliffe Hall, Birstwith, Harrogate, North Yorkshire HG3 2JG
Tel: 01423 771029
Fax: 01423 772600
email: admin@belmontgrosvenor.co.uk
website: www.belmontgrosvenor.co.uk

Chair of Governors: Mrs Frances Trowell

Head: **Mrs Jane Merriman**, BEd, MA, NPQH

Age Range. 3 months–11 years Co-educational.
Number of Pupils. 221.
Fees per term (2014–2015). Prep £3,013, Pre-Prep £2,547, Pre-Reception £1,172–£2,547. Nursery: Under 2s £26–£52 per session; Over 2s £24–£46 per session.

Belmont Grosvenor School is set in 20 acres of beautiful countryside in Birstwith, near Harrogate.

The school, for boys and girls up to the age of 11, has a warm and friendly atmosphere where children learn and grow both inside and outside the classroom. Belmont Grosvenor School provides everything that you would expect for a quality education for boys and girls aged 3 months to 11 years.

The ethos of the School is characterised by the trusting and supportive relationships that exist between staff, children and parents. We create an environment that is safe and happy where academic and social skills, individual talents, consideration and sensitivity to the needs of others are developed. In this secure and friendly setting, learning becomes a pleasure and is its own reward. One of the school's greatest strengths is the continuity of education and care that it offers.

It is not just school-aged children who benefit from Belmont Grosvenor's caring and nurturing environment – the school's Magic Tree Day Care Nursery cares for children from the age of three months. The nursery is divided into two main areas, one for the under twos and the other for the over twos. There is a smooth transition from the Magic Tree Day Care Nursery to the Early Years Department at Belmont Grosvenor.

The school offers a firm academic foundation and develops the children as individuals, preparing them for the future. Sport, Music, Drama and Art are all essential elements in the balanced education enjoyed by the children at BGS.

Children at Belmont Grosvenor School have access to specialist teachers and facilities and enjoy a wide range of extra-curricular activities, educational visits and residential trips.

The school has undergone a series of improvements, including the opening of an outdoor classroom, amphitheatre and adventure trail as well as the redevelopment of the libraries, art and design studio and upgrades of whiteboards and computer software enabling interactive teaching across each subject area. This allows us to deliver a broad curriculum to the highest standard with the children achieving well above National standards in KS1 and KS2 tests. The children are thoroughly prepared for transfer to secondary schools, where academic, music, sport and art scholarships are common.

Charitable status. Belmont-Birklands School Trust Limited is a Registered Charity, number 529584.

Belmont School

Feldemore, Holmbury St Mary, Dorking, Surrey RH5 6LQ
Tel: 01306 730852
Fax: 01306 731220
email: admissions@belmont-school.org
website: www.belmont-school.org
Twitter: @BelmontPrep

Chairman of the Governors: Mr N Butcher

Headmistress: **Mrs H Skrine**, BA Hons Exeter, PGCE London, NPQH, FRSA

Age Range. 2–13.
Number of Pupils. 220 Boys and Girls: Day, Weekly and Flexible Boarding.
Fees per term (2014–2015). Day Pupils: Little Belmont £2,645 (10 sessions, pro-rata for fewer sessions), Reception £2,645, Years 1–2 £2,965, Years 3–4 £4,400, Years 5–8 £4,450. Boarding: £470 (1 night pw), £940 (2 nights), £1,395 (3 nights), £1,810 (4 nights, Monday to Thursday), £2,015 (5 nights, Sunday to Thursday).

Founded in London in 1880, the School is now established in 65 acres of wooded parkland overlooking the picturesque village of Holmbury St Mary, between Guildford and Dorking. The main house, Feldemore, was completely refurbished in the early 1990s so that the school now boasts an historic building with a purpose-built interior. Outstanding facilities include a brand new Early Years building, impressive sports hall, a well-equipped theatre, two state-of-the-art computer suites, newly-refurbished Science lab and woodland adventure courses. These, together with our friendly, talented staff and confident, happy boys and girls, make Belmont the very best choice you could make for your child.

We offer co-educational day education for boys and girls aged 2 to 13, and optional weekly boarding or flexible boarding arrangements. We prepare children for Common Entrance and Scholarship examinations to a wide range of schools, and will assist children in preparing for other Senior Schools that have their own admissions procedures.

Here, every child matters and we look to develop children as individuals, seeking to inspire and to unfurl the hidden strengths of every boy or girl. There is a happy, industrious atmosphere and high expectations pervade throughout all aspects of school life. In addition, we have a challenging curriculum and an extensive array of extra-curricular opportunities which together are designed to captivate the imagination. Creativity is a particular strength of the school. The teaching staff is well qualified and healthy pupil: staff ratios have enabled us to develop a flexible setting system within a relatively small school.

The curriculum covers all the required Common Entrance subjects plus Drama, Art, DT, IT, Music, PSHCE, PE and

Games. Sports include Netball, Rugby, Football, Cross-Country, Hockey, Tennis, Swimming, Cricket, Athletics and Rounders.

Children in Year 1 and above attend for a half day or full day visit prior to entry. Further details can be obtained from the Registrar, Mrs Sarah Brinton.

Charitable status. Belmont School (Feldemore) Educational Trust Limited is a Registered Charity, number 312077.

Berkhampstead School, Cheltenham

Pittville Circus Road, Cheltenham, Glos GL52 2QA
Tel: 01242 523263
email: office@berkhampsteadschool.co.uk
website: www.berkhampsteadschool.co.uk

Chairman of Governors: Mrs R Hope

Headmaster: **R P Cross**, BSc Hons, PGCE

Age Range. 3 months–11 years co-educational.
Number of Pupils. 250 day pupils plus 60 in Day Nursery.
Fees per term (2014–2015). Kindergarten: £1,166 (5 mornings), £1,619 (5 full days); Pre-Prep: £2,028 (Reception), £2,110 (Year 1), £2,309 (Year 2); Prep: £2,513 (Year 3), £2,698 (Year 4), £2,857 (Years 5), £2,935 (Year 6). Lunches: £205.

Children are capable of remarkable things and achieve these at Berkhampstead, Cheltenham.

Enthusiastic and imaginative teaching of small classes allows our pupils to gain skills and confidence – they emerge with the characteristic 'can-do' attitude of the Berkhampstead pupil. Our outstanding record of Independent School Scholarships and Grammar School places speaks for itself – it is second to none. Berkhampstead equips children to thrive at their chosen next school.

Our academic record is impressive – children have huge opportunities to achieve – but there is much more than this to Berkhampstead. From the very youngest age, children are engaged in a happy and positive environment, surrounded by supportive adults and they embrace all that's on offer. Specialist staff in French, Music and PE enrich the Early Years curriculum; specialists teach throughout Prep. Creative teaching is the norm and it inspires – our superb staff write and produce musicals and plays, devise experiments and plan experiences to make lessons memorable and fun.

Our bright Day Nursery is a place of play and creativity for the very smallest – from 3 months – a fun-filled preparation for more formal learning to come. Moving on, the qualified teachers in our School Nursery support and stretch, stimulate and inspire. Their collaborative approach pays dividends and the children are really involved in their learning.

Berkhampstead's non-pressurised yet purposeful environment allows children to flourish academically. Art and Drama are impressive. Pupils excel in music – most play an instrument, from the popular double bass to the trombone – regular Recitals, Concerts and ensemble groups give all the opportunity to perform.

Sport is excellent, with specialist coaching from the earliest age. Every child will represent the school in competitive fixtures, children play sportingly and the Berkhampstead team spirit often shines through to give victory against larger opponents.

Berkhampstead is a purposeful place crammed with opportunities where each pupil's talents are celebrated. Our outstanding Pastoral Care and respectful staff/pupil relationships ensure that we have happy children – a real priority.

Our talented staff, with many male teachers, help the individual to move on to senior school; secure, confident and having achieved remarkable things.

Small classes. Happy children. Excellent results.

Berkhamsted Pre-Preparatory School

Chesham Road, Berkhamsted, Herts HP4 2SZ
Tel: 01442 358188
          01442 358276 (Berkhamsted Day Nursery)
email: preprepoffice@berkhamstedschool.org
website: www.berkhamstedschool.org
Twitter: @berkopreprep
Facebook: /berkhamstedschool

Chairman of Governors: Mr G C Laws

Principal: Mr M S Steed, MA Cantab, MA Nottingham

Head: **Ms S Jaspal**, BA QTS

Age Range. 3–7 years Co-educational. Day Nursery: 5 months–3 years.
Number in School. 170.
Fees per term (2014–2015). £3,160–£3,255 (including lunch).

Berkhamsted School's Pre-Preparatory School caters for children from the ages of three to seven. The School is set in a tastefully converted Georgian coach house and stables in eight acres of grass and woodland, conveniently located on the Herts-Bucks border, 10 kms from the M25 and M1 motorways, at the Chesham exit of the A41. It has a walled garden, a woodland trail, an outdoor classroom and a large Sports Hall. The site provides a beautiful, safe environment – the ideal place for children to start their educational journey.

Berkhamsted Pre-Prep is a caring, vibrant community. It endeavours to create an extended family atmosphere where happy children enjoy learning and each child is encouraged to reach his or her full potential. The school offers a broad-based, stimulating education, including Spanish and French, Music, Drama, Dance, Sport, Sciences and Art. Children progress to the next stage of their education and into the world beyond, making the most of their strengths and achieving at the highest possible levels across the curriculum. Because of our small numbers, adults have time to listen and appreciate each child as a unique person. The children learn to communicate confidently with people of all ages.

There is a wide variety of after-school clubs and children participate in outings and trips. Before- and after-school clubs provide wrap-around care from 7.30 am to 6.30 pm, with homework supervision where required. Mini BASE-CAMP, our holiday activities camp at the school designed for 3–5 year olds, is also available every holiday from 7.30 am to 6.30 pm.

Berkhamsted Day Nursery (0–3+ years) is open 50 weeks per year from 7.30 am to 6.30 pm, and is situated on the school site. Children can join Berkhamsted Day Nursery from five months of age and can move on to Berkhamsted Pre-Prep, which is just next door. Berkhamsted Day Nursery caters for children up to the September that they begin in the Stepping Stones Nursery class at Berkhamsted Pre-Prep (when they can use the school's out-of-hours clubs).

Berkhamsted Preparatory School

Doctors Commons Road, Berkhamsted, Hertfordshire HP4 3DW
Tel: 01442 358201/2
Fax: 01442 358203
email: prepadmin@berkhamstedschool.org
website: www.berkhamstedschool.org
Twitter: @berkhamstedprep
Facebook: /berkhamstedschool

Chairman of Governors: Mr G C Laws

Principal: Mr M S Steed, MA Cantab, MA Nottingham

Head: Mr J Hornshaw, BEd, MEd, NPQH

Deputy Curriculum: Mr P D Whitby, BA, MA

Deputy Pastoral: Mr D Brown, BA

Age Range. 7–11.
Number of Pupils. 164 boys, 187 girls.
Fees per term (2014–2015). £4,175–£4,350.

Berkhamsted Preparatory School is part of Berkhamsted School, a school with a 'Diamond' structure that combines single-sex and co-educational teaching. Boys and girls are taught together at the Pre-Preparatory (Haresfoot site) from age 3 to 7, and at the Preparatory (Doctors Commons Road site) from age 7 to 11. They are then taught separately from age 11 to 16 (Berkhamsted Boys and Berkhamsted Girls), before coming back together again in a joint Sixth Form.

Berkhamsted Preparatory School offers first-class facilities for the 7 to 11 age group, in conjunction with the highest standards of teaching and educational development. All classes offer a happy, caring environment where children are encouraged to investigate and explore the world around them. Classes at all levels have access to computers. Key features include a multi-purpose hall, modern dining facilities and a full range of specialist classrooms (e.g. Science laboratory, 2 ICT suites, new Drama Studio and Art classrooms). The beginning of the 2014–15 academic year saw the addition of a netball court, fives courts and an outdoor learning area. The Preparatory School also has use of Senior School facilities including extensive playing fields, tennis and netball courts, a Sports Centre, a swimming pool and a 500-seat theatre.

All children are encouraged to develop to their full potential and grow in confidence and independence. The School's general approach is progressive, while retaining traditional values and standards; courtesy and politeness towards others are expected at all times. Academic achievement is of great importance, but the emphasis on other activities such as sports and music ensures that pupils receive a well-rounded education.

The most recent ISI Inspection Report (November 2012) noted that the school offers a high quality educational experience to its pupils, whose achievement was excellent because of their highly positive attitude to learning. Personal development of pupils was also found to be excellent, exemplified in the pupils' high levels of interpersonal skills, confidence and self-esteem. It was also reported that the pupils feel happy, secure and well cared for due to the school's exemplary pastoral care.

A wide range of voluntary extra-curricular activities is offered at lunch-time, the end of the school day, including art, drama, music and sport. Choirs and orchestras perform in concerts and services throughout the year and school teams compete successfully in a variety of sports.

Berkhamsted Schools Group is committed to supporting working parents and offers wrap-around care from 7.30 am to 6.30 pm each day. In addition, the school operates a holiday care facility, BASECAMP, which offers a variety of courses from multi-activity to specialist sports and cookery each holiday. The core day runs from 9.30 am to 4.30 pm and extended care is available from 7.30 am and to 6.30 pm each day.

Charitable status. Berkhamsted Schools Group is a Registered Charity, number 310630. It is a leading Charitable School in the field of Junior and Secondary Education.

Bickley Park School

24 Page Heath Lane, Bickley, Bromley, Kent BR1 2DS
Tel: 020 8467 2195
Fax: 020 8325 5511
email: info@bickleyparkschool.co.uk
website: www.bickleyparkschool.co.uk

Chairman of Governors: Mr M Hansra

Headmaster: P Wenham, MA Cantab, PGCE

Age Range. Boys 2½–13, Girls 2½–4.
Number of Pupils. 320 Boys, 20 Girls.
Fees per term (2014–2015). From £1,680 (Nursery) to £4,380 (Boys in Years 7 & 8). There are no compulsory extras.

Bickley Park School, founded in 1918, occupies two sites in Bickley, the Prep Department at 24 Page Heath Lane and the Pre-Prep Department at 14 Page Heath Lane. The school has excellent modern facilities to complement the original Victorian buildings. Both sites are extremely attractive and the school's sports field is on the opposite side of the road.

The EYFS Department (recently rated as outstanding) provides a very caring and stimulating environment for children to start their school lives. At Key Stage 1, the children are cared for by a class teacher with the addition of specialist teaching for Music and Games. Classes are kept small with none exceeding 18 in total.

In the Prep Department, the children are introduced to more specialist teaching and setting for Mathematics, English, Science and French is introduced. The curriculum is broad with the emphasis being placed on encouraging the children to develop their potential to the full in a very caring environment. There is a wide range of extra-curricular activities and a full sports programme. The major sports played are football, rugby and cricket, whilst athletics and tennis are also offered.

The majority of children leave at 13+ through the Common Entrance or Scholarship examinations whilst a small number leave at 11 to join local Grammar Schools.

The Parents Association, run by parents and staff, arrange events, both social and fundraising, during the year.

Visitors are made very welcome.

Charitable status. Bickley Park School Limited is a Registered Charity, number 307915. It exists to provide a broad curriculum for boys aged 2½–13 and girls aged 2½–4.

Bilton Grange

Dunchurch, Rugby, Warwickshire CV22 6QU
Tel: 01788 810217
Fax: 01788 816922
email: admissions@biltongrange.co.uk
website: www.biltongrange.co.uk

The school is registered as an Educational Trust under the Charities Act and is controlled by a Board of Governors.

Chairman of Governors: Jeremy Greenhalgh

Headmaster: Alex Osiatynski, MA Oxon, PGCE

Deputy Headmaster: Paul Nicholson, BA Hons, PGCE
Bursar: Murdo Urquhart, OBE
Assistant Head Pastoral: Sue Warner, BA Hons
Assistant Head Academic: Greg Das Gupta, BSc, BCom, PGCE
Head of Pre Prep: Adrian Brindley, BSc, MA, PGCE
Registrar: Rebecca Bantoft, BA Hons

Age Range. 4–13.
Number of Pupils. 304 boys and girls of whom 50 are boarders. Preparatory (8–13 year olds): 199 pupils; Pre-Preparatory (4–8 year olds): 105 pupils.

Bilton Grange School, which was established in 1887, is one of the foremost co-educational prep schools in the country. Set in 100 secure acres of sports fields, woods, and landscaped gardens dominated by a 19th Century Pugin mansion, the school prides itself on bringing out the very best in every child. Children are extremely happy, and in a nurturing, inspiring and caring environment, confidently find their true potential. Bilton Grange offers a diverse range of opportunities all designed to support individual accomplishments. Here, children share common values of respect, awareness of others and courtesy. They are usually 'all-rounders', willing to take advantage of all the opportunities open to them – be it on the sports field, on an adventure weekend or in the classroom. Not academically selective, class sizes rarely exceed 16 and all classrooms are fitted with interactive whiteboards and the highest level of IT resources. Children are entered for the Common Entrance Examination, and go on to top senior schools across the UK from Rugby, Repton and Oundle to Eton, Wycombe Abbey and Millfield. A good number of pupils each year win awards and scholarships to senior schools, and in recent years, 100% of leavers have gone on to the senior school of their choice.

Inspections of Bilton Grange by Ofsted and Independent Schools Inspectorate (ISI) validate the school's success. In 2011 ISI inspectors reported: '*The excellent curriculum presents the pupils with a substantial breadth of opportunity academically, in the sports, in the arts and in technology*'. Commenting on the extra-curricular programme, the inspectors remarked: '*The excellent extra-curricular programme encourages children to take responsibility for a proportion of their time and select activities in which to participate*' …'*the provision goes beyond the traditional to include Zumba dancing, orienteering and campcraft, which makes good use of the excellent grounds in which the school is set*'. The Early Years setting at Bilton Grange was described as '*an outstanding setting, meeting the needs of all children whilst fully appreciating their individual differences*'. Within the school grounds there is also a Montessori Nursery, which takes babies and children up to the age of 4.

Full, weekly and flexible boarding are offered – with well over 50 boarders divided equally between boys and girls. Ofsted concluded in 2011 that '*The pastoral care given to boarding children [at Bilton Grange] is another outstanding feature of this school.*' …'*Children are cared for in a warm, friendly and safe atmosphere.*'.

Facilities for the children are outstanding, and include a new astroturf within the Pugin Walled Garden, a 9-hole golf course, shooting range, theatre, indoor heated pool and a chapel. The school has seen great sporting success in recent years at a regional and national level. The creative arts are a big part of school life with scholarship successes and creative achievement across music, art, drama and design technology.

Fees per term (from April 2014). Preparatory: Full Boarding £8,045, Weekly Boarding £7,470, Day £5,210–£5,905. Pre-Preparatory: £3,060–£3,670.

There are fee discounts for Service children and third child.

Bursaries and academic scholarships are awarded annually, with the scholarship competition open to internal and external candidates over the age of 7. Bursaries are awarded on the basis of financial need, and are available to families with children aged between 4–11. This annual application process gets under way in January and details are available on the school website.

We encourage all prospective parents and children to visit the school to see and experience teaching and learning of the highest standards in an inspiring setting.

Charitable status. Bilton Grange Trust is a Registered Charity, number 528771. It exists to provide education for boys and girls.

Birchfield School

Albrighton, Wolverhampton, Shropshire WV7 3AF
Tel: 01902 372534
Fax: 01902 373516
email: office@birchfieldschool.co.uk
website: www.birchfieldschool.co.uk

Chairman of the Governors: P J Cotter

Headmaster: **Hugh Myott**, BA Hons, PGCE

Age Range. 4–13.
Number of Pupils. 134: Pre-Prep (age 4–7) 44, Prep (age 8–10) 70, Senior (age 11–13) 20.
Fees per term (2014–2015). Under 5s £2,115; Reception & Year 1 £2,715; Year 2 £3,645; Years 3 to 8 £4,415.

Birchfield School is now fully co-educational with 57 girls and 77 boys. The last Independent Schools Inspectorate report in March 2012 highlighted the first-class education delivered by the School. The School obtained the highest descriptor, 'excellent' in the following key areas: Boarding; Extra-curricular provision, Pastoral Care, Leadership and Management; Overall achievements of the Pupils; Pupils' Personal Development and Quality of the Pupil's Learning and Achievements.

Birchfield's academic staff consists of many subject specialists who operate from well-equipped classrooms and modern facilities such as a music suite, science laboratory, design and technology workshop and art studio, and library. There are two ICT suites with networked PCs.

Sport is a fundamental part of school life and with superb playing fields and a recently refurbished outdoor swimming pool, Birchfield enjoys an excellent sporting reputation. Birchfield also has a floodlit synthetic sports surface which is used for a variety of sports and by all age groups.

Birchfield also encourages self-expression through music, drama, art and design technology. Art is a considerable strength of the School. The Music Department holds regular concerts and our musicians have performed with professional bodies in major productions. The pupils are also involved in a wide range of extra-curricular activities.

The School has a well-resourced Learning Enhancement department with two members of staff who provide excellent support for pupils with special educational needs. For those demonstrating strong academic prowess a scholarship form is in place during the final years.

In recent years senior pupils have achieved numerous scholarships and awards. One in three leavers at 13+ leaves with an award. There is a rich and challenging programme for pupils up to the age of 13, including the opportunity to board in the final years. When the time comes to say goodbye, senior pupils are prepared for entry into a wide range of independent senior schools and local grammar schools which suit best the individual's needs.

The Headmaster's wife is actively involved in school life and there is a full-time school nurse. Birchfield has a fine reputation for its all-round holistic education.

Set in 20 acres of attractive grounds and playing fields, Birchfield School is close to Wolverhampton and Telford and boasts excellent transport links.

Co-educational nursery Prepcare (managed by Prepcare LLP) operates on the Birchfield School site and welcomes children from 6 weeks to 4 years old, all year round (except weekends and Bank Holidays) from 8.00 am until 6.00 pm.

Charitable status. Birchfield School is a Registered Charity, number 528420.

Birkdale Prep School

Clarke House, Clarke Drive, Sheffield S10 2NS
Tel: 0114 267 0407
Fax: 0114 268 2929
email: prepschool@birkdaleschool.org.uk
website: www.birkdaleschool.org.uk

Chairman of Governors: Dr J R Goepel, MBChB, FRCPath

Head of Prep School: **C J Burch**, BA, PGCE

Age Range. 4–11.
Number of Boys. 250 day boys.
Fees per term (2014–2015). Pre-Prep Department £2,600; Prep Department £3,150. Lunch included.

Birkdale Prep School is Sheffield's only school specialising in quality education and care exclusively for boys. Continuous education is offered from 11–18 at Birkdale Senior School (Co-educational Sixth Form).

Birkdale Prep School is based at Clarke House, situated in a pleasant residential area near the University and close to the Senior School. The school has a firm Christian tradition and this, coupled with the size of the school, ensures that the boys develop their own abilities, whether academic or otherwise, to the full.

The Pre-Prep Department is based in a new building, Belmayne House. The facilities are outstanding and designed specifically to meet the needs of 4–7 year olds. Specialist subject teaching across the curriculum starts at the age of 7 and setting in the core subjects in the final two years enhances, still further, the pupil/teacher ratio.

The school has its own Matron and pastoral care is given high priority. Boys are encouraged to join a wide variety of clubs and societies in their leisure time. Music plays a significant part in school life, both in and out of the timetable. There is a large choir, brass band and orchestra and there are strong choral links with Sheffield Cathedral where many of the choristers are Birkdalians.

Cricket, Association and Rugby Football are played on the School's own substantial playing fields, which are within easy reach of the school. A broad range of activities is available as part of the extensive extra-curricular programme.

The majority of boys pass into the Senior School.

Charitable status. Birkdale School is a Registered Charity, number 1018973, and a Company Limited by Guarantee, registered in England, number 2792166. It exists to provide education for boys.

Bishop's Stortford College Prep School

Maze Green Road, Bishop's Stortford, Herts CM23 2PH
Tel: 01279 838607
Fax: 01279 306110
email: psadmissions@bishopsstortfordcollege.org
website: www.bishopsstortfordcollege.org

Twitter: @BSCollege
Facebook: /bishopsstortfordcollege

Chairman of Governors: P J Hargrave, BSc, PhD

Head: **W J Toleman**, BA

Age Range. 4–13.
Number of Pupils. 54 boarders and 573 day pupils.
Fees per term (2014–2015). Full Boarders £5,814–£6,307; Overseas Boarders £6,074–£6,569; Weekly Boarders £5,751–£6,245; Day £4,042–£4,531; Pre-Prep £2,618–£2,669. There are no compulsory extras.

Bishop's Stortford College is a friendly, co-educational, day and boarding community providing high academic standards, good discipline and an excellent all-round education.

There are 50 full-time members of staff, and a small number of Senior School staff also teach in the Prep School. Being on the same campus as the Senior School, many College facilities (design and technology centre, music school, sports hall, swimming pool, all-weather pitches, dining hall, medical centre) are shared. The Prep School also has its own buildings containing a multi-purpose Hall, laboratories, IT centre, library, art room and classrooms. An innovative, interactive science centre was opened in 2006. A major new development opened in 2013, enhancing and extending the Prep School facilities.

The Prep School routine and curriculum are appropriate to the 7–13 age range, with pupils being prepared for Common Entrance and Senior Schools' Scholarships, although most children proceed to the College Senior School. There are 23 forms streamed by general ability and setted for Maths. High standards of work and behaviour are expected and the full development, within a happy and friendly atmosphere, of each child's abilities in sport and the Arts is actively encouraged. A strong swimming tradition exists and many of the Staff are expert coaches of the major games (rugby, hockey, cricket, netball, rounders, tennis and swimming). The choirs and orchestra flourish throughout the year, and two afternoons of Activities provide opportunities for pupils to participate in many minor sports, outdoor pursuits, crafts, computing and chess. Six major dramatic productions occur every year.

A Pre-Prep for 4–6 year olds was opened in 1995 and new purpose-built accommodation was opened in September 2005.

The Prep School is run on boarding lines with a six-day week and a 5.00 pm finish on four days with Wednesdays ending at 4.00 pm and Saturdays at 3.00 pm. The 7 and 8 year olds have a slightly shorter day and their own dedicated building.

Entry tests for 7, 8, 9, 10, 11 year olds are held each January. Scholarships are available at 10+ (Academic and Music) and 11+ (Academic, Music and Art), as is Financial Assistance.

Charitable status. The Incorporated Bishop's Stortford College Association is a Registered Charity, number 311057. Its aims and objectives are to provide high quality Independent Boarding and Day education for boys and girls from age 4 to 18.

Bishopsgate School

Englefield Green, Surrey TW20 0YJ
Tel: 01784 430460 (Admissions)
             01784 432109 (School Office)
email: headmaster@bishopsgate.surrey.sch.uk
             admissions@bishopsgate.surrey.sch.uk
website: www.bishopsgate-school.co.uk

Chairman of Governors: Mr A Taee

Headmaster: Mr A H Cowell, BEd

Age Range. 3–13.
Number of Pupils. 372.
Fees per term (2014–2015). £4,489 (Years 5–8), £3,971 (Years 3–4), £3,324 (Years 1–2), £2,930 (Reception), Nursery: £1,590 (5 mornings), £1,260 (5 afternoons).

Set in beautiful woodland, close to Windsor Great Park, Bishopsgate is blessed with a glorious learning environment. The heart of the school remains a large, Victorian house, but recent developments have included a multi-purpose sports hall, brand new classroom blocks for both Lower and Upper Schools and an all-weather pitch. A new library and performing arts centre opened in 2007 and in 2010 a state-of-the-art Design Technology studio was added. Other specialist facilities include a Science laboratory, Art and Design studio, Music School, ICT suite and extensive playing fields. Our magnificent new 25-metre indoor swimming pool opened in November 2013 and swimming is now incorporated into our curriculum from Nursery.

Children may enter Bishopsgate from the age of 3 into our Nursery. Our trained staff and well-equipped rooms ensure that each child is given the best possible start to life. There is a warm family atmosphere as we recognise how important it is for children to feel happy and secure. We place great emphasis on building a solid foundation of social skills and a love of learning, which will enable each child to settle confidently to school life. A wide variety of activities is on offer with plenty of opportunities for healthy outdoor learning, including Forest School.

Beyond Nursery, a class teacher remains at the core of each child's learning. Emphasis is placed on establishing a firm foundation in literacy and numeracy, but the curriculum is broad with a range of educational visits planned to enrich and extend the children's learning. Good use is made of our glorious grounds as a learning resource. The teaching of French, Music, PE, Singing and Dance is provided by specialist teachers.

Form-based teaching continues in Years Three and Four, but by Year Five all teaching is by subject specialists. Programmes of study in Upper School are full and varied, covering the traditional academic subjects as well as Art, Design, Music, Computer Studies, PSHE and Physical Education. The children are prepared carefully for entrance to a range of senior schools and we are proud of our record of success. We prepare children for 11+ entry to senior schools, but we hope our children will remain with us to 13 and participate in the exciting Prep School Baccalaureate.

In Upper School, opportunities to represent the school in sports teams, plays, choirs and instrumental groups are all part of the 'Bishopsgate Experience'. In addition, a busy programme of extra-curricular activities ensures that all children have the opportunity to shine at something.

Music plays an essential part in the life of the school with many of our pupils enjoying individual music lessons. There are choirs and ensembles. Participation by children of all abilities, with ample opportunities to perform, is our aim. Dramatic productions, dance and public speaking events all provide additional occasions when the children can develop their presentation skills.

Our vibrant Art and Design Department occupies a spacious studio equipped with a kiln for ceramics and a printing press for design projects. There is an annual art exhibition for both Lower and Upper School and the children's work is displayed proudly around the school and in our annual school magazine. There is a popular after-school Art club for children and regular weekend workshops with professional artists.

Team Games, Rowing, Athletics, Dance, Tennis, Gymnastics, Judo, Taekwondo, Swimming and much more are all included in a varied and exciting sporting programme within the school day. An extensive programme of inter-school fixtures is arranged each term and we like to see as many parents in support as possible! We like to win, but our priorities are participation, enjoyment and teamwork.

A prospectus and further details can be obtained from the Admissions Office.

Charitable status. Bishopsgate School is a Registered Charity, number 1060511. It aims to provide a broad and sound education for its pupils with thorough and personal pastoral care.

Blackheath Preparatory School

4 St German's Place, London SE3 0NJ
Tel: 020 8858 0692
Fax: 020 8858 7778
email: info@blackheathprepschool.com
website: www.blackheathprepschool.com

Co-educational Day School.

Chairman of Governors: Mr Hugh Stallard

Headmistress: Mrs P J Thompson, BA Hons, PGCE, BDA Dip

Age Range. 3–11.
Number of Pupils. 200 Girls, 181 Boys.
Fees per term (2014–2015). Nursery: £2,030–£3,280; Reception–Year 2 £3,295; Years 3–6 £3,590.

The school is located in an attractive residential area close to Blackheath village, overlooking the heath itself and borders of Greenwich Park. The five-acre site includes attractive playing fields, cricket nets, tennis courts and two playgrounds, providing enviable sporting opportunities and room for children to play.

A most attractive learning environment includes specialist rooms for Science, ICT, Art, DT, Maths and Music. A spacious multi-purpose hall and music suite enhance the opportunities for Music, Drama, Sport and leisure activities. Over 40 activities are offered in a wide-ranging extra-curricular programme.

Most children join the school in the nursery at the age of three and progress through the Pre-Prep (4–7) and Prep (7–11) before leaving to transfer to selective senior schools. Academic standards are high and pupils are well prepared for selection at 11 and achieve consistent success in obtaining places at their first choice of grammar or independent senior school. Over 50% of Year 6 pupils are awarded academic scholarships each year and a plethora of pupils are awarded scholarships in Art, Music, Drama and Sport.

The form teacher of every class is responsible for the pastoral welfare of each child. In the Nursery and the Pre-Prep the key worker and the form teacher are primarily responsible for teaching the children. However, there is a strong emphasis on specialist teaching from the very beginning. Music, French, PE, Drama and Dance are introduced in the Nursery. As the children progress through the school, more specialist teachers are responsible for Art, ICT, Design Technology, Maths, English and Science. The quality of teaching has been recognised as one of the many strengths of the school and pupils display real pleasure in their learning.

The school positively encourages parental involvement in the daily life of the school. The strong ethos and vision of the school is underpinned by the vibrant enthusiasm of all involved and by the very strong sense of community.

The Blue Coat School

Somerset Road, Edgbaston, Birmingham B17 0HR
Tel: 0121 410 6800
Fax: 0121 454 7757
email: admissions@thebluecoatschool.com
website: www.thebluecoatschool.com

Founded 1722. Co-educational Day Preparatory School.

Chairman of Governors: Mr B H Singleton

Headmaster: **Mr A D J Browning**, MA Cantab, PGCE

Age Range. 2–11.
Number of Pupils. The total enrolment is 558 children. Buttons Nursery and Pre-Prep have 266 girls and boys from 2–7 years, while Prep has 292 from 7–11 years.

There is a graduate and qualified full-time teaching staff of 42, and 8 part-time teachers.

Fees per term (2014–2015). Pre-Prep: £2,455–£3,090; Prep: £3,645–£3,775. The fees quoted include lunches and morning and afternoon breaks. Over 50 extra-curricular activities are available, some of which are charged as extras.

Assisted Places are available at reduced charges to children with a demonstrable need.

Scholarships are offered for academic and musical excellence at age 7.

The School is set in 15 acres of grounds and playing fields just 2 miles from the centre of Birmingham. Its well-designed buildings and facilities comprise the Chapel, the Administrative Building, the Prep Teaching Centre, the Pre-Prep Department, the Pre-School (Buttons Nursery), sports pitches, short tennis courts and a superb multi-purpose Sports Centre with a heated 25m swimming pool. After-school care is available. In Prep this is provided in two spacious, purpose-designed Houses.

Additional features include the Library Resource Centre and specialist facilities for Science, Art, Design and Technology, Music, Media Studies and ICT. All the classrooms have an IWB, and the school is very well equipped with Apple and Windows computers including desktops, laptops and tablets.

Children are prepared for scholarships and examinations to prestigious local schools. The school enjoys particular success in the 11+ examinations to Birmingham's grammar schools and the schools of the King Edward VI Foundation. The Statutory Framework for the Early Years Foundation Stage is followed for children aged 2 to 5, and the National Curriculum is incorporated at Key Stages 1 and 2 as part of a wider academic structure.

The school places great emphasis on Music. The robed Chapel Choir is affiliated to the RSCM, and there are five further choirs and a significant number of instrumental groups and ensembles. The school benefits from Sibelius software, used in the teaching of composition, and from a Steinway concert grand housed in the spacious auditorium. Musicals, concerts and recitals feature in abundance, involving the great majority of the children. Over 250 instrumental lessons are given weekly.

The main sports are Hockey, Netball, Rounders, Rugby, Soccer, Cricket, Athletics and Swimming. The teams enjoy considerable success in inter-school competitions and all children have the opportunity to develop their skills.

Extra-curricular activities include Gymnastics, Judo, Ballet, Drama, Speech Training and Chess. A Ski Trip, French Trip, excursions and field courses are available each year, together with a leadership training programme run in association with Outward Bound.

Charitable status. The Blue Coat School Birmingham Limited is a Registered Charity, number 1152244, and a Company Limited by Guarantee, registered in England, number 8502615.

Blundell's Preparatory School

Milestones House, Blundell's Road, Tiverton, Devon EX16 4NA
Tel: 01884 252393
Fax: 01884 232333
email: prep@blundells.org
website: www.blundells.org

Chairman of Governors: Mr C M Clapp, FCA

Headmaster: **Mr A D Southgate**, BA Ed Hons

Age Range. 3–11 years.
Numbers of Pupils. Boys and Girls: Prep (aged 7–11) 140 Pre-Prep (aged 3–7) 80.
Fees per term (2014–2015). Prep: £3,495–£3,575 (Lunch £275); Pre-Prep: £2,020–£2,575 (Lunch £240); Nursery: £465 (3 sessions, lunch £144), £155 per additional session (lunch £48).

Blundell's Preparatory School is a family school and all the staff adopt a personal interest in every child and work in partnership with the parents. The school places great emphasis on children being happy, secure and confident, thus offering individuals every opportunity to achieve their full potential within a caring family atmosphere.

The School has been established for over seventy years and is part of the Blundell's Charitable Trust. It enjoys its own separate site within the very extensive Blundell's campus. This rural setting is within easy reach of the market town of Tiverton and is conveniently placed less than ten minutes from the M5 motorway and Tiverton Parkway Station.

The School has an excellent reputation for providing the essentials. Sound academic standards are based on providing the core subjects of Maths, English and Science taught to an extremely high standard. Added to this is the bonus of a wide range of supplementary subjects, well taught by specialist teachers. The School has recently had a major redevelopment and a significant extension. This includes a fully-equipped Art & Design Centre and a new Food Technology Suite.

Drama, music and art flourish at Blundell's Preparatory School with all the children participating fully both in lessons and as part of extra-curricular activities. Specialist music teachers offer an extensive variety of different instruments. The Drama and Music department have their own dedicated facility.

The sports department has an enviable reputation of producing good all-round sporting pupils, as well as nurturing and extending those with talent. Amongst the sports offered are rugby, football, netball, hockey and cross-country in the winter and cricket, rounders, tennis, athletics and swimming in the summer. The Preparatory School has access to the extensive sporting facilities within Blundell's campus.

There is an comprehensive choice of extra-curricular activities offered to the pupils which includes ballet, chess, fencing, golf, art, judo, bushcraft club and woodwork.

Priority entrance to Blundell's is given to its Preparatory School pupils but the school's autonomous position ensures that, if wished for, the pupils are prepared for entrance, including scholarships, to a variety of other senior schools.

(*See also Blundell's School entry in HMC section.*)

Charitable status. Blundell's School is a Registered Charity, number 1081249. It exists to provide education for children.

Bootham Junior School

Rawcliffe Lane, York YO30 6NP
Tel: 01904 655021
email: junior@boothamschool.com
website: www.boothamschool.com

Clerk to the School Committee: Chris Petrie

Head: **Helen Todd**, BA Hons, MA Ed, QTS

Age Range. 3–11 Co-educational.
Number of Pupils. 150.
Fees per term (2014–2015). £2,200–£3,200 inc lunch for full-time pupils.

Bootham Junior School stands apart by treating each member of its community, in a practical application of Quaker principles, as equally important. We welcome all faiths or none, encouraging our children to develop their own convictions while learning to respect those of others. The Independent Schools Inspectorate reports '*A sense of calm and a quiet pace to the working of the school that enables individuals to flourish*'. Although our children are as boisterous as any others, and, indeed, enjoy a tolerance to behave as children, quietness is important. The values of cooperation, community, and quietness grow from the Quaker tradition, but they resonate with the modern world of work, where teams find solutions individuals can't, where knowledge is seen as interrelated and not separate, and where values-driven responses earn our respect.

At Bootham Junior School, we aim to encourage a life-long love of learning and inspirational teaching is a good place to start. Equally important is the mutual high regard and understanding that children and teachers enjoy. This relationship provides the very best environment for learning to take place. High standards are achieved because children feel happy, confident, motivated and respected. Education is more than examination preparation; it is about unlocking potential skills and aptitudes. We want our children to find their particular strengths: through sport, through music, through the Arts, through outdoor education, through social debate and action.

Bootham Junior School has a beautiful sports field, a swimming pool at the senior school dating from 1912 and hard courts for tennis and netball. The range of sports taught include: gymnastics, dance, athletics, netball, tennis, swimming, football, basketball, cricket and rounders. Our Director of Music has a range of musical groups including: two choirs, orchestra, flute group, string group, clarinet group and recorder group. Individual music lessons are also available in all instruments should parents wish it. Engagement with the community is in line with a Quaker sense of responsibility and extends to children's activities too. Drama flourishes both within and beyond the formal curriculum. Regular productions of plays and musicals cater for different age groups and allow talents to be explored, nurtured and showcased. Children also take part in LAMDA schemes for recital and public speaking. Our Outdoor Classroom is an extremely well-used resource and all children have the opportunity to take part in residential experiences, from nursery age onwards. We believe in building adaptable, resilient young people who can respond to the world around them. Whatever their interests, this is the place where all our children can find inspiration and where they will be inspired. The small size of our school means that everyone has the chance to try something new. The result is a sense of personal achievement both in and outside the classroom.

Charitable status. Bootham School is a Registered Charity, number 513645.

Boundary Oak School

Roche Court, Wickham Road, Fareham, Hampshire PO17 5BL
Tel: 01329 280955
Fax: 01329 827656
email: registrar@boundaryoak.co.uk
            office@boundaryoak.co.uk
website: www.boundaryoak.co.uk
Twitter: @boundaryoak
Facebook: /boundaryoak

Headmistress: **Mrs Hazel Kellett**, BSc Hons, PGCE

Age Range. 2–13.
Number of Pupils. 8 Boarders, 84 Day Pupils.
Fees per term (2014–2015). Full Boarders £5,315–£6,535; Weekly Boarders £4,740–£5,960 Day Pupils: £2,720–£4,170 (Reception–Year 8), Nursery £1,280–£2,500 (all day).

The school was founded in 1918 and moved to Roche Court in 1960. A new 99 year lease was secured in 1994. The school is set in 22 acres of pleasant, self-contained grounds between Fareham and Wickham in Hampshire and enjoys extensive views of the countryside around.

The Nursery Department takes children from the age of 2 to rising 5 and this group is housed in a purpose-built centre offering the most up-to-date facilities. This department is structured to the needs of this age group and the day can extend from 8.00 am to either 12 noon or 5.30 pm.

The Pre-Prep Department has its own purpose-built buildings and other facilities within the school, and caters for children from rising 5 to 8 years of age.

At 8 years the children move to the Preparatory Department where they remain until they are 13+. Full, weekly and flexi boarding are offered to all from the age of 7 years and the school has a policy of admitting boarders in a flexible system that is of great benefit to all. Pupils are prepared for a wide number of independent schools throughout the United Kingdom in a friendly and caring environment.

Apart from the historic main house of Roche Court where the boarders live, there is the Jubilee Block of classrooms, two laboratories and a Geography room in a separate building, the Widley Block, Library and the Music Centre, which incorporates a computer centred music generating complex. The School has a new ICT Suite and a purpose-built Art and Design Technology Centre that incorporates work areas for Photography, Pottery and Carpentry. The school has a fine Assembly Hall that is also used for Drama and Physical Education.

As well as extensive playing fields with woods beyond for cross country, three new astroturf tennis courts and a netball court, there is an outdoor swimming pool and the indoor Fareham Pool is within very easy reach with our three mini-buses.

Most sports are taught and there is a wide selection of clubs and activities run in the school for both day and boarding pupils including judo, horse riding, art, camp craft, chess and shooting.

For a copy of the prospectus and full details of scholarships, please apply to the Headmistress, or view us on the internet at www.boundaryoakschool.co.uk.

Bradford Grammar Junior School

Keighley Road, Bradford, West Yorkshire BD9 4JP
Tel: 01274 553742
Fax: 01274 553745
email: chsec@bradfordgrammar.com
website: www.bradfordgrammar.com
Twitter: @GabrielNhg

Chairman of the Board of Governors: Lady L Morrison, LLB

Headmaster: **N H Gabriel**, BA, Dip Arch

Age Range. 6–11.
Number of Pupils. 101 boys, 87 girls.
Fees per annum (2014–2015). £9,225.

Bradford Grammar Junior School is a selective school for boys and girls aged 6–11, holding no catchment boundaries and a strong reputation for specialist teaching.

The school seeks to inspire happy, respectful and grounded children, who are ready for the transition to Senior School. The school's aim is to provide exceptional care in a relaxed atmosphere so that each child can thrive.

Location. Bradford Grammar Junior School is located at the same site as the Senior School at Keighley Road, Bradford. It is housed in an original seventeenth century manor house called Clock House.

Specialist facilities. The school offers pupils a wide range of specialist facilities, including a swimming pool, theatre, instrumental music tuition and dedicated Computer Science and Design Technology rooms. Full use is made of the Senior School facilities including Science laboratories, Sports facilities and Art rooms.

Specialist teaching. In Years 2, 3 and 4 (age 6–9) pupils are taught the majority of subjects by form teachers and are based in their classrooms, with specialist teaching for Art, Modern Foreign Languages, Music Computing, and Games. In Years 5 and 6 pupils have increasing input from specialist teachers utilising the extensive facilities throughout the whole school.

Co-curricular Activities. There is a long tradition of excellence in sport, music and drama. Co-curricular activities take place during lunchtimes. Sports include rugby, netball, hockey, swimming, cross-country, cricket, rounders and athletics. Societies and clubs include dance, gymnastics, animation and Design Technology.

Pastoral Care. The school's aim is to provide young boys and girls with a wide range of educational experiences and to develop the right attitude to learning so that they fulfil their potential. The school is a safe, friendly, tolerant and caring environment.

After Care. Bradford Grammar Junior School provides before and after school care from 8.00 am to 6.00 pm.

Transport Links. The school organises private coach transport for pupils travelling to and from Huddersfield, Halifax, Bramhope, Horsforth, Rawdon, Wharfedale and Oxenhope. It is situated a short walk from Frizinghall Railway Station, which is on the Airedale and Wharfedale lines. There are half hourly rail services, taking approximately 30 minutes, to Leeds, Skipton, Ilkley and Apperley Bridge from 2015.

Entry. The school is selective and takes a number of pupils each year for entry from Year 2 (age 6–7) through to Year 6 (age 10–11).

Entry to Years 2, 3 and 4 (age 6, 7 and 8) is by assessment. Entry to Years 5 and 6 (age 9 and 10) is by entrance examination and involves tests in Maths and English.

Pupils who progress from Bradford Grammar School Junior School to the Senior School are not required to sit the 11+ entrance exam. The close relationship between the two schools enables a smooth transition from Junior to Senior School.

Charitable status. Bradford Grammar School (The Free Grammar School of King Charles II at Bradford) is a Registered Charity, number 529113. It exists to provide education for children.

Brambletye

East Grinstead, West Sussex RH19 3PD
Tel: 01342 321004
Fax: 01342 770197
email: schooloffice@brambletye.com
website: www.brambletye.co.uk

Chairman of Governors: A J Hynard, Esq

Headmaster: **N T Westlake**, LLB, PGCE

Age Range. 2½–13 Co-educational.
Number of Pupils. 272 day/boarding pupils.
Fees per term (2014–2015). Boarders £7,390–£7,700; Day Pupils £5,570–£6,330, Pre-Prep (Years 1 & 2) £2,995. Nursery £2,490 (5 full days).

Brambletye is an independent day and boarding Preparatory School for boys and girls aged 7–13 years, situated in beautiful grounds in rural Sussex. There is a Pre-Preparatory/Nursery department which takes boys and girls from the age of 2½ years to the age of 7 years.

Brambletye is a large country house in its own wooded estate of 140 acres, overlooking Ashdown Forest and Weir Wood Reservoir. The school stands one mile south of East Grinstead. Gatwick Airport is only 20 minutes by car and Heathrow is an hour away. London is 30 miles by road and 50 minutes by rail. There is escorted travel to and from London at the beginning and end of all exeat weekends and half-term holidays.

The school has outstanding academic, sporting, music, drama and arts facilities. These include a new modern classroom block, 2 redeveloped science laboratories, an up-to-date Arts Room and Design Technology workshop, an extensive Library, an ICT room, a large theatre and music rooms. There is also a Sports Hall, tennis and netball courts, two squash courts, a swimming pool, a golf course and several playing fields. We aim to produce happy, confident, well-rounded children who work hard, enjoy drama, games and music, play a part in some of the numerous societies and hobbies, and take a full share in the daily life of the school. These facilities in conjunction with high quality teaching staff, generate regular awards for the children from the schools that inherit them.

Brambletye has always been run along family lines, with a distinctive warm and friendly atmosphere. Traditional values such as high standards of manners and good behaviour provide a platform for academic and personal development. As a co-educational day and boarding school, pupils enjoy and benefit from living and working in a community. At weekends, there is a full programme of activities for the boarders and children are encouraged to make constructive use of their spare time. The environment is inspirational and pupils develop a love of learning which creates a positive interaction with the staff and a curiosity about the world around us.

The Nursery and Pre-Preparatory Department is situated in a self-contained purpose-built state-of-the-art building. The main aim of the Department is to provide a secure, friendly and structured environment in which all children are encouraged to achieve their full potential and to develop at their own rate.

Children may join the Nursery class at the age of two and a half before progressing to Reception at four. Boys and girls transfer to the Preparatory Department at the age of seven. All children acquire the basic skills, while following the breadth of the National Curriculum. Religious Studies, Physical Education, Art, Music, Science and Technology are all integrated into the weekly timetable. Children have swimming lessons throughout the year in the indoor pool, and teachers from the Preparatory Department visit regularly to teach Music and to coach games. The Pre-Prep has an exciting School in the Woods project.

Enquiries about admissions, our scholarships and bursary programme are welcomed throughout the year. Brambletye offers generous discounts for Armed Services Families. Please contact the Headmaster's Secretary for a prospectus.

Charitable status. Brambletye School Trust Limited is a Registered Charity, number 307003. It aims to provide an all-round education for the children in its care.

Bramcote Junior School
Junior School to Scarborough College

Filey Road, Scarborough, North Yorkshire YO11 3BA
Tel: 01723 380606
Fax: 01723 380607
email: juniorschool@scarboroughcollege.co.uk
website: www.scarboroughcollege.co.uk
Twitter: @Scarboroughcol1
Facebook: /Scarborough College

Chairman of the Governors: Dr John Renshaw

Head of School: **D Davey**, BEd Hons

Age Range. 3–11 Co-educational.
Number of Pupils. 110.
Fees per term (2014–2015). Tuition: Years 5–6 £3,546, Years 3–4 £3,298, Years 1–2 £2,782, Reception £2,207. Pre-School: £18.50 (per half-day session), £36.00 (full day with lunch).

Wrap-around School Care (3–7 year olds) is all-inclusive. Holiday Clubs (8 am to 6 pm) operate throughout the main school holidays (closed for Christmas and Easter): £14 per half day, £27 per full day.

Bramcote Junior School was formed from the merger of Bramcote Preparatory School with Scarborough College Junior School in 2012. The origins of both schools date back to the 19th Century.

The Junior School now occupies superb purpose-built premises on the Scarborough College site with an outlook over Oliver's Mount, the South Bay and Scarborough Castle. Facilities include a self-contained pre-school, early years and junior suites, an administration unit together with a school hall and a fully dedicated design and technology/art workshop. Classrooms are well equipped including many with interactive whiteboards and all classroom computers are networked to the schools' two ICT suites with intranet and internet facilities. The Junior School shares many impressive resources and amenities with the Senior School: science laboratories, drama studio, main sports/drama hall, music school, sports fields, a full-size all-weather pitch, swimming pool and school minibuses.

The breadth of opportunity on offer does not detract from the solid grounding pupils receive in the core subjects. Class teaching – with thoughtfully introduced specialist support where this is advantageous – is the pattern until Year 4. This is then advanced by full subject specialist teaching in the last two years, in readiness for transfer to the Senior School. The full complement of well-qualified staff ensures a generous teacher-pupil ratio. Provision is further enhanced by a Special Educational Needs Coordinator who oversees the school's learning support unit.

The standard of pastoral care at the school is very high. The Junior School seeks to nurture well-rounded, confident and competent pupils who are ready for the challenges of secondary education at Scarborough College.

Bramley School

Chequers Lane, Walton-on-the-Hill, Tadworth, Surrey KT20 7ST
Tel: 01737 812004
Fax: 01737 819945
email: office@bramleyschool.co.uk
website: www.bramleyschool.co.uk
Twitter: @BramleySchool
Facebook: /Bramley-School

Chairman of Governors: Mr Mark Nallen

Headmistress: **Ms P Burgess**, MA, BEd Hons, NPQH, IAPS

Age Range. 3–11.
Number in School. 90 Girls.
Fees per term (2014–2015). £1,625 (mornings only) to £3,630.

Bramley was founded in 1945 as an independent pre-preparatory and preparatory day school and became an Educational Trust in 1972. A registered charity, the school is administered by a Trust Council and all income is used for educational purposes.

The strength of Bramley School lies in its commitment to developing happy, confident, self-motivated pupils with a lifelong love of learning. An excellent teacher/pupil ratio; a caring friendly atmosphere; highly qualified, specialised and enthusiastic staff, and a genuine concern for each child's welfare contribute to academic success. Bramley achieves excellent examination results at 11+ and many girls gain places and scholarships to prestigious senior schools within both the independent and maintained sectors. Alongside this, children are encouraged to develop their own interests and talents and a wide range of extra-curricular activities are offered.

Throughout the school girls work in small classes, according to their age group, with particular attention being paid to meeting the specific needs of individuals. All children in the Pre-Preparatory Department are taught by dedicated class teachers who have full responsibility for their classes, whilst older children benefit from specialised teaching staff, for example in Mathematics, English, Science, Computing, Music, PE and Art. A specialist teacher teaches French from the age of 5. The Preparatory Curriculum is constantly being developed to keep abreast of educational changes in the National Curriculum, whilst retaining the excellence of well-tried methods.

The Little Bramley Nursery Department is an ideal starting point for school life with literacy and numeracy skills fostered through play in a safe and nurturing environment. Children from three years of age settle quickly and happily and the impressive outdoor facilities allow the early curriculum to take place outdoors as well as indoors.

Open Mornings take place twice in the academic year – details can be found on the school website.

Charitable status. Bramley Educational Trust Limited is a Registered Charity, number 270046. Its aim is to provide an excellent educational establishment for 3–11 year old girls.

Brandeston Hall
Framlingham College's Preparatory School

Brandeston, Woodbridge, Suffolk IP13 7AH
Tel: 01728 685331
Fax: 01728 685437
email: admissions@brandestonhall.co.uk
website: www.brandestonhall.co.uk
Twitter: @brandestonhall
Facebook: /framcollege

Chairman of Governors: A W M Fane, MA, FCA

Headmaster: **M K Myers-Allen**, BSc Hons, PGCE

Deputy Head: R Sampson, BA Hons, PGCE

Senior Team:
Head of Junior Prep: Mrs J Loveridge, BA Hons, PGCE
Head of Pre-Prep & Nursery: Mrs R Steggles, BA Hons, EYPS
Head of Pastoral Care/Tutor: Ms S Thomson, BEd Hons
Head of Co-Curricular: B Wilson, BEd Hons

Age Range. 2½–13 Co-educational.
Number of Pupils. 249: Boarders 70, Day 134; Pre-Prep 45, Nursery 23.
Fees per term (2014–2015). Full Boarding £34 per night, Day £4,524 (inc lunch), Pre-Prep: Day £2,600 (inc lunch), Nursery: £35 (full day session inc lunch), £17 (half day session exc lunch).

All students are prepared for the ISEB Common Entrance Examination at 13 and it is worth noting that in the past 5 years all pupils leaving Brandeston have gained entry to the senior school of their choice, with a significant number choosing to make the transition to Framlingham College (*see HMC entry*)

A recent ISI Inspection Report described the children at Brandeston as *unfailingly polite to visitors* and pupils' social, moral, spiritual and cultural development was described as *outstanding*.

The ISI Inspection Report also recognised the *excellent standard* of boarding at Brandeston, which was recently backed up with an Ofsted Inspection that described the provision of boarding and pastoral care as *outstanding*. The girls and boys boarding accommodation is warm and welcoming and found on separate floors of the old manor house. The school has a core of full-time boarders and an increasing number of children who board on a flexible and occasional basis. All boarders enjoy a wide range of exciting evening and weekend activities.

Facilities include a library, sports hall, a Centre for Music and The Performing Arts, an Art and Design Centre, as well as two full-size floodlit all-weather pitches (hockey/tennis/netball courts) and a nine-hole golf course. In addition the parish church is enclosed in the grounds providing a focus for community activities, as well as a shooting range and covered swimming pool. Pupils also have use of all of the facilities at Framlingham College including the 20m indoor swimming pool, theatre, artificial pitches and castle.

Major games include rugby, hockey, cricket, netball, tennis, rounders and athletics. Skilled coaching is given and a full programme of matches is arranged at all levels in major and minor sports.

Music and Drama provide the perfect opportunity to star in a number of productions as well as performing in music recitals and attending drama workshops with visiting artists.

Pupils also enjoy many residential opportunities including camping trips throughout the UK, sports tours, adventure training camps and a biennial expedition to the Atlas Mountains. In addition Brandeston Hall has the use of a European Education Centre, Chateau de la Baudonnière, in Normandy, France. Senior pupils are encouraged to develop their French language skills as well as understanding and appreciating another culture.

Scholarships are available for 11+ entrants in Music, Academic and Sports.

Charitable status. Albert Memorial College is a Registered Charity, number 1114383. It exists for the purpose of educating children.

Brentwood Preparatory School

Middleton Hall, Middleton Hall Lane, Brentwood, Essex CM15 8EQ
Tel: 01277 243239 (ages 3–7)
           01277 243333 (ages 7–11)
Fax: 01277 243340
email: prep@brentwood.essex.sch.uk
           prep3-7@brentwood.essex.sch.uk
           prep7-11@brentwood.essex.sch.uk
website: www.brentwoodschool.co.uk

Chairman of Governors: C J Finch, FRICS

Headmaster: **Mr K J Whiskerd**, BA, PGCE

Head of Early Years and Key Stage 1: Mrs V Audas, BEd

Age Range. 3–11.
Number of Children. Prep 411.
Fees per term (2014–2015). Nursery £2,041, Prep £4,035.

Brentwood Preparatory School has its own buildings and grounds quite distinct from Brentwood School (qv) but close enough to share the use of its chapel, indoor swimming pool, Sports Centre and world-class athletics track.

The co-educational Preparatory School, which opened in 1892, educates children from age 3 to 7 in the spacious Higgs Building with very well-equipped classrooms. Entrance is by an informal assessment at age 3.

Older children, aged 7 to 11, are based in Middleton Hall, an elegant building which has its own extensive grounds, sports pitches and all-weather Astroturf. Entrance is at age 7 by an academically-selective test and candidates come from a wide range of schools. Small class sizes and a team of well-qualified teachers provide a caring and challenging environment. Specialist rooms for art, design technology, drama, French, ICT, music and science provide outstanding facilities and a stimulating environment in which children can thrive.

There is an extensive programme of house and inter-school sports matches. Three choirs, two orchestras and a variety of ensembles perform regularly both in and out of school. Every child has the opportunity to take part in a major drama production. There is a wide range of lunchtime and after-school clubs, and a late stay scheme for children to complete homework at school. Many day visits to museums and places of interest complement school-based work and children enjoy annual residential trips in the holidays.

The Preparatory School has a strong academic tradition and a reputation for providing an excellent all-round education. The vast majority of pupils transfer to the Senior School (founded in 1557) at age 11.

The Preparatory School was last inspected in 2013 by the ISI and received a superb report with inspectors giving 'excellent' findings in every category of school life. Inspectors reported that *"the School is successful in meeting its aims and offers a high quality educational experience to its pupils …The pupils' achievements are particularly notable in mathematics, literacy, music, art and drama"*. The School fulfils its aims *"to encourage pupils to develop a lifelong love of learning and to strive for the highest academic stan-*

dards in the classroom ...*Teaching is well planned with a high degree of awareness of the differing needs of all the pupils ...Extremely well planned, lively lessons ensure pupils of all ages thoroughly enjoy their learning and provide stimulus and challenge*".

The report continued: "*The teachers' subject knowledge is excellent in all subjects and pupils benefit from specialised teaching in a wide range of subjects. Teachers have very high expectations for pupils, and praise and encouragement are used to good effect. All staff know their pupils well and the excellent relationships are marked by mutual respect, creating an environment conducive to learning and exemplary behaviour from pupils in class.*"

Charitable status. Brentwood School (part of Sir Antony Browne's School Trust, Brentwood) is a Registered Charity, number 310864. It exists for the purpose of educating children.

Bricklehurst Manor

Bardown Road, Stonegate, Wadhurst, East Sussex TN5 7EL
Tel: 01580 200448
Fax: 01580 200998
email: office@bricklehurst.co.uk
website: www.bricklehurst.co.uk

Headmistress: **Mrs C Flowers**, CertEd, BEd Hons

Deputy Head: Mrs K Elliott, BA Hons, QTS, SEN accredited.

Age Range. 3–11.
Number of Pupils. 115.
Fees per term (2014–2015). Kindergarten sessional; Reception and Year 1 £2,700; Year 2 £2,900; Years 3–4 £3,300, Years 5–6 £3,600.

Bricklehurst Manor was founded in 1959. It now operates as a co-educational school for boys and girls from 3 years old. Children are prepared for Common Entrance or equivalent standard entrance examinations at 11.

Bricklehurst stands in 3 acres of mature gardens and grounds. Previously a private house, the school retains many home-like characteristics, not least a friendly, family atmosphere which helps young children bridge the gap between home and school, and build up their confidence in the comfort and security of familiar surroundings.

The school has a purpose-built Kindergarten. The school hall is used for PE, Dance, Drama, Music and any other activity requiring space. There is an Art/Science room, a reference library and a Music Room. Computers are used in all classrooms.

For outdoor playtime there is an orchard with an Adventure Playground, an all-weather grass area, swings and sandpit. In the games periods the older children play hockey, netball, football, tag rugby, rounders and cricket; tennis coaching is available all year round and all the children learn to swim in our own heated and covered pool.

Curriculum. In the Kindergarten 3 and 4 year olds are given a happy introduction to school life learning to mix with others of the same age, to play contentedly together as one of a group, and generally to act in an orderly manner. Through play and active learning, they also learn their letters and numbers, and make a start at reading and understanding simple number concepts.

From Reception Class onwards children stay all day. Gradually their curriculum is extended, subjects such as History, Geography, Religious Studies, Science and project work are introduced, and there are specialist teachers for Art and CDT, Drama and all musical activities. French is taught from Year 1. A variety of after-school activities are offered, including Spanish, LAMDA and Dance. Mathematics is set

by ability from Year 3 and reasoning skills are introduced from Year 4.

Bricklehurst has a reputation for sending children on to their next schools with a sensible attitude towards learning, and the ability to work independently and with enjoyment. A high standard of behaviour is expected, with emphasis on the gradual development of self-control, a sense of responsibility and real consideration for the needs of others.

Brighton & Hove High School Junior School
GDST

Radinden Manor Road, Hove, East Sussex BN3 6NH
Tel: 01273 280200
Fax: 01273 280201
email: enquiries@bhhs.gdst.net
website: www.bhhs.gdst.net
Twitter: @BHHSJuniors
Facebook: /BHHSJuniors

Chair of Local Governors: Mrs J Smith

Head: **Mrs S Cattaneo**

Age Range. Girls 3–11.
Number of Pupils. 245.
Fees per term (2014–2015). £2,495–£2,960, Nursery £2,055.

The Junior School of Brighton & Hove High School stands on a large site in Hove. It benefits from an extensive purpose-built site which provides many specialist areas such as a well-equipped IT suite, a large science lab, bright and airy art room, and a spacious music room with several practice rooms. Despite our urban site we make the most of our green areas including a pond and our large astroturf and netball courts are great additions to the PE opportunities.

Our Pre-School, which takes girls from age three, is very much part of the BHHS community and almost all girls transfer to the Reception class. We have a significant intake at Year Three and girls are then prepared for transfer to our Senior School at the end of Year Six. (*See Senior School entry in GSA section.*)

The ethos of the school is firmly centred on the benefits of a girls-only education. We believe that girls are more independent, focused and self-motivated and that relationships are more positive in a girl-centred setting. We put a strong emphasis on a rounded education and believe that confidence built at an early age with a range of opportunities and experiences provides a great platform for girls for the future. We currently run several choirs, an orchestra and other musical opportunities. We offer a wide PE curriculum which includes the opportunity to be involved in inter-school matches. Drama and Art are also well resourced and girls often get involved in local events such as the Brighton Festival.

We pride ourselves on having a strong relationship with parents and readily involve them in the life of the school. We continue to build positive links with the community and the wider world particularly through our link with Kenya. We are the holder of the prestigious Green Flag which reflects our eco work and commitment to energy saving and eco awareness. Despite the short distance between the sites we often use the opportunity to have whole-school events, such as an annual dance show for Years 3–13.

Charitable status. Brighton & Hove High School is part of The Girls' Day School Trust, which is a Registered Charity, number 306983.

Brighton College Prep School

Walpole Lodge, Walpole Road, Brighton, East Sussex BN2 0EU

Tel: 01273 704210
email: paprep@brightoncollege.net
website: www.brightoncollege.net

Chairman of Governors: Professor Lord Skidelsky, FBA

Headmaster: **Harry Hastings**, BA, MEd

Deputy Heads:
Jane Ashfold, BSc
Lois Griffiths, BPharm

Headmistress of Pre-Prep: Jo Williams, BEd

Head of Admissions, Prep and Pre-Prep: Rebecca Cahill, BA Hons

Age Range. 3–13.
Number of Pupils. Prep 302, Pre-Prep 224.
Fees per term (2014–2015). From £2,920 (Reception) to £5,650 (Year 8).

Brighton College Prep School is a co-educational school, which offers a broad curriculum taught to high standards by dedicated and energetic staff. The Pre-Prep School cares for children from 3–7 years in a nearby purpose-built building with playing fields, overlooking the sea. The Prep School is situated adjacent to the Senior School on its own site. The site is urban, but enjoys close proximity to the sea, the Downs and the vibrant sports and culture of Brighton, where an annual arts festival is held in May.

The excellent facilities provided by Brighton College are shared by the Prep School. These include the Chapel, swimming pool, a sports hall, two areas of playing fields, a purpose-built Performing Arts Centre and The Great Hall, which doubles as a large theatre for the Prep School's annual senior musical. The Prep School itself has many specialist rooms including a well-equipped ICT suite, a large design technology room, art room, science laboratories, home economics room, library and hall. Art and DT are both key subjects on the timetable for all year groups. The Pre-Prep School offers specialist lessons in art, music, French, Mandarin, PE and games on its own well-equipped site.

Academic standards are high and are one of the foundations upon which school life is built, along with the broad range of subjects and activities. A variety of teaching methods is used – the key principle being that children enjoy their lessons and thus develop a love for learning.

The school caters for able dyslexic pupils who are fully integrated into classes. The Dyslexia Centre attached to the school provides specialist teaching; dyslexic pupils are given extra support in small groups and may be withdrawn from French.

Sport is a very important part of the life at the school. Major girls' games are netball, hockey, athletics and rounders. Major boys' games are football, rugby, cricket and athletics. Swimming is on the curriculum for all pupils.

The Prep School is well known for its musical strength with a suite of specially designed music rooms and practice areas. Two orchestras, a concert band and three choirs are organised by the Director of Music and thirty-five visiting music teachers provide tuition for the large number of pupils who learn a wide variety of instruments including piano, violin, harp, saxophone, clarinet and drums.

Drama clubs and coaching are available for every year group and there are opportunities for children to perform during the academic year through assemblies, recitals, chapel services and also through annual drama productions and musicals.

The Brighton College School of Dance, based in the Performing Arts Centre, is thriving and many pupils attend classes on Saturdays and after school during the week.

The Prep School runs a large number of clubs and activities after school and at lunchtimes. There is a range of school bus routes. For details of assessment procedures, scholarships available at 13+ and bus routes, please contact the Director of Admissions.

Charitable status. Brighton College is a Registered Charity, number 307061. It exists to provide high quality education for boys and girls aged 3–18.

BGS Infants and Juniors

Elton Road, Bristol BS8 1SR

Tel: 0117 973 6109
Fax: 0117 974 1941
email: recruitment@bgs.bristol.sch.uk
website: www.bristolgrammarschool.co.uk

Chairman of Governors: Mr N Reeve, FCA

Headmaster: **Mr Peter R Huckle**, BA, MEd

Age Range. 4–11.
Number of Pupils. 327: 206 Boys, 121 Girls (all day children).
Fees per term (2014–2015). Juniors: Years 3–6 £2,960. Infants: Years 1 & 2 £2,750, Reception £2,325. Fees include Lunch.

BGS Infants and Juniors is an independent co-educational day school. It was founded in 1900 and since 2010 has offered Infant as well as Junior provision. The school occupies self-contained buildings on the same site as the Senior School, Bristol Grammar School (*see entry in HMC section*). Its own facilities include a Hall, Library, Music, Art, Science and technology rooms. Some facilities are shared with the Senior School, particularly the Sports Hall, Theatre and Dining Hall. The school now thrives on the happy and purposeful demands of approximately 320 girls and boys aged 4–11 years.

Entry into BGS Infants is by an informal assessment session. Entry for the Junior School is by test and is normally at seven or nine years old (entry to other age groups is subject to the availability of places). Peloquin bursaries are awarded annually and are means tested. Children who have been members of the School since the start of Year 5 or earlier are offered places in the Senior School following continuous assessment of their progress. Other children take the normal Senior School entrance test.

The school aims to provide a rich, broad and balanced curriculum while also maintaining a nurturing environment for children to flourish. BGS Infants and Juniors encourages all students to develop their own ideas, giving support so they gain skills and confidence, and offering challenges to stretch their thinking. Many subjects are taught by subject specialists, including specialists from the Senior School. Music, Art, Dance and Drama are particularly encouraged with the annual MADD Evening a particular highlight. There are many clubs and activities including Craft, Lego, Gardening, Fencing, Orchestra, Chess, Ukelele and extra sports. In addition all children in the Infant School, and many Juniors, take part in Forest School and have violin tuition. The children have many opportunities to develop leadership and responsibility. The Infant and Junior School Councils meet regularly with the Headmaster and there is a Charity Committee.

A wide range of sports is offered to the pupils at the School's superb playing fields at Failand with its state-of-the-art sports pavilion. The impressive purpose-built sports hall on the main campus provides facilities for indoor PE. Pastoral care is provided by the Form Tutors and Assistant

Heads, supported by all teaching staff and the Headmaster. Form Tutors take a lead in ensuring that children are learning and progressing well. A prosperous House system produces many friendships between age groups, with mentors and buddies showing new pupils the ropes, making sure that things are running smoothly for them. This leads to a strong sense of family and community within the school owing much to the warm and trusting relationships between children with each other and with their teachers.

Charitable status. Bristol Grammar School is a Registered Charity, number 1104425. The object of the Charity is the provision and conduct in or near the City of Bristol of a day school for boys and girls.

Brockhurst School

Hermitage, Newbury, Berkshire RG18 9UL
Tel: 01635 200293
email: registrar@brockmarl.org.uk
website: www.brockmarl.org.uk

Headmaster: **D J W Fleming**, MA Oxon, MSc

Age Range. 3 to 13.
Number of Boys. 154 Boys (including 74 Boarders).
Fees per term (2014–2015). Boarding £6,950, Day £4,865–£5,175. Pre-Prep School (Ridge House): £3,090 (full-time). Temporary Overseas Boarders £7,500.

Established in 1884, Brockhurst is situated in 500 acres of its own grounds in countryside of outstanding beauty, but is only four miles from access to the M4. The school is located on the same site as Marlston House Girls' Preparatory School which occupies separate, listed buildings. Boys and Girls are educated separately, but the two schools join forces for drama, music and many hobbies. In this way, Brockhurst and Marlston House aim to combine the best features of the single-sex and co-educational systems: academic excellence and social mixing. The schools have built up a fine reputation for high standards of pastoral care given to each pupil within a caring, family establishment. (*See also entry for Marlston House School.*)

The Pre-Prep School, Ridge House, is a co-educational department for 75 children aged 3 to 6½.

Boys are prepared for entry to all Independent Senior Schools and there is an excellent scholarship record.

All boys play Soccer, Rugby, Hockey and Cricket and take part in Athletics, Cross Country and Swimming (25m indoor heated pool). Additional activities include Riding (own ponies), Fencing, Judo, Shooting (indoor rifle range) and Tennis (indoor court and three hard courts). Facilities for gymnastics and other sporting activities are provided in a purpose-built Sports Hall. Year 7 pupils make a week-long visit to a Château in France as part of their French language studies.

The school is currently building a new dedicated Music School and Theatre to open in the Summer Term 2014. Music and art are important features of the curriculum and a good number of pupils have won scholarships to senior schools in recent years.

Where appropriate, pupils can be transported by members of staff to and from airports if parents are serving in the armed forces or otherwise working overseas.

Bromsgrove Preparatory & Pre-Preparatory School

Prep:
Old Station Road, Bromsgrove, Worcs B60 2BU
Tel: 01527 579679
Fax: 01527 576177

Pre-Prep & Nursery:
Avoncroft House, Hanbury Road, Bromsgrove, Worcs B60 4JS
Tel: 01527 579679
Fax: 01527 576177

email :   admissions@bromsgrove-school.co.uk
website: www.bromsgrove-school.co.uk
Twitter: @BromsSchool
Facebook: /BromsgroveSchool

Chairman of Governors: S Towe, CBE

Headmistress: **Mrs Jacquelyne Deval-Reed**, BEd

Age Range. 3–13.
Number of Pupils. Prep School (7–13): 213 day boys, 217 day girls, 47 boy boarders, 23 girl boarders. Pre-Preparatory & Nursery (3–7): 111 boys, 101 girls.
Fees per term (2014–2015). Nursery: £2,450 full-time; Pre-Prep: £2,200–£2,600; Prep: £3,375–£4,385 day, £6,845–£8,440 full boarding, £4,990–£6,040 weekly boarding.

Forces Bursaries and, from 11+, scholarships are available.

Bromsgrove Preparatory School feeds the adjacent 900-strong Senior School. (*See Bromsgrove School entry in HMC section.*) The sites covering 100 acres offer exclusive and shared facilities, with over £25 million pounds having been invested in the last ten years. The most recent addition to the School's facilities is a new purpose-converted boarding house for 70 boys and girls which now allows the school's youngest boarders to live together in modern and comfortable surroundings. Other recent improvements include a new science laboratory, refurbishment of the library, main hall and sports hall. Pupils have access to a flourishing Forest School. Teachers working in both Senior and Preparatory Schools ensure continuity of ethos and expectation.

Academic, sporting and cultural facilities are extensive and outstanding.

Pupils are admitted at the age of 7+ with another substantial intake at 11+, but pupils including boarders are admitted throughout the age range up to 13. Admission to the school is by Entrance Test (English and Maths) supported by a report from the current school. Year 5 and 6 pupils are assessed during the course of the year; the outcome of these assessments allow them to be guaranteed a place in Bromsgrove Senior School two years later. Pupils admitted at age 11 are also guaranteed entry to the Senior School.

Prep School boarding is flourishing and the junior boarding house is a lively, homely environment where pupils are cared for by resident houseparents and a team of tutors. The school aims to make a boarder's first experience of life away from home enjoyable and absorbing.

Parents can choose either a five or six day week for their children. All academic lessons are timetabled from Monday to Friday with Saturdays offering an optional and flexible programme of activities and sports fixtures. The school has a national reputation in a number of sports.

The aim of the school is to provide a first-class education, which identifies and develops the potential of individual pupils, academically, culturally and socially. It prepares them to enter the Senior School with confidence.

In the Preparatory School there is a purposeful and lively atmosphere. Mutual trust, respect and friendship exist between staff and pupils. The high-quality and dedication of the teaching staff, favourable teacher/pupil ratio and regular monitoring of performance ensure that the natural spontaneity and inquisitiveness of this age group are directed purposefully. The pastoral care system, rated as 'outstanding' in the 2010 ISI Inspection, is rooted in the school's Christian heritage and firmly founded on the form tutor. It is designed to ensure that every pupil is recognised as an important individual and that their development is nurtured.

The School has its own feeder Nursery and Pre-Preparatory School which takes children from the age of 3. The clear majority of children transfer to the Prep School at the end of Year 2. Situated just a mile away in the spacious tree-lined grounds of an old manor house, the Pre-Preparatory School has spacious and light classrooms, equipped with interactive whiteboards. High teacher to pupil ratios and small class sizes ensure each pupil's individual needs are met.

Charitable status. Bromsgrove School is a Registered Charity, number 1098740. It exists to provide education for boys and girls.

Brontë House
The Junior School of Woodhouse Grove

Apperley Bridge, Bradford, West Yorkshire BD10 0PQ
Tel: 0113 250 2811
Fax: 0113 250 0666
email: enquiries@brontehouse.co.uk
website: www.woodhousegrove.co.uk

Chairman of Governors: A Wintersgill, FCA

Headmaster: S Dunn, BEd

Age Range. 3–11 Co-educational.
Number of Pupils. 304 Boys and Girls.
Fees per term (2014–2015). £2,875–£3,450 (day). Ashdown Lodge Nursery and Reception: £2,620 (full day), £1,620 (half day).

These are graduated according to age. The day fee covers an extended day from 7.30 am to 6 pm; there are no extra charges for breakfast, tea and the majority of supervised activities after lessons.

The School is situated in its own grounds, a short distance from the Senior School, on the slopes of the Aire Valley at the edge of the urban area of Bradford and Leeds. The moors are within view and access to the Dales National Park and the international Leeds/Bradford Airport is swift.

At Brontë House we welcome children to Ashdown Lodge, our Early Years setting, during the term that they turn three.

During their time in Foundation Stage, we aim to develop a child's ability and self-confidence, encouraging good behaviour and consideration for others. Children are provided with a stimulating programme of learning and play within a calm and relaxed atmosphere, providing a framework for every individual to fulfil their potential ready for the next stage of their education.

The EYFS curriculum is followed, beginning in the Nursery and lasting for two years. Language and literacy, mathematics, knowledge and understanding of the world, physical and creative development are promoted in preparation for the transfer to Key Stage One.

By encouraging a child's intellectual, creative, sporting and personal development, we aim to get the best from our children in the classroom, on the games field, in music, drama and all other activities. The broad curriculum covers a wide range of subjects, including foreign languages, but with particular emphasis on ensuring a strong foundation in reading, writing, mathematics and science.

As children progress through the school they are encouraged to take increasing responsibility and to show consideration for others. Friendship, trust and courtesy are promoted so our children have a sound foundation as they move up to The Grove at the end of Year 6.

We aim to encourage every pupil to develop his or her potential by participating in a variety of activities both as part of the curriculum and extra-curricular. As they progress through the school, sport plays an increasingly significant role in the life of the children and there are plenty of opportunities for pupils to be involved in team games and individual sports, which encourage not only physical achievement but also a healthy outlook for enjoying school life to the full.

As with sports, music and drama play an important part of life at Brontë House. All children are encouraged to learn a instrument. The music curriculum is a mixture of traditional and modern with opportunities for composing and performing. There are many choirs and ensembles and the children are regularly offered the chance to take part in concerts and festivals. Housed in spacious rooms on the top floor of Brontë House, our children are given excellent opportunities to develop musically and creatively.

Charitable status. Woodhouse Grove School is a Registered Charity, number 529205. It exists to provide education for children.

Brooke Priory School

Station Approach, Oakham, Rutland LE15 6QW
Tel: 01572 724778
email: info@brooke.rutland.sch.uk
website: www.brooke.rutland.sch.uk
Twitter: @BrookePrioryS

Headmistress: Mrs E S Bell, BEd Hons

Age Range. 2 to 11 years (co-educational).
Number of Pupils. 192: 163 (age 4+ to 11); 29 (Nursery, age 2 to 4).
Fees per term (2014–2015). £2,255–£2,810.
Staff. There are 20 graduate and qualified members of the teaching staff.

Brooke Priory is a day Preparatory School for boys and girls. The school was founded in 1989 and moved into its own purpose-built building in February 1995. Since then it has doubled its classroom provision, established a Nursery, fully-networked Computer Suite, well-resourced Library, Theatre, Art & DT Studios, individual Music Practice Rooms and Sports Changing Rooms.

Brooke Priory provides a stimulating, caring environment in which children are encouraged to attain their highest potential. Class sizes are optimally 16, in parallel forms, and children are grouped according to ability in Mathematics and English.

The school delivers a broad and varied curriculum, where every child will participate in Art, Drama, French and Music. Over 60% of children in the Prep Department enjoy individual music lessons and are encouraged to join the Choir and Ensemble.

Brooke Priory enjoys a high success rate at Common Entrance and Senior Independent School Entry Examinations, with many children being awarded scholarships. With this solid foundation pupils move confidently on to their chosen senior schools.

Sport is an important part of the curriculum. Children swim weekly throughout the year and are coached in a wide variety of games by specialist staff. The main sports are Soccer, Rugby, Hockey, Netball, Cricket, Rounders, Tennis and Athletics.

The original Brooke Priory, which is situated just 1 mile outside Oakham, is set in 30 undulating acres and everyone, from the Nursery to Year VI, visits regularly for Welly Days.

The school offers a wide choice of extra-curricular activities.

Before and after school care is available and holiday clubs are enjoyed by many children at the end of every term.

Broomwood Hall

74 Nightingale Lane, London SW12 8NR
Tel: 020 8682 8800
Fax: 020 8675 0136
email: admissions@northwoodschools.com
website: www.broomwood.co.uk

Principal: Sir Malcolm & Lady Colquhoun

Head of Upper School: Mrs Carole Jenkinson
Head of Lower School: Mrs Sarah Graham

Age Range. Girls 4–13, Boys 4–8.
Number of Pupils. Lower School (4–8): 210 girls, 180 boys; Upper School (8–13): 220 girls.
Fees per term (2014–2015). £4,560 Lower School, £5,605 Upper School.

Broomwood Hall is an independent pre-prep and preparatory school for boys and girls from the ages of 4–8 (boys) and 4–13 (girls). Boys have an automatic right of entry at 8 to Northcote Lodge (day preparatory school on Wandsworth Common, in the same ownership as Broomwood Hall) subject to an interview with the Headmaster.

Broomwood Hall has expanded from 12 children to over 600 in five substantial Victorian Houses sprinkled round the south side of Clapham and Tooting Commons, but the school's approach and values have remained constant. Broomwood believes that a young child does not benefit from long drives across London (hence the catchment rule), that single-sex education works best after 8, and that the traditional virtues of self-discipline, a sense of responsibility and good manners are the core of a good education. The Upper School is unique in London in providing an education for girls specifically aiming for boarding at 13.

There are four separate sites: a pre-prep of 140 children at Garrad's Road SW16, another pre-prep of 250 – subdivided into two neighbouring buildings – at 192 Ramsden Road and 50 Nightingale Lane, SW12. And finally, the Upper School – 210 girls aged 8–13 – based in the gracious Victorian mansion at 68–74 Nightingale Lane, SW12.

Teaching (in small groups) is strong throughout. Mixed-ability classes, but setting in maths and English. An extended day for the Upper School because homework is done at school. A variety of clubs – karate, mini-rugby, chess, pottery among many others – are on offer.

Art is particularly lively. Strong music, with two music lessons a week, a Chamber choir, wind ensemble and brass band. Lots of drama – everyone takes part in two productions a year. Netball, hockey, PE, football, touch rugby, athletics, cricket, rounders and tennis taught on site or nearby (five courts within walking distance), with inter-house competitions and external matches. Swimming at local baths, with swim squad once a week. Very good library. Sophisticated ICT, with state-of-the-art computers, interactive whiteboards, permanent high-speed internet connection and an email account for every child above class 2.

A Christian school with regular RE, morning assembly and church attendance once a week. Happy to welcome all faiths (special arrangements for Catholics to attend Mass and days of obligation), but all pupils must attend services. Pastoral care extremely well thought through at every level. From class 5 girls have a personal tutor (chosen by themselves), whom they meet weekly to discuss social and personal issues as well as work. The tutor liaises with parents, helps plan revision, sorts out friendships and writes reports. Social skills as important as academic ones and manners definitely a priority.

One compulsory, though much enjoyed, course is the weekly Leiths cookery lessons for girls in years 7 and 8. Lunches, prepared on site, are accompanied by the teachers for the younger children to ensure that table manners are observed and food is finished.

Entry requirements. Entry takes place in September following a child's fourth birthday. Parents initially register on a Provisional Form and must attend either an open day or an individual tour before completing the Formal Registration form. Children attend a school readiness assessment the year before they are due to start school. Parents must live locally (Clapham, Battersea, Wandsworth, Tooting or Streatham). For entry to the school for older classes, parents are invited to visit the school and the child attends an assessment morning.

Examinations offered. Boys' preparatory schools, girls' Common Entrance and Scholarship examinations at 11+ and 13+ (12+ where applicable) and London day schools' examinations. Pupils may also take Associated Board examinations (music).

Broughton Manor Preparatory School

Newport Road, Broughton, Milton Keynes, Buckinghamshire MK10 9AA
Tel: 01908 665234
Fax: 01908 692501
email: info@bmprep.co.uk
website: www.bmprep.co.uk

Chairman of the Governors: Mr Peter Squire, MA

Headmaster: Mr James Canwell, BA Hons, PGCE

Deputy Head: Mrs Rachel Smith, BA Hons PGCE

Age Range. Nursery 2 months–2½ years. Pre-Prep 2½–7 years. Preparatory Department 7+–11 years.
Number of Pupils. 350 Day Pupils.
Fees per term (2014–2015). Nursery (per week): £241 (babies under 1 year), £252 (1–2½ years). Pre-Preparatory: £3,460 (2½–5 years), £3,560 (6–7 years). Preparatory £3,900 (8–11 years).

Broughton Manor Preparatory School is a well-established, family-owned school, with two sister Pre-Preparatory and Preparatory schools based across Milton Keynes.

Opening hours are 7.30 am to 6.30 pm for a 35-week academic year and a total of 46 weeks per year, enabling children of working parents to join playschemes in school holidays and to be cared for outside normal daily school hours.

Staff are highly qualified and committed to delivering the very best teaching and levels of care. Academic standards are "excellent", as rated in the most recent ISI Inspection, with pupils being prepared for entry to senior independent schools locally and nationally and to grammar schools. Teaching is structured to take into account the requirements of the National Curriculum, with constant evaluation and assessment for each pupil. Scholarships are offered for those with all-round academic and sporting abilities from the ages of 7+.

Housed in a modern purpose-built building, all departments also have their own outside soft play and extensive playground areas; there is a multi-purpose sports hall and brand new Astroturf.

State-of-the-art facilities include a newly developed Art workshop and recently completed high-tech ICT Suite, Science laboratory, Assembly hall and further Prep classrooms.

The additional facilities at The Farm include a fully-equipped fitness room, dance studio, music hall, and computer room. The superb in and outdoor learning resource centre, weather station, large pond and growing poly-tunnels allow the very best environmental studies programme.

Music and Sport play an important part in the life of the school. Concerts are held, and a wide variety of sports is played, with teams competing regularly against other schools, and additional clubs are held for those wanting to learn specialist activities such as judo and ballet.

The school aims to incorporate the best of modern teaching methods and traditional values in a friendly, caring and busy environment, where good work habits and a concern for the needs of others are paramount.

Bruern Abbey School

Chesterton House, Chesterton, Oxfordshire OX26 1UY
Tel: 01869 242448
Fax: 01869 243949
email: secretary@bruernabbey.org
website: www.bruernabbey.org

Chair of Governors: Mrs Sarah Austen, BA Hons

Headmaster: **Mr J Floyd**, MA, PGCE

Age Range. Boys 7–13.
Number of Pupils. 111.
Fees per term (2014–2015). Day £6,949, Boarding £8,361, Flexi Boarding £49 per night.

Bruern Abbey is situated in twenty acres of Oxfordshire countryside, ten miles north-west of Oxford and within easy commuting distance of London, from where a bus brings boys to school on Monday morning and takes them back on Friday afternoon. The School's raison d'être is to prepare boys with learning difficulties for Common Entrance to the major English and Scottish independent senior schools. Bruern boys graduate to a range of independent schools, which have included in recent years, Winchester College, Tonbridge, Stowe, Harrow, Bryanston, Rugby, Shrewsbury, Shiplake, Milton Abbey and Uppingham.

Its purpose is to provide quality education in safe and pleasant surroundings, to ensure that the work of every child is recognised and appreciated, and to build confidence, in the firm belief that confidence is the key to academic success.

Bruern believes that it has found the right balance between the traditional and the progressive. All boys use laptops, and for those who have difficulty in expressing themselves as swiftly or as coherently on paper as they do in speech, this proves a godsend. There is a focus on literacy and numerical work, with up to ten periods of English and Mathematics each a week, but with little or no withdrawal, classes are ten boys or less taught by subject specialists also trained in the field of dyslexia, dyspraxia and dyscalculia. The School is steadfast in the teaching of traditional values, dear to all, and places an emphasis on good manners and self-discipline, and encourages boys to share their aspirations.

The Buchan School

Castletown, Isle of Man IM9 1RD
Tel: 01624 820481
Fax: 01624 820403

email: sarah.charlton@kwc.im
website: www.kwc.im

Chairman of the Governors: N H Wood, ACA, TEP

Headteacher: **Miss R J Corlett**, MEd

Age Range. 2–11.
Number of Pupils. 208 (113 boys, 95 girls).
Fees per term (2014–2015). Day only: £3,048 (P1–P3), £3,827 (Forms 1–2), £3,975 (Forms 3–4).

After more than a century of independence, mainly as a Girls' School, The Buchan School amalgamated, in 1991, with King William's College to form a single continuous provision of Independent Education on the Isle of Man.

As the Preparatory School to King William's College (*see entry in HMC section*), The Buchan School provides an education of all-round quality for boys and girls until the age of 11 when most pupils proceed naturally to the Senior School although the curriculum meets the needs of Common Entrance, Scholarship and Entrance Examinations to other Independent Senior Schools.

The school buildings are clustered round Westhill House, the centre of the original estate, in fourteen acres of partly wooded grounds. The whole environment, close to the attractive harbour of Castletown, is ideally suited to the needs of younger children. They are able to work and play safely and develop their potential in every direction.

Classes are small throughout, providing considerable individual attention. A well-equipped Nursery provides Pre-School education for up to 65 children. At the age of 5, boys and girls are accepted into the Pre-Preparatory Department. They work largely in their own building in bright, modern classrooms and also make use of the specialist Preparatory School facilities where they proceed three years later.

The School is particularly well-equipped with ICT facilities extending down to the Pre-Prep Department. There is a Pavilion with fields marked out for a variety of team games and a multi-purpose area which is used for Netball, Tennis and Hockey.

There is emphasis on traditional standards in and out of the classroom, with an enterprising range of activities outside normal lessons. Music is strong – both choral and instrumental – and there is energetic involvement in Art, Drama, Sport.

The school strives for high academic standards, aiming to ensure that all pupils enjoy the benefits of a rounded education, giving children every opportunity to develop their individual talents from an early age.

Entry is usually by Interview and School report and the children may join The Buchan School at any time, providing there is space. The School is a happy, friendly community where new pupils integrate quickly socially and academically.

Charitable status. King William's College is a Registered Charity, number 615. It exists for the provision of high quality education for boys and girls.

Buckingham College Preparatory School

458 Rayners Lane, Pinner, Middlesex HA5 5DT
Tel: 020 8866 2737
Fax: 020 8868 3228
email: office@buckprep.org
website: www.buckprep.org

Chairman of Governors: Mr Robert Brock

Headmistress: **Mrs Loraine Cavanagh**, MA, Dip CE, FRSA

Age Range. Boys 4–11.
Number of Pupils. 100.
Fees per term (2014–2015). £2,596–£3,399. Lunches £247.

Buckingham College Preparatory School (BCPS) is a small school which offers its pupils an extremely high level of pastoral care. This was confirmed by the Independent Schools Inspection in June 2011 which found that '*the standard of pastoral care provided and support for pupils is excellent*'. In the EYFS Inspection of 2014, the provision was judged to be 'outstanding' overall.

With a maximum class size of 20 throughout the school, individual attention is guaranteed.

BCPS pupils consistently achieve excellent academic results, due to the inspirational teaching, commitment and professionalism of its highly qualified teaching staff. Each year, Year 6 pupils gain offers to the major Independent and Grammar schools in the area and beyond. In the majority of cases, this is to the boys' first-choice schools, often with scholarships.

BCPS also prides itself in its results in other areas of the curriculum; areas which are vital in building confidence and self-esteem. Achievement in sport, music and drama is excellent. The pupils regularly take part in local fixtures, often winning interschool tournaments in cricket, unihoc, football, rugby swimming and cross-country, and other sports. A thriving choir and orchestra, school concerts and plays allow the pupils plentiful opportunities for performance. 70% of pupils play an orchestral instrument.

The Expressive Arts Week, when pupils have the opportunity of participating in approximately 14 categories of events, is also a focal point of the academic year allowing all boys from the very youngest to demonstrate their individual talents.

The School also believes in forging a strong Parent/Teacher partnership so that parents feel they have a vital role to play in the education of their child. The Inspectors found that '*the School has excellent relationships with parents*'. A thriving Parent/Teacher Association also organises as many as three major fundraising events during the academic year which are always well supported and are highlights of the year.

Charitable status. The E Ivor Hughes Educational Foundation is a Registered Charity, number 293623.

Burgess Hill School for Girls – Junior School

Keymer Road, Burgess Hill, West Sussex RH15 0EG
Tel: 01444 233167
Fax: 01444 243538
email: registrar@burgesshill-school.com
website: www.burgesshill-school.com
Twitter: @BHSfG
Facebook: /BurgessHillSchoolforGirls
LinkedIn: /burgess-hill-school-for-girls

Chairman of Governors: Mr C Cooper, BSc, MEd, MBPsS

Headmistress: Mrs K Bell, BSc Hons, PGCE

Head of Junior School: **Mrs H Miller**, BA Hons

Deputy Head of Junior School: Mrs T Pearson-Rujas, BSc Hons, PGCE, QTS, Cert Mgmt

Age Range. Girls 2½–11.
Number of Pupils. 172.
Fees per term (2014–2015). £2,340–£4,130.

Burgess Hill School for Girls is a day and boarding school for girls between 2½ and 18 years. We welcome boys into our Nursery (2½ to 4 years).

The school stands in 14 acres of beautiful grounds close to the centre of Burgess Hill town. It is a five minute walk from Burgess Hill railway station and coaches and mini-buses collect girls from outlying areas of East and West Sussex.

It is small enough that pupils are known as individuals yet large enough to offer breadth, choice and opportunity. Girls are able to strive for excellence wherever their talents lie and the mix of ages, working together on the same site, gives the school a special character. The aim of the school is to provide each girl with the opportunity to realise her potential and the focus is firmly on girls and the way they learn.

The Junior School provides a broad, varied and stimulating curriculum within a warm and caring environment. Every girl is helped to reach her full potential socially, physically, emotionally and intellectually. Whilst academic achievement is important, the school aims to educate young people for life, providing education in the broadest sense.

"*The highly effective teaching and the excellence of the whole educational experience inspire a love of learning and exceptional motivation to achieve the highest possible standards in academic work, sport, drama and music.*" (ISI Inspection Report, March 2009)

The Junior School offers small classes and specialist teachers for music, sport and languages. It has an excellent reputation for Music and the Junior School Choir has been invited to sing at St Paul's and Chichester Cathedrals and their recording of 'Ding Dong Merrily on High' was broadcast on Christmas Day on BBC Sussex and BBC Surrey radio stations.

All Junior pupils take part in sports, with PE lessons most days of the week. There are many opportunities to play against other schools in a range of sports and many pupils achieve sports success at local, county and national level.

The Junior School offers fully-equipped subject-specific classrooms for Music, ICT, Art, Science and Technology and access to all the sports facilities on the school campus plus a Learning Hub incorporating a library – a large learning space with access to iPads and an interactive electronic screen.

The Infants are based in the Little Oaks building with bright, open classrooms and have their own hall and library. The Infants and Juniors have an exciting playground with a wooden adventure trail and outdoor classroom.

ISI Inspection. The 2009 inspection reports clearly confirm that the school has a great many strengths in all aspects of its provision. The Early Years provision was judged to be outstanding. Moving through into the Junior School the inspectors commented that, "*The highly effective teaching and excellence of the whole educational experience inspire a love of learning and exceptional motivation to achieve the highest possible standards in academic work, sport, drama and music*".

The Junior School was also delighted to note that the inspectors picked up on the happy atmosphere of the school commenting that, "*The quality of relations between staff and pupils is excellent. Respect and courtesy are evident and so is humour; relations are clearly warm and relaxed and there is an air of happiness and purpose*".

"*The Junior School accomplishes outstandingly successfully its aims to provide opportunities for all pupils to find and develop their talents within a safe environment which values everyone in it.*" (ISI Inspection Report, March 2009)

The full report can be viewed on www.isi.net.

Entrance Procedures. Entrance to either the Junior School is by examination and school reference. Scholarships are awarded each year for academic and/or musical excellence into Years 3–6 inclusive.

Charitable status. Burgess Hill School for Girls is a Registered Charity, number 307001.

Bute House Preparatory School for Girls

Bute House, Luxemburg Gardens, Hammersmith, London W6 7EA
Tel: 020 7603 7381
Fax: 020 7371 3446
email: mail@butehouse.co.uk
website: www.butehouse.org

Chairman of Governors: Mr S Wathen

Head: **Mrs Helen Lowe**, BA LGSM

Age Range. 4–11.
Number of Pupils. 311 Day Girls.
Fees per term (2014–2015). £4,439 inclusive of lunches.
Bute House overlooks extensive playing fields and is housed in a large bright modern building. Facilities include a science laboratory, art room, technology room, music hall, 2 drama studios, multi-purpose hall and a large well-stocked library. A well-qualified, enthusiastic and experienced staff teach a broad curriculum which emphasises both the academic and the aesthetic. Information Technology is an integral part of the curriculum and the school has a wireless network. The classrooms are all equipped with multimedia machines. Laptops are also widely used for individual or class work. Monitored access to the internet is available. French is taught from Reception, Spanish from Year 4 and Latin from Year 5.

Sports include swimming, gymnastics, dance, tennis, lacrosse, netball and athletics which are taught on excellent on-site facilities. Full use is made of all that London has to offer and residential trips further afield are also offered to older girls.

Girls are encouraged to take full part in the school life from an early age. There is a democratically elected School Council and regular school meetings run by the girls when all pupils are able to put forward their views as well as to volunteer for duties around the school. A wide variety of extra-curricular activities is available.

The school aims at academic excellence in a non competitive, happy environment where girls are encouraged to be confident, articulate and independent and where courtesy and consideration are expected. There is a flourishing Parents Association. Entry is by ballot at age 4 and by assessment at age 7.

Caldicott

Crown Lane, Farnham Royal, Bucks SL2 3SL
Tel: 01753 649300
email: registrar@caldicott.com
website: www.caldicott.com

Chairman of the Board of Governors: M S Swift

Headmaster: **Simon Doggart**, BA

Age Range. 7–13.
Number of Boys. 104 Boarders and 184 Day Boys.
Fees per term (2014–2015). Boarders £7,805; Day Boys: Middle School £5,395, Junior School £4,925.
Caldicott, founded in 1904, is an educational trust. The school is situated in over 40 acres of grounds and playing fields and is adjacent to more than five hundred acres of Burnham Beeches. It is conveniently placed close to London, between the M4 and M40 motorways and is within 20 minutes of Heathrow Airport.

The school's ethos is based on traditional values with a modern outlook. These are underpinned by an excellent teaching and pastoral staff, many of whom live on-site, non-teaching staff and a governing body which is both highly valued and supportive.

The school's buildings and extensive sports grounds are constantly maintained and upgraded. Classrooms are spacious, well-planned and light and these have been enhanced recently by a modernised art and design technology department and music department as well as a new science block. The latest IT technology is used in all classrooms.

The new performing arts centre, with its very good acoustics, provides a drama, music and entertaining space and the indoor sports centre houses two squash courts, a climbing wall, indoor cricket nets, basketball and other sports facilities next to the outdoor swimming pool.

All boys board at school in the last two years (some may choose to board a year earlier) in preparation for boarding at their senior schools. They are prepared for the Common Entrance and Scholarship examinations to the top UK independent senior schools.

The school has a Christian foundation. The day begins with a short chapel service on most weekdays and on Sundays parents are welcome to join in the evening services. There is a strong tutorial system and much emphasis is placed on extra-curricular education. Each boy is encouraged to learn how to use his leisure time sensibly.

The principal games are rugby, football and cricket. Other sporting activities include athletics, swimming, tennis, cross-country, basketball, squash, martial arts, as well as rowing, sailing and fencing for smaller groups. All boys get the option to represent the school in sporting competition.

The prospectus is available online or on application to the Registrar. The Headmaster is always pleased to meet parents and to show them round the school.

Charitable status. Caldicott is a Registered Charity, number 310631. Its purpose is to provide education for the young.

Cameron House

4 The Vale, London SW3 6AH
Tel: 020 7352 4040
Fax: 020 7352 2349
email: info@cameronhouseschool.org
website: www.cameronhouseschool.org

Founded in 1980.

Principal: Miss Josie Cameron Ashcroft, BSc, DipEd

Headmistress: **Mrs Lucie Moore**, BEd Hons

Age Range. 4–11 Co-educational.
Number of Pupils. 118
Fees per term (2014–2015). £5,500.
Based in a beautifully designed Edwardian building, just steps from London King's Road, Cameron House School prides itself on sending pupils to some of the most sought-after schools in the country.

At 11, boys go on to Latymer, Emanuel, Alleyn's, City of London, Colet Court, Westminster Under and other day and boarding schools, and girls leave for St Paul's, Godolphin and Latymer, Queen's Gate, Francis Holland and City of London, as well as a number of other day and boarding schools.

The school is designed to be completely child-centred, modern and warm, creating the right atmosphere for learning. Yet it is not a hot house: its programme is designed to develop each child's personality and to stretch his or her individual talents. A high teacher/pupil ratio is essential to Cameron House's success. Excellent provision is made for children of exceptionally high IQ, or unusual ability, eg a Native French Speakers' Club, and Artists' Group.

The aim is to instil a firm sense of self, a passion for exploration and a freedom to express creativity, balanced by good manners, kindness and a selfless interest in others.

One of the first tasks is to foster a joy of reading, which Cameron House believes is the best foundation in each class. All pupils can access the school's own intranet, interactive whiteboards, class sets of laptops and the extensive computer suite.

From their earliest years, music, art, drama and sport form an integral part of the children's school life and excellent local facilities allow the pupils to engage in a wide variety of sports. Unusually, a large majority of children learn karate, which builds physical confidence. Verbal communication skills are also developed, leading to English Speaking Board Examinations or Guildhall Examinations. Other popular clubs are Lunchtime Latin, Touch Typing, Tennis, Chess, Ballet, Tap and Fencing, to name just a few.

Three active choirs, as well as singing and percussion classes, composition and musical appreciation classes, and individual instrument lessons, lead to grade examinations of the Association Board of the Royal Schools of Music.

There is a genuinely open dialogue between parents and teachers, also fostered by The Friends of Cameron House. This contributes to the welcoming feel of the school. The Headmistress of Cameron House is always delighted to give parents a tour of the school so that they can experience its special qualities for themselves.

Cargilfield

45 Gamekeeper's Road, Edinburgh EH4 6HU
Tel: 0131 336 2207
Fax: 0131 336 3179
email: admin@cargilfield.com
website: www.cargilfield.com

Chairman of the Board of Governors: Lady Janice Gammell, BComm, FRSA

Headmaster: Mr Rob Taylor, BA, PGCE
Assistant Headmaster: Mr David Walker, BA Hons

Deputy Heads:
Mrs Emma Buchanan, MEd
Mr Ross Murdoch, BEd

Age Range. 3–13.
Number of Children. 300.
Fees per term (2014–2015). Boarding: £6,150 (two-weekly), £5,915 (weekly). Day Pupils: £4,430–£4,775, Pre-Prep £3,025, Nursery £1,780–£3,025.

Founded in 1873, the first and oldest Prep School in Scotland, Cargilfield is a small, friendly Prep School for around 300 boys and girls from the age of 3 to 13 years. It is situated on the outskirts of Edinburgh by the lovely village of Cramond, not far from Edinburgh airport, with easy access over the Forth Road Bridge and down to the Borders and the North of England.

Cargilfield is a place of hard work, challenge, courtesy, humour and above all, a great deal of fun; it is a very special school, and it is a tremendous privilege to work in such a dynamic, purposeful and caring place, where we are proud of our academic record, but we are also proud of what happens outside the classroom: in drama, music, sport and in over 70 activities which take place in the evenings and at weekends.

We are a wholly independent school with no ties to any senior school, preparing boys and girls for secondary education both in Scotland but also down in England. Pupils, who are taught in small groups (between 12 and 18), move onto a variety of schools: Ampleforth, Downe House, Cheltenham Ladies' College, Eton, Fettes, Glenalmond, Gordonstoun, Harrow, Loretto, Merchiston, Oundle, Queen Margaret's York, Rugby, Shrewsbury, Winchester and Wycombe Abbey amongst others. We are extremely proud of our academic record: over 145 Scholarship awards being gained since 2006, a 100% pass rate at Common Entrance, and awards also won in Music, Art and Sport.

There is a choice of day, flexi and weekly boarding and also two-weekly boarding to fit in with the modern parent. This choice means that there is something for everyone and we are delighted that so many boys and girls opt for one type of the boarding options. Many of the Cargilfield children will be day children and their education can be a full twelve hour one from 8.00 am to 8.00 pm from the age of 8, but over 90% of our leavers go on to Senior Boarding Schools at the age of 13.

In addition to the normal academic curriculum, we offer a tremendous range of out-of-school activities which numbers over 70 throughout the week, during break, after supper and also throughout our exciting two day weekends. All of these activities cater for both boys and girls, little ones and older ones; they range from fly tying to Ancient Greek, Judo to Cooking – something for everyone, and an opportunity to kindle that fire of enthusiasm.

There is also a thriving Music Department with over 200 teaching lessons per week and all children can be in a play at some stage during the year with drama for all taught within the academic timetable. We have no Prep at the school, and all work is done within classroom time which allows the evenings free for activities.

There is sport for all, five days a week, with matches played at every age group and at all levels, allowing the elite to thrive and also the keen enthusiast to play sport at their own level against other schools.

Over the past ten years, Cargilfield has begun an exciting modernisation programme: a new Pre-Prep Department was opened in 2003; two new ICT Suites and Science Department were opened in 2004 while in 2006, a new two-floor teaching block was built, in addition to a purpose built new Music School, new ICT suites and classrooms, a new girls' boarding wing and in 2013, a new changing room facility for boys and girls. The recent HMI and National Care Inspections grade the school very highly: we are all very proud of the way that the children and teachers contribute so much to the friendly and supportive community that is Cargilfield, and this is something which makes the school so special.

The challenge of youth is ever-present here and, although we do have plenty of new buildings and modern equipment, a boarding and day Preparatory School is about so much more: to learn to help others; to make the most of each talent; to be courteous and kind; and to have a sense of humour – these are our top priorities.

Charitable status. Cargilfield School is a Registered Charity, number SC005757.

Carrdus School

Overthorpe Hall, Nr Banbury, Oxon OX17 2BS
Tel: 01295 263733
Fax: 01295 254644
email: office@carrdusschool.co.uk
website: www.carrdusschool.co.uk

Headmaster: Mr Edward Way, BSc Hons

Age Range. Boys 3–8, Girls 3–11, Nursery Class for children 3–4½.
Number of Day Pupils. 135 (114 girls, 21 boys)

Fees per term (from April 2014). £426–£3,380. Compulsory extras: Insurance £3.75; PTA membership £5.

Carrdus School is a day school for girls and a pre-preparatory school for boys. The large house stands in 11 acres of beautiful grounds.

The teaching staff consists of nine full-time qualified teachers and fifteen part-time specialists. Boys are given a good grounding for their preparatory schools and 7+ or 8+ entry exams. Girls take 11+ Common Entrance and all other 11 year old transitional tests. The school has an excellent record of success in examinations, regularly sending girls to many well-known independent senior schools.

There is a heated outdoor swimming pool, two tennis courts and a purpose-built Sports Hall. Sport, music, drama and art are highly valued in the curriculum.

The aim of the school is to produce confident, well-disciplined and happy children, who have the satisfaction of reaching their own highest academic and personal standards. This is possible for an organisation run by teachers for children, flexible enough to achieve a balance between new methods of teaching and sound traditional disciplines.

Charitable status. Carrdus School is part of Tudor Hall School, which is a Registered Charity, number 1042783.

Casterton, Sedbergh Preparatory School

Kirkby Lonsdale, Cumbria LA6 2SG
Tel: 015242 79200
email: hm@sedberghprep.org
website: www.sedberghprep.org
Twitter: @Sedbergh_Prep
Facebook: /SedberghPrep

Chairman of Governors: Hugh M Blair

Headmaster: **Mr Scott G Carnochan**, BEd

Age Range. 6 months – 13 years Co-educational.
Number of Pupils. 190.
Fees per term (2014–2015). Day £2,645–£4,730, Full Boarding £6,025–£7,140, Weekly Boarding £5,675–£6,790.

Casterton, Sedbergh Preparatory School, is situated in a spectacular rural location in the Lune Valley. This is an ideal location for living out the ethos of allowing children to be children. There is no rush to grow up here, but the foundations are laid for nurturing the resilience our children will need as young adults and the tenacity essential to achieving high standards in all that they do.

This is evident in the unrivalled activities programme and around-the-clock pastoral care. Allied to all that happens in the classroom, it is perhaps the breadth of opportunity and depth of involvement that sets us apart. From pony care to caving, mountain biking (on mountains!) to kayaking, ballet to ghyll scrambling, we incubate a sense of success and achievement in each and every one of our children. We awaken in them, at an early age, the joy of a challenge met.

The school's facilities are outstanding: state-of-the-art Science laboratories, with teachers who are no strangers to explosions and dissections, a floodlit Astroturf and tennis courts, a theatre, heated indoor swimming pool and stables. Balancing the academic with outdoor learning, we are creating a school farm – pupils already consult with our Chef to grow vegetables and herbs and this involvement is set to increase.

The new school has a roll of 85 girls and 105 boys; day, full boarding, weekly boarding and flexi boarding are possible. Parents can visit both Sedbergh School and Casterton, Sedbergh Preparatory School at any time; every day is an open day! Visit the website or telephone for further information.

Charitable status. Sedbergh School is a Registered Charity, number 1080672.

Castle Court Preparatory School

The Knoll House, Knoll Lane, Corfe Mullen, Wimborne, Dorset BH21 3RF
Tel: 01202 694438
Fax: 01202 659063
email: office@castlecourt.com
website: www.castlecourt.com
Facebook: /Castle-Court-School

Chairman of the Governors: Michael J Cuthbertson, MA

Headmaster: **Richard D P Stevenson**, BA Hons, PGCE

Deputy Headmaster: John F Gilmour, BA Hons, PGCE

Age Range. 2–13.
Number of Pupils. 342 (201 boys, 141 girls) including Pre-Prep, Reception and Badgers (Nursery).
Teaching Staff. 25 full time, 31 part time.
Fees per term (2014–2015). £2,595 (Reception to Year 2), £4,690 (Years 3 to 8). Nursery fees on application.

Castle Court is a day prep school for girls and boys aged 2 to 13, situated in 35 acres of beautiful grounds and woodlands within easy reach of Bournemouth, Poole, Blandford, Dorchester and the Isle of Purbeck. A gracious Regency house forms the heart of the school and contains the reception rooms, dining rooms, offices and some of the junior classrooms, as well as the formal rooms used for entertaining parents and visiting school teams. The Badgers, Reception and Pre-Prep departments (for 2 to 7 year olds) are all self-contained and, like the senior classrooms, are all purpose-built. There is a spacious hall for school plays, concerts, drama and gymnastics, as well as school assemblies. Adjacent to the hall is the music department, which includes classrooms and practice rooms, as well as a dance and drama studio. A science and art complex provides laboratories, art studios, design and technology room and the central IT centre (although all classrooms are networked, plus there is Wi-Fi across the site and the junior part of the school has their own banks of computers). The library is situated in the heart of the school and offers the children from all age groups the opportunity to explore and expand their reading. Other facilities include poolside sports changing rooms, an academic block with four classrooms, and office space, as well as smaller quieter rooms where individual learning support can be provided. There is an outdoor heated swimming pool and extensive playing fields including an all-weather astro hockey pitch, which is also used for tennis in the summer, as well as cricket practice.

To take full advantage of the fabulous site the school has become an accredited Forest School, to ensure that the outdoor space is used fully in all the children's learning. The Forest School has just been given a tipi by the Parents and Friends to enable them to make full use of the woods throughout the year. The teaching programme is used across all areas of the school.

While Castle Court is a day school, from the age of seven children are able to stay on for tea and prep or explore various activities before going home at 5.45 pm. This is totally voluntary. Activities vary from term to term but include athletics, lego robotics, Ancient Greek, swimming, drama, dance, cookery, cross-country, chess, orchestra, band, choir, squash, rugby and reasoning. Younger children can stay on until the same time in the Cookie Club, where they are looked after in a home-from-home environment. There is also a breakfast club, which is open from 7.45 am each day for children from Badger Cubs upwards. From Year 3, there is no extra charge for the breakfast and the majority of the after-school clubs. There is a small charge for the younger children for pre- and post-school care. Please contact our Admissions Registrar for more information.

The normal curriculum includes English, mathematics, science, French, Latin, history, geography, religious studies, information technology, design and technology, art, music, and sport, drama and dance. All the children are prepared for the Common Entrance or Scholarship exams to senior independent schools, as well as for entry to local grammar schools. The school has a strong musical tradition with its own Orchestra, Band, Choir and various ensembles. Sport also forms an important part in the life of the children with rugby, soccer, hockey and cricket for the boys, and netball, rounders and hockey for the girls, with athletics, cross-country, gymnastics, dance, swimming and tennis for all. There are opportunities for sailing instruction, riding and golf. Trips include visits to local places of interest, camping weekends, and expeditions to the continent.

Our goal at Castle Court is to provide an outstanding day education based upon strong Christian values, and ensure that all the children here do the best they can and find their natural talents. The children have one childhood, it has to be the best.

A prospectus (with details of the school bus service if required) will be sent on application to the Admissions Registrar; further information may be found on our school website, Facebook page or You Tube channel.

Charitable status. Castle Court School Educational Trust Limited is a Registered Charity, number 325028. It aims to provide a first class education for local children.

Caterham Preparatory School

Harestone Valley Road, Caterham, Surrey CR3 6YB
Tel: 01883 342097
Fax: 01883 341230
email: prep-enquiries@caterhamschool.co.uk
website: www.caterhamprepschool.co.uk

Chairman of Governors: J W Bloomer

Head Teacher: **H W G Tuckett**, MA

Age Range. 3–11 years.
Number of Pupils. 287: 151 Boys, 136 Girls.
Fees per term (2014–2015). Pre-Preparatory £1,673–£2,806, Preparatory £3,581–£4,305. Lunch £200.

The School stands in 200 acres of grounds in the green belt on the slopes of the North Downs, approximately 1 mile outside Caterham.

The curriculum offers the normal range of subjects including Technology and Science in well equipped laboratories. In addition, French is taught from age 4. There is a full PE programme including Soccer, Netball, Cricket, Rounders, Athletics, Tennis, Swimming and Gymnastics. Regular use is made of the sports hall, astroturf and 25m indoor swimming pool. Drama is taught in a purpose-built drama studio.

Over 30 clubs and extra-curricular activities take place each week including Computer Club, Sailing, Drama, Short Tennis, Taekwondo, Needlework, Choir, Orchestra and facilities for instrumental tuition.

All classrooms are equipped with their own multimedia computers and are fully networked with screened internet access. There are also separate ICT Suites in both Prep and Pre-Prep with 20 computers each.

The Preparatory School enjoys close liaison with Caterham School, to which pupils normally proceed at age 11. In 1995 Caterham School became fully co-educational and a member of United Learning. This heralded an exciting series of developments providing the facilities for all pupils

to continue achieving the high standards for which the School is well known.

Charitable status. Caterham School is an Associate School of United Learning and is a Registered Charity, number 1109508.

The Cavendish School

31 Inverness Street, London NW1 7HB
Tel: 020 7485 1958
Fax: 020 7267 0098
email: admissions@cavendish-school.co.uk
website: www.cavendishschool.co.uk

Chairman of Governors: Mrs M Robey

Head: **Mrs Teresa Dunbar**, BSc Hons, PGCE, NPQH

Age Range. 3–11.
Number of Children. 258 Day Pupils.
Fees per term (2014–2015) Reception–Year 6: £4,250; Nursery £2,350–£4,050 depending upon number of sessions. Fees include lunch.

The Cavendish School is a small, friendly IAPS school for girls aged three to eleven and sibling boys aged three to seven. The school is situated near Regent's Park but still in the heart of Camden Town with its excellent public transport links. The Cavendish has a Christian ethos and welcomes pupils of all faiths.

Strong yet informal links between home and school are maintained and we pride ourselves on the high level of pastoral care and attention to each child's individual needs.

The school is non-selective at entry. We provide manageable class sizes and high teacher-pupil ratios so that the foundations of a good education and effective study habits are laid from the beginning.

Through a broad and balanced curriculum we provide personalised learning and much specialised teaching which allows our pupils to flourish and many gain entry and scholarships to top senior schools at 11+.

There is an extensive programme of extra-curricular activities, after-school care services and flexible arrangements for nursery-age pupils.

Our strengths in music, drama and art are reflected in the renewal of our Artsmark Gold in 2012 by Arts Council England. Class music is taught by specialists, instruction is available in a wide variety of instruments and we have a thriving orchestra and choirs.

The school is housed in well maintained Victorian buildings and a modern wing with purpose-built ICT facilities.

The school maintains close links with the local community in a variety of ways both charitable and educational.

Our most recent inspection report by the Independent Schools Inspectorate is very complimentary and well worth reading.

Charitable status. The Cavendish School is a Registered Charity, number 312727.

Chafyn Grove School

33 Bourne Avenue, Salisbury, Wiltshire SP1 1LR
Tel: 01722 333423
Fax: 01722 323114
email: office@chafyngrove.co.uk
website: www.chafyngrove.co.uk

Chairman of Governors: Annie Parnell

Headmaster: **Eddy Newton**, BA Hons, PGCE Cantab

Age Range. 3–13.
Number of Pupils. 305: 189 Boys, 116 Girls.
Fees per term (2014–2015). Boarding supplement £1,940. Day Children: Main School (Years 4–8) £5,095, Transition (Year 3) £3,855, Pre-Prep (Years 1–2) £2,570, Reception £2,070, Nursery £18.67 per session.

Chafyn Grove is set in 14 acres of grounds on the edge of the historic city of Salisbury – just an hour and a half from London by road, with easy access to air and rail links. The children thrive in an ambitious academic environment, where good sports facilities; extensive Art, Music and Drama opportunities and a commitment to extra-curricular activities encourage your child to discover their interests and their strengths.

Chafyn Grove has a happy family atmosphere that is created by a caring pastoral system and a team of talented and committed teachers. Pupils at Chafyn Grove School enjoy a good relationship with our staff; there is mutual friendship and a healthy respect. Our children also develop good relationships with other pupils, whether younger or older. Assemblies, chapel and tutor time all foster an understanding of how people should treat one another.

We have a mix of day and boarding pupils. Our boarding enhances the sense of community and is all about making the most of your time at school, developing independence and making friends for life – our aim is to provide a caring and happy environment in which children thrive and grow. Our boarders benefit from a secure and homely atmosphere and are accommodated in cosy, brightly decorated dormitories, often creatively decorated with their own pictures and posters, their own bedding and of course a teddy or two! There is a full weekly activity programme for boarders as well as a full weekend programme where both boarding and teaching staff are fully involved with the children creating a strong bond between staff and pupils.

Small class sizes (maximum 16 for Pre-Prep and 18 for Main School) and a commitment to high standards allow our pupils to perform impressively in the classroom. In 2014 all pupils achieved entry to the senior school of their choice and 12 Scholarships to Monkton Combe, Hampshire Collegiate, Godolphin, Bryanston, Canford, Claysemore, Charterhouse and Dauntsey's were awarded.

Pupils are also prepared for the 11+ entrance exam to the two Grammar Schools in Salisbury with many children winning places there, although some still opt to stay at Chafyn!

Scholarships to Chafyn are awarded in Years 2, 4, and 6, and take place in at the end of January or early February.

Our facilities include ten acres of playing fields, a large astroturf pitch, 25-metre heated swimming pool, 2 tennis courts, 2 squash courts, sports hall, music school, creative arts centre, two science laboratories and a computer centre. A library block with a computerised resource centre and 8 classrooms and a new Pre-Prep building opened in June 2011.

Charitable status. Chafyn Grove School is a Registered Charity, number 309483. It exists to provide an excellent education for children.

Charlotte House Preparatory School for Girls

88 The Drive, Rickmansworth, Herts WD3 4DU
Tel: 01923 772101
email: office@charlottehouseprepschool.co.uk
website: www.charlottehouseprepschool.co.uk
Facebook: /CharlotteHousePrepSchool

Chairman of Governors: Miss C Smith, MA Hons

Headmistress: Miss J Mitchell, BEd, MEd Cantab, MBPsS

Age Range. 3–11.
Number of Pupils. 140 Girls.
Fees per term (2014–2015). £1,206–£3,575.

Charlotte House is a Nursery and Preparatory School for girls aged 3–11 years, which achieves excellent results across the board (but particularly at 11+) in an atmosphere which feels both comfortable and familiar. Charlotte House girls aspire to be the best that they can and to that end, we offer a wide curriculum and begin specialist teaching in French, Spanish, Science, Music and PE at Pre-Prep.

Girls join the school at age three, and can choose to stay for as much (or as little) of the school day as they like, while they are in Nursery in order that the transition to school is made as easy as possible for them. Early Years pupils enjoy the freedom of our beautiful garden whilst also having access to the Sports Hall, the IT suite and the Library. Older girls are encouraged to develop their dramatic talents by putting on plays, concerts and assemblies for parents each term. Science is taught in our Science Lab and the school has enjoyed phenomenal success in the Haileybury Science challenge, Young Voices Festival, Maths challenges and Thinking Skills days, along with numerous sporting achievements.

Charlotte House sports teams play harder and more competitively because we place an emphasis on cooperation and responsibility as well as giving all girls the chance to play in a team.

Charlotte House staff are strongly committed to the school's ethos and work hard to ensure that pupils have high expectations of themselves, enjoy learning and become responsible and responsive individuals.

The school's excellent record at Secondary Transfer means that girls leave us at 11 to join one of the first class maintained or independent schools which have come to value the calibre of Charlotte House girls.

Charitable status. Charlotte House School Limited is a Registered Charity, number 311075. It exists to provide an enjoyable education that will develop the full potential of each child.

Cheam School

Headley, Newbury, Berkshire RG19 8LD
Tel: 01635 268381
          Registrar: 01635 267822
Fax: 01635 269345
email: registrar@cheamschool.co.uk
website: www.cheamschool.com

The School, originally founded in 1645, is a charitable trust controlled by a Board of Governors.

Chairman of Governors: R Boycott, Esq

Headmaster: M R Johnson, BEd College of St Mark & St John, Plymouth

Assistant Headmaster: T C Haigh, BA Birmingham, PGCE

Age Range. 3–13.
Number of Pupils. 90 boarders, 425 day children.
Fees per term (2014–2015). £8,415 Boarders; £3,555–£6,220 Day children.

The School became co-educational in September 1997. A merger with Inhurst House School, formerly situated at Baughurst, and which relocated to the Headley site in 1999, offers parents the opportunity for education from 3–13+ for their sons and daughters.

Bursaries are offered annually for 8 year olds.

Classes are small (maximum 18) and pupils are prepared for the major senior independent schools with Eton, Harrow, Radley, Marlborough, Sherborne, Wellington, Downe

House, St Mary's Ascot, St Mary's Calne and Sherborne Girls' featuring frequently. Recent improvements include excellent facilities for Design Technology and Information Technology, a dedicated Science Building, a refurbished Chapel and Teaching Block, a Music School, a Sports Hall and much improved boarding facilities. Dormitories are comfortable, carpeted and curtained. A new Art & Design Centre and Pre-Prep classrooms and Assembly Hall opened in September 2012.

Rugby, Soccer and Cricket are the major team games for boys; Netball, Rounders and Hockey for girls. A heated outdoor swimming pool, 6 all-weather tennis courts and a 9-hole golf course in the extensive 80-acre grounds allow a wide range of other sports and pastimes to be enjoyed.

The School is situated half way between Newbury and Basingstoke on the A339 and is within easy reach of the M3 and M4 motorways and the A34 trunk route from Portsmouth, Southampton and Winchester to Oxford and the Midlands. London Heathrow Airport is within an hour's drive.

Charitable status. Cheam School Educational Trust is a Registered Charity, number 290143. It provides high-class education for boarding and day pupils; traditional values; modern thinking; education for the 21st century.

Cheltenham College Preparatory School

Thirlestaine Road, Cheltenham, Gloucestershire GL53 7AB
Tel: 01242 522697
Fax: 01242 265620
email: prep.reception@cheltenhamcollege.org
website: www.cheltenhamcollege.org

President of Council: The Revd J C Horan

Headmaster: **Mr J F Whybrow**, BEd Exeter

Age Range. 3–13.
Number of Pupils. 400 (40 boarders, 360 day boys and girls).
Fees per term (2014–2015). Boarders £5,424–£7,074; Day Boys and Girls £2,421–£5,442.

Cheltenham College Preparatory School is a co-educational preparatory school from 3 to 13. The Pre-Prep Department, Kingfishers, is located in a separate purpose-built wing.

The school stands in a beautiful 15-acre parkland site near the centre of Regency Cheltenham; the town itself being well served by both motorway and rail networks. Excellent facilities include: art and CDT studios, extensive ICT suites, music school, large multi-purpose Assembly Hall, and Woodland School. It also benefits from the College's amenities including the stunning College Chapel, spacious sports complex with a 25m indoor swimming pool, floodlit astroturf all-weather pitches, athletics track, squash courts, tennis courts, and fully-equipped Science laboratories.

The curriculum is wide and stimulating with all pupils being prepared for 11+, 13+ Common Entrance and Scholarship examinations. In addition to the normal academic subjects, all pupils study Art, Music, PE, Information Technology, CDT and Drama, all led by a team of professional and dedicated teachers.

A wide range of sports are available including: rugby, cricket, hockey, cross-country, netball, badminton, athletics, golf, gymnastics, squash, ballet, sailing, skiing, horse riding, mountain biking, swimming, tennis and orienteering. Sporting skills are taught from an early age and include swimming for the whole school.

The school offers a well-rounded education in preparation for senior school. The environment is secure and caring with vast opportunities for pupils to fulfil their potential, from academic and sporting success to artistic and creative excellence. The Boarding House aims to provide a 'home from home', with excellent pastoral care and a wide range of extra-curricular activities under the supervision of the House Parents. The boarding facilities themselves are large and airy, with plenty of pictures, toys and colourful duvets making the place warm and homely. Regular contact with parents is encouraged with frequent exeat weekends, with flexi boarding being a popular option for children from Year 3 up. Progress reports are issued three times a term and either formal parent/teacher meetings are held or full reports issued at the end of each term.

Visitors are warmly welcomed and further information is available from the Registrar, Jennifer Bailey, who arranges school tours, Taster Days and assessments and meetings with the Headmaster, Jonathan Whybrow.

Charitable status. Cheltenham College is a Registered Charity, number 311720. It exists to provide education for boys and girls.

Chesham Preparatory School

Two Dells Lane, Chesham, Bucks HP5 3QF
Tel: 01494 782619
Fax: 01494 791645
email: secretary@cheshamprep.co.uk
      registrar@cheshamprep.co.uk
website: www.cheshamprep.co.uk

Chairman of Governors: Mr Nick Baker, BA Hons, PGCE

Headmaster: **Mr Michael Davies**, BA, PGCE

Age Range. 3–13.
Numbers of Pupils. 395 boys and girls.
Fees per term (2014–2015). £2,640–£4,100 (incl lunch).

Chesham Preparatory School has a well justified reputation for being an incredibly friendly school where boys and girls work hard, behave well and achieve wonderful things. The most recent ISI report (2010) is glowing in its praise for a school in which, "the pupils' achievement is excellent. Children enjoy an outstanding start to their education".

Founded in 1938, Chesham Prep has developed into a flourishing co-educational school. As a non-selective school which educates pupils from 3 to 13 years of age, it champions the strong belief that boys and girls of Prep school age should be educated together. They thrive in the holistic, caring environment and there is a real emphasis on ensuring that every child fulfils his or her potential whatever their varied strengths.

In September 2011 the school was delighted to announce the opening of its nursery – extending the provision offered to children rising 3 years old. From that early age, the children are well prepared for a smooth transition into their Reception class and, very importantly, they feel part of the Chesham Prep family.

The school boasts excellent success rates at 11+ and 12+ Grammar school entry, as well as 13+ Common Entrance to senior independent schools. All pupils benefit enormously from the wonderful years of personal development at Chesham Prep.

Sports teams are highly skilled and competitive, while there is a fabulous choir and orchestra, as well as a wide range of opportunities for involvement in the creative arts. Children are encouraged to express themselves with joy and passion!

Above all, it is the aim of Chesham Preparatory School to inspire children with a love of learning and a confidence to make the most of their abilities.

To find out more or to arrange to visit the school, please visit our website.

Charitable status. Chesham Preparatory School is a Registered Charity, number 310642. It exists to provide education for boys and girls.

Chigwell Junior School

Chigwell, Essex IG7 6QF
Tel: 020 8501 5721
Fax: 020 8501 5723
email: admissions@chigwell-school.org
website: www.chigwell-school.org

Chairman of the Governors: Mrs S Aliker, BA, MBA, ACMA

Head of the Junior School: **Mr S C James**, BA Hons, PGCE

Age Range. 4–13.
Number of Pupils. 460 Day Pupils.
Fees per term (2014–2015). £3,215–£5,115 inc Lunch/Tea.

The Junior School is housed in a purpose-built building on the same site as the Senior School only 7 miles from the heart of London. It shares the use of a wide range of activities and facilities including Chapel, Science laboratories, Music School, Arts and Technology Centre, Theatre, Gymnasium, Swimming Pool, Sports Hall and 100 acres of playing fields.

The curriculum and administration of the Senior and Junior Schools are very closely linked and are overseen by the Headmaster.

Pupils sit a written test for entry to the Junior School and are normally admitted to the Senior School without further examination. (*See Chigwell School entry in HMC section.*)

A Pre-Prep opened in September 2013 for 4–7 year old children in a purpose-built building. Entry is by assessment.

Charitable status. Chigwell School is a Registered Charity, number 1115098. It exists to provide a rounded education of the highest quality for its pupils.

Chinthurst School

Tadworth, Surrey KT20 5QZ
Tel: 01737 812011
Fax: 01737 814835
email: info@chinthurstschool.co.uk
website: www.chinthurstschool.co.uk

The School is an Educational Trust, administered by a Board of Governors.

Chairman of Governors: A Bisset, Esq

Headmaster: **D Williams**

Deputy Headmaster: T Button, BEd

Age Range. Rising 3–13.
Number of Pupils. 130
Fees per term (2014–2015). Nursery: £290 per session, £2,900 (full-time); Pre-Prep £2,910 (Lunch £265); Preparatory £4,030 (Lunch £270).

The School is set in modern and attractive rural surroundings with spacious games facilities including a swimming pool and astroturf area.

Pupils are prepared for all Senior Independent Schools, by way of the Common Entrance or Scholarships. A very experienced and well-qualified staff ensures a high standard is achieved both academically and on the games field. Chinthurst has a 'family' ethos, aimed at the achievement of high academic standards allied to a purposeful and active school life within a happy environment.

Charitable status. Chinthurst School is a Registered Charity, number 271160 A/1.

The Chorister School

Durham DH1 3EL
Tel: 0191 384 2935
Fax: 0191 383 1275
email: secretary@thechoristerschool.com
website: www.thechoristerschool.com

Chairman of Governors: The Dean of Durham, The Very Revd Michael Sadgrove

Headteacher: **Mrs Y F S Day**, BMus Cape Town, MMus London, GDL College of Law

Age Range. 3–13.
Number of Pupils. 220 (40 Boarders, 180 day pupils, including 69 in the Nursery and the Pre-Prep.) The school became co-educational in 1995 and there are girls in every year group.
Fees per term (2014–2015). Choristers (including piano lessons) £3,390 Full/Weekly Boarders £6,480, Day Pupils £3,745, Pre-Prep £2,780, Nursery £21 per half day session. Reductions are available for children of CofE clergy, serving members of the armed forces, children of Durham University staff, children of former pupils and for younger siblings. Scholarships available at entry to Years 3 and 6 Fees are inclusive of all normal requirements; there are no compulsory extras.

The Chorister School is in an outstanding situation in a World Heritage Site tucked behind Durham Cathedral. Quiet and secluded it is a haven in the centre of Durham City. Whilst it is the school for the choristers who sing in the renowned Cathedral Choir over eighty per cent of pupils are not choristers.

Pastoral care is the responsibility of all members of staff. The needs of the boarders are attended to by a dedicated team led by the Housemistress, Housemaster and Headmistress. Before and After School Care is available from the Nursery onwards and there is a wide range of after-school activities including: Art, Embroidery, Choirs, Dance, Film Club, Sports, Speech and Drama, Music Ensembles and World Challenge. Flexible boarding is also available.

Our curriculum introduces French from Pre-Prep level, where each of the classes has its own class teacher. In the Prep School class-teaching of the core curriculum is gradually replaced by subject-specialist teaching as children are prepared for Common Entrance and Scholarship examinations to senior schools. The school has a reputation for academic success, but cherishes all its pupils, whatever their academic attainment. The curriculum, which includes RE, PE, swimming, Art, Technology and Music, is designed to ensure that academic edge does not lead to academic narrowness.

Games are an important element in the curriculum. The Chorister School competes at various levels with other schools in athletics, cricket, netball, hockey, rounders, rugby, football and swimming. Badminton, volleyball, basketball, tennis, indoor football and netball (in our large Sports Hall) are also played. The Chorister School has its own sports fields, tennis court and play areas, and uses the indoor swimming pool at Durham School.

Individual instrumental music lessons are available in almost all instruments, and all pupils take class music in which they sing and learn about musical history, musical instruments, simple analysis and some famous pieces.

Entry is by English and Maths test graded according to age or by informal assessment during a 'taster' day, as seems best for the age of the individual child. Competitive auditions for aspiring Choristers are held regularly, with pre-audition training sessions offered by appointment.

Next School. Children move from The Chorister School to a wide range of maintained and independent secondary schools throughout the North East and further afield. The school advises and guides parents in the appropriate choice of next school and aims to secure a successful transition for every pupil. In the past ten years every child has won a place to the senior school of choice, with an average of 60% winning an academic or subject scholarship or a competitive entry place.

Charitable status. The Chorister School and Durham Cathedral enjoy charitable status (exempt from registration) and the school exists to provide boarding education for the choristers of Durham Cathedral and day or boarding education for other children aged 3–13.

Christ Church Cathedral School

3 Brewer Street, Oxford OX1 1QW
Tel: 01865 242561
Fax: 01865 202945
email: schooloffice@cccs.org.uk
website: www.cccs.org.uk

Governors: The Dean and Canons of Christ Church Cathedral

Headmaster: **Richard Murray**, BA, MA

Age Range. 3–13.
Number of Boys. About 21 boarders, all of whom are Cathedral Choristers (who must board) and 130 day boys.
Fees per term (2014–2015). Day boys (including lunch) £4,720; Pre-Prep £3,287 (including lunch); Cathedral Choristers £2,972–£3,287 (fees are subsidised by the Cathedral); Nursery £840–£2,120.

Christ Church Cathedral School is a day Preparatory, Pre-Preparatory and Nursery School for boys.

The School provides Choristers for the choirs of Christ Church Cathedral and Worcester College, and is governed by the Dean and Canons of Christ Church, with the assistance of lay members drawn from the city's professional community, some of whom are past or current parents.

It was founded in 1546 when provision was made for the education of eight Choristers on King Henry VIII's foundation of Christ Church on the site of Cardinal Wolsey's earlier foundation of Cardinal College. In the latter half of the nineteenth century, at the initiative of Dean Liddell, father of Alice Liddell, the inspiration for 'Alice in Wonderland', the boarding house was established at No 1 Brewer Street, and in 1892, during the Headship of the Reverend Henry Sayers, father of Dorothy L Sayers, the Italian Mediaeval scholar and creator of Lord Peter Wimsey, the present building was erected.

The School is centrally situated off St Aldates, and two hundred yards from Christ Church. It therefore not only enjoys the unique cultural background provided by Oxford itself, but also has the advantage of excellent recreational facilities on Christ Church Meadow. Buildings include a former residence of Cardinal Wolsey and the Sir William Walton Centre which contains a recital hall in addition to spacious classrooms.

Charitable status. Christ Church Cathedral School Education Trust is a Registered Charity, number 1114828.

Churcher's College Junior School

Midhurst Road, Liphook, Hampshire GU30 7HT
Tel: 01730 236870
Fax: 01428 722550
email: ccjsoffice@churcherscollege.com
website: www.churcherscollege.com

Chairman of Governors: M J Gallagher, Esq, Dip Arch Hons, RIBA, MIoD, FIMgt

Head: **I Adams**, BSc, PGCE, MBA

Age Range. 4–11 Co-educational.
Number of Pupils. 230.
Fees per term (2014–2015). £2,769–£2,954 excluding lunch.

Churcher's College Junior School provides a happy, stimulating, safe and secure environment in which every child feels valued and is able to develop personally, socially and academically. Each child is nurtured and taught to hold a high regard for others and themselves.

We view education as a joint partnership between teachers, parents and pupils, and strive to develop a team spirit in which every member gives of their best. We hold high expectations of staff and pupils and aim to create an environment that values individuals, applauds success, strives to encourage questioning, lets pupils explore, be controversial and be special.

The Junior School is sited in Liphook approximately 8 miles from the College, but continues to have strong links with the Senior School in Petersfield.

The school is set in beautiful rural surroundings providing extensive grounds for sports practices, three separate playing areas and a nature garden. Latest computer technology, networked classroom computers and interactive whiteboards are all used by staff and pupils to enhance curriculum studies. The school has a fully-equipped ICT suite, science laboratory, dedicated music and art rooms and a Performing Arts wing.

The wider curriculum is valued, offering additional depth and scope in all subjects and pupils are encouraged to take part in a broad range of experiences both in and out of the classroom. The Sensory Garden and external Education and Activity Trail enhance the quality of outdoor learning.

Churcher's College Junior School provides pupils with:

- a broad-based and challenging curriculum that enables all pupils to achieve their individual potential in all areas and caters for their individual abilities, needs and interests.
- a functional education in which pupils are able to develop transferable skills and a love of learning that will enable them to succeed in the ever-changing world.
- experiences of an aesthetic, creative and spiritual nature.

Teaching and learning activities cater for the varying needs of our pupils and allow all to achieve their full potential in a wide variety of areas – academic, creative, sporting, etc.

We maintain a broad and balanced curriculum in which pupils experience a wide range of activities to maximise their learning opportunities. Teaching is grounded in pupils past experiences and they are helped to see the importance of each area of study.

The school is seen as a continually evolving organisation and we constantly reflect upon practice as a means of self-improvement.

Charitable status. Churcher's College is a Registered Charity, number 307320.

City of London Freemen's Junior School

Ashtead Park, Surrey KT21 1ET
Tel: 01372 822474 (Secretary)
            01372 822423 (Admissions)
Fax: 01372 822415
            01372 822416 (Admissions)
email: admissions@clfs.surrey.sch.uk
website: www.clfs.surrey.sch.uk

Co-educational Day and Boarding School.

Chairman of Governors: Mr Stuart Fraser, CBE
--
Head: **Mr Matthew Robinson**, MA

Age Range. 7–13.
Number of Pupils. 390.
Fees per term (2014–2015). Tuition £3,864–£4,122.
The City of London Freemen's Junior School was established formally in 1988 as an integral part of CLFS and it prepares girls and boys for entry to the Senior School in Year 9. The School is located on a magnificent 57-acre site in Ashtead Park, Surrey, where the many outstanding facilities are available to all pupils (*see separate entry in HMC section*).

With its broad based curriculum and modern purpose-built facilities, the Junior School offers a challenging and unique atmosphere for all. There is a Junior School Head with specialist teaching staff and a clearly defined academic and pastoral structure to ensure that all pupils know what is expected of them. The Junior School encourages young pupils to develop their strengths and discover new skills and passions in an environment of trust, kindness and fun. There are 20 pupils in each of the three parallel classes in each year group. In Year 7 the year groups rises to four classes. Junior pupils benefit greatly from seeing their Form Prefects, who are Sixth Formers from the Senior School, on a daily basis.

For the first four years, in Key Stage 2, Heads of Year work in liaison with the subject coordinators and the Heads of Senior School Departments to ensure that the programmes of work are compatible and progressive. The aim is to establish a secure foundation in traditional core subjects within a curriculum which will broaden experience and excite the imagination of each child. In Years 7 and 8 the teaching programme is managed by the Heads of the Senior School Departments using specialist teachers for all of the subjects. Whilst academic excellence throughout the Junior School is still a major aim, there is also an enrichment programme and a very full programme of extra-curricular activities including drama, music and sports.

Fully integrated into whole school routines, the Junior School takes full advantage of Ashtead Park's facilities. Extensive playing fields, the floodlit all-weather pitch and the sports hall ensure that the sports facilities available are second to none.

There are three Houses in the School providing pastoral care and supervision whilst also promoting healthy competition in many activities. In both the Senior and the Junior School outstanding work and good progress, inside and outside the classroom, are recognised by the award of appropriate merits and distinctions.

Admission to the Junior School is through entrance examination, interview and feeder school report. Progression to the Senior School is based on continuous assessment with no separate qualifying entrance test and as such is almost always automatic for Junior School pupils. Pupils are constantly reviewed and can be assured that they will move through to the Senior School with many familiar faces around them.

Claremont Fan Court Pre-Preparatory and Nursery School

Claremont Drive, Esher, Surrey KT10 9LY
Tel: 01372 463695
email: preprepschool@claremont.surrey.sch.uk
            info@claremont.surrey.sch.uk
website: www.claremont-school.co.uk

Chairman of Governors: Mr Gordon Hunt, MA Kingston, Adv Dip Ed Exeter, Cert Ed Belfast

Head: **Mrs Louise Fox**, BEd Hons

Age Range. 2½–7 Co-educational.
Number of Pupils. 145.
The Pre-Preparatory and Nursery School ensures that the beginning of each child's education is a happy and fulfilling experience. We combine enthusiasm for learning in a stimulating, creative environment with dedicated teachers and assistants. Values for life are taught in a supportive, caring atmosphere with shared aims and aspirations between home and School.

The School is situated in wooded parkland where children have the freedom to grow and develop in a secure and healthy environment. Here we care for the needs of Claremont Fan Court's youngest children in spacious classrooms with excellent facilities and resources.

We place a strong emphasis on the children acquiring sound knowledge and skills in literacy and numeracy, whilst providing every opportunity to explore and develop each child's potential in creative, sporting and musical activities.

Fees per term (2014–2015). Pre-Nursery (2 mornings per week) £645; Nursery (5 mornings per week) £1,525; Nursery (2 afternoons per week) £610; Nursery (full time), Reception, Years 1 & 2 £3,040.

Charitable status. The Claremont Fan Court Foundation Limited is Registered Charity, number 274664.

Claremont Fan Court Preparatory School

Claremont Drive, Esher, Surrey KT10 9LY
Tel: 01372 465380
email: prepschool@claremont.surrey.sch.uk
            info@claremont.surrey.sch.uk
website: www.claremont-school.co.uk

Chairman of Governors: Mr Gordon Hunt, MA Kingston, Adv Dip Ed Exeter, Cert Ed Belfast

Head: **Mr Duncan Murphy**, BA Hons, MEd, FRSA, FCMI, FCollT

Age Range. 7–11 Co-educational.
Number of Pupils. 160.
The Preparatory School is housed in the historic Stable Court and backs onto an idyllic Walled Garden, originally built by Sir John Vanbrugh in 1708. Whilst there is a rich cultural and historical heritage that permeates every aspect of their day-to-day life, pupils also benefit from a progressive educational philosophy which incorporates the very best of contemporary practice.

Life here is busy, engaging and fulfilling. An atmosphere of conviviality underpins our dynamic curriculum, which offers each child the opportunity to develop their unlimited potential in and out of the classroom. The ethos of our school promotes tolerance, respect and friendship; children settle in and become a valued member of our tight-knit community very quickly.

We are fortunate to be situated within a hundred acres of beautiful Grade One listed landscape; this spectacular setting provides the backdrop to a hive of industry where children thrive in a stimulating environment. No two days are ever the same! Friendships flourish and confidence is nurtured by a rich educational experience which overflows with energy and excitement.

There is a forward-thinking curriculum which incorporates the latest ICT thinking, careful pastoral care and a broad range of co-curricular activities. A keenly contested House system with points available for effort, academic performance and a range of competitions throughout the school year captures the imagination of the children and provides an additional sense of camaraderie.

Each child is closely monitored by a vigilant team of staff; the form teacher is initially responsible for the academic development and general well-being of the children in their class whilst the Director of Studies and Deputy Head oversee the academic and pastoral implementation of the curriculum respectively. The Head plays an active role in the day-to-day life of the pupils and maintains a keen interest in, as well as overall responsibility for, their academic progress and pastoral well-being.

Fees per term (2014–2015). £3,915.

Charitable status. The Claremont Fan Court Foundation Limited is Registered Charity, number 274664.

Clayesmore Preparatory School

Iwerne Minster, Blandford Forum, Dorset DT11 8PH

Tel:	01747 813155
Fax:	01747 811692
email:	prepadmissions@clayesmore.com
website:	www.clayesmore.com
Twitter:	@clayesmoreprep

Chairman of Governors: Mr J Andrews, LLB

Headmaster: **Mr W G Dunlop**, BA

Age Range. Rising 3–13 years.
Number of Pupils. 217 (Boarders 56, Day 161).
Fees per term (2014–2015). Boarders: £6,954 (Year 3), £7,622 (Years 4–8). Day Pupils: £2,317 (Pre-Prep), £5,303 (Year 3), £5,661 (Years 4–8).

Filled with a warm, friendly atmosphere, Clayesmore Prep offers excitement and opportunity at every turn with the aim of developing the unique gifts of every pupil. Founded in 1929 at Charlton Marshall House by R A L Everett, the Prep School moved to Iwerne Minster in 1974 and now nestles side by side with the thriving Senior School. There is also a Nursery and Pre-Prep, with their own snug self-contained home, where little ones learn and develop through play and via a host of activities led by specialist teachers.

An ongoing development programme has provided this fully co-educational school with outstanding facilities for sport, music, drama and the arts, while the 62-acre parkland campus, in beautiful rural Dorset, is the ideal environment for young ones to experience a true childhood as they grow. A state-of-the-art building was opened in 2008 comprising five classrooms and two Science laboratories. An adventure playground, complete with pirate ship, has recently been built, and the ballpark has been updated.

The 'all through' provision means there is a comfortable transition between schools and Prep pupils can make a worry-free step up to Senior School accompanied by a soothing sense of familiarity.

Day children can join Pre-Prep at the start of the term in which they are 3 and the youngest boarders usually arrive at age 7/8. The boarders enjoy welcoming boarding facilities with nurturing pastoral care, friendly staff and a real family feel.

Admission is normally by interview and a report from a child's previous school. Academic, Art, Music, Sporting and All-Rounder Scholarships are offered each year, together with 11+ Continuity Scholarships for candidates intending to go on to the dynamic Clayesmore Sixth Form in the Senior School.

The school is proud of its long association with HM Forces and offers a number of service bursaries. There are also children from expatriate families and the school is well versed in handling overseas travel arrangements.

Small classes and individual attention ensure speedy progress and each day at Clayesmore is further enriched by the superb facilities and exciting activities. Younger children spend most of their time with their Form Teacher but by age 10, children are taught by specialist subject teachers. In the upper school the children are put in sets for Mathematics and English, with some streaming taking place in Science, Humanities and Languages, to allow them to proceed at their own pace. Though the pressure of academic work increases as examinations approach, every child experiences a full range of Art, Music, ICT, Design Technology and Games as well as vital play and relaxation time.

There is a strong sporting life at Clayesmore with the main games for boys being rugby, hockey, football and cricket and for girls: netball, hockey, tennis and rounders. A well-equipped Sports Centre with a 25-metre heated pool, a floodlit all-weather hockey pitch and extensive playing fields provide every opportunity for pupils to reach the highest standards. The school also enjoys considerable success at athletics, swimming and orienteering, and numerous other sports are also available.

Music is highly regarded and many children are encouraged to learn an instrument. The Chapel Choir has toured in Italy, France, Germany, USA, Spain, South Africa and Prague. As well as Prep School orchestras there are several instrumental ensembles and the Concert Band that draws the best instrumentalists from both schools, is in hot demand locally, as well having toured abroad. There is also excellent Art provision and the Prep School has its own dedicated Art Department with separate pottery.

Clayesmore has an outstanding reputation for supporting pupils with dyslexia. Regular staff training means that the work of the Learning Support specialists is understood and reinforced by subject staff and form teachers.

When they are ready to move on to the next stage of their education, pupils are prepared for Common Entrance and Senior School Scholarship examinations.

Charitable status. Clayesmore School Limited is a Registered Charity, number 306214. It exists for the purpose of educating children.

Clevelands Preparatory School

425 Chorley New Road, Bolton, Lancashire BL1 5DH

Tel:	01204 843898
Fax:	01204 848007
email:	secretary@clevelandsprepschool.co.uk
website:	www.clevelandsprepschool.co.uk

Co-educational Day School.

Headteacher: **Mrs L Parlane**

Age Range. 2¾–11.
Number of Pupils. 120: 72 boys, 48 girls.
Fees per term (2014–2015). Tuition £2,286; Lunch £199.

Clevelands Nursery and Preparatory School offers a traditional academic education in a caring, stimulating environment. The school and nursery department is open to boys and girls between the ages of 2¾ and 11 years.

We aim to give our pupils a stimulating and challenging curriculum linking strong, traditional values with the best of new educational initiatives. The range of experiences on offer ensures that our pupils have a broad curriculum which combines the National Curriculum with our own successful Educational programme. It also ensures that emphasis is placed on developing and celebrating each child's individual talents.

The school's family values are built on kindness, a sense of belonging, mutual respect and consideration of one another. The pupils spend each day in a happy, caring, work orientated environment in which their needs are prioritised and catered for by dedicated and highly qualified teachers.

Pupils have a proud record of academic success in entrance examinations and scholarships for entry into the leading day senior schools.

They also excel in other fields such as art, drama, music and sport. A significant number of pupils play at least one musical instrument.

Clevelands children compete successfully in local, regional and national sporting competitions.

Pupils are taught by specialist teachers from Nursery upwards. This teaching increases as the pupils move through the school.

Facilities at Clevelands include a fully networked Computer Suite. In the art/design and technology studio pupils can explore all media. The science laboratory is fully equipped with the latest technology. Our sporting facilities include a netball court and football pitch.

A myriad of extra-curricular activities takes place during lunchtimes and after school. A thriving programme of external Educational and Theatre visits exists as well as the opportunity for the children to encounter a variety of new and exciting experiences internally. Skiing trips take place annually.

Our pupils develop into well rounded, self-assured, competent young people who will meet the challenges of life with enthusiasm and vigour.

Before and after school care is available to all.

Most pupils enter the main school in September of any year, but the Headteacher is happy to consider requests for admission for children of any age during the academic year, should circumstances so warrant.

Entry to the Nursery is ongoing throughout the year as a child reaches the appropriate age.

terms of running and organisation. However, it benefits from being governed by the same Council and enjoys the considerable advantages of sharing many of the College's extensive facilities. These include the swimming pool, sports hall, gymnasium, multi-activity hall, Chapel and Theatre. The School is situated in two buildings either side of a superb playground with a variety of play equipment.

The School caters for children in the Foundation Stage (Nursery and Reception), Key Stage 1 (Years 1 and 2) and Year 3, the first year of Key Stage 2. The Nursery has up to 50 children on roll, with a staff-pupil ratio of 1–8. Attendance in the Nursery may be either five mornings, three days or full-time. Morning sessions include lunch at no extra cost. Clifton College Pre-Preparatory School is a member of the Bristol Early Years Partnership and accepts the government's nursery grant for the majority of 3 and 4 year olds. The Nursery staff are either qualified teachers or Early Years practitioners.

There are three classes of 16 children in Reception and in Years 1, 2 and 3, each with a class teacher and teaching assistant. In all there are 22 full-time and 15 part-time staff. Qualified specialist class teachers deliver a topic-based curriculum, with specialist teachers for Music, Dance (Ballet, Jazz Dance, Tap), Sport, French, Mandarin and IT. Piano and instrumental lessons are available from Year 2, and all children in Years 2 and 3 learn the recorder, strings and sing in the choir. Some sports activity takes place every day.

Life at the Pre-Preparatory is busy and challenging. Year 2 and 3 pupils may take part in a range of co-curricular activities at lunchtimes or after school, when around sixteen clubs and societies are held. These change termly and include a variety of sports, sewing, puppet-making, junior detectives, zoo club, chess etc. Termly services and concerts are held in the Chapel, and an annual musical is performed in the Redgrave Theatre. There is a full programme of visits and outings for all ages, including a youth hostelling trip for Year 3.

Recent investment has seen the creation of an outdoor area leading from the reception classrooms. This is designed to give reception classes easy access to an outdoor space which they can use to extend and enhance their learning.

Another exciting provision is the Forest School at our Beggar's Bush Sports Ground. All year groups, from Nursery to Year 3, visit the School and it provides a range of stimulating outdoor experiences for the children, enabling them to learn, achieve and develop confidence through curriculum-linked activities and free exploration of the natural woodland.

Charitable status. Clifton College is a Registered Charity, number 311735. It provides boarding and day education for boys and girls aged 3–18.

Clifton College Pre-Preparatory School

Guthrie Road, Clifton, Bristol BS8 3EZ
Tel: 0117 315 7160
Fax: 0117 315 7592
email: hwilliams@cliftoncollege.com
website: www.cliftoncollege.com
Twitter: @Clifton_College
Facebook: /CliftonCollegeUK
LinkedIn: /clifton-college

Chairman of College Council: Mr Richard Morgan, MA

Headmistress: **Joanne Newman**, BSc, MSc, PGCE

Age Range. 3–8.
Number of Pupils. 220.
Fees per term (2014–2015). £1,900–£3,950.

Clifton College Pre-Preparatory School, part of the main Preparatory School, is independent of Clifton College in

Clifton College Preparatory School

The Avenue, Clifton, Bristol BS8 3HE
Tel: +44 (0)117 315 7503
Fax: +44 (0)117 315 7504
email: abrereton@cliftoncollege.com
website: www.cliftoncollege.com
Twitter: @Clifton_College
Facebook: /CliftonCollegeUK
LinkedIn: /clifton-college

Chairman of College Council: Mr Richard Morgan, MA

Headmaster: **J Milne**, BA, MBA

Age Range. 8–13.
Number of Pupils. 310.
Fees per term (2014–2015). Boarders (from Year 4) £8,900; Weekly Boarders (from Year 4) £7,950; Flexi

Boarders (from Year 4) £5,975–£6,425; Day Pupils £4,975–£5,425.

There is a full time teaching staff of 58, all of whom are qualified. A wide range of subjects is included in the normal curriculum.

The majority of pupils go on to the Upper School with whom there is cooperation on curriculum matters, but a number are prepared for and win scholarships to other schools. Over 60 awards have been won in the past three years. Pupils can be prepared for the Common Entrance examination to other schools.

The administration of the School is entirely separate from the Upper School, but some facilities are shared, including the Chapel, Theatre, Sports Complex and Indoor Swimming Pool, the Gymnasium, Squash and Rackets Courts and 83 acres of playing fields, which include an Olympic-standard water-based Hockey pitch, a 3G pitch, an indoor Tennis and Netball Centre and a new Activity Centre. The School has its own Art & Design Centre and possesses one of the most advanced Information Technology Centres in the West of England.

The House system operates for both boarders and day pupils. Two Houses cater for the boarders, each under the supervision of a Housemaster or Housemistress assisted by wife or husband, House Tutor and Matron. The remaining seven Houses cater specifically for day pupils with boys and girls in separate Houses. In September 2012 a new substantial building opened, purpose-built and in keeping within the local Conservation area containing two Houses, with a whole level having a dance studio with light-rigging and sprung-floor. All other Houses are fully renovated.

Out-of-school activities supplementing the main School games are many and varied, the aim being to give every child an opportunity to participate in an activity from which he or she gains confidence and a sense of achievement.

The youngest boys and girls (aged 3–8) work separately in the Pre-Preparatory School next door, under the care of their own Head and teachers. (*See separate IAPS entry for Clifton College Pre-Preparatory School.*)

Charitable status. Clifton College is a Registered Charity, number 311735. It provides boarding and day education for boys and girls aged 3–18 years.

Clifton School and Nursery
The Pre-prep School of St Peter's School, York

Clifton, York YO30 6AB
Tel: 01904 527361
Fax: 01904 527304
email: enquiries@cliftonyork.org.uk
website: www.cliftonyork.org.uk
Twitter: @PhilHardyCPS
Facebook: /clifton.school.and.nursery

Chairman of the Governors: Mr W Woolley

Head: **Mr Philip Hardy**, BA Northumbria, PGCE

Age Range. 3–8 co-educational.
Number of Pupils. 129 boys, 80 girls.
Fees per term (2014–2015). Nursery (full time) £2,435; Reception, Years 1 & 2: £2,530; Year 3: £2,630. Nursery Education Grant accepted for 3 and 4 year olds.

Clifton School and Nursery is the Pre-prep of St Peter's School, York. The school has large modern buildings on the St Peter's School site which occupies 47 acres in the centre of York. There are new outdoor play surfaces and 25m swimming pool.

Curriculum. An exciting and dynamic thematic skills based curriculum is covered, which offers breath and chal-

lenge to all of its pupils. There is a Thinking Skills lesson each week where children are encouraged to be independent. Small classes, individual attention and after-school activities enable high standards to be achieved. French is offered to all children from Nursery upwards.

Music and Drama. Nursery children have a session of music and movement, and all other classes have weekly lessons with a specialist teacher. From Year 2, children have the opportunity to learn to play the recorder, piano, violin or guitar at school. Each year there are opportunities for children to participate in performances to a wider audience. All classes have weekly drama lessons, and there is the opportunity for Y2 and Y3 to do speech and drama as an after school activity.

Sport and Co-Curricular Activities. Physical Education starts in the Nursery. As children grow older, games and swimming are added. The pupils at Clifton School and Nursery have access to the sports facilities at St Peter's School. Co-curricular activities include Board Games, Chess, Swim Squad, Badminton, Team Games, Football and Tag Rugby, Tennis, Choir, Speech and Drama, Art Clubs, Explorers Club, Library Club, K'Nex & Lego Clubs and Cookery.

Assessments. Throughout Nursery and Reception children work towards achieving the Early Learning Goals, culminating in the completion of the Foundation Stage Profile. Work is assessed continuously and children's progress is discussed at monthly staff meetings. Incas is used in Years 1 to 3 for assessment purposes which informs future planning. There is ongoing communication between parents and staff through a reports system, invitations to visit the school and parent evenings.

After the recent ISI inspection, the inspectors reported that: "The School provides a high-quality education, which is outstanding in several important respects".

Charitable status. St Peter's School, York, is a Registered Charity, number 1141329. It exists to provide education for boys and girls.

Cokethorpe Junior School

Witney, Oxfordshire OX29 7PU
Tel: 01993 703921
Fax: 01993 773499
email: admin@cokethorpe.org
website: www.cokethorpe.org.uk
Twitter: @cokethorpe

Chairman of Governors: Sir John Allison, KCB, CBE, FRAeS

Head: **Mrs C A Cook**, BEd Hons

Deputy Head: Mr M J P O'Connor, BEd Hons

Age Range. 4–11 Co-educational.
Number of Pupils. 142.
Fees per term (2014–2015). £3,825 including lunch.
Staff. 17 full-time and 6 part-time qualified and enthusiastic staff teach the 11 classes.

Location. Cokethorpe Junior School is set in 150 acres of beautiful Oxfordshire parkland, two miles from Witney and ten from Oxford. It was established in 1994 and occupies the elegant Queen Anne Mansion House that is at the heart of Cokethorpe School. The Junior School retains its own identity, independence and distinct character, allowing the children to flourish, develop confidence and feel valued, whilst having the advantage of being part of a wider community with the Senior School.

Facilities. Whilst self-sufficient in most respects, the Junior School benefits from having access to the Senior School facilities, especially the all-weather pitches, Sports

Hall and other sports facilities, performing arts, science laboratories, ICT resources and the splendid Dining Hall. There is also a dedicated play area, library, art room and music room.

Aims. Cokethorpe Junior School is a small, friendly and ambitious school that places a large emphasis on striving for high academic standards as well as on its pastoral care, sense of community and family atmosphere. It aims to provide an insight into a world that is rich and varied, exciting and stimulating and puts its pupils on a journey of discovery. As they progress through the School they are equipped with the necessary academic and social skills to enable them to develop into confident children who are able to cope with all that school life offers. Children make the most of being in an environment which encourages them to aim higher, try harder, and expect more of themselves.

Curriculum. The Junior School offers a fully balanced curriculum with the focus on developing high standards and providing intellectual challenges. Children receive vital foundations for study in small classes and in a positive and purposeful learning environment. Whilst the National Curriculum is followed, the freedom to offer breadth is fully embraced. Trips and events support work done in the classroom and also help children meet the School's high academic, behavioural and social expectations.

Enrichment. Sport and The Arts play a strong part in the Junior School. Children participate in team sports on two afternoons a week, including competitive fixtures, and time is also found for other sports such as swimming, tennis, judo, golf, modern dance and ballet. There are drama productions each year and it is often the case that every child has a speaking or singing role. In addition they have the opportunity to take part in concerts and recitals throughout the year. The dedicated art room is a riot of colour and creativity with displays decorating the corridors and classroom walls.

The School enjoys a particularly close relationship with parents and there is a strong Parents' Association.

Entry. There is no formal assessment for entry to the Reception although children will be invited to spend either the day or half day in School. For entry to Years 1 to 6, children are invited to an Assessment Day, during which they will complete an assessment appropriate to their age. Individual arrangements for assessment can be made throughout the academic year. Reports are also requested from the child's current school or nursery. Early registration is recommended as places are limited. The majority of pupils continue to Cokethorpe Senior School, with many going on to achieve scholarships in the Senior School. (*See Cokethorpe School entry in HMC section.*)

Charitable status. Cokethorpe Educational Trust Limited is a Registered Charity, number 309650.

Colet Court (St Paul's Preparatory School)

Lonsdale Road, London SW13 9JT
Tel: 020 8748 3461
Fax: 020 8746 5357
email: hmpacc@stpaulsschool.org.uk
website: www.coletcourt.org.uk

Chairman of Governors: J M Robertson

Headmaster: T A Meunier, MA, CChem, FRSC, PGCE

Deputy Headmaster: C G Howes, MA, PGCE

Age Range. 7–13.
Number of Boys. 440.
Fees per term (2014–2015). £5,807.

Colet Court, founded in 1881, is the preparatory school for St Paul's School (*see entry in HMC section*). Nearly all pupils at Colet Court transfer to St Paul's at 13. The two schools are in separate, but adjacent modern buildings on the south bank of the Thames, and share many amenities, including the dining hall, sports complex, design & technology workshops and playing fields. Colet Court has its own main teaching block, hall/theatre, library, art & design room, two computer rooms and music school. A drama studio and three science laboratories are situated in a separate building.

There is close consultation with St Paul's in matters of curriculum to ensure the benefit of continuity. Some members of staff teach in both schools. Boys are not specifically prepared for scholarships to senior schools other than St Paul's. Our aim is to give every pupil the opportunity to enjoy a broad education and a wide range of activities. Music, Art, Drama and Sport are all strong.

There are two Year 3 classes and four forms per year group from Years 4 to 8. Boys join the School at 7+ and 8+ and approximately 20 places are also available at 11+. Up to 10 of these places may be offered to pupils who sit an examination in Year 5 and defer their arrival for one year. This mode of entry is available to boys from maintained primary schools only. Entrance at all levels is by competitive examination and interview. Means-tested bursaries are available at all points of entry.

Charitable status. St Paul's School is a Registered Charity, number 1119619. The object of the charity is to promote the education of boys in Greater London.

Colfe's Preparatory School

Horn Park Lane, London SE12 8AW
Tel: 020 8463 8240 Prep
           020 8463 8266 Pre-Prep & Nursery
Fax: 020 8297 2941
email: prep@colfes.com
website: www.colfes.com

Chairman of the Governors: Mr Ian Russell, MBE

Head of the Preparatory School: **Mrs Sarah Marsh**, BEd Hons, MA

Head of the Pre-Prep & Nursery: Mrs Sarah Redman, BEd

Age Range. 3–11.
Number of Pupils. 397 boys and girls.
Fees per term (2014–2015). Prep School £3,987 (excluding lunch); Pre-Prep £3,768 (including lunch); Nursery £3,609 (including lunch).

Colfe's Preparatory School is a co-educational day school under the general direction of the Governors and Headmaster of Colfe's School (founded in 1652). It is academically selective, offers a broad curriculum and aims to provide an excellent all-round education. Children normally enter at the ages of 3, 4 or 7 although the occasional vacancy arises at other times.

The Preparatory School is housed in modern purpose-built accommodation with spacious and well-equipped classrooms. Small class sizes and a team of well-qualified teachers provide a caring and vibrant environment. Excellent library facilities and specialist accommodation for art and design, ICT and science provide boys and girls with a stimulating environment in which to learn. Full use is made of the school's swimming pool, sports centre, visual and performing arts centre and extensive on-site playing fields.

PE specialists teach a wide range of sports. There is an extensive programme of house and inter-school sports matches. A school choir, orchestra, strings group and numerous ensembles perform frequently both in and out of school. Drama productions normally take place each term.

There is a wide range of after-school clubs on offer (over 50 each week for the 7–11 year olds) and a late school scheme until 6 pm. A very successful Breakfast Club is in operation from 7.30 am until 8.00 am each day.

The school has a strong reputation in the local area for excellence within a friendly and caring atmosphere.

A large building programme is ongoing which has expanded the provision of the Pre-Prep & Nursery from September 2014 and will provide a new Sixth Form Centre from September 2015.

Charitable status. Colfe's School is a Registered Charity, number 1109650. It exists to provide education for children.

Collingwood School

Springfield Road, Wallington, Surrey SM6 0BD
Tel: 020 8647 4607
email: secretary@collingwoodschool.org.uk
website: www.collingwoodschool.org.uk

Headmaster: **Mr D P G Cobb**, CertEd, BA Hons, MA

Age Range. 3–11 Co-educational.
Number in School. Day: 110.
Fees per term (2014–2015). £1,340–£2,490 (reduction for siblings).

Collingwood was founded in 1928 and became an Educational Trust in 1978.

It is a school that has deliberately remained small in order to foster a very friendly and caring environment.

Our aim is to give children a first-class academic and sporting education while at the same time instilling the virtues of courtesy, respect and consideration for others. These traditional values, coupled with a modern, relevant education, make Collingwood the happy, purposeful and unique place that it is.

We offer an exciting range of subjects including ICT, French and Spanish. Currently we have over twelve extra-curricular activities taking place each week including street dance, drama, football, gardening, gymnastics and Latin. Children are also able to learn to play a musical instrument such as piano, keyboard, drums, violin, cello, guitar or recorder. We also offer a breakfast, after-school and holiday club.

Although we are a non-selective school, many of our children over the years have gained entry into the local Grammar or Independent Selective Schools.

For a prospectus or to arrange a visit, call Mrs King, the Headmaster's PA, on 020 8647 4607.

Charitable status. Collingwood School Educational Trust Ltd is a Registered Charity, number 277682. It exists to promote and foster a sound education for boys and girls aged 3–11 years.

Colston's Lower School

Park Road, Stapleton, Bristol BS16 1BA
Tel: 0117 965 5297
Fax: 0117 965 6330
email: admissions@colstons.bristol.sch.uk
website: www.colstons.bristol.sch.uk

Chair of Governors: Mr R Bernays

Head of Lower School: **Mr S M Smart**, BA Hons, MSc, PGCE

Age Range. 3–11.

Number of Pupils. 220 Day Pupils.

Fees per term (from January 2015). Reception, Year 1 and 2 £2,210; Years 3 and 4 £2,795; Years 5 and 6 £3,090. Lunch: £195. Nursery: £29.40 per morning (8.30 am–12.30 pm incl lunch); £20.50 per afternoon (12.30–3.30 pm). Scholarships are offered from 7+.

Colston's Lower School is located in Stapleton village which is within the city of Bristol. It is less than one mile from Junction 2 of the M32 and therefore easily accessible from north Bristol and South Gloucestershire. In addition to its own specialist facilities for Science, ICT, Music, Design & Technology, Art and Games, the Lower School has full use of facilities at the neighbouring Upper School including 30 acres of playing fields, theatre, concert hall and sports centre.

At the end of Year 6 pupils move from the Lower to the Upper School (*see entry in HMC section*). They work in small classes on a broad and engaging curriculum that extends beyond the requirements of the National Curriculum. It incorporates the full range of academic subjects together with French, German, Design and Technology, ICT, Art and Music. There is also a Learning Support Unit for those needing additional support on their learning journey.

The creative arts flourish in the Lower School, with a choir and orchestra, regular concerts, school plays and music competitions. A large number of children also play musical instruments, with specialist teachers providing weekly tuition.

In addition to PE lessons there are two afternoons of junior games each week. The boys principally play rugby, hockey and cricket, and the girls play hockey, netball and rounders. Pupils also enjoy opportunities to take part in football, tennis, swimming, athletics and badminton. All juniors are encouraged to take part in competitive sports fixtures, and sports tours are also arranged.

The school also has its own excellent Forest School site which is used every week for outdoor learning.

Colston's Lower School offers a wide range of clubs and activities, and pupils are able to stay on at school under supervision for an extended day or start with Breakfast Club. There are numerous visits and trips including skiing and adventure activities.

Charitable status. Colston's School is a Registered Charity, number 1079552. Its aims and objectives are the provision of education.

Combe Bank Preparatory School

Combe Bank Drive, Sundridge, Kent TN14 6AE
Tel: 01959 564320
Fax: 01959 560456
email: enquiries@combebank.co.uk
website: www.combebankschool.co.uk

Council of Management:
Chairman: Mr P Dickinson

Headmistress: Mrs Julie Tricks, BA Hons, PGCE

Head of Preparatory School: **Miss Esther Wright**, MA Hons, PGCE (*Prep ICT Coordinator*)

Age Range. 3–11 Co-educational.
Number of Pupils. 101.
Fees per term (2014–2015). Preparatory School £2,935–£4,050; Nursery £1,090–£2,100 (according to number of sessions).

Combe Bank School was founded in 1924. The Preparatory School is a flourishing independent school that stands in 27 acres of gardens and grounds, on the Kent/Surrey borders within easy reach of the centre Sevenoaks. The school forms part of the Combe Bank School Educational Trust. (*See also Combe Bank School entry in GSA section.*)

The Preparatory School is housed in an original stable block and affords a unique environment in which the children feel secure and comfortable. Specialist teaching rooms include those dedicated to ICT, French, Music, PE, Speech and Drama. The Hall includes a permanent stage with sound and lighting systems. The older pupils have access to a purpose-built Technology Room and to the Senior School Science labs. The ICT suite, networked to all classrooms, allows full class access at any time.

EYFS Nursery classes are housed within the courtyard area, which has recently undergone refurbishment to provide first-class facilities for both indoor and outdoor activities, including a specially designed Secret Garden.

Beech Walk with its secure adventure play area gives the children greater freedom at break times. There are two playing fields and five outdoor tennis and netball courts. A purpose-built Jubilee Sports Hall allows for the teaching of multi-sporting activities and inter-school fixtures. All pupils, including the Nursery, use the indoor heated swimming pool weekly throughout the year.

Academic standards are high. The pupils between the ages of 7–11 are prepared for scholarship and entrance examinations. Year 6 pupils sit the entrance examinations to the Senior School and compete with other potential Year 7 candidates for Academic, Art, Sports and Music Scholarships with high levels of success. They are also successfully prepared for the Kent Assessment Procedure at 11+ (100% pass rate for those girls recommended) and entrance into other Independent schools.

Drama and Music flourish in the school. Pupils have many opportunities to perform throughout their time in the Prep from large drama productions to musical ensembles. The majority of study at least one musical instrument from Year 3.

A highly dedicated staff team takes care of the academic, physical, pastoral and extra-curricular needs of the pupils. We are committed to academic excellence for all our pupils. We work together to raise the self-esteem of each child. We pay particular attention to the development of thinking skills and positively encourage independent learning. We actively promote the development of a strong home-school partnership through parent consultation, information evenings and social events. We also recognise the impact of Music Speech and Drama, Art and sport in the life of the developing child. The school is distinguished by the high standard of pastoral care it offers. We nurture the individual.

Combe Bank is committed to safeguarding and promoting the welfare of children.

Charitable status. Combe Bank School Educational Trust Limited is a Registered Charity, number 1007871.

Copthorne School

Effingham Lane, Copthorne, West Sussex RH10 3HR
Tel:　　01342 712311
Fax:　　01342 714014
email:　office@copthorneprep.co.uk
website:　www.copthorneprep.co.uk

Chairman of Governors: James Abdool

Headmaster: **C J Jones**, BEd Hons

Deputy Head: S King

Age Range. 2–13.
Number of Boys and Girls. 359 (20 Boarders).
Fees per term (2014–2015). Day: Pre-Prep £2,800, Year 3 £3,765, Year 4 £4,130, Years 5–8 £4,735. Weekly Boarding £5,010. Occasional Boarding £25 per night.

Copthorne is a flourishing IAPS Prep School with approximately 359 boys and girls aged from 2 to 13. The school has grown by over 75% within the last 5 years. Children are prepared for Independent School Scholarships or Common Entrance. In the last 5 years Copthorne children have been awarded 48 Scholarships or Awards to a variety of Senior Schools.

We believe that, in order to learn, children must be happy and feel secure in their environment. Copthorne Prep School is full of happy children and the environment is caring but still allows children the freedom to develop as individuals.

The school helps to develop each child's confidence, to raise self-esteem and to make children feel good about themselves. Nothing does this more than children enjoying success in all areas of school life. This is why Art, Music, ICT, DT, Drama and Sport are all just as important as the pursuit of academic excellence.

We provide opportunities for children to achieve success in all areas of the curriculum and we always celebrate their achievements.

We recognise that all children have talents, and every child is encouraged to realise their true potential, whatever that may be, in whatever area of school life.

We demand and set high standards, and our children respond by always giving of their best.

Put simply, our mission is to:

Develop **C**onfidence – Provide **O**pportunity – Realise **P**otential – in every single child.

The school is very proud of its history of over 100 years, and retains all the important traditions of the past whilst developing a very forward thinking approach. The children receive a "child-centred" education, where their individual needs come first, in an environment that is "parent-friendly", with very high levels of communication and pastoral care.

Charitable status. Copthorne School Trust Limited is a Registered Charity, number 270757. It exists to provide education to boys and girls.

Cottesmore School

Buchan Hill, Pease Pottage, West Sussex RH11 9AU
Tel:　　01293 520648
Fax:　　01293 614784
email:　office@cottesmoreschool.com
website:　www.cottesmoreschool.com

Independent Co-educational Preparatory Boarding School.

Headmaster: **T F Rogerson**, BA, PGCE

Age Range. 4–13.
Number of Pupils. 100 Boys, 50 Girls.
Fees per term (2014–2015). Prep: £5,130 (Day), £7,010 (Boarding); Pre-Prep: £2,740–£3,655.

Cottesmore is a preparatory school offering Day, Weekly and Full Boarding. In September 2009 the school opened a Pre-Prep Department.

Cottesmore is situated a mile from Exit 11 of the M23, ten minutes from Gatwick Airport and one hour from Central London and Heathrow Airport.

Curriculum. Boys and girls are taught together in classes averaging 14 in number. The teacher/pupil ratio is 1:9. Children are fully prepared for Common Entrance and Scholarship examinations.

Music. The musical tradition is strong – more than 80% of children learn a variety of instruments; there are three Choirs, a School Orchestra and several musical ensembles.

Sport. The major games are Association and Rugby Football, Cricket, Hockey, Netball and Rounders. Numerous other sports are taught and encouraged. They include Tennis, Squash, Golf, Riding, Athletics, Cross-Country Running, Swimming, Windsurfing, Fishing, Boating, Gymnastics, Shooting, Judo and Archery. The School competes at a national level in several of these sports.

Recent Developments. Our Technology Centre houses a constantly developing Information Technology Suite, a Design Technology room for metal, woodwork, plastic and pneumatics, a Craft room, Kiln, two Science laboratories and Art Studio.

Hobbies and Activities. These include Pottery, Photography, Stamp Collecting, Chess, Bridge, Model-Making, Model Railway, Tenpin Bowling, Gardening, Rollerblading, Ballet, Modern Dancing, Drama, Craft, Carpentry, Printing, Cooking and Debating.

The boys and girls lead a full and varied life and are all encouraged to take part in as wide a variety of activities as possible. Weekends are a vital part of the school life and are made busy and fun for all.

Entry requirements. Entry is by Headmaster's interview and a report from the previous school. For a prospectus and more information, please write or telephone the Registrar, Lottie Rogerson.

Coworth Flexlands School

Valley End, Chobham, Woking, Surrey GU24 8TE
Tel: 01276 855707
Fax: 01276 856043
email: secretary@coworthflexlands.co.uk
            registrar@coworthflexlands.co.uk
website: www.coworthflexlands.co.uk

Chairman of Governors: Mr Gordon Hague

Headmistress: **Mrs Anne Sweeney**, MA, DipEd

Age Range. Girls 3–11 years; Boys 3–7.
Number of Pupils. 132 day girls, 16 day boys.
Fees per term (2014–2015). £879–£3,975.

If you are looking for a friendly, caring school where children hold on to their childhood and achieve high academic results in a relaxed setting, then Coworth Flexlands is the school for you.

Situated in delightful rural surroundings on the outskirts of Chobham Common, and nestling in 13 acres of Surrey countryside, our lovely Edwardian house has been enhanced by a large, purpose-built extension, offering the best modern facilities.

On arrival you will immediately sense a happy, purposeful atmosphere and see classes engrossed in their studies or outside making use of our extensive grounds. Good-sized year groups provide lots of friends to play with and small teaching groups ensure that each child has the individual attention that they need to do really well academically. Our cheerful Learning Support department works closely with all the teachers to support those who need specific help and provide extended thinking skills for those who are particularly gifted.

In addition to all the usual National Curriculum subjects, Sport, Drama, Dance, Technology, Music, French, and Art feature strongly in a broad curriculum, with our specialist teachers working with the children throughout the whole school to ensure progression and the best possible experience right from the word go. Classes enjoy outings and visits to enhance the curriculum and residential trips are arranged for the older children. For those who enjoy an extended day, we are open from breakfast at 7.30 am until 6 pm after tea, Clubs and Prep. Our extra-curricular activities include various sporting clubs and squads, chess, dance, Rainbows, orchestra, art, choir, gymnastics and Spanish and an after-school Homework Club for older children. There is a strong emphasis on pastoral care throughout the school

and we are small enough for every child to be known to every teacher. In addition we have a thriving House system and the opportunities for children to contribute to school decision-making through the School Council and Eco Council.

We are particularly proud of our Eco-School achievements, Gold Artsmark and our strong academic record. Last year over half of our Year 6 girls achieved scholarships or awards, with all securing places at their Senior Schools of choice, including Tormead, Sir William Perkins and St George's Ascot

There is an active Social Committee which arranges many events throughout the year, adding to the lovely family feel as older and younger siblings come along and join in with us. Prospective parents are warmly invited to tour the school with the Head. All enquiries and appointments should be made via the School Admissions Registrar on 01276 855707.

Charitable status. Coworth-Flexlands School is a Registered Charity, number 309109 and Christian Foundation school, which welcomes pupils from all faiths. It exists to provide an excellent education and preparation for the next stage of schooling for all our pupils.

Crackley Hall School

St Joseph's Park, Kenilworth, Warwickshire CV8 2FT
Tel: 01926 514444
Fax: 01926 514455
email: post@crackleyhall.co.uk
website: www.crackleyhall.co.uk

Co-educational Nursery and Junior School

Headmaster: **Mr Robert Duigan**, BComEd, MEd

Age Range. 2–11 years.
Number of Pupils. 275 (163 boys, 112 girls).
Fees per term (2014–2015). Junior School: £2,612–£2,758. Nursery: £215 per week (full time, term time).

Crackley Hall is a co-educational independent Catholic day school which welcomes pupils of all denominations. The school is part of The Princethorpe Foundation and is the Junior School to Princethorpe College.

Situated on the outskirts of Kenilworth, Crackley Hall occupies a pleasant and safe setting with playing fields a short distance across the road. An extended day facility is offered; pupils may be dropped off from 7.50 am and can stay at school until 6.00 pm. Nursery attendance times are flexible, with term time and year round places available.

Crackley Hall bases its care for individuals on the sound Christian principles of love and forgiveness; children become strong in the understanding of themselves and others. There is a keen sense of community between pupils, staff and parents. We encourage fairness, freedom, friendship and fun.

Small class sizes promote individual attention. The curriculum is based on national guidelines, but pupils are encouraged to achieve well beyond these targets. During the early years, great emphasis is placed on developing key skills in reading, writing, speaking, listening, mathematics and science. The learning of tables and spellings is actively developed through simple homework tasks. Specialists teach Art, Design Technology, French, Music, Games, ICT and RE. Recent investment has resulted in specialist teaching rooms for Art and Music, greatly enhanced IT, Science and Technology suites and improved sports changing facilities.

Football, rugby, cricket, hockey, netball, tennis, athletics, swimming, rounders, trampolining and judo are all available. There is a strong and thriving music department and all pupils together with members of the choir, choral group and orchestra participate in concerts and stage productions to enrich their learning and to build confidence and self-esteem. Pupils have the opportunity to study a wide range of individual instruments under the guidance of a team of peripatetic staff and specialist teachers offer classes in music theatre, speech and drama and dance. Other activities are offered before and after school as well as during lunch breaks including art, chess, craft, ICT, gardening, steel band, food and textiles.

Admission is through interview with the Head, assessments in English and Mathematics, and a taster day at the school. We also ask for a reference from the child's current school. The admission information is considered as a whole so that as accurate a picture as possible of the child can be obtained. The pastoral elements are as important to us as academic ability.

Parents are welcomed into school for Friday morning assembly when the children's good work is celebrated. An active Parent Teacher Association organises social and fundraising events. Pupils are encouraged to maintain their links with the school by joining the Past Pupils' Association.

Charitable status. The Princethorpe Foundation is a Registered Charity, number 1087124. It exists solely for the purpose of educating children.

Craigclowan School

Edinburgh Road, Perth PH2 8PS
Tel: 01738 626310
Fax: 01738 440349
email: headmaster@craigclowan-school.co.uk
website: www.craigclowan-school.co.uk

Chairman of Governors: James Bax

Interim Co-Heads: **Patrick Borderie and Liz Henderson**

Age Range. 3–13.
Number of Pupils. 248: 137 boys, 111 girls
Fees per term (2014–2015). £3,710.

Craigclowan is a co-educational, day school situated in 15 acres of its own grounds on the outskirts of Perth. It is administered by a Charitable Trust.

Boys and girls are prepared for Common Entrance and scholarship for independent schools in both England and Scotland. In the recent past children have entered Glenalmond, Strathallan, Loretto, Merchiston Castle, Fettes, Gordonstoun, St Leonards, Ampleforth, Queen Margaret's York, Heathfield Ascot, Harrow and Eton as a result of Common Entrance or Scholarship. In the last eight years a total of 115 Scholarships have been gained covering academic, music, art, sport and all rounders.

Much attention is paid to each individual child in their preparation for academic success throughout the school and much energy is directed to a wide range of extra-curricular activities with games, music, drama, debating and art high on the list. The games played include rugby, hockey and cricket for boys and tennis, hockey and netball for girls. Instrumental tuition takes in all the orchestral areas and children regularly participate in productions at the local Repertory Company. The children have won National Competitions in Rugby, Netball, Swimming, Skiing, Debating and Choir. The school's dry ski slope and full-size astroturf for hockey and tennis are in daily use.

The 2014 HMIE Inspection Report gave significant praise to the school for the very high standards achieved in key areas of school life. The inspectors were particularly impressed with the school's "*welcoming, caring and stimulating environment for learning*" and praised the "*purposeful leadership*" and "*visionary plan for the future development of the school*". The broad curriculum was commended along with the inspirational extra-curricular programme. Children were recognised as "*articulate and enthusiastic learners at all stages*" who "*produce work of a very high standard across different areas of their learning*".

In addition, the Care Commission has inspected the Preschool four times in the past three years, endorsing all that is being achieved within the Pre-school.

Charitable status. Craigclowan School Limited is a Registered Charity, number SC010817. It exists to promote education generally and for that purpose to establish, carry on and maintain a school within Scotland.

Cranford House Junior School

Moulsford, Wallingford, Oxfordshire OX10 9HT
Tel: 01491 651218
Fax: 01491 652557
email: admissions@cranfordhouse.net
website: www.cranfordhouse.net
Twitter: @CHSMoulsford

The School is a Charitable Trust run by a Board of Governors.

Chair of Governors: Mrs Natalie Scott-Ely

Head of the Junior School: **Dr James Raymond**

Head of Nursery : Mrs Samantha Pritchard

Age Range. Girls 3–11, Boys 3–7.
Number of Pupils. 205.
Fees per term (2014–2015). £3,470–£4,115.

Children are admitted from the age of 3 into Little Willows, Cranford House Nursery School. The large, spacious purpose-built Nursery offers plenty of green space for free-flow play and learning. With a Forest School on site, weekly swimming lessons and specialist coaches for sports, the children thrive and make great progress in their learning. In the September of the year they turn 5 children move into Reception on the main school site. Nursery and Reception children follow the Early Years Foundation Stage curriculum.

The curriculum in Years 1 to 6 is founded on the National Curriculum, but supplemented to ensure children learn to develop resilience, independence, collaborative, reasoning and reflective skills. Junior pupils benefit from Senior School facilities and specialist subject teachers are increasingly used in a variety of subjects. Results in the Junior School are excellent.

There is a full choir, chamber choir and orchestra and pupils are encouraged to take an active role musically as well as in school drama productions. An extensive programme of extra-curricular clubs and activities ensures the all-round development of our pupils. From Year 3 all pupils compete in sporting fixtures both at home and away.

Responsibility is offered at a young age through posts such as Junior Head Girl and team captains.

Charitable status. Cranford House School Trust Limited is a Registered Charity, number 280883.

Cranleigh Preparatory School

Horseshoe Lane, Cranleigh, Surrey GU6 8QH
Tel: 01483 542058
Fax: 01483 277136
email: fmjb@cranprep.org
website: www.cranprep.org

Chairman of Governors: J A V Townsend, MA

Head: **M T Wilson**, BSc

Age Range. 7–13.

Number of Pupils. 300 (50 Boarders, 250 Day).

Fees per term (2014–2015). Boarders £7,170; Day Pupils: £4,460 (Forms 1 & 2), £5,790 (Forms 3–6). These are genuinely inclusive and there are no hidden or compulsory extras.

The school stands in its own beautiful and spacious grounds of 35 acres. Cranleigh Preparatory School is a co-educational boarding and day school. A teaching staff of 40 enables classes to be small. The Head and his wife live in the school, as do the boys' boarding master and his family and the girls' housemistress and her family. They are fully involved with the health and happiness of the boys and girls, together with pastoral staff, including matrons. A great source of strength is the close partnership with Cranleigh School 'across the road'. The Preparatory School has use of Senior School sports facilities, including an indoor pool, artificial pitches, the stables and golf course.

The boys and girls are prepared for Common Entrance and many Scholarships are won. Through these exams about three quarters of the children move on to Cranleigh School and the remaining one quarter to a wide variety of other independent senior schools.

Boarding life is busy and fun. Pupils return home every weekend. There is also the opportunity to flexi board for two or more nights during the week.

The curriculum is broad, balanced and covers all and more than that laid down by the National Curriculum. The school teaches computing, and technological problem solving is encouraged. Art (including design, pottery, woodwork and various craft skills) and Music are included in the curriculum at all level. Individual instrumental lessons are available and peripatetic music staff teach at both schools. There are choirs, orchestras, a band and several ensembles. Boys and girls are given every incentive to develop spare time interests and a choice of activities is built into the timetable.

The school is fortunate to have excellent facilities including a full-sized artificial pitch, a large sports and drama hall, a dance studio, a music school, very light airy classrooms and laboratories. The school has recently undergone a very large refurbishment programme and all facilities are extensive and modern. Boarding accommodation is bright and cheerful and fully modernised. Additions and improvements to the facilities are ongoing.

Rugby, football, hockey, netball, cricket, athletics, tennis, swimming, rounders, squash, cross country, basketball, fencing, riding, golf, Eton Fives, archery and badminton, are among the sports.

Normal entry age is at seven or eleven. Places are sometimes available in the intervening year groups.

Charitable status. Cranleigh School is a Registered Charity, number 1070856, whose Preparatory School exists to provide education for boys and girls aged 7–13.

The School is equidistant between Leatherhead and Guildford and is easily accessible from Cobham, Esher, Weybridge, Dorking and Woking with school transport available. Normal entry points are Nursery, Reception and Year 3 (7+); entry is non-selective in the early years and assessments are held for 7+ entry. There is a Scholarship programme for 7+ entry offering Academic, Sport and Music Scholarships. The most recent Inspection awarded the school top grades in every category including 'Outstanding' for the Early Years (Nursery and Reception).

Bright Stars Nursery (from age 2½) offers both term-time and all-year-round attendance. It has its own dedicated accommodation which includes several rooms and adjacent playground. The Junior Department (4–8 years) offers all children access to tremendous resources including the sports hall, gymnasium, swimming pool and music facilities. Pupils enter the Senior Department at 8+ years and are taught by specialist subject teachers. For National Curriculum Year 7 we create a Scholarship class and two parallel Common Entrance classes. Cranmore's academic standards are high and pupil development enables all pupils to fulfil their individual potential.

Boys are prepared for entry to a wide range of senior schools. We have an impressive track record in Common Entrance and in our pupils gaining Scholarships to a wide variety of prestigious schools. Boys at the upper end of the school (Years 7 and 8) are given significant additional opportunities culminating in an impressive post-Common Entrance programme.

An ongoing programme of investment over several years has given the school many outstanding facilities based on the extensive 25-acre site. These include a forest school, a senior teaching block with three large well-equipped science laboratories, a second ICT laboratory and a chapel. The sports facilities include: a sports hall; gymnasium; swimming pool; four astro tennis courts; large playground with rubberised surface for tennis, hockey and football; three squash courts and fitness room plus extensive playing fields.

Sports teams compete in galas, tournaments, Inter-School and Inter-House competitions to allow all pupils to take part. All boys have the opportunity to represent the school at one of the three main sports: cricket, football and rugby. Rowing, golf, tennis, ski and many other sporting clubs operate. There is a thriving extra-curricular programme ranging from Archery to Sci Tech. Many other out-of-school activities are offered including annual PGL and skiing trips.

The Drama, Speech and Music school offers every pupil the opportunity to learn an instrument, sing in a choir and play in a wide variety of ensembles and orchestras.

Cranmore is a Catholic school with children of all denominations warmly welcomed.

Charitable status. Cranmore School is a Registered Charity, number 1138636. It exists to provide education for children.

Cranmore School

Epsom Road, West Horsley, Surrey KT24 6AT

Tel:	01483 280340
Fax:	01483 280341
email:	admissions@cranmoreprep.co.uk
website:	www.cranmoreprep.co.uk

Chairman of Governors: M J G Henderson, FCA

Headmaster: **M P Connolly**, BSc, BA, MA, MEd

Age Range. Girls 2½–7, Boys 2½–13

Number of Pupils. 465 Day Pupils.

Fees per term (from January 2015). Nursery (term time) £2,040–£3,400; Junior Department £3,650; Senior Department £4,375.

Crescent School

Bawnmore Road, Bilton, Rugby, Warwickshire CV22 7QH

Tel:	01788 521595
Fax:	01788 816185
email:	admin@crescentschool.co.uk
website:	www.crescentschool.co.uk

Chair of Governors: Mrs P Lines

Headmaster: **Mr R H Marshall**, BSc Hons Wales, PGCE

Age Range. 3–11.

Number of Pupils. 154 Day Boys and Girls (85 boys, 70 girls).

Fees per term (2014–2015). £2,531–£2,734.

The Crescent School is an independent co-educational preparatory school for day pupils aged 4–11 years. In addition, there is a Nursery for children from the age of 3. The school was founded in 1947, originally to provide a place of education for the young children of the masters of Rugby School. Over the years the school has steadily expanded, admitting children from Rugby and the surrounding area. In 1988, having outgrown its original premises, the school moved into modern, purpose-built accommodation in Bilton, about a mile to the south of Rugby town centre. The buildings provide large and bright teaching areas, with a separate annexe housing the Nursery and Reception classes. There are specialist rooms for Science, Art, Design Technology, ICT and the Performing Arts. In addition there is also a spacious Library and Resource Area. The multi-purpose hall provides a venue for daily assemblies, large-scale music making, is fully equipped for physical education and has all the necessary equipment to turn it into a theatre for school productions. The school is surrounded by its own gardens, play areas and sports field.

The requirements of the National Curriculum are fully encompassed by the academic programme and particular emphasis is placed on English and mathematics in the early years. All pupils receive specialist tuition in Information and Communication Technology, Music and Physical Education. Specialist teaching in other subjects is introduced as children move upwards through the school. Spanish is introduced in Reception, followed by French in Year 4 and Latin in Year 5. The pupils are prepared for the local 11+ examination for entry to maintained secondary schools, including local grammar schools, and specific entrance examinations also at 11+ for independent senior schools.

The performing arts are a particular strength of the school and lessons are given in speech and drama, singing, percussion, musical theory and appreciation and recorder playing. Instrumental lessons (piano, brass, woodwind and strings) are offered as an optional extra. There is a school choir, orchestra, brass, string and wind ensembles and recorder groups.

Charitable status. The Crescent School Trust is a Registered Charity, number 1120628. The object of the charity shall be the provision and conduct of a day school for children of the inhabitants of Rugby and the surrounding district.

The Croft Preparatory School

Alveston Hill, Loxley Road, Stratford-upon-Avon, Warwickshire CV37 7RL
Tel: 01789 293795
email: office@croftschool.co.uk
website: www.croftschool.co.uk

Principal: Mrs L K M Thornton, CertEd London

Chairman of the School's Governing Committee: Mrs J Russ

Headmaster: **Mr M Cook**, BSc Hons, PGCE

Deputy Headmaster: Mr E Bolderston, BSc Hons, PGCE
Head of Pre-Prep: Mrs N Badger, BEd Hons

Age Range. 2–11.
Number of Pupils. 403: 215 boys, 188 girls.
Fees per term (2014–2015). £530–£3,672.
The Croft is a co-educational day school for children from 2 to 11 years old, situated on the outskirts of Stratford upon Avon. Founded in 1933, the School occupies a large rural site with superb facilities and extensive playing fields, offering children some of the most exciting educational opportunities in the area. There is also a nature conservation area with lake.

A family-based school, The Croft provides specialist teaching in small groups, where good discipline and a wider knowledge of the world around us, both spiritual and geographical, is encouraged. Music, Sport and Drama each play an important part in the curriculum. The resulting high educational standards provide the all-round excellence which is at the heart of the School.

In March 2012, the School opened its 600-seat Theatre and fully-equipped 400m^2 Sports Hall. Mundell Court was completed in 2009 – a two-storey building providing additional, spacious teaching areas for ICT, DT and Mathematics. It also incorporates a small-scale performance space.

Children are prepared for 11+ entry either to the local Grammar Schools or Senior Independent Day Schools, or to go on to Boarding Schools.

Entrance requirements. Children can be accepted in the Nursery from the age of 2 years. Children above Reception age are assessed.

Crosfields School

Shinfield Road, Reading, Berks RG2 9BL
Tel: 0118 9871810
email: office@crosfields.com
website: www.crosfields.com

Chairman of Governors: Mr C Bradfield

Headmaster: **Mr J P Wansey**, BA, CertEd

Deputy Headmaster: S C Dinsdale, MA Ed Open, BA Hons Chichester, FLCM, LTCL, LLCM, PGCE Open

Age Range. 3–13.
Number of Pupils. 535.
Fees per term (2014–2015). £2,773–£4,356 including lunches, school visits and after-school care for Years 1–8. There is an additional charge for children in Nursery and Reception who remain in school after 4.15 pm.

Crosfields School is a co-educational day preparatory school based in Shinfield, Reading. It offers a first-class education with opportunities for all for boys and girls aged 3–13 years. Academically the school is excellent. Pupils progress quickly in small class sizes where they receive individual attention from dedicated teaching staff. Pupils move on to a range of senior schools and there have been a good number of scholarships and exhibitions in recent years and also an excellent record of entry to Reading School.

Facilities within the 40 acres of grounds are unrivalled at prep school level in the area, with a modern library, ICT suite, theatre and music complex, sports hall, indoor swimming pool, cricket nets and even a 6-hole golf course. The main sports for boys are Football, Rugby and Cricket with Netball, Hockey and Rounders for girls. Mixed football and tag rugby are played by both girls and boys and there is a wide range of extra-curricular hobbies and clubs from Year 3 upwards including Cookery, Golf, Drama, Judo, Dance and Fencing. A new Food Technology room opened in May 2009.

The school offers bursary awards of up to 100% of the fees at 11+ entry.

Charitable status. Crosfields School Trust Limited is a Registered Charity, number 584278. The aim of the School is solely to provide education for children between the ages of 3 and 13.

Independent Association of Prep Schools

Culford Preparatory School

Bury St Edmunds, Suffolk IP28 6TX
Tel: 01284 728615
Fax: 01284 728631
email: admissions@culford.co.uk
website: www.culford.co.uk
Twitter: @CulfordSchool

Chairman of Governors: Air Vice Marshall S Abbott, CBE, MPhil, BA

Headmaster: **M Schofield**, BEd

(For a full list of staff, please see Culford School entry in HMC section.)

Age Range. Co-educational 7–13.
Number of Pupils. 181 (Day), 45 (Boarders).
Fees per term (2014–2015). Day £3,500–£4,595, Boarding £6,760–£7,270.
Admission is by entrance examination at all ages, though the majority of pupils enter at age 7 or 11 and scholarships are available at 11+.
Culford Prep School has its own staff and Headmaster, but remains closely linked to the Senior School. This allows the School to enjoy a significant degree of independence and the ability to focus on the particular needs of prep school age children while benefiting from the outstanding facilities and community spirit of Culford.
Facilities. Culford Prep is situated in its own grounds, within Culford Park. The heart of the School is the impressive quadrangle at the centre of which lies the Jubilee Library. Other facilities include two science laboratories and two state-of-the-art ICT suites which, in common with the rest of the Prep School's classrooms, have networked interactive whiteboards.
Outside Prep have a mix of playing fields for all the major sports and the perennially-popular adventure playground. Prep School pupils also have free access to Culford's magnificent Sports and Tennis Centre with its 25m indoor pool, indoor tennis courts, squash courts, fitness suite and sports hall.
Teaching & Learning. Prep School pupils are given a thorough grounding in the essential learning skills of Mathematics and English and the curriculum broadens beyond the confines of the National Curriculum. Work in the classrooms is augmented by an extensive Activities Programme which offers pupils a wide range of opportunities and experiences, including trips out and visits from guest authors and experts in their field.
Music and drama play a significant part in Culford Prep School life, and a variety of theatrical performances, choirs and ensembles are performed each year, either in Prep's own hall or in Culford's purpose-built Studio Theatre. Specialist speech and drama lessons are also offered.
Boarding. Prep School boarders live in Cadogan House, a mixed boarding house located next to the School overlooking the playing fields. Boarders are able to take advantage of a comprehensive programme of weekend activities and are looked after by a team of dedicated staff under the direction of the Housemaster. Recent trips have included visiting Harry Potter World, the Oasis Camel Park and the North Norfolk Coast.
Religious affiliation. Methodist: pupils from all faiths, and those of none, are welcome.
Charitable status. Culford School is a Registered Charity, number 310486. It exists to provide education for boys and girls.

Cumnor House School
Cognita Schools Group

Boys School:
168 Pampisford Road, South Croydon, Surrey CR2 6DA
Tel: 020 8660 3445
Fax: 020 8645 2619

Girls School:
1 Woodcote Lane, Purley, Surrey CR8 3HB
Tel: 020 8660 3445
Fax: 020 8660 9687

email: registrar@cumnorhouse.com
website: www.cumnorhouse.com
Twitter: @WeAreCumnor
Facebook: /WeAreCumnor

Headmaster – Boys School: **P Clare-Hunt**, MA, CertEd

Headmaster – Girls School: **P Kelly**, DipEd

Nursery Manager – Mrs Charlotte Figueira

Age Range. Boys 4–13, Girls 4–11. Co-educational Nursery 2–4 years.
Number of Pupils. Prep & Pre-Prep: 440 Boys, 175 Girls. Nursery: 150.
Fees per term (2014–2015) £2,945–£3,735 (including lunch and school trips).
Cumnor House School for Boys is one of Surrey's leading Preparatory Schools. Pleasantly and conveniently situated, the School prepares boys for scholarships and common entrance examinations to leading senior independent schools and local grammar schools.
Scholarships have been won recently to Dulwich, Epsom, Westminster, Charterhouse, Tonbridge and the local senior independent schools, Whitgift, Trinity and Caterham.
Music, Sports, Art and Drama play a large part in the life of the School and all contribute to the busy, happy atmosphere.
Choir, sports tours and matches, ski trips, regular stage productions and a broad spectrum of clubs and options, give the boys the opportunity to pursue a wide range of interests.
Entry requirements: Assessment test and interview.
At **Cumnor House School for Girls** our main aim is to give parents and their daughters as much choice as possible when selecting their senior schools in Year 6. This journey starts in the Early Years; by developing confidence and a positive attitude to learning, we lay vital foundations for the future.
Practical experiences complement the curriculum and encourage the love of learning needed to embrace the academic, cultural, sporting and musical opportunities that Cumnor House School for Girls provides. The girls are encouraged to develop all their interests and talents, both within the extensive curriculum and through involvement in a wide range of clubs and activities.

Cumnor House School

Danehill, Haywards Heath, West Sussex RH17 7HT
Tel: 01825 790347
Fax: 01825 790910
email: office@cumnor.co.uk
website: www.cumnor.co.uk

Chairman of Governors: S Cockburn, MA Oxon

Headmaster: **C St J S Heinrich**, BA Hons, PGCE

Deputy Headmaster: M N P Mockridge, BSc Hons, PGCE

Age Range. 4–13.
Number of Pupils. 365: 185 boys, 180 girls; 95 in the Pre-Prep; 60 boarders.
Fees per term (from April 2014). £7,105 (Boarding), £5,970 (Day); £3,160 (Pre-Preparatory).

We aim to provide a happy and purposeful atmosphere in which children learn to set themselves high standards. Individuality is encouraged and equal esteem is given to achievements in and out of class.

The School has a strong tradition of scholarship, and many awards have been won at a wide range of senior schools, primarily academic but also in art, music, sport, drama and technology.

Out of school we offer children many opportunities for sports and cultural activities. Girls and boys in the Prep school all play sport every day. Each term children are given a choice of 20 or so supervised hobbies, from which they choose three. Much music and drama take place: 95% of pupils in the Prep school learn an individual instrument and the choirs perform regularly. There are two orchestras and a wind band, as well as much singing and ensemble work. Each Summer term 50 or more children are involved in the annual production of a Shakespearean play in our open air theatre. Our rebuilt Sussex barn is used as a Music School. A purpose-built theatre complex operates as a local arts centre for concerts, lectures, exhibitions and winter term plays. Set in 50 acres of fields and woodland, the school has a Sports Hall, four tennis courts and a heated outdoor pool, as well as a 25m indoor pool. Football, Rugby, Cricket, Netball, Hockey, Rounders and Athletics are all part of the sporting mix with 20 or so teams involved every Wednesday and/or Saturday. Old farm buildings have been converted into blocks for science, music, art, ICT and home economics whilst additions of new boarding wings, new kitchens and laundry are all recent. A new barn conversion in 2006 has provided 6 additional classrooms and a design technology centre and all classrooms have interactive whiteboards. The boarding staff includes a full-time qualified nurse. Boarding, entirely elective, is on a bi-weekly basis, allowing time for full weekends both at home and at school.

Charitable status. Cumnor House School Trust is a Registered Charity, number 801924. It exists for the advancement of education.

Dair House School

Bishop's Blake, Beaconsfield Road, Farnham Royal, Buckinghamshire SL2 3BY
Tel: 01753 643964
Fax: 01753 642376
email: info@dairhouse.co.uk
website: www.dairhouse.org.uk

Chairman of Governors: Mr J O'Brien

Headmaster: **Mr Terence Wintle**, BEd Hons

Age Range. 3–11 Co-educational.
Number in School. 114 Day pupils.
Fees per term (2014–2015). £1,600–£3,700.

Located on the A355 at Farnham Royal we are conveniently placed for the Farnhams, Gerrards Cross, Beaconsfield, Stoke Poges and surrounding villages.

Dair House offers an exciting and personalised education to boys and girls from 3–11. We take pride in our warm, friendly, individual care, catering for each child's abilities. We provide our children with a firm sense of belonging and a sure foundation from the start in classes which are no larger than 16. The school has excellent facilities with a new ICT suite, a new dining room, new office, a recently updated library and Learning Support Department. Each class is fully resourced with interactive whiteboards and computers.

Dair House is situated in wonderful tree lined grounds with a large sports field, multi-purpose gym and all-weather sports surface.

We offer a breakfast club from 8.00 am and an after-school tea club until 5.00 pm, as well as a plethora of lunchtime and after-school activities.

Charitable status. Dair House School Trust Limited is a Registered Charity, number 270719. Its aim is to provide 'a sure foundation from the start'.

Dame Bradbury's School

Ashdon Road, Saffron Walden, Essex CB10 2AL
Tel: 01799 522348
email: dbsoffice@stephenperse.com
website: www.damebradburys.com
Twitter: @DameBradburys

Dame Bradbury's is a co-educational day school, founded in 1525. It is a member school of the Stephen Perse Foundation, Cambridge.

Chairman of Governors of the Stephen Perse Foundation: Dr G Sutherland

Head: **Mrs Tracy Handford**, MA

Age Range. 3–11.
Number of Pupils. 220 Day Boys and Girls.
Fees per term (2014–2015). Kindergarten: £210 (per am session), £200 (per pm session). A minimum of 3 morning sessions a week is recommended. Reception: £3,220; Years 1–2 £3,495; Years 3–4 £3,820; Years 5–6 £3,970. Except for the Kindergarten, fees include lunch. Bursaries are available.

Children are accepted from 3–11 years and are prepared for Common Entrance and entry into both independent and state schools.

A high teacher/pupil ratio is maintained and the fully qualified staff, augmented by specialist teachers and in the younger forms by teachers' assistants, work as a team to provide a stimulating educational environment. The curriculum is designed to give a broad general education of a high standard and covers the National Curriculum. French is introduced at the age of 3 and taught by a specialist. The school has a strong musical tradition and creative potential is encouraged in all the arts.

The spacious buildings provide room for the Kindergarten, large classrooms, a Performing Arts Theatre (created 2006), a multi-purpose Sports Hall (opened 2003), a well-equipped Science Laboratory and environmental garden with dipping pond (created 2007), a Teaching Garden (2008), a DT area, Music and Art Rooms, a spacious Library and Individual Needs teaching rooms and a main Dining Room. IT is fully integrated within the school with a wireless network, interactive whiteboards and an extensive Apple IT suite (opened in 2004). The School also runs a weekly Forest School in nearby woods.

There are spacious grounds and playing fields, 2 hard tennis/netball courts and an Astroturf court (September 2007). Physical Education features strongly in the curriculum and includes gymnastics, tennis, netball, football, rugby, hockey, cricket, athletics, rounders and swimming. There is an extensive programme of extra-curricular activities which includes orchestra, choir, football, cricket, netball, drama, chess and philosophy.

The Headmistress will be pleased to provide further details and meet interested parents.

Charitable status. Dame Bradbury's School is part of the Stephen Perse Foundation, which is a Registered Charity, number 1120608. Dame Bradbury's School provides education for boys and girls.

Danes Hill

Leatherhead Road, Oxshott, Surrey KT22 0JG
Tel: 01372 842509
Fax: 01372 844452
email: registrar@daneshillschool.co.uk
website: www.daneshillschool.co.uk

Chair of Governors: Mr Geoff Toms

Headmaster: **Mr William Murdock**, BA, PGCE

Age Range. 3–13 co-educational.
Number of Children. 880.
Fees per term (2014–2015). £1,940–£5,370.

As a co-educational school, Danes Hill prepares boys and girls for Scholarship and Common Entrance examinations to senior schools. A high academic record (55 scholarships to senior schools awarded in 2014) combines happily with a strong tradition of sporting prowess, to ensure that all children are exposed to a kaleidoscope of opportunity on a peaceful 55-acre site set well back from the main Esher-Leatherhead road. The Pre-Preparatory Department takes children from 3 to 6 years and is situated separately, but within easy walking distance of the Main School. There is a transport system available to take children both to and from Main School.

Extensive facilities include 2 state-of-the-art IT suites, a science block with 4 fully-equipped laboratories, a high-tech Art and DT centre, and new studio theatre. Both Pre-Prep and Main School sites have covered swimming pools.

The curriculum is broad and a wide range of extra-curricular activity is encouraged. Languages are a particular strength of the school. All children learn French from age 3 and Spanish from Year 4. All scholars and some Common Entrance pupils also study Latin. Scholars are encouraged to sit one or more modern foreign languages at GCSE in their final year.

Pastoral care and pupil welfare are closely monitored. The school's Learning Support Centre provides a high level of support both for those with specific learning difficulties as well as running a programme for the exceptionally gifted and talented.

Residential and day trips are seen as an essential part of the school experience. The school operates language trips to centres in Spain and France. The annual Trips Week is a very special feature of the school calendar with over 500 children leaving the site to a range of residential destinations in the UK and abroad. There are also annual ski trips, as well as choir, rugby, netball and hockey tours.

Sport is a major strength and specialist games staff ensure that all the major sports are expertly coached. A floodlit astroturf pitch allows all-weather training and team spirit is valued alongside ability. There are extensive programmes of inter-school fixtures for all age groups. Every child is encouraged to participate. We also arrange annual games dinners for the senior teams and their parents to celebrate the end of each season. In-house Easter and Summer holiday activity courses are also very popular options with pupils.

Charitable status. Danes Hill School (administered by The Vernon Educational Trust Ltd) is a Registered Charity, number 269433. It exists to provide high-quality education for boys and girls.

Daneshill School

Stratfield Turgis, Hook, Hampshire RG27 0AR
Tel: 01256 882707
Fax: 01256 882007

email: office@daneshillprepschool.com
website: www.daneshillprepschool.com

Headmaster & Proprietor: **Simon V Spencer**, Cert Ed, Dip PhysEd

Age Range. 2½–13.
Number of Pupils. Day Boys 118, Day Girls 122.
Fees per term (2014–2015). Nursery on application; Reception £3,250, Year 1 £3,350, Year 2 & Year 3 £3,650, Years 4–8 £4,150. Lunch included. There are no compulsory extras.

Founded in 1950, Daneshill has always prided itself on the collective qualities of its teaching staff and their ability to interact with pupils and deliver a stimulating learning experience.

Set in a beautiful, rural location close to the Hampshire-Berkshire border the School provides the perfect environment and atmosphere for each pupil to grow and prosper as an individual with a strong set of core values.

Academically the Daneshill curriculum has always maintained the expectations of the national curriculum while also offering so much more in respect of what we would regard as real education. Traditional values form the basis of a learning experience that engenders an enthusiasm for knowledge and encourages hard work as a means to academic success. This broadly-based curriculum also allows the development of high academic achievement to sit comfortably alongside our enthusiasm for pupils to become actively involved in all areas of the performing arts as well as the pursuit of sporting excellence.

Our aim has always been to develop enthusiastic learners who will make a strong contribution to their senior schools as good citizens and as pupils who are prepared to work hard in order to achieve success. This is certainly made easier by the children at Daneshill who possess a self-confidence and natural carefree joy which makes them a pleasure to teach. Each of them is a living testament to our belief that self-esteem is crucial to their development and success. We are also justifiably proud of the way our pupils exude courtesy, honesty, warmth and respect for others. They develop responsible attitudes to learning and life, and are a credit to themselves and their families.

Visitors to the School will be made very welcome and straight away they will experience the atmosphere that makes Daneshill unique.

Davenies School

Beaconsfield, Bucks HP9 1AA
Tel: 01494 685400
Fax: 01494 685408
email: office@davenies.co.uk
website: www.davenies.co.uk

Chairman: S Dodds

Headmaster: **C Watson**, BEd, MA

Age Range. 4–13.
Number of Boys. 330 (Day Boys only).
Fees per term (2014–2015). £3,895–£4,975.

Davenies is situated in the heart of Beaconsfield, a Georgian town on the edge of the Chiltern Hills, close to the M40 and only thirty minutes from the centre of London by rail and car. Founded in 1940, the school aims to provide a broad education for day boys between the ages of 4 and 13. It enjoys a 'family' atmosphere, confident and courteous pupils and enthusiastic and committed staff.

The large site includes modern, airy classrooms, a purpose-built Science Laboratory, DT facility and Art Studio and a fully modernised IT Suite and Music Wing. A state-of-the-art Sports Complex incorporates an indoor swimming pool, Sports Hall and Performing Arts Centre. Boys are taught Rugby, Football, Cricket, Hockey, Athletics and Swimming and compete regularly against other schools.

Davenies follows a broad curriculum and there is a strong emphasis on numeracy and literacy from an early age. Specialist subject teaching begins in Year 3. French is taught from Year 1 and Latin from Year 6. There is an exciting array of over fifty extra-curricular activities each week which cater for individual interests; these include jazz band, mountain biking, rock climbing, snowboarding, photography, electronics, cookery and media. The school also has its own Cub Pack.

Once they leave the Pre-Prep Department, the academic and pastoral welfare of the boys is undertaken by a network of form teachers. The Deputy Head and two of the Assistant Heads oversee the management of this care and ensure that regular, detailed communication with parents takes place, both formally and informally.

Some pupils move on to local Grammar Schools at the end of Year 6, although many choose to stay on to enjoy the hugely popular programme that Davenies offers its senior pupils before they move on to Senior Independent Schools at 13. As well as individual attention in the classroom, senior boys take part in the Davenies Award Scheme (DAS) which introduces them to challenging, often unusual activities, whilst promoting team building and character development. DAS activities include paintballing, go-karting, sailing, skiing, water skiing and golf. Senior boys also have opportunities to go on skiing and adventure holidays, outward bound weekend and a wide variety of education trips. They also have the opportunity to participate in various sports tours, both at home and abroad.

Developing the whole individual is paramount at Davenies, where great emphasis is placed on the value of courtesy, good manners and consideration for others, encapsulated in the school's motto: 'singulus pro fraternitate laborans' (one working for the good of all).

Charitable status. Beaconsfield Educational Trust Ltd is a Registered Charity, number 313120. It exists to provide high standards and the fulfilment of each child's potential.

Dean Close Pre-Preparatory School

Lansdown Road, Cheltenham, Gloucestershire GL51 6QS
Tel: 01242 258079
Fax: 01242 258005
email: squirrels@deanclose.org.uk
website: www.deanclose.org.uk
Twitter: @DeanCloseSchool
Facebook: /DeanCloseSchool

Chairman of Governors: Mrs K Carden

Headmistress: **Dr C A Shelley**, BEd, PhD

Age Range. 2.9–7 Co-educational.
Number of Pupils. 150.
Fees per term (2014–2015). £2,470–£2,550.

The Pre-Preparatory School of Dean Close is a co-educational, Christian family school which occupies the same campus as Dean Close Preparatory and Dean Close School and is, therefore, able to share such outstanding facilities as the swimming pool, sports hall, tennis courts, theatre and art block.

The Pre-Preparatory School moved into a new, purpose-built school building opened by Lord Robert Winston in June 2004. The school has a large hall surrounded by classrooms on two floors. There are two playgrounds – one for the Nursery and Kindergarten and one for Reception and Years 1 and 2.

The curriculum within the Pre-Preparatory school offers a wide range of learning opportunities aimed at stimulating and nurturing a child's development and interests in an intellectual, physical, spiritual, social and emotional sense. Speech and Drama, Dance, Tennis, Music, Orchestra and Choir are some of the available extra-curricular activities. All children participate in Forest School, which inspires creativity, thinking skills and cooperation, together with a love of the natural world.

Charitable status. Dean Close School is a Registered Charity, number 1086829.

Dean Close Preparatory School

Lansdown Road, Cheltenham, Gloucestershire GL51 6QS
Tel: 01242 258000
email: dcpsoffice@deanclose.org.uk
website: www.deanclose.org.uk
Twitter: @DeanCloseSchool
Facebook: /DeanCloseSchool

Chairman of Governors: Mrs K Carden

Headmaster: **Mr Roger Jones**

Age Range. 7–13.
Number of Pupils. 281: Boarding Boys 38, Boarding Girls 33, Day Boys 125, Day Girls 85.
Fees per term (2014–2015). Boarders £5,985–£7,580, Day Boarders £4,195–£5,855, Day Pupils £3,495–£5,155.

The Preparatory School of Dean Close is a fully co-educational, Christian, family school which occupies the same campus as Dean Close School and is, therefore, able to share such outstanding facilities as the Chapel, swimming pool, amphitheatre, shooting range, Performance Hall, 550-seater Performance Hall and extensive playing fields, including hard tennis courts, floodlit astroturf hockey pitches and the new sports hall. The sports hall has indoor tennis and cricket nets, as well as a large gymnasium and dance studio.

The Prep School also has its own teaching blocks and Music School, and a new £4.5m building which opened in Autumn 2013, containing an additional theatre and 8 teaching areas located over two floors, with a dedicated IT suite and Drama rooms.

The new building also contains a music suite, which links to the existing Music School, and comprises 6 music practice rooms including a dedicated guitar room. The building also features a formal reception area where parents and visitors are welcomed into the School.

The other main classroom block consists of 10 specialist teaching rooms including 2 laboratories and a computer centre. This building is joined to another teaching block by the admin centre. This block has 7 purpose-built classrooms, together with day house facilities, a staff Common Room, a new Library and an Art and Technology block. There is also a separate dining hall and kitchens.

The purpose-built Pre-Prep School was opened in 2004. (*See separate entry for Dean Close Pre-Preparatory School.*)

Although the Preparatory School is administered by the same Board of Governors as the Pre-Prep and Senior School, it has its own Headmaster and staff. The staff complement consists of 48 who either hold degrees or diplomas in education. As well as a dedicated Director of Music, there is also a team of excellent peripatetic music teachers specialising in a variety of instruments.

There are three boarding houses, each with resident Houseparents, 2 House Tutors and a resident matron.

The day pupils are accommodated in three purpose-built houses. Each is run by a Housemaster/Housemistress, assisted by House Tutors.

The School follows a curriculum which embraces the National Curriculum and Common Entrance, preparing boys and girls for entry to the Senior School at 13+ by CE and internal transfer procedures. A few transfer to other independent senior schools.

The main games for boys are rugby, hockey and cricket, and for girls, hockey, netball, cricket, rounders and tennis. Swimming, athletics and cross-country running are also taught and use is made of the School's Covered Playing Area. Golf is available at a nearby course and shooting is available within school grounds. Riding is also available at a nearby riding school.

Camping, canoeing, hillwalking and orienteering are catered for and a wide range of activities is available including, among others, riding, judo, climbing, cooking, watercolour painting and all forms of dance. Special activity courses are part of the curriculum.

The Prep School provides the choristers for Tewkesbury Abbey – the Schola Cantorum. Boys can apply to join the Schola Cantorum from age 7.

Charitable status. Dean Close School is a Registered Charity, number 1086829. It exists to provide education for children.

Denmead

Wensleydale Road, Hampton, Middlesex TW12 2LP
Tel: 020 8979 1844
Fax: 020 8941 8773
email: secretary@denmeadschool.org.uk
website: www.denmeadschool.org.uk

Chairman of Governors: N J Spooner, BA

Headmaster: **Mr Tim Smith**, BA, NZ Dip Tchg, MBA

Age Range. Boys 3–11, Girls 3–7.
Number of Pupils. 224.
Fees per term (2014–2015). Kindergarten (3–4 years): £1,665 (mornings), £3,330 (all day). Pre-Prep (4–7 years): £3,575. Prep (7–11 years): £3,860 including lunch for full day pupils.

The School is situated in a quiet, leafy part of Hampton and is easily accessible by road and rail. The School merged with Hampton School in September 1999 to become the Hampton School Trust's preparatory school. Although there is still no expectation for pupils to select Hampton as their first-choice secondary school, at least 50 per cent on average each year transfer there. Both schools are served by the same Board of Governors and the Headmaster of Denmead now reports to the Headmaster of Hampton School. The amalgamation produces economies of scale from which Denmead benefits.

Boys transfer to senior schools at 11+. The Prep School is a two-form entry with 18 pupils per class, who are set for English, Maths and Reasoning. Since September 2004 Hampton has been offering Assured Places for 11+ entry. This is done from Year 2 through Denmead's ongoing programme of assessment of the boys and is also open to those starting in the Preparatory Department. In addition, those boys who perform very well in the 11+ Hampton entry exams, but who do not gain an award from Hampton, will be considered for the W D James Award made by Denmead, which will be in the form of a reduction in the child's first term's fees at Hampton.

The Pre-Prep is housed on its own site in the homely atmosphere of two linked residential houses offering space and security. Rooms are well-appointed and there is one class per year group of 22 pupils. The Preparatory section

which backs on to an attractive public park, boasts its own games field and a multi-purpose hall. Planning permission has been granted for the School to replace its present accommodation with a modern two-storey block with excellent facilities for which work is due to start towards the end of 2014. Major school sports are Football, Rugby, Cricket and Athletics. An extensive programme of extra-curricular activities includes art clubs, chess, drama, judo, computing, Warhammer/Lego and a variety of minor sports. There is a School choir, an orchestra, and a flourishing tradition of drama. Individual music tuition is also provided.

Parents share in the life of the School as fully as possible and there exists a very active parents' association.

Please contact the School Office for a prospectus.

Charitable status. Denmead School is part of the Hampton School Trust, which is a Registered Charity, number 1120005. It exists to provide a school in Hampton.

Denstone College Preparatory School at Smallwood Manor
A Woodard School

Uttoxeter, Staffs ST14 8NS
Tel: 01889 562083
Fax: 01889 568682
email: enquiries@denstoneprep.co.uk
website: www.denstoneprep.co.uk

Custos: S Varley

Headmaster: **Jeremy Gear**, BEd Hons

Age Range. 3–11.
Number of Pupils: 83 Boys, 55 Girls
Fees per term (2014–2015): £2,875–£3,675.

Denstone College Preparatory School at Smallwood Manor is a co-educational Nursery and Day School for children aged 3 to 11, set in 50 acres of beautiful woods and parkland just south of Uttoxeter on the Staffordshire/Derbyshire border.

The aims of the school are:

- To ensure that every child enjoys coming to school and that each individual's potential is fully realized.
- To educate the whole child so that academic achievement goes hand in hand with developing spiritual, cultural and physical maturity.
- To emphasize traditional Christian values of good manners and responsible behaviour.
- To provide a stimulating programme of activities to encourage children to develop skills and interests which will make their school careers successful and rewarding.
- To lay a firm foundation for further education.

As a Woodard School, Denstone College Preparatory School has strong ties with Denstone College and has enjoyed an excellent reputation for preparing children for 11+ Entrance Examinations and Scholarships. Our pupils enjoy excellent sports facilities which include: a covered heated swimming pool, a gymnasium, superb sports' pitches and two hard tennis courts. Rugby, Hockey, Football and Netball are the main winter games; Cricket and Rounders are the main summer games.

Denstone College Preparatory School has a fine modern Chapel and our award-winning choir sings regularly in Music Festivals and local churches. Each child learns the violin for a year and a large percentage of our pupils learn at least one musical instrument to a high standard. Our peripatetic music team provide opportunities for pupils to learn brass, woodwind, strings, piano and voice. The school has a string group, wind band and various musical ensembles.

Many of our pupils, past and present, sing in the National Children's Choir of Great Britain.

We offer an exciting range of clubs and activities after school including: Forest School, LAMDA, French, Table Tennis, Cookery, Art and Crafts, Chess, Board Games, Hockey, Dodge Ball and Computers. Our after-school care extends from 8 am until 6 pm.

Charitable status. Smallwood Manor Preparatory School Limited is a Registered Charity, number 1102929. It aims to provide a Christian education for boys and girls aged 3 to 11.

Derwent Lodge
The Schools at Somerhill

Somerhill, Tonbridge, Kent TN11 0NJ
Tel: 01732 352124
Fax: 01732 363381
email: office@somerhill.org
website: www.somerhill.org

Derwent Lodge is one of the three Schools at Somerhill under the care and control of The Somerhill Charitable Trust.

Chairman of Governors: Mr Philip Thomas

Principal: Mr J T Coakley, MA

Headmistress: **Mrs S Michau**, MA Oxon, PGCE

Age Range. Girls 7–11.
Number of Pupils. 130 Day Girls.
Fees per term (2014–2015). £4,535 inclusive of lunch. There are no compulsory extras.

Extras: individual music lessons, recreational outings, minibus service from Tunbridge Wells, West Malling and Brenchley area, residential study visits.

Derwent Lodge was founded in central Tunbridge Wells in 1952 and moved to its present parkland setting on the southern outskirts of Tonbridge in 1993.

The school is noted for its strong academic tradition and for its caring, happy atmosphere. High standards of work, manners and courtesy are expected of each girl. There are specialist facilities for science, art, music, IT and sport.

The curriculum is designed to give a stimulating and rich general education which will prepare pupils well for entry to the grammar or independent schools chosen by their parents. Pupils regularly gain scholarships to secondary schools.

An optional extended day is offered. There is a full programme of extra-curricular clubs and activities. Girls are offered residential visits to the Isle of Wight and France.

Admission to Derwent Lodge follows girls spending a taster day at the school for informal assessment before the offer of a place is confirmed. Girls from the pre-preparatory school at Somerhill may proceed to Derwent Lodge automatically.

Charitable status. The Somerhill Charitable Trust Limited is a Registered Charity, number 1002212. It exists for the purpose of providing education for children.

Devonshire House Preparatory School

2 Arkwright Road, Hampstead, London NW3 6AE
Tel: 020 7435 1916
Fax: 020 7431 4787

email: enquiries@devonshirehouseprepschool.co.uk
website: www.devonshirehouseschool.co.uk

Headmistress: **Mrs S Piper**, BA Hons

Age Range. Boys 2½–13, Girls 2½–11.
Number in School. 637: 340 Boys, 297 Girls.
Fees per term (2014–2015). £2,925–£5,360.

Devonshire House School is for boys and girls from three to thirteen years of age and the School's nursery department, the Oak Tree Nursery, takes children from two and a half. The academic subjects form the core curriculum and the teaching of music, art, drama, computer studies, design technology and games helps to give each child a chance to excel. At the age of eleven for girls and thirteen for boys the children go on to their next schools, particularly the main independent London day schools.

Devonshire House pursues high academic standards whilst developing enthusiasm and initiative. It is considered important to encourage pupils to develop their own individual personalities and a good sense of personal responsibility. A wide variety of clubs and tuition are available in ballet, judo, yoga, Mandarin, chess, speech and communication and in a range of musical instruments. High standards and individual attention for each child are of particular importance.

The School is located on the crest of the hill running into Hampstead Village and has fine Victorian premises with charming grounds and walled gardens.

Dolphin School

Waltham Road, Hurst, Berkshire RG10 0FR
Tel: 0118 934 1277
Fax: 0118 934 4110
email: omnes@dolphinschool.com
website: www.dolphinschool.com

Founded in 1970.

Head: **Tom Lewis**, BA, PGCE

Registrar: Jan Vernon

Age Range. 3–13.
Number of Pupils. 203: 112 Day Boys, 91 Day Girls.
Fees per term (2014–2015). Nursery £3,006 (9 am to 3 pm, 5 days); Reception £3,200; Years 1 and 2 £3,538; Years 3–8 £4,160.

"An exciting, challenging, dynamic learning environment" according to the 2004 ISI Inspection Report of Dolphin School. *"The warmth of the greeting everywhere is striking and genuine"*, noted the Good Schools Guide review.

We believe that children have special gifts and talents, which too often remain hidden forever. Dolphin School offers an environment which encourages these gifts to flourish. Children leave Dolphin with confidence in themselves, a strong sense of individualism, the ability to adjust well in school and social situations, at least one area in which they can feel pride in their own achievement and a strong sense of curiosity and enjoyment in learning. Throughout life, in an ever more quickly changing world, they will have the skills and the confidence successfully to pursue their ambitions and interests and to lead happy and fulfilled lives.

Dolphin children are allowed to develop as individuals and encouraged to fulfil their various potentials in small classes under the careful guidance of specialist teachers. Abundant academic, artistic, social and sporting stimulation is provided through an extremely broad, well-rounded programme. We encourage lateral thinking and the ability to cross reference. Expectations for all children are high and academic rigour is a key component in all lessons.

Dolphin School provides the friendly, family atmosphere of a small school. All members of staff are actively concerned with the pastoral care of all the children, but each form teacher assumes special responsibility for the daily well-being and the overall progress of a very small group of children. In addition children in their final three years have a personal mentor. Class sizes average sixteen. Children learn both to talk and listen to each other, to evaluate and tolerate the opinions of others and to take pride in each other's achievements. They are also encouraged to accept responsibility and to develop their leadership abilities.

Courses offered. Children are taught by graduate specialists from age six in most subjects. In the early years we provide a firm grounding in English-based skills throughout all humanities subjects. French begins in Nursery, Mandarin in Year Five, Latin in Year Six and German, Spanish and Greek in Year Seven. Laboratory science is taught from age seven. Mathematics, geography, history, ICT, classical studies, art, design technology, drama, music and PE are taught throughout the upper school. Architecture, astronomy, philosophy, thinking skills, religious education, current affairs, environmental studies and cultural studies are included in some years.

Activities. A unique strength of Dolphin School is our residential field trip programme in which all children participate from age seven. The work related to these trips forms major sections of all departmental syllabuses. Principal annual field trips visit East Sussex, Dorset, Ironbridge, North Wales, Northumbria, Normandy and Italy, while departments organise residential trips to Boulogne and Stratford. We also offer an extensive mountain-walking programme. We have a large number of trained British Mountain Leaders. Staff and children participate in a graded fell walking programme. Locations range from the Lake District and Brecon Beacons to Snowdonia and the Alps. We also organise sports tours and a "custom made" adventure week in North Wales.

We believe in 'hands-on' learning, whether in or outside the classroom, and children participate in a very wide range of day trips to museums, theatres, archaeological sites and many other venues.

Almost all costs associated with field, walking and day trips are included in the fees, as are lunch-time and after-school clubs which include: athletics, tennis, short tennis, judo, rounders, cricket, embroidery, computing, swimming, football, netball, gymnastics, craft, hockey, chess, cross-country, rugby, art, table tennis, orchestra, windband, string group, choir, orienteering, gardening, cookery and drama.

We field teams at all levels in football, rugby, cricket, chess, netball, rounders, tennis, swimming, cross-country, athletics, hockey and judo. We are well represented at county level.

Facilities. Our hall offers a splendid venue for school concerts and plays. We stage several major productions each year. Grounds include a swimming pool, all-weather tennis, hockey and netball courts, and playing fields. Cricket matches are played at Hurst, a neighbouring county standard ground.

Entry. Nursery at age 3+, Reception at age 4+, and throughout the Upper School as places become available.

Internal and external scholarships are available to children aged 12–13 in the performing arts, art, creative writing and sport. Academic bursaries are also available.

Examination results. Our examination results are outstanding and we regularly win major scholarships to senior independent schools, including St Paul's, Eton, Harrow and Winchester. We have a thriving Old Delphinian organisation. Most past pupils gain good degrees and a high proportion attend Oxbridge colleges.

The Downs Malvern

Colwall, Malvern, Worcs WR13 6EY
Tel: 01684 544 100
Fax: 01684 544 105
email: registrar@thedownsmalvern.org.uk
website: www.thedownsmalvern.org.uk

Chairman of Governors: Reverend Kenneth E Madden, BA, PGCE

Headmaster: Alastair S Cook, BEd Hons, FRGS, IAPS

Age Range. 3–13 years Co-educational.

Number of Pupils. 194 children.

Fees per term (2014–2054). Full Boarding £5,150–£6,786; Weekly boarding £4,531–£5,972; Flexi boarding £35.16 per night; Day £3,642–£5,127; Pre-Preparatory £2,135–£2,889; Early Years: £21.91 per am/pm session, £43.82 per day (8.30–3.30), £47.77 per day (8.30–5.00).

The Downs Malvern is a busy, vibrant and successful co-educational preparatory school for boarding and day children aged between 3 and 13 years, offering an outstanding education.

Located 3 miles west of Malvern, 4 miles east of Ledbury, 15 miles from the M5 motorway, on the main line from Paddington and served by Malvern College transport, the Downs is situated on the Herefordshire side of the Malvern Hills on a striking rural 55-acre campus in Colwall.

The Downs Malvern strives to exceed the confines of the National Curriculum in academic, as well as cultural, sporting and social accomplishments. The school offers a broad curriculum challenging the academically gifted and supporting those with special needs. The School was subjected to a full Independent Schools Inspectorate (ISI) inspection in May 2012 and was considered to be "*an excellent School*". The full inspection report is available on the School website.

The Early Years and Pre-Prep have now settled into their newly refurbished building and, after a seamless move over to the Prep Department at 7 years old, pupils will move on to Malvern College, or to their preferred senior school at 13 to complete their school education.

Year 8 pupils have moved on to a variety of independent senior schools on the basis of scholarship or Common Entrance examinations and, whilst the option to go on to a wide variety of independent schools is still there, the direction has changed. The Downs is the main feeder school for Malvern College and the emphasis in Years 7 and 8 is not only a preparation for scholarships and Common Entrance, but also to allow a smooth transition to the College academically and socially.

Sports, especially team games, are a significant part of the curriculum, as are Music and Art. 80% of the pupils learn to play a musical instrument. There is also a wide and expanding Hobbies programme that includes Railway Engineering as well as Speech and Drama, Dance, Design Technology and Art.

Boarding. The newly refurbished Boarding House provides a home for up to 60 boarders. Boarding can be full, flexi or a one-off experience with a published programme of evening and weekend activities. All boarders are looked after by a caring staff, dedicated to their welfare. A boarding inspection carried out by the ISI in May 2012 found the provision of boarding care at The Downs to be "*excellent*".

Facilities. There is a wide range of facilities including a 300-seat capacity Concert Hall, self-contained Music and Art buildings; new Science laboratories; a new Design and Technology suite, Pottery studio and wired computer network with whiteboards. A new sports complex is supplemented by an astroturf Hockey pitch, 3 Netball/Tennis courts and 55 acres of grounds set aside for games pitches,

Forest School lessons and relaxation. The school has its own narrow gauge steam railway!

11+ Scholarships and Exhibitions, as well as being awarded to pupils who show academic excellence, are also awarded to pupils who show academic competence as well as having a particular talent in Art, Music, Drama or Sport.

Bursaries are available offering assistance to parents subject to completion of a means test form.

Charitable status. The Downs, Malvern College Prep School, trading as The Downs Malvern, is a Registered Charity, number 1120616. It exists to provide education for girls and boys from 3–13 years.

The Downs School

Wraxall, Bristol BS48 1PF
Tel: 01275 852008
Fax: 01275 855840
email: office@thedownsschool.co.uk
website: www.thedownsschool.co.uk

Chairman of Governors: A M J Currie

Head Master: **Marcus Gunn**, MA Ed, BA, PGCE, IAPS

Age Range. 4–13.
Number of Pupils. 282: 178 boys, 104 girls.
Fees per term (2014–2015). £3,225–£4,895 including lunch.

The Downs was founded in 1894 on the parklands of Bristol, otherwise known as the Downs. The school moved to the estate of Charlton House, its present site, in 1927. The Headmaster at the time, Mr Wilfred Harrison, stated that the relocation was because of the "incessant roar of traffic" and the "nerve-racking turmoil of the city". As a consequence of his vision, today at the end of a long meandering drive, three miles from the turmoil of a busy city, approximately two hundred and eighty children excel in the stunning rural environment of The Downs School.

Our children enjoy a vibrant all-round education that is stimulating, challenging and exciting. Academic study is important and we expect all our pupils to adopt a healthy work ethic and achieve high standards, but we believe that to truly educate it is essential to embrace the creative, the physical and the spiritual as much as the intellectual.

At The Downs we embrace a strong set of traditional values and expectations. Childhood is cherished; our young children wear wellies, climb trees and make dens. They make elaborate daisy chains, delight in playing conkers and relish bushcraft cooking. The sophisticated world of mobile devices and adolescence remains at the front entrance for later life. Within this healthy, happy and wholesome environment we seek to nurture unaffected good manners, we embrace grace and humility, and we applaud the qualities of friendship, excellence and respect. We encourage and have high regard for individuality, we endorse aspiration and we celebrate success. Essentially, however, quality of character is considered equally as important as achievement.

Class sizes are small (maximum 18). Pupils are prepared for the major independent senior schools with Badminton, Clifton College, Bristol Grammar School, Queen Elizabeth's Hospital, Millfield, Marlborough, Sherborne, King's College Taunton and Winchester featuring regularly. The pupils follow the Common Entrance Syllabus, a programme that enables the school to make the most of its independence to the benefit of the pupils. The traditional disciplines of English, Maths, Science and French form the core studies. The Foundation subjects of History, Geography and Religious Education are taught independently. These are complemented by a range of contemporary subjects such as Computer Science, Spanish, (Latin optional) and the Theory of Music and Etiquette.

Sport is of an exceptional standard, but there is a team for everyone; it is not unusual to field twenty teams or more at one time. All the major team sports are played. The Performing Arts are valued highly and standards are impressive: 85% of pupils play instruments, choir is compulsory in the Prep School, over 50% of the school attend Speech and Drama lessons, productions are continual, Dance in its many forms is popular and the vibrant Art Department provides for all styles.

Excellent facilities include a purpose-built Pre-Prep, new classroom block, theatre, two IT suites, woodwork centre, extensive playing fields, Forest School, huge Sports Hall, 2 astroturf pitches, and outdoor swimming pool. Significant work to extend the facilities for the Performing Arts is under way.

An independent Prep School, The Downs does not feed any particular senior school. Over the last decade our children have moved on to numerous schools including the best and most demanding in the country. Considerable time is taken to get to know these schools in order that we can provide constructive and objective advice to interested parents. This consultative process is evidently successful, as it is extremely unusual for a child not to gain entry to a school of their first choice, indeed many of our pupils are awarded scholarships.

Visitors are warmly welcomed. The School Registrar, Caroline Crew, is very happy to assist interested parents at their convenience.

For further information or to arrange a visit to see the children at work and play, please contact The School Office on 01275 852008.

Charitable Status. The Downs School is a Registered Charity, number 310279. It was established for the education of boys and girls aged 4–13.

Downsend
Cognita Schools Group

1 Leatherhead Road, Leatherhead, Surrey KT22 8TJ
Tel: 01372 372311
Fax: 01372 363367
email: admissions@downsend.co.uk
website: www.downsend.co.uk
Twitter: @DownsendSchool
Facebook: /DownsendSchool

Headmaster: **I D Thorpe**, BA Ed, MA Ed

Age Range. 2–13 co-educational.
Number of Pupils. Day: 500 (aged 6–13), 250 (aged 2–6).
Fees per term (2014–2015). Pre-Preparatory £870–£3,235, including lunch for full-time pupils and Early Bird and 'Little Lates' facilities. Preparatory: £3,565 (Year 2), £4,315 (Years 3–8), including lunch. Sibling discounts apply for more than one child in Reception or above.

Downsend is a co-educational day school for children aged between 2 and 13 years.

The preparatory school stands on a pleasant, open site just outside the town, surrounded by its own playing fields, tennis courts and all-weather pitch. The Sports Complex includes a large indoor swimming pool and sports hall. The comfortable and vibrant library, expanded networked ICT provision, bespoke facilities for Design Technology, Textiles and Food Technology, and the new Music Suite (complete with sound proof practice rooms) extend the curriculum to support children's learning and development.

Pre-Preparatory (age 2 to 6). There are three co-educational pre-preparatory departments in Ashtead, Epsom and Leatherhead. Here, pupils work in a welcoming and stimulating environment, in small classes, where a strong focus on education builds solid foundations in Numeracy and Literacy. Dance and Drama, French, Music and Swimming are all taught by specialists and enhance the curriculum across all year groups. An enhanced afternoon programme, further supported by a wide range of after school clubs including Spanish, is also on offer. An extended day facility provides complimentary 'Early Bird' and 'Little Lates' facilities each day from 8.30 am to 5.30 pm (6.00 pm at Epsom & Leatherhead Pre-Prep), which is especially useful for working parents. At 6, the children automatically move on to Downsend Preparatory School where they are joined by children from other local independent and state schools.

Preparatory (age 6 to 13). Founded in 1891, Downsend is not only an established academic prep school which prepares children for Common Entrance, Scholarship and High School examinations, but also a thriving community where many other opportunities are provided.

The standard of work is high and the school is particularly proud of its scholarship record. An average of 36 scholarship awards is achieved each year to some of the top senior schools in the area.

There is a broad and engaging curriculum and the children study, in addition to the normal Common Entrance subjects, Art, Drama, Food Technology, ICT, Music, Design Technology, Textiles and PSHE. Parents are kept informed of their children's progress through regular parents' evenings and termly reports, and are welcome at all times to communicate with members of staff.

The school has a strong reputation for its music, with regular concerts throughout the year, as well as orchestras and choirs for each section of the school. A large number of children learn a variety of musical instruments. Drama is equally important and there are several productions each year. Pupils can take part in a full range of sports not only in school but also at local, regional and national level. Regular visits occur outside school and trips abroad are also arranged.

A holiday care activity scheme, Downsend+, gives pupils access to exciting and absorbing workshops and courses, themed days and thrilling days out. Run by qualified Downsend staff, this provision is available to children aged 5–13 from 8 am to 5.30 pm, including breakfast, lunch and tea as appropriate. Downsend Pre-Prep+ is also available as a dedicated facility for children aged 2–5 at Leatherhead Pre-Prep.

Dragon School

Bardwell Road, Oxford OX2 6SS
Tel: 01865 315400
Fax: 01865 311664
email: admissions@dragonschool.org
website: www.dragonschool.org
Twitter: @thedragonschool
Facebook: /DragonSchoolOxford

Chairman of Governors: Chris Jones

Headmaster: **John Baugh**, BEd

Age Range. 4–8 (Lynams Pre-Prep), 8–13 (Dragon).
Number of Pupils. Total: 845. Lynams (Pre-Prep): 212 (120 boys, 92 girls); Bardwell Road (Prep): Day 391(224 boys, 167 girls), Boarders 242 (163 boys, 79 girls).
Fees per term (2014–2015). Day £3,320–£5,990; Boarding £8,630.

The Dragon School, just north of Oxford city centre, enjoys a leafy setting on the banks of the River Cherwell. Traditional buildings, contemporary facilities and extensive playing fields are the setting for an exceptional all-round academic education for boarding and day pupils. Dragons are noted for a spirited informality and a confident, enthusi-

ast approach to all they do. A culture of learning how to learn and the appreciation of effort of every kind, result in all-round academic, sporting and cultural excellence. A non-selective school, the Dragon regularly achieves an impressive list of scholarships and awards (44 in 2012) and children go on to the country's finest Independent Senior Schools.

The Dragon is composed of small, friendly communities. A dedicated building for Year 4 (E block) with its own playground offers children a gentle introduction to a preparatory school that is large enough to grow with them. Boarding is the heart of the school where warm support and a caring ethos are enjoyed by boarders from the local community and around the world. Homely boarding houses of varying sizes provide a gradual transition to life at senior schools; an additional house for girls opened in 2009/10.

The extensive curriculum is taught by highly qualified and individual staff whose innovative lessons and high standards led to the Dragon being deemed 'outstanding' on many fronts in its 2011 Inspection. A very strong sporting tradition is mirrored by rich creativity in drama, music and art.

Extra-curricular activities encompass games, languages, sports, debates, drama, music and much more. Dragons are seasoned travellers and many expeditions and trips are made to destinations ranging from local woodlands to Brazil and including Sri Lanka, Switzerland, South Africa and Morocco. There is a regular exchange programme with schools in New York and Tokyo.

The Dragon Pre-Prep Lynams is a short distance away in Summertown with its own staff and facilities for Reception and Years 1, 2 and 3. The Ofsted report for Reception was 'Outstanding'.

Bursaries of up to 100% of fees are offered for boarding or day places. Academic awards worth up to 50% of fees are also offered.

For further information or to arrange a visit please contact the Registrar on 01865 315405.

Charitable status. The Dragon School Trust Ltd is a Registered Charity, number 309676. It aims to provide education for boys and girls between the ages of 4 and 13.

Duke of Kent School

Peaslake Road, Ewhurst, Surrey GU6 7NS
Tel: 01483 277313
Fax: 01483 273862
email: office@dukeofkentschool.org.uk
website: www.dukeofkentschool.org.uk

Chairman of the Governing Body: Mr Richard Brocksom

Head: **Mrs J Fremont-Barnes**, MA Oxon, MEd

Age Range. 3–16 co-educational.
Number of Pupils. 256.

Set in inspirational grounds high in the Surrey Hills, surrounded by forest land, Duke of Kent School provides an excellent co-educational option for pupils from 3 to 16 years. Coming from Guildford, Horsham, Dorking and a host of local villages, many pupils use the School minibus service.

Extended day arrangements for those pupils who wish to arrive before or stay beyond the end of lessons (7.30 am to 7.30 pm) provide families with exceptional flexibility. At the end of the School day, pupils can choose to complete their Prep at school under supervision or at home, and can also choose from a varied programme of sport, academic and social activities.

The small size of the School enables us to know our pupils very well and to ensure that all pupils can reach their potential. With a maximum class size of 18, all pupils receive the appropriate combination of academic challenge and support to enable them to achieve. A Duke of Kent School pupil is expected to contribute and participate to the very best of his or her ability, take an active role in community life and take responsibility for his or her learning. Our able and committed teaching and support staff work in partnership with pupils and their families. The expectation is that each pupil will strive to achieve a string of 'personal bests': in the classroom, on the sports field, in personal development, in exploring the arts and in a wide range of activities.

Pupils are prepared for Common Entrance and GCSE/IGCSE examinations in the context of a curriculum which aims to take pupils above and beyond exam preparation. There is a focus throughout the School of encouraging pupils to adopt a growth mindset in order to become successful learners. Recent innovations have included the development of Forest School activities and whole-class violin tuition in our Pre-Prep, the development of a Creative Curriculum in the Prep Section and rigorous GCSE programme, preparing pupils for A Level and university study and sparking what may be lifelong intellectual passions. Learning beyond the classroom, whether on educational visits or through outdoor learning on site, is a crucial aspect of our pupils' experience.

The School maintains a busy fixtures calendar at all ages. We have extensive playing fields, a swimming pool, all-weather tennis courts and a full-sized sports hall. More than half of our pupils are learning a musical instrument. Music and Drama activities take place in a purpose-built Performing Arts Hall with facilities for Music Technology. The quality of Art on display and in production is a particular strength of the School.

This year's cohort of Duke of Kent School leavers achieved extremely good results relative to their ability on intake, including our highest ever number of A and A* grades. In total 44% of grades were awarded at A*–A, 74% at A*–B. 59% of Mathematics grades, 41% of English Language and 56% of English Literature grades were awarded at A*–A. Science students also scored highly, with A–A* grades running at 48% in Biology, 47% in Chemistry and 62% in Physics. 100% of pupils achieved an A* to C pass in English and 96% in Mathematics. Pupils are prepared for the transition to Sixth Form or Sixth Form college in both the independent and state sector and all our students have gone on to study at a wide range of schools and colleges.

Prospective pupils are invited to attend a trial day during which they will be interviewed by the Head or another senior member of staff, and will be given tests in English and Mathematics for setting purposes. Scholarships and bursaries are available for admission to the Main School.

Fees per term (2014–2015). £1,695–£5,175.

Charitable status. The Duke of Kent School is a Registered Charity, number 1064183.

Dulwich Prep London

42 Alleyn Park, Dulwich, London SE21 7AA
Tel: 020 8670 3217
Fax: 020 8766 7586
email: registrar@dulwichpreplondon.org
website: www.dulwichpreplondon.org

The School was founded in 1885 and became a charitable trust in 1957 with a board of governors.

Chairman of Governors: Mr D Pennock

Headmaster: **M Roulston**, MBE, MEd

Age Range. Boys 3–13, Girls 3–5.

Number of Boys. 798 day boys, 18 girls, 7 weekly boarders (aged 8–13).

Fees per term (2014–2015). Tuition: Day boys £3,470-£5,395 (inclusive of lunch – there are no compulsory extras). Weekly boarders: £150 per week in addition to tuition fee.

Dulwich Prep London (formerly known as DCPS) is an independent prep school with a national reputation for excellence.

While we are essentially a boys' school, with about 810 pupils aged between 3 and 13, we start with the Early Years Department which also caters for girls. There are four other sections to the school: the Pre-Prep (Years 1 & 2), the Lower School (Years 3 & 4) and the Middle & Upper Schools (Years 5 & 6 and 7 & 8). In addition we have a well-equipped boarding house set in 13 acres of grounds with tennis courts and playing fields. We are delighted to offer weekly boarding.

At 13+ our boys go on to more than fifty excellent day and boarding schools throughout the country. Alleyn's, Charterhouse, Dulwich College, Eton College, Marlborough College, Tonbridge, St Paul's, Wellington College, Westminster and Winchester College are just a selection of our leavers' destination schools. In the 2012–13 academic year our leavers gained more than 40 academic, musical, artistic and sporting scholarships and awards.

Situated in SE21, we have the very best in educational facilities. These include very spacious classrooms, 4 science labs, a dedicated music school, a large sports hall, a studio theatre, 3 ICT suites, a superb art studio, a six-lane 25m swimming pool and more than 25 acres of playing fields, quite unique given our privileged location.

Some of the opportunities available to our pupils are:

- We run more than 25 sports teams each term with the top teams regularly doing well in national competitions. Recent sports tours include cricket to South Africa, football to Italy, swimming in the USA and rugby to Portugal and Ireland.

- More than 700 individual music lessons take place every week and boys have opportunity to perform regularly in a range of groups and ensembles.

- Approaching 30 groups perform regularly in our own 300 seat concert hall. Many also appear on the programme for our gala concerts at prestigious venues such as St John's, Smith Square and Southwark Cathedral.

- We provide more than 100 clubs and extra-curricular activities, stimulating boys' intellectual and sporting interests.

- We run residential trips for pupils in Years 5–8 within the curriculum that are built in to the fee structure. 14 more trips, ranging from cultural visits to skiing, are offered during the holidays.

- Drama productions are staged by forms and year groups from Reception to Year 8.

Charitable status. Dulwich College Preparatory School Trust is a Registered Charity, number 312715. It exists to provide education for boys.

Dulwich Preparatory School

Coursehorn, Cranbrook, Kent TN17 3NP
Tel: 01580 712179
Fax: 01580 715322
email: registrar@dcpskent.org
website: www.dcpskent.org

Chairman of Governors: D R M Pennock

Headmaster: **Mr Paul David**, BEd Hons

Age Range. 3–13.

Number of Boys and Girls. Day and Boarding: 279 (Upper School), 191 (Little Stream), 64 (Pre-Prep).

Fees per term (2014–2015). Day: £5,165 (Years 5–8), £4,400 (Years 2–4), £3,325 (Year 1 & Reception), Nursery: £2,795 (full day), £1,748 (mornings). Boarders: £40.75–£45.00 per night.

The School, which is one mile from the country town of Cranbrook, has extensive grounds (50 acres) and offers a broad and varied education to boys and girls from 3 to 13+. To ensure that children receive the personal attention that is vital for this age range the School is divided up into three separate, self-contained, departments. These are Nash House (3–5 year olds), Little Stream (5–9 year olds) and Upper School (9–13 year olds). Each department has its own staff, teaching equipment, sports facilities, playgrounds, swimming pools, etc. Pupils are prepared for Common Entrance or Scholarship examinations to any school of their parents' choice, and there is a strong emphasis on up-to-date teaching methods. The wide scope for sporting activities – Football, Rugby, Cricket, Hockey, Netball, Rounders, Athletics, Cross-country, Swimming, Tennis – is balanced by the importance attached to Art, DT, Drama, ICT and Music. Over 200 pupils learn the full range of orchestral instruments. There are two Orchestras, Wind and Brass Bands, Jazz Band, and four Choirs. The boarders are divided into two houses, boys and girls, each under the care of House staff. The happiness of the boarders is a particular concern and every effort is made to establish close and friendly contact between the School and the parents. There is a flourishing Parents Association, and regular meetings are held between staff and parents.

The School is a Charitable Trust, under the same Governing Body as Dulwich College Preparatory School, London, although in other respects the two schools are quite separate. The link with Dulwich College is historical only.

Charitable status. Dulwich College Preparatory School Trust is a Registered Charity, number 312715. It exists for the provision of high quality education in a Christian environment.

Dumpton School

Deans Grove House, Deans Grove, Wimborne, Dorset BH21 7AF

Tel: 01202 883818
Fax: 01202 848760
email: secretary@dumpton.com
website: www.dumpton.com

Chairman of Governors: Mr B Davies

Headmaster: **A W Browning**, BSc, PGCE, MA Ed, CChem, MRSC

Age Range. 2½–13.

Number of Pupils. Girls and Boys: 224 aged 7–13 and 147 aged 2½–7.

Fees per term (2014–2015). £4,656 for the Prep School (Years 3–8) and £2,599 for the Pre-Prep (Reception, Years 1 & 2). Nursery on application. The school week is from Monday to Friday with some Saturday fixtures. All fees include meals and there are no compulsory extras.

Dumpton School is a co-educational day school for pupils aged 2½ to 13 years. The school is set in a beautiful rural setting with 26 acres of grounds, but is nevertheless only one mile from Wimborne and school buses run daily to and from the nearby towns of Bournemouth, Poole, Wareham, Ringwood and Blandford.

Despite record numbers in the school, class sizes are small. Children enjoy excellent teaching as well as incomparable opportunities for Music, Art, Drama and Sport in which the school excels. Dumpton is renowned for its caring

approach in which every child is encouraged to identify and develop his or her abilities and personal qualities as fully as possible. This safe and supportive environment sees the children thrive and reach their full potential. The framework of family and Christian values emphasises the importance of teamwork and mutual respect that pervades the school. It is a very happy and successful school and children regularly win scholarships to their Senior Schools or places at the local Grammar Schools. Over the past five years Dumpton pupils have been awarded over 100 scholarships to schools such as Bryanston, Canford, Clayesmore, Millfield, Talbot Heath and Sherborne.

Recent developments have included a new Science and Maths Block, a full-size floodlit Astroturf, a covered swimming pool, a new Art, Design and Food Technology Centre, an outdoor classroom, climbing wall and environmental area, complete with ponds, pontoons, beehives and pupil allotments. In addition the school has recently been awarded Green Flag status by Eco Schools.

The school motto 'You can because you think you can', lies at the cornerstone of teaching at Dumpton and our aim is for pupils to leave us having reached their full potential, as confident communicators and appreciating good manners and tolerance.

For a copy of the prospectus, please apply to the Headmaster's Secretary.

Charitable status. Dumpton School is a Registered Charity, number 306222. It exists to provide education for boys and girls.

Dunhurst
Bedales Prep School

Alton Road, Steep, Petersfield, Hampshire GU32 2DR

Tel: 01730 300200
Fax: 01730 711820
email: jjarman@bedales.org.uk
website: www.bedales.org.uk

Chairman of Governors: M Rice, BA

Head: **Mrs J Grubb**, BA

Age Range. 8–13.

Number of Pupils. 192: 94 girls (49 day, 45 boarders), 98 boys (71 day, 27 boarders).

Fees per term (2014–2015). Boarders £7,510; Half Boarding (3 nights) £6,690; Day: £5,850 (Year 4), £5,885 (Years 5 and 6), £5,915 (Years 7 and 8); Flexi Boarding: £40 per night.

John Badley founded Bedales School in 1893 to educate through head, heart and hand. When Dunhurst was added in 1902 as the prep school, Badley's philosophy on education continued. It is apparent from the moment you enter Dunhurst that it is a unique school. This ethos spearheads thinking in education today and is distinctive because of the following key elements:

Inquisitiveness – We recognise that key to opening a child's joy for learning is to encourage them to question.

Relationships – Children are confident in their learning and have the support to develop because relationships between pupils and teachers at Dunhurst are built on trust and mutual respect.

Informality – A friendly and inclusive atmosphere helps every individual to thrive with room for their personality to grow. Our approach is underpinned by a clear structure which channels young people to flourish with guidance.

Choice – Our environment celebrates individuality by encouraging pupils to make choices about who they are and how they shape their learning in and out of the classroom.

Preparation for life – We produce young people with a determination to keep learning, happy in their own skins, and equipped with the skills to succeed.

We are proud of our environment at Dunhurst, our teachers and our academic results. Most important to the school is how to ensure children's learning thrives. Children respond to lessons that challenge their thinking. Dunhurst engenders inquisitiveness in pupils so they are prepared for the academic rigour of IGCSEs, Bedales Assessed Courses (BACs), A Levels and beyond. It isn't all about getting results; there is depth to pupils' learning because of Dunhurst's diverse curriculum. The creative and performing arts, sport, the outdoor work programme and the wealth of activities on offer ensure that every pupil can develop new interests and skills.

Matches against other schools take place regularly in Athletics, Cricket, Football, Hockey, Netball, Rounders, Rugby and occasionally Swimming and Tennis. A wide range of other sports and outdoor activities is also offered, including judo and golf.

Dunhurst makes full use of the first-rate facilities at Bedales which include the Bedales Olivier Theatre, a Sports Hall, floodlit netball and tennis courts, an all-weather pitch and covered swimming pool. This and the similarity of ethos, makes for an easy transition for pupils moving from Dunhurst to the Senior School at the age of thirteen.

There is a strong boarding community at Dunhurst. Many of the older pupils are full boarders and provision is made for flexible boarding for day pupils.

Applicants for both boarder and day places sit residential entrance tests. The main points of entry are at 8+ and 11+. Entry at other ages is dependent on the availability of places.

For information about Dunannie, the Pre-Prep (3–8 years), see the Bedales entry in HMC section.

Charitable status. Bedales School is a Registered Charity, number 307332. It exists to provide a sound education and training for children and young persons of both sexes.

Durlston Court

Becton Lane, Barton-on-Sea, New Milton, Hampshire BH25 7AQ
Tel:　　01425 610010
Fax:　　01425 622731
email:　secretary@durlstoncourt.co.uk
website:　www.durlstoncourt.co.uk

Chairman of Governors: Mr Chandra Ashfield

Headmaster: D C Wansey, MA Ed, CertEd

Age Range. 2–13 Co-educational.
Number of Pupils. 300 Day Pupils.
Fees per term (2014–2015). Kindergarten £25.02 per morning or afternoon session, £46.47 a day, £2,695 (Reception–Year 2), £3,995 (Year 3), £4,835 (Years 4–8).

Durlston Court Preparatory School, founded in 1903, is a happy and successful day school set in a beautiful campus with impressive facilities.

Durlston Court Prep School prides itself on preparing its pupils fully for Senior School and enabling pupils to reach their potential in all areas. This is demonstrated in the range of Scholarships awarded to pupils who transferred to senior schools in 2014. In addition to academic performance, scholarships were awarded to pupils excelling in Sports, Performing Arts and as All-rounders. Results also included a 100% pass rate to King Edward VI School, Southampton.

Durlston offers:
- Over 50 extra-curricular clubs such as STEM (Science, Technology, Engineering and Maths), Golf, Sailing and Den Activities providing unlimited opportunity.
- Purpose built facilities, such as the Art and Design Centre and the Music School, alongside specialist teachers to inspire pupils in all areas of the Arts.
- Daily sports coaching and regular opportunities to compete in sporting fixtures to help instil team spirit and confidence.

This exciting environment combined with a focus on traditional values makes Durlston Court Prep School an extremely happy place where pupils truly thrive!

Bus services cover routes from the Beaulieu, Bournemouth, Brockenhurst, Burley, Christchurch, Ringwood, Lymington, Lyndhurst and Sway.

Parents are most welcome to visit the school by making an appointment or by attending an Open Morning.

Further details of the school are available by visiting the school's website or by contacting the Headmaster's Secretary by phone or email, as above.

Charitable status. Durlston Court School is a Registered Charity, number 307325, which exists to provide quality education for children from 2–13 years.

Durston House

12 Castlebar Road, Ealing, London W5 2DR
Tel:　　020 8991 6532
Fax:　　020 8991 6547
email:　info@durstonhouse.org
website:　www.durstonhouse.org

Chairman of Governors: A J Allen, MA, FCA

Headmaster: N I Kendrick, MA, BEd Hons

Deputy Head: W J Murphy, BA, DipTch
Director of Studies: Ms J Sparks, Diplom-Kaufmann, PGCE
Head of Junior School: S W Perkins, BEd Hons
Head of Pre-Prep: Mrs H L Wyatt, MA, PGCE

Age Range. 4–13.
Number of Boys. 408 Day Boys.
Fees per term (2014–2015). £3,580–£4,460.

Durston House is an Educational Trust with charitable status. The school has a long history of academic success reflected in Scholarships won at many of the leading senior schools. The emphasis is on high standards of work and targets that are commensurate with each pupil's personal development.

Pre-Prep and Junior School (boys aged 4–8) cater for three classes of about sixteen boys in each year group. There is generous ancillary staffing and learning support for specific needs.

In Middle and Upper School (boys aged 9–13) the Headmaster is helped by a Deputy Head, a Director of Studies and a team comprising graduate specialist Heads of Department for English, Classics, Mathematics, Modern Languages, Science, ICT, History, Geography, Music, Art, Physical Education and Religious Studies.

Throughout the school there are Activities Programmes offering a wide range of cultural, recreational and sporting pursuits. Both playing field complexes have floodlit all-weather facilities and there has been much sporting success in recent years. Extensive use is made of local facilities, especially for drama and swimming. There are fixtures with other prep schools, full participation in IAPS events, and regular expeditions at home and abroad.

Entry into the Reception year is in order of registration. For all other years entry assessment procedures take place some six months before boys are due to enter, which is usually in November, or later if there are vacancies. Durston House is currently seeking to increase its provision of bursaries for boys who would benefit from an education at the school.

Charitable status. Durston House School Educational Trust Limited is a Registered Charity, number 294670. Its aim is the provision and promotion of education.

Eagle House

Crowthorne Road, Sandhurst, Berkshire GU47 8PH
Tel: 01344 772134
Fax: 01344 779039
email: info@eaglehouseschool.com
website: www.eaglehouseschool.com
Twitter: @EagleHouseSch
Facebook: /EagleHouse

Chairman of Governors: H W Veary, Esq

Headmaster: **A P N Barnard**, BA Hons, PGCE

Age Range. 3–13.
Number of Children. 380: 60 Boarders, 320 Day Children.

Fees per term (2014–2015). Prep School: £7,165 (boarders), £5,335 (day pupils). Pre-Prep: £3,400. Nursery: £2,025 (5 mornings including lunch).

Eagle House was founded in 1820, and has been on its present site since 1886. The School is administered by a board of governors under the overall control of Wellington College.

Children are prepared for Scholarship and Common Entrance examinations to senior Independent Schools. There are 65 members of staff and two matrons. The average class size is 15.

The school is situated between Sandhurst and Crowthorne in over 30 acres of playing fields which include a large all-weather sports area, a Sports Hall, an indoor heated swimming pool, extensive woodlands, adventure playground and a small lake. The principal games are rugby, netball, hockey, soccer, rounders and cricket. Other sports include athletics, swimming, tennis, cross country, squash, judo, basketball, archery, golf, riding and badminton.

Much emphasis is placed on the Arts and there are excellent facilities for music, art, design and drama. Music scholarships are available for outstanding young musicians.

The school has its own chapel.

Recent major building works have provided a new Sports and Performing Arts Centre, Design and Food Technology facilities, a Science Laboratory and Library.

Charitable status. Wellington College is a Registered Charity, number 309093. Eagle House School is owned by Wellington College and is part of the same charity registration.

Eaton House The Manor Girls' School

58 Clapham Common Northside, London SW4 9RU
Tel: 020 7924 6000
Fax: 020 7924 1530
email: admin@eatonhouseschools.com
website: www.eatonhouseschools.com

Principal: Mrs H Harper

Headmistress: **Mrs Sarah Segrave**

Deputy Head: Mrs Nicola Borthwick

Age Range. 4–11.

Number of Pupils. 147 Girls.
Fees per term (2014–2015). £4,610.

Eaton House The Manor Girls' School is a single-sex school, conveniently situated on Clapham Common, which offers an excellent education to girls aged 4–11. The Headmistress, Mrs Segrave, has a distinguished career as an educator with over 15 years experience as a Headmistress.

Our girls are encouraged to achieve their full potential in the academic, sporting and artistic fields. They are taught good manners and respect for others and themselves.

Each girl is treated as an individual; Eaton House The Manor Girls' School is intimate and nurturing, and offers state-of-the-art facilities in its new buildings, including a large gymnasium, library, ICT laboratory and new theatre.

All pupils at schools in the Eaton House Group enter Reception (or Kindergarten) on a first-come, first-served basis, and for many years all have achieved entry to their first choice of Senior Day or Boarding school.

Eaton House The Manor Pre-Preparatory School

58 Clapham Common Northside, London SW4 9RU
Tel: 020 7924 6000
Fax: 020 7924 1530
email: admin@eatonhouseschools.com
website: www.eatonhouseschools.com

Principal: Mrs H Harper

Headmaster: **Mr Huw May**, LWCMD, ADWCMD, PGCE, MA Ed, NPQH

Age Range. 4–8.
Number of Pupils. 215 Boys.
Fees per term (2014–2015). £4,610.

The quality of an Eaton House The Manor education means that all of the boys leaving the Pre-Prep and Preparatory Schools go on to their first choice of senior school with several winning scholarships. Our approach, which teaches according to ability in small groups, means that we succeed in bringing out the best in each child, fostering a lifelong enthusiasm for learning and attaining the highest academic results. Pupils go on to the most prestigious independent schools including Eaton House The Manor Prep, Westminster Under School, Colet Court, Dulwich College Prep, Westminster Cathedral School, The Dragon School, Ludgrove and Summer Fields.

The curriculum at Eaton House The Manor Pre-Prep is traditional. Strong moral values and a concern for others are emphasised in the classroom and through the House system. Care is taken to develop each child's confidence, and instil a healthy pride in achieving personal goals as well as participating in team games and competitions.

Pupils are taught in a vibrant environment on an exceptionally large site opposite Clapham Common. A recent multimillion pound investment to extend and improve facilities means they benefit from the latest computer technology in the new ICT lab, lavish art and design rooms, an extended library and extremely good music facilities.

The children enjoy many day and weekend trips as part of the curriculum and are encouraged to take part in a host of extra-curricular activities. Displays, concerts and dramatic performances in the school theatre and gym always prove popular, as do the many parent vs pupils sporting events. Parents are encouraged to be closely involved in their children's education, and to take part in many of the children's activities.

Admission to Eaton House The Manor Pre-Preparatory School is non-selective and on a first-come, first-served basis into the Reception (Kindergarten) Year. Parents wishing to enrol their children in the School are advised to register them at birth.

Eaton House The Manor Preparatory School

58 Clapham Common Northside, London SW4 9RU
Tel: 020 7924 6000
Fax: 020 7924 1530
email: admin@eatonhouseschools.com
website: www.eatonhouseschools.com

Principal: Mrs H Harper

Headmaster: **Mr Jeremy P Edwards**, BA Hons, MA

Deputy Head: Mr Peter Rixham

Age Range. 8–13.
Number of Pupils. 190 Boys.
Fees per term (2014–2015). £5,640.

The quality of an Eaton House The Manor education means that all of the boys leaving the Prep School go on to their first choice of senior school, with several winning scholarships. Our approach, which teaches according to ability in small groups, means that we succeed in bringing out the best in each child, fostering a lifelong enthusiasm for learning and attaining the highest academic results. Pupils go on to the most prestigious independent schools including Westminster, St Paul's, Eton, Harrow, Radley, Charterhouse, Marlborough, King's Wimbledon and Dulwich College.

The curriculum at Eaton House The Manor Prep is traditional. Strong moral values and a concern for others are emphasised in the classroom and through the House system. Care is taken to develop each child's confidence, and instil a healthy pride in achieving personal goals as well as participating in team games and competitions. Every day, children at the Prep School enjoy a reading period after lunch and can attend a supervised homework club at the end of the day.

Pupils are taught in a vibrant environment on an exceptionally large site opposite Clapham Common. A recent multimillion pound investment to extend and improve facilities means they benefit from the latest computer technology in the new ICT lab, lavish art and design rooms, an extended library and extremely good music facilities.

The children enjoy many day and weekend trips as part of the curriculum and are encouraged to take part in a host of extra-curricular activities. Displays, concerts and dramatic performances in the school theatre and gym always prove popular, as do the many parent vs pupils sporting events. Parents are encouraged to be closely involved in their children's education, and to take part in many of the children's activities.

Entry to the Preparatory School is at 8 years of age by examination and interview. Places are offered at 7+ and 8+. 8+ assessments will occur in the academic year before the child's projected start date, backed up by a report from their current Pre-Preparatory School.

Eaton Square School

79 Eccleston Square, London SW1V 1PP
Tel: 020 7931 9469
Fax: 020 7828 0164
email: admissions@eatonsquareschool.com
website: www.eatonsquareschool.com

Headmaster: **Mr S Hepher**

Age Range. 2½–13 Co-educational.
Number of Pupils. 510: 253 boys, 257 girls.
Fees per term (2014–2015). Nursery £1,360–£5,230, Pre-Prep £6,150, Prep £6,350.

Contact. *Pre-Prep & Prep*: Penelope Stitcher, Registrar, email: admissions@eatonsquareschool.com.
Nursery: Lyndsay Salaman, Nursery Registrar, email: lyndsay.salaman@eatonsquareschool.com.

Ethos. Eaton Square School is one of the few co-educational day schools in the heart of London offering nursery, pre-preparatory and preparatory education. The School maintains high standards and encourages in every child an enthusiasm for learning, good manners, self-discipline and, in all things, a determination to do their best and realise their potential. The 2010 ISI inspection report indicated that the "pupils' personal development is outstanding". The School offers a stretching, challenging approach to learning that emphasises achievement and builds confidence. Great emphasis is placed on experiential learning including ski trips, classical tours of Rome and Pompeii, survival skills in the mountains of Scotland and a week's French immersion spent in a French château in Normandy in Year Seven.

Academic Life. The Class Teachers teach general subjects to their classes up to the age of 10. Thereafter, specialist subject teachers continue the curriculum in preparation for the Common Entrance Examinations for senior English Independent Schools, for girls at age 11 and for both boys and girls at age 13. A wide range of subjects are encompassed in the curriculum. ICT is introduced from the age of 3 and it is an integral part of the syllabus. In addition, all Prep School classrooms are equipped with interactive whiteboards and data projectors.

Pupils are prepared for entry into both selective London Day schools and leading Boarding schools through London Day School examinations at 11+ and Common Entrance examinations at 13+.

Sport & the Arts. Sport and Physical Education include Swimming, Fencing, Gymnastics, Football, Rugby, Cricket, Hockey, Sailing, Skiing and Tennis and the School has successful teams competing against other London and national schools. Music is a flourishing department within the School. Appreciation of music, singing, composition, music theory and recorder tuition are taught by specialists at all ages. There are active School Choirs, an orchestra and a variety of ensembles that rehearse throughout the week. Instruction in Music, Art and Design Technology is included for all children from Nursery School upwards, as part of the Curriculum. Drama is integrated within the curriculum and each child takes part in at least two public productions every year. The Prep School production for children in Years 5–8 is held at a West End Theatre during the Summer Term.

Eaton Square School is part of the Minerva Education group which owns a number of private schools in London, East and South East England. Through Minerva's "Inspiring Learning" programme, we seek to share best practice and ensure the continuing improvement in every child's education.

Edge Grove

Aldenham Village, Radlett, Herts WD25 8NL
Tel: 01923 855724
Fax: 01923 859920
email: office@edgegrove.com
website: www.edgegrove.com

The school is a non-profit making Trust administered by a Board of Governors.

Chairman of Governors: P A Haworth

Headmaster: **B Evans**, BA Hons

Age Range. 3–13.

Number of Pupils. Day: 130 (Pre-Prep), 214 (Prep); Boarders 50.

Fees per term (2014–2015). Day: Pre-Prep £2,055–£3,700; Prep £4,250–£4,945; Boarding supplements: Full/Weekly Boarding £1,860; Flexi Boarding: £460–£1,700.

Edge Grove is situated in 28 acres of glorious Hertfordshire countryside. We are approximately 5 minutes' drive from both the M1 and M25 motorways and only 15 miles from Central London. Heathrow and Luton airports are 30 minutes' drive by car.

The Pre-Prep (Hart House) caters for children between the ages of 3 and 7 and is situated within the grounds, close to the main Preparatory school. Children are placed in mixed-ability classes of no more than 20, supervised by a teacher and teaching assistant. A broad curriculum is offered with French, Music and Sport taught by specialist teachers. The children use many of the main Preparatory School's facilities, particularly the outdoor space. The main points of entry are at Nursery (3+) and Reception (4+).

Boys and girls normally join the Preparatory department at 7+ and all are prepared for the Common Entrance and Scholarship Examinations. Pupils are taught in co-educational classes and they move on to a wide variety of Senior Independent schools across the country. There is an excellent record of Scholarship and Common Entrance success; with over 68 scholarships awarded in the past five years to top senior schools. Music and Art are also particularly strong and Edge Grove is a leading player in the world of prep school sport. There is a great range of extra-curricular activities on offer, including a new Activities Programme with a wide range of after-school activities running every day until 6 pm and on Saturday mornings.

Facilities include a modern teaching block, purpose-built Pre-Prep, Science Laboratories, School Chapel, Music School, Sports Hall and two ICT suites. Our facilities for sport include acres of playing fields, a 3-court badminton Sports Hall, a 20-metre outdoor swimming pool, an Astroturf hockey pitch, 2 tennis courts and 8 outdoor cricket nets. Edge Grove offers pupils over 25 sports during the year. The main sports are Netball, Rounders and Hockey for girls and Football, Rugby, Cricket and Hockey for boys. Swimming, Cross-Country, Archery, Tennis and Table-Tennis and Squash are also popular and are played by both boys and girls.

Charitable status. Edge Grove School Trust Ltd is a Registered Charity, number 311054.

Edgeborough

Frensham, Farnham, Surrey GU10 3AH

Tel:	01252 792495
Fax:	01252 795156
email:	office@edgeborough.co.uk
website:	www.edgeborough.co.uk

Chairman of Governors: T Elliott, FCA

Headmaster: **C J Davies**, BA, PGCE

Age Range. 2–13.

Number of Children. Boarders 47, Day 174, Pre Prep 77, Nursery 46.

Fees per term (2014–2015). Years 6–8 £5,305, Years 3–5 £4,760, Pre Prep Years R–2 £3,250. Weekly Boarding (4 nights): £28.50 per night.

Edgeborough is a co-educational IAPS School, for 2–13 year olds, situated on a 50-acre estate in Frensham, near Farnham, Surrey.

The excellent all-round education offered to approx 300 girls and boys is based upon outstanding teaching, wonder-

ful facilities, space and fun. One of the main strengths is the 'value added' input to all children which means that high standards can be achieved by pupils of all abilities. Pupils are prepared for entry both to the local Grammar Schools and to local and National Boarding schools.

The curriculum puts a strong emphasis on the development of learning skills. Languages are also strongly promoted. There is an exciting exchange system with a French language school, where pupils are encouraged to visit frequently. Part of the middle school curriculum is taught in French.

The strong boarding community gives the school its family atmosphere. In addition to weekly boarding, flexi boarding is offered so that girls and boys can enjoy their first experiences of boarding at an early age with their friends. Breakfast and After School care clubs offer logistical help to parents of Day Pupils.

Edgeborough enjoys equally proud records of achievement in sports and in the expressive and performing arts. Scholarships to Senior Schools are frequently awarded for academic work, sports, art, drama music and all round leadership skills.

Day and residential trips both at home and abroad are a regular feature of the school term as is an active, healthy lifestyle.

As well as the spacious grounds and playing fields, the range of facilities is a strength of the school. They include well-equipped classrooms for all the departments, a stunning Science and Technology Building, Art and Pottery Centre, fully-equipped Theatre, Dance and Drama Studio, Sports Hall, Astroturf, Swimming Pool and Golf Course. This enables the school to pursue a wide and varied programme of extra-curricular activities. In addition to the main sports of rugby, football, cricket, hockey, netball, rounders, lacrosse and athletics pupils can enjoy golf, badminton, tennis, swimming, climbing, gymnastics, canoeing, fencing and karate. There are numerous school visits organised for the pupils, including a residential week in France, an annual ski trip, and sporting and cultural tours to South Africa, Spain and Gibraltar.

Charitable status. Edgeborough Educational Trust is a Registered Charity, number 312051.

Elm Green Preparatory School

Parsonage Lane, Little Baddow, Chelmsford, Essex CM3 4SU

Tel:	01245 225230
Fax:	01245 226008
email:	admin@elmgreen.essex.sch.uk
website:	www.elmgreen.essex.sch.uk

Principal: **Mrs A E Milner**, BTech Hons, MSc, PGCE

Age Range. Co-educational 4–11 years.

Number of Day Pupils. 220.

Fees per term (from April 2014). £2,483.

Religious affiliation. Non-denominational.

Elm Green was founded in 1944 and enjoys a lovely rural setting, surrounded by National Trust woodland.

Children enter in the September after their fourth birthday and in their final year are prepared for scholarships, entry to other independent schools and for entry to maintained schools. Many of the pupils take the Essex 11+ and the school has an excellent record of success in this examination.

The school maintains a high standard of academic education giving great emphasis to a secure foundation in the basic subjects whilst offering a wide curriculum with specialist teaching in many areas.

Information technology and design technology form an integral part of the curriculum and there are flourishing art, music and PE departments. The school competes successfully in a wide range of sports – football, rugby, netball, swimming, cricket, gymnastics, athletics, rounders and tennis.

There are many extra-curricular activities and all the children are encouraged to work and to play hard in order to fulfil their potential.

The school aims to foster intellectual curiosity and to encourage individual and corporate work. Kindness and thought for others are given a high priority.

The Elms

Colwall, Malvern, Worcestershire WR13 6EF
Tel: 01684 540344
Fax: 01684 541174
email: office@elmsschool.co.uk
website: www.elmsschool.co.uk

Founded 1614.

Chairman of the Governors: T N Hone, MA, MBA

Head Master: **A Thomas**, BA Hons, PGCE

Age Range. 3–13.
Number of Pupils. Main School: 137: 70 Boys, 67 Girls. 45 boarders. Pre-Prep: 43.
Fees per term (2014–2015). Full board £7,065; Day board £6,290; Pre-Prep (3–7) £2,460–£4,125. Fees are payable termly. There are no compulsory extras.

The Elms is run as a charitable, non-profit making company with a Board of Governors. Children are taken in the Main School from the age of rising 8 and there is a Pre-Preparatory Department for 3–7 year olds.

An experienced staff and small classes ensure attention to each pupil's special needs and a high academic standard is maintained to CE and Scholarship levels. Small numbers help to create a family atmosphere with comfortable accommodation and a resident Headmaster and staff.

Gardens, fields and woodland with stream in 150 acres surround the school, beautifully set at the foot of the Malvern Hills, and include fine playing fields for Rugby, Association Football, Hockey, Cricket, Athletics, Netball and Rounders. Facilities include a Floodlit AstroTurf, Theatre, Sports Hall, Tennis Courts, Laboratory, Computer Rooms, new teaching block, CDT Centre and an Art Room with facilities for Pottery. There is also a heated indoor swimming pool. The children manage a small farming enterprise and many ride on school ponies or bring their own.

Bursaries available for sons and daughters of Services personnel, the Clergy and Teachers; there are also competitive awards.

Charitable status. The Elms (Colwall) Limited is a Registered Charity, number 527252. It exists to provide education for boys and girls.

Eton End School

35 Eton Road, Datchet, Slough, Berkshire SL3 9AX
Tel: 01753 541075
email: admin@etonend.org
website: www.etonend.org

Chairman of Board of Governors: J Clark, Esq

Headmistress: **Mrs S Stokes**, BA Hons, PGCE

Age Range. Girls 3–11, Boys 3–7.
Number of Pupils. 200: 165 girls, 35 boys.
Fees per term (2014–2015). Nursery: £1,600–£2,575; Pre-Prep £2,815–£3,030; Prep £3,340–£3,605. Fees exclude lunch.

The school is a day school set within six acres of spacious grounds. All the classrooms are purpose built and modern, offering excellent facilities, including specialist rooms, e.g. Art & Craft, Music, Science Laboratory, School Library and IT Suite with touch-screen computers. There is a large well-equipped gymnasium, two hard tennis/netball courts, a football and sports field. Boys are prepared for all preparatory schools in the area. Girls leave after the 11+ Entrance Examination often gaining Scholarships. Small classes allow each child to reach their maximum potential in a happy caring environment.

The school's origins lie in the traditions inspired by educationalist, Charlotte Mason, who founded the PNEU movement.

Charitable status. Eton End School Trust (Datchet) Limited is a Registered Charity, number 310644. The aim of the charity is to provide a well-balanced education for children whose parents wish them to attend Eton End School.

Eversfield Preparatory School

Warwick Road, Solihull, West Midlands B91 1AT
Tel: 0121 705 0354
Fax: 0121 709 0168
email: enquiries@eversfield.co.uk
website: www.eversfield.co.uk

Chairman of Governors: Mr D Adamson

Headmaster: **Mr R Yates**, BA, PGCE, LPSH

Age Range. 2¾–11 Co-educational.
Number of Pupils. 300.
Fees per term (2014–2015). £1,515–£3,164 according to age and inclusive of lunch, books and swimming lessons.

Eversfield is a Day Preparatory School on an attractive site in the centre of Solihull preparing boys and girls for entry to the leading Senior Schools in the West Midlands and beyond.

The curriculum values academic excellence and prepares pupils for National Curriculum Tests and 11+ examinations. At the same time it nurtures the creative, sporting, technical and social skills of each pupil. There are excellent facilities and opportunities for sports, music, the arts, and a varied programme of extra-curricular and holiday activities.

On-site facilities include specialist rooms for art, design & technology, science, cookery, music and computing. Sporting facilities comprise a gymnasium, extensive playing fields and all-weather courts. A brand new Sports and Performing Arts Centre with indoor pool is currently under construction, and is due for completion in summer 2015.

The School encourages a strong sense of community where small classes, a well-ordered routine and good pastoral support help pupils to feel secure and develop their self-confidence. Eversfield promotes high moral standards and responsible attitudes based on clear and relevant Christian teaching.

Charitable status. Eversfield Preparatory School Trust Limited is a Registered Charity, number 528966. It is under the direction of a Board of Governors and exists to carry out the work of an Independent Preparatory School.

Ewell Castle Junior School

Glyn House, Church Street, Ewell, Surrey KT17 2AP
Tel: 020 8394 3579
Fax: 020 8394 2220
email: enquiries@ewellcastle.co.uk
website: www.ewellcastle.co.uk
Twitter: @EwellCastleUK

Chairman of Governors: Mr P Durnford-Smith, BA, MCIM

Principal: Mr P Harris, MSc, BSc, PGCE

Head of Junior School: Mrs M Phillips, BEd

Age Range. 3–11.
Number of Pupils. 200 Boys and Girls.
Fees per term (2014–2015). £1,365–£3,130.

Ewell Castle Junior School is a co-educational day school, located on two sites in the heart of Ewell Village. Nursery to Year 2 pupils (3–7 years) are based at Chessington Lodge in Spring Street, while Years 3 to 6 (7–11 years) are based at Glyn House in Church Street, opposite the Senior School (boys 11–18 years, girls 16–18 years), with which a close liaison is maintained.

Those entering the Nursery may attend for a half-day (minimum three sessions per week) until they are ready for full-time education. There are no entry requirements for Nursery children, but older pupils attend the school for a day's assessment, which will include tests in Mathematics and English. Many pupils proceed to the Senior School which from September 2015 will be welcoming girls into Year 7 and Year 9, its normal entry points and a number of aided places and scholarships are available at 11+ entry. All pupils are prepared for entry at 11+ to selective state schools. The National Curriculum is incorporated within a broad curriculum.

The creative arts play an important part in school life. Apart from the timetabled music lessons, there is the opportunity for pupils to learn a variety of instruments under professional teachers. Drama productions take place regularly. Pupils' art work can be seen on display in the local community and is always to be found decorating the school walls. All pupils join in various sporting activities as part of the weekly curriculum. In addition, a wide variety of activities are available after school and during the holidays.

All pupils use the five acres of attractive gardens and playing fields at Glyn House for outdoor play and games lessons. In addition, Junior School pupils benefit from full access to the excellent sporting facilities, including a sports hall and playing fields, on the 15-acre site at The Castle. The main games are football, netball, hockey, cricket and tennis. There are also athletics and cross country events, including a school sports day. All pupils receive swimming instruction.

Outside speakers include police liaison officers and actors and authors who conduct workshops with pupils. A number of visits occur to places of interest which are relevant to a particular area of study. There are regular school visits abroad.

The school also enjoys close links with St Mary's Church, where regular assemblies are held throughout the year.

The Junior School aims to provide a caring, responsive and stimulating environment in which pupils are able to fulfil their potential. Hard work and high standards together with courtesy and consideration to others are of prime importance.

Charitable status. Ewell Castle School is a Registered Charity, number 312079. It exists to provide education for boys and girls.

Exeter Cathedral School

The Chantry, Palace Gate, Exeter, Devon EX1 1HX
Tel: 01392 255298
Fax: 01392 422718
email: reception@exetercs.org
website: www.exetercs.org

Chairman of Governors: The Dean of Exeter

Headmaster: Stephen G Yeo, BMus Hons, LTCL MusEd, NPQH

Age Range. 3–13.
Number of Pupils. 8 full boarders, 7 flexi boarders, 285 day pupils.
Fees per term (2014–2015). Day Pupils (excluding lunches): £2,120–£3,535. Boarding (in addition to Day fees): £2,206 (full). Flexi boarding is also available.

Founded in 1159, the Cathedral School provides 36 Boy and Girl Choristers for Exeter Cathedral and educates 249 other pupils to the same high standard.

Entry is normally at age 3 into the Nursery (the School is a member of the Government's Early Years Funding Scheme) or at age 7 or 8 years into the Prep School, though pupils may join the school at any stage, subject to place availability.

Voice Trials for Cathedral Choristers are usually held in February each year, or by arrangement. There are 18 scholarships available for Boy Choristers and 18 for Girl Choristers to the value of 25% of the tuition fee.

Pupils are prepared for senior school entry to both independent and maintained schools and the School has a proven track record of academic, music, art, drama and sports scholarship success.

There are no Saturday lessons, though day pupils sometimes join boarders in weekend or after school activities. The curriculum encompasses all National Curriculum and Common Entrance subjects, including Modern Foreign Languages, Latin and Greek.

In the Michaelmas Term, rugby football and netball are the team sports. Netball, soccer and hockey are played in the Lent Term. During the Trinity Term, cricket, rounders, athletics and swimming are all pursued competitively. Swimming takes place all year round.

Musical activities, including school choir, orchestra and ensembles for string, woodwind, brass and jazz instrumentalists are available to all pupils in the prep school.

Daily morning worship takes place in the Cathedral or in The Chapter House led by the Headmaster, School Chaplain or a member of the Cathedral Clergy.

The buildings are located around the Close and include a Science Laboratory, a gym, music and drama school, as well as a large portion of the 14th Century Deanery. There is a Food Technology Centre, Design and Technology Department and Computer Centre.

For games, use is made of first-class facilities at Exeter University as well as other playing fields and swimming baths situated short distances away in the city.

Charitable status. Exeter Cathedral School is a Registered Charity, number 1151444.

Exeter Junior School

Victoria Park Road, Exeter, Devon EX2 4NS
Tel: 01392 258738 Headmistress
01392 273679 Registrar
Fax: 01392 498144
email: admissions@exeterschool.org.uk
website: www.exeterschool.org.uk

Co-educational Day School.

Chairman of Board of Governors: Mrs B Meeke, LLB

Headmistress: Mrs Alison J Turner, MA

Age Range. 7–11.
Number of Pupils. 199: 124 Boys, 75 Girls.
Fees per term (2014–2015). £3,395 (includes lunch which is compulsory).

Exeter Junior School is housed in a spacious, Victorian building in the grounds of Exeter School. The close proximity of the Junior School to the Senior School enables the pupils to take full advantage of the facilities on site, which include a chapel, music centre, science laboratories, sports hall with dance studio, fitness suite and squash courts, outdoor heated swimming pool, playing fields, all-weather astroturf arena and tennis courts.

In addition to this the Junior School retains its own playground and green space, therefore giving the School a separate and clearly recognisable identity.

Liaison between Junior and Senior staff is a positive feature of this thriving Junior School.

The School aims to offer, in academic, cultural and sporting terms, the widest possible range of opportunities thus helping each pupil to identify the activities which will give the greatest scope for development and fulfilment in years to come. Music, drama, art, sport and expeditions all have an important part to play in the life of the school.

The majority of pupils enter the school at age 7 or 8, and entrance is by informal assessment in January. This includes a report from the child's previous school, classroom sessions in the company of other prospective pupils, and literacy, numeracy and general intelligence tasks. Pupils may enter the school at age 9 or 10 where space is available.

Pupils are offered an academic programme which incorporates the National Curriculum model with the addition of French which is introduced from Year 3.

Specialist teaching is offered from the outset, with the additional support of Senior School staff in Science, French, Music and ICT.

A wide variety of clubs are available during the week including art & craft, dance, modern languages, calligraphy, sewing, football, hockey, netball, rugby, chess and drama. After-school care is available until 5.30pm.

(*For further information about the Senior School, see Exeter School entry in HMC section.*)

Charitable status. Exeter School is a Registered Charity, number 1093080. It exists to provide education for children.

Fairfield Preparatory School

Leicester Road, Loughborough, Leics LE11 2AE
Tel: 01509 215172
Fax: 01509 238648
email: admin@lesfairfield.org
website: www.lesfairfield.org

Chairman of the Governors: Mr H Michael Pearson, BA Econ, LLB, ACIS

Head: **Mr A R Earnshaw**, BA Lancaster, NPQH

Age Range. 4–11.
Number of Pupils. 268 Boys, 220 Girls (all day)
Fees per term (2014–2015). Pre-Prep £2,998, Prep £3,026. Lunches and individual music lessons extra.

Fairfield School is the Preparatory School of the Loughborough Endowed Schools, the two Upper Schools being Loughborough Grammar School for Boys (*see HMC entry*) and Loughborough High School for Girls (*see GSA entry*).

The three Schools are governed by the same Governing Body and share a fine campus to the west of the Leicester Road, with their private roads free of through traffic.

The aim of Fairfield is to give a broad-based education appropriate for the needs of the children in our care. In the process, they will be prepared for their secondary education. For most this will mean either Loughborough Grammar School or High School, although some children move elsewhere.

Our intention is also to teach children how to live together in a community and to show respect for the property and feelings of others. We hope that time spent at Fairfield will be thoroughly enjoyable.

Whilst our children are prepared for entry to the Upper Schools, this is certainly not our only goal. In addition to all National Curriculum subjects French, Spanish and German are taught and there are specialist rooms for ICT, Science and Music. Our Gymnasium is extremely well equipped.

The children are introduced to a wide variety of sporting and recreational activities. Team games are encouraged for the spirit of cooperation and working together which the School aims to foster. Activities of a more individual nature also play an increasing part in the life of the School. Winter games include Football, Rugby, Netball, Cross-Country Running and Hockey. In the summer Cricket, Tennis, Rounders, Athletics and Short Tennis are played. The children swim throughout the year in the Endowed Schools' indoor, heated pool.

Music and Drama are considered very important areas of School life. In addition to class music lessons, children have the opportunity to receive tuition on a variety of musical instruments and many take advantage of this. The School Orchestras perform on a regular basis and there are also two Choirs, two Recorder Groups and numerous additional instrumental ensembles. The £4 million state-of-the-art whole school Music School opened in September 2006.

Music is coordinated by the Loughborough Endowed Schools Director of Music and the music curriculum includes traditional music teaching, using extensive ICT in the modern facilities.

Dramatic productions play a major part in the life of the School. Here children are given the opportunity to express themselves and experience the excitement of performing before an audience.

There is a whole range of other activities in which children are given the opportunity to participate. Success and enjoyment in these invariably help to boost confidence and widen horizons generally.

Lunchtime and after-school clubs include Brownies, Rainbows, Cubs, Beavers, Drama, Technology, Green Fingers Club, LAMDA and Mind Sports (Chess, Mini Bridge, Go), as well as the sporting and musical activities already mentioned.

The main ages for entry to the School are at 4+ and 7+ although a few places are available at other ages.

The examination for entry at 7+, 8+, 9+ and 10+ takes place in January each year and also assessments for entry at 4+.

The Prospectus and further details can be obtained from the Registrar and the Headmaster will be happy to show prospective parents around the School and more information can be found on the school website www.lesfairfield.org.

Charitable status. Loughborough Endowed Schools is a Registered Charity, number 1081765, and a Company Limited by Guarantee, registered in England, number 4038033.

Fairstead House School

Fordham Road, Newmarket, Suffolk CB8 7AA
Tel: 01638 662318
email: registrar@fairsteadhouse.co.uk
website: www.fairsteadhouse.co.uk

Chair of Governors: Dr Patrick Round

Headmaster: Gareth Williams, BEd Hons

Age Range. Co-educational 3–11.
Number of Children. 88.
Fees per term (2014–2015). Nursery: £23 per session (minimum 3 sessions per week, lunches £2.10 per day). Main School (including lunches): Reception & Year 1 £2,785, Years 2 & 3 £2,950, Years 4, 5 & 6 £2,999.

Fairstead House is situated in the heart of Newmarket and offers a combination of an excellent academic education with an emphasis on creativity and imagination in a caring, happy community with a unique family ethos, closely linked to the local community.

From Nursery onwards, we offer a broad and stimulating curriculum which provides the children with a solid foundation for their onward journeys to senior schools in both Independent and State sectors. The curriculum is complemented by Art, DT, Music, Drama and Sports.

Pupils take part in a variety of sports such as rugby, football and cricket for boys and hockey and netball for girls. All children play rounders and take part in cross country running and athletics.

Extra-curricular Speech & Drama lessons are available, as is private tuition in a wide selection of musical instruments. Children may join the Fairstead House Orchestra or Choir and take part in the many theatrical productions that are held at School.

A programme of development has ensured the provision of first-class facilities throughout the School including a state-of-the-art Music & Drama Centre with specialist facilities, an ICT suite, iPads, interactive whiteboards in every classroom and a dedicated Science & DT area.

As well as a breakfast club and after-school care club providing wrap-around care, there is a diverse range of after-school activity clubs available offering such activities as yoga, aikido, pottery and strategy games together with the major sports.

Throughout the year, pupils go on a variety of trips and excursions, both day and residential. The residential trips to Norfolk and Snowdonia for the older pupils are designed to encourage independence and cultivate a spirit of adventure as well as personal responsibility and development.

Charitable Status. Fairstead House School Trust Limited is a Registered Charity, number 276787. It exists to provide education for boys and girls.

The Falcons Schools
Alpha Plus Group

Boys Nursery and Pre-Prep:
2 Burnaby Gardens, London W4 3DT
Tel: 020 8747 8393
Fax: 020 8995 3903
email: admin@falconschool.com

Boys Prep:
41 Kew Foot Road, Richmond, Surrey TW9 2SS
Tel: 020 8948 9490
Fax: 020 8948 9491

email: admin@falconsprep.co.uk

Girls School:
11 Woodborough Road, Putney, London SW15 6PY
Tel: 020 8992 5189
Fax: 020 8752 1635
email: admin@falconsgirls.co.uk

website: www.falconschool.com

Head Teacher, Girls School: Miss Joan McGillewie

Head Teacher, Boys School: **Mr Gordon Milne**, BEd Hons, CertEd, MCollP, FRSA

Age Range. Boys School: 3–7 (Pre-Prep), 8–13 (Prep); Girls School 3–11.
Number of Pupils. 355 Boys; 85 Girls.
Fees per term (2014–2015). Boys School: £2,560–£5,120. Girls School: £2,500–£4,500.

The Falcons Schools enjoy a well-deserved reputation for excellence. Results to the leading London Day Schools are impressive, as too is the specialist teaching on offer throughout the schools. The schools provide a safe outdoor space for play and sport and a school hall for gym, assemblies and lunch. Nearby sports facilities are used to enhance an exciting sports program. There are well-equipped libraries, music rooms, ICT suites, with a much-admired art and science facility. Our overriding emphasis is on achieving excellence in numeracy and literacy whilst offering a broad and creative curriculum. The Falcons is a uniquely caring and stimulating environment, where learning is seen as fun and the pursuit of excellence is embraced by all.

Farleigh School

Red Rice, Andover, Hampshire SP11 7PW
Tel: 01264 710766
Fax: 01264 710070
email: office@farleighschool.co.uk
website: www.farleighschool.com

Chairman of Governors: Mr Tim Syder

Headmaster: **Fr Simon Everson**

Age Range. 3–13. Boarding from age 7.
Number of Pupils. 76 boarders (45 boys, 31 girls), 250 day, including 33 flexi boarders; 104 in Kindergarten and Pre-Prep.
Fees per term (2014–2015). Senior boarders (Years 7 and 8) £7,490; Junior boarders (Years 3–6) £6,745; HM Forces boarders (Years 3–8) £6,367; Day pupils £1,580–£5,755.

Celebrating its Diamond Jubilee in 2013, Farleigh was originally founded in 1953 as a Roman Catholic boys' boarding school. Today, it is a fully co-educational boarding and day school, welcoming children of all faiths. Situated in a stunning Georgian country house standing in 60 acres of magnificent parkland and landscaped woodland in the Test Valley of Hampshire, Farleigh is just over an hour from London and within easy reach of Southampton and London airports.

High standards are achieved both in and out of the classroom and excellent academic results are the norm, with leavers going to a large number of leading senior schools and many obtaining scholarships.

Farleigh has outstanding facilities, including spacious and light Art and Design Technology building, computer rooms with state-of-the-art Apple Macs and mobile technology, a theatre with tiered seating, music suite, spacious recreation rooms, a fine Chapel, gymnasium, 22-metre heated indoor swimming pool, five tennis courts, squash courts and purpose-built Pre-Prep and Kindergarten. Opened in September 2012 were two new buildings, which accommodate four new classrooms, three new science laboratories and a food technology room, as well as additional circulation space with a well-lit ball play area and a small amphitheatre to the rear of the existing Farleigh theatre.

The teaching staff is complemented by a committed pastoral team including Year Heads, House Parents and two matrons who are qualified nurses. Many staff are resident, giving the school a welcoming family atmosphere, often commented upon by visitors. The latest Ofsted inspection (2010) of the school's boarding provision was "Outstanding" in all six areas inspected, "with no recommendations". The inspectors added, "This is a very caring school that is child-centred and achieves high standards throughout."

The school provides a vibrant and active evening and weekend activity programme for boarders. Regular dinner nights, barbecue parties, X-Factor competitions, theatre trips, quiz nights, bowling are just some of the weekend events organised for pupils. Weekday activities include building dens in the woods, cycling, judo, winter cricket nets, community service, swimming, water polo, tennis, football, unihockey, jewellery making, art and craft.

Drama, music and art have important places in school life with two-thirds of the school learning at least one musical instrument and a third of the school taking up LAMDA drama lessons. A programme of major musical productions and informal concerts take place throughout the year and the children's artwork is displayed around the school.

The major sports for boys are rugby, football, cricket, athletics and cross-country; for girls they are netball, hockey, rounders, athletics and cross-country. Swimming lessons and extra tennis coaching are offered throughout the year.

Charitable status. Farleigh School is a Registered Charity, number 307340. It exists for the purpose of educating children.

Farlington Preparatory School

Strood Park, Horsham, West Sussex RH12 3PN
Tel: 01403 282566
Fax: 01403 272258
email: prepheadmistress@farlingtonschool.net
website: www.farlingtonschool.net
Twitter: @Farlington_Sch
Facebook: FarlingtonSchool

Chairman of Governors: Mrs Sue Mitchell, BA, MA, PGCE

Headmistress: **Mrs Frances Mwale**, BSc, PGCE

Registrar: Mrs J Coveney, BEng

Age Range. 3–11.
Number of Girls. 150.
Fees per term (2014–2015). Tuition: Prep School £2,350–£4,515. Boarding (in addition to Tuition fees): £3,150 (weekly), £3,505 (full).

The Early Years Foundation Stage and Pre-Prep Departments at Farlington are housed in an impressive courtyard building opened in September 2008. This purpose-built accommodation comprises nursery, large infant classrooms, an infant library, a separate junior library, and two innovative play areas. The spacious hall and dining facilities are enjoyed by all of our Prep Pupils. The Junior School girls are also housed in purpose-built classrooms that mirror the architecture of the Mansion House in the School grounds. Younger children quickly feel at home in this close-knit community, and the older girls have the opportunity to learn responsibility and have status in "their" school by becoming Prefects, House Captains and Monitors.

Early school days that are happy and secure, provide a sound basis for learning and for life. At Farlington, we aim to achieve high academic standards in our Preparatory School, with the emphasis on encouragement: we educate for confidence! The philosophy of the School is based on Christian ethics, but we welcome girls from a wide range of religious and cultural backgrounds.

We have a staff of well-qualified and dedicated teachers. They form a wonderfully good-humoured team, who support fully the ethos of the School. Literacy and numeracy are the building blocks of education, and these form the foundation of our curriculum in the Pre-Prep Department.

We follow the National Curriculum, but offer much more in terms of subject content, and, of course, individual attention. As girls become older, they are taught most subjects by specialist teachers (for example, English, Mathematics, Science, French, Spanish, Latin, PE/Games, Drama, Music and Art). In Prep 6, Science skills are developed in a challenging way, using exploration and experiment, as well as practice and problem-solving. Science is taught in the well-equipped laboratories in the Senior School. There is also a strong emphasis on Music and individual tuition can be arranged for most instruments. Girls can progress from the Training Orchestra to the Concert Orchestra.

All girls enjoy the beautiful 33-acre parkland setting for recreation and for learning. Farlington embraces the Forest School Initiatives and we enjoy the benefits of having our own trained instructor on the staff. We run weekly sessions using our wonderful outdoor environment, opening up the amazing natural world through the seasons, giving the children a programme filled with discovery and difference.

The Prep School offers a wide range of extra-curricular activities which take place at lunchtimes and after school. These range from sporting clubs such as tennis, trampolining, golf and judo to musical activities which include choir, orchestra, recorder ensembles and a samba band. We offer chess tuition, ballet, jazz dance, fencing and many more. Farlington Prep has its own Morris Side too! Although school finishes at 3.20 pm for girls in Reception to Prep 2, they can stay on at school until 5.00 pm supervised by members of staff. There is no charge for this after-school care. The older girls finish their lessons at 3.45 pm and can do activities and supervised homework until 5.45 pm.

At Farlington we believe that education is a partnership between home and school, and we hope that parents will take an active part in their daughter's education. Parents are invited to join their daughters on educational outings and visits, and they are keen supporters of our sports teams. Farlington has a very active PTA and a Parents' Round Table (a focus group to develop ideas throughout the school).

Boarding is available to girls from the age of 8. Our Boarding House is small and friendly and run on family lines.

Prospective parents are always welcome to come to meet the Headmistress and have a tour of the School. Please telephone for an appointment and we will be delighted to forward a current prospectus.

For further information on the Senior School, see Farlington School entry in the GSA section.

Charitable status. Farlington Preparatory School is a Registered Charity, number 307048. It exists solely for the purpose of educating girls.

Felsted Preparatory School

Felsted, Essex CM6 3JL
Tel: 01371 822610
Fax: 01371 822617
email: rmw@felstedprep.org
website: www.felsted.org

Chairman of the Governors: Mr J H Davies

Head: **Mrs J M Burrett**, BA Dunelm, MEd Cantab, PGCE

Deputy Head: T J Searle, BSc Loughborough, PGCE

Age Range. 4–13 Co-educational.
Number of Pupils. 468 pupils (of which 15 are full-time boarders, plus 73 flexi boarders).
Fees per term (2014–2015). Preparatory: £3,995–£5,250; Pre-Preparatory: £2,750; Boarding £6,895.

The staff, excluding the Headmistress, consists of 50 full-time qualified teachers and there are additional part-time teachers for instrumental music and games. There are six matrons and two sisters in charge of the Medical Centre.

The School was rated 'excellent' in every category by the Independent School Inspectorate at its latest inspection, in addition to a legacy rating of 'Outstanding' by Ofsted for EYFS and Boarding.

The Preparatory School, set in its own grounds, is separate from Felsted School itself, with all its own facilities, including a modern well-equipped library, an excellent theatre/assembly hall, music practice rooms, a new multi-purpose sports hall, open-air heated swimming pool and floodlit, multi-purpose, hard play/games area. Use is made of Felsted School's extra amenities at regular times so that indoor swimming, two Astroturf hockey pitches, small-bore rifle shooting, squash courts, a new state-of-the-art Music School and another indoor sports hall are also available to the pupils.

Rugby, football, netball, hockey, cricket, tennis, swimming, rounders, athletics and cross-country are the major sports. Music plays an important part in the School's life, and there is an excellent Chapel Choir. Regular instrumental, orchestral and rock concerts are given. The School has a deserved reputation for its drama productions, while Art, Design and Technology, PSHE, and Computing are part of the weekly timetable. Out-of-class activities include public speaking and debating opportunities, horse riding, chess, fencing, golf, public speaking, aerobics, cookery and dance/ballet, among others.

Pupils joining at 11+ can be guaranteed assured transfer to Felsted School at 13, as can pupils of a similar age already at the Preparatory School, following successful completion of assessment tests. The majority of pupils proceed to Felsted School itself, but a number regularly move on to other major independent senior schools, having taken Common Entrance, and there is an excellent record of academic, art, music, sport, drama and Design & Technology scholarships. (*For further information about Felsted, see entry in HMC section.*)

Academic and Music Scholarships and Mary Skill Awards are open to pupils joining Felsted Preparatory School at ages of 11+ in the September of the year of entry. Top-up bursaries may also be available on a means-tested basis. One 100% bursary is available each year to a child who meets the right criteria and is given at the discretion of the Head.

Charitable status. Felsted School is a Registered Charity, number 310870. It exists to provide education for boys and girls.

Feltonfleet School

Cobham, Surrey KT11 1DR
Tel: 01932 862264
Fax: 01932 860280
email: office@feltonfleet.co.uk
           admissions@feltonfleet.co.uk
website: www.feltonfleet.co.uk

Chair of Governors: Mrs M Jenner, MBE, JP

Headmaster: **A G Morrison**, BA, PGCE

Registrar: Mrs Jackie Williams

Age Range. 3–13.
Number of Pupils. Nursery/Pre-Prep 80, Years 3–8 318, of whom 48 are Boarders.
Fees per term (2014–2015). Boarders £7,160 Day Pupils £3,540–£5,210; Nursery £1,895.

Feltonfleet School was founded in 1903 and became an Educational Trust in 1967. The School is situated in 20 acres of scenic grounds close to the M25 between Heathrow and Gatwick Airports. There are 56 full-time and 4 Gap Year members of the teaching staff. The School became fully co-educational in September 1994 and offers both weekly boarding (Monday to Friday) and day education, as well as a flexible boarding option. There is a flourishing, purpose-built Pre-Preparatory Department, Calvi House.

Ethos. It is the School's strongly held belief that if children are happy they will fulfil their potential, and by recognising the individual in a child this is more likely to happen, which is why it is committed to fostering a small school atmosphere centred on family values. The School does its best to place the children first, to meet each child's needs on an individual basis, to encourage and nurture the positive aspects of 'self': self-discipline, self-confidence, self-motivation, self-reliance and self-esteem. High-achieving children, irrespective of their real potential, are those who have a high self-esteem – without it very little can be achieved.

Pastoral. Caring for each other matters at Feltonfleet. From a child's first day, the adult community provides care, direction and confidence. The form tutor is the welcoming face on a daily basis and a secure link with daily routine, a familiar and reassuring presence, a trusted confidant and role model. Small classes make quality pastoral care much more certain. Once pupils join the Main School, the Head of Year provides further direction and guidance. The boarding house is run by two house parents, seven boarding house tutors and two matrons who promote the personal, family atmosphere on which Feltonfleet prides itself.

Entry. Children are admitted from the age of three into the Nursery in the Pre-Preparatory Department and, having moved into the Main School at the age of seven, are prepared for Common Entrance or Scholarship examinations to a wide range of independent senior schools. In the Main School there is a staff : pupil ratio of 9.5:1, with the average class size of 16.

For entry into the Main School pupils are required to sit an entrance assessment and interview. Academic, Art, Music, Drama, DT, All-Rounder and Sports Scholarships are offered at 11+.

Facilities. Well-equipped Science, Art, DT and Digital Learning Departments, Library and Performing Arts Centre, where dramatic productions are performed by all year groups. The Pre-Prep, Calvi House, has its own hall, gardens and ICT suite. There are landscaped play areas throughout the school and a stunning tree-house, pond and wildlife area with bird-hide.

Sport. The Sports Department prides itself that is able to encompass both excellence and sport for all within a very busy prep school environment. All pupils receive high quality teaching and coaching in a variety of sports and activities in a positive and safe learning environment. Facilities include a magnificent sports hall, sports fields, two squash courts, a 15m indoor swimming pool, a shooting range for air weapon and .22 rifle, a large floodlit astro pitch and a climbing wall.

Games played are rugby, football, hockey, netball, lacrosse, athletics and cricket.

Extra-Curricular Activities. The School has an active policy of preparing children for the challenges of today's world and an exceptional activities programme is offered to all pupils during the school day as often as possible. Pupils in the main school are offered the opportunity to attend residential activity courses as well as subject-related overseas trips. In the final two years pupils attend residential leadership courses. After Common Entrance examinations, Year 8 pupils take part in a varied programme of activities, lectures and trips in preparation for leaving Feltonfleet and moving on to their senior schools.

In recent years sporting teams have visited Belgium, Spain, Qatar and Dubai.

Charitable status. Feltonfleet School Trust Limited is a Registered Charity, number 312070.

Fettes College Preparatory School

East Fettes Avenue, Edinburgh EH4 1QZ
Tel: 0131 332 2976
Fax: 0131 332 4724
email: prepschool@fettes.com
website: www.fettes.com
Twitter: @fettes_college

Chairman of Governors: Lord C Tyre

Chairman of Preparatory School Committee: Mrs J A Campbell

Headmaster: **A A Edwards**, BA Hons, PGCE

Age Range. 7–13.
Number of Pupils. 195 (51 boarders, 144 day pupils), 104 boys, 91 girls.
Fees per term (2014–2015). Boarders £7,730, Day Pupils £4,655, including all meals and textbooks.

Fettes Prep School lies within the Fettes College grounds – 80 acres of parkland in the heart of Edinburgh. Although housed in separate buildings about 200m away from the main Fettes College building, the Prep School has all the advantages of the excellent facilities of Fettes College but with the ability to be a complete campus in its own right. Due to expansion in the school roll, William House was completed in 2009 – a state-of-the-art teaching block with superb eco credentials.

Their HMIe inspection had superb results with both Fettes Prep and Fettes College deemed as 'sector-leading'.

The Boarding houses of Iona (girls) and Arran (boys) offer a safe, secure and happy environment. The pastoral staff; housemaster, housemistress, matron and resident tutor, are of the highest calibre and dedicate themselves to creating a secure and happy home.

The curriculum is structured to reflect the strengths of the Curriculum for Excellence, the National Curriculum of England and Wales and IAPS guidance. A strong emphasis is placed on a sound and thorough grounding in the traditionally important subjects of Maths and English as well as specialists subjects such as Science, Art and Languages being taught by specialist teachers. Class sizes remain small to allowing individual attention for each child – the absolute maximum class size is 18.

Formal coaching is given to boys in rugby, hockey, athletics and cricket and to girls in hockey, netball, rounders, athletics and tennis. Each year pupils from the school represent their district in these sports and others. Swimming is also taught as are judo, fencing, squash and shooting (the vast majority taking place on campus). There are over 30 activities and clubs ranging from climbing to origami.

Music and Drama flourish. The School Choir and School Orchestra give concerts each term, and choirs and instrumental groups participate successfully in musical competitions. Year group concerts, too, are regularly held. Each year there is a large-production School Play, younger pupils produce their own pantomime, and shorter plays are performed in French and Latin. The art department continues to excel and every pupil within the school has their work displayed.

There are annual trips abroad to bring learning to life and other tours are regularly organised. All twelve year olds receive leadership training and the top two year groups are involved in a programme designed at the school to increase and improve skills in various areas including resourcefulness, initiative and personal challenge.

Entrance. Entrance at the age of seven, eight or nine is by assessment tests and at 10+, 11+ and 12+ by the Entrance Examinations, taken in late Jan/early Feb. All applicants can apply for a means-tested bursary which can cover up to 100% of the fees. There is a finite amount of funding available each year and therefore not all applicants will be successful. Bursaries are awarded independently of any Scholarship or Award.

All candidates who are applying for entry into the 1st Form at 11+ years of age, will automatically be considered for a Junior Scholarship. The results of the Entrance Examinations will determine who receives a Junior Scholarship.

These Scholarships are awarded for academic or all-round excellence and there is great kudos associated with being a scholar of The College. They can also attract reductions of up to 5% of the fees and these reductions are not related to parents' financial circumstances. A Music award can also be applied for at 11+ and 12+ entry.

Further information and a prospectus can be obtained from the Registrar (Tel: 0131 311 6744, email: admissions@fettes.com) who will be very happy to arrange a visit.

Charitable status. The Fettes Trust is a Registered Charity, number SC017489.

Finton House

171 Trinity Road, London SW17 7HL
Tel: 020 8682 0921
Fax: 020 8767 5017
email: admissions@fintonhouse.org.uk
website: www.fintonhouse.org.uk

Co-Founders: Terry O'Neill and Finola Stack founded Finton House in 1987.

Chair of Governors: Mr Mark Chilton

Headmaster: **Mr A E Floyd**, BSc, PGCE

Age Range. 4–11.
Number of Pupils. 109 Boys, 196 Girls.
Fees per term (2014–2015). £4,335–£4,640.
Entrance. No testing – first come/first served.
Exit. Boys at 11 for both London Day and Prep. Girls at 11 for London Day and Boarding.

Strong policy of inclusion with a percentage of children with Special Needs. Employs a full-time Speech and Language Therapist, an Occupational Therapist and Special Needs Assistants. Aims to give an all-round education, developing the whole child with individual teaching to fulfil each child's potential. Music, Art and Sports are all taught to a very high standard. A stimulating environment which encourages all children to learn and gain confidence in their own abilities. Non-denominational but teaches a moral belief encouraging respect and self-discipline.

Charitable status. Finton House is a Registered Charity, number 296588. It exists to provide an broad, inclusive education for children.

Foremarke Hall
Repton Preparatory School

Milton, Derbyshire DE65 6EJ
Tel: 01283 707100
Fax: 01283 702957
email: registrar@foremarke.org.uk
website: www.foremarke.org.uk
Twitter: @foremarkehall

Chairman of Governors: Sir Henry Every

Head: R P Merriman, MA, BSc Hons, FCollP

Age Range. 3–13.
Number of Pupils. 449: Boys: 39 boarders, 198 day; Girls: 24 boarders, 188 day.
Fees per term (2014–2015). Prep: £7,011 boarding, £5,280 day; Termly Flexi Boarding also available – prices available on application. Pre-Prep: Years 1 & 2 £3,183, Reception £2,871, Nursery £2,729 (full-time), £273 (part-time per session).

Foremarke Hall is under the control of the Governors of Repton School. Boys and girls are prepared for all Independent Schools but about two-thirds choose to continue to Repton.

The school is situated in a fine Georgian mansion surrounded by 55 acres of woods, playing fields and a lake. The facilities include all that the school requires including a new classroom building to house mathematics, three science laboratories, sophisticated computer technology with full-time IT specialist, an extensive library run by a chartered librarian, an indoor competition-sized swimming pool, a sports hall and a floodlit sports artificial turf surface.

The £6m Quad Development was opened by HRH The Duke of Kent KG in September 2013. This facility houses a contemporary music facility, a new language laboratory, many new classrooms, a new art block complete with kiln, a designated ICT suite for design and technology and a Green-power garage for Foremarke's award-winning electric cars.

Great importance is attached to pastoral care where boarders have their own dedicated staff and space for themselves. There is an imaginative and varied programme of activities making most use of the grounds including outdoor pursuits. The games programme is extensive and includes athletics, cricket, football, rugby, hockey, rounders, swimming and tennis. We also have an extensive and varied after-school activities programme.

We seek to bring out the most in every pupil, to provide a rounded education and a range of experience and skills that will be a preparation for life. We value our 'family atmosphere' and strong sense of community, the spacious grounds and happy environment.

Foremarke is situated in undisturbed countryside in the centre of England. It is easily reached by the M1, M42 and Birmingham and East Midlands airports.

Charitable status. Repton Preparatory School is a Registered Charity, number 1093165. It exists to provide high quality education for boys and girls.

Forest Preparatory School

College Place, Snaresbrook, London E17 3PY
Tel: 020 8520 1744
Fax: 020 8520 3656
email: prep@forest.org.uk
website: www.forest.org.uk
Twitter: @ForestSchoolE17

Co-educational Day School.

Chairman of Governors: J W Matthews, FCA

Head: Mr A Noakes, BA Hons De Montfort, MA Ed Open University

Age Range. 4–11.
Number of Pupils. 272.
Fees per term (2014–2015). £3,543–£4,109.

Forest Preparatory School is part of Forest School (HMC), with which it shares a 30-acre site at the foot of Epping Forest on the East London/Essex border. Its aims are to offer an education of high quality, and to encourage and develop each child academically, physically and creatively. In the Pre-Prep, pupils are taught in small co-educational classes. From the age of 7, pupils are taught in single-sex classes, and at age 11 they proceed to the Boys' and Girls' sections of Forest School (*see separate entry in HMC section*).

Entry to the school is by selection at age 4 by means of informal assessment and, at age 7, by entrance examination.

The Pre-Prep Department is co-educational, with forms of 16 pupils who are taught predominantly by form teachers and supported by classroom assistants. Music, Drama and PE are taught by specialist teachers. From the age of 7, forms become single-sex and number around 22 pupils. Form teachers teach the main curriculum subjects, while specialists teach modern foreign languages – Mandarin, French, Spanish and German – ICT, music, drama, dance, design and technology, physical education and games. In the final two years an element of setting is introduced in mathematics and English Grammar. Scholarship and music awards are available to pupils for entry at age 11 to the Boys' and Girls' Schools at Forest.

Sport and music are strengths of the school. The main sports played are football, cricket, netball and rounders, and teams compete locally and regionally. Athletics, swimming and cross-country are all coached to a high standard. The musical life of the school is enriched by its choirs, orchestra and several chamber groups, and all pupils in Years 3 and 4 are provided with free tuition in a musical instrument. There are endless opportunities for pupils to perform in concerts or recitals throughout the year, and Chapel services, form assemblies and school competitions provide occasions for public speaking and performance. Activities take place at lunchtime and after school, with a wide variety of extra-curricular clubs on offer. Breakfast club opens at 7.30 am, after-school care is available up to 6.00 pm, and an extensive school bus service is in operation.

Charitable status. Forest School, Essex is a Registered Charity, number 312677. The objective of the school is education.

Forres Sandle Manor

Sandleheath, Fordingbridge, Hampshire SP6 1NS
Tel: 01425 653181
Fax: 01425 655676
email: office@fsmschool.com
website: www.fsmschool.com

Headmaster: M N Hartley, BSc Hons, PGCE

Age Range. 3–13.
Number of Pupils. Prep: 162 (100 boarders, 94 boys, 68 girls). Pre-Prep: 58 (all are day children, 33 boys, 25 girls).
Fees per term (2014–2015). Boarders: £7,192 (Years 4–8), £5,900 (Year 3); Day pupils: £5,268 (Years 4–8), £4,450 (Year 3), £2,800 (Years 1 & 2), £2,670 (Reception). Early Years Education Entitlement provider.

At Forres Sandle Manor, we believe that "Happy Children Succeed".

You may imagine, with a line like that, Forres Sandle Manor (or FSM as we are known) is some kind of holiday club dedicated to keep the children smiling and entertained. However, this is a surface sort of happiness. The sort of happiness FSM means comes from knowing that you are liked and respected by your peers and your teachers. It comes from knowing that no matter what your skills and talents, or indeed your lack of them, you will be helped and supported to do the best that you can in order to reach your own particular star.

From the Nursery all the way up to Year 8 there are many stars at FSM. Naturally there are those who excel in particular areas of the curriculum or indeed one of the many extra-curricular activities, and these children are enrolled into our Gifted and Talented Programme. Some of these children may also attend the fabulous, nationally renowned, Learning Support Centre which also provides essential support for those who learn differently when and where required. Not all children are all-rounders after all.

At FSM each and every child is supported by our skills based, creative curriculum which allows every single child to contribute to the plans of what they will be learning as a class. We believe that it is only when children have some ownership of their learning that they are able to fully engage with it so that it is meaningful and relevant to them

None of this happens by accident. FSM have exceptional resources; at the heart of the school is the manor house, which is surrounded by 35 acres of playing fields, woods and streams. Our facilities are the same as you would expect to find at a leading prep school; an astro pitch, a multi-purpose sports and performance hall, our Forest School, a 25-metre heated swimming pool as well as much more! Our most important resource, however, is our staff. The teachers at FSM are passionate about what they do and in all areas they actively seek out and nurture raw talent in whatever field that may be.

Life at FSM starts at the Pre-Prep, where children can join the Nursery during the half-term when they turn 3. The first years of school are vital and it's fundamental that they are of the very highest standard. It is at this time that children learn how to learn; that their curiosity is harnessed through meaningful and purposeful play and that they develop the neural pathways that will serve them for the rest of their lives. It is in these valuable years that a child's dispositions and attitudes to learning are developed and that children learn to take risks, to persevere, to explore and to ask questions, as well as the social and communication skills which can only develop through being with others.

FSM provides an environment which nurtures and encourages the developing child at this special time in their lives. We don't believe in hot-housing. We feel that's the way to produce rapid, but weak growth. Instead we allow children the most precious thing of all – time. It is only through sustained, active learning, that a child is able to become absorbed, make connections to past experiences, develop higher order thinking skills and truly learn.

The Music school produces amazing results and every child is encouraged to try an instrument and experience performance in many different areas. Drama is timetabled for all children from Year 3 and above. We encourage all the children to get up and perform as often as they can. It's a fantastic way of building up their self-confidence and by the time they get to Year 8, standing up in front of an audience becomes second nature.

FSM's sporting reputation is becoming stronger every term. All children play sport every afternoon in our beautiful grounds; the recent addition of an astroturf has seen the standard in Hockey reach dizzying heights. The U11 Boys team, in 2012, scooped three successive tournament titles in as many weeks and the children often represent us nationally.

Academically, FSM leads the way in its innovative approach to teaching. Many of the techniques used here have now been adopted by Prep Schools across the country and we are justifiably proud of the fact that every Year 8 has always been successful in achieving their first choice senior school. Always! Not only that, but the children win more than their fair share of scholarships and awards. We spend much time liaising with senior schools, children and parents to ensure that we match the child to the senior school, academically, pastorally, creatively, on the sports field and socially. As we are not a feeder school, we have the freedom to do just that – the children come first.

Much of the family atmosphere surrounding the school comes from the fact that at its heart, FSM is a boarding school; almost two thirds of the children in Years 3 to 8 are full or weekly boarders, and we have a waiting list of children eager to try! The recent Ofsted report supports our claim to have 'the Best Boarding House in the World' by grading it as "outstanding". The level of care shown by the pastoral team isn't just saved for the boarders though. The Senior Houseparent, and her team, extend their support not only to all the children but their parents as well. There is no segmentation between day children and boarders. Day children can also take part in the numerous hobbies and activities on offer at the end of the school day and we often invite our day children in to join in our legendary Wednesday nights; our boarders also get invited out to stay with day children at the weekends.

FSM excels in their care of children from HM Forces families as well as other overseas based families and have done for many, many years. We always have a large number of children staying in at the weekend who look forward to the planned activities as well as having a bit of "chill time"! The school office is excellent at, and very used to, handling any overseas travel arrangements.

FSM now offer several scholarships each year for children entering the school at Year 3 and Year 7 as well as a number of means-tested bursaries.

It is difficult to single out any one particular area and be able to say that FSM excels in this or that; perhaps this is where the uniqueness of FSM lies. We hope that to really get a feel for the school, you will come and visit us and as you walk around the beautiful manor house and amazing grounds you will also think that, actually, "Happy Children Succeed" isn't a clever advertising gimmick after all. It really is at the heart of everything we do.

Charitable status. Forres Sandle Manor Education Trust Ltd is a Registered Charity, number 284260. It exists to provide first-class education for boys and girls.

Fosse Bank School

Mountains Country House, Noble Tree Road, Hildenborough, Kent TN11 8ND
Tel: 01732 834212
Fax: 01732 834884
email: admissions@fossebankschool.co.uk
website: www.fossebankschool.co.uk

Chair of Governors: Mrs Vicky Grimshaw

Headmistress: **Miss Alison Cordingley**, LTCL, PGCE, NPQH

Admissions & Marketing Officer: Mrs Nicki Mulligan

Age Range. 3–11 Co-educational.
Number of Pupils. 74.
Fees per term (2014–2015). £538–£3,681.
Founded in 1892, Fosse Bank School and Kindergarten (available from the term in which the child turns 3 years old) offers an excellent academic education combined with a

truly supportive, friendly and stimulating environment in which your child can learn, grow and flourish. Our school has a positive ethos which celebrates success and encourages each child to be the best that they can be. The importance of good manners is emphasised and our children have a reputation for being confident, articulate and well-behaved. The school has a strong family community and is located in a beautiful Grade II listed building, only 10 minutes' walk from Hildenborough Station, within 26 acres of parkland and boasting a range of wonderful facilities including a state-of-the-art ICT Suite, indoor heated swimming pool, tennis courts, sports hall and extremely well-resourced Kindergarten. There are extensive playing fields and wooded areas with a pond for field-studies, and ample, safe parking.

Academic Studies. In the Kindergarten and Foundation Stage we give the children a solid foundation based on the Early Years Foundations Stage Profile. Further up the school, we follow and extend the National Curriculum, offering broad, enriched learning experiences. ICT, Music, PE and French are taught by specialists so that high standards are achieved in all subject areas and the children are given frequent opportunities to perform and share their talents. Our children achieve excellent academic results accepting offers of places at selective state and independent schools every year, including scholarships to Sevenoaks School and Walthamstow Hall. Our Kent 11+ results are excellent.

Extra-Curricular. A wealth of activities are available after school for all children, such as sewing, cross-country running, ballet, football, choir, iPad Club, Lego and construction and many others. We also have a dynamic after-school care facility, the Phoenix Club which provides top-quality childcare from 3.30 to 6.00 pm.

Entry Procedure. Fosse Bank is not academically selective at entry, although the Headmistress reserves the right to make a decision as to whether the applicant's learning needs can be managed within the School's normal provision. All children are required to attend a Taster Day before a place may be offered.

Charitable status. Fosse Bank New School is a Registered Charity, number 1045435.

Friends' Junior School

Mount Pleasant Road, Saffron Walden, Essex CB11 3EB
Tel: 01799 525351
Fax: 01799 523808
email: admissions@friends.org.uk (Years 3–6)
           adminjs@friends.org.uk (Nursery-Year 2)
website: www.friends.org.uk

Clerk to the Board of Governors: Sue Garratt

Head: **Ruth Darvill**, BEd Cantab

Age Range. 3–11 Co-educational.
Number of Pupils. 111.
Fees per term (2014–2015). £2,375–£3,405 inc. lunch. Nursery: £21 per am session, £15 per pm session, £37 all day inc. lunch. £42.50 all day with before and after school care.

Friends' Junior School opened in 1992 and has grown from small beginnings to a thriving school in the heart of Saffron Walden. The school prides itself on its Quaker roots and a strong sense of community, combined with a friendly, family feel.

Children are nurtured, supported and encouraged to reach their full potential in all aspects of school life. They are encouraged to stretch themselves to ensure they produce their very best results both in academic and pastoral pursuits. Our aim is to foster a real love of learning and thirst for knowledge that will see them through their whole school career and beyond.

The high teacher/pupil ratio delivers a broad and balanced curriculum, enhanced by the use of Senior School facilities and expertise. This includes French from age 3 and Spanish as an additional language from Year 5 (age 9/10).

Music and sport opportunities are abundant at Friends' and there is an extensive range of extra-curricular activities, including chess, cookery, Latin, orchestra, choir, drama, journalism, football, netball, hockey, cross country and cricket.

The school has outstanding facilities, including an indoor swimming pool, a floodlit all-weather mini Astroturf pitch, hard tennis/netball courts, grass tennis courts and is set in extensive grounds, including our own Forest School which every child attends at least twice a term.

Charitable status. Friends' School Saffron Walden is a Registered Charity, number 1000981.

The Froebelian School

Clarence Road, Horsforth, Leeds LS18 4LB
Tel: 0113 258 3047
Fax: 0113 258 0173
email: office@froebelian.co.uk
website: www.froebelian.com

Chair of Governors: Mr R Naru, BSc, MCOptom

Headmaster: **Mr J Tranmer**, MA, PGCE, FCollP

Age Range. 3+ to 11+ years (3–4 years half days, optional afternoons).
Number of Pupils. 183 (83 boys, 100 girls).
Fees per term (2014–2015). £1,480–£2,210. Compulsory extras for full-time pupils, such as lunches and swimming, amount to approximately £225 per term.

Bursaries (income-related fee reduction) may be available.

Religious Affiliation: Christian, non-denominational.

Entry Requirements: Interview and assessment; written tests for older children.

Entry is usually at 3+, but limited places are sometimes available throughout the school.

Every child is respected as an individual and pupils are encouraged to reach their full potential in the purposeful atmosphere of this caring, disciplined school. High standards are achieved in all areas of the school – academic work, creative arts, music, sport, behaviour and manners. Early progress in language and mathematics is sustained and broadened in the junior curriculum, which includes French, information and design technology, drama and outdoor pursuits.

The school enjoys an envied reputation for success in entrance and scholarship examinations at 11+. Froebelian is the only school in Leeds to appear consistently in The Sunday Times list of 'Top 100' schools. A flourishing Parent Teacher Association supports the school and a growing database helps to keep former pupils in touch.

Situated to the north-west of Leeds, and close to Bradford, the school is well served by major transport links. 'Wrap-around' care is available from 7.30 am to 6.00 pm in the form of Breakfast Club, Little Acorns and Homework and Activities Club and there is a holiday club during the summer break.

Charitable status. The Froebelian School is a Registered Charity, number 529111. It exists to provide education of the highest quality at affordable fee levels.

Garden House School

Turk's Row, London SW3 4TW
Tel: 020 7730 1652 (Girls)
            020 7730 6652 (Boys)
email: info@gardenhouseschool.co.uk
website: www.gardenhouseschool.co.uk

Principal: Mrs J K Oddy

Headmistress – Upper School: **Mrs Charlotte Crofton**
Headmistress – Lower School: **Mrs Wendy Challen**, CertEd Froebel
Headmaster – Boys' School: **Mr Christian Warland**, BA Hons

Age Range. 3–11 Girls, 3–11 Boys.
Number of Pupils. 290 girls, 208 boys, taught in single-sex classes.
Fees per term (2014–2015). Kindergarten £4,180, Reception–Year 6 £6,500–£6,700. There is a 10% reduction for siblings.
Buildings and facilities. The School is housed in a charming, light and airy listed building. Original artwork hangs in every classroom, and facilities include libraries for different age groups, a ballet/performance/drama hall and dedicated science and art rooms.

The school has its own garden within the grounds of the Royal Hospital where children enjoy science lessons and attend a Gardening Club.

School drama productions are ambitiously staged at the Royal Court Theatre in Sloane Square.

Aims, ethos and values. Garden House provides a thorough and balanced education in a lively and purposeful environment. Our children achieve high academic results in a calm and constructive manner, being encouraged to have inquiring and independent minds. Emphasis is placed not only on academic, sporting and artistic ability but on manners and consideration to others. Our Kindness Code is adhered to and constantly re-emphasised.

Curriculum. Literacy, Numeracy, Science, History, Geography, Religious Education, French (from Kindergarten), Latin, ICT, PSCHE, Art, Drama, Singing and Music, Dancing, Fencing and Physical Education (netball, tennis, rounders, gymnastics, swimming, athletics, cricket, hockey, pop lacrosse, rugby and football). We have many sports squads, sports clubs and matches. Children with learning difficulties are catered for in small groups, taught by two full-time and many visiting specialist teachers. 80% of children learn at least one musical instrument. The school runs four choirs and a chamber orchestra.

A diverse range of early morning and after-school clubs include Chess, Mandarin, Sculpture, Taekwondo and Touch-Typing.

Benefiting from our central London location, visits to museums, galleries and churches form an essential part of the curriculum, as do annual field study and outward bound trips. Girls spend a week in France after CE and boys enjoy a camping expedition. The choir sings in Canterbury Cathedral.

School Successes. Girls are prepared for the Common Entrance, with the majority leaving for the premier girls' schools, 60% to leading London senior schools, 40% to major boarding schools. Some boys leave us at 8, having been well prepared for entrance to leading London prep schools and 10% to top boarding preps. Other boys remain at Garden House, being educated to the age of 11. Our children achieve several scholarships each year.

Entrance. We encourage you to visit the school. Girls and boys join Garden House in the September after they reach 3 or 4 years of age. An Application Form can be obtained from the School Office and once completed, and returned with the relevant fee, your child's name is placed on the waiting list. Entry interview is held one year before entry. We look forward to welcoming you and your children to Garden House School.

Gatehouse School

Sewardstone Road, Victoria Park, London E2 9JG
Tel: 020 8980 2978
Fax: 020 8983 1642
email: admin@gatehouseschool.co.uk
website: www.gatehouseschool.co.uk

Headmaster: **Mr Robert Francis**

Age Range. 3–11 Co-educational.
Number in School. 381 Day Pupils.
Fees per term (2014–2015). £2,580–£3,180.
Gatehouse School is an Independent Co-educational School for girls and boys aged 3 to 11.

Founded by Phyllis Wallbank, in May 1948, in the gatehouse of St Bartholomew, the Great Priory Church near Smithfield London, the School was a pioneer of much that is now generally accepted in education. Gatehouse is based on the Wallbank plan whose guiding principle is that children of any race, colour, creed, background and intellect shall be accepted as pupils and work side by side without streaming or any kind of segregation with the aim that each child shall get to know and love God, and develop their own uniqueness of personality, to enable them to appreciate the world and the world to appreciate them.

Gatehouse is now located in Sewardstone Road close to Victoria Park and continues to follow this philosophy.

The Nursery is accommodated in a large sunny space with its own outdoor play area. They follow a balanced curriculum of child-initiated and teacher-led activities.

Lower Juniors are taught most subjects by their own qualified teacher and assistant, but have French, PE and Music with a specialist teacher.

In Upper Juniors from the age of 7, teaching is by subject and is conducted by a highly qualified specialist staff. This is a special feature of Gatehouse and gives children from an early age, contact with subject specialists, not available to many children until secondary school.

Our classes average around 22 pupils.

We send children to schools such as City of London boys and girls, Forest, Bancroft's and Highgate, often with scholarships.

Charitable status. Gatehouse Educational Trust Limited is a Registered Charity, number 282558.

Gayhurst School

Bull Lane, Gerrards Cross, Bucks SL9 8RJ
Tel: 01753 882690
Fax: 01753 887451
email: gayhurst@gayhurstschool.co.uk
website: www.gayhurstschool.co.uk

Chair of Governors: Mrs C Shorten Conn

Headmaster: **Mr A Sims**, MA Cantab

Age Range. 3–11 Co-educational.
Number of Children. 353.
Fees per term (2014–2015). £3,460–£4,400 (inclusive of lunch). Nursery: £27–£60 per session.
Gayhurst is a happy, thriving and vibrant independent preparatory school for girls and boys aged 3–11. For over

100 years the school has endeavoured to bring out the best in every child in its care by focusing on individual talents and supporting children to achieve their full potential. Since becoming co-educational in 2008, Gayhurst has built a reputation as a family school, providing first-class co-education in Gerrards Cross.

Life at Gayhurst is engaging and exciting with regular activities organised to enrich the education of its pupils. Children are encouraged to participate in sport, with a busy programme of fixtures against other schools. Creativity is evident throughout the school with opportunities to learn an instrument, become a member of one of the many musical ensembles or take part in the annual year group drama productions. There are also numerous visits to places of interest on both day and residential trips.

Gayhurst strives to ensure that pupils are given every opportunity to achieve the best start in life. The school's commitment to continual improvement and development means that the children benefit greatly from the facilities offered on the school's five acre site, including IT rooms, Science laboratories, woodland adventure playground and an all-weather AstroTurf.

Pupils consistently achieve strong academic results progressing to both local Grammar Schools and to Senior Schools, day and boarding, in the Independent sector.

"Our aims are clear," explains Headmaster Andrew Sims, "we provide a wide range of opportunities in music, drama, art and on the playing fields as well as through the curriculum. We want every girl and boy to discover and develop their particular talents and support them wholeheartedly in their aspirations for the future."

For more information about the school, or to arrange a visit, please contact the Registrar on 01753 279140 or email registrar@gayhurstschool.co.uk.

Charitable status. Gayhurst School Trust is a Registered Charity, number 298869.

Giggleswick Junior School

Giggleswick, Settle, North Yorkshire BD24 0DG
Tel: 01729 893100
Fax: 01729 893150
email: juniorschool@giggleswick.org.uk
website: www.giggleswick.org.uk

Chairman of Governors: Mrs H J Hancock, LVO, MA

Head: **M Brotherton**, BEd Hons, NPQH

Age Range. 3–11 Co-educational.
Number of Pupils. 80.
Fees per term (2014–2015). Boarders (Years 5–6): £6,205 (full), £4,787 (3-night flexi). Day Pupils: £2,329–£3,726.

Giggleswick Junior School offers a co-educational day and boarding education within a secure, happy, family atmosphere. Day pupils are fully integrated into the life and ethos of the school. The Head and his family live on site and the Boarding Housemaster and his family live in the boarding house. There is an experienced team of academic staff and matrons to care for the children.

In its inspection report published February 2010, ISI adjudged both the Junior School and its Early Years Unit as '*outstanding*' in every category and subheading, stating, "*The school prepares pupils extremely well for the next stage of their education through an outstanding educational experience and through outstanding teaching*".

There is a clear sense of purpose and development. Facilities are excellent: the Junior School and its Early Years Unit share a bright, modern, purpose-designed building with a full range of facilities, set within extensive grounds and playing fields. In addition to sharing the Senior School's

swimming pool, Chapel, Food Technology and Design Centre, and all-weather pitch, the Junior School has its own purpose-built sports hall. Our ICT facilities, including email and supervised internet access, are constantly upgraded. The modern dining room serves particularly good food. The great majority of pupils progress to Giggleswick (*see HMC entry*).

In the centre of Britain, in the Yorkshire Dales, Giggleswick is within 75 minutes' drive of Manchester and Leeds, their airports and railway stations. Airport transfers are organised. The School also provides morning and evening bus services from Skipton, Grassington, Colne and Kirkby Lonsdale for the benefit of Day pupils.

Music and drama are integral to school life, as is participation in major team and individual sports and outdoor pursuits. The annual drama production is a highlight of the school year and involves all pupils from Year 1 through to Year 6. Pupils with particular educational needs are offered private individual or group lessons with the on-site specialists.

Visits and "taster" stays are warmly encouraged and contribute to new pupils' sense of involvement while part of the living school.

Charitable status. Giggleswick School is a Registered Charity, number 1109826. It exists to provide education for boys and girls.

Glebe House School

Cromer Road, Hunstanton, Norfolk PE36 6HW
Tel: 01485 532809
Fax: 01485 533900
email: ghsoffice@glebehouseschool.co.uk
website: www.glebehouseschool.co.uk
Twitter: @GlebeHS

Chairman of the Governors: Mr Lloyd Sandy

Headmaster: **Mr John Crofts**, BA, PGCE

Age Range. 6 months to 13 years.
Number of Children. 42 Boys, 46 Girls, Nursery 95.
Fees per term (2014–2015). Prep £4,640; Pre-Prep £3,095. Weekly boarding: £300–£765 (1–4 nights).

Glebe House School and Nursery was founded in 1874 as a preparatory school and is surrounded by 12 acres of playing fields.

The Junior School children are accommodated in a purpose-built building. The Senior School has specialist areas for all academic subjects and music, sport and drama are a significant part of a child's life at Glebe House. Our 25-metre indoor heated swimming pool, astroturf pitch for hockey, tennis and netball, adventure playground, gym, music school and performance hall all help to ensure that the core academic subjects are supported by a balanced and stimulating curriculum. Lessons finish at 3.30 pm (Pre-Prep), 4.10 pm (Prep) but breakfast club, after-school activities, cooked tea and supervised prep provide day care from 7.30 am to 6.30 pm.

Aims and Values. At the heart of Glebe House is our emphasis on supporting and valuing the individual. We encourage the traditional values of courtesy, consideration for others, self discipline and a desire to contribute to society.

Academic Life. We are committed to the achievement of high academic standards, harnessing the best of modern educational practice. Class sizes remain small and every child is encouraged to achieve their full potential. Close supervision, with one-to-one support where necessary, is maintained and progress is carefully monitored through regular standardised testing and classroom assessments. The broad curriculum both incorporates and exceed national requirements, including offering a second modern language in addition to French from year six. Glebe House enjoys a high success rate at Common Entrance and in Independent Scholarship Examinations and with this solid foundation our pupils move confidently on to a wide range of senior schools.

Sport and Activities. We offer a wide sporting programme aimed to encourage fitness and a healthy enjoyment of sport that will remain with the children for life. Rugby, hockey and cricket are the main sports for boys and hockey, netball and rounders for girls. We also encourage involvement in many activities including athletics, cross country, football, golf, swimming and tennis. The lunchtime and after-school activity programme is varied and includes sporting, dramatic, artistic and musical groups as well as others such as Mandarin Chinese. We offer a wide range of activities during the summer holidays, including ball sports, swimming, craft, music and drama workshops, tennis, and sailing.

Pastoral Care and Boarding. Relations between children and staff are respectful but relaxed and the children know they are free to talk to all staff, one of the great advantages of a school this size. All pupils belong to one of three houses and have a tutor who sees them each morning and is the first point of contact for parents. Good communication is crucial and we operate an open door policy to parents. The school offers 35 weekly boarding places and flexibility in choosing from one to four nights.

Travel. Our minibus picks up in the morning and takes home at 4.15 pm and 6 pm to Kings Lynn and surrounding areas.

Further Information. Prospective parents and children are most welcome to contact the School Administrator to meet the Headmaster and tour the school.

Charitable status. Glebe House School Trust Limited is a Registered Charity, number 1018815.

The Gleddings Preparatory School

Birdcage Lane, Savile Park, Halifax, West Yorkshire HX3 0JB
Tel: 01422 354605
Fax: 01422 356263
email: TheGleddings@aol.com
website: www.TheGleddings.co.uk

Headmistress: **Mrs P J Wilson**, CBE

Age Range. 3–11 Co-educational.
Number of Pupils. 194: 98 Boys, 96 Girls.
Fees per term (2014–2015). £2,210.
"The Gleddings is very special. It is precious to several generations of families in the locality and beyond. We are now educating the children of our past pupils. We consider it a great privilege to do so.

The staff and I remember, all of the time, the trust that parents bestow in us. We promise our best efforts for every child.

Our academic results speak for themselves but The Gleddings is about much more. We develop self-discipline, self-respect and confidence within The Gleddings' unique "YOU CHOOSE" ethos. We encourage children to THINK! and to learn how to learn."
Jill Wilson, Headteacher.

The Godolphin Preparatory School

Laverstock Road, Salisbury, Wiltshire SP1 2RB
Tel: 01722 430652
Fax: 01722 430651
email: prep@godolphin.wilts.sch.uk
website: www.godolphinprep.org

Chairman of the Governors: M J Nicholson, Esq

Headmistress: **Miss J Miller**, BA, MEd

Age Range. 3–11.
Number of Pupils. 85 Day Girls.
Fees per term (2014–2015). Full Boarding £7,234, 5-day Boarding £6,177, 3-day Boarding £5,367; Day: Years 4–6 £3,997, Year 3 £3,181, Years 1–2 £2,076, Reception £2,069.

Godolphin Prep is a purpose-built, compact school for girls aged from three to eleven. It is a mainstream academic school which focuses on the strengths of its pupils, values their potential as individuals and nurtures the girls to become caring members of society.

Many of the varied visitors to the school comment on the friendly atmosphere which they encounter. It is within such an environment that the girls are encouraged to have high expectations, good work habits and an active desire to take advantage of all that is on offer to them. Early specialist teaching across the curriculum is available from the age of 7, taught by people who are both dedicated and enthusiastic about their subjects. The high standard of teaching is reflected in the National Curriculum assessment results, as well as the scholarship awards gained by a significant number of pupils at eleven. There is an ambience of learning which comes from the 'work hard–play hard' ethic.

Courtesy and good manners are an implicit part of daily life at Godolphin; the basic precept is *'Never be the cause of another's unhappiness'*.

The school opened in 1993 as a part of the development plan of the Godolphin School. Following an inspection in 1996, which resulted in IAPS accreditation and then Department for Education registration two years later, the Prep has continued to thrive.

Godolphin Prep is a day school where outside interests are encouraged and weekends are perceived as family time, however, there is a programme of after-school activities which creates opportunities for those who travel considerable distances to school by bus. This arrangement offers an element of choice which ensures that the girls develop as well-balanced individuals. Godolphin Prep introduced boarding for Years five and six in September 2011. Girls are accommodated in bright and cheerful rooms and benefit from a tailor-made enrichment programme. There is also be a Breakfast club for day girls.

About 60% of the pupils move to the Godolphin School, following Common Entrance. Others move to boarding schools slightly farther afield or transfer to the local girls' grammar school.

Charitable status. The Godolphin School is a Registered Charity, number 309488. Its object is to provide and conduct in or near Salisbury a boarding and day school for girls.

Godstowe Preparatory School

Shrubbery Road, High Wycombe, Bucks HP13 6PR
Tel: 01494 529273
            01494 429006 Registrar
Fax: 01494 429009

email: schooloffice@godstowe.org
website: www.godstowe.org
Facebook: Godstowe-Preparatory-School

Motto: *Finem Respice*
Founded 1900.

Chairman of the Governors: K Allner, BA Econ

Headmaster: Mr David Gainer, BEd Hons London

Age Range. Girls 3–13, Boys 3–7.
Number of Pupils. Preparatory: 307 (boarding and day). Pre-Preparatory: 118.
Fees per term (2014–2015). Boarders £7,080, Day Children £3,090–£4,820. Nursery: £1,395–£2,790.

The School. Since its foundation in 1900, Godstowe Preparatory School has been at the forefront of education. It has a distinguished tradition as the first British boarding preparatory school for girls, in a foundation that includes Wycombe Abbey, Benenden and St Leonards.

Today, Godstowe is a flourishing boarding and day school with 416 pupils, enjoying an unparalleled academic reputation. It has a Pre-Prep department for boys and girls aged between three and seven, and a Preparatory School for girls from seven to thirteen years old. Class sizes are small allowing children to benefit from individual attention.

A new multi-purpose sports hall as well as a theatre and drama suite have recently been completed. The school recently underwent an independent inspection and was regarded as outstanding in every respect.

Academic Record. Godstowe enjoys an excellent and unparalleled academic reputation amongst British independent schools. Despite its non-selective entry policy, Godstowe consistently achieves unrivalled academic results. An average of 20 scholarships have been won each year for the last five years. By the age of nine, pupils are taught by specialists in 16 subjects across the curriculum. Language teaching includes French, Spanish and Latin. Sport, ICT, art and music are all outstandingly taught within first-rate facilities.

Boarding. Girls' boarding life is focused within three houses in the grounds, one of which is a dedicated junior house. Each has three resident staff and a warm and supportive atmosphere. A combination of professional and caring staff and beautifully refurbished accommodation ensures a safe and relaxing environment. Each house has its own garden and tennis court, reinforcing the feeling of 'going home' at the end of the school day. Weekends are packed full of activity and fun, with many weekly boarders often choosing to stay at School for the weekend.

The **Enrichment Curriculum** is an extended school day from 7.30 am to 7.00 pm, with some 50 after-school activities scheduled each week. The 'E-Curriculum' gives children the chance to try many exciting and challenging new pursuits including poetry writing, rock climbing, watersports, football and debating. In addition, supervised homework sessions are offered every evening. Day children may join the boarders for breakfast and supper. Other than those sessions supervised by outside instructors all activities are offered free of charge. An Enrichment programme is also in place for Pre-Prep children.

Charitable status. The Godstowe Preparatory School Company Limited is a Registered Charity, number 310637. It exists to provide education and training for young girls and boys.

Grace Dieu Manor School

Grace Dieu, Thringstone, Leics LE67 5UG
Tel: 01530 222276
Fax: 01530 223184

email: registrar@gracedieu.com
website: www.gracedieu.com

Chairman of Governors: Mrs C Armitage

Headmaster: Mr P S Fisher, BA Hons, MA, PGCE

Age Range. 3–13 Co-educational.
Number of Pupils. 270: Pre-Prep 93, Seniors 177.
Fees per term (2014–2015). £2,724–£3,884.

Grace Dieu is a modern, vibrant, Catholic, co-educational day school for pupils aged 3 to 13; a happy school where children are encouraged to work hard, play hard and care for each other.

The purpose-built area designed specifically for our 3–7 year olds provides an inspiring, fun and safe environment. Classrooms are bright and colourful and provide easy access to a spacious and secure outdoor area. Small class sizes and a team of qualified teachers and nursery nurses ensure that children have an outstanding start to their education.

A warm, family atmosphere based upon Christian values and traditions welcomes families, whatever their denomination or faith. Staff share a close interest and involvement in the development of every child and experience shows pupils and parents very quickly become part of the school family.

The academic life of the school is central and outstanding results in Key Stage tests and senior school entry exams are evidence of this. A broad range of natural ability is welcomed and celebrated at Grace Dieu. Inspirational teaching, combined with small class sizes, provides an environment where rigorous demands are made of the intellectually gifted while practical support and encouragement are offered to those who are less able. In the older year groups teaching is carried out almost exclusively by subject specialists delivering a diverse and stimulating timetable. This specialism filters down to the younger age groups as well, providing a unique richness of academic experience.

Pupils find many opportunities for fun and friendship. Grace Dieu offers ample space for pupils to participate in the full range of team games on our sports fields, in our indoor heated swimming pool and in our sports hall Weekly sporting fixtures give pupils opportunity to compete locally and nationally. Situated in 120 acres of beautiful grounds in the heart of the Leicestershire countryside.

The arts are a key part to Grace Dieu life, and regular music and drama performances feature in the termly diary.

After-school activities are offered and these greatly enrich the lives of the children. Working parents will be delighted to know that children may be cared for from 8 am until 6 pm.

Charitable status. Grace Dieu Manor School is a Registered Charity, number 1115976.

The Grange
Monmouth Preparatory School

Hadnock Road, Monmouth NP25 3NG
Tel: 01600 715930
email: thegrange@monmouthschool.org
website: www.habs-monmouth.org

Chairman of Governors: J B S Swallow, MA, FCA

Head: Mrs E G Thomas, BA

Age Range. 7–11.
Number of Pupils. 129 boys.
Fees per term (2014–2015). Day £3,317, Boarding £6,239.

The Grange provides the friendliness and close pastoral care of a small school together with the outstanding resources of a large school through its association with

Monmouth School, a Haberdashers' school for boys aged 11 to 18. There are also strong links with the other schools in the area belonging to the family of Haberdashers' Monmouth Schools – Haberdashers' Agincourt School (for boys and girls aged 3 to 7), Inglefield House (for girls aged 7 to 11) and Haberdashers' Monmouth School for Girls (for girls aged 11 to 18). In their final year at The Grange boys take the General Entry Assessment for Monmouth School. Almost without exception there is a 100% pass rate and a significant number of boys gain scholarships and other awards – academic, music and sport. A wide and very popular extra-curricular programme combines with high academic achievement to provide a vibrant and stimulating educational experience. In 2011 independent research carried out by RSAcademics showed that the school was one of the very best they had surveyed in terms of how highly the parents regarded the school. Details are on the website.

Aims. The aims of The Grange are to provide an excellent education as the foundation for future achievement and to develop personal qualities of confidence, independence and social conscience.

Location. In February 2009 The Grange moved into brand new purpose-built premises on a Monmouth School site, situated next to Monmouth School Sports Complex with its own 25-metre swimming pool.

Facilities. Its new building has light, spacious, well-equipped classrooms, each of which opens out onto the play area, as well as a large hall, library, art studio, science laboratory, computer suite, music room and music studios. The Grange also has its own newly-equipped kitchens. The grounds provide a safe, spacious area for recreation, games and outdoor projects. In addition, The Grange shares the facilities of Monmouth School which include the School Chapel, large playing fields (25 acres), Sports Complex, new Sports Pavilion, Drama Studio and Performing Arts Centre – the Blake Theatre.

Staffing. 8 full-time and 9 part-time staff teach the 8 classes, in addition to peripatetic teachers and specialist coaches for extra-curricular activities.

Curriculum. The curriculum is broad and varied and takes account of, though is not constrained by, the National Curriculum. Subjects include English, Mathematics, Science, Information and Communication Technology, History, Geography, Religious Education, Art, Design Technology, Music, Physical Education, Games, Drama and French. There is subject specialist teaching throughout. A part-time learning support teacher provides extra help on an individual or small group basis for boys who would benefit from it.

Extra-Curricular Activities. There is a full programme of activities which take place both in the lunch break and after school. These vary slightly according to the season though in any one year would normally include rugby, football, cricket, tennis, swimming, golf, cross-country running, string orchestra, wind band, choir, fencing, art, gardening, modern foreign languages, computing and chess. There is a good record of boys playing at county and national level in rugby, cricket, fencing and chess.

Entry. Entry is usually at 7+ following assessment, though due to the larger new premises recruitment is currently across all year groups.

Charitable status. William Jones's Schools Foundation is a Registered Charity, number 525616. Its aims and objectives are to provide an all-round education for boys and girls at reasonable fees.

Grange Park Preparatory School

13 The Chine, Grange Park, London N21 2EA
Tel: 020 8360 1469
Fax: 020 8360 4869

email: office@gpps.org.uk
website: www.gpps.org.uk

Day School for Girls.

Chair of Governors: Mr Nigel Barnes

Headteacher: Mrs Bernadette McLaughlin, BA Ed Hons

Age Range. 4–11.
Number of Girls. 95.
Fees per term (2014–2015). £3,150.
Grange Park Preparatory School is a long established, happy and successful school that provides a broad and stimulating education. It is situated in the pleasant residential area of Grange Park.

Hidden behind what was once a residential house lies a purpose-built school with excellent facilities for the modern curriculum, including a fully-equipped ICT suite and facilities for science, art and design technology. There are two libraries, one for KS1 and the other for KS2. The younger children are taught PE and games within the school grounds. Years 5 and 6 make use of off-site facilities for netball and rounders/athletics. From Year 3 girls swim at a local pool.

Classes are small and the school has an excellent reputation for pastoral care and for nurturing the individual child.

We have a very broad curriculum and encourage excellence throughout, academically, in sport, art, dance and drama and in music.

In KS1 the children are taught mostly by form teachers with specialist teaching being introduced gradually in KS2. From Year 1 specialist teachers teach games, French, music and dance. Individual music tuition is available.

The girls are taught by experienced and well qualified staff.

The curriculum is enriched by a comprehensive programme of visits, which take advantage of the artistic and cultural opportunities of London, as well as local facilities for field studies. A ski trip takes place annually and Year 6 girls go on an outdoor pursuits weekend.

Girls are prepared for examinations for a wide range of secondary schools, both selective state schools and independent schools.

The school has a healthy eating policy. Lunches are cooked in school using only fresh ingredients. No processed food is used. There is always a vegetarian option and salads and fresh fruit are available daily.

The school is non-selective and places in Reception are offered after the Head has met with parents and daughters. Children taking up chance vacancies in other classes will be invited to spend a day in school to ensure they will fit into the class successfully.

Charitable status. Grange Park Preparatory School is a Registered Charity, number 268328.

The Granville School

2 Bradbourne Park Road, Sevenoaks, Kent TN13 3LJ
Tel: 01732 453039
Fax: 01732 743634
email: secretary@granvilleschool.org
website: www.granvilleschool.org

Chairman of Governors: Mr J Sorrell

Headmistress: Mrs Jane Scott, BEd Hons Cantab

Age Range. Girls 3–11, Boys 3–5.
Number of Pupils. 200.
Fees per term (2014–2015). Nursery (mornings only) £1,685, Transition (all day) £2,896, Reception, Years 1 & 2

£3,412, Years 3 & 4 £3,859, Years 5 & 6 £4,348. Lunch included for Transition to Year 6.

Extras: Private Lessons: Pianoforte, Violin, Cello, Oboe, Clarinet, Flute £211 per term. Shared Lessons: Recorder £32.50, Ballet £63.50 per term.

The Granville School was founded on VE Day, 8th May 1945, with the Dove of Peace and Churchill's victory sign chosen to form the school crest.

The Granville is an exceptional school which combines the very best of a Prep school tradition with a vibrant, forward-looking outlook where change is embraced and innovation celebrated. Girls aged three to eleven, and boys aged three to four, thrive on individual attention and achieve their best in a happy, secure and stimulating environment. Our highly-qualified, specialist teachers make learning enjoyable, develop enquiring minds and raise levels of expectation.

The school maintains Christian principles and traditional values within a broad and stimulating curriculum. The Granville has a strong record of academic achievement and children are prepared for 11+ entry into independent schools and state grammar schools. Granville pupils excel in music, art, drama and sport. There is a wide range of extra-curricular activities available for all age groups and the school runs an early morning breakfast club.

The school is set in five acres of garden and woodland close to Sevenoaks Station. The original house and new buildings enable pupils to enjoy a high-quality learning environment with light and airy classrooms. The Granville has its own indoor heated Swimming Pool, a Sports Hall, Science Lab, Studio for Music and Drama, French rooms, ICT Suite, individual teaching rooms and Junior and Senior Libraries. A new building, opened in January 2014, provides high-quality Early Years facilities together with a large Art and DT room. Outside facilities include three netball/tennis courts, sports/playing field, junior activity playgrounds and a woodland classroom.

Means-tested bursaries are available on request.

Charitable status. The Ena Makin Educational Trust Limited is a Registered Charity, number 307931. Its aim is to run any school as an educational charity for the promotion of education generally.

fit from our family-centred community and are able to enjoy their first overseas boarding experience in a small, friendly, family atmosphere.

Outdoor activities include: Soccer, Rugby, Hockey, Cricket, Netball, Rounders, Tennis, Athletics, Swimming, Golf, Mountain Biking, Trampolining, Volleyball and Forest School.

Facilities include: gym, libraries, a computerised science laboratory, hall and dance/drama studio, indoor heated pool, extensive sports fields and an astro practice area. ICT facilities are in the main ICT suite and throughout the school. A range of clubs and activities are enjoyed and there are also regular visits to France for intensive language studies.

Children showing real potential in Art, Drama or Music are able to take advantage of excellence classes, a range of instruments are taught and with choirs and various ensemble groups, many children participate in festivals, sit musical exams and enjoy performing in concerts.

Drama is a timetabled subject and every child appears in a form play at some time during the year. LAMDA classes are also offered.

Art is a strength of the school; many children build up quality portfolios to take to their next school and scholarships are won regularly. The constantly changing displays throughout the school show both the quality of work and the children's enthusiasm for Art.

The Pre-Prep Department, for children aged 2–7, is housed in a walled garden area with plenty of space for play activities. The curriculum is delivered by well-qualified, enthusiastic form teachers with extra input from Prep School specialists in PE, music, swimming and drama.

The 'After-hours' club, for children from Nursery age upwards, enables parents to work a full day.

Boarding remains popular and many children take advantage of the flexible arrangements. Boarding facilities are in the Grade II listed House in small cosy dormitories. The Headmaster and his family together with other members of staff live in the House, giving the boarding community a very homely feeling.

The happiness and safety of our children remain priorities. This is supported by the ISI Inspection report that states that "*the quality of relationships between the pupils and staff is outstanding*".

Great Ballard

Eartham, Chichester, West Sussex PO18 0LR
Tel: 01243 814236
Fax: 01243 814586
email: office@greatballard.co.uk
website: www.greatballard.co.uk
Twitter: @greatballard

Headmaster: Mr Richard Morgan, BA, PGCE

Age Range. 2–13 co-educational.
Number of Children. 128: 70 Boys, 58 Girls (including 59 in Pre-Prep and approx 35 flexi boarders).
Fees per term (2014–2015). Day: Prep School £4,000–£4,550, Pre-Prep £2,600–£2,850. Boarding: Weekly (4 nights) £5,000, Full (7 nights) £7,000 Nursery: £30 (morning or afternoon), £35 (including lunch), £45 (all day including lunch). Boarding fees discounts for HM Forces.

The school is situated in 30 acres of wonderful countryside in the South Downs National Park between Chichester and Arundel.

Children prepare for the Common Entrance and Scholarship examinations to Independent Senior Schools, but the emphasis is on ensuring that children achieve to their potential both in and out of the classroom. The average number of children in a teaching group in the prep school is 14. Small numbers of International Students are welcomed who bene-

Great Walstead School

East Mascalls Lane, Lindfield, Haywards Heath, West Sussex RH16 2QL
Tel: 01444 483528
Fax: 01444 482122
email: admin@greatwalstead.co.uk
website: www.greatwalstead.co.uk
Twitter: @greatwalstead

Chairman of the Board of Governors: J Lee

Headmaster: C Baty, BEd, DipT, CPP Boarding Hons, NPQH

Deputy Head (Academic): S Smith MSc, BSc Hons, CertEd
Deputy Head (Pastoral): J Sutherland, BEd

Age Range. 2½–13.
Number of Pupils. 429: Main School 263; Pre-Prep 113; Nursery 53.
Fees per term (2014–2015). Tuition: EYFS £305–£2,405, Pre-Prep £2,915–£3,430, Main School £4,305–£4,685. Boarding (in addition to Tuition): £280–£915 (1–4 nights).

Founded in 1925 by Mr R J Mowll in Enfield, the school moved to its present location in the heart of Sussex two years later. Staff and pupils came to a large country house

set in over 260 acres of fields and woodland, where children could learn and play in unspoilt surroundings.

From these beginnings, Great Walstead has developed into a thriving co-educational prep school, catering for children from 2½ to 13 years of age. It is a school which values children as individuals and regards it as vital that each child develops his or her potential – academically, creatively, socially and spiritually. Above all, the school is built on the strong values of Christian Faith, Success, Communication, Environment and Dedication, creating an essential foundation for the whole of a pupil's education and life.

The Nursery welcomes children from the age of 2½ until it is time to enter the Pre-Prep at 4. It provides a full, rich and varied nursery education, laying firm foundations in basic skills and understanding for future learning.

The Pre-Prep covers the years from 4 to 7 within its own section of the school. It has its own library, ICT suite and play area. The aim here is to ensure that the foundation skills of reading, writing and maths are taught while, at the same time, teachers add a breadth of interest through specialist lead classes in French, computer skills, PE and Music.

Children enter the Junior School at 7. For the next two years they will have a class teacher who supervises them closely for a good proportion of the day, but have specialist teachers for French, music, ICT, art, craft, design technology, sport and PE. They have games or outdoor activities each day and gradually learn to become more independent.

Children in the senior age group, from 9 to 13 years of age, are taught by graduate specialist teachers in preparation for the Common Entrance examination and senior school scholarships at 13. In the past ten years, Great Walstead pupils have won over 200 scholarships or awards to senior schools and in the last four years over 50% of pupils gained such success. Facilities in the Senior School include two computer rooms with 21 linked PCs, a well-equipped science laboratory, and a fine Library.

The 269 acres of farmland, playing fields and woodland make many outdoor activities possible. The woods host learning activities in Eco-School and Forest School and fun exercises in camp-building, as well as teddy bear picnics for the younger children. In the summer, the older children camp out overnight. In addition, the purpose-built challenge course gives enormous pleasure all year round for all ages.

The Art, Craft and Design Technology department is housed in old farm buildings, which have been adapted to make workshops and studios. Lessons here form an integral part of the curriculum for all children.

The school's extensive grounds allow a wide range of sports, from rugby and hockey to cricket and rounders. Swimming is possible all year round in our own heated pool. We have a superbly equipped sports hall and facilities, which allow large numbers of both team and individual sports to be played.

The school has a Learning Development department where specialist staff are able to give the extra support required. The department helps children with all their learning needs whether helping with a specific difficulty or extending those children who are gifted and talented.

Music has long been a strength at Great Walstead, with a high proportion of the children learning instruments and playing in groups, bands and orchestras. Singing is encouraged from Nursery upwards. Drama is also an important part of the Arts here. All children are given the opportunity to act, with both major productions and form performances.

Great Walstead offers weekly boarding on a flexible basis (Monday to Thursday). The boarding areas provide a comfortable home under the care of a boarding family and assisted by other boarding staff. Matron, the school nurse, tends to the health of the children in the whole school. The school, through the Keep, provides flexible holiday, pre- and after-school care, as well as other holiday activities to meet the needs of today's parents.

Parents are always made most welcome at the school. There is a thriving parents' organisation called FOGWA (Friends of Great Walstead Association) which provides a number of successful social events and raises substantial sums for the benefit of the school.

Academic awards are offered at 7+, Academic, Music and Sports Scholarships at 9+, and Academic, All-Rounder, Art, Drama, Music, Performing Arts and Sport Scholarships at 11+.

Charitable status. Great Walstead School is a Registered Charity, number 307002. It exists to provide a good education on Christian foundations.

Greenfield

Brooklyn Road, Woking, Surrey GU22 7TP
Tel: 01483 772525
email: schooloffice@greenfield.surrey.sch.uk
website: www.greenfield.surrey.sch.uk

Chairman of Governors: Mrs Janet Day

Headteacher: **Mrs Tania Botting**, BEd

Age Range. 3–11 years.
Number of Pupils. 76 girls, 116 day boys.
Fees per term (2014–2015). £1,726–£4,041.

Greenfield is a non-selective co-educational school for children aged from rising 3 to 11 years. We aim to offer every possible opportunity for children to reach their full potential and recognise that all children have talents and strengths in many different areas. We are proud of our academic and non-academic successes and have a strong track record of achieving scholarships to a wide range of senior schools for music, art, sport, and academic excellence.

At Greenfield we believe that a happy child will learn. Therefore, we provide a secure and caring environment working closely with our parents, to enable the children to develop their confidence and self-esteem and prepare them for the next stage of their education and future.

We attach importance to traditional values, promoting courtesy, respect, tolerance, empathy, humility and consideration for others.

Greenfield has high standards but we also appreciate the need to strike a happy balance between work and play and the formal and informal. There is an excellent ratio of adults to children throughout the school enabling children to receive individual attention and children are often taught in small groups. Visitors are welcome to visit the school at any time and appointments can be made by calling the school office. To request a copy of the prospectus, please visit the school website or call the school office.

Charitable status. Greenfield is a Registered Charity, number 295145. It aims to offer an excellent all-round education to children of all abilities.

Gresham's Prep School

Holt, Norfolk NR25 6EY
Tel: 01263 714600
            01263 714575 (Pre-Prep School)
Fax: 01263 714060
email: prep@greshams.com
website: www.greshams.com

Chairman of Governors: A Martin Smith

Headmaster: **J H W Quick**, BA Hons Durham, PGCE

Age Range. 3–13.

Number of Pupils. 314: 42 Boarders, 272 Day pupils.

Fees per term (2014–2015). Boarders £7,450, Day £5,500. Pre-Prep School: £2,900–£3,300.

Gresham's Prep School is part of the family of Gresham's Schools, which are located in the busy market town of Holt in a beautiful and tranquil part of North Norfolk. Some pupils enter the school from the Pre-Prep School, which is based on a separate site a quarter of a mile from the Prep School, but many others enter the school from elsewhere. Most pupils move on to Gresham's Senior School, but the school has a very good record of winning scholarships and gaining entry to other major Independent Schools.

The school has excellent facilities including extensive playing fields, an Art and Technology Centre, a Drama Hall and a modern and well-equipped Music School. Use of the Theatre, Chapel, two Astroturf pitches, swimming pool, sports hall and other excellent sports facilities is shared with the Senior School.

Boarders are accommodated in modern, comfortable bedrooms in Crossways House (girls) or Kenwyn House (boys). Flexible boarding is available and is extremely popular.

The school prides itself on the breadth of its curriculum. Sport, Drama and Music play an important part in the lives of all pupils. The school has built up a considerable reputation in these areas in recent years. There is a wide range of extra-curricular activities available in the evenings.

Above all the school wants children to enjoy the process of growing up and developing their talents to the full and to establish the strong roots that will help them become self-assured and well-balanced adults.

Entry Requirements. Entry is by assessment in Mathematics and English and the recommendation of the child's previous school. Entry is possible into all year groups. Scholarships are available for entry into Year 7. Headmaster's Awards are occasionally awarded to those entering other year groups.

Pre-Prep School. Co-educational, age 3–7, Day pupils only.

Headmistress: Mrs J Davidson

The Pre-Prep School is housed in the beautiful setting of Old School House. It is a vibrant and dynamic school that puts great emphasis on the development of the whole child as well giving children an excellent academic grounding.

Charitable status. Gresham's School is a Registered Charity, number 1105500. It exists for the purpose of educating children.

Grimsdell
Mill Hill Pre-Preparatory School

Winterstoke House, Wills Grove, Mill Hill, London NW7 1QR

Tel: 020 8959 6884
Fax: 020 8959 4626
email: office@grimsdell.org.uk
website: www.grimsdell.org.uk

Co-educational Pre-Preparatory Day School.

Chairman of Court of Governors: Dr R G Chapman, BSc, MB BS, FRCGP

Head: **Mrs Kate Simon**, BA, PGCE

Age Range. 3–7.

Number of Pupils. 184: 111 Boys, 73 Girls.

Fees per term (2014–2015). £4,285 (full day), Nursery: £2,324 (mornings only), £1,971 (afternoons only).

Grimsdell is situated in the Green Belt on the borders of Hertfordshire and Middlesex but only ten miles from central London. It stands adjacent to Mill Hill School's 120 acres of land, enjoying the advantages of a rural environment. Grimsdell is part of the Mill Hill School Foundation. It provides a happy, secure and rich learning environment for boys and girls aged 3 to 7. Belmont, the Mill Hill Preparatory School, is less than a quarter of a mile away and educates pupils from 7 to 13, the majority of whom move on to the senior school, Mill Hill.

The boys and girls at Grimsdell learn through hands-on experience. With the support and guidance of professional, caring staff and excellent resources and equipment, each child is encouraged to reach their full potential. Our approach combines traditional skills of reading, writing and mathematics with the breadth and balance offered by an enhanced Early Years Foundation Stage and KS1 Curriculum. Every pupil can enjoy many opportunities offered by learning through Science, Technology and Computing. They also gain much from Art, Drama, Music, PE and French lessons.

The school is housed in a large Victorian building with its own secure play areas and adventure playgrounds, taking advantage of further facilities on the Mill Hill site including a Forest School area, sports fields, swimming pool and theatre.

The usual age of entry is at 3 and 4 years, but 5 and 6 year olds are considered as vacancies occur. It is expected that most children will pass to Belmont at the end of Year 2.

Charitable status. The Mill School Foundation is a Registered Charity, number 1064758. It exists to provide education for boys and girls.

Guildford High School Junior School
United Learning

London Road, Guildford, Surrey GU1 1SJ

Tel: 01483 561440
Fax: 01483 306516
email: guildford-admissions@guildfordhigh.co.uk
website: www.guildfordhigh.surrey.sch.uk
Twitter: @GuildfordHigh

Chairman of Local Governing Body: Mr D Perrett

Headmistress: **Mrs S J Phillips**, BA Hons Reading

Age Range. Girls 4–11.

Number of Pupils. 285.

Fees per term (2014–2015). Reception £3,015, Years 1 and 2 £3,085, Years 3–6 £4,035.

The Junior School at Guildford High School is situated on the same site as the Senior School. It is a modern, bright, self-contained school with the third floor especially designed for art, music, science, IT and the Library.

The girls normally start in the Reception classes (4 years) or at Year 3 (7 years), however, they are welcome in any year group depending on spaces available, and work their way through the Junior School with natural progression on to the Senior School at Year 7 (11 years).

The breadth and depth of the curriculum encompasses 15 fast paced subjects, with an embedded thinking skills programme. Three modern foreign languages are included, with Spanish starting in Year 1 for the five year olds. Music, drama and sport play an important part in the curricular and co-curricular programmes. Specialist teachers and resources are employed throughout the Junior School. Parents and teachers work closely together to ensure excellent differentiation and a nurturing environment with strong pastoral care.

Guildford High Junior School girls of all abilities and temperaments are confident, happy and well-prepared for entry to the Senior School. (*See Guildford High School entry in HMC section.*)

Charitable status. Guildford High Junior School is part of United Learning which comprises: UCST (a Company Limited by Guarantee, Registered in England, number 2780748, and a Registered Charity, number 1016538) and ULT (a Company Limited by Guarantee, Registered in England, number 4439859, and an Exempt Charity).

The Haberdashers' Aske's Boys' Preparatory & Pre-Preparatory School

Butterfly Lane, Elstree, Hertfordshire WD6 3AF
Tel: 020 8266 1779
Fax: 020 8266 1808
email: prepoffice@habsboys.org.uk
website: www.habsboys.org.uk

Chairman of Governors: Sir Robert Fulton, KBE

Head: **Miss Y M Mercer**, BEd, Adv Dip Ed

Deputy Head: Mr M G Brown, BSc

Age Range. Prep 7–11; Pre-Prep 5–7.
Number of Boys. Prep 218, Pre-Prep 72.
Fees per term (2014–2015). Pre-Prep £4,187 (including lunch); Prep £5,554.

The Preparatory School is vibrant with the energy and curiosity of over two hundred boys aged 7–11 from a wide range of local schools and communities. It is a very special place to work and play.

It is housed in a purpose-designed building, opened by HRH The Princess Margaret, Citizen and Haberdasher, in 1983, on the same campus as the Main School. The bright, cheerful classrooms provide a welcoming and stimulating environment. The Prep enjoys a unique mix of family atmosphere and close links with the Main School. The boys are able to share the wonderful facilities and grounds of the Main School, including the Sports Centre, the heated indoor Swimming Pool, the Music School and the Dining Room. The Pre-Prep School is located 6 miles north of the school at How Wood, near St Albans.

The relationship between the Preparatory staff and their forms is close and friendly, within a context of firm discipline. In this environment, brimming with opportunities, the school ensures an education of breadth and depth extending well beyond national guidelines.

Sport and games play a major role in the boys' week, offering fitness and fun to all. Indeed the sporting ethos of team spirit and fair play underpins the whole structure of Prep School life.

The arts spring to life in a wealth of musical, dramatic and artistic activity, guided by specialists whose passion for their subject is matched by the enthusiasm of their pupils.

Every boy is a musician for at least one year when he studies an orchestral instrument of his choice, free of charge, through the Music Scheme; many of these fledgling musicians eventually make their way into the Main School's First Orchestra.

There are many clubs and societies; however boys with some special interest often start their own, supported by staff, and eagerly attended by those of like mind. Some boys also stay on to enjoy extra play time with their friends or to do their homework and to have tea. The After School Care Facility is equipped with bean bags, games and sports equipment.

Boys are admitted each September after assessments to the Pre-Prep at the age of 5+ and to the Prep at 7+. Boys are expected to move into the Main School at 11. Most boys will flourish in the Main School as they have in the Prep, and the transition is made as natural as possible. A qualifying examination assures candidates that the Main School is right for them and they are given help preparing for the different pace and rhythms they will find there. (*For further details, please see entry in HMC section.*)

Charitable status. The Haberdashers' Aske's Charity is a Registered Charity, number 313996. It exists to promote education.

The Hall

23 Crossfield Road, Hampstead, London NW3 4NU
Tel: 020 7722 1700
Fax: 020 7483 0181
email: office@hallschool.co.uk
website: www.hallschool.co.uk

Chairman of Governors: H Davies Jones, Esq

Headmaster: **C Godwin**, BSc, MA

Age Range. 4–13.
Number of Pupils. 464 Day Boys.
Fees per term (2014–2015). £4,820–£5,480 (inclusive of lunch)

Founded in 1889, the school is on three sites within close proximity. The majority of boys join Reception or Year 1 at the age of 4 or 5, but a few places are occasionally available in later years. The average class size is 18.

The school's buildings are spacious and well-appointed, and resources are good. There has been considerable investment over the last ten years in the school's fabric and facilities, and there is a continuing programme of improvements planned, including a well-advanced programme of ICT development. The Junior School (Years 1–3) is undergoing a programme of continuous refurbishment and provides up-to-date computing, science and music facilities. The Senior School boasts a modern library, spacious music, ICT, pottery, computing facilities and changing rooms. Boys in the Junior School use the sports hall, located in the Senior School, and have lunch in the dining hall which serves the whole school.

From the Junior School, boys transfer to the Middle School for Years 4 and 5. During that time they make the transition from classroom based teaching to subject based teaching. Boys are taught by subject specialists from Year 5.

The Hall prides itself on the breadth of education it offers. Senior School boys study Life Skills, Art, Drama, Music, Pottery, ICT, Design Technology and Current Affairs within the timetable and there is a broad range of after-school activities. Music and Drama are considerable strengths within the school. Team games, soccer, rugby and cricket are played mainly at the Wilf Slack Memorial Ground, and in recent years fencing has developed as a sporting strength. A major development of the Wilf Slack Playing Fields has recently been completed, including the installation of two all–weather surfaces, the upgrading of all the pitches and a significant refurbishment of the pavilion to provide a high-quality facility. Hockey, squash, athletics, golf and other sports are also offered.

The school is not linked with any particular senior school. Over half the boys proceed to London day schools, such as Westminster, St Paul's, Highgate, City of London and UCS, and others proceed to leading boarding schools such as Eton, Harrow, Winchester and Tonbridge. In recent years numerous academic scholarships have been won at these and other schools. Other awards have been won in areas such as music and sport.

Means-tested bursaries are available at 10+ and 11+, and a number of boys apply at this entry point from London primary schools.

The school was last inspected in 2010 and the report may be found on the school's website.

Charitable status. The Hall School Charitable Trust is a Registered Charity, number 312722. It exists entirely for the purposes of education.

Hall Grove

London Road, Bagshot, Surrey GU19 5HZ
Tel: 01276 473059
Fax: 01276 452003
email: office@hallgrove.co.uk
website: www.hallgrove.co.uk

Headmaster: **A R Graham**, BSc, PGCE

Age Range. 4–13.
Number of Children. Pre-Preparatory (age 4–7) 102. Preparatory (age 7–13) 301.
Fees per term (2014–2015). Pre-Preparatory £3,020; Preparatory: £3,815 (Years 3–5), £4,240 (Years 6–8). Fees inclusive of meals and all essential extras including field trips.

Hall Grove is a thriving co-educational school for 4–13 year olds. Weekly/Flexi boarding is offered for up to 12 pupils. The main entry ages are 4, 7 and 11. There is a separate nursery in the grounds for children from the age of 2.

The school was founded in 1957 by the parents of the current Headmaster. At its centre is a most attractive Georgian house set in beautiful gardens and parkland. Recent additions have provided some modern rooms and specialist teaching areas, an impressive computer facility and new classroom blocks. Despite this building programme, the character and atmosphere of a family home has been retained.

The academic standards are high and there is a very strong emphasis on Sport and Music. A wide range of activities flourish; woodwork, ceramics, food technology, drama and a host of major and minor sports including soccer, rugby, hockey, netball, rounders, cricket, tennis, athletics, swimming, golf, judo, basketball, badminton and dance. Riding and stable management is an added attraction.

The school day continues until 5.40 pm for Years 7 and 8 and older children may stay overnight on a regular basis. There is also provision for after-school care and a full programme of evening activities.

Hall Grove has its own residential field study centre situated on the South Devon coast called Battisborough House and there are many field trips and expeditions both in Devon and overseas. Battisborough is available for hire by other schools and can accommodate up to 30 in comfort.

Hallfield School

Church Road, Edgbaston, Birmingham B15 3SJ
Tel: 0121 454 1496
Fax: 0121 454 9182
email: admissions@hallfieldschool.co.uk
website: www.hallfieldschool.co.uk

Founded 1879.

Governing Body: The Hallfield School Trust

Chairman of Governors: K Uff, MA, BCL of Gray's Inn, Barrister

Headmaster: **R Outwin-Flinders**, BEd Hons

Deputy Head: J P Thackway, BA Hons, PGCE

Age Range. 3 months to 11 years.
Number of Pupils. 567 Day Boys and Girls: Upper School (7–11 years) 230; Pre-Preparatory Department (2–7 years) 289; Hallfield*first* (3 months to 2 years) 48.
Fees per term (2014–2015). Hallfield*first* on application; Pre-Prep: Transition £2,713 (5 days); Foundation to Year 2 £3,192; Upper School (Year 3 to Year 6), £3,796. Lunches are included in the fees.

Since 1879, Hallfield School has offered an exceptional education for boys (and since 1995, boys and girls) which makes it the leading preparatory school in the Midlands and possibly the country. It is now a flourishing and highly successful co-educational day school.

However, the success of a school should not be judged simply on academic results. To the contrary, the School has always nurtured a strong 'hidden curriculum' which cannot be measured by league tables – where courtesy, manners, self-discipline and respect are valued and reinforced. It is this strong hidden curriculum which underpins everything that takes place at the School: 'happy children are successful children'.

The School's aims are clear and concise:

- To provide a safe, caring, happy and high achieving inclusive environment based on Christian principles, whilst welcoming children of all faiths to the School.
- To develop each child's full potential in academic, social, emotional, cultural and sporting areas.

Since becoming Headmaster of Hallfield in 2012, Roger Outwin-Flinders has steered the School through a successful inspection in January 2013, but he still continues to 'raise the bar' with his expectations for the children and staff.

In the last 2 years, 62 scholarships to the leading independent Schools in the Midlands have been awarded to the Year 6 Leavers and, last year, 91% of Leavers were successfully offered places to selective Local Authority Grammar Schools.

However, Hallfield is more than just successful results at 11+ Examinations. In 2013, the boys were Regional Champions in the Independent Schools Football Association U11 Seven-a-Side Tournament and qualified for the National Finals held at St George's Park, the National Training Centre in Burton-upon-Trent, where they finished a creditable 13th in the country. In 2013, the chess team became National IAPS champions for the 3rd time in four years and in 2014, Year 6 worked with the Young Shakespeare Company and produced their own version of Macbeth in just one week – to great acclaim from everyone.

There is something for everyone at Hallfield, but high standards are expected in everything the children take part in. Excellence and success are celebrated at every opportunity through Year group or School assemblies and, of course, the end of year School Prize Giving.

Charitable status. Hallfield School Trust is a Registered Charity, number 528956. It exists for the purpose of providing education for children.

Halstead Preparatory School for Girls

Woodham Rise, Woking, Surrey GU21 4EE
Tel: 01483 772682
email: registrar@halstead-school.org.uk
website: www.halstead-school.org.uk

Chairman of Governors: Mr J Olsen

Headmistress: **Mrs P A Austin**, BA Hons London, LTCL Trinity College of Music, PGCE, NPQH

Age Range. Nursery–11.
Number of Pupils. 220 Girls.

Fees per term (2014–2015). Nursery (flexible) from £891; Reception (Kindergarten) to Year 2 £3,463; Years 3–6 £4,054.

Girls thrive in the calm, purposeful and happy atmosphere at Halstead with a good balance of study and fun and the opportunities to establish friends and many happy memories.

Halstead is delighted to have been recognised as 'excellent' in every aspect by the Independent Schools Inspectorate in January 2014:

"The school meets its aims very successfully, providing a comfortable and homely environment where pupils are well known, treated as individuals and gain the confidence to thrive and fulfil their potential. From the Early Years Foundation Stage onwards, they achieve highly both in their academic work and in their activities outside the classroom, and have a great appetite for learning. This is thanks to the relevant and interesting curriculum and enthusiasm and expertise of teachers."

"Relationships throughout the school are excellent, and both pupils and their parents say it feels like a happy family."

"The school has a strong track record of success in entrance exams for prestigious local schools. Almost all pupils consistently gain places at their first choice of (senior) schools, with a considerable number being awarded scholarships."

Established in 1927 Halstead is situated in a leafy part of residential Woking. The main school building is a large Edwardian house to which modern facilities have been added including a purpose-built Food Technology, Design Technology and Art Room.

Prospective parents are very welcome to attend an Open Morning or, if more convenient, please make an appointment to meet Mrs Austin and see our happy, nurturing and secure school in action.

Charitable status. Halstead (Educational Trust) Limited is a Registered Charity, number 270525. It exists to provide a high quality all-round education for girls aged 2+–11.

Hampshire Collegiate Prep School
United Learning

Embley Park, Romsey, Hampshire SO51 6ZA
Tel: 01794 515737
email: info@hampshirecs.org.uk
website: www.hampshirecs.org.uk
Twitter: @hampshireschool
Facebook: facebook.com/hampshireschool

Chairman of the Governors: Mr D A d'Arcy Hughes

Principal: Mrs E-K Henry, BA

Head of Prep School: Mrs H Donnelly, BA, BEd

Deputy Head of Prep School: Mr P Brady, BEd

Age Range. 2½–11 Co-educational.
Number of Pupils. 181 Day Pupils: 93 Boys, 88 Girls.
Fees per term (2014–2015). Nursery: £2,590 (full time). Payment by Termly Direct Debit: Prep School £2,989–£3,373.

The school operates an extended day from 8.00 am to 6.00 pm offering comprehensive care to support busy, modern family living.

The school has its own nursery (The Nightingale Nursery) taking children from 2½ years and is very flexible in session bookings to suit parents' working patterns and family life. The nursery operates for 48 weeks of the year and there is also holiday cover for Reception Class, which can extend to Year 2 pupils if there is sufficient interest.

Reception to Year 2 pupils enjoy small class sizes with an emphasis on careful monitoring of progress in the core subjects and early intervention in the event of any identified learning needs. A broad curriculum is offered, including French, Music, IT, DT and PE taught by specialists.

Within Years 3 to 6 the focus is on careful monitoring of progress and the development of potential in each child alongside preparation senior schooling and associated scholarships. The school seeks to provide, through small class sizes, teaching expertise and support staff, a broad education tailored to the individual needs of the children in the school. There is both a clear and effective learning support structure and policy to help children experiencing difficulties, as well as challenge those who are our most able children. The school has three clear aims:

- At HCS we focus on the individual
- We believe that every child has special qualities – it is our responsibility to define and refine these
- We support a broad vision of excellence for our children and our teachers

Throughout the school the children take part in Learning Outside the Classroom (LOC). This is part of the curriculum and introduces the children to learning experiences that engage them in finding out more about their environment, making use of the school orchards, allotments, an outdoor classroom and an amphitheatre, all within our 130 parkland grounds.

There is a strong tradition of musical achievement in the school with choir, an orchestra, and a rock band. Children compete in a wide range of sports within curriculum time and as part of the busy House and fixture programme. Drama is promoted via its inclusion within the weekly timetable for all children, annual LAMDA preparation and regular productions. Our annual art exhibition showcases artistic talent in the school and regular linked work with local artists encourages enthusiasm for the visual arts. Each year our 10 and 11 year olds undertake residential visits. Year 5 experience geographical studies and outdoor pursuits on the Isle of Wight, whilst Year 6 travel to a Normandy château to experience a week's immersion in a wide variety of activities, all enjoyed in French.

The school seeks to achieve a high standard of academic achievement and to encourage attitudes of tolerance, adaptability, invention, persistence, responsibility, confidence, compassion, flexibility and creativity coupled with a lifelong love of learning and endeavour. Our last ISI inspection highlighted the personal development of pupils as 'outstanding'.

Charitable status. Hampshire Collegiate Prep School is part of United Learning which comprises: UCST (a Company Limited by Guarantee, Registered in England, number 2780748, and a Registered Charity, number 1016538) and ULT (a Company Limited by Guarantee, Registered in England, number 4439859, and an Exempt Charity).

Handcross Park School

Handcross, Haywards Heath, West Sussex RH17 6HF
Tel: 01444 400526
Fax: 01444 400527
email: info@handxpark.com
website: www.handcrossparkschool.co.uk
Twitter: @HandcrossPark
Facebook: /handcrosspark

Where potential is nurtured and success is celebrated in a friendly learning environment.

Chairman of Governors: L Tomlinson

Headmaster: G R Owton, BA Hons QTS

Head of Nursery & Pre-Prep: Mr J Gayler, BSc Hons QTS
Senior Deputy Head (Pastoral): Mrs N Bartholomew, BA Hons QTS
Deputy Head (Academic): Mr A Falkus, BSc Hons QTS

Age Range. 2–13 Co-educational.
Number of Pupils. 320: Boys 168, Girls 152.
Fees per term (2014–2015). Nursery according to number of sessions; Pre-Prep £2,860–£3,060; Prep £3,780–£5,640; Weekly boarding £4,750–£6,610; Full boarding £5,340–£7,200.

Handcross Park is one of the Brighton College family of schools offering a pre-preparatory and preparatory school education, set in beautiful surroundings but conveniently located just off the A23 and close to Haywards Heath, Horsham, Gatwick and Crawley. The School provides a first-class education for children from 2 to 13 in a happy family atmosphere within a caring Christian framework.

The School unashamedly takes pride in the pursuit of excellence for all its pupils. Alongside academic endeavours staff believe ardently in educating children to become well-rounded, compassionate and articulate citizens.

The modern Nursery, situated in the Pre-Prep and accommodated in well-designed and purpose-built classrooms, offers a wonderful environment in which to begin the exciting adventure of a child's school career. Activities are specially designed to help young minds investigate and find solutions for themselves and the cleverly planned classrooms allow children the opportunity to pursue interests both inside and outdoors. With an excellent staff to pupil ratio throughout the Early Years and small class sizes right the way through the school, the emphasis is on helping the individual to flourish as part of a supportive, vibrant and happy community.

Handcross Park has a proven academic record with many Year 8 pupils gaining scholarships to Brighton College and other top Senior Schools both locally and further afield. We are proud of our 100% pass rate at Common Entrance and our excellent scholarship success over the years. But as well as a deep and broad knowledge of the curriculum, pupils also develop an understanding of the role they can play in society as informed and caring citizens.

Alongside the provision of a high quality academic education for all children, the School's well-qualified, friendly staff focus on nourishing the creative, musical and sporting aptitudes of the pupils. With a vibrant Music Department, inspiring Art Studio, excellent sports coaching and facilities and well-equipped Science, IT and Design Technology Rooms, pupils are offered the best opportunities to foster and showcase their talents.

The 'home away from home' accommodation at Handcross Park has been refurbished, revamped and rejuvenated resulting in growing boarding numbers and a necessary extension to the Boarding House to cater for these additional numbers. With a variety of activities to choose from the focus is on having fun in a structured environment. Both weekly (Monday–Friday) and full boarding options are available and flexible pre and after school care offered to day parents.

Handcross Park was inspected in June 2014 and in the resulting inspection report we achieved top rating across every area.

Charitable status. Newells School Trust is a Registered Charity, number 307038. Handcross Park School exists to provide a high-quality education to children aged 2 to 13.

Hanford School

Child Okeford, Blandford Forum, Dorset DT11 8HN
Tel: 01258 860219
Fax: 01258 861255

email: office@hanford.dorset.sch.uk
website: www.hanfordschool.co.uk

Chairman of Governors: Mrs L Sunnucks

Headmaster: Mr R Johnston, BA

Age Range. 7–13.
Number of Girls. 100.
Fees per term (2014–2015). Boarders £6,950, Day Girls £5,700.

Hanford School, which was founded in 1947 by the Revd and Mrs C B Canning, is an early 17th Century manor house standing in about 45 acres and situated in the Stour valley, half way between Blandford and Shaftesbury. The amenities include a Chapel, Laboratories, a Computer Room, a Music School, an Art School, a Gymnasium, a Swimming Pool, a Handwork Room, two Netball/Tennis Courts (hard) and a covered Riding School. Pupils are prepared for entry to all Independent Senior Schools.

Charitable status. The Hanford School Charitable Trust Ltd is a Registered Charity, number 1001751.

Haslemere Preparatory School

Hill Road, Haslemere, Surrey GU27 2JP
Tel: 01428 642350
Fax: 01428 645314
email: office@haslemereprep.co.uk
website: www.haslemereprep.co.uk
Twitter: @HaslemerePrep

Chairman of Governors: Mr A Gardner

Headmaster: R W H Smith, BEd

Age Range. Boys 3–13, Girls 3–4.
Number of Pupils. 153.
Fees per term (2014–2015). £2,850–£3,995. The school offers sibling discounts and Scholarships in academic subjects, sport and the arts.

Haslemere Preparatory School is committed to giving each individual boy the best possible start to his education.

The school is a boys' independent day school for 4 to 13 year olds, with a Nursery Department catering for boys and girls from the term they turn 3 years. The school is set in a stunning location, within walking distance of Haslemere town centre.

Academically it has an excellent reputation for producing well rounded, well mannered, confident young men. The majority of boys move on to senior schools such as the Royal Grammar School, King Edward's School, Churcher's College, Lord Wandsworth College, Portsmouth Grammar School, Charterhouse and Cranleigh. The school seeks to encourage all boys to find the best within themselves by creating a safe and stimulating environment in which they can learn. A highly dedicated and professional staff teaches a well balanced curriculum that includes not only the core subjects but also a wide range of extra-curricular activities. Each individual's performance is closely monitored. Class sizes are small, with a maximum of 16 boys in each. Minibus travel is provided from local areas and Haslemere railway station. After school care is provided until 6 pm. Haslemere Preparatory School encourages the active involvement of parents in achieving its pupils' success.

The school formed a federation with St Ives girls' school in January 2009 but remains committed to single-sex education.

For a prospectus, please contact the Headmaster's Secretary or visit www.haslemereprep.co.uk.

Charitable status. Haslemere Preparatory School Trust is a Registered Charity, number 294944.

Hatherop Castle Preparatory School

Hatherop, Cirencester, Glos GL7 3NB
Tel: 01285 750206
Fax: 01285 750430
email: admissions@hatheropcastle.co.uk
website: www.hatheropcastle.co.uk

Headmaster: **Mr P Easterbrook**, BEd

Age Range. 2½–13. Kindergarten/Transition 2½–4½.
Number of Pupils. 158, including 17 Boarders (boarding from age 7).
Fees per term (2014–2015). £2,645–£4,385 (Day), £6,410–£6,770 (Boarding), Overseas boarders £7,325.
Founded in 1947, Hatherop Castle is a co-educational day and boarding prep school for children between the ages of 2½ and 13. Children are prepared for Common Entrance and Scholarship Examinations at 11+ and 13+; the children move on to a wide range of senior independent schools. Weekly boarders are accepted and the boarding facilities are homely and well furnished. A family atmosphere exists throughout the school. The curriculum spans a wide range of subjects and there is a great variety of sports and extra-curricular activities.
Set in 22 acres of beautiful Cotswold countryside, Hatherop Castle enjoys a superb setting and is a happy environment in which the pupils learn. The classes are housed in well-equipped rooms and the pre-prep and kindergarten/transition have their own self-contained areas where the pupils enjoy playing and working in a welcoming and stimulating atmosphere. The ICT Suite impacts across the curriculum. The Independent Curriculum has been introduced for the upper school.
The report of the ISI Inspection in March 2010 can be viewed on the school website. The EYFS setting and Boarding House were inspected in 2013 and these reports can also be viewed on the school website.
In April 2014 the school became part of the Wishford Schools group, www.wishford.co.uk.

Hawkesdown House School

27 Edge Street, Kensington, London W8 7PN
Tel: 020 7727 9090
Fax: 020 7727 9988
email: admin@hawkesdown.co.uk
website: www.hawkesdown.co.uk

Pre-Preparatory Day School for Boys.

Head: **Mrs C Bourne**, MA Cantab

Age Range. 3–8.
Number of Pupils. 145 Boys.
Fees per term (2014–2015). £4,695 (age 3), £5,095 (age 4), £5,395 (age 5–8).
The previous Head was the first Head of a free-standing pre-preparatory school to be elected to membership of IAPS (Independent Association of Prep Schools) and IAPS membership has continued under the leadership of the new Head, Mrs Claire Bourne.
Early literacy and numeracy are of prime importance and the traditional academic subjects form the core curriculum. A balanced education helps all aspects of learning and a wide range of interests is encouraged. The School finds and fosters individual talents in each pupil. Boys are prepared for entry at eight to the main London and other preparatory schools. The Head places the greatest importance on matching boys happily and successfully to potential schools and spends time with parents ensuring that the transition is smooth and free of stress.
Sound and thorough early education is important for success, and also for self-confidence. The thoughtful and inspirational teaching and care at Hawkesdown House ensures high academic standards and promotes initiative, kindness and courtesy. Hawkesdown is a school with fun and laughter, where boys develop their own personalities together with a sense of personal responsibility.
The School provides an excellent traditional education, with the benefits of modern technology, in a safe, happy and caring atmosphere. Many of the boys coming to the School live within walking distance and the School is an important part of the Kensington community.
There are clear expectations and the boys are encouraged by positive motivation and by the recognition and praise of their achievements, progress and effort. Individual attention and pastoral care for each of the boys is of great importance.
Hawkesdown House has a fine building in Edge Street, off Kensington Church Street.
Religious Denomination: Non-denominational; Christian ethos.
Parents who would like further information or to visit the School and meet the Head, should contact the School Office for a prospectus or an appointment.

The Hawthorns

Pendell Court, Bletchingley, Surrey RH1 4QJ
Tel: 01883 743048 (Prep); 01883 743718 (Pre-Prep)
Fax: 01883 744256
email: admissions@hawthorns.com
website: www.hawthorns.com

Motto: *Love God, Love Your Neighbour*
The School is an Educational Trust controlled by a Board of Governors.

Chair of Governors: Mrs Z S Creighton

Headmaster: **T R Johns**, BA, PGCE, FRGS
From September 2015: A E Floyd, BSc, PGCE

Age Range. 2–13.
Number of Pupils. 530 Day Pupils.
Fees per term (2014–2015). From £640 (Nursery 2 mornings) to £4,200.
Founded in 1926 near Redhill, The Hawthorns moved in 1961 to the haven of its present impressive site, a Jacobean manor set in 35 acres below the North Downs, with a catchment area from Lingfield to Coulsdon and Dorking to Westerham.
The prospectus and website reflect the rich and diverse nature of our School. Recent developments include an innovative eco-friendly Pre-Prep building housing Reception to Year 2 pupils to complement the Nursery Ark, Sports and Swimming complex.
Boys and girls join as day pupils between the ages of 2 and 13 years and are prepared for the Common Entrance examination and/or Scholarships at 11+ and 13+. An outstanding 49 Scholarships and Awards were gained last year at 11+ and 13+. The curriculum, incorporating the National Curriculum, Common Entrance and Scholarship goals, blends modern and traditional methods with emphasis on thorough grounding in English, Maths, Science, ICT and Languages. In Music, DT, Art and Textiles specialist centres are very well equipped. The strong Music Department fields three choirs, an orchestra and a variety of ensembles, with a wide range of individual instrumental tuition available. Public recitals and regular competition entries are encouraged.

The co-educational commitment to PE and Games is of great importance with major sports including soccer, netball, lacrosse, rugby, hockey, cricket, tennis, athletics and swimming. The grounds contain four sports areas, tennis courts, astroturf and 5 acres of woodland for outdoor pursuits. An extensive programme of co-curricular activities is offered including sailing, high wires, squash, survival, model-making, badminton and film-making.

A flourishing Parent/Toddler group runs during term time with Extended Day facilities and a comprehensive Holiday Activity Programme.

We believe firmly in hard work encouraging excellent results and providing breadth of opportunity. This includes trips, exchanges, and Schools of Swimming and Dance (open to the local community). Life Skills such as touchtyping, time management, teamwork and service are all taught. Equal opportunities, enjoyment and success are sought for every child. "Happy children learn."

The school is a living, happy, working community and a visit is essential.

Charitable status. The Hawthorns Educational Trust Limited is a Registered Charity, number 312067. It exists to provide education for girls and boys of 2 to 13 years.

Hazelwood School

Wolfs Hill, Limpsfield, Oxted, Surrey RH8 0QU
Tel: 01883 712194
Fax: 01883 716135
email: bursar@hazelwoodschool.com
website: www.hazelwoodschool.co.uk
            www.the-larks.co.uk

Chair of Governors: Mrs Jo Naismith, BA Hons, ACA

Head Teacher: **Mrs Maxine Shaw**, BSc Hons, PGCE, NPQH, EYPS

Age Range. 3 months–13 years.
Number of Pupils. 500 co-educational.
Fees per term (2014–2015). Day Pupils from £2,895 (Reception) to £4,775.

Founded in 1890, Hazelwood stands in superb grounds, commanding a magnificent view over the Kent and Sussex Weald.

Pupils enter at age 4 into the Pre-Prep or at 7+ to the Prep School, joining those pupils transferring from the Pre-Prep to the Prep School. Entry at other ages is possible if space permits. The Larks Nursery School, open all year round for children from 3 months to 4 years, opened in September 2009 on the Laverock site which offers unrivalled accommodation and facilities.

A gradual transition is made towards subject specialist tuition in the middle and upper forms. Pupils are prepared for the Common Entrance examinations at 11+ and 13+, and also for Scholarships to Senior Schools. Over 170 academic, all-rounder, sporting, music and art awards have been gained since 1995.

Extramural activity is an important part of every pupil's education. Excellent sports facilities, which include games fields, heated indoor swimming pool, gymnasium and many games pitches, tennis courts and other hard surfaces, allow preparation of school teams at various age and ability levels in a wide range of sports. A fully-equipped Sports Hall was completed in May 2004. Our aim is that every pupil has an opportunity to represent the School.

Art, Technology, Music and Drama are on the curriculum as well as being lively extramural activities. Our Centenary Theatre incorporates a 200-seat theatre, music school and Chapel. All our pupils are encouraged to play an instrument and join one of the music groups catering for all interests and abilities. Further extramural activities include tap, ballet and jazz dance, judo, art, gymnastics, warhammer, computing, modelling and chess.

Our pupils develop a curiosity about the world in which they live and a real passion for learning. Most importantly of all they become confident learners, mature and articulate individuals who love coming to school each day.

Charitable status. Hazelwood School Limited is a Registered Charity, number 312081. It exists to provide excellent preparatory school education for girls and boys in Oxted, Surrey.

Hazlegrove

Sparkford, Yeovil, Somerset BA22 7JA
Tel: 01963 440314
Fax: 01963 440569
email: office@hazlegrove.co.uk
website: www.hazlegrove.co.uk
Twitter: @Hazlegrove_Prep
Facebook: /hazlegrove

Senior Warden: Lt General [Ret'd] A M D Palmer CB CBE

Headmaster: **Richard Fenwick**, BEd, MA

Deputy Headmaster: Martin Davis, BEd

Head of Pre-Preparatory Department: Eleanor Lee, BEd

Age Range. 2½–13.
Number of Pupils. 373 boys and girls of whom 102 are boarders. Preparatory (7–13 year olds) 302 pupils; Pre-Preparatory (2½–7 year olds) 71 pupils.
Fees per term (2014–2015). Preparatory: Boarders £5,973–£7,621 (fees are inclusive, with few compulsory extras); Day pupils £4,135–£5,275. Pre-Preparatory: £2,602. Nursery: on application
Scholarships and Bursaries. Academic Scholarships are available for entry at 7+ and 11+. Armed Forces Bursaries are also available to serving members.

Hazlegrove is located within a 200 acre park and is based around a country house built by Carew Hervey Mildmay in 1730. The entrance to the school is situated on the A303 at the Sparkford roundabout opposite the turning to Yeovil and Sherborne. The Preparatory School has a strong boarding ethos and was awarded "Outstanding" status by Ofsted 2010/2011. This is reflected in the full days, Saturday morning lessons from Year Four and the full range of activities for boarders, and those day pupils who wish to join in, during the evenings and at weekends.

Hazlegrove is a happy and purposeful school with a strong tutor system. The curriculum provides a varied and exciting experience for pupils as they progress through the school and includes specialist taught Art, Design and Technology, Drama, Music and Outdoor Education. Specialist teaching is extended to all subjects from Year Five when Latin is also introduced. The main sports are Rugby, Hockey, Cricket, Netball, Rounders, Tennis, Athletics and Swimming. Squash, Golf, Horse Riding and Kayaking are also available amongst other activities.

Streaming and setting is introduced as pupils progress through the school with a scholarship stream in the top two years. Pupils are entered for Common Entrance or Scholarship Examinations. About half go to the senior school, King's School Bruton (*see entry in HMC section*). Others move on to major secondary schools such as Canford, Eton, Sherborne, Sherborne School for Girls, Millfield, King's College Taunton, Bryanston, Marlborough and Winchester. Between 25 and 30 scholarships and awards are gained by pupils each year. Extra support is available to those pupils who have specific learning difficulties or who are gifted.

Pupils have achieved considerable success at regional and national level in recent years through sport, in team and individual performances, and in music.

Hazlegrove has outstanding facilities. These include a state-of-the-art new Teaching and Learning Centre, a Theatre, a Sports Hall, a 25m Indoor Heated Pool, two Squash Courts, the Design Centre, three award-winning Libraries, an extensive Music School a comprehensive Computer Network with fibre optic broadband connectivity and classroom sets of iPads. Outside, the extensive playing fields are complemented by two synthetic pitches, tennis courts, eight all-weather cricket nets and for golf, a 6-hole course, a putting green and driving nets. The addition of a full-time tennis coach to the staff has ensured best use of the new hard tennis courts and second synthetic playing surface – both with flood lighting. The mini-farm now has pigs, chickens and raised vegetable beds and the adventure playground has been refurbished with new equipment including a timing device so pupils can compete for the Tarzan award.

Pastoral care for Boarders, which is overseen by the Headmaster's wife, is provided by three sets of House Parents, four Matrons and a Nurse. The school has considerable experience of meeting the needs of pupils whose parents are in the Services or who live in expat communities working overseas. Flexible boarding can also be arranged to meet individual needs.

The school shop, which is on site, provides most necessary clothing and games kit.

Pre-Preparatory Department. Located in a purpose-built facility within the grounds, the Pre-Prep provides a carefully structured curriculum which encourages the development of the basic skills within a balanced programme of learning and play. The innovative curriculum includes Forest School and specialist taught drama, music, games and tennis. In addition to making full use of the Prep School facilities, the Pre-Prep enjoys its own Rainbow Room dedicated to Science, Art and Investigation, an adjacent gardening area and extensive climbing equipment in the playground. After school care is available.

Charitable status. King's School, Bruton is a Registered Charity, number 1071997. It exists to provide education for children.

Headington Preparatory School

26 London Road, Headington, Oxford OX3 7PB
Tel: 01865 759400
Fax: 01865 761774
email: admissions@headington.org
website: www.headington.org

Chairman of Board of Governors: Mrs H Batchelor, BSc

Headmistress: **Mrs J Crouch**, BA Hons Keele, MA Hons London, NPQH

Age Range. Girls 3–11.
Number of Pupils. 250.
Fees per term (2014–2015). Day: £1,135–£3,960. Boarding (from age 9): £8,000–£8,250 (full boarding); £7,300–£7,550 (weekly boarding).

Headington Preparatory School occupies its own three-acre site just two minutes' walk from Headington School and one mile from the centre of Oxford.

The Prep School's friendly, family atmosphere means girls develop as happy individuals with a sense of responsibility and self-awareness, enjoying a wealth of experiences inside and out of the classroom as part of an outstanding education.

In September 2013, we completed our ambitious multi-million-pound building project designed to enhance our extra-curricular activities. The new facilities include a brand new gym and specialist art and design facilities, as well as a substantial new performance space for music and drama, a new dining hall and kitchens and a refurbished library.

Our adventurous art and design curriculum allows girls to explore their imaginations through painting, drawing, claywork and model-building and there are many exciting opportunities for girls in drama and music. We want all our girls to enjoy a variety of musical activities and we are quick to spot and nurture talent. From the age of seven, girls have the chance to learn at least one musical instrument and many of our girls play at a very high standard. All girls are taught to read music in Key Stage 2.

In sport, specialist staff deliver a broad and balanced programme with a total of 12 different sports on offer. Girls are encouraged to try new activities and discover new talents to achieve their full potential, with many taking part in county level tournaments.

The school day runs from 8.30 am to 3.30 pm, with an extended day from 8.00 am to 5.45 pm. There are a large number of after-school clubs and activities from fencing to touch typing and trampolining to African drumming and aftercare runs every day incorporating a range of activities, tea and prep.

Entry to the Prep School is in order of application from nursery to 6+, with priority given to girls with siblings already at Headington, and by examination from 7+. The majority of pupils continue to Headington School, with a number of girls awarded scholarships every year. (*See Headington School entry in GSA section.*)

Charitable status. Headington School Oxford Limited is a Registered Charity, number 309678. It exists to provide quality education for girls.

Heath Mount School

Woodhall Park, Watton-at-Stone, Hertford, Hertfordshire SG14 3NG
Tel: 01920 830230
Fax: 01920 830357
email: registrar@heathmount.org
website: www.heathmount.org

The school became a Trust in September 1970, with a Board of Governors.

Chairman of Governors: Mrs L Haysey

Headmaster: **Mr C Gillam**, BEd Hons

Senior Deputy Head: Mr M Dawes

Age Range. 3–13.
Number of Pupils. 249 Boys, 184 Girls. Flexi/Sleepover boarding offered.
Fees per term (2013–2014). Boarding (1–4 nights): £400–£1,880. Tuition: Nursery £1,995–£3,335, Pre-Prep £3,850, Years 3–6 £4,975, Years 7–8 £5,145.

There is a reduction in fees for the second and subsequent children attending the School at the same time.

Heath Mount School is situated five miles from Hertford, Ware and Knebworth, at Woodhall Park – a beautiful Georgian mansion with 40 acres of grounds set in a large private park. A dedicated Nursery and Pre-Prep is situated in woods a short walk from the main house. The fabulous facilities are inspiring – excellent sports facilities include a sports hall, covered swimming pool, an all-weather pitch for hockey and tennis, netball courts and cricket nets. The main house contains an imaginatively developed lower ground floor housing modern science laboratories and rooms for art, pottery, textiles, film making, food technology and design technology. There is a further information technology room and well-stocked research and fiction libraries. The boys board in a wing of the main house and the girls in a dedicated house in the adjoining park. Resident boarding house parents provide a welcoming environment for both the boys and girls.

The School has an excellent academic record, as well as outstanding art and sport and some of the finest school music in the Country. Illustrating this, in 2014, three quarters of the 13+ leavers achieved scholarships to their senior schools across a range of areas.

Charitable status. Heath Mount School is a Registered Charity, number 311069.

Heatherton House School

Copperkins Lane, Chesham Bois, Amersham, Bucks HP6 5QB
Tel: 01494 726433
Fax: 01494 729628
email: enquiries@heathertonhouse.co.uk
website: www.heathertonhouse.co.uk
Twitter: @HeathertonHouse

Chairman of the Governors: Mr G C Laws (*Chairman of Berkhamsted Schools Group*)

Headmaster: **Mr P H Rushforth**, MA, BEd

Age Range. Girls 3–11.
Number of Pupils. 140 Girls.
Fees per term (2014–2015). £1,725–£3,990 inclusive of all but optional subjects.

Founded in 1912, Heatherton is set in an attractive green and leafy location on the outskirts of Amersham.

Heatherton provides an excellent all-round education. Very high-quality facilities combined with an experienced staff of specialist teachers encourage each child's individual academic and emotional development. High standards are achieved across a broad curriculum with small classes (max 20), a caring ethos and a close relationship with parents.

At 11 pupils progress to both local independent girls' senior schools and Buckinghamshire grammar schools. Excellent results are produced at all stages of school performance tests.

Musical, artistic and sporting talents flourish at Heatherton. A thriving orchestra, individual instrument lessons and many drama, ballet and music productions are an important part of life in a school year. Art and design skills are celebrated in display and exhibitions, both internally and externally. Each pupil is offered a wide range of sporting activities – swimming, netball, gymnastics, dance, athletics, tennis, lacrosse, hockey, with opportunities for cricket and tag rugby.

An extensive range of educational visits and activities in the UK and Europe are organised each year.

Following a merger with Berkhamsted School in 2011, Heatherton pupils are increasingly enjoying the benefits of initiatives such as joint curriculum days, music and drama workshops, sports coaching and residential trips in partnership with Berkhamsted Prep, as well as access to the significant resources and infrastructure of the Berkhamsted Schools Group.

Charitable status. Heatherton House School is a member of the Berkhamsted Schools Group, which is a Registered Charity, number 310630.

Heathfield
The Junior School to Rishworth School

Rishworth, West Yorkshire HX6 4QF
Tel: 01422 823564
Fax: 01422 820880
email: admin@heathfieldjunior.co.uk
website: www.rishworth-school.co.uk

Motto: *Deeds Not Words*

Chairman of the Board of Governors: Dr C A G Brooks

Head: **Mr A M Wilkins**, BA, MA, MA

Age Range. 3–11 co-educational.
Number of Pupils. 120 day boys/girls and 50-place Foundation Stage Unit.
Fees per term (from April 2014). Reception–Year 2 £1,935; Years 3–6 £2,840.
Staffing. 10 full-time teaching and 5 part-time teaching; 2 NNEB staff and 6 teaching assistants; additional teaching support in Physical Education and specialist teaching in music, art, PE, dance, ICT and drama; 9 specialist peripatetic staff provide expert individual tuition in Music and the Arts.

Location. Heathfield stands in its own grounds and enjoys an outstanding rural position in a beautiful Pennine location with easy access via the motorways to Manchester and Leeds.

Facilities. Well-equipped classrooms; Foundation Stage Unit and purpose-built Infant classes; designated teaching rooms for Music, Science, Art and Design Technology; modern ICT Suite; Library; a multi-purpose Hall for assemblies and productions; heated indoor swimming pool; netball court and football/rugby pitch; Pre/After School Care and Holiday School available.

Aims. To provide a stimulating and challenging environment in which individual attainment is nurtured, recognised and celebrated.

To ensure each child receives their full entitlement to a broad, balanced curriculum which builds on a solid foundation in Literacy and Numeracy.

Curriculum. An extensive programme of study which incorporates the Foundation Stage, Key Stage 1 and Key Stage 2. An emphasis on developing an independence in learning and analytical thinking through Literacy, Numeracy, Science, French, History, Geography, Religious Studies, Design Technology, Information and Communications Technology, Music, Art and Physical Education.

Extra-Curricular Activities. Drama, Choir, Orchestra, Brass, Recorder and String Groups, Steel Pans, Art, Board Games; Sports include Swimming, Rounders, Netball, Football, Rugby, Cross-Country, Cricket, Fencing, Pistol shooting, Athletics, Hockey and Biathlon.

Extensive fixtures list of sports for boys and girls.

Each term there are plays and musical concerts incorporating most children in the School. Residentials include Outdoor Pursuits, Camping and Environmental Studies.

Charitable status. Rishworth School is a Registered Charity, number 1115562. It exists to provide education for boys and girls.

Hereford Cathedral Junior School

28 Castle Street, Hereford HR1 2NW
Tel: 01432 363511
email: enquiry@hcjs.org
website: www.herefordcs.com

Established 1898.

Chairman of Governors: R Haydn Jones, BSc, MRICS

Headmaster: **C Wright**, BSc, MSc, PGCE

Age Range. 3–11.
Number of children. 238: 143 boys and 95 girls.
Fees per term (2014–2015). £1,415–£2,025 (Nursery), £2,548 (Reception–Year 2), £3,163 (Years 3–6).

The school is the Junior School for Hereford Cathedral School and has the same board of Governors. Games facilities, including the new sports hall opened in 2009, are shared and there is close cooperation between the two sections of the school, although the Junior School has its own specialist teaching staff.

Entry is generally via the Nursery or Reception but a number of children also enter at 7+ and above. Almost all children continue through to the senior school.

The School occupies listed Georgian and Medieval buildings in Castle Street at the East End of the Cathedral with facilities including specialist music rooms, a new Art and DT centre, an ICT suite and an extensive library. The Moat, a nine-classroom building to house the Pre-Prep, opened in 2003.

The quality of relationships between staff and children is a great strength and a positive and friendly atmosphere characterises the whole school. There is a full and broad curriculum with the School noted for the strength of its music, drama and games. French is taught from the age of 4.

The staff are well qualified and the maximum class size is 18. In the junior forms all subjects are taught by specialists.

Music plays an important part in the life of the school with the Cathedral Choristers being educated at the school and a team of over twenty peripatetic music teachers. There are two school choirs and an orchestra.

An extensive programme of clubs and activities is offered during lunchtime and after school aimed at giving all children opportunities to develop their talents. After school care is also available.

The games fields are on the banks of the River Wye with expert coaching being given in the main sports of cricket, football, rugby, hockey, netball, rounders, athletics and swimming.

There is an active PTA organising a wide programme of social and fundraising activities.

The Little Princess Trust founded in memory of former pupil, Hannah Tarplee, is based at the school and provides hair pieces for children who lose their hair through cancer treatment.

Charitable status. Hereford Cathedral School is a Registered Charity, number 518889. Its aims and objectives are to promote the advancement of education.

Hereward House School

14 Strathray Gardens, London NW3 4NY
Tel: 020 7794 4820
email: office@herewardhouse.co.uk
website: www.herewardhouse.co.uk

Headmaster: **Mr P J E V Evans**, MA

Age Range. 4–13.
Number of Pupils. 176 Day Boys.
Fees per term (2014–2015). £4,700–£4,965.

Hereward House provides a warm and welcoming atmosphere in which every child feels valued, secure and thrives. The school works hard to create a stimulating, purposeful and happy community, within which boys are encouraged and assisted to develop academically, morally, emotionally, culturally and physically. The school's aim is for boys to enjoy their school days yet at the same time be well prepared for the demands of Common Entrance and Scholarship examinations.

The school's academic success is built upon excellent teaching and the highly individual educational teaching programmes created to meet individual boy's needs. Great care is taken to ensure that a boy gains a place at the school which is right for him.

Boys are prepared for the Common Entrance and Scholarship examinations to highly sought after independent schools, both day and boarding. Two-thirds of boys proceed to London Day Schools, such as City of London, Highgate, St Paul's, UCS and Westminster, others to leading boarding schools such as Eton, Harrow, Radley, Rugby and Winchester. Scholarships and Awards have been won by our boys to several of the above schools.

The school takes pride in the breadth of education it offers. Music plays a major role in the boys' education. Almost all boys learn at least one instrument, most of them two or even three. There is a full school orchestra which gives a performance each term. Weekly concerts are held throughout the year.

Team Games play an integral part in the sports syllabus. We regularly field teams against other schools and have an enviable record of success in cricket, football and cross-country running. Swimming, hockey and athletics are included in our sports programme.

Art, pottery and drama have a valued place in the syllabus. Chess, fencing, ICT, tennis and music theory are among the clubs available to the boys.

Herries Preparatory School

Dean Lane, Cookham Dean, Berks SL6 9BD
Tel: 01628 483350
Fax: 01628 483329
email: office@herries.org.uk
website: www.herries.org.uk

Chair of Governors: Miss N Coombs

Headmistress: **Ms S Green**, BSc Econ, PGCE

Age Range. 3–11 Co-educational.
Number of Pupils. 80 Day Boys and Girls.
Fees per term (2014–2015). £2,630–£3,085.

Herries has a delightful location alongside National Trust land and is close to Maidenhead and Marlow. Small class sizes enable each child to receive individual attention and to flourish in a secure environment. The curriculum is broad and balanced and there is a wide range of extra-curricular clubs including football coaching with Wycombe Wanderers, Gymnastics, Judo, Cookery, Table Tennis and ICT programming. Instrumental Music lessons are available. Extended Day is available to all pupils from 8 am to 6 pm Monday to Friday. Herries has a distinctive family atmosphere and happy pupils who progress to the grammar and independent secondary schools of their choice.

Curriculum. The National Curriculum is covered and we teach beyond the levels expected of children in each age group. Class teachers deliver the core and foundation subjects in Key Stage 1 while there is subject specialist teaching in all subjects in KS2.

Examinations. Children are assessed through the NFER testing scheme and a variety of standardised tests. Emphasis is placed on preparing pupils for their next school of choice and the timetable includes 'Thinking Skills' which helps pupils learn to cope with a variety of different tests and exams.

Facilities. Set in a beautiful building which was the house in which Kenneth Grahame wrote 'The Wind in the Willows', the Nursery occupies a purpose-built and spacious suite of rooms. ICT is taught in a specialist room with the latest computers and software. Class rooms are equipped with interactive Smart Boards and there is an excellent library. Games are played at the National Sports Centre at Bisham Abbey, only a few minutes away by coach. Swimming and tennis are based at Court Garden in Marlow. Athletics events are held at Braywick Sports Centre.

High March School

23 Ledborough Lane, Beaconsfield, Bucks HP9 2PZ
Tel: 01494 675186
Fax: 01494 675377
email: office@highmarch.bucks.sch.uk
            admissions@highmarch.bucks.sch.uk
website: www.highmarch.co.uk

Established 1926.

Chairman of the Governing Board: Mr C Hayfield, BSc, FCA

Headmistress: **Mrs S J Clifford**, BEd Hons Oxon, MA London

Age Range. Girls 3–11, Boys 3–4.
Number of Pupils. 294 day pupils.
Fees per term (2014–2015). £905–£4,170 inclusive of books, stationery and lunches, but excluding optional subjects.

High March consists of 3 school houses set in pleasant grounds. Junior House comprises Nursery and Key Stage 1 classes, ages 3–7 years, whilst Upper School covers Key Stage 2, ages 7–11 years. Class sizes are limited. Facilities include a state-of-the-art 20-metre indoor heated swimming pool opened in September 2009, a well-equipped Gymnasium, as well as Science, Music, Art, Poetry, Design Technology, Drama, Information Technology rooms and a Library. Recent refurbishments include large extensions to the Art Room and Science Laboratory and re-landscaping of all the outside space at Upper School to include a new Adventure Playground, new Netball courts and an outdoor learning classroom.

High March is within easy reach of London, High Wycombe, Windsor and within a few minutes' walk of Beaconsfield Station.

Under a large and highly-qualified staff and within a happy atmosphere, the children are prepared for Common Entrance and Scholarships to Independent Senior Schools and for the 11+ County Selection process. All subjects including French, Latin, Music, Art, Technology, Speech and Drama, Dancing, Gymnastics, Games and Swimming are in the hands of specialists. The academic record is high but each child is nevertheless encouraged to develop individual talents.

There is an Annual Open Scholarship to the value of one-third of the annual fee tenable for 3 years.

Highfield & Brookham Schools

Highfield Lane, Liphook, Hampshire GU30 7LQ
Tel: 01428 728000 (Highfield Prep)
            01428 722005 (Brookham Pre-Prep)
email: office@highfieldschool.org.uk
            office@brookhamschool.co.uk
website: www.highfieldschool.org.uk

Chairman of Directors: W S Mills, Esq

Headteacher, Highfield (*Prep*): Mr Phillip Evitt

Headteacher, Brookham (*Pre-Prep*): Mrs Diane Gardiner

Age Range. 3–13.
Number of Children. 450.
Fees per term (2014–2015). Day Pupils £3,275–£6,300; Boarders £6,825–£7,575.

Discounts are available for siblings and Forces families.

Highfield and Brookham are purpose-built, co-educational day and boarding schools set in 175 acres of superb grounds on the Hampshire/Sussex border, 15 miles south of Guildford with easy access (under an hour) to London and Heathrow Airport.

The aim of the schools is to provide children with a keen sense of their own individual identity and to help them to develop a sense of responsibility towards others and fulfil their potential in a happy and caring environment. Highfield and Brookham children are encouraged to have high expectations, good work habits and a desire to benefit from all that the school offers.

The curriculum is broad, stimulating and highly creative. Strong emphasis is placed on cross-curricular and outdoor learning, including Forest School, providing for all styles of learner. Sport, Drama, Music, Design Technology and Art all enjoy generous provision in the Timetable, providing every pupil with the opportunity to explore and develop their talents and interests. The aim is to develop enthusiastic, enquiring, rounded and adaptable independent thinkers who recognise that learning is both a joy and lifelong.

The major sports on offer are rugby, soccer, hockey and cricket for the boys, whilst girls play netball, lacrosse, hockey and rounders. All the children take part in athletics, swimming, tennis and cross country. Activities take place in the evenings and weekends and include judo, ballet, chess, golf, drama, modelling, pottery, sewing and story telling.

Highfield children have a distinguished record of success at Common Entrance and Scholarships to all the major senior schools including Eton, Winchester, Marlborough, Bryanston, Canford, Wycombe Abbey, St Swithun's and Downe House to name but a few.

Highfield Prep School

West Road, Maidenhead, Berkshire SL6 1PD
Tel: 01628 624918
Fax: 01628 635747
email: office@highfieldprep.org
website: www.highfieldprep.org

Educational Charitable Trust Primary Day School with Nursery.

Chairman of Governors: Mr W Bradley

Head: **Ms Annie Lee**, BA, PGCE, MA
From April 2015: Mrs Joanna Leach, BEd, NPQH

Age Range. 3–11.
Number of Pupils. Approximately 160 Girls (brothers in Nursery). Class sizes: average 19, maximum 22.

Highfield Preparatory School, the leading independent girls' school in Maidenhead, offers a great start to the life of learning that we want our girls to enjoy. In the Nursery (3 and 4 year olds) and Reception classes (5 year olds) right through to Year 6 (11 year olds) the girls are taught to love learning and are inspired to achieve their very best. We genuinely want every girl to have the opportunity to shine and be proud, to learn who they are, and have the confidence to have a go with the belief that they can succeed.

We believe, that in the important primary years, girls learn best in girls' schools. They learn by doing, listening, exploring and experimenting. The girls are given daily opportunities to explore, question, try, investigate, discover, apply and have fun! This all starts in the Nursery, which was graded Excellent at inspection in 2013, where the girls learn to develop confidence and independence.

Our girls achieve well beyond national expectations and move on to some of the best schools in the area at 11+, often achieving academic, sports and music scholarships. We also offer a wide range of after-school clubs ranging from watercolours to cookery.

We offer wonderful resources in a happy, secure and stimulating environment where all girls learn and develop at their own pace. Highfield Prep School is a local school, 5 minutes' walk from the town centre, on the same site since 1918, and really is Maidenhead's best kept secret!

From Nursery to Year 6, we offer extended day care from 7.45 am to 6.00 pm, have an all-year round holiday club, serve hot lunches every day and our fees are highly competitive.

The entry process is non-selective.

Come and see for yourself why Highfield Prep is first for girls. A prospectus is available on request from the School Secretary.

Fees per term (2014–2015). Reception to Year 6: £2,640–£3,180; Lunch £295. Nursery: £2,625 (full-time inc lunch), £290 per morning session, £235 per afternoon session (inc lunch).

Charitable status. Highfield School is a Registered Charity, number 309103. It exists to provide an all-round education for girls.

Highgate Junior School

Cholmeley House, 3 Bishopswood Road, London N6 4PL
Tel: 020 8340 9193
Fax: 020 8342 7273
email: jsoffice@highgateschool.org.uk
            pre-prep@highgateschool.org.uk
website: www.highgateschool.org.uk

Chairman of Governors: J F Mills, CBE, MA, BLitt

Principal of Junior School: **S M James**, BA, MA

Principal of Pre-Preparatory School: Mrs D Hecht, PDCE

Age Range. 3–11 Co-educational.
Number of Day Pupils. Junior (age 7–11): 320 boys and girls; Pre-Prep (age 3–7): 130 boys and girls.
Fees per term (2014–2015). Junior School: £5,555; Pre-Preparatory School: £5,245 (Reception–Year 2), £2,620 (Nursery).

Fees are inclusive of lunch (exc Nursery) and the use of books.

Pupils are prepared for Highgate School only. (*See entry in HMC section.*)

Entry to the Pre-Preparatory School is by individual assessment for entry at 3+. Entry to the Junior School is by test and interview at the age of 7. Transfer to the Senior School is at 11+.

The Pre-Preparatory School and the Junior School are both housed in self-contained buildings, located in Bishopswood Road, N6.

The School is well situated close to Hampstead Heath and has excellent facilities as the result of an ongoing development programme. There are several acres of playing fields attached; the Mallinson Sports Centre (which includes a 25-metre indoor pool) is shared with the Senior School, and a newly completed all-weather sports pitch.

A broad and balanced curriculum is followed with art, drama, music, games, ICT and design technology all playing an important part.

Charitable status. Sir Roger Cholmeley's School at Highgate is a Registered Charity, number 312765. The aims and objectives of the charity are educational, namely the maintenance of a school.

Hilden Grange School
Alpha Plus Group

Dry Hill Park Road, Tonbridge, Kent TN10 3BX
Tel: 01732 351169 / 01732 352706
Fax: 01732 377950 / 01732 773360
email: office@hildengrange.co.uk
website: www.hildengrange.co.uk
Facebook: Hilden-Grange-Preparatory-School

Headmaster: **J Withers**, BA Hons

Deputy Head: Mrs R Jubber, BSc, HDE

Age Range. 3–13 Co-educational.
Number of Pupils. 340: 240 Boys and 100 Girls.
Fees per term (2014–2015). Prep School £4,317, Pre-Prep £3,260, Nursery: £43.75 per day, £28.20 per morning, £21.90 per afternoon. Lunches are provided at £218–£248 per term.

Hilden Grange provides a friendly, secure and stimulating environment where children enjoy learning and participating in all aspects of school life.

We offer high standards of teaching and learning, excellent pastoral care and outstanding opportunities in art, music, drama and sport. Both inside and outside the classroom we strive to help each child achieve their own level of excellence – to do their best.

Though links are especially strong with Tonbridge and Sevenoaks boys and girls are prepared for all Independent Senior Schools and Grammar Schools at 11+ and 13+. We have an impressive record of success in this area. Examination results rank among the highest in Kent, and in the past ten years, all pupils gained entry to their chosen school at 13. Boys and girls who show special promise sit for scholarships to the school of their choice, and our track record in this area is excellent. 135 scholarships have been gained in the past thirteen years in areas as diverse as music, drama, technology and sport as well as traditional academic scholarships. Pupils benefit from specialist teaching in all subjects from Year 3, dedicated staff, and class sizes that average 16.

The School stands in about eight acres of attractive grounds in the residential area of North Tonbridge. Boys and girls are accepted into the Nursery at 3+ or at 4+ into the Pre-Preparatory Department within the school grounds, and at 7 into the main school. Tonbridge School Chorister awards may be gained; at present there are ten Choristers.

There is an outdoor heated swimming pool, a dedicated Sports Hall, all-weather tennis courts, Science Laboratories, Music Rooms, an Art and Design area, a Library, a Learning Support Area, a dining hall and two Information Technology Rooms, with networks of personal computers. An extensive building program was completed in September 2012 providing new education and communal facilities which are enjoyed by the whole school.

The Headmaster, staff and children welcome visitors and are pleased to show them around the School.

Hilden Oaks School & Nursery

38 Dry Hill Park Road, Tonbridge, Kent TN10 3BU
Tel: 01732 353941
Fax: 01732 353942

email: secretary@hildenoaks.co.uk
website: www.hildenoaks.co.uk
Twitter: @HildenOaks

Chair of Governors: Mr D Walker

Headmistress: Mrs S A Webb, MA, NPQH

Age Range. 3 months–11 years Co-educational.
Number of Children. 212.
Fees per term (2014–2015). Nursery (5 mornings 8.30 am to 12 noon): Under 2s £1,650, Over 2s £1,545, Over 3s £1,490. Reception £2,775, Years 1 & 2 £3,125, Years 3 & 4 £3,475, Years 5 & 6 £3,700

Hilden Oaks School, founded in 1919, became an Educational Trust in 1965. It is located in a quiet, residential area of north Tonbridge and the Trust owns all the land and buildings.

The Main School incorporates classrooms, the School Hall and an extensive, welcoming Library. The Acorn Building incorporates Music and Drama facilities and also provides spacious rooms for the Nursery and the youngest children in the school. The Stable Block has been developed as a self-contained unit for Reception. The Salmon Building houses the Pre-Prep and Prep Department and specialist Science and Art rooms. The site is a pleasant, enclosed garden setting with hard and grassed playing areas for netball, hockey and football and the school also uses the facilities of neighbouring Tonbridge School for swimming and athletics.

Hilden Oaks prides itself on being a happy, family school where every child is helped and encouraged to develop their potential and independent learning in a caring, stimulating and purposeful environment. We maintain high academic standards while expecting good manners and consideration to others at all times. This is reflected in the active parents' association, close liaison between parents and staff and the school's close involvement with the local community.

In the Pre-School and Pre-Preparatory Departments, children are given a solid foundation upon which they can build, with additional specialist teachers for ICT, French, Music and PE. The Preparatory Department has specialist teachers for Science, ICT, French, Art, Music and PE. All forms are taught by form teachers for the core subjects.

Our pupils enjoy taking part in Music and Drama with regular opportunities to perform. They also enjoy competitive sport in house matches and against other schools. Extracurricular activities include Choir, Drama, Art, ICT and Games. A late room operates for infants and juniors where children are provided with tea. Prep is supervised for the older children while the younger children can relax and play.

All pupils are prepared for both the Common Entrance examination at 11 and the 11+ examination for entry to grammar schools. Our results in these examinations put us among the top schools in Kent.

Hilden Oaks offers a challenging and supportive environment designed to inspire children to life-long learning.

Charitable status. Hilden Oaks School is a Registered Charity, number 307935. It exists to provide education for children.

Hoe Bridge School

Hoe Place, Old Woking, Surrey GU22 8JE
Tel: Prep School: 01483 760018/760065
  Pre-Prep: 01483 772194
Fax: 01483 757560
email: enquiriesprep@hoebridgeschool.co.uk
  enquiriespreprep@hoebridgeschool.co.uk
website: www.hoebridgeschool.co.uk

Co-educational Preparatory and Pre-Preparatory School.

Chairman of Governors: Ian Katté

Headmaster: **N Arkell**, BSc

Deputy Headmaster: G D P Scott, BEd Exeter

Head of Pre-Prep: Mrs Linda Renfrew, MA, PGCE

Age Range. 2½–14.
Number of Children. Prep 280, Pre-Prep 220.
Fees per term (2014–2015). Day: Prep £3,920–£4,540 (including lunch); Pre-Prep £640–£3,160 (including lunch).

Hoe Bridge School is set in a perfect location on the outskirts of Woking surrounded by 22 acres of beautiful grounds and woodland and is only 20 minutes from London.

At the heart of Hoe Bridge stands the stunning 17th century mansion, Hoe Place. Hoe Place is steeped in history and was once the favourite retreat for Lady Castlemaine, one of the mistresses of King Charles II. Major development has taken place over the past few years and the school now boasts outstanding 21st century facilities. These facilities are second to none and we are immensely proud of the successes and achievements of our children as they take full advantage of all that is available to them here. The children are equally proud to call Hoe Bridge their school.

The Pre-Prep department is located in its own purpose-built building and achieved "Outstanding" throughout at our last inspection. From Nursery to Year 2 the creative curriculum followed at the Pre-Prep enables the children to learn through play, adventure, discovery and experience.

Transition to the Prep Department is seamless and as children mature they become increasingly independent learners in preparation for the move to senior school. The results achieved by the children across the ability range are outstanding leading to success at some of the country's leading schools. The pupils are inspired by dedicated staff, lessons are rigorous and interactive and achievement is excellent.

Alongside the academics sport, music, art and drama play a major part throughout the school and children excel in many areas: end-of-year productions; sporting excellence achieving national success in netball and hockey, county success in cricket and football; individual musical success in national youth orchestras and choirs and a spectacular annual art exhibition. Scholarships in all these areas are won every year to a variety of schools across the country. "The pupils' successes in academic work, sport and music, both individually and in groups, are due to their excellent attitudes to learning." Latest ISI Inspection Report.

Senior pupils in Years 7 and 8 take part in regular extracurricular activities such as Bush Craft weekends, French trips, cricket and netball tours and are challenged by preparing and presenting a gourmet meal to their parents. It is at this stage of their time at Hoe Bridge that they take on extra responsibility becoming prefects and role models to the younger children.

The atmosphere of every school is unique and we consider the strength and attraction of Hoe Bridge to lie in the atmosphere here. Created by the staff and children it combines warmth, care, good relations and pride in achievement. The children spend ten years at Hoe Bridge. These are formative years and they should be ten happy and rewarding ones and our aim is to do the very best for each child. Standards and targets are realistic, though set as high as possible. The bright are challenged and the less able supported; we endeavour to instil confidence in all our children. Visitors are amazed how happy the children are, how determined they are to succeed and how much they care about each other.

The School has an extremely good reputation and we are constantly striving to preserve the atmosphere, improve our results and explore all possibilities for enriching both the School and the children.

Charitable status. Hoe Bridge School is a Registered Charity, number 295808. It exists to provide a rounded education for children aged 2½–14.

Holme Grange School

Heathlands Road, Wokingham, Berkshire RG40 3AL
Tel: 0118 9781566
Fax: 0118 9770810
email: school@holmegrange.org
website: www.holmegrange.org
Twitter: @HolmeGrangeHead

Chairman of Governors: A Finch, Former Company
Director

Head: **Mrs Claire Robinson**, BA, PGCE, NPQH

Age Range. 3–13 Co-educational (3–16 from September
2015).
Number of Pupils. 310: 185 boys, 125 girls.
Fees per term (2014–2015). Little Grange Nursery
£1,765–£2,995; Pre-Preparatory: £3,200 (Reception),
£3,250 (Years 1–2); Prep: £4,100 (Years 3–4), £4,200 (Years
5–8), £4500 (Years 9–11) with an option to pay over 10
months. Reductions for second and subsequent children.

The School is a Day School receiving pupils from a wide
catchment area and holiday care is available throughout the
school holidays.

The School occupies a large country mansion, to which
many additional facilities have been added, most recently,
an outdoor classroom, additional science laboratory and a 5-
classroom block. Plans are currently in place to build a 300-
seat theatre, music school and drama suite in 2015.

The School is set in just over 20 acres of grounds comprising grass pitches, all-weather surfaces and woodland
walks for the children to explore. Specialist teaching and
facilities for Music, Art and Technology, Dance, Performing
Arts, Science, ICT and Sport enhance our provision and support the individual development of all our pupils. Holme
Grange is one of the first schools in the area to have gained
Forest School status and has three qualified Forest Leaders
on the Staff, thus allowing opportunities for children to
achieve and develop confidence through hands-on learning
in a woodland environment. The recently erected Polytunnel
provides opportunities for pupils to learn about sustainable
education while the chickens and ducks not only supply to
the school kitchens but also enable the pupils to learn about
lifecycles in a very hands-on manner.

Little Grange is an established Nursery for 3 and 4 year
olds in its own safe, secure environment within the School
grounds, providing flexible education either part or full day
including lunch and tea. All children may stay to 6.00 pm.

We are non-selective and both welcome and cater for
pupils of a wide range of ability. We aim to foster confidence and a love of learning across the age range. Pupils are
accepted from the start of the term in which they turn 3 providing continuous education until they take the Common
Entrance or Scholarship examinations (Academic, Art,
Music) for Senior Independent Schools. At both there is an
enviable record of success. From September 2015, following requests from parents, we will be admitting our first
Year 9 pupils and preparing students for their GCSE examinations in Year 11.

The Headteacher is assisted by a highly qualified and
experienced teaching staff with classroom assistants in the
Pre-Prep and NNEB assistants in Little Grange. There is an
Accelerated Learning Centre giving help to those children
with special needs.

The School's policy is to set high standards, to establish
good all-round personalities and to give inspiration for each
pupil's life. Our aim is to create an environment where
every child can thrive. We appreciate children's differences
and respond to their individual needs. In 2013 we were
awarded the prestigious NACE Challenge Award for More
Able, Gifted and Talented Pupils in recognition of the high
quality work by the whole school in challenging all pupils to
achieve their best.

At Holme Grange we offer excellence in personalised
learning – a rare school that caters equally well for pupils at
both ends of the academic continuum. We believe in our
pupils and instil a belief in themselves.

We develop intellectual character through our learning
habits and the ethos throughout the school is one of warmth
and friendliness – questioning; divergent thinking and the
freedom to learn from mistakes are all encouraged. Pupils
are inspired to take responsibility for their own learning,
develop good work habits and gain a sense that learning can
thrill and invigorate.

We deliver a rounded education by providing opportunities in sport, the arts, languages, technology and a wide
range of activities, maximising opportunities for success for
all. We hope to inspire your child both in and outside of the
classroom. At Holme Grange School, we foster self-reliance, self-discipline and self-confidence in a caring community where children gain interests and characteristics that
give them a head start for life.

At Holme Grange we will not only unlock your child's
potential but will also foster within them, a passion for
learning. Our pupils are prepared to succeed in an ever
changing, competitive world. We offer challenge, we strive
to inspire, develop confidence, provide opportunity and
realise potential in every child – and now up to the age of 16.

We are committed to providing the very best education.
Academic standards are excellent. We provide our pupils
with a toolkit to live their lives and when they eventually
enter the adult world, we can be confident they will do so
well prepared with a real life foundation for every challenge
they will face.

Life in our school is a journey of exploration, and discovery. We are a holistic school offering an all-round education,
bursting with life and vitality.

The School is a Trust, administered by a board of Governors who have considerable experience in education and
business.

Charitable status. Holme Grange Limited is a Registered Charity, number 309105. It exists to serve the local
community in providing an all-round education for boys and
girls.

Holmewood House

**Barrow Lane, Langton Green, Tunbridge Wells, Kent
TN3 0EB**
Tel: 01892 860000
Fax: 01892 863970
email: admin@holmewoodhouse.co.uk
             registrar@holmewoodhouse.co.uk
website: www.holmewoodhouse.co.uk

Chairman of the Governors: M A Evans

Headmaster: **J D B Marjoribanks**, BEd Hons, Dip d'Et Fr

Deputy Headmaster: J Wyld, BA Hons, PGCE

Age Range. 3–13.
Number of Pupils. 462 Boys and Girls.
Fees per term (2014–2015). Day Pupils: Years 5–8
£5,650, Years 3 & 4 £5,535, Pre-Prep £3,250–£3,750, Nursery £1,750–£2,575. Boarders: £6,680. There are reductions
for third and fourth siblings, and children of Old Holme-
woodians. Scholarships are available for entry into Years
3–7; sports, art and music awards are also available for children showing talent in these areas and entering Years 5–8.

The school was founded in 1945 as a boys' school. Girls
were admitted in 1989 and we have been fully co-educational for many years. The school is a Charitable Educa-

tional Trust with a Board of Governors. Holmewood stands in over 30 acres of beautiful grounds on the Kent/Sussex border, just outside Tunbridge Wells, which is one hour by rail from London.

The pastoral side of the school is carefully set in place to ensure there is a member of staff responsible for every child. ISI Inspectors have described our pastoral care as *exemplary. The family atmosphere of the school is outstanding. Pupils have a strong sense of well-being and security.*

The breadth and quality of pupils' achievements are outstanding. Thanks to our highly qualified, dedicated and enthusiastic staff, Holmewood has an outstanding scholastic record in Common Entrance and Scholarship examinations. Despite being essentially a non-selective school, every year our Year 8 pupils gain a large number of scholarships (Academic, Music, Art, DT, Drama and Sport) to senior schools. A strong Learning Support Department (ISI Inspection: *a strength of the school*) provides additional support for less able pupils and we are proud of the achievements of those children who may require some additional support.

Children follow a broad curriculum throughout the school. For example, French is taught from the Nursery; pupils have separate teaching of Physics, Chemistry and Biology from Year 6; all children learn Latin for two years and Ancient Greek is also available. Year 7 and 8 have the opportunity to study Mandarin, Philosophy, Reasoning, Critical Thinking and Debating.

Holmewood leads the way in the use of educational ICT. The school has 250 networked computers and three networked computer rooms. All classrooms have interactive whiteboards. Pupils have timetabled ICT lessons from Reception.

ISI Inspection: *Outstanding creative development is promoted in Art, Design Technology and Music. A wealth of extra-curricular activities enriches the experience of pupils.*

Our state-of-the-art Jubilee Theatre provides a showcase for the many concerts and stunning productions staged by our excellent music and drama departments. Children are encouraged to start learning an instrument in Year 1 (whatever they like the sound of!) and the Pre-Prep Orchestra produces a sound to be proud of! From these first musical notes, each year a number of our pupils progress on to win music scholarships to their senior schools.

The Art Department consists of one large studio classroom and a pottery, equipped with kiln, potter's wheel and slab roller. There are after-school Art activities throughout the week, including a ceramics club, and the Community Art Project runs for two terms of the year, involving pupils from five local primary schools and culminating in an exciting final exhibition. Pupils wishing to apply for an art scholarship are encouraged and supported.

The resources in our large Design Technology Department are on a par with senior schools. In DT, children undertake a range of exciting projects and acquire skills which enable them to produce pieces of practical work way beyond their age. Several pupils have won DT scholarships to senior schools in recent years.

Expert coaching is given in a wide variety of sports and these include rugby, soccer, hockey, gymnastics, netball, cricket, tennis and table tennis, shooting, athletics, cross-country, golf, archery, climbing, judo, basketball, dance, squash, rounders and swimming. We regularly play at national level in most sports. There is a large Sports Hall, an indoor swimming pool, hard tennis courts, three squash courts, an astro surface hockey/football pitch and running track, and an indoor .22 shooting range.

An extensive activity programme which is part of every school day in the Prep School provides all children with the opportunity to 'have a go' at a wide range of activities. We encourage all the children to try something different – many of our boys love cooking!

Weekly and flexi boarding are becoming increasingly popular.

Holmewood is an inspiring place for children. ISI Inspection: *Pupils clearly enjoy coming to school and revel in the opportunities the school provides.*

Charitable status. Holmewood House is a Registered Charity, number 279267.

Holmwood House Preparatory School

Chitts Hill, Lexden, Colchester, Essex CO3 9ST
Tel: 01206 574305
Fax: 01206 768269
email: headmaster@holmwood.essex.sch.uk
website: www.holmwood.essex.sch.uk

Headmaster: **Alexander Mitchell**, BA Hons, LLCM, PGCE

Age Range. 4–13 Co-educational. Nursery: 6 months to 4 years.

Number of Pupils. 300.

Fees per term (2014–2015). Day Pupils £2,930–£5,170; Boarding: £30 per night. 5 nights boarding for the price of 4. All fees are inclusive; there are no compulsory extras. Nursery fees dependent on hours attended.

Holmwood House was founded in 1922 and stands in 34 acres of grounds only 2 kms from Colchester town centre. Children of all abilities are welcomed and are prepared for the Common Entrance examination and for scholarships to senior independent schools both locally and nationally.

The principal aim of the school is genuine all-round education with high academic standards at its core. Small class sizes, well-qualified staff, superb facilities and high-quality leadership ensure pupils at all levels make excellent progress. The Pre-Prep department enjoys spacious and modern accommodation and with the introduction of *Forest School*, the children benefit even more from the beautiful grounds through a programme of outdoor learning. Specialist teaching starts in Reception (French, music, PE, games, swimming) and this increases by age 6/7 (art, science, sports teams). In the Prep school, specialist teaching in all subjects offers pupils an outstanding range and depth of curriculum. Children are increasingly encouraged to take personal ownership of their learning through creative, collaborative and independent activities in all subjects. Pupils' progress is carefully monitored and the relationship between parents and school is an important partnership. Excellent Learning Support is available when required and all teachers have a highly developed understanding of learning styles, ability levels and strategies to enhance progress.

Facilities include 20 acres of sports fields; vibrant, well-equipped classrooms; five squash courts; indoor heated swimming pool; state-of-the-art sports hall; seven tennis courts (two covered); floodlit tarmac play area; 2 adventure playgrounds; a permanent stage with sound and lighting systems; superb Art and Design facilities incorporating print and ceramic workshop; separate Music facilities. The majority of pupils study at least one musical instrument. There are four well-equipped science laboratories. The ICT facilities, networked to all classrooms including two ICT suites and iPads, also supports pupils' learning.

The extensive sports programme in which every child takes part from age 7, is delivered through generous scheduled sessions of instruction in afternoons and evenings and weekly matches against other schools are a strong feature of the week. Classes and compulsory games are all timetabled conventionally; as are 'preps' – supervised homework. An impressive activities programme provides opportunities for pupils to experience a wide range of options; e.g. archery, fencing, kung-fu, design technology, cookery, knitting, jewellery design, athletics, squash, tennis, badminton, dance and much more. Music and drama flourish particularly, ranging from the large-scale productions to the smaller ensembles.

Flexi boarding is a popular option open to all pupils from Year 5 upwards and is a great start for those children who plan to go on to a senior boarding school, where they can gain a boarding experience in familiar surroundings with their friends, to develop the necessary confidence. There is a wide range of opportunities and activities for boarders to explore and during boarding time, pupils have use of all of the school's facilities, as well as a large cinema-type TV screen for special sports events and lectures, pool tables, table football, air hockey, safe darts and table tennis.

Pastoral care is excellent and the family atmosphere is palpable. Pupils enjoy exceptionally good relationships with their teachers and the supportive atmosphere encourages them to make the most of their abilities and the abundance of opportunities on offer. Children at Holmwood House are comfortably confident, display excellent manners and have a thirst for learning. The school's guiding principles of care, courtesy and consideration provide a framework in which children can develop their values, emotional intelligence and sense of citizenship within this and the wider community.

Wraparound care is offered as an option for children from Reception to Year 3 from 7.30 am, up until 6.00 pm, with one member of staff for every 8 children. Pupils in Year 4 upwards also have the option to be dropped off at 7.30 am and all Prep pupils have the option to stay until 6.10 pm at no extra cost.

Holmwood House Nursery caters for children from 6 months to 4 years. A flexible service is offered so that children can attend either during Holmwood House term only, or for any number of different sessions and options. The Nursery is open for 48 weeks in the year.

We would be pleased to send our prospectus and to welcome visitors to the school.

Holy Cross Preparatory School

George Road, Kingston-upon-Thames, Surrey KT2 7NU
Tel: 020 8942 0729
Fax: 020 8336 0764
email: admissions@holycrossprep.com
website: www.holycrossprepschool.co.uk

Headmistress: **Mrs S Hair**

Age Range. 4–11.
Number of Girls. 250.
Fees per term (2014–2015). £3,600. Lunch: £208.
Location. The school is situated on a private estate in an attractive area of Kingston Hill.
Facilities. The building, the former home of John Galsworthy, is of both historical and literary interest and provides excellent accommodation for two classes in each year group through the school from Reception to Year Six. The school contains a state-of-the-art sports and performing arts hall, library, Design and Technology Centre, Music suite, ICT suite, science and cookery room, art room and 14 classrooms all with computers.

The 8 acres of stunning grounds include two tennis/netball courts, hockey pitch, running track and three large playing areas which have play equipment, including adventure climbing frames. There is a nature trail and ecology area, together with a fountain within the ornamental lawns and a pond which is well used in science lessons.
Educational Philosophy. The school was founded by the Sisters of the Holy Cross, an international teaching order who have been engaged in the work of education since

1844. A sound Christian education is given in an Ecumenical framework. The children are happy, cared for and well disciplined. The emphasis is on developing the God-given gifts of each child to their fullest potential, in a stimulating, friendly atmosphere where high standards of work, behaviour and contribution to the well being of the school community are expected.
Curriculum. There is a broad and relevant curriculum providing a high standard of education. Specialist teaching in French, Music, Physical Education, drama, art and Information Technology. The school has a first rate record of success in Common Entrance and in preparing pupils for top Senior Independent, High and Grammar Schools. The varied extra-curricular activities include ballet and dance, Speech & Drama, pottery, Art and Design, cello, piano, flute, clarinet, violin, guitar, sports, technology, French, debating, judo, tennis, origami and chess.
Charitable status. Holy Cross Preparatory School is a Registered Charity, number 238426. It is a Roman Catholic School providing excellence in Christian education to local children.

Homefield Preparatory School

Western Road, Sutton, Surrey SM1 2TE
Tel: 020 8642 0965
Fax: 020 8642 0965
email: registrar@homefield.sutton.sch.uk
website: www.homefield.sutton.sch.uk
Twitter: @HomefieldSchool
Facebook: /homefield.school

"I don't believe we could have found a better school in the country to bring out the best in both our sons."

Chairman of Governors: Dr Inderpreet Dhingra, BSc Hons, PhD, MBA, FSI

Head: **Mr John Towers**, MA, PGCE, NPQH

Age Range. 3–13.
Number of Boys. 400.
Fees per term (2014–2015). Senior Department £3,950; Junior Department: 3rd Year £3,750, 2nd Year £3,350, 1st Year £2,850; Early Years Unit: Reception £2,670, Nursery: £2,570 (full day), £1,710 (mornings only). Lunches: £305 (Seniors and Juniors), £265 (Nursery and Reception).
Homefield is a preparatory school for 400 boys aged 3 to 13, and 50 staff, housed in an extensive purpose-built complex with well-equipped science laboratories, large Art, DT and Music suites, complemented by a spacious Early Years' Unit and a two-acre adjoining playing field.
Founded in 1870, Homefield has its roots in the 19th century and its branches in the twenty-first. The School has cemented its powerful academic reputation by continuing to achieve a 100% pass rate at Common Entrance to 46 senior schools over the last 10 years. 50 scholarships have been won to senior independent schools for academic, musical, sporting, artistic and all-round accomplishment in the last two years.
Throughout the School's development it has been very careful to preserve the original family ethos and intimacy, together with its reputation for academic excellence, the breadth of extra-curricular sporting, musical and artistic provision and first-class pastoral care. We pride ourselves on achieving fulfilment of individual potential, the openness of communication, the provision of specialist teaching at the earliest appropriate opportunity (French, ICT, Music and Sport from the Foundation Stage), our commitment to best practice and all-round academic, musical, dramatic, sporting and artistic achievements. *"Pupils make a strong contribution to their learning through their highly motivated and*

enthusiastic attitudes. The quality of pupils' achievements and learning is excellent." (ISI Inspection, March 2013.)

The school has county or national representatives in table tennis, squash, tennis, athletics, swimming, soccer, rugby, cricket and chess.

Awareness of others is encouraged and the pupils are involved in many fundraising charity events, raising over £11,000 last year.

A wide range of opportunities are available to extend gifted pupils and learning support is available for children with special needs.

We offer academic, sporting, art and music scholarships as well as occasional bursaries.

Daily minibuses run to and from Wimbledon and other areas.

Breakfast and after school clubs are available.

Charitable status. Homefield Preparatory School Trust Limited is a Registered Charity, number 312753. It exists to provide education for boys.

Hornsby House School

Hearnville Road, London SW12 8RS
Tel: 020 8673 7573
Fax: 020 8673 6722
email: school@hornsbyhouse.org.uk
website: www.hornsbyhouse.org.uk

Chair of Governors: Mr Huw Davies

Headmaster: **Mr Edward Rees**, BA Ed Hons

Age Range. 4–11.
Number of Pupils. 209 Girls, 208 Boys.
Fees per term (2014–2015). £4,125 (Reception to Year 2), £4,435 (Years 3 to 6). Lunch: £215.

Hornsby House is a thriving IAPS co-educational prep school in Wandsworth, southwest London. At their most recent inspection in November 2010, the Independent Schools Inspectorate judged Hornsby House pupils' overall achievement as "excellent" and found that "pupils achieve high academic standards within a wide and creative curriculum". Pupils' personal development was described as "excellent and a strength of the school".

Hornsby House provides a nurturing environment where attainment and happiness are key aims and the children achieve outstanding educational outcomes as a result. Results for the latest group of 51 Year 6 children included 17 scholarships and awards.

There are three classes in each year group, a generous staff : pupil ratio and around 420 pupils in the school. Entry into Reception classes is unassessed and is on a first-come, first-served basis with priority being given to siblings. Children wishing to enter the school in year groups above Reception are required to attend an assessment.

There is an extensive co-curricular programme with over 50 clubs, as well as before and after school care. Over half the children in the school play a musical instrument and a third sing in one of the three choirs. Sport is a central part of the curriculum, the staffing level is excellent and the benefits of teamwork are seen clearly in school life as a whole. The school has outstanding ICT infrastructure, with four classrooms set up as e-learning suites.

The majority of leavers go to one of six London day schools: Dulwich College, JAGS, Alleyn's, Emanuel, Streatham & Clapham High School and Whitgift. The remainder move on to other day or boarding schools.

To arrange a visit to see the children at work, please contact the Registrar.

Charitable status. Hornsby House Educational Trust is a Registered Charity, number 800284.

Horris Hill

Newtown, Newbury, Berks RG20 9DJ
Tel: 01635 40594
email: info@horrishill.com
website: www.horrishill.com

Chairman of Governors: C J Ball, Esq

Headmaster: **G F Tollit**, BA Hons

Deputy Headmaster: F J Beardmore-Gray, BA Hons, PGCE

Age Range. 7–13.
Number of Boys. Boarders 100, Day 15.
Fees per term (2014–2015). Boarders £8,000; Day £5,935. (No compulsory Extras)

Horris Hill is one of the leading boys' prep schools in the UK. 115 boys live in the most spectacular grounds just south of Newbury; most are boarders, but we enjoy having our few dayboys. Small means that we know the boys and their parents very well and our latest Inspection Reports (see www.horrishill.com) emphasise the fact that pastoral care is outstanding. High expectations in everything ensure a first-class prep school education with confident, charming boys going on to the top independent schools. Most Horris Hill parents choose boys-only schools for the next stage and over half our boys go on to Winchester, Radley and Eton; the remainder going to Sherborne, Harrow, Milton Abbey, Shrewsbury, Bradfield, Marlborough and many others.

2014 Results: Three boys have won Academic Scholarships to Winchester and one has been awarded an academic exhibition. In addition, one Horris Hill boy has won a King's Scholarship to Eton.

Busy weekends, high academic standards, superb music and art, brilliant sport make this a wonderful school to work in for both staff and boys. Come and see for yourselves.

Charitable status. Horris Hill Preparatory School Trust Limited is a Registered Charity, number 307331. It exists to prepare boys for the Senior Independent Schools.

Hunter Hall School

Frenchfield, Penrith, Cumbria CA11 8UA
Tel: 01768 891291
Fax: 01768 899161
email: office@hunterhall.cumbria.sch.uk
website: www.hunterhall.co.uk

Chairman of Governors: Mr Mike Bauer

Head: **Mrs Donna Vinsome**, BEd Hons, MA

Age Range. 3–11 co-educational.
Number of Pupils. 105.
Fees per term (2014–2015). £2,225 Lower School (Reception to Year 2) £2,575 Upper School (Year 3 to Year 6) including after-school activities. Nursery paid per hour.

Hunter Hall School has grown rapidly from its inception 28 years ago into a thriving and vibrant community, providing high quality education for children aged 3 to 11. Its location is idyllic, in imaginatively converted farm buildings on the outskirts of Penrith and only 2 km from the M6, providing easy access to the attractions of the Lake District and the north of England generally.

It is providing a range of experiences that is important at Hunter Hall and staff recognise that effective learning can take place in a variety of situations. Within the classroom, creativity is emphasised, and the objective is to provide the children with the knowledge, skills and confidence to prosper, not only whilst at Hunter Hall, but also in the schools that they will subsequently join. In the Foundation Stage, the activities that are undertaken are determined by the children, originating from their own interests and needs, then facilitated by the staff. The aim is to stimulate curiosity, interest and excitement in learning, and to encourage self-discipline and develop confidence. These qualities extend as the children move through the school, with the emphasis on providing them with a range of skills to help them to recognise that they have the ability (and courage) to think. In addition, perseverance and co-operation are especially valued, creating a warm, friendly and almost tangible sense of community within the school.

The curriculum is broad, and specialist subject teaching is provided from Year 3. Class sizes are small. Teaching facilities are very good, with ICT featuring prominently in learning. Pupils are encouraged to take responsibility for their own progress and to set themselves challenging targets.

Children at Hunter Hall spend a great deal of time outdoors and, indeed, beyond the school boundaries. The environment in the local area lends itself admirably to geographical and historical investigation, as well as providing an unrivalled stage for exploration and adventure as part of our Outdoor learning sessions. Participation in Art, Drama and Music is extremely active, with extensive representation at local festivals. The variety and quality of sport that is on offer is equally remarkable, and Hunter Hall children have received wide-ranging recognition at local and national level in recent years.

This is a happy school, in which a Christian ethos is present, but never over-dominant. Children (and their parents) and staff enjoy spending time here and contributing to the development of the community.

Charitable status. Hunter Hall School Ltd is a Registered Charity, number 1059098.

Hurlingham School

122 Putney Bridge Road, Putney, London SW15 2NQ
Tel: 020 8874 7186
Fax: 020 8875 0372
email: office@hurlinghamschool.co.uk
website: www.hurlinghamschool.co.uk

Headmaster: **Mr Jonathan Brough**, BEd Hons Cantab, NPQH, FCollT

Age Range. 4–11 Co-educational.
Number of Pupils. 326.
Fees per term (2014–2015). £4,620–£4,820.
Location and Facilities. Hurlingham is a non-selective independent preparatory school in Putney, in very close proximity to Wandsworth Park. The modern and spacious building provides excellent facilities which include bright classrooms, a large gym and a dance and drama studio, as well as a science laboratory, art studio, two ICT suites and several music rooms. Recreational space includes a large playground with climbing wall and a nature garden.

Ethos. The School's ethos is to provide a happy, secure atmosphere in which children flourish both academically and personally. Experienced and enthusiastic teachers provide opportunities for the children that strongly promote creativity and independence of thought, essential attributes for a child growing up in the 21st Century. Self-confidence, self-discipline, self-motivation, self-esteem and above all a thirst and enjoyment for learning are nurtured.

Academic. The curriculum is broad, with the aim of providing a balanced and rounded education in which every child is treated as an individual and is encouraged to make the most of their particular talents. The important skills of reading, writing and numeracy are given a high priority in

everyday teaching; these are delivered through many exciting cross-curricular topics which bring the children's learning alive and allow them to make sense of the world around them. All children learn French and Spanish in Reception, then choose one for the remainder of their time in school. Latin is taught from Form IV; pottery and philosophy are also greatly enjoyed across the school.

Sport. Hurlingham children are fit and healthy, and all boys and girls participate enthusiastically. Seasonal team games skills are taught in football, rugby, hockey, netball, cricket, rounders, gym and athletics. Numerous matches are organised with other local schools throughout the sporting year. Every Summer Term the whole school joins in the traditional Sports Day activities, and a family picnic lunch.

Music. Hurlingham has an excellent music department. The youngest children are encouraged to sing, play simple instruments and enjoy performing. For older pupils there are many opportunities to learn individual instruments, play in ensembles and participate in music concerts. There are several, very popular and talented, choirs and ensemble groups.

Pastoral Care. Strong pastoral care is a very important feature of life at Hurlingham. All staff foster an intimate and welcoming environment centred on family values, with a clear focus on good manners and respect for one another. The House System, School Council and various pupil committees provide the children with wonderful opportunities to support each other and express their views about their own school.

Clubs. Children are encouraged to participate in a wide range of clubs which include: art, ballet, chess, drama, Japanese, karate, music, modern dance, pottery and science. Older children are able to do their homework in school at homework club.

Starting Out. Children begin their life at Hurlingham in Reception which, although contained within the school building, is a separate area allowing children to feel part of the whole school but not overwhelmed by it. The three parallel classrooms (divided according to the children's age) all have direct access on to the playground, thus enabling the teaching of the curriculum to extend outside. There is also a cosy dedicated Hall which provides space for all three forms to join together for group activities, regular access to computers and a quiet place for reading.

Entry. For entry to Reception there is no entrance test or interview. Places are offered in order of registration, although siblings, and those living within 1.2 km of the school, are given priority. Older children are invited to spend a day at Hurlingham and take part in lessons in order to assess their academic ability. Scholarships are available for children joining from 7+ onwards.

School Visits. Appointments should be arranged with the School Office. There is an underground car park which visitors are welcome to use.

Hurstpierpoint College Preparatory School
A Woodard School

Chalker's Lane, Hurstpierpoint, West Sussex BN6 9JS
Tel: 01273 834975 (Prep and Pre-Prep)
Fax: 01273 836900
email: prepadmissions@hppc.co.uk
website: www.hppc.co.uk

Chairman of Governors: Mr A Jarvis, BEd, MA, FRSA

Head of Prep and Pre-Prep School: **I D Pattison**, BSc

Age Range. 4–13 Co-educational.
Number of Pupils. Prep 292; Pre-Prep 54.

Fees per term (2014–2015). Prep: Years 7–8 £4,895, Years 4–6 £4,765, Year 3 £4,145. Pre-Prep: £2,690–£2,895. There are no compulsory extras.

The Prep and Pre-Prep Schools of Hurstpierpoint College (*see entry in HMC section*) share a beautiful 140-acre campus with the College. Although both Schools operate independently of the Senior School, having their own timetable, staff, buildings and Heads, the schools work closely together to offer a first-class programme of education for boys and girls from the age of 4 to 18.

Hurst's Pre-Prep School for children aged 4–7 opened in 2001. It occupies a self-contained unit with reception area and well-equipped classrooms, with its own extensive, fenced hard and grass play areas. There is one class in each year group.

The Prep School has joint use of many of the College's superb facilities (including 25m indoor swimming pool, fully-equipped modern CDT centre, theatre, drama and dance studios, music school, large sports hall, full-size Astroturf hockey pitch, tennis courts and squash courts). A new 15-classroom extension to the College teaching block in 2009 provided new accommodation for Prep School Years 7 and 8 along with the Senior School. New science laboratories for both schools opened in 2011.

The aim of the schools is to provide an outstanding education in a secure and happy environment. The staff's overriding priority is to guide and inspire young people to develop their potential to the full, striving for the highest possible standards in the classroom, on the sports field, in the creative and performing arts and in a wide range of skills and activities.

The Prep School has a 5-day academic week with a Saturday afternoon match programme that runs throughout the school year.

The academic programme is exciting and innovative, with independent learning and mobile technology at the heart of our teaching and learning. The children are provided with an excellent grounding in the more traditional subjects and, as they progress through the school, they are encouraged to take more responsibility for their learning in order to develop the qualities and skills required for academic success in the Senior School.

The Sports programme is extensive: Football, Netball, Rounders, Rugby, Cricket, Hockey, Squash, Swimming, Tennis, Basketball and Athletics. In addition there is a wide-ranging activity programme in place every day which caters for the interests of all pupils.

The Music, Drama and Dance Departments are also very strong; about half the pupils learn musical instruments. The Preparatory School choir performs at the weekly Chapel service. There are at least three musicals or plays each year involving many children throughout the School.

There is always one qualified person on the school site with responsibility for first aid. Prep School children are initially assessed in the School and staff will refer children to the College Medical Centre as necessary.

Each year a number of awards are available for entry into Year 7 (11+): scholarships are available for Music and up to 10 Academic scholarships are awarded at the discretion of the Head.

Charitable status. Hurstpierpoint College is a Registered Charity, number 1076498. The College provides a Christian education to boys and girls between the ages of four and eighteen.

Inglefield House
Haberdashers' Monmouth School for Girls Preparatory School

Hereford Road, Monmouth NP25 5XT
Tel: 01600 711205
          01600 711104 (Admissions)
Fax: 01600 711118 (Admissions)
email: admissions@hmsg.co.uk
website: www.inglefieldhouse.org
          www.habs-monmouth.org

A love of learning and an inquisitive, enthusiastic attitude to life are the cornerstones of our ethos, producing independent, confident girls who also have a very strong sense of responsibility and consideration of others. Girls at Inglefield House are happy and fulfilled, with a sense of fun and a sense of purpose.

Chairman of Governors: Mr J B S Swallow, MA, FCA

Head: Mrs H Phillips, BA, BEd

Age Range. Girls 7–11. Boarding from age 7.
Number of Pupils. 112.
Fees per term (2014–2015). Day £3,317, Boarding £6,239.

Entrance to Inglefield House is selective, but great care is taken to look for potential, not just test performance.

A broad but balanced curriculum captures the imagination and allows girls to thrive in a variety of disciplines. Class-based teaching in Years 3 and 4 offers the core subjects of English, Maths and Science, supplemented by humanities, art, physical education, modern foreign languages, music and drama. In Years 5 and 6, there is more specialist teaching, ensuring that the girls receive the finest tuition and allowing use of the excellent senior school facilities. This includes use of the science laboratories and the ICT suites.

With encouragement and a high degree of personal attention, girls are given every opportunity to maximise their potential and achieve academic excellence. This forms just part of a school life which is vibrant, exciting and outward looking. Our location in the Wye Valley allows us to make educational trips to both Cardiff and Bristol with ease, as well as going further afield. Residential trips are highly effective in broadening horizons and increasing a sense of independence as girls move into Years 5 and 6.

The performing arts are a wonderful method of building self-confidence in the young girls at school. Individual music lessons, the school orchestra, choir and string sections offer a chance to flourish at music, with a wide range of dance being taught as part of PE and within the extended curriculum.

Bringing enjoyment and enthusiasm to sport is another of our central aims. Sport plays a big part in school life, with specialist PE teaching and a number of extra-curricular clubs each week. We aim to nurture a love of team sports and to balance this with other activities which the girls can continue to enjoy into their adult lives. Making the most of our membership of IAPS, teams compete on a national level in a variety of sports, including hockey, netball, gymnastics and fencing. Inglefield girls have the advantage of using the senior school facilities including the 25-metre swimming pool, the gymnasium, a full-size sports hall and astroturf pitches.

There is a relaxed, warm relationship between children and staff, whether boarders or day girls. Boarding creates a real sense of community throughout Inglefield, where girls thrive in a safe, friendly environment which produces thoughtful, intelligent, compassionate girls who are well equipped for senior school life.

A number of scholarships are awarded each year to girls moving on to the senior school. (*For further details see Haberdashers' Monmouth School for Girls entry in the GSA section.*)

Inglefield House enjoys a close relationship with its brother school, The Grange, Monmouth Preparatory School and various joint events take place during the year.

Charitable status. William Jones's Schools Foundation is a Registered Charity, number 525616.

Ipswich Preparatory School

3 Ivry Street, Ipswich, Suffolk IP1 3QW
Tel: 01473 282800
Fax: 01473 400067
email: prepadmissions@ipswich.suffolk.sch.uk
website: www.ipswich.suffolk.sch.uk

Chairman of Governors: Mr K Daniels, ACII, FPMI

Headteacher: **Mrs A H Childs**, BA QTS, PGC PSE, Dip Ed, MA

Age Range. 2–11.
Number of Pupils. 310.
Fees per term (2014–2015). Years 4–6 £3,448; Year 3 (inc lunch) £3,626; Reception, Years 1 & 2 (inc lunch) £3,309; Nursery (inc lunch): £28.96 per am/pm session, £54.75 per whole day.

The Preparatory School has its own staff and Headteacher. It is located just across the road from the senior school (*see Ipswich School entry in HMC section*).

The school seeks to provide a learning environment which allows pupils to develop skills and personal qualities. The curriculum is planned to encourage the children to develop lively, enquiring minds and appropriate emphasis is placed on securing for each child a firm foundation of skills in literacy and numeracy. The broad, balanced curriculum offered provides a breadth of experience which is suitable for children of primary age. High academic standards are reached by the pupils, but in addition, they are encouraged to develop skills in music, art, drama and sport.

Children's happiness is considered essential and the School works closely with parents to ensure a partnership which provides the best possible care for all girls and boys.

The school enjoys the advantage of sharing Senior School facilities such as playing fields, sports hall, swimming pool, theatre/concert hall and the Chapel. The Prep School has its own Art, Design Technology, ICT and Science facilities.

Charitable status. Ipswich Preparatory School is part of Ipswich School, which is a Registered Charity, number 310493. It exists for the purpose of educating children.

James Allen's Preparatory School

East Dulwich Grove, London SE22 8TE
Tel: 020 8693 0374
email: japsadmissions@jags.org.uk
website: www.jags.org.uk

Chair of Governors: Sir Hugh Taylor, BA Hons, KCB

Head: **Miss Finola Stack**, BA Hons, PGCE, Mont Dip

Age Range. Girls 4–11.
Number of Pupils. Day: 300 Girls.
Fees per term (2014–2015). £4,580.

James Allen's Preparatory School (JAPS) is an independent day school for girls aged between 4 and 11.

We see primary education as vital to the success of any child's education. We plan for the children to progress at their own pace, benefiting from working together in small groups. With a well-devised and balanced curriculum, the children reach high standards without the stress of blatant competition and are able to enjoy the many and varied opportunities which we offer, particularly in sport, drama, music and art.

The school has an excellent staff/pupil ratio of approximately 1:10 and provides specialist teachers in Art, DT, ICT, Music, PE and Science. In French the children are taught from 4 years onwards using the immersion method.

The Pre-Prep School (for pupils aged 4–6) is housed in a beautiful Edwardian building. The Middle School (for pupils aged 7–11) is a large, modern building with a first-class Hall and Library, as well as specialist rooms for Science, ICT, DT and Art. Some facilities (the theatre, swimming pool and games fields) are shared with our senior school, James Allen's Girls' School.

JASSPA is the James Allen's Saturday School for the Performing Arts for pupils and siblings and other non-JAPS pupils. This is entirely voluntary and complements the week's activities: music lessons, dance and drama are all offered.

Pupils normally enter the school in the year in which they are 4 or 7 on 1 September. Assessments take place the preceding January. 36 places are available for 4+ entry and up to 15 places available for 7+ entry. At 11, girls normally progress to JAGS by means of an open competitive examination, where JAPS girls regularly win many scholarships. (*See JAGS entry in GSA section.*)

Charitable status. James Allen's Girls' School is a Registered Charity, number 1124853. The purpose of the charity is the conduct at Dulwich of a day school in which there shall be provided a practical, liberal and religious education for girls.

Keble School

Wades Hill, Winchmore Hill, London N21 1BG
Tel: 020 8360 3359
Fax: 020 8360 4000
email: office@kebleprep.co.uk
website: www.kebleprep.co.uk

Chairman of Governors: Mr P Ruocco, MBA, BA Hons, D Inst M

Headmaster: **Mr G P McCarthy**, BSc Hons

Deputy Head: Mr P Gill, BA Hons

Age Range. 4–13.
Number of Boys. 220 Day Boys.
Fees per term (2014–2015). £3,615–£4,490.

As confirmed by the ISI Inspectors in September 2011, the warm and friendly atmosphere that exists at Keble ensures that the boys are well-motivated, keen to learn and able to mature at their own pace. Strong pastoral care is regarded as a key element in the boys' overall development and well-being, along with the encouragement of courteous and considerate behaviour.

The academic staff comprises 23 qualified graduate teachers, 5 classroom assistants and 2 Learning Support teachers. The buildings are well maintained and facilities are regularly updated. The school has an ambitious ICT development programme.

The average class size in the school is 15, although many classes are taught in half-groups and sets as the boys progress through the school. Boys follow the Foundation Stage in Reception. General subject teachers cover the academic curriculum in Years 1 to 4, with subject specialists following on from Year 5 onwards. The National Curriculum is used as a guide to curriculum development. Art, Music, PE, ICT, PSHE and Games are introduced at appropriate stages and are included within the timetable. Boys are encouraged to learn a musical instrument, sing in the choir, perform in plays and concerts, and play an active part in the wide range of sports on offer.

Football, rugby and cricket are the major team games. Further opportunities exist to participate in hockey, swimming, basketball, athletics, cross-country and tennis. There is a wide range of lunchtime and after-school activities and clubs, including drama, gardening and chess. There are also numerous educational outings and four residential trips.

Boys are not required to pass an assessment to gain entry into the school at Reception. Boys wishing to join the school at a later stage in Year 1 or above are assessed in order to ensure that they will fit comfortably into their new surroundings.

Boys are prepared for entry to senior independent schools through Common Entrance and Scholarship examinations at 13+. The school has a strong record of success in placing boys in the senior school which is right for them. In recent years, these schools include Aldenham, City of London, Haberdashers' Aske's, Highgate, Haileybury, Mill Hill, St Albans, St Columba's, University College and Westminster.

Charitable status. Keble Preparatory School (1968) Limited is a Registered Charity, number 312979. It exists to provide education for boys.

Kensington Prep School
GDST

596 Fulham Road, London SW6 5PA
Tel: 020 7731 9300
email: enquiries@kenprep.gdst.net
website: www.kensingtonprep.gdst.net

Founded in 1873.

Kensington Prep School is part of the GDST (Girls' Day School Trust). The GDST is the leading network of independent girls' schools in the UK. As a charity that owns and runs 24 schools and two academies, it reinvests all its income in its schools. For further information about the Trust, see p. xxi or visit www.gdst.net.

A more detailed prospectus may be obtained from the school or on the school's website.

Head: **Mrs P J F Lynch**, MA, PGCE

Age Range. 4–11 years.
Number of Girls. 299.
Fees per term (2014–2015). £4,835.

Since 1997 the School has been based in Fulham. The school is set in an acre of grounds and has large bright classrooms with specialist rooms for ICT, Art, Drama, Music, Science and Design Technology. The large playground provides fantastic play facilities, netball and tennis courts and a pond for environmental studies.

The school aims to provide an excellent, broadly-based but strongly academic curriculum. Independence, individuality and questioning thinkers are encouraged. Girls enjoy challenging and interesting work in a stimulating and caring environment, whilst being prepared for entry to leading boarding and day schools at 11+.

The School was named 'Independent Prep School of the Year' by the Sunday Times Parent Power for 2009–10 in recognition of its "consistently strong academic results, inspiring leadership and innovative curriculum".

Entry to the School is selective and the main entry points are at 4+ with a small intake at 7+. Occasional places do occur throughout the School from time to time.

Charitable status. Kensington Prep School is part of The Girls' Day School Trust, which is a Registered Charity, number 306983.

Kent College Nursery, Infant & Junior School

Harbledown, Canterbury, Kent CT2 9AQ
Tel: 01227 762436
Fax: 01227 763880
email: prepenquiries@kentcollege.co.uk
website: www.kentcollege.com

Chairman of Governors: D Shipton, CertEd Oxon, Dip MathsEd, Mathematical Assoc (*OC*)

Head Master: **A J Carter**, BEd Hons

(*Full staff list can be found on the Kent College website.*)

Age Range. 3–11 Co-educational.
Number of Pupils. Juniors (Day and Boarding) 140, Infants 45, Nursery 20.
Fees per term (2014–2015). Juniors: Boarders £7,615; Day Pupils (including lunch): £4,907 (Years 5–6), £4,816 (Year 4), £4,341 (Year 3). Infants: £3,428 (Years 1–2), £3.160 (Reception). Nursery: £2,608 (5 full days).

GREAT – the foundation stones to educational success.

The GREAT programme (which stands for Gifted, Really Enthusiastic, Able and Talented) offered by the unrestricted curriculum structure at the Nursery, Infant and Junior School at Kent College is key to early success. Setting in core subjects is designed to accelerate progress and gives children the option to develop particular skills, be they academic, art, drama, music or sport. All children are on individualised programmes to maximise their academic potential and are set for English and Maths according to their needs and talents rather than their chronological age.

Parents can also choose for their child to enjoy more focus in a particular area: academic challenge; Kent Test preparation; art; design technology; drama; music or sport. Students do not have to sit the Kent Test, however, those that do enjoy excellent results – 100% pass rate in 2014. Scholarships to senior schools are targeted and in recent years there has been a success rate of over 50%.

Whilst the school day finishes at 4 pm there is a full range of after-school clubs and activities, which all the children can enjoy until 6 pm each evening. There are also holiday activity weeks meaning the school is open for at least 47 weeks a year.

Boarding places are available on a full, weekly or occasional basis and accompanied travel home is available to London's St Pancras station.

All in all a win-win situation resulting in the students being well equipped for senior school education and parents given the peace of mind so that they can focus on their busy working lives.

Charitable status. Kent College, Canterbury is a Registered Charity, number 307844. The School was founded to provide education within a supportive Christian environment and is a member of the Methodist Independent Schools Trust.

Kent College Preparatory School
Pembury

Old Church Road, Pembury, Tunbridge Wells, Kent TN2 4AX
Tel: 01892 820204
Fax: 01892 820214
email: prepschool@kentcollege.kent.sch.uk
website: www.kent-college.co.uk

Chairman of Governors: Mr E Waterhouse

Headmistress: **Mrs A Lawson**, BEd Hons

Age Range. Girls 3–11.
Number of Girls. 200.
Fees per term (2014–2015). Day Girls £2,720–£4,098. Boarders £7,408. All fees include lunches. There are no compulsory extras.

The school has its own purpose-built accommodation on a beautiful 75-acre site, shared with Kent College Pembury (Senior School), and benefits from facilities such as a 300-seater state-of-the-art theatre, specialist Library & Arts Centre, large sports hall, indoor heated swimming pool with small learners pool, dining hall and dance studio.

The school believes that happy, confident children are successful ones and the girls love coming to school. Academic standards are high, but it is never forgotten that there is more to childhood and learning than examinations. Girls are successfully prepared in small classes (average 16) for a wide range of senior schools at age 11, but the school is not a crammer.

The curriculum is broad and balanced, based on the National Curriculum. All pupils benefit from specialist teaching in swimming, dance, drama, ICT, PE and music, with specialist French teaching from Nursery class.

Main intakes are in to the Early Years Department which incorporates the Nursery and Reception classes for girls aged 3–5. The department has its own wing of the School with light, colourful and well-resourced classrooms and its own outside playground areas. The Foundation Stage Curriculum is followed and by the end of the Reception year some of the pupils will be working at the lower stages of Key Stage One.

Performing arts is an important part of the curriculum with opportunities for music, drama and dance at all ages. The youngest pupils, aged 3, can do optional ballet lessons and girls enjoy specialist workshops at the recently launched Kent College Theatre Academy. The school has a choir and an orchestra and there are regular concerts and drama productions. There is a good range of sporting opportunities including The Kent College Gymnastics Academy, netball, hockey, tennis, rounders, cross-country, swimming, trampolining and athletics.

The school prides itself on providing an exciting and varied programme of over 35 clubs and activities and there is a good ethos of participation. The curriculum is supported with interesting trips and days out, and residential holidays for Years 5 and 6. A variety of well-known authors have visited the school to run workshops.

An After School Care facility is available for girls in Nursery upwards and is extremely popular for our working families. Full and weekly boarders are accepted from age 10, with flexi boarders accepted from age 8. All are part of a small, family-run Junior boarding house in which girls have a secure, happy and homely environment. Prospective boarders are invited to spend a day and overnight stay with us to give them a feel for the school. There is a 20% discount for Forces families.

Entry to Nursery, Reception, Years 1 and 2 are based on availability of places. Pupils in Years 3–6 are required to sit entry tests in English and mathematics. The Headmistress is pleased to welcome visitors and to show them around the school.

Charitable status. Kent College Pembury is a Registered Charity, number 307920. It is a Christian school specialising in girls' education.

Kew College

24–26 Cumberland Road, Kew, Surrey TW9 3HQ
Tel: 020 8940 2039
Fax: 020 8332 9945
email: enquiries@kewcollege.com
website: www.kewcollege.com

Chairman of Governors: Mrs Karen Wyatt

Head: **Mrs Marianne Austin**, BSc Hons, MA Hons, ACA, PGCE

Age Range. 3–11 Co-educational.
Number of Pupils. 296.
Fees per term (2014–2015). £2,200–£3,250.

Kew College was established in 1953 and was made into a charitable trust in 1985 by its founder, Elizabeth Hamilton-Spry, to ensure the long-term continuity of the school. The school's ethos is to ensure all pupils have an excellent grounding in the basics, but with a strong emphasis on areas such as art, music, drama and sport to develop the whole child.

Kew College's style is described as traditional, yet imaginative and the atmosphere is happy and lively with a team of enthusiastic, caring and dedicated staff to help fulfil each child's potential. Pupils enjoy excellent facilities including specialist ICT and science labs. The ISI inspection in October 2010 concluded that '*Pupils achieve well across the curriculum and extra-curricular activities, and standards are exceptionally high in all aspects of English and Mathematics. The quality of their reading, writing and mathematical skills is in advance of their years. Pupils also exhibit great creativity, particularly in art work. Pupils display enthusiasm for their lessons and good learning skills. Pupils' personal development and the school's arrangements for welfare, health and safety are outstanding. Pupils develop into exceptionally moral beings. Pupils leave the school as well-balanced personalities. The school is a caring community where pupils are thoughtfully and skilfully looked after by the pastoral care of the whole staff, which contributes strongly to their personal development.*' In the Early Years Foundation Stage the inspectors commented that '*Children are happy and secure and their needs are met well. Careful attention is given to children's welfare and safety; their exemplary behaviour and excellent personal development are strengths.*'

Beyond the core curriculum pupils enjoy participating in lively mixed-year clubs within school on Friday afternoons including graphic design, origami, Sudoku and table tennis. A wide range of weekly after-school clubs includes chess, computer, debating, fencing, Spanish and jazz dance, with arts and crafts and little golfers for the younger pupils. There are also school choirs, a wind band and string orchestra. The school takes full advantage of its London location for educational visits. There are residential field trips in Years 4, 5 and 6. In their final term, Year 6 pupils enjoy a week-long stay at a château in France improving their language skills, cultural knowledge and doing outward bound team activities.

At 11+ pupils not only achieve places through competitive entrance examinations to selective London day schools but also win a good number of awards.

Charitable status. Kew College is a Registered Charity, number 286059.

Kew Green Preparatory School

Layton House, Ferry Lane, Kew Green, Richmond, Surrey TW9 3AF
Tel: 020 8948 5999
Fax: 020 8948 4774
email: secretary@kgps.co.uk
website: www.kgps.co.uk

Chairman of Governors: Dr Helen Ireland

Headmaster: Mr Jem Peck

Age Range. 4–11 Co-educational.
Number of Pupils. 260.
Fees per term (2014–2015). £4,997.
This non-selective school is housed in an attractive building and grounds directly next door to the Royal Botanical Gardens. The front of the school overlooks Kew Green, which is used for games, and the back of the school has a good-sized playground which looks onto the River Thames.

In a non-pressurised, caring environment, KGPS produces excellent academic results, sending its pupils to London's best Independent Senior Schools.

The children are encouraged to use philosophy and ethical thinking throughout the curriculum which includes English, Maths, Science, French, RE, Music, Design & Technology, Art, Games/PE, Computer Studies and Moral & Religious Education. All Upper School children attend a Summer Term Residential Week where cross-curricular studies are applied in a non-urban environment.

There are many after-school clubs and sports activities including three choirs, an orchestra and rock band. Individual tuition is offered in piano, violin, brass, woodwind, cello, saxophone, guitar, drums and singing.

An 8 am to 6 pm All-Day Care service is offered to parents at an extra charge.

The school is noted for its warm, happy atmosphere where parents play a full part in enriching the curriculum and social life. Off-site visits and guest workshops presented by noted visitors are a regular feature of education at Kew Green.

The school is always heavily over-subscribed and registration is recommended from birth. A prospectus and registration form may be obtained from the School Secretary.

Kilgraston Preparatory School

Bridge of Earn, Perthshire PH2 9BQ
Tel: 01738 812257
Fax: 01738 813410
email: prepschool@kilgraston.com
website: www.kilgraston.com
Twitter: @kilgraston
Facebook: /kilgraston

Day and Boarding School for Girls (with boys in the Nursery to age 5).

Chairman of Board of Governors: Mr Timothy Hall

Head: Mrs Kathryn Ebrahim, BSc Hons, PGCE

Age Range. Girls 2½–13, Boys 2½–5.
Number of Pupils. 105 Girls, 8 Boys.
Fees per term (2014–2015). Day £2,995–£4,850, Boarding £7,095.
Kilgraston Preparatory School and Nursery is the junior school for Kilgraston, a leading boarding and day school for girls in Scotland. Located in its own building, the Preparatory School is surrounded by 54 acres of stunning parkland in Bridge of Earn, three miles from the centre of Perth, 45 minutes from Edinburgh and an hour's drive from Glasgow.

The Nursery is an integral part of Kilgraston Prep School providing a flexible and caring pre-school education where boys and girls between the ages of 2½ and 5 years enjoy a secure, happy, creative day. As Kilgraston is an all-through school, the nursery children have the opportunity to benefit from specialist teachers in physical education, swimming, tennis, music and science.

Admission to Kilgraston Preparatory School is by interview. Girls are able to progress into Kilgraston Senior School, or prepare for scholarship exams for Kilgraston and Common Entrance exams for other schools. The academic standard is high with all pupils completing the Preparatory School and achieving a place in their senior school of choice.

Pupils are taught by class teachers until the age of nine, with specialist teachers for PE, French, music and drama. Form teachers hold pastoral responsibility for the pupils and classes are small with provision for additional support needs. From age ten, the curriculum becomes more specialised with increasing input from specialised subject staff and use of the facilities in the Senior School. Pastoral care is the responsibility of a tutor.

The core academic curriculum is enhanced by a wide range of co-curricular subjects. While academic excellence is a priority, art, drama and music flourish and are an important feature of life at Kilgraston. Classrooms are well equipped and modern IT facilities are spread throughout the school. Opportunities are provided throughout the year for pupils to perform in groups or as soloists and they compete successfully in local festivals and events. The girls have the opportunity to take LAMDA, Associated Board and Trinity examinations. There is an annual production involving all pupils.

Sports and recreation thrive within the superb Sports Hall, which includes a climbing wall and gym. Pupils benefit from a 25m indoor swimming pool, 9 floodlit all-weather courts, playing fields and athletics track. Kilgraston is the only school in Scotland with an equestrian facility on campus and also hosts the Scottish Schools Equestrian Championships each year at Gleneagles.

The school's main sports are: hockey, netball, tennis, rounders, swimming and athletics, and fixtures are regularly played against other preparatory schools. The school has a an excellent skiing record.

Kilgraston Preparatory School has a pastoral House system. Inter-House competitions and challenges in games, music and debating provide an opportunity for friendly competition and fun. The family atmosphere in the newly refurbished boarding area, Butterstone, is enhanced by the wide range of weekend activities that make use of the superb local facilities in and around Perthshire.

Charitable status. Kilgraston School Trust is a Registered Charity, number SC029664. It exists to develop a love of learning, a spirit of adventure and openness of heart.

Kimbolton Preparatory School

Kimbolton, Huntingdon, Cambs PE28 0EA
Tel: 01480 860281
Fax: 01480 861874
email: prep@kimbolton.cambs.sch.uk
website: www.kimbolton.cambs.sch.uk

Motto: *Spes Durat Avorum*

Chair of Governors: C A Paull

Headmaster: R J Wells, BEd, BA

Age Range. 4–11 Co-educational.
Number of Children. Approximately 300.
Fees per term (2014–2015). £2,970–£3,770 (including lunch). A 2% discount is applied if fees paid by termly direct debit.

Mission Statement. Kimbolton School creates a caring, challenging environment in which pupils are encouraged to fulfil their potential and are given opportunities to flourish in a wide variety of curricular and extra-curricular interests.

We provide a close family environment where young people are educated to be tolerant, socially responsible and independent of mind, equipping them for our changing world. We are a community that challenges pupils to discover their talents, develop socially and excel.

To the west of Kimbolton village the Preparatory School is located within its own attractive grounds linked to the Senior School by means of a pathway, the 'Duchess Walk', the castle once being the home of Catharine of Aragon. The Preparatory School is partially housed in the old Kimbolton Grammar School buildings which date from 1876.

Boys and girls join the Preparatory School at four years of age. A purpose-built building (Aragon House) encompasses Reception, Year One and Year Two (Lower Prep). It is here that the children are educated in a safe, welcoming and happy environment. The younger children also use the facilities on offer throughout the Preparatory School. The children automatically progress to the Upper Prep. The expectation is that the Year Six children progress to the Senior School. (*See entry in HMC section*)

Children may also join the School when places are available after an assessment/examination and visit.

There is a programme in place for identified gifted and talented children.

The Preparatory School has, on its own site, a Dining Hall, Library, Computer Suite, Assembly Hall, Changing Rooms, Music Teaching and Practice Rooms, Science Room, Art and Design Technology Room, Sports Hall, Academic Support Unit and large, light and airy classrooms, all of which have recently been refurbished as a part of a rolling programme.

There is a qualified full-time nurse on site.

Reception, Year 1 and Year 2 have two classes per year group and Years 3–6 have three classes. Each class has its own class teacher and there is a good deal of specialist teaching throughout the Upper Prep.

The outdoor facilities including the tennis and netball courts, 400m grass athletics track, rounders fields, floodlit all-weather pitches, football, hockey and cricket pitches provide excellent facilities. The Swimming Pool located at the Senior School is used weekly by the Preparatory School.

The majority of children in Years 3–6 have individual music lessons in addition to curricular class music. Year 1 and Year 2 children follow a mini-strings programme. There are an extensive number of excursions, including an annual residential skiing excursion and many visitors and speakers visit the school thereby enriching the curriculum. There is an extensive range of extra-curricular activities.

Children may arrive for breakfast at 7.45 am and the 'Kim Club' facility is available after school until 6.00 pm. Supervised Prep and an extensive list of activities and clubs are also available after school.

We feel that children are given every opportunity to gain a first class education in a family orientated environment situated in superb surroundings. This, allied with strong teaching in small class sizes, prepares a child fully for the future.

Kimbolton Preparatory School was inspected by ISI in 2011.

Charitable status. Kimbolton School Foundation is a Registered Charity, number 1098586.

King Henry VIII Preparatory School

Kenilworth Road, Coventry CV3 6PT
Tel: 024 7627 1307
Fax: 024 7627 1308
email: headmaster@khps.co.uk
website: www.khps.co.uk

Chairman of Governors: Mr Richard Atkins, QC

Headmaster: **Mr Nicholas Lovell**, BA Hons, PGCE

Age Range. 3–11 Co-educational.
Number of Pupils. 500 Day Boys and Girls.
Fees per term (2014–2015). Reception–Year 2 £2,690 (inc lunch); Year 3 £2,750 (inc lunch); Years 4–6 £2,580 (exc lunch).

King Henry VIII Preparatory School is part of Coventry School Foundation, which includes King Henry VIII Senior School and Bablake School (3–18).

The School is situated on two campuses a short distance from each other on the south side of Coventry.

The Swallows Campus, opposite Coventry Memorial Park, educates children aged 3–8 in classes of 16 (from Reception onwards). The campus occupies a beautiful 3½ acre site and has a wealth of facilities, including its own Swimming Pool, Sports Hall, Music Department, Art & Design Centre, All-weather surface and Adventure Playground. Its main building dates to the 17th century. Most teaching is provided by class teachers, giving young children a continuity of approach and providing them with a key individual with whom to build a strong relationship and who will guide them through their daily studies. An increasing number of specialist teachers are provided as children progress through the infant years: Music from age 3, Games and Swimming from age 4 and Art & Design Technology from age 6. There is a strong family atmosphere and the aim is to provide children with a wonderful start to their education.

The Hales Campus is situated just down the road from Swallows and occupies a portion of the main King Henry VIII School site. The main building was purpose-built in 1997 and provides an excellent range of modern facilities for children aged 8–11. From Year 5 at this site children are taught by specialist teachers for all subjects in classes of 20. The Hales Campus has its own Sports Hall, Music Department, Library, Art & Design Room, Science Laboratory and playing areas. Some facilities are shared with the senior school, including games fields and a 25-metre indoor swimming pool.

The School seeks to help its pupils to be happy, confident 'all-rounders'. Academic standards are high and entrance to the School, from the age of 5, is through academic assessment (ages 5–6) and examination (ages 7–10). Children joining the School at the ages of 3 or 4 are not academically selected and names may be registered from birth. The majority of children continue from King Henry VIII Preparatory School to King Henry VIII Senior School at age 11; however, children may sit entrance to a variety of other schools.

The Arts and Sport are very important aspects within the curriculum. The visual and performance Arts are specialist taught from the infant years. Music is strong, with children being able to learn a wide variety of musical instruments from an early age. Drama and performance are aspects of school life which flourish, with all children taking part in a variety of performances during their time at the School. A large number of performance opportunities are available each year.

Games are taught within the timetable from Reception onwards and competitive matches against other schools start in Year 2. The main sports for boys are Rugby, Football and Cricket; for girls Netball, Hockey and Rounders. Beyond the main team sports, there is a range of other sports that may be experienced, both within the timetable and as extra-curricular activities.

Scholarships are awarded from the age of 8, for academic subjects as well as the Arts and All-Rounder awards. Bursaries are available at entrance from Year 3 onwards (7+).

The School has a vibrant extra-curricular activities programme which may be accessed by pupils from Reception onwards, this includes both lunchtime and after school clubs. Before school care (from 7.45 am) and after school care (up to 6.00 pm) are available daily during term time, as well as voluntary Saturday morning sports. There is a full programme of care for children aged from 3–11, starting at 8.30 am and continuing until 5.30 pm, during every school holiday.

School trips and educational visits are regarded as an important aspect of each child's experience at the School. These include visits to local places of interest, usually associated with programmes of study, but also residential trips for each year group from the age of 7 onwards, one of which will be to France in Year 5.

The School's motto *Confide Recte Agens* – have the courage to do what is right – lies at the heart of the School's ethos which encourages children to have the courage of their convictions. The School is a member of the Community of the Cross of Nails, thus having an association with Coventry Cathedral. This stresses tolerance and understanding between people of different creeds and faiths. The School happily accepts children from various faiths and looks to build genuine understanding and tolerance between its pupils.

Overall the School seeks to help its children to be happy, confident people who enjoy learning.

Charitable status. Coventry School Foundation is a Registered Charity, number 528961. Its aim is to advance the education of boys and girls by the provision of a school or schools in or near the City of Coventry.

King's College School

West Road, Cambridge CB3 9DN
Tel: 01223 365814
Fax: 01223 461388
email: office@kcs.cambs.sch.uk
website: www.kcs.cambs.sch.uk

The School is part of King's College and is administered by a Board of Governors.

Chairman of Governors: Professor R Foley

Headmaster: **N J Robinson**, BA

Deputy Heads:
Mrs K Richardson, BEd Hons
Mr T Hales, BA Hons

Age Range. 4–13 Co-educational.
Number of Pupils. 416 day pupils, 35 boy boarders including 16 choristers.
Fees per term (2014–2015). Weekly Boarding: £7,100 Choristers: £2,390 Day Pupils: £4,560; Pre-Prep: £3,585.

The School is administered by Governors appointed by the Council of King's College. King Henry VI's charter founding King's College in 1441 provided for Choristers and their education. In 1878 the School moved to its present site near the University library, across the river from the College. Over the years the facilities have been greatly improved. The main house accommodates the catering facilities and boarding accommodation. A new Wiles Centre for

Technology opened in June 1999 with first class facilities for ICT and DT. The Performing Arts Centre includes 16 new music rooms (opened in 2001) and a multi-purpose hall used for plays and concerts and also a fully-equipped gym. In 2010 an impressive new music wing was added to the department. A new classroom block called the "Briggs Building" was opened in May 2004 by the Duchess of Kent and it contains two very well equipped science labs, two maths classrooms, three modern language classrooms, two English classrooms and a new library. Sports facilities on site include two large playing fields, tennis courts and a heated outdoor swimming pool. A new floodlit astroturf field was laid in May 2005. Two new squash courts were built in 2010. The School also has the use of other nearby sports fields. The Pre-Prep has been expanded to accommodate two-form entry starting from September 2008.

The Headmaster is assisted by 40 full-time and 10 part-time teachers. There are 4 Matrons and a full-time Bursar and Assistant Bursar. There are 40 full- or part-time music staff. In 1976 girls were admitted as day pupils and the ratio of boys to girls is approximately 50:50. In September 1981 the School started a small special centre for dyslexic children of good intelligence which has now become an excellent Learning Support Centre. Pupils are prepared for the Scholarship and Common Entrance examinations of the boys' and girls' Independent Senior Schools. The school broadly follows the National Curriculum subjects, but also teaches French from the age of 4, Latin from 9, and Greek to some older children. The School has a tradition of winning numerous academic, art, music, drama and sports awards annually.

Apart from choral and instrumental music (there are 2 orchestras of some 80 players in each and about 40 chamber groups), activities include Drama, Art, Computing, Touch-typing, Spelling, Gardening, DT, Gymnastics, PE, Chess, Science, Wildlife Explorers, Library, Orienteering, Yoga, Ballet, Spanish, and Mandarin Chinese. Games include Rugby, Football, Hockey, Cricket, Girls' Cricket, Netball, Rounders, Athletics, Tennis, Squash, and Swimming.

Bursaries. King's is pleased to offer a place at the School to a child at a Primary School on a means-tested bursary worth up to 100% of the school fees. The place will usually start from Year 3 or Year 4 and continue until the child leaves King's. This would suit a child with musical potential who would benefit from the wide musical provision offered at King's.

Further information about the School may be obtained from the Headmaster. Enquiries concerning Choristerships should also be addressed to him. Choristership Auditions take place annually, usually in September and January.

Charitable status. King's College School is part of King's College Cambridge, which is a Registered Charity, number 1139422. Its aim is to provide an excellent education for girls and boys of mixed ability aged 4 to 13.

King's College Junior School

Wimbledon Common, London SW19 4TT
Tel: 020 8255 5335
Fax: 020 8255 5339
email: jsadmissions@kcs.org.uk
HMJSsec@kcs.org.uk
website: www.kcs.org.uk

Chairman of the Governing Body: Mrs P L Hughes, CBE

Headmaster: **Dr G A Silverlock**, BEd Hons, MLitt, PhD

Age Range. 7–13.
Number of Boys. 460 (day boys only).
Fees per term (2014–2015). £5,175 (Years 3–4), £5,840 (Years 5–8).

The Junior School was established in 1912 as an integral part of KCS, to prepare boys for the Senior School. It shares with it a common site and many facilities, in particular the Music School, the Art, Design and Technology School, the Dining Hall, the Sports Hall, the swimming pool and extensive playing fields. For the rest, Junior School boys are housed in their own buildings. The Priory, rebuilt in 1980, contains twenty-three classrooms, including specialist rooms for languages, mathematics, history, geography, information technology and multimedia work. The youngest age groups have their own special accommodation in Rushmere, a spacious Georgian house whose grounds adjoin the Junior School. The School also has its own purpose-built library, science laboratories and well-equipped theatre and assembly hall.

The School is separately administered in matters relating to admission, curriculum, discipline and day to day activities. There are thirty-six members of staff in addition to those teaching in specialist departments common to both Schools.

The work and overall programme are organised in close consultation with the Senior School to ensure that boys are educated in a structured and progressive way from 7 to 18, having the benefit of continuity, while enjoying the range and style of learning that are best suited to their age.

Boys come from both maintained and pre-preparatory schools and are admitted at the age of 7, 8, 9, 10 or 11. Entry is by interview and examination.

Charitable status. King's College School is a Registered Charity, number 310024. It exists to provide education for children.

King's Hall School
A Woodard School

Kingston Road, Taunton, Somerset TA2 8AA
Tel: 01823 285920
Fax: 01823 285922
email: schooloffice@kingshalltaunton.co.uk
           admissions@kingshalltaunton.co.uk
website: www.kingshalltaunton.co.uk
Twitter: KingsHallSchool
Facebook: Kings-Hall-School

Chairman of Governors: Roger Knight, Esq, OBE, MA, DipEd

Head: **Justin Chippendale**, BSc Joint Hons

Age Range. 2–13, Co-educational.
Number of Pupils. Preparatory (Years 3–8): 110 boys, 100 girls; including 40 boarders. Pre-Prep (Nursery–Year 2): 40 boys, 45 girls.
Fees per term (2014–2015). Preparatory Day £2,755–£4,900, Full/Weekly Boarding £5,450–£7,090, Pre-Prep £2,165–£2,250.

King's Hall School is a leading Pre-Prep and Prep school with around 300 girls and boys. Set in a beautiful countryside location surrounded by farmland, the school is only a couple of minutes' drive from the centre of Taunton. The school respects traditional values and boarding is a strong feature, which contributes to the tangible family atmosphere that exists in the school. Children enjoy a challenging all-round education in a progressive and stimulating environment. King's Hall has a partner senior school, King's College, Taunton, and the two schools benefit from having their own independent sites, furnished with excellent age-appropriate facilities and attitudes to maximise the opportunities for the children in our care. There is a close working relationship between King's Hall and King's College and the vast majority of pupils move on there at age 13. Scholar-

ships are available for pupils with exceptional ability. These are awarded at 11+ and continue at King's College, Taunton up to age 18.

King's Hawford

Worcester WR3 7SD
Tel: 01905 451292
Fax: 01905 756502
email: hawford@ksw.org.uk
website: www.ksw.org.uk

Chairman of the Governors: H B Carslake, BA, LLB

Headmaster: **J M Turner**, BEd Hons, DipEd, ACP

Age Range. 2–11.
Number of Pupils. 190 Boys, 130 Girls.
Fees per term (2014–2015). £2,065–£3,799 (excluding lunch).

King's Hawford is a junior school to the historic King's School, Worcester, and is set in twenty-three acres of parkland situated on the northern outskirts of Worcester. The school is accommodated within an elegant and recently refurbished Georgian house surrounded by well maintained playing fields, with tennis courts, a heated enclosed swimming pool, a multi-purpose sports hall and secure play area for younger children.

There are extensive opportunities for a wide range of extra-curricular activities and there is a busy calendar of music, drama, sport, clubs. Sports include Rugby, Association Football, Cricket, Hockey, Netball, Rounders, Athletics, Tennis, Cross-Country and Swimming.

The Pre-Prep department accepts children from age 2–6 and the Junior department from age 7–11.

Charitable status. The King's School Worcester is a Registered Charity, number 1098236. It exists to provide a broad education for a wide range of children from 2–11 years.

King's House School

68 King's Road, Richmond, Surrey TW10 6ES
Tel: 020 8940 1878
Fax: 020 8939 2501
email: schooloffice@kingshouseschool.org
website: www.kingshouseschool.org

Established in 1946, the School was constituted as an Educational Trust with a Board of Governors in 1957.

Chairman of the Governors: Mr Tim Sketchley

Head: **M Turner**, BA, PGCE, NPQH

Age Range. Boys 3–13 (Co-educational Nursery).
Number of Pupils. 450.
Fees per term (2014–2015). Nursery Department £2,015–£3,285; Junior Department £3,595–£4,200; Senior Department £4,780 (all fees inclusive of lunch).

We believe the King's House School is a very special place and are very proud of what we have on offer here and what we do.

We are a lively, busy, happy School and one where we feel that the boys (and girls in our wonderful Nursery) thrive. Our aim is to offer a broad education to all our pupils, enabling them to develop their academic, social, sporting and artistic attributes. This breadth and balance on offer is we believe one of the strengths of the School.

The academic side underpins the education here with the emphasis on the core areas in the early years spreading to an increasing range of subjects by the top end of the School. The destination schools of our leavers show that the boys are achieving well academically.

We believe very much that King's House is a community; we pride ourselves on strong pastoral care and an environment where the children feel happy. The positive relationships that we enjoy with our parents and the local community and our links to Rwanda are all key to our sense of responsibility.

The School is based on three sites on Richmond Hill and also benefits from its own extensive playing fields in Chiswick. The three main School sites have spacious state-of-the-art facilities. The School also enjoys the advantages of having close access to London with all the educational opportunities that affords.

King's House is a friendly, caring and supportive School. We have a strong sense of community both within the School and with our parents but we are also keen to play a role in the local and global community and to develop our pupils' sense of awareness of the world around them.

King's House is a lively, busy and happy School and we aim to give each child a broad academic and balanced education. We provide an environment in which the children feel secure and are able to flourish; offering opportunities to take part and develop in all areas, so that the needs of each individual are catered for.

King's House is non-selective at our two main entry points, Nursery and Reception, and this means we have a range of pupils and abilities. We believe that boys benefit from staying in the prep environment until they are 13 years old before moving on. Their final two years here allow them to grow up and develop a sense of responsibility, taking on roles around the school. The boys are well-prepared for the transition to their senior schools.

King's House is proud of its traditions and history. Its principles and standards are founded on Christian values although the school is not aligned to any particular religion, and welcomes pupils of all religions and backgrounds.

For more information visit the school's website or contact our Registrar, Sally Bass, on 020 8940 1878 or bass.s@kingshouseschool.org.

Charitable status. Kings House School Trust (Richmond) Limited is a Registered Charity, number 312669. It exists for the education of children.

King's Junior School Gloucester

Pitt Street, Gloucester GL1 2BG
Tel: 01452 337337
email: office@thekingsschool.co.uk
website: www.thekingsschool.co.uk

Chairman of Governors: Mr C L Major, LLB

Head: **Mrs Anne Haas**, BPrimEd Hons

Age Range. 3–11 Co-educational.
Number of Pupils. 135.
Fees per term (2014–2015). £2,135–£4,075. Kindergarten fees are based on an hourly rate of £6.50 per hour.

The King's Independent Junior School provides a stimulating education for girls and boys aged 3–11 years, enhanced by the inspiring cathedral setting, which develops a rich sense of community and powerful identity. With its small classes, celebrated range of extra-curricular activities and outstanding pastoral care, King's offers a friendly and welcoming start to your child's education.

The unique 'Keystones' approach to learning and pastoral care offered at King's Junior School fosters an inner strength and passion for discovery where children are encouraged to think creatively and explore their potential both inside and outside the classroom – skills which last a lifetime.

The importance of the Cathedral cannot be underestimated on present or past King's Junior School pupils. A haven of peace, the Chapel allows pupils to sit quietly at the start of a school day. Designed to hone and develop moral compasses, the Cathedral is very much the beating heart of this extraordinary school.

King's believe that a good Early Years education lays the foundations for everything that follows. Young children soak up new experiences and information at remarkable speed, and they need a stable environment in which they can develop and grow. King's offers a structured curriculum, designed to balance their need for exploration and play with enjoyable learning activities.

Wardle House provides an early learning experience, which is challenging and fun for young children. At Wardle House the children are cared for by a well-qualified and enthusiastic team of staff in a secure environment dedicated to the Early Years. As well as enjoying spacious classrooms, a large, fully enclosed garden and excellent staffing ratio, the children also benefit from access to the facilities and being part of the wider school community.

King's Junior School shares the grounds with the Senior School and benefits from use of the Design Technology Centre, ICT Suite, brand new Sports Hall and Cookery Centre, as well as taking part in full school assemblies in the Cathedral. There is a close liaison with the specialist teachers in the Senior School to ensure continuity in teaching and the curriculum. After school care is available and Holiday Club which runs for 50 weeks of the year.

There are opportunities for the children to extend their musical ability through participation in an orchestra, and choir, alongside individual extra tuition for those who wish it, specifically focusing on their age group. Games are considered important and opportunities for participation in teams are extensive. King's offers a range of extra-curricular activities, which include cookery, chess, dance and drama.

A high proportion of King's Junior School pupils have achieved the Grammar School entrance level in each of the past ten years and high standards are demanded in all subjects. The Gifted and Talented Programme ensures that the more able pupils are suitably challenged and Learning Support is also provided for the benefit of those who need it.

The King's Junior School has an inclusive admissions policy, but they are academically ambitious for every pupil. Their size does not diminish from their expectations of pupils – giving them big ambitions, compassionate hearts and lively minds.

Charitable status. The King's School, Gloucester is a Registered Charity, number 1080641.

King's St Alban's School

Mill Street, Worcester WR1 2NJ
Tel: 01905 354906
Fax: 01905 763075
email: ksa@ksw.org.uk
website: www.ksw.org.uk

Chairman of the Governors: H B Carslake, BA, LLB

Head: **I R Griffin**, BA Hons QTS

Age Range. 4–11 Co-educational.
Number of Pupils. 220.
Fees per term (2014–2015). Pre-Prep Dept £2,100–£2,426, Junior School £2,482–£3,644 excluding lunch.

Education is about far more than academic learning, although that is still our primary purpose. At King's St

Alban's we aim to develop the whole child, encouraging each girl and boy to explore their capabilities, find fresh challenges and discover spheres in which they can excel.

King's St Alban's, an established school with a purpose-built Pre-Preparatory Department, is located near to Worcester Cathedral on a separate site adjacent to the Senior School. In the grounds stand the Chapel, the main buildings of the Junior School with the Pre-Preparatory Department on an adjacent, self contained site. The school has a large hall, a dedicated Science Laboratory, an IT suite, an Art and Technology Room, well-stocked Libraries and Music Rooms, all of which supplement the usual amenities of a preparatory school. In addition, use is made of Senior School facilities, which include an indoor Swimming Pool, a fully equipped Sports Hall, Dance Studio, Fitness Centre, the Music School, Playing Fields, and a purpose-built Theatre.

We work hard to discover talent and develop it to the full. Music, Art, Dance and Drama play an important part in the life of the school. King's St Alban's supports an Orchestra, Wind Band, Flute Choir and String and Recorder groups with most children playing at least one musical instrument. In the Junior School nearly all children are involved in the school's Choir and there is a smaller Chamber Choir. The annual Carol Service is held in the Cathedral with concerts and musical evenings held each term in the Theatre and Chapel. A major whole-school production is staged annually in the Theatre with several smaller workshop productions taking place during the year.

The staff comprises a mix of men and women, all of whom are experienced and well qualified. In addition there are various visiting music and sport specialists.

The main sports are Rugby, Netball, Soccer, Hockey, Cricket and Rounders with Swimming, Cross-Country, Orienteering and Tennis also featured. Matches are arranged with other schools and excellence is sought, but participation of all girls and boys is the main objective. A thriving inter-House competition provides further opportunities for all to enjoy competition.

Beyond the classroom an extensive programme of after-school activities is available with opportunities varying each term, examples are Art & Craft, Science, Fencing, Ball Skills, Latin, Chess and Swimming. Children from across the school spend time each year at the school's Outdoor Activity Centre in the Black Mountains.

King's St Alban's is academically selective and pupils are expected to progress to the Senior School, subject to a satisfactory performance in their examinations at the age of 11. The main assessment of candidates for the Junior School takes place in early February for entry the following September, but assessments can be arranged on an individual basis throughout the year, when required. The tests cover English, Mathematics and Verbal Reasoning.

There are a small number of Scholarships and Bursaries available from the age of 7, as are Choral Scholarships for Cathedral Choristers.

Charitable status. The King's School, Worcester is a Registered Charity, number 1098236. It exists to provide high quality education for girls and boys.

Junior King's School

Milner Court, Sturry, Canterbury, Kent CT2 0AY
Tel: 01227 714000
email: registrar@junior-kings.co.uk
website: www.junior-kings.co.uk
Twitter: @JuniorKingsSch

Chairman of Governors: The Very Revd Dr R A Willis, BA, Dip Th, FRSA, Dean of Canterbury Cathedral

Headmaster: **Mr P M Wells**, BEd Hons

Age Range. 3–13.

Number of Pupils. 368 (81 Boarders; 287 Day Pupils, including 99 Pre-Prep).

Fees per term (2014–2015). Boarders £7,635; Day Pupils £5,015–£5,580; Pre-Prep £3,315 (including meals).

Junior King's was founded in 1879 as the preparatory school to The King's School Canterbury, which can trace its roots back to the sixth century when St Augustine established a monastery in Kent.

Set in eighty acres of attractive countryside, just two miles from Canterbury city centre, Junior King's pupils enjoy a calm, happy and purposeful atmosphere drawing upon a rich Christian heritage. Girls and boys from the ages of three to thirteen years achieve their potential, both inside and beyond the classroom, whatever their ability.

The school has an outstanding reputation for academic excellence and scholarship due to a varied and stimulating curriculum. This is supported by first class teaching and opportunities to enjoy a wide range of sports, music, drama and extra-curricular activities.

The school is in the grounds of Milner Court, a 16th century Manor House This historic building, along with a Kentish Oast House used by the Pre-Prep, a newly-refurbished Tithe Barn used for theatre and musical productions, and a flint stoned church for services and assemblies has been sensitively augmented over the years. Other impressive facilities include specialist art, science, ICT and design suites.

Spacious and comfortable boarding accommodation for around 80 boarders with social rooms, kitchens and games rooms are at the heart of the school in the main building.

The school has a fine reputation for music, both instrumental and choral, as well as for art, design and drama. The school year includes a programme of concerts, recitals and exhibitions involving children of all ages.

In 2013, Mr Hugh Robertson, MP and Minister of State for Sport, Olympic Legacy and Tourism opened a stunning new all-weather sports pitch and tennis courts.

A large and modern sports hall is used for PE lessons, basketball, volleyball, badminton, and netball, as well as indoor hockey, soccer and tennis. Rowing and sailing take place on nearby lakes. Pupils make use of the large indoor swimming pool at the senior school.

For boys, cricket, soccer hockey and rugby are the main team games, while girls play netball, hockey and rounders. Athletics, tennis and fencing are joint pursuits.

Children can join the Nursery from the age of three in our impressive purpose-built 'Little Barn'. In its delightful Kentish Oast House setting, the Pre-Prep has its own spacious hall, library and seven bright classrooms complete with the latest ICT facilities. Outside, pupils have their own extensive adventure playground as well as sharing the main school facilities such as the sports hall, tithe barn, sports fields and dining hall.

Junior King's pupils progress at 13+ to The King's School Canterbury and other leading public schools, with a sense of achievement, maturity and self-confidence. Academic standards are high and the record of success in Scholarships and Common Entrance is outstanding.

(*See entry for The King's School Canterbury in the HMC section.*)

Charitable status. The King's School of the Cathedral Church of Canterbury is a Registered Charity, number 307942. It exists to provide education for boys and girls.

King's Ely Junior

Ely, Cambridgeshire CB7 4EW
Tel: 01353 660732
Fax: 01353 665281

email: clairerobbins@kingsely.org
website: www.kingsely.org/Junior

Chairman of the Governors: Mr J Hayes

Head: **Mr R J Whymark**, BA Ed Hons

Age Range. 7–13.
Number of Pupils. Boarders: 26 Boys, 8 Girls; Day: 174 Boys, 138 Girls.
Fees per term (2014–2015). Boarding £6,533–£6,896. Day £4,097–£4,471.

King's Ely Junior has its own staff and its own buildings are part of the main school campus. The facilities of King's Ely Senior are freely available to King's Ely Junior boys and girls.

There is a family boarding house for boys and girls up to the age of 13 and a separate boarding house for the boy choristers of Ely Cathedral who are all pupils at King's Ely Junior. Each has its own Housemaster or Housemistress, assisted by House Tutors and experienced Matrons. Both Houses have recently been refurbished and offer excellent boarding facilities.

During the school day all children are divided into four equal-sized co-educational 'Houses' for pastoral and competitive purposes. Each of these 'Houses' is staffed by a Housemaster or Housemistress and several House Tutors.

Entry to King's Ely Junior for boys and girls is through assessment tests and interview. The main two entry points are Year 3 (age 7) and Year 7 (age 11) but pupils may start in any year providing there is space. The main assessment weeks are in January, although it is common to assess for entry at other times of the year. Exceptional children for Year 7 entry may be invited to take the King's Ely Junior Scholarship examination. A broad preparatory school curriculum is followed and all pupils are prepared for the relevant transfer examination. While the great majority proceed to King's Ely Senior in Year 9, pupils can also be prepared for other Independent Schools.

The main games for boys are Rugby, Cricket and Football, and for girls they are Netball, Hockey, Rounders and Tennis. Both boys and girls are involved in Athletics and Cross-Country Running. There is a Swimming Pool, a well-equipped Sports Hall, a full-size all-weather hockey/tennis area, and excellent playing fields. A wide-ranging programme of extra-curricular activities is also offered. All pupils have the opportunity to learn one or more of a wide variety of musical instruments. There are several Junior School Orchestras, and choral and ensemble music are taught. The Junior School musicians regularly tour abroad. The School has its own Music School and Technology Centre, and access to the Senior School's new £1 million Recital Hall and Music School. Years 7 and 8 enjoy a new £1.2m block of seven classrooms and a science laboratory, plus recreational and study facilities.

The School is also justly proud of its art and drama, which are taught in their own studios, and of its excellent computer facilities.

Charitable status. The King's School, Ely is a Registered Charity, number 802427. It exists for the provision of education.

King's Rochester Preparatory School

King Edward Road, Rochester, Kent ME1 1UB
Tel: 01634 888577
Fax: 01634 888507
email: prep@kings-rochester.co.uk
website: www.kings-rochester.co.uk

Chairman of Governors: The Dean of Rochester, The Very Revd Dr M H F Beach

Headmaster: **R P Overend**, BA, FTCL, ARCM, FRSA

Age Range. 8–13.
Number of Pupils. 200.
Fees per term (2014–2015). Boarders £6,425, Day Pupils £3,875–£4,400 (including lunches).

Admission between 8+ to 12+ is by interview and report from present school as well as Entrance Examinations in English, Mathematics and Verbal or Non-Verbal Reasoning. Many children also join at 11+ and sit either our November or March 11+ Assessment Tests in English, Mathematics and Non-Verbal Reasoning.

Scholarships are awarded (partly from the Cathedral, partly from the School) to Cathedral Choristers (boys only) and King's (30%) or Governors' Exhibitions (means-tested up to 100%) to those whose performance in the Entrance Examination merits it.

The Preparatory School is an integral part of King's Rochester, founded in 604 AD by Justus, a Benedictine monk, the first Bishop of Rochester. The Cathedral is at the heart of the School's life with a weekly School service and every day the Choristers maintain the tradition of choral singing at the world's oldest Choir School. When the School is not in the Cathedral a religious assembly is held at the Preparatory School.

The School is a member of the Choir Schools' Association.

The School has been fully co-educational since 1993 and 40% are girls.

Set in Rochester Town Centre, the Preparatory School building overlooks the beautiful Paddock, one of the School's large playing fields. The teaching block consists of 12 classrooms, 2 Science Laboratories, a Computer Suite, Language Laboratory and a Library with over 6,000 volumes. Other facilities such as the Design and Technology Centre, Art Centre, Music School, Indoor Swimming Pool and Sports Halls are shared with the Senior School which virtually all pupils join following the internal Entrance Examination. Chadlington House, the purpose-built Pre-Preparatory School which educates pupils from age 3–8, and a Conference Centre are recent additions to the campus. In September 2012, sport benefited from the acquisition of the King's Rochester Sports Centre adding nine external tennis/netball courts, a large gymnasium, a fitness gym, physio suite and changing rooms to the indoor swimming pool and playing fields already on the 1400 year-old school's town centre site.

The Preparatory School has a small number of boarders who are housed either in School House for boys, or St Margaret's House for girls. Boarding, both full and weekly, is available for boys and girls from 11+.

The curriculum is broad and balanced. In Year 8 science is taught as three separate subjects, French and German are the modern languages, and Latin is taught to the A stream from Year 7. A full programme of CPSHE is given to all pupils. Individual educational support tuition and EFL is available if required.

All pupils enjoy the benefit of two full afternoons a week of Games in addition to a PE lesson for most year groups. Major sports include Rugby, Hockey, Cricket, Netball, Athletics, Rounders and Swimming. There is a wide range of extra-curricular activities at the end of the school day.

Choral and instrumental music is strong throughout the School. Many of our pupils learn one or more musical instruments and strong results are achieved in Associated Board examinations. Each year the Drama Club presents a play or musical held over three nights. Recently productions have required casts in excess of fifty and have been wonderful opportunities for pupils to show their dramatic and musical skills. Amongst latest productions have been *Honk!*, *The Caucasian Chalk Circle*, *Olivia*, *Bendigo Boswell*, *Homer's*

Odyssey, Under Milk Wood, Bugsy Malone, In Holland stands a House and *Little Shop of Horrors*.

Charitable status. King's School, Rochester is a Registered Charity, number 1084266. It is a Charitable Trust for the purpose of educating children.

Kingshott

St Ippolyts, Hitchin, Hertfordshire SG4 7JX
Tel: 01462 432009
Fax: 01462 421652
email: pa2head@kingshottschool.com
website: www.k8.0 ptingshottschool.com

Chairman of Governors: Mr Gavin Hill, MA, FIA

Headmaster: **Mr I Gilmour**, BPrimEd, BEd Hons, MEd

Age Range. 3–13.
Number of Pupils. (All Day) Prep (7–13): 140 Boys, 99 Girls; Pre-Prep (4–7): 72 Boys, 48 Girls; Nursery (3–4): 19 Boys, 13 Girls.
Fees per term (2014–2015). (including Lunch) Nursery £1,750–£2,430, Pre-Prep £3,090, Prep £3,770.

Kingshott, founded in 1930, occupies a large Victorian building, with major recent classroom additions, in 23 acres of attractive grounds on the outskirts of Hitchin. Luton, Letchworth, Baldock, Stevenage, Welwyn and the A1(M) Motorway are all within a 10 mile radius. The school has continued to invest in new facilities including a Pre-Prep, Middle School (for Years 3–5) and most recently a stand-alone Nursery building. Kingshott, a Charitable Educational Trust, with a Board of Governors, welcomes all denominations. Children are encouraged to work towards and realise their individual potential – academic, creative, sporting – and to this end there is a happy friendly atmosphere, with strong emphasis on manners and being part of the wider community.

Kingshott offers a wide range of academic subjects including Latin, French, DT, Drama and ample curriculum time for PE and Games. This is complemented by a full and varied after-school programme.

There is a strong and successful sporting tradition which includes Football, Rugby, Cricket, Hockey, Netball, Rounders, Tennis, Swimming, Cross-Country and Athletics. The School has its own covered, heated swimming pool, astro-turf pitch, hard play areas and extensive playing fields. Many pupils stay for Prep each evening, and there is opportunity for involvement in a wide variety of After-School Hobby activities. The School also offers a Breakfast Club and After-School Care is also available until 5.30 pm for Pre-Prep pupils.

Academic, Music, Art and Sports Scholarships to Senior Independent Schools are gained each year, and Common Entrance results are very sound, with virtually all children accepted by their first-choice schools.

Entry for Reception and beyond is by assessment, appropriate to age.

Registration for Nursery and Pre-Prep is advisable several years before required admission.

Charitable status. Kingshott School Trust Limited is a Registered Charity, number 280626. It exists to provide education for boys and girls.

Kingsmead School

Bertram Drive, Hoylake, Wirral CH47 0LL
Tel: 0151 632 3156
Fax: 0151 632 0302

email: enquiries@kingsmeadschool.com
website: www.kingsmeadschool.com

Chairman of Governors: Mr T J Turvey

Headmaster: **Mr M G Gibbons**, BComm, MSc, QTS

Age Range. 2–16.
Number of Pupils. 124 boys, 56 girls.
Fees per term (2014–2015). £1,938–£3,345.

Academic, Music and Sports Scholarships are available. Scholarship and entrance examinations for Year 7 are held in January each year. Substantial Bursaries are available to the children of Clergy.

Kingsmead School was founded in 1904. It is in a rural setting with extensive playing fields on site, yet is easily accessible by road and rail, and the school provides a bus service. It has a strong Christian tradition, dedicated staff, a reputation for academic rigour, and a happy atmosphere.

There is provision for pupils to go on to Grammar Schools at 11+, although the majority remain at Kingsmead until GCSE (age 16).

Facilities include three Computer Rooms, two well-equipped Science Laboratories, a Food and Nutrition kitchen, a large Gymnasium, a lecture theatre and an indoor heated swimming pool available throughout the year. There is a strong Choir and facilities are available to those wishing to learn a musical instrument. All children have the opportunity to perform in plays, musicals and concerts. The Centenary Building was opened on the campus in February 2003, containing state-of-the-art classrooms for History, Geography, Design Technology (DT), Information and Communications Technology (ICT), Art and French.

Up to the end of Key Stage 1 (Year 2), pupils are taught in their own rooms by Class Teachers. In the Junior Department (Key Stage 2) there is specialist teaching of certain subjects at the appropriate level. Thereafter pupils are based in a Form Room under the care of a Form Teacher but move to the different subject rooms for lessons. For spoken English and Drama, the School has enjoyed excellent results in the English Speaking Board and other examinations. At any level in the school, intelligent children with specific learning difficulties can be given a structured programme of remedial help by a specialist teacher at an extra charge.

Games offered include Football, Rugby, Cricket, Netball, Rounders, Hockey, Athletics, Tennis, and Golf.

Clubs include Ballet, Chess, Gymnastics, Scripture Union, Swimming, Bushcraft, Homework Club, The Duke of Edinburgh's Silver and Bronze Award schemes, Shooting and Dance.

Charitable status. Kingsmead School is a Registered Charity, number 525920.

Kingswood House School

56 West Hill, Epsom, Surrey KT19 8LG
Tel: 01372 723590
Fax: 01372 749081
email: office@kingswoodhouse.org
website: www.kingswoodhouse.org

Founded in 1899, the school moved to its current site, a large Edwardian house in West Hill, Epsom, just outside the town centre in 1920. The school is an educational trust, overseen by a board of governors.

Chairman of Governors: Robert Austen, BSc Eng, CEng, MICE, MIHT

Headmaster: **Peter R Brooks**, MA, BEd Hons, CertEd, IAPS

Age Range. Boys 3–13, Girls 3–7.
Number of Pupils. 200 day pupils.
Fees per term (2014–2015). Pre-Prep £3,100 (part-time Nursery payable by session). Junior 7+ upwards £4,050. Free after-school care provided until 5 pm.

Kingswood House is a thriving day preparatory school for boys aged 3–13 and girls aged 3–7. The school's reputation is based on a friendly and welcoming atmosphere, a positive and supportive ethos and successfully meeting the educational needs of all its pupils. Small classes facilitate individual attention from well-qualified teachers and allow pupils to learn in a relaxed, but stimulating and concentrated environment.

The broad aim of the school is to prepare boys for Common Entrance and Scholarships to senior school at age 13. Development of literacy and numeracy skills is the foundation of the curriculum. English, Maths, Science, History, Geography, French, Religious Education, PE, Music, Art, Design Technology and Information Technology make up the timetable. Study Skills and PSHE courses help prepare boys for senior school life and there is a Study Centre to supplement learning, with excellent provision for children with special educational needs. Kingswood House School is a member of CReSTeD (Council for the Registration of Schools Teaching Dyslexic Pupils) and NAGC (The National Association for Gifted Children).

The senior curriculum is determined by the Common Entrance syllabus with boys being prepared for a wide variety of local senior independent schools, including Epsom College, St John's, Ewell Castle, City of London Freemen's, Reed's, Box Hill and King's College, Wimbledon. Placing boys in the right senior school is of paramount importance and the teachers have wide experience in preparing boys for Common Entrance. There is an excellent success rate at 13+ Common Entrance, with a good proportion obtaining scholarships and awards.

The school prides itself on the quality of teaching, dedicated classrooms and resources provided for Art, Design Technology, Information Technology, Music and Science, all of which have been completely refurbished in the last few years. There are sporting facilities on site, with a playing field, astroturf surface, all-weather cricket nets, adventure playground and climbing wall. Pitches at Ashtead Cricket Club and Epsom College are also used.

Academic Scholarships are awarded at 7+ and there are fee reductions for siblings. The school is registered for the Nursery Education Grant.

Charitable status. Kingswood House School is a Registered Charity, number 312044. It exists to provide educational support in the form of bursaries for the parents of children in need.

Kingswood Preparatory School

College Road, Lansdown, Bath BA1 5SD
Tel: 01225 734460
Fax: 01225 734470
email: kpsreception@kingswood.bath.sch.uk
website: www.kingswood.bath.sch.uk

Chairman of Governors: Mr T Westbrook

Headmaster: **Mr Mark Brearey**, BA Hons, PGCE

Age Range. 3–11.
Number of Pupils. 321: Prep: 107 boys, 98 girls; Pre-Prep: 65 boys, 51 girls. 10 Boarders.
Fees per term (2014–2015). Nursery, Reception, Years 1 and 2: £2,940 (Nursery part-day pro rata); Years 3–4: £3,467; Years 5–6: £3,522. Boarding: £6,936–£7,282 (full), £5,826 (weekly).

Kingswood Preparatory School is the Preparatory School for Kingswood School, Bath. It is part of the Kingswood Foundation and each year over 95% of pupils move on to Kingswood School, through examination in January, at the end of Year 6.

Kingswood School is the oldest Methodist educational institution in the world, having been founded by John Wesley in 1748. Both Preparatory and the Senior Schools have extensive linked sites on Lansdown hill overlooking the world-famous city of Bath.

At Kingswood Preparatory School we are passionate about children's learning and combine high academic standards with a core of kindness that permeates every corner of our school. Our aim is to create a happy, caring community based upon Christian principles in which all individuals can develop respect for themselves and for others.

We provide for the children a rich variety of academic, sporting, creative and social experiences. By doing so we hope to give them the opportunity to develop their personalities and potential in an atmosphere of enthusiasm, enjoyment, security and care for fellow pupils.

As well as our regular Extra-Curricular Programme which currently contains over fifty weekly options, the school offers regular opportunities to participate in Music, Drama and Sport. We are able to use certain senior school facilities such as: the swimming pool, the astroturf hockey pitch and the theatre. The Prep School shares 56 acres of playing fields with the seniors.

The Prep School is situated in the splendid parkland setting of the Summerhill estate. Children of Pre-Preparatory age are educated in the modern, award-winning, purpose-built accommodation and the senior years in the main house, Summerhill. This fine mansion was designed by John Wood the Younger. Before it came into the school's possession in the 1950s it was the home of Ernest Cook, founder of the Ernest Cook Trust. The boarders live in High Vinnalls which offers all types of boarding to boys and girls aged between 7 and 11. Adjacent to the school and superbly situated in large gardens surrounded by woods and parkland, it has been acclaimed as a model for what boarding houses for young children should be like, in terms of its homely atmosphere and facilities. The school enjoys magnificent views over the City of Bath, and is situated only one and half miles from the centre.

There are 66 staff in all: 28 full-time and 6 part-time teachers, 8 ancillary support assistants and a further 20 part-time peripatetic staff.

Charitable status. Kingswood Preparatory School is a Registered Charity, number 309148. It exists for the purpose of educating children.

Knighton House

Durweston, Blandford, Dorset DT11 0PY
Tel: 01258 452065
Fax: 01258 450744
email: admissions@knightonhouse.co.uk
website: www.knightonhouse.com
Twitter: @RedDungarees

Chairman of the Governors: Mrs Camilla Masters

Headmistress: **Mrs S Wicks**, BEd

Age Range. Girls 3–13, Boys 3–7.
Number of Pupils. Prep School: 80; The Orchard, Pre-Prep and Nursery (co-educational): 39.
Fees per term (2014–2015). Boarders £6,995; Day: Prep £4,140–£5,310, Pre-Prep £2,260–£2,685, Nursery: £2,260 (full time but excluding Early Years funding). There are no compulsory extras.

Established in 1950, Knighton House is an exceptional friendly day and boarding school for girls aged 7–13 with an 'outstanding' co-ed pre-prep for children aged 3–7.

Knighton House keeps pace with the expectations of the 21st Century, whilst nurturing its unique traditional values. As one of the few remaining all-girls prep schools, we pride ourselves on our pastoral care and the opportunities we offer girls through a crucial developmental stage of their life. We encourage independent thinking and learning and outdoor play is a key part of the school day. In a delightful country setting, the school provides a safe but challenging environment in which children can discover their strengths, take risks and make friends. Boarding is entirely flexible and ponies and pets are all welcome.

The small classes and high staff/pupil ratio ensures individual attention. The scholarships and awards won from Knighton House reflect academic, musical, artistic and all-rounder prowess; there is a strong artistic and musical tradition. Team sports and swimming have an all-year-round place in the timetable. There are many extra-curricular activities including riding from our own stables, triathlon, tetrathlon, dance, drama and outdoor environmental pursuits.

This careful balance of academic subjects and extra-curricular activities encourages all aspects of personal growth. The size of Knighton House ensures that each pupil is known by everyone; each girl has an identity and is respected for her individuality.

Knighton House feeds a wide range of senior schools, both co-ed and single-sex.

Charitable status. Knighton House School Limited is a Registered Charity, number 306316.

The Lady Eleanor Holles School (Junior Department)

Burlington House, 177 Uxbridge Road, Hampton, Middlesex TW12 1BD

Tel: 020 8979 2173
          Registrar & Senior Department: 020 8979 1601
Fax: 020 8783 1962
email: junior-office@lehs.org.uk
website: www.lehs.org.uk
Twitter: @lehschool

Chairman of Governors: Mr C S Stokes

Head Mistress: Mrs H G Hanbury, MA, MSc

Head of Junior Department: **Mrs F Robinson**, BA Cardiff, MA King's College London

Age Range. 7–11.
Number of Pupils. 188 day girls.
Fees per term (2014–2015). £4,750.

The Lady Eleanor Holles School Junior Department is housed in its own separate building in one corner of the school's spacious thirty-acre grounds. Junior Department pupils make full use of the school's extensive facilities, such as a heated indoor 25m pool, Sports Hall and floodlit netball courts. (*See The Lady Eleanor Holles School's entry in the GSA section for more details.*) They also take advantage of a fleet of school coaches serving most of West London and Surrey.

The school is academically selective, with most girls joining in Year 3. Entrance exams in English and Maths are held the January before entry. The vast majority of Junior Department pupils are given guaranteed places in the Senior Department without having to take the Senior entrance exam.

The school's teaching is firmly based on the National Curriculum and there are specialist teachers for Science, Art, French, IT, Music and PE from the beginning. The school is very well resourced and staff use a wide variety of teaching styles and activities to ensure pace, stimulation and progression.

There is a wide range of extra-curricular activities so girls can develop their own interests and abilities, and all achievements and progress are valued and praised.

Extra-curricular clubs include Drama, Chess, Gardening and various Art, Music and Sports activities.

Whilst LEH is a broadly Christian foundation, it welcomes girls of all faiths, and none. School Assemblies, some of which are performed by the girls for their parents, may feature Hindu, Islamic Sikh or Jewish festivals and stories, as well as Christian.

In 2003, Burlington House, the home of the Junior Department, was the subject of a very extensive programme of extension and renovation, and now boasts superb facilities for a 21st-century education. Amongst the main improvements were four spacious new Practical Rooms for Art, DT and Science; two new Computer suites; a well-stocked and welcoming Library; and larger, brighter classrooms.

The staff work hard to establish and maintain a caring, supportive atmosphere in which girls feel confident to be themselves, to respect and care for everyone in the community, to be proud of their achievements and to persevere with things they find challenging. Pastoral care is a priority and we are proud of the happy, lively, hard-working pupils of the Junior Department.

Charitable status. The Lady Eleanor Holles School is a Registered Charity, number 1130254.

Lambrook

Winkfield Row, Nr Ascot, Berkshire RG42 6LU

Tel: 01344 882717
Fax: 01344 891114
email: registrar@lambrookschool.co.uk
            info@lambrookschool.co.uk
website: www.lambrookschool.co.uk
Twitter: @lambrookschool
Facebook: /lambrook

Chairman of the Governors: Charles Donald, BA Hons, CDipAF

Headmaster: J F Perry, BA Hons, PGCE Cantab

Deputy Headmaster: P P Thacker, BA Hons, PGCE, FRGS

Age Range. 3–13.
Number of Children. 510.
Fees per term (2014–2015). Prep: Weekly Boarding £6,422–£6,878; Day £5,280–£5,736. Pre-Prep: Day £3,430–£3,578.

Lambrook is a happy, lively flexi boarding and day Preparatory school where girls and boys aged 3–13 are immersed in a world of opportunities.

We offer the time-honoured practices and expansive grounds of a country school with outstanding modern facilities, providing the best possible opportunities for our children to develop their feathers to fly to senior school and beyond.

Our facilities include a professional Performing Arts centre, inspiring our children to take to the West End stage and perform at the Edinburgh Fringe. Our talented choristers, dancers and instrumentalists delight at venues from Windsor Castle to Eton College.

Our sector-leading sports facilities include a new aquatic centre, on-site golf course and 50 acres of grounds. With the guidance of Olympic standard mentors, our children enjoy a variety of sports including cricket, rugby, lacrosse and polo.

Founded in 1860, we are one of the oldest preparatory schools in the country. We have a rich history of success with consistently high academic standards resulting in a good number of children attaining top scholarships each year to many of the leading independent senior schools in the country. We are proud also that our children leave us as well-rounded, independent and creative individuals who go on to make significant contributions to the wider world.

On any day, the School is awash with activity on the academic, sporting, musical, theatrical and artistic fronts that seek to draw the best out of each and every one of our pupils. The development of each individual child is at the heart of everything we do allowing them to grow and thrive in a stimulating, challenging and rewarding environment. Through working, playing, learning, living, serving and sharing together our children grow mentally, physically, spiritually and in so doing, appreciate the gifts they have.

The School is situated near Ascot in the heart of the Berkshire countryside in over 50 acres of breathtaking grounds. We are easily accessible from central London, the M4, M3 and M40 motorways and provide transport services across the local area and also to and from West London. We are also close to international transport links with Heathrow a mere 30 minutes away by road.

Charitable status. Lambrook School Trust Limited is a Registered Charity, number 309098. Its purpose is to provide an excellent education for boys and girls.

Lancing College Preparatory School at Hove
A Woodard School

The Droveway, Hove, East Sussex BN3 6LU
Tel: 01273 503452
Fax: 01273 503457
email: hove@lancing.org.uk
website: www.lancingcollege.co.uk

Chairman of Governors: Dr H O Brünjes, BSc, MBBS, DRCOG, FEWI

Headmaster: **A P Laurent**

Age Range. 3–13.
Number of Pupils. 239.
Fees per term (2014–2015). £1,190–£4,765 (including lunch).

Lancing College Preparatory School is situated in an enviable position in Hove overlooking the English Channel.

Much of our ethos is drawn from the fact that we are a Christian based school and central to this is the belief that children must feel happy and secure in their surroundings if they are to succeed. The school is run on family lines, each child being given a sense of their true worth as an individual but also as part of the family.

The school offers an excellent academic education with a modern curriculum preparing for the Common Entrance and Scholarship Examinations at the end of academic year eight. Central to our curriculum beliefs is the idea that all pupils have an area in which they can excel, and to that end we place huge importance on the teaching of Art, Drama, Music and Sport as well as all the subjects that you would expect to find in the National Curriculum.

We have a fully qualified staff of twenty five full and part time teachers who enjoy facilities including a fully equipped science laboratory, an art design and technology room, gymnasium, ICT suite and library. As well as extensive grounds

there is an all-weather area for the coaching of our main sports, cricket, football, rugby, hockey, netball, rounders and tennis.

Charitable status. Lancing College is a Registered Charity, number 1076483. It exists to provide education for boys and girls.

Lanesborough School

Maori Road, Guildford, Surrey GU1 2EL
Tel: 01483 880650
Fax: 01483 880651
email: office@lanesborough.surrey.sch.uk
website: www.lanesborough.surrey.sch.uk

Chairman of Governors: Councillor Mrs S K Creedy, MA Cantab

Head: **Mrs C Turnbull**, BA Hons

Age Range. 3–13.
Number of Boys. 360 Day Boys.
Fees per term (2014–2015). Nursery £2,930 (Surrey County Council Early Years Free Entitlement offsets 3 hours per day for eligible pupils), Reception and Year 1 £3,550, Year 2 £3,750, Years 3–5 £3,950, Years 6–8 £4,070.

Lanesborough is the Preparatory School of the Royal Grammar School and the choir school for Guildford Cathedral. Cathedral choristers qualify for choral scholarships.

The main entry points are Nursery, Reception and Year 3. Many of the pupils gain entry to the Royal Grammar School at age 11 or 13, whilst others are prepared for Scholarship and Common Entrance examination to senior independent schools at 13.

The School is divided into four houses for house competitions. Pastoral care and supervision of academic progress are shared by the Head, Housemasters, Form and subject teachers. Extra-curricular activities include music, art, chess, drama, computer club, judo, fencing, tennis, basketball, science and General Knowledge.

Music is a strong feature of the life of the school, which is a member of the Choir Schools Association. In addition to the Cathedral Choir, there are senior and junior choirs, an orchestra, wind and string groups. Private tuition by qualified peripatetic teachers is available in most instruments. There are music concerts and the School Carol Service at the Cathedral has achieved wide acclaim. Music Scholarships to Independent Senior Schools are gained each year.

Art plays an important part in the curriculum also, with boys receiving tuition throughout the school.

Games are association football, rugby football, cricket, athletics, swimming, basketball, hockey and badminton. There is a school field, gym and astroturf.

Regular school visits are undertaken to local places of interest. School parties also go abroad, eg for skiing, watersports, football and on cultural visits.

The pre-preparatory department (for boys aged 3–7 and including a Nursery unit) is housed in a separate building (Braganza), but shares many of the facilities of the senior part of the School.

There is an active Parents' Association.

Charitable status. Lanesborough is governed by the trustees of The Royal Grammar School of King Edward VI, Guildford which is a Registered Charity, number 312028. It exists for the purpose of educating boys in or near Guildford.

Lathallan School

Brotherton Castle, Johnshaven, Angus DD10 0HN
Tel: 01561 362220
Fax: 01561 361695
email: admissions@lathallan.org.uk
website: www.lathallan.org.uk
Twitter: @lathallanschool
Facebook: /Lathallan-School

Chairman of Board of Directors: Professor Sir Graeme Catto

Headmaster: **Mr Richard Toley**, BA Hons, MPhil, PGCE, FRSA

Age Range. 6 weeks to 18 years.
Number of Pupils. 213, plus 58 in Nursery.
Fees per term (2014–2015). Tuition: J1–J2 £3,230, J3–J4 £4,082, J5–7 £4,626, S1 £4,902, S2–S6 £5,579. Weekly Boarding (in addition to Tuition): £1,337. Full Boarding (inc Tuition): £7,649. Reductions for siblings and Services children. Scholarships and Bursaries available.

With an overall size of just over 200 pupils, class sizes averaged at 12 pupils, high quality academic staff and unique environment are all contributors to fulfilling the claim that every child has the opportunity to develop to their own full potential. Being a non-selective school, there are no entrance exams; they assess each child on his or her own merit.

Recently the school saw pupils reaching national finals in a variety of fields such as drama, science and sports. The diversity of these achievements underpin the Lathallan School ethos that every child deserves to enjoy the success of their individual abilities in whatever field they lie – on the sports field, in the classroom, in the arts, in personal achievement. The school is also capitalizing on its stunning rural coastal location by widening its focus on Outdoor Education and Environmental Studies.

Lathallan School is a place in which challenge, industriousness and maximising individual potential is pivotal in our pupils' educational development. Every individual is made to feel an integral and special part of the school.

Lathallan School, situated in a baronial castle in 62 acres of spectacular grounds overlooking the North Sea is easily accessible. Daily coach runs serve Lathallan School's wide catchment area from Aberdeen and Stonehaven, as well as Forfar and Montrose to the south. Weekly and flexi boarding is available; the only school in the region to offer such a service.

Charitable status. Lathallan School is a Registered Charity, number SC018423. It exists to provide education of the highest standard for boys and girls.

Latymer Prep School

36 Upper Mall, Hammersmith, London W6 9TA
Tel: 0845 638 5700
Fax: 0845 638 5732
email: registrar@latymerprep.org
          admin@latymerprep.org
website: www.latymerprep.org

Chairman of Governors: Mr James Graham, MA, FRSA

Principal: **Mr Stuart P Dorrian**, BA

Age Range. 7–11 Co-educational.
Number of Pupils. 160 Day Pupils.
Fees per term (2014–2015). £5,072.

Latymer Prep School, led by its own Principal, was granted independence by the Governors of the Latymer Foundation in 1995 – the Centenary Year of Latymer Upper School on its present site. Previously the Prep School had been run as a very successful department of the Upper School and the relationship remains an extremely close one with all children usually expected to proceed to the Upper School.

The school is academically selective and pupils are taught the full range of subjects following National Curriculum guidelines, but to an advanced standard. Classes are kept small (20) which allows for close monitoring and evaluation of each pupil's progress and well-being. Means-tested academic scholarships are available.

The school is well resourced and has attractive facilities in two elegant period houses adjacent to the River Thames. Catering, sports and theatre facilities are shared with the Upper School.

A main feature of the school is its friendly and caring atmosphere which offers close pastoral support to each individual pupil. Academic achievement is strong, but in addition, all staff and pupils contribute to an extensive range of activities featuring Sport, Music, Art and Drama. The school has 3 large choirs and its own orchestra. Opportunities exist for all pupils to participate in concerts, plays and inter-school sporting events.

The major sports are soccer, rugby, cricket, tennis, athletics, hockey and netball. There is also a thriving swimming club (the school has its own pool). Karate chess, zumba, drama and bridge are just some of the clubs which take place after school. There is an Arts Week, plus a residential to Norfolk for Y5 and a residential to Italy for Y6 pupils.

There is a Parents' Gild and opportunities occur frequently to meet with staff socially. Visits for prospective parents occur throughout the year and can be arranged by telephoning for an appointment.

Charitable status. The Latymer Foundation is a Registered Charity, number 312714. It exists to provide an opportunity for able pupils from all walks of life to develop their talents to the full.

Laxton Junior – Oundle School

East Road, Oundle, Peterborough PE8 4BX
Tel: 01832 277275
email: info@laxtonjunior.org.uk
website: www.laxtonjunior.org.uk

Governors: The Worshipful Company of Grocers

Chairman: Mr Julian Tregoning

Headmaster: **Mr Mark Potter**, BEd Hons

Deputy Head: Miss Janet Bass, BA Hons, Dip TEFL, PGDPSE

Age Range. 4–11.
Number of Children. 255.
Fees per term (2014–2015). £3,295–£3,615 (including lunches).

Opened in 1973 and part of Oundle School, Laxton Junior is a co-educational day school for children aged 4–11 years. In September 2002 Laxton Junior moved into a new building which caters for 280 pupils. The school has 14 forms of no more than 20 pupils, each with a fully qualified Form Teacher. The curriculum includes Art & Design, Computer Skills, French, Music, PE and Performing Arts as well as the major academic subjects. Emphasis has always been placed on the individual child and the importance of each doing their best at all times, according to their ability. Children are prepared for entrance examinations for Independent

Senior Schools in the area; Kimbolton, Oundle, Oakham and Stamford Schools being the key schools.

The new building has a large multi-purpose hall which is used for PE, Music and Performing Arts as well as concerts, school plays and social events The school has its own games fields and netball courts plus all children receive swimming instruction each week in the Oundle School Pool. The main games are football, rugby, cricket, netball, rounders, hockey and athletics plus coaching in tennis.

In Year 2 all pupils have the opportunity to play the violin or cello as part of the curriculum. From Year 3 the recorder is introduced, plus additional time is given for choir, orchestra and learning other musical instruments. The school also has an Education Support Unit which monitors all pupils' development and helps individuals with specific difficulties.

The aims of the school are to encourage the formation of good work habits and good manners, to lay the foundations for the development of self-discipline, self-confidence and self-motivation and to offer the children the opportunity of experiencing the satisfaction of achievement.

The partnership of home and school in the education of the child is strongly emphasises and all parents are members of the Parents' & Friends' Association.

Laxton Junior School was inspected in March 2008. The report is available on the school website.

Charitable status. Oundle School is a Registered Charity, number 309921. It exists to provide education for boys and girls.

Leaden Hall School

70 The Close, Salisbury, Wiltshire SPI 2EP
Tel: 01722 334700
Fax: 01722 439269
email: admin@leaden-hall.com
website: www.leaden-hall.com

Chair of Governors: Mrs Sara Willan

Headmistress: **Mrs Julia Eager**, MSc

Age Range. Girls 3–11.
Number of Pupils. 160 Girls: 135 Day, 25 Boarders.
Fees per term (2014–2015). Day £2,595–£4,470, Boarding supplement £1,790.

Situated in Salisbury's stunning Cathedral Close, Leaden Hall School provides day and boarding education for girls aged 3–11 in a happy, purposeful atmosphere. In a unique setting, combining historic buildings with contemporary classrooms, studios, laboratories and a performance and sports hall, it is a safe, supportive environment for each pupil to grow at their own pace.

The girls are prepared for Local Authority 11+ examinations, Common Entrance and for individual school assessments, including scholarships for music, drama, art and sport. The breadth of the curriculum, the numerous enrichment activities, a 'sport and music for all' philosophy, together with an academic rigour geared to each pupil's ability, enables them to achieve the best they can.

The principle sports at Leaden Hall are netball, hockey, rounders, athletics, cross country, lacrosse, gymnastics, dance and swimming and as many children as possible are invited to compete in fixtures against other schools both at home and away. There are many opportunities to try other sports through clubs and after-school activities. Musical skills are developed through playing in the orchestra, choirs, string groups, concerts and individual peripatetic music lessons. Each year group participates in at least one annual dramatic production providing the opportunity to develop talent and gain confidence. Art is an important part of the curriculum and the girls study both traditional and contemporary artists as they progress through the school. Every year there

is an exhibition displaying artwork from all year groups and the well-resourced studios have views over the water meadows which also inspired Constable.

Boarding at Leaden Hall is extremely popular and the girls build strong friendships. There is an extensive and varied choice of activities in the evenings and at weekends. As a day and boarding school, children can have wrap-around care from before breakfast to supper time, and day girls can also enjoy the option of flexi boarding.

More information is available on the website, www.leaden-hall.com, but the best way to find out about Leaden Hall is to visit. Contact the Registrar, registrar@leaden-hall.com, to make an appointment.

Scholarships and means-tested bursaries are available.

Charitable status. Leaden Hall School is a Registered Charity, number 309489. It exists to provide education for children.

Leehurst Swan School

19 Campbell Road, Salisbury SP1 3BQ
Tel: 01722 333094
Fax: 01722 330868
email: registrar@leehurstswan.org.uk
            reception@leehurstswan.org.uk
website: www.leehurstswan.org.uk

Chairman of Governors: Mr Michael New

Headmaster: **Mr R N S Leake**, BSc, PGCE, CBiol, MIBiol

Age Range. 2–16 Co-educational.
Number of Children. 332.
Fees per term (2014–2015). Senior School £4,200; Prep School £2,455–£2,965; Pre-School £2,495 (Full time).

Leehurst Swan is an Independent Day School, just 10 minutes' walk from Salisbury city centre, which has been inspiring and educating pupils for 100 years. We are the only independent day school in Salisbury offering education for girls and boys from age 2–16. The benefits of an all-through education are widely recognised, eliminating the problems of transfer between the stages of education. A co-educational environment also encourages the development of excellent social skills. We celebrate the best of the old while embracing the latest innovations and technology.

The school is fully co-educational with over 330 children in the School: 165 children in the Prep School, 140 in the Senior School and 48 in the Pre-Prep. The School has small classes, a family atmosphere, and an environment that inspires and motivates pupils to achieve their best. The individual attention pupils receive reflects the ethos of Christian values and respect for the individual.

We have recently invested in a substantial building project to provide a new Prep school to give state-of-the-art teaching facilities which reflects the thriving and highly successful development of the school in recent years.

Leehurst Swan Pre-Prep was inspected in March 2014 and was graded as "outstanding" in every aspect. The Pre-Prep provides exciting activities and prepares the children fully for formal education. The Pre-Prep welcomes children from the age of two. Set in a purpose-built building, nestling in a wooded glade, the Pre-Prep provides outstanding quality early years education and care in a safe and secure environment. The ethos is one of inclusion with parents as equal partners.

Pupils in the Prep School have specialist teaching in key subjects and use dedicated school facilities in ICT, Science, Music, Art, and Design Technology. The children are prepared for 11+ examinations for entry into the local grammar schools and for entry into the Senior School.

In the Senior School the pupils normally pursue studies in ten GCSE subjects and academic results are excellent. The school equally values and nurtures creative and sporting talent awarding scholarships in these areas in addition to academic scholarships.

Individual lessons are arranged in a wide range of musical instruments leading to Associated Board examinations.

Leehurst Swan welcomes visitors to the school to come and see them at work and play.

Charitable status. Leehurst Swan Limited is a Registered Charity, number 800158. It exists to provide education for children.

Leicester Grammar Junior School

London Road, Great Glen, Leicester LE8 9FL
Tel: 0116 259 1950
Fax: 0116 259 1951
email: friell@leicestergrammar.org.uk
website: www.leicestergrammar.org.uk

Chairman of Governors: I D Patterson, LLB

Headmistress: **Mrs C Rigby**, BA

Age Range. 3–11 Co-educational.
Number of Pupils. 360.
Fees per term (2014–2015). Years 3–6 £3,233; Kinders to Year 2 £3,077.

Leicester Grammar Junior School was founded in 1992 when Leicester Grammar School Trust took over educational responsibility for Evington Hall, an independent school run by the Sisters of Charity of St Paul.

The school is a selective, co-educational day school with a Christian Foundation. It acts as the junior school to Leicester Grammar School and is the first stage in a continuous education from 3 years through to A Level. In September 2008 both the Junior and Senior schools relocated to a new purpose-built campus SW of the city of Leicester. Thus, the school now encompasses the full 3–18 age range on the one site.

The school provides a stimulating, disciplined, happy environment where each child is encouraged to aim for the highest standards in everything they do and take a full and active part in all aspects of school life. It operates as an extension of the family unit within which the staff act with firmness and fairness. Respect and consideration underpin school life. Pupils are encouraged to develop a caring and responsible attitude to others, leading to good manners and acceptable behaviour.

The children benefit from not only academic success and development but also from excellent musical, sporting and dramatic involvement within a broad and well balanced curriculum.

Music is a particular strength of the school and plays an important part in the life of every child. From the beginning as 3 year olds, children are taught by a music specialist. Pupils have the opportunity to learn a variety of instruments and there is a particularly strong Infant String Scheme; children as young as five or six years of age learn to play the violin or cello. The school orchestra and ensembles perform at festivals, concerts and assemblies. There are also many choral opportunities within the Junior and Infant choir which are often linked with Drama. A number of boys and girls are also members of the Leicester Cathedral choir and enjoy weekly training sessions with the Cathedral Master of Music.

In 2004 the school received the Sportsmark Gold Award in recognition of the quality of sport within the curriculum and extra-curricular. The PE and Games provision aims to develop skills in team and individual games, gymnastics, dance, swimming and athletics. The main team games are rugby, football and cricket for the boys and netball, hockey and rounders for the girls. After-school clubs offer additional sporting opportunities such as tennis, badminton, table tennis and cross-country.

Admissions. Pupils are admitted at all ages between 3+ and 10+ although the vast majority enter in the September following their third or fourth birthday (Kinders or Reception). Following a visit to the school an Application Form is offered. When the form is returned a date for assessment is set. Parents wishing their children to be admitted to the Infant Department at times other than in September are invited to bring their child to school to spend part of a day with the class he or she would join. Class teachers then carry out an assessment to determine whether or not the child will be able to integrate into the year group.

Charitable status. Leicester Grammar School Trust is a Registered Charity, number 510809.

Leweston Junior Department

Sherborne, Dorset DT9 6EN
Tel: 01963 210790
Fax: 01963 210648
email: enquiries@leweston.dorset.sch.uk
website: www.leweston.co.uk
Twitter: @LewestonSchool
Facebook: /leweston

Chair of Board of Governors: Mrs M Head

Headmaster: **Mr Adrian Aylward**, MA Oxon

Senior Teacher: Mrs V Bridgeman-Sutton, BA Hons Sheffield, MPhil Sheffield, QTS Dorset, PCES SpLD Southampton

Age Range. 3 months–11 years Co-educational.
Number of Pupils. 69: 47 Girls, 22 Boys.
Fees per term (2014–2015). Nursery: £43 (all day 08.00–18.00 including food); £24 (1 x 5 hr session 08.00–13.00 or 13.00–18.00 including food); Breakfast Club 07.30–08.00: £3; Lunch and Care from 12.00–14.00 for funded children: £5.25 lunch and £5 per hour care; Additional Hourly Rate: £5.
Reception–Year 2 £2,685; Years 3–6 £4,015. Weekly Boarding £5,160, Full Boarding £6,115.

Setting. Leweston Junior Department is an independent Catholic school for boys and girls with boarding provision for girls from age 7. The school is situated in forty-six acres of Dorset parkland three miles south of Sherborne and occupies an enviable setting in a skilfully converted former Coach House providing a unique range of bright spacious classrooms. The beautiful rural site is shared with Leweston School (girls 11–18 years), offering continuity of education for girls right through to A Level. The Junior Department enjoys the benefit of many excellent facilities including a modern, well-equipped Art and Design Centre, an all-weather sports pitch, a heated swimming pool, a large sports hall, tennis courts and extensive playing fields. As a result of the integration with Leweston School in 2014, Junior pupils now take advantage of the specialist teaching in Languages, Art, Maths, Domestic Science, Music and Sport that is provided by the Senior School. The parkland setting offers many opportunities for study and recreation.

Ethos. Traditional excellence in teaching is combined with modern facilities and resources in a stimulating, happy and purposeful Christian environment. The school motto 'Gaudere et Bene Facere' (Rejoice and Do Well) exactly reflects the importance of high academic standards together with artistic, musical and sporting excellence achieved in an atmosphere of joy and vibrancy. Each child is encouraged to develop individual talents within the caring and supportive school community. Small class sizes, a friendly family ethos, and traditional values of work and behaviour are appreciated by parents. Full and flexi boarding options provide flexibility for pupils to enjoy a wide variety of extra-curricular activities, whilst no Saturday morning school allows for rest and relaxation.

Curriculum. Programmes of study encompass the National Curriculum without being constrained by it. Basic subjects are taught to a high standard concentrating on literacy and numeracy acquisition in the early years before expanding into a broader curriculum in Years 3–6. Well-qualified class teachers and specialist subject teachers foster independent learning and encourage the development of problem solving and investigative skills in all areas of the curriculum. Academic standards are high and many pupils gain awards to senior school.

There is a strong tradition in the performing arts. Music, Drama and Dance are taught within the curriculum. A high percentage of pupils learn to play musical instruments and take additional Drama. There is a school orchestra and choir and many opportunities throughout the year for performance and grade examinations in both Music and Drama. All pupils in Years 4–6 undertake English Speaking Board assessments. Individual and team sports are considered important as part of the healthy, active lifestyle and the school enjoys a particular reputation for hockey and cross-country. Art, Ceramics and Design Technology are taught by specialist teachers using the exceptional facilities in the Art and Design Centre.

Charitable status. Leweston School Trust is a Registered Charity, number 295175. It exists to provide for children a contemporary education in the Catholic tradition.

Littlegarth School

Horkesley Park, Nayland, Colchester, Essex CO6 4JR
Tel: 01206 262332
Fax: 01206 263101
email: office@littlegarth.essex.sch.uk
website: www.littlegarth.essex.sch.uk

Chairman of Governors: Mr Stephen Cole, MA

Headmaster: **Mr Peter Jones**, BEd Hons

Deputy Head: Mrs Lynda Turner, BA Hons

Age Range. 2½–11.
Number of Pupils. Day: approx 156 Boys, 160 Girls.
Fees per term (2014–2015). £690–£3,140.
Set in 28 acres of glorious grounds in the beautiful Stour Valley, Littlegarth School was founded in 1940 in Dedham and moved to Horkesley Park in 1994. An accredited Independent School, Littlegarth offers a thorough and successful academic, cultural and sports education within a secure and friendly environment.

There is a flourishing Nursery Department where children are prepared for admission to the Pre-Prep, which they join at 4+, although children are accepted by assessment and interview at all levels, subject to space.

Littlegarth is proud of the broad curriculum offered. The school boasts small class sizes and a friendly atmosphere. French is taught from the age of 4, when specialist teaching is also provided in music and sport. Academic standards are high and progress is monitored closely at all times. Careful attention is given to children as they prepare for scholarships and entrance examinations to Independent Schools and local Grammar Schools. As the children move from the Pre-Prep, specialist teaching is given in each subject.

Music is one of the strengths of the school and a large percentage of our children learn at least one musical instrument as well as the recorder. School choirs perform in a

number of local events and internal concerts are a regular feature of school life. A lunch-time Mandarin Club is open to children from Years 1–6.

The children participate in a wide range of sports throughout the year and the school promotes team participation for all children from the age of 8. As well as boasting a floodlit all-weather area, a substantial new sports hall and changing room complex has been built and a programme to level and extend the sports fields has been completed. An exciting adventure playground has been erected next to the spacious play area and a project to plant an adventure woodland is nearing completion.

The school produces many plays each year and strong drama links with the local community are being forged. As well as running the school library, parents are also actively involved in running a wardrobe department and there is a flourishing 'Friends of Littlegarth' parent body.

A wide variety of clubs, extra-curricular activity and pre and after school care are offered.

Charitable status. Littlegarth School Limited is a Registered Charity, number 325064. It exists to provide education for children.

Lochinver House School

Heath Road, Little Heath, Potters Bar, Herts EN6 1LW
Tel: 01707 653064
Fax: 01707 663828
email: registrar@lochinverhouse.herts.sch.uk
website: www.lochinverhouse.herts.sch.uk

Chairman of the Governors: Stuart Westley, MA, Chair of AGBIS

Headmaster: **Ben Walker**, BA Hons

Age Range. 4–13.
Number of Boys. 350 Day Boys.
Fees per term (2014–2015). £3,214–£4,223 with no compulsory extras.
The academic staff consists of 36 qualified and graduate teachers, Laboratory, ICT, DT technicians, classroom assistants and a Matron.

The school, founded in 1947, is situated in a pleasant residential area on the edge of green belt land in South Hertfordshire, and yet is conveniently placed for access to London. At the heart of the school is a late Victorian house. Facilities on our 8½ acre site are extensive and include a purpose-built Pre-Prep Department, separate Sports Hall, Gymnasium & Theatre, Music Centre, two Science Laboratories and specialist IT, DT, and Art rooms. Lochinver is fully advanced with IT including an exciting project which provides iPads to older boys.

Boys are prepared for Common Entrance and Scholarship examinations to a wide range of top day and boarding Independent Schools.

The school has its own extensive playing fields on site, including an all-weather, Astro pitch. The major sports: Football, Rugby, Cricket, Athletics and Basketball are complemented by opportunities to take part in a very wide range of further sports and physical activity. Some boys choose to play Real Tennis at Hatfield House. All boys learn to swim whilst they are at the School. Residential trips take place both within the UK and overseas, such as skiing in Europe, a Classics trip to Italy and a Rugby Tour to South Africa. During their time at the school each boy will spend some time in France as this is an important and much valued part of the French Curriculum. There are opportunities for the boys to also study Spanish, Latin and Russian.

Music, Art, Drama, Design Technology and PE are part of the timetabled curriculum for all boys. The school encourages boys to learn at least one musical instrument and currently 75% of the children are doing so. There is a School Orchestra, Junior and Senior Choir, together with a variety of instrumental Groups. Parents appreciate our provision of extended care at both ends of the day.

The school is a non-profit making Educational Trust administered by a Board of Governors.

Charitable status. Lochinver House School is a Registered Charity, number 1091045. It aims to provide a quality education.

Lockers Park

Lockers Park Lane, Hemel Hempstead, Hertfordshire HP1 1TL

Tel:	01442 251712
Fax:	01442 234150
email:	secretary@lockerspark.herts.sch.uk
website:	www.lockerspark.herts.sch.uk

Chairman of Governors: C Lister, BSc Hons, MBA

Headmaster: **C Wilson**, BA Cantab, PGCE

Admissions: C R Stephens, BA Hons

Age Range. 5–13.

Number of Pupils. 147 Boys, of whom 70 are boarders or flexi-boarders.

Fees per term (2014–2015). Boarders £7,100, Day Boys £3,200–£5,220. Day fees include the option to have breakfast, stay for supper and participate in evening activities at no extra cost.

Further details are outlined in the prospectus, available on application.

Lockers Park is located in 23 acres of parkland above the town of Hemel Hempstead, only five miles from both the M1 and M25 motorways. It lies within easy access of London (Euston 30 minutes) and all four of its airports; consequently the School is well accustomed to providing the necessary help and support to parents living both in Britain and abroad.

The main school building, purpose-built in 1874, is situated in grounds which are perfect for children, with well-maintained playing fields surrounded by woodland areas which easily occupy even the most active. There has been a steady process of modernisation over the past two decades and the School boasts first-class, all-round facilities: the Mountbatten Centre, which provides eight excellent specialist classrooms including a well-equipped ICT centre; an attached Science and Technology Building, containing two spacious laboratories, technology classroom and fully-fitted workshop; an exceptional art and pottery centre and a well-resourced library.

Sports facilities are of a high calibre and include a fully-fitted sports hall, two squash courts, a recently refurbished heated swimming pool, two tennis courts, an all-weather sports surface and cricket nets, a shooting range and a nine-hole golf course.

Lockers is proud of its academic and musical records; its success in both scholarships and Common Entrance examinations to 45 different schools in the past ten years reflects this well. The average class size is 14 and the pupil : teacher ratio a very healthy 1:7. The Music Department is well known; encouragement is given to every boy to find an instrument which he will enjoy and most gain proficiency in at least one. There is a full orchestra, wind, brass and jazz bands, a string ensemble and two choirs. The number of senior school scholarships of all types awarded to Lockers Park is considered high.

Drama plays a large part in school life with at least two major productions each year together with junior plays,

school assembly productions, charades and public speaking debates.

At Lockers, there is a real family atmosphere, there is always someone to whom a boy can turn and great care is taken to ensure the happiness of every child. Boys are safe, happy, fit and well looked after. While day boys enjoy all the facilities and opportunities of a boarding school, boarding is fun; dormitories are warm and friendly rooms and opportunities for a variety of enjoyable weekend activities are immense. With day boys and boarders alike, great care is taken over the personal development of each individual.

Bursaries. Lockers Park is committed to offering financial help to deserving candidates, subject to financial resources. Bursarial help may be available up to 100% of fees in some circumstances.

Charitable status. Lockers Park School Trust Ltd is a Registered Charity, number 311061. It aims to provide an all round, high quality education on a non-profit making basis.

Longacre School

Shamley Green, Guildford, Surrey GU5 0NQ

Tel:	01483 893225
Fax:	01483 893501
email:	office@longacreschool.co.uk
website:	www.longacreschool.co.uk

Headmistress: **Mrs Alexia Bracewell**, BA Hons, QTS, PCPSE

Age Range. 2½–11.

Number of Pupils. 200+ boys and girls.

Fees per term (from January 2015). £1,445–£4,380.

Are school days really the happiest days of your life? Many Longacre pupils would answer "Yes!" The cheerful and purposeful atmosphere at Longacre is apparent as soon as you enter the school. Here, children are valued as individuals and are encouraged to fulfil their potential in every facet of school life. Personal and social development is highly valued, enabling pupils to grow in confidence as they mature.

The Headmistress and her staff believe that children learn more effectively when they are happy, and that excellent academic results can be achieved without subjecting pupils to hothouse pressure. The fact that Longacre pupils gain a range of scholarships, and that they transfer successfully to senior schools of parental choice, shows that this approach is definitely working.

Academic progress is closely monitored and regularly tested. Small classes (maximum eighteen) enable pupils to be taught at an individual level, with increasing subject specialist tuition as children progress through the school. Alongside the core curriculum, Longacre offers a wide range of sporting opportunities, LAMDA lessons, stimulating off-site visits and exciting workshops. There are after school clubs every evening, ranging from Spanish to judo, and regular masterclasses for able pupils.

Set in a beautiful rural location on the outskirts of the picturesque village of Shamley Green, between Guildford and Cranleigh, the school offers a wonderful environment for young children. The school buildings comprise the original large 1902 house plus modern, purpose-built classrooms standing in nine acres of grounds. Facilities include sports fields, courts, gardens, woodland and an adventure playground.

Longacre is a community where parents are welcome. The school has a thriving and supportive PTA and parents are kept well informed about school events and their children's progress through a weekly newsletter, formal and informal meetings and written reports. The Headmistress and staff work closely with parents to ensure that their children are happy, successful and fulfilled.

To arrange a visit, please call 01483 893225. The Headmistress and her staff look forward to welcoming you to Longacre.

Lorenden Preparatory School

Painter's Forstal, Faversham, Kent ME13 0EN
Tel: 01795 590030
Fax: 01795 538002
email: admin@lorenden.org.uk
website: www.lorenden.org.uk

Chairman of Governors: R Boyd-Powell

Headteacher: **Mrs R Simmonds**, Cert Ed

Age Range. 3–11 Co-educational.
Number of Pupils. 120.
Fees per term (2014–2015). £2,532–£3,667.
Lorenden is situated in the village of Painter's Forstal between Faversham and the North Downs and within easy driving distance of Canterbury, Whitstable, Ashford and Sittingbourne; an idyllic position in the heart of the Kent countryside.

The school's avowed aim is to develop self-disciplined thoughtful children with a cheerful 'can do' attitude to life and a strong sense of fair play.

All round expectations are high and academic results are excellent. At eleven children either transfer to local grammar schools, which in this area are excellent, or continue in independent education. Able children have been awarded major academic, sports or art scholarships. Parents are not directed down one particular route: the choice is theirs.

Music is a great strength of the school and sports results are remarkably good. Every child 'gets a go' and resilience is the name of the game.

This is a school that needs to be experienced to be truly appreciated: it is not particularly well known and visitors are always delighted by what they find.

Enquiries concerning places and admissions should be made to the Secretary.

Charitable status. Lorenden School is a Registered Charity, number 1048805.

Loretto Junior School

North Esk Lodge, 1 North High Street, Musselburgh, East Lothian EH21 6JA
Tel: 0131 653 4570
Fax: 0131 653 4571
email: juniorschool@loretto.com
website: www.loretto.com
Twitter: @lorettohead
Facebook: /lorettoschool

Chairman of Governors: Lt Col S J M Graham

Headmaster: **P Meadows**, MA Cantab, CertEd

Age Range. 3–12.
Number of Pupils. 190.
Fees per term (2014–2015). Day Pupils £2,630–£4,600; Flexi Boarding (3 nights per week) £5,420; Overnighting £45 per night. Bursaries up to 105% of fees are available.

Pupils can enter the Nippers at 3 and are prepared for entrance and scholarship examinations, mostly to Loretto at 12+. Scholarships and Bursaries are available for entry to the Nippers at 10+ and 11+. Occasional and Flexi Boarding

are possible for pupils aged 11 and over. As well as the usual prep school facilities, the Nippers use the Loretto Computer Centre, Squash Courts, Fives Courts, Music School, Theatre, School Chapel, and the Sports Hall. The Nippers have just opened a New Science Lab and all pupils in Years 6 and 7 have their own iPad provided by the School. The school enjoys a fine reputation for Rugby, Hockey, Cricket, Music, Drama and Art. Loretto has its own Art Gallery. A wide range of individual sports is coached. The staff are all University Graduates and each of the thirteen classes can accommodate up to 16 pupils; the average class size is currently 14. Pastoral care is of the highest quality. Catering is in the hands of an experienced Steward.

From an early age children are encouraged to use their initiative and accept responsibility.

A prospectus can be requested from the School.

Charitable status. Loretto School is a Registered Charity, number SC013978. It exists in order to educate young people in mind, body and spirit.

Loyola Preparatory School

103 Palmerston Road, Buckhurst Hill, Essex IG9 5NH
Tel: 020 8504 7372
Fax: 020 8505 5361
email: office@loyola.essex.sch.uk
website: www.loyola.essex.sch.uk

Chair of Governors: Mrs A M Fox

Headmaster: **P G M Nicholson**, BEd London

Age Range. 3–11.
Number of Boys. 190.
Fees per term (2014–2015). £2,830 (incl. lunch)
Loyola Preparatory School is a long established school educating boys for over a century, originally as part of St Ignatius College. As a caring Catholic School it welcomes boys of all denominations offering a weekly mass to celebrate faith, ethos and values.

As a boy's only school, Loyola focuses its teaching techniques to harness the attention of boys by applying the extensive studies made into 'the ways boys learn best'. These practices encourage greater stimulation and enjoyment which is demonstrated by their overall behaviour and results.

Loyola has a high teacher to pupil ratio, facilitated by enthusiastic and committed teachers, supported by a generous quota of quality teaching assistants.

Loyola boys are encouraged to be kind and respect each other, with the older boys acting as role models for the younger boys. Year 6 boys are given "Prefect" responsibilities as well as the opportunity to be elected to the position of "Head Boy" and "Deputy Head Boy". All boys regularly take part in community events including fund raising for national and local charities.

Loyola supports their boy's progression for the next step in their learning journey by preparing them for entrance and scholarship exams with English and Maths being taught in small ability sets from Year 3 upwards.

The curriculum covers all the normal primary subjects and includes German, science and computer studies. There are schola, choir and orchestra opportunities available in school, with additional tuition for piano, strings, woodwind, brass and guitar.

Loyola is proud of its range of sporting activities for the boys, aided by a large all-weather pitch on site. Sporting activities include soccer, cricket, rugby, swimming, athletics and sailing (Year 6) of which many are available during the school day and others offered as an after-school club.

During their time at the school, Loyola boys experience a wide range of trips and activities including a 5-day trip to

Normandy (Year 6), a 3-day trip to Kingswood in Norfolk (Year 4), together with many day trips across the school years selected to stimulate and enrich their learning experience.

The school prospectus is available on the school website and prospective parents are welcome to telephone for an appointment to be given a personal tour of the school.

Charitable status. Loyola Preparatory School is a Registered Charity, number 1085079. The school is established in support of Roman Catholic principles of education.

Lucton School

Lucton, Leominster, Herefordshire HR6 9PN
Tel:	01568 782000
Fax:	01568 782001
email:	admissions@luctonschool.org
website:	www.luctonschool.org
Twitter:	@LuctonSchool
Facebook:	/luctonschool
LinkedIn:	/lucton-school

Headmistress: **Mrs Gill Thorne**, MA, BA Hons, PGCE, LLAM

Deputy Head: Mr D R Styles, JP, BSc Hons, MA, FCIEA, CPhys

Head of Sixth Form: Mr J Goode, MA Cantab, PGCE

Head of Prep School: Mr David Bicker-Caarten, MBA

Age Range. 6 months–19 years.
Number in School. 350.
Fees per term (2014–2015). Day £2,095–£4,110, Weekly Boarding £6,615–£7,810, Full Boarding £9,060.

About Lucton School. Founded in 1708, Lucton provides pupils with an excellent all-round education which aims to bring out their full potential. Pupils benefit from small classes, a friendly atmosphere and an idyllic rural location. There are extensive sports facilities and a good mix of day pupils, weekly boarders and full boarders.

Studying at Lucton School. Lucton has a strong academic record and an established tradition of getting the best possible results from each pupil. Subjects taught to GCSE include English language and literature, mathematics, biology, chemistry, physics, information technology, French, Spanish, German, history, geography, business studies, religious education, design & technology, art, music, drama and PE/games.

All the above GCSE subjects and more are available at AS and A2 Levels. The Sixth Form is housed in a new sixth form centre, including a new senior library and well-equipped IT suite.

School Facilities. The school is set in 45 acres of beautiful Herefordshire countryside. Facilities on site include:

- Junior and senior libraries
- Science laboratories
- ICT rooms
- Design and technology workshop
- Tennis courts
- Indoor swimming pool
- Indoor sports hall
- Games fields
- Equestrian centre.

Boarding pupils are housed in a modern building and all have individual rooms.

Admissions. Admission can take place at any time of the year by interview and assessment. Prospective pupils are always invited to spend a taster day in the school without obligation. Examinations for academic scholarships are held in January each year.

Lucton School is a member of the Independent Schools Association (ISA), The Independent Association of Prep Schools (IAPS) and the Boarding Schools' Association (BSA).

Charitable status. Lucton School is a Registered Charity, number 518076.

Ludgrove

Wixenford, Wokingham, Berks RG40 3AB
Tel:	0118 978 9881
Fax:	0118 979 2973
email:	office@ludgroveschool.co.uk
website:	www.ludgrove.net

Chairman of Governors: P D Edey, QC

Head: **S W T Barber**, BA Durham, PGCE

Age Range. 8–13.
Number of Boys. 185 Boarders.
Fees per term (2014–2015). £8,300.

Ludgrove is a traditional full boarding boys prep school situated in 130 acres of beautiful grounds in Berkshire. Ludgrove was founded in 1892 by Arthur Dunn in Cockfosters, north London. Dunn was one of life's natural enthusiasts and his favourite saying, "Whatsoever thy hand findeth to do, do it with all thy might" remains the school motto today. The principal aims of the school are for boys to grow and develop in a happy caring environment, to explore and expand their potential and to learn to develop an awareness and concern for others around them. We aim to prepare our boys to meet the demanding challenges they will experience at the next stage of their education with confidence and good humour.

Charitable status. Ludgrove School Trust Limited is a Registered Charity, number 309100.

Lyndhurst House Preparatory School

24 Lyndhurst Gardens, Hampstead, London NW3 5NW
Tel:	020 7435 4936
email:	pmg@lyndhursthouse.co.uk
website:	www.lyndhursthouse.co.uk

Headmaster: **A J C Reid**, MA Oxon

Age Range. 4–13.
Number of Day Boys. 165.
Fees per term (2014–2015). £5,440–£6,050 (including lunch and outings).

There is a full-time teaching staff of 20, with classroom assistants for the first four years and learning support across the year-groups. Entry is at 4+, or 7+ following interviews and assessment. All boys stay to 13+, and sit the Common Entrance Exam or Scholarship to the Independent Senior Schools. Lyndhurst is a friendly and lively traditional boys' school, with its own special atmosphere and character. The environment is warm and friendly, small and familiar in feel, yet full of bustle, activity and purpose. Strong foundations laid in the early years are followed by small sets in the top three years to provide the School's excellent record of success in transfers to London day schools and major public schools further afield. In addition to high academic expectations, there is a strong emphasis on sporting activity and achievement, as well as art, music, drama and computing. Lyndhurst House – a full, rich life in a personal, individual and friendly environment.

Magdalene House Preparatory School

Wisbech Grammar School

North Brink, Wisbech, Cambs PE13 1JX
Tel: 01945 586780
Fax: 01945 586781
email: Office@MagdaleneHousePrep.com
website: MagdaleneHousePrep.com
Facebook: /MagdaleneHouse

Chair of Governors: Dr D Barter, MBBS, FRCP, FRCPCH, DCH

Headmaster: **Mr C E Moxon**, BA

Age Range. 4–11 co-educational.
Number of Pupils. 155 day pupils.
Fees per term (2014–2015). £2,733.33. Means-tested bursary support is available.

Magdalene House Preparatory School, which caters for pupils from Reception to Prep 6, has doubled in size since its re-founding in 1997. Great emphasis is placed on reading, writing and numeracy, and the pupils follow a broad-based curriculum. The pupils have access to many of the excellent senior school facilities, including the science laboratory, sports hall and theatre. They also have their own library, a dedicated computer room and a light and spacious hall. Specialist teaching is offered in science, music, design technology, physical education and games, information technology and drama. Many children receive peripatetic music lessons and there are three choirs. Opportunities for performance in drama and music, including class plays, assemblies and informal concerts, are regular features. In January the Prep 6 pupils sit an entrance examination for the senior school. (*See Wisbech Grammar School entry in HMC section.*)

Sporting opportunities abound and a full timetable of fixtures against other schools is arranged. The main boys' team sports are rugby, hockey and cricket, whilst the girls play hockey, netball and rounders. Members of the under 11 rugby and hockey teams enjoy an annual long weekend tour.

A varied after-school programme for both juniors and infants provides the opportunity to develop sports and leisure skills, as well as artistic and musical talents. A supervised homework club also runs each day.

Field trips, activity days at local museums and visits by theatre groups and outside speakers lie at the heart of the curriculum. Prep 4, 5 and 6 enjoy an annual residential visit to an educational activity centre.

Generally children are admitted to the Reception class at the beginning of the school year in which they reach the age of 5, but entry into all year groups is possible throughout the year. All children registering are invited to spend a day in school when they are assessed in a manner appropriate to their age. Candidates for entry are also welcomed at all other stages of the prep school age range.

All enquiries should be made to the Secretary at Magdalene House Preparatory School.

Charitable status. The Wisbech Grammar School Foundation is a Registered Charity, number 1087799. It exists to promote the education of boys and girls.

Maidwell Hall

Maidwell, Northampton NN6 9JG
Tel: 01604 686234
Fax: 01604 686659
email: thesecretary@maidwellhall.co.uk
website: www.maidwellhall.co.uk

Chairman of the Governors: R H Cunningham, Esq

Headmaster: **R A Lankester**, MA Cantab, PGCE

Age Range. 7–13.
Number of Pupils. 111: 100 Boarders, 11 Day pupils.
Fees per term (2014–2015). £7,980 Boarding, £4,920 Day.

Maidwell Hall is a co-educational boarding school with some day pupils. Occupying a substantial 17th Century hall the school is situated in beautiful countryside and is characterized by its rural location and by 44 acres of grounds. It is a Christian school and the teachings of Jesus Christ are central to the moral and spiritual education of the children. Every Sunday morning the school worships in the parish church on the edge of the school grounds. The school aims to encourage all the children to discover and develop all their talents through the academic curriculum, the games programme, Music, Art, Drama and an impressive range of hobbies and activities. The school's happy atmosphere is based on a clear framework of rules and conventions with strong emphasis placed on good manners and a traditional code of behaviour and courtesy.

The school is organized as a 7 day-a-week boarding school with a comprehensive programme of club activities in the evenings supplemented by a choice of outings or school based free-time activities on Sundays. There is a weekly boarding option for Year 4. The children benefit greatly from the freedom and security of the school's spectacular grounds including its famous arboretum (wilderness) and its large lake for fishing and boating. Leave-outs occur every 2 or 3 weeks and run from Friday midday until Monday evening and each term contains a long half-term break. Pastoral care for the boarders is the direct responsibility of the Headmaster and his wife, the Housemaster and the team of Matrons and other residential staff. In addition each pupil has an individual tutor.

Pupils are prepared for Common Entrance to the major independent senior schools (typically Eton, Harrow, Oundle, Radley, Rugby, Shrewsbury, Stowe, Uppingham and Winchester) and every year several sit scholarships. In addition to core subjects all pupils study Art, Design, ICT, Latin, Music and Religious Studies and there are also timetabled lessons in PE, Swimming, PSHE, and Drama. There is a specialist carpentry shop which operates as a club activity.

The school has a strong reputation for sport. The major games for the boys are rugby, football, hockey and cricket and there are also matches against other schools in athletics, cross-country running, golf, squash, swimming and tennis. The major games for girls are hockey, netball, tennis and rounders. Teams are entered for riding events and the Pytchley hunt meets at the school every year. There is a successful school shooting team. In the Summer and Autumn there is sailing once or twice a week. In addition to impressive games pitches, sporting facilities include a multi-purpose sports hall with climbing wall, a squash court, a 6-hole golf course, astroturf, hockey pitch, tennis courts and a heated indoor swimming pool. There is particular emphasis on outward bound activities and leadership. There is a strong musical tradition and most pupils play one or two musical instruments; there is a thriving church choir and strings, wind and guitar groups. There are regular concerts throughout the year and each year there is a major school play.

Charitable status. Maidwell Hall is a Registered Charity, number 309917. It exists for the purpose of educating children.

Maldon Court Preparatory School

Silver Street, Maldon, Essex CM9 4QE
Tel: 01621 853529
Fax: 01621 853529
email: enquiries@maldoncourtschool.org
website: www.maldoncourtschool.org

Head: Mrs L F Guest, BEd Hons

Age Range. 3–11 co-educational.
Number of Pupils. 130 Day Pupils.
Fees per term (2014–2015). £2,854.05 for the first child, with sibling discounts.

The school, founded in 1956, is a co-educational day school of seven classes. The school day begins at 8.45 am and finishes at 3.30 pm. Wrap-around care from 8.00 am until 6.00 pm is available which incorporates homework classes and a variety of clubs. The Pre-Prep department welcomes children from the age of 3. Nursery Education Grants are available and the Pre-Prep is Ofsted registered. The school has the reputation of being a happy, friendly community with a family atmosphere.

Maldon Court's premises comprise the larger part of an eighteenth century town house, a separate four classroom block, separate toilets and a small assembly hall. The grounds consist of 2 playgrounds, gardens and adventure play areas. The premises are very convenient for the town centre. Sports grounds for association football, athletics, hockey and other activities are leased locally. There is a wide variety of after-school clubs including netball, cricket, gymnastics, rounders, athletics, and speech and drama. Swimming is undertaken throughout the year at a nearby sports centre. The school's sporting standard is high; over recent years it has won both national and regional awards in netball, football, swimming and athletics.

Approximately half the children leave the school for independent secondary schools, half enter the maintained sector. Maldon Court's scholarship and entrance record to the independent schools is excellent as is its eleven-plus success rate to Essex grammar schools. Close contact is maintained with both systems of education. Its curriculum covers and goes beyond the National Curriculum.

In 1975 a Parents' Association was formed. It is registered separately with the Charity Commission and has developed into an energetic and lively organisation.

The school had its most recent ISI Inspection in June 2008 where it was recognised that the curriculum and innovative teaching had contributed to the pupils' outstanding personal development.

Within the school motto of "Do it with thy might", the aims of Maldon Court are: to foster a love of learning in which the varied talents and life experiences of each pupil are recognised and valued; to provide a broad and stimulating curriculum through which pupils can flourish and become enthusiastic and independent learners, enabling them to reach their full potential; to promote the traditional values of kindness, respect and courtesy within a happy, nurturing atmosphere; to encourage a social awareness and respect for others through involvement in the local community; and to create confident and happy pupils, ready to face the challenges of the wider world. *ISI Inspection Report 2008*

The Mall School

185 Hampton Road, Twickenham, Middlesex TW2 5NQ
Tel: 020 8977 2523
Fax: 020 8977 8771
email: admissions@themallschool.org.uk
website: www.themallschool.org.uk

Chairman of Governors: R J H Walker, BSc

Headmaster: D Price, BSc, MA, PGCE

Deputy Head: R H A Struck, BA Frankfurt, MA

Age Range. 4–13.
Number of Boys. 324 day boys.
Fees per term (2014–2015). £3,479 (under 8), £3,978 (over 8).

For over 100 years, we have been preparing boys for a range of the leading independent London day and boarding senior schools, such as St Paul's, King's College School, Wimbledon and Hampton School. Many boys have secured scholarships (37 in the last 5 years) to these schools in a wide range of disciplines including Academic, Sport, Art, Drama, Choral, All-rounder and the highly coveted John Colet Award for St Paul's.

Boys are welcomed at 4+, as well as at 7+ and 8+, and are taught by a well-qualified staff consisting of 26 full-time and 2 part-time members, in an average class size of 20. We teach a broad curriculum based on the Common Entrance syllabus, including Art, DT, Music, and Drama, in addition to sport and PE.

Cricket, Rugby, Football, Swimming and Athletics are the main sports played at the school. We have our own outstanding 25m indoor swimming pool and a new state-of-the-art Sports Hall which opened in January 2014.

Music and Drama are warmly encouraged at the Mall School. There are 2 choirs and 2 orchestras with a large variety of ensembles and visiting teachers for piano, strings, guitar, woodwind and brass.

To help working parents, we provide an extensive range of after-school clubs, such as Chess, Judo and Art Clubs, as well as a homework club until 6 pm and a new holiday club.

In addition to bright modern classrooms, facilities include Science Laboratories, Music practice rooms, IT suite, Library and a new Creative and Performing Arts Centre which provides a 160-seat theatre and large-sized Art and Design Technology studios. A morning minibus service is in operation which brings boys to school from the Osterley, Isleworth, Richmond, St Margarets, Twickenham and Kingston areas.

A separate department at Mall Infants, within five minutes' walk, is home to the youngest boys aged 4 and 5 years old.

The Mall School prospectus is available via the website or the Headmaster's Secretary. Early application is advisable.

Charitable status. The Mall School Trust is a Registered Charity, number 295003. It exists to promote and provide for the advancement of the education of children. Established 1872.

Maltman's Green

Maltmans Lane, Gerrards Cross, Bucks SL9 8RR
Tel: 01753 883022
Fax: 01753 891237
email: office@maltmansgreen.com
website: www.maltmansgreen.com

Preparatory School for Girls.

Chairman: Mrs D M Starrs, BA Hons Oxon

Headmistress: Mrs J Pardon, MA, BSc, PGCE

Age Range. 3–11.
Number of Girls. 420.

Fees per term (2014–2015). £1,500 (5 mornings Nursery) to £4,200.

Maltman's Green is a school for girls from 3 to 11. Our girls thrive, working hard and having fun. We believe in the pursuit of excellence whilst maintaining a sense of fun. Our girls are encouraged to take risks in all aspects of school life and are well known for their enthusiasm and confidence. We also nurture old-fashioned values such as courtesy, doing one's best, and respect for others.

Maltman's Green has exceptional facilities including two libraries, specialist teaching classrooms for science, ICT, design and art, music practice rooms, a sports hall and gym and safe and secure traditional playgrounds and a state-of-the-art six-lane indoor swimming pool as well as a new Discovery Garden.

There is plenty of open green space around the School. Sustainability is now at the heart of the School Development Plan and the school has recently been awarded Green Flag Eco-School status for the second time.

Inside, the classrooms are all bright and spacious, with colourful, ever-changing displays. The atmosphere is lively, challenging and happy.

Although we are a non-selective school, our girls have an outstanding track record of winning scholarships to top independent schools and of gaining entrance to the local grammar schools.

The creative and performing arts flourish at Maltman's. The school strongly believes that all children should be given the opportunity to develop their creativity and express themselves.

From Nursery, all girls enjoy specialist Music lessons twice a week and from Reception upwards have weekly drama lessons. All the girls take part in a dramatic production every year.

In addition to the weekly lessons in Art and Design Technology, there are also numerous clubs.

All girls have a lesson of sport every day and, from Nursery. Our girls are frequently local, regional and national champions in swimming, gymnastics, tennis and several team sports.

We provide specialist learning support for girls with learning difficulties, such as dyslexia, and make time to help any girl who might slip behind. Specialist support is also provided for the very able and gifted girls.

Finally, the partnership with parents is not a cliché at Maltman's, but is a genuine joint approach to education. If your daughter knows what is expected of her and is given the expert support and care, and if you are kept informed and involved, the girls have every opportunity to achieve their best.

Charitable status. Maltman's Green School Trust Limited is a Registered Charity, number 310633. It exists to provide a high standard of education for young girls.

Manor Lodge School

Rectory Lane, Ridge Hill, Shenley, Hertfordshire WD7 9BG
Tel: 01707 642424
Fax: 01707 645206
email: enquiries@manorlodgeschool.com
website: www.manorlodgeschool.com

Chair of Governors: Mr D Arnold, MBE

Head: **Mr G Dunn**, Cert Ed

Age Range. 3–11.
Number of Pupils. Nursery (age 3) 24; Infant Department (age 4–7) 182; Junior Department (age 7–11) 229.
Fees per term (2014–2015). Nursery £2,965; Infants £3,175; Juniors £3,595.

There are three forms of approximately 18 children in Years Reception to 6 inclusive. There are specialist teachers for French, PE, IT, CDT, Art and Music as well as numerous peripatetic teachers for brass, woodwind and strings. All staff are fully qualified.

The school consists of a 17th century house and the converted stables offer fifteen classrooms, a French Room, a DT Room and a hall. The classrooms are bright and well-equipped and the standard of work displayed is very high. We aim to provide excellent teaching within an environment characterised by a well-balanced but friendly family atmosphere in which high standards of behaviour and good manners are encouraged and expected. We thus ensure that all pupils achieve their full potential and are prepared for entry to senior schools, both independent and state.

The cottage at the end of the drive houses our Nursery. The children must be siblings of pupils in the main school and are eligible to attend from the term in which they are three.

The dining room was added in 2008 and our caterers, The Brookwood Partnership, provide a delicious selection of fresh lunches, both vegetarian and meat based.

The twelve acres of grounds include woodland, pitches, courts and play areas with climbing activity equipment and other outdoor toys. The children are offered a wide range of sporting activities including football, rugby, hockey, cricket, netball, rounders, swimming and athletics.

Music plays an important part in the life of the school. There are several choirs, an orchestra and almost half the children in school learn an instrument. Music is of course linked into our Drama activities. Reception to Year 5 children take part in at least two performances a year, but in Year 6 a local theatre is hired for 10 days to give the children real theatre experience. Art is of a particularly high standard and the children use a variety of media, producing excellent original work. Our new building, due to be completed in Spring 2015, will house a theatre and additional classrooms to provide more space for music and the performing arts.

Extra activities available at the school include chess, drama and ju-jitsu. There are numerous clubs run by the staff after school until 4.30 pm, for example, sewing, calligraphy, football, rugby, cricket, netball, theatre, athletics and choir.

Charitable status. Manor Lodge School is a Registered Charity, number 1048874. The school exists to provide an education which will maximise the potential of the girls and boys in our care.

The Manor Preparatory School

Faringdon Road, Abingdon, Oxon OX13 6LN
Tel: 01235 858462
Fax: 01235 559593
email: admissions@manorprep.org
website: www.manorprep.org

Chairman of the Governors: Dr A Malmberg

Headmaster: **Mr Piers Heyworth**, MA Oxon, PGCE

Age Range. Girls 2–11, Boys 2–7.
Number of Pupils. 363 Day: 315 Girls, 48 Boys.
Fees per term (2014–2015). £339–£4,385.
The Manor is a Charitable Trust.

A well-qualified staff teaches a full range of subjects. Boys are prepared for entry to preparatory schools and girls for the Common Entrance Examination for Girls' Schools, or for entrance examinations to other senior schools.

The curriculum is broad. Science, Information Communication Technology, Art, Design, Music, Physical Education and Modern Languages are all taught by specialists. All subjects have specialist teaching in the final two years of the preparatory department.

Computers are used throughout the school to supplement the curriculum and ICT skills are taught in three specialist ICT suites.

A vibrant music department of 18 visiting and 2 full-time and 2 part-time members of staff provides tuition in a full range of instruments; all orchestral instruments including harp are available. In addition tuition in singing, drum kit, guitar & saxophone bring the total of pupils receiving instrumental lessons to around 60%. There are two school orchestras, four choirs, three string ensembles, a wind group, brass group, guitar band and harp ensemble. Regular performance opportunities include the annual Carol Service and the spring Manor Concert.

A highly skilled and dedicated PE Department teaches a wide variety of sport including Swimming, Netball, Hockey, Cross Country, Football, Tag Rugby, Rounders and Athletics. Specialist Tennis Coaches provide year-round lessons. The Manor competes at IAPS in Netball, Hockey, Tennis, Cross Country and Swimming, regularly reaching National Finals. The Manor teams have been finalists at the Schools' Biathlon at Crystal Palace and the British Biathlon Championships. A substantial range of "sport for all" clubs take place before school, after school and at lunchtimes. Sports Clubs range from Judo, Gymnastics and Golf to our more traditional sports.

The extra-curricular provision at The Manor is extremely broad and varied with a wide range of activities and clubs. These are run by our own staff together with outside experts before school, at lunchtime and after school. There are approximately 90 extra-curricular activities offered on a weekly basis which include musical groups and ensembles. These challenging and exciting activities support the curriculum in a way that makes our children happy to learn whilst enabling them to make the most of their abilities.

A free Early Birds Club where children can be dropped off at school at 8.00 am is offered. A Breakfast Club operates from 7.30 am to 8.00 am and there is an Extended Day service until 6 pm. There is a charge for these services. Flexible Nursery and Pre-Nursery sessions from the age of 2 are offered.

Bus transport is arranged for pupils travelling from surrounding areas.

The school promotes close cooperation between parents and teachers. Parents' Evenings are a regular feature. "The Friends of The Manor" association is run by parents to welcome new families and to support the school.

Charitable status. The Manor Preparatory School is a Registered Charity, number 900347. It exists to provide education for girls and boys.

The Marist Preparatory School

Kings Road, Sunninghill, Ascot, Berkshire SL5 7PS
Tel: 01344 626137
Fax: 01344 621566
email: admissionsprep@themaristschools.com
website: www.themaristschools.com

Independent Catholic Day School for Girls.

Chair of Governors: Mrs M Cairns

Headteacher: **Miss Jenny Finlayson**, Adv Dip, BEd, MA

Age Range. 2½–11.
Number of Pupils. 200 girls.
Fees per term (2014–2015). £2,900–£3,400.
Mission Statement:
The aim of the school is to:

- provide a caring community where learning is guided by strong Christian values;
- promote excellence where all are encouraged to reach their full potential.

Strengths of the school:

- Early Years, infant and junior departments tailored to the specific needs of the girls at each stage of their education.
- Caring, well qualified and professional staff dedicated to developing happy, secure and stimulated girls.
- Curriculum designed to achieve all the foundation/early year learning goals.
- Able to offer a wide range of both academic and extra-curricular activities.
- High achievement in gym, ballet, art, judo, drama, choir and music.
- Strong emphasis on pastoral care, spiritual and personal development; care and consideration for others.
- Small class sizes to enhance individual progression and recognition.
- The school is renowned for its high standards regarding moral values, community spirit, respect and care. This is in line with the overall ethos of the Marist order which has a worldwide presence, providing a truly international dimension to a girl's education.
- Girls are taught to consider and help those less fortunate than themselves through involvement in a wide range of local, national and international charity projects.

The Marist Preparatory School is able to offer your daughter a complete and fulfilling education in the security of a single sex environment, from the age of 2½ to 11. We welcome all Christians and those supporting its ethos. We are renowned for our happy and caring ethos, where pastoral care is considered paramount. Your daughter will be treated as an individual and encouraged to achieve her full potential in every area. We have a strong academic record but we also place a strong emphasis on extra-curricular activities which help to develop important qualities such as self confidence, individual creativity and teamwork.

We also have a Senior School and Sixth Form on the same campus for girls aged 11–18. *For further details, please see the Marist Senior School entry in the GSA section.*

Charitable status. The Marist Schools is a Registered Charity, number 225485. The principal aims and activities of the Marist Schools are religious and charitable and specifically to provide education by way of an independent day school for girls between the ages of 2½ and 18.

Marlborough House School

High Street, Hawkhurst, Cranbrook, Kent TN18 4PY
Tel: 01580 753555
Fax: 01580 754281
email: registrar@marlboroughhouseschool.co.uk
            frontoffice@marlboroughhouseschool.co.uk
website: www.marlboroughhouseschool.co.uk

Marlborough House was founded in 1874 and is registered as an Educational Trust with a Board of Governors.

Marlborough House School is an independent Preparatory School for boys and girls from 2¾ to 13. We are a community where our values, with mutual respect at their core, are at the heart of everything we do. Happy, confident children are keen to learn, to push themselves and to achieve more. It is our job to help children achieve academically but, much more than this, we also want to nurture children to become well-rounded, enthusiastic, self-confident and fulfilled young people. We believe in high expectations, the value of knowing each child as an individual and providing a breadth of experiences but above all this is our commitment to making sure children here are happy – because we know that only then they will achieve their goals.

Chairman of Governors: H Somerset

Headmaster: **M Ward**, BEd

Deputy Head: P Tooze, BA, PGCE
Assistant Head (Academic): Mrs A Stables, BEd
Head of Senior School: Mrs K Atkins, BEd
Head of Middle School: Mrs C Walker, BA, PGCE
Head of Pre-Prep: Ms V Coatz, BEd

Age Range. 2¾–13 Co-educational.
Number of Pupils. 300.
Fees per term (2014–2015). Prep £5,220, Pre-Prep £2,520–£3,085, Nursery according to number of sessions. Flexi boarding: £36 per night with reduction for consecutive nights. No compulsory extras.

The School is fully co-educational creating a friendly, family atmosphere for children between the ages of 2¾ and 13.

Marlborough House is situated in the village of Hawkhurst in beautiful countryside on the Kent/Sussex border, near the town of Cranbrook. The fine Georgian house is set in 35 acres of superb gardens, playing fields, lawns and woodland. The School has a Chapel, Computer Centre, Sports Hall, 2 Performance/Dance Halls, superbly equipped Science Laboratory, Art, Pottery and Design Technology Department, Music Rooms, Swimming Pool, a .22 Rifle Shooting Range and 2 all-weather games surfaces.

With our 40+ qualified teaching staff we aim to produce well motivated, balanced, confident children who know the value of hard work, and who will thrive in their next schools and the modern world beyond. Our classes are small and the children are prepared for all major Senior Schools, whilst those showing special promise sit scholarships.

Encouragement is given to each child to experience a wide variety of activities. In addition to the traditional sports of Cricket, Rugby, Soccer, Hockey, Athletics, Tennis, Netball and Rounders, opportunities are provided for Music (with around 12 peripatetic music teachers visiting the school each week, children can learn a wide range of instruments and join the orchestra and choirs), Art (in many different media), Pottery, Drama, Ballet, Technology, Computing, Shooting, Sailing, Golf, Swimming, Fencing and Judo.

A copy of the Prospectus together with the annual Review Magazine will be mailed to prospective parents on application to the Registrar.

Charitable status. Marlborough House School is a Registered Charity, number 307793. It exists to provide education for children.

Marlston House School

Hermitage, Newbury, Berkshire RG18 9UL
Tel: 01635 200293
email: registrar@brockmarl.org.uk
website: www.brockmarl.org.uk

Headmistress: **Mrs C E Riley**, MA, BEd, CertEd

Age Range. 3–13.
Number of Girls. 169 Girls (including 65 Boarders).
Fees per term (2014–2015). Boarding £6,950, Day £4,865–£5,175. Pre-Prep School (Ridge House): £3,090 (full-time). Temporary Overseas Boarders £7,500.

Established in 1995, Marlston House is situated in 500 acres of its own grounds in countryside of outstanding beauty, only four miles from access to the M4. The school is situated beside Brockhurst Boys' Preparatory school and occupies separate listed buildings. Boys and girls are taught separately, but the two schools join together for drama music and activities. In this way Brockhurst and Marlston House combine the best features of the single-sex and co-educational systems: academic excellence and social interaction. The schools are proud of the high standard of pastoral care established within a family atmosphere. (*See also entry for Brockhurst School.*)

The Pre-Prep School, Ridge House, is a co-educational department of Brockhurst and Marlston House Schools for 75 children aged 3–6 years, and is situated on the same site in new self-contained, purpose-designed accommodation.

Girls are prepared for entry to a variety of leading Independent Senior Schools through the ISEB Common Entrance and Scholarship Papers at 11+ and 13+.

All girls play Netball (outdoor and indoor courts), Hockey, Rounders and Tennis (outdoor and indoor courts) and take part in Athletics, Cross Country and Swimming (25m indoor heated pool). Additional activities include riding (own equestrian centre), fencing, judo, shooting (indoor rifle range), dance and ballet. Facilities for gymnastics and other sporting activities are provided in a purpose-built Sports Hall. Year 7 pupils make a week-long visit to a Château in France as part of their French studies.

Music and Art are important features of the curriculum and a number of girls have won scholarships and awards to senior schools in these subjects recently. The school is currently building a new dedicated Music School and Theatre to open in the Summer Term 2014.

Transport is provided by the school to and from airports and between Newbury and Paddington stations. Pupils are accompanied by school staff to their destinations.

Mayfield Preparatory School

Sutton Road, Walsall, West Midlands WS1 2PD
Tel: 01922 624107
Fax: 01922 746908
email: info@mayfieldprep.co.uk
website: www.mayfieldprep.co.uk

Administered by the Governors of Queen Mary's Schools.

Chair of Governors: Mrs J Aubrook

Headmaster: **Mr Matthew Draper**, BA, PGCE

Age Range. 2–11 Co-educational.
Number of Pupils. Day: 119 Boys, 93 Girls.
Fees per term (2014–2015). Main School £2,525; Pre-Nursery £1,515.

A co-educational day school for children aged 2 to 11+, set in a listed building with beautiful surroundings and playing fields. A purpose-built Science/Art building opened in November 2000.

The self-contained Nursery Department accepts children at 2+.

A fully qualified Staff with full-time ancillary support throughout KS1 ensures that the individual child receives maximum attention.

The main aim at Mayfield is to encourage intellectual excellence. Children experience a thorough grounding in literacy and numeracy skills.

Through stimulating courses of correctly-paced work the school specialises in the preparation of the children for Grammar and Independent School entrance examinations at 11+.

Our children achieve excellent results, but it is always borne in mind that the individual child's needs are met by matching achievement to potential. All children are expected and encouraged to develop daily in confidence and security.

We believe in a balanced curriculum, and at Mayfield practical and non-academic activities additionally provide interest and varied experiences in Sports, Art, Music, ICT, DT, Dance, Drama and Public Speaking.

Good manners are expected at all times, as well as a happy and whole-hearted participation in the life and studies offered by the school.

Micklefield School

10 Somers Road, Reigate, Surrey RH2 9DU
Tel:　　　01737 224212
Fax:　　　01737 248889
email:　　office@micklefieldschool.co.uk
website:　www.micklefieldschool.co.uk

Chairman of the Council: Mr A B de M Hunter, FCA

Headmistress: **Mrs L Rose**, BEd Hons, Cert Ed, Dip PC

Age Range. Rising 3–11.
Number of Pupils. 282 (141 boys, 141 girls).
Fees per term (2014–2015). £980–£3,445. Lunches £180–£185.

'*Micklefield recognised the individuality in my twins and helped them realise their potential socially and academically.*'

'*Micklefield has helped my boys build confidence and self-esteem in a friendly and secure environment.*'

'*My children have flourished at Micklefield.*'

These quotes from current and former parents sum up the very special education offered at Micklefield School. Established in Reigate over 100 years ago, we offer small classes, taught by qualified staff and qualified subject specialists. We cater for boys and girls from the age of rising 3 up to the age of eleven, preparing them for Common Entrance and other examinations. The children enjoy academic success and have an excellent record in examinations for entrance to senior schools including Scholarship Awards.

After-school care is available for children from Reception age.

In addition to the normal academic subjects, the curriculum includes design technology, information technology, dancing, drama, French, netball, tennis, athletics, swimming, football, rugby, cricket and unihoc.

The children take an active part in a variety of musical and theatrical activities and excel in sports. Dramatic productions and concerts provide opportunities for everyone to display their talents. We encourage participation in drama festivals, sports fixtures, the School's orchestra and choirs. Visits to concerts, theatres and museums are organised together with residential activity holidays for the older children.

The most recent building project provides an excellent art room and music suite with the added benefit of a walkway to our Preparatory Department building. There is a dining room where professional caterers serve high-quality, healthy lunches. The school also has its own sports field within 250 yards in St Albans Road.

Visit the website or telephone for a prospectus on 01737 224212. Mrs Rose, the Headmistress, is always pleased to show prospective parents around by appointment.

Charitable status. Micklefield School (Reigate) Limited is a Registered Charity, number 312069. It exists to provide a first-class education for its pupils.

Millfield Prep School

Edgarley Hall, Glastonbury, Somerset BA6 8LD
Tel:　　　01458 832446
Fax:　　　01458 833679
email:　　office@millfieldprep.com
website:　www.millfieldschool.com

Chair of Governors: Sir J G Reith, KCB, CBE

Head: **Mrs Shirley Shayler**, MA, BSc Hons, PGCE

Tutor for Admissions: Ms Sally Garland-Jones

Age Range. 2–13.
Number of Boys and Girls. 115 Boarders, 220 Day Pupils.
Fees per term (2014–2015). Prep: Full and Weekly Boarding £8,300, Day £4,625–£5,660. Pre-Prep: Day £1,975–£2,575. Flexi Boarding also available.

The school is administered by the same Board of Governors and on the same principles of small-group teaching as Millfield Senior School (made possible by a staffing ratio of approximately 1 to 8) which ensures breadth and flexibility of timetable. It has its own attractive grounds of 185 acres some four miles from the Senior School, and its extensive facilities include games fields, art, design and technology centre, drama hall, music school, science laboratories, sports hall, AstroTurf, gymnasium, golf course, tennis courts, squash courts, equestrian centre on campus, 25 metre indoor swimming pool, three IT laboratories and chapel. The pupils also have access to some of the specialist facilities at Millfield Senior School including water-based astro, Olympic-sized swimming pool, tartan athletics track and indoor tennis centre.

The Pre-Prep department, taking children from 2–7, moved onto the Prep school site in 2004 so that the school now offers an education for children from ages 2–13, after which the majority of pupils transfer to Millfield. The small class sizes allow the individual pupil to be taught at his or her most appropriate pace. The range of ability within the school is comprehensive and setting caters for both the academically gifted and those requiring additional learning support.

The curriculum is broadly based and provides a balance between the usual academic subjects and the aesthetic, musical and artistic fields. Junior pupils study French and in Year 6 there is a choice of Spanish or French plus a taster in Latin for more able pupils. In Years 7 and 8 there is a choice of French, Spanish and Latin. Children may choose either one or two foreign languages, dependent on ability. Pupils are also given a choice of extra-curricular languages: we are currently offering Arabic, Mandarin and Russian (these languages vary depending on demand). Science is taught throughout the school and as three separate subjects from the age of 10.

There is a full games programme organised by qualified teachers of physical education, with the help of other staff. The programme includes Athletics, Canoeing, Caving, Climbing, Cross Country, Cricket, Fencing, Football, Golf, Gymnastics, Hockey, Netball, Riding, Rounders, Rugby, Sailing, Squash, Swimming, Tennis, Outdoor Pursuits and Multi-Sports to name but a few.

Over 45 different clubs are available. Within Music we offer two choices of Choir, an Orchestra, Concert Band and ten music ensembles. Over 250 pupils learn at least one musical instrument. Great emphasis is placed on the inter-house singing competition.

Boys and girls can start from the age of 2 and up to the age of 12 and they come from many lands and widely differing backgrounds. Admission usually depends on interview, assessment and reports from the previous school. Assistance with fees in the form of awards may be available at certain ages to applicants for academic ability, sporting talent, musical, artistic, and skill in chess.

There are five boarding houses (three for boys and two for girls). Each house is under the care of resident houseparents and assistant houseparents. The Medical Centre is staffed by 3 qualified nurses, a physiotherapist, and the School Doctor attends daily.

Charitable status. Millfield is a Registered Charity, number 310283. The Millfield Schools provide a broad and balanced education to boys and girls from widely differing backgrounds, including a significant number with learning difficulties, and many for whom boarding is necessary.

Milton Keynes Preparatory School

Tattenhoe Lane, Milton Keynes, Buckinghamshire MK3 7EG
Tel: 01908 642111
Fax: 01908 366365
email: info@mkps.co.uk
website: www.mkps.co.uk

Chairman of the Governors: Mr Peter Squire, MA

Headmistress: **Hilary Pauley**, BEd

Deputy Heads:
Patricia Cave, Cert Ed
Carl Bates, BA Ed Hons
Simon Driver, BA, PGCE

Age Range. Nursery 2 months–2½ years. Pre-Prep 2½–7 years. Preparatory Department 7+–11 years.
Number of Pupils. 460 Day Pupils.
Fees per term (2014–2015). Nursery (per week): £245 (babies under 1 year), £255 (1–2½ years). Pre-Preparatory: £3,520 (2½–5 years), £3,640 (6–7 years). Preparatory £3,996 (8–11 years).

Milton Keynes Preparatory School is a well-established family-owned school, with two sister Pre-Prep and Preparatory schools based across Milton Keynes.

Opening hours are 7.30 am to 6.30 pm for a 35-week academic year and a total of 46 weeks per year, enabling children of working parents to join play schemes in school holidays and to be cared for outside normal daily school hours.

Staff are highly qualified and committed to delivering the very best teaching and levels of care. Academic standards are "excellent", as awarded by the recent Inspections, with pupils being prepared for entry to senior independent schools locally and nationally and to grammar schools. Teaching is structured to take into account the requirements of the National Curriculum, with constant evaluation and assessment for each pupil. Scholarships are offered for those with all-round, academic and sporting abilities from the ages of 7–11.

Housed in a modern purpose-built building, all departments also have their own outside soft play and extensive playground areas and there is a large multi-purpose sports hall. The newly developed Nursery and Little Prep-Prep departments, with extended artificial grass terraces for year-round activities and learning, is a beautiful addition to the school.

State-of-the-art facilities include fully kitted Music Technology studio, high-tech ICT suite, Science laboratory, interactive DT and Art workshops and a superb new Astro-turf pitch.

The additional facilities at The Farm include a fitness room, dance studio, music hall, arts and crafts and computer room. The superb in and outdoor learning resource centre, weather station, large pond and growing polytunnels allow the very best environmental studies programme.

Music and Sport play an important part in the life of the school. Concerts are held, and a wide variety of sport is played, with teams competing regularly against other schools, and additional clubs are held for those wanting to learn specialist activities as judo and ballet.

The school aims to incorporate the best of modern teaching methods and traditional values in a friendly, caring and busy environment, where good work habits and a concern for the needs of others are paramount.

The Minster School
York

Deangate, York YO1 7JA
Tel: 0844 939 0000
Fax: 0844 939 0001
email: school@yorkminster.org
website: www.minsterschoolyork.co.uk

Chair of Governors: The Very Revd Vivienne Faull, Dean of York Minster

Head Master: **Alex Donaldson**, MA St John's College Cambridge, PGCE King's College London, Cert ICT Cambridge

Age Range. 3–13 Co-educational.
Number of Pupils. Preparatory 115; Pre-Prep Department 65.
Fees per term (2014–2015). Upper School: £3,075. Pre-Prep: £2,011 (full day). Choristers receive substantial Scholarships, ranging between 60%–100%.

The Minster School was originally founded in 627 AD to educate singing boys. It is now a fully co-educational preparatory and pre-preparatory school, which includes a Nursery department. Its most recent ISI inspection report highlighted the Nursery teaching and provision as 'Outstanding' and the school overall was judged to be 'Excellent'. Teaching throughout the whole school was singled out as a particular strength and the achievement, attitude and behaviour of the pupils were warmly praised.

The Nursery and Pre-Prep departments are housed in their own accommodation with gardens, playgrounds and an ICT suite for junior pupils' use. French is taught from Year 2 upwards. In the prep school, teaching is delivered by well-qualified subject specialists. With computers in all classrooms, an IT suite, science lab, art room and DT suite the school is well equipped to deliver a broad curriculum. On our 8-acre sports fields, games are taught by school staff and professional coaches. Regular fixtures for boys and girls teams are arranged throughout the year. The major sports are football, hockey, netball, cricket and athletics. In addition to the normal academic curriculum, there is a flourishing music department and all orchestral instruments are taught. Pupils' levels of musical achievement are very high though there are no academic or musical tests to join the school.

Lunch and after-school care are not charged as extras and a wide variety of extra-curricular activities is available, e.g. sewing, chess, ballet, fencing, judo, art and craft, model-making, drama and sports clubs etc.

Of the 180 children in the School, 20 boys and 20 girls are choristers who sing the services in York Minster in return for a substantial scholarship. Pupils are prepared for Common Entrance and Senior Independent School Scholarships. Many children gain music, art and academic scholarships to their senior schools.

Moira House Junior School

Upper Carlisle Road, Eastbourne, East Sussex
BN20 7TE
Tel: 01323 636800
email: admissions@moirahouse.co.uk
website: www.moirahouse.co.uk
Twitter: @moirahouse1875
Facebook: /moirahouse

Chairman of School Council: Ms J A Jackson-Hill, BA
Hons, FRSA

Principal: **Mr James Sheridan**, BSc, MA

Age Range. Girls 0–11, Boys 0–4.
Number of Pupils. 115.
Fees per term (2014–2015). £2,850–£4,000 (Day
Pupils); £6,680 (Weekly Boarders); £7,180 (Boarders).

Moira House is set within 15 acres of attractively landscaped grounds, on the outskirts of the historic town of Eastbourne on the South Coast of England. Founded in 1875,
Moira House welcomes girls from the age of six months to
eleven in the Junior School and boys in the Nursery, with
full, weekly or flexi boarding offered from the age of 9. The
Junior School shares the site with the Senior School for girls
aged eleven to eighteen. (*See entry in GSA section.*)

The Junior School aims to provide a broad and balanced
curriculum and activity programme, ensuring equal access
and opportunity so that children can celebrate and strive for
excellence. We believe that children will learn if they feel
happy and secure, and if their natural curiosity is aroused.
They learn best when they are actively involved in the learning, with skilled teachers to guide them. As a school our aim
is to provide an atmosphere and a richness of experience
within which each child's unique qualities can flourish. Our
emphasis is on the importance of individual development,
helping each child to realise her maximum potential. We
aim, therefore, to set high standards for each child so that
they are constantly challenged to develop further their skills
and understanding.

Curriculum. The Foundation Stage and National Curriculum form the basis of what is taught but with the flexibility
of specialist teachers and creative learning and teaching
strategies. The curriculum aims to develop critical and creative thinking and self-discipline. Education at this stage is a
foundation for the future and as broad as possible, combining the modern technology of interactive whiteboards and
an ICT suite with all areas of the curriculum. Teaching is in
small groups and is strong throughout. The girls enjoy
mixed-ability classes but are grouped according to ability in
Maths.

EAL, SEN, Sport, Drama, French, Swimming and Music
are all taught or supported to an exceptional level by specialists. The Junior School has three choirs and all the children
are involved in productions, concerts and creative arts presentations across the year. Most of the children take individual music lessons on a variety of instruments.

PE and Swimming form part of the curriculum and the
girls have been particularly successful in competitive challenges. The girls enjoy the facilities of a 25m heated indoor
swimming pool, a sports hall and extensive playing fields
and netball and tennis courts.

The school has recently created a wonderful outdoor
classroom with a pond and large greenhouse where the children begin to understand how important their role is in looking after the natural environment in a more sustainable
world.

Extra-curricular. The school offers daily care from 8 am
until Afternoon Activity Club at 6.00 pm. There is a fleet of
buses which can transport children to and from home each
day.

A wealth of extra-curricular activities enriches the experience of the pupils. The activity programme includes
Dance, Short tennis, Trampolining, Gymnastics, ICT club,
Environmental Studies club, Sewing club, String ensemble
and a wide variety of sporting clubs.

Charitable status. Moira House Girls School is a Registered Charity, number 307072.

Monkton Prep School

Combe Down, Bath BA2 7ET
Tel: 01225 831202
Fax: 01225 840312
email: admin@monktonprep.org.uk
website: www.monktonprep.com
Twitter: @monktonprep

Chairman of Governors: R S Baldock, MA Cantab

Headmaster: **A Marshall-Taylor**, MA, PGCE

Deputy Head: M L Creeth, BEd

Director of Studies: M S Bray, BA, PGCE

Age Range. 2–13.
Number of Pupils. Boarders 35, Day 204, Pre-Prep 89.
Fees per term (2014–2015). Reception £2,954; Years 1
and 2 £3,040; Years 3 to 6 £3,565–£3,672; Years 7 and 8
£5,198. Boarding: Years 3 to 6 £6,885–£7,140; Years 7 and
8 £7,420.

There are no extra charges except for learning a musical
instrument and specialist activities. There are reductions in
fees for the children of clergy and HM Forces.

The School became fully co-educational in September
1993 and has full flexi boarding arrangements that cater for
both boys and girls from the age of 8. It stands in its own
grounds on a magnificent site with the city of Bath on one
side and the Midford valley on the other. The buildings
include a chapel, a modern classroom block, a theatre for
drama and music with 12 music practice rooms, a sports
hall, an indoor 25-metre pool, 2 science laboratories and
dance studio. The Coates Building incorporates an art studio, design technology workshop, a learning resource centre, seminar room and ICT suite. There are 20 acres of
grounds, 3 tennis courts, a hard playing area, an adventure
playground, a nature reserve, as well as an all-weather
hockey pitch. By the end of 2014 there will also be 3 all-
weather netball courts.

The School has a strong musical tradition and flourishing
Art and DT Departments. There are two choirs, an orchestra,
a band and various other instrumental groups. Drama also
plays an important part in school life.

Rugby, Hockey, and Cricket are the major boys' games;
Netball, Hockey and Rounders are the major girls' games.
All pupils take part in Gymnastics, Swimming, Athletics
and Cross-Country. Squash, Badminton, Dance, Judo and
Basketball are also available. There is a full programme of
matches. All pupils take part in a variety of hobbies and
activities sessions which include gardening, animation,
cookery, gymnastics (run by external professionals Basker-
villes Gym) and fun science to name but a few.

Boys and Girls are prepared for Common Entrance and
Scholarship exams to Independent Senior Schools. At least
three-quarters of them proceed to the Senior School and a
quarter to a wide range of other Independent Senior Schools.
90 Scholarships have been won in the past five years.

Over the years Monkton has educated many children
from families who are working overseas, especially HM
Forces families. We make special arrangements for them
and are well used to meeting their various needs.

The School finds its central inspiration and purpose in its
Christian tradition. The caring, family ethos is underpinned

by a large number of resident staff, including the Headmaster and his wife.

Charitable status. Monkton Combe School is a Registered Charity, number 1057185. Its aim is to provide education for girls and boys aged 2 to 18, in accordance with the doctrine and principles of the Church of England.

Moor Park School

Ludlow, Shropshire SY8 4DZ
Tel: 01584 876061
Fax: 01584 877311
email: head@moorpark.org.uk
website: www.moorpark.org.uk
Facebook: /MoorParkSchool

Founded in 1964, Moor Park is a co-educational boarding and day school with strong Christian values for children from 3 to 13 years. A family atmosphere pervades, resulting in happy, rounded and grounded children.

Your children will eventually leave Moor Park, but Moor Park will never leave them.

Chairman of Governors: Maj General A Denaro, CBE, DL

Headmaster: **J R Bartlett**, BSc QTS Brunel

Deputy Head: Mrs J M Morris, Cert Ed
Deputy Head Boarding: S D Gedye, BA

Age Range. 3–13.
Number of Pupils. 266.
Fees per term (2014–2015). Boarding £6,040–£7,255, Day £2,220–£4,955.

The school is built around a magnificent country mansion set in 85 acres of glorious Shropshire countryside. The school campus has a great sense of space and is an oasis of calm and safety. Pupils enjoy the playing fields, pasture, woodland, lake and the assault course.

Facilities include a science/ICT block, art and design block, learning support department, a new Astroturf, sports hall, main hall/theatre, a delightful chapel and a heated pool.

The school has seen considerable investment in recent years with a new structure to the Lower School and remodelled Upper School campus with new classrooms. The Study Centre reflects our emphasis on independent learning and the Design Technology building would be the envy of many a senior school.

Fine facilities are nothing without people: the school is renowned for its warmth, its sense of community, its pastoral care, and the emphasis on the individual development of each pupil. Children of all ages mix with each other comfortably and confidently. There is breadth and depth of opportunity. Pupils go on to a broad range of senior schools all over the country and in the last 7 years, every child has gone to their chosen senior school. The tally of scholarships and awards – academic, sport, art, music, drama and all-round – to senior schools is outstanding, with over 100 achieved in the last ten years. In 2013/2014, 40% of all the children won an award to their senior school.

Boarding is split into two houses; the younger children stay in a purpose-built eco-friendly boarding house, that was completed in 2010, while the older children stay in the main school house, under the care of houseparents and a team of matrons and gap students. Boarders may be full, weekly, or flexi, and day pupils enjoy the opportunities, facilities, activities and pastoral care that such an infrastructure offers, during the week and at weekends. The success of our boarding provision is measured by an increase year on year in the number of children who board and their obvious enjoyment of the experience. A highlight of each term is the Big Week-

end, for which we were shortlisted in the 2014 Independent Schools Awards.

Charitable status. Moor Park School is a Registered Charity, number 511800, which exists to provide education for young people.

Moorfield School

Wharfedale Lodge, 11 Ben Rhydding Road, Ilkley, West Yorkshire LS29 8RL
Tel: 01943 607285
email: enquiries@moorfieldschool.co.uk
website: www.moorfieldschool.co.uk
Twitter: @MoorfieldIlkley

Chairman of Governors: Mrs Lucy Clapham

Headmistress: **Jessica Crossley**

Age Range. 2½–11 Co-educational.
Number of Pupils 100 Girls and Boys.
Fees per term (2014–2015). Nursery £22.20 per session; Main School £2,660–£2,685. Lunches: £3.20 per day.
Staff: 10 full-time, 8 part-time.
Religious affiliation: Interdenominational.

Accommodated in a large house, Moorfield School is situated in a beautiful setting on the edge of Ilkley Moor. The School prides itself on its academic excellence and friendly, caring atmosphere. It has a strong 'family' feel and lays particular emphasis on consideration for others both within and beyond the school community. Independence and individuality are encouraged and confidence nurtured.

High standards of literacy and numeracy are the academic bedrock enabling 100% of our pupils to get into their secondary school of choice. Although non-selective, 70% of our 2013 Year 6 pupils achieved a Level 5 or above. Outstanding teaching from a vibrant staff gives pupils confidence to succeed in all subjects. Success is also achieved in music, art, drama and sport with pupils participating in a wide variety of local events. An all-round broad curriculum is followed with specialist teaching in small classes. A 'Boy Time' every week gives all boys an extra chance to be together. Their sports coach spends an afternoon with them and focuses on what so many boys enjoy: all forms of sport.

Excellent facilities include a purpose-built nursery unit, which gives children a seamless education from rising 3 years, and a fully equipped IT suite, a newly refurbished music department and specialist Science and Art/DT subject rooms. A full range of extra-curricular activities enables each child to develop their interests.

To help busy families we provide wrap around care from 7.45am to 6.00pm and our 'Home from Home' holiday care is offered for 10 weeks a year.

Moorfield is an Education Charitable Trust and the Headmistress is a member of IAPS.

Charitable status. Moorfield School Ltd is a Registered Charity, number 529112.

Moorlands School

Foxhill Drive, Weetwood Lane, Leeds LS16 5PF
Tel: 0113 278 5286
Fax: 0113 203 3193
email: info@moorlands-school.co.uk
website: www.moorlands-school.co.uk

Headmaster: **Martin McElhone**, BEd Hons

Age Range. 2–11 Co-educational.

Number of Pupils. 145 Day Boys and Girls.

Founded in 1898, Moorlands School is dedicated to providing a first-class education for girls and boys aged 2 to 11 years in a warm, friendly environment.

The school is conveniently located off the Ring Road at Weetwood Lane, yet sat in beautiful grounds providing all the outdoor space (and off-road parking) required for children to play in a safe and secure environment. The school boasts fantastic wrap-around care facilities, excellent teaching standards, on-site swimming pool and small class sizes.

In 2012 Moorlands became a full member of the Methodist Independent Schools Trust (MIST) securing its long-term future and bringing with it the benefits of membership of a large network of independent schools.

The aim of the school is to develop the full potential of every child within a happy and caring environment fostered by small classes and the professional skills of a highly qualified staff. Strong links between the parents and the school are encouraged to facilitate the provision of an effective education.

Admission is by assessment and observation. Pupils are accepted at 2 years old for entry into the Nursery and are expected to progress through the school in preparation for entry to senior independent day and boarding schools. The school has a well-developed specialist facility to provide assistance to pupils with any learning issue such as dyslexia or to gifted children.

Blended with this traditional core of academic work is offered a comprehensive range of sporting activities and a wide range of musical and extra-curricular pursuits.

At Moorlands, we have a simple yet beautiful motto, 'Intrepide'!, or 'be brave'! In school, we talk about how being brave or intrepid takes many forms. Being brave isn't always a grand gesture; sometimes it simply means 'having a go', such as attempting that difficult question, offering an answer in class when you're not quite sure or trying something new. This culture of intrepidness allows children to be brave and try new things in a safe, nurturing and stimulating environment.

Religious affiliation: Methodist.

Fees per term (2014–2015). Early Years £2,725; Reception £2,837, Years 1 and 2 £2,847, Lunch £180; Years 3–8 £3,202–£3,227, Lunch £200.

Charitable status. Moorlands School is a Registered Charity, number 529216. It exists to provide children with the finest education possible, using the best resources in an environment of care.

Moreton Hall Preparatory School

Mount Road, Bury St Edmunds, Suffolk IP32 7BJ
Tel: 01284 753532
Fax: 01284 769197
email: office@moretonhallprep.org
website: www.moretonhallprep.org

Chairman of the Board of Governors: Neil Smith

Headmaster: **S Head**, MA Cantab, PGCE, QTS

Age Range. 4–13.
Number of Pupils. Boys 59, Girls 62.
Fees per term (from January 2014). Boarding: £6,285 (full), £5,620 (weekly). Day: £2,510–£4,110.

Moreton Hall is a warm and welcoming school, set in an impressive historic building with 30 acres of attractive grounds. Its latest inspection (2011) assessed both the personal development of the children and their pastoral care as excellent. Sporting standards are high with daily games sessions. Rugby, soccer, hockey, cricket, netball, rounders and swimming form the major sports. There is an outdoor, heated swimming pool and a large sports hall. A second,

indoor swimming pool and squash courts are available for use at the adjacent Health club.

The staff to pupil ratio is high with an average class size of 14 pupils. Some classes are setted, including all Maths lessons, in senior years to improve this ratio still further. Pupils are prepared for Year 9 Scholarship or Common Entrance examination to the full range of Senior schools; prestigious Academic, Music and Sporting awards are all achieved regularly. High importance is also placed upon Music and Drama. The majority of pupils learn a musical instrument and perform regularly in concerts; there are plays in each section of the school and weekly lessons in Speech and Drama available.

The school accepts boarders from the age of 8 and day pupils from the age of 5. Younger children are accepted into the school's on-site day nursery from the age of 6 months. Weekly and flexible boarding arrangements are also popular. The resident Housemaster and his young family are supported by the Headmaster and other staff in addition to gap students. Bury St Edmunds is five minutes away, Cambridge just under an hour away and London is two hours by road or rail. The School can arrange transport to and from airports.

Moreton Hall has a Catholic tradition and welcomes children of all denominations. Financial support is available through means-tested bursaries.

For further information, please access our website or ring the office to arrange a visit or taster day.

The school is a member of CISC.

Charitable status. Moreton Hall School Trust Limited is a Registered Charity, number 280927. It exists to provide high quality education for boys and girls.

Moulsford Preparatory School

Moulsford-on-Thames, Wallingford, Oxfordshire OX10 9HR
Tel: 01491 651438
Fax: 01491 651868
email: pa.registrar@moulsford.com
website: www.moulsford.com

The School is a Charitable Trust controlled by a Board of Governors.

Chairman of the Board of Governors: Mr W Lazarus, FCA

Headmaster: **B Beardmore-Gray**, BA Hons, QTS

Age Range. 4–13.
Number of Boys. 34 Weekly Boarders, 290 Day Boys.
Fees per term (2014–2015). Day Boys £3,280–£4,900, Weekly Boarders £6,150. These fees are all inclusive but individual coaching in music, judo, golf and fencing is charged as an extra.

The School has its own river frontage on the Thames, spacious games fields and lawns and is situated between Wallingford and Reading.

Boys are prepared for the Common Entrance and Scholarship examinations to the top independent schools in the country. An experienced and well qualified staff ensure that a high standard is achieved academically, musically, artistically and on the games field.

The principal games are rugby football, soccer, tennis and cricket. Other sporting activities include athletics, swimming, sailing, judo, golf and gymnastics. The school is proud of its fine academic and sporting reputation which has been built up over many years.

Charitable status. Moulsford Preparatory School is a Registered Charity, number 309643.

The Mount Junior School

Dalton Terrace, York YO24 4DD
Tel: 01904 667500
email: registrar@mountschoolyork.co.uk
website: www.mountschoolyork.co.uk

Management Committee (Board of Governors):
Clerk: Timothy Phillips

Principal of The Mount School: Julie Lodrick, MA, PGCE

Head of Junior School: Rachel Capper, BEd Hons

Age Range. Girls 2–11; Boys 2–7.
Number of Pupils. 80.
Fees per term (2014–2015). Juniors (Years 3–6) £3,316; Infants (Years 1–2) £2,498; Reception £2,451. Pre-School (2–4 years): £49 per extended day (7.30 am to 6 pm). Flexi boarding is available from age 10 at £42 per night.

Children at The Mount Junior School in York benefit from a genuinely remarkable education in an environment which fosters self-belief, independent thought and sensitivity to others.

This Quaker School offers an exclusive 16-acre campus in the heart of York with impressive facilities, a wide range of music disciplines, sports and extra-curricular activities and creative media. We believe our pupils discover potential they never knew existed and grow at their own pace, free from the pressures to conform to stereotypes, and supported to take intellectual risks and to live adventurously.

Our Junior School, for girls aged 7 to 11 years, and Pre-School, for girls and boys aged 2 to 7 years, share the same grounds and educational, recreational, medical, catering and security facilities as our prestigious Senior School.

Academically, the Junior School is admired for the quality and commitment of its teaching staff, and for results produced at critically important stages of a child's education. Even our smallest children enjoy our on-site Forest School and Enchanted Garden weekly where, through free play and structured activities, they learn to be adventurous, inquisitive and proud of their successes. In 2012 and again in 2014 the Junior School achieved 100% Distinctions in the national London Academy of Music and Dramatic Arts (LAMDA) examinations.

For further details about the Senior School, see entry in GSA section.

Charitable status. The Mount School (York) is a Registered Charity, number 513646.

Mount Kelly Preparatory School

Tavistock, Devon PL19 9JL
Tel: 01822 813193
email: admissions@mountkelly.com
website: www.mountkelly.com

Chairman of Governors: Rear Admiral Chris Snow, CBE, DL

Head Master and Principal of the Mount Kelly Foundation: Mr Mark Semmence, BA, MA, MBA, PGCE

Head of Prep: Mr Matthew Foale, BEd Hons, MSc

Age Range. 3–13 Co-educational.
Number of Pupils. 210.
Fees per term (2014–2015). Day: £2,065–£4,200 (lunch included).   Boarding: £4,850–£6,953   (weekly), £5,288–£7,047 (full).

The Prep at Mount Kelly is part of the Mount Kelly Foundation, established in June 2014 following the merger of the Kelly College Foundation and the Mount House School Trust. The Prep at Mount Kelly offers is a co-educational day and boarding school for children from 3–13 years. The School is situated on either side of a beautiful valley (Prep: 3–13 and College: 13–18 years) on the edge of the Dartmoor National Park and is easily accessible from Exeter and Plymouth. Positioned on the outskirts of the attractive market town of Tavistock the school grounds consist of over 100 acres of woodland, forest and green fields. Mount Kelly combines academic excellence with an outstanding range of learning opportunities beyond the classroom and exceptional pastoral care.

Overview. The Prep pupils are nurtured, guided and inspired to develop their own skills and interests with small class sizes offering an exceptional degree of individual focus. In addition to a proven track record of academic excellence based on a broad and challenging Common Entrance curriculum, the School offers an exceptional range of sporting and cultural programmes and facilities.

Mount Kelly is also renowned for its outstanding pastoral care, the result of a close-knit school community with a special emphasis on individual care and support from Nursery through Year 8. Every Prep child is a member of one of four Houses and has a dedicated Form Tutor committed to ensuring that their school career is happy, fulfilling and successful. Family style boarding is available from Year 2 (age 7) at the Prep, with the opportunity to enjoy occasional joint activities with the College. The majority of Mount Kelly pupils progress from the Prep through to the College; for those that do leave, Mount Kelly has an outstanding record in preparing pupils for Common Entrance and a variety of Scholarships to a number of national schools.

Outdoor Learning. Mount Kelly has an excellent year round Outdoor Learning Programme beginning with Forest School in the Pre-Prep and continuing with the Shackleton Scheme from Year 3. The Programme provides hands-on opportunities to learn about their environment on the School site or adjacent Dartmoor National Park as well as a variety of practical skills from basic carpentry, engineering and bush craft to team working and leadership as part of every pupil's weekly curriculum.

The Prep has been established around a beautiful Georgian stately home, stable courtyards and sweeping lawns and is exceptionally well equipped with two libraries, separate art and design technology studios, music school, a performing centre, an ICT suite as well as girls and boys boarding dormitories and common rooms. Also situated at the Prep, the Pre-Prep department is housed in a modern, purpose-built centre offering light, airy accommodation for Nursery through Year 1 with each classroom enjoying direct access to play space (playgrounds, hard standing cycling area and playing fields) as well as relevant Prep facilities.

Enjoying excellent sporting facilities both on site and at the neighbouring College, Prep pupils enjoy the use of an indoor sports hall, eight sports pitches (two Astroturf pitches), 25m indoor and outdoor (heated) swimming pools, a nine-hole golf course, a fishing lake and stream, track and field facilities, cross country course, climbing wall, two Olympic-sized trampolines, an Adventure Centre and the School Farm.

Sport. The School has an outstanding reputation for sporting excellence both as an international elite swimming centre (Mount Kelly swimming has produced competitors in the last five Olympic and Paralympic Games) but also in all school sports particularly rugby, hockey, cricket, netball, athletics and trampoline. The School regularly competes at national and regional levels and fields represented by both teams and individuals. Although the School produces outstanding athletes performing at top Schools' level the Mount Kelly sports programme is broad enough to be inclusive and

1054 Mount Kelly Preparatory School

all children are given the chance to participate in games and matches as well as weekly PE sessions.

Co-Curricular. In addition to organised team sports an extensive variety of sporting and extra-curricular activities are on offer to pupils throughout the year (and often via holiday clubs during the school holidays). These include chess, art, choirs, cookery, current affairs, climbing, dance, debate, golf, photography, and trampoline. Individual music and LAMDA tuition is available and the School is well known for its extensive music programme (over 80% of pupils are involved in the music programme) with individual and group performance opportunities readily available in the form of formal and informal concerts, a weekly assembly "Musician of the Week" and opportunities to join the semi-professional brass band and mixed age Mount Kelly Choral Society. The School offers a rich drama programme including school drama productions, "open stage" evenings, a spoken English competition and LAMDA (Mount Kelly is the largest LAMDA exam centre in the South West and has had a record breaking year at the Plymouth City Festival in 2014 and Mount Kelly pupils feature regularly in regional professional theatrical and broadcast productions). The Art curriculum is rich and varied including scholarship preparation with regular master classes held by professional artists, an annual art exhibition and a pupil "Artist of the Week" celebrated at assembly sessions. Regular excursions and residential trips are also organised for many year groups including the popular annual French experience and school ski tours.

There is an active Parents' Association that organises numerous social and fundraising events throughout the year.

Further details and a prospectus are available from the Admissions Department.

Charitable status. The Mount Kelly Foundation is a Registered Charity, number 306716. It exists to provide education for boys and girls.

Mylnhurst Preparatory School & Nursery

Button Hill, Woodholm Road, Ecclesall, Sheffield S11 9HJ
Tel: 0114 236 1411
Fax: 0114 236 1411
email: enquiries@mylnhurst.co.uk
website: www.mylnhurst.co.uk

A Catholic Foundation Welcoming Families of All Faiths – maximising the potential of your children through partnership within a challenging and supportive Catholic Christian Community.

Headmaster: **Mr C P Emmott**, BSc Hons, MEd, MBA

Age Range. 3–11 Co-educational.
Number of Pupils. 179.
Fees per term (2014–2015). £2,820.

Situated in extensive private grounds, Mylnhurst provides a state-of-the-art teaching environment supported by our outstanding school facilities, which include a 25m pool, dance studio, sports hall and Apple Mac suite.

With a strong emphasis on school-parent partnership, Mylnhurst embraces your high expectations and ensures each child benefits from an exciting and stimulating curriculum.

Be assured of a very warm welcome and the opportunity to work closely with our committed and talented staff. So, whether it be an informal chat or a school open day, we look forward to sharing our vision with you and discussing the exciting future of your children.

Charitable status. Mylnhurst Limited is a Registered Charity, number 1056683.

Naima Jewish Preparatory School

21 Andover Place, London NW6 5ED
Tel: 020 7328 2802
Fax: 020 7624 0161
email: secretary@naimajps.co.uk
website: www.naimajps.co.uk

Chair of Governors: Mr Edward Misrahi

Headmaster: **Mr J W Pratt**, GRSM Hons, CertEd

Age Range. 2–11 Co-educational.
Number of Pupils. 175 girls and boys.
Fees per term (2014–2015). £2,160–£3,990.

Naima JPS is centred on the belief that an excellent secular education and strong Jewish grounding are mutually attainable. As such, our twin goals merge as we aspire to prepare our children for a successful life in society imbued with Torah values. We aim to provide a secular education on a par with the top national private schools with a curriculum that extends beyond the minimum guidelines provided by the National Curriculum. As a private school, we provide both the environment and teaching resources to monitor each individual, and to help children of all abilities to reach their full potential.

Naima JPS challenges all children, together with their parents, no matter what their level of religious observance, to pursue ongoing spiritual growth as individuals. We encourage children on their journey to spiritual maturity in a harmonious and nurturing community environment of tolerance, respect and care for one another.

The school has a one-form entry. Given that class sizes seldom exceed 22 and the favourable ratio of teachers and assistants to children – as little as 1:5 depending on the age and need – programmes of learning have the flexibility for differentiation. The school has a high number of particularly able children with specific intellectual gifts.

During the crucial early years at school it is important that children define themselves by things they can do well. Self-esteem, that essential by-product of success, empowers strength and gifts. Once children understand how their minds work, as they learn in many different ways, they can feel comfortable about entering any environment and mastering it. Children who truly understand, value and like themselves are better equipped to flourish and embrace fresh challenges. Confidence through success contributes to strong identities that welcome new horizons. Resiliency, discovery, independence and spiritual maturity are nurtured at all levels. At Naima JPS education is not about coveting garlands for the few, but ensuring that all children reach their full potential.

Charitable status. Naima JPS is a Registered Charity, number 289066.

The New Beacon

Brittains Lane, Sevenoaks, Kent TN13 2PB
Tel: 01732 452131
Fax: 01732 459509
email: admin@newbeacon.org.uk
website: www.newbeacon.org.uk

Chairman of the Governors: Mr Rupert Horner

Headmaster: **Michael Piercy**, BA Hons

Age Range. 4–13.

Number of Boys. 400. Predominantly Day Pupils, but a small element of flexi boarding is retained from Monday to Thursday.

Fees per term (2014–2015). £3,495–£4,560. Fees include lunches.

Boys are prepared for both grammar and senior independent schools, and enjoy considerable success at 11+ and 13+, with many achieving scholarships (including music, sport, art and drama) to a wide range of first-class senior schools.

The School divides into Senior, Middle and Junior sections in which boys are placed according to age and ability. Initiative is encouraged by organising the School into 4 houses or 'companies'. The well-equipped main School building is complemented by several modern, purpose-built facilities: separate Pre-Prep and Junior School buildings for boys aged 4–9; a Sports Hall with modern changing facilities; a multi-purpose, astroturf sports pitch; a Theatre; a heated indoor Swimming Pool; a centre for Art and Music; and modern facilities for Science and Technology. Soccer, Rugby Union and Cricket are the major games. The School intends to introduce Hockey during 2013. During the summer months Tennis and Athletics are available. Swimming and Shooting are available all year round. A very extensive range of extra-curricular activities is offered (including many interesting and exciting trips) together with a programme of Pre and After School care. Music, sport, art and drama at the School are highly regarded.

A limited number of music and academic bursaries are offered subject to means testing.

Charitable status. The New Beacon is a Registered Charity, number 307925. It exists to provide an all-round education for boys aged 4–13.

New College School

Savile Road, Oxford OX1 3UA
Tel: 01865 285560
Fax: 01865 210277
email: office@newcollegeschool.org
website: www.newcollegeschool.org

Governors: The Warden & Fellows of New College Oxford

Headmaster: **N R Gullifer**, MA, FRSA

Age Range. 4–13 years.

Number of Boys. 160 Day Boys, including 22 Choristers.

Fees per term (2014–2015). Reception £2,877, Year 1 £3,464, Years 2–4 £4,254, Years 5–8 £4,651, Choristers £1,655.

New College School was founded in 1379 when William of Wykeham made provision for the education of 16 Choristers to sing daily services in New College Chapel. Situated in the heart of the city, a few minutes' walk from the College, the school is fortunate in having the use of New College playing fields for sport and New College Chapel for school services.

The staff consists of some 22 full-time teachers and a full complement of visiting music teachers. Boys are prepared for the Common Entrance and Scholarship Examinations for transfer to independent senior schools at age 13. In the final year there is a scholarship form and a common entrance form. The school broadly follows the national curriculum subjects, but also teaches French, Latin, Design Technology and Greek.

Sports, played on New College Sports Ground, include soccer, hockey, cricket, rounders, athletics and rugby. Activities include archery, art, craft, pottery, design, chess, sport,

computer, drama, and science clubs. There is a Choral Society for parents.

Music plays a major part in school life with orchestra, ensembles, concert and junior choirs and form concerts, in addition to individual tuition in a wide range of instruments. A optional Saturday morning music education programme is followed by boys from Year 5 upwards.

Boys are admitted by gentle assessment to the Pre-Prep Department at 4 years and to the Prep School at 7 years. Potential Choristers are tested between the ages of 6 and 7 at annual voice trials.

New Hall Preparatory School

The Avenue, Boreham, Chelmsford, Essex CM3 3HS
Tel: 01245 236192
Fax: 01245 451671
email: prep@newhallschool.co.uk
website: www.newhallschool.co.uk
Twitter: @NewHallSchool
Facebook: /newhallschool

Chair of Governors: Mrs Clare Kershaw, LLB Hons, MCMI

Headteacher: **Mrs S Conrad**, BA Hons, PGCE Dunelm, NPQH

Age Range. 3–11 Co-educational.

Number of Pupils. 343.

Fees per term (2014–2015). Day £1,665.60–£4,203; Boarding (from age 7): £5,620 (weekly), £6,209 (full). There is a Prompt Payment Discount of £100 per term (not included in the Fees shown).

New Hall Preparatory School is a Catholic boarding and day school which welcomes all who are in sympathy with its ethos. The school caters for boys and girls aged 3–11 with boarding available from the age of 7. The school is located in the beautiful, spacious and historic grounds of New Hall School, Chelmsford.

New Hall Preparatory School offers a broad, balanced, differentiated curriculum which aims for academic excellence at all times. We believe that learning should be fun as well as rigorous and engaging as well as disciplined. Our curriculum is based upon the National Curriculum but is greatly enhanced by specialist subject teachers in Music, Drama, French, Swimming, PE, ICT and Latin. An Entrance Examination Programme is built into the curriculum in KS2 which introduces pupils to verbal reasoning skills and prepares them for future entrance examinations and scholarships. Our curriculum is enriched by inspiring speakers and outside visits and supplemented by a rich, varied programme of extra-curricular activities. As a Catholic School, we are dedicated to helping each child to fulfil his/her true potential and to ensure that s/he becomes the very best s/he can be.

The school has outstanding facilities including: a purpose-built Pre-Reception; a well-equipped library; a modern science laboratory; a state-of-the-art computer suite; a theatre; dedicated music rooms; a dance studio; 25m 6-lane indoor swimming pool; 10 floodlit tennis/netball courts; indoor sports hall; floodlit national standard Astroturf hockey pitch; athletics track; football, rugby and cricket pitches and a fitness suite.

Music and sport play an important part in the life of the school. There are choirs and a flourishing School Orchestra which take part in a number of competitions and festivals each year. Concerts and shows are regular features of the school calendar and Year 6 take part in an annual end-of-year production. There are a number of sporting clubs and teams which regularly compete and enjoy successes in a variety of fixtures and competitions.

There is an excellent After School Care facility which provides fun, educational and structured activities in a safe, caring and informal environment. This is run by a dedicated team of After School Care staff.

Charitable status. New Hall School Trust is a Registered Charity, number 1110286.

Newbridge Preparatory School

51 Newbridge Crescent, Wolverhampton, West Midlands WV6 0LH
Tel: 01902 751088
Fax: 01902 751333
email: office@newbridge.wolverhampton.sch.uk
website: www.newbridgeprepschool.org.uk

Chairman of Board: Mrs H M Hughes

Headmistress: **Mrs S Fisher**, BEd Hons

Age Range. Girls 2–11. Boys 2–7.
Number of Pupils. 147.
Fees per term (2014–2015). £1,630–£2,500 including dance, recorder, drama, gym, netball, singing for various year groups.

Newbridge Preparatory School, founded in 1937, occupies a super site on the outskirts of Wolverhampton, convenient for parents travelling from Telford, Bridgnorth, Shropshire, and Stafford.

The school is divided into Lower School (Pre-Nursery–Year 2) and Upper School (Years 3–6). Upper School is housed in the main building which is a substantial house set in huge, beautiful mature gardens. There are specialist facilities in Art and Design, ICT, Science, Music and PE. The school also has netball and tennis courts.

Staff : pupil ratio is high. Specialist teaching takes place in Key Stage Two in English, Mathematics, Music, Science, French, PE, Dance and Drama. In Key Stage One: Dance, PE, Music and French.

Lower School enjoys a separate Nursery and a new building for Pre-Nursery to Year 2. There is a sports hall.

Children with Special Needs are well supported and nurtured.

Upper School girls take drama and dance and enter examinations. They also enter the annual local festival for Music and Drama.

The school offers an Early Morning Club, After School Care and a Holiday Club. It is a very popular school; there are waiting lists for many classes.

Standards are high in all areas of the curriculum – academic, PE and Music. Senior School results are excellent. Places are gained at local selective Independent and Maintained Schools but also Boarding Schools. Sporting, Academic and Speech and Drama Scholarships are attained for entrance into Senior School. Once examinations are complete, Year 6 follow an exciting STAR (Summer Term Activities Refreshed) curriculum using and developing skills previously taught. Girls leave Newbridge well equipped to face the challenges of a Senior School.

Educational visits take place each term. Nursery children enjoy a Forest School experience. Residential visits occur in Years 3–6. The visits vary from outdoor activities and challenges, environmental study to a visit to London.

Emphasis is placed on traditional values, personal development and responsibility. The curriculum is very broad, including many opportunities in Sport, Dance, Drama and Music.

Our school mission statement is: Aiming High, Building Bridges and Preparing for Life.

Children are taught to do their best in all areas, strive for a challenge and succeed at their own level.

Emphasis is placed on self-discipline, inclusion, equal opportunity and respect.

Charitable status. Newbridge Preparatory School is a Registered Charity, number 1019682. It exists to advance the education of children by conducting the school known as Newbridge Preparatory School.

Newcastle Preparatory School

6 Eslington Road, Jesmond, Newcastle-upon-Tyne NE2 4RH
Tel: 0191 281 1769
Fax: 0191 281 5668
email: enquiries@newcastleprepschool.org.uk
website: www.newcastleprepschool.org.uk

The School was founded in 1885 and is now a Charitable Trust with a Board of Governors.

Chair of Governors: Mrs C Wood

Head: **Margaret Coates**, BEd Oxon

Age Range. 3–11.
Number of Pupils. 280 Day Pupils (180 boys, 100 girls).
Fees per term (2014–2015). Reception & Year 1: £3,115, Years 2 & 3: £3,170, Years 4–6: £3,220.

The School is situated in a residential part of Newcastle with easy access from all round the area.

Newcastle Preparatory School is a fully co-educational day school for children aged 3 to 11 years. It is a warm, caring environment in which all pupils are encouraged to reach their full potential.

Children may join 'First Steps' at NPS from the age of 3 years. 'First Steps' is an exciting and colourful nursery with excellent resources and well qualified staff who look after the needs of each individual.

At age 4, children make the easy step into School where they experience many 'steps to success'.

The curriculum offered throughout school is broad and balanced so that children enjoy learning in a variety of ways. French is taught from the age of 4 with music and PE being taught by specialist teachers. As children progress through School they become independent learners, following a varied timetable and class sizes are small to provide individual attention.

Music is an important part of life at NPS. There is a choir and a lively swing band.

Sporting achievements too are very good. There is a purpose-built Sports Hall and a wide range of sport is offered with extra-curricular activities including rugby, football, cricket, hockey, netball, athletics, tennis and swimming.

Also there are many clubs and activities to enrich the curriculum, eg Drama, Dance, Chess, Philosophy, Art, ICT, Design, Food Technology and there is an effective School Council as well as a Buddy System.

The variety of opportunities ensures that the children leave NPS well equipped for an easy transition into senior schools. The academic results are very good and the children receive an all-round education, so that they are confident, eager learners.

Charitable status. Newcastle Preparatory School is a Registered Charity, number 528152. It exists to provide education for boys and girls.

Newland House School

Waldegrave Park, Twickenham TW1 4TQ
Tel: 020 8865 1234
Fax: 020 8744 0399
email: admissions@newlandhouse.net
website: www.newlandhouse.net

Founded in 1897, the school was privately owned until 1971 when the Newland House School Trust was formed. It is a charitable Educational Trust with a Board of Governors.

Chairman of Governors: S Musgrave

Headmaster: D A Alexander, BMus, Dip NCOS

Deputy Headmaster: D S Arnold, BA

Age Range. 4–13.
Number of Pupils. 247 Boys, 161 Girls.
Fees per term (2014–2015). Pre-Prep £3,395, Prep £3,795. Lunch is included in the Fees.

Newland House School is a co-educational day preparatory school set in a residential area on the Twickenham-Teddington border. The school is ideally situated for parents in the Richmond, Kingston and Hampton areas and is very close to the river Thames.

The school currently occupies approximately 5 acres across two properties with grounds that provide sports facilities, including an all-weather pitch. The school is also fortunate to have daily access to the nearby Imperial College Sports Ground.

The school is divided into Pre-Prep, which currently has its own site and provides for children in Reception (EYFS) to Year 2, and Prep for children in Years 3 to 8. A new school for the Pre-Prep is in the process of being built and in summer 2016 the Pre-Prep will move into brand new premises immediately adjacent to the Prep School. The new school will provide an innovative and unique learning environment for pupils using leading sustainable design and the latest technology.

The school's main intakes are at the age of 4 (Reception) which is non-selective and Year 3 via a 7+ assessment. From autumn 2016 the school will be able to offer 20 additional places in Reception following the move to the new premises. Places may also become available in other age groups throughout the school year.

The Prep School has well-appointed, airy classrooms with a traditional feel, a large gymnasium/assembly hall, dining room, separate senior and junior libraries and two well-equipped science laboratories. There is an Art and Design Technology block, as well as a purpose-built Music block. The school has a substantial computer network, including a state-of-the-art computer suite.

The staff currently consists of 33 full-time teachers, and 10 classroom assistants, mostly in the Pre-Prep School. Children are well prepared for the Common Entrance and Scholarship examinations to Independent Schools. During the ISI Inspection in 2013, the school was found to be 'excellent' in many areas. In particular, the opportunities which the school provides for academic achievement and learning, as well as pastoral care and pupils' personal development, were clearly recognised.

There is a strong music department staffed by 19 visiting music staff who teach a variety of instruments. There are 5 choirs, several wind and brass ensembles, 2 orchestras and a jazz band who have the opportunity to perform at a variety of external venues.

The main games for boys are Rugby, Soccer and Cricket with Netball, Hockey and Rounders for girls. All children from the age of 7 have the opportunity to swim throughout the year. The teams take part in a range of leagues and competitions and there is an annual cricket tour to South Africa.

The school is committed to providing a broad and balanced curriculum and an environment that fosters enquiring minds. A wide variety of extra-curricular activities is available including, fencing, golf, chess, and badminton. The school also provides a Breakfast Club from 7.30 am each morning and an After-School Club until 6 pm.

Charitable status. The Newland House School Trust Limited is a Registered Charity, number 312670. It exists to promote and provide for the advancement of education for children of either sex or both sexes.

Newton Prep

149 Battersea Park Road, London SW8 4BX
Tel: 020 7720 4091
Fax: 020 7498 9052
email: admin@newtonprep.co.uk
website: www.newtonprepschool.co.uk

Chairman of Council: Dr Farouk Walji

Head: Mrs A E Fleming, BA, MA

Administration & Finance Manager: Mr P Farrelly

Age Range. 3–13.
Number of Pupils. 600+: 50% Boys, 50% Girls.
Fees per term (2014–2015). £2,690–£5,700.
Average size of class: <20.
The current teacher/pupil ratio is 1:11.
Religious denomination: Non-denominational.

Newton Prep is a vibrant school which offers a challenging education for inquisitive children who are eager to engage fully with the world in which they are growing up. The school aims to:

- inspire children to be adventurous and committed in their learning;
- provide balance and breadth in all aspects of a child's education: intellectual, aesthetic, physical, moral and spiritual;
- encourage initiative, individuality, independence, creativity and enquiry;
- promote responsible behaviour and respect for others in a happy, safe and caring environment.

Entry requirements: Siblings are given priority when allocating nursery places; other nursery places are awarded by lottery, while ensuring an even balance of boys and girls; children joining Reception are assessed individually: a gentle process, with offers made by October half term in the year before entry. Older children come to an assessment morning in the Spring Term (on a case-by-case basis at other times) during which they will be assessed in reading, maths and some diagnostic, age-appropriate reasoning tests. Scholarships and means-tested top-up bursaries are available in and after Year 3.

Examinations offered: All entrance examinations to senior schools, Common Entrance and scholarships at 11, 12 and 13. Most children leave to go to London day schools though a significant minority leave to go boarding. We pride ourselves on the quality of guidance offered and, every 2 years, we organise a Senior Schools Fair attended by over 60 schools.

First-time visitors to the school are invariably impressed by the scale and range of our facilities and by the wide open outdoor spaces enjoyed by the children.

Newton Prep occupies an early 20th-century elementary school building, which has been extensively remodelled internally, and behind which stands modern extensions containing classrooms, the dining hall and kitchen, two gymnasiums, a 300-seat auditorium and a recital hall. The top floor of the Edwardian building provides one large general-purpose space as well as two art studios. Newton Prep has two huge outdoor spaces for PE/Games and free play: behind the school, an all-weather pitch and, in front, a large playground. The school also has a large garden with a wildlife area and an activity area with a pirate boat.

An extensive programme of refurbishment and new building lasted from 2009 to 2013. In the first phase, the Library was enlarged and three new ICT suites located adjacent to it. In addition, three new science laboratories were constructed on the second floor of the Edwardian building. Each teaching space and classroom is now equipped with an interactive whiteboard. In the second phase, the old Orchard Building was demolished and then replaced by a new Lower School including two new nurseries, eight new classrooms and an assembly hall. In the third phase, a new Sports Hall and Music School were completed, with changing facilities, music classrooms and practice rooms, a recording studio and music technology studio, a 120-seat recital hall and three dance studios. In addition the all-weather pitch has been replaced, a new adventure playground has been installed and the IT network has been upgraded.

Norland Place School

162/166 Holland Park Avenue, London W11 4UH
Tel: 020 7603 9103
Fax: 020 7603 0648
email: office@norlandplace.com
website: www.norlandplace.com

Headmaster: **Mr P Mattar**

Age Range. Girls 4–11, Boys 4–8.
Number of Children. 240.
Fees per term (2014–2015). £4,185–£5,110.
A Preparatory school founded in 1876 and still standing on the original site in Holland Park Avenue. Children are prepared for competitive London day schools and top rate boarding schools. The curriculum is well balanced with an emphasis on English, Mathematics and Science. Music, Art and Games are strong. The school contains a Library in addition to specialist Music, IT, Science and Art Rooms.

Early registration is essential.

Northbourne Park

Betteshanger, Deal, Kent CT14 0NW
Tel: 01304 611215
Fax: 01304 619020
email: admissions@northbournepark.com
website: www.northbournepark.com

Chairman of Governors: Mr Brian Semple, OBE, MA, MSc

Headmaster: **Edward Balfour**, BA Hons, PGCE

Age Range. 3–13 Co-educational.
Number of Pupils. 150 boys and girls. There are approximately 50 boarders.
Fees per term (2014–2015). Boarders: £6,240 (weekly), £7,250 (full); French Programme £7,990. Day Pupils: £2,770–£3,190 (Pre-Prep), £3,880–£5,020 (Years 3–8). Sleepover £39 per night. Fees include customary extras and many extra-curricular activities.

Northbourne Park is a happy, thriving and well-established school committed to inspiring in every child the confidence to succeed. Its ethos is that happy children take an active role in and out of the classroom, learning to be confident and balanced young people. We place a strong emphasis on personal development and pastoral care and our pupils are wonderful ambassadors for all that we do.

Set in over 100 acres of beautiful parkland and woods, the school has easy access to London, and to France and Belgium via Eurotunnel. The school provides a fortnightly bus service to central London and an accompanied Eurostar service to Paris and Brussels. School minibuses provide an excellent service for many local families.

Pupils achieve excellent academic standards as a result of inspiring teaching and learning in small classes. Pupils progress confidently on to a wide range of Grammar Schools at 11+ and senior schools at 13+ via Common Entrance, over half of them with scholarships.

We teach French from the age of 3 and modern European languages are a real strength of the school.

Our long-established and well-reputed Learning Support Department offers a wide range of individual support and is particularly successful with bright dyslexic children.

Our Sports, Music, Drama and Outdoor Education programmes play an important part in School life, encouraging self-confidence as well as life skills.

Boarders enjoy a home-from-home atmosphere with a brand new boarding ethos which encourages independence in every boarder and which is fantastic fun.

The school's most recent Independent Schools Inspection report was an excellent assessment of all that we do as a school.

We are happy to discuss scholarships with you. Sibling, HM Forces and Clergy discounts are generous and popular.

Charitable status. Northbourne Park is a Registered Charity, number 280048, and exists to inspire excellence in education.

Northcote Lodge

26 Bolingbroke Grove, London SW11 6EL
Tel: 020 8682 8888
Fax: 020 8682 8879
email: admissions@northwoodschools.com
website: www.northcotelodge.co.uk

Day Preparatory School for Boys.

Principals: Sir Malcolm & Lady Colquhoun

Headmaster: **Mr J Hansford**

Age Range. 8–13.
Number of Pupils. 220 Boys.
Fees per term (2014–2015). £5,605.
Northcote Lodge was founded in 1993 and occupies a large mid-Victorian building overlooking Wandsworth Common, with its own grounds of over one acre.

The school is run along similar lines to a country prep school with a longer day at the end of which all 'homework' is done as prep at school. There is a broad and balanced curriculum leading to Common Entrance or scholarship to all major independent senior schools, usually boarding. Games are played, in one form or another, each day. Karate is on the curriculum and the school has a significant record of success in this field. There are thriving music and arts departments, frequent dramatic productions, a strong Chapel Choir and numerous extra-curricular activities ranging from cookery to golf, debating to pottery, and model-making to basketball. The school has a state-of-the-art computing system which is networked throughout the school.

There is a fully qualified and enthusiastic staff all of whom are totally committed to the aims and values of the school. There is a full-time Matron who shares responsibility with the Deputy Head for the pastoral care. During the first two years the boys have a form teacher and thereafter they are assigned to a tutor with whom they will stay until they leave.

We believe that in a disciplined and happy environment, boys will succeed academically and do not need to feel under constant academic pressure. They know that they are at school to work but it is crucial that they look on their time at school as an enjoyable experience. They will grow up all too soon; they must be allowed to be boys, to enjoy childhood and to mature at their own pace.

High standards are expected of the boys in every area of life at school. Manners, courtesy, self-respect and consideration for others are key values. Once a week the boys attend a service at the local Church. There is considerable value to be gained from being a member of a small and caring community where every boy has the opportunity to shine. A great emphasis is placed on developing self-confidence which is the key to success at school.

Entry Requirements. Entry is in September following their eight birthday, although places for older boys can sometimes become available. Admission is by means of assessment and interview when the boy is 7. Siblings have automatic right of entry into school or to nearby Broomwood Hall (our associate school for boys aged 4–8 and girls aged 4–13). Places are also sometimes available at 9+, 10+ and 11+. Parents should contact the school if interested in such a place.

Northwood College for Girls – Junior School
GDST

Maxwell Road, Northwood, Middlesex HA6 2YE

Tel:	01923 845067
Fax:	01923 836526
email:	juniorschool@nwc.gdst.net
	c.kelly@nwc.gdst.net
website:	www.northwoodcollege.co.uk

In September 2014, Northwood College and Heathfield School for Girls in Pinner merged to form North West London's leading new school for girls aged 3–18 years. The merged school is part of the Girls' Day School Trust (GDST).

The GDST is the leading network of independent girls' schools in the UK. As a charity that owns and runs 24 schools and two academies, it reinvests all its income in its schools. For further information about the Trust, see p. xxi or visit www.gdst.net.

Chairman of Governing Council: Mr G Hudson

Head Mistress: **Mrs H Thaker**, BA Hons East London, PGCE North London

Age Range. Girls 3–11.
Number of Pupils. 406 Girls.
Fees per term (2014–2015). £3,100–£4,142.

Ethos. Our aim is to raise young women who know their own minds and are creative and flexible thinkers, as well as being able to achieve outstanding exam results. We are academically selective, but not narrowly exclusive. We value girls for more than simple academic performance, because our unique approach to advanced thinking skills means that we can develop, stretch and challenge every single one of them. We think that makes for an interesting and vibrant school community – and it's what makes Northwood College for Girls special.

Results show that Junior School girls reach standards far above national norms for the age group. All National Curriculum subjects are taught, plus Latin, Ballet and Drama. In addition, girls in Year 3 to 5 study French and girls in Year 6 study Spanish, Mandarin and German.

Thinking Skills. Our approach to thinking skills is another one of our defining characteristics. It sets Northwood College for Girls apart and gives our girls an edge in the way they approach any task or challenge. Through the programme, we ensure our girls start to understand and develop the way they think from the day they join Nursery through to the end of the Sixth Form. Over the years, they build up their reasoning skills, improve their creativity and acquire strategies for tackling complex problems and decisions. It gives them a life skill that will be as useful at university and in the workplace as it is at school.

Pupil Well-being. We take the challenge of turning out happy, confident and generous young women very seriously. Northwood College for Girls creates an atmosphere in which courtesy, respect and self-respect thrive. Girls are taught to understand and respect the other person's point of view and to show good manners at all times. In keeping with this ethos, the Junior School operates a system of recognition and reward for good behaviour and attitude, as well as work.

Come and visit us. The Junior School is housed in three separate buildings, including an innovative Early Years Centre which has been designed to allow for both indoor and outdoor learning to take place in an exciting and challenging environment.

We enjoy showing parents and girls around Northwood College for Girls. *For more information please see our entry in the GSA section.*

Charitable status. Northwood College for Girls is part of The Girls' Day School Trust, which is a Registered Charity, number 306983.

Northwood Prep

Moor Farm, Sandy Lodge Road, Rickmansworth, Herts WD3 1LW

Tel:	01923 825648
Fax:	01923 835802
email:	office@northwoodprep.co.uk
website:	www.northwoodprep.co.uk

Founded as a private school in 1910 by Mr Francis Terry, NP has a long history and proud traditions. It is still known within the locality as "Terry's" after its founder. In 1954 it became an educational charitable trust administered by a Board of Governors.

Co-Chairs of Governors:
Mr Alan Eastwood, BComm, ACA
Mrs Jane Redman, LLB

Headmaster: **Dr Trevor Lee**, BEd Hons Exon, MEd Jesus College Cambridge, EdD Hull

Deputy Heads:
Mr Ian Rice, CertEd Carnegie, NPQH
Mr Andrew Crook, BA Lancaster, PGCE King's College London

Age Range. 3–13.
Number of Pupils. 300 Day Boys.
Fees per term (2014–2015). £3,086 (Nursery full-time), £4,410 (Reception, Years 1 and 2), £4,628 (Years 3–8).

The School is located amidst 14 acres on a former farm in an ideal park and woodland setting. The Grade II listed buildings have been skilfully converted to provide a complete and unique range of classrooms and ancillary facilities. The mediaeval Manor of the More, once owned by King Henry VIII and used as a palace by Cardinal Wolsey, was originally located within the grounds and provides some interesting and historical associations.

The School is divided into four sections: an off-site Nursery School for children aged 3+, the Junior School (Reception to Year 2), Key Stage 2 (Years 3–6) and Key Stage 3 (Years 7 and 8). These all have their own teaching areas while making use of the same dining, games, extra-curricular and recreational facilities.

Boys are admitted to the school after an assessment by Heads of Section. The main entry is into Nursery at 3+ when boys are admitted in the September after their third birthday. Older boys may also be accepted further up the School if a chance vacancy occurs. Boys are expected to remain until the age of thirteen, being prepared for entry at that stage to independent senior schools by way of Common Entrance. The School has also built up a fine record of Scholarship results over the years.

Work of a traditionally high standard is expected of all boys. The curriculum is interpreted as richly as possible and includes Technology, Music, Art, Drama, Physical Education and Games. The School has modern teaching facilities and the fully qualified and experienced staff is generously resourced. The Sir Christopher Harding Building for Science and Technology, comprising two state-of-the-art laboratories, an ICT Suite and technology workshop was opened in November 2000. A Learning Resource Centre was created in September 2001. A centre for the Performing Arts was commissioned by Mr Kevin Spacey in April 2008 and a music school was opened in May 2008. A nursery school was opened in the grounds of Merchant Taylors' School in April 2008. Additional sports changing facilities were opened in February 2008. Additional classrooms have been added as part of our centenary celebrations in 2010. A new Centenary trail accommodates a range of outdoor learning activities. In 2014 a new kitchen, dining hall and common room were added.

Swift access to London by train from nearby Moor Park Station means that staff often arrange for boys to visit places of historical and cultural interest and attend concerts and lectures.

While the Christian tradition on which the life of the School is based is that of the Church of England, boys from all Christian denominations and other faiths are welcomed.

There is an extensive programme of extra-curricular activities in which all boys are encouraged to take part. A key feature of the School's ethos is a strong tradition of caring, both for those within the community of the school, and those whom the boys can help through regular charitable activities.

Rugby Football, Association Football and Cricket are the principal team games. Tennis, Athletics, Judo and other sports are also coached. A fully equipped Sports Hall was opened in November 1996. The School has the benefit of a floodlit astroturf facility.

The School has a flourishing Parents' Association which arranges social and fundraising activities, and an active association for former pupils, The Old Terryers.

Charitable status. Northwood Preparatory School Trust (Terry's) Limited is a Registered Charity, number 312647. The aims of the charity are the education and development of boys aged 3–13.

Norwich School, The Lower School

Bishopgate, Norwich NR1 4AA
Tel: 01603 728439
email: L.School@norwich-school.org.uk
website: www.norwich-school.org.uk

Chairman of Governors: P J E Smith, MA, FIA

Master of the Lower School: **J K Ingham**, BA

Second Master: C C G Cordy, BA

Deputy Head (Academic): C M W Parsons, BSc

Age Range. 7–11.
Number of Pupils. 182.
Fees per term (2014–2015). £4,159.

The Lower School is the Junior Day School for Norwich School (*see entry in HMC section*). It is delightfully located in the Cathedral Close, between the East End of the Cathedral and the River Wensum. The Cathedral Choristers are educated at Norwich School, which is a member of the Choir Schools' Association.

The Lower School provides depth and breadth of education through a challenging curriculum. It seeks to recognise, nurture and develop each pupil's potential within an environment which encourages all-round emotional, physical, social and spiritual growth and to foster positive relations between pupils, teachers and parents. The dedicated teaching staff is committed to providing a stimulating programme of active learning which has rigour and discipline but avoids unnecessary pressure.

With two forms in each of its four year groups, the Lower School is the ideal size for ensuring a lively environment within a warm family atmosphere. The main building has bright, spacious areas for activities and lessons. As well as the library, there are specialised facilities for science, art, technology and ICT. There is an excellent play area in addition to the adjacent, extensive playing fields. A £750,000 extension for Science and Music opened in January 2014.

A wide range of extra-curricular activities and school trips is offered. Music is a strong feature of school life. Many pupils choose to learn a musical instrument and participate in the various instrumental music groups. Rugby, netball, hockey, cricket, rounders and tennis are taught and the games programme is designed to encourage pupils of all abilities to enjoy games and physical activity.

The School aims to attract pupils who will thrive in a challenging academic environment and is therefore selective. Prospective pupils are assessed in English, mathematics and non-verbal reasoning. There is a two-form entry at 7+ and a small number of places is available each year at 8+, 9+ and 10+. The prospectus and application forms are available from the Admissions Registrar, Tel: 01603 728442.

The vast majority of pupils from the Lower School progress to the Senior School at age eleven, and the curriculum is designed to prepare the pupils effectively for the next stage of their Norwich School education.

Charitable status. Norwich School is a Registered Charity, number 311280.

Notre Dame School
Preparatory School

Burwood House, Cobham, Surrey KT11 1HA
Tel: 01932 869990
email: registrar@notredame.co.uk
website: www.notredame.co.uk
Twitter: @NotreDameCobham
Facebook: /notredamecobham

Chair of Governors: Mr Gerald Russell

Principal: Mr David Plummer, BEd Hons, Dip HE, FRSA

Head of Prep: **Miss Merinda D'Aprano**, BEd Hons, MA, FRSA

Head of Pre-Prep: Mrs Sally Palmer, Cert Ed

Age Range. Girls 2–11, Boys 2–4.
Number of Pupils. 350 Girls, 12 boys.

Fees per term (2014–2015). Nursery £1,035–£2,955, Reception £3,225, Prep 1 & 2 £3,595, Prep 3–6 £3,995.

Bursaries. A limited number of assisted places and bursaries are offered subject to income and asset tests.

Notre Dame School is an independent Roman Catholic day school for approximately 700 girls aged 2–18. Set in 17 acres of beautiful, rural parkland, our school is part of a worldwide educational organisation, founded in Bordeaux in the 17th century by Saint Jeanne de Lestonnac. The Company of Mary Our Lady is the oldest recognised educational order, devoted to the teaching of girls and a belief in the unique contribution they make to society. We welcome families, of all faiths, who wish their daughters to grow spiritually, academically and socially in a dynamic, challenging yet caring environment.

Notre Dame School has:

- An environment which educates, including 17 acres of park lands, sports pitches, swimming pool, forest school area, treehouse, and dedicated specialist teaching rooms.
- A vibrant, bespoke humanities curriculum to develop thinking skills, moral foundation and knowledge.
- A wide range of co-curricular activities to enhance the educational experience.
- Highly-qualified teaching staff including subject specialists for music, PE, drama, Spanish, swimming, upper junior science, and dance.
- A friendly, vibrant, mixed-ability community of happy girls.

The discovery of self is especially important during the Prep years. We draw out individual talents, develop personal strengths and positively address weaknesses. This is undertaken both in class and in a wide range of internal clubs and workshops. The Prep at Notre Dame explores every facet of academic life and the school is especially proud of its strengths in drama, art, music, sport and languages. These are subjects at the very core of self-expression and you will find them enthusiastically carried through to the Senior, where they are taken to an even higher level.

Curriculum. The curriculum has breadth, depth and relevance. It is an enhanced version of the National Curriculum, strong in literacy and numeracy, and designed to provide a truly rounded, challenging preparatory education. The girls learn how to get the best from themselves and grow in motivation to excel, enjoy and achieve. The development of learning skills continues to be an important theme, as pupils tackle more advanced work. Knowing how to learn will forever remain one of life's most valuable lessons. Social, sporting and leisure interests are also encouraged to blossom in an atmosphere of mutual cooperation. A comprehensive range of extra-curricular activities is offered, including: ballet, golf, French, badminton, enthusiasts' swimming, orchestra, jazz, dance, yoga, fencing, Scrabble, chess, choirs, speech and drama, craft, tennis and art appreciation.

Notre Dame girls enjoy high levels of success in all areas of Sport, including swimming, while the professional, 370-seat bespoke Theatre gives pupils a really unique opportunity to tread the boards from a very young age: in drama, singing, ballet and dance or playing their individual instrument of choice.

Transport. Notre Dame is really easy to get to – just two minutes from the A3, less than 10 minutes from Walton, Weybridge, Cobham or Esher, and rarely more than 20 minutes from Guildford. Private coaches from: Barnes, Fulwell, Mortlake, Putney Bridge, Putney Heath, Richmond, Sheen, Teddington, Twickenham, Wandsworth, Wimbledon and all over Surrey offering flexible single/return journeys.

ISI Inspection 2011. Following an outstanding report in 2007, Notre Dame Preparatory School has continued to excel in all areas. '*The pupils' overall achievement from the EYFS onwards is outstanding and represents the successful fulfilment of the school's aim to strive for personal academic excellence.*'

Every aspect of the school from learning and teaching to extra-curricular events was scrutinised and evidence confirmed that: '*Pupils follow a demanding and imaginative curriculum and are successful in entry to the senior schools of their choice, including the award of scholarships*' and '*Their personal development benefits from a carefully planned programme of personal, social and health education. Parents and pupils commend the wide range of clubs and opportunities outside the classroom*'.

Teaching was again praised as being of the highest quality: '*Teachers know their pupils well and care is taken to ensure that they build on what they have already learnt. The pupils' successes are due, in large part, to the excellent teaching.*'

The school was particularly proud that the ethos of the school was reflected in the Inspectors' findings: '*Relationships between staff and pupils, and amongst the pupils themselves, are excellent. Parents appreciate the care provided for their children. Pupils are confident, caring and keen to celebrate the success of others. Pupils of all ages have outstandingly well-developed personal qualities. Excellent leadership and management are reflected in the pupils' outstanding overall achievement and personal development. The hallmark of the management is that nothing is left to chance, with meticulous attention to detail. Teamwork is of a high order.*'

In the words of the Chair of Governors: *This report is a credit to all and recognition of the effort everyone puts in. To be rated so highly in every area is an important external validation*".

Admission. The usual entry points in the Preparatory School are at Early Years (age 2), Reception (age 4) and Year 3 (age 7) although pupils may be accepted at other points as occasional places often become available in other year groups and throughout the year. Children attend an observation/assessment day at the School. During this day they will be assessed in mathematics, English and reading at the appropriate age level, and have a chance to meet new friends.

Senior School. For further information about the Senior School, please see entry in GSA section.

Charitable status. Notre Dame School Cobham is a Registered Charity, number 1081875. It exists to provide education for girls.

Notting Hill Preparatory School

95 Lancaster Road, London W11 1QQ

Tel: 020 7221 0727
Fax: 020 7221 0332
email: admin@nottinghillprep.com
          j.devlin@nottinghillprep.com
website: www.nottinghillprep.com

Co-Chairs of Governing Body:
Mr John Mackay
Mr John Morton Morris

Headmistress: Mrs Jane Cameron, BEd Hons

Age Range. 4–13 Co-educational.
Number of Pupils. 305.
Fees per term (2014–2015). £5,510.

Founded in 2003, NHP is a co-ed Prep School in the heart of Notting Hill, West London. It was created through the cooperation of parents and teachers and this partnership with parents is a cornerstone of the philosophy of the school. It operates on a split-site, Reception to Year 3 being housed in a fine Victorian School House and Years 4–8 in a magnificent new building providing, in addition, school hall/dining room, music room and music practice rooms, Science lab and ICT suite.

Our aim is to 'educate' children in the true sense of the word so that they develop an excitement and passion for learning. A broad-based curriculum ensures that academic subjects are balanced with ample time being dedicated to sport and subjects such as art, music and drama where the emphasis is on enjoyment and self-expression. Subjects are taught by specialist teachers in the Upper School, as are French, music, drama and PE from Reception. Latin is introduced in Year 5. Children are fully prepared for the competitive entrance examinations to London day schools and country boarding schools at 11+ and 13+.

Music and performance are particular features at the school, with creative staff producing original material for plays and concerts. There are two choirs and an orchestra and over two-thirds of the pupils learn a musical instrument.

A wide and varied sports programme using local facilities as well as our own on site gym ensures that children develop and perfect skills in the major sports (football, netball, hockey, rugby, cricket, athletics and swimming). Opportunities for displaying these skills are provided by frequent fixtures arranged with local schools.

Regular school trips enhance all aspects of the curriculum. Full use is made of the many and varied opportunities London offers to extend children's knowledge of their environment, their culture and their history.

We believe there are essential thinking skills that are crucial to learning and life beyond school. Through our curriculum, we strive to develop in our pupils the ability to think critically, collaboratively and creatively and to take ownership of their learning. We aim to develop responsible, reflective and resilient individuals who have a good sense of community and their role in the wider world. We do this in a caring and supportive environment by providing practical ways of developing good thinking, questioning and communication skills.

We are a 'thinking school' in which all members of our community share in a common language where strategies and tools are used in all aspects of school life enabling teachers, pupils and parents to have a deep understanding of how to learn and think effectively and efficiently. Pupils develop an awareness of themselves as learners and thinkers and put into practice ways to develop the dispositions and learning habits that are needed for lifelong learning.

The 'NHP Thinking Skills Toolbox' provides everyone with a framework to articulate their thoughts effectively and to develop good habits of learning. Teachers, children and parents can dip into the toolbox and, depending on the problem or task, pull out a range of strategies to support their thinking from De Bono's Six Thinking Hats to Habits of Mind, Thinking Maps, questioning techniques, graphic organisers, Bloom's taxonomy and so on.

NHP is noted for its open, friendly and happy atmosphere and its strong sense of being part of a wider community. Courtesy, kindness and appreciation of a diversity of talents, abilities and needs are defining values of the school's ethos.

The school is heavily oversubscribed and places are offered following a ballot. The School Secretary tries to keep waiting lists within reasonable limits.

Nottingham High Infant and Junior School

Waverley Mount, Nottingham NG7 4ED
Tel: 0115 845 2214
email: juniorinfo@nottinghamhigh.co.uk

Lovell House Infant School:
13 Waverley Street, Nottingham NG7 4DX
Tel: 0115 845 2222
email: lovellinfo@nottinghamhigh.co.uk

website: www.nottinghamhigh.co.uk

Chairman of Governors: Paul Balen

Head: **Mrs C Bruce**, MA

Age Range. 4–11.
Number of Boys. 257 Day Boys.
Fees per term (2014–2015). Infant School £2,931; Junior School £3,410.

The **Junior School** is housed in purpose-built premises on the main school site, having its own Classrooms, ICT Suite, Library, Art Room, Science Laboratory, Dining Hall and Assembly Hall.

Entrance Assessments are held in January, based around the core subjects of Mathematics and English, including reading, along with some measures of general ability. The tests are all set at National Curriculum ability levels appropriate for each age group.

The Junior School has an experienced and well-qualified staff. The curriculum is designed for those who expect to complete their education at Nottingham High School. The subjects taught are Religious Education, English, Mathematics, History, Geography, Science, French and PSHE. Full provision is made for Music, Art, Design Technology, Information Communication Technology, Swimming, Physical Education and Games.

The Junior School has its own Orchestra and about 100 boys receive instrumental tuition. All Year 3 boys play an instrument of their choice. A Concert and School Plays are performed annually. A wide range of supervised activities and hobbies takes place during every lunch time.

School games are Association Football and Rugby with some Hockey and Cross Country in the winter, Cricket and Tennis in the summer.

Lovell House Infant School opened in September 2008 for boys in Reception, Year 1 and Year 2. Lovell House is situated across the road from the main High School in its own secure and self-contained grounds. The school has been completely refurbished and upgraded recently to provide state-of-the-art classrooms and facilities, and extensive play areas, all in a friendly, home-from-home surrounding. In fact, the main school building is very much like a large house, making the transition between nursery and the early stages of a formal school education so much easier.

Classes are deliberately kept small (a maximum class size of 18), so that our teachers are able to devote time to the boys as individuals. The majority of subjects are taught by class teachers, although specialist teachers are used for ICT, Swimming, Music, French and Spanish. All subjects are taught in an integrated curriculum to allow time for play and problem-solving activities to take place.

Beyond the classroom we offer an excellent range of extra-curricular activities giving real breadth to our curriculum. We make full use of some of the Nottingham High School facilities, such as the swimming pool, the extensive games fields and both the music and drama facilities. Thus whilst Lovell House is largely self-contained we are also able to use the High School's wider facilities to expand the horizons of the boys in our care.

Entry to Lovell House is by assessment; the admissions process is designed to assess the numeracy and literacy skills of the boys applying for a place in Years 1 and 2, and a range of activities are used to assess the potential for learning for boys applying for a place in Reception. In addition, all boys are invited to school for a final classroom-based assessment where they are observed completing practical activities.

In the January of Year 2 all boys sit the entrance assessment for Nottingham High Junior School, with the vast majority transferring not only through to the Junior School at Year 3, but also later to the Senior School at Year 7.

As part of Nottingham High School, Lovell House not only benefits from the continuity of education and community from entry at age 4 right through to A Level at age 18, but also from the extensive recreational and cultural facilities provided by the High School.

Charitable status. Nottingham High School is a Registered Charity, number 1104251. It exists to provide education for boys between the ages of 4 and 18 years.

Oakwood Preparatory School

Chichester, West Sussex PO18 9AN

Tel:	01243 575209
Fax:	01243 575433
email:	office@oakwoodschool.co.uk
website:	www.oakwoodschool.co.uk

Headteacher: **Mrs G Proctor**, CertEd

Age Range. Co-educational 2½ to 11.
Number of Pupils. 260 Day boys and girls.
Fees per term (2014–2015). Pre-Prep £1,750–£3,180; Prep School £4,030–£4,385.

Oakwood was founded in 1912 and has grown into a thriving co-educational preparatory school.

Set in 160 acres of glorious park and woodland between the South Downs and the coast, Oakwood's home is a large Georgian country house.

The children learn in a wonderfully safe and spacious environment in the heart of beautiful Sussex countryside only three miles from Chichester. The school prides itself on its family atmosphere and the happiness of its children.

Oakwood is well-equipped with spacious classrooms, Science and Design Technology Studio, Art Room, Library, Music and Theatre Complex and ICT Centre. There is a Gymnasium and 3 floodlit tennis courts. The playing fields extend over nine acres, there is an indoor heated swimming pool and two adventure playgrounds.

The Pre-Prep, though fully integrated into the Oakwood community, enjoys its own spacious site with a safe and enclosed play area. The setting is particularly cosy and attractive, the classrooms having been sympathetically converted from a stable block.

There is a warm family atmosphere, as the school recognises the importance of children feeling happy and secure. Great emphasis is placed on building a solid foundation of social skills and a love of learning, thus enabling each child to settle confidently to school life.

There is a strong academic curriculum with small class sizes, ensuring that each child receives the closest possible attention. In the Prep School, children are set for English and Mathematics. The curriculum is broad with each child's timetable including Design Technology, Science, Humanities, French, ICT, PE, Drama and Music.

Form tutoring is of prime importance, the form teacher overseeing the development of each child – academically, socially and emotionally. Contact with parents is frequent and encouraged.

Opportunities to represent the school in sports teams, plays, choirs and instrument groups are all part of the "Oakwood Experience".

Music is very much a part of Oakwood life. The children enjoy music lessons each week and there is every opportunity to learn an instrument. The school has three choirs, recorder ensembles, guitar groups, a mini orchestra and a wind band. Each term there are music assemblies, and there are concerts every year for both Prep School and Pre-Prep children. The summer term ends with a musical production by the departing Year 6 pupils. In addition, children are encouraged to perform in Assembly.

The Physical Education and Sports programme has an exciting mix to offer every child. Games are played three times each week and are coached by members of staff with

an expertise and enthusiasm for their sport or by outside coaches.

In winter the boys enjoy a taste of all the major sports – Soccer, Rugby and Hockey, while the girls play netball and hockey. Judo, fencing, yoga, modern dance and ballet are also on offer to the boys and girls. In summer the boys play cricket and the girls play rounders, but the school also offers swimming, lacrosse, athletics and tennis. An extensive programme of inter-school fixtures is arranged each term for all sports teams.

Early arrivals care, after school clubs and activities all ensure that busy parents can benefit from a flexible school day.

There is an excellent record of examination, scholarship and academic award success to a variety of senior schools.

Oakwood School

59 Godstone Road, Purley, Surrey CR8 2AN

Tel:	020 8668 8080
Fax:	020 8668 2895
email:	enquiries@oakwoodschool.org.uk
website:	www.oakwoodschool.org.uk

Chair of Governors: Ella Leonard

Headmaster: **Mr Ciro Candia**, BA Hons, PGCE

Age Range. 3–11 Co-educational.
Number of Pupils. 178.
Fees per term (2014–2015). £1,336–£2,810.
Charitable status. PACT Educational Trust Limited is a Registered Charity, number 1053810.

Old Buckenham Hall School

Brettenham Park, Ipswich, Suffolk IP7 7PH

Tel:	01449 740252
Fax:	01449 740955
email:	admissions@obh.co.uk
website:	www.obh.co.uk
Twitter:	@OBHSchool

Chairman of Governors: N Bullen, BA Hons

Headmaster: **T O'Sullivan**, LLB Hons Durham, PGCE Cambridge

Deputy Head: Mrs J A Campbell, Adv Dip CSN, CertEd

Age Range. 3–13.
Number of Pupils. 81 Boarders; 63 Day Pupils; 39 Pre-Prep; 15 Nursery.
Fees per term (2014–2015). Full and Weekly Boarders £6,500–£7,400; Transitional Boarding: 2 consecutive nights £5,240–£6,420; 3 set nights £5,610–£6,790; 4 set nights £6,920–£7,160; Day £4,500–£5,680; Pre-Prep inc Nursery £349–£2,800.

The School, founded in Lowestoft as South Lodge in 1862, moved in 1937 to Old Buckenham, Norfolk and in 1956 to Brettenham Park, Suffolk, 4 miles from Lavenham and 18 from Ipswich. It became an Educational Trust in 1967.

The pupils go on to a wide range of Senior Independent Schools via Common Entrance and Scholarship Examinations.

The Staff/Pupil ratio is approximately 1:8, giving an average class-size of 14. All members of Staff, including part-time Staff, contribute to the provision of a wide range of extra-curricular activities in which every child has a chance to participate. The major sports are Rugby, Hockey, Soccer, Netball, Cricket and Rounders, but all pupils also take part in Athletics and Swimming (heated open air pool). In addition there are opportunities for Tennis (6 courts including 3 astro courts), Golf (9-hole course), Squash (2 courts) and a wide range of activities including: Table Tennis, Woodwork & Metalwork, Pets, Arts & Craft, Cookery, Clay Pigeon Shooting, Orienteering, Bushcraft, Fencing, Archery. Art, Music and Drama particularly flourish. A full-size Astroturf has recently been installed enhancing the school's sports provision.

The 11-day academic cycle established in September 2013 is proving to be a successful model making more effective use of the school day with the boarding children going home every other weekend. The re-drafting of the school day has given the school the ability to focus on what is fundamental – delivering a high-quality curriculum where every pupil has the best possible opportunity to succeed.

Boarding continues to be popular with refurbished dormitories including separate boys' and girls' common rooms and a separate common room for Year 8. An enhanced evening and weekend activity programme has been devised together with a new Enrichment programme exposing the children to a wide range of Life Skills. Outdoor classrooms have recently been introduced which are particularly popular at weekends together with a specially designed play area. The Science Department has been completely refurbished and was re-opened in 2010.

A School Prospectus can be obtained on application to the Registrar.

Charitable status. Old Buckenham Hall (Brettenham) Educational Trust Limited is a Registered Charity, number 310490. It exists to provide education for boarding and day pupils.

The Old Hall School

Stanley Road, Wellington, Shropshire TF1 3LB
Tel: 01952 223117
Fax: 01952 222674
email: admissions@oldhall.co.uk
            enq@oldhall.co.uk
website: www.oldhall.co.uk
Twitter: @oldhallschool

Chairman of the Governors: Mr H W Campion, ACA, CTA

Headmaster: **Mr Martin C Stott**, BEd Hons

Age Range. 4–11.
Number of Pupils. 231: 132 boys, 99 girls.
Fees per term (2014–2015). Lower School (Reception–Year 2) £2,458; Upper School (Years 3–6) £3,805.

Founded in 1845, The Old Hall School is a co-educational day school (4–11 years), which is housed in spectacular premises, located alongside Wrekin College. The school offers first-class facilities; a double sports hall, 25-metre indoor swimming pool, Astroturf and grass pitches offer an excellent sports and games environment, whilst specialist music and drama help to promote high standards in the performing arts. A suite of specialist learning support rooms reflects the School's commitment to the needs of the individual. First-class facilities have also been created for pre-school care and the education of children from the age of three months.

The broad curriculum is enriched by a dedicated team of professionals who encourage pupils to fulfil their potential in a happy and secure environment.

Through the academic curriculum and caring pastoral system, the school aims to lay solid foundations in the development of well-motivated, confident and happy indi-

viduals who are always willing to give of their best on the road to high achievement.

Charitable status. Wrekin Old Hall Trust Limited is a Registered Charity, number 528417.

The Old School Henstead

Toad Row, Henstead, Nr Beccles, Suffolk NR34 7LG
Tel: 01502 741150
email: office@theoldschoolhenstead.co.uk
website: www.theoldschoolhenstead.co.uk

Headmaster: **Mr W J McKinney**, MA Hons, PG Dip, MA Ed

Age Range. 2½–11.
Number in School. 90 Day Boys and Girls.
Fees per term (2014–2015). £2,035–£2,935.

The Old School Henstead and Nursery offers a traditional style of education in a caring family environment. It is well staffed with small classes throughout the school. Children are prepared for entrance examinations to all local senior schools, many winning scholarships. The curriculum is broad and balanced with facilities for Music, ICT, Science, Art & Drama and Physical Education. There is a wide variety of after-school clubs on offer as well as care before and after school.

Charitable status. The Old School Henstead Educational Trust Limited is a Registered Charity, number 279265. It exists to provide education for boys and girls.

Old Vicarage School

48 Richmond Hill, Richmond, Surrey TW10 6QX
Tel: 020 8940 0922
Fax: 020 8948 6834
email: office@oldvicarageschool.com
website: www.oldvicarageschool.com

Chairman of Governors: Mr M Townsin

Headmistress: **Mrs G Linthwaite**, MA Oxon, PGCE

Age Range. 4–11.
Number of Pupils. 195 girls.
Fees per term (2014–2015). £3,935.

The Old Vicarage school is a non-selective girls' prep school based in a beautiful Grade 2* listed "castle" on Richmond Hill. The School was established in 1881 and became a Charitable Educational Trust in 1973. Whilst retaining traditional values, there is a clear vision for the future and teaching and facilities combine the very best of the old and the new. Girls are admitted to the school into one of the two Reception forms in September following their fourth birthday. Older girls may be admitted further up the school if a vacancy arises, following a day spent at the school to ensure it is a good fit for them. Girls are expected to remain until the age of 11, being prepared for Common Entrance Examinations at 11+ and for entry to the London Day Schools. A good range of academic, sporting, drama and arts scholarships to senior schools has been awarded to girls over the years.

Work of a traditionally high standard is expected of the girls and they are challenged and supported in classes of 14 girls, encouraging self esteem and enabling them to fulfil their potential. Girls in the Lower School are taught by a Form Teacher, with some specialist input. Girls in the Upper School are taught by subject specialists who impart a real enthusiasm and love for their subject areas. They will also have a form tutor to provide the pastoral support the school is known for. A system of older buddies, prefects and the Student Council ensures that all girls feel an integral part of the school from the beginning.

Music and drama are active throughout the school. Individual music tuition is provided in a wide range of instruments in purpose-built facilities and active choirs sing at numerous competitions and collaborations. All girls take part in at least one dramatic production a year, as well as in assemblies to which parents are invited.

The major sports are netball, hockey, rounders, athletics and swimming and the school has close access to state-of-the-art facilities in the surrounding area as well as our own gym and playground. Girls compete in fixtures against other schools from Year 3 and have had notable successes in recent years in borough-wide championships.

Extra-curricular activities cater to a range of interests and include art, photography, sports, Adventure Service Challenge, computing, cooking, craft and drama clubs. All girls in the Upper School attend a residential trip to Sussex, Dorset, Oxfordshire or France and up to fifty join the biennial ski trip to Italy.

Charitable status. The Old Vicarage School is a Registered Charity, number 312671.

The Oratory Preparatory School

Goring Heath, Reading, South Oxfordshire RG8 7SF
Tel: 0118 9844511
Fax: 0118 9844806
email: office@oratoryprep.co.uk
website: www.oratoryprep.co.uk
Twitter: @OPS_OratoryPrep

Chairman of the Board of Governors: M H R Hasslacher

Headmaster: **J J Smith**, BA, PGCE

Age Range. 2–13.
Number of Pupils. 400 (250 boys and 150 girls), including 50 full-time, weekly or flexi-boarders and 125 in the Pre-Prep department.
Fees per term (2014–2015). Boarders: £5,950 (weekly), £6,900 (full); Day £4,650; Pre-Prep: £2,850 (all day), Kindergarten (5 sessions) £1,415; 'Little Oaks' Nursery £60 per day, £30.50 per pre-booked morning session.

A Roman Catholic preparatory school, founded by John Henry Cardinal Newman, which prepares boys for The Oratory School and boys and girls for other independent senior schools. The OPS welcomes children of all denominations and faiths and aims to identify and develop their individual talents and gifts in all aspects of their school lives.

The well-qualified and experienced staff of 56 full-time and 65 part-time and visiting teachers and teaching assistants form a strong and supportive team who deliver a broad curriculum characterised by an unusually wide range of subjects, activities and sports. A friendly and secure environment fosters the welfare of every child. Spiritual and pastoral needs are met by the chaplain, a nursing sister, three matrons, and a large and dedicated team of boarding and day staff operating a comprehensive pastoral and academic tutorial system.

The school has an excellent record of achievement, with pupils gaining many academic, art, music, sports and all-rounder awards to The Oratory School and other major schools. Choral and instrumental music, drama and art play a major part in school life. The school is also very proud of its competitive success in rugby, rugby sevens (once national champions and three times runners-up, most recently in 2012), football, cricket, cross-country, hockey, netball and rounders as well as tennis, swimming, archery, squash, golf, badminton, basketball and table tennis. In addition there is an extensive range of activities to suit and stretch every child. The school also organises frequent educational, cultural and sporting tours, both within this country and overseas, to widen further pupils' horizons.

The school's facilities have been extensively developed, with a large theatre, sports hall, indoor swimming pool and trainer pool, all-weather tennis and hockey surfaces, as well as well-equipped science and art departments and a well-stocked library. The music school contains two large spaces for performance and class teaching and seven smaller practice rooms for individual tuition. ICT provision is considerable and forms an integral part of the educational experience offered. The thriving Pre-Prep department is housed in an attractive courtyard setting on the same site.

The school stands in its own 60-acre estate, high above the Thames and easily accessible by train and road (via the M4 from London and Heathrow airport).

Charitable status. The Oratory Schools Association is a Registered Charity, number 309112. It exists to provide general, physical, moral and religious education for boys and girls.

Orchard House School

16 Newton Grove, London W4 1LB
Tel: 020 8742 8544
email: info@orchardhs.org.uk
website: www.orchardhs.org.uk

Chairman of Governors: Mr Anthony Rentoul

Headmistress: **Mrs S A B Hobbs**, BA Hons Exon, PGCE, AMBDA Mont Dip

Age Range. Girls and Boys 3–11.
Number of Pupils. 291: 171 Girls, 120 Boys.
Fees per term (2014–2015). Nursery (5 mornings) £2,510, Pre-Prep £5,020, Prep £5,240.

Orchard House School, with Bassett House and Prospect House, is part of the House Schools Group. It provides an excellent all-round education for boys and girls from 3 to 11, preparing them for the competitive entry examinations for the London day and country boarding schools whilst maintaining a happy, purposeful atmosphere. In 2010 the school became fully co-educational with boys able to remain until 11, alongside the girls.

There is an emphasis on teaching traditional values tailored for children growing up in the 21st century. Uniform is worn and good manners are expected at all times. Children shake hands with the staff at the end of each day and are encouraged to take part, with the deputy head or headmistress, in describing the school to prospective parents and other visitors. Appetising lunches are provided and children are involved in growing vegetables and salad in the school garden.

The main premises were designed by the well-known architect Norman Shaw and built around 1880; the building is Grade 2 listed. The school enjoys a corner site in Bedford Park and the classrooms have good natural lighting as well as overlooking a large playground/garden. Additional classrooms and associated study areas have been gained through the acquisition of another attractive building within 5 minutes' walk of the main school.

Children aged 3 or 4 are admitted on a first come, first served basis. Occasional places higher up are filled following assessment. The Montessori method is used to deliver the Early Years Foundation Stage curriculum; at KS1 and KS2 the curriculum is based on the National Curriculum and the demands of the future schools. Specialist teachers are employed for many subjects and support teachers provide on-one or small group tuition where necessary. Staff turnover is low.

Orchard House is proud of the excellent results the children achieve at their future schools which include many of the most academic schools in this country. The school is within easy reach of St Paul's schools, Latymer Upper, Notting Hill & Ealing High School and Godolphin & Latymer and many pupils have taken up places at one of these schools. Links with boys' schools such as Latymer Upper and Hampton School at 11+ will grow over the coming years.

The school boasts state-of-the-art ICT resources and attractive playgrounds/garden with all-weather surfaces. The children make good use of additional local facilities to enhance their Sport and Drama lessons.

Orchard House participates in the Nursery Education Grant. There are occasional academic scholarships, through the House Schools Trust, and a bursary scheme for children entering Year 4. See www.houseschoolstrust.org.

Orchard School

Higham Road, Barton-le-Clay, Bedfordshire MK45 4RB
Tel: 01582 882054
email: admin@orchardschool.org.uk
website: www.orchardschool.org.uk

Chair of Friends: Mrs Jenny Devile

Head Teacher: **Mrs Anne Burton**, MEd Cantab, Cert Ed, HV SRN

Deputy Head: Miss Louise Burton, BEd Hons Cantab, QTS

Co-educational Day School.
Age Range. 4–9 years; Nursery for children aged 0–4.
Number of Pupils. Preparatory School 56; Nursery 50.
Fees per term (2014–2015). Tuition (inc lunch) £2,397. Breakfast Club £3.50 per day. After School Club (inc tea) £7.50 per day.

Orchard School is a Preparatory School for boys and girls situated on the outskirts of a large village in south Bedfordshire. The School has been established for 12 years, the Nursery for 22 years. Located in a beautiful setting the School and Pre-Prep is surrounded by rolling countryside with the abundance of wildlife that this brings. The Nursery has its own Deputy Head and specialist team. The children aged 0–4 are located in the charming setting of a Georgian house less than a mile from the main school.

At Orchard we aim to enable each child to value and strive for the highest levels of achievement, creating a culture of pride in success, one in which pupils are proud and have a strong sense of belonging. Praise and encouragement are the motivational tools we employ and we recognise that every child develops at their own pace.

Learning at Orchard is not compartmentalised; trust, motivation, interest, enjoyment as well as physical and social skills are as important as purely cognitive gains. Skillful and careful observations are undertaken across the Orchard teaching team and are key to helping the children learn.

The aim of the school is to develop a passion for learning – to be the best that I can be. We use praise and encouragement as the core motivating factors in school life and are pleased to have built a school of which pupils are proud and have a sense of belonging. We seek to encourage the moral, social and personal development of all pupils building their confidence and self-esteem.

The school boasts an excellent academic record with the majority of our pupils successfully entering the Harpur Trust schools in Bedford. The combination of a progressive, structured, yet genuinely friendly, family atmosphere creates an ideal environment for our children to thrive both academically and in other activities that they pursue.

Encouragement is given to each child to experience a wide range of activities. Music, choir, dance, philosophy and a comprehensive sporting programme including swimming and rugby are all included within the well-rounded curriculum we offer. Further opportunities from Ballet to craftwork, running and badminton to recorder are offered in addition via lunchtime and after-school clubs. There are several visits a term across all year groups to complement topic learning and enhance the children's confidence and provide real-life context to topics being studied. For Years 3 and 4 we embark on residential trips to specialist adventure-based facilities. The children experience a range of activities including abseiling, kayaking and raft building to develop team spirit and confidence.

The School has historically been effective in building partnerships with parents on an individual basis. Together we encourage mutual respect and are mindful of our shared responsibilities. Orchard has had a very strong and supportive parent base and there is a well-established 'Friends of Orchard School' group who organise social gatherings as well as fundraising events which enhances our family-feel.

Orchard's pupils develop into well-motivated, balanced and confident children who are considerate to others, well-mannered, who know the value of hard work and who go on to excel at their next schools.

Orley Farm School

South Hill Avenue, Harrow on the Hill, Middlesex HA1 3NU
Tel: 020 8869 7600
Fax: 020 8869 7601
email: office@orleyfarm.harrow.sch.uk
website: www.orleyfarm.harrow.sch.uk

The school is a Charitable Trust administered by a Board of Governors.

Chairman of Governors: Mr C J Hayfield

Headmaster: **Mr T Calvey**, BA Ed Hons

Age Range. 4–13 Co-educational.
Number of Pupils. 494 Day pupils, including 180 in Pre-Prep (age 4 to 7).
Fees per term (2014–2015). Pre-Prep £4,107; Years 3–4 £4,373; Years 5–8 £4,747 (inclusive of lunch).

At Orley Farm School we are in the fortunate position of being a London day school blessed with boarding school acreage and facilities. Founded in 1850, the school has grown and developed to become one of the leading and largest co-educational prep schools in Greater London. Entry is by assessment at 4+ and at 11+. The academic journey of the children begins in Reception and ends when pupils transfer successfully to their senior schools – at the end of Year 6 for some of our girls and Year 8 for both girls and boys attending more traditional senior schools. Pupils enter a range of very impressive senior schools, including Eton, Godolphin and Latymer, Haberdashers' Aske's Boys and Girls, Harrow, John Lyon, Merchant Taylors', Northwood College, North London Collegiate, Notting Hill and Ealing, St Helen's, St Paul's, Westminster and Wycombe Abbey to name but a few. However, most impressively, Orley Farm has served over 41 senior schools over the past 5 years. We pride ourselves in finding the right future step for every child. Scholarships are regularly awarded to our senior pupils – 47 awards were offered in 2013–2014.

Success, happiness and future fulfilment start with a deep love of learning. So firmly do we believe in this philosophy, that we are investing £11 million in our facilities (a Music and Drama School, three state of the art Science Laboratories, a new Humanities department, a new Dining Hall and at the very heart, a cutting edge Library). Whilst some schools are binning books, we are buying more, and investing heavily in our environment to accompany a focused drive on study skills for life. Solid foundations are setting, not only in our new buildings, but also in the hearts and minds of a generation of young learners.

'Breadth, Balance & Excellence ...The Orley Farm Way!'

Alongside academic excellence, we pride ourselves on giving pupils experiences and opportunities that foster a lifetime and love of learning. All pupils are expected to contribute to the broader curriculum and a packed programme of Drama, Art and Music and Design & Technology. Over 200 individual music lessons take place each week and are supported by many musical groups and choirs. Productions, concerts and competitions offer all pupils the chance to showcase their talents and dedication in a variety of different settings.

Sport plays a very large part in our school life. We have over thirty six acres of land and full use is made of this in providing a venue for training and matches. Pupils will compete internally and externally in athletics, cricket, football, hockey, netball, rounders and rugby. In addition basketball, cross-country, fencing, fives, gymnastics and tennis also thrive through activities, clubs and matches. A Gym, Sports Hall and full-sized AstroTurf pitch enable our strong PE and Games Department to help our pupils develop their sporting talents.

This rich blend of curricular and co-curricular education is exemplified by our Expeditions Week. All pupils and staff from Year 4 and above travel to a variety of venues to spend a week extending their curriculum in a host of new challenges and adventures.

Orley Farm School is located in North West London close to Harrow on the Hill and is only twenty minutes on the Metropolitan Line from Baker Street Station.

Entry to this exciting place of learning is by assessment. For further details contact the Registrar, Mrs Julie Jago, on 0208 869 7634.

Charitable status. Orley Farm School is a Registered Charity, number 312637.

Orwell Park

Nacton, Ipswich, Suffolk IP10 0ER
Tel: 01473 659225
Fax: 01473 659822
email: headmaster@orwellpark.org
website: www.orwellpark.co.uk

Chairman of Governors: James Davison, BA

Headmaster: **Adrian Brown**, MA Cantab

Age Range. 2½–13.
Number of Pupils. Prep: 273: 121 Boarders (52 girls, 69 boys); 131 Day Pupils (51 girls, 80 boys). Pre-Prep: 61 (21 girls, 40 boys).
Fees per term (2014–2015). Prep School: Full and Weekly Boarders: £7,145 (Years 4–8), £6,435 (Year 3); Day Pupils: £5,570 (Years 4–8); £5,025 (Year 3). Pre-Prep Day Pupils: £26 per session (Nursery), £2,200 (Reception), £2,655 (Year 1), £3,395 (Year 2).
Flexible Boarding (ie 1–3 nights a week) is also possible – £40 per night.
Pupils are prepared for all Independent Senior Schools (local day and national boarding) via the Scholarship or Common Entrance Examinations (71 awards in the last 5 years). The school has a thriving Pre-Prep School, which is housed in a brand new, state-of-the-art building containing a large hall, four classrooms and music and ICT rooms.

The ratio of pupils to full-time staff is 10:1. The timetable is especially designed to be very flexible, with setting in most subjects, a potential scholars' set in Year 7 and a scholarship set in Year 8. The curriculum, both in and out of the classroom, is unusually broad. Children are encouraged to enjoy their learning and good learning support is offered. Thinking Skills and other opportunities for academic enrichment are also offered, including a weekly evening lecture programme to challenge the older children. There is a host of extra-curricular activities (just under 100) run by permanent or visiting staff.

About 90% of the school learn a musical instrument and the school has a number of orchestral and ensemble groups. Drama is strong and all children have opportunities to perform regularly in school productions. All children take part in annual Reading and Public Speaking Competitions.

The very large Georgian style building and 110 acres of grounds (sandy soil) on the banks of the River Orwell have the following special features: 21 recently refurbished themed dormitories, 22 bright classrooms with modern audio-visual equipment, beautiful Orangery used as an Assembly and Lecture Hall, 2 ICT suites, large Design Centre including metal, wood and plastic workshop plus electronics, mechanics, home economics, radio and model-making areas, Music Technology Room, Music Room and 40 Practice rooms, 2 Laboratories plus associated areas, Library and Resources Centre, Art Room including large pottery area and kiln, Observatory with 10' Refractor Telescope, Photographic Room, 17 Games pitches and one Astroturf pitch, one Multi-Use Games Area, large Sports Hall with permanent stage, Climbing Wall, Games Room, large heated Swimming Pool, 3 Squash Courts, 5 Hard Tennis Courts, Nine-hole Golf Course (approx 1,800 yds) and a purpose-built Assault Course.

Good sports coaching is given and fixtures are arranged in the following sports: Rugby, Hockey, Cricket, Netball, Rounders, Tennis, Athletics, Squash, Sailing, Swimming and Cross-Country Running. Emphasis is also placed on individual physical activities and we offer a wide range including Gymnastics, Fencing, Ballet, Canoeing, Sailing, Modern Dance, Karate, Riding and Clay Pigeon Shooting. The school owns its own canoes and dinghies.

The School aims to introduce the pupils to a broad and varied set of experiences and opportunities. It tries to see that every activity, whether academic, sporting, social or character building, is properly taught using the best possible facilities and that each is conducted in an atmosphere which is friendly but disciplined. Core values include courage, compassion, commitment, compromise and courtesy. Children are encouraged to feel comfortable taking risks and to be confident without being arrogant.

Charitable status. Orwell Park School is a Registered Charity, number 310481. It exists to provide education for boys and girls.

Our Lady's Abingdon Junior School

St John's Road, Abingdon, Oxfordshire OX14 2HB
Tel: 01235 523147
Fax: 01235 530387
email: officejs@olab.org.uk
website: www.olab.org.uk
Twitter: @OLAabingdon
Facebook: /OLAabingdon

Chairman of Governors: Mr Edward McCabe, MA Oxon, MBA

Headteacher: **Mr Brendan O'Neill**, BEd Hons, NPQH

Deputy Headteacher: Miss Brigid Meadows, GTCL Hons, PGCE

Age Range. 3–11 Co-educational.
Number of Pupils. 130.
Fees per term (2014–2015). Years 5 and 6 £3,563 Year 3 and 4 £2,969, Years 1 and 2 £2,565. Early Years (Nursery/Reception) £2,565 or £226.50 per session per term.
Staff: 16 full time and 5 part time. Specialist teaching in Mathematics, English, Science, French, PE, Art and Music.

Our Lady's Abingdon Junior School is a 'family' school with relationships firmly based on an ethos of care and dedication to the teaching of Christian values through which we aim to develop and foster a loving, caring and welcoming community. Children are at the very centre of all that we do at OLA and we encourage them to be confident, articulate members of the school community. The children are given an excellent all-round education and high academic standards are achieved. A love of learning and a positive attitude are both important elements of the way they are prepared for their future lives.

The 2010 Inspection Report was most complimentary, noting in particular that:

Pupils achieve excellent results in a range of extra-curricular activities, especially in sport.

Pupils make exceptional progress in their academic studies in relation to their ability profile.

Pupils' spiritual, moral, social and cultural development is excellent.

The outstanding pastoral care does much to ensure their safeguarding, and to foster their personal development and academic achievement.

In the EYFS Inspection of 2010 it was noted that:

Good provision enables the achievement of the aim to develop a loving, caring and welcoming community.

Teachers provide very well for the acquisition of essential skills and have forged very strong links with parents and carers.

The leadership and management of the setting are outstanding.

Children's achievements are considerable.

Location. Our Lady's Abingdon Junior School is part of the larger Our Lady's Abingdon, which is a 3–18 school located in the market town of Abingdon. The school occupies its own buildings adjacent to the Senior School and has the advantage of maintaining its own distinct character and ethos, whilst being able to share the extensive facilities and specialist staff on offer in the Senior School. (*See also Senior School entry in The Society of Heads section.*)

Facilities. Bright, spacious classrooms, a well-equipped library, a recently refurbished ICT suite and other specialist rooms provide a stimulating environment conducive to the teaching and learning of our pupils. Sports facilities include a number of tennis courts, a Junior School gymnasium, a sports field and a recently-refurbished 25-metre indoor swimming pool. The Junior School has the advantage of sharing a number of the Senior School facilities, including science laboratories and D&T rooms, as well as benefiting from shared teaching by Senior School staff. The Nursery area is a well-resourced provision on two floors – a peaceful and relaxed classroom area on the first floor and a purpose-built kitchen and "wet" area on the ground floor leading to a large and excitingly resourced outdoor garden area. This provides a gentle yet exciting introduction to school where the children learn through play and discovery to develop their social and learning skills.

Curriculum. Throughout the school we believe that all children have the right to experience a broad and balanced programme of subjects, which provides continuity and progression, and takes into account pupils' individual differences and needs. Planning is based on the requirements of the Primary Framework and encompasses all the core subjects of Mathematics, English and Science as well as a wide range of others, including MFL (French), RE, Music, History and Geography, PE/Games/Swimming, Art/Craft, PSHE and ICT. In the older year groups, much of this teaching is done by specialist staff. We also provide support for those children who have Special Educational Needs or for whom English is not the mother tongue.

Children in the EYFS setting follow the Early Years Foundation Stage curriculum and are assessed according to the EYFS profiles. We are members of the Local Authority Early Years Partnership which enables parents to receive a grant that can be offset against school fees.

Extra-curricular activities. The Junior School provides a wide programme of extra-curricular activities including drama, music, art, many forms of sport, ICT, D&T, cooking, creative play and Thinking Skills to name but a few. These clubs operate from 3.20 pm until 4.00 pm each evening and are available to all children from Reception through to Year Six. A supervised homework session is also available for those who require it. The School Council, which meets regularly each term, is an integral part of the way in which we involve the pupils in the decision making process in the school and the Eco-Council works very hard to ensure we have an awareness of our local environment and how we should care for it. The school has gained the Eco-Schools Silver Award and is working towards the "Green Flag".

Admissions. Our Lady's Abingdon Junior School considers for admission any pupil for whom it is able to provide an appropriate education. The main intake is at the age of 3 or 4, although pupils may be accepted into any Year Group where there are vacancies, at the discretion of the Headteacher. Pupils are selected on the basis of application, previous reports (where applicable) and parents' interview. Pupils may also be asked to visit the school on one or more days prior to the term in which the place is required. The school will wish to ascertain the previous attainment of pupils entering years Four, Five and Six and this is done by formal testing in Mathematics, English and Verbal Reasoning.

Charitable status. Our Lady's Abingdon Trustees Limited is a Registered Charity, number 1120372, and a Company Limited by Guarantee, registered in England and Wales, number 6269288.

Packwood Haugh

Ruyton XI Towns, Shrewsbury, Shropshire SY4 1HX
Tel: 01939 260217
Fax: 01939 262077
email: enquiries@packwood-haugh.co.uk
website: www.packwood-haugh.co.uk

Chairman of Governors: Mrs E Lewis

Headmaster: **C N Smith-Langridge**, BA Hons, QTS

Deputy Heads
N R Jones, BEd, CertEd
Mrs S Rigby, BA, PGCE, Dip SpLD

Age Range. Co-educational 4–13.
Number of Children. 208. Boarding: 57 boys, 24 girls. Day: 64 boys, 33 girls. Pre-Prep 30.
Fees per term (2014–2015). Boarding £6,738, Day £4,005–£5,340, Pre-Prep (Acorns) £2,450. No compulsory extras. Extras available on request.

Set in the heart of the Shropshire countryside, between Shrewsbury and Oswestry, Packwood Haugh is a co-educational day (4–13) and boarding (7–13) school which provides an excellent all-round education in a happy and caring environment. Children benefit from a wide range of academic, sporting, musical, artistic and cultural activities which encourage them to develop enquiring minds and an enthusiasm for learning. The school espouses an atmosphere of co-operation and understanding between pupils, staff and parents and encourages good manners and consideration towards others at all times.

Packwood has always striven for academic excellence; class sizes are small (average 13) and children are prepared for all the major independent schools across the country winning a number of academic, music, sports, art and all-rounder scholarships and awards each year. The school has a thriving pre-prep department (Packwood Acorns), which takes children from Reception.

The school's facilities are superb; a state-of-the-art sports hall allows for indoor tennis, badminton, indoor cricket, fencing and five-a-side football. Incorporated in the building are fully equipped CDT and Art departments and a linked computer suite. A 280-seat theatre is used for assemblies, concerts and drama productions throughout the year.

As well as the classrooms in the main school buildings and a purpose-built new block, there are three science laboratories and two further computer suites. Park House, which accommodates Packwood Acorns and girls' boarding, is a short distance from the main school building.

Packwood has a very strong sporting tradition. As well as a large area of grass playing fields, there is a newly resurfaced full-size, floodlit Astroturf pitch, an additional hard court area, 10 tennis courts, two squash courts, an indoor, heated swimming pool and a 9-hole golf course. In the winter terms the boys play rugby, football and hockey while the girls play netball, hockey and lacrosse. There is also cross country running on a course within the grounds. In the summer the boys play cricket, the girls play rounders and cricket, and all take part in tennis, athletics and swimming.

Additional facilities include a shooting range and an equestrian cross country course as well as an adventure playground.

Charitable status. Packwood Haugh is a Registered Charity, number 528411. It exists to provide day and boarding education for boys and girls from the age of 4 to 13.

Papplewick

Windsor Road, Ascot, Berks SL5 7LH
Tel: 01344 621488
Fax: 01344 874639
email: schoolsec@papplewick.org.uk
              registrar@papplewick.org.uk
website: www.papplewick.org.uk

Chairman of Board of Governors: Brigadier [Retd] A R E Hutchinson, JP

Headmaster: T W Bunbury, BA University College Durham, PGCE

Age Range. 6–13.
Number of Boys. 209: 95 Boarders, 114 day boys.
Fees per term (2014–2015). Boarders £8,650; Day Boys: £4,785 (Year 2), £6,265 (Years 3–4), £6,640 (Years 5–6).

Papplewick is a boys-only, day, weekly and full boarding school with an exceptional Scholarship record to top Independent Schools. Day boys do prep at school and come into board from the Summer term of Year 6. Happy, confident boys abound, and a modern, family-friendly approach to boarding is adopted. Two very popular daily transport services runs to/from West London, one from Chiswick and one from Brook Green. Situated between M3 and M4, the school boasts easy access to London airports.

Papplewick exists to provide a high-quality education where – for all our academic, cultural and sporting success – the happiness of the boys come first.

Charitable status. The Papplewick Educational Trust is a Registered Charity, number 309087.

The Paragon
Junior School of Prior Park College

Lyncombe House, Lyncombe Vale, Bath BA2 4LT
Tel: 01225 310837
Fax: 01225 427980
email: reception.paragon@thepriorfoundation.com
               rbraithwaite@thepriorfoundation.com
website: www.thepriorfoundation.com
Twitter: @ParagonBath
Facebook: The Prior Foundation

Chair of Governors: Mr Michael King

Headmaster: Mr Andrew Harvey, BA Hons, PGCE

Registrar: Mrs Rebecca Braithwaite

Age Range. 3–11 years.
Number of Pupils. 150 Boys, 120 Girls.
Fees per term (2014–2015). Juniors (Years 3–6) £3,040 including lunch; Infants (Years 1 & 2) £2,895 including lunch; Reception £2,730 including lunch. Nursery according to sessions. Sibling discounts available. Registration Fee (non-refundable) £100.

25 experienced and qualified teachers.

The Paragon is an independent, co-educational day school based in a beautiful Georgian house situated a mile from the centre of Bath. The school is set in eight acres of beautiful grounds with woodland, conservation areas, lawns and streams. It's the perfect 'outdoor classroom' and we use it right across the curriculum. We also enjoy regular access to the superb sport, science and drama facilities at our Senior School, Prior Park College.

Several factors help create the 'distinctive Paragon atmosphere'. One is undoubtedly the homely feel that comes from being based in a beautiful, former family home. Then there's our Christian ethos and strong pastoral care, as well as our belief that school at this age is about being stimulated and inspired, about laughter and spontaneity – in short, about having fun. We may be a private school and we certainly expect high standards of behaviour but we're anything but stuffy and grey.

We offer a broad curriculum taught in small classes by teachers with real passion. Academic life at The Paragon cultivates a love of learning and encourages independent and creative thinking. Our results are impressive. Our children consistently achieve well above the national average and many Year 6 children win senior school scholarships. Our facilities include a library, large gymnasium/dining hall, ICT suite, nursery with secure indoor and outdoor play areas, art studio, modern languages and music rooms.

Sport is particularly strong at The Paragon. Our sports teams take part, with considerable success, in a wide range of tournaments and festivals. We also offer a vast range of sports clubs that all children can join regardless of ability. Prior Park College offers us an indoor swimming pool, astroturf and grass pitches, tennis courts, athletics track, sports hall, and dance studio.

The Paragon's extra-curricular programme is extensive. Staff run more than 60 lunchtime and after-school clubs that range from pottery and chess to Mandarin and cross-country running. The school also enjoys an enviable reputation for Music. All children receive weekly music lessons from a specialist teacher. In addition, visiting instrumental teachers offer tuition in a wide range of instruments. We offer an excellent choice of extra-curricular music activities including the orchestra, two choirs, a wind band, brass group, flute choir, saxophone group and string ensemble.

The Paragon is proud of its consistently impressive academic results but we strive for much more than success in exams. We believe in developing the whole person – physically, spiritually, and emotionally as well as intellectually. As W B Yeats said: "Education is not filling a bucket but lighting a fire."

Charitable status. Prior Park Educational Trust is a Registered Charity, number 281242.

Parkside

The Manor, Stoke d'Abernon, Cobham, Surrey KT11 3PX
Tel: 01932 862749
Fax: 01932 860251
email: office@parkside-school.co.uk
website: www.parkside-school.co.uk
Twitter: @parksideprep
Facebook: /parksideprep

Chairman of Governors: G West

Headmaster: **M J Beach**, BA Hons, Adv DipEd, MA Ed

Deputy Head: Mrs H Sayer, BEd Hons

Age Range. Boys 2½–13. Co-educational Nursery.
Numbers. Day Boys 230, Pre-Prep 90, Nursery 85.
Fees per term (from January 2015). Day Boys £4,950, Pre-Prep £3,700, Nursery £415–£3,300.

Parkside was founded in 1879 and became a Charitable Trust in 1960. The School moved from East Horsley to its present site of over 40 acres in 1979, its centenary year. Since the move the Governors have implemented a continual development programme which has included a purpose-built, well-equipped Science Block, extending the main building to provide more Pre-Prep accommodation and a Music School with a large classroom and six practice rooms. An excellent Swimming Pool and Sports Hall complex with a stage for drama offers unrivalled facilities in the area. In addition, a £2m Classroom Block was built about 10 years ago to further enhance the facilities in the school. The Design Technology Department, Nursery and ICT suite are housed in a delightful Grade II Listed Barn which has been completely and skilfully refurbished to provide spacious, well-lit classrooms and workshops. A second Computer Room has been linked to the main network in recent years and the Art and Music facilities have been further expanded.

The school is large enough to be flexible and offer setting in major subjects yet small enough for each pupil to be known and treated as an individual. On average there are 15 pupils in a Set and the teacher : pupil ratio is 1:8. All teaching staff are highly qualified and there is a low staff turnover. Each boy is a member of a House and this helps to stimulate friendly competition for work points and many other inter-house contests.

The National Curriculum is followed to prepare all boys for entry to Senior Independent Schools by Common Entrance and Scholarship examinations. All boys pass to their first choice Senior Schools and our results in these examinations are impressive. Over the past few years many Academic, Art, Music and Sporting Scholarships have been won. Our curriculum is broad based and all boys are taught Art, Music, PE and Technology in addition to the usual Common Entrance subjects. There is a School Choir, a School Orchestra and several smaller musical groups, and over one third of the boys are receiving individual tuition in a wide variety of musical instruments. During the year, there are many opportunities for boys to perform in musical and dramatic productions.

The School has a fine sporting record and, over the past few years, many tournaments in different sports and at different age groups have been won. In addition, a number of boys have gone on to represent their County and Country in various sports. The main sports are football, hockey and cricket, but boys are able to take part in rugby, swimming, athletics, tennis, cross-country running, basketball and judo. An extensive Wednesday afternoon and After School Activity Programme (including supervised homework sessions) is available with over 40 different activities on offer, from gardening to kayaking, and table tennis to golf. Many boys have also represented the school at a high level in chess. The beautiful estate and the River Mole, which runs through the grounds, are also used to contribute to the all round education each pupil receives both in and out of the classroom.

Unusually for a Preparatory School, Parkside has a large and active Old Boys Association which runs many sporting and social events during the year.

Further details and a prospectus are available on application to the Headmaster's Secretary.

Charitable status. Parkside School is a Registered Charity, number 312041. It exists to provide education for children between the ages of 2½ and 13 years.

Pembridge Hall School
Alpha Plus Group

18 Pembridge Square, London W2 4EH
Tel: 020 7229 0121
email: contact@pembridgehall.co.uk
website: www.pembridgehall.co.uk

Headmaster: Mr Henry Keighley-Elstub, BA Hons, PGCE

Age Range. 4½–11.
Number of Girls. 413.
Fees per term (2014–2015). £6,170.

Girls are prepared for entry into independent London day schools and for the Independent Schools Common Entrance examination.

The school aims to create a happy and contented atmosphere in which girls may learn to work with concentration and enthusiasm. The curriculum is designed to give a thorough grounding in English and Mathematics. The girls' interest and desire to learn are stimulated through History, Geography, Religious Instruction, French, Science, Music, Drama, Art, ICT and Physical Education. A wide range of after-school activities is also on offer.

Pennthorpe School

Rudgwick, Horsham, West Sussex RH12 3HJ
Tel: 01403 822391
Fax: 01403 822438
email: enquiries@pennthorpe.com
website: www.pennthorpe.com
Twitter: @PennthorpeHead
Facebook: /PennthorpeSchool

Putting the fun into the fundamentals

Chairman of the Governors: Mr Mark Lucas

Headmaster: **Mr Matthew King**, BA Hons

Age Range. Co-educational 2–13.
Number of Pupils. 315 Day Pupils.
Fees per term (2014–2015). £546–£4,890.

Pennthorpe School in West Sussex lies close to the Surrey border, midway between Guildford and Horsham. The school is committed to high standards in all it does. Pennthorpe also recognises that putting the fun into the fundamentals of school life encourages the children to maximise their learning potential.

Pennthorpe has an outstanding record of 13+ Common Entrance successes, with regular academic, art, music and Performing Arts scholarships won to a number of senior schools in Sussex, Surrey and beyond. Many have also won all-rounder scholarships which reflects the school's commitment to developing its pupils into well-balanced youngsters and it is this outlook, along with the principle of putting the fun into the fundamentals, that drives Pennthorpe forward.

Developing all-rounders means offering choice, and from the very earliest stages when the two year-olds join the Pennthorpe Kindergarten, the emphasis is on breadth, both academic and outside the classroom.

The Pennthorpe Sports Department offers a wealth of sporting activities and competitive opportunities: soccer, netball, rugby, hockey, rounders, cricket and athletics are regular features on the termly fixtures calendar, while gymnastics, climbing, judo, tennis, basketball, archery and many others are available as part of the huge range of after-school options.

Pennthorpe is committed to the Arts. From the age of five, every pupil enjoys weekly Performing Arts lessons in our own dance and drama studio. There are also specialist-taught music lessons for all, including access to composition programs such as Garage Band in the iMac suite; these, along with four choirs, an orchestra, individual instrumental tuition, termly concerts and various productions involving every child in the school, provide many performing opportunities.

Pennthorpe also enjoys a cutting edge Art and Design Centre outstandingly equipped to fire the creative spirits of its pupils. The school's long-standing reputation for artistic excellence is now backed up by a 21-station iMac suite, photography studio and design room. With animation, web design, advanced programming and photo editing all embedded within the curriculum, all children can find their own ways to express their imaginations.

Complementing and building upon the classroom work, Pennthorpe's Flexiday programme of after-school activities aims to bring even more chances for every boy and girl to find their strengths and shine. Whether it is developing their computer skills, throwing a pot, scaling the climbing wall or tapping to the rhythm in the dance studio, there's something for everybody.

A continuous programme of major capital investment is under way. A recently completed Pre-Prep building with 6 new classrooms, a state-of-the-art kindergarten and large multi-purpose hall has transformed the academic life of our younger pupils. In addition to this, our new Art and Design Centre opened its doors in February 2012 and plans are already laid for a new Performing Arts and Music Centre. This is a school that never stands still!

If you would like to see how your child could thrive in this busy, happy and successful school, ask for a prospectus, visit our website (details above) and then book a visit: the Headmaster and all the staff and children will make you very welcome. There are two Open Mornings each term and the Headmaster is also happy to welcome parents for individual visits at any time.

Charitable status. Pennthorpe School is a Registered Charity, number 307043. It exists to provide an excellent education for boys and girls and to benefit the community.

Perrott Hill

North Perrott, Crewkerne, Somerset TA18 7SL
Tel: 01460 72051
Fax: 01460 78246

email: headmaster@perrotthill.com
website: www.perrotthill.com

Chairman of Governors: Lord Bradbury

Headmaster: Mr R J Morse, BEd Hons

Age Range. 3–13.
Number of Pupils. 134 boys and 93 girls, of whom 41 are full, weekly or flexi boarders.
Fees per term (2014–2015). Boarders: £6,920 (full), £5,640 (weekly); Day pupils £1,985–£4,850.

Perrott Hill is a co-educational day and boarding school and is registered as an Educational Trust. Set in 25 acres of beautiful grounds in the heart of the countryside, near Crewkerne on the Somerset/Dorset border, it is served by excellent road and rail networks.

Perrott Hill is a thriving country preparatory school where children settle quickly and learn in confidence. Class sizes are small, with an average of 15 children to a form; the pupils being streamed from Year 5 onwards. Staff are dedicated and highly qualified. Facilities now include an all-weather sports area, a purpose-built sports hall, a theatre, a DT/art school, a computer centre, a music school, games fields, swimming pool and woodland area.

The Montessori Nursery and Pre-Prep are housed within the converted stable courtyard next to the main school buildings, which gives the younger children their own safe, secure environment whilst allowing them to take advantage of the grounds and facilities of the Prep School.

Music, Drama and Art are taught within the timetable alongside core curriculum subjects. The choir and orchestra perform at charity concerts, in competitions and school functions. There are drama productions every term.

Teaching is class-based until Year 5 and subject-based in the upper school, where all lessons are taught by specialist teachers. French, Music, IT and PE, however, are taught by specialists throughout the school.

Each child, boarding or day, has his or her own pastoral and academic tutor, while the welfare of the boarders is supervised by Mr and Mrs Finch, the house master and house mistress. They are ably assisted by a dedicated and enthusiastic boarding staff (twelve of whom live on site).

Sport is played every day, and matches take place on most Wednesdays as well as on Saturdays for the senior part of the school. Emphasis is placed upon skills and team work, as well as the achievement of results. Games played include rugby, football, hockey, netball, cricket, tennis, rounders, swimming and cross-country running. The school takes part in national events, such as the IAPS Ski Championships, IAPS Sailing Regatta and the National Small Schools Rugby Sevens. Optional extras include fencing, carpentry, archery, karate, horse riding, ballet, speech and drama, cookery, Spanish, golf and craft.

Perrott Hill combines extremely high standards of academic and pastoral care. In the last 4 years the 117 children leaving school at the end of Year 8 have secured 63 awards to senior schools and all children were offered a place at the school of their choice. Scholarships have been awarded for academic, artistic, sporting, dramatic, musical, equine and all-round ability. Academic, music, sport, art, drama and all-rounder Scholarships are offered annually in February to children in Years 3–6.

The combination of countryside, space, a family atmosphere and a forward-looking academic programme creates an ideal environment for children to thrive both academically and in their leisure pursuits – we warmly invite you to come and see the school in action.

Charitable status. Perrott Hill School Trust Limited is a Registered Charity, number 310278. It exists to give high quality education to boys and girls.

The Perse Pelican Nursery and Pre-Preparatory School

92 Glebe Road, Cambridge CB1 7TD
Tel: 01223 403940
Fax: 01223 403941
email: pelicanschoolsec@perse.co.uk
website: www.perse.co.uk

Chairman of Governors: Sir David J Wright, GCMG, LVO, MA

Headmistress: **Mrs S Waddington**, BSc, MA

Age Range. 3–7.
Number of Pupils. 153.
Ethos. Our aim is to ensure that the children in our care are sociable, rounded, confident and inquisitive. We are proud of our broad, challenging, enticing curriculum and the spirit with which our pupils approach their learning.

Admissions. The main entry point for the Pelican is Nursery, which is for children who are three years old by 1 September in the year of entry. There are only a few spaces available for extra children in Reception. Selection takes place in the January of the year of intended entry.

History. The buildings of the Nursery and Pre-Prep began life in 1911 as a boarding house for the Upper School. The School has been sympathetically extended inside and out, so that it provides exceptional space and excellent facilities, yet still feels like a home from home.

School life. Classroom routines are quickly established from the start of a child's time at the Pelican, and from day one they feel they belong. Every class benefits from a full-time teaching assistant who works alongside the teacher. This staffing ratio is used flexibly to ensure the individual needs of each child are met. There is one member of staff to every eight children in Nursery, and one to ten in all other years. Dance, Games, French and Music are all taught by specialist teachers. An inclusive choir is open to everyone in Years 1 and 2 and a range of music ensembles are formed each year appropriate to the needs of the children in those year groups at the time. Our musicians regularly perform at the MFY Festival, both regionally and nationally.

Children use 'Pelican Behaviour', our child-friendly guidelines used to manage behaviour within school. In all areas of school life they learn to share, negotiate and collaborate. Every child's achievements, great and small, are celebrated in a variety of ways. Excellent work or a significant achievement outside school may be awarded a Golden Brick in our Wall of Achievements, and celebrated by taking Golden Tea with the Headmistress. The children relish challenge and aim high, knowing that there is always someone to support them. We work in partnership with parents to nurture children's interests and provide opportunities to develop their potential. Pupils begin to acquire essential skills through play, topic work and a wide range of experiences and activities.

A rounded education. Regular school trips bring learning to life and being close to the centre of Cambridge the School is able to take advantage of trips to local museums and wildlife parks.

Out of school care. Children may be dropped at school from 8 am and may stay until 5.30 pm each day. We run an extended range of after school clubs catering to all tastes, from ballet to science, chess to football, and drama to gymnastics. In addition, children may attend our own holiday club, known as Club Pelican, which runs for 6 weeks of the year: four weeks in the summer holidays and one week in each of the Christmas and Lent holidays.

Moving on. By the end of Year 2, children are ready to move onto the Prep with confidence and enthusiasm. Their move is gradual and carefully managed.

Fees per term (2014–2015). Full-time (Reception, Years 1 and 2) £3,880. Part-time Nursery (five sessions per week) £2,180. Additional Nursery sessions: £36 per session. Nursery children attend a minimum of five sessions per week (two of which must be afternoons) but may attend up to 10 sessions per week.

Charitable status. The Perse School is a charitable company limited by guarantee (company number 5977683, registered charity number 1120654) registered in England and Wales whose registered office is situated at The Perse School, Hills Road, Cambridge CB2 8QF.

The Perse Preparatory School

Trumpington Road, Cambridge CB2 8EX
Tel: 01223 403920
Fax: 01223 403921
email: prephmsec@perse.co.uk
website: www.perse.co.uk

Chairman of Governors: Sir David J Wright, GCMG, LVO, MA

Head: **James Piper**, BA Hons, PGCE

Age Range. 7–11.
Number of Pupils. 281.
Ethos. The Prep aims to provide the best all-round education for the children of Cambridgeshire and its surrounding area, providing a firm foundation for educational success. We help our children to reach their academic potential and encourage their intellectual curiosity to flourish. They thrive on challenges both inside and outside the classroom. Pupils at the Prep benefit from being a part of the wider Perse community. Their educational experience, in an environment where academic and pastoral structures are dovetailed, ensures continuity between the schools.

Admissions. The main entry point to the Prep is Year 3 (7+). Admissions to Years 4, 5 and 6 is dependent on availability of places. Entrance tests assess the applicant's abilities in English, Maths and reasoning, and a reference from the child's current school is also sought. Selection for all year groups takes place in mid-January of the year of intended entry.

Facilities. The Perse Prep School is a co-educational preparatory school in Cambridge. It is set in spacious, mature parkland just outside the city centre. The School is proud of its specialist facilities which include outstanding classrooms, a purpose-built art and design technology suite, science laboratories, a drama studio, first-rate games fields and an all-weather pitch.

Educational success. The School aims to achieve high academic standards and a wide range of achievements in cultural, sporting and artistic endeavours. The depth of academic ability throughout the School allows intellectual curiosity to flourish and pupils thrive on challenges both inside and outside the classroom. Enjoyment of learning, mutual respect and the celebration of achievement characterise life at the Prep. As a result children become independent, confident and responsible. Pupils enjoy each other's success and have the quiet confidence to be at ease with new ideas. As they grow the School aims to develop the qualities of reliability, consideration for others, good manners and self-discipline which they need to complement their academic success. Pupils experience the enthusiasm of teachers passionate about their subjects and who inspire rather than spoon-feed. Our first-rate subject specialists have the knowledge that enables them to stretch bright children while finding creative ways to explain complex concepts. The time between the ages of seven and 11 is a precious stage when pupils begin to flourish; their confidence as learners grows and they begin to discover the excitement of study.

A supportive environment. Form teachers keep in close contact with parents and the Head of Pastoral Care is available to pupils, parents, and staff at all times to ensure the general well-being of pupils.

A rounded education. Excellent facilities enable us to offer a wide variety of sporting and recreational pursuits. The games programme (football, rugby, cricket, netball, rounders, athletics, tennis and hockey) is designed to encourage all pupils to enjoy games and physical exercise. Music plays an important part in the curriculum and wider life of the School. The majority of pupils learn a musical instrument, and there are choirs, orchestras and numerous instrumental groups, where there are many opportunities for the children to perform publicly. After-school activities are an important part of the Prep experience and it is through these extra-curricular interests that many of our pupils develop lasting interests. Regular activities at lunchtime or after school include media clubs in which students can write for the Perse Prep Paper or direct a film; creative clubs such as art, poetry and cinema; sports clubs such as running, multi-sports, dance, kung fu and table tennis; and clubs in which to develop thinking, among them chess and countdown.

Moving on. The School plans carefully for a smooth transition to the Upper. Year 5 and 6 pupils spend days on the Upper site as part of their subject learning, helping to prepare them for the move up.

Fees per term (2014–2015). £4,506.

Bursaries. Means-tested bursaries are available for families of limited means, ranging from 5% to 100% of annual tuition fees.

Charitable status. The Perse School is a charitable company limited by guarantee (company number 5977683, registered charity number 1120654) registered in England and Wales whose registered office is situated at The Perse School, Hills Road, Cambridge CB2 8QF.

Pilgrims Pre-Preparatory School

Brickhill Drive, Bedford MK41 7QZ
Tel: 01234 369555
Fax: 01234 369556
email: enquiries@pilgrims-school.org.uk
website: www.pilgrims-school.info

Chair of Governors: Mrs S Clark

Headteacher: **Mrs J Webster**, BEd Hons, EYPS

Co-educational Day School.
Age Range. 3 months–7 years.
Number of Pupils. 388: 199 Boys, 189 Girls.
Fees per term (2014–2015). £1,170–£2,865.

Pilgrims Pre-Preparatory School is the newest addition to the Harpur Trust family of schools. We opened in 2000 in spacious, purpose-built accommodation with extensive playing fields. The majority of our children continue their education within the three other Harpur Trust schools.

Pilgrims is a vibrant, stimulating environment where we pride ourselves on providing a rich and varied curriculum that offers plenty of opportunities to develop each child's self-esteem and confidence, whilst giving the support to enable them to become independent learners and to achieve their full potential. We use the EYFS and the best of the National Curriculum, developing the curriculum further to meet the needs of our children. In addition, we take advantage of our experienced staff and excellent facilities to provide specialist weeks on a range of topics including Healthy

Heart week, Art Week and Science Week. Good manners are valued and celebrated throughout the school.

Children are taught in small classes with specialist teachers. Emphasis is placed upon English and Mathematics to ensure that solid foundations are laid for success across the whole curriculum. School trips are arranged to a variety of local museums, wildlife centres and villages to further enrich the children's learning.

Academic standards are high and children who are identified as gifted and able are offered specific tuition in small groups to ensure their needs are met.

We have a strong music department with a successful choir and orchestra who regularly take part in the Bedfordshire Music Festival. Specialist music teaching begins in the toddler room and continues throughout the school. Individual instrumental tuition is available from Year 1 with over 60% of children learning one or more instruments.

We encourage the children to enjoy a healthy school life. Our menus are planned in conjunction with a nutritionist, and the children have a range of homemade biscuits, fruit and crudités provided for snacks each day. Sport is most important within the school; in addition to gymnastics, dance and outdoor games, from 2 years of age the children use our indoor swimming pool every week, and from Nursery they swim twice each week. Our tennis academy regularly produces county players.

The school is open 46 weeks a year with holiday clubs running outside term time. We also offer a huge range of after-school clubs and a breakfast club. Parents are welcomed into the school and work in partnership with the staff to create a warm, caring, purposeful and fun environment in which our children thrive.

Charitable status. Pilgrims Pre-Preparatory School is part of the Harpur Trust which is a Registered Charity, number 1066861.

The Pilgrims' School

Winchester, Hampshire SO23 9LT
Tel: 01962 854189
Fax: 01962 843610
email: admissions@pilgrims-school.co.uk
         info@pilgrims-school.co.uk
website: www.thepilgrims-school.co.uk

Chairman of Governors: The Very Revd James Atwell, Dean of Winchester

Headmaster: **T Burden**, MA Oxon

Age Range. Boys 4–13.
Number of Pupils. 200 Boys (87 boarders/weekly boarders, 120 day boys). Pre-Prep: 54.
Fees per term (2014–2015). Boarders £7,225, Day boys £5,725, Pre-Prep £3,290.

Preparing boys for a broad portfolio of independent schools, with a significant number moving to Winchester College each year. Cathedral Choristers and Winchester College Quiristers are educated at the school and receive scholarships and bursaries up to the value of the full boarding fee together with free tuition in one musical instrument. All boys whether musical or not receive excellent academic and musical tuition, and the sporting tradition is equally strong. The school is noted for its happy family atmosphere, and a major recent building programme has ensured the highest standard of facilities possible. All enquiries about the school or singing auditions should be addressed to the Registrar.

Charitable status. The Pilgrims' School is a Registered Charity, number 1091579.

Pinewood

Bourton, Shrivenham, Wiltshire SN6 8HZ
Tel: 01793 782205
Fax: 01793 783476
email: office@pinewoodschool.co.uk
website: www.pinewoodschool.co.uk

Headmaster: **Philip Hoyland**, BEd Exeter

Deputy Head: C J Acheson-Gray, BEd

Age Range. 2–13.
Number of Pupils. 400 Boys and Girls (67 flexi boarders, 52 weekly boarders) of which Nursery and Pre-Prep: 119.
Fees per term (2014–2015). Day £2,590–£5,285 inclusive, with no compulsory extras. Weekly Boarding supplement: £1,290.

Pinewood is set in 84 acres of rolling countryside. The School offers a quality, family-based environment where children are encouraged to think for themselves and a strong emphasis is placed on self-discipline, manners, trust and selflessness. Resources include a purpose-built Music School and Science Labs, a flourishing Pre-Prep and Nursery, Art and Design Workshops, Research and Reference Library, ICT Rooms, Astroturf and a state-of-the-art Sports Hall, opened in May 2014.

Excellent academic results are achieved through a mixture of traditional and forward-thinking teaching within a happy, friendly and stimulating learning atmosphere. Outside trips are frequent and visiting speakers prominent. Music, art and drama are encouraged.

Sport is keenly coached and matches are played at all levels on our picturesque playing fields, which incorporate a nine-hole golf course. There is a wide range of activities and clubs both for day children and, in the evening, for boarders.

Pinewood is a school where staff, parents and children work together to find and realise the potential in every child.

Exit Schools: Marlborough, Radley, Cheltenham College, St Edward's Oxford, Cheltenham Ladies, Stowe, Downe House, St Mary's Calne, Dean Close, Monkton Combe, Tudor Hall.

Charitable status. Pinewood is a Registered Charity, number 309642. It exists to provide high quality education for boys and girls.

Plymouth College Preparatory School

St Dunstan's Abbey, The Millfields, Plymouth, Devon PL1 3JL
Tel: 01752 201352
Fax: 01752 831929
email: prepschool@plymouthcollege.com
          jlearmouth@plymouthcollege.com
website: www.plymouthcollege.com

Chairman of Governors: D R Woodgate, BSc, MBA

Headmaster: **C D M Gatherer**, BA Keele

Age Range. 3–11 Co-educational.
Number of Pupils. 232.
Fees per term (2014–2015). Infant Department: Kindergarten £2,360, Reception £2,470, Years 1 & 2 £2,860. Junior Department: Years 3–4 £3,050, Years 5–6 £3,200.

Plymouth College Preparatory School is a co-educational school for children from 3–11 years. The school was founded in 1877 and is within a few minutes' drive of Plymouth College senior school.

The primary academic aim of the school is to prepare children for entry to Plymouth College at the age of 11, ensuring that they are articulate and have taken full advantage of an education designed to stimulate the development of each child both intellectually and socially.

There are thirty full-time and three part-time members of staff, including specialist teachers in Mathematics, English, Science, Information Technology, Design Technology, Geography, History, Art, Music and French. There is a wide range of extra-curricular activities.

There are two libraries, a computer room, a well-equipped laboratory, art room, theatre, music room and a sports centre.

Further information and application forms can be obtained from the Registrar, direct on 01752 831911, and appointments to view the school are welcomed.

Charitable status. Plymouth College is a Registered Charity, number 1105544. It exists to help children fulfil their wish to achieve a higher standard of education.

Pocklington Prep School (formerly Lyndhurst School)
The Prep School of Pocklington School Foundation

West Green, Pocklington, York, East Riding of Yorkshire YO42 2NH
Tel: +44 (0)1759 321228
Fax: +44 (0)1759 306366
email: enquiry@pocklingtonprepschool.com
website: www.pocklingtonschool.com
Twitter: @PockSchool

Chairman of Governors: Mr C M Oughtred, MA, DL

Headmaster: I D Wright, BSc Hons, PGCE, NPQH

Age Range. 4–11 co-educational.
Number of Pupils. 186:101 Boys, 85 Girls.
Fees per term (2014–2015). Day Pupils £2,792–£3,601; Full Boarders £6,551; 5-day Boarders £6,081.

Pocklington Prep School (formerly Lyndhurst School) is the Prep School of the Pocklington School Foundation, a supportive and caring community that has been thriving in the heart of rural Yorkshire for 500 years. The school shares a 65-acre rural site on the edge of the market town of Pocklington with Pocklington School. This gives even the youngest pupils (as appropriate) access to specialist teaching facilities for sports (astroturf pitches), music and the arts (purpose-built theatre) and plenty of space to play. Classes at Pocklington Prep School are intentionally small, ensuring good individual support.

Good road and bus services from York and Hull are supplemented by the school's own minibus services. Full and flexible and casual boarding options are available. Junior boarders live in modern single-sex houses. Boarders have a dedicated programme of weekend and after-school activities in addition to the normal school calendar.

Inspired for Life. We aim to give our pupils the care and encouragement they need to flourish into confident boys and girls who are inspired for lifelong learning so that when our pupils move on to their senior schools they are well prepared for the challenges ahead.

The formal curriculum reflects the new Primary School Review with the emphasis on creativity and enjoyment. Pocklington Prep School offers a secure and happy environment in which pupils are actively encouraged to express their natural talents and curiosity while developing their confidence in the core skills of reading, writing and numeracy to meet the challenges ahead.

Core subjects include English, maths and science but history, geography, art and design technology, music, ICT, religious studies and Modern Languages also play a prominent part, together with swimming, PE and Games. Initially forms are balanced in ability, with teachers taking care to ensure that individual children can progress at a pace according to need. From Year 5 onwards pupils are taught in ability groups in maths and English.

A wide range of sporting, cultural and other activities supports the curriculum. Pupils visit an outdoor education centre in the Yorkshire Dales, take part in fieldwork and leadership/team challenges and make full use of the excellent attractions in the area.

Games played include rugby, hockey, football, netball, cricket, tennis and rounders – with clubs and teams in athletics, swimming and trampoline also. PE and swimming form part of the weekly timetable for all pupils.

House competitions include music, art, drama, chess, creative writing, general knowledge and sport.

Extra activities take place at lunchtimes and after school and include art, computing, choir, drama, chess, orchestra, trampoline, language clubs, swimming and team coaching.

Pocklington Prep School has a strong musical tradition with a successful choir and orchestra. Individual music tuition takes place throughout the age range. Full use is made of the Theatre to perform in concerts, plays, sketches and musicals – some jointly with the senior school.

Entry Requirements: Entry to the Pre-Prep at 4+ is by informal interview and assessment. All pupils internal and external are assessed at 7+ to ensure that they are progressing in line with their peer group. Nearly all pupils go on to Pocklington School at the end of Year 6 (age 11+). Progress is automatic for Prep School applicants provided there are no concerns about a child's behaviour or ability, which have previously been communicated to parents prior to the date of the entrance assessment. New entrants are required to sit the Pocklington School 11+ Entrance Examination.

Charitable status. The Pocklington School Foundation is a Registered Charity, number 529834.

Port Regis

Motcombe Park, Shaftesbury, Dorset SP7 9QA

Tel:	01747 857800
Fax:	01747 857810
email:	office@portregis.com
website:	www.portregis.com
Twitter:	@PortRegisSchool
Facebook:	/PortRegis

Chairman of the Governors: Mrs J Nelson

Headmaster: Benedict H Dunhill, BA Hons

Deputy Head (Pastoral): William Brooks, BA Hons Durham

Deputy Head (Academic): James Webb, MA Oxford, MSc, PGCE, MLitt

Age Range. 3–13.
Number of Pupils. Boarders: 141 (Boys 94, Girls 47); Day Boarders: 164 (Boys 109, Girls 55).
Fees per term (2014–2015). Boarders £7,250–£8,100 (no compulsory extras); Day Boarders £2,890–£5,999 (meals included). Weekly Boarding is available.

Port Regis is highly regarded for its academic, sporting and extra-curricular successes, and these are clearly important aspects of what the school sets out to do. However, none of these could be achieved without happy and well-motivated children, and for Benedict Dunhill (Port Regis's

Headmaster), this is the most fundamental aspect of the education the school provides.

Port Regis is a well-established prep school that aims to equip its children not only with good grades and important academic skills, but also with qualities of character to see them through their lives beyond school. The school's most significant goal is that Port Regis children should learn how to acquire a perspective on life, allowing them to feel at ease with themselves, their fellows, their teachers and their families. It focuses in particular on five values: **Hospitality, Perseverance, Reconciliation, Generosity and Respect**. These values for life are put at the heart of everything that the school does.

The school is located in 150 acres of magnificent parkland in the stunning Dorset countryside; a beautiful campus with superior buildings which are second to none in the prep school world. Extensive ancient woodland with nature trails sits alongside formal and kitchen gardens, lawns, several ponds and a lake, so that the children can enjoy the space and freedom of the grounds. There are also 35 acres of games pitches, a nine-hole (18 tees) golf course, hockey pitch (Astroturf), hard tennis and netball courts, a 25m indoor swimming pool, a rifle range and an indoor sports complex, which includes two sports halls (including badminton and squash courts). These outstanding facilities enable the school to find an interest for every child, and the school day allows plenty of opportunities for these to be pursued. An equestrian centre is conveniently situated close to the School.

The main building is an Elizabethan-style mansion with elegant oak-panelled reception rooms and a splendid galleried Hall with a large feature-fireplace. Younger pupils are accommodated in bright, cosy dormitories in the Mansion House, while the older pupils enjoy the comfort of splendid senior boarding houses. The boys' house has 60 individual study-bedrooms, each provided with its own washbasin, desk, cupboard and drawers. There are also two common rooms and separate kitchen areas as well as a generous provision of showers, baths and toilets. This house complements the senior girls' house, similar in design with 48 study-bedrooms.

A Pre-Prep and Nursery opened in September 1993 in the secure and beautiful environment of the Motcombe Park grounds with full use of the Prep School's facilities.

The school's enviable campus attracts the best teaching staff from all over the country, encompassing the entire spectrum, from the wise and experienced to the newly qualified, each with their own teaching style. All children can find teachers in the school who make them tick, and they will come across them in the classroom, in hobbies or on the games field. Most staff live either on the estate or in the main building, so personal guidance and a family atmosphere has been created. Port Regis is extremely proud of its 100% Common Entrance success record and the high number of scholarships and awards won to senior schools every year. Learning Support is available for children with mild-to-moderate specific learning difficulties.

Extensive opportunities are provided for Music (about three-quarters of the School learn an instrument), Drama (there are up to six productions a year), and Art (in a wide choice of media), with Woodwork, Electronics, Riding, .22 Rifle Shooting, Karate, Gymnastics and Canoeing included in a list of over 70 hobby options. Major team games are Rugby, Hockey, Soccer, Netball, Cricket and Rounders. Inter-school, county and national standard competitions are entered. Home and abroad expeditions take place.

Children who join between the ages of three and nine are looked after by their form teacher. Once they join the C form (Year 6), children choose, with guidance, a member of staff to be their personal Tutor. The Tutor's role is to encourage and assist his or her tutees in all aspects of school life so that parents can be confident that there is a dedicated adult who takes a personal interest in their child's well-being at all times. The Tutor is readily available to talk to parents about any matter, pastoral or academic. This system is closely modelled on a senior school system and is rare in prep schools, but the school believes it is the key to the happiness of the child and the success of the pastoral care at Port Regis.

The high standard of boarding provision is an impressively strong feature of the school, which explains why well over two thirds of the boys and girls choose to board (awarded 'outstanding' by Ofsted following their recent boarding inspection). The school was inspected by the Independent Schools Inspectorate (ISI) in June 2014 and was rated 'Excellent' in every single judgement.

Benedict Dunhill and his wife Elizabeth welcome visitors to the school at any time and very much enjoy showing parents around the school. Open Mornings take place in March and October every year and include tours of the school with pupils, a welcome address and question and answer session with the Headmaster and other key members of staff.

Academic, Music, Gymnastic, Sport and All-Rounder entrance scholarships may be awarded annually. The School also has a wealth of experience in dealing with HM Services Families (approx 15% of pupils) and offers special awards to children of HM Services Families.

Charitable status. Port Regis School Limited is a Registered Charity, number 306218. It exists to provide an all-round education to the highest standard for boys and girls from the ages of 3 to 13.

The Portsmouth Grammar Junior School

High Street, Portsmouth, Hampshire PO1 2LN
Tel: 023 9236 4219
Fax: 023 9236 4263
email: juniorschool@pgs.org.uk
website: www.pgs.org.uk

Chairman of the Governors: B S Larkman, BSc, ACIB

Headmaster of the Junior School: **P S Hopkinson**, BA, PGCE

Deputy Headmaster: J Ashcroft, BSc, PGCE
Assistant Headmistress: Mrs P Giles, BA, PGCE
Head of Nursery: Mrs L Johnson, BEd, PG Dip Early Years

Age Range. 4–11. Nursery: 2½–4.
Number of Day Pupils. 252 boys, 169 girls.
Fees per term (2014–2015). Reception, Years 1 and 2: £2,930; Years 3 and 4: £3,089; Years 5 and 6: £3,249. (Fees quoted include direct debit discount.)

The Junior School is an integral part of The Portsmouth Grammar School under the general direction of the Governors and Headmaster. Children from 4–9 years are educated within bright and spacious classrooms that occupy a discreet space on the whole school site. The 9–11 year old pupils are educated in the historic original school building which stands in splendid isolation in close proximity to the whole school site.

The Junior School's organisation is distinct under its own Headmaster, with 31 full-time, 15 part-time members of staff, and 18 learning support assistants.

The main three-form entry is at 4+ with an additional class formed in KS2. Pupils leave at 11 years, the majority moving on to The Portsmouth Grammar Senior School.

Whilst emphasis is placed on literacy and numeracy there is a broad curriculum which includes; Science, Geography, History, Religious Studies, ICT, Modern Foreign Languages, Music, Design Technology, Art, Drama, Physical Education, Games and PSHE. In addition, many pupils receive tuition in a wide range of musical instruments.

The school also provides a wide choice of co-curricular activities to all pupils. Currently over 30 different club activities are offered. The most recent innovations are a week's sailing instruction for all pupils in Year 4 and a French Trip for all pupils in Year 6. There are specialist rooms for Art, DT, Music and Drama, plus a Science Laboratory and two Information Technology Centres. An innovative string scheme enables all Year 3 pupils to experience a free term's tuition in learning the violin or cello and a brass scheme offers a similar opportunity in Year 4.

Games include Association and Rugby Football, Netball, Hockey, Rounders, Cricket, Athletics, Tennis and Swimming. The Junior School has its own learner swimming pool and uses the Grammar School's excellent 16 acre playing fields at Hilsea, which include a Floodlit astro turf pitch. It also has access to the Grammar School's Sports Hall, Music School and Theatre.

In September 2001 a Nursery School was opened offering up to 60 places in any one session. The architect designed building provides the children, aged from two years six months, with exciting opportunities to learn through play and exploration. All staff have early years specialism, the Head of Nursery being a fully qualified primary teacher with Early Years expertise. The Nursery School offers provision for 45 weeks a year.

Charitable status. The Portsmouth Grammar School is a Registered Charity, number 1063732. It exists to provide education for boys and girls.

Pownall Hall

Carrwood Road, Wilmslow, Cheshire SK9 5DW
Tel: 01625 523141
Fax: 01625 525209
email: headmaster@pownallhallschool.co.uk
website: www.pownallhallschool.co.uk

Chair of Governors: Mrs Eileen MacAulay

Head: **Mr D Goulbourn**, BA Hons, PGCE Distinction

Age Range. 2–11 Co-educational.
Number of Boys and Girls. 200 (Day Children)
Fees per term (2014–2015). £2,450–£2,875.

Pownall Hall, a preparatory day school for children aged 2 to 11 and set in its own beautiful and extensive grounds, has been established for over 100 years. It is situated on the north-western side of Wilmslow, 12 miles from Manchester and within easy reach of motorway, rail and air travel.

The school has highly-trained teaching staff, who prepare children for the Entrance Examinations to the Independent Day schools in the area. A thorough grounding is given in all academic subjects extending well beyond the confines of the National Curriculum. An excellent mixture of traditional and modern techniques is used through the implementation of cutting-edge technology in and around every classroom. In Key Stage 2 each major subject has specialist teaching staff and subject rooms including a fully-equipped Science Laboratory, Maths, English, Information Technology and French rooms and, in addition, a computer-aided Library. French and German are taught from the age of two.

Pownall Hall School has two pre-school years with children entering the Nursery from the age of 2 and transferring to Kindergarten at the age of 3. From here the pupils then enter Reception and go through the school to Year 6 by which point the school will have guided parents as to where best for their child to continue their education at the age of 11.

At Pownall Hall there is an excellent staff to pupil ratio throughout the school, ensuring that pastoral care is of a very high level and also supporting the learning of children of all abilities, in conjunction with a specialist SEND provision. Children are taught in small class sizes, gaining from the individual attention they receive.

Great importance is attached to Sport, Music and Drama in order to develop the rounded education that allows all children to achieve, wherever their ability lies. The school has its own well-equipped theatre where all children perform on stage during the year. Music is offered as part of the curriculum and also additionally through a full range of peripatetic teaching staff, providing chances for the children to perform in and outside school. As well as subject specialist rooms with an outstanding range of specialist equipment, the implementation of mobile technology and 1–1 devices for both staff and children provides opportunity for outstanding teaching and learning across the school.

The facilities for sport are very impressive with the school having its own extensive grounds, alongside a fully-equipped Sports Hall and both outdoor and indoor facilities for Netball, Tennis and Football.

All children experience outdoor learning, with day and residential trips arranged as well as utilising our on-site woods for free-flow teaching and learning at all ages. Children in Years 4 to 6 also experience outdoor pursuits at a range of well-equipped sites which enhance their learning experiences. There is an extensive provision of co-curricular clubs, complementing our out-of-hours Breakfast Club and After School Care. Holiday Club runs on site throughout the year.

The school received an outstanding Full inspection Report in 2011 and an outstanding EYFS Inspection in 2014.

Charitable status. Pownall Hall School is a Registered Charity, number 525929. It exists to provide education for boys and girls, aged 2–11 yrs.

The Prebendal School

52–55 West Street, Chichester, West Sussex PO19 1RP
Tel: 01243 772220
Fax: 01243 780963
email: office@prebendalschool.org.uk
website: www.prebendalschool.org.uk

Chairman of Governors: The Acting Dean of Chichester

Headmaster: **Mr T R Cannell**, MA Ed Man, BEd Winchester

Age Range. 3–13.
Number of Pupils. 195 pupils in total which includes 63 in the Pre-Prep and 21 boarders (full & weekly).
Fees per term (2014–2015). Full Boarders £6,200. Day Pupils: Years 5–8 £4,550; Years 3–4 £4,250. Weekly Boarding: £1,350 in addition to Day Fee. Pre-Prep £2,400–£2,800. Nursery/Kindergarten: £7 per hour. Compulsory extras: laundry and linen for Full Boarders.

The Prebendal is the oldest school in Sussex and has occupied its present building at the west end of the Cathedral (though with later additions) for over 500 years. The Cathedral Choristers are among the boys educated at the School and they receive Choral Scholarships in reduction of fees. Annual Music and Academic Scholarships are open to boys and girls entering the school. Sibling Bursaries are awarded to brothers and sisters. Open and Music Scholarships to Independent Senior Schools are gained regularly.

There are excellent playing fields in the heart of the city. Association Football, Hockey and Netball are played in the Michaelmas and Lent Terms and Cricket, Athletics, Tennis and Rounders in the Summer Term.

Approximately 95% of the children learn to play musical instruments and the School has more than 20 weekly ensembles, several orchestras, two concert bands and three choirs. There are many optional extras and after-school clubs, for example Magic Club and Mandarin Club. Occasional or flexi boarding is available and is a popular choice for many pupils.

Former pupils, parents and staff are known as The Prebendal Associates and events are held regularly throughout each academic year. The School also has its own Toddler Group which takes place every Wednesday morning during term-time.

Charitable status. The Prebendal School is a Registered Charity, number 307370. Its aim is to promote education.

Prestfelde
A Woodard School

London Road, Shrewsbury, Shropshire SY2 6NZ
Tel: 01743 245400
Fax: 01743 241434
email: office@prestfelde.co.uk
website: www.prestfelde.co.uk

Chairman of Governors: B Newman, MA, MBA, CEng, MIMechE, MIEE, FIOD

Headmaster: **M C Groome**, MA London, BEd Leeds

Age Range. 3–13.
Number of Pupils. 282 (4 boarders, 192 day pupils, and 86 children in Little Prestfelde).
Fees per term (2014–2015). Weekly Boarders £6,075. Day: Year 8 £4,720; Years 6–7 £4,695; Year 5 £4,650; Year 4 £4,465; Year 3 £3,795; Year 2 £2,920; Year 1 £2,860; Reception £2,820; Nursery £1,490 (5 mornings).

Pupils at Prestfelde are well known for their cheerful and purposeful attitude. The school aims to maximise the potential of every individual by providing them with significant opportunities for excelling academically, and in musical, sporting and dramatic performances. A well-qualified, loyal, enthusiastic and dedicated staff form the backbone of the school's success. The use of subject specialist teachers for pupils from the age of eight adds greatly to the quality of the teaching and the enthusiasm of the pupils.

Prestfelde has excellent facilities. There has been an extensive building programme over recent years giving all age ranges the benefit of purpose-built class and specialist teaching rooms. This year two well-equipped modern science laboratories have been added. The school enjoys the benefits of thirty acres of delightful parkland playing fields on the edge of Shrewsbury. There are ample, well-maintained facilities for football, rugby, cricket, netball, rounders, lacrosse, tennis and swimming in a covered heated pool.

Although the school is non-selective, the academic standards of the school are excellent. Setting is used for pupils from the age of eight so that the curriculum meets the needs of all our children. Equally, pupils who require support have the benefit of an exceptionally successful learning support department. The great majority of pupils stay to thirteen, and talented pupils are encouraged to attempt scholarship exams to their chosen senior school. The school has an excellent reputation and 20 scholarships were gained this year to senior independent schools. 29 boys have gained academic scholarships to Shrewsbury School in the last five years with other academic awards to Westminster, Bloxham, Repton, Moreton Hall, Wrekin College and Concord College. A number of boys and girls have gained music, art, sport and all-rounder scholarships.

Prestfelde is a Woodard School, with its own Chaplain and a clear stance in promoting spiritual and moral values within the school.

Charitable status. Prestfelde School is a Registered Charity, number 1102931. It aims to provide education for boys and girls.

Prince's Mead School

Worthy Park House, Kings Worthy, Winchester, Hampshire SO21 1AN
Tel: 01962 888000
email: admin@princesmeadschool.org.uk
website: www.princesmeadschool.org.uk

Chairman of Governors: Mr B Welch

Headmistress: **Miss P Kirk**, BEd Exeter

Age Range. 4–11 co-educational.
Number of Children. 271 Day Boys and Girls.
Fees per term (2014–2015). £3,150–£4,690.
Established in 1949, Prince's Mead is a Day Preparatory School on the outskirts of Winchester. The school follows an innovative curriculum that prepares young people for what lies ahead in an every changing world. Children are encouraged to acquire sound working habits, an enthusiasm and zest for knowledge and a desire to achieve their full potential. The pleasures and responsibilities of school life are an integral part of development and we encourage collaboration, independence and leadership qualities. Extensive playing fields and a strong sporting ethos encourage children to participate in competitive sport. The Performing Arts Department is also significant in developing the skills of all our children. The school is alive to the children's needs both now and in the future; the aim is to provide education for life.

Girls are prepared for 11+ Common Entrance and Scholarships to a wide variety of Independent Schools. Boys are prepared for entry to local Independent Day and Boarding schools at age 11. In 2014 children achieved a significant number of scholarships and were all offered places at their first-choice senior schools. Our children also enter the excellent Secondary Schools in the Winchester area.

The curriculum is built around the core subjects and looks to provide education for the 21st Century. An extensive range of extra-curricular activities enhance and enrich development.

Bursaries (financial assistance) are available from Year 3 upwards.

Charitable status. Prince's Mead School is a Registered Charity, number 288675. It exists to provide education for boys and girls.

Prior Park Preparatory School

Calcutt Street, Cricklade, Wiltshire SN6 6BB
Tel: 01793 750275
Fax: 01793 750910
email: prep@thepriorfoundation.com
website: www.thepriorfoundation.com
Twitter: @PriorParkPrep
Facebook: /The Prior Foundation

Chair of Governors: Mr Michael King

Headmaster: **M Pearce**, BA Hons, QTS

Age Range. 3–13.
Number of Pupils. 225 (60 Boarders, 165 Day).
Fees per term (2014–2015). Full Boarding £5,995–£6,970; Weekly Boarding £5,185–£6,160; Day Pupils £2,455–£4,710.

Prior Park Preparatory School is a thriving school situated in rural Wiltshire on the edge of the Cotswolds. Established in 1946, it forms part of the Prior Park Educational Trust with its senior school, Prior Park College in Bath. Awarded "Outstanding" in its recent ISI Inspection, Prior Park Prep provides a nurturing yet challenging school environment which ably prepares our children for life's journey. As a non-selective Catholic Christian school for children aged 3–13, we carefully nurture and encourage our children to flourish through identifying their gifts and talents. Our broad, balanced curriculum enable children to develop lively and enquiring young minds and our carefully planned cultural excursions broaden educational horizons. Our secure and friendly learning environment inspires individual excellence and ensures that children progress to their chosen senior school as confident, capable and independently-minded children.

We pride ourselves on small class sizes with pupils taught in classes of between 10 and 20. Our broad-based Pre-Prep curriculum gives children an excellent start to learning with French taught to the youngest pupils as well as an exciting programme of Forest School. Our modern first-class facilities include a large multi-use sports hall, ICT suite with 20 flat screen computers, art studio with pottery kiln, music studio, extensive playing fields, astroturf and 25m outdoor heated swimming pool. A wide-ranging enrichment programme exists for both day and boarding pupils. Some of the most popular activities include judo, dance, golf, tennis, fencing, debating, choir and orchestra, business enterprise, Eco club and archery.

Children have the chance to represent school in sports fixtures ranging from rugby, hockey and netball to tennis, swimming and athletics. Regular foreign sports tours take place, the most recent being to Barbados, South Africa, Jersey and Paris.

We have a proven track record of academic excellence with the majority of our children gaining scholarship awards to their chosen senior school. Our Learning Support Department is CReSTeD registered and offers support for pupils with mild to moderate dyslexia. We also support children who do not have English as their first language.

A strong boarding community lies at the heart of the school with a third of the pupils boarding from Year 3 (age 7). This includes both full and flexi boarding. The school's philosophy towards boarding is to create a stable family atmosphere in which pupils feel happy and secure. Our most recent inspection highlighted the happy and caring atmosphere which pervades the whole school. Boarders are cared for by very experienced full time members of staff who live within the boarding houses. A range of activities is organised for boarders with pupils having a say in how they spend their free time. The trip out on Sunday is always one of the highlights of the week. We are located only just over an hour from several major airports as well as having excellent road and rail links to major cities.

A limited number of HM Forces bursaries is available.

Charitable status. Prior Park Educational Trust is a Registered Charity, number 281242.

Priory Preparatory School

Bolters Lane, Banstead, Surrey SM7 2AJ
Tel: 01737 366920
Fax: 01737 366921
email: office@prioryprep.co.uk
website: www.prioryprep.co.uk

Chair of Governors: Mr Ashley Head

Headmaster: **Graham D Malcolm**, BEd, MA, FRSA, IAPS

Age Range. 2–13.
Number of Boys. 200 Day Boys.
Fees per term (2014–2015). Nursery £1,905–£2,500; Pre-Prep £2,950; Preparatory £3,800.

Priory Prep is a small, friendly school where every boy is valued and contributes fully to the various activities organised in the school. A strong pastoral framework supports the boys' learning and enjoyment of what is on offer. The boys are prepared for senior independent schools selected by their parents in consultation with the Headmaster. The aim is to provide a sound, well-balanced course designed to prepare boys for a smooth transfer to their next school. The curriculum reflects this aim and in so doing includes all school games and physical activities as a normal and necessary part of every boy's life, irrespective of ability. Soccer, Rugby, Cricket, Athletics, Basketball and Swimming are coached extensively. Gymnastics is particularly strong. A multi-purpose Sports Hall greatly enhances the facilities, as does a large sports field. In 2012 an impressive Early Years outdoor play area was opened. There is specialist accommodation for Art, Science and ICT and a library. There is a strong emphasis on Music and Drama.

The Pre-Preparatory Department is highly successful having had excellent inspection reports. The Preparatory School has also had excellent reviews in recent inspections, being cited as 'Outstanding' in every section (ISI Inspection 2011).

Although most boys are prepared for the Common Entrance Examination, a large number of Scholarships has been won in recent years. The essential groundwork of a good education lies in the experienced Pre-Preparatory Department which the School possesses. Traditional values, skills and standards run parallel with modern teaching methods and an extensive range of educational visits is arranged throughout the year.

Charitable status. The Priory School (Banstead) Trust Limited is a Registered Charity, number 312035. It exists for the education of boys aged two to thirteen years.

Prospect House School

75 Putney Hill, London SW15 3NT
Tel: 020 8780 0456
Fax: 020 8780 3010
email: info@prospecths.org.uk
website: www.prospecths.org.uk

Chairman of Governors: Mr Anthony Rentoul

Headmistress: **Mrs D Barratt**, MEd Newcastle-upon-Tyne

Age Range. 3–11 co-educational.
Number of Pupils. 300 day pupils.
Fees per term (2014–2015). Nursery (5 mornings) £2,560 Reception–Year 2 £4,930, Year 3 £5,040, Years 4–6 £5,120.

Prospect House School occupies two large buildings on Putney Hill situated just a short walk apart. Children aged 3 to 7 years occupy the Lower School building at 76 Putney Hill and children aged 7 to 11 years are based in the Upper School at 75 Putney Hill. They both have large grounds, including an all-weather sports pitch. There are multi-purpose halls where assemblies, music recitals, gymnastics and drama productions take place. There are dedicated rooms for music, ICT and special needs with art and DT also having provision within the school.

Most children join the school at 3 or 4 years of age, although occasionally there are places for older children. Selection for entry at 3 is by date of registration, with preference being given to brothers and sisters of children already in the school. An equal balance of boys and girls is kept

throughout the school. There is also a good balance of male and female staff.

Although the school does not have selective entry at age 3 or 4, the academic track record is very strong. The curriculum includes all National Curriculum subjects, with the addition of French from the age of three. There are numerous specialist teachers and children from Nursery are taught by specialists for music, PE, French, ICT and dance. Children are prepared for a wide range of leading day and boarding schools for entry at 11 years of age, with some children taking academic, music and sports scholarships. There is a wide and varied sports programme with many fixtures against other preparatory schools and children from Year 3 upwards attend training sessions at a nearby sports ground under the guidance of qualified teachers.

The school was awarded 'Best Primary School' in the UK in 2009–10 for the teaching and use of ICT.

Clubs after school cater for many interests and visiting teachers also provide a wide range of individual music lessons. Children are taken on educational visits to London and the surrounding area every term, with residential field study trips being undertaken in the final three years.

Quainton Hall School

Hindes Road, Harrow, Middlesex HA1 1RX
Tel: 020 8861 8861
email: admin@quaintonhall.org.uk
website: www.quaintonhall.org.uk
Twitter: @QuaintonHall

Chairman of Governors: Mrs Barbara Marlow

Headmaster: **Mr Simon Ford**, BEd Hons

Age Range. Boys 2½–13, Girls 2½–11.
Number of Pupils. 180.
Fees per term (2014–2015). £3,025–£3,325.

Established in Central Harrow at the end of the nineteenth century, Quainton Hall is an IAPS Preparatory School for children between the ages of two and a half and thirteen. We have our own Nursery for girls and boys from two and a half to four, our Pre-Prep for girls and boys from four to seven and our Middle and Senior School for girls from seven to eleven and boys from seven to thirteen. Boys continue on to take 13+ entrance examinations and transfer at the end of Year 8 to a range of senior schools, mostly in North and North West London, though some go further afield and into boarding, where desired. To assist them in doing this, they undertake the Common Entrance (CE) curriculum, starting in Year 6. Professional contact with a range of feeder schools for girls at 11+ has been made and support for them to make a successful transfer at 11+ will be as thorough as it is for our 13+ boys.

Quainton Hall provides a broad and balanced education, within a secure and caring environment and with a definite Christian ethos. Our children are valued as individuals and their learning experiences are stimulating. We recognise that children need to feel safe and secure in order to be motivated to learn. However, our curriculum is designed to do much more than prepare children for the next stage in their education; we teach skills and foster attitudes and values which will be of lasting benefit throughout their lives. We provide an extensive extra-curricular programme of activities, visits to places of interest and we invite speakers and theatre groups into school during the course of the school year.

Creativity, communication, teamwork, determination and a sense of the value and dignity of others are just some of the attributes we prize at Quainton Hall and where children grow to develop an understanding of the wider world, of those in need and have opportunities to raise funds for a range of charitable causes.

The life and work of the school is planned to enable children to shine in those areas and activities that they are good at and to reach their full potential. All members of staff have this objective as their aim. We also encourage the notion that learning is fun and that the acquisition of knowledge brings its own rewards. All that we do is conducted in an atmosphere and ethos that is personal, caring and family-orientated. We promote good order and self-discipline, consideration and tolerance towards others as well as personal motivation and group endeavour.

Charitable status. Quainton Hall School, under the Trusteeship of Walsingham College (Affiliated Schools) Limited, is a Registered Charity, number 312638. It exists to provide a sound education within a definite Christian framework.

Queen Elizabeth's Hospital (QEH) – Junior School

Berkeley Place, Clifton, Bristol BS8 1JX
Tel: 0117 930 3087
Fax: 0117 929 3106
email: juniors@qehbristol.co.uk
website: www.qehbristol.co.uk

Chairman of Governors: N J Tyrrell, BA

Junior School Headmaster: **M J Morris**, BEd, BA

Age Range. Boys 7–11.
Number of Pupils. 100 day boys.
Fees per term (2014–2015). £2,765. Fees include pre- and after-school supervision until 5.00 pm.

The QEH Junior School was opened in September 2007 and is located in gracious Georgian town houses in Upper Berkeley Place backing onto the Senior School, which means it can share its first-class facilities including science, drama, music and sport. The cultural facilities of the city, such as the city museum and art gallery, are also on its doorstep.

Pupils travel to the school from across the region and there is a hub for public transport on the nearby Clifton Triangle. The school also offers timed parking facilities for parents in the adjacent West End multi-storey car park, to pick up and drop off pupils, at no extra cost.

As part of the only all-boys' school in the city, QEH Juniors is unique in Bristol. Being small, it focuses on the individual, fostering a love of learning whilst nurturing the interests and talents of each boy. In addition there is a wealth of extra-curricular and holiday activities available.

The school is a happy place with strong pastoral care, academic excellence, and high standards where the educational experience is designed to be relevant and meaningful for every single child. Each boy leaves recognising himself as a lifelong learner.

There is one class per Year group until Year 5 and Year 6 when there are two classes, each with a maximum of 20 pupils. Offers of places are subject to an entrance examination.

Boys can therefore enter in Year 3 or Year 5 though places occasionally become available in other Years. Boys are expected to move into the Main School at 11. (*See QEH entry in HMC section.*)

Charitable status. Queen Elizabeth's Hospital is a Registered Charity, number 1104871, and a Company Limited by Guarantee, number 5164477.

Queen's College Junior School
Taunton

Trull Road, Taunton, Somerset TA1 4QS
Tel: 01823 340830
Fax: 01823 323811
email: admissions@queenscollege.org.uk
website: www.queenscollege.org.uk
Twitter: @QueensTaunton
Facebook: /queenstaunton

Chairman of Governors: Mr Stephen Lawson

Headmistress: **Mrs Tracey Khodabandehloo**

Head of Pre-Prep: Mrs Janet Williams
Head of Nursery: Miss Elizabeth Hayes

Age Range. 3–11.
Number of Pupils. 207 of whom 9 are boarders.
Fees per term (2014–2015). £4,100–£6,200 (boarders); £5,100–£7,200 (overseas boarders); £1,895–£3,840 (day).

Queen's College is a co-educational boarding and day school on the outskirts of Taunton with fine views across the playing fields to the surrounding hills.

The Pre-Prep School educates pupils up to the age of 7 and the Junior School educates pupils up to the end of Key Stage 2 (NC Year 6). Children aged 11+ will usually be admitted directly to the Senior School (*see Queen's College entry in HMC section*).

The Junior School is run as an independent unit and shares many of the excellent facilities of the adjacent Senior School. Known especially for its outstanding pastoral care and real focus on individual children, there is no doubt that pupils here are extremely happy. Specialist subject teachers, high academic standards and a sense of fun are setting this school apart from its competitors and the outstanding Headmistress whose excellent communication skills are admired universally means that parents are flocking towards this lovely, friendly school with its excellent facilities. Definitely on the up.

Junior boarding here is growing and the House parents are kind, sympathetic and organise a wealth of activities for those away from home. Matrons read bedside stories and arrange fun weekend trips and with lots to do in the evenings the children are kept really busy and involved. Many children come from Armed Forces families and Queen's is well versed in settling pupils whose families have been posted abroad and keeping in contact. Emphasis is made on creating a family-style, homely atmosphere in which the pupils can relax and unwind. Lovely, bright bedrooms and living areas with lots of games.

For every pupil the aim of the School is to find areas in which each child can succeed and develop self-confidence to help them really shine. Using different learning styles, reinforcing classroom learning with external trips and visits and a practical approach means that the children here are really inspired and enjoy their school and make excellent friendships.

The principal games are rugby, hockey and cricket for the boys, with hockey, netball and rounders for the girls. Tennis, swimming and athletics matches also take place. Fullest use is made of the excellent sporting facilities of the School, particularly the Sports Hall, tennis courts, heated indoor swimming pool and floodlit Astroturf. The school has achieved national success in hockey, cross country, swimming, athletics and riding this year and all abilities are welcomed. A new hockey academy opened last year.

After-school activities include Board Games, Cookery, Chess, Computer Club, Drama, Gardening, Specialist Music Groups, Model Making, Photography, Puppets, and Fun Swim. Also arranged at an extra charge are Dancing, Speech and Drama, Climbing and Riding. Junior music is outstanding with many opportunities to play in groups and festivals and the performing arts is a real strength of the school with the Taunton Speech and Drama Festival run at Queen's.

Free before and after-school care is available every day until 5.45 pm and holiday clubs operate.

The Pre-Prep day school is in its own purpose-built building and there is a Nursery School for children aged 3–4 years. Nursery and Reception are rated as outstanding and it is not difficult to see why. Outdoor gardens and facilities are superb with plenty of room to run and climb and many different things are happening at once in the classrooms. Innovative teaching methods, getting the children involved as well as teaching the foundations in small class sizes with specialist teachers means that the children have tremendous attention and support and really do achieve their potential.

Nearly all the children move on from one section of Queen's College to the next; there is no further qualifying examination.

Parent and toddler groups are held from Tuesday to Thursday.

Charitable status. Queen's College, Taunton is a Registered Charity, number 310208.

Ramillies Hall School

Cheadle Hulme, Cheadle, Cheshire SK8 7AJ
Tel: 0161 485 3804
email: study@ramillieshall.co.uk
website: www.ramillieshall.co.uk

Headteacher & Joint Principal: Miss D M Patterson, BA, PGCE
Joint Principal: Mrs A L Poole

Age Range. 6 months to 16 years.
Number of Children. Day: 65 boys, 11 girls. Nursery: 75 children.
Fees per term (2014–2015). Day pupils: Reception–Year 6 £2,710, Years 7–9 £2,936, Years 10–11 £2,998. Nursery from £5.10 per hour.

Ramillies Hall, founded in 1884, is a small family-run school for children aged 6 months to 16 years. In our small classes (average 15 pupils) we bring together the best of traditional methods and modern multi-sensory teaching. We follow, and in some areas extend, the National Curriculum and offer a range of practical and vocational GCSEs along with the core subjects. Our well-structured learning programmes build confidence and encourage our pupils to become independent learners.

Our specialism is in dyslexia, dyspraxia and similar learning difficulties, and a high proportion of our pupils come to Ramillies for that reason. When they arrive, many children are lacking in self-esteem because of their previous experience of the education system. Our first task is often to find their strengths and build on them to increase their confidence. We offer tuition and support from specialist trained teachers in our Learning Support Department, to enable pupils to access the full curriculum. This has brought external recognition of our expertise in this field, with accreditation by CReSTeD (Council for the Registration of Schools Teaching Dyslexics). To maintain this, the School is subject to rigorous and regular inspection, and Ramillies is the only school in the Manchester area with the accreditation. Recently, the School has gained specialist status under the Department for Education for SPLDs, ASC & Speech and Language difficulties.

An extended day (until 5.50 pm, Mondays to Thursdays) enables us to offer a wide variety of sports and extra-curricular activities, and homework can be completed during this time under the supervision of a teacher.

Ramillies also has a Nursery, open from 8.00 am to 6.00 pm, Monday to Friday throughout the year, for babies and children up to Reception age. We are proud of our high standards of care, and our qualified and experienced staff provide a stimulating and exciting environment for our youngest children.

Easily accessible by road and rail, the School is set in its own spacious grounds with extensive playing fields and heated outdoor swimming pool.

For more information, visit our website as given above.

Ravenscourt Park Preparatory School

16 Ravenscourt Avenue, Chiswick, London W6 0SL
Tel: 020 8846 9153
Fax: 020 8846 9413
email: secretary@rpps.co.uk
website: www.rpps.co.uk

Chairman of Governors: Mr Kevin Darlington

Headmistress: **Mrs Kate O'Shaughnessy**, BA Hons QTS

Age Range. 4–11 co-educational.
Number of Pupils. 380 boys and girls.
Fees per term (2014–2015). £4,997.

This non-selective school provides education of the highest quality for boys and girls, preparing them for transfer to the best Independent Schools at 11 years of age. The Lower School caters for pupils aged 4–7 and the Upper School, 7–11 years. All pupils are housed in one of the three main buildings that make up the RPPS site. The recent addition of the Gardener Building is home to a theatre, a state-of-the-art science laboratory and an art studio. The secure site includes a large play area and the school makes use of the extensive facilities of Ravenscourt Park which it adjoins.

The curriculum includes French, Humanities, Music, Art and Craft, RE and PE for all pupils in addition to the usual core subjects. In the Upper School the majority of subjects are taught by specialists. All Upper School pupils attend a Residential Week where studies across the curriculum are applied to a non-urban environment.

There are many after-school clubs and sports activities, as well as two choirs and an orchestra. Individual tuition is offered in piano, violin, brass, woodwind, cello, saxophone, percussion and singing. The Drama productions are a highlight of each school year.

A Day Care service, before and after school, is offered to parents at an extra charge.

The school is noted for its warm, happy atmosphere where parents play a full part in enriching the curriculum and social life. Off-site visits and guest workshops presented by noted visitors are a regular feature of education at RPPS.

The school is always heavily over-subscribed and registration is strongly recommended on the child's first birthday. A prospectus and registration form may be obtained from the School Secretary.

The Red Maids' Junior School

Grange Court Road, Westbury-on-Trym, Bristol BS9 4DP
Tel: 0117 962 9451
Fax: 0117 989 8286
email: juniors@redmaids.bristol.sch.uk
website: www.redmaids.co.uk
Twitter: @RedMaidsSchool
Facebook: /redmaidsschool

Chairman of Governors: Mrs J MacFarlane, BSc, MA

Headteacher: **Mrs L Brown**, BSc Hons Leicester, PGCE Oxford Brookes

Age Range. 7–11.
Number of Girls. 120 Day Girls.
Fees per term (2014–2015). £2,780 plus lunches.

The Red Maids' Junior School was established in 1986 alongside the Senior School which was founded in 1634. It occupies a wonderful new building, including a library and ICT suite, at the very heart of the school. There is a wonderful atmosphere for learning and a large garden for outdoor play. The lofty art and music studios inspire creativity and the large modern hall is a fabulous all-purpose space for whole-school activities.

The school is equipped for approximately 120 girls aged 7–11 organised into six classes. In Years 3 and 4, each class is taught by their own class teacher for the majority of their timetable. In Years 5 and 6, girls are taught by more specialist teachers but we take care to ensure that they are nurtured within each year group unit. There are frequent opportunities built into the timetable for girls to work and make friends with children in all year groups. Since the girls know each other and every member of staff well, a strong community feeling is promoted within the school where girls can develop their confidence and self-esteem.

All the girls are encouraged to explore their individual talents and achieve their best through the school's broad and balanced curriculum, including Mandarin. Whole school planning is an essential feature of every subject area, ensuring continuity and progression; assessment is an integral part of this. Year 6 girls sit National Curriculum Key Stage 2 Standard Assessment Tests (SATs).

In addition there is a strong emphasis on the pastoral care of the children. Through school meetings and class activities, the school teaches a sense of good citizenship as girls are encouraged to share responsibility for the care of their community and their environment.

Close links are fostered between the Junior and Senior Red Maids through joint activities and visits. Pupils benefit from use of a science laboratory, extensive PE facilities including an all-weather pitch and shared dining facilities. At age 11, Junior Red Maids transfer to the Senior School (conditions apply) having achieved outstanding success in the entrance examination. (*See Red Maids' School entry in GSA section*.)

Extra-curricular activities are an essential part of every girl's school experience and there is a strong commitment to outdoor education.

The school enjoys close relationships with parents on a daily basis and generous support is offered to the school through a thriving Friends' Association.

Admission to Junior School: The main points of entry to the Junior School are in Year 3 and Year 5. Girls are assessed during a day visit when they also spend time with their peer group.

Charitable status. The Red Maids' School is a Registered Charity, number 1105017.

Redcliffe School

47 Redcliffe Gardens, London SW10 9JH
Tel: 020 7352 9247
Fax: 020 7352 6936
email: admissions@redcliffeschool.com
website: www.redcliffeschool.com

Chairman of the Board of Governors: Mr Roger Flynn

Headmistress: **Mrs Susan Bourne**, BSc, PGCE

Age Range. Boys 3–8, Girls 3–11.
Number of Pupils. 169 Day Pupils (69 boys, 100 girls)
Fees per term (2014–2015). £4,640. Nursery: £2,615 (morning class), £1,745 (afternoon class), £4,375 (full day).

Easily accessible from all parts of central and West London, Redcliffe is a small, friendly school with highly motivated, confident and happy children. Emphasis is placed on a good combination of hard work and plenty of fun within a framework of discipline and good manners. The balanced curriculum includes Mathematics, English, History, Geography, Science, IT, Art and Craft, Scripture, Current Affairs, Music, Physical Education and Drama. French is taught throughout the school. Individual attention encourages the pursuit of high academic standards and we are proud that our children gain places at their first choice of senior or prep school, including Colet Court, Sussex House, St Philip's, Downe House, Benenden, Queen's Gate, Godolphin and Latymer and Francis Holland. Every class has some form of Physical Education each day; in the gym or playground, local netball court or park. All pupils participate in a wide range of sports and activities including: rugby, hockey, cricket and swimming. After school activities include cookery, ballet, computer skills and drama. Music is strength of the school with visiting instrumental staff and a high standard of performance. Parents are encouraged to be involved with the school through Open Assemblies, Parents' Discussion Groups, the Parents' Committee and regular meetings with the teachers.

Redcliffe Robins is our nursery class for children between the ages of 3 and 4 years with a specialist Montessori-trained teacher and access to all of Recliffe's resources and facilities to help prepare the children for entry to the main school. Each day has a balanced timetable of language work, mathematical skills, art and craft, music, drama and PE with ample opportunity for structured free play and the development of social skills.

Children are assessed at three years of age for entry to the main school at four. Entry for subsequent years by test. Tours of the school are held weekly during term time by appointment with the school office.

Charitable status. Redcliffe School Trust Ltd is a Registered Charity, number 312716. It exists to provide a high standard of education for children within a caring environment.

Reddiford School

38 Cecil Park, Pinner, Middlesex HA5 5HH
Tel: 020 8866 0660
Fax: 020 8866 4847
email: office@reddiford.org.uk
website: www.reddiford.org.uk

Chairman of Governors: Mr G Jukes

Head: **Mrs J Batt**, CertEd, NPQH

Age Range. 2 years 9 months to 11.
Number of Pupils. Prep: 91 Boys, 78 Girls; Pre-Prep: 39 Boys, 29 Girls; Early Years: 53 Boys, 34 Girls.
Fees per term (2014–2015). Nursery: £1,410 (mornings only), £2,500 (all day), Foundation £3,010, Reception £3,265, Pre-Prep £3,280, Prep £3,365.

Reddiford School has been established in Cecil Park, Pinner since 1913. Whilst the school maintains its Church of England status, children from all faiths and cultures are welcomed. Throughout the school the ethos is on respect for one another. Reddiford prides itself on being a town school based in the heart of Pinner; a few minutes' walk from local transport facilities.

Reddiford possesses a fine academic record, preparing its pupils for entrance at 11+ into major independent schools, many at scholarship level. There is a high teacher pupil ratio ensuring small classes leading to a friendly caring environment where all children are valued.

The Early Years Department is situated in its own building and caters for children from 2 years nine months to rising 5 years. It offers a stimulating and attractive environment where children are encouraged to be independent and active learners. The Early Years Department follows the Early Years Foundation Stage Curriculum. There is a choice of full or half day provision.

The Pre-Prep Department builds on the knowledge and skills acquired in the Early Years placing the emphasis on developing confidence and the ability to learn and work independently and with others. The Pre-Prep Department has its own computer suite and interactive whiteboards in classrooms. There is specialist teaching in French, Music and PE from reception upwards and all children are taught to swim.

In the Prep Department children are taught by specialist teachers in properly resourced subject rooms. There is a fully-equipped science laboratory, dedicated art and music rooms and an ICT suite. Pupils are prepared for entry to the many prestigious senior schools in the area, a process which involves consultation with parents from an early stage.

There is an extensive programme of extra-curricular activities throughout the school including: sports (football, cricket, netball, gymnastics), languages (French, Latin, Mandarin), art, science, and ballet. We also offer before and after school care, with a prep club for older children.

Entry to the Nursery is possible in any term once a child has reached 2 years and 9 months. Most children move from the Nursery to the Reception classes at 4+, but there are spaces for outside applicants in the Reception classes. An assessment day for these places is held on application for September entry. Means-tested bursaries may be available.

Charitable status. Reddiford School is a Registered Charity, number 312641. It exists to provide education for boys and girls.

Redland High School for Girls Junior School

Redland Court, Bristol BS6 7EF
Tel: 0117 924 5796
email: admissions@redlandhigh.com
website: www.redlandhigh.com

Chairman of Governors: Dr T L Chambers, OBE, JP, FRCP

Head: **Mr J P Eyles**, BEd Bath Spa, MEd Bristol

Age Range. Girls 3–11, Boys 3–6.
Number of Pupils. 150.
Fees per term (2014–2015). Lower Foundation £21.75 per half day; Upper Foundation, Years 1 & 2 £2,400; Years 3–6 £2,750.

Redland High Junior School is situated in two Victorian houses close to the Senior School in a very pleasant residential area of Bristol. The School is easily reached from the surrounding districts.

Children are taught by well-qualified and highly-motivated teachers who are very well supported by a number of excellent classroom assistants.

The School aims to provide each child with the opportunity to develop fully his or her particular talents within a stimulating and supportive environment. We try to create a friendly, family atmosphere within which high standards are expected in all areas of the curriculum.

While emphasis is placed on numeracy and literacy, children also respond to high expectations in science, ICT,

drama, history, geography, RE, art, PE and modern languages. Music is a particular strength of the school with most pupils learning to play an instrument or joining in choral or orchestral activities. Our curriculum embraces the principal areas of study appropriate for Primary School education. It is based on the National Curriculum requirements and the Early Learning Goals for the Under Fives. However, we aim to give our pupils more than these minimum requirements so that they have a head start when they reach senior school. Our high standards and expectations ensure that the brighter pupils can be stretched to their full potential, whilst those who need extra help get additional support.

There are a number of extra-curricular activities available, including outdoor pursuits (canoeing, abseiling etc), orienteering, judo, computer clubs, netball, short tennis, recorder groups, dance and art clubs.

During each school year there are a number of educational visits and workshops. Most of these visits are a way of enabling pupils to consolidate knowledge acquired in lessons. Other outings are of a more cultural nature and often include visits to concerts and theatres. Pupils are encouraged to nominate and support charities, and each term sees an event designed to raise money for the chosen charity.

At the end of Year 2, boys transfer seamlessly to QEH Boys' School and girls continue to Year 3 in the Junior School. At the age of 11, most girls move on to our Senior School where they experience new challenges and choices. The girls from the Junior School are well prepared and ready to embrace the next stage of their education with enthusiasm and confidence.

Charitable status. Redland High School for Girls is a Registered Charity, number 311734. It exists to provide education for girls.

Reigate St Mary's Preparatory and Choir School

Chart Lane, Reigate, Surrey RH2 7RN
Tel: 01737 244880
Fax: 01737 221540
email: office@reigatestmarys.org
website: www.reigatestmarys.org

Chairman of Governors: Mr Alan Walker

Headmaster: **Marcus Culverwell**, MA Ed

Age Range. 3–11.
Number of Pupils. 330 (180 boys 150 girls).
Fees per term (2014–2015). Kindergarten £1,580 (5 mornings), Reception to Year 2 £3,425, Years 3–6 £4,190.

Reigate St Mary's is an independent day school for boys and girls aged 3–11. It is the nursery and junior school of Reigate Grammar School. Set in 15 acres of beautiful parkland and sports fields. We are proud of our reputation as a lively, happy, family friendly school where each child is encouraged and known as an individual.

Reigate St Mary's aims to provide an education of considerable depth and breadth within a disciplined, happy and caring environment, incorporating a tradition of choral excellence and Christian values. All pupils are encouraged to be ambitious, to reach the best standards they can in their academic studies, in sport, in art, in music and in other performing arts. The school aims to engender a love of learning, a zest for life and to develop a caring and understanding attitude towards other people. The school places a very high value on good relationships and developing inter-personal skills in our pupils to enable them to become responsible, adaptable, independent people in a changing world. At Reigate St Mary's we believe that all children should feel valued for who they are, not just for what they achieve.

As a member of the Choir Schools' Association Reigate St Mary's is one of only a small number of schools, not attached to a cathedral or college, which maintain a traditional choir of boys and men under the direction of a Master of Choristers. The choir sings regular school and church services with a repertoire of music from the 16th Century to the present day. Entrance to the choir is by voice trial, and choral scholarships are offered by the Godfrey Searle Choir Trust.

RGS Springfield

Britannia Square, Worcester WR1 3DL
Tel: 01905 24999
email: springfield@rgsw.org.uk
website: www.rgsw.org.uk
Twitter: @RGSWorcester

Chairman of Governors: Mrs R F Ham

Headmistress: **Mrs L Brown**, BA

Age Range. 2–11 Co-educational.
Number of Pupils. 145.
Fees per term (2014–2015). £2,274–£3,474 including lunch.
Introduction from the Headmistress. "I am delighted to have this opportunity to welcome you to RGS Springfield, with its wonderful family atmosphere and nurturing co-educational environment, which together creates a uniquely friendly school.

Our aim is to ensure that children develop their full potential academically, socially and emotionally in a safe, caring environment.

All our pupils benefit from individual care, small class sizes, professional and dedicated teaching; all of which help children become confident, secure and considerate of the needs of others.

The school has scored highly in recent inspections, rated as consistently outstanding by Ofsted, ECERS and ISI inspectors. There are a wealth of academic and extra-curricular opportunities to provide children with an enriching and stimulating environment, preparing them for the challenges of the 21st century, underpinned by traditional family values. The new digital learning programme adds a new dimension to classroom learning.

The school has wonderful grounds, which allow pupils to play outside in all weathers, learn from the natural environment and take part in all the fun that Forest School offers; wellies are very much encouraged!

The school, tucked away within the beautiful Georgian Britannia Square in the heart of Worcester, will provide a safe and happy place for your child to grow and develop. This website conveys only some of the ethos and spirit of RGS Springfield. Please visit us and see for yourself the happy, smiling faces of children having fun and learning in a stimulating environment. We are very much a happy family. I look forward to welcoming you in person to our school."

Overview. RGS Springfield is the co-educational junior school for RGS Worcester (*see HMC entry*). The school educates children between the ages of 2 and 11 and is situated within a large, beautiful Georgian Town House and gardens in the centre of Worcester.

High academic standards are expected as the children are prepared to enter RGS Worcester at 11. There is a wide range of extra-curricular activities on offer and, while the school is noted for academic, creative and sporting excellence, it is of the greatest importance that the children are encouraged to be kind, considerate and well-mannered.

In 2009 an extensive refurbishment was undertaken to restore and develop the original historic site, Springfield, providing excellent modern facilities including art, design technology, science and ICT rooms alongside large, airy and warm well-equipped classrooms.

The school is set in six acres of maintained grounds and offers fantastic games facilities and outdoor space, including an extended Forest School, Walled Garden and Paddock Play Area.

Charitable status. The Royal Grammar School Worcester is a Registered Charity, number 1120644.

RGS The Grange

Grange Lane, Claines, Worcester WR3 7RR
Tel: 01905 451205
Fax: 01905 757917
email: grange@rgsw.org.uk
website: www.rgsw.org.uk
Twitter: @RGSWorcester

Chairman of Governors: Mrs R F Ham

Headmaster: **G W Hughes**, BEd Hons

Age Range. 2–11 Co-educational.
Number of Pupils. 387.
Fees per term (2014–2015). £2,274–£3,474 including lunch.
Introduction from the Headmaster. "Welcome to a nurturing school with a big personality.

Giving a child the best possible foundations for a bright future is a true privilege. Our fantastic facilities give pupils tremendous scope for achieving the academic, sporting and creative excellence that we encourage. Just as important is the safe, secure and caring framework that we provide, giving children the support and self-belief they need to make their own individual strides forward.

I get huge satisfaction from seeing each one cross barriers and shine in a way that is uniquely theirs and with two children myself, I know the pride parents feel when they see their child thriving.

I look forward to helping your child thrive too."

Overview. RGS The Grange is the co-educational junior school for RGS Worcester (*see HMC entry*). The school educates children between the ages of 2 and 11 and is situated in open countryside three miles north of Worcester in Claines.

High academic standards are expected as the children are prepared to enter RGS Worcester at 11. There is a wide range of extra-curricular activities on offer and, while the school is noted for academic, creative and sporting excellence, it is of the greatest importance that the children are encouraged to be kind, considerate and well-mannered.

In 2004 a multimillion pound extension was added to the original country house, The Grange, providing excellent modern facilities including specialist art, design technology, science and ICT rooms alongside large, airy, well-equipped classrooms.

The school is set in 48 acres of grounds and offers exceptional games facilities and outdoor space, including a full-sized floodlit Astroturf, cricket pavilion, wilderness garden and adventure play area.

Charitable status. The Royal Grammar School Worcester is a Registered Charity, number 1120644.

The Richard Pate School

Southern Road, Leckhampton, Cheltenham, Glos GL53 9RP

Tel: 01242 522086
Fax: 01242 524035
email: hm@richardpate.co.uk
website: www.richardpate.co.uk

Chairman of Trustees: C Mourton, Esq

Headmaster: R A MacDonald, MEd, BA

Deputy Heads:
Mrs S Wade
P Lowe

Age Range. 3–11 Co-educational.

Number of Pupils. 300 (approximately an equal number of boys and girls).

Fees per term (2014–2015). Nursery: £1,000 (5 mornings), £1,326 (any 3 full days), £1,768 (any 4 full days), £2,210 (5 full days). Preparatory: £2,245 (Reception), £2,410 (Year 1), £2,575 (Year 2). Junior: £2,690 (Year 3), £2,795 (Year 4), £2,985 (Year 5), £3,120 (Year 6).

Hot lunches are provided and included in the fees, except for 'mornings only' nursery.

The School, occupying an 11½ acre semi-rural site at the foot of the Cotswold escarpment, is part of the Pate's Grammar School Foundation which is a charity founded by Richard Pate, a Recorder of Gloucester, in 1574.

It is a non-denominational Christian school which in its present form began in 1946. The aim of the school is to provide a high academic standard and continuity of education up to the age of 11 years. The curriculum is broadly based with strong emphasis being attached to music, art, drama and sport, for these activities are seen as vital if a child's full potential is to be realised.

Facilities include a music centre with individual practice rooms; a fully equipped computer suite; an all-weather astroturf with floodlights and an enclosed pond for environmental studies. There is also a specialist wing with science labs, language suite and art studio. After-school care is available through until 5.30 pm.

At present the School is divided into three sections: Nursery 3–4½ years; Preparatory Department 5–7 and Junior 7–11. Entrance is dependent upon the availability of places but most pupils join the school at the commencement of the Nursery, Preparatory or Junior Departments.

No entry tests are taken by younger pupils but interviews and selective tests are used for assessing pupils aged 6 years and upwards. A small number of 7+ scholarships are awarded each year.

The teaching takes full account of national curriculum guidelines with children in the upper part of the school following the normal preparatory school curriculum leading to Common Entrance and Scholarship at 11+. Pupils leave at age 11 for local Grammar Schools and a variety of independent secondary schools, particularly those in Cheltenham.

The Headmaster is assisted by two deputies and 18 fully qualified teachers including specialists in Latin, French, History, Art/Design, Science, Music and Learning Support. The School employs music and dance teachers, who prepare children for participation in various competitions, in particular the Cheltenham Festival.

Charitable status. The Pate's Grammar School Foundation is a Registered Charity, number 311707.

Richmond House School

170 Otley Road, Leeds, West Yorkshire LS16 5LG

Tel: 0113 2752670
Fax: 0113 2304868
email: enquiries@rhschool.org
website: www.rhschool.org

Chairman of the Board of Governors: Ms C Shuttleworth

Headmistress: Mrs Jane Disley, BA Hons

Age Range. 3–11.

Number of Day Pupils. 207 boys and girls.

Fees per term (2014–2015). Nursery: £1,715 (half days only), £2,675 (full time, including lunch), Reception to Year 6 £2,675, Lunches £183.

Richmond House School is an independent co-educational preparatory school providing a high standard of education for children aged 3 to 11 years within a happy, stimulating, family environment.

At Richmond House School, a team of dedicated staff is committed to giving each child the opportunity to develop into confident, hard-working and successful individuals.

All pupils are given the chance to learn and achieve across a broad range of activities and subject areas and the talents of each child are nurtured. The breadth of activities offered aims to challenge pupils, build self-confidence and lead pupils to discover new interests and skills.

The School boasts outstanding 11+ exam success with pupils having their choice of senior school and a substantial number being awarded scholarships.

In addition to strong academic credentials, Richmond House School is committed to providing all pupils with the opportunity to excel in other areas. The School is situated in 10 acres of land, providing excellent sports facilities and offering pupils a wide range of sports to choose from. The School also provides specialist teaching in Music, Art, Design Technology, Information Communication Technology, Languages and Science.

Pastoral Care is an important aspect of school life at Richmond House School. Our Deputy Head Teacher is responsible for leading Pastoral Care and works closely with staff, pupils and parents to ensure the well-being and progress of all pupils.

Excellent Pre and After School Care and an easily accessible car park and drop-off zone are available for busy families.

Charitable status. Richmond House School is a Registered Charity, number 505630. It exists to provide high quality education for boys and girls aged 3–11 years.

Riddlesworth Hall Preparatory School

Nr Diss, Norfolk IP22 2TA

Tel: 01953 681246
Fax: 01953 688124
email: ljc@riddlesworth-hall.co.uk
website: www.riddlesworthhall.com

Headmaster: Mr P I Cochrane, CertEd

Age Range. Girls 2–13, Boys 2–13. Girls Boarding from age 7–13. Boys boarding from age 7–13.

Number of Pupils. 17 Boarders, 72 Day, 12 Nursery.

Fees per term (2014–2015). Full Boarders £6,020; Weekly Boarders £5,665; Day (inc Lunch): Years 3–8

£3,685; Years 1–2 £2,585; Nursery & Reception: £236.50 per am/pm session, lunch £165, £2,530 full-time inc lunch.

Riddlesworth Hall, situated in a magnificent country house on the Norfolk/Suffolk border, provides an excellent all-round education. The aim is to develop each child's potential to the full in all areas – academic, sport and creative arts. The boys and girls are prepared for Common Entrance and Scholarship examinations to independent senior schools.

Riddlesworth Hall has excellent art and pottery studios, science, domestic science and technology laboratories, a computer room, music and drama rooms and a refurbished gymnasium. French is taught from Reception. A range of sports is taught to all levels and good-quality teams are regularly produced.

The care of the children is in the hands of the Headmaster and his wife who are resident, supported by a team of matrons.

The school enjoys CreSTeD status and is specifically staffed to welcome dyslexic children. IEPs are prepared for these children, who enjoy all the benefits of full integration into main school activities.

Extras include speech and drama, ballet and riding. There is a very active music department with choirs, orchestra, various ensembles and a recorder group. Senior school music, drama and academic scholarships have been recently achieved.

There is a wide variety of clubs and activities including skiing, dance, ball skills, gym and cookery. A feature of Riddlesworth Hall is its Pets Corner which houses a variety of small animals brought from home and permanently resident at school.

Self-reliance, self-discipline, and tolerance are encouraged, and good manners are expected.

Ripley Court School

Rose Lane, Ripley, Surrey GU23 6NE
Tel:	01483 225217
Fax:	01483 223854
email:	head@ripleycourt.co.uk
website:	www.ripleycourt.co.uk

Chairman of Governors: P Armitage, BA, FCA

Headmaster: **A J Gough**, BSc UED, MA

Deputy Head: D M Cockerill, BA Hons

Age Range. 3–13 Co-educational.
Number of Day Pupils. 272: Main School (age 7–13) 177; Little Court (age 4–7) 66; Nursery (age 3+) 29.
Fees per term (2014–2015). Main School £3,985–£4,135; Little Court £2,990–£3,050; Nursery £2,800 full-time (part-time pro rata).

Pupils start at any time from age 3, with main intakes at 3, 7 and 11 if there is room. They are prepared for Common Entrance and Scholarship Examinations for all the Boys' and Girls' Senior Independent Schools. There is a high academic standard and many Scholarships are won including for Sport, Music and Art, but there is a studious avoidance of cramming. In addition, PE, Music, Art and Craft and Food Technology are a part of every child's timetable. There are opportunities for all in orchestral, choral and dramatic productions – the school prides itself on ensuring every child can participate in all areas, including competitive sports fixtures.

Facilities include a library, science laboratories, a gymnasium, computer suite, art, music and food tech rooms. There are 20 acres of playing fields. Games and sports are Football (Association and Rugby), Hockey, Netball, Cricket, Tennis (2 hard, 2 grass courts), Athletics, Rounders, Volleyball,

Stoolball; Swimming and Life Saving are taught in a large, covered, heated swimming pool.

Little Court is the Pre-Prep Department which also uses the main playing field, swimming pool and gymnasium and other specialist facilities.

The nursery, known as "The Ark", also uses all school facilities and nursery children receive specialist tuition in French, music, swimming and dance.

School transport serves Woking, Pyrford and West Byfleet.

Charitable status. Ripley Court School is a Registered Charitable Trust, number 312084. It aims to educate children and prepare them well for entry to their next school and for adult life. It offers scholarships as well as bursarial scholarships and bursaries on a means-tested basis. It is not-for-profit and all surplus funds are used to improve provision and facilities.

Rockport School

15 Rockport Road, Craigavad, Holywood, Co Down BT18 0DD, Northern Ireland
Tel:	028 9042 8372
Fax:	028 9042 2608
email:	info@rockportschool.com
	schooloffice@rockportschool.com
website:	www.rockportschool.com

Chairman of Governors: M J Burke, Esq

Headmaster: **George Vance**, BEd, LLB

Age Range. 3–16.
Number of Pupils. 98 Girls, 84 Boys.
Fees per term (2014–2015). Day: £3,040–£4,120; Pre-Prep (from age 3): £1,700–£2,710. Boarding (in addition to Day fee): £2,550–£2,700.

Rockport School is the only independent preparatory and senior school in Northern Ireland. It is situated in and around a fine Victorian mansion in twenty-five acres of beautiful surroundings overlooking Belfast Lough and prides itself on bringing out the best in pupils of all abilities and talents.

The Pre-Prep and Nursery Schools are located in purpose-built buildings close to the main school. Children from ages 3 to 8 are placed in small mixed-ability classes of no more than 16 and are offered a broad curriculum, with French, Music and Sport taught by specialist teachers. The children enjoy use of all the school's facilities, particularly the outdoor space, woods and shore, whilst having their own dedicated play areas.

Pupils in the Preparatory School are prepared for 11+ examinations for transfer to local Grammar Schools or for Common Entrance and Scholarship examinations at 13+. There is an excellent record of pupils moving on to top independent schools throughout the UK.

The majority of pupils remain at the school until 16 and are prepared for GCSE examinations; the school offers 22 subjects. The school's relatively small size enables teaching to be highly individualised and annual results consistently outperform national averages and CAT predictions. The school's small and supportive Learning Support department assists this process.

Boarding is central to the life of the school and pupils are looked after by a caring staff dedicated to their welfare. With full, weekly and flexi boarding options, boarding pupils come from Northern Ireland, the rest of the UK and overseas, adding diversity to the Rockport community.

Games & Extra-curricular activities. Sport, especially team games, are a significant part of the curriculum, as are Art, Music and Drama. The school takes full advantage of its beautiful location and has as varied a range of activities as any school of its size. Particular emphasis is placed on service to the environment and to others. There is a 100% participation in the Duke of Edinburgh's Award Scheme in the senior school; the school's own coastal path and woodland, and the Mourne Mountains beyond are used extensively by the school.

Scholarships & Bursaries. Scholarships are awarded at 11+ to pupils who show academic excellence and Bursaries are available to children of HM Forces.

Charitable status. Rockport School Limited is a Registered Charity, number XN48119. It exists to provide education for boys and girls.

Rokeby

George Road, Kingston-upon-Thames, Surrey KT2 7PB
Tel: 020 8942 2247
Fax: 020 8942 5707
email: hmsec@rokeby.org.uk
website: www.rokebyschool.co.uk
Twitter: @RokebyPrep

Maxim: *Smart, Skilful and Kind*

Chairman of the Governors: Mr Charles Carter

Headmaster: **Mr J R Peck**

Age Range. 4–13.
Number of Boys. 370.
Fees per term (2014–2015). £3,974–£4,948 (including lunch, books and all compulsory extras).

Rokeby has an outstanding record of success in Common Entrance and Scholarships to leading Independent Schools. Boys are accepted at 4+ to the Pre-Prep and at 7+ to the Prep School. There is a number of scholarships available to the Prep School at 7+.

This year a fabulous two-storey, energy-efficient new building was opened by HRH Princess Alexandra. It has six spacious classrooms, a multi-purpose Performing Arts Hall, as well as other lovely space built to house Reception, Year 1 and Year 2 Rokeby boys. The spacious and exciting playground area is enjoyed by all year groups and includes an outside classroom, an adventure playground with balance wall and an area for gardening club to grow seeds and encourage wildlife.

Science is taught in two well-equipped Laboratories. There is a large Computer Room and a very spacious Art and Design Technology Centre. Football, Rugby, and Cricket are played while other sports include Swimming, Athletics, Hockey and Basketball. There are two large Halls and an Astroturf. A full activities programme is available for boys from Chess Club to Golf. The Music Department provides Orchestra, Ensembles and two Choirs and there are fourteen visiting peripatetic teachers, who work within a sound-proofed music block.

There is a number of educational school trips arranged as well as trips overseas, including Italy, Greece and Skiing. The school operates a bus service to the Wimbledon and Putney areas.

Charitable status. Rokeby Educational Trust Limited is a Registered Charity, number 312653. It exists to provide an excellent education for boys aged 4–13.

Rose Hill School

Coniston Avenue, Tunbridge Wells, Kent TN4 9SY
Tel: 01892 525591
Fax: 01892 533312
email: admissions@rosehillschool.co.uk
website: www.rosehillschool.co.uk
Twitter: @rosehillschool

Chairman of Governing Body: Mr Charles Arthur

Headmaster: **P D Westcombe**, BA, PGCE

Deputy Head: W R Skottowe, BSc Hons, PGCE

Age Range. 3–13.
Number of Pupils. 173 Boys, 135 Girls.
Fees per term (2014–2015). £4,489 (Years 3–8); £3,355 (Reception–Year 2); £1,947–£2,204 (Kindergarten).

The school is situated in seventeen acres of beautiful grounds adjacent to the green belt, but within five minutes of the centre of the town. A superb Pre-Preparatory building was opened in 1991, followed by a new ICT centre. A Sports Hall was completed in 1998 and a new dining room and kitchen in 1999. Facilities also include an outdoor heated swimming pool and 6-hole golf course. A new block, comprising six classrooms, library and changing rooms, was completed in 2003 and linked to a superb Theatre and Creative Arts Centre in September 2008. An astroturf pitch was completed in 2010 and a £2.2m new teaching facility was opened in 2013. The building took 12 months to complete and is packed with state-of-the-art facilities, including a 95m^2 science laboratory, six teaching classrooms, two ICT suites, a learning skills suite and a surgery for the school nurse.

Children are prepared for Common Entrance and Scholarship entry to Independent Senior Schools and for competitive entry into local grammar schools at 11+ and 13+. Small classes, combined with an enriching curriculum, specialist teachers and exceptional pastoral care, ensure the pupils find and fulfil their potential.

Rose Hill was judged to be 'excellent' in all areas at its last inspection, with pastoral care particularly highlighted. The friendly and supportive atmosphere means children feel happy and secure.

Sport and the Creative Arts are highly valued. Hockey, Football, Rugby, Netball, Cricket, Rounders and Athletics are the main team games and they are supported by a range of individual sports. There is a junior and senior choir and many children receive instrumental tuition. Two major drama productions take place every year.

A full range of extra-curricular clubs, including Cubs and Brownies, ensures breadth of experience. Within a secure environment, based on clear Christian principles, children are encouraged to meet new challenges with confidence.

Charitable status. Rose Hill School is a Registered Charity, number 270158. It aims to provide a high quality education to boys and girls aged 3–13.

Rosemead Preparatory School

70 Thurlow Park Road, Dulwich, London SE21 8HZ
Tel: 020 8670 5865
Fax: 020 8761 9159
email: admin@rosemeadprepschool.org.uk
website: www.rosemeadprepschool.org.uk

Headteacher: **Mr A Bray**, Cert Ed

Age Range. 3–11.
Number of Pupils. Day: 170 Boys, 196 Girls.
Fees per term (2014–2015). £1,997–£3,618.

Rosemead is a well-established preparatory school with a fine record of academic achievement. Children are prepared for entrance to leading independent London day schools and local grammar schools at age 11, many gaining awards and scholarships. The school has a happy, family atmosphere with boys and girls enjoying a varied, balanced curriculum which includes maths, English, science, French, Spanish, information and communication technology, arts, physical education and humanities. Music and drama are strong subjects with tuition available in most orchestral instruments and various music groups meeting frequently. A full programme of physical education includes gymnastics, most major games, dance and (from age 6) swimming. Classes make regular visits to places of interest. Two residential field studies courses are arranged for children in the Prep department and activity courses are arranged during school holidays. Main entry to the school is at Nursery (age 3), following an informal assessment, and at National Curriculum Year 3, following a formal assessment. The school is administered by a board of governors elected annually by the parents.

All religious denominations welcome.

A small number of bursaries are available from Year 3.

Charitable status. Rosemead Preparatory School (The Thurlow Educational Trust) is a Registered Charity, number 1186165. It exists to provide a high standard of education in a happy, caring environment.

Rowan Preparatory School
United Learning

6 Fitzalan Road, Claygate, Esher, Surrey KT10 0LX
Tel: 01372 462627
Fax: 01372 470782
email: school.office@rowanprepschool.co.uk
website: www.rowanprepschool.co.uk

Chairman of the Local Governing Body: Mrs Karen Bowles

Headteacher: **Mrs Susan Clarke**, BEd, NPQH

Age Range. 3–11 (Pre-Preparatory age 3–7, Preparatory age 7–11).

Number of Pupils. 316 Day Girls.

Fees per term (2014–2015). Nursery (5 mornings) £1,280; Kindergarten (5 mornings) £1,672; Reception–Year 6 £3,268–£4,335.

In 1936, Miss Katherine Millar was determined to breathe new life into the English educational system. She wished to create an environment which inspired a passion for learning. The doors of Rowan were opened wide to enable girls to develop a strong sense of self and establish lasting friendships. Three quarters of a century on, Katherine Millar's core values are firmly established in the school. Girls achieve personal excellence in a warm, family environment.

As our motto says 'Hic Feliciter Laboramus'. Here we work happily.

The school is located on two sites very close to each other in a leafy part of Claygate. Rowan Brae accommodates the Nursery and Pre-Prep and Rowan Hill, the Prep.

Upon entering the Brae you cannot fail to notice the warm, friendly and happy atmosphere. The stimulating learning environment, both indoors and outdoors, creates an inspiring and engaging place to learn. Outstanding lessons and excellent resources allow all pupils to thrive and reach their potential. Girls in Year 2 are fully prepared for the seamless transition and exciting challenges which lay ahead at the Hill.

Girls at the Hill develop a thirst for knowledge, an appreciation of all subject areas and a deeper understanding of how to analyse and apply information across different areas of learning and in everyday life. The varied creative and outdoor curriculum continues to stimulate and inspire in all subject areas of day-to-day learning. Dynamic and challenging lessons, adapted to suit the girls' needs ensure that they

can truly achieve personal excellence. There is a superb ICT Suite, which was funded by the very supportive parents association, The Friends of Rowan, and well-equipped playgrounds and adventure walkways with a wooded area called The Spinney, which is held in great affection by the girls.

Admission in the Early Years is non-selective. Early registration is advisable if a place in the pre-prep is to be assured. Girls wishing to enter at other stages will be invited for a Taster Day where they will experience a day in the life of Rowan, involving assessments in maths and English.

Girls are prepared for entry to a wide variety of senior independent day and boarding schools. There is an excellent record of girls gaining places at their senior school of choice, including each year a number of girls being offered academic, music, sports or art scholarships.

Rowan offers a broad-based curriculum of work so that each pupil is able to develop her own talents and maximize her potential through an adventurous learning approach. The school welcomes visiting speakers and performers to enhance the curriculum. Day trips are also included in each term and the annual residential trips to Sayers Croft, The Isle of Wight, European ski resorts and France are both popular and highly educational in content. In addition, a wide variety of clubs are offered before and after school and at lunchtimes; they include drama, chess, art, science, foreign languages and a host of sports and musical activities. In addition, breakfast club and after-school prep clubs are available to support families.

Rowan has an excellent Music Department with all girls singing in a choir and playing the recorder. In addition, three-quarters of girls at the Hill play a further instrument. There are various ensembles, which the girls can also join in preparation for the orchestra. Girls at Rowan Brae are invited to play the violin or 'cello as part of the school's String Initiative during Year 1, a fantastic opportunity to learn about music and performance.

The school has excellent sporting opportunities and achievements. Girls have the chance to represent the school both locally and nationally for sports such as swimming, gymnastics, tennis and biathlon. Games are developed throughout the school with girls taking part in their first matches from Year 2.

Rowan is very proud of its art, providing stunning displays around both the Brae and the Hill expressing the girls' individuality and excellent capabilities.

With small classes on both sites and strong pastoral care it is Rowan's aim to provide the essential early grounding in a happy, stimulating and secure environment where every child's needs are catered for.

Prospective parents are asked to make an appointment to view the school during a normal working day or to attend one of the Open Mornings held each term. Girls entering the school at 7+ will be invited to take part in an assessment day in January.

Assisted places and Scholarships are available and details may be obtained upon request from the school Registrar.

Charitable status. Rowan Preparatory School has a Local Governing Body who play an active and supportive role in the school. Rowan is part of United Learning which is an educational trust controlled by a Board of Governors and chaired by Lord Carey which comprises: UCST (a Company Limited by Guarantee, Registered in England, number 2780748, and a Registered Charity, number 1016538) and ULT (a Company Limited by Guarantee, Registered in England, number 4439859, and an Exempt Charity).

The Rowans School

19 Drax Avenue, Wimbledon, London SW20 0EG
Tel: 020 8946 8220
email: office@rowans.org.uk
website: www.rowans.org.uk

Chairman of Governors: Mrs P L Hughes, CBE

Head: Mrs S Wingrove

Age Range. 3–7 Co-educational.
Number of Pupils. 130.
Fees per term (2014–2015). Nursery and Kindergarten £1,875, Reception, Year 1 and Year 2 £3,680.

The Rowans School was inspected by the Independent Schools Inspectorate (ISI) in October 2013 and was given a rating of "Excellent" in every area, the highest rating possible.

The school is one of the few independent co-educational schools in the area and is situated in a quiet road in Wimbledon, with beautiful grounds and large landscaped gardens, including its own tennis court. We pride ourselves on providing a nurturing, welcoming and happy start to school life. We have a long-standing reputation for academic and all-round excellence and sport, music and the creative arts contribute strongly to the school's lively curriculum.

The focus of our curriculum is to build strong academic foundations, encouraging a love of learning and enabling our children to discover and develop their personal strengths and talents. We prepare children for the 7+ examinations to many of the London Day Schools and have a highly successful track record of sending to the top local prep schools. Class sizes are kept to a maximum of 24 children, with at least one teaching assistant in every class. Music and sport are taught by specialist teachers and children are offered the opportunity of learning violin and piano.

The school takes full advantage of its location with frequent outings for each year group to museums, theatres and the local environment.

The school is very much a family school, with a warm, friendly, child-centred atmosphere.

Charitable status. The Rowans School is owned by King's College School, which is a Registered Charity, number 310024.

The Royal Masonic School for Girls
Pre-School, Pre-Prep and Prep Departments

Rickmansworth Park, Rickmansworth, Herts WD3 4HF
Tel: 01923 773168
Fax: 01923 896729
email: enquiries@royalmasonic.herts.sch.uk
website: www.royalmasonic.herts.sch.uk

Chairman of Governors: Mr J Gould

Headmistress: Mrs D Rose, MA Cantab

***Head of Cadogan House Pre-Prep & Prep Departments*:**
Mr I Connors, BA Hons, NPQH

Head of Ruspini House Pre-School: Mrs K Woodhead, BA

Age Range. Ruspini House: 2–4 Co-educational. Cadogan House: Girls 4–11.
Number of Pupils. Ruspini House 62; Cadogan House 235.

Fees per term (2014–2015). Cadogan House: Boarders (Years 3–6): £5,720 (Full), £5,510 (Weekly); Day Pupils: £3,120 (Reception, Years 1 and 2), £3,620 (Years 3–6). Ruspini House: please visit our website for range of fees.

Ruspini House is a small, friendly, caring community within the larger RMS family, guided by the same inclusive and nurturing ethos.

Housed in totally refurbished, modern and bespoke facilities and sharing our stunning grounds, Ruspini House welcomes boys and girls from 2 to 4 years. The youngest RMS pupils quickly settle into the stimulating, happy and supportive environment where all children are encouraged to reach their full potential through a healthy balance of learning and play.

We follow the principles of the Early Years Foundation Stage Curriculum and focus on each child's individual needs and talents. We encourage each child to develop at their own pace and they are well prepared for entry into their first school.

Recognised by the ISI as outstanding (2014), Ruspini House lays firm foundations for a love of learning. Boys and girls develop independence, curiosity and enthusiasm, learn good manners, courtesy and consideration for others within a busy and supportive framework, where they are challenged and have fun at the same time.

Cadogan House is the stunning, spacious and refurbished home of the RMS Pre-Preparatory and Preparatory Departments for girls aged 4 to 11 years. Recognised as excellent in all areas, Cadogan House is a warm and vibrant community alive with the buzz of happy, enthusiastic and motivated young learners, each of whom is valued as an individual.

The girls benefit from all of the facilities afforded by our magnificent site, including a designated Outdoor Learning Area. We have Forest School status, giving pupils experiences which complement traditional classroom learning, while building self-esteem, confidence and well-being.

The learning opportunities are exceptionally broad with outstanding teaching from both subject specialists and class teachers. Small class sizes ensure that teachers quickly get to know the girls and focus on nurturing their individual talents and strengths to enable them to become well-rounded independent young people. In Pre-Prep, English and Maths are taught each day as individual subject areas, whilst Science and Humanities are covered through cross-curricular work. In Years 3 to 6, girls study English, Mathematics, Science, Art, DT, French, Geography, History, Computing, Music, PE, PSHCE and Religious Studies, with several subjects taught by subject specialists.

Extra-curricular activities abound and sport and Performing Arts have a high profile; girls receive five PE lessons per week, including Swimming, Gymnastics and Dance, and all girls receive music and singing lessons each week, with most playing at least one musical instrument.

Above all, Cadogan House girls learn to exemplify the core RMS values of courtesy, compassion, and respect for others.

Charitable status. The Royal Masonic School Limited is a Registered Charity, number 276784.

Royal Russell Junior School

Coombe Lane, Croydon, Surrey CR9 5BX
Tel: 020 8651 5884
Fax: 020 8651 4169
email: juniorschool@royalrussell.co.uk
website: www.royalrussell.co.uk
Twitter: @Royal_Russell; @RRS_Sport

Patron: Her Majesty The Queen

Chairman of Governors: Mr K Young

Headmaster: Mr James C Thompson, BA QTS St Mary's Twickenham

Age Range. 3–11.
Number of Pupils. 174 Boys, 134 Girls.
Fees per term (2014–2015). Upper Juniors (Years 3–6) £3,915, Lower Juniors (Reception–Year 2) £3,200, Nursery £1,795–£3,200.

The Junior School stands on a magnificent wooded campus extending to over 100 acres, which it shares with Royal Russell Senior School (11–18 years). (*See Royal Russell School entry in HMC section.*)

The school is well served by road, tram and rail links and is one of the few co-educational schools in the Croydon area.

There is a fully-qualified teaching staff of 28. The school has a broad curriculum which seeks to blend the highest standards of academic work with a wide range of co-curricular activities. There are opportunities for all pupils to participate in football, netball, hockey, rounders, cross-country and cricket as team sports, and as individuals to be coached in athletics, swimming, tennis, gymnastics, trampolining and table tennis. There is an extensive fixture list of matches against other schools. Artistic development extends to include full dramatic and musical productions, and many pupils learn musical instruments. All forms of art, design and technology are actively encouraged. There are excellent teaching facilities which are complemented by an Assembly Hall, Science Laboratories, Music School, Art Room, Computer Suite, School Chapel and a Performing Arts Centre with a 200-seat auditorium. For sport, the impressive facilities include a large Sports Hall, Gymnasium, floodlit all-weather pitch for hockey and tennis, multi-use games area, netball courts, 4 grass pitches for athletics, football and cricket and an indoor swimming pool. All Junior School pupils receive weekly swimming lessons from qualified instructors.

The majority of the pupils join the school at 3 years into our Nursery, and transfer to the Senior School at 11+. Candidates for entry to the Lower Juniors and Early Years are interviewed informally, while all other entrants sit assessments in English, Mathematics and Cognitive Ability appropriate to their ages.

Prospective parents are very welcome to come and meet the Headmaster and to tour the school, by appointment.

Charitable status. Royal Russell School is a Registered Charity, number 271907. It exists solely to provide education to girls and boys.

Rudston Preparatory School

59/63 Broom Road, Rotherham, South Yorkshire S60 2SW
Tel: 01709 837774
Fax: 01709 837975
email: office@rudstonschool.com
website: www.rudstonschool.com

Co-educational Day School. The school is a charitable educational trust with a Board of Trustees.

Chairman of Trustees: Mrs H Yarlett, BA Hons, PGCE

Principal: Mr Guy Willatt, BEd Hons Cantab

Age Range. 3–11 years.
Number of Pupils. 78 Boys, 63 Girls.
Fees per term (2014–2015). £2,415 (Age 4–11).
There are 15 members of staff.

Rudston Preparatory School is Rotherham's only independent school, situated in the residential area of Broom. We offer specialist primary education for boys and girls aged three to eleven years.

At Rudston children are provided with a caring, safe and stimulating environment in which they can strive for academic excellence. Very high standards of behaviour are expected and children are taught the value of good manners, respect and friendship.

Charitable status. Rudston Preparatory School is a Registered Charity, number 529438. It exists to provide education for boys and girls.

Rupert House School

90 Bell Street, Henley-on-Thames, Oxon RG9 2BN
Tel: 01491 574263
Fax: 01491 573988
email: office@ruperthouse.oxon.sch.uk
website: www.ruperthouse.org

Chairman of Governors: Mrs A Collinson, MA Oxon

Headmistress: Mrs C Lynas, MA Hons English St Andrews, PGCE, MA Child Development London, NPQH

Age Range. Girls 3–11, Boys 3–7.
Number of Pupils. Girls 164, Boys 42.
Fees per term (2014–2015). £1,635 mornings only for 3 year olds) to £3,875 (inclusive).

Rupert House School, a Charitable Trust, is a day preparatory school for girls aged 3–11 and boys aged 3–7. The school is set in its own large garden in the centre of Henley-on-Thames. The pre-preparatory school is housed in a purpose-built unit and the older children work in a large Georgian House. Specialist facilities include a laboratory, art room, French room, music studio, IT suite and learning support room. There are all-weather games facilities on the site and a sports ground within a short walk.

The staff are fully qualified and experienced. They aim to give a sound and stimulating education in the basic subjects required for 11+ Common Entrance but are concerned also with the wider curriculum. Extra-curricular activities, which can include maths club, martial arts, Latin, netball, dance, swimming, art, craft, football, hockey and computers, are offered after school hours. Individual music lessons in piano, string and wind instruments are offered as an extra.

Within a disciplined framework, where courtesy and consideration are expected, there is a friendly, family atmosphere in which the individual nature of each child is respected. The pupils are encouraged to match their performance to potential and to meet all challenges with enthusiasm and determination. There are regular consultation evenings and twice yearly reports. Parents may consult the Headmistress at any time by appointment.

Care is taken to ensure that pupils are well prepared for transfer to a school suited to their academic ability and personal qualities. In recent years girls have gained admission to well respected Independent Senior Schools and boys to excellent Prep Schools.

Charitable status. Rupert House School is a Registered Charity, number 309648. It exists to provide quality education for boys and girls.

Russell House

Station Road, Otford, Sevenoaks, Kent TN14 5QU
Tel: 01959 522352
email: head@russellhouse.kent.sch.uk
website: www.russellhouseschool.co.uk

Head: Mr Craig McCarthy

Age Range. Co-educational 2–11+.
Number of Pupils. Boys 100, Girls 100.
Fees per term (2014–2015). Nursery Department (mornings) £1,785, Transition £1,835, Reception £3,045, Years 1–3 £3,520, Years 4–6 £4,030 (including lunch).

Russell House is a small, friendly school for boys and girls aged from 2 to 11.

We have a reputation for achieving excellent academic results in a friendly, caring and inclusive atmosphere where every child has access to myriad opportunities for extra-curricular activities.

Many of our pupils are successful in the 11+ examination, gaining entry to the local grammar schools, and others pass on to independent schools such as Sevenoaks. We have a consistently good record in gaining scholarships, both academic and music which goes hand in hand with an ethos which encourages individuality, self-expression, curiosity to learn and the ability to challenge accepted wisdom.

The school is careful to cultivate a calm, happy atmosphere and there is also a strong emphasis on building skills for the future and developing a sensitive awareness of the world beyond the school.

Rydal Penrhos Preparatory School

Pwllycrochan Avenue, Colwyn Bay, North Wales LL29 7BP
Tel: 01492 530381
Fax: 01492 539720
email: prep@rydalpenrhos.com
website: www.rydalpenrhos.com
Twitter: @RydalPenrhos

Chairman of Governors: The Revd J P Atkinson

Headmaster: Roger McDuff, BEd Hons, MA

Age Range. 2½–11.
Number of Pupils. 170 (93 boys, 77 girls).
Fees per term (2014–2015). Nursery: £625 (2 mornings) – £2,250 (5 full days); Reception–Year 2 £2,250–£2,590; Years 3–6 £2,590–£2,990.

Rydal Penrhos Preparatory School is a welcoming, vibrant school for young boys and girls aged 2½ to 11 years.

Ethos. As a Christian school with a Methodist foundation, it seeks to provide a firm but sympathetic moral framework in which care, support, respect, tolerance and responsibility for oneself and for others is accepted as fundamental. The School has a strong family atmosphere and concern for every aspect of a child's development. Parental support is encouraged and welcomed.

Environment. Set on a 12-acre site, the magnificent school building offers breathtaking views to the sea across playing fields and woodland. Maximum advantage is taken of the coastal aspect, the close proximity of the Snowdonia National Park and rich historic and cultural resources in the locality.

Curriculum. The School curriculum is very broad and is based on the National Curriculum. Teaching is mainly class based from the ages of 2½ to 8 and subject-based from 8 to 11, with input from subject specialists throughout. All children have the opportunity to develop their special interests and skills through a varied programme of extra-curricular activities.

Opportunities. Although the syllabus has rigorous academic elements, specialist provision is available within the School for those with learning difficulties. Sport, Music, Drama, Art, Design and Information Technology feature strongly and provide real opportunities for every child to explore and develop individual talents, not always expressed through academic work. Most pupils proceed through to Rydal Penrhos Senior School (*see entry in HMC section*).

Bursaries and Awards to the Senior School are offered at 11+. Parents appreciate the educational continuity between the junior and senior schools and the integrated curriculum ensures a smooth transition between the Schools.

Facilities at the Prep School are excellent, including science laboratories, a recently refurbished Information Technology suite, art studio, Design Technology room, gymnasium and a 25m indoor swimming pool. The large multi-purpose hall with stage provides for dance, drama, gymnastics and regular musical and dramatic productions. An orchestra is formed from class ensembles in Years 3–6 along with a variety of other instrumental ensembles. Choral singing is also of a high standard with all pupils singing together and two choirs. The School has an excellent reputation for both girls' and boys' sport.

The pupils make full use of the superb Astroturf and sports hall at the Senior School.

Positive Reinforcement. Discipline is clear and fair. Staff make sure that pupils are fully informed about their progress and take particular care to praise them for good work.

Playscheme/Holiday Club. A holiday club is also run by staff for many weeks of the school holidays.

Location. The Headmaster, colleagues and pupils assure visitors of a warm welcome at the school, which is easily accessed from the A55.

Charitable status. Rydal Penrhos Limited is a Registered Charity, number 1063489. It exists to provide education for boys and girls.

Ryde Junior School

Queen's Road, Ryde, Isle of Wight PO33 3BE
Tel: 01983 612901
email: juniorhead@rydeschool.org.uk
website: www.rydeschool.org.uk
Twitter: @rydeschool
Facebook: /rydeschool2013

Chairman of the Board of Governors: Dr C J Martin, BSc, DPhil, MBA, FIChemE, CEng

Head: H Edwards, BSc, PGCE

Age Range. 3–11.
Number of Pupils. 112 Boys, 113 Girls.
Fees per term (from January 2015). Tuition: Foundation Stage: £1,998–£2,218 (full day), £1,010 (half day); Pre-Prep £2,408–£3,068; Junior School £3,725. Boarding (excluding tuition): £4,255 (full), £3,720 (weekly). Rates for payment by Direct Debit. Lunch included.

Ryde School Assisted Places/Scholarships are awarded annually for pupils entering Year 3 and Year 5.

The school provides a good, civilised environment that does well academically for a wide range of ability. The pupils are well-motivated and work hard with evident enjoyment in both lessons and activities. By paying careful attention to all aspects of school life, pupils are able to flourish within a supportive community. In this environment, where regular contact between parents and staff is considered to be of paramount importance, children develop confidence and happily give of their best.

Ryde Junior School caters for children aged 3–11 years. Fiveways, just across the road from the main site, is home to the Foundation Stage and Early Years. Through creative and imaginative teaching in new purpose-built classrooms, a sound foundation of key skills is established. At the end of Key Stage 1 pupils are ready to move to the 'senior' part of the Junior School, having already benefited from some specialist teaching in the Junior School. Here they continue to receive the support of a well qualified and dedicated staff, enjoying a full range of specialist facilities including a continually upgraded ICT facility, with Internet access across the school, a Creative Centre, Science Laboratory, Music room and Theatre.

A broad, balanced and rich curriculum is followed. This is based on the National Curriculum, but is greatly enhanced with children working towards ISEB 11+ examinations. A wealth of trips and outings is offered, enriching the curriculum still further, making use not only of the beautiful sites on the Island, but on the mainland and abroad. Pupils are encouraged to develop their full range of talents, with Music, Drama and Sports enjoying equally high profiles. The school maintains a consistently successful record in all areas of team and individual sports. The major sports offered are: Athletics, Cricket, Cross-Country, Hockey, Netball, Rounders, Rugby, Soccer, Swimming and Tennis, with fixtures being arranged both locally and on the mainland (at no extra charge). There is a full and wide ranging programme of clubs and activities (which changes each term) during lunchtime and after school, offering something for everyone.

Our Senior School is on the same campus, enabling us to benefit from the use of a Sports Hall and pitches. Careful liaison between the staff and induction days in the summer term effect a smooth transition for our pupils to the Senior School (*see entry in HMC section*).

The Junior School takes weekly and full boarders who, together with Senior School boarders, have use of the range of facilities available at the Bembridge campus, situated in some 100 acres on a beautiful cliff top site approximately six miles from Ryde. Transport is provided to and from the school during the week.

Charitable status. Ryde School with Upper Chine is a Registered Charity, number 307409. The aims and objectives of the Charity are the education of boys and girls.

Rydes Hill Preparatory School

Rydes Hill House, Aldershot Road, Guildford, Surrey GU2 8BP
Tel: 01483 563160
email: admissions@rydeshill.com
website: www.rydeshill.com

Chairman of the Governors: Mr Dermot Gleeson, MA Cantab

Headmistress: **Mrs Stephanie Bell**, MA Oxon

Age Range. Girls 3–11, Boys 3–7. Nursery class for children 3–4.
Number of Day Pupils. 210.
Fees per term (2014–2015). £2,381–£3,771 including lunch.

Rydes Hill Preparatory School and Nursery has an exceptionally caring, family atmosphere. It has a thriving Nursery and is a Catholic School which welcomes children from all denominations and offers an excellent start academically and socially.

Although Rydes Hill Preparatory School and Nursery is non-selective academically, it achieves outstanding results

and received the top rating in every category in the most recent ISI Inspection in June 2011. "*The pupils' achievements, attitudes and skills are excellent*", "*The teaching is excellent*", "*Pupils are keen to learn and they make excellent progress*", "*The pupils' moral awareness is excellent*".

Experienced and dedicated teachers encourage self-esteem and help pupils excel. Year after year, a high percentage of Year Six pupils are awarded scholarships to leading senior schools. Music, French, Ballet, Drama, Science, Sport including swimming, ICT and Art are taught by specialist teachers. Every pupil performs in one of the school's productions and the creative arts are major strengths of the School.

Extra-Curricular activities include: Speech and Drama, Ballet, Junior and Senior Choirs, Orchestra, Gymnastics, Instrumental Music Tuition (Pianoforte, Clarinet, Flute, Violin, Trumpet, Harp, Guitar, Cornet, and Cello), Tennis, French, Italian, as well as Mathematical Challenge, Netball and Cross Country Clubs. An extended school day is available from the 7.30 am Breakfast Club to the 5.30 pm Stay & Play Club, which includes a healthy afternoon tea. Supervised homework sessions are also offered every day.

Rydes Hill Preparatory School and Nursery is located in a beautiful Georgian house with a panelled Library, vaulted Dining Hall, Victorian Conservatory and galleried, panelled Entrance Hall. Facilities also include a large Science Laboratory, ICT Suite, Netball and Tennis Courts and a purpose-built Music and Performing Arts Studio.

Charitable status. Rydes Hill Preparatory School and Nursery is a Registered Charity, number 299411. It exists to ensure excellence in all aspects of education.

The Ryleys

Alderley Edge, Cheshire SK9 7UY
Tel: 01625 583241
Fax: 01625 581900
email: info@theryleys.com
website: www.theryleys.com
Twitter: @TheRyleys
Facebook: /The-Ryleys

Chairman of Governors: Mr B Staples

Headteacher: **Mrs Claire Hamilton**, BSc Hons, PGCE

Age Range. 3–11/13.
Number of Pupils. 206 Day Boys, 64 Day Girls.
Fees per term (2014–2015). Nursery: £2,116.80 (full day); Reception, Years 1–2 £3,087, Years 3–4 £3,197, Years 5–6 £3,473, Years 7 and 8 £3,584.

Having a long history dating back to the 1870s, The Ryleys has developed a reputation as one of the best independent preparatory schools in the North West, with places at the School being much sought after. Situated in the idyllic village of Alderley Edge, the popular school lies in the heart of the leafy Cheshire countryside, just 15 miles south of the city of Manchester, within easy reach of the motorway and rail networks and close to Manchester Airport.

Starting at age 3, the extremely popular Pre-School gently prepares its pupils for the start of their educational journey, and provides the boys and girls with the advantage of familiarity with the school when they come to take the next step on to formal education.

As the children move through the school, the small class sizes and subject specialist teaching ensures that each and every child receives the individual attention, motivation and encouragement necessary to fulfil their potential. Headteacher Claire Hamilton hopes to send children on to the next stage of their education as confident, enthusiastic and caring individuals who are ready to grasp every opportunity available to them.

The Ryleys provides so much more than just an academic education; it provides unrivalled opportunities to discover and nurture talents outside of the classroom, including music, sport, art and drama.

Children are thoroughly prepared for entry via examination into Independent Day Schools at 11 and 13 or into Boarding Schools at 13 via the Common Entrance or Scholarship examinations. The school has an excellent academic record.

By the time they leave The Ryleys, pupils are equipped with the skills, character and confidence to see them achieve their future goals. All leavers go on to achieve places at highly regarded independent day and boarding schools of their choice, with many winning prestigious music, sports or academic scholarships.

Football, Rugby, Cricket, Athletics, Hockey, Rounders and Netball are the main team games and there is an extensive fixture list of matches against other schools at various ages. The school has undertaken sports tours to Italy and Spain in the last few years and there is an annual skiing trip to Europe or North America. Outdoor pursuits are encouraged and the school organises a regular expedition to Rua Fiola in Scotland.

Music is another of the school's great strengths with well over 130 children receiving individual instrumental tuition from a highly-qualified staff of 9 visiting teachers. The school has a fine reputation for its concerts and musical productions. These performances take place on a full proscenium stage and every child is involved in one of the four productions each year. There are three choirs involving over 70 children.

Children are accepted into the school at various ages providing places are available and are informally assessed upon entry so that the correct educational provision can be made in order to ensure that each pupil achieves his/her full potential. Scholarships and Bursaries are available.

The school places great emphasis upon such personal qualities as good manners and consideration for others.

Charitable status. The Ryleys School Limited is a Registered Charity, number 525915. It exists to provide a quality education for children from 3 to 13 years of age.

St Albans High School for Girls Preparatory School

Wheathampstead House, Codicote Road, Wheathampstead, Hertfordshire AL4 8DJ
Tel: 01582 839270
Fax: 01582 839271
email: WHOffice@stahs.org.uk
website: www.stahs.org.uk
Twitter: @STAHSPrep

Chair of School Council: Miss Dorothy Henderson, MA Cantab, MA Birkbeck

Head of the Preparatory School: Ms G M Bradnam, BEd, MA Ed Mgmt, NPQH

Age Range. Girls 4–11.
Number of Pupils. 300.
Fees per term (2014–2015). Reception (age 4) £3,795 (inc Lunch), Years 1 and 2 (age 5–6) £4,005 (inc Lunch); Years 3–6 (age 7–11) £4,005 (exc Lunch).

The Preparatory School for St Albans High School for Girls is a very popular, academically selective school, with a welcoming family atmosphere, offering outstanding pastoral care. St Albans High School is uniquely placed in being able to offer all the advantages of a continuous education in two very different settings. From the ages of 4–11, the girls have the freedom to grow and develop in an attractive rural envi-

ronment, before moving on to the more urban setting of the Senior School, close to the heart of the City of St Albans.

The Preparatory School, Wheathampstead House, is set in 18 acres of grounds, within the village of Wheathampstead. The extensive site includes play areas, an adventure playground, woods and an outdoor learning classroom.

The curriculum extends beyond the National Curriculum in all year groups; French is taught from Year 3. State-of-the-art facilities support innovative teaching and the development of independent, creative thinkers, who are confident in the use of new technologies. There are specialist rooms for Science, Art, DT and ICT with a very extensive library. Pupils at the Preparatory School use the school swimming pool located at the Senior School.

It is a happy and exciting school with a wide variety of activity days and educational visits throughout the school year. There is an extensive range of clubs including Science, Art, Speech and Drama, Puzzles, Dancing, Sports, Orienteering through to Latin, Mandarin and Spanish. Music is a real strength of the school and there are plenty of orchestras, bands and choirs. Enrichment groups extend and support learning and there are opportunities for highly talented pupils to join with Senior School girls for Music and Sport events.

The School provides a supportive, challenging and creative environment, where girls work hard, are very successful academically and enjoy learning. It provides support for mild dyslexia and mild dyspraxia, all screened in Year 3.

Open Days. Friday 10 October 2014; Saturday 15 November 2014; Friday 5 June 2015.

Charitable status. St Albans High School for Girls is a Registered Charity, number 311065.

St Andrew's Prep

Meads, Eastbourne, East Sussex BN20 7RP
Tel: 01323 733203
Fax: 01323 646860
email: admissions@standrewsprep.co.uk
website: www.standrewsprep.co.uk

Chairman of the Governing Body: Admiral Sir Ian Forbes, KCB, CBE

Head: S Severino, BA Hons, PGCE

Age Range. 1–13.
Number of Pupils. 269 (Prep School), 151 (Pre-Prep and Nursery).
Fees per term (2014–2015). Full boarding £7,320; Weekly Boarding £6,495; Flexible boarding – prices on application; Day children: £5,155 (Years 4–8), £4,680 (Year 3), Pre-Prep £2,960. Nursery sessions: please enquire at the school for session costs and EYEE discounts.

Situated in 12 acres of grounds at the foot of the South Downs, St Andrew's, founded in 1877, has a highly qualified teaching staff and children are taught in classes with a maximum size of 20 and an average number of approximately 16. A number of children in the Prep department are boarders and the school operates a popular scheme of 'sleepover' boarding allowing day children to stay any number of nights during the week on a flexible basis.

The Head is supported by a Deputy Head and a strong management team. All children in the school have a Form Teacher or Form Tutor who is responsible for their pastoral welfare and academic progress. Each section of the school has its own Head (Nursery and Pre-Prep, Junior, Middle and Senior), who coordinates, together with the Deputy Head and Academic Directors, the overall pastoral and academic work of the staff.

In addition to the expanse of playing fields, St Andrew's benefits from its own indoor swimming pool and a well-equipped gymnasium. There are three computer suites equipped with up-to-date software and hardware including a wireless network connection and interactive whiteboards. The equipment in the Pre-Prep suite is designed specifically for children from 3 to 7 years of age. Other facilities include a modern purpose-built music block, an extensively equipped research and resource centre, a chapel and a creative arts centre with an art studio and design and technology facilities. The school strongly encourages music and drama and more than two-thirds of the children play instruments and participate in orchestras, bands and choirs. As well as music, drama is a timetabled subject and plays take place every term.

From the age of nine, children are taught by subject specialists. French is taught from the age of 5 and Latin is introduced from the age of 9. Children are introduced to working on computers at the age of two. The breadth of the curriculum means that, while the requirements of the National Curriculum are fulfilled, the children are able to experience a variety of other stimulating activities.

Accelerated sets exist from Year 5 to provide more challenging opportunities for those who are academically gifted. Academic, art, music, and sports awards have been achieved to many major senior schools and over the past five years more than 150 scholarships have been won by St Andrew's pupils. The school amalgamated with Eastbourne College in 2010 and benefits from the College facilities and staff with approximately half the leavers each year progressing there. Where necessary, extra Specific Needs teaching is provided as well as ESL support.

There is a wide range of activities on offer. The Co-Curricular programme, which runs for children in Years 5 to 8, offers opportunities for all children to develop areas of interest and strength or to discover new ones. Each activity offered has its own educational objectives and challenges designed to improve children's skills and broaden their horizons. An extensive programme of after-school activities has always been a strong feature of St Andrew's. This starts at the Pre-Prep and runs through to Year 8. The school also operates various activity weeks and courses during the school holidays, which are run by our own staff, including art, cricket, rugby, football, swimming, tennis, netball and hockey.

The school's strong sporting reputation manifests itself in national honours regularly achieved in many different sports. Specialist coaches are employed to teach the skills required for all to enjoy participating in team games and opportunities are available to anyone wishing to represent the school.

Charitable status. Eastbourne College Incorporated is a Registered Charity, number 307071. The aim of the Charity is the promotion of Education.

St Andrew's School

Buckhold, Pangbourne, Reading, Berks RG8 8QA
Tel: 0118 974 4276
email: admin@standrewspangbourne.co.uk
website: www.standrewspangbourne.co.uk
Twitter: @StAndrewsSch

The School is an Educational Trust controlled by a Board of Governors.

Chairman of Governors: Mrs Felicity M Rutland

Headmaster: **Dr D Livingstone**, BSc, PhD, NPQH

Age Range. 3–13. Weekly Boarding from age 7.
Number of Pupils. 300 including weekly boarders.

Fees per term (2014–2015). Boarders £5,630–£6,110; Day Pupils £3,095–£5,175. Nursery from £1,465 (5 mornings).

The School is fully co-educational and set in over 50 acres of private wooded estate and parkland.

The Curriculum includes all the traditional CE and Scholarship subjects and there is emphasis on Music, Speech and Drama and Modern Languages. Study Skills are an important part of the senior pupils' timetable and Information Technology is well resourced.

Academic and Sporting standards are high.

Charitable status. St Andrew's (Pangbourne) School Trust Limited is a Registered Charity, number 309090. It exists to provide education for boys and girls.

St Andrew's School, Woking

Church Hill House, Wilson Way, Horsell, Woking, Surrey GU21 4QW
Tel: 01483 760943
Fax: 01483 740314
email: hmsec@st-andrews.woking.sch.uk
           admin@st-andrews.woking.sch.uk
website: www.st-andrews.woking.sch.uk
Twitter: @StAndrewsWoking
Facebook: /standrewsschoolwoking

Chairman of Governors: Mrs Jenny Way

Headmaster: **Mr Adrian Perks**, MSc

Deputy Head: Mr Jonathan Spooner, MA Hons

Age Range. 3–13 co-educational.
Number of Pupils. Total: 313 Day pupils. Pre-Prep and Nursery 144.
Fees per term (2014–2015). Prep £3,830–£4,480. Pre-Prep £1,140–£3,300.

Average Class Size: 16–18.

St Andrew's School was founded in 1937 and is an established, respected and thriving co-educational prep school, set in 11 acres of grounds within a quiet residential area approximately half a mile from Woking town centre. The School seeks to create a nurturing and happy environment of trust and support in which all pupils are encouraged and enabled to develop their skills, talents, interests and potential to the full – intellectually, physically and spiritually, regardless of social circumstances, age or religion.

Within St Andrew's walls children feel secure and confident and are highly motivated to perform to the best of their ability in all aspects of school life. They are competitive without losing sight of their responsibility to share and they are justifiably proud of their school and their own personal achievements. In a world of changing values, self-confidence and a solid grounding are essential building blocks for life. St Andrew's hopes to provide all their children with this basic foundation as they prepare for the bigger challenges that follow. Children are prepared for entrance and scholarship exams to a wide range of independent senior schools and there are specialist teaching facilities for all subjects including science, ICT, music and art. The curriculum is broad and the school places great emphasis on music, sport and the arts.

St Andrew's is very proud of its excellent on-site facilities including an all-weather sports surface, sports pitches, tennis courts, cricket nets and outdoor heated swimming pool. We are very fortunate to enjoy the benefits of carefully designed school grounds that incorporate facilities to meet the needs of the children's physical and social development. Main school games are football, hockey, cricket, netball and rounders. Other activities include, cross-country running, swimming, tennis and athletics.

Children can be supervised at school from 8 am and, through our extensive after-school activities programme for Year 3 and above, until 6/6.30 pm most evenings during the week. There is also an after-school club from 4 pm to 6 pm (chargeable) for Pre-Prep and Year 3 children.

Children are assessed for entry into Year 2 and above. Contact the School for more information regarding scholarships and bursaries.

Charitable status. St Andrew's (Woking) School Trust is a Registered Charity, number 297580, established to promote and provide for the advancement of education of children.

S. Anselm's

Stanedge Road, Bakewell, Derbyshire DE45 1DP
Tel: 01629 812734
Fax: 01629 814742
email: headmaster@anselms.co.uk
website: www.sanselms.co.uk
Twitter: @SAnselmsPrep

The School is an Educational Trust.

Chairman of Governors: R Howard

Headmaster: **P Phillips**, BH Hons London, MA Ed, PG Cert SpLD, NPQH

Age Range. 3–13.
Numbers. Prep School (age 7 to 13) 79 boys, 56 girls. Pre-Prep (age 3 to 7) 60 boys and girls.
Fees per term (2014–2015). Boarders: £6,810. Day: Prep £4,570–£5,660; Pre-Prep £2,960.

Welcome to S. Anselm's School, the only independent co-educational prep school in Derbyshire. Situated in the heart of the glorious Peak District it offers outstanding academic, sporting and extra-curricular opportunities to all pupils. We actively welcome children of all abilities at the school and pride ourselves on cherishing each individual child and allowing their full potential to shine through.

S. Anselm's sits on the crest of a hill in the heart of the Peak National Park – a beacon of excellence in all it does. All parents seek an environment where their children can remain children for as long as possible. Here at S. Anselm's it is just so. Through everything we do this ethos remains steadfast. We are proud of our tradition and are not ashamed to say that the values we hold dear are the very reason this school is quite unique.

With an 18-acre campus in the Peak District the children are surrounded by beauty and opportunities to explore. We have 5 netball courts, an indoor swimming pool, a recently renovated sports hall, a theatre with a permanent stage, a dedicated music block, 2 fully equipped science laboratories, a new DT facility and a newly developed library for 2014. The school is forward looking in its approach to IT having invested heavily in it over the last 2 years with iPads for learning, fully interactive whiteboards and Wi-Fi throughout the school.

The boarders enjoy a varied programme of activities including the debating club and fiercely fought tournaments of dodgeball. Those who learn music practise for 20 minutes every evening and cocoa and toast every night give a homely feel to bedtime.

Here our pupils are encouraged to be themselves; they are genuinely excited about learning and have a real thirst for knowledge. They thrive in the music and art rooms, and on the games field and stage. Pupils adore this school and are justly proud of all they do. They love learning and there is a true sense of fun.

Our small class sizes mean our staff can plan their teaching to ensure every pupil is treated as an individual. Each child is cared for and nurtured in every way they need. Our teaching staff simply want the very best for all our pupils and will do all they can to help them achieve their own personal best.

At the very centre of our values is creativity – whether through the individual or the community. It is creativity in thought and every aspect of life that sets a S. Anselm's pupil apart from others. We encourage our children to be creative in their thinking and their play and strongly believe in the importance of nurturing an environment where they can fully and confidently explore their individuality. This is a kind, caring and tolerant school and we are quite sure this wonderful environment will make a lasting impression on all who visit.

Charitable status. S. Anselm's is a Registered Charity, number 527179. It exists to provide an excellent all-round education for boys and girls.

St Anthony's Preparatory School
Alpha Plus Group

90 Fitzjohns Avenue, Hampstead, London NW3 6AA
Tel: 020 7435 3597 (Junior House)
          020 7435 0316 (Senior House)
          020 7431 1066 (Admissions)
Fax: 020 7435 9223
email: headmaster@stanthonysprep.co.uk
website: www.stanthonysprep.org.uk

Headmaster: **P M Keyte**, MA Oxon

Age Range. 4–13.
Number of Boys. 295 Day Boys.
Fees per term (2014–2015). £5,320–£5,430 including lunches.

Founded in the 19th century and set in the heart of Hampstead village, St Anthony's is an academic IAPS preparatory school for boys between the ages of 4 and 13. It is Roman Catholic but welcomes boys of other faiths. The majority of boys transfer at 13, via scholarship or CE, to leading independent senior schools including Westminster, University College, Habs, Merchant Taylors, St Paul's, Mill Hill, Highgate, Harrow, Eton, City of London, Ampleforth, and Oundle. It is now part of the prestigious Alpha Plus Group of schools. Its CEO is Graham Able, former Chairman of HMC and Headmaster of Dulwich College. The school has just finished a major rebuilding and refurbishment programme spearheaded through its new Governance.

The school accommodation consists of two large Victorian houses in close proximity. Both have their own grounds and separate playgrounds. There are eight forms in the Junior House, where boys range in age from four to eight, and ten forms in the Senior House, where boys range in age from eight to thirteen. The Senior House has a specialist Design and Technology room, a Music room, a Dance & Drama studio, wireless network, a Science laboratory and a swimming pool. Games fields are close by.

All boys receive Religious Education lessons twice a week. The course, which centres on Catholic beliefs and practices, but includes aspects of other faiths, is followed by all pupils. The school's spiritual dimension is regarded as highly important and it exists within a liberal and inclusive atmosphere. Most pupils attend mass about three times each term.

The school curriculum is stimulating and challenging and, for example, it is possible for boys to study five foreign languages. All pupils must study three, including French and Mandarin from Year 1. The arts have an important place in the school with a majority of boys learning to play a musical instrument and all boys involved in drama. Sport is a further strength of the school with some pupils achieving success on a national stage.

St Anthony's still retains a slightly bohemian tradition with former pupils making their mark in the fields of rock music and art. Recently, pupils have been awarded music scholarships to Eton, Highgate and UCS. Academic awards were also achieved at St Paul's, Habs & City.

The school works hard to instil in its pupils a sense of social responsibility and charity fundraising is a feature of school life. A former pupil was awarded the Gusi Peace Prize (Asian equivalent of the Nobel) and the school has just financed the building of a kindergarten for a school in southern India. Much work is also done with local charities.

St Aubyn's School

Bunces Lane, Woodford Green, Essex IG8 9DU
Tel: 020 8504 1577
Fax: 020 8504 2053
email: school@staubyns.com
website: www.staubyns.com

The School was founded in 1884 and is governed by a Charitable Trust.

Chairman of the Governors: Mrs E Ruff, LLB

Headmaster: **Len Blom**, BEd Hons, BA, HDE Phys Ed, NPQH

Deputy Head: Marcus Shute, BEd

Age Range. 3–13+.
Number of Children. 510 Day.
Fees per term (from April 2014). £1,537 (Nursery) to £3,483 (Seniors) fully inclusive.

St Aubyn's provides an all-round preparatory education for children aged 3–13. The School is non-selective at its main point of entry for children aged 3 and 4. There are assessment tests for older children, principally at ages 7+ and 11+.

Classes are small, taught by well-qualified, dedicated staff. Nursery and Reception children are also supported by nursery nurses and teaching assistants. A full-time qualified nurse deals with all medical issues and emergencies.

The School offers a wide-ranging curriculum within a traditional framework, encompassing all National Curriculum and Common Entrance requirements. French is taught from 4+ and Latin from 10+. French, Music and PE are specialist-taught from an early age. All subjects are specialist-taught from Year 6.

Children progress to a range of independent and state schools at 11+ and 13+. Pupils gain a range of scholarships at both 11 and 13. Recent awards include several academic scholarships as well as awards in Sport, Technology, Music and Drama. In 2014 a total of 11 awards were gained by a total of 7 children.

The School is pleasantly situated on the borders of Epping Forest, yet is close both to the North Circular and the M11. There are three departments within the School: Pre Prep (3+, 4+, 5+, 6+); Middle School (7+, 8+, 9+) and Seniors (10+, 11+ and 12+) and each has its own base and resources. Facilities are extensive with 8 acres of grounds, large Sports Centre, all-weather pitch, fully-equipped Performing Arts Centre and Music School, Science Laboratory, Art and Design and Technology Base, a Library and two IT Suites. A computer network runs throughout the school. Games include football, cricket, hockey, rugby, tennis, netball, athletics and swimming, all coached to a high standard.

The Director of Music leads a thriving department, with a school orchestra and various instrumental groups and choirs. Children are regularly involved in performances both within and outside the School. St Aubyn's has also gained the British Council's International School Award.

Most recently the School has benefited from the creation of a new dining facility and second performance space. The old dining hall has now become the designated Art and Design and Technology Base.

St Aubyn's School is a registered charity. All income from fees is for the direct benefit of its pupils. Two scholarships are available at 11+. The primary criterion for the award of a scholarship is academic ability, though special talent in music, technology, art, sport, etc may be taken into account. There is a bursary scheme at 7+.

Charitable status. St Aubyn's (Woodford Green) School Trust is a Registered Charity, number 270143. It exists to provide education for children.

St Bede's Preparatory School

Bishton Hall, Wolseley Bridge, Nr Stafford,
Staffordshire ST17 0XN
Tel: 01889 881277
Fax: 01889 882749
email: admin@saintbedes.com
website: www.saintbedes.com

(Under the patronage of His Grace the Archbishop of Birmingham)

Headmaster: **C W H Stafford Northcote**, BA

Age Range. 3–13.
Number of Pupils. 122 Boys and Girls.
Fees per term (2014–2015). £4,500 Boarders and Weekly Boarders, £2,250–£3,725 Day Pupils. Compulsory Extras Nil.

Saint Bede's is a Catholic Preparatory School, in which other faiths and denominations are welcomed.

Saint Bede's was founded in 1936 by the Grandparents of the current Headmaster. Since then, the Northcote family has educated young people as additions to their own family, treating each child with care and respect. This has helped to create an educational atmosphere unlike any other.

Bishton Hall is a Grade II* listed Georgian Mansion, surrounded by 25 acres of beautifully kept gardens and woodland and 7 acres of professionally levelled playing fields. The school has its own Chapel, hard tennis courts, indoor heated swimming pool, gymnasium/theatre and science laboratory. Situated on the edge of Cannock Chase, this rural setting provides children with a happy and safe environment in which to learn.

Pupils are prepared for all Independent Schools and many Scholarships have been won.

There is a teaching staff of 13 with visiting teachers for violin, brass instruments and guitar. A specialist Drama Teacher teaches Performing Arts to a highly proficient standard.

The Craft, Design and Technology Centre incorporates metal work and metal casting, carpentry, pottery, enamelling, jewellery making, computers, art and stone polishing.

Tennis, Rugby, Cricket, Rounders, Hockey, Netball and Volleyball are played in season.

The Headmaster is personally responsible for the health and welfare of the children. Individual care is taken of each child and good manners and consideration for others insisted upon. An acknowledged feature of the School is its family atmosphere.

For further particulars, please contact the School Office.

St Benedict's Junior School

5 Montpelier Avenue, Ealing, London W5 2XP
Tel: 020 8862 2050
Fax: 020 8862 2058
email: enquiries@stbenedicts.org.uk
website: www.stbenedicts.org.uk
Twitter: @stbenedicts
Facebook: /StBenedictsSchool
LinkedIn: /st-benedicts-school

Governing Body:
The Governing Board of St Benedict's School

Headmaster: Mr R G Simmons, BA Hons, PGCE

Age Range. 3–11 Co-educational.
Number of Pupils. 304.
Fees per term (2014–2015). Pre-Prep: £3,660; Junior School: £4,070.

Our ethos is firmly based in the Benedictine Catholic tradition, and the pastoral and spiritual care of our pupils is central to all that we do. It is the School's mission to '*teach a way of living*' that goes beyond the acquisition of formal academic qualifications and ensures a holistic approach to education from the Nursery through to Sixth Form.

St Benedict's provides a stimulating academic education within a broad, balanced and progressive curriculum. Great importance is placed on achievements in Art, Design Technology, Drama, Information and Communications Technology, Music and Sport. In addition, we offer a wide range of co-curricular activities, including Choir and Orchestra, Dance, Eco Gardening, Fencing, Ju-Jitsu, and Swimming. High-quality teaching, exceptional pastoral care, small classes and a broad curriculum ensure that all pupils have the opportunity to achieve their potential. Interactive whiteboards are present in every classroom and the Library is very well-resourced.

Girls and boys are taught together throughout their time at St Benedict's (3–18), with the exception of traditional single-sex sports. Specialist teachers provide tuition in French, Information and Computing Technology, Science, Music and Art Design Technology. Excellent academic results across the School are matched by equally impressive value-added scores, reflecting the strong and effective partnership between pupils, parents and the staff. We rejoice in the successes of all of our pupils.

The natural points of entry in the Junior School and Nursery are at 3+, 4+ and 7+. Entry is possible at other ages subject to the availability of places.

Charitable status. St Benedict's School Ealing is a Registered Charity, number 1148512, and a Charitable Company Limited by Guarantee, number 8093330.

St Bernard's Preparatory School

Hawtrey Close, Slough, Berkshire SL1 1TB
Tel: 01753 521821
Fax: 01753 552364
email: registrar@stbernardsprep.org
website: www.stbernardsprep.org

Headteacher: Mr N S Cheesman, BEd

Age Range. 2½–11 co-educational.
Number of Pupils. 261.
Fees per term (2014–2015). £2,430–£2,940.
St Bernard's Preparatory has a unique ethos. We are a Catholic school, teaching the Catholic faith and living out the Gospel values which are shared by all faiths and are the foundation of all our relationships and the daily life of our school. We welcome and embrace children of all faiths and we recognise and celebrate our similarities and differences, developing mutual respect, understanding and tolerance.

We recognise the value and uniqueness of each individual, both child and adult. We celebrate the talents and gifts of each child and enable them to develop to their full potential spiritually, morally, academically, socially and physically. Our children are happy, courteous, confident, articulate young citizens, committed to the ideal of service to others.

We work in partnership with parents, recognising that they are the first and best educators of their child. We consider ourselves to be very privileged that parents have entrusted us with the care and education of their child. We ensure that parents are kept fully informed of their child's progress.

We are committed to offering a broad, balanced, creative and challenging curriculum, enriched by experiences and opportunities which enhance and consolidate the learning process. Small class sizes enable our team of highly qualified, caring, committed and enthusiastic teachers to be responsive to the needs of the individual child ensuring continuity and progression for all our children. We have developed a wide and varied range of after-school activities which broaden the curriculum and enrich the children's lives. Children are encouraged to develop new skills.

We are proud of our reputation as a school with a strong ethos and nurturing pastoral care coupled with academic excellence reflected in consistently outstanding results in local and national tests.

Our school motto 'Dieu Mon Abri' meaning 'God is my Shelter', is an inspiring reminder of God's love for each one of us. The three swords represent 'Love, Work and Prayer' which underpin and permeate the life of our school.

St Catherine's Preparatory School

Bramley, Guildford, Surrey GU5 0DF
Tel: 01483 899665; Senior School: 01483 893363
Fax: 01483 899669
email: prepschool.office@stcatherines.info
website: www.stcatherines.info
Twitter: @stcatsbramley

Chairman of the Governing Body: Mr Peter J Martin, BA, FRGS, FCCA

Headmistress: Mrs Alice Phillips, MA Cantab

Head of Preparatory School: Miss Naomi Bartholomew, MA London, BEd Cantab

Age Range. 4–11.
Number of Pupils. 264 Day Girls.
Fees per term (from January 2015). Pre-Prep 1 £2,720, Pre-Prep 2 £3,295, Pre-Prep 3 £3,890; Prep School £4,595.

Girls are accepted from the age of 4 to 11 when they take the Entrance Examinations for entry to Senior Schools.

Charitable status. St Catherine's School Bramley is a Registered Charity, number 1070858, which exists to provide education for girls in accordance with the principles of the Church of England.

St Cedd's School

178a New London Road, Chelmsford, Essex CM2 0AR
Tel: 01245 392810
Fax: 01245 392815
email: info@stcedds.org.uk
website: www.stcedds.org.uk

Chairman of Governors: Mr D Thompson

Head: **Dr P A Edmonds**, EdD, MEd, BEd Hons

Age Range. 3–11 Co-educational.
Number of Pupils. 400.
Fees per term (2014–2015). £2,790–£2,980 including lunch.

St Cedd's School, founded in 1931, is a leading co-educational day school for children aged three to 11. The grounds and purpose-built facilities create a vibrant and purposeful learning environment where children are encouraged to become independent, confident and caring individuals. A St Cedd's School education focuses on high standards of literacy and numeracy within an expansive academic broad and balanced curriculum, supplemented by a superb programme of sport and an extraordinary creative output of drama and the performing arts. PE, Music, Art and French are taught by specialist teachers from Nursery; Swimming and Recorders are introduced in Year 2 and International Studies is studied in Years 5 and 6. Following the 11+ entry and independent school examinations, a baccalaureate-style curriculum in Year 6 leads to the Hold Fast award which celebrates the breadth of children's achievements and talents. Music is a particular strength of the school with outstanding individual instrumental examination results. St Cedd's School is a member of the Chelmsford Choral Foundation and this link to Chelmsford Cathedral provides opportunity for our choirs to perform at Choral Evensong.

The grounded confidence the pupils have as a result of differentiated teaching and learning in a happy and supported environment, where children have fun and are encouraged to take risks, results in great personal achievements. Our boys and girls aspire to the highest levels of attainment and we can boast a successful track record of outstanding results at entry to grammar schools and scholarships to independent senior schools. As a school with the International School Award (ISA) we have international links with schools in India.

Breakfast is available from 0730 and there is a very extensive array of after-school activities until 1700 with wrap-around care in our TLC club until 1800.

Charitable status. St Cedd's School Educational Trust Ltd is a Registered Charity, number 310865. It exists to provide education for boys and girls.

Saint Christina's RC Preparatory School

25 St Edmund's Terrace, London NW8 7PY
Tel: 020 7722 8784
Fax: 020 7586 4961
email: secretary@saintchristinas.org.uk
website: www.saintchristinas.org.uk

Headteacher: **Mrs Paula Mortimer**, BEd

Age Range. Girls 3–11, Boys 3–7.
Number of Pupils. 175 girls, 47 boys.
Fees per term (2014–2015). £3,519 (inclusive).

Saint Christina's was founded in 1949 by the Handmaids of the Sacred Heart of Jesus. At Saint Christina's, children experience the joy of learning and the wonder of God and His Creation. Our purpose at Saint Christina's is to create an environment where children enjoy learning and where each individual experiences respect and acceptance enabling them to become the balanced person they are called to be.

As a School we take pride in the excellent examination results which we achieve. We value most of all our strong sense of community. We seek to ensure that children feel appreciated for themselves as individuals as much as their achievements. We believe that confidence can only grow in an atmosphere of trust and safety.

Boys are prepared for entrance tests for day and boarding schools.

Girls are prepared for Common Entrance Examination and entrance exams to day and boarding schools.

The School is purpose built in a pleasant location within a short walk of Primrose Hill and Regent's Park. Prospective parents are warmly invited to visit the School.

Charitable status. Saint Christina's is a Registered Charity, number 221319.

St Christopher's School
Hampstead

32 Belsize Lane, Hampstead, London NW3 5AE
Tel: 020 7435 1521
Fax: 020 7431 6694
email: admissions@st-christophers.hampstead.sch.uk
website: www.st-christophers.hampstead.sch.uk

Preparatory school for girls.

Chairman of Governors: Graham Hinton, BSc, MIPA

Headmistress: **Mrs S A West**, BA, PGCE, MEd

Age Range. 4–11.
Number of Girls. 238 Day Pupils.
Fees per term (2014–2015). £4,325 inclusive of lunch and all outings, except residential.

The School employs a fully-qualified teaching staff of 16 full-time, 6 part-time, and 7 peripatetic music teachers. Strong emphasis is placed on music. There are three choirs, quartets, ensembles and 2 orchestras; instrumental lessons are arranged within the school timetable. Whilst maintaining high standards in numeracy and literacy, the curriculum provides a wide range of subjects including art, science, computer studies, design and technology, Spanish, Latin, drama, chess, gymnastics and games.

Extra-curricular activities over the year include art, dance, debating, drama, football, gym, language, Mandarin, netball, science, sewing, striking/fielding games and yoga.

All applicants are assessed for entry. 100% means-tested scholarships are available, as well as 50% bursaries. The girls are prepared for entrance examinations to the major London day schools and for 11+ Common Entrance to boarding schools.

Charitable status. St Christopher's School (Hampstead) Limited is a Registered Charity, number 312999. It exists to provide education for girls.

St Christopher's School
Hove

33 New Church Road, Hove, East Sussex BN3 4AD
Tel: 01273 735404
Fax: 01273 747956
email: hmsec@stchristophershove.org.uk
website: www.stchristophershove.org.uk

Chairman of Governors: Mr A J Symonds, FCIS

Headmaster: Mr J A S Withers, BEd Cantab

Age Range. 4–13 co-educational.
Number of Pupils. 293.
Fees per term (2013–2014). £2,549–£3,714.

Since its foundation in 1927, St Christopher's School has expanded to become a highly successful academic preparatory school, located in the middle of Brighton & Hove, England's youngest and most vibrant city.

St Christopher's School aims to provide a traditional academic education within a supportive family environment where individual talents are developed to produce confident, articulate and well-balanced children. Pupils regularly obtain top academic scholarships and awards for art, music, drama and sport. St Christopher's is a Member of the Brighton College Family of Schools and many of its pupils go on to Brighton College.

Entry to the School is at 4+, however, places are occasionally available in other age groups. In the Lower School, pupils are taught mainly by their form teachers. Particular emphasis is placed upon reading, writing and mathematics, but the curriculum is broad and a wide range of subjects is taught by specialist teachers, including French, Mandarin, Latin, Science, Music, Art, ICT, PE and Games.

Pupils move into the Middle School in Year 4, where the curriculum reflects the syllabuses of the Common Entrance and Brighton College Academic Scholarship Examinations. Formal homework is introduced at this stage. In the Upper School (Years 7 and 8), all subjects are taught by specialists, who make full use of the interactive ICT suite, music technology suite, science laboratory, art studio and library. A variety of educational day trips, an annual residential visit to France and sports trips ensure that children receive a broad and stimulating educational experience.

The boys achieve an enviable record of success in football, rugby and cricket and the girls match that success in hockey, netball and rounders. The musical life of St Christopher's is enriched by three choirs and the choice of a wide variety of instrumental and vocal tuition. All pupils are encouraged to perform on stage as part of a wide programme of drama and the development of confidence is a central aim of the school. A wide range of extra-curricular activities is on offer. After-school care is available until 5.30 pm each evening.

The Headmaster is always delighted to welcome prospective parents. Please contact the Registrar to arrange a visit.

Charitable status. St Christopher's School, Hove is a member of the Brighton College Family of Schools, which is a Registered Charity, number 307061.

St Columba's College Preparatory School

King Harry Lane, St Albans, Hertfordshire AL3 4AW
Tel: 01727 862616
Fax: 01727 892025
email: headofprep@stcolumbascollege.org
website: www.stcolumbascollege.org

Chairman of the Governors: Mrs J Harrison, BEd

Dean: Brother Daniel St Jacques SC, BA, PGF HG Dip Counselling, MBACP

Head: **Mrs R Loveman**, BSc

Age Range. 4–11.
Number of Pupils. 255 Boys.
Fees per term (2014–2015). Reception–Prep 2 £3,095, Prep 3 £3,495, Prep 4–6 £3,855. Fees include personal accident insurance. Additional charges are made for coaches and consumables.

The Prep School is an academically selective Catholic Day School which strives to create a welcoming community in which each boy is valued as an individual and endeavours to promote positive relationships based on mutual respect and understanding. There is a rigorous academic curriculum with an extensive range of extra-curricular opportunities. A full curriculum and sports programme is offered at Key Stage 1 and 2.

Admissions at age 4 and 7 years. Entry requirements of the school is by assessment; at age 7+ assessment is via maths, mental arithmetic, perceptual reasoning, creative writing and reading; at age 4 assessment takes place informally using a standardised test and in context in a classroom situation. Subjects include: English, Mathematics, Science, Drama, RE, French, History, Geography, IT, PE, Games, Music, Art and Design Technology.

Examinations: Pupils progress at 11+ to St Columba's College on the same site, or to other senior schools.

Academic facilities include: modern form rooms with specialist facilities for Science, IT, ADT, Music, PE, Games, RE and French, and a professionally staffed extensive library.

Sports facilities include: Rugby/Football pitches, Cricket nets and square. A swimming pool and athletics track are adjacent to the site.

There are means-tested bursaries at Prep level and a number of scholarships available to Prep School boys on entry to St Columba's College. These include academic and music scholarships.

(*See also St Columba's College entry in HMC section.*)

Charitable status. St Columba's College is a Registered Charity, number 1088480. It exists to provide a well-rounded Roman Catholic education for pupils from 4–18 years of age.

St Dunstan's College Junior School

Stanstead Road, London SE6 4TY
Tel: 020 8516 7225
Fax: 020 8516 7300
email: rscard@sdmail.org.uk
website: www.stdunstans.org.uk

Chairman of Governors: Alderman & Sheriff Sir Paul Judge, MA, MBA, LLD Hon

Head of Junior School: **Miss J H Bate**, BEd, NPQH

Age Range. Co-educational 3–11.
Number of Pupils. Pre-Preparatory (3–7) 136, Preparatory (7–11) 154.
Fees per term (2014–2015). Nursery £2,957, Pre-Preparatory £3,769, Preparatory £3,769–£4,749. Fees include lunch.

The Junior School is an integral part of St Dunstan's College and prepares boys and girls for the Senior School (age 11–18) (*see entry in HMC section*). It shares with it a common site and many facilities. In particular the Music Centre, Refectory, Great Hall, Sports Hall, indoor Swimming Pool and playing fields increase the opportunities for all pupils in curricular and extra-curricular activities. For other work the Junior School pupils have their own buildings. The Pre-Preparatory Department is located in a Victorian house which has been beautifully converted for the specific needs of the 3–7 year olds. The Preparatory Department has its own teaching area with a library, ICT Suite, art room and activity room.

We provide an excellent all-round education with special emphasis upon the development of a high level of literacy and numeracy. The curriculum is also designed to promote learning and appreciation of Science, Humanities, Music, Art, Design and Technology, Information Technology, Drama, Languages and Study Skills. Games and Physical Education play an important part in the growth and development of each pupil and the children follow an extensive programme of activities. The children's learning is enhanced by a variety of visits and residential school journeys.

Boys and girls are encouraged to take part in various clubs and activities after school hours and at lunch times. Opportunities range from music, art and sport groups to ICT and drama.

A caring and friendly environment is provided by small class sizes and a dedicated team of well-qualified class teachers and support staff. In addition to being taught many subjects by their class teacher, Preparatory Department pupils have the advantage of being educated by specialists in Art, Music, Languages, Physical Education and Games.

An effective strong partnership exists between the home and school and parents are encouraged to participate in their children's education and the life of the Junior School. Regular contact is maintained between school and the home to ensure that parents are aware of their child's academic and social progress.

Boys and Girls are admitted at all ages from 3+ to 10+ but principally at 3+ and 4+ (Nursery and Reception) and at 7+ (Year 3).

Charitable status. St Dunstan's Educational Foundation is a Registered Charity, number 312747. It exists to provide education for boys and girls.

St Edmund's Junior School
Canterbury

Canterbury, Kent CT2 8HU
Tel: 01227 475601 (Admissions)
              01227 475600 (General Enquiries)
Fax: 01227 471083
email: admissions@stedmunds.org.uk
website: www.stedmunds.org.uk

Chairman of Governors: M C W Terry, FCA

Master of the Junior School: **R G Bacon**, BA Durham
From September 2015: M Jelley, BA Hons UEA, PGCE

Head of the Pre-Prep School: Mrs J E P Exley, BEd Hons CCCU

(Full staff list is available on the school's website)

Age Range. 3–13.
Numbers of Pupils. 240. Boarders: School House 21, Choir House 25; Day Pupils: Boys 97, Girls 97.
Fees per term (2014–2015). Junior School: Boarders £6,939, Weekly Boarders £6,323, Choristers £6,651, Day pupils: Years 7 & 8 £4,737, Years 3–6 £4,655. Pre-Prep: Forms 1 & 2 £3,298, Reception £2,853, Nursery £2,323.

Pupils may enter at any age from 3 to 12. Boarding begins at the age of 8.

The Junior School and the Pre-Prep School are closely linked with the Senior School (*see entry in HMC section*) but has an identity of its own. The Junior School uses some Senior School specialist staff, particularly in the teaching of Science, Music, Art, Technology and shares with the Senior School such amenities as the Chapel, concert theatre, sports facilities and swimming pool. There is a full-time school Chaplain. Domestic arrangements, including health and catering, are under centralised administration.

Boarding in School House offers a family experience in a stimulating environment where the individual is valued. The Canterbury Cathedral Choristers, who are St Edmund's pupils, live in the Choir House which is under the care of a married Housemaster and is situated in the precincts of Canterbury Cathedral.

Scholarships and bursaries. Academic, music, drama, sport, and all-rounder awards are available for applicants aged 11. Cathedral choristerships are available for boys from age 7. Fee concessions are also available as detailed in the Senior School entry in HMC section.

Charitable status. St Edmund's School Canterbury is a Registered Charity, number 1056382. It exists to educate the children in its care.

St Edmund's Prep School

Old Hall Green, Ware, Herts SG11 1DS
Tel: 01920 824239
Fax: 01920 822278
email: prep@stedmundscollege.org
website: www.stedmundscollege.org
Twitter: @stedmundsware

Chairman of Governors: Mr Patrick J Mitton, MSc

Head: **Mr S Cartwright**, BSc Hons Surrey

Age Range. 3–11 Co-educational.
Number of Pupils. 209.
Fees per term (2014–2015). Day (inc Lunch): £1,418–£4,165.

St Edmund's Prep, founded in 1874, is a co-educational, independent Catholic Nursery, Pre-Prep and Prep school, situated in beautiful surroundings of wood and parkland in Old Hall Green, easily accessible from the main thoroughfares of Hertfordshire. The school embraces family values to lay the foundation for a happy and successful life. Education is seen as a joint venture involving staff, parents and children.

When you arrive at the Prep you will experience a welcome from us all that invites you and your child to be part of a very special community.

Guided by the principles of our Catholic faith and acknowledging Christ as our leader and teacher, we strive for excellence and creativity in forward-thinking education. We commit ourselves to the preparation of our children by instilling in them a sense of responsibility and attempting to ensure that they leave St Edmund's Prep with a solid foundation on which to build their future in the College and beyond.

Small class sizes allow focused attention to ensure that your child becomes a confident learner both inside and outside the classroom. Our facilities shared with the College and our committed teachers ensure our pupils have the experiences they need to develop fully in all aspects of their lives. With a heritage and ethos deeply rooted in the Catholic tradition, we welcome families from all faiths who will appreciate the all-round education that we offer.

The school has a broad, balanced curriculum and it seeks to cater for the individual child at the different stages of their development. The curriculum offered is intended to improve the learners' knowledge, introduce them to a wide range of educational experiences and develop skills needed to deal critically and creatively with the world.

A breakfast and tea time club is offered and a school bus service runs for children over 7 in year 3.

We are fortunate to share facilities with St Edmund's College and as a result the Prep children have an opportunity to use the floodlit astroturf, all year round use of the indoor swimming pool and the large gymnasium.

We are committed to being leaders in education in these changing times. We invite you to join us as a member of St Edmund's Prep.

Charitable status. St Edmund's College is a Registered Charity, number 311073.

St Edmund's School

Portsmouth Road, Hindhead, Surrey GU26 6BH
Tel: 01428 609875
Fax: 01428 607898
email: registrar@saintedmunds.co.uk
website: www.saintedmunds.co.uk

Chairman of Governors: Mrs J Alliss

Headmaster: **A J Walliker**, MA Cantab, MBA, PGCE

Age Range. Boys and Girls 2–16.
Number of Pupils. Senior, Prep and Lower School: 265 day pupils; Nursery: 30.
Fees per term (2014–2015). Lower School and Prep £3,075–£4,125; Seniors £4,750; Flexi Boarding Fee: £35–£40 per night; Nursery from £651 (three afternoons) to £2,295 (full week).

The fees are inclusive of all ordinary extras including supervised prep, orchestra/choirs, games, swimming, lectures, optional Saturday activities etc.

Scholarships and means-tested bursaries are available.

"I like St Ed's. I can be myself." These words, from one of our children, capture much of what we strive to do at St Edmund's: to instil in every child a sense of self-esteem and belonging by building on their own talents, opening their eyes to new ones and giving them focused and personal support whenever it is needed.

Academically, it is an approach that continues to pay dividends, with our pupils going on to a wide range of senior schools, both boarding and day. Yet of equal importance are the discoveries, excitements and good old-fashioned fun that St Edmund's creates inside our 40 beautiful acres. These include an immaculate 9-hole golf course, indoor pool and astro pitch, and a wealth of activities ranging from cooking and the chapel choir to campfire building and language masterclasses. A thriving and optional Saturday morning school activity programme allows us to introduce a greater breadth of ideas and new experiences.

We are a fully co-educational school with an unusual flexible boarding option, from one-off nights to regular midweek boarding. Our new senior section for children in Years 9 to 11 opened in September 2014, taking us up to GCSE/IGCSE. The senior section continues our culture, academic standards, exceptional pastoral care, and strengths in sport, music and the arts up to the age of 16. It also offers significantly smaller class sizes than the norm (around 15 per class) and provides a high standard of education at a reasonable cost. Senior pupils have their own common room, kitchen and study areas, the opportunity for flexi midweek boarding and participation in a rich variety of co-curricular and leadership activities.

Charitable status. St Edmund's School Trust Limited is a Registered Charity, number 278301. Its aim is the education of children.

St Edward's Preparatory School

London Road, Charlton Kings, Cheltenham, Glos GL52 6NR
Tel: 01242 538900
Fax: 01242 538901
email: headmaster@stedwardsprep.co.uk
website: www.stedwards.co.uk

Co-educational Day School.

Chairman of Governors: Mr P Goatley

Headmaster: **Mr S McKernan**, BA Hons, MEd, NPQH

Age Range. 2–11 years.
Number of Pupils. 430.
Fees per term (2014–2015). £2,250–£3,600.

St Edward's Preparatory School is an independent co-educational Catholic Foundation welcoming pupils of all denominations from 2 to 11 years. We provide a supportive family atmosphere in which pupils are encouraged to develop their individual potential – academic, social, physical, creative and spiritual – in preparation for their secondary education. The school is situated on the edge of Cheltenham in forty-five acres of beautiful parkland. Our facilities are truly exceptional and give our pupils opportunities for practical experience rarely available in a preparatory school, as well as enabling us to provide an unusually wide range of after-school activities. Class sizes are small which ensures the pupils receive plenty of individual attention. With a strong focus on mathematics, science, English and ICT results are good with children going to local grammar schools, successful entrance into St Edward's Senior School, many obtaining scholarships, and other independent schools. Sport is particularly strong as is music, drama and art. A new Drama Studio has enhanced our provision in this area.

Our Kindergarten is open all year round and provides a secure and stimulating introduction to school life. A new playground built on the Reggio theme uses wood and natural materials to encourage the children to develop imagination and creativity. Kindergarten children have their own ICT area where they can use dedicated software packages and explore creativity using iPads. Children move from here into our purpose-built Pre-Prep School with small classes and a rich range of extra-curricular activities. St Edward's Preparatory School provides the best possible start for a child's educational journey. In 2013 our Early Years Foundation Stage was awarded an "Outstanding" classification in every area – an exceptional achievement.

Charitable status. St Edward's School is a Registered Charity, number 293360.

St Edward's School

64 Tilehurst Road, Reading, Berkshire RG30 2JH
Tel: 0118 957 4342
Fax: 0118 950 3736
email: admin@stedwards.org.uk
website: www.stedwards.org.uk

Chairman of Governors: Mrs S Pellow

Principal: **G Mottram**, HDipEd SA, MA Ed, NPQH

Age Range. 4–13.
Number of Boys. 130 day boys.

Fees per term (2014–2015). £2,680–£3,440. Dayboarding (until 5.55 pm): £650 (Reception, Years 1 & 2), £560 (Years 3–8). There are no compulsory extras.

St Edward's School, situated on the west side of Reading, Berkshire, is a small independent day preparatory school for boys aged 4 to 13, founded in 1947.

St Edward's prides itself on being a small, caring prep school. Traditional values of good manners, respect for others and an excellent understanding of right and wrong make for a very positive environment in which to grow up. Our boys leave us as bright, happy, well-rounded and confident individuals, ready to make the most of their time at their chosen senior school.

The 'Outstanding' Pre-prep department accepts boys from 4 and offers a caring and positive environment in which children can thrive and learn.

The Prep School's curriculum is broadly based and incorporates the best of the National Curriculum, but we seek to offer more, and in greater depth.

Boys study English, Maths, Science, French, History, Geography, RS, Music, Art, Design Technology, PSHE and PE. Drama, Study skills and Latin are optional, depending on year groups.

On entry to the prep school at 7+, the boys are taught for the bulk of the time by one teacher, with specialist teaching for Mathematics, Science, Information Technology, Music, PE and Sport.

In subsequent years the boys are taught exclusively by subject specialists, and are placed in one of two sets within the year group for the core curriculum subjects. Acknowledging the increasing future importance of foreign languages, spoken French is introduced at age 4.

The curriculum also includes *Information and Communications Technology* which is taught as a skill in its own right. The school computers, which are networked together with permanent internet access, are in regular daily use across the curriculum.

The boys are prepared for 13+ entrance to Independent Senior Schools, either by the Common Entrance examination, or by Scholarship. The school has had a fine record of winning Scholarships throughout its history, including success at Reading Grammar School.

St Edward's promotes sound and clearly defined moral values in a learning environment where boys work together enjoying the challenge and rigour of quality teaching. Each child is treated as an individual and strives to achieve their potential whether in academia, sport or the arts.

Charitable status. St Edward's and Highlands School Ltd is a Registered Charity, number 309147.

St Faith's School

Trumpington Road, Cambridge CB2 8AG
Tel: 01223 352073
Fax: 01223 314757
email: info@stfaiths.co.uk
website: www.stfaiths.co.uk
Twitter: @st_faiths

Chair of Governors: Mrs J Plows, BA

Headmaster: **N L Helliwell**, MA, BEd Hons

Deputy Head: Mrs L M Dennis, BEd Southampton

Age Range. 4–13.
Number of Pupils. 540.
Fees per term (2014–2015). £3,650 (Pre-Prep), £4,435 (Years 3 and 4) £4,605 (Years 5 to 8).

St Faith's, founded in 1884, is a co-educational day school set in 9 acres of grounds on the south side of Cambridge, approximately one mile from the city centre. It is situated close to the A10 and M11 and the Park and Ride facilities and operates a school minibus from the Trumpington Road Park and Ride site to the school each morning. Boys and girls enter the school at age 4 and stay until they are 13. Interviews and assessments for places occur throughout the year and scholarships are available at 7+.

St Faith's is very highly regarded in Cambridge and beyond. The 2011 ISI Report rated as 'Outstanding' the high quality of teaching, excellent academic achievements, the huge range of extra-curricular activities, the very effective links with parents and the special care and attention given to each individual child. Pupils are encouraged to develop their talents to the full by following a curriculum which is broadly based and rigorous in its requirement. Classes are small. Teaching in the early years is principally class based, while, from Year 5, pupils work with specialist subject teachers. St Faith's prides itself on the pastoral care of the children, which operates through a House-based tutorial system. The facilities and educational resources at St Faith's are up to the minute and excellent. The Keynes building provides enviable facilities for the teaching of Design and Technology, Music, Digital Literacy and Computer Science. The Ashburton building houses Science labs, well-equipped Art rooms, an extensive library and a Drama studio, as well as a spacious Hall, where Music concerts, Drama productions and whole-school assemblies take place. In addition to the excellent sports facilities on site, including a state-of-the-art Sports Hall opened in 2011, the school has the use of the swimming pool and astroturf nearby at The Leys School.

Learning languages is a way of life at St Faith's. The School is one of ten UK schools awarded 'Associate Status' by the Spanish Embassy in recognition of the excellent teaching provided.

St Faith's has an excellent sporting tradition with rugby, netball, hockey, cricket, tennis, rounders, football and athletics being the main outdoor games. Basketball, cross-country running and other games are also organised, but on a less formal basis. Our sports programme involves inter-House competitions and a strong fixture list with numerous matches against other schools. Music and drama are also important at St Faith's and the school has a flourishing music department with the emphasis placed upon enjoyment as well as good performance. Pupils are able to participate in class and whole school concerts and a large number of instrumental groups, choirs and the school orchestra perform regularly. Drama is timetabled for all forms; there are performances of plays or musicals by each Year group throughout the year and the standard of performance is high.

As an Eco-School, St Faith's has earned its coveted Green Flag award and in 2014 won the Ashden Schools Award for our Eco initiatives.

Extra-curricular activities range from chess, reading, art and model making to more energetic sporting pursuits. In addition there are Play Clubs and Multi-Activity Courses during the holidays and teambuilding activity holidays, language trips and a ski trip for older children. Late Stay facilities operate and families wishing to miss the Cambridge traffic are able to enjoy breakfast in the school's dining room from 07:30 each morning.

St Faith's is part of The Leys and St Faith's Foundation and although each year approximately half of the children move on to The Leys at the end of Year 8, others prepare for entry to a variety of schools, mainly independent, many of them with scholarships.

Charitable status. The Leys and St Faith's Schools Foundation is a Registered Charity, number 1144035. The aim of the charity is the provision of first-class education.

St Francis School

Marlborough Road, Pewsey, Wilts SN9 5NT

Tel:	01672 563228
email:	admissions@st-francis.wilts.sch.uk
	schooloffice@st-francis.wilts.sch.uk
website:	www.st-francis.wilts.sch.uk
Twitter:	@stfrancispewsey

Chair of Governors: Mrs S Soar

Headmaster: **D W T Sibson**, BA Ed Hons Durham

Age Range. 2–13.

Number of Boys and Girls. 231: 113 Boys, 118 Girls.

Fees per term (2014–2015). Reception–Year 8: £2,594–£3,934 including lunch. Nursery £222 per half day session excluding lunch.

St Francis is a co-educational day school which takes children from the age of 2 to 13. Established in 1941, the School which is a charitable trust with a board of governors, is situated alongside the Kennet and Avon Canal in the lovely Vale of Pewsey some five miles south of Marlborough. Pupils travel from a wide area of mid-Wiltshire; daily minibus services operate from Marlborough and Devizes. Wrap-around care is available for all pupils, from 7.45 am until 6 pm.

Providing every child with the opportunity to fulfil his or her full potential is a feature of the school. Staff ensure that they are very positive and encouraging in their teaching. Should a child be found to need some form of specific learning assistance then appropriate help will be given. The facilities are constantly being improved. The modern Burden Block provides a Library, Design Technology room, ICT room and specialist subject teaching rooms, as well as form rooms.

The curriculum is delightfully diverse enabling the older pupils to have, for instance, CDT, Pottery, Drama, Computing, Choir and Swimming all in their normal weekly timetable. Languages are also a key part of the curriculum: French is taught from the age of three, Latin is introduced in Year 6 and Spanish in Year 7. The majority of the pupils take up individual musical tuition and a wide range of instruments is available. Many pupils enter local music and public and choral speaking competitions.

The pupils are offered plenty of opportunity to develop and excel in their sport. All the major sports are taught both outdoors on the playing fields and also inside the Hemery Hall which doubles as a sports hall and a drama theatre. Regular matches take place against other schools and a policy of 'sport for all' allows all pupils to be involved.

Little Saints Nursery caters for children from 2 to 4 years of age. With the Reception class, this makes up the EYFS department of the school which makes use of all the facilities including the school's garden playground and woods.

The school grounds are also home to some more unexpected residents; last year sheep and chickens were introduced to the site, joined more recently by pygmy goats and a flock of ducks.

Results are excellent. The pupils are mainly entered for the local senior schools, St Mary's Calne, Godolphin, Dauntsey's, Marlborough College, Stonar and Warminster, but scholarships and common entrance are also taken for boarding schools further afield. Awards are regularly achieved to all of the aforementioned.

Please write, telephone or email for a prospectus, or ask to visit and tour round the school. The Headmaster will be happy to oblige.

Charitable status. St Francis is a Registered Charity, number 298522. It exists solely to provide education for boys and girls.

St Gabriel's
Junior School

Sandleford Priory, Newbury, Berkshire RG20 9BD

Tel:	01635 555680
Fax:	01635 555698
email:	info@stgabriels.co.uk
website:	www.stgabriels.co.uk

Chairman of Governors: Mr N Garland, BSc Hons

Principal: Mr A Jones, LTCL, LWCMD

Head of Junior School: **Mr P Dove**, BA Hons, PGCE

Age Range. 6 months – 11 years Co-educational

Number of Pupils. 150.

Fees per term (2014–2015). £3,640–£4,085.

In September 2014, Sandleford (Nursery & Reception) and the Junior School became fully co-educational.

Sandleford lies at the heart of St Gabriel's and provides high-quality nursery care and Early Years education for children aged 6 months to 5 years. Sandleford offers flexible full or part-time care with an extended day provision across 50 weeks a year.

The Junior School is situated adjacent to the Senior School in 54 acres of parkland on the southern outskirts of Newbury.

Subjects taught include English, Mathematics, Science, Art, Drama, Humanities (History, Geography), ICT, Modern Foreign Languages (French, Spanish, Italian, Mandarin), Music, PE, Religious Studies, Technology (Textiles, Food Technology, Design Technology) and Thinking Skills.

The excellent range of facilities includes a multi-discipline sports hall, digital theatre, dance studio, junior science laboratory, library, orienteering courses and woodland trails. All Junior School ICT lessons take place in the recently built ICT and MFL block.

Sport plays an important and integral role in the life of the school and there is a comprehensive fixtures list from Year 3 to Year 6. Athletics, Basketball, Cross-Country, Dance, Football, Gymnastics, Hockey, Netball, Rugby, Rounders and Tennis are included in the curriculum for all pupils. Swimming takes place during the Summer Term in the outdoor heated swimming pool.

Music holds an equally high profile. As well as curriculum Music lessons, there is a wide range of extra-curricular music-making for all pupils with an interest in the subject. Many pupils learn instruments in school and they are given numerous opportunities to perform at concerts ranging from informal lunchtime events to major end of term extravaganzas.

In addition, pupils are offered a wide range of extra-curricular activities, including Art Club, Ballet, Chess Club, Choir, Climbing Club, Creative Writing Club, Cricket, Drama, Fencing, Film Making Club, Gardening Club, ICT Club, Judo, Music Theory, Recorder, Science Club, Trampolining Club and Training Orchestra.

From Year 3, entry to the Junior School is by assessment. Maximum class size is 20 pupils.

Boys are prepared for Common Entrance Examinations and the majority of girls progress through to the Senior School at the age of 11, at which point entry is by entrance examination and interview. (*For further information about the Senior School, see St Gabriel's entry in GSA section.*)

Charitable status. The St Gabriel Schools Foundation is a Registered Charity, number 1062748. It exists to provide education for girls and boys from age 6 months to 11 years.

St George's Junior School

Thames Street, Weybridge, Surrey KT13 8NL
Tel: 01932 839400
Fax: 01932 839401
email: contact@stgeorgesweybridge.com
website: www.stgeorgesweybridge.com

Chairman of Board of Governors: Mr M Davie

Headmaster: Mr A J W Hudson, MA Cantab, PGCE, NPQH

Age Range. 3–11.
Number of Pupils. 635.
Fees per term (2014–2015). Nursery: £1,560 (mornings only), £2,550 (full days); Reception–Year 2 £2,940; Years 3–6 £4,040. Lunches: £230.

St George's Junior School is a fully co-ed Roman Catholic Day School and all pupils attending the Junior School normally belong to one of the mainstream Christian traditions. The School was established in 1950 by a Religious Order of Priests and Brothers known as "The Josephites" who maintain a keen interest in the future of the School. Only pupils who are 'rising three' are admitted into the Nursery.

While the majority of the pupils at the school come from around North Surrey, some 13% of the pupils are from countries as far away as Australia, New Zealand, Hong Kong, South Africa, Brazil, Canada, USA as well as from most European countries including Russia. The School operates a very extensive bus service and an option for parents using cars to drop off their children at either the Junior or Senior School.

In September 2000 the Junior School moved from its previous co-located site with St George's College one mile down the road to its present 12½ acre site on the outskirts of Weybridge close to the River Thames. Since then a £1.5 million refurbishment programme has been completed involving the upgrading of most of the classrooms, the science teaching room, the library, the music room, playground equipment, an Astroturf pitch, cricket nets and the creation of a school wide computer network including three computer resources rooms, each classroom has an interactive whiteboard. In 2006, a new Development Launch focused on providing a new state-of-the-art Nursery classroom and a totally refurbished Kitchen and Dining Area, called 'The Mulberry Hall', which opened in January 2008. A new Lower Years building will be in place for September 2015 as the first part of a Master Plan which will see a Performing Arts Centre and Sports Hall erected over the coming years.

The Junior School has a genuinely happy atmosphere in which every pupil is respected and treated as an individual. The Headmaster considers the staff, pupils and parents to be constituent parts of an extended family. The School has always placed great emphasis on the importance of maintaining excellent channels of communication between members of staff, parents and pupils.

The size of classes ensures that the School is a learning community by creating the correct balance between pupil interaction and pupil-teacher contact. The pupils in the top two years of the School are taught by subject specialists. French is offered to all pupils from Year 1. The School was described in its most recent ISI report (2011) as having pupils whose "personal qualities are excellent and the emphasis on promoting the values of the Josephite tradition results in pupils who are well mannered, polite and welcoming".

All pupils are assessed on entry and when they leave at the end of Year 6 nearly all transfer to St George's College. Well over 150 scholarships, including music scholarships, have been won by pupils in Year 6 since 1989; in 2013, 7 academic, 2 Sports and 2 Music Scholarships were awarded.

While the pursuit of academic excellence is highly valued, the Mission Statement of the School stresses the importance of pupils having high personal self-esteem as well as emphasising the importance of their religious, spiritual, social and physical development. The School requires its pupils to have high moral values especially those of its school motto "Honesty and Compassion".

The Junior School has four Houses which compete against each other across a wide range of activities inside and outside the classroom including Music, Public Speaking and Sport.

Extra-curricular and other enrichment activities are, likewise, considered to play an important role in the educational development of children. The extensive range of activities includes dance (ballet, modern and tap), gymnastics and clubs based on the academic subjects taught in the School. Since September 2013, Mandarin has been offered to Year 3 pupils as an after-school club. Pupils are taken to places of educational interest regularly including theatre, music and art trips and there is an annual Book Week during which pupils meet and listen to visiting authors and story-tellers.

Considerable emphasis is placed on the Creative and Performing Arts. Pupils have dance lessons throughout the school with specialist ballet and tap dance lessons being a compulsory part of the curriculum for all pupils up to the end of Reception Year. The School stages six major drama productions a year. All children from Year 2 have two lessons of music each week. Children in Year 2 learn the violin and recorder as part of the music curriculum. There is an Orchestra, Chapel Choir and Year 3 Choir which rehearse on a weekly basis as well as Violin, Brass, Guitar and Recorder ensembles. Individual music lessons are very popular with over 50% of the children in Years 2–6 learning at least one additional instrument. Concerts happen at least once every term and music lessons are supported by the use of the latest computer-based technology. Pupils have achieved considerable success at Public Speaking Competitions and achieve a very high level of attainment in their external Spoken English, Lamda and instrumental music exams. In 2013, 56 Year 6 pupils achieved 14 Distinctions and 42 Merits in their LAMDA exams, while all 29 Year 5 pupils gained Distinctions in their ESB exams.

Apart from its own sports facilities on site comprising an artificial sports pitch, netball and tennis courts, a sprung floor gymnasium and a swimming pool, the School has the use of 20 acres of outstanding sports facilities at the College including three floodlit netball/tennis courts, a floodlit artificial surface for hockey about to be completely refurbished, a four-court indoor tennis centre, three floodlit French clay courts, a sports hall and gym, three cricket squares, a tartan athletics track and six large grass fields.

The Junior School has a track record of great sporting success. In Rugby in 2013, the boys were U11 National Finalists, U10 National Quarter Finalists and the U9s were Plate Semi Finalists at the Regional Finals. In Hockey, the boys were U11 IAPS London and South East Regional Champions. In girls' Hockey, the U11s were IAPS London and South East Regional Champions and Quarter Finalists in the IAPS National Finals as well as coming second in the Surrey Cup competition.

In the midst of all this tangible success, the Junior School prides itself on ensuring that all children from Year 3 upwards have the opportunity to represent the School at least once each term in one of the mainstream sports i.e. Rugby, Hockey and Cricket for boys and Netball, Hockey and Rounders for girls.

School lunches are compulsory from Reception Year, are prepared on site and eaten in the dining rooms which can seat 320 people. The School offers a free supervised homework facility each weekday evening during term time until 4.45 pm for those children in Reception and Years 1 and 2.

Children in Years 3–6 can sign up for clubs which continue until 5.00 pm.

For the last few years the school has usually had more applications for places than it can accommodate in all year groups. When vacancies do occur, pupils are admitted if they meet the School's entry criteria and successfully complete an assessment day at the School as well as receiving a satisfactory report from the current school where this is appropriate. Priority is afforded to siblings and Roman Catholics.

Charitable status. St George's College, Weybridge is a Registered Charity, number 1017853. The aims and objectives of the charity are the Christian education of young people.

St George's School

Windsor Castle, Windsor, Berks SL4 1QF
Tel: 01753 865553
Fax: 01753 842093
email: enqs@stgwindsor.co.uk
website: www.stgwindsor.co.uk

Patron: Her Majesty The Queen

Visitor: The Lord Chancellor

Chairman of the Governors: The Dean of Windsor

Head Master: **Mr Christopher McDade**, BA Hons, FCollT, LTCL, PGCE

Deputy Head: Mr Kevin Wills, BSc Hons, PGCE

   Age Range. 3–13 Co-educational.
   Number of Pupils. 335 (25 boarders).
   Fees per term (2014–2015). Weekly Boarders £6,655, Day Pupils £4,365–£4,890, Choristers (Boarding) £3,145, Pre-Prep £2,945–£3,340, Nursery £1,240–£1,540.

St George's School was established as part of the foundation of the Order of the Garter in 1348 when provision was made for the education of the first choristers. In 1893 the School moved into the Georgian building of the former College of the Naval Knights of Windsor situated between the mound of the Castle and the Home Park. Expansion followed with the admission of supernumerary (non-chorister) pupils. Extensions were made to the buildings in 1988 and 1996, the latter of which allowed for the opening of a Pre-Preparatory Department and Nursery. In 1997 Girls were admitted to the School for the first time, entering both the Pre-Prep and the main school, and five years later the school became fully co-educational. A new Middle School building accommodating pupils in Years 3, 4 and 5, was opened in Spring 2006 by HRH Princess Alexandra. The school remains part of the Foundation of the College of St George, within the Castle and it enjoys strong links with the Royal Family.

St George's School boasts a long tradition of academic and musical excellence alongside impressive art, drama and sport. Many pupils gain academic, all-rounder and music awards to some of the country's leading independent schools. The curriculum is broad and varied. In addition to core teaching subjects, French is introduced to Nursery children with the addition of Latin in Year 5 and Spanish in Year 6. Specialist teaching in PE and Music is provided from the Nursery upwards and in Art, DT and Drama from Year 3.

Facilities for games are excellent with pitches and playing fields on the Home Park, an indoor swimming pool, a recently resurfaced tennis and netball court and a gymnasium. Several areas of the school buildings have recently undergone refurbishment, including the creation of a Design Technology workshop, a significant updating of the ICT suite and brand new Science laboratories opened in 2010 by HRH The Earl of Wessex. In 2013, a new Food Technology teaching room was opened.

The School seeks to pursue the highest standards and aims to develop happy, confident young people who achieve their potential whilst at St George's. There is a strong family ethos within the school community where each child's talents and skills are identified and nurtured. Pastoral care is excellent and each class teacher and form tutor knows the children in their care extremely well. Parents evenings are held regularly and parents are always invited into school to support the children in plays, concerts and sports fixtures and to attend regular school services in St George's Chapel, Windsor Castle.

Communications are excellent: two railway stations, the M25, M3, M4 and M40 are all close by and Heathrow is just fifteen minutes away.

Charitable status. St George's School, Windsor Castle is a Registered Charity, number 1100392. Its purpose is the education, either as boarding or day pupils, of children of pre-preparatory and preparatory school age and of the choristers who maintain the worship in the Queen's Free Chapel of Our Lady, St George and St Edward the Confessor in Windsor Castle.

St Helen's College

Parkway, Hillingdon, Middlesex UB10 9JX
Tel: 01895 234371
Fax: 01895 206948
email: info@sthelenscollege.com
website: www.sthelenscollege.com

Headmaster: **Mr D A Crehan**, ARCS, BA, BSc, MSc, CPhys, MEd
Headmistress: **Mrs G R Crehan**, BA, MA, PGCE

   Age Range. 3–11 co-educational.
   Number of Pupils. 359 Day Pupils.
   Fees per term (2014–2015). £1,720–£2,870.

The aims of St Helen's College are to develop as fully as possible each child's academic potential, to provide a wide, balanced, stimulating and challenging curriculum, and to foster true values and good character based on moral and spiritual principles. The children enjoy a purposeful and happy 'family' atmosphere and are taught by committed professional teachers.

Children are prepared for independent senior schools and local grammar schools, and records of success are very good indeed. In addition to the academic subjects, sport, music and drama play an important part in the lives of the children.

A wide range of extra-curricular activities is offered, and pupils enjoy outings, day and residential, to many places of interest. There is an after-school club and summer school, and a holiday club which runs throughout the year.

St Hilary's School

Holloway Hill, Godalming, Surrey GU7 1RZ
Tel: 01483 416551
Fax: 01483 418325
email: registrar@sthilarysschool.com
website: www.sthilarysschool.com
Twitter: @StHilarysSchool

Chair of Governors: Mrs V J Gillman, DMS, MCMI

Headmistress: **Mrs J Whittingham**, BEd, Cert Prof Prac SpLD

Age Range. Girls 2–11, Boys 2–7.

Number of Pupils. 260 Day Pupils.

Fees per term (from January 2015). Including lunch: Reception £3,005, Year 1 £3,295, Year 2 £3,865, Year 3 £3,980, Years 4–6 £4,440. Kindergarten: £26.50 & Nursery: £27.80 per am/pm session with lunch extra.

St Hilary's is an independent preparatory day school which provides a stimulating, safe environment in which boys up to 7+ and girls up to 11+ can develop, be happy and flourish.

Situated in the heart of Godalming, St Hilary's prides itself in providing an outstanding all-round education, equipping pupils not only with strong academic standards but also the essential qualities and skills required beyond their time at our school. Ultimately we strive to ensure that all our pupils develop a real thirst for learning.

The Independent Schools Inspectorate judged our Early Years Foundation Stage 'Outstanding' in all areas in 2013/ 2014 and the main school achieved an outstanding school inspection report in November 2010.

Every child enjoys the benefits of well-qualified, enthusiastic staff and a broad curriculum combined with splendid facilities. Amenities include well-equipped classrooms, music wing, spacious hall for the performing arts, science lab, library, modern ICT suite, design & technology and art studios, all-weather pitch, and the Hiorns Centre for drama, ballet and cooking. Small class sizes allow children to achieve their best in a dynamic and vibrant environment.

Outside the classroom, pupils can enjoy the woodland and play opportunities with the very popular Taurus Trail and exciting adventure play area. Pupils share a love of growing things with our gardens and appreciate the safe, beautiful surroundings.

Physical Education features highly at St Hilary's. The department gives all pupils equality of opportunity to participate in a broad range of activities. All pupils experience a variety of competitive and challenging situations. Our House system encourages healthy competition with matches, a swimming gala and sports days.

Children are given the opportunity to participate in a wide, varied number of extra-curricular activities, such as, gardening, football skills, drama, science, art, pottery, textiles, debating, First Aid, French, chess, gym, cross country, judo, cricket, dance, tap, choirs, woodwind, string ensemble, percussion, orchestra, recorder groups and Suzuki violin.

Speech & Drama is a highly popular option for many with pupils preparing for LAMDA (London Academy of Music and Dramatic Art) examinations. The school takes advantage of its ideal location and access to London for visits to galleries, museums and theatres.

Parents are guided in next school options and have the opportunity to make informed choices at a time when a child's true academic potential can be accurately predicted and talents in other areas identified. We have an excellent reputation in securing first-choice schools for our pupils when they leave. Boys in Year 2 and girls in Year 6 successfully move on to prestigious schools; every year many obtain academic, art, music, sport and drama scholarships.

Please do come and visit us; we will be delighted to welcome you and discuss your child's education. We hold a number of Open Days throughout the year when you can see the school in action; please visit our website for more details.

Charitable status. St Hilary's is a Registered Charity, number 312056. It exists to provide education for children.

St Hilda's School

High Street, Bushey, Hertfordshire WD23 3DA

Tel:	020 8950 1751
Fax:	020 8420 4523

email:	secretary@sthildasbushey.co.uk
	registrar@sthildasbushey.co.uk
website:	www.sthildas-school.co.uk

Chairman of Governors: Mr T Barton, LLB Hons

Headmistress: **Miss S J Styles**, BA, MA

Age Range. Girls 2–11, Boys 2–4.

Number of Pupils. 130 Day Girls. Co-ed Nursery.

Fees per term (2014–2015). Prep School: £3,407–£3,663. Nursery fees upon application according to sessions chosen.

St Hilda's is an Independent Day School for girls aged 4–11, with a full-time nursery for boys and girls aged 2–4. It was founded in 1918 and has occupied its present 5-acre site since 1928. The Victorian house at the centre of the school has been continually improved, adapted and extended to provide an excellent educational environment. This includes a nature garden area, tennis courts, an indoor heated swimming pool, a large all-purpose hall, science laboratory, technology laboratory and computer suite. We teach a wide range of subjects to a high academic standard in a secure and happy environment in which every pupil can develop their academic and personal potential. We offer a broad and challenging curriculum in which art, drama and music play an important role. There is also a wide range of extra-curricular activities, including ballet, tap, seasonal sports activities, ICT, languages and drama. Pre-school and after-school care is offered from 07.30 until 18.30 Monday to Friday during term time.

Charitable status. St Hilda's School is a Registered Charity, number 298140. It exists to provide education for girls.

St Hugh's

Carswell Manor, Faringdon, Oxon SN7 8PT

Tel:	01367 870700
Fax:	01367 870707
email:	headmaster@st-hughs.co.uk
	registrar@st-hughs.co.uk
website:	www.st-hughs.co.uk

Chairman of Governors: J M Guillum Scott

Headmaster: **A J P Nott**, BA Hons, PGCE

Age Range. 3–13.

Number of Pupils. 330: 20 Weekly Boarders, 212 Day Pupils (of whom many flexi board); Pre-Prep (including Nursery) 98. (Boy-Girl ratio approximately 3:2, both boarding and day).

Fees per term (2014–2015). Upper School: Weekly Boarders £6,895, Day £5,760; Middle School: Weekly Boarders £6,450, Day £5,315; Pre-Prep £3,395–£3,705. (All fees inclusive, with very few compulsory extras.)

The School's main building is a fine Jacobean house with extensive grounds. Boys and girls are prepared for Common Entrance and Scholarship examinations to senior independent schools. The school is organised into four departments: Nursery (3–4), Pre-Prep (4–6), Middle School (7–8) and Upper School (9–13). Careful liaison ensures a strong thread of continuity throughout the school. The main entry points are at 3, 4, 7, 9 and 11.

We are non-selective and both welcome and cater for pupils of a wide range of ability. We aim to foster confidence and a love of learning across this range: an impressive scholarship and CE record and the provision of integral specialist support both bear testimony to our inclusive approach. The arts and sport feature strongly and pupils are encouraged to develop their talents and interests as broadly as possible.

St Hugh's is described by the Good Schools Guide as a school which "personifies what is best in prep school education".

Charitable status. St Hugh's is a Registered Charity, number 309640. It exists to provide a centre of excellence for the education of children.

St Hugh's

Cromwell Avenue, Woodhall Spa LN10 6TQ
Tel: 01526 352169
Fax: 01526 351520
email: office@st-hughs.lincs.sch.uk
website: www.st-hughs.lincs.sch.uk

Chairman of Governors: M Harrison

Headmaster: **C A Ward**, BEd Hons

Age Range. 2–13.
Number of Pupils. 182. Boarders: 13 boys, 6 girls. Day: 53 boys, 50 girls. Pre-Prep: 16 boys, 11 girls. Nursery: 21 children.
Fees per term (2014–2015). Boarding £6,366; Day: £4,049–£4,498; Pre-Prep: £2,581.

St Hugh's School was founded by the Forbes family in 1925, became a Charitable Trust in 1964 and has continued to prosper over the years administered by a forward-thinking Governing Body.

Today the School is fully co-educational, offering both day and boarding places. The Headmaster is assisted by 21 qualified and experienced teachers. Through its Headmaster the School is a member of IAPS (The Independent Association of Prep Schools) as well as the Boarding Schools' Association.

Boys and girls are prepared for the Common Entrance and Scholarship examinations. The School's academic record is excellent, with regular awards being gained to major Independent Schools, as well as places in Lincolnshire Grammar Schools. Children with special learning needs are treated sympathetically within the mainstream, with support from specialist staff. The aim of the School is to give every child a good all-round education and to discover and develop his or her own particular talents.

The major school games for boys are rugby, hockey and cricket, and for girls netball, hockey and rounders. Both boys and girls can also enjoy cross-country, tennis, athletics and swimming. There is an annual Sports Day. All children have PE each week with time set aside for instruction in gymnastics and swimming. Skills in games such as basketball and badminton also form the basis of these lessons.

The school lays heavy emphasis on extra-curricular activities, sport of various kinds, music, the visual arts and drama. All teachers are expected to help in some way with this. There is also a strong and continuing Christian tradition at St Hugh's, where children are encouraged to consider what they believe and develop a faith of their own within the context of regular acts of Christian Worship.

The school has excellent facilities including a modern sports hall, an assembly hall with stage and lighting, a heated indoor swimming pool, extensive playing fields, a fine library, dedicated classrooms and a large Music, Design and ICT studios. The facilities are continually being updated and added to.

Boarders are accommodated in a well-appointed House under the close supervision of Houseparents. Dormitories and common rooms are bright and cheerful and recognition is given to the importance of children having a place where they can feel at home and relaxed at the end of the day. Contact with parents and guardians is well maintained. Every

half term is punctuated by an exeat weekend and arrangements are made for boarders whose parents live abroad. Minibus transport for day pupils is provided from Boston, Louth, Skegness and Lincoln.

The Pre-Preparatory department caters for approximately 40 children, aged from 4 to 7, and is located in its own building with separate play area and staff.

The Nursery for children between 2 and 4 is attached to the Pre-Prep and accommodates approximately 45 children.

Half-fee bursaries are available for the sons and daughters of clergymen. There are also reductions for brothers and sisters as well as bursaries for the children of service personnel. The fees are fully inclusive.

Charitable status. St Hugh's School (Woodhall Spa) Limited is a Registered Charity, number 527611. It exists to provide a high standard of education and care to pupils from the age of 2 to 13.

St Ives School
United Learning

Three Gates Lane, Haslemere, Surrey GU27 2ES
Tel: 01428 643734
Fax: 01428 644788
email: admin@stiveshaslemere.com
website: www.stiveshaslemere.com

Chairman of Governors: Mr Graham Harvey-Browne

Headmistress: **Miss Kay Goldsworthy**

Age Range. Girls 2–11, Boys 2–5.
Number of Children. 150 (Day).
Fees per term (2014–2015). Reception & Year 1 £2,600, Year 2 £3,100, Years 3–4 £3,750, Years 5–6 £4,450. Lunch included.

St Ives is a Preparatory Day School situated within half a mile of the centre of Haslemere and stands in its own attractive and spacious grounds of eight acres.

The school aims to provide a broad and balanced curriculum whilst retaining academic excellence, and a traditional prep school education is combined with the best of modern teaching methods. Each child is encouraged to work hard in a secure, relaxed and happy environment. Individual needs are catered for and high standards of manners, discipline and appearance are encouraged. Classes are small and in addition to class teachers, qualified teaching assistants are provided in each of the Pre-Prep classes.

Our children are prepared for a variety of senior schools and we are very proud of our strong academic achievements. Whilst the basic skills of Numeracy and Literacy are at the heart of our curriculum, the girls also enjoy a wide range of experiences and opportunities.

Competitive sport is played in good spirit with an emphasis on enjoyment, involvement and working together whilst attaining high standards. The school enjoys regional and national sporting success and a large variety of extra-curricular activities is offered including speech and drama, ballet, instrumental lessons and tennis coaching. Annual residential field studies are organised for the upper school and a ski trip is normally organised on alternate years during the Easter holidays.

The school is well resourced including Maths and IT suites, purpose-built Nursery, Pre-Prep classrooms, Science, Art and Music rooms. Two new netball courts and enlarged grassed areas have enhanced the sporting facilities.

Girls are prepared for the Common Entrance and senior school examinations at 11+ and the school has a strong record for gaining scholarships to a wide range of well known senior independent schools. St Ives' full independence from any senior school enables parents and the Head to select the most appropriate senior school for their child.

The St Ives bus provides a daily service, the route currently covering the Haslemere, Liphook, Hindhead, Grayshott, Churt, Witley, Milford and Frensham areas.

For a copy of the prospectus please apply to the Registrar.

Charitable status. St Ives School is a Registered Charity, number 312080. Its aim is the advancement of education for girls.

St John's Beaumont

Priest Hill, Old Windsor, Berkshire SL4 2JN
Tel: 01784 494053
Fax: 01784 494048
email: admissions@stjohnsbeaumont.co.uk
website: www.stjohnsbeaumont.org.uk

Chairman of Governors: M C Brenninkmeyer

Headmaster: G E F Delaney, BA Hons, PGCE

Age Range. 3½–13.
Number of Boys. 310 (60 Full and Weekly Boarders; 250 Day Boys).
Fees per term (2014–2015). Boarding £8,140, Weekly Boarding £6,965, Day Boys £3,655–£5,365, Pre-Preparatory (Nursery–Year 1) £2,805.

St John's is a Jesuit School. Classes are small, and boys can receive individual attention according to their needs and abilities. Although following the Common Entrance syllabus for senior independent schools, St John's also promotes the National Curriculum and boys are assessed at Key Stages 1 and 2, audited by the Local Education Authority. Boys are prepared for entry to some of the top independent schools in the country and have won many scholarships in recent years.

The imposing Victorian building stands in spacious grounds on the edge of Windsor Great Park, with extensive facilities for outdoor sports. It has a large gymnasium and considerable sports fields. Several facilities have been opened in recent years, including two ICT suites, technology block science and art block, music school, concert hall and 25-metre indoor swimming pool. A purpose-built sports complex was opened by HM The Queen in October 2009. Wireless technology is available in classrooms enabling access to individual laptops and there are interactive whiteboards in all classrooms. On top of their daily curriculum schedules, each member of staff offers an extra activity after school. These include rock climbing, chess, polo, drama, art, self-defence and mandarin. Games are played every day and the school particularly excels at rugby, cricket, tennis and swimming. The school's swimming pool is also used by other schools and the local community.

The boys have daily opportunity for religious practice, as well as formal instruction and informal guidance.

An illustrated prospectus is available from the Headmaster, who is always pleased to meet parents and to show them round the school.

Charitable status. St John's is a Registered Charity, number 230165. It exists to provide education for boys.

St John's College Infant and Junior School

Grove Road South, Southsea, Hampshire PO5 3QW
Tel: 023 9281 5118
Fax: 023 9287 3603

email: info@stjohnscollege.co.uk
website: www.stjohnscollege.co.uk

Chairman of Governors: Mr T Forer

Head Master: Mr R A Shrubsall, MA Ed

Age Range. Co-educational 2–11 years.
Number of Pupils. 150.
Fees per term (2014–2015). Day: £2,710 (Reception, Years 1 & 2), £2,770 (Years 3 & 4), £2,895 (Years 5 & 6). UK Boarding £7,690, Overseas Boarding £8,240.

St John's College is an independent school founded to provide an academic education in a Christian environment. The College is fully co-educational, day and boarding, with over 600 pupils and students ranging in age from 2 to over 18. We offer a continuous range of education, starting in the Nursery and progressing through the Junior and Senior schools to the Sixth Form. We are a Catholic foundation but welcome pupils of all faiths and also those with no religious beliefs.

The Junior School is a self-contained unit but located on the main College campus. The Junior School enjoys the use of many excellent facilities: a sports centre, theatre, computer suite, library, science laboratory and music room. The attractive site is complemented by 42 acres of well-maintained playing fields, located on the outskirts of the city.

A broadly balanced and extended curriculum is offered, encompassing all aspects of the National Curriculum at Key Stages 1 and 2. Close staff liaison ensures a smooth automatic transition for pupils into the Senior School at age 11. The Early Years Foundation Stage is covered in Nursery and Reception Year.

The Junior School has a fine academic, musical and sporting tradition and there is a wide range of extra-curricular clubs which run during lunchtimes and after school. Educational and character-building residential trips are offered at holiday times.

St John's is committed to developing the whole person, but at the very heart of all that we do is teaching and learning. Our academic record is a very good one and the commitment of our staff to each pupil is outstanding.

A prospectus and further details are available from the Admissions Registrar.

St John's College School

75 Grange Road, Cambridge, Cambs CB3 9AA
Tel: 01223 353532 Headmaster
            01223 353652 Admissions Secretary
            01223 272701 Bursar
Fax: 01223 355846
email: shoffice@sjcs.co.uk
            bhoffice@sjcs.co.uk
website: www.sjcs.co.uk

Chairman of Governors: The Reverend Mr Duncan Dormor

Headmaster: **Mr K L Jones**, MA Gonville and Caius College Cambridge

Age Range. 4–13.
Number of Children. 455 girls and boys (including 19 Chorister and 16 Non-Chorister boy and girl boarders).
Fees per term (2014–2015). Choristers £2,402; Day Boys and Girls (4–13) £3,460–£4,563 (according to age); Boarders £7,207. Bursaries available for Choristers.

Profile. St John's prides itself on the quality of the academic and pastoral care it provides for each child. Through relaxed and friendly relations with children in a well-structured environment rich with opportunity; through close monitoring of progress; through communication and cooperation with parents; through expert staffing and, above all, through a sense of community that cares for the strengths and weaknesses of each of its members, St John's has consistently achieved outstanding results exemplified by over 70 scholarships during the last three years. Whilst its Choristers maintain the tradition of choral services and tour the world, St John's status as an Expert Centre for ICT, and other innovations, ensure the school's commitment to the future. Headmaster, Mr Kevin Jones, was recently awarded the title of national Tatler's 'Best Head of a Prep School'. Mr Jones's award concludes an exceptional year for the school. The major redevelopment of its site to provide state-of-the-art facilities was completed and this was followed by an inspection report hailed as the best ever achieved by an independent school.

Entry. At 4–7 by parental interview; at 7–12 by parental interview, report from previous school and, as appropriate, assessment.

Curriculum. The curriculum surrounds the core of formal skills teaching with a breadth of enrichment and extension for each child's talents. In addition to the usual subjects including specialist taught DT, ICT, Art, Music, Dance and Drama, and PE for all pupils, the following are also available: French (from 4+), Latin (from 9+), Greek (optional from 11+), Spanish (11+). Pupils prepared for CE and Scholarship examinations. Philosophy and Study Skills are now regularly taught to pupils in certain year groups and all pupils are being introduced to Mindfulness.

Leavers. Virtually all go to senior independent day or boarding schools. The School works closely with parents to assist them in finding the best school for their child.

Consultation. Tutorial system (1 teacher to 10 pupils) with daily tutorial session timetabled. Half yearly academic assessments, end of year examinations, termly Parents' Evenings and weekly staff 'surgery' times.

Sports. Athletics, Badminton, Basketball, Cricket, Cross Country, Football, Golf, Gymnastics, Hockey, Netball, Rounders, Rowing, Rugby, Short Tennis, Squash, Swimming, Table Tennis, Tennis. All games are timetabled and therefore given significant status. All major sports strong.

Activities. Numerous clubs including Art, Chess, Dance, Drama, Pottery, Sketching, Design Technology, Craft, Information Technology, Maths games and puzzles, Magic, Touch-typing, Cycling Proficiency, General Knowledge, Debating, Poetry, Sewing and Wardrobe. College Choir of international status, Chamber Groups, Orchestras, School Chapel Choir, Junior Chamber Choir, Parents' Choir, Major theatrical productions, eg *The Sound of Music, Hamlet*, and theatrical opportunities for all children. A range of visits relating to curriculum plus French, Classics, skiing and outward bound trips.

Facilities. School on two sites with facilities used by all pupils. *Byron House (4–8).* Outstanding facilities including Science, DT Centre, two large suites of networked PCs, computerised Library, Drama Studio, Gym, Hall, and specialist Music wing.

Senior House (9–13). The Senior House site has been completely redeveloped. In addition to existing facilities such as the Chapel, Theatre, Gymnasium Science Laboratory, Art Room, ICT Room, Swimming Pool and Music School, the site now boasts 14 new classrooms, an outstanding Library, a new DT and Computer Control and Graphics facility, a second Science Laboratory, a new Drama Studio, new Music facilities, a Quiet Garden, a new Multi-Sports Court and changing block, extensive new storage and excellent staff facilities.

Boarding. From age 8. Girl and boy boarders form an integral part of life at St John's and benefit from all the School's facilities whilst living in the homely, caring atmosphere of a brand new Boarding House which was completed in Spring 2011. The Boarding House accommodates up to 40 boys and girls. These improved facilities include recreation areas, a library, TV, table tennis and use of all

Senior House facilities. Day boarding and 'Waiters' facilities allow the School to be flexible to the needs of parents and children alike.

Charitable status. St John's College School is part of St John's College Cambridge, which is a Registered Charity, number 1137428.

St John's International School

Broadway, Sidmouth, Devon EX10 8RG
Tel: 01395 513984
Fax: 01395 514539
email: contact.stjohns@iesmail.com
website: www.stjohnsdevon.co.uk

Head: **Mr Simon Larter**, BA Hons, PGCE

Age Range. 2–18 Co-educational.
Number of Pupils. Main School 200, of whom 40–50 are Boarders. The Nursery (up to 5 years) has up to 50 children. Girl/boy ratio 50:50.
Fees per term (2014–2015). Day: £2,215–£3,600; UK Boarding: £5,810–£6,105; International Boarding: £6,725–£7,050; International Study Centre: £8,950. Full fee details are available on our website.

About St John's. St John's School is an independent day and boarding school for girls and boys aged 2–18. The school is located on a hill overlooking the sea in Sidmouth and benefits from excellent facilities, including beautiful historic buildings, extensive grounds and playing fields, a large, outdoor swimming pool, indoor sports hall, adventure playground and tennis courts. With its warm, happy atmosphere, St John's prides itself on providing a caring and safe environment for all its students. Most importantly it is large enough to provide a broad study programme yet small enough to retain a special family feel that is valued by our students, parents and staff alike.

Our School is part of the wider organisation of International Education Systems (IES) and combines traditional values with a contemporary, international approach to learning.

Structure of St John's. St John's offers an 'all-through' education for girls and boys aged 2–18.

Nursery (Age 2–4). St John's Nursery provides a high-quality day care facility through its Early Bird department and a more structured pre-school environment in its nursery class. Nursery is located in a separate area of School but is able to benefit from the main school facilities including the swimming pool, sports hall and dining hall. Early Years Vouchers are accepted.

Junior School (Reception to Year 6). In the Junior School, the children follow an exciting 'cross-curricular' way of learning, underpinned by traditional values. We have recently become one of only 14 schools in the UK to be authorised to teach the International Baccalaureate Primary Years Programme and we are the only school in the South West of the UK to offer it.

Senior School (Year 7 to Year 11). The Senior School offers an integrated programme based on the National Curriculum, combined with a series of individual and theme-based projects to investigate and extend all topics, culminating in IGCSEs in Year 11.

Sixth Form (Years 12 and 13). As a result of the success of our Senior School, St John's opened a Sixth Form in September 2013. Our teachers are fully trained to be able to deliver a comprehensive range of A and AS Level courses across a wide range of subjects, in a small class, tutorial-style environment. Please see website for further information. A/AS Level English Language, A/AS Level English Literature, A/AS Level Mathematics, A/AS Level Physics, A/AS Level Biology, A/AS Level Chemistry, A/AS Level

Applied ICT, A/AS Level Geography, A/AS Level Business Studies, A/AS Level Psychology, A/AS Level French, A/AS Level Spanish, AS Marine Science (one year only), AS Global Perspectives (one year only), A/AS Level Art, A Level Music.

Entrance Requirements. We accept students with a broad range of abilities as our focus is on providing education that is designed to challenge the individual. All students will be asked to take a small Placement Test and we would request sight of at least one School Report. Each student will be invited for a short meeting with the Headmaster.

Transport. A number of bus routes are in place across the county.

Boarding. Weekly or full boarding is available.

St John's School

Potter Street Hill, Northwood, Middlesex HA6 3QY
Tel: 020 8866 0067
Fax: 020 8868 8770
email: office@st-johns.org.uk
website: www.st-johns.org.uk
Twitter: @stjsnorthwood

Chairman of Governors: Mr J Armstrong, Esq

Headmaster: **Mr M S Robinson**, BSc, PGCE
Loughborough

Age Range. 3–13.
Number of Boys. 350 Day Boys (Prep 223; Pre-Prep and Nursery 127).
Fees per annum (2014–2015). Nursery £9,000; Pre-Preparatory £12,280; Preparatory £13,250.

Facing South, on a 35-acre site, we have outstanding views over London. Since the Merchant Taylors' Educational Trust took the School under its wing, impressive development has taken place. St John's has gained a gymnasium and changing block, two science laboratories, a six classroom Pre-Prep Department and a Junior classroom block. Another major development provided an Assembly Hall/Theatre, an Art Studio, Design & Technology Workshop, ICT Centre and a new Music Department. At the same time, other areas of the School were refurbished creating specialist teaching areas for English, French, History, Geography and Mathematics. We also acquired an area of grassland and woodland for ecological and environmental study, to add to our extensive playing fields and formal gardens.

A major extension of our Pre-Preparatory Department provided Nursery facilities, an Information Technology Suite and Library. Extra play area, including an 'indoor quiet area' and a Forest School, have also been created for our Pre-Prep and Nursery pupils. Our playing fields have been transformed with the construction of a large, all-weather multi-purpose sports area. At the same time, our four rugby pitches and athletics track were levelled and provided with excellent drainage and irrigation. Most recently, we have created a small Golf Course.

Most of the boys enter the School at either the age of three into the Nursery or at four into the Pre-Prep and there is a separate entry into the Prep School at seven. St John's has an excellent record of success in scholarship and senior school entrance examinations. Boys are prepared for all independent schools, however, our links with Merchant Taylors' School, Northwood, are particularly strong.

Although the School was originally a Church of England foundation, boys of all religions and denominations are welcome.

Charitable status. St John's School, part of the Merchant Taylors' Educational Trust, is a Registered Charity, number 1063738. It exists for the purpose of educating boys.

St Joseph's In The Park School

St Mary's Lane, Hertingfordbury, Hertfordshire SG14 2LX
Tel: 01992 581378
email: admin@stjosephsinthepark.co.uk
           marketing@stjosephsinthepark.co.uk
website: www.stjosephsinthepark.co.uk
Twitter: @fromthepark

Chair of Governors: Mrs Janet Goldsmith

Headmaster: **Mr Neil Jones**, BSc, MSc, PGCE

Age Range. 3–11 Co-educational.
Number of Pupils. 150.
Fees per term (2014–2015). Nursery (minimum 5 sessions) £1,810, Kindergarten (minimum 7 sessions) £2,402, Pre School (full-time) £2,900 (fees are pro-rata for more or fewer sessions), Infants £3,604, Lower Juniors Y3 to Y4 £3,711, Upper Juniors Y5 to Y6 £3,732, Woodlands Learning Support Centre Y3 to Y6 £5,132. All fees are inclusive of books, stationery and lunches.

St Joseph's In The Park is a single-form entry, co-educational school for children between the ages of 3 and 11 years. Founded in 1898, it is one of the oldest Independent Schools in the area.

Set within 40 acres of Hertingfordbury Park on the outskirts of Hertford, St Joseph's In The Park has not only a celebrated reputation for valuing support for learning and high academic standards, but also a particularly outstanding tradition in pastoral care and a family environment. Our recent ISI inspection report bears out this belief and judged us to be 'Excellent' in all areas. This is the highest possible accolade from the largest inspection body for independent schools. The Inspectors noted that "*the pupils' achievement is excellent. It is underpinned by high quality teaching and a vibrant curriculum*"; in addition, the "*pupils thrive in the school's atmosphere of hard work, enjoyment and effort*".

Through each Key Stage the children experience an exciting curriculum. The core focus on Literacy, Mathematics and Science is supported by a themed approach to some of the Foundation Subjects.

A school that thrives on values and tradition can also boast an environment that permits children to develop and learn in a contemporary educational setting which includes:

* an extended day starting with Breakfast Club from 7.45 am and After School Care until 6 pm with a light tea at 4.30 pm;
* the Woodlands Department of Learning, established in 1998, providing differentiated education for children between Years 3 and 6 who need extra learning support;
* Juniors are involved in a Wednesday afternoon programme of technology, art and sport which changes every half term during the year and may be enriched to include film making, textiles, photography, cookery, golf, forest school, skiing and street dance delivered by specialists. After exams Junior 4 (Year 6) are offered Social Responsibility and Self Awareness Week, which is intended to prepare them for life beyond St Joseph's and support their individual development;
* two choirs and music lessons in dedicated music rooms that include singing, ukulele, guitar, drums, saxophone, violin and piano, ensuring that music is enjoyed throughout the school;
* a dedicated ICT room, wireless network across the school, interactive whiteboards in every classroom;
* an Art room and newly-built DT room provide bespoke areas for creativity;
* a newly-refurbished Science Room providing space for discovery, taught by a dedicated Science Teacher;

- healthy-eating menus on a three-week rotation providing nut-free, nutritious and varied meals all prepared in the school kitchen by experienced and long-standing catering staff;
- extensive woodland setting within beautiful parkland;
- an outdoor heated swimming pool, sports field and large, multi-purpose hall for drama, dance, concerts and sports;
- on-site dedicated car park.

A prospectus which further illustrates the distinctiveness of the school is available on request.

Charitable status. St Joseph's In The Park School is a Registered Charity, number 1111064.

St Lawrence College Junior School

Ramsgate, Kent CT11 7AF
Tel: 01843 572912
Fax: 01843 572913
email: hjs@slcuk.com
website: www.slcuk.com

Chairman of the Council: Mr David W Taylor, MA Oxon, PGCE, FRSA

Head: **Mr Simon J E Whittle**, BA Hons, PGCE

Age Range. 3–11.
Number of Pupils. 180 boys and girls, a few of whom are boarders.
Fees per term (2014–2015). Boarders £7,505, Day £2,281–£3,565.

St Lawrence College Junior School offers a supportive, caring environment, based on traditional Christian values, in which children are given every opportunity to fulfil their potential. Academic expectations are high, but realistic and open-minded. Personal attention is given within small classes where talents are recognised and needs are catered for. There is a strong belief that education, in its truest sense, is measured not just in a student's exam results but by its ability to open young people's minds.

Most pupils transfer to the Senior School at 11+, and scholarships are regularly earned. There is also an excellent record of success at securing places in the highly-selective local grammar schools.

The Junior School is based in an attractive Victorian building in a peaceful corner of the 150-acre St Lawrence College campus. Its own independent facilities include a Music Department and Performance Hall, two fully-networked ICT Suites, adventure playgrounds, tennis courts and spacious playing fields. These have recently been enhanced by the addition of a new Science Lab and Art Studio. Membership of the wider College community gives pupils the best of both worlds, and they are able to share many of the Senior School's excellent specialist facilities, including new Sports Centre and Theatre. Boarders enjoy living in Kirby House, an ultra-modern, eco-friendly development which offers accommodation of an exceptional quality.

A wide range of extra-curricular opportunities includes sports such as football, rugby, hockey, cricket, lacrosse, rounders, netball, basketball, athletics, cross-country running, swimming and dance. There are plenty of fixtures against other schools, but, most importantly, children learn the value of fitness, cooperative teamwork and good sportsmanship. There is a proud musical tradition, and plenty of scope for drama and the creative arts. Some Activities take place at the end of the school day, but most are concentrated into the popular, informal Saturday morning programme.

St Lawrence's Christian heritage underpins all that the Junior School stands for. An atmosphere of trust and mutual respect is based on kindness, forgiveness and consideration for others. There is a strong emphasis placed on thoughtful

conduct, courtesy and good manners, and on endowing young people with a clear sense of moral responsibility.

Charitable status. The Corporation of St Lawrence College is a Registered Charity, number 307921. It exists to provide education for boys and girls.

St Leonards Junior School

St Andrews, Fife KY16 9QJ
Tel: 01334 472126
Fax: 01334 476152
email: slnp@stleonards-fife.org
website: www.stleonards-fife.org

Chairman of the St Leonards Council: James Murray

Headmaster: **Andrew Donald**, BSc Aberdeen

Age Range. 5–12.
Number of Pupils. 180 (85 girls, 95 boys).
Fees per term (2014–2015). £2,929 (Years 1–5), £3,283 (Years 6–7).

St Leonards Junior School in St Andrews is the co-educational junior school of St Leonards. The school is administered by the St Leonards Council and educates children between the ages of 5 and 12, from Year 1 to Year 7.

Pupils are prepared for entry to St Leonards Senior School. With specialist teachers and small class sizes, children benefit from individual attention. In addition to a strong academic tradition, drama, music, art, ICT and PE are included in the timetable.

Outside the classroom, a wide variety of sports are available; netball, rugby, hockey, lacrosse, tennis and cricket being the main team activities. Tuition in golf, judo and swimming is also offered. Outdoor education activities include watersports. There are also classes in Scottish Country Dancing and ballet.

Charitable status. St Leonards School is a Registered Charity, number SC010904. It exists to provide education to children between the ages of 5 and 18.

St Margaret's Preparatory School

Curzon Street, Calne, Wiltshire SN11 0DF
Tel: 01249 857220
Fax: 01249 857227
email: office@stmargaretsprep.org.uk
website: www.stmargaretsprep.org.uk
Twitter: @StMargaretsPrep

Chairman of Governors: Mr S Knight, FRICS

Headmistress: **Mrs K E Cordon**, GLCM, LLCM TD, ALCM

Age Range. 3–11.
Number of Pupils. 220 Day: 122 girls, 98 boys.
Fees per term (2014–2015). £1,442–£3,970.

St Margaret's is an independent day preparatory school for boys and girls aged 3–11 based in Calne, Wiltshire.

The school has an ethos that is based on traditional values combined with an innovative approach, providing a happy environment for all children in a friendly, caring community. Within this context, it is hoped that boys and girls will learn the value of hard work and how to accept discipline and responsibility.

The St Margaret's curriculum comprises an extensive range of activities, designed to promote not only learning, but also personal growth and development. It is based around the subjects of the National Curriculum which are delivered, in the main, by class teachers, all of whom are experts in the relevant ages. This is then enhanced by specialist tuition in Sport, Music, Latin, ICT and Modern Foreign Languages, as well as the extensive extra-curricular programme, designed to enrich every child's experience whilst at the school; this includes the 'hidden curriculum' – what the children learn from the way they are treated and how they are expected to behave. It is important that the pupils learn to grow into positive, responsible adults who can work and cooperate with others, whilst at the same time developing their knowledge and skills in order to achieve their true potential.

Sport plays an important part at St Margaret's and the school is fortunate to share a 25-acre site with St Mary's, Calne. Consequently, the children benefit from a wide range of facilities not always available to preparatory school pupils. These include a 25m indoor swimming pool and an all-weather surface astroturf offering facilities for hockey, tennis, football and lacrosse. Every child enjoys up to five timetabled sessions of sport in school each week; these include swimming, PE and Games. The main games for the boys are rugby, hockey and cricket and for the girls, netball, hockey and rounders. St Margaret's competes throughout the year with other schools in Bath, Wiltshire, Oxfordshire and Somerset at various inter-school matches and festivals. All children are encouraged to improve their physical coordination and to compete with confidence on the games field. The school has recently been awarded the Youth Sports Trust Gold Quality Mark.

The Performing Arts have a high profile and there are Music and Drama opportunities at every age group. The children are encouraged to enter for external examinations, as well as competing in local festivals, in which their success rate is high. The school is especially proud of its award-winning Chamber Choir. There is a comprehensive performance programme in place, which is enjoyed by both performers and spectators alike!

School hours are between 8.25 am and 3.30/4.30 pm each day. There is an optional early morning drop-off facility at 8.00 am and the school has its own After School Club which is staffed by three fully-trained child carers and is available until 6 pm, five days a week. Whilst at the club, the children participate in a physical activity, craft and creative work, and a quiet time is set aside to enable them to do their homework. Tea is also provided. This facility is also open for a number of weeks during the Easter and Summer holidays.

St Margaret's is extremely proud of its pupils' academic achievements. The children are thoroughly prepared for entrance examinations to senior schools and they enjoy an impressive record of success in academic and specialist subject scholarships, as well as consistently gaining entry to first-choice schools.

Good manners and consideration for the needs of others are expectations, but at the same time the children are inspired, not afraid to take risks and above all, have fun and enjoy learning!

Charitable status. St Mary's School (Calne) is a Registered Charity, number 309482. It exists to provide education for boys and girls.

St Margaret's Preparatory School
Bushey

Merry Hill Road, Bushey, Hertfordshire WD23 1DT
Tel: 020 8416 4400
Fax: 020 8416 4401
email: prepoffice@smbushey.com
website: www.stmargaretsbushey.co.uk
Twitter: @stmargsbushey
Facebook: /StMargaretsBushey
LinkedIn: /St Margaret's School, Bushey

Chair of Governors: Miss M Rudland

Headmistress: Mrs R Hardy, MA Oxon, MEd, FRSA

Head of Preparatory School: Mrs C Aisthorpe, BEd Hons, LRAM

Age Range. Girls 4–11.
Number of Pupils. 118.
Fees per term (2014–2015). Years 4–6 £4,100, Transition (Year 3) £3,730, Reception, Years 1 & 2 £3,110.

St Margaret's School in Bushey, Hertfordshire is among the oldest girls' schools in the UK, established in 1749. It has an excellent record of academic success, which is attributed to the School's emphasis upon providing the very best pastoral care. The School is set within 74 acres of stunning Hertfordshire countryside which offers girls abundant space to grow and be inspired in safety. St Margaret's educates girls all the way through from ages 4 to 18. It is predominantly a day school; however, boarding facilities are available for up to 90 girls from the age of 11.

St Margaret's Preparatory School is distinct from the wider School. It is a day school offering a warm and nurturing environment for girls in their primary school years. Through this environment the school prides itself upon its consistent ability to stimulate and challenge girls to reach their potential and become confident members of society. Girls achieve in a myriad of ways as the school works to ensure that each fulfills her academic potential and is inspired to have a love of learning.

The Preparatory School's curriculum is challenging and broad in variety. It aims to identify and develop each girl's unique skill, talent and curiosity, extending her horizons and expectations. Within the School there are numerous opportunities to thrive through house, class and school-wide activities. There is a choir, an orchestra, opportunities for speech and drama through annual productions and concerts, sport, dance, numerous leadership opportunities, workshops, field trips and many other co-curricular activities. Equipped within this happy and secure education girls move confidently and seamlessly from the Preparatory School to the Senior School with independent and inquiring minds, a positive attitude to learning and an appetite for new experiences and challenges.

School surveys consistently feature comments from parents saying that St Margaret's is a happy, friendly and vibrant family community filled with the cheerful chatter of lively minds and the hum of purposeful activity. An exceptional team of dedicated staff are committed to bringing out the best in every girl, focusing on each as an individual.

There are also plenty of opportunities for parents to engage with life at St Margaret's, particularly through the School's parents' association, called Connections.

To find out more or to arrange to visit the school, please visit our website: www.stmargaretsbushey.co.uk.

Charitable status. St Margaret's School Bushey is a Registered Charity, number 1056228.

St Martin's Ampleforth

Gilling Castle, Gilling East, York YO62 4HP
Tel: 01439 766600
Fax: 01439 788538
email: headmaster@stmartins.ampleforth.org.uk
website: www.stmartins.ampleforth.org.uk

Chairman of the Trustees: Rt Rev Cuthbert Madden

Headmaster: Mr Mark O'Donnell, BA, MA, EdM, PGDE

Age Range. 3+ to 13+ years.
Number of Pupils. 167 (47 Boarders, 120 Flexi Boarders and Day Children).

Fees per term (2014–2015). Boarding £7,044; Day £2,526–£4,682.

St Martin's Ampleforth is a boarding and day preparatory school which takes boys and girls from the age of 3+ years and prepares them for Common Entrance and Scholarship examinations. It is expected most of the pupils will enter Ampleforth College at 13+.

St Martin's Ampleforth is based in a 14th century castle with spacious and secluded gardens, 18 miles north of York and close to the North Yorkshire Moors National Park.

All Faiths are made most welcome in this Benedictine school. The Chaplaincy team is led by a monk of Ampleforth Abbey.

The highest academic standards are aimed for, within a broad and challenging curriculum. Each pupil's ability is taken into account. Very able children are provided for and coached for scholarships to Ampleforth College and other leading independent senior schools, whilst those with learning difficulties, including dyslexia, are given qualified specialist help. Each form of approximately 15 children has a tutor responsible for overall progress and pastoral support. Setting is in place from Year 6 and beyond.

There is a striking variety of extra-curricular pursuits including horse riding, fencing, golf, shooting, drama, swimming and debating. The School has an enviable reputation for games and fields highly successful teams in rugby, netball, cricket, rounders, hockey, track and field and cross-country running.

Music is strong. Typically, 80% of pupils learn musical instruments and perform regularly. The School provides the trebles for the acclaimed Ampleforth College Schola Cantorum and there is an increasingly successful girls' Schola too. A purpose-built performing arts centre enhances the current provision for choral and instrumental performance as well as fostering drama throughout the school.

Parents are considered part of the School community. They are welcome at any time, especially for matches, other organised events and, of course, for Mass on Sundays and feast days.

Facilities include a sports hall, ICT room, Music School, Language School, all-weather cricket nets, a 9-hole golf course and all-weather floodlit astroturf. The extensive grounds, including woods, lakes and gardens, combine a sense of space and freedom with unrivalled beauty.

Bursaries are available.

Daily transport is provided to and from Pickering, Malton, Kirkbymoorside, Boroughbridge, Easingwold, York and Helmsley.

Charitable status. St Martin's Ampleforth, as part of the St Laurence Trust, is a registered charity, number 1063808 and exists to provide education for boys and girls.

St Martin's School

40 Moor Park Road, Northwood, Middlesex HA6 2DJ
Tel: 01923 825740
Fax: 01923 835452
email: office@stmartins.org.uk
website: www.stmartins.org.uk

Chairman of Governors: Roy Jakes

Headmaster: David T Tidmarsh, BSc Hons, PGCE

Age Range. 3–13.
Number of Boys. 400 Day Boys.
Fees per term (2014–2015). Main School £4,440; Pre-Prep £4,075; Kindergarten £1,620 (mornings). Bursaries are available, details on request.

St Martin's aims to provide boys aged 3–13 with the breadth of education and experience necessary for them to realise their full potential in a safe and friendly environment.

An enthusiastic staff of 40 experienced and well-qualified teachers maintains high academic standards and provides broad sporting, musical and cultural opportunities. The atmosphere is friendly and lively with great emphasis on pastoral care.

The School, which is an Educational Trust, administered by a Board of Governors, prepares boys for entry to all the Independent Senior Schools. Fifty-eight Scholarship awards have been won to senior schools during the last five years. The School, which is in a pleasant residential area, stands in 12 acres of grounds. Facilities include a Kindergarten and separate Pre-Preparatory building; two Science Laboratories; a Performing Arts Centre; a Sports Centre including an indoor swimming pool; a playground; two ICT suites; an Art Studio with facilities for Design Technology; 3 Tennis Courts.

ICT, Art, DT, and Music are included in the curriculum for all boys, and a large proportion of the boys in the School learn a musical instrument. There is a varied after-school activity programme for boys to pursue their interests.

There is a pre-school and after-school club from Kindergarten age upwards enabling parents to work a full day.

The School is divided into Patrols for competitions in work and games, and senior boys make a responsible contribution towards the running of the School. Boys are taught football, rugby, cross-country running, hockey, cricket, swimming, athletics and tennis. The school has a fine reputation in inter-school matches.

Charitable status. St Martin's (Northwood) Preparatory School Trust Limited is a Registered Charity, number 312648. It exists to provide education for boys.

St Mary's School

Hampstead

47 Fitzjohn's Avenue, London NW3 6PG
Tel: 020 7435 1868
Fax: 020 7794 7922
email: enquiries@stmh.co.uk
website: www.stmh.co.uk

Chairman of Governors: Mrs Susan McCarron

Headmistress: Miss A M Rawlinson, MA Hons, Dip Tchng

Age Range. Girls 2¾–11, Boys 2¾–7.
Number in School. 284 Girls, 17 Boys. Nursery: 37 Girls, 15 Boys.
Fees per term (2014–2015). Nursery £2,235 (5 mornings a week), £36 each additional afternoon per week; Reception to Year 6 £4,140.

Surrounded by mature woodland and gardens, unmatched by any other school in the area, St Mary's has been established in Hampstead since 1926. Founded by the Institute of the Blessed Virgin Mary as a Roman Catholic School for Girls, the school remains true to the ideals of the IBVM foundress, Mary Ward who believed in the provision of a thoroughly grounded academic and spiritual education as a foundation for an enriched and confident adulthood.

The school has a thriving Pre-Nursery, Nursery and Pre-Prep for girls and boys. Boys are prepared for transfer to popular London Boys Preparatory Schools and the girls are prepared for Common Entrance and the entrance examinations for top London Senior Schools. The girls transfer at the age of 11 years, many gaining awards and scholarships.

In addition to a broad curriculum, a wider range of activities is seen as essential to the rounded development of a healthy child. Importance is attached to physical education, drama and the arts. There are extra-curricular classes such as ballet and languages. There is a school choir and a chapel choir. Tuition is offered for many musical instruments. School trips abroad are arranged for older children.

There is an enthusiastic and dedicated staff of 40 experienced and well qualified teachers. There are specialist staff for Science, French, Art, Design and Technology, Music, PE and Special Needs. St Mary's aims to develop and fulfil the maximum potential of each child and this objective is fostered within a happy and caring environment which recognises the needs and importance of children of all abilities.

Bursaries are available (100%). Contact the Bursar for further details.

Charitable status. St Mary's School, Hampstead is a Registered Charity, number 1006411. It exists to provide education for girls and boys. It is managed by a majority of Lay Trustees and Governors.

St Mary's Preparatory School
Melrose

Abbey Park, Melrose, Roxburghshire TD6 9LN
Tel: 01896 822517
Fax: 01896 823550
email: office@stmarysmelrose.org.uk
website: www.stmarysmelrose.org.uk

Founded 1895.

Chairman of Governors: Mr G T G Baird

Headmaster: **William J Harvey**, BEd Hons

Age Range. 2–13 co-educational.
Number of Pupils. 188.
Fees per term (2014–2015). Day: Pre-Prep £3,804, Prep £4,754. Weekly Boarding: £5,554.

Curriculum. A healthy variety of subjects including traditional core subjects reflecting both the Scottish and English Curriculums (English, Maths, Science, Computer Studies, French, Geography, History, Classics, Latin, RE, Art, Music, Drama and PE). The School's intention is to provide a genuinely nourishing environment allowing for the development of the whole child.

Entry requirements. Application by letter or telephone, followed by a visit to the school, if possible, and a tour guided by senior pupils. All pupils can be offered an 'In-day' to help with placement.

Examinations offered. Common Entrance to Scholarship for independent senior schools in Scotland and England.

Academic, sports, games and leisure facilities. Classroom computers, Science Laboratory and a big open Art Room. Theatre-Arts and Assembly Hall for concerts and drama. Spacious games pitches supporting a strong tradition in rugby, cricket, hockey, netball and rounders. There is a cross-curricular Study Support Programme for talented and gifted children as well as for children with Specific Learning Difficulties.

Religious activities. Morning Assembly with hymn-singing and readings, stressing pupil participation and contribution through drama and music.

Charitable status. St Mary's School, Melrose is a Registered Charity, number SC009352. Its aim is to provide education for primary school children.

St Michael's Preparatory School

La Rue de la Houguette, Five Oaks, St Saviour, Jersey, Channel Islands JE2 7UG
Tel: 01534 856904
Fax: 01534 856620
email: tr@stmichaels.je
           office@stmichaels.je
website: www.stmichaelsschool.je
Twitter: @stmichaelsprep
Facebook: /St-Michaels-Preparatory-School-Jersey

Headmaster: **Michael Rees**, DipEd, MEd

Deputy Head: L McAviney, Cert Ed, BEd Hons

Senior Master: G Riddell, Cert Ed

Age Range. 3–14.
Number of Pupils. 165 Boys, 137 Girls.
Fees per term (2014–2015). Pre-Prep £2,918–£3,277; Forms 1 and 2 £4,055; Form 3 £4,177; Form 4 £4,476; Forms 5 and 6 £4,497. Lunch £280.

Boys and girls are prepared for scholarship and entrance to all Independent Senior Schools. Hockey, rugby football, soccer, gymnastics, netball, rounders, cricket, athletics and tennis are taught on spacious playing fields with pavilion and hard tennis courts which adjoin the school. The school also has a purpose-built Sports Hall (4 badminton court size), indoor swimming pool, gymnasium and dance/drama studio. Regular tours are made to Guernsey and England for sporting fixtures.

The school has flourishing and well equipped computer, art and design technology departments, in addition to networked computers in every classroom. A large variety of clubs and hobbies function within the school and many out-of-door activities, including surfing, sailing and photography, are enjoyed by the children. Music, drama and art (including pottery), are all encouraged and a wide range of musical instruments are taught. There are three school choirs, two orchestras and a number of ensemble groups. The choirs participate locally and nationally in events and competitions.

For senior children there is an annual Activities Week. Year 6 have overnight trips to neighbouring islands and France, while Year 7 go to Brittany and Year 8 to the south of France. Each winter a party of children from Years 3 to 8 ski in Switzerland.

Care, consideration, courtesy and good manners are important aspects of behaviour that the school holds dear.

The academic and physical development, in addition to the spiritual, moral and cultural growth, of the whole child is the main aim of the school and every child is encouraged to do "a little better" than anyone thought possible.

St Michael's Preparatory School

198 Hadleigh Road, Leigh-on-Sea, Essex SS9 2LP
Tel: 01702 478719
Fax: 01702 710183
email: info@stmichaelsschool.com
website: www.stmichaelsschool.com

Chairman of Governors: The Revd Ian Booth

Head: **Mr S Tompkins**, BSc Hons Sunderland, PGCE Leeds, MA York, NPQH

Age Range. Co-educational 3–11 years.
Number of Pupils. 271 day pupils (133 boys, 138 girls).
Fees per term (2014–2015). £1,300–£2,860.

St Michael's is a Church of England Preparatory (IAPS) School founded in 1922 to provide pupils with a well-rounded education based on Christian principles, with children welcomed from other Christian traditions and faiths. The school has its own Chapel.

The school is situated in a popular residential area in Leigh-on-Sea within easy reach of public transport. London is accessible by rail and Fenchurch Street Station is approximately 40 minutes away.

The curriculum offered is broad, balanced and tailored towards the children's needs and it aims to contribute to the intellectual, physical, creative, social and spiritual development of each child. All the children, from Nursery through to Form 6, receive specialist teaching in Music, French and PE with additional specialist teaching in the Prep department. Pupils are prepared for the end of Key Stage standardised attainment tests, 11+ entry to local grammar schools and Entrance or Scholarship examinations for independent schools. High academic standards are achieved throughout the school and the children thrive in a happy but disciplined environment.

St Michael's has a dedicated and well-qualified staff team. Class sizes are small to enable personal attention to be given. The school is well resourced with many specialist areas. Nearby playing fields are used for Games. There is a wide range of extra-curricular activities available, with Music and Drama as particular strengths.

Visits to the school are warmly welcomed.

Charitable status. St Michael's Preparatory School is a Registered Charity, number 280688. It exists to provide education.

St Michael's Prep School
Otford

Otford Court, Row Dow, Otford, Kent TN14 5SA
Tel: 01959 522137
Fax: 01959 522137
email: office@stmichaels.kent.sch.uk
website: www.stmichaels.kent.sch.uk

Chair of Governors: Ms Paula Carter

Head: **Mrs J Aisher**, BA Oxon, PGCE London, MCIL

Head of Pre-Prep Department: Mrs C Hookes-Gosney, BEd

Age Range. 2–13 Co-educational.
Number of Pupils. 472.
Fees per term (2014–2015). £344–£4,185.

St Michael's is a thriving, friendly school in a superb setting. We offer a fully co-educational, all-round preparatory education of the highest standard in a caring, family community. With a generous staff to pupil ratio and small classes, St Michael's achieves excellent results at every stage. Boys and girls share all activities; everyone is encouraged to try their best and to take part, perform and enjoy every aspect of school life.

The school's Christian roots support its modern ethos. St Michael's was founded in 1872 by London vicar Arthur Tooth who used his own fortune to create a school. The simple, egalitarian style of the founder has strong echoes today in a community where children from a wide variety of backgrounds and every faith are welcome.

St Michael's provides a unique environment for learning and enjoyment. The distinguished Victorian architecture of the original estate has been thoughtfully extended and upgraded. Spacious facilities for learning now include modern science, music, drama and art rooms, a large sports hall and splendid indoor 25m swimming pool. The school's wonderful wooded grounds on the slopes of the North Downs provide outdoor inspiration and extensive space for exploration, sport and play. They are also a truly memorable backdrop to a well-balanced education which allows every pupil to flourish.

The school prepares pupils for senior independent schools and local grammar schools (at 11+ and 13+) and has a proven academic record with many pupils gaining prestigious awards. It also has a high reputation for music, games (rugby, cricket, soccer, netball, hockey and athletics), drama and art.

A thriving Nursery, Kindergarten and Pre-Prep Department is self-contained and housed in a new purpose-built facility which opened in February 2013. Children play in the secure environment of the old walled garden, which has recently been equipped with an adventure playground.

An extensive out of school extra-curricular activity programme is offered to all pupils on a weekly basis and all classes participate in an integral programme of visits, workshops and field trips.

An active Parents and Friends Association is a strong supporter of the school and the Old Michaelian Society is one of the longest established in the Prep School world.

Charitable status. St Michael's is a Registered Charity, number 1076999. It exists to provide education for boys and girls.

St Neot's Preparatory School

St Neot's Road, Eversley, Hook, Hampshire RG27 0PN
Tel: Office: 0118 973 2118
            Admissions: 0118 973 9650
Fax: 0118 973 9949
email: office@stneotsprep.co.uk
            admissions@stneotsprep.co.uk
website: www.st-neots-prep.co.uk
Facebook: /stneotsprep

Chairman of Governors: Mr P Smith

Co Heads: **Mr Peter Withers and Mrs Maria Lloyd**

Age Range. 3 months–13 years co-educational.
Number of Pupils. 310.
Fees per term (2014–2015). Boarders: £5,798; Day pupils: Years 4–8 £4,998, Year 3 £3,778, Reception–Year 2 £3,090, Nursery from £8.15 per hour, Tiny Tuskers £6.60 per hour.

St Neot's is a co-educational independent preparatory school situated on the border of Hampshire, Surrey and Berkshire in its own 70-acre peaceful site, comprising many grass pitches, all-weather surfaces and woodland. The 'essence' of the school is about genuine care for each other, commitment, community and truly focusing on the individual child so that everyone achieves their potential. Children between the ages of 3 months and 13 years receive an outstanding education in a family environment, where happiness is seen as the key to success. Extensive use is made of the stunning grounds and independent learning and creativity are reinforced in the Forest school, whilst activity challenge stations help with team building and confidence.

Pupils are taught in two parallel classes, based with a class Teacher and supported by a classroom assistant, up to and including Year 4. Some specialist teaching is introduced from Reception and by the time pupils reach Year 5 they are taught by specialists across all subject areas. A broad academic programme covers all core subjects whilst taking full advantage of the outstanding setting and facilities to work beyond the classroom in subjects such as art, ICT, music, drama, design and food technology. The programme is based on the National Curriculum, appropriately extended to meet the rigorous requirements of senior school entrance exams via either Common Entrance or Scholarship with over 50 Scholarships being attained in the last 5 years.

A wide-ranging enrichment programme takes full advantage of the grounds and builds on the school's ethos, promoting teamwork, leadership and creative skills. Whilst doing so, some impressive academic results are achieved too!

All children from Year 3 take part in matches and an extensive sports enrichment programme is also offered making use of the school's enclosed swimming pool, rifle range, mountain biking course and traversing wall.

Although predominantly a day school, weekly, flexi or occasional boarding is offered in the school's Scandinavian-style boarding house. Children in Tuskers Nursery and Tiny Tuskers Crèche learn and play in their own purpose-built facility, with gardens and play area, whilst having access to the facilities and grounds of the school itself.

The school aims to ensure that all pupils receive the best possible training for life in a hard-working, but happy family atmosphere.

Charitable status. St Neot's (Eversley) Limited is a Registered Charity, number 307324. The aim of the Charity is to try to provide the best all-round education possible to as many pupils as possible, with bursarial help according to need.

St Olave's Prep School

106–110 Southwood Road, New Eltham, London SE9 3QS
Tel: 020 8294 8930
Fax: 020 8294 8939
email: office@stolaves.org.uk
website: www.stolaves.org.uk

Chairman of Trustees: Mr M D Ireland, MIoD, FRSA

Head: Mr James Tilly, BA Hons QTS

Age Range. 3–11.
Number of Pupils. 220 Day Boys and Girls.
Fees per term (2014–2015). Pre-Prep £1,424–£2,848; Reception & Year 1 £3,000; Years 2–6 £3,250.

In a single sentence, the school aims to bring out the best in everyone. It seeks to achieve this aim by providing an all-round education for both boys and girls aged 3 to 11 in a warm and caring environment in which each child can thrive and be happy knowing that each is accepted for who they are.

A Christian ethos permeates the pastoral life of the school, where care for others through thoughtful and responsible behaviour is expected. Praise and encouragement, rather than punishment and restriction, are emphasised and relationships between staff and pupils are relaxed and friendly. A close partnership with parents is sought.

The children in the Lower School are taught in mixed-ability classes where each child's progress is carefully monitored by the Class Teacher. In the Upper School the children are set across the year group for Mathematics. Throughout the school individual differences are appropriately met, with the very able and those with mild learning difficulties receiving additional support where this is thought beneficial. The school is noted for the broad curriculum it offers and for its excellent achievements in Music and Drama. A range of sporting activities is taught as part of the curriculum and there is a wide range of after school clubs and activities. Music and PE are taught by specialist teachers from the age of three and French is introduced at 6 years old. The classrooms are equipped with computers and there is a networked suite which supports all areas of the curriculum. A specialist ICT teacher teaches all year groups from Reception to Year

6. Digital panels (replacing interactive whiteboards) and portable devices are used to enhance learning.

St Olave's feeds a wide range of secondary schools and parents are given help in choosing the school most appropriate to meet the needs of their child.

Charitable status. St Olave's School is a Registered Charity, number 312734. It exists to provide high quality education for boys and girls.

St Olave's School, York
The Prep School of St Peter's School, York

York YO30 6AB
Tel: 01904 527416
Fax: 01904 527303
email: enquiries@stolavesyork.org.uk
website: www.stolavesyork.org.uk
Twitter: @StOlavesYork
Facebook: /stolavesyork

Chairman of the Governors: Mr W Woolley

Master: **Mr A I Falconer**, BA Hons Lancaster, MBA Leicester

Age Range. 8–13 co-educational.
Number of Pupils. 201 Boys, 138 Girls.
Fees per term (2014–2015). Day £3,630–£4,390. Boarding: £7,465 (Years 7 & 8), £6,770 (Year 6). Weekly and Flexi boarding are available. Tuition fees include the costs of stationery and textbooks. There are no compulsory extras except for examination fees. Lunches are included in day fees.

St Olave's was founded in 1876. With its own halls, music school, practical subjects workshops, sports hall and magnificently appointed specialist teaching rooms, St Olave's enjoys some of the best facilities for a prep school of its type.

The school puts praise, encouragement and pastoral care of the individual as its highest priority. There is a demanding wide curriculum from the earliest age with specialist subject areas – modern foreign languages, information technology, science and music, amongst others – being taught by specialist teachers from Year 4. Progress is monitored through a regular system of effort grades, and attainment is measured through internal and externally moderated tests.

Boarding is a flourishing aspect of the school, with a co-educational House under the constant care of resident House parents and their own family. Weekly and flexi boarding are also available. There are also five Day Houses.

Music plays an important part in the life of the school with 22 music teachers, two orchestras, a wind band and 14 ensembles playing and practising weekly. Over 200 pupils learn individual instruments, and all are encouraged to join larger groups. Sport has an equally high profile where rugby football, hockey, cricket, netball, tennis and swimming are major sports. Athletics, cross-country running, squash, badminton, basketball and volleyball are also available for all. The boys have won the National Schools' Seven-a-Side rugby tournament four times in the last eleven years and won the National Cricket JET cup. The school has 23 tennis courts, a synthetic pitch and a 25m 6-lane swimming pool.

Drama has an increasing profile, and out-of-school activities flourish through such clubs as science society, chess, photography, art and trampoline.

The vast majority of boys and girls move on to St Peter's and are not required to take the Common Entrance examination.

Entrance assessments are held in January/February each year, and assessments can also be arranged at other times. Entry is possible in most year groups, although the school is heavily oversubscribed at most stages. Means-tested bursaries are available from age 11.

Charitable status. St Peter's School, York, is a Registered Charity, number 1141329. It exists to provide education for boys and girls.

St Paul's Cathedral School

2 New Change, London EC4M 9AD
Tel: 020 7248 5156
Fax: 020 7329 6568
email: office@spcs.london.sch.uk
website: www.spcslondon.com

Chairman of Governors: The Very Revd Dr David Ison, Dean of St Paul's Cathedral

Headmaster: **Mr Neil R Chippington**, MA, MEd, FRCO

Age Range. 4–13 Co-educational.
Number of Pupils. Boarding Choristers 34, Day Boys 118, Day Girls 100, Pre-Prep 62.
Fees per term (2014–2015). Choristers £2,595; Day pupils £4,167–£4,487.

There have been choristers at St Paul's for over nine centuries. The present school is a Church of England Foundation dating back over 100 years and is governed by the Dean and Chapter of St Paul's Cathedral and 7 Lay Governors. The broadening of educational expectations and the challenge of curricular developments led the Dean and Chapter to agree to expand the school in 1989 by admitting non-chorister day-boys for the first time; a decision which continues to enrich the life of the school and Cathedral. In September 1998, the school admitted girls as well as boys into its new pre-prep department for 4–7 year olds. The school became fully co-educational in September 2002. It offers a broad curriculum leading to scholarship and Common Entrance examinations. In the first three years the work is tailored to individual needs bearing in mind the wide variety of educational backgrounds from which pupils come. The school has an excellent record in placing pupils in the senior schools of their choice, many with music scholarships. Every opportunity is taken to make use of the school's proximity to museums, libraries, galleries, theatres and the numerous attractions which London has to offer.

The 33 chorister boarders are housed on the School site and are fully integrated with the day pupils for all their academic studies and games. The choristers' cathedral choral training offers them a unique opportunity to participate in the rich musical life of St Paul's and the City.

The school was rehoused in the 60s in purpose-built premises on the eastern end of the Cathedral site. Refurbishment projects have added a new music school, art room, IT room, three pre-prep classrooms and games rooms to the existing facilities which include a hall/gymnasium, science laboratory, common room and a TV/video room. All pupils are encouraged to play a musical instrument (most pupils play two) and there are music and theory lessons with school orchestras and chamber groups.

A wide variety of games is offered including field sports at local playing fields and weekly swimming lessons. The children have their own playground and the use of the hall for indoor games and gymnastics.

Admissions procedure. Prospective pupils of 7+ years in September are given academic tests in verbal and non-verbal reasoning, usually in January of the previous academic year.

Pre-Prep children (4+) are assessed in an informal play situation in the November prior to entry.

Voice trials and tests for chorister places are held throughout the year for boys between 6½ and 8½ years old.

St Peter and St Paul School

Brambling House, Hady Hill, Chesterfield, Derbyshire S41 0EF
Tel: 01246 278522
email: head@spsp.org.uk
website: www.spsp.org.uk

Chairman of Board of Trustees: Mrs Dawn Graham

Headmaster: **Mr Andrew Lamb**, Cert Ed

Age Range. 4–11 years.
Number of Pupils. 130.
Fees per term (2014–2015). £2,655–£2,808.

Laughter, self-esteem, family, being cherished, awe and wonder, security, opportunity, preparation, independence and success are all part of the St Peter and St Paul School experience.

The school is set in 12 acres of park and woodland in walking distance of the town centre. The school has undergone enormous changes since 2002 under the current Headmaster, including joining the ranks of IAPS in 2006. As well as the school itself which caters for children from 4 to 11, there is a flourishing Nursery run by Children 1st in partnership with the school. This enables provision to be made for care and education throughout the year from birth to 11. There are no formal entry requirements and a number of bursaries are available.

Through five simple aims that involve us being dedicated to providing the best education, the best standard of care, the best opportunities, the best possible preparation for life for children while at the same time providing exceptional value for parents we are able to achieve our mission of providing a challenging and supportive environment where every child is valued as an individual and can reach their full potential.

Combining traditional teaching methods, family values, care from 7.30 am to 6.00 pm in a safe, secure and happy environment ensures that all our children meet with success. Our modern facilities designed to provide the greatest opportunities for children help us to achieve our aims.

The school's academic standard is exceptionally high and pupils are prepared for entry to a range of both independent and state schools. Recently pupils have gained a variety of awards to independent schools.

The school has a dedicated staff team who provide the children with stimulating and enjoyable learning experiences. Whether in the classroom, on the games field, in the concert hall or on the school stage, staff give all children the opportunity to shine. Our unique Life Skills programme has been designed to develop skills in teamwork and leadership as well as to enable children to make healthy life style choices. We live in an ever-changing world and the programme also involves managing and coping with change. Within the programme children experience such activities as Indoor Climbing, Orienteering, First Aid, Aerobic Dance, Archery and much more.

While achieving our aims, our pupils develop honesty, good manners, confidence, independence, motivation, the ability to succeed as well as the value of helping others.

Never being satisfied and always expecting a lot from both children and staff ensures that the school continues to thrive and develop in this modern world.

Charitable status. The St Peter and St Paul School Trust is a Registered Charity, number 516113.

St Piran's

Gringer Hill, Maidenhead, Berkshire SL6 7LZ
Tel: 01628 594302
Fax: 01628 594301
email: registrar@stpirans.co.uk
website: www.stpirans.co.uk

Chairman of Governors: Mr Edward Parrott

Headmaster: **J Carroll**, BA Hons, BPhilEd, PGCE, NPQH

Age Range. 3–11 Co-educational.
Number of Pupils. 350 day pupils.
Fees per term (2014–2015). £3,200–£4,550. Nursery – 5 full days: £282.35 per week

St Piran's is a thriving co-educational IAPS day school set amid 10 delightful acres just to the north of Maidenhead town centre. In 2005 we celebrated our bicentenary, having been founded as a small school in Blackheath, London in 1805.

Class sizes are small. Boys and girls benefit from individual attention in all subjects. They are provided with a wide range of exciting opportunities both inside and outside the classroom. Numerous trips to castles and museums, theatres and shows, history re-enactments, geographical fieldwork and religious sites extend the children's understanding of the world around them. In addition to the academic subjects, pupils take part in a wide range of other activities each week. These include music and art as well as pursuits as diverse as riding, website design, technology, cycling and even fishing.

Academically, the school supports a broad curriculum at all levels in the school. French starts with our youngest classes where confidence in the spoken language is encouraged. By Year 6 we are introducing Latin and Spanish. The children enjoy specialist teaching in art, games and PE, ICT, swimming and music from an early age. By the age of 10, all lessons are taught by extremely well qualified subject specialists. We support children with their entrance exams at 11+ to Grammar Schools or other Senior independent schools. Our results over the years have been excellent, supporting our desire to encourage independent thinkers, confident individuals and strong leaders of the future.

The main sports that pupils take part in are rugby, soccer, netball, hockey, cricket, rounders and swimming. The school has its own indoor swimming pool and large sports hall. St Piran's also has a dance studio and pupils are encouraged to take an active part in the performing arts. We are blessed with wonderful facilities which serve to enhance the varied sports programmes that we offer the children at all levels.

The school has its own Leadership programme and regular visits off site are arranged for all the children, including residential trips.

Pupils may enter the school at any age, although the main intakes occur at Nursery, Reception and Year 3. Scholarships and bursaries may be offered after assessment. Please contact the school and an appointment can be arranged to talk to the Headmaster about financial support.

The school is proud of its outstanding record of achievement and the fully rounded education that it provides within a friendly caring atmosphere. We are proud of our Christian tradition and family ethos which foster high expectations and successful, happy children.

Children and parents are warmly invited to visit St Piran's to see for themselves the excellent facilities that we offer and to meet some of the staff and pupils.

Charitable status. St Piran's School Limited is a Registered Charity, number 309094.

St Pius X Prep School

200 Garstang Road, Fulwood, Preston, Lancashire PR2 8RD
Tel: 01772 719937
Fax: 01772 787535
email: enquiries@st-piusx.lancs.sch.uk
website: www.stpiusx.co.uk

Chairman of Governors: P Clegg

Headmistress: **Miss B Banks**, MA

Age Range. 2–11.
Number of Children. 255 Day Girls and Boys.
Fees per term (2014–2015). Main School £2,441.25, Nursery £235 per week.

The School is administered as a non-profit-making educational trust by a Board of Governors, providing education from 2–11. The children are prepared for entrance examination to independent schools and local high schools. The school has an excellent record of scholarships to senior schools and SATS results at KS1 and KS2. The school has a large Nursery division which covers the EYFS in recently-refurbished Nursery rooms. The school is in four acres of its own grounds in a pleasant suburb of Preston. All preparatory curriculum subjects covered.

Sports taught are Association Football, Cricket, Tennis, Hockey, Netball, Rugby, Table Tennis, Rounders, Athletics and Cross-Country.

Ballet, piano, clarinet, flute, violin, guitar and singing lessons are some of the optional extras offered. The school has a thriving music centre.

Charitable status. St Pius X School is a Registered Charity, number 526609. Its purpose is to equip the children with an outstanding academic and social education in a Catholic Christian environment, which will enable them to achieve their full potential – the school welcomes pupils of all faiths.

St Richard's

Bredenbury Court, Bromyard, Herefordshire HR7 4TD
Tel: 01885 482491
email: schooloffice@st-richards.org.uk
website: www.st-richards.org.uk

Headmaster: **Mr Fred de Falbe**, BA Hons, PGCE

Age Range. 3–13 Co-educational.
Number of Pupils. 114.
Fees per term (2014–2015). Prep: £6,525 Boarders, £6,050 Weekly Boarders, £4,390 Day. Pre-Prep: £1,650–£2,045. No compulsory extras.

St Richard's is a Catholic Preparatory School which welcomes all denominations and takes full advantage of its superb rural position and 35 acres of parkland. St Richard's aims to encourage all pupils to discover their talents and to develop them to the full. Each child is known individually by staff and fellow pupils alike in what is a very nurturing family atmosphere.

Children are prepared for entrance and scholarship examinations to a wide range of senior schools, yielding an excellent record of results. 100% of pupils win places at their first-choice schools and in 2014 60% of leavers won a scholarship or award. Entry to the prep school is normally between the ages of 7 and 8, but there is a Nursery and Pre-Prep Department which welcomes children from rising 3, with nursery vouchers accepted.

The school's facilities and small classes (average 15) allow for devoted individual care, where every child can take part in every activity. Art, pottery, music, CDT and drama flourish. There are nine separate music groups, including string quartets, woodwind and brass groups and an orchestra. The Chapel Choir sings plainsong at weekly Mass, as well as a Chamber Choir and Carol Choir which features staff alongside children.

Local arts and music events and competitions are regularly supported and entered. Cross country is particularly strong (the school hosting numerous events and winning many more) but in all co-curricular activities the school consistently punches above its weight.

The usual team games are played (rugby and hockey, cricket and rounders, football and netball), with cross-country running, athletics and riding featuring strongly on the timetable and many children playing for county teams. Evening activities enable children to sample and develop a wide range of skill-based tasks, including cookery, gardening, film-making, chess, table tennis, model-building, photography, card-making, golfing, hand puppet production, treasure-hunting, felt-making, canoeing and orienteering.

There are three levels of boarding: flexi, weekly and full boarding. 'Big fun' weekends are arranged each term with organised Saturday and Sunday programmes; highlights are dry ski slopes and theme parks. There are also dedicated weekends arranged for the younger children to help with confidence and enjoyment of boarding.

The school is experienced in looking after the needs of those from abroad. There is a long allegiance to generations of families from Spain, Austria and France. Children are escorted to and from London Heathrow, Birmingham, Bristol, etc.

Birthdays are celebrated with special 'Birthday teas' arranged by the Matrons.

An illustrated prospectus including details of recent scholarships, staff and other particulars and the school magazine are available from the school office (schooloffice@strichards.org.uk).

Charitable status. St Richard's School Bredenbury Court is a Registered Charity, number 1113203.

Saint Ronan's

Water Lane, Hawkhurst, Kent TN18 5DJ
Tel: 01580 752271
Fax: 01580 754882
email: info@saintronans.co.uk
website: www.saintronans.co.uk

Chairman of Governors: Mr Colin Willis

Headmaster: W E H Trelawny-Vernon, BSc Hons

Deputy Head (Pastoral): R Andrew
Deputy Head (Academic): G Vincendeau

Age Range. 3–13 fully co-educational.
Number of Children. 320.
Fees per term (2014–2015). Day £3,108–£5,328. We also operate a flexi boarding system (£34 per night) which can be tailored to individual needs.

Saint Ronan's is a family school as it has been since it was started in Worthing in 1883. It occupies a fine Victorian Mansion set in 249 acres of beautiful Weald of Kent countryside. There are numerous games pitches, hard tennis courts, a golf course and a swimming pool as well as a hundred-acre wood.

By deliberately remaining small the school has developed a unique and special atmosphere in which staff and children work together to achieve their aims. Our small size helps the transition from home to school and small class sizes enable children to gain confidence and interact positively with their peers and the staff.

Academically we have an excellent pass rate at CE and many pupils gain Scholarships to major senior independent schools such as Eton, Sevenoaks, Benenden, Tonbridge, Harrow, King's Canterbury and Eastbourne College; we also prepare children for entry to local Grammar Schools and boast an enviable record here too.

Music and art play a vital role at Saint Ronan's. We have two choirs: the Chamber choir and the Chapel choir, and over three-quarters of the children learn at least one musical instrument. We have an excellent orchestra and ensembles for most instruments. Music is thriving and scholarships to King's Canterbury, The Purcell School and Eastbourne College are amongst recent notable achievements. The Art department is flourishing and the children have the option to learn pottery and woodwork in addition to their timetabled Art lessons. In 2012–3, we obtained five Art Scholarships to Senior schools.

The major sports at Saint Ronan's are rugby, football, hockey, cricket and netball but we also offer coaching in athletics, tennis, swimming, dance, rounders, judo, golf, archery, fencing, lacrosse, sailing and cross-country. Sports scholarships are also regularly achieved.

The Nursery and Pre-Prep are very much part of the school, in both location and ethos, and are thriving and dynamic departments taking children from age 3 to 7.

In 2006 we opened a new Nursery, Pre-Prep, Music school and IT suite, in 2010 a new Sports Hall and in 2012 a new DT suite and School Farm. Our swimming pool has been renovated and there are many new and exciting projects afoot, including building an astroturf.

Charitable status. Saint Ronan's School is a Registered Charity, number 1066420. It exists for the advancement of education of its children.

St Swithun's Junior School

Alresford Road, Winchester, Hampshire SO21 1HA
Tel: 01962 835750
Fax: 01962 835781
email: office.juniorschool@stswithuns.com
website: www.stswithuns.com
Twitter: @stswithunsjs
Facebook: /StSwithunsJuniorSchool

Established 1884. Girls day preparatory school with pre-preparatory boys. Church of England.

Work is currently in progress to create a new St Swithun's Junior School. The new school will replace the existing school buildings and will enable the Junior School to increase its pupil numbers to 256 in response to an increased demand for places whilst also allowing smaller class sizes. The development will include specialist teaching rooms, a science laboratory, an art studio, a media/computing room and a new performing arts space and gym. The new school main building will be open in September 2015.

School Council:
Chairman: Professor Natalie Lee, LLB

Headmistress: Mrs P Grimes, BA Hons Sussex, PGCE King Alfred's College

Age Range. Girls 3–11, Boys 3–7.
Number of Pupils. 183 Girls, 3 Boys. Average class size 25. Pupil : teacher ratio 12:1.
Fees per term (2014–2015). Nursery: £1,560 (mornings inc lunch), £3,120 (all day); Reception, Years 1 & 2 £3,120; Years 3–6 £4,020.

Profile. At St Swithun's we believe a child's education should be about discovery, a sense of adventure and a spirit of excitement and fun; that good academic success and a great deal more is achieved as a result of this ethos.

We are a non-selective independent day school and, as such, our academic success is achieved through good teaching in small groups, excellent resources and facilities, supportive parents and motivated children who enjoy coming to school.

It is the children that we are most proud of and we spend a lot of time building their self-esteem. All children have different talents and skills and the teaching staff are committed to finding and developing these. Success in one area leads to a boost in confidence elsewhere and this helps our pupils feel secure enough to explore and take risks.

When searching for a school, we believe parents look for a number of qualities – confident and engaging pupils; staff who are dedicated to ensuring that the pupils are successful and happy; an understanding that every child is different; exceptional facilities. You will find these at St Swithun's.

Entry. At 3.

Curriculum. Usual subjects taught plus French (from Nursery), art, technology, drama, ICT, music and PE, with due regard for National Curriculum requirements.

Leavers. Boys leave for various preparatory schools, including The Pilgrims' and Twyford. Girls go on to a range of senior independent schools, with the majority going to St Swithun's Senior School.

Consultation. Biannual reports, regular parents' evenings and PTA.

Sports. Gymnastics, netball, rounders, tennis, short tennis, swimming, and athletics.

Activities. These include tennis, art, drama, gymnastics, judo, science, cookery, swimming, football and dance.

Musical concerts and productions are regularly held. Three annual residential trips in Years 4–6, and regular visits from Nursery to Year 6 take place.

Special needs. Qualified Learning Support teacher.

Charitable status. St Swithun's School Winchester is a Registered Charity, number 307335.

Salisbury Cathedral School

1 The Close, Salisbury, Wilts SP1 2EQ
Tel: 01722 555300
Fax: 01722 410910
email: headsec@salisburycathedralschool.com
website: www.salisburycathedralschool.com

Founded in 1091. Co-educational Preparatory, Pre-Preparatory and Choir School.

Chairman of Governors: The Dean of Salisbury

Head Master: **C Marriott**

Age Range. 3–13.

Number of Pupils. Preparatory: 133 boys and girls (35 boarders); Pre-Prep Department 55 boys and girls.

Fees per term (2014–2015). Pre-Prep: £3.71 per hour (Nursery), £2,460 (Reception, Years 1 & 2), £3,890 (Year 3). Preparatory School: £4,670 (day), £6,865 (boarding).

The school was founded in 1091 and is situated in the former Bishop's Palace on a 25-acre site in the beautiful Cathedral Close. There is a self-contained Pre-Prep Department for boys and girls between the ages of three and seven.

High academic standards, excellent music and drama. An impressive array of scholarships are gained to senior schools. Although the main thrust of the academic work leads towards examinations at 13+, some children sit the 11+ tests for the local Grammar Schools. The school also has a fully qualified Individual Needs team.

Facilities include: refurbished science laboratory, IT centre, music technology room, gymnasium, large all-weather pitch, extensive playing fields, heated outdoor swimming pool.

Talented sports staff coach all the major team sports and there are regular fixtures.

There are many after-school clubs open to all children in the Preparatory School. (Quality before and after school care is available for children in the Pre-Prep). The boarding house staff operate an "open door" policy to parents, organise many outings and activities and have achieved an enviable reputation for running a truly happy and caring boarding house.

For a prospectus and/or to arrange a visit to the school, please telephone or visit our website.

Charitable status. Salisbury Cathedral School is a Registered Charity, number 309485. It exists to provide high quality education for children.

Sandroyd School

Rushmore, Tollard Royal, Salisbury, Wiltshire SP5 5QD
Tel: 01725 516264
Fax: 01725 516441
email: office@sandroyd.com
website: www.sandroyd.org

Chairman of Governors: R G L Thomas, MRICS, FAAV

Headmaster: **M J S Harris**, BSc, PGCE

Age Range. 3–13 co-educational.

Number of Pupils. 110 boarders, 60 day, plus 34 in Pre-Prep, The Walled Garden.

Fees per term (2014–2015). Boarding £7,638, Day £6,304. Year 3: Boarding £6,049, Day £4,684. Pre-Prep £2,688, Nursery: £28 (per morning), £48 (all day).

Sandroyd is a co-educational boarding and day school set in 900 acres of beautiful parkland in the heart of the Cranborne Chase on the Wiltshire/Dorset border.

The facilities which the school has to offer are second to none. They include an indoor swimming pool, all-weather hockey/tennis surfaces, cross-country riding course, squash court, extensive games fields and access to a golf course and driving range. A new Sports Hall has just been completed, with specialist gymnastic equipment, badminton courts and 4 indoor cricket nets, providing space for dance, football, indoor hockey, netball, martial arts, shooting and squash, as well as access to the indoor swimming pool.

Pets such as ponies, ferrets, hens, ducks, rabbits and hamsters are welcome. The school owns a number of mild-mannered ponies, but there are liveries available too.

On the academic side, high standards are expected and achieved. The children are prepared for Common Entrance and Scholarships to all the leading independent senior schools and, together with a number of Academic Scholarships, awards have been won in recent years for Art, Music, Sport and all-round ability. A specialist Learning Support department is in place to assist those who need extra help with their studies. The school is well known for the excellence of its music, both choral and instrumental and a new theatre caters for the many productions which the pupils put on throughout the year across all age ranges.

Pastoral care is five star. Puppet shows in the Junior dorms are a regular occurrence. Academic staff help upstairs in the evenings and the Headmaster's wife is very popular when it comes to reading bedtime stories.

Excellent opportunity: in conjunction with Bryanston, Sandroyd offers an annual full-fee bursary for academic years 7 to 13. Other bursaries are available on request.

Visitors are always welcome to meet the Headmaster and to look round the school and its exceptional grounds.

Charitable status. Sandroyd School Trust Limited is a Registered Charity, number 309490. It exists for the purpose of providing education.

Sarum Hall School

15 Eton Avenue, London NW3 3EL
Tel: 020 7794 2261
Fax: 020 7431 7501
email: admissions@sarumhallschool.co.uk
website: www.sarumhallschool.co.uk

The School, which has a Christian (Church of England) foundation, is an educational trust with a Board of Governors.

Chairman of Governors: Mr B Gorst

Headmistress: **Mrs Christine Smith**, BA Open, CertEd, RSA SpLD

Age Range. 3–11.
Number of Pupils. 175 Day Girls.
Fees per term (2014–2015). £4,015–£4,350.

Founded in 1929, the school has, since 1995, been housed in new purpose-built premises which provide excellent, spacious facilities, including a large playground, gym, dining room and specialist art, IT, music and science rooms, in addition to a French room, changing room, multi-purpose room and three individual music teaching rooms.

Girls are prepared for senior London day schools and for 11+ Common Entrance. Girls entering at age 3 are not assessed, but those joining from Year 1 are tested in English and maths. The school is ambitious for its girls and believes that in a caring, supportive and imaginative environment, every girl can achieve her potential. They are encouraged to develop a love and interest of learning for itself and awareness that their success in all fields is dependent on their own efforts. Consequently the school has a well-established record of scholarship and examination success. Destination schools include Channing, Cheltenham Ladies' College, City of London School for Girls, Downe House, Francis Holland, Highgate, King's Canterbury, Mill Hill Foundation, North London Collegiate, Oundle School, Queen's College, Queenswood, South Hampstead High School, St Helen's, St Paul's Girls and Wycombe Abbey.

A broad curriculum is followed and a major investment in IT ensures that each girl has access to the latest technology. French is taught from Reception and Mandarin from Year 4, and a comprehensive games programme, which takes place on site, ensures that girls have the opportunity to experience a variety of sports. Strong emphasis is placed on music, art, design and drama. Woodwind, violin, piano, cello and singing are offered. There are also two choirs, an orchestra and ensemble groups. Other extra-curricular activities include theory of music, fencing, junior and senior football, gardening, netball, tennis, ICT, yoga, philosophy, photography, drama, craft, chess, cooking, classical civilisations, board games and performance.

Charitable status. Sarum Hall School is a Registered Charity, number 312721. Its purpose is education.

Seaford College Prep School
Wilberforce House

Lavington Park, Petworth, West Sussex GU28 0ND
Tel: 01798 867893
Fax: 01798 867802

email: wilberforce@seaford.org
           jmackay@seaford.org
website: www.seafordprep.org

Seaford College Prep School (Wilberforce House) is an integral part of Seaford College with its own buildings, playground and corporate organisation. Wilberforce House is named after Samuel Wilberforce, the son of the anti-slavery campaigner William Wilberforce. Samuel is buried in the grounds of the School's chapel. The School is set in a magnificent 400-acre site adjacent to the South Downs National Park.

Chairman of Governors: R Venables Kyrke

Head of Prep School: **S Rees**, BA Hons, PGCE, NPQH

Age Range. 6–13 Co-educational.
Number of Pupils. 180.
Fees per term (2014–2015). Day: £2,950–£4,950. Weekly Boarding: £6,130 (Year 6), £6,550 (Years 7 & 8).

This is the Prep School for Seaford College and has the same board of governors. There is very close cooperation between the two schools and there are many shared facilities such as the games fields, the Music School, Science Department, and Art & Design Department.

The Prep School educates boys and girls from the age of 6 and the vast majority of children continue their education at Seaford College until 16 or 18. The main entry points for the Prep School are at 7+ and 11+ although children are welcome to join the school at any age.

The school aims to nurture a love of learning through a broadly based curriculum and classroom activities are often complemented by day and residential visits. In Years 2, 3, 4 and 5, the majority of lessons are taught by form teachers with subjects such as Music, French, PE/Games and Design and Technology taught by specialist staff. From Year 6 upwards all subjects are taught by specialist staff, many of whom also teach in the Senior School. All classrooms are equipped with interactive whiteboards while a Special Educational Needs Coordinator oversees the school's learning support provision which further enhances learning and achievement. The majority of children complete most of their homework in school and the school day finishes at 5.20 pm.

Boarding provision, from Year 6 upwards, is an important aspect of life in the school with the aim being to be as flexible as possible in order to meet parents' and pupils' needs as well as providing a warm and caring home-from-home atmosphere.

Pupils are able to benefit from the impressive range of games facilities on site, including an astroturf hockey pitch, swimming pool and a 9-hole golf course, with practice greens and driving range as well as the services of a golf professional. Expert coaching is provided in the main sports of football, rugby, hockey, cricket, netball, rounders, tennis, athletics and swimming. The school also has excellent facilities for music, art and design and technology.

The standard of pastoral care is high and the school has its own Chaplain who takes a weekly assembly in the school chapel. The Prep School aims to treat each pupil as an individual and to establish the firm foundations necessary for success in the Senior School and beyond. (*See Seaford College entry in HMC section.*)

Charitable status. Seaford College is a Registered Charity, number 277439.

Seaton House School

67 Banstead Road South, Sutton, Surrey SM2 5LH
Tel: 020 8642 2332
Fax: 020 8642 2332
email: office@seatonhouse.sutton.sch.uk
website: www.seatonhouse.sutton.sch.uk

Chair of Governors: Mrs J Evans

Headmistress: **Mrs D Morrison**, RSA HDipEd

Age Range. Girls 3–11, Boys 3–4 (Nursery only).
Number of Pupils. Main School 130; Nursery 35.
Fees per term (2014–2015). £684–£2,871.

Seaton House School was founded in 1930 by Miss Violet Henry and there is a strong tradition of family loyalty to the school. The School aims to provide children with a thorough educational grounding to give them a good start in their school lives and to instil sound learning habits in a secure, disciplined but friendly atmosphere. The girls, from Year 4, are prepared for various entrance examinations at 11+, both in the London Borough of Sutton and those required by independent day schools with a high percentage of our girls securing grammar school places at Nonsuch High School and Wallington Girls Grammar School. Our highly qualified and committed staff create a stimulating learning environment and small classes ensure that all children have the necessary individual attention and encouragement to achieve the highest standards.

We follow the broad outlines of the National Curriculum with generous provision for Music, French and Physical Education. There is a School Orchestra and Choir and, each year, all children have the opportunity to take part in dramatic productions. School sports teams enjoy considerable success when they compete regularly against neighbouring schools and each Spring we host our own Netball Tournament. Years 5 and 6 have the opportunity to experience outdoor pursuits during their annual week's residential course. The School has excellent Library and ICT resources, while the range of extra-curricular activities offered is extremely varied, complementing the established provision of after-school care.

Pastoral care is of the highest calibre with form staff taking a keen interest in all their pupils. Courtesy, good manners and kindness are expected as the norm and children are encouraged to develop initiative, independence and confidence. There is a strong house system in the main school which stimulates good community awareness.

The prospectus is available upon request and the Headmistress is always happy to meet parents and arrange for them to look around the School.

Charitable status. Seaton House School is a Registered Charity, number 800673. It exists to provide education for children.

Sevenoaks Preparatory School

Godden Green, Sevenoaks, Kent TN15 0JU
Tel: 01732 762336
Fax: 01732 764279
email: admin@theprep.org.uk
website: www.theprep.org.uk

Chairman of Governors: Jan Berry

Headmaster: **Luke Harrison**, BA Hons, PGCE

Head of Junior School: Nik Pears, BEd Hons

Age Range. 2½ to 13.

Number of Children. 200 Boys, 180 Girls.
Fees per term (2014–2015). Nursery & Kindergarten £305 per session, Reception £2,933, Years 1–2 £3,380 Years 3–8 £4,130.

Founded in 1919, Sevenoaks Prep School stands on a spacious 25-acre site of playing fields and woodland bordering the 1,000-acre Knole Estate. We welcome girls and boys from 2½ to 13 years of age. Our small class sizes and family atmosphere enables us to build special relationships with the children and their parents.

The curriculum is tailored to the needs of the pupils and their future aspirations. Whilst due regard is paid to the National Curriculum, our children are taught to the highest standard achievable by the individual. To this end, our teachers enhance their Programmes of Study to ensure that every pupil is motivated, challenged and prepared for 11+ or 13+ entry tests to local grammar schools or via Common Entrance examinations and scholarships to independent schools. Our academic achievements are consistently high and our pupils compete successfully for academic, music and other scholarships.

Throughout the school all classes regularly participate in a programme of visits, workshops and field trips to support their learning. Education at Sevenoaks Prep is for life not just the classroom – it is the balance of academic study and co-curricular activities that prepare the children for their future.

The school comprises the Junior School (Nursery–Year 2), and the Senior School (Years 3–8).

Nursery and Kindergarten are staffed by teachers who are specially qualified in Early Years education, with a high teacher to pupil ratio. The education provided is specifically designed to match each child's needs, so that child-initiated play and teacher-directed activities are thoughtfully planned and carefully balanced.

Full-time education starts in the Reception class and from this point, through Years 1 and 2, class teachers and their assistants provide a rich and stimulating environment where curiosity and enthusiasm to learn are fostered.

On entering the Senior School in Year 3, class teaching is continued for core subjects (with specialist teaching for drama, languages, music, ICT, PE and games). By the age of ten, our pupils are taught by specialist teachers in all subjects whilst each class continues to have a form teacher who monitors their progress. Years 7 and 8 are the secondary school years and this is reflected in the teaching and levels of responsibility offered to the children. At Sevenoaks Prep they are at the top of the school and are provided with leadership opportunities and responsibilities. Heads of our destination schools say that children from the Prep enter Year 9 as rounded individuals, confident both academically and socially.

Facilities include a large multi-purpose sports hall, a state-of-the-art drama and music suite as well as a modern restaurant and kitchen. Our location provides a useful and natural extension to our teaching facilities and provide a vast playground, where children are trusted and encouraged to explore safely.

The school provides after-school care until 6.00 pm each evening and the extra-curricular activities are extensive. The school is supported by an active Social Events Committee who regularly arrange social events for parents to meet each other and to raise money for the school.

Sherborne Preparatory School

Acreman Street, Sherborne, Dorset DT9 3NY
Tel: 01935 812097
email: registrar@sherborneprep.org
website: www.sherborneprep.org

Chair of Governors: Mr P Jones

Headmaster: **P S Tait**, MA, FRSA

Age Range. 3–13.
Number of Boys and Girls. 240 (Pre-Prep 58, Prep 182).
Fees per term (2014–2015). Boarders: £7,070–£7,400.
Day: Nursery £1,340–£2,795; Pre-Prep £2,795; Prep:
£4,225 (Year 3), £5,165 (Years 4–8). Generous discounts
available for Forces families and a range of scholarships
available from Year 3 upwards (scholarship assessment in
February each year). Bursaries available on a means-tested
basis.

Sherborne Prep School aims to foster independent learning through the teaching of a broader enquiry-based curriculum with an emphasis on study and thinking skills, designed
to meet the individual learning styles of the pupils.

The school is an independent co-educational day and
boarding school for children aged 3–13 years. Founded in
1885, the School is set in twelve acres of attractive grounds
and gardens in the centre of Sherborne and is well served by
road and rail links. Although fully independent, it enjoys a
long and close association with its neighbours, Sherborne
School and Sherborne Girls.

The Prep School (Years 3–8) offers a broad education,
leading to Common Entrance and Scholarship examinations
in the penultimate and final year groups. There is a strong
emphasis on languages (the school offers French, Latin,
German, Spanish, Italian and Mandarin at various levels),
art and design technology, and on independent thinking. In
recent years the Prep has led the way in curriculum development in Geography and History, and this has been extremely
well received by senior schools.

Despite being non-selective ourselves, over the last five
years an impressive 38% of leavers have won scholarships
or awards to leading independent schools, including Sherborne School, Sherborne Girls, Cheltenham College, Bryanston, Sedbergh School, Radley, Taunton School, Wells
Cathedral School, Abingdon School, Monmouth School, St
Swithun's School, St Mary's Shaftesbury, Milton Abbey,
Canford School, Blundell's, King's College Taunton and
Leweston School.

The Prep also offers a distinctive Saturday morning programme of various sporting, artistic, musical and cultural
activities, including introductory language classes and informative lectures, to which the parents are warmly invited.

The Pre-Prep Department is housed in a fully-equipped
and purpose-built classroom building, with experienced and
well-qualified staff, providing an excellent ratio of teachers
to children. The children enjoy weekly swimming lessons
and a varied programme of after-school activities, including
fun fitness, dance, music, and circus skills, and there is a
thriving weekly toddler group ("Little Preppers") for children between 0 and 3.

The School's ISI report in November 2006 was outstanding and praised the School for its success in many areas,
notably in developing independent learning and positive
attitudes to work and study. The Ofsted Inspection Report
for Boarding in 2010 was also outstanding.

Charitable status. Sherborne Preparatory School is a
Registered Charity, number 1071494. It exists to provide an
all-round education for children.

Shrewsbury High Prep School
GDST

Old Roman Road, Shrewsbury, Shropshire SY3 9AH
Tel: 01743 494200
Fax: 01743 494213
email: enquiries@shr.gdst.net
website: www.shrewsburyhigh.gdst.net
Twitter: @ShrewsburyHigh
Facebook: Shrewsbury High School

Shrewsbury High School has an unrivalled record of
academic achievement. The Prep School is just a few
minutes' walk away from the Senior School and accepts
girls from age 3 to 11 and boys from 3 to 13.

Acting Head: **Miss C James**, BA Hons University of
   Central England

Age Range. Girls 3–11, Boys 3–13.
Number of Pupils. 200.
Fees per term (2014–2015). Years 7–8: £4,089; Years
4–6: £3,330; Year 3: £3,057; Kindergarten (Phase 2, ages
4–5) to Year 2: £2,845; Kindergarten (Phase 1 from age 3):
£2,227 (full-time).

The fees cover tuition across the regular curriculum,
school books, games and swimming, stationery, choral
music and other materials. They also cover non-residential
curriculum trips and activities. They do not cover lunches,
optional extra subjects or the cost of travel to school. Lunch
costs are £176 per term. Lunches are compulsory for all prep
pupils.

Shrewsbury High Prep School is located close to the A5
ring road, the town centre and Shrewsbury High School's
Senior School. Occupying a delightful 14-acre site the
school has extensive playing fields and a large natural
woodland.

Outstanding facilities include its own Science laboratory,
Design Technology workshop, Music School and purpose-
built outdoor areas.

Small class sizes ensure as much individual attention as
possible. The four to eight year-old pupils have a class
teacher responsible for teaching and pastoral care. Subject
specialists are introduced from the age of eight years. The
school curriculum is continually upgraded and developed to
meet the modern needs of education whilst still employing
tried and tested traditional learning methods. At 11+ girls
are expected to move up to the renowned Shrewsbury High
School Senior School. The boys move on to senior independent schools at 13+, mostly by way of Common Entrance or
Scholarship examinations. Every year several boys gain
scholarships to leading schools.

We supplement the academic subjects with a timetable of
Design and Technology, Art, Music, Drama and Information
Technology. The vast majority of pupils study a musical
instrument. We have a School choir and our boys supply the
treble voices for the Shrewsbury School Choir. Athletics,
Swimming and Cross-Country feature for all pupils, with
Soccer, Rugby and Cricket for the boys and Netball, Round-
ers and Hockey for the girls. Additional activities include
Chess, Outward Bound, Canoeing, Mountain-biking and
Tennis. These take place at lunchtimes and after school,
within an extended school day.

Annual trips abroad include a French Adventure trip,
French City visit and a Ski Trip. Extra-curricular visits and
invited speakers/performers are a normal part of the school
life. Pupils take English Speaking Board examinations, and
regularly take part in Festivals of Poetry and Verse Speaking
with great success. There is an annual musical and dramatic
production.

Charitable status. Shrewsbury High School is part of The Girls' Day School Trust, which is a Registered Charity, number 306983.

Shrewsbury House

107 Ditton Road, Surbiton, Surrey KT6 6RL
Tel: 020 8399 3066
Fax: 020 8339 9529
email: office@shspost.co.uk
website: www.shrewsburyhouse.net

Chairman of the Governors: G Corbett

Headmaster: **K A Doble**, BA, PDM HR, PGCE

Deputy Head: S Ford, BEd Hons, DipIT

Age Range. 7–13.
Number of Boys. 320 Day Boys.
Fees per term (2014–2015). £5,275.
Shrewsbury House was founded in 1865. In 1979 it became an Educational Trust and is administered by a Board of Governors.

Boys are admitted from 7 years of age and are prepared for entry at 13+, either by Scholarship or Common Entrance, to any of the Independent Senior Schools. There are 43 full-time staff, as well as visiting music staff.

The School aims to provide both an academic and broad education; to give a comprehensive preparation for the various examinations required by independent Senior Schools; to develop sound work attitudes and habits; to promote spiritual, moral, social and cultural development and to foster individual development, including instilling self-esteem, confidence and wholeheartedness.

The School is particularly committed to offering every boy a truly broad education. Regardless of his ability – not only on the academic side but also on the non-academic – every boy is taught/coached by someone with expertise. The aims are to foster and discover talents, to aid boys to fulfil them, and, for those not so talented in a pursuit, to give them nevertheless a chance to develop an interest in and/or enjoyment for it. To this end, for instance: every boy is in a team with its own coach; every boy who wishes to be individually tutored in Music may be (currently over 80% learn at least one musical instrument); every boy is in at least one concert each year and every boy is in a play every year (there are 6 plays a year).

The School is fortunate in its extensive land, including an on-site newly completed 4G, Premiership Standard Astro-Turf facility. The original building is Victorian; its interior has been adapted, furnished and decorated for modern educational needs. There is a covered heated swimming pool, further playing fields nearby which include a further, flood-lit all-weather playing surface.

Facilities are constantly being updated and improved. In recent years, the following facilities were added: a new Music centre, a new Theatre, a new Dining hall, a new Library and Resources room, a new Pottery room, a new Technology room, 2 new Science Laboratories, a new Art room and 8 further new Classrooms. The School has invested considerably in computer equipment in every desk and we seek to remain at the forefront of ICT good practice.

The main sports are Association Football, Rugby Football, Cricket and Athletics. Hockey is a new addition to the match schedule. At the same time boys are encouraged to try a variety of the more individual sports such as Swimming, Tennis, Skiing, Golf, Shooting and Sailing. In addition, there is ample opportunity for boys to discover other abilities and talents through activities in Music, technical activities and Drama.

Shrewsbury House has pupils join from many pre-prep schools including Shrewsbury Lodge, its own pre-prep School (*see Shrewsbury Lodge entry*).

Charitable status. Shrewsbury House School Trust Limited is a Registered Charity, number 277324. It seeks to provide the best possible learning environment for boys aged between 7 and 13 who have the potential for above-average academic achievement.

Shrewsbury Lodge School

22 Milbourne Lane, Esher, Surrey KT10 9EA
Tel: 01372 462781
Fax: 01372 469914
email: admin@shrewsburylodge.com
website: www.shrewsburylodge.com

Chairman of Governors: Mr Gavin Corbett

Head: **Mrs G Hope**, BEd, CertEd

Age Range. 3–7 years.
Number of Children. 150 Co-educational.
Fees per term (2014–2015). £2,475–£3,945.
Shrewsbury Lodge is an independent day school for boys and girls aged from 3 to 7 years. It is the pre-prep school for Shrewsbury House, the prestigious preparatory school for boys in nearby Surbiton.

We aim to develop the whole child within an environment of academic excellence. High standards of success are achieved through individual attention, provided by highly qualified professionals in a nurturing and caring family atmosphere. We create a secure, purposeful and happy atmosphere where the children learn positive attitudes to work and play, and develop self-confidence and a respect for others.

We welcome children from different faiths and ethnic backgrounds. Together we respect our many differences. Our curriculum sets out to encourage the diverse talents of the children fostering intellectual, physical, cultural moral and spiritual development.

Shrewsbury Lodge has extensive facilities including modern purpose-built classrooms, a well-stocked library, a hall, a gym, a heated swimming pool, as well as specialist facilities for ICT, Art, Design and Technology, Forest School and Music. There is a soft surface playground with climbing frames and a variety of outdoor equipment. The school also owns a large sports field and pavilion.

When children leave us, they are equipped for the next stage of their education, having acquired sound work habits and a caring attitude. Our girls and boys are prepared for entry to a number of Prep schools, although the majority of the boys move on to Shrewsbury House. (*See separate entry.*)

Charitable status. Shrewsbury House School Trust is a Registered Charity, number 277324. It exists to provide education for children.

Solefield School

Solefields Road, Sevenoaks, Kent TN13 1PH
Tel: 01732 452142
email: admissions@solefieldschool.org
            office@solefieldschool.org
website: www.solefieldschool.org

Chairman of the Governors: Mr R Clewley

Headmaster: **D A Philps**, BSc

Age Range. 4–13.

Number of Boys. 180.

Fees per term (2014–2015). £3,330–£4,020 including lunch.

Solefield is a day Preparatory School for boys from 4 to 13, located in the heart of Sevenoaks. Through exceptional teaching, learning and care it prepares boys for entry to independent schools such as Sevenoaks and Tonbridge at 13, along with Grammar School entry at 11. The curriculum is comprehensive and, along with core subjects and Humanities, also includes subjects such as Latin, Thinking Skills and Politics, Philosophy and Ethics. Extra-curricular endeavours are an essential part of life at Solefield and are well catered for with extensive opportunities in Sport, Drama, Music and Art. Solefield has a strong tradition of academic excellence. In the early years emphasis is placed on teaching the three Rs in a caring yet well-structured atmosphere, whilst senior boys gain numerous awards each year to secondary schools. Links between parents and the school are a particular strength.

Enquiries concerning places and admissions should be made to the Registrar, Mrs Barbara Volpato.

Charitable status. Solefield School is a Registered Charity, number 293466. It aims to provide a high quality education to boys aged 4–13.

Sompting Abbotts

Church Lane, Sompting, West Sussex BN15 0AZ
Tel: 01903 235960
Fax: 01903 210045
email: office@somptingabbotts.com
website: www.somptingabbotts.com

Principal: Mrs P M Sinclair

Headmaster: **S J Douch**, BA Hons, MA

Bursar: D A Sinclair

Age Range. 2–13 Co-educational.

Number of Pupils. 120.

Fees per term (2014–2015). Day £2,620–£3,365 (including lunches).

The only independent, family-run school in the area!

Set in a magnificent site on the edge of the South Downs, Sompting Abbotts overlooks the English Channel with views towards Beachy Head and the Isle of Wight. The imposing Victorian House has some 30 acres of sports fields, woodlands, gardens and activity areas.

The aim of the school is to provide a well-balanced education in a caring environment, recognizing and developing the individual needs of each child, so that maximum potential academic achievement may be gained. Within the community of the school an emphasis is laid on the cultivation of courtesy, self-discipline and respect for one another in order to engender a happy atmosphere.

The school has a vibrant Pre-Preparatory Department, which includes lively Early Years classes. In the Preparatory Department well-equipped Science Laboratory and Computer Room are enjoyed by all ages. The Art and Drama departments offer wide scope for creativity, and peripatetic teachers provide tuition for a range of musical instruments. Free wrap-around care is provided from 8 am to 6 pm.

Book your child in for a Taster Day to see what life is like at our wonderful school!

South Lee School

Nowton Road, Bury St Edmunds, Suffolk IP33 2BT
Tel: 01284 754654
Fax: 01284 706178
email: office@southlee.co.uk
website: www.southlee.co.uk

Chairman of the Governors: Mr A Holliday

Headmaster: **Mr Derek Whipp**, MA, CertEd

Age Range. 2–13.

Number of Pupils. 275 Boys and Girls.

Fees per term (2014–2015). £2,760–£3,420 including lunches.

South Lee enjoys an excellent reputation for its friendly, family atmosphere. The school provides a stimulating and caring environment where children have every opportunity to learn and develop. From an early age, pupils are taught the traditional subjects, emphasising mathematics, science and English but within a wider curriculum that incorporates the use of the latest developments in technology and educational resources.

The school is situated close to the A14, has purpose-built, modern classrooms and specialist teaching areas. Sport is an important part of the curriculum and the school has the use of excellent local facilities

South Lee offers its pupils opportunities for self-expression and individual development through study of the Arts, drama, music and a broad range of outdoor, sporting and extra-curricular activities.

The **Nursery**, which caters for children from 2 to 4 years of age, makes learning a fun experience from the very start.

The **Pre-Prep** is essentially class-based, though specialist staff teach French, music, ICT and Physical education.

The **Prep School** is well staffed with experienced teachers. The full range of academic subjects is taught, encompassing the national curriculum and preparing pupils for the Common Entrance 13+ examination.

Charitable status. South Lee exists to educate children from 2–13 years of age. Control is vested in a Board of Governors, the majority of whom are current parents. The school is run as a non-profit making Limited Company and is a Registered Charity, number 310491.

Spratton Hall

Smith Street, Spratton, Northampton NN6 8HP
Tel: 01604 847292
Fax: 01604 820844
email: office@sprattonhall.com
website: www.sprattonhall.com

Chairman: Mr James Coley

Head Master: **Mr Simon Clarke**, BA

Deputy Head Master: Mr Robert Dow, BA Hons, PGCE

Age Range. 4–13 Co-educational.

Number of Pupils. 400+.

Fees per term (2014–2015). Prep £4,175–£4,400, Pre-Prep £3,100. Fees include stationery, lunch, all academic books and most extra-curricular activities.

Set in 50 acres of Northamptonshire countryside, Spratton Hall is a fully co-educational day school for 4 to 13 years old.

Through highly skilled teaching we create an exciting and stimulating environment for learning, and by developing the talents of each child we believe that every pupil can succeed. The children are encouraged to become independent thinkers and to use their own initiative with confidence.

In the happy, caring Pre-Prep Department (from 4 to 7 years old) the girls and boys play imaginatively and grow in confidence. Each child is nurtured to establish a sound social and academic foundation for their future education.

Spratton has an enviable record of success at Common Entrance. Scholarships and awards are frequently won to many of the leading Independent Senior Schools.

The children enjoy a truly all-round education, achieving high academic standards as well as being recognised nationally for their success in sports and the Arts.

There are excellent facilities for Music, Art and Drama. The Performing Arts Centre provides Spratton Hall with a stage, tiered seating and a state-of-the-art sound and lighting system enabling each and every performance to be seen at its best. A wide variety of concerts, productions and exhibitions are enjoyed by all age groups throughout the year.

The Science laboratories, catering facilities and Dining Hall have been completely refurbished. Technology is constantly kept up to date and modernised to reflect the present advances in our society. The Townsend Library and Media centre incorporates books and technology exceptionally well.

The extensive playing fields together with the Jubilee Sports Dome, two all-weather surfaces and a full-size floodlit Astroturf enable all pupils to enjoy a range of sports including rugby, hockey, cricket, netball, rounders, athletics, cross-country and tennis with the Dome allowing for indoor tennis, badminton, gymnastics, dance and ballet.

In November 2010 Spratton Hall's successes were confirmed by an '*excellent*' and '*outstanding*' school inspection report in every respect by the Independent Schools Inspectorate.

For further information or to arrange a visit to see the children at work and play, please contact The Registrar on 01604 847292 or email afj@sprattonhall.com.

Charitable status. Spratton Hall is a Registered Charity, number 309925. It exists to provide education for boys and girls.

Spring Grove School

Harville Road, Wye, Kent TN25 5EZ
Tel: 01233 812337
email: office@springgroveschool.co.uk
website: www.springgroveschool.co.uk

Chairman of Governors: Mr Hugo Fenwick

Headmaster: **Mr W J B Jones**, BMus Hons, PGCE

Age Range. 2–11 Co-educational.
Number of Pupils. 199.
Fees per term (2014–2015). £2,350–£3,650.

Spring Grove is a co-educational Day Preparatory School from age 2 to 11. The school was founded in 1967 and is situated on the outskirts of the beautiful village of Wye. The main building is an inspiring late 17th Century house. The facilities include an outstanding Early Years department, Science Room, School Hall, Art Room, a brand new Music Room (2014), well-equipped Classrooms, Computer Room and Changing Rooms. The grounds contain the main school buildings and 15 acres of playing fields. Qualified and graduate staff help prepare the children for entry to Independent Senior and Grammar Schools. Spring Grove has a strong tradition of academic excellence, exceptionally lively music, drama and art departments and children who are inspired with a sense of wonder about the world. Emphasis is placed on innovative and creative teaching in a caring yet well-structured atmosphere with close contact maintained

between parents and teachers. 15 senior school scholarships have been awarded in the past two years.

The curriculum includes Music, Drama, Dance, Art and Technology, PE and extra-curricular activities. Athletics, Cricket, Cross-Country (National U11 IAPS Champions in 2011), Football, Hockey, Netball, Rounders and Rugby are the principal games.

Enquiries concerning places and admissions should be made to the Registrar, Tel: 01233 812337.

Charitable status. Spring Grove School 2003 is a Registered Charity, number 1099823.

Staines Preparatory School

3 Gresham Road, Staines upon Thames, Middlesex TW18 2BT
Tel: 01784 450909
email: admissions@stainesprep.co.uk
website: www.stainesprep.co.uk
Twitter: @StainesPrep
Facebook: /Stainesprep

Co-educational Day School founded in 1935.

Chairman of Governors: Mr M Bannister

Head Teacher: **Ms Samantha Sawyer**, BEd Hons, NPQH

Bursar: Mrs S Rogers

Admissions Manager: Mrs N Tait

Age Range. 2½–11 Co-educational.
Number of Pupils. 212 Day Boys, 179 Day Girls.
Fees per term (2014–2015). £2,915–£3,350.

Throughout its history SPS has maintained a reputation for high standards of education and care. The School aims for all pupils to attain their potential within a secure and happy environment and strives to produce boys and girls who are confident, honest, considerate and courteous.

The School believes in traditional values but is committed to providing the very best in terms of modern facilities and educational methods.

The School's philosophy of '*Educating Today's Children for the Challenges of Tomorrow*' is highlighted by the outstanding achievements of former SPS pupils in their secondary schools, with many attaining positions of responsibility as well as enjoying academic, sporting, musical and artistic success.

As Headmistress Sam Sawyer said recently, "It is vitally important to the School that all our pupils have the chance to flourish both educationally and personally. Staines Prep provides the foundations for each and every child to strive towards their full potential and enjoy themselves in the process."

The curriculum is based upon the National Curriculum with a sharp focus on the acquisition of literacy and numeracy skills. However, it is given additional breadth by the inclusion of French from Year 2 and Latin/Classical Studies in Years 5 and 6. Sport plays an important role at SPS and there is a regular programme of fixtures against other preparatory schools. Whilst the School believes in competitive sport and has won a number of local tournaments in soccer, netball, cricket and swimming in recent years, it also believes that as many pupils as possible should be given the opportunity to play in matches at various levels. Development of abilities in the Arts is also considered highly important with opportunities provided throughout the School both in the classroom and as extra activities. Subject specialist teaching commences in Year 4 following a series of assessments at the end of Year 3. A regular programme of trips and visits enhance the curriculum and the annual Ski Trip, trip to Melun and Field Trip are much enjoyed.

The new Multi-Sports Hall, state-of-the-art teaching and performance facilities along with the The Jubilee Wing, Library, and ICT Suite all indicate the School's commitment to providing the very best facilities as well as education. In addition to the general teaching classrooms there are special facilities for Science, Art, Design and Technology and Special Needs. Hard surfaced playground areas, an all-weather floodlit court and the adjoining playing fields and environmental area provide ample space for sport and recreation. Headmistress Ms Sawyer said: "The School is exceptionally proud of its new facilities. It has been a long-awaited dream which has now come to fruition and is enjoyed by everyone, including our local community."

The School welcomes contact with parents and has a flourishing Friends' Association whose activities strengthen the links between home and school. SPARKS, the School's Child Minding facility, operates from 7.30 am and remains open until 5.30 pm and is available for pupils of all ages.

There is also a Holiday Club on the school premises which is run by The Academies. They have a fun, active and inspirational programme of activities which we hope all children will enjoy in the safe and secure surrounds of the School. The Club runs for all holidays, including Christmas.

Stamford Junior School

Stamford, Lincolnshire PE9 2LR
Tel: 01780 484400
Fax: 01780 484401
email: headjs@ses.lincs.sch.uk
website: www.ses.lincs.sch.uk

Stamford Junior School, along with Stamford High School (girls) and Stamford School (boys), is one of three schools in the historic market town of Stamford comprising the Stamford Endowed Schools Educational Charity. The schools are under a single Governing Body and overall management and leadership of the Principal and allow continuity of education for boys and girls from 2 to 18, including boarding from age 8. Each school has its own Head and staff.

Chairman of Governors: Malcolm Desforges, Esq

Principal of the Stamford Endowed Schools: S C Roberts, MA

Headmistress: **Mrs E Smith**, BEd Hons

Age Range. 2–11.
Number of Children. 334.
Fees per term (2014–2015). Day: Year 0 £2,754; Year 1–2 £2,926; Year 3–6 £3,542. Full Boarding £6,382; Weekly Boarding £5,785; Three Night Boarding £5,084.

The Junior School educates boys and girls up to the age of 11 (including boarders from age 8), when boys move on to Stamford School and girls to Stamford High School. Admission from the Junior School to the two senior schools is based on progress and without further entrance testing.

The Junior School occupies its own spacious grounds, bordering the River Welland, overlooking the sports fields and open countryside, the boarding houses, the sports hall, floodlit artificial hockey pitch and the swimming pool on the same site. It is on the south west outskirts of Stamford within easy reach of the A1.

Entry to the School is according to registration at 4+ and assessment and interview in all other age groups.

The attractive and varied curriculum is designed to establish firm foundations in oracy, literacy and numeracy whilst providing excellent opportunities for music, drama, art and design and for acquiring technical and physical skills. The aims of the school are to develop the talents and potential of all the children.

There are 26 full-time staff, with specialist teachers in physical education, swimming, art and music, and visiting teachers offering a variety of sports, dance, speech and drama.

There is a purpose-built nursery in the grounds of the school – Stamford Nursery School – offering first-class care and early learning for children aged 2–4. Pupils then head to the adjacent Early Years Reception Classes.

Boarding. The co-educational Boarding House (St Michael's) is run in a homely, family style under the experienced leadership of Mr and Mrs Burns. Boys and girls are accepted as full or weekly boarders from the age of 8. Occasional or flexi boarding is accommodated where possible and according to family need. A full programme of activities takes place at weekends so that boarders enjoy a rich and varied week.

Stockport Grammar Junior School

Buxton Road, Stockport, Cheshire SK2 7AF
Tel: 0161 419 2405
Fax: 0161 419 2435
email: sgs@stockportgrammar.co.uk
website: www.stockportgrammar.co.uk

Chairman of Governors: C Dunn, MA

Headmaster: **T C Wheeler**, BA, MA

Age Range. 3–11.
Number of Pupils. 400: 217 boys, 183 girls.
Fees per term (2014–2015). £2,661, plus lunch.

Entry is mainly at 3+ and 4+ following assessment, with occasional places available at other ages. Stockport Grammar Junior School is a happy school, where children are encouraged to develop their strengths. A broad curriculum is taught and academic standards are very high. There are specialist facilities and teaching in science, ICT, physical education, music, art and design technology. A large number of pupils learn to play a musical instrument and tuition is available for many orchestral instruments. French is taught throughout. All children have swimming lessons in the School's pool. Infant and junior children can choose to join in the numerous lunch-time and after-school clubs and activities.

The Junior School and the Senior School share the same site. The vast majority of pupils move into the Senior School at 11, having passed the Entrance Examinations. (*See also Stockport Grammar School entry in HMC section.*)

Hockey, netball, football, cricket and athletics are the main sports. Swimming, tennis, rounders, cross-country, rugby, archery, canoeing and fencing are also offered. There is a full range of sporting fixtures and regular music and drama productions. All junior pupils have the opportunity to participate in residential visits, which include outdoor pursuits.

Before and after school care is available and holiday play schemes are run at Easter and in the summer.

Facilities are excellent. In addition to specialist teaching rooms, which include a computer room and a science laboratory, there are extensive playing fields, a large all-weather area, new sports hall and drama studio.

Charitable status. Stockport Grammar School is a Registered Charity, number 1120199. It exists to advance education by the provision and conduct, in or near Stockport, of a school for boys and girls.

Stonar Preparatory School

Cottles Park, Atworth, Wiltshire SN12 8NT
Tel: 01225 701762
Fax: 01225 790830
email: office@stonarschool.com
website: www.stonarschool.com

Chairman of Board of Directors:
Mr A McEwen, NACE UK Ltd

Headmaster: **Mr M Brain**, BA Ed Hons Exeter

Age Range. 2–11 Co-educational.
Number of Pupils. 95.
Fees per term (2014–2015). Day £2,555–£3,545; Boarding £6,020.

Stonar Prep School is a vibrant and exciting place to be. We pride ourselves on our genuinely small classes which enable us to offer individual care for girls and boys. Happy children are the feature of our school rather than an added extra, as we strive to develop everyone's confidence in a secure and caring atmosphere. Uniquely for a school of our size we are blessed with outstanding facilities in a beautiful environment; we make the most of these to offer a wide-reaching curriculum abounding with purpose and new experiences.

There are plenty of clubs and sports coaching on offer throughout the year, including Judo, Football, Ballet, Orchestra, Trampoline, Gymnastics and Yoga, plus all the traditional team sports and riding lessons.

Boarders are welcomed from 8 years and upwards. They live in a warm and cosy farmhouse known as Fuller House, where they are looked after by a House Parent and her assistant. Weekends are lively and there are plenty of trips and activities for the boarders.

Stonar Pre-Prep is for girls and boys aged 2–7. The children begin their 'Early Years' in Nursery before progressing through the transition stage of Kindergarten and on into the Reception class and more formal learning. The Pre-Prep is a lively and exciting area of the school where small groups allow individual attention to be given to each child at this most crucial developmental stage. A wide variety of experiences is enabled through our excellent facilities and generous staff ratios.

Stonar Prep and Pre-Prep benefit from the excellent facilities shared with the senior school, set in 80 acres of parkland and gardens. These include a range of grass and all-weather and sports pitches, a multi-purpose indoor sports hall, indoor heated swimming pool, music school, theatre, brand new art facility and of course Stonar's renowned equestrian centre which has stabling for up to 60 horses, indoor and outdoor arenas and 4 levels of cross country courses.

Minibuses operate throughout Wiltshire and South Gloucestershire and the Prep School provides a free before and after-school club with breakfast available for those who require it.

Governance. Stonar is a part of NACE Educational Services Limited, Company Registration No. 8441252, Registered Address: 17 Hanover Square, London, United Kingdom W1S 1HU.

Stonyhurst St Mary's Hall
Preparatory School for Stonyhurst College

Stonyhurst, Clitheroe, Lancashire BB7 9PU
Tel: 01254 827073
Fax: 01254 827136
email: admissions@stonyhurst.ac.uk
website: www.stonyhurst.ac.uk

Chairman of Governors: John Cowdall

Headmaster: **Mr Ian Murphy**, BA, PGCE

Age Range. 3–13 (Boarders from age 8).
Number of Pupils. Day 172, Boarding 42.
Fees per term (2014–2015). Day £2,363–£4,709; Weekly Boarding £6,144; Full Boarding £7,251.

Stonyhurst St Mary's Hall provides a co-educational preparatory education in the Jesuit Catholic tradition for boarders (age 8–13) and day pupils (age 3–13). Stonyhurst, founded in 1593, is one of the oldest Jesuit schools in the world, and the College and Preparatory School are set within two thousand acres of outstanding natural beauty. We have impressive facilities and buildings, however, it will always be our people – children, staff, parents and families that breathe life into Stonyhurst St Mary's Hall. The positive and optimistic vision within our school community is tangible. This is an exciting time for us and our school is thriving. This is a special place where children want to be and where relationships between all members of the community are remarkable.

The children receive a high-quality rounded education. St Mary's Hall has its own dedicated teaching facilities and resources for all preparatory subjects, including French, Spanish and Latin. A new state-of-the-art Science laboratory was recently opened, and the school also enjoys the benefit of very extensive games fields, a sports hall, a fully equipped modern theatre, as well as shared use with the College of a large indoor swimming pool, and one of the finest all-weather pitches in the North. St Mary's Hall has a national reputation for rugby, but at the same time many other boys' and girls' sports flourish, as do a wide variety of cultural pursuits including drama and music. Many educational and recreational excursions take place both at home and abroad.

All pupils receive pastoral care and academic tutoring through their Class teachers and Playroom (Head of Year) Staff, who meet regularly to monitor closely pupils' progress. Early Years and Key Stage 1 pupils are taught in their own purpose-built building. The teaching staff are also closely supported by a resident Chaplaincy team, which leads the largely lay staff in the religious life of the School. Pupils of other denominations are very welcome at St Mary's Hall.

Boarders are under the care of the resident Housemaster and his wife, supported by a fantastic resident pastoral team, which ensures one of the best staff to student ratios in the country. The boarders enjoy a stimulating and wide-ranging programme of lunchtime, evening, and weekend activities. St Mary's Hall, like Stonyhurst College, provides a seven-day week boarding environment, in which the day pupils are able to participate to a great extent if they wish.

The main sports played are Rugby, Cross Country, Netball, Rounders, Hockey, Cricket, Athletics and Tennis. The wide range of extra-curricular activities available for the children in their recreational time includes Chess, Model Making, Camping (Summer), Art, Photography, Fencing, Gymnastics, Computing, Theatre Workshop, Modern Dance, Ballet, and Skiing.

Admission to St Mary's Hall of pupils from age 3 to 10+ is by previous school report (where applicable) and interview. At 11+ there is also an entrance test. Academic Scholarships are also awarded at 11+, as is an annual music scholarship. The Academic provision at the school is overseen by College Heads of Department from the age of 11 as part of a seamless transition preparing the pupils for national examinations, and whilst the pastoral care of the pupils remains in a supportive prep school environment, all pupils are effectively admitted to the College from age 11 onwards and are taught by KS3 teaching staff.

Further details and a prospectus may be obtained from the Registrar.

Charitable status. St Mary's Hall is a Registered Charity, number 230165. It exists to promote Catholic Independent Jesuit Education within the Christian Community. It also runs its own registered, pupil-led charity, Children for Children, which raises funds for a school in Zimbabwe and other worthy causes.

Stormont

The Causeway, Potters Bar, Herts EN6 5HA
Tel: 01707 654037
email: admin@stormont.herts.sch.uk
website: www.stormont.herts.sch.uk

The school is administered by a Board of Governors.

Chairman of Board of Governors: Mr J H Salmon, FCA

Headmistress: **Mrs S E Martin**, BSc

Age Range. 4–11.
Number of Pupils. 170 Day Girls.
Fees per term (2014–2015). £3,560–£3,720 (including lunch). There are no compulsory extras.

The School was founded in 1944 and has occupied its attractive Victorian House since then. There is a spacious, bright, purpose-built Lower School Building, which adjoins the Assembly Hall and Dining Room. Old stables have been converted to provide well-equipped rooms for Art, Pottery, Design Technology, Science and French. A Millennium Building houses a Drama/Music Studio and an Information and Communications Technology Suite. The school has two tennis courts and a playground. It has use of a two-acre playing field and a swimming pool. A well-equipped Sports Hall was opened in the Summer Term 2009.

Well-qualified and experienced staff prepare the girls for entry to a wide range of senior schools at the age of eleven.

Charitable status. Stormont School is a Registered Charity, number 311079. It exists to establish and carry on a school where children may receive a sound education.

Stover Preparatory School

Newton Abbot, South Devon TQ12 6QG
Tel: 01626 354505 or 01626 331451
Fax: 01626 361475
email: mail@stover.co.uk
website: www.stover.co.uk

Chairman of Governors: Mr S Killick, ND, ARB

Head: **Mrs C Coyle**, BEd, MA

Age Range. 3–11 Co-educational.
Number of Pupils. 165.
Fees per term (2014–2015). Preparatory School: Day: Reception–Year 2 £2,462, Year 3 £2,678, Years 4–5 £3,049,

Year 6 £3,327. Weekly Boarding: Year 3 £5,243, Years 4–5 £5,614, Year 6 £5,892. Full Boarding: Years 3–5 £6,438, Year 6 £6,716.

"The school very successfully fulfils its aim of providing a high quality education in which the individual needs of the pupils are paramount... The contribution of teaching is excellent. Throughout the school, teaching promotes effective learning, catering extremely well for the full range of pupils. Positive, supportive relationships stimulate and motivate the pupils so that they make good progress" ISI Inspection Report 2008.

Stover Preparatory School enjoys a beautiful rural setting on the edge of Dartmoor National Park and close to the south Devon coast. Set in 64 acres there is ample space for pupils of all ages to experience the great outdoors; be that through play, nature walks, sport, orienteering, building an outdoor classroom, researching the history of the fine old buildings and much more. Stover Preparatory School shares its fine site with Stover Senior School making transfer at aged 11 years a smooth process for our pupils.

We pride ourselves on our warm, welcoming atmosphere where each individual is nurtured and encouraged to reach their full potential. Visitors frequently comment on the positive, happy feeling they experience upon entering the school. Teachers are aware of pupils' individual needs and provide support in an approachable and friendly manner.

We offer a broad, balanced curriculum with high academic standards complemented by a wide range of extra-curricular activities. Spanish begins in Reception with French also introduced at Year 3. Years 5 and 6 are taught all subjects by specialist teachers whilst in the younger age groups there is a balance between specialist teaching and class teaching, depending upon the age of the pupils. Sport and the Performing Arts play a vital role in each child's development. We have a full fixture list for our U9 and U11 teams as well as involvement with the local Schools' Sports Partnership. Our regular school performances and concerts are a highlight of the calendar. More than 80% of our Prep School pupils choose to participate in the Prep School Choir. In addition we offer a Pre-Prep Choir and a Chamber Choir for talented pupils in Years 5 and 6. Residential and day trips into our beautiful local environment further complement the curriculum.

Facilities include an extensive Sports Fields, Tennis Courts, Art room, Music room, Multi-Purpose Hall, Library and ICT suite.

Flexi, weekly and full boarding are available from the age of 7 years. Scholarships are offered at 11+. The majority of our pupils move on to Stover Senior School or local grammar Schools.

See also Stover School senior entry in The Society of Heads section.

Charitable status. Stover School Association is a Registered Charity, number 306712.

Stroud School
King Edward VI Preparatory School

Highwood House, Highwood Lane, Romsey, Hampshire SO51 9ZH
Tel: 01794 513231
Fax: 01794 514432
email: enquiries@stroud-kes.org.uk
website: www.stroud-kes.org.uk

Chairman of Governors: Mr B Richards

Headmaster: **A J L Dodds**, MA Cantab, DMS

Deputy Head: Miss R M Lyons

Director of Studies: Mr C Jackson

Age Range. 3–13.
Number of Pupils. 318: 186 Boys, 146 Girls.
Fees per term (2014–2015). Upper School £4,925, Middle School £4,470, Pre-Preparatory £3,020, Nursery £7.00 per hour.

Stroud is a co-educational day school for children aged 2 years 9 months to 13 years. Pupils are prepared for entrance to senior Independent or Grammar Schools.

The School stands on the outskirts of Romsey in its own grounds of 20 acres, which include playing fields, a full-sized sports hall, a heated outdoor swimming pool, tennis courts, riding arena, lawns and gardens. The main team games for boys are cricket, hockey, rugby and soccer, and for girls hockey, rounders and netball. Both boys and girls play tennis.

Music and drama play an important part in the life of the School. A wide variety of instruments is taught and children are encouraged to join the school orchestra. Each year there is a musical production and the Carol Service is held in Romsey Abbey.

The Stroud School Association, run by the parents, holds many social activities and helps to raise money for amenities, but its main function is to generate goodwill.

A new Early Years building was completed in 2007.

In 2014 a £2.5 million investment included a new kitchen, dining room, as well as an art/dt/mfl block. Included in this projects was a £300K Bio Mass Heating System.

The Study Preparatory School

Wilberforce House, Camp Road, Wimbledon Common, London SW19 4UN
Tel: 020 8947 6969
Fax: 020 8944 5975
email: wilberforce@thestudyprep.co.uk
website: www.thestudyprep.co.uk

Chairman of Governors: Mr Nick Brookes

Headmistress: **Mrs Susan Pepper**, MA Oxon

Age Range. 4–11.
Number of Girls. 320 (approximately).
Fees per term (2014–2015). £3,790.

The Study Preparatory School provides a happy and stimulating learning environment for girls from 4 to 11 on two very attractive and well-equipped sites close to Wimbledon Common.

The girls enjoy a rich diversity of experiences, both in and out of the classroom. The school is renowned for its creative ethos, and has been awarded Artsmark Gold status by Arts Council England for the second time in 2012. Each girl is encouraged to do her best academically, and excellent teaching standards encourage academic rigour and challenge. Music and sport are exceptionally strong, while drama, public speaking and a varied clubs programme play an important part. Guest speakers, fundraising events, workshops and school trips all help the children to understand important issues beyond the school gates. Good manners and consideration for others are encouraged at all times. Girls leave at 11+, very well prepared for the next stage of their education, with a zest for learning and many happy memories. Girls receive offers from leading day and boarding senior schools, many with academic or performance scholarships. A record number of eighteen scholarships were awarded in 2012, with 44 scholarships having been offered over the last three years.

Entry is by ballot. The Study has an assisted places scheme for girls aged 7+. For details contact Joint Educational Trust (JET) on 020 3217 1100.

Charitable status. The Study (Wimbledon) Ltd is a Registered Charity, number 271012. It exists to provide education for girls from 4 to 11.

Summer Fields

Mayfield Road, Oxford OX2 7EN
Tel: 01865 459204
Fax: 01865 459200
email: admissions@summerfields.com
website: www.summerfields.com

Chairman of Governors: A E Reekes, MA, FRSA

Headmaster: **David Faber**, MA Oxon

Age Range. 8–13.
Number of Boys. 210 boarders and 45 day.
Fees per term (2014–2015). £8,651 Boarding, £6,699 Day.

Set in 70 acres of delightful grounds which lead down to the river Cherwell and yet only a few miles from the city centre, Summer Fields is often known as Oxford's *Secret Garden*.

The School has always had a strong academic reputation. In 2012, Summerfieldians secured 9 scholarships and awards to top independent schools, including three academic scholarships to Winchester. Each year, boys pass Common Entrance to their first-choice senior schools including Eton, Harrow, Radley, Winchester, and St Edward's.

Huge emphasis is placed on providing the highest standards of pastoral care. Each boy has a personal tutor, who is responsible for his academic progress and social welfare and will be in regular contact with the boy's parents. The boarders live in comfortable Lodges within the school grounds and are looked after by an experienced and dedicated husband and wife team of Lodgeparents. More than 90% of the staff live on site, making a significant contribution to school life both in and out of the classroom.

The Music, Art, Drama, Design Technology, ICT and Sport departments are all impressive. The Choir has recently sung in Westminster and Christ Church Cathedrals and at Keble, Magdalen, Exeter and New College, Oxford. They also regularly tour abroad, most recently visiting Vienna in May 2014. At least one Drama production takes place every term in the Macmillan Theatre with DVDs available of the major productions. Every summer an Art Exhibition of boys' work is held at the School and is open to the public.

The facilities are outstanding, including a fine library, theatre and chapel; purpose-built classrooms; Art, Design & Technology, Music and ICT Centres and a magnificent Sports Hall, with squash and Eton fives courts, a shooting gallery and swimming pool. In 2011, Summer Fields build a new Astroturf and tennis courts and new all-weather cricket nets, to add to the extensive outdoor facilities including a nine-hole golf course, an adventure playground and an outdoor swimming pool. A huge range of sports, activities and hobbies is on offer throughout the week and at weekends.

100% scholarships and bursaries are available.

For further information or to arrange a visit, please contact Mrs Christine Berry, Tel: 01865 459204.

Charitable status. Summer Fields is a Registered Charity, number 309683.

Sunningdale School

Dry Arch Road, Sunningdale, Berks SL5 9PY
Tel: 01344 620159
Fax: 01344 873304
email: headmaster@sunningdaleschool.co.uk
website: www.sunningdaleschool.co.uk

Headmaster: **T A C N Dawson**, MA, PGCE

Deputy Headmaster: A J Logue, BSc, PGCE

Age Range. 8–13.
Number of Boys. 100.
Fees per term (2014–2015). Boarding £7,070 (no compulsory extras).

Sunningdale is a small, mainly boarding school of around 100 boys. The unique family atmosphere means that the boys feel happy and secure and as a result are able to achieve their full potential. Our aim is to find each boy's strengths and give him the opportunity to shine in different areas of school life.

Our academic record speaks for itself, with scholarships gained on a regular basis to senior schools. The structure of our forms means that boys move through the school at their own pace, constantly challenged or supported where necessary.

Three-quarters of the boys play at least one musical instrument; many play two or even three. The chapel choir sings on Sundays and occasionally at old boys' weddings and there is a pipe band which plays on Sports Day and at other events. As well as other drama productions we produce a musical each year in which every boy appears. The art department puts on a large exhibition every year and often wins awards at senior schools.

We have a good reputation on the sports field and one of the benefits of being a small school is that almost all the boys get to represent the school in a team. This does wonders for their confidence. There is a wide range of activities on offer from judo to juggling, clay pigeons to clay modelling.

The school has a strong boarding ethos and boys can weekly board in their first year. Weekends are packed with activities to keep the boys stimulated and entertained.

Sunninghill Prep School

South Court, South Walks, Dorchester, Dorset DT1 1EB
Tel: 01305 262306
Fax: 01305 261254
email: office@sunninghill.dorset.sch.uk
website: www.sunninghillprep.co.uk

Chair of Governors: Mr Richard Miller, Chartered Surveyor

Acting Headmaster: **Mr John Thorpe**, BSc Hons, PGCE

Age Range. 3 months–13 years.
Number of Children. Baby unit (3 months–2 years 9 months) 3 girls, 5 boys, Nursery (2 years 9 months–4 years) 13 girls, 11 boys; Reception (4–5 years) 4 girls, 5 boys; Pre-Prep (5–8 years) 27 girls, 30 boys; Main School (8–13 years) 36 girls, 47 boys.
Fees per term (2014–2015). £2,642–£4,278. There are no compulsory extras. Nursery: £720 (based on 5 sessions per week, inclusive of Early Years Grant).

Sunninghill is a co-educational day school. There are 14 full-time and 16 part-time fully qualified staff.

Founded in 1939, Sunninghill Prep became a Charitable Trust in 1969. It moved to its present site in January 1997 and has its own swimming pool, tennis courts and extensive grounds. Children are prepared for the Common Entrance examination to any Independent Senior School, and those with particular ability may be entered for scholarships. Over the years the school has attained many academic successes, but the broad curriculum also includes drama, art, craft, music and physical education. Friday Enrichments allow greater cross-curricular links for years 1–8, enhancing their learning further.

Team and individual sports played with PE and Games at least three times a week from years 3–8 and these include hockey, netball, lacrosse and rounders for the girls, and hockey, rugby, association football and cricket for the boys. In the summer term both boys and girls participate in athletics, swimming and tennis.

Out-of-school activities include academic clubs preparing for scholarships, such as the core subjects, humanities and art, plus debating, chess, creative arts, ballet, dance, LAMDA and various music clubs including choir and string quartet. We offer multi sports across a wide age group, all pentathlon sports and swimming and we are a member of the National Sailing Academy, with our own race team. Sunninghill Prep prides itself on its nurturing, family ethos. The school's flourishing Parents' Association ensures that parents and staff all know each other and work together for the good of the children and the School.

The prospectus is available on request.

Charitable status. Sunninghill Preparatory School is a Registered Charity, number 1024774. It exists to provide education for boys and girls.

Sunny Hill Preparatory School
Bruton School for Girls

Sunny Hill, Bruton, Somerset BA10 0NT
Tel: 01749 814400
Fax: 01749 812537
email: info@brutonschool.co.uk
website: www.brutonschool.co.uk

Chairman of Governors: Mr D H C Batten

Head of Preparatory School: **Mrs Helen Snow**, BEd

Age Range. Day places for Girls and Boys aged 2–7. Day and Boarding places for Girls aged 8–11. No Saturday school.
Numbers of Pupils. 70.
Fees per term (2014–2015). Day: £3,480–£3,580 (Preparatory School), £1,740–£2,319 (Pre-Preparatory School), £20 per session (Nursery).

Boarding (from Year 4): £6,348–£6,448 (full), £5,755–£5,855 (weekly boarding), £53.50 per day (casual boarding).

Ethos. Sunny Hill Prep aims to create a happy, caring and vibrant atmosphere where children build strong academic foundations and develop personal confidence. Pupils are encouraged to think of others in a community based on mutual respect.

Location. Situated in 40 acres in beautiful countryside, the school is conveniently located on the Somerset, Wiltshire and Dorset borders with easy access to the A303. It shares the campus with the senior school and pupils benefit from specialist teachers and facilities.

Curriculum. A carefully structured and broad curriculum, delivered using an exciting variety of teaching and learning styles ensures good foundations are laid and high standards are achieved by all. Pupils thrive on a rich mix of activities – including themed curriculum weeks, a comprehensive outdoor education programme, imaginative topic work and educational visits – all encouraging curiosity and a love of learning. Food Technology modules in specialist rooms are an integral part of Years 5 and 6 DT work. Creative and enthusiastic teachers inspire and stretch pupils. Pupils are nurtured by an excellent system of pastoral care. Children in the Nursery and Early Years Class follow the Early Years Foundation Stage curriculum with emphasis on learning through play.

A love of creative and performing arts is encouraged as are opportunities to perform – facilities include a modern theatre and an amphitheatre. Other facilities include a library, a nature reserve and a meadow. There is a wide variety of extra-curricular activities, for example Latin, rugby, gymnastics, yoga, Eco club and folk group.

Sport. Hockey, netball, rounders, gymnastics, tennis, swimming and athletics are integral to the curriculum taught by specialist PE teachers. Facilities include an astroturf pitch, dance studio and heated outdoor swimming pool. Pupils participate in inter-school competitions and in addition pupils can try activities such as riding, indoor rowing, dance and trampolining.

Boarding. A high standard of care and comfort is provided in a self-contained junior boarding house with well-equipped facilities and grounds. In the evenings and at weekends, pupils enjoy a full programme of activities.

Spiritual Life. The school has a Christian ethos and welcomes pupils from all faiths or none.

Medical Care. The school has its own medical centre with a qualified nursing Sister.

Charitable status. Bruton School for Girls is a Registered Charity, number 1085577, and a Company Limited by Guarantee.

Surbiton High Boys' Preparatory School
United Learning

3 Avenue Elmers, Surbiton, Surrey KT6 4SP
Tel: 020 8390 6640
Fax: 020 8255 3049
email: boysprep@surbitonhigh.com
website: www.surbitonhigh.com
Twitter: @SHSBoysPrep
Facebook: /SurbitonHigh

Chair of Local Governing Body: Mr Eggie Kock

Head: **Miss C Bufton**, BA Hons Wales, PGCE Kingston

Age Range. 4–11.
Number of Pupils. 136 day boys.
Fees per term (2014–2015). £3,007 (Reception, Years 1–2); £4,021 (Years 3–6). Lunch: £229. Fee rates apply to payment by termly direct debit. A reduction in fees applies when two or more children from the same family attend the Preparatory and either the Junior or Senior Girls' Schools. Reductions are also made for children of members of the clergy.

Established in 1862, the School became the Boys' Preparatory School of Surbiton High School and thus part of United Learning in 1987. Situated in a large Victorian villa in Avenue Elmers, the School shares the facilities offered at the Senior School including access to those in the Surbiton Assembly Rooms and Hinchley Wood Playing Fields.

Boys join the School at 4+ (Reception), although places in other forms are occasionally available. The School is single-form entry and at the 11+ stage all pupils take entrance examinations to their chosen senior school.

At Surbiton High Boys' Preparatory School we have contact with some 20 Senior Schools in south-west London and north Surrey. All of these schools have strong academic traditions and reputations and those in the maintained sector are established selective boys' secondary schools. Regularly, the boys' success in entrance examinations allows the opportunity to choose between three or more senior schools, and many pupils gain scholarship awards. The Boys' Prep offers a broad and balanced curriculum that closely follows the National Curriculum. It is enhanced and enriched in order to provide every pupil with the opportunity to reach his potential. English, Mathematics, Science and ICT are the core subjects taught, and formal SATs tests are carried out in Years 2 and 6. In addition to these subjects, we also teach History, Geography, Religious Education, French, Spanish, Music, Drama, Games, Art, Design Technology and Personal, Social and Health Education. The Prep offers three languages: Reception to Year 2 start with Spanish, with French being introduced in Year 3 and Mandarin in Year 4. Furthermore, we have a very caring Learning Support teacher who is able to provide the boys with any individual attention they may require to succeed within School. There is specialist teaching throughout the School for Music, Languages and PE. Years 5 and 6 are introduced to subject-based teaching for all subjects, which prepares them for their senior school experiences.

There are many opportunities for the boys to perform within Music and Drama. They take part in a range of plays and musical concerts throughout the year. We celebrate Christmas with a Carol Service in St Mark's Church every year.

In addition to the computer suite, each classroom has its own interactive whiteboard and laptops are available for use and facilitated through a wireless network.

Teaching is frequently supported by visits to outside venues and by visits from speakers, theatre groups and musicians. Further opportunities to develop interests are provided by a wide range of extra-curricular activities.

There are extensive sports grounds at Hinchley Wood and Oaken Lane, which include a pavilion, all-weather netball/tennis courts, two all-weather hockey pitches and a multi-use games area.

At Surbiton High Boys' Preparatory School we work with parents to ensure that each child develops intellectually, physically, socially, morally and spiritually into a confident, happy individual. The boys are introduced to a variety of different experiences in a secure, caring and stimulating environment. The natural curiosity of every child is fostered and developed within a traditional academically based environment. We hope, thus, to encourage a positive attitude towards education and develop boys' self-motivation.

Charitable status. Surbiton High Boys' Preparatory School is part of United Learning which comprises: UCST (a Company Limited by Guarantee, Registered in England, number 2780748, and a Registered Charity, number 1016538) and ULT (a Company Limited by Guarantee, Registered in England, number 4439859, and an Exempt Charity).

Surbiton High Junior Girls' School
United Learning

95–97 Surbiton Road, Kingston-upon-Thames, Surrey KT1 2HW
Tel: 020 8546 9756
Fax: 020 8974 6293
email: juniorgirls@surbitonhigh.com
website: www.surbitonhigh.com
Twitter: @SHSJnrGirls
Facebook: /SurbitonHigh

Chair of Local Governing Body: Mr Eggie Kock

Head: Miss C Bufton, BA Hons Wales, PGCE Kingston

Age Range. 4–11.
Number of Pupils. 290 Day Girls.
Fees per term (2014–2015). £3,007 (Reception, Years 1–2); £4,021 (Years 3–6). Lunch: £229. Fee rates apply to payment by termly direct debit. Sibling discount applies to families with 2 or more children in the School and for children of members of the Clergy.

The main age of entry is at 4+, with a second intake joining the School at the age of 7, however the school does admit girls at other age groups dependent on the availability of places. We have approximately 24 girls in a class.

Surbiton High Junior Girls' School is a vibrant school which balances excellent academic achievement and learning with a broad co-curricular programme. It is a warm and welcoming school where staff inspire, encourage and empower pupils to achieve their very best both inside and outside the classroom.

Surbiton girls become independent learners and decision-makers from the earliest age. We encourage them to think for themselves and to recognise their own styles of work and learning. We also understand the importance of strong foundations in numeracy and literacy. From mental arithmetic to grammar and punctuation, our girls are exceptionally well-prepared for the demands of modern education.

There is a natural progression to the Senior School and the Junior School prepares girls well for the next stage in learning at our Senior School.

The Junior School building is spacious, well planned and well resourced. In addition to the classroom accommodation there is a Library, Hall/Gym, Computer Room, Music Studio, Drama Studio, a large Science/Art laboratory and an outdoor learning area for Reception.

The School has interactive whiteboards in all classrooms and also has a wireless network to facilitate the laptops available for use. The boards enable the curriculum to be taught with the most up-to-date resources and methods, keeping the pace and stimulus appropriate for children of today. We offer a broad and balanced curriculum that closely follows the National Curriculum. It is enhanced and enriched in order to provide every pupil with the opportunity to reach her potential. English, Mathematics, Science and ICT are the core subjects taught and formal SATs tests are carried out in Years 2 and 6. In addition to these subjects, we also teach History, Geography, Religious Education, French, Spanish, Music, Drama, Gymnastics, Dance, Games, Art, Design Technology and Personal, Social and Health Education. Furthermore, we have a very caring Learning Support teacher who is able to provide the girls with any individual attention they may require to succeed within School. There is specialist teaching throughout the School for Music, Languages and PE. Years 5 and 6 are introduced to subject-based teaching for all subjects, which prepares them for their Senior School experiences.

There are many opportunities for the girls to perform within Music and Drama. They present Form Assemblies for the School and their parents, and also take part in a range of plays and musical concerts throughout the year. We celebrate Christmas with a Carol Service in St Mark's Church every year.

One of the strengths of the School is its pastoral care which is reflected in the warmth of its atmosphere. We try to ensure that we give each child social, emotional and academic support and opportunities for growth. The successful School Council and 'pupil voice' is another way in which this strength can be identified. The girls leave Surbiton High Junior Girls' School as contented, articulate and capable young ladies ready for the challenges of Senior School life.

The School has beautiful playing fields at Hinchley Wood nearby on a 33-acre site, to which the girls are transported by coach for their lessons. There is also an additional sports facility in Oaken Lane which includes an all-weather hockey pitch, three netball/tennis courts and a multi-use games area.

There are School teams for Netball, Tennis and Rounders and thriving after-school Gymnastics Club and Ski Club where the children can soon reach extremely high standards. We have national champions at Junior level.

Charitable status. Surbiton High Junior Girls' School is part of United Learning which comprises: UCST (a Company Limited by Guarantee, Registered in England, number 2780748, and a Registered Charity, number 1016538) and ULT (a Company Limited by Guarantee, Registered in England, number 4439859, and an Exempt Charity).

Sussex House

68 Cadogan Square, London SW1X 0EA
Tel: 020 7584 1741
Fax: 020 7589 2300
email: schoolsecretary@sussexhouseschool.co.uk
website: www.sussexhouseschool.co.uk

Chairman of the Governors: John Crewe, Esq

Headmaster: Nicholas Kaye, MA Magdalene College Cambridge, ACP, FRSA, FRGS

Deputy Headmaster: Martin Back, BA, PGCE Sussex

Age Range. 8–13.
Number of Boys. 182.
Fees per term (2014–2015). £5,610.
Founded in 1952, Sussex House is situated in the heart of Chelsea in a fine Norman Shaw house in Cadogan Square. Its Gymnasium and Music School are housed in a converted chapel in Cadogan Street. The school is an independent charitable trust. At Common Entrance and Scholarship level it has achieved a record of consistently strong results to academically demanding schools. The school enjoys its own entirely independent character and the style is traditional yet imaginative.

There is a full-time teaching staff of 22. Creative subjects are given strong emphasis and throughout the school boys take Music and Art. Team sports take place at a nearby site and the school's football teams have an impressive record. Cricket is the main summer sport and there are opportunities for tennis, swimming, basketball, indoor football and indoor hockey. All boys have physical education classes and Sussex House is a centre of excellence for fencing and its international records are well known.

Cultural and creative activities play a major role, including theatrical productions in a West End theatre, a major annual exhibition of creative work featuring large-scale architectural models and an annual competition of poetry written by boys. There is a strong bias towards music and an ambitious programme of choral and orchestral concerts. A large number of pupils play musical instruments and there is an impressive record of music awards to senior schools. The school provides a range of sporting and cultural trips.

The school has a Church of England affiliation. There is a school chaplain and weekly services are held in St Simon Zelotes Church, Chelsea. Boys of all religions and denominations are welcomed.

Charitable status. Sussex House is a Registered Charity, number 1035806. It exists to provide education for boys.

Sutton Valence Preparatory School

**Church Road, Chart Sutton, Maidstone, Kent
ME17 3RF**
Tel: 01622 842117
Fax: 01622 844201
email: enquiries@svprep.svs.org.uk
website: www.svs.org.uk

Chairman of Governors: B F W Baughan, Esq

Head: Malcolm Gough, BA, LLB Rhodes, LLM Cape
Town, PGCE OU

Deputy Head: Miss C L Corkran, MEd, BEd Hons Cantab
Head of Pre-Prep: Miss P McCarmick, MA, BSc QTS,
AMBDA
Director of Studies: Mrs R Harrison, BEd Hons

Age Range. 3–11.
Number of Day Pupils. Prep (7–11): 104 boys, 80 girls.
Pre-Prep (3–6): 55 boys, 47 girls.
Fees per term (2014–2015). £2,670–£4,095. Lunch £233.
The school is fully co-educational with its Pre-Prep
department housed in a new purpose-built facility. Central to
everything are the values of the school community and the
happiness of our children. These provide pupils with a
strong feeling of structure and security which enables them
to work effectively.

The school has a passion for reaching for the highest possible standards inside and out of the classroom. That, however, does not come at the expense of childhood and we
believe that what Sutton Valence Prep does so successfully
is find that balance between delivering in terms of education, and yet doing so kindly and with many broad and interesting opportunities. The school is very proud of its
articulate and confident pupils who move on equipped to
work things out for themselves, so crucial in our increasingly challenging world.

To achieve this we have dedicated Art, Science and ICT
facilities and a new Library. Classes are small throughout
the school. The 40 teaching staff are all well qualified and
there is an extensive peripatetic staff for music. Special
needs are addressed by the SENCO and 3 part-time teachers.
The Kindergarten to Year 2 classes all have qualified classroom assistants.

The school is situated in 18 acres of countryside overlooking the Weald and includes a hard and grass play areas,
heated outdoor swimming pool, four hard tennis courts, a
Sports Hall, a 13-acre games field, a full-size Astroturf and
a newly established 'forest school' area, all of which support
our co-curricular programme.

A solid foundation in the core subjects of English, Mathematics, Science and ICT is supplemented by Languages,
Music, Drama, Art, Design Technology and Sport which are
all taught by specialist teaching staff. The co-curricular programme is wide and varied providing many opportunities
for children to perform in drama productions and in concerts, occasionally in conjunction with the senior school.
Children are prepared for our senior school, Sutton Valence,
the local Grammar schools and other independent schools
with an 11+ entry.

Cricket, football, hockey, netball, rugby and rounders are
the major sports, with athletics, swimming and cross-country also being available. The proximity of the senior school,
Sutton Valence, allows the children to benefit from their
staffing and facilities, including the use of the Sports Hall,
athletics track and the indoor swimming pool. After-school
activities include chess club, art, 5-a-side football, gymnastics, drama, craft, croquet, science club, ballet and judo.

The school is a Christian foundation. Assemblies, for celebration, and the use of the local church are an important
facet of our lives, with the schools' Chaplain visiting regu-

larly. The school provides a fulfilling education for all its
children, a thriving network for its parents and a happy
workplace for all who dedicate their lives to it.

Charitable status. United Westminster Schools Foundation is a Registered Charity, number 309267. It exists to provide education for boys and girls and provides valuable
resources and support.

Swanbourne House School

**Swanbourne, Milton Keynes, Buckinghamshire
MK17 0HZ**
Tel: 01296 720264
Fax: 01296 728089
email: office@swanbourne.org
website: www.swanbourne.org

The School is a Charitable Trust, administered by a Board of
Governors.

Chairman of Governors: J Leggett

Headmaster: S Hitchings, MA Oxon

Age Range. 3–13.
Number of Pupils. Prep: 126 Boys, 103 Girls (26 full/
weekly boarders, 24 flexi boarders). Pre-Prep: 42 Girls, 62
Boys. Nursery: 11 Girls, 16 Boys.
Fees per term (2014–2015). Full/Weekly boarding
£6,940; Day: Prep £5,450; Pre-Prep £3,100, Nursery
£385–£1,716.
The house, which was once the home of the Cottesloe
family, is a Grade II listed building, standing in 40 acres of
wooded grounds and commanding extensive views of the
surrounding countryside. Swanbourne has been described
by Gabbitas Guardianship as 'a school you would just dream
of'.

There are 40 full-time members of teaching staff, many
of whom are resident. They are assisted by several peripatetic specialist teachers. The well-being of the boarders is in
the hands of a resident Housemaster and his wife: they are
assisted by our daily RGN staff and an Assistant Housemaster and Assistant Housemistress.

A strong musical tradition has been established. There are
three choirs, an orchestra and various ensembles. Musical
concerts are held throughout the school year and all pupils
are encouraged to participate in drama and the Inter-House
music competition. The school has its own chapel.

Boys and girls are prepared for entry to independent
senior schools, usually at 13+, with 33 Common Entrance
passes and 14 scholarships awarded last year. The majority
of boys and girls go on to leading senior independent
schools, where the pass rate in recent years has been 100%.
From age 9, pupils are taught by specialist teachers in well-
equipped subject rooms. There are 2 Modern Language Laboratories and all senior pupils have the opportunity to spend
a week in France.

The more practical side of the Curriculum is fully catered
for in the Fremantle Hall of Technology. Art, Design Technology, Science and Information Technology are taught in
this attractive building: more than 200 computers are in use
throughout the school. We have two computer rooms and
internet access in every classroom.

A House system operates to encourage healthy competition in work and games. The Housemasters and Housemistresses have a special responsibility and concern for the
welfare of the children in their House.

For boys, the main school games are Rugby, Hockey,
Football and Cricket, and for girls Hockey, Netball and
Rounders. Coaching and matches are also arranged in Athletics. Both winter and summer Tennis is played. Further
opportunities include Cross-country, Archery, Dance and

Squash. A very wide range of extra-curricular activities is available in the evenings, at weekends and on certain afternoons. Tennis and Golf facilities are excellent.

The Bridget More Hall offers outstanding facilities for Drama, Music and PE. Other facilities include a rifle range, an indoor swimming pool, two astroturf pitches, and a squash court. There are various holiday sports clubs and time to offer camping and outward-bound activities, such as canoeing, climbing, riding, skiing and leadership training.

School Prefects are taught to foster a caring concern for the well-being of every member of our community.

Children are prepared for Senior Independent Schools through lectures and workshops on international education, drugs, first aid and senior school life. All leavers at 13+ take part in a residential week of outdoor education. Our Leadership Training is first-rate and has led to the regular winning of all-rounder scholarships and the Gordonstoun Challenge.

The Pre-Preparatory Department occupies an Elizabethan Manor House, adjoining the school grounds. Whilst retaining a separate identity, the younger children are able to use the Main School facilities throughout the year.

Charitable status. Swanbourne House School is a Registered Charity, number 310640. It seeks to provide a continuous structured education for children aged 3–13 years.

Talbot Heath Junior School

Rothesay Road, Bournemouth BH4 9NJ
Tel: 01202 763360
Fax: 01202 768155
email: jsoffice@talbotheath.org
website: www.talbotheath.org

Chairman of Governors: Mr Graham Exon

Head Teacher: **Mrs Karen Leahy**, BA Hons, MA Ed

Age Range. Girls 3–11.
Number of Pupils. 200.
Our Ethos. We are immensely proud of our pupils and the happy atmosphere, where there is a genuine love of learning that permeates the school. The school, unique in the area in catering for girls from 3–18, is one where each individual really matters and is nurtured and valued. The School's motto is 'Honour Before Honours' and this underpins our community. We care for each other and support one another. Integrity and character lie at the heart of who we are.

We have a strong family atmosphere where all have a chance to achieve at their own level across every area of the broad curriculum. Perhaps, more importantly, the girls are happy and see coming to school as something enjoyable and great fun.

Talbot Heath girls are confident but not arrogant, knowledgeable but not complacent, able to express their opinions but willing to listen to those of others, independent yet supportive, strong yet compassionate, principled but fun. They value what they have and they value others. They are original but can work as a team, are keen to play a role in the wider world but have a strong sense of community.

The academic tradition and ethos of the school depends on both the encouragement of hard work and diligence and the creation of a caring community. Pupils are from a wide range of abilities and emphasis is placed on becoming rounded individuals, experiencing the full breadth of an extensive curriculum and achieving at their own personal level. Home school links are strong and positive which helps to create the caring and supportive environment of which we are so proud. Our results, right from the first steps in EYFS, are outstanding but the school places value on so much more than just results.

Facilities. The Junior School, housed in its own buildings on our woodland campus, is split into two departments, Pre-Prep (age 3–7) and Junior (age 7–11). Apart from large, spacious classrooms, Juniors have their own hall, two dining rooms, three computer suites, two libraries, a studio, a Science room and large outdoor play facilities including woodland trails, playgrounds and an adventure playground.

In addition to this they make use of all the Senior School facilities as they progress through school including the dedicated Music School, the Sports' Hall, athletics track, all-weather pitches, courts and gym, Science Centre and Creative Arts block. The girls are taught by subject specialists for Music and PE from Reception onwards. Once the girls reach Year 4 they are taught by academic subject specialists for the majority of their curriculum.

Fees per term (2014–2015). £1,886–£3,355.

Charitable status. Talbot Heath School Trust Limited is a Registered Charity, number 283708.

Taunton Preparatory School

Staplegrove Road, Taunton, Somerset TA2 6AE
Tel: 01823 703307; Admissions: 01823 703303
email: tpsenquiries@tauntonschool.co.uk
website: www.tauntonschool.co.uk

Chairman of the Governors: Mrs Jane E Barrie, OBE, BSc, ARCS, FSI

Headmaster: **Mr Duncan Sinclair**, MA, HDE

Deputy Headmaster: Mr William Newman, MA
Assistant Head – Teaching and Learning: Mrs Marian Drew, MA
Senior Master: Mr Chris Coleman, BA Hons

Age Range. 0–13.
Number of Pupils. Day 420; Boarders 33.
Fees per term (2014–2015). Prep: Boarders £4,150–£7,520; Day £2,450–£4,610 Pre-Preparatory & Nursery (full-time) £2,130.

Taunton Preparatory School is the Preparatory School of Taunton School (q.v.) and shares its aim to prepare young people to shape a changing world in the 21st century. The School offers a broad and balanced and forward-thinking education in a friendly, Christian community, in which pupils can develop their confidence, talents and interests. Classes and academic sets are small, allowing close personal attention to each child. All children are encouraged to mix easily with each other and with adults, and it is a principle of the School's teaching that learning is best achieved through the fostering of enthusiasm and the development of an enquiring mind. Kindness and courtesy are highly prized qualities.

The Preparatory School was almost entirely rebuilt in 1994 to provide outstanding academic, cultural and athletic facilities. The new teaching facilities include 4 dedicated Science laboratories, Art, Design Technology and IT suites, a well-resourced library and spacious classrooms. A second Junior Art/Technology room, a further ICT suite and a dance studio are recent additions.

Boarding care of a high standard is provided and the School prides itself on its high standards of catering and individual care for all its pupils. Full and Flexi boarding are on offer. An ambitious weekend programme of activities is organised. The School welcomes pupils from overseas, enjoying a close relationship with Taunton School's own International Middle School. The School has close links with the Armed Services – a generous Bursary scheme is well established.

Music, Drama and Dance are highly valued and the School received Artsmark Gold accreditation in 2012. The school offers opportunities to join nine instrumental ensembles, String Orchestra, Wind Band and seven Choirs. Over 200 children learn an instrument. There is an annual choir tour abroad – to Rome in 2012. Pupils are encouraged to participate in festivals, concerts and to take examinations.

Sporting facilities at Taunton School are quite exceptional. The Preparatory School enjoys its own Sports Centre comprising an indoor heated 25 metre Swimming Pool and Sports Hall. The main boys' games are Rugby, Hockey and Cricket whilst girls are offered Netball, Hockey, Tennis and Rounders. Athletics, Swimming and Biathlon are all particularly strong. All-weather playing surfaces and extensive grass pitches are available within the campus.

The broad curriculum is supported by a full programme of extra-curricular activities including Street Dance, Thinking Games, Fencing, Squash, Horse Riding, Debating, Drama, golf, Modelling and Filmakers. The School is a keen supporter of the Scout movement, with its own dedicated camping facility off site.

A thorough grounding is given in core subjects and all children learn three modern languages during their time in the School. The requirements of an extended National Curriculum are met by enthusiastic and committed staff. There are scholarships at 11+ and 13+ (for entry to the Senior School). Art, Sports, Music and All-Rounder Scholarships and Awards are also offered. There are a number of ministerial bursaries and awards at 11+.

There is a purpose-built Nursery and Pre-Prep, which enjoys its own excellent classrooms, hall, library, computers and recreational facilities and has full access to the Preparatory School's Sports Centre. Each nursery teacher is supported by nursery practitioners and all infant class teachers are supported by a teaching assistant.

A comprehensive prospectus is available from The Admissions Secretary.

Charitable status. Taunton School is a Registered Charity, number 1081420. It exists to provide a high standard of education for children.

Taverham Hall Preparatory School

Taverham, Norwich, Norfolk NR8 6HU
Tel: 01603 868206
Fax: 01603 861061
email: enquire@taverhamhall.co.uk
website: www.taverhamhall.co.uk

Chair of Governors: Mrs Sharon Turner

Headmaster: **M A Crossley**, NPQH, BEd Hons

Deputy Headmaster: J Worrall, BSc, Dip Teach, EIHC Level 3 Health and Safety

Age Range. 2½–13.
Number of Pupils. 289: Prep 165, Pre-Prep 84, Nursery 40.
Fees per term (2014–2015). Weekly Boarding £5,750; Day (including lunch): Prep £3,700–£4,450; Pre-Prep £3,200.

Nursery (per session): £32.50 (morning), £45.50 (all day), Lunch £2.50 per day.

Taverham Hall Preparatory School was founded in 1921 and is a co-educational IAPS day and flexi/weekly boarding school which offers an exceptional education in an idyllic 100-acre woodland location with excellent facilities for children aged 2½–13. The school is situated in Norfolk's well-known Ringland area which is easily accessible via the A47 north-west of Norwich.

There is an educational focus firmly on the individual and personalised learning along with a continued commitment to small class sizes. The high standards achieved by pupils are

recognised by both senior schools and inspection teams. Since 2010 the school has received four outstanding inspection reports in as many years as well as the Healthy Schools Award, demonstrating the importance Taverham Hall places on emotional health and well-being. The school is dedicated to providing outstanding pastoral care combined with personalised, academic learning programmes and investigative hands-on Forest School experiences. Taverham Hall offers a breadth of opportunities together with a focus on how children learn rather than what they learn. The school's inspiring teaching staff identify learning styles, set personalised targets and tailor teaching to the individual, ensuring that each child has every opportunity to achieve their personal best. Through small classes and individual academic guidance and a carefully thought out PSHE program, pupils are encouraged to analyse their strengths and target their weaknesses.

Specialist teachers throughout the school ensure children flourish in the school's vibrant, warm and friendly atmosphere. Pupils are heard to read every day in the Pre-Prep department whilst pupils in the Nursery and Reception classes follow a new bespoke curriculum which draws on the strengths of the Early Years curriculum whilst crucially offering children, who are ready, the opportunity to read and write at a younger age and to develop their mathematical skills beyond the current levels of expectation. The introduction of this bespoke curriculum has only been possible as a result of Taverham Hall's two excellent inspections with an 'outstanding' grading from Ofsted – the basis on which the school has been allowed to exit the EYFS framework whilst maintaining the funding. This is a fabulous time for the school to build on such solid foundations.

High pupil achievements contribute to the school's excellent record for placing Year 8 pupils at senior schools as well as obtaining senior school scholarships each year.

As pupils approach Common Entrance and Scholarship examinations, there is a greater move towards independence. Pupils take increased responsibility for their learning and conduct, as well as obtaining leadership roles within the school, including Prefect status and mentoring Year 3 pupils when in Year 8. Both the School's Council and Boarders' Forum provide pupils with a voice and an opportunity to play an active role in the school's community as well as enhancing ways in which pupils can communicate with staff and the school in general. In their top two years pupils are taught life skills which culminate in an exciting post-Common Entrance programme with a clear focus on fun, adventure and teamwork.

Inspection Reports and Awards can be viewed via the school's website: www.taverhamhall.co.uk.

Taverham Hall's Open Mornings take place in October, January and May.

Charitable status. Taverham Hall is a Registered Charity, number 311272. It exists for the purpose of educating children.

Terra Nova School

Jodrell Bank, Holmes Chapel, Cheshire CW4 8BT
Tel: 01477 571251
Fax: 01477 571646
email: office@tnschool.co.uk
website: www.tnschool.co.uk

Chairman of Governors: M C Hallam

Headmaster: **Mark Mitchell**, BSc, PGCE

Age Range. 3–13 Co-educational.
Number of Pupils. 304.
Fees per term (2014–2015). Seniors: Day £3,550–£4,440, Flexi boarding £33 per night, Weekly boarding £99

per week. Juniors: £2,990*. Nursery: £1,450* (*Free Early Education Entitlement for three and four year olds).

Terra Nova School is nestled in 36 acres of the Cheshire countryside and caters for children from Nursery through to Year 8. Children are encouraged to aim high and believe in themselves; happiness, confidence and excellent personal achievement are our priorities.

Results from Reception to Year 8 indicate that pupils are typically working significantly higher than national levels of achievements. We have a 100% pass rate at 11+ and 13+.

Our Early Years Foundation Stage and Junior School experience is unrivalled and we have the results to prove it! Facilities include a large outdoor learning environment with woodland, outdoor classrooms, willow theatre, adventure play area, and multi-sensory zones giving children the freedom to explore beyond the classroom in a safe environment.

In the Seniors children are given opportunities to excel academically, socially and physically through our extensive sporting activities, all of which take place in our stunning grounds. They are also introduced to boarding or 'staying the night', with our flexible boarding options from Year 3.

Our Years 7 & 8 experience gives pupils great preparation for life at senior day or boarding school, as well as an extra two years in which to develop academically at a crucial time in their emotional and social development.

Based six and a half miles from Alderley Edge our location is rural but our technology connects children to the world whilst they benefit from a peaceful environment in which to thrive.

2014 was a remarkable year for Terra Nova with our Year 8 pupils moving on to some of the UK's leading independent day and boarding schools, such as Fettes College, Malvern College, Radley College, Repton School, Rugby School, Sedbergh School, Shrewsbury School, Stowe School, and Uppingham School.

For more information call Melanie Machin on 01477 572261.

Charitable status. Terra Nova School Trust Limited is a Registered Charity, number 525919. It is dedicated to all round educational excellence for children.

Terrington Hall

Terrington, York YO60 6PR
Tel: 01653 648227
Fax: 01653 648458
email: office@terringtonhall.com
website: www.terringtonhall.com

Chairman of Governors: Mr Roger Hobson

Headmaster: **Mr Stephen Mulryne**

Age Range. 3–13 years.
Number of Children. 150: 80 boys, 70 girls (Boarding 15, Day 135).
Fees per term (2014–2015). Boarding: £6,000; Day (including lunch): £4,220 (Years 5–8), £4,100 (Year 4), £4,000 (Year 3), £2,630 (Year 2), £2,490 (Year 1), £2,350 (Reception & Nursery). Day Pupils in Years 3 to 8 receive two free nights' boarding per term.

Terrington is a co-educational school situated in beautiful countryside in the Howardian Hills (an area designated to be of Outstanding Natural Beauty) some fifteen miles from the City of York.

Terrington is busy and vibrant seven days a week but all activities are available to day pupils, many of whom convert to boarding in their final years in preparation for the next stage of their education.

Terrington prepares pupils for all the leading independent schools in the North and further afield and is particularly

proud of the twenty scholarships and exhibitions won by its pupils in the last three years.

The school enjoys excellent sporting facilities, with eight acres of playing fields, tennis courts, indoor heated swimming pool and Sports Hall. All major sports are played and, in addition, Athletics, Cross Country, Fencing, Gymnastics, Judo, Riding, Orienteering, Sailing, Canoeing and Clay Pigeon Shooting are available. There is an extensive outdoor education programme with all children learning to canoe/kayak. The school has its own climbing wall.

Teaching facilities are modern and well-equipped and they include a Computer Suite, two Science Labs and a Middle School Block. Music, Art and Drama all form an important part of the curriculum. Tuition is available for most instruments and children can be prepared for Associated Board exams. There are two choirs and a very successful Wind Band, which has recently toured overseas. There are at least two major drama productions each year.

The School Chaplain is the local Rector and boarders attend the village Church most Sundays. Each day starts with a short act of worship.

The Headmaster, his wife and children live in the school and the pupils are very much part of an extended family. A wide range of activities is followed at weekends and full use is made of the surrounding countryside. Parents are fully involved in the life of the school and there is a flourishing social committee.

The school welcomes children whose parents live overseas and an escort service is provided to collect and deliver the children from airports at the beginning and end of term. There is a bus service to the Salisbury area available at half-terms.

A number of Entrance Scholarships are available for children under eleven and there are Bursaries for sons and daughters of Clergy and HM Forces Personnel.

Charitable status. Terrington Hall is a Registered Charity, number 532362. It exists to provide a quality education for boys and girls.

Thorngrove School

The Mount, Pantings Lane, Highclere, Newbury, Berkshire RG20 9PS
Tel: 01635 253172
Fax: 01635 254135
email: admin@thorngroveschool.co.uk
website: www.thorngroveschool.co.uk

Headmaster: **Mr Adam King**, BA Hons QTS Leeds, PG Dip Ed

Age Range. 2½–13 Co-educational.
Number of Pupils. 220 Day Pupils.
Fees per term (2014–15). Reception–Year 2 £4,060; Year 3 and 4 £4,560; Year 5–8 £5,080.

Thorngrove School was founded in 1988 by Nick and Connie Broughton, the Principals. It is a co-educational day school for children aged 2½ to 13 years. The purpose-built facilities are set in former farmland in the village of Highclere, 5 miles south of Newbury and 12 miles north of Andover.

The school started with just 14 children. Due to its success and unique atmosphere the school flourished and grew in size year on year. There are currently 220 pupils at Thorngrove. Over the years facilities have been built and extended. In 1996 The Old Hall was enlarged to provide more space for Physical Education and lunches and staff accommodation was built adjacent to the Main Building. In 2000 The Senior Block was built. This provided exceptional facilities including a large Music Room with numerous individual practice rooms; a fully resourced Science Laboratory;

a light and airy Art Room as well as several teaching classrooms. In 2007 an architect-designed Sports Hall was built. This magnificent building not only has a large multi-purpose hall, but also houses an IT suite, changing rooms and several teaching classrooms and offices.

The beautiful grounds have always been a key feature of the school. These have also been extended and now stretch over 25 acres. The children are lucky enough to have access to woodland areas and a small stream runs through the campus. The extensive playing fields are the envy of many a visiting team. The latest addition, partly funded by the children's school council, is an Adventure Play Area which has been positioned beside the tennis courts and astroturf pitch.

In the summer of 2009 Mr and Mrs Broughton stepped back from running the school and appointed Adam King as Headmaster. In 2010 a D&T centre was opened to provide a facility for children in Year 4 and above to work with resistant materials. In addition to this, a unique eco-garden was created just behind the Senior Block with chickens, raised beds and a fruit cage (much of the produce is used by the kitchens). In 2012 a new Nursery was opened next to the Reception Form in the main building to create a wonderful Early Years setting. The latest project is the creation of an outdoor education programme in the beautiful woods involving every child in the school.

Thorpe House School

Oval Way, Gerrards Cross, Bucks SL9 8QA
Tel: 01753 882474
Fax: 01753 889755
email: office@thorpehouse.co.uk
website: www.thorpehouse.co.uk

Chairman of the Governors: Mr Richard Coward, MA

Headmaster: **Mr T Ayres**, BA Hons, PGCE

Age Range. Boys 3–16.
Numbers of Pupils. 299 Day Pupils.
Fees per term (2014–2015). Y7–11 £4,635, Y3–6 £3,940, Y1&2 £3,150, Reception £3,000, Nursery £1,500–£2,400.

Thorpe House was founded as a Boys' Prep School in 1923 with the Pre-Prep department established in 1964. The School became a Charitable Trust in 1986 and in 2006 it increased its age range to become a school catering for boys between the ages of 3 and 16.

Situated in an urban setting on the outskirts of Gerrards Cross the School thrives on its 'small school' environment and caters for boys of all abilities and interests. The Nursery class takes boys in the September following their 3rd birthday and then many others join Reception the following year. At the end of the pre-prep stage boys move to the Junior School in the main school building where they start to be taught by the specialist staff in music, ICT, DT, French and PE/Games: specialist teaching in all subjects starts in Year 5. At the end of Year 6 around half the boys leave to enter local grammar schools. Those who stay on are joined by an equal number of new entrants who then form the class groups who will progress through to GCSE, although some move on to independent senior schools at 13 via the Common Entrance or scholarship examinations. Class sizes throughout the school never exceed 16. The school's examination record at GCSE is very strong with a 100% record to date of pupils gaining at least 6 passes at C or above and pupils often gaining a full set of A and A* passes.

Although academic progress and excellence is a fundamental aspect of school life it is far from being the only focus. The boys excel at a variety of cultural activities. Music, drama, art and design technology are popular GCSE courses and boys of all ages enjoy studying these subjects and taking part in practical activities. Well over half of all recent Associated Board Music examination passes have been at Merit or Distinction level and following the latest GCSE Art exhibition one of the pupils was given a commission. The school works closely with the nearby St Mary's Girls' School to give both sets of pupils the opportunity to work together in a number of different cultural activities.

Sport is another central aspect of school life. The school has a seven-acre playing field and an outdoor swimming pool. The main team sports are rugby, football, cricket and athletics and the school puts out teams from Under 8 to Under 16 level against a wide variety of schools from the local area and further afield. These teams are very successful but the school is very proud of its Sport for All ethos and bringing on the less sporty boys is another important aspect of school life.

When the school extended its age range an extensive programme of new building and refurbishment was undertaken and the school now has improved facilities for Science, Art, Design Technology and ICT The school is now able to offer a full and modern range of facilities and all normal school experiences can take place on site. In addition the school runs a very extensive programme of extra-curricular clubs and activities, some of which such as sailing, golf and tennis involve taking advantage of local amenities.

The school offers before and after school care and arrangements to take this up are completely flexible. A bus service is also available to pick up and take home boys from certain areas.

Charitable status. Thorpe House School Trust is a Registered Charity, number 292683. It exists to provide education to boys.

Thorpe House Langley Preparatory School and Nursery

7 Yarmouth Road, Thorpe St Andrew, Norwich, Norfolk NR7 0EA
Tel: 01603 433055
Fax: 01603 436323
email: jberry@thlps.co.uk
website: www.thlps.co.uk

Chairman of the Governors: Mrs M Alston, JP

Headmaster: **P Oldroyd**, BA, PGCE

Age Range. 2–11 co-educational.
Number of Pupils. 230.
Fees per term (2014–2015). £2,315 (Reception–Year 2), £2,805 (Years 3–6). Nursery (per session): £42 (full day), £28 (half day).

The school is situated in 10 acres of gardens, woodlands and playing fields and is close to the city centre. Facilities include an indoor swimming pool, fully-equipped gymnasium, a large sports hall, dance studio, library, art studio, cookery room, science laboratory, IT suite and technology workshop. The entire site is networked with secure internet access.

Pupils are taken from the age of 2 into Nursery or at age 4 into Reception Class. Entry into school thereafter is dependent upon availability and follows a trial day and receipt of a satisfactory report from the previous school.

Children are prepared for many schools, but principally for entry to Langley School at the age of 11+. (*See Langley School entry in The Society of Heads section.*) Qualified and experienced staff maintain a purposeful academic atmosphere, but there is a friendly and caring family environment where children can discover individual talents and abilities so that they will be well prepared for the secondary stage of their education. A broad curriculum is followed, and classes rarely exceed 16. English, Mathematics, Science and ICT form the core of the curriculum, but from Year 3 subject specialists teach Design Technology, Art, Drama, French, Music and Humanities.

Hockey, rugby, soccer, netball, cricket, rounders and tennis are the main team games. Activities operate at the end of the school day and offer the chance for children to try numerous other sports, music and drama activities, including sailing, ten pin bowling, dry slope skiing, archery, golf, orienteering, karate, and so on. The school is particularly strong at chess with many pupils representing the county and country.

There is a fine tradition of drama and public speaking. We participate in local speech, drama and music festivals and there are many opportunities for performances in music and drama every year.

Experienced and qualified staff run the Nursery, which caters for 2 to 4 year olds. It is well equipped and has a large secure outside learning environment. Nursery hours are flexible and a child-minding service is offered after school hours. The Nursery has been Ofsted inspected and is a registered provider under the government scheme. It is open during school term time and some of the holidays.

Charitable status. Langley School is a Registered Charity, number 311270.

Tockington Manor

Washingpool Hill Road, Tockington, Bristol BS32 4NY
Tel: 01454 613229
Fax: 01454 613676
email: admin@tockingtonmanorschool.com
website: www.tockingtonmanorschool.com

Chairman of Governors: G Sheppard

Headmaster: **Stephen Symonds**, BA Ed Hons

Age Range. Boys and Girls aged 2–13+.
Number of Pupils. 20 Boarders, 80 Day, 65 Infants, 80 Nursery.
Fees per term (2014–2015). Boarders £6,000–£6,600 (inclusive); Day £4,000–£4,600 (including meals); Lower School £2,995; Nursery £47.30 per day.

Tockington Manor School is an independent co-educational Preparatory school set in 28 acres of lovely countryside in the picturesque village of Tockington, South Gloucestershire. Pupils are welcomed from age 2 to 14 with boarding available from age 7.

We pride ourselves in delivering a varied timetable in small classes geared to the needs of each pupil but with emphasis on the core subjects of English, Mathematics and Science. We aim to provide an environment that is positive, supportive and disciplined within a warm, caring family atmosphere. Pupils are encouraged to be confident, considerate and accomplished free thinkers. All pupils take part in all aspects of school life, academic or otherwise, making the most of every moment. The boarding house has a real family atmosphere and aims to provide a caring environment which promotes the values of honesty, sharing and trust between the children.

Tormead Junior School

Cranley Road, Guildford, Surrey GU1 2JD
Tel: 01483 796073
Fax: 01483 450592
email: head@tormeadschool.org.uk
website: www.tormeadschool.org.uk
Twitter: @Tormead_JS

Chairman of Governors: C W M Herbert, Esq, BSc Hons

Head of Junior School: **Mrs Louise Salmond Smith**, BA East Anglia, MMus Hull, PGCE Gloucestershire, MBA Keele

Age Range. Girls 4–11.
Number of Girls. 205.
Fees per term (2014–2015). £2,330–£3,890.

Of all the gifts a girl can receive, none has more lasting value than a first-rate education, at a school in which she will be happy and successful. We believe this is achieved at Tormead. We encourage each girl to develop her talents to the full, instilling a life-long love of learning. The curriculum offers breadth and challenge, and ensures that each girl gains a fine foundation to her education – providing her with core skills and knowledge that will stand her in good stead for the future. Academic expectations are high but our aim is to achieve this through stimulating, enjoyable and well-taught lessons in a happy, friendly and relaxed school.

Entry is selective at age 4 and 7 by assessment. When space is available, entrance at all other year groups is considered. When the girls come for assessment into the Reception class they are invited to a 'Party' and we hope this provides an environment where we can see the potential for learning in the girls, whilst they enjoy a selection of fun activities. As the girls get older, assessment becomes more academically based. All the junior girls sit the entrance examination for the senior school and have priority on places over the external candidates.

The school prides itself on its high academic standards and expectation of the girls whilst ensuring teaching and learning is 'fun' including many first-hand experiences. The Early Years Foundation stage and National Curriculum are extended and enriched by skilled, enthusiastic staff. French is taught from Year 2 and Latin is added to the girls' timetable in Year 5. All girls enjoy specialist teaching in music, games and gymnastics and from Year 2 also in Design Technology. The ICT curriculum gradually builds up the skills of the girls, and by the end of the Junior School they are confidently using computers as a tool for learning in other subjects. SEN provision is provided on an individual needs basis, is not an issue in school and holds no stigma.

The girls enjoy numerous opportunities to be involved in extra-curricular activities. The aim of the school is to offer a comprehensive range of activities to allow each girl to find something during the week that she would like to participate in and so develop her talents in this area, regardless of their ability. Girls with a particular talent are taken on further in their chosen activity with additional practices. Extra-curricular activities (in addition to sports) include; art, LAMDA, Jazz band, instrumental ensembles, two orchestras, two choirs, gardening, computers, cookery and board games.

All the girls enjoy specialist teaching in all aspects of PE including swimming and gymnastics. All sport except swimming is catered for by facilities on the Junior or Senior School site and includes the use of the sprung floor gymnasium. The school enjoys success at the highly competitive GISGA gymnastics competition. The girls have regular fixtures in numerous sports, throughout the year, with neighbouring schools. The ethos of the school means that all girls have an opportunity to be involved in sporting (in fact, all) extra-curricular activities regardless of their ability. There are high expectations of behaviour both in and outside the classroom, but as this is the accepted norm the need for strong discipline is rare. When there are difficulties with friendships the girls know to seek help and all concerns are taken seriously by staff. Time is given to ensure any problem is resolved in a fair and lasting manner.

There are numerous opportunities during the year when parents enjoy seeing their girls 'in action'; weekly sporting fixtures, termly informal music concerts, an annual open afternoon, carol service, nativity, formal concert and summer play. In addition, parents help in the library, and organise special class social events.

Charitable status. Tormead Limited is a Registered Charity, number 312057.

Tower House School

188 Sheen Lane, East Sheen, London SW14 8LF
Tel: 020 8876 3323
Fax: 020 8876 3321
email: secretary@thsboys.org.uk
website: www.thsboys.org.uk

Chairman of Governors: Mr Jamie Forsyth

Headmaster: **Mr G Evans**, BSc, MA, PGCE

Age Range. 4–13.
Number of Boys. 180.
Fees per term (2014–2015). Reception and Year 1 £3,691, Years 2 and 3 £4,076, Senior School £4,186 (including residential trips and all school lunches).

Tower House is a day school established in 1931. The school stands in its own grounds and is conveniently situated near a number of bus routes and the local station.

Entry is at the age of 4+. Admission of boys after the age of 4+ depends very much on the availability of places. There is an entry test at this later stage and the Deputy Head interviews all boys.

The school prepares boys for Common Entrance and Scholarships to appropriate Independent Senior Schools.

The staff is fully qualified and includes specialists in art, music and games, which together with drama play an important part in the school curriculum. In addition to the full time staff, there are visiting teachers for piano, violin, woodwind, brass and guitar.

The school is well supplied with modern teaching aids, including computers. There is a well-equipped science laboratory, an art and technology room, library, and an ICT Room.

The principal games are rugby, soccer and cricket. Other sports include athletics, cross country, squash, swimming, tennis and watersports. There are many fixtures arranged with other schools.

A prospectus is available on application to the School Secretary.

Charitable status. Tower House School is a Registered Charity, number 1068844.

Town Close School

14 Ipswich Road, Norwich, Norfolk NR2 2LR
Tel: 01603 620180 (Prep)
             01603 626718 (Pre-Prep)
Fax: 01603 618256 (Prep)
             01603 599043 (Pre-Prep)
email: admissions@townclose.com
website: www.townclose.com

Chairman of Governors: Mr David Bolton, BSc, Dip FBA, FRAgS, FAAV

Headmaster: **Nicholas Bevington**, BA Hons, PGCE

Age Range. 3–13 Co-educational.
Number of Pupils. Prep 275, Pre-Prep 185.

Fees per term (2014–2015). £2,532–£3,953 including lunch and all single-day educational excursions. No compulsory extras.

Town Close School was founded in 1932 and became a Charitable Trust in 1968. The School is fully co-educational and is situated on a beautiful wooded site near the centre of Norwich. This location provides pupils with space and freedom and contributes substantially to Town Close's reputation as an outstandingly happy school.

There is a team of 57 talented teachers who aim to produce well-motivated, balanced, confident children, who are caring and sociable and who know the value of hard work. The children receive excellent teaching and are prepared for all major senior schools. In recent years, pupils have achieved highly in entrance and scholarship assessments to a range of the country's leading senior schools.

A modern teaching building stands at the heart of the School, containing a large, well-equipped library, an art room, an IT centre and 16 purpose-built classrooms. There are many other outstanding facilities including an indoor heated swimming pool, a new high-specification sports hall completed in July 2009, a new performance hall completed in January 2010 and a new, full-size, floodlit Astroturf opened in May 2011. Science and DT are taught in specialist buildings and the school places a high value on innovation, engineering and scientific discovery. The Pre-Prep occupies a magnificent converted house on the campus and also contains a multi-purpose hall, kitchens and a purpose-built Nursery wing opening onto fantastic outdoor facilities.

Nursery and Reception classes follow the Foundation Stage curriculum, an important element of which is outdoor learning. Children progress through a broad and varied programme of activities with a strong emphasis on the development of personal and social skills and on establishing positive attitudes to learning and to school life. Swimming, music and dance are taught by specialist teachers, while the rest of the curriculum is delivered by class teachers, ably supported by well-qualified teaching assistants.

Throughout the children's time at Town Close particular attention is paid to the teaching of good handwriting and spelling. Traditional core skills are valued very highly in addition to promoting children's use of digital technology. IT provision is extensive allowing children to become confident and proficient users. The Pre-Prep pupils use a range of children's software to develop key skills and Prep Department children build on this foundation using more sophisticated software, either in the computer room or on laptops and tablets. All sections of the School have filtered access to the internet across the network. The School Intranet contains interactive activities, images, lesson material and links to carefully selected websites. Interactive whiteboards are used throughout the School to support the curriculum.

Town Close has an excellent academic reputation and is also known for the quality of its sport, music, art, drama and its extensive co-curricular programme. Trips and expeditions form a valuable part of what is offered, and provide the balance essential for a full and rounded education. Activities take place during the lunch hour, after school, and occasionally at weekends. In terms of music, the School has a full orchestra, a variety of choirs and a wide range of ensembles. All children are encouraged to perform with regular high-quality concerts and plays.

Physical Education plays an important part in the development of each child, be they in the Nursery or in Year 8. Emphasis is placed on fostering healthy exercise, as well as encouraging a positive, competitive attitude, individual skills and teamwork. As well as providing all the usual opportunities for the major sports (rugby, netball, hockey, cricket and athletics), coaching is offered in many other sports.

A copy of the School's prospectus is available on request, while a visit to www.townclose.com will provide a fuller picture of the School, including a sight of the most recent inspection report, in which the Town Close was given the highest rating in every area.

Charitable status. Town Close House Educational Trust Limited is a Registered Charity, number 311293. It exists to provide education for children.

Truro Preparatory School

Highertown, Truro, Cornwall TR1 3QN
Tel: 01872 272616
Fax: 01872 222377
email: enquiries@truroprep.com
          admissions@truroprep.com
website: www.truroprep.com

Chairman of the Governors: Mr K Conchie

Headmaster of Truro School: Mr A S Gordon-Brown, BCom Hons, MSc, CA SA

Headmaster of Preparatory School: **Mr M J Lovett**, BA Ed Hons

Head of Pre-Prep: Mrs S Hudson, MA, BEd Hons

Age Range. 3–11.
Number of Pupils. 260: 152 Boys, 108 Girls.
Fees per term (2014–2015). Prep (including lunch): £3,740 (Years 3–4), £3,885 (Years 5–6). Pre-Prep (including lunch): £2,850 (Nursery and Reception). £2,965 (Years 1 and 2).

Optional extras: Individual music lessons, fencing, dance, judo.

Truro School Prep was opened as Treliske School in 1936 in the former residence and estate of Sir George Smith. The school lies in extensive and secluded grounds to the west of the cathedral city of Truro, three miles from Truro School. The grounds command fine views of the neighbouring countryside. The drive to the school off the main A390 is almost 800 metres and Truro Golf Course also surrounds the school, so producing a campus of beauty and seclusion.

The keynote of the school is a happy, caring atmosphere in which children learn the value of contributing positively to the school community through the firm and structured framework of academic study and extra-curricular interests. The approach is based firmly in Christian beliefs and the school is proud of its Methodist foundation.

Building development has kept pace with modern expectations and Truro School Prep has its own large sports hall, an indoor heated swimming pool, a design and technology workshop with a computer room adjoined and purpose-built Pre-Prep.

The games programme is designed to encourage all children, from the keenest to the least athletic, to enjoy games and physical exercise. Our excellent facilities and the diverse skill of our staff enable us to offer a rich variety of sporting and recreational pursuits. There are over 20 popular clubs and activities run each week from 4.00 pm to 5.00 pm.

There is a strong school tradition in music and drama and the arts. Children may choose to learn a musical instrument from the full orchestral range. Each year the November concert, with Truro School, allows the school to show the community the excellent talents, which flourish in both schools.

Close links are maintained with the Senior School and nearly all pupils progress through at age 11 on the Headmaster's recommendation to Truro School which is the only Independent Headmasters' and Headmistresses' Conference School in Cornwall (*see entry in HMC section*).

The prospectus and further details can be obtained from the Headmaster's Secretary, and the Headmaster will be pleased to show prospective parents around the school.

Charitable status. Truro School is a Registered Charity, number 306576. It is a charitable foundation established for the purpose of education.

Twickenham Preparatory School

Beveree, 43 High Street, Hampton, Middlesex TW12 2SA
Tel: 020 8979 6216
Fax: 020 8979 1596
email: office@twickenhamprep.co.uk
website: www.twickenhamprep.co.uk

Chairman of Governors: Mr H Bates

Headmaster: **Mr D Malam**, BA Hons Southampton, PGCE Winchester

Age Range. 4–13.
Number of Pupils. Boys 145, Girls 130.
Fees per term (2014–2015). £3,225–£3,490. Lunch £175–£190.

Founded in 1969, Twickenham Prep is an independent school for boys and girls situated in Hampton. We are a happy, vibrant, and thriving school where every child is valued as an individual and inspired to achieve their full potential, personally, socially and academically. The pupils benefit from small classes, first-class facilities, specialist subject teaching and excellent pastoral care.

The children enter the Pre-Prep, a light and spacious purpose-built building, at the age of 4. They then automatically transfer at age 7 into the Prep which is located in a Grade II listed building in the Hampton Conservation area.

The girls sit entrance exams at 11+ and the boys Common Entrance at 13+ and all move on to some of the leading senior schools in the area, many with scholarships.

Our curriculum is based on the National Curriculum with specialist teaching of PE, Games, ICT, French, Music and Mind Lab (an innovative thinking skills programme) from Reception ensuring a balanced educational experience. Art/Design and Technology is introduced in Year 3 and from Year 4 pupils have specialist teaching in all subjects, with Latin being introduced in Year 5. Class sizes are about 18, developing each pupil to their full academic potential and promoting high academic standards. The school is well equipped to cover the full range of subjects, with purpose-built Art/DT, Science and Music facilities and a modern sports hall used for PE and termly productions.

Strong emphasis is placed on participation by all in sporting, musical and extra-curricular activities. The school plays a wide range of sports and has recently formed an affiliation with Kempton Cricket Club to provide 10 acres of dedicated sporting facilities for rugby, football, cricket and rounders. The girls also play netball and hockey, with athletics and swimming also part of the sporting curriculum. Music and drama play a large part in the school with full-scale productions and concerts annually involving all pupils. There is a school choir and individual instrumental lessons are taught by visiting specialists.

Twickenham Prep are recent National Independent Chess Champions and the current National Mind Lab Champions; we represented the UK at the 2014 Mind Lab Olympics, held in Budapest, winning the first ever individual Gold Medal.

There are also many extra-curricular clubs during and after school to choose from and from September 2014 we have extended our wrap-around care provision from 8 am to 6 pm.

A morning minibus service is available from Kew, Richmond, Twickenham, Teddington, St Margaret's, Hampton Wick and Isleworth.

Regular Open Days are held and personal tours are available – the pupils and Headmaster would be delighted to show you around. Please contact the school office.

Charitable Status. Twickenham Preparatory School is a Registered Charity, number 1067572. It exists to provide education for boys and girls.

Twyford School

Winchester, Hampshire SO21 1NW
Tel: 01962 712269
Fax: 01962 712100
email: registrar@twyfordschool.com
website: www.twyfordschool.com

Chairman of Governors: Mr S P Kelly

Headmaster: **Dr S J Bailey**, BEd, PhD, FRSA

Age Range. 3–13.
Number of Children. 403. Main School: 281 (145 boys, 140 girls, of whom 91 are weekly and flexi boarders); Pre-Prep: 122 (71 boys, 51 girls).
Fees per term (2014–2015). Weekly Boarding £7,415; Day £5,892; Year 3 £4,914; Pre-Prep £2,876–£3,307. Fees are inclusive of all outings/trips run during the term. Bursaries are available.

Twyford School is situated at the edge of the beautiful South Downs just two miles from the historic city of Winchester and the M3. Twyford is a family school that aims to offer an all-round top-rate education with a Christian ethos. Boarding is central to life at Twyford. Most pupils start as day pupils, but by the end of their last year over 80% are weekly boarding through the school's flexi boarding system, which makes an excellent preparation for their move to senior school. The contrast between the modern facilities (classrooms, laboratories, music school, creative arts and ICT block, swimming pool and sports centre) and the Victorian chapel and hall creates a rich and stimulating environment.

The school regularly achieves scholarships – 77 awards (academic, art, design, sport and music) in the last 5 years – to major senior schools such as Winchester, St Swithun's, Canford, Marlborough, Harrow, Cheltenham Ladies' College, Wycombe Abbey, Radley and Sherborne.

Charitable status. Twyford School is a Registered Charity, number 307425. It exists to provide education for children.

Unicorn School

238 Kew Road, Richmond, Surrey TW9 3JX
Tel: 020 8948 3926
email: registrar@unicornschool.org.uk
website: ~www.unicornschool.org.uk

Chairs of Governors: Mrs Anne Fowler and Mr Paul Rathbone

Headmaster: **Mr Kit Thompson**

Age Range. 3–11.
Number of Children. 172 Day Pupils: 85 boys, 87 girls.
Fees per term (2014–2015). £2,000–£3,670.
Unicorn is a parent-owned IAPS prep school founded in 1970. Situated opposite Kew Gardens, the school occupies a large Victorian house and converted coach house with a spacious, superbly-equipped new playground and garden.

The school has free and unrestricted access to Kew Gardens and the sports facilities at the nearby Old Deer Park are used for games and swimming.

There are 10 full-time teachers, supported by 13 part-time assistants and specialist teachers, with visiting teachers for music, individual tuition and clubs. Classes average 21 children.

Unicorn aims to give children a firm foundation and a broad education. A variety of teaching methods are used and the children are regularly assessed. Importance is placed upon the development of the individual and high academic standards are achieved. The main point of entry is to nursery at 3+ and the majority of children stay the full eight years. Children are prepared for entry at 11+ to the leading London Day Schools, as well as a variety of boarding schools.

There is a specialist IT room and networked computers in every classroom. At nine years old all children take an intensive touch-typing course. In addition, there is a Science and Design Technology suite with interactive whiteboard technology in all classrooms.

The curriculum includes Drama, French (from age 5), Art and Music – with individual music lessons offered in piano, violin, cello, clarinet, saxophone, flute, guitar and trumpet, as well as singing. Recorder groups, choirs, an orchestra and a wind band also flourish.

In addition to the major games of football, rugby, hockey, netball, cricket, rounders and athletics, there are optional clubs for tennis, squash, badminton, ice skating, golf, riding, sailing and self-defence. Other club activities include arts and crafts, cookery, mini Glee, mosaic, pottery, riding, sailing and trampolining. There are regular visits to the theatre and museums as well as the galleries of Central London. All children, from the age of seven upwards, participate in residential field study trips.

An elected School Council, with representatives from each age group, meets weekly with the Headmaster and a weekly newsletter for parents is also produced.

A happy, caring environment prevails and importance is placed on producing kind, responsible children who show awareness and consideration for the needs of others.

Charitable status. Unicorn School is a Registered Charity, number 312578. It exists to provide education for boys and girls.

University College School – Junior Branch

11 Holly Hill, Hampstead, London NW3 6QN
Tel: 020 7435 3068
Fax: 020 7435 7332
email: juniorbranch@ucs.org.uk
website: www.ucs.org.uk

Chairman of Council of Governors: The Rt Hon Sir Brian Leveson, MA, LLD Hon

Headmaster: **Mr L R J Hayward**, MA

Age Range. 7–11.
Number of Boys. 250.
Fees per term (2014–2015). £5,495.
The School was founded in 1891 by the Governors of University College, London. The present building was opened in 1928, but retains details from the Georgian house first used. It stands near the highest point of Hampstead Heath and the hall and classrooms face south. Facilities include a Science Laboratory, Library, Drama Studio, Music and Computer Rooms, and a Centre for Art and Technology. Boys receive their Swimming and PE lessons in the pool and Sports Hall at the Senior School, 5 minutes' walk away. The

Junior School has full use of the 27 acres of playing fields on games days.

Boys enter at 7+ each year and they are prepared for transfer to the Senior School at 11+. (*See entry in HMC section.*)

Charitable status. University College School, Hampstead is a Registered Charity, number 312748. The Junior Branch exists to provide education for boys aged 7+ to 11 years.

University College School – The Phoenix

36 College Crescent, Hampstead, London NW3 5LF
Tel: 020 7722 4433
Fax: 020 7722 4601
email: thephoenix@ucs.org.uk
website: www.ucs.org.uk/The-Phoenix-School

Chairman of Council: The Rt Hon Sir Brian Leveson, MA, LLD Hon

Headmistress: **Miss Caroline Froud**, MA

Age Range. 3–7 Co-educational.
Number of Pupils. 126.
Fees per term (2014–2015). £3,570–£4,010.

At The Phoenix, we firmly believe that happiness and self-esteem are the keys to success in every pupil's learning journey. The well-qualified and highly-supportive staff accompany each child on a voyage of educational and social discovery during the first years of school life.

The Phoenix School joined the UCS Foundation of Schools in 2002 and fully supports the aims and ethos of UCS: intellectual curiosity and independence of mind are developed, self-discovery and self-expression are fostered and a cooperative and collaborative approach to learning is of great importance.

For every child in our care, we provide a continuously positive and creative learning environment that allows the individual the opportunity to develop personal qualities and talents. We are able to cater for up to 140 pupils aged 3–7 in our well-resourced classrooms. At the end of Year 2, both girls and boys transfer to a range of local independent schools. Whilst it is hoped that most boys will transfer to the Junior Branch of UCS this is not automatic and is subject to meeting the required standard in the entrance examination. (*See separate Junior Branch entry.*)

Charitable status. The Phoenix School Limited is a Registered Charity, number 1098657.

Upton House School

115 St Leonard's Road, Windsor, Berkshire SL4 3DF
Tel: 01753 862610
Fax: 01753 621950
email: info@uptonhouse.org.uk
             registrar@uptonhouse.org.uk
website: www.uptonhouse.org.uk

Chairman of the Council: Mr G O J Story

Headmistress: **Mrs Madeleine Collins**, BA Hons, PGCE Oxon

Age Range. Girls 2–11 years, Boys 2–7 years.
Number of Pupils. 258 Day: 196 Girls, 62 Boys.
Fees per term (2014–2015). £1,084–£4,395 (inclusive).

The aim of Upton House is to foster a happy and stimulating environment in which each child can prosper academically, socially and emotionally. The school will prepare all children for their continuing education and enhance their awareness of the world in which they live.

Upton House School was founded in 1936 by benefactors and has evolved over the years to provide a well-equipped environment where children can thrive. The extensive facilities include music rooms, state-of-the-art ICT suite, science laboratory, two libraries, a fully-equipped gymnasium, a drama studio, a purpose-built food technology room and a new arts block which includes a media room, music room and art studio. The school aims to motivate every child to develop their potential to the full in a happy, lively and caring community. We believe in the importance of small classes taken by well-qualified, caring members of staff. In our broad, inclusive curriculum the children are taught from Nursery by subject specialists. They have the opportunity to benefit from the best possible teaching, and to be inspired by teachers who love their subjects and who are able to get the best from their pupils. Boys are prepared for entry to preparatory schools in the area at 7+. Girls leaving gain places at a wide range of senior schools and regularly win scholarships.

Entry is non-selective and means-tested bursaries (up to 100%) are available for those entering the school.

We provide care from 8.00 am in Early Birds until the end of the official teaching day. Children from the age of 3 are able to enjoy a late programme until 5.45 pm. A wide variety of clubs are offered in the late programmes as well as teacher-supervised prep.

We have an active PTA who organise many fundraising events through the year and help forge close links between the school and parents.

Charitable status. Upton House School is a Registered Charity, number 309095. It exists to provide an excellent all-round educational foundation for boys and girls.

Ursuline Preparatory School
Wimbledon

18 The Downs, Wimbledon, London SW20 8HR
Tel: 020 8947 0859
Fax: 020 8947 0885
email: admissions@ursuline-prep.merton.sch.uk
website: www.ursuline-prep.merton.sch.uk

A Catholic Independent day school.

Chair of Governors: Mr Francis Bacon

Headmistress: **Mrs Anne Farnish**, MA, PGCE, NPQH

Age Range. Girls 3–11, Boys 3–4.
Number of Pupils. 250+.
Fees per term (2014–2015). £3,016 full-time, £1,869 for part-time Nursery.

The Ursuline Preparatory School provides a happy and stimulating environment for girls aged 3–11 years and boys aged 3–4 years in our nursery unit.

The children enjoy a rich diversity of experiences both inside and outside of the classroom. Guest speakers, fundraising opportunities and school trips also provide valuable experiences. Each girl is strongly encouraged to give of her best academically and to take advantage of the opportunities provided during her time at The Ursuline Preparatory School. An extensive range of extra-curricular activities are available to suit different skills and talents. A thriving after-school care facility is also available.

Girls at 11+ leave very well prepared for the next stage of their educational career with a love of learning. In the spirit of our school motto Serviam pupils show care and concern for others and strive to achieve their personal best and look to the future with confidence keen to make a difference in the world.

We are a thriving IAPS school with a vibrant Catholic ethos welcoming pupils of all faiths who would benefit from our rigorous but nurturing learning environment.

Charitable status. Ursuline Preparatory School Wimbledon Trust is a Registered Charity, number 1079754.

The Ursuline Preparatory School Ilford

2–8 Coventry Road, Ilford, Essex IG1 4QR
Tel: 020 8518 4050
Fax: 020 8518 2060
email: urspsi@urspsi.org.uk
website: www.urspsi.org.uk

Chair of Governors: Mr Peter Nicholson

Head: **Ms Lisa Sevilla**

Age Range. 3–11 Co-educational.
Number of Pupils. 197.
Fees per term (2014–2015). Nursery: £159 per week full-time including lunch, pre- and after-school care, holiday care, £59 per week part-time including lunch. Reception–Year 6 £2,834 including lunch, pre- and after-school care, holiday care.

The Ursuline Preparatory School Ilford is a Roman Catholic day school in the trusteeship of the Ursuline Sisters. The Ursuline Sisters first came to England in 1862 settling at Forest Gate from where they established the school in Ilford in 1903 at 73 Cranbrook Road. The school has since flourished. Formerly part of The Ursuline Academy, The Ursuline Preparatory School Ilford is now a fully independent school in its own right, but continues to share close and valued links with the Academy.

As a Catholic school we firmly believe that Religious Education is the foundation of the entire educational process. Prayers and liturgical celebrations are an important aspect of school life, unifying the hearts and minds of all associated with the school and ensuring we are all working to achieve the best possible education for the children in our care.

We provide a safe, secure and stimulating environment for our pupils to thrive. We recognise each child's unique value and are committed to encouraging self-esteem and developing each child's potential. We encourage the children to become independent learners by building on their curiosity and desire to learn and developing their skills, concepts and understanding.

While the school continues to set its own high standards, we complement these with the integration of the best of the National Curriculum. English and mathematics form the core subjects together with Religious Education, science, history, geography, ICT, PE, drama, design technology, art, music, MFL and stimulating project work. The Performing Arts have a high profile in school and the children are regularly given the opportunity to develop their talents. Well-stocked libraries, audio-visual aids and a state-of-the-art specialist Information Communication Technology department are all available throughout the nursery and school.

We offer a wide range of extra-curricular activities including ballet, speech and drama and Irish Dancing. Other clubs and sports clubs including football, cricket, basketball, gymnastics and trampolining are held weekly. Individual instrumental tuition can be arranged for piano, violin, flute, clarinet and saxophone. There is also an award-winning school choir.

All teaching staff are fully qualified, experienced and dedicated to the ideals of the school. They work in close partnership with parents to ensure that each child's special individual needs are recognised. In addition, we have the help of experienced general assistants. Our pupil : teacher ratio is excellent and we are able to engage in small group teaching.

Pre- and after-school care and a holiday club are available. A variety of structured activities is planned for the children enrolled and refreshments are provided.

Charitable status. The Ursuline Preparatory School Ilford is a Registered Charity, number 245661.

Victoria College Preparatory School

Jersey, Channel Islands JE2 4RR
Tel: 01534 723468
Fax: 01534 780596
email: admin@vcp.sch.je
website: www.vcp.sch.je

Chairman of Governors: C Barton

Headmaster: **Russell Price**, BSc, MPhil

Age Range. 7–11.
Number of Boys. 300 Day Boys.
Fees per term (2014–2015). £1,600 (inclusive).
Victoria College Preparatory School was founded in 1922 as an integral part of Victoria College and is now a separate School under its own Headmaster, who is responsible for such matters as staffing, curriculum and administration. The Preparatory School shares Governors with Victoria College whose members are drawn from the leaders of the Island of Jersey with a minority representation from the States of Jersey Education Committee. Members of staff are all experienced and well-qualified teachers, including specialists in Music, Dance, Art, PE and French. Entry to the Prep School is at 7 and boys normally leave to enter Victoria College at the age of 11. The school games are cricket, football, athletics, swimming, hockey, cross-country and rugby. Sporting facilities are shared with Victoria College. Special features of the school are exceptionally high standards of sport, drama, music and French. Many visits, both sporting and educational, are arranged out of the Island.

A separate Pre-Preparatory School (5 to 7 years) is incorporated in a co-educational school situated at JCG Prep and offers places for boys whose parents wish them to be educated at both Victoria College and the Preparatory School. Candidates for Pre-Prep entry should be registered at JCG Prep, St Helier, Jersey.

Vinehall School

Robertsbridge, East Sussex TN32 5JL
Tel: 01580 880413
Fax: 01580 882119
email: office@vinehallschool.com
website: www.vinehallschool.com

Chairman of Governors: Mr W Foster-Kemp, LLB, ACA

Headmaster: **Richard Follett**, BA

Age Range. 2–13 co-educational.
Number of Children. 255: 30 boarders, 225 day children.

Fees per term (2014–2015). Day Pupil: Years 3–5 £5,195, Years 6–8 £5,352; Boarder: Years 3–5 £6,815 (full boarding), £6,295 (weekly boarding), Years 6–8 £6,981 (full boarding), £6,421 (weekly boarding); Pre-Prep: Reception, Years 1 & 2 £2,871; Nursery (without Early Years funding): £31.90 per morning session, £17.70 per afternoon session, £49.50 per full day session; Nursery (with Early Years funding): £28.30 per full day session.

Founded in 1938, Vinehall School is set within 47 acres of countryside in an area of outstanding natural beauty on the East Sussex/Kent border. A flourishing Pre-Prep for boys and girls aged 2 to 7 is situated in a modern, well-resourced and purpose-built building on the same site as the Prep School.

The School's first-class facilities include a magnificent Millennium Building, comprising classrooms, IT suite and library, a science block, music building, art, design and technology centre, a purpose-built theatre with seating for 250, a sports hall and adjoining indoor swimming pool, an Astro-Turf pitch, an adventure playground and a nine-hole golf course.

The curriculum, which is based on the National Curriculum but which extends far beyond, prepares pupils for Common Entrance, local grammar school entrance and scholarship entrance to a variety of independent senior schools. The innovative 'Learning Journey' curriculum (which begins in Year 3), stimulates enquiring young minds. The academic day finishes at 4.30 pm, with a wide range of clubs and enrichment activities until 5.20 pm when school buses leave. On Saturday mornings (apart from exeat weekends) there are optional Clubs and Enrichment activities for pupils in Years 3 to 8. A SENCO is available for those children who require additional support.

Games and the Arts are an integral part of the Vinehall timetable. Pupils participate in all major team sports and everyone has a chance to represent the School. Major girls games are netball, hockey, rounders and tennis and for boys, football, rugby, hockey, cricket and tennis. Swimming, gymnastics and athletics are also important sports throughout the year. Creative Arts are also strong, with flourishing Art, Music and Drama departments, all of which exhibit/perform regularly both inside and outside School. Carpentry and wood-turning are also offered.

Boarding is at the very heart of the School and Vinehall has a well-established boarding community, the majority being from Sussex, Kent and London. Weekly and full boarding are offered, as well as 'temp' boarding. There is a Junior boarding option for Years 3–6 (four nights per week) with children moving on to full or weekly boarding in Years 7 and 8. There are regular exeat weekends and a full and varied programme of weekend activities.

Charitable status. Vinehall School is a Registered Charity, number 307014. It exists to provide a secure, quality education, in particular for those in need of residential schooling.

Walhampton School

Lymington, Hampshire SO41 5ZG
Tel: 01590 613300
Fax: 01590 678498
email: office@walhampton.com
website: www.walhampton.com

Chairman of Governors: N A McGrigor

Headmaster: Mr Titus Mills, BA Hons

Age Range. 2–13.
Number of Pupils. Boarding boys 28, Boarding girls 14, Day children 157, Pre-Prep 137.

Fees per term (2014–2015). Boarding £6,930; Day £3,825–£5,185; Pre-Preparatory £2,675; Kindergarten & Nursery £24 per am/pm session. The only extras are: After-School Club, Riding, Individual Music, Learning Support tuition and Expeditions.

An independent day and boarding school for boys and girls aged 2–13, Walhampton lies in ancient woodland on the southern edge of the New Forest, on the coast near Lymington in Hampshire. With big vistas and broad horizons set within one hundred acres of lawns, lakes and woodland, the school's location is truly remarkable. Few prep schools can match Walhampton's setting.

Our pupils achieve consistently impressive academic results, taking their learning to the next level as they prepare for the country's leading senior schools. With small classes and outstanding teaching we prepare our boys and girls for 13+ Common Entrance and scholarships to senior independent schools including Winchester, Eton, St Swithun's, Canford, Clayesmore, Harrow, Radley and Bryanston. Academic standards at Walhampton are excellent and were strongly endorsed in our recent ISI report. We have enjoyed 100% success rate in Common Entrance for a number of years.

Our location and facilities enable us to offer a broad and dynamic curriculum, which stretches beyond the classroom. Lessons are taught in our kitchen garden, fields and woodland bringing Maths, English and Science to life while making sure sports, music and the arts flourish alongside academic disciplines. In how many other schools would you find the Battles of Trafalgar staged on a lake, or Hastings re-enacted with children in armour on horses?

As well as rigorous academic standards, Walhampton is passionate about breadth. It offers over 60 on-site extra-curricular activities including beekeeping, model railways, fishing, dance, archery, and shooting. There is a distinct 'Swallows and Amazons' spirit that burns brightly here. Sailing lessons take place on our lakes and horse riding is also popular in our equestrian centre.

Full, weekly and flexi boarders enjoy the relaxed and homely atmosphere of Bradfield House. Flexi boarding enables children to enjoy all that the school has to offer, while supporting families with busy lives.

At Walhampton, parents and children will find a school in a stunning location, with a distinctive ethos and tremendous spirit. A warm welcome awaits you at our Open Mornings on October 10th 2014, January 30th and 8th May 2015 from 10:00 to 12:30. Please contact the School Registrar on 01590 613 303 or at registrar@walhampton.com.

Walthamstow Hall Junior School

Bradbourne Park Road, Sevenoaks, Kent TN13 3LD
Tel: 01732 453815
Fax: 01732 456980
email: registrar@walthamstowhall.kent.sch.uk
website: www.walthamstow-hall.co.uk

Chairman of Governors: Ian Philip Esq, FCA

Head of the Junior School: Mrs Diane Wood, BSc Hons Durham, PGCE

Day School for Girls.
Age Range. 3–11.
Number of Girls. 220.
Fees per term (2014–2015). Kindergarten £270 per session (2–10 sessions per week); Reception–Year 2 £3,370, Years 3–6 £4,250.

Walthamstow Hall Junior School is a happy and vibrant school with a proud tradition of providing the highest quality education for girls aged 3–11 years.

From Reception upwards pupils benefit from being in small classes (up to 18 per class) with two parallel classes in each year group. Optimum-sized classes throughout the Junior School guarantee individual attention, with obvious benefits including a seamless and highly effective preparation for Senior School entrance exams without last-minute cramming and changes to routine.

A well-planned programme of education brings out the potential of each child as she progresses through the Junior School. A broad curriculum is enriched with many extra-curricular activities and clubs. After-school care is offered until 6 pm.

Girls are well prepared for a range of senior schools and have won awards to prestigious independent schools, including Walthamstow Hall Senior School (*see entry in GSA section*). Entry to our Senior School is from 11+, 13+ and 16+ with Awards, Scholarships and Bursaries offered. Equally, our track record in the Kent test is excellent.

Walthamstow Hall was founded in 1838 and is one of the oldest girls' schools in the country. It has built a reputation for 'all-round' excellence and achievements by girls are outstanding. Over recent years, many new facilities have been added including nursery classrooms, a library with computerised lending facility and a science laboratory. Girls have access to facilities at the nearby Senior School including the recently refurbished 'Ship Theatre' and swimming pool. A new Dining Hall and Pre-Prep facilities opened at the Junior School in 2014. The school is situated in the centre of Sevenoaks within easy reach of road and rail networks. Minibuses operate from surrounding towns and villages.

Warminster Preparatory School

Vicarage Street, Warminster, Wiltshire BA12 8JG
Tel: 01985 224800
Fax: 01985 218850
email: prep@warminsterschool.org.uk
website: www.warminsterschool.org.uk
Facebook: /Warminster-Prep
LinkedIn: /WarminsterSchool

Co-educational, Day & Boarding.

Chairman of Governors: The Right Hon Sir David Latham, QC

Headmaster: **David A H Edwards**, BEd, MA

Age Range. 3–11 co-educational.
Number of Pupils. 140.
Fees per term (2014–2015). Day: Reception £2,320; Years 1 & 2 £2,505; Year 3 £2,960; Year 4 £3,305; Years 5 & 6 £3,710. Boarding: £6,560.

Conveniently situated on the edge of Salisbury Plain with easy access to London and the South-West, Warminster Prep is a thriving school with a friendly, family atmosphere. Together with our Senior School, we make up Warminster School, providing exciting, high-quality education for children from 3 to 18 years old.

Fully-qualified and dedicated teaching staff deliver a vibrant and stimulating curriculum enriched with many trips and theme days. Our teaching in the Prep School is rich and varied in its styles to suit the diverse variety of children who thrive in our inclusive and holistic environment. We have Learning Support for those who may need it and an 'Able & Talented' club to ensure that all our children are achieving their potential in a supportive and caring atmosphere.

The curriculum is broad and balanced reflecting an ethos that values the development of skills and achievement in all subjects and areas of school life. Whilst the pursuit of excellence in core subjects is very important, Art, Sport, Music, Drama and Technologies are also vital areas in building confidence and self-esteem. Scholarships are available from Year 3 upwards as well as for Years 7 and 9 in the Senior School.

Totally flexible boarding arrangements exist for children from 7 years upwards. Under the auspices of our experienced, dedicated Matrons and House Parents, children enjoy a very high standard of Pastoral care with weekend trips and outings being a highlight of the week. A number of children are full boarders, but weekly and hotel boarding are very popular with, and a cost-effective service for, busy working parents. The Boarding Schools Allowance is available for serving members of HM Forces.

Sport is an important part of life at Warminster Prep, with a busy programme of inter-school fixtures in Rugby, Soccer, Hockey and Cricket for boys, and Hockey, Netball and Rounders for girls. In the summer term, children also swim and enjoy Tennis and Athletics.

Warminster Prep School has a strong creative tradition in the Arts; performing art in Music, Speech and Drama, visual art in a wide range of media including sculpture and fired clay.

The Prep (and Pre-Prep) School is well-equipped with its own catering and Dining Hall, modern fully-equipped Science lab, ICT suite, sports pitches, AstroTurf, Art and DT studio, well-equipped stage, tennis courts, Music and practice rooms and Library. This is in addition to the superb facilities we share with our adjacent Senior School such as the newly-opened Thomas Arnold Hall, swimming pool, Library, Chapel and Sports Hall. The Courtyard Nursery was opened in 2007 and provides superb accommodation for the Early Years Foundation Stage. The Nursery is oversubscribed and parents are advised to register for places in plenty of time.

We provide, for Day and Boarding children, a wide choice of clubs and activities. These augment our timetabled curriculum and ensure that children can develop their individual tastes and interests alongside more traditionally academic abilities. We include opportunities for foreign travel with our French Trip and Ski Trip.

Interested parents are invited to ring the Headmaster's Secretary for a prospectus and to arrange a visit and free taster-day.

For information about the Senior School, please see entry in HMC section.

Charitable status. Warminster School is Registered Charity, number 1042204, providing education for boys and girls.

Warwick Junior School

Myton Road, Warwick CV34 6PP
Tel: 01926 776418
Fax: 01926 776478
email: enquiries@warwickschool.org
website: www.warwickschool.org

Chairman of Governors: R M Dancey, MA

Head of Junior School: **G R G Canning**, BA, PGCE

Age Range. 7–11.
Number of Pupils. 250 boys.
Fees per term (2014–2015). Tuition: £2,948 (7+); £3,348 (8+/9+), £3,749 (10+).

The School is the Junior School of Warwick School. The Junior School is situated on a site on the outskirts of Warwick Town adjacent to Warwick Senior School. The buildings are contained within a four-acre site and enjoy the use of the Sports and other facilities of Warwick Senior School. A new extension to the school, providing six classrooms and a library, was completed in May 2002. A programme of refurbishment in the existing Junior School building was completed in September 2002 and this includes new ICT and DT rooms.

The aim of the School is to provide a good general education based on Christian principles. Academic standards are high and in particular participation in a range of activities is encouraged. Each pupil is encouraged to develop his own personality and to realise his own potential.

The curriculum gives a good grounding in English, Mathematics, Science, Technology, ICT, History, Geography, Religious Education, French, Art, Music, Performing Arts, Drama and PE. Many sporting activities are available on the fifty acre campus of Warwick School, which includes a sports hall and indoor swimming pool. Rugby and Soccer are the main winter sports, with Cricket in the summer, plus Athletics, Swimming, Tennis, Squash and Cross Country. Since 2008 the School has won six national sporting championships.

The School's creative activities, dramatic productions and musical performances provide a useful focus in the development of many talents within the School.

Boys benefit from an extensive extra-curricular programme of activity.

Warwick Junior School provides a schedule of Curriculum Support. This support is available both for boys who need some additional assistance in English and/or Maths and also for boys with specific learning difficulties such as dyslexia or dyspraxia.

Extended day facilities are available until 5.30 pm when pupils can either do their homework or enrol in the extensive clubs and activity programme.

Boys are prepared for the Entrance Examination to Warwick Senior School at age 11. The majority of pupils who leave Warwick Junior School gain a place in the Senior School at Warwick. (*See Warwick School entry in HMC section*)

Charitable status. Warwick Independent Schools Foundation is a Registered Charity, number 1088057. It exists to provide quality education for boys.

Warwick Preparatory School

Bridge Field, Banbury Road, Warwick CV34 6PL
Tel: 01926 491545
Fax: 01926 403456
email: info@warwickprep.com
website: www.warwickprep.com

Chairman of the Governors: Miss K A Parr

Headmaster: **Mr M Turner**, BA Hons, PGCE, NPQH

Age Range. Boys 3–7, Girls 3–11.
Number of Children. 122 Boys, 335 Girls.
Fees per term (2014–2015). Nursery: £1,993 (full time, after Nursery Education Funding). Lower School (4–6 years) £3,069; Middle and Upper Schools (7–11 years) £3,391. (Lunch included.)

Instrumental music tuition optional extra.

Warwick Preparatory School is an Independent School, purpose built on a 4½ acre site on the outskirts of Warwick. It is part of the Warwick Independent Schools Foundation, which includes Warwick School and the King's High School for Girls.

The Prep School has an exceptionally large staff, with specialist tuition in Art, French, Science, Music, Drama, DT, Physical Education and Computing.

Boys and girls are admitted from the age of 3+, subject to the availability of places. At the age of 7, the majority of boys continue to Warwick School, whilst the girls normally remain with us until they are 11.

Entry to King's High School is by a competitive examination and girls at the Prep School are prepared for this.

Girls are also prepared for the Common Entrance and any other appropriate examinations for their secondary education.

Early registration is advised if a place in the Pre-Preparatory Dept is to be ensured. Entry to the School at the age of 7 and later requires a satisfactory level of attainment in the basic skills and may be competitive.

Charitable status. Warwick Independent Schools Foundation is a Registered Charity, number 1088057.

Waverley School

Waverley Way, Finchampstead, Wokingham, Berkshire RG40 4YD
Tel: 0118 973 1121
Fax: 0118 973 1131
email: info@waverleyschool.co.uk
website: www.waverleyschool.co.uk

Chairman of Governors: Blair Jenkins

Head Teacher: **Tammy Howard**, BSc Hons, PGCE

Age Range. 3 months–11 years.
Number of Pupils. 120.
Fees per term (2014–2015). Reception–Year 6 Core day: £2,625–£3,810. Extended day package also available. Nursery according to the broad range of flexible sessions attended. Wrap-around care available from 7.30 am to 6.00 pm.

Waverley is a co-educational day school, founded in 1945. Waverley School is located in purpose-built premises just south of Wokingham. This prestigious development in a superb location offers children outstanding opportunities in and out of the classroom. Waverley's curriculum provides children with a solid foundation, particularly in the areas of literacy and numeracy. An excellent network of computers provides outstanding opportunities for Information and Communications Technology. All subjects of the National Curriculum are taught, with the addition of French from Reception. Team games include soccer, rugby, netball, cricket and rounders. Swimming and athletics are included in the physical education programme. Children's self-confidence is developed through their involvement in drama. Music, both choral and instrumental, is a particular strength of the School.

Waverley School welcomes visiting specialists for French, Swimming, Piano, Violin, Clarinet, Flute, Guitar, Ballet, Judo, Chess, and Speech & Drama. There is specialist help for pupils with specific learning difficulties.

Waverley successfully prepares boys and girls for entrance to Independent Senior Schools and Reading's grammar schools at 11+. An integral Nursery offers a carefully balanced introduction to the School, and ensures both social and educational continuity from 3–11 years.

Waverley School offers an extended day and year facility, a full and active clubs programme, and a Holiday Club offering care 51 weeks of the year.

There is also a thriving Friends' Association.

Charitable status. Waverley School (Crowthorne) Limited is a Registered Charity, number 309102. It exists to provide education for boys and girls between 3 months and 11 years.

Wellesley House

114 Ramsgate Road, Broadstairs, Kent CT10 2DG
Tel: 01843 862991
Fax: 01843 602068
email: hmsec@wellesleyhouse.net
website: www.wellesleyhouse.org

Chairman of the Governors: P J Woodhouse, Esq

Headmaster: S T P O'Malley, MA Hons, PGCE

Age Range. 7–13.
Number of Pupils. 81 Boys, 55 Girls.
Fees per term (2014–2015). Boarding £7,865; Day £5,950; Year 3 Day £5,220.

Location. The school, which is run by an Educational Trust, stands in its own grounds of 20 acres and was purpose-built in 1898.

Trains run hourly from Victoria Station, London with a high-speed rail link from St Pancras which takes as little as 1 hour 15 minutes or under two hours by road. At the beginning of each term, and at most exeats and half-terms, the school operates coach services between Broadstairs and London via the M2 services and also to Birchanger services on the M11 via Brentwood. The school also operates a minibus at exeats and half-terms to Charing, near Ashford, and Benenden.

Facilities. The school has a science and technology building, which includes modern science laboratories, an ICT laboratory and a craft room. Other facilities include a library, an indoor heated swimming pool, four hard tennis courts, two squash courts, a modelling room, art room, a music wing, a .22 shooting range, fitness trail, outdoor stage and separate recreation rooms, all of which are in the school grounds. There is a spacious sports hall. The main team games are cricket, Association and rugby football, hockey, netball and rounders. Tuition is also given in squash, shooting, golf, tennis, archery, judo, scuba and swimming. Ballet, tap, modern dancing, riding and sailing are also available.

A special feature of the school is that boys between the ages of 7 and 9 live in a junior wing. This is linked to the main school, but self-contained under the care of resident house staff and a resident matron.

The girls live in a separate house, The Orchard, within the school grounds, under the care of a housemaster and his wife. The house was recently refurbished with a new conservatory added.

Education. Boys and girls are prepared for all independent senior schools. Those who show sufficient promise are prepared for scholarships and the school has a fine record of success on this front with a third of leavers gaining scholarships in recent years. The curriculum is designed to enable all children to reach the highest standard possible by sound teaching along carefully thought out lines to suit the needs of the individual.

The Headmaster and his wife are assisted by 23 teaching staff.

Charitable status. Wellesley House and St Peter Court School Education Trust Ltd is a Registered Charity, number 307852. It exists solely to provide education to boys and girls.

Wellingborough Preparatory School

London Road, Wellingborough, Northamptonshire NN8 2BX
Tel: 01933 222698
Fax: 01933 233474
email: prep-head@wellingboroughschool.org
website: www.wellingboroughschool.org
Twitter: @WboroPrepSchool

Chairman of the Governors: Dr J K Cox, MA Cantab, MB BChir, BA Hons

Headmaster: **R J Mitchell**, BEd

Deputy Headmaster: T J Gray, BEd, Dip Ed

Age Range. 8–13.
Number of Pupils. 179 Boys, 115 Girls.
Fees per term (2014–2015). £4,188 (Years 4–6), £4,293 (Years 7–8) (including lunch).

The School is the Preparatory School of Wellingborough School (a registered charity). Girls and boys are admitted from 8 years old. The Preparatory School is self-contained with its own teaching centre, library, two science laboratories, computer suite and purpose-built Art Atrium. Music, sports and design technology facilities are shared with the Senior School.

The School offers a broad, well-balanced curriculum with Foundation Scholarships available at 11+, Entrance Scholarships at 13+ and an enrichment programme.

The School enjoys a strong sporting reputation which combines a desire for excellence with an 'all-inclusive sports' ethos. Games played are rugby, football, and cricket for the boys. Hockey, netball and rounders are the games played by the girls. The children are also able to represent the school at athletics, tennis and cross-country. There is an equestrian team whose fixture list continues to grow and Year 8 pupils can participate in sailing during the Trinity term.

The creative arts are highly valued, with termly drama productions and a flourishing Art Department that has exhibited nationally. The School boast two orchestras and a wide variety of groups and ensembles. All the pupils have an opportunity to learn a brass instrument in Year 5 as well as learning composition and keyboard skills in other year groups. There are around 50 to 60 after-school activities to choose from during the week, as well as an optional Weekend Activities programme, which varies from term to term; some activities which might be included are: indoor skiing, equestrian, golf, dance, film school, masterclass cricket, clay pigeon shooting and white water rafting.

The pastoral care of pupils is of paramount importance. The School is organised into six Clubs. Each Club is headed by a member of staff who oversees the academic and social progress of the girls and boys within their club.

The children work in a stimulating environment. The School aims for the pupils to become successful learners, confident individuals and responsible citizens, with parents working together in partnership with the School in the education of their children.

Almost 100% of Year 8 pupils make the transition into the Senior School with only one or two going to alternative Independent schools.

Charitable status. Wellingborough School is a Registered Charity, number 309923. It exists to provide education for girls and boys.

Wellington Prep School

South Street, Wellington, Somerset TA21 8NT
Tel: 01823 668700
email: prep@wellington-school.org.uk
website: www.wellington-school.org.uk

Chairman of Governors: Mr Phil Nunnerley, BA, FCIB

Headmaster: **Mr Adam Gibson**, BSc Hons, PGCE, NPQH, Cert Ed

Age Range. 3–11 Co-educational.
Number of Pupils. 220.
Fees per term (2014–2015). Day: £1,895–£3,450; Year 6 Boarding £7,012; Year 6 Weekly Boarding £5,607.

Wellington Prep School opened in September 1999 in purpose-built accommodation to provide one of the most modern and stimulating educational environments for young children anywhere in the country.

Wellington Prep School provides an education of unrivalled quality which both complements and enhances the national reputation of Wellington School and enables us to deliver educational excellence from nursery level through to university entrance.

The School Chapel is central to the ethos of the school and the School Chaplain visits the Prep School at the start of each week to take an assembly. At Wellington traditional Christian values combine with the bests of modern innovation to give children the best possible of starts in a wonderfully happy and purposeful atmosphere. Flexi boarding is available from Year 5 and full boarding is available from Year 6.

Each class in Nursery and Reception operates a key-worker system with highly-qualified and experienced support staff working alongside teachers. In all classes specialist support is available to help gifted children as well as to support those who might need additional input. The school uses a dedicated area of Woodland on the nearby Blackdown Hills (an area of Outstanding Natural Beauty) for weekly forest school sessions for children aged 4 to 7 years.

Encouragement and reward systems promote hard work and good behaviour.

Our superb facilities include:

- Eighteen purpose-designed, modern classrooms;
- A large, attractive, central school hall;
- The most modern and up-to-date education resources;
- Purpose-built ICT suite and library;
- Spacious grounds including a large playground with wooden amphitheatre;
- Sports hall, astro pitch and sports fields (shared facilities with the Senior School)

Situated on the same campus as the Senior School, the Prep School has full access to the facilities of the Senior School which include the Princess Royal Sports Complex, numerous rugby pitches, tennis courts, netball courts, hockey pitches (including an all-weather pitch), cricket pitches, swimming pool, athletics track and field events area.

Specialist teaching in ICT and Music begins in Nursery and from Year 1 French and Religious Education are also taught as specialist subjects. The use of subject specialists increases as the children move through the Prep School so that in Years 5 and 6 children follow a senior school style timetable and receive Senior School teaching in Science, Drama, Sport, Art, Design and Technology, as well as Prep School subject specialist teaching.

There is an extensive clubs programme each afternoon followed by the STAR club which is available to all children from 5–6 pm term time. Holiday clubs operate at Christmas, Easter and for six weeks during the summer holidays to accommodate busy working families.

A comprehensive prospectus is available from the School Registrar.

Charitable status. Wellington School is a Registered Charity, number 310268.

Wellow House School

Wellow, Newark, Notts NG22 0EA
Tel: 01623 861054
Fax: 01623 836665
email: office@wellowhouseschool.co.uk
website: www.wellowhouse.notts.sch.uk

Chairman of the Governors: Steve Cooling

Headmaster: **Peter Cook**, BEd

Age Range. 3–13.
Number of Pupils. 150.
Fees per term (2014–2015). Pre-Prep pupils £2,270; Day pupils £3,655–£3,875; Boarding £20 per night. Fees include meals and normal extras.

Wellow House School was founded in 1971 by the Stewart General Charitable Trust. Since 1994 it has been managed as an educational charity by the Directors and administered by a Board of Governors. This co-educational school has an established reputation for high academic standards, a successful sporting record, broad cultural interests and a happy family atmosphere. Weekly and occasional boarding has become an increasingly popular means of encouraging self-reliance within a supportive community and as a preparation for senior school and university.

The teaching staff of 8 men and 12 women is well qualified and experienced. A distinctive teaching style places great emphasis on the rapport between teacher and pupil in small classes, without slavish reliance on worksheets and textbooks. Each pupil maintains a file of notes, as a record and for reference. All take pride in honest hard work, confidence through encouragement, courtesy and fair discipline, and a strong sense of belonging. The thriving house points' system encourages much voluntary study and is the basis of the disciplinary process.

The Headmaster, Matron and Boarding Parents look after the boarders. They are assisted by a team of resident and non-resident tutors, one of whom oversees the evening activity programme. Qualified Catering Manager and Matron supervise the pupils' boarding, catering and medical needs. There are visiting teachers for instrumental tuition, table tennis, judo and drama.

The school is attractively set in 20 acres of parkland and playing fields on the fringe of the Sherwood Forest village of Wellow. There is easy road access to this heart of Nottinghamshire from Worksop and Sheffield to the north, Mansfield and Chesterfield to the west, Nottingham and Grantham to the south, and Lincoln and Newark to the east. Newark lies on north-south and east-west main line rail routes.

A continuous programme of development has provided purpose-built classrooms, science laboratory, networked computer room, music rooms, library, assembly hall and dining hall to add to the original country house. The boarding accommodation was refurbished in 1997 and 2000 with further refinements and updates in 2006 to 2008. Recent additions to the school include studios for art and ceramics and a sports hall with indoor cricket nets. There is an indoor heated swimming pool, an all-weather cricket net, and an all-weather tennis court. The Pre-Prep classes are housed in their own building, which was totally refurbished and extended in September 2006 and is surrounded by play-time facilities. There are close links with the village church.

Children enter the school after an interview visit and a trial day at any age from 3 to 11+ – the oldest often transferring from primary schools. Six Entrance Scholarships may be awarded annually and Bursaries can give financial assistance. Pupils are prepared for Common Entrance and Scholarships to a wide range of Senior Independent Schools, both boarding and day, and there is a continuous programme of assessment and reporting.

There is a broad physical education programme, with school matches in Rugby, Netball, Soccer, Hockey, Cricket, Rounders, Cross Country, Swimming and Tennis. The school is renowned for its pupils' prowess in Archery and Table Tennis. Weekend and holiday expeditions for Outdoor Pursuits in the Peak District, Yorkshire, Scotland and beyond are popular.

There is encouragement to participate in Natural History, the Visual Arts, Dance, Drama and Music, and more than half of the pupils learn a musical instrument. Most are involved in the much enjoyed regular concerts.

The school provides activity week cover during the holiday periods on Monday, Wednesday and Friday in the Pre Prep (to include pupils in Y3 and Y4). The Prep run activity weeks for 7–13 year olds for 2 full weeks in the summer.

Charitable status. Wellow House School is a Registered Charity, number 528234. It exists solely to provide a high standard of all-round education for children aged 3 to 13 years.

Wells Cathedral Junior School

Jocelyn House, 11 The Liberty, Wells, Somerset BA5 2ST
Tel: 01749 834400
Fax: 01749 834401
email: juniorschool@wells-cathedral-school.com
website: www.wells-cathedral-school.com

Chairman of Governors: The Very Revd John Clarke, MA, BD (*Dean of Wells*)

Head of the Junior School: **Mrs J Barrow**, BEd

Age Range. 3–11 years.
Number of Boys and Girls. 152: 81 Boys and 71 Girls.
Fees per term (2014–2015). Boarders £7,514; Day £4,320; Pre-Prep £2,333. Nursery: Morning with lunch £19; Afternoon with lunch £23; Afternoon £19; All day with lunch £33.

The Junior School is made up of the Pre-Prep department (age 3–7) and the Junior School (age 7–11). Pupils accepted into the Junior School normally make a smooth transfer to the Senior School at 11 and academic, music and sports scholarships are awarded.

Academic Work. The Junior School prepares children for the academic work in the senior school and takes part in the national tests at the end of KS2, however, the school is not restricted by the demands of the National Curriculum. The aim of the school is to ensure high academic standards within a friendly and stimulating environment.

Children are assessed regularly for both academic achievement and effort, and parents have many opportunities to meet staff and receive information on their child's progress.

Pastoral Care. The form teacher is responsible for the pastoral care of pupils; in addition each pupil is allocated to a House which has an assembly once a week. Work and sports competitions take place in houses and pupils are able to develop a good relationship not only with their own peer group but with pupils from across the Junior School.

Creativity. Set in beautiful grounds just to the north of the Cathedral, pupils from the school provide the boy and girl choristers at the Cathedral. In addition, a number of pupils are specialist musicians enjoying the expert tuition of the music department at the school which is one of the four in England designated and grant-aided by the Government's Music and Dance Scheme. Scholarships are available for both the choristers and the musicians.

Drama, music and dance are considered vital activities to bring out the best in children. A full programme of concerts, both formal and informal, takes place during the year for all age groups as well as big productions and small year group dramas. The school takes its production to the Edinburgh Festival in alternate years and it has established drama exchange links with schools in other European countries.

A whole school arts week each summer allows all aspects of creativity to come to the fore for every pupil. Themes have included the Caribbean, Somerset and China; pupils experience workshops in the areas of art, dance, drama and music. Regular exhibitions and performances are a feature of the school. The school has received the Artsmark Gold award from Arts Council England.

Sport. The school has many excellent facilities, such as the sports hall, dance studio, astroturf pitch and swimming pool. Pupils experience a wide range of activities on the games field. Sport is played to a high standard with rugby, cross country, netball, hockey, cricket, swimming, athletics and gymnastics being the main sports, more recently basketball and badminton have been introduced. A full programme of inter-school matches and house matches is available for all pupils in Year 3 to 6. Many clubs and activities run at lunchtimes or after school.

Charitable status. Wells Cathedral School is a Registered Charity, number 310212. It has existed since AD 909 to provide education for its pupils.

West Hill Park

St Margarets Lane, Titchfield, Hants PO14 4BS
Tel: 01329 842356
Fax: 01329 842911
email: admissions@westhillpark.com
website: www.westhillpark.com

Chairman of Governors: Mrs B Worsley, BA Hons, ACA

Headmaster: **A P Ramsay**, BEd, MSc

Age Range. 3–13.
Number of Pupils. Prep School (age 5–13): 25 Boarders (10 girls, 15 boys); 235 Day Pupils (95 girls, 105 boys). Early Years (age rising 3 to 5): 30 boys, 27 girls.
Fees per term (2014–2015). Prep School: Day £3,335–£5,590, Boarding supplement £1,400. Early Years: according to sessions attended.

At West Hill Park pupils are prepared for Scholarships and Common Entrance to all Independent Schools.

The main building is Georgian, originally a shooting lodge for the Earls of Southampton, and provides spacious and comfortable boarding accommodation for boys and girls under the supervision of resident Houseparents. Resident matrons, academic staff and a qualified school nurse complete the Boarding team. Also in the main building are the administrative offices, the Library, the Dining Hall and the Assembly Hall with fully equipped sound and lighting equipment and stage. Further excellent facilities include the Art and Design Technology Studios, the Music School, a 25m heated indoor Swimming Pool, a fully-equipped Sports Hall, 2 Computing Suites, two Computing Suites, the French, History, Maths and Geography Departments with Interactive Whiteboards and the purpose-built Early Years Department with its Outdoor Play Area and Woodland Classroom. West Hill Park stands in its own grounds of nearly 40 acres on the edge of Titchfield village. There are sports fields, 5 hard, 3 grass and 5 Astro tennis courts, a floodlit Riding School, a floodlit Astroturf, a cross-country course and in summer a nine-hole golf course.

There are 28 fully-qualified members of the teaching staff. 13 members of staff are resident, either in the main building or in houses in the school grounds, giving a great sense of community to the school.

A strong pastoral care system monitors the individual child's well-being regularly. There is a wide range of activities available in order to encourage children to develop individual skills and talents: choirs, orchestra, dance, aerobics, carpentry, judo, ballet, drama, golf, life-saving, computer club, string group, squash, chess, sailing, fly fishing, riding on school ponies and public speaking, as well as the more intensive training available in the Swim Squad, Tennis Squad and other sporting clubs. The Boarders enjoy many expeditions at weekends as well as fun events at school, such as orienteering, theatre workshops, cycle marathons and games evenings.

Games played include rugby, football, cricket, hockey, tennis, athletics, netball and rounders.

Charitable status. West Hill School Trust is a Registered Charity, number 307343. It exists to educate children.

West House School

24 St James Road, Edgbaston, Birmingham B15 2NX
Tel: 0121 440 4097
Fax: 0121 440 5839
email: secretary@westhouseprep.com
website: www.westhouseprep.com
Twitter: @westhouseschool

Chairman of Governors: S T Heathcote, FCA

Headmaster: **A M J Lyttle**, BA Hons Birmingham, PGCE Birmingham, NPQH

Age Range. Boys: 4–11 years; Co-educational Nursery: 12 months to 4 years.

Number of Pupils. A maximum 220 boys aged 4–11 (Reception to Year 6) plus 90 boys and girls aged 12 months–4 years.

Fees per term (2014–2015). 4–11 year olds: £2,445–£3,500 according to age. The fees include lunches and breaktime drinks. Under 4: fees according to number of sessions attended per week. Fee list on application.

West House was founded in 1895 and since 1959 has been an Educational Trust controlled by a Board of Governors. The school has a strong academic reputation and pupils are regularly awarded scholarships to senior schools at 11+. The well-qualified and experienced staff provides a sound education for boys of all abilities. The National Curriculum has been adapted to suit the aptitudes and interests of pupils and to ensure that it provides an outstanding preparation for entry into selective senior schools. Pupils are taught in small classes which ensures that they receive much individual attention. Specialist help is available for children with Dyslexia or who require learning support. Music teachers visit the school to give individual music tuition.

The school occupies a leafy five-acre site a mile from Birmingham city centre. As well as the main teaching blocks there are two well-equipped science laboratories and a sports hall.

The Centenary Building, opened in 1998, accommodates the art and design technology department, ICT room and senior Library. Extensive playing fields, two all-weather tennis courts and all-weather cricket nets enable pupils to participate in many games and sports. Pupils also enjoy a wide range of hobby activities, and drama and music play important roles in school life.

The school is open during term time between 8 am and 6 pm. On-site Holiday Clubs are run by members of staff during the holidays.

Charitable status. West House School is a Registered Charity, number 528959. It exists to provide education for boys.

Westbourne House

Shopwyke, Chichester, West Sussex PO20 2BH
Tel: 01243 782739
Fax: 01243 770759
email: office@westbournehouse.org
website: www.westbournehouse.org

Chairman of the Governors: J A Ashworth, BSc Hons

Headmaster: **Martin Barker**

Age Range. 3–13.
Number of Pupils. 436: Boarders 93; Prep Day 221; Pre-Prep 122.
Fees per term (2014–2015). Boarders £6,470; Day £5,280; Pre-Prep £3,120.

Westbourne House School was founded in 1907 and became a Charitable Trust in 1967. It has been co-educational since 1992. There is a well-qualified teaching staff of 54, plus 26 visiting music staff and 38 support staff; all play important roles in the care of the children. The School has a strong boarding ethos.

Situated in a beautiful parkland setting of 100+ acres, Westbourne House offers a warm, happy environment, which fosters learning and development. Pupils are prepared for the Common Entrance and many Scholarships (20 in 2014) have been won at an impressive list of Senior Independent Schools in recent years; virtually all children go on to their first-choice school at 13+. Individual academic progress is carefully monitored and the school has recently invested in the latest database technology to enhance this process. The average class size (16) allows plenty of individual attention, differentiation and pastoral care. The broad curriculum includes the full quota of academic subjects as well as Music, Art, Design Technology, Ceramics, Food Technology, Drama, Physical Education & Games, and Information Technology. Individual Needs, as well as the Gifted & Talented, are nurtured by a highly-qualified SENCO.

Children are encouraged to discover their talents within the wide range of activities on offer, with the aim of developing these talents to the full. Westbourne enjoys a proud record of sporting achievement and the children have access to excellent facilities: extensive playing fields, including a new astroturf pitch, host the major sports (football, rugby, hockey and cricket for boys; netball, hockey, pop lacrosse and rounders for girls) and the children also engage in athletics, swimming (25-metre indoor heated pool), squash (2 courts), tennis (16 courts), as well as golf, fencing, judo and dance (new dance studio). A large, well-equipped Sports Hall caters for indoor sports. Music is outstanding: the children enjoy excellent facilities and teaching, with a wide range of instruments, orchestras, bands and choirs on offer. All children are encouraged to perform from an early age. Art and Technology are housed within the original stable block of the Georgian house, providing a delightful environment for the children to develop their creative skills. Drama is encouraged through a number of productions involving most of the children.

An extensive building programme has been undertaken in recent years. A new Junior Teaching block for Years 3, 4 and 5 was built in 1997, a purpose-built Science Department in 1999 and a Theatre seating 300 was completed in 2001. A new Dining Room, catering facilities and three new classrooms were completed in 2004, as were improvements to the library and recreational facilities; a new dance studio (2008) and full-size astroturf all-weather surface (2009). Development in 2011 included a new 30-acre lake on the school grounds for canoeing, as well as Pre-Prep extensions to accommodate 3-form entry. The most recent development was in September 2014: 2 new boarding houses, a new Food Tech room and a new Science Lab.

Charitable status. Westbourne House is a Registered Charity, number 307034.

Westbourne School

60 Westbourne Road, Sheffield S10 2QT
Tel: 0114 266 0374
Fax: 0114 263 8176
email: admin@westbourneschool.co.uk
website: www.westbourneschool.co.uk

Chairman of the Governors: Mr S Hinchliffe

Headmaster: **John Hicks**, MEd Kingston, BEd Hons Exeter

Age Range. 3–16.
Number of Pupils. 345 day pupils, boys and girls.
Fees per term (2014–2015). £2,795–£3,830.

The fully co-educational School, founded in 1885, is an Educational Trust with a Board of Governors, some of whom are Parents. The number of entries is limited to maintain small class sizes – with an average class size of 14 throughout the school with a staff/pupil ratio of less than 1:10.

The Pre-School and Junior School are housed in a specially designed and equipped building, staffed by qualified and experienced teachers. Music and Games are taught by specialists. Specialist Science and Technology are introduced from Year 4 (8+), as well as specialist teaching in Information Technology, Art and Design, and RE. French, Science and Computers are introduced from the age of 4.

In the Junior School, some lessons are taught by specialists in Subject Rooms. There is also a Science Laboratory and ICT, Art and Music Rooms, Fiction and Reference Libraries, and a Hall with Stage.

The Senior School provides teaching to GCSE from Year 7 to 11 up to age 16. It has its own campus immediately adjacent to the Junior School. Years 7 and 8 have the benefit of their own designated building with access to all the facilities available in Senior School. The school has a 3-form entry in Year 7 with a scholarship class. External and internal scholarships are taken in January of Year 6. All children are placed in sets in Maths and English from Year 5.

The main aim of the school is to bring out the best in every pupil according to their ability. There is a Department catering for those with Specific Learning Difficulties. Great emphasis is laid on courtesy and a mutual respect for each other.

Art, Music and Drama are strongly encouraged throughout the school, with regular concerts, plays and art exhibitions. Tuition in several instruments is available.

The main sports are Rugby, Football, Hockey, Cricket, Athletics, Netball, Rounders and Cross-Country Running with regular matches against other schools. There are also opportunities for Short Tennis, Swimming, Basketball, Volleyball, Fencing, Skiing, Badminton, Climbing, Golf and Scuba Diving. Numerous educational visits are on offer with annual trips abroad.

A supervised breakfast club runs from 7.45 am to 8.30 am. Breakfast for pupils and parents is available from 7.45 am and, while the length of day depends on the age of the child, there are after-school facilities for all pupils until 5.15 pm. There is no school on Saturdays.

Charitable status. Westbourne School is a Registered Charity, number 529381. It exists to provide education for boys and girls.

Westbrook Hay

London Road, Hemel Hempstead, Herts HP1 2RF
Tel: 01442 256143/230099
Fax: 01442 232076
email: admin@westbrookhay.co.uk
website: www.westbrookhay.co.uk

Chairman of Governors: Andrew Newland

Headmaster: **Keith D Young**, BEd Hons Exeter

Age Range. Boys 3–13, Girls 3–11.
Number of Pupils. Day: 221 Boys, 107 Girls.
Fees per term (2014–2015). £2,627–£4,425. Flexi Boarding £34.50 per night.

Westbrook Hay is an outstanding independent prep school which educates boys and girls from rising 3–13 years. The school's beautiful location boasts 26 acres of parkland overlooking the Bourne valley in Hertfordshire, and is just off the A41, between Berkhamsted and Hemel Hempstead. This unique setting offers a secure environment, within which children explore and enjoy all that childhood has to offer.

Through visionary teaching in small classes and with a wonderful mixture of purpose-built facilities and historic surroundings, our children achieve excellent results, enjoy a broad curriculum, and have the all-important confidence to succeed.

The Independent Schools Inspectorate (ISI) carried out a very successful inspection recently and regarded our school as 'Excellent' and 'Outstanding', the highest possible recognition from the ISI for both age groups.

"Pupil's achievement is excellent and they are very well educated in accordance with the school's aim for pupils to realise their intellectual, social and physical potential."

"The quality of the provision is outstanding. Through excellent understanding of differing developmental stages and careful observations, staff plan challenging and enjoyable work for each child across all learning areas."

Classes are small and each individual is encouraged and helped to achieve their potential. Individuality, honesty, a sense of humour and self-reliance are attributes which are stimulated and valued in this most friendly school, which maintains a caring, family atmosphere.

Lower and Middle School departments prepare children from rising three to eight for entry into the Upper School. Children in Years 3 and 4 are class taught primarily by their form teacher, before a move to a subject-based curriculum in Year 5. The academic focus is provided by the goals of the Common Entrance and Scholarship examinations as most children go on to independent senior schools. All children follow the National Curriculum subject areas and in many cases extend them.

The facilities of the school have benefited from significant recent improvements including a £2 million lower school building, an art studio with pottery kiln and a two new fully equipped Information Technology rooms. A Performing Arts Centre, with a 300-seat theatre and full music practice and performance facilities is planned for September 2015.

Extensive playing fields give ample room for rugby, soccer, hockey, cricket, golf, rounders and athletics. All-weather netball and tennis courts and a heated swimming pool are complemented by a purpose-built Sports Hall which provides for badminton, table tennis, cricket nets, five-a-side football, gymnastics and a galaxy of other indoor sports.

A breakfast club, after-school care and a school bus service are also offered to accommodate the needs of working parents.

Charitable status. Westbrook Hay School is a Registered Charity, number 292537. It exists to provide education for boys and girls.

Westminster Abbey Choir School

Dean's Yard, London SW1P 3NY
Tel: 020 7654 4918
Fax: 020 7222 1548
email: headmaster@westminster-abbey.org
website: www.westminster-abbey.org

Chairman of Governors: The Dean of Westminster

Headmaster: **J H Milton**, BEd

Age Range. 8–13.
Number of Boys. Up to 35 all chorister boarders.
Fees per term (2014–2015). £2,468 inclusive of tuition on two instruments. Additional bursaries may be available in cases of real financial need.

Westminster Abbey Choir School is the only school in Britain exclusively devoted to the education of boy choristers. Boys have been singing services in the Abbey since at least 1384 and the 35 boys in the school maintain this tradition.

Westminster Abbey Choir School is a special place, offering boys from eight to thirteen a unique and exciting opportunity to be a central part of one of our great national institutions. Boys sing daily in the Abbey and also take part in many special services and celebrations both in the UK and abroad.

The small size of the school, the fact that all boys are boarders and the high proportion of staff who live on the premises, allow the School to have an extended family atmosphere.

A full academic curriculum is taught by specialist staff and boys are prepared for the Common Entrance and academic scholarship examinations; most boys win valuable scholarships to secondary independent schools when they leave at 13.

Music obviously plays a central part in the school. Every boy learns the piano and at least one orchestral instrument and there are 15 visiting music teachers. Concerts, both inside and outside school, are a regular feature of the year.

Besides music and academic lessons there is a thriving programme of other activities and there are many opportunities for boys to develop interests outside music.

Sports played include football, cricket, rugby, athletics, hockey, sailing, canoeing and tennis.

Entry is by voice trial and academic tests. Further details are available from Thérèse Gordon-Duffy (Headmaster's Secretary and Admissions). The Headmaster is always pleased to hear from parents who feel that their son might have the potential to become a chorister.

Charitable status. Westminster Abbey is a Registered Charity, number X8259. It is a religious establishment incorporated by Royal Charter in 1560.

Westminster Cathedral Choir School

Ambrosden Avenue, London SW1P 1QH
Tel: 020 7798 9081
Fax: 020 7630 7209

email: office@choirschool.com
website: www.choirschool.com

President: The Most Reverend Vincent Nichols, Archbishop of Westminster

Chairman of Governors: John Gibbs

Headmaster: **Neil McLaughlan**, BA Hons

Age Range. 7–13.
Number of Boys. 160 (28 Choristers, 132 Day Boys).
Fees per term (2014–2015). Chorister Boarders £2,861; Day Boys £5,350.

Founded in 1901, Westminster Cathedral Choir School is a Day Prep School and Boarding Choir School concerned with the development of the whole person. Choristers must be Roman Catholic, but Day Boys of all denominations are welcome.

The school forms part of the precincts of Westminster Cathedral and enjoys such facilities as a large playground and a Grade 1 listed Library. The school has recently undergone a £1.3 million refurbishment, including a brand new playground and boarding facilities.

Choristers and Day Boys alike achieve a high level of music making. The Choristers sing the daily capitular liturgy in the Cathedral and are regularly involved in broadcasts, recordings and tours abroad. There is also a Day Boy Choir, two orchestras and a substantial programme of chamber music. Boys can learn the piano and any orchestral instrument in school.

The major sports played at the Choir School include football, rugby and cricket and the boys travel to Vincent Square, Battersea Park and the Queen Mother Sports Centre for Games.

There is a wide range of extra-curricular activities available including: chess, computing, debating, fencing, football, judo, drama and a Saturday rugby club.

The school is justly famed for its fantastic food!

Assessment for Choristers is by academic assessment and voice trial, generally in November and February. Day Boy assessments are held in January.

Charitable status. Westminster Cathedral Choir School is a Registered Charity, number 1063761. It exists to provide a musical education for Roman Catholic boys.

Westminster Under School

Adrian House, 27 Vincent Square, London SW1P 2NN
Tel: 020 7821 5788
Fax: 020 7821 0458
email: under.school@westminster.org.uk
website: www.westminsterunder.org.uk

Chairman of Governors: The Dean of Westminster, The Very Reverend Dr John Hall

Master: **Mrs E A Hill**, MA

Deputy Master: D S C Bratt, BA

Age Range. 7–13.
Number of Boys. 286 (day boys only).
Fees per term (2014–2015). £5,460 (inclusive of lunches and stationery).

The Under School is closely linked to Westminster School, sharing the same Governing Body, although it has its own building overlooking the beautiful school playing fields in Vincent Square. The school's premises were extended in 2011 with a new dining hall and a specialist suite of Art rooms located in the adjacent building. The current site was also extensively refurbished.

Boys are prepared, though not exclusively, for Westminster through the Common Entrance examinations and "The

Challenge", Westminster School's scholarship examinations. Most boys proceed to Westminster, but entry into the Under School does not guarantee a place at the "Great School". Each year some boys will go on to leading senior schools including Eton and Winchester.

There is a strong musical tradition at the Under School, with a junior and senior choir, an orchestra, and string, brass and jazz groups. Art is equally strong with new facilities for all kinds of creative activity. The Art department also organises competitions in photography and model-making. In addition to these we have school competitions in public speaking and creative writing, chess and Scrabble. Drama is also popular with the boys and there are plays for each year group at different times in the year.

Games are played on the school grounds adjacent to Adrian House in Vincent Square and although football and cricket are the main sports, there are opportunities to participate in athletics, basketball, cross-country, hockey, rugby, swimming and tennis. Our new sports centre, recently opened in September 2012, provides excellent facilities for all sports and after-school clubs in fencing, judo, karate, climbing and table tennis.

Approximately 20 new boys are admitted at 7+, 8+ and up to 28 at 11+ in September. Means-tested bursaries are available at 11+, as are music scholarships, and many boys apply at this entry point from London primary schools.

Charitable status. St Peter's College (otherwise known as Westminster School) is a Registered Charity, number 312728. It exists to provide education for boys.

Westonbirt Prep School

Westonbirt, Tetbury, Gloucestershire GL8 8QG
Tel: 01666 881375
Fax: 01666 881391
email: prep@westonbirt.org
website: www.westonbirt.org
Twitter: @westonbirtprep

Chairman of Governors: Mr D McMeekin, MBA

Headmaster: **Mr N Shaw**, MA

Age Range. 3–11.
Number of Pupils. 130 day pupils.
Fees per term (2014–2015). £2,475–£3,570.
Westonbirt Prep School is a Preparatory Day School and Nursery for Boys and Girls aged 3–11.

Location. The school's idyllic setting in 210 acres of beautiful rural park and woodland in Gloucestershire (shared with Westonbirt School, an independent boarding and day school for girls) allows pupils the freedom to play and explore in a safe and natural environment, developing imagination and confidence. The school is located close to the village of Tetbury and is within half an hour of the M4 and M5 and within easy reach of the surrounding towns of Cirencester, Gloucester, Swindon, Bath and Bristol.

Philosophy. Westonbirt Prep School is committed to enhancing children's broader personal development, as well as preparing them for senior independent, grammar and secondary maintained schools. Its most recent ISI inspection report praised how Westonbirt Prep School is *"successful in meeting its aims to encourage every pupil, educating the whole child and celebrating the individual"*. The school fosters a strong family and Christian ethos. This combination of care and overriding sense of community creates a happy, secure and stimulating environment in which the boys and girls thrive. *"Westonbirt Prep is a caring, friendly school with a real local, family feel."* Good Schools Guide 2014.

The emphasis of the staff is on achieving the highest academic standards whilst encouraging participation in a full programme of sport and creative activities such as art, drama, and music.

Prep School pupils receive specialist coaching in a wide variety of games using the exceptional sporting facilities. These include a 25m swimming pool, well-maintained pitches, netball and tennis courts. The boys play rugby, football, hockey and cricket and the girls' main sports are hockey, netball and rounders. During the inter-house competitions mixed teams participate in these sports. Both girls and boys take part in track and field athletics, swimming, tennis, golf and cross-country activities.

Westonbirt Prep School is accredited by Forest Schools and successfully incorporates an Outdoor Education Programme into the curriculum. Pupils enjoy one double lesson per week in the spinney, where children are encouraged to explore the unique environment in order to support and develop their learning. *"It's great for self-esteem. It can bring out unexpected talents from a child who may not shine in the classroom."* Good Schools Guide 2014.

The school has a thriving Music Department (including a state-of-the-art Music Technology Centre) and pupils have at least two periods of singing and music per week. Children can also have individual music lessons in a range of instruments.

"Teachers at Westonbirt Prep School know their pupils very well and provide high-quality support and guidance, enabling the pupils to learn and understand effectively." ISI 2011. When pupils leave Westonbirt Prep School at 11+, they are fully prepared having acquired an excellent educational foundation. They are happy, accomplished and caring individuals motivated to make the best of their prospects wherever they go.

Charitable status. Westonbirt School Limited is a Registered Charity, number 311715. It exists to provide quality education in a demanding world.

Westville House School

Carter's Lane, Middleton, Ilkley, West Yorkshire LS29 0DQ
Tel: 01943 608053
Fax: 01943 817410
email: office@westvillehouseschool.co.uk
website: www.westvillehouseschool.co.uk
Twitter: @WestvilleHouseS

Chairman of Trustees: Mr A N Brown

Headteacher: **Mrs R James**, BSc Hons, PGCE

Age Range. 3–11.
Number of Pupils. 130.
Fees per term (2014–2015). £1,600–£2,775.
Perched on the top of a stunning hillside location, with views across to The Cow and Calf, lies Westville House School, Ilkley's foremost provider of independent education. The gleaming white school building stands proud in acres of grounds and exudes fun, strong values, pride in tradition and a strong belief in the Westville family.

Originally based down in the town centre, the school relocated to its current site over 20 years ago and has gone from strength to strength, developing fantastic education facilities. Inspirational classrooms are to be seen throughout the school; specialist science, art and music classrooms along with a sophisticated IT suite, a state-of-the-art sports hall with attached playing fields and most recently a forest classroom stimulate learning and encourage fun.

From the minute a child begins their journey at Westville house they are valued for who they are. The Early Years Unit, which takes children from 3 years, devotes masses of energy to building foundations that will set the children up for life. Each child has education tailored to their needs – for those who are very able there is masses to challenge, whilst for those who need a little bit of extra help there is huge encouragement and a clear development of an excitement about learning.

Children progress through the Pre-Prep department (ages 3–7) and then on through the Prep department (ages 7–11). They emerge as well-rounded, confident, and above all very happy children whose memories of their time at Westville prompt them to return year after year.

Academics are brilliant here and the school is consistently ranked in the Sunday Times Top 50 Prep Schools in the UK – a fantastic achievement for a small non-selective school. Children regularly achieve scholarships to many independent senior schools and gain entrance to the local selective grammar schools.

Academics aside, there is a whole host of extra-curricular activities designed to have something to suit every child. The school is particularly strong in swimming and cross country; drama and dance produce some excellent school productions. Music, in the form of choirs and instrumental lessons, is encouraged and the school ensemble is always seen as great fun. As the children progress through the school new activities and experiences are opened up to them – canoeing, fencing, first aid, street dancing – all geared to ensure that Westville children are totally prepared for their journey on to the senior school of their choice.

The school's motto '*Quotidie Opus Novum – something new every day*' really does sum up the excitement of coming to Westville House – the beginning of a lifelong education where an appetite for learning is something to be nurtured and enjoyed.

Charitable status. Westville House School is a Registered Charity, number 1086711.

Wetherby Pre-Preparatory School
Alpha Plus Group

11 Pembridge Square, London W2 4ED
Tel: 020 7727 9581
Fax: 020 7221 8827
email: learn@wetherbyschool.co.uk
website: www.wetherbyschool.co.uk

Headmaster: **Mr Mark Snell**, BA Hons, PGCE

Age Range. Boys 4–8.
Number of Pupils. 274.
Fees per term (2014–2015). £6,170.
Wetherby School is situated at 11 Pembridge Square and 19 Pembridge Villas. The four Reception classes and Little Wetherby (a boys-only nursery opened in September 2014) are based at 19 Pembridge Villas. Each class occupies a whole floor level and there is a playground at the back for the boys to run around in. The rest of the school in based at 11 Pembridge Square.

Whilst proud of its academic attainments for London Day School entry at 7+ and 8+ and top Boarding Schools, the priority is in producing happy, respectful, thoughtful, sociable and motivated boys. The curriculum is well balanced, with excellent sport, music and art opportunities including specialist teaching rooms for art, ICT, library and music. There is also a wide range of extra-curricular activities available. Wetherby operates a non-selective admissions procedure; registration is at birth.

Wetherby Preparatory School
Alpha Plus Group

48 Bryanston Square, London W1H 2EA
Tel: 020 7535 3520
Fax: 020 7535 3523
email: admin@wetherbyprep.co.uk
website: www.wetherbyprep.co.uk

Headmaster: **Mr Nick Baker**, BA Hons, PGCE

Age Range. Boys 7–13.
Number of Pupils. 318.
Fees per term (2014–2015). £6,035.
The school's motto, *Participes Civitatis* (being part of a community), exemplifies life at Wetherby Preparatory School. Boys, teachers and parents work closely together to create a unique educational experience. The quality of communication with parents and a strong PTA demonstrate the high level of partnership and cooperation at the school.

Every boy at Wetherby Prep finds the opportunity to shine, be it for academic scholarship, sporting excellence, choral or instrumental accomplishment or involvement in the vast array of clubs offered. This is not a school for an apathetic boy: enthusiasm, application and self-motivation are applauded and actively encouraged.

Wetherby Prep boys experience a varied and challenging academic curriculum. Boys enjoy their lessons and core subjects of Maths, English and Science are strongly emphasised. With subject-specialist teaching from Year 5 onwards, boys are educated by experienced and enthusiastic teachers, guiding them forwards and preparing them for the 13+ Common Entrance examinations.

Classroom learning is enhanced regularly by guest speakers and wide-ranging visits. All boys participate in an annual residential excursion, ranging from outdoor pursuits to language and other study trips.

Some boys spend their lunchtimes playing in nearby Hyde Park. The lunch menu includes a choice of hot and cold dishes, cooked on site, and includes numerous themed days for breakfast and lunch. Good table manners and healthy eating are clearly promoted.

Sport enjoys a high profile at Wetherby Prep at the recently acquired Wetherby Sports Grounds in Acton, with two Games afternoons a week, as well as PE, Swimming and Senior School Rowing classes. In addition, boys can develop their skills and learn new ones by attending after-school clubs including football training, cricket nets and fencing. Numerous fixtures and tournaments against other schools are held, along with eagerly awaited inter-house competitions.

Widford Lodge

Widford Road, Chelmsford, Essex CM2 9AN
Tel: 01245 352581
email: admin@widfordlodge.co.uk
            headmaster@widfordlodge.co.uk
website: www.widfordlodge.co.uk

Principal: Mrs Louise Gear

Headmaster: **S C Trowell**, BHum Hons, PGCE London

Age Range. 2½–11 years.
Number of Pupils. Prep 140; Pre-Prep & EYFS Kindergarten 80; Pre-School Nursery: varies according to number of sessions.

Fees per term (from April 2014). Pre-Prep £2,196, Main School £2,840. All fees include lunch, textbooks, stationery, etc.

Widford Lodge is a co-educational day school situated on the southern fringe of Chelmsford. Founded in 1935 the school aims to provide an all-round education within a happy, caring environment. Children are encouraged to enjoy their time at school, while also learning a sense of responsibility and a positive approach to their role in school and the wider community.

An enthusiastic staff prepare the children for grammar school via the 11+, entrance into senior independent schools through examination or scholarship and local secondary schools. A combination of form tutors, subject specialists and small classes ensure a good academic standard. The curriculum is broadly based and aims to develop a variety of interests, academic, aesthetic and sporting. The school has a well-equipped computer suite and the children are encouraged to use their IT skills in many different ways.

The main part of the school stands in 5 acres of wooded grounds that include an outdoor Swimming Pool, a Floodlit Tennis Court, Cricket Nets, Science Laboratory, Design Technology Centre and a Performing Arts Centre. There is plenty of space for the children to play and to use their imagination. The school also owns 9 acres of playing fields.

The children have the opportunity to play cricket, netball, rugby, hockey, soccer, athletics, swimming, cross-country, tennis, golf and rounders. Although a small school we are proud of our sporting tradition, which is underpinned by our belief that sport is for all and is ultimately played for fun.

Music, drama and art are all encouraged and a wide range of musical instruments are taught. There is a busy school choir and an annual concert.

There are many after-school activities which the children are encouraged to get involved in. These range from sports coaching in all the major games to art & crafts. The children can stay at school until 5.30 pm to do their Prep under the supervision of a member of staff.

Willington Independent Preparatory School

Worcester Road, Wimbledon, London SW19 7QQ
Tel: 020 8944 7020
Fax: 020 8944 9596
email: office@willingtonschool.co.uk
website: www.willingtonschool.co.uk

Chairman of the Council: B Whitmore, BSc, PhD

Headmaster: **M Chanter**, BSc Hons, PGCE, MA

Age Range. 4–13.
Number of Boys. 263 (all day boys).
Fees per term (2014–2015). £3,340–£4,070 according to age.

Willington Independent Preparatory School is a day school for boys aged 4–13. The school is set in the heart of Wimbledon and draws on a very local catchment area. Following the opening of the Johnson Building in 1999, which houses Art and History specialist rooms, the school in 2007 embarked on a major upgrading of our Worcester Road site and the rebuilding programme has created new centres for Maths, Science and Languages, a multi-purpose ICT suite, library and studio theatre and much improved Music provision. We also have our own extensive playing fields less than 10 minutes away by coach, which all boys use.

We aim to provide a nurturing environment, where each boy is inspired to reach his full potential, not only in terms of academic, creative and sporting attainments, but also in terms of his self-confidence and happiness as a 13 year old boy, ready to meet the demands of his future life. In 2010, Willington celebrated its 125th anniversary. Throughout its history, Willington has been a welcoming independent preparatory school for boys. We take pupils from age 4 in Reception and they normally leave us at the end of Year 8 after Common Entrance, when they are 13.

We pride ourselves on small class sizes; they average 15 across the school, with a maximum of 18. Our main intake is at Reception where we are currently over-subscribed. For over 100 years, Willington was in Putney and we moved to our present site in 1990. The school has been a charitable trust since 1961. We have recently been re-elected as a member of IAPS. We are keen to promote the highest academic standards and the number of scholarships gained over recent years is testament to this. However, we do not see this pursuit to be exclusive of a wide approach to prep school education, which involves the boys in a host of sporting and cultural opportunities.

Willington is a forward thinking school, which has traditional prep school values at heart. There is great stress here on individuality, but within a disciplined environment. We want our boys to be socially adept, confident and, not least, pleasant to each other and to the people around them. The school is founded on Christian values and is very much a family school, where parents are encouraged to participate in the day-to-day running of school life. Boys move on to a wide variety of Senior Schools on leaving Willington, including the traditional public schools. We work very closely with parents to find the right secondary school for each individual boy. It is testament to the school's unique place in Willingtonians' hearts that so many boys come back to visit.

Charitable status. Willington School Foundation Limited is a Registered Charity, number 312733. Its aim is to devote itself to the continuation and development of the School.

Wilmslow Preparatory School

Grove Avenue, Wilmslow, Cheshire SK9 5EG
Tel: 01625 524246
Fax: 01625 536660
email: secretary@wilmslowprep.co.uk
website: www.wilmslowprep.co.uk
Twitter: @wilmslowprep
Facebook: /wilmslowprep

Co-ed Day School founded 1909.

Chairman of Board of Trustees: Mr N Rudgard, MA Oxon

Headteacher: **Mrs H Rigby**, BEd Hons, NPQH

Age Range. 3–11.
Number of Pupils. 118 day pupils.
Fees per term (2014–2015). £855–£3,200 (lunches extra).

The School is registered as an Educational Trust. It is purpose built and is situated in the centre of Wilmslow in its own spacious grounds. The facilities include an Assembly Hall, new Sports Hall, a Science Room, Computer Room with networked PCs, a specialist Art Room, two well-stocked libraries and a Classroom Block with its own outdoor area for 3–5 year olds. There is a Tennis/Netball Court, a Sports field with its own stand-alone Sports Hall, and ample play areas.

The School aims to provide wide educational opportunities for all its pupils. It has a long-established excellent academic record and caters for a wide variety of entrance examinations to Independent Senior Day and Boarding Schools.

Wilmslow Preparatory School offers a variety of activities which include Music, Art and Drama. Principal sports include gymnastics, netball, football, cricket, hockey, tennis, athletics and swimming.

There are fourteen qualified and experienced teachers on the staff.

Charitable status. Wilmslow Preparatory School is a Registered Charity, number 525924. It exists to provide full-time education for pupils aged between 5 and 11, and part-time or full-time education to kindergarten children from the age of 3.

Wimbledon Common Prep School

113 Ridgway, Wimbledon, London SW19 4TA
Tel: 020 8946 1001
email: info@wimbledoncommonprep.co.uk
website: www.wimbledoncommonprep.co.uk

Chairman of Governors: Mrs P L Hughes, CBE

Head Teacher: **Mrs Tracey Buck**, BEd Hons

Age Range. Boys 4–7.
Number of Pupils. 168.
Wimbledon Common Preparatory School is a pre-prep school for boys situated in Wimbledon village, south-west London. It was founded in 1919 as a preparatory school for King's College School and other public schools, and moved to its present site in 1957. In 2006 it was bought by King's College School and is now part of their foundation and run by their board of governors.

The school's aims are to provide challenging and exciting teaching; to develop a love of learning; to encourage good study skills; to offer a variety of extra-curricular activities; to create a culture which encourages self-confidence and values tolerance, generosity, respect for others and a strong sense of community; to help boys acquire the social skills which will enable them to make a positive contribution to society; to develop sound parent partnerships, and to provide opportunities for boys to reflect upon their relationships with one another, the wider world and their God.

The school educates boys aged from four to seven years, offering Early Years Foundation Stage (EYFS) provision in its Reception classes.

Fees per term (2014–2015). £3,680.
Charitable status. Wimbledon Common Prep School is owned by King's College School, which is a Registered Charity, number 310024.

Winchester House School

High Street, Brackley, Northants NN13 7AZ
Tel: 01280 702483
Fax: 01280 706400
email: office@winchester-house.org
website: www.winchester-house.org

Chairman of Governors: G E S Seligman

Head: **Mrs Emma Goldsmith**, BA

Age Range. 3–13.
Number of Children. 319. Pre-Prep: 90 (60 Boys, 30 Girls); Upper School: 210 (135 Boys, 75 Girls).
Fees per term (2014–2015). Pre-Prep: £2,575–£3,240. Upper School: Day £4,505–£5,675; Boarders £5,940–£7,495 inclusive.
"The quality of pupils' achievements and learning is excellent." ISI Inspection Report March 2013.

Winchester House School is a fully co-educational independent school for boys and girls aged 3–13 offering day, weekly boarding and flexi boarding.

Winchester House School sits in its own 18 acres of sports fields and gardens in the market town of Brackley, midway between Oxford and Northampton and close to the borders of Buckinghamshire, Oxfordshire and Northamptonshire. Lying just 10 minutes from the M40 and 20 minutes from the M1, it is also serviced with good rail links to London.

The boys and girls are taught by dedicated specialist teachers. Children in the middle and upper school are placed in streamed sets for all academic subjects and potential scholars are carefully prepared for the scholarship examinations to all major independent senior schools. Over the last few years, excellent examination performance has resulted in a 100% success rate in gaining entry to first-choice senior schools and a significant number of senior school entrance awards.

"Pupils who receive extra support for SEND (Special Educational Needs or Disabilities) make excellent progress in reading and writing tasks both in the classroom and in additional booster groups." ISI Inspection Report March 2013.

Many children enter the school in the nursery or reception classes while others join in Year 3 at seven years old. The day children and the weekly boarders follow the same timetable during the day and many convert from day to weekly boarding during their time at the school. The school operates two minibus services for day children in the local area.

Winchester House has magnificent facilities that include an extensive information and communication technology suite, well-equipped art and design studios, a well-stocked library and dedicated science laboratories and performing arts studio. Sports facilities include numerous rugby, hockey and cricket pitches, a full-size AstroTurf, tennis courts, a heated swimming pool, squash courts, a rifle range, and a fully-fitted sports hall with indoor cricket nets. In more recent years, Winchester House School has introduced riding lessons into the after-school curriculum and has hosted a successful inter-school Hunter Trials, involving more than 55 schools.

Winchester House is dedicated to a fully-rounded education. In addition to the academic timetable, extensive instrumental music teaching and team sports, a broad range of further activities is offered. Activities include brass group, chamber choir, chess, cookery, dance, drama, gymnastics, golf, judo, orchestra and speech & drama. Recent major dramatic productions have included The Odyssey, The Lion, The Witch & The Wardrobe and Romeo & Juliet.

The school is also committed to teaching leadership skills to all pupils. This takes place both on the school grounds and on expeditions in the UK and Europe. Winchester House is the first prep school to introduce such a programme to all its pupils under the banner 'Learn to Lead' in conjunction with The Bushcraft Company.

Charitable status. Winchester House School Trust Limited is a Registered Charity, number 309912.

Windermere Preparatory School
Preparatory School of Windermere School

Ambleside Road, Windermere, The Lake District, Cumbria LA23 1AP
Tel: 015394 43308
Fax: 015394 46803
email: admissions@windermereschool.co.uk
website: www.windermereschool.co.uk
Twitter: @windermeresc
Facebook: /Windermere-School

Chairman of Governors: Mr Michael Dwan

Headmaster: **Mr B C Freeman**, BEd Hons Bristol, PG Dip

Deputy Head: Mrs R Thomas, BA Hons Music Huddersfield, PGCE Newcastle

Type of School. Co-educational Day and Boarding School.

Age Range. 2–11.

Number of Pupils. 48 girls, 52 boys.

Fees per term (2014–2015). *Average* Day Fees (including lunch): Reception £2,410, Years 1–2 £3,227, Years 3–6 £4,767. *Average* Boarding Fees: £7,653 (weekly), £8,085 (full).

International Students: Years 3–6 £8,980 (payable in all 3 terms).

Discounts are available for Forces families eligible for the MOD Continuity of Education Allowance (CEA). Government Nursery Education Grants accepted.

The Purpose of the School. Windermere School and Windermere Preparatory School promote academic excellence and challenge through adventure. It has an international outlook which develops courageous, responsible and inspiring individuals. Windermere Preparatory School is an Independent Preparatory School for boys and girls from 2–11 years, set in 17 acres of grounds in the heart of the English Lake District, and a lakeside watersports centre.

Adventure activities and watersports opportunities are provided for each pupil with nationally recognised certificates from organisations including the Royal Yachting Association and the British Canoe Union. The School's watersports centre, Hodge Howe, has been awarded RYA Champion Club status for its race training and is the first School in the UK to receive this. This combined with the rich literary and cultural heritage of the Lake District provides a unique setting for academic study and self-development; thus the motto Vincit qui se Vincit, *One conquers, who conquers oneself*.

The school aims to ensure that children enjoy the excitement of learning, and benefit from their outstanding location, where adventure skills support academic confidence. Individuality is praised and encouraged. It has a friendly and family-like atmosphere, where children are given the opportunity to use the great outdoors as an inspirational classroom. The school has its own Adventure! Programme built into the daily curriculum.

Academic Ethos. Windermere Preparatory School offers an enhanced curriculum which has science at its core, and includes French in Year 1. Children learn presentation skills and hold regular exhibitions to showcase their work. There are spacious classrooms – most with spectacular views of the lake and fells. All Form Tutors are specialist primary teachers and there is both Extension Learning through the Gifted and Talented programme and Special Educational Needs support. The majority of pupils achieve results well ahead of the national average in the Standard Attainment Tests at seven and eleven years, and are successful in winning places at Windermere School or other secondary schools in the UK or abroad. Subject specialists teach Art, Drama, Dance, French, Games, Design and Technology, Music, Physical Education, and the unique Adventure! lessons. There are progressive camping trips, first on the school grounds, and when children are older, on staff-led expeditions throughout the Lake District.

Sport for All. Windermere Preparatory School offers a wide range of challenging and competitive sports, available every day after school. They are taught by specialist staff and include Athletics, Badminton, GymClub, Cricket, Dance (tap, jazz, modern, ballet), Fell walking, Football, Netball, Rounders, Sailing, Swimming, Tennis, Tag Rugby, Rugby, Adventure Club, Dens, Kayaking, Canoeing,

Hockey, Adventure Playground, Gymnastics, and Cross-Country Running.

Clubs and Activities. *The Arts*: Art Club, Choir, ICT, Video Club, Drama, Infant Cookery, Individual Music lessons including piano, strings, woodwind, brass and guitar, Le Club Francais, Library, Orchestra, Recorder groups, Craft Club.

Uniform. Girls wear blue kilt and striped blazer plus light blue blouses in the winter. In the summer the kilt is worn with a blue and white flowered short-sleeved blouse and blue sleeveless slipover. Boys wear grey trousers, pale blue shirts and sweater, the school tie and blazer.

Pastoral and Boarding. Windermere Preparatory School accepts boarders from the age of eight. They reside at Windermere School just minutes away. The boys reside in Langdale House, and the girls reside in Browhead with children in their age group. There are qualified Housemasters and Housemistresses to offer care and supervision. All meals are provided, along with laundry and transportation by dedicated school drivers. There are after school, early evening and weekend activities, as well as supervised prep with academic staff available for advice and assistance at all times.

Leadership and teamworking skills are continually developed and there is a thriving School Council and House System. Thoughtfulness towards others, and a strong ethos of service and contribution towards society are all part of the Windermere Preparatory School spirit.

Charitable status. Windermere Educational Trust Limited is a Registered Charity, number 526973. It exists to provide education of the highest quality.

Windlesham House School

Washington, Pulborough, West Sussex RH20 4AY
Tel: 01903 874700
Fax: +44 (0)1903 874702
email: whsadmissions@windlesham.com
website: www.windlesham.com

Chairman of Governors: Christina Maude, BA Hons, BArch RIBA

Head: **Richard Foster**, BEd Hons

Age Range. 4–13.

Number of Pupils. 194 boarders, 158 day (c. 50/50 boys and girls). Children can board from Year 4.

Fees per term (2014–2015). Prep: Day £5,065–£6,945, Boarding £7,850–£8,080; Pre-Prep: Day £2,810–£3,265.

Windlesham nestles in 65 glorious acres of the South Downs countryside in West Sussex and gives every child the opportunity to reach their potential in whatever sphere of life that may be. Established in 1837 Windlesham was the first school in the country to be established as a preparatory school and in 1967 became the first IAPS co-educational school. Windlesham is one of the few prep schools to have no uniform and our children are not confined to a playground; they make dens, climb trees and camp in the woods and are free to choose what they want to do in their break times.

Today we educate approximately 352 pupils with a broad range of ability. Windlesham traditionally receives outstanding Ofsted and ISI reports which underlines our position as one of the leading prep schools in the world today. We give every child the opportunity to reach his or her full potential in whatever sphere of learning that may be. Although academic excellence is key we also encourage success in sport, music, drama and the arts whilst nurturing a friendly, family-orientated atmosphere with wonderful pastoral care.

With us children have the time and space to be children, away from the pressures of competition and urban hothousing. Windlesham is set in exceptionally beautiful grounds with magnificent buildings and facilities where children are encouraged to try a host of sports and extra-curricular activities after the academic day and at weekends. The children learn about independence, interdependence and cooperation.

At the top end of the school our overriding aim is to ensure that each child achieves the highest grades they can in their Common Entrance or Scholarship exams to some of the best senior schools in the country, as well as ensuring they follow a balanced and enjoyable curriculum. This year saw a record number of scholarships to senior schools and a 100% success rate at Common Entrance with all candidates gaining places at their first choice of school.

When the time comes to leave Windlesham children do so as confident, curious, clever and above all, kind people who are ready to make a difference in their world. Senior Schools often comment on how well prepared Windlesham children are for the next stage. Some even admit they've got a hard act to follow.

Charitable status. Windlesham House School is a Registered Charity, number 307046. It exists to provide education for girls and boys aged 4–13.

Winterfold House

Chaddesley Corbett, Worcestershire DY10 4PW
Tel: 01562 777234
Fax: 01562 777078
email: linda@winterfoldhouse.co.uk
website: www.winterfoldhouse.co.uk

Chairman of Governors: Mrs M Chapman, MA

Headmaster: **W C R Ibbetson-Price**, MA, NPQH

Age Range. 3–13 Co-educational.
Number of Pupils. 350 Day Boys and Girls.
Fees per term (2014–2015). Preparatory £3,400–£3,950; Pre-Prep £2,310–£2,540; Kindergarten: £31.60 per day (inc Nursery Education Funding), £47.40 per day (excluding Nursery Education Funding).

Winterfold is centred around a spacious Georgian house set in nearly 40 acres of attractive grounds, surrounded by beautiful and unspoilt Worcestershire countryside. However, we are only half an hour from the centre of Birmingham, Worcester is just 10 miles away, and we are a mere 10 minutes from the M5 and M42.

Winterfold is a Roman Catholic co-educational day preparatory school but children of all faiths are warmly welcomed and made to feel valued members of the community.

The school has an excellent academic record at all levels including National Curriculum Key Stage Tests, Common Entrance and Scholarship. Children are prepared for entrance to both local independent day schools (such as RGS Worcester, Holy Trinity, King's Worcester, and the King Edward's schools in Birmingham) and to independent schools of national renown (such as Shrewsbury, Cheltenham Ladies' College, Malvern College, Stonyhurst, Ampleforth Cheltenham College and Bromsgrove). We have a highly regarded Learning Support Unit which provides one to one help for children with specific learning difficulties such as dyslexia. In the last 3 years our children have gained 69 scholarships to senior schools.

Winterfold places a great emphasis upon educating the whole child and aims to produce well rounded and confident boys and girls with high moral standards and good manners. In order to develop self-belief we encourage every child to achieve success in some area and thus the school fields a great number of teams and not just in the main sports of rugby, soccer, cricket, netball, hockey and rounders; but also in the minor sports which include fishing, golf, archery, tennis, swimming, athletics, basketball, fencing, judo, chess and shooting. There are also a large number of clubs and societies and regular visits to theatres and concerts and other places of educational interest which gives fullness and breadth to the educational experience.

In recent years there has been considerable investment into the school which has seen the development of a new sports hall, ICT suite, entrance hall and offices, classrooms, a chapel, library and three adventure playgrounds. A brand new classroom block has just been completed, with eight new classrooms, Science labs and Art and CDT rooms. A new Performing Arts Centre is currently under construction and will be completed for 2012.

Charitable status. Winterfold House School is a Registered Charity, number 1063133. It exists solely to provide education for boys and girls.

Witham Hall

Witham-on-the-Hill, Bourne, Lincolnshire PE10 0JJ
Tel: 01778 590222
Fax: 01778 590606
email: office@withamhall.com
website: www.withamhall.com

The school was founded in 1959 and was formed into an Educational Trust in 1978.

Chairman of Governors: Mr J W Sharman

Headmaster: **Mr A C Welch**, BEd

Age Range. 4–13.
Number of Pupils. 248: Prep (age 8–13): 90 Boys (55 boarders, 35 day pupils); 72 Girls (50 boarders, 22 day pupils); Pre-Prep (age 4–8): 86 pupils.
Fees per term (2014–2015). Boarders £6,255, Day pupils £4,650, Pre-Prep £2,830–£3,030.

The school is situated in a superb country house setting in the village of Witham on the Hill, close to the Lincolnshire-Rutland border. Boarding is very popular (weekly and flexi are available from Year 4) and benefits from first-class provision within the original Queen Anne house, at the heart of the school.

There is a teaching staff of 40, and additional visiting teachers for instrumental music. The maximum class size is 17 and pupils benefit from outstanding pastoral care across the school. The majority of pupils join at the Pre-Prep stage, and then continue through to Common Entrance. Pupils progress to their first-choice senior school both locally (Oundle, Oakham, Uppingham and Stamford) and further afield (Eton, Rugby, Repton, Shrewsbury and Stowe). The school has an enviable scholarship record (17 awards from a cohort of 34 in 2014 retaining a proud tradition) across a range of disciplines, including academic, art, drama, music and sport.

Facilities are outstanding with modern, purpose-built Prep and Pre-Prep teaching areas. Significant developments have taken place in the last three years, including a new ICT suite, two new state-of-the-art Science laboratories, and a new Library and Resource Centre. The Stimson Hall, a superb Concert Hall and Theatre, underpins a strong commitment to both Creative and Performing Arts. Most of the children learn one instrument or more and there are three bands and four choirs. Inclusivity is strong; within sport all Prep pupils represent the school on a regular basis each term. The standard is high, with teams regularly reaching National Finals in rugby, hockey, netball, cricket and rounders. Pupils benefit from a multi-purpose sports hall, an Olympic-size all-weather astroturf, high-quality tennis and netball courts, a squash court and magnificently maintained grass surfaces, including county-standard cricket facilities and a 9-hole golf course. The school has seen considerable growth in numbers and in almost every year group early registration is recommended.

Charitable status. Witham Hall School Trust is a Registered Charity, number 507070. It exists for the purpose of educating children.

Woodbridge School – The Abbey

Church Street, Woodbridge, Suffolk IP12 1DS
Tel: 01394 382673
Fax: 01394 383880
email: office@theabbeyschool-suffolk.org.uk
website: www.woodbridge.suffolk.sch.uk/the_abbey

Chairman of the Governors: R Finbow, MA Oxon

The Master: **N J Garrett**, BA, PGCE

Head of Pre-Prep: Mrs J King, BEd

Age Range. Co-educational 4–11.
Number of Pupils. 330 Day pupils.
Fees per term (2014–2015). Pre-Prep £2,647; Prep £4,082.

The Abbey is the Preparatory School for Woodbridge School for which boys and girls are prepared for entry. A small number of pupils go elsewhere. There is a highly qualified teaching staff of thirty, with additional visiting music and other specialist teachers. The academic record has been consistently good: scholarships are won regularly both to Woodbridge and to other schools. The teaching is linked to the National Curriculum and emphasis is placed on pupils reaching their full academic potential whilst also benefiting from a broad education. The school enjoys strong links with a number of European schools and exchange visits take place, and pupils learn four European languages. Music is regarded as an important part of school life with a large number of pupils receiving individual music lessons and in Year Four all pupils receive strings tuition as well as their class music lessons. In Games lessons boys play soccer, rugby, hockey and cricket and girls play netball, hockey and rounders. Children also have the opportunity to swim, play tennis and take part in athletics, cross-country, horse riding and sailing. In lunch breaks and after school, pupils are able to participate in a whole range of extra-curricular activities and hobbies.

The School is set in its own beautiful grounds of 30 acres in the middle of the town. As well as a fine Tudor Manor house, it has a well-planned and high-quality classroom and changing room block. Another major development includes a multi-purpose hall and classroom block. Recent developments have included an upgrade of Music, ICT, Art, DT and Science facilities. The grounds are extensive and include playing fields, an all-weather surface games area and a science garden. The Pre-Prep Department is at Queen's House, situated within the Senior School's grounds, a short walk from The Abbey. Here the pupils enjoy spacious accommodation and excellent facilities.

Parents of Abbey pupils are eligible to join the Parents' Association and there is a close contact maintained between parents and school.

Religious affiliation: Church of England (other denominations welcome).

Charitable status. The Seckford Foundation is a Registered Charity, number 1110964. It exists to provide education for boys and girls.

Woodcote House

Windlesham, Surrey GU20 6PF
Tel: 01276 472115
Fax: 01276 472890
email: info@woodcotehouseschool.co.uk
website: www.woodcotehouseschool.co.uk

Headmaster: **Henry Knight**, BA, PGCE

Age Range. 7–13.
Number of Boys. 105 (80 boarders, 25 day).
Fees per term (from April 2014). £6,900 (Boarding), £5,200 (Day). No compulsory extras. Annual Scholarship Day in March.

Location. Originally a Coaching Inn on the old London to Portsmouth Road, Woodcote enjoys a beautiful, rural setting in 30 acres of grounds. The school is easily accessible from London and runs a bus service from the top of the A3. We are only 25 miles from Fulham via the M3 (Junction 3), 25 minutes from Heathrow and 40 minutes from Gatwick.

Pastoral Care. Woodcote House has been owned and run by the Paterson family for over 75 years. Four years ago they promoted Henry Knight to be the new Headmaster and he, along with his wife Susannah and their three young children, will maintain the strong family ethos for which Woodcote has become so well known. With a settled and committed staff, most of whom live on site with their own families, Woodcote provides an exceptionally caring and supportive environment for both Boarders and Day Boys. Our unique, graduated approach to boarding has helped solve the modern boarding conundrum faced by parents torn between Full and Weekly options. A strong emphasis is placed on manners, consideration and respect for others. The school has its own Chapel in the woods and parents are welcome to Sunday services, as well as to school matches on Wednesdays and Saturdays (after which legendary Match Teas are served), so there is plenty of opportunity to see their boys and talk to staff and fellow parents.

Academic. There are two forms in each year group, with an average of 10 boys in each class, enabling the staff to offer all boys an enormous degree of individual attention. With SEN and EFL teaching also available, academic standards are high and the school is proud of its 100% Common Entrance and excellent Scholarship record. Woodcote boys go on to a wide variety of independent senior schools and Mr Knight takes particular care in assisting parents to choose the right school for their son.

Music and Drama. 80% of boys learn at least one musical instrument, and the young and innovative Director of Music has ensured that it is considered 'cool' to be in the excellent choir. There is an orchestra and a jazz band and the school holds regular concerts so that the boys are comfortable with public performance, both individually and as part of a group. The school produces a Junior and a Senior Play each year, in which all boys are involved one way or another.

Sports. Rugby, football, cricket and hockey are coached to a high standard and there are teams at all levels of age and ability, with a high success rate for a small school. Individual sports include tennis (the school has five courts), swimming, athletics, golf, judo, riding, squash, rifle-shooting and polo.

Hobbies and Free Time. With 'prep' done first thing in the morning, there are numerous opportunities for the boys to pursue hobbies after lessons and games, and each member of staff offers a 'club' during Hobbies Hour on Wednesday afternoons. These activities are also available at weekends, along with the traditional activities of 'hutting' (camp building in the woods), 'cooking' (frying potatoes on camp fires), and overnight camping in the grounds. Boys are also offered the opportunity to be involved in the CCF. Boys are encouraged to read and have a quiet time after lunch each day for this as well as before lights out in the evening.

Ethos. The school motto, "Vive ut Discas et Disce ut Vivas" (Live to Learn and Learn to Live), embodies the school's aim to give all boys a love of learning and to discover and nurture their individual talents in a happy and positive atmosphere.

Woodford Green Preparatory School

Glengall Road, Woodford Green, Essex IG8 0BZ
Tel: 020 8504 5045
email: admin@wgprep.co.uk
website: www.wgprep.co.uk

The School is an Educational Charity, controlled by a Board of Governors.

Chairman of Governors: Mr D Paterson

Head: Mrs J Hart, MA, BEd, MSc, Adv Dip RE

Age Range. 3–11.
Number of Pupils. 384 (Boys and Girls).
Fees per term (2014–2015). £2,772.
The school provides an outstanding learning environment in which children achieve their best feeling valued and secure. The School also has an outstanding record of success in 11+ examinations to Senior Independent and Grammar Schools and demand for places far outstrips availability. Parents are advised to make a very early application to the school.

Means-tested Bursaries, of up to 100% of the full fees, are available for 7+ entry.

Charitable status. Woodford Green Preparatory School is a Registered Charity, number 310930.

Worksop College Preparatory School, Ranby House
A Woodard School

Retford, Nottinghamshire DN22 8HX
Tel: 01777 703138; Bursary: 01777 714391
Fax: 01777 702813
email: admissionsprep@wsnl.co.uk
website: www.wsnl.co.uk
Twitter: @worksopcollege

Chairman of the School Council: C J D Anderson, MA

Headmaster: C S J Pritchard, MA, BA Hons QTS

Age Range. 3–13 years.
Number of Pupils. 165: 85 boys, 80 girls.
Fees per term (2014–2015). Boarders £5,560, Day Children £197.50–£4,070.
Worksop College Preparatory School, Ranby House is situated in 60 acres of outstanding countryside. The Pre-Prep takes children from 3 to 7 years with a seamless transition to the Prep School for ages 7 to 13. The facilities are excellent and include: a Performing Arts Centre which houses a 300-seat Theatre and Music School, a large Sports Centre with Sports Hall and changing rooms, three ICT suites to complement the school's fully networked intranet, a Design Technology Centre, modern Library, two Science Laboratories, a well-equipped Art Studio, a dedicated Chapel, four floodlit all-weather netball/tennis courts, and extensive level playing fields.

Pupils are encouraged to take on responsibility at all levels: on the School Council, the Eco Committee, as Librarians and as Year 8 Leaders.

The prep school fosters a special sense of community, instilling values and standards which are often overlooked in the twenty-first century. With awareness of each other and society in general, pupils grow up with confidence within a framework based on Christian values. Above all, the prep school is a very happy school.

At the centre of life in this Woodard School (see www.woodard.co.uk) is our modern Chapel. The teaching of Christian values helps the children to learn to live and respect one another within our community and also in the wider world through supporting a number of charities and good causes. Children from families of Christian faith, different faith or no faith are all welcome, and everyone attends Chapel services.

The purpose-built Pre-Prep Department, with its Nursery School and Forest Learning, takes children from 3 to 7 years after which they transfer to the Prep School for ages 7 to 13. At 13 the majority of pupils transfer to Worksop College, our senior school within Woodard Schools (Nottinghamshire) Ltd, although pupils are prepared for entry to a variety of independent senior schools.

There is flexi boarding from Year 3 to 8 Mondays to Thursday evening. Spacious, colourful bedrooms, wholesome food and caring houseparents are important elements of the Prep School boarding experience. Boarding is flexible and is dependent upon the needs of the individual family; weekly, flexi and casual boarding are all offered by the school.

Academic standards are high at the Prep School. In the last four years, a total of 57 Awards for academic, musical, sporting, art, all-round excellence and leadership have been gained by pupils transferring to their senior independent school. The school is non-selective and caters for children of all abilities including those with specific learning difficulties.

A wealth of extra-curricular opportunities is on offer and pupils are encouraged to take an active part in all aspects of school life. The school has strong traditions in sport, music and drama.

We are non-selective and believe that education is for life, so whether joining the school in the dedicated Nursery, with its forest school, or following on to The College (ages 13 to 18), your child will be given the chance to discover how our environment would provide an opportunity of a lifetime.

The school is extremely well-situated half a mile from the A1 and close to the A57/A614. Daily bus routes, which the school shares with Worksop College, are available from the surrounding area of Bassetlaw, Rotherham, Doncaster, Tickhill, Mansfield, Newark and Southwell, all providing easy access from a wide area.

You are warmly invited to contact us to arrange to come and visit, meet the Headmaster, staff and pupils and to tour the school, to discover how our environment would inspire your child.

Worksop College is our senior school and the majority of our pupils transfer to the College at age 13. Worksop College is about 4 miles from the Prep School and offers boarding and day education to boys and girls from age 13–18. (*For further details see Worksop College entry in HMC section.*)

Charitable status. Woodard Schools (Nottinghamshire) Limited is a Registered Charity, number 1103326. It exists for the purpose of educating children.

Wycliffe Preparatory School

Stonehouse, Gloucestershire GL10 2LD
Tel: 01453 820470
Fax: 01453 825604
email: prep@wycliffe.co.uk
website: www.wycliffe.co.uk

Chairman of Trustees: Mrs G E Camm, BSc Hons

Headmaster: A Palmer, MA, BEd

Age Range. 2–13.
Number of Pupils. Nursery: 68 pupils; Preparatory: 62 boarding, 282 day pupils.
Fees per term (2014–2015). Day £2,005–£4,055 (Lunch £305), Boarding £5,610–£7,180.

Wycliffe Preparatory School is a co-educational day, boarding and flexi boarding school from 2 to 13 years. The School is administered by the Governors' Advisory Body and the Trustees of Wycliffe (*see Wycliffe College entry in HMC section*), but is a separate unit with its own Headmaster and full-time staff of 30 teachers (all qualified), house staff and matrons.

A range of Scholarships, both academic and non-academic, are offered by competition annually. There are also bursaries available for children from HM Forces families. The vast majority of our pupils go on to the Senior School, however, pupils are prepared for Common Entrance examinations to all schools.

Wycliffe is committed to fostering individual learning in all areas of the curriculum and pupils benefit from small class sizes with a high teacher to pupil ratio. One of Wycliffe's aims is to cultivate each pupil's unique talents and to bring out the best in its pupils by creating a supportive learning environment which promotes individual achievements in all fields. Specialist teachers ensure outstanding teaching delivery across the curriculum and a wide variety of extra-curricular activities enables the school to offer a fully-rounded education designed to develop confidence and self-esteem.

There is also a dedicated CReSTeD registered SEN Department which supports children who have weaknesses in some areas of the curriculum. The school not only promotes success in the classroom, but prides itself on enabling every child to do well, whether on the sports field, in one of the many drama or musical productions or by taking part in the annual Art exhibition, hosted at the Senior School.

Academic excellence is something all pupils are encouraged to attain. Challenge for our Gifted & Talented children is something that we, as a school, provide on a regular basis, through ensuring our more able children are sufficiently stretched in the areas where they have been identified as gifted or talented. In addition to this, we offer further enrichment through the delivery of a number of specific Gifted & Talented events that provide our children with some exciting and unique learning opportunities. We have become a member of the National Association for Gifted Children (NAGC) and have recently gained the Gold Star Award.

The Preparatory School continues with its programme to improve facilities with a state-of-the-art Years 7 and 8 learning centre opening in September 2014. This university-style facility will offer 8 spacious classrooms, with high-tech facilities including touchscreen smart boards, latest computer technology, common room, staff offices and two new tennis courts. A new Reception, Years 1 and 2 teaching block which is situated on the Prep campus with its own adventure playground and the extension of the boys' and girls' boarding houses by a further 16 beds. The school also boasts an all-weather pitch, refurbished Years 3 and 4 classrooms, swimming pool, art studio and craft workshop, extensive playing fields, tennis courts, sports hall, studio theatre and music school, two science laboratories, three computer rooms, a covered playground and cafeteria-style dining room. The Preparatory School uses the College Chapel, Medical Centre and state-of-the-art Sports Centre.

The boarding houses are in the care of House staff and there are members of staff with particular responsibility for the welfare of day pupils. Vegetarian and other dietary specialities can be catered for.

As well as the usual range of sport, drama and music, there are clubs, activities and opportunities for outdoor pursuits. A number of educational trips are also arranged, including a Year 5 residential stay at the Jorvik Viking Centre, team building activity in Wales and a trip to Paris, organised by the languages department.

Charitable status. Wycliffe College Incorporated is a Registered Charity, number 311714. It is a co-educational boarding and day school promoting a balanced education for children between the ages of 2 and 18.

Yardley Court
The Schools at Somerhill

Somerhill, Tonbridge, Kent TN11 0NJ
Tel: 01732 352124
Fax: 01732 363381
email: office@somerhill.org
website: www.somerhill.org

Chairman of Governors: Mr Philip Thomas

Headmaster: John Coakley, BA Hons, PGCE, MA

Age Range. Boys 7–13.
Number of Pupils. 254 Day Boys.
Fees per term (2014–2015). £4,605 inclusive of lunch. There are no compulsory extras.

Yardley Court is one of the three Schools at Somerhill. From a co-educational Pre-Prep of some 270+ children, the seven year old boys join Yardley Court and the girls join our sister school, Derwent Lodge. All three schools are housed in a magnificent Jacobean mansion set within 150 acres of beautiful parkland. Thus we are able to offer single-sex education in the classroom but very much within a co-educational setting.

Yardley Court was founded in 1898 and moved to the Somerhill estate in 1990. We prepare boys for Common Entrance and Scholarships to senior independent schools in the immediate vicinity such as Tonbridge and Sevenoaks and also to schools further afield. Boys are also prepared for 11+ and 13+ entrance to the very strong Grammar Schools in our area: The Judd, Skinners and Tunbridge Wells Grammar School For Boys. Sound foundations are the basis of all the academic teaching with particular emphasis placed on the core subject of Mathematics, English, Science and French.

Music plays an important part in school life with most boys participating in some way, either through the choirs, the orchestra or in solo or group instruction in a wide range of instruments.

The parkland and woods adjoining the school together with our purpose-built playing fields provide an excellent environment for both sport and play. A strong sports programme centres around Football, Rugby, Cross-country, Cricket, Tennis, Swimming and Athletics. All the boys are given the opportunity to represent the school on a regular basis. The school also encourages participation in a wide range of clubs and activities.

As well as our extensive grounds, we are lucky to enjoy excellent facilities including a recently constructed sports hall, indoor swimming pool and dining facility.

Charitable status. The Somerhill Charitable Trust Limited is a Registered Charity, number 1002212. It exists to provide education for children.

Yarlet School

Yarlet, Nr Stafford ST18 9SU
Tel: 01785 286568
email: info@yarletschool.org
website: www.yarletschool.org

Chairman of the Governors: Dr A Primrose

Headmaster: Mr Ian Raybould, BEd Hons, ALCM, NPQH

Age Range. Co-educational 2–13.
Number of Pupils. 151 pupils: 74 Girls and Boys in the Preparatory School (aged 7 to 13) and 77 Girls and Boys in the Nursery and Pre-Preparatory School (aged 2 to 7).
Fees per term (2014–2015). £2,240–£3,755. Flexi boarding available (Wednesday and Thursday nights) at £25 per night.

Established in 1873, Yarlet stands in 33 acres of grounds in unspoilt open countryside 5 miles north of Stafford. The school offers small classes, enthusiastic, qualified teachers, excellent facilities and a warm, friendly environment conducive to learning. All teachers keep fully abreast of the National Curriculum guidelines to Key Stage 3 and beyond.

Pupils have access to the wide range of facilities which include a modern Science Laboratory, an Information Technology Centre, a CDT Centre, a purpose-built Art Studio and an indoor Sports and Performance Hall; and extensive outdoor facilities which include a heated swimming pool, four playing fields (for football, rugby, hockey, cricket and athletics), three tennis courts, a netball court, an all-weather Astroturf pitch (for football, hockey and netball), and a large garden area close to the Pre-Prep. These facilities support an extensive sports curriculum, which features a daily games lesson.

Music and Drama complete the picture of a Yarlet education, with termly performances from the Yarlet Academy of Music and the Academy of Performing Arts. The arts are brought to life at Yarlet, inspiring self-belief and creative confidence in all our pupils. Whatever their talent, Yarlet pupils have the chance to shine. Club and extra-curricular activities are a further feature of Yarlet and include art (painting, sculpture and pottery), model-making, music, drama, French culture, chess, photography and fishing.

Yarlet has high expectations of all its children. Children are prepared for entry to a wide variety of senior schools and their achievements in both Key Stage tests and Common Entrance examinations are a source of great pride, as too is the fact that many children leave with a Scholarship award from their Senior School.

Charitable status. Yarlet is a Registered Charity, number 528618. It exists to provide education for boys and girls from 2 to 13.

Yarm Preparatory School

Grammar School Lane, Yarm, Stockton-on-Tees TS15 9ES
Tel: 01642 781447
Fax: 01642 787425
email: prepschool@yarmschool.org
website: www.yarmschool.org

Chair of Governors: Ms C Evans, MA, MBA, ARCM

Head: **W Sawyer**, BA Hons, PGCE

Age Range. 3–11.
Number of Pupils. 361 Boys and Girls.
Fees per term (2014–2015). Preparatory School £2,917–£3,227; Pre-Prep and Nursery £2,291–£2,331; Pre-Prep and Nursery (with Nursery Grant): £1,568. Lunches are extra.

Yarm Preparatory School is a co-educational day school which educates children from 3–11 years of age (3–7 within the Nursery and Pre-Prep).

Ethos. The Preparatory School is well known as a friendly and stimulating environment that encourages children to flourish educationally whilst also developing valuable social abilities and leadership skills. Through the broad variety of extra-curricular activities, children come to excel in sport and music as well as a wide range of other pastimes.

Organisation. Pastoral care is based on both a year group and a House system. Every pupil belongs to one of four Houses. Houses exist to promote competitions, sporting events, charity and fundraising etc. Pupils have opportunities to represent their form as Form Captains, who also serve on the School Council.

Curriculum. The Preparatory School curriculum is based upon the National Curriculum, although it offers greater breadth and depth in many subject areas. In addition to the core curriculum of English, mathematics and science (in a new laboratory), full weight is given to both history and geography, whilst subjects such as design technology, ICT, art, music, religious education, PSHE, PE and games are fully catered for. Children are also taught French from age 3. Whilst form teachers deliver much of the core curriculum, subject specialist teachers are employed to cover many areas.

Games and Activities. The Preparatory School hosts a whole range of sports. However, rugby and hockey are the school's main winter games. Football and netball are played during the Spring Term, followed by cricket, athletics and rounders in the summer. In addition, cross-country is also pursued at inter-school level throughout the year. There are many school activities including music, dance, drama, orienteering, chess, swimming, badminton, gardening, modelling, crafts, pottery, ICT and quizzes which are timetabled to take place during two lessons, at lunchtimes and after school each week. These activities change at least termly.

Music. The Preparatory School boasts many musical groups, choirs, choristers and a variety of traditional and modern ensembles with well over half of the school learning an instrument.

Educational Visits. A varied programme of educational day visits is undertaken by all year groups to enrich the curriculum, using the locality as a resource. From age 7, pupils have the opportunity to participate in residential trips, including visits to Whitby, York, Robinwood, Ru'a Fiola and Saint-Omer, France.

Admission. Entry to the Preparatory School is by assessment which may be carried out at any time of the year if places are available. Pupils are prepared for entry to the Senior School, sitting transfer papers in January before the September in which they transfer. The results of transfer papers are considered in conjunction with ongoing assessment information made available by teachers in the Preparatory School.

Open Days. The Nursery/Pre-Prep and Preparatory School hold Open Mornings each year, normally in October and January with an Open Week in May. Prospective parents are encouraged to attend at least one Open Morning as this gives excellent opportunity to look around the school at leisure, view the new facilities, see our development plans and chat with staff. Visits are, however, welcome at any time.

Religion. The school is an interdenominational community but follows Christian traditions and ethos.

Charitable status. Yarm School is a Registered Charity, number 1093434. It exists to provide education for boys and girls from 3–18.

Yarrells Preparatory School

Yarrells House, Upton, Poole, Dorset BH16 5EU
Tel: 01202 622229
email: secretary@yarrells.co.uk
website: www.yarrells.co.uk
Facebook: /Yarrells-Preparatory-School

Headmistress: **Mrs C Oosthuizen**, BEd Hons, PGCE

Director of Studies: Mrs L Sharpe, BSc Hons, PGCE

Age Range. 2–13.
Number of Pupils. 250 Boys and Girls.
Fees per term (2014–2015). £1,875–£3,447.

Ethos. Yarrells School offers a unique environment for the early development of intellectual, artistic and sporting potential. Only minutes from Bournemouth and Poole, Yarrells occupies a late Georgian country house surrounded by woods, gardens, playing fields, tennis courts and covered, heated swimming pool. The atmosphere is warm and encouraging while a rigorous approach is taken to the maintenance of each child's highest standards. Well-qualified and committed staff work with the Headmistress to ensure careful character-building, social responsibility and maximum academic performance. The school seeks to identify and develop children's abilities in such a way that the children grow in self-knowledge, self-discipline and self-confidence.

Curriculum. We seek the highest standards of attainment for all our children and we also value a stimulating, creative and broad curriculum that makes the most of all the facilities on offer at Yarrells. We aim to foster creativity in our children, and to help them become independent learners. Above all we believe in making learning a positive experience. We offer excellent education within an enriching environment. The rich school curriculum at Yarrells provides opportunities for all pupils to learn and to achieve. We aim to develop the enjoyment of, and commitment to learning, to encourage the best possible progress and the highest attainment for all pupils. It is our intention to build on pupils' strengths, interests and experiences to help them develop confidence in their capacity to learn, and to work independently and collaboratively. All children have curricular tuition in Art, Music (singing and instrumental), Drama and Dance. There are Recorder Ensembles, a Wind Band, Choir, Choral Societies and an Orchestra. There is a broad PE programme that includes swimming, tennis, football, rugby, netball, rounders, hockey and cross-country. Science, Investigational Mathematics, Design and ICT are areas of study given good accommodation in the timetable. The school is active until 5.45 pm each weekday evening for those children from age 7 who elect to stay for supervised prep and a range of activities which include football, cross-country, ballet, extra swimming and tennis, tap and modern dance, art, drama and music.

Senior Success. Yarrells School has an excellent record of success in Entrance Examinations and Scholarship Awards to senior schools. Most children go on to Grammar Schools or to Senior Independent Schools.

Holiday Activity Weeks. During the holidays, Yarrells offers Activity Weeks, which are led by Yarrells teaching staff. These are attended by pupils of Yarrells as well as non-pupils. These weeks are packed with sport, music, drama, craft and good company. Activities are timetabled depending on children's ages.

Eco. Yarrells is an Eco-School and has been awarded the Green Flag by Eco-Schools England. The school is deeply committed to developing a sustainable environment. Through studies across the curriculum and links with parents, the whole community participates in environmental activities: recycling and re-using, gardening, composting, caring for wildlife and conserving energy.

Yateley Manor Preparatory School

51 Reading Road, Yateley, Hampshire GU46 7UQ
Tel: 01252 405500
Fax: 01252 405504
email: office@yateleymanor.com
website: www.yateleymanor.com

The School is an Educational Trust controlled by a Board of Governors.

Chairman of Governors: Stephen Gorys

Headmaster: **Rob Williams**, MA Hons Edinburgh, PGCE Bedford

Age Range. 3–13.
Number of Pupils. Pre-Prep and Nursery: 55 Girls, 81 Boys; Prep: 103 Girls, 173 Boys.
Fees per term (2014–2015). £1,750–£4,495. Fees are inclusive of all normal activities, extended supervision from 8.00 am until 6.30 pm, meals and residential field trips for Years 5, 6, 7 and 8.

Yateley Manor has a long and successful history of educating girls and boys from the age of 3 to 13.

Innovative, enthusiastic and committed teachers are at the heart of our learning community and they provide the framework for your child's educational, cultural and social development. Nurtured in a warm, friendly and safe environment with excellent facilities and limited class sizes, children are given new experiences to explore, building confidence and stimulating a desire to learn.

Yateley Manor is proud of its impressive examination results and scholarship to senior schools. Being independent of any senior school, pupils proceed to a wide variety of local independent schools, and to many further away.

Yateley Manor is a Prep School Baccalaureate (PSB) School. The PSB incorporates core subjects – English, Mathematics, Science and French – which are assessed through Common Entrance. It also includes a record of achievement in all other subjects such as Humanities, Classics, Sport, Art, DT and Drama. Importantly key life skills: communication, thinking and learning, self-reviewing and improving are all tracked with respect to independence, collaboration and leadership.

A full programme enriches our educational experience giving children the opportunity to reach their full potential. Chess is a very important part of Yateley Manor's programme and the school's results are second to none. There are many other activities to try, including dance and ballet in our specially equipped Studio. Horse riding, athletics and archery are also very popular and we are always looking for new opportunities for pupils to find something they enjoy.

The school has recently completed the purchase of an adjoining seven acres of land which will complement the already impressive facilities. These include a heated indoor swimming pool in use all year round, a spacious sports hall with indoor cricket nets, football, netball and basketball facilities, a gymnasium and several sports pitches. Imaginatively equipped play areas give children the freedom to unwind and play creatively.

In a community that embraces a breadth of cultures centred on Christian values where all relationships are based upon respect, children learn to appreciate the need to be courteous, considerate and to use common sense. At the same time they are encouraged to be creative and courageous as they develop into confident individuals, with a strong foundation for a happy and balanced life. Pupils can only achieve this once they have been given the tools and the self-belief. The Yateley Manor experience does just that.

There is an informal screening assessment for entry to the school and the most common entrance points are at 3 into the Nursery, at 4 into Reception, and at 7 into the main school. Children are welcome to join at all other ages, and many do. Means-tested bursaries are available.

A network of school coaches serves the surrounding areas including, Camberley, Church Crookham, Farnborough, Fleet, Frimley, Hartley Wintney, Hook and Odiham.

Charitable status. Yateley Manor is a Registered Charity, number 307374. It is dedicated to providing the highest quality education for children of the local community.

York House School

Sarratt Road, Croxley Green, Rickmansworth, Herts WD3 4LW

Tel:	01923 772395
Fax:	01923 779231
email:	yhsoffice@york-house.com
website:	www.york-house.com
Twitter:	@schoolYorkHouse; @YHheadmaster

Founded in 1910, York House School is a non-profit making Educational Trust with a Board of Governors.

Chairman of the Governors: Mrs G Noach

Headmaster: **Mr Jon Gray**, BA Ed Hons

Age Range. Boys 3–13, Girls 3–10. Move to co-education commenced in September 2009. Now taking girls up to and including Year 5.

Number of Children. All are Day pupils: 160 Prep, 110 Pre-Prep, 30 Nursery.

Fees per term (2014–2015). Pre-Prep £2,895–£3,500; Middle and Upper Schools £3,980; including lunch. Nursery: £260 per half-day session (minimum 3 sessions per week).

York House School is a well-established, innovative and forward-looking school located in a Queen Anne country house standing in 47 acres of the Hertfordshire countryside. The Headmaster is assisted by a fully-qualified and caring staff. Our extended day arrangements enable pupils to attend early morning clubs and after school clubs between 7.45 am and 6.00 pm (see our website for costs).

The school's aim is to encourage children to achieve the highest academic results in a happy atmosphere while promoting self-discipline and caring for others.

The school has excellent facilities which include a multi-purpose hall, Library, state-of-the-art computer suite, a modern Pre-Prep and Nursery building that opened in 2001. In 2005 a new Junior School, Science Laboratory, Art Design and Technology Rooms were opened. The music centre is large with 6 practice rooms.

Sporting facilities are excellent with brand new all-weather multi-purpose pitches for football, hockey and netball, 15 acres of playing fields for cricket, rugby, soccer, and athletics as well as a 25-metre indoor heated swimming pool.

Our smallholding includes goats, hens, chickens and two Shetland ponies that provide the children with an invaluable opportunity to experience nature first hand. This approach to Outdoor Learning is further enhanced by our 47 acres of countryside, with outdoor classrooms, use of local Woodland Trust forest, activity equipment and orienteering trails, with more to follow.

Pupils are prepared for Common Entrance and Independent Schools Scholarships. There is a Pre-Preparatory Department for children from age 4 to 6+ and a Nursery for children from rising 3 to 5.

Charitable status. York House School is a Registered Charity, number 311076. It exists for the purpose of achieving educational excellence.

Independent Association of Prep Schools
Overseas Members

ALPHABETICAL LIST OF SCHOOLS

PAGE

Aiglon College Junior School, Switzerland 1127

The Banda School, Kenya 1127
The British Embassy School Ankara, Turkey 1127
The British International School, Cairo, Egypt 1128
The British International School of New York, United
States of America 1128
The British School – Al Khubairat, United Arab
Emirates 1129
The British School of Brussels – Primary School,
Belgium 1129
The British School in The Netherlands, Netherlands . 1130
The British School of Paris – Junior School, France . 1130
Brookhouse Preparatory School, Kenya 1130

The English School, Kuwait 1131

The Grange Preparatory School, Chile 1131
Grange School, Nigeria 1132

PAGE

Hillcrest Preparatory School, Kenya 1132
Jerudong International School, Brunei Darussalam . . 1133

Kenton College, Kenya 1133
King's College School, La Moraleja, Spain 1134
King's Infant School, Chamartín, Spain 1134

Lagos Preparatory School, Nigeria 1135

Pembroke House, Kenya 1136
Peponi House, Kenya 1136

The Roman Ridge School, Ghana 1137

St Andrew's Preparatory School, Kenya 1137
St Christopher's School, Bahrain 1138
St Paul's School, Brazil 1138
St Saviour's School, Ikoyi, Nigeria 1139
Tanglin Trust Junior School, Singapore 1139

GEOGRAPHICAL LIST OF SCHOOLS

PAGE

Bahrain
St Christopher's School, Bahrain 1138

Belgium
The British School of Brussels – Primary School . 1129

Brazil
St Paul's School 1138

Brunei Darussalam
Jerudong International School 1133

Chile
The Grange Preparatory School 1131

Egypt
The British International School, Cairo 1128

France
The British School of Paris – Junior School 1130

Ghana
The Roman Ridge School 1137

Kenya
The Banda School 1127
Brookhouse Preparatory School 1130
Hillcrest Preparatory School 1132
Kenton College 1133
Pembroke House 1136
Peponi House 1136
St Andrew's Preparatory School 1137

PAGE

Kuwait
The English School 1131

Netherlands
The British School in The Netherlands 1130

Nigeria
Grange School 1132
Lagos Preparatory School 1135
St Saviour's School, Ikoyi 1139

Singapore
Tanglin Trust Junior School 1139

Spain
King's College School, La Moraleja 1134
King's Infant School, Chamartín 1134

Switzerland
Aiglon College Junior School 1127

Turkey
The British Embassy School Ankara 1127

United Arab Emirates
The British School – Al Khubairat 1129

United States of America
The British International School of New York . . . 1128

Individual School Entries
Overseas Members

Aiglon College Junior School

CH-1885 Chesières-Villars, Switzerland
Tel: 00 41 24 496 6141
Fax: 00 41 24 496 6142
email: junior@aiglon.ch
website: www.aiglon.ch

Chairman of Governors: Pia Atkinson-Davies

Head: Stuart Hamilton

Age Range. 9–13.
Number of Pupils. Boys 35, Girls 35, Boarders 55, Day Children 15.
Fees per annum (2014–2015). Day: CHF 31,150–44,850; Full Boarding: CHF 63,000–69,800.
Setting. The Aiglon College Junior School provides a warm family atmosphere in the beauty and peace of the Swiss Alps for children from all over the world – with around 25 different nationalities. The intimate and caring community spirit encourages self-discipline, thought for others and joy in learning. Aiglon College Junior School's buildings and life are kept quite separate from those of the Senior school. However, it shares part of the campus of Aiglon College, and follows the principles of the founder, John Corlette. Ultimately we aim at ensuring a smooth and well-prepared transition into the Senior School.
Pastoral Care. Having a place of their own allows us to concentrate on issues most significant to this age group, such as creating and developing good habits in a positive and encouraging environment. Our main goal is to create a caring environment and, through carefully chosen experiences, build up the whole person and develop the many talents that all our pupils possess. We also aim at making the transition from Junior to Senior School a comfortable one. Learning to live and grow up with peers, listening to each other, and acquiring a taste for discovery and independence within a supportive environment; all these skills contribute, using moral and spiritual beliefs in a constructive way, to the foundation of a healthy attitude towards the challenges of teenage life. Moral principles are developed within school "meditations" (morning assemblies) especially and spiritual life is encouraged in chapel services.
Curriculum. The school also offers an ESL programme for all non-English speakers aged 9–12. The Junior School curriculum includes English, Maths, French, Science, Geography, History, Art, Music, Physical Education, Drama, Religious Studies and ICT. Strong pastoral care and individual attention allows for a curriculum which has its roots in the British National Curriculum but caters for the international diversity of our recruitment. The Learning Support department aids children with special learning needs and tests all children on a yearly basis.
Sports and expeditions. Sports and "expeditions" form an essential component of a well-rounded approach to the development of our children's personality and character. There is a range of sports teams to choose from and we encourage full participation. "Expeditions" take place at weekends and activities include walking, map reading and orienteering, cycling, canoeing, gorge walking and rock climbing. Children participate in camping, hiking or skiing "expeditions" under expert and qualified supervision. Apart from learning to enjoy and understand nature, being outdoors together, come rain or shine, reinforces children's team spirit and respect for each other and their environment as they learn to live a little closer to nature!

Extra-curricular activities. There is a wide variety of extra-curricular activities called "Options", which encompass sports, art and craft activities, music clubs, choir and bands, as well as quieter pastimes.
Further information. Further information may be obtained from the Headmaster or the Director of Admissions.
Aiglon College is a non-profit making organisation, accredited by ECIS.

The Banda School

PO Box 24722, Nairobi 00502, Kenya
Tel: 00 254 20 8891220 / 8891260 / 3547828 /
           2603929 / 5000728 / 9
           Mobiles: 00 254 20 726–439909 / 737–563438
Fax: 00 254 20 8890004
email: office@bandaschool.com
website: www.bandaschool.com

Chairman of Governors: Mr D G M Hutchison

Headmistress: Mrs A Francombe, BEd Hons

Age Range. 1–13.
Number of Children. 420 (Day and Weekly Boarding).
Fees per term (2014–2015). Tuition: Kshs 477,000 (Years 3–8 including lunches). Weekly Boarding: Kshs 158,000 in addition to Tuition Fees. Sliding fee scale Year 2 and below.
The School was founded in 1966 by Mr and Mrs J A L Chitty. It is 9 miles from Nairobi and stands in its own grounds of 30 acres adjacent to the Nairobi Game Park. Boys and girls are admitted in equal numbers and are prepared for Independent Senior School Scholarship and Common Entrance Examinations to leading secondary schools in the UK, Kenya and South Africa. The Staff consists of 48 teachers with the vast majority being UK trained graduates. The teacher-pupil ratio is about 1:10.
Facilities include a modern Weekly Boarding House, new Pegasus Pre-Prep building, Science laboratories, ICT rooms, Art room, Music rooms, Hall with well-equipped stage, two Libraries, Junior Art Room and a Dance Studio, specialist rooms for Mathematics, French, History and Geography, Design Technology, audio-visual room, Astroturf, two Squash courts and a six-lane 25-metre Swimming Pool with three diving boards.
Sports include Rugby, Football, Hockey, Cricket, Tennis, Swimming, Netball, Rounders, Athletics, Sailing, Squash and Cross-Country. A wide range of other activities including Instrumental lessons, Dancing and LAMDA are also available. Music, Art and Drama are an important part in the life of the school.

The British Embassy School Ankara

Sehit Ersan Caddesi 46/A, Çankaya 06680, Ankara, Turkey
email: admin@besaturkey.org
website: www.besaturkey.org

Head Teacher: **Mr Ken Page**

The British International School, Cairo

The Junior School

Km 38, Alexandria Road, Beverly Hills, Cairo, Egypt
Tel: 00 202 3827 0444
Fax: 00 202 3857 1720
email: info@bisc.edu.eg
website: www.bisc.edu.eg

Chairman of Governors: Mr Yasser Hashem

Head of Junior School: **Mr Michael Higgins**, BEd Hons, MA

Age Range. 3–11 Co-educational.
Number of Pupils. 547.
Fees per term (2014–2015). £2,636–£3,095.

The Junior School of The British International School, Cairo (BISC) is situated alongside its Senior School within a new purpose-built 65,000 square metre campus on the western outskirts of Cairo, having relocated from the School's former city centre position in the summer of 2008. BISC, founded in 1976, is the oldest established of Cairo's British international schools and is academically selective with a strong tradition of excellent academic results. The Junior School has its own dedicated and spacious classroom buildings within the whole school campus, including a large library and multimedia learning centre, science laboratory, art and design technology centres and multi-purpose hall. All classrooms are equipped with interactive 'smart' boards and computer facilities. The Junior School also shares with the Senior School a large sports hall, a gym, a 50-metre and learner swimming pools, several playing fields, an athletics track, outdoor tennis and basketball courts, and a 670-seat theatre.

The British National Curriculum is taught throughout the School and all staff are UK qualified and experienced teachers. Arabic and French are taught by qualified native speakers. Best UK educational practice is also maintained through the School's continuing professional development programme for all staff.

The school's aims are included in its mission statement: to be a first-class school preparing pupils who will eventually progress to positions of leadership in life; to provide a stimulating British education with an appreciation and understanding of Egyptian culture and Arabic; to ensure equal opportunities for pupils to develop their full intellectual, aesthetic, emotional, physical and moral potential; and to provide a broadly based education within a supportive pastoral environment, with the best possible resources and facilities. BISC seeks to foster mutual respect and tolerance and to teach essential human values such as honesty, loyalty, compassion and charity. The positive values promoted at BISC connect to those of families, the local community and the wider world, and embrace a commitment to international cooperation and understanding.

The School has over 40 nationalities represented amongst its pupil body and as such there is no affiliation to any one particular religious system. The School places a strong emphasis on moral education, both within the Personal, Social and Citizenship curriculum programme and in terms of all aspects of the life of the School. Values that characterise and permeate BISC also include a commitment to respect for others' beliefs. Regular assemblies involve participation of all pupils. The pupils' voice and developing sense of responsibility is also expressed within regular meetings of the Pupil Council and other pupil positions such as within the School's House Captaincy system.

The School's pursuit of excellence in education is also expressed in the provision of a wide programme of sporting, cultural, and artistic pursuits for all pupils, both within and as additional to the main curriculum. Concerts, choral productions and drama performances feature in every term and the Junior School has its own dedicated specialist staff for music, drama, PE and modern foreign languages, in addition to its teams of Key Stage class teachers. Junior School pupils throughout Foundation and Key Stages One and Two also enjoy regular opportunities for off-site educational visits. As pupils progress into KS2 these include Humanities trips to Luxor and El Alamein, and overseas trips in Mathematics and Sports competitions. Inter-school sporting and cultural events also take place with other schools in Cairo and Alexandria.

Learning, teaching and pastoral care structures in the Junior School are child-centred. Great importance is attached to the close monitoring of all pupils' academic progress and pastoral well being, and their progress as successful, confident and responsible learners. Regular pupil reports, parent conferences, presentation evenings and opportunities for both formal and informal meetings are all part of the natural rhythm of BISC. There is also an active PTA through which parents encourage and run many family social events, and also help to promote the wider community links of the School. Open Days for prospective parents to view the School are also held each term.

In addition to IAPS membership, BISC is also in membership of COBIS, BSME, and AGBIS. The School's most recent Inspection was undertaken by the Independent Schools Inspectorate (ISI) in November 2008, and this Report is viewable on the ISI and BISC Websites.

BISC is constituted as a not-for-profit organisation of the British International Schools Society, whose elected Board members are all current parents of the School.

The British International School of New York

20 Waterside Plaza, East 23rd Street, Manhattan, New York City 10010, USA
Tel: 00 1 212 481 2700
Fax: 00 1 646 607 5970
email: info@bis-ny.org
website: www.bis-ny.org

Chairman of Board of Directors: Anthony Millard

Headmaster: **William T Phelps**, BA, AKC, PGCE

Age Range. 3–14 Co-educational.
Number of Pupils. 270.
Fees per annum (2014–2015). $40,600.

The British International School is proud to offer a challenging curriculum which combines the inquiry-based, child-centred philosophy of the International Baccalaureate Programme with the rigour and academic quality of the English National Curriculum. As quoted in our most recent Independent Schools Inspectorate report, "The school is highly successful in meeting its ambitious aims to provide an education for pupils to inspire and stimulate a love of learning, within an international community. Standards of achievement are excellent, and pupils have outstanding speaking, listening and literacy skills for their age."

From Nursery through to Year 9, we offer a happy and nurturing environment, where students can develop a genuine love for learning and academic success. BIS-NY cultivates individual enrichment in music, the fine arts, world languages, drama and athletics. Taught by a highly-qualified faculty, content is reinforced by superior technology and resources at a stunning waterside facility on the East River in Manhattan.

BIS-NY's curriculum has been chosen for its rigorous standards of excellence and its adaptability to school systems both here in NYC and across the globe. The education provided by The British International School of New York is designed to be highly portable, preparing children for their next stage of schooling. BIS-NY graduates have enjoyed great success at some of the leading independent schools in Manhattan, the United Kingdom and other parts of the world where they continue to foster the attitudes and traits that promote international mindedness, leadership, and an application of learning that is purposeful, significant, relevant and challenging.

Application requirements for admission can be found on our website.

The British School – Al Khubairat

P O Box 4001, Abu Dhabi, United Arab Emirates
Tel: 00 971 2 446 2280
Fax: 00 971 2 446 1915
email: registrar@britishschool.sch.ae
website: www.britishschool.sch.ae

A member of HMC, IAPS, COBIS and BSME.

Chair of Governors: Mr Marc Jessel

Acting Head: **Mrs Elaine Rawlings**

Age Range. 3–18.
Number of Pupils. 933 Boys, 908 Girls (all day).
Fees per term (2014–2015). Nursery: AED11,919; FS2–Year 6: AED15,456; Years 7–13: AED20,761.

The school's overriding aim is to provide education for English speaking children "in accordance with the best teaching practices, in order to enable children to qualify for normal subsequent education in the United Kingdom within their own age groups, without disadvantage". There is an extensive extra-curricular programme in which sport, music and drama figure prominently. In order to maintain and enhance the school's high standards, all classes are taught by fully-qualified British trained and experienced teachers and the school is inspected on a three-yearly cycle. The ISI report of March 2011 deemed the school excellent in all aspects of its work.

All the buildings are fully air-conditioned, light and spacious. Facilities are outstanding. Our Primary department comprises of 34 classrooms with additional central activity areas. We also have modern electronic libraries, computer suites, assembly/gymnasium halls, a 25-metre, 6-lane, swimming pool, as well as a learner pool, specialist music rooms, specialists rooms for French, Arabic and Special Education Needs. Our Secondary Department caters for students up to and including Sixth Form. Accommodation includes a sports hall, gymnasium, 8 laboratories, 3 Design Technology workshops, 4 ICT suites, 3 Art rooms, a range of Music rooms, a 330-seat theatre, a library, Sixth Form facilities and a range of academic classrooms. Students access top universities in the UK and worldwide as well as an extensive range of top independent and state schools in the UK.

The school is self-supporting, financed by fees paid by parents for the education of their children. It operates as a 'not for profit' concern, the funds being used only for the school's purposes. The British Ambassador appoints several Board members and the Ambassador's representative sits on the Board.

The British School of Brussels – Primary School

Pater Dupierreuxlaan 1, Tervuren 3080, Belgium
Tel: +32 2 766 04 30
Fax: +32 2 767 80 70
email: admissions@britishschool.be
website: www.britishschool.be
Twitter: @BSB_Brussels
Facebook: britishschoolbrussels
LinkedIn: /company/the-british-school-of-brussels

Patron:
Her Excellency the British Ambassador to the King of the Belgians

Chairman of the Board: Mr Ian Backhouse

Principal: Mrs Sue Woodroofe, BA Hons, NPQH

Vice-Principal & Head of Primary School: **Ms Pauline Markey**

Age Range. 1–11 Co-educational.
Number of Pupils. 600.
Fees per annum (2014–2015). €13,500–€25,200.
Introduction. The development of the whole child is at the heart of BSB's primary education programme. Learning in the Primary School is about developing personal, emotional and social skills as well as being an intellectual and academic process. We aim to help children find their voice – their own unique, personal significance. We encourage them to think about what their contribution will be in the world – how they will try to make a difference as responsible and engaged members of the school community as well as citizens of the world.

BSB has high expectations for all its learners. We pride ourselves on knowing each child as an individual in order to help them make progress. Learning opportunities are planned so that all students are challenged appropriately. Above all, we are interested in the learning process – learning how to learn and how to apply skills and knowledge across an ever-increasing spectrum of experience. From the earliest age we ensure that children have an enjoyable experience of school and are motivated to learn and improve. This positive attitude is supported by a team of highly professional teachers who are themselves engaged in lifelong learning and model effective habits of mind.

Curriculum. The curriculum is based on that of the National Curriculum for England adapted to reflect the needs of an increasingly international and multi-cultural student body and to capitalise upon the opportunities of being in Belgium at the heart of Europe. For example, our curriculum includes integrated learning themes (ILTs) unique to BSB. We aim to build on the children's background knowledge and experience to equip them with the skills, strategies and a love of learning that will inspire them to succeed whatever the next step on their educational journey. The Primary Senior Management Team works to ensure coherence, consistency, continuity and progression across the whole primary age range.

Facilities. The Primary School enjoys excellent resources and provides a stimulating and varied environment. The children are spread geographically across the school campus, housed in three buildings.

We seek not only to provide an environment which promotes achievement in learning, but also one of warmth, security and care. The school was purpose-built and laid out to be both light and spacious. Our visitors frequently comment not only on the beautiful site and these excellent facilities but also on the warm and happy atmosphere which infuses the school. This complements the purposeful working environment and enables our children's learning development to flourish.

Children have access to well-resourced classrooms (including computers in every classroom and interactive boards in teaching rooms), dedicated computer suites, a fully equipped gymnasium, differentiated playgrounds, the main 240-seat school theatre for drama productions, a spacious hall, the school playing field, an art, design and technology room, well-stocked libraries and smaller classrooms for additional educational needs (AEN). Rooms are also provided for English as an additional language (EAL) and French teaching. We provide a French/English bilingual programme for children aged 4–14 years in addition to our English medium teaching.

Our Early Learning & Development Centre (Kindercrib) for children aged 1–3 is situated in a separate villa next to the school and provides a caring and stimulating pre-school environment.

(*See also British School of Brussels entry in HMC section.*)

The British School in The Netherlands
Junior School Diamanthorst

Diamanthorst 16, 2592 GH, The Hague, The Netherlands
Tel: 00 31 (0)70 315 7620
Fax: 00 31 (0)70 315 7621
email: junior.diamanthorst@britishschool.nl
website: www.britishschool.nl
Twitter: @BSN_JSD
Facebook: /BSNofficial
LinkedIn: /the-british-school-in-the-netherlands

Chairman of Governors: Mr P Bayliff

Headteacher: **Mrs Angela Parry-Davies**, BEd Hons

Age Range. 3–11 Co-educational.
Number of Pupils. 350.
Fees per annum (2014–2015). Foundation Stage Full Time €13,260, Years 1–2 €13,560, Years 3–6 €13,740.

Junior School Diamanthorst is a place where children can thrive and grow, develop and study, play and perform and, above all, discover the enjoyment of learning. The school aims to help children understand the value of both work and leisure and encourage them to become confident, happy individuals.

The site is located in a residential area in the north of The Hague. The facilities include a Media Library Centre, Food Technology Room, Hall/Gym, Design Technology Room, Dance/Drama Studio, IT suite and Music Room as well as a recently fully-landscaped new Outdoor Learning/Play Area. All classrooms are equipped with interactive whiteboards and computers. The school has a wireless network system throughout.

The learning programme includes the three core subjects Mathematics, English and Science, together with the foundation subjects, geography, history, design and technology, art & music, information technology and PE with the addition of Dutch from entry into the School and taster courses in French, German and Spanish from Year 5.

Our Foundation classes follow the English Foundation Curriculum with particular emphasis on acquiring literacy, numeracy and social skills.

In Key Stages 1 and 2 specific schemes of work outline the progressive skills and knowledge which are taught, and all work is closely monitored to ensure that pupils are making progress matched to their abilities. In the case of children who display unusual talent or ability, extension

material is given to motivate and challenge their intellectual growth. All children enjoy a variety of experiences, visiting places of interest in the immediate locality, performing in dance, drama and choral activities and engaging in a wide range of extra-curricular programmes.

As children progress through the Junior School subject teaching becomes more defined, especially in the core subjects of English, Mathematics and Science. Children are carefully prepared for the subject-orientated approach evident in the Senior School where they are expected to become more independent in the planning and completion of tasks and time management.

The British School of Paris – Junior School

2 rue Hans List, 78290 Croissy sur Seine, France
Tel: 00 33 1 30 15 88 30
Fax: 00 33 1 73 79 15 71
email: junior@britishschool.fr
website: www.britishschool.fr

Chairman of Governors: Mr P Kett

Headmaster: Mr N Hammond

Head of the Junior School: **Ms K Tuckwell**

Age Range. 3–11 Co-educational.
Number of Pupils. 400.
Fees per annum (2014–2015). €15,080–€22,007.

The Junior School caters for pupils aged 3–11 and is located very close to the Senior School along the leafy banks of the river Seine. This brand new facility opened in September 2010; there are 35 classrooms accommodating up to 480 pupils, as well as 4 bespoke classrooms and 2 activity areas that are dedicated to our foundation stage/nursery section. The school was specifically designed to meet the educational and social welfare needs of junior school pupils. It is bristling with new technology and up-to-the-minute IT facilities to assist the pupils' learning and development. The British School of Paris's philosophy of education permeates throughout the Junior School and has at its core the goal of unlocking the potential of all students, by identifying strengths and supporting areas of development, while having fun and enjoying happy and strong social relationships. Studies are based on the British National Curriculum with emphasis on English, Maths and Science, and of course, the French language. Various sports, music, drama and many other extra-curricular activities are also provided.

For further details and applications, please contact the Registrar, email: registrar@britishschool.fr.

Brookhouse Preparatory School

PO Box 24987, Langata, Nairobi 00502, Kenya
Tel: 00 254 20 2430 260–3
Fax: 00 254 20 2430 269
email: info@brookhouse.ac.ke
website: www.brookhouse.ac.ke

Preparatory School Headteacher: **Ms Michelle Forsyth**, BA, PGCE

Age Range. 2–13 Co-educational.
Number of Pupils. 385 boys and girls, including 30 boarders.
Fees per term (2014–2015). Tuition: Kshs 200,000–445,000 (includes lunch, but excludes transport). Transport

to and from school: Kshs 45,000. Boarding: Kshs 300,000 in addition to Tuition Fees.

Established in 1981 in a leafy suburb of Nairobi about 10 minutes from the city centre, Brookhouse Preparatory School is an independent co-educational day and boarding school accredited by the Council of International Schools. Brookhouse benefits from a purpose-built "castle-style" building design that ensures a physical environment for children that is truly inspirational. The school delivers an adapted form of the British National Curriculum, catering mainly for the professional, business and diplomatic communities of the East African region. Brookhouse balances traditional values with an innovative approach to the curriculum. Our philosophy as a Round Square global member school focuses on respect for each child as an individual and the development of leadership through service to others. The school features small classes, and a particular focus on the core areas of numeracy, literacy and computer literacy. The average class size is 15.

With more than 40 nationalities represented on the student roll, the school prides itself on fostering tolerance and understanding, and promotes a diverse programme of extracurricular activities, sports and clubs to ensure the development of the whole child. Teachers are recruited from both UK and East Africa and average nearly fifteen years of classroom experience. They are carefully selected for their ability to provide both a challenging academic environment and a caring pastoral network of support for each child.

Situated on a thirteen-acre campus adjacent to Nairobi National Park, the school has on-site co-educational boarding accommodation. Academic facilities include a 'space station' computer laboratory, purpose-built science and home science laboratories, a three-storey library, Fine Art and Music studios, and a world-class performance theatre where regular drama and musical productions are staged. All classrooms are computer networked, and students have supervised email and internet access. A Learning Support Unit caters for students with Special Educational Needs (SEN) and for students who have English as an Additional Language (EAL) backgrounds, as well as providing an Academic Extension Programme (AEP) for highly able pupils.

Sporting facilities include a gym and aerobics studio, squash courts, swimming pool, indoor sports centre for tennis and basketball and irrigated playing fields to ensure a year round quality playing surface. A varied programme of team and individual sports are available.

The English School
Kuwait

PO Box 379, 13004 Safat, Kuwait, Kuwait
Tel: 00 965 22271385
Fax: 00 965 22271389
email: registrar@tes.edu.kw
website: www.tes.edu.kw

Sponsor: Mr Emad Mohamed Al-Bahar

Chair of the Governing Committee: Brigadier Edward Brown

Headmaster: **Kieron Peacock**

Age Range. 2–13.
Number of Pupils. 620.
Fees per annum (2014–2015). Nursery (Pre-KG and KG) KD1,860; Pre-Preparatory (Rec, Year 1 and Year 2) KD2,720; Preparatory (Years 3–8) KD3,245.

The English School, founded in 1953 under the auspices of the British Embassy, is the longest established school in Kuwait catering for the expatriate community. The school operates as a not-for-profit, private co-educational establishment providing the highest standards in education for children of Pre-Kindergarten to Preparatory school age. The school is registered with the United Kingdom Department for Education (DfE No 703 6052) and the Headmaster is a Member of the Independent Association of Prep Schools. TES is an Accredited Member of BSME and is also accredited as a British School Overseas with the DfE and listed as a "world class British school". Uniquely in Kuwait, the language of the playground is English. The roll is predominantly British, as are the resources and texts. With the exception of foreign language teachers, the teaching staff are also predominantly British and qualified in the United Kingdom. The number of pupils in the school continues to increase although the average class size remains around 20. The school is housed in well-resourced and spacious, fully air-conditioned premises in a pleasant residential suburb of Kuwait City.

The curriculum is British, contemporary and delivers the best of traditional standards within a broad-based structure. Class teachers are supported by specialist coordinators in Art, Design and Technology, Information Technology, Music, Library and PE and Games. Music is taught to all ages and French is introduced from Year 4. The National Curriculum for England is used as the core for the curriculum, although the most able are challenged and those in need of support benefit from individual tuition. Formal end of key stage assessment takes place in Years 2 and 6. In addition the pupils are prepared for entrance tests to other schools including, where appropriate, Common Entrance Examinations at 11+, 12+ and 13+, and scholarship examinations.

Responsibility for the school is vested in the Governing Committee whose members serve in a voluntary capacity. The school provides a learning environment within which children develop their individual capacity for achievement to its fullest potential. The school's core values of Confidence, Empathy, Integrity, Positivity and Respect are at the heart of all that it does. Strong emphasis is placed on academic study, together with a wide range of non-academic activities to provide breadth and balance. The school aims to ensure that, by achieving standards at least equivalent and often better than those of competitive private and state schools in Britain, pupils are well prepared for the subsequent stages of their academic development whether in Britain, Kuwait or elsewhere in the world.

In the first instance application for enrolment should be made online via the website – please see drop-down menu: Parents, Enrolment, Online Registration Form.

The Registrar will confirm receipt of the Online Registration Form. If there are places in the year requested, the Registrar will ask for copies of current academic reports and arrange a date for the child/children to be assessed. Pupils and parents will then be invited to attend one of the school's 'Welcome and Assessment Days' prior to the start of the academic year.

The Grange Preparatory School
Chile

Av Principe de Gales 6154, La Reina, 687067, Santiago, Chile
Tel: 00 562 598 1500
Fax: 00 562 277 0946
email: hmprep@grange.cl
website: www.grange.cl

Co-educational Day School.

Headmaster of The Grange School: Mr Rachid Benammar

Head of the Upper Preparatory School: **Mr Carlos Packer-Comyn**

Head of the Lower Preparatory School: Mrs Carmen Gloria Gomez

Age Range. 4–12.
Number of Pupils. 1,200.
Fees per annum (2014–2015). Approximately £6,000 payable in one annual sum or 11 monthly instalments. There is a one-off incorporation fee payable on entry.

The Grange Preparatory School is the junior section of The Grange, founded in 1928 by John Jackson and based upon the British independent school which he had attended.

The Prep School is divided into the Lower Prep, which takes children from the age of 4 to the age of 8, and the Upper Prep, taking children from 8 to 12. Almost all pupils will transfer into The Grange senior school.

The ethos of the school is strongly based on giving a broad, all-round educational experience to find strengths for each child. The school may be very large but each child is valued as an individual within the team.

Entry to the school is usually at the age of 4, though entry at ages over 4 may be possible as vacancies occur in the course of the year. All teaching is in English except in those areas where the Chilean National Curriculum requires that they be taught in Spanish. The majority of the pupils are Chilean and begin an immersion course in English upon entry.

International assessment criteria are used at various stages of each pupil's career, with NFER testing in English and mathematics. The core curriculum is based largely upon the National Curriculum of England and Wales, fully encompassing and surpassing the local National Curriculum. Teaching is mainly by class teachers, though older children will find themselves being taught by specialists in many subjects. All heads of department are specialists. Approximately 30 of the teachers are expatriates.

Over the last few years strong progress has been made in the areas of Science, ICT, Music, Drama and Art and Design Technology, with new rooms having been dedicated to these subjects. There is a comprehensive after-school extra-curricular programme in which children from the age of 7 upwards are strongly encouraged to take part.

Grange School

Harold Shodipo Crescent, Ikeja GRA, Lagos State, Nigeria
Tel: 00 234 12950493; 00 234 12713886
email: info@grangeschool.com
website: www.grangeschool.com

Chairman of Board of Directors: Mr Dayo Lawuyi MON

CEO/Principal: **Mr Graham J Stothard**, JP, BEd Hons Wales, NPQH Manchester, FRSA, FInstLM, FCollT, MIOD, AISTD

Age Range. 4–16 Co-educational day and boarding.
Number of Pupils. 780.
Fees per annum (2014–2015). Tuition: £5,500 KS1, £6,350 KS2, £8,500 KS3, £8,800 KS4. Boarders (age 9–16): £6,000 in addition to tuition fees.

Founded fifty-six years ago in 1958 Grange is one of the oldest and most prestigious British International Schools in West Africa. With the Deputy British High Commissioner as its Patron, Grange is firmly rooted in British tradition inspired by Nigerian innovation. The school is located in GRA Ikeja on the Lagos mainland. Parents and all stakeholders have high academic and social aspirations for their children almost all of whom graduate to the best of Public

schools in England, America and Canada. The school has a selective admissions policy. In 2014 over 90% of IGCSE grades were A*–B. Currently seventeen subjects are offered at this level.

The majority of the school's 205 staff is Nigerian with the school currently expanding its legal quota of expatriate teacher colleagues, from the UK, America, Australia and China. Approximately 85% of children are Nigerian nationals, therefore in order to acknowledge their cultural identity and heritage, clear evidence exists of using local exemplars to supplement programmes of study. This is further witnessed by the programme of co-curricular clubs and in the many school visits the children undertake both locally and further afield annually to the UK, France, Switzerland and South Africa. The school's executive team is primarily focused on 'quality first learning' across all year groups and this is reflected in Grange's vision.

We acknowledge parental aspirations for their children through a continual drive for reflective practices both within and outside the classroom. There is regular monitoring of the quality of learning and teaching, the school learning environment and pupil progress via homework and termly assessment including optional and 'statutory' Checkpoint examinations administered by the University of Cambridge Examinations Syndicate (UCLES). Children benefit from many co-curricular activities based in classrooms, on our sports field and multipurpose court, our 25 metre swimming pool and tennis courts at the adjoining Country Club.

The school has embarked on an extensive building programme which will see new boarding accommodation commissioned this year; a new multi-purpose hall complex with classrooms and performance areas; a dining room and administration offices; an astroturf football pitch and a cinder running track. There is an active PTA which, in addition to raising substantial amounts of money to assist in purchasing additional resources for the school and local charities, provides a constructive link with the CEO around everything from individual parental concerns to strategic matters.

Hillcrest Preparatory School

PO Box 24282, Karen 00502, Nairobi, Kenya
Tel: 00 254 (0)20 883914/16/17
email: admin_prep@hillcrest.ac.ke
website: www.hillcrest.ac.ke
Facebook: Hillcrest International Schools

Chairman of Governors: Mr Bob Kikuyu

Headmaster: **Mr Ian Rosario-Hopkins**

Age Range. 18 months – 13 years Co-educational.
Number of Pupils. 320.
Fees per term (2014–2015). Tuition in Hillcrest Early Years (HEY) from Play Group to Year 2 (Key Stage 1) ranges from Kshs 66,600 to 350,000 including lunch, excluding transport. Tuition in the Preparatory school from Year 3 (Key Stage 2) to Year 8 (Key Stage 3) ranges from Kshs 411,400 to 429,000. Weekly Boarding: Kshs 226,300 (in addition to Tuition fees). Weekend Boarding: Kshs 9,700 per weekend.

Boarding is available on application from Year 6.

Hillcrest School was founded in 1965 by Mr Frank Thompson as Founding Headmaster. It is located on an attractive, purpose-built, 20-acre campus next to our Secondary School in Karen/Langata.

Boys and girls are accepted from the age of 18 months in HEY and 8 years at the Preparatory. Each year group has two classes of 16–20 pupils with a teaching assistant available up to the end of Year 2 (Key Stage 1). The pupils follow a broad and extensive curriculum which prepares them for Common Entrance Examinations. Some children transfer to

UK Independent Secondary Schools but the majority enter the equivalent in Kenya, Hillcrest Secondary School, which prepares pupils for IGCSE and A Levels. Entry to the Senior School is achieved after successfully writing the Common Entrance.

The school has a multinational feel with its pupils drawn from the Diplomatic and United Nations community, expatriate families on contract, and Kenyan residents. The friendly spirit and strong communication network that exists between staff, pupils and parents are of particular note.

Extensive information can be found at www.hillcrest.ac.ke.

Jerudong International School

PO Box 1408, Bandar Seri Begawan BS8672, Negara Brunei Darussalam

Tel: 00 673 241 1000
Fax: 00 673 241 1010
email: enrol@jis.edu.bn
          office@jis.edu.bn
website: www.jis.edu.bn
Facebook: /JerIntScho

Jerudong International School (JIS) is a British international, co-educational day and boarding school founded in 1997. The Principal is an international member of HMC and the Head of the Junior School is a overseas member of IAPS, while the school is a member of COBIS and BSA. The School consists of a Junior School with Pre-Prep for Nursery to Year 2 and Prep for Years 3 to 6. Following this, students progress to Senior School (Years 7 to 13).

Principal: **Barnaby Sandow**, BSc Eng Durham, PGCE Exeter

Head of Junior School: **Paul Bannister**, BEd Hons Nottingham, NPQH

Age Range. 2–18.
Number of Pupils. 1,675: Junior School (Nursery to Year 6) 600; Senior School: 300 (Years 7–8), 445 (Years 9–11), 330 (Years 12–13 – Sixth Form).
Fees per annum (2014–2015). Nursery: B\$7,968–\$10,600, Kindergarten: B\$10,632–\$13,550, Reception to Year 7: B\$15,912–\$20,650, Year 8–11: B\$16,728–\$22,150, Year 12 and 13: B\$17,496–\$22,750. Boarding: B\$17,688–\$23,500 (weekly boarding); full boarding is B\$6,000 per annum in addition to weekly fees (£1 = B\$2.1 approximately).

Built in 1997, Jerudong International School (JIS) is a large, thriving school with pupils from over 54 nationalities offering a broad, liberal education in the best traditions of western independent schools. It is one of the leading British international schools in South East Asia preparing students for I/GCSEs, A Levels and the IB Diploma. JIS has almost 200 highly-qualified teachers primarily from the UK but also from Australia, New Zealand, France and Brunei.

Facilities. The facilities at JIS are exceptional. The purpose-built ICT networked school occupies 100 acres of a 300-acre single campus in Jerudong, near the coast – a short drive from the capital city. Pupils are able to use the Arts Centre and Music faculty (containing a 725-seat auditorium, dance studios, smaller theatres, rehearsal rooms including individual practice rooms, iMac studios and recording studios), science laboratories, libraries and traditional classrooms. Subjects such as design and technology, art, food technology, textiles and music are taught in specialist workshops / classrooms. Sports facilities include three sports fields, a gymnasium, a shaded 50m swimming pool, tennis and covered netball and basketball courts. The playground areas are extensive and shaded in some areas. The new

Senior Academic and Administration Centre opened in August 2012 and includes an e-Learning Centre and 200-seat Lecture Theatre as well as 10 Science Laboratories and 23 classrooms.

Boarding facilities are purpose designed and built for the community of 280 weekly and full boarders.

Curriculum. At JIS much emphasis is placed on academic achievement. Children are expected to work hard and achieve very high standards. Children transfer to the Senior School from the Junior School at the end of Year 6. The pastoral system is based closely on traditional UK public schools with 16 Houses including 4 Boarding Houses. Much support is given to parents relocating to Brunei and the challenges of expatriate life are well understood.

All Junior School pupils have a class teacher for most of their studies. There are specialist teachers in Design and Technology, ICT, Art, Music, Drama, Malay, French, Urdu and Physical Education. Languages are taught by native speakers. In the Junior School, pupils follow the British National Curriculum and the International Primary Curriculum.

In the Senior School, from Year 7, pupils have specialist teachers in each subject. Students sit for the I/GCSEs at the end of Year 11. JIS introduced the International Baccalaureate Diploma in 2011 alongside the well-established A Level provision in the Sixth Form. A specialist team of higher education advisors guide and prepare students in Years 12 and 13 for e.g. SATS, IELTS and UCAS. A strong House programme exists in Senior School offering many competitive opportunities.

The co-curricular programme offers pupils the opportunity to take part in a variety of activities. More than 200 activities are on offer with Model United Nations (MUN) – for Year 7 and above, Music, Art and Sport all strong. Pupils in Years 10–13 can also join in the extensive Duke of Edinburgh's International Award (Bronze, Silver and Gold). Children acquire good social and communication skills and learn to cooperate with others. There is a lively sporting programme and opportunities to compete locally and internationally at the games organised by the Federation of Independent Schools of South-East Asia (FOBISIA). There is an After School Care Centre for children who cannot be collected immediately at the end of the school day.

Kenton College

PO Box 30017, 00100 Nairobi, Kenya

Tel: 00 254 20 4347000 / 4347532 / 4347371
          Cell: 00 254 722 205038 / 00 254 733 687077
email: admin@kenton.ac.ke
website: www.kentonschoolnairobi.com

Chairman of the Governors: C H Banks, Esq

Headmistress: **Mrs M Cussans**, BA, PGCE, MA

Age Range. 6–13 Co-educational.
Number of Pupils. 295.
Fees per term (2014–2015). Kshs 465,000.
Founded in 1924 and transferred to purpose-built accommodation in 1935, Kenton College is one of the oldest schools in the country. Situated in its own secluded grounds of 35 acres, at an altitude of nearly 6000 feet, some three miles from the centre of one of Africa's most cosmopolitan capitals, Kenton is an oasis of calm amidst the rapidly sprawling urban development of the city of Nairobi.

Kenton College is an independent co-educational preparatory school, entry to which is open to both boys and girls of any race or religious persuasion, who have had their sixth birthday before the beginning of the school year in September. Most pupils remain seven years with us and leave in the July following their thirteenth birthday for senior schools in the UK, Kenya or South Africa, having followed a syllabus in the senior part of the school leading to the ISEB Common Entrance Examination. Kenton pupils frequently obtain scholarships to UK or Kenyan senior schools.

The school is based on a strong Christian foundation which is reflected in the warm and caring environment provided for its pupils, wherein positive encouragement is given towards any aspect of school life. Considerable emphasis is placed on character building, discipline and good manners, within a relaxed and happy atmosphere.

We aim for high academic achievements by offering a full curriculum in which the best of traditional and modern approaches are employed. The British National Curriculum provides the framework for our teaching throughout the school. Use is made of specialist subject teaching rooms in the senior school, to which recent additions are a Modern Languages suite, a Design Studio and two Computer rooms. There are two Science laboratories, a well-stocked Library, a 300-seat Assembly Hall with large stage, and a purpose-built Music Studio.

The academic day is balanced by opportunities for drama and music for all, together with a wide variety of sports and extra-curricular activities. Traditional British sports are played using our first class facilities which include three tennis courts and a heated swimming pool.

Many pupils opt for extra activities such as riding, ballet, karate, music tuition, tennis or swimming coaching, speech and drama awards. Sailing in the school boats on Lake Naivasha is available a few times each term. Trips to facilities found in an international city are combined with expeditions and fieldwork in the unrivalled Kenyan countryside.

Academic subjects are taught by a staff complement of local and expatriate teachers numbering 25. Full use is made of accomplished musicians for music tuition, while recognised Kenyan sportsmen assist with games coaching. The average class size is 18, with 20 the maximum.

King's College School, La Moraleja

Paseo de Alcobendas 5, La Moraleja, Madrid 28109, Spain

Tel: 00 34 916 585 540
Fax: 00 34 916 507 686
email: info.lamoraleja@kingscollege.es
website: www.kingscollegeschools.org
Twitter: @KCSMoraleja
LinkedIn: /King's College Moraleja

King's College School La Moraleja opened in September 2007. It is a co-educational day school and one of three King's Group schools in Madrid, the first of which was founded in 1969. The Headteacher of La Moraleja is an overseas member of IAPS and the Headteacher of King's College is an international member of HMC. King's College Madrid is also a member of COBIS.

The school is governed by the King's Group Board of Directors and the School Council. These governing bodies are composed of distinguished members from the business and academic communities.

Headteacher: Dawn Akyürek, BA Hons, PGCE

Deputy Headteacher: June Donnan, BA Hons Ulster, MEd OU
Upper School Leader: Jacky Walters, BEd Winchester
Lower School Leader: Dhamayanthi Vinthini Sangarabalan, PGCE Edinburgh
Head of Spanish Studies: Maria Dolores Oñoro, Diplomada Magisterio Madrid
Head of Admissions: Nuria Sanz, BA, MBA SIU Madrid

Age Range. 3–14 Co-educational.

Number of Pupils. 500.
Fees per term (2014–2015). €1,978–€3,244 excluding lunch and transport.

This is a day school which caters for children of approximately 35 nationalities between the ages of 3 and 14 years (Nursery to Year 9). Pupil enrolment is approximately 500 boys and girls and there are 33 fully-qualified British staff, and five qualified Spanish language teachers.

The school vision, like its sister schools in Madrid, is to "be at the forefront of British education internationally" and to provide students with an excellent all-round education while fostering tolerance and understanding between young people of different nationalities and backgrounds. It is a happy and inspiring place to learn.

At the age of fourteen, at the end of National Curriculum Year 9, pupils transfer to the school in Soto de Viñuelas to complete their final four years of study. (*See King's College entry in HMC section.*)

Location. This modern, purpose-built school is situated in the superb location of La Moraleja, one of the most highly-regarded residential areas in Madrid. The site is well connected to the city, just off the A1 and a short walk from the La Moraleja Metro station. There is an optional bus service for pupils to the city of Madrid and its outlying residential areas and all routes are supervised by a bus monitor.

Facilities. All classrooms are bright, spacious and house a complement of high-quality resources and technology to encourage interactive learning. The on-site facilities include a library, two ICT suites, science laboratory, music rooms, multi-purpose sports surface, gymnasium and infirmary.

Curriculum. Teachers deliver a broad and balanced curriculum and encourage pupils to put effort into all that they undertake academically, culturally and physically.

Pupils follow the English National Curriculum (leading to IGCSE, GCE AS and A Level examinations once pupils transfer to Soto de Viñuelas). There are Induction English Classes for children over the age of 7 who need to improve their English. There are also Beginners Spanish Classes for international children joining the school. All pupils learn Spanish.

Activities. There are choirs and musical ensembles, which participate in events throughout the year. Pupils are encouraged to explore their capabilities in the areas of music and the arts from a very early age.

Sports play an important role at the school and pupils are encouraged to take part in tournaments and local competitive events, in addition to their normal PE classes. School football and basketball teams compete in the local Alcobendas Leagues and pupils also take part in inter-school championships in athletics and cross-country.

There is a programme of optional classes which includes chess, ballet, judo, Spanish dancing, swimming and tuition in various musical instruments, as well as performing arts, language clubs and craft workshops.

Admission. Pupils wishing to enter Year 3 and above are required to sit entrance tests in English and Mathematics and to present copies of recent school reports. Further information may be obtained from The Head of Admissions, Mrs Nuria Sanz, nuria.sanz@kingsgroup.org.

Senior School. At the age of fourteen, at the end of National Curriculum Year 9, pupils transfer to King's College in Soto de Viñuelas to complete their final four years of study. (*See King's College entry in HMC section.*)

King's Infant School, Chamartín

Prieta Ureña 9–11, Madrid 28016, Spain

Tel: 00 34 913 505 843
email: info.chamartin@kingscollege.es
website: www.kingscollegeschools.org
Twitter: @KISChamartin

LinkedIn: /King's Infant School, Chamartin

King's Infant School is based in the Chamartín area of Madrid city centre. Chamartín was the original site of the first King's College school, which opened in 1969. Today King's Infant School makes up one of seven schools in the King's Group; it is a co-educational day school educating pupils from Nursery to Year 2 (age 3–7).

The Headteacher of Chamartín is an overseas member of IAPS and King's Infant School is also an accredited member of COBIS.

The school is governed by the King's Group Board of Directors and the School Council. These governing bodies are composed of distinguished members from the business and academic communities.

Headteacher: **Kay Seward**, BEd

Deputy Headteacher: Rachel Davies

Head of Admissions: Araceli Losana Vela

Age Range. 3–7 Co-educational.
Number of Pupils. 202.
Fees per term (2014–2015). €1,978–€2,281 excluding lunch and transport.

The Vision of King's Infant School, like its sister schools in King's Group, is to "Be at the forefront of British Education Internationally". The Group's Mission is to provide high-quality British education that delivers a transformative learning experience to all our pupils.

Location. The school occupies a modern, well-equipped and compact campus which caters ideally for young learners. It is well connected by road and public transport and is just a short walk from the nearest Metro station. There is an optional bus service for pupils to and from school which covers the city of Madrid and its outlying residential areas. All routes are supervised by a bus monitor.

Facilities. All classrooms are bright and spacious with high-quality resources and technology to encourage interactive learning. Classrooms are also fully air-conditioned in order to keep pupils cool in the hot summer months.

On-site facilities include:
- Covered play areas for use during summer and winter
- Extended outdoor play areas for Nursery and Reception class
- Mini football and netball pitch
- Music room
- SMART boards in every classroom (Reception–Year 2) IWB for use in Nursery class

Curriculum. Teachers deliver a broad and balanced curriculum, based on the English National Curriculum, and encourage pupils to put effort into all that they undertake academically, culturally and physically. King's Infant School caters for children of a variety of nationalities. There are 10 UK qualified staff, one of whom is a Spanish language teacher, as well as 7 Teaching Assistants and an Educational Psychologist. There are Induction English Classes for children who need to improve their English. There are also Beginners Spanish Classes for international children joining the school. All pupils learn Spanish.

Activities. The school boasts an array of extra-curricular activities to complement those already catered for within the curriculum. Pupils are encouraged to explore their capabilities in the areas of music and the arts from a very early age. Sport plays an important role at the school and pupils are encouraged to take part in activity days to build cooperation and confidence in addition to their normal PE classes.

Optional classes include chess, ballet, judo, modern dance, football, skating, Chinese, swimming and tuition in various musical instruments, as well as performing arts.

Admissions. Parents and pupils are invited to meet with the Head of Admissions and the Head Teacher on their visit to the school. Further information may be obtained from

The Head of Admissions, Mrs Araceli Losana Vela, email: araceli.losana@kingsgroup.org.

At the age of seven, at the end of National Curriculum Year 2, pupils transfer to one of two sister schools in Madrid: King's College, Soto de Viñuelas which caters for pupils from Pre-Nursery to Year 13 (age 2 to 18) or alternatively to King's College School, La Moraleja which caters for pupils from Nursery to Year 9 (age 3 to 15). If pupils transfer to La Moraleja, they will later join the main site in Soto de Viñuelas from Year 10 in order to continue their studies leading to IGCSE, GCE AS and A Level examinations. (*See separate entry for King's College School, La Moraleja in IAPS section and King's College's entry in HMC section.*)

Lagos Preparatory School

36–40 Glover Road, Ikoyi, Lagos, Nigeria
Tel: 00 234 1 740 8325
          00 234 1 740 8323
email: admin@lagosprepikoyi.com.ng
          headteacher@lagosprepikoyi.com.ng
website: www.lagosprepikoyi.com.ng

Headmaster: **Mr John Samuel**

Age Range. 2–13 Co-educational.
Number of Pupils. 440.
Fees per annum (2014–2015). Tuition: US$12,375.00

Our school is an international 13+ preparatory school delivering the British National Curriculum to some 440 pupils of 33 different nationalities. English is the medium of all tuition. The majority of the school's 135 staff is Nigerian with the school having its full legal quota of expatriate teacher colleagues, from the UK; South Africa and India. Each of the 24 classes has (at the very least) a graduate teacher, who also possesses the PGCE qualification, and an assistant teacher. All assistant teachers are graduates, many working towards the PGCE. Y2 classes and below also have a class assistant and a Nanny working in them. The school is located in Ikoyi that part of Lagos regarded as the prime residential area of the city. Our new purpose-built premises opened in September 2011. Parents and all stakeholders have high academic and social aspirations for their children. The school has a selective admissions policy.

Approximately 51% of children are Nigerian nationals therefore in order to acknowledge their cultural identity and heritage, clear evidence exists of using local exemplars to supplement programmes of study. This is further witnessed by the programme of pre and after school clubs and in the many school visits the children undertake. The school's senior leadership team are primarily focused on 'quality first teaching' across the whole school and this is reflected in our mission statement. We acknowledge parental aspirations for their children through a continual drive for reflective practices both within and outside the classroom. There is regular monitoring of the quality of teaching and learning, the school learning environment and pupil progress via homework and bi-weekly testing (including optional and 'statutory' SATs). Children benefit from many co-curricular activities based in classrooms, our multi-purpose hall, our 25m swimming pool and on our astro surface soccer field and tennis court.

There is an active PTA which in addition to raising substantial amounts of money to assist in purchasing additional resources for the school, provides a most useful and constructive link with the Headmaster around everything from individual parental concerns through to strategic whole school development matters. In keeping with the school's mission statement it maintains a proactive stance in relation to community links. Our school has a very active staff training programme and performance management system for all staff. One member of the SLT is responsible for this crucial area of development. Over the last few years a significant number of our graduate teachers and assistant teachers have undertaken the distance learning PGCE course with the University of Sunderland, with much success.

In 2010 the school became the world's first international school to achieve the Every Child Matters Standards Award. In the Lent term of 2011 the school underwent a successful ISI inspection and accordingly became the first British school on the African continent to achieve the DfE's standards for British schools overseas. We remain the only British school in Africa to hold this accolade. The Headmaster is a member of Independent Association of Prep Schools (IAPS) and the school is the only British school in Africa that is an Accredited Member of COBIS.

Pembroke House

PO Box 31, 20116 Gilgil, Kenya
Tel: 00 254 (0)20 231 2323
            00 254 (0)734 480 439
email: headmistress@pembrokehouse.sc.ke
website: www.pembrokehouse.sc.ke

Chairman of Council: Mr Richard Fernandes

Headmistress: **Mrs Deborah Boyd-Moss**, MA Cantab, PGCE

Age Range. 5–13.
Number of Pupils. 122 boy boarders, 101 girl boarders.
Fees per term (2014–2015). Kshs 550,000 (UK£3,930).
The school was founded in 1927 and is presently owned and administered by the Kenya Educational Trust Limited. It is situated in over 40 hectares of well-maintained grounds in the Rift Valley at 2,000 metres and is 120 kms from Nairobi. The climate is sunny throughout the year affording many opportunities for an extensive education.

Facilities include the Chapel, Theatre, Swimming Pool, Music School, Library, Art and Design Technology Centre, Computer Room, two Squash Courts and Tennis Courts, access to a neighbouring Golf Course, and a multi-purpose sports hall. The school has a well-equipped Surgery on site.

The main sports are Cricket, Hockey, Rugby, Rounders and Netball with Tennis, Swimming, Athletics, Squash, Golf, Horse Riding, Sailing, Soccer, Shooting and Taekwondo on offer as well.

A full range of clubs and various extras, including individual music instruction, are also offered. Drama is strong with several productions put on each year. The school also has a vibrant and varied weekend programme to support the full boarding ethos of the school. This involves much camping and other outdoor pursuits as well as many team building and leadership activities.

Children are admitted from five years as full boarders and are prepared, through the British Curriculum, for the ISEB Common Entrance Examinations which qualifies them for entry to Independent Senior Schools in the UK and South Africa as well as Kenyan schools. The School usually gains numerous academic scholarships and awards each year in addition to music and sports awards. The Learning Support Facilities at Pembroke House have been developed over many years and now provide essential help for those who require such assistance. The school currently has children from seven different countries including the United Kingdom.

The average number of pupils in each form is 15, and there are 41 fully qualified members of teaching staff plus three qualified Nurses, a Cateress, an Estate Manager, Registrar and a Commercial Director.

Pembroke has a reputation for producing outstanding pupils. The Headmistress and the staff work together to produce kind, well-mannered, balanced children with integrity and courage who try their best at all times. This is the best preparation a child can have.

Peponi House

PO Box 23203, Lower Kabete, Nairobi 00604, Kenya
Tel: 00 254 20 2585710–712, 734881255,
            722202947
email: secretary@peponihouseschool.co.ke
website: www.peponihouseschool.co.ke

Headmaster: **Mr R J Blake**, BSc Hons, PGCE, NPQH

Age Range. 6–13.
Number of Pupils. 394 boys and girls, all day.
Fees per annum (2014–2015). Kshs 1,455,000.
Founded in 1986, Peponi House has grown to become one of the leading preparatory schools in East Africa. The attractive and spacious site in Lower Kabete houses all that a thriving prep school requires to get the very best out of the children, both in and out of the classroom.

We are a multi-cultural community which encourages respect for self and others. Our emphasis is on excellence, through a broad, balanced education which aims to maximise the potential of each pupil as a whole person. To this end, we have outstanding facilities including a 25-metre swimming pool, three hard tennis courts, purpose-built Art and Design Technology rooms and networked PCs in all rooms. We have two fully-equipped science laboratories and a new music school. Two new classrooms dedicated to History and Geography opened last year, with a senior RS room added in 2014. The school libraries and Computing room occupy an area that is central to the school both geographically and philosophically. These facilities help to complement the excellent work that the children and staff carry out in the well-resourced classrooms. Our extensive use of interactive whiteboards has resulted in the school being elected as a SMART Showcase School.

Whilst always striving for academic excellence, it is central to Peponi's philosophy that education is not limited to the classroom. In addition to the numerous scholarships to senior schools that our pupils have won in the last three years, we have had notable successes in sport, music, art and drama. Peponi teams have won competitions at a national level, with many individuals going on to represent their country.

We follow the British National Curriculum but this is seen very much as a framework for extension. In addition to the core subjects of Literacy, Numeracy, Science and Computing, pupils in the Junior School (Years 2 to 4) also have lessons in Music, PE and Games, Swimming, Kiswahili, Art and DT, tennis and, from Year 3, French. Junior children are taught these subjects by specialist teachers while the class teachers deliver the core subjects and humanities. All children are taught in a way that best suits their individual needs and some children do require additional support. This is carried out by our Learning Support teachers who will help children either individually or in small groups. Our special needs teachers also play a vital role in advising colleagues as to the strengths and weaknesses of particular children so that teaching can be differentiated to suit everyone.

In Year 5, children are taught Humanities and English by their form teachers, who also play a vital pastoral role in preparing the children for life in the senior school. In Year 6, all subjects are delivered by subject specialists. The sciences are taught separately and there is an option for children to study Kiswahili, Spanish or Latin.

We also have a wide and varied range of extra-curricular activities. Seniors have activities twice a week and Juniors once a week.

Our music department flourishes and has recently moved into new purpose-built accommodation. In addition to twice-weekly class music lessons, the children have the opportunity to play in the orchestra or in one of the ensembles, or sing in either the Junior or Senior Choir. As well as the two major school concerts during the year, all children have the opportunity to perform in front of their peers and parents at our termly "Tea-Time Concerts". The Christmas and Easter Services are another chance for our choirs to perform and all the children are encouraged to take part in the plays that are staged in December, March and June.

We have children from many different cultures and ethnic backgrounds and we encourage understanding and above all respect for each other. We are a Christian School and the ethos of "Love one another" is a recurring theme in our Thursday services, but we are proud of our multi-faith society where children learn to appreciate and value their differences as well as their similarities.

The school's motto "A School of Many Nations, a Family of One" encapsulates all that we hold most dear. First and foremost, we are a school and the academic side of things lies at the heart of all that we do. However, we are also a family and that makes itself very clear in the day to day life of the school. We have an open door policy with our parents and encourage them to be very active in their support of what we do, either through our energetic PTA or through close consultation with the staff.

At Peponi House, we believe that our role as educators is to give our children the best possible foundation for what lies ahead. We are, after all, a preparatory school and excellent preparation is what we set out to achieve. By the time they leave us, our pupils will be confident young adults who are ready to face the future with poise and self-belief.

The Roman Ridge School

No. 8 Onyasia Crescent, Roman Ridge, Accra, Ghana
Tel: 00 233 302 780456/780457
Fax: 00 233 302 780458
email: enquiries@theromanridgeschool.com
website: www.theromanridgeschool.com

Postal Address:
PO Box GP 21057, Accra, Ghana

Co-educational Day School.

Governors:
Chairman: Dr Frank B Adu Jnr, BA Hons, MBA
Chair, Academic Board: Dr Joyce Aryee, BA Hons, PG
  Cert Public Administration

Principal: Mrs Valerie Mainoo, BSc Psych, MA Ed

Age Range. 4–18.
Numbers of Pupils. 232 Boys, 249 Girls.
Fees per term (2014–2015). Junior School (Reception–Class 6): US$1,450; Senior School (Forms 1–5) US$1,750; Sixth Form US$1,850.

Established in September 2002, The Roman Ridge School aims to provide the very best of British Education whilst being firmly rooted in Ghanaian life and culture. The school is a unique facility in Ghana as it offers small class sizes (20), individual pupil attention, a family atmosphere, firm discipline, emphasis on good manners, a sound Christian foundation, a caring environment and a full programme of Sports and extra-curricular activities.

The school is noted for its Special Needs and Individual Learning Programmes as well as its dedication to all other pupils including the high ability learners and scholars. Pupils are carefully monitored and assessed regularly in order to achieve academic success, and, parents are encouraged to help in this process.

All teaching is initially based on the English National Curriculum for the Foundation Course and Key Stage One, after which the pupils progress to the 11+ examination, then take the full range of academic subjects at the 13+ Common Entrance & the IGCSE Courses with the Cambridge Board. The school has begun its A Level programme and offers a comprehensive range of Courses.

There are thirty classrooms at present, three ICT suites, a Multimedia Centre with a Language lab, two up-to-date Libraries with full audio-visual facilities, junior & senior Science Labs, a Dance Studio, a specialised Art Room and a climbing wall. A modern clinic is on site staffed by a qualified SRN.

Pupils play Football, Netball, Hockey, Basketball and Rounders and also enjoy a very successful Swimming programme. Scouting is also provided throughout the school for Beavers (6–8), Wolf Cubs (8–11), Scouts (11–16) and Senior Scouts (16+). Pupils keenly attend visits and trips to various places of interest including the Slave Forts, Game Parks, a jungle canopy walk and the Volta Lake.

At weekends, the school offers a full range of Adventure Activities including Mountain-Biking, Canoeing, Climbing, Hiking, Camping and Orienteering which are all led by fully qualified UK instructors.

During the very full school day the pupils take part in many activities such as Choirs, Music Lessons (Piano and Guitar), Drama, Karate, Traditional Drumming and Dancing, and the school has its own Skittle Alley. School productions and concerts take place at the end of each term.

The school is open on Saturdays for extra work programmes, swimming, games, music lessons, art and computer clubs, and special events.

Pupils thrive in The Roman Ridge School and are reluctant to go home at the end of the day.

St Andrew's Preparatory School

Private Bag, Molo 20106, Kenya
Tel: +254 202025708
              +254 735337736
email: officeprep@turimail.co.ke
website: www.standrewsturi.com

Chair of Governors: Mrs Anne Aliker

Headmaster: **Mr Paddy Moss**

Age Range. 3–13.
Number of Pupils. 250: 126 Boys, 124 Girls.
Fees per term (2014–2015). Boarding: Kshs 498,000–576,000. Day: Kshs 249,000–288,000.

St Andrew's Preparatory School, Turi, is an international, multicultural, Christian boarding school offering British Curriculum education of the highest standard. The School aims to provide a happy, stimulating, well-rounded educational experience for children. Pupils are encouraged to grow into well-educated, confident, self-disciplined young adults with the potential to be future leaders.

The Prep School together with its Senior School is situated 200 km north west of Nairobi on a beautiful 300-acre estate at an altitude of over 2,000 metres, where the climate is both healthy and invigorating. The School has its own private airstrip within the grounds.

Boarding pupils are accepted from the age of 5 and follow the British National Curriculum and then the Common Entrance Syllabus which prepares them for entry to St Andrew's Senior School and to other independent senior schools in Britain or elsewhere.

The original School, founded in 1931, was destroyed by fire in 1944. It was completely rebuilt and is superbly designed and equipped as a modern purpose-built preparatory school. There are subject rooms for English, Mathematics, French, History, Geography and Science laboratories. Information Technology is an integral part of the curriculum throughout the School with two ICT suites and most classrooms are equipped with interactive whiteboards and data projectors. An exceptionally large Hall is used for plays, concerts and large functions. The average size of classes is 16.

Sports form a key part of school life at St Andrew's School. The grounds and playing fields are extensive. Boys play cricket and rugby; girls play rounders and netball; all play football, hockey, tennis and take part in athletics and cross-country. In the newly-opened sports centre there are excellent facilities for a wide range of indoor sports including two glass-backed squash courts and a fitness suite. There are seven school tennis courts and a heated swimming pool, as well as a riding school on site where pupils of all abilities are taught by qualified instructors.

The School has a strong musical tradition. In addition to the many and varied opportunities for music within the curriculum over 80 pupils opt for specialist instrumental tuition in a wide range of instruments. Many of these pupils work towards ABRSM examinations. There are also several specialist music groups who practice and perform together and the Junior and Senior choirs.

A large and well-equipped Art Studio as well as Design Technology and Food Technology rooms allow pupils to express themselves creatively. A wealth of arts and crafts, hobbies and outdoor pursuits are actively encouraged. The School has its own Chapel and aims to give a practical Christian education in a community with high standards and in a supportive family atmosphere.

All staff live within the estate. The teaching staff are all qualified and are committed to the Christian ethos of the School.

St Andrew's Senior School offers a three-year course to IGCSE examinations with excellent academic results, and thereafter students can opt for A Levels at the incorporated St Andrew's College. The School has the same Board of Governors, but its own Headmaster, teaching staff and Management Team.

St Christopher's School

PO Box 32052, Isa Town, Kingdom of Bahrain
Tel: +973 17 598 600
Fax: +973 17 598 604
email: admissions.school@st-chris.net
website: www.st-chris.net

Principal: **Mr Ed Goodwin**, BA, MA, MBA, OBE

Head of Infant School: Mr Ian Fellows, BEd, NPQH
Head of Junior School: Mrs Wendy Bataineh, BA, PGCE, MA, NPQH
Head of Senior School: Mr Nick Wilson, BSc, PGCE, NPQH

Age Range. 3–18 Co-educational.
Number of Pupils. 2,264.

St Christopher's first opened in 1961 and has grown to become an internationally renowned school with over 2,200 students from around 70 nations; a school with a fine international reputation and widely recognised as one of the world's top British schools overseas, with exceptional facilities and resources.

With a consistent record of excellent academic success, we also offer a broad programme of extra-curricular activities and personal development opportunities. The school has

been rated "Outstanding" in 3 different inspection regimes – not just overall, but for every aspect of our performance.

St Christopher's is not for profit, with all income from fees being used to run and further develop the School for the benefit of our students, making us the premier choice for those parents who need and demand the very best British-style education for their children in Bahrain.

St Christopher's is a highly successful school, firmly established in the British tradition, yet with an international outlook.

St Christopher's: Caring, Learning and Communicating to give your family the very best in British-International education!

Fees per term (2014–2015). Nursery BD907; Reception–Year 2 BD1,186; Years 3–6 BD1,318; Years 7–8 BD1,607; Years 9–11 BD1,977; Years 12–13 BD2,312.

St Paul's School

Rua Juquiá 166, Jardim Paulistano, São Paulo SP 01440–903, Brazil
Tel: 00 55 11 3087 3399
Fax: 00 55 11 3087 3398
email: head@stpauls.br
website: www.stpauls.br

Chairman of the Board of Governors: Mrs Cristina Betts

***Head*: Ms Louise Simpson**

Deputy Headmaster: Mr Paul Morgan
Head of Senior School: Dr Barry Hallinan
Head of Preparatory School: Mrs Siobhain Allum
Head of Pre-Preparatory School: Dr Anne d'Heursel-Baldisseri

Age Range. 3–18.
Number of Pupils. 1,090: Pre-Preparatory 226, Preparatory 389, Senior 475.

Fees per annum (2013–2014). Pre-Prep and Prep School R$53,496; Senior School R$69,024.

St Paul's School was founded in 1926 and is an independent non-denominational school. It is *the* British School in the São Paulo area, although there are some other English-speaking international schools. St Paul's is situated in the leafy and affluent residential area aptly named *Jardins*.

The Board of Governors is appointed by Trustees of the British and Commonwealth Community Council (B&CCC), and includes parents of current or former pupils, a representative of the B&CCC, ex officio members and the Headmaster. Her Majesty's Ambassador to Brazil is the Honorary President. St Paul's is co-educational with a School roll of 1090 pupils from 3 to 18 years old. There are approximately 30 different nationalities in School. The teaching staff totals 172; around 80 are British or Anglo-Brazilians. The aim of the School is to provide an education for British children in São Paulo, Anglo-Brazilians, Brazilians and other nationalities. The curriculum offered in the Pre-Preparatory and Preparatory Schools is based on the IPC (International Primary Curriculum). Pupils in the Senior School prepare for IGCSEs in Forms 4 and 5, and the International Baccalaureate Bilingual Diploma Programme in the Sixth Form. Pupils normally go on to universities in the UK, in the United States and Canada, as well as to universities in Brazil.

All members of staff are expected to contribute to the Extra-curricular Activities Programme, which includes an extensive range of activities after School. Each part of the School has its own floor in the main building: the Pre-Preparatory School is a self-contained unit on the ground floor, the Preparatory School is situated on the middle floor and the Senior School on the top floor. The general impression when entering the School is that of any other modern British school – it just happens to be in Brazil.

The School has gone through an interesting and challenging period in its development. Classrooms have been refurbished to the highest standards, up-to-date Science facilities have been installed and the computer provision is complete with over 450 networked computers (of which 100 are Net Books). The Library has over 32,000 items on its database, and an excellent selection of magazines and newspapers. The School has an impressive Art Centre, a spacious Theatre and Drama Studio, Music rooms (one with 10 iMacs) as well as an excellent underground Sports centre. The School is about to start a major Development Project to significantly enhance the facilities for Art, Music, the Sciences and Library.

The School is a busy, hard-working place and standards are high. In September 2012 the School underwent an ISI (Independent Schools Inspectorate) inspection as part of the UK Government's Scheme for recognising St Paul's as a British School overseas (the first to do so in South America). St Paul's School is seen as one of the foremost academic establishments in Latin America, capable of holding its own with the best in the UK.

St Saviour's School, Ikoyi
Lagos, Nigeria

54 Alexander Avenue, Ikoyi, Lagos, Nigeria
Tel: 00 234 1 8990153
Fax: 00 234 1 2700255
email: info@stsavioursschikoyi.org
website: www.stsavioursschikoyi.org

St Saviour's is an Associate Member of COBIS.

Chairman of Board of Trustees: Mr L N Mbanefo, SAN

Head Teacher: Mr Craig Heaton, BA Hons

  Age Range. 4–11 Co-educational.
  Number of Pupils. 320.
  Fees per term (2014–2015). Naira 695,000.
  A truly rounded education is a preparation for life. Grounded on our core values, St Saviour's seeks to provide an education that is challenging, relevant, exciting and delivered in a caring and thoroughly professional manner. We look, unashamedly, for academic achievement in each pupil alongside equal progress in spiritual growth, friendship, independence, confidence and some appreciation of their place in the world and their responsibilities towards others.

Christian principles are integrated into the daily life of the school which is an Anglican foundation. Children of a number of denominations and faiths attend the school and are warmly welcomed. Parents are welcomed as part of the learning cycle; communication with them is regular and their support of the school is exceptional.

The development of the whole child is at the heart of education at St Saviour's. Learning is about developing personal, emotional and social skills as well as being an intellectual and academic process. We aim to help children find their voice – their own unique, personal significance. We encourage them to think about what their contribution will be in the world – how they will try to make a difference as responsible and engaged members of the School community as well as citizens of the world.

St Saviour's has high expectations for all its learners. We pride ourselves on knowing each child as an individual in order to help them make progress. Teachers plan to scaffold success for all learners from their point of entry. This means that learning opportunities are planned so that all students are challenged appropriately, sometimes by providing work that is a little too hard and then providing support systems to enable students to work through their difficulties to achieve success.

Above all, we are interested in the learning process – learning how to learn and how to apply skills and knowledge across an ever-increasing spectrum of experience. From the earliest age we ensure that children have an enjoyable experience of school and are motivated to learn and improve. This positive attitude is supported by a team of highly professional teachers who are themselves engaged in lifelong learning and model effective habits of mind. The curriculum is based on that of the National Curriculum for England and Wales and the International Primary Curriculum adapted to reflect the needs of an increasingly international and multicultural student body We aim to build on the children's background knowledge and experience to equip them with the skills, strategies and a love of learning that will inspire them to succeed whatever the next step on their educational journey.

The school has developed and renewed its own sports facilities over the past few years and now has its own 25m swimming pool and extensive sports field, including football pitch and running track as well as informal play areas. Routinely, about 30 extra-curricular Clubs operate after school each week and they are very well supported. Events such as Assemblies, Independence Day, Foundation, KS1 and KS2 Productions, Sports Day, International Week, Flower Show, Fun Day and Harvest Festival add greatly to the school's character. Our support of local orphanages flows from monies raised at some of these events.

Pupils leave the school from Y6 to attend leading Secondary schools in Nigeria and approximately 40% move on to outstanding independent schools in the UK, where they prove to be excellent ambassadors of the holistic education they have received at St Saviour's.

Tanglin Trust Junior School

95 Portsdown Road, Singapore 139299
Tel: 00 65 6778 9000
email: junior.school@tts.edu.sg
website: www.tts.edu.sg
Twitter: @TanglinTrust
Facebook: /TanglinTrustSchool
LinkedIn: /tanglin-trust-school

Chair of Governors: Mr Dominic Nixon

Chief Executive Officer: Mr Peter J Derby-Crook

Head of Junior School: Mr David Ingram

  Age Range. 7–11.
  Number of Pupils. Junior School 770 (2,750 across Infant, Junior, Senior Schools).
  Fees per term (2014–2015). S$10,373.65.
  Building on strong foundations. Tanglin Trust School was formed in 1925 and has nearly 90 years' experience offering British-based learning for expatriates from a wide range of nationalities, who benefit from world-class facilities combined with the highest possible standards of teaching. The school is divided into three distinct entities: Infant (3–7), Junior (7–11) and Senior (11–18) each with their own Head of School and unique set of characteristics; yet all part of the bigger Tanglin 'family'.

Broad and Balanced Curriculum. The Junior School provides a stimulating environment that inspires and motivates students in their academic, sporting, artistic and cultural development from Years 3 to 6. A creative and integrated curriculum is underpinned by a structured approach to teaching the core subjects of English, Mathematics, Science, the Humanities, Chinese and PSHCE (Personal, Social, Health and Citizenship Education) and a commitment to high standards. Alongside academic skills and knowledge, the key drivers of self-awareness and personal development and global awareness and sense of community, lead to an overall focus on students becoming well-rounded, community spirited and responsible, international young citizens. A strong pastoral system nurtures positive relationships, promoting an ethos that values and celebrates students as individuals while fostering a strong sense of community.

Entry. Students entering the School must be fluent in English, residing in Singapore with at least one parent and be able to access the curriculum independently. Prospective students may be required to sit admissions assessments.

Smooth Transition. The transition from Key Stage 1 in Tanglin's Infant School to Key Stage 2 and the Junior School presents students with exciting new challenges. The school day becomes more formally structured and students are encouraged to take on new responsibilities as they work towards becoming independent learners. The Junior School's warm and caring environment facilitates a holistic approach to learning that provides students with a wide range of opportunities to guide their academic, personal, social and physical development.

Creative Learning. All teachers (class and specialist) work creatively to capture the interest of boys and girls and to make their learning personalised, enjoyable and meaningful. A range of contemporary teaching strategies are employed. The school looks to engage and capture the imagination and interest of students right from the start of study, through themed dress-up days or practical activities involving research and collaboration as a class and in groups. The school believes that the quality of the learning experience determines the ability of the students to embrace concepts, to analyse and make connections and to see past the subject to its relevance for them beyond the classroom.

The English National Curriculum provides the basis for the programmes of study but these are enhanced and enriched to reflect the calibre of the students and the school's international setting.

Co-Curricular Activities. Students are encouraged to participate in the extensive range of Co-Curricular Activities (CCAs): over 100 activities range from cooking, cheerleading, rock climbing, soft toy making or Bollywood dancing to more traditional sport and music options. Students can learn to play a wide variety of instruments and take part in an impressive array of choirs, ensembles and orchestras. All students play sport in lesson time and are also encouraged to choose from the many sporting opportunities that are available as CCAs. Junior students are also selected to represent Tanglin in sporting events against other British schools in South and East Asia.

Building Group Identity and House System. Tanglin Junior School understands the value young people place on group membership. It ensures students are well integrated into their classes and encouraged to be part of a wide group of friends.

Each Junior student is also warmly welcomed into a House and special House days feature innovative teambuilding activities. To promote year group identity, students experience learning in large shared spaces that feature computers and comfortable reading areas and are imaginatively transformed each term into a range of settings to enrich learning.

Personal and Social Responsibility. Opportunities abound in the Junior School to build leadership skills and an appreciation of the many cultures that co-exist in Singapore. Juniors act as buddies to Infant students and can participate in the Student Council or become a Library Monitor, Junior Listener, Maths Mentor or Computer Champion. Themed assemblies celebrate cultural festivals and reinforce the importance of self management and personal and social responsibility.

Outdoor Education. Juniors also take part in challenging residential field studies that range from an overnight trip to one of Singapore's islands in Year 4 to a six-day excursion to Sarawak in Malaysia in Year 6. By valuing each individual and the contribution he or she makes and emphasising meaningful learning, self management and responsibility, Junior students are thoroughly prepared for Senior School.

Tanglin Mission. Tanglin Trust School Singapore has a long tradition of providing British-based learning with an international perspective. At Tanglin we strive to make every individual feel valued, happy and successful. Responsibility, enthusiasm and participation are actively encouraged and integrity is prized. Working together in a safe, caring yet stimulating environment, we set high expectations whilst offering strong support, resulting in a community of lifelong learners who can contribute with confidence to our world.

Tanglin's Learner Profile is a set of ten attributes which act as a framework to identify and measure the skills and attributes necessary to achieve the school's mission, in particular, the goal of nurturing 'a community of lifelong learners who can contribute with confidence to Our World.' The ten attributes are: Balanced, Caring, Risk-takers, Knowledgeable, Resilient Inquirers, Communicators, Principled, Open-minded, Thinkers, Reflective.

Not-For-Profit status. Tanglin is a not-for-profit organisation and is registered as an educational charity.

PART V
Schools whose Heads are members of the Independent Schools Association

ALPHABETICAL LIST OF SCHOOLS

PAGE

Abbey College Manchester, Greater Manchester . . . 1147
Abbey Gate Prep School, Cheshire 1147
Abingdon House School, London 1147
ACS Cobham International School, Surrey 1148
ACS Egham International School, Surrey 1148
ACS Hillingdon International School, Middx 1149
Alton Convent School, Hants 1149
Argyle House School, Tyne and Wear 1150
Arts Educational Schools London, London 1150
Ashton House School, Middx 1151
Ayscoughfee Hall School, Lincs 1151

Babington House School, Kent 1151
Beech Hall School, Cheshire 1152
Beech House School, Greater Manchester 1152
Bishop Challoner School, Kent 1152
Bowbrook House School, Worcs 1153
Braeside School for Girls, Essex 1153
Bredon School, Glos 1153
Bridgewater School, Greater Manchester 1154
Brigidine School Windsor, Berks 1154
Bronte School, Kent 1155
Buxlow Preparatory School, Middx 1155

Cambridge Tutors College, Surrey. 1155
Canbury School, Surrey 1156
Cardiff Sixth Form College, Wales 1156
Carleton House Preparatory School, Merseyside . . . 1157
Castle House School, Shropshire 1157
CATS College Cambridge, Cambs. 1158
Chase Grammar School, Staffs 1158
Chilton Cantelo School, Somerset 1159
Claires Court, Berks 1159
Coopersale Hall School, Essex 1160
Copthill School, Lincs 1160
Cransley School, Cheshire 1161
Crowstone Preparatory School, Essex 1161
Cundall Manor School, N Yorks 1161

Dagfa School Nottingham, Notts 1162
Daiglen School, Essex 1162
Ditcham Park School, Hants 1162
The Dixie Grammar School, Leics. 1163
DLD College, London 1163
Dwight School London, London. 1164

Egerton Rothesay School, Herts 1164

Fairfield School, Bristol 1165
Fairley House School, London. 1165
Falkner House, London 1165
Faraday School, London 1166
Ferndale House Preparatory School, Oxon 1166
Finborough School, Suffolk 1166
The Firs School, Cheshire 1167
Firwood Manor Preparatory School, Lancs 1167
Forest Park Preparatory School, Cheshire 1168
Forest Preparatory School, Cheshire. 1168

PAGE

Frewen College & Frewen Preparatory School,
 E Sussex 1168
Fyling Hall School, N Yorks 1169

Gads Hill School, Kent 1169
GEMS Bolitho School, Cornwall 1170
GEMS Hampshire School, London 1170
Gidea Park College, Essex 1171
Gosfield School, Essex 1171
Grangewood Independent School, London 1172
Grantham Preparatory International School, Lincs . . 1172
Greenbank Preparatory School and Day Nursery,
 Cheshire. 1172
Greenfields School, E Sussex 1173
The Gregg School, Hants 1173
The Grove Independent School, Bucks 1173

Hale Preparatory School, Cheshire 1173
The Hammond, Cheshire 1174
Harvington Prep School, London 1174
Hawley Place School, Surrey 1174
Heathcote School, Essex. 1175
Heathfield School and Day Nursery, Worcs 1175
Hemdean House School, Berks 1175
Herne Hill School, London 1176
Heywood Prep, Wilts 1176
Highclare School, W Midlands 1177
Highfield Priory School, Lancs 1177
Highfields School, Notts. 1178
Hipperholme Grammar School, W Yorks 1178
Hopelands Preparatory School, Glos 1179
Howe Green House School, Herts 1179
Hulme Hall Grammar School, Cheshire 1179
Hurst Lodge School, Berks 1179
Hurtwood House School, Surrey 1180

Ibstock Place School, London 1180
The Italia Conti Academy of Theatre Arts, London . . 1181

King Alfred School, London. 1181
Kings Monkton School, Wales. 1181
Kirkstone House School, Lincs 1182
Knightsbridge School, London 1182
The Knoll School, Worcs 1182

Lady Barn House School, Cheshire 1183
Lime House School, Cumbria 1183
Lingfield Notre Dame, Surrey 1183
Loreto Preparatory School, Cheshire 1184
Lyndhurst School, Surrey 1185
Lyonsdown School, Herts 1185

Mander Portman Woodward (MPW), London. 1185
Manor House School, Leics 1186
Maple Hayes Hall School for Dyslexics, Staffs 1186
Maple Walk School, London. 1186
Mark College, Somerset 1187
Mayville High School, Hants 1187

PAGE

Mead School, Kent. 1188
The Moat School, London 1188
Moffats School, Worcs. 1189
Moon Hall School for Dyslexic Children, Surrey . . . 1189
Moorland School, Lancs 1189
More House School, Surrey 1190
Moyles Court School, Hants 1190

New Eccles Hall School, Norfolk 1190
Norfolk House School, W Midlands. 1191
Normanhurst School, London 1191
Northease Manor School, E Sussex 1191
Notre Dame Preparatory School, Norfolk 1192

Oakfield Preparatory School, London 1192
Oakhill College, Lancs. 1192
Oakhyrst Grange School, Surrey. 1193
Oaklands School, Essex 1193
OLCS – Our Lady's Convent School, Leics. 1194

Park School, Dorset 1194
Park School for Girls, Essex 1194
The Park School, Somerset 1195
Polwhele House School, Cornwall. 1195
Prenton Preparatory School, Merseyside 1196
Priory School, W Midlands 1196

Queen Ethelburga's Collegiate Foundation, N Yorks . 1196

Raphael Independent School, Essex 1197
Rastrick Independent School, W Yorks 1197
Ravenstone Preparatory & Pre-Preparatory
   Schools, London 1198
Red House School, Cleveland 1198
Redcourt – St Anselm's, Merseyside 1199
Riverston School, London 1199
Rochester Independent College, Kent 1200
Rookwood School, Hants 1200
Roselyon School, Cornwall 1200
Ruckleigh School, W Midlands 1201
Rushmoor School, Beds 1201

Sackville School, Kent. 1201
Sacred Heart School, Norfolk 1202
Sacred Heart School, E Sussex 1202
St Andrew's School, Beds 1203
St Anne's Preparatory School, Essex 1203
St Christopher's School, Surrey 1203
St Christopher's School, Devon 1204
St Christopher's School, Middx 1204
St Clare's, Oxford, Oxon. 1204
St David's College, Kent. 1205
St David's School, Surrey 1205
St Gerard's School, Wales 1205
St Hilda's School, Herts 1206
St James Junior School, London 1206
St James' School, Lincs 1206
St John's School, Essex 1207
St Joseph's Convent School, London 1207

PAGE

St Joseph's Park Hill School, Lancs 1207
St Joseph's Preparatory School, Staffs. 1207
St Joseph's School, Cornwall 1207
St Joseph's School, Notts 1208
St Margaret's Preparatory School, Essex 1208
St Martin's Preparatory School, Lincs 1208
St Michael's School, Wales 1209
St Nicholas House School, Norfolk 1209
Saint Nicholas School, Essex 1209
St Peter's School, Northants 1210
St Philomena's Catholic School, Essex 1210
St Piran's School, Cornwall 1210
St Teresa's Catholic Independent School & Nursery,
   Bucks 1211
St Winefride's Convent School, Shropshire 1211
St Winifred's School, Hants 1211
St Wystan's School, Derbyshire 1212
Salesian College, Hants 1212
Salterford House School, Notts 1212
Sancton Wood School, Cambs. 1213
Scarisbrick Hall School & College, Lancs. 1213
Shapwick School, Somerset 1213
Sherborne House School, Hants 1214
Sherborne International, Dorset 1214
Sherfield School, Hants 1214
Sherrardswood School, Herts 1215
Shoreham College, W Sussex 1215
Slindon College, W Sussex 1215
Snaresbrook Preparatory School, London 1216
Steephill School, Kent. 1216
Stoke College, Suffolk 1216
Stratford Preparatory School, Warwicks 1217
Study School, Surrey. 1217
The Swaminarayan School, London 1217
Sylvia Young Theatre School, London 1218

Thames Christian College, London 1218
Thorpe Hall School, Essex. 1219
Tower College, Merseyside 1219
The Towers Convent School, E Sussex 1219
Trevor-Roberts School, London 1220
Trinity School, Essex 1220

Ursuline Preparatory School, Essex 1220

Vernon Lodge Preparatory School, Staffs 1221
Virgo Fidelis Preparatory School, London. 1221
Vita et Pax Preparatory School, London. 1221

The Webber Independent School, Bucks 1222
West Lodge School, Kent 1222
Westbourne School, Wales. 1223
Westward School, Surrey 1223
Whitehall School, Cambs 1223
Windrush Valley School, Oxon 1223
Woodlands School, Essex 1224
Woodlands School, Essex 1224

The following schools, whose Heads are members of both ISA and HMC, can be found in the HMC section:

The Grange School
Princethorpe College

The following schools, whose Heads are members of both ISA and GSA, can be found in the GSA section:

Adcote School
Alderley Edge School for Girls
Dodderhill School
Northwood College for Girls
St Catherine's School, Twickenham

St Dominic's Brewood
St Dominic's Priory School
St James Senior Girls' School
St Martha's

The following schools, whose Heads are members of both ISA and The Society of Heads, can be found in The Society of Heads section:

Abbey Gate College
Bedstone College
Derby Grammar School
Hull Collegiate School
LVS Ascot (The Licensed Victuallers' School)
North Cestrian Grammar School
Pitsford School

Portland Place School
St Edward's School
St James Senior Boys' School
Stafford Grammar School
Tring Park School for the Performing Arts
Trinity School

The following schools, whose Heads are members of both ISA and IAPS, can be found in the IAPS section:

Abercorn School
Alleyn Court Preparatory School
Ballard School
Berkhamsted Pre-Preparatory School
Collingwood School
Crackley Hall School
Cumnor House School
Gatehouse School
Hatherop Castle Preparatory School
Leehurst Swan School
Littlegarth School

Lucton School
Mylnhurst Preparatory School & Nursery
The Old School Henstead
Pilgrims Pre-Preparatory School
Reddiford School
Rosemead Preparatory School
St Edward's Preparatory School
Shrewsbury Lodge School
The Study Preparatory School
Wilmslow Preparatory School

GEOGRAPHICAL LIST OF ISA SCHOOLS

PAGE   PAGE

ENGLAND

Bedfordshire
Rushmoor School 1201
St Andrew's School 1203

Berkshire
Brigidine School Windsor 1154
Claires Court 1159
Hemdean House School 1175
Hurst Lodge School 1179

Bristol
Fairfield School 1165

Buckinghamshire
The Grove Independent School 1173
St Teresa's Catholic Independent School &
   Nursery 1211
The Webber Independent School 1222

Cambridgeshire
CATS College Cambridge 1158
Sancton Wood School 1213
Whitehall School 1223

Cheshire
Abbey Gate Prep School 1147
Beech Hall School 1152
Cransley School 1161
The Firs School 1167
Forest Park Preparatory School 1168
Forest Preparatory School 1168
Greenbank Preparatory School and Day Nursery . . 1172
Hale Preparatory School 1173
The Hammond 1174
Hulme Hall Grammar School 1179
Lady Barn House School 1183
Loreto Preparatory School 1184

Cleveland
Red House School 1198

Cornwall
GEMS Bolitho School 1170
Polwhele House School 1195
Roselyon School 1200
St Joseph's School 1207
St Piran's School 1210

Cumbria
Lime House School 1183

Derbyshire
St Wystan's School 1212

Devon
St Christopher's School 1204

Dorset
Park School 1194
Sherborne International 1214

Essex
Braeside School for Girls 1153

Coopersale Hall School 1160
Crowstone Preparatory School 1161
Daiglen School 1162
Gidea Park College 1171
Gosfield School 1171
Heathcote School 1175
Oaklands School 1193
Park School for Girls 1194
Raphael Independent School 1197
St Anne's Preparatory School 1203
St John's School 1207
St Margaret's Preparatory School 1208
Saint Nicholas School 1209
St Philomena's Catholic School 1210
Thorpe Hall School 1219
Trinity School 1220
Ursuline Preparatory School 1220
Woodlands School 1224
Woodlands School 1224

Gloucestershire
Bredon School 1153
Hopelands Preparatory School 1179

Greater Manchester
Abbey College Manchester 1147
Beech House School 1152
Bridgewater School 1154

Hampshire
Alton Convent School 1149
Ditcham Park School 1162
The Gregg School 1173
Mayville High School 1187
Moyles Court School 1190
Rookwood School 1200
St Winifred's School 1211
Salesian College 1212
Sherborne House School 1214
Sherfield School 1214

Hertfordshire
Egerton Rothesay School 1164
Howe Green House School 1179
Lyonsdown School 1185
St Hilda's School 1206
Sherrardswood School 1215

Kent
Babington House School 1151
Bishop Challoner School 1152
Bronte School 1155
Gads Hill School 1169
Mead School 1188
Rochester Independent College 1200
Sackville School 1201
St David's College 1205
Steephill School 1216
West Lodge School 1222

Lancashire
Firwood Manor Preparatory School 1167
Highfield Priory School 1177
Moorland School 1189

PAGE

Oakhill College 1192
St Joseph's Park Hill School 1207
Scarisbrick Hall School & College 1213

Leicestershire
The Dixie Grammar School. 1163
Manor House School 1186
OLCS – Our Lady's Convent School. 1194

Lincolnshire
Ayscoughfee Hall School 1151
Copthill School 1160
Grantham Preparatory International School 1172
Kirkstone House School 1182
St James' School 1206
St Martin's Preparatory School 1208

London (see also Essex, Middlesex, Surrey)
Abingdon House School 1147
Arts Educational Schools London 1150
DLD College 1163
Dwight School London 1164
Fairley House School 1165
Falkner House. 1165
Faraday School 1166
GEMS Hampshire School. 1170
Grangewood Independent School. 1172
Harvington Prep School. 1174
Herne Hill School. 1176
Ibstock Place School 1180
The Italia Conti Academy of Theatre Arts 1181
King Alfred School 1181
Knightsbridge School 1182
The Lyceum. 1184
Mander Portman Woodward (MPW) 1185
Maple Walk School 1186
The Moat School 1188
Normanhurst School 1191
Oakfield Preparatory School 1192
Ravenstone Preparatory & Pre-Preparatory Schools 1198
Riverston School 1199
St James Junior School 1206
St Joseph's Convent School. 1207
Snaresbrook Preparatory School 1216
The Swaminarayan School 1217
Sylvia Young Theatre School 1218
Thames Christian College. 1218
Trevor-Roberts School 1220
Virgo Fidelis Preparatory School 1221
Vita et Pax Preparatory School 1221

Merseyside
Carleton House Preparatory School. 1157
Prenton Preparatory School. 1196
Redcourt – St Anselm's. 1199
Tower College. 1219

Middlesex
ACS Hillingdon International School. 1149
Ashton House School 1151
Buxlow Preparatory School. 1155
St Christopher's School. 1204

Norfolk
New Eccles Hall School 1190
Notre Dame Preparatory School 1192
Sacred Heart School 1202
St Nicholas House School 1209

PAGE

Northamptonshire
St Peter's School 1210

Nottinghamshire
Dagfa School Nottingham 1162
Highfields School. 1178
St Joseph's School 1208
Salterford House School 1212

Oxfordshire
Ferndale House Preparatory School 1166
St Clare's, Oxford. 1204
Windrush Valley School 1223

Shropshire
Castle House School 1157
St Winefride's Convent School 1211

Somerset
Chilton Cantelo School 1159
Mark College 1187
The Park School 1195
Shapwick School 1213

Staffordshire (see also West Midlands)
Chase Grammar School. 1158
Maple Hayes Hall School for Dyslexics 1186
St Joseph's Preparatory School 1207
Vernon Lodge Preparatory School 1221

Suffolk
Finborough School 1166
Stoke College 1216

Surrey
ACS Cobham International School 1148
ACS Egham International School 1148
Cambridge Tutors College 1155
Canbury School 1156
Hawley Place School 1174
Hurtwood House School 1180
Lingfield Notre Dame. 1183
Lyndhurst School 1185
Moon Hall School for Dyslexic Children. 1189
More House School 1190
Oakhyrst Grange School 1193
St Christopher's School. 1203
St David's School. 1205
Study School 1217
Westward School 1223

Sussex (East)
Frewen College & Frewen Preparatory School. . . 1168
Greenfields School 1173
Northease Manor School 1191
Sacred Heart School 1202
The Towers Convent School 1219

Sussex (West)
Shoreham College 1215
Slindon College. 1215

Tyne and Wear
Argyle House School 1150

Warwickshire
Stratford Preparatory School 1217

	PAGE
West Midlands	
Highclare School	1177
Norfolk House School	1191
Priory School	1196
Ruckleigh School	1201
Wiltshire	
Heywood Prep	1176
Worcestershire	
Bowbrook House School	1153
Heathfield School and Day Nursery	1175
The Knoll School	1182
Moffats School	1189

	PAGE
Yorkshire (North)	
Cundall Manor School	1161
Fyling Hall School	1169
Queen Ethelburga's Collegiate Foundation	1196
Yorkshire (West)	
Hipperholme Grammar School	1178
Rastrick Independent School	1197
WALES	
Cardiff Sixth Form College	1156
Kings Monkton School	1181
St Gerard's School	1205
St Michael's School	1209
Westbourne School	1223

Individual School Entries

Abbey College Manchester
Alpha Plus Group Limited

5–7 Cheapside, King Street, Manchester M2 4WG
Tel: 0161 817 2700
Fax: 0161 817 2705
email: admin@abbeymanchester.co.uk
website: www.abbeymanchester.co.uk
Twitter: @AbbeyManchester
Facebook: /Abbey College Manchester

Principal: **Ms L Elam**

Age Range. 15–19.
Number of Pupils. 230.
GCSE, A Level, BTEC and One Year A Level Retake
An independent day school with a college environment
- Year 11, Lower Sixth and Upper Sixth entry
- Very small classes (an average 7 students in each) ensure excellent progress
- Unique one year GCSEs and A Levels for those sitting for the first time or retaking
- High levels of personal support and individual responsibility gives good preparation for university life
- Expert advice is delivered for entry onto all university courses leading to strong relationships with the top universities in Britain
- City centre location means students will benefit from the unlimited arts, business, science, sports and music resources on offer

Flexible learning programmes mean that students can join at any time during the academic year, not just September.

Fees per annum (2014–2015). Lower Sixth (AS Level or BTEC) £11,500; Upper Sixth (A2 Level or BTEC) £11,500; One Year A Level (1 subject) £6,000; One Year A Level (2 subjects) £11,500; One Year GCSE (6–8 subjects) £11,000; One Year GCSE (up to 5 subjects) £8,750.

Fees are inclusive of exam fees.

Abbey Gate Prep School

Clare Avenue, Hoole, Chester CH2 3HR
Tel: 01244 319649
email: abbeygateschool@talk21.com
           headteacher.abbeygateschool@live.co.uk
website: www.abbeygateschool.org.uk
Twitter: @AbbeyGatePrep
Facebook: /Abbey-Gate-Prep-School

Head: **Mrs S A Rhodes-Leader**, BA Hons, PGCE

Age Range. 3–11.
Number in School. Day: 60 Boys and Girls.
Fees per term (2014–2015). £2,375–£2,535.
Abbey Gate Prep School, founded in 1910, is a small, exclusive Christian school, comprising around 60 children and a dedicated, well-qualified staff. Small class sizes allow each child to flourish and excel as an individual. This culminates in excellent 11+ success.

It offers a broad and well-balanced curriculum and has a proven tradition of academic success both locally and nationally, as well as a growing reputation for excellence in the performing arts. Tuition is offered in a variety of musical instruments and in speech & drama and dance. Some scholarships and bursaries are available.

Specialist help is available for children with specific learning difficulties.

Extra-curricular activities include chess, judo, ballet, modern dance, football, construction, computer, rhythmic gymnastics, Glee, craft, running and science clubs.

A forward-looking school, it aims to create exciting and challenging opportunities to develop academic, creative and physical skills, to produce confident and self-disciplined young people of the future. Excellent links have been established with the local community and with other schools in the area, both independent and maintained.

School opens at 8 am and has an After-School Club until 6 pm each day.

Abingdon House School
Alpha Plus Group

Broadley Terrace, London NW1 6LG
Tel: 0845 2300426
email: ahs@abingdonhouseschool.co.uk
website: www.abingdonhouseschool.co.uk

Head: **Mr Roy English**, MA, PGCE, Adv Dip SEN

Assistant Head – Pastoral Care: Mr Adrian Groves
Director of Studies: Mrs Claire Bredahl
SENCO: Mrs Laura Piper

Age Range. 5–13 Co-educational.
Number of Pupils. 57.
Fees per term (2014–2015). £9,200.
Abingdon House School is located in a refurbished Victorian building in London NW1 on four levels with facilities to educate up to 90 pupils aged between 5–13 years of age (Years 1–9). The school has specific expertise in the education of children who have Specific Learning Difficulties. This includes children with Dyslexia, Dyspraxia, Dyscalculia, Speech and Language Difficulties, Sensory Integration Difficulties, high-functioning Autism and so on.

The school provides a warm, nurturing environment in which the specific individual learning needs of our pupils are addressed through a multi-disciplinary approach. We provide an integrated, whole-school approach to meeting the needs of pupils who are diagnosed with a specific learning difficulty. When diagnosed early in their education, children generally respond well to intense intervention for a period of time, after which it is anticipated they would be able to return to the mainstream.

Effective learning and teaching is based on understanding a child's individual needs, nurturing a child's academic and social development and caring for a child's well-being. The environment is therefore warm and friendly and we are committed to each child's holistic development.

We aim to prepare the children for a return to mainstream schooling through:
- The provision of a holistic and individually tailored education programme.
- A whole-school teaching regime of small classes with teaching assistants, therapists and trained staff using a range of teaching strategies and therapeutic interventions. There is an appropriately low pupil to teacher ratio. Many

pupils have integrated successfully into various London day schools.

- Developing, monitoring and implementing an IEP (Individual Education Plan) for each pupil, which details SMART (Specific, Measurable, Achievable, Realistic and Timely) targets and describes the strategies and supports required to achieve those targets.
- Monitoring pupil progress through a rigorous system of assessment and tracking.
- Implementing a consistent system of positive behaviour support.
- Facilitating pupil-centred active learning.
- Placing special emphasis on the development of literacy and numeracy, social skills, language and communication and coordination, sequencing and movement.

Effort and achievement are praised and rewarded to build self-esteem. Merits and stickers are awarded daily. Certificates and rosettes are awarded each week. Pupils are given the opportunity for their efforts and achievements to be recognised and celebrated on a regular basis culminating in an end-of-term Musical Performance and Prize Giving.

We offer a full curriculum. PE/Games take place on a weekly basis at school and in local community facilities. Reading, Literacy and Maths lessons are ability grouped to enable pupils to progress as soon as they are ready. After-school clubs are offered several times a week, for example, ICT, Music, Games and Swimming.

We value teamwork and the partnership between parents and staff. Parent/Teacher meetings are held several times a term. Special Provision staff are available in weekly drop-in sessions.

ACS Cobham International School

Heywood, Portsmouth Road, Cobham, Surrey KT11 1BL

Tel:	01932 867251
Fax:	01932 869789
email:	CobhamAdmissions@acs-schools.com
website:	www.acs-schools.com

Head: Tony Eysele

Age Range. 2–18.
Number in School. Day: 827 Boys, 654 Girls; 107 Boarders.
Tuition Fees (2014–2015) per semester (2 semesters). £3,565–£12,125.
Boarding Fees (2014–2015) per semester (2 semesters). In addition to tuition fees: 7 day £9,025 (grades 7–13); 5 day £6,585 (grades 7–13).

Founded in 1967 to serve the needs of international and local families, ACS International Schools now educates 3,500 students up to age 18, from more than 70 countries, at three London area campuses in England and one in Doha, Qatar. All our schools are non-sectarian and co-educational.

The success of the programme at ACS Cobham is based on teamwork, collaboration, and the broad participation of its international community. All students are treated as unique individuals, with equal potential to make a positive contribution to the school. The goal is to instil an enthusiasm for lifelong learning and a sense of global awareness in each student, along with the necessary skills to prepare them for the challenges and changes which lie ahead.

The academic programme offers both the International Baccalaureate (IB) Diploma and Advanced Placement (AP) courses, creating a curriculum that meets the needs of a broad international student body. ACS graduates have established a tradition of attaining excellent exam results, enabling them to continue their studies at top universities around the world, including the US and UK.

Situated on 128 acres approximately 30 minutes by train from Central London, ACS Cobham enrols over 1,400 students. Exceptional facilities include an Early Childhood village; purpose-built Lower, Middle, and High School buildings; gymnasium and cafeteria complex and a Dormitory. All Lower, Middle and High School buildings have separate classrooms, science labs, libraries, computer labs, art and music studios and access to the school's state-of-the-art Interactive Learning Centre.

ACS Cobham offers extensive and varied extra-curricular clubs and community service activities both locally and internationally, which encourage students to participate in the richness of school life. Students also participate in international theatre arts programmes, maths, literature and music competitions in the UK and across Europe.

The campus sports programme runs three seasons fielding teams in football, volleyball, cross-country, basketball, rugby, swimming, dance, tennis, track & field, baseball, softball and golf. Sports facilities include six tennis courts, an Olympic-sized track, playing fields for football, rugby and baseball, a six-hole golf course, and a Sports Centre with 25-metre competition indoor swimming pool, basketball/volleyball show courts, dance and fitness studios, and a café.

The Dormitory provides a home-away-from-home for up to 110 students, aged 12–18. Boarders share two-person rooms with ensuite facilities and wireless internet connections; there are student lounges, kitchens, computer and study rooms. Six full-time Dormitory houseparents and over ten resident teaching staff ensure an active yet well-considered programme of pastoral care, friendship and advisor groups, house activities and weekend trips.

The admissions team is available throughout the year to answer questions, book campus visits, and assist families through the enrolment process. Students are accepted in all grades throughout the year, on non-selective criteria.

ACS Egham International School

Woodlee, London Road (A30), Egham, Surrey TW20 0HS

Tel:	01784 430800
Fax:	01784 430626
email:	EghamAdmissions@acs-schools.com
website:	www.acs-schools.com
Twitter:	@ACSEgham

Head of School: Mr Jeremy Lewis

Age Range. 3–18.
Number in School. Day only: 317 Boys, 273 Girls.
Tuition Fees (2014–2015) per semester (2 semesters). £3,420–£11,400.

Founded in 1967 to serve the needs of international and local families, ACS International Schools now educates 3,500 students up to age 18, from more than 70 countries, at three London area campuses in England and one in Doha, Qatar. All our schools are non-sectarian and co-educational.

ACS Egham offers all four International Baccalaureate (IB) programmes – the IB Primary Years Programme (3–11), the IB Middle Years Programme (11–16), the IB Diploma Programme (16–18) as well as the Career-related Programme (16–18). These programmes share a common philosophy and common characteristics: they develop the whole student, helping them to grow socially, physically, aesthetically, and culturally; and provide a broad and balanced education that includes science and the humanities, languages and mathematics, technology, physical education, and the arts.

This academic programme challenges students to fulfil their potential, and offers a broad-based selection of courses and levels to meet individual needs and interests. An important characteristic of ACS Egham is individual attention to students' needs facilitated by an exceptionally well-qualified, experienced, and sympathetic faculty; many of whom are IB examiners, moderators, and teacher trainers. The success of our programme is reflected in our IB Diploma pass rate over the last six years, which has enabled our graduates to continue their studies at top universities around the world, including the US and UK.

Situated on a 20-acre campus approximately 25 miles from central London, ACS Egham enrols more than 600 students. The school has purpose-built computer labs, libraries, spacious classrooms, playgrounds and sports fields. To further enhance the teaching programme there is a 21st century Visual Arts & Design Technology Centre and a new Science wing. A new sports centre opened in September 2012.

ACS Egham runs small class sizes which afford a greater opportunity for individual attention and support for various learning styles so that students are encouraged and challenged accordingly. Child Study Teams meet with individual student's teachers, administrators and parents, to ensure that every child is appropriately challenged and supported. A Language Coordinator assists families in organising native language lessons after-school or, if possible, during the school day.

ACS Egham offers extensive and varied extra-curricular clubs and community service activities both locally and internationally, which encourage students to participate in the richness of school life. Students also participate in international theatre arts programmes, maths, literature and music competitions in the UK and across Europe. The Campus sports programme runs three seasons fielding teams in football, volleyball, cross-country, basketball, rugby, swimming, dance, tennis, athletics, baseball, softball and golf.

The admissions team is available throughout the year to answer questions, book campus visits, and assist families through the enrolment process. Students are accepted in all grades throughout the year.

ACS Hillingdon International School

Hillingdon Court, 108 Vine Lane, Hillingdon, Middlesex UB10 0BE
Tel: 01895 259771
Fax: 01895 818404
email: HillingdonAdmissions@acs-schools.com
website: www.acs-schools.com

Head of School: **Linda LaPine**

Age Range. 4–18.
Number in School. Day only: 317 Boys, 263 Girls.
Tuition Fees (2014–2015) per semester (2 semesters). £4,990–£11,025.

Founded in 1967 to serve the needs of international and local families, ACS International Schools now educates 3,500 students up to age 18, from more than 70 countries, at three London area campuses in England and one in Doha, Qatar. All our schools are non-sectarian and co-educational.

The ACS Hillingdon philosophy:

- encourages a positive attitude toward education and lifelong learning
- provides meaningful educational experiences that enable students to acquire and apply knowledge, concepts, and skills
- helps each student realise his/her academic, creative, and physical potential
- provides opportunities for students to understand, appreciate, and develop sensitivity for other cultures

- encourages participation in community service, and support of local and international charities
- promotes a partnership with parents to meet the needs of students, and offer programmes that addresses issues associated with a highly mobile population
- promotes students to become lifelong learners in a global community

The academic programme offers both the International Baccalaureate (IB) Middle Years and Diploma Programmes as well as Advanced Placement (AP) courses, creating a curriculum that meets the needs of our entire international student body. IB scores regularly rank it among the highest achieving non-selective schools in the UK, enabling graduates to continue their studies at top universities around the world, including the US and UK.

ACS Hillingdon accepts over 600 students aged between 4 and 18. The campus is situated on an 11-acre estate less than 15 miles from central London. A door-to-door busing service covers much of London. The campus combines Grade II listed stately mansion with a modern wing housing classrooms, computer labs, an integrated IT network, libraries, cafeteria, gymnasium, auditorium, and the Harmony House Centre for international music which houses a digital recording studio, rehearsal rooms, practice studios and a computer lab for music technology.

The campus has on-site playing fields, tennis courts and playgrounds, and off-site playing fields for football, rugby and athletics. Local swimming and golf facilities are also used by our students. The sports programme runs three seasons fielding teams in football, volleyball, cross-country, basketball, rugby, swimming, dance, tennis, track & field, baseball, softball and golf.

ACS Hillingdon also offers extensive and varied extra-curricular clubs and community service activities both locally and internationally, which encourage students to participate in the richness of school life. Students also participate in international theatre arts programmes, maths, literature and music competitions in the UK and across Europe.

The admissions team is available throughout the year to answer questions, book campus visits, and assist families through the enrolment process. Students are accepted in all grades throughout the year.

Alton Convent School

Anstey Lane, Alton, Hampshire GU34 2NG
Tel: 01420 82070
Fax: 01420 541711
email: enquiries@altonconvent.org.uk
website: www.altonconvent.org.uk
Twitter: @AltonConventSch
Facebook: alton.conventschool

Motto: *Vita dulcedo spes nostra salve*

Chairman of Governors: Mr Kevin Ryan

Headmaster: **Mr Graham Maher**, BA Hons, PGCE, MA

Deputy Head (Pastoral): Mrs Elizabeth Hoyes, BA Hons, PGCE

Deputy Head (Curriculum): Mrs Sally Webb, BEd Hons

Age Range. Girls 6 months–18 years, Boys 6 months–11 years.
Number in School. Day: 425 Girls, 125 Boys.
Fees per term (2014–2015). Reception–Year 1 £2,885, Preparatory £3,490, Senior School £4,095. Garden House Nursery (daily charge): 6–14 months £54.60; 15 months–2+ £57.60; 3+ £69.90. EYE grants applicable.

Alton Convent School, situated in north east Hampshire, is an independent Catholic day school welcoming pupils from all faiths. It has a stimulating, friendly community promoting mutual tolerance, courtesy, care for others, a sense of self worth and personal discipline. Inspectors noted that pupils' personal development is excellent and a strength of the school, enhanced by excellent pastoral care integral to the school's ethos. Pupils are happy, confident, courteous and articulate. There is excellence of pupils' achievements, learning, attitudes and basic skills. High standards are fostered by good quality teaching, excellent monitoring and a changing, varied curriculum. Visitors comment on the calm, happy, purposeful working environment. This September the school created two further classrooms in the preparatory school to accommodate increasing numbers and proudly opened restructured, redesigned and newly equipped science laboratories in the senior school, a further encouragement to senior girls to consider the full range of scientific careers. An 'Inspirational Speaker' programme regularly exposes girls to the exciting opportunities in the world of work.

The Garden House Nursery, a purpose-built facility, is open 51 weeks a year from 8.00 am to 6.00 pm. It takes babies from 6 months and EYE grants are applicable. The quality of provision is rated as 'outstanding'.

Entry at the beginning of the prep school is non-selective but entry to the senior school is by entrance examination taken in January for September entry. The school accepts girls in other years up to and including Year 10. Entry to the Sixth Form is by GCSE results and interview. Whilst academically selective, we seek to admit pupils in sympathy with our ethos who will flourish in our community. The curriculum is broad and balanced for all ages with a wide range of science, sports, languages, and expressive arts. Academic standards are high, with pupils encouraged to think for themselves and take responsibility for their own development. Boys and girls are prepared for entry into their senior schools. Senior girls take an average ten GCSEs and continue to A Level in our Sixth Form, currently selecting five AS subjects with three or four subjects continued to A2 Level.

Inspectors affirmed that A Level performance is impressive and above the national average for girls in maintained and selective schools year on year, and results at GCSE are consistently above national averages. Girls progress to prestigious universities.

Co-curricular activities include a wide range of competitive sporting opportunities, artistic activities and study workshops. Musical and dramatic opportunities are strong in both schools, with thriving choirs, orchestras, ensembles, jazz group and drama productions. All pupils are encouraged to become involved in the major music and drama productions: additional tuition in sport, dance, LAMDA and music is offered. Art is strong and has been recognised nationally in various awards. The school has retained its Gold status for the Artsmark Award marking the high expectations and provision offered in the school.

Parents have regular opportunities for consultation with staff. Open Mornings, newsletters and the school website keep parents up to date. The school is noted as having a clear vision for the future.

A range of academic scholarships are available in Years 7 (by examination) and 12 (by results and interview).

Charitable status. The Alton Convent School Charity is a Registered Charity, number 1071684.

Argyle House School

19/20 Thornhill Park, Tunstall Road, Sunderland, Tyne & Wear SR2 7LA
Tel: 0191 510 0726
Fax: 0191 567 2209
email: info@argylehouseschool.co.uk
website: www.argylehouseschool.co.uk

Head: **Mr C Johnson**

Age Range. 2½–16.
Number in School. 200 Boys and Girls.
Fees per term (2014–2015). £2,030–£2,420.
Argyle House School was established in 1884 as a small independent day school for boys and girls, situated in the centre of Sunderland. Students travel from all parts of the region, by our buses, or local forms of transport. The school has maintained its high standards of academic achievement, whilst catering for a wide variety of abilities.

At Argyle House, we believe in the individual, and work with him or her to enable the achievement of each student's potential. This is due to attention to detail by fully qualified and dedicated staff, who help to mould the individual into a well-mannered and accomplished young individual, who will be able to meet future challenges.

Small class sizes and a friendly environment facilitate learning, but not all work is academic, as the school takes an active part in many sporting leagues, both within the school, and locally with other schools. We aim to offer all the facilities of a much larger school, whilst remaining at present student levels to keep the intimacy and friendliness of a smaller school, for both parents and students.

Arts Educational Schools London

Cone Ripman House, 14 Bath Road, Chiswick, London W4 1LY
Tel: 020 8987 6600
Fax: 020 8987 6601
email: rjones@artsed.co.uk
website: www.artsed.co.uk
Twitter: @ArtsEdLondon
Facebook: /artseducational

Founded in 1919.

Headteacher: **Mr Adrian Blake**

Age Range. 11–18 Co-educational.
Number in School. Day: 176 Girls, 57 Boys.
Fees per term (2014–2015). £4,600–£4,900.
"The UK's Leading Specialist Performing Arts Institution in Academic Achievement" Sunday Times, Parent Power 2007.

100% A Level Pass Rate and outstanding GCSE results.
The Arts Educational Schools London are committed to developing the full potential of each and every pupil. High quality vocational, academic and social education, in a warm, friendly, caring environment, ensures that our pupils feel challenged and fulfilled throughout the whole of their exciting careers at the school.

The school has been educating young performing artists since 1919, and there is no comparable school in the UK. Dancers learn to act and sing, actors learn to sing and dance, musicians learn to do more than play their instruments well, and everyone has the opportunity to be grounded in the visual arts, languages, humanities, sciences, and mathematics.

From Year 7 all pupils follow a course leading to eight or nine GCSEs. All pupils have access to the outstanding performance facilities, rehearsal rooms, proscenium and studio theatres. At Year 12 pupils follow a course of four AS Levels, leading to three or four A Levels, whilst receiving outstanding training in dance, drama, music and musical theatre.

In addition, students in Year 12 can opt to take a Level 3 BTEC in Musical Theatre, Acting, Dance or Production Arts, along with two A Levels as additional courses of study, where they benefit from all the expertise and excellence of the professional performance departments along with the academic reputation and pastoral guidance of the Secondary School.

Former Students of the schools include: Julie Andrews, Samantha Barks, Sarah Brightman, Darcey Bussell, Martin Clunes, Joan Collins, Adam Cooper, Bonnie Langford, Jane Seymour, Hugo Speer, Summer Strallen and Will Young.

Admission is at 11+ and 16+ and occasionally at other ages if places become available.

Charitable status. The Arts Educational Schools is a Registered Charity, number 311087. It exists solely for educational purposes.

Ashton House School

50–52 Eversley Crescent, Isleworth, Middlesex TW7 4LW
Tel: 020 8560 3902
Fax: 020 8568 1097
email: principal@ashtonhouse.com
website: www.ashtonhouse.com

Principal: Mr S J Turner, BSc

Head Teacher: Dr James Heslop

Age Range. 3–11.
Number in School. 119 Day Pupils: 71 Boys, 48 Girls.
Fees per term (2014–2015). £2,357–£3,401.
Founded 1930. Proprietors: P A, G B & S J Turner. Entry by interview and assessment. Prospectus on request.

Choosing a school for your child is one of the most important decisions you will be making on their behalf and we fully understand that you want to get it right. At Ashton House we do our very best to deliver a first-class education in a calm and happy atmosphere, where children learn and develop while still enjoying their childhood. Our results at 11 indicate that we are succeeding while our pupils have grown into confident, caring young people ready for the next phase in their education. Our most recent inspection judged the personal development of our pupils to be "outstanding".

Ayscoughfee Hall School

Welland Hall, London Road, Spalding, Lincs PE11 2TE
Tel: 01775 724733
Fax: 01775 769669
email: admin@ahs.me.uk
website: www.ahs.me.uk

Head: Mrs Clare Ogden

Age Range. 3–11 Co-educational.
Number of Pupils. 145 Day Pupils.
Fees per term (2014–2015). £1,315–£1,945.
Founded in 1920, Ayscoughfee Hall School is centred around a beautiful Georgian family home. A purpose-built

extension complements the already spacious accommodation. The School houses a Kindergarten, Infant and Junior Departments and has further developed its facilities to include enlarged classrooms, a dedicated Science/Art Room, a Music Department, a large Sports Hall and a Foreign Language Room.

The guidelines and principles of the National Curriculum are followed in all subjects but go far beyond the basic requirements in order to give each child a broader, more varied understanding. Academic standards are high and progress is well monitored throughout the school. The vast majority of pupils are successful in the Lincolnshire County Council selection examination and progress to secondary selective school education very well equipped to tackle all subjects. The curriculum is continually reviewed and class teachers are supported by specialist teachers for PE, ICT, languages and music. French is taught from Reception class.

iPads support learning in the classrooms and pupils receive weekly, dedicated ICT tuition in our up-to-date ICT suite.

The School excels with its music and drama productions over the academic year, in which all children perform in front of their parents and guests.

The school competes successfully in local and regional sports activities, including football, rugby, hockey, netball, cross-country and athletics.

There is a thriving programme of extra-curricular activities, including sport, drama, cookery, poetry, textiles, choir, instrumental groups and ICT. A wide variety of educational visits is offered, with the older children having the opportunity to participate in alternate foreign and activity trips, accompanied by the staff. Furthermore, regular visits by professional groups and individuals take place in school.

As a small school with classes limited to 20, we aim to provide a happy and caring environment where the individual child may flourish. We are proud of our academic standards but we also strive to give a broad and balanced education. Above all, we want our boys and girls to use and develop their different abilities and to enjoy the success this brings.

Charitable status. Ayscoughfee Hall School Limited is a Registered Charity, number 527294. It exists to provide education for boys and girls.

Babington House School

Grange Drive, Chislehurst, Kent BR7 5ES
Tel: 020 8467 5537
Fax: 020 8295 1175
email: enquiries@babingtonhouse.com
website: www.babingtonhouse.com
Twitter: @babingtonbr7
LinkedIn: /Babington House Sch

Headmaster: Mr T W A Lello, MA, FRSA, NPQH

Age Range. Boys 3–11, Girls 3–18
Number in School. Day: 86 Boys, 215 Girls
Fees per term (2014–2015). £2,760–£4,700.
A day school that in the last inspection was praised by the ISI for achieving outstanding academic success at all key stages and providing exemplary pastoral care. The boys and girls receive a first-class education in a nurturing and supportive environment, set in pleasant suburban surroundings. Full range of courses for examinations at all levels. Schools Curriculum Award. ISA Excellence Award. "Outstanding and Excellent" in all areas of school (ISI report November 2010).

Specialist facilities for Science, Music, Drama, Art, Sport, ICT, Languages, Maths & English.

Small classes: Maximum size 20 pupils. Careers guidance by a specialist.

Wide range of sports (Athletics, Swimming, Tennis, Netball, Gymnastics, Hockey, Football, Cross Country) and extra-curricular activities (Drama, Gym Club, Horse Riding, Cookery, Rock Climbing, Archaeology Club, Choir, Ballet, Tap, Golf, Elocution and Instrumental Tuition).

Charitable status. Babington House School is a Registered Charity, number 307914. It exists to provide exemplary education.

Beech Hall School

Tytherington, Macclesfield, Cheshire SK10 2EG
Tel: 01625 422192
Fax: 01625 502424
email: secretary@beechhallschool.org
website: www.beechhallschool.org

Chairman of Board of Governors: Mr E McGrath

Head: **Mrs G Yandell**, BA Hons, PGCE

Age Range. 6 months–16 years.
Number of Pupils. 206.
Fees per term (2014–2015). Infants £2,515, Transition £2,930, Junior School £3,380, Senior School £3,445. Lunches and snacks are charged at £160 per term.

Kindergarten, Infant, Junior and Senior departments offer education between 8.30 am and 4.00 pm with further supervised sporting and leisure activities available until 5.00 pm. If required, there is supervised care up until 6.00 pm for all children.

Beech Hall is a co-educational Day school situated in spacious and attractive grounds with extensive playing fields, a heated outdoor swimming pool and many other facilities.

Boys and girls are prepared for entry to a wide variety of Independent Schools and Sixth Form Colleges. Classes are kept small – the school has a maximum class size policy of 18 pupils – making individual attention possible in every lesson.

There is a very popular Kindergarten and Reception department, consisting of children between the ages of 6 months and 5 years under the care of their own specialist teachers. These classes were started with the objective of giving boys and girls a good grounding in reading, writing and arithmetic.

Beech Hall aims to provide a sound all-round education and children are encouraged to sit for academic, music and art scholarships. There is a school choir, a high standard of drama and the children produce their own school magazine.

Rugby, football, hockey and netball are played in the winter terms and in summer, cricket, athletics, rounders and tennis are taught. There is an extensive sporting fixture list covering all sports with children playing representative sport from Year 3 upwards. Swimming is taught throughout the year and other activities include squash, badminton and judo.

The school is situated off the main Stockport–Macclesfield road, within easy reach of Manchester International Airport and the M6 and M62 motorways.

Further details and illustrated prospectus are obtainable from the school or via the school's website.

Charitable status. Beech Hall School Trust Limited is a Registered Charity, number 525922. It exists to provide education for boys and girls.

Beech House School

184 Manchester Road, Rochdale, Greater Manchester OL11 4JQ
Tel: 01706 646309
email: info@beechhouseschool.co.uk
website: www.beechhouseschool.co.uk

Headmaster: **Mr Kevin Sartain**, BSc Hons, PGCE, Dip Spo Psy, CBiol, FIBiol

Age Range. 2–16 Co-educational.
Number of Pupils. 199.
Fees per term (2014–2015). £890–£1,942.

Beech House School is a co-educational day school for pupils aged from two to sixteen. The aim of the school is to blend the best of traditional education with the skills and resources of the modern system to ensure that pupils' talents are exercised to the full. To this end, class sizes are kept small, with 20 or fewer pupils per form at preparatory level and 16 or fewer in each secondary class. The school upholds traditional values and behaviour, providing a secure, caring and academically challenging environment. This gives Beech House its unique character as a 'family-centred' school.

The Independent Schools Association held their annual conference at Coombe Abbey, Warwickshire. During this conference they held their awards ceremony. Nobody was more surprised and delighted than our Headmaster, when guest host, TV Presenter Juliet Morris, announced that the winner of School of the Year was Beech House School of Rochdale. The trophy was presented by Lord Lexden (OBE), the ISA President. It is a great honour for the school.

The ninth Education Business Awards, sponsored by Rathbones, were held this year at The Grange Hotel, St Paul's, London. The hotel is famous for being the place where Winston Churchill planned the D Day landings. Beech House School was shortlisted for the 'Outstanding Progress Award for Independent Schools' category. The award is presented to the Independent school that has made outstanding progress and can demonstrate an increase in the educational performance of the school. Beech House was joint runners-up and Kevin Sartain, the Headmaster of the school received their award from the Olympic swimmer and television personality, Sharron Davies MBE.

For the second year running the school's Nursery was presented with the highest level in Rochdale's Early Years quality assurance award.

Bishop Challoner School

228 Bromley Road, Shortlands, Bromley, Kent BR2 0BS
Tel: 020 8460 3546
Fax: 020 8466 8885
email: admissions@bishopchallonerschool.com
website: www.bishopchallonerschool.com

Headteacher: **Mrs Paula Anderson**, BSc Hons, MBA

Age Range. 3–18.
Number in School. 420 Day Pupils.
Fees per term (from April 2014). Seniors £3,291, Juniors £2,633, Infants £2,374, Nursery £735–£2,343.

This is a Roman Catholic Independent Co-educational School with Nursery, Infants and Junior sections for ages 3–11 years and a Senior School and Sixth Form Department for ages 11–18 years.

The School is Catholic and welcomes all Faiths.

The School curriculum includes all National Curriculum subjects and others leading to GCSE and A Levels. Admissions to the Senior School at any age follows the successful completion of an entrance examination and an interview with the Headteacher.

Bishop Challoner has Outstanding Pastoral Care.

Charitable status. Bishop Challoner School is a Registered Charity, number 235468. It exists to provide an excellent education for boys and girls.

Bowbrook House School

Peopleton, Nr Pershore, Worcs WR10 2EE
Tel: 01905 841242/841843
Fax: 01905 840716
email: enquiries@bowbrookhouseschool.co.uk
website: www.bowbrookhouseschool.co.uk

Headmaster: **Mr C D Allen**, BSc Hons, CertEd, DipSoc

Age Range. 3½–16.
Number in School. Day: 112 Boys, 67 Girls.
Fees per term (2014–2015). £1,925–£3,305.

Bowbrook House is set in 14 acres of picturesque Worcestershire countryside yet within easy reach of Worcester, Pershore and Evesham. The school caters for the academic child and also those of average ability, who can benefit from the small classes. All pupils are able to take full advantage of the opportunities offered and are encouraged to participate in all activities. As well as the academic subjects, the school has a flourishing art department, a computer room, hard tennis courts and an open air swimming pool in addition to extensive games fields.

The Pre-Prep department of 3½–8 year olds is a self-contained unit but enjoys the use of the main school facilities.

Whilst stressing academic achievement, the school aims to provide a structured and disciplined environment in which children of all abilities can flourish, gain confidence and achieve their true potential. The small school size enables the head and staff to know all pupils well, to be able to accurately assess their strengths and weaknesses it enables each pupil to be an important part of the school and to feel that their individual attitudes, behaviour, efforts and achievements are important.

There is an extended school day from 8.15 am to 5.30 pm, with supervised prep sessions. There is also an extensive and varied extra-curricular programme run by specialist coaches from basketball, gym and dance to kickboxing and fencing.

Braeside School for Girls

130 High Road, Buckhurst Hill, Essex IG9 5SD
Tel: 020 8504 1133
Fax: 020 8505 6675
email: enquiries@braesideschool.co.uk
website: www.braesideschool.co.uk

Headteacher: **Mrs G Haddon**, BA Hons, PGCE

Age Range. 3–16.
Number in School. 200 Day Girls.
Fees per term (2014–2015). £1,800–£3,770.

Braeside School is dedicated to the education and well-being of girls. We recognise that girls can be encouraged and supported to learn in a much more practical way by being in a single-sex environment.

We understand that choosing the right school for your daughter is not easy. Changes in education and the way that these are interpreted by schools can mean that it is hard to find a school that combines traditional values and high standards of discipline with excellent teaching in a stable and caring environment.

At Braeside School our small community allows everyone to feel valued. We consider the needs of every student as they move through the school, providing the necessary challenge and opportunity for each individual at different stages of their lives, so that they can achieve their academic potential.

Our Early Years Department welcomes girls from the age of 3 and focus is on the seven learning areas. We fully understand the issues of maturity linked to birthdays and operate a flexible programme of activities within our Lower Kindergarten and Kindergarten classes to meet all educational needs.

Infant and Junior class teachers are supported by specialist teachers in French, Music, ICT and PE and have the benefit of dedicated Music and Art rooms and an ICT suite.

At Braeside Senior School a combination of the best in traditional and contemporary teaching methods in a full range of subjects can be seen. Class sizes are small and some subjects are delivered in half class groups with correspondingly successful grades being achieved at GCSE. Academic class work is well balanced by activities such as sport, music and drama; enhancement programmes for enrichment of the curriculum are well established. Citizenship is taught throughout the school and is linked to community events.

We have always believed that an important part of our undertaking to our girls, and their parents, is to prepare them for when they leave Braeside. We were therefore delighted to read the following comment made in the ISI School Inspection report in September 2014, *"The personal development of the pupils is excellent. From the youngest age, pupils exhibit confidence and friendliness towards their peers and visitors. Over time, the pupils develop into responsible young individuals who are self-aware and thoughtful."*

Entry, at every age apart from 3 and 4, is by test and interview.

Bredon School

Pull Court, Bushley, Tewkesbury, Gloucestershire GL20 6AH
Tel: 01684 293156
Fax: 01684 298008
email: enquiries@bredonschool.co.uk
website: www.bredonschool.org
Twitter: @BredonSchool

Executive Officer of Governors: Mr Paul Albrecht

Headmaster: **Mr David A T Ward**, BEd, MA

Age Range. 3–18.
Number of Pupils. 229. Boarders: 71 Boys, 18 Girls. Day: 104 Boys, 36 Girls.

Bredon School is situated in a magnificent 84-acre rural estate and delivers a broad-based education centring upon individual attention and personal recognition. Since the school was founded 52 years ago, it has set out to discover and nurture children's strengths and talents and to support them in overcoming any weaknesses.

Ethos. Bredon educates the whole child through sound realistic academic provision, sympathetic pastoral care, regular leadership challenges and a varied sports programme. The small and friendly environment allows children of all ages to thrive and achieve more than they thought possible.

Learning Support. The school is internationally-renowned for its expertise in supporting children with specific learning difficulties, such as dyslexia and dyspraxia. Within the dedicated Access Centre, an extensive range of specialist software and specialist tuition allows pupils to organise their thoughts, practice their skills and use voice-activation to enhance their individual progress.

Curriculum. Bredon provides a broad academic curriculum at all Key Stages through to GCSE and A Level. In addition Bredon offers extensive vocational programmes at Foundation, Intermediate and Advanced levels. The School Farm offers a vocational route for those interested in pursuing a career in agriculture or animal care. Class sizes across the school average 10 in number and the teacher/pupil ratio is 1:7.

Physical & Outdoor Education. In addition to the many sporting opportunities on offer; including frequent competitive fixtures with local schools, a fully-equipped gymnasium, a 30-metre sports hall and numerous outdoor sports pitches and cross country running trails, Bredon also has a forest school and thriving School Farm with pigs, ponies, cattle and small animals, which add to the amount of time children spend learning outdoors and through practical activity. The school also organises an extensive range of trips and expeditions through the Duke of Edinburgh's Award Scheme.

Clubs and Activities. There are many thriving lunchtime clubs including model making and music activities. In addition, once a week, the afternoon lessons are given over to activities and the children can choose from activities as varied as sailing, cycling, dancing, music, art, cookery, magic club, fencing, engineering, farming and clay pigeon/air rifle shooting.

Boarders. There is provision for full-time, weekly or flexi-boarders from age seven and they are cared for by house parents, creating a real home from home environment. Accommodation is in dormitory-style rooms until Year 11 when boys move into individual study-bedrooms. Girls from Year 11 can choose to have a small individual room or share with a friend. Boarders have an extensive range of after school activities to participate in and there is a lively schedule of weekend events too.

Admissions. Admission is by potential not just attainment, and specialist support is available to pupils with learning difficulties. There is no entrance examination, instead school reports and any specialist reports will be requested and assessed, followed by a 3-day guest visit to the school to assess suitability. A place is usually offered upon completion of a satisfactory guest stay.

Fees per term (2014–2015). Day £2,150–£5,845. Weekly boarding £6,310–£8,995 Full Boarding £6,475–£9,165.

Bridgewater School

Drywood Hall, Worsley Road, Worsley, Manchester M28 2WQ

Tel: 0161 794 1463
Fax: 0161 794 3519
email: admin@bwslive.co.uk
website: www.bridgewater-school.co.uk
Twitter: @BridgewaterScho
Facebook: /BridgewaterConnected

Chair of Governors: Mrs J A Close, CMIOSH

Headmistress: Mrs J A T Nairn, CertEd Distinction

Age Range. 3–18 Co-educational.
Number of Pupils. 414: 214 Boys, 200 Girls.
Fees per term (2014–2015). £2,375–£3,167. Lunch is included.

Bridgewater School is a co-educational, independent day school for pupils aged between 3 and 18 years. Established

as a boys' school in 1950 and having moved to its present, delightful, semi-rural setting soon afterwards, the school has since grown considerably – admitting girls and developing a sixth form. We draw pupils from the immediate locality, but also from a much wider area, well served as we are by the motorway network and by other major road links.

Bridgewater is by design not a large school. This enables us to provide small classes and high levels of attention to the needs of individual pupils. We seek to maximise education attainment all through a child's development, not least in the years of external examinations at GCSE and A Level.

In addition to its academic goals Bridgewater seeks to retain the intimate atmosphere it has had since its inception. We greatly value our capacity to offer provision across the full age range, from the nursery years to university entrance, for families wanting this continuity of individual attention for their children.

At the same time, however, pupils must look outward to the wider community and to the society in which they will live as adults. We see it as an integral part of Bridgewater's role to foster high standards of behaviour and self-discipline, as well as to develop an awareness of personal and social responsibility. Vital, too, are the many activities which take place outside the classroom – sport, music, drama clubs and societies, language exchange visits and outdoor activity breaks to name but a sample of the range available.

Entrusting your child's education to a school is a very big decision. We are mindful of our responsibility to justify a parent's decision to send their child to us, and of the need for that child's education to be a partnership between school and home. We aim, by the end of this partnership, to produce rounded, articulate young people who are well prepared for the challenges of adult and business life.

The School governors, staff and pupils share a sense of excitement about Bridgewater's future. The school has developed rapidly in recent years, with splendid new buildings and facilities and a considerable increase in pupil numbers. We have a commitment to continual development and improvement. If you have not yet visited us then may we recommend that you do so soon. We would be delighted to meet you and to show you how much Bridgewater School has to offer you and your child.

Charitable status. Bridgewater School is a Registered Charity, number 1105547.

Brigidine School Windsor

Queensmead, King's Road, Windsor, Berkshire SL4 2AX

Tel: 01753 863779
email: registrar@brigidine.org.uk
website: www.brigidine.org.uk

Chair of Governors: Dr H Miller

Head of Education: Mrs Sue Manser, BEd Hons

Head of Business Affairs: Mrs Dawn Fleming

Age Range. Girls: 2–18 years; Boys: 2–11 years.
Number of Pupils. 150 day pupils.
School Hours. 2–11 years: 8.30 am–3.30 pm. 11+–18 years: 8.30 am–4.10 pm. Extended day from 7.30 am to 6.30 pm.

There is an on-site Chef and Uniform Shop.

Brigidine School Windsor is an independent, non-selective school. Founded in 1948 as a Catholic school by sisters of the Order of St Brigid, Brigidine welcomes all faiths and abilities. The school is located on the M4 corridor, standing in 5 acres of beautiful grounds.

Mission Statement. The quality of learning and teaching is at the centre of any school's success and both teachers and support staff work together to ensure that all students at this school have an appropriately challenging curriculum, matched to their ability. Students are encouraged to think independently while being guided to achieve excellence in external examinations, participate fully in the life of the school and decide wisely on their future pathways.

Brigidine School is a happy, caring and inspirational environment in which children enjoy and develop a lifelong love of learning and want to achieve their full potential. A rich and rewarding curriculum has been planned, encouraging each child to make the most of special talents in the Preparatory and Senior School.

Curriculum. The full curriculum is available to all students with girls studying, on average, nine GCSE subjects in Years 10 and 11. Our Sixth Form offers a wide range of subjects at A Level. Sixth Form tutors liaise closely with the Careers Specialist which forms an integral part of the curriculum.

There is a Learning Support Department and mentoring for students with specific needs.

Extra-Curricular Activities. Our students enjoy 5 acres of grounds, excellent facilities, a range of languages, sporting, musical (chamber choir), drama (students actively participate taking on acting, directing, producing and backstage roles) and artistic opportunities. We offer a rich and exciting programme of extra-curricular activities including aerobics, ballet, street dance, tennis coaching, badminton, self-defence, fitness training, swimming, netball, football, hockey, golf, rounders, athletics, cross-country running, indoor climbing and equestrian lessons enjoyed in the most beautiful learning environments Windsor Great Park. The students compete locally and nationally and a "sport for all" policy provides many opportunities to take part for fun and recreation. Brigidine students were Champions of the U15 and U16 Ascot Schools Borough Rounders in July 2014. Other opportunities include: The Duke of Edinburgh's Award scheme, Young Enterprise, LAMDA, Rotary Club Youth Speaks Competition and a variety of overseas trips including World Challenge.

Care. The form tutor is responsible for welfare and progress. Parents' meetings are held annually, students receive written reports and grade cards. Year 7 students are assigned to an older student who will act as a peer mentor. Every student is a member of a House and the older students work with the younger ones in a variety of House competitions.

Examination and Results. If the evidence of a good school is in its examination results, then Brigidine School scores highly. Students at Brigidine achieve outstanding Value Added results at GCSE and A Level. Our dedicated staff and framework of pastoral care ensure that students achieve their full potential. In 2014 at GCSE 100% of students gained 5 or more passes at grades A*–C; 91% of passes overall were grades A*–C. The A Level pass rate was 92%, of which 64% were grades A*–C. The majority of the leavers went to their first-choice university.

ISI Inspection Report. "Strong and effective teaching, enables students of all abilities to make good progress. Throughout the school students' attitudes to their learning are excellent. The personal development of students is outstanding, resulting in confident, articulate and well-rounded young people."

Other opportunities available. Brigidine School offers all year round holiday club, adult ballet, zumba, football, Chinese lessons, NCT classes and 11+ tuition on site. Please visit our website for further details.

Admission. Entry can be at any stage. From Year 7 upwards, the pupils are interviewed and assessed prior to entry.

Registration fee (non-returnable): £25.

Fees per term (2014–2015). Senior School: £3,400–£4,385, Sixth Form £4,440. Junior School: £2,275–£2,695.

Early Years: Reception £2,210, Nursery: £2,605 (full day), £1,455 (mornings only). Lunch: £285 (£195 for full day Nursery).

PTA. The Association exists to further the interests of the School in the broadest possible way and does much to strengthen the links between staff, parents and students.

Charitable status. Brigidine School Windsor is a Registered Charity, number 1104042. It exists to provide quality education for boys and girls.

Bronte School

Mayfield, 7 Pelham Road, Gravesend, Kent DA11 0HN
Tel: 01474 533805
Fax: 01474 352003
email: enquiry@bronteschool.co.uk
website: www.bronteschool.co.uk

Headmaster: **Mr Nicholas Clements**, MA, BSc

Age Range. 4–11.
Number in School. 122 Day Pupils: 74 Boys, 48 Girls.
Fees per term (2014–2015). £2,795 (£90 discount for those paying on or before first day of term). Compulsory extras: Swimming from Year 1.

Bronte is a small, friendly, family-orientated, co-educational day school serving Gravesend and surrounding villages. The children are taught in small classes and are prepared for all types of secondary education. In 1999 the school moved to its present building which has since been expanded to accommodate specialist teaching rooms. A broadly-based curriculum and an extensive number of activity clubs provide the children with every opportunity to develop their individual interests and abilities.

The school was awarded Artsmark Gold status in 2013.

Entry is preferred at 4 following a parental visit to the school and an interview with the Head. Children joining at a later stage are assessed informally prior to entry.

Buxlow Preparatory School

5/6 Castleton Gardens, East Lane, Wembley, Middlesex HA9 7QJ
Tel: 020 8904 3615
Fax: 020 8904 3606
email: admin@buxlowschool.org.uk
website: www.buxlowschool.com

Headmaster: **Mr Charlie Cook**, BA Hons, PGCE

Age Range. 4–11 Co-educational.
Number of Pupils. 95.
Fees per term (2014–2015). £2,695.

Cambridge Tutors College

Water Tower Hill, Croydon, Surrey CR0 5SX
Tel: 020 8688 5284
Fax: 020 8686 9220
email: info@ctc.ac.uk
website: www.ctc.ac.uk

Principal: **Mr Mark Eagers**, MA Bath, PGCE Cantab

Age Range. 15–19.
Number of Pupils. 200.

Fees per annum (2014–2015). £19,800 excluding accommodation; approximately £24,000 with accommodation.

Since 1958 Cambridge Tutors College (CTC) has been offering high quality education to young people from the United Kingdom and from across the world. Fundamental to the College's ethos is small group teaching – no group is larger than 9 – and regular testing – students sit weekly tests in every subject, under examination conditions. This combination of small classes and regular testing has proved to be highly successful in giving students the confidence to succeed.

The College's most recent ISI Inspection report in 2011 was outstanding as was the very recent 2014 Student Welfare inspection.

CTC offers 2 year A Level courses, accelerated (18 month) A Level courses and fast-track 1-year IGCSE courses.

The college enjoys a particularly strong reputation for helping students to gain entry to the UK's most prestigious universities and to medical schools.

Situated in a pleasant parkside location in South Croydon, CTC is just a few minutes' walk from the town centre, East Croydon station and bus and tram routes. It is close to Central London, just 15 minutes away by train, but surrounded by parkland and quiet residential streets.

Facilities and resources are modern and extremely well-appointed. The Osborne Centre offers state-of-the-art ICT technology as well as a comfortable library, reading room and lecture theatre. An all-day café provides a wide variety of fresh food and drinks.

The College's welfare provision includes a team of trained professionals and all students have a personal tutor. A varied weekly programme of sporting and other activities is offered, as well as weekend excursions.

Charitable status. Cambridge Tutors Educational Trust Limited is a Registered Charity, number 312878.

Canbury School

Kingston Hill, Kingston-upon-Thames, Surrey KT2 7LN
Tel: 020 8549 8622
Fax: 020 8974 6018
email: lclancy@canburyschool.co.uk
website: www.canburyschool.co.uk

Founded in 1982, Canbury School is a mainstream, co-educational, independent day school. It is non-denominational.

Head: **Ms L Clancy**, BEd

Age Range. 11–16.
Number in School. 65 boys and girls.
Fees per term (2014–2015). £4,830.

Bursaries are available at the discretion of the School and are subject to satisfactory completion of the School's Bursary Form.

Entry requirements. There are standardised tests in Reasoning, Reading and Mathematics. The Headmistress interviews each candidate. A trial day or two at the school can be arranged prior to entry.

Curriculum. We cover a full range of GCSE subjects, most pupils taking a total of eight or nine.

In Years 7, 8 and 9 we emphasise English, Mathematics and Science in line with the requirements of the National Curriculum. Our extended curriculum includes Spanish, Geography, History, Information Technology, Art, Design & Technology, Performing Arts, PE and Games, Music, and Personal, Social and Health Education. Later, Physics, Chemistry and Biology are taken as doubly-certificated

GCSE subjects. Individual arrangements can be made for pupils to prepare for GCSE in Japanese, German, Chinese and other languages. Business Studies is offered in Years 10 and 11 leading to the GCSE.

We run a wide range of extra-curricular activities and clubs including natural history, drama, art, dance, karate, computing, basketball, football and table-tennis.

Canbury School is different in placing emphasis on small classes. No class has more than 16 pupils. Full concentration is placed on bringing out the talents of each pupil. Pupils participate in the school council which makes decisions in some areas of school life. The School runs an English Language programme (ESOL) for pupils arriving from abroad with limited skills in spoken English.

Facilities. A small, friendly school with well-equipped classrooms. We have up-to-date computer facilities, science laboratory, classrooms and Art/DT Studio with pottery area and kiln. There is also a playground and a garden area. We access local facilities for a wide range of sporting activities including athletics, cricket, netball, softball, swimming, watersports, badminton, soccer, hockey, basketball and rock climbing.

Charitable status. Canbury School is a Registered Charity, number 803766. It exists to provide education to a broad range of children including some of various nationalities who stand to benefit from being in a small school.

Cardiff Sixth Form College

1&3 Trinity Court, 21–27 Newport Road, Cardiff CF24 0AA
Tel: 02920 493121
email: enquiries@ccoex.com
website: www.ccoex.com

Motto: Inspire, Reach and Achieve

Principal: **Dr Liam Hughes**, BA Hons, PGCE, PhD

Vice Principal: Mrs Lindsay Thompson

Executive Director: Mrs Yasmin Sarwar

Director of Studies: Mr Imran Farzal

Age Range. 16–19 Co-educational.
Number of Students. 303.

With a reputation for outstanding educational achievements, excellent facilities and enriching extra-curricular activities, Cardiff Sixth Form College (CSFC) focuses on individual care, and inspires students to make the most of their unique talents.

CSFC celebrates its 10th Anniversary this year as a co-educational independent school. CSFC was established in 2004 and started with just a handful of students. We have established ourselves as a leading Sixth Form College in the UK with over 300 students. In 2014, CSFC was ranked top of the A Level league tables by results, cited in The Times and the Daily Telegraph, achieving 59% A*, 95% A*–A, 99% A*–B. In 2013 our results were equally excellent with 100% A*–B grades achieved. Within that was an amazing 95.01% A*–A grades. In 2012 we were placed first in the UK League Table by Best School and Best A Level results by The Spectator magazine, a sister publication of The Daily Telegraph. In February 2014 the College won three Crystal awards from The Education Advisers, the first for Top Private School in The UK, Top Private Co-educational Boarding School and Top Private Sixth Form College by A Level results for 2013.

Our A Level programme offers a range of subjects including, Biology, Chemistry, Physics, Mathematics and Further Mathematics, Business and Economics, History, Geography, English Literature, French, Philosophy and Psychology. We also provide compulsory IELTS tuition and examination as part of our study plans. Our programmes are delivered by an exceptional team of teaching staff, many of whom are examiners or chief examiners in their subjects. From September 2015 GCSEs will be introduced to the academic programme; students can choose 6 subjects from the range of topics available on a one-year course; minimum age for the programme is 15.

Since 2007, CSFC has enjoyed exceptional success in placing its students on high-demand courses of their choice such as medicine, dentistry, veterinary science, law, engineering and economics. Our successful applications have been submitted to the most prestigious universities in the UK, including Oxford and Cambridge. Students are provided with expert guidance through each stage of the UCAS process.

We host a range of in-house extra-curricular activities which foster team work and discipline, including sports, music, debates and the arts. Our aim is to prepare students for a well-balanced, modern life. CSFC appointed David Lloyd as our sports facilitator who provides our students with state of the art facilities including, swimming pools, racquet activities, gym and exercise classes, sauna and steam rooms as well as sporting clubs. David Lloyd is a private leisure and sporting facility in Cardiff. Students are able to access the facilities at David Lloyds on a daily basis, with a free bus shuttle provided by the college during evenings and weekends.

Cardiff Sixth Form prides itself on providing students with first-class facilities and our accommodation is no different. All CSFC students reside at Student Castle, which is a purpose-built state-of-the-art student accommodation within walking distance of the teaching facility at Trinity Court. This salubrious accommodation consists of 218 single rooms, tastefully furnished with double beds, en suite shower and fitted kitchens. There are 41 studio flats with kitchen facilities, TV and en suite. In addition there is an on-site self-service laundry facility. Our accommodation is bright and modern throughout, with a large common room to relax in – to watch TV or play pool or other social activities. All rooms have ultra-fast broadband/Wi-Fi so our students can always stay connected. There is CCTV, 24-hour security and a concierge. Students can feel relaxed; enjoy themselves in a safe, comfortable and thoroughly modern environment.

Fees per annum (2014–2015). Day £12,000; Boarding £29,700–£32,400.

Charitable status. Cardiff Sixth Form College is Registered Charity, number: 1123262.

Carleton House Preparatory School

145 Menlove Avenue, Liverpool L18 3EE
Tel: 0151 722 0756
email: info@carletonhouse.co.uk
website: www.carletonhouse.co.uk

Chair of Governors: Mr M N Amiry

Head Teacher: **Mrs A Daniels**, BA Hons, PGCE

Age Range. 3+–11 Co-educational.
Number in School. 175.
Fees per term (2014–2015). £2,370 inclusive of lunch, day trips, Spanish lessons and personal insurance cover.

Located in the leafy suburbs of south Liverpool, Carleton House is Merseyside's leading co-ed Preparatory School (8th in the Sunday Times Parent Power 2014). It is a Catholic school that welcomes children of all denominations.

They can because they think they can truly embodies the spirit of Carleton House. Our school is a lively, vibrant community that gives its pupils a first-class education for the 21st century.

Small class sizes (we endeavour to keep to a maximum of 23) and a high ratio of teaching staff to pupils enable the well-qualified and experienced staff to provide individual attention in a friendly, caring atmosphere. We nurture the development of the whole child – academically, spiritually and in the sporting and cultural aspects of their lives. Through excellent teaching and the close relationship that exists between school and home, our pupils are challenged, encouraged and supported to achieve their very best.

The implementation of all ten National Curriculum subjects ensures a broad, well-balanced curriculum is followed, but great importance is given to Maths and English as success in these subjects is central to development in other areas. Additional specialist teaching is provided for children requiring support in the basic subjects.

French has been successfully introduced in all classes including Reception with Spanish in the upper years.

All children receive music lessons and individual piano and guitar lessons are also available.

Emphasis is placed on high academic standards with children being prepared for a variety of Entrance examinations at 11 and more than 90% of pupils gain places at selective schools of their choice.

A wide range of sports and extra-curricular activities is offered to both boys and girls, including football, netball, cricket, rounders, swimming, chess, lacrosse, singing and speech choir. The children compete in local sporting events as well as choral festivals.

Theatre and educational visits are encouraged along with a residential trip to Shropshire, and Paris for older pupils, which provide field and adventure activities that help build confidence and self-esteem.

Close contact with parents is promoted through regular parent/teacher meetings and reports on pupils progress.

A thriving Parent Teacher Association provides social functions for parents while raising funds for extra equipment.

After-school provision is provided by the 'Kids Club'. This operates daily from 3.30 pm until 6.00 pm and school is open from 8 am for early drop-offs.

Parents are welcome to visit the school by appointment.

Further information available from the Head Teacher.

Charitable status. Carleton House Preparatory School is a Registered Charity, number 505310. It exists to provide education for boys and girls.

Castle House School

Chetwynd End, Newport, Shropshire TF10 7JE
Tel: 01952 811035
Fax: 01952 810022
email: admin@castlehouseschool.co.uk
website: www.castlehouseschool.co.uk

Chairman of Governors: Dr Martin Deahl

Headmaster: **Richard Walden**, MA Hons Downing College Cambridge, CertEd, MEd Hons, FCollP

Type of School. Co-educational day preparatory school.
Age Range. 2–11.
Number of Pupils. 105: 55 girls, 50 boys.
Fees per term (2014–2015). £2,050–£2,356.

Castle House is a friendly day preparatory school with a family feel. It is small enough for everybody to know and be known by everybody else, but offers a full and busy programme.

The school aims to bring the best out of every pupil by providing opportunities to excel and developing confidence to try.

Much importance is attached to the children being kind and considerate to each other, in the belief that happy children work best. We develop positive and courteous behaviour.

Since 1980 the school has been a charitable trust, run by a board of governors with varied talents and local interests. It was founded in 1944 by Miss Zellah Pitchford. The current head is the fourth.

The school's Georgian house, set in delightful gardens, is in the conservation area of Newport in east Shropshire. It serves urban and rural areas, including west Staffordshire, Market Drayton, Eccleshall, Telford and Shifnal.

Pupils are prepared for entrance exams to independent schools and to local grammar schools of which the two in Newport are unique in Shropshire. There is an excellent record of passes and scholarships, from a mixed ability intake, with children achieving their potential and beyond.

The curriculum covers all major subjects, and Art, DT, French, Music, Spanish, ICT, PE, Games, Swimming, Gymnastics and Drama. RE and assemblies are Christian, but non-denominational, encouraging all to join in.

Our flourishing educational nursery, CHerubS, for two to four year olds, is open all year from 8.00 am to 6.00 pm. Holiday care is available all day for children up to eleven, every holiday.

A rich range of after-school activities includes build-it, art, crafts, choirs, computers, cookery, gymnastics, chess, radio, football, netball, short tennis, cricket and rounders.

Matches are played in traditional team games, cross-country and swimming. Particular success has been achieved in schools' gymnastics, with girls' teams winning silver medals at national level in GISGA (independent schools) competitions. Boys' teams have three times won national under 9 titles and the school team has twice won the BSGA under 11 mixed teams Floor and Vault national title. The teams are ISA national champions.

We see education as a cooperative venture with parents. There are regular progress reports and feedback meetings. Parents are encouraged to bring their concerns to the teachers. There is a lively Parents' Association.

Further information can be obtained on our website or by telephoning the Registrar at the school.

Charitable status. Castle House School Trust Ltd is a Registered Charity, number 510515. It exists for the provision of high quality education for boys and girls.

CATS College Cambridge

Round Church Street, Cambridge CB5 8AD
Tel: 01223 345698
Fax: 01223 346181
email: admissions@ceg-uk.com
website: www.catscollege.com/en
Facebook: /CatsCollegeCambs

Acting Principal: **Mr Tim Joseph**, BA Hons, RSA Dip, MA

Vice Principal: Mr Darren Coxon, BA Hons, PGCE

Age Range. 14–19+.
Number of Students. 365.
Fees per annum (2014–2015). Tuition: £16,380–£28,350. Accommodation: £7,815–£12,245.

CATS College is one of Britain's most established and distinguished independent education providers. Founded in 1952, we have helped thousands of students achieve their ambitions and progress to some of the world's most prestigious universities.

By studying at CATS College you will enjoy all the benefits of the high-quality education for which the British independent system is renowned, in the international environment of your choice: choose the academic heart of Cambridge, this historic city steeped in tradition is an inspiring location with a lively student community.

CATS College offers a broad range of academic programmes; GCSEs, Pre: Programme, A Levels, University Foundation Programme, International Baccalaureate, Academic English and Summer School Programmes.

We offer a wide variety of study pathways and subjects: over 30 A Level subjects and specialised career pathways to ensure students are on the right track. Stretch exercises such as Olympiads, STEP examinations and academic competitions are in place to enhance the university applications of our gifted and talented students applying for Oxbridge or other top universities. CATS College had a record year for Oxbridge success, with 4 students gaining a place at the University of Cambridge and the University of Oxford.

At the heart of our ethos is recognition of the fact that everyone is different and as such has different aims, aspirations and desires. At CATS College we encourage ambition, recognise potential and allow you to stretch your abilities – all within a challenging but supportive atmosphere that is right for you as an individual.

Our personalised learning approach, regular assessments and one-to-one tuition ensure you are equipped with the study skills to achieve the best grades possible for you. Teachers and students have a joint commitment to achieving students' aims and work as a team to achieve success. Small class sizes of up to 10 students and bespoke learning plans ensure students are on track to exceed their academic goals.

Top universities require students to be motivated, well-balanced, team-playing individuals – not just good academics. We equip you with all the necessary skills to ensure you stand out. CATS College provide a wide range of extra-curricular activities: sports, drama, music, debates, cultural events and excursions to ensure students broaden their horizons.

CATS College works in partnership with you, to help you prepare for and select the best degree programme at the best university to suit your personal strengths and career aspirations. Mock interviews, personal statement guidance and subject specialist reading are all standard practice.

We are experts in welcoming international students to our college and a comprehensive support network is in place. Choose from a range of accommodation and Homestay options, varying in occupancy and cost. All our residences are supervised, safe and secure and located within easy reach of the campus offering single, shared and en-suite bedrooms, catered or self-catered and fully-furnished communal areas.

Chase Grammar School
(formerly Chase Academy)

Convent Close, Cannock, Staffordshire WS11 0UR
Tel: 01543 501800
Fax: 01543 501801
email: info@chasegrammar.com
website: www.chasegrammar.com

Principal: Mr Mark Ellse, MA, CPhys, MInstP, PGCE

Vice-Principal/Headmistress: **Mrs Jackie Williams**, BA Hons, PGCE

Head of Preparatory Department: Mr Ian Sterling, BEd

Age Range. 3–18.
Number in School. 6 Boarders, 197 Day.

Fees per term (2014–2015). Day £1,020–£3,496; Boarding £4,600–£8,400. Fees include lunches and most extras.

Independent day and boarding school for boys and girls from nursery to A Level.

Formerly a convent, founded in 1879, the senior school was added in 1980.

Extensive modern school on spacious urban site. Excellent science, technology, computing and language facilities, and Music School. Extensive sports facilities, including 3 floodlit astroturf pitches.

Academic work. Small classes allow attention to the individual student. The National Curriculum is shadowed throughout. Common core up to Year 9. GCSE, AS and A2 Level in: English, Mathematics, Physics, Chemistry, Biology, Design and Technology, Business Studies, History, Geography, French, German, Physical Education, Music, Drama, Art, Dance, Accounting, Latin.

A programme of early GCSE in Maths, English, Science and DT and our Grammar stream allow us to tailor timetables to individual needs.

Boarding. Delightful modern rooms, the majority of which are single or double study-bedrooms. The associated International Study Centre makes provision for overseas students who need to learn or improve their English.

Dyslexia. Support for intelligent dyslexics from a Dyslexia Institute trained teacher and within the small classes.

Sport. Football, cricket, hockey and netball are the principal sports with school facilities for tennis, volleyball, basketball, badminton and table tennis.

Music and Drama. A strong team of professional performers and first-rate teachers producing big uptake in the performing arts.

School day. 08.50–15.50. Prep/Clubs until 16.45. Facilities for early drop-off and late pick-up.

Chilton Cantelo School
Cognita Schools Group

Chilton Cantelo, Yeovil, Somerset BA22 8BG
Tel:　　　01935 850555
email:　　info@chiltoncanteloschool.co.uk
website:　www.chiltoncanteloschool.co.uk

Headmistress: **Mrs Verity White**, MEd

Age Range. Co-educational 3–18.

Number of Pupils. 165 Boys, 123 Girls; 54 Boarding, 234 Day.

Fees per term (2014–2015). Reception £1,820, Pre-Prep (Years 1–2): £1,945–£1,995; Prep (Year 3–6): £2,965 (day), £5,795 (boarding); Senior School (Years 7–11): £3,835 (day), £7,620–£7,475 (boarding), £4,605 (international tuition) +£515 (EAL support) +£3,640 (international boarding); Sixth Form (Year 12–13): £4,140 (day), £7,720 (boarding), £4,995 (international tuition) +£515 (EAL support) +£3,640 (international boarding).

Set in twenty acres of parkland, Chilton Cantelo School is located near Sherborne and Yeovil in the idyllic and beautiful Somerset countryside.

Chilton Cantelo is a small school with a big heart which provides a caring, attentive and loving atmosphere in which pupils thrive and flourish. First-time visitors often comment on the warmth and mutual respect they come across as they walk around the school and visit classrooms.

The school provides an Individualised Learning approach from Early Years to Sixth Form in which the teachers create tailored programmes of learning for each pupil. Appropriate targets are set after regular reviews to ensure each pupil progresses with the right amount of challenge. We hold true to our non-selective ethos and aspire to enrich and add value to each pupil's learning regardless of ability.

GCSE results for 2013/14 produced 80% of pupils achieving A* to C grades with an overall pass rate of 98%. Sciences and Languages were particular areas of good performance. Biology and Physics pupils achieved a 100% pass rate with 93% gaining A* to B in Biology and 87% of Physics pupils gaining A* to B.

Our A Level curriculum is designed to focus mainly, but not exclusively, on academic courses. In addition to the 17 A Level subjects offered, the school also provides pupils with the opportunity to undertake the Extended Project Qualification (EPQ), a project that gains extra UCAS points giving pupils an added edge when applying to a university. We have a Sixth Form Centre including a fully-equipped Common Room and dedicated classrooms.

As part of Cognita Group of Schools, Chilton Cantelo offers exchange opportunities with sister schools. Cognita is committed to raising standards of education in each and every school and to ensure that best practice is adopted in all aspects of the schools' curricula, teaching and learning and school management.

Both day pupils and boarders benefit from excellent tuition in a range of activities such as archery, athletics, cricket, football, hockey, horse riding, netball, rounders, and rugby.

Visit our website and our lively and fun Facebook pages, but the best way to really get a feel for the school is to come and see it in person.

We have Open Days and Evenings throughout the year, as well as tours on request if that is more convenient for our visitors. We look forward to welcoming you.

Claires Court

1 College Avenue, Maidenhead, Berkshire SL6 6AW
Tel:　　　01628 411470; Registrar: 01628 411472
Fax:　　　01628 411466
email:　　registrar@clairescourt.com
website:　www.clairescourt.com

Principals:
H StJ Wilding, BA, MCIM, FRSA
J T Wilding, BSc, FRSA

Head of Claires Court Senior Boys: J M Rayer, BSc, PGCE
Head of Claires Court Junior Boys: J M Spanswick, BSc, PGCE
Head of Claires Court Girls: P A J Bevis, CertEd
Head of Claires Court Sixth Form: A R Giles, BSc
Head of Nursery: Mrs S Wilding, BA, DPP

Age Range. 3–18.

Number of Pupils. 578 Boys; 264 Girls. Sixth Form: 76 Boys, 36 Girls.

Fees per term (2014–2015). £2,565–£4,575.

Teaching Staff: 75 full time, 36 part time, 20 visiting.

Claires Court is a school on three sites – Claires Court Senior Boys, Claires Court Junior Boys, and the third site comprises Claires Court Senior Girls, Claires Court Junior Girls, Nursery and Sixth Form. The ethos of the School lies in the provision for its pupils of a broad and thorough education in all senses, so that in time the challenges of the future will be met with confidence.

A rich and full programme of study and activity leads to academic success, sports accomplishment and cultural fulfilment, within a firm structure based on friendship and self-discipline. All pupils follow an exciting and diverse curriculum and participate in the main sports for boys and girls as well as a wide variety of additional opportunities.

Claires Court Junior Boys (4+ to 11) is situated to the west of the town centre in its own extensive grounds which include a purpose-built sports hall together with a refurbished and now year-round swimming pool. The classroom accommodation has been considerably extended to provide additional space for art, science and ICT.

At 11+ boys transfer to Claires Court Senior Boys which is located near Boulters Lock in a pleasant residential area of the town. Here the facilities include a technology wing housing science laboratories as well as facilities for art, ICT and technology. The Nicholas Watson Sports Centre opened in 2003 with an extended gallery area for physiological testing and additional teaching space. A wide range of subjects is offered at GCSE as well as PSCHE and careers advice being available.

The Girls, together with Nursery and Sixth Form, are based close to the town centre of Maidenhead, with its own pleasant grounds housing a covered year-round heated swimming pool, tennis courts and its own sports grounds. The Nursery based here is co-ed for children from 3 to 4+ years from where girls transfer into the main school on the same site and boys move to Junior Boys. As with Senior Boys, a wide range of subjects is available for study at GCSE together with quality facilities for all subjects throughout the age range.

The Sixth Form is co-ed with boys and girls transferring from Senior Boys and Girls as well as accepting external candidates. A wide range of A Level subjects is available for study with considerable pastoral, higher education and careers guidance available.

All parts of the School participate in extensive after-school activities programmes and, whilst boys and girls are academically taught on separate sites, they meet for many social, extra-curricular and aesthetic activities.

The School is multi-denominational. A prospectus containing further information may be obtained from the School or the website and prospective parents are always welcome to visit. Open Mornings are held throughout the year.

Coopersale Hall School

Flux's Lane, Epping, Essex CM16 7PE
Tel: 01992 577133
Fax: 01992 571544
email: info@coopersalehallschool.co.uk
website: www.coopersalehallschool.co.uk

Headmistress: **Miss Kaye Lovejoy**, AD BEd, CertEd, BEd Hons

Age Range. 2½–11.
Number in School. 275 Day Pupils.
Fees per term (2014–2015). £1,200–£3,220.

Coopersale Hall School is a thriving, caring local independent school with a high standard of academic achievement and a wide range of activities.

The School offers small class sizes and specialist teachers for ICT, Science, PE, Sport, Music and Drama. We provide a high standard of education and enjoy success in Entrance Examinations at 11 years to a wide choice of Secondary Schools.

We encourage our pupils to develop self-confidence and to take on roles of responsibility as they move up through the school. Creativity is nurtured within a disciplined environment and traditional values such as self-discipline are promoted to maximise our pupils' effectiveness in an ever-changing world.

Coopersale Hall is situated in a large country house that is pleasantly located on the outskirts of Epping, just off Stewards Green Road and only two minutes from Epping High Street. The School has its own private road and stands in some seven acres of landscaped gardens and playing fields.

Entry requirements: Interview and assessment.

Copthill School

Barnack Road, Uffington, Stamford, Lincolnshire PE9 3AD
Tel: 01780 757506
email: admissions@copthill.com
website: www.copthill.com
Twitter: @copthill
Facebook: /Copthill-School

Headmaster: **Mr J A Teesdale**, BA Hons, PGCE

Deputy Head: Mrs Helen Schofield, BA Hons, PGCE
Head of Lower School: Mrs A Teesdale, BEd Hons
Head of Early Years: Mrs J Dimbleby, BSc, PGCE

Age Range. Co-educational 2–11 years.
Number of Pupils. 300: Main School (age 4+ to 11) 240; Nursery and Pre-School (age 2 to 4) 60.
Fees per term (2014–2015). £2,790–£3,060.
Educational Aims.

- A welcoming, stimulating and happy environment which is friendly, caring and well disciplined, in which every pupil is encouraged to achieve and motivated to succeed.
- An open-door policy, providing the foundations for effective communication and co-operation between Home and School.
- A broad curriculum emphasising the importance of literacy and numeracy and designed to develop lifelong knowledge, skills and attitudes that allow our children to become responsible citizens, independent explorers, creative thinkers, problem solvers, team players and reflective learners.
- An emphasis on using the outdoor environment to engage and inspire our pupils, developing their knowledge, skills and attitudes across the curriculum.
- An excellent preparation for entrance to a wide range of state and independent secondary schools.

Location. Purpose-built, modern facilities set within 350 acres of farmland, including river and woodland. 2 miles from Stamford and the A1 and 15 miles from Peterborough.

School Day. Monday to Friday. School Day – 8.35 am to 3.40 pm. Crèche hours from 7.45 am to 6.00 pm. Breakfast and Tea available.

Facilities. Creative Suite, Library, Languages Suite, Sports Hall and playing fields including AstroTurf and a well-established on-site Forest School. High-quality catering facilities offering delicious, nutritionally balanced meals.

Pastoral Care. In addition to their forms, pupils from Year 5 onwards are also placed in small tutor groups in which their progress is closely monitored in preparation for senior school entrance. There is a genuine 'open door policy' throughout the School. Parents' Evenings and reports given twice a year.

Curriculum. A modern curriculum based on the National Curriculum. Combines traditional and innovative teaching methods. Learning support offered throughout the school where a specific need has been assessed.

Music, Speech & Drama. Music and Drama are taught as part of the curriculum. Regular drama productions encourage all pupils to participate. Pupils can also receive expert individual tuition and perform at school concerts, assemblies and in local music and drama festivals.

Sport. Athletics, Cricket, Football, Hockey, Netball, Cross-Country, Rounders, Rugby, Swimming, Tennis. All pupils encouraged to be in teams.

Future Schools. Pupils leave Copthill at 11 years old with great confidence and the ability to think for themselves. Copthill is a truly independent school, offering thorough preparation to a wide variety of independent and state senior schools, both local and national, achieving a large number of scholarships and awards.

Cransley School

Belmont Hall, Great Budworth, Nr Northwich, Cheshire CW9 6HN
Tel: 01606 891747
Fax: 01606 892122
email: admin@cransleyschool.org.uk
website: www.cransleyschool.org

Headmaster: **Mr Simon Leyshon**

Deputy Head: Mrs Beverley Crumpton
Deputy Head, Head of Juniors: Mr Richard Pollock

Age Range. Co-educational 3–16.
Number in School. Day: 121 Girls, 26 Boys.
Fees per term (2014–2015). £1,896–£3,280. Lunches £241.

Cransley School near Great Budworth is a very special place. Set in the midst of the beautiful Cheshire Countryside, it has a warm, friendly atmosphere in which all students are encouraged to fulfil their potential. Well-qualified, dedicated staff work hard to make the 'Cransley Experience' a rewarding, happy one. Small class sizes and a positive environment encourages academic success at every level.

GCSE results are always good. This year 93% of our final year students achieved at least 5 GCSEs at grades A*–C and all went on to A Level studies in the Sixth Forms of their choice. In fact we were ranked as the 5th small Independent School in the country by the Sunday Times Parent Power Survey 2010.

2014 celebrates 80 years of experience of educating and nurturing talented individuals, Cransley School has entered an exciting new chapter in its history and now welcomes boys into its Senior School. At Cransley our focus is on your child's individual achievements and success – ensuring they have a happy and rewarding experience.

Life is never dull at Cransley. There is a wide variety of extra-curricular activities available throughout the school – there are three choirs, a thriving orchestra and regular drama performances. Students have a choice of clubs – gymnastics, gardening, languages, football and rugby to name but a few. There are many sporting opportunities and Cransley teams regularly compete against other schools in the area.

Cransley students enjoy many visits to enrich the curriculum. We also play hosts to visiting theatre groups. We offer residential opportunities – groups have been overnight in London for theatre and museum visits; GCSE Geography students visit the Lake District; activity weekends are particular favourites for both Senior and Junior Department pupils; foreign travel is also on the menu.

Cransley also has a thriving PTA – they organise regular events throughout the year which raise valuable funds to support staff and students and also offer a fantastic opportunity for parents to get to know each other.

Crowstone Preparatory School

121/123 Crowstone Road, Westcliff-on-Sea, Essex SS0 8LH
Tel: 01702 346758
email: info@crowstoneprepschool.com
website: www.crowstoneprepschool.com

Headmaster: **Mr J P Thayer**, TCert London

Age Range. 2½–11.
Number in School. Day: 28 Boys, 46 Girls.
Fees per term (from January 2015). £1,060–£3,055 excluding lunch and insurance.

Crowstone Preparatory School is an independent day school for boys and girls between the ages of 2½ and 11 years.

The aim of the school is to obtain the highest possible achievement from each individual pupil in a happy relaxed atmosphere in all areas of school work.

We are especially concerned in providing extra stimulus for children of high ability but also provide extra facilities for slower learners.

Cundall Manor School

Cundall, North Yorkshire YO61 2RW
Tel: 01423 360200
Fax: 01423 360754
email: head@cundallmanor.org.uk
website: www.cundallmanorschool.com
Twitter: @CundallManor

Joint Heads:
Mr John Sample, BSc Hons, PGCE
Mrs Amanda Kirby, BA Hons, PGCE, NPQH

Age Range. 2½–16 Co-educational.
Number of Pupils. 330.

Cundall Manor School is a thriving independent co-educational boarding school, catering for nearly 400 boys and girls from two and a half to sixteen years of age. Described by Ofsted as 'Outstanding', it is ranked in the top 9% of independent schools in the UK. Set in 50 acres of beautiful grounds between Harrogate, Ripon and York, it is easily accessed from the A1M and A19.

Cundall Manor School blends the best traditions of honour, integrity and courtesy with up-to-the-minute teaching facilities and approaches. The school has developed a reputation for ensuring that each and every child feels happy, safe, supported and celebrated. Within this environment, children engage fully with the educational challenges and risks that maximise learning and achievement. The rural setting allows pupils to embrace their childhoods while the innovative and unique curriculum provides opportunity for all to develop the confidence, judgement and personal skills that will benefit their futures.

Children are encouraged to participate in a number of sports and events outside of the curriculum including outward bound courses, travel, charity/community work and extra-curricular sports. Whilst many children do achieve top standards and awards across academia, sports and music, competing and succeeding at area, county and national level, our aim is to ensure every child has the opportunity to participate in the full range of activities, whatever their level of ability and experience. We do this by cultivating a 'yes' mentality amongst our pupils, encouraging them to engage with the wider world and to think and act independently and without inhibition.

Fees per term (2014–2015). Nursery: £362–£1,810; Reception to Year 2 £2,925; Years 3–4: Day £4,610, Weekly Boarding £6,085, Full Boarding £7,530; Years 5–11: Day £4,675, Weekly Boarding £6,150, Full Boarding £7,595, Non UK Resident Boarding £8,220 Occasional Boarding £35 per night.

Charitable status. Cundall Manor Limited is a Registered Charity, number 529540.

Dagfa School Nottingham

57 Broadgate, Beeston, Nottingham NG9 2FU
Tel: 0115 913 8330
Fax: 0115 913 8331
email: headmaster@dagfaschool.notts.sch.uk
website: www.dagfaschool.notts.sch.uk

Head: **Dr P Woodroffe**, PhD, MMath, PGCE

Age Range. 2–16.
Number in School. Day: Boys 101, Girls 71.
Fees per term (2014–2015). £2,508–£3,360.

Dagfa School is situated in pleasant gardens in a quiet neighbourhood adjacent to University Park, and it enjoys easy access from all areas of the city and county. Small classes are taught by caring and dedicated staff, creating a purposeful learning environment where each pupil is treated as an individual and their talents encouraged to flourish.

Our Vision is to see pupils leaving Dagfa with excellent exam results backed up with a character deserving of respect able to cope and positively influence the ever-changing world in which we live. Our core values are respect, integrity, humility, responsibility, positivity, sociability and independence, and building everything we do on these values allows us to fulfil our vision.

For a non-selective school, Dagfa enjoys amazing exam results, with 85% of pupils achieving 5 or more A*–C grades over the last three years. Predictions of the pupils' grades based on national tests showed that only 65% were likely to achieve this and so the improvement of 20% is very impressive. In addition, this year, the predictions showed that 3.5% of exams would be passed at A or A*, but on results day we discovered that 24% were at A or A* grade. This shows that Dagfa School does a very good job at helping struggling pupils to get the 5 passes they need for college, but also can inspire and enthuse the more gifted pupils to stretch themselves further.

As well as having a broad range of options to choose from, including Drama, Sociology and Computing as well as all the standard subjects, Dagfa offers extra subjects for those pupils who are keen and willing. Additional Maths is available for those pupils gifted at Maths, and Religious Studies is offered as a lunchtime club for those interested in philosophy and ethics. This year, some pupils will leave with 13 GCSE qualifications! Alternatively, we can restrict the number of subjects taken to allow pupils to have extra, supported time to improve their core subjects.

At Dagfa School, we pride ourselves on being able to treat every pupil as an individual, knowing their needs, desires and abilities, and being able to add value to every single pupil, without adding unpleasant stress or pressure. We can do this because of our small class sizes and caring family atmosphere.

Daiglen School

68 Palmerston Road, Buckhurst Hill, Essex IG9 5LG
Tel: 020 8504 7108
Fax: 020 8502 9608
email: admin@daiglenschool.co.uk
website: www.daiglenschool.co.uk

Perstare et Praestare – Persevere and Excel

Head Teacher: **Mrs M Bradfield**, BA, CertEd, DipNatSci

Age Range. 3–11.
Number in School. 156.

Fees per term (2014–2015). £2,310–£2,410, sibling discount available. Extras: lunch, swimming, drama (infants).

Daiglen School is a small preparatory school which provides a happy and secure environment for all pupils. Kindness to others is valued above all, and pupils are polite and considerate with each other as well as with adults. We have a strong sense of family and community, underpinned by warm supportive relationships and mutual respect, which ensures that all pupils are valued and given the chance to shine.

Confident children relish challenge and the school promotes a culture of excellence. We celebrate individual and group successes as children learn the importance of pursuing their ambitions with determination and perseverance. They are inspired to do well both by the infectious enthusiasm of their excellent teachers and by the example of older children who become their role models. Our pupils flourish in this environment and leave as caring, confident, articulate and well-mannered young people, fully prepared for the next stage in their journey through life. We are justifiably proud of our pupils' academic achievements, as well as those on the sports field and other areas, and a good proportion leave with scholarships to selective independent and state secondary schools.

Founded in 1916, Daiglen School is rich in history and tradition. The school is built around an elegant Victorian house with much of its stained glass and cornices intact. Modern features include a purpose-built gymnasium/hall, art room, science laboratory and ICT suite. It is pleasantly situated on the borders of Epping Forest and is well served by public transport.

Inspection: Daiglen School was inspected in September 2010 and received the highest accolades from the Independent Schools Inspectorate. The team praised Daiglen in glowing terms, awarding the highest possible rating in areas that include pupils' all-round achievement, personal development and the quality of teaching, and declaring the school's Early Years Foundation Stage setting to be outstanding in every respect. The full report is available to read on our website.

Choosing a school is arguably the most difficult decision you will make for your child, and one which will have the greatest consequences in his or her life. Most of our pupils come to Daiglen on personal recommendation from parents of past or present pupils. We encourage a close and mutually supportive partnership with parents. To find out more about us, you can visit our website or make arrangements to visit the school; you will receive a warm welcome.

Charitable status. The Daiglen School Trust Limited is a Registered Charity, number 273015.

Ditcham Park School

Ditcham Park, Petersfield, Hampshire GU31 5RN
Tel: 01730 825659
Fax: 01730 825070
email: admissions@ditchampark.com
website: www.ditchampark.com

Head Teacher: **Mr A P N Rowley**, BSc Hons, PGCE

Age Range. 4–16.
Number in School. Day: 181 Boys, 167 Girls.
Fees per term (2014–2015). £2,508–£4,206 excluding lunch.

Situated high on the South Downs, the School achieves excellent results in a happy purposeful atmosphere.

Charitable status. Ditcham Park School is a Registered Charity, number 285244R. It exists for educational purposes.

The Dixie Grammar School

Market Bosworth, Leicestershire CV13 0LE
Tel: 01455 292244
Fax: 01455 292151
email: info@dixie.org.uk
website: www.dixie.org.uk

Headmaster: **Mr Richard J Lynn**, BA Cardiff

Age Range. 3–18.
Number in School. 452.
Fees per term (2014–2015). Nursery: Daily Rate (inc lunch) £44.50; Reception, Years 1 and 2 £2,520, Years 3 to 5 £2,890, Year 6 to Sixth Form £3,460. Scholarships, Bursaries, Vouchers/Government Funding, Monthly Payment Scheme available.

The earliest records we have of the School's existence date from 1320, but the School gained its present name when it was re-founded in 1601 under the will of an Elizabethan merchant and Lord Mayor of London, Sir Wolstan Dixie.

The most distinguished of the School's former pupils is Thomas Hooker, founder of Hartford, Connecticut, and Father of American Democracy. The best known of its teachers is undoubtedly Dr Johnson, moralist, poet and author of the famous dictionary, who taught at the School in the mid-eighteenth century.

The main building of today's School was built in 1828 and faces the historic market square of Market Bosworth, making a distinctive landmark. However, in 1969 the School was closed, as new, much larger comprehensive schools found favour.

It was to revive the best aspects of the grammar school tradition that the Leicestershire Independent Educational Trust was formed in 1983, and four years later the School was re-opened as a selective, independent, day school for boys and girls of all backgrounds between the ages of 10 and 18. Three years later our Junior School opened, moving to its present premises, Temple Hall in Wellsborough, in 2001.

The emphasis remains the same as it ever was: to provide an excellent academic education that will be of lasting value to our children as they face the challenges of the future.

Both schools are selective and have academic achievement as their central aim. Music, drama, sport and service are also an integral part of the education offered. Both schools have an interdenominational Christian basis. The relative smallness of the schools ensures that they combine great friendliness with excellent discipline, providing a secure and well-ordered framework in which children can confidently achieve their full potential.

The Grammar School offers academic, music, art, sports and sixth form scholarships.

Charitable status. The Leicestershire Independent Educational Trust is a Registered Charity, number 514407. It exists to provide a grammar school education.

DLD College
Alpha Plus Group

100 Marylebone Lane, London W1U 2QB
Tel: 020 7935 8411
Fax: 020 7935 0755
email: dld@dld.org
website: www.dldcollege.co.uk
Twitter: @DLDcollege
Facebook: /DLDcollege

Principal: **Ms Rachel Borland**

Age Range. 14+ Co-educational.
Number of Pupils. 430 Day.
Fees per annum (2014–2015). £18,000.

Our oldest College, DLD, was established in 1931. After 10 years located in Marylebone, the College has merged with its younger sister, Abbey College, and moved in 2015 to brand new, purpose-built facilities in the centre of London, looking over the River Thames to the Houses of Parliament. With bright, state-of-the-art teaching facilities and secure, on-site student accommodation, all in the centre of the amazing, historic and vibrant city of London, DLD College London is a truly unique college campus, with facilities including:

- 220 secure, ensuite student bedrooms within the College
- Restaurant facilities on site, including a Starbucks franchise
- 6 high specification laboratories
- A creative arts and media faculty featuring art rooms, photography, drama, music and media suites, including a 100+ seat theatre
- Nearly 40 tutorial rooms
- Open plan library, study and ICT facilities
- Access to shared swimming pool and gymnasium facilities

DLD College is a co-educational London day school accepting pupils from the ages of 14+. There are over 430 students in the Sixth Form studying A Levels or BTECs from a choice of 40 subjects. Most are doing A Levels in the normal way over a two-year period with another cohort joining at the start of Upper Sixth. There are no subject restrictions at A Level. GCSE courses are taught over a one-year period so pupils are able to join at the beginning of Year 11. The average class size is between 6 and 8 students. The College offers a 2-year GCSE Programme for SEN students. The college also offers two BTEC programmes in Business and Media Studies.

At DLD we offer an extensive range of extra-curricular activities, which include many traditional options such as Sport, Music, Drama and Art. Our wide enrichment programme supports our academic curriculum and forms an integral part of the wider education and college experience we offer our students. Our vision is to create all-rounded students, who excel academically and develop further their emotional, inter-personal and social skills. All students are encouraged to participate in one or more of our range of extra-curricular activities. This participation is important for students both as an opportunity for recreation and as an effective way to improve the quality of their UCAS personal statement and CV in the future.

While the atmosphere at DLD is more informal than in mainstream independent schools, rules regarding academic performance are strictly enforced with an emphasis on attendance and punctuality. There are fortnightly tests in each subject and three weekly reports. Parents receive five reports each year and there are two parents' evenings and a parents' social evening.

The teaching staff are highly qualified and chosen not just for their expertise but also for their ability to relate positively to young people. The college aims to make learning interesting, active and rigorous. While clear guidelines are very important to ensure pupils establish a good working routine, the college believes strongly that pupils respond best when there is a culture of encouragement. Effort, progress, achievement and courtesy are regularly acknowledged and formally rewarded.

Dwight School London
formerly North London International School

6 Friern Barnet Lane, London N11 3LX
Tel: 020 8920 0600
Fax: 020 8211 4605
email: admissions@dwightlondon.org
website: www.dwightlondon.org

Head of School: **Mr David Rose**, BA, CertEd, MA Ed, FRSA

Age Range. 3–18.
Number in School. 350 Boys and Girls.
Fees per term (2014–2015). £1,280–£6,130. Homestay and Boarding available from age 16.

Dwight School London provides a secure, well-ordered and happy environment with the learning process at its core, offering the finest possible education for all pupils in order for them to reach their full potential. Serving a cosmopolitan and diverse North London community, great importance is attached to respect, understanding and empathy with every-one's cultures, religions and backgrounds. Emphasis is placed on development of the individual student with aca-demic, artistic, sporting, creative, practical and social skills being encouraged and individual talents nurtured. Every child has a spark of genius, we aim to ignite it!

Students follow the International Baccalaureate curric-ulum, starting at aged 3 with the Primary Years Programme, moving onto the Middle Years Programme at age 11 and the International Baccalaureate Diploma Programme at age 16. The programmes are designed to encourage the develop-ment of learning skills and to meet a child's academic, social, physical, emotional and cultural needs. Through enquiry-based learning and various disciplines, subject interrelatedness is accentuated, preparing students for the pre-university Diploma Programme. Within the programme students must study six subjects, a research project, leading to a 4000 word essay, The Theory of Knowledge course, and Creativity, Action, Service (CAS). The CAS programme is a fundamental part of the Diploma programme, requiring stu-dents to participate in 150 hours of activities both in and out of school.

The Quest Programme is designed for students who need help developing strategies to assist them to study effectively. Through one-to-one tuition from specialist staff in skills such as effective reading, time management, planning of work and revision and exam techniques, students can reach their full potential, further enhanced by the school's teacher : student ratio.

Entry requirements. Students are accepted for entry at any time throughout the school year.

Kindergarten and Lower School (ages 3–11): Students are invited to attend for half a day and may be asked to com-plete a basic assessment.

Upper School (ages 11–16): Students attend an interview with the Head of the school, are invited to visit the school for a day and may be required to complete a basic assess-ment.

Entry to the Upper School is automatic for students in the Lower School.

Upper School (ages 16–19): Diploma programme appli-cants are invited for interview with the programme coordi-nator. Students would be expected to have 5 or 6 GCSE passes, with B, A or A* grades for subjects to be studied at Higher Level. Students arriving from overseas without GSCE qualifications need to demonstrate a sound academic background and understanding of English. The school is able to offer a Foundation Year to students whose command of the English language or subject area knowledge is not

sufficient to enable them to start the full programme, includ-ing specialist English as an Alternative Language support.

Any decision regarding the offering of a place to a pro-spective student from overseas who is unable to visit for interview or assessment, will be made by the Head of the respective department, referring to school reports and scho-lastic references.

Examinations offered. Key Stages 1, 2 and 3; GCSE; International Baccalaureate.

Facilities. The school has dedicated IT, music, art and Design Technology facilities for all students. The commit-ment to the use of Information and Communications Tech-nology in all subject areas is highlighted by IT and graphics suites, individual student home drives and email accounts, student dedicated laptops and wireless network.

Music tuition is incorporated into the curriculum with the addition of individual lessons in a wide variety of instru-ments such as piano, guitar, drums, saxophone and violin with composition and singing also available. The school has a number of bands and groups with varying styles from jazz to rock and regular concerts highlight the very real talent within the student body.

Student's physical development is considered as import-ant as academic development and the school's sports fields provide excellent facilities for football, cricket, athletics, hockey, tennis and softball. The school's hall, playgrounds and local amenities are also utilised to offer further activities such as basketball, badminton, squash, swimming, table ten-nis, ice skating and skiing. Matches and tournaments between local schools are regular fixtures.

The school's close proximity to central London allows for numerous trips to the capital's museums, galleries and theatres. A variety of overseas trips are offered, both aca-demic and leisure, including France, Spain, skiing and our sister school, The Dwight, in New York while Diploma stu-dents are given the opportunity to attend the Model United Nations conferences at The Hague.

Scholarships and Bursaries. A number of scholarships are offered each year to students with a high ability in aca-demic, sporting, musical or artistic areas. For students wish-ing to enter the Diploma Programme, a scholarship award of up to 30% will be considered for candidates who show a high level of academic achievement. Bursaries are consid-ered on application.

Egerton Rothesay School

Durrants Lane, Berkhamsted, Herts HP4 3UJ
Tel: 01442 865275
Fax: 01442 864977
email: admin.dl@eger-roth.co.uk
website: www.eger-roth.co.uk

A School with a Difference

Headteacher: **Mr Colin Parker**, BSc Hons, Dip Ed, PGCE, CMath

Age Range. 5–19 years: Poplar 5–11 years; Senior School 11–16 years; Sixth Form 16–19 years.
Number in School. 104 boys, 48 girls.
Fees per term (2014–2015). £4,770–£6,790 (lunches included).

When you visit Egerton Rothesay in Berkhamsted you soon see that it is a school that is different.

ERS aims to provide an exciting and relevant educational experience for pupils who need that little bit more support from their school.

It focuses especially on students who have found, or would find, it difficult to make progress and succeed within another school – perhaps because of an earlier, negative, educational experience or perhaps because of a specific learning difficulty, such as dyslexia or dyspraxia or a speech and language difficulty. If your child has other educational difficulties the school may also be able to help with these.

Children come with a variety of learning styles and use is made of a wide range of teaching strategies in order to match these. The school provides additional levels of support both in the classroom and on an individual basis, varying to suit the need of the child. Throughout the school children are taught in small classes to match their need for support, to the level of teaching and support staff provided. In addition there are also two special groups with a specific focus: Rowan (a base for senior-aged pupils with complex needs) and Rainbow Classes (for some of our younger children with speech and language difficulties).

In September 2012 the school launched a new Sixth Form provision for students who continue to mature beyond the age of 16 and require an additional amount of support and time in order to enable them to transfer successfully into a further education establishment or employment. The school has developed both one and two year educational programmes within a high-quality, secure and supportive environment, in which students are able to continue to mature, develop and learn.

Every child at Egerton Rothesay is seen as a unique person and an individual student. The school aims to make an excellent contribution into the life of each one ensuring that they can be supported in the way that they personally need to maximise their individual learning potential.

The school wants more than just to deliver a curriculum and has a learning skills approach throughout the school – aiming to prepare students not just for school and exams but for life in today's complex society and an ever changing world of work.

A child can often be able and talented in one aspect of the curriculum yet find it difficult to make good progress in another. Some students will need support for the duration of their time in school whilst others may only need a short amount of support to address a specific problem or to give a boost.

All activities takes place within an environment offering exceptional pastoral care and spiritual development that is driven and informed by the school's Christian foundation.

Transport: Egerton Rothesay is also more than just a local school – students travel to the school from all directions, many using the comprehensive bus service that the school runs over a 35-mile radius.

If you think this may be the right type of school for your child you can obtain more information from the Registrar on 01442 877060 or visit the website at www.eger-roth.co.uk.

Fairfield School

Fairfield Way, Backwell, Bristol BS48 3PD
Tel: 01275 462743
email: secretary@fairfieldschool.org.uk
website: www.fairfieldschool.org.uk

Headteacher: **Mrs Lesley Barton**, BA Hons, PGCE

Age Range. 3–11.
Number in School. 60 Boys, 51 Girls.
Fees per term (2014–2015). Nursery (full-time), Reception, Years 1–2 £2,420; Years 3–6 £2,665.

Fairfield is an independent day school for boys and girls aged 3–11. The school was founded in 1935 and aims to provide a broad, traditional education. We encourage each child to maximise his or her potential through creating a family ethos in which children feel happy, secure and valued. A fundamental aspect of our ethos is our commitment to small classes, usually of 18–20. Fairfield offers a broad and balanced curriculum, informed by the National Curriculum. Teachers and visiting coaches provide a wide range of extra-curricular lessons including music, dance, sport, drama and creative activities. Pupils are prepared for entry into all local independent senior schools as well as for the local maintained sector schools.

For further details please apply to the School Secretary.
Charitable status. Fairfield PNEU School (Backwell) Limited is a Registered Charity, number 310215.

Fairley House School

Junior Department:
218–220 Lambeth Road, London SE1 7JY
Tel: 020 7976 5456
Fax: 020 7620 1069
email: junior@fairleyhouse.org.uk

Senior Department:
30 Causton Street, London SW1P 4AU
Tel: 020 7976 5456
Fax: 020 7976 5905
email: senior@fairleyhouse.org.uk

website: www.fairleyhouse.org.uk

Headmaster: **Michael Taylor**, BA Hons, PGCE, FRGS

Age Range. 5–14.
Number of Pupils. 173 (123 Boys, 50 Girls).
Fees per term (2014–2015). £9,797.

Fairley House School is a school for children with specific learning difficulties, dyslexia and dyspraxia. The aim of the school is to provide intensive support to help children to overcome difficulties, coupled with a full, rich curriculum designed to bring out children's strengths and talents. Most children return to mainstream schooling after two to three years. Children's learning styles have often not been catered for in their previous school, leading to failure and loss of confidence, but Fairley House offers them a 'level playing field' where everyone has similar difficulties. Children receive a stimulating educational experience integrated with therapy and specialist teaching. Teaching is multi-sensory and children learn Science, Spelling, Geography and History through interesting, hands-on activities. There is a staff: pupil ratio of 1: 3.5. This integration is one of the many things that sets us apart as a specialist day school for children with specific learning difficulties.

We emphasise the development of the whole child, helping him or her to gain confidence and self-esteem through an encouraging and nurturing ethos. The children have plenty of opportunities to develop sound academic and social skills and to become independent. At Fairley House, everyone succeeds.

Falkner House

19 Brechin Place, London SW7 4QB
Tel: 020 7373 4501
Fax: 020 7835 0073
email: office@falknerhouse.co.uk
website: www.falknerhouse.co.uk

Headmistress: **Mrs Anita Griggs**, BA Hons, PGCE

Age Range. Girls 4–11, Co-educational Nursery (ages 3–4).
Number of Girls. 200.
Fees per term (2014–2015). Main School £5,350, Nursery £2,675.

Falkner House is unashamedly academically ambitious and pupils achieve notable success at 11+ to the very top day and boarding schools. This is all within a naturally self-policing, civilised atmosphere where the development of self-confidence and happiness are seen as key goals. There is a busy yet friendly environment and as a result pupils have an engaging openness, intellectual curiosity and courtesy beyond their years. "We like them to have ability and oomph" says Mrs Griggs, "but not to be sassy or precocious."

Excellent facilities include a science laboratory, art room, library and playground. State-of-the-art IT facilities now include individual iPads integrated into the curriculum. A strong musical tradition lies alongside an excellent sporting record. Pre/post school care is offered, as well as a wide range of after-school activities.

Entrance at 4+ is by assessment and interview.

Falkner House Nursery caters for boys and girls aged 3–4 years. Children thrive in a stimulating atmosphere under the care of professional and thoughtful teachers. Children are encouraged to be curious, to experiment and to learn through play. Specialist staff teach subjects such as music and PE to enrich the nursery curriculum.

Entrance at rising 3 is by date of registration.

Faraday School

Old Gate House, 7 Trinity Buoy Wharf, London E14 0FH
Tel: 020 7719 9342
          020 8965 7374 (Admissions)
email: admissions@faradayschool.co.uk
          head@faradayschool.co.uk
website: www.faradayschool.co.uk

Headmistress: **Miss Susan Stark**

Age Range. 4–11 Co-educational.
Number of Pupils. 80.
Founded in 2009, Faraday is a small but growing independent school in East London located at the unique setting of Trinity Buoy Wharf.

Here at Faraday we offer a traditional approach to primary education with a strong emphasis on the core skills of literacy and numeracy. Although we believe in a traditional approach, our lessons reflect modern thinking on how children learn most effectively and our small classes and quality staff allow for a very personal approach to learning.

Opportunities outside the classroom abound. Through sporting activities, first-class music, art and drama, we encourage every child to find their own particular strength. A wide range of after-school clubs, after-school care and school bus service is attractive to many working parents.

Termly school trips extend the curriculum and develop social skills. Our location on the historic wharf, home to the Faraday lighthouse, Container City and a wealth of creative tenants offers us excellent opportunities for partnerships to extend our pupils' learning. Our partially-covered playground roof, with views over the Thames to the O2 Centre, allows for all-weather play.

Entry into Reception is non selective and based on the date the completed registration form is returned to our Registrar, with siblings given priority. Entry higher up the school is by interview and informal assessment in the classroom. We offer regular open days and welcome private tours.

Faraday was the second of the New Model School Company's schools, offering a low-fee model, based on traditional teaching methods and with a Christian ethos, although we accept children of all faiths or none.

Fees per term (2014–2015). £2,666.

Ferndale House Preparatory School

5–7 Bromsgrove, Faringdon, Oxon SN7 7JF
Tel: 01367 240618
email: info@ferndalehouseschool.co.uk
website: www.ferndaleschool.co.uk
Twitter: @ferndalehouse
Facebook: /ferndaleprep

Headteacher: **Mrs Fiona Shires**, Dip Eur Hum, BA Hons, PGCE

Age Range. 2½–11 years.
Number in School. Day: 33 Girls, 45 Boys.
Fees per term (2014–2015). Nursery: Morning £30.00 (inc lunch), Afternoon £18.00 (exc lunch), Whole Day £48.00 (inc lunch); Lower School (Reception to Year 2): £2,695; Upper School (Years 3–6): £3,195.

Ferndale House is a small, thriving co-educational prep school, occupying pleasant Georgian buildings in the historic market town of Faringdon. Its size means that each child receives individual attention and its family atmosphere provides a secure and supportive environment where confidence and exceptional results are achieved.

There is no formal test, but an interview, with a "taster" day may help ensure that a child is appropriately placed. Entry is age 2½ into the Nursery and in succeeding years subject to place availability. Ferndale welcomes children of all faiths, though broadly Christian values underpin an ethos where social responsibility and habits of courtesy and consideration for others are much in evidence.

Ferndale House has a remarkable record of success in entrance to schools of first choice, amongst them several in the highest league. Scholarships and other awards have regularly been won at target independent schools from Cheltenham to Abingdon and from Bath to Oxford, while places have also been gained at Grammar and maintained schools.

In recent years most of our boys have been offered places at Abingdon School or Magdalen College, Oxford; our girls have mainly gone to the School of St Helen & St Katharine or boys and girls to Our Lady's Abingdon. Other schools have included Oxford High, Headington, Wychwood, Cokethorpe, Grittleton House, Pate's Grammar, King Edward's Bath, Warneford, Farmor's, Faringdon, Rendcomb and Kingham Hill.

The arts flourish at Ferndale. Music and the visual arts are strong, and drama and dance are highly regarded. Games from rugby and netball to chess are another success story and a wide range of extra-curricular activities includes such activities as art, football, gardening, rugby, ICT and swimming at Faringdon's Leisure Centre.

Specialist teaching at a young age is a strength of the school. There are specialist rooms for music, art, science and ICT which perfectly complement the homely, child-friendly classrooms in the original buildings; these also house a custom-designed nursery department. The school employs its own chef who provides excellent and varied lunches with an impressive range of choices.

Finborough School

The Hall, Great Finborough, Stowmarket, Suffolk IP14 3EF
Tel: 01449 773600
Fax: 01449 773601
email: admin@finborough.suffolk.sch.uk
website: www.finboroughschool.co.uk

Principal: Mr James Sinclair

Head of Senior School: Miss Vivienne Davies

Head of Preparatory School: Mr Ashley Martin, BEd Hons

Age Range. Co-educational 2½–18.

Number of Pupils. Boarders 59, Day 167.

Fees per term (2014–2015). Full Boarding £5,765–£7,735, Weekly Boarding £4,640–£6,205, Day £2,475–£3,825. The Montessori Nursery has its own fee structure. Fees are fully inclusive of all meals, educational materials and extended day care for day pupils. Flexible and occasional boarding facilities for day pupils are available at additional cost.

Location. Finborough School is two miles west of Stowmarket, which is on the main London-Norwich line and is 5 minutes' drive from the A14. The school operates a local bus service for day pupils.

Facilities. Founded in 1977, the School moved to its present site in 1980 since when it has consistently reinvested in improved facilities, including a new Art Studio and Apple Mac suite. Well-maintained playing fields and hard courts for tennis, netball and basketball. The woodland provides an adventure playground, camping site and a stretch of river for canoeing and fishing. An equestrian centre has been opened with a floodlit arena.

Aims. By acknowledging each pupil as an individual and by nurturing their individual talents, our aim is to prepare them for life after school. The School Development Plan allows for planned growth to around 400 pupils in total. The number permits retention of our small school family atmosphere whilst providing a unit where viability will allow the provision of first-rate facilities in all areas.

Education. Classes are small, with an average of 15 pupils and are taught by highly-qualified professional staff. The curriculum covers the full range of traditional subjects, as well as technology and ICT through to GCSE and A Level. All pupils receive trained advice on careers and university entry.

Examination results are good, reflecting not only pupil ability but their hard work and the expertise and commitment of teaching staff.

Music, Drama and Art. Pupils receive expert tuition and perform at School concerts, assemblies, and in the local music and drama festivals. A wide range of instrumental tuition is available at additional cost. The School regularly has successes in Art competitions and a wide range of work is displayed around the premises.

Sport. Competitive but well-mannered – Rugby, Netball, Hockey, Soccer, Rounders, Cricket, Golf, Cross-country, Athletics, Swimming, Tennis etc.

Entry. Following application, previous schools reports and school references are received and interview arranged. All candidates attend trial sessions for 2 or 3 days before making up their minds about the school. Entry tests in Mathematics and English are taken during trial days.

General. Day pupils can be accommodated from 8.00 am to 5.30 pm and there is no Saturday school. A weekly assembly in the village church is an important social as well as spiritual occasion.

The Firs School

45 Newton Lane, Chester CH2 2HJ
Tel: 01244 322443
Fax: 01244 400450
email: admin@firsschool.org
           s.hunt@firsschool.org
website: www.firsschool.net

Headmistress: **Mrs L Davies**, BA Hons, PGCE, PGDCL, NPQH

Age Range. 3–11 Co-educational.

Number in School. 191: 110 Boys, 81 Girls.

Fees per term (2014–2015). £500–£2,590.

The Firs School is an independent co-educational primary school set in attractive grounds about a mile and a half north of the city of Chester. It was founded in 1945 by Mrs F A Longman.

The aim of the Firs is to help children achieve their academic potential in the context of a caring environment based upon Christian principles. Children of all faiths are welcome and we respect and learn from their beliefs and cultures. Our strengths lie in the individual attention we are able to give, a carefully planned curriculum and an effective partnership with parents. Specialist teaching for dyslexia and other educational needs is available. We have a proven record of success in preparing children for entrance to local independent and state schools. The school is well resourced with a continuous programme of investment, including our technology and pottery rooms.

Whilst placing great emphasis on the core subjects, our curriculum is enhanced through the teaching of French, Spanish, drama, the opportunity for sport and the quality of our provision of art and music throughout the school.

Our objective is to encourage the development of the whole child so that each will leave The Firs School with an understanding of the wider world and an awareness of his or her responsibility to others.

Firwood Manor Preparatory School

Broadway, Chadderton, Oldham, Lancs OL9 0AD
Tel: 0161 620 6570
email: secretary@firwoodmanorschool.co.uk
website: www.firwoodmanorschool.co.uk
Facebook: /firwoodmanorschool

Head Teacher: **Mrs Caroline Greenwood**, BEd Hons

Age Range. 2¾–11 Co-educational.

Number of Pupils. 100.

Fees per term (2014–2015). £1,505–£2,090 plus £160 for lunch.

Firwood Manor Preparatory School opened in September 2002 and is an independent, co-educational day school for children aged from 2¾ to 11 years. It is situated on Broadway in Chadderton, Oldham close to the beginning of the A627M. This location makes it very accessible from a number of places in Greater Manchester and Lancashire, including Bury, Rochdale, North Manchester and Ashton. It is also an easy dropping-off point for parents who commute to work. The school is open from 7.30 am to 6.00 pm to care for your child.

The school has grown through teamwork, close interaction, open communication and collaborative planning and has a hard working, dedicated, well-qualified and experienced staff. The last ISI inspection in October 2011 described the school as being outstanding, particularly in the pastoral care of children and their personal, social and moral development.

At Firwood Manor we are very aware of our responsibility to provide children with the very best educational possibilities and to optimise the opportunities for children to reach their full potential, so that their years of primary education culminate in the maximum appropriate outcomes.

Our exceptional facilities certainly help us to realise these aims. They include a fully equipped nursery, purpose-built classrooms from Reception to Year 6, specialist rooms for Science and Art, Design and Technology, an ICT suite, a hall for sport, gymnastics, dance, music and drama, extensive grounds with facilities for football, hockey and netball and on-site catering facilities. Children also learn Spanish and French from the age of 3.

The starting point of every teacher is the infinite worth of each child. Every day our aim is to provide each and every child with exciting and challenging learning experiences, which are both traditional and innovative.

Our children are encouraged to be independent, confident, responsible and compassionate with a strong sense of purpose and self-discipline. They have a love of learning for its own sake with enquiring minds and the ability to freely express their likes and dislikes. We aim to give them opportunities to develop skills to enable them to be good team players, to solve problems, both academically and in their daily lives, and to enable them to manage change, risk and uncertainty. And above all, they have a strong belief in themselves and in what they can achieve.

Forest Park Preparatory School

Lauriston House, 27 Oakfield, Sale, Cheshire M33 6NB
Tel: 0161 973 4835
email: post@forestparkprep.co.uk
website: www.forestparkschool.co.uk
Twitter: @ForestParkPrep
Facebook: /Forest-Park-School

Headteacher: **Mrs Karen Horrocks**, BA, MA, PGCE

Age Range. 3–11.
Number in School. 63 Day Boys, 65 Day Girls.
Fees per term (2014–2015). £1,957–£2,127.

Forest Park occupies a pleasant site in a quiet road surprisingly close to the centre of Sale, easily accessible from motorways and surrounding areas.

The school aims to discover and develop each child's particular abilities by offering a varied curriculum in a stimulating and happy atmosphere. Forest Park has a good pupil teacher ratio and offers a wide range of subjects with priority given to the traditional disciplines of English, Mathematics and Science. Pupils from three years of age are taught Information Technology by specialist staff. Swimming is taught from the age of five and games offered are Football, Cricket, Netball, Tennis and Hockey. Pupils are taught French from an early age, the older children having the opportunity to visit a language study centre in France.

The confidence and social ease one expects of a private education is a product of the school. Our aim is to develop skills and knowledge through a habit of hard work in a secure and happy environment within a disciplined framework. The school prepares pupils for all independent grammar school examinations and has an excellent record in this respect.

The school prides itself on strong links and communication with a most supportive Parents' Association.

Forest Preparatory School

Moss Lane, Timperley, Altrincham, Cheshire WA15 6LJ
Tel: 0161 980 4075
Fax: 0161 903 9275
email: headteacher@forestschool.co.uk
website: www.forestschool.co.uk

Headmaster: **Mr R Hyde**

Age Range. 2–11.
Number in School. Day: 90 Boys, 95 Girls.
Fees per term (2014–2015). £1,940–£2,190.

An independent, co-educational school that is rich in tradition.

Excellent pastoral care is built on the teachers' knowledge of every child as an individual. With its 'open door' policy, strong links are formed with the parents and excellent two-way communication takes place between home and school.

Family values and discipline are important codes of practice at the school, which has an excellent reputation for preparing the children for state and independent grammar schools.

There is before and after-school care provided for the working parent and a comprehensive list of after-school activities offered to the children.

Pupils begin their education in the school's thriving pre-prep department, where children may start from the age of two.

Though the school is not selective at infant level, Forest Prep has great expectations and as a result the aspirations of the children are high, with great achievements occurring in and out of the classroom.

The pupils are renowned for the standards that they achieve musically and in the sporting arena and for their polite and well-mannered behaviour when taking part in a myriad of out-of-school activities and events.

Frewen College & Frewen Preparatory School

Brickwall, Northiam, Nr Rye, East Sussex TN31 6NL
Tel: 01797 252494
Fax: 01797 252567
email: office@frewencollege.co.uk
website: www.frewencollege.co.uk

Principal: **Mr Nick Goodman**, BA Hons, PGCE, NPQH

Prep Headmistress: Miss Jeannette Bidder, BA Hons, PGCE, Adv Dip SpLD

Age Range. 7–19 Co-educational.
Number in School. Full Boarders: 12 boys, 9 girls; Weekly Boarders: 15 boys, 7 girls; Day: 52 boys, 20 girls.
Fees per term (2014–2015). Day £4,821–£7,679; Full and Weekly Boarding £7,223–£10,660.

Frewen College is a small friendly independent specialist school catering for children with Specific Learning Difficulties (dyslexia, dyspraxia, dyscalculia) and related speech and language and sensory integration problems. We are inspected by Ofsted and rated *Good with many outstanding features* for education.

The school adopts a holistic approach to teaching, designed to enhance pupils' confidence and self-esteem, allowing them to build on their strengths while learning to cope with their difficulties. Each pupil has a comprehensive 'Provision Map' so that teaching can be tailored to individual needs. About half the children have statements of special educational need and are funded, currently by 14 different Local Authorities. Services children are also welcome and their fees are fully covered by the SEN Allowance, and we have a growing number of international students from all Continents.

The number of girls increases each year. Boarding for girls was introduced in September 2009 and has already been extended twice. Our very friendly Houseparents run boarding very much like an extended family, with bedrooms of 1–4 pupils, all with en-suite facilities. Catering is 'in house', and rated by all-comers as 'excellent'! A very wide range of recreational activities is available, and transport is available to and from London each weekend.

Our separate junior school, Frewen Preparatory School, has all the benefits of a small independent school while being able to make use of specialist facilities on the adjacent senior school site. Frewen Prep employs the 'creative curriculum' approach to teaching, which has been extremely successful in engaging children in the delights of learning. As a result of the re-launch numbers are now up, with almost all pupils privately funded.

Newly launched in 2014, our Sixth Form offers a very wide range of courses, both in house, and through two partner Colleges. Applications are welcome from both internal and external students and we expect to be at full capacity in 2015.

Frewen College has excellent facilities, based around a historic house located in 60 acres of playing fields, gardens and parkland. Educational provision includes three modern IT suites, a drama workshop, food and nutrition kitchens, pottery, music and music practice rooms, two newly refitted Science labs, Design & Technology workshop and an art studio. English lessons are supplemented by intensive daily reading sessions.

Outdoor facilities include a large open-air swimming pool, tennis and netball court, all-weather five-a-side and hockey pitch, newly refurbished fitness suite, as well as extensive playing fields. Our cricket pitch is rated one of the best village pitches in the County. We also have access to another 100 acres of ancient parkland for cross-country runs, camping, and orienteering. All Year 9 pupils are entered for the Duke of Edinburgh's Award Scheme. A recent addition to the facilities is a mountain bike trail largely designed and built by the senior pupils.

All classroom staff have specialist dyslexia training. We are Department for Education approved, a supporting corporate member of the BDA, and rated 'Dyslexia Specialist Provision' by CReSTeD.

Charitable status. The Frewen Educational Trust Limited is a Registered Charity, number 307019.

Fyling Hall School

Robin Hood's Bay, Whitby, North Yorkshire YO22 4QD
Tel: 01947 880353
Fax: 01947 881097
email: office@fylinghall.org
website: www.fylinghall.org

Headmaster: **Mr Steven Allen**, BA Hons, QTS

Age Range. 4–18.
Number of Pupils. Boarders: Boys 50, Girls 30; Day: Boys 60, Girls 40.
Fees per term (2014–2015). Day: £2,184–£2,912; Weekly Boarding: £5,096–£5,928; Full Boarding: £5,304–£6,344.

Fyling Hall School is one of the oldest recognised co-educational schools in the country. It occupies a spectacular coastal setting within the North York Moors National Park.

Pupils may safely enjoy freedom in this beautiful and peaceful rural area.

The buildings centre on a grade two listed Georgian country house in delightfully landscaped gardens incorporating an outdoor theatre overlooking Robin Hood's Bay. Recent expansion has included two new boarding houses, science laboratories and dining room in addition to the purpose-built Junior School. We have also built a spacious multi-functional sports hall and an astroturf recently.

The school is intentionally small due to its desire to educate pupils as individuals. The advantageous pupil-teacher ratio encourages effective learning. The teaching is along traditional lines with an emphasis on 'doing one's best' within a supportive yet challenging environment. A broadly based and well resourced curriculum is followed which reflects recent national initiatives, particularly in the scientific and information technology fields. A wide range of GCSE and A Level courses are offered.

Fyling Hall is a closely knit society with an emphasis on pastoral care and a real sense of communal responsibility. The chief feature is a spirit of confidence and cooperation between staff and pupils in an atmosphere which is natural for growth.

There is no entrance examination, but an interview and a report from the current school are integral parts of the admission process.

Many of the pupils stay to join the Sixth Form, where freedom and responsibility present a balance and are a useful preparation for university life.

The school takes advantage of its natural surroundings in the provision of numerous extra-curricular activities. Fyling Hall has its own ponies and these constitute a much loved part of school life. Climbing, Karate, Duke of Edinburgh's Award and Riding are all popular. The main games are rugby, hockey, cricket and tennis, each with a full fixture list. Music enjoys a good reputation and individual tuition is available in all the usual musical instruments.

Robin Hood's Bay is remarkably accessible despite its rural splendour. Nearby Whitby and Scarborough are both railheads. Teesside Airport and the ferry port of Hull, with their frequent continental connections, are both easily reached. An experienced Secretary is able to advise on all travel arrangements.

Academic standards are high, but other abilities are valued, and aided by the small size of classes it is hoped that all pupils can be encouraged to achieve their maximum potential.

Charitable status. Fyling Hall School Trust Ltd is a Registered Charity, number 507857. It exists for the provision of high quality education for boys and girls.

Gads Hill School

Higham, Rochester, Kent ME3 7PA
Tel: 01474 822366
Fax: 01474 822977
email: admissions@gadshillschool.org
website: www.gadshill.org

Headmaster: **Mr D G Craggs**, BSc, MA, FCollP, FRSA

Age Range. Co-educational 3–16.
Number in School. 394.
Fees per term (2014–2015). £2,969–£3,555.
Entry requirements. Interview and assessment.
Aim. To provide a good all-round education, to build confidence, establish friendships, to reward success (however small) and to ensure our students leave as mature, self-reliant young people who depart Gads for the career or University placement of their choice.

Kindergarten (3–6 years). From the very early years in Kindergarten the children are encouraged to learn through play, music and drama. Basic letter and number work is introduced within the nursery and reception class as the children concentrate on the Early Learning Goals. In Year 1 and Year 2 they largely follow Key Stage One of the National Curriculum although in addition; from Reception upwards, all of our children are taught French and also Information and Communications Technology.

Junior School (7–11 years). Our Junior School curriculum seeks to build upon the children's undaunted love of adventure. Literacy, Numeracy and Humanities continue to be taught by Form Tutors however, the children begin to benefit from more lessons delivered by specialist tutors particularly in French, Information Technology, Design & Technology, RE, Games and Drama.

Senior School (11–16 years). Senior School concentrates very much on the preparation for GCSE success and our classes are kept to a maximum of 20 children per class. This way the children benefit from smaller class sizes and consequently our tutors get to know each child as an individual and this enables them to provide the right level of support and assistance. This goes a long way to helping them achieve their goals for GCSEs and A Levels.

Location. Gads Hill School is centred on the former home of Charles Dickens and is surrounded by beautiful grounds, playing fields and countryside. It is a few minutes' drive from the A2 and M2, with good access to the Medway Towns, Dartford and Gravesend.

Curriculum. At Gads we largely follow the National Curriculum although we place a strong emphasis on "communication" with all of our children benefiting from lessons in French, Information and Communications Technology and Drama as well as English. Senior School children progress to take GCSEs in English, English Literature, Maths, French, Design & Technology, Combined Science (Double Award), Geography and GNVQ ICT (4 GCSEs).

Sports and Activities. We concentrate very much on team games (rugby, hockey, soccer, netball, cricket, athletics and rounders) to ensure that our children learn the values of team work and communication. In the Kindergarten and Junior Schools all students take part in weekly swimming lessons. Because of our small class sizes almost all of our children have the opportunity to represent the school in competitive fixtures against other schools. Gad's Hill also has a thriving Combined Cadet Force. Students join the CCF in Year 8 and take part in weekly training sessions as well as termly field days and an annual camp. The CCF allows children to experience fantastic outdoor pursuits, adventurous training and leadership courses and is essentially about doing something different and challenging. Gad's Hill pupils are also able to take part in a variety of after-school activities. These range from academic pursuits to a variety of other sports and Performing Arts.

Charitable status. Gads Hill School is a Registered Charity, number 803153. It exists for the purpose of educating children aged 3–16.

GEMS Bolitho School
GEMS Education

Polwithen Road, Penzance, Cornwall TR18 4JR
Tel: 01736 363271
Fax: 01736 330960
email: enquiries@bolithoschool.co.uk
website: www.bolithoschool.co.uk

Head: Mr Gordon McGinn

Co-educational Day and Boarding School.
Age Range. 4–18 years.

Number of Pupils. Boys: 2 Boarders, 82 Day; Girls: 1 Boarder, 62 Day.

Fees per term (2014–2015). Day £2,565-£4,265 inc lunch; Boarding Fees: Weekly Boarding (Year 7 to 11) £2,650; Full Boarding (Year 7 to 11) £3,500; Sixth Form Boarding £3,600.

GEMS Bolitho School is a small, co-educational school catering for pupils of all ages and for day pupils, weekly and full boarders. It deservedly has a national and international reputation for its pioneering and forward-looking approach. Distinctive educational features include: an accelerated national curriculum strategy, whereby pupils take the Key Stage 2 and 3 SATs tests a year early; there is a bilingual section, unique to the UK, where pupils can take around 30% of the syllabus through the medium of French; in the sixth form, students take the internationally prestigious International Baccalaureate – welcomed and recognised by all UK universities, all EU and USA universities, and most other universities worldwide. Set sizes average 12 for children between the ages of 5 years old and 13 years old. Above all, however, the school is a very happy school indeed.

The school's stated aim is to 'bring out the potential of every child and to offer a rounded education that aims at the highest academic standards'. At the heart of the school's philosophy lies the belief that children have extraordinary potential in a great many directions. If this potential is not realised during childhood, it fades; if it is identified and nourished, a child can be galvanised into a dynamic and motivated personality. If a child is to receive a genuinely rounded education, then it must hold that art, drama, music and sports should be embedded firmly into the curriculum – and this the school has done. In addition, there are a great many clubs, activities, outings and expeditions catering for all age groups.

The school prides itself on its European and international outlook. International students from all over the world are warmly welcomed and encouraged to apply. Penzance, in Cornwall, is the warmest locality of the UK. It is also one of the safest and most beautiful parts of the country. This not only attracts pupils of excellence: the location, combined with the school's strong reputation, attracts large numbers of applications for teaching posts, and in consequence the teaching at the school is genuinely excellent.

GEMS Hampshire School
GEMS Education

15 Manresa Road, Chelsea, London SW3 6NB
Tel: 020 7352 7077
Fax: 020 7351 3960

Little GEMS:
5 Wetherby Place, London SW7 4NX

email: info@ghs.gemsedu.co.uk
website: www.ths.westminster.sch.uk

Headmaster: Mr Donal Brennan

Age Range. 3–13.
Number in School. Day: 150 Boys, 150 Girls.
Fees per term (2014–2015). £3,755-£5,320.

Founded in 1928 and located in the London Borough of Kensington and Chelsea, just a stone's throw from the Kings Road, GEMS Hampshire School provides the top class education one would expect from a traditional British Preparatory school, combined with a caring approach and family feel. An independent, interdenominational day school, we cater for boys and girls between the ages of rising 3 and 13. Through personal attention from their dedicated staff and a stimulating curriculum, they ensure that learning is fun and that every child feels confident and valued.

In January 2009, the Pre-Preparatory and Preparatory sections made a successful move to a spacious and beautiful new site in Chelsea's old Public Library at 15 Manresa Road, London SW3.

A broad-based and balanced curriculum is provided by dedicated staff. Children are given every opportunity to develop individual talents as fully as possible – a broad range of academic subjects being supported by a high level of instruction in music, art, physical education as well as the core subjects. Children are encouraged to study the history and development of their environment and culture by means of regular visit to museums, art galleries, exhibitions and places of interest.

The main school's excellent facilities include a galleried library, gymnasium, science laboratory, art and design studio, fully equipped stage, and garden.

There are a wide range of extra-curricular activities offered, from judo, gymnastics, horse riding and dancing to art, languages and music, as well as many in between, such as media, radio station, ukulele and cross stitch.

The School has been successful in preparing pupils for examination and scholarship entry into leading day and boarding senior independent schools. Great emphasis is placed on developing each child's individual talents. Children excel academically at GEMS Hampshire School. In recent years, pupils successfully navigate the 8+, 11+ or 13+ Common Entrance Examinations to gain entry to their first choice schools.

We are also able to offer younger children and siblings a fantastic start through our Little GEMS Nursery, which is situated a mile away from the main school and is a newly renovated classical London town house, providing children with the 'home away from home' secure and nurturing environment they need at this tender young age. The EYFS curriculum is followed, with the school putting emphasis on the children becoming happy, confident and polite learners who are engaged and enthusiastic in their education.

Gidea Park College

2 Balgores Lane, Gidea Park, Romford, Essex RM2 5JR
Tel: 01708 740381
Fax: 01708 740381
email: office@gideaparkcollege.co.uk
website: www.gideaparkcollege.co.uk

Headmistress: **Mrs Susan Gooding**, BA Hons Dunelm

Age Range. 3–11 Co-educational.
Number in School. 175 Day Pupils.
Fees per term (2014–2015). £2,845.

An established Preparatory school founded in 1924, the current Directors are the granddaughters of the founders.

The main building, a substantial Georgian/Victorian house, accommodates the 7–11 year old children, the school library, assembly room and IT room plus the kitchens. In separate outside classrooms, bounded by lawns and playgrounds, is the small Pre-school unit and accommodation for 4–7 year old pupils.

All children are known and treated as individuals with specific talents which are valued and developed. Likewise, identified areas needing extra help and encouragement are recognised.

The broad-based curriculum is delivered by highly qualified, full-time classroom staff using traditional methods, assisted by qualified support staff.

Results in selection procedures at 11+ are of a consistently high standard with scholarships and places awarded at local Independent and Grammar Schools. Our KS1 and KS2 National Assessment Testing reveals standards above the National expectations.

All National Curriculum areas are covered using whole-class teaching methods. Latin and French are introduced in the higher year groups.

A school choir performs on formal occasions and visits local care homes to sing.

Local facilities are used for PE, swimming and games lessons. Our House system fosters team spirit and enables each individual to participate in a variety of inter-house competitions as well as inter-school events.

The school has a Christian Foundation and strong links with our local parish church. However, within our diverse community those of other faiths are welcomed and their beliefs respected and festivals celebrated. Our pupils are encouraged to think of others less fortunate than themselves and arrange a variety of fundraising events for charity.

The staff supervise an early Morning and After School Club for the convenience of working parents. Those staying relax and then complete homework assignments giving quality time for parents and children at home.

New parents are made welcome by our thriving Parents' Association and encouraged to join in the various social events arranged providing a friendship base for them whilst at the school. Their fundraising provides extra equipment and fun occasions for the children.

We encourage all prospective parents to visit the school prior to applying so they may see classes in action and have an opportunity to ask any questions. We consider the partnership between pupils, parents and school to be of paramount importance in enabling each child to reach his/her potential.

Gosfield School

Halstead, Essex CO9 1PF
Tel: 01787 474040
Fax: 01787 478228
email: enquiries@gosfieldschool.org.uk
website: www.gosfieldschool.org.uk

Chair of Governors: Mr Peter Sakal

Principal: **Dr Sarah J Welch**, MA, PhD

Age Range. 4–18 Boys and Girls.
Number in School. Boarders 12, Day 208.
Fees per term (2014–2015). Day £1,710–£4,840; Boarding: £5,315–£5,995 (5 nights), £5,995–£6,995 (7 nights).

Founded in 1929, Gosfield occupies a gracious, listed country house which was built in 1870 for Lady Courtauld. The school is set in a glorious 110 acre estate which borders ancient woodland and is a haven for wildlife and rare species. There are conservation areas and nature trails within the grounds.

Recent building developments include a brand new Sixth Form Centre, Sports Hall, IT Suite and an all-weather sports surface. Boarding accommodation has also been completely upgraded.

The school is deliberately small in numbers and provides a caring family atmosphere in which every pupil will be able to develop his or her own potential to the full. Classes are small, and standards are high. The system of personal tutors ensures that every child's needs are properly looked after both in academic work and in the sporting and cultural activities in which the school encourages all pupils to participate.

There is a wide range of activities including sports, music, drama and conservation work. The programme changes termly and provides something for everyone. There are no weekend lessons.

The school day is from 8.30 am to 3.45 pm with the Pre-Prep department finishing at 3.10 pm. On Monday to Thursday there are after-school games and activities which run until 4.45 pm. All our pupils are encouraged to participate in these activities. On Friday school ends at 3.45 pm. Games fixtures are all in midweek.

The whole structure – daily and weekly – aims to be flexible and helpful to parents and pupils. The school sees education as a partnership, so parents are always welcome to visit, to talk to staff, and to be involved in the school's activities.

Gosfield is situated in rural North Essex only 20 miles from Stansted Airport and thirty miles from the M25. The nearest town, Halstead, is a mile away and the nearest train station is just five miles away at Braintree.

There is a daily minibus service to and from Chelmsford, Sudbury, Braintree and Colchester.

Charitable status. Gosfield School is a Registered Charity, number 310871. It exists to provide education for boys and girls.

Grangewood Independent School

Chester Road, Forest Gate, London E7 8QT
Tel: 020 8472 3552
Fax: 020 8552 8817
email: admin@grangewoodschool.com
website: www.grangewoodschool.com

Head: **Mrs Beverley Roberts**, BEd Hons

Age Range. 3–11.
Number in School. 41 boys, 29 girls.
Fees per term (2014–2015). £1,384–£1,719.
Grangewood is a Christian Day School which welcomes children from any faith background. We offer a secure, friendly and caring environment in small classes where children can achieve their potential in a setting of excellence.

Charitable status. Grangewood Educational Association is a Registered Charity, number 803492.

Grantham Preparatory International School
An IES School

Gorse Lane, Grantham, Lincolnshire NG31 7UF
Tel: 01476 593293
email: contact.grantham@iesmail.com
website: www.tgps.co.uk

Head: **Mrs Kathryn Korcz**, BSc Hons, CertEd

Age Range. 3–11 Co-educational.
Number of Pupils. 105.
Fees per term (2014–2015). £2,300–£2,810.
The Grantham Preparatory School is a non-denominational independent day school for boys and girls between the ages of three and eleven. The school was established in 1981 and moved to a modern purpose-built building in 1987. It is set in nearly four acres of grounds and playing fields and, being close to the A1, it is easily accessible.

The school is now owned by International Education Systems. IES is a network of eight schools (three in South Africa, three in the UK, one in Hungary and one in the United States). IES's mission is to provide excellence in education provision within an international perspective. Here at The Grantham Preparatory School we are "committed" to excellence in all areas of the curriculum, and we aim to provide the best for all our children in a happy family environment. We are now delighted to be a member of the ISA family after being accredited in November 2011.

Our children are prepared for entrance examinations to Independent senior schools and for Grammar school selection examinations. Children benefit from many specialist teachers who bring their own enthusiasm and knowledge to a particular subject. This ensures high academic standards and our broad and balanced curriculum enables our children to experience sport, art, music and drama and have the opportunity to pursue and develop their strengths, achieving their full potential. Specialist music teachers provide individual tuition in a wide variety of instruments.

Gold Artsmark was awarded in May 2010 in recognition of the very high standards achieved in music, drama and art. The school wind band, choir and recital groups continue to delight audiences with their stunning performances. The school was awarded the PE Kitemark – Gold Award for Sport (2012–2013).

Within our foundation stage there is a strong emphasis upon learning through play. We provide a stimulating and exciting curriculum which is delivered through a combination of whole-class, adult-led and child-initiated activities. There is a successful phonics programme, which begins in the Early Years classroom and continues throughout the Infant Department.

We believe that every child is an important unique individual that should be valued and nurtured during their time with us. We expect our children to leave us at age 11 as independent, confident individuals, tolerant of others and well prepared for the next stage of their education.

Greenbank Preparatory School and Day Nursery

Heathbank Road, Cheadle Hulme, Cheadle, Cheshire SK8 6HU
Tel: 0161 485 3724
Fax: 0161 485 5519
email: info@greenbankschool.co.uk
website: www.greenbankschool.co.uk

Headmistress: **Mrs Janet Lowe**, CertEd

Age Range. 6 months–11 years.
Number in School. Day: 106 Boys, 66 Girls. Daycare: 70.
Fees per term (2014–2015). £2,497 including lunches from Reception to Year Six.

Greenbank is an independent co-educational school for pupils aged three to eleven years. A separate Nursery, open fifty weeks of the year, cares for babies and children from six months to four years old.

Greenbank School was founded in 1951 by Karl and Linda Orsborn. Since 1971 the School has been administered by an Educational Trust and is registered with the Department for Education.

Greenbank is situated within extensive grounds, comprises a mixture of traditional and modern buildings including an IT Suite and Library, separate play areas for Foundation, Infant and Junior children, playing fields with a cricket pavilion, an Astroturf area and netball court. 2009 saw the opening of state-of-the-art Science, Art and Music classrooms within a new administration building. Further developments in 2012 include a brand new Preschool offering greater flexibility to parents.

The school day begins at 8.40 am and ends at 3.30 pm, however we provide wrap-around care from 7.30 am until 6.00 pm. The school also runs activity and sports clubs in the holidays.

Through its varied curricula and extra-curricular activities the School provides pupils with the opportunity of expanding their natural abilities to the full. Music, drama, sport, computing and educational visits are some of the activities which play their part in providing a well-rounded programme of education. We strive to meet the social, emotional and intellectual needs of all pupils and the success of this philosophy is proven by the consistently outstanding examination results throughout the school, particularly at age eleven.

Charitable status. Greenbank School Limited is a Registered Charity, number 525930.

Greenfields School

Priory Road, Forest Row, East Sussex RH18 5JD
Tel: 01342 822189
Fax: 01342 825289
email: admissions@greenfieldsschool.com
website: www.greenfieldsschool.com

Headteacher: **Mr G Hudson**, BA

Age Range. 2–18.
Number in School. Day: 70 Boys, 65 Girls. Boarding: 10 Boys, 8 Girls.
Fees per term (2014–2015). Day £1,020–£3,631, Boarding £5,506–£6,697. *In July 2012 Greenfields introduced a radical new fees scheme which makes private schooling available for as little as £59 per week (subject to review).*

Greenfields is a non-denominational private day and boarding school. It is located on the edge of the Ashdown Forest and has a fully licensed and accredited Montessori-based Kindergarten, Elementary and Middle School and Sixth Form.

The school utilizes proven study methods and a strong moral code ensuring happy students, no bullying, no drugs and successful graduates. Students receive an all-round education for life, including National Curriculum. It also has its own English Language College.

The main difference between Greenfields and other schools is the unique teaching method it uses. This method isolates the barriers preventing or hindering a child from learning and then provides precise tools to deal with them. Its use allows any child of any ability to learn anything.

There is a high level of open communication between students and staff that helps to prevent failure, bullying or drugs.

Every student is individually programmed and targeted to ensure each one achieves the success they are capable of.

The classes are small and an excellent curriculum, providing core subjects and peripheral studies, is available up to GCSE and Advanced Levels.

A "qualifications" department exists for checking that students have fully understood each step of their studies, and also provides extra help for any student having any trouble in class. There is also an "ethics" department that helps to resolve any personal problems the student may have.

The pre-school has Montessori trained staff who use Montessori materials to ensure the best foundation for the rest of a student's education.

Entry is by tests for literacy and numeracy. There is a pre-entry section for those who need a short programme to catch up and be ready to join their correct class.

Trains take under an hour from London to East Grinstead, which is a ten minute car ride from the school. Gatwick Airport is a twenty minute car ride away.

Charitable status. Greenfields Educational Trust is a Registered Charity, number 287037. The object for which the trust is established is the advancement of education.

The Gregg School

Townhill Park House, Cutbush Lane, Southampton SO18 2GF
Tel: 023 8047 2133
Fax: 023 8047 1080
email: office@gregg.southampton.sch.uk
website: www.gregg.southampton.sch.uk

Chairman of Board of Trustees: Mr John W Watts, MCIPS, MILT, AIGEM

Headteacher: **Mrs S Sellers**, MSc, BSc Hons, NPQH, PGCE

Age Range. 11–16 years.
Number in School. 325.
Fees per term (2014–2015). £3,700.

The Gregg School is situated to the east of Southampton and set in 23 acres of beautifully landscaped grounds. The School has a unique family atmosphere and an excellent reputation for its outstanding pastoral care. A high value is placed on identifying and developing each child's individual talents and abilities, and small classes, taught by experienced and dedicated staff, ensure that every student has the opportunity to achieve their very best.

A broad and balanced curriculum is supplemented by a wide range of extra-curricular clubs and activities, ranging from orienteering to off-road buggy building.

The School's music and drama departments provide a host of opportunities for students to perform to a range of audiences, and the School regularly achieves success in sporting disciplines at both city and county level.

A comprehensive transport service is provided for students living within a 15 mile radius of the School.

Our Trust Partner, St Winifred's School, offers a high-quality educational experience for children aged 3–11.

The Grove Independent School

Redland Drive, Loughton, Milton Keynes, Buckinghamshire MK5 8HD
Tel: 01908 690590
Fax: 01908 694043
email: office@groveschool.co.uk
website: www.groveschool.co.uk

Principal: **Mrs Deborah Berkin**

Age Range. 3 months – 13 years Co-educational.
Number of Pupils. 247.
Fees per term (2014–2015). £4,210 (47 weeks all inclusive), £3,983 (term time). Nursery: £950 per month (full time).

Hale Preparatory School

Broomfield Lane, Hale, Cheshire WA15 9AS
Tel: 0161 928 2386
email: mail@haleprepschool.com
website: www.haleprepschool.com

Headmaster: **J Connor**, JP, BSc, FCP

Age Range. 4–11.
Number in School. Day: 103 Boys, 97 Girls.
Fees per term (2014–2015). £2,270.

Hale Preparatory School is a completely independent, co-educational school for children from the age of 4 to 11.

The school's most recent ISI inspection was in the summer of 2014. The overall summary of the report reads, "*Hale Prep is a very successful school. Throughout, the teaching is excellent and the pupils' industrious approach to their studies is reflected in their rapid progress and substantial academic achievement at all levels. Indeed, in some cases, levels of progress and achievement are exceptional. The pupils reach high standards of personal fulfilment and participate enthusiastically in a wide range of extra-curricular activities. The quality of the pupils' personal development is excellent, reflecting the school's highly effective emphasis on their welfare, safeguarding and wellbeing.*"

In recent years, the school was considered the Prep School of the Year by the Sunday Times and was referred to in two studies presented to the Department of Education: firstly, on "Best Practice in the Independent Sector" and secondly, as one of five examples of successful private schools.

One of the aims of the school is to develop each child to his or her fullest potential. This can only be achieved in a situation that emphasises a disciplined approach to school work. Teaching is carried out in a formal, traditional manner but one which also incorporates modern teaching aids. Homework is set every night.

The curriculum of the school is designed to create well-rounded children. Thus, whilst 50% of the curriculum is devoted to the core subjects of maths, English and science, all children have weekly lessons in drama, music, dance, art and design, information technology, history, geography, French, Spanish, ethics, physical education/games and Latin in year 6. Additionally, the school offers a range of extra-curricular activities including a dance club, theatre club, fencing, chess, sewing, gardening, choir, orchestra, a range of sports, outdoor pursuit holidays and continental ski trips.

The Hammond

Hoole Bank House, Mannings Lane, Chester, Cheshire CH2 4ES
Tel: 01244 305350
Fax: 01244 305351
email: info@thehammondschool.co.uk
website: www.thehammondschool.co.uk

The Hammond is the leading provider for performing arts education in the North West. Recognised and funded as a centre of excellence by the Department for Education (DfE) under the Music and Dance Scheme (MDS) and also receiving support through the Education Funding Agency's (EFA) Dance and Drama Award (DaDA) Scheme. Accredited by the CDET (Council for Dance Education and Training), The Hammond caters for a wide range of talents and interests. The Hammond has a place amongst the leading schools specialising in the field of dance, drama and music providing pupils with an academic education and training at the highest level in all aspects of the curriculum.

Principal: **Mrs M Evans**, BA, MA, PGCE, NPQH, FRSA

Age Range. 3–19+.
Number in School. 100 Boarders, 162 Day Pupils.
Fees per term (2014–2015). £3,550 for education only. Boarding extra £2,600. Prep Department £2,575.
Prep Department takes girls and boys from age 3 to 11.
Education Department takes girls and boys from 11 years to GCSE level.
Drama Department takes girls and boys from 11 years joining the Education Department with additional Drama.

Dance Department takes girls and boys from 11 years joining the Education Department with a Vocational Dance training.
Music Department takes girls and boys from 11 years joining the Education Department with additional Music.
Sixth Form takes boys and girls into the Education Department to study for A/AS Levels, also BTEC in Performing Arts (Acting), as well as those wishing to specialise in Dance, Musical Theatre and Drama.
Full boarding is available.
Outreach Programme. The School is acknowledged for its commitment to the community and its varied outreach projects include:
• Hammond Dance Associates – Specialist classes for talented children, selected by audition, 9–16 years.
• Hammond Youth Theatre – weekend drama classes for 4–16 year olds.
• The Hammond's Easter and Summer schools, working with participants drawn from the community.
For a prospectus apply to The School Secretary.

Harvington Prep School

20 Castlebar Road, Ealing, London W5 2DS
Tel: 020 8997 1583
Fax: 020 8810 4756
email: admin@harvingtonschool.com
website: www.harvingtonschool.com

Headmistress: **Mrs Anna Evans**, BA Hons, PGCE

Age Range. Girls 3–11, Boys 3–4.
Number in School. 106 Girls, 9 Boys (in nursery).
Fees per term (2014–2015). Early Years £3,100; Years 1–6 £4,040. Fees include lunch and a snack at break. No compulsory extras.
The School was founded in 1890 and made into an Educational Trust in 1970. Harvington is known for its high standards and happy atmosphere. Classes are small so that individual attention can be given by qualified and experienced staff. An academic education is offered preparing girls for senior school entrance examinations. The school continues to improve specialist facilities and also to provide a mixed nursery class for 3–4 year olds.
It is close to Ealing Broadway station and a number of bus routes.
Prospectus available from the Secretary.
Charitable status. Harvington School Education Trust Ltd is a Registered Charity, number 312621. It aims to subscribe to traditional values in behaviour and academic standards in a happy environment; to encourage a high standard of academic achievement for girls across a broad range of abilities; to encourage girls to develop their potential to the full, both in personal and academic terms; and to create an environment in which pupils will want to learn.

Hawley Place School

Fernhill Road, Blackwater, Camberley, Surrey GU17 9HU
Tel: 01276 32028
Fax: 01276 609695
email: office@hawleyplace.com
website: www.hawleyplace.com

Principal: **Mr Michael Stone**, BA Hons Dunelm, MA, PGCE Cantab

Age Range. Girls 2–16; Boys 2–11.

Number in School. 370 Day Pupils.

Fees per term (2014–2015). Juniors (Reception to Year 4) £3,192; Seniors (Years 5 to 11) £3,990.

Hawley Place School is based in an imposing Victorian building situated in a beautiful 18 acre park. Our Nursery School provides full and part-time care and education to boys and girls aged 2–4. Our Junior School provides education for boys and girls aged 4 to 11 and our Senior School educates girls aged 11–16.

Throughout the school, pupils are taught in small groups with an excellent teacher/pupil ratio ensuring that individual needs are met effectively in a unique family atmosphere where children can develop, thrive and succeed. We offer a broad and stimulating curriculum, a wealth of opportunities in Sport, Art, Drama and Music, which, combined with the three 'C's (Courtesy, Kindness and Consideration), all help to mould a well-rounded and well-balanced young person.

Girls achieve consistently high GCSE results in the Senior School. Indeed, consistent academic excellence is one of the cornerstones of the school's success and popularity. Over the 5 year period 2008–2012, 91% of the girls on average obtained 5 or more passes at A*–C including English/Maths/Science. An average of 80% obtained their EBac (English, Maths, Science, a language, a Humanities subject) and 79% of grades overall fell into the A*/A/B range. Boys are also extremely successful in achieving entry to the Senior School of their choice.

In the 2012 Early Years Inspection, the school received the highest ranking judgment possible of Outstanding. In the latest ISI Inspection, the school was described as "full of happy purposeful young people and committed, caring staff, who are all very proud of Hawley Place". The school was praised for its outstanding levels of pastoral care and links with parents, for its high standards of education and its high quality of spiritual, moral, social and cultural development of pupils.

Hawley Place pupils not only excel within but also beyond the classroom. The school has built a strong reputation in public speaking, swimming, cross-country running and athletics and has won numerous trophies in Regional and National Finals.

Hawley Place School is part of the Minerva Education group which owns a number of private schools in London, East and South East England. Through Minerva's "Inspiring Learning" programme, we seek to share best practice and ensure the continuing improvement in every child's education.

Heathcote School

Eves Corner, Danbury, Essex CM3 4QB
Tel: 01245 223131
email: enquiries@heathcoteschool.co.uk
website: www.heathcoteschool.co.uk

Head Teacher: **Miss H Petersen**, BA Open University

Age Range. 2–11+.
Number in School. 105.
Fees per term (2014–2015). £2,570.

Founded in 1935, Heathcote School has achieved a high reputation as a school where every child matters. It is a small, village school that encourages excellence in all areas. However, there is room in this happy school for children of all abilities and parents can be sure that their child's education, at all levels, will be designed to develop their particular potential.

Children may start in our Nursery from 2 years old. We offer wrap-around care from 7.30 am to 6.00 pm and have many extra-curricular activities.

Specialist subject teachers ensure the success of the high teaching standards expected at this school. Many children are prepared for scholarships, entrance examinations and the Essex Selective Schools Examination at 11+. A very high pass rate is attained in these examinations.

Pupils are expected to show courtesy and consideration at all times and encouraged to develop self-discipline and pride in themselves and their environment. Parents are asked to support the school in this. Regular consultations with parents are held and the Head Teacher is always available for any discussions that parents consider necessary. We have an active and dedicated "Friends of Heathcote School" who regularly hold social events and raise funds for charity and for the school.

For more information please contact us or visit our website.

Heathfield School and Day Nursery

Wolverley, Kidderminster, Worcestershire DY10 3QE
Tel: 01562 850204
Fax: 01562 852609
email: info@heathfieldschool.co.uk
website: www.heathfieldschool.co.uk
Twitter: @heathfieldsch

Headmaster: **R H Brierly**, BEd

Age Range. 3–16. Baby Unit for children 3 months plus.
Number in School. 205 Day pupils.
Fees per term (2014–2015). £2,093–£3,469. Pre School: £20.10 per session, £30.65 per half day, £45.00 per full day. Nursery from £20.75 (part day) to £49.10 (full day).

Heathfield is a co-educational day school with nursery provision, governed by an Educational Trust. The School is situated in spacious grounds in a green belt area north of Kidderminster, within easy reach of Worcestershire, West Midlands and Shropshire.

The curriculum is broadly based and pupils are prepared for GCSE. We also prepare children for the Common Entrance Examination at 13+. Pupils in our Junior School move up to our own Senior School at 11+. Classes are small. Careers guidance is available to senior pupils.

The school is strong in Drama, Music, Art and Sport. A wide variety of team and individual sports is offered with some pupils achieving regional and national standards.

Prospectus available from Headmaster's Secretary.

Charitable status. Heathfield Educational Trust is a Registered Charity, number 1098940. It exists to provide excellent educational opportunities at a reasonable cost.

Hemdean House School

Hemdean Road, Caversham, Reading, Berks RG4 7SD
Tel: 0118 9472590
Fax: 0118 9464474
email: office@hemdeanhouse.co.uk
website: www.hemdeanhouse.co.uk

Headmistress: **Mrs Debbie Lee**, BEd Hons, MA Ed

Age Range. Girls 3–16, Boys 3–11.
Number in School. 108 Girls, 48 Boys.
Fees per term (2014–2015). £2,270–£3,000.

Founded in 1859, Hemdean House is a school where traditional educational concepts are highly valued. We look for personal achievement in academic and other spheres, responsible behaviour and consideration for others. We aim to develop the varied talents of each and every child within our structured and caring environment; individual attention has high priority. Small classes help us to achieve our aims. We believe that school and family should work together and have opportunities to meet.

The school is organised and operated as one complete unit; many of the specialist staff teach in both the Senior and Junior schools.

The self-contained Nursery unit offers children aged 3–4 the opportunity to begin the learning process and to develop their skills in a secure and happy environment.

We follow the National Curriculum throughout the school; Mathematics, Science, Information Technology, the Humanities and the Expressive Arts, Modern Languages, Technology and Physical Education are taught throughout the age range. French lessons begin at age 5 and recorder lessons begin at age 7 and many children learn at least one other musical instrument. Drama and Public Speaking, Music and Art head a wide range of extra-curricular activities. For the working parent, after-school and holiday care are available if required.

Examination results including GCSE and National Curriculum Key Stage Tests are excellent with pupils achieving well in excess of the national average. Over the last five years an average of 90% of our GCSE grades were A* to C.

The school has always been committed to Christian ethics and values, but all faiths are welcomed and understanding and appreciation of the beliefs of others is encouraged.

The most recent inspection report made some of the following statements:

Hemdean House School provides outstanding pastoral care throughout the school, where pupils are educated well and achieve their full academic potential.

The pupils are friendly, forthcoming and assured, their manners are excellent, and their behaviour throughout the school is exemplary.

Teachers know their pupils extremely well and this creates a happy, supportive environment in which the pupils thrive.

Nursery children are curious and eager to investigate.

The school successfully builds confidence and self-esteem in pupils.

Admission. Assessment during a day or half-day spent in school according to age. An entrance exam is taken by prospective Year 7 pupils. Scholarships and bursaries are available throughout the school.

Charitable status. Hemdean House is a Registered Charity, number 309146. Its aims include academic achievement, the development of every pupil's potential, Christian values and care for others.

Herne Hill School

The Old Vicarage, 127 Herne Hill, London SE24 9LY
Tel: 020 7274 6336
Fax: 020 7924 9510
email: enquiries@hernehillschool.co.uk
website: www.hernehillschool.co.uk

Headteacher: **Mrs Jane Beales**

Age Range. 3–7.
Number in School. 260 boys and girls.
Fees per term (2014–2015). £1,580–£3,985.

Herne Hill School has much to offer – caring and enthusiastic staff, happy and confident children, and excellent results at 7+ years. Children usually join Nursery, Kindergarten or Reception with occasional chance vacancies in Years 1 and 2.

The school is well known as an oasis of happy learning and as the largest feeder into the Dulwich Foundation Schools. It lies tucked away behind St Paul's Church on Herne Hill and operates out of an Old Vicarage and a new purpose-built building. These facilities and the grounds combine to provide a 'homely', safe and nurturing feel while at the same time being open, green and deceptively large – the perfect environment for young children to blossom and enjoy discovering how to learn.

By focusing on Early Years education, Herne Hill School has developed a strong expertise in making the critical transition from Nursery to School seamless. Children joining the Nursery or Kindergarten can avoid the disruption of a 4+ change and have continuity for up to five years in what are arguably their most important formative years. Children joining in Reception also benefit from the smooth progression from a play-based learning approach to more structured lessons.

"Herne Hill School – love, care and excellence" encapsulates the school philosophy that love, nurture and a caring environment foster the children's self-confidence, sense of achievement and happiness, thereby stimulating their curiosity and desire to learn. The school's atmosphere lives this philosophy. It is a caring, friendly and fun place, and at the same time there is an air of achievement, respect and discipline.

The curriculum is finely balanced to take account of each child's individual needs as well as the requirements of the 7+ entry tests – and to make learning fun! It is designed to develop the skills of independent learning and to sustain the children's innate joy of learning. Music, drama, gym, dancing and French are emphasised and taught by specialists.

The latest ISI inspection report delivered a strong endorsement of the school's ethos, staff, curriculum, *modus operandi* and infrastructure by giving the highest possible rating of 'excellent' or 'outstanding' to *every* aspect of the school. The inspectors deemed overall achievement to be excellent and that pupils are very well educated and achieve very high standards in both their learning and personal development. The full report can be found on www.isi.net.

The school holds two open mornings a year, typically in March and September. Prospective parents may also see the school 'in action' by joining one of the regular tours held during school hours. The school's website contains relevant information about life at the school, its curriculum, the destination of its leavers and some useful links.

Heywood Prep

The Priory, Corsham, Wiltshire SN13 0AP
Tel: 01249 713379
Fax: 01249 701757
email: admissions@heywoodprep.com
website: heywoodprep.com

Headmaster: **Guy Barrett**, BSc Hons

Age Range. 2–11 Co-educational.
Number in School. Day: 70 Boys, 70 Girls.
Fees per term (2014–2015). £2,250–£2,580.

Heywood Prep is a friendly community in which happy children discover a love of learning, the confidence to succeed and are supported and challenged to fulfil their academic, creative and sporting potential.

Located on a two-acre site in the heart of the historical market town of Corsham, the school combines the nurturing feel of a village school with the success of a much larger school. Children at Heywood Prep develop enquiring minds while exploring the school's gardens and grounds. Good manners and a caring approach are highly prized and the older children at the school enthusiastically support and engage with the younger members of the school community.

The school is housed in a handsome Georgian manor house, with its own nursery school located in the town's former fire station, on the same site. Children can join the nursery from the age of two. As one of the few truly independent prep schools in the area, Heywood Prep is well placed to assist parents in choosing the right senior school for their child at age 11. Pupils from Heywood Prep have an excellent track record in entrance and scholarship exams and thrive in their senior schools having developed the self-confidence to succeed.

The headmaster, Guy Barrett, who joined Heywood Prep in September 2012, is leading a programme of investment and improvement as the school seeks to build upon the fantastic successes which were highlighted in a recent inspection report. Published in June 2014, the report described Heywood Prep as "a welcoming, friendly and open community. As a result of feeling safe and well looked after, pupils thrive and challenge themselves to reach their full potential."

Mr Barrett is delighted to welcome prospective parents to the school throughout the year.

Highclare School

10 Sutton Road, Erdington, Birmingham B23 6QL
Tel: 0121 373 7400
Fax: 0121 373 7445
email: abbey@highclareschool.co.uk
website: www.highclareschool.co.uk

Founded 1932.

Chair of Governors: Mrs L Flowith

Head: **Dr Richard Luker**, BA, MA, PhD, PGCE

Age Range. 18 months to 18 years Co-educational.
Number of Pupils. 700.
Fees per term (2014–2015). £2,075–£3,750.
Location. The School is situated on three sites on the main road (A5127) between Four Oaks, Sutton Coldfield and Birmingham. The Senior Department (girls and boys in Year 7 from September 2011, becoming fully co-educational in 2015) and co-educational Sixth Form, is on direct train and bus routes from Birmingham City Centre, Tamworth, Lichfield and Walsall as well as being serviced by our own buses. There are two Primary Schools, known as Highclare Woodfield and Highclare St Paul's. Wrap-around care operates from 7.30 am until 6.00 pm for the parents who require it, including holiday cover. The ethos of the school lies in the encouragement of individual excellence for each pupil, outstanding pastoral care and a belief in the education of the 'whole person'.
Organisation. Four departments:
Nursery and Preparatory Department (age 18 months to 7 years, Girls and Boys). The Nursery caters for children from 18 months to 3 years and although an independent unit it has the support of facilities and resources of the Preparatory Department. French is taught from Reception.
Junior Departments (age 7+ to 11 years, Two Co-educational Departments). The Junior Departments, with classes of up to a maximum of 22 pupils, follow National Curriculum guidelines. Pupils also have the benefit of specialist tuition in French, PE and Music. Other foundation subjects are taught by subject and by class teachers. Entry by School's own assessment procedure.
Senior Department (age 11 to 16, Girls and Boys). The full curriculum is covered at KS3. At GCSE all students study English Language and English Literature, Mathematics, Science and Additional Science, with the opportunity to study separate sciences, and a modern foreign language, either French, German or Spanish with a wide choice of options. In addition pupils also study PSHCE and take the ECDL qualification in Information Technology. Physical

Education, Music and Performing Arts also form important parts of the curriculum. Through a wide programme of enrichment activities every child has the opportunity to enjoy activities beyond the academic. Entry by School's own assessment procedure.
Co-educational Sixth Form (age 16+). The Sixth Form is co-educational and accepts external candidates as well as pupils transferring from Highclare Senior School. A wide range of A Level subjects is available for study with excellent pastoral, higher education and careers guidance available. The timetable is structured to meet the individual requirements of each student.

All parts of the School participate in extensive lunchtime and after-school activities.

The School is multi-denominational. Further information may be obtained from the School or the website and prospective parents are always welcome to visit. Open mornings are held throughout the year.

Charitable status. Highclare School is a Registered Charity, number 528940.

Highfield Priory School

Fulwood Row, Fulwood, Preston, Lancashire PR2 5RW
Tel: 01772 709624
email: schooloffice@highfieldpriory.co.uk
website: www.highfieldpriory.co.uk

Headmaster: **Mr J Duke**

Age Range. 6 months–11 years.
Number in School. Day: 130 Boys, 120 Girls.
Fees per term (2014–2015). £2,290.
Highfield is set in 8 acres of landscaped gardens, woodlands and playing fields and is a co-educational preparatory school for children aged 6 months to 11+ years. It is fully equipped with its own established Nursery and prepares children for all Independent, Grammar and Senior Schools in Lancashire, for which it has an excellent academic record.

Class numbers average 20 and children are taught by fully-qualified and experienced staff. Specialist facilities and teachers ensure that children are challenged and fulfilled across the curriculum, most notably in Art and CDT with a new studio in 2005, an ICT suite (since 1994), a Science Laboratory (2006) and, most recently, a Performing Arts Studio in 2013. Children from Nursery through to Year Six are also able to enjoy the school Library, Sports Hall and the school's own nature reserve, Highfield Haven.

The school has strong musical, dramatic and sporting traditions. Every child in the Junior School is given the opportunity to take part in competitive sporting fixtures and to perform in a full-scale dramatic production each year. In addition, Highfield examines the Junior children in the disciplines of Public Speaking, Elocution and Drama twice a year thereby greatly improving the children's eloquence and confidence.

Highfield holds a Step into Quality Award for its Early Years and Foundation Stage and Potential Plus UK's Three Star Gold Membership for its work with Gifted and Talented children. Highfield encourages its pupils to "Aim High" and gives them every opportunity to achieve this.

Highfield offers an extended day from 7.15 am until 6.00 pm. Extra-curricular activities include Ballet, Gardening, Choir, Design, Dance, Judo, Public Speaking, Chess, Spanish, Cookery, Homework Club and Instrument Tuition. The school is well supported by an enthusiastic Parents Association. Prospective parents, and children, are encouraged to visit the school, have a tour with the Headmaster and to experience a school day.

Charitable status. Highfield Priory School is a Registered Charity, number 532262. It exists to provide independent education to all children between the ages of 6 months and 11 years within Preston and surrounding areas for all who wish to participate and to provide access to the community at large to all sporting, musical and artistic provision within the school.

Highfields School

London Road, Newark, Nottinghamshire NG24 3AL
Tel: 01636 704103
Fax: 01636 680919
email: office@highfieldsschool.co.uk
website: www.highfieldsschool.co.uk

Headteacher: **Mrs C L Fraser**, BEd Hons

Age Range. 2–11.
Number in School. Day: 51 Boys, 47 Girls.
Fees per term (2014–2015). £2,720 including lunch. Day Nursery from £16 per half day session.

Highfields School is situated in ten acres of mature parkland and sports field, an enviable setting for children to enjoy their education. It provides a happy, lively, caring community which allows the children to experience a sense of pride and fulfilment that comes from working to their full potential. Basic subjects need to be mastered but children learn to react in different ways and need to be treated as individuals. Personal responsibility, initiative, good manners and smart appearance are encouraged and developed, thereby fulfilling the School's pledge to combine modern methods with traditional values.

Children enter a structured course of Nursery Education in the term in which they reach the age of three. Children enter the Reception Class before their fifth birthday and proceed through the School in year groups. Each class is taught by its own teacher in the basic subjects. The maximum class size is twenty. All members of staff are fully qualified and specialist teachers assist with Art, ICT, Music, PE and Games throughout the School.

The curriculum is balanced and broadly based with the emphasis on English, Mathematics and Science. The full range of National Curriculum subjects is covered in order that the varying interests and skills of the children may be fully developed. Highfields has a fully deserved reputation for the quality of its pastoral care.

All children are encouraged to be creative and exhibit a delight in learning. There are ample opportunities for speech and drama, ballet and music with recorder ensembles, choir and an orchestra. Peripatetic staff offer lessons in trumpet, saxophone, violin, cello, flute and clarinet. The School offers a wide range of extra-curricular activities and sports teams compete against local authority and independent schools. Highfields has fully qualified staff who teach tennis, hockey, cricket, football, rugby and netball. The School holds an Activemark Gold Award. All children have a swimming lesson each week.

Highfields pursues a non-selective admissions policy but has an excellent academic record sending most pupils to local selective independent schools or to Grammar Schools in Lincolnshire through 11+ entry.

The School is administered by a Board of Governors, including parent governors.

Charitable status. Newark Preparatory School Company Limited is a Registered Charity, number 528261. It exists to provide and further the education of children.

Hipperholme Grammar School

Bramley Lane, Hipperholme, Halifax, West Yorkshire HX3 8JE
Tel: 01422 202256
Fax: 01422 204592
email: secretary@hgsf.org.uk
           info@hgsf.org.uk
website: www.hgsf.org.uk
Twitter: @HipperholmeGS

Hipperholme Grammar School Foundation was founded in 1648 by Matthew Broadley, Paymaster General to Charles I (our Alumni are known as Brodleians).

The Foundation provides a small, caring setting in which children are educated to be the very best they can be. Alongside high academic standards, all children are provided with outstanding opportunities for leadership and personal enrichment. A love of learning is developed alongside traditional values of politeness, good manners and strong moral code. The atmosphere that pervades through the School from Nursery to Sixth Form is welcoming yet challenging: all visitors to the School are given a very warm welcome. All students are provided with a range of academic and personal development challenges.

Chairman of Governors: Mr C D Redfearn, BSc, DMS, MBIM

Headmaster: **Mr J D Williams**, BSc, PGCE

Organisation. The Hipperholme Grammar School Foundation is a co-educational day school comprising Junior School for children aged 3–11 years and Senior School for children aged 11–18 years.

The pupil roll stands at around 350 pupils, with 18 in each Form in the Junior School and an average of 20 in each Form group in the Senior School. Our school is small enough to ensure individual attention for all children, yet large enough to provide a full range of subjects to GCSE and A Level. Class sizes at GCSE and A Level vary from 3 to 18 dependent on pupil choice.

Pupil Welfare. A great strength of our School is the strong commitment to provide outstanding pastoral care. Our small teaching groups, individual attention, teachers who genuinely care and excellent relationships with parents enable all children to blossom and fulfil their potential. Where necessary, individual learning programmes are devised and learning support staff ensure children make excellent progress.

Teaching and Learning. Our teachers enjoy teaching: they are enthusiastic, dedicated and exceptionally caring. Our curriculum is broadly in line with the National Curriculum to Year 9, after which students choose from a range of subjects leading to GCSE and later to A Level.

Personal Enrichment. Our Personal Enrichment programme builds self-confident and well-balanced young people with strong leadership skills. A wide range of activities is provided, including sports, music and drama, as well as a varied outdoor education programme and The Duke of Edinburgh's Award scheme.

Admission. Admission to the Junior School is non-selective and places are offered following an interview with the Headteacher and individual classroom-based assessments, if appropriate. Entry to the Senior School at 11+ follows assessment in our Entrance Examination, primary school report and interview with the Headmaster. The Senior School also selects children for their personal qualities and desire to attend the Senior School as well as academic performance. Entry to the Senior School for other year groups depends on availability and assessment during a two-day taster visit.

Fees per term (2014–2015). Junior School: Nursery £19.20 per am/pm session plus £9.30 lunchtime session; Reception to Year 6 £2,882; Senior School £3,915. Fees include lunch at both Schools. Senior School fees for 2015–16 will be reduced by an average of 10%

The Foundation operates a number of schemes which enable parents to spread the cost of School fees throughout the year. Transport, SEN and Individual Music Tuition are charged separately.

Bursaries and Scholarships. A number of Scholarships are awarded for entry at both Year 7 and Year 12 (Lower Sixth) for academic, musical and sporting achievement. Our Junior School children receive a fee reduction on transfer to the Senior School. Bursaries may be available throughout the School to families in financial need.

Charitable status. Hipperholme Grammar School Foundation is a Registered Charity, number 517152. It exists to provide high-quality education for boys and girls aged 3–18 in the local area and to assist those who cannot afford full fees, to finance such education.

Hopelands Preparatory School

38/40 Regent Street, Stonehouse, Gloucestershire GL10 2AD
Tel: 01453 822164
Fax: 01453 827288
email: enquiries@hopelands.org.uk
website: www.hopelands.org.uk

Chairman of Governors: Mr R D James

Head: **Mrs Sheila Bradburn**, BA Hons, PGCE

Age Range. 3–11 Co-educational.
Number of Pupils. 75.
Fees per term (2014–2015). £1,975–£2,490.
Charitable status. Hopelands Preparatory School is a Registered Charity, number 1007707.

Howe Green House School

Great Hallingbury, Bishop's Stortford, Herts CM22 7UF
Tel: 01279 657706
Fax: 01279 501333
email: info@howegreenhouseschool.co.uk
website: www.howegreenhouseschool.co.uk

Headmistress: **Mrs Deborah Mills**, BA Hons, QTS

Age Range. 2–11 years.
Number in School. 158.
Fees per term (2014–2015). Kindergarten £2,364, Infants £2,733, Juniors £3,388.

Howe Green House offers an education of the highest quality in the widest sense. Facilities are excellent being sited in 8 acres of countryside adjacent to Hatfield Forest. It is a single-stream school which works broadly to the National Curriculum, offering additional French, Latin, Music, Drama and Sport. There is a strong parental involvement within the school whereby parents are actively encouraged to be part of their children's education. The school is seen as a community which fosters an understanding of children's development within both school and home. Children sit external examinations to senior schools both boarding and day and have been highly successful.

Entry to the school is mainly via Acorns Nursery but children are considered for entry to the Junior School by assessment and interview.

Charitable status. The Howe Green Educational Trust Ltd is a Registered Charity, number 297106. It exists to promote and provide for the advancement of education for the public benefit and in connection therewith to conduct a day school for the education of boys and girls.

Hulme Hall Grammar School

Hulme Hall Road, Cheadle Hulme, Stockport, Cheshire SK8 6LA
Tel: 0161 485 3524/0161 485 4638
Fax: 0161 485 5966
email: secretary@hulmehallschool.org
website: www.hulmehallschool.org

Headteacher: **Miss Rachael Allen**, BA Hons, MEd, PGCE

Age Range. 2–16 Co-educational.
Number in School. 300.
Fees per term (2014–2015). £1,530–£2,836.
Junior School. We cater for girls and boys from 2 to 11 years in our Nursery, Kindergarten, Infant and Junior classes. At every stage of the learning process, we provide a caring and stimulating environment.

Given excellent resources, small classes and teachers of high calibre, children derive considerable satisfaction from their school work and experience no difficulty in realising their academic potential.

Senior School (11–16 years). The school is well staffed and equipped to deliver a curriculum covering a wide range of academic, creative and practical subjects. An extensive choice of GCSE and other external examination options enables pupils at Key Stage 4 to target optimum qualifications reflecting their personal choice of programme. The staff are consistent in the emphasis they place upon the encouragement of pupils who respond with a highly conscientious approach to their studies, which in turn ensures steady progress and excellent results.

Communication between school and home is given high priority and the regular issue of reports enables parents to monitor closely their child's educational development. At the age of 16, almost all pupils continue with A Level studies.

The school operates a bus service in conjunction with Elite Coaches, offering an extensive network of services covering a 15 mile radius of the school.

For further information please contact the School Secretary.

Charitable status. Hulme Hall Educational Trust is a Registered Charity, number 525931. The school aims to promote personal, moral, social and academic development of all pupils.

Hurst Lodge School

Bagshot Road, Ascot, Berkshire SL5 9JU
Tel: 01344 622154
Fax: 01344 627049
email: admissions@hurstlodgesch.co.uk
website: www.hurstlodge.co.uk

Principal: **Miss V S Smit**, BSc Hons

Age Range. Girls 3–18; Boys 3–11. Weekly Boarding from age 9.
Number in School. Day: 71 Boys, 129 Girls; 17 Weekly Boarders.

Fees per term (2014–2015). Tuition: Years 7–13 £4,725, Years 3–6 £3,700; Foundation–Year 2 £3,020, Kindergarten (5 mornings) £1,421. Weekly Boarding Fee: £2,935.

Hurst Lodge is a small, well-established day and boarding school which successfully combines an academic and creative education. We aspire to help our students realise their potential by encouraging learning for life and celebrating all achievements equally.

Small teaching groups ensure high standards, individual attention and excellent pastoral care.

We have a strong dyslexia department.

Hurst Lodge offers a wide breadth of academic and vocational subjects to GCSE and A Level. We specialise in Art, Textiles, Drama, Music and Dance at all levels but also have excellent academic results.

Students have Form and Personal Tutors to ensure a high level of pastoral care and support.

The Sixth Form is small and offers a full range of A Levels.

Hurtwood House School

Holmbury St Mary, Dorking, Surrey RH5 6NU
Tel: 01483 279000
Fax: 01483 267586
email: info@hurtwood.net
website: www.hurtwoodhouse.com

Headmasters: C M Jackson, BEd; K R B Jackson, MA

Age Range. 16–18.
Number in School. 330 (170 girls, 160 boys).
Fees per term (2014–2015). £12,740–£14,651.

Hurtwood House is the only independent boarding school specialising exclusively in the Sixth Form. It concentrates on the 16–18 age range and offers students a caring, residential structure and a commitment to a complete education where culture, sport, friendship and a full range of extra-curricular activities all play an important part. Hugely successful across the whole range of academic subjects, Hurtwood House is also widely recognised as having the best Creative and Performing Arts and Media departments in the country and is therefore especially attractive to aspiring actors, directors, film directors, dancers, singers, artists and fashion designers.

Many students now want to leave the traditional school system at 16. They are seeking an environment which is structured and safe, but which is less institutional and better equipped to provide the challenge and stimulation which they are now ready for, and which is therefore better placed to develop their potential. They also require teaching methods which will prepare them for an increasingly competitive world by developing their initiative and encouraging them to think for themselves.

Hurtwood House has 330 boys and girls. It is a small and personal school, but it is a large and powerful sixth form which benefits from having specialised A level teachers. The examination results put Hurtwood House in the top independent school league tables, but it is equally important to the school that the students develop energy, motivation and self-confidence.

In short, Hurtwood House is a stepping-stone between school and university for students who are all in the same age group and who share the same maturity and the same ambitions.

The school is situated in its own grounds high up in the Surrey Hills and offers excellent facilities in outstandingly beautiful surroundings.

Ibstock Place School

Clarence Lane, London SW15 5PY
Tel: General Enquiries: 020 8876 9991
            Headmistress's PA: 020 8392 5802
            Bursar's Office: 020 8392 5804
            Registrar: 020 8392 5803
email: office@ibstockplaceschool.co.uk
website: www.ibstockplaceschool.co.uk

Chairman of Governors: Michael Gibbins, LVO, FCA

Headmistress: **Mrs Anna Sylvester-Johnson**, BA Hons, PGCE

Deputy Headmaster: Mr Huw Daniel, BSc Hons London, PGCE
Second Master: Mr Christopher Wolsey, MA Nottingham, MEd Buckingham
Head of Pastoral Care: Dr Trevor Addenbrooke, BEng, AGCI Imperial, MSc, DIC, PhD
Tutor for Admissions: Mr Christopher Banfield, MA Leeds, MSc Open
Heads of Houses:
Mr Andrew Copeman, BA Newcastle, MSc
Mr Charles Janz, MA Oxon
Mr John-Daniel Price, BSc Exeter
Mr Samuel Robinson, BA Sussex
Head of Pre-Prep and Preparatory School: Miss Diana Wynter, BA, CertEd

Age Range. 4–18 Co-educational.
Number in School. 950: 494 Boys, 456 Girls.
Fees per term (2014–2015). £4,570–£5,890 (including lunches).

Ibstock Place School is located in spacious grounds of some eight acres adjacent to Richmond Park and with easy access to Putney, Barnes, Richmond and Hammersmith. The school offers a balanced education combining a traditional academic curriculum with an extensive range of co-curricular opportunities.

This co-educational school has grown and prospered with significant building development in recent years. A new Sports Hall opened in 2008. New School, occupying Clarence Lane and Priory wings and comprising twenty-one classrooms, six laboratories and two computer suites, opened in 2011. Additional facilities include: a new Library accommodated over two floors, a Music Technology studio, AstroTurf and sports pitches on the adjacent Lawrence House campus site, and a swimming pool. Construction work on a new Performing Arts Centre is well under way and will be completed in 2015.

The Preparatory Department and the Senior School remain distinctive and are housed separately, so that each child benefits from a small-school ambience and the younger pupils gain from many of the facilities enjoyed by the Senior School. The Prep School, which incorporates Pre-Prep, provides a rich and stimulating environment, with a wide range of curricular activity carefully planned to realise each child's abilities and talents.

The Senior School, age 11–18, offers a full range of Arts, Humanities, Languages, Science and Technology subjects. All pupils follow a core curriculum which includes a requirement to study two languages at (I)GCSE, along with many opportunities for enrichment. Co-curricular emphasis is placed on Music, Drama and Sports, and recent tours have taken pupils to China, Iceland, India, South Africa and the USA, as well as language visits to European destinations closer to home. There is an outstanding programme of outdoor education, a wide range of after-school clubs, as well as the Duke of Edinburgh's Award Scheme. All pupils are supported by a strong and effective pastoral system which operates through four houses. House Groups are vertically organised and are aspirational as well as companionable.

In 2014, 60% of pupils attained A Level entries at A* or A grades, propelling IPS to 81st position in The Daily Telegraph's independent schools' A Level results ranking. Three pupils took up places at Oxbridge colleges, to read Mathematics, English Literature and Natural Sciences, while another secured a place at the prestigious Johns Hopkins University in the USA. There are now 124 pupils in the Sixth Form. 82% of pupils' entries at (I)GCSE were graded either A* or A. The Daily Telegraph placed IPS 47th out of 366 in its annual ranking of UK independent schools' GCSE performance.

Entry to the Pre-Prep is by date of Registration and for subsequent years by assessment. There is no guaranteed transfer from the Prep School to the Senior School. All candidates for Senior School entry are interviewed and take examinations in Mathematics, English and Reasoning. A satisfactory report from the entrant's current school is also required.

Further information is available from the Registrar and Open Mornings and Evenings are held regularly through the year. Occasional places may arise from time to time (e.g. at 13+).

Charitable status. Ibstock Place School is a Registered Charity, number 1145565.

The Italia Conti Academy of Theatre Arts

Italia Conti House, 23 Goswell Road, London EC1M 7AJ
Tel: 020 7608 0047/8
Fax: 020 7253 1430
email: admin@italiaconti.co.uk
website: www.italiaconti.com

Principal: Mrs A Sheward

Head: **Mrs Karen Dwyer-Burchill**, MA, HDipEd, MEd

Age Range. 10–16.
Number in School. Day: 79.
Fees per term (2014–2015). £4,325.

For over a hundred years the Academy has been preparing young people for successful careers in the performing arts it has been aware that the profession expects excellent standards of education and training of its new entrants. Today's Producers and Directors demand that performers entering the industry be versatile and be able to take direction within the theatre, television or film studio.

The five courses offered by the Academy seek to expose students to a wide range of disciplines and techniques in the Dance, Drama and Singing fields working in the mediums of stage, television and recording studio under the careful tuition of highly qualified professional staff.

The courses are as follows:
The Theatre Arts School. For 10 to 16 year olds providing a balanced traditional academic education leading to nine GCSEs with broadly based vocational training in dance, drama and singing. Sixth Form Studies within the Performing Arts Course allows two A Levels to be studied alongside a full professional dance, drama and singing theatre arts course.

Performing Arts Course. A three-year course for students aged 16+. Accredited by the National Council for Dance Education and Training. Leading to the award of The National Diploma in Musical Theatre or a Foundation Degree in the Performing Arts

One Year Foundation Course. From age 16. Drama & Dance Award Scholarships are available for this Course.

Entry Requirements. Entry for all the above courses is by audition and assessment.

In addition to the above the Academy offers part-time Saturday classes to children aged 3½ to 18 years in Dance, Drama and Singing. Entry is by interview. Also offered is a Summer School, one week Performing Arts or Drama courses for those aged 9 to 19.

Charitable status. The Italia Conti Academy Trust is a Registered Charity, number 290261. It exists to promote education in the Performing Arts through both teaching and the provision of scholarships.

King Alfred School

Manor Wood, 149 North End Road, London NW11 7HY
Tel: 020 8457 5200
Fax: 020 8457 5249
email: admissions@kingalfred.org.uk
website: www.kingalfred.org.uk

Head: **Mrs Dawn Moore**, MA London

Age Range. 4–18.
Number in School. Primary: approx 300; Secondary: approx 320.
Fees per term (2014–2015). Reception, Years 1–2 £4,397, Years 3–6 £5,066, Middle & Upper School £5,301.

King Alfred School is unique among independent schools in North London. Apart from being all-age (4–18), co-ed and secular, it takes in a wide range of ability as opposed to its academically selective neighbours in the private sector.

KAS's beginnings are unusual: it was founded (in 1898) by a group of Hampstead parents and its large governing body comprises only current and ex-parents. Visitors tend to comment on the pretty site (on the edge of Hampstead Garden Suburb), the "village" layout (carefully preserved by a succession of architects), and the friendly atmosphere – this is a no-uniform establishment and all are on first-name terms. The recent purchase of property across the road has enabled the school to extend classroom facilities.

Academic results are consistently impressive and constantly improving and almost 100% of the KAS Sixth Form go on to university or Art Foundation courses or music colleges and conservatoires. The school prides itself on its reputation as a relaxed, informal and vibrant community that achieves academic success within a non-pressured environment.

Bursaries for the Sixth Form and Year 7 are available.
Charitable status. King Alfred School is a Registered Charity, number 312590. It exists to provide quality education for boys and girls.

Kings Monkton School

6 West Grove, Cardiff CF24 3XL
Tel: 029 2048 2854
Fax: 029 2049 0484
email: mail@kingsmonkton.org.uk
website: www.kingsmonkton.org.uk

Principal: **Mr Paul Norton**

Age Range. 2–18.
Number in School. 220.
Fees per term (2014–2015). £2,334–£4,000.

Kings Monkton School is a co-educational day school for children from nursery age right up to university entrance. The school is owned by Heathfield Independent Schools and is renowned for its caring and inclusive ethos.

Kings Monkton is one of South Wales's oldest independent schools, having educated generations of local pupils since its foundation in 1870. The school prides itself on its consistent record of academic success, its system of pastoral care and its relations with parents. Pupils are drawn from a wide catchment area including Cardiff, the Vale of Glamorgan, the Valleys and Monmouth, as well as having a number of CAS Sponsored International Pupils on Tier 4 Visas. The school is housed in purpose-built accommodation in the centre of Cardiff, close to Queen Street station and to all amenities.

Kings Monkton's primary school has small classes in which young children can receive individual care and guidance. Pupils follow a well-balanced curriculum, designed to develop and stimulate young minds to the full. Children are taught both French and Mandarin and have extensive access to sports.

In the secondary school, pupils pursue a wide curriculum with their progress being carefully monitored and receive strong pastoral support throughout their adolescent years. All pupils are encouraged to strive for high standards in their work and to contribute to the well-being of the community to which they belong. Entry to the school is non-selective, with a strict 15 pupils per class to ensure that all achieve their highest potential.

In the school's A Level college, students are taught in small tutorial groups and in addition to their academic studies participate in a number of other activities including Young Enterprise, Welsh Baccalaureate and the Extended Project Qualification as part of the school's philosophy of giving its pupils a thorough preparation for life. The minimum entry requirements to the College are five GCSE passes at grades A–C.

In 2003 the school opened its new purpose-built sixth form centre with upgraded facilities for physics, technology and music.

The school works in partnership with Oxford Royale Academy, Dragon Career Associates and Wonderland Studios, as well as having close links with China and Spain.

Kirkstone House School

Baston, Peterborough, Lincolnshire PE6 9PA
Tel: 01778 560350
Fax: 01778 560547
email: info@kirkstonehouseschool.co.uk
website: www.kirkstonehouseschool.co.uk

Co-Principals: Mrs B K Wyman, Mr E G Wyman, Mr J W R Wyman

Head: **Mrs C Jones**

Age Range. 3–18.
Number in School. 171: 100 boys, 71 girls.
Fees per term (2014–2015). £2,645–£3,304.
Kirkstone House prides itself on being a family run nonselective school where children of all abilities can achieve their full potential in a caring environment. The atmosphere is characterised by its supportive nature and sense of community. Classes are small and pupils and staff know each other well.

There are high aspirations for pupils and the school aims to provide the highest quality of education throughout all years by catering for the full academic range and offering a wide curriculum. Strong emphasis is placed on choice with a wide range of GCSEs and BTEC courses being offered up to the age of 18. There is also a very well established Learning Support Department providing tailored additional assistance including helping pupils to cope with dyslexia.

A wealth of extra-curricular activities are enjoyed by many pupils including The Duke of Edinburgh's Award, a thriving Youth Theatre and a range of sporting pursuits. Additionally, a 60-acre site of woodlands and lakes has specific scientific interest and is used for environmental and land-based study.

Knightsbridge School

67 Pont Street, London SW1X 0BD
Tel: 020 7590 9000
Fax: 020 7589 9055
email: registrar@knightsbridgeschool.com
website: www.knightsbridgeschool.com

Headmaster: **Mr Magoo Giles**

Age Range. 4–13.
Number in School. 390.
Fees per term (2014–2015). £5,408–£5,755.
Knightsbridge School is a preparatory school offering a broad, balanced and challenging curriculum to prepare both boys and girls for entry to senior day and boarding schools.

Pupils are encouraged to play hard, work hard in the Junior School and work hard, play hard in the Senior School, and make the most of every opportunity open to them to achieve their full potential. They are taught all National Curriculum subjects to a high standard, and modern languages from nursery age upwards.

The school fosters a strong sense of community, and provides a supportive and warm environment. Small classes, overseen by highly qualified, dynamic and enthusiastic staff, will ensure that boys and girls benefit not only academically but also personally. By developing their self-esteem and confidence they will grow into happy, independent all-rounders of healthy body and healthy mind.

Located in the heart of Central London, the school is housed in two magnificent mansions. The premises have undergone an extensive renovation and upgrade programme. Teaching facilities include well-equipped and modern classrooms, a new science laboratory, an information and communication technology suite, music rooms, and a performing arts studio and a new library, as well as a fully catered kitchen and dining area.

Sports facilities include a gymnasium on site and the diverse and challenging sports programme makes use of local venues such as Burton's Court, Battersea Park, St Luke's recreational grounds, the Queen Mother Sports Centre and Hyde Park.

Entry to Knightsbridge School is by informal interview of both parents and children at the appropriate level. Prospective boys and girls for Year 1 and above will be expected to spend a day of assessment at the school in their relevant year group, and a report from the Head of the applicant's current school will be required.

Charitable status. Knightsbridge School Education Foundation is a Registered Charity, number 1120970.

The Knoll School

Manor Avenue, Kidderminster, Worcestershire DY11 6EA
Tel: 01562 822622
Fax: 01562 865686
email: info@knollschool.co.uk
           head@knollschool.co.uk
website: www.knollschool.co.uk
Facebook: /KnollSchool

Headmaster: **N J Humphreys**, BEd Hons

Age Range. Co-educational 3 months–11 years.
Number in School. Day: 70 Boys, 55 Girls.
Fees per term (2014–2015). £636–£2,731.

The Knoll School is a small independent school situated on the outskirts of Kidderminster. It was founded in 1917. Children start at The Knoll School in our First Steps Nursery, opened in 2003, which caters for children from 3 months to rising 3 years and is open 50 weeks of the year. Rising 3s move into our Nursery Class in the main school. All our staff in the nursery are NVQ3 or higher qualified and well experienced. The environment at The Knoll is that of a large, caring family. Pastoral care is of utmost importance to us and we employ a full-time Matron.

Pre- and after-school care is available from 7.30 am to 6 pm every day. We operate a very active holiday club during all of the school holidays, and go out regularly on trips.

The school has a busy calendar and has achieved a Gold Sing Up Award – music plays a large part at The Knoll. The children go out of school on a variety of educational outings and we offer a wide range of sporting activities, including swimming, hockey and tennis. The children enter various sporting competitions throughout the year.

We have high expectations of our pupils in all aspects of their education and our Year 6 children's achievements have enabled them to gain places at top independent schools in our area.

We are currently ranked in the top 100 independent schools in the country, being the only one in Worcestershire.

Charitable status. The Knoll School Educational Trust Limited is a Registered Charity, number 527600.

Lady Barn House School

Schools Hill, Cheadle, Cheshire SK8 1JE
Tel: 0161 428 2912
Fax: 0161 428 5798
email: info@ladybarnhouse.stockport.sch.uk
website: www.ladybarnhouse.org
Twitter: @LadyBarnHouse

Headmistress: **Mrs S Marsh**

Age Range. 3–11.
Number in School. Day: 250 Boys, 216 Girls.
Fees per term (2014–2015). Nursery: £2,021 (all day), £1,344 (mornings only); KS1 & KS2 £2,308. Lunches per term £145.

W H Herford, minister and educational pioneer, founded the school in 1873. His vision was to establish a co-educational school that promoted happiness, academia, whilst embracing a Christian ethos. Today, Herford's vision still drives our thriving, family-orientated community. Boys and girls flourish, learning side by side, in an exceptional educational setting.

We combine the latest educational thinking with tried and tested traditional methods. Pupils are gradually nurtured and developed so that they can confidently face their future with knowledge, understanding and the ability to be independent. Music, sport, drama, languages, outdoor adventure and a wide range of other clubs, trips and residential visits enhance our curriculum.

Pupils are prepared and supported for their 11+ entrance exams; they then move on to the best and most appropriate senior schools.

Lady Barn House School is a truly special educational institution where each and every pupil experiences success and reaches their potential. It remains one of the North West's most prestigious independent primary schools.

The School is a Charitable Trust. Bursaries are available at Year 2 and Year 3.

Charitable status. Lady Barn House School Limited is a Registered Charity, number 1042587. It exists to provide education for boys and girls.

Lime House School

Holm Hill, Dalston, Nr Carlisle, Cumbria CA5 7BX
Tel: 01228 710225
Fax: 01228 710508
email: lhsoffice@aol.com
headmaster@limehouseschool.co.uk
website: www.limehouseschool.co.uk

Headmaster: **N A Rice**, MA, BA, CertEd

Age Range. 3+–18+. Boarders from age 9.
Number in School. Day: 28 Boys, 22 Girls; Boarding: 50 Boys, 25 Girls.
Fees per term (2014–2015). Boarding £6,500–£8,000; Day £1,500–£3,300.
Compulsory extras: Activities, Laundry.

Lime House School is a fully independent co-educational boarding and day school for pupils aged 3½ to 18. Our aim is to ensure that each pupil achieves his or her potential both academically and socially, with each child treated individually. Our pupils are cared for in a safe rural environment and every possible attempt is made to ensure that they develop confidence and self-esteem. Boarding is available to all pupils, with the majority being full boarders.

Foreign students whose first language is not English add to the cosmopolitan atmosphere of the school. They are prepared for Cambridge English examinations (KET, PET & IELTS) and follow the same curriculum as all other students.

Games and sport form an important part of school life. All students participate and a wide range of team and individual sports is offered. Most pupils take games to GCSE level, with many continuing to A Level. In 2012 the GCSE pass rate was 100% and at A Level 83% of grades were A* to C.

We would welcome a visit to our school to see it in action. Simply contact the school and we will arrange a time convenient for you.

Lingfield Notre Dame

St Piers Lane, Lingfield, Surrey RH7 6PH
Tel: 01342 832407
email: office@lingfieldnd.co.uk
website: www.lingfieldnd.co.uk
Twitter: @lingfieldnd

Headmaster: **Mr Richard Bool**, BA, MBA

Age Range. 2½–18.
Number in School. 927.
Fees per term (2014–2015). £3,125–£4,050. Nursery according to sessions attended.

Entry. Junior School: Nursery and Reception through registration alone; Year 1 upwards by assessment, subject to vacancies.

Senior School: at 11+ and 13+ by Entrance Examination, interview and report from previous school. At 16+ by 6+ GCSEs at A grade, and interview.

Scholarships. Available to existing students from Y4. To existing and external students at 11+ (Academic, Art, Music and Sporting Scholarships) and at 13+ (Academic, Art, Drama, Music and Sporting Scholarships). Means-tested Bursaries may also be available to Scholars. Scholarships are also available for the Sixth Form.

Curriculum. In the Junior School the usual primary subjects are taught, including French, Dance, Speech and Drama. In the Senior School a wide curriculum of academic and practical subjects is offered to GCSE and A Level. The National Curriculum is incorporated throughout the school.

Reports and Consultations. In the Junior School, written reports are sent home every term. In the Senior School, detailed written reports are sent home once a year and interim report sheets are issued at appropriate stages throughout the year. Parent/Teacher interviews are held annually. Parents are always welcome to discuss progress with the appropriate Head of Year. There is a well developed pastoral system.

Leavers. The majority of pupils in the Junior School progress to the Senior School. Ninety percent of Sixth Form leavers go on to further education courses at University, including Oxbridge, resulting in a wide variety of careers.

Sport. In the Junior School sports include Gym, Golf, Hockey, Cricket, Rugby, Football, Cross Country, Dance, Netball, Karate, Rounders and Short Tennis.

In the Senior School, Tennis, Netball, Trampolining, Rounders, Fitness Suite, Volleyball, Gymnastics, Dance, Basketball, Football, Hockey, Rugby, Squash, Badminton, and Athletics are all played.

Annual Ski Trips are arranged for Senior School pupils.

Extra-Curricular Activities. In the Junior School, there are over 50 extra-curricular clubs available for students before, during and after the School Day. The following are a few of the activities offered: Choir and Orchestra, Language Clubs, Cookery, Sewing, Debating, Technology, Squash, Philosophy, Golf, Karate, Tap Dancing, Computer, Drama, Gardening, Art and Craft, and Eco Club.

In the Senior School an extensive range of activities is offered (in excess of 140 activities and Clubs) including Duke of Edinburgh's Award Scheme, Outward Bound, Drama, Music and Science Clubs, Public Speaking, Chef's Club, Sports fixtures, Choir, Orchestra and Ensembles.

In the Sixth Form a wide programme of activities is arranged such as Salsa Dancing, Ballroom Dancing, Self Defence, Car Maintenance, Orienteering, Cooking, Youth Parliament, Debating, Public Speaking, Critical Thinking, Safe Driving Talks plus an extensive range of outside speakers.

In addition, the School has participated in expeditions to destinations near and far.

Religious Services. Regular school, house, form and year assemblies are held.

Lingfield Notre Dame transferred to a lay management in 1987. It maintains its Christian ethos and welcomes students and staff of all faiths, and of none. Its philosophy is based on a strong belief in the development of the whole person. The school has a tradition of providing a caring, friendly and disciplined environment.

Charitable status. Lingfield Notre Dame is a Registered Charity, number 295598. It exists to provide education.

Loreto Preparatory School

Dunham Road, Altrincham, Cheshire WA14 4GZ
Tel: 0161 928 8310
Fax: 0161 929 5801
email: info.loretoprep@btconnect.com
website: www.loretoprep.org.uk

Headteacher: **Mrs Helen Norwood**, BA Hons, PGCE

Age Range. Girls 3–11.
Number in School. 160 Day Girls.
Fees per term (2014–2015). £1,890.

Loreto Preparatory School, founded in 1909, is a modern, purpose-built school (1971), standing in pleasant grounds

and offering an all-round education by well-qualified staff. Religious education and moral training are central to our teaching, based on Gospel principles. Our recent ISI Inspection stated that the school "maintains its traditional values, yet incorporates some modern thinking in the curriculum".

Music plays an important part in the life of the school. All aspects of class music are taught by a specialist. We have a school orchestra, and private individual lessons are available in most instruments. The children's dramatic ability and interest are developed through class lessons, theatre visits and regular productions. Gymnastics, swimming, netball, badminton and athletics, taught by a PE specialist, are important elements of our physical education programme and the school participates fully in local and national competitions.

Our ICT facilities are excellent and include a computer suite and interactive whiteboards in every class. There is a well-stocked, computerised library, allowing pupils to select, issue and return their own books.

We offer a wide range of extra-curricular activities including Drama, Art Club, Zumbatomic and Street Dance.

Of equal importance is social development and each child is encouraged to reach her full potential and to care for others.

Loreto is a Catholic independent school and is one of many Loreto schools built on the foundations laid by Mary Ward, foundress of the Institute of the Blessed Virgin Mary, according to the vision of St Ignatius of Loyola.

Visits to the school are welcome by appointment. Admission at 3+ is usually by interview and by interview and Entrance Examination for those wishing to join at 7+.

Charitable status. Loreto Preparatory School is a Registered Charity, number 250607.

The Lyceum

6 Paul Street, City of London, London EC2A 4JH
Tel: 020 7247 1588
email: admin@lyceumschool.co.uk
website: www.lyceumschool.co.uk

Headmaster: **Mr Edwin Brown**, BEd Hons, MA

Age Range. 3–11 Co-educational.
Number of Pupils. 111.
Fees per term (2014–2015). £3,000–£4,600.

The Lyceum is a non-selective independent co-educational school conveniently based near Old Street station. At The Lyceum they believe that all children have the potential to achieve and excel. The school provides children with an educational atmosphere and experiences that stimulate, motivate and encourage them to achieve beyond what may be expected.

The Lyceum is a small school with a family atmosphere where children are happy, excited and challenged daily. The children in their care are offered a broad and balanced curriculum with equal emphasis on the arts, physical education, moral and spiritual education as well as academic subjects. They believe that involvement in the arts helps to build confidence and self-esteem, and that a good all-round education leads to high standards.

The Lyceum aims:

- To ensure that each child's talents are discovered and nurtured and they achieve their potential in terms of spiritual awareness, academic achievement and aesthetic appreciation.
- To ensure children go on to a suitable secondary school that matches their academic, emotional and social needs, and where their talents can be nurtured.

- To develop in children the skills which will equip them for the next stage of their lives and to enable them to positively influence their own lives.
- That children and parents look back on their time at The Lyceum as a positive and happy one.
- To ensure all children have access to a broad and balanced curriculum and a range of extra-curricular activities.
- To develop tolerance and understanding towards each other and all members of the wider community.
- To develop curiosity, a drive to learn, confidence, independence and a strong work ethic.
- To develop a positive attitude to behaviour based on traditional manners.
- To develop a responsible and independent attitude towards work and their future roles in society.
- To encourage curiosity and a positive attitude to learning.

The curriculum has a strong emphasis on using local resources, as well as the school's link to a wide range of study centres, experiences of living history and a Year 6 residential visit to a European City, usually Paris or Amsterdam.

Children who attend the Lyceum get to take advantage of their central location including the large range of museums, galleries and concert halls nearby. Children undertake at least one educational visit per half term related to the curriculum. From Year 3 (age 7) upwards children go on residential trips including 'living history' events. In addition to this authors, artists and speakers are invited to speak at the school, to enhance the curriculum.

The Lyceum is part of the Minerva Education group which owns a number of private schools in London, East and South East England. Through Minerva's "Inspiring Learning" programme, we seek to share best practice and ensure the continuing improvement in every child's education.

Lyndhurst School

36 The Avenue, Camberley, Surrey GU15 3NE
Tel: 01276 22895
email: office@lyndhurstschool.co.uk
website: www.lyndhurstschool.co.uk

Headmaster: **Mr Andrew Rudkin**

Deputy Head: Mrs Nicola Price
PA to the Headmaster/School Business Manager: Mrs Lesley McCready

Age Range. 3–11 years.
Number in School. Day: 76 Boys, 64 Girls.
Fees per term (2014–2015). Main School £2,870–£3,865. Little Lyndhurst: £1,540–£3,200 (five full days 8.00 am to 6.00 pm). Fees include tuition, hot lunches, 2 afterschool clubs from a selective list, wrap-around care from 8.00 am to 6.00 pm and all school trips.

We are a small friendly co-educational school with a wonderful family feel. Parents and pupils comment on the 'home from home' atmosphere.

Boys and girls are accepted from the age of 3 years into the happy and friendly Early Years Department, situated in a beautiful house within the school grounds. From here until they leave the school at the age of 11, every care is taken to realise the full potential of each child.

Small class sizes ensure that, whilst teachers really know their pupils and are able to tailor the curriculum to the individual child's needs, pupils are also able to learn from each other in a challenging yet supportive environment. Our experienced staff inspire the children and set high academic standards, we achieve excellent 11+ examination results, including academic scholarships.

We make full use of the excellent local sporting facilities and the Royal Military Academy, Sandhurst. All pupils take weekly swimming lessons and are involved in a wide range of sporting activities.

Music and Drama have a significant presence within the school. We have two choirs and an orchestra, many plays throughout the year and pupils are prepared for the examinations of the Associated Board of Music. We offer an extensive after school activities programme and wrap-around care from 8.00 am to 6.00 pm.

Entry to the school can be at any age if there is a vacancy.

Happiness is the key ingredient and every child at Lyndhurst is given the chance to shine at something, whether academic, music, sport or art.

Lyonsdown School

3 Richmond Road, New Barnet, Hertfordshire EN5 1SA
Tel: 020 8449 0225
Fax: 020 8441 4690
email: enquiries@lyonsdownschool.co.uk
website: www.lyonsdownschool.co.uk

Headmistress: **Mrs Lynn Maggs-Wellings**, BEd

Age Range. Girls 3–11, Boys 3–7.
Number of Pupils. 200.
Fees per term (2014–2015). Pre-Reception: £1,152–£2,090; Reception–Year 2 £2,662; Years 3–6 £2,930.

Lyonsdown School has built on its past inheritance since its foundation in 1906, to embrace the needs of education for children of the 21st Century. Pupils are nurtured by our well-qualified, experienced and caring staff who help them to maximise their potential. The school has a tradition of high academic standards and achievements within a broad curriculum.

The personal development of each child is a high priority. A wide variety of extra-curricular activities allows pupils to extend their experiences and learn new skills.

A balanced academic, physical and cultural education, together with a high level of pastoral care, enables pupils to grow and look forward to being part of the modern world.

Entry into Pre-Reception and Reception is non-selective. Pupils are considered for entry at other ages if places become available.

We aim to allow each child to move easily into the next stage of their education by preparing them for schools which best suit their needs.

Charitable status. Lyonsdown School Trust Ltd is a Registered Charity, number 312591.

Mander Portman Woodward (MPW)
London

90–92 Queen's Gate, London SW7 5AB
Tel: 020 7835 1355
Fax: 020 7259 2705
email: london@mpw.co.uk
website: www.mpw.co.uk

Principal: **Steven Boyes**, BA, MSc, PGCE

Age Range. 14–19.
Number in School. Day: 289 Boys, 253 Girls.
Fees per term (2014–2015). £7,991–£8,391.

Mander Portman Woodward (MPW) is a co-educational London day school accepting pupils from the first year of

GCSE onwards. Approximately 150 new pupils join each year at the start of the sixth form. We offer a very wide range of subjects (42 at A Level and 26 at GCSE) and there are no restrictions on subject combinations at A Level. At all levels the absolute maximum number of pupils in any one class is eight.

The school has completely refurbished its Queen's Gate premises with modern facilities tastefully blended in with the traditional architecture of the buildings. There are five well equipped laboratories for Science subjects and specialist studios for Art, Ceramics, Photography, Media Studies and Drama. The school also has extensive facilities for independent study, including two supervised reading rooms and an internet library.

There is a range of compulsory extra-curricular activities for GCSE pupils, including sport, and a variety of voluntary extra-curricular activities is offered at A Level. In keeping with our founding principles, our primary focus at all age levels is on academic goals. Entry into the sixth form is dependent on a student's academic record and performance at interview. Almost all pupils proceed to university after leaving, with about 10 each year going to read Medicine. Over the past four years an average of 7 of our full-time pupils each year have won places at the Universities of Oxford or Cambridge.

We insist on strict punctuality in the attendance of lessons and the submission of homework and there is a formal system of monthly examinations in each subject throughout a pupil's career at the school. This system is designed to ensure that sensible, cumulative revision becomes a study habit not only at school but also later on at university. We require pupils to have a strong commitment to academic discipline but our reputation is based on having created a framework in which pupils can enjoy working hard. The environment is friendly, the teachers experienced and enthusiastic and the atmosphere positive and conducive to success.

Manor House School

South Street, Ashby-de-la-Zouch, Leics LE65 1BR
Tel: 01530 412932
Fax: 01530 417435
email: enquiries@manorhouseashby.co.uk
website: www.manorhouseashby.co.uk

Headteacher: **Mrs E A Scrine**, MEd, BA Hons, PGCE

Age Range. 4–16 Co-educational.
Number of Pupils. 114 Day Pupils: 52 Boys, 62 Girls.
Fees per term (2014–2015). £2,023–£2,942, including meals.

Manor House is an independent co-educational school for children ranging in age from 4 to 16. It is situated in a magnificent setting between the impressive ruins of Ashby Castle and the ancient Parish Church, and is within easy reach of Derby, Leicester, Birmingham and Nottingham.

The school caters for mixed ability children with a maximum class size of twenty and one class per year group.

From the age of 8 children have access to the school's fully-equipped Science Laboratory, Computer Suite, Art Room, and two libraries. Children are taught French from the age of 4 and German from the age of 11. A wide range of extra-curricular activities is also on offer, as well as a Breakfast Club and an After-School Club.

The school has a wide reputation for both its academic achievements and its genuinely friendly and happy atmosphere. We deliver a curriculum that stimulates and challenges children to produce their best. We also provide an environment where children can develop self-discipline, responsibility, and self-motivation with a respect for others.

The main aim is to unlock the potential of all pupils, whatever their aptitude or ability.

Maple Hayes Hall School for Dyslexics

Abnalls Lane, Lichfield, Staffordshire WS13 8BL
Tel: 01543 264387
Fax: 01543 262022
email: office@dyslexia.gb.com
website: www.dyslexia.gb.com

Principal: **Dr E N Brown**, PhD, MSc, BA, MSCME, MINS, AFBPsS, CPsychol

Headmaster: Dr D J Brown, DPhil, MEd Psychology of SpLD, MA Oxon, PGCE

Age Range. 7–17.
Number in School. 120 Day Boys and Girls.
Fees per term (2014–2015). £4,635–£6,200.

Maple Hayes is a specialist independent day school approved under the 1996 Education Act as a co-educational school for children of average to very high intelligence who are not achieving their intellectual potential by normal teaching methods.

This school is under the direction of Dr E Neville Brown whose work in the field of learning strategies has achieved international recognition and includes a major breakthrough in the teaching of dyslexic children. Attention is paid to the individual child by teaching the basic literacy and numeracy skills required for the child to benefit from a full curriculum (with the exception of a foreign language). The school had an excellent Ofsted report.

The very favourable teacher-pupil ratio of 1:10 or better ensures a high standard of educational and pastoral care. The children's learning is under the supervision and guidance of a qualified educational psychologist.

Maple Walk School

62A Crownhill Road, London NW10 4EB
Tel: 020 8963 3890
             020 8965 7374 (Admissions)
email: admin@maplewalkschool.co.uk
website: www.maplewalkschool.co.uk

Head Teacher: **Mrs Sarah Gillam**

Age Range. 4–11 Co-educational.
Number of Pupils. 200.

Maple Walk is a happy, thriving and vibrant independent primary school, for girls and boys aged 4–11, in North West London.

We provide a secure and supportive environment for effective learning and personal development. High standards are pursued in all subjects including English and Maths using traditional teaching methods, alongside an innovative curriculum.

We have a friendly, well-resourced, purpose-built environment with small class sizes, in which children learn and flourish.

Opportunities outside the classroom abound. Through sporting activities, first class music, art and drama, we encourage every child to find their own particular strength.

Termly school trips and residential experiences in Years 5 and 6 extend the curriculum and develop social skills.

Year 6 leavers have been offered places at a range of independent and maintained schools, including Godolphin and Latymer, Christ's Hospital, John Lyon, Frances Holland, Slough Grammar, Notting Hill & Ealing High School, Latymer Upper, Henrietta Barnett and Highgate, to name just a few.

Founded in 2004, Maple Walk was the first of the New Model School Company's schools, offering a low-fee model, based on traditional teaching methods and with a Christian ethos.

Entry into Reception is non selective and based on the date the completed registration form is returned to our Registrar, with siblings given priority. Entry higher up the school is by interview and informal assessment in the classroom. We offer regular open days and welcome private tours.

Fees per term (2014–2015). £2,590.

Mark College

Mark, Highbridge, Somerset TA9 4NP
Tel: 01278 641632
Fax: 01278 641426
email: markcollege@priorygroup.com
website: www.priorygroup.com

Principal: Mr Chris Sweeney

Head Teacher: Robert Helliar-Moore

Age Range. 9–19.
Number in School. Boarding: 38 Boys, 5 Girls; Day: 29 Boys, 3 Girls.
Fees per term (2014–2015). Full Boarding from £9,179; Weekly Boarding from £8,831; Day from £6,496.

Mark College is a Department for Education and CReSTeD approved school for boys and girls with specific learning difficulties including dyslexia, dyspraxia, dyscalculia, and language disorders. The College offers a full curriculum with specialist help so that boys and girls enter for 6 to 8 GCSEs, BTECs or other examinations in Year 11. The Sixth Form allows pupils to gain further independence skills whilst studying for a range of qualifications including A Levels and ASDAN (CoPE).

Accommodation, including a full-sized sports hall, is of a high standard. The College is well resourced and the atmosphere is relaxed and purposeful.

The College's provision for mathematics is recognised internationally, and its English provision involves the use of the latest work in information technology.

After a very good Ofsted report, the College received a commendation and was listed in the HMCI Annual Report, described as a "significant achievement" by the Secretary of State. Mark College is a Beacon school. It received the ISA "Award for Excellence" in May 2000. In 2003 the College was awarded a Sportsmark with Distinction. The 2011 Ofsted Education inspection report commented on the high standard of education, the outstanding sports provision and the high quality of personal care afforded to the students by the staff. The Ofsted Social Care inspection in 2012 gave the overall judgement of "good".

Mayville High School

35 St Simon's Road, Southsea, Hants PO5 2PE
Tel: 023 9273 4847
Fax: 023 9229 3649
email: enquiries@mayvillehighschool.net
website: www.mayvillehighschool.com

Mayville High School – Excellence through nurture

Headteacher: Mrs R H K Parkyn, MA Oxon, MA, PGCE, MCIL

Age Range. 2+ to 16 years.
Number in School. Day Pupils: 246 Boys, 215 Girls.
Fees per term (2014–2015). £2,200–£3,230.

Mayville High School can offer your child a place from the age of 2+ to 16 years. Our close-knit community is divided into the Early Years, Pre-Prep, Junior and Senior Schools. We have a renowned Dyslexia Unit, recognised by CReSTeD, and offer a Gifted and Talented Programme. Our pupils star in numerous ways, and the Mayville family includes pupils, teachers, parents, carers and grandparents.

Mayville, a co-educational day school in Southsea, Hampshire was founded in 1897. There is a strong emphasis on traditional skills, yet Mayville adopts innovative teaching methods to help promote your child's learning. Our size is our strength, big enough to offer pupils a wide range of opportunities, we are small enough to truly treat and know each pupil as an individual.

Mayville provides a learning environment where your child is able to achieve their goals. At Mayville we want children to feel secure and valued: this enables them to take advantage of every opportunity, whether it is academic, social, physical, creative or spiritual.

Mayville sets high standards in all areas. Small class sizes encourage academic success. Boys and girls are taught separately throughout, to best meet their individual learning styles. Over the years Mayville pupils have consistently achieved high standards in GCSE examinations. Flexible teaching, varied resources, support and extension programmes coupled with high expectations help to meet the needs of each individual learner. Art, drama, dance, music and sport play an important part in school life, the latter now enhanced by new playing fields. There are a number of clubs and after-school activities. There is something available to interest everyone.

Early Years (2+ to 5+ years). Our Early Years at Mayville encompass the statutory curriculum of the Foundation Stage; the youngest children are the 2+ year olds (Swans) who are situated in the "Cottage". In the September following their 3rd birthday the Swans graduate to the Kestrels where they complete the second year of their Foundation Stage. Our aim is to ensure that all children feel cherished and secure in a "home-from-home" environment. Our Swan and Kestrels areas have also been awarded the much coveted Flying High for Early Years Accreditation that stamps a seal of excellence on the care we provide.

When you leave your young child for the first time you want them to be cared for as they would at home. In our cosy bright buildings with their own safety surface playgrounds, children are nurtured by qualified Early Years staff. Children sit down together at lunchtime and enjoy freshly cooked nutritious meals. Close proximity to the seafront and local amenities means children are regularly taken out for trips. Our Swan and Kestrel classes are open 50 weeks of the year, 8 am to 6 pm.

For their third and final year of the Foundation Stage the children move into the Reception Class (Lower I) this class provides an early start to literacy and numeracy, and a wide range of activities designed to help them become active independent learners.

Pre-Prep Dept (6–7 years) Key Stage One. The Pre-Prep Department includes Upper I and Lower II. In these classes the curriculum widens to include science, geography, history and ICT as separate subjects. Upper I staff work closely with Lower I in order to affect a smooth transition from the Foundation stage to Key Stage One, while Lower II work closely with the Junior school in order to prepare children for Key Stage Two. All pupils in the Foundation Stage and Pre-Prep benefit from use of the the school's halls for drama, dance and PE. French and Music are taught throughout the Foundation Stage and Pre-Prep Departments.

Junior and Senior Schools. The Junior School accepts boys and girls from the age of 7+. We offer bright airy surroundings, a caring yet disciplined environment and small class sizes. While a strong emphasis is placed on the traditional skills of reading writing and numeracy, children in the Junior School enjoy a varied curriculum. Pupils are taught to appreciate that education is as much about attitudes and values, as it is about academic and sporting success. In the senior school this ethos continues, and pupils are given a wide range of opportunities to excel in: academic, creative, sporting and social settings. Pupils at KS3 follow a full curriculum. This includes thinking skills and first aid, and study skills seminars. It is Mayville's policy to enter all pupils for their GCSE providing they have completed the course of study and any coursework. Therefore our results, which have been well above the national average for the past ten years, are a true reflection of the efforts of pupils and staff.

At Mayville we believe that confidence is the central building block to success in future life. Our commitment to Global Rock Challenge and membership of our own St John Ambulance cadet unit, allows pupils to develop teamwork and leadership skills. At Mayville we celebrate the many successes of our pupils and encourage their competitive spirit. With three houses, there are a number of inter-house competitions which also promote this. Trips to local, national and international locations are encouraged to broaden the experiences begun in the classroom.

Transport. There are good public transport links into the city from the surrounding areas. School minibuses pick up pupils from the local ferry terminals and train stations.

If you would like a prospectus, to book a tour of the school with the Head teacher, Mr Castle, or to find out about our taster days and entrance procedures, please telephone the school or visit our website. Scholarships are available from Year 2.

Charitable status. Mayville High School is a Registered Charity, number 286347. It exists to provide a traditional education to children from a wide range of academic backgrounds within a caring environment.

Mead School

16 Frant Road, Tunbridge Wells, Kent TN2 5SN
Tel: 01892 525837
email: office@themeadschool.co.uk
website: www.meadschool.info

Headmistress: **Mrs A Culley**

Age Range. 3–11.
Number in School. 190.
Fees per term (2014–2015). Kindergarten £1,625; Infants £2,990; Juniors £3,315.

The Mead is an independent, co-educational preparatory school situated in the centre of Tunbridge Wells. We prepare children for both Kent Selection into Grammar School and for Common Entrance to a wide range of Independent Schools at 11+.

We aim to create a happy, secure and enthusiastic atmosphere in which every individual can develop his or her all round potential and thereby become well motivated, interesting and hard working members of society.

Academic standards are high and based on National Curriculum requirements. Strong emphasis is placed on individual attention and close cooperation between school and parents is encouraged.

We offer a broad range of extra-curricular activities including sport, drama, music, dance, judo, swimming.

A copy of our Prospectus and outstanding recent ISI report are available on request.

The Moat School

Bishop's Avenue, Fulham, London SW6 6EG
Tel: 020 7610 9018
email: office@moatschool.org.uk
website: www.moatschool.org.uk

Chair of Governors: Simon Goldhill

Headmistress: **Clare King**, EMBA, BA Hons, PGCE, Cert SpLD

Co-educational Day School.
Age Range. 11–16.
Number of Pupils. 58 Boys, 14 Girls.
Fees per term (2014–2015). £8,783.

Set within the historic conservation area of Fulham Palace, The Moat School is a specialist school for secondary-age SpLD pupils. Mainstream in structure and specialist in nature, The Moat caters successfully for the needs of pupils with specific learning difficulties. Alongside the curriculum, the school also offers expertise in speech and language therapy, occupational therapy and a school counsellor.

All teachers complete a post-graduate BDA approved course in teaching students with SpLD within their first 2 years of appointment. Qualified Learning Support Assistants accompany pupils throughout their lessons at Key Stage 3, where class sizes are a maximum of 10. Class sizes are even smaller at Key Stage 4.

Multi-sensory teaching is combined with advanced IT provision, each pupil being provided with a laptop computer for use in school and at home. Touch-typing is taught in Year 7 and there is a state-of-the-art wireless network which enables staff and pupils to access the school intranet with its wide range of learning resources and data, as well as the internet.

At Key Stage 3, pupils follow a mainstream curriculum (with the exception of foreign languages) before selecting their GCSE options alongside the core subjects of English, Mathematics and Single or Dual Award Science. The Moat offers excellent facilities for learning, with a suite of Design Technology workshops offering state-of-the-art facilities for Food Technology, Resistant Materials and Graphics. Art, Music, Drama, ICT and Business Studies each have dedicated studios or specialist classrooms.

The Moat has an extensive enrichment programme of extra-curricular activities designed to widen experience and develop self-confidence. In Drama, all Year 9 pupils take part in an annual Shakespeare play and there are several productions and workshop performances each year. The Moat's proximity to the River Thames enables pupils to experience rowing as a sport, swimming is popular and 2012 saw the introduction of Martial Arts and boxing. The Duke of Edinburgh's Award encourages pupils to test their own limits and each summer pupils in Years 7, 8 and 9 make a residential visit to an outdoor activity centre to develop independence and leadership skills.

Charitable status. The Constable Educational Trust is a Registered Charity, number 1068445. It exists to establish and support The Moat School so that it can provide education and opportunity for SpLD learners (dyslexic & dyspraxic).

Moffats School

Kinlet Hall, Bewdley, Worcs DY12 3AY
Tel: 01299 841230
Fax: 01299 841444
email: office@moffats.co.uk
website: www.moffats.co.uk

Head: **Mrs Robin McCarthy**, MA Oxon

Age Range. 3–13+.
Number of Children. 67.
Fees per term (2014–2015). Boarding £5,700, Day £2,160–£3,320.

Moffats is a co-educational boarding and day school in a Grade 1 historic house set in its own hundred acres of park and farmland, a glorious environment a mile from any public road. There are equal numbers of boys and girls who share the same opportunities and responsibilities in all activities. We are proud of our record since 1934, but this is not limited to academic awards or A grades in the Common Entrance Examination. Our joy and satisfaction is in bringing out the best in every child. Their achievements in music, speech and drama are outstanding. All usual games are coached daily, including athletics and cross-country running, and, with our own stables, riding is professionally taught. Weekends and spare time are filled with a multitude of activities and the annual sailing camp takes older pupils to Cornwall. Moffats is a truly family school; the personal touch of members of the same family which founded Moffats ensures the well-being and happiness of all the children in their care.

Moon Hall School for Dyslexic Children

Pasturewood Road, Holmbury St Mary, Dorking, Surrey RH5 6LQ
Tel: 01306 731464
Fax: 01306 731504
email: enquiries@moonhallschool.co.uk
website: www.moonhallschool.co.uk

Chairman of Governors: Mr David Baker

Headmistress: **Mrs Pamela Loré**, BA Hons Psych, MA Ed, DipSpLD

Age Range. 7–13.
Number of Children. Approximately 60.
Fees per term (2014–2015). Day Pupils £5,995–£6,180; Boarding Pupils £8,010–£8,195

Religious denomination: Church of England.
Moon Hall School, Holmbury St Mary caters for boys and girls with SpLD. Accredited by CReSTeD (SP), it has a unique relationship with Belmont Preparatory School (*see separate entry*), sharing its site and excellent facilities. Uniform is common to both schools, and pupils are fully integrated at assembly, lunch and break. They also join together for sport/teams and in dramatic and musical productions. Moon Hall pupils may transfer to Belmont classes when ready, usually into Year 7.

MHS's specialist qualified, multi-disciplinary staff deliver a full curriculum to dyslexic children from Year 3. All are taught to touch-type and are successfully entered for OCR examinations normally taken by those aged 16+. Within the well-designed, purpose-built accommodation, classes contain a maximum of 14 children, subdivided for English and Mathematics. One-to-one tuition is available as needed. Literacy and numeracy teaching is structured and multi-sensory, incorporating material devised by acknowledged experts in the field. The Phono-Graphix Programme is employed at all levels. Study/Thinking Skills are an integral part of our teaching. Great emphasis is placed upon re-building self-esteem.

Entry requirements: A full report by an independent Educational Psychologist showing the child to be dyslexic and of at least average intelligence. Assessment and interview at MHS.

After Year 6 children may transfer to a number of suitable mainstream senior schools, or continue their education at Moon Hall College, our own Senior School located in Leigh, near Reigate.

Charitable status. Moon Hall School is a Registered Charity, number 803481.

Moorland School

Ribblesdale Avenue, Clitheroe, Lancashire BB7 2JA
Tel: 01200 423833
Fax: 01200 429339
email: enquiries@moorlandschool.co.uk
website: www.moorlandschool.co.uk
Twitter: @MoorlandSchool1
Facebook: /Moorland-Private-School

Headteacher: **Mr Jonathan Harrison**, BA Hons, PGCE

Age Range. 3 months – 18 years.
Number of Pupils. 165 including 51 boarders.
Fees per term (2014–2015). Day (Reception–Year 13): £1,950–£3,000 (inc Lunch); Full Boarding: £6,000–£7,250; Weekly Boarding: £4,775–£6,500.

Moorland School is a thriving co-educational day and boarding school located in the historic town of Clitheroe within the picturesque Ribble Valley, in the North-West of England. The school enjoys excellent transport links to Manchester. We have an outstandingly beautiful site with more than 15 acres of grounds. Around one third of children at Moorland are boarders and we find it makes for a good social mix with our day pupils from the surrounding area. The opening of our purpose-built new building means our boarders can enjoy modern and spacious facilities, fully equipped with satellite television and Wi-Fi. Moorland can now offer the seamless transition from GCSE to A Level study, through our thriving new Sixth Form Centre, which provides our students with the opportunity to settle in one place rather than having to move from school to school. Furthermore, the School boasts an outstanding elite football, elite ballet and elite music curriculum, unique to any British boarding school. These courses are led by field professionals in their respective areas.

Admission to Moorland. Parents and children are encouraged to visit the school to meet the Principal and see the school in action. Boarding or Day children are also welcome to attend Moorland for a one or two day 'taster visit'.

Kindergarten & Nursery. As well as having its own indoor soft-play area, the nursery also has a large outdoor play area within its extensive grounds, with unbroken views over Waddington Fell. The Nursery's superb layout of colourful rooms and equipment make it an ideal and exceptional learning environment.

Junior School. The Preparatory Department takes children between the ages of 4 and 11. The children have their own play area and IT suite and benefit from using the facilities of the Senior School such as science laboratories and sports hall.

The children follow Key Stages 1 and 2 of the National Curriculum with particular emphasis on numeracy and literacy. Our small class sizes allow every child to read to the

Teacher on a daily basis. French is also included in the Junior curriculum.

The Senior School follows the criteria set down in the National Curriculum. We enter our pupils for the Standard Attainment Tests and for GCSE at the end of Key stage 4.

Football at Moorland. Our FA approved coach, Charles Jackson, is one of the UK's most innovative and well-respected football coaches. He teaches to a Premier League standard. He has worked at Moorland since November 2002. He also worked at the Manchester United Advanced Coaching Centre up to July 2005 and is now the Under 14 academy technical skills Development Coach at Manchester City FC. He spends 4 days per week at Moorland School teaching children from age 4–18.

Pastoral Care. At Moorland children benefit from continuous pastoral support within a friendly family environment. By day, teaching staff provide continual support within small classes. Evening and weekend care is undertaken by the teaching staff and House Parent team.

More House School

Frensham, Farnham, Surrey GU10 3AP
Tel: 01252 792303
           Admissions: 01252 797600
Fax: 01252 797601
email: schooloffice@morehouseschool.co.uk
website: www.morehouseschool.co.uk
Twitter: @MHSFrensham
Facebook: /morehouseschoolfrensham

Headmaster: **B Huggett**, BA Hons, QTS, FSB

Age Range. 8 to 18.
Number in School. 447: 100 Boarders, 347 Day Boys.
Fees per term (2014–2015). Full Boarding £6,885–£8,718; Weekly Boarding £6,232–£8,050; Day £3,998–£5,602

More House School occupies a unique position in helping boys with specific learning difficulties in that multi-sensory remediation is applied across the curriculum, through carefully targeted and maintained intervention, and extra help is available in our Learning Development Centre, so that proper support is always available and individual needs met.

It is approved by the Department for Education and has been listed by CReSTeD in their Specialist Schools category. No school can help every child, so we have a very careful selection assessment to ensure that we really can help those who finally enter the school.

Founded 75 years ago, the school is a centre of excellence and prides itself in using the best modern practice to increase confidence and make children feel valued, happy and to fulfil their potential at GCSE, AS, A Level and other public examinations.

Boarding is run by caring staff and is situated in beautiful grounds with ample opportunities for outdoor pursuits. Our activities programme, which offers 18 options each day, encourages all day boys and boarders to make good use of their leisure time. There is a strong sense of community.

There is an ongoing building programme and the facilities are very good in all departments.

The 2013 full Ofsted inspection described More House as offering "an outstanding curriculum, which is highly tailored to meet the needs of each boy". The 2014 Ofsted Welfare inspection concluded that "the residential provision is outstanding and and contributes remarkably effectively to the personal, social and educational development of each boarder.

We have a comprehensive information pack, and always welcome visitors. Please do call us.

Charitable status. More House School is a Registered Charity, number 311872. A Catholic foundation, open to all denominations, helping boys to succeed.

Moyles Court School

Moyles Court, Ringwood, Hampshire BH24 3NF
Tel: 01425 472856/473197
Fax: 01425 474715
email: info@moylescourt.co.uk
website: www.moylescourt.co.uk

Headmaster: **Mr Richard Milner-Smith**

Age Range. 2½–16.
Number in School. Boarders: 20 boys, 16 girls. Day: 62 boys, 56 girls.
Fees per term (2014–2015). Boarders: £6,370–£7,932; Senior Day: £4,220–£4,352; Junior Day £2,029*–£4,305; Nursery: £5.50 per hour (Early Years Pathfinder Scheme Funding available*).

Moyles Court is a small and successful co-educational boarding and day school for children from 2½ to 16 years. A strong pastoral ethos with traditional family values supports a broad and balanced curriculum. Academic achievement is very good.

The school is administered by a Board of Governors and is registered as an Educational Charitable Trust. The trust has passed the Charity Commission Public Benefit Test.

The school is situated two miles north east of Ringwood in beautiful grounds on the edge of the New Forest, surrounded by heath, woodlands and streams. The fourteen acres provide ideal playing areas for the children and they use these extensively in their free time.

At Moyles Court, we aim to enthuse and encourage children of all academic abilities to maximise their potential in preparation for the challenging and competitive world, which lies outside the security of home and school. Education means development of the 'whole' person and this is the aim at Moyles Court.

It is the school's policy to follow the National Curriculum, within which a comprehensive range of GCSE subjects are offered. The National Curriculum is enriched in the Junior School by the International Primary Curriculum.

Moyles Court has a thriving sporting and outdoor education programme. An extensive selection of extra-curricular activities is available throughout the year including the Duke of Edinburgh's Award Scheme.

Discounts apply for Service families. Sibling discounts, Scholarships and Bursaries are available. Admission is through personal interview with the Headmaster, report from previous school and a taster day at Moyles Court, during which Literacy and Numeracy assessments are conducted.

For further details visit the website at www. moylescourt.co.uk or contact Chris Young, Admissions Secretary. A warm welcome awaits you.

Charitable status. Moyles Court School is a Registered Charity, number 307347.

New Eccles Hall School

Quidenham, Nr Norwich, Norfolk NR16 2NZ
Tel: 01953 887217
Fax: 01953 887397
email: admin@neweccleshall.com
website: www.neweccleshall.com

Headmaster: **R W Allard**, Cert Ed

Age Range. 5–18.
Number in School. 38 Boarders, 80 Day.
Fees per term (2014–2015). Day £2,315–£3,790, Boarding £5,580–£6,595.
The school offers:

- Excellent standard of teaching in small classes.
- Curriculum that covers the national requirements and more.
- Caring for the pupil as an individual is at the centre of the school's ethos.
- Large country estate providing a perfect learning environment.
- Exceptional games facilities combined with an extensive leisure programme.
- Successful Individual Teaching Unit for Specific Learning Difficulties.
- Happy relaxed atmosphere for teaching and learning.
- Attractive and comfortable boarding accommodation.
- Learning respect for each other considered essential.
- Length of the day suits working families.

Visitors to the school are welcome when the school is in session.

Norfolk House School

4 Norfolk Road, Edgbaston, Birmingham B15 3PS
Tel: 0121 454 7021
Fax: 0121 455 7657
email: info@norfolkhouseschool.co.uk
website: www.norfolkhouseschool.co.uk

Headmistress: **Mrs Sarah L Morris**, BA Hons, PGCE

Age Range. 3–11.
Number in School. 150.
Fees per term (from April 2014). £2,110–£2,747 (including Prompt Payment Discount).

Norfolk House School is a Christian Independent day school situated in the pleasant suburb of Edgbaston and is ideally located for pupils and parents all over Birmingham and the surrounding areas.

The school aims to provide individual attention to each pupil, thus enabling each child to fulfil his or her potential. Small class sizes and favourable pupil : teacher ratios culminate in the best possible academic results. Many pupils move on to the various King Edward Schools, or to other Grammar Schools or senior Independent Schools as the direct result of the high standards achieved at Norfolk House.

The syllabus is designed to give each child a general academic education over a wide range of subjects – in line with the National Curriculum; the requirements of the Eleven Plus and the various Entrance Examinations are also taken into consideration.

In addition to education, Norfolk House School aims to instil in each child good manners, consideration and respect for others, and recognition of personal responsibility. Norfolk House is a small school with an emphasis on caring and traditional values, yet forward thinking in outlook. It is a happy school with high attainment, competitive fees and a family atmosphere.

Normanhurst School

68–74 Station Road, North Chingford, London E4 7BA
Tel: 020 8529 4307
Fax: 020 8524 7737
email: info@normanhurstschool.co.uk
website: www.normanhurstschool.co.uk

Headmistress: **Mrs Claire Osborn**, BA Hons, MSc, PGCE

Age Range. 2½–16.
Number in School. 245 Day Pupils.
Fees per term (2014–2015). £1,125–£4,055.

Normanhurst School is a thriving, caring, local independent school with a warm, friendly atmosphere and a wide range of activities offered. The School boasts a high standard of academic achievement with excellent SATs and GCSE results.

We encourage our pupils to develop self-confidence and to take on roles of responsibility as they move up through the school. Creativity is nurtured within a disciplined environment and traditional values such as self-discipline are promoted to maximise our pupils' effectiveness in an ever-changing world.

The School offers small class sizes and a wide range of core and optional subjects up to GCSE, including English, Science, Maths, French, Spanish, Design Technology, Art, History, Geography, ICT, Business Studies, PE, Sport, Music and Drama.

Numerous clubs are provided to strengthen the important social aspect of schooling. These include Football, Netball, Gymnastics, Chess, French, Cross-country, Dance, and ICT. Homework club and Teatime club are available to all pupils, while tuition on various musical instruments takes place either as an extra-curricular activity during the day or after school.

The School is located in the centre of a tree-lined suburban street with good parking, two minutes from a mainline British Rail station and well-connected bus station.

Entry requirements: Interview and assessment.

Northease Manor School

Rodmell, Lewes, East Sussex BN7 3EY
Tel: 01273 472915
Fax: 01273 472202
email: office@northease.co.uk
           pa2headteacher@northease.co.uk
website: www.northease.co.uk

Chairman of Governors: David Boys

Head: **Mrs C Harvey-Browne**, BA, PGCE

Type of School. Co-educational day and weekly boarding school.
Age Range. 10–17.
Number of Pupils. 96: 13 Girls, 83 Boys.
Fees per term (2014–2015). Day £6,784, Boarding £9,232.

Northease Manor School is a co-educational special school for pupils, aged ten to seventeen, who have specific learning difficulties. It caters for both weekly boarders and day pupils. It is approved by the Department for Education and is accredited by CReSTeD. It is set in the South Downs with Grade II listed buildings.

It provides a holistic approach to Specific Learning Difficulties within small teaching groups and provides on-site access to Speech and Language Therapy and Occupational

Therapy. Most of the staff have specialist qualifications and benefit from in-house training.

Northease caters for potentially able pupils who have not realised their true potential at previous schools due to their Specific Learning Difficulties which normally results in a deficit in literacy skills but sometimes in numeracy skills as well. They receive full access to the National Curriculum and benefit from an intensive multi-sensory input which provides for all their literacy and language needs. Detailed pastoral support is given to enable pupils to feel secure and become independent learners. Everything that happens at the school is geared to the needs of the child and to ensure that each pupil experiences success in order to raise self-esteem and self-confidence.

The most recent Ofsted report (2011) says 'the quality of education is good and, as a result of the good teaching, pupils make good progress in their learning'. This is also evident in the value added that students achieve in their GCSE results.

A CReSTeD Inspection concluded that "the school has a clear and focused objective to remain one of the best schools in its field".

The ethos of the school is based upon respect for the individual and the celebration of success and achievement. All pupils have abilities and talents and it is the school's role to enable every pupil to discover and develop these talents. Pupils are encouraged to "work hard, play hard" and to have a sense of ownership. It is "our school" and everybody contributes to its well-being and development. High standards of behaviour are expected, with the onus on partnership between pupils and adults. Mistakes are seen as part of the learning process.

Charitable status. Northease Manor School Trust Ltd is a Registered Charity, number 307005. It exists for the provision of high-quality education for pupils with Specific Learning Difficulties.

Notre Dame Preparatory School

147 Dereham Road, Norwich, Norfolk NR2 3TA
Tel: 01603 625593
Fax: 01603 444139
email: info@notredameprepschool.co.uk
website: www.notredameprepschool.co.uk

Chairman of Governors: Mr Richard Bailey

Headmaster: **Mr K O'Herlihy**, BA, HDipEd

Age Range. 2–11 Co-educational.
Number of Pupils. 204 Day.
Fees per term (2014–2015). £1,800–£1,950.

Notre Dame Prep School was originally founded by the Sisters of Notre Dame de Namur in 1865. The school transferred to its present site in 1971 and is now a Company with charitable status. The school maintains the traditions and the spirit of the Sisters of Notre Dame and the former name and uniform.

As a Catholic school the school and staff endeavour to nurture a love of God through Jesus Christ in all the children. The school has an ethos of love and care and embraces children of all faiths.

Children are treated as individuals, respected, nurtured and encouraged to embrace and fulfil their potential in all areas of school life. We have excellent links with High Schools in both the maintained and independent sectors.

The school achieves well above average results in external tests and has a strong academic reputation. Children are prepared for entry to selective independent schools on request. Subjects include English, Maths, Science, ICT, Design and Technology, Art, Geography, PE, History,

Music, RE, French and Personal, Social and Health Education.

The school has a very strong musical tradition and has a wide range of extra-curricular musical activities on offer including Choir, Music Ensemble, Recorder, Piano, Guitar, Flute, Violin, Saxophone and Clarinet lessons.

Sports include Football, Cricket, Rugby, Netball, Hockey, Tennis and Swimming.

The school has a wide range of extra-curricular activities including Dance, Speech and Drama, Chess, ICT, Arts and Crafts, Gardening and Basketball.

We have an After School Activities Club which runs until 5.40 pm incorporating homework club and games activities for younger children. A cooked meal is provided. Holiday clubs run throughout most of the holidays.

Charitable status. Notre Dame Preparatory School (Norwich) Limited is a Registered Charity, number 269003.

Oakfield Preparatory School

125–128 Thurlow Park Road, West Dulwich, London SE21 8HP
Tel: 020 8670 4206
Fax: 020 8766 6744
email: info@oakfield.dulwich.sch.uk
               admissions@oakfield.dulwich.sch.uk
website: www.oakfield.dulwich.sch.uk

Principal: **Mrs Jane Stevens**, BA Hons, PGCE, NPQH

Age Range. 2–11.
Number in School. Day: 230 Boys, 187 Girls.
Fees per term (2014–2015). £1,538–£3,930 including lunch.

Oakfield School was founded in 1887 and is today a modern co-educational prep school which prepares children for the entrance examinations of London and countrywide independent senior schools.

The School is arranged into three groups, the Nursery (age 2–3), Foundation Years and Year 1 (age 3–6) and Years 2–6 (age 6–11). Each age group has its own self-contained building and facilities. The School site of nearly three acres allows space for play and games and older children use the nearby playing field where games sessions are played. Children aged five to eleven swim once a week under instruction.

Entry to the Nursery is by observation. Once accepted the child will progress automatically into the Foundation Years (subject to the admissions policy) and Main School. Entry at 3+ and 4+ is also by observation and children should have a good idea of colours, shapes, matching, sorting and simple counting. Entry at 7+ follows an assessment and observation in a class setting.

Prospective parents – and children – would be very welcome to visit Oakfield during a school day on an Open Morning.

Oakhill College

Wiswell Lane, Whalley, Clitheroe, Lancashire BB7 9AF
Tel: 01254 823546
Fax: 01254 822662
email: enquiries@oakhillcollege.co.uk
website: www.oakhillcollege.co.uk
Twitter: @oakhillcollege
Facebook: /OakhillCollege1
LinkedIn: /Oakhill-College

Chairman of Governors: Mr Tony Baron

Principal: **Mrs Carmel Riley**, BA, PGCE, MA

Age Range. 0–16 Co-educational.
Number of Pupils. 225 pupils.
Fees per term (2014–2015). Lower Prep (Reception–Year 2) £2,272; Upper Prep (Years 3–6) £2,559; Senior School (Years 7–11) £3,517. Nursery: £42 per full day, £24.50 per half day.

Oakhill College is a small, independent Roman Catholic day school, warmly welcoming all faiths. We provide a Catholic education for school life and beyond for children of all abilities aged 0–16. We are committed to providing a happy, safe and stimulating education within a family environment.

We seek to develop spiritual awareness; encourage a sense of self-worth; challenge students to achieve; instil mutual respect and understanding; and teach the value of service to others.

We are a family community where honesty, humour and commitment help us to achieve these aims.

Oakhill College has excellent teaching facilities within a mixture of traditional and new buildings which include the extensive sporting facilities of Oakhill Academy. The large grounds offer attractive seating areas, all-weather pitches, playing fields and a nature trail along a small stream through woodlands.

The curriculum at Oakhill College is broad and well balanced with pupils being offered a range of subjects for GCSE including individual award sciences, French, Spanish, Latin, Music, Art, ICT and Business Studies. All pupils in Year 10 take part in the Duke of Edinburgh's Bronze Award and some go on to complete the Silver Award in Year 11. There is an extensive programme of educational visits for all of the year groups and a wide range of extra-curricular activities offered. The main sports played at Oakhill are Tennis, Badminton, Football, Netball, Hockey, Basketball, Cross Country Running and Orienteering.

We encourage parents and their children to visit the school, meet the Principal and experience school life for two or more taster days. Scholarships are available for entry into Year 7 and awarded following the Entrance Examination in the Easter Term prior to Senior School entry. Bursaries are also available.

Charitable status. Oakhill College Charitable Trust is a Registered Charity, number 1048514.

Oakhyrst Grange School

Stanstead Road, Caterham, Surrey CR3 6AF
Tel: 01883 343344
Fax: 01883 342021
email: office@oakhyrstgrangeschool.co.uk
website: www.oakhyrstgrangeschool.co.uk

Headmaster: **Mr A Gear**, BEd

Age Range. 4–11.
Number in School. 142 Day Boys and Girls.
Fees per term (2014–2015). £1,140–£2,511.

Oakhyrst Grange School is an independent, co-educational preparatory day school for boys and girls between 4 and 11 years.

The School was established in 1950 and moved to its present premises in Stanstead Road in 1957. Since September 1973 the School has been administered by a non-profit making trust.

Standing in five acres of open country and woodland surrounded by the Green Belt, the School enjoys a fine position amongst the Surrey Hills.

The school has a wide and imaginative curriculum, which includes traditional teaching combined with innovative ideas. Small class sizes, with a maximum of 20 pupils, and an excellent teacher/pupil ratio enable pupils to work at their own rate and capabilities whilst being encouraged to meet new challenges.

Our pupils secure the offer of places at prominent senior schools, including scholarships and awards across the range of academic, all-rounder, music, sports and art.

There are many sporting opportunities offered and particularly high standards have been reached in cross-country, swimming, football, judo and athletics where ISA National level has been achieved. The pupils compete in many inter house, inter school and area competitions. The school also has its own heated indoor swimming pool, all-weather tennis, netball, hockey and 5-a-side court, sports pitch, cross-country course and gymnasium.

Extra-curricular music lessons are offered and much music making also takes place as part of the normal school timetable. The school has an orchestra in addition to clarinet, flute, guitar, saxophone, violin and trumpet ensembles and a choir, all of whom perform regularly. In 2014, the school was the winner of the National ISA Award for Excellence in the Arts.

In addition to the curriculum the pupils can enjoy an extensive range of clubs and activities throughout the week.

Academic excellence is encouraged and achieved, every child is expected to attain his or her individual potential. The School helps children to develop into caring, thoughtful and confident adults.

Charitable status. Oakhyrst Grange School Educational Trust is a Registered Charity, number 325043. It exists to provide an all-round education, to give the children success and the best possible start.

Oaklands School

8 Albion Hill, Loughton, Essex IG10 4RA
Tel: 020 8508 3517
Fax: 020 8508 4454
email: info@oaklandsschool.co.uk
website: www.oaklandsschool.co.uk

Headmistress: **Mrs Cheryl Macnair**, BA, PGCE

Age Range. 2½–11 Co-educational.
Number in School. 248 Day Pupils.
Fees per term (2014–2015). £1,000–£3,220.

Oaklands is a long-established preparatory school, founded in 1937, and delightfully situated in extensive grounds on the edge of Epping Forest. It provides a firm foundation for girls and boys aged 2½ to 11. Great care is taken in preparing pupils for entrance examinations to their next schools.

A broad curriculum is offered, with early emphasis on literacy and numeracy, ensuring high standards, and great importance is placed on fully developing each child's potential in a secure and caring atmosphere. We have small class sizes and specialist teachers for Science, French, Music, PE, Dancing, ICT, Sport and Drama. A wide range of extra-curricular activities is offered and breakfast club operates from 7.45 am and tea time club continues after school until 6 pm. Parents enjoy easy access to their child's teachers and the headmistress has an open-door policy. Individual music tuition is available, including piano and woodwind instrumental lessons, and singing lessons.

Oaklands is a friendly, happy school where children can enjoy learning and take pride in both their own success and the achievements of others. In addition to the attainment of high standards, pupils build personal qualities of confidence, self-reliance and respect for others, in preparation for the challenges and opportunities of the modern world.

OLCS – Our Lady's Convent School

Gray Street, Loughborough, Leics LE11 2DZ
Tel: 01509 263901
Fax: 01509 236193
email: office@olcs.leics.sch.uk
website: www.olcs.leics.sch.uk

Headteacher: **Mrs Patricia Hawley**, BA, PGCE

Age Range. Girls 3–18, Boys 3–11.
Number of Pupils. Approximately 250.
Fees per term (2014–2015). Nursery £2,720, Infants £2,865, Juniors £2,950, Seniors £3,515.
OLCS is a Catholic day school that extends a warm welcome to children of all faiths and denominations. It educates girls from 3 to 18 and boys from 3 to 11. The focus is very much on the individual child and their personal progress and achievement at all levels. Our next Open Day would be an excellent time to see our Senior and Primary School Departments in action on a normal working day, view our facilities and meet our Headteacher.

At all stages of their education, our students receive individual attention in guaranteed small classes. They are helped, encouraged and supported rather than pressured, stretched and not stressed. Academic achievement is high at all levels. Recently Year 13 achieved a pass rate of 100 per cent with 89 per cent of students gaining A* to C grades whilst Year 11 had 100 per cent of students achieving grades A* to C. A wide variety of GCSE and A Levels are offered in the Senior department. Academic Support is excellent for all students in all areas. 99 per cent of our students go on to university to study a wide range of subjects. In addition there are numerous cultural, musical and sporting activities. Music and Drama have a high profile in the school; girls have taken part in the national Shakespeare Festival. A wide variety of extra-curricular activities is on offer. The school successfully participates in The Duke of Edinburgh's Award and Young Enterprise schemes.

The school is a registered charity and its policy is to continually enhance the facilities available to our students and to improve our service to them and their parents. All departments are well resourced and ICT facilities are excellent and updated regularly. Our most recent developments include a refurbished and re-equipped Early Years/Infant Department, play and recreation areas and library for primary children, and a refurbished sixth form suite.

The School campus is an attractive walled area; an oasis of calm, near the centre of Loughborough. Open Days are held during working school days and visitors continually note the happy classroom environment and the mutual respect between students, staff and visitors. Some of our students are with us from 3 to 18 but others are very welcome to join at other stages of their education.

The Pelican Club provides before and after school care for a small additional cost.

For further information visit our website www.olcs.leics.sch.uk.

Charitable status. Our Lady's Convent School is a Registered Charity, number 1110802.

Park School

Queens Park South Drive, Bournemouth BH8 9BJ
Tel: 01202 396640
Fax: 01202 237640
email: office@parkschool.co.uk
website: www.parkschool.co.uk

Headmaster: **Mr Andrew D Edwards**, BA Hons, PGCE

Age Range. 2–11.
Number in School. Day: 157 Boys, 132 Girls.
Fees per term (2014–2015). £1,910–£2,670. (Fee rates apply to payment by direct debit.)
The Park is a co-educational junior day school occupying a quiet location overlooking Queens Park Golf course in a pleasant residential area near the town centre.

Pupils are taught in small classes in a caring, happy environment. The school is geared principally towards academic achievement although we do provide special help for a limited number of children with specific learning difficulties. The emphasis is on nurturing individual and academic progress whilst fostering a positive ethos and the development of the all-round child. This covers not only work in the classroom but also all other aspects of school life: games, music, the Arts and many practical activities. Pupils are prepared for entry to Senior Independent Schools and to Bournemouth and Poole Grammar Schools through their tests at 11+ years. Many children gain scholarships to Senior Independent Schools.

Many pupils join us in the Nursery at 2 years old, but there are occasional vacancies at other ages. Offer of a place is made only after prospective pupils have been formally assessed.

Parents with pupils in our Nursery classes can take advantage of our extended working day and the longer school terms should they so wish.

Park School for Girls

20–22 Park Avenue, Ilford, Essex IG1 4RS
Tel: Office: 020 8554 2466
          Bursar: 020 8554 6022
Fax: 020 8554 3003
email: admin@parkschool.org.uk
website: www.parkschool.org.uk

Head Teacher: **Mrs E Gallagher**, BA Hons, PGCE

Age Range. 4–16.
Number in School. 170 Day Girls.
Fees per term (2014–2015). Reception £1,990, Pre-Prep £2,275, Prep School £2,375, Senior School £3,090.
The School is situated near Valentine's Park in Ilford. It is convenient for road, rail and Central Line tube services.

Our basic aim is to provide a full educational programme leading to recognised external examinations at the age of 16.

We create a caring, well-ordered atmosphere. Our pupils are encouraged to achieve their full academic and social potential. The well-qualified staff and the policy of small classes produce well above the national average GCSE results. We do not offer a sixth form, but the majority of our leavers from Year 11 move to another school to study subjects to A Level.

In addition, the staff and I stress the development of each child as a whole person. We expect every girl to strive for self-confidence in her ability to use her talents to the full and to respect individuality. She is encouraged to make decisions and to accept responsibility for her own actions. The poise that comes from good manners and correct speech, we consider to be highly important. Honesty, reliability, courtesy and consideration for others are prime factors in the educative system.

Interested parents are welcome to visit the school, where the Head Teacher will be pleased to answer their queries.

Charitable status. Park School for Girls is a Registered Charity, number 269936. It exists to provide a caring environment in which we develop our pupils' potential to the full.

The Park School
Yeovil

The Park, Yeovil, Somerset BA20 1DH
Tel: 01935 423514
Fax: 01935 411257
email: admin@parkschool.com
website: www.parkschool.com

Head: **Mrs J Huntington**, ARAM, GRSM, LRAM, CPSEd

Age Range. 3–18 Co-educational.
Number in School. 203: 106 Boys, 97 Girls; 29 Boarders.

Fees per term (2014–2015). Day £1,928-£3,350 (including lunch); Weekly Boarding £6,500–£6,930; Full Boarding £6,720–£7,250.

The Park School, Yeovil is an Independent day and boarding school founded in 1851. It aims to provide a sound education based on Christian principles. It is a non-denominational Evangelical Christian school and has strong connections with a number of different local churches.

The School is pleasantly situated near the centre of Yeovil with easy access to surrounding towns and villages, from which day pupils are drawn, and to the main line station, Yeovil Junction, for London Waterloo. There is also a rail connection to Bristol and Weymouth from Yeovil, Pen Mill station. Transport to London Heathrow and other airports is arranged for boarders travelling abroad.

Our 'Saplings' EYFS Unit has recently been re-modelled with outdoor learning space and two classrooms for our 3–5 year olds.

Pupils flourish in a friendly, caring environment where, in small classes, they benefit from well-qualified staff. There is a wide and varied curriculum which encourages each pupil to develop their own abilities and interests to the full. In line with the National Curriculum guidelines, senior pupils choose from a range of subjects at GCSE and A Level, including: English, RE, History, Drama, Geography, French, German, Spanish, Mathematics, Science, Art, Music, Design Technology, Food Technology, ICT, Sports Studies and English for overseas pupils. Physics, Chemistry and Biology are studied as separate Sciences. Chinese is offered subject to demand. Additional subjects studied at A Level include: Business Studies, Sports Studies, Further Mathematics, Economics, Psychology and Classical Civilisation.

Physical Education is also an essential part of the curriculum. Pupils participate in a varied programme of sporting activities including: Athletics, Badminton, Basketball, Cricket, Football, Gymnastics, Hockey, Netball, Squash, Swimming, Tennis, Table Tennis, Volleyball and Cross-Country. Many Senior pupils also take part in the Duke of Edinburgh's Award Scheme as well as Young Enterprise.

A wide range of musical instruments are taught by the Director of Music and visiting staff. There are School Choirs and an Orchestra as well as a jazz band, rock group and a baroque ensemble. Music and drama productions are regular features of School life.

Boarders live in a newly refurbished, purpose-built School House and Bennet House. Many students occupy single study-bedrooms. They are cared for in a homely, family atmosphere by resident houseparents and assistants. At weekends a variety of interesting activities is available. On Sundays all boarders are encouraged to attend the church of their choice.

Academic standards in the School are high with The Park being consistently well placed in the GCSE league tables. However, the School is non-selective and pupils are encouraged to develop their talents as individuals with extremely favourable pupil : teacher ratios.

The school offers scholarships which may be given for academic, music, art, sport or drama ability. These are awarded by examination and interview in January of each year for entry to Years 4, 7 and 9. Sixth Form scholarship exams are held in December. Bursaries are available for children of those parents who are engaged in full-time Christian work or are members of HM Forces. In addition means-tested bursaries are available for parents on low incomes.

Charitable status. The Park School (Yeovil) Limited is a Registered Charity, number 310214. It exists to provide Christian education and care for children aged 3–18 years.

Polwhele House School

Truro, Cornwall TR4 9AE
Tel: 01872 273011
email: office@polwhelehouse.co.uk
website: www.polwhelehouse.co.uk

Headmaster: **Alex McCullough**, BA Hons Dunelm, PGCE, NPQH

Age Range. 3–13+.
Number in School. 90.
Fees per term (2014–2015). Day: £505–£3,995, Lunch £172–£193; Flexi Boarding (1–4 nights per week): £400–£1,600.

Polwhele House is a beautiful and historic listed building, set in over 30 acres of garden, playing fields, park and woodland. The school enjoys a glorious and secure environment only 1¼ miles from Truro Cathedral.

Uninterrupted education is provided for boys and girls during those important early years from three to thirteen. There is flexible attendance for under-fives who are taught by qualified professionals in Nursery and Reception. The school has an established reputation for high levels of care and excellent teaching.

Although mainly a day-school, weekly boarding, day boarding, and after-school care are growing in popularity. The boarders live in the Main House in comfortable surroundings which include a TV lounge, en-suite facilities, quiet areas and garden. The well-being and happiness of each child is the top priority.

This flourishing family school was founded in 1976 and has a continual programme of development, building and refurbishment. Accommodation now includes a separate Pre-Prep and Prep School, built and equipped for art and craft, design technology, sciences, languages and ICT. More recently the EYFS provision was extended with larger rooms and greater free-flow access to the outdoors.

Twenty years ago an equestrian centre was built. There are now five ponies at school and over a third of the pupils enjoy riding lessons and some attend competitions.

The school combines modern teaching methods with the best of traditional values. The social development of the child is carefully nurtured to help them to become confident, considerate and polite young people. Polwhele House values each child and a very strong team of skilled and caring staff is able to devote a great deal of time to every pupil in small classes.

Drama flourishes with each child participating in at least one of eight productions a year. Music is an important part of the school life with all pupils singing, and the majority playing an instrument. There are Truro Cathedral Chorister-ships for boys and Polwhele House Music Scholarships for girls. All the usual team games are coached and there are regular outstanding successes in athletics and cross-country running at school, county and national levels.

Polwhele House is a Christian, non-denominational school and assembly is considered to be an important part of the day. The school motto is 'Karenza Whelas Karenza', Cornish for 'Love Begets Love'. Boys and girls share the same opportunities and responsibilities in all areas of school life.

The school has a fine record of academic achievement. There is a wide variety of sporting and extra-curricular activities to bring out the best in every child. Pupils are pre-pared for a broad range of schools, and win numerous schol-arships, bursaries and exhibitions to senior independent schools.

Mr McCullough takes great pleasure in meeting prospec-tive parents and showing them around personally. Polwhele House is not just a school, more a way of life.

Prenton Preparatory School

Mount Pleasant, Oxton, Wirral CH43 5SY
Tel: 0151 652 3182
email: enquiry@prentonprep.co.uk
website: www.prentonprep.co.uk

Headteacher: **Mr M T R Jones**

Age Range. 2½–11.
Number in School. Day: 54 Boys, 45 Girls.
Fees per term (from January 2015). £2,200 Infants; £2,300 Juniors; from £680 part-time in Foundation Stage.
Founded in 1935.

Prenton Preparatory School is a co-educational day school for children aged 2½–11 years, situated about a mile from Junction 3 of the M53.

The building is a large Victorian house which has been carefully converted into the uses of a school. There is a large playground and gardens. Facilities include an ICT/Science block and an Art block and Pre-School outdoor play area are recent additions to the school.

The children benefit from small classes and individual attention in a disciplined environment which enable them to realise their full potential.

The school offers a wide range of academic subjects with emphasis on the three main National Curriculum core sub-jects: English, Mathematics and Science. French is taught from an early age.

Children are prepared for entrance examinations to county, independent and grant-maintained grammar schools, gaining well above-average pass rates.

Child care facilities are available from 8 am to 6 pm. Clubs are provided at lunchtime and after school. They include football, cricket, computers and technology, karate, swimming, gymnastics, ballet, netball, music group, speech & drama, handchimes and musical instruments.

Priory School

Sir Harry's Road, Edgbaston, Birmingham B15 2UR
Tel: 0121 440 4103/0256
Fax: 0121 440 3639

email: enquiries@prioryschool.net
website: www.prioryschool.net

Chairman of Governors: Mr S Gilmore, LLB

Headmaster: **Mr Jonathan Cramb**, BA Hons, PGCE MEd

Age Range. 6 months – 18 years.
Number in School. 440.
Fees per term (2014–2015). £2,840–£4,290.

The school, founded on its present site in 1936 by the Sis-ters of the Society of the Holy Child Jesus, stands in 17 acres of parkland in the pleasant suburb of Edgbaston, only 2 miles from the centre of Birmingham. The school has exten-sive playing fields, excellent astroturf tennis courts, athletics facilities and football and cricket pitches. There are coaches running to and from school and frequent bus services to all parts of the city.

The school has an excellent Nursery on site which offers care for 51 weeks per annum and accepts children from the age of 6 months. All pupils are able to remain in After Care until 6.00 pm if parents so wish.

The school has a culturally diverse pupil community, based on catholic values, but welcomes all faiths. Pupils are taught by specialist teachers from the age of 9 and in the Senior School the curriculum is broad and balanced and pupils benefit from small class sizes and individual attention enabling the to make excellent progress in their academic development.

The school, whilst remaining proudly multi-ability, is justly proud of the academic achievements of the pupils. A wide range of subjects is available for GCSE, with good facilities, including well-equipped Science Laboratories, Language Resources rooms, Information Technology facili-ties, Sports Centre, Performing Arts Suite and Learning Resources Centre. The school offers support for children with special needs, particularly dyslexia, with specially qualified staff.

A wide range of extra-curricular opportunities are offered in both Prep. and Senior School. These currently include photography, debating, chess, Duke of Edinburgh's Award scheme to name just a few. Private tuition is also offered in Speech, singing and a wide range of musical instruments.

Entry to the school is by interview, assessment and day visit. Scholarships are awarded at 11+. Bursaries may be awarded in cases of special need.

Parents are warmly welcomed into the school to discuss individual needs. Full details prior to the visit may be obtained from the Admissions Registrar.

Charitable status. Priory School is a Registered Charity, number 518009.

Queen Ethelburga's Collegiate Foundation

Thorpe Underwood Hall, York YO26 9SS
Tel: 01423 333330
Fax: 01423 333754
email: info@QE.org
           pj@QE.org
website: www.QE.org

Co-educational Day and Boarding School.

Chairman of Governors: Brian R Martin, FCMI, FInstD, FFA

Headmaster: **Steven Jandrell**, BA

Head of The Faculty: **Mrs Denise Willis**, MA, CertEd

Age Range. 3 months–18 years.

Number of Pupils. 771: 126 day boys, 143 day girls, 235 boy boarders, 263 girl boarders.

Fees per term (2014–2015). Day: £1,060–£4,320; Boarding: £8,880–£11,095 (UK students), £10,860–£13,685 (International students).

Queen Ethelburga's is located at Thorpe Underwood, situated between Harrogate and York. The College is co-educational, for students in the age range 11 to 19. The Faculty provides more vocational/professional courses and courses for students who need support in the English Language and is for students aged 14 to 19 and Chapter House Preparatory School has children up to age 11. The schools are supported by the Queen Ethelburga's Charitable Foundation which provides many bursaries, scholarships and awards, and investment in the yearly capital projects.

The campus is exceptional. Set in 100 acres of manicured country park in the Vale of York, the Foundation maintains an excellent quality of provision with huge investments in the last 10 years. Set around a Grade 2* Listed country house there are Science, Modern Language, Art and Technology suites, together with Sports Hall, excellent floodlit pitches for Rugby, Hockey and Football, floodlit tennis courts and a swimming pool. The Equestrian Centre is probably unique in Europe with stabling for 60 horses, an Olympic-size indoor arena and acres of all-weather floodlit arenas. Many students take advantage of the Foundation Riding Award, which allows students to bring their own horses to school with free livery. Planned projects include a second, and much larger Sports Hall, additional Classroom areas, extra sports facilities and Sixth Form Boarding and Leisure Accommodation. There will also be a new Art, Fashion and Design Technology area and extensive library provision.

We are proud that we have been able to maintain a broad access school with students obtaining very good academic results. The overriding ethos is "to be the best that I can with the gifts that I have". The College and Faculty offer a broad ranging curriculum up to GCSE based around the NC, with small classes and a wide range of extra-curricular activities. Sixth Form students have the choice of 22 different A Levels, IB and BTech.

Boarding is based around three boys' houses and three girls' houses with excellent facilities including most bedrooms being en suite and equipped with TV, hi-fi, telephone and other modern electrical equipment (albeit on timers). The strong pastoral care is centred on House Parents and Tutors, who work closely with the Heads of Year and the Head of Pastoral Care.

Entry is via our own entrance examination and interview with the Headmaster. Applicants are expected to have achieved the equivalent of at least Level 4 at Key Stage 2, Level 5 at Key Stage 3, at least 4 B Grades and 2 C Grades for the College and have attained at least 4 GCSE passes at C Grade and above for the Faculty. The Foundation contributes over £1,000,000 each year in awards for academic excellence, sport, music, drama, equestrian and many others. All boarders of HM Forces families attract a Forces Bursary of 20%.

Charitable status. Queen Ethelburga's College Foundation is a Registered Charity, number 1012924.

Raphael Independent School

Park Lane, Hornchurch, Essex RM11 1XY
Tel: 01708 744735
Fax: 01708 722432
email: admin@raphaelschool.com
website: www.raphaelschool.com

Headmistress: **Mrs J Lawrence**, BEd Hons

Age Range. Co-educational 4–16.

Number of Pupils. Day: 100 boys, 50 girls.

Fees per term (2014–2015). £1,915–£2,760.

Entry requirements. Interview for Early Years and Infants. Informal assessment for Juniors. Entry Tests in English and Maths for Seniors.

Aims. To develop the academic, social, artistic and sporting potential of each individual within a caring and welcoming school community.

To foster respect for each other within a multi-cultural school.

To offer a broad range of educational visits and extra-curricular activities.

Location. Raphael is a ten minute walk from Romford Main Line Station, and a fifteen minute drive from the A12 or A127 junctions of the M25.

School day. Infants from 8.40 am, Juniors until 3.25 pm and Seniors until 4.00 pm. Our After School Club looks after pupils until 5.45 pm.

Curriculum strengths. ICT, French and Spanish, English and Drama, Maths.

Sport. We believe in competitive sport, and we offer Soccer, Rugby, Netball, Cross-Country, Swimming, Cricket and Tennis amongst others.

A prospectus containing further information may be obtained from our Office Manager, Carolyn Carter, and all prospective parents are most welcome to visit the school.

Rastrick Independent School

Ogden Lane, Rastrick, Brighouse, West Yorkshire HD6 3HF
Tel: 01484 400344
Fax: 01484 718318
email: info@rastrick-independent.co.uk
website: www.rastrick-independent.co.uk

Headmistress: **Mrs S A Vaughey**

Age Range. 0–16 co-educational. Tutorial College 16+.

Number of Pupils. 200.

Fees per term (2014–2015). £2,310–£3,431.

The philosophy of this Independent School is to provide a first-class education for all ages combined with academic excellence. This School and College are also renowned for their superb pastoral care. Situated in a small village in the heart of Yorkshire, this educational campus is flourishing in a historic and beautiful location. A 19th Century Manor House and grounds with extensive, well stocked gardens frame a collection of exquisite buildings which accommodate children and students from birth to eighteen. The academic achievement at Rastrick has been acknowledged as 'Excellent' by ISI and Ofsted. The School has achieved 100% Pass rate at 11+ and 100% A*–C at GCSE. The SATS results are outstanding at all key stages. When it comes to examination results, Rastrick succeeds far above the national and local averages.

The highly qualified team create a vibrant, exciting environment for learning. The pupils have a reputation for manners and discipline which has produced confident, happy, well adjusted young people. Life at this Independent School is extremely successful academically and daily school life is rich and rewarding. There is something very special about the atmosphere and the team at Rastrick.

Walking into the Main School, visitors experience something quite unique. The architecture and design of Rastrick has maintained the atmosphere of the historic buildings and incorporates light, air and space to create a superb learning environment. Children and Students greet invited guests, each other, their teachers and parents with a natural warmth and charm. There is a sense of mutual respect. The structure of a day here is ordered and classes for all ages take place in rooms designed to stimulate learning as well as to showcase the work being undertaken. Every child learns to take care of themselves and their peers. The pastoral care at Rastrick is outstanding.

In partnership with families, pupils achieve their potential academically but also flourish in Sports and The Arts. The School and College are open all year round to accommodate working parents. The School has taken its place in the centre of the community, taking pride in activities which reflect the daily life of the village of Rastrick.

This educational establishment has experienced a sustained record of academic success and pastoral care. The rapid growth and development of Rastrick has seen considerable investment in buildings and first-class facilities. Rastrick now welcomes Boarders, International Students and students to the Tutorial College for full or part time education beyond age the age of 16. In addition Rastrick is an Examination Centre for Private Candidates.

This environment offers an education which expects success. There is an expectation that discipline, self-worth and good manners will lead to the development of a confident, happy child.

Ravenstone Preparatory & Pre-Preparatory Schools

Preparatory School:
24 Elvaston Place, London SW7 5NL
Tel: 020 7225 3131
Fax: 020 7590 9745
email: registrar@ravenstoneschools.com

Pre-Preparatory School:
The Long Garden, St George's Fields, Albion Street, London W2 2AX
Tel: 020 7262 1190
Fax: 020 7724 6980
email: admissions@ravenstoneschools.com

website: www.ravenstoneschools.com

Headmaster: **Dr Ronald Pritchard**, PhD, BSc, PGCE

Age Range. Co-educational: Prep 2¾–11, Pre-Prep 1–7.
Number of Pupils. Prep 120, Pre-Prep 80.
Fees per term (2014–2015). £3,760–£5,625.

Ravenstone Prep School and Ravenstone Pre-Prep occupy two separate and very different sites: the prep is housed in an elegant Victorian building in an excellent location in the heart of South Kensington; the pre-prep is situated in a wonderful large garden in W2, just north of Hyde Park. The prep school takes children aged 2¾ to 11 years and the pre-prep takes children from 1 to 7 years. The schools have traditional values and our staff expect high standards of both work and behaviour, with kindness and consideration for others being of paramount importance. At the same time, the schools are well resourced with modern equipment and the children are safe, secure and exceptionally well cared for. Both schools are small, cosy, friendly establishments where no individual becomes lost in the crowd. Delicious healthy lunches are prepared by our own cooks who cater for all dietary needs.

One of the main purposes of the prep school is to prepare children for entry into the senior school of their choice. The curriculum consists of all the customary subjects plus our own additions: French from Nursery upwards and Mandarin from Form 4. We more than compensate for our limited outside space with an extensive PE curriculum including swimming from Reception and games afternoons at Battersea Park from Form 2. The children participate in regular trips

to the nearby museums and Hyde Park or to places of interest further afield. There is a residential trip in Forms 4, 5 and 6. We offer a wide range of after-school activities including chess, karate, drama, yoga, flamenco dancing, cookery and Arabic. The children may also take ballet classes as an optional extra and there is excellent provision at both schools for children who do not have English as their first language.

The pre-prep in W2 is a paradise for young children with its wonderful garden and vast sandpit. Whatever the weather, the children have a huge array of resources to exercise their minds and bodies, and the freedom to investigate and experiment under the watchful eyes of our well-qualified and highly-experienced staff. Children who attend the pre-prep are guaranteed places at the prep school and can opt to travel between the sites by school minibus if they wish.

Ravenstone Schools are part of Minerva Education group which owns a number of private schools in London, East and South East England. Through Minerva's "Inspiring Learning" programme, we seek to share best practice and ensure the continuing improvement in every child's education.

Red House School

36 The Green, Norton, Stockton-on-Tees, Cleveland TS20 1DX
Tel: 01642 553370
Fax: 01642 361031
email: headmaster@redhouseschool.co.uk
website: www.redhouseschool.co.uk

Chairman of Governors: Mr Vinay Bedi

Headmaster: **Mr Alex R W Taylor**, BSc, MSc, CBiol, MSB

Head of Nursery & Infant School: Miss Jo Everington, BEd

Age Range. 3–16.
Number in School. Approx 215 girls and 218 boys.
Fees per term (2014–2015). Nursery £1,620*; Reception £1,690*; Years 1–2 £2,340; Years 3–6 £2,910; Years 7–11 £3,340. Lunches £190.

*Nursery and Reception (under 5 years) fees are shown net of the Early Years Funding Grant. The grant is claimed by the school on behalf of the parents and is available from the term following the child's third birthday (for a total of 6 terms) until they reach their 5th birthday.

Red House School is a 3–16 co-educational independent day school. Situated on the picturesque village green at Norton, Stockton-on-Tees, Red House School has the enviable reputation as being the region's premier co-educational independent school, offering a first-class education and helping children to reach their full potential since 1929.

Our commitment to pupils and parents is summarized below:

- To provide a happy, stimulating and well disciplined environment in which children succeed.
- To encourage each child to reach their full potential and strive for excellence in all areas of school life.
- To develop pupil's self-esteem so that they have the confidence to use their individual talents, skills and knowledge effectively.
- To develop their skills of communication, analysis and independent thinking so that children are equipped to be lifelong learners prepared for a rapidly changing society.
- To develop a positive partnership between staff, parents, pupils and the wider community.

The Nursery and Infant School (Pre-Nursery to Year 3) is housed in and around the Old Vicarage, a beautiful listed building. This site has been further developed with the construction of purpose-built nursery facilities, additional classrooms and the redevelopment of 'The Barn' to provide an assembly hall and dining room. There is an ICT suite and all classrooms have interactive whiteboards. Close links are maintained with Red House Preparatory and Senior School.

The Preparatory and Senior School (Years 4–11) are housed in a beautiful Victorian building, which has been augmented over the years with purpose-built sports and assembly halls, classrooms and laboratories. The school has its own playing fields, including tennis courts. ICT is well developed within the teaching and learning across the school.

Although a selective school, Red House caters for pupils with a wide range of abilities and backgrounds. Small class sizes mean that teaching can be tailored to the needs of the individual child allowing them to reach their full potential. GCSE results have been consistently amongst the best, if not the best, of any school within the area. In 2014 over 98% of pupils gained A*-C grades. The academic side of the school is balanced by an extensive programme of games and activities. Pupils have regularly achieved representational honours at county, regional and national level.

Charitable status. Red House School Limited is a Registered Charity, number 527377. It exists to provide education for children and for the advancement of education for the benefit of the community.

Redcourt – St Anselm's

7 Devonshire Place, Oxton, Birkenhead, Wirral CH43 1TX
Tel: 0151 652 5228
Fax: 0151 653 5883
email: admin@redcourt.net
website: www.redcourtstanselms.com

Chairman of Governors: Mrs L Scholes

Headmaster: Mr K S Davey, MA, PGCE

Age Range. 3–11 Co-educational.
Number of Pupils. 220.
Fees per term (2014–2015). £2,000.

Redcourt – St Anselm's is an inclusive school welcoming all children of all abilities. There is no formal entrance examination. Prospective pupils are invited into Redcourt for a day's visit. During the day, Staff will assess the level at which the visiting child is currently working. However, most children join at nursery level. Our aim is to provide each and every child with a sound academic education in an environment which is explicitly Christian and where discipline and care go hand in hand. We endeavour to be aware of each child as an individual and we seek to encourage the development of the whole person. The school operates in an open and friendly manner, becoming something of a second home for its pupils.

The core national curriculum subjects plus RE, History, Geography, Art and Design, PE and Games, Music, ICT and French form the basis of what is taught. Children are prepared for the eleven plus and entrance examinations to grammar and selective independent schools with most children proceeding to Grammar Schools.

Charitable status. Redcourt St Anselm's is part of the Congregation of Christian Brothers which is a Registered Charity, number 254312.

Riverston School

63–69 Eltham Road, Lee Green, London SE12 8UF
Tel: 020 8318 4327
email: office@riverstonschool.co.uk
website: www.riverstonschool.co.uk

Principal: Professsor D M Lewis

Headteacher: Mrs S E Salathiel

Deputy Headmaster, Director of SEN: Mr J D Allen

Age Range. 9 months – 19 years.
Number in School. Day: 140 Boys, 85 Girls.
Fees per term (2014–2015). £2,691–£4,309.

Riverston School is a small, co-educational, independent day school in South East London for up to 250 children between the ages of 9 months and 19 years. Riverston was founded in the early 1900s, and in 1927 moved to its present site in Eltham Road, Lee Green. It is centrally located on the A20, close to the A2 and South Circular Roads, served by numerous bus routes and is convenient for mainline railway stations being 20 minutes from London Bridge.

The school stands in nearly three acres of carefully maintained grounds and is built around four imposing Victorian houses. It has modern purpose-built units, incorporating specialist teaching rooms, library, science laboratories, general-purpose hall, ICT suite and dance studio. The school has a fully-equipped Sports Hall, two large playground areas, the use of extensive playing fields and tennis courts. The Nursery and Pre School Departments have their own separate and fully-equipped outdoor play area.

In September 2012, the school opened a Sixth Form and pupils are able to continue their education at Riverston until the age of 19. The emphasis is on "Bespoke Learning for Life" and to this end a new Life Skills Centre has been opened which includes a brand new Food Technology laboratory and a Student Flat which enables students to prepare for independent living when school life has ended. Vocational studies are at the core of the Sixth Form curriculum with BTEC courses available in various subjects as well as A Levels being delivered to students who are academically able. We have forged an educational link with Hadlow College in Mottingham where students can study Animal Management and Horticulture.

The school has a well-earned reputation for its teaching of children of all abilities including those who may require learning support or have special learning difficulties. There is a dedicated Riverston Plus department providing excellent specialist provision. Whilst many pupils may require additional help with their academic work, wherever possible they attend full-time mainstream lessons except for those periods determined by their individual educational programmes when they are taught individually or in small groups.

Riverston has a lively, friendly and cheerful ethos with ideals which are as strong today as they were when first conceived. A traditional school with the mission statement "Bespoke Learning for Life", Riverston endeavours to provide each pupil with an individualised curriculum, promoting a positive self-image and ensuring that all have the chance of maximising their academic potential, whilst encouraging their sporting ability. There is a considerable emphasis on pastoral care for personal happiness and a real sense of community in an environment where staff and pupils know each other very well across the year groups.

Parents are invited to visit the school on Open Mornings and by appointment only. Details can be found on our website at www.riverstonschool.co.uk

Rochester Independent College

Star Hill, Rochester, Kent ME1 1XF
Tel: 01634 828115
Fax: 01634 405667
email: admissions@rochester-college.org
website: www.rochester-college.org
Twitter: @RICollege
Facebook: /Rochester-Independent-College

Co-Principals:
Pauline Bailey, HND, PgDip, MA
Alistair Brownlow, MA Hons, MPhil
Brian Pain, BSc Hons, PGDip

Age Range. 11–19 Co-educational.
Number of Pupils. 300 (including 65 boarders).
Fees per term (2014–2015). Tuition: £4,000–£5,500. Weekly Boarding £3,200; Full Boarding: £3,600–£4,200.

Rochester Independent College is an alternative to conventional secondary education with a happily distinctive ethos. Accepting day students from the age of 11 and boarders from 16 the focus is on examination success in a lively, supportive and informal atmosphere. Students are encouraged to be themselves and achieve exam results that often exceed their expectations. There is no uniform, no bells ring and everybody is on first name terms. The average class size is eight. Our January 2008 Ofsted report judged that "the quality of education is outstanding".

Students enjoy being here and are treated as young adults. We encourage them to search for their own answers, to voice their opinions, to think critically, creatively and independently. They leave not only with excellent examination results but with enthusiasm for the future and new confidence about themselves and their education.

Personal Tutors work closely with students on all courses to give advice about course combinations and help students to ensure that their courses are designed to meet the requirements of university entrance. With such small class sizes individual attention is not only available, it's practically inescapable.

The College has particular academic strengths in Science, Mathematics, English Literature and the Creative and Visual Arts including Film, Photography and Media.

The College's reputation for academic excellence is founded on 30 years' experience of rigorous teaching. Students come to us for a variety of reasons and from many different backgrounds. We are not academically selective; our only entrance qualification is an honest determination to work hard. Our results however are always ranked among the best of the academically selective and students secure places at top UK universities. Direct entry into any year group is possible and the College also offers intensive one year GCSE and A Level courses as well as retake programmes. International students benefit from specialised English Language teaching support.

The College Halls combine the informality of a university residence with the supervision and pastoral support appropriate for young adults. The College offers students the opportunity to thrive in an atmosphere of managed independence and acts as a stepping stone between school and university. All accommodation is on campus and in either single or double rooms.

Rookwood School

Weyhill Road, Andover, Hampshire SP10 3AL
Tel: 01264 325900
Fax: 01264 325909

email: office@rookwood.hants.sch.uk
website: www.rookwood.hants.sch.uk

Headmistress: Mrs L Whetstone, MA, BA Hons, PGCE

Age Range. Co-educational 3–16 with Boarders from age 8.
Number in School. 320: 169 girls, 151 Boys (39 in the Nursery).
Fees per term (2014–2015). Boarding: £7,005–£8,205. Day: £2,785–£4,585. Nursery: £9.00 per hour (Early Years Education Funding accepted).

Recently hailed by the ISI as a place "where pupils flourish", Rookwood is an independent day & boarding school for girls and boys, successfully nurturing children from their very first steps in the nursery all the way through to their GCSEs.

Described as "Warm", "Friendly" and "Caring", Rookwood is known for its family atmosphere and strong pastoral care and prides itself on encouraging each and every child to achieve their very best – with outstanding results; over a third of all GCSEs taken in 2014 were awarded an A*/ A with 98% of the pupils achieving at least 5 GCSEs at grades A*–C – testament to Rookwood's small class sizes and dedicated teaching.

Set in 8 acres of private grounds Rookwood has an impressive range of amenities including a state-of-the-art sports hall, a lovely outdoor swimming pool, excellent art and science facilities and a wonderful purpose-built Pre-Prep (currently deemed educationally '*Outstanding*' by the ISI). Both Music and Drama thrive at Rookwood, with every child encouraged to take part, whilst the Physical Education department is equally busy (with several pupils advancing to represent their favourite sports at national level in recent years).

In addition to its many tangible achievements Rookwood remains dedicated to developing courteous and caring pupils with a strong sense of right and wrong and a natural respect for those around them – just one of the reasons why the school's boarding houses run so smoothly. A stone's throw from the main site, Rookwood boarders enjoy a unique 'home-from-home' experience. Family-style meal times, experienced and supportive boarding staff and busy weekends all combine to ensure that Rookwood's boarders receive the very best of care.

As the ISI recently observed, pupils at Rookwood '*take great pride in their school and the value placed on everyone's contribution*'. It is, as one pupil commented, '*Just like having another family*'.

Prospective pupils and their parents are warmly invited to attend one of Rookwood's open days (please see website for latest information). Alternatively, if you require any further information or would like to make an individual appointment, please do not hesitate to contact the Registrar directly.

Admission is by school reports and individual visits.

Charitable status. Rookwood School is a Registered Charity, number 307322. It exists to provide education for children.

Roselyon School

Par, Cornwall PL24 2HZ
Tel: 01726 812110
Fax: 01726 812110
email: secretary@roselyonschool.com
website: www.roselyonschool.com

Head: Mrs Hilary Mann, MBA, BEd

Age Range. 2½–11.
Number in School. Day: 39 Boys, 37 Girls.

Fees per term (2014–2015). £2,795.

Roselyon School, formerly the Victorian manor house in the village of Par, near St Austell, stands in 5 acres of beautiful woodland. A new multi-purpose gymnasium and hall recently built in the centre of the campus has added greatly to the school's facilities. Roselyon is fully co-educational, taking pupils in the full time Nursery from 2½ and joining the Main School from 5–11.

The school is proud of its academic strengths and excellent examination results to local senior independent schools. It offers a broad curriculum, a variety of sports, music and drama and has an extensive range of extra-curricular activities.

Academic and Music Scholarships and Bursaries are available for pupils in Years 3 to 6, and assessments are usually taken in the Summer Term.

Roselyon is a small, friendly school where a warm family atmosphere is maintained by the committed team of caring staff.

Charitable status. Roselyon School Limited is a Registered Charity, number 306583. It exists to provide quality education to boys and girls.

Ruckleigh School

17 Lode Lane, Solihull, West Midlands B91 2AB
Tel: 0121 705 2773
Fax: 0121 704 4883
email: admin@ruckleigh.co.uk
website: www.ruckleigh.co.uk

Headmistress: **Mrs B M Forster**

Age Range. 3–11.
Number in School. Day: 120 Boys, 105 Girls.
Fees per term (2014–2015). £924–£2,662.

Ruckleigh is an independent day school offering education to boys and girls between the ages of 4 and 11 with a Nursery Department catering for children from the age of 3.

Although a high standard of work is expected this is related to the individual child, and the school is able to provide opportunities within a wide range of academic ability. Each child has every chance to develop his or her talents to the full, often resulting in achievements beyond initial expectations.

The comparatively small classes mean that every child is well known individually throughout the school creating a friendly environment.

Pupils are guided into habits of clear thinking, self-reliance and courtesy. Sound practical judgement, sensitivity towards the needs of others, and a willingness to "have a go" are the qualities that the school seeks to promote.

Rushmoor School

58–60 Shakespeare Road, Bedford MK40 2DL
Tel: 01234 352031
email: admissions@rushmoorschool.co.uk
website: www.rushmoorschool.co.uk

Chair of Governors: G M Bates, OBE, JP

Head Teacher: **I M Daniel**, BA, NPQH

Age Range. Boys 2–16, Girls 2–11.
Number in School. 320 Day Pupils.
Fees per term (2014–2015). £1,980–£3,330.

Rushmoor has grown and improved by investing greatly to provide excellent facilities. In September 2006 a major new building was opened which comprises a second ICT suite, Art rooms, Library, Drama studio, and an additional eight classrooms. In September 2011 we opened the Food Technology room and new cricket facilities.

At Rushmoor we appreciate the importance of selecting the right school for your son or daughter; childhood is something which can be experienced only once. With this in mind, and the belief that children learn best when they feel happy and secure, we aim to develop in our pupils a lifelong interest in learning – one which encompasses the full range of intellectual, cultural, artistic and sporting achievements of our society.

We believe in individual care and attention. Visitors to the school are impressed by the friendly, positive attitude of the pupils and their energetic sense of purpose. The staff are caring and understanding, yet know the importance of effort and personal discipline in enabling pupils to achieve the highest academic standards.

At the school we ensure that all children have opportunities to develop their intellectual, physical and creative gifts, across a broad and balanced curriculum. Children in Reception and Junior classes benefit greatly from a wide range of specialist teachers.

We emphasise the individual, recognizing that all children are different and value each child in their own right. Encouraging children to develop their strengths improves their self-esteem, enabling them to find their role in the community. We promote children's personal development, encouraging lively and enquiring minds, respect for others and a high regard for truth. The stability of continuous education, spanning the ages 2–16 years, is a major factor in helping us achieve this.

At Rushmoor we pride ourselves on our ability to integrate children with Specific Learning Differences within mainstream school life, whilst still providing extended challenges for our gifted and talented pupils. We believe that every child should be allowed to embrace any aspect of the curriculum. Enabling children to receive support without undermining their confidence amongst their peers is of primary importance.

Rushmoor has a fine reputation in sport and boasts a highly successful record with many pupils gaining county and national honours. Children have also gained much success in national and local drama competitions and festivals.

In 2014 Rushmoor was a finalist in the ISA Awards for excellence and winner of the 'Financial Innovation' category.

Prospective parents and children can tour the school at any time and 'taster days' can be arranged. Come and experience our caring ethos which enables our children to develop the confidence and flexibility which allows them to face the demands of modern life. To view our excellent inspection report please visit our website.

Charitable status. Rushmoor School Limited is a Registered Charity, number 307530. It exists to provide education.

Sackville School
Cognita Schools Group

Tonbridge Road, Hildenborough, Kent TN11 9HN
Tel: 01732 838888
Fax: 01732 836404
email: office@sackvilleschool.com
website: www.sackvilleschool.co.uk

Headmaster: **Mr John Hewitt**, BA, MBA

Age Range. 11–18.
Number in School. 160.
Fees per term (2014–2015). £4,540.

Sackville School is situated in Hildenborough, midway between Tonbridge and Sevenoaks. The main school building, which dates back to 1866, is set in 28 acres of magnificent parkland. The school has a newly refurbished Science block with four specialised laboratories, two dedicated Computer rooms, an impressive Sports Hall, an Art/Photography building and a new Design Suite, a modern Food Technology area, a new Drama/Music studio offering a performance area, a beautiful oak panelled Library, plus the usual range of specialist teaching rooms.

We are a mixed-ability school and our philosophy is based upon the individual and their unique learning needs. Individualised teaching is strong and successful at Sackville and all pupils benefit from this form of teaching. By concentrating on excellence the school ensures that each child has the opportunity to fulfil their true potential, and develop their gifts and talents at all levels. Students achieve excellent GCSE results and the Sixth Form offers one of the widest ranges of A Level courses, plus Young Enterprise, Duke of Edinburgh's Award and many other life-enriching opportunities.

Our students go on to a wide variety of universities including Oxford and other Russell Group universities.

Sackville students are cheerful, confident children who work hard and enjoy aiming high and achieving their very best – they are expected to take a full part in the life of the school. The Headmaster and staff encourage a warm, friendly working atmosphere, whilst promoting pride in achievement. Every student is valued, and their talents recognised.

The full range of academic, cultural and sporting activities are offered and all students are encouraged to try all activities. All major team games, and minor sports, are played and Sackville students have represented their County as well as National Squads. The school has a lively Music Department and over three quarters of the students are engaged in music making. The Creative Arts are particularly well represented. Art is exceptionally strong and Drama/Dance have a huge reputation for excellence. The Activities programme is an integral part of the school day and includes Orchestra, Choir, Duke of Edinburgh's Award, Drama, Golf, Film Unit, Windsurfing, Boules, Dry Slope Skiing, Archery, Self Defence, Community Service, Horse Riding, Computing, Photography and many other activities.

The school fosters the qualities of honour, care for others, thoughtfulness and tolerance. The Headmaster is always delighted to meet with prospective parents with their sons and daughters to discuss the educational opportunities available at Sackville.

Sacred Heart School

Mangate Street, Swaffham, Norfolk PE37 7QW
Tel: 01760 721330/724577
Fax: 01760 725557
email: info@sacredheartschool.co.uk
website: www.sacredheartschool.co.uk

Headteacher: **Sister Francis Ridler**, FDC, BEd Hons, EYPS

Age Range. 3–16 Co-educational.
Number in School. 103 Day Pupils, 4 Girl Boarders.
Fees per term (2014–2015). Boarders: Termly £6,950, Weekly £5,360–£5,745; Day: £2,525 (Juniors); £3,360–£3,750 (Seniors).
Assistance with fees: Academic, Music, Art, Sport, All Rounder (Boarder) Scholarships for Year 7 (11+). Some bursaries available.
Entry requirements: Non-selective, Assessments, School Report and Interview.

Religious Affiliation: Roman Catholic (other denominations welcome).
Staff: 12 Full Time, 12 Part Time, 6 Learning Support.
The Sacred Heart School was founded by the Daughters of Divine Charity in 1914. The Sisters and lay staff work together to provide a safe and caring environment where Christian values are upheld.

Principally a day school, the school is now co-educational. Pupils study for eight to eleven GCSEs gaining consistently high A–C grades. At 16, the pupils have gained the confidence and self-possession which makes them much sought after by all Sixth Form Centres and other Independent Schools. There is a limited number of boarding places for girls aged 8–16 as well as the opportunity for flexi boarding.

All pupils are encouraged to develop their gifts in Music, Drama, Art and Sport, and the School has a fine record of success in all these areas.

Facilities include a Sports Hall, Swimming Pool and Arts Centre with Theatre, Art and Music Rooms and a Pottery Workshop.

A very active Parents' Association, loyal past pupils and parents network, together with highly-qualified Staff provide the energy, enthusiasm and friendly atmosphere which characterises the school community.

Before and after school care is available and Nursery Vouchers are accepted for the Little Pedlars Pre-School.

Charitable status. The Daughters of Divine Charity is a Registered Charity, number 237760.

Sacred Heart School

Mayfield Lane, Durgates, Wadhurst, East Sussex TN5 6DQ
Tel: 01892 783414
email: admin@sacredheartwadhurst.org.uk
website: www.sacredheartwadhurst.org.uk

Chair of Governors: Mrs Maureen Hughes

Head Teacher: **Mrs Hilary Blake**, BA, PGCE

Age Range. 3–11 Co-educational.
Number of Pupils. 120.
Fees per term (2014–2015). £2,175.
Sacred Heart School is a small independent Catholic primary school and Nursery, nestling in the heart of the Sussex countryside.

We welcome boys and girls from 3–11 and with pupil numbers around 100 we have the opportunity to know each child individually, to recognise and encourage their strengths and support them in overcoming areas of difficulty.

Our pupils enjoy a high degree of academic success, regularly obtaining places at their first choice of school, including passes at 11+ and Scholarships.

Courtesy and care for each other are important values nurtured at Sacred Heart School where children play and work well together.

Charitable status. Sacred Heart School, as part of the Arundel and Brighton Diocesan Trust, is a Registered Charity, number 252878.

St Andrew's School
Bedford

Kimbolton Road, Bedford MK40 2PA
Tel: 01234 267272
email: standrews@standrewsschoolbedford.com
website: www.standrewsschoolbedford.com

Chairman of Governors: Mr G Bates

Principal: Mr I M Daniel, BA, NPQH

Head of School: **Mrs H Ryan**, BEd Hons

Age Range. 6 weeks–16 years.
Number of Pupils. 250.
Fees per term (2014–2015). £1,680–£3,680.

Founded in 1896, as a boarding school for girls, St Andrew's School is a charitable trust run by a Board of Governors. It is now a day school and nursery for girls between 6 weeks and 16, and for boys from six weeks to 11. St Andrew's School is located in central Bedford and is based around two large Victorian houses that have seen modernisation and various additions to meet the needs of our pupils. Most recently a complete refurbishment of the Physics Laboratory has been undertaken to support the strong interest of our pupils in science. In September 2013 a close working partnership between St Andrew's School and Rushmoor School was formalised to increase educational opportunities, joint ventures and the sharing of best practice.

Our vision is to continually combine the best of traditional values with being at the forefront of educational advancement. Children in Reception and Junior classes benefit from a wide range of specialist teachers. By Year 9 our pupils are fully prepared to make informed choices for GCSE study.

The school's key aim is to provide the best possible standard of education and an appropriate level of challenge and support to allow each individual pupil to develop fully both academically and personally. Our GCSE results invariably demonstrate a very high degree of "value added". The high achievement at GCSE allows girls to study at competitive entry Sixth Forms, upper schools and colleges.

The older and younger girls form strong bonds outside the classroom through vertical tutor groups in Years 7–9, a pupil led House system, School Council and a wide range of co-curricular opportunities. These include team and individual sports, music, drama, science, ICT and art clubs. We offer a full range of outdoor and residential opportunities including the Blue Peris Mountain Centre and the Duke of Edinburgh's Award scheme.

Our community is a safe and peaceful environment which is both dynamic and caring, and which promotes strong values and mutual respect. To view our excellent inspection report, please visit our website.

We offer a limited number of means-tested bursaries and scholarships for pupils who excel in a particular field.

Charitable status. St Andrew's School (Bedford) Limited is a Registered Charity, number 307531.

St Anne's Preparatory School

154 New London Road, Chelmsford, Essex CM2 0AW
Tel: 01245 353488
Fax: 01245 353488
email: headmistress@stannesprep.essex.sch.uk
website: www.stannesprep.essex.sch.uk

Headmistress: **Mrs F Pirrie**, BSc, PGCE

Age Range. 3+–11+.
Number of Children. 160.
Fees per term (2014–2015). £2,275–£2,385.

St Anne's is a co-educational day school, with its own excellent nursery facility. Established in 1925, the school is conveniently situated in the centre of Chelmsford. The building is a large Victorian house, which has been carefully converted into the uses of a school. Extensive lawned areas, astroturf, playground and Nursery play area provide ample space for both recreation and games lessons. In addition, older pupils benefit from the use of the excellent sports facilities at the nearby Essex County Cricket Club.

The children benefit from small classes and individual attention in a disciplined but happy environment, which enables them to realise their full potential. Provision is made in the school for the gifted as well as those pupils less educationally able. Classrooms are bright and well equipped and the teachers are chosen for their qualifications, experience and understanding of the needs of their pupils.

St Anne's combines modern teaching with the best of traditional values. The school maintains a high standard of academic education giving great emphasis to a secure foundation in the basic subjects whilst offering a wide curriculum with specialist teaching in many areas.

Examination results at both KS1 and KS2 levels are excellent and many pupils gain places at the prestigious Grammar and Independent schools in the county.

The school offers a wide range of extra-curricular activities and an excellent after-care facility is available for all age groups. St Anne's is rightly recognised for its friendly and supportive ethos. Parents are particularly supportive of all aspects of school life. Visitors are always welcome.

St Christopher's School

6 Downs Road, Epsom, Surrey KT18 5HE
Tel: 01372 721807
Fax: 01372 726717
email: office@st-christophers.surrey.sch.uk
website: www.st-christophers.surrey.sch.uk

Headteacher: **Mrs A Thackray**, MA, BA, Dip Mus

Age Range. 3–7.
Number in School. 170.
Fees per term (2014–2015). £2,736 (Full time including lunch), £1,392 (5 mornings).

St Christopher's School (founded in 1938) is a co-educational nursery and pre-preparatory school for children from 3–7 years.

Set in a quiet residential area a short distance from the centre of Epsom, famous for the annual Derby and horse racing traditions, it has attractive secure grounds with gardens and play areas.

St Christopher's main purpose is to support children and parents through the early years of education. We offer a carefully managed induction programme to school life and, subsequently, a broad and challenging education within a happy, caring and secure family environment. Above all we aim to offer your child the best possible start to their education.

The children are prepared to enter a wide range of Surrey schools and we maintain a very high pass rate in a variety of entrance tests.

Breakfast Club opens at 8 am and After-School Care is available until 6 pm Monday to Friday. There are also a number of after-school clubs.

St Christopher's enjoys the support of an active parents association that organises a wide variety of social and fundraising events.

For further information and a prospectus please contact the school. Parents are welcome to visit the school by appointment with the Headteacher.

Charitable status. St Christopher's School Trust (Epsom) Limited is a Registered Charity, number 312045. It aims to provide a Nursery and Pre-Preparatory education in Epsom and district.

St Christopher's School

Mount Barton, Staverton, Totnes, Devon TQ9 6PF
Tel: 01803 762202
Fax: 01803 762202
email: office@st-christophers.devon.sch.uk
website: www.st-christophers.devon.sch.uk

Headmistress: **Mrs Victoria Kennington**

Age Range. 3–11 Co-educational.
Number of Pupils. 100.
Fees per term (2014–2015). Nursery: £215 per am/pm session; Reception £2,260; Years 1–6 £2,495.

St Christopher's School is a proprietorial school owned by Mrs Jane Kenyon, the Principal, and Mr Gregory Kenyon, the Bursar. It is a non-selective school with a Christian ethos. Admission is on completion of a Registration Form by the child's parents or guardians. We are a small, co-educational Prep School providing for children aged 3 to 11 years.

St Christopher's was established in 1991 and moved to its present site at Staverton in 1993. The school occupies 19th Century stables and barns converted to provide a delightful setting in which to learn, surrounded by the beautiful South Hams countryside.

At St Christopher's we treat your son or daughter as an individual, striving to discover their needs and abilities while giving them security and a sense of belonging to the community of the school family. In preparing children not only for the next stage of education, but for the wider world, we aim to provide solid foundations based on a clear Christian ethos, resulting in sound values and the ability to make clear judgements. Education is a team effort. We need and expect strong support from home. The family atmosphere at St Christopher's encourages a happy, cooperative approach including parental access to the teaching staff on an informal basis. Our formal reporting system lies in providing short quarterly reports two or three times a term and a full subject-based report at the end of each term. Formal parents' evenings are held in the Autumn and Summer Terms.

All pupils are prepared for entrance to Secondary Education and great care is taken to ensure that their transfer to the next stage of education is as smooth and positive as possible. The School has a long record of successfully preparing pupils for 11+ Entrance Examinations to the excellent local grammar schools and Common Entrance Examinations to Independent Senior Schools.

St Christopher's School

71 Wembley Park Drive, Wembley Park, Middlesex HA9 8HE
Tel: 020 8902 5069
Fax: 020 8903 5939
email: admin@stchristophersschool.org.uk
website: www.stchristophersschool.org.uk

Headteacher: **Mrs A McNeill**

Age Range. 4–11.

Number in School. 45 Boys, 36 Girls.
Fees per term (2014–2015). £2,500–£2,865. Discount for siblings 10%.

Entry requirements: Interview and Assessment.

St Christopher's School, a large Victorian building on Wembley Park Drive, offers a caring family atmosphere coupled with an equal emphasis on good manners, enthusiastic endeavour and academic excellence. The School, originally a Christian foundation dating from 1928, welcomes children of all faiths and cultures.

Caring and supportive staff provide a well-structured, disciplined and stimulating environment in which children are nurtured and encouraged to develop the necessary skills – academic, social and cultural – so that when they leave us at the age of 11 they can be certain of future success. All children at St Christopher's are equal and we emphasise the qualities of equality, justice and compassion. Children benefit from a curriculum that offers both breadth and depth, an activity programme that teaches skills and develops talents, and a pastoral programme that develops social responsibility.

The full range of academic subjects is taught based on an enriched National Curriculum. Sports and Music are seen as central elements in school life with sports matches, regular concerts and an annual carol service. In addition there is a variety of clubs and activities both at lunchtime and after school; these include Book Club, Booster Club, Choir, Cookery, First Aid, Gardening, Judo, Needlecraft, Netball and Recorders.

Children are prepared for the full range of examinations at 11 years. Eleven scholarships were awarded in 2013.

Recent leavers have gained entry to a wide range of excellent schools including Haberdasher's Boys and Girls, Merchant Taylors', Northwood College, Heathfield, St Helen's, North London Collegiate, City of London Boys and Girls, Henrietta Barnet, Queen Elizabeth's Boys Barnet, UCS, Aldenham School, John Lyon, St Paul's Girls' School and South Hampstead High.

St Christopher's offers both Pre-School and After-School Care, from 8:00 am until 5:30 pm.

Please phone for an appointment to view the school. We look forward to welcoming you.

St Clare's, Oxford

139 Banbury Road, Oxford OX2 7AL
Tel: 01865 552031
Fax: 01865 513359
email: admissions@stclares.ac.uk
website: www.stclares.ac.uk/ib

Principal: **Mrs Paula Holloway**, BSc, PGCE, MSc Oxon, DipPM

Age Range. 15–19 Co-educational.
Number of Students. 270.
Fees per term (2014–2015). Boarding £11,363, Day £5,569.

Established over 60 years St Clare's is an international college with a mission "To advance international education and understanding", something it has been doing successfully ever since. The College embraces internationalism and academic excellence as core values. It is a co-educational day and residential college which has been offering the International Baccalaureate Diploma for over 35 years, longer than any other school or college in England. Students have achieved the maximum 45 points for the past 10 consecutive years.

Students from over 45 countries study at St Clare's with a core group of British students. The atmosphere is informal and friendly with an equal emphasis on hard work and developing personal responsibility. Each student has a Personal tutor who oversees welfare and progress.

St Clare's has an especially wide range of subjects on offer at Higher and Standard level and, in addition, currently teaches 28 different languages. The College takes a small number of transfer students each year. For students not yet ready to begin the IB Diploma, a Pre-IB course is offered with regular entry points throughout the year. There is an extensive programme of social, cultural and sporting activities and students are encouraged to take full advantage of the opportunities that Oxford provides.

The College also runs a 3-week introduction to the IB Diploma in July and August. St Clare's is also authorised to run IB workshops for teachers.

St Clare's is located in an elegant residential area which is part of the North Oxford Conservation Area. It occupies 28 large Victorian and Edwardian houses to which purpose-built facilities have been added. These include a beautiful library building (over 35,000 volumes, an IT suite and a Careers and Higher Education Information Centre), six science laboratories and three mathematics classes in a stunning new building on the campus, art and music studios, dining room and the popular Sugar House café. Students live in College houses close to the central campus under the care of residential staff.

The College welcomes applications from international and UK students. Entry is based on academic results, interview and confidential school report. There is a competitive scholarship and bursary programme awarded by examination, interview and group exercises.

St Clare's had a highly successful ISI inspection in March 2013; the full Report can be accessed via the College website. The College was awarded the highest rating for the quality of its boarding after its Ofsted inspection in March 2009.

Charitable status. St Clare's, Oxford is a Registered Charity, number 294085.

St David's College

Justin Hall, Beckenham Road, West Wickham, Kent BR4 0QS
Tel: 020 8777 5852
Fax: 020 8777 9549
email: StDavids@dial.pipex.com
          sarah.handy@btconnect.com
website: www.stdavidscollege.com

Principal: **Mrs A Wagstaff**, BA Hons London, FHA Cert IT & Comp Open

Head Teacher: Mrs J Foulger, BA Hons, PGCE

Deputy Head: Mrs J Grainge, Foundation Degree Early Years, Cert Ed, Dip Nursery Nursing

Bursar: Mrs R Smith, MA Hons Edinburgh, ACA

Age Range. 4–11.
Number in School. Day: 80 Boys, 71 Girls.
Fees per term (2014–2015). £2,350–£2,400. Reduction in fees for all siblings.

A full-time staff of nine teachers, all fully qualified, is supplemented by ten part-time specialist teachers. Entry is by interview and informal test. Pupils are prepared for entrance to independent schools at age 11, as well as for the Kent grammar schools and for places at the London Boroughs of Bexley, Bromley and Sutton selective schools. Many scholarships and awards are gained each year. The school offers before and after-school care.

Speech and Drama, Cello, Clarinet, Dance, Flute, Music Theory, Piano, Recorder, Solo Singing, Recorder, Trumpet and Violin lessons are available. Sports include Athletics,

Cricket, Cross-Country, Football, Hockey, Netball, Rounders, Swimming and Tennis. There is a Chess Club, Computing Club, Dance, School Choir and a School Orchestra.

There are separate infant and junior schools, set within extensive and beautiful grounds. The school is positioned close to bus routes and to the mid-Kent and Hayes railway line, and is within easy reach of Bromley South and East Croydon stations.

The Principal and Head Teacher are always pleased to show the school to visitors.

St David's School

23–25 Woodcote Valley Road, Purley, Surrey CR8 3AL
Tel: 020 8660 0723
Fax: 020 8645 0426
email: office@stdavidsschool.co.uk
website: www.stdavidsschool.co.uk

Head Teacher: **Miss Cressida Mardell**

Age Range. 3+–11.
Number in School. 156 Day: 87 boys, 69 girls.
Fees per term (2014–2015). £1,615–£2,895 (including lunch).

We look forward to welcoming you to our happy and creative school, where we aim to achieve the highest academic standards. At St David's we offer a rich and stimulating curriculum, delivered by a talented and caring staff, giving your child the best possible start. The School has undergone many changes and developments since its foundation in 1912 and we have recently celebrated our 100th birthday! Please visit our recently re-launched website to find out more about all the exciting things that have been going on.

The small school atmosphere is, we believe, a strength and reassuring to parents and children alike. We aim to balance nurture with independence to equip your child to succeed academically and we are extremely proud of our results. Please do contact us to experience the warm inspiring environment that is the "St David's Family". Please telephone the School Office to arrange an appointment and I look forward to showing you round our school.

St David's participates fully in the Government Nursery Vouchers Scheme.

Charitable status. St David's (Purley) Educational Trust is a Registered Charity, number 312613. It aims to provide a quality education for boys and girls from 3+ to 11 years old. Bursaries are awarded in cases of financial hardship.

St Gerard's School
Bangor

Ffriddoedd Road, Bangor, Gwynedd LL57 2EL
Tel: 01248 351656
Fax: 01248 351204
email: sgadmin@st-gerards.org
website: www.st-gerards.org

Chairman of the Governing Body: Mr D Breslin

Headteacher: **Miss Anne Parkinson**, BA

Age Range. 3–18.
Number in School. Day: 85 Boys, 92 Girls.
Fees per term (2014–2015). £2,030–£3,070.
Founded in 1915 by the Congregation of the Sisters of Mercy, this co-educational school is now a lay trust. The school welcomes pupils of all denominations and traditions

and has an excellent reputation locally. It has consistently attracted a high profile in national league tables also.

Class sizes in both junior and senior schools ensure close support and individual attention in order to enable all pupils to achieve their full academic potential, within an environment which promotes their development as well-rounded individuals with a keen social conscience.

The curriculum is comprehensive – pupils in the senior section usually achieve 9/10 good GCSE grades, going on to A Level and to university.

Charitable status. St Gerard's School Trust is a Registered Charity, number 1001211.

St Hilda's School

28 Douglas Road, Harpenden, Hertfordshire AL5 2ES
Tel: 01582 712307
email: office@sthildasharpenden.co.uk
website: www.sthildasharpenden.co.uk

Head: **Mr D Sayers**, BA Hons, QTS

Age Range. 3–11.
Number in School. 180 approx.
Fees per term (2014–2015). £3,325 (Forms II to VI including lunch), £3,295 (Reception & Form I including lunch), Nursery: £1,905–£2,785 (including lunch if appropriate).

St Hilda's School, situated in a residential site of 1¼ acres, has its own swimming pool, hard tennis/netball court and adjacent playing field. It also has a fully-equipped stage, a suite of music rooms, a dedicated computer suite, a science lab, a purpose-built EYFS unit, an art room, and six new classrooms.

A broad, well-balanced curriculum covering the requirements of the National Curriculum prepares girls for the Common Entrance and other senior independent school entrance examinations. Girls also enter State secondary schools if desired. Latin and French are taught to all pupils, and German and Spanish sessions are also available.

The school is well known for its high musical standards with almost all pupils learning an instrument, many two or three. The standards in drama, art and sport are also consistently high.

A prospectus is available on application to the School Secretary.

St James Junior School

Earsby Street, London W14 8SH
Tel: 020 7348 1794
email: admissions@stjamesjunior.org
website: www.stjamesjuniors.co.uk

Chair of Governors: Mr Jeremy Sinclair

Headmistress: **Mrs Catherine Thomlinson**, BA Hons

Age Range. Boys 4–11+. Boys can then transfer to St James Senior Boys' School (*see entry in The Society of Heads section*) or other senior schools.
Girls 4–10+. Girls then transfer to Year 6 at St James Senior Girls' School (*see entry in GSA section*).
Number in School. 125 Boys and 127 Girls.
Fees per term (2014–2015). £4,610.

St James provides an inspiring education. The Junior School is situated on a large Central London site and the beautiful Victorian building provides an Assembly Hall/

Theatre, Gym and large airy classrooms. The playground has a climbing wall and pretty cloister gardens.

The curriculum is imaginatively and carefully balanced and, together with the impressive level of commitment from the teaching staff, high academic standards of reading, writing and arithmetic are achieved and above all a love of knowledge. Art, Drama and Music are taught with enthusiasm and results are outstanding; children sing daily and morning assemblies bring joy and a sense of unity throughout the school.

An interest and knowledge in that which is common to all traditions is cultivated. Every class has a weekly Philosophy lesson during which they explore virtues such as consideration, friendship and truthfulness. The school's philosophy curriculum is available on the website, together with curriculum details of all subjects taught.

Team sports, gymnastics or athletics are played daily and full use is made of good facilities both within school and locally. A rota of after-school clubs offers a rich choice of activities, including Ballet, French, Fencing, Cricket, Netball, Ornithology, Rugby and Yoga.

Creative residential holidays are organised each year for children in the Upper Junior School (7+ years) to places such as New Barn in Dorset, Chartres in France and to Northumberland, where History, Geography and Geometry become a living experience and time is enjoyed out of London with their friends and teachers.

Boys and girls are taught separately with frequent joint activities such as plays, concerts and outings. Educating the children about the environment is part of the school's wider curriculum. The Reception classes are involved with the Forest Schools programme and from Year 3 the children visit Minstead Study Centre in Dorset, where they learn about the environment and look after livestock.

The obvious happiness of the children flows from the full education offered and a level of attention and care from teachers that has become a St James trademark.

Charitable status. The Independent Educational Association Limited is a Registered Charity, number 270156. It exists to provide education for boys and girls.

St James' School
A Woodard School

22 Bargate, Grimsby, North East Lincolnshire DN34 4SY
Tel: 01472 503260
Fax: 01472 503275
email: enquiries@saintjamesschool.co.uk
website: www.saintjamesschool.co.uk
Twitter: @StJamesSchoolGY
Facebook: /stjamesschoolgrimsby

Headmaster: **Dr John Price**, BSc Hons, PhD

Age Range. 2–18.
Number in School. Boarders: Boys 25, Girls 14. Day: Boys 133, Girls 118.
Fees per term (2014–2015). Tuition: Prep School: Reception £1,535 to Year 6 £2,419. Senior School Day Pupils: £2,870–£3,689. Boarding: £2,100 (weekly), £2,550 (termly).

St James' School, Grimsby provides an excellent day and boarding education for children aged 2 to 18 years. The School is co-educational and a fully incorporated Member of the Woodard Corporation.

Pupils benefit from an extremely supportive environment that creates a rich and rewarding educational experience. Our highly qualified and dedicated teaching staff have the ability and experience necessary to be able to inspire and enthuse every pupil. This teaching excellence, along with the small class sizes, equips our pupils with the knowledge, skills and understanding they require to reach their academic potential.

All pupils are given the opportunity to take part in a vast range of extra-curricular activities above and beyond the traditional sporting programme: from Sailing, to Archery, Horse Riding and Golf. Every pupil has a talent and such experiences ensure that we are able to discover that talent and ultimately develop the most important things, which are confidence and self-esteem.

The School offers academic scholarships and also bursaries for Choristers and candidates within the Academy Girls' Choir (both subject to voice trials).

The School operates a morning bus service calling in at villages from the Louth and Brigg areas.

Charitable status. St James' School Grimsby Ltd is a Registered Charity, number 1099060. It exists to provide education for boys and girls.

St John's School

47–49 Stock Road, Billericay, Essex CM12 0AR
Tel: 01277 623070
Fax: 01277 651288
email: registrar@stjohnsschool.net
           a.fleming@stjohnsschool.net
website: www.stjohnsschool.net
Twitter: @StJBillericay
Facebook: /StJBillericay

Headteacher: **Mrs Fiona Armour**, BEd Hons

Age Range. 3–16.
Number in School. Day: 167 Boys, 146 Girls.
Fees per term (2014–2015). £1,600–£3,895.
St John's School enjoys a beautiful setting in 8 acres overlooking Lake Meadows Park in Billericay. It is ideally located for public transport links and is only a five-minute walk from Billericay station.

St John's School is an independent school which is known for its excellent levels of pastoral care and its friendly atmosphere. Pupils are taught in small classes by dedicated teachers. A range of extra-curricular activities and clubs is offered, including skiing, bowling, street dancing and rock school. All pupils are valued as individuals and their individual talents and strengths are nurtured in a supportive and happy environment.

Means-tested scholarships are available. For more information and to arrange a tour of the school, please contact the Mrs Philpott on 01277 623070 or by email to registrar@stjohnsschool.net.

St Joseph's Convent School

59 Cambridge Park, Wanstead, London E11 2PR
Tel: 020 8989 4700
Fax: 020 8989 4700
email: enquiries@stjosephsconventschool.co.uk

Chair of Governors: Sr Catherine Quane

Headteacher: **Ms Christine Glover**

Age Range. 3–11.
Number in School. 174 Day Girls.
Fees per term (2014–2015). £1,950.
Charitable status. Institute of Our Lady of Mercy is a Registered Charity, number 290544.

St Joseph's Park Hill School

Padiham Road, Burnley, Lancashire BB12 6TG
Tel: 01282 455622
Fax: 01282 435375
email: office@parkhillschool.co.uk
website: www.parkhillschool.co.uk

Chairman of Governors: Mrs Catherine McDermott

Head Teacher: **Mrs A Robinson**, BEd Hons

Age Range. 3–11 Co-educational.
Number of Pupils. 99.
Fees per term (2014–2015). £1,916.
St Joseph's was founded by the Sisters of Mercy in 1913 and has operated from its present site since 1957.

It is a small school with a warm, friendly atmosphere where the children are known personally by all the staff. We have a broad, enriched curriculum which provides many activities and opportunities, both sporting and musical. The children enjoy their learning experience and are encouraged to do their best, achieving excellent results.

The Catholic ethos permeates all areas of the school. Pupils learn to care for each other, and respect different cultures. We welcome children from all faiths.

The school has the benefit of extensive grounds and offers a morning and after-school service as well as a 4-week summer school.

Charitable status. St Joseph's School is owned by The Institute of our Lady of Mercy which is a Registered Charity, number 290544.

St Joseph's Preparatory School

Rookery Lane, Trent Vale, Stoke-on-Trent, Staffordshire ST4 5RF
Tel: 01782 417533
Fax: 01782 849327
email: enquiries@stjosephsprepschool.co.uk
website: www.stjosephsprepschool.co.uk

Chair of Governors: Mr S Hulme

Head: **Mrs S D Hutchinson**, BEd

Age Range. 3–11 Co-educational.
Number of Pupils. 160 Day Pupils.
Fees per term (2014–2015). £1,750–£2,300.
Charitable status. The Congregation of Christian Brothers is a Registered Charity, number 254312.

St Joseph's School

St Stephens Hill, Launceston, Cornwall PL15 8HN
Tel: 01566 772580
email: registrar@stjosephscornwall.co.uk
website: www.stjosephscornwall.co.uk

Head Teacher: **Mrs Sue Rowe**

Deputy Head: Mrs Elisabeth Mann
Junior Head: Mrs Sue Marks
Director of Studies: Mr Oliver Scott
Bursar: Mr Ian Barton
Registrar: Miss Rebecca Walker

Age Range. 3–16 Co-educational.
Number in School. 220.

Fees per term (2014–2015). £1,560–£4,095.

St Joseph's School, Launceston is an award-winning Independent Day School for boys and girls from 3–16.

St Joseph's has a truly unique atmosphere. The school's small size means that it is possible to keep sight of strong family values, which gives children the confidence necessary to succeed, and to allow both staff and pupils to work happily together. Due to the high teacher-pupil ratio, St Joseph's is able to encourage each pupil to reach his or her full potential through positive encouragement and commendation.

The school provides an excellent academic education for all, regardless of ability and background, with a wide variety of extra-curricular activities to provide balance and insight into opportunity. It offers equal prospects to all and inspires them to respond positively to challenges through encouragement and commendation.

In 2013 GCSE pupils achieved a superb set of results with 100% gaining five A*–C grades including Maths and English, 42% of which were A* or A grades. This is a remarkable achievement as St Joseph's is a non-selective school, meaning that there is no entrance exam and admission is possible at any time throughout a child's education. Fees are set at levels which offer tremendous value for money, particularly in light of what is on offer to all the pupils at the school and our excellent academic results.

National Honours have been gained in many areas including athletics, swimming and music. The senior chamber choir is a "flagship" choir for the South West, having appeared on both local and national television.

Academic and Sports Scholarships are offered from age 7+ and Music Scholarships from 11+. Bursaries are available and considered on an individual basis.

An extensive daily bus service (7 bus routes) allows pupils from a wide area of Devon and Cornwall to attend St Joseph's.

St Joseph's School offers a number of open events throughout the year for prospective parents or to arrange an individual visit please contact the Registrar. Further information can be found at www.stjosephscornwall.co.uk or by contacting the Registrar on 01566 772580, registrar@stjosephscornwall.co.uk.

Charitable status. St Joseph's School is a Registered Charity, number 289048.

St Joseph's School

33 Derby Road, Nottingham NG1 5AW
Tel: 0115 941 8356
email: office@st-josephs.nottingham.sch.uk
website: www.st-josephs.nottingham.sch.uk

Head Teacher: **Mr Ian Eastwood**, BEd Hons

Age Range. 1–11 years.
Number in School. 90 Boys, 60 Girls.
Fees per term (2014–2015). £2,576 (Main School Reception to Year 6). Nursery fees on application.

A co-educational day school providing the very highest standards to children of all abilities. Children receive individual attention in small classes. The curriculum is planned to encourage children to develop lively, enquiring minds with emphasis on literacy and numeracy. Music and Drama have a high profile in the school.

Sports include Football, Netball, Cricket, Rounders, Tag Rugby, Swimming, and Squash.

Extra-curricular activities include Karate, Archery, Dance, Speech and Drama, Chess, Piano, Drums, Violin, and Guitar.

It provides a happy and caring environment in which children can develop their full potential both socially and academically. The school is Roman Catholic but welcomes children of all faiths.

Charitable status. St Joseph's School Nottingham is a Registered Charity, number 1003916.

St Margaret's Preparatory School
Cognita Schools Group

Gosfield Hall Park, Gosfield, Halstead, Essex CO9 1SE
Tel: 01787 472134
Fax: 01787 478207
email: admin@stmargaretsprep.com
website: www.stmargaretsprep.com

Principal: **Mrs E Powling**

Age Range. 2–11.
Number of Pupils. Day: 131 Boys, 124 Girls.
Fees per term (2014–2015). £2,775–£3,335.

St Margaret's is an ISA accredited school which specializes in the needs of children from 2 to 11 years. Academically, we provide excellence beyond the National Curriculum, stretching each child to the best of their individual ability, but not at the expense of a full and varied childhood. Although we regularly gain academic, music, art and sports scholarships to Senior schools, the emphasis is on an all-round education, encompassing the academic needs, enriching aspects such as social integration and encouraging other interests of each individual. Typically, a child at St Margaret's will have two afternoons a week of coached sport as well as a PE lesson, extra coaching sessions at lunchtime for the keen and able, and numerous after-school clubs. These clubs encompass a whole range of activities including fencing, archery, all major sports, speech and drama, martial arts, ballet, country dancing, chess, Forensic Science – the list goes on. They are regarded as an important and integral part of school, broadening their horizons. With a purpose-built ICT Suite and Art Studio, along with Music Rooms, Science Lab and gymnasium, the children have every opportunity to excel in their chosen sphere.

Naturally, the school has choirs, ensembles, an orchestra and numerous concerts and plays throughout the year. There are trips to Art Galleries, concerts, museums, as well as taking part in Festivals, competitions and local events.

Our extensive curriculum provides the children with the social confidence and academic ability to achieve their potential.

St Martin's Preparatory School

63 Bargate, Grimsby, N E Lincolnshire DN34 5AA
Tel: 01472 878907
email: secretary@stmartinsprep.co.uk
            headmaster@stmartinsprep.co.uk
website: www.stmartinsprep.co.uk

Headmaster: **Mr S Thompson**, BEd

Age Range. 2–11.
Number in School. Day: 58 Boys, 64 Girls.
Fees per term (2014–2015). £1,690–£2,080.

St Martin's was founded in 1930. It aims to foster an interest in learning from an early age. A fully qualified and dedicated staff ensure that a high standard in Primary School subjects is attained throughout the school. French is taught from the age of 3 and Spanish from the age of 7. Children are taught in small classes and great attention is given to individual development. Specialist teaching is also available for children who need specific support or extension.

The purpose-built Early Years block is a modern building full of light and colour, which enhances the already excellent education provided by the main school.

Girls and boys are prepared for Common Entrance and the 11+ examination. The vast majority of children transfer to the local Grammar schools. The school offers a range of clubs, including Yoga, Art, Football, Netball, Boules, Chess, Table Tennis, Computer and Drama. The school has an orchestra and two choirs. A happy and friendly atmosphere prevails throughout the school.

St Michael's School

Bryn, Llanelli, Carmarthenshire SA14 9TU
Tel: 01554 820325
Fax: 01554 821716
email: office@stmikes.co.uk
          bursar@stmikes.co.uk
website: www.stmikes.co.uk
Facebook: /St-Michaels-School

Headteacher: **Alun J Millington**, MA Oxon, PGCE

Head of Senior School: Kay Francis, BSc Hons, PGCE
Head of Prep School: Mari Davies, BA Ed Hons, PG Dip Ed

Age Range. 3–18.
Number in School. 383: 207 boys, 176 girls.
Fees per term (from January 2015). Tuition: Preparatory School £1,654–£2,686; Senior School £3,557–£3,885. Sibling allowances available. Boarding per annum (2014–2015): Twin room: Years 7–8 £19,600, Year 9 £20,100, Years 10–11 (GCSE) £21,600. Years 9–11 single room supplement £1,000. Sixth Form (A Level) £25,000 (single room).

St Michael's is very much in the pattern of the small well-disciplined grammar schools. The school has a traditional approach to learning, which does not mean it lives in the past, but places emphasis on the importance of hard work and homework in the school curriculum. The high academic standards of the school are reflected in the National League Tables. In 2013 the school was ranked 37th in The Times Top 100 Co-Educational Schools in the UK.

No school can build up such a strong reputation without a competitive, but well-disciplined atmosphere and a highly-qualified and dedicated staff. This is where we feel St Michael's is particularly fortunate.

In 2013 the school began an exciting new phase with the commissioning of two brand new developments. In addition to Park House, which is a handsome and historic mansion set in an acre of grounds in the village of Llangennech, our new, on-site, purpose-built, state-of-the-art, 31-bedroom boarding house, 'Ty Mawr', was commissioned. Both houses offer a high standard of comfort where every pupil feels safe, happy and protected. Pupils are accommodated in well-furnished and equipped, single en-suite or shared study-bedrooms. The houses provide spacious recreation rooms and pleasant grounds in which pupils may relax, play or watch TV. The Early Learning Centre for pupils aged between 3 and 7 also opened its doors for the first time in January 2013.

We have well-equipped computer laboratories where pupils have access to a computer each from 3 years of age. Languages taught in the school are French, Spanish, Welsh and Chinese (Mandarin).

The school has an envied reputation for its academic achievement but is also proud of the wide range of traditional games and activities it offers. Pupils from Year 10 onwards pupils can also take part in the Duke of Edin-

burgh's Award Scheme to Gold Award standard. We have a large choir and school orchestra and pupils may take music examinations at GCSE and A Level.

One of the main reasons behind the school's success is the thorough grounding that pupils receive in the 'basics' – English, Mathematics, ICT and Science in the school's Preparatory Department.

We have enjoyed outstanding sporting success over the last few years in netball, rugby, football, tennis, cricket and athletics.

Every pupil is encouraged to develop their full potential whether in academic work or in all the extra-curricular activities on offer.

St Nicholas House School

Yarmouth Road, North Walsham, Norfolk NR28 9AT
Tel: 01692 403143
email: office@stnicholashouse.com
website: www.stnicholashouse.com

Headmaster: **Mr M Castle**, BA, PGCE

Age Range. 2–11 co-educational.
Number of Pupils. 66.
Fees per term (2014–2015). £1,675.

St Nicholas House School is a small caring happy environment where children are encouraged to try their best and provided with the opportunity to thrive.

In small classes children benefit from a wide and varied curriculum giving a solid grounding and foundation in English and Maths, in addition to history, geography, art, craft, RE and ICT. Subject specialists teach French and Music from Reception to Year 6. In addition Peripatetic teachers offer a wide variety of musical instruments, speech and drama, dancing and singing.

Children are encouraged to try as many activities as possible through Clubs and after-school activities such as skiing, golf and chess. Sport plays an important part in the curriculum and in a child's time in the school, they will have the opportunity to try football, hockey, swimming, netball, cricket, rounders and short tennis in addition to seasonal sports.

The school enjoys an excellent success rate in entrance examinations to Senior independent schools obtaining numerous academic, sporting and drama scholarships.

Please telephone for an appointment to come and see us at work and play.

Saint Nicholas School

Hillingdon House, Hobbs Cross Road, Old Harlow, Essex CM17 0NJ
Tel: 01279 429910
Fax: 01279 450224
email: office@saintnicholasschool.net
          admissions@saintnicholasschool.net
website: www.saintnicholasschool.net
Twitter: @SaintNicksSch
Facebook: /saintnicholasschoolharlow

Headmaster: **Mr K M Knight**, BEd Hons, MA, NPQH

Age Range. 3–16.
Number in School. 351 Day Pupils: 185 Boys, 166 Girls.
Fees per term (from April 2014). £1,700-£3,320.

Saint Nicholas School is celebrating 75 years of excellence and is situated in a delightful rural location. Saint

Nicholas combines a fresh and enthusiastic approach to learning with a firm belief in traditional values.

The academic record of the school is excellent, reflected in high pupil success rates in all competitive examinations. The dedicated team of staff involves itself closely with all aspects of pupils' educational progress and general development. High standards of formal teaching are coupled with positive encouragement for pupils to reason for themselves and develop a high degree of responsibility.

As part of the school's commitment to providing affordable, quality care to children in the community, Little Saints Pre-School for 3 and 4 year olds opened its doors in September 2014. Recent building developments include magnificent junior and infant department buildings, theatre, science and technology centre, swimming pool and sports hall, and new on-site catering facilities are on schedule to open in January 2015.

Main sports include hockey, netball, tennis, football, rugby, cricket, swimming, athletics and gymnastics. Optional extras include ballet, individual instrumental lessons, karate, performing arts and Spanish classes.

Charitable status. Saint Nicholas School (Harlow) Limited is a Registered Charity, number 310876. It exists to provide and promote educational enterprise by charitable means.

St Peter's School

52 Headlands, Kettering, Northamptonshire NN15 6DJ
Tel: 01536 512066
Fax: 01536 416469
email: st-petersschool@btconnect.com
website: www.st-peters.org.uk

Headmistress: **Mrs M Chapman**, MA Ed, BA Hons, PGCE

   Age Range. 2 years 9 months – 11.
   Number in School. Day: 47 Boys, 56 Girls.
   Fees per term (2014–2015). £2,075–£3,185.
   Established in 1946, St Peter's is a small day school set in pleasant grounds on the outskirts of Kettering. It offers a sound education for boys and girls aged 2 years 9 months to 11. Pupils are thoroughly prepared for entry into their senior schools and a high rate of success in Entrance and Scholarship Examinations is regularly achieved. In addition to fulfilling the requirements of the National Curriculum the school emphasises the importance of Music, Art, Sport and Information Technology in its programme. French is introduced at Nursery.

St Peter's School is a lively, friendly school with a strong family atmosphere where children are encouraged to develop to the full their individual strengths and talents. It aims to promote, through Christian teaching, a respect for traditional values, a sense of responsibility and a concern for the needs of others.

   Charitable status. St Peter's School is a Registered Charity, number 309914. It exists to maintain and manage a school for boys and girls in the town of Kettering.

St Philomena's Catholic School

Hadleigh Road, Frinton-on-Sea, Essex CO13 9HQ
Tel: 01255 674492
Fax: 01255 674459
email: generalenquiries@stphilomenas.com
website: www.stphilomenas.com

Co-educational Day School.

Chair of Governors: Mrs Josephine Geldard

Headteacher: **Mrs Barbara McKeown**, DipEd, CTC

   Age Range. 3–11.
   Number of Pupils. 113: 75 girls, 38 boys.
   Fees per term (2014–2015). £1,810–£2,200.
   St Philomena's is situated in a pleasant coastal area close to the beach. The school is dedicated to providing sound education based on Gospel values of the Whole Child within a Christian environment. Children flourish in the tangible family atmosphere throughout the school.

Very good attitudes to learning are promoted for the mixed ability intake. Pupils strive for high academic standards and have achieved a very good record in 11+ selection examinations for both the grammar schools in the maintained sector and secondary schools in the independent sector.

Staff are fully qualified, experienced and dedicated professionals who communicate well with parents. Very high standards in pupil behaviour are maintained – pupils are caring and courteous with each other and towards adults.

There is a wide range of extra-curricular activities including sports clubs, science club, Scrabble, chess, art, cycling proficiency and ICT. Tuition is offered for a wide range of musical instruments including, piano, violin, drums, guitar, flute, clarinet, trumpet and saxophone. Music lessons with a music specialist take place throughout the school and there are recorder lessons for whole classes. There are weekly swimming lessons and French lessons available for Key Stage 2. The school choirs and drama groups have achieved outstanding success in local and national competitions in recent years.

Emphasis is given to physical education. There are representative teams for football, hockey, cricket, rounders, netball, and cross country (numbers permitting). Tennis is taught to the senior children.

All children are encouraged to speak confidently and to express themselves clearly. All children from 7+ participate in an annual oral communication assessment adjudicated externally. Parents are invited to regular concerts, plays, class presentations and class assemblies.

   Charitable status. St Philomena's Preparatory School is a Registered Charity, number 298635. It exists to provide Roman Catholic children and those of other denominations with the opportunity to reach the highest possible standards in every area of school life.

St Piran's School

14 Trelissick Road, Hayle, Cornwall TR27 4HY
Tel: 01736 752612
Fax: 01736 759446
email: admin@stpirans.net
website: www.stpiranshayle.net

Headteacher: **Mrs Carol A de Labat**, BEd Hons, CertEd

   Age Range. 3–16.
   Number of Pupils. 63.
   Fees per term (2014–2015). £870–£2,225.
   Established in 1988, St Piran's School is set in attractive and well-maintained premises which, at present, accommodate around seventy children, aged from three to sixteen. It is a friendly, well-ordered community with a positive ethos where pupils make good friendships with each other and relate well to staff. Pupils are treated with respect and valued equally. They have a clear sense of right and wrong. There is a good sense of community within the school and new pupils are quickly made to feel welcome. The school places a strong emphasis on good manners and politeness.

The curriculum is broad and balanced and helps to prepare the children for the next stage in their education. A wide variety of after school and lunchtime clubs provide additional activities and experiences for pupils of all ages. Educational visits to local places of interest and annual residential visits (for Year 5 and up) further enrich the curriculum.

From Years Five and Six there is greater emphasis on subjects being taught by specialists. Class size remains low, with the maximum class size being twelve. Well-qualified, conscientious and hard-working staff teach children in a supportive learning environment. Children are given the opportunity to explain their ideas and be involved in activities. There is a very well-equipped and effectively-organised computer suite, which ensures that the children are at the cutting edge of technology.

Results for our 2014 GCSE examinations were good and we were delighted by their achievement.

St Teresa's Catholic Independent School & Nursery

Aylesbury Road, Princes Risborough, Buckinghamshire HP27 0JW
Tel: 01844 345005
Fax: 01844 345131
email: office@st-teresas.bucks.sch.uk
website: www.st-teresas.bucks.sch.uk

Head Teacher: **Mrs T Milton**, CertEd

Age Range. 3–11.
Number in School. 51 Boys, 70 Girls. Nursery School: 11 Boys, 10 Girls.
Fees per term (2014–2015). £2,818.77 (first child), £2,645.37 (siblings).

St Teresa's School is primarily a Catholic School, but is open to boys and girls of all religions or none.

A full programme of clubs includes Wrap-Around Care 7.45 am to 6 pm, kwik cricket, rounders, tennis, football, netball, cross-country, athletics, swimming, chess, choir, orchestra and others.

A well-qualified and caring staff prepares the children for independent and state senior schools. The school has an excellent academic record of achievement and our pupils leave as confident and well-mannered individuals.

The children are encouraged to live out the school motto, *Fidelity* – faith in God, faith in others and faith in oneself.

Charitable status. St Teresa's is a Registered Charity, number 310645. It exists to provide a broad education enfolded by the Catholic faith.

St Winefride's Convent School
Shrewsbury

Belmont, Shrewsbury, Shropshire SY1 1TE
Tel: 01743 369883
Fax: 01743 369883
email: st.winefrides@btconnect.com
website: www.stwinefrides.com

Headmistress: **Sister M Felicity**, BA Hons

Age Range. 4+–11. Nursery: 3+–4.
Number in School. Day: 83 Boys, 81 Girls.
Fees per term (from April 2014). £1,295–£1,370.

St Winifred's School

17–19 Winn Road, Portswood, Southampton SO17 1EJ
Tel: 023 8055 7352
email: office@stwinifreds.southampton.sch.uk
website: www.stwinifreds.southampton.sch.uk

Chairman of Board of Trustees: Mr John W Watts, MCIPS, MILT, AIGEM

Head: **Mrs C A Pearcey**, BEd

Age Range. 3–11 Co-educational.
Number of Pupils. 100.
Fees per term (2014–2015). £2,410 (Lunch £145).

St Winifred's is a small school, on a pleasant, urban road in central Southampton, close to the university. It exists to make *the most of Individual Talent – nurturing every child*. The school caters for children aged 4–11; the pre-school takes children from age three, including those receiving Nursery Education Funding. The school provides before and after care from 8.00 am until 6.00 pm.

The School aims to provide for the whole child through a varied curriculum, with a wide programme of study and opportunities to develop all aspects of every pupil's talents. The core subjects, English, Maths and Science, as well as the development of ICT skills, are at the centre of learning throughout the school. Pupils are encouraged and helped to develop a disciplined approach to personal study skills at all ages. Group and class activities help everyone to experience cooperative work and gain useful understanding of others skills and feelings.

Details of the curriculum can be found on our website. A structured academic program is covered by all age groups. This is delivered by specialist staff that enable every pupil to achieve their potential. Continuous assessment and tests prepare the upper school pupils for their entrance exams and for further achievement at secondary school.

The School provides regular feedback about pupils' progress at Parents' Evenings and through reports. Weekly newsletters are emailed to parents informing them of events pupils are involved in as well as activities happening within the school. Parents are encouraged to be involved in their children's education where ever possible.

The School is proud of its achievements in music, drama, games, swimming and dance. As well as our own two indoor hall spaces and playground, the school takes advantage of The Gregg School's sporting facilities. Weekly games, swimming and gym/dance sessions with qualified staff are provided, as well as a variety of after-school activities.

Upper school pupils gain valuable experience whilst preparing for Communication examinations. Each year many pupils achieve distinctions and merits but, most importantly, all gain much personal satisfaction and confidence that will help them in later life.

Further opportunities are provided, through extra-curricular activities, to develop pupils' individual talents and personal strengths and interests. Monthly Achievement Assemblies celebrate individual and group interests in and out of school as well as focusing on pupils Endeavour and Courtesy within school. These are an opportunity for every individual to learn their own self-worth.

For taster days and further information, please contact the school secretary or visit our website.

Charitable status. The Gregg and St Winifred's Schools Trust is a Registered Charity, number 1089055.

St Wystan's School

High Street, Repton, Derbyshire DE65 6GE
Tel: 01283 703258
Fax: 01283 703258
email: head@stwystans.org.uk
website: www.stwystans.org.uk

Headmaster: **Mr P Soutar**, BEd Hons

Age Range. 2½–11.
Number in School. Day: Boys 56, Girls 53.
Fees per term (2014–2015). £2,455. Compulsory extras: Lunch £250.

A small number of scholarships are offered for 7+ entry to Year 3.

Situated in the historic village of Repton, only a short distance from Burton-on-Trent and the city of of Derby, St Wystan's is ideally placed to serve a wide catchment area. Both Nottingham and Uttoxeter are within 25 minutes of the school, though the majority of pupils come from Derby, Burton and surrounding villages.

St Wystan's prides itself on a family atmosphere in which every child can grow in confidence and develop to his or her full potential as an individual. Great emphasis is placed on courtesy and good manners and a pastoral system, centred on the four School Houses, promotes a caring environment and develops teamwork and commitment.

Academic expectations are high, though the school serves a wide ability range and is non-selective. Small classes enable the children to receive individual attention and work at a pace appropriate to their ability. As a freestanding junior school, St Wystan's prepares pupils for a large number of senior schools and pupils have won a significant number of academic, sport and music scholarships recently.

The pre-school department provides a Nursery, headed by a fully qualified teacher and a reception class which both accept pupils on government subsidised "Early Years" places. The main school covers Key Stages 1 and 2 but is not restricted by the National Curriculum, offering a broad range of subjects and a blend of form teacher based teaching at the lower end and subject specialist teaching further up the school.

St Wystan's enjoys an excellent reputation in music and sport, with pupils progressing to regional and national championships, recently in football, swimming, cross-country and athletics. Many pupils have instrumental tuition and there is a thriving school choir and orchestra, together with a broad range of other extra-curricular activities.

St Wystan's runs a very popular pre-school and after-school care facility. Children can be delivered to school from 7.30 am and looked after at school until 6.30 pm.

Charitable status. St Wystan's School (Repton) Limited is a Registered Charity, number 527181. It exists to provide a quality education for boys and girls.

Salesian College

Reading Road, Farnborough, Hampshire GU14 6PA
Tel: 01252 893000
Fax: 01252 893032
email: office@salesiancollege.com
website: www.salesiancollege.com

Headmaster: **Mr Patrick A Wilson**, BA Hons, MA, CertEd

Age Range. Boys 11–16 years; Co-educational Sixth Form.
Number in School. 625.
Fees per term (2014–2015). £3,353.

Salesian College at Farnborough in Hampshire was founded in 1901 and is an Independent Catholic Grammar School of about 600 students aged 11 to 18 years. Members of all Christian faiths are welcomed into the school which is part of a worldwide organisation of educational foundations run by the Salesians, a religious Order founded in the last century in Italy by St John Bosco specifically for the formation of young people, spiritually, academically, culturally, physically and emotionally. This continues to be our aspiration for each student.

Our aim is to send out from the school at 18 years young men and women who are confident without being arrogant, comfortable with themselves and all those around them, good Christians, honest citizens, and good individuals, well equipped to take their place in, and make a significant contribution to society.

This is achieved by the use of The Preventive System of Education promoted by St John Bosco and based on the three principles of Reason, Religion and Kindness. These principles encourage the students to develop a strong sense of responsibility and a caring attitude towards each other and the Community at large.

Academic achievements at GCSE and A Level, and sporting achievements are outstanding and highly valued. The friendliness and mutual respect that exist between staff and pupils provides a family and Christian ethos conducive to good order, confidence and scholarship.

The recent ISI Inspection report stated: "*Salesian College produces well-educated, confident, courteous and kind young men and women who are ready to take on responsibility and to serve*". The new co-educational Sixth Form has enhanced this.

We regard education to be a tripartite process involving the school, the family and the student and in order to produce the desired result all three must work in harmony.

Public speaking, music, orchestra, chess, drama and debating all flourish and there are many other extra-curricular activities.

The school has its own chapel, chaplaincy and resident chaplain.

Prospective parents are always welcome to make an appointment to visit the College while in session. Please see our website for up-to-date details.

Charitable status. Salesian College Farnborough Limited is a Registered Charity, number 1130166. It exists to provide education in North East Hampshire and neighbouring counties.

Salterford House School

Salterford Lane, Calverton, Nottinghamshire NG14 6NZ
Tel: 0115 965 2127
email: office@salterfordhouseschool.co.uk
website: www.salterfordhouseschool.co.uk

Principal: **Mrs Marlene Venables**

Age Range. 3–11.
Number in School. Main School 79: 40 Boys, 39 Girls. Kindergarten and Pre-Prep 18: 6 Boys, 12 Girls.
Fees per term (2014–2015). £2,170–£2,200.

Salterford House is situated in rural Nottinghamshire, in a 4.5 acre woodland setting, and aims to provide a happy, family atmosphere with small classes, in order to equip children academically and socially to cope with the demands of any type of education which might follow.

Although the school is mainly Church of England, all faiths are accepted. 75% of pupils go on to senior independent schools such as Nottingham Boys' High School, Nottingham Girls' High School, Trent College and Hollygirt.

Sports include Cricket, Tennis, Swimming, Rounders, Rugby, Lacrosse, Netball, Climbing, Football, Hockey, Golf and Skiing.

The school produces 3 concerts a year and there is a recorder Group and Choir. Individual tuition in Speech and Drama, Piano, Flute, Clarinet, Guitar, Violin and Percussion is available.

Dance lessons including Ballet and Jazz/Street Dance are available.

All classrooms are equipped with computers.

Staff are easily available for discussion. Regular contact is maintained with parents via Parents Evening and newsletters.

Sancton Wood School

2 St Paul's Road, Cambridge CB1 2EZ
Tel: 01223 359488
Fax: 01223 471703
email: Office@sanctonwood.co.uk
website: www.sanctonwood.co.uk
Twitter: @SanctonWood
Facebook: /SanctonWood

Headmaster: **Mr Richard J Settle**, BA, PGCE

Age Range. 1–16 Co-educational.
Number of Pupils. 200.
Fees per term (2014–2015). £1,182–£3,668.

Sancton Wood is a school where every child finds their niche. Our small, supportive and close-knit community of just 200 boys and girls is often likened to a family – a kind, tolerant, school where everyone can find their place and be valued.

Our class sizes are similarly small at just 16 pupils, creating fabulous learning environments, where our teachers have time for individual pupils, where they feel comfortable airing their ideas, where imaginations soar.

Our exam results are excellent by any measure. In recent years they have been second to none in some league tables. But the school is not just about exam results; art, music, sport and a wealth of other activities are all important aspects of life here, and play their part in making well-rounded students with their lives in balance.

Sancton Wood School is part of the Minerva Education group which owns a number of private schools in London, East and South East England. Through Minerva's "Inspiring Learning" programme, we seek to share best practice and ensure the continuing improvement in every child's education.

Scarisbrick Hall School & College

Southport Road, Ormskirk, Lancashire L40 9RQ
Tel: 01704 841151
Fax: 0845 505 7890
email: enquiries@scarisbrickhallschool.co.uk
website: www.scarisbrickhallschool.co.uk

Head of Middle School & College: **Mr Jeff Shaw**

Head of Nursery & First School: **Mr Tony McCoy**

Age Range. 0–16.
Number of Pupils. 408.

Fees per term (2014–2015). Reception £1,713, Years 1–2 £2,066, Years 3–6 £2,298, Years 7–9 £2,979, Years 10–12 £3,286.

The essential elements of Scarisbrick Hall School are: the daily efforts of staff to provide an ambience where spiritual and cultural gifts can develop, the quality of teaching in the classroom, and the commitment of staff to extra-curricular activities.

The school follows the guidelines of the National Curriculum, but enhances these through an impressive selection of options to present a breadth and depth for all the pupils. The aim is to provide equal opportunities for all and to cater for the needs of the individual.

Throughout the school the size of classes is restricted to approximately 21 so that each pupil may receive close attention and be treated as an individual, encouraged to develop his/her abilities to the full in a friendly, caring environment.

High standards are set and expected from the pupils, with the emphasis on self-discipline. The school rules have been compiled from principles which are necessary for good order. The utmost importance is attached to the cultivation of good manners and consideration for others.

The Headteachers and staff consider the school as a partner with parents in the education of their children.

Shapwick School

Shapwick Prep (age 8–13):
Mark Road, Burtle, Bridgwater, Somerset TA7 8NJ
Tel: 01278 722012
Fax: 01278 723312
email: prep@shapwickschool.com

Shapwick Senior & Sixth Form (age 13–19):
Shapwick Manor, Shapwick, Bridgwater, Somerset TA7 9NJ
Tel: 01458 210384
Fax: 01458 210111
email: office@shapwickschool.com
        sixthform@shapwickschool.com

website: www.shapwickschool.com

Headmaster: **Mr M Lee**, BA Hons, PGCE

Age Range. 8–18.
Number in School. Boarders: 73 boys, 32 girls; Day: 37 boys, 13 girls.
Fees per term (2014–2015). Boarders £7,458–£8,564, Day £5,693–£5,960.

Shapwick is a specialist school for boys and girls whose education would otherwise be impaired by dyslexia. The School provides a caring and supportive atmosphere, staffed by specialist teachers across a wide curriculum offering the structured help needed by students who have dyslexia. Students take up to 8 GCSE subjects and the aim is to teach to their strengths whilst their weaknesses are being overcome and their confidence grows. Supplementary courses, such as Study Skills, Keyboard Skills, and careers advice are also taken. The School has a full range of specialist classrooms, including four laboratories, computing rooms, design centre, art rooms, library, sports hall, recreation room and games field. Students are involved in a wide range of extra-curricular activities, the Duke of Edinburgh's Award, and games fixtures, to complement the formal curriculum.

Prospective entrants need an Educational Psychologist's report diagnosing dyslexia and at least average intellectual potential together with a current Head's report, and interview.

Sherborne House School
GEMS Education

39 Lakewood Road, Chandler's Ford, Hants SO53 1EU
Tel: 023 8025 2440
email: info@shs.gemsedu.co.uk
website: www.sherbornehouse.co.uk

Head: **Mrs Heather Hopson-Hill**, BEd Hons

Age Range. 2¾–11 Co-educational.
Number of Pupils. 284 (all day pupils).
Fees per term (2014–2015). £2,500–£2,910 including lunches. Nursery Grants (vouchers and salary sacrifice schemes) available for 3–4 year olds.

Sherborne House School, founded in 1933, takes children from Chandler's Ford, Winchester, Romsey, Southampton and the surrounding villages.

Sherborne House occupies an attractive four-acre site within the Hiltingbury area of Chandler's Ford. Boys and girls between 2¾ and 11 years of age are admitted through informal assessment. Scholarships in academic subjects, art, sport and music are available.

We have an enviable reputation for excellent Common Entrance and SATs results and regularly secure scholarships to established senior schools. Our outstanding results are achieved as a result of highly qualified staff, small classes and specialist learning support. Our broad curriculum emphasises literacy, numeracy and science but not at the expense of other subjects. Performing Arts is a particular strength of the school, with all children being encouraged to perform in both musical and dramatic activities, with additional peripatetic lessons are offered on a wide range of instruments. Art and CDT are taught in a specialist craft facility and all classrooms have interactive whiteboards to support work undertaken in the IT suite. A wide variety of sports is offered, including soccer, rugby, cricket, netball, hockey, short tennis, basketball and volleyball and the school has an extensive fixtures programme. French is offered from Pre-School and Spanish is added to the curriculum in the upper school. Sherborne House also provides a strong Learning Support network for those with special needs and individual programmes are drawn up and delivered by our SENCO in collaboration with the appropriate teaching staff. School trips and workshops and specialists curriculum days are arranged for all children as are residential visits for Key Stage 2 pupils. A wide range of after-school activities and clubs is also available.

At Sherborne House we believe that a child's self-esteem is paramount. We expect children to work and play and we take pride in our multi-sensory teaching methods, high but realistic expectations and our broad, engaging curriculum to accelerate our pupils' learning. The pastoral care at Sherborne House is outstanding and the pupils are confident, disciplined, purposeful and happy.

School hours: The school day runs from 8.30 am to 3.45 pm (Reception) and 4.00 pm (pre-prep and prep). Additional supervised care is available from 7.30 am until 6.00 pm.

We are always delighted to show prospective parents around the school and have regular Open Days.

Sherborne International

Newell Grange, Sherborne, Dorset DT9 4EZ
Tel: 01935 814743
Fax: 01935 816863
email: reception@sherborne-international.org
website: www.sherborne-international.org

Principal: **Mrs M A Arnal**, BA, MSc, PGCE, FRSA

Age Range. Co-educational 11–17 (Boarding 11–17).
Number in School. 160 boarders: 80 boys, 80 girls.
Fees per term (2014–2015). £12,500.

Sherborne International, formerly the International College was set up by Sherborne School in 1977. It has grown to become a separate institution and is now separately recognised by the Department for Education and the Independent Schools Association.

The School aims to be the best starting point for children from non-English speaking, non-British educational backgrounds who wish to join the British educational system. Students normally stay at the School for one academic year. During this time the School aims to equip each student to take his or her place successfully at a traditional British independent boarding school.

While the full academic curriculum is provided, all teachers of all subjects at Sherborne International are trained or qualified in teaching English as a foreign language. Each student is prepared for any appropriate public examinations, for example GCSEs and IGCSEs, or Cambridge English language examinations. Each year the group taking GCSEs records very impressive results – in 2014, nearly 83% of the entries achieved A–C grades.

The School has no entry requirements and no entry examinations for most courses. All students are non-native speakers of English, and some are complete beginners in English. However, the popular one-year GCSE/IGCSE course requires all applicants to have at least lower-intermediate standard English (IELTS 4+) or B2.

The School is housed in a purpose-built campus close to the centre of Sherborne. Its boarding houses are nearby. Students are taught in classes of up to eight students.

The School is also a member of the Boarding Schools Association, the European Council of International Schools and the British Association of International Study Centres and is also accredited by the British Council.

Charitable status. Sherborne International is owned by Sherborne School, which is a Registered Charity, number 1081228. It exists to provide education to school-aged children.

Sherfield School
GEMS Education

Sherfield-on-Loddon, Hook, Hampshire RG27 0HT
Tel: 01256 884800
Fax: 01256 883172
email: info@gss.gemsedu.co.uk
website: www.sherfieldschool.co.uk

Head Master: **Mr R G Jaine**, MA, FRGS

Age Range. 3 months – 18 years Co-educational.
Number in School. 425.
Fees per term (2014–2015). Day: £2,970–£4,963; Boarding: £8,333.

We offer a first-class academic education within a forward-looking and enriched curriculum to pupils aged from 3 months to 18 years, with a wraparound from 7.30 am to 6.00

pm for 48 weeks of the year. Provision includes a range of holiday activities so that pupils can continue to extend and develop their talents. Pupils may be full or flexi boarders from Year 5.

Teaching methods are a blend of the traditional and the very best of new ideas, based upon research and an understanding of how the brain develops and functions. Along with the core subjects for all pupils there is a range of options to meet the needs of each individual student. The flexible approach allows some students to take examinations early if appropriate. Our sixth form offers a range of subject choices which are studied in Years 12 and 13.

Sherfield offers Partnership Programmes in Equestrianism, Flying, Golf, Gymnastics, Ice Skating, Performing Arts and Tennis. Our partnerships are with locally-based, nationally-recognised organisations who work with us in order to provide a balance of academic studies combined with specialist training.

Setting high standards, developing self-discipline and meeting the needs of each individual pupil ensure that each child meets their full potential. As part of the school's commitment to achievement they offer outstanding opportunities for talented individuals. Scholarships are offered in sports, music, arts and academic excellence for pupils at Year 7 and upwards.

The Sherfield website provides vital information about the school to parents, the community and the media.

Sherfield prides itself on not just specialising in one area, but in all aspects of academic and sporting life.

Sherrardswood School

Lockleys, Welwyn, Hertfordshire AL6 0BJ
Tel: 01438 714282
Fax: 01438 840616
email: mimram@sherrardswood.herts.sch.uk
website: www.sherrardswood.co.uk

Headteacher: **Mrs L E Corry**

Age Range. 2–18.
Number in School. Day: 161 Boys, 117 Girls.
Fees per term (2013–2014). £3,000–£4,970.

Sherrardswood, founded in 1928, is a co-educational day school for pupils aged 2–18. The School is set in 25 acres of attractive parkland two miles north of Welwyn Garden City. The Junior Department is housed in a fine 18th century building whilst the Senior Department occupies a purpose-built facility. Games fields, tennis courts and woodlands trail are available on the Lockleys site for both departments.

Entry to the school is by interview or by interview and examination according to age. A broad curriculum is offered to GCSE level and a wide range of A Level subjects is available. A range of sport and extra-curricular opportunities is available, both within the school day and out of school hours.

The recent ISI inspection confirmed that Sherrardswood is achieving its aims and that the quality of education and pastoral care is outstanding.

Charitable status. Sherrardswood School is a Registered Charity, number 311070. It exists solely to provide independent education for boys and girls aged 2–18.

Shoreham College

St Julian's Lane, Shoreham-by-Sea, West Sussex BN43 6YW
Tel: 01273 592681
Fax: 01273 591673
email: info@shorehamcollege.co.uk
website: www.shorehamcollege.co.uk

Headmaster: **Richard Taylor-West**, MA, AKC

Age Range. 3–16.
Number in School. 258 Day Boys, 111 Day Girls.
Fees per term (2014–2015). £2,750–£4,450.

Founded in 1852 and set mainly in a Tudor manor house within 11 acres of beautiful grounds between the sea and Sussex Downs, Shoreham College is a leading independent, non-selective school for both girls and boys aged 3–16.

Our dedicated and highly qualified staff ensure children of all abilities are provided a good all-round education and encouraged to not only achieve but exceed their potential. With our blend of spirited children, inspiring teachers and supportive parents we are able to achieve something special; we achieve a school full of happiness and joy.

Shoreham College challenges, supports and inspires to give every child the confidence to excel. The environment is friendly and open and the welfare, safety and happiness of the child is paramount.

We know that our school is exceptional; the teachers are passionate and the children thrive. We invite you to take a tour around the school with the Headmaster; talk to the staff, meet the pupils and see the beautiful setting in which they are nurtured and experience the unique atmosphere of our school for yourself.

We look forward to welcoming you.

Charitable status. Shoreham College (The Kennedy Independent School Trust Limited) is a Registered Charity, number 307045. It exists to provide high-quality education for boys and girls.

Slindon College

Slindon, Arundel, West Sussex BN18 0RH
Tel: 01243 814320
Fax: 01243 814702
email: registrar@slindoncollege.co.uk
website: www.slindoncollege.co.uk

Headmaster: **Mr David Quick**

Age Range. 8–18.
Number in School. 40 Boarders, 40 Day Boys.
Fees per term (2014–2015). Boarders £9,445, Day Boys £5,900.

A small school for up to 100 boys whose classes have a maximum of 12 pupils. The National Curriculum is followed where appropriate and in Years 4–9 a broad-based, balanced curriculum is provided. GCSE courses include PE, photography, art, music and design technology – all practical based and "hands-on". BTEC Food Skills & Horticulture also offered. The excellent Learning Support Department helps boys with specific learning difficulties, including dyslexia and ADD/ADHD.

A wide range of extra-curricular activities is offered, including car mechanics, farm club and stagecraft.

The school is non-denominational but has firm links with the local Anglican church.

Some bursaries are available and discount is available for Service families and second sons.

Charitable status. Slindon College is a Registered Charity, number 1028125. It aims to provide for the academic, social and personal development of each boy in a caring and purposeful environment.

Snaresbrook Preparatory School

75 Woodford Road, South Woodford, London E18 2EA
Tel: 020 8989 2394
Fax: 020 8989 4379
email: office@snaresbrookprep.org
website: www.snaresbrookprep.org
Twitter: @snaresbrookprep
Facebook: /Snaresbrook-Prep

Head: **Mr Christopher M Curl**, MA, BEd

Age Range. 3½–11.
Number in School. 160.
Fees per term (2014–2015). £2,520–£3,368.
Snaresbrook Preparatory School is a vibrant independent
day school for boys and girls aged from 3½ to 11 years.
Founded in the 1930s, the school occupies a substantial Victorian building, once a large private family home – something that contributes to the strong community spirit within
the school. We aim to cultivate an intimate, caring family
atmosphere in which children feel secure and valued. Most
children join the school at age 3½ and stay with us until they
reach 11 when they leave for their senior schools.

We provide a rounded education covering every aspect of
your child's early development. The curriculum is designed
to prepare pupils for entrance and scholarship examinations
to senior independent and grammar schools. The curriculum
includes Mathematics, English, Science, Current Affairs,
ICT, Art, DT, Music, Drama, French, PE/Games and PSHE.
Latin and Swimming are introduced in the Juniors. Year 6
undertake the Adventure Service Challenge in preparation
for The Duke of Edinburgh's Award undertaken at senior
school.

At age 11, we find that Snaresbrook children are confident, cheerful and courteous, with a good sense of community and a readiness to care for each other and the world
around them. They have learned how to work in the ways
that suit them best, are receptive to teaching and are well
prepared for the next stage of their education and development.

We see ourselves as joint trustees, with parents, of the
young lives in our care, bearing equal responsibility for their
happiness, well being and development.

Steephill School

off Castle Hill, Fawkham, Longfield, Kent DA3 7BG
Tel: 01474 702107
Fax: 01474 706011
email: secretary@steephill.co.uk
website: www.steephill.co.uk

Head Teacher: **Mrs Caroline Birtwell**, BSc, MBA, PGCE

Age Range. 3–11 co-educational.
Number of Pupils. 120.
Fees per term (2014–2015). £2,750. Nursery days are
pro rata.
Steephill School is a very successful School based on its
academic, sporting and musical achievements. In 2014 it
had 87% entry into selective schools, won many awards at
music festivals and had numerous successes at inter-school
sports. In its 2013 ISI inspection report the school was given
an "excellent" rating in Pastoral Care, Curriculum, Extra-
Curriculum and the Spiritual, Moral, Social and Cultural
Development of pupils.

The School believes in high-quality teaching within a disciplined but relaxed atmosphere. The School holds traditional values and beliefs; working with and supporting each
other is an important part of the ethos. There are close links
with the church opposite the School. Four services per year
are held there and the Rector takes a fortnightly assembly.
The setting is very rural despite being only a few minutes'
drive from the M2 and 5 miles from the M20 and M25. The
School enjoys beautiful views of the countryside with very
little traffic nearby.

The classes are a maximum of 16 and with only 120
pupils in the School, there is a close liaison between all
members of the school community: children, staff, family
members and governors. Parents are welcomed into the
School and work closely with the teachers. There is regular
feedback to parents on children's progress. Parents are also
active in Friends of Steephill School, the Parents Association, to provide social and fundraising activities.

The children join the School aged 3½ in the Nursery and
they leave at age 11. The curriculum is designed to support
all abilities to achieve academically and in all the broader
aspects of education such as drama, the arts and sports.
Information Technology has been developed well over the
last few years and is being continually updated.

There is a large selection of extra-curricular activities at
lunchtime and after school. Our Gardening Club is one of
the more popular together with the choir, instruction on
musical instruments, dance and football. We are very fortunate to have large grounds with a superb sports field, despite
being a small school.

There is a care facility both before and after school so we
are open from 7 am to 5.30 pm. The School is also very
proud of the lunches. All the food is sourced from local
shops: butcher, baker and greengrocer. The meals are carefully balanced and freshly made.

Charitable status. Steephill School is a Registered Charity, number 803152.

Stoke College

Stoke-by-Clare, Sudbury, Suffolk CO10 8JE
Tel: 01787 278141
Fax: 01787 277904
email: office@stokecollege.co.uk
website: www.stokecollege.co.uk

Headmaster: **Mr M Parker**, MEd, BEd, CPhys, MInstP

Age Range. 3–16+ Co-educational.
Number in School. Total 230: 131 Boys, 99 Girls.
Boarders: 5 Boys, 1 Girl.
Fees per term (2014–2015). Day: £975–£4,370. Weekly
Boarding: £6,080–£7,070.
Stoke College provides a broad, balanced and relevant
curriculum up to GCSE. Weekly boarders or day pupils
enjoy a caring environment in an idyllic rural situation with
small classes yielding excellent results in public examinations. The College has a strong tradition in athletics and
cross-country and in Music and Drama. The school benefits
from a new Sports/Assembly Hall, Junior School Teaching
Block, Technology Rooms, a Performing Arts Centre, a
swimming pool, hard tennis courts and a Nursery Department. The College aims to develop the individual's
strengths and to produce a well rounded young adult to take
his or her place in society.

Charitable status. Stoke College is a Registered Charity,
number 310487. It is devoted to providing a full and relevant education to its pupils.

Stratford Preparatory School

Church House, Old Town, Stratford-upon-Avon, Warwickshire CV37 6BG
Tel: 01789 297993
Fax: 01789 263993
email: secretary@stratfordprep.co.uk
website: www.stratfordprep.co.uk

Motto: *Lux et Scientia*

Principal: Mrs C Quinn, MBA, BEd Hons

Headmaster: Mr Neil Musk, MA, BA Hons, PGCE

Age Range. Preparatory School 4–11 years. Montessori Nursery School 2–4 years.
Number in School. Main School: 39 Boys, 58 Girls; Nursery School: 11 Boys, 9 Girls.
Fees per term (2014–2015). Junior School £3,310; Infant School £3,020; Nursery School: £2,450 (full-time), £1,300 (5 mornings). Compulsory extras: Lunch £135.

Stratford Preparatory School is situated in the heart of the historic town of Stratford-upon-Avon. The Preparatory school opened in September 1989 and has developed around a large town house. An additional detached house within the school's grounds provides accommodation for the Reception and Nursery children, a gymnasium, a science room and design and technology room.

The school was judged 'Outstanding' in all areas in its 2011 ISI Inspection.

The Nursery implements the Montessori philosophy of learning which encourages a structured learning environment. French and ballet are taught from the age of 2 years.

The main school offers a broad balanced learning plan adapted to the individual needs of the children using traditional teaching methods and with specific reference to the National Curriculum. All children are entered for the 11+ and independent school entrance examinations.

The school offers a high level of pastoral care and attention to personal development.

Physical education activities include: sailing, swimming, football, cricket, tennis, netball, rounders, ballet, athletics and judo.

There are opportunities for the children to learn a variety of musical instruments. The school has two choirs and an orchestra.

Reduction in fees is offered for families with two or more children in the School.

The Headmaster is pleased to provide further details and meet prospective parents.

Study School

57 Thetford Road, New Malden, Surrey KT3 5DP
Tel: 020 8942 0754
Fax: 020 8942 0754
email: info@thestudyschool.co.uk
website: www.thestudyschool.co.uk

Headmistress: Mrs Donna Brackstone-Drake, BA Hons, PGCE, NPQH, MBA

Age Range. Rising 3–11 Co-educational.
Number in School. Day: 74 Boys, 61 Girls.
Fees per term (2014–2015). Nursery (mornings only) £1,443, Reception & Year 1 £2,938, Years 2–6 £3,358. Additional Nursery afternoon sessions available each day of the week: £228 per afternoon per term. All fees include a cooked school lunch. The school belongs to the Early Years Funding Scheme for 3 and 4 year olds.

Since 1923 we have successfully given our children a firm foundation in reading, writing and number skills, whilst also teaching French, Spanish, Music, Art and Games. Science, Geography, History, Design and Technology and ICT play an important part in the curriculum, with interactive whiteboards in every classroom and a full set of iPads and laptops which augment the curriculum.

Small classes allow us to stretch the most able pupils, whilst giving all our children individual attention.

Popular After School Clubs include Football, Art, Computer Coding, Drama, Dance, Fencing and Cookery. Individual instrumental music tuition is also available. We have Before School Care from 7.45 am and After School Care until 6.15 pm. All classes go on a school trip once a term and Years Four, Five and Six attend residential activity and field study courses and language trips abroad.

We provide a caring and stimulating atmosphere in which our children thrive. After Year Six they leave us to enter such schools at Kingston Grammar School, Wallington Boys' School, Non-Such Girls' School, Hampton School, the High Schools at Wimbledon, Sutton, Putney and Surbiton and both Tiffin Schools.

Please visit our website: www.thestudyschool.co.uk.

The Swaminarayan School

260 Brentfield Road, Neasden, London NW10 8HE
Tel: 020 8965 8381
Fax: 020 8961 4042
email: admin@tssuk.org
website: www.swaminarayan.brent.sch.uk

Chairman of Governors: Mr Piyush Amin

Headteacher, Senior School: Mr Nilesh Manani, BSc Hons, FRSA, PGCE

Headteacher, Prep School: Mr Umesh Raja, BSc, PGCE, NLP Masters, NPQH

Age Range. 2½–18.
Number of Pupils. 497: 254 boys, 243 girls.
Fees per term (2014–2015). £2,905–£3,906.

The Swaminarayan School was founded in 1991 by His Holiness Shree Pramukh Swami Maharaj to provide education along the lines of independent British schools, whilst reinforcing Hindu culture and tradition. It is a non-profit making, co-educational school for children aged two and a half to eighteen years.

The school admitted its first eighty or so Prep School pupils in September 1992 and the Senior School took its first intake the following September. Now there are just under 500 pupils in the school and already students from the school have gained admission to Cambridge, Oxford, Imperial, Warwick, UCL, LSE and King's.

Since those early days excellent progress has been made in all areas. The most striking aspect that always attracts comment from visitors is the purposeful atmosphere, both in classrooms and throughout the school. Teachers are able to help pupils achieve their full potential because of the generous staffing ratio, excellent behaviour of pupils and commitment from parents.

Resources and premises have also improved beyond recognition with modern libraries and computer rooms for each school. Former students from those early days dropping in to meet their teachers are amazed by the transformation!

On the curriculum front, the school has taken up the most desirable elements of the National Curriculum while developing the best practices of independent education. The cultural subjects unique to the school give it a special dimension – students have lessons in the Indian Performing Arts up to Year 8 and all students whose mother tongue is Gujarati study it up GCSE and all study Religious Education in Hinduism up to GCSE level.

In addition to their timetabled LAMDA lessons, PE lessons and club afternoons, pupils are involved in a range of extra-curricular activities such as public speaking, sports, drama, dance and much more. An extensive programme of instrumental lessons, both Indian and European, is also on offer to all pupils. The school arranges regular day trips to museums, parks and other places of educational interest. The Duke of Edinburgh's Award Scheme and residential outings are also a feature of the school. Whilst continuing to deliver a value based, broad and balanced curriculum, the school excels academically. Each year its excellent GCSE and A Level results put it at the top of Brent Performance tables. In The Daily Telegraph list of top independent schools, TSS has been consistently placed amongst the top ten performing schools in the country. Twenty years of vision, investment and hard work from trustees and governors, teaching and non-teaching staff as well as commitment from parents and pupils have made this a school to be proud of. The next ten years will see the school reaching even greater heights.

Charitable status. The Akshar Educational Trust is a Registered Charity, number 1023731.

Sylvia Young Theatre School

1 Nutford Place, London W1H 5YZ
Tel: 020 7258 2330
Fax: 020 7724 8371
email: info@sylviayoungtheatreschool.co.uk
website: www.syts.co.uk

Principal: Mrs Sylvia Young, OBE

Headteacher: **Ms Frances Chave**, BSc, PGCE, NPQH

Age Range. 10–16.
Number in School. Day: Boys 86, Girls 154. Weekly boarding is available with host families at an additional cost.
Fees per term (2014–2015). Junior Department £3,100; Years 7, 8 and 9 £4,145; Years 10 and 11 £4,250. There is a compulsory school lunch costing £180 per term in addition to these fees.

The School has a junior department (Year 6 only) and a secondary department (Years 7–11). We aim to provide an appropriately balanced academic and vocational experience for our students. We are proud of the caring and well disciplined environment that prevails and promotes a very positive climate of individual success.

Academic subjects are delivered by highly qualified staff to the end of Key Stage 4.

GCSE Examination subjects include English, English Literature, Mathematics, Science, Additional Science, Art, Drama, Expressive Arts, Music, Media Studies, Spanish and History.

Theatrical training is given by experienced professional teachers. Pupils are prepared for examinations in Speech and Drama – LAMDA (London Academy of Music and Dramatic Art). Entry is by audition with academic ability assessed.

Thames Christian College

Wye Street, London SW11 2HB
Tel: 020 7228 3933
Fax: 020 7924 1112
email: info@thameschristiancollege.org.uk
website: www.thameschristiancollege.org.uk

Executive Head: **Dr Stephen Holsgrove**, PhD

Age Range. 11–16 Co-educational.
Number of Pupils. 125.

Thames Christian College is a small independent secondary school for girls and boys in Battersea, South West London. Included in the Good Schools Guide, we are recognised for our strong Christian ethos.

In our rapidly changing world, pupils need a thorough and well-rounded education to succeed and enjoy life. Refreshingly independent, not only do our pupils achieve top grades, but they also leave with the depth of character and steadfast values that set them apart from other young people competing for school places and jobs. When a Thames pupil goes on to their chosen sixth form college, they flourish due to the strong foundations developed during their time with us.

We achieve this with small classes, consistent discipline based on mutual respect, courtesy and a dedicated, highly-qualified staff team, many of whom have real world experience and specialist knowledge of their subjects. We avoid just 'teaching to the test', preferring to stretch our pupils' imaginations and abilities in a stimulating environment. Our size allows us to be flexible – we can and do tailor our curriculum to enable pupils to develop their skills, realise their strengths and become highly motivated, successful young people. Without compromising our ethos of valuing the individual, we are making plans to have two streams of entry by 2019, as well as a sixth form in new state-of-the-art, purpose-built premises.

We believe that it is important that pupils have the option to take creative subjects alongside Technology, Sciences, Maths, Languages and Humanities, as this gives them a broad platform and keeps career options open. Typically half our Year 11s take separate Biology, Chemistry and Physics GCSEs. They can also study Additional Maths along with creative subjects such as Art, Graphics, Drama and Music. All pupils take practical qualifications in computer skills and Personal Finance to ensure they are fully equipped for the world of work.

We never have to resort to being 'just an exam factory'. As a result, not only do our pupils achieve excellent examinations results, they also develop into confident, perceptive and mature young adults ready to succeed in their chosen future.

Pupils take part in national competitions such as the UK Maths Challenge and excel in many areas of competitive sport, particularly in football, cross country and athletics. Our most talented footballers gain places at professional sports academies. Music and Drama are highly valued with an annual whole-school production performed at a professional theatre. In recent years we have put on the musicals *Thoroughly Modern Millie*, *Evita* and *Oliver*. Our choir develops links within the community by performing at local sheltered housing and care homes. Our most talented musicians are entered for local competitions and some have performed at the Royal Festival Hall. Senior pupils have the opportunity to be professionally trained as mentors for young children at a local primary school and excellent use is made of the museums, theatres, galleries and other learning environments in London, on camps and overseas trips. Through our links with the charity Go MAD in Tanzania, we support projects relating to education, health and income generation in north-west Tanzania, and provide opportunities for teams of pupils to visit and contribute as volunteers.

Thames Christian College was created for pupils who want to make the most of their potential. When considering a pupil for admission to Thames we consider how he or she will support our ethos. Our pupils are well behaved and show a willingness to learn. They have a high regard for the school's Christian values, especially those of honesty and integrity.

Given that we are just 5 minutes' walk from Clapham Junction, you may be surprised that a 30-minute travel time covers a significant part of London and surrounding counties.

Our Value Add score is consistently in the top 5% of schools as we seek to see every child fulfil their academic potential.

The best way to find out if our school is suitable for your child is to visit us on one of our Open Days. Individual appointments to view the school should be made if you wish to apply for immediate entry.

For a full list of open mornings, enrolment and fee details contact: 020 7228 3933 or visit www.thameschristiancollege.org.uk.

Fees per term (2014–2015). £4,240.

Charitable status. Thames Christian College Ltd is Registered Charity, number 1081666.

Thorpe Hall School

Wakering Road, Thorpe Bay, Essex SS1 3RD
Tel: 01702 582340
Fax: 01702 587070
email: sec@thorpehall.southend.sch.uk
website: www.thorpehall.southend.sch.uk

Headmaster: **A Hampton**, BA Hons, LTCL, MEd, NPQH

Age Range. 2–16 years.
Number in School. Approximately 300 girls and boys.
Fees per term (2014–2015). £1,111–£3,540.

Thorpe Hall School is a co-educational independent day school, pleasantly situated on green belt land on the outskirts of Southend-on-Sea, Essex. The buildings are modern and purpose-built.

Communications to London are good via the A13 and A127 and the Liverpool/Fenchurch Street railway lines. The nearest station is approximately 10 minutes' walk.

Founded in 1925, the school has been educating children for 80 years and consistently achieves excellent academic results at Key Stage 1, 2, 3 and GCSE with special emphasis being placed on the traditional values of good manners, behaviour, dress and speech.

On Monday, Tuesday and Thursday each week the school day is extended by one hour to enable all children to access library and computer facilities as well as having the opportunities to participate in Sport, Music, Drama, Mathematics and French or simply to do their homework in a suitable and supervised environment.

Refurbishment of the Science, Modern Languages, Information Systems and Resources Centre facilities has greatly enhanced the learning opportunities for all pupils.

A new building was recently completed, which houses a Theatre, Technology rooms, an extra ICT suite and an excellent Modern Art area. These new facilities ensure that Thorpe Hall School has the most modern, up-to-date and technologically advanced facilities of any independent school in South East Essex.

Thorpe Hall School has an orderly, disciplined and caring ethos that caters for the social and academic needs of children – Pre-Nursery, Nursery, Reception, Infant, Junior and Senior – not only between the hours of 9 am to 4 pm but also offers sporting opportunities in golf, tennis, karate, netball, horse riding and football at weekends and during holiday times. Youngsters have the opportunity to join our Beavers, Cubs and Scout groups while senior pupils can become involved in the Duke of Edinburgh's Award Scheme.

The Charitable Trust status enables fees, which are very competitive, to be kept to a minimum. Nursery vouchers are accepted and some bursaries are available. The School is regularly inspected by the Independent Schools Inspectorate.

Charitable status. Thorpe Hall School is a Registered Charity, number 298155. It exists to provide good quality education for boys and girls in South East Essex.

Tower College

Mill Lane, Rainhill, Merseyside L35 6NE
Tel: 0151 426 4333
Fax: 0151 426 3338
email: missoxley@towercollege.com
          mrtaylor@towercollege.com
          mrsknox@towercollege.com
website: www.towercollege.com

Principal: **Miss R J Oxley**

Vice-Principal: Mrs P Knox
Bursar: Mr M Taylor

Age Range. 3 months – 16 years.
Number in School. Day: 192 Boys, 205 Girls.
Fees per term (from April 2014). £1,880–£2,262.

Tower College is a non-denominational Christian Day School housed in a beautiful Victorian mansion set in 11 acres.

Our emphasis is on academic excellence and good behaviour. We have a strong musical tradition.

Five coaches cover a 25-mile radius including South Liverpool, Widnes, Warrington, Runcorn, St Helens, Prescot, Rainford and Ormskirk. Breakfast and after school clubs are available.

Academic and music scholarships are available.

Charitable status. Tower College is a Registered Charity, number 526611. It aims to provide a sound education based on Christian beliefs, with an emphasis on good behaviour and academic excellence.

The Towers Convent School

Upper Beeding, Steyning, West Sussex BN44 3TF
Tel: 01903 812185
Fax: 01903 813858
email: admin@thetowersconventschool.org
website: www.thetowersconventschool.org
Twitter: @TowersConvent
Facebook: /TheTowersConvent

Headmistress: **Mrs Clare Trelfa**

Age Range. Girls 2–16, Boys 2–8.
Number in School. 320 including accommodation for 10 flexi-boarders.
Fees per term (2014–2015). Tuition: £2,370–£3,300. Flexi boarding: £40 per night.

The Towers Convent School, a Roman Catholic school for girls aged 2–16 and boys aged 2–8 years in the beautiful setting of the South Downs, is owned by a Community of Sisters. At the heart of The Towers Community is Christian love; all people of whatever race, colour, creed or status are welcome, and have equal worth and opportunity. We aim to celebrate the dignity of each individual pupil. Our motto "Always Faithful" upholds the qualities of honesty and trust, responsibility, self-discipline and forgiveness. Pupils are encouraged to achieve their full potential in everything they do, developing a love of learning and seeking "wholeness". Mathematics and science subjects are particular strengths, and the school has three times won the Whitbread Prize for GCSE results. The GCSE pass rate is consistently high and reflects a quest for high academic standards. There is a keen interest in music and drama and a major musical is produced annually. The school's achievements in sport bear witness to a fine tradition, especially in tennis, where the school has won the Sussex Shield five times; netball and gymnastics are also very strong. The on-site covered and heated pool is a real asset and is enjoyed by all ages including the nursery children.

Find enjoyment and fulfilment at affordable fees!

Charitable status. The Towers Convent School is a Registered Charity, number 229394. It exists to provide quality education for girls and boys.

Trevor-Roberts School

55–57 Eton Avenue, London NW3 3ET
Tel: 020 7586 1444
Fax: 020 7483 1473
email: trsenior@trevor-robertsschool.co.uk

Headteacher: **Mr Simon Trevor-Roberts**, BA

Age Range. 5–13 Co-educational.
Number in School. 170 Day Pupils: 100 boys, 70 girls.
Fees per term (2014–2015). £4,270–£4,870.

Trevor-Roberts School was founded in Hampstead in 1955 by the headmaster's late father and moved to its present site in 1981. The school is made up of two departments but operates as one school and occupies two adjacent much-adapted late Victorian houses in Belsize Park. In addition to on-site facilities, the school makes use of nearby playing fields and a leisure centre swimming pool.

Central to the education provided is the school's aim for all pupils to become happy and confident individuals who fulfil their potential. Strong emphasis is placed on personal organisation and pupils are encouraged to develop a love of learning for its own sake. In a happy, non-competitive atmosphere, pupils are well cared for and teachers' responses are tailored to the individual needs of pupils. It is the School's strong belief that much can be expected of a child if he or she is given self-confidence and a sense of personal worth and does not feel judged too early in life against the attainment of others.

High success rates throughout the school are achieved through small classes, individual attention and specialist teachers. The standards achieved enable almost all pupils to gain places in their first choice of school at either 11+ or 13+ into the main London day schools and academically selective independent boarding schools. In recent years a number of pupils have been awarded academic, art and music scholarships to these schools. The school aims to make pupils prepared for this process and give them the confidence to enjoy the academic challenges they will be offered.

The school provides a broad range of curricular and extra-curricular activities, contributing to pupils' linguistic, mathematical, scientific, technological, social and physical development in a balanced way. Aesthetic and creative development is strongly encouraged through art, drama and music. In the Senior Department the syllabus is extended to include Classical History, Latin and Greek. The curriculum is enriched at all stages by a variety of one-day educational visits as well as by residential trips for Years 6–8 for activity weekends, geography field trips and visits to France.

A range of extra-curricular activities and sporting opportunities, appropriate for boys and girls of all ages, is offered on two afternoons a week and after school. The school's founder believed passionately in music and drama as a means of developing pupils' confidence and self-esteem and both subjects are a strong feature of the school today. All classes prepare and perform two drama performances each year in which every pupil has a speaking part.

Pupils thrive in a caring family atmosphere where the emphasis is on individual progress and expectation, and where improvement is rewarded as highly as success. It has a broadly Christian tradition, but welcomes pupils of all faiths and of none.

Trinity School

Brizes Park, Ongar Road, Kelvedon Hatch, Brentwood, Essex CM14 5TB
Tel: 01277 374123
Fax: 01277 373596
email: enquiries@trinityschool.ac
website: www.trinityschool.ac

Headmaster: **Mr Rob Whitaker**, MA Cantab, DMS, PGCE

Age Range. 3–18 co-educational.
Number of Pupils. 114.
Fees per term (2014–2015). £1,312–£2,112.

Trinity School is situated in Brizes Park, a 73-acre site of magnificent parkland on the outskirts of Brentwood. An elegant Georgian mansion houses the senior section while the primary section is in modern classrooms in a beautifully landscaped walled garden.

Trinity School has a distinctively Christian ethos, and aims for its pupils to develop as grounded and successful individuals. The academic results at GCSE and A Level are consistently strong, and sporting achievements are excellent. Most pupils go on to gain good university degrees and then proceed to top jobs and careers. Many former students regularly give back to the school in various ways as a thank you for all they received here.

The school has a warm family atmosphere with many of the parents fulfilling roles in teaching, administration and support. The school is closely linked to Trinity Church, Brentwood, and one of the secrets of its success is the principle established from its foundation that the pupils should find the same standards in the school, the church and the home. This has produced happy, secure and well-motivated children who have a strong sense of service as well as a platform for success throughout life.

Charitable status. The school is a Registered Charity, number 1112705.

Ursuline Preparatory School

Great Ropers Lane, Warley, Brentwood, Essex CM13 3HR
Tel: 01277 227152
Fax: 01277 202559
email: headmistress@ursulineprepwarley.co.uk
website: www.ursulineprepwarley.co.uk

Headmistress: **Mrs Pauline Wilson**, MSc

Age Range. 3–11.
Number in School. Day 160.
Fees per term (2014–2015). £1,740–£3,250.

Founded in the early 1930s, the Ursuline Preparatory School enjoys a reputation as a happy family school, where pupils strive to give of their best in all areas of school life. Consequently, much emphasis is placed on encouraging the children to develop to the full their individual talents and interests, as well as fostering in each pupil a strong sense of well-being, self-reliance and team spirit. This is achieved by the frequent use of praise, by adherence to an agreed policy of consistent and fair discipline, and by the high standards, moral code and caring attitudes deriving from the strongly Catholic ethos which underpins the life of the whole school.

The Ursuline Preparatory School has well qualified and very experienced teachers and support staff. It is committed to offering to all its pupils the distinct advantages of a broad and balanced curriculum. This includes following the National Curriculum, in addition to affording many other opportunities such as the provision of French and Information Technology to all children from 4 years upwards, Swimming Lessons, and also Extension classes where this is deemed appropriate.

A comprehensive range of extra-curricular activities are offered to the pupils. These are often taught by specialist staff and include subjects such as Theatre Club, Art Appreciation, Computing, Photography, Forest Skills, Spanish, Sewing, Chess, and Speech and Drama as well as many Instrumental Classes and Sporting Activities, with which the School has considerable success in gaining individual and team awards at competition level.

The School successfully prepares children for entry to local and national independent schools, Grammar Schools or local Secondary Schools, including the Ursuline High School.

The relatively small size of the School allows for very close contact between staff, pupils and parents and provides each child with the opportunity to fulfil his or her academic potential. The pupils are encouraged to follow their own interests and to develop a sense of self-confidence and self-worth which will hopefully remain with them throughout their lives, allowing them to reflect the school motto: *A Caring School that strives for excellence.*

Charitable status. The Ursuline Preparatory School is a Registered Charity, number 1058282, which is non-profit making and managed by an independent board of voluntary trustees. It exists to provide Roman Catholic children and those of other denominations with the opportunity to reach the highest individual standards possible in every area of School life.

Vernon Lodge Preparatory School

School Lane, Stretton, Near Brewood, Staffordshire ST19 9LJ
Tel: 01902 850568
Fax: 01902 850568
email: info@vernonlodge.co.uk
website: www.vernonlodge.co.uk

Directors: Mr G Barker, Mr D Whipps

Headteacher: **Mrs P Sills**, BEd Birmingham, CertEd, RSA Cert SpLD

Age Range. Nursery 2+–4+, Prep School 4+–11.
Number of Children. 31.
Fees per term (2014–2015). £950–£2,488.

Situated in a lovely country garden, Vernon Lodge with its small classes provides individual attention and a happy atmosphere. We are a very active school with pupils participating in music, LAMDA, drama and sporting events; our all-weather court and playing field enables pupils to participate in tennis, football, netball, rounders and athletics. Pupils are offered swimming lessons and enjoy entering swimming galas.

The Early Years Department provides young children with an excellent foundation to learning. In our well equipped Nursery, children flourish as they enjoy a creative curriculum where they are stimulated and encouraged to develop reading, writing and number work which are introduced as a natural progression.

We make no apology for our traditional teaching methods, in fact we are proud of them as, together with up-to-date resources, excellent results of passes and scholarships to senior schools are achieved each year.

Our facilities have expanded over recent years. In addition to an IT suite, there has been a substantial investment in laptops, tablets and interactive whiteboards; a purposely designed library and music room provides the opportunity for personal study.

All pupils learn a modern language. There are outward bound residential visits which are always enjoyed.

The popularity of Vernon Lodge Preparatory School is evident from its wide catchment area: children travel from Wolverhampton, Stafford, Cannock, Telford, Newport and the surrounding villages.

Virgo Fidelis Preparatory School

147 Central Hill, Upper Norwood, London SE19 1RS
Tel: 020 8653 2169
Fax: 020 8771 0317
email: office@vfps.org
website: www.vfps.org

Headmistress: **Mrs Meg Baines**, BA, MBA, FRSA, NPQH

Age Range. 3–11.
Number in School. Day: 166 Boys and Girls.
Fees per term (2014–2015). £2,057–£2,788.

The school is a Roman Catholic Foundation with a strong ecumenical outlook. Pupils are received from various religious backgrounds. Emphasis is placed on the pursuit of high educational standards and on the development of personal responsibility.

Charitable status. Our Lady of Fidelity at Upper Norwood, London is a Registered Charity, number 245644.

Vita et Pax Preparatory School

6A Priory Close, Green Road, Southgate, London N14 4AT
Tel: 020 8449 8336
Fax: 020 8440 0483
email: info@vitaetpax.co.uk
website: www.vitaetpax.co.uk

Chair of Governors: Ms Pamela Clear-Doughty

Headteacher: **Mrs Margaret O'Connor**, BEd Hons, MSc

Co-educational Day School.
Age Range. 3–11 years.
Number of Pupils. 96 Boys, 95 Girls.
Fees per term (2014–2015). £2,750.

Vita et Pax is an 'outstanding' school (ISI 2011) where staff work in close partnership with parents and children to provide a happy environment where everyone feels valued and cared for.

The school was founded 77 years ago by the Benedictine Olivetan Sisters in a spirit of ecumenism. Over the last 30 years it has evolved under lay leadership into a modern environment where pupils are prepared to be tomorrow's citizens, facing all the challenges that brings.

The school aims to instil in its pupils a love of learning from the outset. The curriculum offered encompasses the Early Years Foundation and National Curriculum with additional challenge and pace.

The school is not academically selective but has been judged (ISI 2011) to achieve exceptional standards both in academic and extra-curricular activities.

Pupils are prepared for transfer to both Independent and maintained grammar schools at age 11 and achieve considerable success through academic selection and scholarship offers.

Our highly qualified and dedicated staff nurture the pupils to become confident and considerate members of the wider community.

Charitable status. Vita et Pax School (Cockfosters) Ltd is a Registered Charity, number 281566. It exists to promote and provide for the advancement of education of infant and junior school age children.

The Webber Independent School
GEMS Education

Soskin Drive, Stantonbury Fields, Milton Keynes, Bucks MK14 6DP

Tel: 01908 574740
Fax: 01908 574741
email: info@wis.gemsedu.co.uk
website: www.webberindependentschool.com

Principal: Mrs Sue Vig

Vice-Principal: Mrs Hilary Marsden

Age Range. 3–18.
Number in School. 252: 130 boys, 122 girls.
Fees per term (2014–2015). Little GEMS (ages 3–5) £1,384–£2,720; Years 1 and 2 (ages 5–7) £2,762; Years 3 and 4 (ages 7–9) £2,860; Years 5 and 6 (ages 9–11) £3,070; Years 7–13 (ages 11–18) £3,690.

All inclusive Fees (7:30 am to 6:00 pm termly): This fee option includes breakfast, lunch and tea. Little GEMS (ages 3–5) £3,905–£4,074; Years 1 and 2 (ages 5–7) £4,130; Years 3 and 4 (ages 7–9) £4,269; Years 5 and 6 (ages 9–11) £4,556; Years 7–13 (ages 11–18) £5,412.

The Webber Independent School is an exceptional private co-educational day school for students aged 3 to 18 in Milton Keynes. The school is located in attractive private grounds on a single site. It is the only private 3–18 school in Central Milton Keynes with easy access to the station, from where the school operates a pick up and drop off service.

The School inspires and supports students in achieving the highest possible standards. The School offers an exciting, challenging and enriching curriculum within a supportive community in order to promote a love of learning, which benefits students throughout their lives. They discover and nurture individual talents and promote values of respect, responsibility, effort and empathy, which enhances independent learning, academic progress and emotional well-being. The School encourages in their young people the skills, ambition and confidence required to become successful global citizens and to meet the challenges of the modern world. The Webber Independent School focuses on the attributes that are highly prized in higher education and the workplace, such as initiative, confidence, perseverance, teamwork and leadership.

The Webber Independent School offers:
• Little GEMS International – a unique revolutionary Early Years educational programme
• Pre-Prep – the best possible start and the best possible future
• Prep School – to get your child off to a Flying Start
• Sixth Form – with over 24 A Level courses
• Excellent Value Added Results at GCSE and A Level
• A stimulating 21st Century learning environment
• Highly individualised and personalised learning

• Inspirational Teaching in small classes
• Expert advice on entry to top Universities
• A record 100% of Sixth Form gaining their first-choice University place
• Exceptional Pastoral care in a well-ordered environment
• Excellent Parental Engagement
• Door-to-door minibus service
• Pick up from Central Milton Keynes Station
• A culture of success and an ethos of excellence
An outstanding ISI Inspection Report was received in 2011.

West Lodge School

36 Station Road, Sidcup, Kent DA15 7DU

Tel: 020 8300 2489
Fax: 020 8308 1905
email: info@westlodge.org.uk
website: www.westlodge.org.uk

Chair of Governors: Mrs Chris Head-Rapson

Head Teacher: **Mrs Susan Webb**, MA

Age Range. 3–11.
Number of Pupils. 161 Day Boys and Girls.
Fees per term (2014–2015). £1,665–£2,785.

West Lodge was founded in 1940 and is now an educational trust. The main building is an extended Victorian house, well adapted to use as a school, whilst still retaining its homely atmosphere. Facilities include a newly-built extension, incorporating a science/cookery room and art room/crèche, which can also be used together as an additional hall facility, a fully-equipped gymnasium, Astroturf surface, music rooms and a computer suite. There are eight classes of up to 21 pupils, one class in each year group from Nursery through to Year 6. The staff-pupil ratio is extremely high and the children are taught in smaller groups by specialist teachers for many subjects. The school is open from 8.15 am and an after-school crèche and homework club operate until 5.30 pm.

The school has a strong academic tradition and a purposeful atmosphere permeates each class. The National Curriculum is at the core of our teaching, but it is enhanced and enriched by the inclusion of a wider range of subjects. These include: English, mathematics, science, French, information technology, design technology, history, geography, religious education, music, art and craft, physical education and games, swimming and drama.

Great emphasis is placed on a thorough grounding in basic learning skills, with literacy and numeracy seen as key elements in the foundation, upon which future learning will be built. Particular care is taken to extend the most gifted children and support the less able. West Lodge has a consistent record of a high level of entry to local authority selective schools and independent schools.

Music has a particularly high profile within the school and all of the children are encouraged to develop their talents. Well-qualified peripatetic staff teach both group and individual lessons and children of all ages are encouraged to join the school orchestras and choir. Concerts and dramatic performances are staged regularly and parents are warmly invited to attend.

The school promotes a caring attitude between all its members and aims to help each child towards the achievement of self-control and self-discipline. The Head Teacher and the class teachers know each of the children well and the excellent pastoral care and family atmosphere are major features of the school.

Home-school links are strong and the open door policy gives parents immediate access to members of staff should worries occur. The school also has strong contacts with the local community.

Extra-curricular activities are given the highest priority and clubs run each afternoon after school. Regular school outings form part of the curriculum for all children, the older pupils enjoying residential visits.

Charitable status. West Lodge School Educational Trust is a Registered Charity, number 283627. It exists for the provision of high quality education for boys and girls between 3 and 11 years.

Westbourne School

Hickman Road, Penarth, Vale of Glamorgan CF64 2AJ
Tel: 029 2070 5705
email: enquiries@westbourneschool.com
website: www.westbourneschool.com
Twitter: @WestbourneS
Facebook: /Westbourne School

Principal: **Mr K W Underhill**, BA Ed Hons

Head of Junior School: Mrs Carol Clint
Deputy Head of Senior School (Pastoral): Mr Colin Laity
Deputy Head of Senior School (Academic): Mr Mark Silcock
Finance Director: Mr Gary Hughes
Admissions Manager: Miss Catrin Cooper

Age Range. 3–18.
Number in School. 92 Boys, 80 Girls.
Fees per term (2014–2015). £2,250–£3,900 (payable in advance). Fees include textbooks, sporting activities and examination charges. Boarding and Homestay £26,850 per year, fully inclusive of tuition fees, single or shared room during term time, daily breakfast, lunch and dinner, guardianship costs and annual airport transfers.

We are an Independent Co-educational school for children from Nursery age to Sixth Form, with continuity in teaching methods throughout the School, and a stable context for study. Since September 2008 we have offered the IB Diploma Programme in a brand new Sixth Form Building. A wide and flexible range of subjects is offered at GCSE, and results are consistently excellent. The staff is well-qualified and settled and pupils are known individually to all teachers and also to the Head of School; education takes place in a happy, family-like environment.

A disciplined, caring context is maintained and ample opportunity is given for a variety of sporting activities.

Entry into Year 12 is based on GCSE Results and an interview with the Head of School; entry into Year 9 is by Common Entrance at which a 50% pass is required. Otherwise entrance is by interview and two day induction.

Penarth is a small seaside town on the outskirts of Cardiff, and pupils are normally drawn from Penarth, Sully, Cardiff, Barry, Cowbridge and the Vale of Glamorgan. There is a convenient train service to Penarth and the School has minibuses running each day from The Vale of Glamorgan, Cowbridge, Barry and Cardiff.

Westward School

47 Hersham Road, Walton-on-Thames, Surrey KT12 1LE
Tel: 01932 220911
Fax: 01932 242891
email: admin@westwardschool.co.uk
website: www.westwardschool.co.uk

Principals: Mr & Mrs David Townley

Headmistress: **Mrs Shelley Stevenson**, BEd Hons

Age Range. 3–11 Co-educational.
Number of Pupils. 150.
Fees per term (from April 2014). £1,073–£2,300.

Whitehall School

117 High Street, Somersham, Cambs PE28 3EH
Tel: 01487 840966
Fax: 01487 840966
email: office@whitehallschool.com
website: www.whitehallschool.com

Headmaster: **Mr Jon Willcocks**, BA Hons, PGCE, NPQH

Age Range. 10 months to 11 years.
Number in School. 90 Day children: 43 boys, 47 girls.
Fees per term (from April 2014). £822–£2,322.
'A Unique School in Rural Cambridgeshire: A Dynamic, Forward-Thinking environment.'

Set in extensive grounds with excellent facilities, Whitehall School provides a small, family environment where children are supported to achieve their best academically whilst also developing personality, creativity and social consciousness.

The school consists of an Edwardian house and 18th Century coach house and is set within approximately 1.5 acres of stunning grounds. Facilities include a covered heated swimming pool, playground, sensory garden, games field, library and iPad suite.

Small class sizes to a maximum of 16 allow us to support children to access the curriculum at their own pace on a 'Vertical Pathway', catering for the specific needs of each child so that they excel. Our Individual Performance Programme allows us to work in partnership with parents to encourage children to become active, independent learners.

Windrush Valley School

The Green, London Lane, Ascott-under-Wychwood, Oxfordshire OX7 6AN
Tel: 01993 831793
email: info@windrushvalleyschool.co.uk
website: www.windrushvalleyschool.co.uk

Headmaster: **Mr G A Wood**, MEd, TCert, DipSpEd, ACP, FCollP

Age Range. 3–11 Co-educational.
Number of Pupils. 118.
Fees per term (2014–2015). £1,999.

Windrush Valley School is a lively, happy community in which boys and girls thrive. Its rural location provides access to all the amenities of a beautiful Cotswold village including the 12th century church and playing fields. The school is non-selective; admission is by interview with the Headmaster. Before- and after-school care extend the school day from 8 am to 6 pm with a wide range of after-school clubs/societies. The small number of children with special educational needs are taught under the supervision of specialist staff. The school plays competitive sports in a wide range of games. Class groups are organised on a chronological age basis and the curriculum exceeds the requirements of the National Curriculum. Excellent examination results enable pupils to achieve their first choice of school on transfer to secondary education and help maintain its listing as a 'Times' top 100 preparatory school.

Woodlands School
Great Warley

Warley Street, Great Warley, Brentwood, Essex
CM13 3LA
Tel: 01277 233288
Fax: 01277 232715
email: info@woodlandsschools.co.uk
website: www.woodlandsschools.co.uk

Headmistress: **Mrs B Harding**
From September 2015: Mrs K Mansfield

Age Range. 3 months–11.
Number in School. 127: 60 boys, 67 girls.
Fees per term (2014–2015). £2,545–£4,060.
Admission is by interview.

Woodlands School at Great Warley is set in attractive, spacious grounds, with excellent facilities for outdoor activities. The school also uses the extensive facilities of our sister school at Hutton Manor.

It is the School's principle aim to ensure that all the children are happy and secure and are as successful as possible. They are encouraged to work hard and to show kindness and consideration to their peers. The resulting ethos of the School is one of warmth, support and mutual respect.

The School provides an exciting learning experience which enables the pupils to achieve full academic potential and to develop qualities of curiosity, independence and fortitude. Classes are small. The school aims to develop high levels of self-esteem and a good attitude to learning. The School has an excellent record in public examinations. Pupils are highly successful in gaining places at the schools of their choice. Examination results in Music and LAMDA are also excellent.

A varied programme of team and individual sports aims to offer something for everyone.

There is a strong music tradition and a variety of dramatic and musical concerts and productions are staged throughout the year for children of each age group.

Modern languages are taught to a very high standard, with French introduced at the age of 3 and Spanish in the Upper School.

Pastoral care is a major feature. An 'Open House' policy is in place for parents, which results in any concern being dealt with promptly and effectively.

It is the School's view that the education of the whole child is the most important priority and is confident that the learning experience it provides is fun, truly stimulating and memorable.

The school has recently added a nursery facility offering places for children from 3 months to 3 years who will then progress automatically into Early Years.

Woodlands School
Hutton Manor

428 Rayleigh Road, Hutton, Brentwood, Essex
CM13 1SD
Tel: 01277 245585
Fax: 01277 221546
email: info@woodlandshutton.co.uk
website: www.woodlandsschools.co.uk

Head Teacher: **Mrs Paula Hobbs**, BEd

Age Range. 3–11 Co-educational.
Number of Pupils. 140.
Fees per term (2014–2015). £3,315–£4,530.

PART VI
Schools in membership of the
Council of British International Schools

ALPHABETICAL LIST OF SCHOOLS

PAGE

ABC International School, Vietnam 1227
Al Khor International School, Qatar 1230
The Alice Smith School, Malaysia 1226
Aloha College, Spain 1229

The British Embassy School Ankara, Turkey 1227
British International Primary School of Stockholm,
  Sweden 1230
The British International School of Brussels, Belgium 1227
The British International School, Cairo, Egypt 1230
The British International School, Istanbul, Turkey . . 1227
British International School of Ljubljana, Slovenia . . 1229
The British International School of New York,
  United States of America 1227
British International School of Stavanger, Norway . . 1229
British Junior Academy of Brussels, Belgium 1227
The British School of Amsterdam, Netherlands 1228
British School in Baku, Azerbaijan 1226
The British School of Beijing, Sanlitun, China 1226
The British School of Beijing, Shunyi, China 1226
British School of Bucharest, Romania 1229
British School of Gran Canaria, Spain 1229
The British School Kathmandu, Nepal 1227
The British School of Milan, Italy 1228
British School Muscat, Oman 1230
The British School in The Netherlands, Netherlands . 1228
The British School of Paris, France 1228
The British School in Tokyo, Japan 1226
Byron College, Greece 1228

Campion School, Greece 1228

Doha College, Qatar 1230
Dubai College, United Arab Emirates 1230

The Edron Academy, Mexico 1227
The English College in Prague, Czech Republic . . . 1227

GEMS Jumeirah Primary School, United Arab
  Emirates 1230
GEMS Royal Dubai School, United Arab Emirates . . 1230
GEMS Wellington Academy – Silicon Oasis, United
  Arab Emirates 1231
GEMS Wellington International School, United
  Arab Emirates 1231

GEMS Wellington Primary School, United Arab
  Emirates 1231
Geneva English School, Switzerland 1230

Haileybury Almaty, Kazakhstan 1226
Halcyon London International School, United
  Kingdom 1230
Hillcrest International Schools, Kenya 1226

Independent Bonn International School, Germany . . 1228
International British School of Bucharest, Romania . 1229
International School of Moscow, Russia 1229
International School Olomouc, Czech Republic 1227

Jerudong International School, Brunei Darussalam . . 1226

King's College, Spain 1229
King's College, Spain 1229
King's College School, La Moraleja, Spain 1229
King's Infant School, Chamartín, Spain 1229

Lagos Preparatory School, Nigeria 1226

Maadi British International School, Egypt 1230
Mougins School, France 1228

New Cairo British International School, Egypt 1230

Oporto British School, Portugal 1229

Park Lane International School, Czech Republic . . . 1227
Poznan British International School, Poland 1229
The Prague British School Kamýk, Czech Republic . 1227
The Prague British School Vlastina, Czech Republic . 1228

Radnor House School, United Kingdom 1230
Riverside School, Czech Republic 1228
Rygaards School, Denmark 1228

St Catherine's British School, Greece 1228
St George's British International School, Italy 1228
St George's International School, Luxembourg 1228
St Paul's British Primary School, Belgium 1227
St Paul's School, Brazil 1227
Sherborne Qatar, Qatar 1230

Transylvania College, Romania 1229
Two Boats School, Ascension Island 1231

Member Schools

Africa

Kenya

Hillcrest International Schools
PO Box 24819, Karen 00502, Nairobi, Kenya
email: admin@hillcrest.ac.ke
website: www.hillcrest.ac.ke

Principal & CEO: **Mr Chris Wheeler**

Headteacher, Secondary School: Mr Leon Bareham

Headteacher, Preparatory School: Mrs Karen Morey

Nigeria

Lagos Preparatory School
36–40 Glover Road, Ikoyi, Lagos, Nigeria
email: admin@lagosprepikoyi.com.ng
website: www.lagosprepikoyi.com.ng

Headmaster: **Mr John Samuel**

(*See entry in IAPS section*)

Asia

Azerbaijan

British School in Baku
13 Koroglu Rahimov Str, Odlar Yurdu University, Baku
AZ1072, Azerbaijan
email: office@bsb-azeri.org.uk
website: www.bsb-edu.org.uk

Head of Secondary School: **Robert Ellis**
Head of Primary School: **Andrew Haynes**

Brunei Darussalam

Jerudong International School
PO Box 1408, Bandar Seri Begawan BS8672, Negara
Brunei Darussalam
email: enrol@jis.edu.bn
website: www.jis.edu.bn

Principal: **Barnaby Sandow**, BSc Eng Durham, PGCE
Exeter

(*See entry in IAPS section*)

China

The British School of Beijing, Sanlitun
5 Xiliujie, Sanlitun Road, Chaoyang District, Beijing
100027, China
email: sltadmissions@britishschool.org.cn
website: www.nordangliaeducation.com/our-schools/
beijing/sanlitun

Principal: **Lisa Milanec**

The British School of Beijing, Shunyi
South Side, No.9 An Hua Street, Shunyi District, Beijing
101318, China
email: admissions@britishschool.org.cn
website: www.nordangliaeducation.com/our-schools/
beijing/shunyi

Principal: **Andy Puttock**

Head of Primary: Phil Allman
Head of Secondary: Steve Lewis

Japan

The British School in Tokyo
1-21-18 Shibuya, Shibuya-ku, Tokyo 150-0002, Japan
email: admissions@bst.ac.jp
website: www.bst.ac.jp

Principal: **Brian Christian**

Kazakhstan

Haileybury Almaty
112 Al-Farabi Avenue, Almaty 050040, Kazakhstan
email: info@haileyburyalmaty.kz
website: www.haileyburyalmaty.kz

Headmaster: **Mr Craig Halsall**

Malaysia

The Alice Smith School
2 Jalan Bellamy, 50460 Kuala Lumpur, Malaysia
email: klass@alice-smith.edu.my
website: www.alice-smith.edu.my

Head of School: **Mr Roger Schulz**

Nepal

The British School Kathmandu
PO Box 566, Jhamsikhel, Patan, Kathmandu, Nepal
email: tbs@tbs.edu.np
website: www.tbskathmandu.org

Principal: Mr John Moore

Turkey

The British Embassy School Ankara
Sehit Ersan Caddesi 46/A, Çankaya 06680, Ankara,
Turkey
email: admin@besaturkey.org
website: www.besaturkey.org

Head Teacher: Mr Ken Page

The British International School, Istanbul
Dilhayat Sokak No 18, Etiler, Istanbul 34337, Turkey
email: bisadmin@bis.k12.tr
website: www.bis.k12.tr

Secondary School Director: William Bradley

Pre School & Primary School Director: Richard I'Anson

Vietnam

ABC International School
2 1E Street, KDC Trung Son, Binh Hung, Binh Chanh,
Ho Chi Minh City, Vietnam
email: abcintschoolss@vnn.vn
website: www.theabcis.com

Headmaster: Mr Gary Benfield, BEd Hons, MIMgt

Central, North and South America

Brazil

St Paul's School
Rua Juquiá 166, Jardim Paulistano, São Paulo SP 01440-903, Brazil
email: spshead@stpauls.br
website: www.stpauls.br

Head: Ms Louise Simpson

(*See entry in IAPS section*)

Mexico

The Edron Academy
Calz Desierto de los Leones 5578, Col Olivar de los
Padres Mexico, DF Mexico, Mexico
email: information@edron.edu.mx
website: www.edron.edu.mx

Headteacher: Mr Eamonn Mullally

United States of America

The British International School of New York
20 Waterside Plaza, East 23rd Street, Manhattan, New
York City 10010, USA
email: info@bis-ny.org
website: www.bis-ny.org

Headmaster: William T Phelps, BA, AKC, PGCE

(*See full entry in IAPSO section*)

Europe

Belgium

The British International School of Brussels
163 Avenue Emile Max, 1030 Brussels, Belgium
email: schooloffice@bisb.org
website: www.bisb.org

Headteacher: Stephen Prescott, BEng, PGCE, MA
EdMgt

British Junior Academy of Brussels
83 Boulevard St Michel, 1040 Brussels, Belgium
email: bjabrussels@yahoo.com
website: www.bjab.org

Head Teacher: Mrs Sarah White

St Paul's British Primary School
Stationsstraat 3, Vossem, 3080 Tervuren, Belgium
email: secretary@britishprimary.com
website: www.britishprimary.com

Headteacher: Brett Neilson

Czech Republic

The English College in Prague
Sokolovska 320, 190-00 Praha 9, Czech Republic
email: headmaster@englishcollege.cz
website: www.englishcollege.cz

Headmaster: Mr Simon Marshall, MA, MA, MPhil

International School Olomouc
Rooseveltova 101, Olomouc 779 00, Czech Republic
email: info@ischool.cz
website: www.ischool.cz

Director: Mr Petr Pospisil

Park Lane International School
Norbertov 3, Praha 6, Czech Republic
email: info@parklane-is.com
website: www.parklane-is.com

Principal: Paul Ingarfield

The Prague British School Kamýk
K Lesu 558/2, 142 00 Prague 4, Czech Republic
email: admissions@pbschool.cz
website: www.pbschool.cz

Head of Senior School: Tim Roberts

Head of Kamýk Primary School: Paul Baker

The Prague British School Vlastina
Vlastina 19, Prague 6, Czech Republic
email: admissions@pbschool.cz
website: www.pbschool.cz

Head of Primary Schools: John Bagust

Riverside School
Roztocka 9, Sedlec, 160 00 Prague 6, Czech Republic
email: administration@riverside school.cz
website: www.riversideschool.cz

Director: Peter Daish

Denmark

Rygaards School
Bernstorffsvej 54, 2900 Hellerup, Denmark
email: admin@rygaards.com
website: www.rygaards.com

Principal: Charles Dalton

France

The British School of Paris
38 Quai de l'Ecluse, 78290 Croissy-Sur-Seine, France
email: registrar@britishschool.fr
website: www.britishschool.fr

Headmaster: Mr N Hammond

(*See entry in HMC section*)

Mougins School
615 Avenue Dr Maurice Donat, Font de l'Orme, BP 401, 06251 Mougins Cedex, France
email: information@mougins-school.com
website: www.mougins-school.com

Headmaster: Brian Hickmore

Germany

Independent Bonn International School
Tulpenbaumweg 42, 53177 Bonn, Germany
email: ibis@ibis-school.com
website: www.ibis-school.com

Headmistress: Irene Bolik

Greece

Byron College
7 Filolaou Street & Aristotelous, Gerakas, Athens 153 44, Greece
email: info@byroncollege.gr
website: www.byroncollege.gr

Head of School: Matthew Burfield

Campion School
PO Box 67484, Pallini, Athens 153 02, Greece
email: dbaker@campion.edu.gr
website: www.campion.edu.gr

Headmaster: Stephen W Atherton, MA Oxon, MSc Open, LRSM, ARCO

St Catherine's British School
PO Box 51019, Kifissia GR 145 10, Greece
email: headmaster@stcatherines.gr
website: www.stcatherines.gr

Headmaster: Mr Stuart Smith

Italy

The British School of Milan
Via Pisani Dossi 16, 20134 Milan, Italy
email: info@sjhschool.com
website: www.sjhschool.com

Principal: Dr Carlo Ferrario

St George's British International School
Via Cassia, La Storta, 00123 Rome, Italy
email: secretary@stgeorge.school.it
website: www.stgeorge.school.it

Principal: Martyn J Hales, BSc

Luxembourg

St George's International School
11 rue des Peupliers, L-2328, Luxembourg
email: info@st-georges.lu
website: www.st-georges.lu

Principal: Dr Christian Barkei

Head Teacher - Secondary: Mark Fleet
Head Teacher - Primary: Heather Duxbury

Netherlands

The British School of Amsterdam
Anthonie van Dijckstraat 1, Amsterdam 1077 ME, Netherlands
email: info@britams.nl
website: www.britishschoolofamsterdam.nl

Principal: Mrs Jonnie Goyer, MA

The British School in The Netherlands
Boerderij Rosenburgh, Rosenburgherlaan 2, 2252 BA Voorschoten, Netherlands
email: principal@britishschool.nl
website: www.britishschool.nl

Principal: Martin Coles

(*See entry in HMC section*)

Norway

British International School of Stavanger
Gauselbakken 107, N-4032 Stavanger, Norway
email: principal@biss.no
website: www.biss.no

Principal: **Anne Howells**, BA, PGCE, CertEd

Poland

Poznan British International School
Ul. Darzyborska 1A, 61-303 Poznan, Poland
email: office@pbis.edu.pl
website: www.pbis.edu.pl

Principal: **Mrs Danuta Kościńska-Michalczuk**

Portugal

Oporto British School
Rua da Cerca 326/350, 4150-201 Porto, Portugal
email: school@obs.edu.pt
website: www.obs.edu.pt

Head Master: **Mr Tom McGrath**

Romania

British School of Bucharest
42 Erou Iancu Nicolae Street, 077190 Voluntari, Ilfov
County, Romania
email: office@britishschool.ro
website: www.britishschool.ro

Principal: **Joanne Puddy-Wells**

International British School of Bucharest
Str Agricultori Nr 21, Sector 2, Bucharest, Romania
email: office@ibsb.ro
website: www.ibsb.ro

Head of School: **Mr Kendall Peet**

Transylvania College
Str Baisoara 2A, Cluj-Napoca 400445, Romania
email: office@transylvania-college.ro
website: www.transylvania-college.ro

Head of School: **Mrs Gillian Greenwood**

Russia

International School of Moscow
12 Krylatskaya Street, Buildings 5 & 6, Moscow
121552, Russia
email: info@internationalschool.ru
website: www.internationalschool.ru

Headmaster: **Paul Seedhouse**

Slovenia

British International School of Ljubljana
Podmilscakova ulica 24, 1000 Ljubljana, Slovenia
email: enquiries@britishschool.si
website: www.britishschool.si

Principal: **Mr David Cooksey**

Spain

Aloha College
Urb. El Angel, Nueva Andalucia, 29660 Marbella,
Málaga, Spain
email: info@aloha-college.com
website: www.aloha-college.com

Principal & Headteacher, Secondary School: **Mrs
Elizabeth Batchelor**

Headteacher, *Primary School*: **Mrs Kathryn Salmon**

British School of Gran Canaria
Crta Tafira a Marzagán s/n, El Sabinal, 35017 Las
Palmas de Gran Canaria, Spain
email: hardes@bs-gc.net
website: www.bs-gc.com

Director: **Julian M Clark**

King's College
The British School of Alicante
Glorieta del Reino Unido 5, 03008 Alicante, Spain
email: info@bsalicante.com
website: www.bsalicante.com

Head Teacher: **Derek Laidlaw**, DipT Mus, NPQH

King's College
The British School of Madrid
Paseo de los Andes 35, 28761 Soto de Viñuelas, Madrid,
Spain
email: info@kingscollege.es
website: www.kingscollege.es

Headteacher: **Andrew Rattue**, MA Oxon, MA London,
PGCE London

(*See entry in HMC section*)

King's College School, La Moraleja
Paseo de Alcobendas 5, 28109 La Moraleja, Madrid,
Spain
email: info.lamoraleja@kingscollege.es
website: www.kingscollege.es

Headteacher: **Dawn Akyürek**, BA Hons, PGCE

King's Infant School, Chamartín
Prieto Ureña 9-11, Chamartín, 28016 Madrid, Spain
email: info.chamartin@kingscollege.es
website: www.kingscollege.es

Headteacher: **Kay Seward**, BEd

Sweden

British International Primary School of Stockholm

Östra Valhallavägen 17, S182 68 Djursholm, Sweden
email: borgen@britishinternationalprimaryschool.se
website: www.britishinternationalprimaryschool.se

Principal: Carl Hutson

Switzerland

Geneva English School

36 route de Malagny, 1294 Genthod, Geneva,
Switzerland
email: admin@geschool.ch
website: www.geneva-english-school.ch

Headmaster: Stephen Baird

United Kingdom

Halcyon London International School

33 Seymour Place, London W1H 5AU, UK
email: hello@halcyonschool.com
          join@halcyonschool.com
website: halcyonschool.com

Head: Mr Duncan Partridge

Radnor House School

Pope's Villa, Cross Deep, Twickenham TW1 4QG, UK
email: info@radnorhouse.org
website: www.radnorhouse.org

Head: Mr David Paton

Middle East

Egypt

The British International School, Cairo

PO Box 137, Gezira 11211, Cairo, Egypt
email: info@bisc.edu.eg
website: www.bisc.edu.eg

Principal: Simon O'Grady

(*See Junior School entry in IAPS section*)

Maadi British International School

4th District, Next to Wadi Degla Club, Zahraa El Maadi,
Cairo, Egypt
email: mbis@mbisegypt.com
website: www.mbisegypt.com

Headmaster: Richard White, BSc, PGCE

New Cairo British International School

PO Box 9057, Nasr City, Cairo, Egypt
email: info@ncbis.net
website: www.ncbis.net

Principal: Mr Raymond Williams

Oman

British School Muscat

PO Box 1907, Ruwi, Muscat PC112, Sultanate of Oman
email: admissionsoffice@britishschoolmuscat.com
website: www.britishschoolmuscat.com

Principal: Mr Kai Vacher

Qatar

Al Khor International School

PO Box 22166, Doha, Qatar
email: enquiries@akis.sch.qa
website: www.akis.sch.qa

Headmaster: Gerard MacMahon

Doha College

PO Box 7506, Doha, State of Qatar
email: seniorexec@dohacollege.com
website: www.dohacollege.com

Principal: Mark Leppard

Sherborne Qatar

PO Box 1108, Doha, Qatar
email: office@sherborneqatar.org
website: www.sherborneqatar.org

Senior Headmaster: Mr Michael Weston

Prep School Headmaster: Mr Nick Prowse

United Arab Emirates

Dubai College

PO Box 837, Dubai, United Arab Emirates
email: dcadmin@dubaicollege.org
website: www.dubaicollege.org

Headmaster: Mr Peter Hill

GEMS Jumeirah Primary School

19th Street, Al Safa, PO Box 29093, Dubai, United Arab
Emirates
email: info_jps@gemsedu.com
website: www.jumeirahprimaryschool.com

Principal: Miss Catherine McKeever

GEMS Royal Dubai School

Al Mizhar 1, Street 11A, PO Box 121310, Dubai, United
Arab Emirates
email: principal_rds@gemsedu.com
website: www.royaldubaischool.com

Principal/CEO: Mr Kevin Loft

GEMS Wellington Academy – Silicon Oasis
Dubai Silicon Oasis, Dubai, United Arab Emirates
email: contactus_wso@gemsedu.com
website: www.gemswellingtonacademy-dso.com

CEO & Principal: **Mr Michael Gernon**

GEMS Wellington International School
Al Sufouh Area, Sheikh Zayed Road, PO Box 37486,
Dubai, United Arab Emirates
email: reception_wis@gemsedu.com
website: www.wellingtoninternationalschool.com

Principal & CEO: **Mr Keith Miller**

GEMS Wellington Primary School
PO Box 114652, Dubai, United Arab Emirates
email: principal_wps@gemsedu.com
website: www.gemswps.com

Principal: **Mr Stephen J Chynoweth**

South Atlantic

Ascension Island

Two Boats School
Two Boats Village ASCN 1ZZ, Ascension Island
email: enquiries@tbschool.edu.ac
website: www.ascension-island.gov.ac/government/
             school

Headteacher: **Mr David Blunt**

PAGE

Abberley Hall, Worcs (IAPS). 872
Abbey College Manchester, Greater Manchester
(ISA). 1147
Abbey Gate College, Cheshire (Society of Heads,
ISA) 761
Abbey Gate Prep School, Cheshire (ISA) 1147
The Abbey School, Berks (GSA). 561
Abbots Bromley School, Staffs (GSA) 562
Abbot's Hill School, Herts (GSA) 563
Abbotsholme School, Derbyshire (Society of
Heads) 763
ABC International School, Vietnam (COBIS) . . 1227
Abercorn School, London (IAPS, ISA). 872
Aberdour School, Surrey (IAPS) 872
Abingdon House School, London (ISA) 1147
Abingdon Preparatory School, Oxon (IAPS). . . . 873
Abingdon School, Oxon (HMC) 7
Ackworth School, W Yorks (HMC, Society of
Heads) 9
ACS Cobham International School, Surrey
(ISA). 1148
ACS Egham International School, Surrey (ISA) . 1148
ACS Hillingdon International School, Middx
(ISA). 1149
Adcote School, Shropshire (GSA, ISA) 564
Aiglon College Junior School, Switzerland
(IAPSO) 1127
Aiglon College, Switzerland (HMCI) 555
AKS, Lancs (HMC). 10
Al Khor International School, Qatar (COBIS) . . . 1230
Aldenham Preparatory School, Herts (IAPS). . . . 873
Aldenham School, Herts (HMC) 11
Alderley Edge School for Girls, Cheshire (GSA,
ISA) 566
Aldro, Surrey (IAPS) 874
Aldwickbury School, Herts (IAPS). 874
The Alice Smith School, Malaysia (COBIS) 1226
All Hallows School, Somerset (IAPS) 875
Alleyn Court Preparatory School, Essex (IAPS,
ISA) 875
Alleyn's Junior School, London (IAPS) 876
Alleyn's School, London (HMC). 13
Aloha College, Spain (COBIS). 1229
Alpha Preparatory School, Middx (IAPS) 876
Alton Convent School, Hants (ISA) 1149
Altrincham Preparatory School, Cheshire (IAPS) . 877
Amesbury, Surrey (IAPS). 877
Ampleforth College, N Yorks (HMC) 15
Anglican Church Grammar School, Australia
(HMCI) 553
Ardingly College, W Sussex (HMC) 17
Ardingly College Prep & Pre-Prep Schools,
W Sussex (IAPS) 877
Ardvreck, Scotland (IAPS) 878
Argyle House School, Tyne and Wear (ISA) 1150
Arnold House School, London (IAPS) 879
Arts Educational Schools London, London
(ISA) 1150
Ashdell Preparatory School, S Yorks (IAPS). . . . 879
Ashdown House, E Sussex (IAPS) 879
Ashfold School, Bucks (IAPS) 880
Ashford Prep School, Kent (IAPS) 880

PAGE

Ashford School, Kent (HMC). 18
Ashton House School, Middx (ISA) 1151
Ashville College, N Yorks (HMC) 19
Ashville College Junior School, N Yorks (IAPS). . 881
Ashville College Pre-Prep School, N Yorks
(IAPS) 881
Austin Friars St Monica's Junior School, Cumbria
(IAPS) 882
Austin Friars St Monica's School, Cumbria
(Society of Heads) 764
Avenue House School, London (IAPS). 882
Avenue Nursery & Pre-Preparatory School, London
(IAPS) 883
Ayscoughfee Hall School, Lincs (ISA) 1151
Aysgarth School, N Yorks (IAPS) 883

Babington House School, Kent (ISA) 1151
Babington House School – Preparatory
Department, Kent (IAPS) 884
Bablake Junior School and Pre Prep, W Midlands
(IAPS) 884
Bablake School, W Midlands (HMC) 21
Badminton Junior School, Bristol (IAPS) 885
Badminton School, Bristol (GSA) 567
Ballard School, Hants (ISA, IAPS) 885
Bancroft's Preparatory School, Essex (IAPS) . . . 885
Bancroft's School, Essex (HMC) 22
The Banda School, Kenya (IAPSO) 1127
Bangor Grammar School, Northern Ireland
(HMC) 24
Barfield School & Nursery, Surrey (IAPS). 886
Barlborough Hall School, Derbyshire (IAPS) . . . 886
Barnard Castle Preparatory School, Durham
(IAPS) 887
Barnard Castle School, Durham (HMC) 25
Barnardiston Hall Preparatory School, Suffolk
(IAPS) 887
Barrow Hills School, Surrey (IAPS) 888
Bassett House School, London (IAPS) 888
Beachborough, Northants (IAPS). 888
The Beacon, Bucks (IAPS) 889
Beaudesert Park, Glos (IAPS) 889
Bedales School, Hants (HMC, Society of Heads) . 27
Bede's Preparatory School, E Sussex (IAPS). . . . 890
Bede's Senior School, E Sussex (HMC) 29
Bedford Girls' School Junior School, Beds
(IAPS) 890
Bedford Girls' School, Beds (GSA) 569
Bedford Modern Junior School, Beds (IAPS) . . . 891
Bedford Modern School, Beds (HMC) 30
Bedford Preparatory School, Beds (IAPS) 891
Bedford School, Beds (HMC) 33
Bedstone College, Shropshire (Society of Heads,
ISA) 766
Beech Hall School, Cheshire (ISA). 1152
Beech House School, Greater Manchester (ISA) . 1152
Beechwood Park, Herts (IAPS). 892
Beechwood Sacred Heart School, Kent (Society of
Heads) 768
Beeston Hall School, Norfolk (IAPS) 892
Beijing Dulwich International School, China
(HMCI). 552
Belfast Royal Academy, Northern Ireland (HMC) . 35

PAGE

Belhaven Hill, Scotland (IAPS) 892
Belmont, London (IAPS) 893
Belmont Grosvenor School, N Yorks (IAPS) . . . 894
Belmont School, Surrey (IAPS) 894
Benenden School, Kent (HMC, GSA) 37
Berkhampstead School, Cheltenham, Glos (IAPS) . 895
Berkhamsted Pre-Preparatory School, Herts (IAPS, ISA) 895
Berkhamsted Preparatory School, Herts (IAPS) . . 896
Berkhamsted School, Herts (HMC, GSA) 41
Bethany School, Kent (Society of Heads) . . . 769
Bickley Park School, Kent (IAPS) 896
Bilton Grange, Warwicks (IAPS) 896
Birchfield School, Shropshire (IAPS) 897
Birkdale Prep School, S Yorks (IAPS) 898
Birkdale School, S Yorks (HMC) 44
Birkenhead School, Merseyside (HMC) 46
Bishop Challoner School, Kent (ISA) 1152
Bishop's Stortford College, Herts (HMC) 47
Bishop's Stortford College Prep School, Herts (IAPS) 898
Bishopsgate School, Surrey (IAPS) 898
Blackheath High School, London (GSA) 569
Blackheath Preparatory School, London (IAPS) . . 899
Bloxham School, Oxon (HMC) 50
The Blue Coat School, W Midlands (IAPS) 900
Blundell's Preparatory School, Devon (IAPS) . . . 900
Blundell's School, Devon (HMC) 52
Bolton School Boys' Division, Lancs (HMC) 54
Bolton School Girls' Division, Lancs (GSA) . . . 570
Bootham Junior School, N Yorks (IAPS) 901
Bootham School, N Yorks (HMC) 55
Boundary Oak School, Hants (IAPS) 901
Bournemouth Collegiate School, Dorset (Society of Heads, IAPS) 770
Bowbrook House School, Worcs (ISA) 1153
Box Hill School, Surrey (Society of Heads) . . . 770
Bradfield College, Berks (HMC) 57
Bradford Grammar Junior School, W Yorks (IAPS) 902
Bradford Grammar School, W Yorks (HMC) 59
Braeside School for Girls, Essex (ISA) 1153
Brambletye, W Sussex (IAPS) 902
Bramcote Junior School, N Yorks (IAPS) 903
Bramley School, Surrey (IAPS) 903
Brandeston Hall, Suffolk (IAPS) 904
Bredon School, Glos (ISA) 1153
Brentwood Preparatory School, Essex (IAPS) . . . 904
Brentwood School, Essex (HMC) 62
Bricklehurst Manor, E Sussex (IAPS) 905
Bridgewater School, Greater Manchester (ISA) . . 1154
Brighton & Hove High School, E Sussex (GSA) . . 572
Brighton & Hove High School Junior School, E Sussex (IAPS) 905
Brighton College, E Sussex (HMC) 64
Brighton College Prep School, E Sussex (IAPS) . . 906
Brigidine School Windsor, Berks (ISA) 1154
Bristol Grammar School, Bristol (HMC, Society of Heads) 66
BGS Infants and Juniors, Bristol (IAPS) 906
The British Embassy School Ankara, Turkey (COBIS, IAPSO) 1227
British International Primary School of Stockholm, Sweden (COBIS) 1230

The British International School of Brussels, Belgium (COBIS) 1227
The British International School, Cairo, Egypt (IAPSO) 1128
The British International School, Cairo, Egypt (COBIS) 1230
The British International School, Istanbul, Turkey (COBIS) 1227
British International School of Ljubljana, Slovenia (COBIS) 1229
The British International School of New York, United States of America (COBIS) 1227
The British International School of New York, United States of America (IAPSO) 1128
British International School of Stavanger, Norway (COBIS) 1229
British Junior Academy of Brussels, Belgium (COBIS) 1227
The British School – Al Khubairat, United Arab Emirates (IAPSO) 1129
The British School of Amsterdam, Netherlands (COBIS) 1228
British School in Baku, Azerbaijan (COBIS) . . . 1226
The British School of Barcelona, Spain (HMCI) . . 555
The British School of Beijing, Sanlitun, China (COBIS) 1226
The British School of Beijing, Shunyi, China (COBIS) 1226
The British School of Brussels – Primary School, Belgium (IAPSO) 1129
The British School of Brussels, Belgium (HMCE) . 548
British School of Bucharest, Romania (COBIS) . . 1229
British School of Gran Canaria, Spain (COBIS) . . 1229
The British School Kathmandu, Nepal (COBIS) . . 1227
The British School of Milan, Italy (HMCI) 555
The British School of Milan, Italy (COBIS) 1228
British School Muscat, Oman (COBIS) 1230
The British School in The Netherlands, Netherlands (COBIS) 1228
The British School in The Netherlands, Netherlands (HMCE) 549
The British School in The Netherlands, Netherlands (IAPSO) 1130
The British School, New Delhi, India (HMCI) . . . 552
The British School of Paris, France (COBIS) . . . 1228
The British School of Paris, France (HMCE) . . . 550
The British School of Paris – Junior School, France (IAPSO) 1130
The British School in Tokyo, Japan (COBIS) . . . 1226
Brockhurst School, Berks (IAPS) 907
Bromley High School, Kent (GSA) 572
Bromsgrove Preparatory & Pre-Preparatory School, Worcs (IAPS) 907
Bromsgrove School, Worcs (HMC) 68
Brontë House, W Yorks (IAPS) 908
Bronte School, Kent (ISA) 1155
Brooke Priory School, Rutland (IAPS) 908
Brookhouse Preparatory School, Kenya (IAPSO) 1130
Broomwood Hall, London (IAPS) 909
Broughton Manor Preparatory School, Bucks (IAPS) 909
Bruern Abbey School, Oxon (IAPS) 910
Bruton School for Girls, Somerset (GSA) 574
Bryanston School, Dorset (HMC) 72

PAGE

The Buchan School, Isle of Man (IAPS) 910
Buckingham College Preparatory School, Middx
(IAPS) 910
Burgess Hill School for Girls – Junior School,
W Sussex (IAPS) 911
Burgess Hill School for Girls, W Sussex (GSA,
Society of Heads) 575
Bury Grammar School Boys, Lancs (HMC) 74
Bury Grammar School Girls, Lancs (GSA) 576
Bute House Preparatory School for Girls, London
(IAPS) 912
Buxlow Preparatory School, Middx (ISA) 1155
Byron College, Greece (COBIS) 1228

Caldicott, Bucks (IAPS) 912
Camberwell Grammar School, Australia (HMCI) . 553
Cambridge Tutors College, Surrey (ISA) 1155
Cameron House, London (IAPS) 912
Campbell College, Northern Ireland (HMC) 75
Campion School, Greece (HMCI) 555
Campion School, Greece (COBIS) 1228
Canbury School, Surrey (ISA) 1156
Canford School, Dorset (HMC) 77
Cardiff Sixth Form College, Wales (ISA) 1156
Cargilfield, Scotland (IAPS) 913
Carleton House Preparatory School, Merseyside
(ISA) 1157
Carrdus School, Oxon (IAPS) 913
Casterton, Sedbergh Preparatory School, Cumbria
(IAPS) 914
Castle Court Preparatory School, Dorset (IAPS) . 914
Castle House School, Shropshire (ISA) 1157
Caterham Preparatory School, Surrey (IAPS) . . . 915
Caterham School, Surrey (HMC) 80
The Cathedral & John Connon School, India
(HMCI) 552
The Cathedral School Llandaff, Wales (Society of
Heads, IAPS) 772
CATS College Cambridge, Cambs (ISA) 1158
The Cavendish School, London (IAPS) 915
Chafyn Grove School, Wilts (IAPS) 915
Channing School, London (GSA) 577
Charlotte House Preparatory School for Girls, Herts
(IAPS) 916
Charterhouse, Surrey (HMC) 83
Chase Grammar School, Staffs (ISA) 1158
Cheadle Hulme School, Cheshire (HMC) 85
Cheam School, Berks (IAPS) 916
Cheltenham College, Glos (HMC) 86
Cheltenham College Preparatory School, Glos
(IAPS) 917
Cheltenham Ladies' College, Glos (GSA) 579
Chesham Preparatory School, Bucks (IAPS) 917
Chetham's School of Music, Greater Manchester
(HMC) 89
Chigwell Junior School, Essex (IAPS) 918
Chigwell School, Essex (HMC) 91
Chilton Cantelo School, Somerset (ISA) 1159
Chinthurst School, Surrey (IAPS) 918
The Chorister School, Durham (IAPS) 918
Christ Church Cathedral School, Oxon (IAPS) . . . 919
Christ Church Grammar School, Australia
(HMCI) 553
Christ College, Wales (HMC) 93
Christ's College, New Zealand (HMCI) 554

PAGE

Christ's Hospital, W Sussex (HMC) 95
Churcher's College, Hants (HMC) 96
Churcher's College Junior School, Hants (IAPS) . 919
City of London Freemen's Junior School, Surrey
(IAPS) 920
City of London Freemen's School, Surrey (HMC) . . 98
City of London School, London (HMC) 101
City of London School for Girls, London (HMC,
GSA) 103
Claires Court, Berks (ISA) 1159
Claremont Fan Court Pre-Preparatory and Nursery
School, Surrey (IAPS) 920
Claremont Fan Court Preparatory School, Surrey
(IAPS) 920
Claremont Fan Court School, Surrey (Society of
Heads) 772
Clayesmore Preparatory School, Dorset (IAPS) . . 921
Clayesmore School, Dorset (HMC, Society of
Heads) 104
Clevelands Preparatory School, Lancs (IAPS) . . . 921
Clifton College, Bristol (HMC) 106
Clifton College Pre-Preparatory School, Bristol
(IAPS) 922
Clifton College Preparatory School, Bristol
(IAPS) 922
Clifton High School, Bristol (Society of Heads) . . 773
Clifton School and Nursery, N Yorks (IAPS) 923
Clongowes Wood College, Ireland (HMC) 108
Cobham Hall, Kent (GSA) 580
Cokethorpe Junior School, Oxon (IAPS) 923
Cokethorpe School, Oxon (HMC, Society of
Heads) 109
Colet Court (St Paul's Preparatory School), London
(IAPS) 924
Colfe's Preparatory School, London (IAPS) 924
Colfe's School, London (HMC) 110
Collingwood School, Surrey (IAPS, ISA) 925
Colston's Lower School, Bristol (IAPS) 925
Colston's School, Bristol (HMC) 112
Combe Bank Preparatory School, Kent (IAPS) . . 925
Concord College, Shropshire (Society of Heads) . . 776
Coopersale Hall School, Essex (ISA) 1160
Copthill School, Lincs (ISA) 1160
Copthorne School, W Sussex (IAPS) 926
Cottesmore School, W Sussex (IAPS) 926
Coworth Flexlands School, Surrey (IAPS) 927
Crackley Hall School, Warwicks (IAPS, ISA) . . . 927
Craigclowan School, Scotland (IAPS) 928
Cranford House Junior School, Oxon (IAPS) . . . 928
Cranford House School, Oxon (GSA) 582
Cranleigh, Surrey (HMC) 113
Cranleigh Preparatory School, Surrey (IAPS) . . . 928
Cranmore School, Surrey (IAPS) 929
Cransley School, Cheshire (ISA) 1161
Crescent School, Warwicks (IAPS) 929
The Croft Preparatory School, Warwicks (IAPS) . . 930
Crosfields School, Berks (IAPS) 930
Crowstone Preparatory School, Essex (ISA) 1161
Croydon High School, Surrey (GSA) 583
Culford Preparatory School, Suffolk (IAPS) 931
Culford School, Suffolk (HMC) 116
Cumnor House School, Surrey (IAPS, ISA) 931
Cumnor House School, W Sussex (IAPS) 931
Cundall Manor School, N Yorks (ISA) 1161

PAGE

Dagfa School Nottingham, Notts (ISA) 1162
Daiglen School, Essex (ISA) 1162
Dair House School, Bucks (IAPS) 932
Dame Allan's Boys' School, Tyne and Wear
  (HMC) 119
Dame Allan's Girls' School, Tyne and Wear
  (GSA) 584
Dame Bradbury's School, Essex (IAPS) 932
Danes Hill, Surrey (IAPS) 933
Daneshill School, Hants (IAPS) 933
Dauntsey's School, Wilts (HMC) 120
Davenies School, Bucks (IAPS) 933
Dean Close Pre-Preparatory School, Glos (IAPS) . 934
Dean Close Preparatory School, Glos (IAPS) . . . 934
Dean Close School, Glos (HMC) 121
Denmead, Middx (IAPS) 935
Denstone College, Staffs (HMC) 123
Denstone College Preparatory School at Smallwood
  Manor, Staffs (IAPS) 935
Derby Grammar School, Derbyshire (Society of
  Heads, ISA) 777
Derby High School, Derbyshire (GSA) 585
Derwent Lodge, Kent (IAPS) 936
Devonshire House Preparatory School, London
  (IAPS) 936
Ditcham Park School, Hants (ISA) 1162
The Dixie Grammar School, Leics (ISA) 1163
DLD College, London (ISA) 1163
Dodderhill School, Worcs (GSA, ISA) 587
Doha College, Qatar (HMCI) 555
Doha College, Qatar (COBIS) 1230
Dollar Academy, Scotland (HMC) 125
Dolphin School, Berks (IAPS) 936
The Doon School, India (HMCI) 552
Dover College, Kent (Society of Heads) 778
d'Overbroeck's College, Oxon (Society of Heads) . 780
Downe House, Berks (HMC, GSA) 127
The Downs Malvern, Worcs (IAPS) 937
The Downs School, Bristol (IAPS) 938
Downsend, Surrey (IAPS) 938
Dragon School, Oxon (IAPS) 939
Dubai College, United Arab Emirates (HMCI) . . 555
Dubai College, United Arab Emirates (COBIS) . . 1230
Duke of Kent School, Surrey (IAPS) 939
Dulwich College, London (HMC, IAPS) 129
Dulwich Prep London, London (IAPS) 940
Dulwich Preparatory School, Kent (IAPS) 940
Dumpton School, Dorset (IAPS) 941
The High School of Dundee, Scotland (HMC) . . 131
Dunhurst, Hants (IAPS) 941
Dunottar School, Surrey (Society of Heads) . . . 782
Durham High School for Girls, Durham (GSA) . . 588
Durham School, Durham (HMC, IAPS) 132
Durlston Court, Hants (IAPS) 942
Durston House, London (IAPS) 942
Dwight School London, London (ISA) 1164

Eagle House, Berks (IAPS) 943
Eastbourne College, E Sussex (HMC) 134
Eaton House The Manor Girls' School, London
  (IAPS) 943
Eaton House The Manor Pre-Preparatory School,
  London (IAPS) 943
Eaton House The Manor Preparatory School,
  London (IAPS) 944

PAGE

Eaton Square School, London (IAPS) 944
Edgbaston High School, W Midlands (GSA) . . . 589
Edge Grove, Herts (IAPS) 944
Edgeborough, Surrey (IAPS) 945
The Edinburgh Academy, Scotland (HMC) . . . 136
The Edron Academy, Mexico (COBIS) 1227
Egerton Rothesay School, Herts (ISA) 1164
Elizabeth College, Channel Islands (HMC) . . . 138
Ellesmere College, Shropshire (HMC) 139
Elm Green Preparatory School, Essex (IAPS) . . . 945
The Elms, Worcs (IAPS) 946
Eltham College, London (HMC) 141
Emanuel School, London (HMC) 143
The English College in Prague, Czech Republic
  (COBIS) 1227
The English College in Prague, Czech Republic
  (HMCI) 555
The English School, Cyprus (HMCI) 554
The English School, Kuwait (IAPSO) 1131
Epsom College, Surrey (HMC) 145
Eton College, Berks (HMC) 149
Eton End School, Berks (IAPS) 946
Eversfield Preparatory School, W Midlands
  (IAPS) 946
Ewell Castle Junior School, Surrey (IAPS) 947
Ewell Castle School, Surrey (Society of Heads) . . 783
Exeter Cathedral School, Devon (IAPS) 947
Exeter Junior School, Devon (IAPS) 947
Exeter School, Devon (HMC) 151

Fairfield Preparatory School, Leics (IAPS) 948
Fairfield School, Bristol (ISA) 1165
Fairley House School, London (ISA) 1165
Fairstead House School, Suffolk (IAPS) 949
The Falcons Schools, London (IAPS) 949
Falkner House, London (ISA) 1165
Faraday School, London (ISA) 1166
Farleigh School, Hants (IAPS) 949
Farlington Preparatory School, W Sussex (IAPS) . 950
Farlington School, W Sussex (GSA) 592
Farnborough Hill, Hants (GSA) 593
Farringtons School, Kent (Society of Heads) . . . 784
Felsted Preparatory School, Essex (IAPS) 950
Felsted School, Essex (HMC) 154
Feltonfleet School, Surrey (IAPS) 951
Ferndale House Preparatory School,
  Oxon (ISA) 1166
Fettes College, Scotland (HMC) 156
Fettes College Preparatory School, Scotland
  (IAPS) 952
Finborough School, Suffolk (ISA) 1166
Finton House, London (IAPS) 952
The Firs School, Cheshire (ISA) 1167
Firwood Manor Preparatory School, Lancs (ISA) . 1167
Foremarke Hall, Derbyshire (IAPS) 953
Forest Park Preparatory School, Cheshire (ISA) . . 1168
Forest Preparatory School, Cheshire (ISA) 1168
Forest Preparatory School, London (IAPS) 953
Forest School, London (HMC) 159
Forres Sandle Manor, Hants (IAPS) 953
Fosse Bank School, Kent (IAPS) 954
Framlingham College, Suffolk (HMC) 162
Francis Holland School, London (HMC, GSA) . . 163
Francis Holland School, London (GSA, Society of
  Heads) 594

PAGE

Frensham Heights, Surrey (HMC) 164
Frewen College & Frewen Preparatory School,
   E Sussex (ISA). 1168
Friends' Junior School, Essex (IAPS) 955
Friends' School, Essex (Society of Heads) 785
The Froebelian School, W Yorks (IAPS). 955
Fulneck School, W Yorks (Society of Heads,
   IAPS). 787
Fyling Hall School, N Yorks (ISA) 1169

Gads Hill School, Kent (ISA). 1169
Garden House School, London (IAPS) 956
Gatehouse School, London (IAPS, ISA) 956
Gateways School, W Yorks (GSA) 596
Gayhurst School, Bucks (IAPS) 956
Geelong Grammar School, Australia (HMCI) . . . 553
GEMS Bolitho School, Cornwall (ISA) 1170
GEMS Hampshire School, London (ISA) 1170
GEMS Jumeirah Primary School, United Arab
   Emirates (COBIS) 1230
GEMS Royal Dubai School, United Arab
   Emirates (COBIS) 1230
GEMS Wellington Academy –Silicon Oasis,
   United Arab Emirates (COBIS) 1231
GEMS Wellington International School, United
   Arab Emirates (COBIS) 1231
GEMS Wellington Primary School, United Arab
   Emirates (COBIS) 1231
Geneva English School, Switzerland (COBIS). . . 1230
George Heriot's School, Scotland (HMC) 167
Gidea Park College, Essex (ISA). 1171
Giggleswick Junior School, N Yorks (IAPS). . . . 957
Giggleswick School, N Yorks (HMC) 169
The Glasgow Academy, Scotland (HMC) 171
The High School of Glasgow, Scotland (HMC) . . 172
Glebe House School, Norfolk (IAPS) 957
The Gleddings Preparatory School, W Yorks
   (IAPS) 958
Glenalmond College, Scotland (HMC). 174
The Godolphin and Latymer School, London
   (HMC, GSA). 176
The Godolphin Preparatory School, Wilts (IAPS) . 958
The Godolphin School, Wilts (HMC, GSA) 179
Godstowe Preparatory School, Bucks (IAPS) . . . 958
Gosfield School, Essex (ISA). 1171
Grace Dieu Manor School, Leics (IAPS). 959
The Grange, Wales (IAPS) 959
Grange Park Preparatory School, London (IAPS) . 960
The Grange Preparatory School, Chile (IAPSO) . . 1131
The Grange School, Chile (HMCI). 554
The Grange School, Cheshire (HMC, ISA). 180
Grange School, Nigeria (IAPSO). 1132
Grangewood Independent School, London (ISA) . 1172
Grantham Preparatory International School, Lincs
   (ISA). 1172
The Granville School, Kent (IAPS). 960
Great Ballard, W Sussex (IAPS) 961
Great Walstead School, W Sussex (IAPS) 961
Greenacre School for Girls, Surrey (GSA) 598
Greenbank Preparatory School and Day Nursery,
   Cheshire (ISA). 1172
Greenfield, Surrey (IAPS) 962
Greenfields School, E Sussex (ISA) 1173
The Gregg School, Hants (ISA) 1173
Gresham's Prep School, Norfolk (IAPS) 962

PAGE

Gresham's School, Norfolk (HMC). 183
Grimsdell, London (IAPS) 963
The Grove Independent School, Bucks (ISA) . . . 1173
Guildford High School, Surrey (HMC). 186
Guildford High School Junior School, Surrey
   (IAPS) 963

The Haberdashers' Aske's Boys' Preparatory &
   Pre-Preparatory School, Herts (IAPS) 964
The Haberdashers' Aske's Boys' School, Herts
   (HMC) 188
Haberdashers' Aske's School for Girls, Herts
   (GSA) 599
Haberdashers' Monmouth School for Girls, Wales
   (GSA) 601
Haileybury, Herts (HMC) 191
Haileybury, Australia (HMCI) 553
Haileybury Almaty, Kazakhstan (COBIS) 1226
Halcyon London International School, United
   Kingdom (COBIS). 1230
Hale Preparatory School, Cheshire (ISA). 1173
The Hall, London (IAPS). 964
Hall Grove, Surrey (IAPS) 965
Hallfield School, W Midlands (IAPS) 965
Halliford School, Middx (HMC, Society of
   Heads) 194
Halstead Preparatory School for Girls, Surrey
   (IAPS) 965
The Hammond, Cheshire (ISA). 1174
Hampshire Collegiate Prep School, Hants (IAPS) . 966
Hampshire Collegiate School, Hants (Society of
   Heads) 788
Hampton School, Middx (HMC) 196
Handcross Park School, W Sussex (IAPS) 966
Hanford School, Dorset (IAPS). 967
Harrogate Ladies' College, N Yorks (GSA) 603
Harrow School, Middx (HMC) 200
Harvington Prep School, London (ISA) 1174
Haslemere Preparatory School, Surrey (IAPS). . . 967
Hatherop Castle Preparatory School, Glos (IAPS,
   ISA) 968
Hawkesdown House School, London (IAPS) . . . 968
Hawley Place School, Surrey (ISA) 1174
The Hawthorns, Surrey (IAPS) 968
Hazelwood School, Surrey (IAPS) 969
Hazlegrove, Somerset (IAPS). 969
Headington Preparatory School, Oxon (IAPS) . . . 970
Headington School, Oxon (GSA) 605
Heath Mount School, Herts (IAPS). 970
Heathcote School, Essex (ISA) 1175
Heatherton House School, Bucks (IAPS). 971
Heathfield, W Yorks (IAPS) 971
Heathfield School and Day Nursery, Worcs
   (ISA) 1175
Heathfield School, Berks (GSA) 607
Hemdean House School, Berks (ISA) 1175
Hereford Cathedral Junior School, Herefordshire
   (IAPS) 971
Hereford Cathedral School, Herefordshire (HMC) . 202
Hereward House School, London (IAPS) 972
Herne Hill School, London (ISA). 1176
Herries Preparatory School, Berks (IAPS) 972
Hethersett Old Hall School, Norfolk (GSA) 609
Heywood Prep, Wilts (ISA). 1176
High March School, Bucks (IAPS) 973

PAGE

Highclare School, W Midlands (ISA) 1177
Highfield & Brookham Schools, Hants (IAPS) . . 973
Highfield Priory School, Lancs (ISA) 1177
Highfield Prep School, Berks (IAPS) 973
Highfields School, Notts (ISA). 1178
Highgate Junior School, London (IAPS). 974
Highgate School, London (HMC) 203
Hilden Grange School, Kent (IAPS) 974
Hilden Oaks School & Nursery, Kent (IAPS) . . . 974
Hill House School, S Yorks (Society of Heads,
    IAPS) 790
Hillcrest International Schools, Kenya (HMCI) . . 552
Hillcrest International Schools, Kenya (COBIS). . 1226
Hillcrest Preparatory School, Kenya (IAPSO) . . . 1132
Hoe Bridge School, Surrey (IAPS). 975
Holme Grange School, Berks (IAPS) 976
Holmewood House, Kent (IAPS). 976
Holmwood House Preparatory School, Essex
    (IAPS) 977
Holy Cross Preparatory School, Surrey (IAPS) . . 978
Homefield Preparatory School, Surrey (IAPS). . . 978
Hopelands Preparatory School, Glos (ISA) 1179
Hornsby House School, London (IAPS). 979
Horris Hill, Berks (IAPS). 979
Howe Green House School, Herts (ISA) 1179
Howell's School Llandaff, Wales (GSA). 610
Hull Collegiate School, E Yorks (Society of Heads,
    ISA) 790
Hulme Hall Grammar School, Cheshire (ISA). . . 1179
Hunter Hall School, Cumbria (IAPS) 979
Hurlingham School, London (IAPS) 980
Hurst Lodge School, Berks (ISA) 1179
Hurstpierpoint College, W Sussex (HMC). 207
Hurstpierpoint College Preparatory School,
    W Sussex (IAPS) 980
Hurtwood House School, Surrey (ISA) 1180
Hutchesons' Grammar School, Scotland (HMC). . 209
Hymers College, E Yorks (HMC) 211
Ibstock Place School, London (ISA) 1180
Immanuel College, Herts (HMC). 212

Independent Bonn International School, Germany
    (COBIS). 1228
Inglefield House, Wales (IAPS) 981
International British School of Bucharest, Romania
    (COBIS). 1229
The International School Bangalore, India
    (HMCI) 552
International School of Moscow, Russia
    (COBIS) 1229
International School Olomouc, Czech Republic
    (COBIS). 1227
Ipswich High School, Suffolk (GSA) 611
Ipswich Preparatory School, Suffolk (IAPS). . . . 982
Ipswich School, Suffolk (HMC) 214
The Italia Conti Academy of Theatre Arts, London
    (ISA) 1181

James Allen's Girls' School (JAGS), London
    (HMC, GSA) 216
James Allen's Preparatory School, London
    (IAPS) 982
Jerudong International School, Brunei Darussalam
    (HMCI) 552

PAGE

Jerudong International School, Brunei Darussalam
    (IAPSO) 1133
Jerudong International School, Brunei Darussalam
    (COBIS) 1226
The John Lyon School, Middx (HMC) 218
Jumeirah English Speaking School, United Arab
    Emirates (HMCI) 555

Keble School, London (IAPS) 982
Kelvinside Academy, Scotland (HMC). 219
Kensington Prep School, London (IAPS) 983
Kent College, Kent (HMC). 220
Kent College Nursery, Infant & Junior School,
    Kent (IAPS) 983
Kent College Pembury, Kent (HMC, GSA) 222
Kent College Preparatory School, Kent (IAPS) . . 984
Kenton College, Kenya (IAPSO). 1133
Kew College, Surrey (IAPS) 984
Kew Green Preparatory School, Surrey (IAPS) . . 985
Kilgraston, Scotland (GSA) 612
Kilgraston Preparatory School, Scotland (IAPS). . 985
Kimbolton Preparatory School, Cambs (IAPS) . . 985
Kimbolton School, Cambs (HMC) 225
Kincoppal-Rose Bay School of the Sacred Heart,
    Australia (HMCI) 553
King Alfred School, London (ISA). 1181
King Edward VI High School for Girls,
    W Midlands (GSA, Society of Heads). 613
King Edward VI School, Hants (HMC) 227
King Edward's School, Somerset (HMC) 228
King Edward's School, W Midlands (HMC). . . . 231
King Edward's, Surrey (HMC) 232
King Henry VIII Preparatory School, W Midlands
    (IAPS) 986
King Henry VIII School, W Midlands (HMC) . . . 234
King William's College, Isle of Man (HMC). . . . 235
Kingham Hill School, Oxon (Society of Heads) . . 792
King's College, New Zealand (HMCI) . . . .
King's College, Spain (COBIS) 1229
King's College, Spain (COBIS) 1229
King's College, Spain (HMCE). 550
King's College School, London (HMC) 237
King's College School, Cambs (IAPS) 987
King's College School, La Moraleja, Spain
    (IAPSO) 1134
King's College School, La Moraleja, Spain
    (COBIS) 1229
King's College Junior School, London (IAPS). . . 987
King's College, Somerset (HMC) 241
King's Hall School, Somerset (IAPS) 988
King's Hawford, Worcs (IAPS). 988
King's High School, Warwicks (GSA) 615
The King's Hospital, Ireland (HMC) 242
King's House School, Surrey (IAPS). 988
King's Infant School, Chamartín, Spain
    (COBIS) 1229
King's Infant School, Chamartín, Spain
    (IAPSO) 1134
King's Junior School Gloucester, Glos (IAPS). . . 989
Kings Monkton School, Wales (ISA). 1181
King's St Alban's School, Worcs (IAPS). 989
The King's School, Australia (HMCI) 553
King's School, Somerset (HMC) 243
The King's School, Canterbury, Kent (HMC) . . . 245
Junior King's School, Canterbury, Kent (IAPS) . . 990

PAGE

The King's School, Chester, Cheshire (HMC) . . . 248
King's Ely, Cambs (HMC, Society of Heads) . . . 249
King's Ely Junior, Cambs (IAPS). 990
The King's School, Glos (HMC) 252
The King's School, Macclesfield, Cheshire (HMC) 255
King's Rochester, Kent (HMC). 256
King's Rochester Preparatory School, Kent
 (IAPS) 991
The King's School, Worcs (HMC) 258
Kingshott, Herts (IAPS) 992
The Kingsley School, Warwicks (GSA, IAPS). . . 617
Kingsley School, Devon (Society of Heads) 793
Kingsmead School, Merseyside (IAPS) 992
Kingston Grammar School, Surrey (HMC). 260
Kingswood House School, Surrey (IAPS) 992
Kingswood Preparatory School, Somerset (IAPS). 993
Kingswood School, Somerset (HMC) 262
Kirkham Grammar School, Lancs (HMC, Society
 of Heads). 265
Kirkstone House School, Lincs (ISA) 1182
Knighton House, Dorset (IAPS) 993
Knightsbridge School, London (ISA). 1182
The Knoll School, Worcs (ISA) 1182
Knox Grammar School, Australia (HMCI). 553
Kolej Tuanku Ja'afar, Malaysia (HMCI) 553

Lady Barn House School, Cheshire (ISA) 1183
The Lady Eleanor Holles School, Middx (GSA) . . 618
The Lady Eleanor Holles School (Junior
 Department), Middx (IAPS). 994
Lagos Preparatory School, Nigeria (IAPSO). . . . 1135
Lagos Preparatory School, Nigeria (COBIS). . . . 1226
Lambrook, Berks (IAPS). 994
Lancing College, W Sussex (HMC) 266
Lancing College Preparatory School at Hove,
 E Sussex (IAPS). 995
Lanesborough School, Surrey (IAPS) 995
Langley School, Norfolk (Society of Heads). . . . 795
Lathallan School, Scotland (IAPS) 996
Latymer Prep School, London (IAPS) 996
Latymer Upper School, London (HMC) 268
Lavant House, W Sussex (GSA) 621
The Lawrence School, India (HMCI). 552
Laxton Junior – Oundle School, Northants (IAPS). 996
Leaden Hall School, Wilts (IAPS) 997
The Grammar School at Leeds, W Yorks (HMC,
 IAPS). 270
Leehurst Swan School, Wilts (IAPS, ISA) 997
Leicester Grammar Junior School, Leics (IAPS). . 998
Leicester Grammar School, Leics (HMC) 271
Leicester High School for Girls, Leics (GSA) . . . 623
Leighton Park School, Berks (HMC, Society of
 Heads). 273
Leweston Junior Department, Dorset (IAPS). . . . 998
Leweston School, Dorset (GSA). 624
The Leys School, Cambs (HMC). 275
Lichfield Cathedral School, Staffs (Society of
 Heads) 797
Lime House School, Cumbria (ISA) 1183
Lincoln Minster School, Lincs (HMC, Society of
 Heads, IAPS). 277
Lingfield Notre Dame, Surrey (ISA) 1183
Littlegarth School, Essex (IAPS, ISA) 999
Lochinver House School, Herts (IAPS) 999
Lockers Park, Herts (IAPS). 1000

PAGE

Lomond School, Scotland (HMC) 278
Longacre School, Surrey (IAPS) 1000
Longridge Towers School, Northumberland
 (Society of Heads) 798
Lord Wandsworth College, Hants (HMC) 280
Lorenden Preparatory School, Kent (IAPS) 1001
Loreto Preparatory School, Cheshire (ISA). . . . 1184
Loretto Junior School, Scotland (IAPS) 1001
Loretto School, Scotland (HMC) 281
Loughborough Grammar School, Leics (HMC) . . 284
Loughborough High School, Leics (GSA) 626
Loyola Preparatory School, Essex (IAPS) 1001
Luckley House School, Berks (GSA). 628
Lucton School, Herefordshire (ISA, IAPS). . . . 1002
Ludgrove, Berks (IAPS) 1002
LVS Ascot (The Licensed Victuallers' School),
 Berks (Society of Heads, ISA). 800
The Lyceum, London (ISA). 1184
Lyndhurst House Preparatory School, London
 (IAPS) 1002
Lyndhurst School, Surrey (ISA) 1185
Lyonsdown School, Herts (ISA) 1185

Maadi British International School, Egypt
 (COBIS) 1230
Magdalen College School, Oxon (HMC). 287
Magdalene House Preparatory School, Cambs
 (IAPS) 1003
Maidwell Hall, Northants (IAPS). 1003
Maldon Court Preparatory School, Essex (IAPS) 1004
The Mall School, Middx (IAPS) 1004
Maltman's Green, Bucks (IAPS) 1004
Malvern College, Worcs (HMC) 289
The Manchester Grammar School, Greater
 Manchester (HMC) 291
Manchester High School for Girls, Greater
 Manchester (GSA) 629
Mander Portman Woodward (MPW), London
 (ISA) 1185
Manor House School, Leics (ISA) 1186
Manor House School, Surrey (GSA) 630
Manor Lodge School, Herts (IAPS) 1005
The Manor Preparatory School, Oxon (IAPS) . . 1005
Maple Hayes Hall School for Dyslexics, Staffs
 (ISA) 1186
Maple Walk School, London (ISA). 1186
The Marist Preparatory School, Berks (IAPS) . . 1006
The Marist Senior School, Berks (GSA) 631
Mark College, Somerset (ISA) 1187
Marlborough College, Wilts (HMC) 293
Marlborough House School, Kent (IAPS) 1006
Marlston House School, Berks (IAPS) 1007
The Mary Erskine School, Scotland (GSA) 632
Marymount International School, Surrey (GSA) . . 634
Mayfield Preparatory School, W Midlands
 (IAPS) 1007
The Maynard School, Devon (GSA) 636
Mayville High School, Hants (ISA) 1187
Mead School, Kent (ISA). 1188
Melbourne Grammar School, Australia (HMCI) . . 553
Mentone Grammar School, Australia (HMCI) . . . 553
Merchant Taylors' Boys' School, Merseyside
 (HMC) 296
Merchant Taylors' Girls' School, Merseyside
 (GSA) 638

PAGE

Merchant Taylors' School, Middx (HMC) 297
Merchiston Castle School, Scotland (HMC) 300
Methodist Ladies' College, Australia (HMCI) . . . 553
Michaelhouse, South Africa (HMCI). 552
Micklefield School, Surrey (IAPS). 1008
Mill Hill School, London (HMC) 303
Millfield, Somerset (HMC) 308
Millfield Prep School, Somerset (IAPS) 1008
Milton Abbey School, Dorset (Society of Heads) . 801
Milton Keynes Preparatory School, Bucks
  (IAPS). 1009
The Minster School, N Yorks (IAPS) 1009
The Moat School, London (ISA) 1188
Moffats School, Worcs (ISA). 1189
Moira House Girls School, E Sussex (GSA) 639
Moira House Junior School, E Sussex (IAPS) . . . 1010
Monkton Combe School, Somerset (HMC) 309
Monkton Prep School, Somerset (IAPS) 1010
Monmouth School, Wales (HMC) 312
Moon Hall School for Dyslexic Children, Surrey
  (ISA) 1189
Moor Park School, Shropshire (IAPS) 1011
Moorfield School, W Yorks (IAPS) 1011
Moorland School, Lancs (ISA). 1189
Moorlands School, W Yorks (IAPS) 1011
More House School, Surrey (ISA) 1190
More House School, London (GSA) 642
Moreton Hall, Shropshire (GSA, Society of
  Heads) 644
Moreton Hall Preparatory School, Suffolk
  (IAPS). 1012
Morrison's Academy, Scotland (HMC) 314
Mougins School, France (COBIS) 1228
Moulsford Preparatory School, Oxon (IAPS) . . . 1012
The Mount Junior School, N Yorks (IAPS) 1013
Mount Kelly, Devon (HMC) 316
Mount Kelly Preparatory School, Devon (IAPS) . 1013
Mount St Mary's College, Derbyshire (HMC) . . . 318
The Mount School, N Yorks (GSA) 646
Moyles Court School, Hants (ISA) 1190
Mylnhurst Preparatory School & Nursery, S Yorks
  (IAPS, ISA) 1014

Naima Jewish Preparatory School, London
  (IAPS). 1014
The New Beacon, Kent (IAPS). 1014
New Cairo British International School, Egypt
  (COBIS) 1230
New College School, Oxon (IAPS) 1015
New Eccles Hall School, Norfolk (ISA) 1190
New Hall Preparatory School, Essex (IAPS). . . . 1015
New Hall School, Essex (HMC, GSA) 320
Newbridge Preparatory School, W Midlands
  (IAPS). 1016
Newcastle High School for Girls, Tyne and Wear
  (GSA) 648
Newcastle Preparatory School, Tyne and Wear
  (IAPS). 1016
Newcastle School for Boys, Tyne and Wear (Society
  of Heads). 803
Newcastle-under-Lyme School, Staffs (HMC) . . . 322
Newland House School, Middx (IAPS) 1017
Newton Prep, London (IAPS) 1017
Norfolk House School, W Midlands (ISA). 1191
Norland Place School, London (IAPS). 1018

PAGE

Normanhurst School, London (ISA) 1191
North Cestrian Grammar School, Cheshire (Society
  of Heads, ISA). 803
North London Collegiate School, Middx (GSA) . . 649
Northampton High School, Northants (GSA) . . . 650
Northbourne Park, Kent (IAPS) 1018
Northcote Lodge, London (IAPS) 1018
Northease Manor School, E Sussex (ISA) 1191
Northwood College for Girls, Middx (GSA, ISA) . 652
Northwood College for Girls – Junior School,
  Middx (IAPS) 1019
Northwood Prep, Herts (IAPS) 1019
Norwich High School, Norfolk (GSA) 653
Norwich School, Norfolk (HMC) 323
Norwich School, The Lower School, Norfolk
  (IAPS) 1020
Notre Dame Preparatory School, Norfolk (ISA) . 1192
Notre Dame School, Surrey (IAPS) 1020
Notre Dame School, Surrey (GSA). 654
Notting Hill and Ealing High School, London
  (GSA) 657
Notting Hill Preparatory School, London
  (IAPS) 1021
Nottingham Girls' High School, Notts (GSA) . . . 658
Nottingham High Infant and Junior School, Notts
  (IAPS) 1022
Nottingham High School, Notts (HMC) 326

Oakfield Preparatory School, London (ISA) 1192
Oakham School, Rutland (HMC). 328
Oakhill College, Lancs (ISA). 1192
Oakhyrst Grange School, Surrey (ISA). 1193
Oaklands School, Essex (ISA) 1193
Oakwood Preparatory School, W Sussex (IAPS) . 1023
Oakwood School, Surrey (IAPS) 1023
Ockbrook School, Derbyshire (Society of Heads,
  IAPS) 804
Old Buckenham Hall School, Suffolk (IAPS) . . . 1023
The Old Hall School, Shropshire (IAPS). 1024
The Old School Henstead, Suffolk (IAPS, ISA) . . 1024
Old Vicarage School, Surrey (IAPS) 1024
Oldham Hulme Grammar School, Lancs (HMC) . 329
Oporto British School, Portugal (HMCI). 555
Oporto British School, Portugal (COBIS) 1229
The Oratory Preparatory School, Oxon (IAPS) . . 1025
The Oratory School, Oxon (HMC) 331
Orchard House School, London (IAPS) 1025
Orchard School, Beds (IAPS) 1026
Orley Farm School, Middx (IAPS) 1026
Orwell Park, Suffolk (IAPS) 1027
Oswestry School, Shropshire (Society of Heads) . 806
Oundle School, Northants (HMC) 333
Our Lady's Abingdon Senior School, Oxon
  (Society of Heads) 807
Our Lady's Abingdon Junior School, Oxon
  (IAPS) 1027
OLCS – Our Lady's Convent School, Leics
  (ISA) 1194
Oxford High School, Oxon (GSA) 659

Packwood Haugh, Shropshire (IAPS) 1028
Palmers Green High School, London (GSA). . . . 659
Pangbourne College, Berks (HMC) 336
Papplewick, Berks (IAPS) 1029
The Paragon, Somerset (IAPS) 1029

PAGE

Park Lane International School, Czech Republic
(COBIS) 1227
Park School, Dorset (ISA) 1194
Park School for Girls, Essex (ISA) 1194
The Park School, Somerset (ISA) 1195
Parkside, Surrey (IAPS) 1030
Pembridge Hall School, London (IAPS) 1030
Pembroke House, Kenya (IAPSO) 1136
Pennthorpe School, W Sussex (IAPS) 1030
Peponi House, Kenya (IAPSO) 1136
Peponi School, Kenya (HMCI) 552
Perrott Hill, Somerset (IAPS) 1031
The Perse Pelican Nursery and Pre-Preparatory
School, Cambs (IAPS) 1032
The Perse Preparatory School, Cambs (IAPS) . . . 1032
The Perse Upper School, Cambs (HMC) 338
The Peterborough School, Cambs (Society of
Heads) 808
Peterhouse, Zimbabwe (HMCI) 552
Pilgrims Pre-Preparatory School, Beds (IAPS, ISA) . .
1033
The Pilgrims' School, Hants (IAPS) 1033
Pinewood, Wilts (IAPS) 1034
Pipers Corner School, Bucks (GSA, IAPS) 661
Pitsford School, Northants (Society of Heads,
ISA) 810
Plymouth College, Devon (HMC) 339
Plymouth College Preparatory School, Devon
(IAPS) 1034
Pocklington Prep School (formerly Lyndhurst
School), E Yorks (IAPS) 1034
Pocklington School, E Yorks (HMC) 341
Polwhele House School, Cornwall (ISA) 1195
Port Regis, Dorset (IAPS) 1035
Portland Place School, London (Society of Heads,
ISA) 811
The Portsmouth Grammar Junior School, Hants
(IAPS) 1036
The Portsmouth Grammar School, Hants (HMC) . 343
Portsmouth High School, Hants (GSA) 661
Pownall Hall, Cheshire (IAPS) 1036
Poznan British International School, Poland
(COBIS) 1229
The Prague British School, Czech Republic
(HMCI) 555
The Prague British School Kamýk, Czech
Republic (COBIS) 1227
The Prague British School Vlastina, Czech
Republic (COBIS) 1228
The Prebendal School, W Sussex (IAPS) 1037
Prenton Preparatory School, Merseyside (ISA) . . 1196
Prestfelde, Shropshire (IAPS) 1037
Prince's Mead School, Hants (IAPS) 1038
Princess Helena College, Herts (GSA) 662
Princethorpe College, Warwicks (HMC, ISA) . . . 346
Prior Park College, Somerset (HMC) 350
Prior Park Preparatory School, Wilts (IAPS) . . . 1038
Prior's Field, Surrey (GSA) 664
Priory Preparatory School, Surrey (IAPS) 1038
Priory School, W Midlands (ISA) 1196
Prospect House School, London (IAPS) 1039
The Purcell School, Herts (Society of Heads) . . . 813
Putney High School, London (GSA) 665

Quainton Hall School, Middx (IAPS) 1039

PAGE

Queen Anne's School, Berks (HMC, GSA) 353
Queen Elizabeth's Hospital (QEH), Bristol
(HMC) 354
Queen Elizabeth's Hospital (QEH) – Junior
School, Bristol (IAPS) 1040
Queen Ethelburga's Collegiate Foundation,
N Yorks (ISA) 1196
Queen Margaret's School, N Yorks (GSA) 668
Queen Mary's School, N Yorks (GSA) 671
Queen's College Junior School, Somerset
(IAPS) 1040
Queen's College, London, London (GSA) 672
Queen's College, Somerset (HMC) 355
Queen's Gate School, London (GSA) 673
Queenswood School, Herts (GSA) 675

Radley College, Oxon (HMC) 358
Radnor House School, United Kingdom
(COBIS) 1230
Ramillies Hall School, Cheshire (IAPS) 1041
Raphael Independent School, Essex (ISA) 1197
Rastrick Independent School, W Yorks (ISA) . . . 1197
Ratcliffe College, Leics (HMC, IAPS) 360
Ravenscourt Park Preparatory School, London
(IAPS) 1041
Ravenstone Preparatory & Pre-Preparatory
Schools, London (ISA) 1198
The Read School, N Yorks (Society of Heads) . . . 815
Reading Blue Coat School, Berks (HMC, Society
of Heads) 362
Red House School, Cleveland (ISA) 1198
The Red Maids' Junior School, Bristol (IAPS) . . 1041
The Red Maids' School, Bristol (GSA) 676
Redcliffe School, London (IAPS) 1042
Redcourt – St Anselm's, Merseyside (ISA) 1199
Reddam House Bearwood, Berks (Society of
Heads) 816
Reddiford School, Middx (IAPS, ISA) 1042
Redland High School for Girls, Bristol (GSA) . . . 678
Redland High School for Girls Junior School,
Bristol (IAPS) 1043
Reed's School, Surrey (HMC, Society of Heads) . . 364
Reigate Grammar School, Surrey (HMC) 365
Reigate St Mary's Preparatory and Choir School,
Surrey (IAPS) 1043
Rendcomb College, Glos (HMC, Society of
Heads) 367
Repton School, Derbyshire (HMC) 370
RGS Springfield, Worcs (IAPS) 1044
RGS The Grange, Worcs (IAPS) 1044
The Richard Pate School, Glos (IAPS) 1045
Richmond House School, W Yorks (IAPS) 1045
Riddlesworth Hall Preparatory School, Norfolk
(IAPS) 1045
Ridley College, Canada (HMCI) . . . .
Ripley Court School, Surrey (IAPS) 1046
Rishworth School, W Yorks (Society of Heads) . . 818
Riverside School, Czech Republic (COBIS) . . . 1228
Riverston School, London (ISA) 1199
Robert Gordon's College, Scotland (HMC) 372
Rochester Independent College, Kent (ISA) . . . 1200
Rockport School, Northern Ireland (IAPS) 1046
Roedean School, E Sussex (HMC, GSA) 375
Rokeby, Surrey (IAPS) 1047
The Roman Ridge School, Ghana (IAPSO) . . . 1137

	PAGE
Rookwood School, Hants (ISA)	1200
Rose Hill School, Kent (IAPS)	1047
Roselyon School, Cornwall (ISA)	1200
Rosemead Preparatory School, London (IAPS, ISA)	1047
Rossall School, Lancs (HMC)	377
Rougemont School, Wales (HMC)	379
Rowan Preparatory School, Surrey (IAPS)	1048
The Rowans School, London (IAPS)	1049
Royal Grammar School, Surrey (HMC)	380
Royal Grammar School, Tyne and Wear (HMC)	382
RGS Worcester, Worcs (HMC)	384
The Royal High School Bath, Somerset (GSA)	680
The Royal Hospital School, Suffolk (HMC)	386
The Royal Masonic School for Girls, Herts (HMC)	388
The Royal Masonic School for Girls, Herts (IAPS)	1049
Royal Russell Junior School, Surrey (IAPS)	1049
Royal Russell School, Surrey (HMC)	389
The Royal School Dungannon, Northern Ireland (HMC)	391
The Royal School, Wolverhampton, W Midlands (Society of Heads)	820
Ruckleigh School, W Midlands (ISA)	1201
Rudston Preparatory School, S Yorks (IAPS)	1050
Rugby School, Warwicks (HMC)	393
Rupert House School, Oxon (IAPS)	1050
Rushmoor School, Beds (ISA)	1201
Russell House, Kent (IAPS)	1051
Ruthin School, Wales (Society of Heads)	822
Rydal Penrhos Preparatory School, Wales (IAPS)	1051
Rydal Penrhos School, Wales (HMC, Society of Heads)	396
Ryde Junior School, Isle of Wight (IAPS)	1051
Ryde School with Upper Chine, Isle of Wight (HMC)	398
Rydes Hill Preparatory School, Surrey (IAPS)	1052
Rye St Antony, Oxon (GSA)	682
Rygaards School, Denmark (COBIS)	1228
The Ryleys, Cheshire (IAPS)	1052
Sackville School, Kent (ISA)	1201
Sacred Heart School, Norfolk (ISA)	1202
Sacred Heart School, E Sussex (ISA)	1202
St Albans High School for Girls, Herts (HMC, GSA)	400
St Albans High School for Girls Preparatory School, Herts (IAPS)	1053
St Albans School, Herts (HMC)	402
St Aloysius' College, Scotland (HMC)	404
St Andrew's Preparatory School, Kenya (IAPSO)	1137
St Andrew's School, Beds (ISA)	1203
St Andrew's Prep, E Sussex (IAPS)	1053
St Andrew's School, Berks (IAPS)	1054
St Andrew's School, Woking, Surrey (IAPS)	1054
St Andrew's Scots School, Argentina (HMCI)	554
St Anne's Preparatory School, Essex (ISA)	1203
S. Anselm's, Derbyshire (IAPS)	1055
St Anthony's Preparatory School, London (IAPS)	1055
St Aubyn's School, Essex (IAPS)	1056

	PAGE
St Augustine's Priory School, London (GSA, Society of Heads)	684
St Bede's Preparatory School, Staffs (IAPS)	1056
St Bede's College, Greater Manchester (HMC)	404
St Bees School, Cumbria (Society of Heads)	823
St Benedict's Junior School, London (IAPS)	1057
St Benedict's School, London (HMC)	406
St Bernard's Preparatory School, Berks (IAPS)	1057
St Catherine's School, Surrey (GSA)	687
St Catherine's Preparatory School, Surrey (IAPS)	1057
St Catherine's British School, Greece (COBIS)	1228
St Catherine's British School, Greece (HMCI)	555
St Catherine's School, Middx (GSA, ISA)	689
St Cedd's School, Essex (IAPS)	1058
Saint Christina's RC Preparatory School, London (IAPS)	1058
St Christopher School, Herts (Society of Heads)	825
St Christopher's School, Bahrain (IAPSO)	1138
St Christopher's School, Bahrain (HMCI)	555
St Christopher's School, Surrey (ISA)	1203
St Christopher's School, London (IAPS)	1058
St Christopher's School, E Sussex (IAPS)	1059
St Christopher's School, Devon (ISA)	1204
St Christopher's School, Middx (ISA)	1204
St Clare's, Oxford, Oxon (ISA)	1204
St Columba's College, Ireland (HMC)	407
St Columba's College, Herts (HMC, Society of Heads)	408
St Columba's College Preparatory School, Herts (IAPS)	1059
St Columba's School, Scotland (HMC)	410
St David's College, Kent (ISA)	1205
St David's School, Surrey (ISA)	1205
St Dominic's Brewood, Staffs (GSA, ISA)	690
St Dominic's Priory School, Staffs (GSA, ISA)	691
St Dunstan's College, London (HMC)	411
St Dunstan's College Junior School, London (IAPS)	1059
St Edmund's College, Herts (HMC)	412
St Edmund's Junior School, Kent (IAPS)	1060
St Edmund's Prep School, Herts (IAPS)	1060
St Edmund's School, Kent (HMC)	416
St Edmund's School, Surrey (IAPS)	1061
St Edward's, Oxford, Oxon (HMC)	418
St Edward's Preparatory School, Glos (IAPS, ISA)	1061
St Edward's School, Glos (Society of Heads, ISA)	827
St Edward's School, Berks (IAPS)	1061
St Faith's School, Cambs (IAPS)	1062
Saint Felix School, Suffolk (Society of Heads)	828
St Francis School, Wilts (IAPS)	1063
St Gabriel's, Berks (GSA)	692
St Gabriel's, Berks (IAPS)	1063
St George's British International School, Italy (COBIS)	1228
St George's British International School, Italy (HMCI)	555
St George's College, Surrey (HMC, Society of Heads)	421
St George's College, Zimbabwe (HMCI)	552
St George's College North, Argentina (HMCI)	554
St George's College Quilmes, Argentina (HMCI)	554
St George's International School, Luxembourg (COBIS)	1228

	PAGE
St George's Junior School, Surrey (IAPS)	1064
St George's School, W Midlands (Society of Heads)	830
St George's School, Berks (IAPS)	1065
St George's, Ascot, Berks (GSA)	694
St Gerard's School, Wales (ISA)	1205
St Helen & St Katharine, Oxon (GSA)	696
St Helen's College, Middx (IAPS)	1065
St Helen's School, Middx (GSA)	698
St Hilary's School, Surrey (IAPS)	1065
St Hilda's School, Herts (IAPS)	1066
St Hilda's School, Herts (ISA)	1206
St Hugh's, Oxon (IAPS)	1066
St Hugh's, Lincs (IAPS)	1067
St Ives School, Surrey (IAPS)	1067
St James Junior School, London (ISA)	1206
St James' School, Lincs (ISA)	1206
St James Senior Boys' School, Surrey (Society of Heads, ISA)	832
St James Senior Girls' School, London (GSA, ISA)	701
St John's Beaumont, Berks (IAPS)	1068
St John's College Infant and Junior School, Hants (IAPS)	1068
St John's College School, Cambs (IAPS)	1068
St John's College, Hants (Society of Heads)	833
St John's International School, Devon (IAPS)	1069
St John's School, Surrey (HMC)	423
St John's School, Essex (ISA)	1207
St John's School, Middx (IAPS)	1070
St Joseph's College, Suffolk (Society of Heads, IAPS)	834
St Joseph's Convent School, London (ISA)	1207
St Joseph's In The Park School, Herts (IAPS)	1070
St Joseph's Park Hill School, Lancs (ISA)	1207
St Joseph's Preparatory School, Staffs (ISA)	1207
St Joseph's School, Cornwall (ISA)	1207
St Joseph's School, Notts (ISA)	1208
St Julian's School, Portugal (HMCI)	555
St Lawrence College, Kent (HMC)	425
St Lawrence College Junior School, Kent (IAPS)	1071
St Leonard's College, Australia (HMCI)	553
St Leonards Junior School, Scotland (IAPS)	1071
St Leonards-Mayfield School, E Sussex (GSA)	702
St Leonards School, Scotland (HMC)	427
St Margaret's School for Girls, Scotland (GSA)	704
St Margaret's School, Herts (GSA)	706
St Margaret's Preparatory School, Essex (ISA)	1208
St Margaret's School, London (GSA)	707
St Margaret's Preparatory School, Wilts (IAPS)	1071
St Margaret's Preparatory School, Herts (IAPS)	1072
St Martha's, Herts (GSA, ISA)	707
St Martin's Ampleforth, N Yorks (IAPS)	1072
St Martin's Preparatory School, Lincs (ISA)	1208
St Martin's School, Middx (IAPS)	1073
Saint Martin's, W Midlands (GSA)	709
St Mary's Calne, Wilts (HMC, GSA)	429
St Mary's School, Cambs (GSA, IAPS)	710
St Mary's School, Essex (GSA)	713
St Mary's College, Merseyside (HMC)	430
St Mary's School, Bucks (GSA)	714
St Mary's School, London (IAPS)	1073
St Mary's Preparatory School, Scotland (IAPS)	1074
St Mary's School Ascot, Berks (HMC, GSA)	431
St Mary's School, Dorset (GSA)	715
St Michael's Preparatory School, Channel Islands (IAPS)	1074
St Michael's Preparatory School, Essex (IAPS)	1074
St Michael's School, Wales (ISA)	1209
St Michael's Prep School, Kent (IAPS)	1075
St Neot's Preparatory School, Hants (IAPS)	1075
St Nicholas House School, Norfolk (ISA)	1209
St Nicholas' School, Hants (GSA)	717
Saint Nicholas School, Essex (ISA)	1209
St Olave's Prep School, London (IAPS)	1076
St Olave's School, York, N Yorks (IAPS)	1076
St Paul's British Primary School, Belgium (COBIS)	1227
St Paul's Cathedral School, London (IAPS)	1077
St Paul's Girls' School, London (HMC, GSA)	434
St Paul's School, London (HMC)	436
St Paul's School, Brazil (HMCI)	554
St Paul's School, Brazil (COBIS)	1227
St Paul's School, Brazil (IAPSO)	1138
St Peter and St Paul School, Derbyshire (IAPS)	1077
St Peter's School, Northants (ISA)	1210
St Peter's School, York, N Yorks (HMC)	439
St Philomena's Catholic School, Essex (ISA)	1210
St Piran's, Berks (IAPS)	1078
St Piran's School, Cornwall (ISA)	1210
St Pius X Prep School, Lancs (IAPS)	1078
St Richard's, Herefordshire (IAPS)	1078
Saint Ronan's, Kent (IAPS)	1079
St Saviour's School, Ikoyi, Nigeria (IAPSO)	1139
St Swithun's Junior School, Hants (IAPS)	1079
St Swithun's School, Hants (GSA)	719
St Teresa's Catholic Independent School & Nursery, Bucks (ISA)	1211
St Winefride's Convent School, Shropshire (ISA)	1211
St Winifred's School, Hants (ISA)	1211
St Wystan's School, Derbyshire (ISA)	1212
Salesian College, Hants (ISA)	1212
Salisbury Cathedral School, Wilts (IAPS)	1080
Salterford House School, Notts (ISA)	1212
Sancton Wood School, Cambs (ISA)	1213
Sandroyd School, Wilts (IAPS)	1080
Sarum Hall School, London (IAPS)	1081
Scarborough College, N Yorks (Society of Heads)	835
Scarisbrick Hall School & College, Lancs (ISA)	1213
Scotch College, Australia (HMCI)	553
The Scots College, Australia (HMCI)	553
Seaford College, W Sussex (HMC, Society of Heads)	440
Seaford College Prep School, W Sussex (IAPS)	1081
Seaton House School, Surrey (IAPS)	1082
Sevenoaks Preparatory School, Kent (IAPS)	1082
Sevenoaks School, Kent (HMC)	442
Shapwick School, Somerset (ISA)	1213
Shawnigan Lake School, Canada (HMCI)	554
Shebbear College, Devon (Society of Heads)	837
Sheffield High School, S Yorks (GSA)	723
Sherborne Girls, Dorset (HMC, GSA)	444
Sherborne House School, Hants (ISA)	1214
Sherborne International, Dorset (ISA)	1214
Sherborne Preparatory School, Dorset (IAPS)	1083

PAGE

Sherborne Qatar, Qatar (COBIS). 1230
Sherborne School, Dorset (HMC) 446
Sherfield School, Hants (ISA) 1214
Sherrardswood School, Herts (ISA) 1215
Shiplake College, Oxon (HMC, Society of
    Heads). 448
Shore School, Australia (HMCI) 554
Shoreham College, W Sussex (ISA) 1215
Shrewsbury High Prep School, Shropshire
    (IAPS) 1083
Shrewsbury High School, Shropshire (GSA). . . . 723
Shrewsbury House, Surrey (IAPS) 1084
Shrewsbury International School, Thailand
    (HMCI) 553
Shrewsbury Lodge School, Surrey (IAPS, ISA) . 1084
Shrewsbury School, Shropshire (HMC) 450
Sibford School, Oxon (Society of Heads) 838
Sidcot School, Somerset (HMC, Society of
    Heads). 452
Silcoates School, W Yorks (HMC, Society of
    Heads). 453
Slindon College, W Sussex (ISA) 1215
Snaresbrook Preparatory School, London (ISA) . . 1216
Solefield School, Kent (IAPS) 1084
Solihull School, W Midlands (HMC, IAPS) 454
Sompting Abbotts, W Sussex (IAPS) 1085
South Hampstead High School, London (GSA) . . . 725
South Lee School, Suffolk (IAPS) 1085
Spratton Hall, Northants (IAPS) 1085
Spring Grove School, Kent (IAPS) 1086
Stafford Grammar School, Staffs (Society of
    Heads, ISA) 840
Staines Preparatory School, Middx (IAPS) 1086
Stamford High School, Lincs (GSA) 726
Stamford Junior School, Lincs (IAPS) 1087
Stamford School, Lincs (HMC) 457
Steephill School, Kent (ISA) 1216
The Stephen Perse Foundation, Cambs (HMC) . . 458
Stewart's Melville College, Scotland (HMC) . . . 459
Stockport Grammar Junior School, Cheshire
    (IAPS). 1087
Stockport Grammar School, Cheshire (HMC) . . . 461
Stoke College, Suffolk (ISA). 1216
Stonar Preparatory School, Wilts (IAPS). 1088
Stonar, Wilts (GSA, Society of Heads). 728
Stonyhurst College, Lancs (HMC) 463
Stonyhurst St Mary's Hall, Lancs (IAPS) 1088
Stormont, Herts (IAPS). 1089
Stover Preparatory School, Devon (IAPS) 1089
Stover School, Devon (Society of Heads) 841
Stowe School, Bucks (HMC). 465
Stratford Preparatory School, Warwicks (ISA). . . 1217
Strathallan School, Scotland (HMC) 468
Streatham & Clapham High School, London
    (GSA, IAPS). 729
Stroud School, Hants (IAPS) 1089
The Study Preparatory School, London (IAPS,
    ISA) 1090
Study School, Surrey (ISA). 1217
Summer Fields, Oxon (IAPS) 1090
Sunderland High School, Tyne and Wear (Society
    of Heads). 843
Sunningdale School, Berks (IAPS) 1091
Sunninghill Prep School, Dorset (IAPS) 1091

PAGE

Sunny Hill Preparatory School, Somerset
    (IAPS) 1091
Surbiton High Boys' Preparatory School, Surrey
    (IAPS) 1092
Surbiton High Junior Girls' School, Surrey
    (IAPS) 1092
Surbiton High School, Surrey (HMC) 470
Sussex House, London (IAPS) 1093
Sutton High School, Surrey (GSA). 731
Sutton Valence Preparatory School, Kent
    (IAPS) 1094
Sutton Valence School, Kent (HMC). 474
The Swaminarayan School, London (ISA) 1217
Swanbourne House School, Bucks (IAPS) 1094
Sydenham High School, London (GSA) 733
Sydney Grammar School, Australia (HMCI). . . . 554
Sylvia Young Theatre School, London (ISA) . . . 1218

Talbot Heath, Dorset (GSA) 734
Talbot Heath Junior School, Dorset (IAPS) . . . 1095
Tanglin Trust Junior School, Singapore
    (IAPSO) 1139
Tanglin Trust School, Singapore (HMCI) 553
Taunton Preparatory School, Somerset (IAPS). . . 1095
Taunton School, Somerset (HMC) 477
Taverham Hall Preparatory School, Norfolk
    (IAPS) 1096
Terra Nova School, Cheshire (IAPS) 1096
Terrington Hall, N Yorks (IAPS) 1097
Tettenhall College, W Midlands (Society of Heads,
    IAPS) 844
Thames Christian College, London (ISA) 1218
Thetford Grammar School, Norfolk (Society of
    Heads) 846
Thorngrove School, Berks (IAPS) 1097
Thorpe Hall School, Essex (ISA). 1219
Thorpe House School, Bucks (IAPS). 1098
Thorpe House Langley Preparatory School and
    Nursery, Norfolk (IAPS). 1098
Tockington Manor, Glos (IAPS) 1099
Tonbridge School, Kent (HMC) 479
Tormead Junior School, Surrey (IAPS). 1099
Tormead School, Surrey (GSA) 734
Tower College, Merseyside (ISA) 1219
Tower House School, London (IAPS) 1100
The Towers Convent School, E Sussex (ISA) . . . 1219
Town Close School, Norfolk (IAPS) 1100
Transylvania College, Romania (COBIS) 1229
Trevor-Roberts School, London (ISA) 1220
Tring Park School for the Performing Arts, Herts
    (Society of Heads, ISA) 847
Trinity Grammar School, Australia (HMCI) 554
Trinity School, Essex (ISA) 1220
Trinity School, Surrey (HMC) 481
Trinity School, Devon (Society of Heads, ISA) . . 848
Truro High School for Girls, Cornwall (GSA,
    IAPS) 736
Truro Preparatory School, Cornwall (IAPS) . . . 1101
Truro School, Cornwall (HMC) 483
Tudor Hall, Oxon (GSA) 737
Twickenham Preparatory School, Middx (IAPS). 1101
Two Boats School, Ascension Island (COBIS). . 1231
Twyford School, Hants (IAPS) 1102

Unicorn School, Surrey (IAPS). 1102
University College School, London (HMC) 485

PAGE

University College School – Junior Branch, London (IAPS). 1102
University College School – The Phoenix, London (IAPS). 1103
Upper Canada College, Canada (HMCI) 554
Uppingham School, Rutland (HMC) 487
Upton House School, Berks (IAPS) 1103
Ursuline Preparatory School, Essex (ISA) 1220
Ursuline Preparatory School, London (IAPS) . . 1103
The Ursuline Preparatory School Ilford, Essex (IAPS) 1104

Vernon Lodge Preparatory School, Staffs (ISA) . 1221
Victoria College, Channel Islands (HMC) 491
Victoria College Preparatory School, Channel Islands (IAPS) 1104
Vinehall School, E Sussex (IAPS) 1104
Virgo Fidelis Preparatory School, London (ISA). . 1221
Vita et Pax Preparatory School, London (ISA) . . . 1221

Walhampton School, Hants (IAPS). 1105
Walthamstow Hall, Kent (GSA) 739
Walthamstow Hall Junior School, Kent (IAPS) . . 1105
Warminster Preparatory School, Wilts (IAPS) . . 1106
Warminster School, Wilts (HMC, Society of Heads) 492
Warwick Junior School, Warwicks (IAPS) 1106
Warwick Preparatory School, Warwicks (IAPS) . . 1107
Warwick School, Warwicks (HMC) 493
Waverley School, Berks (IAPS) 1107
The Webber Independent School, Bucks (ISA). . . 1222
Welbeck – The Defence Sixth Form College, Leics (Society of Heads). 849
Wellesley House, Kent (IAPS) 1108
Wellingborough Preparatory School, Northants (IAPS) 1108
Wellingborough School, Northants (HMC). 495
Wellington College, Berks (HMC) 498
Wellington Prep School, Somerset (IAPS) 1109
Wellington School, Somerset (HMC). 501
Wellow House School, Notts (IAPS) 1109
Wells Cathedral Junior School, Somerset (IAPS) 1110
Wells Cathedral School, Somerset (HMC) 502
Wesley College, Australia (HMCI). 554
West Buckland School, Devon (HMC, IAPS) . . . 504
West Hill Park, Hants (IAPS). 1110
West House School, W Midlands (IAPS). 1111
West Lodge School, Kent (ISA) 1222
Westbourne House, W Sussex (IAPS) 1111
Westbourne School, S Yorks (IAPS) 1112
Westbourne School, Wales (ISA). 1223
Westbrook Hay, Herts (IAPS) 1112
Westfield School, Tyne and Wear (GSA). 741
Westholme School, Lancs (GSA, Society of Heads) 743
Westminster Abbey Choir School, London (IAPS) 1113
Westminster Cathedral Choir School, London (IAPS) 1113
Westminster School, London (HMC). 506
Westminster Under School, London (IAPS) 1113
Westonbirt School, Glos (GSA) 743

Westonbirt Prep School, Glos (IAPS). 1114
Westville House School, W Yorks (IAPS) 1114
Westward School, Surrey (ISA). 1223
Wetherby Pre-Preparatory School, London (IAPS) 1115
Wetherby Preparatory School, London (IAPS) . . 1115
Whitehall School, Cambs (ISA) 1223
Whitgift School, Surrey (HMC) 508
Widford Lodge, Essex (IAPS) 1115
Willington Independent Preparatory School, London (IAPS). 1116
Wilmslow Preparatory School, Cheshire (IAPS, ISA) 1116
Wimbledon Common Prep School, London (IAPS) 1117
Wimbledon High School, London (GSA) 745
Winchester College, Hants (HMC) 511
Winchester House School, Northants (IAPS). . . . 1117
Windermere Preparatory School, Cumbria (IAPS) . 1117
Windermere School, Cumbria (Society of Heads) . 850
Windlesham House School, W Sussex (IAPS) . . . 1118
Windrush Valley School, Oxon (ISA) 1223
Winterfold House, Worcs (IAPS) 1119
Wisbech Grammar School, Cambs (HMC, Society of Heads) 513
Witham Hall, Lincs (IAPS) 1119
Withington Girls' School, Greater Manchester (HMC, GSA). 515
Woldingham School, Surrey (GSA) 746
Wolverhampton Grammar School, W Midlands (HMC) 516
Woodbridge School, Suffolk (HMC) 518
Woodbridge School – The Abbey, Suffolk (IAPS) 1120
Woodcote House, Surrey (IAPS) 1120
Woodford Green Preparatory School, Essex (IAPS) 1121
Woodhouse Grove School, W Yorks (HMC) 520
Woodlands School, Essex (ISA) 1224
Woodlands School, Essex (ISA) 1224
Woodstock School, India (HMCI) 552
Worksop College, Notts (HMC) 521
Worksop College Preparatory School, Ranby House, Notts (IAPS) 1121
Worth School, W Sussex (HMC) 523
Wrekin College, Shropshire (HMC) 526
Wychwood School, Oxon (GSA) 748
Wycliffe College, Glos (HMC) 528
Wycliffe Preparatory School, Glos (IAPS) 1122
Wycombe Abbey, Bucks (HMC, GSA). 531
Wykeham House School, Hants (GSA). 749

Yardley Court, Kent (IAPS). 1122
Yarlet School, Staffs (IAPS) 1123
Yarm Preparatory School, Cleveland (IAPS) . . . 1123
Yarm School, Cleveland (HMC) 532
Yarrells Preparatory School, Dorset (IAPS) . . . 1124
Yateley Manor Preparatory School, Hants (IAPS) 1124
The Yehudi Menuhin School, Surrey (Society of Heads) 851
York House School, Herts (IAPS) 1125